R.H. Leach

DOCUMENTA GEIGY

SCIENTIFIC TABLES · SEVENTH EDITION

The following Supplements to the Documenta Geigy Scientific Tables are available:

I F.A. Schaub, 'Fundamentals of Clinical Electrocardiography' (1966)

II J.G. Baer, E. Berger, H. Brodhage, L.P. Garrod, R. Geigy, O. Gsell and H.P.R. Seeliger, 'Pathogenic Organisms and Infectious Diseases' (in preparation)

DOCUMENTA
GEIGY

SCIENTIFIC TABLES

SEVENTH EDITION

EDITED BY K. DIEM AND C. LENTNER

PUBLISHED BY J.R. GEIGY S.A., BASLE, SWITZERLAND

DISTRIBUTED BY GEIGY (U.K.) LIMITED
PHARMACEUTICALS DIVISION
MACCLESFIELD

Publisher's Foreword

This 7th edition of the *Geigy Scientific Tables* pursues the aim of earlier editions, namely to provide doctors and biologists with basic data in a concise form and thus spare them much searching in the literature.

In the 6th edition the main changes from the previous edition consisted of an extension of the mathematical, physical and chemical data and a new chapter devoted to biochemistry; in this edition the principal difference is the greatly expanded medical part of the book. The increasing extent to which physical, physicochemical and biochemical methods are finding application in medicine has resulted in the last few years in an immense accumulation of new data whose proper evaluation can be undertaken only by specialists. For this reason we have been compelled in this edition to enlist the cooperation of outside experts to a much greater degree than in the past. Here we would like to thank all those who have contributed in this way – whether in the form of original article or expert advice – for their invaluable help. Their names are listed overleaf.

We would also like to express our appreciation once again of the assistance of all those who have made suggestions or drawn our attention to errors. If we have been unable to adopt all the suggestions put to us, this has been due to the limits set us by the physical compass of the *Scientific Tables*. Users can rest assured that we shall continue to do our best to meet their wishes in the future.

J.R. GEIGY S.A., Basle

Geigy (U.K.) Limited
Pharmaceuticals Division
Macclesfield

Editors' Foreword

All the fields covered by the 6th edition of the *Scientific Tables* are again represented in this new edition with the exception of 'Infectious Diseases', the chapter on which appears separately as a supplement. The thoroughgoing revision of the remaining chapters has resulted in a number of major changes, of which the following are worthy of special mention.

The data on units of measurement and the physical constants take account of decisions and recommendations adopted by the various international commissions up to March 1969, in particular those concerned with the introduction of the International System of Units. The adoption of the unified scale of atomic weights based on the isotope carbon-12 has involved the recalculation of molecular weights throughout the book. In the physicochemical part of the book a chapter on pH standards has been added, and the data on buffer solutions have been recalculated to the pH scale of the National Bureau of Standards.

'Biochemistry' has been greatly enlarged, particularly by the inclusion of more data on nucleic acids and protein and fatty-acid synthesis as well as by the addition of a new chapter on 'Inborn Errors of Metabolism'. Throughout this section – as in the other sections – the recommendations on nomenclature made by the International Union of Pure and Applied Chemistry and the International Union of Biochemistry have been largely adhered to.

In the section on nutrition due regard has been paid to the considerable advances made in recent years in knowledge of the nutritional significance of the vitamins; and important new sources have been utilized in revising the data on the composition of foods.

Of the chapters comprising the section on 'Composition and Functions of the Body', those on the composition of the body, renal function and respiration in particular have been greatly extended. Under the heading of body fluids the subject of blood enzymes has been given much more thorough treatment, and chapters on the synovial fluid and sweat have been added.

Under body measurements the normal data of pregnancy have been completely revised, and the chapter now includes tables of weights of the organs.

The final section of the book is now that on hormones, an arrangement that has permitted the inclusion of more recent endocrinological data from this rapidly advancing field than would otherwise have been possible.

K. Diem
C. Lentner

Acknowledgments

The editors are indebted to the following for their invaluable assistance in compiling this edition of the Geigy Scientific Tables:

Dr. M. ALIAPOULOS, Peter Bent Brigham Hospital, Boston, Mass.
Prof. M. ALLGÖWER, University Dept. of Surgery, Municipal Hospital, Basle
Dr. G. BECKER, Braunschweig
Dr. S. BÖHME, Institute of Astronomical Computation, Heidelberg
Dr. C.G. VON BOROVICZÉNY, Dept. of Medicine, University of Freiburg i. Br.
Dr. L. BRAVERMAN, St.Elizabeth's Hospital, Boston, Mass.
Dr. A. BRÜGGER, Zurich
Dr. R.B. CLAYTON, Dept. of Psychiatry, Stanford University, Palo Alto
Dr. E.R. COHEN, North American Rockwell Science Center, Thousand Oaks, Calif.
Dr. R.A. COOPER, Dept. of Biochemistry, University of Leicester
Dr. D.P. DEARNALEY, Dept. of Pharmacology, University of Oxford
Dr. J.W.T. DICKERSON, Dept. of Experimental Medicine, University of Cambridge
Prof. W. FRITZ, Braunschweig
Prof. W. FURRER, Swiss Federal Institute of Technology, Zurich
Prof. MARIA-PIA GEPPERT, Dept. of Medical Statistics, University of Tübingen
Dr. H.M. GOODMAN, Harvard Medical School, Boston, Mass.
Dr. U.F. GRUBER, University Dept. of Surgery, Municipal Hospital, Basle
Dr. M.J. HERRERA, Joslin Research Laboratory, Boston, Mass.
Prof. H. HERZOG, Dept. of Respiratory Diseases, Municipal Hospital, Basle
Prof. W.H. HITZIG, Children's Hospital, Zurich
Prof. L.P. HOLLÄNDER, Blood Donor Centre of the Swiss Red Cross, Basle
J. HOPPE-BLANK, Braunschweig
Prof. W. HÜBNER, Braunschweig
Dr. F.E. HYTTEN, Reproduction and Growth Research Unit, University of Newcastle-upon-Tyne
Prof. M.J. JAEGER, Dept. of Physiology, University of Fribourg (Switzerland)
Prof. E. KALLEE, Isotope Laboratory, Dept. of Medicine, University of Tübingen
Dr. H.J. KAUFMANN, Dept. of Radiology, Children's Hospital, Basle
Dr. F. KOHLER, Dept. of Physical Chemistry, University of Vienna
Prof. H.L. KORNBERG, F.R.S., Dept. of Biochemistry, University of Leicester
Professor Sir HANS KREBS, F.R.S., Metabolic Research Laboratory, Nuffield Dept. of Clinical Medicine, Oxford
Dr. J.M. LOWENSTEIN, Graduate Dept. of Biochemistry, Brandeis University, Waltham, Mass.
Dr. PATRICIA LUND, Metabolic Research Laboratory, Nuffield Dept. of Clinical Medicine, Oxford
Dr. H. LÜTHY, University Dept. of Radiology, Municipal Hospital, Basle
Dr. C. MONTIGEL, Scientific Laboratories, J.R. Geigy S.A., Basle
Prof. D.P. MERTZ, Dept. of Medicine, University of Freiburg i. Br.
Dr. G. NAGELSCHMIDT, London
Dr. E.A. NEWSHOLME, Dept. of Biochemistry, University of Oxford
Dr. C.V. PERRIER, University Dept. of Therapeutics, Cantonal Hospital, Geneva
Prof. J.R. QUAYLE, Dept. of Microbiology, University of Sheffield
Dr. R.R. RACE, Medical Research Council, Blood Group Research Unit, London
Dr. P.R. RAGGATT, Dept. of Biochemistry, University of Oxford
Prof. S. RAUCH, Dept. of Biochemistry, Academy of Medicine, Düsseldorf
Dr. W.J. REDDY, Harvard Medical School, Boston, Mass.
Dr. CHARLOTTE RHONHEIMER, Zurich
Prof. W. RICK, Municipal Hospital, Düsseldorf
Dr. H.P. RIEDER, Dept. of Neurology, University of Basle
Dr. W. ROTH, Harvard Medical School, Boston, Mass.
Prof. G. RUHENSTROTH, Max Planck Institute of Biochemistry, Munich
Dr. R. SANGER, Medical Research Council, Blood Group Research Unit, London
Prof. H. SARRE, Dept. of Medicine, University of Freiburg i. Br.
Dr. P. SCHMID, Federal Institute of Forestry, Birmensdorf, Zurich
Dr. E. SCHMIDT and Prof. F.W. SCHMIDT, Dept. of Medicine, College of Medicine, Hanover
Dr. W. SCHOOP, Aggerter Clinic, Engelskirchen (Germany)
Dr. J. SOLOMON, Chestnut Hill, Mass.
Dr. J. STEINKE, Joslin Research Laboratory, Boston, Mass.
Prof. U. STILLE, Braunschweig
Dr. E. STREHLER, Feldbach, Zurich
Prof. H. STUDER, Dept. of Medicine, University of Berne
Dr. R. VEYRAT, Dept. of Int. Medicine, Cantonal Hospital, Geneva
Dr. I.O. WALKER, Dept. of Biochemistry, University of Oxford
E. WECHSELBERGER, Isotope Laboratory, Dept. of Medicine, University of Tübingen
Prof. H. WEICKER, Dept. of Human Genetics, University of Bonn
Dr. H.-M. WEISS, Braunschweig
Dr. ELSIE M. WIDDOWSON, Dept. of Experimental Medicine, University of Cambridge
Dr. J.R. WILLIAMSON, Dept. of Biophysics and Physical Biochemistry, The Johnson Foundation, Philadelphia, Pa.
Prof. O. WISS, F. Hoffmann-La Roche & Co., Ltd., Basle
Dr. L.I. WOOLF, Faculty of Medicine, University of British Columbia, Vancouver

---

The publisher and editors wish to thank the following scientific bodies, journals and publishing houses for permission to reproduce data or illustrations (on the pages given):

Academic Press Inc., New York (757); Acta Medica Scandinavica, Stockholm (548, 549); Acta Paediatrica Scandinavica, Stockholm (549); American Dental Association, Chicago, Ill. (709); American Medical Association, Chicago, Ill. (745); American Physiological Society, Bethesda, Md. (528, 547); American Review of Respiratory Disease, New York (550); American Society for Clinical Investigation, New York (557); American Statistical Association, Washington, D.C. (53, 56, 57); Association of American Physicians, Baltimore, Md. (535); Bell Telephone Laboratories, Murray Hill, N.J. (130); The Biometric Society, Tucson, Ariz. (50, 53, *Folia medica*); Biometrika, London (47, 48, 49, 51, 52, 53); Birkhäuser Verlag, Basle (131, *Folia medica*); British Medical Bulletin, London (734); J. & A. Churchill Ltd., London (678, 715); Columbia University Press, New York (64, 65, 69); Federation of American Societies for Experimental Biology, Bethesda, Md. (541); Charles Griffin & Co. Ltd., London (66); Institute of Mathematical Statistics, Hayward, Calif. (53, 58, 129, 130); International Civil Aviation Organization, Montreal (252–254); The Lancet, London (534, 736); Lea & Febiger, Philadelphia, Pa. (565, 621); Smith-Corona Marchant, Inc., Oakland, Calif. (24); McGraw-Hill Book Company, New York (45, 46, 256); Masson & Cie, Editeurs, Paris (249); Methuen & Co. Ltd., London (686); The C.V. Mosby Company, St.Louis, Mo. (618); National Academy of Sciences, Washington, D.C. (256); National Research Council, Washington, D.C. (256); National Bureau of Standards, Washington, D.C. (29, 31, 64, 65, 69); Oliver & Boyd Ltd., Edinburgh (31, 54, 55, 616); Pathological Society of Great Britain and Ireland, London (616); Periodica, Copenhagen (748); Pitman Medical Publishing Company Limited, London (749); The Radiological Society of North America, Inc., New York (708); Royal College of Obstetricians and Gynaecologists, London (754); Schwabe & Co., Verlag, Basle (529); Skandinavisk Aktuarietidskrift, Stocksund, Sweden (36, 37); Smithsonian Institution Press, Washington, D.C. (256–258); E. & F.N. Spon Limited, London (18–20, 23, 284); Springer-Verlag, Berlin, Heidelberg, New York (40, 41, 532, 533, 534, 535, 546, 548, 752); Stichting Mathematisch Centrum, Amsterdam (124–126); Georg Thieme Verlag, Stuttgart (292, 293, 707, *Folia medica*); The University of Chicago Press, Chicago, Ill. (528); Urban & Schwarzenberg, Munich (484); Virginia Polytechnic Institute, Blacksburg, Va. (50); World Health Organization, Geneva (759–764); John Wiley & Sons, Inc., New York (279, 556); The Williams & Wilkins Company, Baltimore, Md. (547, 562, 569).

Contents

Mathematics and statistics

Constants ... 9
Logarithms ... 10
Reciprocals, powers and roots ... 18
Binomial coefficients ... 25
Factorials ... 26
Statistical tables ... 28
Mathematical symbols, definitions and formulae ... 132
Statistical methods
  Contents ... 145
  Introduction ... 146
  Index ... 197

Physics

Symbols of units ... 199
Mechanical and thermal units ... 200
Electrical and magnetic units ... 215
Radioactivity and radiation dosimetry ... 217
Electromagnetic radiation and light units ... 222
Acoustical units ... 224
Unit of amount of substance ... 226
Physical constants ... 228

Physical chemistry

Elements
  Periodic system ... 231
  Alphabetical tables ... 232
  Properties, abundance, isotopes ... 234
  Electronic configurations ... 249
  Multiples of atomic weights ... 250
Chemical conversion factors ... 251
ICAO normal atmosphere ... 252
Mercury barometer correction ... 255
Saturation pressure of water vapour ... 256
Vapour pressure and boiling point of water ... 257
Reduction of gas volumes ... 259
Aqueous solutions
  Introduction ... 270
  Calculation of freezing-point depression and osmotic pressure ... 272
  Calculation of salt and glucose concentrations ... 273
  Conversion factors for electrolytes ... 274
  Decinormal solutions ... 277
pH standards ... 278
Buffer solutions ... 280
Acid–base indicators ... 283
Flame photometry lines ... 284
Radioactive nuclides
  Principles ... 285
  Diagnostic uses ... 287
  Therapeutic uses ... 290
  Characteristics ... 292
  Decay tables ... 294

Biochemistry

Contents ... 307
Constituents of living matter ... 308
Metabolism ... 387
Inborn errors of metabolism ... 446

Nutrition

Vitamins
  Vitamin A ... 457
  Vitamin D ... 461
  Vitamin E ... 464
  Vitamin K ... 467
  Thiamine ... 469
  Riboflavin ... 471
  Vitamin B_6 ... 473
  Nicotinic acid ... 476
  Folic acid group ... 478
  Vitamin B_{12} group ... 482
  Biotin ... 486
  Pantothenic acid ... 487
  Ascorbic acid ... 489
  Vitaminoids ... 491
Nutritional standards ... 493
Foods
  Principal nutrients and minerals ... 498
  Amino acids ... 516

Composition and functions of the body

Chemical composition of the body ... 517
Water and electrolyte balance ... 523
Renal function values ... 531
Body surface area ... 537
Basal metabolism ... 539
Respiration ... 541
Blood pressure ... 553
Blood volume ... 554

Body fluids

Blood
  Physicochemical data ... 557
  Inorganic substances ... 561
  Blood gases ... 568
  Nitrogenous substances ... 572
  Proteins ... 579
  Enzymes ... 584
  Lipids ... 600
  Carbohydrates ... 604
  Non-nitrogenous metabolites ... 606
  Vitamins ... 609
Blood cells
  Erythroblasts ... 612
  Reticulocytes ... 612
  Erythrocytes ... 613
  Leucocytes ... 618
  Thrombocytes ... 620
  Bone marrow ... 621
Blood coagulation ... 622
Blood groups ... 626
Serum groups ... 634
Cerebrospinal fluid ... 635
Synovial fluid ... 640
Saliva ... 643
Gastric juice ... 647
Pancreatic juice ... 651
Bile ... 653
Intestinal juice ... 656
Faeces ... 657
Urine
  Physicochemical data ... 661
  Inorganic substances ... 662
  Nitrogenous substances ... 665

Contents

Enzymes ... 672
Carbohydrates ... 673
Non-nitrogenous metabolites ... 674
Vitamins ... 676
Sediments ... 677
Sweat ... 679
Semen ... 682
Spermatozoa ... 686
Breast milk ... 687

Body measurements

Pregnancy ... 690
Normal measurements during growth ... 692
Appearance of secondary ossification centres ... 706
Development of the teeth ... 709
Weights of the organs ... 710
Average and desirable weights of adults ... 711

Hormones

Gonadotropins of the anterior pituitary ... 713
Chorionic gonadotropin ... 715
Corticotropin ... 716
Thyrotropin ... 718
Prolactin ... 718
Growth hormone ... 719
Placental lactogen ... 721
Melanotropin ... 721
Oxytocin and vasopressin ... 722
Hypothalamic pituitary-regulating factors ... 725
Thyroid hormones ... 725
Parathyroid hormone ... 728
Calcitonin ... 729
Thymus hormone ... 730
Hormones of the pineal gland ... 730
Catecholamines ... 730
Insulin ... 734
Glucagon ... 737
Hormones of the gastrointestinal tract ... 739
Erythropoietin ... 740
Renin-angiotensin system ... 740
Plasma kinins ... 742
Corticosteroids ... 742
Androgens ... 751
Progesterone ... 753
Oestrogens ... 755
Function of the sex hormones ... 758

International biological standards and reference preparations ... 759

Index ... 765

Addenda and errata ... 809

Folia medica Geigy ... (inside back cover)

Notes for the guidance of users

Apart from the main contents (above) and general index (pages 765 et seq.) the user will find the contents of the chapter on 'Statistical Methods' on page 145, that of the chapters on 'Constituents of Living Matter' and 'Metabolism' on page 307; in addition there is a separate detailed index to the chapter on 'Statistical Methods' on pages 197–198.

Zero values are indicated by the figure 0 throughout the book. A dash (–) signifies that the value is unknown, and this sign should on no account be interpreted as a zero value.

As a rule, the meanings of symbols and abbreviations are given where they first occur. For units of measurement an alphabetical list is available on page 199.

In the numerical tables, a point over the last figure (or figures) indicates a recurring figure (or figures), thus

$$1.\dot{6} = 1.666666\ldots$$
$$1.65\dot{2}7\dot{8} = 1.65278278278\ldots$$

In general the number of places given has been dictated by the space available. The user should abstract as many as he needs and round off accordingly.

Exact values have been distinguished from rounded-off values by printing the last figure in **bold-face** type. Thus, 1.1257 would be the rounded-off value of, say, 1.1257354..., while 1.125**7** is an exact number. This notation is used in particular for the arbitrarily defined values of constants.

When they have been calculated according to statistical procedures (usually as mean value ± 2 standard deviations), normal ranges are given under the heading '95% range' (note that this practice differs from that adopted in previous editions).

For obvious reasons we have had to restrict bibliographical references to a representative selection of recently published original papers and reviews. In fields where research activity is currently high a rather fuller bibliography is given. The abbreviations used in the literature references are those recommended by the UNESCO and WHO (*World Medical Periodicals*, World Medical Association, New York, 1961).

Additional copies of the *Folia medica Geigy* in the inside back cover of this book may be obtained by application to J.R. Geigy S.A., CH-4000 Basle 18, Switzerland.

Mathematical constants

Bernoulli numbers	
n	B_n
1	1/ 6
2	1/ 30
3	1/ 42
4	1/ 30
5	5/ 66
6	691/2730
7	7/ 6
8	3617/ 510
9	43867/ 798
10	1 74611/ 330
11	8 54513/ 138
12	2363 64091/2730
13	85 53103/ 6

Euler numbers	
n	E_n
1	1
2	5
3	61
4	1385
5	50521
6	27 02765
7	1993 60981
8	1 93915 12145
9	240 48796 75441
10	37037 11882 37525
11	69 34887 43931 37901
12	15514 53416 35570 86905
13	40 87072 50929 31238 92361

Prime numbers < *100*	
Number	$\log_{10}$ (mantissa)
2	30102 99956 63981 19521
3	47712 12547 19662 43730
5	69897 00043 36018 80479
7	84509 80400 14256 83071
11	04139 26851 58225 04075
13	11394 33523 06836 76921
17	23044 89213 78273 92854
19	27875 36009 52828 96154
23	36172 78360 17592 87887
29	46239 79978 98956 08733
31	49136 16938 34272 67967
37	56820 17240 66994 99681
41	61278 38567 19735 49451
43	63346 84555 79586 52641
47	67209 78579 35717 46441
53	72427 58696 00789 04563
59	77085 20116 42144 19026
61	78532 98350 10767 03389
67	82607 48027 00826 43415
71	85125 83487 19075 28609
73	86332 28601 20455 90107
79	89762 70912 90441 42799
83	91907 80923 76073 90383
89	94939 00066 44912 78472
97	98677 17342 66244 85178

Constants

Constant	Value	$\log_{10}$
π	3.14159 26535 89793 23846	0.49714 98726 94133 85435
π^2	9.86960 44010 89358 61883	0.99429 97453 88267 70870
$(2\pi)^{-1/2}$	0.39894 22804 01432 67794	0.60091 00658 20942 47522–1
e	2.71828 18284 59045 23536	= M
$M = \log_{10} e = \lg e$	0.43429 44819 03251 82765	
$1/M = \log_e 10 = \ln 10$	2.30258 50929 94045 68402	
γ (EULER's constant)	0.57721 56649 01532 86061	0.76133 81087 83167 61054–1

Greek alphabet

Greek character		Greek name	Roman equivalent
Α α	*Α α*	alpha	A a
Β β	*Β β*	beta	B b
Γ γ	*Γ γ*	gamma	G g
Δ δ	*Δ δ*	delta	D d
Ε ε, ϵ	*Ε ε, ϵ*	epsilon	Ĕ ĕ
Ζ ζ	*Ζ ζ*	zeta	Z z
Η η	*Η η*	eta	Ē ē
Θ ϑ, θ	*Θ ϑ, θ*	theta	Th th
Ι ι	*Ι ι*	iota	I i
Κ ϰ, κ	*Κ ϰ, κ*	kappa	K k
Λ λ	*Λ λ*	lambda	L l
Μ μ	*Μ μ*	mu	M m
Ν ν	*Ν ν*	nu	N n
Ξ ξ	*Ξ ξ*	xi	X x
Ο ο	*Ο ο*	omicron	Ŏ ŏ
Π π, ϖ	*Π π, ϖ*	pi	P p
Ρ ρ	*Ρ ϱ*	rho	R r
Σ σ, ς	*Σ σ, ς*	sigma	S s
Τ τ	*Τ τ*	tau	T t
Υ υ	*Υ υ*	upsilon	Y y
Φ φ, ϕ	*Φ φ, ϕ*	phi	Ph ph
Χ χ	*Χ χ*	chi	Ch ch
Ψ ψ	*Ψ ψ*	psi	Ps ps
Ω ω	*Ω ω*	omega	Ō ō

Prefixes and symbols for decimal multiples and submultiples of units[1]

Power of ten	Prefix	Symbol
10^{12}	tera	T
10^{9}	giga	G
10^{6}	mega	M
10^{3}	kilo	k
10^{2}	hecto	h
10^{1}	deca*	da
10^{-1}	deci	d
10^{-2}	centi	c
10^{-3}	milli	m
10^{-6}	micro	μ
10^{-9}	nano	n
10^{-12}	pico	p
10^{-15}	femto	f
10^{-18}	atto	a

* Also 'deka'.

[1] Conférence générale des Poids et Mesures, *Comptes rendus des séances de la 11e Conférence générale des Poids et Mesures*, Paris 1960, Gauthier-Villars, Paris, 1961, page 87; *Comptes rendus des séances de la 12e Conférence générale des Poids et Mesures*, Paris 1964, Gauthier-Villars, Paris, 1964, page 94.

	log x										Proportional parts								
x	0	1	2	3	4	5	6	7	8	9	1	2	3	4	5	6	7	8	9
100	0000	0004	0009	0013	0017	0022	0026	0030	0035	0039	0	1	1	2	2	3	3	3	4
101	0043	0048	0052	0056	0060	0065	0069	0073	0077	0082	0	1	1	2	2	3	3	3	4
102	0086	0090	0095	0099	0103	0107	0111	0116	0120	0124	0	1	1	2	2	3	3	3	4
103	0128	0133	0137	0141	0145	0149	0154	0158	0162	0166	0	1	1	2	2	3	3	3	4
104	0170	0175	0179	0183	0187	0191	0195	0199	0204	0208	0	1	1	2	2	2	3	3	4
105	0212	0216	0220	0224	0228	0233	0237	0241	0245	0249	0	1	1	2	2	2	3	3	4
106	0253	0257	0261	0265	0269	0273	0278	0282	0286	0290	0	1	1	2	2	2	3	3	4
107	0294	0298	0302	0306	0310	0314	0318	0322	0326	0330	0	1	1	2	2	2	3	3	4
108	0334	0338	0342	0346	0350	0354	0358	0362	0366	0370	0	1	1	2	2	2	3	3	4
109	0374	0378	0382	0386	0390	0394	0398	0402	0406	0410	0	1	1	2	2	2	3	3	4
↓ **10**	0000	0043	0086	0128	0170	0212	0253	0294	0334	0374	4	8	12	17	21	25	29	33	37
11	0414	0453	0492	0531	0569	0607	0645	0682	0719	0755	4	8	11	15	19	23	26	30	34
12	0792	0828	0864	0899	0934	0969	1004	1038	1072	1106	3	7	10	14	17	21	24	28	31
13	1139	1173	1206	1239	1271	1303	1335	1367	1399	1430	3	6	10	13	16	19	23	26	29
14	1461	1492	1523	1553	1584	1614	1644	1673	1703	1732	3	6	9	12	15	18	21	24	27
15	1761	1790	1818	1847	1875	1903	1931	1959	1987	2014	3	6	8	11	14	17	20	22	25
16	2041	2068	2095	2122	2148	2175	2201	2227	2253	2279	3	5	8	11	13	16	18	21	24
17	2304	2330	2355	2380	2405	2430	2455	2480	2504	2529	2	5	7	10	12	15	17	20	22
18	2553	2577	2601	2625	2648	2672	2695	2718	2742	2765	2	5	7	9	12	14	16	19	21
19	2788	2810	2833	2856	2878	2900	2923	2945	2967	2989	2	4	7	9	11	13	16	18	20
20	3010	3032	3054	3075	3096	3118	3139	3160	3181	3201	2	4	6	8	11	13	15	17	19
21	3222	3243	3263	3284	3304	3324	3345	3365	3385	3404	2	4	6	8	10	12	14	16	18
22	3424	3444	3464	3483	3502	3522	3541	3560	3579	3598	2	4	6	8	10	12	14	15	17
23	3617	3636	3655	3674	3692	3711	3729	3747	3766	3784	2	4	6	7	9	11	13	15	17
24	3802	3820	3838	3856	3874	3892	3909	3927	3945	3962	2	4	5	7	9	11	12	14	16
25	3979	3997	4014	4031	4048	4065	4082	4099	4116	4133	2	3	5	7	9	10	12	14	15
26	4150	4166	4183	4200	4216	4232	4249	4265	4281	4298	2	3	5	7	8	10	11	13	15
27	4314	4330	4346	4362	4378	4393	4409	4425	4440	4456	2	3	5	6	8	9	11	13	14
28	4472	4487	4502	4518	4533	4548	4564	4579	4594	4609	2	3	5	6	8	9	11	12	14
29	4624	4639	4654	4669	4683	4698	4713	4728	4742	4757	1	3	4	6	7	9	10	12	13
30	4771	4786	4800	4814	4829	4843	4857	4871	4886	4900	1	3	4	6	7	9	10	11	13
31	4914	4928	4942	4955	4969	4983	4997	5011	5024	5038	1	3	4	6	7	8	10	11	12
32	5051	5065	5079	5092	5105	5119	5132	5145	5159	5172	1	3	4	5	7	8	9	11	12
33	5185	5198	5211	5224	5237	5250	5263	5276	5289	5302	1	3	4	5	6	8	9	10	12
34	5315	5328	5340	5353	5366	5378	5391	5403	5416	5428	1	3	4	5	6	8	9	10	11
35	5441	5453	5465	5478	5490	5502	5514	5527	5539	5551	1	2	4	5	6	7	9	10	11
36	5563	5575	5587	5599	5611	5623	5635	5647	5658	5670	1	2	4	5	6	7	8	10	11
37	5682	5694	5705	5717	5729	5740	5752	5763	5775	5786	1	2	3	5	6	7	8	9	10
38	5798	5809	5821	5832	5843	5855	5866	5877	5888	5899	1	2	3	5	6	7	8	9	10
39	5911	5922	5933	5944	5955	5966	5977	5988	5999	6010	1	2	3	4	5	7	8	9	10
40	6021	6031	6042	6053	6064	6075	6085	6096	6107	6117	1	2	3	4	5	6	8	9	10
41	6128	6138	6149	6160	6170	6180	6191	6201	6212	6222	1	2	3	4	5	6	7	8	9
42	6232	6243	6253	6263	6274	6284	6294	6304	6314	6325	1	2	3	4	5	6	7	8	9
43	6335	6345	6355	6365	6375	6385	6395	6405	6415	6425	1	2	3	4	5	6	7	8	9
44	6435	6444	6454	6464	6474	6484	6493	6503	6513	6522	1	2	3	4	5	6	7	8	9
45	6532	6542	6551	6561	6571	6580	6590	6599	6609	6618	1	2	3	4	5	6	7	8	9
46	6628	6637	6646	6656	6665	6675	6684	6693	6702	6712	1	2	3	4	5	6	7	7	8
47	6721	6730	6739	6749	6758	6767	6776	6785	6794	6803	1	2	3	4	5	5	6	7	8
48	6812	6821	6830	6839	6848	6857	6866	6875	6884	6893	1	2	3	4	4	5	6	7	8
49	6902	6911	6920	6928	6937	6946	6955	6964	6972	6981	1	2	3	4	4	5	6	7	8
50	6990	6998	7007	7016	7024	7033	7042	7050	7059	7067	1	2	3	3	4	5	6	7	8
51	7076	7084	7093	7101	7110	7118	7126	7135	7143	7152	1	2	3	3	4	5	6	7	8
52	7160	7168	7177	7185	7193	7202	7210	7218	7226	7235	1	2	2	3	4	5	6	7	7
53	7243	7251	7259	7267	7275	7284	7292	7300	7308	7316	1	2	2	3	4	5	6	6	7
54	7324	7332	7340	7348	7356	7364	7372	7380	7388	7396	1	2	2	3	4	5	6	6	7
55	7404	7412	7419	7427	7435	7443	7451	7459	7466	7474	1	2	2	3	4	5	5	6	7
56	7482	7490	7497	7505	7513	7520	7528	7536	7543	7551	1	2	2	3	4	5	5	6	7
57	7559	7566	7574	7582	7589	7597	7604	7612	7619	7627	1	2	2	3	4	5	5	6	7
58	7634	7642	7649	7657	7664	7672	7679	7686	7694	7701	1	1	2	3	4	4	5	6	7
59	7709	7716	7723	7731	7738	7745	7752	7760	7767	7774	1	1	2	3	4	4	5	6	7
60	7782	7789	7796	7803	7810	7818	7825	7832	7839	7846	1	1	2	3	4	4	5	6	6
61	7853	7860	7868	7875	7882	7889	7896	7903	7910	7917	1	1	2	3	4	4	5	6	6
62	7924	7931	7938	7945	7952	7959	7966	7973	7980	7987	1	1	2	3	3	4	5	6	6
63	7993	8000	8007	8014	8021	8028	8035	8041	8048	8055	1	1	2	3	3	4	5	5	6
64	8062	8069	8075	8082	8089	8096	8102	8109	8116	8122	1	1	2	3	3	4	5	5	6
65	8129	8136	8142	8149	8156	8162	8169	8176	8182	8189	1	1	2	3	3	4	5	5	6
66	8195	8202	8209	8215	8222	8228	8235	8241	8248	8254	1	1	2	3	3	4	5	5	6
67	8261	8267	8274	8280	8287	8293	8299	8306	8312	8319	1	1	2	3	3	4	5	5	6
68	8325	8331	8338	8344	8351	8357	8363	8370	8376	8382	1	1	2	3	3	4	4	5	6
69	8388	8395	8401	8407	8414	8420	8426	8432	8439	8445	1	1	2	2	3	4	4	5	6
70	8451	8457	8463	8470	8476	8482	8488	8494	8500	8506	1	1	2	2	3	4	4	5	6
71	8513	8519	8525	8531	8537	8543	8549	8555	8561	8567	1	1	2	2	3	4	4	5	5
72	8573	8579	8585	8591	8597	8603	8609	8615	8621	8627	1	1	2	2	3	4	4	5	5
73	8633	8639	8645	8651	8657	8663	8669	8675	8681	8686	1	1	2	2	3	4	4	5	5
74	8692	8698	8704	8710	8716	8722	8727	8733	8739	8745	1	1	2	2	3	4	4	5	5
75	8751	8756	8762	8768	8774	8779	8785	8791	8797	8802	1	1	2	2	3	3	4	5	5
76	8808	8814	8820	8825	8831	8837	8842	8848	8854	8859	1	1	2	2	3	3	4	5	5
77	8865	8871	8876	8882	8887	8893	8899	8904	8910	8915	1	1	2	2	3	3	4	4	5
78	8921	8927	8932	8938	8943	8949	8954	8960	8965	8971	1	1	2	2	3	3	4	4	5
79	8976	8982	8987	8993	8998	9004	9009	9015	9020	9025	1	1	2	2	3	3	4	4	5
80	9031	9036	9042	9047	9053	9058	9063	9069	9074	9079	1	1	2	2	3	3	4	4	5
81	9085	9090	9096	9101	9106	9112	9117	9122	9128	9133	1	1	2	2	3	3	4	4	5
82	9138	9143	9149	9154	9159	9165	9170	9175	9180	9186	1	1	2	2	3	3	4	4	5
83	9191	9196	9201	9206	9212	9217	9222	9227	9232	9238	1	1	2	2	3	3	4	4	5
84	9243	9248	9253	9258	9263	9269	9274	9279	9284	9289	1	1	2	2	3	3	4	4	5
85	9294	9299	9304	9309	9315	9320	9325	9330	9335	9340	1	1	2	2	3	3	4	4	5
86	9345	9350	9355	9360	9365	9370	9375	9380	9385	9390	1	1	2	2	3	3	4	4	5
87	9395	9400	9405	9410	9415	9420	9425	9430	9435	9440	0	1	1	2	2	3	3	4	4
88	9445	9450	9455	9460	9465	9469	9474	9479	9484	9489	0	1	1	2	2	3	3	4	4
89	9494	9499	9504	9509	9513	9518	9523	9528	9533	9538	0	1	1	2	2	3	3	4	4
90	9542	9547	9552	9557	9562	9566	9571	9576	9581	9586	0	1	1	2	2	3	3	4	4
91	9590	9595	9600	9605	9609	9614	9619	9624	9628	9633	0	1	1	2	2	3	3	4	4
92	9638	9643	9647	9652	9657	9661	9666	9671	9675	9680	0	1	1	2	2	3	3	4	4
93	9685	9689	9694	9699	9703	9708	9713	9717	9722	9727	0	1	1	2	2	3	3	4	4
94	9731	9736	9741	9745	9750	9754	9759	9763	9768	9773	0	1	1	2	2	3	3	4	4
95	9777	9782	9786	9791	9795	9800	9805	9809	9814	9818	0	1	1	2	2	3	3	4	4
96	9823	9827	9832	9836	9841	9845	9850	9854	9859	9863	0	1	1	2	2	3	3	4	4
97	9868	9872	9877	9881	9886	9890	9894	9899	9903	9908	0	1	1	2	2	3	3	4	4
98	9912	9917	9921	9926	9930	9934	9939	9943	9948	9952	0	1	1	2	2	3	3	4	4
99	9956	9961	9965	9969	9974	9978	9983	9987	9991	9996	0	1	1	2	2	3	3	3	4

	x										Proportional parts								
log x	0	1	2	3	4	5	6	7	8	9	1	2	3	4	5	6	7	8	9
.00	1000	1002	1005	1007	1009	1012	1014	1016	1019	1021	0	0	1	1	1	1	2	2	2
.01	1023	1026	1028	1030	1033	1035	1038	1040	1042	1045	0	0	1	1	1	1	2	2	2
.02	1047	1050	1052	1054	1057	1059	1062	1064	1067	1069	0	0	1	1	1	1	2	2	2
.03	1072	1074	1076	1079	1081	1084	1086	1089	1091	1094	0	0	1	1	1	1	2	2	2
.04	1096	1099	1102	1104	1107	1109	1112	1114	1117	1119	0	1	1	1	1	2	2	2	2
.05	1122	1125	1127	1130	1132	1135	1138	1140	1143	1146	0	1	1	1	1	2	2	2	2
.06	1148	1151	1153	1156	1159	1161	1164	1167	1169	1172	0	1	1	1	1	2	2	2	2
.07	1175	1178	1180	1183	1186	1189	1191	1194	1197	1199	0	1	1	1	1	2	2	2	2
.08	1202	1205	1208	1211	1213	1216	1219	1222	1225	1227	0	1	1	1	1	2	2	2	3
.09	1230	1233	1236	1239	1242	1245	1247	1250	1253	1256	0	1	1	1	1	2	2	2	3
.10	1259	1262	1265	1268	1271	1274	1276	1279	1282	1285	0	1	1	1	1	2	2	2	3
.11	1288	1291	1294	1297	1300	1303	1306	1309	1312	1315	0	1	1	1	2	2	2	2	3
.12	1318	1321	1324	1327	1330	1334	1337	1340	1343	1346	0	1	1	1	2	2	2	2	3
.13	1349	1352	1355	1358	1361	1365	1368	1371	1374	1377	0	1	1	1	2	2	2	3	3
.14	1380	1384	1387	1390	1393	1396	1400	1403	1406	1409	0	1	1	1	2	2	2	3	3
.15	1413	1416	1419	1422	1426	1429	1432	1435	1439	1442	0	1	1	1	2	2	2	3	3
.16	1445	1449	1452	1455	1459	1462	1466	1469	1472	1476	0	1	1	1	2	2	2	3	3
.17	1479	1483	1486	1489	1493	1496	1500	1503	1507	1510	0	1	1	1	2	2	2	3	3
.18	1514	1517	1521	1524	1528	1531	1535	1538	1542	1545	0	1	1	1	2	2	2	3	3
.19	1549	1552	1556	1560	1563	1567	1570	1574	1578	1581	0	1	1	1	2	2	3	3	3
.20	1585	1589	1592	1596	1600	1603	1607	1611	1614	1618	0	1	1	1	2	2	3	3	3
.21	1622	1626	1629	1633	1637	1641	1644	1648	1652	1656	0	1	1	2	2	2	3	3	3
.22	1660	1663	1667	1671	1675	1679	1683	1687	1690	1694	0	1	1	2	2	2	3	3	3
.23	1698	1702	1706	1710	1714	1718	1722	1726	1730	1734	0	1	1	2	2	2	3	3	4
.24	1738	1742	1746	1750	1754	1758	1762	1766	1770	1774	0	1	1	2	2	2	3	3	4
.25	1778	1782	1786	1791	1795	1799	1803	1807	1811	1816	0	1	1	2	2	2	3	3	4
.26	1820	1824	1828	1832	1837	1841	1845	1849	1854	1858	0	1	1	2	2	3	3	3	4
.27	1862	1866	1871	1875	1879	1884	1888	1892	1897	1901	0	1	1	2	2	3	3	3	4
.28	1905	1910	1914	1919	1923	1928	1932	1936	1941	1945	0	1	1	2	2	3	3	4	4
.29	1950	1954	1959	1963	1968	1972	1977	1982	1986	1991	0	1	1	2	2	3	3	4	4
.30	1995	2000	2004	2009	2014	2018	2023	2028	2032	2037	0	1	1	2	2	3	3	4	4
.31	2042	2046	2051	2056	2061	2065	2070	2075	2080	2084	0	1	1	2	2	3	3	4	4
.32	2089	2094	2099	2104	2109	2113	2118	2123	2128	2133	0	1	1	2	2	3	3	4	4
.33	2138	2143	2148	2153	2158	2163	2168	2173	2178	2183	0	1	1	2	2	3	3	4	4
.34	2188	2193	2198	2203	2208	2213	2218	2223	2228	2234	1	1	2	2	3	3	4	4	5
.35	2239	2244	2249	2254	2259	2265	2270	2275	2280	2286	1	1	2	2	3	3	4	4	5
.36	2291	2296	2301	2307	2312	2317	2323	2328	2333	2339	1	1	2	2	3	3	4	4	5
.37	2344	2350	2355	2360	2366	2371	2377	2382	2388	2393	1	1	2	2	3	3	4	4	5
.38	2399	2404	2410	2415	2421	2427	2432	2438	2443	2449	1	1	2	2	3	3	4	4	5
.39	2455	2460	2466	2472	2477	2483	2489	2495	2500	2506	1	1	2	2	3	3	4	5	5
.40	2512	2518	2523	2529	2535	2541	2547	2553	2559	2564	1	1	2	2	3	4	4	5	5
.41	2570	2576	2582	2588	2594	2600	2606	2612	2618	2624	1	1	2	2	3	4	4	5	5
.42	2630	2636	2642	2649	2655	2661	2667	2673	2679	2685	1	1	2	2	3	4	4	5	6
.43	2692	2698	2704	2710	2716	2723	2729	2735	2742	2748	1	1	2	3	3	4	4	5	6
.44	2754	2761	2767	2773	2780	2786	2793	2799	2805	2812	1	1	2	3	3	4	4	5	6
.45	2818	2825	2831	2838	2844	2851	2858	2864	2871	2877	1	1	2	3	3	4	5	5	6
.46	2884	2891	2897	2904	2911	2917	2924	2931	2938	2944	1	1	2	3	3	4	5	5	6
.47	2951	2958	2965	2972	2979	2985	2992	2999	3006	3013	1	1	2	3	3	4	5	5	6
.48	3020	3027	3034	3041	3048	3055	3062	3069	3076	3083	1	1	2	3	4	4	5	6	6
.49	3090	3097	3105	3112	3119	3126	3133	3141	3148	3155	1	1	2	3	4	4	5	6	6
.50	3162	3170	3177	3184	3192	3199	3206	3214	3221	3228	1	1	2	3	4	4	5	6	7
.51	3236	3243	3251	3258	3266	3273	3281	3289	3296	3304	1	2	2	3	4	5	5	6	7
.52	3311	3319	3327	3334	3342	3350	3357	3365	3373	3381	1	2	2	3	4	5	5	6	7
.53	3388	3396	3404	3412	3420	3428	3436	3443	3451	3459	1	2	2	3	4	5	6	6	7
.54	3467	3475	3483	3491	3499	3508	3516	3524	3532	3540	1	2	2	3	4	5	6	6	7
.55	3548	3556	3565	3573	3581	3589	3597	3606	3614	3622	1	2	2	3	4	5	6	7	7
.56	3631	3639	3648	3656	3664	3673	3681	3690	3698	3707	1	2	3	3	4	5	6	7	8
.57	3715	3724	3733	3741	3750	3758	3767	3776	3784	3793	1	2	3	3	4	5	6	7	8
.58	3802	3811	3819	3828	3837	3846	3855	3864	3873	3882	1	2	3	4	4	5	6	7	8
.59	3890	3899	3908	3917	3926	3936	3945	3954	3963	3972	1	2	3	4	5	5	6	7	8
.60	3981	3990	3999	4009	4018	4027	4036	4046	4055	4064	1	2	3	4	5	6	6	7	8
.61	4074	4083	4093	4102	4111	4121	4130	4140	4150	4159	1	2	3	4	5	6	7	8	9
.62	4169	4178	4188	4198	4207	4217	4227	4236	4246	4256	1	2	3	4	5	6	7	8	9
.63	4266	4276	4285	4295	4305	4315	4325	4335	4345	4355	1	2	3	4	5	6	7	8	9
.64	4365	4375	4385	4395	4406	4416	4426	4436	4446	4457	1	2	3	4	5	6	7	8	9
.65	4467	4477	4487	4498	4508	4519	4529	4539	4550	4560	1	2	3	4	5	6	7	8	9
.66	4571	4581	4592	4603	4613	4624	4634	4645	4656	4667	1	2	3	4	5	6	7	9	10
.67	4677	4688	4699	4710	4721	4732	4742	4753	4764	4775	1	2	3	4	5	7	8	9	10
.68	4786	4797	4808	4819	4831	4842	4853	4864	4875	4887	1	2	3	4	6	7	8	9	10
.69	4898	4909	4920	4932	4943	4955	4966	4977	4989	5000	1	2	3	5	6	7	8	9	10
.70	5012	5023	5035	5047	5058	5070	5082	5093	5105	5117	1	2	4	5	6	7	8	9	11
.71	5129	5140	5152	5164	5176	5188	5200	5212	5224	5236	1	2	4	5	6	7	8	10	11
.72	5248	5260	5272	5284	5297	5309	5321	5333	5346	5358	1	2	4	5	6	7	9	10	11
.73	5370	5383	5395	5408	5420	5433	5445	5458	5470	5483	1	3	4	5	6	8	9	10	11
.74	5495	5508	5521	5534	5546	5559	5572	5585	5598	5610	1	3	4	5	6	8	9	10	12
.75	5623	5636	5649	5662	5675	5689	5702	5715	5728	5741	1	3	4	5	7	8	9	10	12
.76	5754	5768	5781	5794	5808	5821	5834	5848	5861	5875	1	3	4	5	7	8	9	11	12
.77	5888	5902	5916	5929	5943	5957	5970	5984	5998	6012	1	3	4	5	7	8	10	11	12
.78	6026	6039	6053	6067	6081	6095	6109	6124	6138	6152	1	3	4	6	7	8	10	11	13
.79	6166	6180	6194	6209	6223	6237	6252	6266	6281	6295	1	3	4	6	7	9	10	11	13
.80	6310	6324	6339	6353	6368	6383	6397	6412	6427	6442	1	3	4	6	7	9	10	12	13
.81	6457	6471	6486	6501	6516	6531	6546	6561	6577	6592	2	3	5	6	8	9	11	12	14
.82	6607	6622	6637	6653	6668	6683	6699	6714	6730	6745	2	3	5	6	8	9	11	12	14
.83	6761	6776	6792	6808	6823	6839	6855	6871	6887	6902	2	3	5	6	8	9	11	13	14
.84	6918	6934	6950	6966	6982	6998	7015	7031	7047	7063	2	3	5	6	8	10	11	13	15
.85	7079	7096	7112	7129	7145	7161	7178	7194	7211	7228	2	3	5	7	8	10	12	13	15
.86	7244	7261	7278	7295	7311	7328	7345	7362	7379	7396	2	3	5	7	8	10	12	13	15
.87	7413	7430	7447	7464	7482	7499	7516	7534	7551	7568	2	3	5	7	9	10	12	14	16
.88	7586	7603	7621	7638	7656	7674	7691	7709	7727	7745	2	4	5	7	9	11	12	14	16
.89	7762	7780	7798	7816	7834	7852	7870	7889	7907	7925	2	4	5	7	9	11	13	14	16
.90	7943	7962	7980	7998	8017	8035	8054	8072	8091	8110	2	4	6	7	9	11	13	15	17
.91	8128	8147	8166	8185	8204	8222	8241	8260	8279	8299	2	4	6	8	9	11	13	15	17
.92	8318	8337	8356	8375	8395	8414	8433	8453	8472	8492	2	4	6	8	10	12	14	15	17
.93	8511	8531	8551	8570	8590	8610	8630	8650	8670	8690	2	4	6	8	10	12	14	16	18
.94	8710	8730	8750	8770	8790	8810	8831	8851	8872	8892	2	4	6	8	10	12	14	16	18
.95	8913	8933	8954	8974	8995	9016	9036	9057	9078	9099	2	4	6	8	10	12	15	17	19
.96	9120	9141	9162	9183	9204	9226	9247	9268	9290	9311	2	4	6	8	11	13	15	17	19
.97	9333	9354	9376	9397	9419	9441	9462	9484	9506	9528	2	4	7	9	11	13	15	17	20
.98	9550	9572	9594	9616	9638	9661	9683	9705	9727	9750	2	4	7	9	11	13	16	18	20
.99	9772	9795	9817	9840	9863	9886	9908	9931	9954	9977	2	5	7	9	11	14	16	18	20

x	0.000	0.001	0.002	0.003	0.004	0.005	0.006	0.007	0.008	0.009
0.000	−∞	−6.90776	−6.21461	−5.80914	−5.52146	−5.29832	−5.11600	−4.96185	−4.82831	−4.71053
010	−4.60517	−4.50986	−4.42285	−4.34281	−4.26870	−4.19971	−4.13517	−4.07454	−4.01738	−3.96332
020	−3.91202	−3.86323	−3.81671	−3.77226	−3.72970	−3.68888	−3.64966	−3.61192	−3.57555	54046
030	50656	47377	44202	41125	38139	35241	32424	29684	27017	24419
040	21888	19418	17009	14656	12357	10109	07911	05761	03655	01593
0.050	−2.99573	−2.97593	−2.95651	−2.93746	−2.91877	−2.90042	−2.88240	−2.86470	−2.84731	−2.83022
060	81341	79688	78062	76462	74887	73337	71810	70306	68825	67365
070	65926	64508	63109	61730	60369	59027	57702	56395	55105	53831
080	52573	51331	50104	48891	47694	46510	45341	44185	43042	41912
090	40795	39690	38597	37516	36446	35388	34341	33304	32279	31264
0.100	−2.30259	−2.29263	−2.28278	−2.27303	−2.26336	−2.25379	−2.24432	−2.23493	−2.22562	−2.21641
110	20727	19823	18926	18037	17156	16282	15417	14558	13707	12863
120	12026	11196	10373	09557	08747	07944	07147	06357	05573	04794
130	04022	03256	02495	01741	00992	00248	−1.99510	−1.98777	−1.98050	−1.97328
140	−1.96611	−1.95900	−1.95193	−1.94491	−1.93794	−1.93102	92415	91732	91054	90381
0.150	−1.89712	−1.89048	−1.88387	−1.87732	−1.87080	−1.86433	−1.85790	−1.85151	−1.84516	−1.83885
160	83258	82635	82016	81401	80789	80181	79577	78976	78379	77786
170	77196	76609	76026	75446	74870	74297	73727	73161	72597	72037
180	71480	70926	70375	69827	69282	68740	68201	67665	67131	66601
190	66073	65548	65026	64507	63990	63476	62964	62455	61949	61445
0.200	−1.60944	−1.60445	−1.59949	−1.59455	−1.58964	−1.58475	−1.57988	−1.57504	−1.57022	−1.56542
210	56065	55590	55117	54646	54178	53712	53248	52786	52326	51868
220	51413	50959	50508	50058	49611	49165	48722	48281	47841	47403
230	46968	46534	46102	45672	45243	44817	44392	43970	43548	43129
240	42712	42296	41882	41469	41059	40650	40242	39837	39433	39030
0.250	−1.38629	−1.38230	−1.37833	−1.37437	−1.37042	−1.36649	−1.36258	−1.35868	−1.35480	−1.35093
260	34707	34323	33941	33560	33181	32803	32426	32051	31677	31304
270	30933	30564	30195	29828	29463	29098	28735	28374	28013	27654
280	27297	26940	26585	26231	25878	25527	25176	24827	24479	24133
290	23787	23443	23100	22758	22418	22078	21740	21402	21066	20731
0.300	−1.20397	−1.20065	−1.19733	−1.19402	−1.19073	−1.18744	−1.18417	−1.18091	−1.17766	−1.17441
310	17118	16796	16475	16155	15836	15518	15201	14885	14570	14256
320	13943	13631	13320	13010	12701	12393	12086	11780	11474	11170
330	10866	10564	10262	09961	09661	09362	09064	08767	08471	08176
340	07881	07587	07294	07002	06711	06421	06132	05843	05555	05268
0.350	−1.04982	−1.04697	−1.04412	−1.04129	−1.03846	−1.03564	−1.03282	−1.03002	−1.02722	−1.02443
360	02165	01888	01611	01335	01060	00786	00512	00239	−0.99967	−0.99696
370	−0.99425	−0.99155	−0.98886	−0.98618	−0.98350	−0.98083	−0.97817	−0.97551	97286	97022
380	96758	96496	96233	95972	95711	95451	95192	94933	94675	94418
390	94161	93905	93649	93395	93140	92887	92634	92382	92130	91879
0.400	−0.91629	−0.91379	−0.91130	−0.90882	−0.90634	−0.90387	−0.90140	−0.89894	−0.89649	−0.89404
410	89160	88916	88673	88431	88189	87948	87707	87467	87227	86988
420	86750	86512	86275	86038	85802	85567	85332	85097	84863	84630
430	84397	84165	83933	83702	83471	83241	83011	82782	82554	82326
440	82098	81871	81645	81419	81193	80968	80744	80520	80296	80073
0.450	−0.79851	−0.79629	−0.79407	−0.79186	−0.78966	−0.78746	−0.78526	−0.78307	−0.78089	−0.77871
460	77653	77436	77219	77003	76787	76572	76357	76143	75929	75715
470	75502	75290	75078	74866	74655	74444	74234	74024	73814	73605
480	73397	73189	72981	72774	72567	72361	72155	71949	71744	71539
490	71335	71131	70928	70725	70522	70320	70118	69917	69716	69515
0.500	−0.69315	−0.69115	−0.68916	−0.68717	−0.68518	−0.68320	−0.68122	−0.67924	−0.67727	−0.67531
510	67334	67139	66943	66748	66553	66359	66165	65971	65778	65585
520	65393	65201	65009	64817	64626	64436	64245	64055	63866	63677
530	63488	63299	63111	62923	62736	62549	62362	62176	61990	61804
540	61619	61434	61249	61065	60881	60697	60514	60331	60148	59966
0.550	−0.59784	−0.59602	−0.59421	−0.59240	−0.59059	−0.58879	−0.58699	−0.58519	−0.58340	−0.58161
560	57982	57803	57625	57448	57270	57093	56916	56740	56563	56387
570	56212	56037	55862	55687	55513	55339	55165	54991	54818	54645
580	54473	54300	54128	53957	53785	53614	53444	53273	53103	52933
590	52763	52594	52425	52256	52088	51919	51751	51584	51416	51249
0.600	−0.51083	−0.50916	−0.50750	−0.50584	−0.50418	−0.50253	−0.50088	−0.49923	−0.49758	−0.49594
610	49430	49266	49102	48939	48776	48613	48451	48289	48127	47965
620	47804	47642	47482	47321	47160	47000	46840	46681	46522	46362
630	46204	46045	45887	45728	45571	45413	45256	45099	44942	44785
640	44629	44473	44317	44161	44006	43850	43696	43541	43386	43232
0.650	−0.43078	−0.42925	−0.42771	−0.42618	−0.42465	−0.42312	−0.42159	−0.42007	−0.41855	−0.41703
660	41552	41400	41249	41098	40947	40797	40647	40497	40347	40197
670	40048	39899	39750	39601	39453	39304	39156	39008	38861	38713
680	38566	38419	38273	38126	37980	37834	37688	37542	37397	37251
690	37106	36962	36817	36673	36528	36384	36241	36097	35954	35810
0.700	−0.35667	−0.35525	−0.35382	−0.35240	−0.35098	−0.34956	−0.34814	−0.34672	−0.34531	−0.34390
710	34249	34108	33968	33827	33687	33547	33408	33268	33129	32989
720	32850	32712	32573	32435	32296	32158	32021	31883	31745	31608
730	31471	31334	31197	31061	30925	30788	30653	30517	30381	30246
740	30111	29975	29841	29706	29571	29437	29303	29169	29035	28902
0.750	−0.28768	−0.28635	−0.28502	−0.28369	−0.28236	−0.28104	−0.27971	−0.27839	−0.27707	−0.27575
760	27444	27312	27181	27050	26919	26788	26657	26527	26397	26266
770	26136	26007	25877	25748	25618	25489	25360	25231	25103	24974
780	24846	24718	24590	24462	24335	24207	24080	23953	23826	23699
790	23572	23446	23319	23193	23067	22941	22816	22690	22565	22439
0.800	−0.22314	−0.22189	−0.22065	−0.21940	−0.21816	−0.21691	−0.21567	−0.21443	−0.21319	−0.21196
810	21072	20949	20825	20702	20579	20457	20334	20212	20089	19967
820	19845	19723	19601	19480	19358	19237	19116	18995	18874	18754
830	18633	18513	18392	18272	18152	18032	17913	17793	17674	17554
840	17435	17316	17198	17079	16960	16842	16724	16605	16487	16370
0.850	−0.16252	−0.16134	−0.16017	−0.15900	−0.15782	−0.15665	−0.15548	−0.15432	−0.15315	−0.15199
860	15032	14966	14850	14734	14618	14503	14387	14272	14156	14041
870	13926	13811	13697	13582	13467	13353	13239	13125	13011	12897
880	12783	12670	12556	12443	12330	12217	12104	11991	11878	11766
890	11653	11541	11429	11317	11205	11093	10981	10870	10759	10647
0.900	−0.10536	−0.10425	−0.10314	−0.10203	−0.10093	−0.09982	−0.09872	−0.09761	−0.09651	−0.09541
910	09431	09321	09212	09102	08992	08883	08774	08665	08556	08447
920	08338	08230	08121	08013	07904	07796	07688	07580	07472	07365
930	07257	07150	07042	06935	06828	06721	06614	06507	06401	06294
940	06188	06081	05975	05869	05763	05657	05551	05446	05340	05235
0.950	−0.05129	−0.05024	−0.04919	−0.04814	−0.04709	−0.04604	−0.04500	−0.04395	−0.04291	−0.04186
960	04082	03978	03874	03770	03666	03563	03459	03356	03252	03149
970	03046	02943	02840	02737	02634	02532	02429	02327	02225	02122
980	02020	01918	01816	01715	01613	01511	01410	01309	01207	01106
990	01005	00904	00803	00702	00602	00501	00401	00300	00200	00100

* To find the natural logarithm ($\log_e$) of a number which is a power of ten less or greater than a number given in the table: if the number concerned is *less*, e.g., $^1/_{10}$ (10^{-1}), $^1/_{100}$ (10^{-2}), $^1/_{1000}$ (10^{-3}), etc., *subtract* from the given logarithm $\log_e 10$, $2 \log_e 10$, $3 \log_e 10$, etc.; if the number concerned is *greater*, e.g., 10 times (10^1), 100 times (10^2), 1000 times (10^3), etc., *add* to the given logarithm $\log_e 10$, $2 \log_e 10$, $3 \log_e 10$, etc. Examples: $\log_e 0.02 = \log_e 0.2 - \log_e 10$; $\log_e 2000 = \log_e 200 + \log_e 10$.

x	0.00	0.01	0.02	0.03	0.04	0.05	0.06	0.07	0.08	0.09
1.00	0.00000	0.00995	0.01980	0.02956	0.03922	0.04879	0.05827	0.06766	0.07696	0.08618
10	09531	10436	11333	12222	13103	13976	14842	15700	16551	17395
20	18232	19062	19885	20701	21511	22314	23111	23902	24686	25464
30	26236	27003	27763	28518	29267	30010	30748	31481	32208	32930
40	33647	34359	35066	35767	36464	37156	37844	38526	39204	39878
1.50	0.40547	0.41211	0.41871	0.42527	0.43178	0.43825	0.44469	0.45108	0.45742	0.46373
60	47000	47623	48243	48858	49470	50078	50682	51282	51879	52473
70	53063	53649	54232	54812	55389	55962	56531	57098	57661	58222
80	58779	59333	59884	60432	60977	61519	62058	62594	63127	63658
90	64185	64710	65233	65752	66269	66783	67294	67803	68310	68813
2.00	0.69315	0.69813	0.70310	0.70804	0.71295	0.71784	0.72271	0.72755	0.73237	0.73716
10	74194	74669	75142	75612	76081	76547	77011	77473	77932	78390
20	78846	79299	79751	80200	80648	81093	81536	81978	82418	82855
30	83291	83725	84157	84587	85015	85442	85866	86289	86710	87129
40	87547	87963	88377	88789	89200	89609	90016	90422	90826	91228
2.50	0.91629	0.92028	0.92426	0.92822	0.93216	0.93609	0.94001	0.94391	0.94779	0.95166
60	95551	95935	96317	96698	97078	97456	97833	98208	98582	98954
70	99325	99695	1.00063	1.00430	1.00796	1.01160	1.01523	1.01885	1.02245	1.02604
80	1.02962	1.03318	03674	04028	04380	04732	05082	05431	05779	06126
90	06471	06815	07158	07500	07841	08181	08519	08856	09192	09527
3.00	1.09861	1.10194	1.10526	1.10856	1.11186	1.11514	1.11841	1.12168	1.12493	1.12817
10	13140	13462	13783	14103	14422	14740	15057	15373	15688	16002
20	16315	16627	16938	17248	17557	17865	18173	18479	18784	19089
30	19392	19695	19996	20297	20597	20896	21194	21491	21788	22083
40	22378	22671	22964	23256	23547	23837	24127	24415	24703	24990
3.50	1.25276	1.25562	1.25846	1.26130	1.26413	1.26695	1.26976	1.27257	1.27536	1.27815
60	28093	28371	28647	28923	29198	29473	29746	30019	30291	30563
70	30833	31103	31372	31641	31909	32176	32442	32708	32972	33237
80	33500	33763	34025	34286	34547	34807	35067	35325	35584	35841
90	36098	36354	36609	36864	37118	37372	37624	37877	38128	38379
4.00	1.38629	1.38879	1.39128	1.39377	1.39624	1.39872	1.40118	1.40364	1.40610	1.40854
10	41099	41342	41585	41828	42070	42311	42552	42792	43031	43270
20	43508	43746	43984	44220	44456	44692	44927	45161	45395	45629
30	45862	46094	46326	46557	46787	47018	47247	47476	47705	47933
40	48160	48387	48614	48840	49065	49290	49515	49739	49962	50185
4.50	1.50408	1.50630	1.50851	1.51072	1.51293	1.51513	1.51732	1.51951	1.52170	1.52388
60	52606	52823	53039	53256	53471	53687	53902	54116	54330	54543
70	54756	54969	55181	55393	55604	55814	56025	56235	56444	56653
80	56862	57070	57277	57485	57691	57898	58104	58309	58515	58719
90	58924	59127	59331	59534	59737	59939	60141	60342	60543	60744
5.00	1.60944	1.61144	1.61343	1.61542	1.61741	1.61939	1.62137	1.62334	1.62531	1.62728
10	62924	63120	63315	63511	63705	63900	64094	64287	64481	64673
20	64866	65058	65250	65441	65632	65823	66013	66203	66393	66582
30	66771	66959	67147	67335	67523	67710	67896	68083	68269	68455
40	68640	68825	69010	69194	69378	69562	69745	69928	70111	70293
5.50	1.70475	1.70656	1.70838	1.71019	1.71199	1.71380	1.71560	1.71740	1.71919	1.72098
60	72277	72455	72633	72811	72988	73166	73342	73519	73695	73871
70	74047	74222	74397	74572	74746	74920	75094	75267	75440	75613
80	75786	75958	76130	76302	76473	76644	76815	76985	77156	77326
90	77495	77665	77834	78002	78171	78339	78507	78675	78842	79009
6.00	1.79176	1.79342	1.79509	1.79675	1.79840	1.80006	1.80171	1.80336	1.80500	1.80665
10	80829	80993	81156	81319	81482	81645	81808	81970	82132	82294
20	82455	82616	82777	82938	83098	83258	83418	83578	83737	83896
30	84055	84214	84372	84530	84688	84845	85003	85160	85317	85473
40	85630	85786	85942	86097	86253	86408	86563	86718	86872	87026
6.50	1.87180	1.87334	1.87487	1.87641	1.87794	1.87947	1.88099	1.88251	1.88403	1.88555
60	88707	88858	89010	89160	89311	89462	89612	89762	89912	90061
70	90211	90360	90509	90658	90806	90954	91102	91250	91398	91545
80	91692	91839	91986	92132	92279	92425	92571	92716	92862	93007
90	93152	93297	93442	93586	93730	93874	94018	94162	94305	94448
7.00	1.94591	1.94734	1.94876	1.95019	1.95161	1.95303	1.95445	1.95586	1.95727	1.95869
10	96009	96150	96291	96431	96571	96711	96851	96991	97130	97269
20	97408	97547	97685	97824	97962	98100	98238	98376	98513	98650
30	98787	98924	99061	99198	99334	99470	99606	99742	99877	2.00013
40	2.00148	2.00283	2.00418	2.00553	2.00687	2.00821	2.00956	2.01089	2.01223	01357
7.50	2.01490	2.01624	2.01757	2.01890	2.02022	2.02155	2.02287	2.02419	2.02551	2.02683
60	02815	02946	03078	03209	03340	03471	03601	03732	03862	03992
70	04122	04252	04381	04511	04640	04769	04898	05027	05156	05284
80	05412	05540	05668	05796	05924	06051	06179	06306	06433	06560
90	06686	06813	06939	07065	07191	07317	07443	07568	07694	07819
8.00	2.07944	2.08069	2.08194	2.08318	2.08443	2.08567	2.08691	2.08815	2.08939	2.09063
10	09186	09310	09433	09556	09679	09802	09924	10047	10169	10291
20	10413	10535	10657	10779	10900	11021	11142	11263	11384	11505
30	11626	11746	11866	11986	12106	12226	12346	12465	12585	12704
40	12823	12942	13061	13180	13298	13417	13535	13653	13771	13889
8.50	2.14007	2.14124	2.14242	2.14359	2.14476	2.14593	2.14710	2.14827	2.14943	2.15060
60	15176	15292	15409	15524	15640	15756	15871	15987	16102	16217
70	16332	16447	16562	16677	16791	16905	17020	17134	17248	17361
80	17475	17589	17702	17816	17929	18042	18155	18267	18380	18493
90	18605	18717	18830	18942	19054	19165	19277	19389	19500	19611
9.00	2.19722	2.19834	2.19944	2.20055	2.20166	2.20276	2.20387	2.20497	2.20607	2.20717
10	20827	20937	21047	21157	21266	21375	21485	21594	21703	21812
20	21920	22029	22138	22246	22354	22462	22570	22678	22786	22894
30	23001	23109	23216	23324	23431	23538	23645	23751	23858	23965
40	24071	24177	24284	24390	24496	24601	24707	24813	24918	25024
9.50	2.25129	2.25234	2.25339	2.25444	2.25549	2.25654	2.25759	2.25863	2.25968	2.26072
60	26176	26280	26384	26488	26592	26696	26799	26903	27006	27109
70	27213	27316	27419	27521	27624	27727	27829	27932	28034	28136
80	28238	28340	28442	28544	28646	28747	28849	28950	29051	29152
90	29253	29354	29455	29556	29657	29757	29858	29958	30058	30158

* To find the natural logarithm ($\log_e$) of a number which is a power of ten less or greater than a number given in the table: if the number concerned is *less*, e.g., $^1/_{10}$ (10^{-1}), $^1/_{100}$ (10^{-2}), $^1/_{1000}$ (10^{-3}), etc., *subtract* from the given logarithm $\log_e 10$, $2 \log_e 10$, $3 \log_e 10$, etc.; if the number concerned is *greater*, e.g., 10 times (10^1), 100 times (10^2), 1000 times (10^3), etc., *add* to the given logarithm $\log_e 10$, $2 \log_e 10$, $3 \log_e 10$, etc. Examples: $\log_e 0.02 = \log_e 0.2 - \log_e 10$; $\log_e 2000 = \log_e 200 + \log_e 10$.

x	0.0	0.1	0.2	0.3	0.4	0.5	0.6	0.7	0.8	0.9
10.0	2.30259	2.31254	2.32239	2.33214	2.34181	2.35138	2.36085	2.37024	2.37955	2.38876
11.0	39790	40695	41591	42480	43361	44235	45101	45959	46810	47654
12.0	48491	49321	50144	50960	51770	52573	53370	54160	54945	55723
13.0	56495	57261	58022	58776	59525	60269	61007	61740	62467	63189
14.0	63906	64617	65324	66026	66723	67415	68102	68785	69463	70136
15.0	2.70805	2.71469	2.72130	2.72785	2.73437	2.74084	2.74727	2.75366	2.76001	2.76632
16.0	77259	77882	78501	79117	79728	80336	80940	81541	82138	82731
17.0	83321	83908	84491	85071	85647	86220	86790	87356	87920	88480
18.0	89037	89591	90142	90690	91235	91777	92316	92852	93386	93916
19.0	94444	94969	95491	96011	96527	97041	97553	98062	98568	99072
20.0	2.99573	3.00072	3.00568	3.01062	3.01553	3.02042	3.02529	3.03013	3.03495	3.03975
21.0	3.04452	04927	05400	05871	06339	06805	07269	07731	08191	08649
22.0	09104	09558	10009	10459	10906	11352	11795	12236	12676	13114
23.0	13549	13983	14415	14845	15274	15700	16125	16548	16969	17388
24.0	17805	18221	18635	19048	19458	19867	20275	20680	21084	21487
25.0	3.21888	3.22287	3.22684	3.23080	3.23475	3.23868	3.24259	3.24649	3.25037	3.25424
26.0	25810	26194	26576	26957	27336	27714	28091	28466	28840	29213
27.0	29584	29953	30322	30689	31054	31419	31782	32143	32504	32863
28.0	33220	33577	33932	34286	34639	34990	35341	35690	36038	36384
29.0	36730	37074	37417	37759	38099	38439	38777	39115	39451	39786
30.0	3.40120	3.40453	3.40784	3.41115	3.41444	3.41773	3.42100	3.42426	3.42751	3.43076
31.0	43399	43721	44042	44362	44681	44999	45316	45632	45947	46261
32.0	46574	46886	47197	47507	47816	48124	48431	48738	49043	49347
33.0	49651	49953	50255	50556	50856	51155	51453	51750	52046	52342
34.0	52636	52930	53223	53515	53806	54096	54385	54674	54962	55249
35.0	3.55535	3.55820	3.56105	3.56388	3.56671	3.56953	3.57235	3.57515	3.57795	3.58074
36.0	58352	58629	58906	59182	59457	59731	60005	60278	60550	60821
37.0	61092	61362	61631	61899	62167	62434	62700	62966	63231	63495
38.0	63759	64021	64284	64545	64806	65066	65325	65584	65842	66099
39.0	66356	66612	66868	67122	67377	67630	67883	68135	68387	68638
40.0	3.68888	3.69138	3.69387	3.69635	3.69883	3.70130	3.70377	3.70623	3.70868	3.71113
41.0	71357	71601	71844	72086	72328	72569	72810	73050	73290	73529
42.0	73767	74005	74242	74479	74715	74950	75185	75420	75654	75887
43.0	76120	76352	76584	76815	77046	77276	77506	77735	77963	78191
44.0	78419	78646	78872	79098	79324	79549	79773	79997	80221	80444
45.0	3.80666	3.80888	3.81110	3.81331	3.81551	3.81771	3.81991	3.82210	3.82428	3.82647
46.0	82864	83081	83298	83514	83730	83945	84160	84374	84588	84802
47.0	85015	85227	85439	85651	85862	86073	86283	86493	86703	86912
48.0	87120	87328	87536	87743	87950	88156	88362	88568	88773	88978
49.0	89182	89386	89589	89792	89995	90197	90399	90600	90801	91002
50.0	3.91202	3.91402	3.91602	3.91801	3.91999	3.92197	3.92395	3.92593	3.92790	3.92986
51.0	93183	93378	93574	93769	93964	94158	94352	94546	94739	94932
52.0	95124	95316	95508	95700	95891	96081	96272	96462	96651	96840
53.0	97029	97218	97406	97594	97781	97968	98155	98341	98527	98713
54.0	98898	99083	99268	99452	99636	99820	4.00003	4.00186	4.00369	4.00551
55.0	4.00733	4.00915	4.01096	4.01277	4.01458	4.01638	4.01818	4.01998	4.02177	4.02356
56.0	02535	02714	02892	03069	03247	03424	03601	03777	03954	04130
57.0	04305	04480	04655	04830	05004	05178	05352	05526	05699	05872
58.0	06044	06217	06389	06560	06732	06903	07073	07244	07414	07584
59.0	07754	07923	08092	08261	08429	08598	08766	08933	09101	09268
60.0	4.09434	4.09601	4.09767	4.09933	4.10099	4.10264	4.10429	4.10594	4.10759	4.10923
61.0	11087	11251	11415	11578	11741	11904	12066	12228	12390	12552
62.0	12713	12875	13036	13196	13357	13517	13677	13836	13996	14155
63.0	14313	14472	14630	14789	14946	15104	15261	15418	15575	15732
64.0	15888	16044	16200	16356	16511	16667	16821	16976	17131	17285
65.0	4.17439	4.17592	4.17746	4.17899	4.18052	4.18205	4.18358	4.18510	4.18662	4.18814
66.0	18965	19117	19268	19419	19570	19720	19870	20020	20170	20320
67.0	20469	20618	20767	20916	21065	21213	21361	21509	21656	21804
68.0	21951	22098	22244	22391	22537	22683	22829	22975	23120	23266
69.0	23411	23555	23700	23844	23989	24133	24276	24420	24563	24707
70.0	4.24850	4.24992	4.25135	4.25277	4.25419	4.25561	4.25703	4.25845	4.25986	4.26127
71.0	26268	26409	26549	26690	26830	26970	27110	27249	27388	27528
72.0	27667	27805	27944	28082	28221	28359	28496	28634	28772	28909
73.0	29046	29183	29320	29456	29592	29729	29865	30000	30136	30271
74.0	30407	30542	30676	30811	30946	31080	31214	31348	31482	31615
75.0	4.31749	4.31882	4.32015	4.32149	4.32281	4.32413	4.32546	4.32678	4.32810	4.32942
76.0	33073	33205	33336	33467	33598	33729	33860	33990	34120	34251
77.0	34381	34510	34640	34769	34899	35028	35157	35286	35414	35543
78.0	35671	35800	35927	36055	36182	36310	36437	36564	36691	36818
79.0	36945	37071	37198	37324	37450	37576	37701	37827	37952	38078
80.0	4.38203	4.38328	4.38452	4.38577	4.38701	4.38826	4.38950	4.39074	4.39198	4.39321
81.0	39445	39568	39692	39815	39938	40060	40183	40305	40428	40550
82.0	40672	40794	40916	41037	41159	41280	41401	41522	41643	41764
83.0	41884	42004	42125	42245	42365	42485	42604	42724	42843	42963
84.0	43082	43201	43319	43438	43557	43675	43793	43912	44030	44147
85.0	4.44265	4.44383	4.44500	4.44617	4.44735	4.44852	4.44969	4.45085	4.45202	4.45318
86.0	45435	45551	45667	45783	45899	46014	46130	46245	46361	46476
87.0	46591	46706	46820	46935	47050	47164	47278	47392	47506	47620
88.0	47734	47847	47961	48074	48187	48300	48413	48526	48639	48751
89.0	48864	48976	49088	49200	49312	49424	49536	49647	49758	49870
90.0	4.49981	4.50092	4.50203	4.50314	4.50424	4.50535	4.50645	4.50756	4.50866	4.50976
91.0	51086	51196	51305	51415	51525	51634	51743	51852	51961	52070
92.0	52179	52287	52396	52504	52613	52721	52829	52937	53045	53152
93.0	53260	53367	53475	53582	53689	53796	53903	54010	54116	54223
94.0	54329	54436	54542	54648	54754	54860	54966	55071	55177	55282
95.0	4.55388	4.55493	4.55598	4.55703	4.55808	4.55913	4.56017	4.56122	4.56226	4.56331
96.0	56435	56539	56643	56747	56851	56954	57058	57161	57265	57368
97.0	57471	57574	57677	57780	57883	57985	58088	58190	58292	58395
98.0	58497	58599	58701	58802	58904	59006	59107	59208	59310	59411
99.0	59512	59613	59714	59815	59915	60016	60116	60217	60317	60417

* To find the natural logarithm ($\log_e$) of a number which is a power of ten less or greater than a number given in the table: if the number concerned is *less*, e.g., $^1/_{10}$ (10^{-1}), $^1/_{100}$ (10^{-2}), $^1/_{1000}$ (10^{-3}), etc., *subtract* from the given logarithm $\log_e 10$, $2 \log_e 10$, $3 \log_e 10$, etc.; if the number concerned is *greater*, e.g., 10 times (10^1), 100 times (10^2), 1000 times (10^3), etc., *add* to the given logarithm $\log_e 10$, $2 \log_e 10$, $3 \log_e 10$, etc. Examples: $\log_e 0.02 = \log_e 0.2 - \log_e 10$; $\log_e 2000 = \log_e 200 + \log_e 10$.

x	0	1	2	3	4	5	6	7	8	9
00	∞	0.00000	0.69315	1.09861	1.38629	1.60944	1.79176	1.94591	2.07944	2.19722
10	2.30259	2.39790	2.48491	2.56495	2.63906	2.70805	2.77259	2.83321	89037	94444
20	99573	3.04452	3.09104	3.13549	3.17805	3.21888	3.25810	3.29584	3.33220	3.36730
30	3.40120	43399	46574	49651	52636	55535	58352	61092	63759	66356
40	68888	71357	73767	76120	78419	80666	82864	85015	87120	89182
50	3.91202	3.93183	3.95124	3.97029	3.98898	4.00733	4.02535	4.04305	4.06044	4.07754
60	4.09434	4.11087	4.12713	4.14313	4.15888	17439	18965	20469	21951	23411
70	24850	26268	27667	29046	30407	31749	33073	34381	35671	36945
80	38203	39445	40672	41884	43082	44265	45435	46591	47734	48864
90	49981	51086	52179	53260	54329	55388	56435	57471	58497	59512
100	4.60517	4.61512	4.62497	4.63473	4.64439	4.65396	4.66344	4.67283	4.68213	4.69135
110	70048	70953	71850	72739	73620	74493	75359	76217	77068	77912
120	78749	79579	80402	81218	82028	82831	83628	84419	85203	85981
130	86753	87520	88280	89035	89784	90527	91265	91998	92725	93447
140	94164	94876	95583	96284	96981	97673	98361	99043	99721	5.00395
150	5.01064	5.01728	5.02388	5.03044	5.03695	5.04343	5.04986	5.05625	5.06260	5.06890
160	07517	08140	08760	09375	09987	10595	11199	11799	12396	12990
170	13580	14166	14749	15329	15906	16479	17048	17615	18178	18739
180	19296	19850	20401	20949	21494	22036	22575	23111	23644	24175
190	24702	25227	25750	26269	26786	27300	27811	28320	28827	29330
200	5.29832	5.30330	5.30827	5.31321	5.31812	5.32301	5.32788	5.33272	5.33754	5.34233
210	34711	35186	35659	36129	36598	37064	37528	37990	38450	38907
220	39363	39816	40268	40717	41165	41610	42053	42495	42935	43372
230	43808	44242	44674	45104	45532	45959	46383	46806	47227	47646
240	48064	48480	48894	49306	49717	50126	50533	50939	51343	51745
250	5.52146	5.52545	5.52943	5.53339	5.53733	5.54126	5.54518	5.54908	5.55296	5.55683
260	56068	56452	56834	57215	57595	57973	58350	58725	59099	59471
270	59842	60212	60580	60947	61313	61677	62040	62402	62762	63121
280	63479	63835	64191	64545	64897	65249	65599	65948	66296	66643
290	66988	67332	67675	68017	68358	68698	69036	69373	69709	70044
300	5.70378	5.70711	5.71043	5.71373	5.71703	5.72031	5.72359	5.72685	5.73010	5.73334
310	73657	73979	74300	74620	74939	75257	75574	75890	76205	76519
320	76832	77144	77455	77765	78074	78383	78690	78996	79301	79606
330	79909	80212	80513	80814	81114	81413	81711	82008	82305	82600
340	82895	83188	83481	83773	84064	84354	84644	84932	85220	85507
350	5.85793	5.86079	5.86363	5.86647	5.86930	5.87212	5.87493	5.87774	5.88053	5.88332
360	88610	88888	89164	89440	89715	89990	90263	90536	90808	91080
370	91350	91620	91889	92158	92426	92693	92959	93225	93489	93754
380	94017	94280	94542	94803	95064	95324	95584	95842	96101	96358
390	96615	96871	97126	97381	97635	97889	98141	98394	98645	98896
400	5.99146	5.99396	5.99645	5.99894	6.00141	6.00389	6.00635	6.00881	6.01127	6.01372
410	6.01616	6.01859	6.02102	6.02345	02587	02828	03069	03309	03548	03787
420	04025	04263	04501	04737	04973	05209	05444	05678	05912	06146
430	06379	06611	06843	07074	07304	07535	07764	07993	08222	08450
440	08677	08904	09131	09357	09582	09807	10032	10256	10479	10702
450	6.10925	6.11147	6.11368	6.11589	6.11810	6.12030	6.12249	6.12468	6.12687	6.12905
460	13123	13340	13556	13773	13988	14204	14419	14633	14847	15060
470	15273	15486	15698	15910	16121	16331	16542	16752	16961	17170
480	17379	17587	17794	18002	18208	18415	18621	18826	19032	19236
490	19441	19644	19848	20051	20254	20456	20658	20859	21060	21261
500	6.21461	6.21661	6.21860	6.22059	6.22258	6.22456	6.22654	6.22851	6.23048	6.23245
510	23441	23637	23832	24028	24222	24417	24611	24804	24998	25190
520	25383	25575	25767	25958	26149	26340	26530	26720	26910	27099
530	27288	27476	27664	27852	28040	28227	28413	28600	28786	28972
540	29157	29342	29527	29711	29895	30079	30262	30445	30628	30810
550	6.30992	6.31173	6.31355	6.31536	6.31716	6.31897	6.32077	6.32257	6.32436	6.32615
560	32794	32972	33150	33328	33505	33683	33859	34036	34212	34388
570	34564	34739	34914	35089	35263	35437	35611	35784	35957	36130
580	36303	36475	36647	36819	36990	37161	37332	37502	37673	37843
590	38012	38182	38351	38519	38688	38856	39024	39192	39359	39526
600	6.39693	6.39859	6.40026	6.40192	6.40357	6.40523	6.40688	6.40853	6.41017	6.41182
610	41346	41510	41673	41836	41999	42162	42325	42487	42649	42811
620	42972	43133	43294	43455	43615	43775	43935	44095	44254	44413
630	44572	44731	44889	45047	45205	45362	45520	45677	45834	45990
640	46147	46303	46459	46614	46770	46925	47080	47235	47389	47543
650	6.47697	6.47851	6.48004	6.48158	6.48311	6.48464	6.48616	6.48768	6.48920	6.49072
660	49224	49375	49527	49677	49828	49979	50129	50279	50429	50578
670	50728	50877	51026	51175	51323	51471	51619	51767	51915	52062
680	52209	52356	52503	52649	52796	52942	53088	53233	53379	53524
690	53669	53814	53959	54103	54247	54391	54535	54679	54822	54965
700	6.55108	6.55251	6.55393	6.55536	6.55678	6.55820	6.55962	6.56103	6.56244	6.56386
710	56526	56667	56808	56948	57088	57228	57368	57508	57647	57786
720	57925	58064	58203	58341	58479	58617	58755	58893	59030	59167
730	59304	59441	59578	59715	59851	59987	60123	60259	60394	60530
740	60665	60800	60935	61070	61204	61338	61473	61607	61740	61874
750	6.62007	6.62141	6.62274	6.62407	6.62539	6.62672	6.62804	6.62936	6.63068	6.63200
760	63332	63463	63595	63726	63857	63988	64118	64249	64379	64509
770	64639	64769	64898	65028	65157	65286	65415	65544	65673	65801
780	65929	66058	66185	66313	66441	66568	66696	66823	66950	67077
790	67203	67330	67456	67582	67708	67834	67960	68085	68211	68336
800	6.68461	6.68586	6.68711	6.68835	6.68960	6.69084	6.69208	6.69332	6.69456	6.69580
810	69703	69827	69950	70073	70196	70319	70441	70564	70686	70808
820	70930	71052	71174	71296	71417	71538	71659	71780	71901	72022
830	72143	72263	72383	72503	72623	72743	72863	72982	73102	73221
840	73340	73459	73578	73697	73815	73934	74052	74170	74288	74406
850	6.74524	6.74641	6.74759	6.74876	6.74993	6.75110	6.75227	6.75344	6.75460	6.75577
860	75693	75809	75926	76041	76157	76273	76388	76504	76619	76734
870	76849	76964	77079	77194	77308	77422	77537	77651	77765	77878
880	77992	78106	78219	78333	78446	78559	78672	78784	78897	79010
890	79122	79234	79347	79459	79571	79682	79794	79906	80017	80128
900	6.80239	6.80351	6.80461	6.80572	6.80683	6.80793	6.80904	6.81014	6.81124	6.81235
910	81344	81454	81564	81674	81783	81892	82002	82111	82220	82329
920	82437	82546	82655	82763	82871	82979	83087	83195	83303	83411
930	83518	83626	83733	83841	83948	84055	84162	84268	84375	84482
940	84588	84694	84801	84907	85013	85118	85224	85330	85435	85541
950	6.85646	6.85751	6.85857	6.85961	6.86066	6.86171	6.86276	6.86380	6.86485	6.86589
960	86693	86797	86901	87005	87109	87213	87316	87420	87523	87626
970	87730	87833	87936	88038	88141	88244	88346	88449	88551	88653
980	88755	88857	88959	89061	89163	89264	89366	89467	89568	89669
990	89770	89871	89972	90073	90174	90274	90375	90475	90575	90675

* To find the natural logarithm ($\log_e$) of a number which is a power of ten less or greater than a number given in the table: if the number concerned is *less*, e.g., $^1/_{10}$ (10^{-1}), $^1/_{100}$ (10^{-2}), $^1/_{1000}$ (10^{-3}), etc., *subtract* from the given logarithm $\log_e 10$, $2 \log_e 10$, $3 \log_e 10$, etc.; if the number concerned is *greater*, e.g., 10 times (10^1), 100 times (10^2), 1000 times (10^3), etc., *add* to the given logarithm $\log_e 10$, $2 \log_e 10$, $3 \log_e 10$, etc. Examples: $\log_e 0.02 = \log_e 0.2 - \log_e 10$; $\log_e 2000 = \log_e 200 + \log_e 10$.

x	e^x	$\log_{10}(e^x)$	e^{-x}	x	e^x	$\log_{10}(e^x)$	e^{-x}	x	e^x	$\log_{10}(e^x)$	e^{-x}
0.00	1.0000	0.00000	1.000000	**1.00**	2.7183	0.43429	0.367879	**2.00**	7.3891	0.86859	0.135335
0.01	1.0101	00434	0.990050	1.01	2.7456	43864	364219	2.01	7.4633	87293	133989
0.02	1.0202	00869	980199	1.02	2.7732	44298	360595	2.02	7.5383	87727	132655
0.03	1.0305	01303	970446	1.03	2.8011	44732	357007	2.03	7.6141	88162	131336
0.04	1.0408	01737	960789	1.04	2.8292	45167	353455	2.04	7.6906	88596	130029
0.05	1.0513	0.02171	0.951229	**1.05**	2.8577	0.45601	0.349938	**2.05**	7.7679	0.89030	0.128735
0.06	1.0618	02606	941765	1.06	2.8864	46035	346456	2.06	7.8460	89465	127454
0.07	1.0725	03040	932394	1.07	2.9154	46470	343009	2.07	7.9248	89899	126186
0.08	1.0833	03474	923116	1.08	2.9447	46904	339596	2.08	8.0045	90333	124930
0.09	1.0942	03909	913931	1.09	2.9743	47338	336216	2.09	8.0849	90768	123687
0.10	1.1052	0.04343	0.904837	**1.10**	3.0042	0.47772	0.332871	**2.10**	8.1662	0.91202	0.122456
0.11	1.1163	04777	895834	1.11	3.0344	48207	329559	2.11	8.2482	91636	121238
0.12	1.1275	05212	886920	1.12	3.0649	48641	326280	2.12	8.3311	92070	120032
0.13	1.1388	05646	878095	1.13	3.0957	49075	323033	2.13	8.4149	92505	118837
0.14	1.1503	06080	869358	1.14	3.1268	49510	319819	2.14	8.4994	92939	117655
0.15	1.1618	0.06514	0.860708	**1.15**	3.1582	0.49944	0.316637	**2.15**	8.5849	0.93373	0.116484
0.16	1.1735	06949	852144	1.16	3.1899	50378	313486	2.16	8.6711	93808	115325
0.17	1.1853	07383	843665	1.17	3.2220	50812	310367	2.17	8.7583	94242	114178
0.18	1.1972	07817	835270	1.18	3.2544	51247	307279	2.18	8.8463	94676	113042
0.19	1.2092	08252	826959	1.19	3.2871	51681	304221	2.19	8.9352	95110	111917
0.20	1.2214	0.08686	0.818731	**1.20**	3.3201	0.52115	0.301194	**2.20**	9.0250	0.95545	0.110803
0.21	1.2337	09120	810584	1.21	3.3535	52550	298197	2.21	9.1157	95979	109701
0.22	1.2461	09554	802519	1.22	3.3872	52984	295230	2.22	9.2073	96413	108609
0.23	1.2586	09989	794534	1.23	3.4212	53418	292293	2.23	9.2999	96848	107528
0.24	1.2712	10423	786628	1.24	3.4556	53853	289384	2.24	9.3933	97282	106459
0.25	1.2840	0.10857	0.778801	**1.25**	3.4903	0.54287	0.286505	**2.25**	9.4877	0.97716	0.105399
0.26	1.2969	11292	771052	1.26	3.5254	54721	283654	2.26	9.5831	98151	104350
0.27	1.3100	11726	763379	1.27	3.5609	55155	280832	2.27	9.6794	98585	103312
0.28	1.3231	12160	755784	1.28	3.5966	55590	278037	2.28	9.7767	99019	102284
0.29	1.3364	12595	748264	1.29	3.6328	56024	275271	2.29	9.8749	99453	101266
0.30	1.3499	0.13029	0.740818	**1.30**	3.6693	0.56458	0.272532	**2.30**	9.9742	0.99888	0.100259
0.31	1.3634	13463	733447	1.31	3.7062	56893	269820	2.31	10.074	1.00322	099261
0.32	1.3771	13897	726149	1.32	3.7434	57327	267135	2.32	10.176	00756	098274
0.33	1.3910	14332	718924	1.33	3.7810	57761	264477	2.33	10.278	01191	097296
0.34	1.4049	14766	711770	1.34	3.8190	58195	261846	2.34	10.381	01625	096328
0.35	1.4191	0.15200	0.704688	**1.35**	3.8574	0.58630	0.259240	**2.35**	10.486	1.02059	0.095369
0.36	1.4333	15635	697676	1.36	3.8962	59064	256661	2.36	10.591	02493	094420
0.37	1.4477	16069	690734	1.37	3.9354	59498	254107	2.37	10.697	02928	093481
0.38	1.4623	16503	683861	1.38	3.9749	59933	251579	2.38	10.805	03362	092551
0.39	1.4770	16937	677057	1.39	4.0149	60367	249075	2.39	10.913	03796	091630
0.40	1.4918	0.17372	0.670320	**1.40**	4.0552	0.60801	0.246597	**2.40**	11.023	1.04231	0.090718
0.41	1.5068	17806	663650	1.41	4.0960	61236	244143	2.41	11.134	04665	089815
0.42	1.5220	18240	657047	1.42	4.1371	61670	241714	2.42	11.246	05099	088922
0.43	1.5373	18675	650509	1.43	4.1787	62104	239309	2.43	11.359	05534	088037
0.44	1.5527	19109	644036	1.44	4.2207	62538	236928	2.44	11.473	05968	087161
0.45	1.5683	0.19543	0.637628	**1.45**	4.2631	0.62973	0.234570	**2.45**	11.588	1.06402	0.086294
0.46	1.5841	19978	631284	1.46	4.3060	63407	232236	2.46	11.705	06836	085435
0.47	1.6000	20412	625002	1.47	4.3492	63841	229925	2.47	11.822	07271	084585
0.48	1.6161	20846	618783	1.48	4.3929	64276	227638	2.48	11.941	07705	083743
0.49	1.6323	21280	612626	1.49	4.4371	64710	225373	2.49	12.061	08139	082910
0.50	1.6487	0.21715	0.606531	**1.50**	4.4817	0.65144	0.223130	**2.50**	12.182	1.08574	0.082085
0.51	1.6653	22149	600496	1.51	4.5267	65578	220910	2.51	12.305	09008	081268
0.52	1.6820	22583	594521	1.52	4.5722	66013	218712	2.52	12.429	09442	080460
0.53	1.6989	23018	588605	1.53	4.6182	66447	216536	2.53	12.554	09877	079659
0.54	1.7160	23452	582748	1.54	4.6646	66881	214381	2.54	12.680	10311	078866
0.55	1.7333	0.23886	0.576950	**1.55**	4.7115	0.67316	0.212248	**2.55**	12.807	1.10745	0.078082
0.56	1.7507	24320	571209	1.56	4.7588	67750	210136	2.56	12.936	11179	077305
0.57	1.7683	24755	565525	1.57	4.8066	68184	208045	2.57	13.066	11614	076536
0.58	1.7860	25189	559898	1.58	4.8550	68619	205975	2.58	13.197	12048	075774
0.59	1.8040	25623	554327	1.59	4.9037	69053	203926	2.59	13.330	12482	075020
0.60	1.8221	0.26058	0.548812	**1.60**	4.9530	0.69487	0.201897	**2.60**	13.464	1.12917	0.074274
0.61	1.8404	26492	543351	1.61	5.0028	69921	199888	2.61	13.599	13351	073535
0.62	1.8589	26926	537944	1.62	5.0531	70356	197899	2.62	13.736	13785	072803
0.63	1.8776	27361	532592	1.63	5.1039	70790	195930	2.63	13.874	14219	072078
0.64	1.8965	27795	527292	1.64	5.1552	71224	193980	2.64	14.013	14654	071361
0.65	1.9155	0.28229	0.522046	**1.65**	5.2070	0.71659	0.192050	**2.65**	14.154	1.15088	0.070651
0.66	1.9348	28663	516851	1.66	5.2593	72093	190139	2.66	14.296	15522	069948
0.67	1.9542	29098	511709	1.67	5.3122	72527	188247	2.67	14.440	15957	069252
0.68	1.9739	29532	506617	1.68	5.3656	72961	186374	2.68	14.585	16391	068563
0.69	1.9937	29966	501576	1.69	5.4195	73396	184520	2.69	14.732	16825	067881
0.70	2.0138	0.30401	0.496585	**1.70**	5.4739	0.73830	0.182684	**2.70**	14.880	1.17260	0.067206
0.71	2.0340	30835	491644	1.71	5.5290	74264	180866	2.71	15.029	17694	066537
0.72	2.0544	31269	486752	1.72	5.5845	74699	179066	2.72	15.180	18128	065875
0.73	2.0751	31703	481909	1.73	5.6407	75133	177284	2.73	15.333	18562	065219
0.74	2.0959	32138	477114	1.74	5.6973	75567	175520	2.74	15.487	18997	064570
0.75	2.1170	0.32572	0.472367	**1.75**	5.7546	0.76002	0.173774	**2.75**	15.643	1.19431	0.063928
0.76	2.1383	33006	467666	1.76	5.8124	76436	172045	2.76	15.800	19865	063292
0.77	2.1598	33441	463013	1.77	5.8709	76870	170333	2.77	15.959	20300	062662
0.78	2.1815	33875	458406	1.78	5.9299	77304	168638	2.78	16.119	20734	062039
0.79	2.2034	34309	453845	1.79	5.9895	77739	166960	2.79	16.281	21168	061421
0.80	2.2255	0.34744	0.449329	**1.80**	6.0496	0.78173	0.165299	**2.80**	16.445	1.21602	0.060810
0.81	2.2479	35178	444858	1.81	6.1104	78607	163654	2.81	16.610	22037	060205
0.82	2.2705	35612	440432	1.82	6.1719	79042	162026	2.82	16.777	22471	059606
0.83	2.2933	36046	436049	1.83	6.2339	79476	160414	2.83	16.945	22905	059013
0.84	2.3164	36481	431711	1.84	6.2965	79910	158817	2.84	17.116	23340	058426
0.85	2.3396	0.36915	0.427415	**1.85**	6.3598	0.80344	0.157237	**2.85**	17.288	1.23774	0.057844
0.86	2.3632	37349	423162	1.86	6.4237	80779	155673	2.86	17.462	24208	057269
0.87	2.3869	37784	418952	1.87	6.4883	81213	154124	2.87	17.637	24643	056699
0.88	2.4109	38218	414783	1.88	6.5535	81647	152590	2.88	17.814	25077	056135
0.89	2.4351	38652	410656	1.89	6.6194	82082	151072	2.89	17.993	25511	055576
0.90	2.4596	0.39087	0.406570	**1.90**	6.6859	0.82516	0.149569	**2.90**	18.174	1.25945	0.055023
0.91	2.4843	39521	402524	1.91	6.7531	82950	148080	2.91	18.357	26380	054476
0.92	2.5093	39955	398519	1.92	6.8210	83385	146607	2.92	18.541	26814	053934
0.93	2.5345	40389	394554	1.93	6.8895	83819	145148	2.93	18.728	27248	053397
0.94	2.5600	40824	390628	1.94	6.9588	84253	143704	2.94	18.916	27683	052866
0.95	2.5857	0.41258	0.386741	**1.95**	7.0287	0.84687	0.142274	**2.95**	19.106	1.28117	0.052340
0.96	2.6117	41692	382893	1.96	7.0993	85122	140858	2.96	19.298	28551	051819
0.97	2.6379	42127	379083	1.97	7.1707	85556	139457	2.97	19.492	28985	051303
0.98	2.6645	42561	375311	1.98	7.2427	85990	138069	2.98	19.688	29420	050793
0.99	2.6912	42995	371577	1.99	7.3155	86425	136695	2.99	19.886	29854	050287

x	e^x	$\log_{10}(e^x)$	e^{-x}
3.00	20.086	1.30288	0.049787
3.01	20.287	1.30723	049292
3.02	20.491	1.31157	048801
3.03	20.697	1.31591	048316
3.04	20.905	1.32026	047835
3.05	21.115	1.32460	0.047359
3.06	21.328	1.32894	046888
3.07	21.542	1.33328	046421
3.08	21.758	1.33763	045959
3.09	21.977	1.34197	045502
3.10	22.198	1.34631	0.045049
3.11	22.421	1.35066	044601
3.12	22.646	1.35500	044157
3.13	22.874	1.35934	043718
3.14	23.104	1.36368	043283
3.15	23.336	1.36803	0.042852
3.16	23.571	1.37237	042426
3.17	23.807	1.37671	042004
3.18	24.047	1.38106	041586
3.19	24.288	1.38540	041172
3.20	24.533	1.38974	0.040762
3.21	24.779	1.39409	040357
3.22	25.028	1.39843	039955
3.23	25.280	1.40277	039557
3.24	25.534	1.40711	039164
3.25	25.790	1.41146	0.038774
3.26	26.050	1.41580	038388
3.27	26.311	1.42014	038006
3.28	26.576	1.42449	037628
3.29	26.843	1.42883	037254
3.30	27.113	1.43317	0.036883
3.31	27.385	1.43751	036516
3.32	27.660	1.44186	036153
3.33	27.938	1.44620	035793
3.34	28.219	1.45054	035437
3.35	28.503	1.45489	0.035084
3.36	28.789	1.45923	034735
3.37	29.079	1.46357	034390
3.38	29.371	1.46792	034047
3.39	29.666	1.47226	033709
3.40	29.964	1.47660	0.033373
3.41	30.265	1.48094	033041
3.42	30.569	1.48529	032712
3.43	30.877	1.48963	032387
3.44	31.187	1.49397	032065
3.45	31.500	1.49832	0.031746
3.46	31.817	1.50266	031430
3.47	32.137	1.50700	031117
3.48	32.460	1.51134	030807
3.49	32.786	1.51569	030501
3.50	33.115	1.52003	0.030197
3.51	33.448	1.52437	029897
3.52	33.784	1.52872	029599
3.53	34.124	1.53306	029305
3.54	34.467	1.53740	029013
3.55	34.813	1.54175	0.028725
3.56	35.163	1.54609	028439
3.57	35.517	1.55043	028156
3.58	35.874	1.55477	027876
3.59	36.234	1.55912	027598
3.60	36.598	1.56346	0.027324
3.61	36.966	1.56780	027052
3.62	37.338	1.57215	026783
3.63	37.713	1.57649	026516
3.64	38.092	1.58083	026252
3.65	38.475	1.58517	0.025991
3.66	38.861	1.58952	025733
3.67	39.252	1.59386	025476
3.68	39.646	1.59820	025223
3.69	40.045	1.60255	024972
3.70	40.447	1.60689	0.024724
3.71	40.854	1.61123	024478
3.72	41.264	1.61558	024234
3.73	41.679	1.61992	023993
3.74	42.098	1.62426	023754
3.75	42.521	1.62860	0.023518
3.76	42.948	1.63295	023284
3.77	43.380	1.63729	023052
3.78	43.816	1.64163	022823
3.79	44.256	1.64598	022596
3.80	44.701	1.65032	0.022371
3.81	45.150	1.65466	022148
3.82	45.604	1.65900	021928
3.83	46.063	1.66335	021710
3.84	46.525	1.66769	021494
3.85	46.993	1.67203	0.021280
3.86	47.465	1.67638	021068
3.87	47.942	1.68072	020858
3.88	48.424	1.68506	020651
3.89	48.911	1.68941	020445
3.90	49.402	1.69375	0.020242
3.91	49.899	1.69809	020041
3.92	50.400	1.70243	019841
3.93	50.907	1.70678	019644
3.94	51.419	1.71112	019448
3.95	51.935	1.71546	0.019255
3.96	52.457	1.71981	019063
3.97	52.985	1.72415	018873
3.98	53.517	1.72849	018686
3.99	54.055	1.73283	018500

x	e^x	$\log_{10}(e^x)$	e^{-x}
4.00	54.598	1.73718	0.018316
4.01	55.147	1.74152	018133
4.02	55.701	1.74586	017953
4.03	56.261	1.75021	017774
4.04	56.826	1.75455	017597
4.05	57.397	1.75889	0.017422
4.06	57.974	1.76324	017249
4.07	58.557	1.76758	017077
4.08	59.145	1.77192	016907
4.09	59.740	1.77626	016739
4.10	60.340	1.78061	0.016573
4.11	60.947	1.78495	016408
4.12	61.559	1.78929	016245
4.13	62.178	1.79364	016083
4.14	62.803	1.79798	015923
4.15	63.434	1.80232	0.015764
4.16	64.072	1.80667	015608
4.17	64.715	1.81101	015452
4.18	65.366	1.81535	015299
4.19	66.023	1.81969	015146
4.20	66.686	1.82404	0.014996
4.21	67.357	1.82838	014846
4.22	68.033	1.83272	014699
4.23	68.717	1.83707	014552
4.24	69.408	1.84141	014408
4.25	70.105	1.84575	0.014264
4.26	70.810	1.85009	014122
4.27	71.522	1.85444	013982
4.28	72.240	1.85878	013843
4.29	72.966	1.86312	013705
4.30	73.700	1.86747	0.013569
4.31	74.440	1.87181	013434
4.32	75.189	1.87615	013300
4.33	75.944	1.88050	013168
4.34	76.708	1.88484	013037
4.35	77.478	1.88918	0.012907
4.36	78.257	1.89352	012778
4.37	79.044	1.89787	012651
4.38	79.838	1.90221	012525
4.39	80.640	1.90655	012401
4.40	81.451	1.91090	0.012277
4.41	82.269	1.91524	012155
4.42	83.096	1.91958	012034
4.43	83.931	1.92392	011914
4.44	84.775	1.92827	011796
4.45	85.627	1.93261	0.011679
4.46	86.488	1.93695	011562
4.47	87.357	1.94130	011447
4.48	88.235	1.94564	011333
4.49	89.121	1.94998	011221
4.50	90.017	1.95433	0.011109
4.51	90.922	1.95867	010998
4.52	91.836	1.96301	010889
4.53	92.759	1.96735	010781
4.54	93.691	1.97170	010673
4.55	94.632	1.97604	0.010567
4.56	95.583	1.98038	010462
4.57	96.544	1.98473	010358
4.58	97.514	1.98907	010255
4.59	98.494	1.99341	010153
4.60	99.484	1.99775	0.010052
4.61	100.48	2.00210	009952
4.62	101.49	2.00644	009853
4.63	102.51	2.01078	009755
4.64	103.54	2.01513	009658
4.65	104.58	2.01947	0.009562
4.66	105.64	2.02381	009466
4.67	106.70	2.02816	009372
4.68	107.77	2.03250	009279
4.69	108.85	2.03684	009187
4.70	109.95	2.04118	0.009095
4.71	111.05	2.04553	009005
4.72	112.17	2.04987	008915
4.73	113.30	2.05421	008826
4.74	114.43	2.05856	008739
4.75	115.58	2.06290	0.008652
4.76	116.75	2.06724	008566
4.77	117.92	2.07158	008480
4.78	119.10	2.07593	008396
4.79	120.30	2.08027	008312
4.80	121.51	2.08461	0.008230
4.81	122.73	2.08896	008148
4.82	123.97	2.09330	008067
4.83	125.21	2.09764	007987
4.84	126.47	2.10199	007907
4.85	127.74	2.10633	0.007828
4.86	129.02	2.11067	007750
4.87	130.32	2.11501	007673
4.88	131.63	2.11936	007597
4.89	132.95	2.12370	007521
4.90	134.29	2.12804	0.007447
4.91	135.64	2.13239	007372
4.92	137.00	2.13673	007299
4.93	138.38	2.14107	007227
4.94	139.77	2.14541	007155
4.95	141.17	2.14976	0.007083
4.96	142.59	2.15410	007013
4.97	144.03	2.15844	006943
4.98	145.47	2.16279	006874
4.99	146.94	2.16713	006806

x	e^x	$\log_{10}(e^x)$	e^{-x}
5.00	148.41	2.17147	0.006738
5.01	149.90	2.17582	006671
5.02	151.41	2.18016	006605
5.03	152.93	2.18450	006539
5.04	154.47	2.18884	006474
5.05	156.02	2.19319	0.006409
5.06	157.59	2.19753	006346
5.07	159.17	2.20187	006282
5.08	160.77	2.20622	006220
5.09	162.39	2.21056	006158
5.10	164.02	2.21490	0.006097
5.11	165.67	2.21924	006036
5.12	167.34	2.22359	005976
5.13	169.02	2.22793	005917
5.14	170.72	2.23227	005858
5.15	172.43	2.23662	0.005799
5.16	174.16	2.24096	005742
5.17	175.91	2.24530	005685
5.18	177.68	2.24965	005628
5.19	179.47	2.25399	005572
5.20	181.27	2.25833	0.005517
5.21	183.09	2.26267	005462
5.22	184.93	2.26702	005407
5.23	186.79	2.27136	005354
5.24	188.67	2.27570	005300
5.25	190.57	2.28005	0.005248
5.26	192.48	2.28439	005195
5.27	194.42	2.28873	005144
5.28	196.37	2.29307	005092
5.29	198.34	2.29742	005042
5.30	200.34	2.30176	0.004992
5.31	202.35	2.30610	004942
5.32	204.38	2.31045	004893
5.33	206.44	2.31479	004844
5.34	208.51	2.31913	004796
5.35	210.61	2.32348	0.004748
5.36	212.72	2.32782	004701
5.37	214.86	2.33216	004654
5.38	217.02	2.33650	004608
5.39	219.20	2.34085	004562
5.40	221.41	2.34519	0.004517
5.41	223.63	2.34953	004472
5.42	225.88	2.35388	004427
5.43	228.15	2.35822	004383
5.44	230.44	2.36256	004339
5.45	232.76	2.36690	0.004296
5.46	235.10	2.37125	004254
5.47	237.46	2.37559	004211
5.48	239.85	2.37993	004169
5.49	242.26	2.38428	004128
5.5	244.69	2.38862	0.004087
5.6	270.43	2.43205	003698
5.7	298.87	2.47548	003346
5.8	330.30	2.51891	003028
5.9	365.04	2.56234	002739
6.0	403.43	2.60577	0.002479
6.1	445.86	2.64920	002243
6.2	492.75	2.69263	002029
6.3	544.57	2.73606	001836
6.4	601.85	2.77948	001662
6.5	665.14	2.82291	0.001503
6.6	735.10	2.86634	001360
6.7	812.41	2.90977	001231
6.8	897.85	2.95320	001114
6.9	992.27	2.99663	001008
7.0	1096.6	3.04006	0.000912
7.1	1212.0	3.08349	000825
7.2	1339.4	3.12692	000747
7.3	1480.3	3.17035	000676
7.4	1636.0	3.21378	000611
7.5	1808.0	3.25721	0.000553
7.6	1998.2	3.30064	000501
7.7	2208.3	3.33407	000453
7.8	2440.6	3.38750	000410
7.9	2697.3	3.43093	000371
8.0	2981.0	3.47436	0.000336
8.1	3294.5	3.51779	000304
8.2	3641.0	3.56121	000275
8.3	4023.9	3.60464	000249
8.4	4447.1	3.64807	000225
8.5	4914.8	3.69150	0.000204
8.6	5431.7	3.73493	000184
8.7	6002.9	3.77836	000167
8.8	6634.2	3.82179	000151
8.9	7332.0	3.86522	000136
9.0	8103.1	3.90865	0.000123
9.1	8955.3	3.95208	000112
9.2	9897.1	3.99551	000101
9.3	10938	4.03894	000091
9.4	12088	4.08237	000083
9.5	13360	4.12580	0.000075
9.6	14765	4.16923	000068
9.7	16318	4.21266	000061
9.8	18034	4.25609	000056
9.9	19930	4.29952	000050
10.0	22026	4.34294	0.000045

Reciprocals[1] of the Integers 1–999

Reciprocal of $n = 1/n$

n	0	1	2	3	4	5	6	7	8	9
0		1.0 000 0000	0.5 000 0000	0.3 333 3333	0.2 500 0000	0.2 000 0000	0.1 666 6667	0.1 428 5714	0.1 250 0000	0.1 111 1111
10	0.1 000 0000	0.0 909 0909	0.0 833 3333	0.0 769 2308	0.0 714 2857	0.0 666 6667	0.0 625 0000	0.0 588 2353	0.0 555 5556	0.0 526 3158
20	0.0 500 0000	476 1905	454 5455	434 7826	416 6667	400 0000	384 6154	370 3704	357 1429	344 8276
30	333 3333	322 5806	312 5000	303 0303	294 1176	285 7143	277 7778	270 2703	263 1579	256 4103
40	250 0000	243 9024	238 0952	232 5581	227 2727	222 2222	217 3913	212 7660	208 3333	204 0816
50	0.0 200 0000	0.0 196 0784	0.0 192 3077	0.0 188 6792	0.0 185 1852	0.0 181 8182	0.0 178 5714	0.0 175 4386	0.0 172 4138	0.0 169 4915
60	166 6667	163 9344	161 2903	158 7302	156 2500	153 8462	151 5152	149 2537	147 0588	144 9275
70	142 8571	140 8451	138 8889	136 9863	135 1351	133 3333	131 5789	129 8701	128 2051	126 5823
80	125 0000	123 4568	121 9512	120 4819	119 0476	117 6471	116 2791	114 9425	113 6364	112 3596
90	111 1111	109 8901	108 6957	107 5269	106 3830	105 2632	104 1667	103 0928	102 0408	101 0101
100	0.0 100 0000	0.00 990 0990	0.00 980 3922	0.00 970 8738	0.00 961 5385	0.00 952 3810	0.00 943 3962	0.00 934 5794	0.00 925 9259	0.00 917 4312
110	0.00 909 0909	900 9009	892 8571	884 9558	877 1930	869 5652	862 0690	854 7009	847 4576	840 3361
120	833 3333	826 4463	819 6721	813 0081	806 4516	800 0000	793 6508	787 4016	781 2500	775 1938
130	769 2308	763 3588	757 5758	751 8797	746 2687	740 7407	735 2941	729 9270	724 6377	719 4245
140	714 2857	709 2199	704 2254	699 3007	694 4444	689 6552	684 9315	680 2721	675 6757	671 1409
150	0.00 666 6667	0.00 662 2517	0.00 657 8947	0.00 653 5948	0.00 649 3506	0.00 645 1613	0.00 641 0256	0.00 636 9427	0.00 632 9114	0.00 628 9308
160	625 0000	621 1180	617 2840	613 4969	609 7561	606 0606	602 4096	598 8024	595 2381	591 7160
170	588 2353	584 7953	581 3953	578 0347	574 7126	571 4286	568 1818	564 9718	561 7978	558 6592
180	555 5556	552 4862	549 4505	546 4481	543 4783	540 5405	537 6344	534 7594	531 9149	529 1005
190	526 3158	523 5602	520 8333	518 1347	515 4639	512 8205	510 2041	507 6142	505 0505	502 5126
200	0.00 500 0000	0.00 497 5124	0.00 495 0495	0.00 492 6108	0.00 490 1961	0.00 487 8049	0.00 485 4369	0.00 483 0918	0.00 480 7692	0.00 478 4689
210	476 1905	473 9336	471 6981	469 4836	467 2897	465 1163	462 9630	460 8295	458 7156	456 6210
220	454 5455	452 4887	450 4505	448 4305	446 4286	444 4444	442 4779	440 5286	438 5965	436 6812
230	434 7826	432 9004	431 0345	429 1845	427 3504	425 5319	423 7288	421 9409	420 1681	418 4100
240	416 6667	414 9378	413 2231	411 5226	409 8361	408 1633	406 5041	404 8583	403 2258	401 6064
250	0.00 400 0000	0.00 398 4064	0.00 396 8254	0.00 395 2569	0.00 393 7008	0.00 392 1569	0.00 390 6250	0.00 389 1051	0.00 387 5969	0.00 386 1004
260	384 6154	383 1418	381 6794	380 2281	378 7879	377 3585	375 9398	374 5318	373 1343	371 7472
270	370 3704	369 0037	367 6471	366 3004	364 9635	363 6364	362 3188	361 0108	359 7122	358 4229
280	357 1429	355 8719	354 6099	353 3569	352 1127	350 8772	349 6503	348 4321	347 2222	346 0208
290	344 8276	343 6426	342 4658	341 2969	340 1361	338 9831	337 8378	336 7003	335 5705	334 4482
300	0.00 333 3333	0.00 332 2259	0.00 331 1258	0.00 330 0330	0.00 328 9474	0.00 327 8689	0.00 326 7974	0.00 325 7329	0.00 324 6753	0.00 323 6246
310	322 5806	321 5434	320 5128	319 4888	318 4713	317 4603	316 4557	315 4574	314 4654	313 4796
320	312 5000	311 5265	310 5590	309 5975	308 6420	307 6923	306 7485	305 8104	304 8780	303 9514
330	303 0303	302 1148	301 2048	300 3003	299 4012	298 5075	297 6190	296 7359	295 8580	294 9853
340	294 1176	293 2551	292 3977	291 5452	290 6977	289 8551	289 0173	288 1844	287 3563	286 5330
350	0.00 285 7143	0.00 284 9003	0.00 284 0909	0.00 283 2861	0.00 282 4859	0.00 281 6901	0.00 280 8989	0.00 280 1120	0.00 279 3296	0.00 278 5515
360	277 7778	277 0083	276 2431	275 4821	274 7253	273 9726	273 2240	272 4796	271 7391	271 0027
370	270 2703	269 5418	268 8172	268 0965	267 3797	266 6667	265 9574	265 2520	264 5503	263 8522
380	263 1579	262 4672	261 7801	261 0966	260 4167	259 7403	259 0674	258 3979	257 7320	257 0694
390	256 4103	255 7545	255 1020	254 4529	253 8071	253 1646	252 5253	251 8892	251 2563	250 6266
400	0.00 250 0000	0.00 249 3766	0.00 248 7562	0.00 248 1390	0.00 247 5248	0.00 246 9136	0.00 246 3054	0.00 245 7002	0.00 245 0980	0.00 244 4988
410	243 9024	243 3090	242 7184	242 1308	241 5459	240 9639	240 3846	239 8082	239 2344	238 6635
420	238 0952	237 5297	236 9668	236 4066	235 8491	235 2941	234 7418	234 1920	233 6449	233 1002
430	232 5581	232 0186	231 4815	230 9469	230 4147	229 8851	229 3578	228 8330	228 3105	227 7904
440	227 2727	226 7574	226 2443	225 7336	225 2252	224 7191	224 2152	223 7136	223 2143	222 7171
450	0.00 222 2222	0.00 221 7295	0.00 221 2389	0.00 220 7506	0.00 220 2643	0.00 219 7802	0.00 219 2982	0.00 218 8184	0.00 218 3406	0.00 217 8649
460	217 3913	216 9197	216 4502	215 9827	215 5172	215 0538	214 5923	214 1328	213 6752	213 2196
470	212 7660	212 3142	211 8644	211 4165	210 9705	210 5263	210 0840	209 6436	209 2050	208 7683
480	208 3333	207 9002	207 4689	207 0393	206 6116	206 1856	205 7613	205 3388	204 9180	204 4990
490	204 0816	203 6660	203 2520	202 8398	202 4291	202 0202	201 6129	201 2072	200 8032	200 4008
500	0.00 200 0000	0.00 199 6008	0.00 199 2032	0.00 198 8072	0.00 198 4127	0.00 198 0198	0.00 197 6285	0.00 197 2387	0.00 196 8504	0.00 196 4637
510	196 0784	195 6947	195 3125	194 9318	194 5525	194 1748	193 7984	193 4236	193 0502	192 6782
520	192 3077	191 9386	191 5709	191 2046	190 8397	190 4762	190 1141	189 7533	189 3939	189 0359
530	188 6792	188 3239	187 9699	187 6173	187 2659	186 9159	186 5672	186 2197	185 8736	185 5288
540	185 1852	184 8429	184 5018	184 1621	183 8235	183 4862	183 1502	182 8154	182 4818	182 1494
550	0.00 181 8182	0.00 181 4882	0.00 181 1594	0.00 180 8318	0.00 180 5054	0.00 180 1802	0.00 179 8561	0.00 179 5332	0.00 179 2115	0.00 178 8909
560	178 5714	178 2531	177 9359	177 6199	177 3050	176 9912	176 6784	176 3668	176 0563	175 7469
570	175 4386	175 1313	174 8252	174 5201	174 2160	173 9130	173 6111	173 3102	173 0104	172 7116
580	172 4138	172 1170	171 8213	171 5266	171 2329	170 9402	170 6485	170 3578	170 0680	169 7793
590	169 4915	169 2047	168 9189	168 6341	168 3502	168 0672	167 7852	167 5042	167 2241	166 9449
600	0.00 166 6667	0.00 166 3894	0.00 166 1130	0.00 165 8375	0.00 165 5629	0.00 165 2893	0.00 165 0165	0.00 164 7446	0.00 164 4737	0.00 164 2036
610	163 9344	163 6661	163 3987	163 1321	162 8664	162 6016	162 3377	162 0746	161 8123	161 5509
620	161 2903	161 0306	160 7717	160 5136	160 2564	160 0000	159 7444	159 4896	159 2357	158 9825
630	158 7302	158 4786	158 2278	157 9779	157 7287	157 4803	157 2327	156 9859	156 7398	156 4945
640	156 2500	156 0062	155 7632	155 5210	155 2795	155 0388	154 7988	154 5595	154 3210	154 0832
650	0.00 153 8462	0.00 153 6098	0.00 153 3742	0.00 153 1394	0.00 152 9052	0.00 152 6718	0.00 152 4390	0.00 152 2070	0.00 151 9757	0.00 151 7451
660	151 5152	151 2859	151 0574	150 8296	150 6024	150 3759	150 1502	149 9250	149 7006	149 4768
670	149 2537	149 0313	148 8095	148 5884	148 3680	148 1481	147 9290	147 7105	147 4926	147 2754
680	147 0588	146 8429	146 6276	146 4129	146 1988	145 9854	145 7726	145 5604	145 3488	145 1379
690	144 9275	144 7178	144 5087	144 3001	144 0922	143 8849	143 6782	143 4720	143 2665	143 0615
700	0.00 142 8571	0.00 142 6534	0.00 142 4501	0.00 142 2475	0.00 142 0455	0.00 141 8440	0.00 141 6431	0.00 141 4427	0.00 141 2429	0.00 141 0437
710	140 8451	140 6470	140 4494	140 2525	140 0560	139 8601	139 6648	139 4700	139 2758	139 0821
720	138 8889	138 6963	138 5042	138 3126	138 1215	137 9310	137 7410	137 5516	137 3626	137 1742
730	136 9863	136 7989	136 6120	136 4256	136 2398	136 0544	135 8696	135 6852	135 5014	135 3180
740	135 1351	134 9528	134 7709	134 5895	134 4086	134 2282	134 0483	133 8688	133 6898	133 5113
750	0.00 133 3333	0.00 133 1558	0.00 132 9787	0.00 132 8021	0.00 132 6260	0.00 132 4503	0.00 132 2751	0.00 132 1004	0.00 131 9261	0.00 131 7523
760	131 5789	131 4060	131 2336	131 0616	130 8901	130 7190	130 5483	130 3781	130 2083	130 0390
770	129 8701	129 7017	129 5337	129 3661	129 1990	129 0323	128 8660	128 7001	128 5347	128 3697
780	128 2051	128 0410	127 8772	127 7139	127 5510	127 3885	127 2265	127 0648	126 9036	126 7427
790	126 5823	126 4223	126 2626	126 1034	125 9446	125 7862	125 6281	125 4705	125 3133	125 1564
800	0.00 125 0000	0.00 124 8439	0.00 124 6883	0.00 124 5330	0.00 124 3781	0.00 124 2236	0.00 124 0695	0.00 123 9157	0.00 123 7624	0.00 123 6094
810	123 4568	123 3046	123 1527	123 0012	122 8501	122 6994	122 5490	122 3990	122 2494	122 1001
820	121 9512	121 8027	121 6545	121 5067	121 3592	121 2121	121 0654	120 9190	120 7729	120 6273
830	120 4819	120 3369	120 1923	120 0480	119 9041	119 7605	119 6172	119 4743	119 3317	119 1895
840	119 0476	118 9061	118 7648	118 6240	118 4834	118 3432	118 2033	118 0638	117 9245	117 7856
850	0.00 117 6471	0.00 117 5088	0.00 117 3709	0.00 117 2333	0.00 117 0960	0.00 116 9591	0.00 116 8224	0.00 116 6861	0.00 116 5501	0.00 116 4144
860	116 2791	116 1440	116 0093	115 8749	115 7407	115 6069	115 4734	115 3403	115 2074	115 0748
870	114 9425	114 8106	114 6789	114 5475	114 4165	114 2857	114 1553	114 0251	113 8952	113 7656
880	113 6364	113 5074	113 3787	113 2503	113 1222	112 9944	112 8668	112 7396	112 6126	112 4859
890	112 3596	112 2334	112 1076	111 9821	111 8568	111 7318	111 6071	111 4827	111 3586	111 2347
900	0.00 111 1111	0.00 110 9878	0.00 110 8647	0.00 110 7420	0.00 110 6195	0.00 110 4972	0.00 110 3753	0.00 110 2536	0.00 110 1322	0.00 110 0110
910	109 8901	109 7695	109 6491	109 5290	109 4092	109 2896	109 1703	109 0513	108 9325	108 8139
920	108 6957	108 5776	108 4599	108 3424	108 2251	108 1081	107 9914	107 8749	107 7586	107 6426
930	107 5269	107 4114	107 2961	107 1811	107 0664	106 9519	106 8376	106 7236	106 6098	106 4963
940	106 3830	106 2699	106 1571	106 0445	105 9322	105 8201	105 7082	105 5966	105 4852	105 3741
950	0.00 105 2632	0.00 105 1525	0.00 105 0420	0.00 104 9318	0.00 104 8218	0.00 104 7120	0.00 104 6025	0.00 104 4932	0.00 104 3841	0.00 104 2753
960	104 1667	104 0583	103 9501	103 8422	103 7344	103 6269	103 5197	103 4126	103 3058	103 1992
970	103 0928	102 9866	102 8807	102 7749	102 6694	102 5641	102 4590	102 3541	102 2495	102 1450
980	102 0408	101 9368	101 8330	101 7294	101 6260	101 5228	101 4199	101 3171	101 2146	101 1122
990	101 0101	100 9082	100 8065	100 7049	100 6036	100 5025	100 4016	100 3009	100 2004	100 1001

[1] Values from COMRIE, L. J. (Ed.), *Barlow's Tables of Squares, Cubes, Square Roots, Cube Roots and Reciprocals of All Integers up to 12,500*, 4th ed., Spon, London, 1958. Reprinted by kind permission of the editor and publishers.

Cubes[1] of the Integers 1–999

n	0	1	2	3	4	5	6	7	8	9
0	0	1	8	27	64	125	216	343	512	729
10	1 000	1 331	1 728	2 197	2 744	3 375	4 096	4 913	5 832	6 859
20	8 000	9 261	10 648	12 167	13 824	15 625	17 576	19 683	21 952	24 389
30	27 000	29 791	32 768	35 937	39 304	42 875	46 656	50 653	54 872	59 319
40	64 000	68 921	74 088	79 507	85 184	91 125	97 336	103 823	110 592	117 649
50	125 000	132 651	140 608	148 877	157 464	166 375	175 616	185 193	195 112	205 379
60	216 000	226 981	238 328	250 047	262 144	274 625	287 496	300 763	314 432	328 509
70	343 000	357 911	373 248	389 017	405 224	421 875	438 976	456 533	474 552	493 039
80	512 000	531 441	551 368	571 787	592 704	614 125	636 056	658 503	681 472	704 969
90	729 000	753 571	778 688	804 357	830 584	857 375	884 736	912 673	941 192	970 299
100	1 000 000	1 030 301	1 061 208	1 092 727	1 124 864	1 157 625	1 191 016	1 225 043	1 259 712	1 295 029
110	1 331 000	1 367 631	1 404 928	1 442 897	1 481 544	1 520 875	1 560 896	1 601 613	1 643 032	1 685 159
120	1 728 000	1 771 561	1 815 848	1 860 867	1 906 624	1 953 125	2 000 376	2 048 383	2 097 152	2 146 689
130	2 197 000	2 248 091	2 299 968	2 352 637	2 406 104	2 460 375	2 515 456	2 571 353	2 628 072	2 685 619
140	2 744 000	2 803 221	2 863 288	2 924 207	2 985 984	3 048 625	3 112 136	3 176 523	3 241 792	3 307 949
150	3 375 000	3 442 951	3 511 808	3 581 577	3 652 264	3 723 875	3 796 416	3 869 893	3 944 312	4 019 679
160	4 096 000	4 173 281	4 251 528	4 330 747	4 410 944	4 492 125	4 574 296	4 657 463	4 741 632	4 826 809
170	4 913 000	5 000 211	5 088 448	5 177 717	5 268 024	5 359 375	5 451 776	5 545 233	5 639 752	5 735 339
180	5 832 000	5 929 741	6 028 568	6 128 487	6 229 504	6 331 625	6 434 856	6 539 203	6 644 672	6 751 269
190	6 859 000	6 967 871	7 077 888	7 189 057	7 301 384	7 414 875	7 529 536	7 645 373	7 762 392	7 880 599
200	8 000 000	8 120 601	8 242 408	8 365 427	8 489 664	8 615 125	8 741 816	8 869 743	8 998 912	9 129 329
210	9 261 000	9 393 931	9 528 128	9 663 597	9 800 344	9 938 375	10 077 696	10 218 313	10 360 232	10 503 459
220	10 648 000	10 793 861	10 941 048	11 089 567	11 239 424	11 390 625	11 543 176	11 697 083	11 852 352	12 008 989
230	12 167 000	12 326 391	12 487 168	12 649 337	12 812 904	12 977 875	13 144 256	13 312 053	13 481 272	13 651 919
240	13 824 000	13 997 521	14 172 488	14 348 907	14 526 784	14 706 125	14 886 936	15 069 223	15 252 992	15 438 249
250	15 625 000	15 813 251	16 003 008	16 194 277	16 387 064	16 581 375	16 777 216	16 974 593	17 173 512	17 373 979
260	17 576 000	17 779 581	17 984 728	18 191 447	18 399 744	18 609 625	18 821 096	19 034 163	19 248 832	19 465 109
270	19 683 000	19 902 511	20 123 648	20 346 417	20 570 824	20 796 875	21 024 576	21 253 933	21 484 952	21 717 639
280	21 952 000	22 188 041	22 425 768	22 665 187	22 906 304	23 149 125	23 393 656	23 639 903	23 887 872	24 137 569
290	24 389 000	24 642 171	24 897 088	25 153 757	25 412 184	25 672 375	25 934 336	26 198 073	26 463 592	26 730 899
300	27 000 000	27 270 901	27 543 608	27 818 127	28 094 464	28 372 625	28 652 616	28 934 443	29 218 112	29 503 629
310	29 791 000	30 080 231	30 371 328	30 664 297	30 959 144	31 255 875	31 554 496	31 855 013	32 157 432	32 461 759
320	32 768 000	33 076 161	33 386 248	33 698 267	34 012 224	34 328 125	34 645 976	34 965 783	35 287 552	35 611 289
330	35 937 000	36 264 691	36 594 368	36 926 037	37 259 704	37 595 375	37 933 056	38 272 753	38 614 472	38 958 219
340	39 304 000	39 651 821	40 001 688	40 353 607	40 707 584	41 063 625	41 421 736	41 781 923	42 144 192	42 508 549
350	42 875 000	43 243 551	43 614 208	43 986 977	44 361 864	44 738 875	45 118 016	45 499 293	45 882 712	46 268 279
360	46 656 000	47 045 881	47 437 928	47 832 147	48 228 544	48 627 125	49 027 896	49 430 863	49 836 032	50 243 409
370	50 653 000	51 064 811	51 478 848	51 895 117	52 313 624	52 734 375	53 157 376	53 582 633	54 010 152	54 439 939
380	54 872 000	55 306 341	55 742 968	56 181 887	56 623 104	57 066 625	57 512 456	57 960 603	58 411 072	58 863 869
390	59 319 000	59 776 471	60 236 288	60 698 457	61 162 984	61 629 875	62 099 136	62 570 773	63 044 792	63 521 199
400	64 000 000	64 481 201	64 964 808	65 450 827	65 939 264	66 430 125	66 923 416	67 419 143	67 917 312	68 417 929
410	68 921 000	69 426 531	69 934 528	70 444 997	70 957 944	71 473 375	71 991 296	72 511 713	73 034 632	73 560 059
420	74 088 000	74 618 461	75 151 448	75 686 967	76 225 024	76 765 625	77 308 776	77 854 483	78 402 752	78 953 589
430	79 507 000	80 062 991	80 621 568	81 182 737	81 746 504	82 312 875	82 881 856	83 453 453	84 027 672	84 604 519
440	85 184 000	85 766 121	86 350 888	86 938 307	87 528 384	88 121 125	88 716 536	89 314 623	89 915 392	90 518 849
450	91 125 000	91 733 851	92 345 408	92 959 677	93 576 664	94 196 375	94 818 816	95 443 993	96 071 912	96 702 579
460	97 336 000	97 972 181	98 611 128	99 252 847	99 897 344	100 544 625	101 194 696	101 847 563	102 503 232	103 161 709
470	103 823 000	104 487 111	105 154 048	105 823 817	106 496 424	107 171 875	107 850 176	108 531 333	109 215 352	109 902 239
480	110 592 000	111 284 641	111 980 168	112 678 587	113 379 904	114 084 125	114 791 256	115 501 303	116 214 272	116 930 169
490	117 649 000	118 370 771	119 095 488	119 823 157	120 553 784	121 287 375	122 023 936	122 763 473	123 505 992	124 251 499
500	125 000 000	125 751 501	126 506 008	127 263 527	128 024 064	128 787 625	129 554 216	130 323 843	131 096 512	131 872 229
510	132 651 000	133 432 831	134 217 728	135 005 697	135 796 744	136 590 875	137 388 096	138 188 413	138 991 832	139 798 359
520	140 608 000	141 420 761	142 236 648	143 055 667	143 877 824	144 703 125	145 531 576	146 363 183	147 197 952	148 035 889
530	148 877 000	149 721 291	150 568 768	151 419 437	152 273 304	153 130 375	153 990 656	154 854 153	155 720 872	156 590 819
540	157 464 000	158 340 421	159 220 088	160 103 007	160 989 184	161 878 625	162 771 336	163 667 323	164 566 592	165 469 149
550	166 375 000	167 284 151	168 196 608	169 112 377	170 031 464	170 953 875	171 879 616	172 808 693	173 741 112	174 676 879
560	175 616 000	176 558 481	177 504 328	178 453 547	179 406 144	180 362 125	181 321 496	182 284 263	183 250 432	184 220 009
570	185 193 000	186 169 411	187 149 248	188 132 517	189 119 224	190 109 375	191 102 976	192 100 033	193 100 552	194 104 539
580	195 112 000	196 122 941	197 137 368	198 155 287	199 176 704	200 201 625	201 230 056	202 262 003	203 297 472	204 336 469
590	205 379 000	206 425 071	207 474 688	208 527 857	209 584 584	210 644 875	211 708 736	212 776 173	213 847 192	214 921 799
600	216 000 000	217 081 801	218 167 208	219 256 227	220 348 864	221 445 125	222 545 016	223 648 543	224 755 712	225 866 529
610	226 981 000	228 099 131	229 220 928	230 346 397	231 475 544	232 608 375	233 744 896	234 885 113	236 029 032	237 176 659
620	238 328 000	239 483 061	240 641 848	241 804 367	242 970 624	244 140 625	245 314 376	246 491 883	247 673 152	248 858 189
630	250 047 000	251 239 591	252 435 968	253 636 137	254 840 104	256 047 875	257 259 456	258 474 853	259 694 072	260 917 119
640	262 144 000	263 374 721	264 609 288	265 847 707	267 089 984	268 336 125	269 586 136	270 840 023	272 097 792	273 359 449
650	274 625 000	275 894 451	277 167 808	278 445 077	279 726 264	281 011 375	282 300 416	283 593 393	284 890 312	286 191 179
660	287 496 000	288 804 781	290 117 528	291 434 247	292 754 944	294 079 625	295 408 296	296 740 963	298 077 632	299 418 309
670	300 763 000	302 111 711	303 464 448	304 821 217	306 182 024	307 546 875	308 915 776	310 288 733	311 665 752	313 046 839
680	314 432 000	315 821 241	317 214 568	318 611 987	320 013 504	321 419 125	322 828 856	324 242 703	325 660 672	327 082 769
690	328 509 000	329 939 371	331 373 888	332 812 557	334 255 384	335 702 375	337 153 536	338 608 873	340 068 392	341 532 099
700	343 000 000	344 472 101	345 948 408	347 428 927	348 913 664	350 402 625	351 895 816	353 393 243	354 894 912	356 400 829
710	357 911 000	359 425 431	360 944 128	362 467 097	363 994 344	365 525 875	367 061 696	368 601 813	370 146 232	371 694 959
720	373 248 000	374 805 361	376 367 048	377 933 067	379 503 424	381 078 125	382 657 176	384 240 583	385 828 352	387 420 489
730	389 017 000	390 617 891	392 223 168	393 832 837	395 446 904	397 065 375	398 688 256	400 315 553	401 947 272	403 583 419
740	405 224 000	406 869 021	408 518 488	410 172 407	411 830 784	413 493 625	415 160 936	416 832 723	418 508 992	420 189 749
750	421 875 000	423 564 751	425 259 008	426 957 777	428 661 064	430 368 875	432 081 216	433 798 093	435 519 512	437 245 479
760	438 976 000	440 711 081	442 450 728	444 194 947	445 943 744	447 697 125	449 455 096	451 217 663	452 984 832	454 756 609
770	456 533 000	458 314 011	460 099 648	461 889 917	463 684 824	465 484 375	467 288 576	469 097 433	470 910 952	472 729 139
780	474 552 000	476 379 541	478 211 768	480 048 687	481 890 304	483 736 625	485 587 656	487 443 403	489 303 872	491 169 069
790	493 039 000	494 913 671	496 793 088	498 677 257	500 566 184	502 459 875	504 358 336	506 261 573	508 169 592	510 082 399
800	512 000 000	513 922 401	515 849 608	517 781 627	519 718 464	521 660 125	523 606 616	525 557 943	527 514 112	529 475 129
810	531 441 000	533 411 731	535 387 328	537 367 797	539 353 144	541 343 375	543 338 496	545 338 513	547 343 432	549 353 259
820	551 368 000	553 387 661	555 412 248	557 441 767	559 476 224	561 515 625	563 559 976	565 609 283	567 663 552	569 722 789
830	571 787 000	573 856 191	575 930 368	578 009 537	580 093 704	582 182 875	584 277 056	586 376 253	588 480 472	590 589 719
840	592 704 000	594 823 321	596 947 688	599 077 107	601 211 584	603 351 125	605 495 736	607 645 423	609 800 192	611 960 049
850	614 125 000	616 295 051	618 470 208	620 650 477	622 835 864	625 026 375	627 222 016	629 422 793	631 628 712	633 839 779
860	636 056 000	638 277 381	640 503 928	642 735 647	644 972 544	647 214 625	649 461 896	651 714 363	653 972 032	656 234 909
870	658 503 000	660 776 311	663 054 848	665 338 617	667 627 624	669 921 875	672 221 376	674 526 133	676 836 152	679 151 439
880	681 472 000	683 797 841	686 128 968	688 465 387	690 807 104	693 154 125	695 506 456	697 864 103	700 227 072	702 595 369
890	704 969 000	707 347 971	709 732 288	712 121 957	714 516 984	716 917 375	719 323 136	721 734 273	724 150 792	726 572 699
900	729 000 000	731 432 701	733 870 808	736 314 327	738 763 264	741 217 625	743 677 416	746 142 643	748 613 312	751 089 429
910	753 571 000	756 058 031	758 550 528	761 048 497	763 551 944	766 060 875	768 575 296	771 095 213	773 620 632	776 151 559
920	778 688 000	781 229 961	783 777 448	786 330 467	788 889 024	791 453 125	794 022 776	796 597 983	799 178 752	801 765 089
930	804 357 000	806 954 491	809 557 568	812 166 237	814 780 504	817 400 375	820 025 856	822 656 953	825 293 672	827 936 019
940	830 584 000	833 237 621	835 896 888	838 561 807	841 232 384	843 908 625	846 590 536	849 278 123	851 971 392	854 670 349
950	857 375 000	860 085 351	862 801 408	865 523 177	868 250 664	870 983 875	873 722 816	876 467 493	879 217 912	881 974 079
960	884 736 000	887 503 681	890 277 128	893 056 347	895 841 344	898 632 125	901 428 696	904 231 063	907 039 232	909 853 209
970	912 673 000	915 498 611	918 330 048	921 167 317	924 010 424	926 859 375	929 714 176	932 574 833	935 441 352	938 313 739
980	941 192 000	944 076 141	946 966 168	949 862 087	952 763 904	955 671 625	958 585 256	961 504 803	964 430 272	967 361 669
990	970 299 000	973 242 271	976 191 488	979 146 657	982 107 784	985 074 875	988 047 936	991 026 973	994 011 992	997 002 999

[1] Values from COMRIE, L. J. (Ed.), *Barlow's Tables of Squares, Cubes, Square Roots, Cube Roots and Reciprocals of All Integers up to 12,500*, 4th ed., Spon, London, 1958. Reprinted by kind permission of the editor and publishers.

$\sqrt{100n} = 10\sqrt{n}$ $\sqrt{1000n} = 10\sqrt{10n}$ $\sqrt{0.1n} = 0.1\sqrt{10n}$ $\sqrt{0.01n} = 0.1\sqrt{n}$ $\sqrt{0.001n} = 0.01\sqrt{10n}$

n	n^2	$\sqrt{n}$	$\sqrt{10n}$	n	n^2	$\sqrt{n}$	$\sqrt{10n}$	n	n^2	$\sqrt{n}$	$\sqrt{10n}$	n	n^2	$\sqrt{n}$	$\sqrt{10n}$
				100	1 00 00	10.000 0000	31.622 777	**200**	4 00 00	14.142 1356	44.721 360	**300**	9 00 00	17.320 5081	54.772 256
1	1	1.000 0000	3.162 2777	101	1 02 01	10.049 8756	31.780 497	201	4 04 01	14.177 4469	44.833 024	301	9 06 01	17.349 3516	54.863 467
2	4	1.414 2136	4.472 1360	102	1 04 04	10.099 5049	31.937 439	202	4 08 04	14.212 6704	44.944 410	302	9 12 04	17.378 1472	54.954 527
3	9	1.732 0508	5.477 2256	103	1 06 09	10.148 8916	32.093 613	203	4 12 09	14.247 8068	45.055 521	303	9 18 09	17.406 8952	55.045 436
4	16	2.000 0000	6.324 5553	104	1 08 16	10.198 0390	32.249 031	204	4 16 16	14.282 8569	45.166 359	304	9 24 16	17.435 5958	55.136 195
5	25	2.236 0680	7.071 0678	**105**	1 10 25	10.246 9508	32.403 703	**205**	4 20 25	14.317 8211	45.276 926	**305**	9 30 25	17.464 2492	55.226 805
6	36	2.449 4897	7.745 9667	106	1 12 36	10.295 6301	32.557 641	206	4 24 36	14.352 7001	45.387 223	306	9 36 36	17.492 8557	55.317 267
7	49	2.645 7513	8.366 6003	107	1 14 49	10.344 0804	32.710 854	207	4 28 49	14.387 4946	45.497 253	307	9 42 49	17.521 4155	55.407 581
8	64	2.828 4271	8.944 2719	108	1 16 64	10.392 3048	32.863 353	208	4 32 64	14.422 2051	45.607 017	308	9 48 64	17.549 9288	55.497 748
9	81	3.000 0000	9.486 8330	109	1 18 81	10.440 3065	33.015 148	209	4 36 81	14.456 8323	45.716 518	309	9 54 81	17.578 3958	55.587 768
10	1 00	3.162 2777	10.000 0000	**110**	1 21 00	10.488 0885	33.166 248	**210**	4 41 00	14.491 3767	45.825 757	**310**	9 61 00	17.606 8169	55.677 644
11	1 21	3.316 6248	10.488 0885	111	1 23 21	10.535 6538	33.316 662	211	4 45 21	14.525 8390	45.934 736	311	9 67 21	17.635 1921	55.767 374
12	1 44	3.464 1016	10.954 4512	112	1 25 44	10.583 0052	33.466 401	212	4 49 44	14.560 2198	46.043 458	312	9 73 44	17.663 5217	55.856 960
13	1 69	3.605 5513	11.401 7543	113	1 27 69	10.630 1458	33.615 473	213	4 53 69	14.594 5195	46.151 923	313	9 79 69	17.691 8060	55.946 403
14	1 96	3.741 6574	11.832 1596	114	1 29 96	10.677 0783	33.763 886	214	4 57 96	14.628 7388	46.260 134	314	9 85 96	17.720 0451	56.035 703
15	2 25	3.872 9833	12.247 4487	**115**	1 32 25	10.723 8053	33.911 650	**215**	4 62 25	14.662 8783	46.368 092	**315**	9 92 25	17.748 2393	56.124 861
16	2 56	4.000 0000	12.649 1106	116	1 34 56	10.770 3296	34.058 773	216	4 66 56	14.696 9385	46.475 800	316	9 98 56	17.776 3888	56.213 877
17	2 89	4.123 1056	13.038 4048	117	1 36 89	10.816 6538	34.205 263	217	4 70 89	14.730 9199	46.583 259	317	10 04 89	17.804 4938	56.302 753
18	3 24	4.242 6407	13.416 4079	118	1 39 24	10.862 7805	34.351 128	218	4 75 24	14.764 8231	46.690 470	318	10 11 24	17.832 5545	56.391 489
19	3 61	4.358 8989	13.784 0488	119	1 41 61	10.908 7121	34.496 377	219	4 79 61	14.798 6486	46.797 436	319	10 17 61	17.860 5711	56.480 085
20	4 00	4.472 1360	14.142 1356	**120**	1 44 00	10.954 4512	34.641 016	**220**	4 84 00	14.832 3970	46.904 158	**320**	10 24 00	17.888 5438	56.568 542
21	4 41	4.582 5757	14.491 3767	121	1 46 41	11.000 0000	34.785 054	221	4 88 41	14.866 0687	47.010 637	321	10 30 41	17.916 4729	56.656 862
22	4 84	4.690 4158	14.832 3970	122	1 48 84	11.045 3610	34.928 498	222	4 92 84	14.899 6644	47.116 876	322	10 36 84	17.944 3584	56.745 044
23	5 29	4.795 8315	15.165 7509	123	1 51 29	11.090 5365	35.071 356	223	4 97 29	14.933 1845	47.222 876	323	10 43 29	17.972 2008	56.833 089
24	5 76	4.898 9795	15.491 9334	124	1 53 76	11.135 5287	35.213 634	224	5 01 76	14.966 6295	47.328 638	324	10 49 76	18.000 0000	56.920 998
25	6 25	5.000 0000	15.811 3883	**125**	1 56 25	11.180 3399	35.355 339	**225**	5 06 25	15.000 0000	47.434 165	**325**	10 56 25	18.027 7564	57.008 771
26	6 76	5.099 0195	16.124 5155	126	1 58 76	11.224 9722	35.496 479	226	5 10 76	15.033 2964	47.539 457	326	10 62 76	18.055 4701	57.096 410
27	7 29	5.196 1524	16.431 6767	127	1 61 29	11.269 4277	35.637 059	227	5 15 29	15.066 5192	47.644 517	327	10 69 29	18.083 1413	57.183 914
28	7 84	5.291 5026	16.733 2005	128	1 63 84	11.313 7085	35.777 088	228	5 19 84	15.099 6689	47.749 346	328	10 75 84	18.110 7703	57.271 284
29	8 41	5.385 1648	17.029 3864	129	1 66 41	11.357 8167	35.916 570	229	5 24 41	15.132 7460	47.853 944	329	10 82 41	18.138 3571	57.358 522
30	9 00	5.477 2256	17.320 5081	**130**	1 69 00	11.401 7543	36.055 513	**230**	5 29 00	15.165 7509	47.958 315	**330**	10 89 00	18.165 9021	57.445 626
31	9 61	5.567 7644	17.606 8169	131	1 71 61	11.445 5231	36.193 922	231	5 33 61	15.198 6842	48.062 459	331	10 95 61	18.193 4054	57.532 599
32	10 24	5.656 8542	17.888 5438	132	1 74 24	11.489 1253	36.331 804	232	5 38 24	15.231 5462	48.166 378	332	11 02 24	18.220 8672	57.619 441
33	10 89	5.744 5626	18.165 9021	133	1 76 89	11.532 5626	36.469 165	233	5 42 89	15.264 3375	48.270 074	333	11 08 89	18.248 2876	57.706 152
34	11 56	5.830 9519	18.439 0889	134	1 79 56	11.575 8369	36.606 010	234	5 47 56	15.297 0585	48.373 546	334	11 15 56	18.275 6669	57.792 733
35	12 25	5.916 0798	18.708 2869	**135**	1 82 25	11.618 9500	36.742 346	**235**	5 52 25	15.329 7097	48.476 799	**335**	11 22 25	18.303 0052	57.879 185
36	12 96	6.000 0000	18.973 6660	136	1 84 96	11.661 9038	36.878 178	236	5 56 96	15.362 2915	48.579 831	336	11 28 96	18.330 3028	57.965 507
37	13 69	6.082 7625	19.235 3841	137	1 87 69	11.704 6999	37.013 511	237	5 61 69	15.394 8043	48.682 646	337	11 35 69	18.357 5598	58.051 701
38	14 44	6.164 4140	19.493 5887	138	1 90 44	11.747 3401	37.148 351	238	5 66 44	15.427 2486	48.785 244	338	11 42 44	18.384 7763	58.137 767
39	15 21	6.244 9980	19.748 4177	139	1 93 21	11.789 8261	37.282 704	239	5 71 21	15.459 6248	48.887 626	339	11 49 21	18.411 9526	58.223 707
40	16 00	6.324 5553	20.000 0000	**140**	1 96 00	11.832 1596	37.416 574	**240**	5 76 00	15.491 9334	48.989 795	**340**	11 56 00	18.439 0889	58.309 519
41	16 81	6.403 1242	20.248 4567	141	1 98 81	11.874 3421	37.549 967	241	5 80 81	15.524 1747	49.091 751	341	11 62 81	18.466 1853	58.395 205
42	17 64	6.480 7407	20.493 9015	142	2 01 64	11.916 3753	37.682 887	242	5 85 64	15.556 3492	49.193 496	342	11 69 64	18.493 2420	58.480 766
43	18 49	6.557 4385	20.736 4414	143	2 04 49	11.958 2607	37.815 341	243	5 90 49	15.588 4573	49.295 030	343	11 76 49	18.520 2592	58.566 202
44	19 36	6.633 2496	20.976 1770	144	2 07 36	12.000 0000	37.947 332	244	5 95 36	15.620 4994	49.396 356	344	11 83 36	18.547 2370	58.651 513
45	20 25	6.708 2039	21.213 2034	**145**	2 10 25	12.041 5946	38.078 866	**245**	6 00 25	15.652 4758	49.497 475	**345**	11 90 25	18.574 1756	58.736 701
46	21 16	6.782 3300	21.447 6106	146	2 13 16	12.083 0460	38.209 946	246	6 05 16	15.684 3871	49.598 387	346	11 97 16	18.601 0752	58.821 765
47	22 09	6.855 6546	21.679 4834	147	2 16 09	12.124 3557	38.340 579	247	6 10 09	15.716 2336	49.699 095	347	12 04 09	18.627 9360	58.906 706
48	23 04	6.928 2032	21.908 9023	148	2 19 04	12.165 5251	38.470 768	248	6 15 04	15.748 0157	49.799 598	348	12 11 04	18.654 7581	58.991 525
49	24 01	7.000 0000	22.135 9436	149	2 22 01	12.206 5556	38.600 518	249	6 20 01	15.779 7338	49.899 900	349	12 18 01	18.681 5417	59.076 222
50	25 00	7.071 0678	22.360 6798	**150**	2 25 00	12.247 4487	38.729 833	**250**	6 25 00	15.811 3883	50.000 000	**350**	12 25 00	18.708 2869	59.160 798
51	26 01	7.141 4284	22.583 1796	151	2 28 01	12.288 2057	38.858 718	251	6 30 01	15.842 9795	50.099 900	351	12 32 01	18.734 9940	59.245 253
52	27 04	7.211 1026	22.803 5085	152	2 31 04	12.328 8280	38.987 177	252	6 35 04	15.874 5079	50.199 602	352	12 39 04	18.761 6630	59.329 588
53	28 09	7.280 1099	23.021 7289	153	2 34 09	12.369 3169	39.115 214	253	6 40 09	15.905 9737	50.299 105	353	12 46 09	18.788 2942	59.413 803
54	29 16	7.348 4692	23.237 9001	154	2 37 16	12.409 6736	39.242 834	254	6 45 16	15.937 3775	50.398 413	354	12 53 16	18.814 8877	59.497 899
55	30 25	7.416 1985	23.452 0788	**155**	2 40 25	12.449 8996	39.370 039	**255**	6 50 25	15.968 7194	50.497 525	**355**	12 60 25	18.841 4437	59.581 876
56	31 36	7.483 3148	23.664 3191	156	2 43 36	12.489 9960	39.496 835	256	6 55 36	16.000 0000	50.596 443	356	12 67 36	18.867 9623	59.665 736
57	32 49	7.549 8344	23.874 6728	157	2 46 49	12.529 9641	39.623 226	257	6 60 49	16.031 2195	50.695 167	357	12 74 49	18.894 4436	59.749 477
58	33 64	7.615 7731	24.083 1892	158	2 49 64	12.569 8051	39.749 214	258	6 65 64	16.062 3784	50.793 700	358	12 81 64	18.920 8879	59.833 101
59	34 81	7.681 1457	24.289 9156	159	2 52 81	12.609 5202	39.874 804	259	6 70 81	16.093 4769	50.892 043	359	12 88 81	18.947 2953	59.916 609
60	36 00	7.745 9667	24.494 8974	**160**	2 56 00	12.649 1106	40.000 000	**260**	6 76 00	16.124 5155	50.990 195	**360**	12 96 00	18.973 6660	60.000 000
61	37 21	7.810 2497	24.698 1781	161	2 59 21	12.688 5775	40.124 805	261	6 81 21	16.155 4944	51.088 159	361	13 03 21	19.000 0000	60.083 276
62	38 44	7.874 0079	24.899 7992	162	2 62 44	12.727 9221	40.249 224	262	6 86 44	16.186 4141	51.185 936	362	13 10 44	19.026 2976	60.166 436
63	39 69	7.937 2539	25.099 8008	163	2 65 69	12.767 1453	40.373 258	263	6 91 69	16.217 2747	51.283 526	363	13 17 69	19.052 5589	60.249 481
64	40 96	8.000 0000	25.298 2213	164	2 68 96	12.806 2485	40.496 913	264	6 96 96	16.248 0768	51.380 930	364	13 24 96	19.078 7840	60.332 413
65	42 25	8.062 2577	25.495 0976	**165**	2 72 25	12.845 2326	40.620 192	**265**	7 02 25	16.278 8206	51.478 151	**365**	13 32 25	19.104 9732	60.415 230
66	43 56	8.124 0384	25.690 4652	166	2 75 56	12.884 0987	40.743 098	266	7 07 56	16.309 5064	51.575 188	366	13 39 56	19.131 1265	60.497 934
67	44 89	8.185 3528	25.884 3582	167	2 78 89	12.922 8480	40.865 633	267	7 12 89	16.340 1346	51.672 043	367	13 46 89	19.157 2441	60.580 525
68	46 24	8.246 2113	26.076 8096	168	2 82 24	12.961 4814	40.987 803	268	7 18 24	16.370 7055	51.768 716	368	13 54 24	19.183 3261	60.663 004
69	47 61	8.306 6239	26.267 8511	169	2 85 61	13.000 0000	41.109 610	269	7 23 61	16.401 2195	51.865 210	369	13 61 61	19.209 3727	60.745 370
70	49 00	8.366 6003	26.457 5131	**170**	2 89 00	13.038 4048	41.231 056	**270**	7 29 00	16.431 6767	51.961 524	**370**	13 69 00	19.235 3841	60.827 625
71	50 41	8.426 1498	26.645 8252	171	2 92 41	13.076 6968	41.352 146	271	7 34 41	16.462 0776	52.057 660	371	13 76 41	19.261 3603	60.909 769
72	51 84	8.485 2814	26.832 8157	172	2 95 84	13.114 8770	41.472 883	272	7 39 84	16.492 4225	52.153 619	372	13 83 84	19.287 3015	60.991 803
73	53 29	8.544 0037	27.018 5122	173	2 99 29	13.152 9464	41.593 269	273	7 45 29	16.522 7116	52.249 402	373	13 91 29	19.313 2079	61.073 726
74	54 76	8.602 3253	27.202 9410	174	3 02 76	13.190 9060	41.713 307	274	7 50 76	16.552 9454	52.345 009	374	13 98 76	19.339 0796	61.155 539
75	56 25	8.660 2540	27.386 1279	**175**	3 06 25	13.228 7566	41.833 001	**275**	7 56 25	16.583 1240	52.440 442	**375**	14 06 25	19.364 9167	61.237 244
76	57 76	8.717 7979	27.568 0975	176	3 09 76	13.266 4992	41.952 354	276	7 61 76	16.613 2477	52.535 702	376	14 13 76	19.390 7194	61.318 839
77	59 29	8.774 9644	27.748 8739	177	3 13 29	13.304 1347	42.071 368	277	7 67 29	16.643 3170	52.630 789	377	14 21 29	19.416 4878	61.400 326
78	60 84	8.831 7609	27.928 4801	178	3 16 84	13.341 6641	42.190 046	278	7 72 84	16.673 3320	52.725 705	378	14 28 84	19.442 2221	61.481 705
79	62 41	8.888 1944	28.106 9386	179	3 20 41	13.379 0882	42.308 392	279	7 78 41	16.703 2931	52.820 451	379	14 36 41	19.467 9223	61.562 976
80	64 00	8.944 2719	28.284 2712	**180**	3 24 00	13.416 4079	42.426 407	**280**	7 84 00	16.733 2005	52.915 026	**380**	14 44 00	19.493 5887	61.644 140
81	65 61	9.000 0000	28.460 4989	181	3 27 61	13.453 6240	42.544 095	281	7 89 61	16.763 0546	53.009 433	381	14 51 61	19.519 2213	61.725 197
82	67 24	9.055 3851	28.635 6421	182	3 31 24	13.490 7376	42.661 458	282	7 95 24	16.792 8556	53.103 672	382	14 59 24	19.544 8203	61.806 149
83	68 89	9.110 4336	28.809 7206	183	3 34 89	13.527 7493	42.778 499	283	8 00 89	16.822 6038	53.197 744	383	14 66 89	19.570 3858	61.886 994
84	70 56	9.165 1514	28.982 7535	184	3 38 56	13.564 6600	42.895 221	284	8 06 56	16.852 2995	53.291 650	384	14 74 56	19.595 9179	61.967 734
85	72 25	9.219 5445	29.154 7595	**185**	3 42 25	13.601 4705	43.011 626	**285**	8 12 25	16.881 9430	53.385 391	**385**	14 82 25	19.621 4169	62.048 368
86	73 96	9.273 6185	29.325 7566	186	3 45 96	13.638 1817	43.127 717	286	8 17 96	16.911 5345	53.478 968	386	14 89 96	19.646 8827	62.128 898
87	75 69	9.327 3791	29.495 7624	187	3 49 69	13.674 7943	43.243 497	287	8 23 69	16.941 0743	53.572 381	387	14 97 69	19.672 3156	62.209 324
88	77 44	9.380 8315	29.664 7939	188	3 53 44	13.711 3092	43.358 967	288	8 29 44	16.970 5627	53.665 631	388	15 05 44	19.697 7156	62.289 646
89	79 21	9.433 9811	29.832 8678	189	3 57 21	13.747 7271	43.474 130	289	8 35 21	17.000 0000	53.758 720	389	15 13 21	19.723 0829	62.369 865
90	81 00	9.486 8330	30.000 0000	**190**	3 61 00	13.784 0488	43.588 989	**290**	8 41 00	17.029 3864	53.851 648	**390**	15 21 00	19.748 4177	62.449 980
91	82 81	9.539 3920	30.166 2063	191	3 64 81	13.820 2750	43.703 547	291	8 46 81	17.058 7221	53.944 416	391	15 28 81	19.773 7199	62.529 993
92	84 64	9.591 6630	30.331 5018	192	3 68 64	13.856 4065	43.817 805	292	8 52 64	17.088 0075	54.037 024	392	15 36 64	19.798 9899	62.609 903
93	86 49	9.643 6508	30.495 9014	193	3 72 49	13.892 4440	43.931 765	293	8 58 49	17.117 2428	54.129 474	393	15 44 49	19.824 2276	62.689 712
94	88 36	9.695 3597	30.659 4194	194	3 76 36	13.928 3883	44.045 431	294	8 64 36	17.146 4282	54.221 767	394	15 52 36	19.849 4332	62.769 419
95	90 25	9.746 7943	30.822 0700	**195**	3 80 25	13.964 2400	44.158 804	**295**	8 70 25	17.175 5640	54.313 902	**395**	15 60 25	19.874 6069	62.849 025
96	92 16	9.797 9590	30.983 8668	196	3 84 16	14.000 0000	44.271 887	296	8 76 16	17.204 6505	54.405 882	396	15 68 16	19.899 7487	62.928 531
97	94 09	9.848 8578	31.144 8230	197	3 88 09	14.035 6688	44.384 682	297	8 82 09	17.233 6879	54.497 706	397	15 76 09	19.924 8588	63.007 936
98	96 04	9.899 4949	31.304 9517	198	3 92 04	14.071 2473	44.497 191	298	8 88 04	17.262 6765	54.589 376	398	15 84 04	19.949 9373	63.087 241
99	98 01	9.949 8744	31.464 2654	199	3 96 01	14.106 7360	44.609 416	299	8 94 01	17.291 6165	54.680 892	399	15 92 01	19.974 9844	63.166 447

[1] Values from COMRIE, L. J. (Ed.), *Barlow's Tables of Squares, Cubes, Square Roots, Cube Roots and Reciprocals of All Integers up to 12,500*, 4th ed., Spon, London, 1958. Reprinted by kind permission of the editor and publishers.

$\sqrt{100n} = 10\sqrt{n}$ $\sqrt{1000n} = 10\sqrt{10n}$ $\sqrt{0.1n} = 0.1\sqrt{10n}$ $\sqrt{0.01n} = 0.1\sqrt{n}$ $\sqrt{0.001n} = 0.01\sqrt{10n}$

n	n^2	$\sqrt{n}$	$\sqrt{10n}$
400	16 00 00	20.000 0000	63.245 553
401	16 08 01	20.024 9844	63.324 561
402	16 16 04	20.049 9377	63.403 470
403	16 24 09	20.074 8599	63.482 281
404	16 32 16	20.099 7512	63.560 994
405	16 40 25	20.124 6118	63.639 610
406	16 48 36	20.149 4417	63.718 129
407	16 56 49	20.174 2410	63.796 552
408	16 64 64	20.199 0099	63.874 878
409	16 72 81	20.223 7484	63.953 108
410	16 81 00	20.248 4567	64.031 242
411	16 89 21	20.273 1349	64.109 282
412	16 97 44	20.297 7831	64.187 226
413	17 05 69	20.322 4014	64.265 076
414	17 13 96	20.346 9899	64.342 832
415	17 22 25	20.371 5488	64.420 494
416	17 30 56	20.396 0781	64.498 062
417	17 38 89	20.420 5779	64.575 537
418	17 47 24	20.445 0483	64.652 920
419	17 55 61	20.469 4895	64.730 209
420	17 64 00	20.493 9015	64.807 407
421	17 72 41	20.518 2845	64.884 513
422	17 80 84	20.542 6386	64.961 527
423	17 89 29	20.566 9638	65.038 450
424	17 97 76	20.591 2603	65.115 282
425	18 06 25	20.615 5281	65.192 024
426	18 14 76	20.639 7674	65.268 675
427	18 23 29	20.663 9783	65.345 237
428	18 31 84	20.688 1609	65.421 709
429	18 40 41	20.712 3152	65.498 092
430	18 49 00	20.736 4414	65.574 385
431	18 57 61	20.760 5395	65.650 590
432	18 66 24	20.784 6097	65.726 707
433	18 74 89	20.808 6520	65.802 736
434	18 83 56	20.832 6667	65.878 676
435	18 92 25	20.856 6536	65.954 530
436	19 00 96	20.880 6130	66.030 296
437	19 09 69	20.904 5450	66.105 976
438	19 18 44	20.928 4495	66.181 568
439	19 27 21	20.952 3268	66.257 075
440	19 36 00	20.976 1770	66.332 496
441	19 44 81	21.000 0000	66.407 831
442	19 53 64	21.023 7960	66.483 081
443	19 62 49	21.047 5652	66.558 245
444	19 71 36	21.071 3075	66.633 325
445	19 80 25	21.095 0231	66.708 320
446	19 89 16	21.118 7121	66.783 231
447	19 98 09	21.142 3745	66.858 059
448	20 07 04	21.166 0105	66.932 802
449	20 16 01	21.189 6201	67.007 462
450	20 25 00	21.213 2034	67.082 039
451	20 34 01	21.236 7606	67.156 534
452	20 43 04	21.260 2916	67.230 945
453	20 52 09	21.283 7967	67.305 275
454	20 61 16	21.307 2758	67.379 522
455	20 70 25	21.330 7290	67.453 688
456	20 79 36	21.354 1565	67.527 772
457	20 88 49	21.377 5583	67.601 775
458	20 97 64	21.400 9346	67.675 697
459	21 06 81	21.424 2853	67.749 539
460	21 16 00	21.447 6106	67.823 300
461	21 25 21	21.470 9106	67.896 981
462	21 34 44	21.494 1853	67.970 582
463	21 43 69	21.517 4348	68.044 103
464	21 52 96	21.540 6592	68.117 545
465	21 62 25	21.563 8587	68.190 908
466	21 71 56	21.587 0331	68.264 193
467	21 80 89	21.610 1828	68.337 398
468	21 90 24	21.633 3077	68.410 526
469	21 99 61	21.656 4078	68.483 575
470	22 09 00	21.679 4834	68.556 546
471	22 18 41	21.702 5344	68.629 440
472	22 27 84	21.725 5610	68.702 256
473	22 37 29	21.748 5632	68.774 995
474	22 46 76	21.771 5411	68.847 658
475	22 56 25	21.794 4947	68.920 244
476	22 65 76	21.817 4242	68.992 753
477	22 75 29	21.840 3297	69.065 187
478	22 84 84	21.863 2111	69.137 544
479	22 94 41	21.886 0686	69.209 826
480	23 04 00	21.908 9023	69.282 032
481	23 13 61	21.931 7122	69.354 164
482	23 23 24	21.954 4984	69.426 220
483	23 32 89	21.977 2610	69.498 201
484	23 42 56	22.000 0000	69.570 109
485	23 52 25	22.022 7155	69.641 941
486	23 61 96	22.045 4077	69.713 700
487	23 71 69	22.068 0765	69.785 385
488	23 81 44	22.090 7220	69.856 997
489	23 91 21	22.113 3444	69.928 535
490	24 01 00	22.135 9436	70.000 000
491	24 10 81	22.158 5198	70.071 392
492	24 20 64	22.181 0730	70.142 712
493	24 30 49	22.203 6033	70.213 959
494	24 40 36	22.226 1108	70.285 134
495	24 50 25	22.248 5955	70.356 236
496	24 60 16	22.271 0575	70.427 267
497	24 70 09	22.293 4968	70.498 227
498	24 80 04	22.315 9136	70.569 115
499	24 90 01	22.338 3079	70.639 932

n	n^2	$\sqrt{n}$	$\sqrt{10n}$
500	25 00 00	22.360 6798	70.710 678
501	25 10 01	22.383 0293	70.781 353
502	25 20 04	22.405 3565	70.851 958
503	25 30 09	22.427 6615	70.922 493
504	25 40 16	22.449 9443	70.992 957
505	25 50 25	22.472 2051	71.063 352
506	25 60 36	22.494 4438	71.133 677
507	25 70 49	22.516 6605	71.203 932
508	25 80 64	22.538 8553	71.274 119
509	25 90 81	22.561 0283	71.344 236
510	26 01 00	22.583 1796	71.414 284
511	26 11 21	22.605 3091	71.484 264
512	26 21 44	22.627 4170	71.554 175
513	26 31 69	22.649 5033	71.624 018
514	26 41 96	22.671 5681	71.693 793
515	26 52 25	22.693 6114	71.763 500
516	26 62 56	22.715 6334	71.833 140
517	26 72 89	22.737 6340	71.902 712
518	26 83 24	22.759 6134	71.972 217
519	26 93 61	22.781 5715	72.041 655
520	27 04 00	22.803 5085	72.111 026
521	27 14 41	22.825 4244	72.180 330
522	27 24 84	22.847 3193	72.249 567
523	27 35 29	22.869 1933	72.318 739
524	27 45 76	22.891 0463	72.387 844
525	27 56 25	22.912 8785	72.456 884
526	27 66 76	22.934 6899	72.525 857
527	27 77 29	22.956 4806	72.594 766
528	27 87 84	22.978 2506	72.663 608
529	27 98 41	23.000 0000	72.732 386
530	28 09 00	23.021 7289	72.801 099
531	28 19 61	23.043 4372	72.869 747
532	28 30 24	23.065 1252	72.938 330
533	28 40 89	23.086 7928	73.006 849
534	28 51 56	23.108 4400	73.075 304
535	28 62 25	23.130 0670	73.143 694
536	28 72 96	23.151 6738	73.212 021
537	28 83 69	23.173 2605	73.280 284
538	28 94 44	23.194 8270	73.348 483
539	29 05 21	23.216 3735	73.416 619
540	29 16 00	23.237 9001	73.484 692
541	29 26 81	23.259 4067	73.552 702
542	29 37 64	23.280 8935	73.620 649
543	29 48 49	23.302 3604	73.688 534
544	29 59 36	23.323 8076	73.756 356
545	29 70 25	23.345 2351	73.824 115
546	29 81 16	23.366 6429	73.891 813
547	29 92 09	23.388 0311	73.959 448
548	30 03 04	23.409 3998	74.027 022
549	30 14 01	23.430 7490	74.094 534
550	30 25 00	23.452 0788	74.161 985
551	30 36 01	23.473 3892	74.229 374
552	30 47 04	23.494 6802	74.296 702
553	30 58 09	23.515 9520	74.363 970
554	30 69 16	23.537 2046	74.431 176
555	30 80 25	23.558 4380	74.498 322
556	30 91 36	23.579 6522	74.565 408
557	31 02 49	23.600 8474	74.632 433
558	31 13 64	23.622 0236	74.699 398
559	31 24 81	23.643 1808	74.766 303
560	31 36 00	23.664 3191	74.833 148
561	31 47 21	23.685 4386	74.899 933
562	31 58 44	23.706 5392	74.966 659
563	31 69 69	23.727 6210	75.033 326
564	31 80 96	23.748 6842	75.099 933
565	31 92 25	23.769 7286	75.166 482
566	32 03 56	23.790 7545	75.232 971
567	32 14 89	23.811 7618	75.299 402
568	32 26 24	23.832 7506	75.365 775
569	32 37 61	23.853 7209	75.432 089
570	32 49 00	23.874 6728	75.498 344
571	32 60 41	23.895 6063	75.564 542
572	32 71 84	23.916 5215	75.630 682
573	32 83 29	23.937 4184	75.696 763
574	32 94 76	23.958 2971	75.762 788
575	33 06 25	23.979 1576	75.828 754
576	33 17 76	24.000 0000	75.894 664
577	33 29 29	24.020 8243	75.960 516
578	33 40 84	24.041 6306	76.026 311
579	33 52 41	24.062 4188	76.092 050
580	33 64 00	24.083 1892	76.157 731
581	33 75 61	24.103 9416	76.223 356
582	33 87 24	24.124 6762	76.288 924
583	33 98 89	24.145 3929	76.354 437
584	34 10 56	24.166 0919	76.419 893
585	34 22 25	24.186 7732	76.485 293
586	34 33 96	24.207 4369	76.550 637
587	34 45 69	24.228 0829	76.615 925
588	34 57 44	24.248 7113	76.681 158
589	34 69 21	24.269 3222	76.746 335
590	34 81 00	24.289 9156	76.811 457
591	34 92 81	24.310 4916	76.876 524
592	35 04 64	24.331 0501	76.941 536
593	35 16 49	24.351 5913	77.006 493
594	35 28 36	24.372 1152	77.071 395
595	35 40 25	24.392 6218	77.136 243
596	35 52 16	24.413 1112	77.201 036
597	35 64 09	24.433 5834	77.265 775
598	35 76 04	24.454 0385	77.330 460
599	35 88 01	24.474 4765	77.395 090

n	n^2	$\sqrt{n}$	$\sqrt{10n}$
600	36 00 00	24.494 8974	77.459 667
601	36 12 01	24.515 3013	77.524 190
602	36 24 04	24.535 6883	77.588 659
603	36 36 09	24.556 0583	77.653 075
604	36 48 16	24.576 4115	77.717 437
605	36 60 25	24.596 7478	77.781 746
606	36 72 36	24.617 0673	77.846 002
607	36 84 49	24.637 3700	77.910 205
608	36 96 64	24.657 6560	77.974 355
609	37 08 81	24.677 9254	78.038 452
610	37 21 00	24.698 1781	78.102 497
611	37 33 21	24.718 4142	78.166 489
612	37 45 44	24.738 6338	78.230 429
613	37 57 69	24.758 8368	78.294 317
614	37 69 96	24.779 0234	78.358 152
615	37 82 25	24.799 1935	78.421 936
616	37 94 56	24.819 3473	78.485 667
617	38 06 89	24.839 4847	78.549 348
618	38 19 24	24.859 6058	78.612 976
619	38 31 61	24.879 7106	78.676 553
620	38 44 00	24.899 7992	78.740 079
621	38 56 41	24.919 8716	78.803 553
622	38 68 84	24.939 9278	78.866 977
623	38 81 29	24.959 9679	78.930 349
624	38 93 76	24.979 9920	78.993 671
625	39 06 25	25.000 0000	79.056 942
626	39 18 76	25.019 9920	79.120 162
627	39 31 29	25.039 9681	79.183 332
628	39 43 84	25.059 9282	79.246 451
629	39 56 41	25.079 8724	79.309 520
630	39 69 00	25.099 8008	79.372 539
631	39 81 61	25.119 7134	79.435 508
632	39 94 24	25.139 6102	79.498 428
633	40 06 89	25.159 4913	79.561 297
634	40 19 56	25.179 3566	79.624 117
635	40 32 25	25.199 2063	79.686 887
636	40 44 96	25.219 0404	79.749 608
637	40 57 69	25.238 8589	79.812 280
638	40 70 44	25.258 6619	79.874 902
639	40 83 21	25.278 4493	79.937 476
640	40 96 00	25.298 2213	80.000 000
641	41 08 81	25.317 9778	80.062 476
642	41 21 64	25.337 7189	80.124 902
643	41 34 49	25.357 4447	80.187 281
644	41 47 36	25.377 1551	80.249 611
645	41 60 25	25.396 8502	80.311 892
646	41 73 16	25.416 5301	80.374 125
647	41 86 09	25.436 1947	80.436 310
648	41 99 04	25.455 8441	80.498 447
649	42 12 01	25.475 4784	80.560 536
650	42 25 00	25.495 0976	80.622 577
651	42 38 01	25.514 7016	80.684 571
652	42 51 04	25.534 2907	80.746 517
653	42 64 09	25.553 8647	80.808 415
654	42 77 16	25.573 4237	80.870 266
655	42 90 25	25.592 9678	80.932 070
656	43 03 36	25.612 4969	80.993 827
657	43 16 49	25.632 0112	81.055 537
658	43 29 64	25.651 5107	81.117 199
659	43 42 81	25.670 9953	81.178 815
660	43 56 00	25.690 4652	81.240 384
661	43 69 21	25.709 9203	81.301 906
662	43 82 44	25.729 3607	81.363 382
663	43 95 69	25.748 7864	81.424 812
664	44 08 96	25.768 1975	81.486 195
665	44 22 25	25.787 5939	81.547 532
666	44 35 56	25.806 9758	81.608 823
667	44 48 89	25.826 3431	81.670 068
668	44 62 24	25.845 6960	81.731 267
669	44 75 61	25.865 0343	81.792 420
670	44 89 00	25.884 3582	81.853 528
671	45 02 41	25.903 6677	81.914 590
672	45 15 84	25.922 9628	81.975 606
673	45 29 29	25.942 2435	82.036 577
674	45 42 76	25.961 5100	82.097 503
675	45 56 25	25.980 7621	82.158 384
676	45 69 76	26.000 0000	82.219 219
677	45 83 29	26.019 2237	82.280 010
678	45 96 84	26.038 4331	82.340 755
679	46 10 41	26.057 6284	82.401 456
680	46 24 00	26.076 8096	82.462 113
681	46 37 61	26.095 9767	82.522 724
682	46 51 24	26.115 1297	82.583 291
683	46 64 89	26.134 2687	82.643 814
684	46 78 56	26.153 3937	82.704 293
685	46 92 25	26.172 5047	82.764 727
686	47 05 96	26.191 6017	82.825 117
687	47 19 69	26.210 6848	82.885 463
688	47 33 44	26.229 7541	82.945 765
689	47 47 21	26.248 8095	83.006 024
690	47 61 00	26.267 8511	83.066 239
691	47 74 81	26.286 8789	83.126 410
692	47 88 64	26.305 8929	83.186 537
693	48 02 49	26.324 8932	83.246 622
694	48 16 36	26.343 8797	83.306 662
695	48 30 25	26.362 8527	83.366 660
696	48 44 16	26.381 8119	83.426 614
697	48 58 09	26.400 7576	83.486 526
698	48 72 04	26.419 6896	83.546 394
699	48 86 01	26.438 6081	83.606 220

n	n^2	$\sqrt{n}$	$\sqrt{10n}$
700	49 00 00	26.457 5131	83.666 003
701	49 14 01	26.476 4046	83.725 743
702	49 28 04	26.495 2826	83.785 440
703	49 42 09	26.514 1472	83.845 095
704	49 56 16	26.532 9983	83.904 708
705	49 70 25	26.551 8361	83.964 278
706	49 84 36	26.570 6605	84.023 806
707	49 98 49	26.589 4716	84.083 292
708	50 12 64	26.608 2694	84.142 736
709	50 26 81	26.627 0539	84.202 138
710	50 41 00	26.645 8252	84.261 498
711	50 55 21	26.664 5833	84.320 816
712	50 69 44	26.683 3281	84.380 092
713	50 83 69	26.702 0598	84.439 327
714	50 97 96	26.720 7784	84.498 521
715	51 12 25	26.739 4839	84.557 673
716	51 26 56	26.758 1763	84.616 783
717	51 40 89	26.776 8557	84.675 853
718	51 55 24	26.795 5220	84.734 881
719	51 69 61	26.814 1754	84.793 868
720	51 84 00	26.832 8157	84.852 814
721	51 98 41	26.851 4432	84.911 719
722	52 12 84	26.870 0577	84.970 583
723	52 27 29	26.888 6593	85.029 407
724	52 41 76	26.907 2481	85.088 190
725	52 56 25	26.925 8240	85.146 932
726	52 70 76	26.944 3872	85.205 634
727	52 85 29	26.962 9375	85.264 295
728	52 99 84	26.981 4751	85.322 916
729	53 14 41	27.000 0000	85.381 497
730	53 29 00	27.018 5122	85.440 037
731	53 43 61	27.037 0117	85.498 538
732	53 58 24	27.055 4985	85.556 999
733	53 72 89	27.073 9727	85.615 419
734	53 87 56	27.092 4344	85.673 800
735	54 02 25	27.110 8834	85.732 141
736	54 16 96	27.129 3199	85.790 442
737	54 31 69	27.147 7439	85.848 704
738	54 46 44	27.166 1554	85.906 926
739	54 61 21	27.184 5544	85.965 109
740	54 76 00	27.202 9410	86.023 253
741	54 90 81	27.221 3152	86.081 357
742	55 05 64	27.239 6769	86.139 422
743	55 20 49	27.258 0263	86.197 448
744	55 35 36	27.276 3634	86.255 435
745	55 50 25	27.294 6881	86.313 383
746	55 65 16	27.313 0006	86.371 292
747	55 80 09	27.331 3007	86.429 162
748	55 95 04	27.349 5887	86.486 993
749	56 10 01	27.367 8644	86.544 786
750	56 25 00	27.386 1279	86.602 540
751	56 40 01	27.404 3792	86.660 256
752	56 55 04	27.422 6184	86.717 934
753	56 70 09	27.440 8455	86.775 573
754	56 85 16	27.459 0604	86.833 173
755	57 00 25	27.477 2633	86.890 736
756	57 15 36	27.495 4542	86.948 260
757	57 30 49	27.513 6330	87.005 747
758	57 45 64	27.531 7998	87.063 195
759	57 60 81	27.549 9546	87.120 606
760	57 76 00	27.568 0975	87.177 979
761	57 91 21	27.586 2284	87.235 314
762	58 06 44	27.604 3475	87.292 611
763	58 21 69	27.622 4546	87.349 871
764	58 36 96	27.640 5499	87.407 094
765	58 52 25	27.658 6334	87.464 278
766	58 67 56	27.676 7050	87.521 426
767	58 82 89	27.694 7648	87.578 536
768	58 98 24	27.712 8129	87.635 609
769	59 13 61	27.730 8492	87.692 645
770	59 29 00	27.748 8739	87.749 644
771	59 44 41	27.766 8868	87.806 606
772	59 59 84	27.784 8880	87.863 531
773	59 75 29	27.802 8775	87.920 419
774	59 90 76	27.820 8555	87.977 270
775	60 06 25	27.838 8218	88.034 084
776	60 21 76	27.856 7766	88.090 862
777	60 37 29	27.874 7197	88.147 603
778	60 52 84	27.892 6514	88.204 308
779	60 68 41	27.910 5715	88.260 977
780	60 84 00	27.928 4801	88.317 609
781	60 99 61	27.946 3772	88.374 204
782	61 15 24	27.964 2629	88.430 764
783	61 30 89	27.982 1372	88.487 287
784	61 46 56	28.000 0000	88.543 774
785	61 62 25	28.017 8515	88.600 226
786	61 77 96	28.035 6915	88.656 641
787	61 93 69	28.053 5203	88.713 020
788	62 09 44	28.071 3377	88.769 364
789	62 25 21	28.089 1438	88.825 672
790	62 41 00	28.106 9386	88.881 944
791	62 56 81	28.124 7222	88.938 181
792	62 72 64	28.142 4946	88.994 382
793	62 88 49	28.160 2557	89.050 547
794	63 04 36	28.178 0056	89.106 678
795	63 20 25	28.195 7444	89.162 773
796	63 36 16	28.213 4720	89.218 832
797	63 52 09	28.231 1884	89.274 856
798	63 68 04	28.248 8938	89.330 846
799	63 84 01	28.266 5881	89.386 800

Squares and Square Roots of the Integers 800—1199

$\sqrt{100n} = 10\sqrt{n}$ $\sqrt{1000n} = 10\sqrt{10n}$ $\sqrt{0.1n} = 0.1\sqrt{10n}$ $\sqrt{0.01n} = 0.1\sqrt{n}$ $\sqrt{0.001n} = 0.01\sqrt{10n}$

n	n^2	$\sqrt{n}$	$\sqrt{10n}$	n	n^2	$\sqrt{n}$	$\sqrt{10n}$	n	n^2	$\sqrt{n}$	$\sqrt{10n}$	n	n^2	$\sqrt{n}$	$\sqrt{10n}$
800	64 00 00	28.284 2712	89.442 719	**900**	81 00 00	30.000 0000	94.868 330	**1000**	1 00 00 00	31.622 777	100.000 000	**1100**	1 21 00 00	33.166 248	104.880 885
801	64 16 01	28.301 9434	89.498 603	901	81 18 01	30.016 6620	94.921 020	1001	1 00 20 01	31.638 584	100.049 988	1101	1 21 22 01	33.181 320	104.928 547
802	64 32 04	28.319 6045	89.554 453	902	81 36 04	30.033 3148	94.973 681	1002	1 00 40 04	31.654 384	100.099 950	1102	1 21 44 04	33.196 385	104.976 188
803	64 48 09	28.337 2546	89.610 267	903	81 54 09	30.049 9584	95.026 312	1003	1 00 60 09	31.670 175	100.149 888	1103	1 21 66 09	33.211 444	105.023 807
804	64 64 16	28.354 8938	89.666 047	904	81 72 16	30.066 5928	95.078 915	1004	1 00 80 16	31.685 959	100.199 800	1104	1 21 88 16	33.226 495	105.071 404
805	64 80 25	28.372 5219	89.721 792	**905**	81 90 25	30.083 2179	95.131 488	**1005**	1 01 00 25	31.701 735	100.249 688	**1105**	1 22 10 25	33.241 540	105.118 980
806	64 96 36	28.390 1391	89.777 503	906	82 08 36	30.099 8339	95.184 032	1006	1 01 20 36	31.717 503	100.299 551	1106	1 22 32 36	33.256 578	105.166 535
807	65 12 49	28.407 7454	89.833 179	907	82 26 49	30.116 4407	95.236 548	1007	1 01 40 49	31.733 263	100.349 390	1107	1 22 54 49	33.271 610	105.214 068
808	65 28 64	28.425 3408	89.888 820	908	82 44 64	30.133 0383	95.289 034	1008	1 01 60 64	31.749 016	100.399 203	1108	1 22 76 64	33.286 634	105.261 579
809	65 44 81	28.442 9253	89.944 427	909	82 62 81	30.149 6269	95.341 491	1009	1 01 80 81	31.764 760	100.448 992	1109	1 22 98 81	33.301 652	105.309 069
810	65 61 00	28.460 4989	90.000 000	**910**	82 81 00	30.166 2063	95.393 920	**1010**	1 02 01 00	31.780 497	100.498 756	**1110**	1 23 21 00	33.316 662	105.356 538
811	65 77 21	28.478 0617	90.055 538	911	82 99 21	30.182 7765	95.446 320	1011	1 02 21 21	31.796 226	100.548 496	1111	1 23 43 21	33.331 667	105.403 985
812	65 93 44	28.495 6137	90.111 043	912	83 17 44	30.199 3377	95.498 691	1012	1 02 41 44	31.811 947	100.598 211	1112	1 23 65 44	33.346 664	105.451 411
813	66 09 69	28.513 1549	90.166 513	913	83 35 69	30.215 8899	95.551 033	1013	1 02 61 69	31.827 661	100.647 901	1113	1 23 87 69	33.361 655	105.498 815
814	66 25 96	28.530 6852	90.221 949	914	83 53 96	30.232 4329	95.603 347	1014	1 02 81 96	31.843 367	100.697 567	1114	1 24 09 96	33.376 639	105.546 198
815	66 42 25	28.548 2048	90.277 350	**915**	83 72 25	30.248 9669	95.655 632	**1015**	1 03 02 25	31.859 065	100.747 208	**1115**	1 24 32 25	33.391 616	105.593 560
816	66 58 56	28.565 7137	90.332 718	916	83 90 56	30.265 4919	95.707 889	1016	1 03 22 56	31.874 755	100.796 825	1116	1 24 54 56	33.406 586	105.640 901
817	66 74 89	28.583 2119	90.388 052	917	84 08 89	30.282 0079	95.760 117	1017	1 03 42 89	31.890 437	100.846 418	1117	1 24 76 89	33.421 550	105.688 221
818	66 91 24	28.600 6993	90.443 352	918	84 27 24	30.298 5148	95.812 317	1018	1 03 63 24	31.906 112	100.895 986	1118	1 24 99 24	33.436 507	105.735 519
819	67 07 61	28.618 1760	90.498 619	919	84 45 61	30.315 0128	95.864 488	1019	1 03 83 61	31.921 779	100.945 530	1119	1 25 21 61	33.451 457	105.782 796
820	67 24 00	28.635 6421	90.553 851	**920**	84 64 00	30.331 5018	95.916 630	**1020**	1 04 04 00	31.937 439	100.995 049	**1120**	1 25 44 00	33.466 401	105.830 052
821	67 40 41	28.653 0976	90.609 050	921	84 82 41	30.347 9818	95.968 745	1021	1 04 24 41	31.953 091	101.044 545	1121	1 25 66 41	33.481 338	105.877 287
822	67 56 84	28.670 5424	90.664 216	922	85 00 84	30.364 4529	96.020 831	1022	1 04 44 84	31.968 735	101.094 016	1122	1 25 88 84	33.496 268	105.924 501
823	67 73 29	28.687 9766	90.719 347	923	85 19 29	30.380 9151	96.072 889	1023	1 04 65 29	31.984 371	101.143 462	1123	1 26 11 29	33.511 192	105.971 694
824	67 89 76	28.705 4002	90.774 446	924	85 37 76	30.397 3683	96.124 919	1024	1 04 85 76	32.000 000	101.192 885	1124	1 26 33 76	33.526 109	106.018 866
825	68 06 25	28.722 8132	90.829 511	**925**	85 56 25	30.413 8127	96.176 920	**1025**	1 05 06 25	32.015 621	101.242 284	**1125**	1 26 56 25	33.541 020	106.066 017
826	68 22 76	28.740 2157	90.884 542	926	85 74 76	30.430 2481	96.228 894	1026	1 05 26 76	32.031 235	101.291 658	1126	1 26 78 76	33.555 923	106.113 147
827	68 39 29	28.757 6077	90.939 540	927	85 93 29	30.446 6747	96.280 839	1027	1 05 47 29	32.046 841	101.341 008	1127	1 27 01 29	33.570 821	106.160 256
828	68 55 84	28.774 9891	90.994 505	928	86 11 84	30.463 0924	96.332 757	1028	1 05 67 84	32.062 439	101.390 335	1128	1 27 23 84	33.585 711	106.207 344
829	68 72 41	28.792 3601	91.049 437	929	86 30 41	30.479 5013	96.384 646	1029	1 05 88 41	32.078 030	101.439 637	1129	1 27 46 41	33.600 595	106.254 412
830	68 89 00	28.809 7206	91.104 336	**930**	86 49 00	30.495 9014	96.436 508	**1030**	1 06 09 00	32.093 613	101.488 916	**1130**	1 27 69 00	33.615 473	106.301 458
831	69 05 61	28.827 0706	91.159 201	931	86 67 61	30.512 2926	96.488 341	1031	1 06 29 61	32.109 189	101.538 170	1131	1 27 91 61	33.630 343	106.348 484
832	69 22 24	28.844 4102	91.214 034	932	86 86 24	30.528 6750	96.540 147	1032	1 06 50 24	32.124 757	101.587 401	1132	1 28 14 24	33.645 208	106.395 489
833	69 38 89	28.861 7394	91.268 834	933	87 04 89	30.545 0487	96.591 925	1033	1 06 70 89	32.140 317	101.636 608	1133	1 28 36 89	33.660 065	106.442 473
834	69 55 56	28.879 0582	91.323 600	934	87 23 56	30.561 4136	96.643 675	1034	1 06 91 56	32.155 870	101.685 791	1134	1 28 59 56	33.674 916	106.489 436
835	69 72 25	28.896 3666	91.378 334	**935**	87 42 25	30.577 7697	96.695 398	**1035**	1 07 12 25	32.171 416	101.734 950	**1135**	1 28 82 25	33.689 761	106.536 379
836	69 88 96	28.913 6646	91.433 036	936	87 60 96	30.594 1171	96.747 093	1036	1 07 32 96	32.186 954	101.784 085	1136	1 29 04 96	33.704 599	106.583 301
837	70 05 69	28.930 9523	91.487 704	937	87 79 69	30.610 4557	96.798 760	1037	1 07 53 69	32.202 484	101.833 197	1137	1 29 27 69	33.719 431	106.630 202
838	70 22 44	28.948 2297	91.542 340	938	87 98 44	30.626 7857	96.850 400	1038	1 07 74 44	32.218 007	101.882 285	1138	1 29 50 44	33.734 256	106.677 083
839	70 39 21	28.965 4967	91.596 943	939	88 17 21	30.643 1069	96.902 012	1039	1 07 95 21	32.233 523	101.931 349	1139	1 29 73 21	33.749 074	106.723 943
840	70 56 00	28.982 7535	91.651 514	**940**	88 36 00	30.659 4194	96.953 597	**1040**	1 08 16 00	32.249 031	101.980 390	**1140**	1 29 96 00	33.763 886	106.770 783
841	70 72 81	29.000 0000	91.706 052	941	88 54 81	30.675 7233	97.005 155	1041	1 08 36 81	32.264 532	102.029 408	1141	1 30 18 81	33.778 692	106.817 602
842	70 89 64	29.017 2363	91.760 558	942	88 73 64	30.692 0185	97.056 684	1042	1 08 57 64	32.280 025	102.078 401	1142	1 30 41 64	33.793 490	106.864 400
843	71 06 49	29.034 4623	91.815 031	943	88 92 49	30.708 3051	97.108 187	1043	1 08 78 49	32.295 511	102.127 371	1143	1 30 64 49	33.808 283	106.911 178
844	71 23 36	29.051 6781	91.869 473	944	89 11 36	30.724 5830	97.159 662	1044	1 08 99 36	32.310 989	102.176 318	1144	1 30 87 36	33.823 069	106.957 936
845	71 40 25	29.068 8837	91.923 882	**945**	89 30 25	30.740 8523	97.211 110	**1045**	1 09 20 25	32.326 460	102.225 242	**1145**	1 31 10 25	33.837 849	107.004 673
846	71 57 16	29.086 0791	91.978 258	946	89 49 16	30.757 1130	97.262 531	1046	1 09 41 16	32.341 923	102.274 141	1146	1 31 33 16	33.852 622	107.051 390
847	71 74 09	29.103 2644	92.032 603	947	89 68 09	30.773 3651	97.313 925	1047	1 09 62 09	32.357 379	102.323 018	1147	1 31 56 09	33.867 388	107.098 086
848	71 91 04	29.120 4396	92.086 915	948	89 87 04	30.789 6086	97.365 292	1048	1 09 83 04	32.372 828	102.371 871	1148	1 31 79 04	33.882 149	107.144 762
849	72 08 01	29.137 6046	92.141 196	949	90 06 01	30.805 8436	97.416 631	1049	1 10 04 01	32.388 269	102.420 701	1149	1 32 02 01	33.896 903	107.191 418
850	72 25 00	29.154 7595	92.195 445	**950**	90 25 00	30.822 0700	97.467 943	**1050**	1 10 25 00	32.403 703	102.469 508	**1150**	1 32 25 00	33.911 650	107.238 053
851	72 42 01	29.171 9043	92.249 661	951	90 44 01	30.838 2879	97.519 229	1051	1 10 46 01	32.419 130	102.518 291	1151	1 32 48 01	33.926 391	107.284 668
852	72 59 04	29.189 0390	92.303 846	952	90 63 04	30.854 4972	97.570 487	1052	1 10 67 04	32.434 549	102.567 051	1152	1 32 71 04	33.941 125	107.331 263
853	72 76 09	29.206 1637	92.357 999	953	90 82 09	30.870 6981	97.621 719	1053	1 10 88 09	32.449 961	102.615 788	1153	1 32 94 09	33.955 854	107.377 838
854	72 93 16	29.223 2784	92.412 120	954	91 01 16	30.886 8904	97.672 924	1054	1 11 09 16	32.465 366	102.664 502	1154	1 33 17 16	33.970 576	107.424 392
855	73 10 25	29.240 3830	92.466 210	**955**	91 20 25	30.903 0743	97.724 101	**1055**	1 11 30 25	32.480 764	102.713 193	**1155**	1 33 40 25	33.985 291	107.470 926
856	73 27 36	29.257 4777	92.520 268	956	91 39 36	30.919 2497	97.775 252	1056	1 11 51 36	32.496 154	102.761 861	1156	1 33 63 36	34.000 000	107.517 440
857	73 44 49	29.274 5623	92.574 294	957	91 58 49	30.935 4166	97.826 377	1057	1 11 72 49	32.511 536	102.810 505	1157	1 33 86 49	34.014 703	107.563 934
858	73 61 64	29.291 6370	92.628 289	958	91 77 64	30.951 5751	97.877 474	1058	1 11 93 64	32.526 912	102.859 127	1158	1 34 09 64	34.029 399	107.610 408
859	73 78 81	29.308 7018	92.682 253	959	91 96 81	30.967 7251	97.928 545	1059	1 12 14 81	32.542 280	102.907 726	1159	1 34 32 81	34.044 089	107.656 862
860	73 96 00	29.325 7566	92.736 185	**960**	92 16 00	30.983 8668	97.979 590	**1060**	1 12 36 00	32.557 641	102.956 301	**1160**	1 34 56 00	34.058 773	107.703 296
861	74 13 21	29.342 8015	92.790 086	961	92 35 21	31.000 0000	98.030 607	1061	1 12 57 21	32.572 995	103.004 854	1161	1 34 79 21	34.073 450	107.749 710
862	74 30 44	29.359 8365	92.843 955	962	92 54 44	31.016 1248	98.081 599	1062	1 12 78 44	32.588 341	103.053 384	1162	1 35 02 44	34.088 121	107.796 104
863	74 47 69	29.376 8616	92.897 793	963	92 73 69	31.032 2413	98.132 563	1063	1 12 99 69	32.603 681	103.101 891	1163	1 35 25 69	34.102 786	107.842 478
864	74 64 96	29.393 8769	92.951 600	964	92 92 96	31.048 3494	98.183 502	1064	1 13 20 96	32.619 013	103.150 376	1164	1 35 48 96	34.117 444	107.888 832
865	74 82 25	29.410 8823	93.005 376	**965**	93 12 25	31.064 4491	98.234 414	**1065**	1 13 42 25	32.634 338	103.198 837	**1165**	1 35 72 25	34.132 096	107.935 166
866	74 99 56	29.427 8779	93.059 121	966	93 31 56	31.080 5405	98.285 299	1066	1 13 63 56	32.649 655	103.247 276	1166	1 35 95 56	34.146 742	107.981 480
867	75 16 89	29.444 8637	93.112 835	967	93 50 89	31.096 6236	98.336 158	1067	1 13 84 89	32.664 966	103.295 692	1167	1 36 18 89	34.161 382	108.027 774
868	75 34 24	29.461 8397	93.166 518	968	93 70 24	31.112 6984	98.386 991	1068	1 14 06 24	32.680 269	103.344 085	1168	1 36 42 24	34.176 015	108.074 049
869	75 51 61	29.478 8059	93.220 169	969	93 89 61	31.128 7648	98.437 798	1069	1 14 27 61	32.695 565	103.392 456	1169	1 36 65 61	34.190 642	108.120 303
870	75 69 00	29.495 7624	93.273 791	**970**	94 09 00	31.144 8230	98.488 578	**1070**	1 14 49 00	32.710 854	103.440 804	**1170**	1 36 89 00	34.205 263	108.166 538
871	75 86 41	29.512 7091	93.327 381	971	94 28 41	31.160 8729	98.539 332	1071	1 14 70 41	32.726 136	103.489 130	1171	1 37 12 41	34.219 877	108.212 753
872	76 03 84	29.529 6461	93.380 940	972	94 47 84	31.176 9145	98.590 060	1072	1 14 91 84	32.741 411	103.537 433	1172	1 37 35 84	34.234 486	108.258 949
873	76 21 29	29.546 5734	93.434 469	973	94 67 29	31.192 9479	98.640 762	1073	1 15 13 29	32.756 679	103.585 713	1173	1 37 59 29	34.249 088	108.305 125
874	76 38 76	29.563 4910	93.487 967	974	94 86 76	31.208 9731	98.691 438	1074	1 15 34 76	32.771 939	103.633 971	1174	1 37 82 76	34.263 683	108.351 281
875	76 56 25	29.580 3989	93.541 435	**975**	95 06 25	31.224 9900	98.742 088	**1075**	1 15 56 25	32.787 193	103.682 207	**1175**	1 38 06 25	34.278 273	108.397 417
876	76 73 76	29.597 2972	93.594 872	976	95 25 76	31.240 9987	98.792 712	1076	1 15 77 76	32.802 439	103.730 420	1176	1 38 29 76	34.292 856	108.443 534
877	76 91 29	29.614 1858	93.648 278	977	95 45 29	31.256 9992	98.843 310	1077	1 15 99 29	32.817 678	103.778 611	1177	1 38 53 29	34.307 434	108.489 631
878	77 08 84	29.631 0648	93.701 654	978	95 64 84	31.272 9915	98.893 883	1078	1 16 20 84	32.832 910	103.826 779	1178	1 38 76 84	34.322 005	108.535 708
879	77 26 41	29.647 9342	93.755 000	979	95 84 41	31.288 9757	98.944 429	1079	1 16 42 41	32.848 135	103.874 925	1179	1 39 00 41	34.336 569	108.581 766
880	77 44 00	29.664 7939	93.808 315	**980**	96 04 00	31.304 9517	98.994 949	**1080**	1 16 64 00	32.863 353	103.923 048	**1180**	1 39 24 00	34.351 128	108.627 805
881	77 61 61	29.681 6442	93.861 600	981	96 23 61	31.320 9195	99.045 444	1081	1 16 85 61	32.878 564	103.971 150	1181	1 39 47 61	34.365 681	108.673 824
882	77 79 24	29.698 4848	93.914 855	982	96 43 24	31.336 8792	99.095 913	1082	1 17 07 24	32.893 768	104.019 229	1182	1 39 71 24	34.380 227	108.719 823
883	77 96 89	29.715 3159	93.968 080	983	96 62 89	31.352 8308	99.146 356	1083	1 17 28 89	32.908 965	104.067 286	1183	1 39 94 89	34.394 767	108.765 803
884	78 14 56	29.732 1375	94.021 274	984	96 82 56	31.368 7743	99.196 774	1084	1 17 50 56	32.924 155	104.115 321	1184	1 40 18 56	34.409 301	108.811 764
885	78 32 25	29.748 9496	94.074 439	**985**	97 02 25	31.384 7097	99.247 166	**1085**	1 17 72 25	32.939 338	104.163 333	**1185**	1 40 42 25	34.423 829	108.857 705
886	78 49 96	29.765 7521	94.127 573	986	97 21 96	31.400 6369	99.297 533	1086	1 17 93 96	32.954 514	104.211 324	1186	1 40 65 96	34.438 351	108.903 627
887	78 67 69	29.782 5452	94.180 677	987	97 41 69	31.416 5561	99.347 874	1087	1 18 15 69	32.969 683	104.259 292	1187	1 40 89 69	34.452 866	108.949 530
888	78 85 44	29.799 3289	94.233 752	988	97 61 44	31.432 4673	99.398 189	1088	1 18 37 44	32.984 845	104.307 238	1188	1 41 13 44	34.467 376	108.995 413
889	79 03 21	29.816 1030	94.286 797	989	97 81 21	31.448 3704	99.448 479	1089	1 18 59 21	33.000 000	104.355 163	1189	1 41 37 21	34.481 879	109.041 277
890	79 21 00	29.832 8678	94.339 811	**990**	98 01 00	31.464 2654	99.498 744	**1090**	1 18 81 00	33.015 148	104.403 065	**1190**	1 41 61 00	34.496 377	109.087 121
891	79 38 81	29.849 6231	94.392 796	991	98 20 81	31.480 1525	99.548 983	1091	1 19 02 81	33.030 289	104.450 945	1191	1 41 84 81	34.510 868	109.132 946
892	79 56 64	29.866 3690	94.445 752	992	98 40 64	31.496 0315	99.599 197	1092	1 19 24 64	33.045 423	104.498 804	1192	1 42 08 64	34.525 353	109.178 753
893	79 74 49	29.883 1056	94.498 677	993	98 60 49	31.511 9025	99.649 385	1093	1 19 46 49	33.060 551	104.546 640	1193	1 42 32 49	34.539 832	109.224 539
894	79 92 36	29.899 8328	94.551 573	994	98 80 36	31.527 7655	99.699 549	1094	1 19 68 36	33.075 671	104.594 455	1194	1 42 56 36	34.554 305	109.270 307
895	80 10 25	29.916 5506	94.604 440	**995**	99 00 25	31.543 6206	99.749 687	**1095**	1 19 90 25	33.090 784	104.642 248	**1195**	1 42 80 25	34.568 772	109.316 056
896	80 28 16	29.933 2591	94.657 277	996	99 20 16	31.559 4677	99.799 800	1096	1 20 12 16	33.105 891	104.690 019	1196	1 43 04 16	34.583 233	109.361 785
897	80 46 09	29.949 9583	94.710 084	997	99 40 09	31.575 3068	99.849 887	1097	1 20 34 09	33.120 990	104.737 768	1197	1 43 28 09	34.597 688	109.407 495
898	80 64 04	29.966 6481	94.762 862	998	99 60 04	31.591 1380	99.899 950	1098	1 20 56 04	33.136 083	104.785 495	1198	1 43 52 04	34.612 137	109.453 186
899	80 82 01	29.983 3287	94.815 611	999	99 80 01	31.606 9613	99.949 987	1099	1 20 78 01	33.151 169	104.833 201	1199	1 43 76 01	34.626 579	109.498 858

Reciprocals[1] of Square Roots of the Integers 1—999

Reciprocal of $\sqrt{n} = 1/\sqrt{n}$

n	0	1	2	3	4	5	6	7	8	9
0	0.0000000	0.0000000	0.7071068	0.5773503	0.5000000	0.4472136	0.4082483	0.3779645	0.3535534	0.3333333
10	3162278	3015113	2886751	2773501	2672612	2581989	2500000	2425356	2357023	2294157
20	2236068	2182179	2132007	2085144	2041241	2000000	1961161	1924501	1889822	1856953
30	1825742	1796053	1767767	1740777	1714986	1690309	1666667	1643990	1622214	1601282
40	1581139	1561738	1543034	1524986	1507557	1490712	1474420	1458650	1443376	1428571
50	0.1414214	0.1400280	0.1386750	0.1373606	0.1360828	0.1348400	0.1336306	0.1324532	0.1313064	0.1301889
60	1290994	1280369	1270001	1259882	1250000	1240347	1230915	1221694	1212678	1203859
70	1195229	1186782	1178511	1170411	1162476	1154701	1147079	1139606	1132277	1125088
80	1118034	1111111	1104315	1097643	1091089	1084652	1078328	1072113	1066004	1059998
90	1054093	1048285	1042572	1036952	1031421	1025978	1020621	1015346	1010153	1005038
100	0.1000000	0.0995037	0.0990148	0.0985329	0.0980581	0.0975900	0.0971286	0.0966736	0.0962250	0.0957826
110	0953463	0949158	0944911	0940721	0936586	0932505	0928477	0924500	0920575	0916698
120	0912871	0909091	0905357	0901670	0898027	0894427	0890871	0887357	0883883	0880451
130	0877058	0873704	0870388	0867110	0863868	0860663	0857493	0854358	0851257	0848189
140	0845154	0842152	0839181	0836242	0833333	0830455	0827606	0824786	0821995	0819232
150	0.0816497	0.0813788	0.0811107	0.0808452	0.0805823	0.0803219	0.0800641	0.0798087	0.0795557	0.0793052
160	0790569	0788110	0785674	0783260	0780869	0778499	0776151	0773823	0771517	0769231
170	0766965	0764719	0762493	0760286	0758098	0755929	0753778	0751646	0749532	0747435
180	0745356	0743294	0741249	0739221	0737210	0735215	0733236	0731272	0729325	0727393
190	0725476	0723575	0721688	0719816	0717958	0716115	0714286	0712470	0710669	0708881
200	0.0707107	0.0705346	0.0703598	0.0701862	0.0700140	0.0698430	0.0696733	0.0695048	0.0693375	0.0691714
210	0690066	0688428	0686803	0685189	0683586	0681994	0680414	0678844	0677285	0675737
220	0674200	0672673	0671156	0669650	0668153	0666667	0665190	0663723	0662266	0660819
230	0659380	0657952	0656532	0655122	0653720	0652328	0650945	0649570	0648204	0646846
240	0645497	0644157	0642824	0641500	0640184	0638877	0637577	0636285	0635001	0633724
250	0.0632456	0.0631194	0.0629941	0.0628695	0.0627456	0.0626224	0.0625000	0.0623783	0.0622573	0.0621370
260	0620174	0618984	0617802	0616626	0615457	0614295	0613139	0611990	0610847	0609711
270	0608581	0607457	0606339	0605228	0604122	0603023	0601929	0600842	0599760	0598684
280	0597614	0596550	0595491	0594438	0593391	0592349	0591312	0590281	0589256	0588235
290	0587220	0586210	0585206	0584206	0583212	0582223	0581238	0580259	0579284	0578315
300	0.0577350	0.0576390	0.0575435	0.0574485	0.0573539	0.0572598	0.0571662	0.0570730	0.0569803	0.0568880
310	0567962	0567048	0566139	0565233	0564333	0563436	0562544	0561656	0560772	0559893
320	0559017	0558146	0557278	0556415	0555556	0554700	0553849	0553001	0552158	0551318
330	0550482	0549650	0548821	0547997	0547176	0546358	0545545	0544735	0543928	0543125
340	0542326	0541530	0540738	0539949	0539164	0538382	0537603	0536828	0536056	0535288
350	0.0534522	0.0533761	0.0533002	0.0532246	0.0531494	0.0530745	0.0529999	0.0529256	0.0528516	0.0527780
360	0527046	0526316	0525588	0524864	0524142	0523424	0522708	0521996	0521286	0520579
370	0519875	0519174	0518476	0517780	0517088	0516398	0515711	0515026	0514345	0513665
380	0512989	0512316	0511645	0510976	0510310	0509647	0508987	0508329	0507673	0507020
390	0506370	0505722	0505076	0504433	0503793	0503155	0502519	0501886	0501255	0500626
400	0.0500000	0.0499376	0.0498755	0.0498135	0.0497519	0.0496904	0.0496292	0.0495682	0.0495074	0.0494468
410	0493865	0493264	0492665	0492068	0491473	0490881	0490290	0489702	0489116	0488532
420	0487950	0487370	0486792	0486217	0485643	0485071	0484502	0483934	0483368	0482805
430	0482243	0481683	0481125	0480569	0480015	0479463	0478913	0478365	0477818	0477274
440	0476731	0476190	0475651	0475114	0474579	0474045	0473514	0472984	0472456	0471929
450	0.0471405	0.0470882	0.0470360	0.0469841	0.0469323	0.0468807	0.0468293	0.0467780	0.0467269	0.0466760
460	0466252	0465746	0465242	0464739	0464238	0463739	0463241	0462745	0462250	0461757
470	0461266	0460776	0460287	0459800	0459315	0458831	0458349	0457869	0457389	0456912
480	0456435	0455961	0455488	0455016	0454545	0454077	0453609	0453143	0452679	0452216
490	0451754	0451294	0450835	0450377	0449921	0449467	0449013	0448561	0448111	0447661
500	0.0447214	0.0446767	0.0446322	0.0445878	0.0445435	0.0444994	0.0444554	0.0444116	0.0443678	0.0443242
510	0442807	0442374	0441942	0441511	0441081	0440653	0440225	0439799	0439375	0438951
520	0438529	0438108	0437688	0437269	0436852	0436436	0436021	0435607	0435194	0434783
530	0434372	0433963	0433555	0433148	0432742	0432338	0431934	0431532	0431131	0430730
540	0430331	0429934	0429537	0429141	0428746	0428353	0427960	0427569	0427179	0426790
550	0.0426401	0.0426014	0.0425628	0.0425243	0.0424859	0.0424476	0.0424094	0.0423714	0.0423334	0.0422955
560	0422577	0422200	0421825	0421450	0421076	0420703	0420331	0419961	0419591	0419222
570	0418854	0418487	0418121	0417756	0417392	0417029	0416667	0416305	0415945	0415586
580	0415227	0414870	0414513	0414158	0413803	0413449	0413096	0412744	0412393	0412043
590	0411693	0411345	0410997	0410651	0410305	0409960	0409616	0409273	0408930	0408589
600	0.0408248	0.0407909	0.0407570	0.0407231	0.0406894	0.0406558	0.0406222	0.0405887	0.0405554	0.0405220
610	0404888	0404557	0404226	0403896	0403567	0403239	0402911	0402585	0402259	0401934
620	0401610	0401286	0400963	0400642	0400320	0400000	0399680	0399362	0399043	0398726
630	0398410	0398094	0397779	0397464	0397151	0396838	0396526	0396214	0395904	0395594
640	0395285	0394976	0394669	0394362	0394055	0393750	0393445	0393141	0392837	0392534
650	0.0392232	0.0391931	0.0391630	0.0391330	0.0391031	0.0390732	0.0390434	0.0390137	0.0389841	0.0389545
660	0389249	0388955	0388661	0388368	0388075	0387783	0387492	0387202	0386912	0386622
670	0386334	0386046	0385758	0385472	0385186	0384900	0384615	0384331	0384048	0383765
680	0383482	0383201	0382920	0382639	0382360	0382080	0381802	0381524	0381246	0380970
690	0380693	0380418	0380143	0379869	0379595	0379322	0379049	0378777	0378506	0378235
700	0.0377964	0.0377695	0.0377426	0.0377157	0.0376889	0.0376622	0.0376355	0.0376089	0.0375823	0.0375558
710	0375293	0375029	0374766	0374503	0374241	0373979	0373718	0373457	0373197	0372937
720	0372678	0372419	0372161	0371904	0371647	0371391	0371135	0370879	0370625	0370370
730	0370117	0369863	0369611	0369358	0369107	0368856	0368605	0368355	0368105	0367856
740	0367607	0367359	0367112	0366864	0366618	0366372	0366126	0365881	0365636	0365392
750	0.0365148	0.0364905	0.0364662	0.0364420	0.0364179	0.0363937	0.0363696	0.0363456	0.0363216	0.0362977
760	0362738	0362500	0362262	0362024	0361787	0361551	0361315	0361079	0360844	0360609
770	0360375	0360141	0359908	0359675	0359443	0359211	0358979	0358748	0358517	0358287
780	0358057	0357828	0357599	0357371	0357143	0356915	0356688	0356462	0356235	0356009
790	0355784	0355559	0355335	0355110	0354887	0354663	0354441	0354218	0353996	0353775
800	0.0353553	0.0353333	0.0353112	0.0352892	0.0352673	0.0352454	0.0352235	0.0352017	0.0351799	0.0351581
810	0351364	0351147	0350931	0350715	0350500	0350285	0350070	0349856	0349642	0349428
820	0349215	0349002	0348790	0348578	0348367	0348155	0347945	0347734	0347524	0347314
830	0347105	0346896	0346688	0346479	0346272	0346064	0345857	0345651	0345444	0345238
840	0345033	0344828	0344623	0344418	0344214	0344010	0343807	0343604	0343401	0343199
850	0.0342997	0.0342796	0.0342594	0.0342393	0.0342193	0.0341993	0.0341793	0.0341593	0.0341394	0.0341196
860	0340997	0340799	0340601	0340404	0340207	0340010	0339814	0339618	0339422	0339227
870	0339032	0338837	0338643	0338449	0338255	0338062	0337869	0337676	0337484	0337292
880	0337100	0336909	0336718	0336527	0336336	0336146	0335957	0335767	0335578	0335389
890	0335201	0335013	0334825	0334637	0334450	0334263	0334077	0333890	0333704	0333519
900	0.0333333	0.0333148	0.0332964	0.0332779	0.0332595	0.0332411	0.0332228	0.0332045	0.0331862	0.0331679
910	0331497	0331315	0331133	0330952	0330771	0330590	0330409	0330229	0330049	0329870
920	0329690	0329511	0329332	0329154	0328976	0328798	0328620	0328443	0328266	0328089
930	0327913	0327737	0327561	0327385	0327210	0327035	0326860	0326686	0326512	0326338
940	0326164	0325991	0325818	0325645	0325472	0325300	0325128	0324956	0324785	0324614
950	0.0324443	0.0324272	0.0324102	0.0323932	0.0323762	0.0323592	0.0323423	0.0323254	0.0323085	0.0322917
960	0322749	0322581	0322413	0322245	0322078	0321911	0321745	0321578	0321412	0321246
970	0321081	0320915	0320750	0320585	0320421	0320256	0320092	0319928	0319765	0319601
980	0319438	0319275	0319113	0318950	0318788	0318626	0318465	0318304	0318142	0317982
990	0317821	0317660	0317500	0317340	0317181	0317021	0316862	0316703	0316544	0316386

[1] Values from COMRIE, L. J. (Ed.), *Barlow's Tables of Squares, Cubes, Square Roots, Cube Roots and Reciprocals of All Integers up to 12,500*, 4th ed., Spon, London, 1958. Reprinted by kind permission of the editor and publishers.

Extraction of Square Roots with Calculators[1]

This table is applicable to any calculating machine with which division can be made.

First adjust the number *n* of which the root is desired by moving its decimal point to the right or left two places at a time until it has a value between 1 and 100. Now look for the two numbers nearest to this in column A of the table and note the values in columns B and C lying between these numbers.

The square root of *n* is then equal to $\frac{n+B}{C}$

The result is correct to 6 significant places and deviates in the 7th decimal place only by 5 units from the correct value.

The decimal point of the root is located as follows:

(a) Values of *n* greater than 1:

Count the numbers of pairs of digits lying before the decimal point and add one to this number if an odd digit remains. The result gives the number of digits before the decimal point in the root.

Example: A number with 5 digits before the decimal point yields 2 groups of two plus 1 odd digit. In the root there are therefore 3 digits before the decimal point.

(b) Values of *n* less than 1:

Count the numbers of pairs of ciphers following the decimal point and ignore an odd cipher which may remain. This number is then the number of ciphers following the decimal point in the root.

Example: A number less than 1 with 5 ciphers following the decimal point yields 2 groups of two. In the root there are therefore 2 ciphers following the decimal point.

Examples

$\sqrt{0.00678934 5}$
=(67.89345+68):1649243
=8239746962
Desired square root: 0.0823974

$\sqrt{129.3456}$
=(1.293456+1.3):228036
=1137301127
Desired square root: 11.3730

A	B	C
1.00	1	200
1.005	1.01	200 998
1.015	1.02	201 99
1.025	1.03	202 978
1.035		
	1.04	203 961
1.045	1.05	204 939
1.055	1.06	205 913
1.065	1.07	206 882
1.075	1.08	207 846
1.085		
	1.09	208 806
1.095	1.1	209 762
1.105	1.11	210 713
1.115	1.12	211 66
1.125	1.13	212 603
1.135		
	1.14	213 542
1.145	1.15	214 476
1.155	1.16	215 407
1.165	1.17	216 333
1.175	1.18	217 256
1.185		
	1.19	218 174
1.195	1.2	219 089
1.205	1.21	220
1.215	1.22	220 907
1.225	1.23	221 811
1.235		
	1.24	222 711
1.245	1.25	223 607
1.255	1.26	224 500 2
1.27	1.28	226 275
1.29	1.3	228 036
1.31		
	1.32	229 783 3
1.33	1.34	231 517 5
1.35	1.36	233 239
1.37	1.38	234 947 6
1.39	1.4	236 644
1.41		
	1.42	238 328
1.43	1.44	240 001
1.45	1.46	241 661 6
1.47	1.48	243 311
1.49	1.5	244 949 7
1.51		
	1.52	246 577
1.53	1.54	248 194
1.55	1.56	249 800 6
1.57	1.58	251 397
1.59	1.6	252 983
1.61		
	1.62	254 559
1.63	1.64	256 125 6
1.65	1.66	257 682 6
1.67	1.68	259 23
1.69	1.7	260 769
1.71		
	1.72	262 298
1.73	1.74	263 819
1.75	1.76	265 330 5
1.77	1.78	266 834
1.79	1.8	268 329
1.81		
	1.82	269 815
1.83	1.84	271 294
1.85	1.86	272 764
1.87	1.88	274 227
1.89	1.9	275 681
1.91		
	1.92	277 129
1.93	1.94	278 568
1.95	1.96	280
1.97	1.98	281 425
1.99	2	282 843
2.01		
	2.02	284 254
2.03	2.04	285 658
2.05	2.06	287 054
2.07	2.08	288 445
2.09	2.1	289 828
2.11		
	2.12	291 205 3

A	B	C
2.135	2.15	293 258 5
2.165	2.18	295 297 4
2.195	2.21	297 322 3
2.225	2.24	299 333 5
2.255		
	2.27	301 331 2
2.285	2.3	303 316
2.315	2.33	305 287 7
2.345	2.36	307 246 6
2.375	2.39	309 193 3
2.405		
	2.42	311 127 7
2.435	2.45	313 05
2.465	2.48	314 961
2.495	2.51	316 860 4
2.525	2.54	318 748 4
2.555		
	2.57	320 625
2.585	2.6	322 491
2.615	2.63	324 346
2.645	2.66	326 191
2.675	2.69	328 025
2.705		
	2.72	329 849
2.735	2.75	331 663
2.765	2.78	333 467
2.795	2.81	335 262
2.825	2.84	337 046 6
2.855		
	2.87	338 822
2.885	2.9	340 588
2.915	2.93	342 345
2.945	2.96	344 093 7
2.975	2.99	345 833
3.005		
	3.02	347 563 6
3.035	3.05	349 285 6
3.065	3.08	350 999
3.095	3.11	352 704
3.125	3.14	354 401 6
3.155		
	3.17	356 09
3.185	3.2	357 771 7
3.22	3.24	360 001
3.26	3.28	362 216 2
3.30	3.32	364 418 2
3.34		
	3.36	366 607
3.38	3.4	368 782 6
3.42	3.44	370 945 6
3.46	3.48	373 096
3.50	3.52	375 234
3.54		
	3.56	377 36
3.58	3.6	379 474
3.62	3.64	381 576 3
3.66	3.68	383 667 3
3.70	3.72	385 747
3.74		
	3.76	387 815
3.78	3.8	389 872 5
3.82	3.84	391 919
3.86	3.88	393 955
3.90	3.92	395 980 5
3.94		
	3.96	397 995 6
3.98	4	400 001
4.02	4.04	401 996
4.06	4.08	403 981
4.10	4.12	405 956
4.14		
	4.16	407 922
4.18	4.2	409 879
4.225	4.25	412 311 5
4.275	4.3	414 729 7
4.325	4.35	417 134
4.375		
	4.4	419 524 4
4.425	4.45	421 901 3
4.475	4.5	424 265
4.525	4.55	426 615 4
4.575	4.6	428 953
4.625		
	4.65	431 278

A	B	C
4.675	4.7	433 590 4
4.725	4.75	435 890 6
4.775	4.8	438 179
4.825	4.85	440 455
4.875		
	4.9	442 719 5
4.925	4.95	444 972 7
4.975	5	447 214
5.025	5.05	449 445
5.075	5.1	451 664
5.125		
	5.15	453 873
5.175	5.2	456 071
5.225	5.25	458 258
5.275	5.3	460 435
5.325	5.35	462 602
5.375		
	5.4	464 759
5.425	5.45	466 905
5.475	5.5	469 042
5.525	5.55	471 169
5.575	5.6	473 287
5.625		
	5.65	475 395
5.675	5.7	477 494
5.725	5.75	479 584
5.775	5.8	481 664
5.825	5.85	483 736
5.875		
	5.9	485 799
5.925	5.95	487 853
5.975	6	489 898 5
6.025	6.05	491 935 5
6.075	6.1	493 964
6.125		
	6.15	495 984
6.175	6.2	497 996
6.225	6.25	500 001
6.275	6.3	501 996 5
6.325	6.35	503 985
6.375		
	6.4	505 965
6.425	6.45	507 937
6.475	6.5	509 902
6.525	6.55	511 86
6.575	6.6	513 81
6.625		
	6.65	515 752
6.675	6.7	517 688
6.725	6.75	519 616
6.775	6.8	521 537
6.825	6.85	523 45
6.875		
	6.9	525 357
6.925	6.95	527 257
6.975	7	529 151
7.025	7.05	531 037
7.075	7.1	532 917
7.125		
	7.15	534 79
7.175	7.2	536 657
7.225	7.25	538 517
7.275	7.3	540 371
7.325	7.35	542 218
7.375		
	7.4	544 059
7.425	7.45	545 894
7.475	7.5	547 723
7.525	7.55	549 546
7.575	7.6	551 362
7.625		
	7.65	553 173
7.675	7.7	554 978
7.725	7.75	556 777
7.775	7.8	558 57
7.825	7.85	560 357
7.875		
	7.9	562 139
7.925	7.95	563 915
7.975	8	565 686
8.025	8.05	567 451
8.075	8.1	569 21
8.125		
	8.15	570 964

A	B	C
8.175	8.2	572 713
8.225	8.25	574 457
8.275	8.3	576 195
8.325	8.35	577 928
8.375		
	8.4	579 655
8.425	8.45	581 378
8.475	8.5	583 096
8.525	8.55	584 808
8.575	8.6	586 516
8.625		
	8.65	588 218
8.675	8.7	589 916
8.725	8.75	591 608
8.775	8.8	593 296
8.825	8.85	594 979
8.875		
	8.9	596 658
8.925	8.95	598 331
8.975	9	600
9.025	9.05	601 665
9.075	9.1	603 324
9.125		
	9.15	604 98
9.175	9.2	606 63
9.225	9.25	608 276
9.275	9.3	609 918
9.325	9.35	611 556
9.375		
	9.4	613 189
9.425	9.45	614 817
9.475	9.5	616 442
9.525	9.55	618 062
9.575	9.6	619 678
9.625		
	9.65	621 289
9.675	9.7	622 897
9.725	9.75	624 5
9.775	9.8	626 099
9.825	9.85	627 694
9.875		
	9.9	629 286
9.925	9.95	630 873
9.975	9.99	632 139
10.00*	10	632 456
10.025	10.05	634 035
10.075		
	10.1	635 61
10.125	10.15	637 181
10.175	10.2	638 749
10.225	10.25	640 313
10.275	10.3	641 872
10.325		
	10.35	643 429
10.375	10.4	644 981
10.425	10.45	646 529
10.475	10.5	648 074
10.525	10.55	649 615
10.575		
	10.6	651 153 7
10.65	10.7	654 218
10.75	10.8	657 268
10.85	10.9	660 303 8
10.95	11	663 326
11.05		
	11.1	666 334
11.15	11.2	669 329
11.25	11.3	672 310 3
11.35	11.4	675 278 6
11.45	11.5	678 233 8
11.55		
	11.6	681 176 2
11.65	11.7	684 106
11.75	11.8	687 023 3
11.85	11.9	689 928 4
11.95	12	692 821
12.05		
	12.1	695 702
12.15	12.2	698 570 7
12.25	12.3	701 428
12.35	12.4	704 273 3
12.45	12.5	707 107 5
12.55		
	12.6	709 93

A	B	C
12.65	12.7	712 742
12.75	12.8	715 542 5
12.85	12.9	718 332
12.95	13	721 111
13.05		
	13.1	723 879
13.15	13.2	726 637
13.25	13.3	729 384
13.35	13.4	732 121
13.45	13.5	734 848
13.55		
	13.6	737 564
13.65	13.7	740 271
13.75	13.8	742 968
13.85	13.9	745 655
13.95	14	748 332
14.05		
	14.1	751
14.15	14.2	753 658
14.25	14.3	756 307
14.35	14.4	758 947
14.45	14.5	761 578
14.55		
	14.6	764 199 5
14.65	14.7	766 812
14.75	14.8	769 416
14.85	14.9	772 011
14.95	15	774 597
15.05		
	15.1	777 175
15.15	15.2	779 744
15.25	15.3	782 305
15.35	15.4	784 857
15.45	15.5	787 401
15.55		
	15.6	789 937
15.65	15.7	792 465
15.75	15.8	794 985
15.85	15.9	797 496 6
15.95	16	800
16.05		
	16.1	802 497
16.15	16.2	804 985
16.25	16.3	807 466
16.35	16.4	809 939
16.45	16.5	812 404
16.55		
	16.6	814 862
16.65	16.7	817 313
16.75	16.8	819 756
16.85	16.9	822 193
16.95	17	824 622
17.05		
	17.1	827 043
17.15	17.2	829 458
17.25	17.3	831 866
17.35	17.4	834 266
17.45	17.5	836 66
17.55		
	17.6	839 047
17.65	17.7	841 428
17.75	17.8	843 801
17.85	17.9	846 168
17.95	18	848 529
18.05		
	18.1	850 882
18.15	18.2	853 23
18.25	18.3	855 57
18.35	18.4	857 905
18.45	18.5	860 233
18.55		
	18.6	862 555
18.65	18.7	864 87
18.75	18.8	867 18
18.85	18.9	869 483
18.95	19	871 78
19.05		
	19.1	874 071
19.15	19.2	876 356
19.25	19.3	878 636
19.35	19.4	880 909
19.45	19.5	883 176
19.55		
	19.6	885 438

A	B	C
19.65	19.7	887 694
19.75	19.8	889 944
19.85	19.9	892 189
19.95	20	894 428
20.05		
	20.1	896 661
20.15	20.2	898 889
20.25	20.3	901 111
20.35	20.4	903 328
20.45	20.5	905 539
20.55		
	20.6	907 745
20.65	20.7	909 945
20.75	20.8	912 141
20.85	20.9	914 331
20.95	21	916 516
21.05		
	21.1	918 695
21.15	21.2	920 87
21.25	21.3	923 039
21.35	21.4	925 203
21.45	21.5	927 362
21.55		
	21.6	929 516
21.65	21.7	931 666
21.75	21.8	933 81
21.85	21.9	935 949
21.95	22	938 084
22.05		
	22.1	940 213
22.15	22.2	942 338
22.25	22.3	944 458
22.35	22.4	946 573
22.45	22.5	948 683
22.55		
	22.6	950 789
22.65	22.7	952 891
22.75	22.8	954 987
22.85	22.9	957 079
22.95	23	959 167
23.05		
	23.1	961 249
23.15	23.2	963 328
23.25	23.3	965 402
23.35	23.4	967 471
23.45	23.5	969 536
23.55		
	23.6	971 597
23.65	23.7	973 653
23.75	23.8	975 705
23.85	23.9	977 753
23.95	24	979 796
24.05		
	24.1	981 835
24.15	24.2	983 87
24.25	24.3	985 901
24.35	24.4	987 927
24.45	24.5	989 95
24.55		
	24.6	991 968
24.65	24.7	993 982
24.75	24.8	995 992
24.85	24.9	997 998
24.95	25	100
25.05		
	25.1	100 199 8
25.15	25.2	100 399 2
25.25	25.3	100 598 2
25.35	25.4	100 796 8
25.45	25.5	100 995 1
25.55		
	25.6	101 192 9
25.65	25.7	101 390 4
25.75	25.8	101 587 4
25.85	25.9	101 784 1
25.95	26	101 980 4
26.05		
	26.1	102 176 3
26.15	26.2	102 371 9
26.25	26.3	102 567 1
26.35	26.4	102 761 9
26.45	26.5	102 956 3
26.55		
	26.6	103 150 4

* For $\sqrt{10.00}$ use the values in the table between 10.00 and 10.025.

[1] Reproduced from Marchant Table 81 by permission of the copyright owner, Marchant Calculators Division of Smith-Corona Marchant, Inc., Oakland (Calif.), USA.

A	B	C
26.65	26.7	103 344 1
26.75	26.8	103 537 5
26.85	26.9	103 730 4
26.95	27	103 923 13
27.10	27.2	104 307 33
27.30	27.4	104 690 1
27.50	27.6	105 071 5
27.7	27.8	105 451 5
27.9	28	105 830 15
28.1	28.2	106 207 42
28.3	28.4	106 583 4
28.5	28.6	106 958 02
28.7	28.8	107 331 34
28.9	29	107 703 38
29.1	29.2	108 074 13
29.3	29.4	108 443 6
29.5	29.6	108 811 84
29.7	29.8	109 178 8
29.9	30	109 544 6
30.1	30.2	109 909 14
30.3	30.4	110 272 48
30.5	30.6	110 634 6
30.7	30.8	110 995 57
30.9	31	111 355 35
31.1	31.2	111 714
31.3	31.4	112 071 5
31.5	31.6	112 427 83
31.7	31.8	112 783 05
31.9	32	113 137 15
32.1	32.2	113 490 14
32.3	32.4	113 842 07
32.5	32.6	114 192 9
32.7	32.8	114 542 6
32.9	33	114 891 3
33.1	33.2	115 238 95
33.3	33.4	115 585 5
33.5	33.6	115 931 1
33.7	33.8	116 275 6
33.9	34	116 619 1
34.1	34.2	116 961 6
34.3	34.4	117 303 1
34.5	34.6	117 643 6
34.7		

A	B	C
34.7	34.8	117 983 1
34.9	35	118 321 66
35.1	35.2	118 659 24
35.3	35.4	118 995 86
35.5	35.6	119 331 5
35.7	35.8	119 666 3
35.9	36	120 000 1
36.1	36.2	120 332 9
36.3	36.4	120 664 9
36.5	36.6	120 995 9
36.7	36.8	121 326 1
36.9	37	121 655 3
37.1	37.2	121 983 7
37.3	37.4	122 311 1
37.5	37.6	122 637 7
37.7	37.8	122 963 5
37.9	38	123 288 3
38.1	38.2	123 612 4
38.3	38.4	123 935 5
38.5	38.6	124 257 9
38.7	38.8	124 579 4
38.9	39	124 9
39.1	39.2	125 219 9
39.3	39.4	125 538 9
39.5	39.6	125 857 1
39.7	39.8	126 174 5
39.9	40	126 491 1
40.1	40.2	126 807
40.3	40.4	127 122
40.5	40.6	127 436 3
40.7	40.8	127 749 8
40.9	41	128 062 5
41.1	41.2	128 374 5
41.3	41.4	128 685 7
41.5	41.6	128 996 2
41.7	41.8	129 305 9
41.9	42	129 614 9
42.1	42.2	129 923 1
42.3	42.4	130 230 6
42.5	42.6	130 537 4
42.7	42.8	130 843 5
42.9	43	131 148 8
43.1		

A	B	C
43.1	43.2	131 453 5
43.3	43.4	131 757 4
43.5	43.6	132 060 6
43.7	43.8	132 363 2
43.9	44	132 665 1
44.1	44.2	132 966 2
44.3	44.4	133 266 7
44.5	44.6	133 566 5
44.7	44.8	133 865 6
44.9	45	134 164 1
45.1	45.2	134 461 9
45.3	45.4	134 759 1
45.5	45.6	135 055 6
45.7	45.8	135 351 4
45.9	46	135 646 6
46.1	46.2	135 941 2
46.3	46.4	136 235 1
46.5	46.6	136 528 4
46.70	46.8	136 821 1
46.90	47	137 113 2
47.15	47.3	137 550 1
47.45	47.6	137 985 6
47.75	47.9	138 419 75
48.05	48.2	138 852 53
48.35	48.5	139 283 96
48.65	48.8	139 714 08
48.95	49.1	140 142 86
49.25	49.4	140 570 35
49.55	49.7	140 996 55
49.85	50	141 421 44
50.15	50.3	141 845 07
50.45	50.6	142 267 43
50.75	50.9	142 688 55
51.05	51.2	143 108 44
51.35	51.5	143 527 1
51.65	51.8	143 944 5
51.95	52.1	144 360 74
52.25	52.4	144 775 76
52.55	52.7	145 189 6
52.85	53	145 602 27
53.15	53.3	146 013 77
53.45	53.6	146 424 1
53.75		

A	B	C
53.75	53.9	146 833 3
54.05	54.2	147 241 37
54.35	54.5	147 648 3
54.65	54.8	148 054 1
54.95	55.1	148 458 8
55.25	55.4	148 862 4
55.55	55.7	149 264 9
55.85	56	149 666 4
56.15	56.3	150 066 73
56.45	56.6	150 466
56.75	56.9	150 864 25
57.05	57.2	151 261 4
57.35	57.5	151 657 6
57.65	57.8	152 052 7
57.95	58.1	152 446 8
58.25	58.4	152 839 85
58.55	58.7	153 231 9
58.85	59	153 623
59.15	59.3	154 013 05
59.45	59.6	154 402 14
59.75	59.9	154 790 24
60.05	60.2	155 177 4
60.35	60.5	155 563 6
60.65	60.8	155 948 8
60.95	61.1	156 333
61.25	61.4	156 716 4
61.55	61.7	157 098 8
61.85	62	157 480 2
62.15	62.3	157 860 8
62.45	62.6	158 240 4
62.75	62.9	158 619 1
63.05	63.2	158 996 9
63.35	63.5	159 373 8
63.65	63.8	159 749 9
63.95	64.1	160 125
64.25	64.4	160 499 3
64.55	64.7	160 872 7
64.85	65	161 245 2
65.15	65.3	161 616 9
65.45	65.6	161 987 7
65.75	65.9	162 357 7
66.05	66.2	162 726 8
66.35		

A	B	C
66.35	66.5	163 095 1
66.65	66.8	163 462 6
66.95	67.1	163 829 2
67.25	67.4	164 195 1
67.55	67.7	164 560 1
67.85	68	164 924 3
68.2	68.4	165 408 67
68.6	68.8	165 891 62
69.0	69.2	166 373 17
69.4	69.6	166 853 3
69.8	70	167 332 1
70.2	70.4	167 809 5
70.6	70.8	168 285 56
71.0	71.2	168 760 27
71.4	71.6	169 233 65
71.8	72	169 705 7
72.2	72.4	170 176 46
72.6	72.8	170 645 92
73.0	73.2	171 114 08
73.4	73.6	171 580 96
73.8	74	172 046 6
74.2	74.4	172 510 95
74.6	74.8	172 974 06
75.0	75.2	173 435 95
75.4	75.6	173 896 6
75.8	76	174 356 04
76.2	76.4	174 814 26
76.6	76.8	175 271 3
77.0	77.2	175 727 14
77.4	77.6	176 181 8
77.8	78	176 635 3
78.2	78.4	177 087 6
78.6	78.8	177 538 8
79.0	79.2	177 988 84
79.4	79.6	178 437 74
79.8	80	178 885 5
80.2	80.4	179 332 16
80.6	80.8	179 777 7
81.0	81.2	180 222 15
81.4	81.6	180 665 5
81.8	82	181 107 8
82.2	82.4	181 548 96
82.6		

A	B	C
82.6	82.8	181 989 1
83.0	83.2	182 428 1
83.4	83.6	182 866 14
83.8	84	183 303 1
84.2	84.4	183 739
84.6	84.8	184 173 9
85.0	85.2	184 607 76
85.4	85.6	185 040 6
85.8	86	185 472 4
86.2	86.4	185 903 3
86.6	86.8	186 333 1
87.0	87.2	186 761 94
87.4	87.6	187 189 8
87.8	88	187 616 7
88.2	88.4	188 042 6
88.6	88.8	188 467 6
89.0	89.2	188 891 6
89.4	89.6	189 314 6
89.8	90	189 736 7
90.2	90.4	190 157 9
90.60	90.8	190 578 1
91.00	91.2	190 997 4
91.40	91.6	191 415 8
91.80	92	191 833 35
92.25	92.5	192 353 93
92.75	93	192 873 1
93.25	93.5	193 390 88
93.75	94	193 907 29
94.25	94.5	194 422 3
94.75	95	194 935 96
95.25	95.5	195 448 3
95.75	96	195 959 26
96.25	96.5	196 468 9
96.75	97	196 977 24
97.25	97.5	197 484 26
97.75	98	197 989 98
98.25	98.5	198 494 4
98.75	99	198 997 57
99.20	99.4	199 399 1
99.60	99.8	199 799 9
100.0		

Binomial Coefficients*

$$\binom{n}{x} = \frac{n!}{x!\,(n-x)!}$$

n	$\binom{n}{0}$	$\binom{n}{1}$	$\binom{n}{2}$	$\binom{n}{3}$	$\binom{n}{4}$	$\binom{n}{5}$	$\binom{n}{6}$	$\binom{n}{7}$	$\binom{n}{8}$	$\binom{n}{9}$	$\binom{n}{10}$	$\binom{n}{11}$	$\binom{n}{12}$	$\binom{n}{13}$	$\binom{n}{14}$	$\binom{n}{15}$
0	1															
1	1	1														
2	1	2	1													
3	1	3	3	1												
4	1	4	6	4	1											
5	1	5	10	10	5	1										
6	1	6	15	20	15	6	1									
7	1	7	21	35	35	21	7	1								
8	1	8	28	56	70	56	28	8	1							
9	1	9	36	84	126	126	84	36	9	1						
10	1	10	45	120	210	252	210	120	45	10	1					
11	1	11	55	165	330	462	462	330	165	55	11	1				
12	1	12	66	220	495	792	924	792	495	220	66	12	1			
13	1	13	78	286	715	1287	1716	1716	1287	715	286	78	13	1		
14	1	14	91	364	1001	2002	3003	3432	3003	2002	1001	364	91	14	1	
15	1	15	105	455	1365	3003	5005	6435	6435	5005	3003	1365	455	105	15	1
16	1	16	120	560	1820	4368	8008	11440	12870	11440	8008	4368	1820	560	120	16
17	1	17	136	680	2380	6188	12376	19448	24310	24310	19448	12376	6188	2380	680	136
18	1	18	153	816	3060	8568	18564	31824	43758	48620	43758	31824	18564	8568	3060	816
19	1	19	171	969	3876	11628	27132	50388	75582	92378	92378	75582	50388	27132	11628	3876
20	1	20	190	1140	4845	15504	38760	77520	125970	167960	184756	167960	125970	77520	38760	15504
21	1	21	210	1330	5985	20349	54264	116280	203490	293930	352716	352716	293930	203490	116280	54264
22	1	22	231	1540	7315	26334	74613	170544	319770	497420	646646	705432	646646	497420	319770	170544
23	1	23	253	1771	8855	33649	100947	245157	490314	817190	1144066	1352078	1352078	1144066	817190	490314
24	1	24	276	2024	10626	42504	134596	346104	735471	1307504	1961256	2496144	2704156	2496144	1961256	1307504
25	1	25	300	2300	12650	53130	177100	480700	1081575	2042975	3268760	4457400	5200300	5200300	4457400	3268760
26	1	26	325	2600	14950	65780	230230	657800	1562275	3124550	5311735	7726160	9657700	10400600	9657700	7726160
27	1	27	351	2925	17550	80730	296010	888030	2220075	4686825	8436285	13037895	17383860	20058300	20058300	17383860
28	1	28	378	3276	20475	98280	376740	1184040	3108105	6906900	13123110	21474180	30421755	37442160	40116600	37442160
29	1	29	406	3654	23751	118755	475020	1560780	4292145	10015005	20030010	34597290	51895935	67863915	77558760	77558760
30	1	30	435	4060	27405	142506	593775	2035800	5852925	14307150	30045015	54627300	86493225	119759850	145422675	155117520
31	1	31	465	4495	31465	169911	736281	2629575	7888725	20160075	44352165	84672315	141120525	206253075	265182525	300540195
32	1	32	496	4960	35960	201376	906192	3365856	10518300	28048800	64512240	129024480	225792840	347373600	471435600	565722720
33	1	33	528	5456	40920	237336	1107568	4272048	13884156	38567100	92561040	193536720	354817320	573166440	818809200	1037158320
34	1	34	561	5984	46376	278256	1344904	5379616	18156204	52451256	131128140	286097760	548354040	927983760	1391975640	1855967520
35	1	35	595	6545	52360	324632	1623160	6724520	23535820	70607460	183579396	417225900	834451800	1476337800	2319959400	3247943160
36	1	36	630	7140	58905	376992	1947792	8347680	30260340	94143280	254186856	600805296	1251677700	2310789600	3796297200	5567902560
37	1	37	666	7770	66045	435897	2324784	10295472	38608020	124403620	348330136	854992152	1852482996	3562467300	6107086800	9364199760
38	1	38	703	8436	73815	501942	2760681	12620256	48903492	163011640	472733756	1203322288	2707475148	5414950296	9669554100	15471286560
39	1	39	741	9139	82251	575757	3262623	15380937	61523748	211915132	635745396	1676056044	3910797436	8122425444	15084504396	25140840660

* For logarithms of binomial coefficients up to $\binom{n}{100}$ see pages 70–77. Reproduction of values from this table only by permission of the publishers of these *Scientific Tables.*

Common Logarithms* of Factorials of the Integers 1—999

Factorial of $n = n! = n \times (n-1) \times \cdots \times 3 \times 2 \times 1$; factorial of $0 = 1$

n	0	1	2	3	4	5	6	7	8	9
0	0.00000	0.00000	0.30103	0.77815	1.38021	2.07918	2.85733	3.70243	4.60552	5.55976
10	6.55976	7.60116	8.68034	9.79428	10.94041	12.11650	13.32062	14.55107	15.80634	17.08509
20	18.38612	19.70834	21.05077	22.41249	23.79271	25.19065	26.60562	28.03698	29.48414	30.94654
30	32.42366	33.91502	35.42017	36.93869	38.47016	40.01423	41.57054	43.13874	44.71852	46.30959
40	47.91165	49.52443	51.14768	52.78115	54.42460	56.07781	57.74057	59.41267	61.09391	62.78410
50	64.48307	66.19064	67.90665	69.63092	71.36332	73.10368	74.85187	76.60774	78.37117	80.14202
60	81.92017	83.70550	85.49790	87.29724	89.10342	90.91633	92.73587	94.56195	96.39446	98.23331
70	100.07841	101.92966	103.78700	105.65032	107.51955	109.39461	111.27543	113.16192	115.05401	116.95164
80	118.85473	120.76321	122.67703	124.59610	126.52038	128.44980	130.38430	132.32382	134.26830	136.21769
90	138.17194	140.13098	142.09476	144.06325	146.03638	148.01410	149.99637	151.98314	153.97437	155.97000
100	157.97000	159.97433	161.98293	163.99576	166.01280	168.03398	170.05929	172.08867	174.12210	176.15952
110	178.20092	180.24624	182.29546	184.34854	186.40544	188.46614	190.53060	192.59878	194.67067	196.74621
120	198.82539	200.90818	202.99454	205.08444	207.17787	209.27478	211.37515	213.47895	215.58616	217.69675
130	219.81069	221.92797	224.04854	226.17239	228.29950	230.42983	232.56337	234.70009	236.83997	238.98298
140	241.12911	243.27833	245.43062	247.58595	249.74432	251.90568	254.07004	256.23735	258.40762	260.58080
150	262.75689	264.93587	267.11771	269.30240	271.48993	273.68026	275.87338	278.06928	280.26794	282.46933
160	284.67345	286.88028	289.08980	291.30198	293.51683	295.73431	297.95442	300.17713	302.40244	304.63033
170	306.86078	309.09378	311.32930	313.56735	315.80790	318.05094	320.29645	322.54442	324.79484	327.04770
180	329.30297	331.56065	333.82072	336.08317	338.34799	340.61516	342.88467	345.15651	347.43067	349.70713
190	351.98589	354.26692	356.55022	358.83578	361.12358	363.41362	365.70587	368.00034	370.29700	372.59586
200	374.89689	377.20008	379.50544	381.81293	384.12256	386.43432	388.74818	391.06415	393.38222	395.70236
210	398.02458	400.34887	402.67520	405.00358	407.33400	409.66643	412.00089	414.33735	416.67580	419.01625
220	421.35867	423.70306	426.04942	428.39772	430.74797	433.10015	435.45426	437.81029	440.16822	442.52806
230	444.88978	447.25340	449.61888	451.98624	454.35546	456.72652	459.09944	461.47418	463.85076	466.22916
240	468.60937	470.99139	473.37520	475.76081	478.14820	480.53737	482.92830	485.32100	487.71545	490.11165
250	492.50959	494.90926	497.31066	499.71378	502.11862	504.52516	506.93340	509.34333	511.75495	514.16825
260	516.58322	518.99986	521.41816	523.83812	526.25972	528.68297	531.10785	533.53436	535.96250	538.39225
270	540.82361	543.25658	545.69115	548.12731	550.56506	553.00439	555.44530	557.88778	560.33183	562.77743
280	565.22459	567.67330	570.12354	572.57533	575.02865	577.48349	579.93986	582.39774	584.85713	587.31803
290	589.78043	592.24432	594.70971	597.17657	599.64492	602.11474	604.58603	607.05879	609.53301	612.00868
300	614.48580	616.96436	619.44437	621.92581	624.40869	626.89299	629.37871	631.86585	634.35440	636.84436
310	639.33572	641.82848	644.32263	646.81818	649.31511	651.81342	654.31310	656.81416	659.31659	661.82038
320	664.32553	666.83204	669.33989	671.84910	674.35964	676.87152	679.38474	681.89929	684.41516	686.93236
330	689.45087	691.97070	694.49184	697.01428	699.53803	702.06307	704.58941	707.11704	709.64596	712.17616
340	714.70764	717.24039	719.77442	722.30971	724.84627	727.38409	729.92317	732.46350	735.00508	737.54790
350	740.09197	742.63728	745.18382	747.73160	750.28060	752.83083	755.38228	757.93495	760.48883	763.04392
360	765.60023	768.15773	770.71644	773.27635	775.83745	778.39974	780.96323	783.52789	786.09374	788.66077
370	791.22897	793.79834	796.36888	798.94059	801.51347	804.08750	806.66268	809.23903	811.81652	814.39516
380	816.97494	819.55587	822.13793	824.72113	827.30546	829.89092	832.47751	835.06522	837.65405	840.24400
390	842.83507	845.42724	848.02053	850.61492	853.21042	855.80701	858.40471	861.00350	863.60338	866.20436
400	868.80642	871.40956	874.01379	876.61909	879.22547	881.83293	884.44146	887.05105	889.66171	892.27343
410	894.88622	897.50006	900.11496	902.73091	905.34791	907.96595	910.58505	913.20518	915.82636	918.44857
420	921.07182	923.69611	926.32142	928.94776	931.57512	934.20351	936.83292	939.46335	942.09480	944.72725
430	947.36072	949.99520	952.63068	955.26717	957.90466	960.54315	963.18263	965.82312	968.46459	971.10705
440	973.75051	976.39495	979.04037	981.68677	984.33415	986.98251	989.63185	992.28216	994.93344	997.58568
450	1000.23889	1002.89307	1005.54821	1008.20431	1010.86136	1013.51937	1016.17834	1018.83825	1021.49912	1024.16093
460	1026.82369	1029.48739	1032.15203	1034.81761	1037.48413	1040.15158	1042.81997	1045.48929	1048.15953	1050.83071
470	1053.50280	1056.17582	1058.84977	1061.52463	1064.20041	1066.87710	1069.55471	1072.23322	1074.91265	1077.59299
480	1080.27423	1082.95637	1085.63942	1088.32337	1091.00821	1093.69395	1096.38059	1099.06812	1101.75654	1104.44585
490	1107.13604	1109.82712	1112.51909	1115.21194	1117.90566	1120.60027	1123.29575	1125.99211	1128.68934	1131.38744
500	1134.08641	1136.78624	1139.48695	1142.18851	1144.89094	1147.59424	1150.29839	1153.00339	1155.70926	1158.41598
510	1161.12355	1163.83197	1166.54124	1169.25135	1171.96232	1174.67412	1177.38677	1180.10026	1182.81459	1185.52976
520	1188.24576	1190.96260	1193.68027	1196.39877	1199.11810	1201.83826	1204.55925	1207.28106	1210.00369	1212.72715
530	1215.45142	1218.17652	1220.90243	1223.62916	1226.35670	1229.08505	1231.81422	1234.54419	1237.27497	1240.00656
540	1242.73896	1245.47215	1248.20615	1250.94095	1253.67655	1256.41295	1259.15014	1261.88813	1264.62691	1267.36648
550	1270.10684	1272.84799	1275.58993	1278.33266	1281.07617	1283.82046	1286.56554	1289.31139	1292.05803	1294.80544
560	1297.55363	1300.30259	1303.05232	1305.80283	1308.55411	1311.30616	1314.05898	1316.81256	1319.56691	1322.32202
570	1325.07790	1327.83453	1330.59193	1333.35008	1336.10899	1338.86866	1341.62908	1344.39026	1347.15219	1349.91487
580	1352.67829	1355.44247	1358.20739	1360.97306	1363.73948	1366.50663	1369.27453	1372.04317	1374.81254	1377.58266
590	1380.35351	1383.12510	1385.89742	1388.67048	1391.44426	1394.21878	1396.99403	1399.77000	1402.54670	1405.32413
600	1408.10228	1410.88115	1413.66075	1416.44107	1419.22210	1422.00386	1424.78633	1427.56952	1430.35343	1433.13804
610	1435.92337	1438.70941	1441.49617	1444.28363	1447.07179	1449.86067	1452.65025	1455.44054	1458.23152	1461.02322
620	1463.81561	1466.60870	1469.40249	1472.19698	1474.99216	1477.78804	1480.58462	1483.38188	1486.17984	1488.97849
630	1491.77784	1494.57787	1497.37858	1500.17999	1502.98208	1505.78485	1508.58831	1511.39245	1514.19727	1517.00277
640	1519.80895	1522.61581	1525.42334	1528.23155	1531.04044	1533.85000	1536.66023	1539.47114	1542.28271	1545.09496
650	1547.90787	1550.72145	1553.53570	1556.35061	1559.16619	1561.98243	1564.79933	1567.61690	1570.43513	1573.25401
660	1576.07356	1578.89376	1581.71461	1584.53613	1587.35830	1590.18112	1593.00459	1595.82872	1598.65350	1601.47892
670	1604.30500	1607.13172	1609.95909	1612.78710	1615.61576	1618.44507	1621.27501	1624.10560	1626.93683	1629.76870
680	1632.60121	1635.43436	1638.26814	1641.10256	1643.93762	1646.77331	1649.60964	1652.44659	1655.28418	1658.12240
690	1660.96125	1663.80073	1666.64083	1669.48157	1672.32293	1675.16491	1678.00752	1680.85075	1683.69461	1686.53909
700	1689.38418	1692.22990	1695.07624	1697.92320	1700.77077	1703.61896	1706.46776	1709.31718	1712.16721	1715.01786
710	1717.86912	1720.72099	1723.57347	1726.42656	1729.28026	1732.13456	1734.98948	1737.84500	1740.70112	1743.55785
720	1746.41518	1749.27312	1752.13165	1754.99079	1757.85053	1760.71087	1763.57181	1766.43334	1769.29547	1772.15820
730	1775.02152	1777.88544	1780.74995	1783.61505	1786.48075	1789.34704	1792.21391	1795.08138	1797.94944	1800.81808
740	1803.68731	1806.55713	1809.42754	1812.29853	1815.17010	1818.04225	1820.91499	1823.78831	1826.66222	1829.53670
750	1832.41176	1835.28740	1838.16362	1841.04041	1843.91778	1846.79573	1849.67425	1852.55335	1855.43302	1858.31326
760	1861.19407	1864.07546	1866.95741	1869.83994	1872.72303	1875.60669	1878.49092	1881.37571	1884.26108	1887.14700
770	1890.03349	1892.92055	1895.80816	1898.69634	1901.58508	1904.47439	1907.36425	1910.25467	1913.14565	1916.03718
780	1918.92928	1921.82193	1924.71514	1927.60890	1930.50321	1933.39808	1936.29351	1939.18948	1942.08601	1944.98308
790	1947.88071	1950.77889	1953.67761	1956.57689	1959.47671	1962.37707	1965.27799	1968.17944	1971.08145	1973.98399
800	1976.88708	1979.79072	1982.69489	1985.59961	1988.50486	1991.41066	1994.31699	1997.22387	2000.13128	2003.03922
810	2005.94771	2008.85673	2011.76629	2014.67638	2017.58700	2020.49816	2023.40985	2026.32207	2029.23482	2032.14811
820	2035.06192	2037.97626	2040.89114	2043.80654	2046.72246	2049.63892	2052.55590	2055.47340	2058.39143	2061.30999
830	2064.22906	2067.14867	2070.06879	2072.98943	2075.91060	2078.83229	2081.75449	2084.67722	2087.60046	2090.52422
840	2093.44850	2096.37330	2099.29861	2102.22444	2105.15078	2108.07764	2111.00501	2113.93289	2116.86129	2119.79019
850	2122.71961	2125.64954	2128.57998	2131.51093	2134.44239	2137.37435	2140.30683	2143.23981	2146.17330	2149.10729
860	2152.04179	2154.97679	2157.91230	2160.84831	2163.78482	2166.72184	2169.65936	2172.59737	2175.53589	2178.47491
870	2181.41443	2184.35445	2187.29497	2190.23598	2193.17749	2196.11950	2199.06200	2202.00500	2204.94850	2207.89249
880	2210.83697	2213.78195	2216.72741	2219.67338	2222.61983	2225.56677	2228.51420	2231.46213	2234.41054	2237.35944
890	2240.30883	2243.25871	2246.20908	2249.15993	2252.11126	2255.06309	2258.01540	2260.96819	2263.92146	2266.87522
900	2269.82947	2272.78419	2275.73940	2278.69509	2281.65125	2284.60790	2287.56503	2290.52264	2293.48072	2296.43929
910	2299.39833	2302.35785	2305.31784	2308.27831	2311.23926	2314.20068	2317.16258	2320.12495	2323.08779	2326.05111
920	2329.01489	2331.97915	2334.94388	2337.90909	2340.87476	2343.84090	2346.80751	2349.77459	2352.74214	2355.71015
930	2358.67864	2361.64759	2364.61700	2367.58688	2370.55723	2373.52804	2376.49932	2379.47106	2382.44326	2385.41593
940	2388.38906	2391.36265	2394.33670	2397.31121	2400.28618	2403.26161	2406.23750	2409.21385	2412.19066	2415.16793
950	2418.14565	2421.12383	2424.10247	2427.08156	2430.06111	2433.04112	2436.02157	2439.00249	2441.98385	2444.96567
960	2447.94794	2450.93066	2453.91384	2456.89747	2459.88154	2462.86607	2465.85105	2468.83647	2471.82235	2474.80867
970	2477.79545	2480.78266	2483.77033	2486.75844	2489.74700	2492.73601	2495.72546	2498.71535	2501.70569	2504.69647
980	2507.68770	2510.67937	2513.67148	2516.66403	2519.65703	2522.65047	2525.64434	2528.63866	2531.63342	2534.62861
990	2537.62425	2540.62032	2543.61683	2546.61378	2549.61117	2552.60899	2555.60725	2558.60595	2561.60508	2564.60464

Common Logarithms* of Reciprocal Factorials of the Integers 1–999

Reciprocal factorial of $n = 1/n!$. The bold figures are negative characteristics; the mantissae are positive

n	0	1	2	3	4	5	6	7	8	9
0	00000	00000	1 69897	1 22185	2 61979	3 92082	3 14267	4 29757	5 39448	6 44024
10	7 44024	8 39884	9 31966	10 20572	11 05959	13 88350	14 67938	15 44893	16 19366	18 91491
20	19 61388	20 29166	22 94923	23 58751	24 20729	26 80935	27 39438	29 96302	30 51586	31 05346
30	33 57634	34 08498	36 57983	37 06131	39 52984	41 98577	42 42946	44 86126	45 28148	47 69041
40	48 08835	50 47557	52 85232	53 21885	55 57540	57 92219	58 25943	60 58733	62 90609	63 21590
50	65 51693	67 80936	68 09335	70 36908	72 63668	74 89632	75 14813	77 39226	79 62883	81 85798
60	82 07983	84 29450	86 50210	88 70276	90 89658	91 08367	93 26413	95 43805	97 60554	99 76669
70	101 92159	102 07034	104 21300	106 34968	108 48045	110 60539	112 72457	114 83808	116 94599	117 04836
80	119 14527	121 23679	123 32297	125 40390	127 47962	129 55020	131 61570	133 67618	135 73170	137 78231
90	139 82806	141 86902	143 90524	145 93675	147 96362	149 98590	150 00363	152 01686	154 02563	156 03000
100	158 03000	160 02567	162 01707	164 00424	167 98720	169 96602	171 94071	173 91133	175 87790	177 84048
110	179 79908	181 75376	183 70454	185 65146	187 59456	189 53386	191 46940	193 40122	195 32933	197 25379
120	199 17461	201 09182	203 00546	206 91556	208 82213	210 72522	212 62485	214 52105	216 41384	218 30325
130	220 18931	222 07203	225 95146	227 82761	229 70050	231 57017	233 43663	235 29991	237 16003	239 01702
140	242 87089	244 72167	246 56938	248 41405	250 25568	252 09432	255 92996	257 76265	259 59238	261 41920
150	263 24311	265 06413	268 88229	270 69760	272 51007	274 31974	276 12662	279 93072	281 73206	283 53067
160	285 32655	287 11972	290 91020	292 69802	294 48317	296 26569	298 04558	301 82287	303 59756	305 36967
170	307 13922	310 90622	312 67070	314 43265	316 19210	319 94906	321 70355	323 45558	325 20516	328 95230
180	330 69703	332 43935	334 17928	337 91683	339 65201	341 38484	343 11533	346 84349	348 56933	350 29287
190	352 01411	355 73308	357 44978	359 16422	362 87642	364 58638	366 29413	369 99966	371 70300	373 40414
200	375 10311	378 79992	380 49456	382 18707	385 87744	387 56568	389 25182	392 93585	394 61778	396 29764
210	399 97542	401 65113	403 32480	406 99642	408 66600	410 33357	413 99911	415 66265	417 32420	420 98375
220	422 64133	424 29694	427 95058	429 60228	431 25203	434 89985	436 54574	438 18971	441 83178	443 47194
230	445 11022	448 74660	450 38112	452 01376	455 64454	457 27348	460 90056	462 52582	464 14924	467 77084
240	469 39063	471 00861	474 62480	476 23919	479 85180	481 46263	483 07170	486 67900	488 28455	491 88835
250	493 49041	495 09074	498 68934	500 28622	503 88138	505 47484	507 06660	510 65667	512 24505	515 83175
260	517 41678	519 00014	522 58184	524 16188	527 74028	529 31703	532 89215	534 46564	536 03750	539 60775
270	541 17639	544 74342	546 30885	549 87269	551 43494	554 99561	556 55470	558 11222	561 66817	563 22257
280	566 77541	568 32670	571 87646	573 42467	576 97135	578 51651	580 06014	583 60226	585 14287	588 68197
290	590 21957	593 75568	595 29029	598 82343	600 35508	603 88526	605 41397	608 94121	610 46699	613 99132
300	615 51420	617 03564	620 55563	622 07419	625 59131	627 10701	630 62129	632 13415	635 64560	637 15564
310	640 66428	642 17152	645 67737	647 18182	650 68489	652 18658	655 68690	657 18584	660 68341	662 17962
320	665 67447	667 16796	670 66011	672 15090	675 64036	677 12848	680 61526	682 10071	685 58484	687 06764
330	690 54913	692 02930	695 50816	698 98572	700 46197	703 93693	705 41059	708 88296	710 35404	713 82384
340	715 29236	718 75961	720 22558	723 69029	725 15373	728 61591	730 07683	733 53650	736 99492	738 45210
350	741 90803	743 36272	746 81618	748 26840	751 71940	753 16917	756 61772	758 06505	761 51117	764 95608
360	766 39977	769 84227	771 28356	774 72365	776 16255	779 60026	781 03677	784 47211	787 90626	789 33923
370	792 77103	794 20166	797 63112	799 05941	802 48653	805 91250	807 33732	810 76097	812 18348	815 60484
380	817 02506	820 44413	823 86207	825 27887	828 69454	830 10908	833 52249	836 93478	838 34595	841 75600
390	843 16493	846 57276	849 97947	851 38508	854 78958	856 19299	859 59529	862 99650	864 39662	867 79564
400	869 19358	872 59044	875 98621	877 38091	880 77453	882 16707	885 55854	888 94895	890 33829	893 72657
410	895 11378	898 49994	901 88504	903 26909	906 65209	908 03405	911 41495	914 79482	916 17364	919 55143
420	922 92818	924 30389	927 67858	929 05224	932 42488	935 79649	937 16708	940 53665	943 90520	945 27275
430	948 63928	950 00480	953 36932	956 73283	958 09534	961 45685	964 81737	966 17688	969 53541	972 89295
440	974 24949	977 60505	980 95963	982 31323	985 66585	987 01749	990 36815	993 71784	995 06656	998 41432
450	1001 76111	1003 10693	1006 45179	1009 79569	1011 13864	1014 48063	1017 82166	1019 16175	1022 50088	1025 83907
460	1027 17631	1030 51261	1033 84797	1035 18239	1038 51587	1041 84842	1043 18003	1046 51071	1049 84047	1051 16929
470	1054 49720	1057 82418	1059 15023	1062 47537	1065 79959	1067 12290	1070 44529	1073 76678	1075 08735	1078 40701
480	1081 72577	1083 04363	1086 36058	1089 67663	1092 99179	1094 30605	1097 61941	1100 93188	1102 24346	1105 55415
490	1108 86396	1110 17288	1113 48091	1116 78806	1118 09434	1121 39973	1124 70425	1126 00789	1129 31066	1132 61256
500	1135 91359	1137 21376	1140 51305	1143 81149	1145 10906	1148 40576	1151 70161	1154 99661	1156 29074	1159 58402
510	1162 87645	1164 16803	1167 45876	1170 74865	1172 03768	1175 32588	1178 61323	1181 89974	1183 18541	1186 47024
520	1189 75424	1191 03740	1194 31973	1197 60123	1200 88190	1202 16174	1205 44075	1208 71894	1211 99631	1213 27285
530	1216 54858	1219 82348	1221 09757	1224 37084	1227 64330	1230 91495	1232 18578	1235 45581	1238 72503	1241 99344
540	1243 26104	1246 52785	1249 79385	1251 05905	1254 32345	1257 58705	1260 84986	1262 11187	1265 37309	1268 63352
550	1271 89316	1273 15201	1276 41007	1279 66734	1282 92383	1284 17954	1287 43446	1290 68861	1293 94197	1295 19456
560	1298 44637	1301 69741	1304 94768	1306 19717	1309 44589	1312 69384	1315 94102	1317 18744	1320 43309	1323 67798
570	1326 92210	1328 16547	1331 40807	1334 64992	1337 89101	1339 13134	1342 37092	1345 60974	1348 84781	1350 08513
580	1353 32171	1356 55753	1359 79261	1361 02694	1364 26052	1367 49337	1370 72547	1373 95683	1375 18746	1378 41734
590	1381 64649	1384 87490	1386 10258	1389 32952	1392 55574	1395 78122	1397 00597	1400 23000	1403 45330	1406 67587
600	1409 89772	1411 11885	1414 33925	1417 55893	1420 77790	1423 99614	1425 21367	1428 43048	1431 64657	1434 86196
610	1436 07663	1439 29059	1442 50383	1445 71637	1448 92821	1450 13933	1453 34975	1456 55946	1459 76848	1462 97678
620	1464 18439	1467 39130	1470 59751	1473 80302	1475 00784	1478 21196	1481 41538	1484 61812	1487 82016	1489 02151
630	1492 22216	1495 42213	1498 62142	1501 82001	1503 01792	1506 21515	1509 41169	1512 60755	1515 80273	1518 99723
640	1520 19105	1523 38419	1526 57666	1529 76845	1532 95956	1534 15000	1537 33977	1540 52886	1543 71729	1546 90504
650	1548 09213	1551 27855	1554 46430	1557 64939	1560 83381	1562 01757	1565 20067	1568 38310	1571 56487	1574 74599
660	1577 92644	1579 10624	1582 28539	1585 46387	1588 64170	1591 81888	1594 99541	1596 17128	1599 34650	1602 52108
670	1605 69500	1608 86828	1610 04091	1613 21290	1616 38424	1619 55493	1622 72499	1625 89440	1627 06317	1630 23130
680	1633 39879	1636 56564	1639 73186	1642 89744	1644 06238	1647 22669	1650 39036	1653 55341	1656 71582	1659 87760
690	1661 03875	1664 19927	1667 35917	1670 51843	1673 67707	1676 83509	1679 99248	1681 14925	1684 30539	1687 46091
700	1690 61582	1693 77010	1696 92376	1698 07680	1701 22923	1704 38104	1707 53224	1710 68282	1713 83279	1716 98214
710	1718 13088	1721 27901	1724 42653	1727 57344	1730 71974	1733 86544	1735 01052	1738 15500	1741 29888	1744 44215
720	1747 58482	1750 72688	1753 86835	1755 00921	1758 14947	1761 28913	1764 42819	1767 56666	1770 70453	1773 84180
730	1776 97848	1778 11456	1781 25005	1784 38495	1787 51925	1790 65296	1793 78609	1796 91862	1798 05056	1801 18192
740	1804 31269	1807 44287	1810 57246	1813 70147	1816 82990	1819 95775	1821 08501	1824 21169	1827 33778	1830 46330
750	1833 58824	1836 71260	1839 83638	1842 95959	1844 08222	1847 20427	1850 32575	1853 44665	1856 56698	1859 68674
760	1862 80593	1865 92454	1867 04259	1870 16006	1873 27697	1876 39331	1879 50908	1882 62429	1885 73892	1888 85300
770	1891 96651	1893 07945	1896 19184	1899 30366	1902 41492	1905 52561	1908 63575	1911 74533	1914 85435	1917 96282
780	1919 07072	1922 17807	1925 28486	1928 39110	1931 49679	1934 60192	1937 70649	1940 81052	1943 91399	1945 01692
790	1948 11929	1951 22111	1954 32239	1957 42311	1960 52329	1963 62293	1966 72201	1969 82056	1972 91855	1974 01601
800	1977 11292	1980 20928	1983 30511	1986 40039	1989 49514	1992 58934	1995 68301	1998 77613	2001 86872	2004 96078
810	2006 05229	2009 14327	2012 23371	2015 32362	2018 41300	2021 50184	2024 59015	2027 67793	2030 76518	2033 85189
820	2036 93808	2038 02374	2041 10886	2044 19346	2047 27754	2050 36108	2053 44410	2056 52660	2059 60857	2062 69001
830	2065 77094	2068 85133	2071 93121	2073 01057	2076 08940	2079 16771	2082 24551	2085 32278	2088 39954	2091 47578
840	2094 55150	2097 62670	2100 70139	2103 77556	2106 84922	2109 92236	2112 99499	2114 06711	2117 13871	2120 20981
850	2123 28039	2126 35046	2129 42002	2132 48907	2135 55761	2138 62565	2141 69317	2144 76019	2147 82670	2150 89271
860	2153 95821	2155 02321	2158 08770	2161 15169	2164 21518	2167 27816	2170 34064	2173 40263	2176 46411	2179 52509
870	2182 58557	2185 64555	2188 70503	2191 76402	2194 82251	2197 88050	2200 93800	2203 99500	2205 05150	2208 10751
880	2211 16303	2214 21805	2217 27259	2220 32662	2223 38017	2226 43323	2229 48580	2232 53787	2235 58946	2238 64056
890	2241 69117	2244 74129	2247 79092	2250 84007	2253 88874	2256 93691	2259 98460	2261 03181	2264 07854	2267 12478
900	2270 17053	2273 21581	2276 26060	2279 30491	2282 34875	2285 39210	2288 43497	2291 47736	2294 51928	2297 56071
910	2300 60167	2303 64215	2306 68216	2309 72169	2312 76074	2315 79932	2318 83742	2321 87505	2324 91221	2327 94889
920	2330 98511	2332 02085	2335 05612	2338 09091	2341 12524	2344 15910	2347 19249	2350 22541	2353 25786	2356 28985
930	2359 32136	2362 35241	2365 38300	2368 41312	2371 44277	2374 47196	2377 50068	2380 52894	2383 55674	2386 58407
940	2389 61094	2392 63735	2395 66330	2398 68879	2401 71382	2404 73839	2407 76250	2410 78615	2413 80934	2416 83207
950	2419 85435	2422 87617	2425 89753	2428 91844	2431 93889	2434 95888	2437 97843	2440 99751	2442 01615	2445 03433
960	2448 05206	2451 06934	2454 08616	2457 10253	2460 11846	2463 13393	2466 14895	2469 16353	2472 17765	2475 19133
970	2478 20455	2481 21734	2484 22967	2487 24156	2490 25300	2493 26399	2496 27454	2499 28465	2502 29431	2505 30353
980	2508 31230	2511 32063	2514 32852	2517 33597	2520 34297	2523 34953	2526 35566	2529 36134	2532 36658	2535 37139
990	2538 37575	2541 37968	2544 38317	2547 38622	2550 38883	2553 39101	2556 39275	2559 39405	2562 39492	2565 39536

Integral → Deviation* c

$\int_{-\infty}^{c}$	0.000	0.001	0.002	0.003	0.004	0.005	0.006	0.007	0.008	0.009
0.00	—	*3.0902*	*2.8782*	*2.7478*	*2.6521*	*2.5758*	*2.5121*	*2.4573*	*2.4089*	*2.3656*
0.01	*2.3263*	*2.2904*	*2.2571*	*2.2262*	*2.1973*	*2.1701*	*2.1444*	*2.1201*	*2.0969*	*2.0749*
0.02	*2.0537*	*2.0335*	*2.0141*	*1.9954*	*1.9774*	*1.9600*	*1.9431*	*1.9268*	*1.9110*	*1.8957*
0.03	*1.8808*	*1.8663*	*1.8522*	*1.8384*	*1.8250*	*1.8119*	*1.7991*	*1.7866*	*1.7744*	*1.7624*
0.04	*1.7507*	*1.7392*	*1.7279*	*1.7169*	*1.7060*	*1.6954*	*1.6849*	*1.6747*	*1.6646*	*1.6546*
0.05	*1.6449*	*1.6352*	*1.6258*	*1.6164*	*1.6072*	*1.5982*	*1.5893*	*1.5805*	*1.5718*	*1.5632*
0.06	*1.5548*	*1.5464*	*1.5382*	*1.5301*	*1.5220*	*1.5141*	*1.5063*	*1.4985*	*1.4909*	*1.4833*
0.07	*1.4758*	*1.4684*	*1.4611*	*1.4538*	*1.4466*	*1.4395*	*1.4325*	*1.4255*	*1.4187*	*1.4118*
0.08	*1.4051*	*1.3984*	*1.3917*	*1.3852*	*1.3787*	*1.3722*	*1.3658*	*1.3595*	*1.3532*	*1.3469*
0.09	*1.3408*	*1.3346*	*1.3285*	*1.3225*	*1.3165*	*1.3106*	*1.3047*	*1.2988*	*1.2930*	*1.2873*
0.10	*1.2816*	*1.2759*	*1.2702*	*1.2646*	*1.2591*	*1.2536*	*1.2481*	*1.2426*	*1.2372*	*1.2319*
0.11	*1.2265*	*1.2212*	*1.2160*	*1.2107*	*1.2055*	*1.2004*	*1.1952*	*1.1901*	*1.1850*	*1.1800*
0.12	*1.1750*	*1.1700*	*1.1650*	*1.1601*	*1.1552*	*1.1503*	*1.1455*	*1.1407*	*1.1359*	*1.1311*
0.13	*1.1264*	*1.1217*	*1.1170*	*1.1123*	*1.1077*	*1.1031*	*1.0985*	*1.0939*	*1.0893*	*1.0848*
0.14	*1.0803*	*1.0758*	*1.0714*	*1.0669*	*1.0625*	*1.0581*	*1.0537*	*1.0494*	*1.0450*	*1.0407*
0.15	*1.0364*	*1.0322*	*1.0279*	*1.0237*	*1.0194*	*1.0152*	*1.0110*	*1.0069*	*1.0027*	*0.9986*
0.16	*0.9945*	*0.9904*	*0.9863*	*0.9822*	*0.9782*	*0.9741*	*0.9701*	*0.9661*	*0.9621*	*0.9581*
0.17	*0.9542*	*0.9502*	*0.9463*	*0.9424*	*0.9385*	*0.9346*	*0.9307*	*0.9269*	*0.9230*	*0.9192*
0.18	*0.9154*	*0.9116*	*0.9078*	*0.9040*	*0.9002*	*0.8965*	*0.8927*	*0.8890*	*0.8853*	*0.8816*
0.19	*0.8779*	*0.8742*	*0.8705*	*0.8669*	*0.8633*	*0.8596*	*0.8560*	*0.8524*	*0.8488*	*0.8452*
0.20	*0.8416*	*0.8381*	*0.8345*	*0.8310*	*0.8274*	*0.8239*	*0.8204*	*0.8169*	*0.8134*	*0.8099*
0.21	*0.8064*	*0.8030*	*0.7995*	*0.7961*	*0.7926*	*0.7892*	*0.7858*	*0.7824*	*0.7790*	*0.7756*
0.22	*0.7722*	*0.7688*	*0.7655*	*0.7621*	*0.7588*	*0.7554*	*0.7521*	*0.7488*	*0.7454*	*0.7421*
0.23	*0.7388*	*0.7356*	*0.7323*	*0.7290*	*0.7257*	*0.7225*	*0.7192*	*0.7160*	*0.7128*	*0.7095*
0.24	*0.7063*	*0.7031*	*0.6999*	*0.6967*	*0.6935*	*0.6903*	*0.6871*	*0.6840*	*0.6808*	*0.6776*
0.25	*0.6745*	*0.6713*	*0.6682*	*0.6651*	*0.6620*	*0.6588*	*0.6557*	*0.6526*	*0.6495*	*0.6464*
0.26	*0.6433*	*0.6403*	*0.6372*	*0.6341*	*0.6311*	*0.6280*	*0.6250*	*0.6219*	*0.6189*	*0.6158*
0.27	*0.6128*	*0.6098*	*0.6068*	*0.6038*	*0.6008*	*0.5978*	*0.5948*	*0.5918*	*0.5888*	*0.5858*
0.28	*0.5828*	*0.5799*	*0.5769*	*0.5740*	*0.5710*	*0.5681*	*0.5651*	*0.5622*	*0.5592*	*0.5563*
0.29	*0.5534*	*0.5505*	*0.5476*	*0.5446*	*0.5417*	*0.5388*	*0.5359*	*0.5330*	*0.5302*	*0.5273*
0.30	*0.5244*	*0.5215*	*0.5187*	*0.5158*	*0.5129*	*0.5101*	*0.5072*	*0.5044*	*0.5015*	*0.4987*
0.31	*0.4959*	*0.4930*	*0.4902*	*0.4874*	*0.4845*	*0.4817*	*0.4789*	*0.4761*	*0.4733*	*0.4705*
0.32	*0.4677*	*0.4649*	*0.4621*	*0.4593*	*0.4565*	*0.4538*	*0.4510*	*0.4482*	*0.4454*	*0.4427*
0.33	*0.4399*	*0.4372*	*0.4344*	*0.4316*	*0.4289*	*0.4261*	*0.4234*	*0.4207*	*0.4179*	*0.4152*
0.34	*0.4125*	*0.4097*	*0.4070*	*0.4043*	*0.4016*	*0.3989*	*0.3961*	*0.3934*	*0.3907*	*0.3880*
0.35	*0.3853*	*0.3826*	*0.3799*	*0.3772*	*0.3745*	*0.3719*	*0.3692*	*0.3665*	*0.3638*	*0.3611*
0.36	*0.3585*	*0.3558*	*0.3531*	*0.3505*	*0.3478*	*0.3451*	*0.3425*	*0.3398*	*0.3372*	*0.3345*
0.37	*0.3319*	*0.3292*	*0.3266*	*0.3239*	*0.3213*	*0.3186*	*0.3160*	*0.3134*	*0.3107*	*0.3081*
0.38	*0.3055*	*0.3029*	*0.3002*	*0.2976*	*0.2950*	*0.2924*	*0.2898*	*0.2871*	*0.2845*	*0.2819*
0.39	*0.2793*	*0.2767*	*0.2741*	*0.2715*	*0.2689*	*0.2663*	*0.2637*	*0.2611*	*0.2585*	*0.2559*
0.40	*0.2533*	*0.2508*	*0.2482*	*0.2456*	*0.2430*	*0.2404*	*0.2378*	*0.2353*	*0.2327*	*0.2301*
0.41	*0.2275*	*0.2250*	*0.2224*	*0.2198*	*0.2173*	*0.2147*	*0.2121*	*0.2096*	*0.2070*	*0.2045*
0.42	*0.2019*	*0.1993*	*0.1968*	*0.1942*	*0.1917*	*0.1891*	*0.1866*	*0.1840*	*0.1815*	*0.1789*
0.43	*0.1764*	*0.1738*	*0.1713*	*0.1687*	*0.1662*	*0.1637*	*0.1611*	*0.1586*	*0.1560*	*0.1535*
0.44	*0.1510*	*0.1484*	*0.1459*	*0.1434*	*0.1408*	*0.1383*	*0.1358*	*0.1332*	*0.1307*	*0.1282*
0.45	*0.1257*	*0.1231*	*0.1206*	*0.1181*	*0.1156*	*0.1130*	*0.1105*	*0.1080*	*0.1055*	*0.1030*
0.46	*0.1004*	*0.0979*	*0.0954*	*0.0929*	*0.0904*	*0.0878*	*0.0853*	*0.0828*	*0.0803*	*0.0778*
0.47	*0.0753*	*0.0728*	*0.0702*	*0.0677*	*0.0652*	*0.0627*	*0.0602*	*0.0577*	*0.0552*	*0.0527*
0.48	*0.0502*	*0.0476*	*0.0451*	*0.0426*	*0.0401*	*0.0376*	*0.0351*	*0.0326*	*0.0301*	*0.0276*
0.49	*0.0251*	*0.0226*	*0.0201*	*0.0175*	*0.0150*	*0.0125*	*0.0100*	*0.0075*	*0.0050*	*0.0025*
0.50	0.0000	0.0025	0.0050	0.0075	0.0100	0.0125	0.0150	0.0175	0.0201	0.0226
0.51	0.0251	0.0276	0.0301	0.0326	0.0351	0.0376	0.0401	0.0426	0.0451	0.0476
0.52	0.0502	0.0527	0.0552	0.0577	0.0602	0.0627	0.0652	0.0677	0.0702	0.0728
0.53	0.0753	0.0778	0.0803	0.0828	0.0853	0.0878	0.0904	0.0929	0.0954	0.0979
0.54	0.1004	0.1030	0.1055	0.1080	0.1105	0.1130	0.1156	0.1181	0.1206	0.1231
0.55	0.1257	0.1282	0.1307	0.1332	0.1358	0.1383	0.1408	0.1434	0.1459	0.1484
0.56	0.1510	0.1535	0.1560	0.1586	0.1611	0.1637	0.1662	0.1687	0.1713	0.1738
0.57	0.1764	0.1789	0.1815	0.1840	0.1866	0.1891	0.1917	0.1942	0.1968	0.1993
0.58	0.2019	0.2045	0.2070	0.2096	0.2121	0.2147	0.2173	0.2198	0.2224	0.2250
0.59	0.2275	0.2301	0.2327	0.2353	0.2378	0.2404	0.2430	0.2456	0.2482	0.2508
0.60	0.2533	0.2559	0.2585	0.2611	0.2637	0.2663	0.2689	0.2715	0.2741	0.2767
0.61	0.2793	0.2819	0.2845	0.2871	0.2898	0.2924	0.2950	0.2976	0.3002	0.3029
0.62	0.3055	0.3081	0.3107	0.3134	0.3160	0.3186	0.3213	0.3239	0.3266	0.3292
0.63	0.3319	0.3345	0.3372	0.3398	0.3425	0.3451	0.3478	0.3505	0.3531	0.3558
0.64	0.3585	0.3611	0.3638	0.3665	0.3692	0.3719	0.3745	0.3772	0.3799	0.3826
0.65	0.3853	0.3880	0.3907	0.3934	0.3961	0.3989	0.4016	0.4043	0.4070	0.4097
0.66	0.4125	0.4152	0.4179	0.4207	0.4234	0.4261	0.4289	0.4316	0.4344	0.4372
0.67	0.4399	0.4427	0.4454	0.4482	0.4510	0.4538	0.4565	0.4593	0.4621	0.4649
0.68	0.4677	0.4705	0.4733	0.4761	0.4789	0.4817	0.4845	0.4874	0.4902	0.4930
0.69	0.4959	0.4987	0.5015	0.5044	0.5072	0.5101	0.5129	0.5158	0.5187	0.5215
0.70	0.5244	0.5273	0.5302	0.5330	0.5359	0.5388	0.5417	0.5446	0.5476	0.5505
0.71	0.5534	0.5563	0.5592	0.5622	0.5651	0.5681	0.5710	0.5740	0.5769	0.5799
0.72	0.5828	0.5858	0.5888	0.5918	0.5948	0.5978	0.6008	0.6038	0.6068	0.6098
0.73	0.6128	0.6158	0.6189	0.6219	0.6250	0.6280	0.6311	0.6341	0.6372	0.6403
0.74	0.6433	0.6464	0.6495	0.6526	0.6557	0.6588	0.6620	0.6651	0.6682	0.6713
0.75	0.6745	0.6776	0.6808	0.6840	0.6871	0.6903	0.6935	0.6967	0.6999	0.7031
0.76	0.7063	0.7095	0.7128	0.7160	0.7192	0.7225	0.7257	0.7290	0.7323	0.7356
0.77	0.7388	0.7421	0.7454	0.7488	0.7521	0.7554	0.7588	0.7621	0.7655	0.7688
0.78	0.7722	0.7756	0.7790	0.7824	0.7858	0.7892	0.7926	0.7961	0.7995	0.8030
0.79	0.8064	0.8099	0.8134	0.8169	0.8204	0.8239	0.8274	0.8310	0.8345	0.8381
0.80	0.8416	0.8452	0.8488	0.8524	0.8560	0.8596	0.8633	0.8669	0.8705	0.8742
0.81	0.8779	0.8816	0.8853	0.8890	0.8927	0.8965	0.9002	0.9040	0.9078	0.9116
0.82	0.9154	0.9192	0.9230	0.9269	0.9307	0.9346	0.9385	0.9424	0.9463	0.9502
0.83	0.9542	0.9581	0.9621	0.9661	0.9701	0.9741	0.9782	0.9822	0.9863	0.9904
0.84	0.9945	0.9986	1.0027	1.0069	1.0110	1.0152	1.0194	1.0237	1.0279	1.0322
0.85	1.0364	1.0407	1.0450	1.0494	1.0537	1.0581	1.0625	1.0669	1.0714	1.0758
0.86	1.0803	1.0848	1.0893	1.0939	1.0985	1.1031	1.1077	1.1123	1.1170	1.1217
0.87	1.1264	1.1311	1.1359	1.1407	1.1455	1.1503	1.1552	1.1601	1.1650	1.1700
0.88	1.1750	1.1800	1.1850	1.1901	1.1952	1.2004	1.2055	1.2107	1.2160	1.2212
0.89	1.2265	1.2319	1.2372	1.2426	1.2481	1.2536	1.2591	1.2646	1.2702	1.2759
0.90	1.2816	1.2873	1.2930	1.2988	1.3047	1.3106	1.3165	1.3225	1.3285	1.3346
0.91	1.3408	1.3469	1.3532	1.3595	1.3658	1.3722	1.3787	1.3852	1.3917	1.3984
0.92	1.4051	1.4118	1.4187	1.4255	1.4325	1.4395	1.4466	1.4538	1.4611	1.4684
0.93	1.4758	1.4833	1.4909	1.4985	1.5063	1.5141	1.5220	1.5301	1.5382	1.5464
0.94	1.5548	1.5632	1.5718	1.5805	1.5893	1.5982	1.6072	1.6164	1.6258	1.6352
0.95	1.6449	1.6546	1.6646	1.6747	1.6849	1.6954	1.7060	1.7169	1.7279	1.7392
0.96	1.7507	1.7624	1.7744	1.7866	1.7991	1.8119	1.8250	1.8384	1.8522	1.8663
0.97	1.8808	1.8957	1.9110	1.9268	1.9431	1.9600	1.9774	1.9954	2.0141	2.0335
0.98	2.0537	2.0749	2.0969	2.1201	2.1444	2.1701	2.1973	2.2262	2.2571	2.2904
0.99	2.3263	2.3656	2.4089	2.4573	2.5121	2.5758	2.6521	2.7478	2.8782	3.0902

* Italic figures are negative values.

[1] Calculated by the editors of these *Scientific Tables* from N. B. S. tables (see footnote page 29).

Deviation c → Integral

c	0.00	0.01	0.02	0.03	0.04	0.05	0.06	0.07	0.08	0.09
	0.	0.	0.	0.	0.	0.	0.	0.	0.	0.
−3.2	00069	00066	00064	00062	00060	00058	00056	00054	00052	00050
−3.1	00097	00094	00090	00087	00084	00082	00079	00076	00074	00071
−3.0	00135	00131	00126	00122	00118	00114	00111	00107	00104	00100
−2.9	00187	00181	00175	00169	00164	00159	00154	00149	00144	00139
−2.8	00256	00248	00240	00233	00226	00219	00212	00205	00199	00193
−2.7	00347	00336	00326	00317	00307	00298	00289	00280	00272	00264
−2.6	00466	00453	00440	00427	00415	00402	00391	00379	00368	00357
−2.5	00621	00604	00587	00570	00554	00539	00523	00508	00494	00480
−2.4	00820	00798	00776	00755	00734	00714	00695	00676	00657	00639
−2.3	01072	01044	01017	00990	00964	00939	00914	00889	00866	00842
−2.2	01390	01355	01321	01287	01255	01222	01191	01160	01130	01101
−2.1	01786	01743	01700	01659	01618	01578	01539	01500	01463	01426
−2.0	02275	02222	02169	02118	02068	02018	01970	01923	01876	01831
−1.9	02872	02807	02743	02680	02619	02559	02500	02442	02385	02330
−1.8	03593	03515	03438	03362	03288	03216	03144	03074	03005	02938
−1.7	04457	04363	04272	04182	04093	04006	03920	03836	03754	03673
−1.6	05480	05370	05262	05155	05050	04947	04846	04746	04648	04551
−1.5	06681	06552	06426	06301	06178	06057	05938	05821	05705	05592
−1.4	08076	07927	07780	07636	07493	07353	07215	07078	06944	06811
−1.3	09680	09510	09342	09176	09012	08851	08691	08534	08379	08226
−1.2	11507	11314	11123	10935	10749	10565	10383	10204	10027	09853
−1.1	13567	13350	13136	12924	12714	12507	12302	12100	11900	11702
−1.0	15866	15625	15386	15151	14917	14686	14457	14231	14007	13786
−0.9	18406	18141	17879	17619	17361	17106	16853	16602	16354	16109
−0.8	21186	20897	20611	20327	20045	19766	19489	19215	18943	18673
−0.7	24196	23885	23576	23270	22965	22663	22363	22065	21770	21476
−0.6	27425	27093	26763	26435	26109	25785	25463	25143	24825	24510
−0.5	30854	30503	30153	29806	29460	29116	28774	28434	28096	27760
−0.4	34458	34090	33724	33360	32997	32636	32276	31918	31561	31207
−0.3	38209	37828	37448	37070	36693	36317	35942	35569	35197	34827
−0.2	42074	41683	41294	40905	40517	40129	39743	39358	38974	38591
−0.19	42465	42426	42387	42348	42309	42270	42231	42191	42152	42113
−0.18	42858	42818	42779	42740	42701	42661	42622	42583	42544	42505
−0.17	43251	43211	43172	43133	43093	43054	43015	42975	42936	42897
−0.16	43644	43605	43565	43526	43487	43447	43408	43369	43329	43290
−0.15	44038	43999	43959	43920	43880	43841	43802	43762	43723	43683
−0.14	44433	44393	44354	44315	44275	44236	44196	44157	44117	44078
−0.13	44828	44789	44749	44710	44670	44631	44591	44552	44512	44473
−0.12	45224	45185	45145	45105	45066	45026	44987	44947	44907	44868
−0.11	45620	45581	45541	45502	45462	45422	45383	45343	45303	45264
−0.10	46017	45978	45938	45898	45858	45819	45779	45739	45700	45660
−0.09	46414	46375	46335	46295	46255	46216	46176	46136	46097	46057
−0.08	46812	46772	46732	46693	46653	46613	46573	46534	46494	46454
−0.07	47210	47170	47130	47090	47051	47011	46971	46931	46891	46852
−0.06	47608	47568	47528	47488	47449	47409	47369	47329	47289	47249
−0.05	48006	47966	47926	47887	47847	47807	47767	47727	47687	47648
−0.04	48405	48365	48325	48285	48245	48205	48166	48126	48086	48046
−0.03	48803	48763	48724	48684	48644	48604	48564	48524	48484	48445
−0.02	49202	49162	49122	49083	49043	49003	48963	48923	48883	48843
−0.01	49601	49561	49521	49481	49441	49402	49362	49322	49282	49242
−0.00	50000	49960	49920	49880	49840	49801	49761	49721	49681	49641
+0.00	50000	50040	50080	50120	50160	50199	50239	50279	50319	50359
+0.01	50399	50439	50479	50519	50559	50598	50638	50678	50718	50758
+0.02	50798	50838	50878	50917	50957	50997	51037	51077	51117	51157
+0.03	51197	51237	51276	51316	51356	51396	51436	51476	51516	51555
+0.04	51595	51635	51675	51715	51755	51795	51834	51874	51914	51954
+0.05	51994	52034	52074	52113	52153	52193	52233	52273	52313	52352
+0.06	52392	52432	52472	52512	52551	52591	52631	52671	52711	52751
+0.07	52790	52830	52870	52910	52949	52989	53029	53069	53109	53148
+0.08	53188	53228	53268	53307	53347	53387	53427	53466	53506	53546
+0.09	53586	53625	53665	53705	53745	53784	53824	53864	53903	53943
+0.10	53983	54022	54062	54102	54142	54181	54221	54261	54300	54340
+0.11	54380	54419	54459	54498	54538	54578	54617	54657	54697	54736
+0.12	54776	54815	54855	54895	54934	54974	55013	55053	55093	55132
+0.13	55172	55211	55251	55290	55330	55369	55409	55448	55488	55527
+0.14	55567	55607	55646	55685	55725	55764	55804	55843	55883	55922
+0.15	55962	56001	56041	56080	56120	56159	56198	56238	56277	56317
+0.16	56356	56395	56435	56474	56513	56553	56592	56631	56671	56710
+0.17	56749	56789	56828	56867	56907	56946	56985	57025	57064	57103
+0.18	57142	57182	57221	57260	57299	57339	57378	57417	57456	57495
+0.19	57535	57574	57613	57652	57691	57730	57769	57809	57848	57887
+0.2	57926	58317	58706	59095	59483	59871	60257	60642	61026	61409
+0.3	61791	62172	62552	62930	63307	63683	64058	64431	64803	65173
+0.4	65542	65910	66276	66640	67003	67364	67724	68082	68439	68793
+0.5	69146	69497	69847	70194	70540	70884	71226	71566	71904	72240
+0.6	72575	72907	73237	73565	73891	74215	74537	74857	75175	75490
+0.7	75804	76115	76424	76730	77035	77337	77637	77935	78230	78524
+0.8	78814	79103	79389	79673	79955	80234	80511	80785	81057	81327
+0.9	81594	81859	82121	82381	82639	82894	83147	83398	83646	83891
+1.0	84134	84375	84614	84849	85083	85314	85543	85769	85993	86214
+1.1	86433	86650	86864	87076	87286	87493	87698	87900	88100	88298
+1.2	88493	88686	88877	89065	89251	89435	89617	89796	89973	90147
+1.3	90320	90490	90658	90824	90988	91149	91309	91466	91621	91774
+1.4	91924	92073	92220	92364	92507	92647	92785	92922	93056	93189
+1.5	93319	93448	93574	93699	93822	93943	94062	94179	94295	94408
+1.6	94520	94630	94738	94845	94950	95053	95154	95254	95352	95449
+1.7	95543	95637	95728	95818	95907	95994	96080	96164	96246	96327
+1.8	96407	96485	96562	96638	96712	96784	96856	96926	96995	97062
+1.9	97128	97193	97257	97320	97381	97441	97500	97558	97615	97670
+2.0	97725	97778	97831	97882	97932	97982	98030	98077	98124	98169
+2.1	98214	98257	98300	98341	98382	98422	98461	98500	98537	98574
+2.2	98610	98645	98679	98713	98745	98778	98809	98840	98870	98899
+2.3	98928	98956	98983	99010	99036	99061	99086	99111	99134	99158
+2.4	99180	99202	99224	99245	99266	99286	99305	99324	99343	99361
+2.5	99379	99396	99413	99430	99446	99461	99477	99492	99506	99520
+2.6	99534	99547	99560	99573	99585	99598	99609	99621	99632	99643
+2.7	99653	99664	99674	99683	99693	99702	99711	99720	99728	99736
+2.8	99744	99752	99760	99767	99774	99781	99788	99795	99801	99807
+2.9	99813	99819	99825	99831	99836	99841	99846	99851	99856	99861
+3.0	99865	99869	99874	99878	99882	99886	99889	99893	99896	99900
+3.1	99903	99906	99910	99913	99916	99918	99921	99924	99926	99929
+3.2	99931	99934	99936	99938	99940	99942	99944	99946	99948	99950

Integral → Deviation *c*

$\int_{-c}^{c}$	0.000	0.001	0.002	0.003	0.004	0.005	0.006	0.007	0.008	0.009
0.00	0.0000	0.0013	0.0025	0.0038	0.0050	0.0063	0.0075	0.0088	0.0100	0.0113
0.01	0.0125	0.0138	0.0150	0.0163	0.0175	0.0188	0.0201	0.0213	0.0226	0.0238
0.02	0.0251	0.0263	0.0276	0.0288	0.0301	0.0313	0.0326	0.0338	0.0351	0.0364
0.03	0.0376	0.0389	0.0401	0.0414	0.0426	0.0439	0.0451	0.0464	0.0476	0.0489
0.04	0.0502	0.0514	0.0527	0.0539	0.0552	0.0564	0.0577	0.0589	0.0602	0.0615
0.05	0.0627	0.0640	0.0652	0.0665	0.0677	0.0690	0.0702	0.0715	0.0728	0.0740
0.06	0.0753	0.0765	0.0778	0.0790	0.0803	0.0816	0.0828	0.0841	0.0853	0.0866
0.07	0.0878	0.0891	0.0904	0.0916	0.0929	0.0941	0.0954	0.0967	0.0979	0.0992
0.08	0.1004	0.1017	0.1030	0.1042	0.1055	0.1067	0.1080	0.1093	0.1105	0.1118
0.09	0.1130	0.1143	0.1156	0.1168	0.1181	0.1193	0.1206	0.1219	0.1231	0.1244
0.10	0.1257	0.1269	0.1282	0.1295	0.1307	0.1320	0.1332	0.1345	0.1358	0.1370
0.11	0.1383	0.1396	0.1408	0.1421	0.1434	0.1446	0.1459	0.1472	0.1484	0.1497
0.12	0.1510	0.1522	0.1535	0.1548	0.1560	0.1573	0.1586	0.1598	0.1611	0.1624
0.13	0.1637	0.1649	0.1662	0.1675	0.1687	0.1700	0.1713	0.1726	0.1738	0.1751
0.14	0.1764	0.1776	0.1789	0.1802	0.1815	0.1827	0.1840	0.1853	0.1866	0.1878
0.15	0.1891	0.1904	0.1917	0.1929	0.1942	0.1955	0.1968	0.1981	0.1993	0.2006
0.16	0.2019	0.2032	0.2045	0.2057	0.2070	0.2083	0.2096	0.2109	0.2121	0.2134
0.17	0.2147	0.2160	0.2173	0.2186	0.2198	0.2211	0.2224	0.2237	0.2250	0.2263
0.18	0.2275	0.2288	0.2301	0.2314	0.2327	0.2340	0.2353	0.2366	0.2378	0.2391
0.19	0.2404	0.2417	0.2430	0.2443	0.2456	0.2469	0.2482	0.2495	0.2508	0.2521
0.20	0.2533	0.2546	0.2559	0.2572	0.2585	0.2598	0.2611	0.2624	0.2637	0.2650
0.21	0.2663	0.2676	0.2689	0.2702	0.2715	0.2728	0.2741	0.2754	0.2767	0.2780
0.22	0.2793	0.2806	0.2819	0.2832	0.2845	0.2858	0.2871	0.2885	0.2898	0.2911
0.23	0.2924	0.2937	0.2950	0.2963	0.2976	0.2989	0.3002	0.3015	0.3029	0.3042
0.24	0.3055	0.3068	0.3081	0.3094	0.3107	0.3121	0.3134	0.3147	0.3160	0.3173
0.25	0.3186	0.3200	0.3213	0.3226	0.3239	0.3252	0.3266	0.3279	0.3292	0.3305
0.26	0.3319	0.3332	0.3345	0.3358	0.3372	0.3385	0.3398	0.3411	0.3425	0.3438
0.27	0.3451	0.3465	0.3478	0.3491	0.3505	0.3518	0.3531	0.3545	0.3558	0.3571
0.28	0.3585	0.3598	0.3611	0.3625	0.3638	0.3651	0.3665	0.3678	0.3692	0.3705
0.29	0.3719	0.3732	0.3745	0.3759	0.3772	0.3786	0.3799	0.3813	0.3826	0.3840
0.30	0.3853	0.3867	0.3880	0.3894	0.3907	0.3921	0.3934	0.3948	0.3961	0.3975
0.31	0.3989	0.4002	0.4016	0.4029	0.4043	0.4056	0.4070	0.4084	0.4097	0.4111
0.32	0.4125	0.4138	0.4152	0.4166	0.4179	0.4193	0.4207	0.4220	0.4234	0.4248
0.33	0.4261	0.4275	0.4289	0.4303	0.4316	0.4330	0.4344	0.4358	0.4372	0.4385
0.34	0.4399	0.4413	0.4427	0.4441	0.4454	0.4468	0.4482	0.4496	0.4510	0.4524
0.35	0.4538	0.4552	0.4565	0.4579	0.4593	0.4607	0.4621	0.4635	0.4649	0.4663
0.36	0.4677	0.4691	0.4705	0.4719	0.4733	0.4747	0.4761	0.4775	0.4789	0.4803
0.37	0.4817	0.4831	0.4845	0.4860	0.4874	0.4888	0.4902	0.4916	0.4930	0.4944
0.38	0.4959	0.4973	0.4987	0.5001	0.5015	0.5029	0.5044	0.5058	0.5072	0.5086
0.39	0.5101	0.5115	0.5129	0.5144	0.5158	0.5172	0.5187	0.5201	0.5215	0.5230
0.40	0.5244	0.5258	0.5273	0.5287	0.5302	0.5316	0.5330	0.5345	0.5359	0.5374
0.41	0.5388	0.5403	0.5417	0.5432	0.5446	0.5461	0.5476	0.5490	0.5505	0.5519
0.42	0.5534	0.5548	0.5563	0.5578	0.5592	0.5607	0.5622	0.5636	0.5651	0.5666
0.43	0.5681	0.5695	0.5710	0.5725	0.5740	0.5754	0.5769	0.5784	0.5799	0.5814
0.44	0.5828	0.5843	0.5858	0.5873	0.5888	0.5903	0.5918	0.5933	0.5948	0.5963
0.45	0.5978	0.5993	0.6008	0.6023	0.6038	0.6053	0.6068	0.6083	0.6098	0.6113
0.46	0.6128	0.6143	0.6158	0.6174	0.6189	0.6204	0.6219	0.6234	0.6250	0.6265
0.47	0.6280	0.6295	0.6311	0.6326	0.6341	0.6357	0.6372	0.6387	0.6403	0.6418
0.48	0.6433	0.6449	0.6464	0.6480	0.6495	0.6511	0.6526	0.6542	0.6557	0.6573
0.49	0.6588	0.6604	0.6620	0.6635	0.6651	0.6666	0.6682	0.6698	0.6713	0.6729
0.50	0.6745	0.6761	0.6776	0.6792	0.6808	0.6824	0.6840	0.6855	0.6871	0.6887
0.51	0.6903	0.6919	0.6935	0.6951	0.6967	0.6983	0.6999	0.7015	0.7031	0.7047
0.52	0.7063	0.7079	0.7095	0.7111	0.7128	0.7144	0.7160	0.7176	0.7192	0.7209
0.53	0.7225	0.7241	0.7257	0.7274	0.7290	0.7306	0.7323	0.7339	0.7356	0.7372
0.54	0.7388	0.7405	0.7421	0.7438	0.7454	0.7471	0.7488	0.7504	0.7521	0.7537
0.55	0.7554	0.7571	0.7588	0.7604	0.7621	0.7638	0.7655	0.7671	0.7688	0.7705
0.56	0.7722	0.7739	0.7756	0.7773	0.7790	0.7807	0.7824	0.7841	0.7858	0.7875
0.57	0.7892	0.7909	0.7926	0.7943	0.7961	0.7978	0.7995	0.8012	0.8030	0.8047
0.58	0.8064	0.8082	0.8099	0.8116	0.8134	0.8151	0.8169	0.8186	0.8204	0.8221
0.59	0.8239	0.8257	0.8274	0.8292	0.8310	0.8327	0.8345	0.8363	0.8381	0.8398
0.60	0.8416	0.8434	0.8452	0.8470	0.8488	0.8506	0.8524	0.8542	0.8560	0.8578
0.61	0.8596	0.8614	0.8633	0.8651	0.8669	0.8687	0.8705	0.8724	0.8742	0.8761
0.62	0.8779	0.8797	0.8816	0.8834	0.8853	0.8871	0.8890	0.8909	0.8927	0.8946
0.63	0.8965	0.8983	0.9002	0.9021	0.9040	0.9059	0.9078	0.9097	0.9116	0.9135
0.64	0.9154	0.9173	0.9192	0.9211	0.9230	0.9249	0.9269	0.9288	0.9307	0.9327
0.65	0.9346	0.9365	0.9385	0.9404	0.9424	0.9443	0.9463	0.9483	0.9502	0.9522
0.66	0.9542	0.9561	0.9581	0.9601	0.9621	0.9641	0.9661	0.9681	0.9701	0.9721
0.67	0.9741	0.9761	0.9782	0.9802	0.9822	0.9842	0.9863	0.9883	0.9904	0.9924
0.68	0.9945	0.9965	0.9986	1.001	1.003	1.005	1.007	1.009	1.011	1.013
0.69	1.015	1.017	1.019	1.022	1.024	1.026	1.028	1.030	1.032	1.034
0.70	1.036	1.039	1.041	1.043	1.045	1.047	1.049	1.052	1.054	1.056
0.71	1.058	1.060	1.063	1.065	1.067	1.069	1.071	1.074	1.076	1.078
0.72	1.080	1.083	1.085	1.087	1.089	1.092	1.094	1.096	1.098	1.101
0.73	1.103	1.105	1.108	1.110	1.112	1.115	1.117	1.119	1.122	1.124
0.74	1.126	1.129	1.131	1.134	1.136	1.138	1.141	1.143	1.146	1.148
0.75	1.150	1.153	1.155	1.158	1.160	1.163	1.165	1.168	1.170	1.172
0.76	1.175	1.177	1.180	1.183	1.185	1.188	1.190	1.193	1.195	1.198
0.77	1.200	1.203	1.206	1.208	1.211	1.213	1.216	1.219	1.221	1.224
0.78	1.227	1.229	1.232	1.235	1.237	1.240	1.243	1.245	1.248	1.251
0.79	1.254	1.256	1.259	1.262	1.265	1.267	1.270	1.273	1.276	1.279
0.80	1.282	1.284	1.287	1.290	1.293	1.296	1.299	1.302	1.305	1.308
0.81	1.311	1.314	1.317	1.320	1.323	1.326	1.329	1.332	1.335	1.338
0.82	1.341	1.344	1.347	1.350	1.353	1.356	1.359	1.363	1.366	1.369
0.83	1.372	1.375	1.379	1.382	1.385	1.388	1.392	1.395	1.398	1.402
0.84	1.405	1.408	1.412	1.415	1.419	1.422	1.426	1.429	1.433	1.436
0.85	1.440	1.443	1.447	1.450	1.454	1.457	1.461	1.465	1.468	1.472
0.86	1.476	1.480	1.483	1.487	1.491	1.495	1.499	1.502	1.506	1.510
0.87	1.514	1.518	1.522	1.526	1.530	1.534	1.538	1.542	1.546	1.551
0.88	1.555	1.559	1.563	1.567	1.572	1.576	1.580	1.585	1.589	1.594
0.89	1.598	1.603	1.607	1.612	1.616	1.621	1.626	1.630	1.635	1.640
0.90	1.645	1.650	1.655	1.660	1.665	1.670	1.675	1.680	1.685	1.690
0.91	1.695	1.701	1.706	1.711	1.717	1.722	1.728	1.734	1.739	1.745
0.92	1.751	1.757	1.762	1.768	1.774	1.780	1.787	1.793	1.799	1.806
0.93	1.812	1.818	1.825	1.832	1.838	1.845	1.852	1.859	1.866	1.873
0.94	1.881	1.888	1.896	1.903	1.911	1.919	1.927	1.935	1.943	1.951
0.95	1.960	1.969	1.977	1.986	1.995	2.005	2.014	2.024	2.034	2.044
0.96	2.054	2.064	2.075	2.086	2.097	2.108	2.120	2.132	2.144	2.157
0.97	2.170	2.183	2.197	2.212	2.226	2.241	2.257	2.273	2.290	2.308
0.98	2.326	2.346	2.366	2.387	2.409	2.432	2.457	2.484	2.512	2.543
0.99	2.576	2.612	2.652	2.697	2.748	2.807	2.878	2.968	3.090	3.291

Deviation *c* → Integral

c	0.000	0.001	0.002	0.003	0.004	0.005	0.006	0.007	0.008	0.009
	0.	0.	0.	0.	0.	0.	0.	0.	0.	0.
0.00	00000	00080	00160	00239	00319	00399	00479	00559	00638	00718
0.01	00798	00878	00957	01037	01117	01197	01277	01356	01436	01516
0.02	01596	01675	01755	01835	01915	01995	02074	02154	02234	02314
0.03	02393	02473	02553	02633	02712	02792	02872	02951	03031	03111
0.04	03191	03270	03350	03430	03510	03589	03669	03749	03828	03908
0.05	03988	04067	04147	04227	04306	04386	04466	04545	04625	04705
0.06	04784	04864	04944	05023	05103	05183	05262	05342	05421	05501
0.07	05581	05660	05740	05819	05899	05979	06058	06138	06217	06297
0.08	06376	06456	06535	06615	06694	06774	06853	06933	07012	07092
0.09	07171	07251	07330	07410	07489	07569	07648	07727	07807	07886
0.10	07966	08045	08124	08204	08283	08362	08442	08521	08600	08680
0.11	08759	08838	08918	08997	09076	09155	09235	09314	09393	09472
0.12	09552	09631	09710	09789	09868	09948	10027	10106	10185	10264
0.13	10343	10422	10502	10581	10660	10739	10818	10897	10976	11055
0.14	11134	11213	11292	11371	11450	11529	11608	11687	11766	11845
0.15	11924	12002	12081	12160	12239	12318	12397	12476	12554	12633
0.16	12712	12791	12869	12948	13027	13106	13184	13263	13342	13420
0.17	13499	13578	13656	13735	13813	13892	13971	14049	14128	14206
0.18	14285	14363	14442	14520	14599	14677	14756	14834	14912	14991
0.19	15069	15147	15226	15304	15382	15461	15539	15617	15695	15774
0.20	15852	15930	16008	16086	16165	16243	16321	16399	16477	16555
0.21	16633	16711	16789	16867	16945	17023	17101	17179	17257	17335
0.22	17413	17491	17569	17646	17724	17802	17880	17958	18035	18113
0.23	18191	18269	18346	18424	18502	18579	18657	18734	18812	18889
0.24	18967	19044	19122	19199	19277	19354	19432	19509	19587	19664
0.25	19741	19819	19896	19973	20050	20128	20205	20282	20359	20436
0.26	20514	20591	20668	20745	20822	20899	20976	21053	21130	21207
0.27	21284	21361	21438	21515	21592	21668	21745	21822	21899	21976
0.28	22052	22129	22206	22282	22359	22436	22512	22589	22665	22742
0.29	22818	22895	22971	23048	23124	23201	23277	23353	23430	23506
0.30	23582	23659	23735	23811	23887	23963	24040	24116	24192	24268
0.31	24344	24420	24496	24572	24648	24724	24800	24876	24952	25027
0.32	25103	25179	25255	25330	25406	25482	25558	25633	25709	25784
0.33	25860	25936	26011	26087	26162	26237	26313	26388	26464	26539
0.34	26614	26690	26765	26840	26915	26991	27066	27141	27216	27291
0.35	27366	27441	27516	27591	27666	27741	27816	27891	27966	28040
0.36	28115	28190	28265	28340	28414	28489	28563	28638	28713	28787
0.37	28862	28936	29011	29085	29160	29234	29308	29383	29457	29531
0.38	29605	29680	29754	29828	29902	29976	30050	30124	30198	30272
0.39	30346	30420	30494	30568	30642	30716	30789	30863	30937	31011
0.40	31084	31158	31232	31305	31379	31452	31526	31599	31673	31746
0.41	31819	31893	31966	32039	32113	32186	32259	32332	32405	32478
0.42	32551	32624	32697	32770	32843	32916	32989	33062	33135	33208
0.43	33280	33353	33426	33499	33571	33644	33716	33789	33861	33934
0.44	34006	34079	34151	34223	34296	34368	34440	34512	34585	34657
0.45	34729	34801	34873	34945	35017	35089	35161	35233	35305	35377
0.46	35448	35520	35592	35664	35735	35807	35878	35950	36022	36093
0.47	36164	36236	36307	36379	36450	36521	36593	36664	36735	36806
0.48	36877	36948	37019	37090	37161	37232	37303	37374	37445	37516
0.49	37587	37657	37728	37799	37869	37940	38011	38081	38152	38222
0.50	38292	38363	38433	38504	38574	38644	38714	38785	38855	38925
0.51	38995	39065	39135	39205	39275	39345	39415	39484	39554	39624
0.52	39694	39763	39833	39903	39972	40042	40111	40181	40250	40319
0.53	40389	40458	40527	40597	40666	40735	40804	40873	40942	41011
0.54	41080	41149	41218	41287	41356	41425	41493	41562	41631	41699
0.55	41768	41837	41905	41974	42042	42111	42179	42247	42316	42384
0.56	42452	42520	42588	42657	42725	42793	42861	42929	42997	43064
0.57	43132	43200	43268	43336	43403	43471	43538	43606	43674	43741
0.58	43809	43876	43943	44011	44078	44145	44212	44280	44347	44414
0.59	44481	44548	44615	44682	44749	44816	44882	44949	45016	45083
0.60	45149	45216	45283	45349	45416	45482	45549	45615	45681	45748
0.61	45814	45880	45946	46012	46078	46145	46211	46277	46342	46408
0.62	46474	46540	46606	46672	46738	46803	46869	46934	47000	47065
0.63	47131	47196	47261	47327	47392	47457	47522	47588	47653	47718
0.64	47783	47848	47913	47978	48042	48107	48172	48237	48302	48366
0.65	48431	48495	48560	48624	48689	48753	48818	48882	48946	49010
0.66	49075	49139	49203	49267	49331	49395	49459	49523	49587	49650
0.67	49714	49778	49842	49905	49969	50032	50096	50159	50223	50286
0.68	50350	50413	50476	50539	50602	50666	50729	50792	50855	50918
0.69	50981	51043	51106	51169	51232	51294	51357	51420	51482	51545
0.7	51607	52230	52848	53461	54070	54675	55275	55870	56461	57047
0.8	57629	58206	58778	59346	59909	60467	61021	61570	62114	62653
0.9	63188	63718	64243	64763	65278	65789	66294	66795	67291	67783
1.0	68269	68750	69227	69699	70166	70628	71086	71538	71986	72429
1.1	72867	73300	73729	74152	74571	74986	75395	75800	76200	76595
1.2	76986	77372	77754	78130	78502	78870	79233	79592	79945	80295
1.3	80640	80980	81316	81648	81975	82298	82617	82931	83241	83547
1.4	83849	84146	84439	84728	85013	85294	85571	85844	86113	86378
1.5	86639	86896	87149	87398	87644	87886	88124	88358	88589	88817
1.6	89040	89260	89477	89690	89899	90106	90309	90508	90704	90897
1.7	91087	91273	91457	91637	91814	91988	92159	92327	92492	92655
1.8	92814	92970	93124	93275	93423	93569	93711	93852	93989	94124
1.9	94257	94387	94514	94639	94762	94882	95000	95116	95230	95341
2.0	95450	95557	95662	95764	95865	95964	96060	96155	96247	96338
2.1	96427	96514	96599	96683	96765	96844	96923	96999	97074	97148
2.2	97219	97289	97358	97425	97491	97555	97618	97679	97739	97798
2.3	97855	97911	97966	98019	98072	98123	98173	98221	98269	98315
2.4	98360	98405	98448	98490	98531	98571	98611	98649	98686	98723
2.5	98758	98793	98826	98859	98891	98923	98953	98983	99012	99040
2.6	99068	99095	99121	99146	99171	99195	99219	99241	99264	99285
2.7	99307	99327	99347	99367	99386	99404	99422	99439	99456	99473
2.8	99489	99505	99520	99535	99549	99563	99576	99590	99602	99615
2.9	99627	99639	99650	99661	99672	99682	99692	99702	99712	99721
3.0	99730	99739	99747	99755	99763	99771	99779	99786	99793	99800
3.1	99806	99813	99819	99825	99831	99837	99842	99848	99853	99858
3.2	99863	99867	99872	99876	99880	99885	99889	99892	99896	99900
3.3	99903	99907	99910	99913	99916	99919	99922	99925	99928	99930

3.4: 99933; 3.5: 99953; 3.6: 99968; 3.7: 99978; 3.8: 99986; 3.891: 99990

[1] Values abridged from National Bureau of Standards, *Tables of Normal Probability Functions*, Applied Mathematics Series 23, Washington, 1953. Reproduction of values on this and the preceding page only by permission of the publishers of these *Scientific Tables*.

2 *P* = twice the integral between *c* and infinity

Integral[1] 2 *P* (outside minus *c* and *c*)

Deviation c → Integral

c	0.000	0.001	0.002	0.003	0.004	0.005	0.006	0.007	0.008	0.009
	0.	0.	0.	0.	0.	0.	0.	0.	0.	0.
0.00	00000*	99920	99840	99761	99681	99601	99521	99441	99362	99282
0.01	99202	99122	99043	98963	98883	98803	98723	98644	98564	98484
0.02	98404	98325	98245	98165	98085	98005	97926	97846	97766	97686
0.03	97607	97527	97447	97367	97288	97208	97128	97049	96969	96889
0.04	96809	96730	96650	96570	96490	96411	96331	96251	96172	96092
0.05	96012	95933	95853	95773	95694	95614	95534	95455	95375	95295
0.06	95216	95136	95056	94977	94897	94817	94738	94658	94579	94499
0.07	94419	94340	94260	94181	94101	94021	93942	93862	93783	93703
0.08	93624	93544	93465	93385	93306	93226	93147	93067	92988	92908
0.09	92829	92749	92670	92590	92511	92431	92352	92273	92193	92114
0.10	92034	91955	91876	91796	91717	91638	91558	91479	91400	91320
0.11	91241	91162	91082	91003	90924	90845	90765	90686	90607	90528
0.12	90448	90369	90290	90211	90132	90052	89974	89894	89815	89736
0.13	89657	89578	89498	89419	89340	89261	89182	89103	89024	88945
0.14	88866	88787	88708	88629	88550	88471	88392	88313	88234	88155
0.15	88076	87998	87919	87840	87761	87682	87603	87524	87446	87367
0.16	87288	87209	87131	87052	86973	86894	86816	86737	86658	86580
0.17	86501	86422	86344	86265	86187	86108	86029	85951	85872	85794
0.18	85715	85637	85558	85480	85401	85323	85244	85166	85088	85009
0.19	84931	84853	84774	84696	84618	84539	84461	84383	84305	84226
0.20	84148	84070	83992	83914	83835	83757	83679	83601	83523	83445
0.21	83367	83289	83211	83133	83055	82977	82899	82821	82743	82665
0.22	82587	82509	82431	82354	82276	82198	82120	82042	81965	81887
0.23	81809	81731	81654	81576	81498	81421	81343	81266	81188	81111
0.24	81033	80956	80878	80801	80723	80646	80568	80491	80413	80336
0.25	80259	80181	80104	80027	79950	79872	79795	79718	79641	79564
0.26	79486	79409	79332	79255	79178	79101	79024	78947	78870	78793
0.27	78716	78639	78562	78485	78408	78332	78255	78178	78101	78024
0.28	77948	77871	77794	77718	77641	77564	77488	77411	77335	77258
0.29	77182	77105	77029	76952	76876	76799	76723	76647	76570	76494
0.30	76418	76341	76265	76189	76113	76037	75960	75884	75808	75732
0.31	75656	75580	75504	75428	75352	75276	75200	75124	75048	74973
0.32	74897	74821	74745	74670	74594	74518	74442	74367	74291	74216
0.33	74140	74064	73989	73913	73838	73763	73687	73612	73536	73461
0.34	73386	73310	73235	73160	73085	73009	72934	72859	72784	72709
0.35	72634	72559	72484	72409	72334	72259	72184	72109	72034	71960
0.36	71885	71810	71735	71660	71586	71511	71437	71362	71287	71213
0.37	71138	71064	70989	70915	70840	70766	70692	70617	70543	70469
0.38	70395	70320	70246	70172	70098	70024	69950	69876	69802	69728
0.39	69654	69580	69506	69432	69358	69284	69211	69137	69063	68989
0.40	68916	68842	68768	68695	68621	68548	68474	68401	68327	68254
0.41	68181	68107	68034	67961	67887	67814	67741	67668	67595	67522
0.42	67449	67376	67303	67230	67157	67084	67011	66938	66865	66792
0.43	66720	66647	66574	66501	66429	66356	66284	66211	66139	66066
0.44	65994	65921	65849	65777	65704	65632	65560	65488	65415	65343
0.45	65271	65199	65127	65055	64983	64911	64839	64767	64695	64623
0.46	64552	64480	64408	64336	64265	64193	64122	64050	63978	63907
0.47	63836	63764	63693	63621	63550	63479	63407	63336	63265	63194
0.48	63123	63052	62981	62910	62839	62768	62697	62626	62555	62484
0.49	62413	62343	62272	62201	62131	62060	61989	61919	61848	61778
0.50	61708	61637	61567	61496	61426	61356	61286	61215	61145	61075
0.51	61005	60935	60865	60795	60725	60655	60585	60516	60446	60376
0.52	60306	60237	60167	60097	60028	59958	59889	59819	59750	59681
0.53	59611	59542	59473	59403	59334	59265	59196	59127	59058	58989
0.54	58920	58851	58782	58713	58644	58575	58507	58438	58369	58301
0.55	58232	58163	58095	58026	57958	57889	57821	57753	57684	57616
0.56	57548	57480	57412	57343	57275	57207	57139	57071	57003	56936
0.57	56868	56800	56732	56664	56597	56529	56462	56394	56326	56259
0.58	56191	56124	56057	55989	55922	55855	55788	55720	55653	55586
0.59	55519	55452	55385	55318	55251	55184	55118	55051	54984	54917
0.60	54851	54784	54717	54651	54584	54518	54451	54385	54319	54252
0.61	54186	54120	54054	53988	53922	53855	53789	53723	53658	53592
0.62	53526	53460	53394	53328	53263	53197	53131	53066	53000	52935
0.63	52869	52804	52739	52673	52608	52543	52478	52412	52347	52282
0.64	52217	52152	52087	52022	51958	51893	51828	51763	51698	51634
0.65	51569	51505	51440	51376	51311	51247	51182	51118	51054	50990
0.66	50925	50861	50797	50733	50669	50605	50541	50477	50413	50350
0.67	50286	50222	50158	50095	50031	49968	49904	49841	49777	49714
0.68	49650	49587	49524	49461	49398	49334	49271	49208	49145	49082
0.69	49019	48957	48894	48831	48768	48706	48643	48580	48518	48455
0.7	48393	47770	47152	46539	45930	45325	44725	44130	43539	42953
0.8	42371	41794	41222	40654	40091	39533	38979	38430	37886	37347
0.9	36812	36282	35757	35237	34722	34211	33706	33205	32709	32217
1.0	31731	31250	30773	30301	29834	29372	28914	28462	28014	27571
1.1	27133	26700	26271	25848	25429	25014	24605	24200	23800	23405
1.2	23014	22628	22246	21870	21498	21130	20767	20408	20055	19705
1.3	19360	19020	18684	18352	18025	17702	17383	17069	16759	16453
1.4	16151	15854	15561	15272	14987	14706	14429	14156	13887	13622
1.5	13361	13104	12851	12602	12356	12114	11876	11642	11411	11183
1.6	10960	10740	10523	10310	10101	09894	09691	09492	09296	09103
1.7	08913	08727	08543	08363	08186	08012	07841	07673	07508	07345
1.8	07186	07030	06876	06725	06577	06431	06289	06148	06011	05876
1.9	05743	05613	05486	05361	05238	05118	05000	04884	04770	04659
2.0	04550	04443	04338	04236	04135	04036	03940	03845	03753	03662
2.1	03573	03486	03401	03317	03235	03156	03077	03001	02926	02852
2.2	02781	02711	02642	02575	02509	02445	02382	02321	02261	02202
2.3	02145	02089	02034	01981	01928	01877	01827	01779	01731	01685
2.4	01640	01595	01552	01510	01469	01429	01389	01351	01314	01277
2.5	01242	01207	01174	01141	01109	01077	01047	01017	00988	00960
2.6	00932	00905	00879	00854	00829	00805	00781	00759	00736	00715
2.7	00693	00673	00653	00633	00614	00596	00578	00561	00544	00527
2.8	00511	00495	00480	00465	00451	00437	00424	00410	00398	00385
2.9	00373	00361	00350	00339	00328	00318	00308	00298	00288	00279
3.0	00270	00261	00253	00245	00237	00229	00221	00214	00207	00200
3.1	00194	00187	00181	00175	00169	00163	00158	00152	00147	00142
3.2	00137	00133	00128	00124	00120	00115	00111	00108	00104	00100
3.3	00097	00093	00090	00087	00084	00081	00078	00075	00072	00070

3.4: 00067; 3.5: 00047; 3.6: 00032; 3.7: 00022; 3.8: 00014; 3.891: 00010

Integral[1] between zero and c

Deviation c → Integral

c	0.000	0.001	0.002	0.003	0.004	0.005	0.006	0.007	0.008	0.009
	0.	0.	0.	0.	0.	0.	0.	0.	0.	0.
0.00	00000	00040	00080	00120	00160	00200	00240	00280	00319	00359
0.01	00399	00439	00479	00519	00559	00599	00639	00678	00718	00758
0.02	00798	00838	00878	00918	00958	00998	01037	01077	01117	01157
0.03	01197	01237	01277	01317	01356	01396	01436	01476	01516	01556
0.04	01596	01635	01675	01715	01755	01795	01835	01875	01914	01954
0.05	01994	02034	02074	02114	02153	02193	02233	02273	02313	02353
0.06	02392	02432	02472	02512	02552	02592	02631	02671	02711	02751
0.07	02791	02830	02870	02910	02950	02990	03029	03069	03109	03149
0.08	03188	03228	03268	03308	03347	03387	03427	03467	03506	03546
0.09	03586	03626	03665	03705	03745	03785	03824	03864	03904	03943
0.10	03983	04023	04062	04102	04142	04181	04221	04261	04300	04340
0.11	04380	04419	04459	04499	04538	04578	04618	04657	04697	04736
0.12	04776	04816	04855	04895	04934	04974	05013	05053	05093	05132
0.13	05172	05211	05251	05291	05330	05370	05409	05449	05488	05528
0.14	05567	05607	05646	05686	05725	05765	05804	05844	05883	05923
0.15	05962	06001	06041	06080	06120	06159	06199	06238	06277	06317
0.16	06356	06396	06435	06474	06514	06553	06592	06632	06671	06710
0.17	06750	06789	06828	06868	06907	06946	06986	07025	07064	07103
0.18	07143	07182	07221	07260	07300	07339	07378	07417	07456	07496
0.19	07535	07574	07613	07652	07691	07731	07770	07809	07848	07887
0.20	07926	07965	08004	08043	08083	08122	08161	08200	08239	08278
0.21	08317	08356	08395	08434	08473	08512	08551	08590	08629	08668
0.22	08707	08746	08785	08823	08862	08901	08940	08979	09018	09057
0.23	09096	09135	09173	09212	09251	09290	09329	09367	09406	09445
0.24	09484	09522	09561	09600	09639	09677	09716	09755	09794	09832
0.25	09871	09910	09948	09987	10025	10064	10103	10141	10180	10218
0.26	10257	10296	10334	10373	10411	10450	10488	10527	10565	10604
0.27	10642	10681	10719	10758	10796	10834	10873	10911	10950	10988
0.28	11026	11065	11103	11141	11180	11218	11256	11295	11333	11371
0.29	11409	11448	11486	11524	11562	11601	11639	11677	11715	11753
0.30	11791	11830	11868	11906	11944	11982	12020	12058	12096	12134
0.31	12172	12210	12248	12286	12324	12362	12400	12438	12476	12514
0.32	12552	12590	12628	12665	12703	12741	12779	12817	12855	12892
0.33	12930	12968	13006	13044	13081	13119	13157	13194	13232	13270
0.34	13307	13345	13383	13420	13458	13496	13533	13571	13608	13646
0.35	13683	13721	13758	13796	13833	13871	13908	13946	13983	14020
0.36	14058	14095	14133	14170	14207	14245	14282	14319	14357	14394
0.37	14431	14468	14506	14543	14580	14617	14654	14692	14729	14766
0.38	14803	14840	14877	14914	14951	14988	15025	15062	15099	15136
0.39	15173	15210	15247	15284	15321	15358	15395	15432	15469	15506
0.40	15542	15579	15616	15653	15690	15726	15763	15800	15837	15873
0.41	15910	15947	15983	16020	16057	16093	16130	16166	16203	16239
0.42	16276	16312	16349	16385	16422	16458	16495	16531	16568	16604
0.43	16640	16677	16713	16750	16786	16822	16858	16895	16931	16967
0.44	17003	17040	17076	17112	17148	17184	17220	17256	17293	17329
0.45	17365	17401	17437	17473	17509	17545	17581	17617	17653	17689
0.46	17724	17760	17796	17832	17868	17904	17939	17975	18011	18047
0.47	18082	18118	18154	18190	18225	18261	18297	18332	18368	18403
0.48	18439	18474	18510	18545	18581	18616	18652	18687	18723	18758
0.49	18794	18829	18864	18900	18935	18970	19006	19041	19076	19111
0.50	19146	19182	19217	19252	19287	19322	19357	19393	19428	19463
0.51	19498	19533	19568	19603	19638	19673	19708	19742	19777	19812
0.52	19847	19882	19917	19952	19986	20021	20056	20091	20125	20160
0.53	20195	20229	20264	20299	20333	20368	20402	20437	20471	20506
0.54	20540	20575	20609	20644	20678	20713	20747	20781	20816	20850
0.55	20884	20919	20953	20987	21021	21056	21090	21124	21158	21192
0.56	21226	21260	21294	21329	21363	21397	21431	21465	21499	21532
0.57	21566	21600	21634	21668	21702	21736	21769	21803	21837	21871
0.58	21905	21938	21972	22006	22039	22073	22106	22140	22174	22207
0.59	22241	22274	22308	22341	22375	22408	22441	22475	22508	22542
0.60	22575	22608	22642	22675	22708	22741	22775	22808	22841	22874
0.61	22907	22940	22973	23006	23039	23073	23106	23139	23171	23204
0.62	23237	23270	23303	23336	23369	23402	23435	23467	23500	23533
0.63	23566	23598	23631	23664	23696	23729	23761	23794	23827	23859
0.64	23892	23924	23957	23989	24021	24054	24086	24119	24151	24183
0.65	24216	24248	24280	24312	24345	24377	24409	24441	24473	24505
0.66	24538	24570	24602	24634	24666	24698	24730	24762	24794	24825
0.67	24857	24889	24921	24953	24985	25016	25048	25080	25112	25143
0.68	25175	25207	25238	25270	25301	25333	25365	25396	25428	25459
0.69	25491	25522	25553	25585	25616	25647	25679	25710	25741	25773
0.7	25804	26115	26424	26731	27035	27338	27638	27935	28231	28524
0.8	28815	29103	29389	29673	29955	30234	30511	30785	31057	31327
0.9	31594	31859	32122	32382	32639	32895	33147	33398	33646	33892
1.0	34135	34375	34614	34850	35083	35314	35543	35769	35993	36215
1.1	36434	36650	36865	37076	37286	37493	37698	37900	38100	38298
1.2	38493	38686	38877	39065	39251	39435	39617	39796	39973	40148
1.3	40320	40490	40658	40824	40988	41149	41309	41466	41621	41774
1.4	41925	42073	42220	42364	42507	42647	42786	42922	43057	43189
1.5	43320	43448	43575	43699	43822	43943	44062	44179	44295	44409
1.6	44520	44630	44739	44845	44950	45053	45155	45254	45352	45449
1.7	45544	45637	45729	45819	45907	45994	46080	46164	46246	46328
1.8	46407	46485	46562	46638	46712	46785	46856	46926	46995	47062
1.9	47129	47194	47257	47320	47381	47441	47500	47558	47615	47671
2.0	47725	47779	47831	47882	47933	47982	48030	48078	48124	48169
2.1	48214	48257	48300	48342	48383	48422	48462	48500	48537	48574
2.2	48610	48645	48679	48713	48746	48778	48809	48840	48870	48899
2.3	48928	48956	48983	49010	49036	49062	49087	49111	49135	49158
2.4	49180	49203	49224	49245	49266	49286	49306	49325	49343	49362
2.5	49379	49397	49413	49430	49446	49462	49477	49492	49506	49520
2.6	49534	49548	49561	49573	49586	49598	49610	49621	49632	49643
2.7	49654	49664	49674	49684	49693	49702	49711	49720	49728	49737
2.8	49745	49753	49760	49768	49775	49782	49788	49795	49801	49808
2.9	49814	49820	49825	49831	49836	49841	49846	49851	49856	49861
3.0	49865	49870	49874	49878	49882	49886	49890	49893	49897	49900
3.1	49903	49907	49910	49913	49916	49919	49921	49924	49927	49929
3.2	49932	49934	49936	49938	49940	49943	49945	49946	49948	49950
3.3	49952	49954	49955	49957	49958	49960	49961	49963	49964	49965

3.4: 49967; 3.5: 49977; 3.6: 49984; 3.7: 49989; 3.8: 49993; 3.891: 49995

* To be read as 1.000 00.

[1] Values abridged from National Bureau of Standards, *Tables of Normal Probability Functions*, Applied Mathematics Series 23, Washington, 1953. Reproduction only by permission of the publishers of these *Scientific Tables*.

Deviation |c| → Ordinate f(c)

|c|	0.000	0.001	0.002	0.003	0.004	0.005	0.006	0.007	0.008	0.009
	0.	0.	0.	0.	0.	0.	0.	0.	0.	0.
0.00	39894	39894	39894	39894	39894	39894	39894	39893	39893	39893
0.01	39892	39892	39891	39891	39890	39890	39889	39888	39888	39887
0.02	39886	39885	39885	39884	39883	39882	39881	39880	39879	39877
0.03	39876	39875	39874	39873	39871	39870	39868	39867	39865	39864
0.04	39862	39861	39859	39857	39856	39854	39852	39850	39848	39846
0.05	39844	39842	39840	39838	39836	39834	39832	39829	39827	39825
0.06	39822	39820	39818	39815	39813	39810	39807	39805	39802	39799
0.07	39797	39794	39791	39788	39785	39782	39779	39776	39773	39770
0.08	39767	39764	39760	39757	39754	39750	39747	39744	39740	39737
0.09	39733	39729	39726	39722	39718	39715	39711	39707	39703	39699
0.10	39695	39691	39687	39683	39679	39675	39671	39667	39662	39658
0.11	39654	39649	39645	39640	39636	39631	39627	39622	39617	39613
0.12	39608	39603	39598	39594	39589	39584	39579	39574	39569	39564
0.13	39559	39553	39548	39543	39538	39532	39527	39522	39516	39511
0.14	39505	39500	39494	39488	39483	39477	39471	39466	39460	39454
0.15	39448	39442	39436	39430	39424	39418	39412	39406	39399	39393
0.16	39387	39381	39374	39368	39361	39355	39348	39342	39335	39329
0.17	39322	39315	39308	39302	39295	39288	39281	39274	39267	39260
0.18	39253	39246	39239	39232	39225	39217	39210	39203	39195	39188
0.19	39181	39173	39166	39158	39151	39143	39135	39128	39120	39112
0.20	39104	39096	39089	39081	39073	39065	39057	39049	39041	39032
0.21	39024	39016	39008	38999	38991	38983	38974	38966	38957	38949
0.22	38940	38932	38923	38915	38906	38897	38888	38880	38871	38862
0.23	38853	38844	38835	38826	38817	38808	38799	38789	38780	38771
0.24	38762	38752	38743	38734	38724	38715	38705	38696	38686	38676
0.25	38667	38657	38647	38638	38628	38618	38608	38598	38588	38578
0.26	38568	38558	38548	38538	38528	38518	38508	38497	38487	38477
0.27	38466	38456	38445	38435	38424	38414	38403	38393	38382	38371
0.28	38361	38350	38339	38328	38317	38306	38296	38285	38274	38263
0.29	38251	38240	38229	38218	38207	38196	38184	38173	38162	38150
0.30	38139	38127	38116	38104	38093	38081	38070	38058	38046	38034
0.31	38023	38011	37999	37987	37975	37963	37951	37939	37927	37915
0.32	37903	37891	37879	37867	37854	37842	37830	37817	37805	37793
0.33	37780	37768	37755	37743	37730	37717	37705	37692	37679	37667
0.34	37654	37641	37628	37615	37602	37589	37576	37563	37550	37537
0.35	37524	37511	37498	37484	37471	37458	37445	37431	37418	37405
0.36	37391	37378	37364	37351	37337	37323	37310	37296	37282	37269
0.37	37255	37241	37227	37213	37199	37186	37172	37158	37144	37129
0.38	37115	37101	37087	37073	37059	37044	37030	37016	37002	36987
0.39	36973	36958	36944	36929	36915	36900	36886	36871	36856	36842
0.40	36827	36812	36797	36783	36768	36753	36738	36723	36708	36693
0.41	36678	36663	36648	36633	36618	36603	36587	36572	36557	36542
0.42	36526	36511	36496	36480	36465	36449	36434	36418	36403	36387
0.43	36371	36356	36340	36324	36309	36293	36277	36261	36245	36229
0.44	36213	36198	36182	36166	36150	36133	36117	36101	36085	36069
0.45	36053	36036	36020	36004	35988	35971	35955	35938	35922	35906
0.46	35889	35873	35856	35839	35823	35806	35789	35773	35756	35739
0.47	35723	35706	35689	35672	35655	35638	35621	35604	35587	35570
0.48	35553	35536	35519	35502	35485	35468	35450	35433	35416	35399
0.49	35381	35364	35347	35329	35312	35294	35277	35259	35242	35224
0.50	35207	35189	35171	35154	35136	35118	35100	35083	35065	35047
0.51	35029	35011	34993	34975	34958	34940	34922	34904	34885	34867
0.52	34849	34831	34813	34795	34777	34758	34740	34722	34703	34685
0.53	34667	34648	34630	34612	34593	34575	34556	34538	34519	34500
0.54	34482	34463	34445	34426	34407	34388	34370	34351	34332	34313
0.55	34294	34276	34257	34238	34219	34200	34181	34162	34143	34124
0.56	34105	34085	34066	34047	34028	34009	33990	33970	33951	33932
0.57	33912	33893	33874	33854	33835	33815	33796	33777	33757	33738
0.58	33718	33698	33679	33659	33640	33620	33600	33581	33561	33541
0.59	33521	33502	33482	33462	33442	33422	33402	33382	33362	33342
0.60	33322	33302	33282	33262	33242	33222	33202	33182	33162	33142
0.61	33121	33101	33081	33061	33040	33020	33000	32980	32959	32939
0.62	32918	32898	32878	32857	32837	32816	32796	32775	32754	32734
0.63	32713	32693	32672	32651	32631	32610	32589	32569	32548	32527
0.64	32506	32485	32465	32444	32423	32402	32381	32360	32339	32318
0.65	32297	32276	32255	32234	32213	32192	32171	32150	32129	32108
0.66	32086	32065	32044	32023	32002	31980	31959	31938	31916	31895
0.67	31874	31852	31831	31810	31788	31767	31745	31724	31702	31681
0.68	31659	31638	31616	31595	31573	31551	31530	31508	31487	31465
0.69	31443	31421	31400	31378	31356	31334	31313	31291	31269	31247

|c|	0.000	0.001	0.002	0.003	0.004	0.005	0.006	0.007	0.008	0.009
	0.	0.	0.	0.	0.	0.	0.	0.	0.	0.
0.70	31225	31204	31182	31160	31138	31116	31094	31072	31050	31028
0.71	31006	30984	30962	30940	30918	30896	30874	30852	30829	30807
0.72	30785	30763	30741	30719	30696	30674	30652	30630	30607	30585
0.73	30563	30540	30518	30496	30473	30451	30429	30406	30384	30361
0.74	30339	30316	30294	30272	30249	30227	30204	30181	30159	30136
0.75	30114	30091	30069	30046	30023	30001	29978	29955	29933	29910
0.76	29887	29865	29842	29819	29796	29774	29751	29728	29705	29682
0.77	29659	29637	29614	29591	29568	29545	29522	29499	29476	29453
0.78	29431	29408	29385	29362	29339	29316	29293	29270	29246	29223
0.79	29200	29177	29154	29131	29108	29085	29062	29039	29015	28992
0.80	28969	28946	28923	28900	28876	28853	28830	28807	28783	28760
0.81	28737	28714	28690	28667	28644	28620	28597	28574	28550	28527
0.82	28504	28480	28457	28433	28410	28387	28363	28340	28316	28293
0.83	28269	28246	28223	28199	28176	28152	28129	28105	28081	28058
0.84	28034	28011	27987	27964	27940	27917	27893	27869	27846	27822
0.85	27798	27775	27751	27728	27704	27680	27657	27633	27609	27586
0.86	27562	27538	27514	27491	27467	27443	27419	27396	27372	27348
0.87	27324	27301	27277	27253	27229	27205	27182	27158	27134	27110
0.88	27086	27063	27039	27015	26991	26967	26943	26919	26896	26872
0.89	26848	26824	26800	26776	26752	26728	26704	26680	26656	26632
0.90	26609	26585	26561	26537	26513	26489	26465	26441	26417	26393
0.91	26369	26345	26321	26297	26273	26249	26225	26201	26177	26153
0.92	26129	26105	26081	26056	26032	26008	25984	25960	25936	25912
0.93	25888	25864	25840	25816	25792	25768	25744	25719	25695	25671
0.94	25647	25623	25599	25575	25551	25527	25502	25478	25454	25430
0.95	25406	25382	25358	25333	25309	25285	25261	25237	25213	25189
0.96	25164	25140	25116	25092	25068	25044	25019	24995	24971	24947
0.97	24923	24899	24874	24850	24826	24802	24778	24754	24729	24705
0.98	24681	24657	24633	24608	24584	24560	24536	24512	24487	24463
0.99	24439	24415	24391	24366	24342	24318	24294	24270	24245	24221
1.00	24197	24173	24149	24124	24100	24076	24052	24028	24003	23979
1.01	23955	23931	23907	23883	23858	23834	23810	23786	23762	23737
1.02	23713	23689	23665	23641	23616	23592	23568	23544	23520	23496
1.03	23471	23447	23423	23399	23375	23351	23326	23302	23278	23254
1.04	23230	23206	23181	23157	23133	23109	23085	23061	23036	23012
1.05	22988	22964	22940	22916	22892	22868	22843	22819	22795	22771
1.06	22747	22723	22699	22675	22651	22626	22602	22578	22554	22530
1.07	22506	22482	22458	22434	22410	22386	22362	22338	22313	22289
1.08	22265	22241	22217	22193	22169	22145	22121	22097	22073	22049
1.09	22025	22001	21977	21953	21929	21905	21881	21857	21833	21809
1.1	21785	21546	21307	21069	20831	20594	20357	20121	19886	19652
1.2	19419	19186	18954	18724	18494	18265	18037	17810	17585	17360
1.3	17137	16915	16694	16474	16256	16038	15822	15608	15395	15183
1.4	14973	14764	14556	14350	14146	13943	13742	13542	13344	13147
1.5	12952	12758	12566	12376	12188	12001	11816	11632	11450	11270
1.6	11092	10915	10741	10567	10396	10226	10059	09893	09728	09566
1.7	09405	09246	09089	08933	08780	08628	08478	08329	08183	08038
1.8	07895	07754	07614	07477	07341	07206	07074	06943	06814	06687
1.9	06562	06438	06316	06195	06077	05959	05844	05730	05618	05508
2.0	05399	05292	05186	05082	04980	04879	04780	04682	04586	04491
2.1	04398	04307	04217	04128	04041	03955	03871	03788	03706	03626
2.2	03547	03470	03394	03319	03246	03174	03103	03034	02965	02898
2.3	02833	02768	02705	02643	02582	02522	02463	02406	02349	02294
2.4	02239	02186	02134	02083	02033	01984	01936	01888	01842	01797
2.5	01753	01709	01667	01625	01585	01545	01506	01468	01431	01394
2.6	01358	01323	01289	01256	01223	01191	01160	01130	01100	01071
2.7	01042	01014	00987	00961	00935	00909	00885	00861	00837	00814
2.8	00792	00770	00748	00727	00707	00687	00668	00649	00631	00613
2.9	00595	00578	00562	00545	00530	00514	00499	00485	00470	00457
3.0	00443	00430	00417	00405	00393	00381	00370	00358	00348	00337
3.1	00327	00317	00307	00298	00288	00279	00271	00262	00254	00246
3.2	00238	00231	00224	00216	00210	00203	00196	00190	00184	00178
3.3	00172	00167	00161	00156	00151	00146	00141	00136	00132	00127
3.4	00123	00119	00115	00111	00107	00104	00100	00097	00094	00090
3.5	00087	00084	00081	00079	00076	00073	00071	00068	00066	00063
3.6	00061	00059	00057	00055	00053	00051	00049	00047	00046	00044
3.7	00042	00041	00039	00038	00037	00035	00034	00033	00031	00030
3.8	00029	00028	00027	00026	00025	00024	00023	00022	00021	00021
3.9	00020	00019	00018	00018	00017	00016	00016	00015	00014	00014
4.0	00013	00013	00012	00012	00011	00011	00011	00010	00010	00009

Probability[2] 2 P → Deviation c

2 P = twice the integral between c and infinity

2 P	0.00	0.01	0.02	0.03	0.04	0.05	0.06	0.07	0.08	0.09
	Deviation c									
0.0	∞	2.575829	2.326348	2.170090	2.053749	1.959964	1.880794	1.811911	1.750686	1.695398
0.1	1.644854	1.598193	1.554774	1.514102	1.475791	1.439531	1.405072	1.372204	1.340755	1.310579
0.2	1.281552	1.253565	1.226528	1.200359	1.174987	1.150349	1.126391	1.103063	1.080319	1.058122
0.3	1.036433	1.015222	0.994458	0.974114	0.954165	0.934589	0.915365	0.896473	0.877896	0.859617
0.4	0.841621	0.823894	0.806421	0.789192	0.772193	0.755415	0.738847	0.722479	0.706303	0.690309
0.5	0.674490	0.658838	0.643345	0.628006	0.612813	0.597760	0.582842	0.568051	0.553385	0.538836
0.6	0.524401	0.510073	0.495850	0.481727	0.467699	0.453762	0.439913	0.426148	0.412463	0.398855
0.7	0.385320	0.371856	0.358459	0.345126	0.331853	0.318639	0.305481	0.292375	0.279319	0.266311
0.8	0.253347	0.240426	0.227545	0.214702	0.201893	0.189118	0.176374	0.163658	0.150969	0.138304
0.9	0.125661	0.113039	0.100434	0.087845	0.075270	0.062707	0.050154	0.037608	0.025069	0.012533

Very small values of P

2 P	.	.	.	0.001	0.000 1	0.000 01	0.000 001	0.000 000 1	0.000 000 01	0.000 000 001
c	.	.	.	3.29053	3.89059	4.41717	4.89164	5.32672	5.73073	6.10941

[1] Values abridged from National Bureau of Standards, *Tables of Normal Probability Functions*, Applied Mathematics Series 23, Washington, 1953. Reproduction only by permission of the publishers of these *Scientific Tables*.

[2] Values from Fisher and Yates, *Statistical Tables for Biological, Agricultural and Medical Research*, 6th ed., Oliver and Boyd, Edinburgh, 1963, page 44. Reprinted by kind permission of the authors and publishers.

Significance Limits* of the Student Distribution ν=1—50

$P = P$ (right) = integral between t and infinity. P (left) = P (right)

2 P	0.9995	0.999	0.995	0.99	0.98	0.975	0.95	0.90	0.80	0.70	0.60	0.50	0.40	0.30	0.20	0.10	0.05	0.025	0.02	0.01	0.005	0.001
P	0.49975	0.4995	0.4975	0.495	0.49	0.4875	0.475	0.45	0.40	0.35	0.30	0.25	0.20	0.15	0.10	0.05	0.025	0.0125	0.01	0.005	0.0025	0.0005
ν																						
1	0.0008	0.0015	0.0077	0.0154	0.030	0.0385	0.0770	0.1580	0.3250	0.5100	0.7270	1.0000	1.376	1.963	3.078	6.3138	12.706	25.452	31.821	63.657	127.32	636.619
2	0.0007	0.0014	0.0071	0.0141	0.028	0.0353	0.0707	0.1419	0.2885	0.4448	0.6172	0.8165	1.061	1.386	1.886	2.9200	4.3027	6.2053	6.965	9.9248	14.089	31.598
3	0.0007	0.0014	0.0068	0.0136	0.027	0.0340	0.0681	0.1366	0.2766	0.4243	0.5840	0.7649	0.978	1.250	1.638	2.3534	3.1825	4.1765	4.541	5.8409	7.4533	12.924
4	0.0007	0.0013	0.0067	0.0133	0.026	0.0333	0.0667	0.1338	0.2707	0.4143	0.5692	0.7407	0.941	1.190	1.533	2.1318	2.7764	3.4954	3.747	4.6041	5.5976	8.610
5	0.0007	0.0013	0.0066	0.0132	0.026	0.0329	0.0659	0.1322	0.2672	0.4083	0.5598	0.7267	0.920	1.156	1.476	2.0150	2.5706	3.1634	3.365	4.0321	4.7733	6.869
6	0.0007	0.0013	0.0065	0.0131	0.026	0.0327	0.0654	0.1311	0.2648	0.4044	0.5536	0.7176	0.906	1.134	1.440	1.9432	2.4469	2.9687	3.143	3.7074	4.3168	5.959
7	0.0006	0.0013	0.0065	0.0130	0.025	0.0325	0.0650	0.1303	0.2632	0.4016	0.5493	0.7111	0.896	1.119	1.415	1.8946	2.3646	2.8412	2.998	3.4995	4.0293	5.408
8	0.0006	0.0013	0.0065	0.0129	0.025	0.0323	0.0647	0.1297	0.2619	0.3995	0.5461	0.7064	0.889	1.108	1.397	1.8595	2.3060	2.7515	2.896	3.3554	3.8325	5.041
9	0.0006	0.0013	0.0064	0.0129	0.025	0.0322	0.0645	0.1293	0.2610	0.3979	0.5436	0.7027	0.883	1.100	1.383	1.8331	2.2622	2.6850	2.821	3.2498	3.6897	4.781
10	0.0006	0.0013	0.0064	0.0129	0.025	0.0321	0.0643	0.1289	0.2602	0.3966	0.5416	0.6998	0.879	1.093	1.372	1.8125	2.2281	2.6338	2.764	3.1693	3.5814	4.587
11	0.0006	0.0013	0.0064	0.0128	0.025	0.0321	0.0642	0.1286	0.2596	0.3956	0.5400	0.6975	0.876	1.088	1.363	1.7959	2.2010	2.5931	2.718	3.1058	3.4966	4.437
12	0.0006	0.0013	0.0064	0.0128	0.025	0.0320	0.0640	0.1283	0.2590	0.3947	0.5387	0.6955	0.873	1.083	1.356	1.7823	2.1788	2.5600	2.681	3.0545	3.4284	4.318
13	0.0006	0.0013	0.0064	0.0128	0.025	0.0319	0.0639	0.1281	0.2586	0.3940	0.5375	0.6938	0.870	1.079	1.350	1.7709	2.1604	2.5326	2.650	3.0123	3.3725	4.221
14	0.0006	0.0013	0.0064	0.0128	0.025	0.0319	0.0638	0.1280	0.2582	0.3933	0.5366	0.6924	0.868	1.076	1.345	1.7613	2.1448	2.5096	2.624	2.9768	3.3257	4.140
15	0.0006	0.0013	0.0064	0.0127	0.025	0.0319	0.0638	0.1278	0.2579	0.3928	0.5358	0.6912	0.866	1.074	1.341	1.7530	2.1315	2.4899	2.602	2.9467	3.2860	4.073
16	0.0006	0.0013	0.0064	0.0127	0.025	0.0318	0.0637	0.1277	0.2576	0.3923	0.5350	0.6901	0.865	1.071	1.337	1.7459	2.1199	2.4729	2.583	2.9208	3.2520	4.015
17	0.0006	0.0013	0.0064	0.0127	0.025	0.0318	0.0636	0.1276	0.2574	0.3919	0.5344	0.6892	0.863	1.069	1.333	1.7396	2.1098	2.4581	2.567	2.8982	3.2225	3.965
18	0.0006	0.0013	0.0064	0.0127	0.025	0.0318	0.0636	0.1274	0.2571	0.3915	0.5338	0.6884	0.862	1.067	1.330	1.7341	2.1009	2.4450	2.552	2.8784	3.1966	3.922
19	0.0006	0.0013	0.0063	0.0127	0.025	0.0318	0.0635	0.1274	0.2569	0.3912	0.5333	0.6876	0.861	1.066	1.328	1.7291	2.0930	2.4334	2.539	2.8609	3.1737	3.883
20	0.0006	0.0013	0.0063	0.0127	0.025	0.0317	0.0635	0.1273	0.2567	0.3909	0.5329	0.6870	0.860	1.064	1.325	1.7247	2.0860	2.4231	2.528	2.8453	3.1534	3.850
21	0.0006	0.0013	0.0063	0.0127	0.025	0.0317	0.0635	0.1272	0.2566	0.3906	0.5325	0.6864	0.859	1.063	1.323	1.7207	2.0796	2.4138	2.518	2.8314	3.1352	3.819
22	0.0006	0.0013	0.0063	0.0127	0.025	0.0317	0.0634	0.1271	0.2564	0.3904	0.5321	0.6858	0.858	1.061	1.321	1.7171	2.0739	2.4055	2.508	2.8188	3.1188	3.792
23	0.0006	0.0013	0.0063	0.0127	0.025	0.0317	0.0634	0.1271	0.2563	0.3902	0.5318	0.6853	0.858	1.060	1.319	1.7139	2.0687	2.3979	2.500	2.8073	3.1040	3.767
24	0.0006	0.0013	0.0063	0.0127	0.025	0.0317	0.0634	0.1270	0.2562	0.3900	0.5315	0.6849	0.857	1.059	1.318	1.7109	2.0639	2.3910	2.492	2.7969	3.0905	3.745
25	0.0006	0.0013	0.0063	0.0127	0.025	0.0317	0.0633	0.1269	0.2561	0.3898	0.5312	0.6844	0.856	1.058	1.316	1.7081	2.0595	2.3846	2.485	2.7874	3.0782	3.725
26	0.0006	0.0013	0.0063	0.0127	0.025	0.0316	0.0633	0.1269	0.2560	0.3896	0.5309	0.6841	0.856	1.058	1.315	1.7056	2.0555	2.3788	2.479	2.7787	3.0669	3.707
27	0.0006	0.0013	0.0063	0.0126	0.025	0.0316	0.0633	0.1269	0.2559	0.3895	0.5307	0.6837	0.855	1.057	1.314	1.7033	2.0518	2.3734	2.473	2.7707	3.0565	3.690
28	0.0006	0.0013	0.0063	0.0126	0.025	0.0316	0.0633	0.1268	0.2558	0.3893	0.5304	0.6834	0.855	1.056	1.313	1.7011	2.0484	2.3685	2.467	2.7633	3.0469	3.674
29	0.0006	0.0013	0.0063	0.0126	0.025	0.0316	0.0633	0.1268	0.2557	0.3892	0.5302	0.6830	0.854	1.055	1.311	1.6991	2.0452	2.3638	2.462	2.7564	3.0380	3.659
30	0.0006	0.0013	0.0063	0.0126	0.025	0.0316	0.0632	0.1267	0.2556	0.3890	0.5300	0.6828	0.854	1.055	1.310	1.6973	2.0423	2.3596	2.457	2.7500	3.0298	3.646
31	0.0006	0.0013	0.0063	0.0126	0.025	0.0316	0.0632	0.1267	0.2555	0.3889	0.5298	0.6825	0.8535	1.0541	1.3095	1.6955	2.0395	2.3556	2.453	2.7441	3.0222	3.6338
32	0.0006	0.0013	0.0063	0.0126	0.025	0.0316	0.0632	0.1267	0.2555	0.3888	0.5297	0.6823	0.8531	1.0536	1.3086	1.6939	2.0370	2.3519	2.449	2.7385	3.0150	3.6221
33	0.0006	0.0013	0.0063	0.0126	0.025	0.0316	0.0632	0.1266	0.2554	0.3887	0.5295	0.6820	0.8527	1.0531	1.3078	1.6924	2.0345	2.3484	2.445	2.7333	3.0083	3.6111
34	0.0006	0.0013	0.0063	0.0126	0.025	0.0316	0.0632	0.1266	0.2553	0.3886	0.5294	0.6818	0.8524	1.0526	1.3070	1.6909	2.0323	2.3451	2.441	2.7284	3.0020	3.6011
35	0.0006	0.0013	0.0063	0.0126	0.025	0.0316	0.0632	0.1266	0.2553	0.3885	0.5292	0.6816	0.8521	1.0521	1.3062	1.6896	2.0301	2.3420	2.438	2.7239	2.9962	3.5915
36	0.0006	0.0013	0.0063	0.0126	0.025	0.0316	0.0631	0.1266	0.2552	0.3884	0.5291	0.6814	0.8518	1.0516	1.3055	1.6883	2.0281	2.3391	2.434	2.7195	2.9905	3.5824
37	0.0006	0.0013	0.0063	0.0126	0.025	0.0316	0.0631	0.1265	0.2552	0.3883	0.5290	0.6812	0.8515	1.0512	1.3049	1.6871	2.0262	2.3364	2.431	2.7155	2.9853	3.5741
38	0.0006	0.0013	0.0063	0.0126	0.025	0.0315	0.0631	0.1265	0.2551	0.3883	0.5288	0.6810	0.8512	1.0508	1.3042	1.6860	2.0244	2.3338	2.428	2.7116	2.9804	3.5661
39	0.0006	0.0013	0.0063	0.0126	0.025	0.0315	0.0631	0.1265	0.2551	0.3882	0.5287	0.6808	0.8510	1.0504	1.3037	1.6849	2.0227	2.3313	2.426	2.7079	2.9757	3.5586
40	0.0006	0.0013	0.0063	0.0126	0.025	0.0315	0.0631	0.1265	0.2550	0.3881	0.5286	0.6807	0.8507	1.0501	1.3031	1.6839	2.0211	2.3290	2.423	2.7045	2.9713	3.5511
41	0.0006	0.0013	0.0063	0.0126	0.025	0.0315	0.0631	0.1264	0.2550	0.3880	0.5285	0.6805	0.8505	1.0498	1.3026	1.6829	2.0196	2.3268	2.421	2.7012	2.9671	3.5446
42	0.0006	0.0013	0.0063	0.0126	0.025	0.0315	0.0631	0.1264	0.2550	0.3880	0.5284	0.6804	0.8503	1.0494	1.3020	1.6820	2.0181	2.3247	2.418	2.6981	2.9631	3.5383
43	0.0006	0.0013	0.0063	0.0126	0.025	0.0315	0.0631	0.1264	0.2549	0.3879	0.5283	0.6803	0.8501	1.0491	1.3016	1.6811	2.0167	2.3226	2.416	2.6952	2.9592	3.5323
44	0.0006	0.0013	0.0063	0.0126	0.025	0.0315	0.0631	0.1264	0.2549	0.3879	0.5282	0.6801	0.8499	1.0488	1.3011	1.6802	2.0154	2.3207	2.414	2.6923	2.9556	3.5264
45	0.0006	0.0013	0.0063	0.0126	0.025	0.0315	0.0631	0.1264	0.2549	0.3878	0.5281	0.6800	0.8497	1.0485	1.3007	1.6794	2.0141	2.3189	2.412	2.6896	2.9522	3.5207
46	0.0006	0.0013	0.0063	0.0126	0.025	0.0315	0.0631	0.1264	0.2548	0.3877	0.5281	0.6799	0.8495	1.0483	1.3002	1.6787	2.0129	2.3172	2.410	2.6870	2.9489	3.5153
47	0.0006	0.0013	0.0063	0.0126	0.025	0.0315	0.0630	0.1263	0.2548	0.3877	0.5280	0.6798	0.8494	1.0480	1.2998	1.6779	2.0118	2.3155	2.408	2.6846	2.9457	3.5104
48	0.0006	0.0013	0.0063	0.0126	0.025	0.0315	0.0630	0.1263	0.2548	0.3876	0.5279	0.6796	0.8492	1.0478	1.2994	1.6772	2.0106	2.3139	2.406	2.6822	2.9427	3.5053
49	0.0006	0.0013	0.0063	0.0126	0.025	0.0315	0.0630	0.1263	0.2547	0.3876	0.5278	0.6795	0.8490	1.0476	1.2991	1.6766	2.0096	2.3124	2.405	2.6800	2.9398	3.5010
50	0.0006	0.0013	0.0063	0.0126	0.025	0.0315	0.0630	0.1263	0.2547	0.3875	0.5278	0.6794	0.8489	1.0473	1.2987	1.6759	2.0086	2.3109	2.403	2.6778	2.9370	3.4965

Significance Limits* of the Student Distribution ν = 51–100

$P = P$ (right) = integral between t and infinity. P (left) = P (right)

2 P	0.9995	0.999	0.995	0.99	0.98	0.975	0.95	0.90	0.80	0.70	0.60	0.50	0.40	0.30	0.20	0.10	0.05	0.025	0.02	0.01	0.005	0.001
P	0.49975	0.4995	0.4975	0.495	0.49	0.4875	0.475	0.45	0.40	0.35	0.30	0.25	0.20	0.15	0.10	0.05	0.025	0.0125	0.01	0.005	0.0025	0.0005
ν																						
51	0.0006	0.0013	0.0063	0.0126	0.025	0.0315	0.0630	0.1263	0.2547	0.3875	0.5277	0.6793	0.8488	1.0471	1.2984	1.6753	2.0077	2.3096	2.402	2.6758	2.9344	3.4924
52	0.0006	0.0013	0.0063	0.0126	0.025	0.0315	0.0630	0.1263	0.2547	0.3875	0.5276	0.6792	0.8486	1.0469	1.2981	1.6747	2.0067	2.3082	2.400	2.6738	2.9318	3.4883
53	0.0006	0.0013	0.0063	0.0126	0.025	0.0315	0.0630	0.1263	0.2547	0.3875	0.5276	0.6792	0.8485	1.0467	1.2978	1.6742	2.0058	2.3070	2.399	2.6719	2.9295	3.4845
54	0.0006	0.0013	0.0063	0.0126	0.025	0.0315	0.0630	0.1263	0.2546	0.3874	0.5275	0.6791	0.8484	1.0465	1.2975	1.6736	2.0049	2.3057	2.397	2.6700	2.9271	3.4807
55	0.0006	0.0013	0.0063	0.0126	0.025	0.0315	0.0630	0.1263	0.2546	0.3874	0.5275	0.6790	0.8483	1.0463	1.2972	1.6731	2.0041	2.3045	2.396	2.6683	2.9249	3.4770
56	0.0006	0.0013	0.0063	0.0126	0.025	0.0315	0.0630	0.1262	0.2546	0.3873	0.5274	0.6789	0.8481	1.0461	1.2969	1.6725	2.0033	2.3033	2.395	2.6666	2.9226	3.4733
57	0.0006	0.0013	0.0063	0.0126	0.025	0.0315	0.0630	0.1262	0.2546	0.3873	0.5274	0.6789	0.8480	1.0460	1.2967	1.6721	2.0025	2.3022	2.393	2.6650	2.9205	3.4702
58	0.0006	0.0013	0.0063	0.0126	0.025	0.0315	0.0630	0.1262	0.2545	0.3872	0.5273	0.6788	0.8479	1.0458	1.2964	1.6716	2.0017	2.3011	2.392	2.6633	2.9184	3.4670
59	0.0006	0.0013	0.0063	0.0126	0.025	0.0315	0.0630	0.1262	0.2545	0.3872	0.5273	0.6787	0.8478	1.0457	1.2962	1.6712	2.0010	2.3001	2.391	2.6618	2.9165	3.4638
60	0.0006	0.0013	0.0063	0.0126	0.025	0.0315	0.0630	0.1262	0.2545	0.3872	0.5272	0.6786	0.8477	1.0455	1.2959	1.6707	2.0003	2.2991	2.390	2.6603	2.9146	3.4606
61	0.0006	0.0013	0.0063	0.0126	0.025	0.0315	0.0630	0.1262	0.2545	0.3872	0.5272	0.6786	0.8476	1.0454	1.2957	1.6703	1.9997	2.2982	2.389	2.6590	2.9128	3.4577
62	0.0006	0.0013	0.0063	0.0126	0.025	0.0315	0.0630	0.1262	0.2544	0.3871	0.5271	0.6785	0.8475	1.0452	1.2954	1.6698	1.9990	2.2972	2.388	2.6576	2.9110	3.4548
63	0.0006	0.0013	0.0063	0.0126	0.025	0.0315	0.0630	0.1262	0.2544	0.3871	0.5271	0.6785	0.8474	1.0451	1.2952	1.6694	1.9984	2.2963	2.387	2.6563	2.9094	3.4521
64	0.0006	0.0013	0.0063	0.0126	0.025	0.0315	0.0630	0.1262	0.2544	0.3871	0.5270	0.6784	0.8473	1.0449	1.2950	1.6690	1.9977	2.2954	2.386	2.6549	2.9077	3.4494
65	0.0006	0.0013	0.0063	0.0126	0.025	0.0315	0.0630	0.1262	0.2544	0.3871	0.5270	0.6783	0.8472	1.0448	1.2948	1.6687	1.9972	2.2946	2.385	2.6537	2.9061	3.4470
66	0.0006	0.0013	0.0063	0.0126	0.025	0.0315	0.0629	0.1261	0.2544	0.3870	0.5270	0.6782	0.8471	1.0447	1.2945	1.6683	1.9966	2.2937	2.384	2.6525	2.9045	3.4445
67	0.0006	0.0013	0.0063	0.0126	0.025	0.0315	0.0629	0.1261	0.2544	0.3870	0.5270	0.6782	0.8471	1.0446	1.2944	1.6680	1.9961	2.2929	2.383	2.6513	2.9031	3.4423
68	0.0006	0.0013	0.0063	0.0126	0.025	0.0315	0.0629	0.1261	0.2543	0.3870	0.5269	0.6781	0.8470	1.0444	1.2942	1.6676	1.9955	2.2921	2.382	2.6501	2.9016	3.4400
69	0.0006	0.0013	0.0063	0.0126	0.025	0.0315	0.0629	0.1261	0.2543	0.3870	0.5269	0.6781	0.8469	1.0443	1.2940	1.6673	1.9950	2.2914	2.381	2.6491	2.9002	3.4378
70	0.0006	0.0013	0.0063	0.0126	0.025	0.0315	0.0629	0.1261	0.2543	0.3869	0.5268	0.6780	0.8468	1.0442	1.2938	1.6669	1.9945	2.2907	2.381	2.6480	2.8988	3.4355
71	0.0006	0.0013	0.0063	0.0126	0.025	0.0315	0.0629	0.1261	0.2543	0.3869	0.5268	0.6780	0.8468	1.0441	1.2936	1.6666	1.9940	2.2900	2.380	2.6470	2.8976	3.4333
72	0.0006	0.0013	0.0063	0.0126	0.025	0.0314	0.0629	0.1261	0.2543	0.3869	0.5267	0.6779	0.8467	1.0440	1.2934	1.6663	1.9935	2.2893	2.379	2.6459	2.8963	3.4310
73	0.0006	0.0013	0.0063	0.0126	0.025	0.0314	0.0629	0.1261	0.2543	0.3869	0.5267	0.6779	0.8466	1.0439	1.2933	1.6660	1.9931	2.2887	2.378	2.6450	2.8950	3.4291
74	0.0006	0.0013	0.0063	0.0126	0.025	0.0314	0.0629	0.1261	0.2543	0.3868	0.5267	0.6778	0.8465	1.0438	1.2931	1.6657	1.9926	2.2880	2.378	2.6440	2.8937	3.4272
75	0.0006	0.0013	0.0063	0.0126	0.025	0.0314	0.0629	0.1261	0.2543	0.3868	0.5267	0.6778	0.8465	1.0437	1.2930	1.6655	1.9922	2.2874	2.377	2.6431	2.8925	3.4253
76	0.0006	0.0013	0.0063	0.0126	0.025	0.0314	0.0629	0.1261	0.2542	0.3868	0.5266	0.6777	0.8464	1.0436	1.2928	1.6652	1.9917	2.2867	2.376	2.6421	2.8913	3.4234
77	0.0006	0.0013	0.0063	0.0126	0.025	0.0314	0.0629	0.1261	0.2542	0.3868	0.5266	0.6777	0.8464	1.0435	1.2927	1.6649	1.9913	2.2861	2.376	2.6413	2.8903	3.4217
78	0.0006	0.0013	0.0063	0.0126	0.025	0.0314	0.0629	0.1261	0.2542	0.3867	0.5266	0.6777	0.8463	1.0434	1.2925	1.6646	1.9909	2.2855	2.375	2.6404	2.8892	3.4200
79	0.0006	0.0013	0.0063	0.0126	0.025	0.0314	0.0629	0.1261	0.2542	0.3867	0.5266	0.6777	0.8463	1.0433	1.2924	1.6644	1.9905	2.2850	2.374	2.6396	2.8882	3.4185
80	0.0006	0.0013	0.0063	0.0126	0.025	0.0314	0.0629	0.1261	0.2542	0.3867	0.5265	0.6776	0.8462	1.0432	1.2922	1.6641	1.9901	2.2844	2.374	2.6388	2.8871	3.4169
81	0.0006	0.0013	0.0063	0.0126	0.025	0.0314	0.0629	0.1261	0.2542	0.3867	0.5265	0.6776	0.8461	1.0431	1.2921	1.6639	1.9897	2.2839	2.373	2.6380	2.8861	3.4152
82	0.0006	0.0013	0.0063	0.0126	0.025	0.0314	0.0629	0.1261	0.2542	0.3867	0.5265	0.6775	0.8460	1.0430	1.2920	1.6637	1.9893	2.2833	2.372	2.6372	2.8851	3.4135
83	0.0006	0.0013	0.0063	0.0126	0.025	0.0314	0.0629	0.1261	0.2542	0.3867	0.5265	0.6775	0.8460	1.0430	1.2919	1.6635	1.9890	2.2828	2.372	2.6365	2.8842	3.4121
84	0.0006	0.0013	0.0063	0.0126	0.025	0.0314	0.0629	0.1260	0.2542	0.3866	0.5264	0.6774	0.8459	1.0429	1.2917	1.6632	1.9886	2.2823	2.371	2.6357	2.8832	3.4106
85	0.0006	0.0013	0.0063	0.0126	0.025	0.0314	0.0629	0.1260	0.2542	0.3866	0.5264	0.6774	0.8459	1.0428	1.2916	1.6630	1.9883	2.2818	2.371	2.6350	2.8823	3.4091
86	0.0006	0.0013	0.0063	0.0126	0.025	0.0314	0.0629	0.1260	0.2541	0.3866	0.5264	0.6774	0.8458	1.0427	1.2915	1.6628	1.9880	2.2813	2.370	2.6343	2.8814	3.4076
87	0.0006	0.0013	0.0063	0.0126	0.025	0.0314	0.0629	0.1260	0.2541	0.3866	0.5264	0.6774	0.8458	1.0427	1.2914	1.6626	1.9877	2.2809	2.370	2.6336	2.8805	3.4063
88	0.0006	0.0013	0.0063	0.0126	0.025	0.0314	0.0629	0.1260	0.2541	0.3866	0.5263	0.6773	0.8457	1.0426	1.2913	1.6624	1.9873	2.2804	2.369	2.6329	2.8796	3.4050
89	0.0006	0.0013	0.0063	0.0126	0.025	0.0314	0.0629	0.1260	0.2541	0.3866	0.5263	0.6773	0.8457	1.0426	1.2912	1.6622	1.9870	2.2800	2.369	2.6323	2.8788	3.4036
90	0.0006	0.0013	0.0063	0.0126	0.025	0.0314	0.0629	0.1260	0.2541	0.3866	0.5263	0.6772	0.8457	1.0425	1.2910	1.6620	1.9867	2.2795	2.368	2.6316	2.8779	3.4022
91	0.0006	0.0013	0.0063	0.0126	0.025	0.0314	0.0629	0.1260	0.2541	0.3866	0.5263	0.6772	0.8457	1.0424	1.2909	1.6618	1.9864	2.2791	2.368	2.6310	2.8772	3.4010
92	0.0006	0.0013	0.0063	0.0126	0.025	0.0314	0.0629	0.1260	0.2541	0.3865	0.5262	0.6772	0.8456	1.0423	1.2908	1.6616	1.9861	2.2787	2.367	2.6303	2.8764	3.3997
93	0.0006	0.0013	0.0063	0.0126	0.025	0.0314	0.0629	0.1260	0.2541	0.3865	0.5262	0.6772	0.8456	1.0423	1.2907	1.6614	1.9859	2.2783	2.367	2.6298	2.8757	3.3986
94	0.0006	0.0013	0.0063	0.0126	0.025	0.0314	0.0629	0.1260	0.2541	0.3865	0.5262	0.6771	0.8455	1.0422	1.2906	1.6612	1.9856	2.2779	2.366	2.6292	2.8749	3.3975
95	0.0006	0.0013	0.0063	0.0126	0.025	0.0314	0.0629	0.1260	0.2541	0.3865	0.5262	0.6771	0.8455	1.0422	1.2905	1.6611	1.9853	2.2775	2.366	2.6286	2.8742	3.3964
96	0.0006	0.0013	0.0063	0.0126	0.025	0.0314	0.0629	0.1260	0.2541	0.3865	0.5262	0.6771	0.8454	1.0421	1.2904	1.6609	1.9850	2.2771	2.366	2.6280	2.8734	3.3952
97	0.0006	0.0013	0.0063	0.0126	0.025	0.0314	0.0629	0.1260	0.2541	0.3865	0.5262	0.6771	0.8454	1.0421	1.2904	1.6608	1.9848	2.2768	2.365	2.6275	2.8728	3.3940
98	0.0006	0.0013	0.0063	0.0126	0.025	0.0314	0.0629	0.1260	0.2540	0.3865	0.5261	0.6770	0.8453	1.0420	1.2903	1.6606	1.9845	2.2764	2.365	2.6270	2.8721	3.3928
99	0.0006	0.0013	0.0063	0.0126	0.025	0.0314	0.0629	0.1260	0.2540	0.3865	0.5261	0.6770	0.8453	1.0419	1.2902	1.6604	1.9843	2.2761	2.364	2.6265	2.8714	3.3919
100	0.0006	0.0013	0.0063	0.0126	0.025	0.0314	0.0629	0.1260	0.2540	0.3864	0.5261	0.6770	0.8452	1.0418	1.2901	1.6602	1.9840	2.2757	2.364	2.6260	2.8707	3.3909

Significance Limits* of the Student Distribution ν = 101—150

$P = P$ (right) = integral between t and infinity. P (left) = P (right)

2 P	0.9995	0.999	0.995	0.99	0.98	0.975	0.95	0.90	0.80	0.70	0.60	0.50	0.40	0.30	0.20	0.10	0.05	0.025	0.02	0.01	0.005	0.001
P	0.49975	0.4995	0.4975	0.495	0.49	0.4875	0.475	0.45	0.40	0.35	0.30	0.25	0.20	0.15	0.10	0.05	0.025	0.0125	0.01	0.005	0.0025	0.0005
ν																						
101	0.0006	0.0013	0.0063	0.0126	0.025	0.0314	0.0629	0.1260	0.2540	0.3864	0.5261	0.6770	0.8452	1.0418	1.2900	1.6601	1.9838	2.2754	2.364	2.6255	2.8701	3.3899
102	0.0006	0.0013	0.0063	0.0126	0.025	0.0314	0.0629	0.1260	0.2540	0.3864	0.5261	0.6769	0.8452	1.0417	1.2899	1.6599	1.9835	2.2750	2.363	2.6249	2.8695	3.3888
103	0.0006	0.0013	0.0063	0.0126	0.025	0.0314	0.0629	0.1260	0.2540	0.3864	0.5261	0.6769	0.8452	1.0417	1.2899	1.6598	1.9833	2.2747	2.363	2.6245	2.8689	3.3879
104	0.0006	0.0013	0.0063	0.0126	0.025	0.0314	0.0629	0.1260	0.2540	0.3864	0.5260	0.6769	0.8451	1.0416	1.2898	1.6596	1.9831	2.2743	2.363	2.6240	2.8682	3.3870
105	0.0006	0.0013	0.0063	0.0126	0.025	0.0314	0.0629	0.1260	0.2540	0.3864	0.5260	0.6769	0.8451	1.0416	1.2897	1.6595	1.9829	2.2740	2.362	2.6236	2.8677	3.3860
106	0.0006	0.0013	0.0063	0.0126	0.025	0.0314	0.0629	0.1260	0.2540	0.3864	0.5260	0.6768	0.8450	1.0415	1.2896	1.6594	1.9826	2.2737	2.362	2.6231	2.8671	3.3850
107	0.0006	0.0013	0.0063	0.0126	0.025	0.0314	0.0629	0.1260	0.2540	0.3864	0.5260	0.6768	0.8450	1.0415	1.2895	1.6593	1.9824	2.2734	2.362	2.6227	2.8665	3.3840
108	0.0006	0.0013	0.0063	0.0126	0.025	0.0314	0.0629	0.1260	0.2540	0.3864	0.5260	0.6768	0.8450	1.0414	1.2894	1.6591	1.9822	2.2731	2.361	2.6222	2.8659	3.3830
109	0.0006	0.0013	0.0063	0.0126	0.025	0.0314	0.0629	0.1260	0.2540	0.3864	0.5260	0.6768	0.8450	1.0414	1.2894	1.6590	1.9820	2.2728	2.361	2.6218	2.8654	3.3823
110	0.0006	0.0013	0.0063	0.0126	0.025	0.0314	0.0629	0.1260	0.2540	0.3863	0.5259	0.6767	0.8449	1.0414	1.2893	1.6588	1.9818	2.2725	2.361	2.6213	2.8648	3.3816
111	0.0006	0.0013	0.0063	0.0126	0.025	0.0314	0.0629	0.1260	0.2540	0.3863	0.5259	0.6767	0.8449	1.0414	1.2893	1.6587	1.9816	2.2723	2.360	2.6209	2.8643	3.3808
112	0.0006	0.0013	0.0063	0.0126	0.025	0.0314	0.0628	0.1259	0.2540	0.3863	0.5259	0.6767	0.8449	1.0413	1.2892	1.6586	1.9814	2.2720	2.360	2.6205	2.8638	3.3800
113	0.0006	0.0013	0.0063	0.0126	0.025	0.0314	0.0628	0.1259	0.2540	0.3863	0.5259	0.6767	0.8449	1.0413	1.2891	1.6585	1.9812	2.2717	2.360	2.6201	2.8633	3.3791
114	0.0006	0.0013	0.0063	0.0126	0.025	0.0314	0.0628	0.1259	0.2539	0.3863	0.5259	0.6767	0.8448	1.0412	1.2890	1.6583	1.9810	2.2714	2.359	2.6197	2.8627	3.3782
115	0.0006	0.0013	0.0063	0.0126	0.025	0.0314	0.0628	0.1259	0.2539	0.3863	0.5259	0.6767	0.8448	1.0412	1.2890	1.6582	1.9808	2.2712	2.359	2.6193	2.8623	3.3775
116	0.0006	0.0013	0.0063	0.0126	0.025	0.0314	0.0628	0.1259	0.2539	0.3863	0.5259	0.6766	0.8447	1.0411	1.2889	1.6581	1.9806	2.2709	2.359	2.6189	2.8618	3.3767
117	0.0006	0.0013	0.0063	0.0126	0.025	0.0314	0.0628	0.1259	0.2539	0.3863	0.5259	0.6766	0.8447	1.0411	1.2889	1.6580	1.9805	2.2707	2.359	2.6186	2.8613	3.3760
118	0.0006	0.0013	0.0063	0.0126	0.025	0.0314	0.0628	0.1259	0.2539	0.3863	0.5258	0.6766	0.8447	1.0410	1.2888	1.6579	1.9803	2.2704	2.358	2.6182	2.8608	3.3752
119	0.0006	0.0013	0.0063	0.0126	0.025	0.0314	0.0628	0.1259	0.2539	0.3863	0.5258	0.6766	0.8447	1.0410	1.2888	1.6578	1.9801	2.2702	2.358	2.6179	2.8604	3.3744
120	0.0006	0.0013	0.0063	0.0126	0.025	0.0314	0.0628	0.1259	0.2539	0.3862	0.5258	0.6765	0.8446	1.0409	1.2887	1.6577	1.9799	2.2699	2.358	2.6175	2.8599	3.3736
121	0.0006	0.0013	0.0063	0.0126	0.025	0.0314	0.0628	0.1259	0.2539	0.3862	0.5258	0.6765	0.8446	1.0409	1.2886	1.6576	1.9798	2.2697	2.357	2.6172	2.8595	3.3729
122	0.0006	0.0013	0.0063	0.0126	0.025	0.0314	0.0628	0.1259	0.2539	0.3862	0.5258	0.6765	0.8446	1.0409	1.2885	1.6575	1.9796	2.2694	2.357	2.6168	2.8591	3.3721
123	0.0006	0.0013	0.0063	0.0126	0.025	0.0314	0.0628	0.1259	0.2539	0.3862	0.5258	0.6765	0.8446	1.0409	1.2885	1.6574	1.9795	2.2692	2.357	2.6165	2.8587	3.3715
124	0.0006	0.0013	0.0063	0.0126	0.025	0.0314	0.0628	0.1259	0.2539	0.3862	0.5258	0.6765	0.8445	1.0408	1.2884	1.6573	1.9793	2.2690	2.357	2.6161	2.8582	3.3709
125	0.0006	0.0013	0.0063	0.0126	0.025	0.0314	0.0628	0.1259	0.2539	0.3862	0.5258	0.6765	0.8445	1.0408	1.2884	1.6572	1.9792	2.2688	2.356	2.6158	2.8578	3.3702
126	0.0006	0.0013	0.0063	0.0126	0.025	0.0314	0.0628	0.1259	0.2539	0.3862	0.5257	0.6765	0.8445	1.0407	1.2883	1.6571	1.9790	2.2685	2.356	2.6155	2.8574	3.3694
127	0.0006	0.0013	0.0063	0.0126	0.025	0.0314	0.0628	0.1259	0.2539	0.3862	0.5257	0.6765	0.8445	1.0407	1.2883	1.6570	1.9789	2.2683	2.356	2.6152	2.8570	3.3690
128	0.0006	0.0013	0.0063	0.0126	0.025	0.0314	0.0628	0.1259	0.2539	0.3862	0.5257	0.6764	0.8445	1.0407	1.2882	1.6569	1.9787	2.2681	2.356	2.6148	2.8566	3.3685
129	0.0006	0.0013	0.0063	0.0126	0.025	0.0314	0.0628	0.1259	0.2539	0.3862	0.5257	0.6764	0.8445	1.0407	1.2882	1.6568	1.9786	2.2679	2.355	2.6145	2.8562	3.3679
130	0.0006	0.0013	0.0063	0.0126	0.025	0.0314	0.0628	0.1259	0.2539	0.3862	0.5257	0.6764	0.8444	1.0406	1.2881	1.6567	1.9784	2.2677	2.355	2.6142	2.8558	3.3673
131	0.0006	0.0013	0.0063	0.0126	0.025	0.0314	0.0628	0.1259	0.2539	0.3862	0.5257	0.6764	0.8444	1.0406	1.2881	1.6566	1.9783	2.2675	2.355	2.6139	2.8555	3.3667
132	0.0006	0.0013	0.0063	0.0126	0.025	0.0314	0.0628	0.1259	0.2539	0.3862	0.5257	0.6764	0.8444	1.0405	1.2880	1.6565	1.9781	2.2673	2.355	2.6136	2.8551	3.3661
133	0.0006	0.0013	0.0063	0.0126	0.025	0.0314	0.0628	0.1259	0.2539	0.3862	0.5257	0.6764	0.8444	1.0405	1.2880	1.6564	1.9780	2.2671	2.355	2.6134	2.8548	3.3655
134	0.0006	0.0013	0.0063	0.0126	0.025	0.0314	0.0628	0.1259	0.2539	0.3862	0.5257	0.6763	0.8443	1.0405	1.2879	1.6563	1.9778	2.2669	2.354	2.6131	2.8544	3.3648
135	0.0006	0.0013	0.0063	0.0126	0.025	0.0314	0.0628	0.1259	0.2539	0.3862	0.5257	0.6763	0.8443	1.0405	1.2879	1.6563	1.9777	2.2667	2.354	2.6128	2.8540	3.3642
136	0.0006	0.0013	0.0063	0.0126	0.025	0.0314	0.0628	0.1259	0.2538	0.3861	0.5256	0.6763	0.8443	1.0404	1.2878	1.6562	1.9776	2.2665	2.354	2.6125	2.8536	3.3636
137	0.0006	0.0013	0.0063	0.0126	0.025	0.0314	0.0628	0.1259	0.2538	0.3861	0.5256	0.6763	0.8443	1.0404	1.2878	1.6561	1.9775	2.2664	2.354	2.6123	2.8533	3.3631
138	0.0006	0.0013	0.0063	0.0126	0.025	0.0314	0.0628	0.1259	0.2538	0.3861	0.5256	0.6763	0.8442	1.0403	1.2877	1.6560	1.9773	2.2662	2.354	2.6120	2.8529	3.3626
139	0.0006	0.0013	0.0063	0.0126	0.025	0.0314	0.0628	0.1259	0.2538	0.3861	0.5256	0.6763	0.8442	1.0403	1.2877	1.6559	1.9772	2.2660	2.353	2.6117	2.8526	3.3621
140	0.0006	0.0013	0.0063	0.0126	0.025	0.0314	0.0628	0.1259	0.2538	0.3861	0.5256	0.6763	0.8442	1.0403	1.2876	1.6558	1.9771	2.2658	2.353	2.6114	2.8523	3.3615
141	0.0006	0.0013	0.0063	0.0126	0.025	0.0314	0.0628	0.1259	0.2538	0.3861	0.5256	0.6763	0.8442	1.0403	1.2876	1.6558	1.9770	2.2657	2.353	2.6112	2.8520	3.3611
142	0.0006	0.0013	0.0063	0.0126	0.025	0.0314	0.0628	0.1259	0.2538	0.3861	0.5256	0.6762	0.8442	1.0402	1.2876	1.6557	1.9768	2.2655	2.353	2.6109	2.8516	3.3606
143	0.0006	0.0013	0.0063	0.0126	0.025	0.0314	0.0628	0.1259	0.2538	0.3861	0.5256	0.6762	0.8442	1.0402	1.2876	1.6556	1.9767	2.2653	2.353	2.6107	2.8513	3.3600
144	0.0006	0.0013	0.0063	0.0126	0.025	0.0314	0.0628	0.1259	0.2538	0.3861	0.5256	0.6762	0.8441	1.0402	1.2875	1.6555	1.9766	2.2651	2.352	2.6104	2.8510	3.3594
145	0.0006	0.0013	0.0063	0.0126	0.025	0.0314	0.0628	0.1259	0.2538	0.3861	0.5256	0.6762	0.8441	1.0402	1.2875	1.6555	1.9765	2.2650	2.352	2.6102	2.8507	3.3590
146	0.0006	0.0013	0.0063	0.0126	0.025	0.0314	0.0628	0.1259	0.2538	0.3861	0.5256	0.6762	0.8441	1.0401	1.2874	1.6554	1.9764	2.2648	2.352	2.6099	2.8504	3.3585
147	0.0006	0.0013	0.0063	0.0126	0.025	0.0314	0.0628	0.1259	0.2538	0.3861	0.5256	0.6762	0.8441	1.0401	1.2874	1.6553	1.9763	2.2647	2.352	2.6097	2.8501	3.3581
148	0.0006	0.0013	0.0063	0.0126	0.025	0.0314	0.0628	0.1259	0.2538	0.3861	0.5255	0.6762	0.8441	1.0401	1.2873	1.6552	1.9762	2.2645	2.352	2.6095	2.8498	3.3576
149	0.0006	0.0013	0.0063	0.0126	0.025	0.0314	0.0628	0.1259	0.2538	0.3861	0.5255	0.6762	0.8441	1.0401	1.2873	1.6552	1.9761	2.2644	2.352	2.6093	2.8495	3.3572
150	0.0006	0.0013	0.0063	0.0126	0.025	0.0314	0.0628	0.1259	0.2538	0.3861	0.5255	0.6761	0.8440	1.0400	1.2872	1.6551	1.9759	2.2642	2.351	2.6090	2.8492	3.3567

Significance Limits* of the Student Distribution ν = 151—200

P = *P* (right) = integral between *t* and infinity. *P* (left) = *P* (right)

2 *P*	0.9995	0.999	0.995	0.99	0.98	0.975	0.95	0.90	0.80	0.70	0.60	0.50	0.40	0.30	0.20	0.10	0.05	0.025	0.02	0.01	0.005	0.001
P	0.49975	0.4995	0.4975	0.495	0.49	0.4875	0.475	0.45	0.40	0.35	0.30	0.25	0.20	0.15	0.10	0.05	0.025	0.0125	0.01	0.005	0.0025	0.0005
ν																						
151	0.0006	0.0013	0.0063	0.0126	0.025	0.0314	0.0628	0.1259	0.2538	0.3861	0.5255	0.6761	0.8440	1.0400	1.2872	1.6551	1.9758	2.2641	2.351	2.6088	2.8490	3.3563
152	0.0006	0.0013	0.0063	0.0126	0.025	0.0314	0.0628	0.1259	0.2538	0.3861	0.5255	0.6761	0.8440	1.0400	1.2872	1.6550	1.9757	2.2639	2.351	2.6086	2.8487	3.3559
153	0.0006	0.0013	0.0063	0.0126	0.025	0.0314	0.0628	0.1259	0.2538	0.3861	0.5255	0.6761	0.8440	1.0400	1.2872	1.6549	1.9756	2.2638	2.351	2.6084	2.8484	3.3554
154	0.0006	0.0013	0.0063	0.0126	0.025	0.0314	0.0628	0.1259	0.2538	0.3860	0.5255	0.6761	0.8440	1.0399	1.2871	1.6548	1.9755	2.2636	2.351	2.6082	2.8481	3.3548
155	0.0006	0.0013	0.0063	0.0126	0.025	0.0314	0.0628	0.1259	0.2538	0.3860	0.5255	0.6761	0.8440	1.0399	1.2871	1.6548	1.9754	2.2635	2.351	2.6080	2.8478	3.3545
156	0.0006	0.0013	0.0063	0.0126	0.025	0.0314	0.0628	0.1259	0.2538	0.3860	0.5255	0.6761	0.8439	1.0399	1.2870	1.6547	1.9753	2.2633	2.350	2.6077	2.8475	3.3541
157	0.0006	0.0013	0.0063	0.0126	0.025	0.0314	0.0628	0.1259	0.2538	0.3860	0.5255	0.6761	0.8439	1.0399	1.2870	1.6547	1.9752	2.2632	2.350	2.6075	2.8473	3.3538
158	0.0006	0.0013	0.0063	0.0126	0.025	0.0314	0.0628	0.1259	0.2538	0.3860	0.5255	0.6761	0.8439	1.0398	1.2869	1.6546	1.9751	2.2630	2.350	2.6073	2.8471	3.3535
159	0.0006	0.0013	0.0063	0.0126	0.025	0.0314	0.0628	0.1259	0.2538	0.3860	0.5255	0.6761	0.8439	1.0398	1.2869	1.6546	1.9750	2.2629	2.350	2.6072	2.8468	3.3531
160	0.0006	0.0013	0.0063	0.0126	0.025	0.0314	0.0628	0.1259	0.2538	0.3860	0.5255	0.6760	0.8439	1.0398	1.2869	1.6545	1.9749	2.2627	2.350	2.6070	2.8465	3.3527
161	0.0006	0.0013	0.0063	0.0126	0.025	0.0314	0.0628	0.1259	0.2538	0.3860	0.5255	0.6760	0.8439	1.0398	1.2869	1.6544	1.9748	2.2626	2.350	2.6068	2.8463	3.3524
162	0.0006	0.0013	0.0063	0.0126	0.025	0.0314	0.0628	0.1259	0.2538	0.3860	0.5254	0.6760	0.8439	1.0398	1.2868	1.6543	1.9747	2.2625	2.349	2.6066	2.8461	3.3521
163	0.0006	0.0013	0.0063	0.0126	0.025	0.0314	0.0628	0.1259	0.2538	0.3860	0.5254	0.6760	0.8439	1.0398	1.2868	1.6543	1.9747	2.2624	2.349	2.6064	2.8459	3.3517
164	0.0006	0.0013	0.0063	0.0126	0.025	0.0314	0.0628	0.1259	0.2538	0.3860	0.5254	0.6760	0.8438	1.0397	1.2868	1.6542	1.9746	2.2622	2.349	2.6062	2.8456	3.3512
165	0.0006	0.0013	0.0063	0.0126	0.025	0.0314	0.0628	0.1259	0.2538	0.3860	0.5254	0.6760	0.8438	1.0397	1.2868	1.6542	1.9745	2.2621	2.349	2.6060	2.8454	3.3509
166	0.0006	0.0013	0.0063	0.0126	0.025	0.0314	0.0628	0.1259	0.2538	0.3860	0.5254	0.6760	0.8438	1.0397	1.2867	1.6541	1.9744	2.2619	2.349	2.6058	2.8451	3.3506
167	0.0006	0.0013	0.0063	0.0126	0.025	0.0314	0.0628	0.1259	0.2538	0.3860	0.5254	0.6760	0.8438	1.0397	1.2867	1.6541	1.9743	2.2618	2.349	2.6057	2.8449	3.3502
168	0.0006	0.0013	0.0063	0.0126	0.025	0.0314	0.0628	0.1259	0.2538	0.3860	0.5254	0.6760	0.8438	1.0396	1.2866	1.6540	1.9742	2.2617	2.349	2.6055	2.8447	3.3497
169	0.0006	0.0013	0.0063	0.0126	0.025	0.0314	0.0628	0.1259	0.2538	0.3860	0.5254	0.6760	0.8438	1.0396	1.2866	1.6540	1.9741	2.2616	2.348	2.6053	2.8445	3.3493
170	0.0006	0.0013	0.0063	0.0126	0.025	0.0314	0.0628	0.1259	0.2537	0.3860	0.5254	0.6759	0.8438	1.0396	1.2866	1.6539	1.9740	2.2615	2.348	2.6051	2.8442	3.3489
171	0.0006	0.0013	0.0063	0.0126	0.025	0.0314	0.0628	0.1259	0.2537	0.3860	0.5254	0.6759	0.8438	1.0396	1.2866	1.6539	1.9740	2.2614	2.348	2.6050	2.8440	3.3486
172	0.0006	0.0013	0.0063	0.0126	0.025	0.0314	0.0628	0.1258	0.2537	0.3860	0.5254	0.6759	0.8437	1.0396	1.2865	1.6538	1.9739	2.2612	2.348	2.6048	2.8438	3.3482
173	0.0006	0.0013	0.0063	0.0126	0.025	0.0314	0.0628	0.1258	0.2537	0.3860	0.5254	0.6759	0.8437	1.0396	1.2865	1.6538	1.9738	2.2611	2.348	2.6046	2.8436	3.3479
174	0.0006	0.0013	0.0063	0.0126	0.025	0.0314	0.0628	0.1258	0.2537	0.3860	0.5254	0.6759	0.8437	1.0395	1.2865	1.6537	1.9737	2.2610	2.348	2.6044	2.8434	3.3476
175	0.0006	0.0013	0.0063	0.0126	0.025	0.0314	0.0628	0.1258	0.2537	0.3860	0.5254	0.6759	0.8437	1.0395	1.2865	1.6537	1.9737	2.2609	2.348	2.6043	2.8432	3.3474
176	0.0006	0.0013	0.0063	0.0126	0.025	0.0314	0.0628	0.1258	0.2537	0.3860	0.5254	0.6759	0.8437	1.0395	1.2864	1.6536	1.9736	2.2608	2.348	2.6041	2.8430	3.3471
177	0.0006	0.0013	0.0063	0.0126	0.025	0.0314	0.0628	0.1258	0.2537	0.3860	0.5254	0.6759	0.8437	1.0395	1.2864	1.6536	1.9735	2.2607	2.347	2.6040	2.8428	3.3467
178	0.0006	0.0013	0.0063	0.0126	0.025	0.0314	0.0628	0.1258	0.2537	0.3859	0.5253	0.6759	0.8437	1.0395	1.2863	1.6535	1.9734	2.2605	2.347	2.6038	2.8426	3.3462
179	0.0006	0.0013	0.0063	0.0126	0.025	0.0314	0.0628	0.1258	0.2537	0.3859	0.5253	0.6759	0.8437	1.0395	1.2863	1.6535	1.9734	2.2604	2.347	2.6037	2.8424	3.3459
180	0.0006	0.0013	0.0063	0.0126	0.025	0.0314	0.0628	0.1258	0.2537	0.3859	0.5253	0.6759	0.8436	1.0394	1.2863	1.6534	1.9733	2.2603	2.347	2.6035	2.8421	3.3456
181	0.0006	0.0013	0.0063	0.0126	0.025	0.0314	0.0628	0.1258	0.2537	0.3859	0.5253	0.6759	0.8436	1.0394	1.2863	1.6534	1.9732	2.2602	2.347	2.6034	2.8419	3.3453
182	0.0006	0.0013	0.0063	0.0126	0.025	0.0314	0.0628	0.1258	0.2537	0.3859	0.5253	0.6758	0.8436	1.0394	1.2862	1.6533	1.9731	2.2601	2.347	2.6032	2.8417	3.3450
183	0.0006	0.0013	0.0063	0.0126	0.025	0.0314	0.0628	0.1258	0.2537	0.3859	0.5253	0.6758	0.8436	1.0394	1.2862	1.6533	1.9731	2.2600	2.347	2.6031	2.8416	3.3447
184	0.0006	0.0013	0.0063	0.0126	0.025	0.0314	0.0628	0.1258	0.2537	0.3859	0.5253	0.6758	0.8436	1.0394	1.2862	1.6532	1.9730	2.2599	2.347	2.6029	2.8414	3.3444
185	0.0006	0.0013	0.0063	0.0126	0.025	0.0314	0.0623	0.1258	0.2537	0.3859	0.5253	0.6758	0.8436	1.0394	1.2862	1.6532	1.9729	2.2598	2.346	2.6028	2.8412	3.3441
186	0.0006	0.0013	0.0063	0.0126	0.025	0.0314	0.0623	0.1258	0.2537	0.3859	0.5253	0.6758	0.8436	1.0393	1.2861	1.6531	1.9728	2.2597	2.346	2.6026	2.8410	3.3438
187	0.0006	0.0013	0.0063	0.0126	0.025	0.0314	0.0623	0.1258	0.2537	0.3859	0.5253	0.6758	0.8436	1.0393	1.2861	1.6531	1.9728	2.2596	2.346	2.6025	2.8408	3.3435
188	0.0006	0.0013	0.0063	0.0126	0.025	0.0314	0.0623	0.1258	0.2537	0.3859	0.5253	0.6758	0.8435	1.0393	1.2861	1.6530	1.9727	2.2595	2.346	2.6023	2.8406	3.3432
189	0.0006	0.0013	0.0063	0.0126	0.025	0.0314	0.0623	0.1258	0.2537	0.3859	0.5253	0.6758	0.8435	1.0393	1.2861	1.6530	1.9727	2.2594	2.346	2.6022	2.8405	3.3429
190	0.0006	0.0013	0.0063	0.0126	0.025	0.0314	0.0623	0.1258	0.2537	0.3859	0.5253	0.6758	0.8435	1.0393	1.2860	1.6529	1.9726	2.2593	2.346	2.6020	2.8403	3.3426
191	0.0006	0.0013	0.0063	0.0126	0.025	0.0314	0.0623	0.1258	0.2537	0.3859	0.5253	0.6758	0.8435	1.0393	1.2860	1.6529	1.9725	2.2592	2.346	2.6019	2.8401	3.3424
192	0.0006	0.0013	0.0063	0.0126	0.025	0.0314	0.0623	0.1258	0.2537	0.3859	0.5253	0.6758	0.8435	1.0392	1.2860	1.6528	1.9724	2.2591	2.346	2.6017	2.8399	3.3421
193	0.0006	0.0013	0.0063	0.0126	0.025	0.0314	0.0623	0.1258	0.2537	0.3859	0.5253	0.6758	0.8435	1.0392	1.2860	1.6528	1.9724	2.2591	2.346	2.6016	2.8397	3.3418
194	0.0006	0.0013	0.0063	0.0126	0.025	0.0314	0.0623	0.1258	0.2537	0.3859	0.5253	0.6758	0.8435	1.0392	1.2859	1.6528	1.9723	2.2590	2.346	2.6015	2.8395	3.3415
195	0.0006	0.0013	0.0063	0.0126	0.025	0.0314	0.0628	0.1258	0.2537	0.3859	0.5253	0.6758	0.8435	1.0392	1.2859	1.6528	1.9723	2.2589	2.345	2.6014	2.8394	3.3414
196	0.0006	0.0013	0.0063	0.0126	0.025	0.0314	0.0628	0.1258	0.2537	0.3859	0.5253	0.6758	0.8435	1.0392	1.2859	1.6527	1.9722	2.2588	2.345	2.6012	2.8392	3.3412
197	0.0006	0.0013	0.0063	0.0126	0.025	0.0314	0.0628	0.1258	0.2537	0.3859	0.5253	0.6758	0.8435	1.0392	1.2859	1.6527	1.9721	2.2587	2.345	2.6011	2.8391	3.3409
198	0.0006	0.0013	0.0063	0.0126	0.025	0.0314	0.0628	0.1258	0.2537	0.3859	0.5253	0.6757	0.8435	1.0392	1.2859	1.6526	1.9720	2.2586	2.345	2.6009	2.8389	3.3406
199	0.0006	0.0013	0.0063	0.0126	0.025	0.0314	0.0628	0.1258	0.2537	0.3859	0.5253	0.6757	0.8435	1.0392	1.2859	1.6526	1.9720	2.2585	2.345	2.6008	2.8388	3.3403
200	0.0006	0.0013	0.0063	0.0125	0.025	0.0314	0.0628	0.1258	0.2537	0.3859	0.5252	0.6757	0.8434	1.0391	1.2858	1.6525	1.9719	2.2584	2.345	2.6006	2.8386	3.3400

Significance Limits[1] of the χ^2 Distribution $\nu = 1-50$

$\int_r$ = integral between χ^2 and infinity ($1 \int_r = 2\alpha$, $\frac{1}{2}\int_r = \alpha$ in χ^2 tests), $\int_1$ = integral between zero and χ^2

$\int_r$ 1	0.99950	0.9990	0.9950	0.990	0.9750	0.950	0.90	0.80	0.70	0.60	0.50	0.40	0.30	0.20	0.10	0.050	0.0250	0.010	0.0050	0.0010	0.00050
$\int_r$ ½	0.49975	0.4995	0.4975	0.495	0.4875	0.475	0.45	0.40	0.35	0.30	0.25	0.20	0.15	0.10	0.05	0.025	0.0125	0.005	0.0025	0.0005	0.00025
$\int_1$ 1	0.00050	0.0010	0.0050	0.010	0.0250	0.050	0.10	0.20	0.30	0.40	0.50	0.60	0.70	0.80	0.90	0.950	0.9750	0.990	0.9950	0.9990	0.99950
$\int_1$ ½	0.00025	0.0005	0.0025	0.005	0.0125	0.025	0.05	0.10	0.15	0.20	0.25	0.30	0.35	0.40	0.45	0.475	0.4875	0.495	0.4975	0.4995	0.49975
ν																					
1	0.000000393	0.00000157	0.0000393	0.000157	0.000982	0.00393	0.0158	0.0642	0.148	0.275	0.455	0.708	1.074	1.642	2.706	3.841	5.024	6.635	7.879	10.828	12.116
2	0.00100	0.00200	0.0100	0.0201	0.0506	0.103	0.211	0.446	0.713	1.022	1.386	1.833	2.408	3.219	4.605	5.991	7.378	9.210	10.597	13.816	15.202
3	0.0153	0.0243	0.0717	0.115	0.216	0.352	0.584	1.005	1.424	1.869	2.366	2.946	3.665	4.642	6.251	7.815	9.348	11.345	12.838	16.266	17.730
4	0.0639	0.0908	0.207	0.297	0.484	0.711	1.064	1.649	2.195	2.753	3.357	4.045	4.878	5.989	7.779	9.488	11.143	13.277	14.860	18.467	19.998
5	0.158	0.210	0.412	0.554	0.831	1.145	1.610	2.343	3.000	3.655	4.351	5.132	6.064	7.289	9.236	11.070	12.832	15.086	16.750	20.515	22.105
6	0.299	0.381	0.676	0.872	1.237	1.635	2.204	3.070	3.828	4.570	5.348	6.211	7.231	8.558	10.645	12.592	14.449	16.812	18.548	22.458	24.103
7	0.485	0.598	0.989	1.239	1.690	2.167	2.833	3.822	4.671	5.493	6.346	7.283	8.383	9.803	12.017	14.067	16.013	18.475	20.278	24.322	26.018
8	0.710	0.857	1.344	1.646	2.180	2.733	3.490	4.594	5.527	6.423	7.344	8.351	9.524	11.030	13.362	15.507	17.535	20.090	21.955	26.125	27.868
9	0.972	1.153	1.735	2.088	2.700	3.325	4.168	5.380	6.393	7.357	8.343	9.414	10.656	12.242	14.684	16.919	19.023	21.666	23.589	27.877	29.666
10	1.265	1.479	2.156	2.558	3.247	3.940	4.865	6.179	7.267	8.295	9.342	10.473	11.781	13.442	15.987	18.307	20.483	23.209	25.188	29.588	31.419
11	1.587	1.834	2.603	3.053	3.816	4.575	5.578	6.989	8.148	9.237	10.341	11.530	12.899	14.631	17.275	19.675	21.920	24.725	26.757	31.264	33.136
12	1.934	2.214	3.074	3.571	4.404	5.226	6.304	7.807	9.034	10.182	11.340	12.584	14.011	15.812	18.549	21.026	23.336	26.217	28.300	32.909	34.821
13	2.305	2.617	3.565	4.107	5.009	5.892	7.042	8.634	9.926	11.129	12.340	13.636	15.119	16.985	19.812	22.362	24.736	27.688	29.819	34.528	36.478
14	2.697	3.041	4.075	4.660	5.629	6.571	7.790	9.467	10.821	12.079	13.339	14.685	16.222	18.151	21.064	23.685	26.119	29.141	31.319	36.123	38.109
15	3.108	3.483	4.601	5.229	6.262	7.261	8.547	10.307	11.721	13.030	14.339	15.733	17.322	19.311	22.307	24.996	27.488	30.578	32.801	37.697	39.719
16	3.536	3.942	5.142	5.812	6.908	7.962	9.312	11.152	12.624	13.983	15.338	16.780	18.418	20.465	23.542	26.296	28.845	32.000	34.267	39.252	41.308
17	3.980	4.416	5.697	6.408	7.564	8.672	10.085	12.002	13.531	14.937	16.338	17.824	19.511	21.615	24.769	27.587	30.191	33.409	35.718	40.790	42.879
18	4.439	4.905	6.265	7.015	8.231	9.390	10.865	12.857	14.440	15.893	17.338	18.868	20.601	22.760	25.989	28.869	31.526	34.805	37.156	42.312	44.434
19	4.912	5.407	6.844	7.633	8.907	10.117	11.651	13.716	15.352	16.850	18.338	19.910	21.689	23.900	27.204	30.144	32.852	36.191	38.582	43.820	45.973
20	5.398	5.921	7.434	8.260	9.591	10.851	12.443	14.578	16.266	17.809	19.337	20.951	22.775	25.038	28.412	31.410	34.170	37.566	39.997	45.315	47.498
21	5.896	6.447	8.034	8.897	10.283	11.591	13.240	15.445	17.182	18.768	20.337	21.991	23.858	26.171	29.615	32.671	35.479	38.932	41.401	46.797	49.010
22	6.405	6.983	8.643	9.542	10.982	12.338	14.041	16.314	18.101	19.729	21.337	23.031	24.939	27.301	30.813	33.924	36.781	40.289	42.796	48.268	50.511
23	6.924	7.529	9.260	10.196	11.688	13.091	14.848	17.187	19.021	20.690	22.337	24.069	26.018	28.429	32.007	35.172	38.076	41.638	44.181	49.728	52.000
24	7.453	8.085	9.886	10.856	12.401	13.848	15.659	18.062	19.943	21.652	23.337	25.106	27.096	29.553	33.196	36.415	39.364	42.980	45.558	51.179	53.479
25	7.991	8.649	10.520	11.524	13.120	14.611	16.473	18.940	20.867	22.616	24.337	26.143	28.172	30.675	34.382	37.652	40.646	44.314	46.928	52.620	54.947
26	8.538	9.222	11.160	12.198	13.844	15.379	17.292	19.820	21.792	23.579	25.336	27.179	29.246	31.795	35.563	38.885	41.923	45.642	48.290	54.052	56.407
27	9.093	9.803	11.808	12.879	14.573	16.151	18.114	20.703	22.719	24.544	26.336	28.214	30.319	32.912	36.741	40.113	43.194	46.963	49.645	55.476	57.858
28	9.656	10.391	12.461	13.565	15.308	16.928	18.939	21.588	23.647	25.509	27.336	29.249	31.391	34.027	37.916	41.337	44.461	48.278	50.993	56.892	59.300
29	10.227	10.986	13.121	14.256	16.047	17.708	19.768	22.475	24.577	26.475	28.336	30.283	32.461	35.139	39.087	42.557	45.722	49.588	52.336	58.302	60.734
30	10.804	11.588	13.787	14.953	16.791	18.493	20.599	23.364	25.508	27.442	29.336	31.316	33.530	36.250	40.256	43.773	46.979	50.892	53.672	59.703	62.161
31	11.389	12.196	14.458	15.655	17.539	19.281	21.434	24.255	26.440	28.409	30.336	32.349	34.598	37.359	41.422	44.985	48.232	52.191	55.003	61.098	63.582
32	11.979	12.811	15.134	16.362	18.291	20.072	22.271	25.148	27.373	29.376	31.336	33.381	35.665	38.466	42.585	46.194	49.480	53.486	56.328	62.487	64.995
33	12.576	13.431	15.815	17.073	19.047	20.867	23.110	26.042	28.307	30.344	32.336	34.413	36.731	39.572	43.745	47.400	50.725	54.776	57.648	63.870	66.402
34	13.179	14.057	16.501	17.789	19.806	21.664	23.952	26.938	29.242	31.313	33.336	35.444	37.795	40.676	44.903	48.602	51.966	56.061	58.964	65.247	67.803
35	13.788	14.688	17.192	18.509	20.569	22.465	24.797	27.836	30.178	32.282	34.336	36.475	38.859	41.778	46.059	49.802	53.203	57.342	60.275	66.619	69.198
36	14.401	15.324	17.887	19.233	21.336	23.269	25.643	28.735	31.115	33.252	35.336	37.505	39.922	42.879	47.212	50.998	54.437	58.619	61.581	67.985	70.588
37	15.020	15.965	18.586	19.960	22.106	24.075	26.492	29.635	32.053	34.222	36.336	38.535	40.984	43.978	48.363	52.192	55.668	59.892	62.883	69.346	71.972
38	15.644	16.611	19.289	20.691	22.878	24.884	27.343	30.537	32.992	35.192	37.335	39.564	42.045	45.076	49.513	53.384	56.895	61.162	64.181	70.703	73.351
39	16.273	17.261	19.996	21.426	23.654	25.695	28.196	31.441	33.932	36.163	38.335	40.593	43.105	46.173	50.660	54.572	58.120	62.428	65.476	72.055	74.725
40	16.906	17.916	20.707	22.164	24.433	26.509	29.051	32.345	34.872	37.134	39.335	41.622	44.165	47.269	51.805	55.758	59.342	63.691	66.766	73.402	76.095
41	17.544	18.575	21.421	22.906	25.215	27.326	29.907	33.251	35.813	38.105	40.335	42.651	45.224	48.363	52.949	56.942	60.561	64.950	68.053	74.745	77.459
42	18.186	19.238	22.138	23.650	25.999	28.144	30.765	34.157	36.755	39.077	41.335	43.679	46.282	49.456	54.090	58.124	61.777	66.206	69.336	76.084	78.820
43	18.832	19.905	22.859	24.398	26.785	28.965	31.625	35.065	37.698	40.050	42.335	44.706	47.339	50.548	55.230	59.304	62.990	67.459	70.616	77.418	80.176
44	19.482	20.576	23.584	25.148	27.575	29.787	32.487	35.974	38.641	41.022	43.335	45.734	48.396	51.639	56.369	60.481	64.201	68.709	71.893	78.749	81.528
45	20.136	21.251	24.311	25.901	28.366	30.612	33.350	36.884	39.585	41.995	44.335	46.761	49.452	52.729	57.505	61.656	65.410	69.957	73.166	80.077	82.876
46	20.794	21.929	25.041	26.657	29.160	31.439	34.215	37.795	40.529	42.968	45.335	47.787	50.507	53.818	58.641	62.830	66.617	71.201	74.437	81.400	84.220
47	21.456	22.610	25.774	27.416	29.956	32.268	35.081	38.708	41.474	43.942	46.335	48.814	51.562	54.906	59.774	64.001	67.821	72.443	75.704	82.720	85.560
48	22.121	23.295	26.511	28.177	30.755	33.098	35.949	39.621	42.420	44.915	47.335	49.840	52.616	55.993	60.907	65.171	69.023	73.683	76.969	84.037	86.897
49	22.789	23.983	27.249	28.941	31.555	33.930	36.818	40.534	43.366	45.889	48.335	50.866	53.670	57.079	62.038	66.339	70.222	74.919	78.231	85.350	88.231
50	23.461	24.674	27.991	29.707	32.357	34.764	37.689	41.449	44.313	46.864	49.335	51.892	54.723	58.164	63.167	67.505	71.420	76.154	79.490	86.661	89.561

[1] Values from HALD and SINKBÆK, *Skand. Aktuar Tidskr.*, 33, 168 (1950). Reprinted by kind permission of the authors and publishers.

Significance Limits[1] of the χ^2 Distribution $\nu = 51–100$

$\int_r$ = integral between χ^2 and infinity ($1\int_r = 2\alpha$, $\frac{1}{2}\int_r = \alpha$ in χ^2 tests), $\int_1$ = integral between zero and χ^2

$\int_r$ 1	0.99950	0.9990	0.9950	0.990	0.9750	0.950	0.90	0.80	0.70	0.60	0.50	0.40	0.30	0.20	0.10	0.050	0.0250	0.010	0.0050	0.0010	0.00050
$\int_r$ ½	0.49975	0.4995	0.4975	0.495	0.4875	0.475	0.45	0.40	0.35	0.30	0.25	0.20	0.15	0.10	0.05	0.025	0.0125	0.005	0.0025	0.0005	0.00025
$\int_1$ 1	0.00050	0.0010	0.0050	0.010	0.0250	0.050	0.10	0.20	0.30	0.40	0.50	0.60	0.70	0.80	0.90	0.950	0.9750	0.990	0.9950	0.9990	0.99950
$\int_1$ ½	0.00025	0.0005	0.0025	0.005	0.0125	0.025	0.05	0.10	0.15	0.20	0.25	0.30	0.35	0.40	0.45	0.475	0.4875	0.495	0.4975	0.4995	0.49975
ν																					
51	24.136	25.368	28.735	30.475	33.162	35.600	38.560	42.365	45.261	47.838	50.335	52.917	55.775	59.248	64.295	68.669	72.616	77.386	80.747	87.968	90.887
52	24.814	26.065	29.481	31.246	33.968	35.437	39.433	43.281	46.209	48.813	51.335	53.942	56.827	60.332	65.422	69.832	73.810	78.616	82.001	89.272	92.211
53	25.495	26.765	30.230	32.018	34.776	37.276	40.308	44.199	47.157	49.788	52.335	54.967	57.879	61.414	66.548	70.993	75.002	79.843	83.253	90.573	93.532
54	26.179	27.468	30.981	32.793	35.586	38.116	41.183	45.117	48.106	50.764	53.335	55.992	58.930	62.496	67.673	72.153	76.192	81.069	84.502	91.872	94.849
55	26.866	28.173	31.735	33.570	36.398	38.958	42.060	46.036	49.056	51.739	54.335	57.016	59.980	63.577	68.796	73.311	77.380	82.292	85.749	93.167	96.163
56	27.556	28.881	32.490	34.350	37.212	39.801	42.937	46.955	50.005	52.715	55.335	58.040	61.031	64.658	69.918	74.468	78.567	83.513	86.994	94.460	97.475
57	28.248	29.592	33.248	35.131	38.027	40.646	43.816	47.876	50.956	53.691	56.335	59.064	62.080	65.737	71.040	75.624	79.752	84.733	88.236	95.751	98.784
58	28.943	30.305	34.008	35.913	38.844	41.492	44.696	48.797	51.906	54.667	57.335	60.088	63.129	66.816	72.160	76.778	80.936	85.950	89.477	97.039	100.090
59	29.640	31.021	34.771	36.698	39.662	42.339	45.577	49.718	52.857	55.643	58.335	61.111	64.178	67.894	73.279	77.931	82.117	87.166	90.715	98.324	101.394
60	30.340	31.739	35.535	37.485	40.482	43.188	46.459	50.641	53.809	56.620	59.335	62.135	65.226	68.972	74.397	79.082	83.298	88.379	91.952	99.607	102.695
61	31.043	32.459	36.301	38.273	41.303	44.038	47.342	51.564	54.761	57.597	60.335	63.158	66.274	70.049	75.514	80.232	84.476	89.591	93.186	100.888	103.993
62	31.748	33.181	37.068	39.063	42.126	44.889	48.226	52.487	55.714	58.574	61.335	64.181	67.322	71.125	76.630	81.381	85.654	90.802	94.419	102.166	105.289
63	32.455	33.906	37.838	39.855	42.950	45.741	49.111	53.411	56.666	59.551	62.335	65.204	68.369	72.201	77.745	82.529	86.830	92.010	95.649	103.442	106.583
64	33.165	34.633	38.610	40.649	43.776	46.595	49.996	54.336	57.619	60.528	63.335	66.226	69.416	73.276	78.860	83.675	88.004	93.217	96.878	104.716	107.874
65	33.877	35.362	39.383	41.444	44.603	47.450	50.883	55.262	58.573	61.506	64.335	67.249	70.462	74.351	79.973	84.821	89.177	94.422	98.105	105.988	109.164
66	34.591	36.093	40.158	42.240	45.431	48.305	51.770	56.188	59.527	62.484	65.335	68.271	71.508	75.425	81.086	85.965	90.349	95.626	99.330	107.258	110.451
67	35.307	36.826	40.935	43.038	46.261	49.162	52.659	57.115	60.481	63.461	66.335	69.293	72.554	76.498	82.197	87.108	91.519	96.828	100.554	108.525	111.735
68	36.025	37.561	41.713	43.838	47.092	50.020	53.548	58.042	61.436	64.440	67.334	70.315	73.600	77.571	83.308	88.250	92.688	98.028	101.776	109.791	113.018
69	36.745	38.298	42.494	44.639	47.924	50.879	54.438	58.970	62.391	65.418	68.334	71.337	74.645	78.643	84.418	89.391	93.856	99.227	102.996	111.055	114.299
70	37.467	39.036	43.275	45.442	48.758	51.739	55.329	59.898	63.346	66.396	69.334	72.358	75.689	79.715	85.527	90.531	95.023	100.425	104.215	112.317	115.577
71	38.192	39.777	44.058	46.246	49.592	52.600	56.221	60.827	64.302	67.375	70.334	73.380	76.734	80.786	86.635	91.670	96.189	101.621	105.432	113.577	116.854
72	38.918	40.520	44.843	47.051	50.428	53.462	57.113	61.756	65.258	68.353	71.334	74.401	77.778	81.857	87.743	92.808	97.353	102.816	106.648	114.835	118.129
73	39.646	41.264	45.629	47.858	51.265	54.325	58.006	62.686	66.214	69.332	72.334	75.422	78.822	82.927	88.850	93.945	98.516	104.010	107.862	116.091	119.402
74	40.376	42.010	46.417	48.666	52.103	55.189	58.900	63.616	67.170	70.311	73.334	76.443	79.865	83.997	89.956	95.081	99.678	105.202	109.074	117.346	120.673
75	41.107	42.757	47.206	49.475	52.942	56.054	59.795	64.547	68.127	71.290	74.334	77.464	80.908	85.066	91.061	96.217	100.839	106.393	110.286	118.599	121.942
76	41.841	43.506	47.998	50.286	53.782	56.920	60.690	65.478	69.084	72.270	75.334	78.485	81.951	86.135	92.166	97.351	101.999	107.583	111.495	119.851	123.209
77	42.576	44.257	48.788	51.097	54.623	57.786	61.586	66.409	70.042	73.249	76.334	79.505	82.994	87.203	93.270	98.484	103.158	108.771	112.704	121.100	124.475
78	43.313	45.010	49.582	51.910	55.466	58.654	62.483	67.341	70.999	74.228	77.334	80.526	84.036	88.271	94.374	99.617	104.316	109.958	113.911	122.348	125.739
79	44.051	45.764	50.376	52.725	56.309	59.522	63.380	68.274	71.957	75.208	78.334	81.546	85.078	89.338	95.476	100.749	105.473	111.144	115.117	123.594	127.001
80	44.791	46.520	51.172	53.540	57.153	60.391	64.278	69.207	72.915	76.188	79.334	82.566	86.120	90.405	96.578	101.879	106.629	112.329	116.321	124.839	128.261
81	45.533	47.277	51.969	54.357	57.998	61.261	65.176	70.140	73.874	77.168	80.334	83.586	87.161	91.472	97.680	103.009	107.783	113.512	117.524	126.083	129.520
82	46.276	48.036	52.767	55.174	58.845	62.132	66.076	71.074	74.833	78.148	81.334	84.606	88.202	92.538	98.780	104.139	108.937	114.695	118.726	127.324	130.777
83	47.021	48.796	53.567	55.993	59.692	63.004	66.976	72.008	75.792	79.128	82.334	85.626	89.243	93.604	99.880	105.267	110.090	115.876	119.927	128.565	132.033
84	47.767	49.557	54.368	56.813	60.540	63.876	67.876	72.943	76.751	80.108	83.334	86.646	90.284	94.669	100.980	106.395	111.242	117.057	121.126	129.804	133.287
85	48.515	50.320	55.170	57.634	61.389	64.749	68.777	73.878	77.710	81.089	84.334	87.665	91.325	95.734	102.079	107.522	112.393	118.236	122.325	131.041	134.540
86	49.264	51.085	55.973	58.456	62.239	65.623	69.679	74.813	78.670	82.069	85.334	88.685	92.365	96.799	103.177	108.648	113.544	119.414	123.522	132.277	135.792
87	50.015	51.850	56.777	59.279	63.089	66.498	70.581	75.749	79.630	83.050	86.334	89.704	93.405	97.863	104.275	109.773	114.693	120.591	124.718	133.512	137.042
88	50.767	52.617	57.582	60.103	63.941	67.373	71.484	76.685	80.590	84.031	87.334	90.723	94.445	98.927	105.372	110.898	115.841	121.767	125.912	134.745	138.290
89	51.521	53.386	58.389	60.928	64.793	68.249	72.387	77.622	81.550	85.012	88.334	91.742	95.484	99.991	106.469	112.022	116.989	122.942	127.106	135.977	139.537
90	52.276	54.155	59.196	61.754	65.647	69.126	73.291	78.558	82.511	85.993	89.334	92.761	96.524	101.054	107.565	113.145	118.136	124.116	128.299	137.208	140.783
91	53.032	54.926	60.005	62.581	66.501	70.003	74.196	79.496	83.472	86.974	90.334	93.780	97.563	102.116	108.661	114.268	119.282	125.289	129.491	138.438	142.027
92	53.790	55.698	60.815	63.409	67.356	70.882	75.101	80.433	84.433	87.955	91.334	94.799	98.602	103.179	109.756	115.390	120.427	126.462	130.681	139.666	143.270
93	54.549	56.471	61.625	64.238	68.211	71.760	76.006	81.371	85.394	88.936	92.334	95.818	99.641	104.242	110.850	116.511	121.571	127.633	131.871	140.893	144.511
94	55.309	57.246	62.437	65.068	69.068	72.640	76.912	82.309	86.356	89.917	93.334	96.836	100.679	105.303	111.944	117.632	122.715	128.803	133.059	142.119	145.751
95	56.070	58.022	63.250	65.898	69.925	73.520	77.818	83.248	87.317	90.899	94.334	97.855	101.717	106.364	113.038	118.752	123.858	129.973	134.247	143.343	146.990
96	56.833	58.799	64.063	66.730	70.783	74.400	78.725	84.187	88.279	91.881	95.334	98.873	102.755	107.425	114.131	119.871	125.000	131.141	135.433	144.567	148.228
97	57.597	59.577	64.878	67.562	71.642	75.282	79.633	85.126	89.241	92.862	96.334	99.892	103.793	108.486	115.223	120.990	126.141	132.309	136.619	145.789	149.464
98	58.362	60.356	65.694	68.396	72.501	76.164	80.541	86.065	90.204	93.844	97.334	100.910	104.831	109.547	116.315	122.108	127.282	133.476	137.803	147.010	150.699
99	59.128	61.136	66.510	69.230	73.361	77.046	81.449	87.005	91.166	94.826	98.334	101.928	105.868	110.607	117.406	123.225	128.422	134.642	138.987	148.230	151.934
100	59.897	61.919	67.328	70.065	74.222	77.930	82.358	87.945	92.129	95.808	99.334	102.946	106.906	111.667	118.498	124.342	129.561	135.806	140.169	149.448	153.165

[1] Values from HALD and SINKBÆK, *Skand. Aktuar Tidskr.*, 33, 168 (1950). Reprinted by kind permission of the authors and publishers.

Significance Limits* of the χ^2 Distribution $\nu = 101$—150

$\int_r$ = integral between χ^2 and infinity ($1\int_r = 2\alpha$, $\frac{1}{2}\int_r = \alpha$ in χ^2 tests), $\int_1$ = integral between zero and χ^2

$\int_r$ 1 / ½	0.99950 0.49975	0.9990 0.4995	0.9950 0.4975	0.990 0.495	0.9750 0.4875	0.950 0.475	0.90 0.45	0.80 0.40	0.70 0.35	0.60 0.30	0.50 0.25	0.40 0.20	0.30 0.15	0.20 0.10	0.10 0.05	0.050 0.025	0.0250 0.0125	0.010 0.005	0.0050 0.0025	0.0010 0.0005	0.00050 0.00025
$\int_1$ 1 / ½	0.00050 0.00025	0.0010 0.0005	0.0050 0.0025	0.010 0.005	0.0250 0.0125	0.050 0.025	0.10 0.05	0.20 0.10	0.30 0.15	0.40 0.20	0.50 0.25	0.60 0.30	0.70 0.35	0.80 0.40	0.90 0.45	0.950 0.475	0.9750 0.4875	0.990 0.495	0.9950 0.4975	0.9990 0.4995	0.99950 0.49975
ν																					
101	60.666	62.702	68.147	70.901	75.084	78.813	83.267	88.886	93.092	96.790	100.334	103.964	107.943	112.726	119.589	125.458	130.700	136.971	141.351	150.666	154.397
102	61.436	63.485	68.966	71.738	75.946	79.698	84.177	89.826	94.055	97.772	101.334	104.982	108.980	113.786	120.679	126.574	131.837	138.134	142.532	151.883	155.628
103	62.207	64.270	69.786	72.575	76.809	80.582	85.088	90.767	95.018	98.754	102.334	105.999	110.017	114.845	121.769	127.689	132.975	139.297	143.712	153.098	156.857
104	62.978	65.056	70.607	73.413	77.672	81.468	85.998	91.709	95.981	99.737	103.334	107.017	111.053	115.903	122.858	128.804	134.111	140.459	144.891	154.313	158.086
105	63.752	65.842	71.429	74.252	78.537	82.354	86.909	92.650	96.945	100.719	104.334	108.035	112.090	116.962	123.947	129.918	135.247	141.620	146.069	155.527	159.313
106	64.526	66.630	72.252	75.092	79.401	83.240	87.821	93.592	97.909	101.701	105.334	109.052	113.126	118.020	125.035	131.031	136.382	142.780	147.246	156.739	160.539
107	65.301	67.419	73.075	75.933	80.267	84.127	88.733	94.534	98.873	102.684	106.334	110.070	114.162	119.078	126.123	132.144	137.517	143.940	148.423	157.951	161.765
108	66.077	68.208	73.899	76.774	81.133	85.015	89.645	95.477	99.837	103.667	107.334	111.087	115.198	120.135	127.211	133.257	138.650	145.099	149.599	159.161	162.989
109	66.854	68.999	74.725	77.616	82.000	85.903	90.558	96.419	100.801	104.649	108.334	112.104	116.233	121.193	128.298	134.369	139.784	146.257	150.774	160.371	164.212
110	67.632	69.791	75.551	78.459	82.867	86.792	91.471	97.362	101.766	105.632	109.334	113.121	117.269	122.250	129.385	135.480	140.916	147.414	151.948	161.580	165.434
111	68.412	70.583	76.377	79.302	83.735	87.681	92.385	98.306	102.730	106.615	110.334	114.138	118.304	123.306	130.472	136.591	142.048	148.571	153.121	162.787	166.655
112	69.192	71.377	77.205	80.146	84.604	88.570	93.299	99.249	103.695	107.598	111.334	115.156	119.340	124.363	131.558	137.701	143.180	149.727	154.294	163.994	167.875
113	69.973	72.171	78.033	80.991	85.473	89.461	94.213	100.193	104.660	108.581	112.334	116.172	120.375	125.419	132.643	138.811	144.311	150.882	155.466	165.200	169.094
114	70.755	72.966	78.862	81.837	86.343	90.351	95.128	101.137	105.625	109.564	113.334	117.189	121.410	126.475	133.729	139.921	145.441	152.036	156.637	166.405	170.312
115	71.538	73.762	79.692	82.683	87.213	91.242	96.043	102.081	106.590	110.547	114.334	118.206	122.444	127.531	134.813	141.030	146.571	153.190	157.807	167.609	171.530
116	72.322	74.559	80.523	83.530	88.084	92.134	96.958	103.025	107.556	111.531	115.334	119.223	123.479	128.587	135.898	142.138	147.700	154.344	158.977	168.812	172.746
117	73.107	75.357	81.354	84.377	88.955	93.026	97.874	103.970	108.521	112.514	116.334	120.239	124.513	129.642	136.982	143.246	148.829	155.496	160.146	170.015	173.961
118	73.893	76.156	82.186	85.225	89.827	93.918	98.790	104.915	109.487	113.497	117.334	121.256	125.548	130.697	138.066	144.354	149.957	156.648	161.314	171.216	175.176
119	74.680	76.956	83.019	86.074	90.700	94.811	99.707	105.860	110.453	114.481	118.334	122.273	126.582	131.752	139.149	145.461	151.084	157.799	162.481	172.417	176.389
120	75.468	77.756	83.852	86.924	91.573	95.705	100.624	106.806	111.419	115.465	119.334	123.289	127.616	132.806	140.233	146.567	152.211	158.950	163.648	173.617	177.602
121	76.256	78.557	84.686	87.774	92.446	96.599	101.541	107.751	112.385	116.448	120.334	124.305	128.650	133.861	141.315	147.673	153.338	160.100	164.814	174.815	178.813
122	77.046	79.360	85.521	88.624	93.320	97.493	102.458	108.697	113.351	117.432	121.334	125.322	129.684	134.915	142.398	148.779	154.464	161.249	165.979	176.014	180.024
123	77.836	80.162	86.356	89.476	94.195	98.388	103.376	109.643	114.317	118.416	122.334	126.338	130.717	135.969	143.480	149.885	155.589	162.398	167.144	177.211	181.234
124	78.627	80.966	87.193	90.328	95.070	99.283	104.295	110.589	115.284	119.399	123.334	127.354	131.751	137.022	144.562	150.989	156.714	163.546	168.308	178.407	182.443
125	79.419	81.771	88.029	91.180	95.946	100.178	105.213	111.536	116.250	120.383	124.334	128.370	132.784	138.076	145.643	152.094	157.838	164.694	169.471	179.603	183.652
126	80.212	82.576	88.867	92.033	96.822	101.074	106.132	112.483	117.217	121.367	125.334	129.386	133.817	139.129	146.724	153.198	158.962	165.841	170.634	180.798	184.859
127	81.006	83.382	89.705	92.887	97.699	101.971	107.051	113.430	118.184	122.351	126.334	130.402	134.850	140.182	147.805	154.301	160.086	166.987	171.796	181.992	186.066
128	81.800	84.189	90.544	93.741	98.576	102.867	107.971	114.377	119.151	123.335	127.334	131.418	135.883	141.235	148.885	155.405	161.209	168.133	172.957	183.186	187.272
129	82.595	84.996	91.383	94.596	99.453	103.765	108.891	115.324	120.118	124.320	128.334	132.434	136.916	142.288	149.965	156.507	162.331	169.278	174.118	184.378	188.477
130	83.391	85.805	92.223	95.451	100.331	104.662	109.811	116.272	121.086	125.304	129.334	133.450	137.949	143.340	151.045	157.610	163.453	170.423	175.278	185.570	189.681
131	84.188	86.614	93.063	96.307	101.210	105.560	110.732	117.219	122.053	126.288	130.334	134.465	138.981	144.392	152.125	158.712	164.575	171.567	176.437	186.761	190.885
132	84.985	87.423	93.905	97.164	102.089	106.459	111.652	118.167	123.021	127.272	131.334	135.481	140.014	145.444	153.204	159.814	165.696	172.711	177.596	187.952	192.087
133	85.784	88.234	94.746	98.021	102.968	107.357	112.573	119.116	123.988	128.257	132.334	136.497	141.046	146.496	154.283	160.915	166.816	173.854	178.755	189.141	193.289
134	86.583	89.045	95.589	98.878	103.848	108.257	113.495	120.064	124.956	129.241	133.334	137.512	142.078	147.548	155.361	162.016	167.936	174.996	179.912	190.330	194.490
135	87.383	89.857	96.432	99.736	104.729	109.156	114.416	121.012	125.924	130.226	134.334	138.528	143.110	148.599	156.440	163.116	169.056	176.138	181.069	191.519	195.691
136	88.183	90.669	97.275	100.595	105.609	110.056	115.338	121.961	126.892	131.210	135.334	139.543	144.142	149.651	157.518	164.216	170.175	177.280	182.226	192.706	196.890
137	88.984	91.483	98.119	101.454	106.491	110.956	116.261	122.910	127.860	132.195	136.334	140.559	145.174	150.702	158.595	165.316	171.294	178.420	183.382	193.893	198.089
138	89.786	92.297	98.964	102.314	107.372	111.857	117.183	123.859	128.829	133.180	137.334	141.574	146.206	151.753	159.673	166.415	172.412	179.561	184.537	195.080	199.288
139	90.589	93.111	99.809	103.174	108.254	112.758	118.106	124.809	129.797	134.164	138.334	142.589	147.237	152.803	160.750	167.514	173.530	180.701	185.692	196.265	200.485
140	91.393	93.926	100.655	104.035	109.137	113.659	119.029	125.758	130.766	135.149	139.334	143.604	148.269	153.854	161.827	168.613	174.648	181.840	186.846	197.450	201.682
141	92.197	94.742	101.502	104.896	110.020	114.561	119.953	126.708	131.734	136.134	140.334	144.619	149.300	154.904	162.904	169.711	175.765	182.979	188.000	198.634	202.878
142	93.001	95.559	102.349	105.757	110.903	115.463	120.876	127.658	132.703	137.119	141.334	145.635	150.331	155.954	163.980	170.809	176.881	184.117	189.153	199.818	204.073
143	93.807	96.376	103.196	106.620	111.787	116.366	121.800	128.608	133.672	138.104	142.334	146.650	151.362	157.004	165.056	171.907	177.998	185.255	190.306	201.001	205.268
144	94.613	97.194	104.044	107.482	112.671	117.268	122.724	129.558	134.641	139.089	143.334	147.665	152.393	158.054	166.132	173.004	179.114	186.393	191.458	202.183	206.462
145	95.420	98.012	104.892	108.345	113.556	118.171	123.649	130.508	135.610	140.074	144.334	148.680	153.424	159.104	167.207	174.101	180.229	187.530	192.610	203.365	207.656
146	96.227	98.832	105.741	109.209	114.441	119.075	124.574	131.459	136.579	141.059	145.334	149.694	154.455	160.153	168.283	175.198	181.344	188.666	193.761	204.546	208.848
147	97.035	99.651	106.591	110.073	115.326	119.979	125.499	132.409	137.548	142.044	146.334	150.709	155.486	161.202	169.358	176.294	182.459	189.802	194.911	205.726	210.040
148	97.844	100.472	107.441	110.937	116.212	120.883	126.424	133.360	138.518	143.029	147.334	151.724	156.516	162.251	170.432	177.390	183.573	190.938	196.061	206.906	211.232
149	98.654	101.293	108.292	111.802	117.098	121.787	127.349	134.311	139.487	144.015	148.334	152.739	157.547	163.300	171.507	178.485	184.687	192.073	197.211	208.085	212.422
150	99.464	102.114	109.143	112.668	117.985	122.692	128.275	135.263	140.457	145.000	149.334	153.753	158.577	164.349	172.581	179.581	185.800	193.207	198.360	209.264	213.613

Significance Limits* of the χ^2 Distribution ν=151—200

$\int_r$ = integral between χ^2 and infinity ($1\int_r = 2\alpha$, $\frac{1}{2}\int_r = \alpha$ in χ^2 tests), $\int_1$ = integral between zero and χ^2

$\int_r$ 1 / ½	0.99950 / 0.49975	0.9990 / 0.4995	0.9950 / 0.4975	0.990 / 0.495	0.9750 / 0.4875	0.950 / 0.475	0.90 / 0.45	0.80 / 0.40	0.70 / 0.35	0.60 / 0.30	0.50 / 0.25	0.40 / 0.20	0.30 / 0.15	0.20 / 0.10	0.10 / 0.05	0.050 / 0.025	0.0250 / 0.0125	0.010 / 0.005	0.0050 / 0.0025	0.0010 / 0.0005	0.00050 / 0.00025
$\int_1$ 1 / ½	0.00050 / 0.00025	0.0010 / 0.0005	0.0050 / 0.0025	0.010 / 0.005	0.0250 / 0.0125	0.050 / 0.025	0.10 / 0.05	0.20 / 0.10	0.30 / 0.15	0.40 / 0.20	0.50 / 0.25	0.60 / 0.30	0.70 / 0.35	0.80 / 0.40	0.90 / 0.45	0.950 / 0.475	0.9750 / 0.4875	0.990 / 0.495	0.9950 / 0.4975	0.9990 / 0.4995	0.99950 / 0.49975
ν																					
151	100.274	102.936	109.994	113.534	118.872	123.597	129.201	136.214	141.427	145.985	150.334	154.768	159.608	165.398	173.655	180.676	186.913	194.342	199.508	210.442	214.802
152	101.086	103.759	110.846	114.400	119.759	124.502	130.127	137.165	142.396	146.971	151.334	155.783	160.638	166.446	174.729	181.770	188.026	195.475	200.656	211.619	215.991
153	101.898	104.582	111.699	115.267	120.646	125.408	131.054	138.117	143.366	147.956	152.334	156.797	161.668	167.495	175.803	182.865	189.139	196.609	201.804	212.796	217.179
154	102.710	105.406	112.552	116.134	121.535	126.314	131.980	139.069	144.336	148.942	153.334	157.812	162.698	168.543	176.876	183.959	190.251	197.742	202.951	213.973	218.367
155	103.523	106.230	113.405	117.001	122.423	127.220	132.907	140.021	145.306	149.927	154.334	158.826	163.728	169.591	177.949	185.052	191.362	198.874	204.098	215.148	219.554
156	104.337	107.055	114.259	117.870	123.312	128.127	133.835	140.973	146.277	150.913	155.334	159.841	164.758	170.639	179.022	186.146	192.473	200.006	205.244	216.323	220.740
157	105.151	107.881	115.114	118.738	124.201	129.034	134.762	141.925	147.247	151.898	156.334	160.855	165.787	171.686	180.094	187.239	193.584	201.138	206.389	217.498	221.926
158	105.966	108.707	115.968	119.607	125.090	129.941	135.690	142.878	148.217	152.884	157.334	161.869	166.817	172.734	181.167	188.332	194.695	202.269	207.535	218.672	223.111
159	106.782	109.534	116.824	120.476	125.980	130.848	136.618	143.831	149.188	153.870	158.334	162.883	167.847	173.781	182.239	189.424	195.805	203.400	208.679	219.845	224.296
160	107.598	110.361	117.680	121.346	126.870	131.756	137.546	144.783	150.158	154.856	159.334	163.898	168.876	174.828	183.311	190.516	196.915	204.530	209.824	221.018	225.480
161	108.415	111.189	118.536	122.216	127.761	132.664	138.474	145.736	151.129	155.841	160.334	164.912	169.905	175.875	184.382	191.608	198.025	205.660	210.967	222.191	226.663
162	109.232	112.017	119.393	123.086	128.651	133.573	139.403	146.689	152.100	156.827	161.334	165.926	170.935	176.922	185.454	192.700	199.134	206.789	212.111	223.363	227.846
163	110.050	112.846	120.250	123.957	129.543	134.481	140.331	147.643	153.070	157.813	162.334	166.940	171.964	177.969	186.525	193.791	200.243	207.919	213.254	224.534	229.029
164	110.868	113.675	121.107	124.829	130.434	135.390	141.260	148.596	154.041	158.799	163.334	167.954	172.993	179.016	187.596	194.883	201.351	209.047	214.396	225.705	230.211
165	111.687	114.505	121.965	125.700	131.326	136.299	142.190	149.549	155.012	159.785	164.334	168.968	174.022	180.062	188.667	195.973	202.459	210.176	215.538	226.875	231.392
166	112.506	115.335	122.824	126.572	132.218	137.209	143.119	150.503	155.984	160.771	165.334	169.982	175.051	181.109	189.737	197.064	203.567	211.304	216.680	228.045	232.573
167	113.326	116.166	123.683	127.445	133.111	138.118	144.049	151.457	156.955	161.757	166.334	170.996	176.079	182.155	190.808	198.154	204.675	212.431	217.821	229.214	233.753
168	114.147	116.998	124.542	128.318	134.003	139.028	144.979	152.411	157.926	162.743	167.334	172.010	177.108	183.201	191.878	199.244	205.782	213.558	218.962	230.383	234.932
169	114.968	117.829	125.401	129.191	134.897	139.939	145.909	153.365	158.897	163.729	168.334	173.024	178.137	184.247	192.948	200.334	206.889	214.685	220.102	231.551	236.111
170	115.790	118.662	126.262	130.065	135.790	140.849	146.839	154.319	159.869	164.716	169.334	174.037	179.165	185.293	194.017	201.423	207.995	215.812	221.242	232.719	237.290
171	116.612	119.495	127.122	130.939	136.684	141.760	147.769	155.273	160.840	165.702	170.334	175.051	180.194	186.338	195.087	202.513	209.102	216.938	222.382	233.886	238.468
172	117.434	120.328	127.983	131.813	137.578	142.671	148.700	156.228	161.812	166.688	171.334	176.065	181.222	187.384	196.156	203.601	210.208	218.063	223.521	235.053	239.646
173	118.257	121.162	128.844	132.688	138.472	143.582	149.631	157.182	162.784	167.675	172.334	177.079	182.250	188.429	197.225	204.690	211.313	219.189	224.660	236.219	240.823
174	119.081	121.996	129.706	133.563	139.367	144.494	150.562	158.137	163.755	168.661	173.334	178.092	183.279	189.475	198.294	205.779	212.419	220.314	225.798	237.385	241.999
175	119.905	122.831	130.568	134.438	140.262	145.406	151.493	159.092	164.727	169.647	174.334	179.106	184.307	190.520	199.363	206.867	213.524	221.438	226.936	238.550	243.175
176	120.730	123.666	131.431	135.314	141.157	146.318	152.425	160.047	165.699	170.634	175.334	180.119	185.335	191.565	200.432	207.955	214.628	222.562	228.073	239.715	244.351
177	121.555	124.502	132.294	136.190	142.053	147.230	153.356	161.002	166.671	171.620	176.334	181.133	186.363	192.610	201.500	209.042	215.733	223.686	229.210	240.880	245.526
178	122.381	125.338	133.157	137.067	142.949	148.143	154.288	161.957	167.643	172.607	177.334	182.146	187.391	193.654	202.568	210.130	216.837	224.810	230.347	242.043	246.700
179	123.207	126.175	134.021	137.943	143.845	149.056	155.220	162.913	168.616	173.593	178.334	183.160	188.418	194.699	203.636	211.217	217.941	225.933	231.484	243.207	247.874
180	124.033	127.012	134.885	138.821	144.741	149.969	156.153	163.868	169.588	174.580	179.334	184.173	189.446	195.743	204.704	212.304	219.044	227.056	232.620	244.370	249.048
181	124.860	127.849	135.749	139.698	145.638	150.882	157.085	164.824	170.560	175.567	180.334	185.187	190.474	196.788	205.771	213.391	220.148	228.178	233.755	245.533	250.221
182	125.688	128.687	136.614	140.576	146.535	151.796	158.018	165.780	171.533	176.553	181.334	186.200	191.501	197.832	206.839	214.477	221.250	229.301	234.890	246.695	251.393
183	126.516	129.526	137.479	141.454	147.432	152.709	158.950	166.735	172.505	177.540	182.334	187.213	192.529	198.876	207.906	215.563	222.353	230.423	236.025	247.856	252.565
184	127.344	130.364	138.345	142.333	148.330	153.624	159.883	167.691	173.478	178.527	183.334	188.226	193.556	199.920	208.973	216.649	223.456	231.544	237.160	249.018	253.737
185	128.173	131.204	139.211	143.211	149.228	154.538	160.817	168.647	174.450	179.513	184.334	189.240	194.584	200.964	210.040	217.735	224.558	232.665	238.294	250.178	254.908
186	129.003	132.043	140.077	144.091	150.126	155.452	161.750	169.604	175.423	180.500	185.334	190.253	195.611	202.008	211.106	218.820	225.660	233.786	239.428	251.339	256.079
187	129.833	132.884	140.944	144.970	151.025	156.367	162.684	170.560	176.396	181.487	186.334	191.266	196.638	203.052	212.173	219.906	226.761	234.907	240.561	252.499	257.249
188	130.663	133.724	141.811	145.850	151.923	157.282	163.617	171.517	177.369	182.474	187.334	192.279	197.665	204.095	213.239	220.991	227.862	236.027	241.694	253.658	258.419
189	131.494	134.565	142.678	146.730	152.822	158.197	164.551	172.473	178.342	183.461	188.334	193.292	198.692	205.139	214.305	222.076	228.964	237.147	242.827	254.817	259.588
190	132.325	135.407	143.546	147.611	153.721	159.113	165.485	173.430	179.315	184.448	189.334	194.305	199.719	206.182	215.371	223.160	230.064	238.266	243.959	255.976	260.757
191	133.157	136.248	144.414	148.491	154.621	160.028	166.419	174.387	180.288	185.435	190.334	195.318	200.746	207.225	216.437	224.245	231.165	239.385	245.091	257.134	261.925
192	133.989	137.091	145.282	149.372	155.521	160.944	167.354	175.343	181.261	186.422	191.334	196.331	201.773	208.268	217.502	225.329	232.265	240.504	246.223	258.292	263.093
193	134.821	137.933	146.151	150.254	156.421	161.860	168.288	176.301	182.234	187.409	192.334	197.344	202.800	209.311	218.568	226.413	233.365	241.623	247.354	259.449	264.261
194	135.654	138.776	147.020	151.136	157.321	162.776	169.223	177.258	183.207	188.396	193.334	198.357	203.827	210.354	219.633	227.496	234.465	242.741	248.485	260.606	265.428
195	136.488	139.620	147.889	152.018	158.222	163.693	170.158	178.215	184.181	189.383	194.334	199.370	204.853	211.397	220.698	228.580	235.564	243.859	249.616	261.763	266.595
196	137.322	140.464	148.759	152.900	159.122	164.610	171.093	179.172	185.154	190.370	195.334	200.383	205.880	212.439	221.763	229.663	236.663	244.977	250.746	262.919	267.761
197	138.156	141.308	149.629	153.783	160.023	165.527	172.029	180.130	186.128	191.358	196.334	201.395	206.906	213.482	222.828	230.746	237.762	246.095	251.876	264.075	268.927
198	138.990	142.153	150.499	154.665	160.925	166.444	172.964	181.087	187.101	192.345	197.334	202.408	207.933	214.524	223.892	231.829	238.861	247.212	253.006	265.230	270.092
199	139.826	142.998	151.370	155.549	161.826	167.361	173.900	182.045	188.075	193.332	198.334	203.421	208.959	215.567	224.957	232.912	239.960	248.328	254.135	266.385	271.257
200	140.661	143.843	152.241	156.432	162.728	168.279	174.835	183.003	189.049	194.319	199.334	204.434	209.985	216.609	226.021	233.994	241.058	249.445	255.264	267.540	272.422

Upper Significance Limits[1] of the *F*-Distribution $P=0.05$

$P = P(\text{right}) =$ integral between F and infinity

ν_2 \ ν_1	1	2	3	4	5	6	7	8	9	10	11	12	13	14	15	16	17	18	19	20	22	24	26	28	30	40	50	60	80	100
1	161.44	200	216	225	230	234	237	239	241	242	243	244	245	245	246	246	247	247	248	248	249	249	249	250	250	251	252	252	252	253
2	18.51	19.0	19.2	19.2	19.3	19.3	19.4	19.4	19.4	19.4	19.4	19.4	19.4	19.4	19.4	19.4	19.4	19.4	19.4	19.4	19.5	19.5	19.5	19.5	19.5	19.5	19.5	19.5	19.5	19.5
3	10.13	9.55	9.28	9.12	9.01	8.94	8.89	8.85	8.81	8.79	8.76	8.74	8.73	8.71	8.70	8.69	8.68	8.67	8.67	8.66	8.65	8.64	8.63	8.62	8.62	8.59	8.58	8.57	8.56	8.55
4	7.71	6.94	6.59	6.39	6.26	6.16	6.09	6.04	6.00	5.96	5.94	5.91	5.89	5.87	5.86	5.84	5.83	5.82	5.81	5.80	5.79	5.77	5.76	5.75	5.75	5.72	5.70	5.69	5.67	5.66
5	6.61	5.79	5.41	5.19	5.05	4.95	4.88	4.82	4.77	4.74	4.70	4.68	4.66	4.64	4.62	4.60	4.59	4.58	4.57	4.56	4.54	4.53	4.52	4.50	4.50	4.46	4.44	4.43	4.41	4.41
6	5.99	5.14	4.76	4.53	4.39	4.28	4.21	4.15	4.10	4.06	4.03	4.00	3.98	3.96	3.94	3.92	3.91	3.90	3.88	3.87	3.86	3.84	3.83	3.82	3.81	3.77	3.75	3.74	3.72	3.71
7	5.59	4.74	4.35	4.12	3.97	3.87	3.79	3.73	3.68	3.64	3.60	3.57	3.55	3.53	3.51	3.49	3.48	3.47	3.46	3.44	3.43	3.41	3.40	3.39	3.38	3.34	3.32	3.30	3.29	3.27
8	5.32	4.46	4.07	3.84	3.69	3.58	3.50	3.44	3.39	3.35	3.31	3.28	3.26	3.24	3.22	3.20	3.19	3.17	3.16	3.15	3.13	3.12	3.10	3.09	3.08	3.04	3.02	3.01	2.99	2.97
9	5.12	4.26	3.86	3.63	3.48	3.37	3.29	3.23	3.18	3.14	3.10	3.07	3.05	3.03	3.01	2.99	2.97	2.96	2.95	2.94	2.92	2.90	2.89	2.87	2.86	2.83	2.80	2.79	2.77	2.76
10	4.96	4.10	3.71	3.48	3.33	3.22	3.14	3.07	3.02	2.98	2.94	2.91	2.89	2.86	2.85	2.83	2.81	2.80	2.78	2.77	2.75	2.74	2.72	2.71	2.70	2.66	2.64	2.62	2.60	2.59
11	4.84	3.98	3.59	3.36	3.20	3.09	3.01	2.95	2.90	2.85	2.82	2.79	2.76	2.74	2.72	2.70	2.69	2.67	2.66	2.65	2.63	2.61	2.59	2.58	2.57	2.53	2.51	2.49	2.47	2.46
12	4.75	3.89	3.49	3.26	3.11	3.00	2.91	2.85	2.80	2.75	2.72	2.69	2.66	2.64	2.62	2.60	2.58	2.57	2.56	2.54	2.52	2.51	2.49	2.48	2.47	2.43	2.40	2.38	2.36	2.35
13	4.67	3.81	3.41	3.18	3.03	2.92	2.83	2.77	2.71	2.67	2.63	2.60	2.58	2.55	2.53	2.51	2.50	2.48	2.47	2.46	2.44	2.42	2.41	2.39	2.38	2.34	2.31	2.30	2.27	2.26
14	4.60	3.74	3.34	3.11	2.96	2.85	2.76	2.70	2.65	2.60	2.57	2.53	2.51	2.48	2.46	2.44	2.43	2.41	2.40	2.39	2.37	2.35	2.33	2.32	2.31	2.27	2.24	2.22	2.20	2.19
15	4.54	3.68	3.29	3.06	2.90	2.79	2.71	2.64	2.59	2.54	2.51	2.48	2.45	2.42	2.40	2.38	2.37	2.35	2.34	2.33	2.31	2.29	2.27	2.26	2.25	2.20	2.18	2.16	2.14	2.12
16	4.49	3.63	3.24	3.01	2.85	2.74	2.66	2.59	2.54	2.49	2.46	2.42	2.40	2.37	2.35	2.33	2.32	2.30	2.29	2.28	2.25	2.24	2.22	2.21	2.19	2.15	2.12	2.11	2.08	2.07
17	4.45	3.59	3.20	2.96	2.81	2.70	2.61	2.55	2.49	2.45	2.41	2.38	2.35	2.33	2.31	2.29	2.27	2.26	2.24	2.23	2.21	2.19	2.17	2.16	2.15	2.10	2.08	2.06	2.03	2.02
18	4.41	3.55	3.16	2.93	2.77	2.66	2.58	2.51	2.46	2.41	2.37	2.34	2.31	2.29	2.27	2.25	2.23	2.22	2.20	2.19	2.17	2.15	2.13	2.12	2.11	2.06	2.04	2.02	1.99	1.98
19	4.38	3.52	3.13	2.90	2.74	2.63	2.54	2.48	2.42	2.38	2.34	2.31	2.28	2.26	2.23	2.21	2.20	2.18	2.17	2.16	2.13	2.11	2.10	2.08	2.07	2.03	2.00	1.98	1.96	1.94
20	4.35	3.49	3.10	2.87	2.71	2.60	2.51	2.45	2.39	2.35	2.31	2.28	2.25	2.22	2.20	2.18	2.17	2.15	2.14	2.12	2.10	2.08	2.07	2.05	2.04	1.99	1.97	1.95	1.92	1.91
21	4.32	3.47	3.07	2.84	2.68	2.57	2.49	2.42	2.37	2.32	2.28	2.25	2.22	2.20	2.18	2.16	2.14	2.12	2.11	2.10	2.07	2.05	2.04	2.02	2.01	1.96	1.94	1.92	1.89	1.88
22	4.30	3.44	3.05	2.82	2.66	2.55	2.46	2.40	2.34	2.30	2.26	2.23	2.20	2.17	2.15	2.13	2.11	2.10	2.08	2.07	2.05	2.03	2.01	2.00	1.98	1.94	1.91	1.89	1.86	1.85
23	4.28	3.42	3.03	2.80	2.64	2.53	2.44	2.37	2.32	2.27	2.23	2.20	2.18	2.15	2.13	2.11	2.09	2.07	2.06	2.05	2.02	2.00	1.99	1.97	1.96	1.91	1.88	1.86	1.84	1.82
24	4.26	3.40	3.01	2.78	2.62	2.51	2.42	2.36	2.30	2.25	2.21	2.18	2.15	2.13	2.11	2.09	2.07	2.05	2.04	2.03	2.00	1.98	1.97	1.95	1.94	1.89	1.86	1.84	1.82	1.80
25	4.24	3.39	2.99	2.76	2.60	2.49	2.40	2.34	2.28	2.24	2.20	2.16	2.14	2.11	2.09	2.07	2.05	2.04	2.02	2.01	1.98	1.96	1.95	1.93	1.92	1.87	1.84	1.82	1.80	1.78
26	4.23	3.37	2.98	2.74	2.59	2.47	2.39	2.32	2.27	2.22	2.18	2.15	2.12	2.09	2.07	2.05	2.03	2.02	2.00	1.99	1.97	1.95	1.93	1.91	1.90	1.85	1.82	1.80	1.78	1.76
27	4.21	3.35	2.96	2.73	2.57	2.46	2.37	2.31	2.25	2.20	2.17	2.13	2.10	2.08	2.06	2.04	2.02	2.00	1.99	1.97	1.95	1.93	1.91	1.90	1.88	1.84	1.81	1.79	1.76	1.74
28	4.20	3.34	2.95	2.71	2.56	2.45	2.36	2.29	2.24	2.19	2.15	2.12	2.09	2.06	2.04	2.02	2.00	1.99	1.97	1.96	1.93	1.91	1.90	1.88	1.87	1.82	1.79	1.77	1.74	1.73
29	4.18	3.33	2.93	2.70	2.55	2.43	2.35	2.28	2.22	2.18	2.14	2.10	2.08	2.05	2.03	2.01	1.99	1.97	1.96	1.94	1.92	1.90	1.88	1.87	1.85	1.81	1.77	1.75	1.73	1.71
30	4.17	3.32	2.92	2.69	2.53	2.42	2.33	2.27	2.21	2.16	2.13	2.09	2.06	2.04	2.01	1.99	1.98	1.96	1.95	1.93	1.91	1.89	1.87	1.85	1.84	1.79	1.76	1.74	1.71	1.70
32	4.15	3.29	2.90	2.67	2.51	2.40	2.31	2.24	2.19	2.14	2.10	2.07	2.04	2.01	1.99	1.97	1.95	1.94	1.92	1.91	1.88	1.86	1.85	1.83	1.82	1.77	1.74	1.71	1.69	1.67
34	4.13	3.28	2.88	2.65	2.49	2.38	2.29	2.23	2.17	2.12	2.08	2.05	2.02	1.99	1.97	1.95	1.93	1.92	1.90	1.89	1.86	1.84	1.82	1.80	1.80	1.75	1.71	1.69	1.66	1.65
36	4.11	3.26	2.87	2.63	2.48	2.36	2.28	2.21	2.15	2.11	2.07	2.03	2.00	1.98	1.95	1.93	1.92	1.90	1.88	1.87	1.85	1.82	1.81	1.79	1.78	1.73	1.69	1.67	1.64	1.62
38	4.10	3.24	2.85	2.62	2.46	2.35	2.26	2.19	2.14	2.09	2.05	2.02	1.99	1.96	1.94	1.92	1.90	1.88	1.87	1.85	1.83	1.81	1.79	1.77	1.76	1.71	1.68	1.65	1.62	1.61
40	4.08	3.23	2.84	2.61	2.45	2.34	2.25	2.18	2.12	2.08	2.04	2.00	1.97	1.95	1.92	1.90	1.89	1.87	1.85	1.84	1.81	1.79	1.77	1.76	1.74	1.69	1.66	1.64	1.61	1.59
42	4.07	3.22	2.83	2.59	2.44	2.32	2.24	2.17	2.11	2.06	2.03	1.99	1.96	1.93	1.91	1.89	1.87	1.86	1.84	1.83	1.80	1.78	1.76	1.74	1.73	1.68	1.65	1.62	1.59	1.57
44	4.06	3.21	2.82	2.58	2.43	2.31	2.23	2.16	2.10	2.05	2.01	1.98	1.95	1.92	1.90	1.88	1.86	1.84	1.83	1.81	1.79	1.77	1.75	1.73	1.72	1.67	1.63	1.61	1.58	1.56
46	4.05	3.20	2.81	2.57	2.42	2.30	2.22	2.15	2.09	2.04	2.00	1.97	1.94	1.91	1.89	1.87	1.85	1.83	1.82	1.80	1.78	1.76	1.74	1.72	1.71	1.65	1.62	1.60	1.57	1.55
48	4.04	3.19	2.80	2.57	2.41	2.29	2.21	2.14	2.08	2.03	1.99	1.96	1.93	1.90	1.88	1.86	1.84	1.82	1.81	1.79	1.77	1.75	1.73	1.71	1.70	1.64	1.61	1.59	1.56	1.54
50	4.03	3.18	2.79	2.56	2.40	2.29	2.20	2.13	2.07	2.03	1.99	1.95	1.92	1.89	1.87	1.85	1.83	1.81	1.80	1.78	1.76	1.74	1.72	1.70	1.69	1.63	1.60	1.58	1.54	1.52
60	4.00	3.15	2.76	2.53	2.37	2.25	2.17	2.10	2.04	1.99	1.95	1.92	1.89	1.86	1.84	1.82	1.80	1.78	1.76	1.75	1.72	1.70	1.68	1.66	1.65	1.59	1.56	1.53	1.50	1.48
70	3.98	3.13	2.74	2.50	2.35	2.23	2.14	2.07	2.02	1.97	1.93	1.89	1.86	1.84	1.81	1.79	1.77	1.75	1.74	1.72	1.70	1.67	1.65	1.64	1.62	1.57	1.53	1.50	1.47	1.45
80	3.96	3.11	2.72	2.49	2.33	2.21	2.13	2.06	2.00	1.95	1.91	1.88	1.84	1.82	1.79	1.77	1.75	1.73	1.72	1.70	1.68	1.65	1.63	1.62	1.60	1.54	1.51	1.48	1.45	1.43
90	3.95	3.10	2.71	2.47	2.32	2.20	2.11	2.04	1.99	1.94	1.90	1.86	1.83	1.80	1.78	1.76	1.74	1.72	1.70	1.69	1.66	1.64	1.62	1.60	1.59	1.53	1.49	1.46	1.43	1.41
100	3.94	3.09	2.70	2.46	2.31	2.19	2.10	2.03	1.97	1.93	1.89	1.85	1.82	1.79	1.77	1.75	1.73	1.71	1.69	1.68	1.65	1.63	1.61	1.59	1.57	1.52	1.48	1.45	1.41	1.39
125	3.92	3.07	2.68	2.44	2.29	2.17	2.08	2.01	1.96	1.91	1.87	1.83	1.80	1.77	1.75	1.72	1.70	1.69	1.67	1.65	1.63	1.60	1.58	1.57	1.55	1.49	1.45	1.42	1.39	1.36
150	3.90	3.06	2.66	2.43	2.27	2.16	2.07	2.00	1.94	1.89	1.85	1.82	1.79	1.76	1.73	1.71	1.69	1.67	1.66	1.64	1.61	1.59	1.57	1.55	1.53	1.48	1.44	1.41	1.37	1.34
200	3.89	3.04	2.65	2.42	2.26	2.14	2.06	1.98	1.93	1.88	1.84	1.80	1.77	1.74	1.72	1.69	1.67	1.66	1.64	1.62	1.60	1.57	1.55	1.53	1.52	1.46	1.41	1.39	1.35	1.32
300	3.87	3.03	2.63	2.40	2.24	2.13	2.04	1.97	1.91	1.86	1.82	1.78	1.75	1.72	1.70	1.68	1.66	1.64	1.62	1.61	1.58	1.55	1.53	1.51	1.50	1.43	1.39	1.36	1.32	1.30
500	3.86	3.01	2.62	2.39	2.23	2.12	2.03	1.96	1.90	1.85	1.81	1.77	1.74	1.71	1.69	1.66	1.64	1.62	1.61	1.59	1.56	1.54	1.52	1.50	1.48	1.42	1.38	1.34	1.30	1.28
1000	3.85	3.00	2.61	2.38	2.22	2.11	2.02	1.95	1.89	1.84	1.80	1.76	1.73	1.70	1.68	1.65	1.63	1.61	1.60	1.58	1.55	1.53	1.51	1.49	1.47	1.41	1.36	1.33	1.29	1.26

[1] Values from VAN DER WAERDEN, B. L., *Mathematische Statistik*, Springer, Berlin, 1957, page 340. Reprinted by kind permission of the author and publishers.

Upper Significance Limits[1] of the *F*-Distribution $P = 0.01$

$P = P$ (right) = integral between F and infinity

ν_2 \ ν_1	1	2	3	4	5	6	7	8	9	10	11	12	13	14	15	16	17	18	19	20	22	24	26	28	30	40	50	60	80	100
2	98.50	99.0	99.2	99.2	99.3	99.3	99.4	99.4	99.4	99.4	99.4	99.4	99.4	99.4	99.4	99.4	99.4	99.4	99.4	99.4	99.5	99.5	99.5	99.5	99.5	99.5	99.5	99.5	99.5	99.5
3	34.12	30.8	29.5	28.7	28.2	27.9	27.7	27.5	27.3	27.2	27.1	27.1	27.0	26.9	26.9	26.8	26.8	26.8	26.7	26.7	26.6	26.6	26.6	26.5	26.5	26.4	26.4	26.3	26.3	26.2
4	21.20	18.0	16.7	16.0	15.5	15.2	15.0	14.8	14.7	14.5	14.4	14.4	14.3	14.2	14.2	14.2	14.1	14.1	14.0	14.0	14.0	13.9	13.9	13.9	13.8	13.7	13.7	13.7	13.6	13.6
5	16.26	13.3	12.1	11.4	11.0	10.7	10.5	10.3	10.2	10.1	9.96	9.89	9.82	9.77	9.72	9.68	9.64	9.61	9.58	9.55	9.51	9.47	9.43	9.40	9.38	9.29	9.24	9.20	9.16	9.13
6	13.75	10.9	9.78	9.15	8.75	8.47	8.26	8.10	7.98	7.87	7.79	7.72	7.66	7.60	7.56	7.52	7.48	7.45	7.42	7.40	7.35	7.31	7.28	7.25	7.23	7.14	7.09	7.06	7.01	6.99
7	12.25	9.55	8.45	7.85	7.46	7.19	6.99	6.84	6.72	6.62	6.54	6.47	6.41	6.36	6.31	6.27	6.24	6.21	6.18	6.16	6.11	6.07	6.04	6.02	5.99	5.91	5.86	5.82	5.78	5.75
8	11.26	8.65	7.59	7.01	6.63	6.37	6.18	6.03	5.91	5.81	5.73	5.67	5.61	5.56	5.52	5.48	5.44	5.41	5.38	5.36	5.32	5.28	5.25	5.22	5.20	5.12	5.07	5.03	4.99	4.96
9	10.56	8.02	6.99	6.42	6.06	5.80	5.61	5.47	5.35	5.26	5.18	5.11	5.05	5.00	4.96	4.92	4.89	4.86	4.83	4.81	4.77	4.73	4.70	4.67	4.65	4.57	4.52	4.48	4.44	4.42
10	10.04	7.56	6.55	5.99	5.64	5.39	5.20	5.06	4.94	4.85	4.77	4.71	4.65	4.60	4.56	4.52	4.49	4.46	4.43	4.41	4.36	4.33	4.30	4.27	4.25	4.17	4.12	4.08	4.04	4.01
11	9.65	7.21	6.22	5.67	5.32	5.07	4.89	4.74	4.63	4.54	4.46	4.40	4.34	4.29	4.25	4.21	4.18	4.15	4.12	4.10	4.06	4.02	3.99	3.96	3.94	3.86	3.81	3.78	3.73	3.71
12	9.33	6.93	5.95	5.41	5.06	4.82	4.64	4.50	4.39	4.30	4.22	4.16	4.10	4.05	4.01	3.97	3.94	3.91	3.88	3.86	3.82	3.78	3.75	3.72	3.70	3.62	3.57	3.54	3.49	3.47
13	9.07	6.70	5.74	5.21	4.86	4.62	4.44	4.30	4.19	4.10	4.02	3.96	3.91	3.86	3.82	3.78	3.75	3.72	3.69	3.66	3.62	3.59	3.56	3.53	3.51	3.43	3.38	3.34	3.30	3.27
14	8.86	6.51	5.56	5.04	4.69	4.46	4.28	4.14	4.03	3.94	3.86	3.80	3.75	3.70	3.66	3.62	3.59	3.56	3.53	3.51	3.46	3.43	3.40	3.37	3.35	3.27	3.22	3.18	3.14	3.11
15	8.68	6.36	5.42	4.89	4.56	4.32	4.14	4.00	3.89	3.80	3.73	3.67	3.61	3.56	3.52	3.49	3.45	3.42	3.40	3.37	3.33	3.29	3.26	3.24	3.21	3.13	3.08	3.05	3.00	2.98
16	8.53	6.23	5.29	4.77	4.44	4.20	4.03	3.89	3.78	3.69	3.62	3.55	3.50	3.45	3.41	3.37	3.34	3.31	3.28	3.26	3.22	3.18	3.15	3.12	3.10	3.02	2.97	2.93	2.89	2.86
17	8.40	6.11	5.18	4.67	4.34	4.10	3.93	3.79	3.68	3.59	3.52	3.46	3.40	3.35	3.31	3.27	3.24	3.21	3.18	3.16	3.12	3.08	3.05	3.03	3.00	2.92	2.87	2.83	2.79	2.76
18	8.29	6.01	5.09	4.58	4.25	4.01	3.84	3.71	3.60	3.51	3.43	3.37	3.32	3.27	3.23	3.19	3.16	3.13	3.10	3.08	3.03	3.00	2.97	2.94	2.92	2.84	2.78	2.75	2.70	2.68
19	8.18	5.93	5.01	4.50	4.17	3.94	3.77	3.63	3.52	3.43	3.36	3.30	3.24	3.19	3.15	3.12	3.08	3.05	3.03	3.00	2.96	2.92	2.89	2.87	2.84	2.76	2.71	2.67	2.63	2.60
20	8.10	5.85	4.94	4.43	4.10	3.87	3.70	3.56	3.46	3.37	3.29	3.23	3.18	3.13	3.09	3.05	3.02	2.99	2.96	2.94	2.90	2.86	2.83	2.80	2.78	2.69	2.64	2.61	2.56	2.54
21	8.02	5.78	4.87	4.37	4.04	3.81	3.64	3.51	3.40	3.31	3.24	3.17	3.12	3.07	3.03	2.99	2.96	2.93	2.90	2.88	2.84	2.80	2.77	2.74	2.72	2.64	2.58	2.55	2.50	2.48
22	7.95	5.72	4.82	4.31	3.99	3.76	3.59	3.45	3.35	3.26	3.18	3.12	3.07	3.02	2.98	2.94	2.91	2.88	2.85	2.83	2.78	2.75	2.72	2.69	2.67	2.58	2.53	2.50	2.45	2.42
23	7.88	5.66	4.76	4.26	3.94	3.71	3.54	3.41	3.30	3.21	3.14	3.07	3.02	2.97	2.93	2.89	2.86	2.83	2.80	2.78	2.74	2.70	2.67	2.64	2.62	2.54	2.48	2.45	2.40	2.37
24	7.82	5.61	4.72	4.22	3.90	3.67	3.50	3.36	3.26	3.17	3.09	3.03	2.98	2.93	2.89	2.85	2.82	2.79	2.76	2.74	2.70	2.66	2.63	2.60	2.58	2.49	2.44	2.40	2.36	2.33
25	7.77	5.57	4.68	4.18	3.86	3.63	3.46	3.32	3.22	3.13	3.06	2.99	2.94	2.89	2.85	2.81	2.78	2.75	2.72	2.70	2.66	2.62	2.59	2.56	2.54	2.45	2.40	2.36	2.32	2.29
26	7.72	5.53	4.64	4.14	3.82	3.59	3.42	3.29	3.18	3.09	3.02	2.96	2.90	2.86	2.82	2.78	2.74	2.72	2.69	2.66	2.62	2.58	2.55	2.53	2.50	2.42	2.36	2.33	2.28	2.25
27	7.68	5.49	4.60	4.11	3.78	3.56	3.39	3.26	3.15	3.06	2.99	2.93	2.87	2.82	2.78	2.75	2.71	2.68	2.66	2.63	2.59	2.55	2.52	2.49	2.47	2.38	2.33	2.29	2.25	2.22
28	7.64	5.45	4.57	4.07	3.75	3.53	3.36	3.23	3.12	3.03	2.96	2.90	2.84	2.79	2.75	2.72	2.68	2.65	2.63	2.60	2.56	2.52	2.49	2.46	2.44	2.35	2.30	2.26	2.22	2.19
29	7.60	5.42	4.54	4.04	3.73	3.50	3.33	3.20	3.09	3.00	2.93	2.87	2.81	2.77	2.73	2.69	2.66	2.63	2.60	2.57	2.53	2.49	2.46	2.44	2.41	2.33	2.27	2.23	2.19	2.16
30	7.56	5.39	4.51	4.02	3.70	3.47	3.30	3.17	3.07	2.98	2.91	2.84	2.79	2.74	2.70	2.66	2.63	2.60	2.57	2.55	2.51	2.47	2.44	2.41	2.39	2.30	2.25	2.21	2.16	2.13
32	7.50	5.34	4.46	3.97	3.65	3.43	3.26	3.13	3.02	2.93	2.86	2.80	2.74	2.70	2.66	2.62	2.58	2.55	2.53	2.50	2.46	2.42	2.39	2.36	2.34	2.25	2.20	2.16	2.11	2.08
34	7.44	5.29	4.42	3.93	3.61	3.39	3.22	3.09	2.98	2.89	2.82	2.76	2.70	2.66	2.62	2.58	2.55	2.51	2.49	2.46	2.42	2.38	2.35	2.32	2.30	2.21	2.16	2.12	2.07	2.04
36	7.40	5.25	4.38	3.89	3.57	3.35	3.18	3.05	2.95	2.86	2.79	2.72	2.67	2.62	2.58	2.54	2.51	2.48	2.45	2.43	2.38	2.35	2.32	2.29	2.26	2.17	2.12	2.08	2.03	2.00
38	7.35	5.21	4.34	3.86	3.54	3.32	3.15	3.02	2.92	2.83	2.75	2.69	2.64	2.59	2.55	2.51	2.48	2.45	2.42	2.40	2.35	2.32	2.28	2.26	2.23	2.14	2.09	2.05	2.00	1.97
40	7.31	5.18	4.31	3.83	3.51	3.29	3.12	2.99	2.89	2.80	2.73	2.66	2.61	2.56	2.52	2.48	2.45	2.42	2.39	2.37	2.33	2.29	2.26	2.23	2.20	2.11	2.06	2.02	1.97	1.94
42	7.28	5.15	4.29	3.80	3.49	3.27	3.10	2.97	2.86	2.78	2.70	2.64	2.59	2.54	2.50	2.46	2.43	2.40	2.37	2.34	2.30	2.26	2.23	2.20	2.18	2.09	2.03	1.99	1.94	1.91
44	7.25	5.12	4.26	3.78	3.47	3.24	3.08	2.95	2.84	2.75	2.68	2.62	2.56	2.52	2.47	2.44	2.40	2.37	2.35	2.32	2.28	2.24	2.21	2.18	2.15	2.06	2.01	1.97	1.92	1.89
46	7.22	5.10	4.24	3.76	3.44	3.22	3.06	2.93	2.82	2.73	2.66	2.60	2.54	2.50	2.45	2.42	2.38	2.35	2.33	2.30	2.26	2.22	2.19	2.16	2.13	2.04	1.99	1.95	1.90	1.86
48	7.19	5.08	4.22	3.74	3.43	3.20	3.04	2.91	2.80	2.72	2.64	2.58	2.53	2.48	2.44	2.40	2.37	2.33	2.31	2.28	2.24	2.20	2.17	2.14	2.12	2.02	1.97	1.93	1.88	1.84
50	7.17	5.06	4.20	3.72	3.41	3.19	3.02	2.89	2.79	2.70	2.63	2.56	2.51	2.46	2.42	2.38	2.35	2.32	2.29	2.27	2.22	2.18	2.15	2.12	2.10	2.01	1.95	1.91	1.86	1.82
55	7.12	5.01	4.16	3.68	3.37	3.15	2.98	2.85	2.75	2.66	2.59	2.53	2.47	2.42	2.38	2.34	2.31	2.28	2.25	2.23	2.18	2.15	2.11	2.08	2.06	1.97	1.91	1.87	1.81	1.78
60	7.08	4.98	4.13	3.65	3.34	3.12	2.95	2.82	2.72	2.63	2.56	2.50	2.44	2.39	2.35	2.31	2.28	2.25	2.22	2.20	2.15	2.12	2.08	2.05	2.03	1.94	1.88	1.84	1.78	1.75
70	7.01	4.92	4.08	3.60	3.29	3.07	2.91	2.78	2.67	2.59	2.51	2.45	2.40	2.35	2.31	2.27	2.23	2.20	2.18	2.15	2.11	2.07	2.03	2.01	1.98	1.89	1.83	1.78	1.73	1.70
80	6.96	4.88	4.04	3.56	3.26	3.04	2.87	2.74	2.64	2.55	2.48	2.42	2.36	2.31	2.27	2.23	2.20	2.17	2.14	2.12	2.07	2.03	2.00	1.97	1.94	1.85	1.79	1.75	1.69	1.66
90	6.93	4.85	4.01	3.54	3.23	3.01	2.84	2.72	2.61	2.52	2.45	2.39	2.33	2.29	2.24	2.21	2.17	2.14	2.11	2.09	2.04	2.00	1.97	1.94	1.92	1.82	1.76	1.72	1.66	1.62
100	6.90	4.82	3.98	3.51	3.21	2.99	2.82	2.69	2.59	2.50	2.43	2.37	2.31	2.26	2.22	2.19	2.15	2.12	2.09	2.07	2.02	1.98	1.94	1.92	1.89	1.80	1.73	1.69	1.63	1.60
125	6.84	4.78	3.94	3.47	3.17	2.95	2.79	2.66	2.55	2.47	2.39	2.33	2.28	2.23	2.19	2.15	2.11	2.08	2.05	2.03	1.98	1.94	1.91	1.88	1.85	1.76	1.69	1.65	1.59	1.55
150	6.81	4.75	3.92	3.45	3.14	2.92	2.76	2.63	2.53	2.44	2.37	2.31	2.25	2.20	2.16	2.12	2.09	2.06	2.03	2.00	1.96	1.92	1.88	1.85	1.83	1.73	1.66	1.62	1.56	1.52
200	6.76	4.71	3.88	3.41	3.11	2.89	2.73	2.60	2.50	2.41	2.34	2.27	2.22	2.17	2.13	2.09	2.06	2.02	2.00	1.97	1.93	1.89	1.85	1.82	1.79	1.69	1.63	1.58	1.52	1.48
300	6.72	4.68	3.85	3.38	3.08	2.86	2.70	2.57	2.47	2.38	2.31	2.24	2.19	2.14	2.10	2.06	2.03	1.99	1.97	1.94	1.89	1.85	1.82	1.79	1.76	1.66	1.59	1.55	1.48	1.44
500	6.69	4.65	3.82	3.36	3.05	2.84	2.68	2.55	2.44	2.36	2.28	2.22	2.17	2.12	2.07	2.04	2.00	1.97	1.94	1.92	1.87	1.83	1.79	1.76	1.74	1.63	1.56	1.52	1.45	1.41
1000	6.66	4.63	3.80	3.34	3.04	2.82	2.66	2.53	2.43	2.34	2.27	2.20	2.15	2.10	2.06	2.02	1.98	1.95	1.92	1.90	1.85	1.81	1.77	1.74	1.72	1.61	1.54	1.50	1.43	1.38

[1] Values from VAN DER WAERDEN, B. L., *Mathematische Statistik*, Springer, Berlin, 1957, page 342. Reprinted by kind permission of the author and publishers.

$P=2\alpha$	0.20	0.10	0.05	0.02	0.01	0.005	0.001	$P=2\alpha$	0.20	0.10	0.05	0.02	0.01	0.005	0.001
½ $P=\alpha$	0.10	0.05	0.025	0.01	0.005	0.0025	0.0005	½ $P=\alpha$	0.10	0.05	0.025	0.01	0.005	0.0025	0.0005
ν								ν							
1	9.474	39.864	161.442	1012.576	4052.214	16210.382	405283.751	101	1.664	2.756	3.935	5.589	6.893	8.237	11.491
2	3.557	8.526	18.513	48.511	98.502	198.500	998.434	102	1.664	2.755	3.934	5.587	6.890	8.234	11.484
3	2.683	5.538	10.128	20.621	34.116	55.552	167.030	103	1.664	2.755	3.933	5.585	6.888	8.231	11.478
4	2.350	4.545	7.708	14.040	21.198	31.333	74.132	104	1.664	2.754	3.933	5.583	6.885	8.227	11.472
5	2.179	4.060	6.608	11.323	16.258	22.784	47.183	**105**	1.663	2.754	3.932	5.582	6.883	8.224	11.465
6	2.074	3.776	5.987	9.878	13.745	18.635	35.510	106	1.663	2.754	3.931	5.580	6.881	8.220	11.458
7	2.002	3.590	5.591	8.988	12.247	16.235	29.246	107	1.663	2.753	3.930	5.579	6.879	8.217	11.451
8	1.952	3.458	5.318	8.387	11.259	14.688	25.412	108	1.663	2.753	3.929	5.577	6.876	8.213	11.445
9	1.913	3.360	5.118	7.958	10.561	13.614	22.858	109	1.663	2.752	3.928	5.575	6.874	8.211	11.440
10	1.882	3.285	4.964	7.640	10.044	12.826	21.041	**110**	1.662	2.752	3.928	5.574	6.871	8.207	11.435
11	1.858	3.225	4.844	7.388	9.646	12.226	19.687	111	1.662	2.751	3.927	5.572	6.869	8.204	11.430
12	1.839	3.177	4.747	7.188	9.330	11.754	18.645	112	1.662	2.751	3.926	5.571	6.867	8.201	11.424
13	1.823	3.136	4.667	7.023	9.074	11.374	17.817	113	1.662	2.751	3.925	5.570	6.865	8.198	11.418
14	1.809	3.102	4.600	6.885	8.861	11.060	17.140	114	1.662	2.750	3.924	5.568	6.863	8.195	11.412
15	1.798	3.073	4.543	6.770	8.683	10.798	16.589	**115**	1.662	2.750	3.924	5.567	6.861	8.193	11.408
16	1.788	3.048	4.494	6.672	8.531	10.576	16.120	116	1.661	2.749	3.923	5.565	6.859	8.190	11.402
17	1.777	3.026	4.451	6.589	8.400	10.385	15.721	117	1.661	2.749	3.922	5.564	6.857	8.187	11.397
18	1.769	3.007	4.414	6.513	8.285	10.218	15.382	118	1.661	2.749	3.922	5.563	6.855	8.184	11.392
19	1.764	2.990	4.381	6.447	8.185	10.072	15.078	119	1.661	2.748	3.921	5.561	6.853	8.182	11.387
20	1.756	2.975	4.351	6.391	8.096	9.944	14.823	**120**	1.661	2.748	3.920	5.560	6.851	8.179	11.381
21	1.750	2.961	4.325	6.340	8.017	9.829	14.585	121	1.660	2.748	3.920	5.559	6.850	8.177	11.376
22	1.745	2.948	4.301	6.290	7.946	9.727	14.379	122	1.660	2.747	3.919	5.558	6.848	8.174	11.371
23	1.740	2.937	4.280	6.250	7.881	9.635	14.190	123	1.660	2.747	3.918	5.556	6.846	8.172	11.367
24	1.737	2.927	4.260	6.210	7.823	9.551	14.025	124	1.660	2.747	3.918	5.555	6.844	8.169	11.363
25	1.732	2.918	4.242	6.175	7.770	9.475	13.876	**125**	1.660	2.746	3.917	5.554	6.842	8.167	11.358
26	1.729	2.909	4.225	6.145	7.721	9.406	13.742	126	1.660	2.746	3.916	5.553	6.841	8.165	11.353
27	1.727	2.901	4.210	6.116	7.677	9.342	13.616	127	1.660	2.746	3.916	5.552	6.839	8.162	11.350
28	1.724	2.894	4.196	6.086	7.636	9.284	13.498	128	1.659	2.745	3.915	5.551	6.837	8.160	11.347
29	1.719	2.887	4.183	6.061	7.598	9.229	13.388	129	1.659	2.745	3.915	5.550	6.836	8.158	11.343
30	1.716	2.881	4.171	6.037	7.563	9.180	13.293	**130**	1.659	2.745	3.914	5.549	6.834	8.156	11.339
31	1.715	2.875	4.160	6.015	7.530	9.134	13.205	131	1.659	2.744	3.914	5.547	6.832	8.154	11.335
32	1.712	2.869	4.149	5.995	7.499	9.090	13.120	132	1.659	2.744	3.913	5.546	6.831	8.152	11.331
33	1.710	2.864	4.139	5.976	7.471	9.050	13.040	133	1.659	2.744	3.912	5.545	6.830	8.150	11.327
34	1.708	2.859	4.130	5.958	7.444	9.012	12.968	134	1.659	2.743	3.912	5.544	6.828	8.148	11.322
35	1.706	2.855	4.121	5.941	7.420	8.977	12.899	**135**	1.659	2.743	3.911	5.543	6.827	8.145	11.318
36	1.704	2.850	4.113	5.925	7.396	8.943	12.834	136	1.658	2.743	3.911	5.542	6.825	8.143	11.314
37	1.703	2.846	4.105	5.911	7.374	8.912	12.774	137	1.658	2.743	3.911	5.541	6.824	8.141	11.310
38	1.701	2.843	4.098	5.897	7.353	8.883	12.717	138	1.658	2.742	3.910	5.540	6.823	8.139	11.307
39	1.700	2.839	4.091	5.883	7.333	8.855	12.664	139	1.658	2.742	3.909	5.540	6.821	8.137	11.304
40	1.698	2.836	4.085	5.871	7.314	8.829	12.610	**140**	1.658	2.742	3.909	5.539	6.819	8.136	11.300
41	1.697	2.832	4.079	5.859	7.296	8.804	12.564	141	1.658	2.742	3.909	5.538	6.818	8.134	11.297
42	1.695	2.829	4.073	5.848	7.280	8.780	12.520	142	1.658	2.741	3.908	5.537	6.817	8.132	11.294
43	1.694	2.826	4.067	5.837	7.264	8.757	12.477	143	1.658	2.741	3.907	5.536	6.816	8.130	11.290
44	1.693	2.823	4.062	5.827	7.248	8.736	12.435	144	1.658	2.741	3.907	5.535	6.814	8.128	11.286
45	1.692	2.820	4.057	5.817	7.234	8.715	12.395	**145**	1.658	2.741	3.907	5.534	6.813	8.126	11.283
46	1.691	2.818	4.052	5.808	7.220	8.696	12.357	146	1.657	2.740	3.906	5.533	6.812	8.125	11.280
47	1.689	2.815	4.047	5.799	7.207	8.677	12.323	147	1.657	2.740	3.906	5.532	6.811	8.123	11.277
48	1.688	2.813	4.043	5.791	7.194	8.659	12.287	148	1.657	2.740	3.905	5.532	6.809	8.121	11.273
49	1.688	2.811	4.038	5.783	7.182	8.642	12.257	149	1.657	2.740	3.905	5.531	6.808	8.120	11.271
50	1.687	2.809	4.034	5.775	7.171	8.626	12.226	**150**	1.657	2.739	3.904	5.530	6.807	8.118	11.267
51	1.686	2.807	4.031	5.767	7.160	8.611	12.197	151	1.657	2.739	3.904	5.529	6.806	8.117	11.265
52	1.685	2.805	4.027	5.760	7.149	8.595	12.168	152	1.657	2.739	3.903	5.528	6.805	8.115	11.262
53	1.684	2.803	4.023	5.753	7.139	8.582	12.142	153	1.657	2.739	3.903	5.528	6.804	8.113	11.259
54	1.684	2.801	4.020	5.747	7.129	8.568	12.115	154	1.657	2.738	3.903	5.527	6.803	8.112	11.255
55	1.683	2.799	4.016	5.740	7.120	8.555	12.090	**155**	1.657	2.738	3.902	5.526	6.802	8.110	11.253
56	1.682	2.797	4.013	5.734	7.111	8.542	12.064	156	1.656	2.738	3.902	5.525	6.800	8.108	11.250
57	1.681	2.796	4.010	5.728	7.102	8.529	12.042	157	1.656	2.738	3.901	5.525	6.799	8.107	11.248
58	1.681	2.794	4.007	5.723	7.093	8.517	12.020	158	1.656	2.738	3.901	5.524	6.798	8.106	11.246
59	1.680	2.793	4.004	5.717	7.085	8.506	11.998	159	1.656	2.738	3.901	5.523	6.797	8.104	11.243
60	1.679	2.791	4.001	5.712	7.077	8.495	11.976	**160**	1.656	2.737	3.900	5.522	6.796	8.103	11.241
61	1.679	2.790	3.999	5.707	7.070	8.484	11.956	161	1.656	2.737	3.900	5.522	6.795	8.101	11.239
62	1.678	2.788	3.996	5.702	7.063	8.474	11.936	162	1.656	2.737	3.899	5.521	6.794	8.100	11.237
63	1.678	2.787	3.994	5.698	7.056	8.465	11.917	163	1.656	2.737	3.899	5.520	6.793	8.099	11.234
64	1.677	2.786	3.991	5.693	7.048	8.455	11.898	164	1.656	2.736	3.899	5.520	6.792	8.097	11.231
65	1.677	2.785	3.989	5.689	7.042	8.445	11.882	**165**	1.656	2.736	3.899	5.519	6.791	8.096	11.229
66	1.676	2.783	3.986	5.684	7.036	8.436	11.865	166	1.656	2.736	3.898	5.518	6.790	8.095	11.227
67	1.675	2.782	3.984	5.680	7.029	8.428	11.849	167	1.656	2.736	3.898	5.518	6.790	8.093	11.224
68	1.675	2.781	3.982	5.676	7.023	8.419	11.834	168	1.655	2.736	3.897	5.517	6.789	8.092	11.220
69	1.674	2.780	3.980	5.672	7.018	8.411	11.818	169	1.655	2.736	3.897	5.516	6.788	8.091	11.218
70	1.674	2.779	3.978	5.668	7.012	8.403	11.803	**170**	1.655	2.735	3.897	5.516	6.787	8.089	11.215
71	1.673	2.778	3.976	5.665	7.007	8.396	11.788	171	1.655	2.735	3.897	5.515	6.786	8.088	11.213
72	1.673	2.777	3.974	5.661	7.001	8.389	11.772	172	1.655	2.735	3.896	5.515	6.785	8.087	11.210
73	1.673	2.776	3.972	5.658	6.996	8.381	11.759	173	1.655	2.735	3.896	5.514	6.784	8.086	11.208
74	1.672	2.775	3.970	5.654	6.991	8.373	11.746	174	1.655	2.735	3.895	5.513	6.783	8.085	11.206
75	1.672	2.774	3.969	5.651	6.986	8.367	11.733	**175**	1.655	2.735	3.895	5.513	6.782	8.084	11.205
76	1.671	2.773	3.967	5.648	6.981	8.360	11.720	176	1.655	2.734	3.895	5.512	6.781	8.083	11.203
77	1.671	2.772	3.965	5.645	6.976	8.354	11.708	177	1.655	2.734	3.895	5.512	6.781	8.082	11.200
78	1.671	2.771	3.964	5.642	6.972	8.347	11.696	178	1.655	2.734	3.894	5.511	6.780	8.080	11.197
79	1.670	2.770	3.962	5.639	6.967	8.342	11.686	179	1.655	2.734	3.894	5.511	6.779	8.079	11.195
80	1.670	2.769	3.960	5.636	6.963	8.335	11.675	**180**	1.655	2.734	3.894	5.510	6.778	8.078	11.193
81	1.670	2.769	3.959	5.633	6.959	8.330	11.664	181	1.655	2.734	3.894	5.509	6.778	8.076	11.191
82	1.669	2.768	3.957	5.630	6.955	8.324	11.652	182	1.654	2.733	3.893	5.509	6.777	8.075	11.189
83	1.669	2.767	3.956	5.628	6.951	8.319	11.642	183	1.654	2.733	3.893	5.508	6.776	8.075	11.187
84	1.668	2.766	3.955	5.625	6.947	8.313	11.632	184	1.654	2.733	3.893	5.508	6.775	8.074	11.185
85	1.668	2.766	3.953	5.622	6.943	8.308	11.622	**185**	1.654	2.733	3.892	5.507	6.775	8.072	11.183
86	1.668	2.765	3.952	5.620	6.940	8.302	11.612	186	1.654	2.733	3.892	5.507	6.774	8.071	11.181
87	1.668	2.764	3.951	5.618	6.936	8.297	11.603	187	1.654	2.733	3.892	5.506	6.773	8.070	11.179
88	1.667	2.764	3.949	5.615	6.932	8.292	11.594	188	1.654	2.732	3.892	5.506	6.772	8.069	11.177
89	1.667	2.763	3.948	5.613	6.929	8.287	11.584	189	1.654	2.732	3.892	5.505	6.771	8.068	11.175
90	1.667	2.762	3.947	5.611	6.925	8.282	11.575	**190**	1.654	2.732	3.891	5.505	6.770	8.067	11.173
91	1.666	2.762	3.946	5.608	6.922	8.278	11.567	191	1.654	2.732	3.891	5.504	6.770	8.066	11.172
92	1.666	2.761	3.945	5.606	6.918	8.274	11.558	192	1.654	2.732	3.890	5.504	6.769	8.065	11.170
93	1.666	2.760	3.944	5.604	6.916	8.270	11.550	193	1.654	2.732	3.890	5.503	6.768	8.064	11.168
94	1.666	2.760	3.943	5.602	6.913	8.265	11.543	194	1.654	2.732	3.890	5.503	6.768	8.063	11.166
95	1.665	2.759	3.941	5.600	6.910	8.261	11.536	**195**	1.654	2.732	3.890	5.502	6.767	8.062	11.165
96	1.665	2.759	3.940	5.598	6.906	8.256	11.527	196	1.654	2.731	3.890	5.502	6.766	8.061	11.164
97	1.665	2.758	3.939	5.596	6.904	8.253	11.519	197	1.654	2.731	3.889	5.501	6.766	8.060	11.162
98	1.665	2.758	3.938	5.594	6.901	8.249	11.511	198	1.654	2.731	3.889	5.501	6.765	8.059	11.160
99	1.665	2.757	3.937	5.592	6.899	8.245	11.505	199	1.654	2.731	3.889	5.500	6.764	8.059	11.158
100	1.664	2.756	3.936	5.590	6.896	8.241	11.498	**200**	1.653	2.731	3.888	5.500	6.763	8.058	11.156

Confidence limits for μ: $\bar{x} \pm k_2 s$; k_2 is given in the table. N = size of the sample from which $\bar{x}$ and s are calculated

100 (1−2α) = 95%

N	0	1	2	3	4	5	6	7	8	9
0			8.9845	2.4842	1.5913	1.2416	1.0494	0.9248	0.8360	0.7687
10	0.7154	0.6718	0.6354	0.6043	0.5774	0.5538	0.5329	5142	4973	4820
20	4680	4552	4434	4324	4223	4128	4039	3956	3878	3804
30	3734	3668	3605	3546	3489	3435	3384	3334	3287	3242
40	3198	3156	3116	3078	3040	3004	2970	2936	2904	2872
50	0.2842	0.2813	0.2784	0.2756	0.2730	0.2703	0.2678	0.2653	0.2629	0.2606
60	2583	2561	2540	2519	2498	2478	2458	2439	2421	2402
70	2385	2367	2350	2333	2317	2301	2285	2270	2255	2240
80	2225	2211	2197	2184	2170	2157	2144	2131	2119	2107
90	2095	2083	2071	2060	2048	2037	2026	2016	2005	1995
100	0.1984	0.1974	0.1964	0.1954	0.1945	0.1935	0.1926	0.1917	0.1908	0.1899
110	1890	1881	1872	1864	1856	1847	1839	1831	1823	1815
120	1808	1800	1792	1785	1778	1770	1763	1756	1749	1742
130	1735	1729	1722	1715	1709	1702	1696	1690	1683	1677
140	1671	1665	1659	1653	1647	1642	1636	1630	1625	1619
150	0.1614	0.1608	0.1603	0.1597	0.1592	0.1587	0.1582	0.1577	0.1571	0.1566
160	1561	1556	1552	1547	1542	1537	1533	1528	1523	1519
170	1514	1510	1505	1501	1496	1492	1488	1483	1479	1475
180	1471	1467	1463	1459	1455	1451	1447	1443	1439	1435
190	1431	1427	1424	1420	1416	1412	1409	1405	1402	1398
200	0.1394	0.1391	0.1379	0.1376	0.1372	0.1369	0.1366	0.1362	0.1359	0.1356
210	1353	1349	1346	1343	1340	1337	1334	1331	1328	1324
220	1321	1318	1315	1313	1310	1307	1304	1301	1298	1295
230	1292	1290	1287	1284	1281	1279	1276	1273	1271	1268
240	1265	1263	1260	1257	1255	1252	1250	1247	1245	1242
250	0.1240	0.1237	0.1235	0.1232	0.1230	0.1227	0.1225	0.1223	0.1220	0.1218
260	1216	1213	1211	1209	1206	1204	1202	1200	1197	1195
270	1193	1191	1188	1186	1184	1182	1180	1178	1176	1173
280	1171	1169	1167	1165	1163	1161	1159	1157	1155	1153
290	1151	1149	1147	1145	1143	1141	1139	1137	1135	1134
300	0.1132	0.1130	0.1128	0.1126	0.1124	0.1122	0.1120	0.1119	0.1117	0.1115
310	1113	1111	1110	1108	1106	1104	1103	1101	1099	1097
320	1096	1094	1092	1091	1089	1087	1086	1084	1082	1081
330	1079	1077	1076	1074	1072	1071	1069	1068	1066	1065
340	1063	1061	1060	1058	1057	1055	1054	1052	1051	1049
350	0.1048	0.1046	0.1045	0.1043	0.1042	0.1040	0.1039	0.1037	0.1036	0.1034
360	1033	1032	1030	1029	1027	1026	1025	1023	1022	1020
370	1019	1018	1016	1015	1014	1012	1011	1009	1008	1007
380	1005	1004	1003	1002	1000	0999	0998	0996	0995	0994
390	0993	0991	0990	0989	0987	0986	0985	0984	0982	0981
400	0.0980	0.0979	0.0978	0.0976	0.0975	0.0974	0.0973	0.0972	0.0970	0.0969
410	0968	0967	0966	0964	0963	0962	0961	0960	0959	0958
420	0956	0955	0954	0953	0952	0951	0950	0949	0947	0946
430	0945	0944	0943	0942	0941	0940	0939	0938	0937	0935
440	0934	0933	0932	0931	0930	0929	0928	0927	0926	0925
450	0.0924	0.0923	0.0922	0.0921	0.0920	0.0919	0.0918	0.0917	0.0916	0.0915
460	0914	0913	0912	0911	0910	0909	0908	0907	0906	0905
470	0904	0903	0902	0901	0900	0899	0898	0897	0897	0896
480	0895	0894	0893	0892	0891	0890	0889	0888	0887	0886
490	0885	0885	0884	0883	0882	0881	0880	0879	0878	0877
500	0.0877	0.0876	0.0875	0.0874	0.0873	0.0872	0.0871	0.0871	0.0870	0.0869
510	0868	0867	0866	0865	0865	0864	0863	0862	0861	0860
520	0860	0859	0858	0857	0856	0855	0855	0854	0853	0852
530	0851	0851	0850	0849	0848	0847	0847	0846	0845	0844
540	0843	0843	0842	0841	0840	0840	0839	0838	0837	0837
550	0.0836	0.0835	0.0834	0.0834	0.0833	0.0832	0.0831	0.0831	0.0830	0.0829
560	0828	0828	0827	0826	0825	0825	0824	0823	0822	0822
570	0821	0820	0820	0819	0818	0817	0817	0816	0815	0815
580	0814	0813	0812	0812	0811	0810	0810	0809	0808	0808
590	0807	0806	0806	0805	0804	0804	0803	0802	0802	0801
600	0.0800	0.0800	0.0799	0.0798	0.0798	0.0797	0.0796	0.0796	0.0795	0.0794
610	0794	0793	0792	0792	0791	0790	0790	0789	0788	0788
620	0787	0787	0786	0785	0785	0784	0783	0783	0782	0782
630	0781	0780	0780	0779	0778	0778	0777	0777	0776	0775
640	0775	0774	0774	0773	0772	0772	0771	0771	0770	0769
650	0.0769	0.0768	0.0768	0.0767	0.0766	0.0766	0.0765	0.0765	0.0764	0.0764
660	0763	0762	0762	0761	0761	0760	0760	0759	0758	0758
670	0757	0757	0756	0756	0755	0754	0754	0753	0753	0752
680	0752	0751	0751	0750	0749	0749	0748	0748	0747	0747
690	0746	0746	0745	0745	0744	0744	0743	0742	0742	0741
700	0.0741	0.0740	0.0740	0.0739	0.0739	0.0738	0.0738	0.0737	0.0737	0.0736
710	0736	0735	0735	0734	0734	0733	0733	0732	0732	0731
720	0730	0730	0729	0729	0728	0728	0727	0727	0726	0726
730	0725	0725	0724	0724	0723	0723	0723	0722	0722	0721
740	0721	0720	0720	0719	0719	0718	0718	0717	0717	0716
750	0.0716	0.0715	0.0715	0.0714	0.0714	0.0713	0.0713	0.0712	0.0712	0.0711
760	0711	0711	0710	0710	0709	0709	0708	0708	0707	0707
770	0706	0706	0705	0705	0705	0704	0704	0703	0703	0702
780	0702	0701	0701	0700	0700	0700	0699	0699	0698	0698
790	0697	0697	0696	0696	0696	0695	0695	0694	0694	0693
800	0.0693	0.0693	0.0692	0.0692	0.0691	0.0691	0.0690	0.0690	0.0690	0.0689
810	0689	0688	0688	0687	0687	0687	0686	0686	0685	0685
820	0684	0684	0684	0683	0683	0682	0682	0682	0681	0681
830	0680	0680	0680	0679	0679	0678	0678	0678	0677	0677
840	0676	0676	0675	0675	0675	0674	0674	0674	0673	0673
850	0.0672	0.0672	0.0672	0.0671	0.0671	0.0670	0.0670	0.0670	0.0669	0.0669
860	0668	0668	0668	0667	0667	0666	0666	0666	0665	0665
870	0665	0664	0664	0663	0663	0663	0662	0662	0662	0661
880	0661	0660	0660	0660	0659	0659	0659	0658	0658	0657
890	0657	0657	0656	0656	0656	0655	0655	0654	0654	0654
900	0.0653	0.0653	0.0653	0.0652	0.0652	0.0652	0.0651	0.0651	0.0650	0.0650
910	0650	0649	0649	0649	0648	0648	0648	0647	0647	0647
920	0646	0646	0646	0645	0645	0644	0644	0644	0643	0643
930	0643	0642	0642	0642	0641	0641	0641	0640	0640	0640
940	0639	0639	0639	0638	0638	0638	0637	0637	0637	0636
950	0.0636	0.0636	0.0635	0.0635	0.0635	0.0634	0.0634	0.0634	0.0633	0.0633
960	0633	0632	0632	0632	0631	0631	0631	0630	0630	0630
970	0629	0629	0629	0628	0628	0628	0627	0627	0627	0626
980	0626	0626	0625	0625	0625	0625	0624	0624	0624	0623
990	0623	0623	0622	0622	0622	0621	0621	0621	0620	0620
1000	0.0620									

100 (1−2α) = 99%

N	0	1	2	3	4	5	6	7	8	9
0			45.012	5.7301	2.9205	2.0590	1.6461	1.4013	1.2373	1.1185
10	1.0277	0.9556	0.8966	0.8472	0.8051	0.7686	0.7367	0.7084	0.6831	0.6604
20	0.6397	6209	6037	5878	5730	5594	5467	5348	5236	5131
30	5033	4939	4851	4767	4688	4612	4540	4471	4405	4342
40	4282	4224	4168	4115	4063	4013	3966	3919	3875	3832
50	0.3790	0.3750	0.3711	0.3673	0.3636	0.3600	0.3566	0.3532	0.3499	0.3467
60	3436	3406	3377	3348	3320	3293	3267	3241	3215	3190
70	3166	3143	3120	3097	3075	3053	3032	3011	2991	2971
80	2951	2932	2913	2895	2877	2859	2841	2824	2807	2791
90	2775	2759	2743	2728	2712	2698	2683	2668	2654	2640
100	0.2627	0.2613	0.2600	0.2586	0.2574	0.2561	0.2548	0.2536	0.2524	0.2512
110	2500	2488	2477	2465	2454	2443	2432	2421	2411	2400
120	2390	2380	2370	2360	2350	2340	2330	2321	2312	2302
130	2293	2284	2275	2266	2258	2249	2241	2232	2224	2216
140	2207	2199	2191	2183	2176	2168	2160	2153	2145	2138
150	0.2131	0.2123	0.2116	0.2109	0.2102	0.2095	0.2088	0.2081	0.2074	0.2068
160	2061	2055	2048	2042	2035	2029	2023	2016	2010	2004
170	1998	1992	1986	1980	1975	1969	1963	1957	1952	1946
180	1941	1935	1930	1924	1919	1914	1909	1903	1898	1893
190	1888	1883	1878	1873	1868	1863	1858	1853	1849	1844
200	0.1839	0.1834	0.1812	0.1808	0.1803	0.1799	0.1795	0.1790	0.1786	0.1782
210	1778	1773	1769	1765	1761	1757	1753	1749	1745	1741
220	1737	1733	1729	1725	1721	1717	1713	1710	1706	1702
230	1699	1695	1691	1688	1684	1680	1677	1673	1670	1666
240	1663	1659	1656	1652	1649	1646	1642	1639	1636	1632
250	0.1629	0.1626	0.1623	0.1619	0.1616	0.1613	0.1610	0.1607	0.1604	0.1601
260	1598	1594	1591	1588	1585	1582	1579	1576	1573	1571
270	1568	1565	1562	1559	1556	1553	1551	1548	1545	1542
280	1539	1537	1534	1531	1529	1526	1523	1521	1518	1515
290	1513	1510	1507	1505	1502	1500	1497	1495	1492	1490
300	0.1487	0.1485	0.1482	0.1480	0.1477	0.1475	0.1473	0.1470	0.1468	0.1465
310	1463	1461	1458	1456	1454	1451	1449	1447	1445	1442
320	1440	1438	1436	1433	1431	1429	1427	1424	1422	1420
330	1418	1416	1414	1412	1409	1407	1405	1403	1401	1399
340	1397	1395	1393	1391	1389	1387	1385	1383	1381	1379
350	0.1377	0.1375	0.1373	0.1371	0.1369	0.1367	0.1365	0.1363	0.1361	0.1360
360	1358	1356	1354	1352	1350	1348	1346	1345	1343	1341
370	1339	1337	1336	1334	1332	1330	1328	1327	1325	1323
380	1321	1320	1318	1316	1315	1313	1311	1309	1308	1306
390	1304	1303	1301	1299	1298	1296	1294	1293	1291	1290
400	0.1288	0.1286	0.1285	0.1283	0.1282	0.1280	0.1278	0.1277	0.1275	0.1274
410	1272	1271	1269	1268	1266	1264	1263	1261	1260	1258
420	1257	1255	1254	1252	1251	1250	1248	1247	1245	1244
430	1242	1241	1239	1238	1236	1235	1234	1232	1231	1229
440	1228	1227	1225	1224	1222	1221	1220	1218	1217	1216
450	0.1214	0.1213	0.1212	0.1210	0.1209	0.1208	0.1206	0.1205	0.1204	0.1202
460	1201	1200	1198	1197	1196	1195	1193	1192	1191	1189
470	1188	1187	1186	1184	1183	1182	1181	1179	1178	1177
480	1176	1175	1173	1172	1171	1170	1168	1167	1166	1165
490	1164	1163	1161	1160	1159	1158	1157	1155	1154	1153
500	0.1152	0.1151	0.1150	0.1149	0.1147	0.1146	0.1145	0.1144	0.1143	0.1142
510	1141	1140	1138	1137	1136	1135	1134	1133	1132	1131
520	1130	1129	1127	1126	1125	1124	1123	1122	1121	1120
530	1119	1118	1117	1116	1115	1114	1113	1112	1111	1110
540	1109	1107	1106	1105	1104	1103	1102	1101	1100	1099
550	0.1098	0.1097	0.1096	0.1095	0.1094	0.1093	0.1092	0.1091	0.1090	0.1090
560	1089	1088	1087	1086	1085	1084	1083	1082	1081	1080
570	1079	1078	1077	1076	1075	1074	1073	1072	1071	1071
580	1070	1069	1068	1067	1066	1065	1064	1063	1062	1061
590	1061	1060	1059	1058	1057	1056	1055	1054	1053	1053
600	0.1052	0.1051	0.1050	0.1049	0.1048	0.1047	0.1046	0.1046	0.1045	0.1044
610	1043	1042	1041	1040	1040	1039	1038	1037	1036	1035
620	1035	1034	1033	1032	1031	1030	1030	1029	1028	1027
630	1026	1025	1025	1024	1023	1022	1021	1021	1020	1019
640	1018	1017	1017	1016	1015	1014	1013	1013	1012	1011
650	0.1010	0.1010	0.1009	0.1008	0.1007	0.1007	0.1006	0.1005	0.1004	0.1003
660	1003	1002	1001	1000	1000	0999	0998	0997	0997	0996
670	0995	0994	0994	0993	0992	0991	0991	0990	0989	0989
680	0988	0987	0986	0986	0985	0984	0984	0983	0982	0981
690	0981	0980	0979	0979	0978	0977	0976	0976	0975	0974
700	0.0974	0.0973	0.0972	0.0972	0.0971	0.0970	0.0969	0.0969	0.0968	0.0967
710	0967	0966	0965	0965	0964	0963	0963	0962	0961	0961
720	0960	0959	0959	0958	0957	0957	0956	0955	0955	0954
730	0953	0953	0952	0951	0951	0950	0950	0949	0948	0948
740	0947	0946	0946	0945	0944	0944	0943	0942	0942	0941
750	0.0941	0.0940	0.0939	0.0939	0.0938	0.0937	0.0937	0.0936	0.0936	0.0935
760	0934	0934	0933	0933	0932	0931	0931	0930	0930	0929
770	0928	0928	0927	0927	0926	0925	0925	0924	0924	0923
780	0922	0922	0921	0921	0920	0919	0919	0918	0918	0917
790	0916	0916	0915	0915	0914	0914	0913	0912	0912	0911
800	0.0911	0.0910	0.0910	0.0909	0.0908	0.0908	0.0907	0.0907	0.0906	0.0906
810	0905	0905	0904	0903	0903	0902	0902	0901	0901	0900
820	0900	0899	0898	0898	0897	0897	0896	0896	0895	0895
830	0894	0894	0893	0893	0892	0891	0891	0890	0890	0889
840	0889	0888	0888	0887	0887	0886	0886	0885	0885	0884
850	0.0884	0.0883	0.0883	0.0882	0.0881	0.0881	0.0880	0.0880	0.0879	0.0879
860	0878	0878	0877	0877	0876	0876	0875	0875	0874	0874
870	0873	0873	0872	0872	0871	0871	0870	0870	0869	0869
880	0868	0868	0867	0867	0866	0866	0865	0865	0864	0864
890	0863	0863	0863	0862	0862	0861	0861	0860	0860	0859
900	0.0859	0.0858	0.0858	0.0857	0.0857	0.0856	0.0856	0.0855	0.0855	0.0854
910	0854	0853	0853	0853	0852	0852	0851	0851	0850	0850
920	0849	0849	0848	0848	0847	0847	0847	0846	0846	0845
930	0845	0844	0844	0843	0843	0842	0842	0842	0841	0841
940	0840	0840	0839	0839	0838	0838	0838	0837	0837	0836
950	0.0836	0.0835	0.0835	0.0834	0.0834	0.0834	0.0833	0.0833	0.0832	0.0832
960	0831	0831	0831	0830	0830	0829	0829	0828	0828	0828
970	0827	0827	0826	0826	0825	0825	0825	0824	0824	0823
980	0823	0822	0822	0822	0821	0821	0820	0820	0820	0819
990	0819	0818	0818	0817	0817	0817	0816	0816	0815	0815
1000	0.0815									

$\beta_p = (1 - 2\alpha_p)$ = tolerance probability; $\beta_t = (1 - 2\alpha_t)$ = confidence probability; N = size of the sample from which $\bar{x}$ and s are calculated

	A									B									
	k_3 for $(\bar{x} \pm k_3\sigma)$				k_4 for $(\bar{x} \pm k_4 s)$				$\sqrt{\frac{N+1}{N}}$	k_5 for $(\bar{x} \pm k_5\sigma)$				k_6 for $(\mu \pm k_6 s)$					
										$\beta_t = 0.95$		$\beta_t = 0.99$		$\beta_t = 0.95$		$\sqrt{\frac{N-1}{\chi^2(N-1;0.95)}}$	$\beta_t = 0.99$		$\sqrt{\frac{N-1}{\chi^2(N-1;0.99)}}$
N \ β_p	0.90	0.95	0.98	0.99	0.90	0.95	0.98	0.99		0.90	0.95	0.95	0.99	0.90	0.95		0.95	0.99	
2	2.0145	2.4005	2.8492	3.1547	7.7328	15.562	38.973	77.964	1.224745	2.667	3.031	3.466	4.147	26.231	31.256	15.947	156.38	205.52	79.789
3	1.8993	2.2632	2.6862	2.9743	3.3717	4.9683	8.042	11.460	154701	2.415	2.776	3.132	3.813	7.263	8.654	4.4155	19.550	25.694	9.9749
4	1.8390	2.1913	2.6009	2.8799	2.6312	3.5581	5.077	6.5303	118034	2.265	2.626	2.933	3.614	4.803	5.723	2.9199	10.018	13.166	5.1113
5	1.8018	2.1470	2.5484	2.8217	2.3353	3.0414	4.105	5.0435	1.095445	2.165	2.525	2.797	3.478	3.902	4.650	2.3724	7.191	9.451	3.6692
6	7766	1170	5127	7822	2.1764	2.7766	3.635	4.3552	080123	2.093	450	698	3.370	3.437	4.095	2.0893	5.887	7.736	3.0034
7	7584	0953	4870	7537	2.0774	2.6158	3.360	3.9634	069045	2.038	394	620	3.301	3.151	3.754	1.9154	5.141	6.756	2.6230
8	7446	0789	4675	7321	2.0095	2.5080	3.180	3.7118	060660	1.995	349	558	3.238	2.956	3.522	1.7971	4.659	6.122	2.3769
9	7338	0660	4522	7152	1.9601	2.4307	3.053	3.5369	054092	1.961	313	507	3.186	2.814	3.354	1.7110	4.320	5.678	2.2043
10	1.7251	2.0556	2.4399	2.7016	1.9226	2.3726	2.959	3.4084	1.048809	1.932	2.283	2.465	3.143	2.706	3.225	1.6452	4.069	5.348	2.0762
11	7180	0471	4298	6904	8931	3272	887	3.3102	044466	909	258	428	3.105	620	3.122	5931	3.875	5.093	1.9771
12	7120	0400	4213	6810	8692	2909	829	3.2326	040833	889	236	397	3.075	551	3.039	5506	3.720	4.889	1.8980
13	7069	0340	4142	6731	8496	2610	782	3.1698	037749	872	218	369	3.044	492	2.970	5153	3.593	4.722	1.8332
14	7026	0288	4080	6662	8331	2362	743	3.1180	035098	856	201	345	3.018	443	2.911	4854	3.487	4.583	1.7792
15	1.6988	2.0242	2.4026	2.6603	1.8191	2.2151	2.710	3.0744	1.032796	1.843	2.186	2.324	2.996	2.401	2.861	1.4597	3.397	4.464	1.7332
16	6955	0203	3979	6551	8070	1971	682	3.0374	030776	832	174	309	976	364	817	4373	3.319	4.361	6936
17	6925	0168	3938	6505	7965	1814	658	3.0055	028991	821	162	287	958	332	778	4176	3.252	4.274	6592
18	6899	0137	3901	6464	7873	1676	637	2.9776	027402	812	153	272	941	303	744	4001	3.192	4.196	6288
19	6876	0109	3868	6427	7791	1555	618	2.9532	025978	804	143	258	926	277	714	3845	3.140	4.126	6019
20	1.6855	2.0084	2.3838	2.6394	1.7718	2.1447	2.602	2.9315	1.024695	1.796	2.134	2.245	2.912	2.254	2.686	1.3704	3.092	4.064	1.5777
21	6836	0061	3811	6364	7653	1351	587	9123	023533	789	127	233	899	233	661	3576	3.050	4.008	5560
22	6818	0040	3786	6337	7594	1263	575	8950	022475	783	120	222	887	214	638	3460	3.011	3.957	5363
23	6802	0021	3764	6312	7540	1185	562	8794	021508	777	113	212	876	196	617	3353	2.976	3.911	5184
24	6788	0004	3743	6289	7492	1114	552	8652	020621	772	107	202	866	180	598	3255	2.944	3.869	5020
25	1.6774	1.9988	2.3724	2.6268	1.7448	2.1048	2.541	2.8523	1.019804	1.767	2.101	2.193	2.856	2.165	2.580	1.3165	2.914	3.830	1.4868
26	6762	9973	3707	6249	7406	0987	532	8405	019049	762	096	185	847	152	564	3081	887	794	4729
27	6750	9959	3690	6231	7369	0932	524	8297	018350	758	092	178	839	139	548	3002	861	761	4600
28	6740	9947	3675	6214	7334	0881	517	8197	017700	754	087	171	831	127	534	2929	838	730	4479
29	6730	9935	3661	6199	7302	0834	509	8105	017095	751	083	164	823	115	521	2861	816	701	4367
30	1.6720	1.9924	2.3648	2.6184	1.7272	2.0790	2.503	2.8020	1.016530	1.747	2.079	2.158	2.816	2.105	2.508	1.2797	2.795	3.674	1.4262
31	6712	9913	3636	6170	7245	0750	496	7940	016001	744	075	153	810	095	496	2737	776	648	4164
32	6704	9904	3624	6158	7218	0711	491	7866	015505	741	072	147	803	086	485	2680	758	625	4072
33	6696	9894	3613	6146	7194	0676	486	7797	015039	738	069	142	797	077	475	2626	741	602	3985
34	6689	9886	3603	6134	7171	0642	481	7732	014599	736	066	137	792	069	465	2576	725	581	3903
35	1.6682	1.9878	2.3593	2.6124	1.7149	2.0611	2.476	2.7671	1.014185	1.733	2.063	2.132	2.786	2.061	2.455	1.2528	2.710	3.561	1.3825
36	6675	9870	3584	6114	7129	0581	472	7615	013794	731	060	127	781	053	446	2482	695	542	3751
37	6669	9863	3576	6104	7110	0553	467	7560	013423	728	057	123	776	046	438	2438	682	524	3681
38	6664	9856	3568	6095	7092	0527	463	7510	013072	726	055	119	772	039	430	2397	669	507	3615
39	6658	9849	3560	6086	7075	0502	459	7461	012740	724	053	115	767	033	422	2358	656	491	3552
40	1.6653	1.9843	2.3552	2.6078	1.7058	2.0478	2.456	2.7415	1.012423	1.722	2.051	2.112	2.763	2.026	2.415	1.2320	2.644	3.475	1.3492
41	6648	9837	3545	6071	7043	0456	452	7373	012122	720	048	108	759	020	408	2284	633	460	3434
42	6643	9832	3539	6063	7028	0435	450	7332	011835	718	046	105	755	015	401	2249	622	446	3379
43	6639	9826	3532	6056	7014	0414	446	7293	011561	717	044	102	752	009	394	2216	612	433	3326
44	6634	9821	3526	6049	7001	0395	443	7257	011300	715	042	099	748	004	388	2184	602	420	3276
45	1.6630	1.9816	2.3521	2.6043	1.6988	2.0377	2.441	2.7220	1.011050	1.714	2.040	2.096	2.745	1.999	2.382	1.2154	2.593	3.407	1.3227
46	6626	9812	3515	6037	6976	0359	438	7187	010811	712	039	093	742	994	376	2124	583	395	3181
47	6623	9807	3510	6031	6965	0342	436	7154	010582	711	037	091	738	990	371	2096	575	384	3136
48	6619	9803	3505	6025	6953	0326	433	7124	010363	710	036	088	735	985	365	2069	566	373	3093
49	6616	9799	3500	6020	6942	0310	430	7094	010152	708	034	086	732	981	360	2043	558	361	3052
50	1.6612	1.9795	2.3495	2.6015	1.6933	2.0296	2.429	2.7066	1.009951	1.707	2.033	2.083	2.729	1.977	2.355	1.2017	2.550	3.352	1.3012
51	6609	9791	3490	6010	6923	0282	426	7039	009756	706	031	081	727	973	351	1993	543	342	2974
52	6606	9787	3486	6005	6913	0269	425	7014	009569	705	030	079	724	969	346	1969	536	332	2936
53	6603	9784	3482	6000	6904	0255	423	6989	009390	704	029	077	722	965	341	1946	528	323	2900
54	6600	9780	3478	5996	6896	0243	421	6965	009217	703	028	075	719	961	337	1924	522	314	2866
55	1.6597	1.9777	2.3474	2.5991	1.6887	2.0230	2.419	2.6942	1.009050	1.702	2.026	2.073	2.717	1.958	2.333	1.1903	2.515	3.305	1.2832
56	6595	9774	3470	5987	6879	0219	417	6920	008889	701	025	071	714	954	329	1882	509	297	2800
57	6592	9771	3467	5983	6871	0208	416	6899	008734	700	024	069	712	951	325	1862	503	289	2768
58	6590	9768	3463	5979	6864	0197	414	6878	008584	699	023	067	710	948	321	1842	497	281	2738
59	6587	9765	3460	5976	6857	0186	412	6858	008439	698	022	065	708	945	317	1823	491	273	2708
60	1.6585	1.9762	2.3457	2.5972	1.6850	2.0176	2.411	2.6839	1.008299	1.697	2.021	2.064	2.706	1.942	2.314	1.1805	2.485	3.266	1.2680
61	6583	9760	3453	5969	6843	0166	410	6820	008164	696	020	062	704	939	310	1787	480	259	2652
62	6581	9757	3450	5965	6837	0157	408	6803	008032	695	019	060	702	936	307	1769	474	252	2625
63	6579	9755	3447	5962	6830	0148	407	6785	007906	694	018	059	700	933	303	1752	469	245	2598
64	6577	9752	3445	5959	6824	0139	406	6769	007782	694	017	057	698	930	300	1736	464	239	2573
65	1.6575	1.9750	2.3442	2.5956	1.6818	2.0130	2.404	2.6753	1.007663	1.693	2.016	2.056	2.696	1.928	2.297	1.1720	2.459	3.232	1.2548
66	6573	9748	3439	5953	6813	0122	403	6737	007547	692	016	055	695	925	294	1704	455	226	2524
67	6571	9745	3436	5950	6807	0114	402	6722	007435	691	015	053	693	923	291	1689	450	220	2500
68	6569	9743	3434	5947	6802	0107	400	6707	007326	691	014	052	692	920	288	1674	445	214	2477
69	6567	9741	3431	5944	6796	0099	399	6692	007221	690	013	051	690	918	285	1660	441	208	2455
70	1.6566	1.9739	2.3429	2.5942	1.6791	2.0092	2.398	2.6679	1.007118	1.689	2.012	2.049	2.689	1.916	2.282	1.1645	2.437	3.203	1.2433
71	6564	9737	3427	5939	6786	0085	398	6666	007018	689	012	048	687	913	280	1632	433	197	2411
72	6562	9735	3424	5937	6781	0078	396	6653	006920	688	011	047	686	911	277	1618	429	192	2391
73	6561	9733	3422	5934	6777	0071	395	6640	006826	688	010	046	684	909	275	1605	425	186	2370
74	6559	9732	3420	5932	6772	0065	394	6628	006734	687	010	045	683	907	272	1592	421	181	2350
75	1.6558	1.9730	2.3418	2.5929	1.6768	2.0058	2.394	2.6616	1.006645	1.686	2.009	2.044	2.681	1.905	2.270	1.1579	2.417	3.176	1.2331
76	6556	9728	3416	5927	6764	0052	393	6604	006558	686	009	043	680	903	267	1567	413	171	2312
77	6555	9727	3414	5925	6760	0046	391	6592	006473	685	008	042	679	901	265	1555	410	167	2294
78	6554	9725	3412	5923	6755	0040	391	6582	006390	685	007	041	678	899	263	1543	406	162	2276
79	6552	9723	3410	5921	6751	0035	390	6571	006309	685	007	040	677	897	260	1532	403	158	2258
80	1.6551	1.9722	2.3408	2.5919	1.6747	2.0029	2.389	2.6560	1.006231	1.684	2.006	2.039	2.676	1.895	2.258	1.1521	2.399	3.153	1.2241
81	6550	9720	3407	5917	6743	0023	389	6550	006154	684	006	038	674	893	256	1509	396	149	2224
82	6549	9719	3405	5915	6740	0018	387	6540	006079	683	005	037	673	891	254	1499	393	144	2207
83	6547	9717	3403	5913	6737	0012	386	6530	006006	683	004	036	672	890	252	1488	389	140	2191
84	6546	9716	3402	5911	6734	0007	386	6521	005934	682	004	035	671	888	250	1478	386	136	2175
85	1.6545	1.9715	2.3400	2.5909	1.6730	2.0003	2.385	2.6512	1.005865	1.682	2.004	2.034	2.670	1.886	2.248	1.1468	2.383	3.132	1.2159
86	6544	9713	3398	5908	6726	1.9998	385	6503	005797	681	003	033	669	885	246	1458	380	128	2144
87	6543	9712	3397	5906	6723	9994	384	6494	005731	681	002	032	668	883	244	1448	377	124	2129
88	6542	9711	3395	5904	6720	9989	383	6485	005666	680	002	032	667	881	242	1438	374	121	2115
89	6541	9709	3394	5903	6717	9985	382	6476	005602	680	002	031	666	880	240	1429	372	117	2100
90	1.6540	1.9708	2.3392	2.5901	1.6714	1.9980	2.382	2.6468	1.005541	1.680	2.001	2.030	2.665	1.878	2.238	1.1419	2.369	3.113	1.2086
91	6539	9707	3391	5899	6711	9976	381	6460	005480	679	000	029	664	877	236	1410	366	110	2072
92	6538	9706	3390	5898	6708	9972	381	6452	005420	679	000	029	664	875	235	1401	363	106	2059
93	6537	9705	3388	5896	6705	9968	380	6444	005362	678	000	028	663	874	233	1393	361	103	2045
94	6536	9704	3387	5895	6702	9964	380	6437	005305	678	1.999	027	662	873	231	1384	358	099	2032
95	1.6535	1.9703	2.3386	2.5893	1.6699	1.9960	2.378	2.6430	1.005249	1.678	1.999	2.026	2.661	1.871	2.230	1.1376	2.356	3.096	1.2019
96	6534	9701	3384	5892	6697	9956	378	6423	005195	677	999	026	660	870	228	1367	353	093	2007
97	6533	9700	3383	5891	6694	9952	378	6416	005141	677	998	025	659	868	226	1359	351	090	1994
98	6532	9699	3382	5889	6692	9949	377	6409	005090	677	998	024	658	867	225	1351	348	086	1982
99	6531	9698	3381	5888	6689	9945	377	6402	005038	677	997	024	657	866	223	1343	346	083	1970
100	1.6531	1.9697	2.3380	2.5887	1.6687	1.9942	2.376	2.6396	1.004988	1.676	1.997	2.023	2.657	1.865	2.222	1.1336	2.344	3.080	1.1958
∞	1.6449	1.9600	2.3263	2.5758	1.6449	1.9600	2.326	2.5758	1.000000	1.645	1.960	1.960	2.576	1.645	1.960	1.0000	1.960	2.576	1.0000

Tolerance Factors[7]

Tolerance factors k_7 for determination of the tolerance interval $\bar{x} \pm k_7 s$. $\beta_p = (1-2\alpha_p)$ = tolerance probability; $\beta_t = (1-2\alpha_t)$ = confidence probability; N = size of the sample from which $\bar{x}$ and s are calculated

	$\beta_t = 0.75$					$\beta_t = 0.90$					$\beta_t = 0.95$					$\beta_t = 0.99$				
β_p / N	0.75	0.90	0.95	0.99	0.999	0.75	0.90	0.95	0.99	0.999	0.75	0.90	0.95	0.99	0.999	0.75	0.90	0.95	0.99	0.999
2	4.498	6.301	7.414	9.531	11.920	11.407	15.978	18.800	24.167	30.227	22.858	32.019	37.674	48.430	60.573	114.363	160.193	188.491	242.300	303.054
3	2.501	3.538	4.187	5.431	6.844	4.132	5.847	6.919	8.974	11.309	5.922	8.380	9.916	12.861	16.208	13.378	18.930	22.401	29.055	36.616
4	2.035	2.892	3.431	4.471	5.657	2.932	4.166	4.943	6.440	8.149	3.779	5.369	6.370	8.299	10.502	6.614	9.398	11.150	14.527	18.383
5	1.825	2.599	3.088	4.033	5.117	2.454	3.494	4.152	5.423	6.879	3.002	4.275	5.079	6.634	8.415	4.643	6.612	7.855	10.260	13.015
6	1.704	2.429	2.889	3.779	4.802	2.196	3.131	3.723	4.870	6.188	2.604	3.712	4.414	5.775	7.337	3.743	5.337	6.345	8.301	10.548
7	1.624	2.318	2.757	3.611	4.593	2.034	2.902	3.452	4.521	5.750	2.361	3.369	4.007	5.248	6.676	3.233	4.613	5.488	7.187	9.142
8	1.568	2.238	2.663	3.491	4.444	1.921	2.743	3.264	4.278	5.446	2.197	3.136	3.732	4.891	6.226	2.905	4.147	4.936	6.468	8.234
9	1.525	2.178	2.593	3.400	4.330	1.839	2.626	3.125	4.098	5.220	2.078	2.967	3.532	4.631	5.899	2.677	3.822	4.550	5.966	7.600
10	1.492	2.131	2.537	3.328	4.241	1.775	2.535	3.018	3.959	5.046	1.987	2.839	3.379	4.433	5.649	2.508	3.582	4.265	5.594	7.129
11	1.465	2.093	2.493	3.271	4.169	1.724	2.463	2.933	3.849	4.906	1.916	2.737	3.259	4.277	5.452	2.378	3.397	4.045	5.308	6.766
12	1.443	2.062	2.456	3.223	4.110	1.683	2.404	2.863	3.758	4.792	1.858	2.655	3.162	4.150	5.291	2.274	3.250	3.870	5.079	6.477
13	1.425	2.036	2.424	3.183	4.059	1.648	2.355	2.805	3.682	4.697	1.810	2.587	3.081	4.044	5.158	2.190	3.130	3.727	4.893	6.240
14	1.409	2.013	2.398	3.148	4.016	1.619	2.314	2.756	3.618	4.615	1.770	2.529	3.012	3.955	5.045	2.120	3.029	3.608	4.737	6.043
15	1.395	1.994	2.375	3.118	3.979	1.594	2.278	2.713	3.562	4.545	1.735	2.480	2.954	3.878	4.949	2.060	2.945	3.507	4.605	5.876
16	1.383	1.977	2.355	3.092	3.946	1.572	2.246	2.676	3.514	4.484	1.705	2.437	2.903	3.812	4.865	2.009	2.872	3.421	4.492	5.732
17	1.372	1.962	2.337	3.069	3.917	1.552	2.219	2.643	3.471	4.430	1.679	2.400	2.858	3.754	4.791	1.965	2.808	3.345	4.393	5.607
18	1.363	1.948	2.321	3.048	3.891	1.535	2.194	2.614	3.433	4.382	1.655	2.366	2.819	3.702	4.725	1.926	2.753	3.279	4.307	5.497
19	1.355	1.936	2.307	3.030	3.867	1.520	2.172	2.588	3.399	4.339	1.635	2.337	2.784	3.656	4.667	1.891	2.703	3.221	4.230	5.399
20	1.347	1.925	2.294	3.013	3.846	1.506	2.152	2.564	3.368	4.300	1.616	2.310	2.752	3.615	4.614	1.860	2.659	3.168	4.161	5.312
21	1.340	1.915	2.282	2.998	3.827	1.493	2.135	2.543	3.340	4.264	1.599	2.286	2.723	3.577	4.567	1.833	2.620	3.121	4.100	5.234
22	1.334	1.906	2.271	2.984	3.809	1.482	2.118	2.524	3.315	4.232	1.584	2.264	2.697	3.543	4.523	1.808	2.584	3.078	4.044	5.163
23	1.328	1.898	2.261	2.971	3.793	1.471	2.103	2.506	3.292	4.203	1.570	2.244	2.673	3.512	4.484	1.785	2.551	3.040	3.993	5.098
24	1.322	1.891	2.252	2.959	3.778	1.462	2.089	2.489	3.270	4.176	1.557	2.225	2.651	3.483	4.447	1.764	2.522	3.004	3.947	5.039
25	1.317	1.883	2.244	2.948	3.764	1.453	2.077	2.474	3.251	4.151	1.545	2.208	2.631	3.457	4.413	1.745	2.494	2.972	3.904	4.985
26	1.313	1.877	2.236	2.938	3.751	1.444	2.065	2.460	3.232	4.127	1.534	2.193	2.612	3.432	4.382	1.727	2.469	2.941	3.865	4.935
27	1.309	1.871	2.229	2.929	3.740	1.437	2.054	2.447	3.215	4.106	1.523	2.178	2.595	3.409	4.353	1.711	2.446	2.914	3.828	4.888
28	1.305	1.865	2.222	2.920	3.728	1.430	2.044	2.435	3.199	4.085	1.514	2.164	2.579	3.388	4.326	1.695	2.424	2.888	3.794	4.845
29	1.301	1.860	2.216	2.911	3.718	1.423	2.034	2.424	3.184	4.066	1.505	2.152	2.564	3.368	4.301	1.681	2.404	2.864	3.763	4.805
30	1.297	1.855	2.210	2.904	3.708	1.417	2.025	2.413	3.170	4.049	1.497	2.140	2.549	3.350	4.278	1.668	2.385	2.841	3.733	4.768
31	1.294	1.850	2.204	2.896	3.699	1.411	2.017	2.403	3.157	4.032	1.489	2.129	2.536	3.332	4.256	1.656	2.367	2.820	3.706	4.732
32	1.291	1.846	2.199	2.890	3.690	1.405	2.009	2.393	3.145	4.016	1.481	2.118	2.524	3.316	4.235	1.644	2.351	2.801	3.680	4.699
33	1.288	1.842	2.194	2.883	3.682	1.400	2.001	2.385	3.133	4.001	1.475	2.108	2.512	3.300	4.215	1.633	2.335	2.782	3.655	4.668
34	1.285	1.838	2.189	2.877	3.674	1.395	1.994	2.376	3.122	3.987	1.468	2.099	2.501	3.286	4.197	1.623	2.320	2.764	3.632	4.639
35	1.283	1.834	2.185	2.871	3.667	1.390	1.988	2.368	3.112	3.974	1.462	2.090	2.490	3.272	4.179	1.613	2.306	2.748	3.611	4.611
36	1.280	1.830	2.181	2.866	3.660	1.386	1.981	2.361	3.102	3.961	1.455	2.081	2.479	3.258	4.161	1.604	2.293	2.732	3.590	4.585
37	1.278	1.827	2.177	2.860	3.653	1.381	1.975	2.353	3.092	3.949	1.450	2.073	2.470	3.246	4.146	1.595	2.281	2.717	3.571	4.560
38	1.275	1.824	2.173	2.855	3.647	1.377	1.969	2.346	3.083	3.938	1.446	2.068	2.464	3.237	4.134	1.587	2.269	2.703	3.552	4.537
39	1.273	1.821	2.169	2.850	3.641	1.374	1.964	2.340	3.075	3.927	1.441	2.060	2.455	3.226	4.120	1.579	2.257	2.690	3.534	4.514
40	1.271	1.818	2.166	2.846	3.635	1.370	1.959	2.334	3.066	3.917	1.435	2.052	2.445	3.213	4.104	1.571	2.247	2.677	3.518	4.493
41	1.269	1.815	2.162	2.841	3.629	1.366	1.954	2.328	3.059	3.907	1.430	2.045	2.437	3.202	4.090	1.564	2.236	2.665	3.502	4.472
42	1.267	1.812	2.159	2.837	3.624	1.363	1.949	2.322	3.051	3.897	1.426	2.039	2.429	3.192	4.077	1.557	2.227	2.653	3.486	4.453
43	1.266	1.810	2.156	2.833	3.619	1.360	1.944	2.316	3.044	3.888	1.422	2.033	2.422	3.183	4.065	1.551	2.217	2.642	3.472	4.434
44	1.264	1.807	2.153	2.829	3.614	1.357	1.940	2.311	3.037	3.879	1.418	2.027	2.415	3.173	4.053	1.545	2.208	2.631	3.458	4.416
45	1.262	1.805	2.150	2.826	3.609	1.354	1.935	2.306	3.030	3.871	1.414	2.021	2.408	3.165	4.042	1.539	2.200	2.621	3.444	4.399
46	1.261	1.802	2.148	2.822	3.605	1.351	1.931	2.301	3.024	3.863	1.410	2.016	2.402	3.156	4.031	1.533	2.192	2.611	3.431	4.383
47	1.259	1.800	2.145	2.819	3.600	1.348	1.927	2.297	3.018	3.855	1.406	2.011	2.396	3.148	4.021	1.527	2 184	2.602	3.419	4.367
48	1.258	1.798	2.143	2.815	3.596	1.345	1.924	2.292	3.012	3.847	1.403	2.006	2.390	3.140	4.011	1.522	2.176	2.593	3.407	4.352
49	1.256	1.796	2.140	2.812	3.592	1.343	1.920	2.288	3.006	3.840	1.399	2.001	2.384	3.133	4.002	1.517	2.169	2.584	3.396	4.337
50	1.255	1.794	2.138	2.809	3.588	1.340	1.916	2.284	3.001	3.833	1.396	1.996	2.379	3.126	3.993	1.512	2.162	2.576	3.385	4.323
51	1.253	1.792	2.135	2.806	3.584	1.338	1.913	2.279	2.995	3.826	1.393	1.992	2.373	3.119	3.984	1.507	2.155	2.568	3.374	4.310
52	1.252	1.790	2.133	2.803	3.581	1.336	1.910	2.276	2.990	3.820	1.390	1.988	2.368	3.112	3.975	1.503	2.148	2.560	3.364	4.297
53	1.251	1.789	2.131	2.801	3.577	1.334	1.907	2.272	2.985	3.813	1.387	1.984	2.363	3.106	3.967	1.498	2.142	2.552	3.354	4.284
54	1.250	1.787	2.129	2.798	3.574	1.331	1.904	2.268	2.981	3.807	1.384	1.980	2.359	3.100	3.959	1.494	2.136	2.545	3.344	4.272
55	1.249	1.785	2.127	2.795	3.571	1.329	1.901	2.265	2.976	3.801	1.382	1.976	2.354	3.094	3.951	1.490	2.130	2.538	3.335	4.260
56	1.247	1.784	2.125	2.793	3.567	1.327	1.898	2.261	2.972	3.796	1.379	1.972	2.350	3.088	3.944	1.486	2.124	2.531	3.326	4.249
57	1.246	1.782	2.123	2.790	3.564	1.325	1.895	2.258	2.967	3.790	1.377	1.968	2.345	3.082	3.937	1.482	2.119	2.524	3.318	4.238
58	1.245	1.781	2.122	2.788	3.561	1.323	1.892	2.255	2.963	3.785	1.374	1.965	2.341	3.076	3.930	1.478	2.113	2.518	3.309	4.227
59	1.244	1.779	2.120	2.786	3.558	1.322	1.890	2.252	2.959	3.779	1.372	1.961	2.337	3.071	3.923	1.474	2.108	2.512	3.301	4.216
60	1.243	1.778	2.118	2.784	3.556	1.320	1.887	2.248	2.955	3.774	1.369	1.958	2.333	3.066	3.916	1.471	2.103	2.506	3.293	4.206
61	1.242	1.776	2.117	2.781	3.553	1.318	1.885	2.245	2.951	3.769	1.367	1.955	2.329	3.061	3.909	1.467	2.098	2.500	3.285	4.196
62	1.241	1.775	2.115	2.779	3.550	1.316	1.882	2.243	2.947	3.765	1.365	1.951	2.325	3.056	3.903	1.464	2.093	2.494	3.278	4.187
63	1.240	1.774	2.113	2.777	3.548	1.315	1.880	2.240	2.944	3.760	1.363	1.948	2.322	3.051	3.897	1.461	2.089	2.489	3.271	4.178
64	1.240	1.772	2.112	2.775	3.545	1.313	1.878	2.237	2.940	3.755	1.361	1.945	2.318	3.046	3.891	1.458	2.084	2.483	3.264	4.169
65	1.239	1.771	2.110	2.773	3.543	1.312	1.875	2.235	2.937	3.751	1.359	1.943	2.315	3.042	3.886	1.455	2.080	2.478	3.257	4.160
66	1.238	1.770	2.109	2.771	3.540	1.310	1.873	2.232	2.933	3.747	1.357	1.940	2.311	3.037	3.880	1.452	2.076	2.473	3.250	4.152
67	1.237	1.769	2.108	2.770	3.538	1.309	1.871	2.229	2.930	3.742	1.355	1.937	2.308	3.033	3.874	1.449	2.071	2.468	3.244	4.143
68	1.236	1.768	2.106	2.768	3.536	1.307	1.869	2.227	2.927	3.738	1.353	1.934	2.305	3.029	3.869	1.446	2.067	2.463	3.237	4.135
69	1.235	1.766	2.105	2.766	3.533	1.306	1.867	2.225	2.923	3.734	1.351	1.932	2.302	3.025	3.864	1.443	2.063	2.459	3.231	4.127
70	1.235	1.765	2.104	2.764	3.531	1.304	1.865	2.222	2.920	3.730	1.349	1.929	2.299	3.021	3.859	1.440	2.060	2.454	3.225	4.120
71	1.234	1.764	2.102	2.763	3.529	1.303	1.863	2.220	2.917	3.727	1.347	1.927	2.296	3.017	3.854	1.438	2.056	2.450	3.219	4.112
72	1.233	1.763	2.101	2.761	3.527	1.302	1.861	2.218	2.915	3.723	1.346	1.924	2.293	3.013	3.849	1.435	2.052	2.445	3.214	4.105
73	1.233	1.762	2.100	2.760	3.525	1.300	1.859	2.216	2.912	3.719	1.344	1.922	2.290	3.009	3.844	1.433	2.049	2.441	3.208	4.098
74	1.232	1.761	2.099	2.758	3.523	1.299	1.858	2.214	2.909	3.716	1.343	1.920	2.287	3.006	3.840	1.430	2.045	2.437	3.203	4.091
75	1.231	1.760	2.098	2.757	3.521	1.298	1.856	2.211	2.906	3.712	1.341	1.917	2.285	3.002	3.835	1.428	2.042	2.433	3.197	4.084
76	1.230	1.759	2.096	2.755	3.519	1.297	1.854	2.209	2.904	3.709	1.339	1.915	2.282	2.999	3.831	1.426	2.039	2.429	3.192	4.078
77	1.230	1.758	2.095	2.754	3.517	1.296	1.853	2.207	2.901	3.706	1.338	1.913	2.279	2.996	3.826	1.423	2.035	2.425	3.187	4.071
78	1.229	1.758	2.094	2.752	3.516	1.295	1.851	2.206	2.898	3.702	1.336	1.911	2.277	2.992	3.822	1.421	2.032	2.421	3.182	4.065
79	1.229	1.757	2.093	2.751	3.514	1.293	1.849	2.204	2.896	3.699	1.335	1.909	2.274	2.989	3.818	1.419	2.029	2.418	3.177	4.059
80	1.228	1.756	2.092	2.749	3.512	1.292	1.848	2.202	2.894	3.696	1.334	1.907	2.272	2.986	3.814	1.417	2.026	2.414	3.173	4.053
81	1.227	1.755	2.091	2.748	3.510	1.291	1.846	2.200	2.891	3.693	1.332	1.905	2.270	2.983	3.810	1.415	2.023	2.411	3.168	4.047
82	1.227	1.754	2.090	2.747	3.509	1.290	1.845	2.198	2.889	3.690	1.331	1.903	2.267	2.980	3.806	1.413	2.020	2.407	3.163	4.041
83	1.226	1.753	2.089	2.746	3.507	1.289	1.843	2.196	2.887	3.687	1.329	1.901	2.265	2.977	3.803	1.411	2.017	2.404	3.159	4.035
84	1.226	1.753	2.088	2.744	3.506	1.288	1.842	2.195	2.884	3.684	1.328	1.899	2.263	2.974	3.799	1.409	2.014	2.400	3.155	4.030
85	1.225	1.752	2.087	2.743	3.504	1.287	1.841	2.193	2.882	3.682	1.327	1.897	2.261	2.971	3.795	1.407	2.012	2.397	3.150	4.024
86	1.225	1.751	2.086	2.742	3.503	1.286	1.839	2.191	2.880	3.679	1.326	1.896	2.259	2.968	3.792	1.405	2.009	2.394	3.146	4.019
87	1.224	1.750	2.086	2.741	3.501	1.285	1.838	2.190	2.878	3.676	1.324	1.894	2.257	2.966	3.788	1.403	2.007	2.391	3.142	4.014
88	1.224	1.749	2.085	2.740	3.500	1.284	1.837	2.188	2.876	3.674	1.323	1.892	2.255	2.963	3.785	1.402	2.004	2.388	3.138	4.009
89	1.223	1.749	2.084	2.738	3.498	1.284	1.835	2.187	2.874	3.671	1.322	1.890	2.253	2.960	3.781	1.400	2.001	2.385	3.134	4.004
90	1.223	1.748	2.083	2.737	3.497	1.283	1.834	2.185	2.872	3.669	1.321	1.889	2.251	2.958	3.778	1.398	1.999	2.382	3.130	3.999
91	1.222	1.747	2.082	2.736	3.495	1.282	1.833	2.184	2.870	3.666	1.320	1.887	2.249	2.955	3.775	1.396	1.997	2.379	3.127	3.994
92	1.222	1.747	2.081	2.735	3.494	1.281	1.832	2.182	2.868	3.664	1.319	1.886	2.247	2.953	3.772	1.395	1.994	2.376	3.123	3.989
93	1.221	1.746	2.081	2.734	3.493	1.280	1.830	2.181	2.866	3.661	1.318	1.884	2.245	2.950	3.769	1.393	1.992	2.373	3.119	3.985
94	1.221	1.745	2.080	2.733	3.491	1.279	1.829	2.180	2.864	3.659	1.317	1.882	2.243	2.948	3.766	1.392	1.990	2.371	3.116	3.980
95	1.220	1.745	2.079	2.732	3.490	1.278	1.828	2.178	2.863	3.657	1.315	1.881	2.241	2.945	3.763	1.390	1.987	2.368	3.112	3.976
96	1.220	1.744	2.078	2.731	3.489	1.278	1.827	2.177	2.861	3.654	1.314	1.880	2.240	2.943	3.760	1.388	1.985	2.366	3.109	3.971
97	1.219	1.743	2.077	2.730	3.488	1.277	1.826	2.175	2.859	3.652	1.313	1.878	2.238	2.941	3.757	1.387	1.983	2.363	3.105	3.967
98	1.219	1.743	2.077	2.729	3.486	1.276	1.825	2.174	2.857	3.650	1.312	1.877	2.236	2.939	3.754	1.385	1.981	2.360	3.102	3.963
99	1.219	1.742	2.076	2.728	3.485	1.275	1.824	2.173	2.856	3.648	1.311	1.875	2.234	2.936	3.751	1.384	1.979	2.358	3.099	3.958

[7] Values from Bowker, A.H., in Eisenhart et al. (Eds.), *Selected Techniques of Statistical Analysis for Scientific and Industrial Research and Production and Management Engineering*, McGraw-Hill, New York and London, 1947, page 102. Reprinted by kind permission of the author and publishers.

Tolerance factors k_7 for determination of the tolerance interval $\bar{x} \pm k_7 s$. $\beta_p = (1 - 2\alpha_p)$ = tolerance probability; $\beta_t = (1 - 2\alpha_t)$ = confidence probability; N = size of the sample from which $\bar{x}$ and s are calculated

	$\beta_t = 0.75$					$\beta_t = 0.90$					$\beta_t = 0.95$					$\beta_t = 0.99$				
N \ β_p	0.75	0.90	0.95	0.99	0.999	0.75	0.90	0.95	0.99	0.999	0.75	0.90	0.95	0.99	0.999	0.75	0.90	0.95	0.99	0.999
100	1.218	1.742	2.075	2.727	3.484	1.275	1.822	2.172	2.854	3.646	1.311	1.874	2.233	2.934	3.748	1.383	1.977	2.355	3.096	3.954
101	1.218	1.741	2.075	2.726	3.483	1.274	1.821	2.170	2.852	3.644	1.310	1.872	2.231	2.932	3.746	1.381	1.975	2.353	3.092	3.950
102	1.217	1.741	2.074	2.726	3.482	1.273	1.820	2.169	2.851	3.642	1.309	1.871	2.230	2.930	3.743	1.380	1.973	2.351	3.089	3.946
104	1.217	1.739	2.073	2.724	3.480	1.272	1.818	2.167	2.848	3.638	1.307	1.869	2.227	2.926	3.738	1.377	1.969	2.346	3.083	3.939
106	1.216	1.738	2.071	2.722	3.477	1.270	1.816	2.164	2.845	3.634	1.305	1.866	2.224	2.922	3.733	1.374	1.965	2.342	3.077	3.931
108	1.215	1.737	2.070	2.721	3.475	1.269	1.815	2.162	2.842	3.630	1.303	1.864	2.221	2.918	3.728	1.372	1.962	2.337	3.072	3.924
110	1.214	1.736	2.069	2.719	3.473	1.268	1.813	2.160	2.839	3.626	1.302	1.861	2.218	2.915	3.723	1.369	1.958	2.333	3.066	3.917
112	1.214	1.735	2.068	2.717	3.471	1.267	1.811	2.158	2.836	3.623	1.300	1.859	2.215	2.911	3.719	1.367	1.955	2.329	3.061	3.910
114	1.213	1.734	2.067	2.716	3.469	1.265	1.809	2.156	2.833	3.619	1.299	1.857	2.212	2.908	3.714	1.365	1.951	2.325	3.056	3.904
116	1.212	1.733	2.065	2.714	3.468	1.264	1.808	2.154	2.831	3.616	1.297	1.855	2.210	2.904	3.710	1.363	1.948	2.321	3.051	3.897
118	1.212	1.733	2.064	2.713	3.466	1.263	1.806	2.152	2.828	3.613	1.296	1.852	2.207	2.901	3.706	1.360	1.945	2.318	3.046	3.891
120	1.211	1.732	2.063	2.712	3.464	1.262	1.804	2.150	2.826	3.610	1.294	1.850	2.205	2.898	3.702	1.358	1.942	2.314	3.041	3.885
122	1.210	1.731	2.062	2.710	3.462	1.261	1.803	2.148	2.823	3.607	1.293	1.848	2.203	2.895	3.698	1.356	1.939	2.311	3.037	3.879
124	1.210	1.730	2.061	2.709	3.461	1.260	1.801	2.147	2.821	3.604	1.291	1.847	2.200	2.892	3.694	1.354	1.936	2.307	3.032	3.873
126	1.209	1.729	2.060	2.708	3.459	1.259	1.800	2.145	2.819	3.601	1.290	1.845	2.198	2.889	3.690	1.352	1.934	2.304	3.028	3.868
128	1.209	1.728	2.060	2.707	3.458	1.258	1.799	2.143	2.816	3.598	1.289	1.843	2.196	2.886	3.686	1.350	1.931	2.301	3.024	3.862
130	1.208	1.728	2.059	2.705	3.456	1.257	1.797	2.141	2.814	3.595	1.288	1.841	2.194	2.883	3.683	1.349	1.928	2.298	3.019	3.857
132	1.208	1.727	2.058	2.704	3.455	1.256	1.796	2.140	2.812	3.592	1.286	1.839	2.192	2.880	3.679	1.347	1.926	2.295	3.015	3.852
134	1.207	1.726	2.057	2.703	3.453	1.255	1.795	2.138	2.810	3.590	1.285	1.838	2.190	2.878	3.676	1.345	1.923	2.292	3.012	3.847
136	1.207	1.725	2.056	2.702	3.452	1.254	1.793	2.137	2.808	3.587	1.284	1.836	2.188	2.875	3.673	1.343	1.921	2.289	3.008	3.842
138	1.206	1.725	2.055	2.701	3.450	1.253	1.792	2.135	2.806	3.585	1.283	1.834	2.186	2.873	3.669	1.342	1.918	2.286	3.004	3.837
140	1.206	1.724	2.054	2.700	3.449	1.252	1.791	2.134	2.804	3.582	1.282	1.833	2.184	2.870	3.666	1.340	1.916	2.283	3.000	3.833
142	1.205	1.723	2.054	2.699	3.448	1.252	1.790	2.132	2.802	3.580	1.281	1.831	2.182	2.868	3.663	1.338	1.914	2.280	2.997	3.828
144	1.205	1.723	2.053	2.698	3.446	1.251	1.788	2.131	2.801	3.578	1.280	1.830	2.180	2.865	3.660	1.337	1.912	2.278	2.993	3.824
146	1.204	1.722	2.052	2.697	3.445	1.250	1.787	2.130	2.799	3.575	1.279	1.828	2.178	2.863	3.657	1.335	1.909	2.275	2.990	3.820
148	1.204	1.722	2.051	2.696	3.444	1.249	1.786	2.128	2.797	3.573	1.278	1.827	2.177	2.861	3.654	1.334	1.907	2.273	2.987	3.815
150	1.204	1.721	2.051	2.695	3.443	1.248	1.785	2.127	2.795	3.571	1.277	1.825	2.175	2.859	3.652	1.332	1.905	2.270	2.983	3.811
152	1.203	1.720	2.050	2.694	3.441	1.248	1.784	2.126	2.794	3.569	1.276	1.824	2.173	2.856	3.649	1.331	1.903	2.268	2.980	3.807
154	1.203	1.720	2.049	2.693	3.440	1.247	1.783	2.125	2.792	3.567	1.275	1.823	2.172	2.854	3.646	1.330	1.901	2.265	2.977	3.803
156	1.202	1.719	2.049	2.692	3.439	1.246	1.782	2.123	2.791	3.565	1.274	1.821	2.170	2.852	3.644	1.328	1.899	2.263	2.974	3.799
158	1.202	1.719	2.048	2.691	3.438	1.246	1.781	2.122	2.789	3.563	1.273	1.820	2.169	2.850	3.641	1.327	1.897	2.261	2.971	3.796
160	1.202	1.718	2.047	2.691	3.437	1.245	1.780	2.121	2.787	3.561	1.272	1.819	2.167	2.848	3.638	1.326	1.896	2.259	2.968	3.792
162	1.201	1.718	2.047	2.690	3.436	1.244	1.779	2.120	2.786	3.559	1 271	1.818	2.166	2.846	3.636	1.324	1.894	2.256	2.965	3.788
164	1.201	1.717	2.046	2.689	3.435	1.244	1.778	2.119	2.785	3.557	1.270	1.816	2.164	2.844	3.634	1.323	1.892	2.254	2.963	3.785
166	1.201	1.717	2.045	2.688	3.434	1.243	1.777	2.118	2.783	3.555	1.269	1.815	2.163	2.843	3.631	1.322	1.890	2.252	2.960	3.781
168	1.200	1.716	2.045	2.687	3.433	1.242	1.776	2.117	2.782	3.553	1.269	1.814	2.162	2.841	3.629	1.321	1.888	2.250	2.957	3.778
170	1.200	1.716	2.044	2.687	3.432	1.242	1.775	2.116	2.780	3.552	1.268	1.813	2.160	2.839	3.627	1.320	1.887	2.248	2.955	3.774
172	1.199	1.715	2.044	2.686	3.431	1.241	1.775	2.115	2.779	3.550	1.267	1.812	2.159	2.837	3.624	1.318	1.885	2.246	2.952	3.771
174	1.199	1.715	2.043	2.685	3.430	1.240	1.774	2.114	2.778	3.548	1.266	1.811	2.158	2.835	3.622	1.317	1.884	2.244	2.950	3.768
176	1.199	1.714	2.043	2.684	3.429	1.240	1.773	2.113	2.776	3.547	1.266	1.810	2.156	2.834	3.620	1.316	1.882	2.243	2.947	3.765
178	1.199	1.714	2.042	2.684	3.428	1.239	1.772	2.112	2.775	3.545	1.265	1.809	2.155	2.832	3.618	1.315	1.880	2.241	2.945	3.762
180	1.198	1.713	2.042	2.683	3.427	1.239	1.771	2.111	2.774	3.543	1.264	1.808	2.154	2.831	3.616	1.314	1.879	2.239	2.942	3.759
185	1.197	1.712	2.040	2.681	3.425	1.237	1.769	2.108	2.771	3.539	1.262	1.805	2.151	2.827	3.611	1.311	1.875	2.234	2.937	3.751
190	1.197	1.711	2.039	2.680	3.423	1.236	1.767	2.106	2.768	3.536	1.261	1.803	2.148	2.823	3.606	1.309	1.872	2.230	2.931	3.744
195	1.196	1.710	2.038	2.678	3.421	1.235	1.766	2.104	2.765	3.532	1.259	1.800	2.145	2.819	3.601	1.307	1.868	2.226	2.926	3.738
200	1.195	1.709	2.037	2.677	3.419	1.234	1.764	2.102	2.762	3.529	1.258	1.798	2.143	2.816	3.597	1.304	1.865	2.222	2.921	3.731
205	1.195	1.708	2.036	2.675	3.418	1.233	1.762	2.100	2.760	3.526	1.256	1.796	2.140	2.812	3.593	1.302	1.862	2.219	2.916	3.725
210	1.194	1.708	2.035	2.674	3.416	1.231	1.761	2.098	2.757	3.522	1.255	1.794	2.138	2.809	3.589	1.300	1.859	2.215	2.911	3.719
215	1.194	1.707	2.034	2.673	3.414	1.230	1.759	2.096	2.755	3.519	1.253	1.792	2.135	2.806	3.585	1.298	1.856	2.212	2.907	3.713
220	1.193	1.706	2.033	2.671	3.413	1.229	1.758	2.095	2.753	3.516	1.252	1.790	2.133	2.803	3.581	1.296	1.854	2.209	2.903	3.708
225	1.192	1.705	2.032	2.670	3.411	1.228	1.756	2.093	2.750	3.514	1.251	1.788	2.131	2.800	3.577	1.294	1.851	2.205	2.898	3.703
230	1.192	1.704	2.031	2.669	3.409	1.227	1.755	2.091	2.748	3.511	1.249	1.787	2.129	2.798	3.574	1.293	1.848	2.202	2.894	3.697
235	1.191	1.704	2.030	2.668	3.408	1.226	1.754	2.090	2.746	3.508	1.248	1.785	2.127	2.795	3.571	1.291	1.846	2.199	2.890	3.692
240	1.191	1.703	2.029	2.667	3.407	1.226	1.752	2.088	2.744	3.506	1.247	1.783	2.125	2.792	3.567	1.289	1.843	2.197	2.887	3.688
245	1.190	1.702	2.028	2.666	3.405	1.225	1.751	2.087	2.742	3.503	1.246	1.782	2.123	2.790	3.564	1.288	1.841	2.194	2.883	3.683
250	1.190	1.702	2.028	2.665	3.404	1.224	1.750	2.085	2.740	3.501	1.245	1.780	2.121	2.788	3.561	1.286	1.839	2.191	2.880	3.678
255	1.190	1.701	2.027	2.664	3.403	1.223	1.749	2.084	2.739	3.499	1.244	1.779	2.119	2.785	3.558	1.284	1.837	2.189	2.876	3.674
260	1.189	1.700	2.026	2.663	3.401	1.222	1.748	2.083	2.737	3.496	1.243	1.777	2.118	2.783	3.555	1.283	1.835	2.186	2.873	3.670
265	1.189	1.700	2.025	2.662	3.400	1.222	1.747	2.081	2.735	3.494	1.242	1.776	2.116	2.781	3.552	1.282	1.833	2.184	2.870	3.666
270	1.188	1.699	2.025	2.661	3.399	1.221	1.746	2.080	2.734	3.492	1.241	1.774	2.114	2.779	3.550	1.280	1.831	2.181	2.867	3.662
275	1.188	1.699	2.024	2.660	3.398	1.220	1.745	2.079	2.732	3.490	1.240	1.773	2.113	2.777	3.547	1.279	1.829	2.179	2.864	3.658
280	1.188	1.698	2.023	2.659	3.397	1.219	1.744	2.078	2.730	3.488	1.239	1.772	2.111	2.775	3.544	1.278	1.827	2.177	2.861	3.655
285	1.187	1.698	2.023	2.658	3.396	1.219	1.743	2.076	2.729	3.486	1.238	1.771	2.110	2.773	3.542	1.276	1.825	2.175	2.858	3.651
290	1.187	1.697	2.022	2.658	3.395	1.218	1.742	2.075	2.727	3.484	1.237	1.769	2.108	2.771	3.540	1.275	1.823	2.173	2.855	3.647
295	1.186	1.697	2.022	2.657	3.394	1.217	1.741	2.074	2.726	3.482	1.237	1.768	2.107	2.769	3.537	1.274	1.822	2.170	2.853	3.644
300	1.186	1.696	2.021	2.656	3.393	1.217	1.740	2.073	2.725	3.481	1.236	1.767	2.106	2.767	3.535	1.273	1.820	2.169	2.850	3.641
310	1.185	1.695	2.020	2.655	3.391	1.216	1.738	2.071	2.722	3.477	1.234	1.765	2.103	2.764	3.531	1.271	1.817	2.165	2.845	3.634
320	1.185	1.694	2.019	2.653	3.389	1.215	1.737	2.069	2.719	3.474	1.233	1.763	2.100	2.760	3.526	1.268	1.814	2.161	2.840	3.628
330	1.184	1.693	2.018	2.652	3.388	1.213	1.735	2.067	2.717	3.471	1.231	1.761	2.098	2.757	3.522	1.266	1.811	2.158	2.836	3.623
340	1.184	1.693	2.017	2.651	3.386	1.212	1.734	2.066	2.715	3.468	1.230	1.759	2.096	2.754	3.519	1.265	1.808	2.154	2.831	3.617
350	1.183	1.692	2.016	2.649	3.384	1.211	1.732	2.064	2.713	3.465	1.229	1.757	2.094	2.752	3.515	1.263	1.805	2.151	2.827	3.612
360	1.183	1.691	2.015	2.648	3.383	1.210	1.731	2.062	2.710	3.463	1.228	1.755	2.092	2.749	3.512	1.261	1.803	2.148	2.823	3.607
370	1.182	1.690	2.014	2.647	3.382	1.210	1.730	2.061	2.708	3.460	1.227	1.754	2.090	2.746	3.508	1.259	1.801	2.146	2.820	3.602
380	1.182	1.690	2.013	2.646	3.380	1.209	1.728	2.059	2.707	3.458	1.225	1.752	2.088	2.744	3.505	1.258	1.798	2.143	2.816	3.598
390	1.181	1.689	2.013	2.645	3.379	1.208	1.727	2.058	2.705	3.455	1.224	1.751	2.086	2.742	3.502	1.256	1.796	2.140	2.813	3.593
400	1.181	1.688	2.012	2.644	3.378	1.207	1.726	2.057	2.703	3.453	1.223	1.749	2.084	2.739	3.499	1.255	1.794	2.138	2.809	3.589
425	1.180	1.687	2.010	2.642	3.375	1.205	1.723	2.054	2.699	3.448	1.221	1.746	2.080	2.734	3.492	1.251	1.789	2.132	2.802	3.579
450	1.179	1.686	2.009	2.640	3.372	1.204	1.721	2.051	2.695	3.443	1.219	1.743	2.077	2.729	3.486	1.248	1.785	2.127	2.795	3.570
475	1.178	1.685	2.007	2.638	3.370	1.202	1.719	2.048	2.692	3.438	1.217	1.740	2.073	2.725	3.481	1.245	1.781	2.122	2.788	3.562
500	1.177	1.683	2.006	2.636	3.368	1.201	1.717	2.046	2.689	3.434	1.215	1.737	2.070	2.721	3.475	1.243	1.777	2.117	2.783	3.555
525	1.177	1.682	2.005	2.635	3.366	1.199	1.715	2.043	2.686	3.431	1.213	1.735	2.067	2.717	3.471	1.240	1.773	2.113	2.777	3.548
550	1.176	1.681	2.004	2.633	3.364	1.198	1.713	2.041	2.683	3.427	1.212	1.733	2.065	2.713	3.466	1.238	1.770	2.109	2.772	3.541
575	1.175	1.681	2.003	2.632	3.362	1.197	1.712	2.039	2.680	3.424	1 210	1.731	2.062	2.710	3.462	1.236	1.767	2.106	2.767	3.535
600	1.175	1.680	2.002	2.631	3.360	1.196	1.710	2.038	2.678	3.421	1.209	1.729	2.060	2.707	3.458	1.234	1.764	2.102	2.763	3.530
625	1.174	1.679	2.001	2.629	3.359	1.195	1.709	2.036	2.676	3.418	1.208	1.727	2.058	2.704	3.455	1.232	1.762	2.099	2.759	3.525
650	1.174	1.678	2.000	2.628	3.357	1.194	1.707	2.034	2.674	3.416	1.207	1.725	2.056	2.702	3.451	1.230	1.759	2.096	2.755	3.520
675	1.173	1.678	1.999	2.627	3.356	1.193	1.706	2.033	2.672	3.413	1.205	1.724	2.054	2.699	3.448	1.229	1.757	2.094	2.752	3.515
700	1.173	1.677	1.998	2.626	3.355	1.192	1.705	2.032	2.670	3.411	1.204	1.722	2.052	2.697	3.445	1.227	1.755	2.091	2.748	3.511
725	1.172	1.676	1.998	2.625	3.354	1.192	1.704	2.030	2.668	3.408	1.203	1.721	2.050	2.694	3.442	1.226	1.753	2.089	2.745	3.507
750	1.172	1.676	1.997	2.624	3.352	1.191	1.703	2.029	2.667	3.406	1.202	1.719	2.049	2.692	3.439	1.225	1.751	2.086	2.742	3.503
800	1.171	1.675	1.996	2.623	3.350	1.189	1.701	2.027	2.663	3.402	1.201	1.717	2.046	2.688	3.434	1.222	1.747	2.082	2.736	3.495
850	1.171	1.674	1.994	2.621	3.348	1.188	1.699	2.025	2.661	3.399	1.199	1.714	2.043	2.685	3.430	1.220	1.744	2.078	2.731	3.489
900	1.170	1.673	1.993	2.620	3.347	1.187	1.697	2.023	2.658	3.396	1.198	1.712	2.040	2.682	3.426	1.218	1.741	2.075	2.726	3.483
950	1.169	1.672	1.992	2.619	3.345	1.186	1.696	2.021	2.656	3.393	1.196	1.710	2.038	2.679	3.422	1.216	1.738	2.071	2.722	3.477
1000	1.169	1.671	1.992	2.617	3.344	1.185	1.695	2.019	2.654	3.390	1.195	1.709	2.036	2.676	3.418	1.214	1.736	2.068	2.718	3.472
∞	1.150	1.645	1.960	2.576	3.291	1.150	1.645	1.960	2.576	3.291	1.150	1.645	1.960	2.576	3.291	1.150	1.645	1.960	2.576	3.291

[1] Values from BOWKER, A.H., in EISENHART et al. (Eds.), *Selected Techniques of Statistical Analysis for Scientific and Industrial Research and Production and Management Engineering*, McGraw-Hill, New York and London, 1947, page 102. Reprinted by kind permission of the author and publishers.

For explanation see page 48

Correction factors[1] and confidence factors[2] for σ

ν	k_s	$1-2\alpha=0.90$	$1-2\alpha=0.95$	$1-2\alpha=0.98$	$1-2\alpha=0.99$
1	1.2533	0.5102–15.947	0.4463–31.910	0.3882–79.789	0.3562–159.58
2	1284	5777– 4.416	5207– 6.285	4660– 9.974	4344– 14.124
3	0854	6196– 2.920	5665– 3.729	5142– 5.111	4834– 6.468
4	0638	6493– 372	5991– 2.874	5489– 3.669	5188– 4.396
5	1.0509	0.6720– 2.089	0.6242– 2.453	0.5757– 3.003	0.5464– 3.485
6	0424	6903– 1.915	6444– 202	5974– 2.623	5688– 2.980
7	0362	7054– 797	6612– 035	6155– 377	5875– 660
8	0317	7183– 711	6755– 1.916	6310– 204	6036– 439
9	0281	7293– 645	6878– 826	6445– 076	6177– 278
10	1.0253	0.7391– 1.593	0.6987– 1.755	0.6564– 1.977	0.6301– 2.154
11	0230	7477– 551	7084– 698	6670– 898	6412– 056
12	0210	7555– 515	7171– 651	6765– 833	6512– 1.976
13	0194	7625– 485	7250– 611	6852– 779	6603– 910
14	0180	7688– 460	7321– 577	6931– 733	6686– 854
15	1.0168	0.7747– 1.437	0.7387– 1.548	0.7004– 1.694	0.6762– 1.806
16	0157	7800– 418	7448– 522	7071– 659	6833– 764
17	0148	7850– 400	7504– 499	7133– 629	6899– 727
18	0140	7896– 384	7556– 479	7191– 602	6960– 695
19	0132	7939– 370	7604– 461	7246– 578	7018– 666
20	1.0126	0.7980– 1.358	0.7651– 1.444	0.7297– 1.556	0.7071– 1.640
21	0120	8017– 346	7694– 429	7344– 536	7122– 617
22	0114	8053– 335	7734– 415	7390– 518	7170– 596
23	0109	8087– 326	7772– 403	7432– 502	7215– 576
24	0105	8118– 316	7808– 391	7473– 487	7258– 558
25	1.0100	0.8148– 1.308	0.7843– 1.380	0.7511– 1.473	0.7299– 1.542
26	0097	8177– 300	7875– 370	7548– 460	7338– 526
27	0093	8204– 293	7906– 361	7582– 448	7375– 512
28	0090	8230– 286	7936– 352	7616– 437	7410– 499
29	0087	8255– 280	7964– 344	7647– 426	7444– 487
30	1.0084	0.8279– 1.274	0.7991– 1.337	0.7678– 1.416	0.7476– 1.475
31	0081	8301– 268	8017– 329	7707– 407	7507– 464
32	0078	8323– 263	8042– 323	7735– 399	7537– 454
33	0076	8344– 258	8066– 316	7762– 390	7566– 445
34	0074	8364– 253	8089– 310	7788– 382	7594– 435
35	1.0072	0.8383– 1.248	0.8111– 1.304	0.7813– 1.375	0.7620– 1.427
36	0070	8402– 244	8132– 299	7837– 368	7646– 419
37	0068	8420– 240	8153– 294	7860– 362	7671– 411
38	0066	8437– 236	8172– 289	7882– 355	7695– 404
39	0064	8454– 232	8192– 284	7904– 349	7718– 397
40	1.0063	0.8470– 1.228	0.8210– 1.279	0.7925– 1.343	0.7740– 1.390
41	0061	8485– 225	8228– 275	7945– 338	7762– 383
42	0060	8501– 222	8245– 271	7965– 333	7783– 377
43	0058	8515– 218	8262– 267	7984– 328	7803– 372
44	0057	8529– 215	8279– 263	8002– 323	7823– 366
45	1.0056	0.8543– 1.212	0.8294– 1.260	0.8020– 1.318	0.7842– 1.361
46	0055	8556– 210	8310– 256	8038– 314	7861– 355
47	0053	8569– 207	8325– 253	8055– 309	7879– 350
48	0052	8582– 204	8339– 249	8071– 305	7897– 346
49	0051	8594– 202	8353– 246	8087– 301	7914– 341
50	1.0050	0.8606– 1.199	0.8367– 1.243	0.8103– 1.297	0.7931– 1.337
51	0049	8618– 197	8380– 240	8118– 294	7947– 332
52	0048	8629– 195	8394– 237	8133– 290	7963– 328
53	0047	8640– 192	8406– 235	8147– 287	7979– 324
54	0046	8651– 190	8419– 232	8161– 283	7994– 320
55	1.0046	0.8662– 1.188	0.8431– 1.229	0.8175– 1.280	0.8009– 1.316
56	0045	8672– 186	8443– 227	8189– 277	8023– 313
57	0044	8682– 184	8454– 224	8202– 274	8037– 309
58	0043	8692– 182	8465– 222	8215– 271	8051– 306
59	0043	8701– 180	8476– 220	8227– 268	8065– 303
60	1.0042	0.8710– 1.179	0.8487– 1.217	0.8239– 1.265	0.8078– 1.299
61	0041	8719– 177	8498– 215	8251– 262	8091 296
62	0040	8728– 175	8508– 213	8263– 260	8103– 293
63	0040	8737– 174	8518– 211	8275– 257	8116– 290
64	0039	8746– 172	8528– 209	8286– 255	8128– 287
65	1.0039	0.8754– 1.170	0.8537– 1.207	0.8297– 1.252	0.8140– 1.285
66	0038	8762– 169	8547– 205	8308– 250	8151– 282
67	0037	8770– 167	8556– 203	8318– 248	8163– 279
68	0037	8778– 166	8565– 202	8329– 245	8174– 277
69	0036	8786– 165	8574– 200	8339– 243	8185– 274
70	1.0036	0.8793– 1.163	0.8583– 1.198	0.8349– 1.241	0.8196– 1.272
71	0035	8801– 162	8591– 197	8359– 239	8206– 269
72	0035	8808– 160	8600– 195	8368– 237	8217– 267
73	0034	8815– 159	8608– 193	8378– 235	8227– 265
74	0034	8822– 158	8616– 192	8387– 233	8237– 263
75	1.0033	0.8829– 1.157	0.8624– 1.190	0.8396– 1.231	0.8247– 1.260
76	0033	8836– 156	8632– 189	8405– 229	8256– 258
77	0033	8842– 154	8640– 187	8414– 228	8266– 256
78	0032	8849– 153	8647– 186	8422– 226	8275– 254
79	0032	8855– 152	8655– 184	8431– 224	8284– 252
80	1.0031	0.8861– 1.151	0.8662– 1.183	0.8439– 1.222	0.8293– 1.250
81	0031	8868– 150	8669– 182	8447– 221	8302– 248
82	0031	8874– 149	8676– 180	8455– 219	8311– 247
83	0030	8880– 148	8683– 179	8463– 218	8319– 245
84	0030	8885– 147	8690– 178	8471– 216	8328– 243
85	1.0030	0.8891– 1.146	0.8696– 1.177	0.8479– 1.214	0.8336– 1.241
86	0029	8897– 145	8703– 175	8486– 213	8344– 240
87	0029	8902– 144	8709– 174	8494– 211	8352– 238
88	0029	8908– 143	8716– 173	8501– 210	8360– 236
89	0028	8913– 142	8722– 172	8508– 209	8368– 235
90	1.0028	0.8919– 1.141	0.8728– 1.171	0.8515– 1.207	0.8375– 1.233
91	0028	8924– 140	8734– 170	8522– 206	8383– 231
92	0027	8929– 139	8740– 169	8529– 205	8390– 230
93	0027	8934– 138	8746– 168	8536– 203	8398– 228
94	0027	8939– 138	8752– 167	8543– 202	8405– 227
95	1.0026	0.8944– 1.137	0.8758– 1.166	0.8549– 1.201	0.8412– 1.226
96	0026	8949– 136	8764– 165	8556– 199	8419– 224
97	0026	8954– 135	8769– 164	8562– 198	8426– 223
98	0026	8959– 134	8775– 163	8569– 197	8433– 221
99	0025	8963– 134	8780– 162	8575– 196	8440– 220
100	1.0025	0.8968– 1.133	0.8785– 1.161	0.8581– 1.195	0.8446– 1.219
∞	1.0000	1.0000	1.0000	1.0000	1.0000

Mean extreme range[3] as multiple of σ

n	0	1 10	2 20	3 30	4 40	5 50	6 60	7 70	8 80	9 90
0	—	—	1.1284	1.6926	2.0588	2.3259	2.5344	2.7044	2.8472	2.9700
10	3.0775	3.1729	3.2585	3.3360	3.4068	3.4718	3.5320	3.5879	3.6401	3.6890
20	3.7350	3.7783	3.8194	3.8583	3.8954	3.9306	3.9643	3.9965	4.0274	4.0570
30	4.0855	4.1129	4.1393	4.1648	4.1894	4.2132	4.2363	4.2586	4.2802	4.3012
40	4.3216	4.3414	4.3606	4.3794	4.3976	4.4154	4.4328	4.4497	4.4662	4.4824
50	4.4982	4.5136	4.5286	4.5434	4.5578	4.5720	4.5858	4.5994	4.6127	4.6258
60	4.6386	4.6511	4.6635	4.6756	4.6875	4.6992	4.7107	4.7219	4.7331	4.7440
70	4.7547	4.7653	4.7757	4.7860	4.7960	4.8060	4.8158	4.8254	4.8349	4.8443
80	4.8536	4.8627	4.8717	4.8805	4.8893	4.8979	4.9064	4.9148	4.9231	4.9313
90	4.9394	4.9474	4.9553	4.9631	4.9708	4.9784	4.9859	4.9934	5.0007	5.0080
100	5.0152	5.0223	5.0293	5.0363	5.0432	5.0500	5.0567	5.0634	5.0700	5.0765
110	5.0830	5.0893	5.0957	5.1020	5.1082	5.1143	5.1204	5.1264	5.1324	5.1383
120	5.1442	5.1500	5.1557	5.1614	5.1671	5.1727	5.1782	5.1837	5.1892	5.1946
130	5.2000	5.2053	5.2106	5.2158	5.2210	5.2261	5.2312	5.2363	5.2413	5.2462
140	5.2512	5.2561	5.2609	5.2658	5.2705	5.2753	5.2800	5.2847	5.2893	5.2939
150	5.2985	5.3030	5.3075	5.3120	5.3165	5.3209	5.3252	5.3296	5.3339	5.3382
160	5.3424	5.3467	5.3509	5.3550	5.3592	5.3633	5.3674	5.3714	5.3755	5.3795
170	5.3834	5.3874	5.3913	5.3952	5.3991	5.4030	5.4068	5.4106	5.4144	5.4181
180	5.4219	5.4256	5.4293	5.4329	5.4366	5.4402	5.4438	5.4474	5.4509	5.4545
190	5.4580	5.4615	5.4650	5.4684	5.4719	5.4753	5.4787	5.4821	5.4854	5.4888
200	5.4921	5.4954	5.4987	5.5020	5.5052	5.5084	5.5117	5.5149	5.5180	5.5212
210	5.5244	5.5275	5.5306	5.5337	5.5368	5.5399	5.5429	5.5459	5.5490	5.5520
220	5.5550	5.5579	5.5609	5.5639	5.5668	5.5697	5.5726	5.5755	5.5784	5.5812
230	5.5841	5.5869	5.5898	5.5926	5.5954	5.5981	5.6009	5.6037	5.6064	5.6091
240	5.6119	5.6146	5.6173	5.6199	5.6226	5.6253	5.6279	5.6305	5.6332	5.6358
250	5.6384	5.6410	5.6435	5.6461	5.6487	5.6512	5.6537	5.6563	5.6588	5.6613
260	5.6638	5.6662	5.6687	5.6712	5.6736	5.6760	5.6785	5.6809	5.6833	5.6857
270	5.6881	5.6905	5.6928	5.6952	5.6975	5.6999	5.7022	5.7045	5.7068	5.7091
280	5.7114	5.7137	5.7160	5.7183	5.7205	5.7228	5.7250	5.7273	5.7295	5.7317
290	5.7339	5.7361	5.7383	5.7405	5.7427	5.7448	5.7470	5.7491	5.7513	5.7534
300	5.7555	5.7577	5.7598	5.7619	5.7640	5.7661	5.7681	5.7702	5.7723	5.7743
310	5.7764	5.7784	5.7805	5.7825	5.7845	5.7865	5.7886	5.7906	5.7926	5.7945
320	5.7965	5.7985	5.8005	5.8024	5.8044	5.8063	5.8083	5.8102	5.8121	5.8141
330	5.8160	5.8179	5.8198	5.8217	5.8236	5.8255	5.8273	5.8292	5.8311	5.8329
340	5.8348	5.8367	5.8385	5.8403	5.8422	5.8440	5.8458	5.8476	5.8494	5.8512
350	5.8530	5.8548	5.8566	5.8584	5.8602	5.8619	5.8637	5.8655	5.8672	5.8690
360	5.8707	5.8724	5.8742	5.8759	5.8776	5.8793	5.8810	5.8827	5.8844	5.8861
370	5.8878	5.8895	5.8912	5.8929	5.8945	5.8962	5.8979	5.8995	5.9012	5.9028
380	5.9045	5.9061	5.9077	5.9094	5.9110	5.9126	5.9142	5.9158	5.9174	5.9190
390	5.9206	5.9222	5.9238	5.9254	5.9270	5.9286	5.9301	5.9317	5.9333	5.9348
400	5.9364	5.9517	5.9666	5.9811	5.9952	6.0090	6.0225	6.0357	6.0485	6.0611
500	6.0734	6.0854	6.0972	6.1087	6.1200	6.1311	6.1420	6.1526	6.1631	6.1733
600	6.1834	6.1933	6.2030	6.2126	6.2219	6.2312	6.2402	6.2492	6.2579	6.2666
700	6.2751	6.2835	6.2917	6.2999	6.3079	6.3158	6.3235	6.3312	6.3388	6.3462
800	6.3536	6.3608	6.3680	6.3751	6.3820	6.3889	6.3957	6.4025	6.4091	6.4156
900	6.4221	6.4285	6.4348	6.4411	6.4473	6.4534	6.4594	6.4754	6.4713	6.4771

σ as fraction of the mean extreme range[4]

n	0	1 10	2 20	3 30	4 40	5 50	6 60	7 70	8 80	9 90
	0.	0.	0.	0.	0.	0.	0.	0.	0.	0.
0	—	—	88623	59082	48573	42994	39457	36977	35122	33670
10	32494	31517	30689	29976	29353	28803	28313	27872	27472	27108
20	26774	26467	26182	25918	25672	25441	25225	25022	24830	24649
30	24477	24314	24158	24011	23870	23735	23606	23482	23364	23249
40	23140	23034	22932	22834	22739	22648	22559	22473	22390	22310
50	22231	22155	22082	22010	21940	21872	21806	21742	21679	21618
60	21558	21500	21443	21388	21333	21280	21228	21178	21128	21079
70	21032	20985	20939	20894	20851	20807	20765	20724	20683	20643
80	20603	20565	20527	20490	20453	20417	20382	20347	20312	20279
90	20245	20213	20180	20149	20118	20087	20056	20027	19997	19968
100	19939	19911	19883	19856	19829	19802	19776	19750	19724	19699
110	19674	19649	19624	19600	19577	19553	19530	19507	19484	19462
120	19439	19418	19396	19374	19353	19332	19312	19291	19271	19251
130	19231	19211	19192	19173	19154	19135	19116	19098	19079	19061
140	19043	19026	19008	18991	18973	18956	18939	18923	18906	18890
150	18873	18857	18841	18825	18810	18794	18779	18763	18748	18733
160	18718	18703	18689	18674	18660	18645	18631	18617	18603	18589
170	18575	18562	18548	18535	18522	18508	18495	18482	18469	18457
180	18444	18431	18419	18406	18394	18382	18370	18357	18345	18334
190	18322	18310	18298	18287	18275	18264	18253	18241	18230	18219
200	18208	18197	18186	18175	18165	18154	18143	18133	18122	18112
210	18102	18091	18081	18071	18061	18051	18041	18031	18021	18012
220	18002	17992	17983	17973	17964	17954	17945	17936	17926	17917
230	17908	17899	17890	17881	17872	17863	17854	17845	17837	17828
240	17819	17811	17802	17794	17785	17777	17769	17760	17752	17744
250	17736	17727	17719	17711	17703	17695	17687	17680	17672	17664
260	17656	17648	17641	17633	17625	17618	17610	17603	17595	17588
270	17581	17573	17566	17559	17551	17544	17537	17530	17523	17516
280	17509	17502	17495	17488	17481	17474	17467	17460	17454	17447
290	17440	17433	17427	17420	17414	17407	17400	17394	17387	17381
300	17375	17368	17362	17355	17349	17343	17337	17330	17324	17318
310	17312	17306	17300	17294	17287	17281	17275	17270	17264	17258
320	17252	17246	17240	17234	17228	17223	17217	17211	17205	17200
330	17194	17188	17183	17177	17172	17166	17160	17155	17149	17144
340	17139	17133	17128	17122	17117	17112	17106	17101	17096	17090
350	17085	17080	17075	17070	17064	17059	17054	17049	17044	17039
360	17034	17029	17024	17019	17014	17009	17004	16999	16994	16989
370	16984	16979	16974	16970	16965	16960	16955	16951	16946	16941
380	16936	16932	16927	16922	16918	16913	16908	16904	16899	16895
390	16890	16886	16881	16876	16872	16868	16863	16859	16854	16850
400	16845	16802	16760	16719	16680	16642	16604	16568	16533	16499
500	16465	16433	16401	16370	16340	16310	16281	16253	16226	16199
600	16172	16146	16121	16096	16072	16048	16025	16002	15980	15958
700	15936	15915	15894	15873	15853	15833	15814	15795	15776	15757
800	15739	15721	15704	15686	15669	15652	15636	15619	15603	15587
900	15571	15556	15540	15525	15510	15496	15481	15443	15453	15439

For footnotes see page 48.

$\sigma_{\bar{x}}$ **as fraction of the mean extreme range**[4] (for explanation see below)

m \ *n*	2	3	4	5	6	7	8	9	10	11	12	13	14	15	16	17	18	19	20
	0. *0.0*	0. *0.0*	0. *0.0*	0. *0.0*	0. *0.0*	0. *0.0*	0. *0.0*	0. *0.0*	0. *0.0*	0.0	0.0	0.0	0.0	0.0	0.0	0.0 *0.00*	0.0 *0.00*	0.0 *0.00*	0.0 *0.00*
1	*62666*	*34111*	*24287*	*19227*	*16108*	*13976*	*12418*	*11223*	*10275*	95027	88592	83139	78450	74370	70782	67599	64752	62190	59869
2	*44311*	*24120*	*17173*	*13596*	*11390*	98826	87806	79360	72658	67195	62644	58788	55473	52587	50050	47799	45787	43975	42334
3	*36180*	*19694*	*14022*	*11101*	93001	80691	71693	64797	59325	54864	51149	48000	45293	42937	40866	39028	37385	35905	34565
4	*31333*	*17055*	*12143*	96137	80541	69548	62088	56116	51377	47514	44296	41569	39225	37185	35391	33799	32376	31095	29934
5	*28025*	*15255*	*10861*	85987	72038	62503	55533	50192	45953	42498	39620	37181	35084	33259	31655	30231	28958	27812	26774
6	*25583*	*13926*	99150	78495	65762	57057	50695	45819	41949	38795	36168	33941	32027	30361	28897	27597	26435	25389	24441
7	*23685*	*12893*	91795	72672	60883	52825	46934	42420	38838	35917	33485	31424	29651	28109	26753	25550	24474	23506	22628
8	*22156*	*12060*	85866	67979	56951	49413	43903	39680	36329	33597	31322	29394	27736	26294	25025	23900	22893	21987	21167
9	*20889*	*11370*	80955	64091	53694	46587	41392	37411	34251	31676	29531	27713	26150	24790	23594	22533	21584	20730	19956
10	*19817*	*10787*	76801	60802	50939	44196	39268	35491	32494	30050	28015	26291	24808	23518	22383	21377	20476	19666	18932
11	*18894*	*10285*	73227	57973	48568	42140	37440	33839	30982	28652	26712	25067	23654	22423	21342	20382	19524	18751	18051
12	*18090*	98470	70109	55504	46500	40346	35846	32399	29663	27432	25574	24000	22647	21469	20433	19514	18692	17953	17283
13	*17380*	94607	67359	53327	44676	38763	34440	31128	28499	26356	24571	23059	21758	20626	19631	18748	17959	17248	16605
14	*16748*	91165	64909	51387	43051	37353	33187	29995	27462	25397	23677	22220	20967	19876	18917	18066	17306	16621	16001
15	*16180*	88074	62708	49645	41591	36086	32062	28978	26531	24536	22874	21466	20256	19202	18276	17454	16719	16057	15458
16	*15666*	85277	60716	48068	40271	34940	31044	28058	25689	23757	22148	20785	19613	18592	17695	16900	16188	15547	14967
17	*15199*	82731	58904	46633	39068	33897	30117	27220	24922	23048	21487	20164	19027	18037	17167	16395	15705	15083	14520
18	*14770*	80400	57244	45319	37967	32942	29269	26453	24219	22398	20881	19596	18491	17529	16683	15933	15262	14658	14111
19	*14376*	78256	55717	44110	36955	32063	28488	25748	23573	21801	20325	19073	17998	17062	16238	15508	14855	14267	13735
20	*14012*	76274	54306	42994	36019	31252	27767	25096	22977	21249	19810	18590	17542	16630	15827	15115	14479	13906	13387
21	*13675*	74436	52998	41957	35151	30498	27097	24491	22423	20737	19332	18142	17119	16229	15446	14751	14130	13571	13064
22	*13360*	72725	51779	40993	34343	29797	26474	23928	21907	20260	18888	17725	16726	15856	15091	14412	13805	13259	12764
23	*13067*	71126	50641	40092	33588	29142	25892	23402	21426	19815	18473	17336	16358	15507	14759	14095	13502	12967	12483
24	*12792*	69628	49575	39248	32881	28529	25347	22909	20975	19397	18084	16971	16014	15181	14448	13799	13218	12694	12220
25	*12533*	68222	48573	38455	32216	27952	24835	22446	20551	19006	17718	16628	15690	14874	14156	13520	12950	12438	11974
26	*12290*	66897	47630	37708	31591	27409	24353	22011	20152	18637	17374	16305	15385	14585	13881	13257	12699	12196	11741
27	*12060*	65646	46740	37003	31000	26897	23898	21599	19775	18288	17050	16000	15098	14312	13622	13009	12462	11968	11522
28	*11843*	64463	45897	36336	30442	26412	23467	21210	19419	17959	16742	15712	14826	14055	13377	12775	12237	11753	11314
29	*11637*	63342	45099	35704	29912	25953	23059	20841	19081	17646	16451	15439	14568	13810	13144	12553	12024	11548	11117
30	*11441*	62278	44341	35104	29409	25517	22671	20491	18760	17350	16175	15179	14323	13578	12923	12342	11822	11354	10930
31	*11255*	61265	43620	34533	28931	25102	22303	20158	18455	17068	15912	14932	14090	13357	12713	12141	11630	11170	10753
32	*11078*	60300	42932	33989	28476	24707	21951	19840	18165	16799	15661	14697	13868	13147	12513	11950	11447	10994	10583
33	*10909*	59379	42277	33470	28041	24329	21616	19537	17887	16542	15422	14473	13656	12946	12322	11767	11272	10826	10422
34	*10747*	58500	41651	32975	27625	23969	21296	19248	17622	16297	15193	14258	13454	12754	12139	11593	11105	10665	10267
35	*10592*	57658	41052	32500	27228	23624	20990	18971	17369	16063	14975	14053	13261	12571	11964	11426	10945	10512	10120
36	*10444*	56851	40478	32046	26847	23294	20696	18705	17126	15838	14765	13856	13075	12395	11797	11266	10792	10365	*99781*
37	*10302*	56078	39927	31610	26482	22977	20414	18451	16893	15623	14565	13668	12897	12226	11636	11113	10645	10224	*98424*
38	*10166*	55335	39398	31191	26131	22672	20144	18206	16669	15416	14372	13487	12726	12064	11482	10966	10504	10089	*97120*
39	*10035*	54621	38890	30788	25794	22380	19884	17972	16454	15217	14186	13313	12562	11909	11334	10824	10369	*99583*	*95867*
40	99083	53934	38400	30401	25469	22098	19634	17745	16247	15025	14008	13145	12404	11759	11192	10688	10238	*98331*	*94661*
41	97867	53272	37929	30028	25157	21827	19393	17528	16048	14841	13836	12984	12252	11615	11054	10557	10113	*97124*	*93499*
42	96695	52634	37475	29668	24856	21566	19161	17318	15855	14663	13670	12829	12105	11476	10922	10431	*99915*	*95961*	*92380*
43	95564	52019	37037	29321	24565	21313	18937	17115	15670	14492	13510	12679	11964	11341	10794	10309	*98746*	*94839*	*91299*
44	94472	51424	36613	28986	24284	21070	18720	16920	15491	14326	13356	12534	11827	11212	10671	10191	*97618*	*93755*	*90256*
45	93416	50849	36204	28662	24013	20834	18511	16731	15318	14166	13207	12394	11695	11086	10552	10077	*96527*	*92707*	*89247*
46	92395	50294	35809	28349	23750	20607	18309	16548	15150	14011	13062	12258	11567	10965	10436	*99668*	*95472*	*91694*	*88272*
47	91407	49756	35426	28046	23496	20386	18113	16371	14988	13861	12923	12127	11443	10848	10325	*98603*	*94451*	*90713*	*87328*
48	90450	49235	35055	27752	23250	20173	17923	16199	14831	13716	12787	12000	11323	10734	10216	*97570*	*93462*	*89763*	*86413*
49	89522	48730	34695	27468	23012	19966	17739	16033	14679	13575	12656	11877	11207	10624	10112	*96569*	*92503*	*88843*	*85527*
50	88623	48240	34346	27192	22780	19765	17561	15872	14532	13439	12529	11758	11095	10517	10010	*95599*	*91574*	*87950*	*84667*

Explanation (pages 47–49)

Correction factors[1] and confidence factors[2] for σ (page 47)

(a) The estimation of σ^2 from s^2 is unbiased, but not that of σ from s. This bias is eliminated by multiplying s by the factor k_s.

(b) Confidence limits for σ. Columns 3–6 give the confidence factors by which s must be multiplied in order to obtain the confidence limits that include σ with a probability of $(1 - 2\alpha)$.

Extreme range

If x_1 is the lowest and x_n the highest value of a sample of size n, then $(x_n - x_1)$ is the extreme range w_n of this sample.

The standardized extreme range of a sample of size n from a population with standard deviation σ is

$$W_n = \frac{w_n}{\sigma} = \frac{x_n - x_1}{\sigma}$$

The mean extreme range of m samples of size n from one and the same population is

$$\overline{w}_{m,n} = \frac{\sum_1^m w_n}{m} = \frac{\sum_1^m (x_n - x_1)}{m}$$

The standardized mean extreme range is

$$\overline{W}_{m,n} = \frac{\overline{w}_{m,n}}{\sigma} = \frac{\sum_1^m w_n}{m\sigma} = \frac{\sum_1^m (x_n - x_1)}{m\sigma}$$

Since the extreme range w_n is merely a special case of the mean extreme range $\overline{w}_{m,n}$ with $m = 1$, only the mean extreme range will be referred to in the text that follows.

Mean extreme range[3] as a multiple of σ (page 47)

The expected value $\boldsymbol{W}_n$ of the extreme range of random samples of size n from a normally distributed population with unit standard deviation satisfies the relation

$$\overline{W}_{m,n} \underset{(m \to \infty)}{\longrightarrow} \boldsymbol{W}_n$$

The table gives values of $\boldsymbol{W}_n$ for the standardized normal distribution as multiples of σ. (Many authors use d_n instead of $\boldsymbol{W}_n$.)

σ as a fraction of the mean extreme range[4] (page 47)

The quotient $\dfrac{\overline{w}_{m,n}}{\boldsymbol{W}_n} = \overline{w}_{m,n} \times \boldsymbol{A}_n$

gives an unbiased estimate of σ that improves as m increases but rapidly worsens as the size n of the individual samples increases. Its variance is also greater than s.

With small samples (n between 5 and 10), however, there is practically no difference between the accuracy of the two estimates, even for $m = 1$.

$\sigma_{\bar{x}}$ as a fraction of the mean extreme range[4]

The quotient $\dfrac{\overline{w}_{m,n}}{\boldsymbol{W}_n \sqrt{m\,n}} = \overline{w}_{m,n} \times \boldsymbol{A}_{m,n}$

where $m\,n$ = sample size N, gives an unbiased estimate of the standard deviation $\sigma_{\bar{x}}$ of the estimate $\bar{x}$. See remarks in the previous paragraph. Values of the factor $\boldsymbol{A}_{m,n}$ are given in the table above.

Significance limits for the difference between two means based on the extreme range

The table on page 49 gives the 2α significance limits for u:

(a) $u = \dfrac{(\bar{x} - \mu)\, m}{\sum (x_n - x_1)\, \boldsymbol{A}_{m,n}}$

(b) $u = \dfrac{(\bar{x}' - \bar{x}'')\sqrt{m' m''}}{\left[\sum (x'_n - x'_1) + \sum (x''_n - x''_1)\right] \boldsymbol{A}_{m,n}}$

$(m = m' + m'')$

(a): When $m = 1$, the test is much simpler. See page 53.

(b): When $m' = m'' = 1$, the test is much simpler. See page 53.

See also (**618**) and (**619**), page 173.

[1] Calculated from values in Pearson and Hartley (Eds.), *Biometrika Tables for Statisticians*, vol. 1, Cambridge University Press, 1954.

[2] Confidence factors calculated from χ^2-values in Pearson and Hartley, *loc. cit.*, and from data of Hald and Sinkbæk, *Skand. Aktuar Tidskr.*, **33**, 168 (1950). Reproduction only by permission of the publishers of these *Scientific Tables*.

[3] Values from Tippett, L. H. C., *Biometrika*, **17**, 364 (1925). Reprinted by kind permission of the author and publishers.

[4] Calculated from values of Tippett, L. H. C., *loc. cit.* Reproduction only by permission of the publishers of these *Scientific Tables*.

Significance Limits[1] for the Difference Between Two Means Based on the Extreme Range

For explanation see page 48

2α = 0.10

m \ n	2	3	4	5	6	7	8	9	10	11	12	13	14	15	16	17	18	19	20
1	5.04	2.59	2.18	2.02	1.94	1.88	1.85	1.82	1.81	1.79	1.78	1.77	1.76	1.75	1.75	1.74	1.74	1.73	1.73
2	2.62	02	1.88	1.81	78	76	74	73	72	71	71	71	70	70	70	69	69	69	69
3	20	1.88	79	75	73	72	71	70	70	69	69	69	68	68	68	68	68	67	67
4	03	81	75	73	71	70	69	69	68	68	68	68	67	67	67	67	67	67	67
5	1.94	1.77	1.73	1.71	1.70	1.69	1.68	1.68	1.68	1.68	1.67	1.67	1.67	1.67	1.67	1.67	1.66	1.66	1.66
6	89	75	72	70	69	68	68	67	67	67	67	67	66	66	66	66	66	66	66
7	85	73	71	69	68	67	67	67	66	66	66	66	66	66	66	66	66	66	66
8	82	72	70	68	68	67	67	67	66	66	66	66	66	66	66	66	66	66	66
9	80	71	69	68	67	67	67	66	66	66	66	66	66	66	66	66	66	66	66
10	1.78	1.71	1.69	1.68	1.67	1.67	1.66	1.66	1.66	1.66	1.66	1.66	1.66	1.66	1.65	1.65	1.65	1.65	1.65
11	77	71	68	68	67	67	66	66	66	66	66	66	66	66	65	65	65	65	65
12	76	70	68	68	66	66	66	66	65	65	65	65	65	65	65	65	65	65	65
13	75	70	67	67	66	66	66	66	65	65	65	65	65	65	65	65	65	65	65
14	74	69	67	67	66	66	66	66	65	65	65	65	65	65	65	65	65	65	65
15	1.73	1.69	1.67	1.67	1.66	1.66	1.66	1.66	1.65	1.65	1.65	1.65	1.65	1.65	1.65	1.65	1.65	1.65	1.65
16	72	69	67	67	66	66	66	66	65	65	65	65	65	65	65	65	65	65	65
17	72	68	67	67	66	66	66	66	65	65	65	65	65	65	65	65	65	65	65
18	72	68	67	66	66	66	65	65	65	65	65	65	65	65	65	65	65	65	65
19	71	67	67	66	66	66	65	65	65	65	65	65	65	65	65	65	65	65	65
20	1.71	1.67	1.67	1.66	1.66	1.66	1.65	1.65	1.65	1.65	1.65	1.65	1.65	1.65	1.65	1.65	1.65	1.65	1.65
30	69	66	66	66	65	65	65	65	65	65	65	65	65	65	65	65	65	65	65
60	67	66	65	65	65	65	65	65	65	65	65	65	65	65	65	65	65	65	65
120	66	65	65	65	65	65	65	65	65	65	65	65	65	65	65	65	65	65	65

2α = 0.05

m \ n	2	3	4	5	6	7	8	9	10	11	12	13	14	15	16	17	18	19	20
1	10.14	3.82	2.95	2.63	2.48	2.38	2.32	2.27	2.24	2.21	2.19	2.17	2.16	2.15	2.14	2.13	2.12	2.11	2.11
2	3.87	2.64	37	25	19	15	13	11	09	08	07	06	06	05	05	04	04	03	03
3	2.98	37	22	15	11	09	07	06	05	04	03	02	02	02	02	01	01	01	01
4	66	25	15	10	07	05	04	03	02	01	01	01	01	00	00	00	00	00	00
5	2.49	2.19	2.11	2.07	2.05	2.03	2.02	2.02	2.01	2.01	2.00	2.00	2.00	1.99	1.99	1.99	1.99	1.99	1.99
6	38	14	08	05	03	02	01	01	00	00	00	00	1.99	99	99	99	99	99	99
7	31	11	06	04	02	02	01	00	1.99	1.99	1.99	1.99	99	98	98	98	98	98	98
8	26	09	05	03	01	01	00	00	99	99	99	99	98	98	98	98	98	98	98
9	23	08	04	02	01	00	1.99	1.99	99	99	98	98	98	98	98	98	98	98	98
10	2.20	2.07	2.03	2.01	2.00	2.00	1.99	1.99	1.98	1.98	1.98	1.98	1.98	1.98	1.98	1.98	1.98	1.97	1.97
11	17	06	02	01	00	1.99	99	99	98	98	98	98	98	98	98	98	98	97	97
12	15	05	02	01	00	99	98	99	98	98	97	97	97	97	97	97	97	97	97
13	14	04	02	00	1.99	98	98	98	98	98	97	97	97	97	97	97	97	97	97
14	12	04	01	00	99	98	98	98	98	98	97	97	97	97	97	97	97	97	97
15	2.11	2.03	2.01	2.00	1.99	1.98	1.98	1.98	1.98	1.98	1.97	1.97	1.97	1.97	1.97	1.97	1.97	1.97	1.97
16	10	03	01	00	99	98	98	98	98	98	97	97	97	97	97	97	97	97	97
17	09	02	01	00	99	98	98	98	98	98	97	97	97	97	97	97	97	97	97
18	08	02	00	1.99	98	98	98	97	97	97	97	97	97	97	97	97	97	97	97
19	08	01	00	99	98	98	98	97	97	97	97	97	97	97	97	97	97	97	97
20	2.07	2.01	2.00	1.99	1.98	1.98	1.98	1.97	1.97	1.97	1.97	1.97	1.97	1.97	1.97	1.97	1.97	1.97	1.97
30	03	1.99	1.98	98	97	97	97	97	97	97	97	97	97	97	97	97	97	96	96
60	00	98	97	97	97	97	97	96	96	96	96	96	96	96	96	96	96	96	96
120	1.98	97	97	96	96	96	96	96	96	96	96	96	96	96	96	96	96	96	96

2α = 0.02

m \ n	2	3	4	5	6	7	8	9	10	11	12	13	14	15	16	17	18	19	20
1	25.39	6.19	4.21	3.56	3.25	3.07	2.95	2.87	2.81	2.76	2.72	2.69	2.67	2.65	2.63	2.61	2.60	2.59	2.58
2	6.27	3.56	3.05	2.84	2.73	2.66	61	58	55	53	51	50	49	48	47	46	46	45	45
3	4.27	05	2.77	65	58	54	51	49	47	46	45	44	43	43	42	42	41	41	41
4	3.60	2.84	65	56	51	48	46	45	44	43	42	42	41	41	40	40	39	39	39
5	3.27	2.72	2.58	2.51	2.47	2.45	2.43	2.42	2.41	2.41	2.40	2.40	2.39	2.39	2.38	2.38	2.38	2.37	2.37
6	08	65	53	48	45	43	42	41	40	39	39	38	38	38	37	37	37	37	37
7	2.95	60	50	46	43	41	40	40	39	38	38	37	37	37	36	36	36	36	36
8	86	56	48	44	42	40	39	39	38	38	37	37	37	37	36	36	36	36	36
9	79	53	46	43	41	39	38	38	37	37	37	36	36	36	35	35	35	35	35
10	2.73	2.51	2.45	2.42	2.40	2.39	2.38	2.37	2.37	2.37	2.36	2.36	2.36	2.36	2.35	2.35	2.35	2.35	2.35
11	69	49	44	41	39	38	37	37	36	36	36	36	36	36	35	35	35	35	35
12	66	48	43	41	38	38	37	37	36	36	36	36	36	36	35	35	35	35	34
13	63	47	42	40	38	38	37	36	36	36	35	35	35	35	35	34	34	34	34
14	61	46	42	40	37	37	36	36	35	35	35	35	35	35	35	34	34	34	34
15	2.59	2.45	2.41	2.39	2.37	2.37	2.36	2.36	2.35	2.35	2.35	2.35	2.35	2.35	2.35	2.34	2.34	2.34	2.34
16	57	44	41	39	37	37	36	36	35	35	35	35	35	35	35	34	34	34	34
17	56	44	40	38	36	37	36	36	35	35	35	35	35	35	35	34	34	34	34
18	54	43	40	38	36	36	35	35	35	34	34	34	34	34	34	34	34	34	34
19	53	42	39	37	36	36	35	35	35	34	34	34	34	34	34	34	34	34	34
20	2.52	2.42	2.39	2.37	2.36	2.36	2.35	2.35	2.35	2.34	2.34	2.34	2.34	2.34	2.34	2.34	2.34	2.34	2.34
30	45	39	37	36	35	35	34	34	34	34	34	34	34	34	34	33	33	33	33
60	39	36	35	34	34	34	34	33	33	33	33	33	33	33	33	33	33	33	33
120	36	34	34	33	33	33	33	33	33	33	33	33	33	33	33	33	33	33	33

2α = 0.01

m \ n	2	3	4	5	6	7	8	9	10	11	12	13	14	15	16	17	18	19	20
1	50.79	8.82	5.42	4.38	3.90	3.63	3.45	3.33	3.24	3.17	3.12	3.08	3.05	3.02	2.99	2.97	2.95	2.93	2.92
2	8.93	4.34	3.60	3.29	13	03	2.97	2.92	2.88	2.85	2.83	2.81	2.80	2.79	78	77	76	75	74
3	5.49	3.60	20	02	2.93	2.87	83	80	78	76	74	73	72	71	71	70	70	69	69
4	4.43	30	02	2.90	83	79	76	74	72	71	70	69	69	68	67	66	66	66	66
5	3.93	3.14	2.92	2.83	2.78	2.75	2.72	2.71	2.69	2.68	2.68	2.67	2.66	2.66	2.65	2.65	2.65	2.64	2.64
6	64	03	86	79	74	72	70	68	67	66	66	65	65	64	64	64	63	63	63
7	46	2.96	82	75	72	70	68	67	66	65	65	64	64	63	63	63	62	62	62
8	32	91	79	73	70	68	67	66	65	64	64	63	63	62	62	62	62	62	62
9	21	87	77	71	68	67	66	65	64	63	63	63	62	62	62	62	61	61	61
10	3.14	2.84	2.74	2.70	2.67	2.66	2.65	2.64	2.63	2.63	2.62	2.62	2.62	2.62	2.61	2.61	2.61	2.61	2.61
11	08	82	72	69	66	65	64	64	63	62	62	62	62	61	61	61	61	61	61
12	03	80	71	68	66	64	63	63	62	62	62	62	61	61	61	61	61	61	61
13	2.99	78	70	67	65	64	63	63	62	62	61	61	61	60	60	60	60	60	60
14	96	76	69	67	65	63	62	62	61	61	61	61	60	60	60	60	60	60	60
15	2.93	2.75	2.68	2.66	2.64	2.63	2.62	2.62	2.61	2.61	2.61	2.61	2.60	2.60	2.60	2.60	2.60	2.60	2.60
16	91	74	68	66	64	63	62	62	61	61	61	61	60	60	60	60	60	60	60
17	89	73	67	65	63	63	61	62	61	61	61	61	60	60	60	60	60	60	60
18	87	72	67	65	63	62	61	61	60	60	60	60	60	60	60	59	59	59	59
19	85	71	66	64	62	62	61	61	60	60	60	60	60	60	60	59	59	59	59
20	2.84	2.70	2.66	2.64	2.62	2.62	2.61	2.61	2.60	2.60	2.60	2.60	2.60	2.60	2.60	2.59	2.59	2.59	2.59
30	75	66	63	62	61	60	60	60	59	59	59	59	59	59	59	59	59	59	59
60	66	62	60	60	59	59	59	59	59	58	58	58	58	58	58	58	58	58	58
120	62	60	59	59	58	58	58	58	58	58	58	58	58	58	58	58	58	58	58

[1] Values from LORD, E., *Biometrika*, **34**, 41 (1947), reprinted by kind permission of the author and publishers. Interpolated values calculated by the editors of these *Scientific Tables*.

For explanation see page 174

ν \ n	2	3	4	5	6	7	8	9	10	11	12	13	14	15	16	17	18	19	20	22	24	26	28	30	32	34	36	38	40	50	60
$2\alpha = 0.05$																															
1	17.97	17.97	17.97	17.97	17.97	17.97	17.97	17.97	17.97	17.97	17.97	17.97	17.97	17.97	17.97	17.97	17.97	17.97	17.97	17.97	17.97	17.97	17.97	17.97	17.97	17.97	17.97	17.97	17.97	17.97	17.97
2	6.085	6.085	6.085	6.085	6.085	6.085	6.085	6.085	6.085	6.085	6.085	6.085	6.085	6.085	6.085	6.085	6.085	6.085	6.085	6.085	6.085	6.085	6.085	6.085	6.085	6.085	6.085	6.085	6.085	6.085	6.085
3	4.501	4.516	4.516	4.516	4.516	4.516	4.516	4.516	4.516	4.516	4.516	4.516	4.516	4.516	4.516	4.516	4.516	4.516	4.516	4.516	4.516	4.516	4.516	4.516	4.516	4.516	4.516	4.516	4.516	4.516	4.516
4	3.927	4.013	4.033	4.033	4.033	4.033	4.033	4.033	4.033	4.033	4.033	4.033	4.033	4.033	4.033	4.033	4.033	4.033	4.033	4.033	4.033	4.033	4.033	4.033	4.033	4.033	4.033	4.033	4.033	4.033	4.033
5	3.635	3.749	3.797	3.814	3.814	3.814	3.814	3.814	3.814	3.814	3.814	3.814	3.814	3.814	3.814	3.814	3.814	3.814	3.814	3.814	3.814	3.814	3.814	3.814	3.814	3.814	3.814	3.814	3.814	3.814	3.814
6	3.461	3.587	3.649	3.680	3.694	3.697	3.697	3.697	3.697	3.697	3.697	3.697	3.697	3.697	3.697	3.697	3.697	3.697	3.697	3.697	3.697	3.697	3.697	3.697	3.697	3.697	3.697	3.697	3.697	3.697	3.697
7	3.344	3.477	3.548	3.588	3.611	3.622	3.626	3.626	3.626	3.626	3.626	3.626	3.626	3.626	3.626	3.626	3.626	3.626	3.626	3.626	3.626	3.626	3.626	3.626	3.626	3.626	3.626	3.626	3.626	3.626	3.626
8	3.261	3.399	3.475	3.521	3.549	3.566	3.575	3.579	3.579	3.579	3.579	3.579	3.579	3.579	3.579	3.579	3.579	3.579	3.579	3.579	3.579	3.579	3.579	3.579	3.579	3.579	3.579	3.579	3.579	3.579	3.579
9	3.199	3.339	3.420	3.470	3.502	3.523	3.536	3.544	3.547	3.547	3.547	3.547	3.547	3.547	3.547	3.547	3.547	3.547	3.547	3.547	3.547	3.547	3.547	3.547	3.547	3.547	3.547	3.547	3.547	3.547	3.547
10	3.151	3.293	3.376	3.430	3.465	3.489	3.505	3.516	3.522	3.525	3.526	3.526	3.526	3.526	3.526	3.526	3.526	3.526	3.526	3.526	3.526	3.526	3.526	3.526	3.526	3.526	3.526	3.526	3.526	3.526	3.526
11	3.113	3.256	3.342	3.397	3.435	3.462	3.480	3.493	3.501	3.506	3.509	3.510	3.510	3.510	3.510	3.510	3.510	3.510	3.510	3.510	3.510	3.510	3.510	3.510	3.510	3.510	3.510	3.510	3.510	3.510	3.510
12	3.082	3.225	3.313	3.370	3.410	3.439	3.459	3.474	3.484	3.491	3.496	3.498	3.499	3.499	3.499	3.499	3.499	3.499	3.499	3.499	3.499	3.499	3.499	3.499	3.499	3.499	3.499	3.499	3.499	3.499	3.499
13	3.055	3.200	3.289	3.348	3.389	3.419	3.442	3.458	3.470	3.478	3.484	3.488	3.490	3.490	3.490	3.490	3.490	3.490	3.490	3.490	3.490	3.490	3.490	3.490	3.490	3.490	3.490	3.490	3.490	3.490	3.490
14	3.033	3.178	3.268	3.329	3.372	3.403	3.426	3.444	3.457	3.467	3.474	3.479	3.482	3.484	3.484	3.485	3.485	3.485	3.485	3.485	3.485	3.485	3.485	3.485	3.485	3.485	3.485	3.485	3.485	3.485	3.485
15	3.014	3.160	3.250	3.312	3.356	3.389	3.413	3.432	3.446	3.457	3.465	3.471	3.476	3.478	3.480	3.481	3.481	3.481	3.481	3.481	3.481	3.481	3.481	3.481	3.481	3.481	3.481	3.481	3.481	3.481	3.481
16	2.998	3.144	3.235	3.298	3.343	3.376	3.402	3.422	3.437	3.449	3.458	3.465	3.470	3.473	3.477	3.478	3.478	3.478	3.478	3.478	3.478	3.478	3.478	3.478	3.478	3.478	3.478	3.478	3.478	3.478	3.478
17	2.984	3.130	3.222	3.285	3.331	3.366	3.392	3.412	3.429	3.441	3.451	3.459	3.465	3.469	3.473	3.475	3.476	3.476	3.476	3.476	3.476	3.476	3.476	3.476	3.476	3.476	3.476	3.476	3.476	3.476	3.476
18	2.971	3.118	3.210	3.274	3.321	3.356	3.383	3.405	3.421	3.435	3.445	3.454	3.460	3.465	3.470	3.472	3.474	3.474	3.474	3.474	3.474	3.474	3.474	3.474	3.474	3.474	3.474	3.474	3.474	3.474	3.474
19	2.960	3.107	3.199	3.264	3.311	3.347	3.375	3.397	3.415	3.429	3.440	3.449	3.456	3.462	3.467	3.470	3.472	3.473	3.474	3.474	3.474	3.474	3.474	3.474	3.474	3.474	3.474	3.474	3.474	3.474	3.474
20	2.950	3.097	3.190	3.255	3.303	3.339	3.368	3.391	3.409	3.424	3.436	3.445	3.453	3.459	3.464	3.467	3.470	3.472	3.473	3.474	3.474	3.474	3.474	3.474	3.474	3.474	3.474	3.474	3.474	3.474	3.474
24	2.919	3.066	3.160	3.226	3.276	3.315	3.345	3.370	3.390	3.406	3.420	3.432	3.441	3.449	3.456	3.461	3.465	3.469	3.471	3.475	3.477	3.477	3.477	3.477	3.477	3.477	3.477	3.477	3.477	3.477	3.477
30	2.888	3.035	3.131	3.199	3.250	3.290	3.322	3.349	3.371	3.389	3.405	3.418	3.430	3.439	3.447	3.454	3.460	3.466	3.470	3.477	3.481	3.484	3.486	3.486	3.486	3.486	3.486	3.486	3.486	3.486	3.486
40	2.858	3.006	3.102	3.171	3.224	3.266	3.300	3.328	3.352	3.373	3.390	3.405	3.418	3.429	3.439	3.448	3.456	3.463	3.469	3.479	3.486	3.492	3.497	3.500	3.503	3.504	3.504	3.504	3.504	3.504	3.504
60	2.829	2.976	3.073	3.143	3.198	3.241	3.277	3.307	3.333	3.355	3.374	3.391	3.406	3.419	3.431	3.442	3.451	3.460	3.467	3.481	3.492	3.501	3.509	3.515	3.521	3.525	3.529	3.531	3.534	3.537	3.537
120	2.800	2.947	3.045	3.116	3.172	3.217	3.254	3.287	3.314	3.337	3.359	3.377	3.394	3.409	3.423	3.435	3.446	3.457	3.466	3.483	3.498	3.511	3.522	3.532	3.541	3.548	3.555	3.561	3.566	3.585	3.596
∞	2.772	2.918	3.017	3.089	3.146	3.193	3.232	3.265	3.294	3.320	3.343	3.363	3.382	3.399	3.414	3.428	3.442	3.454	3.466	3.486	3.505	3.522	3.536	3.550	3.562	3.574	3.584	3.594	3.603	3.640	3.668
$2\alpha = 0.01$																															
1	90.03	90.03	90.03	90.03	90.03	90.03	90.03	90.03	90.03	90.03	90.03	90.03	90.03	90.03	90.03	90.03	90.03	90.03	90.03	90.03	90.03	90.03	90.03	90.03	90.03	90.03	90.03	90.03	90.03	90.03	90.03
2	14.04	14.04	14.04	14.04	14.04	14.04	14.04	14.04	14.04	14.04	14.04	14.04	14.04	14.04	14.04	14.04	14.04	14.04	14.04	14.04	14.04	14.04	14.04	14.04	14.04	14.04	14.04	14.04	14.04	14.04	14.04
3	8.261	8.321	8.321	8.321	8.321	8.321	8.321	8.321	8.321	8.321	8.321	8.321	8.321	8.321	8.321	8.321	8.321	8.321	8.321	8.321	8.321	8.321	8.321	8.321	8.321	8.321	8.321	8.321	8.321	8.321	8.321
4	6.512	6.677	6.740	6.756	6.756	6.756	6.756	6.756	6.756	6.756	6.756	6.756	6.756	6.756	6.756	6.756	6.756	6.756	6.756	6.756	6.756	6.756	6.756	6.756	6.756	6.756	6.756	6.756	6.756	6.756	6.756
5	5.702	5.893	5.989	6.040	6.065	6.074	6.074	6.074	6.074	6.074	6.074	6.074	6.074	6.074	6.074	6.074	6.074	6.074	6.074	6.074	6.074	6.074	6.074	6.074	6.074	6.074	6.074	6.074	6.074	6.074	6.074
6	5.243	5.439	5.549	5.614	5.655	5.680	5.694	5.701	5.703	5.703	5.703	5.703	5.703	5.703	5.703	5.703	5.703	5.703	5.703	5.703	5.703	5.703	5.703	5.703	5.703	5.703	5.703	5.703	5.703	5.703	5.703
7	4.949	5.145	5.260	5.334	5.383	5.416	5.439	5.454	5.464	5.470	5.472	5.472	5.472	5.472	5.472	5.472	5.472	5.472	5.472	5.472	5.472	5.472	5.472	5.472	5.472	5.472	5.472	5.472	5.472	5.472	5.472
8	4.746	4.939	5.057	5.135	5.189	5.227	5.256	5.276	5.291	5.302	5.309	5.314	5.316	5.317	5.317	5.317	5.317	5.317	5.317	5.317	5.317	5.317	5.317	5.317	5.317	5.317	5.317	5.317	5.317	5.317	5.317
9	4.596	4.787	4.906	4.986	5.043	5.086	5.118	5.142	5.160	5.174	5.185	5.193	5.199	5.203	5.205	5.206	5.206	5.206	5.206	5.206	5.206	5.206	5.206	5.206	5.206	5.206	5.206	5.206	5.206	5.206	5.206
10	4.482	4.671	4.790	4.871	4.931	4.975	5.010	5.037	5.058	5.074	5.088	5.098	5.106	5.112	5.117	5.120	5.122	5.124	5.124	5.124	5.124	5.124	5.124	5.124	5.124	5.124	5.124	5.124	5.124	5.124	5.124
11	4.392	4.579	4.697	4.780	4.841	4.887	4.924	4.952	4.975	4.994	5.009	5.021	5.031	5.039	5.045	5.050	5.054	5.057	5.059	5.061	5.061	5.061	5.061	5.061	5.061	5.061	5.061	5.061	5.061	5.061	5.061
12	4.320	4.504	4.622	4.706	4.767	4.815	4.852	4.883	4.907	4.927	4.944	4.958	4.969	4.978	4.986	4.993	4.998	5.002	5.006	5.010	5.011	5.011	5.011	5.011	5.011	5.011	5.011	5.011	5.011	5.011	5.011
13	4.260	4.442	4.560	4.644	4.706	4.755	4.793	4.824	4.850	4.872	4.889	4.904	4.917	4.928	4.937	4.944	4.950	4.956	4.960	4.966	4.970	4.972	4.972	4.972	4.972	4.972	4.972	4.972	4.972	4.972	4.972
14	4.210	4.391	4.508	4.591	4.654	4.704	4.743	4.775	4.802	4.824	4.843	4.859	4.872	4.884	4.894	4.902	4.910	4.916	4.921	4.929	4.935	4.938	4.940	4.940	4.940	4.940	4.940	4.940	4.940	4.940	4.940
15	4.168	4.347	4.463	4.547	4.610	4.660	4.700	4.733	4.760	4.783	4.803	4.820	4.834	4.846	4.857	4.866	4.874	4.881	4.887	4.897	4.904	4.909	4.912	4.914	4.914	4.914	4.914	4.914	4.914	4.914	4.914
16	4.131	4.309	4.425	4.509	4.572	4.622	4.663	4.696	4.724	4.748	4.768	4.786	4.800	4.813	4.825	4.835	4.844	4.851	4.858	4.869	4.877	4.883	4.887	4.890	4.892	4.892	4.892	4.892	4.892	4.892	4.892
17	4.099	4.275	4.391	4.475	4.539	4.589	4.630	4.664	4.693	4.717	4.738	4.756	4.771	4.785	4.797	4.807	4.816	4.824	4.832	4.844	4.853	4.860	4.865	4.869	4.872	4.873	4.874	4.874	4.874	4.874	4.874
18	4.071	4.246	4.362	4.445	4.509	4.560	4.601	4.635	4.664	4.689	4.711	4.729	4.745	4.759	4.772	4.783	4.792	4.801	4.808	4.821	4.832	4.839	4.846	4.850	4.854	4.856	4.857	4.858	4.858	4.858	4.858
19	4.046	4.220	4.335	4.419	4.483	4.534	4.575	4.610	4.639	4.665	4.686	4.705	4.722	4.736	4.749	4.761	4.771	4.780	4.788	4.802	4.812	4.821	4.828	4.833	4.838	4.841	4.843	4.844	4.845	4.845	4.845
20	4.024	4.197	4.312	4.395	4.459	4.510	4.552	4.587	4.617	4.642	4.664	4.684	4.701	4.716	4.729	4.741	4.751	4.761	4.769	4.784	4.795	4.805	4.813	4.818	4.823	4.827	4.830	4.832	4.833	4.833	4.833
24	3.956	4.126	4.239	4.322	4.386	4.437	4.480	4.516	4.546	4.573	4.596	4.616	4.634	4.651	4.665	4.678	4.690	4.700	4.710	4.727	4.741	4.752	4.762	4.770	4.777	4.783	4.788	4.791	4.794	4.802	4.802
30	3.889	4.056	4.168	4.250	4.314	4.366	4.409	4.445	4.477	4.504	4.528	4.550	4.569	4.586	4.601	4.615	4.628	4.640	4.650	4.669	4.685	4.699	4.711	4.721	4.730	4.738	4.744	4.750	4.755	4.772	4.777
40	3.825	3.988	4.098	4.180	4.244	4.296	4.339	4.376	4.408	4.436	4.461	4.483	4.503	4.521	4.537	4.553	4.566	4.579	4.591	4.611	4.630	4.645	4.659	4.671	4.682	4.692	4.700	4.708	4.715	4.740	4.754
60	3.762	3.922	4.031	4.111	4.174	4.226	4.270	4.307	4.340	4.368	4.394	4.417	4.438	4.456	4.474	4.490	4.504	4.518	4.530	4.553	4.573	4.591	4.607	4.620	4.633	4.645	4.655	4.665	4.673	4.707	4.730
120	3.702	3.858	3.965	4.044	4.107	4.158	4.202	4.239	4.272	4.301	4.327	4.351	4.372	4.392	4.410	4.426	4.442	4.456	4.469	4.494	4.516	4.535	4.552	4.568	4.583	4.596	4.609	4.619	4.630	4.673	4.703
∞	3.643	3.796	3.900	3.978	4.040	4.091	4.135	4.172	4.205	4.235	4.261	4.285	4.307	4.327	4.345	4.363	4.379	4.394	4.408	4.434	4.457	4.478	4.497	4.514	4.530	4.545	4.559	4.572	4.584	4.635	4.675

[1] Values from HARTER, H. L., *Biometrics*, **16**, 671 (1960). Reprinted by kind permission of the author and publishers.

Upper Significance Limits[1] of the Studentized Extreme Range

Test quotient: $\dfrac{x_{N_1} - x_1}{s}$ where x_{N_1} is the highest and x_1 the lowest value of the sample of size N_1 to be tested; s = standard deviation with degrees of freedom $\nu = N_2 - 1$ of a sample of size N_2 *independent* of the sample of size N_1

$2\alpha = 0.05$

ν \ N_1	2	3	4	5	6	7	8	9	10	11	12	13	14	15	16	17	18	19	20
1	17.969	26.98	32.82	37.08	40.41	43.12	45.40	47.36	49.07	50.59	51.96	53.20	54.33	55.36	56.32	57.22	58.04	58.83	59.56
2	6.085	8.33	9.80	10.88	11.74	12.44	13.03	13.54	13.99	14.39	14.75	15.08	15.38	15.65	15.91	16.14	16.37	16.57	16.77
3	4.501	5.91	6.82	7.50	8.04	8.48	8.85	9.18	9.46	9.72	9.95	10.15	10.35	10.52	10.69	10.84	10.98	11.11	11.24
4	3.926	5.04	5.76	6.29	6.71	7.05	7.35	7.60	7.83	8.03	8.21	8.37	8.52	8.66	8.79	8.91	9.03	9.13	9.23
5	3.635	4.60	5.22	5.67	6.03	6.33	6.58	6.80	6.99	7.17	7.32	7.47	7.60	7.72	7.83	7.93	8.03	8.12	8.21
6	460	34	4.90	30	5.63	5.90	12	32	49	6.65	6.79	6.92	03	14	24	34	7.43	7.51	7.59
7	344	16	68	06	36	61	5.82	00	16	30	43	55	6.66	6.76	6.85	6.94	02	10	17
8	261	04	53	4.89	17	40	60	5.77	5.92	05	18	29	39	48	57	65	6.73	6.80	6.87
9	199	3.95	41	76	02	24	43	59	74	5.87	5.98	09	19	28	36	44	51	58	64
10	3.151	3.88	4.33	4.65	4.91	5.12	5.30	5.46	5.60	5.72	5.83	5.93	6.03	6.11	6.19	6.27	6.34	6.40	6.47
11	113	82	26	57	82	03	20	35	49	61	71	81	5.90	5.98	06	13	20	27	33
12	081	77	20	51	75	4.95	12	27	39	51	61	71	80	88	5.95	02	09	15	21
13	055	73	15	45	69	88	05	19	32	43	53	63	71	79	86	5.93	5.99	05	11
14	033	70	11	41	64	83	4.99	13	25	36	46	55	64	71	79	85	91	5.97	03
15	3.014	3.67	4.08	4.37	4.59	4.78	4.94	5.08	5.20	5.31	5.40	5.49	5.57	5.65	5.72	5.78	5.85	5.90	5.96
16	2.998	65	05	33	56	74	90	03	15	26	35	44	52	59	66	73	79	84	90
17	984	63	02	30	52	70	86	4.99	11	21	31	39	47	54	61	67	73	79	84
18	971	61	00	28	49	67	82	96	07	17	27	35	43	50	57	63	69	74	79
19	960	59	3.98	25	47	65	79	92	04	14	23	31	39	46	53	59	65	70	75
20	2.950	3.58	3.96	4.23	4.45	4.62	4.77	4.90	5.01	5.11	5.20	5.28	5.36	5.43	5.49	5.55	5.61	5.66	5.71
21	941	56	94	21	43	60	74	87	4.98	08	17	25	33	40	46	52	58	62	67
22	933	55	93	20	41	58	72	85	96	05	15	23	30	37	43	49	55	59	64
23	926	54	91	18	39	56	70	83	94	03	12	20	27	34	40	46	52	57	62
24	919	53	90	17	37	54	68	81	92	01	10	18	25	32	38	44	49	55	59
25	2.913	3.52	3.89	4.16	4.36	4.52	4.66	4.79	4.90	4.99	5.08	5.16	5.23	5.30	5.36	5.42	5.48	5.52	5.57
26	907	51	88	14	34	51	65	78	89	97	06	14	21	28	34	40	46	50	55
27	902	51	87	13	33	50	63	76	87	96	04	12	19	26	32	38	43	48	53
28	897	50	86	12	32	48	62	75	86	94	03	11	18	24	30	36	42	46	51
29	892	49	85	11	31	47	61	73	84	93	01	09	16	23	29	35	40	44	49
30	2.888	3.49	3.85	4.10	4.30	4.46	4.60	4.72	4.82	4.92	5.00	5.08	5.15	5.21	5.27	5.33	5.38	5.43	5.47
31	884	48	83	09	29	45	59	71	82	91	4.99	07	14	20	26	32	37	41	46
32	881	48	83	09	28	44	58	70	81	89	98	06	13	19	24	30	35	40	45
33	877	47	82	08	27	44	57	69	80	88	97	04	11	17	23	29	34	39	44
34	874	47	82	07	27	43	56	68	79	87	96	03	10	16	22	28	33	37	42
35	2.871	3.46	3.81	4.07	4.26	4.42	4.55	4.67	4.78	4.86	4.95	5.02	5.09	5.15	5.21	5.27	5.32	5.36	5.41
36	868	46	81	06	25	41	55	66	77	85	94	01	08	14	20	26	31	35	40
37	865	45	80	05	25	41	54	65	76	84	93	00	08	14	19	25	30	34	39
38	863	45	80	05	24	40	53	64	75	84	92	00	07	13	18	24	29	33	38
39	861	44	79	04	24	40	53	64	75	83	92	4.99	06	12	17	23	28	32	37
40	2.858	3.44	3.79	4.04	4.23	4.39	4.52	4.63	4.73	4.82	4.90	4.98	5.04	5.11	5.16	5.22	5.27	5.31	5.36
50	841	41	76	00	19	34	47	58	69	76	85	92	4.99	05	10	15	20	24	29
60	829	40	74	3.98	16	31	44	55	65	73	81	88	94	00	06	11	15	20	24
120	800	36	68	92	10	24	36	47	56	64	71	78	84	4.90	4.95	00	04	09	13
∞	772	31	63	86	03	17	29	39	47	55	62	68	74	80	85	4.89	4.93	4.97	01

$2\alpha = 0.01$

ν \ N_1	2	3	4	5	6	7	8	9	10	11	12	13	14	15	16	17	18	19	20
1	90.025	135.0	164.3	185.6	202.2	215.8	227.2	237.0	245.6	253.2	260.0	266.2	271.8	277.0	281.8	286.3	290.4	294.3	298.0
2	14.036	19.02	22.29	24.72	26.63	28.20	29.53	30.68	31.69	32.59	33.40	34.13	34.81	35.43	36.00	36.53	37.03	37.50	37.95
3	8.260	10.62	12.17	13.33	14.24	15.00	15.64	16.20	16.69	17.13	17.53	17.89	18.22	18.52	18.81	19.07	19.32	19.55	19.77
4	6.511	8.12	9.17	9.96	10.58	11.10	11.55	11.93	12.27	12.57	12.84	13.09	13.32	13.53	13.73	13.91	14.08	14.24	14.40
5	5.702	6.98	7.80	8.42	8.91	9.32	9.67	9.97	10.24	10.48	10.70	10.89	11.08	11.24	11.40	11.55	11.68	11.81	11.93
6	243	33	03	7.56	7.97	8.32	8.61	8.87	9.10	9.30	9.48	9.65	9.81	9.95	10.08	10.21	10.32	10.43	10.54
7	4.949	5.92	6.54	01	37	7.68	7.94	17	8.37	8.55	8.71	8.86	00	12	9.24	9.35	9.46	9.55	9.65
8	745	64	20	6.62	6.96	24	47	7.68	7.86	03	18	31	8.44	8.55	8.66	8.76	8.85	8.94	03
9	596	43	5.96	35	66	6.91	13	33	49	7.65	7.78	7.91	03	13	23	33	41	49	8.57
10	4.482	5.27	5.77	6.14	6.43	6.67	6.87	7.05	7.21	7.36	7.49	7.60	7.71	7.81	7.91	7.99	8.08	8.15	8.23
11	392	15	62	5.97	25	48	67	6.84	6.99	13	25	36	46	56	65	73	7.81	7.88	7.95
12	320	05	50	84	10	32	51	67	81	6.94	06	17	26	36	44	52	59	66	73
13	260	4.96	40	73	5.98	19	37	53	67	79	6.90	01	10	19	27	35	42	48	55
14	210	89	32	63	88	08	26	41	54	66	77	6.87	6.96	05	13	20	27	33	39
15	4.167	4.84	5.25	5.56	5.80	5.99	6.16	6.31	6.44	6.55	6.66	6.76	6.84	6.93	7.00	7.07	7.14	7.20	7.26
16	131	79	19	49	72	92	08	22	35	46	56	66	74	82	6.90	6.97	03	09	15
17	099	74	14	43	66	85	01	15	27	38	48	57	66	73	81	87	6.94	00	05
18	071	70	09	38	60	79	5.94	08	20	31	41	50	58	65	73	79	85	6.91	6.97
19	045	67	05	33	55	73	89	02	14	25	34	43	51	58	65	72	78	84	89
20	4.024	4.64	5.02	5.29	5.51	5.69	5.84	5.97	6.09	6.19	6.28	6.37	6.45	6.52	6.59	6.65	6.71	6.77	6.82
21	004	61	4.99	26	47	65	80	92	04	14	24	32	39	47	53	59	65	70	76
22	3.986	58	96	22	43	61	76	88	00	10	19	27	35	42	48	54	60	65	70
23	970	56	93	20	40	57	72	84	5.96	06	15	23	30	37	43	49	55	60	65
24	955	55	91	17	37	54	69	81	92	02	11	19	26	33	39	45	51	56	61
25	3.942	4.52	4.89	5.15	5.34	5.51	5.66	5.78	5.89	5.99	6.07	6.15	6.22	6.29	6.35	6.41	6.47	6.52	6.57
26	930	50	87	12	32	49	63	75	86	95	04	12	19	26	32	38	43	48	53
27	918	49	85	10	30	46	61	72	83	93	01	09	16	22	28	34	40	45	50
28	908	47	83	08	28	44	58	70	80	90	5.98	06	13	19	25	31	37	42	47
29	898	46	82	07	26	42	56	67	78	87	95	03	10	17	23	29	34	39	44
30	3.889	4.45	4.80	5.05	5.24	5.40	5.54	5.65	5.76	5.85	5.93	6.01	6.08	6.14	6.20	6.26	6.31	6.36	6.41
31	881	44	79	03	22	38	52	63	74	83	91	5.99	06	12	18	23	29	34	38
32	873	43	78	02	21	37	50	61	72	81	89	97	03	09	16	21	26	31	36
33	865	42	76	01	19	35	48	59	70	79	87	95	01	07	13	19	24	29	34
34	859	41	75	4.99	18	34	47	58	68	77	86	93	5.99	05	12	17	22	27	31
35	3.852	4.41	4.74	4.98	5.16	5.33	5.45	5.56	5.67	5.76	5.84	5.91	5.98	6.04	6.10	6.15	6.20	6.25	6.29
36	846	40	73	97	15	31	44	55	65	74	82	90	96	02	08	13	18	23	28
37	841	39	72	96	14	30	43	54	64	73	81	88	94	00	06	12	17	22	26
38	835	38	72	95	13	29	41	52	62	72	80	87	93	5.99	05	10	15	20	24
39	830	38	71	94	12	28	40	51	61	70	78	85	91	97	03	08	13	18	23
40	3.825	4.37	4.70	4.93	5.11	5.26	5.39	5.50	5.60	5.69	5.76	5.83	5.90	5.96	6.02	6.07	6.12	6.16	6.21
50	787	32	64	86	04	19	30	41	51	59	67	74	80	86	5.91	5.96	01	06	09
60	762	28	59	82	4.99	13	25	36	45	53	60	67	73	78	84	89	5.93	5.97	01
120	702	20	50	71	87	01	12	21	30	37	44	50	56	61	66	71	75	79	5.83
∞	643	12	40	60	76	4.88	4.99	08	16	23	29	35	40	45	49	54	57	61	65

[1] Values from MAY, J. M., *Biometrika*, **39**, 192 (1952), with corrections from Table 29 in PEARSON and HARTLEY (Eds.), *Biometrika Tables for Statisticians*, vol. 1, Cambridge University Press, 1954, page 176, and from PACHARES, J., *Biometrika*, **46**, 461 (1959). Reprinted by kind permission of the authors and publishers. Values in column 2 and interpolated values calculated by the editors of these *Scientific Tables*.

Upper significance limits* of the standardized extreme range

Test quotient: $\frac{x_N - \mu}{\sigma}$ or $\frac{\mu - x_1}{\sigma}$, where x_N is the highest and x_1 the lowest value of the sample

N \ α	0.10	0.05	0.025	0.01	0.005	0.001	0.0005
1	1.282	1.645	1.960	2.326	2.576	3.090	3.291
2	632	955	2.239	575	807	290	481
3	818	2.121	391	712	935	403	588
4	943	234	494	806	3.023	481	662
5	2.036	2.319	2.572	2.877	3.090	3.540	3.719
6	111	386	635	934	143	588	765
7	172	442	687	981	188	628	803
8	224	490	731	3.022	227	662	836
9	269	531	769	057	260	692	865
10	2.309	2.568	2.803	3.089	3.290	3.719	3.891
11	344	601	834	117	317	743	914
12	376	630	862	143	341	765	935
13	406	657	887	166	363	785	954
14	432	682	910	187	383	803	971
15	2.457	2.705	2.932	3.207	3.402	3.820	3.988
16	480	726	952	226	420	836	4.003
17	502	746	970	243	436	851	017
18	522	765	988	259	452	865	031
19	541	783	3.004	275	466	878	044
20	2.559	2.799	3.020	3.289	3.480	3.890	4.056
21	576	815	034	303	493	902	067
22	592	830	048	316	506	914	078
23	607	844	062	328	517	924	088
24	621	858	075	340	529	934	098
25	2.635	2.870	3.087	3.351	3.539	3.944	4.107
26	648	883	098	362	550	954	116
27	661	895	109	373	560	963	125
28	673	906	120	383	569	971	134
29	685	917	130	392	578	980	142
30	2.696	2.928	3.140	3.402	3.587	3.988	4.149
31	707	938	150	411	596	996	157
32	718	948	159	419	604	4.003	164
33	728	957	168	428	612	010	171
34	738	966	177	436	620	017	178
35	2.747	2.975	3.185	3.444	3.627	4.024	4.185
36	756	984	193	451	635	031	191
37	765	992	201	459	642	037	197
38	774	3.000	209	466	648	044	203
39	782	008	216	473	655	050	209

N \ α	0.10	0.05	0.025	0.01	0.005	0.001	0.0005
40	2.791	3.016	3.224	3.479	3.662	4.056	4.215
41	799	023	231	486	668	061	220
42	806	031	238	493	674	067	226
43	814	038	244	499	680	072	231
44	821	045	251	505	686	078	236
45	2.828	3.051	3.257	3.511	3.692	4.083	4.241
46	835	058	263	517	697	088	246
47	842	064	270	522	703	093	251
48	849	071	276	528	708	098	256
49	856	077	281	533	713	103	260
50	2.862	3.083	3.287	3.539	3.718	4.107	4.265
51	868	089	293	544	723	112	269
52	875	094	298	549	728	116	274
53	880	100	303	554	733	121	278
54	886	106	309	559	738	125	282
55	2.892	3.111	3.314	3.564	3.742	4.129	4.286
56	898	116	319	569	747	134	290
57	903	122	324	573	751	138	294
58	909	127	329	578	756	142	298
59	914	132	333	582	760	146	302
60	2.919	3.137	3.338	3.587	3.764	4.149	4.305
61	924	141	343	591	768	153	309
62	929	146	347	595	772	157	313
63	934	151	352	599	776	160	316
64	939	155	356	603	780	164	320
65	2.944	3.160	3.360	3.607	3.784	4.168	4.323
66	949	164	364	611	788	171	326
67	953	169	369	615	792	175	330
68	958	173	373	619	795	178	333
69	962	177	377	623	799	181	336
70	2.967	3.182	3.381	3.627	3.803	4.184	4.339
71	971	186	384	630	806	188	342
72	976	190	388	634	810	191	346
73	980	194	392	637	813	194	349
74	984	198	396	641	816	197	352
75	2.988	3.201	3.400	3.644	3.820	4.200	4.355
76	992	205	403	648	823	203	357
77	996	209	407	651	826	206	360
78	3.000	213	410	655	829	209	363
79	004	216	414	658	832	212	366

N \ α	0.10	0.05	0.025	0.01	0.005	0.001	0.0005
80	3.008	3.220	3.417	3.661	3.835	4.215	4.369
81	011	224	421	664	839	217	371
82	015	227	424	667	842	220	374
83	019	231	427	670	845	223	377
84	022	234	430	673	847	226	379
85	3.026	3.237	3.434	3.676	3.850	4.228	4.382
86	030	241	437	679	853	231	384
87	033	244	440	682	856	234	387
88	037	247	443	685	859	236	389
89	040	250	446	688	862	239	392
90	3.043	3.254	3.449	3.691	3.864	4.241	4.394
91	047	257	452	694	867	244	397
92	050	260	455	697	870	246	399
93	053	263	458	699	872	249	401
94	056	266	461	702	875	251	404
95	3.060	3.269	3.464	3.705	3.878	4.253	4.406
96	063	272	466	707	880	256	408
97	066	275	469	710	883	258	411
98	069	278	472	713	885	260	413
99	072	281	475	715	888	263	415
100	3.075	3.283	3.477	3.718	3.890	4.265	4.417
200	276	474	659	889	4.055	417	565
300	389	581	762	987	149	504	649
400	467	656	833	4.054	214	565	708
500	3.526	3.713	3.888	4.106	4.264	4.611	4.754
600	574	758	932	148	305	649	790
700	614	797	968	183	339	681	821
800	649	830	4.000	214	368	708	848
900	679	859	028	240	394	732	871
1000	3.706	3.884	4.053	4.264	4.417	4.754	4.892

Upper significance limits[1] of the studentized extreme range

Test quotients: $\frac{x_{N_1} - \bar{x}}{s}$ or $\frac{\bar{x} - x_1}{s}$ $(\nu < \infty)$ and $\frac{x_{N_1} - \bar{x}}{\sigma}$ or $\frac{\bar{x} - x_1}{\sigma}$ $(\nu = \infty)$

where x_{N_1} is the highest value, x_1 the lowest value and $\bar{x}$ the mean of the sample of size N_1 to be tested; s = standard deviation with degrees of freedom $\nu = N_2 - 1$ of a sample of size N_2 *independent* of the sample of size N_1

$\alpha = 0.1$

ν \ N_1	3	4	5	6	7	8	9
10	1.68	1.92	2.09	2.23	2.33	2.42	2.50
11	1.66	1.90	2.07	2.20	2.30	2.39	2.46
12	1.65	1.88	2.05	2.17	2.28	2.36	2.44
13	1.63	1.86	2.03	2.16	2.26	2.34	2.41
14	1.62	1.85	2.01	2.14	2.24	2.32	2.39
15	1.61	1.84	2.00	2.12	2.22	2.31	2.38
16	1.61	1.83	1.99	2.11	2.21	2.29	2.36
17	1.60	1.82	1.98	2.10	2.20	2.28	2.35
18	1.59	1.82	1.97	2.09	2.19	2.27	2.34
19	1.59	1.81	1.96	2.08	2.18	2.26	2.33
20	1.58	1.80	1.96	2.08	2.17	2.25	2.32
24	1.57	1.78	1.94	2.05	2.15	2.22	2.29
30	1.55	1.77	1.92	2.03	2.12	2.20	2.26
40	1.54	1.75	1.90	2.01	2.10	2.17	2.23
60	1.52	1.73	1.87	1.98	2.07	2.14	2.20
120	1.51	1.71	1.85	1.96	2.05	2.12	2.18
∞	1.50	1.70	1.83	1.94	2.02	2.09	2.15

$\alpha = 0.05$

ν \ N_1	3	4	5	6	7	8	9
10	2.01	2.27	2.46	2.60	2.72	2.81	2.89
11	1.98	2.24	2.42	2.56	2.67	2.76	2.84
12	1.96	2.21	2.39	2.52	2.63	2.72	2.80
13	1.94	2.19	2.36	2.50	2.60	2.69	2.76
14	1.93	2.17	2.34	2.47	2.57	2.66	2.74
15	1.91	2.15	2.32	2.45	2.55	2.64	2.71
16	1.90	2.14	2.31	2.43	2.53	2.62	2.69
17	1.89	2.13	2.29	2.42	2.52	2.60	2.67
18	1.88	2.11	2.28	2.40	2.50	2.58	2.65
19	1.87	2.11	2.27	2.39	2.49	2.57	2.64
20	1.87	2.10	2.26	2.38	2.47	2.56	2.63
24	1.84	2.07	2.23	2.34	2.44	2.52	2.58
30	1.82	2.04	2.20	2.31	2.40	2.48	2.54
40	1.80	2.02	2.17	2.28	2.37	2.44	2.50
60	1.78	1.99	2.14	2.25	2.33	2.41	2.47
120	1.76	1.96	2.11	2.22	2.30	2.37	2.43
∞	1.74	1.94	2.08	2.18	2.27	2.33	2.39

$\alpha = 0.025$

ν \ N_1	3	4	5	6	7	8	9
10	2.34	2.63	2.83	2.98	3.10	3.20	3.29
11	2.30	2.58	2.77	2.92	3.03	3.13	3.22
12	2.27	2.54	2.73	2.87	2.98	3.08	3.16
13	2.24	2.51	2.69	2.83	2.94	3.03	3.11
14	2.22	2.48	2.66	2.79	2.90	2.99	3.07
15	2.20	2.45	2.63	2.76	2.87	2.96	3.04
16	2.18	2.43	2.61	2.74	2.84	2.93	3.01
17	2.17	2.42	2.59	2.72	2.82	2.91	2.98
18	2.15	2.40	2.57	2.70	2.80	2.89	2.96
19	2.14	2.39	2.56	2.68	2.78	2.87	2.94
20	2.13	2.37	2.54	2.67	2.77	2.85	2.92
24	2.10	2.34	2.50	2.62	2.72	2.80	2.87
30	2.07	2.30	2.46	2.58	2.67	2.75	2.81
40	2.04	2.27	2.42	2.53	2.62	2.70	2.76
60	2.01	2.23	2.38	2.49	2.58	2.65	2.71
120	1.98	2.20	2.34	2.45	2.53	2.60	2.66
∞	1.95	2.16	2.30	2.41	2.49	2.56	2.61

$\alpha = 0.01$

ν \ N_1	3	4	5	6	7	8	9
10	2.78	3.10	3.32	3.48	3.62	3.73	3.82
11	2.72	3.02	3.24	3.39	3.52	3.63	3.72
12	2.67	2.96	3.17	3.32	3.45	3.55	3.64
13	2.63	2.92	3.12	3.27	3.38	3.48	3.57
14	2.60	2.88	3.07	3.22	3.33	3.43	3.51
15	2.57	2.84	3.03	3.17	3.29	3.38	3.46
16	2.54	2.81	3.00	3.14	3.25	3.34	3.42
17	2.52	2.79	2.97	3.11	3.22	3.31	3.38
18	2.50	2.77	2.95	3.08	3.19	3.28	3.35
19	2.49	2.75	2.93	3.06	3.16	3.25	3.33
20	2.47	2.73	2.91	3.04	3.14	3.23	3.30
24	2.42	2.68	2.84	2.97	3.07	3.16	3.23
30	2.38	2.62	2.79	2.91	3.01	3.08	3.15
40	2.34	2.57	2.73	2.85	2.94	3.02	3.08
60	2.29	2.52	2.68	2.79	2.88	2.95	3.01
120	2.25	2.48	2.62	2.73	2.82	2.89	2.95
∞	2.22	2.43	2.57	2.68	2.76	2.83	2.88

$\alpha = 0.005$

ν \ N_1	3	4	5	6	7	8	9
10	3.12	3.46	3.70	3.87	4.02	4.14	4.24
11	3.04	3.37	3.59	3.76	3.90	4.01	4.11
12	2.98	3.29	3.51	3.67	3.80	3.91	4.00
13	2.93	3.23	3.44	3.60	3.72	3.83	3.92
14	2.88	3.18	3.38	3.54	3.66	3.76	3.85
15	2.84	3.13	3.33	3.48	3.60	3.70	3.78
16	2.81	3.10	3.29	3.44	3.56	3.65	3.73
17	2.78	3.07	3.26	3.40	3.52	3.61	3.68
18	2.76	3.04	3.23	3.37	3.48	3.57	3.64
19	2.74	3.01	3.20	3.34	3.45	3.54	3.61
20	2.72	2.99	3.17	3.31	3.42	3.51	3.58
24	2.66	2.92	3.10	3.23	3.33	3.42	3.49
30	2.60	2.86	3.03	3.15	3.25	3.33	3.40
40	2.55	2.79	2.96	3.08	3.17	3.25	3.31
60	2.50	2.73	2.89	3.01	3.10	3.17	3.23
120	2.45	2.67	2.83	2.94	3.02	3.09	3.15
∞	2.40	2.62	2.76	2.87	2.95	3.02	3.07

$\alpha = 0.001$

ν \ N_1	3	4	5	6	7	8	9
10	4.0	4.3	4.6	4.8	5.0	5.2	5.3
11	3.8	4.2	4.5	4.7	4.8	5.0	5.1
12	3.7	4.1	4.3	4.5	4.7	4.8	4.9
13	3.6	4.0	4.2	4.4	4.5	4.6	4.7
14	3.5	3.9	4.1	4.3	4.4	4.5	4.6
15	3.5	3.8	4.0	4.2	4.3	4.4	4.5
16	3.4	3.7	4.0	4.1	4.3	4.4	4.5
17	3.4	3.7	3.9	4.1	4.2	4.3	4.4
18	3.3	3.6	3.9	4.0	4.1	4.2	4.3
19	3.3	3.6	3.8	4.0	4.1	4.2	4.3
20	3.3	3.6	3.8	3.9	4.0	4.1	4.2
24	3.2	3.5	3.7	3.8	3.9	4.0	4.1
30	3.1	3.4	3.6	3.7	3.8	3.9	4.0
40	3.0	3.3	3.5	3.6	3.7	3.7	3.8
60	2.9	3.2	3.4	3.5	3.6	3.6	3.7
120	2.9	3.1	3.3	3.4	3.5	3.5	3.6
∞	2.8	3.0	3.2	3.3	3.4	3.4	3.5

* Reproduction only by permission of the publishers of these *Scientific Tables*.

[1] Values from NAIR, K.R., *Biometrika*, **39**, 189 (1952), corrected by DAVID, H.A., *Biometrika*, **43**, 449 (1956). Reprinted by kind permission of the authors and publishers.

Significance limits[1] for testing extreme values of a sample

$x_1 \leqq x_2 \leqq x_3 \ldots \leqq x_N$

N \ α	0.30	0.20	0.10	0.05	0.02	0.01	0.005	Test quotient
3	0.684	0.781	0.886	0.941	0.976	0.988	0.994	$\frac{x_N - x_{N-1}}{x_N - x_1}$
4	471	560	679	765	846	889	926	
5	373	451	557	642	729	780	821	
6	318	386	482	560	644	698	740	
7	281	344	434	507	586	637	680	
8	0.318	0.385	0.479	0.554	0.631	0.683	0.725	$\frac{x_N - x_{N-1}}{x_N - x_2}$
9	288	352	441	512	587	635	677	
10	265	325	409	477	551	597	639	
11	0.391	0.442	0.517	0.576	0.638	0.679	0.713	$\frac{x_N - x_{N-2}}{x_N - x_2}$
12	370	419	490	546	605	642	675	
13	351	399	467	521	578	615	649	
14	0.370	0.421	0.492	0.546	0.602	0.641	0.674	$\frac{x_N - x_{N-2}}{x_N - x_3}$
15	0.353	0.402	0.472	0.525	0.579	0.616	0.647	
16	338	386	454	507	559	595	624	
17	325	373	438	490	542	577	605	
18	314	361	424	475	527	561	589	
19	304	350	412	462	514	547	575	
20	0.295	0.340	0.401	0.450	0.502	0.535	0.562	
21	287	331	391	440	491	524	551	
22	280	323	382	430	481	514	541	
23	274	316	374	421	472	505	532	
24	268	310	367	413	464	497	524	
25	0.262	0.304	0.360	0.406	0.457	0.489	0.516	

Significance limits[2] for the difference between the mean of a sample and a hypothetical mean μ

Test quotient: $\frac{\bar{x} - \mu}{x_N - x_1}$; where x_N is the highest and x_1 the lowest value of a sample of size N

N \ 2α	0.10	0.05	0.02	0.01	0.002	0.001
2	3.157	6.353	15.910	31.828	159.16	318.31
3	0.885	1.304	2.111	3.008	6.77	9.58
4	0.529	0.717	1.023	1.316	2.29	2.85
5	0.388	0.507	0.685	0.843	1.32	1.58
6	0.312	0.399	0.523	0.628	0.92	1.07
7	0.263	0.333	0.429	0.507	0.71	0.82
8	0.230	0.288	0.366	0.429	0.59	0.67
9	0.205	0.255	0.322	0.374	0.50	0.57
10	0.186	0.230	0.288	0.333	0.44	0.50
11	0.170	0.210	0.262	0.302	0.40	0.44
12	0.158	0.194	0.241	0.277	0.36	0.40
13	0.147	0.181	0.224	0.256	0.33	0.37
14	0.138	0.170	0.209	0.239	0.31	0.34
15	0.131	0.160	0.197	0.224	0.29	0.32
16	0.124	0.151	0.186	0.212	0.27	0.30
17	0.118	0.144	0.177	0.201	0.26	0.28
18	0.113	0.137	0.168	0.191	0.24	0.26
19	0.108	0.131	0.161	0.182	0.23	0.25
20	0.104	0.126	0.154	0.175	0.22	0.24

Significance limits[2] for the difference between the means of two samples of the same size

Test quotient: $\frac{\bar{x}' - \bar{x}''}{x_N' - x_1' + x_N'' - x_1''}$; where x_N is the highest and x_1 the lowest value of the two samples of size $N' = N'' = N$

N \ 2α	0.10	0.05	0.02	0.01	0.002	0.001
2	1.161	1.714	2.777	3.958	8.91	12.62
3	0.487	0.636	0.857	1.047	1.64	2.09
4	0.322	0.407	0.524	0.619	0.87	1.00
5	0.247	0.307	0.386	0.448	0.61	0.68
6	0.203	0.250	0.311	0.357	0.47	0.52
7	0.174	0.213	0.263	0.300	0.39	0.43
8	0.153	0.187	0.230	0.261	0.34	0.37
9	0.137	0.167	0.205	0.232	0.30	0.32
10	0.125	0.152	0.186	0.210	0.27	0.29
11	0.117	0.140	0.170	0.192	0.24	0.26
12	0.107	0.130	0.158	0.178	0.22	0.24
13	0.101	0.122	0.147	0.166	0.21	0.22
14	0.095	0.114	0.138	0.156	0.20	0.21
15	0.090	0.108	0.131	0.147	0.18	0.20
16	0.085	0.103	0.124	0.139	0.17	0.19
17	0.081	0.098	0.118	0.132	0.17	0.18
18	0.078	0.094	0.113	0.126	0.16	0.17
19	0.075	0.090	0.108	0.121	0.15	0.16
20	0.072	0.086	0.104	0.116	0.15	0.16

[1] Values from DIXON, W. J., *Biometrics*, **9**, 74 (1953).

[2] Values from LORD, E., *Biometrika*, **34**, 41 (1947), but recalculated from the simplified test quotient given.

[3] Values from WALSH, J. E., *Ann. math. Statist.*, **20**, 257 (1949).

Significance limits for the difference between the mean of a sample and a hypothetical mean μ

$\bar{x}$ does not need to be calculated in these tests. The values x are so arranged that $x_1 \leqq x_2 \leqq x_3 \ldots \leqq x_N$. Test B is also suitable for symmetrical distributions that are not normal distributions

A[3]

Test quotient: $\frac{x_N + x_1 - 2\mu}{x_N - x_1}$

N \ 2α	0.10	0.05	0.02	0.01
2	6.32	12.70	31.82	63.66
3	1.80	2.60	4.22	6.04
4	1.11	1.48	2.08	2.74
5	0.85	1.04	1.42	1.70
6	0.70	0.86	1.12	1.32
7	0.60	0.75	0.95	1.10
8	0.53	0.66	0.84	0.95
9	0.48	0.60	0.76	0.85
10	0.45	0.55	0.70	0.78

B[4]

N	$\bar{x} \neq \mu\ (2\alpha)$, when: either $\bar{x} < \mu\ (\alpha)$, when	or $\bar{x} > \mu\ (\alpha)$, when	2α
4	$1.055\,x_4 - 0.055\,x_1 < \mu$	$1.055\,x_1 - 0.055\,x_4 > \mu$	0.10
5	$0.63\,x_5 + 0.37\,x_4 < \mu$	$0.63\,x_1 + 0.37\,x_2 > \mu$	0.10
	$1.02\,x_5 - 0.02\,x_1 < \mu$	$1.02\,x_1 - 0.02\,x_5 > \mu$	0.05
6	$0.63\,x_6 + 0.37\,x_5 < \mu$	$0.63\,x_1 + 0.37\,x_2 > \mu$	0.05
	$1.06\,x_6 - 0.06\,x_1 < \mu$	$1.06\,x_1 - 0.06\,x_6 > \mu$	0.02
7	$0.785\,x_7 + 0.215\,x_6 < \mu$	$0.785\,x_1 + 0.215\,x_2 > \mu$	0.02
	$1.05\,x_7 - 0.05\,x_1 < \mu$	$1.05\,x_1 - 0.05\,x_7 > \mu$	0.01
8	the *greater* of the values x_7 or $(0.5\,x_8 + 0.28\,x_6 + 0.22\,x_7) < \mu$	the *smaller* of the values x_2 or $(0.5\,x_1 + 0.28\,x_3 + 0.22\,x_2) > \mu$	$\cong 0.02$
	$0.785\,x_6 + 0.215\,x_7 < \mu$	$0.785\,x_1 + 0.215\,x_2 > \mu$	0.01
9	the *greater* of the values x_8 or $0.5\,(x_5 + x_9) < \mu$	the *smaller* of the values x_2 or $0.5\,(x_1 + x_5) > \mu$	0.02
	the *greater* of the values x_8 or $(0.5\,x_9 + 0.28\,x_7 + 0.22\,x_8) < \mu$	the *smaller* of the values x_2 or $(0.5\,x_1 + 0.28\,x_3 + 0.22\,x_2) > \mu$	$\cong 0.01$
10	the *greater* of the values x_9 or $0.5\,(x_6 + x_{10}) < \mu$	the *smaller* of the values x_2 or $0.5\,(x_1 + x_5) > \mu$	0.01
11	the *greater* of the values x_7 or $0.5\,(x_4 + x_{11}) < \mu$	the *smaller* of the values x_5 or $0.5\,(x_1 + x_8) > \mu$	$\cong 0.10$
	the *greater* of the values x_9 or $0.5\,(x_7 + x_{11}) < \mu$	the *smaller* of the values x_3 or $0.5\,(x_1 + x_5) > \mu$	$\cong 0.01$
12	the *greater* of the values x_9 or $0.5\,(x_6 + x_{12}) < \mu$	the *smaller* of the values x_4 or $0.5\,(x_1 + x_7) > \mu$	0.02
13	the *greater* of the values x_{10} or $0.5\,(x_7 + x_{13}) < \mu$	the *smaller* of the values x_4 or $0.5\,(x_1 + x_7) > \mu$	0.01
14	the *greater* of the values x_{10} or $0.5\,(x_6 + x_{14}) < \mu$	the *smaller* of the values x_5 or $0.5\,(x_1 + x_9) > \mu$	0.02
15	the *greater* of the values x_{11} or $0.5\,(x_7 + x_{15}) < \mu$	the *smaller* of the values x_5 or $0.5\,(x_1 + x_9) > \mu$	0.01

[4] Values from WALSH, J. E., *loc. cit.*, and from WALSH, J. E., *J. Amer. statist. Ass.*, **44**, 342 (1949). All values reprinted by kind permission of the authors and publishers.

Probit Transformation[1]

The percentages correspond to 100 times the area under the normal distribution curve between minus infinity and c
The probits are the normal deviates c increased by 5

%	0.0	0.1	0.2	0.3	0.4	0.5	0.6	0.7	0.8	0.9	1	2	3	4	5
	Probits														
0	...	1.9098	2.1218	2.2522	2.3479	2.4242	2.4879	2.5427	2.5911	2.6344					
1	2.6737	2.7096	2.7429	2.7738	2.8027	2.8299	2.8556	2.8799	2.9031	2.9251					
2	2.9463	2.9665	2.9859	3.0046	3.0226	3.0400	3.0569	3.0732	3.0890	3.1043					
3	3.1192	3.1337	3.1478	3.1616	3.1750	3.1881	3.2009	3.2134	3.2256	3.2376					
4	3.2493	3.2608	3.2721	3.2831	3.2940	3.3046	3.3151	3.3253	3.3354	3.3454					
5	3.3551	3.3648	3.3742	3.3836	3.3928	3.4018	3.4107	3.4195	3.4282	3.4368	9	18	27	36	45
6	3.4452	3.4536	3.4618	3.4699	3.4780	3.4859	3.4937	3.5015	3.5091	3.5167	8	16	24	32	40
7	3.5242	3.5316	3.5389	3.5462	3.5534	3.5605	3.5675	3.5745	3.5813	3.5882	7	14	21	28	36
8	3.5949	3.6016	3.6083	3.6148	3.6213	3.6278	3.6342	3.6405	3.6468	3.6531	6	13	19	26	32
9	3.6592	3.6654	3.6715	3.6775	3.6835	3.6894	3.6953	3.7012	3.7070	3.7127	6	12	18	24	30
10	3.7184	3.7241	3.7298	3.7354	3.7409	3.7464	3.7519	3.7574	3.7628	3.7681	6	11	17	22	28
11	3.7735	3.7788	3.7840	3.7893	3.7945	3.7996	3.8048	3.8099	3.8150	3.8200	5	10	16	21	26
12	3.8250	3.8300	3.8350	3.8399	3.8448	3.8497	3.8545	3.8593	3.8641	3.8689	5	10	15	20	24
13	3.8736	3.8783	3.8830	3.8877	3.8923	3.8969	3.9015	3.9061	3.9107	3.9152	5	9	14	18	23
14	3.9197	3.9242	3.9286	3.9331	3.9375	3.9419	3.9463	3.9506	3.9550	3.9593	4	9	13	18	22
15	3.9636	3.9678	3.9721	3.9763	3.9806	3.9848	3.9890	3.9931	3.9973	4.0014	4	8	13	17	21
16	4.0055	4.0096	4.0137	4.0178	4.0218	4.0259	4.0299	4.0339	4.0379	4.0419	4	8	12	16	20
17	4.0458	4.0498	4.0537	4.0576	4.0615	4.0654	4.0693	4.0731	4.0770	4.0808	4	8	12	16	19
18	4.0846	4.0884	4.0922	4.0960	4.0998	4.1035	4.1073	4.1110	4.1147	4.1184	4	8	11	15	19
19	4.1221	4.1258	4.1295	4.1331	4.1367	4.1404	4.1440	4.1476	4.1512	4.1548	4	7	11	15	18
20	4.1584	4.1619	4.1655	4.1690	4.1726	4.1761	4.1796	4.1831	4.1866	4.1901	4	7	11	14	18
21	4.1936	4.1970	4.2005	4.2039	4.2074	4.2108	4.2142	4.2176	4.2210	4.2244	3	7	10	14	17
22	4.2278	4.2312	4.2345	4.2379	4.2412	4.2446	4.2479	4.2512	4.2546	4.2579	3	7	10	13	17
23	4.2612	4.2644	4.2677	4.2710	4.2743	4.2775	4.2808	4.2840	4.2872	4.2905	3	7	10	13	16
24	4.2937	4.2969	4.3001	4.3033	4.3065	4.3097	4.3129	4.3160	4.3192	4.3224	3	6	10	13	16
25	4.3255	4.3287	4.3318	4.3349	4.3380	4.3412	4.3443	4.3474	4.3505	4.3536	3	6	9	12	16
26	4.3567	4.3597	4.3628	4.3659	4.3689	4.3720	4.3750	4.3781	4.3811	4.3842	3	6	9	12	15
27	4.3872	4.3902	4.3932	4.3962	4.3992	4.4022	4.4052	4.4082	4.4112	4.4142	3	6	9	12	15
28	4.4172	4.4201	4.4231	4.4260	4.4290	4.4319	4.4349	4.4378	4.4408	4.4437	3	6	9	12	15
29	4.4466	4.4495	4.4524	4.4554	4.4583	4.4612	4.4641	4.4670	4.4698	4.4727	3	6	9	12	14
30	4.4756	4.4785	4.4813	4.4842	4.4871	4.4899	4.4928	4.4956	4.4985	4.5013	3	6	9	11	14
31	4.5041	4.5070	4.5098	4.5126	4.5155	4.5183	4.5211	4.5239	4.5267	4.5295	3	6	8	11	14
32	4.5323	4.5351	4.5379	4.5407	4.5435	4.5462	4.5490	4.5518	4.5546	4.5573	3	6	8	11	14
33	4.5601	4.5628	4.5656	4.5684	4.5711	4.5739	4.5766	4.5793	4.5821	4.5848	3	5	8	11	14
34	4.5875	4.5903	4.5930	4.5957	4.5984	4.6011	4.6039	4.6066	4.6093	4.6120	3	5	8	11	14
35	4.6147	4.6174	4.6201	4.6228	4.6255	4.6281	4.6308	4.6335	4.6362	4.6389	3	5	8	11	13
36	4.6415	4.6442	4.6469	4.6495	4.6522	4.6549	4.6575	4.6602	4.6628	4.6655	3	5	8	11	13
37	4.6681	4.6708	4.6734	4.6761	4.6787	4.6814	4.6840	4.6866	4.6893	4.6919	3	5	8	11	13
38	4.6945	4.6971	4.6998	4.7024	4.7050	4.7076	4.7102	4.7129	4.7155	4.7181	3	5	8	10	13
39	4.7207	4.7233	4.7259	4.7285	4.7311	4.7337	4.7363	4.7389	4.7415	4.7441	3	5	8	10	13
40	4.7467	4.7492	4.7518	4.7544	4.7570	4.7596	4.7622	4.7647	4.7673	4.7699	3	5	8	10	13
41	4.7725	4.7750	4.7776	4.7802	4.7827	4.7853	4.7879	4.7904	4.7930	4.7955	3	5	8	10	13
42	4.7981	4.8007	4.8032	4.8058	4.8083	4.8109	4.8134	4.8160	4.8185	4.8211	3	5	8	10	13
43	4.8236	4.8262	4.8287	4.8313	4.8338	4.8363	4.8389	4.8414	4.8440	4.8465	3	5	8	10	13
44	4.8490	4.8516	4.8541	4.8566	4.8592	4.8617	4.8642	4.8668	4.8693	4.8718	3	5	8	10	13
45	4.8743	4.8769	4.8794	4.8819	4.8844	4.8870	4.8895	4.8920	4.8945	4.8970	3	5	8	10	13
46	4.8996	4.9021	4.9046	4.9071	4.9096	4.9122	4.9147	4.9172	4.9197	4.9222	3	5	8	10	13
47	4.9247	4.9272	4.9298	4.9323	4.9348	4.9373	4.9398	4.9423	4.9448	4.9473	3	5	8	10	13
48	4.9498	4.9524	4.9549	4.9574	4.9599	4.9624	4.9649	4.9674	4.9699	4.9724	3	5	8	10	13
49	4.9749	4.9774	4.9799	4.9825	4.9850	4.9875	4.9900	4.9925	4.9950	4.9975	3	5	8	10	13
50	5.0000	5.0025	5.0050	5.0075	5.0100	5.0125	5.0150	5.0175	5.0201	5.0226	3	5	8	10	13
51	5.0251	5.0276	5.0301	5.0326	5.0351	5.0376	5.0401	5.0426	5.0451	5.0476	3	5	8	10	13
52	5.0502	5.0527	5.0552	5.0577	5.0602	5.0627	5.0652	5.0677	5.0702	5.0728	3	5	8	10	13
53	5.0753	5.0778	5.0803	5.0828	5.0853	5.0878	5.0904	5.0929	5.0954	5.0979	3	5	8	10	13
54	5.1004	5.1030	5.1055	5.1080	5.1105	5.1130	5.1156	5.1181	5.1206	5.1231	3	5	8	10	13
55	5.1257	5.1282	5.1307	5.1332	5.1358	5.1383	5.1408	5.1434	5.1459	5.1484	3	5	8	10	13
56	5.1510	5.1535	5.1560	5.1586	5.1611	5.1637	5.1662	5.1687	5.1713	5.1738	3	5	8	10	13
57	5.1764	5.1789	5.1815	5.1840	5.1866	5.1891	5.1917	5.1942	5.1968	5.1993	3	5	8	10	13
58	5.2019	5.2045	5.2070	5.2096	5.2121	5.2147	5.2173	5.2198	5.2224	5.2250	3	5	8	10	13
59	5.2275	5.2301	5.2327	5.2353	5.2378	5.2404	5.2430	5.2456	5.2482	5.2508	3	5	8	10	13
60	5.2533	5.2559	5.2585	5.2611	5.2637	5.2663	5.2689	5.2715	5.2741	5.2767	3	5	8	10	13
61	5.2793	5.2819	5.2845	5.2871	5.2898	5.2924	5.2950	5.2976	5.3002	5.3029	3	5	8	10	13
62	5.3055	5.3081	5.3107	5.3134	5.3160	5.3186	5.3213	5.3239	5.3266	5.3292	3	5	8	11	13
63	5.3319	5.3345	5.3372	5.3398	5.3425	5.3451	5.3478	5.3505	5.3531	5.3558	3	5	8	11	13
64	5.3585	5.3611	5.3638	5.3665	5.3692	5.3719	5.3745	5.3772	5.3799	5.3826	3	5	8	11	13
65	5.3853	5.3880	5.3907	5.3934	5.3961	5.3989	5.4016	5.4043	5.4070	5.4097	3	5	8	11	14
66	5.4125	5.4152	5.4179	5.4207	5.4234	5.4261	5.4289	5.4316	5.4344	5.4372	3	5	8	11	14
67	5.4399	5.4427	5.4454	5.4482	5.4510	5.4538	5.4565	5.4593	5.4621	5.4649	3	6	8	11	14
68	5.4677	5.4705	5.4733	5.4761	5.4789	5.4817	5.4845	5.4874	5.4902	5.4930	3	6	8	11	14
69	5.4959	5.4987	5.5015	5.5044	5.5072	5.5101	5.5129	5.5158	5.5187	5.5215	3	6	9	11	14
70	5.5244	5.5273	5.5302	5.5330	5.5359	5.5388	5.5417	5.5446	5.5476	5.5505	3	6	9	12	14
71	5.5534	5.5563	5.5592	5.5622	5.5651	5.5681	5.5710	5.5740	5.5769	5.5799	3	6	9	12	15
72	5.5828	5.5858	5.5888	5.5918	5.5948	5.5978	5.6008	5.6038	5.6068	5.6098	3	6	9	12	15
73	5.6128	5.6158	5.6189	5.6219	5.6250	5.6280	5.6311	5.6341	5.6372	5.6403	3	6	9	12	15
74	5.6433	5.6464	5.6495	5.6526	5.6557	5.6588	5.6620	5.6651	5.6682	5.6713	3	6	9	12	16
75	5.6745	5.6776	5.6808	5.6840	5.6871	5.6903	5.6935	5.6967	5.6999	5.7031	3	6	10	13	16
76	5.7063	5.7095	5.7128	5.7160	5.7192	5.7225	5.7257	5.7290	5.7323	5.7356	3	7	10	13	16
77	5.7388	5.7421	5.7454	5.7488	5.7521	5.7554	5.7588	5.7621	5.7655	5.7688	3	7	10	13	17
78	5.7722	5.7756	5.7790	5.7824	5.7858	5.7892	5.7926	5.7961	5.7995	5.8030	3	7	10	14	17
79	5.8064	5.8099	5.8134	5.8169	5.8204	5.8239	5.8274	5.8310	5.8345	5.8381	4	7	11	14	18
80	5.8416	5.8452	5.8488	5.8524	5.8560	5.8596	5.8633	5.8669	5.8705	5.8742	4	7	11	14	18
81	5.8779	5.8816	5.8853	5.8890	5.8927	5.8965	5.9002	5.9040	5.9078	5.9116	4	7	11	15	19
82	5.9154	5.9192	5.9230	5.9269	5.9307	5.9346	5.9385	5.9424	5.9463	5.9502	4	8	12	15	19
83	5.9542	5.9581	5.9621	5.9661	5.9701	5.9741	5.9782	5.9822	5.9863	5.9904	4	8	12	16	20
84	5.9945	5.9986	6.0027	6.0069	6.0110	6.0152	6.0194	6.0237	6.0279	6.0322	4	8	13	17	21
85	6.0364	6.0407	6.0450	6.0494	6.0537	6.0581	6.0625	6.0669	6.0714	6.0758	4	9	13	18	22
86	6.0803	6.0848	6.0893	6.0939	6.0985	6.1031	6.1077	6.1123	6.1170	6.1217	5	9	14	18	23
87	6.1264	6.1311	6.1359	6.1407	6.1455	6.1503	6.1552	6.1601	6.1650	6.1700	5	10	15	19	24
88	6.1750	6.1800	6.1850	6.1901	6.1952	6.2004	6.2055	6.2107	6.2160	6.2212	5	10	15	21	26
89	6.2265	6.2319	6.2372	6.2426	6.2481	6.2536	6.2591	6.2646	6.2702	6.2759	5	11	16	22	27
90	6.2816	6.2873	6.2930	6.2988	6.3047	6.3106	6.3165	6.3225	6.3285	6.3346	6	12	18	24	29
91	6.3408	6.3469	6.3532	6.3595	6.3658	6.3722	6.3787	6.3852	6.3917	6.3984	6	13	19	26	32
92	6.4051	6.4118	6.4187	6.4255	6.4325	6.4395	6.4466	6.4538	6.4611	6.4684	7	14	21	28	35
93	6.4758	6.4833	6.4909	6.4985	6.5063	6.5141	6.5220	6.5301	6.5382	6.5464	8	16	24	31	39
94	6.5548	6.5632	6.5718	6.5805	6.5893	6.5982	6.6072	6.6164	6.6258	6.6352	9	18	27	36	45

[1] Values from Fisher and Yates, *Statistical Tables for Biological, Agricultural and Medical Research*, 6th ed., Oliver and Boyd, Edinburgh, 1963, page 68. Reprinted by kind permission of the authors and publishers.

(continuation of table on page 54)

%	0.0	0.1	0.2	0.3	0.4	0.5	0.6	0.7	0.8	0.9	1	2	3	4	5
	Probits														
95	6.6449	6.6546	6.6646	6.6747	6.6849	6.6954	6.7060	6.7169	6.7279	6.7392					
	97	100	101	102	105	106	109	110	113	115					
96	6.7507	6.7624	6.7744	6.7866	6.7991	6.8119	6.8250	6.8384	6.8522	6.8663					
	117	120	122	125	128	131	134	138	141	145					
97	6.8808	6.8957	6.9110	6.9268	6.9431	6.9600	6.9774	6.9954	7.0141	7.0335					
	149	153	158	163	169	174	180	187	194	202					
	0.00	0.01	0.02	0.03	0.04	0.05	0.06	0.07	0.08	0.09					
98.0	7.0537	7.0558	7.0579	7.0600	7.0621	7.0642	7.0663	7.0684	7.0706	7.0727	2	4	6	8	11
98.1	7.0749	7.0770	7.0792	7.0814	7.0836	7.0858	7.0880	7.0902	7.0924	7.0947	2	4	7	9	11
98.2	7.0969	7.0992	7.1015	7.1038	7.1061	7.1084	7.1107	7.1130	7.1154	7.1177	2	5	7	9	12
98.3	7.1201	7.1224	7.1248	7.1272	7.1297	7.1321	7.1345	7.1370	7.1394	7.1419	2	5	7	10	12
98.4	7.1444	7.1469	7.1494	7.1520	7.1545	7.1571	7.1596	7.1622	7.1648	7.1675	3	5	8	10	13
98.5	7.1701	7.1727	7.1754	7.1781	7.1808	7.1835	7.1862	7.1890	7.1917	7.1945	3	5	8	11	14
98.6	7.1973	7.2001	7.2029	7.2058	7.2086	7.2115	7.2144	7.2173	7.2203	7.2232	3	6	9	12	14
98.7	7.2262	7.2292	7.2322	7.2353	7.2383	7.2414	7.2445	7.2476	7.2508	7.2539	3	6	9	12	15
98.8	7.2571	7.2603	7.2636	7.2668	7.2701	7.2734	7.2768	7.2801	7.2835	7.2869	3	7	10	13	17
98.9	7.2904	7.2938	7.2973	7.3009	7.3044	7.3080	7.3116	7.3152	7.3189	7.3226	4	7	11	14	18
99.0	7.3263	7.3301	7.3339	7.3378	7.3416	7.3455	7.3495	7.3535	7.3575	7.3615	4	8	12	16	20
99.1	7.3656	7.3698	7.3739	7.3781	7.3824	7.3867	7.3911	7.3954	7.3999	7.4044	4	9	13	17	22
99.2	7.4089	7.4135	7.4181	7.4228	7.4276	7.4324	7.4372	7.4422	7.4471	7.4522	5	10	14	19	24
99.3	7.4573	7.4624	7.4677	7.4730	7.4783	7.4838	7.4893	7.4949	7.5006	7.5063	5	11	16	22	27
99.4	7.5121	7.5181	7.5241	7.5302	7.5364	7.5427	7.5491	7.5556	7.5622	7.5690	6	13	19	25	32
99.5	7.5758	7.5828	7.5899	7.5972	7.6045	7.6121	7.6197	7.6276	7.6356	7.6437					
99.6	7.6521	7.6606	7.6693	7.6783	7.6874	7.6968	7.7065	7.7164	7.7266	7.7370					
99.7	7.7478	7.7589	7.7703	7.7822	7.7944	7.8070	7.8202	7.8338	7.8480	7.8627					
99.8	7.8782	7.8943	7.9112	7.9290	7.9478	7.9677	7.9889	8.0115	8.0357	8.0618					
99.9	8.0902	8.1214	8.1559	8.1947	8.2389	8.2905	8.3528	8.4316	8.5401	8.7190					

Weighting coefficients and probit values to be used for final adjustments

Expected probit Y	Minimum working probit $Y-P/Z$	Range $1/Z$	Maximum working probit $Y+Q/Z$	Weighting coefficient Z^2/PQ
1.1	0.8579	5034	5035	0.00082
1.2	0.9522	3425	3426	00118
1.3	1.0462	2354	2355	00167
1.4	1.1400	1634	1635	00235
1.5	1.2335	1146	1147	0.00327
1.6	1.3266	811.5	812.8	00451
1.7	1.4194	580.5	581.9	00614
1.8	1.5118	419.4	420.9	00828
1.9	1.6038	306.1	307.7	01104
2.0	1.6954	225.6	227.3	0.01457
2.1	1.7866	168.00	169.79	01903
2.2	1.8772	126.34	128.22	02459
2.3	1.9673	95.96	97.93	03143
2.4	2.0568	73.62	75.68	03977
2.5	2.1457	57.05	59.20	0.04979
2.6	2.2340	44.654	46.888	06169
2.7	2.3214	35.302	37.623	07563
2.8	2.4081	28.189	30.597	09179
2.9	2.4938	22.736	25.230	11026
3.0	2.5786	18.522	21.101	0.13112
3.1	2.6624	15.240	17.902	15436
3.2	2.7449	12.666	15.411	17994
3.3	2.8261	10.633	13.459	20774
3.4	2.9060	9.015	11.921	23753
3.5	2.9842	7.721	10.705	0.26907
3.6	3.0606	6.6788	9.7394	30199
3.7	3.1351	5.8354	8.9705	33589
3.8	3.2074	5.1497	8.3571	37031
3.9	3.2773	4.5903	7.8676	40474
4.0	3.3443	4.1327	7.4770	0.43863
4.1	3.4083	3.7582	7.1665	47144
4.2	3.4687	3.4519	6.9206	50260
4.3	3.5251	3.2025	6.7276	53159
4.4	3.5770	3.0010	6.5780	55788
4.5	3.6236	2.8404	6.4640	0.58099
4.6	3.6643	2.7154	6.3797	60052
4.7	3.6982	2.6220	6.3202	61609
4.8	3.7241	2.5573	6.2814	62741
4.9	3.7407	2.5192	6.2599	63431

Expected probit Y	Minimum working probit $Y-P/Z$	Range $1/Z$	Maximum working probit $Y+Q/Z$	Weighting coefficient Z^2/PQ
5.0	3.7467	2.5066	6.2533	0.63662
5.1	3.7401	2.5192	6.2593	63431
5.2	3.7186	2.5573	6.2759	62742
5.3	3.6798	2.6220	6.3018	61609
5.4	3.6203	2.7154	6.3357	60052
5.5	3.5360	2.8404	6.3764	0.58099
5.6	3.4220	3.0010	6.4230	55788
5.7	3.2724	3.2025	6.4749	53159
5.8	3.0794	3.4519	6.5313	50260
5.9	2.8335	3.7582	6.5917	47144
6.0	2.5230	4.1327	6.6557	0.43863
6.1	2.1324	4.5903	6.7227	40474
6.2	1.6429	5.1497	6.7926	37031
6.3	1.0295	5.8354	6.8649	33589
6.4	0.2606	6.6788	6.9394	30199
6.5	−0.705	7.721	7.0158	0.26907
6.6	−1.921	9.015	7.0940	23753
6.7	−3.459	10.633	7.1739	20774
6.8	−5.411	12.666	7.2551	17994
6.9	−7.902	15.240	7.3376	15436
7.0	−11.101	18.522	7.4214	0.13112
7.1	−15.230	22.736	7.5062	11026
7.2	−20.597	28.189	7.5919	09179
7.3	−27.623	35.302	7.6786	07564
7.4	−36.888	44.654	7.7661	06168
7.5	−49.20	57.05	7.8543	0.04979
7.6	−65.68	73.62	7.9432	03977
7.7	−87.93	95.96	8.0327	03143
7.8	−118.22	126.34	8.1228	02458
7.9	−159.79	168.00	8.2134	01903
8.0	−217.3	225.6	8.3046	0.01457
8.1	−297.7	306.1	8.3962	01104
8.2	−410.9	419.4	8.4882	00828
8.3	−571.9	580.5	8.5806	00614
8.4	−802.8	811.5	8.6734	00451
8.5	−1137	1146	8.7666	0.00327
8.6	−1625	1634	8.8600	00235
8.7	−2345	2354	8.9538	00167
8.8	−3416	3425	9.0478	00118
8.9	−5025	5034	9.1421	00082

[1] Values from FISHER and YATES, *Statistical Tables for Biological, Agricultural and Medical Research*, 6th ed., Oliver and Boyd, Edinburgh, 1963, pages 68–71. Reprinted by kind permission of the authors and publishers.

Logits[1] and Antilogits

Numbers in *italics* are negative values

p	0.000	0.001	0.002	0.003	0.004	0.005	0.006	0.007	0.008	0.009
0.00	—	*6.90675*	*6.21261*	*5.80614*	*5.51745*	*5.29330*	*5.10998*	*4.95482*	*4.82028*	*4.70149*
0.01	*4.59512*	*4.49880*	*4.41078*	*4.32972*	*4.25460*	*4.18459*	*4.11904*	*4.05740*	*3.99922*	*3.94413*
0.02	*3.89182*	*3.84201*	*3.79447*	*3.74899*	*3.70541*	*3.66356*	*3.62331*	*3.58455*	*3.54715*	*3.51103*
0.03	*3.47610*	*3.44228*	*3.40950*	*3.37769*	*3.34680*	*3.31678*	*3.28757*	*3.25914*	*3.23143*	*3.20441*
0.04	*3.17805*	*3.15232*	*3.12718*	*3.10260*	*3.07857*	*3.05505*	*3.03202*	*3.00947*	*2.98736*	*2.96569*
0.05	*2.94444*	*2.92358*	*2.90311*	*2.88301*	*2.86326*	*2.84385*	*2.82477*	*2.80601*	*2.78756*	*2.76941*
0.06	*2.75154*	*2.73394*	*2.71662*	*2.69955*	*2.68273*	*2.66616*	*2.64982*	*2.63371*	*2.61783*	*2.60215*
0.07	*2.58669*	*2.57143*	*2.55637*	*2.54149*	*2.52681*	*2.51231*	*2.49798*	*2.48382*	*2.46984*	*2.45601*
0.08	*2.44235*	*2.42884*	*2.41548*	*2.40227*	*2.38920*	*2.37627*	*2.36348*	*2.35083*	*2.33830*	*2.32591*
0.09	*2.31363*	*2.30149*	*2.28946*	*2.27754*	*2.26574*	*2.25406*	*2.24248*	*2.23101*	*2.21965*	*2.20839*
0.10	*2.19722*	*2.18616*	*2.17520*	*2.16433*	*2.15355*	*2.14286*	*2.13227*	*2.12176*	*2.11133*	*2.10100*
0.11	*2.09074*	*2.08057*	*2.07047*	*2.06046*	*2.05052*	*2.04066*	*2.03087*	*2.02115*	*2.01151*	*2.00193*
0.12	*1.99243*	*1.98299*	*1.97363*	*1.96432*	*1.95508*	*1.94591*	*1.93680*	*1.92775*	*1.91876*	*1.90983*
0.13	*1.90096*	*1.89215*	*1.88339*	*1.87469*	*1.86605*	*1.85745*	*1.84892*	*1.84043*	*1.83200*	*1.82362*
0.14	*1.81529*	*1.80701*	*1.79878*	*1.79059*	*1.78246*	*1.77437*	*1.76632*	*1.75833*	*1.75037*	*1.74247*
0.15	*1.73460*	*1.72678*	*1.71900*	*1.71126*	*1.70357*	*1.69591*	*1.68830*	*1.68072*	*1.67318*	*1.66569*
0.16	*1.65823*	*1.65081*	*1.64342*	*1.63607*	*1.62876*	*1.62149*	*1.61425*	*1.60704*	*1.59987*	*1.59273*
0.17	*1.58563*	*1.57856*	*1.57152*	*1.56451*	*1.55754*	*1.55060*	*1.54369*	*1.53681*	*1.52996*	*1.52314*
0.18	*1.51635*	*1.50959*	*1.50286*	*1.49615*	*1.48948*	*1.48283*	*1.47621*	*1.46962*	*1.46306*	*1.45652*
0.19	*1.45001*	*1.44353*	*1.43707*	*1.43063*	*1.42423*	*1.41784*	*1.41148*	*1.40515*	*1.39884*	*1.39256*
0.20	*1.38629*	*1.38006*	*1.37384*	*1.36765*	*1.36148*	*1.35533*	*1.34921*	*1.34310*	*1.33702*	*1.33096*
0.21	*1.32493*	*1.31891*	*1.31291*	*1.30694*	*1.30098*	*1.29505*	*1.28913*	*1.28324*	*1.27736*	*1.27150*
0.22	*1.26567*	*1.25985*	*1.25405*	*1.24827*	*1.24251*	*1.23676*	*1.23104*	*1.22533*	*1.21964*	*1.21397*
0.23	*1.20831*	*1.20267*	*1.19705*	*1.19145*	*1.18586*	*1.18029*	*1.17474*	*1.16920*	*1.16368*	*1.15817*
0.24	*1.15268*	*1.14720*	*1.14175*	*1.13630*	*1.13087*	*1.12546*	*1.12006*	*1.11468*	*1.10931*	*1.10395*
0.25	*1.09861*	*1.09329*	*1.08797*	*1.08268*	*1.07739*	*1.07212*	*1.06686*	*1.06162*	*1.05639*	*1.05117*
0.26	*1.04597*	*1.04078*	*1.03560*	*1.03043*	*1.02528*	*1.02014*	*1.01501*	*1.00990*	*1.00479*	*0.99970*
0.27	*0.99462*	*0.98955*	*0.98450*	*0.97945*	*0.97442*	*0.96940*	*0.96439*	*0.95939*	*0.95440*	*0.94943*
0.28	*0.94446*	*0.93951*	*0.93456*	*0.92963*	*0.92471*	*0.91979*	*0.91489*	*0.91000*	*0.90512*	*0.90025*
0.29	*0.89538*	*0.89053*	*0.88569*	*0.88086*	*0.87604*	*0.87122*	*0.86642*	*0.86162*	*0.85684*	*0.85206*
0.30	*0.84730*	*0.84254*	*0.83779*	*0.83305*	*0.82832*	*0.82360*	*0.81889*	*0.81418*	*0.80949*	*0.80480*
0.31	*0.80012*	*0.79545*	*0.79079*	*0.78613*	*0.78148*	*0.77685*	*0.77222*	*0.76759*	*0.76298*	*0.75837*
0.32	*0.75377*	*0.74918*	*0.74460*	*0.74002*	*0.73545*	*0.73089*	*0.72633*	*0.72179*	*0.71724*	*0.71271*
0.33	*0.70819*	*0.70367*	*0.69915*	*0.69465*	*0.69015*	*0.68566*	*0.68117*	*0.67669*	*0.67222*	*0.66775*
0.34	*0.66329*	*0.65884*	*0.65439*	*0.64995*	*0.64552*	*0.64109*	*0.63667*	*0.63225*	*0.62784*	*0.62344*
0.35	*0.61904*	*0.61465*	*0.61026*	*0.60588*	*0.60150*	*0.59713*	*0.59277*	*0.58841*	*0.58406*	*0.57971*
0.36	*0.57536*	*0.57103*	*0.56669*	*0.56237*	*0.55804*	*0.55373*	*0.54942*	*0.54511*	*0.54081*	*0.53651*
0.37	*0.53222*	*0.52793*	*0.52365*	*0.51937*	*0.51509*	*0.51083*	*0.50656*	*0.50230*	*0.49805*	*0.49379*
0.38	*0.48955*	*0.48531*	*0.48107*	*0.47683*	*0.47260*	*0.46838*	*0.46416*	*0.45994*	*0.45573*	*0.45152*
0.39	*0.44731*	*0.44311*	*0.43891*	*0.43472*	*0.43053*	*0.42634*	*0.42216*	*0.41798*	*0.41381*	*0.40963*
0.40	*0.40547*	*0.40130*	*0.39714*	*0.39298*	*0.38883*	*0.38467*	*0.38053*	*0.37638*	*0.37224*	*0.36810*
0.41	*0.36397*	*0.35983*	*0.35570*	*0.35158*	*0.34745*	*0.34333*	*0.33922*	*0.33510*	*0.33099*	*0.32688*
0.42	*0.32277*	*0.31867*	*0.31457*	*0.31047*	*0.30637*	*0.30228*	*0.29819*	*0.29410*	*0.29002*	*0.28593*
0.43	*0.28185*	*0.27777*	*0.27370*	*0.26962*	*0.26555*	*0.26148*	*0.25741*	*0.25335*	*0.24928*	*0.24522*
0.44	*0.24116*	*0.23710*	*0.23305*	*0.22900*	*0.22494*	*0.22089*	*0.21685*	*0.21280*	*0.20875*	*0.20471*
0.45	*0.20067*	*0.19663*	*0.19259*	*0.18856*	*0.18452*	*0.18049*	*0.17646*	*0.17243*	*0.16840*	*0.16437*
0.46	*0.16034*	*0.15632*	*0.15229*	*0.14827*	*0.14425*	*0.14023*	*0.13621*	*0.13219*	*0.12818*	*0.12416*
0.47	*0.12014*	*0.11613*	*0.11212*	*0.10811*	*0.10409*	*0.10008*	*0.09607*	*0.09206*	*0.08806*	*0.08405*
0.48	*0.08004*	*0.07604*	*0.07203*	*0.06803*	*0.06402*	*0.06002*	*0.05601*	*0.05201*	*0.04801*	*0.04401*
0.49	*0.04001*	*0.03600*	*0.03200*	*0.02800*	*0.02400*	*0.02000*	*0.01600*	*0.01200*	*0.00800*	*0.00400*
0.50	0.00000	0.00400	0.00800	0.01200	0.01600	0.02000	0.02400	0.02800	0.03200	0.03600
0.51	0.04001	0.04401	0.04801	0.05201	0.05601	0.06002	0.06402	0.06803	0.07203	0.07604
0.52	0.08004	0.08405	0.08806	0.09206	0.09607	0.10008	0.10409	0.10811	0.11212	0.11613
0.53	0.12014	0.12416	0.12818	0.13219	0.13621	0.14023	0.14425	0.14827	0.15229	0.15632
0.54	0.16034	0.16437	0.16840	0.17243	0.17646	0.18049	0.18452	0.18856	0.19259	0.19663
0.55	0.20067	0.20471	0.20875	0.21280	0.21685	0.22089	0.22494	0.22900	0.23305	0.23710
0.56	0.24116	0.24522	0.24928	0.25335	0.25741	0.26148	0.26555	0.26962	0.27370	0.27777
0.57	0.28185	0.28593	0.29002	0.29410	0.29819	0.30228	0.30637	0.31047	0.31457	0.31867
0.58	0.32277	0.32688	0.33099	0.33510	0.33922	0.34333	0.34745	0.35158	0.35570	0.35983
0.59	0.36397	0.36810	0.37224	0.37638	0.38053	0.38467	0.38883	0.39298	0.39714	0.40130
0.60	0.40547	0.40963	0.41381	0.41798	0.42216	0.42634	0.43053	0.43472	0.43891	0.44311
0.61	0.44731	0.45152	0.45573	0.45994	0.46416	0.46838	0.47260	0.47683	0.48107	0.48531
0.62	0.48955	0.49379	0.49805	0.50230	0.50656	0.51083	0.51509	0.51937	0.52365	0.52793
0.63	0.53222	0.53651	0.54081	0.54511	0.54942	0.55373	0.55804	0.56237	0.56669	0.57103
0.64	0.57536	0.57971	0.58406	0.58841	0.59277	0.59713	0.60150	0.60588	0.61026	0.61465
0.65	0.61904	0.62344	0.62784	0.63225	0.63667	0.64109	0.64552	0.64995	0.65439	0.65884
0.66	0.66329	0.66775	0.67222	0.67669	0.68117	0.68566	0.69015	0.69465	0.69915	0.70367
0.67	0.70819	0.71271	0.71724	0.72179	0.72633	0.73089	0.73545	0.74002	0.74460	0.74918
0.68	0.75377	0.75837	0.76298	0.76759	0.77222	0.77685	0.78148	0.78613	0.79079	0.79545
0.69	0.80012	0.80480	0.80949	0.81418	0.81889	0.82360	0.82832	0.83305	0.83779	0.84254
0.70	0.84730	0.85206	0.85684	0.86162	0.86642	0.87122	0.87604	0.88086	0.88569	0.89053
0.71	0.89538	0.90025	0.90512	0.91000	0.91489	0.91979	0.92471	0.92963	0.93456	0.93951
0.72	0.94446	0.94943	0.95440	0.95939	0.96439	0.96940	0.97442	0.97945	0.98450	0.98955
0.73	0.99462	0.99970	1.00479	1.00990	1.01501	1.02014	1.02528	1.03043	1.03560	1.04078
0.74	1.04597	1.05117	1.05639	1.06162	1.06686	1.07212	1.07739	1.08268	1.08797	1.09329
0.75	1.09861	1.10395	1.10931	1.11468	1.12006	1.12546	1.13087	1.13630	1.14175	1.14720
0.76	1.15268	1.15817	1.16368	1.16920	1.17474	1.18029	1.18586	1.19145	1.19705	1.20267
0.77	1.20831	1.21397	1.21964	1.22533	1.23104	1.23676	1.24251	1.24827	1.25405	1.25985
0.78	1.26567	1.27150	1.27736	1.28324	1.28913	1.29505	1.30098	1.30694	1.31291	1.31891
0.79	1.32493	1.33096	1.33702	1.34310	1.34921	1.35533	1.36148	1.36765	1.37384	1.38006
0.80	1.38269	1.39256	1.39884	1.40515	1.41148	1.41784	1.42423	1.43063	1.43707	1.44353
0.81	1.45001	1.45652	1.46306	1.46962	1.47621	1.48283	1.48948	1.49615	1.50286	1.50959
0.82	1.51635	1.52314	1.52996	1.53681	1.54369	1.55060	1.55754	1.56451	1.57152	1.57856
0.83	1.58563	1.59273	1.59987	1.60704	1.61425	1.62149	1.62876	1.63607	1.64342	1.65081
0.84	1.65823	1.66569	1.67318	1.68072	1.68830	1.69591	1.70357	1.71126	1.71900	1.72678
0.85	1.73460	1.74247	1.75037	1.75833	1.76632	1.77437	1.78246	1.79059	1.79878	1.80701
0.86	1.81529	1.82362	1.83200	1.84043	1.84892	1.85745	1.86605	1.87469	1.88339	1.89215
0.87	1.90096	1.90983	1.91876	1.92775	1.93680	1.94591	1.95508	1.96432	1.97363	1.98299
0.88	1.99243	2.00193	2.01151	2.02115	2.03087	2.04066	2.05052	2.06046	2.07047	2.08057
0.89	2.09074	2.10100	2.11133	2.12176	2.13227	2.14286	2.15355	2.16433	2.17520	2.18616
0.90	2.19722	2.20839	2.21965	2.23101	2.24248	2.25406	2.26574	2.27754	2.28946	2.30149
0.91	2.31363	2.32591	2.33830	2.35083	2.36348	2.37627	2.38920	2.40227	2.41548	2.42884
0.92	2.44235	2.45601	2.46984	2.48382	2.49798	2.51231	2.52681	2.54149	2.55637	2.57143
0.93	2.58669	2.60215	2.61783	2.63371	2.64982	2.66616	2.68273	2.69955	2.71662	2.73394
0.94	2.75154	2.76941	2.78756	2.80601	2.82477	2.84385	2.86326	2.88301	2.90311	2.92358
0.95	2.94444	2.96569	2.98736	3.00947	3.03202	3.05505	3.07857	3.10260	3.12718	3.15232
0.96	3.17805	3.20441	3.23143	3.25914	3.28757	3.31678	3.34680	3.37769	3.40950	3.44228
0.97	3.47610	3.51103	3.54715	3.58455	3.62331	3.66356	3.70541	3.74899	3.79447	3.84201
0.98	3.89182	3.94413	3.99922	4.05740	4.11904	4.18459	4.25460	4.32972	4.41078	4.49880
0.99	4.59512	4.70149	4.82028	4.95482	5.10998	5.29330	5.51745	5.80614	6.21261	6.90675

l	0.00	0.01	0.02	0.03	0.04	0.05	0.06	0.07	0.08	0.09
	0.	0.	0.	0.	0.	0.	0.	0.	0.	0.
− **4.9**	00739	00732	00725	00717	00710	00703	00696	00690	00683	00676
− 4.8	00816	00808	00800	00792	00785	00777	00769	00761	00754	00747
− 4.7	00901	00892	00884	00875	00866	00858	00849	00841	00833	00824
− 4.6	00995	00985	00976	00966	00957	00947	00938	00929	00919	00910
− **4.5**	01099	01088	01077	01067	01056	01046	01035	01025	01015	01005
− 4.4	01213	01201	01189	01177	01166	01154	01143	01132	01121	01110
− 4.3	01339	01326	01313	01300	01287	01274	01262	01249	01237	01225
− 4.2	01477	01463	01449	01434	01420	01406	01393	01379	01365	01352
− 4.1	01630	01614	01598	01583	01567	01552	01537	01522	01507	01492
− **4.0**	01799	01781	01764	01746	01729	01712	01696	01679	01663	01646
− 3.9	01984	01965	01946	01927	01908	01889	01871	01852	01834	01816
− 3.8	02188	02167	02146	02125	02104	02084	02063	02043	02023	02004
− 3.7	02413	02389	02366	02343	02320	02298	02275	02253	02231	02210
− 3.6	02660	02634	02608	02583	02558	02533	02509	02484	02460	02436
− **3.5**	02931	02903	02875	02847	02820	02792	02765	02738	02712	02686
− 3.4	03230	03198	03168	03137	03107	03077	03047	03018	02989	02960
− 3.3	03557	03523	03489	03456	03422	03390	03357	03325	03293	03261
− 3.2	03917	03879	03842	03805	03769	03733	03697	03661	03626	03592
− 3.1	04311	04270	04229	04189	04149	04109	04070	04031	03993	03954
− **3.0**	04743	04698	04653	04609	04565	04522	04479	04436	04394	04352
− 2.9	05215	05166	05117	05069	05021	04974	04927	04880	04834	04788
− 2.8	05732	05679	05625	05572	05520	05468	05417	05366	05315	05265
− 2.7	06297	06239	06180	06123	06065	06009	05952	05897	05841	05787
− 2.6	06914	06850	06786	06723	06661	06599	06538	06477	06416	06357
− **2.5**	07586	07516	07447	07378	07310	07243	07176	07109	07044	06978
− 2.4	08317	08241	08166	08091	08017	07944	07871	07799	07727	07656
− 2.3	09112	09030	08948	08867	08786	08707	08627	08549	08471	08394
− 2.2	09975	09886	09797	09709	09622	09535	09449	09364	09279	09195
− 2.1	10910	10813	10717	10621	10527	10433	10340	10248	10156	10065
− **2.0**	11920	11816	11712	11609	11507	11405	11305	11205	11106	11007
− 1.9	13011	12898	12786	12675	12565	12455	12347	12239	12132	12026
− 1.8	14185	14064	13943	13824	13705	13587	13470	13354	13239	13124
− 1.7	15447	15316	15187	15059	14931	14805	14679	14554	14430	14307
− 1.6	16798	16659	16520	16383	16247	16111	15976	15842	15710	15578
− **1.5**	18243	18094	17946	17799	17654	17509	17365	17222	17080	16938
− 1.4	19782	19623	19466	19310	19155	19000	18847	18694	18543	18392
− 1.3	21417	21249	21082	20916	20751	20587	20424	20262	20101	19941
− 1.2	23148	22970	22794	22618	22444	22270	22097	21926	21755	21585
− 1.1	24974	24787	24601	24416	24232	24049	23867	23685	23505	23326
− **1.0**	26894	26698	26503	26308	26115	25923	25731	25540	25351	25162
− 0.9	28905	28700	28496	28292	28090	27888	27688	27488	27289	27091
− 0.8	31003	30789	30576	30365	30153	29943	29734	29525	29318	29111
− 0.7	33181	32960	32739	32519	32300	32082	31865	31648	31432	31217
− 0.6	35434	35206	34978	34751	34525	34299	34074	33850	33626	33403
− **0.5**	37754	37519	37285	37052	36819	36586	36355	36124	35893	35663
− 0.4	40131	39891	39652	39413	39174	38936	38699	38462	38225	37989
− 0.3	42556	42311	42068	41824	41581	41338	41096	40854	40613	40372
− 0.2	45017	44769	44522	44275	44029	43782	43536	43291	43045	42800
− 0.1	47502	47253	47004	46755	46506	46257	46009	45760	45512	45264
− **0.0**	50000	49750	49500	49250	49000	48750	48500	48251	48001	47752
+ **0.0**	50000	50250	50500	50750	51000	51250	51500	51749	51999	52248
+ 0.1	52498	52747	52996	53245	53494	53743	53991	54240	54488	54736
+ 0.2	54983	55231	55478	55725	55971	56218	56464	56709	56955	57200
+ 0.3	57444	57689	57932	58176	58419	58662	58904	59146	59387	59628
+ 0.4	59869	60109	60348	60587	60826	61064	61301	61538	61775	62011
+ **0.5**	62246	62481	62715	62948	63181	63414	63645	63876	64107	64337
+ 0.6	64566	64794	65022	65249	65475	65701	65926	66150	66374	66597
+ 0.7	66819	67040	67261	67481	67700	67918	68135	68352	68568	68783
+ 0.8	68997	69211	69424	69635	69847	70057	70266	70475	70682	70889
+ 0.9	71095	71300	71504	71708	71910	72112	72312	72512	72711	72909
+ **1.0**	73106	73302	73497	73692	73885	74077	74269	74460	74649	74838
+ 1.1	75026	75213	75399	75584	75768	75951	76133	76315	76495	76674
+ 1.2	76852	77030	77206	77382	77556	77730	77903	78074	78245	78415
+ 1.3	78583	78751	78918	79084	79249	79413	79576	79738	79899	80059
+ 1.4	80218	80377	80534	80690	80845	81000	81153	81306	81457	81608
+ **1.5**	81757	81906	82054	82201	82346	82491	82635	82778	82920	83062
+ 1.6	83202	83341	83480	83617	83753	83889	84024	84158	84290	84422
+ 1.7	84553	84684	84813	84941	85069	85195	85321	85446	85570	85693
+ 1.8	85815	85936	86057	86176	86295	86413	86530	86646	86761	86876
+ 1.9	86989	87102	87214	87325	87435	87545	87653	87761	87868	87974
+ **2.0**	88080	88184	88288	88391	88493	88595	88695	88795	88894	88993
+ 2.1	89090	89187	89283	89379	89473	89567	89660	89752	89844	89935
+ 2.2	90025	90114	90203	90291	90378	90465	90551	90636	90721	90805
+ 2.3	90888	90970	91052	91133	91214	91293	91373	91451	91529	91606
+ 2.4	91683	91759	91834	91909	91983	92056	92129	92201	92273	92344
+ **2.5**	92414	92484	92553	92622	92690	92757	92824	92891	92956	93022
+ 2.6	93086	93150	93214	93277	93339	93401	93462	93523	93584	93643
+ 2.7	93703	93761	93820	93877	93935	93991	94048	94103	94159	94213
+ 2.8	94268	94321	94375	94428	94480	94532	94583	94634	94685	94735
+ 2.9	94785	94834	94883	94931	94979	95026	95073	95120	95166	95212
+ **3.0**	95257	95302	95347	95391	95435	95478	95521	95564	95606	95648
+ 3.1	95689	95730	95771	95811	95851	95891	95930	95969	96007	96046
+ 3.2	96083	96121	96158	96195	96231	96267	96303	96339	96374	96408
+ 3.3	96443	96477	96511	96544	96578	96610	96643	96675	96707	96739
+ 3.4	96770	96802	96832	96863	96893	96923	96953	96982	97011	97040
+ **3.5**	97069	97097	97125	97153	97180	97208	97235	97262	97288	97314
+ 3.6	97340	97366	97392	97417	97442	97467	97491	97516	97540	97564
+ 3.7	97587	97611	97634	97657	97680	97702	97725	97747	97769	97790
+ 3.8	97812	97833	97854	97875	97896	97916	97937	97957	97977	97996
+ 3.9	98016	98035	98054	98073	98092	98111	98129	98148	98166	98184
+ **4.0**	98201	98219	98236	98254	98271	98288	98304	98321	98337	98354
+ 4.1	98370	98386	98402	98417	98433	98448	98463	98478	98493	98508
+ 4.2	98523	98537	98551	98566	98580	98594	98607	98621	98635	98648
+ 4.3	98661	98674	98687	98700	98713	98726	98738	98751	98763	98775
+ 4.4	98787	98799	98811	98823	98834	98846	98857	98868	98879	98890
+ **4.5**	98901	98912	98923	98933	98944	98954	98965	98975	98985	98995
+ 4.6	99005	99015	99024	99034	99043	99053	99062	99071	99081	99090
+ 4.7	99099	99108	99116	99125	99134	99142	99151	99159	99167	99176
+ 4.8	99184	99192	99200	99208	99215	99223	99231	99239	99246	99253
+ 4.9	99261	99268	99275	99283	99290	99297	99304	99310	99317	99324

[1] Values of *l* (from + 0.0 to + 4.9) and of *p* from Berkson, J., *J. Amer. statist. Ass.*, **48**, 565 (1953). Reprinted by kind permission of the author and publishers.

Logistic Weights[1]

In the upper line are values of $w = pq$, in the lower line those of $wl = pql$. Numbers in *italics* are negative values

p	0.000	0.001	0.002	0.003	0.004	0.005	0.006	0.007	0.008	0.009
	0.	0.	0.	0.	0.	0.	0.	0.	0.	0.
0.00	0000	0010	0020	0030	0040	0050	0060	0070	0079	0089
	—	*0069*	*0124*	*0174*	*0220*	*0263*	*0305*	*0344*	*0383*	*0419*
0.01	0099	0109	0119	0128	0138	0148	0157	0167	0177	0186
	0455	*0489*	*0523*	*0556*	*0587*	*0618*	*0649*	*0678*	*0707*	*0735*
0.02	0196	0206	0215	0225	0234	0244	0253	0263	0272	0282
	0763	*0790*	*0816*	*0842*	*0868*	*0893*	*0918*	*0942*	*0965*	*0989*
0.03	0291	0300	0310	0319	0328	0338	0347	0356	0366	0375
	1012	*1034*	*1056*	*1078*	*1099*	*1120*	*1141*	*1161*	*1181*	*1201*
0.04	0384	0393	0402	0412	0421	0430	0439	0448	0457	0466
	1220	*1239*	*1258*	*1277*	*1295*	*1313*	*1331*	*1348*	*1365*	*1382*
0.05	0475	0484	0493	0502	0511	0520	0529	0538	0546	0555
	1399	*1415*	*1431*	*1447*	*1463*	*1478*	*1493*	*1508*	*1523*	*1538*
0.06	0564	0573	0582	0590	0599	0608	0616	0625	0634	0642
	1552	*1566*	*1580*	*1594*	*1607*	*1620*	*1633*	*1646*	*1659*	*1672*
0.07	0651	0660	0668	0677	0685	0694	0702	0711	0719	0728
	1684	*1696*	*1708*	*1720*	*1731*	*1743*	*1754*	*1765*	*1776*	*1787*
0.08	0736	0744	0753	0761	0769	0778	0786	0794	0803	0811
	1798	*1808*	*1818*	*1828*	*1838*	*1848*	*1858*	*1867*	*1877*	*1886*
0.09	0819	0827	0835	0844	0852	0860	0868	0876	0884	0892
	1895	*1904*	*1913*	*1921*	*1930*	*1938*	*1946*	*1954*	*1962*	*1970*
0.10	0900	0908	0916	0924	0932	0940	0948	0956	0963	0971
	1977	*1985*	*1992*	*2000*	*2007*	*2014*	*2021*	*2027*	*2034*	*2040*
0.11	0979	0987	0995	1002	1010	1018	1025	1033	1041	1048
	2047	*2053*	*2059*	*2065*	*2071*	*2077*	*2083*	*2088*	*2093*	*2099*
0.12	1056	1064	1071	1079	1086	1094	1101	1109	1116	1124
	2104	*2109*	*2114*	*2119*	*2124*	*2128*	*2133*	*2137*	*2142*	*2146*
0.13	1131	1138	1146	1153	1160	1168	1175	1182	1190	1197
	2150	*2154*	*2158*	*2162*	*2165*	*2169*	*2173*	*2176*	*2179*	*2182*
0.14	1204	1211	1218	1226	1233	1240	1247	1254	1261	1268
	2186	*2189*	*2192*	*2194*	*2197*	*2200*	*2202*	*2205*	*2207*	*2209*
0.15	1275	1282	1289	1296	1303	1310	1317	1324	1330	1337
	2212	*2214*	*2216*	*2218*	*2219*	*2221*	*2223*	*2224*	*2226*	*2227*
0.16	1344	1351	1358	1364	1371	1378	1384	1391	1398	1404
	2229	*2230*	*2231*	*2232*	*2233*	*2234*	*2235*	*2236*	*2236*	*2237*
0.17	1411	1418	1424	1431	1437	1444	1450	1457	1463	1470
	2237	*2238*	*2238*	*2238*	*2239*	*2239*	*2239*	*2239*	*2239*	*2238*
0.18	1476	1482	1489	1495	1501	1508	1514	1520	1527	1533
	2238	*2238*	*2237*	*2237*	*2236*	*2236*	*2235*	*2234*	*2233*	*2233*
0.19	1539	1545	1551	1558	1564	1570	1576	1582	1588	1594
	2232	*2231*	*2229*	*2228*	*2227*	*2226*	*2224*	*2223*	*2221*	*2220*
0.20	1600	1606	1612	1618	1624	1630	1636	1642	1647	1653
	2218	*2216*	*2215*	*2213*	*2211*	*2209*	*2207*	*2205*	*2203*	*2200*
0.21	1659	1665	1671	1676	1682	1688	1693	1699	1705	1710
	2198	*2196*	*2193*	*2191*	*2188*	*2186*	*2183*	*2180*	*2178*	*2175*
0.22	1716	1722	1727	1733	1738	1744	1749	1755	1760	1766
	2172	*2169*	*2166*	*2163*	*2160*	*2157*	*2153*	*2150*	*2147*	*2143*
0.23	1771	1776	1782	1787	1792	1798	1803	1808	1814	1819
	2140	*2136*	*2133*	*2129*	*2126*	*2122*	*2118*	*2114*	*2110*	*2106*
0.24	1824	1829	1834	1840	1845	1850	1855	1860	1865	1870
	2102	*2098*	*2094*	*2090*	*2086*	*2082*	*2078*	*2073*	*2069*	*2064*
0.25	1875	1880	1885	1890	1895	1900	1905	1910	1914	1919
	2060	*2055*	*2051*	*2046*	*2041*	*2037*	*2032*	*2027*	*2022*	*2017*
0.26	1924	1929	1934	1938	1943	1948	1952	1957	1962	1966
	2012	*2007*	*2002*	*1997*	*1992*	*1987*	*1982*	*1976*	*1971*	*1966*
0.27	1971	1976	1980	1985	1989	1994	1998	2003	2007	2012
	1960	*1955*	*1949*	*1944*	*1938*	*1933*	*1927*	*1921*	*1916*	*1910*
0.28	2016	2020	2025	2029	2033	2038	2042	2046	2051	2055
	1904	*1898*	*1892*	*1886*	*1880*	*1874*	*1868*	*1862*	*1856*	*1850*
0.29	2059	2063	2067	2072	2076	2080	2084	2088	2092	2096
	1844	*1837*	*1831*	*1825*	*1818*	*1812*	*1805*	*1799*	*1792*	*1786*
0.30	2100	2104	2108	2112	2116	2120	2124	2128	2131	2135
	1779	*1773*	*1766*	*1759*	*1753*	*1746*	*1739*	*1732*	*1725*	*1718*
0.31	2139	2143	2147	2150	2154	2158	2161	2165	2169	2172
	1711	*1704*	*1697*	*1690*	*1683*	*1676*	*1669*	*1662*	*1655*	*1647*
0.32	2176	2180	2183	2187	2190	2194	2197	2201	2204	2208
	1640	*1633*	*1626*	*1618*	*1611*	*1603*	*1596*	*1588*	*1581*	*1573*
0.33	2211	2214	2218	2221	2224	2228	2231	2234	2238	2241
	1566	*1558*	*1551*	*1543*	*1535*	*1527*	*1520*	*1512*	*1504*	*1496*
0.34	2244	2247	2250	2254	2257	2260	2263	2266	2269	2272
	1488	*1481*	*1473*	*1465*	*1457*	*1449*	*1441*	*1433*	*1425*	*1416*
0.35	2275	2278	2281	2284	2287	2290	2293	2296	2298	2301
	1408	*1400*	*1392*	*1384*	*1376*	*1367*	*1359*	*1351*	*1342*	*1334*
0.36	2304	2307	2310	2312	2315	2318	2320	2323	2326	2328
	1326	*1317*	*1309*	*1300*	*1292*	*1283*	*1275*	*1266*	*1258*	*1249*
0.37	2331	2334	2336	2339	2341	2344	2346	2349	2351	2354
	1241	*1232*	*1223*	*1215*	*1206*	*1197*	*1189*	*1180*	*1171*	*1162*
0.38	2356	2358	2361	2363	2365	2368	2370	2372	2375	2377
	1153	*1145*	*1136*	*1127*	*1118*	*1109*	*1100*	*1091*	*1082*	*1073*
0.39	2379	2381	2383	2386	2388	2390	2392	2394	2396	2398
	1064	*1055*	*1046*	*1037*	*1028*	*1019*	*1010*	*1001*	*0991*	*0982*
0.40	2400	2402	2404	2406	2408	2410	2412	2414	2415	2417
	0973	*0964*	*0955*	*0945*	*0936*	*0927*	*0918*	*0908*	*0899*	*0890*
0.41	2419	2421	2423	2424	2426	2428	2429	2431	2433	2434
	0880	*0871*	*0862*	*0852*	*0843*	*0834*	*0824*	*0815*	*0805*	*0796*
0.42	2436	2438	2439	2441	2442	2444	2445	2447	2448	2450
	0786	*0777*	*0767*	*0758*	*0748*	*0739*	*0729*	*0720*	*0710*	*0700*
0.43	2451	2452	2454	2455	2456	2458	2459	2460	2462	2463
	0691	*0681*	*0672*	*0662*	*0652*	*0643*	*0633*	*0623*	*0614*	*0604*
0.44	2464	2465	2466	2468	2469	2470	2471	2472	2473	2474
	0594	*0584*	*0575*	*0565*	*0555*	*0546*	*0536*	*0526*	*0516*	*0506*
0.45	2475	2476	2477	2478	2479	2480	2481	2482	2482	2483
	0497	*0487*	*0477*	*0467*	*0457*	*0448*	*0438*	*0428*	*0418*	*0408*
0.46	2484	2485	2486	2486	2487	2488	2488	2489	2490	2490
	0398	*0388*	*0379*	*0369*	*0359*	*0349*	*0339*	*0329*	*0319*	*0309*
0.47	2491	2492	2492	2493	2493	2494	2494	2495	2495	2496
	0299	*0289*	*0279*	*0269*	*0260*	*0250*	*0240*	*0230*	*0220*	*0210*
0.48	2496	2496	2497	2497	2497	2498	2498	2498	2499	2499
	0200	*0190*	*0180*	*0170*	*0160*	*0150*	*0140*	*0130*	*0120*	*0110*
0.49	2499	2499	2499	2500	2500	2500	2500	2500	2500	2500
	0100	*0090*	*0080*	*0070*	*0060*	*0050*	*0040*	*0030*	*0020*	*0010*

p	0.000	0.001	0.002	0.003	0.004	0.005	0.006	0.007	0.008	0.009
	0.	0.	0.	0.	0.	0.	0.	0.	0.	0.
0.50	2500	2500	2500	2500	2500	2500	2500	2500	2499	2499
	0000	0010	0020	0030	0040	0050	0060	0070	0080	0090
0.51	2499	2499	2499	2498	2498	2498	2497	2497	2497	2496
	0100	0110	0120	0130	0140	0150	0160	0170	0180	0190
0.52	2496	2496	2495	2495	2494	2494	2493	2493	2492	2492
	0200	0210	0220	0230	0240	0250	0260	0269	0279	0289
0.53	2491	2490	2490	2489	2488	2488	2487	2486	2486	2485
	0299	0309	0319	0329	0339	0349	0359	0369	0379	0388
0.54	2484	2483	2482	2482	2481	2480	2479	2478	2477	2476
	0398	0408	0418	0428	0438	0448	0457	0467	0477	0487
0.55	2475	2474	2473	2472	2471	2470	2469	2468	2466	2465
	0497	0506	0516	0526	0536	0546	0555	0565	0575	0584
0.56	2464	2463	2462	2460	2459	2458	2456	2455	2454	2552
	0594	0604	0614	0623	0633	0643	0652	0662	0672	0681
0.57	2451	2450	2448	2447	2445	2444	2442	2441	2439	2438
	0691	0700	0710	0720	0729	0739	0748	0758	0767	0777
0.58	2436	2434	2433	2431	2429	2428	2426	2424	2423	2421
	0786	0796	0805	0815	0824	0834	0843	0852	0862	0871
0.59	2419	2417	2415	2414	2412	2410	2408	2406	2404	2402
	0880	0890	0899	0908	0918	0927	0936	0945	0955	0964
0.60	2400	2398	2396	2394	2392	2390	2388	2386	2383	2381
	0973	0982	0991	1001	1010	1019	1028	1037	1046	1055
0.61	2379	2377	2375	2372	2370	2368	2365	2363	2361	2358
	1064	1073	1082	1091	1100	1109	1118	1127	1136	1145
0.62	2356	2354	2351	2349	2346	2344	2341	2339	2336	2334
	1153	1162	1171	1180	1189	1197	1206	1215	1223	1232
0.63	2331	2328	2326	2323	2320	2318	2315	2312	2310	2307
	1241	1249	1258	1266	1275	1283	1292	1300	1309	1317
0.64	2304	2301	2298	2296	2293	2290	2287	2284	2281	2278
	1326	1334	1342	1351	1359	1367	1376	1384	1392	1400
0.65	2275	2272	2269	2266	2263	2260	2257	2254	2250	2247
	1408	1416	1425	1433	1441	1449	1457	1465	1473	1481
0.66	2244	2241	2238	2234	2231	2228	2224	2221	2218	2214
	1488	1496	1504	1512	1520	1527	1535	1543	1551	1558
0.67	2211	2208	2204	2201	2197	2194	2190	2187	2183	2180
	1566	1573	1581	1588	1596	1603	1611	1618	1626	1633
0.68	2176	2172	2169	2165	2161	2158	2154	2150	2147	2143
	1640	1647	1655	1662	1669	1676	1683	1690	1697	1704
0.69	2139	2135	2131	2128	2124	2120	2116	2112	2108	2104
	1711	1718	1725	1732	1739	1746	1753	1759	1766	1773
0.70	2100	2096	2092	2088	2084	2080	2076	2072	2067	2063
	1779	1786	1792	1799	1805	1812	1818	1825	1831	1837
0.71	2059	2055	2051	2046	2042	2038	2033	2029	2025	2020
	1844	1850	1856	1862	1868	1874	1880	1886	1892	1898
0.72	2016	2012	2007	2003	1998	1994	1989	1985	1980	1976
	1904	1910	1916	1921	1927	1933	1938	1944	1949	1955
0.73	1971	1966	1962	1957	1952	1948	1943	1938	1934	1929
	1960	1966	1971	1976	1982	1987	1992	1997	2002	2007
0.74	1924	1919	1914	1910	1905	1900	1895	1890	1885	1880
	2012	2017	2022	2027	2032	2037	2041	2046	2051	2055
0.75	1875	1870	1865	1860	1855	1850	1845	1840	1834	1829
	2060	2064	2069	2073	2078	2082	2086	2090	2094	2098
0.76	1824	1819	1814	1808	1803	1798	1792	1787	1782	1776
	2102	2106	2110	2114	2118	2122	2126	2129	2133	2136
0.77	1771	1766	1760	1755	1749	1744	1738	1733	1727	1722
	2140	2143	2147	2150	2153	2157	2160	2163	2166	2169
0.78	1716	1710	1705	1699	1693	1688	1682	1676	1671	1665
	2172	2175	2178	2180	2183	2186	2188	2191	2193	2196
0.79	1659	1653	1647	1642	1636	1630	1624	1618	1612	1606
	2198	2200	2203	2205	2207	2209	2211	2213	2215	2216
0.80	1600	1594	1588	1582	1576	1570	1564	1558	1551	1545
	2218	2220	2221	2223	2224	2226	2227	2228	2229	2231
0.81	1539	1533	1527	1520	1514	1508	1501	1495	1489	1482
	2232	2233	2233	2234	2235	2236	2236	2237	2237	2238
0.82	1476	1470	1463	1457	1450	1444	1437	1431	1424	1418
	2238	2238	2239	2239	2239	2239	2239	2238	2238	2238
0.83	1411	1404	1398	1391	1384	1378	1371	1364	1358	1351
	2237	2237	2236	2236	2235	2234	2233	2232	2231	2230
0.84	1344	1337	1330	1324	1317	1310	1303	1296	1289	1282
	2229	2227	2226	2224	2223	2221	2219	2218	2216	2214
0.85	1275	1268	1261	1254	1247	1240	1233	1226	1218	1211
	2212	2209	2207	2205	2202	2200	2197	2194	2192	2189
0.86	1204	1197	1190	1182	1175	1168	1160	1153	1146	1138
	2186	2182	2179	2176	2173	2169	2165	2162	2158	2154
0.87	1131	1124	1116	1109	1101	1094	1086	1079	1071	1064
	2150	2146	2142	2137	2133	2128	2124	2119	2114	2109
0.88	1056	1048	1041	1033	1025	1018	1010	1002	0995	0987
	2104	2099	2093	2088	2083	2077	2071	2065	2059	2053
0.89	0979	0971	0963	0956	0948	0940	0932	0924	0916	0908
	2047	2040	2034	2027	2021	2014	2007	2000	1992	1985
0.90	0900	0892	0884	0876	0868	0860	0852	0844	0835	0827
	1977	1970	1962	1954	1946	1938	1930	1921	1913	1904
0.91	0819	0811	0803	0794	0786	0778	0769	0761	0753	0744
	1895	1886	1877	1867	1858	1848	1838	1828	1818	1808
0.92	0736	0728	0719	0711	0702	0694	0685	0677	0668	0660
	1798	1787	1776	1765	1754	1743	1731	1720	1708	1696
0.93	0651	0642	0634	0625	0616	0608	0599	0590	0582	0573
	1684	1672	1659	1646	1633	1620	1607	1594	1580	1566
0.94	0564	0555	0546	0538	0529	0520	0511	0502	0493	0484
	1552	1538	1523	1508	1493	1478	1463	1447	1431	1415
0.95	0475	0466	0457	0448	0439	0430	0421	0412	0402	0393
	1399	1382	1365	1348	1331	1313	1295	1277	1258	1239
0.96	0384	0375	0366	0356	0347	0338	0328	0319	0310	0300
	1220	1201	1181	1161	1141	1120	1099	1078	1056	1034
0.97	0291	0282	0272	0263	0253	0244	0234	0225	0215	0206
	1012	0989	0965	0942	0918	0893	0868	0842	0816	0790
0.98	0196	0186	0177	0167	0157	0148	0138	0128	0119	0109
	0763	0735	0707	0678	0649	0618	0587	0556	0523	0489
0.99	0099	0089	0079	0070	0060	0050	0040	0030	0020	0010
	0455	0419	0383	0344	0305	0263	0220	0174	0124	0069

[1] Values from BERKSON, J., *J. Amer. statist. Ass.*, **48**, 565 (1953). Reprinted by kind permission of the author and publishers.

Mean square successive difference[1, 3]

N = size of sample. Test quotient: $\Sigma\,(x_{i+1} - x_i)^2 \,/\, \Sigma\,(\bar{x} - x_i)^2$

N	$2\alpha = 0.10$	$2\alpha = 0.02$	N	$2\alpha = 0.10$	$2\alpha = 0.02$
			101	1.676–2.324	1.542–2.458
			102	677– 323	544– 456
			103	679– 321	546– 454
4	0.780–3.220	0.626–3.374	104	680– 320	548– 452
5	0.820–3.180	0.538–3.462	**105**	1.682–2.318	1.550–2.450
6	890– 110	561– 439	106	683– 317	552– 448
7	936– 064	614– 386	107	685– 315	554– 446
8	982– 018	663– 337	108	686– 314	556– 444
9	1.024–2.976	709– 291	109	688– 312	558– 442
10	1.062–2.938	0.752–3.248	**110**	1.689–2.311	1.560–2.440
11	096– 904	791– 209	111	691– 309	562– 438
12	128– 872	828– 172	112	692– 308	564– 436
13	156– 844	862– 138	113	693– 307	566– 434
14	182– 818	893– 107	114	695– 305	568– 432
15	1.205–2.795	0.922–3.078	**115**	1.696–2.304	1.570–2.430
16	227– 773	949– 051	116	697– 303	572– 428
17	247– 753	974– 026	117	698– 302	573– 427
18	266– 734	998– 002	118	700– 300	575– 425
19	283– 717	1.020–2.980	119	701– 299	577– 423
20	1.300–2.700	1.041–2.959	**120**	1.702–2.298	1.579–2.421
21	315– 685	060– 940	121	703– 297	580– 420
22	329– 671	078– 922	122	705– 295	582– 418
23	342– 658	096– 904	123	706– 294	584– 416
24	355– 645	112– 888	124	707– 293	585– 415
25	1.367–2.633	1.128–2.872	**125**	1.708–2.292	1.587–2.413
26	378– 622	142– 858	126	709– 291	589– 411
27	389– 611	157– 843	127	710– 290	590– 410
28	399– 601	170– 830	128	711– 289	592– 408
29	409– 591	183– 817	129	713– 287	593– 407
30	1.418–2.582	1.195–2.805	**130**	1.714–2.286	1.595–2.405
31	426– 574	207– 793	131	715– 285	597– 403
32	435– 565	218– 782	132	716– 284	598– 402
33	443– 557	228– 772	133	717– 283	600– 400
34	451– 549	239– 761	134	718– 282	601– 399
35	1.458–2.542	1.248–2.752	**135**	1.719–2.281	1.602–2.398
36	466– 534	258– 742	136	720– 280	604– 396
37	472– 528	267– 733	137	721– 279	605– 395
38	479– 521	276– 724	138	722– 278	607– 393
39	486– 514	285– 715	139	723– 277	608– 392
40	1.492–2.508	1.293–2.707	**140**	1.724–2.276	1.610–2.390
41	498– 502	302– 698	141	725– 275	611– 389
42	504– 496	310– 690	142	726– 274	612– 388
43	510– 490	317– 683	143	727– 273	614– 386
44	515– 485	325– 675	144	728– 272	615– 385
45	1.521–2.479	1.332–2.668	**145**	1.729–2.271	1.616–2.384
46	526– 474	339– 661	146	730– 270	618– 382
47	530– 470	345– 655	147	730– 270	619– 381
48	535– 465	351– 649	148	731– 269	620– 380
49	539– 461	357– 643	149	732– 268	621– 379
50	1.544–2.456	1.363–2.637	**150**	1.733–2.267	1.623–2.377
51	548– 452	368– 632	151	734– 266	624– 376
52	552– 448	374– 626	152	735– 265	625– 375
53	556– 444	379– 621	153	736– 264	626– 374
54	559– 441	384– 616	154	737– 263	627– 373
55	1.563–2.437	1.390–2.610	**155**	1.737–2.263	1.629–2.371
56	567– 433	395– 605	156	738– 262	630– 370
57	571– 429	400– 600	157	739– 261	631– 369
58	574– 426	405– 595	158	740– 260	632– 368
59	578– 422	410– 590	159	741– 259	633– 367
60	1.581–2.419	1.414–2.586	**160**	1.742–2.258	1.634–2.366
61	584– 416	419– 581	161	742– 258	636– 364
62	587– 413	423– 577	162	743– 257	637– 363
63	590– 410	427– 573	163	744– 256	638– 362
64	593– 407	431– 569	164	745– 255	639– 361
65	1.596–2.404	1.435–2.565	**165**	1.745–2.255	1.640–2.360
66	599– 401	439– 561	166	746– 254	641– 359
67	602– 398	443– 557	167	747– 253	642– 358
68	605– 395	447– 553	168	748– 252	643– 357
69	608– 392	451– 549	169	748– 252	644– 356
70	1.611–2.389	1.454–2.546	**170**	1.749–2.251	1.645–2.355
71	614– 386	458– 542	171	750– 250	646– 354
72	617– 383	461– 539	172	751– 249	647– 353
73	620– 380	465– 535	173	751– 249	648– 352
74	623– 377	468– 532	174	752– 248	649– 351
75	1.625–2.375	1.471–2.529	**175**	1.753–2.247	1.650–2.350
76	628– 372	474– 526	176	753– 247	651– 349
77	630– 370	477– 523	177	754– 246	652– 348
78	632– 368	480– 520	178	755– 245	653– 347
79	635– 365	483– 517	179	755– 245	654– 346
80	1.637–2.363	1.486–2.514	**180**	1.756–2.244	1.655–2.345
81	639– 361	489– 511	181	757– 243	656– 344
82	641– 359	492– 508	182	757– 243	657– 343
83	643– 357	495– 505	183	758– 242	658– 342
84	645– 355	498– 502	184	759– 241	659– 341
85	1.647–2.353	1.501–2.499	**185**	1.759–2.241	1.660–2.340
86	649– 351	504– 496	186	760– 240	661– 339
87	651– 349	507– 493	187	761– 239	662– 338
88	653– 347	510– 490	188	761– 239	662– 338
89	655– 345	512– 488	189	762– 238	663– 337
90	1.657–2.343	1.515–2.485	**190**	1.763–2.237	1.664–2.336
91	659– 341	518– 482	191	763– 237	665– 335
92	661– 339	520– 480	192	764– 236	666– 334
93	662– 338	523– 477	193	764– 236	667– 333
94	664– 336	525– 475	194	765– 235	668– 332
95	1.666–2.334	1.528–2.472	**195**	1.766–2.234	1.668–2.332
96	668– 332	530– 470	196	766– 234	669– 331
97	669– 331	532– 468	197	767– 233	670– 330
98	671– 329	535– 465	198	767– 233	671– 329
99	673– 327	537– 463	199	768– 232	672– 328
100	1.674–2.326	1.539–2.461	**200**	1.768–2.232	1.673–2.327
			∞	2.000–2.000	2.000–2.000

Serial correlation[2, 3] (significance of departure from null hypothesis)

N = size of sample, h = lag. Test quotient: $(\Sigma\,x_i x_{i+h} - \bar{x}\,\Sigma\,x_i) \,/\, \Sigma\,(\bar{x} - x_i)^2$

N	$2\alpha = 0.10$	$2\alpha = 0.02$	N	$2\alpha = 0.10$	$2\alpha = 0.02$
			101	-0.174–+0.154	-0.242–+0.221
			102	173– 153	240– 220
			103	172– 152	239– 219
			104	171– 152	238– 218
5	-0.753–+0.253	-0.798–+0.297	**105**	-0.170–+0.151	-0.237–+0.217
6	708– 345	863– 447	106	169– 150	236– 216
7	674– 370	799– 510	107	168– 150	234– 216
8	625– 371	764– 531	108	167– 149	233– 215
9	593– 366	737– 533	109	167– 148	232– 214
10	-0.564–+0.360	-0.705–+0.525	**110**	-0.166–+0.148	-0.231–+0.213
11	539– 353	679– 515	111	165– 147	230– 212
12	516– 348	655– 505	112	164– 146	229– 211
13	497– 341	634– 495	113	164– 146	228– 210
14	479– 335	615– 485	114	163– 145	227– 209
15	-0.462–+0.328	-0.597–+0.475	**115**	-0.162–+0.145	-0.226–+0.208
16	447– 322	580– 465	116	161– 144	225– 207
17	434– 316	564– 456	117	161– 143	224– 206
18	421– 310	550– 448	118	160– 143	223– 206
19	410– 304	536– 440	119	159– 142	222– 205
20	-0.399–+0.299	-0.524–+0.432	**120**	-0.159–+0.142	-0.221–+0.204
21	389– 294	512– 424	121	158– 141	220– 203
22	380– 289	502– 417	122	157– 141	219– 202
23	372– 285	491– 411	123	157– 140	218– 202
24	364– 280	482– 404	124	156– 140	217– 201
25	-0.356–+0.276	-0.473–+0.398	**125**	-0.155–+0.139	-0.216–+0.200
26	349– 272	464– 392	126	155– 139	215– 199
27	343– 268	456– 386	127	154– 138	214– 199
28	336– 264	448– 380	128	153– 138	214– 198
29	331– 260	440– 375	129	153– 137	213– 197
30	-0.325–+0.257	-0.433–+0.370	**130**	-0.152–+0.137	-0.212–+0.196
31	319– 254	426– 365	131	151– 136	211– 196
32	314– 251	420– 361	132	151– 136	210– 195
33	309– 248	413– 356	133	150– 135	209– 194
34	304– 245	408– 352	134	150– 135	209– 193
35	-0.300–+0.242	-0.402–+0.348	**135**	-0.149–+0.134	-0.208–+0.193
36	295– 239	396– 344	136	148– 134	207– 192
37	291– 236	391– 340	137	148– 133	206– 191
38	287– 234	386– 336	138	147– 133	205– 191
39	283– 231	381– 333	139	147– 132	205– 190
40	-0.279–+0.229	-0.377–+0.330	**140**	-0.146–+0.132	-0.204–+0.189
41	275– 227	372– 326	141	146– 131	203– 189
42	272– 224	368– 323	142	145– 131	202– 188
43	268– 222	364– 320	143	145– 131	202– 188
44	265– 220	360– 317	144	144– 130	201– 187
45	-0.262–+0.218	-0.356–+0.314	**145**	-0.144–+0.130	-0.200–+0.186
46	259– 216	352– 311	146	143– 129	199– 186
47	256– 214	348– 308	147	143– 129	199– 185
48	253– 212	345– 305	148	142– 128	198– 184
49	250– 210	341– 302	149	142– 128	197– 184
50	-0.248–+0.208	-0.338–+0.300	**150**	-0.141–+0.128	-0.197–+0.183
51	245– 206	334– 297	151	141– 127	196– 183
52	242– 205	331– 295	152	140– 127	195– 182
53	240– 203	328– 292	153	140– 126	195– 182
54	238– 201	325– 290	154	139– 126	194– 181
55	-0.235–+0.199	-0.322–+0.287	**155**	-0.139–+0.126	-0.193–+0.180
56	233– 198	319– 285	156	138– 125	193– 180
57	231– 196	316– 283	157	138– 125	192– 179
58	229– 195	314– 281	158	137– 125	191– 179
59	227– 193	311– 279	159	137– 124	191– 178
60	-0.225–+0.192	-0.308–+0.276	**160**	-0.136–+0.124	-0.190–+0.178
61	223– 190	306– 274	161	136– 123	190– 177
62	221– 189	303– 272	162	135– 123	189– 177
63	219– 188	301– 270	163	135– 123	188– 176
64	217– 186	299– 269	164	135– 122	188– 176
65	-0.215–+0.185	-0.296–+0.267	**165**	-0.134–+0.122	-0.187–+0.175
66	213– 184	294– 265	166	134– 122	187– 175
67	212– 182	292– 263	167	133– 121	186– 174
68	210– 181	290– 261	168	133– 121	186– 174
69	208– 180	288– 260	169	133– 121	185– 173
70	-0.207–+0.179	-0.286–+0.258	**170**	-0.132–+0.120	-0.184–+0.173
71	205– 177	284– 256	171	132– 120	184– 172
72	203– 176	282– 255	172	131– 120	183– 172
73	202– 175	280– 253	173	131– 119	183– 171
74	200– 174	278– 252	174	131– 119	182– 171
75	-0.199–+0.173	-0.276–+0.250	**175**	-0.130–+0.119	-0.182–+0.170
76	198– 172	275– 249	176	130– 118	181– 170
77	197– 172	273– 248	177	129– 118	181– 169
78	196– 171	272– 247	178	129– 118	180– 169
79	195– 170	271– 246	179	129– 117	180– 168
80	-0.194–+0.169	-0.269–+0.245	**180**	-0.128–+0.117	-0.179–+0.168
81	193– 169	268– 243	181	128– 117	179– 167
82	192– 168	267– 242	182	127– 116	178– 167
83	191– 167	265– 241	183	127– 116	178– 167
84	190– 166	264– 240	184	127– 116	177– 166
85	-0.189–+0.166	-0.263–+0.239	**185**	-0.126–+0.116	-0.177–+0.166
86	188– 165	261– 238	186	126– 115	176– 165
87	187– 164	260– 237	187	126– 115	176– 165
88	186– 163	259– 236	188	125– 115	175– 164
89	185– 163	257– 234	189	125– 114	175– 164
90	-0.184–+0.162	-0.256–+0.233	**190**	-0.125–+0.114	-0.174–+0.164
91	183– 161	255– 232	191	124– 114	174– 163
92	182– 160	254– 231	192	124– 114	173– 163
93	181– 160	252– 230	193	124– 113	173– 162
94	180– 159	251– 229	194	123– 113	172– 162
95	-0.179–+0.158	-0.249–+0.228	**195**	-0.123–+0.113	-0.172–+0.161
96	178– 157	248– 227	196	123– 112	171– 161
97	177– 157	247– 226	197	122– 112	171– 161
98	177– 156	245– 224	198	122– 112	170– 160
99	176– 155	244– 223	199	122– 112	170– 160
100	-0.175–+0.154	-0.243–+0.222	**200**	-0.121–+0.111	-0.170–+0.160
			1000	-0.053–+0.051	-0.075–+0.073

[1] Values up to $N = 60$ obtained by converting the exact values of HART, B.I., *Ann. math. Statist.*, **13**, 445 (1942), by use of the factor $(N-1)/N$. Reprinted by kind permission of the author and publishers.

[2] Values up to $N = 75$ from the exact values of ANDERSON, R.L., *Ann. math. Statist.*, **13**, 1 (1942), with interpolated values from $N = 16$ to 75. Values reprinted by kind permission of the author and publishers.

[3] Empirical approximation at transition values, then normal approximation.

Functions* of the Correlation Coefficient r: $\sqrt{1-r^2}$, $1-r^2$

$\sqrt{1-r^2}$

r	0.000	0.001	0.002	0.003	0.004	0.005	0.006	0.007	0.008	0.009
	0.	0.	0.	0.	0.	0.	0.	0.	0.	0.
0.000	00000†	00000†	00000†	00000†	99999	99999	99998	99998	99997	99996
010	99995	99994	99993	99992	99990	99989	99987	99986	99984	99982
020	99980	99978	99976	99974	99971	99969	99966	99964	99961	99958
030	99955	99952	99949	99946	99942	99939	99935	99932	99928	99924
040	99920	99916	99912	99908	99903	99899	99894	99889	99885	99880
0.050	99875	99870	99865	99859	99854	99849	99843	99837	99832	99826
060	99820	99814	99808	99801	99795	99789	99782	99775	99769	99762
070	99755	99748	99740	99733	99726	99718	99711	99703	99695	99687
080	99679	99671	99663	99655	99647	99638	99630	99621	99612	99603
090	99594	99585	99576	99567	99557	99548	99538	99528	99519	99509
0.100	99499	99489	99478	99468	99458	99447	99437	99426	99415	99404
110	99393	99382	99371	99359	99348	99337	99325	99313	99301	99289
120	99277	99265	99253	99241	99228	99216	99203	99190	99177	99164
130	99151	99138	99125	99112	99098	99085	99071	99057	99043	99029
140	99015	99001	98987	98972	98958	98943	98928	98914	98899	98884
0.150	98869	98853	98838	98823	98807	98791	98776	98760	98744	98728
160	98712	98695	98679	98663	98646	98629	98613	98596	98579	98562
170	98544	98527	98510	98492	98475	98457	98439	98421	98403	98385
180	98367	98348	98330	98311	98293	98274	98255	98236	98217	98198
190	98178	98159	98139	98120	98100	98080	98060	98040	98020	98000
0.200	97980	97959	97939	97918	97897	97876	97855	97834	97813	97792
210	97770	97749	97727	97705	97683	97661	97639	97617	97595	97572
220	97550	97527	97505	97482	97459	97436	97413	97389	97366	97343
230	97319	97295	97272	97248	97224	97200	97175	97151	97127	97102
240	97077	97053	97028	97003	96978	96952	96927	96902	96876	96850
0.250	96825	96799	96773	96747	96720	96694	96668	96641	96614	96588
260	96561	96534	96507	96480	96452	96425	96397	96370	96342	96314
270	96286	96258	96230	96201	96173	96144	96116	96087	96058	96029
280	96000	95971	95941	95912	95882	95853	95823	95793	95763	95733
290	95703	95672	95642	95611	95581	95550	95519	95488	95457	95425
0.300	95394	95362	95331	95299	95267	95235	95203	95171	95139	95106
310	95074	95041	95008	94975	94942	94909	94876	94843	94809	94775
320	94742	94708	94674	94640	94606	94571	94537	94502	94468	94433
330	94398	94363	94328	94293	94257	94222	94186	94150	94115	94079
340	94043	94006	93970	93934	93897	93860	93823	93787	93749	93712
0.350	93675	93638	93600	93562	93525	93487	93449	93410	93372	93334
360	93295	93257	93218	93179	93140	93101	93061	93022	92983	92943
370	92903	92863	92823	92783	92743	92702	92662	92621	92581	92540
380	92499	92458	92416	92375	92333	92292	92250	92208	92166	92124
390	92081	92039	91997	91954	91911	91868	91825	91782	91739	91695
0.400	91652	91608	91564	91520	91476	91432	91387	91343	91298	91253
410	91209	91164	91118	91073	91028	90982	90936	90891	90845	90799
420	90752	90706	90660	90613	90566	90519	90472	90425	90378	90330
430	90283	90235	90187	90139	90091	90043	89995	89946	89897	89849
440	89800	89751	89702	89652	89603	89553	89503	89453	89403	89353
0.450	89303	89252	89202	89151	89100	89049	88998	88947	88895	88844
460	88792	88740	88688	88636	88584	88531	88478	88426	88373	88320
470	88267	88213	88160	88106	88052	87999	87945	87890	87836	87781
480	87727	87672	87617	87562	87507	87451	87396	87340	87284	87228
490	87172	87116	87060	87003	86946	86889	86832	86775	86718	86660
0.500	86603	86545	86487	86429	86370	86312	86253	86195	86136	86077
510	86017	85958	85899	85839	85779	85719	85659	85599	85538	85477
520	85417	85356	85295	85233	85172	85110	85048	84987	84924	84862
530	84800	84737	84674	84612	84548	84485	84422	84358	84294	84231
540	84167	84102	84038	83973	83909	83844	83779	83713	83648	83582
0.550	83516	83451	83384	83318	83252	83185	83118	83051	82984	82917
560	82849	82782	82714	82646	82577	82509	82441	82372	82303	82234
570	82164	82095	82025	81956	81886	81815	81745	81674	81604	81533
580	81462	81390	81319	81247	81175	81103	81031	80959	80886	80813
590	80740	80667	80594	80520	80447	80373	80298	80224	80150	80075
0.600	80000	79925	79850	79774	79698	79623	79546	79470	79394	79317
610	79240	79163	79086	79008	78931	78853	78775	78696	78618	78539
620	78460	78381	78302	78222	78142	78062	77982	77902	77821	77741
630	77660	77578	77497	77415	77333	77251	77169	77086	77004	76921
640	76837	76754	76670	76587	76503	76418	76334	76249	76164	76079
0.650	75993	75908	75822	75736	75649	75563	75476	75389	75302	75214
660	75127	75039	74950	74862	74773	74684	74595	74506	74416	74326
670	74236	74146	74055	73964	73873	73782	73690	73598	73506	73414
680	73321	73228	73135	73042	72948	72854	72760	72666	72571	72476
690	72381	72285	72190	72094	71997	71901	71804	71707	71610	71512
0.700	71414	71316	71218	71119	71020	70921	70821	70721	70621	70521
710	70420	70319	70218	70116	70015	69912	69810	69707	69604	69501
720	69397	69294	69189	69085	68980	68875	68769	68664	68558	68451
730	68345	68238	68130	68023	67915	67807	67698	67589	67480	67371
740	67261	67151	67040	66929	66818	66706	66595	66482	66370	66257
0.750	66144	66030	65916	65802	65687	65572	65457	65341	65225	65109
760	64992	64875	64758	64640	64522	64403	64284	64165	64045	63925
770	63804	63684	63562	63441	63319	63196	63073	62950	62826	62702
780	62578	62453	62328	62202	62076	61950	61823	61695	61568	61439
790	61311	61182	61052	60922	60792	60661	60530	60398	60266	60133
0.800	60000	59866	59732	59598	59463	59327	59192	59055	58918	58781
810	58643	58505	58366	58226	58086	57946	57805	57664	57522	57379
820	57236	57093	56949	56804	56659	56513	56367	56220	56073	55925
830	55776	55627	55478	55327	55176	55025	54873	54720	54567	54413
840	54259	54104	53948	53791	53634	53477	53318	53159	53000	52839
0.850	52678	52517	52354	52191	52027	51863	51698	51532	51365	51198
860	51029	50860	50691	50520	50349	50177	50004	49831	49656	49481
870	49305	49128	48951	48772	48593	48412	48231	48049	47866	47682
880	47497	47312	47125	46937	46749	46559	46369	46177	45984	45791
890	45596	45400	45204	45006	44807	44607	44405	44203	44000	43795
0.900	43589	43382	43174	42964	42753	42541	42328	42113	41897	41680
910	41461	41241	41019	40796	40571	40345	40118	39889	39658	39426
920	39192	38956	38719	38480	38239	37997	37752	37506	37258	37008
930	36756	36502	36246	35988	35727	35465	35200	34933	34664	34392
940	34117	33841	33561	33279	32995	32707	32417	32123	31827	31528
0.950	31225	30919	30610	30297	29981	29661	29337	29009	28677	28341
960	28000	27655	27305	26950	26590	26225	25854	25478	25095	24706
970	24310	23908	23498	23081	22655	22220	21777	21324	20860	20386
980	19900	19401	18888	18361	17817	17255	16675	16072	15445	14792
990	14107	13386	12624	11811	10938	09987	08935	07740	06321	04471

$1-r^2$

r	0.000	0.001	0.002	0.003	0.004	0.005	0.006	0.007	0.008	0.009
	0.	0.	0.	0.	0.	0.	0.	0.	0.	0.
0.000	00000†	00000†	00000†	99999	99998	99998	99996	99995	99994	99992
010	99990	99988	99986	99983	99980	99978	99974	99971	99968	99964
020	99960	99956	99952	99947	99942	99938	99932	99927	99922	99916
030	99910	99904	99898	99891	99884	99878	99870	99863	99856	99848
040	99840	99832	99824	99815	99806	99798	99788	99779	99770	99760
0.050	99750	99740	99730	99719	99708	99698	99686	99675	99664	99652
060	99640	99628	99616	99603	99590	99578	99564	99551	99538	99524
070	99510	99496	99482	99467	99452	99438	99422	99407	99392	99376
080	99360	99344	99328	99311	99294	99278	99260	99243	99226	99208
090	99190	99172	99154	99135	99116	99098	99078	99059	99040	99020
0.100	99000	98980	98960	98939	98918	98898	98876	98855	98834	98812
110	98790	98768	98746	98723	98700	98678	98654	98631	98608	98584
120	98560	98536	98512	98487	98462	98438	98412	98387	98362	98336
130	98310	98284	98258	98231	98204	98178	98150	98123	98096	98068
140	98040	98012	97984	97955	97926	97898	97868	97839	97810	97780
0.150	97750	97720	97690	97659	97628	97598	97566	97535	97504	97472
160	97440	97408	97376	97343	97310	97278	97244	97211	97178	97144
170	97110	97076	97042	97007	96972	96938	96902	96867	96832	96796
180	96760	96724	96688	96651	96614	96578	96540	96503	96466	96428
190	96390	96352	96314	96275	96236	96198	96158	96119	96080	96040
0.200	96000	95960	95920	95879	95838	95798	95756	95715	95674	95632
210	95590	95548	95506	95463	95420	95378	95334	95291	95248	95204
220	95160	95116	95072	95027	94982	94938	94892	94847	94802	94756
230	94710	94664	94618	94571	94524	94478	94430	94383	94336	94288
240	94240	94192	94144	94095	94046	93998	93948	93899	93850	93800
0.250	93750	93700	93650	93599	93548	93498	93446	93395	93344	93292
260	93240	93188	93136	93083	93030	92978	92924	92871	92818	92764
270	92710	92656	92602	92547	92492	92438	92382	92327	92272	92216
280	92160	92104	92048	91991	91934	91878	91820	91763	91706	91648
290	91590	91532	91474	91415	91356	91298	91238	91179	91120	91060
0.300	91000	90940	90880	90819	90758	90698	90636	90575	90514	90452
310	90390	90328	90266	90203	90140	90078	90014	89951	89888	89824
320	89760	89696	89632	89567	89502	89438	89372	89307	89242	89176
330	89110	89044	88978	88911	88844	88778	88710	88643	88576	88508
340	88440	88372	88304	88235	88166	88098	88028	87959	87890	87820
0.350	87750	87680	87610	87539	87468	87398	87326	87255	87184	87112
360	87040	86968	86896	86823	86750	86678	86604	86531	86458	86384
370	86310	86236	86162	86087	86012	85938	85862	85787	85712	85636
380	85560	85484	85408	85331	85254	85178	85100	85023	84946	84868
390	84790	84712	84634	84555	84476	84398	84318	84239	84160	84080
0.400	84000	83920	83840	83759	83678	83598	83516	83435	83354	83272
410	83190	83108	83026	82943	82860	82778	82694	82611	82528	82444
420	82360	82276	82192	82107	82022	81938	81852	81767	81682	81596
430	81510	81424	81338	81251	81164	81078	80990	80903	80816	80728
440	80640	80552	80464	80375	80286	80198	80108	80019	79930	79840
0.450	79750	79660	79570	79479	79388	79298	79206	79115	79024	78932
460	78840	78748	78656	78563	78470	78378	78284	78191	78098	78004
470	77910	77816	77722	77627	77532	77438	77342	77247	77152	77056
480	76960	76864	76768	76671	76574	76478	76380	76283	76186	76088
490	75990	75892	75794	75695	75596	75498	75398	75299	75200	75100
0.500	75000	74900	74800	74699	74598	74498	74396	74295	74194	74092
510	73990	73888	73786	73683	73580	73478	73374	73271	73168	73064
520	72960	72856	72752	72647	72542	72438	72332	72227	72122	72016
530	71910	71804	71698	71591	71484	71378	71270	71163	71056	70948
540	70840	70732	70624	70515	70406	70298	70188	70079	69970	69860
0.550	69750	69640	69530	69419	69308	69198	69086	68975	68864	68752
560	68640	68528	68416	68303	68190	68078	67964	67851	67738	67624
570	67510	67396	67282	67167	67052	66938	66822	66707	66592	66476
580	66360	66244	66128	66011	65894	65778	65660	65543	65426	65308
590	65190	65072	64954	64835	64716	64598	64478	64359	64240	64120
0.600	64000	63880	63760	63639	63518	63398	63276	63155	63034	62912
610	62790	62668	62546	62423	62300	62178	62054	61931	61808	61684
620	61560	61436	61312	61187	61062	60938	60812	60687	60562	60436
630	60310	60184	60058	59931	59804	59678	59550	59423	59296	59168
640	59040	58912	58784	58655	58526	58398	58268	58139	58010	57880
0.650	57750	57620	57490	57359	57228	57098	56966	56835	56704	56572
660	56440	56308	56176	56043	55910	55778	55644	55511	55378	55244
670	55110	54976	54842	54707	54572	54438	54302	54167	54032	53896
680	53760	53624	53488	53351	53214	53078	52940	52803	52666	52528
690	52390	52252	52114	51975	51836	51698	51558	51419	51280	51140
0.700	51000	50860	50720	50579	50438	50298	50156	50015	49874	49732
710	49590	49448	49306	49163	49020	48878	48734	48591	48448	48304
720	48160	48016	47872	47727	47582	47438	47292	47147	47002	46856
730	46710	46564	46418	46271	46124	45978	45830	45683	45536	45388
740	45240	45092	44944	44795	44646	44498	44348	44199	44050	43900
0.750	43750	43600	43450	43299	43148	42998	42846	42695	42544	42392
760	42240	42088	41936	41783	41630	41478	41324	41171	41018	40864
770	40710	40556	40402	40247	40092	39938	39782	39627	39472	39316
780	39160	39004	38848	38691	38534	38378	38220	38063	37906	37748
790	37590	37432	37274	37115	36956	36798	36638	36479	36320	36160
0.800	36000	35840	35680	35519	35358	35198	35036	34875	34714	34552
810	34390	34228	34066	33903	33740	33578	33414	33251	33088	32924
820	32760	32596	32432	32267	32102	31938	31772	31607	31442	31276
830	31110	30944	30778	30611	30444	30278	30110	29943	29776	29608
840	29440	29272	29104	28935	28766	28598	28428	28259	28090	27920
0.850	27750	27580	27410	27239	27068	26898	26726	26555	26384	26212
860	26040	25868	25696	25523	25350	25178	25004	24831	24658	24484
870	24310	24136	23962	23787	23612	23438	23262	23087	22912	22736
880	22560	22384	22208	22031	21854	21678	21500	21323	21146	20968
890	20790	20612	20434	20255	20076	19898	19718	19539	19360	19180
0.900	19000	18820	18640	18459	18278	18098	17916	17735	17554	17372
910	17190	17008	16826	16643	16460	16278	16094	15911	15728	15544
920	15360	15176	14992	14807	14622	14438	14252	14067	13882	13696
930	13510	13324	13138	12951	12764	12578	12390	12203	12016	11828
940	11640	11452	11264	11075	10886	10698	10508	10319	10130	09940
0.950	09750	09560	09370	09179	08988	08798	08606	08415	08224	08032
960	07840	07648	07456	07263	07070	06878	06684	06491	06298	06104
970	05910	05716	05522	05327	05132	04938	04742	04547	04352	04156
980	03960	03764	03568	03371	03174	02978	02780	02583	02386	02188
990	01990	01792	01594	01395	01196	00998	00798	00599	00400	00200

 † To be read as 1.00000.

n	$\sqrt{\frac{n-1}{n-2}}$	$\frac{n-1}{n-2}$	n	$\sqrt{\frac{n-1}{n-2}}$	$\frac{n-1}{n-2}$	n	$\sqrt{\frac{n-1}{n-2}}$	$\frac{n-1}{n-2}$	n	$\sqrt{\frac{n-1}{n-2}}$	$\frac{n-1}{n-2}$	n	$\sqrt{\frac{n-1}{n-2}}$	$\frac{n-1}{n-2}$
	1.	1.		1.	1.		1.	1.		1.	1.		1.	1.
0	–	–	**50**	01036	02083	**100**	00509	01020	**150**	00337	00676	**200**	00252	00505
1	–	–	51	01015	02041	101	00504	01010	151	00335	00671	201	00251	00503
2	–	–	52	00995	02000	102	00499	01000	152	00333	00667	202	00250	00500
3	41421	00000†	53	00976	01961	103	00494	00990	153	00331	00662	203	00248	00498
4	22474	50000	54	00957	01923	104	00489	00980	154	00328	00658	204	00247	00495
5	15470	33333	**55**	00939	01887	**105**	00484	00971	**155**	00326	00654	**205**	00246	00493
6	11803	25000	56	00922	01852	106	00480	00962	156	00324	00649	206	00245	00490
7	09545	20000	57	00905	01818	107	00475	00952	157	00322	00645	207	00244	00488
8	08012	16667	58	00889	01786	108	00471	00943	158	00320	00641	208	00242	00485
9	06904	14286	59	00873	01754	109	00466	00935	159	00318	00637	209	00241	00483
10	06066	12500	**60**	00858	01724	**110**	00462	00926	**160**	00316	00633	**210**	00240	00481
11	05409	11111	61	00844	01695	111	00458	00917	161	00314	00629	211	00239	00478
12	04881	10000	62	00830	01667	112	00454	00909	162	00312	00625	212	00238	00476
13	04447	09091	63	00816	01639	113	00449	00901	163	00310	00621	213	00237	00474
14	04083	08333	64	00803	01613	114	00445	00893	164	00308	00617	214	00236	00472
15	03775	07692	**65**	00791	01587	**115**	00442	00885	**165**	00306	00613	**215**	00234	00469
16	03510	07143	66	00778	01563	116	00438	00877	166	00304	00610	216	00233	00467
17	03280	06667	67	00766	01538	117	00434	00870	167	00303	00606	217	00232	00465
18	03078	06250	68	00755	01515	118	00430	00862	168	00301	00602	218	00231	00463
19	02899	05882	69	00744	01493	119	00426	00855	169	00299	00599	219	00230	00461
20	02740	05556	**70**	00733	01471	**120**	00423	00847	**170**	00297	00595	**220**	00229	00459
21	02598	05263	71	00722	01449	121	00419	00840	171	00295	00592	221	00228	00457
22	02470	05000	72	00712	01429	122	00416	00833	172	00294	00588	222	00227	00455
23	02353	04762	73	00702	01408	123	00412	00826	173	00292	00585	223	00226	00452
24	02247	04545	74	00692	01389	124	00409	00820	174	00290	00581	224	00225	00450
25	02151	04348	**75**	00683	01370	**125**	00406	00813	**175**	00289	00578	**225**	00224	00448
26	02062	04167	76	00673	01351	126	00402	00806	176	00287	00575	226	00223	00446
27	01980	04000	77	00664	01333	127	00399	00800	177	00285	00571	227	00222	00444
28	01905	03846	78	00656	01316	128	00396	00794	178	00284	00568	228	00221	00442
29	01835	03704	79	00647	01299	129	00393	00787	179	00282	00565	229	00220	00441
30	01770	03571	**80**	00639	01282	**130**	00390	00781	**180**	00281	00562	**230**	00219	00439
31	01710	03448	81	00631	01266	131	00387	00775	181	00279	00559	231	00218	00437
32	01653	03333	82	00623	01250	132	00384	00769	182	00277	00556	232	00217	00435
33	01600	03226	83	00615	01235	133	00381	00763	183	00276	00552	233	00216	00433
34	01550	03125	84	00608	01220	134	00378	00758	184	00274	00549	234	00215	00431
35	01504	03030	**85**	00601	01205	**135**	00375	00752	**185**	00273	00546	**235**	00214	00429
36	01460	02941	86	00593	01190	136	00372	00746	186	00271	00543	236	00213	00427
37	01419	02857	87	00587	01176	137	00370	00741	187	00270	00541	237	00213	00426
38	01379	02778	88	00580	01163	138	00367	00735	188	00268	00538	238	00212	00424
39	01342	02703	89	00573	01149	139	00364	00730	189	00267	00535	239	00211	00422
40	01307	02632	**90**	00567	01136	**140**	00362	00725	**190**	00266	00532	**240**	00210	00420
41	01274	02564	91	00560	01124	141	00359	00719	191	00264	00529	241	00209	00418
42	01242	02500	92	00554	01111	142	00357	00714	192	00263	00526	242	00208	00417
43	01212	02439	93	00548	01099	143	00354	00709	193	00261	00524	243	00207	00415
44	01183	02381	94	00542	01087	144	00351	00704	194	00260	00521	244	00206	00413
45	01156	02326	**95**	00536	01075	**145**	00349	00699	**195**	00259	00518	**245**	00206	00412
46	01130	02273	96	00531	01064	146	00347	00694	196	00257	00515	246	00205	00410
47	01105	02222	97	00525	01053	147	00344	00690	197	00256	00513	247	00204	00408
48	01081	02174	98	00519	01042	148	00342	00685	198	00255	00510	248	00203	00407
49	01058	02128	99	00514	01031	149	00340	00680	199	00253	00508	249	00202	00405
50	01036	02083	**100**	00509	01020	**150**	00337	00676	**200**	00252	00505	**250**	00202	00403

Examples: $s_{y \cdot x} = s_y \sqrt{1-r^2}\sqrt{\frac{n-1}{n-2}}$; $s^2_{y \cdot x} = s^2_y (1-r^2)\frac{n-1}{n-2}$

Explanation of the table on page 61

The table gives the values of

$$r = \sqrt{\frac{t^2}{t^2+\nu}} \quad (\nu = \text{degrees of freedom of } t)$$

thus enabling it to be decided without calculation whether a correlation coefficient differs significantly from zero. The table also allows the corresponding regression coefficients to be tested automatically in the same way. If, for example, r_{xy} is not equal to zero, then b_{xy} and b_{yx} are also not equal to zero.

The degrees of freedom are found as follows: from the number n of pairs of observations, the number 2 is subtracted and, in the case of partial correlation coefficients, also the number of excluded variables.

Examples: (variable 1, 2, ...) r_{12} $\nu = n-2$
$r_{12 \cdot 3}$ $\nu = n-2-1$
$r_{12 \cdot 34}$ $\nu = n-2-2$

* Reproduction only by permission of the publishers of these *Scientific Tables*. † To be read as 2.00000.

Significance Limits* for *r* when the Population Correlation Coefficient is Zero

ν \ 2α	0.1	0.05	0.01	0.001	ν \ 2α	0.1	0.05	0.01	0.001
1	0.9877	0.9969	0.9999	1.0000	101	0.1630	0.1937	0.2528	0.3196
2	9000	9500	9900	0.9990	102	1622	1927	2515	3181
3	8054	8783	9587	9911	103	1614	1918	2504	3166
4	7293	8114	9172	9741	104	1606	1909	2492	3152
5	0.6694	0.7545	0.8745	0.9509	**105**	0.1599	0.1900	0.2480	0.3138
6	6215	7067	8343	9249	106	1591	1891	2469	3123
7	5822	6664	7977	8983	107	1584	1882	2458	3109
8	5494	6319	7646	8721	108	1577	1874	2447	3095
9	5214	6021	7348	8471	109	1569	1865	2436	3082
10	0.4973	0.5760	0.7079	0.8233	**110**	0.1562	0.1857	0.2425	0.3069
11	4762	5529	6835	8010	111	1555	1848	2414	3055
12	4575	5324	6614	7800	112	1548	1840	2404	3042
13	4409	5139	6411	7604	113	1542	1832	2393	3029
14	4259	4973	6226	7419	114	1535	1824	2383	3017
15	0.4124	0.4821	0.6055	0.7247	**115**	0.1528	0.1816	0.2373	0.3004
16	4000	4683	5897	7084	116	1522	1809	2363	2992
17	3887	4555	5751	6932	117	1515	1801	2353	2979
18	3783	4438	5614	6788	118	1509	1793	2343	2967
19	3687	4329	5487	6652	119	1502	1786	2334	2955
20	0.3598	0.4227	0.5368	0.6524	**120**	0.1496	0.1779	0.2324	0.2943
21	3515	4132	5256	6402	121	1490	1771	2315	2932
22	3438	4044	5151	6287	122	1484	1764	2305	2920
23	3365	3961	5052	6177	123	1478	1757	2296	2909
24	3297	3882	4958	6073	124	1472	1750	2287	2897
25	0.3233	0.3809	0.4869	0.5974	**125**	0.1466	0.1743	0.2278	0.2886
26	3172	3739	4785	5880	126	1460	1736	2269	2875
27	3115	3673	4705	5790	127	1455	1730	2261	2864
28	3061	3610	4629	5703	128	1449	1723	2252	2854
29	3009	3550	4556	5620	129	1443	1716	2243	2843
30	0.2960	0.3494	0.4487	0.5541	**130**	0.1438	0.1710	0.2235	0.2832
31	2913	3440	4421	5465	131	1432	1703	2226	2822
32	2869	3388	4357	5392	132	1427	1697	2218	2812
33	2826	3338	4297	5322	133	1422	1690	2210	2801
34	2785	3291	4238	5255	134	1416	1684	2202	2791
35	0.2746	0.3246	0.4182	0.5189	**135**	0.1411	0.1678	0.2194	0.2781
36	2709	3202	4128	5126	136	1406	1672	2186	2771
37	2673	3160	4076	5066	137	1401	1666	2178	2762
38	2638	3120	4026	5007	138	1396	1660	2170	2752
39	2605	3081	3978	4951	139	1391	1654	2163	2742
40	0.2573	0.3044	0.3932	0.4896	**140**	0.1386	0.1648	0.2155	0.2733
41	2542	3008	3887	4843	141	1381	1642	2148	2724
42	2512	2973	3843	4792	142	1376	1637	2140	2714
43	2483	2940	3802	4742	143	1371	1631	2133	2705
44	2455	2907	3761	4694	144	1367	1625	2126	2696
45	0.2428	0.2875	0.3721	0.4647	**145**	0.1362	0.1620	0.2118	0.2687
46	2403	2845	3683	4602	146	1357	1614	2111	2678
47	2377	2816	3646	4558	147	1353	1609	2104	2669
48	2353	2787	3610	4515	148	1348	1603	2097	2660
49	2329	2759	3575	4473	149	1344	1598	2090	2652
50	0.2306	0.2732	0.3541	0.4433	**150**	0.1339	0.1593	0.2083	0.2643
51	2284	2706	3509	4393	151	1335	1587	2077	2635
52	2262	2681	3477	4355	152	1330	1582	2070	2626
53	2241	2656	3445	4317	153	1326	1577	2063	2618
54	2221	2632	3415	4281	154	1322	1572	2057	2610
55	0.2201	0.2609	0.3385	0.4245	**155**	0.1318	0.1567	0.2050	0.2602
56	2181	2586	3357	4210	156	1313	1562	2044	2594
57	2162	2564	3329	4176	157	1309	1557	2037	2586
58	2144	2542	3301	4143	158	1305	1552	2031	2578
59	2126	2521	3274	4111	159	1301	1547	2025	2570
60	0.2108	0.2500	0.3248	0.4079	**160**	0.1297	0.1543	0.2019	0.2562
61	2091	2480	3223	4048	161	1293	1538	2012	2554
62	2075	2461	3198	4018	162	1289	1533	2006	2547
63	2058	2442	3174	3988	163	1285	1529	2000	2539
64	2042	2423	3150	3959	164	1281	1524	1994	2532
65	0.2027	0.2405	0.3127	0.3931	**165**	0.1277	0.1519	0.1988	0.2524
66	2012	2387	3104	3904	166	1273	1515	1982	2517
67	1997	2369	3081	3877	167	1270	1510	1977	2510
68	1982	2352	3060	3850	168	1266	1506	1971	2502
69	1968	2335	3038	3824	169	1262	1501	1965	2495
70	0.1954	0.2319	0.3017	0.3798	**170**	0.1258	0.1497	0.1959	0.2488
71	1940	2303	2997	3773	171	1255	1493	1954	2481
72	1927	2287	2977	3749	172	1251	1488	1948	2474
73	1914	2272	2957	3725	173	1248	1484	1943	2467
74	1901	2257	2938	3701	174	1244	1480	1937	2460
75	0.1889	0.2242	0.2919	0.3678	**175**	0.1240	0.1476	0.1932	0.2453
76	1876	2227	2900	3655	176	1237	1471	1926	2446
77	1864	2213	2882	3633	177	1233	1467	1921	2440
78	1852	2199	2864	3611	178	1230	1463	1915	2433
79	1841	2185	2847	3590	179	1227	1459	1910	2426
80	0.1829	0.2172	0.2830	0.3569	**180**	0.1223	0.1455	0.1905	0.2420
81	1818	2159	2813	3548	181	1220	1451	1900	2413
82	1807	2146	2796	3527	182	1216	1447	1895	2407
83	1796	2133	2780	3507	183	1213	1443	1890	2400
84	1786	2120	2764	3488	184	1210	1439	1885	2394
85	0.1775	0.2108	0.2748	0.3468	**185**	0.1207	0.1435	0.1880	0.2388
86	1765	2096	2733	3449	186	1203	1432	1874	2381
87	1755	2084	2717	3430	187	1200	1428	1870	2375
88	1745	2072	2702	3412	188	1197	1424	1865	2369
89	1735	2061	2688	3394	189	1194	1420	1860	2363
90	0.1726	0.2050	0.2673	0.3376	**190**	0.1191	0.1417	0.1855	0.2357
91	1716	2039	2659	3358	191	1188	1413	1850	2351
92	1707	2028	2645	3341	192	1184	1409	1845	2345
93	1698	2017	2631	3324	193	1181	1406	1841	2339
94	1689	2006	2617	3307	194	1178	1402	1836	2333
95	0.1680	0.1996	0.2604	0.3291	**195**	0.1175	0.1399	0.1831	0.2327
96	1671	1986	2591	3274	196	1172	1395	1827	2321
97	1663	1976	2578	3258	197	1169	1391	1822	2316
98	1654	1966	2565	3242	198	1166	1388	1818	2310
99	1646	1956	2552	3227	199	1164	1384	1813	2304
100	0.1638	0.1946	0.2540	0.3211	**200**	0.1161	0.1381	0.1809	0.2299

r	0.000	0.001	0.002	0.003	0.004	0.005	0.006	0.007	0.008	0.009
0.000	0.00000	0.00100	0.00200	0.00300	0.00400	0.00500	0.00600	0.00700	0.00800	0.00900
010	01000	01100	01200	01300	01400	01500	01600	01700	01800	01900
020	02000	02100	02200	02300	02400	02501	02601	02701	02801	02901
030	03001	03101	03201	03301	03401	03501	03602	03702	03802	03902
040	04002	04102	04202	04303	04403	04503	04603	04703	04804	04904
0.050	0.05004	0.05104	0.05205	0.05305	0.05405	0.05506	0.05606	0.05706	0.05806	0.05907
060	06007	06108	06208	06308	06409	06509	06610	06710	06810	06911
070	07011	07112	07212	07313	07414	07514	07615	07715	07816	07916
080	08017	08118	08218	08319	08420	08521	08621	08722	08823	08924
090	09024	09125	09226	09327	09428	09529	09630	09731	09832	09933
0.100	0.10034	0.10135	0.10236	0.10337	0.10438	0.10539	0.10640	0.10741	0.10842	0.10943
110	11045	11146	11247	11348	11450	11551	11652	11754	11855	11957
120	12058	12160	12261	12363	12464	12566	12667	12769	12871	12972
130	13074	13176	13277	13379	13481	13583	13685	13787	13889	13991
140	14093	14195	14297	14399	14501	14603	14705	14807	14910	15012
0.150	0.15114	0.15216	0.15319	0.15421	0.15524	0.15626	0.15728	0.15831	0.15934	0.16036
160	16139	16241	16344	16447	16549	16652	16755	16858	16961	17064
170	17167	17270	17373	17476	17579	17682	17785	17888	17992	18095
180	18198	18302	18405	18509	18612	18716	18819	18923	19026	19130
190	19234	19338	19441	19545	19649	19753	19857	19961	20065	20169
0.200	0.20273	0.20377	0.20482	0.20586	0.20690	0.20795	0.20899	0.21004	0.21108	0.21213
210	21317	21422	21526	21631	21736	21841	21946	22051	22156	22261
220	22366	22471	22576	22681	22786	22892	22997	23102	23208	23313
230	23419	23525	23630	23736	23842	23948	24053	24159	24265	24371
240	24477	24584	24690	24796	24902	25009	25115	25222	25328	25435
0.250	0.25541	0.25648	0.25755	0.25862	0.25968	0.26075	0.26182	0.26289	0.26396	0.26504
260	26611	26718	26825	26933	27040	27148	27255	27363	27471	27579
270	27686	27794	27902	28010	28118	28226	28335	28443	28551	28660
280	28768	28877	28985	29094	29203	29312	29420	29529	29638	29747
290	29857	29966	30075	30184	30294	30403	30513	30623	30732	30842
0.300	0.30952	0.31062	0.31172	0.31282	0.31392	0.31502	0.31613	0.31723	0.31833	0.31944
310	32055	32165	32276	32387	32498	32609	32720	32831	32942	33053
320	33165	33276	33388	33499	33611	33723	33835	33947	34059	34171
330	34283	34395	34507	34620	34732	34845	34958	35070	35183	35296
340	35409	35522	35636	35749	35862	35976	36089	36203	36317	36430
0.350	0.36544	0.36658	0.36772	0.36887	0.37001	0.37115	0.37230	0.37344	0.37459	0.37574
360	37689	37804	37919	38034	38149	38264	38380	38495	38611	38726
370	38842	38958	39074	39190	39307	39423	39539	39656	39772	39889
380	40006	40123	40240	40357	40474	40592	40709	40827	40944	41062
390	41180	41298	41416	41534	41653	41771	41890	42008	42127	42246
0.400	0.42365	0.42484	0.42603	0.42723	0.42842	0.42962	0.43081	0.43201	0.43321	0.43441
410	43561	43681	43802	43922	44043	44164	44284	44405	44527	44648
420	44769	44891	45012	45134	45256	45378	45500	45622	45745	45867
430	45990	46112	46235	46358	46481	46605	46728	46852	46975	47099
440	47223	47347	47471	47596	47720	47845	47970	48094	48220	48345
0.450	0.48470	0.48595	0.48721	0.48847	0.48973	0.49099	0.49225	0.49351	0.49478	0.49604
460	49731	49858	49985	50112	50240	50367	50495	50623	50751	50879
470	51007	51135	51264	51393	51522	51651	51780	51909	52039	52169
480	52298	52428	52559	52689	52819	52950	53081	53212	53343	53475
490	53606	53738	53870	54002	54134	54266	54399	54531	54664	54797
0.500	0.54931	0.55064	0.55198	0.55331	0.55465	0.55600	0.55734	0.55868	0.56003	0.56138
510	56273	56408	56544	56679	56815	56951	57087	57224	57360	57497
520	57634	57771	57908	58046	58184	58322	58460	58598	58737	58876
530	59015	59154	59293	59433	59572	59712	59853	59993	60134	60274
540	60416	60557	60698	60840	60982	61124	61266	61409	61552	61695
0.550	0.61838	0.61982	0.62125	0.62269	0.62413	0.62558	0.62702	0.62847	0.62992	0.63138
560	63283	63429	63575	63721	63868	64015	64162	64309	64457	64604
570	64752	64901	65049	65198	65347	65496	65646	65795	65945	66096
580	66246	66397	66548	66700	66851	67003	67155	67308	67460	67613
590	67767	67920	68074	68228	68382	68537	68692	68847	69003	69159
0.600	0.69315	0.69471	0.69628	0.69785	0.69942	0.70100	0.70258	0.70416	0.70574	0.70733
610	70892	71052	71211	71371	71532	71692	71853	72015	72176	72338
620	72500	72663	72826	72989	73153	73317	73481	73646	73811	73976
630	74142	74308	74474	74641	74808	74975	75143	75311	75479	75648
640	75817	75987	76157	76327	76498	76669	76840	77012	77184	77357
0.650	0.77530	0.77703	0.77877	0.78051	0.78226	0.78401	0.78576	0.78752	0.78928	0.79104
660	79281	79459	79637	79815	79993	80172	80352	80532	80712	80893
670	81074	81256	81438	81621	81804	81987	82171	82355	82540	82726
680	82911	83098	83284	83472	83659	83847	84036	84225	84415	84605
690	84796	84987	85178	85370	85563	85756	85950	86144	86339	86534
0.700	0.86730	0.86926	0.87123	0.87321	0.87519	0.87717	0.87916	0.88116	0.88316	0.88517
710	88718	88920	89123	89326	89530	89734	89939	90144	90350	90557
720	90765	90972	91181	91390	91600	91811	92022	92233	92446	92659
730	92873	93087	93302	93518	93735	93952	94169	94388	94607	94827
740	95048	95269	95491	95714	95938	96162	96387	96613	96840	97067
0.750	0.97296	0.97524	0.97754	0.97985	0.98216	0.98448	0.98681	0.98915	0.99150	0.99385
760	99622	99859	1.00097	1.00336	1.00575	1.00816	1.01058	1.01300	1.01543	1.01788
770	1.02033	1.02279	02526	02774	03023	03273	03524	03775	04028	04282
780	04537	04793	05050	05308	05567	05827	06088	06350	06613	06878
790	07143	07410	07677	07946	08216	08488	08760	09033	09308	09584
0.800	1.09861	1.10140	1.10419	1.10700	1.10982	1.11266	1.11551	1.11837	1.12124	1.12413
810	12703	12994	13287	13581	13877	14174	14473	14773	15074	15377
820	15682	15988	16295	16604	16915	17227	17541	17857	18174	18493
830	18814	19136	19460	19786	20113	20443	20774	21107	21442	21779
840	22117	22458	22801	23145	23492	23840	24191	24544	24899	25256
0.850	1.25615	1.25977	1.26340	1.26706	1.27075	1.27445	1.27818	1.28194	1.28571	1.28952
860	29334	29720	30108	30498	30891	31287	31686	32087	32491	32898
870	33308	33721	34137	34555	34977	35403	35831	36262	36697	37135
880	37577	38022	38470	38922	39378	39838	40301	40768	41239	41714
890	42193	42676	43163	43654	44150	44651	45156	45665	46179	46698
0.900	1.47222	1.47751	1.48285	1.48824	1.49368	1.49918	1.50473	1.51034	1.51601	1.52174
910	52752	53337	53928	54526	55130	55741	56359	56984	57616	58256
920	58903	59558	60221	60892	61571	62260	62957	63663	64379	65104
930	65839	66584	67340	68107	68885	69674	70475	71288	72114	72953
940	73805	74671	75552	76447	77358	78284	79227	80188	81166	82162
0.950	1.83178	1.84214	1.85270	1.86349	1.87450	1.88574	1.89723	1.90898	1.92100	1.93331
960	94591	95882	97207	98566	99961	2.01395	2.02870	2.04388	2.05952	2.07565
970	2.09230	2.10950	2.12730	2.14574	2.16486	18472	20539	22692	24940	27291
980	29756	32346	35075	37958	41014	44266	47741	51472	55499	59875
990	64665	69958	75873	82574	90307	99448	3.10630	3.25039	3.45338	3.80020

* Reproduction only by permission of the publishers of these *Scientific Tables*.

z-Transformation

When the population correlation coefficients differ significantly from zero, their distribution deviates from the normal distribution to an extent which is the greater the smaller the number n of pairs of observations and the larger the absolute value of r. The z-transformation can be used to normalize the distribution of the correlation coefficients, as follows:

$$z = \tfrac{1}{2} \ln \frac{1+r}{1-r} \quad \text{(see table on this page)}$$

and

$$r = \frac{e^{2z}-1}{e^{2z}+1} = \tanh z = \text{hyperbolic tangent of } z$$

(see tables on pages 64 and 65)

The variance of z is

$$\sigma_z^2 \approx \frac{1}{n-p-3} = \frac{1}{n'-3}$$

where n = number of pairs of observations, p = number of excluded variables. In the case of the correlation coefficient r_{xy}, for example, $p = 0$, whence $n' = n$; in the case of the partial correlation coefficient $r_{xy \cdot z}$, $p = 1$, whence $n' = n - 1$.

The approximate expected value of z (see page 180) is

$$\boldsymbol{z} \approx \tfrac{1}{2} \ln \frac{1+\boldsymbol{r}}{1-\boldsymbol{r}}$$

where $\boldsymbol{r}$ is the population value of r.

$\boldsymbol{z}$ is estimated from z, with k correlation coefficients from $\bar{z}$†:

$$\bar{z} = \frac{\sum_1^k (n_i - 3)\, z_i}{\sum_1^k (n_i - 3)}$$

with the variance

$$\sigma_{\bar{z}}^2 = \frac{1}{\sum_1^k (n_i - 3)}$$

The confidence interval for $\boldsymbol{z}$ is

$$z \pm \frac{|c_\alpha|}{\sqrt{n-3}}; \ \text{(for values of } \frac{|c_\alpha|}{\sqrt{n-3}} \text{ see the table on the opposite page)}$$

or $\bar{z} \pm |c_\alpha| \sigma_{\bar{z}}$

The confidence interval for $\boldsymbol{r}$ is

$$\tanh\left(z - \frac{|c_\alpha|}{\sqrt{n-3}}\right) \leq \boldsymbol{r} \leq \tanh\left(z + \frac{|c_\alpha|}{\sqrt{n-3}}\right)$$

or

$$\tanh(\bar{z} - |c_\alpha| \sigma_{\bar{z}}) \leq \boldsymbol{r} \leq \tanh(\bar{z} + |c_\alpha| \sigma_{\bar{z}})$$

Tests

Testing for population correlation coefficient = $\boldsymbol{r}$

$$c = \frac{z - \boldsymbol{z}}{\sqrt{n-3}}$$

Testing for $\boldsymbol{r}_1 = \boldsymbol{r}_2$

$$c = \frac{z_1 - z_2}{\sqrt{\dfrac{1}{n_1-3} + \dfrac{1}{n_2-3}}}$$

For other tests see page 180.

† $\bar{z}$ can be used for estimating $\boldsymbol{z}$ only when χ^2 is not significant, i.e., when

$$\chi^2 = \sum_1^k (n_i - 3)(z_i - \bar{z})^2$$

does not exceed a chosen upper significance limit with degrees of freedom $\nu = k - 1$.

Confidence Limits* for the Correlation Coefficient r

Confidence limits for $\mathfrak{z} = z \pm c_g$. The table gives the values for $c_g = |c_\alpha| / \sqrt{n-3}$. See page 180

95% limits $(1-2\alpha=0.95)$

n	0	1	2	3	4	5	6	7	8	9
	0.	0.	0.	0.	0.	0.	0.	0.	0.	0.
10	74080	69295	65332	61980	59095	56579	54360	52382	50606	48999
20	47536	46197	44965	43826	42770	41787	40868	40008	39199	38438
30	37720	37040	36396	35784	35202	34648	34119	33613	33129	32666
40	32222	31795	31385	30990	30609	30243	29889	29548	29217	28898
50	28589	28290	27999	27718	27445	27180	26922	26672	26428	26191
60	25960	25736	25517	25303	25095	24892	24693	24500	24310	24125
70	23945	23768	23595	23426	23260	23098	22940	22784	22632	22482
80	22336	22192	22051	21913	21777	21644	21513	21385	21259	21135
90	21013	20893	20776	20660	20546	20434	20324	20215	20109	20004
100	19900	19799	19698	19600	19502	19407	19312	19219	19127	19037
110	18948	18860	18773	18688	18603	18520	18438	18357	18277	18198
120	18120	18043	17967	17892	17818	17745	17672	17601	17530	17461
130	17392	17324	17257	17190	17124	17059	16995	16932	16869	16807
140	16745	16684	16624	16565	16506	16448	16390	16333	16277	16221
150	16166	16111	16057	16003	15950	15897	15845	15794	15743	15692
160	15642	15593	15544	15495	15447	15399	15352	15305	15258	15212
170	15167	15121	15077	15032	14988	14945	14901	14858	14816	14774
180	14732	14691	14649	14609	14568	14528	14488	14449	14410	14371
190	14333	14295	14257	14219	14182	14145	14108	14072	14036	14000
200	13964	13929	13894	13859	13825	13790	13756	13722	13689	13656
210	13623	13590	13557	13525	13493	13461	13429	13398	13367	13336
220	13305	13275	13244	13214	13184	13154	13125	13096	13066	13037
230	13009	12980	12952	12924	12896	12868	12840	12813	12785	12758
240	12731	12705	12678	12652	12625	12599	12573	12547	12522	12496
250	12471	12446	12421	12396	12371	12347	12322	12298	12274	12250
260	12226	12202	12179	12155	12132	12109	12086	12063	12040	12017
270	11995	11972	11950	11928	11906	11884	11862	11841	11819	11798
280	11776	11755	11734	11713	11692	11671	11651	11630	11610	11590
290	11569	11549	11529	11509	11490	11470	11450	11431	11411	11392
300	11373	11354	11335	11316	11297	11278	11260	11241	11223	11204
310	11186	11168	11150	11132	11114	11096	11078	11061	11043	11026
320	11008	10991	10974	10957	10939	10922	10906	10889	10872	10855
330	10839	10822	10806	10789	10773	10757	10741	10724	10708	10692
340	10677	10661	10645	10629	10614	10598	10583	10567	10552	10537
350	10522	10507	10491	10476	10462	10447	10432	10417	10402	10388
360	10373	10359	10344	10330	10316	10301	10287	10273	10259	10245
370	10231	10217	10203	10189	10176	10162	10148	10135	10121	10108
380	10094	10081	10068	10054	10041	10028	10015	10002	09989	09976
390	09963	09950	09937	09925	09912	09899	09887	09874	09862	09849
400	09837	09824	09812	09800	09788	09775	09763	09751	09739	09727
410	09715	09703	09691	09680	09668	09656	09644	09633	09621	09610
420	09598	09586	09575	09564	09552	09541	09530	09518	09507	09496
430	09485	09474	09463	09452	09441	09430	09419	09408	09397	09387
440	09376	09365	09354	09344	09333	09323	09312	09302	09291	09281
450	09270	09260	09250	09239	09229	09219	09209	09199	09188	09178
460	09168	09158	09148	09138	09128	09119	09109	09099	09089	09079
470	09070	09060	09050	09041	09031	09021	09012	09002	08993	08983
480	08974	08965	08955	08946	08937	08927	08918	08909	08900	08891
490	08881	08872	08863	08854	08845	08836	08827	08818	08809	08800
500	08792	08783	08774	08765	08756	08748	08739	08730	08722	08713
510	08705	08696	08687	08679	08670	08662	08653	08645	08637	08628
520	08620	08612	08603	08595	08587	08579	08570	08562	08554	08546
530	08538	08530	08522	08514	08506	08498	08490	08482	08474	08466
540	08458	08450	08442	08434	08427	08419	08411	08403	08396	08388
550	08380	08373	08365	08357	08350	08342	08335	08327	08320	08312
560	08305	08297	08290	08282	08275	08268	08260	08253	08246	08238
570	08231	08224	08217	08209	08202	08195	08188	08181	08174	08167
580	08159	08152	08145	08138	08131	08124	08117	08110	08103	08097
590	08090	08083	08076	08069	08062	08055	08049	08042	08035	08028
600	08022	08015	08008	08002	07995	07988	07982	07975	07968	07962
610	07955	07949	07942	07936	07929	07923	07916	07910	07903	07897
620	07891	07884	07878	07871	07865	07859	07852	07846	07840	07834
630	07827	07821	07815	07809	07802	07796	07790	07784	07778	07772
640	07766	07760	07753	07747	07741	07735	07729	07723	07717	07711
650	07705	07699	07694	07688	07682	07676	07670	07664	07658	07652
660	07647	07641	07635	07629	07623	07618	07612	07606	07600	07595
670	07589	07583	07578	07572	07566	07561	07555	07549	07544	07538
680	07533	07527	07522	07516	07511	07505	07500	07494	07489	07483
690	07478	07472	07467	07461	07456	07451	07445	07440	07435	07429
700	07424	07419	07413	07408	07403	07397	07392	07387	07382	07376
710	07371	07366	07361	07356	07350	07345	07340	07335	07330	07325
720	07320	07315	07309	07304	07299	07294	07289	07284	07279	07274
730	07269	07264	07259	07254	07249	07244	07239	07234	07229	07225
740	07220	07215	07210	07205	07200	07195	07190	07186	07181	07176
750	07171	07166	07162	07157	07152	07147	07143	07138	07133	07128
760	07124	07119	07114	07110	07105	07100	07096	07091	07086	07082
770	07077	07072	07068	07063	07059	07054	07050	07045	07040	07036
780	07031	07027	07022	07018	07013	07009	07004	07000	06995	06991
790	06987	06982	06978	06973	06969	06964	06960	06956	06951	06947
800	06943	06938	06934	06930	06925	06921	06917	06912	06908	06904
810	06899	06895	06891	06887	06882	06878	06874	06870	06865	06861
820	06857	06853	06849	06844	06840	06836	06832	06828	06824	06820
830	06815	06811	06807	06803	06799	06795	06791	06787	06783	06779
840	06775	06771	06767	06763	06758	06754	06750	06746	06742	06738
850	06735	06731	06727	06723	06719	06715	06711	06707	06703	06699
860	06695	06691	06687	06683	06680	06676	06672	06668	06664	06660
870	06656	06653	06649	06645	06641	06637	06633	06630	06626	06622
880	06618	06615	06611	06607	06603	06600	06596	06592	06588	06585
890	06581	06577	06574	06570	06566	06562	06559	06555	06551	06548
900	06544	06540	06537	06533	06530	06526	06522	06519	06515	06512
910	06508	06504	06501	06497	06494	06490	06487	06483	06479	06476
920	06472	06469	06465	06462	06458	06455	06451	06448	06444	06441
930	06437	06434	06430	06427	06424	06420	06417	06413	06410	06406
940	06403	06400	06396	06393	06389	06386	06383	06379	06376	06372
950	06369	06366	06362	06359	06356	06352	06349	06346	06342	06339
960	06336	06332	06329	06326	06322	06319	06316	06313	06309	06306
970	06303	06300	06296	06293	06290	06287	06283	06280	06277	06274
980	06270	06267	06264	06261	06258	06254	06251	06248	06245	06242
990	06239	06235	06232	06229	06226	06223	06220	06217	06214	06210
1000	06207									

99% limits $(1-2\alpha=0.99)$

n	0	1	2	3	4	5	6	7	8	9
	0.	0.	0.	0.	0.	0.	0.	0.	0.	0.
10	97357	91069	85861	81455	77664	74358	71441	68842	66508	64396
20	62473	60713	59094	57597	56209	54917	53710	52579	51517	50516
30	49572	48679	47832	47028	46263	45535	44839	44175	43539	42930
40	42346	41785	41246	40727	40228	39746	39281	38832	38398	37979
50	37572	37179	36798	36428	36069	35720	35382	35053	34732	34421
60	34118	33822	33534	33254	32980	32713	32452	32198	31949	31706
70	31469	31237	31009	30787	30569	30356	30148	29943	29743	29547
80	29354	29166	28980	28799	28620	28445	28273	28105	27939	27776
90	27616	27458	27304	27152	27002	26855	26710	26568	26427	26289
100	26154	26020	25888	25758	25630	25505	25380	25258	25138	25019
110	24901	24786	24672	24560	24449	24339	24231	24125	24020	23916
120	23814	23712	23613	23514	23417	23320	23225	23132	23039	22947
130	22857	22767	22679	22592	22505	22420	22335	22252	22169	22088
140	22007	21927	21848	21770	21692	21616	21540	21465	21391	21318
150	21245	21173	21102	21032	20962	20893	20824	20757	20690	20623
160	20557	20492	20428	20364	20300	20238	20175	20114	20053	19992
170	19932	19873	19814	19756	19698	19641	19584	19527	19471	19416
180	19361	19307	19253	19199	19146	19093	19041	18989	18938	18887
190	18836	18786	18736	18687	18638	18589	18541	18493	18446	18399
200	18352	18306	18260	18214	18168	18123	18079	18034	17990	17947
210	17903	17860	17817	17775	17733	17691	17649	17608	17567	17526
220	17486	17446	17406	17366	17327	17288	17249	17210	17172	17134
230	17096	17059	17022	16985	16948	16911	16875	16839	16803	16767
240	16732	16697	16662	16627	16592	16558	16524	16490	16456	16423
250	16390	16357	16324	16291	16258	16226	16194	16162	16130	16099
260	16068	16036	16005	15975	15944	15914	15883	15853	15823	15793
270	15764	15734	15705	15676	15647	15618	15590	15561	15533	15505
280	15477	15449	15421	15394	15366	15339	15312	15285	15258	15231
290	15205	15178	15152	15126	15100	15074	15048	15023	14997	14972
300	14946	14921	14896	14872	14847	14822	14798	14773	14749	14725
310	14701	14677	14653	14630	14606	14583	14559	14536	14513	14490
320	14467	14445	14422	14399	14377	14355	14332	14310	14288	14266
330	14244	14223	14201	14179	14158	14137	14115	14094	14073	14052
340	14031	14011	13990	13969	13949	13928	13908	13888	13868	13848
350	13828	13808	13788	13768	13749	13729	13710	13690	13671	13652
360	13633	13614	13595	13576	13557	13538	13520	13501	13483	13464
370	13446	13427	13409	13391	13373	13355	13337	13319	13302	13284
380	13266	13249	13231	13214	13196	13179	13162	13145	13128	13111
390	13094	13077	13060	13043	13027	13010	12993	12977	12960	12944
400	12928	12911	12895	12879	12863	12847	12831	12815	12799	12784
410	12768	12752	12737	12721	12706	12690	12675	12660	12644	12629
420	12614	12599	12584	12569	12554	12539	12524	12509	12495	12480
430	12465	12451	12436	12422	12407	12393	12379	12364	12350	12336
440	12322	12308	12294	12280	12266	12252	12238	12224	12211	12197
450	12183	12170	12156	12143	12129	12116	12102	12089	12076	12062
460	12049	12036	12023	12010	11997	11984	11971	11958	11945	11932
470	11920	11907	11894	11881	11869	11856	11844	11831	11819	11806
480	11794	11782	11769	11757	11745	11733	11720	11708	11696	11684
490	11672	11660	11648	11636	11625	11613	11601	11589	11577	11566
500	11554	11543	11531	11519	11508	11496	11485	11474	11462	11451
510	11440	11428	11417	11406	11395	11384	11373	11361	11350	11339
520	11328	11318	11307	11296	11285	11274	11263	11253	11242	11231
530	11220	11210	11199	11189	11178	11168	11157	11147	11136	11126
540	11116	11105	11095	11085	11074	11064	11054	11044	11034	11024
550	11013	11003	10993	10983	10973	10963	10954	10944	10934	10924
560	10914	10904	10895	10885	10875	10865	10856	10846	10837	10827
570	10817	10808	10798	10789	10780	10770	10761	10751	10742	10733
580	10723	10714	10705	10696	10686	10677	10668	10659	10650	10641
590	10632	10623	10614	10605	10596	10587	10578	10569	10560	10551
600	10542	10533	10525	10516	10507	10498	10490	10481	10472	10464
610	10455	10446	10438	10429	10421	10412	10404	10395	10387	10378
620	10370	10362	10353	10345	10336	10328	10320	10312	10303	10295
630	10287	10279	10271	10262	10254	10246	10238	10230	10222	10214
640	10206	10198	10190	10182	10174	10166	10158	10150	10142	10134
650	10127	10119	10111	10103	10095	10088	10080	10072	10065	10057
660	10049	10042	10034	10026	10019	10011	10004	09996	09989	09981
670	09974	09966	09959	09951	09944	09936	09929	09922	09914	09907
680	09900	09892	09885	09878	09871	09863	09856	09849	09842	09835
690	09827	09820	09813	09806	09799	09792	09785	09778	09771	09764
700	09757	09750	09743	09736	09729	09722	09715	09708	09701	09694
710	09687	09681	09674	09667	09660	09653	09647	09640	09633	09626
720	09620	09613	09606	09600	09593	09586	09580	09573	09566	09560
730	09553	09547	09540	09534	09527	09521	09514	09508	09501	09495
740	09488	09482	09475	09469	09463	09456	09450	09443	09437	09431
750	09424	09418	09412	09406	09399	09393	09387	09381	09374	09368
760	09362	09356	09350	09344	09337	09331	09325	09319	09313	09307
770	09301	09295	09289	09283	09277	09271	09265	09259	09253	09247
780	09241	09235	09229	09223	09217	09211	09205	09199	09194	09188
790	09182	09176	09170	09164	09159	09153	09147	09141	09136	09130
800	09124	09118	09113	09107	09101	09096	09090	09084	09079	09073
810	09067	09062	09056	09051	09045	09039	09034	09028	09023	09017
820	09012	09006	09001	08995	08990	08984	08979	08973	08968	08962
830	08957	08952	08946	08941	08935	08930	08925	08919	08914	08909
840	08903	08898	08893	08887	08882	08877	08872	08866	08861	08856
850	08851	08845	08840	08835	08830	08825	08819	08814	08809	08804
860	08799	08794	08789	08784	08778	08773	08768	08763	08758	08753
870	08748	08743	08738	08733	08728	08723	08718	08713	08708	08703
880	08698	08693	08688	08683	08678	08673	08668	08663	08659	08654
890	08649	08644	08639	08634	08629	08625	08620	08615	08610	08605
900	08600	08596	08591	08586	08581	08577	08572	08567	08562	08558
910	08553	08548	08543	08539	08534	08529	08525	08520	08515	08511
920	08506	08502	08497	08492	08488	08483	08478	08474	08469	08465
930	08460	08456	08451	08446	08442	08437	08433	08428	08424	08419
940	08415	08410	08406	08401	08397	08393	08388	08384	08379	08375
950	08370	08366	08361	08357	08353	08348	08344	08340	08335	08331
960	08326	08322	08318	08313	08309	08305	08300	08296	08292	08288
970	08283	08279	08275	08270	08266	08262	08258	08253	08249	08245
980	08241	08237	08232	08228	08224	08220	08216	08211	08207	08203
990	08199	08195	08191	08187	08182	08178	08174	08170	08166	08162
1000	08158									

$z = \tanh^{-1} r$

z	0.000	0.001	0.002	0.003	0.004	0.005	0.006	0.007	0.008	0.009
0.000	0.00000	0.00100	0.00200	0.00300	0.00400	0.00500	0.00600	0.00700	0.00800	0.00900
010	01000	01100	01200	01300	01400	01500	01600	01700	01800	01900
020	02000	02100	02200	02300	02400	02499	02599	02699	02799	02899
030	02999	03099	03199	03299	03399	03499	03598	03698	03798	03898
040	03998	04098	04198	04297	04397	04497	04597	04697	04796	04896
0.050	0.04996	0.05096	0.05195	0.05295	0.05395	0.05494	0.05594	0.05694	0.05794	0.05893
060	05993	06092	06192	06292	06391	06491	06590	06690	06790	06889
070	06989	07088	07188	07287	07387	07486	07585	07685	07784	07884
080	07983	08082	08182	08281	08380	08480	08579	08678	08777	08877
090	08976	09075	09174	09273	09372	09472	09571	09670	09769	09868
0.100	0.09967	0.10066	0.10165	0.10264	0.10363	0.10462	0.10560	0.10659	0.10758	0.10857
110	10956	11055	11153	11252	11351	11450	11548	11647	11746	11844
120	11943	12041	12140	12238	12337	12435	12534	12632	12731	12829
130	12927	13026	13124	13222	13320	13419	13517	13615	13713	13811
140	13909	14007	14105	14203	14301	14399	14497	14595	14693	14791
0.150	0.14889	0.14986	0.15084	0.15182	0.15279	0.15377	0.15475	0.15572	0.15670	0.15767
160	15865	15962	16060	16157	16255	16352	16449	16546	16644	16741
170	16838	16935	17032	17129	17227	17324	17420	17517	17614	17711
180	17808	17905	18002	18098	18195	18292	18388	18485	18582	18678
190	18775	18871	18967	19064	19160	19257	19353	19449	19545	19641
0.200	0.19738	0.19834	0.19930	0.20026	0.20122	0.20218	0.20313	0.20409	0.20505	0.20601
210	20697	20792	20888	20984	21079	21175	21270	21366	21461	21556
220	21652	21747	21842	21938	22033	22128	22223	22318	22413	22508
230	22603	22698	22793	22887	22982	23077	23171	23266	23361	23455
240	23550	23644	23738	23833	23927	24021	24115	24210	24304	24398
0.250	0.24492	0.24586	0.24680	0.24774	0.24868	0.24961	0.25055	0.25149	0.25242	0.25336
260	25430	25523	25617	25710	25803	25897	25990	26083	26176	26269
270	26362	26456	26548	26641	26734	26827	26920	27013	27105	27198
280	27291	27383	27476	27568	27660	27753	27845	27937	28029	28121
290	28213	28305	28397	28489	28581	28673	28765	28856	28948	29040
0.300	0.29131	0.29223	0.29314	0.29406	0.29497	0.29588	0.29679	0.29771	0.29862	0.29953
310	30044	30135	30226	30316	30407	30498	30589	30679	30770	30860
320	30951	31041	31131	31222	31312	31402	31492	31582	31672	31762
330	31852	31942	32032	32121	32211	32301	32390	32480	32569	32658
340	32748	32837	32926	33015	33104	33193	33282	33371	33460	33549
0.350	0.33638	0.33726	0.33815	0.33903	0.33992	0.34080	0.34169	0.34257	0.34345	0.34433
360	34521	34609	34697	34785	34873	34961	35049	35136	35224	35312
370	35399	35487	35574	35661	35749	35836	35923	36010	36097	36184
380	36271	36358	36444	36531	36618	36704	36791	36877	36963	37050
390	37136	37222	37308	37394	37480	37566	37652	37738	37824	37909
0.400	0.37995	0.38080	0.38166	0.38251	0.38337	0.38422	0.38507	0.38592	0.38677	0.38762
410	38847	38932	39017	39102	39186	39271	39356	39440	39524	39609
420	39693	39777	39861	39945	40029	40113	40197	40281	40365	40449
430	40532	40616	40699	40783	40866	40949	41032	41115	41199	41282
440	41364	41447	41530	41613	41695	41778	41861	41943	42025	42108
0.450	0.42190	0.42272	0.42354	0.42436	0.42518	0.42600	0.42682	0.42764	0.42845	0.42927
460	43008	43090	43171	43253	43334	43415	43496	43577	43658	43739
470	43820	43901	43981	44062	44143	44223	44303	44384	44464	44544
480	44624	44704	44784	44864	44944	45024	45104	45183	45263	45342
490	45422	45501	45580	45659	45739	45818	45897	45975	46054	46133
0.500	0.46212	0.46290	0.46369	0.46447	0.46526	0.46604	0.46682	0.46760	0.46839	0.46917
510	46995	47072	47150	47228	47306	47383	47461	47538	47615	47693
520	47770	47847	47924	48001	48078	48155	48232	48308	48385	48462
530	48538	48615	48691	48767	48843	48919	48995	49071	49147	49223
540	49299	49374	49450	49526	49601	49676	49752	49827	49902	49977
0.550	0.50052	0.50127	0.50202	0.50277	0.50351	0.50426	0.50500	0.50575	0.50649	0.50724
560	50798	50872	50946	51020	51094	51168	51242	51315	51389	51462
570	51536	51609	51683	51756	51829	51902	51975	52048	52121	52194
580	52267	52339	52412	52484	52557	52629	52701	52773	52846	52918
590	52990	53061	53133	53205	53277	53348	53420	53491	53562	53634
0.600	0.53705	0.53776	0.53847	0.53918	0.53989	0.54060	0.54131	0.54201	0.54272	0.54342
610	54413	54483	54553	54624	54694	54764	54834	54904	54973	55043
620	55113	55182	55252	55321	55391	55460	55529	55598	55667	55736
630	55805	55874	55943	56011	56080	56149	56217	56285	56354	56422
640	56490	56558	56626	56694	56762	56829	56897	56965	57032	57100
0.650	0.57167	0.57234	0.57301	0.57369	0.57436	0.57503	0.57570	0.57636	0.57703	0.57770
660	57836	57903	57969	58036	58102	58168	58234	58300	58366	58432
670	58498	58564	58629	58695	58760	58826	58891	58957	59022	59087
680	59152	59217	59282	59347	59411	59476	59541	59605	59670	59734
690	59798	59862	59927	59991	60055	60118	60182	60246	60310	60373
0.700	0.60437	0.60500	0.60564	0.60627	0.60690	0.60753	0.60816	0.60879	0.60942	0.61005
710	61068	61130	61193	61255	61318	61380	61443	61505	61567	61629
720	61691	61753	61815	61876	61938	62000	62061	62123	62184	62245
730	62307	62368	62429	62490	62551	62611	62672	62733	62794	62854
740	62915	62975	63035	63095	63156	63216	63276	63336	63395	63455
0.750	0.63515	0.63575	0.63634	0.63694	0.63753	0.63812	0.63871	0.63931	0.63990	0.64049
760	64108	64167	64225	64284	64343	64401	64460	64518	64576	64635
770	64693	64751	64809	64867	64925	64983	65040	65098	65156	65213
780	65271	65328	65385	65443	65500	65557	65614	65671	65727	65784
790	65841	65898	65954	66011	66067	66123	66179	66236	66292	66348
0.800	0.66404	0.66460	0.66515	0.66571	0.66627	0.66682	0.66738	0.66793	0.66849	0.66904
810	66959	67014	67069	67124	67179	67234	67289	67343	67398	67453
820	67507	67561	67616	67670	67724	67778	67832	67886	67940	67994
830	68048	68101	68155	68208	68262	68315	68368	68422	68475	68528
840	68581	68634	68687	68739	68792	68845	68897	68950	69002	69055
0.850	0.69107	0.69159	0.69211	0.69263	0.69315	0.69367	0.69419	0.69471	0.69523	0.69574
860	69626	69677	69729	69780	69831	69882	69934	69985	70036	70087
870	70137	70188	70239	70290	70340	70391	70441	70491	70542	70592
880	70642	70692	70742	70792	70842	70892	70941	70991	71040	71090
890	71139	71189	71238	71287	71336	71385	71434	71483	71532	71581
0.900	0.71630	0.71678	0.71727	0.71776	0.71824	0.71872	0.71921	0.71969	0.72017	0.72065
910	72113	72161	72209	72257	72305	72352	72400	72448	72495	72542
920	72590	72637	72684	72731	72778	72825	72872	72919	72966	73013
930	73059	73106	73153	73199	73245	73292	73338	73384	73430	73476
940	73522	73568	73614	73660	73705	73751	73797	73842	73888	73933
0.950	0.73978	0.74024	0.74069	0.74114	0.74159	0.74204	0.74249	0.74294	0.74338	0.74383
960	74428	74472	74517	74561	74606	74650	74694	74738	74782	74826
970	74870	74914	74958	75002	75046	75089	75133	75176	75220	75263
980	75307	75350	75393	75436	75479	75522	75565	75608	75651	75694
990	75736	75779	75821	75864	75906	75949	75991	76033	76075	76117
1.000	0.76159	0.76201	0.76243	0.76285	0.76327	0.76369	0.76410	0.76452	0.76493	0.76535
010	76576	76618	76659	76700	76741	76782	76823	76864	76905	76946
020	76987	77027	77068	77109	77149	77190	77230	77270	77310	77351
030	77391	77431	77471	77511	77551	77591	77630	77670	77710	77749
040	77789	77828	77868	77907	77946	77985	78025	78064	78103	78142

[1] Values abridged from National Bureau of Standards, *Table of Circular and Hyperbolic Tangents and Cotangents for Radian Arguments*, Columbia University Press, New York, 1947, by kind permission of the authors and publishers.

z-Transformation[1] of the Correlation Coefficient r

$z = \tanh^{-1} r$

z	0.000	0.001	0.002	0.003	0.004	0.005	0.006	0.007	0.008	0.009
1.050	0.78181	0.78219	0.78258	0.78297	0.78336	0.78374	0.78413	0.78451	0.78490	0.78528
060	78566	78605	78643	78681	78719	78757	78795	78833	78871	78908
070	78946	78984	79021	79059	79096	79134	79171	79208	79246	79283
080	79320	79357	79394	79431	79468	79505	79541	79578	79615	79651
090	79688	79724	79761	79797	79833	79870	79906	79942	79978	80014
1.100	0.80050	0.80086	0.80122	0.80157	0.80193	0.80229	0.80264	0.80300	0.80335	0.80371
110	80406	80442	80477	80512	80547	80582	80617	80652	80687	80722
120	80757	80792	80826	80861	80896	80930	80965	80999	81033	81068
130	81102	81136	81170	81204	81238	81272	81306	81340	81374	81408
140	81441	81475	81509	81542	81576	81609	81642	81676	81709	81742
1.150	0.81775	0.81809	0.81842	0.81875	0.81907	0.81940	0.81973	0.82006	0.82039	0.82071
160	82104	82137	82169	82202	82234	82266	82299	82331	82363	82395
170	82427	82459	82491	82523	82555	82587	82619	82650	82682	82714
180	82745	82777	82808	82840	82871	82902	82933	82965	82996	83027
190	83058	83089	83120	83151	83182	83212	83243	83274	83304	83335
1.200	0.83365	0.83396	0.83426	0.83457	0.83487	0.83517	0.83548	0.83578	0.83608	0.83638
210	83668	83698	83728	83758	83788	83817	83847	83877	83906	83936
220	83965	83995	84024	84054	84083	84112	84142	84171	84200	84229
230	84258	84287	84316	84345	84374	84402	84431	84460	84488	84517
240	84546	84574	84603	84631	84659	84688	84716	84744	84772	84800
1.250	0.84828	0.84856	0.84884	0.84912	0.84940	0.84968	0.84996	0.85023	0.85051	0.85079
260	85106	85134	85161	85189	85216	85244	85271	85298	85325	85353
270	85380	85407	85434	85461	85488	85515	85542	85568	85595	85622
280	85648	85675	85702	85728	85755	85781	85808	85834	85860	85886
290	85913	85939	85965	85991	86017	86043	86069	86095	86121	86147
1.300	0.86172	0.86198	0.86224	0.86249	0.86275	0.86300	0.86326	0.86351	0.86377	0.86402
310	86428	86453	86478	86503	86528	86554	86579	86604	86629	86654
320	86678	86703	86728	86753	86778	86802	86827	86851	86876	86900
330	86925	86949	86974	86998	87022	87047	87071	87095	87119	87143
340	87167	87191	87215	87239	87263	87287	87311	87334	87358	87382
1.350	0.87405	0.87429	0.87452	0.87476	0.87499	0.87523	0.87546	0.87570	0.87593	0.87616
360	87639	87662	87686	87709	87732	87755	87778	87801	87824	87846
370	87869	87892	87915	87937	87960	87983	88005	88028	88050	88073
380	88095	88118	88140	88162	88184	88207	88229	88251	88273	88295
390	88317	88339	88361	88383	88405	88427	88448	88470	88492	88514
1.400	0.88535	0.88557	0.88578	0.88600	0.88621	0.88643	0.88664	0.88686	0.88707	0.88728
410	88749	88771	88792	88813	88834	88855	88876	88897	88918	88939
420	88960	88981	89002	89022	89043	89064	89084	89105	89126	89146
430	89167	89187	89208	89228	89248	89269	89289	89309	89329	89350
440	89370	89390	89410	89430	89450	89470	89490	89510	89530	89549
1.450	0.89569	0.89589	0.89609	0.89628	0.89648	0.89668	0.89687	0.89707	0.89726	0.89746
460	89765	89785	89804	89823	89843	89862	89881	89900	89920	89939
470	89958	89977	89996	90015	90034	90053	90072	90090	90109	90128
480	90147	90166	90184	90203	90221	90240	90259	90277	90296	90314
490	90332	90351	90369	90388	90406	90424	90442	90460	90479	90497
1.500	0.90515	0.90533	0.90551	0.90569	0.90587	0.90605	0.90623	0.90641	0.90658	0.90676
510	90694	90712	90729	90747	90765	90782	90800	90817	90835	90852
520	90870	90887	90905	90922	90939	90957	90974	90991	91008	91025
530	91042	91060	91077	91094	91111	91128	91145	91161	91178	91195
540	91212	91229	91246	91262	91279	91296	91312	91329	91345	91362
1.550	0.91379	0.91395	0.91411	0.91428	0.91444	0.91461	0.91477	0.91493	0.91510	0.91526
560	91542	91558	91574	91591	91607	91623	91639	91655	91671	91687
570	91703	91718	91734	91750	91766	91782	91797	91813	91829	91845
580	91860	91876	91891	91907	91922	91938	91953	91969	91984	92000
590	92015	92030	92046	92061	92076	92091	92106	92122	92137	92152
1.600	0.92167	0.92182	0.92197	0.92212	0.92227	0.92242	0.92257	0.92272	0.92286	0.92301
610	92316	92331	92346	92360	92375	92390	92404	92419	92433	92448
620	92462	92477	92491	92506	92520	92535	92549	92563	92578	92592
630	92606	92620	92635	92649	92663	92677	92691	92705	92719	92733
640	92747	92761	92775	92789	92803	92817	92831	92844	92858	92872
1.650	0.92886	0.92899	0.92913	0.92927	0.92940	0.92954	0.92968	0.92981	0.92995	0.93008
660	93022	93035	93049	93062	93075	93089	93102	93115	93129	93142
670	93155	93168	93182	93195	93208	93221	93234	93247	93260	93273
680	93286	93299	93312	93325	93338	93351	93364	93376	93389	93402
690	93415	93427	93440	93453	93465	93478	93491	93503	93516	93528
1.700	0.93541	0.93553	0.93566	0.93578	0.93591	0.93603	0.93615	0.93628	0.93640	0.93652
710	93665	93677	93689	93701	93714	93726	93738	93750	93762	93774
720	93786	93798	93810	93822	93834	93846	93858	93870	93882	93894
730	93906	93917	93929	93941	93953	93964	93976	93988	93999	94011
740	94023	94034	94046	94057	94069	94080	94092	94103	94115	94126
1.750	0.94138	0.94149	0.94160	0.94172	0.94183	0.94194	0.94205	0.94217	0.94228	0.94239
760	94250	94261	94273	94284	94295	94306	94317	94328	94339	94350
770	94361	94372	94383	94394	94405	94415	94426	94437	94448	94459
780	94470	94480	94491	94502	94512	94523	94534	94544	94555	94565
790	94576	94587	94597	94608	94618	94629	94639	94649	94660	94670
1.800	0.94681	0.94691	0.94701	0.94712	0.94722	0.94732	0.94742	0.94753	0.94763	0.94773
810	94783	94793	94803	94814	94824	94834	94844	94854	94864	94874
820	94884	94894	94904	94914	94924	94933	94943	94953	94963	94973
830	94983	94992	95002	95012	95022	95031	95041	95051	95060	95070
840	95080	95089	95099	95108	95118	95127	95137	95146	95156	95165
1.850	0.95175	0.95184	0.95193	0.95203	0.95212	0.95221	0.95231	0.95240	0.95249	0.95259
860	95268	95277	95286	95296	95305	95314	95323	95332	95341	95350
870	95359	95368	95378	95387	95396	95405	95413	95422	95431	95440
880	95449	95458	95467	95476	95485	95493	95502	95511	95520	95529
890	95537	95546	95555	95563	95572	95581	95589	95598	95607	95615
1.900	0.95624	0.95632	0.95641	0.95649	0.95658	0.95666	0.95675	0.95683	0.95692	0.95700
910	95709	95717	95725	95734	95742	95750	95759	95767	95775	95783
920	95792	95800	95808	95816	95825	95833	95841	95849	95857	95865
930	95873	95881	95889	95898	95906	95914	95922	95930	95938	95945
940	95953	95961	95969	95977	95985	95993	96001	96009	96016	96024
1.950	0.96032	0.96040	0.96047	0.96055	0.96063	0.96071	0.96078	0.96086	0.96094	0.96101
960	96109	96117	96124	96132	96139	96147	96155	96162	96170	96177
970	96185	96192	96200	96207	96214	96222	96229	96237	96244	96251
980	96259	96266	96273	96281	96288	96295	96303	96310	96317	96324
990	96331	96339	96346	96353	96360	96367	96374	96382	96389	96396

z	0.0	0.1	0.2	0.3	0.4	0.5	0.6	0.7	0.8	0.9
0.0	0.00000 00000	0.09966 79946	0.19737 53202	0.29131 26125	0.37994 89623	0.46211 71573	0.53704 95670	0.60436 77771	0.66403 67703	0.71629 78702
1.0	76159 41560	80049 90218	83365 46070	86172 31593	88535 16482	90514 82536	92166 85544	93540 90706	94680 60128	95623 74581
2.0	96402 75801	97045 19366	97574 31300	98009 63963	98367 48577	98661 42982	98902 74022	99100 74537	99263 15202	99396 31674
3.0	99505 47537	99594 93592	99668 23978	99728 29601	99777 49279	99817 78976	99850 79423	99877 82413	99899 95978	99918 08657
4.0	99932 92997	99945 08437	99955 03665	99963 18562	99969 85793	99975 32108	99979 79416	99983 45656	99986 45517	99988 91030
5.0	0.99990 92043	0.99992 56621	0.99993 91369	0.99995 01692	0.99995 92018	0.99996 65972	0.99997 26520	0.99997 76093	0.99998 16680	0.99998 49910
6.0	99998 77117	99998 99391	99999 17629	99999 32560	99999 44785	99999 54794	99999 62988	99999 69697	99999 75190	99999 79687
7.0	99999 83369	99999 86384	99999 88852	99999 90873	99999 92527	99999 93882	99999 94991	99999 95899	99999 96642	99999 97251
8.0	99999 97749	99999 98157	99999 98491	99999 98765	99999 98989	99999 99172	99999 99322	99999 99445	99999 99546	99999 99628
9.0	99999 99695	99999 99751	99999 99796	99999 99833	99999 99863	99999 99888	99999 99908	99999 99925	99999 99939	99999 99950

[1] See footnote on previous page.

Significance Limits[1] when the Population Correlation Coefficient is Zero

ΣD^2 = sum of the squared differences between the two ranks for n pairs of observations with exact values for $n = 1$ to 10. Values below in *italics* are values of the tangents through the last exact value ($n = 10$) on the approximation curve $|c_\alpha| / \sqrt{n-1}$ (for $2\alpha = 0.05$, 0.02, 0.01 and 0.001). For $2\alpha = 0.10$ the *italic* values correspond to the extrapolated exponential curve between the two last exact values ($n = 9$ and 10). This ensures being on the safe side with all approximated values.

n	$2\alpha = 0.10$: ΣD^2 lower–upper	R (±)	$2\alpha = 0.05$: ΣD^2 lower–upper	R (±)	$2\alpha = 0.02$: ΣD^2 lower–upper	R (±)	$2\alpha = 0.01$: ΣD^2 lower–upper	R (±)	$2\alpha = 0.001$: ΣD^2 lower–upper	R (±)
5	2–38	0.9000	0–40	1.0000	0–40	1.0000	–	–	–	–
6	6–64	8286	4–66	0.8857	2–68	0.9429	0–70	1.0000	–	–
7	16–96	7143	12–100	7857	6–106	8929	4–108	0.9286	0–112	1.0000
8	30–138	6429	22–146	7381	14–154	8333	10–158	8810	2–166	0.9762
9	48–192	6000	38–202	6833	26–214	7833	20–220	8333	8–232	9333
10	72–258	0.5636	58–272	0.6485	44–286	0.7333	34–296	0.7939	16–314	0.9030
11	*103–337*	*5294*	*83–357*	*6194*	*63–377*	*7110*	*50–390*	*7724*	*24–416*	*8875*
12	*143–429*	*4973*	116–456	5910	*89–483*	*6887*	*71–501*	*7509*	*36–536*	*8720*
13	191–537	4748	158–570	5658	*121–607*	*6634*	*98–630*	*7294*	*52–676*	*8565*
14	247–663	4562	207–703	5436	*161–748*	*6441*	*132–778*	*7080*	*72–838*	*8410*
15	313–807	0.4396	266–854	0.5238	211–909	0.6217	*175–945*	*0.6865*	*97–1023*	*0.8255*
16	391–969	4247	335–1025	5061	271–1089	6007	*227–1133*	*6650*	*129–1231*	*8100*
17	480–1152	4112	416–1216	4900	341–1291	5816	290–1342	6440	*167–1465*	*7945*
18	582–1356	3989	508–1430	4754	422–1516	5642	363–1575	6247	*214–1724*	*7790*
19	698–1582	3877	613–1667	4620	514–1766	5483	447–1833	6071	*269–2011*	*7635*
20	828–1832	0.3774	731–1929	0.4496	620–2040	0.5337	544–2116	0.5909	*335–2325*	*0.7480*
21	973–2107	3678	865–2215	4383	738–2342	5202	653–2427	5760	*412–2668*	*7325*
22	1135–2407	3589	1013–2529	4277	871–2671	5077	775–2767	5621	*501–3041*	*7170*
23	1314–2734	3507	1178–2870	4179	1020–3028	4960	912–3136	5492	*604–3444*	*7015*
24	1511–3089	3430	1360–3240	4087	1184–3416	4851	1064–3536	5371	721–3879	6861
25	1727–3473	0.3358	1559–3641	0.4001	1365–3835	0.4749	1232–3968	0.5258	853–4347	0.6717
26	1962–3888	3290	1778–4072	3920	1564–4286	4653	1418–4432	5152	1000–4850	6581
27	2219–4333	3226	2016–4536	3844	1781–4771	4562	1621–4931	5052	1161–5391	6453
28	2497–4811	3166	2275–5033	3772	2018–5290	4477	1842–5466	4957	1340–5968	6333
29	2797–5323	3108	2556–5564	3704	2275–5845	4396	2083–6037	4868	1535–6585	6219
30	3122–5868	0.3054	2859–6131	0.3640	2553–6437	0.4320	2344–6646	0.4783	1748–7242	0.6110
31	3470–6450	3003	3185–6735	3578	2853–7067	4247	2627–7293	4703	1980–7940	6008
32	3844–7068	2954	3535–7377	3520	3176–7736	4178	2931–7981	4626	2231–8681	5910
33	4244–7724	2908	3910–8058	3465	3523–8445	4112	3259–8709	4553	2503–9465	5817
34	4670–8420	2863	4311–8779	3412	3894–9196	4050	3610–9480	4484	2795–10295	5728
35	5125–9155	0.2821	4740–9540	0.3361	4291–9989	0.3990	3985–10295	0.4418	3110–11170	0.5643
36	5609–9931	2780	5195–10345	3313	4714–10826	3932	4386–11154	4354	3448–12092	5562
37	6123–10749	2741	5680–11192	3267	5165–11707	3877	4814–12058	4293	3809–13063	5484
38	6667–11611	2704	6194–12084	3222	5643–12635	3824	5268–13010	4235	4195–14083	5410
39	7243–12517	2668	6738–13022	3179	6151–13609	3774	5751–14009	4179	4606–15154	5338
40	7852–13468	0.2634	7314–14006	0.3138	6689–14631	0.3725	6263–15057	0.4125	5043–16277	0.5269
41	8494–14466	2601	7922–15038	3099	7257–15703	3678	6804–16156	4073	5507–17453	5203
42	9170–15512	2569	8563–16119	3061	7857–16825	3633	7376–17306	4023	5999–18683	5139
43	9882–16606	2538	9238–17250	3024	8489–17999	3590	7980–18508	3975	6519–19969	5077
44	10630–17750	2508	9948–18432	2989	9155–19225	3548	8616–19764	3928	7069–21311	5018
45	11415–18945	0.2480	10694–19666	0.2955	9856–20504	0.3507	9285–21075	0.3883	7649–22711	0.4961
46	12239–20191	2452	11477–20953	2922	10591–21839	3468	9988–22442	3840	8261–24169	4905
47	13101–21491	2425	12297–22295	2890	11363–23229	3430	10727–23865	3798	8904–25688	4852
48	14003–22845	2399	13156–23692	2859	12172–24676	3393	11501–25347	3757	9580–27268	4800
49	14946–24254	2374	14055–25145	2829	13018–26182	3358	12312–26888	3718	10291–28909	4749
50	15931–25719	0.2350	14994–26656	0.2800	13904–27746	0.3323	13161–28489	0.3680	11035–30615	0.4701
51	16959–27241	2326	15974–28226	2772	14829–29371	3290	14049–30151	3643	11815–32385	4654
52	18030–28822	2303	16996–29856	2744	15794–31058	3258	14976–31876	3607	12632–34220	4608
53	19146–30462	2281	18062–31546	2718	16802–32806	3226	15943–33665	3572	13485–36123	4563
54	20307–32163	2259	19171–33299	2692	17851–34619	3195	16952–35518	3538	14377–38093	4520
55	21515–33925	0.2238	20326–35114	0.2667	18944–36496	0.3166	18003–37437	0.3505	15307–40133	0.4478
56	22770–35750	2218	21527–36993	2643	20081–38439	3137	19097–39423	3473	16277–42243	4437
57	24073–37639	2198	22774–38938	2619	21263–40449	3109	20235–41477	3442	17288–44424	4397
58	25426–39592	2179	24069–40949	2596	22491–42527	3081	21417–43601	3412	18340–46678	4358
59	26829–41611	2160	25413–43027	2574	23767–44673	3055	22646–45794	3382	19434–49006	4321
60	28283–43697	0.2141	26806–45174	0.2552	25089–46891	0.3029	23920–48060	0.3353	20572–51408	0.4284
61	29788–45852	2123	28250–47390	2530	26461–49179	3003	25243–50397	3325	21753–53887	4248
62	31347–48075	2106	29745–49677	2509	27882–51540	2979	26614–52808	3298	22980–56442	4213
63	32960–50368	2089	31293–52035	2489	29354–53974	2954	28034–55294	3271	24252–59076	4179
64	34628–52732	2072	32893–54467	2469	30877–56483	2931	29504–57856	3245	25571–61789	4146
65	36351–55169	0.2056	34549–56971	0.2450	32453–59067	0.2908	31026–60494	0.3220	26938–64582	0.4113
66	38131–57679	2040	36259–59551	2431	34082–61728	2885	32599–63211	3195	28353–67457	4081
67	39969–60263	2025	38025–62207	2413	35765–64467	2864	34226–66006	3171	29817–70415	4050
68	41865–62923	2010	39848–64940	2394	37503–67285	2842	35906–68882	3147	31331–73457	4020
69	43821–65659	1995	41729–67751	2377	39297–70183	2821	37641–71839	3124	32896–76584	3990
70	45837–68473	0.1980	43669–70641	0.2360	41148–73162	0.2801	39431–74879	0.3101	34514–79796	0.3961
71	47914–71366	1966	45668–73612	2343	43056–76224	2781	41278–78002	3079	36183–83097	3933
72	50054–74338	1952	47728–76664	2326	45024–79368	2761	43183–81209	3057	37907–86485	3905
73	52258–77390	1938	49850–79798	2310	47051–82597	2742	45145–84503	3036	39685–89963	3878
74	54525–80525	1925	52035–83015	2294	49139–85911	2723	47167–87883	3015	41519–93531	3851
75	56857–83743	0.1912	54282–86318	0.2278	51288–89312	0.2704	49249–91351	0.2994	43409–97191	0.3825
76	59256–87044	1899	56594–89706	2263	53500–92800	2686	51392–94908	2974	45356–100944	3800
77	61722–90430	1887	58972–93180	2248	55775–96377	2669	53597–98555	2955	47361–104791	3774
78	64255–93903	1874	61416–96742	2234	58114–100044	2651	55865–102293	2935	49425–108733	3750
79	66858–97462	1862	63926–100394	2219	60518–103802	2634	58197–106123	2917	51548–112772	3726
80	69530–101110	0.1851	66505–104135	0.2205	62988–107652	0.2617	60593–110047	0.2898	53733–116907	0.3702
81	72273–104847	1839	69153–107967	2191	65526–111594	2601	63055–114065	2880	55979–121141	3679
82	75088–108674	1828	71871–111891	2178	68131–115631	2585	65584–118178	2862	58287–125475	3656
83	77976–112592	1816	74660–115908	2164	70805–119763	2569	68180–122388	2845	60659–129909	3634
84	80937–116603	1805	77521–120019	2151	73549–123991	2553	70844–126696	2827	63095–134445	3612
85	83973–120707	0.1795	80454–124226	0.2138	76363–128317	0.2538	73577–131103	0.2810	65597–139083	0.3590
86	87084–124906	1784	83461–128529	2126	79249–132741	2523	76381–135609	2794	68164–143826	3569
87	90272–129200	1774	86543–132929	2113	82208–137264	2509	79255–140217	2778	70798–148674	3548
88	93537–133591	1763	89700–137428	2101	85239–141889	2494	82202–144926	2762	73500–153628	3528
89	96880–138080	1753	92934–142026	2089	88346–146614	2480	85221–149739	2746	76271–158689	3508
90	100303–142667	0.1744	96245–146725	0.2078	91527–151443	0.2466	88315–154655	0.2730	79111–163859	0.3488
91	103806–147354	1734	99635–151525	2066	94785–156375	2452	91482–159678	2715	82022–169138	3469
92	107390–152142	1724	103104–156428	2055	98120–161412	2439	94726–164806	2700	85004–174528	3449
93	111057–157031	1715	106653–161435	2043	101533–166555	2425	98046–170042	2685	88058–180030	3431
94	114806–162024	1706	110283–166547	2032	105025–171805	2412	101444–175386	2671	91186–185644	3412
95	118639–167121	0.1697	113996–171764	0.2022	108596–177164	0.2399	104920–180840	0.2657	94387–191373	0.3394
96	122558–172322	1688	117791–177089	2011	112249–182631	2387	108475–186405	2643	97664–197216	3376
97	126562–177630	1679	121671–182521	2000	115983–188209	2374	112110–192082	2629	101016–203176	3358
98	130653–183045	1670	125635–188063	1990	119800–193898	2362	115827–197871	2615	104445–209253	3341
99	134832–188568	1662	129685–193715	1980	123701–199699	2350	119625–203775	2602	107951–215449	3324

[1] Values up to $n = 10$ from KENDALL, M.G., *Rank Correlation Methods*, 3rd ed., Charles Griffin, London, 1962, page 174. Reprinted by kind permission of the author and publishers. Reproduction of other values only by permission of the publishers of these *Scientific Tables*.

Significance Limits* when the Population Correlation Coefficient is Zero

$\sum D^2$ = sum of the squared differences between the two ranks for n pairs of observations. Approximate values from $R = |c_\alpha| / \sqrt{n-1}$ (c_α = corresponding deviation from the standardized normal distribution)

n	$2\alpha = 0.10$		$2\alpha = 0.05$		$2\alpha = 0.02$		$2\alpha = 0.01$		$2\alpha = 0.001$	
	$\sum D^2$ lower upper	R (±)	$\sum D^2$ lower upper	R (±)	$\sum D^2$ lower upper	R (±)	$\sum D^2$ lower upper	R (±)	$\sum D^2$ lower upper	R (±)
100	139100– 194200	0.1653	133822– 199478	0.1970	127686– 205614	0.2338	123507– 209793	0.2589	111537– 221763	0.3307
101	143457– 199943	1645	138047– 205353	1960	131756– 211644	2326	127473– 215927	2576	115201– 228199	3291
102	147905– 205797	1637	142360– 211342	1950	135913– 217789	2315	131523– 222179	2563	118946– 234756	3274
103	152445– 211763	1629	146763– 217445	1941	140157– 224051	2303	135659– 228549	2550	122772– 241436	3258
104	157077– 217843	1621	151257– 223663	1931	144490– 230430	2292	139881– 235039	2538	126680– 248240	3242
105	161803– 224037	0.1613	155842– 229998	0.1922	148911– 236929	0.2281	144192– 241648	0.2526	130671– 255169	0.3227
106	166623– 230347	1605	160520– 236450	1913	153423– 243547	2270	148590– 248380	2514	134746– 262224	3211
107	171539– 236773	1598	165291– 243021	1904	158025– 250287	2260	153078– 255234	2502	138906– 269406	3196
108	176551– 243317	1590	170156– 249712	1895	162720– 257148	2249	157657– 262211	2490	143152– 276716	3181
109	181660– 249980	1583	175116– 256524	1886	167508– 264132	2239	162327– 269313	2479	147484– 284156	3166
110	186868– 256762	0.1575	180173– 263457	0.1877	172389– 271241	0.2228	167088– 276542	0.2467	151904– 291726	0.3152
111	192175– 263665	1568	185327– 270513	1869	177365– 278475	2218	171943– 283897	2456	156412– 299428	3137
112	197582– 270690	1561	190579– 277693	1860	182437– 285835	2208	176892– 291380	2445	161009– 307263	3123
113	203090– 277838	1554	195930– 284998	1852	187605– 293323	2198	181936– 298992	2434	165697– 315231	3109
114	208700– 285110	1547	201381– 292429	1844	192871– 300939	2188	187076– 306734	2423	170476– 323334	3095
115	214413– 292507	0.1541	206932– 299988	0.1836	198235– 308685	0.2179	192313– 314607	0.2412	175347– 331573	0.3082
116	220230– 300030	1534	212586– 307674	1828	203699– 316561	2169	197647– 322613	2402	180310– 339950	3068
117	226152– 307680	1527	218343– 315489	1820	209263– 324569	2160	203080– 330752	2392	185368– 348464	3055
118	232180– 315458	1521	224203– 323435	1812	214928– 332710	2151	208612– 339026	2381	190520– 357118	3042
119	238314– 323366	1514	230168– 331512	1804	220695– 340985	2142	214246– 347434	2371	195768– 365912	3029
120	244557– 331403	0.1508	236238– 339722	0.1797	226566– 349394	0.2133	219980– 355980	0.2361	201113– 374847	0.3016
121	250908– 339572	1502	242415– 348065	1789	232541– 357939	2124	225817– 364663	2351	206554– 383926	3004
122	257369– 347873	1495	248700– 356542	1782	238620– 366622	2115	231757– 373485	2342	212095– 393147	2991
123	263940– 356308	1489	255093– 365155	1774	244806– 375442	2106	237801– 382447	2332	217734– 402514	2979
124	270624– 364876	1483	261595– 373905	1767	251098– 384402	2098	243951– 391549	2323	223474– 412026	2967
125	277419– 373581	0.1477	268208– 382792	0.1760	257499– 393501	0.2089	250206– 400794	0.2313	229315– 421685	0.2955
126	284328– 382422	1471	274932– 391818	1753	264008– 402742	2081	256569– 410181	2304	235258– 431492	2943
127	291352– 391400	1465	281769– 400983	1746	270626– 412126	2072	263039– 419713	2295	241303– 441449	2931
128	298491– 400517	1460	288718– 410290	1739	277355– 421653	2064	269618– 429390	2286	247453– 451555	2920
129	305746– 409774	1454	295782– 419738	1732	284196– 431324	2056	276307– 439213	2277	253707– 461813	2908
130	313119– 419171	0.1448	302961– 429329	0.1726	291149– 441141	0.2048	283107– 449183	0.2268	260067– 472223	0.2897
131	320610– 428710	1443	310255– 439065	1719	298216– 451104	2040	290018– 459302	2259	266533– 482787	2886
132	328220– 438392	1437	317667– 448945	1712	305397– 461215	2033	297042– 469570	2251	273107– 493505	2875
133	335950– 448218	1432	325197– 458971	1706	312693– 471475	2025	304179– 479989	2242	279789– 504379	2864
134	343802– 458188	1426	332845– 469145	1700	320106– 481884	2017	311431– 490559	2234	286581– 515409	2853
135	351775– 468305	0.1421	340614– 479466	0.1693	327635– 492445	0.2010	318798– 501282	0.2225	293482– 526598	0.2843
136	359872– 478568	1416	348503– 489937	1687	335283– 503157	2002	326282– 512158	2217	300495– 537945	2832
137	368093– 488979	1410	356513– 500559	1681	343050– 514022	1995	333882– 523190	2209	307620– 549452	2822
138	376438– 499540	1405	364647– 511331	1675	350937– 525041	1988	341601– 534377	2201	314857– 561121	2811
139	384910– 510250	1400	372904– 522256	1668	358944– 536216	1980	349439– 545721	2193	322209– 572951	2801
140	393508– 521112	0.1395	381285– 533335	0.1662	367074– 547546	0.1973	357397– 557223	0.2185	329675– 584945	0.2791
141	402234– 532126	1390	389792– 544568	1656	375326– 559034	1966	365476– 568884	2177	337256– 597104	2781
142	411089– 543293	1385	398426– 555956	1651	383702– 570680	1959	373676– 580706	2169	344955– 609427	2771
143	420074– 554614	1380	407187– 567501	1645	392203– 582485	1952	382000– 592688	2162	352771– 621917	2761
144	429189– 566091	1375	416076– 579204	1639	400829– 594451	1945	390447– 604833	2154	360705– 634575	2752
145	438436– 577724	0.1371	425095– 591065	0.1633	409582– 606578	0.1939	399019– 617141	0.2147	368758– 647402	0.2742
146	447816– 589514	1366	434243– 603087	1628	418462– 618868	1932	407716– 629614	2139	376932– 660398	2733
147	457329– 601463	1361	443523– 615269	1622	427471– 631321	1925	416540– 642252	2132	385227– 673565	2723
148	466977– 613571	1357	452935– 627613	1617	436609– 643939	1919	425492– 655056	2125	393644– 686904	2714
149	476760– 625840	1352	462481– 640119	1611	445877– 656723	1912	434572– 668028	2117	402184– 700416	2705
150	486680– 638270	0.1348	472160– 652790	0.1606	455277– 669673	0.1906	443781– 681169	0.2110	410848– 714102	0.2696
151	496737– 650863	1343	481974– 665626	1600	464809– 682791	1899	453120– 694480	2103	419636– 727964	2687
152	506933– 663619	1339	491924– 678628	1595	474474– 696078	1893	462591– 707961	2096	428551– 742001	2678
153	517267– 676541	1334	502011– 691797	1590	484273– 709535	1887	472194– 721614	2089	437591– 756217	2669
154	527742– 689628	1330	512236– 705134	1585	494207– 723163	1881	481930– 735440	2082	446760– 770610	2660
155	538359– 702881	0.1325	522600– 718640	0.1579	504277– 736963	0.1875	491800– 749440	0.2076	456057– 785183	0.2652
156	549117– 716303	1321	533103– 732317	1574	514483– 750937	1869	501805– 763615	2069	465483– 799937	2643
157	560019– 729893	1317	543747– 746165	1569	524828– 765084	1863	511945– 777967	2062	475040– 814872	2635
158	571065– 743653	1313	554533– 760185	1564	535311– 779407	1857	522223– 792495	2056	484728– 829990	2626
159	582255– 757585	1309	565461– 774379	1559	545935– 793905	1851	532638– 807202	2049	494548– 845292	2618
160	593592– 771688	0.1304	576533– 788747	0.1554	556698– 808582	0.1845	543192– 822088	0.2043	504500– 860780	0.2610
161	605076– 785964	1300	587750– 803290	1549	567604– 823436	1839	553886– 837154	2036	514587– 876453	2601
162	616708– 800414	1296	599111– 818011	1545	578652– 838470	1833	564720– 852402	2030	524809– 892313	2593
163	628489– 815039	1292	610620– 832908	1540	589843– 853685	1828	575696– 867832	2024	535167– 908361	2585
164	640419– 829841	1288	622275– 847985	1535	601179– 869081	1822	586814– 883446	2018	545661– 924599	2577
165	652500– 844820	0.1284	634079– 863241	0.1530	612660– 884660	0.1817	598075– 899245	0.2011	556293– 941027	0.2569
166	664734– 859976	1281	646032– 878678	1526	624287– 900423	1811	609481– 915229	2005	567064– 957646	2562
167	677120– 875312	1277	658135– 894297	1521	636062– 916370	1806	621032– 931400	1999	577974– 974458	2554
168	689659– 890829	1273	670390– 910098	1517	647985– 932503	1800	632729– 947759	1993	589025– 991463	2546
169	702353– 906527	1269	682797– 926083	1512	660057– 948823	1795	644574– 964306	1987	600216–1008664	2539
170	715203– 922407	0.1265	695356– 942254	0.1508	672279– 965331	0.1789	656566– 981044	0.1981	611550–1026060	0.2531
171	728210– 938470	1262	708070– 958610	1503	684653– 982027	1784	668707– 997973	1976	623028–1043652	2524
172	741374– 954718	1258	720939– 975153	1499	697178– 998914	1779	680999–1015093	1970	634649–1061443	2516
173	754696– 971152	1254	733963– 991885	1494	709856–1015992	1774	693441–1032407	1964	646415–1079433	2509
174	768179– 987771	1251	747145–1008805	1490	722688–1033262	1769	706035–1049915	1958	658328–1097622	2502
175	781821–1004579	0.1247	760484–1025916	0.1486	735675–1050725	0.1764	718782–1067618	0.1953	670387–1116013	0.2495
176	795625–1021575	1243	773982–1043218	1482	748817–1068383	1759	731682–1085518	1947	682594–1134606	2487
177	809591–1038761	1240	787640–1060712	1477	762117–1086235	1754	744737–1103615	1942	694949–1153403	2480
178	823721–1056137	1236	801458–1078400	1473	775573–1104285	1749	757948–1121910	1936	707455–1172403	2473
179	838014–1073706	1233	815438–1096282	1469	789189–1122531	1744	771315–1140405	1931	720110–1191610	2466
180	852473–1091467	0.1229	829581–1114359	0.1465	802964–1140976	0.1739	784840–1159100	0.1925	732918–1211022	0.2459
181	867099–1109421	1226	843887–1132633	1461	816899–1159621	1734	798523–1177997	1920	745877–1230643	2453
182	881891–1127571	1223	858358–1151104	1457	830996–1178466	1729	812365–1197097	1915	758990–1250472	2446
183	896852–1145916	1219	872995–1169773	1453	845256–1197512	1724	826367–1216401	1909	772257–1270511	2439
184	911981–1164459	1216	887797–1188643	1449	859678–1216762	1720	840531–1235909	1904	785680–1290760	2432
185	927281–1183199	0.1213	902767–1207713	0.1445	874265–1236215	0.1715	854857–1255623	0.1899	799258–1311222	0.2426
186	942752–1202138	1209	917906–1226984	1441	889017–1255873	1710	869346–1275544	1894	812994–1331896	2419
187	958394–1221278	1206	933213–1246459	1437	903936–1275736	1706	883999–1295673	1889	826887–1352785	2413
188	974210–1240618	1203	948691–1266137	1433	919021–1295807	1701	898817–1316011	1884	840939–1373889	2406
189	990199–1260161	1200	964341–1286019	1429	934274–1316086	1697	913801–1336559	1879	855151–1395209	2400
190	1006364–1279906	0.1196	980162–1306108	0.1426	949697–1336573	0.1692	928952–1357318	0.1874	869524–1416746	0.2394
191	1022704–1299856	1193	996156–1326404	1422	965289–1357271	1688	944271–1378289	1869	884059–1438501	2387
192	1039221–1320011	1190	1012325–1346907	1418	981052–1378180	1683	959758–1399474	1864	898756–1460476	2381
193	1055915–1340373	1187	1028668–1367620	1414	996987–1399301	1679	975415–1420873	1859	913616–1482672	2375
194	1072789–1360941	1184	1045188–1388542	1411	1013095–1420635	1675	991243–1442487	1854	928641–1505089	2369
195	1089842–1381718	0.1181	1061884–1409676	0.1407	1029377–1442183	0.1670	1007242–1464318	0.1849	943831–1527729	0.2362
196	1107075–1402705	1178	1078758–1431022	1404	1045833–1463947	1666	1023414–1486366	1845	959188–1550592	2356
197	1124491–1423901	1175	1095811–1452581	1400	1062465–1485927	1662	1039759–1508633	1840	974711–1573681	2350
198	1142089–1445309	1172	1113044–1474354	1396	1079274–1508124	1657	1056279–1531119	1835	990403–1596995	2344
199	1159870–1466930	1169	1130458–1496342	1393	1096260–1530540	1653	1072973–1553827	1831	1006264–1620536	2338

Values* of $6/(n^3-n)$ for Calculation of the Spearman Correlation Coefficient R

n	0	1	2	3	4	5	6	7	8	9
0			1.00000	$10^{-1}\times$ 2.50000	$10^{-1}\times$ 1.00000	$10^{-2}\times$ 5.00000	$10^{-2}\times$ 2.85714	$10^{-2}\times$ 1.78571	$10^{-2}\times$ 1.19048	$10^{-3}\times$ 8.33333
10	$10^{-3}\times$ 6.06061	$10^{-3}\times$ 4.54545	$10^{-3}\times$ 3.49650	$10^{-3}\times$ 2.74725	$10^{-3}\times$ 2.19780	$10^{-3}\times$ 1.78571	$10^{-3}\times$ 1.47059	$10^{-3}\times$ 1.22549	$10^{-3}\times$ 1.03199	$10^{-4}\times$ 8.77193
20	$10^{-4}\times$ 7.51880	$10^{-4}\times$ 6.49351	$10^{-4}\times$ 5.64653	$10^{-4}\times$ 4.94071	$10^{-4}\times$ 4.34783	$10^{-4}\times$ 3.84615	$10^{-4}\times$ 3.41880	$10^{-4}\times$ 3.05250	$10^{-4}\times$ 2.73673	2.46305
30	2.22469	2.01613	1.83284	1.67112	1.52788	1.40056	1.28700	1.18540	1.09421	1.01215
40	$10^{-5}\times$ 9.38086	$10^{-5}\times$ 8.71080	$10^{-5}\times$ 8.10307	$10^{-5}\times$ 7.55059	$10^{-5}\times$ 7.04722	$10^{-5}\times$ 6.58762	$10^{-5}\times$ 6.16713	$10^{-5}\times$ 5.78168	$10^{-5}\times$ 5.42770	$10^{-5}\times$ 5.10204
50	4.80192	4.52489	4.26876	4.03161	3.81170	3.60750	3.41763	3.24086	3.07607	2.92227
60	2.77855	2.64410	2.51819	2.40015	2.28938	2.18531	2.08746	1.99537	1.90862	1.82682
70	1.74963	1.67673	1.60782	1.54264	1.48093	1.42248	1.36705	1.31447	1.26456	1.21714
80	1.17206	1.12918	1.08836	1.04949	1.01245	$10^{-6}\times$ 9.77135	$10^{-6}\times$ 9.43441	$10^{-6}\times$ 9.11278	$10^{-6}\times$ 8.80561	$10^{-6}\times$ 8.51209
90	$10^{-6}\times$ 8.23147	$10^{-6}\times$ 7.96305	$10^{-6}\times$ 7.70618	$10^{-6}\times$ 7.46024	$10^{-6}\times$ 7.22465	6.99888	6.78242	6.57479	6.37556	6.18429
100	$10^{-6}\times$ 6.00060	$10^{-6}\times$ 5.82411	$10^{-6}\times$ 5.65448	$10^{-6}\times$ 5.49137	$10^{-6}\times$ 5.33447	$10^{-6}\times$ 5.18350	$10^{-6}\times$ 5.03816	$10^{-6}\times$ 4.89822	$10^{-6}\times$ 4.76340	$10^{-6}\times$ 4.63349
110	4.50826	4.38750	4.27102	4.15863	4.05014	3.94540	3.84423	3.74650	3.65205	3.56075
120	3.47246	3.38707	3.30446	3.22452	3.14713	3.07220	2.99963	2.92932	2.86120	2.79517
130	2.73116	2.66909	2.60888	2.55047	2.49380	2.43879	2.38538	2.33353	2.28316	2.23424
140	2.18670	2.14050	2.09560	2.05194	2.00948	1.96819	1.92803	1.88895	1.85091	1.81389
150	1.77786	1.74277	1.70860	1.67531	1.64289	1.61129	1.58050	1.55049	1.52124	1.49272
160	1.46490	1.43777	1.41131	1.38549	1.36030	1.33572	1.31172	1.28830	1.26543	1.24310
170	1.22129	1.19999	1.17918	1.15885	1.13898	1.11957	1.10059	1.08204	1.06391	1.04618
180	1.02884	1.01188	$10^{-7}\times$ 9.95291	$10^{-7}\times$ 9.79064	$10^{-7}\times$ 9.63187	$10^{-7}\times$ 9.47652	$10^{-7}\times$ 9.32449	$10^{-7}\times$ 9.17569	$10^{-7}\times$ 9.03005	$10^{-7}\times$ 8.88747
190	$10^{-7}\times$ 8.74787	$10^{-7}\times$ 8.61119	8.47733	8.34624	8.21784	8.09206	7.96883	7.84809	7.72977	7.61383
200	$10^{-7}\times$ 7.50019	$10^{-7}\times$ 7.38880	$10^{-7}\times$ 7.27960	$10^{-7}\times$ 7.17255	$10^{-7}\times$ 7.06759	$10^{-7}\times$ 6.96466	$10^{-7}\times$ 6.86372	$10^{-7}\times$ 6.76473	$10^{-7}\times$ 6.66763	$10^{-7}\times$ 6.57237
210	6.47893	6.38725	6.29728	6.20901	6.12237	6.03733	5.95387	5.87194	5.79150	5.71252
220	5.63498	5.55883	5.48405	5.41060	5.33846	5.26759	5.19798	5.12958	5.06238	4.99635
230	4.93146	4.86770	4.80502	4.74342	4.68286	4.62334	4.56481	4.50727	4.45070	4.39506
240	4.34035	4.28655	4.23363	4.18157	4.13037	4.08000	4.03045	3.98169	3.93372	3.88651
250	3.84006	3.79435	3.74935	3.70507	3.66148	3.61857	3.57633	3.53475	3.49380	3.45349
260	3.41380	3.37471	3.33621	3.29830	3.26096	3.22418	3.18796	3.15227	3.11712	3.08248
270	3.04836	3.01474	2.98161	2.94896	2.91679	2.88509	2.85384	2.82304	2.79269	2.76277
280	2.73327	2.70419	2.67553	2.64726	2.61940	2.59192	2.56483	2.53811	2.51177	2.48578
290	2.46015	2.43488	2.40995	2.38536	2.36110	2.33717	2.31356	2.29027	2.26729	2.24462
300	$10^{-7}\times$ 2.22225	$10^{-7}\times$ 2.20017	$10^{-7}\times$ 2.17839	$10^{-7}\times$ 2.15689	$10^{-7}\times$ 2.13568	$10^{-7}\times$ 2.11474	$10^{-7}\times$ 2.09407	$10^{-7}\times$ 2.07368	$10^{-7}\times$ 2.05354	$10^{-7}\times$ 2.03367
310	2.01405	1.99469	1.97557	1.95669	1.93806	1.91966	1.90149	1.88355	1.86584	1.84835
320	1.83107	1.81401	1.79716	1.78052	1.76409	1.74785	1.73182	1.71598	1.70033	1.68487
330	1.66960	1.65452	1.63961	1.62488	1.61033	1.59596	1.58175	1.56771	1.55384	1.54012
340	1.52658	1.51318	1.49995	1.48687	1.47394	1.46116	1.44853	1.43604	1.42370	1.41149
350	1.39943	1.38750	1.37571	1.36405	1.35252	1.34113	1.32986	1.31871	1.30769	1.29679
360	1.28602	1.27536	1.26482	1.25440	1.24409	1.23389	1.22380	1.21383	1.20396	1.19420
370	1.18454	1.17499	1.16554	1.15619	1.14694	1.13779	1.12873	1.11977	1.11091	1.10214
380	1.09346	1.08487	1.07638	1.06797	1.05965	1.05141	1.04326	1.03519	1.02721	1.01931
390	1.01149	1.00375	$10^{-8}\times$ 9.96084	$10^{-8}\times$ 9.88499	$10^{-8}\times$ 9.80992	$10^{-8}\times$ 9.73560	$10^{-8}\times$ 9.66203	$10^{-8}\times$ 9.58920	$10^{-8}\times$ 9.51710	$10^{-8}\times$ 9.44572
400	$10^{-8}\times$ 9.37506	$10^{-8}\times$ 9.30510	$10^{-8}\times$ 9.23583	$10^{-8}\times$ 9.16724	$10^{-8}\times$ 9.09934	$10^{-8}\times$ 9.03210	$10^{-8}\times$ 8.96553	$10^{-8}\times$ 8.89960	$10^{-8}\times$ 8.83432	$10^{-8}\times$ 8.76968
410	8.70567	8.64228	8.57950	8.51733	8.45576	8.39478	8.33439	8.27457	8.21533	8.15665
420	8.09852	8.04095	7.98392	7.92743	7.87147	7.81604	7.76113	7.70673	7.65283	7.59944
430	7.54655	7.49414	7.44222	7.39077	7.33980	7.28930	7.23926	7.18967	7.14054	7.09186
440	7.04361	6.99581	6.94843	6.90148	6.85495	6.80884	6.76315	6.71786	6.67297	6.62849
450	6.58439	6.54069	6.49738	6.45444	6.41189	6.36970	6.32789	6.28644	6.24535	6.20462
460	6.16424	6.12422	6.08453	6.04519	6.00619	5.96753	5.92919	5.89118	5.85350	5.81614
470	5.77909	5.74236	5.70594	5.66983	5.63402	5.59851	5.56330	5.52838	5.49376	5.45942
480	5.42537	5.39160	5.35811	5.32490	5.29197	5.25930	5.22690	5.19477	5.16290	5.13129
490	5.09994	5.06884	5.03800	5.00740	4.97705	4.94695	4.91709	4.88747	4.85808	4.82893

Relationship* Between R and r $r \cong 2 \sin \frac{\pi}{6} R$

R	0.000	0.001	0.002	0.003	0.004	0.005	0.006	0.007	0.008	0.009	R	0,000	0.001	0.002	0.003	0.004	0.005	0.006	0.007	0.008	0.009
0.00	0.000	0.001	0.002	0.003	0.004	0.005	0.006	0.007	0.008	0.009	**0.50**	0.518	0.519	0.520	0.521	0.522	0.523	0.524	0.525	0.526	0.527
01	010	012	013	014	015	016	017	018	019	020	51	528	529	530	531	532	533	534	535	536	537
02	021	022	023	024	025	026	027	028	029	030	52	538	539	540	541	542	543	544	545	546	547
03	031	032	034	035	036	037	038	039	040	041	53	548	549	550	551	552	553	554	555	556	557
04	042	043	044	045	046	047	048	049	050	051	54	558	559	560	561	562	563	564	565	566	567
0.05	0.052	0.053	0.054	0.055	0.057	0.058	0.059	0.060	0.061	0.062	**0.55**	0.568	0.569	0.570	0.571	0.572	0.573	0.574	0.575	0.576	0.577
06	063	064	065	066	067	068	069	070	071	072	56	578	579	580	581	582	583	584	585	586	587
07	073	074	075	076	077	079	080	081	082	083	57	588	589	590	591	592	593	594	595	596	597
08	084	085	086	087	088	089	090	091	092	093	58	598	599	600	601	602	603	604	605	606	607
09	094	095	096	097	098	099	100	102	103	104	59	608	609	610	611	612	613	614	615	616	617
0.10	0.105	0.106	0.107	0.108	0.109	0.110	0.111	0.112	0.113	0.114	**0.60**	0.618	0.619	0.620	0.621	0.622	0.623	0.624	0.625	0.626	0.627
11	115	116	117	118	119	120	121	122	123	125	61	628	629	630	631	632	633	634	635	636	637
12	126	127	128	129	130	131	132	133	134	135	62	638	639	640	641	642	643	644	645	646	647
13	136	137	138	139	140	141	142	143	144	145	63	648	649	650	651	652	653	654	655	656	657
14	146	148	149	150	151	152	153	154	155	156	64	658	659	660	661	662	663	664	665	666	667
0.15	0.157	0.158	0.159	0.160	0.161	0.162	0.163	0.164	0.165	0.166	**0.65**	0.668	0.669	0.670	0.671	0.672	0.673	0.674	0.675	0.676	0.676
16	167	168	169	170	172	173	174	175	176	177	66	677	678	679	680	681	682	683	684	685	686
17	178	179	180	181	182	183	184	185	186	187	67	687	688	689	690	691	692	693	694	695	696
18	188	189	190	191	192	193	194	196	197	198	68	697	698	699	700	701	702	703	704	705	706
19	199	200	201	202	203	204	205	206	207	208	69	707	708	709	710	711	712	713	714	715	716
0.20	0.209	0.210	0.211	0.212	0.213	0.214	0.215	0.216	0.217	0.218	**0.70**	0.717	0.718	0.719	0.720	0.721	0.722	0.723	0.724	0.725	0.726
21	219	221	222	223	224	225	226	227	228	229	71	727	727	728	729	730	731	732	733	734	735
22	230	231	232	233	234	235	236	237	238	239	72	736	737	738	739	740	741	742	743	744	745
23	240	241	242	243	244	245	247	248	249	250	73	746	747	748	749	750	751	752	753	754	755
24	251	252	253	254	255	256	257	258	259	260	74	756	757	758	759	760	761	761	762	763	764
0.25	0.261	0.262	0.263	0.264	0.265	0.266	0.267	0.268	0.269	0.270	**0.75**	0.765	0.766	0.767	0.768	0.769	0.770	0.771	0.772	0.773	0.774
26	271	272	274	275	276	277	278	279	280	281	76	775	776	777	778	779	780	781	782	783	784
27	282	283	284	285	286	287	288	289	290	291	77	785	786	787	788	789	789	790	791	792	793
28	292	293	294	295	296	297	298	299	300	301	78	794	795	796	797	798	799	800	801	802	803
29	303	304	305	306	307	308	309	310	311	312	79	804	805	806	807	808	809	810	811	812	813
0.30	0.313	0.314	0.315	0.316	0.317	0.318	0.319	0.320	0.321	0.322	**0.80**	0.813	0.814	0.815	0.816	0.817	0.818	0.819	0.820	0.821	0.822
31	323	324	325	326	327	328	329	330	331	333	81	823	824	825	826	827	828	829	830	831	832
32	334	335	336	337	338	339	340	341	342	343	82	833	834	834	835	836	837	838	839	840	841
33	344	345	346	347	348	349	350	351	352	353	83	842	843	844	845	846	847	848	849	850	851
34	354	355	356	357	358	359	360	361	362	363	84	852	853	853	854	855	856	857	858	859	860
0.35	0.364	0.366	0.367	0.368	0.369	0.370	0.371	0.372	0.373	0.374	**0.85**	0.861	0.862	0.863	0.864	0.865	0.866	0.867	0.868	0.869	0.870
36	375	376	377	378	379	380	381	382	383	384	86	870	871	872	873	874	875	876	877	878	879
37	385	386	387	388	389	390	391	392	393	394	87	880	881	882	883	884	885	886	886	887	888
38	395	396	397	398	399	400	401	402	404	405	88	889	890	891	892	893	894	895	896	897	898
39	406	407	408	409	410	411	412	413	414	415	89	899	900	901	901	902	903	904	905	906	907
0.40	0.416	0.417	0.418	0.419	0.420	0.421	0.422	0.423	0.424	0.425	**0.90**	0.908	0.909	0.910	0.911	0.912	0.913	0.914	0.915	0.915	0.916
41	426	427	428	429	430	431	432	433	434	435	91	917	918	919	920	921	922	923	924	925	926
42	436	437	438	439	440	441	442	443	444	445	92	927	928	928	929	930	931	932	933	934	935
43	447	448	449	450	451	452	453	454	455	456	93	936	937	938	939	940	940	941	942	943	944
44	457	458	459	460	461	462	463	464	465	466	94	945	946	947	948	949	950	951	952	952	953
0.45	0.467	0.468	0.469	0.470	0.471	0.472	0.473	0.474	0.475	0.476	**0.95**	0.954	0.955	0.956	0.957	0.958	0.959	0.960	0.961	0.962	0.963
46	477	478	479	480	481	482	483	484	485	486	96	964	964	965	966	967	968	969	970	971	972
47	487	488	489	490	491	492	493	494	495	496	97	973	974	975	975	976	977	978	979	980	981
48	497	498	499	500	501	502	503	504	505	507	98	982	983	984	985	985	986	987	988	989	990
49	508	509	510	511	512	513	514	515	516	517	99	991	992	993	994	995	995	996	997	998	999

Values[1] of Arc Sin x

(for arc-sine transformations)

x	0.000	0.001	0.002	0.003	0.004	0.005	0.006	0.007	0.008	0.009
0.000	0.00000	0.00100	0.00200	0.00300	0.00400	0.00500	0.00600	0.00700	0.00800	0.00900
0.010	01000	01100	01200	01300	01400	01500	01600	01700	01800	01900
0.020	02000	02100	02200	02300	02400	02500	02600	02700	02800	02900
0.030	03000	03100	03201	03301	03401	03501	03601	03701	03801	03901
0.040	04001	04101	04201	04301	04401	04502	04602	04702	04802	04902
0.050	0.05002	0.05102	0.05202	0.05302	0.05403	0.05503	0.05603	0.05703	0.05803	0.05903
0.060	06004	06104	06204	06304	06404	06505	06605	06705	06805	06905
0.070	07006	07106	07206	07306	07407	07507	07607	07708	07808	07908
0.080	08009	08109	08209	08310	08410	08510	08611	08711	08811	08912
0.090	09012	09113	09213	09313	09414	09514	09615	09715	09816	09916
0.100	0.10017	0.10117	0.10218	0.10318	0.10419	0.10519	0.10620	0.10721	0.10821	0.10922
0.110	11022	11123	11224	11324	11425	11525	11626	11727	11828	11928
0.120	12029	12130	12230	12331	12432	12533	12634	12734	12835	12936
0.130	13037	13138	13239	13340	13440	13541	13642	13743	13844	13945
0.140	14046	14147	14248	14349	14450	14551	14652	14753	14855	14956
0.150	0.15057	0.15158	0.15259	0.15360	0.15462	0.15563	0.15664	0.15765	0.15866	0.15968
0.160	16069	16170	16272	16373	16474	16576	16677	16779	16880	16981
0.170	17083	17184	17286	17387	17489	17591	17692	17794	17895	17997
0.180	18099	18200	18302	18404	18505	18607	18709	18811	18913	19014
0.190	19116	19218	19320	19422	19524	19626	19728	19830	19932	20034
0.200	0.20136	0.20238	0.20340	0.20442	0.20544	0.20646	0.20749	0.20851	0.20953	0.21055
0.210	21157	21260	21362	21464	21567	21669	21772	21874	21976	22079
0.220	22181	22284	22387	22489	22592	22694	22797	22900	23002	23105
0.230	23208	23311	23413	23516	23619	23722	23825	23928	24031	24134
0.240	24237	24340	24443	24546	24649	24752	24855	24958	25062	25165
0.250	0.25268	0.25371	0.25475	0.25578	0.25681	0.25785	0.25888	0.25992	0.26095	0.26199
0.260	26302	26406	26509	26613	26717	26820	26924	27028	27132	27235
0.270	27339	27443	27547	27651	27755	27859	27963	28067	28171	28275
0.280	28379	28484	28588	28692	28796	28901	29005	29109	29214	29318
0.290	29423	29527	29632	29736	29841	29946	30050	30155	30260	30364
0.300	0.30469	0.30574	0.30679	0.30784	0.30889	0.30994	0.31099	0.31204	0.31309	0.31414
0.310	31519	31625	31730	31835	31940	32046	32151	32256	32362	32467
0.320	32573	32679	32784	32890	32995	33101	33207	33313	33419	33524
0.330	33630	33736	33842	33948	34054	34161	34267	34373	34479	34585
0.340	34692	34798	34904	35011	35117	35224	35330	35437	35544	35650
0.350	0.35757	0.35864	0.35971	0.36078	0.36184	0.36291	0.36398	0.36505	0.36613	0.36720
0.360	36827	36934	37041	37149	37256	37363	37471	37578	37686	37793
0.370	37901	38009	38116	38224	38332	38440	38548	38656	38764	38872
0.380	38980	39088	39196	39304	39412	39521	39629	39738	39846	39955
0.390	40063	40172	40280	40389	40498	40607	40716	40825	40934	41043
0.400	0.41152	0.41261	0.41370	0.41479	0.41589	0.41698	0.41807	0.41917	0.42026	0.42136
0.410	42245	42355	42465	42575	42684	42794	42904	43014	43124	43234
0.420	43345	43455	43565	43675	43786	43896	44007	44117	44228	44339
0.430	44449	44560	44671	44782	44893	45004	45115	45226	45337	45449
0.440	45560	45671	45783	45894	46006	46117	46229	46341	46453	46565
0.450	0.46677	0.46789	0.46901	0.47013	0.47125	0.47237	0.47350	0.47462	0.47574	0.47687
0.460	47800	47912	48025	48138	48251	48363	48476	48590	48703	48816
0.470	48929	49042	49156	49269	49383	49496	49610	49724	49838	49952
0.480	50065	50179	50294	50408	50522	50636	50751	50865	50980	51094
0.490	51209	51324	51439	51553	51668	51783	51899	52014	52129	52244
0.500	0.52360	0.52475	0.52591	0.52707	0.52822	0.52938	0.53054	0.53170	0.53286	0.53402
0.510	53518	53635	53751	53868	53984	54101	54217	54334	54451	54568
0.520	54685	54802	54919	55037	55154	55272	55389	55507	55624	55742
0.530	55860	55978	56096	56214	56332	56451	56569	56688	56806	56925
0.540	57044	57163	57282	57401	57520	57639	57758	57878	57997	58117
0.550	0.58236	0.58356	0.58476	0.58596	0.58716	0.58836	0.58957	0.59077	0.59197	0.59318
0.560	59439	59559	59680	59801	59922	60043	60165	60286	60407	60529
0.570	60651	60772	60894	61016	61138	61260	61383	61505	61628	61750
0.580	61873	61996	62119	62242	62365	62488	62611	62735	62858	62982
0.590	63106	63230	63354	63478	63602	63727	63851	63976	64100	64225
0.600	0.64350	0.64475	0.64600	0.64726	0.64851	0.64977	0.65102	0.65228	0.65354	0.65480
0.610	65606	65732	65859	65985	66112	66239	66365	66492	66620	66747
0.620	66874	67002	67129	67257	67385	67513	67641	67770	67898	68027
0.630	68155	68284	68413	68542	68671	68801	68930	69060	69190	69320
0.640	69450	69580	69710	69841	69972	70102	70233	70364	70496	70627
0.650	0.70758	0.70890	0.71022	0.71154	0.71286	0.71418	0.71551	0.71683	0.71816	0.71949
0.660	72082	72215	72348	72482	72616	72749	72883	73017	73152	73286
0.670	73421	73556	73691	73826	73961	74096	74232	74368	74504	74640
0.680	74776	74913	75049	75186	75323	75460	75598	75735	75873	76011
0.690	76149	76287	76426	76564	76703	76842	76981	77121	77260	77400
0.700	0.77540	0.77680	0.77820	0.77961	0.78101	0.78242	0.78383	0.78525	0.78666	0.78808
0.710	78950	79092	79234	79377	79519	79662	79806	79949	80092	80236
0.720	80380	80524	80669	80813	80958	81103	81249	81394	81540	81686
0.730	81832	81979	82125	82272	82419	82567	82714	82862	83010	83158
0.740	83307	83456	83605	83754	83904	84053	84204	84354	84504	84655
0.750	0.84806	0.84958	0.85109	0.85261	0.85413	0.85565	0.85718	0.85871	0.86024	0.86178
0.760	86331	86485	86640	86794	86949	87104	87260	87415	87571	87728
0.770	87884	88041	88198	88356	88513	88672	88830	88989	89148	89307
0.780	89467	89627	89787	89947	90108	90270	90431	90593	90755	90918
0.790	91081	91244	91408	91572	91736	91901	92066	92231	92397	92563
0.800	0.92730	0.92896	0.93064	0.93231	0.93399	0.93568	0.93736	0.93905	0.94075	0.94245
0.810	94415	94586	94757	94929	95101	95273	95446	95619	95793	95967
0.820	96141	96316	96491	96667	96843	97020	97197	97375	97553	97732
0.830	97911	98090	98270	98451	98632	98813	98995	99178	99361	99544
0.840	99728	99913	1.00098	1.00284	1.00470	1.00657	1.00844	1.01032	1.01220	1.01409
0.850	1.01599	1.01789	1.01979	1.02171	1.02363	1.02555	1.02748	1.02942	1.03136	1.03331
0.860	03527	03723	03920	04118	04316	04515	04715	04915	05116	05318
0.870	05520	05723	05927	06132	06337	06544	06751	06958	07167	07376
0.880	07586	07797	08009	08222	08435	08649	08865	09081	09298	09516
0.890	09735	09954	10175	10397	10619	10843	11068	11294	11520	11748
0.900	1.11977	1.12207	1.12438	1.12670	1.12903	1.13138	1.13374	1.13610	1.13849	1.14088
0.910	14328	14570	14813	15058	15304	15551	15799	16049	16301	16554
0.920	16808	17064	17321	17581	17841	18104	18368	18633	18901	19170
0.930	19441	19714	19989	20266	20545	20826	21109	21394	21681	21971
0.940	22263	22557	22854	23153	23455	23759	24067	24376	24689	25005
0.950	1.25324	1.25645	1.25970	1.26299	1.26631	1.26966	1.27305	1.27648	1.27994	1.28345
0.960	28700	29060	29423	29792	30166	30544	30928	31318	31713	32115
0.970	32523	32938	33360	33789	34226	34672	35127	35591	36065	36550
0.980	37046	37555	38077	38614	39167	39737	40327	40938	41572	42234
0.990	42926	43653	44422	45241	46120	47075	48132	49332	50754	52607
1.000	1.57080									

[1] Abridged from National Bureau of Standards, *Tables of Arc Sin X*, Columbia University Press, New York, 1945, by kind permission of the authors and publishers.

Common Logarithms* of the Binomial Coefficients *C* and Their Reciprocals *N* = 2 — 33

For explanation see page 77

Exponent of $p(q)$	Exponent of $q(p)$	log *C*	log 1/*C*
N = 2			
0	2	0.00000	0 00000
1	1	0.30103	1 69897
N = 3			
0	3	0.00000	0 00000
1	2	0.47712	1 52288
N = 4			
0	4	0.00000	0 00000
1	3	0.60206	1 39794
2	2	0.77815	1 22185
N = 5			
0	5	0.00000	0 00000
1	4	0.69897	1 30103
2	3	1.00000	2 00000
N = 6			
0	6	0.00000	0 00000
1	5	0.77815	1 22185
2	4	1.17609	2 82391
3	3	1.30103	2 69897
N = 7			
0	7	0.00000	0 00000
1	6	0.84510	1 15490
2	5	1.32222	2 67778
3	4	1.54407	2 45593
N = 8			
0	8	0.00000	0 00000
1	7	0.90309	1 09691
2	6	1.44716	2 55284
3	5	1.74819	2 25181
4	4	1.84510	2 15490
N = 9			
0	9	0.00000	0 00000
1	8	0.95424	1 04576
2	7	1.55630	2 44370
3	6	1.92428	2 07572
4	5	2.10037	3 89963
N = 10			
0	10	0.00000	0 00000
1	9	1.00000	2 00000
2	8	1.65321	2 34679
3	7	2.07918	3 92082
4	6	2.32222	3 67778
5	5	2.40140	3 59860
N = 11			
0	11	0.00000	0 00000
1	10	1.04139	2 95861
2	9	1.74036	2 25964
3	8	2.21748	3 78252
4	7	2.51851	3 48149
5	6	2.66464	3 33536
N = 12			
0	12	0.00000	0 00000
1	11	1.07918	2 92082
2	10	1.81954	2 18046
3	9	2.34242	3 65758
4	8	2.69461	3 30539
5	7	2.89873	3 10127
6	6	2.96567	3 03433
N = 13			
0	13	0.00000	0 00000
1	12	1.11394	2 88606
2	11	1.89209	2 10791
3	10	2.45637	3 54363
4	9	2.85431	3 14569
5	8	3.10958	4 89042
6	7	3.23452	4 76548
N = 14			
0	14	0.00000	0 00000
1	13	1.14613	2 85387
2	12	1.95904	2 04096
3	11	2.56110	3 43890
4	10	3.00043	4 99957
5	9	3.30146	4 69854
6	8	3.47756	4 52244
7	7	3.53555	4 46445

Exponent of $p(q)$	Exponent of $q(p)$	log *C*	log 1/*C*
N = 15			
0	15	0.00000	0 00000
1	14	1.17609	2 82391
2	13	2.02119	3 97881
3	12	2.65801	3 34199
4	11	3.13513	4 86487
5	10	3.47756	4 52244
6	9	3.69940	4 30060
7	8	3.80855	4 19145
N = 16			
0	16	0.00000	0 00000
1	15	1.20412	2 79588
2	14	2.07918	3 92082
3	13	2.74819	3 25181
4	12	3.26007	4 73993
5	11	3.64028	4 35972
6	10	3.90352	4 09648
7	9	4.05843	5 94157
8	8	4.10958	5 89042
N = 17			
0	17	0.00000	0 00000
1	16	1.23045	2 76955
2	15	2.13354	3 86646
3	14	2.83251	3 16749
4	13	3.37658	4 62342
5	12	3.79155	4 20845
6	11	4.09258	5 90742
7	10	4.28887	5 71113
8	9	4.38578	5 61422
N = 18			
0	18	0.00000	0 00000
1	17	1.25527	2 74473
2	16	2.18469	3 81531
3	15	2.91169	3 08831
4	14	3.48572	4 51428
5	13	3.93288	4 06712
6	12	4.26867	5 73133
7	11	4.50275	5 49725
8	10	4.64106	5 35894
9	9	4.68681	5 31319
N = 19			
0	19	0.00000	0 00000
1	18	1.27875	2 72125
2	17	2.23300	3 76700
3	16	2.98632	3 01368
4	15	3.58838	4 41162
5	14	4.06551	5 93449
6	13	4.43348	5 56652
7	12	4.70233	5 29767
8	11	4.87842	5 12158
9	10	4.96557	5 03443
N = 20			
0	20	0.00000	0 00000
1	19	1.30103	2 69897
2	18	2.27875	3 72125
3	17	3.05690	4 94310
4	16	3.68529	4 31471
5	15	4.19044	5 80956
6	14	4.58838	5 41162
7	13	4.88941	5 11059
8	12	5.10027	6 89973
9	11	5.22521	6 77479
10	10	5.26660	6 73340
N = 21			
0	21	0.00000	0 00000
1	20	1.32222	2 67778
2	19	2.32222	3 67778
3	18	3.12385	4 87615
4	17	3.77706	4 22294
5	16	4.30854	5 69146
6	15	4.73451	5 26549
7	14	5.06551	6 93449
8	13	5.30854	6 69146
9	12	5.46824	6 53176
10	11	5.54743	6 45257
N = 22			
0	22	0.00000	0 00000
1	21	1.34242	2 65758
2	20	2.36361	3 63639
3	19	3.18752	4 81248
4	18	3.86421	4 13579
5	17	4.42052	5 57948
6	16	4.87281	5 12719
7	15	5.23184	6 76816

Exponent of $p(q)$	Exponent of $q(p)$	log *C*	log 1/*C*
N = 22 (continued)			
8	14	5.50484	6 49516
9	13	5.69672	6 30328
10	12	5.81067	6 18933
11	11	5.84846	6 15154
N = 23			
0	23	0.00000	0 00000
1	22	1.36173	2 63827
2	21	2.40312	3 59688
3	20	3.24822	4 75178
4	19	3.94719	4 05281
5	18	4.52697	5 47303
6	17	5.00409	6 99591
7	16	5.38944	6 61056
8	15	5.69047	6 30953
9	14	5.91232	6 08768
10	13	6.05845	7 94155
11	12	6.13100	7 86900
N = 24			
0	24	0.00000	0 00000
1	23	1.38021	2 61979
2	22	2.44091	3 55909
3	21	3.30621	4 69379
4	20	4.02637	5 97363
5	19	4.62843	5 37157
6	18	5.12903	6 87097
7	17	5.53921	6 46079
8	16	5.86657	6 13343
9	15	6.11644	7 88356
10	14	6.29253	7 70747
11	13	6.39727	7 60273
12	12	6.43203	7 56797
N = 25			
0	25	0.00000	0 00000
1	24	1.39794	2 60206
2	23	2.47712	3 52288
3	22	3.36173	4 63827
4	21	4.10209	5 89791
5	20	4.72534	5 27466
6	19	5.24822	6 75178
7	18	5.68187	6 31813
8	17	6.03406	7 96594
9	16	6.31026	7 68974
10	15	6.51438	7 48562
11	14	6.64908	7 35092
12	13	6.71603	7 28397
N = 26			
0	26	0.00000	0 00000
1	25	1.41497	2 58503
2	24	2.51188	3 48812
3	23	3.41497	4 58503
4	22	4.17464	5 82536
5	21	4.81809	5 18191
6	20	5.36216	6 63784
7	19	5.81809	6 18191
8	18	6.19376	7 80624
9	17	6.49479	7 50521
10	16	6.72524	7 27476
11	15	6.88796	7 11204
12	14	6.98487	7 01513
13	13	7.01706	8 98294
N = 27			
0	27	0.00000	0 00000
1	26	1.43136	2 56864
2	25	2.54531	3 45469
3	24	3.46613	4 53387
4	23	4.24428	5 75572
5	22	4.90703	5 09297
6	21	5.47131	6 52869
7	20	5.94843	6 05157
8	19	6.34637	7 65363
9	18	6.67088	7 32912
10	17	6.92615	7 07385
11	16	7.11521	8 88479
12	15	7.24015	8 75985
13	14	7.30229	8 69771
N = 28			
0	28	0.00000	0 00000
1	27	1.44716	2 55284
2	26	2.57749	3 42251
3	25	3.51534	4 48466
4	24	4.31122	5 68878
5	23	4.99247	5 00753
6	22	5.57604	6 42396
7	21	6.07337	7 92663

Exponent of $p(q)$	Exponent of $q(p)$	log *C*	log 1/*C*
N = 28 (continued)			
8	20	6.49250	7 50750
9	19	6.83928	7 16072
10	18	7.11804	8 88196
11	17	7.33192	8 66808
12	16	7.48318	8 51682
13	15	7.57336	8 42664
14	14	7.60332	8 39668
N = 29			
0	29	0.00000	0 00000
1	28	1.46240	2 53760
2	27	2.60853	3 39147
3	26	3.56277	4 43723
4	25	4.37568	5 62432
5	24	5.07465	6 92535
6	23	5.67671	6 32329
7	22	6.19334	7 80666
8	21	6.63267	7 36733
9	20	7.00065	8 99935
10	19	7.30168	8 69832
11	18	7.53904	8 46096
12	17	7.71513	8 28487
13	16	7.83164	8 16836
14	15	7.88963	8 11037
N = 30			
0	30	0.00000	0 00000
1	29	1.47712	2 52288
2	28	2.63849	3 36151
3	27	3.60853	4 39147
4	26	4.43783	5 56217
5	25	5.15383	6 84617
6	24	5.77362	6 22638
7	23	6.30874	7 69126
8	22	6.76737	7 23263
9	21	7.15555	8 84445
10	20	7.47777	8 52223
11	19	7.73741	8 26259
12	18	7.93698	8 06302
13	17	8.07831	9 92169
14	16	8.16263	9 83737
15	15	8.19066	9 80934
N = 31			
0	31	0.00000	0 00000
1	30	1.49136	2 50864
2	29	2.66745	3 33255
3	28	3.65273	4 34727
4	27	4.49783	5 50217
5	26	5.23022	6 76978
6	25	5.86704	6 13296
7	24	6.41989	7 58011
8	23	6.89701	7 10299
9	22	7.30449	8 69551
10	21	7.64691	8 35309
11	20	7.92774	8 07226
12	19	8.14959	9 85041
13	18	8.31440	9 68560
14	17	8.42354	9 57646
15	16	8.47790	9 52210
N = 32			
0	32	0.00000	0 00000
1	31	1.50515	2 49485
2	30	2.69548	3 30452
3	29	3.69548	4 30452
4	28	4.55582	5 44418
5	27	5.30401	6 69599
6	26	5.95722	6 04278
7	25	6.52710	7 47290
8	24	7.02195	8 97805
9	23	7.44791	8 55209
10	22	7.80964	8 19036
11	21	8.11067	9 88933
12	20	8.35371	9 64629
13	19	8.54080	9 45920
14	18	8.67342	9 32658
15	17	8.75260	9 24740
16	16	8.77893	9 22107
N = 33			
0	33	0.00000	0 00000
1	32	1.51851	2 48149
2	31	2.72263	3 27737
3	30	3.73687	4 26313
4	29	4.61194	5 38806
5	28	5.37536	6 62464
6	27	6.04437	7 95563
7	26	6.63064	7 36936
8	25	7.14252	8 85748
9	24	7.58622	8 41378

Common Logarithms* of the Binomial Coefficients C and Their Reciprocals N = 33 — 49

For explanation see page 77

Exponent of $p(q)$	Exponent of $q(p)$	log C	log $1/C$
	$N = 33$ (continued)		
10	23	7.96643	8 03357
11	22	8.28676	9 71324
12	21	8.55000	9 45000
13	20	8.75828	9 24172
14	19	8.91318	9 08682
15	18	9.01585	10 98415
16	17	9.06700	10 93300
	$N = 34$		
0	34	0.00000	0 00000
1	33	1.53148	2 46852
2	32	2.74896	3 25104
3	31	3.77699	4 22301
4	30	4.66629	5 33371
5	29	5.44444	6 55556
6	28	6.12869	7 87131
7	27	6.73075	7 26925
8	26	7.25903	8 74097
9	25	7.71976	8 28024
10	24	8.11770	9 88230
11	23	8.45651	9 54349
12	22	8.73906	9 26094
13	21	8.96754	9 03246
14	20	9.14363	10 85637
15	19	9.26857	10 73143
16	18	9.34320	10 65680
17	17	9.36803	10 63197
	$N = 35$		
0	35	0.00000	0 00000
1	34	1.54407	2 45593
2	33	2.77452	3 22548
3	32	3.81591	4 18409
4	31	4.71900	5 28100
5	30	5.51139	6 48861
6	29	6.21036	7 78964
7	28	6.82766	7 17234
8	27	7.37173	8 62827
9	26	7.84885	8 15115
10	25	8.26382	9 73618
11	24	8.62037	9 37963
12	23	8.92140	9 07860
13	22	9.16919	10 83081
14	21	9.36548	10 63452
15	20	9.51161	10 48839
16	19	9.60852	10 39148
17	18	9.65682	10 34318
	$N = 36$		
0	36	0.00000	0 00000
1	35	1.55630	2 44370
2	34	2.79934	3 20066
3	33	3.85370	4 14630
4	32	4.77015	5 22985
5	31	5.57633	6 42367
6	30	6.28954	7 71046
7	29	6.92157	7 07843
8	28	7.48087	8 51913
9	27	7.97379	8 02621
10	26	8.40515	9 59485
11	25	8.77873	9 22127
12	24	9.09749	10 90251
13	23	9.36376	10 63624
14	22	9.57936	10 42064
15	21	9.74569	10 25431
16	20	9.86379	10 13621
17	19	9.93437	10 06563
18	18	9.95785	10 04215
	$N = 37$		
0	37	0.00000	0 00000
1	36	1.56820	2 43180
2	35	2.82347	3 17653
3	34	3.89042	4 10958
4	33	4.81984	5 18016
5	32	5.63938	6 36062
6	31	6.36638	7 63362
7	30	7.01265	8 98735
8	29	7.58668	8 41332
9	28	8.09483	9 90517
10	27	8.54199	9 45801
11	26	8.93196	9 06804
12	25	9.26775	10 73225
13	24	9.55175	10 44825
14	23	9.78583	10 21417
15	22	9.97147	10 02853
16	21	10.10977	11 89023
17	20	10.20154	11 79846
18	19	10.24730	11 75270
	$N = 38$		
0	38	0.00000	0 00000
1	37	1.57978	2 42022
2	36	2.84696	3 15304
3	35	3.92614	4 07386
4	34	4.86814	5 13186
5	33	5.70065	6 29935
6	32	6.44102	7 55898
7	31	7.10107	8 89893
8	30	7.68934	8 31066
9	29	8.21222	9 78778
10	28	8.67462	9 32538
11	27	9.08038	10 91962
12	26	9.43256	10 56744
13	25	9.73359	10 26641
14	24	9.98541	10 01459
15	23	10.18953	11 81047
16	22	10.34713	11 65287
17	21	10.45911	11 54089
18	20	10.52605	11 47395
19	19	10.54833	11 45167
	$N = 39$		
0	39	0.00000	0 00000
1	38	1.59106	2 40894
2	37	2.86982	3 13018
3	36	3.96090	4 03910
4	35	4.91514	5 08486
5	34	5.76024	6 23976
6	33	6.51357	7 48643
7	32	7.18698	8 81302
8	31	7.78904	8 21096
9	30	8.32616	9 67384
10	29	8.80328	9 19672
11	28	9.22429	10 77571
12	27	9.59227	10 40773
13	26	9.90969	10 09031
14	25	10.17853	11 82147
15	24	10.40038	11 59962
16	23	10.57647	11 42353
17	22	10.70775	11 29225
18	21	10.79490	11 20510
19	20	10.83837	11 16163
	$N = 40$		
0	40	0.00000	0 00000
1	39	1.60206	2 39794
2	38	2.89209	3 10791
3	37	3.99476	4 00524
4	36	4.96090	5 03910
5	35	5.81823	6 18177
6	34	6.58415	7 41585
7	33	7.27053	8 72947
8	32	7.88595	8 11405
9	31	8.43686	9 56314
10	30	8.92822	9 07178
11	29	9.36395	10 63605
12	28	9.74717	10 25283
13	27	10.08038	11 91962
14	26	10.36562	11 63438
15	25	10.60450	11 39550
16	24	10.79832	11 20168
17	23	10.94808	11 05192
18	22	11.05454	12 94546
19	21	11.11821	12 88179
20	20	11.13940	12 86060
	$N = 41$		
0	41	0.00000	0 00000
1	40	1.61278	2 38722
2	39	2.91381	3 08619
3	38	4.02776	5 97224
4	37	5.00548	6 99452
5	36	5.87471	6 12529
6	35	6.65286	7 34714
7	34	7.35183	8 64817
8	33	7.98022	8 01978
9	32	8.54449	9 45551
10	31	9.04964	10 95036
11	30	9.49961	10 50039
12	29	9.89755	10 10245
13	28	10.24601	11 75399
14	27	10.54704	11 45296
15	26	10.80231	11 19769
16	25	11.01316	12 98684
17	24	11.18065	12 81935
18	23	11.30559	12 69441
19	22	11.38857	12 61143
20	21	11.42996	12 57004
	$N = 42$		
0	42	0.00000	0 00000
1	41	1.62325	2 37675
2	40	2.93500	3 06500
3	39	4.05994	5 94006
4	38	5.04895	6 95105
5	37	5.92976	6 07024
6	36	6.71981	7 28019
7	35	7.43102	8 56898
8	34	8.07199	9 92801
9	33	8.64923	9 35077
10	32	9.16774	10 83226
11	31	9.63150	10 36850
12	30	10.04368	11 95632
13	29	10.40686	11 59314
14	28	10.72313	11 27687
15	27	10.99420	11 00580
16	26	11.22144	12 77856
17	25	11.40596	12 59404
18	24	11.54863	12 45137
19	23	11.65009	12 34991
20	22	11.71079	12 28921
21	21	11.73099	12 26901
	$N = 43$		
0	43	0.00000	0 00000
1	42	1.63347	2 36653
2	41	2.95569	3 04431
3	40	4.09135	5 90865
4	39	5.09135	6 90865
5	38	5.98344	6 01656
6	37	6.78508	7 21492
7	36	7.50818	8 49182
8	35	8.16139	9 83861
9	34	8.75122	9 24878
10	33	9.28270	10 71730
11	32	9.75982	10 24018
12	31	10.18579	11 81421
13	30	10.56321	11 43679
14	29	10.89420	11 10580
15	28	11.18051	12 81949
16	27	11.42354	12 57646
17	26	11.62446	12 37554
18	25	11.78416	12 21584
19	24	11.90335	12 09665
20	23	11.98253	12 01747
21	22	12.02204	13 97796
	$N = 44$		
0	44	0.00000	0 00000
1	43	1.64345	2 35655
2	42	2.97589	3 02411
3	41	4.12202	5 87798
4	40	5.13274	6 86726
5	39	6.03583	7 96417
6	38	6.84875	7 15125
7	37	7.58343	8 41657
8	36	8.24854	9 75146
9	35	8.85060	9 14940
10	34	9.39467	10 60533
11	33	9.88476	10 11524
12	32	10.32409	11 67591
13	31	10.71530	11 28470
14	30	11.06053	12 93947
15	29	11.36156	12 63844
16	28	11.61984	12 38016
17	27	11.83655	12 16345
18	26	12.01264	13 98736
19	25	12.14886	13 85114
20	24	12.24577	13 75423
21	23	12.30376	13 69624
22	22	12.32307	13 67693
	$N = 45$		
0	45	0.00000	0 00000
1	44	1.65321	2 34679
2	43	2.99564	3 00436
3	42	4.15198	5 84802
4	41	5.17317	6 82683
5	40	6.08699	7 91301
6	39	6.91089	7 08911
7	38	7.65686	8 34314
8	37	8.33355	9 66645
9	36	8.94751	9 05249
10	35	9.50382	10 49618
11	34	10.00649	11 99351
12	33	10.45879	11 54121
13	32	10.86336	11 13664
14	31	11.22238	12 77762
15	30	11.53765	12 46235
16	29	11.81065	12 18935
17	28	12.04260	13 95740
18	27	12.23449	13 76551
19	26	12.38710	13 61290
20	25	12.50104	13 49896
21	24	12.57676	13 42324
22	23	12.61455	13 38545
	$N = 46$		
0	46	0.00000	0 00000
1	45	1.66276	2 33724
2	44	3.01494	4 98506
3	43	4.18127	5 81873
4	42	5.21268	6 78732
5	41	6.13696	7 86304
6	40	6.97159	7 02841
7	39	7.72855	8 27145
8	38	8.41653	9 58347
9	37	9.04207	10 95793
10	36	9.61027	10 38973
11	35	10.12518	11 87482
12	34	10.59007	11 40993
13	33	11.00760	12 99240
14	32	11.37999	12 62001
15	31	11.70905	12 29095
16	30	11.99629	12 00371
17	29	12.24296	13 75704
18	28	12.45009	13 54991
19	27	12.61849	13 38151
20	26	12.74883	13 25117
21	25	12.84158	13 15842
22	24	12.89710	13 10290
23	23	12.91558	13 08442
	$N = 47$		
0	47	0.00000	0 00000
1	46	1.67210	2 32790
2	45	3.03383	4 96617
3	44	4.20992	5 79008
4	43	5.25131	6 74869
5	42	6.18581	7 81419
6	41	7.03091	8 96909
7	40	7.79859	8 20141
8	39	8.49756	9 50244
9	38	9.13438	10 86562
10	37	9.71417	10 28583
11	36	10.24098	11 75902
12	35	10.71810	11 28190
13	34	11.14822	12 85178
14	33	11.53357	12 46643
15	32	11.87600	12 12400
16	31	12.17703	13 82297
17	30	12.43794	13 56206
18	29	12.65979	13 34021
19	28	12.84343	13 15657
20	27	12.98956	13 01044
21	26	13.09870	14 90130
22	25	13.17126	14 82874
23	24	13.20747	14 79253
	$N = 48$		
0	48	0.00000	0 00000
1	47	1.68124	2 31876
2	46	3.05231	4 94769
3	45	4.23795	5 76205
4	44	5.28910	6 71090
5	43	6.23358	7 76642
6	42	7.08890	8 91110
7	41	7.86705	8 13295
8	40	8.57674	9 42326
9	39	9.22456	10 77544
10	38	9.81563	10 18437
11	37	10.35402	11 64598
12	36	10.84304	11 15696
13	35	11.28540	12 71460
14	34	11.68334	12 31666
15	33	12.03872	13 96128
16	32	12.35312	13 64688
17	31	12.62782	13 37218
18	30	12.86391	13 13609
19	29	13.06228	14 93772
20	28	13.22364	14 77636
21	27	13.34858	14 65142
22	26	13.43752	14 56248
23	25	13.49077	14 50923
24	24	13.50850	14 49150
	$N = 49$		
0	49	0.00000	0 00000
1	48	1.69020	2 30980
2	47	3.07041	4 92959
3	46	4.26538	5 73462
4	45	5.32608	6 67392
5	44	6.28032	7 71968
6	43	7.14563	8 85437
7	42	7.93400	8 06600
8	41	8.65416	9 34584
9	40	9.31270	10 68730
10	39	9.91476	10 08524
11	38	10.46443	11 53557
12	37	10.96503	11 03497
13	36	11.41929	12 58071
14	35	11.82946	12 17054

Common Logarithms* of the Binomial Coefficients C and Their Reciprocals $N = 49 - 61$

For explanation see page 77

N = 49 (continued)

Exponent of p(q)	q(p)	log C	log 1/C
15	34	12.19744	13 80256
16	33	12.52480	13 47520
17	32	12.81286	13 18714
18	31	13.06274	14 93726
19	30	13.27535	14 72465
20	29	13.45144	14 54856
21	28	13.59162	14 40838
22	27	13.69636	14 30364
23	26	13.76599	14 23401
24	25	13.80075	14 19925

N = 50

Exponent of p(q)	q(p)	log C	log 1/C
0	50	0.00000	0 00000
1	49	1.69897	2 30103
2	48	3.08814	4 91186
3	47	4.29226	5 70774
4	46	5.36229	6 63771
5	45	6.32608	7 67392
6	44	7.20114	8 79886
7	43	7.99950	8 00050
8	42	8.72988	9 27012
9	41	9.39888	10 60112
10	40	10.01167	11 98833
11	39	10.57233	11 42767
12	38	11.08422	12 91578
13	37	11.55006	12 44994
14	36	11.97213	12 02787
15	35	12.35234	13 64766
16	34	12.69229	13 30771
17	33	12.99332	13 00668
18	32	13.25656	14 74344
19	31	13.48296	14 51704
20	30	13.67329	14 32671
21	29	13.82819	14 17181
22	28	13.94817	14 05183
23	27	14.03360	15 96640
24	26	14.08475	15 91525
25	25	14.10178	15 89822

N = 51

Exponent of p(q)	q(p)	log C	log 1/C
0	51	0.00000	0 00000
1	50	1.70757	2 29243
2	49	3.10551	4 89449
3	48	4.31859	5 68141
4	47	5.39777	6 60223
5	46	6.37089	7 62911
6	45	7.25550	8 74450
7	44	8.06362	9 93638
8	43	8.80398	9 19602
9	42	9.48320	10 51680
10	41	10.10645	11 89355
11	40	10.67784	11 32216
12	39	11.20072	12 79928
13	38	11.67784	12 32216
14	37	12.11150	13 88850
15	36	12.50361	13 49639
16	35	12.85579	13 14421
17	34	13.16941	14 83059
18	33	13.44562	14 55438
19	32	13.68538	14 31462
20	31	13.88950	14 11050
21	30	14.05864	15 94136
22	29	14.19334	15 80666
23	28	14.29401	15 70599
24	27	14.36096	15 63904
25	26	14.39438	15 60562

N = 52

Exponent of p(q)	q(p)	log C	log 1/C
0	52	0.00000	0 00000
1	51	1.71600	2 28400
2	50	3.12254	4 87746
3	49	4.34439	5 65561
4	48	5.43253	6 56747
5	47	6.41480	7 58520
6	46	7.30875	8 69125
7	45	8.12641	9 87359
8	44	8.87653	9 12347
9	43	9.56574	10 43426
10	42	10.19921	11 80079
11	41	10.78106	11 21894
12	40	11.31467	12 68533
13	39	11.80278	12 19722
14	38	12.24772	13 75228
15	37	12.65141	13 34859
16	36	13.01549	14 98451
17	35	13.34135	14 65865
18	34	13.63014	14 36986
19	33	13.88287	14 11713
20	32	14.10035	15 89965
21	31	14.28328	15 71672
22	30	14.43222	15 56778
23	29	14.54762	15 45238
24	28	14.62980	15 37020

N = 52 (continued)

Exponent of p(q)	q(p)	log C	log 1/C
25	27	14.67902	15 32098
26	26	14.69541	15 30459

N = 53

Exponent of p(q)	q(p)	log C	log 1/C
0	53	0.00000	0 00000
1	52	1.72428	2 27572
2	51	3.13925	4 86075
3	50	4.36970	5 63030
4	49	5.46661	6 53339
5	48	6.45783	7 54217
6	47	7.36092	8 63908
7	46	8.18792	9 81208
8	45	8.94759	9 05241
9	44	9.64656	10 35344
10	43	10.29001	11 70999
11	42	10.88209	11 11791
12	41	11.42616	12 57384
13	40	11.92500	12 07500
14	39	12.38093	13 61907
15	38	12.79590	13 20410
16	37	13.17157	14 82843
17	36	13.50932	14 49068
18	35	13.81035	14 18965
19	34	14.07567	15 92433
20	33	14.30611	15 69389
21	32	14.50241	15 49759
22	31	14.66514	15 33486
23	30	14.79477	15 20523
24	29	14.89168	15 10832
25	28	14.95614	15 04386
26	27	14.98832	15 01168

N = 54

Exponent of p(q)	q(p)	log C	log 1/C
0	54	0.00000	0 00000
1	53	1.73239	2 26761
2	52	3.15564	4 84436
3	51	4.39452	5 60548
4	50	5.50003	6 49997
5	49	6.50003	7 49997
6	48	7.41208	8 58792
7	47	8.24822	9 75178
8	46	9.01723	10 98277
9	45	9.72574	10 27426
10	44	10.37896	11 62104
11	43	10.98102	11 01898
12	42	11.53530	12 46470
13	41	12.04461	13 95539
14	40	12.51126	13 48874
15	39	12.93723	13 06277
16	38	13.32418	14 67582
17	37	13.67351	14 32649
18	36	13.98644	14 01356
19	35	14.26399	15 73601
20	34	14.50703	15 49297
21	33	14.71629	15 28371
22	32	14.89238	15 10762
23	31	15.03580	16 96420
24	30	15.14695	16 85305
25	29	15.22613	16 77387
26	28	15.27356	16 72644
27	27	15.28935	16 71065

N = 55

Exponent of p(q)	q(p)	log C	log 1/C
0	55	0.00000	0 00000
1	54	1.74036	2 25964
2	53	3.17173	4 82827
3	52	4.41888	5 58112
4	51	5.53282	6 46718
5	50	6.54142	7 45858
6	49	7.46224	8 53776
7	48	8.30734	9 69266
8	47	9.08549	10 91451
9	46	9.80335	10 19665
10	45	10.46611	11 53389
11	44	11.07793	12 92207
12	43	11.64220	12 35780
13	42	12.16172	13 83828
14	41	12.63884	13 36116
15	40	13.07554	14 92446
16	39	13.47348	14 52652
17	38	13.83409	14 16591
18	37	14.15860	15 84140
19	36	14.44805	15 55195
20	35	14.70332	15 29668
21	34	14.92517	15 07483
22	33	15.11423	16 88577
23	32	15.27101	16 72899
24	31	15.39595	16 60405
25	30	15.48937	16 51063
26	29	15.55152	16 44848
27	28	15.58256	16 41744

N = 56

Exponent of p(q)	q(p)	log C	log 1/C
0	56	0.00000	0 00000
1	55	1.74819	2 25181
2	54	3.18752	4 81248
3	53	4.44279	5 55721
4	52	5.56501	6 43499
5	51	6.58204	7 41796
6	50	7.51146	8 48854
7	49	8.36533	9 63467
8	48	9.15244	10 84756
9	47	9.87944	10 12056
10	46	10.55154	11 44846
11	45	11.17290	12 82710
12	44	11.74693	12 25307
13	43	12.27644	13 72356
14	42	12.76378	13 23622
15	41	13.21094	14 78906
16	40	13.61960	14 38040
17	39	13.99122	14 00878
18	38	14.32701	15 67299
19	37	14.62804	15 37196
20	36	14.89521	15 10479
21	35	15.12929	16 87071
22	34	15.33094	16 66906
23	33	15.50069	16 49931
24	32	15.63899	16 36101
25	31	15.74620	16 25380
26	30	15.82259	16 17741
27	29	15.86835	16 13165
28	28	15.88359	16 11641

N = 57

Exponent of p(q)	q(p)	log C	log 1/C
0	57	0.00000	0 00000
1	56	1.75587	2 24413
2	55	3.20303	4 79697
3	54	4.46627	5 53373
4	53	5.59661	6 40339
5	52	6.62191	7 37809
6	51	7.55977	8 44023
7	50	8.42224	9 57776
8	49	9.21812	10 78188
9	48	9.95407	10 04593
10	47	10.63531	11 36469
11	46	11.26602	12 73398
12	45	11.84959	12 15041
13	44	12.38886	13 61114
14	43	12.88619	13 11381
15	42	13.34357	14 65643
16	41	13.76270	14 23730
17	40	14.14503	15 85497
18	39	14.49182	15 50818
19	38	14.80413	15 19587
20	37	15.08288	16 91712
21	36	15.32886	16 67114
22	35	15.54274	16 45726
23	34	15.72508	16 27492
24	33	15.87635	16 12365
25	32	15.99693	16 00307
26	31	16.08710	17 91290
27	30	16.14710	17 85290
28	29	16.17706	17 82294

N = 58

Exponent of p(q)	q(p)	log C	log 1/C
0	58	0.00000	0 00000
1	57	1.76343	2 23657
2	56	3.21827	4 78173
3	55	4.48934	5 51066
4	54	5.62764	6 37236
5	53	6.66107	7 33893
6	52	7.60719	8 39281
7	51	8.47810	9 52190
8	50	9.28258	10 71742
9	49	10.02730	11 97270
10	48	10.71750	11 28250
11	47	11.35735	12 64265
12	46	11.95026	12 04974
13	45	12.49908	13 50092
14	44	13.00616	14 99384
15	43	13.47353	14 52647
16	42	13.90287	14 09713
17	41	14.29567	15 70433
18	40	14.65319	15 34681
19	39	14.97649	15 02351
20	38	15.26653	16 73347
21	37	15.52409	16 47591
22	36	15.74987	16 25013
23	35	15.94444	16 05556
24	34	16.10830	17 89170
25	33	16.24184	17 75816
26	32	16.34538	17 65462
27	31	16.41917	17 58083
28	30	16.46337	17 53663
29	29	16.47809	17 52191

N = 59

Exponent of p(q)	q(p)	log C	log 1/C
0	59	0.00000	0 00000
1	58	1.77085	2 22915
2	57	3.23325	4 76675
3	56	4.51200	5 48800
4	55	5.65813	6 34187
5	54	6.69952	7 30048
6	53	7.65377	8 34623
7	52	8.53294	9 46706
8	51	9.34586	10 65414
9	50	10.09919	11 90081
10	49	10.79816	11 20184
11	48	11.44696	12 55304
12	47	12.04902	13 95098
13	46	12.60717	13 39283
14	45	13.12380	14 87620
15	44	13.60092	14 39908
16	43	14.04026	15 95974
17	42	14.44328	15 55672
18	41	14.81125	15 18875
19	40	15.14528	16 85472
20	39	15.44631	16 55369
21	38	15.71516	16 28484
22	37	15.95252	16 04748
23	36	16.15899	17 84101
24	35	16.33509	17 66491
25	34	16.48121	17 51879
26	33	16.59772	17 40228
27	32	16.68487	17 31513
28	31	16.74286	17 25714
29	30	16.77182	17 22818

N = 60

Exponent of p(q)	q(p)	log C	log 1/C
0	60	0.00000	0 00000
1	59	1.77815	2 22185
2	58	3.24797	4 75203
3	57	4.53428	5 46572
4	56	5.68809	6 31191
5	55	6.73731	7 26269
6	54	7.69952	8 30048
7	53	8.58682	9 41318
8	52	9.40801	10 59199
9	51	10.16977	11 83023
10	50	10.87734	11 12266
11	49	11.53491	12 46509
12	48	12.14593	13 85407
13	47	12.71323	13 28677
14	46	13.23920	14 76080
15	45	13.72586	14 27414
16	44	14.17496	15 82504
17	43	14.58796	15 41204
18	42	14.96616	15 03384
19	41	15.31065	16 68935
20	40	15.62241	16 37759
21	39	15.90225	16 09775
22	38	16.15089	17 84911
23	37	16.36894	17 63106
24	36	16.55693	17 44307
25	35	16.71530	17 28470
26	34	16.84439	17 15561
27	33	16.94451	17 05549
28	32	17.01586	18 98414
29	31	17.05861	18 94139
30	30	17.07285	18 92715

N = 61

Exponent of p(q)	q(p)	log C	log 1/C
0	61	0.00000	0 00000
1	60	1.78533	2 21467
2	59	3.26245	4 73755
3	58	4.55618	5 44382
4	57	5.71755	6 28245
5	56	6.77445	7 22555
6	55	7.74449	8 25551
7	54	8.63976	9 36024
8	53	9.46906	10 53094
9	52	10.23909	11 76091
10	51	10.95510	11 04490
11	50	11.62127	12 37873
12	49	12.24106	13 75894
13	48	12.81732	13 18268
14	47	13.35243	14 64757
15	46	13.84844	14 15156
16	45	14.30707	15 69293
17	44	14.72984	15 27016
18	43	15.11802	16 88198
19	42	15.47273	16 52727
20	41	15.79495	16 20505
21	40	16.08552	17 91448
22	39	16.34515	17 65485
23	38	16.57449	17 42551
24	37	16.77406	17 22594
25	36	16.94432	17 05568
26	35	17.08565	18 91435
27	34	17.19836	18 80164
28	33	17.28268	18 71732

Common Logarithms* of the Binomial Coefficients *C* and Their Reciprocals $N = 61 - 72$

For explanation see page 77

Exponent of p(q)	Exponent of q(p)	log C	log 1/C
N = 61 (continued)			
29	32	17.33879	18 66121
30	31	17.36682	18 63318
N = 62			
0	62	0.00000	0 00000
1	61	1.79239	2 20761
2	60	3.27669	4 72331
3	59	4.57772	5 42228
4	58	5.74651	6 25349
5	57	6.81097	7 18903
6	56	7.78870	8 21130
7	55	8.69179	9 30821
8	54	9.52906	10 47094
9	53	10.30721	11 69279
10	52	11.03148	12 96852
11	51	11.70610	12 29390
12	50	12.33448	13 66552
13	49	12.91951	13 08049
14	48	13.46358	14 53642
15	47	13.96873	14 03127
16	46	14.43671	15 56329
17	45	14.86902	15 13098
18	44	15.26696	16 73304
19	43	15.63166	16 36834
20	42	15.96409	16 03591
21	41	16.26512	17 73488
22	40	16.53548	17 46452
23	39	16.77582	17 22418
24	38	16.98667	17 01333
25	37	17.16851	18 83149
26	36	17.32174	18 67826
27	35	17.44668	18 55332
28	34	17.54359	18 45641
29	33	17.61267	18 38733
30	32	17.65406	18 34594
31	31	17.66785	18 33215
N = 63			
0	63	0.00000	0 00000
1	62	1.79934	2 20066
2	61	3.29070	4 70930
3	60	4.59891	5 40109
4	59	5.77500	6 22500
5	58	6.84688	7 15312
6	57	7.83216	8 16784
7	56	8.74294	9 25706
8	55	9.58804	10 41196
9	54	10.37416	11 62584
10	53	11.10655	12 89345
11	52	11.78943	12 21057
12	51	12.42625	13 57375
13	50	13.01988	14 98012
14	49	13.57272	14 42728
15	48	14.08683	15 91317
16	47	14.56395	15 43605
17	46	15.00560	16 99440
18	45	15.41308	16 58692
19	44	15.78754	16 21246
20	43	16.12997	17 87003
21	42	16.44121	17 55879
22	41	16.72204	17 27796
23	40	16.97310	17 02690
24	39	17.19495	18 80505
25	38	17.38807	18 61193
26	37	17.55288	18 44712
27	36	17.68972	18 31028
28	35	17.79886	18 20114
29	34	17.88053	18 11947
30	33	17.93489	18 06511
31	32	17.96204	18 03796
N = 64			
0	64	0.00000	0 00000
1	63	1.80618	2 19382
2	62	3.30449	4 69551
3	61	4.61976	5 38024
4	60	5.80303	6 19697
5	59	6.88221	7 11779
6	58	7.87491	8 12509
7	57	8.79324	9 20676
8	56	9.64603	10 35397
9	55	10.43997	11 56003
10	54	11.18034	12 81966
11	53	11.87134	12 12866
12	52	12.51643	13 48357
13	51	13.11849	14 88151
14	50	13.67993	14 32007
15	49	14.20281	15 79719
16	48	14.68889	15 31111
17	47	15.13968	16 86032
18	46	15.55651	16 44349
19	45	15.94051	16 05949
N = 64 (continued)			
20	44	16.29269	17 70731
21	43	16.61393	17 38607
22	42	16.90497	17 09503
23	41	17.16649	18 83351
24	40	17.39907	18 60093
25	39	17.60319	18 39681
26	38	17.77928	18 22072
27	37	17.92770	18 07230
28	36	18.04874	19 95126
29	35	18.14265	19 85735
30	34	18.20959	19 79041
31	33	18.24971	19 75029
32	32	18.26307	19 73693
N = 65			
0	65	0.00000	0 00000
1	64	1.81291	2 18709
2	63	3.31806	4 68194
3	62	4.64028	5 35972
4	61	5.83061	6 16939
5	60	6.91697	7 08303
6	59	7.91697	8 08303
7	58	8.84273	9 15727
8	57	9.70307	10 29693
9	56	10.50470	11 49530
10	55	11.25289	12 74711
11	54	11.95186	12 04814
12	53	12.60507	13 39493
13	52	13.21540	14 78460
14	51	13.78528	14 21472
15	50	14.31676	15 68324
16	49	14.81161	15 18839
17	48	15.27135	16 72865
18	47	15.69732	16 30268
19	46	16.09067	17 90933
20	45	16.45239	17 54761
21	44	16.78339	17 21661
22	43	17.08442	18 91558
23	42	17.35616	18 64384
24	41	17.59920	18 40080
25	40	17.81404	18 18596
26	39	18.00113	19 99887
27	38	18.16083	19 83917
28	37	18.29345	19 70655
29	36	18.39926	19 60074
30	35	18.47844	19 52156
31	34	18.53114	19 46886
32	33	18.55747	19 44253
N = 66			
0	66	0.00000	0 00000
1	65	1.81954	2 18046
2	64	3.33143	4 66857
3	63	4.66049	5 33951
4	62	5.85777	6 14223
5	61	6.95119	7 04881
6	60	7.95837	8 04163
7	59	8.89142	9 10858
8	58	9.75918	10 24082
9	57	10.56837	11 43163
10	56	11.32424	12 67576
11	55	12.03104	13 96896
12	54	12.69222	13 30778
13	53	13.31067	14 68933
14	52	13.88882	14 11118
15	51	14.42873	15 57127
16	50	14.93218	15 06782
17	49	15.40070	16 59930
18	48	15.83562	16 16438
19	47	16.23811	17 76189
20	46	16.60918	17 39082
21	45	16.94972	17 05028
22	44	17.26051	18 73949
23	43	17.54223	18 45777
24	42	17.79549	18 20451
25	41	18.02080	19 97920
26	40	18.21861	19 78139
27	39	18.38931	19 61069
28	38	18.53321	19 46679
29	37	18.65060	19 34940
30	36	18.74168	19 25832
31	35	18.80662	19 19338
32	34	18.84554	19 15446
33	33	18.85850	19 14150
N = 67			
0	67	0.00000	0 00000
1	66	1.82607	2 17393
2	65	3.34459	4 65541
3	64	4.68038	5 31962
4	63	5.88450	6 11550
5	62	6.98487	7 01513
6	61	7.99911	8 00089
N = 67 (continued)			
7	60	8.93934	9 06066
8	59	9.81440	10 18560
9	58	10.63101	11 36899
10	57	11.39444	12 60556
11	56	12.10892	13 89108
12	55	12.77793	13 22207
13	54	13.40435	14 59565
14	53	13.99062	14 00938
15	52	14.53880	15 46120
16	51	15.05068	16 94932
17	50	15.52781	16 47219
18	49	15.97150	16 02850
19	48	16.38295	17 61705
20	47	16.76316	17 23684
21	46	17.11304	18 88696
22	45	17.43337	18 56663
23	44	17.72486	18 27514
24	43	17.98810	18 01190
25	42	18.22363	19 77637
26	41	18.43190	19 56810
27	40	18.61332	19 38668
28	39	18.76822	19 23178
29	38	18.89689	19 10311
30	37	18.99955	19 00045
31	36	19.07639	20 92361
32	35	19.12754	20 87246
33	34	19.15310	20 84690
N = 68			
0	68	0.00000	0 00000
1	67	1.83251	2 16749
2	66	3.35755	4 64245
3	65	4.69998	5 30002
4	64	5.91083	6 08917
5	63	7.01804	8 98196
6	62	8.03923	9 96077
7	61	8.98652	9 01348
8	60	9.86876	10 13124
9	59	10.69267	11 30733
10	58	11.46352	12 53648
11	57	12.18556	13 81444
12	56	12.86225	13 13775
13	55	13.49650	14 50350
14	54	14.09073	15 90927
15	53	14.64703	15 35297
16	52	15.16719	16 83281
17	51	15.65274	16 34726
18	50	16.10504	17 89496
19	49	16.52526	17 47474
20	48	16.91442	17 08558
21	47	17.27345	18 72655
22	46	17.60312	18 39688
23	45	17.90415	18 09585
24	44	18.17715	19 82285
25	43	18.42267	19 57733
26	42	18.64116	19 35884
27	41	18.83305	19 16695
28	40	18.99867	19 00133
29	39	19.13833	20 86167
30	38	19.25228	20 74772
31	37	19.34070	20 65930
32	36	19.40375	20 59625
33	35	19.44154	20 55846
34	34	19.45413	20 54587
N = 69			
0	69	0.00000	0 00000
1	68	1.83885	2 16115
2	67	3.37033	4 62967
3	66	4.71928	5 28072
4	65	5.93677	6 06323
5	64	7.05071	8 94929
6	63	8.07874	9 92126
7	62	9.03298	10 96702
8	61	9.92228	10 07772
9	60	10.75337	11 24663
10	59	11.53152	12 46848
11	58	12.26098	13 73902
12	57	12.94523	13 05477
13	56	13.58716	14 41284
14	55	14.18922	15 81078
15	54	14.75349	15 24651
16	53	15.28176	16 71824
17	52	15.77559	16 22441
18	51	16.23632	17 76368
19	50	16.66514	17 33486
20	49	17.06308	18 93692
21	48	17.43105	18 56895
22	47	17.76987	18 23013
23	46	18.08024	19 91976
24	45	18.36279	19 63721
25	44	18.61806	19 38194
26	43	18.84654	19 15346
27	42	19.04865	20 95135
N = 69 (continued)			
28	41	19.22474	20 77526
29	40	19.37512	20 62488
30	39	19.50006	20 49994
31	38	19.59976	20 40024
32	37	19.67440	20 32560
33	36	19.72409	20 27591
34	35	19.74891	20 25109
N = 70			
0	70	0.00000	0 00000
1	69	1.84510	2 15490
2	68	3.38292	4 61708
3	67	4.73830	5 26170
4	66	5.96232	6 03768
5	65	7.08289	8 91711
6	64	8.11766	9 88234
7	63	9.07874	10 92126
8	62	9.97499	10 02501
9	61	10.81314	11 18686
10	60	11.59847	12 40153
11	59	12.33523	13 66477
12	58	13.02690	14 97310
13	57	13.67638	14 32362
14	56	14.28613	15 71387
15	55	14.85822	15 14178
16	54	15.39447	16 60553
17	53	15.89641	16 10359
18	52	16.36542	17 63458
19	51	16.80267	17 19733
20	50	17.20921	18 79079
21	49	17.58596	18 41404
22	48	17.93373	18 06627
23	47	18.25324	19 74676
24	46	18.54513	19 45487
25	45	18.80995	19 19005
26	44	19.04819	20 95181
27	43	19.26028	20 73972
28	42	19.44659	20 55341
29	41	19.60744	20 39256
30	40	19.74310	20 25690
31	39	19.85380	20 14620
32	38	19.93971	20 06029
33	37	20.00098	21 99902
34	36	20.03771	21 96229
35	35	20.04994	21 95006
N = 71			
0	71	0.00000	0 00000
1	70	1.85126	2 14874
2	69	3.39533	4 60467
3	68	4.75705	5 24295
4	67	5.98750	6 01250
5	66	7.11461	8 88539
6	65	8.15600	9 84400
7	64	9.12382	10 87618
8	63	10.02691	11 97309
9	62	10.87200	11 12800
10	61	11.66440	12 33560
11	60	12.40833	13 59167
12	59	13.10730	14 89270
13	58	13.76421	14 23579
14	57	14.38151	15 61849
15	56	14.96130	15 03870
16	55	15.50536	16 49464
17	54	16.01528	17 98472
18	53	16.49240	17 50760
19	52	16.93792	17 06208
20	51	17.35289	18 64711
21	50	17.73824	18 26176
22	49	18.09479	19 90521
23	48	18.42326	19 57674
24	47	18.72429	19 27571
25	46	18.99845	19 00155
26	45	19.24623	20 75377
27	44	19.46808	20 53192
28	43	19.66438	20 33562
29	42	19.83545	20 16455
30	41	19.98157	20 01843
31	40	20.10300	21 89700
32	39	20.19991	21 80009
33	38	20.27246	21 72754
34	37	20.32076	21 67924
35	36	20.34490	21 65510
N = 72			
0	72	0.00000	0 00000
1	71	1.85733	2 14267
2	70	3.40756	4 59244
3	69	4.77554	5 22446
4	68	6.01233	7 98767
5	67	7.14587	8 85413
6	66	8.19379	9 80621

Common Logarithms* of the Binomial Coefficients C and Their Reciprocals N = 72 — 81

For explanation see page 77

N = 72 (continued)

Exponent of p (q)	Exponent of q (p)	log C	log 1/C
7	65	9.16824	10 83176
8	64	10.07806	11 92194
9	63	10.93000	11 07000
10	62	11.72934	12 27066
11	61	12.48034	13 51966
12	60	13.18648	14 81352
13	59	13.85069	14 14931
14	58	14.47542	15 52458
15	57	15.06275	16 93725
16	56	15.61451	16 38549
17	55	16.13225	17 86775
18	54	16.61734	17 38266
19	53	17.07098	18 92902
20	52	17.49422	18 50578
21	51	17.88801	18 11199
22	50	18.25315	19 74685
23	49	18.59040	19 40960
24	48	18.90038	19 09962
25	47	19.18368	20 81632
26	46	19.44081	20 55919
27	45	19.67220	20 32780
28	44	19.87826	20 12174
29	43	20.05931	21 94069
30	42	20.21566	21 78434
31	41	20.34755	21 65245
32	40	20.45518	21 54482
33	39	20.53873	21 46127
34	38	20.59831	21 40169
35	37	20.63403	21 36597
36	36	20.64593	21 35407

N = 73

Exponent of p (q)	Exponent of q (p)	log C	log 1/C
0	73	0.00000	0 00000
1	72	1.86332	2 13668
2	71	3.41963	4 58037
3	70	4.79376	5 20624
4	69	6.03680	7 96320
5	68	7.17668	8 82332
6	67	8.23104	9 76896
7	66	9.21201	10 78799
8	65	10.12847	11 87153
9	64	10.98714	11 01286
10	63	11.79332	12 20668
11	62	12.55127	13 44873
12	61	13.26448	14 73552
13	60	13.93586	14 06414
14	59	14.56789	15 43211
15	58	15.16265	16 83735
16	57	15.72196	16 27804
17	56	16.24738	17 75262
18	55	16.74030	17 25970
19	54	17.20191	18 79809
20	53	17.63327	18 36673
21	52	18.03533	19 96467
22	51	18.40891	19 59109
23	50	18.75475	19 24525
24	49	19.07351	20 92649
25	48	19.36576	20 63424
26	47	19.63203	20 36797
27	46	19.87277	20 12723
28	45	20.08837	21 91163
29	44	20.27918	21 72082
30	43	20.44551	21 55449
31	42	20.58762	21 41238
32	41	20.70572	21 29428
33	40	20.79999	21 20001
34	39	20.87057	21 12943
35	38	20.91757	21 08243
36	37	20.94105	21 05895

N = 74

Exponent of p (q)	Exponent of q (p)	log C	log 1/C
0	74	0.00000	0 00000
1	73	1.86923	2 13077
2	72	3.43152	4 56848
3	71	4.81174	5 18826
4	70	6.06093	7 93907
5	69	7.20706	8 79294
6	68	8.26776	9 73224
7	67	9.25517	10 74483
8	66	10.17816	11 82184
9	65	11.04346	12 95654
10	64	11.85637	12 14363
11	63	12.62116	13 37884
12	62	13.34132	14 65868
13	61	14.01977	15 98023
14	60	14.65897	15 34103
15	59	15.26103	16 73897
16	58	15.82776	16 17224
17	57	16.36074	17 63926
18	56	16.86134	17 13866
19	55	17.33078	18 66922
20	54	17.77011	18 22989
21	53	18.18028	19 81972
22	52	18.56214	19 43786

N = 74 (continued)

Exponent of p (q)	Exponent of q (p)	log C	log 1/C
23	51	18.91641	19 08359
24	50	19.24377	20 75623
25	49	19.54480	20 45520
26	48	19.82002	20 17998
27	47	20.06990	21 93010
28	46	20.29484	21 70516
29	45	20.49520	21 50480
30	44	20.67129	21 32871
31	43	20.82338	21 17662
32	42	20.95170	21 04830
33	41	21.05644	22 94356
34	40	21.13774	22 86226
35	39	21.19573	22 80427
36	38	21.23049	22 76951
37	37	21.24208	22 75792

N = 75

Exponent of p (q)	Exponent of q (p)	log C	log 1/C
0	75	0.00000	0 00000
1	74	1.87506	2 12494
2	73	3.44326	4 55674
3	72	4.82946	5 17054
4	71	6.08474	7 91526
5	70	7.23703	8 76297
6	69	8.30397	9 69603
7	68	9.29772	10 70228
8	67	10.22714	11 77286
9	66	11.09897	12 90103
10	65	11.91852	12 08148
11	64	12.69004	13 30996
12	63	13.41704	14 58296
13	62	14.10244	15 89756
14	61	14.74870	15 25130
15	60	15.35794	16 64206
16	59	15.93197	16 06803
17	58	16.47237	17 52763
18	57	16.98053	17 01947
19	56	17.45765	18 54235
20	55	17.90481	18 09519
21	54	18.32295	19 67705
22	53	18.71292	19 28708
23	52	19.07547	20 92453
24	51	19.41126	20 58874
25	50	19.72089	20 27911
26	49	20.00489	21 99511
27	48	20.26372	21 73628
28	47	20.49780	21 50220
29	46	20.70750	21 29250
30	45	20.89314	21 10686
31	44	21.05499	22 94501
32	43	21.19329	22 80671
33	42	21.30825	22 69175
34	41	21.40002	22 59998
35	40	21.46873	22 53127
36	39	21.51449	22 48551
37	38	21.53735	22 46265

N = 76

Exponent of p (q)	Exponent of q (p)	log C	log 1/C
0	76	0.00000	0 00000
1	75	1.88081	2 11919
2	74	3.45484	4 54516
3	73	4.84696	5 15304
4	72	6.10822	7 89178
5	71	7.26658	8 73342
6	70	8.33969	9 66031
7	69	9.33969	10 66031
8	68	10.27545	11 72455
9	67	11.15371	12 84629
10	66	11.97979	12 02021
11	65	12.75794	13 24206
12	64	13.49167	14 50833
13	63	14.18391	15 81609
14	62	14.83712	15 16288
15	61	15.45342	16 54658
16	60	16.03463	17 96537
17	59	16.58233	17 41767
18	58	17.09791	18 90209
19	57	17.58259	18 41741
20	56	18.03743	19 96257
21	55	18.46340	19 53660
22	54	18.86134	19 13866
23	53	19.23201	20 76799
24	52	19.57607	20 42393
25	51	19.89413	20 10587
26	50	20.18673	21 81327
27	49	20.45434	21 54566
28	48	20.69738	21 30262
29	47	20.91622	21 08378
30	46	21.11120	22 88880
31	45	21.28259	22 71741
32	44	21.43065	22 56935
33	43	21.55559	22 44441
34	42	21.65758	22 34242
35	41	21.73676	22 26324
36	40	21.79325	22 20675

N = 76 (continued)

Exponent of p (q)	Exponent of q (p)	log C	log 1/C
37	39	21.82710	22 17290
38	38	21.83838	22 16162

N = 77

Exponent of p (q)	Exponent of q (p)	log C	log 1/C
0	77	0.00000	0 00000
1	76	1.88649	2 11351
2	75	3.46627	4 53373
3	74	4.86421	5 13579
4	73	6.13139	7 86861
5	72	7.29574	8 70426
6	71	8.37492	9 62508
7	70	9.38108	10 61892
8	69	10.32309	11 67691
9	68	11.20770	12 79230
10	67	12.04020	13 95980
11	66	12.82489	13 17511
12	65	13.56525	14 43475
13	64	14.26422	15 73578
14	63	14.92427	15 07573
15	62	15.54752	16 45248
16	61	16.13579	17 86421
17	60	16.69067	17 30933
18	59	17.21355	18 78645
19	58	17.70565	18 29435
20	57	18.16805	19 83195
21	56	18.60170	19 39830
22	55	19.00747	20 99253
23	54	19.38610	20 61390
24	53	19.73829	20 26171
25	52	20.06462	21 93538
26	51	20.36565	21 63435
27	50	20.64186	21 35814
28	49	20.89367	21 10633
29	48	21.12147	22 87853
30	47	21.32559	22 67441
31	46	21.50632	22 49368
32	45	21.66393	22 33607
33	44	21.79863	22 20137
34	43	21.91060	22 08940
35	42	22.00001	23 99999
36	41	22.06695	23 93305
37	40	22.11153	23 88847
38	39	22.13381	23 86619

N = 78

Exponent of p (q)	Exponent of q (p)	log C	log 1/C
0	78	0.00000	0 00000
1	77	1.89209	2 10791
2	76	3.47756	4 52244
3	75	4.88125	5 11875
4	74	6.15425	7 84575
5	73	7.32451	8 67549
6	72	8.40968	9 59032
7	71	9.42192	10 57808
8	70	10.37009	11 62991
9	69	11.26094	12 73906
10	68	12.09979	13 90021
11	67	12.89091	13 10909
12	66	13.63780	14 36220
13	65	14.34340	15 65660
14	64	15.01019	16 98981
15	63	15.64027	16 35973
16	62	16.23549	17 76451
17	61	16.79744	17 20256
18	60	17.32749	18 67251
19	59	17.82689	18 17311
20	58	18.29671	19 70329
21	57	18.73792	19 26208
22	56	19.15138	20 84862
23	55	19.53784	20 46216
24	54	19.89799	20 10201
25	53	20.23244	21 76756
26	52	20.54174	21 45826
27	51	20.82638	21 17362
28	50	21.08679	22 91321
29	49	21.32337	22 67663
30	48	21.53644	22 46356
31	47	21.72632	22 27368
32	46	21.89327	22 10673
33	45	22.03751	23 96249
34	44	22.15925	23 84075
35	43	22.25863	23 74137
36	42	22.33580	23 66420
37	41	22.39084	23 60916
38	40	22.42385	23 57615
39	39	22.43484	23 56516

N = 79

Exponent of p (q)	Exponent of q (p)	log C	log 1/C
0	79	0.00000	0 00000
1	78	1.89763	2 10237
2	77	3.48869	4 51131
3	76	4.89806	5 10194
4	75	6.17681	7 82319
5	74	7.35291	8 64709

N = 79 (continued)

Exponent of p (q)	Exponent of q (p)	log C	log 1/C
6	73	8.44399	9 55601
7	72	9.46221	10 53779
8	71	10.41645	11 58355
9	70	11.31347	12 68653
10	69	12.15857	13 84143
11	68	12.95602	13 04398
12	67	13.70935	14 29065
13	66	14.42148	15 57852
14	65	15.09490	16 90510
15	64	15.73172	16 26828
16	63	16.33378	17 66622
17	62	16.90267	17 09733
18	61	17.43979	18 56021
19	60	17.94637	18 05363
20	59	18.42349	19 57651
21	58	18.87212	19 12788
22	57	19.29313	20 70687
23	56	19.68727	20 31273
24	55	20.05525	21 94475
25	54	20.39767	21 60233
26	53	20.71509	21 28491
27	52	21.00801	22 99199
28	51	21.27685	22 72315
29	50	21.52202	22 47798
30	49	21.74387	22 25613
31	48	21.94271	22 05729
32	47	22.11880	23 88120
33	46	22.27238	23 72762
34	45	22.40366	23 59634
35	44	22.51281	23 48719
36	43	22.59996	23 40004
37	42	22.66522	23 33478
38	41	22.70869	23 29131
39	40	22.73041	23 26959

N = 80

Exponent of p (q)	Exponent of q (p)	log C	log 1/C
0	80	0.00000	0 00000
1	79	1.90309	2 09691
2	78	3.49969	4 50031
3	77	4.91466	5 08534
4	76	6.19909	7 80091
5	75	7.38093	8 61907
6	74	8.47784	9 52216
7	73	9.50198	10 49802
8	72	10.46221	11 53779
9	71	11.36530	12 63470
10	70	12.21656	13 78344
11	69	13.02027	14 97973
12	68	13.77993	14 22007
13	67	14.49850	15 50150
14	66	15.17845	16 82155
15	65	15.82190	16 17810
16	64	16.43069	17 56931
17	63	17.00642	18 99358
18	62	17.55049	18 44951
19	61	18.06413	19 93587
20	60	18.54843	19 45157
21	59	19.00436	20 99564
22	58	19.43279	20 56721
23	57	19.83449	20 16551
24	56	20.21015	21 78985
25	55	20.56040	21 43960
26	54	20.88579	21 11421
27	53	21.18682	22 81318
28	52	21.46394	22 53606
29	51	21.71754	22 28246
30	50	21.94799	22 05201
31	49	22.15560	23 84440
32	48	22.34065	23 65935
33	47	22.50337	23 49663
34	46	22.64399	23 35601
35	45	22.76268	23 23732
36	44	22.85959	23 14041
37	43	22.93484	23 06516
38	42	22.98853	23 01147
39	41	23.02071	24 97929
40	40	23.03144	24 96856

N = 81

Exponent of p (q)	Exponent of q (p)	log C	log 1/C
0	81	0.00000	0 00000
1	80	1.90849	2 09151
2	79	3.51055	4 48945
3	78	4.93105	5 06895
4	77	6.22109	7 77891
5	76	7.40861	8 59139
6	75	8.51127	9 48873
7	74	9.54123	10 45877
8	73	10.50737	11 49263
9	72	11.41645	12 58355
10	71	12.27379	13 72621
11	70	13.08365	14 91635
12	69	13.84957	14 15043
13	68	14.57447	15 42553
14	67	15.26086	16 73914

Common Logarithms* of the Binomial Coefficients C and Their Reciprocals N=81—89

For explanation see page 77

Exponent of p (q)	q (p)	log C	log 1/C
N = 81 (continued)			
15	66	15.91084	16 08916
16	65	16.52626	17 47374
17	64	17.10873	18 89127
18	63	17.65963	18 34037
19	62	18.18022	19 81978
20	61	18.67158	19 32842
21	60	19.13469	20 86531
22	59	19.57042	20 42958
23	58	19.97955	20 02045
24	57	20.36276	21 63724
25	56	20.72070	21 27930
26	55	21.05391	22 94609
27	54	21.36291	22 63709
28	53	21.64815	22 35185
29	52	21.91003	22 08997
30	51	22.14891	23 85109
31	50	22.36512	23 63488
32	49	22.55894	23 44106
33	48	22.73062	23 26938
34	47	22.88038	23 11962
35	46	23.00841	24 99159
36	45	23.11487	24 88513
37	44	23.19988	24 80012
38	43	23.26355	24 73645
39	42	23.30595	24 69405
40	41	23.32714	24 67286

Exponent of p (q)	q (p)	log C	log 1/C
N = 82			
0	82	0.00000	0 00000
1	81	1.91381	2 08619
2	80	3.52127	4 47873
3	79	4.94724	5 05276
4	78	6.24280	7 75720
5	77	7.43593	8 56407
6	76	8.54427	9 45573
7	75	9.57998	10 42002
8	74	10.55196	11 44804
9	73	11.46694	12 53306
10	72	12.33027	13 66973
11	71	13.14621	14 85379
12	70	13.91828	14 08172
13	69	14.64944	15 35056
14	68	15.34216	16 65784
15	67	15.99858	16 00142
16	66	16.62053	17 37947
17	65	17.20963	18 79037
18	64	17.76727	18 23273
19	63	18.29470	19 70530
20	62	18.79301	19 20699
21	61	19.26318	20 73682
22	60	19.70609	20 29391
23	59	20.12251	21 87749
24	58	20.51315	21 48685
25	57	20.87864	21 12136
26	56	21.21954	22 78046
27	55	21.53636	22 46364
28	54	21.82957	22 17043
29	53	22.09956	23 90044
30	52	22.34672	23 65328
31	51	22.57136	23 42864
32	50	22.77378	23 22622
33	49	22.95424	23 04576
34	48	23.11295	24 88705
35	47	23.25013	24 74987
36	46	23.36592	24 63408
37	45	23.46048	24 53952
38	44	23.53391	24 46609
39	43	23.58629	24 41371
40	42	23.61770	24 38230
41	41	23.62817	24 37183

Exponent of p (q)	q (p)	log C	log 1/C
N = 83			
0	83	0.00000	0 00000
1	82	1.91908	2 08092
2	81	3.53186	4 46814
3	80	4.96323	5 03677
4	79	6.26426	7 73574
5	78	7.46291	8 53709
6	77	8.57686	9 42314
7	76	9.61825	10 38175
8	75	10.59597	11 40403
9	74	11.51679	12 48321
10	73	12.38602	13 61398
11	72	13.20795	14 79205
12	71	13.98610	14 01390
13	70	14.72342	15 27658
14	69	15.42239	16 57761
15	68	16.08515	17 91485
16	67	16.71354	17 28646
17	66	17.30916	18 69084
18	65	17.87343	18 12657
19	64	18.40759	19 59241
20	63	18.91274	19 08726
21	62	19.38986	20 61014
N = 83 (continued)			
22	61	19.83983	20 16017
23	60	20.26344	21 73656
24	59	20.66138	21 33862
25	58	21.03429	22 96571
26	57	21.38274	22 61726
27	56	21.70725	22 29275
28	55	22.00828	23 99172
29	54	22.28625	23 71375
30	53	22.54152	23 45848
31	52	22.77443	23 22557
32	51	22.98529	23 01471
33	50	23.17434	24 82566
34	49	23.34184	24 65816
35	48	23.48796	24 51204
36	47	23.61290	24 38710
37	46	23.71680	24 28320
38	45	23.79977	24 20023
39	44	23.86192	24 13808
40	43	23.90331	24 09669
41	42	23.92400	24 07600

Exponent of p (q)	q (p)	log C	log 1/C
N = 84			
0	84	0.00000	0 00000
1	83	1.92428	2 07572
2	82	3.54233	4 45767
3	81	4.97902	5 02098
4	80	6.28545	7 71455
5	79	7.48956	8 51044
6	78	8.60904	9 39096
7	77	9.65604	10 34396
8	76	10.63944	11 36056
9	75	11.56601	12 43399
10	74	12.44107	13 55893
11	73	13.26891	14 73109
12	72	14.05305	15 94695
13	71	14.79644	15 20356
14	70	15.50157	16 49843
15	69	16.17058	17 82942
16	68	16.80531	17 19469
17	67	17.40737	18 59263
18	66	17.97817	18 02183
19	65	18.51896	19 48104
20	64	19.03084	20 96916
21	63	19.51480	20 48520
22	62	19.97172	20 02828
23	61	20.40238	21 59762
24	60	20.80750	21 19250
25	59	21.18771	22 81229
26	58	21.54359	22 45641
27	57	21.87566	22 12434
28	56	22.18437	23 81563
29	55	22.47016	23 52984
30	54	22.73341	23 26659
31	53	22.97444	23 02556
32	52	23.19356	24 80644
33	51	23.39105	24 60895
34	50	23.56714	24 43286
35	49	23.72205	24 27795
36	48	23.85594	24 14406
37	47	23.96898	24 03102
38	46	24.06129	25 93871
39	45	24.13299	25 86701
40	44	24.18414	25 81586
41	43	24.21481	25 78519
42	42	24.22503	25 77497

Exponent of p (q)	q (p)	log C	log 1/C
N = 85			
0	85	0.00000	0 00000
1	84	1.92942	2 07058
2	83	3.55267	4 44733
3	82	4.99463	5 00537
4	81	6.30638	7 69362
5	80	7.51589	8 48411
6	79	8.64083	9 35917
7	78	9.69336	10 30664
8	77	10.68237	11 31763
9	76	11.61461	12 38539
10	75	12.49543	13 50457
11	74	13.32910	14 67090
12	73	14.11915	15 88085
13	72	14.86853	15 13147
14	71	15.57973	16 42027
15	70	16.25490	17 74510
16	69	16.89588	17 10412
17	68	17.50428	18 49572
18	67	18.08151	19 91849
19	66	18.62883	19 37117
20	65	19.14735	20 85265
21	64	19.63804	20 36196
22	63	20.10180	21 89820
23	62	20.53941	21 46059
24	61	20.95159	21 04841
25	60	21.33898	22 66102
26	59	21.70216	22 29784
N = 85 (continued)			
27	58	22.04165	23 95835
28	57	22.35792	23 64208
29	56	22.65140	23 34860
30	55	22.92246	23 07754
31	54	23.17146	24 82854
32	53	23.39871	24 60129
33	52	23.60447	24 39553
34	51	23.78899	24 21101
35	50	23.95250	24 04750
36	49	24.09516	25 90484
37	48	24.21716	25 78284
38	47	24.31861	25 68139
39	46	24.39965	25 60035
40	45	24.46035	25 53965
41	44	24.50077	25 49923
42	43	24.52098	25 47902

Exponent of p (q)	q (p)	log C	log 1/C
N = 86			
0	86	0.00000	0 00000
1	85	1.93450	2 06550
2	84	3.56289	4 43711
3	83	5.01005	6 98995
4	82	6.32706	7 67294
5	81	7.54191	8 45809
6	80	8.67224	9 32776
7	79	9.73023	10 26977
8	78	10.72477	11 27523
9	77	11.66262	12 33738
10	76	12.54911	13 45089
11	75	13.38853	14 61147
12	74	14.18441	15 81559
13	73	14.93970	15 06030
14	72	15.65690	16 34310
15	71	16.33814	17 66186
16	70	16.98528	17 01472
17	69	17.59993	18 40007
18	68	18.18350	19 81650
19	67	18.73726	19 26274
20	66	19.26230	20 73770
21	65	19.75963	20 24037
22	64	20.23012	21 76988
23	63	20.67457	21 32543
24	62	21.09370	22 90630
25	61	21.48815	22 51185
26	60	21.85851	22 14149
27	59	22.20529	23 79471
28	58	22.52899	23 47101
29	57	22.83002	23 16998
30	56	23.10877	24 89123
31	55	23.36560	24 63440
32	54	23.60081	24 39919
33	53	23.81469	24 18531
34	52	24.00749	25 99251
35	51	24.17942	25 82058
36	50	24.33069	25 66931
37	49	24.46146	25 53854
38	48	24.57187	25 42813
39	47	24.66205	25 33795
40	46	24.73209	25 26791
41	45	24.78206	25 21794
42	44	24.81202	25 18798
43	43	24.82201	25 17799

Exponent of p (q)	q (p)	log C	log 1/C
N = 87			
0	87	0.00000	0 00000
1	86	1.93952	2 06048
2	85	3.57299	4 42701
3	84	5.02529	6 97471
4	83	6.34750	7 65250
5	82	7.56761	8 43239
6	81	8.70328	9 29672
7	80	9.76666	10 23334
8	79	10.76666	11 23334
9	78	11.71005	12 28995
10	77	12.60214	13 39786
11	76	13.44724	14 55276
12	75	14.24887	15 75113
13	74	15.00999	16 99001
14	73	15.73309	16 26691
15	72	16.42033	17 57967
16	71	17.07354	18 92646
17	70	17.69435	18 30565
18	69	18.28417	19 71583
19	68	18.84427	19 15573
20	67	19.37575	20 62425
21	66	19.87960	20 12040
22	65	20.35672	21 64328
23	64	20.80791	21 19209
24	63	21.23388	22 76612
25	62	21.63528	22 36472
26	61	22.01270	23 98730
27	60	22.36666	23 63334
28	59	22.69766	23 30234
29	58	23.00611	24 99389
N = 87 (continued)			
30	57	23.29242	24 70758
31	56	23.55693	24 44307
32	55	23.79997	24 20003
33	54	24.02182	25 97818
34	53	24.22273	25 77727
35	52	24.40294	25 59706
36	51	24.56264	25 43736
37	50	24.70201	25 29799
38	49	24.82120	25 17880
39	48	24.92033	25 07967
40	47	24.99951	25 00049
41	46	25.05882	26 94118
42	45	25.09833	26 90167
43	44	25.11807	26 88193

Exponent of p (q)	q (p)	log C	log 1/C
N = 88			
0	88	0.00000	0 00000
1	87	1.94448	2 05552
2	86	3.58297	4 41703
3	85	5.04035	6 95965
4	84	6.36771	7 63229
5	83	7.59302	8 40698
6	82	8.73394	9 26606
7	81	9.80266	10 19734
8	80	10.80806	11 19194
9	79	11.75690	12 24310
10	78	12.65453	13 34547
11	77	13.50523	14 49477
12	76	14.31254	15 68746
13	75	15.07941	16 92059
14	74	15.80834	16 19166
15	73	16.50148	17 49852
16	72	17.16069	18 83931
17	71	17.78757	18 21243
18	70	18.38356	19 61644
19	69	18.94990	19 05010
20	68	19.48772	20 51228
21	67	19.99801	20 00199
22	66	20.48166	21 51834
23	65	20.93948	21 06052
24	64	21.37218	22 62782
25	63	21.78042	22 21958
26	62	22.16479	23 83521
27	61	22.52582	23 47418
28	60	22.86399	23 13601
29	59	23.17974	24 82026
30	58	23.47347	24 52653
31	57	23.74554	24 25446
32	56	23.99626	24 00374
33	55	24.22594	25 77406
34	54	24.43482	25 56518
35	53	24.62315	25 37685
36	52	24.79112	25 20888
37	51	24.93892	25 06108
38	50	25.06671	26 93329
39	49	25.17461	26 82539
40	48	25.26275	26 73725
41	47	25.33121	26 66879
42	46	25.38006	26 61994
43	45	25.40934	26 59066
44	44	25.41910	26 58090

Exponent of p (q)	q (p)	log C	log 1/C
N = 89			
0	89	0.00000	0 00000
1	88	1.94939	2 05061
2	87	3.59284	4 40716
3	86	5.05524	6 94476
4	85	6.38768	7 61232
5	84	7.61813	8 38187
6	83	8.76426	9 23574
7	82	9.83824	10 16176
8	81	10.84896	11 15104
9	80	11.80320	12 19680
10	79	12.70629	13 29371
11	78	13.56253	14 43747
12	77	14.37544	15 62456
13	76	15.14799	16 85201
14	75	15.88267	16 11733
15	74	16.58164	17 41836
16	73	17.24675	18 75325
17	72	17.87963	18 12037
18	71	18.48169	19 51831
19	70	19.05419	20 94581
20	69	19.59826	20 40174
21	68	20.11489	21 88511
22	67	20.60498	21 39502
23	66	21.06932	22 93068
24	65	21.50866	22 49134
25	64	21.92363	22 07637
26	63	22.31484	23 68516
27	62	22.68281	23 31719
28	61	23.02805	24 97195
29	60	23.35098	24 64902
30	59	23.65201	24 34799
31	58	23.93150	24 06850

Exponent of $p(q)$	Exponent of $q(p)$	log C	log $1/C$
		$N = 89$ (continued)	
32	57	24.18978	25 81022
33	56	24.42714	25 57286
34	55	24.64385	25 35615
35	54	24.84014	25 15986
36	53	25.01623	26 98377
37	52	25.17231	26 82769
38	51	25.30853	26 69147
39	50	25.42503	26 57497
40	49	25.52194	26 47806
41	48	25.59936	26 40064
42	47	25.65735	26 34265
43	46	25.69598	26 30402
44	45	25.71528	26 28472
		$N = 90$	
0	90	0.00000	0 00000
1	89	1.95424	2 04576
2	88	3.60260	4 39740
3	87	5.06996	6 93004
4	86	6.40742	7 59258
5	85	7.64295	8 35705
6	84	8.79422	9 20578
7	83	9.87340	10 12660
8	82	10.88939	11 11061
9	81	11.84896	12 15104
10	80	12.75745	13 24255
11	79	13.61914	14 38086
12	78	14.43759	15 56241
13	77	15.21574	16 78426
14	76	15.95610	16 04390
15	75	16.66082	17 33918
16	74	17.33177	18 66823
17	73	17.97055	18 02945
18	72	18.57860	19 42140
19	71	19.15718	20 84282
20	70	19.70741	20 29259
21	69	20.23028	21 76972
22	68	20.72671	21 27329
23	67	21.19749	22 80251
24	66	21.64336	22 35664
25	65	22.06496	23 93504
26	64	22.46290	23 53710
27	63	22.83772	23 16228
28	62	23.18990	24 81010
29	61	23.51989	24 48011
30	60	23.82810	24 17190
31	59	24.11489	25 88511
32	58	24.38059	25 61941
33	57	24.62551	25 37449
34	56	24.84990	25 15010
35	55	25.05402	26 94598
36	54	25.23808	26 76192
37	53	25.40227	26 59773
38	52	25.54677	26 45323
39	51	25.67171	26 32829
40	50	25.77722	26 22278
41	49	25.86340	26 13660
42	48	25.93035	26 06965
43	47	25.97812	26 02188
44	46	26.00677	27 99323
45	45	26.01631	27 98369
		$N = 91$	
0	91	0.00000	0 00000
1	90	1.95904	2 04096
2	89	3.61225	4 38775
3	88	5.08452	6 91548
4	87	6.42695	7 57305
5	86	7.66749	8 33251
6	85	8.82384	9 17616
7	84	9.90816	10 09184
8	83	10.92935	11 07065
9	82	11.89419	12 10581
10	81	12.80800	13 19200
11	80	13.67509	14 32491
12	79	14.49900	15 50100
13	78	15.28269	16 71731
14	77	16.02865	17 97135
15	76	16.73905	17 26095
16	75	17.41575	18 58425
17	74	18.06036	19 93964
18	73	18.67432	19 32568
19	72	19.25889	20 74111
20	71	19.81519	20 18481
21	70	20.34423	21 65577
22	69	20.84690	21 15310
23	68	21.32402	22 67598
24	67	21.77632	22 22368
25	66	22.20446	23 79554
26	65	22.60903	23 39097
27	64	22.99058	23 00942
28	63	23.34960	24 65040
29	62	23.68654	24 31346
30	61	24.00181	25 99819

Exponent of $p(q)$	Exponent of $q(p)$	log C	log $1/C$
		$N = 91$ (continued)	
31	60	24.29578	25 70422
32	59	24.56878	25 43122
33	58	24.82112	25 17888
34	57	25.05307	26 94693
35	56	25.26488	26 73512
36	55	25.45676	26 54324
37	54	25.62892	26 37108
38	53	25.78153	26 21847
39	52	25.91474	26 08526
40	51	26.02869	27 97131
41	50	26.12347	27 87653
42	49	26.19919	27 80081
43	48	26.25592	27 74408
44	47	26.29371	27 70629
45	46	26.31260	27 68740
		$N = 92$	
0	92	0.00000	0 00000
1	91	1.96379	2 03621
2	90	3.62180	4 37820
3	89	5.09892	6 90108
4	88	6.44625	7 55375
5	87	7.69176	8 30824
6	86	8.85313	9 14687
7	85	9.94253	10 05747
8	84	10.96886	11 03114
9	83	11.93890	12 06110
10	82	12.85798	13 14202
11	81	13.73040	14 26960
12	80	14.55970	15 44030
13	79	15.34885	16 65115
14	78	16.10035	17 89965
15	77	16.81635	17 18365
16	76	17.49872	18 50128
17	75	18.14908	19 85092
18	74	18.76887	19 23113
19	73	19.35935	20 64065
20	72	19.92164	20 07836
21	71	20.45676	21 54324
22	70	20.96559	21 03441
23	69	21.44896	22 55104
24	68	21.90760	22 09240
25	67	22.34217	23 65783
26	66	22.75327	23 24673
27	65	23.14145	24 85855
28	64	23.50721	24 49279
29	63	23.85099	24 14901
30	62	24.17321	25 82679
31	61	24.47424	25 52576
32	60	24.75442	25 24558
33	59	25.01406	26 98594
34	58	25.25343	26 74657
35	57	25.47279	26 52721
36	56	25.67236	26 32764
37	55	25.85235	26 14765
38	54	26.01293	27 98707
39	53	26.15426	27 84574
40	52	26.27647	27 72353
41	51	26.37969	27 62031
42	50	26.46401	27 53599
43	49	26.52951	27 47049
44	48	26.57626	27 42374
45	47	26.60429	27 39571
46	46	26.61363	27 38637
		$N = 93$	
0	93	0.00000	0 00000
1	92	1.96848	2 03152
2	91	3.63124	4 36876
3	90	5.11316	6 88684
4	89	6.46534	7 53466
5	88	7.71576	8 28424
6	87	8.88209	9 11791
7	86	9.97652	10 02348
8	85	11.00792	12 99208
9	84	11.98310	12 01690
10	83	12.90738	13 09262
11	82	13.78507	14 21493
12	81	14.61970	15 38030
13	80	15.41424	16 58576
14	79	16.17120	17 82880
15	78	16.89274	17 10726
16	77	17.58071	18 41929
17	76	18.23675	19 76325
18	75	18.86230	19 13770
19	74	19.45860	20 54140
20	73	20.02680	21 97320
21	72	20.56791	21 43209
22	71	21.08282	22 91718
23	70	21.57235	22 42765
24	69	22.03724	23 96276
25	68	22.47814	23 52186
26	67	22.89568	23 10432
27	66	23.29039	24 70961

Exponent of $p(q)$	Exponent of $q(p)$	log C	log $1/C$
		$N = 93$ (continued)	
28	65	23.66278	24 33722
29	64	24.01329	25 98671
30	63	24.34235	25 65765
31	62	24.65033	25 34967
32	61	24.93757	25 06243
33	60	25.20439	26 79561
34	59	25.45106	26 54894
35	58	25.67784	26 32216
36	57	25.88497	26 11503
37	56	26.07264	27 92736
38	55	26.24105	27 75895
39	54	26.39034	27 60966
40	53	26.52068	27 47932
41	52	26.63217	27 36783
42	51	26.72492	27 27508
43	50	26.79903	27 20097
44	49	26.85454	27 14546
45	48	26.89153	27 10847
46	47	26.91001	27 08999
		$N = 94$	
0	94	0.00000	0 00000
1	93	1.97313	2 02687
2	92	3.64058	4 35942
3	91	5.12725	6 87275
4	90	6.48423	7 51577
5	89	7.73950	8 26050
6	88	8.91074	9 08926
7	87	10.01012	11 98988
8	86	11.04655	12 95345
9	85	12.02681	13 97319
10	84	12.95623	13 04377
11	83	13.83912	14 16088
12	82	14.67901	15 32099
13	81	15.47888	16 52112
14	80	16.24124	17 75876
15	79	16.96824	17 03176
16	78	17.66175	18 33825
17	77	18.32339	19 67661
18	76	18.95461	19 04539
19	75	19.55667	20 44333
20	74	20.13070	21 86930
21	73	20.67771	21 32229
22	72	21.19861	22 80139
23	71	21.69422	22 30578
24	70	22.16527	23 83473
25	69	22.61242	23 38758
26	68	23.03630	24 96370
27	67	23.43744	24 56256
28	66	23.81636	24 18364
29	65	24.17351	25 82649
30	64	24.50930	25 49070
31	63	24.82412	25 17588
32	62	25.11831	26 88169
33	61	25.39219	26 60781
34	60	25.64604	26 35396
35	59	25.88012	26 11988
36	58	26.09467	27 90533
37	57	26.28990	27 71010
38	56	26.46599	27 53401
39	55	26.62311	27 37689
40	54	26.76141	27 23859
41	53	26.88102	27 11898
42	52	26.98205	27 01795
43	51	27.06458	28 93542
44	50	27.12870	28 87130
45	49	27.17446	28 82554
46	48	27.20190	28 79810
47	47	27.21104	28 78896
		$N = 95$	
0	95	0.00000	0 00000
1	94	1.97772	2 02228
2	93	3.64982	4 35018
3	92	5.14118	6 85882
4	91	6.50291	7 49709
5	90	7.76298	8 23702
6	89	8.93907	9 06093
7	88	10.04337	11 95663
8	87	11.08476	12 91524
9	86	12.07004	13 92996
10	85	13.00453	14 99547
11	84	13.89256	14 10744
12	83	14.73766	15 26234
13	82	15.54279	16 45721
14	81	16.31048	17 68952
15	80	17.04287	18 95713
16	79	17.74184	18 25816
17	78	18.40902	19 59098
18	77	19.04584	20 95416
19	76	19.65358	20 34642
20	75	20.23336	21 76664
21	74	20.78621	21 21379
22	73	21.31301	22 68699

Exponent of $p(q)$	Exponent of $q(p)$	log C	log $1/C$
		$N = 95$ (continued)	
23	72	21.81461	22 18539
24	71	22.29173	23 70827
25	70	22.74505	23 25495
26	69	23.17517	24 82483
27	68	23.58266	24 41734
28	67	23.96801	24 03199
29	66	24.33169	25 66831
30	65	24.67411	25 32589
31	64	24.99566	25 00434
32	63	25.29669	26 70331
33	62	25.57752	26 42248
34	61	25.83843	26 16157
35	60	26.07969	27 92031
36	59	26.30154	27 69846
37	58	26.50419	27 49581
38	57	26.68784	27 31216
39	56	26.85265	27 14735
40	55	26.99877	27 00123
41	54	27.12635	28 87365
42	53	27.23550	28 76450
43	52	27.32630	28 67370
44	51	27.39886	28 60114
45	50	27.45321	28 54679
46	49	27.48942	28 51058
47	48	27.50752	28 49248
		$N = 96$	
0	96	0.00000	0 00000
1	95	1.98227	2 01773
2	94	3.65896	4 34104
3	93	5.15497	6 84503
4	92	6.52139	7 47861
5	91	7.78621	8 21379
6	90	8.96710	9 03290
7	89	10.07625	11 92375
8	88	11.12255	12 87745
9	87	12.11279	13 88721
10	86	13.05231	14 94769
11	85	13.94541	14 05459
12	84	14.79565	15 20435
13	83	15.60599	16 39401
14	82	16.37894	17 62106
15	81	17.11666	18 88334
16	80	17.82102	18 17898
17	79	18.49366	19 50634
18	78	19.13602	20 86398
19	77	19.74936	20 25064
20	76	20.33482	21 66518
21	75	20.89342	21 10658
22	74	21.42605	22 57395
23	73	21.93356	22 06644
24	72	22.41667	23 58333
25	71	22.87606	23 12394
26	70	23.31235	24 68765
27	69	23.72608	24 27392
28	68	24.11777	25 88223
29	67	24.48788	25 51212
30	66	24.83684	25 16316
31	65	25.16502	26 83498
32	64	25.47278	26 52722
33	63	25.76045	26 23955
34	62	26.02831	27 97169
35	61	26.27663	27 72337
36	60	26.50566	27 49434
37	59	26.71561	27 28439
38	58	26.90668	27 09332
39	57	27.07904	28 92096
40	56	27.23286	28 76714
41	55	27.36826	28 63174
42	54	27.48537	28 51463
43	53	27.58430	28 41570
44	52	27.66512	28 33488
45	51	27.72791	28 27209
46	50	27.77273	28 22727
47	49	27.79960	28 20040
48	48	27.80855	28 19145
		$N = 97$	
0	97	0.00000	0 00000
1	96	1.98677	2 01323
2	95	3.66801	4 33199
3	94	5.16862	6 83138
4	93	6.53968	7 46032
5	92	7.80920	8 19080
6	91	8.99483	9 00517
7	90	10.10878	11 89122
8	89	11.15993	12 84007
9	88	12.15508	13 84492
10	87	13.09956	14 90044
11	86	13.99769	14 00231
12	85	14.85300	15 14700
13	84	15.66848	16 33152
14	83	16.44663	17 55337
15	82	17.18962	18 81038

Common Logarithms* of the Binomial Coefficients C and Their Reciprocals N=97—100

Exponent of p(q)	Exponent of q(p)	log C	log 1/C
N = 97 (continued)			
16	81	17.89931	**18** 10069
17	80	18.57735	**19** 42265
18	79	19.22516	**20** 77484
19	78	19.84404	**20** 15596
20	77	20.43510	**21** 56490
21	76	20.99937	**21** 00063
22	75	21.53776	**22** 46224
23	74	22.05110	**23** 94890
24	73	22.54012	**23** 45988
25	72	23.00550	**24** 99450
26	71	23.44786	**24** 55214
27	70	23.86775	**24** 13225
28	69	24.26569	**25** 73431
29	68	24.64215	**25** 35785
30	67	24.99753	**25** 00247
31	66	25.33225	**26** 66775
32	65	25.64664	**26** 35336
33	64	25.94104	**26** 05896
34	63	26.21574	**27** 78426
35	62	26.47101	**27** 52899
36	61	26.70710	**27** 29290
37	60	26.92423	**27** 07577
38	59	27.12260	**28** 87740
39	58	27.30239	**28** 69761
40	57	27.46375	**28** 53625
41	56	27.60684	**28** 39316
42	55	27.73178	**28** 26822
43	54	27.83868	**28** 16132
44	53	27.92762	**28** 07238
45	52	27.99868	**28** 00132
46	51	28.05193	**29** 94807
47	50	28.08740	**29** 91260
48	49	28.10513	**29** 89487
N = 98			
0	98	0.00000	**0** 00000
1	97	1.99123	**2** 00877
2	96	3.67697	**4** 32303
3	95	5.18212	**6** 81788
4	94	6.55778	**7** 44222
5	93	7.83194	**8** 16806
6	92	9.02227	**10** 97773
7	91	10.14096	**11** 85904
8	90	11.19691	**12** 80309
9	89	12.19691	**13** 80309
10	88	13.14630	**14** 85370
11	87	14.04939	**15** 95061
12	86	14.90973	**15** 09027
13	85	15.73029	**16** 26971
14	84	16.51358	**17** 48642
15	83	17.26176	**18** 73824
16	82	17.97672	**18** 02328
17	81	18.66009	**19** 33991
18	80	19.31330	**20** 68670
19	79	19.93764	**20** 06236
20	78	20.53423	**21** 46577
21	77	21.10411	**22** 89589
22	76	21.64818	**22** 35182
23	75	22.16726	**23** 83274
24	74	22.66211	**23** 33789
25	73	23.13340	**24** 86660
26	72	23.58175	**24** 41825
27	71	24.00772	**25** 99228
28	70	24.41182	**25** 58818
29	69	24.79452	**25** 20548
30	68	25.15625	**26** 84375
31	67	25.49740	**26** 50260
32	66	25.81832	**26** 18168
33	65	26.11935	**27** 88065
34	64	26.40079	**27** 59921
35	63	26.66290	**27** 33710
36	62	26.90594	**27** 09406
37	61	27.13013	**28** 86987
38	60	27.33567	**28** 66433
39	59	27.52276	**28** 47724
40	58	27.69155	**28** 30845
41	57	27.84220	**28** 15780
42	56	27.97482	**28** 02518
43	55	28.08954	**29** 91046
44	54	28.18645	**29** 81355
45	53	28.26563	**29** 73437
46	52	28.32715	**29** 67285
47	51	28.37106	**29** 62894
48	50	28.39738	**29** 60262
49	49	28.40616	**29** 59384
N = 99			
0	99	0.00000	**0** 00000
1	98	1.99564	**2** 00436
2	97	3.68583	**4** 31417
3	96	5.19548	**6** 80452
4	95	6.57569	**7** 42431
5	94	7.85445	**8** 14555
6	93	9.04942	**10** 95058

Exponent of p(q)	Exponent of q(p)	log C	log 1/C
N = 99 (continued)			
7	92	10.17281	**11** 82719
8	91	11.23351	**12** 76649
9	90	12.23830	**13** 76170
10	89	13.19255	**14** 80745
11	88	14.10054	**15** 89946
12	87	14.96585	**15** 03415
13	86	15.79142	**16** 20858
14	85	16.57979	**17** 42021
15	84	17.33312	**18** 66688
16	83	18.05328	**19** 94672
17	82	18.74191	**19** 25809
18	81	19.40045	**20** 59955
19	80	20.03018	**21** 96982
20	79	20.63224	**21** 36776
21	78	21.20765	**22** 79235
22	77	21.75732	**22** 24268
23	76	22.28208	**23** 71792
24	75	22.78269	**23** 21731
25	74	23.25981	**24** 74019
26	73	23.71407	**24** 28593
27	72	24.14602	**25** 85398
28	71	24.55620	**25** 44380
29	70	24.94506	**25** 05494
30	69	25.31304	**26** 68696
31	68	25.66052	**26** 33948
32	67	25.98788	**26** 01212
33	66	26.29544	**27** 70456
34	65	26.58351	**27** 41649
35	64	26.85235	**27** 14765
36	63	27.10223	**28** 89777
37	62	27.33337	**28** 66663
38	61	27.54598	**28** 45402
39	60	27.74024	**28** 25976
40	59	27.91633	**28** 08367
41	58	28.07440	**29** 92560
42	57	28.21458	**29** 78542
43	56	28.33699	**29** 66301
44	55	28.44172	**29** 55828
45	54	28.52887	**29** 47113
46	53	28.59851	**29** 40149
47	52	28.65069	**29** 34931
48	51	28.68545	**29** 31455
49	50	28.70282	**29** 29718
N = 100			
0	100	0.00000	**0** 00000
1	99	2.00000	**3** 00000
2	98	3.69461	**4** 30539
3	97	5.20871	**6** 79129
4	96	6.59342	**7** 40658
5	95	7.87672	**8** 12328
6	94	9.07630	**10** 92370
7	93	10.20433	**11** 79567
8	92	11.26972	**12** 73028
9	91	12.27926	**13** 72074
10	90	13.23830	**14** 76170
11	89	14.15115	**15** 84885
12	88	15.02136	**16** 97864
13	87	15.85190	**16** 14810
14	86	16.64529	**17** 35471
15	85	17.40370	**18** 59630
16	84	18.12900	**19** 87100
17	83	18.82283	**19** 17717
18	82	19.48664	**20** 51336
19	81	20.12170	**21** 87830
20	80	20.72915	**21** 27085
21	79	21.31002	**22** 68998
22	78	21.86523	**22** 13477
23	77	22.39559	**23** 60441
24	76	22.90187	**23** 09813
25	75	23.38475	**24** 61525
26	74	23.84483	**24** 15517
27	73	24.28270	**25** 71730
28	72	24.69887	**25** 30113
29	71	25.09380	**26** 90620
30	70	25.46794	**26** 53206
31	69	25.82167	**26** 17833
32	68	26.15537	**27** 84463
33	67	26.46937	**27** 53063
34	66	26.76396	**27** 23604
35	65	27.03944	**28** 96056
36	64	27.29605	**28** 70395
37	63	27.53403	**28** 46597
38	62	27.75359	**28** 24641
39	61	27.95491	**28** 04509
40	60	28.13818	**29** 86182
41	59	28.30355	**29** 69645
42	58	28.45115	**29** 54885
43	57	28.58111	**29** 41889
44	56	28.69354	**29** 30646
45	55	28.78851	**29** 21149
46	54	28.86612	**29** 13388
47	53	28.92641	**29** 07359
48	52	28.96945	**29** 03055
49	51	28.99525	**29** 00475
50	50	29.00385	**30** 99615

Explanation of the tables on pages 70–84

The **bold** figures in the tables are negative characteristics. The mantissae are all positive.

Binomial coefficients $C(N, x) = \binom{N}{x} = \dfrac{N!}{x!\,(N-x)!}$

For values of N between 100 and 1000, values of C can be calculated with the help of the tables on pages 26 and 27.

Example:

$\log \binom{54}{6} = 7.41208 \qquad C(54, 6) = 2.583 \times 10^{7}$

$\log 1\Big/\binom{54}{6} = -8 + 0.58792 \qquad 1/C(54, 6) = 3.872 \times 10^{-8}$

Calculation of individual probabilities Prob $(x_1 \mid N, N_1, X)$ **in the hypergeometric distribution**

Given are

x_1	$N_1 - x_1$	N_1
x_2	$N_2 - x_2$	N_2
X	$N - X$	N

$$\text{Prob}\,(x_1 \mid N, N_1, X) = \frac{N_1!\,N_2!\,X!\,(N-X)!}{x_1!\,(N_1-x_1)!\,x_2!\,(N_2-x_2)!\,N!}$$

$$= \dot{P}(x_1) = \binom{N_1}{x_1} \times \binom{N_2}{x_2} \times 1\Big/\binom{N}{X}$$

$$\log \dot{P}(x_1) = \underbrace{\log C(N_1, x_1) + \log C(N_2, x_2) + \log 1/C(N, X)}_{\text{from pages 70–77}}$$

Example:

2	5	7
3	2	5
5	7	12

$\log C(7, 2) \quad + 1 \quad + 0.32222$

$\log C(5, 3) \quad + 1 \quad + 0.00000$

$\log 1/C(12, 5) \quad - 3 \quad + 0.10127$

Sum: $\log \dot{P}(x_1) = -1 + 0.42349$

$\dot{P}(x_1) = 0.2653$

Calculation of individual probabilities $\dot{P}(x)$ **in the binomial distribution**

Required is $\dot{P}(x) = \binom{N}{x} p^{x} q^{N-x}$

Solution: $\log \dot{P}(x) = \underbrace{\log C(N, x)}_{\text{pages 70–77}} + \underbrace{\log p^{x} + \log q^{N-x}}_{\text{pages 78–84}}$

Example:

$N = 32,\ p = 0.06,\ x_1 = 2,\ x_2 = 30$

$\dot{P}_2$		$\dot{P}_{30}$	
$\log C(32, 2)$	$+2 + 0.69548$	$\log C(32, 30)$	$+\ 2 + 0.69548$
$\log p^{2}$	$-3 + 0.55630$	$\log p^{30}$	$-37 + 0.34454$
$\log q^{30}$	$-1 + 0.19384$	$\log q^{2}$	$-\ 1 + 0.94626$
$\log \dot{P}_2$	$-2 + 1.44562$	$\log \dot{P}_{30}$	$-36 + 1.98628$
	$= -1 + 0.44562$		$= -35 + 0.98628$
$\dot{P}_2 =$	0.2790	$\dot{P}_{30} =$	9.690×10^{-35}

For explanation see page 77

n	p (q) 0.01	q (p) 0.99	p (q) 0.02	q (p) 0.98	p (q) 0.03	q (p) 0.97	p (q) 0.04	q (p) 0.96	p (q) 0.05	q (p) 0.95	p (q) 0.06	q (p) 0.94	p (q) 0.07	q (p) 0.93
0	0 00000	0 00000	0 00000	0 00000	0 00000	0 00000	0 00000	0 00000	0 00000	0 00000	0 00000	0 00000	0 00000	0 00000
1	2 00000	1 99564	2 30103	1 99123	2 47712	1 98677	2 60206	1 98227	2 69897	1 97772	2 77815	1 97313	2 84510	1 96848
2	4 00000	1 99127	4 60206	1 98245	4 95424	1 97354	3 20412	1 96454	3 39794	1 95545	3 55630	1 94626	3 69020	1 93697
3	6 00000	1 98691	6 90309	1 97368	5 43136	1 96032	5 80618	1 94681	4 09691	1 93317	4 33445	1 91938	4 53529	1 90545
4	8 00000	1 98254	7 20412	1 96490	7 90849	1 94709	6 40824	1 92908	6 79588	1 91089	5 11261	1 89251	5 38039	1 87393
5	10 00000	1 97818	9 50515	1 95613	8 38561	1 93386	7 01030	1 91136	7 49485	1 88862	7 89076	1 86564	6 22549	1 84241
6	12 00000	1 97381	11 80618	1 94736	10 86273	1 92063	9 61236	1 89363	8 19382	1 86634	8 66891	1 83877	7 07059	1 81090
7	14 00000	1 96945	12 10721	1 93858	11 33985	1 90740	10 21442	1 87590	10 89279	1 84407	9 44706	1 81189	9 91569	1 77938
8	16 00000	1 96508	14 40824	1 92981	13 81697	1 89417	12 81648	1 85817	11 59176	1 82179	10 22521	1 78502	10 76078	1 74786
9	18 00000	1 96072	16 70927	1 92103	14 29409	1 88095	13 41854	1 84044	12 29073	1 79951	11 00336	1 75815	11 60588	1 71635
10	20 00000	1 95635	17 01030	1 91226	16 77121	1 86772	14 02060	1 82271	14 98970	1 77724	13 78151	1 73128	12 45098	1 68483
11	22 00000	1 95199	19 31133	1 90349	17 24833	1 85449	16 62266	1 80498	15 68867	1 75496	14 55966	1 70441	13 29608	1 65331
12	24 00000	1 94762	21 61236	1 89471	19 72546	1 84126	17 22472	1 78725	16 38764	1 73268	15 33782	1 67753	14 14118	1 62180
13	26 00000	1 94326	23 91339	1 88594	20 20258	1 82803	19 82678	1 76953	17 08661	1 71041	16 11597	1 65066	16 98627	1 59028
14	28 00000	1 93889	24 21442	1 87717	22 67970	1 81480	20 42884	1 75180	19 78558	1 68813	18 89412	1 62379	17 83137	1 55876
15	30 00000	1 93453	26 51545	1 86839	23 15682	1 80158	21 03090	1 73407	20 48455	1 66585	19 67227	1 59692	18 67647	1 52724
16	32 00000	1 93016	28 81648	1 85962	25 63394	1 78835	23 63296	1 71634	21 18352	1 64358	20 45042	1 57005	19 52157	1 49573
17	34 00000	1 92580	29 11751	1 85084	26 11106	1 77512	24 23502	1 69861	23 88249	1 62130	21 22857	1 54317	20 36667	1 46421
18	36 00000	1 92143	31 41854	1 84207	28 58818	1 76189	26 83708	1 68088	24 58146	1 59902	22 00672	1 51630	21 21176	1 43269
19	38 00000	1 91707	33 71957	1 83330	29 06530	1 74866	27 43914	1 66315	25 28043	1 57675	24 78487	1 48943	22 05686	1 40118
20	40 00000	1 91270	34 02060	1 82452	31 54243	1 73543	28 04120	1 64542	27 97940	1 55447	25 56303	1 46256	24 90196	1 36966
21	42 00000	1 90834	36 32163	1 81575	32 01955	1 72221	30 64326	1 62770	28 67837	1 53220	26 34118	1 43568	25 74706	1 33814
22	44 00000	1 90397	38 62266	1 80697	34 49667	1 70898	31 24532	1 60997	29 37734	1 50992	27 11933	1 40881	26 59216	1 30662
23	46 00000	1 89961	40 92369	1 79820	36 97379	1 69575	33 84738	1 59224	30 07631	1 48764	29 89748	1 38194	27 43725	1 27511
24	48 00000	1 89524	41 22472	1 78943	37 45091	1 68252	34 44944	1 57451	32 77528	1 46537	30 67563	1 35507	28 28235	1 24359
25	50 00000	1 89088	43 52575	1 78065	39 92803	1 66929	35 05150	1 55678	33 47425	1 44309	31 45378	1 32820	29 12745	1 21207
26	52 00000	1 88652	45 82678	1 77188	40 40515	1 65607	37 65356	1 53905	34 17322	1 42081	32 23193	1 30132	31 97255	1 18056
27	54 00000	1 88215	46 12781	1 76310	42 88227	1 64284	38 25562	1 52132	36 87219	1 39854	33 01008	1 27445	32 81765	1 14904
28	56 00000	1 87779	48 42884	1 75433	43 35940	1 62961	40 85768	1 50359	37 57116	1 37626	35 78824	1 24758	33 66275	1 11752
29	58 00000	1 87342	50 72987	1 74556	45 83652	1 61638	41 45974	1 48587	38 27013	1 35398	36 56639	1 22071	34 50784	1 08601
30	60 00000	1 86906	51 03090	1 73678	46 31364	1 60315	42 06180	1 46814	40 96910	1 33171	37 34454	1 19384	35 35294	1 05449
31	62 00000	1 86469	53 33193	1 72801	48 79076	1 58992	44 66386	1 45041	41 66807	1 30943	38 12269	1 16696	36 19804	1 02297
32	64 00000	1 86033	55 63296	1 71923	49 26788	1 57670	45 26592	1 43268	42 36704	1 28716	40 90084	1 14009	37 04314	2 99145
33	66 00000	1 85596	57 93399	1 71046	51 74500	1 56347	47 86798	1 41495	43 06601	1 26488	41 67899	1 11322	39 88824	2 95994
34	68 00000	1 85160	58 23502	1 70169	52 22212	1 55024	48 47004	1 39722	45 76498	1 24260	42 45714	1 08635	40 73333	2 92842
35	70 00000	1 84723	60 53605	1 69291	54 69924	1 53701	49 07210	1 37949	46 46395	1 22033	43 23529	1 05947	41 57843	2 89690
36	72 00000	1 84287	62 83708	1 68414	55 17637	1 52378	51 67416	1 36176	47 16292	1 19805	44 01345	1 03260	42 42353	2 86539
37	74 00000	1 83850	63 13811	1 67536	57 65349	1 51055	52 27622	1 34404	49 86189	1 17577	46 79160	1 00573	43 26863	2 83387
38	76 00000	1 83414	65 43914	1 66659	58 13061	1 49733	54 87828	1 32631	50 56086	1 15350	47 56975	2 97886	44 11373	2 80235
39	78 00000	1 82977	67 74017	1 65782	60 60773	1 48410	55 48034	1 30858	51 25983	1 13122	48 34790	2 95199	46 95882	2 77083
40	80 00000	1 82541	68 04120	1 64904	61 08485	1 47087	56 08240	1 29085	53 95880	1 10894	49 12605	2 92511	47 80392	2 73932
41	82 00000	1 82104	70 34223	1 64027	63 56197	1 45764	58 68446	1 27312	54 65777	1 08667	51 90420	2 89824	48 64902	2 70780
42	84 00000	1 81668	72 64326	1 63150	64 03909	1 44441	59 28652	1 25539	55 35674	1 06439	52 68235	2 87137	49 49412	2 67628
43	86 00000	1 81231	74 94429	1 62272	66 51621	1 43118	61 88858	1 23766	56 05571	1 04212	53 46050	2 84450	50 33922	2 64477
44	88 00000	1 80795	75 24532	1 61395	68 99334	1 41796	62 49064	1 21993	58 75468	1 01984	54 23866	2 81763	51 18431	2 61325
45	90 00000	1 80358	77 54635	1 60517	69 47046	1 40473	63 09270	1 20221	59 45365	2 99756	55 01681	2 79075	52 02941	2 58173
46	92 00000	1 79922	79 84738	1 59640	71 94758	1 39150	65 69476	1 18448	60 15262	2 97529	57 79496	2 76388	54 87451	2 55022
47	94 00000	1 79485	80 14841	1 58763	72 42470	1 37827	66 29682	1 16675	62 85159	2 95301	58 57311	2 73701	55 71961	2 51870
48	96 00000	1 79049	82 44944	1 57885	74 90182	1 36504	68 89888	1 14902	63 55056	2 93073	59 35126	2 71014	56 56471	2 48718
49	98 00000	1 78612	84 75047	1 57008	75 37894	1 35181	69 50094	1 13129	64 24953	2 90846	60 12941	2 68326	57 40980	2 45566
50	100 00000	1 78176	85 05150	1 56130	77 85606	1 33859	70 10300	1 11356	66 94850	2 88618	62 90756	2 65639	58 25490	2 42415
51	102 00000	1 77739	87 35253	1 55253	78 33318	1 32536	72 70506	1 09583	67 64747	2 86390	63 68571	2 62952	59 10000	2 39263
52	104 00000	1 77303	89 65356	1 54376	80 81031	1 31213	73 30712	1 07810	68 34644	2 84163	64 46387	2 60265	61 94510	2 36111
53	106 00000	1 76867	91 95459	1 53498	81 28743	1 29890	75 90918	1 06038	69 04541	2 81935	65 24202	2 57578	62 79020	2 32960
54	108 00000	1 76430	92 25562	1 52621	83 76455	1 28567	76 51124	1 04265	71 74438	2 79707	66 02017	2 54890	63 63529	2 29808
55	110 00000	1 75994	94 55665	1 51743	84 24167	1 27245	77 11330	1 02492	72 44335	2 77480	68 79832	2 52203	64 48039	2 26656
56	112 00000	1 75557	96 85768	1 50866	86 71879	1 25922	79 71536	1 00719	73 14232	2 75252	69 57647	2 49516	65 32549	2 23505
57	114 00000	1 75121	97 15871	1 49989	87 19591	1 24599	80 31742	2 98946	75 84129	2 73025	70 35462	2 46829	66 17059	2 20353
58	116 00000	1 74684	99 45974	1 49111	89 67303	1 23276	82 91948	2 97173	76 54026	2 70797	71 13277	2 44142	67 01569	2 17201
59	118 00000	1 74248	101 76077	1 48234	90 15015	1 21953	83 52154	2 95400	77 23923	2 68569	73 91092	2 41454	69 86078	2 14049
60	120 00000	1 73811	102 06180	1 47356	92 62728	1 20630	84 12360	2 93627	79 93820	2 66342	74 68908	2 38767	70 70588	2 10898
61	122 00000	1 73375	104 36283	1 46479	93 10440	1 19308	86 72566	2 91855	80 63717	2 64114	75 46723	2 36080	71 55098	2 07746
62	124 00000	1 72938	106 66386	1 45602	95 58152	1 17985	87 32772	2 90082	81 33614	2 61886	76 24538	2 33393	72 39608	2 04594
63	126 00000	1 72502	108 96489	1 44724	96 05864	1 16662	89 92978	2 88309	82 03511	2 59659	77 02353	2 30705	73 24118	2 01443
64	128 00000	1 72065	109 26592	1 43847	98 53576	1 15339	90 53184	2 86536	84 73408	2 57431	79 80168	2 28018	74 08627	3 98291
65	130 00000	1 71629	111 56695	1 42969	99 01288	1 14016	91 13390	2 84763	85 43305	2 55203	80 57983	2 25331	76 93137	3 95139
66	132 00000	1 71192	113 86798	1 42092	101 49000	1 12693	93 73596	2 82990	86 13202	2 52976	81 35798	2 22644	77 77647	3 91987
67	134 00000	1 70756	114 16901	1 41215	103 96712	1 11371	94 33802	2 81217	88 83099	2 50748	82 13613	2 19957	78 62157	3 88836
68	136 00000	1 70319	116 47004	1 40337	104 44425	1 10048	96 94008	2 79444	89 52996	2 48521	84 91429	2 17269	79 46667	3 85684
69	138 00000	1 69883	118 77107	1 39460	106 92137	1 08725	97 54214	2 77672	90 22893	2 46293	85 69244	2 14582	80 31176	3 82532
70	140 00000	1 69446	119 07210	1 38583	107 39849	1 07402	98 14420	2 75899	92 92790	2 44065	86 47059	2 11895	81 15686	3 79381
71	142 00000	1 69010	121 37313	1 37705	109 87561	1 06079	100 74626	2 74126	93 62687	2 41838	87 24874	2 09208	82 00196	3 76229
72	144 00000	1 68573	123 67416	1 36828	110 35273	1 04756	101 34832	2 72353	94 32584	2 39610	88 02689	2 06521	84 84706	3 73077
73	146 00000	1 68137	125 97519	1 35950	112 82985	1 03434	103 95038	2 70580	95 02481	2 37382	90 80504	2 03833	85 69216	3 69926
74	148 00000	1 67700	126 27622	1 35073	113 30697	1 02111	104 55244	2 68807	97 72378	2 35155	91 58319	2 01146	86 53725	3 66774
75	150 00000	1 67264	128 57725	1 34196	115 78409	1 00788	105 15450	2 67034	98 42275	2 32927	92 36134	3 98459	87 38235	3 63622
76	152 00000	1 66827	130 87828	1 33318	116 26122	2 99465	107 75656	2 65261	99 12172	2 30699	93 13950	3 95772	88 22745	3 60470
77	154 00000	1 66391	131 17931	1 32441	118 73834	2 98142	108 35862	2 63488	101 82069	2 28472	95 91765	3 93084	89 07255	3 57319
78	156 00000	1 65955	133 48034	1 31563	119 21546	2 96820	110 96068	2 61716	102 51966	2 26244	96 69580	3 90397	91 91765	3 54167
79	158 00000	1 65518	135 78137	1 30686	121 69258	2 95497	111 56274	2 59943	103 21863	2 24016	97 47395	3 87710	92 76275	3 51015
80	160 00000	1 65082	136 08240	1 29809	122 16970	2 94174	112 16480	2 58170	105 91760	2 21789	98 25210	3 85023	93 60784	3 47864
81	162 00000	1 64645	138 38343	1 28931	124 64682	2 92851	114 76686	2 56397	106 61657	2 19561	99 03025	3 82336	94 45294	3 44712
82	164 00000	1 64209	140 68446	1 28054	125 12394	2 91528	115 36892	2 54624	107 31554	2 17334	101 80840	3 79648	95 29804	3 41560
83	166 00000	1 63772	142 98549	1 27176	127 60106	2 90205	117 97098	2 52851	108 01451	2 15106	102 58655	3 76961	96 14314	3 38408
84	168 00000	1 63336	143 28652	1 26299	128 07819	2 88883	118 57304	2 51078	110 71348	2 12878	103 36471	3 74274	98 98824	3 35257
85	170 00000	1 62899	145 58755	1 25422	130 55531	2 87560	119 17510	2 49305	111 41245	2 10651	104 14286	3 71587	99 83333	3 32105
86	172 00000	1 62463	147 88858	1 24544	131 03243	2 86237	121 77716	2 47533	112 11142	2 08423	106 92101	3 68900	100 67843	3 28953
87	174 00000	1 62026	148 18961	1 23667	133 50955	2 84914	122 37922	2 45760	114 81039	2 06195	107 69916	3 66212	101 52353	3 25802
88	176 00000	1 61590	150 49064	1 22789	135 98667	2 83591	124 98128	2 43987	115 50936	2 03968	108 47731	3 63525	102 36863	3 22650
89	178 00000	1 61153	152 79167	1 21912	136 46379	2 82268	125 58334	2 42214	116 20833	2 01740	109 25546	3 60838	103 21373	3 19498
90	180 00000	1 60717	153 09270	1 21035	138 94091	2 80946	126 18540	2 40441	118 90730	3 99512	110 03361	3 58151	104 05882	3 16347
91	182 00000	1 60280	155 39373	1 20157	139 41803	2 79623	128 78746	2 38668	119 60627	3 97285	112 81176	3 55463	106 90392	3 13195
92	184 00000	1 59844	157 69476	1 19280	141 89516	2 78300	129 38952	2 36895	120 30524	3 95057	113 58992	3 52776	107 74902	3 10043
93	186 00000	1 59407	159 99579	1 18403	142 37228	2 76977	131 99158	2 35122	121 00421	3 92830	114 36807	3 50089	108 59412	3 06891
94	188 00000	1 58971	160 29682	1 17525	144 84940	2 75654	132 59364	2 33350	123 70318	3 90602	115 14622	3 47402	109 43922	3 03740
95	190 00000	1 58534	162 59785	1 16648	145 32652	2 74331	133 19570	2 31577	124 40215	3 88374	117 92437	3 44715	110 28431	3 00588
96	192 00000	1 58098	164 89888	1 15770	147 80364	2 73009	135 79776	2 29804	125 10112	3 86147	118 70252	3 42027	111 12941	4 97436
97	194 00000	1 57661	165 19991	1 14893	148 28076	2 71686	136 39982	2 28031	127 80009	3 83919	119 48067	3 39340	113 97451	4 94285
98	196 00000	1 57225	167 50094	1 14016	150 75788	2 70363	137 00188	2 26258	128 49906	3 81691	120 25882	3 36653	114 81961	4 91133
99	198 00000	1 56788	169 80197	1 13138	151 23500	2 69040	139 60394	2 24485	129 19803	3 79464	121 03697	3 33966	115 66471	4 87981
100	200 00000	1 56352	170 10300	1 12261	153 71213	2 67717	140 20600	2 22712	131 89700	3 77236	123 81513	3 31279	116 50980	4 84829

Common Logarithms* of p^n and q^n ($q=1-p$)

For explanation see page 77

n	p(q) 0.08	q(p) 0.92	p(q) 0.09	q(p) 0.91	p(q) 0.10	q(p) 0.90	p(q) 0.11	q(p) 0.89	p(q) 0.12	q(p) 0.88	p(q) 0.13	q(p) 0.87	p(q) 0.14	q(p) 0.86
0	0 00000	0 00000	0 00000	0 00000	0 00000	0 00000	0 00000	0 00000	0 00000	0 00000	0 00000	0 00000	0 00000	0 00000
1	2 90309	1 96379	2 95424	1 95904	1 00000	1 95424	1 04139	1 94939	1 07918	1 94448	1 11394	1 93952	1 14613	1 93450
2	3 80618	1 92758	3 90849	1 91808	2 00000	1 90849	2 08279	1 89878	2 15836	1 88897	2 22789	1 87904	2 29226	1 86900
3	4 70927	1 89136	4 86273	1 87712	3 00000	1 86273	3 12418	1 84817	3 23754	1 83345	3 34183	1 81856	3 43838	1 80350
4	5 61236	1 85515	5 81697	1 83617	4 00000	1 81697	4 16557	1 79756	4 31672	1 77793	4 45577	1 75808	4 58451	1 73799
5	6 51545	1 81894	6 77121	1 79521	5 00000	1 77121	5 20696	1 74695	5 39591	1 72241	5 56972	1 69760	5 73064	1 67249
6	7 41854	1 78273	7 72546	1 75425	6 00000	1 72546	6 24836	1 69634	6 47509	1 66690	6 68366	1 63712	6 87677	1 60699
7	8 32163	1 74651	8 67970	1 71329	7 00000	1 67970	7 28975	1 64573	7 55427	1 61138	7 79760	1 57663	6 02290	1 54149
8	9 22472	1 71030	9 63394	1 67233	8 00000	1 63394	8 33114	1 59512	8 63345	1 55586	8 91155	1 51615	7 16902	1 47599
9	10 12781	1 67409	10 58818	1 63137	9 00000	1 58818	9 37253	1 54451	9 71263	1 50034	8 02549	1 45567	8 31515	1 41049
10	11 03090	1 63788	11 54243	1 59041	10 00000	1 54243	10 41393	1 49390	10 79181	1 44483	9 13943	1 39519	9 46128	1 34498
11	13 93399	1 60167	12 49667	1 54946	11 00000	1 49667	11 45532	1 44329	11 87099	1 38931	10 25338	1 33471	10 60741	1 27948
12	14 83708	1 56545	13 45091	1 50850	12 00000	1 45091	12 49671	1 39268	12 95017	1 33379	11 36732	1 27423	11 75354	1 21398
13	15 74017	1 52924	14 40515	1 46754	13 00000	1 40515	13 53810	1 34207	12 02936	1 27827	12 48126	1 21375	12 89966	1 14848
14	16 64326	1 49303	15 35940	1 42658	14 00000	1 35940	14 57950	1 29146	13 10854	1 22276	13 59521	1 15327	12 04579	1 08298
15	17 54635	1 45682	16 31364	1 38562	15 00000	1 31364	15 62089	1 24085	14 18772	1 16724	14 70915	1 09279	13 19192	1 01748
16	18 44944	1 42061	17 26788	1 34466	16 00000	1 26788	16 66228	1 19024	15 26690	1 11172	15 82309	1 03231	14 33805	2 95198
17	19 35253	1 38439	18 22212	1 30370	17 00000	1 22212	17 70368	1 13963	16 34608	1 05621	16 93704	2 97183	15 48418	2 88647
18	20 25562	1 34818	19 17637	1 26275	18 00000	1 17637	18 74507	1 08902	17 42526	1 00069	16 05098	2 91135	16 63030	2 82097
19	21 15871	1 31197	20 13061	1 22179	19 00000	1 13061	19 78646	1 03841	18 50444	2 94517	17 16492	2 85087	17 77643	2 75547
20	22 06180	1 27576	21 08485	1 18083	20 00000	1 08485	20 82785	2 98780	19 58362	2 88965	18 27887	2 79039	18 92256	2 68997
21	24 96489	1 23954	22 03909	1 13987	21 00000	1 03909	21 86925	2 93719	20 66281	2 83414	19 39281	2 72990	18 06869	2 62447
22	25 86798	1 20333	24 99334	1 09891	22 00000	2 99334	22 91064	2 88658	21 74199	2 77862	20 50675	2 66942	19 21482	2 55897
23	26 77107	1 16712	25 94758	1 05795	23 00000	2 94758	23 95203	2 83597	22 82117	2 72310	21 62070	2 60894	20 36094	2 49346
24	27 67416	1 13091	26 90182	1 01699	24 00000	2 90182	24 99342	2 78536	23 90035	2 66758	22 73464	2 54846	21 50707	2 42796
25	28 57725	1 09470	27 85606	2 97603	25 00000	2 85606	24 03482	2 73475	24 97953	2 61207	23 84858	2 48798	22 65320	2 36246
26	29 48034	1 05848	28 81031	2 93508	26 00000	2 81031	25 07621	2 68414	24 05871	2 55655	24 96253	2 42750	23 79933	2 29696
27	30 38343	1 02227	29 76455	2 89412	27 00000	2 76455	26 11760	2 63353	25 13789	2 50103	24 07647	2 36702	24 94546	2 23146
28	31 28652	2 98606	30 71879	2 85316	28 00000	2 71879	27 15900	2 58292	26 21707	2 44551	25 19041	2 30654	24 09159	2 16596
29	32 18961	2 94985	31 67303	2 81220	29 00000	2 67303	28 20039	2 53231	27 29626	2 39000	26 30436	2 24606	25 23771	2 10046
30	33 09270	2 91363	32 62728	2 77124	30 00000	2 62728	29 24178	2 48170	28 37544	2 33448	27 41830	2 18558	26 38384	2 03495
31	35 99579	2 87742	33 58152	2 73028	31 00000	2 58152	30 28317	2 43109	29 45462	2 27896	28 53224	2 12510	27 52997	3 96945
32	36 89888	2 84121	34 53576	2 68932	32 00000	2 53576	31 32457	2 38048	30 53380	2 22345	29 64619	2 06462	28 67610	3 90395
33	37 80197	2 80500	35 49000	2 64837	33 00000	2 49000	32 36596	2 32987	31 61298	2 16793	30 76013	2 00414	29 82223	3 83845
34	38 70506	2 76879	36 44425	2 60741	34 00000	2 44425	33 40735	2 27926	32 69216	2 11241	31 87407	3 94365	30 96835	3 77295
35	39 60815	2 73257	37 39849	2 56645	35 00000	2 39849	34 44874	2 22865	33 77134	2 05689	32 98802	3 88317	30 11448	3 70745
36	40 51124	2 69636	38 35273	2 52549	36 00000	2 35273	35 49014	2 17804	34 85052	2 00138	32 10196	3 82269	31 26061	3 64194
37	41 41433	2 66015	39 30697	2 48453	37 00000	2 30697	36 53153	2 12743	35 92971	3 94586	33 21590	3 76221	32 40674	3 57644
38	42 31742	2 62394	40 26122	2 44357	38 00000	2 26122	37 57292	2 07682	35 00889	3 89034	34 32985	3 70173	33 55287	3 51094
39	43 22051	2 58773	41 21546	2 40261	39 00000	2 21546	38 61431	2 02621	36 08807	3 83482	35 44379	3 64125	34 69899	3 44544
40	44 12360	2 55151	42 16970	2 36166	40 00000	2 16970	39 65571	3 97560	37 16725	3 77931	36 55773	3 58077	35 84512	3 37994
41	45 02669	2 51530	43 12394	2 32070	41 00000	2 12394	40 69710	3 92499	38 24643	3 72379	37 67168	3 52029	36 99125	3 31444
42	47 92978	2 47909	44 07819	2 27974	42 00000	2 07819	41 73849	3 87438	39 32561	3 66827	38 78562	3 45981	36 13738	3 24893
43	48 83287	2 44288	45 03243	2 23878	43 00000	2 03243	42 77989	3 82377	40 40479	3 61275	39 89956	3 39933	37 28351	3 18343
44	49 73596	2 40666	47 98667	2 19782	44 00000	3 98667	43 82128	3 77316	41 48397	3 55724	39 01351	3 33885	38 42963	3 11793
45	50 63905	2 37045	48 94091	2 15686	45 00000	3 94091	44 86267	3 72255	42 56316	3 50172	40 12745	3 27837	39 57576	3 05243
46	51 54214	2 33424	49 89516	2 11590	46 00000	3 89516	45 90406	3 67194	43 64234	3 44620	41 24139	3 21789	40 72189	4 98693
47	52 44523	2 29803	50 84940	2 07495	47 00000	3 84940	46 94546	3 62133	44 72152	3 39069	42 35534	3 15740	41 86802	4 92143
48	53 34832	2 26182	51 80364	2 03399	48 00000	3 80364	47 98685	3 57072	45 80070	3 33517	43 46928	3 09692	41 01415	4 85593
49	54 25141	2 22560	52 75788	3 99303	49 00000	3 75788	47 02824	3 52011	46 87988	3 27965	44 58322	3 03644	42 16027	4 79042
50	55 15450	2 18939	53 71213	3 95207	50 00000	3 71213	48 06963	3 46950	47 95906	3 22413	45 69717	4 97596	43 30640	4 72492
51	56 05759	2 15318	54 66637	3 91111	51 00000	3 66637	49 11103	3 41889	47 03824	3 16862	46 81111	4 91548	44 45253	4 65942
52	58 96068	2 11697	55 62061	3 87015	52 00000	3 62061	50 15242	3 36828	48 11742	3 11310	47 92505	4 85500	45 59866	4 59392
53	59 86377	2 08075	56 57485	3 82919	53 00000	3 57485	51 19381	3 31767	49 19661	3 05758	47 03900	4 79452	46 74479	4 52842
54	60 76686	2 04454	57 52910	3 78824	54 00000	3 52910	52 23521	3 26706	50 27579	3 00206	48 15294	4 73404	47 89091	4 46292
55	61 66995	2 00833	58 48334	3 74728	55 00000	3 48334	53 27660	3 21645	51 35497	4 94655	49 26688	4 67356	47 03704	4 39741
56	62 57304	3 97212	59 43758	3 70632	56 00000	3 43758	54 31799	3 16584	52 43415	4 89103	50 38083	4 61308	48 18317	4 33191
57	63 47613	3 93591	60 39182	3 66536	57 00000	3 39182	55 35938	3 11523	53 51333	4 83551	51 49477	4 55260	49 32930	4 26641
58	64 37922	3 89969	61 34607	3 62440	58 00000	3 34607	56 40078	3 06462	54 59251	4 77999	52 60871	4 49212	50 47543	4 20091
59	65 28231	3 86348	62 30031	3 58344	59 00000	3 30031	57 44217	3 01401	55 67169	4 72448	53 72266	4 43164	51 62155	4 13541
60	66 18540	3 82727	63 25455	3 54248	60 00000	3 25455	58 48356	4 96340	56 75087	4 66896	54 83660	4 37116	52 76768	4 06991
61	67 08849	3 79106	64 20879	3 50152	61 00000	3 20879	59 52495	4 91279	57 83006	4 61344	55 95054	4 31067	53 91381	4 00441
62	69 99158	3 75485	65 16304	3 46057	62 00000	3 16304	60 56635	4 86218	58 90924	4 55793	55 06449	4 25019	53 05994	5 93890
63	70 89467	3 71863	66 11728	3 41961	63 00000	3 11728	61 60774	4 81157	59 98842	4 50241	56 17843	4 18971	54 20607	5 87340
64	71 79776	3 68242	67 07152	3 37865	64 00000	3 07152	62 64913	4 76096	59 06760	4 44689	57 29237	4 12923	55 35219	5 80790
65	72 70085	3 64621	68 02576	3 33769	65 00000	3 02576	63 69052	4 71035	60 14678	4 39137	58 40632	4 06875	56 49832	5 74240
66	73 60394	3 61000	70 98001	3 29673	66 00000	4 98001	64 73192	4 65974	61 22596	4 33586	59 52026	4 00827	57 64445	5 67690
67	74 50703	3 57378	71 93425	3 25577	67 00000	4 93425	65 77331	4 60913	62 30514	4 28034	60 63420	5 94779	58 79058	5 61140
68	75 41012	3 53757	72 88849	3 21481	68 00000	4 88849	66 81470	4 55852	63 38432	4 22482	61 74815	5 88731	59 93671	5 54589
69	76 31321	3 50136	73 84273	3 17386	69 00000	4 84273	67 85610	4 50791	64 46351	4 16930	62 86209	5 82683	59 08283	5 48039
70	77 21630	3 46515	74 79698	3 13290	70 00000	4 79698	68 89749	4 45730	65 54269	4 11379	63 97603	5 76635	60 22896	5 41489
71	78 11939	3 42894	75 75122	3 09194	71 00000	4 75122	69 93888	4 40669	66 62187	4 05827	63 08998	5 70587	61 37509	5 34939
72	79 02248	3 39272	76 70546	3 05098	72 00000	4 70546	70 98027	4 35608	67 70105	4 00275	64 20392	5 64539	62 52122	5 28389
73	81 92557	3 35651	77 65970	3 01002	73 00000	4 65970	70 02167	4 30547	68 78023	5 94724	65 31786	5 58491	63 66735	5 21839
74	82 82866	3 32030	78 61395	4 96906	74 00000	4 61395	71 06306	4 25486	69 85941	5 89172	66 43181	5 52442	64 81347	5 15289
75	83 73175	3 28409	79 56819	4 92810	75 00000	4 56819	72 10445	4 20425	70 93859	5 83620	67 54575	5 46394	65 95960	5 08738
76	84 63484	3 24787	80 52243	4 88715	76 00000	4 52243	73 14584	4 15364	70 01777	5 78068	68 65969	5 40346	65 10573	5 02188
77	85 53793	3 21166	81 47667	4 84619	77 00000	4 47667	74 18724	4 10303	71 09696	5 72517	69 77364	5 34298	66 25186	6 95638
78	86 44102	3 17545	82 43092	4 80523	78 00000	4 43092	75 22863	4 05242	72 17614	5 66965	70 88758	5 28250	67 39799	6 89088
79	87 34411	3 13924	83 38516	4 76427	79 00000	4 38516	76 27002	4 00181	73 25532	5 61413	70 00152	5 22202	68 54411	6 82538
80	88 24720	3 10303	84 33940	4 72331	80 00000	4 33940	77 31141	5 95120	74 33450	5 55861	71 11547	5 16154	69 69024	6 75988
81	89 15029	3 06681	85 29364	4 68235	81 00000	4 29364	78 35281	5 90059	75 41368	5 50310	72 22941	5 10106	70 83637	6 69437
82	90 05338	3 03060	86 24789	4 64139	82 00000	4 24789	79 39420	5 84998	76 49286	5 44758	73 34335	5 04058	71 98250	6 62887
83	92 95647	4 99439	87 20213	4 60044	83 00000	4 20213	80 43559	5 79937	77 57204	5 39206	74 45730	6 98010	71 12863	6 56337
84	93 85956	4 95818	88 15637	4 55948	84 00000	4 15637	81 47699	5 74876	78 65122	5 33654	75 57124	6 91962	72 27476	6 49787
85	94 76265	4 92197	89 11061	4 51852	85 00000	4 11061	82 51838	5 69815	79 73041	5 28103	76 68518	6 85914	73 42088	6 43237
86	95 66574	4 88575	90 06486	4 47756	86 00000	4 06486	83 55977	5 64754	80 80959	5 22551	77 79913	6 79866	74 56701	6 36687
87	96 56883	4 84954	91 01910	4 43660	87 00000	4 01910	84 60116	5 59693	81 88877	5 16999	78 91307	6 73817	75 71314	6 30137
88	97 47192	4 81333	93 97334	4 39564	88 00000	5 97334	85 64256	5 54632	82 96795	5 11448	78 02702	6 67769	76 85927	6 23586
89	98 37501	4 77712	94 92758	4 35468	89 00000	5 92758	86 68395	5 49571	82 04713	5 05896	79 14096	6 61721	76 00540	6 17036
90	99 27810	4 74090	95 88183	4 31373	90 00000	5 88183	87 72534	5 44510	83 12631	5 00344	80 25490	6 55673	77 15152	6 10486
91	100 18119	4 70469	96 83607	4 27277	91 00000	5 83607	88 76673	5 39449	84 20549	6 94792	81 36885	6 49625	78 29765	6 03936
92	101 08428	4 66848	97 79031	4 23181	92 00000	5 79031	89 80813	5 34388	85 28467	6 89241	82 48279	6 43577	79 44378	7 97386
93	103 98737	4 63227	98 74455	4 19085	93 00000	5 74455	90 84952	5 29327	86 36386	6 83689	83 59673	6 37529	80 58991	7 90836
94	104 89046	4 59606	99 69880	4 14989	94 00000	5 69880	91 89091	5 24266	87 44304	6 78137	84 71068	6 31481	81 73604	7 84285
95	105 79355	4 55984	100 65304	4 10893	95 00000	5 65304	92 93231	5 19205	88 52222	6 72585	85 82462	6 25433	82 88216	7 77735
96	106 69664	4 52363	101 60728	4 06797	96 00000	5 60728	93 97370	5 14144	89 60140	6 67034	86 93856	6 19385	82 02829	7 71185
97	107 59973	4 48742	102 56152	4 02702	97 00000	5 56152	93 01509	5 09083	90 68058	6 61482	86 05251	6 13337	83 17442	7 64635
98	108 50282	4 45121	103 51577	5 98606	98 00000	5 51577	94 05648	5 04022	91 75976	6 55930	87 16645	6 07289	84 32055	7 58085
99	109 40591	4 41499	104 47001	5 94510	99 00000	5 47001	95 09788	6 98961	92 83894	6 50378	88 28039	6 01241	85 46668	7 51535
100	110 30900	4 37878	105 42425	5 90414	100 00000	5 42425	96 13927	6 93900	93 91812	6 44827	89 39434	7 95193	86 61280	7 44985

Common Logarithms* of p^n and q^n ($q=1-p$)

For explanation see page 77

n	p(q) 0.15	q(p) 0.85	p(q) 0.16	q(p) 0.84	p(q) 0.17	q(p) 0.83	p(q) 0.18	q(p) 0.82	p(q) 0.19	q(p) 0.81	p(q) 0.20	q(p) 0.80	p(q) 0.21	q(p) 0.79
0	0 00000	0 00000	0 00000	0 00000	0 00000	0 00000	0 00000	0 00000	0 00000	0 00000	0 00000	0 00000	0 00000	0 00000
1	1 17609	1 92942	1 20412	1 92428	1 23045	1 91908	1 25527	1 91381	1 27875	1 90849	1 30103	1 90309	1 32222	1 89763
2	2 35218	1 85884	2 40824	1 84856	2 46090	1 83816	2 51055	1 82763	2 55751	1 81697	2 60206	1 80618	2 64444	1 79525
3	3 52827	1 78826	3 61236	1 77284	3 69135	1 75723	3 76582	1 74144	3 83626	1 72546	3 90309	1 70927	3 96666	1 69288
4	4 70437	1 71768	4 81648	1 69712	4 92180	1 67631	3 02109	1 65526	3 11501	1 63394	3 20412	1 61236	3 28888	1 59051
5	5 88046	1 64709	4 02060	1 62140	4 15224	1 59539	4 27636	1 56907	4 39377	1 54243	4 50515	1 51545	4 61110	1 48814
6	5 05655	1 57651	5 22472	1 54568	5 38269	1 51447	5 53164	1 48288	5 67252	1 45091	5 80618	1 41854	5 93332	1 38576
7	6 23264	1 50593	6 42884	1 46996	6 61314	1 43355	6 78691	1 39670	6 95128	1 35940	5 10721	1 32163	5 25554	1 28339
8	7 40873	1 43535	7 63296	1 39423	7 84359	1 35262	6 04218	1 31051	6 23003	1 26788	6 40824	1 22472	6 57775	1 18102
9	8 58482	1 36477	8 83708	1 31851	7 07404	1 27170	7 29745	1 22432	7 50878	1 17637	7 70927	1 12781	7 89997	1 07864
10	9 76091	1 29419	8 04120	1 24279	8 30449	1 19078	8 55273	1 13814	8 78754	1 08485	7 01030	1 03090	7 22219	2 97627
11	10 93700	1 22361	9 24532	1 16707	9 53494	1 10986	9 80800	1 05195	8 06629	2 99334	8 31133	2 93399	8 54441	2 87390
12	10 11310	1 15303	10 44944	1 09135	10 76539	1 02894	9 06327	2 96577	9 34504	2 90182	9 61236	2 83708	9 86663	2 77153
13	11 28919	1 08245	11 65356	1 01563	11 99584	2 94802	10 31854	2 87958	10 62380	2 81031	10 91339	2 74017	9 18885	2 66915
14	12 46528	1 01186	12 85768	2 93991	11 22628	2 86709	11 57382	2 79339	11 90255	2 71879	10 21442	2 64326	10 51107	2 56678
15	13 64137	2 94128	12 06180	2 86419	12 45673	2 78617	12 82909	2 70721	11 18130	2 62728	11 51545	2 54635	11 83329	2 46441
16	14 81746	2 87070	13 26592	2 78847	13 68718	2 70525	12 08436	2 62102	12 46006	2 53576	12 81648	2 44944	11 15551	2 36203
17	15 99355	2 80012	14 47004	2 71275	14 91763	2 62433	13 33963	2 53484	13 73881	2 44425	12 11751	2 35253	12 47773	2 25966
18	15 16964	2 72954	15 67416	2 63703	14 14808	2 54341	14 59491	2 44865	13 01756	2 35273	13 41854	2 25562	13 79995	2 15729
19	16 34573	2 65896	16 87828	2 56131	15 37853	2 46248	15 85018	2 36246	14 29632	2 26122	14 71957	2 15871	13 12217	2 05491
20	17 52183	2 58838	16 08240	2 48559	16 60898	2 38156	15 10545	2 27628	15 57507	2 16970	14 02060	2 06180	14 44439	3 95254
21	18 69792	2 51780	17 28652	2 40987	17 83943	2 30064	16 36072	2 19009	16 85383	2 07819	15 32163	3 96489	15 76661	3 85017
22	19 87401	2 44722	18 49064	2 33414	17 06988	2 21972	17 61600	2 10390	16 13258	3 98667	16 62266	3 86798	15 08882	3 74780
23	19 05010	2 37664	19 69476	2 25842	18 30033	2 13880	18 87127	2 01772	17 41133	3 89516	17 92369	3 77107	16 41104	3 64542
24	20 22619	2 30605	20 89888	2 18270	19 53077	2 05787	18 12654	3 93153	18 69009	3 80364	17 22472	3 67416	17 73326	3 54305
25	21 40228	2 23547	20 10300	2 10698	20 76122	3 97695	19 38181	3 84535	19 96884	3 71213	18 52575	3 57725	17 05548	3 44068
26	22 57837	2 16489	21 30712	2 03126	21 99167	3 89603	20 63709	3 75916	19 24759	3 62061	19 82678	3 48034	18 37770	3 33830
27	23 75446	2 09431	22 51124	3 95554	21 22212	3 81511	21 89236	3 67297	20 52635	3 52910	19 12781	3 38343	19 69992	3 23593
28	24 93056	2 02373	23 71536	3 87982	22 45257	3 73419	21 14763	3 58679	21 80510	3 43758	20 42884	3 28652	19 02214	3 13356
29	24 10665	3 95315	24 91948	3 80410	23 68302	3 65326	22 40290	3 50060	21 08385	3 34607	21 72987	3 18961	20 34436	3 03119
30	25 28274	3 88257	24 12360	3 72838	24 91347	3 57234	23 65818	3 41442	22 36261	3 25455	21 03090	3 09270	21 66658	4 92881
31	26 45883	3 81199	25 32772	3 65266	24 14392	3 49142	24 91345	3 32823	23 64136	3 16304	22 33193	4 99579	22 98880	4 82644
32	27 63492	3 74141	26 53184	3 57694	25 37437	3 41050	24 16872	3 24204	24 92012	3 07152	23 63296	4 89888	22 31102	4 72407
33	28 81101	3 67082	27 73596	3 50122	26 60481	3 32958	25 42399	3 15586	24 19887	4 98001	24 93399	4 80197	23 63324	4 62169
34	29 98710	3 60024	28 94008	3 42550	27 83526	3 24866	26 67927	3 06967	25 47762	4 88849	24 23502	4 70506	24 95546	4 51932
35	29 16319	3 52966	28 14420	3 34978	27 06571	3 16773	27 93454	4 98348	26 75638	4 79698	25 53605	4 60815	24 27768	4 41695
36	30 33929	3 45908	29 34832	3 27405	28 29616	3 08681	27 18981	4 89730	26 03513	4 70546	26 83708	4 51124	25 59989	4 31458
37	31 51538	3 38850	30 55244	3 19833	29 52661	3 00589	28 44508	4 81111	27 31388	4 61395	26 13811	4 41433	26 92211	4 21220
38	32 69147	3 31792	31 75656	3 12261	30 75706	4 92497	29 70036	4 72493	28 59264	4 52243	27 43914	4 31742	26 24433	4 10983
39	33 86756	3 24734	32 96068	3 04689	31 98751	4 84405	30 95563	4 63874	29 87139	4 43092	28 74017	4 22051	27 56655	4 00746
40	33 04365	3 17676	32 16480	4 97117	31 21796	4 76312	30 21090	4 55255	29 15014	4 33940	28 04120	4 12360	28 88877	5 90508
41	34 21974	3 10618	33 36892	4 89545	32 44841	4 68220	31 46617	4 46637	30 42890	4 24789	29 34223	4 02669	28 21099	5 80271
42	35 39583	3 03559	34 57304	4 81973	33 67885	4 60128	32 72145	4 38018	31 70765	4 15637	30 64326	5 92978	29 53321	5 70034
43	36 57192	4 96501	35 77716	4 74401	34 90930	4 52036	33 97672	4 29400	32 98640	4 06486	31 94429	5 83287	30 85543	5 59796
44	37 74802	4 89443	36 98128	4 66829	34 13975	4 43944	33 23199	4 20781	32 26516	5 97334	31 24532	5 73596	30 17765	5 49559
45	38 92411	4 82385	36 18540	4 59257	35 37020	4 35851	34 48726	4 12162	33 54391	5 88183	32 54635	5 63905	31 49987	5 39322
46	38 10020	4 75327	37 38952	4 51685	36 60065	4 27759	35 74254	4 03544	34 82267	5 79031	33 84738	5 54214	32 82209	5 29085
47	39 27629	4 68269	38 59364	4 44113	37 83110	4 19667	36 99781	5 94925	34 10142	5 69880	33 14841	5 44523	32 14431	5 18847
48	40 45238	4 61211	39 79776	4 36541	37 06155	4 11575	36 25308	5 86306	35 38017	5 60728	34 44944	5 34832	33 46653	5 08610
49	41 62847	4 54153	39 00188	4 28969	38 29200	4 03483	37 50835	5 77688	36 65893	5 51577	35 75047	5 25141	34 78875	6 98373
50	42 80456	4 47095	40 20600	4 21396	39 52245	5 95390	38 76363	5 69069	37 93768	5 42425	35 05150	5 15450	34 11096	6 88135
51	43 98065	4 40037	41 41012	4 13824	40 75290	5 87298	38 01890	5 60451	37 21643	5 33274	36 35253	5 05759	35 43318	6 77898
52	43 15675	4 32978	42 61424	4 06252	41 98334	5 79206	39 27417	5 51832	38 49519	5 24122	37 65356	6 96068	36 75540	6 67661
53	44 33284	4 25920	43 81836	5 98680	41 21379	5 71114	40 52944	5 43213	39 77394	5 14971	38 95459	6 86377	36 07762	6 57424
54	45 50893	4 18862	43 02248	5 91108	42 44424	5 63022	41 78472	5 34595	39 05269	5 05819	38 25562	6 76686	37 39984	6 47186
55	46 68502	4 11804	44 22660	5 83536	43 67469	5 54930	41 03999	5 25976	40 33145	6 96668	39 55665	6 66995	38 72206	6 36949
56	47 86111	4 04746	45 43072	5 75964	44 90514	5 46837	42 29526	5 17358	41 61020	6 87516	40 85768	6 57304	38 04428	6 26712
57	47 03720	5 97688	46 63484	5 68392	44 13559	5 38745	43 55053	5 08739	42 88896	6 78365	40 15871	6 47613	39 36650	6 16474
58	48 21329	5 90630	47 83896	5 60820	45 36604	5 30653	44 80581	5 00120	42 16771	6 69213	41 45974	6 37922	40 68872	6 06237
59	49 38938	5 83572	47 04308	5 53248	46 59649	5 22561	44 06108	6 91502	43 44646	6 60062	42 76077	6 28231	40 01094	7 96000
60	50 56548	5 76514	48 24720	5 45676	47 82694	5 14469	45 31635	6 82883	44 72522	6 50910	42 06180	6 18540	41 33316	7 85763
61	51 74157	5 69455	49 45132	5 38104	47 05738	5 06376	46 57162	6 74264	44 00397	6 41759	43 36283	6 08849	42 65538	7 75525
62	52 91766	5 62397	50 65544	5 30532	48 28783	6 98284	47 82690	6 65646	45 28272	6 32607	44 66386	7 99158	43 97760	7 65288
63	52 09375	5 55339	51 85956	5 22960	49 51828	6 90192	47 08217	6 57027	46 56148	6 23456	45 96489	7 89467	43 29982	7 55051
64	53 26984	5 48281	51 06368	5 15387	50 74873	6 82100	48 33744	6 48409	47 84023	6 14304	45 26592	7 79776	44 62203	7 44813
65	54 44593	5 41223	52 26780	5 07815	51 97918	6 74008	49 59271	6 39790	47 11898	6 05153	46 56695	7 70085	45 94425	7 34576
66	55 62202	5 34165	53 47192	5 00243	51 20963	6 65915	50 84799	6 31171	48 39774	7 96001	47 86798	7 60394	45 26647	7 24339
67	56 79811	5 27107	54 67604	6 92671	52 44008	6 57823	50 10326	6 22553	49 67649	7 86850	47 16901	7 50703	46 58869	7 14102
68	57 97421	5 20049	55 88016	6 85099	53 67053	6 49731	51 35853	6 13934	50 95524	7 77698	48 47004	7 41012	47 91091	7 03864
69	57 15030	5 12991	55 08428	6 77527	54 90098	6 41639	52 61380	6 05316	50 23400	7 68547	49 77107	7 31321	47 23313	8 93627
70	58 32639	5 05932	56 28840	6 69955	54 13142	6 33547	53 86908	7 96697	51 51275	7 59395	49 07210	7 21630	48 55535	8 83390
71	59 50248	6 98874	57 49252	6 62383	55 36187	6 25454	53 12435	7 88078	52 79151	7 50244	50 37313	7 11939	49 87757	8 73152
72	60 67857	6 91816	58 69664	6 54811	56 59232	6 17362	54 37962	7 79460	52 07026	7 41092	51 67416	7 02248	49 19979	8 62915
73	61 85466	6 84758	59 90076	6 47239	57 82277	6 09270	55 63489	7 70841	53 34901	7 31941	52 97519	8 92557	50 52201	8 52678
74	61 03075	6 77700	59 10488	6 39667	57 05322	6 01178	56 89017	7 62223	54 62777	7 22789	52 27622	8 82866	51 84423	8 42440
75	62 20684	6 70642	60 30900	6 32095	58 28367	7 93086	56 14544	7 53604	55 90652	7 13638	53 57725	8 73175	51 16645	8 32203
76	63 38294	6 63584	61 51312	6 24523	59 51412	7 84994	57 40071	7 44985	55 18527	7 04486	54 87828	8 63484	52 48867	8 21966
77	64 55903	6 56526	62 71724	6 16951	60 74457	7 76901	58 65598	7 36367	56 46403	8 95335	54 17931	8 53793	53 81089	8 11729
78	65 73512	6 49468	63 92136	6 09378	61 97502	7 68809	59 91126	7 27748	57 74278	8 86183	55 48034	8 44102	53 13311	8 01491
79	66 91121	6 42410	63 12548	6 01806	61 20546	7 60717	59 16653	7 19129	57 02153	8 77032	56 78137	8 34411	54 45532	9 91254
80	66 08730	6 35351	64 32960	7 94234	62 43591	7 52625	60 42180	7 10511	58 30029	8 67880	56 08240	8 24720	55 77754	9 81017
81	67 26339	6 28293	65 53372	7 86662	63 66636	7 44533	61 67707	7 01892	59 57904	8 58729	57 38343	8 15029	55 09976	9 70779
82	68 43948	6 21235	66 73784	7 79090	64 89681	7 36440	62 93235	8 93274	60 85780	8 49577	58 68446	8 05338	56 42198	9 60542
83	69 61557	6 14177	67 94196	7 71518	64 12726	7 28348	62 18762	8 84655	60 13655	8 40426	59 98549	9 95647	57 74420	9 50305
84	70 79167	6 07119	67 14608	7 63946	65 35771	7 20256	63 44289	8 76036	61 41530	8 31274	59 28652	9 85956	57 06642	9 40068
85	71 96776	6 00061	68 35020	7 56374	66 58816	7 12164	64 69816	8 67418	62 69406	8 22123	60 58755	9 76265	58 38864	9 29830
86	71 14385	7 93003	69 55432	7 48802	67 81861	7 04072	65 95344	8 58799	63 97281	8 12971	61 88858	9 66574	59 71086	9 19593
87	72 31994	7 85945	70 75844	7 41230	67 04906	8 95979	65 20871	8 50181	63 25156	8 03820	61 18961	9 56883	59 03308	9 09356
88	73 49603	7 78887	71 96256	7 33658	68 27951	8 87887	66 46398	8 41562	64 53032	9 94668	62 49064	9 47192	60 35530	10 99118
89	74 67212	7 71828	71 16668	7 26086	69 50995	8 79795	67 71925	8 32943	65 80907	9 85517	63 79167	9 37501	61 67752	10 88881
90	75 84821	7 64770	72 37080	7 18514	70 74040	8 71703	68 97453	8 24325	65 08782	9 76365	63 09270	9 27810	62 99974	10 78644
91	75 02430	7 57712	73 57492	7 10942	71 97085	8 63611	68 22980	8 15706	66 36658	9 67214	64 39373	9 18119	62 32196	10 68407
92	76 20040	7 50654	74 77904	7 03369	71 20130	8 55518	69 48507	8 07087	67 64533	9 58062	65 69476	9 08428	63 64418	10 58169
93	77 37649	7 43596	75 98316	8 95797	72 43175	8 47426	70 74034	9 98469	68 92408	9 48911	66 99579	10 98737	64 96639	10 47932
94	78 55258	7 36538	75 18728	8 88225	73 66220	8 39334	71 99562	9 89850	68 20284	9 39759	66 29682	10 89046	64 28861	10 37695
95	79 72867	7 29480	76 39140	8 80653	74 89265	8 31242	71 25089	9 81232	69 48159	9 30608	67 59785	10 79355	65 61083	10 27457
96	80 90476	7 22422	77 59552	8 73081	74 12310	8 23150	72 50616	9 72613	70 76035	9 21456	68 89888	10 69664	66 93305	10 17220
97	80 08085	7 15364	78 79964	8 65509	75 35355	8 15057	73 76143	9 63994	70 03910	9 12305	68 19991	10 59973	66 25527	10 06983
98	81 25694	7 08305	78 00376	8 57937	76 58399	8 06965	73 01671	9 55376	71 31785	9 03153	69 50094	10 50282	67 57749	11 96745
99	82 43303	7 01247	79 20788	8 50365	77 81444	9 98873	74 27198	9 46757	72 59661	10 94002	70 80197	10 40591	68 89971	11 86508
100	83 60913	8 94189	80 41200	8 42793	77 04489	9 90781	75 52725	9 38139	73 87536	10 84850	70 10300	10 30900	68 22193	11 76271

Common Logarithms* of p^n and q^n ($q=1-p$)

For explanation see page 77

n	$p(q)$ 0.22	$q(p)$ 0.78	$p(q)$ 0.23	$q(p)$ 0.77	$p(q)$ 0.24	$q(p)$ 0.76	$p(q)$ 0.25	$q(p)$ 0.75	$p(q)$ 0.26	$q(p)$ 0.74	$p(q)$ 0.27	$q(p)$ 0.73	$p(q)$ 0.28	$q(p)$ 0.72
0	0 00000	0 00000	0 00000	0 00000	0 00000	0 00000	0 00000	0 00000	0 00000	0 00000	0 00000	0 00000	0 00000	0 00000
1	1 34242	1 89209	1 36173	1 88649	1 38021	1 88081	1 39794	1 87506	1 41497	1 86923	1 43136	1 86332	1 44716	1 85733
2	2 68485	1 78419	2 72346	1 77298	2 76042	1 76163	2 79588	1 75012	2 82995	1 73846	2 86273	1 72665	2 89432	1 71466
3	2 02727	1 67628	2 08518	1 65947	2 14063	1 64244	2 19382	1 62518	2 24492	1 60770	2 29409	1 58997	2 34147	1 57200
4	3 36969	1 56838	3 44691	1 54596	3 52084	1 52325	3 59176	1 50025	3 65989	1 47693	3 72546	1 45329	3 78863	1 42933
5	4 71211	1 46047	4 80864	1 43245	4 90106	1 40407	4 98970	1 37531	3 07487	1 34616	3 15682	1 31661	3 23579	1 28666
6	4 05454	1 35257	4 17037	1 31894	4 28127	1 28488	4 38764	1 25037	4 48984	1 21539	4 58818	1 17994	4 68295	1 14399
7	5 39696	1 24466	5 53209	1 20544	5 66148	1 16570	5 78558	1 12543	5 90481	1 08462	4 01955	1 04326	4 13011	1 00133
8	6 73938	1 13676	6 89382	1 09193	5 04169	1 04651	5 18352	1 00049	5 31979	2 95385	5 45091	2 90658	5 57726	2 85866
9	6 08180	1 02885	6 25555	2 97842	6 42190	2 92732	6 58146	2 87555	6 73476	2 82309	6 88227	2 76991	5 02442	2 71599
10	7 42423	2 92095	7 61728	2 86491	7 80211	2 80814	7 97940	2 75061	6 14973	2 69232	6 31364	2 63323	6 47158	2 57332
11	8 76665	2 81304	8 97901	2 75140	7 18232	2 68895	7 37734	2 62567	7 56471	2 56155	7 74500	2 49655	7 91874	2 43066
12	8 10907	2 70514	8 34073	2 63789	8 56253	2 56976	8 77528	2 50074	8 97968	2 43078	7 17637	2 35987	7 36590	2 28799
13	9 45149	2 59723	9 70246	2 52438	9 94275	2 45058	8 17322	2 37580	8 39465	2 30001	8 60773	2 22320	8 81305	2 14532
14	10 79392	2 48932	9 06419	2 41087	9 32296	2 33139	9 57116	2 25086	9 80963	2 16924	8 03909	2 08652	8 26021	2 00265
15	10 13634	2 38142	10 42592	2 29736	10 70317	2 21220	10 96910	2 12592	9 22460	2 03848	9 47046	3 94984	9 70737	3 85999
16	11 47876	2 27351	11 78765	2 18385	10 08338	2 09302	10 36704	2 00098	10 63957	3 90771	10 90182	3 81317	9 15453	3 71732
17	12 82119	2 16561	11 14937	2 07034	11 46359	3 97383	11 76498	3 87604	10 05455	3 77694	10 33318	3 67649	10 60169	3 57465
18	12 16361	2 05770	12 51110	3 95683	12 84380	3 85464	11 16292	3 75110	11 46952	3 64617	11 76455	3 53981	10 04884	3 43198
19	13 50603	3 94980	13 87283	3 84332	12 22401	3 73546	12 56086	3 62616	12 88449	3 51540	11 19591	3 40313	11 49600	3 28932
20	14 84845	3 84189	13 23456	3 72981	13 60422	3 61627	13 95880	3 50123	12 29947	3 38463	12 62728	3 26646	12 94316	3 14665
21	14 19088	3 73399	14 59628	3 61631	14 98444	3 49709	13 35674	3 37629	13 71444	3 25387	12 05864	3 12978	12 39032	3 00398
22	15 53330	3 62608	15 95801	3 50280	14 36465	3 37790	14 75468	3 25135	13 12941	3 12310	13 49000	4 99310	13 83748	4 86131
23	16 87572	3 51818	15 31974	3 38929	15 74486	3 25871	14 15262	3 12641	14 54439	4 99233	14 92137	4 85643	13 28463	4 71865
24	16 21814	3 41027	16 68147	3 27578	15 12507	3 13953	15 55056	3 00147	15 95936	4 86156	14 35273	4 71975	14 73179	4 57598
25	17 56057	3 30237	16 04320	3 16227	16 50528	3 02034	16 94850	4 87653	15 37433	4 73079	15 78409	4 58307	14 17895	4 43331
26	18 90299	3 19446	17 40492	3 04876	17 88549	4 90115	16 34644	4 75159	16 78931	4 60002	15 21546	4 44639	15 62611	4 29064
27	18 24541	3 08655	18 76665	4 93525	17 26570	4 78197	17 74438	4 62665	16 20428	4 46926	16 64682	4 30972	15 07327	4 14798
28	19 58784	4 97865	18 12838	4 82174	18 64591	4 66278	17 14232	4 50172	17 61925	4 33849	16 07819	4 17304	16 52042	4 00531
29	20 93026	4 87074	19 49011	4 70823	18 02613	4 54359	18 54026	4 37678	17 03423	4 20772	17 50955	4 03636	17 96758	5 86264
30	20 27268	4 76284	20 85184	4 59472	19 40634	4 42441	19 93820	4 25184	18 44920	4 07695	18 94091	5 89969	17 41474	5 71997
31	21 61510	4 65493	20 21356	4 48121	20 78655	4 30522	19 33614	4 12690	19 86417	5 94618	18 37228	5 76301	18 86190	5 57731
32	22 95753	4 54703	21 57529	4 36770	20 16676	4 18603	20 73408	4 00196	19 27915	5 81542	19 80364	5 62633	18 30906	5 43464
33	22 29995	4 43912	22 93702	4 25419	21 54697	4 06685	20 13202	5 87702	20 69412	5 68465	19 23500	5 48965	19 75622	5 29197
34	23 64237	4 33122	22 29875	4 14068	22 92718	5 94766	21 52996	5 75208	20 10909	5 55388	20 66637	5 35298	19 20337	5 14930
35	24 98479	4 22331	23 66047	4 02718	22 30739	5 82848	22 92790	5 62714	21 52407	5 42311	20 09773	5 21630	20 65053	5 00664
36	24 32722	4 11541	23 02220	5 91367	23 68760	5 70929	22 32584	5 50221	22 93904	5 29234	21 52910	5 07962	20 09769	6 86397
37	25 66964	4 00750	24 38393	5 80016	23 06782	5 59010	23 72378	5 37727	22 35401	5 16157	22 96046	6 94295	21 54485	6 72130
38	25 01206	5 89959	25 74566	5 68665	24 44803	5 47092	23 12172	5 25233	23 76899	5 03081	22 39182	6 80627	22 99201	6 57863
39	26 35448	5 79169	25 10739	5 57314	25 82824	5 35173	24 51966	5 12739	23 18396	6 90004	23 82319	6 66959	22 43916	6 43597
40	27 69691	5 68378	26 46911	5 45963	25 20845	5 23254	25 91760	5 00245	24 59893	6 76927	23 25455	6 53291	23 88632	6 29330
41	27 03933	5 57588	27 83084	5 34612	26 58866	5 11336	25 31554	6 87751	24 01391	6 63850	24 68591	6 39624	23 33348	6 15063
42	28 38175	5 46797	27 19257	5 23261	27 96887	6 99417	26 71348	6 75257	25 42888	6 50773	24 11728	6 25956	24 78064	6 00796
43	29 72418	5 36007	28 55430	5 11910	27 34908	6 87498	26 11142	6 62763	26 84385	6 37696	25 54864	6 12288	24 22780	7 86530
44	29 06660	5 25216	29 91602	5 00559	28 72929	6 75580	27 50936	6 50270	26 25883	6 24620	26 98001	7 98621	25 67495	7 72263
45	30 40902	5 14426	29 27775	6 89208	28 10951	6 63661	28 90730	6 37776	27 67380	6 11543	26 41137	7 84953	25 12211	7 57996
46	31 75144	5 03635	30 63948	6 77857	29 48972	6 51743	28 30524	6 25282	27 08877	7 98466	27 84273	7 71285	26 56927	7 43729
47	31 09387	6 92845	30 00121	6 66506	30 86993	6 39824	29 70318	6 12788	28 50375	7 85389	27 27410	7 57617	26 01643	7 29463
48	32 43629	6 82054	31 36294	6 55155	30 25014	6 27905	29 10112	6 00294	29 91872	7 72312	28 70546	7 43950	27 46359	7 15196
49	33 77871	6 71264	32 72466	6 43805	31 63035	6 15987	30 49906	7 87800	29 33369	7 59235	28 13682	7 30282	28 91074	7 00929
50	33 12113	6 60473	32 08639	6 32454	31 01056	6 04068	31 89700	7 75306	30 74867	7 46159	29 56819	7 16614	28 35790	8 86662
51	34 46356	6 49682	33 44812	6 21103	32 39077	7 92149	31 29494	7 62812	30 16364	7 33082	30 99955	7 02947	29 80506	8 72396
52	35 80598	6 38892	34 80985	6 09752	33 77098	7 80231	32 69288	7 50319	31 57861	7 20005	30 43092	8 89279	29 25222	8 58129
53	35 14840	6 28101	34 17158	7 98401	33 15120	7 68312	32 09082	7 37825	32 99359	7 06928	31 86228	8 75611	30 69938	8 43862
54	36 49082	6 17311	35 53330	7 87050	34 53141	7 56393	33 48876	7 25331	32 40856	8 93851	31 29364	8 61943	30 14653	8 29595
55	37 83325	6 06520	36 89503	7 75699	35 91162	7 44475	34 88670	7 12837	33 82353	8 80774	32 72501	8 48276	31 59369	8 15329
56	37 17567	7 95730	36 25676	7 64348	35 29183	7 32556	34 28464	7 00343	33 23851	8 67698	32 15637	8 34608	31 04085	8 01062
57	38 51809	7 84939	37 61849	7 52997	36 67204	7 20637	35 68258	8 87849	34 65348	8 54621	33 58773	8 20940	32 48801	9 86795
58	39 86052	7 74149	38 98021	7 41646	36 05225	7 08719	35 08052	8 75355	34 06845	8 41544	33 01910	8 07273	33 93517	9 72528
59	39 20294	7 63358	38 34194	7 30295	37 43246	8 96800	36 47846	8 62861	35 48343	8 28467	34 45046	9 93605	33 38232	9 58262
60	40 54536	7 52568	39 70367	7 18944	38 81267	8 84882	37 87640	8 50368	36 89840	8 15390	35 88183	9 79937	34 82948	9 43995
61	41 88778	7 41777	39 06540	7 07593	38 19289	8 72963	37 27434	8 37874	36 31337	8 02313	35 31319	9 66269	34 27664	9 29728
62	41 23021	7 30987	40 42713	8 96242	39 57310	8 61044	38 67228	8 25380	37 72835	9 89237	36 74455	9 52602	35 72380	9 15461
63	42 57263	7 20196	41 78885	8 84892	40 95331	8 49126	38 07022	8 12886	37 14332	9 76160	36 17592	9 38934	35 17096	9 01195
64	43 91505	7 09405	41 15058	8 73541	40 33352	8 37207	39 46816	8 00392	38 55829	9 63083	37 60728	9 25266	36 61811	10 86928
65	43 25747	8 98615	42 51231	8 62190	41 71373	8 25288	40 86610	9 87898	39 97327	9 50006	37 03864	9 11599	36 06527	10 72661
66	44 59990	8 87824	43 87404	8 50839	41 09394	8 13370	40 26404	9 75404	39 38824	9 36929	38 47001	10 97931	37 51243	10 58394
67	45 94232	8 77034	43 23577	8 39488	42 47415	8 01451	41 66198	9 62910	40 80321	9 23853	39 90137	10 84263	38 95959	10 44128
68	45 28474	8 66243	44 59749	8 28137	43 85436	9 89532	41 05992	9 50417	40 21819	9 10776	39 33274	10 70595	38 40675	10 29861
69	46 62716	8 55453	45 95922	8 16786	43 23458	9 77614	42 45786	9 37923	41 63316	10 97699	40 76410	10 56928	39 85390	10 15594
70	47 96959	8 44662	45 32095	8 05435	44 61479	9 65695	43 85580	9 25429	41 04813	10 84622	40 19546	10 43260	39 30106	10 01327
71	47 31201	8 33872	46 68268	9 94084	45 99500	9 53777	43 25374	9 12935	42 46311	10 71545	41 62683	10 29592	40 74822	11 87061
72	48 65443	8 23081	46 04440	9 82733	45 37521	9 41858	44 65168	9 00441	43 87808	10 58468	41 05819	10 15925	40 19538	11 72794
73	49 99686	8 12291	47 40613	9 71382	46 75542	9 29939	44 04962	10 87947	43 29305	10 45392	42 48955	10 02257	41 64254	11 58527
74	49 33928	8 01500	48 76786	9 60031	46 13563	9 18021	45 44756	10 75453	44 70803	10 32315	43 92092	11 88589	41 08969	11 44260
75	50 68170	9 90710	48 12959	9 48680	47 51584	9 06102	46 84550	10 62959	44 12300	10 19238	43 35228	11 74921	42 53685	11 29994
76	50 02412	9 79919	49 49132	9 37330	48 89605	10 94183	46 24344	10 50466	45 53797	10 06161	44 78365	11 61254	43 98401	11 15727
77	51 36655	9 69128	50 85304	9 25979	48 27627	10 82265	47 64138	10 37972	46 95295	11 93084	44 21501	11 47586	43 43117	11 01460
78	52 70897	9 58338	50 21477	9 14628	49 65648	10 70346	47 03932	10 25478	46 36792	11 80007	45 64637	11 33918	44 87833	12 87193
79	52 05139	9 47547	51 57650	9 03277	49 03669	10 58427	48 43726	10 12984	47 78289	11 66931	45 07774	11 20251	44 32548	12 72927
80	53 39381	9 36757	52 93823	10 91926	50 41690	10 46509	49 83520	10 00490	47 19787	11 53854	46 50910	11 06583	45 77264	12 58660
81	54 73624	9 25966	52 29995	10 80575	51 79711	10 34590	49 23314	11 87996	48 61284	11 40777	47 94046	12 92915	45 21980	12 44393
82	54 07866	9 15176	53 66168	10 69224	51 17732	10 22671	50 63108	11 75502	48 02781	11 27700	47 37183	12 79247	46 66696	12 30126
83	55 42108	9 04385	53 02341	10 57873	52 55753	10 10753	50 02902	11 63008	49 44279	11 14623	48 80319	12 65580	46 11412	12 15860
84	56 76351	10 93595	54 38514	10 46522	53 93774	11 98834	51 42696	11 50515	50 85776	11 01546	48 23456	12 51912	47 56127	12 01593
85	56 10593	10 82804	55 74687	10 35171	53 31796	11 86916	52 82490	11 38021	50 27273	12 88470	49 66592	12 38244	47 00843	13 87326
86	57 44835	10 72014	55 10859	10 23820	54 69817	11 74997	52 22284	11 25527	51 68771	12 75393	49 09728	12 24577	48 45559	13 73059
87	58 79077	10 61223	56 47032	10 12469	54 07838	11 63078	53 62078	11 13033	51 10268	12 62316	50 52865	12 10909	49 90275	13 58793
88	58 13320	10 50433	57 83205	10 01118	55 45859	11 51160	53 01872	11 00539	52 51765	12 49239	51 96001	13 97241	49 34991	13 44526
89	59 47562	10 39642	57 19378	11 89767	56 83880	11 39241	54 41666	12 88045	53 93263	12 36162	51 39138	13 83573	50 79706	13 30259
90	60 81804	10 28851	58 55551	11 78417	56 21901	11 27322	55 81460	12 75551	53 34760	12 23085	52 82274	13 69906	50 24422	13 15992
91	60 16046	10 18061	59 91723	11 67066	57 59922	11 15404	55 21254	12 63057	54 76257	12 10009	52 25410	13 56238	51 69138	13 01726
92	61 50289	10 07270	59 27896	11 55715	58 97943	11 03485	56 61048	12 50564	54 17755	13 96932	53 68547	13 42570	51 13854	14 87459
93	62 84531	11 96480	60 64069	11 44364	58 35965	12 91566	56 00842	12 38070	55 59252	13 83855	53 11683	13 28903	52 58570	14 73192
94	62 18773	11 85689	60 00242	11 33013	59 73986	12 79648	57 40636	12 25576	55 00749	13 70778	54 54819	13 15235	52 03285	14 58925
95	63 53015	11 74899	61 36414	11 21662	59 12007	12 67729	58 80430	12 13082	56 42247	13 57701	55 97956	13 01567	53 48001	14 44659
96	64 87258	11 64108	62 72587	11 10311	60 50028	12 55810	58 20224	12 00588	57 83744	13 44625	55 41092	14 87899	54 92717	14 30392
97	64 21500	11 53318	62 08760	12 98960	61 88049	12 43892	59 60018	13 88094	57 25241	13 31548	56 84229	14 74232	54 37433	14 16125
98	65 55742	11 42527	63 44933	12 87609	61 26070	12 31973	60 99812	13 75600	58 66739	13 18471	56 27365	14 60564	55 82149	14 01858
99	66 89985	11 31737	64 81106	12 76258	62 64091	12 20055	60 39606	13 63107	58 08236	13 05394	57 70501	14 46896	55 26865	15 87592
100	66 24227	11 20946	64 17278	12 64907	62 02112	12 08136	61 79400	13 50613	59 49733	14 92317	57 13638	14 33229	56 71580	15 73325

For explanation see page 77

n	$p(q)$ 0.29	$q(p)$ 0.71	$p(q)$ 0.30	$q(p)$ 0.70	$p(q)$ 0.31	$q(p)$ 0.69	$p(q)$ 0.32	$q(p)$ 0.68	$p(q)$ 0.33	$q(p)$ 0.67	$p(q)$ 0.34	$q(p)$ 0.66	$p(q)$ 0.35	$q(p)$ 0.65
0	0 00000	0 00000	0 00000	0 00000	0 00000	0 00000	0 00000	0 00000	0 00000	0 00000	0 00000	0 00000	0 00000	0 00000
1	1 46240	1 85126	1 47712	1 84510	1 49136	1 83885	1 50515	1 83251	1 51851	1 82607	1 53148	1 81954	1 54407	1 81291
2	2 92480	1 70252	2 95424	1 69020	2 98272	1 67770	1 01030	1 66502	1 03703	1 65215	1 06296	1 63909	1 08814	1 62583
3	2 38719	1 55378	2 43136	1 53529	2 47409	1 51655	2 51545	1 49753	2 55554	1 47822	2 59444	1 45863	2 63220	1 43874
4	3 84959	1 40503	3 90849	1 38039	3 96545	1 35540	2 02060	1 33004	2 07406	1 30430	2 12592	1 27818	2 17627	1 25165
5	3 31199	1 25629	3 38561	1 22549	3 45681	1 19425	3 52575	1 16254	3 59257	1 13037	3 65739	1 09772	3 72034	1 06457
6	4 77439	1 10755	4 86273	1 07059	4 94817	1 03309	3 03090	2 99505	3 11108	2 95645	3 18887	2 91726	3 26441	2 87748
7	4 23679	2 95881	4 33985	2 91569	4 43953	2 87194	4 53605	2 82756	4 62960	2 78252	4 72035	2 73681	4 80848	2 69039
8	5 69918	2 81007	5 81697	2 76078	5 93089	2 71079	4 04120	2 66007	4 14811	2 60860	4 25183	2 55635	4 35254	2 50331
9	5 16158	2 66133	5 29409	2 60588	5 42226	2 54964	5 54635	2 49258	5 66663	2 43467	5 78331	2 37590	5 89661	2 31622
10	6 62398	2 51258	6 77121	2 45098	6 91362	2 38849	5 05150	2 32509	5 18514	2 26075	5 31479	2 19544	5 44068	2 12913
11	6 08638	2 36384	6 24833	2 29608	6 40498	2 22734	6 55665	2 15760	6 70365	2 08682	6 84627	2 01498	6 98475	3 94205
12	7 54878	2 21510	7 72546	2 14118	7 89634	2 06619	6 06180	3 99011	6 22217	3 91290	6 37775	3 83453	6 52882	3 75496
13	7 01117	2 06636	7 20258	3 98627	7 38770	3 90504	7 56695	3 82262	7 74068	3 73897	7 90923	3 65407	6 07288	3 56787
14	8 47357	3 91762	8 67970	3 83137	8 87906	3 74389	7 07210	3 65512	7 25920	3 56505	7 44070	3 47362	7 61695	3 38079
15	9 93597	3 76888	8 15682	3 67647	8 37043	3 58274	8 57725	3 48763	8 77771	3 39112	8 97218	3 29316	7 16102	3 19370
16	9 39837	3 62013	9 63394	3 52157	9 86179	3 42159	8 08240	3 32014	8 29622	3 21720	8 50366	3 11270	8 70509	3 00661
17	10 86077	3 47139	9 11106	3 36667	9 35315	3 26043	9 58755	3 15265	9 81474	3 04327	8 03514	4 93225	8 24916	4 81953
18	10 32316	3 32265	10 58818	3 21176	10 84451	3 09928	9 09270	4 98516	9 33325	4 86935	9 56662	4 75179	9 79322	4 63244
19	11 78556	3 17391	10 06530	3 05686	10 33587	4 93813	10 59785	4 81767	10 85176	4 69542	9 09810	4 57133	9 33729	4 44535
20	11 24796	3 02517	11 54243	4 90196	11 82723	4 77698	10 10300	4 65018	10 37028	4 52150	10 62958	4 39088	10 88136	4 25827
21	12 71036	4 87643	11 01955	4 74706	11 31860	4 61583	11 60815	4 48269	11 88879	4 34757	10 16106	4 21042	10 42543	4 07118
22	12 17276	4 72768	12 49667	4 59216	12 80996	4 45468	11 11330	4 31520	11 40731	4 17365	11 69254	4 02997	11 96950	5 88409
23	13 63515	4 57894	13 97379	4 43725	12 30132	4 29353	12 61845	4 14770	12 92582	5 99972	11 22402	5 84951	11 51357	5 69701
24	13 09755	4 43020	13 45091	4 28235	13 79268	4 13238	12 12360	5 98021	12 44433	5 82580	12 75549	5 66905	11 05763	5 50992
25	14 55995	4 28146	14 92803	4 12745	13 28404	5 97123	13 62875	5 81272	13 96285	5 65187	12 28697	5 48860	12 60170	5 32283
26	14 02235	4 13272	14 40515	5 97255	14 77540	5 81008	13 13390	5 64523	13 48136	5 47794	13 81845	5 30814	12 14577	5 13575
27	15 48475	5 98398	15 88227	5 81765	14 26677	5 64893	14 63905	5 47774	14 99988	5 30402	13 34993	5 12769	13 68984	6 94866
28	16 94714	5 83523	15 35940	5 66275	15 75813	5 48777	14 14420	5 31025	14 51839	5 13009	14 88141	6 94723	13 23391	6 76157
29	16 40954	5 68649	16 83652	5 50784	15 24949	5 32662	15 64935	5 14276	14 03690	6 95617	14 41289	6 76677	14 77797	6 57449
30	17 87194	5 53775	16 31364	5 35294	16 74085	5 16547	15 15450	6 97527	15 55542	6 78224	15 94437	6 58632	14 32204	6 38740
31	17 33434	5 38901	17 79076	5 19804	16 23221	5 00432	16 65965	6 80778	15 07393	6 60832	15 47585	6 40586	15 86611	6 20031
32	18 79674	5 24027	17 26788	5 04314	17 72357	6 84317	16 16480	6 64029	16 59245	6 43439	15 00733	6 22541	15 41018	6 01323
33	18 25913	5 09153	18 74500	6 88824	17 21494	6 68202	17 66995	6 47279	16 11096	6 26047	16 53880	6 04495	16 95425	7 82614
34	19 72153	6 94278	18 22212	6 73333	18 70630	6 52087	17 17510	6 30530	17 62947	6 08654	16 07028	7 86449	16 49831	7 63905
35	19 18393	6 79404	19 69924	6 57843	18 19766	6 35972	18 68025	6 13781	17 14799	7 91262	17 60176	7 68404	16 04238	7 45197
36	20 64633	6 64530	19 17637	6 42353	19 68902	6 19857	18 18540	7 97032	18 66650	7 73869	17 13324	7 50358	17 58645	7 26488
37	20 10873	6 49656	20 65349	6 26863	19 18038	6 03742	19 69055	7 80283	18 18502	7 56477	18 66472	7 32313	17 13052	7 07779
38	21 57112	6 34782	20 13061	6 11373	20 67174	7 87627	19 19570	7 63534	19 70353	7 39084	18 19620	7 14267	18 67459	8 89071
39	21 03352	6 19908	21 60773	7 95882	20 16311	7 71511	20 70085	7 46785	19 22204	7 21692	19 72768	8 96221	18 21865	8 70362
40	22 49592	6 05033	21 08485	7 80392	21 65447	7 55396	20 20600	7 30036	20 74056	7 04299	19 25916	8 78176	19 76272	8 51653
41	23 95832	7 90159	22 56197	7 64902	21 14583	7 39281	21 71115	7 13287	20 25907	8 86907	20 79064	8 60130	19 30679	8 32945
42	23 42072	7 75285	22 03909	7 49412	22 63719	7 23166	21 21630	8 96537	21 77759	8 69514	20 32211	8 42085	20 85086	8 14236
43	24 88311	7 60411	23 51621	7 33922	22 12855	7 07051	22 72145	8 79788	21 29610	8 52122	21 85359	8 24039	20 39493	9 95527
44	24 34551	7 45537	24 99334	7 18431	23 61991	8 90936	22 22660	8 63039	22 81461	8 34729	21 38507	8 05993	21 93899	9 76819
45	25 80791	7 30663	24 47046	7 02941	23 11128	8 74821	23 73175	8 46290	22 33313	8 17337	22 91655	9 87948	21 48306	9 58110
46	25 27031	7 15788	25 94758	8 87451	24 60264	8 58706	23 23690	8 29541	23 85164	9 99944	22 44803	9 69902	21 02713	9 39401
47	26 73271	7 00914	25 42470	8 71961	24 09400	8 42591	24 74205	8 12792	23 37016	9 82552	23 97951	9 51856	22 57120	9 20693
48	26 19510	8 86040	26 90182	8 56471	25 58536	8 26476	24 24720	9 96043	24 88867	9 65159	23 51099	9 33811	22 11527	9 01984
49	27 65750	8 71166	26 37894	8 40980	25 07672	8 10361	25 75235	9 79294	24 40718	9 47767	23 04247	9 15765	23 65933	10 83275
50	27 11990	8 56292	27 85606	8 25490	26 56808	9 94245	25 25750	9 62545	25 92570	9 30374	24 57395	10 97720	23 20340	10 64567
51	28 58230	8 41418	27 33318	8 10000	26 05945	9 78130	26 76265	9 45795	25 44421	9 12981	24 10542	10 79674	24 74747	10 45858
52	28 04470	8 26543	28 81031	9 94510	27 55081	9 62015	26 26780	9 29046	26 96272	10 95589	25 63690	10 61628	24 29154	10 27149
53	29 50709	8 11669	28 28743	9 79020	27 04217	9 45900	27 77295	9 12297	26 48124	10 78196	25 16838	10 43583	25 83561	10 08441
54	30 96949	9 96795	29 76455	9 63529	28 53353	9 29785	27 27810	10 95548	27 99975	10 60804	26 69986	10 25537	25 37967	11 89732
55	30 43189	9 81921	29 24167	9 48039	28 02489	9 13670	28 78325	10 78799	27 51827	10 43411	26 23134	10 07492	26 92374	11 71023
56	31 89429	9 67047	30 71879	9 32549	29 51625	10 97555	28 28840	10 62050	27 03678	10 26019	27 76282	11 89446	26 46781	11 52315
57	31 35669	9 52173	30 19591	9 17059	29 00762	10 81440	29 79355	10 45301	28 55529	10 08626	27 29430	11 71400	26 01188	11 33606
58	32 81908	9 37298	31 67303	9 01569	30 49898	10 65325	29 29870	10 28552	28 07381	11 91234	28 82578	11 53355	27 55595	11 14897
59	32 28148	9 22424	31 15015	10 86078	31 99034	10 49210	30 80385	10 11803	29 59232	11 73841	28 35726	11 35309	27 10001	12 96189
60	33 74388	9 07550	32 62728	10 70588	31 48170	10 33095	30 30900	11 95053	29 11084	11 56449	29 88874	11 17264	28 64408	12 77480
61	33 20628	10 92676	32 10440	10 55098	32 97306	10 16979	31 81415	11 78304	30 62935	11 39056	29 42021	12 99218	28 18815	12 58771
62	34 66868	10 77802	33 58152	10 39608	32 46443	10 00864	31 31930	11 61555	30 14786	11 21664	30 95169	12 81172	29 73222	12 40063
63	34 13107	10 62928	33 05864	10 24118	33 95579	11 84749	32 82445	11 44806	31 66638	11 04271	30 48317	12 63127	29 27629	12 21354
64	35 59347	10 48053	34 53576	10 08627	33 44715	11 68634	32 32960	11 28057	31 18489	12 86879	30 01465	12 45081	30 82035	12 02645
65	35 05587	10 33179	34 01288	11 93137	34 93851	11 52519	33 83475	11 11308	32 70341	12 69486	31 54613	12 27036	30 36442	13 83937
66	36 51827	10 18305	35 49000	11 77647	34 42987	11 36404	33 33990	12 94559	32 22192	12 52094	31 07761	12 08990	31 90849	13 65228
67	37 98067	10 03431	36 96712	11 62157	35 92123	11 20289	34 84505	12 77810	33 74043	12 34701	32 60909	13 90944	31 45256	13 46519
68	37 44306	11 88557	36 44425	11 46667	35 41260	11 04174	34 35020	12 61061	33 25895	12 17309	32 14057	13 72899	32 99663	13 27811
69	38 90546	11 73683	37 92137	11 31176	36 90396	12 88059	35 85535	12 44311	34 77746	13 99916	33 67205	13 54853	32 54070	13 09102
70	38 36786	11 58808	37 39849	11 15686	36 39532	12 71944	35 36050	12 27562	34 29598	13 82524	33 20352	13 36808	32 08476	14 90393
71	39 83026	11 43934	38 87561	11 00196	37 88668	12 55829	36 86565	12 10813	35 81449	13 65131	34 73500	13 18762	33 62883	14 71685
72	39 29266	11 29060	38 35273	12 84706	37 37804	12 39713	36 37080	13 94064	35 33300	13 47739	34 26648	13 00716	33 17290	14 52976
73	40 75505	11 14186	39 82985	12 69216	38 86940	12 23598	37 87595	13 77315	36 85152	13 30346	35 79796	14 82671	34 71697	14 34268
74	40 21745	12 99312	39 30697	12 53725	38 36077	12 07483	37 38110	13 60566	36 37003	13 12954	35 32944	14 64625	34 26104	14 15559
75	41 67985	12 84438	40 78409	12 38235	39 85213	13 91368	38 88625	13 43817	37 88855	14 95561	36 86092	14 46580	35 80510	15 96850
76	41 14225	12 69563	40 26122	12 22745	39 34349	13 75253	38 39140	13 27068	37 40706	14 78169	36 39240	14 28534	35 34917	15 78142
77	42 60465	12 54689	41 73834	12 07255	40 83485	13 59138	39 89655	13 10319	38 92557	14 60776	37 92388	14 10488	36 89324	15 59433
78	42 06704	12 39815	41 21546	13 91765	40 32621	13 43023	39 40170	14 93570	38 44409	14 43383	37 45536	15 92443	36 43731	15 40724
79	43 52944	12 24941	42 69258	13 76275	41 81757	13 26908	40 90685	14 76820	39 96260	14 25991	38 98683	15 74397	37 98138	15 22016
80	44 99184	12 10067	42 16970	13 60784	41 30894	13 10793	40 41200	14 60071	39 48112	14 08598	38 51831	15 56351	37 52544	15 03307
81	44 45424	13 95193	43 64682	13 45294	42 80030	14 94678	41 91715	14 43322	40 99963	15 91206	38 04979	15 38306	37 06951	16 84598
82	45 91664	13 80318	43 12394	13 29804	42 29166	14 78563	41 42230	14 26573	40 51814	15 73813	39 58127	15 20260	38 61358	16 65890
83	45 37903	13 65444	44 60106	13 14314	43 78302	14 62447	42 92745	14 09824	40 03666	15 56421	39 11275	15 02215	38 15765	16 47181
84	46 84143	13 50570	44 07819	14 98824	43 27438	14 46332	42 43260	15 93075	41 55517	15 39028	40 64423	16 84169	39 70172	16 28472
85	46 30383	13 35696	45 55531	14 83333	44 76574	14 30217	43 93775	15 76326	41 07368	15 21636	40 17571	16 66123	39 24578	16 09764
86	47 76623	13 20822	45 03243	14 67843	44 25711	14 14102	43 44290	15 59577	42 59220	15 04243	41 70719	16 48078	40 78985	17 91055
87	47 22863	13 05948	46 50955	14 52353	45 74847	15 97987	44 94805	15 42828	42 11071	16 86851	41 23867	16 30032	40 33392	17 72346
88	48 69102	14 91073	47 98667	14 36863	45 23983	15 81872	44 45320	15 26078	43 62923	16 69458	42 77014	16 11987	41 87799	17 53638
89	48 15342	14 76199	47 46379	14 21373	46 73119	15 65757	45 95835	15 09329	43 14774	16 52066	42 30162	17 93941	41 42206	17 34929
90	49 61582	14 61325	48 94091	14 05882	46 22255	15 49642	45 46350	16 92580	44 66625	16 34673	43 83310	17 75895	42 96612	17 16220
91	49 07822	14 46451	48 41803	15 90392	47 71391	15 33527	46 96865	16 75831	44 18477	16 17281	43 36458	17 57850	42 51019	18 97512
92	50 54062	14 31577	49 89516	15 74902	47 20528	15 17412	46 47380	16 59082	45 70328	17 99888	44 89606	17 39804	42 05426	18 78803
93	50 00301	14 16703	49 37228	15 59412	48 69664	15 01297	47 97895	16 42333	45 22180	17 82496	44 42754	17 21759	43 59833	18 60094
94	51 46541	14 01828	50 84940	15 43922	48 18800	16 85181	47 48410	16 25584	46 74031	17 65103	45 95902	17 03713	43 14240	18 41386
95	52 92781	15 86954	50 32652	15 28431	49 67936	16 69066	48 98925	16 08835	46 25882	17 47711	45 49050	18 85667	44 68646	18 22677
96	52 39021	15 72080	51 80364	15 12941	49 17072	16 52951	48 49440	17 92086	47 77734	17 30318	45 02198	18 67622	44 23053	18 03968
97	53 85261	15 57206	51 28076	16 97451	50 66208	16 36836	49 99955	17 75336	47 29585	17 12926	46 55345	18 49576	45 77460	19 85260
98	53 31500	15 42332	52 75788	16 81961	50 15345	16 20721	49 50470	17 58587	48 81437	18 95533	46 08493	18 31531	45 31867	19 66551
99	54 77740	15 27458	52 23500	16 66471	51 64481	16 04606	49 00985	17 41838	48 33288	18 78141	47 61641	18 13485	46 86274	19 47842
100	54 23980	15 12583	53 71213	16 50980	51 13617	17 88491	50 51500	17 25089	49 85139	18 60748	47 14789	19 95439	46 40680	19 29134

Common Logarithms* of p^n and q^n $(q=1-p)$

For explanation see page 77

n	$p(q)$ 0.36	$q(p)$ 0.64	$p(q)$ 0.37	$q(p)$ 0.63	$p(q)$ 0.38	$q(p)$ 0.62	$p(q)$ 0.39	$q(p)$ 0.61	$p(q)$ 0.40	$q(p)$ 0.60	$p(q)$ 0.41	$q(p)$ 0.59	$p(q)$ 0.42	$q(p)$ 0.58
0	0 00000	0 00000	0 00000	0 00000	0 00000	0 00000	0 00000	0 00000	0 00000	0 00000	0 00000	0 00000	0 00000	0 00000
1	1 55630	1 80618	1 56820	1 79934	1 57978	1 79239	1 59106	1 78533	1 60206	1 77815	1 61278	1 77085	1 62325	1 76343
2	1 11261	1 61236	1 13640	1 59868	1 15957	1 58478	1 18213	1 57066	1 20412	1 55630	1 22557	1 54170	1 24650	1 52686
3	2 66891	1 41854	2 70461	1 39802	2 73935	1 37718	2 77319	1 35599	2 80618	1 33445	2 83835	1 31256	2 86975	1 29028
4	2 22521	1 22472	2 27281	1 19736	2 31913	1 16957	2 36426	1 14132	2 40824	1 11261	2 45114	1 08341	2 49300	1 05371
5	3 78151	1 03090	3 84101	2 99670	3 89892	2 96196	3 95532	2 92665	2 01030	2 89076	2 06392	2 85426	2 11625	2 81714
6	3 33782	2 83708	3 40921	2 79604	3 47870	2 75435	3 54639	2 71198	3 61236	2 66891	3 67670	2 62511	3 73950	2 58057
7	4 89412	2 64326	4 97741	2 59538	3 05849	2 54674	3 13745	2 49731	3 21442	2 44706	3 28949	2 39596	3 36275	2 34400
8	4 45042	2 44944	4 54561	2 39472	4 63827	2 33913	4 72852	2 28264	4 81648	2 22521	4 90227	2 16682	4 98599	2 10742
9	4 00672	2 25562	4 11382	2 19406	4 21805	2 13153	4 31958	2 06797	4 41854	2 00336	4 51505	3 93767	4 60924	3 87085
10	5 56303	2 06180	5 68202	3 99341	5 79784	3 92392	5 91065	3 85330	4 02060	3 78151	4 12784	3 70852	4 23249	3 63428
11	5 11933	3 86798	5 25022	3 79275	5 37762	3 71631	5 50171	3 63863	5 62266	3 55966	5 74062	3 47937	5 85574	3 39771
12	6 67563	3 67416	6 81842	3 59209	6 95740	3 50870	5 09278	3 42396	5 22472	3 33782	5 35341	3 25022	5 47899	3 16114
13	6 23193	3 48034	6 38662	3 39143	6 53719	3 30109	6 68384	3 20929	6 82678	3 11597	6 96619	3 02108	5 10224	4 92456
14	7 78824	3 28652	7 95482	3 19077	6 11697	3 09348	6 27490	4 99462	6 42884	4 89412	6 57897	4 79193	6 72549	4 68799
15	7 34454	3 09270	7 52303	4 99011	7 69675	4 88588	7 86597	4 77995	6 03090	4 67227	6 19176	4 56278	6 34874	4 45142
16	8 90084	4 89888	7 09123	4 78945	7 27654	4 67827	7 45703	4 56528	7 63296	4 45042	7 80454	4 33363	7 97199	4 21485
17	8 45714	4 70506	8 65943	4 58879	8 85632	4 47066	7 04810	4 35061	7 23502	4 22857	7 41733	4 10448	7 59524	5 97828
18	8 01345	4 51124	8 22763	4 38813	8 43610	4 26305	8 63916	4 13594	8 83708	4 00672	7 03011	5 87534	7 21849	5 74170
19	9 56975	4 31742	9 79583	4 18747	8 01589	4 05544	8 23023	5 92127	8 43914	5 78487	8 64289	5 64619	8 84174	5 50513
20	9 12605	4 12360	9 36403	5 98681	9 59567	5 84783	9 82129	5 70660	8 04120	5 56303	8 25568	5 41704	8 46499	5 26856
21	10 68235	5 92978	10 93224	5 78615	9 17546	5 64023	9 41236	5 49193	9 64326	5 34118	9 86846	5 18789	8 08824	5 03199
22	10 23866	5 73596	10 50044	5 58549	10 75524	5 43262	9 00342	5 27726	9 24532	5 11933	9 48124	6 95874	9 71148	6 79542
23	11 79496	5 54214	10 06864	5 38483	10 33502	5 22501	10 59449	5 06259	10 84738	6 89748	9 09403	6 72960	9 33473	6 55884
24	11 35126	5 34832	11 63684	5 18417	11 91481	5 01740	10 18555	6 84792	10 44944	6 67563	10 70681	6 50045	10 95798	6 32227
25	12 90756	5 15450	11 20504	6 98351	11 49459	6 80979	11 77662	6 63325	10 05150	6 45378	10 31960	6 27130	10 58123	6 08570
26	12 46387	6 96068	12 77324	6 78285	11 07437	6 60218	11 36768	6 41858	11 65356	6 23193	11 93238	6 04215	10 20448	7 84913
27	12 02017	6 76686	12 34145	6 58219	12 65416	6 39458	12 95874	6 20391	11 25562	6 01008	11 54516	7 81300	11 82773	7 61256
28	13 57647	6 57304	13 90965	6 38154	12 23394	6 18697	12 54981	7 98924	12 85768	7 78824	11 15795	7 58386	11 45098	7 37598
29	13 13277	6 37922	13 47785	6 18088	13 81372	7 97936	12 14087	7 77457	12 45974	7 56639	12 77073	7 35471	11 07423	7 13941
30	14 68908	6 18540	13 04605	7 98022	13 39351	7 77175	13 73194	7 55990	12 06180	7 34454	12 38352	7 12556	12 69748	8 90284
31	14 24538	7 99158	14 61425	7 77956	14 97329	7 56414	13 32300	7 34522	13 66386	7 12269	13 99630	8 89641	12 32073	8 66627
32	15 80168	7 79776	14 18246	7 57890	14 55308	7 35653	14 91407	7 13055	13 26592	8 90084	13 60908	8 66726	13 94398	8 42970
33	15 35798	7 60394	15 75066	7 37824	14 13286	7 14893	14 50513	8 91588	14 86798	8 67899	13 22187	8 43812	13 56723	8 19312
34	16 91429	7 41012	15 31886	7 17758	15 71264	8 94132	14 09620	8 70121	14 47004	8 45714	14 83465	8 20897	13 19048	9 95655
35	16 47059	7 21630	16 88706	8 97692	15 29243	8 73371	15 68726	8 48654	14 07210	8 23529	14 44743	9 97982	14 81373	9 71998
36	16 02689	7 02248	16 45526	8 77626	16 87221	8 52610	15 27833	8 27187	15 67416	8 01345	14 06022	9 75067	14 43697	9 48341
37	17 58319	8 82866	16 02346	8 57560	16 45199	8 31849	16 86939	8 05720	15 27622	9 79160	15 67300	9 52152	14 06022	9 24684
38	17 13950	8 63484	17 59167	8 37494	16 03178	8 11088	16 46046	9 84253	16 87828	9 56975	15 28579	9 29238	15 68347	9 01026
39	18 69580	8 44102	17 15987	8 17428	17 61156	9 90328	16 05152	9 62786	16 48034	9 34790	16 89857	9 06323	15 30672	10 77369
40	18 25210	8 24720	18 72807	9 97362	17 19134	9 69567	17 64258	9 41319	16 08240	9 12605	16 51135	10 83408	16 92997	10 53712
41	19 80840	8 05338	18 29627	9 77296	18 77113	9 48806	17 23365	9 19852	17 68446	10 90420	16 12414	10 60493	16 55322	10 30055
42	19 36471	9 85956	19 86447	9 57230	18 35091	9 28045	18 82471	10 98385	17 28652	10 68235	17 73692	10 37578	16 17647	10 06398
43	20 92101	9 66574	19 43267	9 37164	19 93069	9 07284	18 41578	10 76918	18 88858	10 46050	17 34971	10 14664	17 79972	11 82740
44	20 47731	9 47192	19 00088	9 17098	19 51048	10 86523	18 00684	10 55451	18 49064	10 23866	18 96249	11 91749	17 42297	11 59083
45	20 03361	9 27810	20 56908	10 97032	19 09026	10 65763	19 59791	10 33984	18 09270	10 01681	18 57527	11 68834	17 04622	11 35426
46	21 58992	9 08428	20 13728	10 76967	20 67005	10 45002	19 18897	10 12517	19 69476	11 79496	18 18806	11 45919	18 66947	11 11769
47	21 14622	10 89046	21 70548	10 56901	20 24983	10 24241	20 78004	11 91050	19 29682	11 57311	19 80084	11 23004	18 29272	12 88112
48	22 70252	10 69664	21 27368	10 36835	21 82961	10 03480	20 37110	11 69583	20 89888	11 35126	19 41363	11 00090	19 91597	12 64454
49	22 25882	10 50282	22 84188	10 16769	21 40940	11 82719	21 96217	11 48116	20 50094	11 12941	19 02641	12 77175	19 53922	12 40797
50	23 81513	10 30900	22 41009	11 96703	22 98918	11 61958	21 55323	11 26649	20 10300	12 90756	20 63919	12 54260	19 16246	12 17140
51	23 37143	10 11518	23 97829	11 76637	22 56896	11 41198	21 14429	11 05182	21 70506	12 68571	20 25198	12 31345	20 78571	13 93483
52	24 92773	11 92136	23 54649	11 56571	22 14875	11 20437	22 73536	12 83715	21 30712	12 46387	21 86476	12 08430	20 40896	13 69826
53	24 48403	11 72754	23 11469	11 36505	23 72853	12 99676	22 32642	12 62248	22 90918	12 24202	21 47754	13 85516	20 03221	13 46168
54	24 04034	11 53372	24 68289	11 16439	23 30831	12 78915	23 91749	12 40781	22 51124	12 02017	21 09033	13 62601	21 65546	13 22511
55	25 59664	11 33990	24 25109	12 96373	24 88810	12 58154	23 50855	12 19314	22 11330	13 79832	22 70311	13 39686	21 27871	14 98854
56	25 15294	11 14608	25 81930	12 76307	24 46788	12 37393	23 09962	13 97847	23 71536	13 57647	22 31590	13 16771	22 90196	14 75197
57	26 70924	12 95226	25 38750	12 56241	24 04767	12 16633	24 69068	13 76380	23 31742	13 35462	23 92868	14 93856	22 52521	14 51540
58	26 26555	12 75844	26 95570	12 36175	25 62745	13 95872	24 28175	13 54913	24 91948	13 13277	23 54146	14 70942	22 14846	14 27882
59	27 82185	12 56462	26 52390	12 16109	25 20723	13 75111	25 87281	13 33446	24 52154	14 91092	23 15425	14 48027	23 77171	14 04225
60	27 37815	12 37080	26 09210	13 96043	26 78702	13 54350	25 46388	13 11979	24 12360	14 68908	24 76703	14 25112	23 39496	15 80568
61	28 93445	12 17698	27 66031	13 75977	26 36680	13 33589	25 05494	14 90512	25 72566	14 46723	24 37982	14 02197	23 01821	15 56911
62	28 49076	13 98316	27 22851	13 55911	27 94658	13 12828	26 64601	14 69045	25 32772	14 24538	25 99260	15 79282	24 64146	15 33254
63	28 04706	13 78934	28 79671	13 35845	27 52637	14 92068	26 23707	14 47578	26 92978	14 02353	25 60538	15 56368	24 26471	15 09596
64	29 60336	13 59552	28 36491	13 15780	27 10615	14 71307	27 82813	14 26111	26 53184	15 80168	25 21817	15 33453	25 88795	16 85939
65	29 15966	13 40170	29 93311	14 95714	28 68593	14 50546	27 41920	14 04644	26 13390	15 57983	26 83095	15 10538	25 51120	16 62282
66	30 71597	13 20788	29 50131	14 75648	28 26572	14 29785	27 01026	15 83177	27 73596	15 35798	26 44373	16 87623	25 13445	16 38625
67	30 27227	13 01406	29 06952	14 55582	29 84550	14 09024	28 60133	15 61710	27 33802	15 13613	26 05652	16 64708	26 75770	16 14968
68	31 82857	14 82024	30 63772	14 35516	29 42528	15 88263	28 19239	15 40243	28 94008	16 91429	27 66930	16 41794	26 38095	17 91310
69	31 38487	14 62642	30 20592	14 15450	29 00507	15 67503	29 78346	15 18776	28 54214	16 69244	27 28209	16 18879	26 00420	17 67653
70	32 94118	14 43260	31 77412	15 95384	30 58485	15 46742	29 37452	16 97309	28 14420	16 47059	28 89487	17 95964	27 62745	17 43996
71	32 49748	14 23878	31 34232	15 75318	30 16464	15 25981	30 96559	16 75842	29 74626	16 24874	28 50765	17 73049	27 25070	17 20339
72	32 05378	14 04496	32 91052	15 55252	31 74442	15 05220	30 55665	16 54375	29 34832	16 02689	28 12044	17 50134	28 87395	18 96682
73	33 61008	15 85114	32 47873	15 35186	31 32420	16 84459	30 14772	16 32908	30 95038	17 80504	29 73322	17 27220	28 49720	18 73024
74	33 16639	15 65732	32 04693	15 15120	32 90399	16 63699	31 73878	16 11441	30 55244	17 58319	29 34601	17 04305	28 12045	18 49367
75	34 72269	15 46350	33 61513	16 95054	32 48377	16 42938	31 32985	17 89974	30 15450	17 36134	30 95879	18 81390	29 74370	18 25710
76	34 27899	15 26968	33 18333	16 74988	32 06355	16 22177	32 92091	17 68507	31 75656	17 13950	30 57157	18 58475	29 36695	18 02053
77	35 83529	15 07586	34 75153	16 54922	33 64334	16 01416	32 51197	17 47040	31 35862	18 91765	30 18436	18 35560	30 99020	19 78396
78	35 39160	16 88204	34 31973	16 34856	33 22312	17 80655	32 10304	17 25573	32 96068	18 69580	31 79714	18 12646	30 61344	19 54738
79	36 94790	16 68822	35 88794	16 14790	34 80290	17 59894	33 69410	17 04106	32 56274	18 47395	31 40992	19 89731	30 23669	19 31081
80	36 50420	16 49440	35 45614	17 94724	34 38269	17 39134	33 28517	18 82639	32 16480	18 25210	31 02271	19 66816	31 85994	19 07424
81	36 06050	16 30058	35 02434	17 74658	35 96247	17 18373	34 87623	18 61172	33 76686	18 03025	32 63549	19 43901	31 48319	20 83767
82	37 61681	16 10676	36 59254	17 54593	35 54225	18 97612	34 46730	18 39705	33 36892	19 80840	32 24828	19 20986	31 10644	20 60110
83	37 17311	17 91294	36 16074	17 34527	35 12204	18 76851	34 05836	18 18238	34 97098	19 58655	33 86106	20 98072	32 72969	20 36452
84	38 72941	17 71912	37 72894	17 14461	36 70182	18 56090	35 64943	19 96771	34 57304	19 36471	33 47384	20 75157	32 35294	20 12795
85	38 28571	17 52530	37 29715	18 94395	36 28161	18 35329	35 24049	19 75304	34 17510	19 14286	33 08663	20 52242	33 97619	21 89138
86	39 84202	17 33148	38 86535	18 74329	37 86139	18 14569	36 83156	19 53837	35 77716	20 92101	34 69941	20 29327	33 59944	21 65481
87	39 39832	17 13766	38 43355	18 54263	37 44117	19 93808	36 42262	19 32370	35 37922	20 69916	34 31220	20 06413	33 22269	21 41824
88	40 95462	18 94384	38 00175	18 34197	37 02096	19 73047	36 01369	19 10903	36 98128	20 47731	35 92498	21 83498	34 84594	21 18166
89	40 51092	18 75002	39 56995	18 14131	38 60074	19 52286	37 60475	20 89436	36 58334	20 25546	35 53776	21 60583	34 46919	22 94509
90	40 06723	18 55620	39 13816	19 94065	38 18052	19 31525	37 19581	20 67969	36 18540	20 03361	35 15055	21 37668	34 09244	22 70852
91	41 62353	18 36238	40 70636	19 73999	39 76031	19 10764	38 78688	20 46501	37 78746	21 81176	36 76333	21 14753	35 71569	22 47195
92	41 17983	18 16856	40 27456	19 53933	39 34009	20 90004	38 37794	20 25034	37 38952	21 58992	36 37611	22 91839	35 33893	22 23538
93	42 73613	19 97474	41 84276	19 33867	40 91987	20 69243	39 96901	20 03567	38 99158	21 36807	37 98890	22 68924	36 96218	23 99880
94	42 29244	19 78092	41 41096	19 13801	40 49966	20 48482	39 56007	21 82100	38 59364	21 14622	37 60168	22 46009	36 58543	23 76223
95	43 84874	19 58710	42 97916	20 93735	40 07944	20 27721	39 15114	21 60633	38 19570	22 92437	37 21447	22 23094	36 20868	23 52566
96	43 40504	19 39328	42 54737	20 73669	41 65923	20 06960	40 74220	21 39166	39 79776	22 70252	38 82725	22 00179	37 83193	23 28909
97	44 96134	19 19946	42 11557	20 53603	41 23901	21 86199	40 33327	21 17699	39 39982	22 48067	38 44003	23 77265	37 45518	23 05252
98	44 51765	19 00564	43 68377	20 33537	42 81879	21 65439	41 92433	22 96232	39 00188	22 25882	38 05282	23 54350	37 07843	24 81594
99	44 07395	20 81182	43 25197	20 13471	42 39858	21 44678	41 51540	22 74765	40 60394	22 03697	39 66560	23 31435	38 70168	24 57937
100	45 63025	20 61800	44 82017	21 93405	43 97836	21 23917	41 10646	22 53298	40 20600	23 81513	39 27839	23 08520	38 32493	24 34280

For explanation see page 77

n	p(q) 0.43	q(p) 0.57	p(q) 0.44	q(p) 0.56	p(q) 0.45	q(p) 0.55	p(q) 0.46	q(p) 0.54	p(q) 0.47	q(p) 0.53	p(q) 0.48	q(p) 0.52	p(q) 0.49	q(p) 0.51	p(q) 0.50	q(p) 0.50
0	0 00000	0 00000	0 00000	0 00000	0 00000	0 00000	0 00000	0 00000	0 00000	0 00000	0 00000	0 00000	0 00000	0 00000	0 00000	0 00000
1	1 63347	1 75587	1 64345	1 74819	1 65321	1 74036	1 66276	1 73239	1 67210	1 72428	1 68124	1 71600	1 69020	1 70757	1 69897	1 69897
2	1 26694	1 51175	1 28691	1 49638	1 30643	1 48073	1 32552	1 46479	1 34420	1 44855	1 36248	1 43201	1 38039	1 41514	1 39794	1 39794
3	2 90041	1 26762	2 93036	1 24456	2 95964	1 22109	2 98827	1 19718	1 01629	1 17283	1 04372	1 14801	1 07059	1 12271	1 09691	1 09691
4	2 53387	1 02350	2 57381	2 99275	2 61285	2 96145	2 65103	2 92958	2 68839	2 89710	2 72496	2 86401	2 76078	2 83028	2 79588	2 79588
5	2 16734	2 77937	2 21726	2 74094	2 26606	2 70181	2 31379	2 66197	2 36049	2 62138	2 40621	2 58002	2 45098	2 53785	2 49485	2 49485
6	3 80081	2 53525	3 86072	2 48913	3 91928	2 44218	3 97655	2 39436	2 03259	2 34566	2 08745	2 29602	2 14118	2 24542	2 19382	2 19382
7	3 43428	2 29112	3 50417	2 23732	3 57249	2 18254	3 63930	2 12676	3 70469	2 06993	3 76869	2 01202	3 83137	3 95299	3 89279	3 89279
8	3 06775	2 04700	3 14762	3 98550	3 22570	3 92290	3 30206	3 85915	3 37678	3 79421	3 44993	3 72803	3 52157	3 66056	3 59176	3 59176
9	4 70122	3 80287	4 79107	3 73369	4 87891	3 66326	4 96482	3 59154	3 04888	3 51848	3 13117	3 44403	3 21176	3 36813	3 29073	3 29073
10	4 33468	3 55875	4 43453	3 48188	4 53213	3 40363	4 62758	3 32394	4 72098	3 24276	4 81241	3 16003	4 90196	3 07570	4 98970	4 98970
11	5 96815	3 31462	4 07798	3 23007	4 18534	3 14399	4 29034	3 05633	4 39308	4 96703	4 49365	4 87604	4 59216	4 78327	4 68867	4 68867
12	5 60162	3 07050	5 72143	4 97826	5 83855	4 88435	5 95309	4 78873	4 06517	4 69131	4 17489	4 59204	4 28235	4 49084	4 38764	4 38764
13	5 23509	4 82637	5 36488	4 72644	5 49176	4 62471	5 61585	4 52112	5 73727	4 41559	5 85614	4 30804	5 97255	4 19841	4 08661	4 08661
14	6 86856	4 58225	5 00834	4 47463	5 14498	4 36508	5 27861	4 25351	5 40937	4 13986	5 53738	4 02405	5 66275	5 90598	5 78558	5 78558
15	6 50203	4 33812	6 65179	4 22282	6 79819	4 10544	6 94137	5 98591	5 08147	5 86414	5 21862	5 74005	5 35294	5 61355	5 48455	5 48455
16	6 13550	4 09400	6 29524	5 97101	6 45140	5 84580	6 60413	5 71830	6 75357	5 58841	6 89986	5 45605	5 04314	5 32112	5 18352	5 18352
17	7 76896	5 84987	7 93870	5 71920	6 10461	5 58617	6 26688	5 45069	6 42566	5 31269	6 58110	5 17206	6 73333	5 02869	6 88249	6 88249
18	7 40243	5 60575	7 58215	5 46738	7 75783	5 32653	7 92964	5 18309	6 09776	5 03697	6 26234	6 88806	6 42353	6 73626	6 58146	6 58146
19	7 03590	5 36162	7 22560	5 21557	7 41104	5 06689	7 59240	6 91548	7 76986	6 76124	7 94358	6 60406	6 11173	6 44383	6 28043	6 28043
20	8 66937	5 11750	8 86905	6 96376	7 06425	6 80725	7 25516	6 64788	7 44196	6 48552	7 62482	6 32007	7 80392	6 15140	7 97940	7 97940
21	8 30284	6 87337	8 51251	6 71195	8 71746	6 54762	8 91791	6 38027	7 11406	6 20979	7 30607	6 03607	7 49412	7 85897	7 67837	7 67837
22	9 93631	6 62925	8 15596	6 46014	8 37068	6 28798	8 58067	6 11266	8 78615	7 93407	8 98731	7 75207	7 18431	7 56654	7 37734	7 37734
23	9 56977	6 38512	9 79941	6 20832	8 02389	6 02834	8 24343	7 84506	8 45825	7 65835	8 66855	7 46808	8 87451	7 27411	7 07631	7 07631
24	9 20324	6 14100	9 44286	7 95651	9 67710	7 76870	9 90619	7 57745	8 13035	7 38262	8 34979	7 18408	8 56471	8 98168	8 77528	8 77528
25	10 83671	7 89687	9 08632	7 70470	9 33031	7 50907	9 56895	7 30984	9 80245	7 10690	8 03103	8 90008	8 25490	8 68925	8 47425	8 47425
26	10 47018	7 65275	10 72977	7 45289	10 98353	7 24943	9 23170	7 04224	9 47454	8 83117	9 71227	8 61609	9 94510	8 39682	8 17322	8 17322
27	10 10365	7 40862	10 37322	7 20108	10 63674	8 98979	10 89446	8 77463	9 14664	8 55545	9 39351	8 33209	9 63529	8 10439	9 87219	9 87219
28	11 73712	7 16450	10 01667	8 94926	10 28995	8 73016	10 55722	8 50703	10 81874	8 27972	9 07475	8 04809	9 32549	9 81196	9 57116	9 57116
29	11 37059	8 92037	11 66013	8 69745	11 94316	8 47052	10 21998	8 23942	10 49084	8 00400	10 75600	9 76410	9 01569	9 51954	9 27013	9 27013
30	11 00405	8 67625	11 30358	8 44564	11 59638	8 21088	11 88273	9 97181	10 16294	9 72828	10 43724	9 48010	10 70588	9 22711	10 96910	10 96910
31	12 63752	8 43212	12 94703	8 19383	11 24959	9 95124	11 54549	9 70421	11 83503	9 45255	10 11848	9 19610	10 39608	10 93468	10 66807	10 66807
32	12 27099	8 18800	12 59049	9 94202	12 90280	9 69161	11 20825	9 43660	11 50713	9 17683	11 79972	10 91211	10 08627	10 64225	10 36704	10 36704
33	13 90446	9 94387	12 23394	9 69020	12 55601	9 43197	12 87101	9 16899	11 17923	10 90110	11 48096	10 62811	11 77647	10 34982	10 06601	10 06601
34	13 53793	9 69975	13 87739	9 43839	12 20923	9 17233	12 53377	10 90139	12 85133	10 62538	11 16220	10 34411	11 46667	10 05739	11 76498	11 76498
35	13 17140	9 45562	13 52084	9 18658	13 86244	10 91269	12 19652	10 63378	12 52343	10 34966	12 84344	10 06012	11 15686	11 76496	11 46395	11 46395
36	14 80486	9 21149	13 16430	10 93477	13 51565	10 65306	13 85928	10 36618	12 19552	10 07393	12 52468	11 77612	12 84706	11 47253	11 16292	11 16292
37	14 43833	10 96737	14 80775	10 68296	13 16886	10 39342	13 52204	10 09857	13 86762	11 79821	12 20593	11 49212	12 53725	11 18010	12 86189	12 86189
38	14 07180	10 72324	14 45120	10 43115	14 82208	10 13378	13 18480	11 83096	13 53972	11 52248	13 88717	11 20813	12 22745	12 88767	12 56086	12 56086
39	15 70527	10 47912	14 09465	10 17933	14 47529	11 87414	14 84756	11 56336	13 21182	11 24676	13 56841	12 92413	13 91765	12 59524	12 25983	12 25983
40	15 33874	10 23499	15 73811	11 92752	14 12850	11 61451	14 51031	11 29575	14 88391	12 97103	13 24965	12 64013	13 60784	12 30281	13 95880	13 95880
41	16 97221	11 99087	15 38156	11 67571	15 78171	11 35487	14 17307	11 02814	14 55601	12 69531	14 93089	12 35614	13 29804	12 01038	13 65777	13 65777
42	16 60568	11 74674	15 02501	11 42390	15 43493	11 09523	15 83583	12 76054	14 22811	12 41959	14 61213	12 07214	14 98824	13 71795	13 35674	13 35674
43	16 23914	11 50262	16 66847	11 17209	15 08814	12 83560	15 49859	12 49293	15 90021	12 14386	14 29337	13 78814	14 67843	13 42552	13 05571	13 05571
44	17 87261	11 25849	16 31192	12 92027	16 74135	12 57596	15 16134	12 22533	15 57231	13 86814	15 97461	13 50415	14 36863	13 13309	14 75468	14 75468
45	17 50608	11 01437	17 95537	12 66846	16 39456	12 31632	16 82410	13 95772	15 24440	13 59241	15 65586	13 22015	14 05882	14 84066	14 45365	14 45365
46	17 13955	12 77024	17 59882	12 41665	16 04778	12 05668	16 48686	13 69011	16 91650	13 31669	15 33710	14 93615	15 74902	14 54823	14 15262	14 15262
47	18 77302	12 52612	17 24228	12 16484	17 70099	13 79705	16 14962	13 42251	16 58860	13 04097	15 01834	14 65216	15 43922	14 25580	15 85159	15 85159
48	18 40649	12 28199	18 88573	13 91303	17 35420	13 53741	17 81238	13 15490	16 26070	14 76524	16 69958	14 36816	15 12941	15 96337	15 55056	15 55056
49	18 03995	12 03787	18 52918	13 66121	17 00741	13 27777	17 47513	14 88729	17 93280	14 48952	16 38082	14 08416	16 81961	15 67094	15 24953	15 24953
50	19 67342	13 79374	18 17263	13 40940	18 66063	13 01813	17 13789	14 61969	17 60489	14 21379	16 06206	15 80017	16 50980	15 37851	16 94850	16 94850
51	19 30689	13 54962	19 81609	13 15759	18 31384	14 75850	18 80065	14 35208	17 27699	15 93807	17 74330	15 51617	16 20000	15 08608	16 64747	16 64747
52	20 94036	13 30549	19 45954	14 90578	19 96705	14 49886	18 46341	14 08448	18 94909	15 66235	17 42454	15 23217	17 89020	16 79365	16 34644	16 34644
53	20 57383	13 06137	19 10299	14 65397	19 62026	14 23922	18 12617	15 81687	18 62119	15 38662	17 10579	16 94818	17 58039	16 50122	16 04541	16 04541
54	20 20730	14 81724	20 74644	14 40215	19 27348	15 97959	19 78892	15 54926	18 29328	15 11090	18 78703	16 66418	17 27059	16 20879	17 74438	17 74438
55	21 84077	14 57312	20 38990	14 15034	20 92669	15 71995	19 45168	15 28166	19 96538	16 83517	18 46827	16 38018	18 96078	17 91636	17 44335	17 44335
56	21 47423	14 32899	20 03335	15 89853	20 57990	15 46031	19 11444	15 01405	19 63748	16 55945	18 14951	16 09619	18 65098	17 62393	17 14232	17 14232
57	21 10770	14 08487	21 67680	15 64672	20 23311	15 20067	20 77720	16 74644	19 30958	16 28372	19 83075	17 81219	18 34118	17 33150	18 84129	18 84129
58	22 74117	15 84074	21 32026	15 39491	21 88633	16 94104	20 43995	16 47884	20 98168	16 00800	19 51199	17 52819	18 03137	17 03907	18 54026	18 54026
59	22 37464	15 59662	22 96371	15 14309	21 53954	16 68140	20 10271	16 21123	20 65377	17 73228	19 19323	17 24420	19 72157	18 74664	18 23923	18 23923
60	22 00811	15 35249	22 60716	16 89128	21 19275	16 42176	21 76547	17 94363	20 32587	17 45655	20 87447	18 96020	19 41176	18 45421	19 93820	19 93820
61	23 64158	15 10837	22 25061	16 63947	22 84596	16 16212	21 42823	17 67602	21 99797	17 18083	20 55572	18 67620	19 10196	18 16178	19 63717	19 63717
62	23 27504	16 86424	23 89407	16 38766	22 49918	17 90249	21 09099	17 40841	21 67007	18 90510	20 23696	18 39221	20 79216	19 86935	19 33614	19 33614
63	24 90851	16 62012	23 53752	16 13585	22 15239	17 64285	22 75374	17 14081	21 34217	18 62938	21 91820	18 10821	20 48235	19 57692	19 03511	19 03511
64	24 54198	16 37599	23 18097	17 88403	23 80560	17 38321	22 41650	18 87320	21 01426	18 35366	21 59944	19 82421	20 17255	19 28449	20 73408	20 73408
65	24 17545	16 13187	24 82442	17 63222	23 45881	17 12357	22 07926	18 60559	22 68636	18 07793	21 28068	19 54022	21 86275	20 99206	20 43305	20 43305
66	25 80892	17 88774	24 46788	17 38041	23 11203	18 86394	23 74202	18 33799	22 35846	19 80221	22 96192	19 25622	21 55294	20 69963	20 13202	20 13202
67	25 44239	17 64362	24 11133	17 12860	24 76524	18 60430	23 40477	18 07038	22 03056	19 52648	22 64316	20 97222	21 24314	20 40720	21 83099	21 83099
68	25 07585	17 39949	25 75478	18 87679	24 41845	18 34466	23 06753	19 80278	23 70265	19 25076	22 32440	20 68823	22 93333	20 11477	21 52996	21 52996
69	26 70932	17 15537	25 39823	18 62497	24 07166	18 08503	24 73029	19 53517	23 37475	20 97504	22 00565	20 40423	22 62353	21 82234	21 22893	21 22893
70	26 34279	18 91124	25 04169	18 37316	25 72488	19 82539	24 39305	19 26756	23 04685	20 69931	23 68689	20 12023	22 31373	21 52991	22 92790	22 92790
71	27 97626	18 66711	26 68514	18 12135	25 37809	19 56575	24 05581	20 99996	24 71895	20 42359	23 36813	21 83624	22 00392	21 23748	22 62687	22 62687
72	27 60973	18 42299	26 32859	19 86954	25 03130	19 30611	25 71856	20 73235	24 39105	20 14786	23 04937	21 55224	23 69412	22 94505	22 32584	22 32584
73	27 24320	18 17886	27 97205	19 61773	26 68451	19 04648	25 38132	20 46474	24 06314	21 87214	24 73061	21 26824	23 38431	22 65262	22 02481	22 02481
74	28 87667	19 93474	27 61550	19 36591	26 33773	20 78684	25 04408	20 19714	25 73524	21 59641	24 41185	22 98425	23 07451	22 36019	23 72378	23 72378
75	28 51013	19 69061	27 25895	19 11410	27 99094	20 52720	26 70684	21 92953	25 40734	21 32069	24 09309	22 70025	24 76471	22 06776	23 42275	23 42275
76	28 14360	19 44649	28 90240	20 86229	27 64415	20 26756	26 36960	21 66193	25 07944	21 04497	25 77433	22 41625	24 45490	23 77533	23 12172	23 12172
77	29 77707	19 20236	28 54586	20 61048	27 29736	20 00793	26 03235	21 39432	26 75154	22 76924	25 45558	22 13226	24 14510	23 48290	24 82069	24 82069
78	29 41054	20 95824	28 18931	20 35867	28 95058	21 74829	27 69511	21 12671	26 42363	22 49352	25 13682	23 84826	25 83529	23 19047	24 51966	24 51966
79	29 04401	20 71411	29 83276	20 10685	28 60379	21 48865	27 35787	22 85911	26 09573	22 21779	26 81806	23 56426	25 52549	24 89804	24 21863	24 21863
80	30 67748	20 46999	29 47621	21 85504	28 25700	21 22902	27 02063	22 59150	27 76783	23 94207	26 49930	23 28027	25 21569	24 60561	25 91760	25 91760
81	30 31094	20 22586	29 11967	21 60323	29 91021	22 96938	28 68338	22 32389	27 43993	23 66635	26 18054	24 99627	26 90588	24 31318	25 61657	25 61657
82	31 94441	21 98174	30 76312	21 35142	29 56343	22 70974	28 34614	22 05629	27 11202	23 39062	27 86178	24 71227	26 59608	24 02075	25 31554	25 31554
83	31 57788	21 73761	30 40657	21 09961	29 21664	22 45010	28 00890	23 78868	28 78412	23 11490	27 54302	24 42828	26 28627	25 72832	25 01451	25 01451
84	31 21135	21 49349	30 05002	22 84779	30 86985	22 19047	29 67166	23 52108	28 45622	24 83917	27 22426	24 14428	27 97647	25 43589	26 71348	26 71348
85	32 84482	21 24936	31 69348	22 59598	30 52306	23 93083	29 33442	23 25347	28 12832	24 56345	28 90551	25 86028	27 66667	25 14347	26 41245	26 41245
86	32 47829	21 00524	31 33693	22 34417	30 17628	23 67119	30 99717	24 98586	29 80042	24 28772	28 58675	25 57629	27 35686	26 85104	26 11142	26 11142
87	32 11176	22 76111	32 98038	22 09236	31 82949	23 41155	30 65993	24 71826	29 47251	24 01200	28 26799	25 29229	27 04706	26 55861	27 81039	27 81039
88	33 74522	22 51699	32 62384	23 84055	31 48270	23 15192	30 32269	24 45065	29 14461	25 73628	29 94923	25 00829	28 73726	26 26618	27 50936	27 50936
89	33 37869	22 27286	32 26729	23 58873	31 13591	24 89228	31 98545	24 18304	30 81671	25 46055	29 63047	26 72430	28 42745	27 97375	27 20833	27 20833
90	33 01216	22 02874	33 91074	23 33692	32 78913	24 63264	31 64820	25 91544	30 48881	25 18483	29 31171	26 44030	28 11765	27 68132	28 90730	28 90730
91	34 64563	23 78461	33 55419	23 08511	32 44234	24 37300	31 31096	25 64783	30 16091	26 90910	30 99295	26 15630	29 80784	27 38889	28 60627	28 60627
92	34 27910	23 54049	33 19765	24 83330	32 09555	24 11337	32 97372	25 38023	31 83300	26 63338	30 67419	27 87231	29 49804	27 09646	28 30524	28 30524
93	35 91257	23 29636	34 84110	24 58149	33 74876	25 85373	32 63648	25 11262	31 50510	26 35766	30 35544	27 58831	29 18824	28 80403	28 00421	28 00421
94	35 54603	23 05224	34 48455	24 32967	33 40198	25 59409	32 29924	26 84501	31 17720	26 08193	30 03668	27 30431	30 87843	28 51160	29 70318	29 70318
95	35 17950	24 80811	34 12800	24 07786	33 05519	25 33446	33 96199	26 57741	32 84930	27 80621	31 71792	27 02032	30 56863	28 21917	29 40215	29 40215
96	36 81297	24 56399	35 77146	25 82605	34 70840	25 07482	33 62475	26 30980	32 52139	27 53048	31 39916	28 73632	30 25882	29 92674	29 10112	29 10112
97	36 44644	24 31986	35 41491	25 57424	34 36161	26 81518	33 28751	26 04219	32 19349	27 25476	31 08040	28 45232	31 94902	29 63431	30 80009	30 80009
98	36 07991	24 07574	35 05836	25 32243	34 01483	26 55554	34 95027	27 77459	33 86559	28 97904	32 76164	28 16833	31 63922	29 34188	30 49906	30 49906
99	37 71338	25 83161	36 70182	25 07061	35 66804	26 29591	34 61303	27 50698	33 53769	28 70331	32 44288	29 88433	31 32941	29 04945	30 19803	30 19803
100	37 34685	25 58749	36 34527	26 81880	35 32125	26 03627	34 27578	27 23938	33 20979	28 42759	32 12412	29 60033	31 01961	30 75702	31 89700	31 89700

N = number of trials, x = number of successes, etc., $100\,p_x = 100\,x/N$

100 (1 − 2α) limits

N = 2

x	$100p_x$	95% $100p_l$ $100p_r$	99% $100p_l$ $100p_r$
0	0.00	0.00- 84.19	0.00- 92.93
1	50.00	1.26- 98.74	0.25- 99.75
2	100.00	15.81-100.00	7.07-100.00

N = 3

x	$100p_x$	95% $100p_l$ $100p_r$	99% $100p_l$ $100p_r$
0	0.00	0.00- 70.76	0.00- 82.90
1	33.33	0.84- 90.57	0.17- 95.86
2	66.67	9.43- 99.16	4.14- 99.83
3	100.00	29.24-100.00	17.10-100.00

N = 4

x	$100p_x$	95% $100p_l$ $100p_r$	99% $100p_l$ $100p_r$
0	0.00	0.00- 60.24	0.00- 73.41
1	25.00	0.63- 80.59	0.13- 88.91
2	50.00	6.76- 93.24	2.94- 97.06
3	75.00	19.41- 99.37	11.09- 99.87
4	100.00	39.76-100.00	26.59-100.00

N = 5

x	$100p_x$	95% $100p_l$ $100p_r$	99% $100p_l$ $100p_r$
0	0.00	0.00- 52.18	0.00- 65.34
1	20.00	0.51- 71.64	0.10- 81.49
2	40.00	5.27- 85.34	2.29- 91.72
3	60.00	14.66- 94.73	8.28- 97.71
4	80.00	28.36- 99.49	18.51- 99.90
5	100.00	47.82-100.00	34.66-100.00

N = 6

x	$100p_x$	95% $100p_l$ $100p_r$	99% $100p_l$ $100p_r$
0	0.00	0.00- 45.93	0.00- 58.65
1	16.67	0.42- 64.12	0.08- 74.60
2	33.33	4.33- 77.72	1.87- 85.64
3	50.00	11.81- 88.19	6.63- 93.37
4	66.67	22.28- 95.67	14.36- 98.13
5	83.33	35.88- 99.58	25.40- 99.92
6	100.00	54.07-100.00	41.35-100.00

N = 7

x	$100p_x$	95% $100p_l$ $100p_r$	99% $100p_l$ $100p_r$
0	0.00	0.00- 40.96	0.00- 53.09
1	14.29	0.36- 57.87	0.07- 68.49
2	28.57	3.67- 70.96	1.58- 79.70
3	42.86	9.90- 81.59	5.53- 88.23
4	57.14	18.41- 90.10	11.77- 94.47
5	71.43	29.04- 96.33	20.30- 98.42
6	85.71	42.13- 99.64	31.51- 99.93
7	100.00	59.04-100.00	46.91-100.00

N = 8

x	$100p_x$	95% $100p_l$ $100p_r$	99% $100p_l$ $100p_r$
0	0.00	0.00- 36.94	0.00- 48.43
1	12.50	0.32- 52.65	0.06- 63.15
2	25.00	3.19- 65.09	1.37- 74.22
3	37.50	8.52- 75.51	4.75- 83.03
4	50.00	15.70- 84.30	9.99- 90.01
5	62.50	24.49- 91.48	16.97- 95.25
6	75.00	34.91- 96.81	25.78- 98.63
7	87.50	47.35- 99.68	36.85- 99.94
8	100.00	63.06-100.00	51.57-100.00

N = 9

x	$100p_x$	95% $100p_l$ $100p_r$	99% $100p_l$ $100p_r$
0	0.00	0.00- 33.63	0.00- 44.50
1	11.11	0.28- 48.25	0.06- 58.50
2	22.22	2.81- 60.01	1.21- 69.26
3	33.33	7.49- 70.07	4.16- 78.09
4	44.44	13.70- 78.80	8.68- 85.39
5	55.56	21.20- 86.30	14.61- 91.32
6	66.67	29.93- 92.51	21.91- 95.84
7	77.78	39.99- 97.19	30.74- 98.79
8	88.89	51.75- 99.72	41.50- 99.94
9	100.00	66.37-100.00	55.50-100.00

N = 10

x	$100p_x$	95% $100p_l$ $100p_r$	99% $100p_l$ $100p_r$
0	0.00	0.00- 30.85	0.00- 41.13
1	10.00	0.25- 44.50	0.05- 54.43
2	20.00	2.52- 55.61	1.09- 64.82
3	30.00	6.67- 65.25	3.70- 73.51
4	40.00	12.16- 73.76	7.68- 80.91
5	50.00	18.71- 81.29	12.83- 87.17
6	60.00	26.24- 87.84	19.09- 92.32
7	70.00	34.75- 93.33	26.49- 96.30
8	80.00	44.39- 97.48	35.18- 98.91
9	90.00	55.50- 99.75	45.57- 99.95
10	100.00	69.15-100.00	58.87-100.00

N = 11

x	$100p_x$	95% $100p_l$ $100p_r$	99% $100p_l$ $100p_r$
0	0.00	0.00- 28.49	0.00- 38.22
1	9.09	0.23- 41.28	0.05- 50.86
2	18.18	2.28- 51.78	0.98- 60.85
3	27.27	6.02- 60.97	3.33- 69.33
4	36.36	10.93- 69.21	6.88- 76.68
5	45.45	16.75- 76.62	11.45- 83.07
6	54.55	23.38- 83.25	16.93- 88.55
7	63.64	30.79- 89.07	23.32- 93.12
8	72.73	39.03- 93.98	30.67- 96.67
9	81.82	48.22- 97.72	39.15- 99.02

N = 11 (continued)

x	$100p_x$	95% $100p_l$ $100p_r$	99% $100p_l$ $100p_r$
10	90.91	58.72- 99.77	49.14- 99.95
11	100.00	71.51-100.00	61.78-100.00

N = 12

x	$100p_x$	95% $100p_l$ $100p_r$	99% $100p_l$ $100p_r$
0	0.00	0.00- 26.46	0.00- 35.69
1	8.33	0.21- 38.48	0.04- 47.70
2	16.67	2.09- 48.41	0.90- 57.29
3	25.00	5.49- 57.19	3.03- 65.52
4	33.33	9.92- 65.11	6.24- 72.75
5	41.67	15.17- 72.33	10.34- 79.15
6	50.00	21.09- 78.91	15.22- 84.78
7	58.33	27.67- 84.83	20.85- 89.66
8	66.67	34.89- 90.08	27.25- 93.76
9	75.00	42.81- 94.51	34.48- 96.97
10	83.33	51.59- 97.91	42.71- 99.10
11	91.67	61.52- 99.79	52.30- 99.96
12	100.00	73.54-100.00	64.31-100.00

N = 13

x	$100p_x$	95% $100p_l$ $100p_r$	99% $100p_l$ $100p_r$
0	0.00	0.00- 24.71	0.00- 33.47
1	7.69	0.19- 36.03	0.04- 44.90
2	15.38	1.92- 45.45	0.83- 54.10
3	23.08	5.04- 53.81	2.78- 62.06
4	30.77	9.09- 61.43	5.71- 69.13
5	38.46	13.86- 68.42	9.42- 75.46
6	46.15	19.22- 74.87	13.83- 81.13
7	53.85	25.13- 80.78	18.87- 86.17
8	61.54	31.58- 86.14	24.54- 90.58
9	69.23	38.57- 90.91	30.87- 94.29
10	76.92	46.19- 94.96	37.94- 97.22
11	84.62	54.55- 98.08	45.90- 99.17
12	92.31	63.97- 99.81	55.10- 99.96
13	100.00	75.29-100.00	66.53-100.00

N = 14

x	$100p_x$	95% $100p_l$ $100p_r$	99% $100p_l$ $100p_r$
0	0.00	0.00- 23.16	0.00- 31.51
1	7.14	0.18- 33.87	0.04- 42.40
2	14.29	1.78- 42.81	0.76- 51.23
3	21.43	4.66- 50.80	2.57- 58.92
4	28.57	8.39- 58.10	5.26- 65.79
5	35.71	12.76- 64.86	8.66- 72.01
6	42.86	17.66- 71.14	12.67- 77.66
7	50.00	23.04- 76.96	17.24- 82.76
8	57.14	28.86- 82.34	22.34- 87.33
9	64.29	35.14- 87.24	27.99- 91.34
10	71.43	41.90- 91.61	34.21- 94.74
11	78.57	49.20- 95.34	41.08- 97.43
12	85.71	57.19- 98.22	48.77- 99.24
13	92.86	66.13- 99.82	57.60- 99.96
14	100.00	76.84-100.00	68.49-100.00

N = 15

x	$100p_x$	95% $100p_l$ $100p_r$	99% $100p_l$ $100p_r$
0	0.00	0.00- 21.80	0.00- 29.76
1	6.67	0.17- 31.95	0.03- 40.16
2	13.33	1.66- 40.46	0.71- 48.63
3	20.00	4.33- 48.09	2.39- 56.05
4	26.67	7.79- 55.10	4.88- 62.73
5	33.33	11.82- 61.62	8.01- 68.82
6	40.00	16.34- 67.71	11.70- 74.39
7	46.67	21.27- 73.41	15.87- 79.49
8	53.33	26.59- 78.73	20.51- 84.13
9	60.00	32.29- 83.66	25.61- 88.30
10	66.67	38.38- 88.18	31.18- 91.99
11	73.33	44.90- 92.21	37.27- 95.12
12	80.00	51.91- 95.67	43.95- 97.61
13	86.67	59.54- 98.34	51.37- 99.29
14	93.33	68.05- 99.83	59.84- 99.97
15	100.00	78.20-100.00	70.24-100.00

N = 16

x	$100p_x$	95% $100p_l$ $100p_r$	99% $100p_l$ $100p_r$
0	0.00	0.00- 20.59	0.00- 28.19
1	6.25	0.16- 30.23	0.03- 38.14
2	12.50	1.55- 38.35	0.67- 46.28
3	18.75	4.05- 45.65	2.23- 53.44
4	25.00	7.27- 52.38	4.55- 59.91
5	31.25	11.02- 58.66	7.45- 65.85
6	37.50	15.20- 64.57	10.86- 71.32
7	43.75	19.75- 70.12	14.71- 76.38
8	50.00	24.65- 75.35	18.97- 81.03
9	56.25	29.88- 80.25	23.62- 85.29
10	62.50	35.43- 84.80	28.68- 89.14
11	68.75	41.34- 88.98	34.15- 92.55
12	75.00	47.62- 92.73	40.09- 95.45
13	81.25	54.35- 95.95	46.56- 97.77
14	87.50	61.65- 98.45	53.72- 99.33
15	93.75	69.77- 99.84	61.86- 99.97
16	100.00	79.41-100.00	71.81-100.00

N = 17

x	$100p_x$	95% $100p_l$ $100p_r$	99% $100p_l$ $100p_r$
0	0.00	0.00- 19.51	0.00- 26.78
1	5.88	0.15- 28.69	0.03- 36.30
2	11.76	1.46- 36.44	0.63- 44.13
3	17.65	3.80- 43.43	2.09- 51.04
4	23.53	6.81- 49.90	4.26- 57.32

N = 17 (continued)

x	$100p_x$	95% $100p_l$ $100p_r$	99% $100p_l$ $100p_r$
5	29.41	10.31- 55.96	6.97- 63.10
6	35.29	14.21- 61.67	10.14- 68.46
7	41.18	18.44- 67.08	13.71- 73.44
8	47.06	22.98- 72.19	17.64- 78.07
9	52.94	27.81- 77.02	21.93- 82.36
10	58.82	32.92- 81.56	26.56- 86.29
11	64.71	38.33- 85.79	31.54- 89.86
12	70.59	44.04- 89.69	36.90- 93.03
13	76.47	50.10- 93.19	42.68- 95.74
14	82.35	56.57- 96.20	48.96- 97.91
15	88.24	63.56- 98.54	55.87- 99.37
16	94.12	71.31- 99.85	63.70- 99.97
17	100.00	80.49-100.00	73.22-100.00

N = 18

x	$100p_x$	95% $100p_l$ $100p_r$	99% $100p_l$ $100p_r$
0	0.00	0.00- 18.53	0.00- 25.50
1	5.56	0.14- 27.29	0.03- 34.63
2	11.11	1.38- 34.71	0.59- 42.17
3	16.67	3.58- 41.42	1.97- 48.84
4	22.22	6.41- 47.64	4.00- 54.92
5	27.78	9.69- 53.48	6.54- 60.55
6	33.33	13.34- 59.01	9.51- 65.79
7	38.89	17.30- 64.25	12.84- 70.68
8	44.44	21.53- 69.24	16.49- 75.26
9	50.00	26.02- 73.98	20.47- 79.53
10	55.56	30.76- 78.47	24.74- 83.51
11	61.11	35.75- 82.70	29.32- 87.16
12	66.67	40.99- 86.66	34.21- 90.49
13	72.22	46.52- 90.31	39.45- 93.46
14	77.78	52.36- 93.59	45.08- 96.00
15	83.33	58.58- 96.42	51.16- 98.03
16	88.89	65.29- 98.62	57.83- 99.41
17	94.44	72.71- 99.86	65.37- 99.97
18	100.00	81.47-100.00	74.50-100.00

N = 19

x	$100p_x$	95% $100p_l$ $100p_r$	99% $100p_l$ $100p_r$
0	0.00	0.00- 17.65	0.00- 24.34
1	5.26	0.13- 26.03	0.03- 33.11
2	10.53	1.30- 33.14	0.56- 40.37
3	15.79	3.38- 39.58	1.86- 46.82
4	21.05	6.05- 45.57	3.78- 52.71
5	26.32	9.15- 51.20	6.17- 58.18
6	31.58	12.58- 56.55	8.95- 63.29
7	36.84	16.29- 61.64	12.07- 68.09
8	42.11	20.25- 66.50	15.49- 72.60
9	47.37	24.45- 71.14	19.19- 76.84
10	52.63	28.86- 75.55	23.16- 80.81
11	57.89	33.50- 79.75	27.40- 84.51
12	63.16	38.36- 83.71	31.91- 87.93
13	68.42	43.45- 87.42	36.71- 91.05
14	73.68	48.80- 90.85	41.82- 93.83
15	78.95	54.43- 93.95	47.29- 96.22
16	84.21	60.42- 96.62	53.18- 98.14
17	89.47	66.86- 98.70	59.63- 99.44
18	94.74	73.97- 99.87	66.89- 99.97
19	100.00	82.35-100.00	75.66-100.00

N = 20

x	$100p_x$	95% $100p_l$ $100p_r$	99% $100p_l$ $100p_r$
0	0.00	0.00- 16.84	0.00- 23.27
1	5.00	0.13- 24.87	0.03- 31.71
2	10.00	1.23- 31.70	0.53- 38.71
3	15.00	3.21- 37.89	1.76- 44.95
4	20.00	5.73- 43.66	3.58- 50.66
5	25.00	8.66- 49.10	5.83- 55.98
6	30.00	11.89- 54.28	8.46- 60.96
7	35.00	15.39- 59.22	11.39- 65.66
8	40.00	19.12- 63.95	14.60- 70.09
9	45.00	23.06- 68.47	18.06- 74.28
10	50.00	27.20- 72.80	21.77- 78.23
11	55.00	31.53- 76.94	25.72- 81.94
12	60.00	36.05- 80.88	29.91- 85.40
13	65.00	40.78- 84.61	34.34- 88.61
14	70.00	45.72- 88.11	39.04- 91.54
15	75.00	50.90- 91.34	44.02- 94.17
16	80.00	56.34- 94.27	49.34- 96.42
17	85.00	62.11- 96.79	55.05- 98.24
18	90.00	68.30- 98.77	61.29- 99.47
19	95.00	75.13- 99.87	68.29- 99.97
20	100.00	83.16-100.00	76.73-100.00

N = 21

x	$100p_x$	95% $100p_l$ $100p_r$	99% $100p_l$ $100p_r$
0	0.00	0.00- 16.11	0.00- 22.30
1	4.76	0.12- 23.82	0.02- 30.43
2	9.52	1.17- 30.38	0.50- 37.18
3	14.29	3.05- 36.34	1.68- 43.22
4	19.05	5.45- 41.91	3.39- 48.76
5	23.81	8.22- 47.17	5.53- 53.92
6	28.57	11.28- 52.18	8.01- 58.78
7	33.33	14.59- 56.97	10.78- 63.37
8	38.10	18.11- 61.56	13.81- 67.72
9	42.86	21.82- 65.98	17.07- 71.85
10	47.62	25.71- 70.22	20.55- 75.76
11	52.38	29.78- 74.29	24.24- 79.45
12	57.14	34.02- 78.18	28.15- 82.93
13	61.90	38.44- 81.89	32.28- 86.19
14	66.67	43.03- 85.41	36.63- 89.22

N = 21 (continued)

x	$100p_x$	95% $100p_l$ $100p_r$	99% $100p_l$ $100p_r$
15	71.43	47.82- 88.72	41.22- 91.99
16	76.19	52.83- 91.78	46.08- 94.47
17	80.95	58.09- 94.55	51.24- 96.61
18	85.71	63.66- 96.95	56.78- 98.32
19	90.48	69.62- 98.83	62.82- 99.50
20	95.24	76.18- 99.88	69.57- 99.98
21	100.00	83.89-100.00	77.70-100.00

N = 22

x	$100p_x$	95% $100p_l$ $100p_r$	99% $100p_l$ $100p_r$
0	0.00	0.00- 15.44	0.00- 21.40
1	4.55	0.12- 22.84	0.02- 29.24
2	9.09	1.12- 29.16	0.48- 35.77
3	13.64	2.91- 34.91	1.60- 41.61
4	18.18	5.19- 40.28	3.23- 46.99
5	22.73	7.82- 45.37	5.26- 52.01
6	27.27	10.73- 50.22	7.61- 56.74
7	31.82	13.86- 54.87	10.24- 61.23
8	36.36	17.20- 59.34	13.10- 65.49
9	40.91	20.71- 63.65	16.18- 69.54
10	45.45	24.39- 67.79	19.46- 73.40
11	50.00	28.22- 71.78	22.93- 77.07
12	54.55	32.21- 75.61	26.60- 80.54
13	59.09	36.35- 79.29	30.46- 83.82
14	63.64	40.66- 82.80	34.51- 86.90
15	68.18	45.13- 86.14	38.77- 89.76
16	72.73	49.78- 89.27	43.26- 92.39
17	77.27	54.63- 92.18	47.99- 94.74
18	81.82	59.72- 94.81	53.01- 96.77
19	86.36	65.09- 97.09	58.39- 98.40
20	90.91	70.84- 98.88	64.23- 99.52
21	95.45	77.16- 99.88	70.76- 99.98
22	100.00	84.56-100.00	78.60-100.00

N = 23

x	$100p_x$	95% $100p_l$ $100p_r$	99% $100p_l$ $100p_r$
0	0.00	0.00- 14.82	0.00- 20.58
1	4.35	0.11- 21.95	0.02- 28.14
2	8.70	1.07- 28.04	0.46- 34.46
3	13.04	2.78- 33.59	1.53- 40.12
4	17.39	4.95- 38.78	3.08- 45.34
5	21.74	7.46- 43.70	5.02- 50.22
6	26.09	10.23- 48.41	7.25- 54.83
7	30.43	13.21- 52.92	9.74- 59.21
8	34.78	16.38- 57.27	12.46- 63.38
9	39.13	19.71- 61.46	15.37- 67.36
10	43.48	23.19- 65.51	18.48- 71.16
11	47.83	26.82- 69.41	21.76- 74.79
12	52.17	30.59- 73.18	25.21- 78.24
13	56.52	34.49- 76.81	28.84- 81.52
14	60.87	38.54- 80.29	32.64- 84.63
15	65.22	42.73- 83.62	36.62- 87.54
16	69.57	47.08- 86.79	40.79- 90.26
17	73.91	51.59- 89.77	45.17- 92.75
18	78.26	56.30- 92.54	49.78- 94.98
19	82.61	61.22- 95.05	54.66- 96.92
20	86.96	66.41- 97.22	59.88- 98.47
21	91.30	71.96- 98.93	65.54- 99.54
22	95.65	78.05- 99.89	71.86- 99.98
23	100.00	85.18-100.00	79.42-100.00

N = 24

x	$100p_x$	95% $100p_l$ $100p_r$	99% $100p_l$ $100p_r$
0	0.00	0.00- 14.25	0.00- 19.81
1	4.17	0.11- 21.12	0.02- 27.13
2	8.33	1.03- 27.00	0.44- 33.24
3	12.50	2.66- 32.36	1.46- 38.73
4	16.67	4.74- 37.38	2.95- 43.79
5	20.83	7.13- 42.15	4.79- 48.55
6	25.00	9.77- 46.71	6.92- 53.04
7	29.17	12.62- 51.09	9.30- 57.32
8	33.33	15.63- 55.32	11.88- 61.40
9	37.50	18.80- 59.41	14.65- 65.30
10	41.67	22.11- 63.36	17.59- 69.04
11	45.83	25.55- 67.18	20.70- 72.62
12	50.00	29.12- 70.88	23.96- 76.04
13	54.17	32.82- 74.45	27.38- 79.30
14	58.33	36.64- 77.89	30.96- 82.41
15	62.50	40.59- 81.20	34.70- 85.35
16	66.67	44.68- 84.37	38.60- 88.12
17	70.83	48.91- 87.38	42.68- 90.70
18	75.00	53.29- 90.23	46.96- 93.08
19	79.17	57.85- 92.87	51.45- 95.21
20	83.33	62.62- 95.26	56.21- 97.05
21	87.50	67.64- 97.34	61.27- 98.54
22	91.67	73.00- 98.97	66.76- 99.56
23	95.83	78.88- 99.89	72.87- 99.98
24	100.00	85.75-100.00	80.19-100.00

N = 25

x	$100p_x$	95% $100p_l$ $100p_r$	99% $100p_l$ $100p_r$
0	0.00	0.00- 13.72	0.00- 19.10
1	4.00	0.10- 20.35	0.02- 26.18
2	8.00	0.98- 26.03	0.42- 32.10
3	12.00	2.55- 31.22	1.40- 37.43
4	16.00	4.54- 36.08	2.82- 42.35
5	20.00	6.83- 40.70	4.59- 46.98
6	24.00	9.36- 45.13	6.63- 51.36
7	28.00	12.07- 49.39	8.89- 55.53
8	32.00	14.95- 53.50	11.35- 59.52

N = number of trials, x = number of successes, etc., $100\,p_x = 100\,x/N$

$N = 25$ (continued)

x	$100p_x$	95% $100p_l$–$100p_r$	99% $100p_l$–$100p_r$
9	36.00	17.97– 57.48	13.99– 63.35
10	40.00	21.13– 61.33	16.79– 67.02
11	44.00	24.40– 65.07	19.74– 70.54
12	48.00	27.80– 68.69	22.83– 73.93
13	52.00	31.31– 72.20	26.07– 77.17
14	56.00	34.93– 75.60	29.46– 80.26
15	60.00	38.67– 78.87	32.98– 83.21
16	64.00	42.52– 82.03	36.65– 86.01
17	68.00	46.50– 85.05	40.48– 88.65
18	72.00	50.61– 87.93	44.47– 91.11
19	76.00	54.87– 90.64	48.64– 93.37
20	80.00	59.30– 93.17	53.02– 95.41
21	84.00	63.92– 95.46	57.65– 97.18
22	88.00	68.78– 97.45	62.57– 98.60
23	92.00	73.97– 99.02	67.90– 99.58
24	96.00	79.65– 99.90	73.82– 99.98
25	100.00	86.28–100.00	80.90–100.00

$N = 26$

x	$100p_x$	95% $100p_l$–$100p_r$	99% $100p_l$–$100p_r$
0	0.00	0.00– 13.23	0.00– 18.44
1	3.85	0.10– 19.64	0.02– 25.29
2	7.69	0.95– 25.13	0.41– 31.04
3	11.54	2.45– 30.15	1.34– 36.21
4	15.38	4.36– 34.87	2.71– 41.00
5	19.23	6.55– 39.35	4.40– 45.50
6	23.08	8.97– 43.65	6.35– 49.77
7	26.92	11.57– 47.79	8.52– 53.85
8	30.77	14.33– 51.79	10.87– 57.75
9	34.62	17.21– 55.67	13.38– 61.50
10	38.46	20.23– 59.43	16.05– 65.10
11	42.31	23.35– 63.08	18.86– 68.57
12	46.15	26.59– 66.63	21.81– 71.91
13	50.00	29.93– 70.07	24.89– 75.11
14	53.85	33.37– 73.41	28.09– 78.19
15	57.69	36.92– 76.65	31.43– 81.14
16	61.54	40.57– 79.77	34.90– 83.95
17	65.38	44.33– 82.79	38.50– 86.62
18	69.23	48.21– 85.67	42.25– 89.13
19	73.08	52.21– 88.43	46.15– 91.48
20	76.92	56.35– 91.03	50.23– 93.65
21	80.77	60.65– 93.45	54.50– 95.60
22	84.62	65.13– 95.64	59.00– 97.29
23	88.46	69.85– 97.55	63.79– 98.66
24	92.31	74.87– 99.05	68.96– 99.59
25	96.15	80.36– 99.90	74.71– 99.98
26	100.00	86.77–100.00	81.56–100.00

$N = 27$

x	$100p_x$	95% $100p_l$–$100p_r$	99% $100p_l$–$100p_r$
0	0.00	0.00– 12.77	0.00– 17.82
1	3.70	0.09– 18.97	0.02– 24.46
2	7.41	0.91– 24.29	0.39– 30.04
3	11.11	2.35– 29.16	1.29– 35.07
4	14.81	4.19– 33.73	2.60– 39.73
5	18.52	6.30– 38.08	4.23– 44.11
6	22.22	8.62– 42.26	6.10– 48.28
7	25.93	11.11– 46.28	8.17– 52.26
8	29.63	13.75– 50.18	10.42– 56.08
9	33.33	16.52– 53.96	12.83– 59.75
10	37.04	19.40– 57.63	15.38– 63.28
11	40.74	22.39– 61.20	18.07– 66.69
12	44.44	25.48– 64.67	20.88– 69.98
13	48.15	28.67– 68.05	23.81– 73.14
14	51.85	31.95– 71.33	26.86– 76.19
15	55.56	35.33– 74.52	30.02– 79.12
16	59.26	38.80– 77.61	33.31– 81.93
17	62.96	42.37– 80.60	36.72– 84.62
18	66.67	46.04– 83.48	40.25– 87.17
19	70.37	49.82– 86.25	43.92– 89.58
20	74.07	53.72– 88.89	47.74– 91.83
21	77.78	57.74– 91.38	51.72– 93.90
22	81.48	61.92– 93.70	55.89– 95.77
23	85.19	66.27– 95.81	60.27– 97.40
24	88.89	70.84– 97.65	64.93– 98.71
25	92.59	75.71– 99.09	69.96– 99.61
26	96.30	81.03– 99.91	75.54– 99.98
27	100.00	87.23–100.00	82.18–100.00

$N = 28$

x	$100p_x$	95% $100p_l$–$100p_r$	99% $100p_l$–$100p_r$
0	0.00	0.00– 12.34	0.00– 17.24
1	3.57	0.09– 18.35	0.02– 23.69
2	7.14	0.88– 23.50	0.38– 29.11
3	10.71	2.27– 28.23	1.25– 33.99
4	14.29	4.03– 32.67	2.51– 38.53
5	17.86	6.06– 36.89	4.07– 42.80
6	21.43	8.30– 40.95	5.86– 46.87
7	25.00	10.69– 44.87	7.86– 50.76
8	28.57	13.22– 48.67	10.02– 54.49
9	32.14	15.88– 52.35	12.32– 58.08
10	35.71	18.64– 55.93	14.77– 61.55
11	39.29	21.50– 59.42	17.33– 64.90
12	42.86	24.46– 62.82	20.02– 68.14
13	46.43	27.51– 66.13	22.82– 71.26
14	50.00	30.65– 69.35	25.72– 74.28
15	53.57	33.87– 72.49	28.74– 77.18
16	57.14	37.18– 75.54	31.86– 79.98
17	60.71	40.58– 78.50	35.10– 82.67

$N = 28$ (continued)

x	$100p_x$	95% $100p_l$–$100p_r$	99% $100p_l$–$100p_r$
18	64.29	44.07– 81.36	38.45– 85.23
19	67.86	47.65– 84.12	41.92– 87.68
20	71.43	51.33– 86.78	45.51– 89.98
21	75.00	55.13– 89.31	49.24– 92.14
22	78.57	59.05– 91.70	53.13– 94.14
23	82.14	63.11– 93.94	57.20– 95.93
24	85.71	67.33– 95.97	61.47– 97.49
25	89.29	71.77– 97.73	66.01– 98.75
26	92.86	76.50– 99.12	70.89– 99.62
27	96.43	81.65– 99.91	76.31– 99.98
28	100.00	87.66–100.00	82.76–100.00

$N = 29$

x	$100p_x$	95% $100p_l$–$100p_r$	99% $100p_l$–$100p_r$
0	0.00	0.00– 11.94	0.00– 16.70
1	3.45	0.09– 17.76	0.02– 22.96
2	6.90	0.85– 22.77	0.36– 28.23
3	10.34	2.19– 27.35	1.20– 32.98
4	13.79	3.89– 31.66	2.42– 37.40
5	17.24	5.85– 35.77	3.92– 41.57
6	20.69	7.99– 39.72	5.65– 45.54
7	24.14	10.30– 43.54	7.56– 49.33
8	27.59	12.73– 47.24	9.64– 52.99
9	31.03	15.28– 50.83	11.85– 56.51
10	34.48	17.94– 54.33	14.20– 59.91
11	37.93	20.69– 57.74	16.66– 63.20
12	41.38	23.52– 61.06	19.23– 66.38
13	44.83	26.45– 64.31	21.91– 69.46
14	48.28	29.45– 67.47	24.69– 72.43
15	51.72	32.53– 70.55	27.57– 75.31
16	55.17	35.69– 73.55	30.54– 78.09
17	58.62	38.94– 76.48	33.62– 80.77
18	62.07	42.26– 79.31	36.80– 83.34
19	65.52	45.67– 82.06	40.09– 85.80
20	68.97	49.17– 84.72	43.49– 88.15
21	72.41	52.76– 87.27	47.01– 90.36
22	75.86	56.46– 89.70	50.67– 92.44
23	79.31	60.28– 92.01	54.46– 94.35
24	82.76	64.23– 94.15	58.43– 96.08
25	86.21	68.34– 96.11	62.60– 97.58
26	89.66	72.65– 97.81	67.02– 98.80
27	93.10	77.23– 99.15	71.77– 99.64
28	96.55	82.24– 99.91	77.04– 99.98
29	100.00	88.06–100.00	83.30–100.00

$N = 30$

x	$100p_x$	95% $100p_l$–$100p_r$	99% $100p_l$–$100p_r$
0	0.00	0.00– 11.57	0.00– 16.19
1	3.33	0.08– 17.22	0.02– 22.27
2	6.67	0.82– 22.07	0.35– 27.40
3	10.00	2.11– 26.53	1.16– 32.03
4	13.33	3.76– 30.72	2.33– 36.34
5	16.67	5.64– 34.72	3.78– 40.40
6	20.00	7.71– 38.57	5.45– 44.28
7	23.33	9.93– 42.28	7.29– 47.99
8	26.67	12.28– 45.89	9.29– 51.56
9	30.00	14.73– 49.40	11.42– 55.01
10	33.33	17.29– 52.81	13.67– 58.34
11	36.67	19.93– 56.14	16.04– 61.57
12	40.00	22.66– 59.40	18.50– 64.70
13	43.33	25.46– 62.57	21.07– 67.73
14	46.67	28.34– 65.67	23.73– 70.67
15	50.00	31.30– 68.70	26.48– 73.52
16	53.33	34.33– 71.66	29.33– 76.27
17	56.67	37.43– 74.54	32.27– 78.93
18	60.00	40.60– 77.34	35.30– 81.50
19	63.33	43.86– 80.07	38.43– 83.96
20	66.67	47.19– 82.71	41.66– 86.33
21	70.00	50.60– 85.27	44.99– 88.58
22	73.33	54.11– 87.72	48.44– 90.71
23	76.67	57.72– 90.07	52.01– 92.71
24	80.00	61.43– 92.29	55.72– 94.55
25	83.33	65.28– 94.36	59.60– 96.22
26	86.67	69.28– 96.24	63.66– 97.67
27	90.00	73.47– 97.89	67.97– 98.84
28	93.33	77.93– 99.18	72.60– 99.65
29	96.67	82.78– 99.92	77.73– 99.98
30	100.00	88.43–100.00	83.81–100.00

$N = 31$

x	$100p_x$	95% $100p_l$–$100p_r$	99% $100p_l$–$100p_r$
0	0.00	0.00– 11.22	0.00– 15.71
1	3.23	0.08– 16.70	0.02– 21.63
2	6.45	0.79– 21.42	0.34– 26.62
3	9.68	2.04– 25.75	1.12– 31.13
4	12.90	3.63– 29.83	2.25– 35.33
5	16.13	5.45– 33.73	3.65– 39.30
6	19.35	7.45– 37.47	5.26– 43.08
7	22.58	9.59– 41.10	7.04– 46.71
8	25.81	11.86– 44.61	8.96– 50.21
9	29.03	14.22– 48.04	11.02– 53.58
10	32.26	16.68– 51.37	13.18– 56.85
11	35.48	19.23– 54.63	15.46– 60.02
12	38.71	21.85– 57.81	17.83– 63.09
13	41.94	24.55– 60.92	20.29– 66.08
14	45.16	27.32– 63.97	22.85– 68.98
15	48.39	30.15– 66.94	25.49– 71.79
16	51.61	33.06– 69.85	28.21– 74.51
17	54.84	36.03– 72.68	31.02– 77.15

$N = 31$ (continued)

x	$100p_x$	95% $100p_l$–$100p_r$	99% $100p_l$–$100p_r$
18	58.06	39.08– 75.45	33.92– 79.71
19	61.29	42.19– 78.15	36.91– 82.17
20	64.52	45.37– 80.77	39.98– 84.54
21	67.74	48.63– 83.32	43.15– 86.82
22	70.97	51.96– 85.78	46.42– 88.98
23	74.19	55.39– 88.14	49.79– 91.04
24	77.42	58.90– 90.41	53.29– 92.96
25	80.65	62.53– 92.55	56.92– 94.74
26	83.87	66.27– 94.55	60.70– 96.35
27	87.10	70.17– 96.37	64.67– 97.75
28	90.32	74.25– 97.96	68.87– 98.88
29	93.55	78.58– 99.21	73.38– 99.66
30	96.77	83.30– 99.92	78.37– 99.98
31	100.00	88.78–100.00	84.29–100.00

$N = 32$

x	$100p_x$	95% $100p_l$–$100p_r$	99% $100p_l$–$100p_r$
0	0.00	0.00– 10.89	0.00– 15.26
1	3.13	0.08– 16.22	0.02– 21.02
2	6.25	0.77– 20.81	0.33– 25.88
3	9.38	1.98– 25.02	1.09– 30.28
4	12.50	3.51– 28.99	2.18– 34.38
5	15.63	5.28– 32.79	3.53– 38.25
6	18.75	7.21– 36.44	5.09– 41.95
7	21.88	9.28– 39.97	6.80– 45.50
8	25.00	11.46– 43.40	8.66– 48.92
9	28.13	13.75– 46.75	10.64– 52.22
10	31.25	16.12– 50.01	12.73– 55.43
11	34.38	18.57– 53.19	14.92– 58.54
12	37.50	21.10– 56.31	17.20– 61.56
13	40.63	23.70– 59.36	19.57– 64.50
14	43.75	26.36– 62.34	22.03– 67.35
15	46.88	29.09– 65.26	24.56– 70.13
16	50.00	31.89– 68.11	27.18– 72.82
17	53.13	34.74– 70.91	29.87– 75.44
18	56.25	37.66– 73.64	32.65– 77.97
19	59.38	40.64– 76.30	35.50– 80.43
20	62.50	43.69– 78.90	38.44– 82.80
21	65.63	46.81– 81.43	41.46– 85.08
22	68.75	49.99– 83.88	44.57– 87.27
23	71.88	53.25– 86.25	47.78– 89.36
24	75.00	56.60– 88.54	51.08– 91.34
25	78.13	60.03– 90.72	54.50– 93.20
26	81.25	63.56– 92.79	58.05– 94.91
27	84.38	67.21– 94.72	61.75– 96.47
28	87.50	71.01– 96.49	65.62– 97.82
29	90.63	74.98– 98.02	69.72– 98.91
30	93.75	79.19– 99.23	74.12– 99.67
31	96.88	83.78– 99.92	78.98– 99.98
32	100.00	89.11–100.00	84.74–100.00

$N = 33$

x	$100p_x$	95% $100p_l$–$100p_r$	99% $100p_l$–$100p_r$
0	0.00	0.00– 10.58	0.00– 14.83
1	3.03	0.08– 15.76	0.02– 20.44
2	6.06	0.74– 20.23	0.32– 25.18
3	9.09	1.92– 24.33	1.05– 29.47
4	12.12	3.40– 28.20	2.11– 33.47
5	15.15	5.11– 31.90	3.42– 37.26
6	18.18	6.98– 35.46	4.92– 40.87
7	21.21	8.98– 38.91	6.58– 44.34
8	24.24	11.09– 42.26	8.38– 47.69
9	27.27	13.30– 45.52	10.29– 50.93
10	30.30	15.59– 48.71	12.31– 54.08
11	33.33	17.96– 51.83	14.42– 57.13
12	36.36	20.40– 54.88	16.62– 60.10
13	39.39	22.91– 57.86	18.90– 62.98
14	42.42	25.48– 60.78	21.27– 65.79
15	45.45	28.11– 63.65	23.71– 68.53
16	48.48	30.80– 66.46	26.22– 71.19
17	51.52	33.54– 69.20	28.81– 73.78
18	54.55	36.35– 71.89	31.47– 76.29
19	57.58	39.22– 74.52	34.21– 78.73
20	60.61	42.14– 77.09	37.02– 81.10
21	63.64	45.12– 79.60	39.90– 83.38
22	66.67	48.17– 82.04	42.87– 85.58
23	69.70	51.29– 84.41	45.92– 87.69
24	72.73	54.48– 86.70	49.07– 89.71
25	75.76	57.74– 88.91	52.31– 91.62
26	78.79	61.09– 91.02	55.66– 93.42
27	81.82	64.54– 93.02	59.13– 95.08
28	84.85	68.10– 94.89	62.74– 96.58
29	87.88	71.80– 96.60	66.53– 97.89
30	90.91	75.67– 98.08	70.53– 98.95
31	93.94	79.77– 99.26	74.82– 99.68
32	96.97	84.24– 99.92	79.56– 99.98
33	100.00	89.42–100.00	85.17–100.00

$N = 34$

x	$100p_x$	95% $100p_l$–$100p_r$	99% $100p_l$–$100p_r$
0	0.00	0.00– 10.28	0.00– 14.43
1	2.94	0.07– 15.33	0.01– 19.90
2	5.88	0.72– 19.68	0.31– 24.52
3	8.82	1.86– 23.68	1.02– 28.71
4	11.76	3.30– 27.45	2.05– 32.62
5	14.71	4.95– 31.06	3.32– 36.31
6	17.65	6.76– 34.53	4.77– 39.85
7	20.59	8.70– 37.90	6.38– 43.24
8	23.53	10.75– 41.17	8.11– 46.52

$N = 34$ (continued)

x	$100p_x$	95% $100p_l$–$100p_r$	99% $100p_l$–$100p_r$
9	26.47	12.88– 44.36	9.96– 49.7
10	29.41	15.10– 47.48	11.91– 52.7
11	32.35	17.39– 50.53	13.95– 55.7
12	35.29	19.75– 53.51	16.07– 58.6
13	38.24	22.17– 56.44	18.28– 61.5
14	41.18	24.65– 59.30	20.56– 64.3
15	44.12	27.19– 62.11	22.91– 67.0
16	47.06	29.78– 64.87	25.33– 69.6
17	50.00	32.43– 67.57	27.82– 72.1
18	52.94	35.13– 70.22	30.38– 74.6
19	55.88	37.89– 72.81	33.00– 77.0
20	58.82	40.70– 75.35	35.70– 79.4
21	61.76	43.56– 77.83	38.47– 81.7
22	64.71	46.49– 80.25	41.31– 83.9
23	67.65	49.47– 82.61	44.22– 86.0
24	70.59	52.52– 84.90	47.22– 88.0
25	73.53	55.64– 87.12	50.30– 90.0
26	76.47	58.83– 89.25	53.48– 91.8
27	79.41	62.10– 91.30	56.76– 93.6
28	82.35	65.47– 93.24	60.15– 95.2
29	85.29	68.94– 95.05	63.69– 96.6
30	88.24	72.55– 96.70	67.38– 97.9
31	91.18	76.32– 98.14	71.29– 98.9
32	94.12	80.32– 99.28	75.48– 99.6
33	97.06	84.67– 99.93	80.10– 99.9
34	100.00	89.72–100.00	85.57–100.0

$N = 35$

x	$100p_x$	95% $100p_l$–$100p_r$	99% $100p_l$–$100p_r$
0	0.00	0.00– 10.00	0.00– 14.0
1	2.86	0.07– 14.92	0.01– 19.3
2	5.71	0.70– 19.16	0.30– 23.8
3	8.57	1.80– 23.06	0.99– 27.9
4	11.43	3.20– 26.74	1.99– 31.8
5	14.29	4.81– 30.26	3.22– 35.4
6	17.14	6.56– 33.65	4.63– 38.8
7	20.00	8.44– 36.94	6.18– 42.2
8	22.86	10.42– 40.14	7.86– 45.4
9	25.71	12.49– 43.26	9.65– 48.5
10	28.57	14.64– 46.30	11.54– 51.5
11	31.43	16.85– 49.29	13.51– 54.4
12	34.29	19.13– 52.21	15.56– 57.3
13	37.14	21.47– 55.08	17.69– 60.1
14	40.00	23.87– 57.89	19.89– 62.8
15	42.86	26.32– 60.65	22.16– 65.5
16	45.71	28.83– 63.35	24.50– 68.1
17	48.57	31.38– 66.01	26.90– 70.0
18	51.43	33.99– 68.62	29.36– 73.1
19	54.29	36.65– 71.17	31.89– 75.5
20	57.14	39.35– 73.68	34.48– 77.8
21	60.00	42.11– 76.13	37.13– 80.
22	62.86	44.92– 78.53	39.86– 82.3
23	65.71	47.79– 80.87	42.65– 84.4
24	68.57	50.71– 83.15	45.51– 86.4
25	71.43	53.70– 85.36	48.45– 88.4
26	74.29	56.74– 87.51	51.48– 90.3
27	77.14	59.86– 89.58	54.59– 92.
28	80.00	63.06– 91.56	57.80– 93.
29	82.86	66.35– 93.44	61.13– 95.
30	85.71	69.74– 95.19	64.58– 96.
31	88.57	73.26– 96.80	68.20– 98.
32	91.43	76.94– 98.20	72.02– 99.
33	94.29	80.84– 99.30	76.11– 99.
34	97.14	85.08– 99.93	80.62– 99.
35	100.00	90.00–100.00	85.95–100.

$N = 36$

x	$100p_x$	95% $100p_l$–$100p_r$	99% $100p_l$–$100p_r$
0	0.00	0.00– 9.74	0.00– 13.
1	2.78	0.07– 14.53	0.01– 18.
2	5.56	0.68– 18.66	0.29– 23.
3	8.33	1.75– 22.47	0.96– 27.
4	11.11	3.11– 26.06	1.93– 31.
5	13.89	4.67– 29.50	3.12– 34.
6	16.67	6.37– 32.81	4.49– 37.
7	19.44	8.19– 36.02	6.00– 41.
8	22.22	10.12– 39.15	7.63– 44.
9	25.00	12.12– 42.20	9.36– 47.
10	27.78	14.20– 45.19	11.19– 50.
11	30.56	16.35– 48.11	13.10– 53.
12	33.33	18.56– 50.97	15.09– 56.
13	36.11	20.82– 53.78	17.14– 58.
14	38.89	23.14– 56.54	19.27– 61.
15	41.67	25.51– 59.24	21.46– 64.
16	44.44	27.94– 61.90	23.72– 66.
17	47.22	30.41– 64.51	26.03– 69.
18	50.00	32.92– 67.08	28.41– 71.
19	52.78	35.49– 69.59	30.84– 73.
20	55.56	38.10– 72.06	33.34– 76.
21	58.33	40.76– 74.49	35.89– 78.
22	61.11	43.46– 76.86	38.51– 80.
23	63.89	46.22– 79.18	41.19– 82.
24	66.67	49.03– 81.44	43.93– 84.
25	69.44	51.89– 83.65	46.75– 86
26	72.22	54.81– 85.80	49.63– 88.
27	75.00	57.80– 87.88	52.60– 90
28	77.78	60.85– 89.88	55.65– 92.
29	80.56	63.98– 91.81	58.80– 94

N = number of trials, x = number of successes, etc., $100\,p_x = 100\,x/N$

x	$100\,p_x$	95% $100p_l$	95% $100p_r$	99% $100p_l$	99% $100p_r$
$N = 36$ (continued)					
30	83.33	67.19	93.63	62.06	95.51
31	86.11	70.50	95.33	65.44	96.88
32	88.89	73.94	96.89	68.98	98.07
33	91.67	77.53	98.25	72.71	99.04
34	94.44	81.34	99.32	76.71	99.71
35	97.22	85.47	99.93	81.11	99.99
36	100.00	90.26	100.00	86.31	100.00
$N = 37$					
0	0.00	0.00	9.49	0.00	13.34
1	2.70	0.07	14.16	0.01	18.42
2	5.41	0.66	18.19	0.28	22.73
3	8.11	1.70	21.91	0.94	26.63
4	10.81	3.03	25.42	1.88	30.28
5	13.51	4.54	28.77	3.04	33.75
6	16.22	6.19	32.01	4.36	37.06
7	18.92	7.96	35.16	5.83	40.25
8	21.62	9.83	38.21	7.41	43.33
9	24.32	11.77	41.20	9.09	46.32
10	27.03	13.79	44.12	10.86	49.24
11	29.73	15.87	46.98	12.71	52.07
12	32.43	18.01	49.79	14.64	54.83
13	35.14	20.21	52.54	16.63	57.53
14	37.84	22.46	55.24	18.69	60.17
15	40.54	24.75	57.90	20.81	62.75
16	43.24	27.10	60.51	22.99	65.26
17	45.95	29.49	63.08	25.22	67.73
18	48.65	31.92	65.60	27.52	70.13
19	51.35	34.40	68.08	29.87	72.48
20	54.05	36.92	70.51	32.27	74.78
21	56.76	39.49	72.90	34.74	77.01
22	59.46	42.10	75.25	37.25	79.19
23	62.16	44.76	77.54	39.83	81.31
24	64.86	47.46	79.79	42.47	83.37
25	67.57	50.21	81.99	45.17	85.36
26	70.27	53.02	84.13	47.93	87.29
27	72.97	55.88	86.21	50.76	89.14
28	75.68	58.80	88.23	53.68	90.91
29	78.38	61.79	90.17	56.67	92.59
30	81.08	64.84	92.04	59.75	94.17
31	83.78	67.99	93.81	62.94	95.64
32	86.49	71.23	95.46	66.25	96.96
33	89.19	74.58	96.97	69.72	98.12
34	91.89	78.09	98.30	73.37	99.06
35	94.59	81.81	99.34	77.27	99.72
36	97.30	85.84	99.93	81.58	99.99
37	100.00	90.51	100.00	86.66	100.00
$N = 38$					
0	0.00	0.00	9.25	0.00	13.01
1	2.63	0.07	13.81	0.01	17.98
2	5.26	0.64	17.75	0.28	22.19
3	7.89	1.66	21.38	0.91	26.01
4	10.53	2.94	24.80	1.83	29.58
5	13.16	4.41	28.09	2.95	32.97
6	15.79	6.02	31.25	4.24	36.21
7	18.42	7.74	34.33	5.67	39.34
8	21.05	9.55	37.32	7.20	42.36
9	23.68	11.44	40.24	8.83	45.30
10	26.32	13.40	43.10	10.55	48.15
11	28.95	15.42	45.90	12.35	50.94
12	31.58	17.50	48.65	14.21	53.65
13	34.21	19.63	51.35	16.14	56.31
14	36.84	21.81	54.01	18.14	58.90
15	39.47	24.04	56.61	20.19	61.44
16	42.11	26.31	59.18	22.30	63.92
17	44.74	28.62	61.70	24.47	66.35
18	47.37	30.98	64.18	26.68	68.72
19	50.00	33.38	66.62	28.95	71.05
20	52.63	35.82	69.02	31.28	73.32
21	55.26	38.30	71.38	33.65	75.53
22	57.89	40.82	73.69	36.08	77.70
23	60.53	43.39	75.96	38.56	79.81
24	63.16	45.99	78.19	41.10	81.86
25	65.79	48.65	80.37	43.69	83.86
26	68.42	51.35	82.50	46.35	85.79
27	71.05	54.10	84.58	49.06	87.65
28	73.68	56.90	86.60	51.85	89.45
29	76.32	59.76	88.56	54.70	91.17
30	78.95	62.68	90.45	57.64	92.80
31	81.58	65.67	92.26	60.66	94.33
32	84.21	68.75	93.98	63.79	95.76
33	86.84	71.91	95.59	67.03	97.05
34	89.47	75.20	97.06	70.42	98.17
35	92.11	78.62	98.34	73.99	99.09
36	94.74	82.25	99.36	77.81	99.72
37	97.37	86.19	99.93	82.02	99.99
38	100.00	90.75	100.00	86.99	100.00
$N = 39$					
0	0.00	0.00	9.03	0.00	12.70
1	2.56	0.06	13.48	0.01	17.56
2	5.13	0.63	17.32	0.27	21.67
3	7.69	1.62	20.87	0.89	25.41
4	10.26	2.87	24.22	1.78	28.90
5	12.82	4.30	27.43	2.87	32.22
$N = 39$ (continued)					
6	15.38	5.86	30.53	4.13	35.40
7	17.95	7.54	33.54	5.51	38.47
8	20.51	9.30	36.46	7.01	41.43
9	23.08	11.13	39.33	8.59	44.31
10	25.64	13.04	42.13	10.26	47.12
11	28.21	15.00	44.87	12.00	49.85
12	30.77	17.02	47.57	13.81	52.52
13	33.33	19.09	50.22	15.69	55.13
14	35.90	21.20	52.82	17.62	57.68
15	38.46	23.36	55.38	19.61	60.18
16	41.03	25.57	57.90	21.66	62.62
17	43.59	27.81	60.38	23.75	65.02
18	46.15	30.09	62.82	25.90	67.36
19	48.72	32.42	65.22	28.10	69.66
20	51.28	34.78	67.58	30.34	71.90
21	53.85	37.18	69.91	32.64	74.10
22	56.41	39.62	72.19	34.98	76.25
23	58.97	42.10	74.43	37.38	78.34
24	61.54	44.62	76.64	39.82	80.39
25	64.10	47.18	78.80	42.32	82.38
26	66.67	49.78	80.91	44.87	84.31
27	69.23	52.43	82.98	47.48	86.19
28	71.79	55.13	85.00	50.15	88.00
29	74.36	57.87	86.96	52.88	89.74
30	76.92	60.67	88.87	55.69	91.41
31	79.49	63.54	90.70	58.57	92.99
32	82.05	66.46	92.46	61.53	94.49
33	84.62	69.47	94.14	64.60	95.87
34	87.18	72.57	95.70	67.78	97.13
35	89.74	75.78	97.13	71.10	98.22
36	92.31	79.13	98.38	74.59	99.11
37	94.87	82.68	99.37	78.33	99.73
38	97.44	86.52	99.94	82.44	99.99
39	100.00	90.97	100.00	87.30	100.00
$N = 40$					
0	0.00	0.00	8.81	0.00	12.41
1	2.50	0.06	13.16	0.01	17.15
2	5.00	0.61	16.92	0.26	21.18
3	7.50	1.57	20.39	0.86	24.84
4	10.00	2.79	23.66	1.73	28.26
5	12.50	4.19	26.80	2.80	31.51
6	15.00	5.71	29.84	4.02	34.63
7	17.50	7.34	32.78	5.37	37.63
8	20.00	9.05	35.65	6.82	40.54
9	22.50	10.84	38.45	8.36	43.37
10	25.00	12.69	41.20	9.98	46.12
11	27.50	14.60	43.89	11.68	48.81
12	30.00	16.56	46.53	13.44	51.43
13	32.50	18.57	49.13	15.26	54.00
14	35.00	20.63	51.68	17.13	56.51
15	37.50	22.73	54.20	19.06	58.97
16	40.00	24.86	56.67	21.05	61.38
17	42.50	27.04	59.11	23.08	63.74
18	45.00	29.26	61.51	25.16	66.05
19	47.50	31.51	63.87	27.29	68.32
20	50.00	33.80	66.20	29.46	70.54
21	52.50	36.13	68.49	31.68	72.71
22	55.00	38.49	70.74	33.95	74.84
23	57.50	40.89	72.96	36.26	76.92
24	60.00	43.33	75.14	38.62	78.95
25	62.50	45.80	77.27	41.03	80.94
26	65.00	48.32	79.37	43.49	82.87
27	67.50	50.87	81.43	46.00	84.74
28	70.00	53.47	83.44	48.57	86.56
29	72.50	56.11	85.40	51.19	88.32
30	75.00	58.80	87.31	53.88	90.02
31	77.50	61.55	89.16	56.63	91.64
32	80.00	64.35	90.95	59.46	93.18
33	82.50	67.22	92.66	62.37	94.63
34	85.00	70.16	94.29	65.37	95.98
35	87.50	73.20	95.81	68.49	97.20
36	90.00	76.34	97.21	71.74	98.27
37	92.50	79.61	98.43	75.16	99.14
38	95.00	83.08	99.39	78.82	99.74
39	97.50	86.84	99.94	82.85	99.99
40	100.00	91.19	100.00	87.59	100.00
$N = 41$					
0	0.00	0.00	8.60	0.00	12.12
1	2.44	0.06	12.86	0.01	16.77
2	4.88	0.60	16.53	0.26	20.71
3	7.32	1.54	19.92	0.84	24.29
4	9.76	2.72	23.13	1.69	27.64
5	12.20	4.08	26.20	2.73	30.83
6	14.63	5.57	29.17	3.92	33.89
7	17.07	7.15	32.06	5.23	36.83
8	19.51	8.82	34.87	6.64	39.69
9	21.95	10.56	37.61	8.14	42.46
10	24.39	12.36	40.30	9.72	45.17
11	26.83	14.22	42.94	11.37	47.81
12	29.27	16.13	45.54	13.08	50.38
13	31.71	18.08	48.09	14.85	52.91
14	34.15	20.08	50.59	16.67	55.38
15	36.59	22.12	53.06	18.55	57.80
16	39.02	24.20	55.50	20.47	60.17
$N = 41$ (continued)					
17	41.46	26.32	57.89	22.44	62.50
18	43.90	28.47	60.25	24.46	64.78
19	46.34	30.66	62.58	26.53	67.02
20	48.78	32.88	64.87	28.63	69.22
21	51.22	35.13	67.12	30.78	71.37
22	53.66	37.42	69.34	32.98	73.47
23	56.10	39.75	71.53	35.22	75.54
24	58.54	42.11	73.68	37.50	77.56
25	60.98	44.50	75.80	39.83	79.53
26	63.41	46.94	77.88	42.20	81.45
27	65.85	49.41	79.92	44.62	83.33
28	68.29	51.91	81.92	47.09	85.15
29	70.73	54.46	83.87	49.62	86.92
30	73.17	57.06	85.78	52.19	88.63
31	75.61	59.70	87.64	54.83	90.28
32	78.05	62.39	89.44	57.54	91.86
33	80.49	65.13	91.18	60.31	93.36
34	82.93	67.94	92.85	63.17	94.77
35	85.37	70.83	94.43	66.11	96.08
36	87.80	73.80	95.92	69.17	97.27
37	90.24	76.87	97.28	72.36	98.31
38	92.68	80.08	98.46	75.71	99.16
39	95.12	83.47	99.40	79.29	99.74
40	97.56	87.14	99.94	83.23	99.99
41	100.00	91.40	100.00	87.88	100.00
$N = 42$					
0	0.00	0.00	8.41	0.00	11.85
1	2.38	0.06	12.57	0.01	16.40
2	4.76	0.58	16.16	0.25	20.26
3	7.14	1.50	19.48	0.82	23.77
4	9.52	2.66	22.62	1.65	27.05
5	11.90	3.98	25.63	2.66	30.18
6	14.29	5.43	28.54	3.82	33.18
7	16.67	6.97	31.36	5.10	36.07
8	19.05	8.60	34.12	6.47	38.87
9	21.43	10.30	36.81	7.94	41.59
10	23.81	12.05	39.45	9.47	44.25
11	26.19	13.86	42.04	11.08	46.84
12	28.57	15.72	44.58	12.74	49.38
13	30.95	17.62	47.09	14.46	51.86
14	33.33	19.57	49.55	16.23	54.29
15	35.71	21.55	51.97	18.06	56.68
16	38.10	23.57	54.36	19.93	59.02
17	40.48	25.63	56.72	21.84	61.31
18	42.86	27.72	59.04	23.80	63.56
19	45.24	29.85	61.33	25.81	65.77
20	47.62	32.00	63.58	27.85	67.94
21	50.00	34.19	65.81	29.93	70.07
22	52.38	36.42	68.00	32.06	72.15
23	54.76	38.67	70.15	34.23	74.19
24	57.14	40.96	72.28	36.44	76.20
25	59.52	43.28	74.37	38.69	78.16
26	61.90	45.64	76.43	40.98	80.07
27	64.29	48.03	78.45	43.32	81.94
28	66.67	50.45	80.43	45.71	83.77
29	69.05	52.91	82.38	48.14	85.54
30	71.43	55.42	84.28	50.62	87.26
31	73.81	57.96	86.14	53.16	88.92
32	76.19	60.55	87.95	55.75	90.53
33	78.57	63.19	89.70	58.41	92.06
34	80.95	65.88	91.40	61.13	93.53
35	83.33	68.64	93.03	63.93	94.90
36	85.71	71.46	94.57	66.82	96.18
37	88.10	74.37	96.02	69.82	97.34
38	90.48	77.38	97.34	72.95	98.35
39	92.86	80.52	98.50	76.23	99.18
40	95.24	83.84	99.42	79.74	99.75
41	97.62	87.43	99.94	83.60	99.99
42	100.00	91.59	100.00	88.15	100.00
$N = 43$					
0	0.00	0.00	8.22	0.00	11.59
1	2.33	0.06	12.29	0.01	16.04
2	4.65	0.57	15.81	0.24	19.82
3	6.98	1.46	19.06	0.80	23.27
4	9.30	2.59	22.14	1.61	26.49
5	11.63	3.89	25.08	2.60	29.55
6	13.95	5.30	27.93	3.73	32.49
7	16.28	6.81	30.70	4.97	35.33
8	18.60	8.39	33.40	6.32	38.08
9	20.93	10.04	36.04	7.74	40.76
10	23.26	11.76	38.63	9.24	43.37
11	25.58	13.52	41.17	10.80	45.92
12	27.91	15.33	43.67	12.42	48.41
13	30.23	17.18	46.13	14.09	50.85
14	32.56	19.08	48.54	15.82	53.25
15	34.88	21.01	50.93	17.59	55.59
16	37.21	22.98	53.27	19.41	57.90
17	39.53	24.98	55.59	21.27	60.16
18	41.86	27.01	57.87	23.18	62.38
19	44.19	29.08	60.12	25.12	64.56
20	46.51	31.18	62.35	27.11	66.70
21	48.84	33.31	64.54	29.13	68.80
22	51.16	35.46	66.69	31.20	70.87
23	53.49	37.65	68.82	33.30	72.89
$N = 43$ (continued)					
24	55.81	39.88	70.92	35.44	74.88
25	58.14	42.13	72.99	37.62	76.82
26	60.47	44.41	75.02	39.84	78.73
27	62.79	46.73	77.02	42.10	80.59
28	65.12	49.07	78.99	44.41	82.41
29	67.44	51.46	80.92	46.75	84.18
30	69.77	53.87	82.82	49.15	85.91
31	72.09	56.33	84.67	51.59	87.58
32	74.42	58.83	86.48	54.08	89.20
33	76.74	61.37	88.24	56.63	90.76
34	79.07	63.96	89.96	59.24	92.26
35	81.40	66.60	91.61	61.92	93.68
36	83.72	69.30	93.19	64.67	95.03
37	86.05	72.07	94 70	67.51	96.27
38	88.37	74.92	96.11	70.45	97.40
39	90.70	77.86	97.41	73.51	98.39
40	93.02	80.94	98.54	76.73	99.20
41	95.35	84.19	99.43	80.18	99.76
42	97.67	87.71	99.94	83.96	99.99
43	100.00	91.78	100.00	88.41	100.00
$N = 44$					
0	0.00	0.00	8.04	0.00	11.34
1	2.27	0.06	12.02	0.01	15.70
2	4.55	0.56	15.47	0.24	19.41
3	6.82	1.43	18.66	0.78	22.79
4	9.09	2.53	21.67	1.57	25.95
5	11.36	3.79	24.56	2.54	28.95
6	13.64	5.17	27.35	3.64	31.84
7	15.91	6.64	30.07	4.85	34.62
8	18.18	8.19	32.71	6.16	37.33
9	20.45	9.80	35.30	7.55	39.96
10	22.73	11.47	37.84	9.01	42.52
11	25.00	13.19	40.34	10.53	45.03
12	27.27	14.96	42.79	12.11	47.48
13	29.55	16.76	45.20	13.74	49.88
14	31.82	18.61	47.58	15.43	52.24
15	34.09	20.49	49.92	17.15	54.55
16	36.36	22.41	52.23	18.92	56.82
17	38.64	24.36	54.50	20.73	59.05
18	40.91	26.34	56.75	22.59	61.24
19	43.18	28.35	58.97	24.48	63.39
20	45.45	30.39	61.15	26.41	65.50
21	47.73	32.46	63.31	28.37	67.58
22	50.00	34.56	65.44	30.38	69.62
23	52.27	36.69	67.54	32.42	71.63
24	54.55	38.85	69.61	34.50	73.59
25	56.82	41.03	71.65	36.61	75.52
26	59.09	43.25	73.66	38.76	77.41
27	61.36	45.50	75.64	40.95	79.27
28	63.64	47.77	77.59	43.18	81.08
29	65.91	50.08	79.51	45.45	82.85
30	68.18	52.42	81.39	47.76	84.57
31	70.45	54.80	83.24	50.12	86.26
32	72.73	57.21	85.04	52.52	87.89
33	75.00	59.66	86.81	54.97	89.47
34	77.27	62.16	88.53	57.48	90.99
35	79.55	64.70	90.20	60.04	92.45
36	81.82	67.29	91.81	62.67	93.84
37	84.09	69.93	93.36	65.38	95.15
38	86.36	72.65	94.83	68.16	96.36
39	88.64	75.44	96.21	71.05	97.46
40	90.91	78.33	97.47	74.05	98.43
41	93.18	81.34	98.57	77.21	99.22
42	95.45	84.53	99.44	80.59	99.76
43	97.73	87.98	99.94	84.30	99.99
44	100.00	91.96	100.00	88.66	100.00
$N = 45$					
0	0.00	0.00	7.87	0.00	11.11
1	2.22	0.06	11.77	0.01	15.38
2	4.44	0.54	15.15	0.23	19.01
3	6.67	1.40	18.27	0.77	22.32
4	8.89	2.48	21.22	1.54	25.43
5	11.11	3.71	24.05	2.48	28.38
6	13.33	5.05	26.79	3.56	31.21
7	15.56	6.49	29.46	4.74	33.95
8	17.78	8.00	32.05	6.02	36.60
9	20.00	9.58	34.60	7.37	39.18
10	22.22	11.20	37.09	8.80	41.71
11	24.44	12.88	39.54	10.28	44.17
12	26.67	14.60	41.94	11.82	46.58
13	28.89	16.37	44.31	13.41	48.95
14	31.11	18.17	46.65	15.05	51.27
15	33.33	20.00	48.95	16.73	53.54
16	35.56	21.87	51.22	18.46	55.78
17	37.78	23.77	53.46	20.22	57.98
18	40.00	25.70	55.67	22.02	60.14
19	42.22	27.66	57.85	23.86	62.26
20	44.44	29.64	60.00	25.74	64.35
21	46.67	31.66	62.13	27.65	66.40
22	48.89	33.70	64.23	29.60	68.42
23	51.11	35.77	66.30	31.58	70.40
24	53.33	37.87	68.34	33.60	72.35
25	55.56	40.00	70.36	35.65	74.26
26	57.78	42.15	72.34	37.74	76.14
27	60.00	44.33	74.30	39.86	77.98

N = number of trials, x = number of successes, etc., $100\,p_x = 100\,x/N$

$N = 45$ (continued)

x	$100p_x$	100(1 − 2α) limits 95% $100p_l$	95% $100p_r$	99% $100p_l$	99% $100p_r$
28	62.22	46.54	76.23	42.02	79.78
29	64.44	48.78	78.13	44.22	81.54
30	66.67	51.05	80.00	46.46	83.27
31	68.89	53.35	81.83	48.73	84.95
32	71.11	55.69	83.63	51.05	86.59
33	73.33	58.06	85.40	53.42	88.18
34	75.56	60.46	87.12	55.83	89.72
35	77.78	62.91	88.80	58.29	91.20
36	80.00	65.40	90.42	60.82	92.63
37	82.22	67.95	92.00	63.40	93.98
38	84.44	70.54	93.51	66.05	95.26
39	86.67	73.21	94.95	68.79	96.44
40	88.89	75.95	96.29	71.62	97.52
41	91.11	78.78	97.52	74.57	98.46
42	93.33	81.73	98.60	77.68	99.23
43	95.56	84.85	99.46	80.99	99.77
44	97.78	88.23	99.94	84.62	99.99
45	100.00	92.13	100.00	88.89	100.00

$N = 46$

x	$100p_x$	95% $100p_l$	95% $100p_r$	99% $100p_l$	99% $100p_r$
0	0.00	0.00	7.71	0.00	10.88
1	2.17	0.06	11.53	0.01	15.07
2	4.35	0.53	14.84	0.23	18.63
3	6.52	1.37	17.90	0.75	21.88
4	8.70	2.42	20.79	1.50	24.93
5	10.87	3.62	23.57	2.42	27.82
6	13.04	4.94	26.26	3.47	30.60
7	15.22	6.34	28.87	4.63	33.29
8	17.39	7.82	31.42	5.88	35.90
9	19.57	9.36	33.91	7.20	38.44
10	21.74	10.95	36.36	8.59	40.92
11	23.91	12.59	38.77	10.04	43.34
12	26.09	14.27	41.13	11.54	45.72
13	28.26	15.99	43.46	13.10	48.04
14	30.43	17.74	45.75	14.69	50.33
15	32.61	19.53	48.02	16.33	52.57
16	34.78	21.35	50.25	18.01	54.77
17	36.96	23.21	52.45	19.73	56.94
18	39.13	25.09	54.63	21.49	59.07
19	41.30	27.00	56.77	23.28	61.16
20	43.48	28.93	58.89	25.11	63.23
21	45.65	30.90	60.99	26.97	65.25
22	47.83	32.89	63.05	28.86	67.25
23	50.00	34.90	65.10	30.79	69.21
24	52.17	36.95	67.11	32.75	71.14
25	54.35	39.01	69.10	34.75	73.03
26	56.52	41.11	71.07	36.77	74.89
27	58.70	43.23	73.00	38.84	76.72
28	60.87	45.37	74.91	40.93	78.51
29	63.04	47.55	76.79	43.06	80.27
30	65.22	49.75	78.65	45.23	81.99
31	67.39	51.98	80.47	47.43	83.67
32	69.57	54.25	82.26	49.67	85.31
33	71.74	56.54	84.01	51.96	86.90
34	73.91	58.87	85.73	54.28	88.46
35	76.09	61.23	87.41	56.66	89.96
36	78.26	63.64	89.05	59.08	91.41
37	80.43	66.09	90.64	61.56	92.80
38	82.61	68.58	92.18	64.10	94.12
39	84.78	71.13	93.66	66.71	95.37
40	86.96	73.74	95.06	69.40	96.53
41	89.13	76.43	96.38	72.18	97.58
42	91.30	79.21	97.58	75.07	98.50
43	93.48	82.10	98.63	78.12	99.25
44	95.65	85.16	99.47	81.37	99.77
45	97.83	88.47	99.94	84.93	99.99
46	100.00	92.29	100.00	89.12	100.00

$N = 47$

x	$100p_x$	95% $100p_l$	95% $100p_r$	99% $100p_l$	99% $100p_r$
0	0.00	0.00	7.55	0.00	10.66
1	2.13	0.05	11.29	0.01	14.77
2	4.26	0.52	14.54	0.22	18.27
3	6.38	1.34	17.54	0.73	21.45
4	8.51	2.37	20.38	1.47	24.44
5	10.64	3.55	23.10	2.37	27.29
6	12.77	4.83	25.74	3.40	30.02
7	14.89	6.20	28.31	4.53	32.66
8	17.02	7.65	30.81	5.75	35.23
9	19.15	9.15	33.26	7.04	37.72
10	21.28	10.70	35.66	8.40	40.16
11	23.40	12.30	38.03	9.81	42.55
12	25.53	13.94	40.35	11.28	44.88
13	27.66	15.62	42.64	12.79	47.17
14	29.79	17.34	44.89	14.35	49.42
15	31.91	19.09	47.12	15.95	51.63
16	34.04	20.86	49.31	17.59	53.80
17	36.17	22.67	51.48	19.27	55.94
18	38.30	24.51	53.62	20.98	58.04
19	40.43	26.37	55.73	22.73	60.11
20	42.55	28.26	57.82	24.51	62.14
21	44.68	30.17	59.88	26.32	64.14
22	46.81	32.11	61.92	28.16	66.11
23	48.94	34.08	63.94	30.04	68.05
24	51.06	36.06	65.92	31.95	69.96
25	53.19	38.08	67.89	33.89	71.84
26	55.32	40.12	69.83	35.86	73.68
27	57.45	42.18	71.74	37.86	75.49

$N = 47$ (continued)

x	$100p_x$	95% $100p_l$	95% $100p_r$	99% $100p_l$	99% $100p_r$
28	59.57	44.27	73.63	39.89	77.27
29	61.70	46.38	75.49	41.96	79.02
30	63.83	48.52	77.33	44.06	80.73
31	65.96	50.69	79.14	46.20	82.41
32	68.09	52.88	80.91	48.37	84.05
33	70.21	55.11	82.66	50.58	85.65
34	72.34	57.36	84.38	52.83	87.21
35	74.47	59.65	86.06	55.12	88.72
36	76.60	61.97	87.70	57.45	90.19
37	78.72	64.34	89.30	59.84	91.60
38	80.85	66.74	90.85	62.28	92.96
39	82.98	69.19	92.35	64.77	94.25
40	85.11	71.69	93.80	67.34	95.47
41	87.23	74.26	95.17	69.98	96.60
42	89.36	76.90	96.45	72.71	97.63
43	91.49	79.62	97.63	75.56	98.53
44	93.62	82.46	98.66	78.55	99.27
45	95.74	85.46	99.48	81.73	99.78
46	97.87	88.71	99.95	85.23	99.99
47	100.00	92.45	100.00	89.34	100.00

$N = 48$

x	$100p_x$	95% $100p_l$	95% $100p_r$	99% $100p_l$	99% $100p_r$
0	0.00	0.00	7.40	0.00	10.45
1	2.08	0.05	11.07	0.01	14.48
2	4.17	0.51	14.25	0.22	17.91
3	6.25	1.31	17.20	0.72	21.04
4	8.33	2.32	19.98	1.44	23.98
5	10.42	3.47	22.66	2.32	26.78
6	12.50	4.73	25.25	3.32	29.46
7	14.58	6.07	27.76	4.43	32.06
8	16.67	7.48	30.22	5.62	34.58
9	18.75	8.95	32.63	6.89	37.03
10	20.83	10.47	34.99	8.21	39.43
11	22.92	12.03	37.31	9.59	41.78
12	25.00	13.64	39.60	11.03	44.08
13	27.08	15.28	41.85	12.51	46.33
14	29.17	16.95	44.06	14.03	48.55
15	31.25	18.66	46.25	15.59	50.72
16	33.33	20.40	48.41	17.19	52.86
17	35.42	22.16	50.54	18.83	54.97
18	37.50	23.95	52.65	20.50	57.04
19	39.58	25.77	54.73	22.20	59.08
20	41.67	27.61	56.79	23.93	61.09
21	43.75	29.48	58.82	25.70	63.07
22	45.83	31.37	60.83	27.50	65.01
23	47.92	33.29	62.81	29.33	66.93
24	50.00	35.23	64.77	31.18	68.82
25	52.08	37.19	66.71	33.07	70.67
26	54.17	39.17	68.63	34.99	72.50
27	56.25	41.18	70.52	36.93	74.30
28	58.33	43.21	72.39	38.91	76.07
29	60.42	45.27	74.23	40.92	77.80
30	62.50	47.35	76.05	42.96	79.50
31	64.58	49.46	77.84	45.03	81.17
32	66.67	51.59	79.60	47.14	82.81
33	68.75	53.75	81.34	49.28	84.41
34	70.83	55.94	83.05	51.45	85.97
35	72.92	58.15	84.72	53.67	87.49
36	75.00	60.40	86.36	55.92	88.97
37	77.08	62.69	87.97	58.22	90.41
38	79.17	65.01	89.53	60.57	91.79
39	81.25	67.37	91.05	62.97	93.11
40	83.33	69.78	92.52	65.42	94.38
41	85.42	72.24	93.93	67.94	95.57
42	87.50	74.75	95.27	70.54	96.68
43	89.58	77.34	96.53	73.22	97.68
44	91.67	80.02	97.68	76.02	98.56
45	93.75	82.80	98.69	78.96	99.28
46	95.83	85.75	99.49	82.09	99.78
47	97.92	88.93	99.95	85.52	99.99
48	100.00	92.60	100.00	89.55	100.00

$N = 49$

x	$100p_x$	95% $100p_l$	95% $100p_r$	99% $100p_l$	99% $100p_r$
0	0.00	0.00	7.25	0.00	10.25
1	2.04	0.05	10.85	0.01	14.21
2	4.08	0.50	13.98	0.21	17.58
3	6.12	1.28	16.87	0.70	20.65
4	8.16	2.27	19.60	1.41	23.53
5	10.20	3.40	22.23	2.27	26.28
6	12.24	4.63	24.77	3.25	28.92
7	14.29	5.94	27.24	4.34	31.47
8	16.33	7.32	29.66	5.50	33.95
9	18.37	8.76	32.02	6.74	36.37
10	20.41	10.24	34.34	8.03	38.73
11	22.45	11.77	36.62	9.39	41.04
12	24.49	13.34	38.87	10.79	43.30
13	26.53	14.95	41.08	12.23	45.52
14	28.57	16.58	43.26	13.72	47.70
15	30.61	18.25	45.42	15.24	49.85
16	32.65	19.95	47.54	16.81	51.96
17	34.69	21.67	49.64	18.40	54.03
18	36.73	23.42	51.71	20.03	56.07
19	38.78	25.20	53.76	21.69	58.09
20	40.82	27.00	55.79	23.39	60.07
21	42.86	28.82	57.79	25.11	62.02
22	44.90	30.67	59.77	26.86	63.95
23	46.94	32.53	61.73	28.64	65.84

$N = 49$ (continued)

x	$100p_x$	95% $100p_l$	95% $100p_r$	99% $100p_l$	99% $100p_r$
24	48.98	34.42	63.66	30.45	67.71
25	51.02	36.34	65.58	32.29	69.55
26	53.06	38.27	67.47	34.16	71.36
27	55.10	40.23	69.33	36.05	73.14
28	57.14	42.21	71.18	37.98	74.89
29	59.18	44.21	73.00	39.93	76.61
30	61.22	46.24	74.80	41.91	78.31
31	63.27	48.29	76.58	43.93	79.97
32	65.31	50.36	78.33	45.97	81.60
33	67.35	52.46	80.05	48.04	83.19
34	69.39	54.58	81.75	50.15	84.76
35	71.43	56.74	83.42	52.30	86.28
36	73.47	58.92	85.05	54.48	87.77
37	75.51	61.13	86.66	56.70	89.21
38	77.55	63.38	88.23	58.96	90.61
39	79.59	65.66	89.76	61.27	91.97
40	81.63	67.98	91.24	63.63	93.26
41	83.67	70.34	92.68	66.05	94.50
42	85.71	72.76	94.06	68.53	95.66
43	87.76	75.23	95.37	71.08	96.75
44	89.80	77.77	96.60	73.72	97.73
45	91.84	80.40	97.73	76.47	98.59
46	93.88	83.13	98.72	79.35	99.30
47	95.92	86.02	99.50	82.42	99.79
48	97.96	89.15	99.95	85.79	99.99
49	100.00	92.75	100.00	89.75	100.00

$N = 50$

x	$100p_x$	95% $100p_l$	95% $100p_r$	99% $100p_l$	99% $100p_r$
0	0.00	0.00	7.11	0.00	10.05
1	2.00	0.05	10.65	0.01	13.94
2	4.00	0.49	13.71	0.21	17.25
3	6.00	1.25	16.55	0.69	20.27
4	8.00	2.22	19.23	1.38	23.11
5	10.00	3.33	21.81	2.22	25.80
6	12.00	4.53	24.31	3.19	28.40
7	14.00	5.82	26.74	4.25	30.91
8	16.00	7.17	29.11	5.39	33.35
9	18.00	8.58	31.44	6.60	35.73
10	20.00	10.03	33.72	7.86	38.05
11	22.00	11.53	35.96	9.19	40.32
12	24.00	13.06	38.17	10.56	42.55
13	26.00	14.63	40.34	11.97	44.74
14	28.00	16.23	42.49	13.42	46.89
15	30.00	17.86	44.61	14.91	49.00
16	32.00	19.52	46.70	16.44	51.08
17	34.00	21.21	48.77	18.00	53.12
18	36.00	22.92	50.81	19.59	55.14
19	38.00	24.65	52.83	21.21	57.13
20	40.00	26.41	54.82	22.87	59.08
21	42.00	28.19	56.79	24.55	61.01
22	44.00	29.99	58.75	26.26	62.91
23	46.00	31.81	60.68	27.99	64.78
24	48.00	33.66	62.58	29.76	66.63
25	50.00	35.53	64.47	31.55	68.45
26	52.00	37.42	66.34	33.37	70.24
27	54.00	39.32	68.19	35.22	72.01
28	56.00	41.25	70.01	37.09	73.74
29	58.00	43.21	71.81	38.99	75.45
30	60.00	45.18	73.59	40.92	77.13
31	62.00	47.17	75.35	42.87	78.79
32	64.00	49.19	77.08	44.86	80.41
33	66.00	51.23	78.79	46.88	82.00
34	68.00	53.30	80.48	48.92	83.56
35	70.00	55.39	82.14	51.00	85.09
36	72.00	57.51	83.77	53.11	86.58
37	74.00	59.66	85.37	55.26	88.03
38	76.00	61.83	86.94	57.45	89.44
39	78.00	64.04	88.47	59.68	90.81
40	80.00	66.28	89.97	61.95	92.14
41	82.00	68.56	91.42	64.27	93.40
42	84.00	70.89	92.83	66.65	94.61
43	86.00	73.26	94.18	69.09	95.75
44	88.00	75.69	95.47	71.60	96.81
45	90.00	78.19	96.67	74.20	97.78
46	92.00	80.77	97.78	76.89	98.62
47	94.00	83.45	98.75	79.73	99.31
48	96.00	86.29	99.51	82.75	99.79
49	98.00	89.35	99.95	86.06	99.99
50	100.00	92.89	100.00	89.95	100.00

$N = 51$

x	$100p_x$	95% $100p_l$	95% $100p_r$	99% $100p_l$	99% $100p_r$
0	0.00	0.00	6.98	0.00	9.87
1	1.96	0.05	10.45	0.01	13.68
2	3.92	0.48	13.46	0.20	16.94
3	5.88	1.23	16.24	0.67	19.90
4	7.84	2.18	18.88	1.35	22.69
5	9.80	3.26	21.41	2.18	25.35
6	11.76	4.44	23.87	3.12	27.90
7	13.73	5.70	26.26	4.16	30.37
8	15.69	7.02	28.59	5.28	32.77
9	17.65	8.40	30.87	6.46	35.11
10	19.61	9.82	33.12	7.70	37.39
11	21.57	11.29	35.32	8.99	39.63
12	23.53	12.79	37.49	10.33	41.82
13	25.49	14.33	39.63	11.72	43.98
14	27.45	15.89	41.74	13.14	46.09
15	29.41	17.49	43.83	14.59	48.18

$N = 51$ (continued)

x	$100p_x$	95% $100p_l$	95% $100p_r$	99% $100p_l$	99% $100p_r$
16	31.37	19.11	45.89	16.09	50.23
17	33.33	20.76	47.92	17.61	52.25
18	35.29	22.43	49.93	19.17	54.23
19	37.25	24.13	51.92	20.75	56.19
20	39.22	25.84	53.89	22.37	58.12
21	41.18	27.58	55.83	24.01	60.03
22	43.14	29.35	57.75	25.68	61.91
23	45.10	31.13	59.66	27.37	63.76
24	47.06	32.93	61.54	29.10	65.58
25	49.02	34.75	63.40	30.84	67.38
26	50.98	36.60	65.25	32.62	69.16
27	52.94	38.46	67.07	34.42	70.90
28	54.90	40.34	68.87	36.24	72.63
29	56.86	42.25	70.65	38.09	74.32
30	58.82	44.17	72.42	39.97	75.99
31	60.78	46.11	74.16	41.88	77.63
32	62.75	48.08	75.87	43.81	79.25
33	64.71	50.07	77.57	45.77	80.83
34	66.67	52.08	79.24	47.75	82.39
35	68.63	54.11	80.89	49.77	83.91
36	70.59	56.17	82.51	51.82	85.41
37	72.55	58.26	84.11	53.91	86.86
38	74.51	60.37	85.67	56.02	88.28
39	76.47	62.51	87.21	58.18	89.67
40	78.43	64.68	88.71	60.37	91.01
41	80.39	66.88	90.18	62.61	92.30
42	82.35	69.13	91.60	64.89	93.54
43	84.31	71.41	92.98	67.23	94.72
44	86.27	73.74	94.30	69.63	95.84
45	88.24	76.13	95.56	72.10	96.88
46	90.20	78.59	96.74	74.65	97.82
47	92.16	81.12	97.82	77.31	98.65
48	94.12	83.76	98.77	80.10	99.33
49	96.08	86.54	99.52	83.06	99.80
50	98.04	89.55	99.95	86.32	99.99
51	100.00	93.02	100.00	90.13	100.00

$N = 52$

x	$100p_x$	95% $100p_l$	95% $100p_r$	99% $100p_l$	99% $100p_r$
0	0.00	0.00	6.85	0.00	9.69
1	1.92	0.05	10.26	0.01	13.44
2	3.85	0.47	13.21	0.20	16.63
3	5.77	1.21	15.95	0.66	19.55
4	7.69	2.14	18.54	1.32	22.29
5	9.62	3.20	21.03	2.13	24.90
6	11.54	4.35	23.44	3.06	27.41
7	13.46	5.59	25.79	4.08	29.84
8	15.38	6.88	28.08	5.17	32.20
9	17.31	8.23	30.33	6.33	34.51
10	19.23	9.63	32.53	7.54	36.76
11	21.15	11.06	34.70	8.81	38.96
12	23.08	12.53	36.84	10.12	41.12
13	25.00	14.03	38.95	11.47	43.24
14	26.92	15.57	41.02	12.86	45.33
15	28.85	17.13	43.08	14.29	47.38
16	30.77	18.72	45.10	15.75	49.40
17	32.69	20.33	47.11	17.24	51.39
18	34.62	21.97	49.09	18.76	53.36
19	36.54	23.62	51.04	20.31	55.29
20	38.46	25.30	52.98	21.89	57.20
21	40.38	27.01	54.90	23.49	59.08
22	42.31	28.73	56.80	25.12	60.93
23	44.23	30.47	58.67	26.78	62.76
24	46.15	32.23	60.53	28.46	64.57
25	48.08	34.01	62.37	30.17	66.35
26	50.00	35.81	64.19	31.90	68.10
27	51.92	37.63	65.99	33.65	69.83
28	53.85	39.47	67.77	35.43	71.54
29	55.77	41.33	69.53	37.24	73.22
30	57.69	43.20	71.27	39.07	74.88
31	59.62	45.10	72.99	40.92	76.51
32	61.54	47.02	74.70	42.80	78.11
33	63.46	48.96	76.38	44.71	79.69
34	65.38	50.91	78.03	46.64	81.24
35	67.31	52.89	79.67	48.61	82.7
36	69.23	54.90	81.28	50.60	84.2
37	71.15	56.92	82.87	52.62	85.71
38	73.08	58.98	84.43	54.67	87.14
39	75.00	61.05	85.97	56.76	88.53
40	76.92	63.16	87.47	58.88	89.8
41	78.85	65.30	88.94	61.04	91.1
42	80.77	67.47	90.37	63.24	92.4
43	82.69	69.67	91.77	65.49	93.6
44	84.62	71.92	93.12	67.80	94.8
45	86.54	74.21	94.41	70.16	95.9
46	88.46	76.56	95.65	72.59	96.9
47	90.38	78.97	96.80	75.10	97.8
48	92.31	81.46	97.86	77.71	98.6
49	94.23	84.05	98.79	80.45	99.3
50	96.15	86.79	99.53	83.37	99.8
51	98.08	89.74	99.95	86.56	99.9
52	100.00	93.15	100.00	90.31	100.0

$N = 53$

x	$100p_x$	95% $100p_l$	95% $100p_r$	99% $100p_l$	99% $100p_r$
0	0.00	0.00	6.72	0.00	9.5
1	1.89	0.05	10.07	0.01	13.2
2	3.77	0.46	12.98	0.20	16.3
3	5.66	1.18	15.66	0.65	19.2

N = number of trials, x = number of successes, etc., $100\,p_x = 100\,x/N$

N = 53 (continued)

x	$100p_x$	95% $100p_l$ – $100p_r$	99% $100p_l$ – $100p_r$
4	7.55	2.09- 18.21	1.30- 21.90
5	9.43	3.13- 20.66	2.09- 24.47
6	11.32	4.27- 23.03	3.00- 26.94
7	13.21	5.48- 25.34	4.00- 29.33
8	15.09	6.75- 27.59	5.07- 31.66
9	16.98	8.07- 29.80	6.20- 33.93
10	18.87	9.44- 31.97	7.39- 36.14
11	20.75	10.84- 34.11	8.63- 38.31
12	22.64	12.28- 36.21	9.92- 40.44
13	24.53	13.76- 38.28	11.24- 42.53
14	26.42	15.26- 40.33	12.60- 44.59
15	28.30	16.79- 42.35	14.00- 46.61
16	30.19	18.34- 44.34	15.43- 48.61
17	32.08	19.92- 46.32	16.89- 50.57
18	33.96	21.52- 48.27	18.37- 52.51
19	35.85	23.14- 50.20	19.89- 54.41
20	37.74	24.79- 52.11	21.43- 56.30
21	39.62	26.45- 54.00	23.00- 58.15
22	41.51	28.14- 55.87	24.59- 59.99
23	43.40	29.84- 57.72	26.21- 61.79
24	45.28	31.56- 59.55	27.86- 63.58
25	47.17	33.30- 61.36	29.52- 65.34
26	49.06	35.06- 63.16	31.21- 67.07
27	50.94	36.84- 64.94	32.93- 68.79
28	52.83	38.64- 66.70	34.66- 70.48
29	54.72	40.45- 68.44	36.42- 72.14
30	56.60	42.28- 70.16	38.21- 73.79
31	58.49	44.13- 71.86	40.01- 75.41
32	60.38	46.00- 73.55	41.85- 77.00
33	62.26	47.89- 75.21	43.70- 78.57
34	64.15	49.80- 76.86	45.59- 80.11
35	66.04	51.73- 78.48	47.49- 81.63
36	67.92	53.68- 80.08	49.43- 83.11
37	69.81	55.66- 81.66	51.39- 84.57
38	71.70	57.65- 83.21	53.39- 86.00
39	73.58	59.67- 84.74	55.41- 87.40
40	75.47	61.72- 86.24	57.47- 88.76
41	77.36	63.79- 87.72	59.56- 90.08
42	79.25	65.89- 89.16	61.69- 91.37
43	81.13	68.03- 90.56	63.86- 92.61
44	83.02	70.20- 91.93	66.07- 93.80
45	84.91	72.41- 93.25	68.34- 94.93
46	86.79	74.66- 94.52	70.67- 96.00
47	88.68	76.97- 95.73	73.06- 97.00
48	90.57	79.34- 96.87	75.53- 97.91
49	92.45	81.79- 97.91	78.10- 98.70
50	94.34	84.34- 98.82	80.79- 99.35
51	96.23	87.02- 99.54	83.66- 99.80
52	98.11	89.93- 99.95	86.80- 99.99
53	100.00	93.28-100.00	90.49-100.00

N = 54

x	$100p_x$	95% $100p_l$ – $100p_r$	99% $100p_l$ – $100p_r$
0	0.00	0.00- 6.60	0.00- 9.35
1	1.85	0.05- 9.89	0.01- 12.97
2	3.70	0.45- 12.75	0.19- 16.06
3	5.56	1.16- 15.39	0.64- 18.88
4	7.41	2.06- 17.89	1.27- 21.53
5	9.26	3.08- 20.30	2.05- 24.06
6	11.11	4.19- 22.63	2.94- 26.49
7	12.96	5.37- 24.90	3.92- 28.84
8	14.81	6.62- 27.12	4.97- 31.13
9	16.67	7.92- 29.29	6.08- 33.36
10	18.52	9.25- 31.43	7.25- 35.55
11	20.37	10.63- 33.53	8.46- 37.69
12	22.22	12.04- 35.60	9.72- 39.78
13	24.07	13.49- 37.64	11.02- 41.85
14	25.93	14.96- 39.65	12.35- 43.87
15	27.78	16.46- 41.64	13.72- 45.87
16	29.63	17.98- 43.61	15.12- 47.83
17	31.48	19.52- 45.55	16.55- 49.77
18	33.33	21.09- 47.47	18.00- 51.68
19	35.19	22.68- 49.38	19.49- 53.56
20	37.04	24.29- 51.26	20.99- 55.42
21	38.89	25.92- 53.12	22.53- 57.26
22	40.74	27.57- 54.97	24.09- 59.07
23	42.59	29.23- 56.79	25.67- 60.85
24	44.44	30.92- 58.60	27.27- 62.62
25	46.30	32.62- 60.39	28.90- 64.36
26	48.15	34.34- 62.16	30.55- 66.08
27	50.00	36.08- 63.92	32.23- 67.77
28	51.85	37.84- 65.66	33.92- 69.45
29	53.70	39.61- 67.38	35.64- 71.10
30	55.56	41.40- 69.08	37.38- 72.73
31	57.41	43.21- 70.77	39.15- 74.33
32	59.26	45.03- 72.43	40.93- 75.91
33	61.11	46.88- 74.08	42.74- 77.47
34	62.96	48.74- 75.71	44.58- 79.01
35	64.81	50.62- 77.32	46.44- 80.51
36	66.67	52.53- 78.91	48.32- 82.00
37	68.52	54.45- 80.48	50.23- 83.45
38	70.37	56.39- 82.02	52.17- 84.88
39	72.22	58.36- 83.54	54.13- 86.28
40	74.07	60.35- 85.04	56.13- 87.65
41	75.93	62.36- 86.51	58.15- 88.98
42	77.78	64.40- 87.96	60.22- 90.28
43	79.63	66.47- 89.37	62.31- 91.54
44	81.48	68.57- 90.75	64.45- 92.75
45	83.33	70.71- 92.08	66.64- 93.92

N = 54 (continued)

x	$100p_x$	95% $100p_l$ – $100p_r$	99% $100p_l$ – $100p_r$
46	85.19	72.88- 93.38	68.87- 95.03
47	87.04	75.10- 94.63	71.16- 96.08
48	88.89	77.37- 95.81	73.51- 97.06
49	90.74	79.70- 96.92	75.94- 97.95
50	92.59	82.11- 97.94	78.47- 98.73
51	94.44	84.61- 98.84	81.12- 99.36
52	96.30	87.25- 99.55	83.94- 99.81
53	98.15	90.11- 99.95	87.03- 99.99
54	100.00	93.40-100.00	90.65-100.00

N = 55

x	$100p_x$	95% $100p_l$ – $100p_r$	99% $100p_l$ – $100p_r$
0	0.00	0.00- 6.49	0.00- 9.18
1	1.82	0.05- 9.72	0.01- 12.75
2	3.64	0.44- 12.53	0.19- 15.79
3	5.45	1.14- 15.12	0.62- 18.56
4	7.27	2.02- 17.59	1.25- 21.17
5	9.09	3.02- 19.95	2.01- 23.66
6	10.91	4.11- 22.25	2.89- 26.05
7	12.73	5.27- 24.48	3.85- 28.37
8	14.55	6.50- 26.66	4.88- 30.62
9	16.36	7.77- 28.80	5.97- 32.82
10	18.18	9.08- 30.90	7.11- 34.97
11	20.00	10.43- 32.97	8.30- 37.08
12	21.82	11.81- 35.01	9.53- 39.15
13	23.64	13.23- 37.02	10.81- 41.18
14	25.45	14.67- 39.00	12.11- 43.18
15	27.27	16.14- 40.96	13.45- 45.15
16	29.09	17.63- 42.90	14.82- 47.08
17	30.91	19.14- 44.81	16.22- 49.00
18	32.73	20.68- 46.71	17.64- 50.88
19	34.55	22.24- 48.58	19.10- 52.74
20	36.36	23.81- 50.44	20.57- 54.57
21	38.18	25.41- 52.27	22.07- 56.39
22	40.00	27.02- 54.09	23.60- 58.17
23	41.82	28.65- 55.89	25.15- 59.94
24	43.64	30.30- 57.68	26.72- 61.68
25	45.45	31.97- 59.45	28.31- 63.40
26	47.27	33.65- 61.20	29.92- 65.10
27	49.09	35.35- 62.93	31.56- 66.78
28	50.91	37.07- 64.65	33.22- 68.44
29	52.73	38.80- 66.35	34.90- 70.08
30	54.55	40.55- 68.03	36.60- 71.69
31	56.36	42.32- 69.70	38.32- 73.28
32	58.18	44.11- 71.35	40.06- 74.85
33	60.00	45.91- 72.98	41.83- 76.40
34	61.82	47.73- 74.59	43.61- 77.93
35	63.64	49.56- 76.19	45.43- 79.43
36	65.45	51.42- 77.76	47.26- 80.90
37	67.27	53.29- 79.32	49.12- 82.36
38	69.09	55.19- 80.86	51.00- 83.78
39	70.91	57.10- 82.37	52.92- 85.18
40	72.73	59.04- 83.86	54.85- 86.55
41	74.55	61.00- 85.33	56.82- 87.89
42	76.36	62.98- 86.77	58.82- 89.19
43	78.18	64.99- 88.19	60.85- 90.47
44	80.00	67.03- 89.57	62.92- 91.70
45	81.82	69.10- 90.92	65.03- 92.89
46	83.64	71.20- 92.23	67.18- 94.03
47	85.45	73.34- 93.50	69.38- 95.12
48	87.27	75.52- 94.73	71.63- 96.15
49	89.09	77.75- 95.89	73.95- 97.11
50	90.91	80.05- 96.98	76.34- 97.99
51	92.73	82.41- 97.98	78.83- 98.75
52	94.55	84.88- 98.86	81.44- 99.38
53	96.36	87.47- 99.56	84.21- 99.81
54	98.18	90.28- 99.95	87.25- 99.99
55	100.00	93.51-100.00	90.82-100.00

N = 56

x	$100p_x$	95% $100p_l$ – $100p_r$	99% $100p_l$ – $100p_r$
0	0.00	0.00- 6.38	0.00- 9.03
1	1.79	0.05- 9.55	0.01- 12.53
2	3.57	0.44- 12.31	0.19- 15.52
3	5.36	1.12- 14.87	0.61- 18.25
4	7.14	1.98- 17.29	1.23- 20.82
5	8.93	2.96- 19.62	1.98- 23.27
6	10.71	4.03- 21.88	2.83- 25.63
7	12.50	5.18- 24.07	3.77- 27.91
8	14.29	6.38- 26.22	4.79- 30.13
9	16.07	7.62- 28.33	5.86- 32.30
10	17.86	8.91- 30.40	6.98- 34.42
11	19.64	10.23- 32.43	8.14- 36.49
12	21.43	11.59- 34.44	9.35- 38.53
13	23.21	12.98- 36.42	10.60- 40.53
14	25.00	14.39- 38.37	11.88- 42.50
15	26.79	15.83- 40.30	13.19- 44.45
16	28.57	17.30- 42.21	14.53- 46.36
17	30.36	18.78- 44.10	15.90- 48.24
18	32.14	20.29- 45.96	17.30- 50.10
19	33.93	21.81- 47.81	18.72- 51.94
20	35.71	23.36- 49.64	20.17- 53.75
21	37.50	24.92- 51.45	21.64- 55.54
22	39.29	26.50- 53.25	23.13- 57.31
23	41.07	28.10- 55.02	24.65- 59.05
24	42.86	29.71- 56.78	26.18- 60.77
25	44.64	31.34- 58.53	27.74- 62.48
26	46.43	32.99- 60.26	29.32- 64.16
27	48.21	34.66- 61.97	30.92- 65.82

N = 56 (continued)

x	$100p_x$	95% $100p_l$ – $100p_r$	99% $100p_l$ – $100p_r$
28	50.00	36.34- 63.66	32.54- 67.46
29	51.79	38.03- 65.34	34.18- 69.08
30	53.57	39.74- 67.01	35.84- 70.68
31	55.36	41.47- 68.66	37.52- 72.26
32	57.14	43.22- 70.29	39.23- 73.82
33	58.93	44.98- 71.90	40.95- 75.35
34	60.71	46.75- 73.50	42.69- 76.87
35	62.50	48.55- 75.08	44.46- 78.36
36	64.29	50.36- 76.64	46.25- 79.83
37	66.07	52.19- 78.19	48.06- 81.28
38	67.86	54.04- 79.71	49.90- 82.70
39	69.64	55.90- 81.22	51.76- 84.10
40	71.43	57.79- 82.70	53.64- 85.47
41	73.21	59.70- 84.17	55.55- 86.81
42	75.00	61.63- 85.61	57.50- 88.12
43	76.79	63.58- 87.02	59.47- 89.40
44	78.57	65.56- 88.41	61.47- 90.65
45	80.36	67.57- 89.77	63.51- 91.86
46	82.14	69.60- 91.09	65.58- 93.02
47	83.93	71.67- 92.38	67.70- 94.14
48	85.71	73.78- 93.62	69.87- 95.21
49	87.50	75.93- 94.82	72.09- 96.23
50	89.29	78.12- 95.97	74.37- 97.17
51	91.07	80.38- 97.04	76.73- 98.02
52	92.86	82.71- 98.02	79.18- 98.77
53	94.64	85.13- 98.88	81.75- 99.39
54	96.43	87.69- 99.56	84.48- 99.81
55	98.21	90.45- 99.95	87.47- 99.99
56	100.00	93.62-100.00	90.97-100.00

N = 57

x	$100p_x$	95% $100p_l$ – $100p_r$	99% $100p_l$ – $100p_r$
0	0.00	0.00- 6.27	0.00- 8.88
1	1.75	0.04- 9.39	0.01- 12.32
2	3.51	0.43- 12.11	0.18- 15.27
3	5.26	1.10- 14.62	0.60- 17.96
4	7.02	1.95- 17.00	1.21- 20.48
5	8.77	2.91- 19.30	1.94- 22.90
6	10.53	3.96- 21.52	2.78- 25.22
7	12.28	5.08- 23.68	3.71- 27.47
8	14.04	6.26- 25.79	4.70- 29.65
9	15.79	7.48- 27.87	5.75- 31.79
10	17.54	8.75- 29.91	6.85- 33.88
11	19.30	10.05- 31.91	7.99- 35.92
12	21.05	11.38- 33.89	9.18- 37.93
13	22.81	12.74- 35.84	10.40- 39.91
14	24.56	14.13- 37.76	11.66- 41.85
15	26.32	15.54- 39.66	12.94- 43.77
16	28.07	16.97- 41.54	14.26- 45.65
17	29.82	18.43- 43.40	15.60- 47.51
18	31.58	19.91- 45.24	16.97- 49.35
19	33.33	21.40- 47.06	18.36- 51.16
20	35.09	22.91- 48.87	19.78- 52.95
21	36.84	24.45- 50.66	21.22- 54.72
22	38.60	26.00- 52.43	22.68- 56.46
23	40.35	27.56- 54.18	24.17- 58.19
24	42.11	29.14- 55.92	25.67- 59.89
25	43.86	30.74- 57.64	27.20- 61.57
26	45.61	32.36- 59.34	28.74- 63.24
27	47.37	33.98- 61.03	30.31- 64.88
28	49.12	35.63- 62.71	31.89- 66.51
29	50.88	37.29- 64.37	33.49- 68.11
30	52.63	38.97- 66.02	35.12- 69.69
31	54.39	40.66- 67.64	36.76- 71.26
32	56.14	42.36- 69.26	38.43- 72.80
33	57.89	44.08- 70.86	40.11- 74.33
34	59.65	45.82- 72.44	41.81- 75.83
35	61.40	47.57- 74.00	43.54- 77.32
36	63.16	49.34- 75.55	45.28- 78.78
37	64.91	51.13- 77.09	47.05- 80.22
38	66.67	52.94- 78.60	48.84- 81.64
39	68.42	54.76- 80.09	50.65- 83.03
40	70.18	56.60- 81.57	52.49- 84.40
41	71.93	58.46- 83.03	54.35- 85.74
42	73.68	60.34- 84.46	56.23- 87.06
43	75.44	62.24- 85.87	58.15- 88.34
44	77.19	64.16- 87.26	60.09- 89.60
45	78.95	66.11- 88.62	62.07- 90.82
46	80.70	68.09- 89.95	64.08- 92.01
47	82.46	70.09- 91.25	66.12- 93.15
48	84.21	72.13- 92.52	68.21- 94.25
49	85.96	74.21- 93.74	70.35- 95.30
50	87.72	76.32- 94.92	72.53- 96.29
51	89.47	78.48- 96.04	74.78- 97.22
52	91.23	80.70- 97.09	77.10- 98.06
53	92.98	83.00- 98.05	79.52- 98.79
54	94.74	85.38- 98.90	82.04- 99.40
55	96.49	87.89- 99.57	84.73- 99.82
56	98.25	90.61- 99.96	87.68- 99.99
57	100.00	93.73-100.00	91.12-100.00

N = 58

x	$100p_x$	95% $100p_l$ – $100p_r$	99% $100p_l$ – $100p_r$
0	0.00	0.00- 6.16	0.00- 8.73
1	1.72	0.04- 9.24	0.01- 12.12
2	3.45	0.42- 11.91	0.18- 15.02
3	5.17	1.08- 14.38	0.59- 17.67
4	6.90	1.91- 16.73	1.18- 20.16

N = 58 (continued)

x	$100p_x$	95% $100p_l$ – $100p_r$	99% $100p_l$ – $100p_r$
5	8.62	2.86- 18.98	1.91- 22.53
6	10.34	3.89- 21.17	2.73- 24.82
7	12.07	4.99- 23.30	3.64- 27.03
8	13.79	6.15- 25.38	4.61- 29.19
9	15.52	7.35- 27.42	5.64- 31.29
10	17.24	8.59- 29.43	6.72- 33.35
11	18.97	9.87- 31.41	7.85- 35.37
12	20.69	11.17- 33.35	9.01- 37.35
13	22.41	12.51- 35.27	10.21- 39.30
14	24.14	13.87- 37.17	11.44- 41.22
15	25.86	15.26- 39.04	12.70- 43.11
16	27.59	16.66- 40.90	13.99- 44.97
17	29.31	18.09- 42.73	15.31- 46.80
18	31.03	19.54- 44.54	16.65- 48.62
19	32.76	21.01- 46.34	18.02- 50.41
20	34.48	22.49- 48.12	19.41- 52.17
21	36.21	23.99- 49.88	20.82- 53.92
22	37.93	25.51- 51.63	22.25- 55.64
23	39.66	27.05- 53.36	23.70- 57.35
24	41.38	28.60- 55.07	25.18- 59.03
25	43.10	30.16- 56.77	26.67- 60.70
26	44.83	31.74- 58.46	28.18- 62.34
27	46.55	33.34- 60.13	29.72- 63.97
28	48.28	34.95- 61.78	31.27- 65.57
29	50.00	36.58- 63.42	32.84- 67.16
30	51.72	38.22- 65.05	34.43- 68.73
31	53.45	39.87- 66.66	36.03- 70.28
32	55.17	41.54- 68.26	37.66- 71.82
33	56.90	43.23- 69.84	39.30- 73.33
34	58.62	44.93- 71.40	40.97- 74.82
35	60.34	46.64- 72.95	42.65- 76.30
36	62.07	48.37- 74.49	44.36- 77.75
37	63.79	50.12- 76.01	46.08- 79.18
38	65.52	51.88- 77.51	47.83- 80.59
39	67.24	53.66- 78.99	49.59- 81.98
40	68.97	55.46- 80.46	51.38- 83.35
41	70.69	57.27- 81.91	53.20- 84.69
42	72.41	59.10- 83.34	55.03- 86.01
43	74.14	60.96- 84.74	56.89- 87.30
44	75.86	62.83- 86.13	58.78- 88.56
45	77.59	64.73- 87.49	60.70- 89.79
46	79.31	66.65- 88.83	62.65- 90.99
47	81.03	68.59- 90.13	64.63- 92.15
48	82.76	70.57- 91.41	66.65- 93.28
49	84.48	72.58- 92.65	68.71- 94.36
50	86.21	74.62- 93.85	70.81- 95.39
51	87.93	76.70- 95.01	72.97- 96.36
52	89.66	78.83- 96.11	75.18- 97.27
53	91.38	81.02- 97.14	77.47- 98.09
54	93.10	83.27- 98.09	79.84- 98.82
55	94.83	85.62- 98.92	82.33- 99.41
56	96.55	88.09- 99.58	84.98- 99.82
57	98.28	90.76- 99.96	87.88- 99.99
58	100.00	93.84-100.00	91.27-100.00

N = 59

x	$100p_x$	95% $100p_l$ – $100p_r$	99% $100p_l$ – $100p_r$
0	0.00	0.00- 6.06	0.00- 8.59
1	1.69	0.04- 9.09	0.01- 11.93
2	3.39	0.41- 11.71	0.18- 14.78
3	5.08	1.06- 14.15	0.58- 17.39
4	6.78	1.88- 16.46	1.16- 19.84
5	8.47	2.81- 18.68	1.87- 22.18
6	10.17	3.82- 20.83	2.69- 24.43
7	11.86	4.91- 22.93	3.58- 26.62
8	13.56	6.04- 24.98	4.53- 28.74
9	15.25	7.22- 26.99	5.54- 30.82
10	16.95	8.44- 28.97	6.60- 32.84
11	18.64	9.69- 30.91	7.71- 34.83
12	20.34	10.98- 32.83	8.85- 36.79
13	22.03	12.29- 34.73	10.03- 38.71
14	23.73	13.62- 36.60	11.24- 40.60
15	25.42	14.98- 38.44	12.47- 42.47
16	27.12	16.36- 40.27	13.74- 44.30
17	28.81	17.76- 42.08	15.03- 46.12
18	30.51	19.19- 43.87	16.35- 47.91
19	32.20	20.62- 45.64	17.69- 49.67
20	33.90	22.08- 47.39	19.05- 51.42
21	35.59	23.55- 49.13	20.43- 53.14
22	37.29	25.04- 50.85	21.84- 54.84
23	38.98	26.55- 52.56	23.26- 56.53
24	40.68	28.07- 54.25	24.70- 58.19
25	42.37	29.61- 55.93	26.17- 59.84
26	44.07	31.16- 57.60	27.65- 61.47
27	45.76	32.72- 59.25	29.15- 63.08
28	47.46	34.30- 60.88	30.67- 64.67
29	49.15	35.89- 62.50	32.20- 66.24
30	50.85	37.50- 64.11	33.76- 67.80
31	52.54	39.12- 65.70	35.33- 69.33
32	54.24	40.75- 67.28	36.92- 70.85
33	55.93	42.40- 68.84	38.53- 72.35
34	57.63	44.07- 70.39	40.16- 73.83
35	59.32	45.75- 71.93	41.81- 75.30
36	61.02	47.44- 73.45	43.47- 76.74
37	62.71	49.15- 74.96	45.16- 78.16
38	64.41	50.87- 76.45	46.86- 79.57
39	66.10	52.61- 77.92	48.58- 80.95
40	67.80	54.36- 79.38	50.33- 82.31
41	69.49	56.13- 80.81	52.09- 83.65

$N=$ number of trials, $x=$ number of successes, etc., $100\,p_x = 100\,x/N$

N = 59 (continued)

x	$100p_x$	95% $100p_l$	95% $100p_r$	99% $100p_l$	99% $100p_r$
42	71.19	57.92	82.24	53.88	84.97
43	72.88	59.73	83.64	55.70	86.26
44	74.58	61.56	85.02	57.53	87.53
45	76.27	63.40	86.38	59.40	88.76
46	77.97	65.27	87.71	61.29	89.97
47	79.66	67.17	89.02	63.21	91.15
48	81.36	69.09	90.31	65.17	92.29
49	83.05	71.03	91.56	67.16	93.40
50	84.75	73.01	92.78	69.18	94.46
51	86.44	75.02	93.96	71.26	95.47
52	88.14	77.07	95.09	73.38	96.42
53	89.83	79.17	96.18	75.57	97.31
54	91.53	81.32	97.19	77.82	98.13
55	93.22	83.54	98.12	80.16	98.84
56	94.92	85.85	98.94	82.61	99.42
57	96.61	88.29	99.59	85.22	99.82
58	98.31	90.91	99.96	88.07	99.99
59	100.00	93.94	100.00	91.41	100.00

N = 60

x	$100p_x$	95% $100p_l$	95% $100p_r$	99% $100p_l$	99% $100p_r$
0	0.00	0.00	5.96	0.00	8.45
1	1.67	0.04	8.94	0.01	11.74
2	3.33	0.41	11.53	0.17	14.55
3	5.00	1.04	13.92	0.57	17.12
4	6.67	1.85	16.20	1.14	19.53
5	8.33	2.76	18.39	1.84	21.84
6	10.00	3.76	20.51	2.64	24.06
7	11.67	4.82	22.57	3.51	26.21
8	13.33	5.94	24.59	4.45	28.31
9	15.00	7.10	26.57	5.45	30.35
10	16.67	8.29	28.52	6.49	32.35
11	18.33	9.52	30.44	7.57	34.31
12	20.00	10.78	32.33	8.69	36.24
13	21.67	12.07	34.20	9.85	38.14
14	23.33	13.38	36.04	11.04	40.00
15	25.00	14.72	37.86	12.25	41.84
16	26.67	16.07	39.66	13.49	43.66
17	28.33	17.45	41.44	14.76	45.45
18	30.00	18.85	43.21	16.05	47.21
19	31.67	20.26	44.96	17.37	48.96
20	33.33	21.69	46.69	18.70	50.68
21	35.00	23.13	48.40	20.06	52.39
22	36.67	24.59	50.10	21.44	54.07
23	38.33	26.07	51.79	22.83	55.73
24	40.00	27.56	53.46	24.25	57.38
25	41.67	29.07	55.12	25.68	59.01
26	43.33	30.59	56.76	27.13	60.62
27	45.00	32.12	58.39	28.60	62.21
28	46.67	33.67	60.00	30.09	63.78
29	48.33	35.23	61.61	31.60	65.34
30	50.00	36.81	63.19	33.12	66.88
31	51.67	38.39	64.77	34.66	68.40
32	53.33	40.00	66.33	36.22	69.91
33	55.00	41.61	67.88	37.79	71.40
34	56.67	43.24	69.41	39.38	72.87
35	58.33	44.88	70.93	40.99	74.32
36	60.00	46.54	72.44	42.62	75.75
37	61.67	48.21	73.93	44.27	77.17
38	63.33	49.90	75.41	45.93	78.56
39	65.00	51.60	76.87	47.61	79.94
40	66.67	53.31	78.31	49.32	81.30
41	68.33	55.04	79.74	51.04	82.63
42	70.00	56.79	81.15	52.79	83.95
43	71.67	58.56	82.55	54.55	85.24
44	73.33	60.34	83.93	56.34	86.51
45	75.00	62.14	85.28	58.16	87.75
46	76.67	63.96	86.62	60.00	88.96
47	78.33	65.80	87.93	61.86	90.15
48	80.00	67.67	89.22	63.76	91.31
49	81.67	69.56	90.48	65.69	92.43
50	83.33	71.48	91.71	67.65	93.51
51	85.00	73.43	92.90	69.65	94.55
52	86.67	75.41	94.06	71.69	95.55
53	88.33	77.43	95.18	73.79	96.49
54	90.00	79.49	96.24	75.94	97.36
55	91.67	81.61	97.24	78.16	98.16
56	93.33	83.80	98.15	80.47	98.86
57	95.00	86.08	98.96	82.88	99.43
58	96.67	88.47	99.59	85.45	99.83
59	98.33	91.06	99.96	88.26	99.99
60	100.00	94.04	100.00	91.55	100.00

N = 61

x	$100p_x$	95% $100p_l$	95% $100p_r$	99% $100p_l$	99% $100p_r$
0	0.00	0.00	5.87	0.00	8.32
1	1.64	0.04	8.80	0.01	11.56
2	3.28	0.40	11.35	0.17	14.33
3	4.92	1.03	13.71	0.56	16.86
4	6.56	1.82	15.95	1.12	19.24
5	8.20	2.72	18.10	1.81	21.51
6	9.84	3.70	20.19	2.59	23.70
7	11.48	4.74	22.22	3.45	25.82
8	13.11	5.84	24.22	4.38	27.88
9	14.75	6.98	26.17	5.35	29.90
10	16.39	8.15	28.09	6.38	31.87
11	18.03	9.36	29.98	7.44	33.81
12	19.67	10.60	31.84	8.54	35.71
13	21.31	11.86	33.68	9.68	37.58

N = 61 (continued)

x	$100p_x$	95% $100p_l$	95% $100p_r$	99% $100p_l$	99% $100p_r$
14	22.95	13.15	35.50	10.84	39.42
15	24.59	14.46	37.29	12.04	41.24
16	26.23	15.80	39.07	13.26	43.03
17	27.87	17.15	40.83	14.50	44.80
18	29.51	18.52	42.57	15.77	46.54
19	31.15	19.90	44.29	17.06	48.26
20	32.79	21.31	46.00	18.37	49.97
21	34.43	22.73	47.69	19.70	51.65
22	36.07	24.16	49.37	21.05	53.31
23	37.70	25.61	51.04	22.42	54.96
24	39.34	27.07	52.69	23.81	56.59
25	40.98	28.55	54.32	25.21	58.20
26	42.62	30.04	55.94	26.64	59.79
27	44.26	31.55	57.55	28.08	61.36
28	45.90	33.06	59.15	29.54	62.92
29	47.54	34.60	60.73	31.01	64.46
30	49.18	36.14	62.30	32.50	65.99
31	50.82	37.70	63.86	34.01	67.50
32	52.46	39.27	65.40	35.54	68.99
33	54.10	40.85	66.94	37.08	70.46
34	55.74	42.45	68.45	38.64	71.92
35	57.38	44.06	69.96	40.21	73.36
36	59.02	45.68	71.45	41.80	74.79
37	60.66	47.31	72.93	43.41	76.19
38	62.30	48.96	74.39	45.04	77.58
39	63.93	50.63	75.84	46.69	78.95
40	65.57	52.31	77.27	48.35	80.30
41	67.21	54.00	78.69	50.03	81.63
42	68.85	55.71	80.10	51.74	82.94
43	70.49	57.43	81.48	53.46	84.23
44	72.13	59.17	82.85	55.20	85.50
45	73.77	60.93	84.20	56.97	86.74
46	75.41	62.71	85.54	58.76	87.96
47	77.05	64.50	86.85	60.58	89.16
48	78.69	66.32	88.14	62.42	90.32
49	80.33	68.16	89.40	64.29	91.46
50	81.97	70.02	90.64	66.19	92.56
51	83.61	71.91	91.85	68.13	93.62
52	85.25	73.83	93.02	70.10	94.65
53	86.89	75.78	94.16	72.12	95.62
54	88.52	77.78	95.26	74.18	96.55
55	90.16	79.81	96.30	76.30	97.41
56	91.80	81.90	97.28	78.49	98.19
57	93.44	84.05	98.18	80.76	98.88
58	95.08	86.29	98.97	83.14	99.44
59	96.72	88.65	99.60	85.67	99.83
60	98.36	91.20	99.96	88.44	99.99
61	100.00	94.13	100.00	91.68	100.00

N = 62

x	$100p_x$	95% $100p_l$	95% $100p_r$	99% $100p_l$	99% $100p_r$
0	0.00	0.00	5.78	0.00	8.19
1	1.61	0.04	8.66	0.01	11.38
2	3.23	0.39	11.17	0.17	14.11
3	4.84	1.01	13.50	0.55	16.60
4	6.45	1.79	15.70	1.11	18.95
5	8.06	2.67	17.83	1.78	21.19
6	9.68	3.63	19.88	2.55	23.35
7	11.29	4.66	21.89	3.40	25.44
8	12.90	5.74	23.85	4.30	27.47
9	14.52	6.86	25.78	5.26	29.46
10	16.13	8.02	27.67	6.27	31.41
11	17.74	9.20	29.53	7.32	33.32
12	19.35	10.42	31.37	8.40	35.20
13	20.97	11.66	33.18	9.51	37.04
14	22.58	12.93	34.97	10.66	38.86
15	24.19	14.22	36.74	11.83	40.65
16	25.81	15.53	38.50	13.03	42.42
17	27.42	16.85	40.23	14.25	44.16
18	29.03	18.20	41.95	15.49	45.89
19	30.65	19.56	43.65	16.76	47.59
20	32.26	20.94	45.34	18.05	49.27
21	33.87	22.33	47.01	19.35	50.93
22	35.48	23.74	48.66	20.68	52.58
23	37.10	25.16	50.31	22.02	54.21
24	38.71	26.60	51.93	23.38	55.81
25	40.32	28.05	53.55	24.76	57.41
26	41.94	29.51	55.15	26.16	58.98
27	43.55	30.99	56.74	27.57	60.54
28	45.16	32.48	58.32	29.00	62.08
29	46.77	33.98	59.88	30.45	63.61
30	48.39	35.50	61.44	31.91	65.12
31	50.00	37.02	62.98	33.39	66.61
32	51.61	38.56	64.50	34.88	68.09
33	53.23	40.12	66.02	36.39	69.55
34	54.84	41.68	67.52	37.92	71.00
35	56.45	43.26	69.01	39.46	72.43
36	58.06	44.85	70.49	41.02	73.84
37	59.68	46.45	71.95	42.59	75.24
38	61.29	48.07	73.40	44.19	76.62
39	62.90	49.69	74.84	45.79	77.98
40	64.52	51.34	76.26	47.42	79.32
41	66.13	52.99	77.67	49.07	80.65
42	67.74	54.66	79.06	50.73	81.95
43	69.35	56.35	80.44	52.41	83.24
44	70.97	58.05	81.80	54.11	84.51
45	72.58	59.77	83.15	55.84	85.75
46	74.19	61.50	84.47	57.58	86.97
47	75.81	63.26	85.78	59.35	88.17

N = 62 (continued)

x	$100p_x$	95% $100p_l$	95% $100p_r$	99% $100p_l$	99% $100p_r$
48	77.42	65.03	87.07	61.14	89.34
49	79.03	66.82	88.34	62.96	90.49
50	80.65	68.63	89.58	64.80	91.60
51	82.26	70.47	90.80	66.68	92.68
52	83.87	72.33	91.98	68.59	93.73
53	85.48	74.22	93.14	70.54	94.74
54	87.10	76.15	94.26	72.53	95.70
55	88.71	78.11	95.34	74.56	96.60
56	90.32	80.12	96.37	76.65	97.45
57	91.94	82.17	97.33	78.81	98.22
58	93.55	84.30	98.21	81.05	98.89
59	95.16	86.50	98.99	83.40	99.45
60	96.77	88.83	99.61	85.89	99.83
61	98.39	91.34	99.96	88.62	99.99
62	100.00	94.22	100.00	91.81	100.00

N = 63

x	$100p_x$	95% $100p_l$	95% $100p_r$	99% $100p_l$	99% $100p_r$
0	0.00	0.00	5.69	0.00	8.07
1	1.59	0.04	8.53	0.01	11.21
2	3.17	0.39	11.00	0.17	13.90
3	4.76	0.99	13.29	0.54	16.36
4	6.35	1.76	15.47	1.09	18.67
5	7.94	2.63	17.56	1.75	20.88
6	9.52	3.58	19.59	2.51	23.00
7	11.11	4.59	21.56	3.34	25.07
8	12.70	5.65	23.50	4.23	27.08
9	14.29	6.75	25.39	5.18	29.04
10	15.87	7.88	27.26	6.17	30.96
11	17.46	9.05	29.10	7.19	32.84
12	19.05	10.25	30.91	8.26	34.70
13	20.63	11.47	32.70	9.35	36.52
14	22.22	12.72	34.46	10.48	38.31
15	23.81	13.98	36.21	11.63	40.08
16	25.40	15.27	37.94	12.81	41.83
17	26.98	16.57	39.65	14.01	43.55
18	28.57	17.89	41.35	15.23	45.25
19	30.16	19.23	43.02	16.47	46.93
20	31.75	20.58	44.69	17.74	48.59
21	33.33	21.95	46.34	19.02	50.24
22	34.92	23.34	47.97	20.32	51.86
23	36.51	24.73	49.60	21.64	53.47
24	38.10	26.15	51.20	22.98	55.06
25	39.68	27.57	52.80	24.33	56.64
26	41.27	29.01	54.38	25.70	58.19
27	42.86	30.46	55.95	27.08	59.74
28	44.44	31.92	57.51	28.49	61.26
29	46.03	33.39	59.06	29.90	62.77
30	47.62	34.88	60.59	31.34	64.27
31	49.21	36.38	62.11	32.79	65.75
32	50.79	37.89	63.62	34.25	67.21
33	52.38	39.41	65.12	35.73	68.66
34	53.97	40.94	66.61	37.23	70.10
35	55.56	42.49	68.08	38.74	71.51
36	57.14	44.05	69.54	40.26	72.92
37	58.73	45.62	70.99	41.81	74.30
38	60.32	47.20	72.43	43.36	75.67
39	61.90	48.80	73.85	44.94	77.02
40	63.49	50.40	75.27	46.53	78.36
41	65.08	52.03	76.66	48.14	79.68
42	66.67	53.66	78.05	49.76	80.98
43	68.25	55.31	79.42	51.41	82.26
44	69.84	56.98	80.77	53.07	83.53
45	71.43	58.65	82.11	54.75	84.77
46	73.02	60.35	83.43	56.45	85.99
47	74.60	62.06	84.73	58.17	87.19
48	76.19	63.79	86.02	59.92	88.37
49	77.78	65.54	87.28	61.69	89.52
50	79.37	67.30	88.53	63.48	90.65
51	80.95	69.09	89.75	65.30	91.74
52	82.54	70.90	90.95	67.16	92.81
53	84.13	72.74	92.12	69.04	93.83
54	85.71	74.61	93.25	70.96	94.82
55	87.30	76.50	94.35	72.92	95.77
56	88.89	78.44	95.41	74.93	96.66
57	90.48	80.41	96.42	77.00	97.49
58	92.06	82.44	97.37	79.12	98.25
59	93.65	84.53	98.24	81.33	98.91
60	95.24	86.71	99.01	83.64	99.46
61	96.83	89.00	99.61	86.10	99.83
62	98.41	91.47	99.96	88.79	99.99
63	100.00	94.31	100.00	91.93	100.00

N = 64

x	$100p_x$	95% $100p_l$	95% $100p_r$	99% $100p_l$	99% $100p_r$
0	0.00	0.00	5.60	0.00	7.95
1	1.56	0.04	8.40	0.01	11.04
2	3.13	0.38	10.84	0.16	13.69
3	4.69	0.98	13.09	0.54	16.12
4	6.25	1.73	15.24	1.07	18.40
5	7.81	2.59	17.30	1.72	20.57
6	9.38	3.52	19.30	2.47	22.67
7	10.94	4.51	21.25	3.29	24.71
8	12.50	5.55	23.15	4.17	26.69
9	14.06	6.64	25.02	5.09	28.62
10	15.63	7.76	26.86	6.07	30.52
11	17.19	8.90	28.68	7.08	32.38
12	18.75	10.08	30.46	8.12	34.21
13	20.31	11.28	32.23	9.20	36.01

N = 64 (continued)

x	$100p_x$	95% $100p_l$	95% $100p_r$	99% $100p_l$	99% $100p_r$
14	21.88	12.51	33.97	10.30	37.7
15	23.44	13.75	35.69	11.44	39.5
16	25.00	15.02	37.40	12.59	41.2
17	26.56	16.30	39.09	13.77	42.9
18	28.13	17.60	40.76	14.97	44.6
19	29.69	18.91	42.42	16.19	46.2
20	31.25	20.24	44.06	17.43	47.9
21	32.81	21.59	45.69	18.69	49.5
22	34.38	22.95	47.30	19.97	51.1
23	35.94	24.32	48.90	21.27	52.7
24	37.50	25.70	50.49	22.58	54.3
25	39.06	27.10	52.07	23.91	55.8
26	40.63	28.51	53.63	25.25	57.4
27	42.19	29.94	55.18	26.61	58.9
28	43.75	31.37	56 72	27.99	60.4
29	45.31	32.82	58.25	29.38	61.9
30	46.88	34.28	59.77	30.79	63.4
31	48.44	35.75	61.27	32.21	64.9
32	50.00	37.23	62.77	33.64	66.3
33	51.56	38.73	64.25	35.10	67.7
34	53.13	40.23	65.72	36.56	69.2
35	54.69	41.75	67.18	38.04	70.6
36	56.25	43.28	68.63	39.54	72.0
37	57.81	44.82	70.06	41.05	73.3
38	59.38	46.37	71.49	42.57	74.7
39	60.94	47.93	72.90	44.11	76.0
40	62.50	49.51	74.30	45.67	77.4
41	64.06	51.10	75.68	47.24	78.7
42	65.63	52.70	77.05	48.83	80.0
43	67.19	54.31	78.41	50.44	81.3
44	68.75	55.94	79.76	52.06	82.57
45	70.31	57.58	81.09	53.71	83.8
46	71.88	59.24	82.40	55.37	85.0
47	73.44	60.91	83.70	57.05	86.2
48	75.00	62.60	84.98	58.75	87.4
49	76.56	64.31	86.25	60.47	88.5
50	78.13	66.03	87.49	62.22	89.7
51	79.69	67.77	88.72	63.99	90.8
52	81.25	69.54	89.92	65.79	91.88
53	82.81	71.32	91.10	67.62	92.92
54	84.38	73.14	92.24	69.48	93.9
55	85.94	74.98	93.36	71.38	94.9
56	87.50	76.85	94.45	73.31	95.8
57	89.06	78.75	95.49	75.29	96.7
58	90.63	80.70	96.48	77.33	97.5
59	92.19	82.70	97.41	79.43	98.2
60	93.75	84.76	98.27	81.60	98.93
61	95.31	86.91	99.02	83.88	99.46
62	96.88	89.16	99.62	86.31	99.84
63	98.44	91.60	99.96	88.96	99.9
64	100.00	94.40	100.00	92.05	100.0

N = 65

x	$100p_x$	95% $100p_l$	95% $100p_r$	99% $100p_l$	99% $100p_r$
0	0.00	0.00	5.52	0.00	7.83
1	1.54	0.04	8.28	0.01	10.88
2	3.08	0.37	10.68	0.16	13.4
3	4.62	0.96	12.90	0.53	15.88
4	6.15	1.70	15.01	1.05	18.1
5	7.69	2.54	17.05	1.70	20.28
6	9.23	3.46	19.02	2.43	22.35
7	10.77	4.44	20.94	3.24	24.36
8	12.31	5.47	22.82	4.10	26.31
9	13.85	6.53	24.66	5.01	28.22
10	15.38	7.63	26.48	5.97	30.0
11	16.92	8.76	28.27	6.96	31.93
12	18.46	9.92	30.03	7.99	33.73
13	20.00	11.10	31.77	9.05	35.51
14	21.54	12.31	33.49	10.14	37.26
15	23.08	13.53	35.19	11.25	38.98
16	24.62	14.77	36.87	12.38	40.69
17	26.15	16.03	38.54	13.54	42.37
18	27.69	17.31	40.19	14.72	44.03
19	29.23	18.60	41.83	15.93	45.67
20	30.77	19.91	43.45	17.14	47.29
21	32.31	21.23	45.05	18.38	48.90
22	33.85	22.57	46.65	19.64	50.49
23	35.38	23.92	48.23	20.91	52.06
24	36.92	25.28	49.80	22.20	53.61
25	38.46	26.65	51.36	23.50	55.15
26	40.00	28.04	52.90	24.82	56.68
27	41.54	29.44	54.44	26.16	58.19
28	43.08	30.85	55.96	27.51	59.68
29	44.62	32.27	57.47	28.88	61.16
30	46.15	33.70	58.97	30.26	62.63
31	47.69	35.15	60.46	31.65	64.08
32	49.23	36.60	61.93	33.06	65.52
33	50.77	38.07	63.40	34.48	66.94
34	52.31	39.54	64.85	35.92	68.35
35	53.85	41.03	66.30	37.37	69.74
36	55.38	42.53	67.73	38.84	71.12
37	56.92	44.04	69.15	40.32	72.49
38	58.46	45.56	70.56	41.81	73.84
39	60.00	47.10	71.96	43.32	75.18
40	61.54	48.64	73.35	44.85	76.50
41	63.08	50.20	74.72	46.39	77.80
42	64.62	51.77	76.08	47.94	79.09
43	66.15	53.35	77.43	49.51	80.36
44	67.69	54.95	78.77	51.10	81.62

'Exact' Confidence Limits* for p $N = 65-71$

N = number of trials, x = number of successes, etc., $100\,p_x = 100\,x/N$

N = 65 (continued)

x	$100p_x$	95% $100p_l$	95% $100p_r$	99% $100p_l$	99% $100p_r$
45	69.23	56.55–	80.09	52.71–	82.86
46	70.77	58.17–	81.40	54.33–	84.07
47	72.31	59.81–	82.69	55.97–	85.28
48	73.85	61.46–	83.97	57.63–	86.46
49	75.38	63.13–	85.23	59.31–	87.62
50	76.92	64.81–	86.47	61.02–	88.75
51	78.46	66.51–	87.69	62.74–	89.86
52	80.00	68.23–	88.90	64.49–	90.95
53	81.54	69.97–	90.08	66.27–	92.01
54	83.08	71.73–	91.24	68.07–	93.04
55	84.62	73.52–	92.37	69.91–	94.03
56	86.15	75.34–	93.47	71.78–	94.99
57	87.69	77.18–	94.53	73.69–	95.90
58	89.23	79.06–	95.56	75.64–	96.76
59	90.77	80.98–	96.54	77.65–	97.57
60	92.31	82.95–	97.46	79.72–	98.30
61	93.85	84.99–	98.30	81.87–	98.95
62	95.38	87.10–	99.04	84.12–	99.47
63	96.92	89.32–	99.63	86.51–	99.84
64	98.46	91.72–	99.96	89.12–	99.99
65	100.00	94.48–	100.00	92.17–	100.00

N = 66

x	$100p_x$	95% $100p_l$	95% $100p_r$	99% $100p_l$	99% $100p_r$
0	0.00	0.00–	5.44	0.00–	7.71
1	1.52	0.04–	8.16	0.01–	10.72
2	3.03	0.37–	10.52	0.16–	13.30
3	4.55	0.95–	12.71	0.52–	15.66
4	6.06	1.68–	14.80	1.04–	17.88
5	7.58	2.51–	16.80	1.67–	19.99
6	9.09	3.41–	18.74	2.39–	22.04
7	10.61	4.37–	20.64	3.19–	24.02
8	12.12	5.38–	22.49	4.03–	25.95
9	13.64	6.43–	24.31	4.93–	27.83
10	15.15	7.51–	26.10	5.87–	29.68
11	16.67	8.62–	27.87	6.85–	31.49
12	18.18	9.76–	29.61	7.86–	33.27
13	19.70	10.93–	31.32	8.90–	35.03
14	21.21	12.11–	33.02	9.97–	36.75
15	22.73	13.31–	34.70	11.07–	38.46
16	24.24	14.54–	36.36	12.18–	40.14
17	25.76	15.78–	38.01	13.32–	41.80
18	27.27	17.03–	39.64	14.49–	43.44
19	28.79	18.30–	41.25	15.67–	45.06
20	30.30	19.59–	42.85	16.86–	46.67
21	31.82	20.89–	44.44	18.08–	48.25
22	33.33	22.20–	46.01	19.31–	49.82
23	34.85	23.53–	47.58	20.56–	51.38
24	36.36	24.87–	49.13	21.83–	52.92
25	37.88	26.22–	50.66	23.11–	54.44
26	39.39	27.58–	52.19	24.41–	55.95
27	40.91	28.95–	53.71	25.72–	57.44
28	42.42	30.34–	55.21	27.05–	58.92
29	43.94	31.74–	56.70	28.39–	60.39
30	45.45	33.14–	58.19	29.74–	61.84
31	46.97	34.56–	59.66	31.11–	63.28
32	48.48	35.99–	61.12	32.49–	64.70
33	50.00	37.43–	62.57	33.89–	66.11
34	51.52	38.88–	64.01	35.30–	67.51
35	53.03	40.34–	65.44	36.72–	68.89
36	54.55	41.81–	66.86	38.16–	70.26
37	56.06	43.30–	68.26	39.61–	71.61
38	57.58	44.79–	69.66	41.08–	72.95
39	59.09	46.29–	71.05	42.56–	74.28
40	60.61	47.81–	72.42	44.05–	75.59
41	62.12	49.34–	73.78	45.56–	76.89
42	63.64	50.87–	75.13	47.08–	78.17
43	65.15	52.42–	76.47	48.62–	79.44
44	66.67	53.99–	77.80	50.18–	80.69
45	68.18	55.56–	79.11	51.75–	81.92
46	69.70	57.15–	80.41	53.33–	83.14
47	71.21	58.75–	81.70	54.94–	84.33
48	72.73	60.36–	82.97	56.56–	85.51
49	74.24	61.99–	84.22	58.20–	86.68
50	75.76	63.64–	85.46	59.86–	87.82
51	77.27	65.30–	86.69	61.54–	88.93
52	78.79	66.98–	87.89	63.25–	90.03
53	80.30	68.68–	89.07	64.97–	91.10
54	81.82	70.39–	90.24	66.73–	92.14
55	83.33	72.13–	91.38	68.51–	93.15
56	84.85	73.90–	92.49	70.32–	94.13
57	86.36	75.69–	93.57	72.17–	95.07
58	87.88	77.51–	94.62	74.05–	95.97
59	89.39	79.36–	95.63	75.98–	96.81
60	90.91	81.26–	96.59	77.96–	97.61
61	92.42	83.20–	97.49	80.01–	98.33
62	93.94	85.20–	98.32	82.12–	98.96
63	95.45	87.29–	99.05	84.34–	99.48
64	96.97	89.48–	99.63	86.70–	99.84
65	98.48	91.84–	99.96	89.28–	99.99
66	100.00	94.56–	100.00	92.29–	100.00

N = 67

x	$100p_x$	95% $100p_l$	95% $100p_r$	99% $100p_l$	99% $100p_r$
0	0.00	0.00–	5.36	0.00–	7.60
1	1.49	0.04–	8.04	0.01–	10.57
2	2.99	0.36–	10.37	0.16–	13.11
3	4.48	0.93–	12.53	0.51–	15.44
4	5.97	1.65–	14.59	1.02–	17.63

N = 67 (continued)

x	$100p_x$	95% $100p_l$	95% $100p_r$	99% $100p_l$	99% $100p_r$
5	7.46	2.47–	16.56	1.65–	19.72
6	8.96	3.36–	18.48	2.36–	21.73
7	10.45	4.31–	20.35	3.14–	23.69
8	11.94	5.30–	22.18	3.97–	25.59
9	13.43	6.33–	23.97	4.86–	27.45
10	14.93	7.40–	25.74	5.78–	29.28
11	16.42	8.49–	27.48	6.74–	31.07
12	17.91	9.61–	29.20	7.74–	32.82
13	19.40	10.76–	30.89	8.76–	34.56
14	20.90	11.92–	32.57	9.82–	36.26
15	22.39	13.11–	34.22	10.89–	37.95
16	23.88	14.31–	35.86	11.99–	39.61
17	25.37	15.53–	37.49	13.11–	41.25
18	26.87	16.76–	39.10	14.25–	42.87
19	28.36	18.01–	40.69	15.41–	44.47
20	29.85	19.28–	42.27	16.59–	46.06
21	31.34	20.56–	43.84	17.79–	47.63
22	32.84	21.85–	45.40	19.00–	49.18
23	34.33	23.15–	46.94	20.23–	50.72
24	35.82	24.47–	48.47	21.47–	52.24
25	37.31	25.80–	49.99	22.73–	53.74
26	38.81	27.14–	51.50	24.01–	55.24
27	40.30	28.49–	53.00	25.30–	56.72
28	41.79	29.85–	54.48	26.60–	58.18
29	43.28	31.22–	55.96	27.92–	59.63
30	44.78	32.60–	57.42	29.25–	61.07
31	46.27	34.00–	58.88	30.59–	62.49
32	47.76	35.40–	60.33	31.95–	63.90
33	49.25	36.82–	61.76	33.32–	65.30
34	50.75	38.24–	63.18	34.70–	66.68
35	52.24	39.67–	64.60	36.10–	68.05
36	53.73	41.12–	66.00	37.51–	69.41
37	55.22	42.58–	67.40	38.93–	70.75
38	56.72	44.04–	68.78	40.37–	72.08
39	58.21	45.52–	70.15	41.82–	73.40
40	59.70	47.00–	71.51	43.28–	74.70
41	61.19	48.50–	72.86	44.76–	75.99
42	62.69	50.01–	74.20	46.26–	77.27
43	64.18	51.53–	75.53	47.76–	78.53
44	65.67	53.06–	76.85	49.28–	79.77
45	67.16	54.60–	78.15	50.82–	81.00
46	68.66	56.16–	79.44	52.37–	82.21
47	70.15	57.73–	80.72	53.94–	83.41
48	71.64	59.31–	81.99	55.53–	84.59
49	73.13	60.90–	83.24	57.13–	85.75
50	74.63	62.51–	84.47	58.75–	86.89
51	76.12	64.14–	85.69	60.39–	88.01
52	77.61	65.78–	86.89	62.05–	89.11
53	79.10	67.43–	88.08	63.74–	90.18
54	80.60	69.11–	89.24	65.44–	91.24
55	82.09	70.80–	90.39	67.18–	92.26
56	83.58	72.52–	91.51	68.93–	93.26
57	85.07	74.26–	92.60	70.72–	94.22
58	86.57	76.03–	93.67	72.55–	95.14
59	88.06	77.82–	94.70	74.41–	96.03
60	89.55	79.65–	95.69	76.31–	96.86
61	91.04	81.52–	96.64	78.27–	97.64
62	92.54	83.44–	97.53	80.28–	98.35
63	94.03	85.41–	98.35	82.37–	98.98
64	95.52	87.47–	99.07	84.56–	99.49
65	97.01	89.63–	99.64	86.89–	99.84
66	98.51	91.96–	99.96	89.43–	99.99
67	100.00	94.64–	100.00	92.40–	100.00

N = 68

x	$100p_x$	95% $100p_l$	95% $100p_r$	99% $100p_l$	99% $100p_r$
0	0.00	0.00–	5.28	0.00–	7.50
1	1.47	0.04–	7.92	0.01–	10.42
2	2.94	0.36–	10.22	0.15–	12.93
3	4.41	0.92–	12.36	0.50–	15.22
4	5.88	1.63–	14.38	1.01–	17.38
5	7.35	2.43–	16.33	1.62–	19.45
6	8.82	3.31–	18.22	2.32–	21.44
7	10.29	4.24–	20.07	3.09–	23.37
8	11.76	5.22–	21.87	3.91–	25.25
9	13.24	6.23–	23.64	4.78–	27.08
10	14.71	7.28–	25.39	5.69–	28.88
11	16.18	8.36–	27.10	6.64–	30.65
12	17.65	9.46–	28.80	7.62–	32.39
13	19.12	10.59–	30.47	8.63–	34.10
14	20.59	11.74–	32.12	9.66–	35.78
15	22.06	12.90–	33.76	10.72–	37.45
16	23.53	14.09–	35.38	11.80–	39.09
17	25.00	15.29–	36.98	12.91–	40.71
18	26.47	16.50–	38.57	14.03–	42.31
19	27.94	17.73–	40.15	15.17–	43.90
20	29.41	18.98–	41.71	16.33–	45.46
21	30.88	20.24–	43.26	17.51–	47.02
22	32.35	21.51–	44.79	18.70–	48.55
23	33.82	22.79–	46.32	19.91–	50.07
24	35.29	24.08–	47.83	21.13–	51.57
25	36.76	25.39–	49.33	22.37–	53.07
26	38.24	26.71–	50.82	23.62–	54.54
27	39.71	28.03–	52.30	24.89–	56.00
28	41.18	29.37–	53.77	26.17–	57.45
29	42.65	30.72–	55.23	27.46–	58.89
30	44.12	32.08–	56.68	28.77–	60.31
31	45.59	33.45–	58.12	30.09–	61.72
32	47.06	34.83–	59.55	31.42–	63.12
33	48.53	36.22–	60.97	32.77–	64.50

N = 68 (continued)

x	$100p_x$	95% $100p_l$	95% $100p_r$	99% $100p_l$	99% $100p_r$
34	50.00	37.62–	62.38	34.12–	65.88
35	51.47	39.03–	63.78	35.50–	67.23
36	52.94	40.45–	65.17	36.88–	68.58
37	54.41	41.88–	66.55	38.28–	69.91
38	55.88	43.32–	67.92	39.69–	71.23
39	57.35	44.77–	69.28	41.11–	72.54
40	58.82	46.23–	70.63	42.55–	73.83
41	60.29	47.70–	71.97	44.00–	75.11
42	61.76	49.18–	73.29	45.46–	76.38
43	63.24	50.67–	74.61	46.93–	77.63
44	64.71	52.17–	75.92	48.43–	78.87
45	66.18	53.68–	77.21	49.93–	80.09
46	67.65	55.21–	78.49	51.45–	81.30
47	69.12	56.74–	79.76	52.98–	82.49
48	70.59	58.29–	81.02	54.54–	83.67
49	72.06	59.85–	82.27	56.10–	84.83
50	73.53	61.43–	83.50	57.69–	85.97
51	75.00	63.02–	84.71	59.29–	87.09
52	76.47	64.62–	85.91	60.91–	88.20
53	77.94	66.24–	87.10	62.55–	89.28
54	79.41	67.88–	88.26	64.22–	90.34
55	80.88	69.53–	89.41	65.90–	91.37
56	82.35	71.20–	90.54	67.61–	92.38
57	83.82	72.90–	91.64	69.35–	93.36
58	85.29	74.61–	92.72	71.12–	94.31
59	86.76	76.36–	93.77	72.92–	95.22
60	88.24	78.13–	94.78	74.75–	96.09
61	89.71	79.93–	95.76	76.63–	96.91
62	91.18	81.78–	96.69	78.56–	97.68
63	92.65	83.67–	97.57	80.55–	98.38
64	94.12	85.62–	98.37	82.62–	98.99
65	95.59	87.64–	99.08	84.78–	99.50
66	97.06	89.78–	99.64	87.07–	99.85
67	98.53	92.08–	99.96	89.58–	99.99
68	100.00	94.72–	100.00	92.50–	100.00

N = 69

x	$100p_x$	95% $100p_l$	95% $100p_r$	99% $100p_l$	99% $100p_r$
0	0.00	0.00–	5.21	0.00–	7.39
1	1.45	0.04–	7.81	0.01–	10.28
2	2.90	0.35–	10.08	0.15–	12.75
3	4.35	0.91–	12.18	0.50–	15.02
4	5.80	1.60–	14.18	0.99–	17.15
5	7.25	2.39–	16.11	1.60–	19.18
6	8.70	3.26–	17.97	2.29–	21.15
7	10.14	4.18–	19.79	3.04–	23.05
8	11.59	5.14–	21.57	3.85–	24.91
9	13.04	6.14–	23.32	4.71–	26.72
10	14.49	7.17–	25.04	5.61–	28.50
11	15.94	8.24–	26.74	6.54–	30.25
12	17.39	9.32–	28.41	7.50–	31.96
13	18.84	10.43–	30.06	8.50–	33.65
14	20.29	11.56–	31.69	9.51–	35.32
15	21.74	12.71–	33.31	10.56–	36.96
16	23.19	13.87–	34.91	11.62–	38.58
17	24.64	15.06–	36.49	12.71–	40.19
18	26.09	16.25–	38.06	13.81–	41.77
19	27.54	17.46–	39.62	14.93–	43.34
20	28.99	18.69–	41.16	16.07–	44.88
21	30.43	19.92–	42.69	17.23–	46.42
22	31.88	21.17–	44.21	18.40–	47.94
23	33.33	22.44–	45.71	19.59–	49.44
24	34.78	23.71–	47.21	20.80–	50.93
25	36.23	25.00–	48.69	22.01–	52.40
26	37.68	26.29–	50.16	23.24–	53.86
27	39.13	27.60–	51.63	24.49–	55.31
28	40.58	28.91–	53.08	25.75–	56.75
29	42.03	30.24–	54.52	27.02–	58.17
30	43.48	31.58–	55.96	28.30–	59.58
31	44.93	32.92–	57.38	29.60–	60.97
32	46.38	34.28–	58.80	30.91–	62.36
33	47.83	35.65–	60.20	32.23–	63.73
34	49.28	37.02–	61.59	33.57–	65.09
35	50.72	38.41–	62.98	34.91–	66.43
36	52.17	39.80–	64.35	36.27–	67.77
37	53.62	41.20–	65.72	37.64–	69.09
38	55.07	42.62–	67.08	39.03–	70.40
39	56.52	44.04–	68.42	40.42–	71.70
40	57.97	45.48–	69.76	41.83–	72.98
41	59.42	46.92–	71.09	43.25–	74.25
42	60.87	48.37–	72.40	44.69–	75.51
43	62.32	49.84–	73.71	46.14–	76.76
44	63.77	51.31–	75.00	47.60–	77.99
45	65.22	52.79–	76.29	49.07–	79.20
46	66.67	54.29–	77.56	50.56–	80.41
47	68.12	55.79–	78.83	52.06–	81.60
48	69.57	57.31–	80.08	53.58–	82.77
49	71.01	58.84–	81.31	55.12–	83.93
50	72.46	60.38–	82.54	56.66–	85.07
51	73.91	61.94–	83.75	58.23–	86.19
52	75.36	63.51–	84.94	59.81–	87.29
53	76.81	65.09–	86.13	61.42–	88.38
54	78.26	66.69–	87.29	63.04–	89.44
55	79.71	68.31–	88.44	64.68–	90.49
56	81.16	69.94–	89.57	66.35–	91.50
57	82.61	71.59–	90.68	68.04–	92.50
58	84.06	73.26–	91.76	69.75–	93.46
59	85.51	74.96–	92.83	71.50–	94.39
60	86.96	76.68–	93.86	73.28–	95.29

N = 69 (continued)

x	$100p_x$	95% $100p_l$	95% $100p_r$	99% $100p_l$	99% $100p_r$
61	88.41	78.43–	94.86	75.09–	96.15
62	89.86	80.21–	95.82	76.95–	96.96
63	91.30	82.03–	96.74	78.85–	97.71
64	92.75	83.89–	97.61	80.82–	98.40
65	94.20	85.82–	98.40	82.85–	99.01
66	95.65	87.82–	99.09	84.98–	99.50
67	97.10	89.92–	99.65	87.25–	99.85
68	98.55	92.19–	99.96	89.72–	99.99
69	100.00	94.79–	100.00	92.61–	100.00

N = 70

x	$100p_x$	95% $100p_l$	95% $100p_r$	99% $100p_l$	99% $100p_r$
0	0.00	0.00–	5.13	0.00–	7.29
1	1.43	0.04–	7.70	0.01–	10.14
2	2.86	0.35–	9.94	0.15–	12.58
3	4.29	0.89–	12.02	0.49–	14.81
4	5.71	1.58–	13.99	0.98–	16.92
5	7.14	2.36–	15.89	1.57–	18.93
6	8.57	3.21–	17.73	2.25–	20.87
7	10.00	4.12–	19.52	3.00–	22.75
8	11.43	5.07–	21.28	3.80–	24.58
9	12.86	6.05–	23.01	4.64–	26.37
10	14.29	7.07–	24.71	5.52–	28.13
11	15.71	8.11–	26.38	6.44–	29.85
12	17.14	9.18–	28.03	7.39–	31.55
13	18.57	10.28–	29.66	8.37–	33.22
14	20.00	11.39–	31.27	9.37–	34.86
15	21.43	12.52–	32.87	10.40–	36.49
16	22.86	13.67–	34.45	11.45–	38.09
17	24.29	14.83–	36.01	12.51–	39.67
18	25.71	16.01–	37.56	13.60–	41.24
19	27.14	17.20–	39.10	14.71–	42.79
20	28.57	18.40–	40.62	15.83–	44.32
21	30.00	19.62–	42.13	16.97–	45.84
22	31.43	20.85–	43.63	18.12–	47.34
23	32.86	22.09–	45.12	19.29–	48.82
24	34.29	23.35–	46.60	20.47–	50.30
25	35.71	24.61–	48.07	21.67–	51.76
26	37.14	25.89–	49.52	22.88–	53.20
27	38.57	27.17–	50.97	24.11–	54.63
28	40.00	28.47–	52.41	25.34–	56.05
29	41.43	29.77–	53.83	26.59–	57.46
30	42.86	31.09–	55.25	27.85–	58.86
31	44.29	32.41–	56.66	29.13–	60.24
32	45.71	33.74–	58.06	30.42–	61.61
33	47.14	35.09–	59.45	31.72–	62.97
34	48.57	36.44–	60.83	33.03–	64.32
35	50.00	37.80–	62.20	34.35–	65.65
36	51.43	39.17–	63.56	35.68–	66.97
37	52.86	40.55–	64.91	37.03–	68.28
38	54.29	41.94–	66.26	38.39–	69.58
39	55.71	43.34–	67.59	39.76–	70.87
40	57.14	44.75–	68.91	41.14–	72.15
41	58.57	46.17–	70.23	42.54–	73.41
42	60.00	47.59–	71.53	43.95–	74.66
43	61.43	49.03–	72.83	45.37–	75.89
44	62.86	50.48–	74.11	46.80–	77.12
45	64.29	51.93–	75.39	48.24–	78.33
46	65.71	53.40–	76.65	49.70–	79.53
47	67.14	54.88–	77.91	51.18–	80.71
48	68.57	56.37–	79.15	52.66–	81.88
49	70.00	57.87–	80.38	54.16–	83.03
50	71.43	59.38–	81.60	55.68–	84.17
51	72.86	60.90–	82.80	57.21–	85.29
52	74.29	62.44–	83.99	58.76–	86.40
53	75.71	63.99–	85.17	60.33–	87.49
54	77.14	65.55–	86.33	61.91–	88.55
55	78.57	67.13–	87.48	63.51–	89.60
56	80.00	68.73–	88.61	65.14–	90.63
57	81.43	70.34–	89.72	66.78–	91.63
58	82.86	71.97–	90.82	68.45–	92.61
59	84.29	73.62–	91.89	70.15–	93.56
60	85.71	75.29–	92.93	71.87–	94.48
61	87.14	76.99–	93.95	73.63–	95.36
62	88.57	78.72–	94.93	75.42–	96.20
63	90.00	80.48–	95.88	77.25–	97.00
64	91.43	82.27–	96.79	79.13–	97.75
65	92.86	84.11–	97.64	81.07–	98.43
66	94.29	86.01–	98.42	83.08–	99.02
67	95.71	87.98–	99.11	85.19–	99.51
68	97.14	90.06–	99.65	87.42–	99.85
69	98.57	92.30–	99.96	89.86–	99.99
70	100.00	94.87–	100.00	92.71–	100.00

N = 71

x	$100p_x$	95% $100p_l$	95% $100p_r$	99% $100p_l$	99% $100p_r$
0	0.00	0.00–	5.06	0.00–	7.19
1	1.41	0.04–	7.60	0.01–	10.00
2	2.82	0.34–	9.81	0.15–	12.41
3	4.23	0.88–	11.86	0.48–	14.62
4	5.63	1.56–	13.80	0.96–	16.69
5	7.04	2.33–	15.67	1.55–	18.68
6	8.45	3.17–	17.49	2.22–	20.59
7	9.86	4.06–	19.26	2.95–	22.45
8	11.27	4.99–	21.00	3.74–	24.26
9	12.68	5.96–	22.70	4.57–	26.03
10	14.08	6.97–	24.38	5.44–	27.77
11	15.49	8.00–	26.03	6.35–	29.47
12	16.90	9.05–	27.66	7.28–	31.14

(Column headings: 100 (1 − 2α) limits; 95% and 99%.)

N = number of trials, x = number of successes, etc., $100p_x = 100x/N$

$N = 71$ (continued)

x	$100p_x$	95% $100p_l$	95% $100p_r$	99% $100p_l$	99% $100p_r$
13	18.31	10.13	29.27	8.24	32.79
14	19.72	11.22	30.87	9.23	34.42
15	21.13	12.33	32.44	10.24	36.02
16	22.54	13.46	34.00	11.27	37.61
17	23.94	14.61	35.54	12.33	39.17
18	25.35	15.77	37.08	13.40	40.72
19	26.76	16.94	38.59	14.48	42.25
20	28.17	18.13	40.10	15.59	43.77
21	29.58	19.33	41.59	16.71	45.27
22	30.99	20.54	43.08	17.84	46.75
23	32.39	21.76	44.55	18.99	48.22
24	33.80	23.00	46.01	20.16	49.68
25	35.21	24.24	47.46	21.34	51.12
26	36.62	25.50	48.90	22.53	52.55
27	38.03	26.76	50.33	23.73	53.97
28	39.44	28.03	51.75	24.95	55.38
29	40.85	29.32	53.16	26.18	56.77
30	42.25	30.61	54.56	27.42	58.15
31	43.66	31.91	55.95	28.67	59.52
32	45.07	33.23	57.34	29.95	60.88
33	46.48	34.55	58.71	31.22	62.23
34	47.89	35.88	60.08	32.50	63.56
35	49.30	37.22	61.44	33.80	64.88
36	50.70	38.56	62.78	35.12	66.20
37	52.11	39.92	64.12	36.44	67.50
38	53.52	41.29	65.45	37.77	68.78
39	54.93	42.66	66.77	39.12	70.06
40	56.34	44.05	68.09	40.48	71.33
41	57.75	45.44	69.39	41.85	72.58
42	59.15	46.84	70.68	43.23	73.82
43	60.56	48.25	71.97	44.62	75.05
44	61.97	49.67	73.24	46.03	76.27
45	63.38	51.10	74.50	47.45	77.47
46	64.79	52.54	75.76	48.88	78.66
47	66.20	53.99	77.00	50.32	79.84
48	67.61	55.45	78.24	51.78	81.01
49	69.01	56.92	79.46	53.25	82.16
50	70.42	58.41	80.67	54.73	83.29
51	71.83	59.90	81.87	56.23	84.41
52	73.24	61.41	83.06	57.75	85.52
53	74.65	62.92	84.23	59.28	86.60
54	76.06	64.46	85.39	60.83	87.67
55	77.46	66.00	86.54	62.39	88.73
56	78.87	67.56	87.67	63.98	89.76
57	80.28	69.13	88.78	65.58	90.77
58	81.69	70.73	89.87	67.21	91.76
59	83.10	72.34	90.95	68.86	92.72
60	84.51	73.97	92.00	70.53	93.65
61	85.92	75.62	93.03	72.23	94.56
62	87.32	77.30	94.04	73.97	95.43
63	88.73	79.00	95.01	75.74	96.26
64	90.14	80.74	95.94	77.55	97.05
65	91.55	82.51	96.83	79.41	97.78
66	92.96	84.33	97.67	81.32	98.45
67	94.37	86.20	98.44	83.31	99.04
68	95.77	88.14	99.12	85.38	99.52
69	97.18	90.19	99.66	87.59	99.85
70	98.59	92.40	99.96	90.00	99.99
71	100.00	94.94	100.00	92.81	100.00

$N = 72$

x	$100p_x$	95% $100p_l$	95% $100p_r$	99% $100p_l$	99% $100p_r$
0	0.00	0.00	4.99	0.00	7.09
1	1.39	0.04	7.50	0.01	9.87
2	2.78	0.34	9.68	0.14	12.25
3	4.17	0.87	11.70	0.48	14.42
4	5.56	1.53	13.62	0.95	16.48
5	6.94	2.29	15.47	1.53	18.44
6	8.33	3.12	17.26	2.19	20.33
7	9.72	4.00	19.01	2.91	22.16
8	11.11	4.92	20.72	3.69	23.95
9	12.50	5.88	22.41	4.51	25.70
10	13.89	6.87	24.06	5.36	27.41
11	15.28	7.88	25.69	6.26	29.09
12	16.67	8.92	27.30	7.18	30.75
13	18.06	9.98	28.89	8.12	32.38
14	19.44	11.06	30.47	9.10	33.99
15	20.83	12.16	32.02	10.09	35.57
16	22.22	13.27	33.56	11.11	37.14
17	23.61	14.40	35.09	12.14	38.69
18	25.00	15.54	36.60	13.20	40.22
19	26.39	16.70	38.10	14.27	41.73
20	27.78	17.86	39.59	15.36	43.23
21	29.17	19.05	41.07	16.46	44.71
22	30.56	20.24	42.53	17.58	46.18
23	31.94	21.44	43.99	18.71	47.64
24	33.33	22.66	45.43	19.86	49.08
25	34.72	23.88	46.86	21.01	50.51
26	36.11	25.12	48.29	22.19	51.92
27	37.50	26.36	49.70	23.37	53.33
28	38.89	27.62	51.11	24.57	54.72
29	40.28	28.88	52.50	25.78	56.10
30	41.67	30.15	53.89	27.00	57.47
31	43.06	31.43	55.27	28.23	58.82
32	44.44	32.72	56.64	29.48	60.17
33	45.83	34.02	58.00	30.73	61.50
34	47.22	35.33	59.35	32.00	62.82
35	48.61	36.65	60.69	33.28	64.13
36	50.00	37.98	62.02	34.57	65.43

$N = 72$ (continued)

x	$100p_x$	95% $100p_l$	95% $100p_r$	99% $100p_l$	99% $100p_r$
37	51.39	39.31	63.35	35.87	66.72
38	52.78	40.65	64.67	37.18	68.00
39	54.17	42.00	65.98	38.50	69.27
40	55.56	43.36	67.28	39.83	70.52
41	56.94	44.73	68.57	41.18	71.77
42	58.33	46.11	69.85	42.53	73.00
43	59.72	47.50	71.12	43.90	74.22
44	61.11	48.89	72.38	45.28	75.43
45	62.50	50.30	73.64	46.67	76.63
46	63.89	51.71	74.88	48.08	77.81
47	65.28	53.14	76.12	49.49	78.99
48	66.67	54.57	77.34	50.92	80.14
49	68.06	56.01	78.56	52.36	81.29
50	69.44	57.47	79.76	53.82	82.42
51	70.83	58.93	80.95	55.29	83.54
52	72.22	60.41	82.14	56.77	84.64
53	73.61	61.90	83.30	58.27	85.73
54	75.00	63.40	84.46	59.78	86.80
55	76.39	64.91	85.60	61.31	87.86
56	77.78	66.44	86.73	62.86	88.89
57	79.17	67.98	87.84	64.43	89.91
58	80.56	69.53	88.94	66.01	90.90
59	81.94	71.11	90.02	67.62	91.88
60	83.33	72.70	91.08	69.25	92.82
61	84.72	74.31	92.12	70.91	93.74
62	86.11	75.94	93.13	72.59	94.64
63	87.50	77.59	94.12	74.30	95.49
64	88.89	79.28	95.08	76.05	96.31
65	90.28	80.99	96.00	77.84	97.09
66	91.67	82.74	96.88	79.67	97.81
67	93.06	84.53	97.71	81.56	98.47
68	94.44	86.38	98.47	83.52	99.05
69	95.83	88.30	99.13	85.58	99.52
70	97.22	90.32	99.66	87.75	99.86
71	98.61	92.50	99.96	90.13	99.99
72	100.00	95.01	100.00	92.91	100.00

$N = 73$

x	$100p_x$	95% $100p_l$	95% $100p_r$	99% $100p_l$	99% $100p_r$
0	0.00	0.00	4.93	0.00	7.00
1	1.37	0.03	7.40	0.01	9.74
2	2.74	0.33	9.55	0.14	12.09
3	4.11	0.86	11.54	0.47	14.24
4	5.48	1.51	13.44	0.94	16.26
5	6.85	2.26	15.26	1.51	18.20
6	8.22	3.08	17.04	2.16	20.07
7	9.59	3.94	18.76	2.87	21.88
8	10.96	4.85	20.46	3.63	23.65
9	12.33	5.80	22.12	4.44	25.37
10	13.70	6.77	23.75	5.29	27.07
11	15.07	7.77	25.36	6.17	28.73
12	16.44	8.79	26.95	7.07	30.37
13	17.81	9.84	28.53	8.01	31.98
14	19.18	10.90	30.08	8.97	33.57
15	20.55	11.98	31.62	9.95	35.13
16	21.92	13.08	33.14	10.95	36.68
17	23.29	14.19	34.65	11.97	38.21
18	24.66	15.32	36.14	13.01	39.73
19	26.03	16.45	37.62	14.06	41.22
20	27.40	17.61	39.09	15.13	42.71
21	28.77	18.77	40.55	16.22	44.17
22	30.14	19.94	42.00	17.32	45.63
23	31.51	21.13	43.44	18.43	47.06
24	32.88	22.33	44.87	19.56	48.49
25	34.25	23.53	46.28	20.70	49.90
26	35.62	24.75	47.69	21.86	51.31
27	36.99	25.97	49.09	23.02	52.70
28	38.36	27.21	50.48	24.20	54.07
29	39.73	28.45	51.86	25.39	55.44
30	41.10	29.71	53.23	26.59	56.79
31	42.47	30.97	54.59	27.80	58.14
32	43.84	32.24	55.95	29.03	59.47
33	45.21	33.52	57.30	30.26	60.79
34	46.58	34.80	58.63	31.51	62.10
35	47.95	36.10	59.96	32.77	63.40
36	49.32	37.40	61.28	34.03	64.69
37	50.68	38.72	62.60	35.31	65.97
38	52.05	40.04	63.90	36.60	67.23
39	53.42	41.37	65.20	37.90	68.49
40	54.79	42.70	66.48	39.21	69.74
41	56.16	44.05	67.76	40.53	70.97
42	57.53	45.41	69.03	41.86	72.20
43	58.90	46.77	70.29	43.21	73.41
44	60.27	48.14	71.55	44.56	74.61
45	61.64	49.52	72.79	45.93	75.80
46	63.01	50.91	74.03	47.30	76.98
47	64.38	52.31	75.25	48.69	78.14
48	65.75	53.72	76.47	50.10	79.30
49	67.12	55.13	77.67	51.51	80.44
50	68.49	56.56	78.87	52.94	81.57
51	69.86	58.00	80.06	54.37	82.68
52	71.23	59.45	81.23	55.83	83.78
53	72.60	60.91	82.39	57.29	84.87
54	73.97	62.38	83.55	58.78	85.94
55	75.34	63.86	84.68	60.27	86.99
56	76.71	65.35	85.81	61.79	88.03
57	78.08	66.86	86.92	63.32	89.05
58	79.45	68.38	88.02	64.87	90.05
59	80.82	69.92	89.10	66.43	91.03

$N = 73$ (continued)

x	$100p_x$	95% $100p_l$	95% $100p_r$	99% $100p_l$	99% $100p_r$
60	82.19	71.47	90.16	68.02	91.99
61	83.56	73.05	91.21	69.63	92.93
62	84.93	74.64	92.23	71.27	93.83
63	86.30	76.25	93.23	72.93	94.71
64	87.67	77.88	94.20	74.63	95.56
65	89.04	79.54	95.15	76.35	96.37
66	90.41	81.24	96.06	78.12	97.13
67	91.78	82.96	96.92	79.93	97.84
68	93.15	84.74	97.74	81.80	98.49
69	94.52	86.56	98.49	83.74	99.06
70	95.89	88.46	99.14	85.76	99.53
71	97.26	90.45	99.67	87.91	99.86
72	98.63	92.60	99.97	90.26	99.99
73	100.00	95.07	100.00	93.00	100.00

$N = 74$

x	$100p_x$	95% $100p_l$	95% $100p_r$	99% $100p_l$	99% $100p_r$
0	0.00	0.00	4.86	0.00	6.91
1	1.35	0.03	7.30	0.01	9.62
2	2.70	0.33	9.42	0.14	11.93
3	4.05	0.84	11.39	0.46	14.06
4	5.41	1.49	13.27	0.92	16.06
5	6.76	2.23	15.07	1.49	17.97
6	8.11	3.03	16.82	2.13	19.81
7	9.46	3.89	18.52	2.83	21.60
8	10.81	4.78	20.19	3.58	23.35
9	12.16	5.71	21.84	4.38	25.06
10	13.51	6.68	23.45	5.21	26.73
11	14.86	7.66	25.04	6.08	28.37
12	16.22	8.67	26.61	6.97	29.99
13	17.57	9.70	28.17	7.89	31.58
14	18.92	10.75	29.70	8.84	33.15
15	20.27	11.81	31.22	9.80	34.70
16	21.62	12.89	32.72	10.79	36.24
17	22.97	13.99	34.21	11.80	37.75
18	24.32	15.10	35.69	12.82	39.25
19	25.68	16.22	37.16	13.86	40.73
20	27.03	17.35	38.61	14.91	42.19
21	28.38	18.50	40.05	15.98	43.64
22	29.73	19.66	41.48	17.07	45.08
23	31.08	20.83	42.90	18.16	46.51
24	32.43	22.00	44.32	19.27	47.92
25	33.78	23.19	45.72	20.40	49.32
26	35.14	24.39	47.11	21.53	50.70
27	36.49	25.60	48.49	22.68	52.08
28	37.84	26.81	49.87	23.84	53.44
29	39.19	28.04	51.23	25.01	54.79
30	40.54	29.27	52.59	26.20	56.14
31	41.89	30.51	53.94	27.39	57.47
32	43.24	31.77	55.28	28.59	58.79
33	44.59	33.02	56.61	29.81	60.10
34	45.95	34.29	57.93	31.03	61.39
35	47.30	35.57	59.25	32.27	62.68
36	48.65	36.85	60.56	33.52	63.96
37	50.00	38.14	61.86	34.77	65.23
38	51.35	39.44	63.15	36.04	66.48
39	52.70	40.75	64.43	37.32	67.73
40	54.05	42.07	65.71	38.61	68.97
41	55.41	43.39	66.98	39.90	70.19
42	56.76	44.72	68.23	41.21	71.41
43	58.11	46.06	69.49	42.53	72.61
44	59.46	47.41	70.73	43.86	73.80
45	60.81	48.77	71.96	45.21	74.99
46	62.16	50.13	73.19	46.56	76.16
47	63.51	51.51	74.40	47.92	77.32
48	64.86	52.89	75.61	49.30	78.47
49	66.22	54.28	76.81	50.68	79.60
50	67.57	55.68	78.00	52.08	80.73
51	68.92	57.10	79.17	53.49	81.84
52	70.27	58.52	80.34	54.92	82.93
53	71.62	59.95	81.50	56.36	84.02
54	72.97	61.39	82.65	57.81	85.09
55	74.32	62.84	83.78	59.27	86.14
56	75.68	64.31	84.90	60.75	87.18
57	77.03	65.79	86.01	62.25	88.20
58	78.38	67.28	87.11	63.76	89.21
59	79.73	68.78	88.19	65.30	90.20
60	81.08	70.30	89.25	66.85	91.16
61	82.43	71.83	90.30	68.42	92.11
62	83.78	73.39	91.33	70.01	93.03
63	85.14	74.96	92.34	71.63	93.92
64	86.49	76.55	93.32	73.27	94.79
65	87.84	78.16	94.29	74.94	95.62
66	89.19	79.81	95.22	76.65	96.42
67	90.54	81.48	96.11	78.40	97.17
68	91.89	83.18	96.97	80.19	97.87
69	93.24	84.93	97.77	82.03	98.51
70	94.59	86.73	98.51	83.94	99.08
71	95.95	88.61	99.16	85.94	99.54
72	97.30	90.58	99.67	88.07	99.86
73	98.65	92.70	99.97	90.38	99.99
74	100.00	95.14	100.00	93.09	100.00

$N = 75$

x	$100p_x$	95% $100p_l$	95% $100p_r$	99% $100p_l$	99% $100p_r$
0	0.00	0.00	4.80	0.00	6.82
1	1.33	0.03	7.21	0.01	9.49
2	2.67	0.32	9.30	0.14	11.78
3	4.00	0.83	11.25	0.46	13.88
4	5.33	1.47	13.10	0.91	15.85

$N = 75$ (continued)

x	$100p_x$	95% $100p_l$	95% $100p_r$	99% $100p_l$	99% $100p_r$
5	6.67	2.20	14.88	1.47	17.74
6	8.00	2.99	16.60	2.10	19.57
7	9.33	3.84	18.29	2.79	21.34
8	10.67	4.72	19.94	3.53	23.06
9	12.00	5.64	21.56	4.32	24.75
10	13.33	6.58	23.16	5.14	26.40
11	14.67	7.56	24.73	5.99	28.03
12	16.00	8.55	26.28	6.88	29.63
13	17.33	9.57	27.81	7.78	31.20
14	18.67	10.60	29.33	8.71	32.75
15	20.00	11.65	30.83	9.67	34.29
16	21.33	12.71	32.32	10.64	35.80
17	22.67	13.79	33.79	11.63	37.30
18	24.00	14.89	35.25	12.64	38.78
19	25.33	15.99	36.70	13.66	40.24
20	26.67	17.11	38.14	14.70	41.69
21	28.00	18.24	39.56	15.75	43.13
22	29.33	19.38	40.98	16.82	44.55
23	30.67	20.53	42.38	17.90	45.96
24	32.00	21.69	43.78	19.00	47.36
25	33.33	22.86	45.17	20.10	48.74
26	34.67	24.04	46.54	21.22	50.11
27	36.00	25.23	47.91	22.35	51.48
28	37.33	26.43	49.27	23.49	52.83
29	38.67	27.64	50.62	24.65	54.16
30	40.00	28.85	51.96	25.81	55.49
31	41.33	30.08	53.30	26.99	56.81
32	42.67	31.31	54.62	28.17	58.12
33	44.00	32.55	55.94	29.37	59.42
34	45.33	33.79	57.25	30.57	60.70
35	46.67	35.05	58.55	31.79	61.98
36	48.00	36.31	59.85	33.02	63.25
37	49.33	37.58	61.14	34.25	64.50
38	50.67	38.86	62.42	35.50	65.75
39	52.00	40.15	63.69	36.75	66.98
40	53.33	41.45	64.95	38.02	68.21
41	54.67	42.75	66.21	39.30	69.43
42	56.00	44.06	67.45	40.58	70.63
43	57.33	45.38	68.69	41.88	71.83
44	58.67	46.70	69.92	43.19	73.01
45	60.00	48.04	71.15	44.51	74.19
46	61.33	49.38	72.36	45.84	75.35
47	62.67	50.73	73.57	47.17	76.51
48	64.00	52.09	74.77	48.52	77.65
49	65.33	53.46	75.96	49.89	78.78
50	66.67	54.83	77.14	51.26	79.90
51	68.00	56.22	78.31	52.64	81.00
52	69.33	57.62	79.47	54.04	82.10
53	70.67	59.02	80.62	55.45	83.18
54	72.00	60.44	81.76	56.87	84.25
55	73.33	61.86	82.89	58.31	85.30
56	74.67	63.30	84.01	59.76	86.34
57	76.00	64.75	85.11	61.22	87.36
58	77.33	66.21	86.21	62.70	88.37
59	78.67	67.68	87.29	64.20	89.36
60	80.00	69.17	88.35	65.71	90.33
61	81.33	70.67	89.40	67.25	91.29
62	82.67	72.19	90.43	68.80	92.22
63	84.00	73.72	91.45	70.37	93.12
64	85.33	75.27	92.44	71.97	94.01
65	86.67	76.84	93.42	73.60	94.86
66	88.00	78.44	94.36	75.25	95.68
67	89.33	80.06	95.28	76.93	96.47
68	90.67	81.71	96.16	78.66	97.21
69	92.00	83.40	97.01	80.43	97.90
70	93.33	85.12	97.80	82.26	98.53
71	94.67	86.90	98.53	84.15	99.09
72	96.00	88.75	99.17	86.12	99.54
73	97.33	90.70	99.68	88.22	99.86
74	98.67	92.79	99.97	90.51	99.99
75	100.00	95.20	100.00	93.18	100.00

$N = 76$

x	$100p_x$	95% $100p_l$	95% $100p_r$	99% $100p_l$	99% $100p_r$
0	0.00	0.00	4.74	0.00	6.73
1	1.32	0.03	7.11	0.01	9.37
2	2.63	0.32	9.18	0.14	11.63
3	3.95	0.82	11.11	0.45	13.71
4	5.26	1.45	12.93	0.90	15.66
5	6.58	2.17	14.69	1.45	17.52
6	7.89	2.95	16.40	2.07	19.33
7	9.21	3.78	18.06	2.76	21.07
8	10.53	4.66	19.69	3.49	22.78
9	11.84	5.56	21.29	4.26	24.45
10	13.16	6.49	22.87	5.07	26.08
11	14.47	7.45	24.42	5.91	27.69
12	15.79	8.43	25.96	6.78	29.27
13	17.11	9.43	27.47	7.68	30.83
14	18.42	10.45	28.97	8.59	32.36
15	19.74	11.49	30.46	9.53	33.88
16	21.05	12.54	31.92	10.49	35.37
17	22.37	13.60	33.38	11.47	36.85
18	23.68	14.68	34.82	12.46	38.32
19	25.00	15.77	36.26	13.47	39.77
20	26.32	16.87	37.68	14.49	41.20
21	27.63	17.99	39.09	15.53	42.62
22	28.95	19.11	40.49	16.58	44.03
23	30.26	20.25	41.87	17.65	45.43
24	31.58	21.39	43.25	18.73	46.81

Column heads as printed: $100(1 - 2\alpha)$ limits, 95% and 99%, each with $100p_l$ and $100p_r$.

N = number of trials, x = number of successes, etc., $100\,p_x = 100\,x/N$

$N = 76$ (continued)

x	$100p_x$	95% $100p_l$	95% $100p_r$	99% $100p_l$	99% $100p_r$
25	32.89	22.54	44.63	19.82	48.18
26	34.21	23.71	45.99	20.92	49.54
27	35.53	24.88	47.34	22.03	50.89
28	36.84	26.06	48.69	23.16	52.22
29	38.16	27.25	50.02	24.29	53.55
30	39.47	28.44	51.35	25.44	54.86
31	40.79	29.65	52.67	26.59	56.17
32	42.11	30.86	53.98	27.76	57.46
33	43.42	32.08	55.29	28.94	58.75
34	44.74	33.31	56.59	30.13	60.02
35	46.05	34.55	57.87	31.32	61.29
36	47.37	35.79	59.16	32.53	62.55
37	48.68	37.04	60.43	33.75	63.79
38	50.00	38.30	61.70	34.97	65.03
39	51.32	39.57	62.96	36.21	66.25
40	52.63	40.84	64.21	37.45	67.47
41	53.95	42.13	65.45	38.71	68.68
42	55.26	43.41	66.69	39.98	69.87
43	56.58	44.71	67.92	41.25	71.06
44	57.89	46.02	69.14	42.54	72.24
45	59.21	47.33	70.35	43.83	73.41
46	60.53	48.65	71.56	45.14	74.56
47	61.84	49.98	72.75	46.45	75.71
48	63.16	51.31	73.94	47.78	76.84
49	64.47	52.66	75.12	49.11	77.97
50	65.79	54.01	76.29	50.46	79.08
51	67.11	55.37	77.46	51.82	80.18
52	68.42	56.75	78.61	53.19	81.27
53	69.74	58.13	79.75	54.57	82.35
54	71.05	59.51	80.89	55.97	83.42
55	72.37	60.91	82.01	57.38	84.47
56	73.68	62.32	83.13	58.80	85.51
57	75.00	63.74	84.23	60.23	86.53
58	76.32	65.18	85.32	61.68	87.54
59	77.63	66.62	86.40	63.15	88.53
60	78.95	68.08	87.46	64.63	89.51
61	80.26	69.54	88.51	66.12	90.47
62	81.58	71.03	89.55	67.64	91.41
63	82.89	72.53	90.57	69.17	92.32
64	84.21	74.04	91.57	70.73	93.22
65	85.53	75.58	92.55	72.31	94.09
66	86.84	77.13	93.51	73.92	94.93
67	88.16	78.71	94.44	75.55	95.74
68	89.47	80.31	95.34	77.22	96.51
69	90.79	81.94	96.22	78.93	97.24
70	92.11	83.60	97.05	80.67	97.93
71	93.42	85.31	97.83	82.48	98.55
72	94.74	87.07	98.55	84.34	99.10
73	96.05	88.89	99.18	86.29	99.55
74	97.37	90.82	99.68	88.37	99.86
75	98.68	92.89	99.97	90.63	99.99
76	100.00	95.26	100.00	93.27	100.00

$N = 77$

x	$100p_x$	95% $100p_l$	95% $100p_r$	99% $100p_l$	99% $100p_r$
0	0.00	0.00	4.68	0.00	6.65
1	1.30	0.03	7.02	0.01	9.26
2	2.60	0.32	9.07	0.14	11.49
3	3.90	0.81	10.97	0.44	13.54
4	5.19	1.43	12.77	0.89	15.47
5	6.49	2.14	14.51	1.43	17.31
6	7.79	2.91	16.19	2.04	19.09
7	9.09	3.73	17.84	2.72	20.82
8	10.39	4.59	19.45	3.44	22.50
9	11.69	5.49	21.03	4.20	24.15
10	12.99	6.41	22.59	5.00	25.77
11	14.29	7.35	24.13	5.83	27.36
12	15.58	8.32	25.64	6.69	28.92
13	16.88	9.31	27.14	7.57	30.46
14	18.18	10.31	28.62	8.48	31.98
15	19.48	11.33	30.09	9.40	33.48
16	20.78	12.37	31.54	10.35	34.96
17	22.08	13.42	32.98	11.31	36.42
18	23.38	14.48	34.41	12.29	37.87
19	24.68	15.56	35.82	13.28	39.31
20	25.97	16.64	37.23	14.29	40.72
21	27.27	17.74	38.62	15.32	42.13
22	28.57	18.85	40.00	16.35	43.52
23	29.87	19.97	41.38	17.40	44.90
24	31.17	21.09	42.74	18.46	46.27
25	32.47	22.23	44.10	19.54	47.63
26	33.77	23.38	45.45	20.62	48.97
27	35.06	24.53	46.78	21.72	50.31
28	36.36	25.70	48.12	22.83	51.63
29	37.66	26.87	49.44	23.95	52.95
30	38.96	28.05	50.75	25.08	54.25
31	40.26	29.23	52.06	26.21	55.54
32	41.56	30.43	53.36	27.36	56.82
33	42.86	31.63	54.65	28.52	58.10
34	44.16	32.84	55.93	29.69	59.36
35	45.45	34.06	57.21	30.87	60.62
36	46.75	35.29	58.48	32.06	61.86
37	48.05	36.52	59.74	33.26	63.10
38	49.35	37.76	61.00	34.46	64.32
39	50.65	39.00	62.24	35.68	65.54
40	51.95	40.26	63.48	36.90	66.74
41	53.25	41.52	64.71	38.14	67.94
42	54.55	42.79	65.94	39.38	69.13
43	55.84	44.07	67.16	40.64	70.31

$N = 77$ (continued)

x	$100p_x$	95% $100p_l$	95% $100p_r$	99% $100p_l$	99% $100p_r$
44	57.14	45.35	68.37	41.90	71.48
45	58.44	46.64	69.57	43.18	72.64
46	59.74	47.94	70.77	44.46	73.79
47	61.04	49.25	71.95	45.75	74.92
48	62.34	50.56	73.13	47.05	76.05
49	63.64	51.88	74.30	48.37	77.17
50	64.94	53.22	75.47	49.69	78.28
51	66.23	54.55	76.62	51.03	79.38
52	67.53	55.90	77.77	52.37	80.46
53	68.83	57.26	78.91	53.73	81.54
54	70.13	58.62	80.03	55.10	82.60
55	71.43	60.00	81.15	56.48	83.65
56	72.73	61.38	82.26	57.87	84.68
57	74.03	62.77	83.36	59.28	85.71
58	75.32	64.18	84.44	60.69	86.72
59	76.62	65.59	85.52	62.13	87.71
60	77.92	67.02	86.58	63.58	88.69
61	79.22	68.46	87.63	65.04	89.65
62	80.52	69.91	88.67	66.52	90.60
63	81.82	71.38	89.69	68.02	91.52
64	83.12	72.86	90.69	69.54	92.43
65	84.42	74.36	91.68	71.08	93.31
66	85.71	75.87	92.65	72.64	94.17
67	87.01	77.41	93.59	74.23	95.00
68	88.31	78.97	94.51	75.85	95.80
69	89.61	80.55	95.41	77.50	96.56
70	90.91	82.16	96.27	79.18	97.28
71	92.21	83.81	97.09	80.91	97.96
72	93.51	85.49	97.86	82.69	98.57
73	94.81	87.23	98.57	84.53	99.11
74	96.10	89.03	99.19	86.46	99.56
75	97.40	90.93	99.68	88.51	99.86
76	98.70	92.98	99.97	90.74	99.99
77	100.00	95.32	100.00	93.35	100.00

$N = 78$

x	$100p_x$	95% $100p_l$	95% $100p_r$	99% $100p_l$	99% $100p_r$
0	0.00	0.00	4.62	0.00	6.57
1	1.28	0.03	6.94	0.01	9.14
2	2.56	0.31	8.96	0.13	11.35
3	3.85	0.80	10.83	0.44	13.37
4	5.13	1.41	12.61	0.88	15.28
5	6.41	2.11	14.33	1.41	17.10
6	7.69	2.88	15.99	2.02	18.86
7	8.97	3.68	17.62	2.68	20.57
8	10.26	4.53	19.21	3.39	22.24
9	11.54	5.41	20.78	4.15	23.87
10	12.82	6.32	22.32	4.94	25.46
11	14.10	7.26	23.83	5.76	27.03
12	15.38	8.21	25.33	6.60	28.58
13	16.67	9.18	26.81	7.47	30.10
14	17.95	10.17	28.28	8.36	31.60
15	19.23	11.18	29.73	9.28	33.09
16	20.51	12.20	31.16	10.21	34.55
17	21.79	13.24	32.59	11.16	36.00
18	23.08	14.29	34.00	12.12	37.43
19	24.36	15.35	35.40	13.10	38.85
20	25.64	16.42	36.79	14.10	40.26
21	26.92	17.50	38.16	15.11	41.65
22	28.21	18.59	39.53	16.13	43.03
23	29.49	19.70	40.89	17.16	44.39
24	30.77	20.81	42.24	18.21	45.75
25	32.05	21.93	43.58	19.27	47.09
26	33.33	23.06	44.92	20.34	48.42
27	34.62	24.20	46.24	21.42	49.74
28	35.90	25.34	47.56	22.51	51.05
29	37.18	26.50	48.87	23.61	52.36
30	38.46	27.66	50.17	24.72	53.65
31	39.74	28.83	51.46	25.85	54.93
32	41.03	30.01	52.75	26.98	56.20
33	42.31	31.19	54.02	28.12	57.46
34	43.59	32.39	55.30	29.27	58.71
35	44.87	33.59	56.56	30.43	59.96
36	46.15	34.79	57.82	31.60	61.19
37	47.44	36.01	59.07	32.78	62.41
38	48.72	37.23	60.31	33.97	63.63
39	50.00	38.46	61.54	35.16	64.84
40	51.28	39.69	62.77	36.37	66.03
41	52.56	40.93	63.99	37.59	67.22
42	53.85	42.18	65.21	38.81	68.40
43	55.13	43.44	66.41	40.04	69.57
44	56.41	44.70	67.61	41.29	70.73
45	57.69	45.98	68.81	42.54	71.88
46	58.97	47.25	69.99	43.80	73.02
47	60.26	48.54	71.17	45.07	74.15
48	61.54	49.83	72.34	46.35	75.28
49	62.82	51.13	73.50	47.64	76.39
50	64.10	52.44	74.66	48.95	77.49
51	65.38	53.76	75.80	50.26	78.58
52	66.67	55.08	76.94	51.58	79.66
53	67.95	56.42	78.07	52.91	80.73
54	69.23	57.76	79.19	54.25	81.79
55	70.51	59.11	80.30	55.61	82.84
56	71.79	60.47	81.41	56.97	83.87
57	73.08	61.84	82.50	58.35	84.89
58	74.36	63.21	83.58	59.74	85.90
59	75.64	64.60	84.65	61.15	86.90
60	76.92	66.00	85.71	62.57	87.88
61	78.21	67.41	86.76	64.00	88.84

$N = 78$ (continued)

x	$100p_x$	95% $100p_l$	95% $100p_r$	99% $100p_l$	99% $100p_r$
62	79.49	68.84	87.80	65.45	89.79
63	80.77	70.27	88.82	66.91	90.72
64	82.05	71.72	89.83	68.40	91.64
65	83.33	73.19	90.82	69.90	92.53
66	84.62	74.67	91.79	71.42	93.40
67	85.90	76.17	92.74	72.97	94.24
68	87.18	77.68	93.68	74.54	95.06
69	88.46	79.22	94.59	76.13	95.85
70	89.74	80.79	95.47	77.76	96.61
71	91.03	82.38	96.32	79.43	97.32
72	92.31	84.01	97.12	81.14	97.98
73	93.59	85.67	97.89	82.90	98.59
74	94.87	87.39	98.59	84.72	99.12
75	96.15	89.17	99.20	86.63	99.56
76	97.44	91.04	99.69	88.65	99.87
77	98.72	93.06	99.97	90.86	99.99
78	100.00	95.38	100.00	93.43	100.00

$N = 79$

x	$100p_x$	95% $100p_l$	95% $100p_r$	99% $100p_l$	99% $100p_r$
0	0.00	0.00	4.56	0.00	6.49
1	1.27	0.03	6.85	0.01	9.03
2	2.53	0.31	8.85	0.13	11.21
3	3.80	0.79	10.70	0.43	13.21
4	5.06	1.40	12.46	0.86	15.10
5	6.33	2.09	14.16	1.39	16.90
6	7.59	2.84	15.80	1.99	18.64
7	8.86	3.64	17.41	2.65	20.33
8	10.13	4.47	18.98	3.35	21.97
9	11.39	5.34	20.53	4.09	23.59
10	12.66	6.24	22.05	4.87	25.17
11	13.92	7.16	23.55	5.68	26.72
12	15.19	8.10	25.03	6.51	28.25
13	16.46	9.06	26.49	7.37	29.75
14	17.72	10.04	27.94	8.25	31.24
15	18.99	11.03	29.38	9.15	32.71
16	20.25	12.04	30.80	10.07	34.16
17	21.52	13.06	32.20	11.01	35.59
18	22.78	14.10	33.60	11.96	37.01
19	24.05	15.14	34.98	12.93	38.41
20	25.32	16.20	36.36	13.91	39.80
21	26.58	17.27	37.72	14.90	41.18
22	27.85	18.35	39.07	15.91	42.54
23	29.11	19.43	40.42	16.93	43.89
24	30.38	20.53	41.75	17.96	45.23
25	31.65	21.63	43.08	19.00	46.56
26	32.91	22.75	44.40	20.06	47.88
27	34.18	23.87	45.71	21.12	49.19
28	35.44	25.00	47.01	22.20	50.49
29	36.71	26.14	48.31	23.29	51.78
30	37.97	27.28	49.59	24.38	53.06
31	39.24	28.44	50.87	25.49	54.33
32	40.51	29.60	52.15	26.60	55.59
33	41.77	30.77	53.41	27.73	56.84
34	43.04	31.94	54.67	28.86	58.08
35	44.30	33.12	55.92	30.00	59.31
36	45.57	34.31	57.17	31.16	60.53
37	46.84	35.51	58.40	32.32	61.75
38	48.10	36.71	59.64	33.49	62.95
39	49.37	37.92	60.86	34.66	64.15
40	50.63	39.14	62.08	35.85	65.34
41	51.90	40.36	63.29	37.05	66.51
42	53.16	41.60	64.49	38.25	67.68
43	54.43	42.83	65.69	39.47	68.84
44	55.70	44.08	66.88	40.69	70.00
45	56.96	45.33	68.06	41.92	71.14
46	58.23	46.59	69.23	43.16	72.27
47	59.49	47.85	70.40	44.41	73.40
48	60.76	49.13	71.56	45.67	74.51
49	62.03	50.41	72.72	46.94	75.62
50	63.29	51.69	73.86	48.22	76.71
51	64.56	52.99	75.00	49.51	77.80
52	65.82	54.29	76.13	50.81	78.88
53	67.09	55.60	77.25	52.12	79.94
54	68.35	56.92	78.37	53.44	81.00
55	69.62	58.25	79.47	54.77	82.04
56	70.89	59.58	80.57	56.11	83.07
57	72.15	60.93	81.65	57.46	84.09
58	73.42	62.28	82.73	58.82	85.10
59	74.68	63.64	83.80	60.20	86.09
60	75.95	65.02	84.86	61.59	87.07
61	77.22	66.40	85.90	62.99	88.04
62	78.48	67.80	86.94	64.41	88.99
63	79.75	69.20	87.96	65.84	89.93
64	81.01	70.62	88.97	67.29	90.85
65	82.28	72.06	89.96	68.76	91.75
66	83.54	73.51	90.94	70.25	92.63
67	84.81	74.97	91.90	71.75	93.49
68	86.08	76.45	92.84	73.28	94.32
69	87.34	77.95	93.76	74.83	95.13
70	88.61	79.47	94.66	76.41	95.91
71	89.87	81.02	95.53	78.03	96.65
72	91.14	82.59	96.36	79.67	97.35
73	92.41	84.20	97.16	81.36	98.01
74	93.67	85.84	97.91	83.10	98.61
75	94.94	87.54	98.60	84.90	99.14
76	96.20	89.30	99.21	86.79	99.57
77	97.47	91.15	99.69	88.79	99.87
78	98.73	93.15	99.97	90.97	99.99
79	100.00	95.44	100.00	93.51	100.00

$N = 80$

x	$100p_x$	95% $100p_l$	95% $100p_r$	99% $100p_l$	99% $100p_r$
0	0.00	0.00	4.51	0.00	6.41
1	1.25	0.03	6.77	0.01	8.92
2	2.50	0.30	8.74	0.13	11.08
3	3.75	0.78	10.57	0.43	13.05
4	5.00	1.38	12.31	0.85	14.92
5	6.25	2.06	13.99	1.37	16.70
6	7.50	2.80	15.61	1.96	18.42
7	8.75	3.59	17.20	2.61	20.09
8	10.00	4.42	18.76	3.31	21.72
9	11.25	5.28	20.28	4.04	23.31
10	12.50	6.16	21.79	4.81	24.87
11	13.75	7.07	23.27	5.61	26.41
12	15.00	8.00	24.74	6.43	27.92
13	16.25	8.95	26.18	7.28	29.41
14	17.50	9.91	27.62	8.14	30.88
15	18.75	10.89	29.03	9.03	32.33
16	20.00	11.89	30.44	9.94	33.77
17	21.25	12.89	31.83	10.86	35.19
18	22.50	13.91	33.21	11.80	36.59
19	23.75	14.95	34.58	12.75	37.98
20	25.00	15.99	35.94	13.72	39.35
21	26.25	17.04	37.29	14.70	40.72
22	27.50	18.10	38.62	15.70	42.07
23	28.75	19.18	39.95	16.70	43.41
24	30.00	20.26	41.28	17.72	44.73
25	31.25	21.35	42.59	18.75	46.05
26	32.50	22.45	43.89	19.79	47.36
27	33.75	23.55	45.19	20.84	48.65
28	35.00	24.67	46.48	21.90	49.94
29	36.25	25.79	47.76	22.97	51.21
30	37.50	26.92	49.04	24.05	52.48
31	38.75	28.06	50.30	25.14	53.74
32	40.00	29.20	51.56	26.24	54.99
33	41.25	30.35	52.82	27.35	56.22
34	42.50	31.51	54.06	28.46	57.45
35	43.75	32.68	55.30	29.59	58.68
36	45.00	33.85	56.53	30.72	59.89
37	46.25	35.03	57.76	31.87	61.09
38	47.50	36.21	58.98	33.02	62.29
39	48.75	37.41	60.19	34.18	63.47
40	50.00	38.60	61.40	35.35	64.65
41	51.25	39.81	62.59	36.53	65.82
42	52.50	41.02	63.79	37.71	66.98
43	53.75	42.24	64.97	38.91	68.13
44	55.00	43.47	66.15	40.11	69.28
45	56.25	44.70	67.32	41.32	70.41
46	57.50	45.94	68.49	42.55	71.54
47	58.75	47.18	69.65	43.78	72.65
48	60.00	48.44	70.80	45.01	73.76
49	61.25	49.70	71.94	46.26	74.86
50	62.50	50.96	73.08	47.52	75.95
51	63.75	52.24	74.21	48.79	77.03
52	65.00	53.52	75.33	50.06	78.10
53	66.25	54.81	76.45	51.35	79.16
54	67.50	56.11	77.55	52.64	80.21
55	68.75	57.41	78.65	53.95	81.25
56	70.00	58.72	79.74	55.27	82.28
57	71.25	60.05	80.82	56.59	83.30
58	72.50	61.38	81.90	57.93	84.30
59	73.75	62.71	82.96	59.28	85.30
60	75.00	64.06	84.01	60.65	86.28
61	76.25	65.42	85.05	62.02	87.25
62	77.50	66.79	86.09	63.41	88.20
63	78.75	68.17	87.11	64.81	89.14
64	80.00	69.56	88.11	66.23	90.06
65	81.25	70.97	89.11	67.67	90.97
66	82.50	72.38	90.09	69.12	91.86
67	83.75	73.82	91.05	70.59	92.72
68	85.00	75.26	92.00	72.08	93.57
69	86.25	76.73	92.93	73.59	94.39
70	87.50	78.21	93.84	75.13	95.19
71	88.75	79.72	94.72	76.69	95.96
72	90.00	81.24	95.58	78.28	96.69
73	91.25	82.80	96.41	79.91	97.39
74	92.50	84.39	97.20	81.58	98.04
75	93.75	86.01	97.94	83.30	98.63
76	95.00	87.69	98.62	85.08	99.15
77	96.25	89.43	99.22	86.95	99.57
78	97.50	91.26	99.70	88.92	99.87
79	98.75	93.23	99.97	91.08	99.99
80	100.00	95.49	100.00	93.59	100.00

$N = 81$

x	$100p_x$	95% $100p_l$	95% $100p_r$	99% $100p_l$	99% $100p_r$
0	0.00	0.00	4.45	0.00	6.33
1	1.23	0.03	6.69	0.01	8.82
2	2.47	0.30	8.64	0.13	10.95
3	3.70	0.77	10.44	0.42	12.90
4	4.94	1.36	12.16	0.84	14.74
5	6.17	2.03	13.82	1.36	16.50
6	7.41	2.77	15.43	1.94	18.21
7	8.64	3.55	17.00	2.58	19.86
8	9.88	4.36	18.54	3.27	21.47
9	11.11	5.21	20.05	3.99	23.04
10	12.35	6.08	21.53	4.75	24.59
11	13.58	6.98	23.00	5.53	26.11
12	14.81	7.90	24.45	6.35	27.60
13	16.05	8.83	25.88	7.18	29.08
14	17.28	9.78	27.30	8.04	30.53

Column heads: $100(1-2\alpha)$ limits, 95% and 99%.

N = number of trials, x = number of successes, etc., $100\,p_x = 100\,x/N$

N = 81 (continued)

x	$100p_x$	100(1 − 2α) limits 95% $100p_l$ $100p_r$	99% $100p_l$ $100p_r$
15	18.52	10.75– 28.70	8.92– 31.97
16	19.75	11.73– 30.09	9.81– 33.39
17	20.99	12.73– 31.46	10.72– 34.79
18	22.22	13.73– 32.83	11.65– 36.18
19	23.46	14.75– 34.18	12.59– 37.55
20	24.69	15.78– 35.53	13.54– 38.92
21	25.93	16.82– 36.86	14.51– 40.27
22	27.16	17.87– 38.19	15.49– 41.60
23	28.40	18.93– 39.50	16.48– 42.93
24	29.63	19.99– 40.81	17.49– 44.24
25	30.86	21.07– 42.11	18.50– 45.55
26	32.10	22.15– 43.40	19.52– 46.84
27	33.33	23.24– 44.68	20.56– 48.12
28	34.57	24.34– 45.96	21.61– 49.40
29	35.80	25.45– 47.23	22.66– 50.66
30	37.04	26.56– 48.49	23.73– 51.92
31	38.27	27.69– 49.74	24.80– 53.16
32	39.51	28.81– 50.99	25.88– 54.40
33	40.74	29.95– 52.23	26.97– 55.62
34	41.98	31.09– 53.46	28.08– 56.84
35	43.21	32.24– 54.69	29.18– 58.05
36	44.44	33.40– 55.91	30.30– 59.26
37	45.68	34.56– 57.13	31.43– 60.45
38	46.91	35.73– 58.33	32.56– 61.64
39	48.15	36.90– 59.53	33.71– 62.81
40	49.38	38.08– 60.73	34.86– 63.98
41	50.62	39.27– 61.92	36.02– 65.14
42	51.85	40.47– 63.10	37.19– 66.29
43	53.09	41.67– 64.27	38.36– 67.44
44	54.32	42.87– 65.44	39.55– 68.57
45	55.56	44.09– 66.60	40.74– 69.70
46	56.79	45.31– 67.76	41.95– 70.82
47	58.02	46.54– 68.91	43.16– 71.92
48	59.26	47.77– 70.05	44.38– 73.03
49	60.49	49.01– 71.19	45.60– 74.12
50	61.73	50.26– 72.31	46.84– 75.20
51	62.96	51.51– 73.44	48.08– 76.27
52	64.20	52.77– 74.55	49.34– 77.34
53	65.43	54.04– 75.66	50.60– 78.39
54	66.67	55.32– 76.76	51.88– 79.44
55	67.90	56.60– 77.85	53.16– 80.48
56	69.14	57.89– 78.93	54.45– 81.50
57	70.37	59.19– 80.01	55.76– 82.51
58	71.60	60.50– 81.07	57.07– 83.52
59	72.84	61.81– 82.13	58.40– 84.51
60	74.07	63.14– 83.18	59.73– 85.49
61	75.31	64.47– 84.22	61.08– 86.46
62	76.54	65.82– 85.25	62.45– 87.41
63	77.78	67.17– 86.27	63.82– 88.35
64	79.01	68.54– 87.27	65.21– 89.28
65	80.25	69.91– 88.27	66.61– 90.19
66	81.48	71.30– 89.25	68.03– 91.08
67	82.72	72.70– 90.22	69.47– 91.96
68	83.95	74.12– 91.17	70.92– 92.82
69	85.19	75.55– 92.10	72.40– 93.65
70	86.42	77.00– 93.02	73.89– 94.47
71	87.65	78.47– 93.92	75.41– 95.25
72	88.89	79.95– 94.79	76.96– 96.01
73	90.12	81.46– 95.64	78.53– 96.73
74	91.36	83.00– 96.45	80.14– 97.42
75	92.59	84.57– 97.23	81.79– 98.06
76	93.83	86.18– 97.97	83.50– 98.64
77	95.06	87.84– 98.64	85.26– 99.16
78	96.30	89.56– 99.23	87.10– 99.58
79	97.53	91.36– 99.70	89.05– 99.87
80	98.77	93.31– 99.97	91.18– 99.99
81	100.00	95.55–100.00	93.67–100.00

N = 82

x	$100p_x$	100(1 − 2α) limits 95% $100p_l$ $100p_r$	99% $100p_l$ $100p_r$
0	0.00	0.00– 4.40	0.00– 6.26
1	1.22	0.03– 6.61	0.01– 8.71
2	2.44	0.30– 8.53	0.13– 10.82
3	3.66	0.76– 10.32	0.42– 12.75
4	4.88	1.34– 12.02	0.83– 14.57
5	6.10	2.01– 13.66	1.34– 16.31
6	7.32	2.73– 15.25	1.92– 18.00
7	8.54	3.50– 16.80	2.55– 19.63
8	9.76	4.31– 18.32	3.22– 21.22
9	10.98	5.14– 19.82	3.94– 22.78
10	12.20	6.01– 21.29	4.69– 24.31
11	13.41	6.89– 22.74	5.46– 25.81
12	14.63	7.80– 24.17	6.27– 27.29
13	15.85	8.72– 25.58	7.09– 28.75
14	17.07	9.66– 26.98	7.94– 30.19
15	18.29	10.62– 28.37	8.80– 31.61
16	19.51	11.58– 29.74	9.68– 33.02
17	20.73	12.57– 31.11	10.58– 34.41
18	21.95	13.56– 32.46	11.50– 35.78
19	23.17	14.56– 33.80	12.42– 37.14
20	24.39	15.58– 35.12	13.37– 38.49
21	25.61	16.60– 36.45	14.32– 39.82
22	26.83	17.64– 37.76	15.29– 41.15
23	28.05	18.68– 39.06	16.27– 42.46
24	29.27	19.74– 40.35	17.26– 43.76
25	30.49	20.80– 41.64	18.26– 45.05
26	31.71	21.87– 42.92	19.27– 46.33
27	32.93	22.94– 44.19	20.29– 47.61
28	34.15	24.03– 45.45	21.32– 48.87

N = 82 (continued)

x	$100p_x$	100(1 − 2α) limits 95% $100p_l$ $100p_r$	99% $100p_l$ $100p_r$
29	35.37	25.12– 46.70	22.36– 50.12
30	36.59	26.22– 47.95	23.41– 51.36
31	37.80	27.32– 49.19	24.47– 52.60
32	39.02	28.44– 50.43	25.54– 53.82
33	40.24	29.56– 51.66	26.61– 55.04
34	41.46	30.68– 52.88	27.70– 56.25
35	42.68	31.82– 54.09	28.79– 57.45
36	43.90	32.95– 55.30	29.89– 58.64
37	45.12	34.10– 56.51	31.00– 59.82
38	46.34	35.25– 57.70	32.12– 61.00
39	47.56	36.41– 58.89	33.25– 62.16
40	48.78	37.58– 60.08	34.38– 63.32
41	50.00	38.75– 61.25	35.53– 64.47
42	51.22	39.92– 62.42	36.68– 65.62
43	52.44	41.11– 63.59	37.84– 66.75
44	53.66	42.30– 64.75	39.00– 67.88
45	54.88	43.49– 65.90	40.18– 69.00
46	56.10	44.70– 67.05	41.36– 70.11
47	57.32	45.91– 68.18	42.55– 71.21
48	58.54	47.12– 69.32	43.75– 72.30
49	59.76	48.34– 70.44	44.96– 73.39
50	60.98	49.57– 71.56	46.18– 74.46
51	62.20	50.81– 72.68	47.40– 75.53
52	63.41	52.05– 73.78	48.64– 76.59
53	64.63	53.30– 74.88	49.88– 77.64
54	65.85	54.55– 75.97	51.13– 78.68
55	67.07	55.81– 77.06	52.39– 79.71
56	68.29	57.08– 78.13	53.67– 80.73
57	69.51	58.36– 79.20	54.95– 81.74
58	70.73	59.65– 80.26	56.24– 82.74
59	71.95	60.94– 81.32	57.54– 83.73
60	73.17	62.24– 82.36	58.85– 84.71
61	74.39	63.55– 83.40	60.18– 85.68
62	75.61	64.88– 84.42	61.51– 86.63
63	76.83	66.20– 85.44	62.86– 87.58
64	78.05	67.54– 86.44	64.22– 88.50
65	79.27	68.89– 87.43	65.59– 89.42
66	80.49	70.26– 88.42	66.98– 90.32
67	81.71	71.63– 89.38	68.39– 91.20
68	82.93	73.02– 90.34	69.81– 92.06
69	84.15	74.42– 91.28	71.25– 92.91
70	85.37	75.83– 92.20	72.71– 93.73
71	86.59	77.26– 93.11	74.19– 94.54
72	87.80	78.71– 93.99	75.69– 95.31
73	89.02	80.18– 94.86	77.22– 96.06
74	90.24	81.68– 95.69	78.78– 96.78
75	91.46	83.20– 96.50	80.37– 97.45
76	92.68	84.75– 97.27	82.00– 98.08
77	93.90	86.34– 97.99	83.69– 98.66
78	95.12	87.98– 98.66	85.43– 99.17
79	96.34	89.68– 99.24	87.25– 99.58
80	97.56	91.47– 99.70	89.18– 99.87
81	98.78	93.39– 99.97	91.29– 99.99
82	100.00	95.60–100.00	93.74–100.00

N = 83

x	$100p_x$	100(1 − 2α) limits 95% $100p_l$ $100p_r$	99% $100p_l$ $100p_r$
0	0.00	0.00– 4.35	0.00– 6.18
1	1.20	0.03– 6.53	0.01– 8.61
2	2.41	0.29– 8.43	0.13– 10.70
3	3.61	0.75– 10.20	0.41– 12.61
4	4.82	1.33– 11.88	0.82– 14.41
5	6.02	1.98– 13.50	1.32– 16.13
6	7.23	2.70– 15.07	1.89– 17.79
7	8.43	3.46– 16.61	2.52– 19.41
8	9.64	4.25– 18.11	3.18– 20.98
9	10.84	5.08– 19.59	3.89– 22.53
10	12.05	5.93– 21.04	4.63– 24.04
11	13.25	6.81– 22.48	5.40– 25.53
12	14.46	7.70– 23.89	6.19– 26.99
13	15.66	8.61– 25.29	7.00– 28.43
14	16.87	9.54– 26.68	7.84– 29.86
15	18.07	10.48– 28.05	8.69– 31.26
16	19.28	11.44– 29.41	9.56– 32.65
17	20.48	12.41– 30.76	10.45– 34.03
18	21.69	13.39– 32.09	11.35– 35.39
19	22.89	14.38– 33.42	12.27– 36.74
20	24.10	15.38– 34.73	13.20– 38.07
21	25.30	16.39– 36.04	14.14– 39.39
22	26.51	17.42– 37.34	15.09– 40.70
23	27.71	18.45– 38.62	16.06– 42.00
24	28.92	19.48– 39.91	17.03– 43.29
25	30.12	20.53– 41.18	18.02– 44.57
26	31.33	21.59– 42.44	19.02– 45.84
27	32.53	22.65– 43.70	20.03– 47.10
28	33.73	23.72– 44.95	21.04– 48.35
29	34.94	24.80– 46.19	22.07– 49.59
30	36.14	25.88– 47.43	23.10– 50.82
31	37.35	26.97– 48.66	24.15– 52.04
32	38.55	28.07– 49.88	25.20– 53.26
33	39.76	29.17– 51.10	26.26– 54.46
34	40.96	30.28– 52.31	27.33– 55.66
35	42.17	31.40– 53.51	28.41– 56.85
36	43.37	32.53– 54.71	29.50– 58.03
37	44.58	33.66– 55.90	30.59– 59.20
38	45.78	34.79– 57.08	31.69– 60.37
39	46.99	35.93– 58.26	32.80– 61.53
40	48.19	37.08– 59.44	33.92– 62.68
41	49.40	38.24– 60.60	35.05– 63.82

N = 83 (continued)

x	$100p_x$	100(1 − 2α) limits 95% $100p_l$ $100p_r$	99% $100p_l$ $100p_r$
42	50.60	39.40– 61.76	36.18– 64.95
43	51.81	40.56– 62.92	37.32– 66.08
44	53.01	41.74– 64.07	38.47– 67.20
45	54.22	42.92– 65.21	39.63– 68.31
46	55.42	44.10– 66.34	40.80– 69.41
47	56.63	45.29– 67.47	41.97– 70.50
48	57.83	46.49– 68.60	43.15– 71.59
49	59.04	47.69– 69.72	44.34– 72.67
50	60.24	48.90– 70.83	45.54– 73.74
51	61.45	50.12– 71.93	46.74– 74.80
52	62.65	51.34– 73.03	47.96– 75.85
53	63.86	52.57– 74.12	49.18– 76.90
54	65.06	53.81– 75.20	50.41– 77.93
55	66.27	55.05– 76.28	51.65– 78.96
56	67.47	56.30– 77.35	52.90– 79.97
57	68.67	57.56– 78.41	54.16– 80.98
58	69.88	58.82– 79.47	55.43– 81.98
59	71.08	60.09– 80.52	56.71– 82.97
60	72.29	61.38– 81.55	58.00– 83.94
61	73.49	62.66– 82.58	59.30– 84.91
62	74.70	63.96– 83.61	60.61– 85.86
63	75.90	65.27– 84.62	61.93– 86.80
64	77.11	66.58– 85.62	63.26– 87.73
65	78.31	67.91– 86.61	64.61– 88.65
66	79.52	69.24– 87.59	65.97– 89.55
67	80.72	70.59– 88.56	67.35– 90.44
68	81.93	71.95– 89.52	68.74– 91.31
69	83.13	73.32– 90.46	70.14– 92.16
70	84.34	74.71– 91.39	71.57– 93.00
71	85.54	76.11– 92.30	73.01– 93.81
72	86.75	77.52– 93.19	74.47– 94.60
73	87.95	78.96– 94.07	75.96– 95.37
74	89.16	80.41– 94.92	77.47– 96.11
75	90.36	81.89– 95.75	79.02– 96.82
76	91.57	83.39– 96.54	80.59– 97.48
77	92.77	84.93– 97.30	82.21– 98.11
78	93.98	86.50– 98.02	83.87– 98.68
79	95.18	88.12– 98.67	85.59– 99.18
80	96.39	89.80– 99.25	87.39– 99.59
81	97.59	91.57– 99.71	89.30– 99.87
82	98.80	93.47– 99.97	91.39– 99.99
83	100.00	95.65–100.00	93.82–100.00

N = 84

x	$100p_x$	100(1 − 2α) limits 95% $100p_l$ $100p_r$	99% $100p_l$ $100p_r$
0	0.00	0.00– 4.30	0.00– 6.11
1	1.19	0.03– 6.46	0.01– 8.51
2	2.38	0.29– 8.34	0.12– 10.57
3	3.57	0.74– 10.08	0.41– 12.46
4	4.76	1.31– 11.75	0.81– 14.24
5	5.95	1.96– 13.35	1.31– 15.95
6	7.14	2.67– 14.90	1.87– 17.59
7	8.33	3.42– 16.42	2.49– 19.19
8	9.52	4.20– 17.91	3.15– 20.75
9	10.71	5.02– 19.37	3.84– 22.28
10	11.90	5.86– 20.81	4.57– 23.77
11	13.10	6.72– 22.22	5.33– 25.25
12	14.29	7.61– 23.62	6.11– 26.69
13	15.48	8.51– 25.01	6.91– 28.12
14	16.67	9.42– 26.38	7.74– 29.53
15	17.86	10.35– 27.74	8.58– 30.92
16	19.05	11.30– 29.08	9.44– 32.30
17	20.24	12.25– 30.41	10.32– 33.66
18	21.43	13.22– 31.74	11.21– 35.01
19	22.62	14.20– 33.05	12.11– 36.34
20	23.81	15.19– 34.35	13.03– 37.66
21	25.00	16.19– 35.64	13.96– 38.97
22	26.19	17.20– 36.93	14.90– 40.27
23	27.38	18.21– 38.20	15.85– 41.56
24	28.57	19.24– 39.47	16.82– 42.83
25	29.76	20.27– 40.73	17.79– 44.10
26	30.95	21.31– 41.98	18.77– 45.35
27	32.14	22.36– 43.22	19.77– 46.60
28	33.33	23.42– 44.46	20.77– 47.84
29	34.52	24.48– 45.69	21.78– 49.07
30	35.71	25.55– 46.92	22.81– 50.29
31	36.90	26.63– 48.13	23.84– 51.50
32	38.10	27.71– 49.34	24.87– 52.70
33	39.29	28.80– 50.55	25.92– 53.90
34	40.48	29.90– 51.75	26.98– 55.09
35	41.67	31.00– 52.94	28.04– 56.27
36	42.86	32.11– 54.12	29.11– 57.44
37	44.05	33.22– 55.30	30.19– 58.60
38	45.24	34.34– 56.48	31.28– 59.76
39	46.43	35.47– 57.65	32.37– 60.90
40	47.62	36.60– 58.81	33.47– 62.04
41	48.81	37.74– 59.96	34.58– 63.18
42	50.00	38.88– 61.12	35.70– 64.30
43	51.19	40.04– 62.26	36.82– 65.42
44	52.38	41.19– 63.40	37.96– 66.53
45	53.57	42.35– 64.53	39.10– 67.63
46	54.76	43.52– 65.66	40.24– 68.72
47	55.95	44.70– 66.78	41.40– 69.81
48	57.14	45.88– 67.89	42.56– 70.89
49	58.33	47.06– 69.00	43.73– 71.96
50	59.52	48.25– 70.10	44.91– 73.02
51	60.71	49.45– 71.20	46.10– 74.08
52	61.90	50.66– 72.29	47.30– 75.13
53	63.10	51.87– 73.37	48.50– 76.16

N = 84 (continued)

x	$100p_x$	100(1 − 2α) limits 95% $100p_l$ $100p_r$	99% $100p_l$ $100p_r$
54	64.29	53.08– 74.45	49.71– 77.19
55	65.48	54.31– 75.52	50.93– 78.22
56	66.67	55.54– 76.58	52.16– 79.23
57	67.86	56.78– 77.64	53.40– 80.23
58	69.05	58.02– 78.69	54.65– 81.23
59	70.24	59.27– 79.73	55.90– 82.21
60	71.43	60.53– 80.76	57.17– 83.18
61	72.62	61.80– 81.79	58.44– 84.15
62	73.81	63.07– 82.80	59.73– 85.10
63	75.00	64.36– 83.81	61.03– 86.04
64	76.19	65.65– 84.81	62.34– 86.97
65	77.38	66.95– 85.80	63.66– 87.89
66	78.57	68.26– 86.78	64.99– 88.79
67	79.76	69.59– 87.75	66.34– 89.68
68	80.95	70.92– 88.70	67.70– 90.56
69	82.14	72.26– 89.65	69.08– 91.42
70	83.33	73.62– 90.58	70.47– 92.26
71	84.52	74.99– 91.49	71.88– 93.09
72	85.71	76.38– 92.39	73.31– 93.89
73	86.90	77.78– 93.28	74.75– 94.67
74	88.10	79.19– 94.14	76.23– 95.43
75	89.29	80.63– 94.98	77.72– 96.16
76	90.48	82.09– 95.80	79.25– 96.85
77	91.67	83.58– 96.58	80.81– 97.51
78	92.86	85.10– 97.33	82.41– 98.13
79	94.05	86.65– 98.04	84.05– 98.69
80	95.24	88.25– 98.69	85.76– 99.19
81	96.43	89.92– 99.26	87.54– 99.59
82	97.62	91.66– 99.71	89.43– 99.88
83	98.81	93.54– 99.97	91.49– 99.99
84	100.00	95.70–100.00	93.89–100.00

N = 85

x	$100p_x$	100(1 − 2α) limits 95% $100p_l$ $100p_r$	99% $100p_l$ $100p_r$
0	0.00	0.00– 4.25	0.00– 6.04
1	1.18	0.03– 6.38	0.01– 8.42
2	2.35	0.29– 8.24	0.12– 10.45
3	3.53	0.74– 9.97	0.40– 12.32
4	4.71	1.30– 11.61	0.80– 14.08
5	5.88	1.94– 13.20	1.29– 15.77
6	7.06	2.64– 14.73	1.85– 17.40
7	8.24	3.38– 16.23	2.46– 18.98
8	9.41	4.15– 17.71	3.11– 20.52
9	10.59	4.96– 19.15	3.80– 22.03
10	11.76	5.79– 20.57	4.52– 23.51
11	12.94	6.64– 21.98	5.26– 24.97
12	14.12	7.51– 23.36	6.04– 26.40
13	15.29	8.40– 24.73	6.83– 27.82
14	16.47	9.31– 26.09	7.64– 29.21
15	17.65	10.23– 27.43	8.48– 30.59
16	18.82	11.16– 28.76	9.33– 31.95
17	20.00	12.10– 30.08	10.19– 33.30
18	21.18	13.06– 31.39	11.07– 34.63
19	22.35	14.03– 32.69	11.96– 35.95
20	23.53	15.00– 33.97	12.87– 37.26
21	24.71	15.99– 35.25	13.78– 38.56
22	25.88	16.99– 36.52	14.71– 39.84
23	27.06	17.99– 37.79	15.65– 41.12
24	28.24	19.00– 39.04	16.61– 42.38
25	29.41	20.02– 40.29	17.57– 43.63
26	30.59	21.05– 41.53	18.54– 44.88
27	31.76	22.08– 42.76	19.52– 46.12
28	32.94	23.13– 43.98	20.51– 47.34
29	34.12	24.18– 45.20	21.51– 48.56
30	35.29	25.23– 46.41	22.51– 49.77
31	36.47	26.29– 47.62	23.53– 50.97
32	37.65	27.36– 48.82	24.55– 52.16
33	38.82	28.44– 50.01	25.59– 53.35
34	40.00	29.52– 51.20	26.63– 54.52
35	41.18	30.61– 52.38	27.68– 55.69
36	42.35	31.70– 53.55	28.73– 56.85
37	43.53	32.80– 54.72	29.80– 58.01
38	44.71	33.91– 55.89	30.87– 59.15
39	45.88	35.02– 57.04	31.95– 60.29
40	47.06	36.13– 58.19	33.03– 61.42
41	48.24	37.26– 59.34	34.13– 62.55
42	49.41	38.39– 60.48	35.23– 63.66
43	50.59	39.52– 61.61	36.34– 64.77
44	51.76	40.66– 62.74	37.45– 65.87
45	52.94	41.81– 63.87	38.58– 66.97
46	54.12	42.96– 64.98	39.71– 68.05
47	55.29	44.11– 66.09	40.85– 69.13
48	56.47	45.28– 67.20	41.99– 70.20
49	57.65	46.45– 68.30	43.15– 71.27
50	58.82	47.62– 69.39	44.31– 72.32
51	60.00	48.80– 70.48	45.48– 73.37
52	61.18	49.99– 71.56	46.65– 74.41
53	62.35	51.18– 72.64	47.84– 75.45
54	63.53	52.38– 73.71	49.03– 76.47
55	64.71	53.59– 74.77	50.23– 77.49
56	65.88	54.80– 75.82	51.44– 78.49
57	67.06	56.02– 76.87	52.66– 79.49
58	68.24	57.24– 77.92	53.88– 80.48
59	69.41	58.47– 78.95	55.12– 81.46
60	70.59	59.71– 79.98	56.37– 82.43
61	71.76	60.96– 81.00	57.62– 83.39
62	72.94	62.21– 82.01	58.88– 84.35
63	74.12	63.48– 83.01	60.16– 85.29
64	75.29	64.75– 84.01	61.44– 86.22

N = number of trials, x = number of successes, etc., $100\,p_x = 100\,x/N$

$N = 85$ (continued)

x	$100p_x$	95% $100p_l$	95% $100p_u$	99% $100p_l$	99% $100p_u$
65	76.47	66.03-	85.00	62.74-	87.13
66	77.65	67.31-	85.97	64.05-	88.04
67	78.82	68.61-	86.94	65.37-	88.93
68	80.00	69.92-	87.90	66.70-	89.81
69	81.18	71.24-	88.84	68.05-	90.67
70	82.35	72.57-	89.77	69.41-	91.52
71	83.53	73.91-	90.69	70.79-	92.36
72	84.71	75.27-	91.60	72.18-	93.17
73	85.88	76.64-	92.49	73.60-	93.96
74	87.06	78.02-	93.36	75.03-	94.74
75	88.24	79.43-	94.21	76.49-	95.48
76	89.41	80.85-	95.04	77.97-	96.20
77	90.59	82.29-	95.85	79.48-	96.89
78	91.76	83.77-	96.62	81.02-	97.54
79	92.94	85.27-	97.36	82.60-	98.15
80	94.12	86.80-	98.06	84.23-	98.71
81	95.29	88.39-	98.70	85.92-	99.20
82	96.47	90.03-	99.26	87.68-	99.60
83	97.65	91.76-	99.71	89.55-	99.88
84	98.82	93.62-	99.97	91.58-	99.99
85	100.00	95.75-	100.00	93.96-	100.00

$N = 86$

x	$100p_x$	95% $100p_l$	95% $100p_u$	99% $100p_l$	99% $100p_u$
0	0.00	0.00-	4.20	0.00-	5.97
1	1.16	0.03-	6.31	0.01-	8.32
2	2.33	0.28-	8.15	0.12-	10.34
3	3.49	0.73-	9.86	0.40-	12.19
4	4.65	1.28-	11.48	0.79-	13.93
5	5.81	1.91-	13.05	1.28-	15.60
6	6.98	2.60-	14.57	1.82-	17.21
7	8.14	3.34-	16.05	2.43-	18.77
8	9.30	4.10-	17.51	3.07-	20.30
9	10.47	4.90-	18.94	3.75-	21.79
10	11.63	5.72-	20.35	4.46-	23.26
11	12.79	6.56-	21.73	5.20-	24.70
12	13.95	7.42-	23.11	5.96-	26.12
13	15.12	8.30-	24.46	6.75-	27.52
14	16.28	9.20-	25.80	7.55-	28.90
15	17.44	10.10-	27.13	8.37-	30.26
16	18.60	11.02-	28.45	9.21-	31.61
17	19.77	11.96-	29.75	10.07-	32.94
18	20.93	12.90-	31.05	10.93-	34.27
19	22.09	13.86-	32.33	11.81-	35.57
20	23.26	14.82-	33.61	12.71-	36.87
21	24.42	15.80-	34.87	13.61-	38.15
22	25.58	16.78-	36.13	14.53-	39.42
23	26.74	17.77-	37.38	15.46-	40.69
24	27.91	18.77-	38.62	16.40-	41.94
25	29.07	19.78-	39.86	17.35-	43.18
26	30.23	20.79-	41.08	18.31-	44.41
27	31.40	21.81-	42.30	19.27-	45.64
28	32.56	22.84-	43.52	20.25-	46.85
29	33.72	23.88-	44.72	21.24-	48.06
30	34.88	24.92-	45.92	22.23-	49.26
31	36.05	25.97-	47.12	23.23-	50.45
32	37.21	27.02-	48.30	24.24-	51.63
33	38.37	28.08-	49.49	25.26-	52.80
34	39.53	29.15-	50.66	26.29-	53.97
35	40.70	30.22-	51.83	27.32-	55.13
36	41.86	31.30-	52.99	28.37-	56.28
37	43.02	32.39-	54.15	29.41-	57.43
38	44.19	33.48-	55.30	30.47-	58.56
39	45.35	34.58-	56.45	31.54-	59.69
40	46.51	35.68-	57.59	32.61-	60.81
41	47.67	36.79-	58.73	33.69-	61.93
42	48.84	37.90-	59.86	34.77-	63.03
43	50.00	39.02-	60.98	35.86-	64.14
44	51.16	40.14-	62.10	36.97-	65.23
45	52.33	41.27-	63.21	38.07-	66.31
46	53.49	42.41-	64.32	39.19-	67.39
47	54.65	43.55-	65.42	40.31-	68.46
48	55.81	44.70-	66.52	41.44-	69.53
49	56.98	45.85-	67.61	42.57-	70.59
50	58.14	47.01-	68.70	43.72-	71.63
51	59.30	48.17-	69.78	44.87-	72.68
52	60.47	49.34-	70.85	46.03-	73.71
53	61.63	50.51-	71.92	47.20-	74.74
54	62.79	51.70-	72.98	48.37-	75.76
55	63.95	52.88-	74.03	49.55-	76.77
56	65.12	54.08-	75.08	50.74-	77.77
57	66.28	55.28-	76.12	51.94-	78.76
58	67.44	56.48-	77.16	53.15-	79.75
59	68.60	57.70-	78.19	54.36-	80.73
60	69.77	58.92-	79.21	55.59-	81.69
61	70.93	60.14-	80.22	56.82-	82.65
62	72.09	61.38-	81.23	58.06-	83.60
63	73.26	62.62-	82.23	59.31-	84.54
64	74.42	63.87-	83.22	60.58-	85.47
65	75.58	65.13-	84.20	61.85-	86.39
66	76.74	66.39-	85.18	63.13-	87.29
67	77.91	67.67-	86.14	64.43-	88.19
68	79.07	68.95-	87.10	65.73-	89.07
69	80.23	70.25-	88.04	67.06-	89.93
70	81.40	71.55-	88.98	68.39-	90.79
71	82.56	72.87-	89.90	69.74-	91.63
72	83.72	74.20-	90.80	71.10-	92.45
73	84.88	75.54-	91.70	72.48-	93.25
74	86.05	76.89-	92.58	73.88-	94.04
75	87.21	78.27-	93.44	75.30-	94.80
76	88.37	79.65-	94.28	76.74-	95.54
77	89.53	81.06-	95.10	78.21-	96.25
78	90.70	82.49-	95.90	79.70-	96.93
79	91.86	83.95-	96.66	81.23-	97.57
80	93.02	85.43-	97.40	82.79-	98.18
81	94.19	86.95-	98.09	84.40-	98.72
82	95.35	88.52-	98.72	86.07-	99.21
83	96.51	90.14-	99.27	87.81-	99.60
84	97.67	91.85-	99.72	89.66-	99.88
85	98.84	93.69-	99.97	91.68-	99.99
86	100.00	95.80-	100.00	94.03-	100.00

$N = 87$

x	$100p_x$	95% $100p_l$	95% $100p_u$	99% $100p_l$	99% $100p_u$
0	0.00	0.00-	4.15	0.00-	5.91
1	1.15	0.03-	6.24	0.01-	8.23
2	2.30	0.28-	8.06	0.12-	10.22
3	3.45	0.72-	9.75	0.39-	12.05
4	4.60	1.27-	11.36	0.78-	13.78
5	5.75	1.89-	12.90	1.26-	15.43
6	6.90	2.57-	14.41	1.80-	17.02
7	8.05	3.30-	15.88	2.40-	18.57
8	9.20	4.05-	17.32	3.03-	20.08
9	10.34	4.84-	18.73	3.71-	21.56
10	11.49	5.65-	20.12	4.41-	23.01
11	12.64	6.48-	21.50	5.14-	24.44
12	13.79	7.34-	22.85	5.89-	25.84
13	14.94	8.20-	24.20	6.67-	27.23
14	16.09	9.09-	25.52	7.46-	28.59
15	17.24	9.98-	26.84	8.27-	29.94
16	18.39	10.89-	28.14	9.10-	31.28
17	19.54	11.81-	29.43	9.94-	32.60
18	20.69	12.75-	30.71	10.80-	33.91
19	21.84	13.69-	31.98	11.67-	35.20
20	22.99	14.64-	33.25	12.55-	36.48
21	24.14	15.60-	34.50	13.45-	37.75
22	25.29	16.58-	35.75	14.35-	39.02
23	26.44	17.55-	36.98	15.27-	40.27
24	27.59	18.54-	38.21	16.20-	41.51
25	28.74	19.54-	39.43	17.13-	42.74
26	29.89	20.54-	40.65	18.08-	43.96
27	31.03	21.55-	41.86	19.04-	45.17
28	32.18	22.56-	43.06	20.00-	46.38
29	33.33	23.58-	44.25	20.97-	47.57
30	34.48	24.61-	45.44	21.95-	48.76
31	35.63	25.65-	46.62	22.94-	49.94
32	36.78	26.69-	47.80	23.94-	51.11
33	37.93	27.74-	48.97	24.95-	52.27
34	39.08	28.79-	50.13	25.96-	53.43
35	40.23	29.85-	51.29	26.98-	54.58
36	41.38	30.92-	52.45	28.01-	55.72
37	42.53	31.99-	53.59	29.04-	56.85
38	43.68	33.06-	54.74	30.09-	57.98
39	44.83	34.15-	55.87	31.13-	59.10
40	45.98	35.23-	57.00	32.19-	60.21
41	47.13	36.33-	58.13	33.26-	61.32
42	48.28	37.42-	59.25	34.33-	62.42
43	49.43	38.53-	60.36	35.40-	63.51
44	50.57	39.64-	61.47	36.49-	64.60
45	51.72	40.75-	62.58	37.58-	65.67
46	52.87	41.87-	63.67	38.68-	66.74
47	54.02	43.00-	64.77	39.79-	67.81
48	55.17	44.13-	65.85	40.90-	68.87
49	56.32	45.26-	66.94	42.02-	69.91
50	57.47	46.41-	68.01	43.15-	70.96
51	58.62	47.55-	69.08	44.28-	71.99
52	59.77	48.71-	70.15	45.42-	73.02
53	60.92	49.87-	71.21	46.57-	74.04
54	62.07	51.03-	72.26	47.73-	75.05
55	63.22	52.20-	73.31	48.89-	76.06
56	64.37	53.38-	74.35	50.06-	77.06
57	65.52	54.56-	75.39	51.24-	78.05
58	66.67	55.75-	76.42	52.43-	79.03
59	67.82	56.94-	77.44	53.62-	80.00
60	68.97	58.14-	78.45	54.83-	80.96
61	70.11	59.35-	79.46	56.04-	81.92
62	71.26	60.57-	80.46	57.26-	82.87
63	72.41	61.79-	81.46	58.49-	83.80
64	73.56	63.02-	82.45	59.73-	84.73
65	74.71	64.25-	83.42	60.98-	85.65
66	75.86	65.50-	84.40	62.25-	86.55
67	77.01	66.75-	85.36	63.52-	87.45
68	78.16	68.02-	86.31	64.80-	88.33
69	79.31	69.29-	87.25	66.09-	89.20
70	80.46	70.57-	88.19	67.40-	90.06
71	81.61	71.86-	89.11	68.72-	90.90
72	82.76	73.16-	90.02	70.06-	91.73
73	83.91	74.48-	90.91	71.41-	92.54
74	85.06	75.80-	91.80	72.77-	93.33
75	86.21	77.15-	92.66	74.16-	94.11
76	87.36	78.50-	93.52	75.56-	94.86
77	88.51	79.88-	94.35	76.99-	95.59
78	89.66	81.27-	95.16	78.44-	96.29
79	90.80	82.68-	95.95	79.92-	96.97
80	91.95	84.12-	96.70	81.43-	97.60
81	93.10	85.59-	97.43	82.98-	98.20
82	94.25	87.10-	98.11	84.57-	98.74
83	95.40	88.64-	98.73	86.22-	99.22
84	96.55	90.25-	99.28	87.95-	99.61
85	97.70	91.94-	99.72	89.78-	99.88
86	98.85	93.76-	99.97	91.77-	99.99
87	100.00	95.85-	100.00	94.09-	100.00

$N = 88$

x	$100p_x$	95% $100p_l$	95% $100p_u$	99% $100p_l$	99% $100p_u$
0	0.00	0.00-	4.11	0.00-	5.84
1	1.14	0.03-	6.17	0.01-	8.14
2	2.27	0.28-	7.97	0.12-	10.11
3	3.41	0.71-	9.64	0.39-	11.92
4	4.55	1.25-	11.23	0.77-	13.63
5	5.68	1.87-	12.76	1.25-	15.26
6	6.82	2.54-	14.25	1.78-	16.84
7	7.95	3.26-	15.70	2.37-	18.37
8	9.09	4.01-	17.13	3.00-	19.87
9	10.23	4.78-	18.53	3.66-	21.33
10	11.36	5.59-	19.91	4.36-	22.77
11	12.50	6.41-	21.27	5.08-	24.18
12	13.64	7.25-	22.61	5.82-	25.57
13	14.77	8.11-	23.94	6.59-	26.94
14	15.91	8.98-	25.25	7.37-	28.29
15	17.05	9.87-	26.55	8.17-	29.63
16	18.18	10.76-	27.84	8.99-	30.95
17	19.32	11.68-	29.12	9.82-	32.26
18	20.45	12.60-	30.39	10.67-	33.55
19	21.59	13.53-	31.65	11.53-	34.84
20	22.73	14.47-	32.89	12.40-	36.11
21	23.86	15.42-	34.14	13.29-	37.37
22	25.00	16.38-	35.37	14.18-	38.61
23	26.14	17.34-	36.59	15.09-	39.85
24	27.27	18.32-	37.81	16.00-	41.08
25	28.41	19.30-	39.02	16.93-	42.30
26	29.55	20.29-	40.22	17.86-	43.51
27	30.68	21.29-	41.42	18.80-	44.71
28	31.82	22.29-	42.61	19.76-	45.91
29	32.95	23.30-	43.79	20.72-	47.09
30	34.09	24.32-	44.97	21.68-	48.27
31	35.23	25.34-	46.14	22.66-	49.44
32	36.36	26.37-	47.31	23.65-	50.60
33	37.50	27.40-	48.47	24.64-	51.75
34	38.64	28.44-	49.62	25.64-	52.90
35	39.77	29.49-	50.77	26.64-	54.04
36	40.91	30.54-	51.91	27.66-	55.17
37	42.05	31.60-	53.05	28.68-	56.29
38	43.18	32.66-	54.18	29.71-	57.41
39	44.32	33.73-	55.30	30.74-	58.52
40	45.45	34.80-	56.42	31.79-	59.63
41	46.59	35.88-	57.54	32.84-	60.72
42	47.73	36.96-	58.65	33.89-	61.81
43	48.86	38.05-	59.75	34.96-	62.90
44	50.00	39.15-	60.85	36.03-	63.97
45	51.14	40.25-	61.95	37.10-	65.04
46	52.27	41.35-	63.04	38.19-	66.11
47	53.41	42.46-	64.12	39.28-	67.16
48	54.55	43.58-	65.20	40.37-	68.21
49	55.68	44.70-	66.27	41.48-	69.26
50	56.82	45.82-	67.34	42.59-	70.29
51	57.95	46.95-	68.40	43.71-	71.32
52	59.09	48.09-	69.46	44.83-	72.34
53	60.23	49.23-	70.51	45.96-	73.36
54	61.36	50.38-	71.56	47.10-	74.36
55	62.50	51.53-	72.60	48.25-	75.36
56	63.64	52.69-	73.63	49.40-	76.35
57	64.77	53.86-	74.66	50.56-	77.34
58	65.91	55.03-	75.68	51.73-	78.32
59	67.05	56.21-	76.70	52.91-	79.28
60	68.18	57.39-	77.71	54.09-	80.24
61	69.32	58.58-	78.71	55.29-	81.20
62	70.45	59.78-	79.71	56.49-	82.14
63	71.59	60.98-	80.70	57.70-	83.07
64	72.73	62.19-	81.68	58.92-	84.00
65	73.86	63.41-	82.66	60.15-	84.91
66	75.00	64.63-	83.62	61.39-	85.82
67	76.14	65.86-	84.58	62.63-	86.71
68	77.27	67.11-	85.53	63.89-	87.60
69	78.41	68.35-	86.47	65.16-	88.47
70	79.55	69.61-	87.40	66.45-	89.33
71	80.68	70.88-	88.32	67.74-	90.18
72	81.82	72.16-	89.24	69.05-	91.01
73	82.95	73.45-	90.13	70.37-	91.83
74	84.09	74.75-	91.02	71.71-	92.63
75	85.23	76.06-	91.89	73.06-	93.41
76	86.36	77.39-	92.75	74.43-	94.18
77	87.50	78.73-	93.59	75.82-	94.92
78	88.64	80.09-	94.41	77.23-	95.64
79	89.77	81.47-	95.22	78.67-	96.34
80	90.91	82.87-	95.99	80.13-	97.00
81	92.05	84.30-	96.74	81.63-	97.63
82	93.18	85.75-	97.46	83.16-	98.22
83	94.32	87.24-	98.13	84.74-	98.75
84	95.45	88.77-	98.75	86.37-	99.23
85	96.59	90.36-	99.29	88.08-	99.61
86	97.73	92.03-	99.72	89.89-	99.88
87	98.86	93.83-	99.97	91.86-	99.99
88	100.00	95.89-	100.00	94.16-	100.00

$N = 89$

x	$100p_x$	95% $100p_l$	95% $100p_u$	99% $100p_l$	99% $100p_u$
0	0.00	0.00-	4.06	0.00-	5.78
1	1.12	0.03-	6.10	0.01-	8.05
2	2.25	0.27-	7.88	0.12-	10.00
3	3.37	0.70-	9.54	0.38-	11.79
4	4.49	1.24-	11.11	0.77-	13.48
5	5.62	1.85-	12.63	1.23-	15.10
6	6.74	2.51-	14.10	1.76-	16.66
7	7.87	3.22-	15.54	2.34-	18.18
8	8.99	3.96-	16.95	2.96-	19.66
9	10.11	4.73-	18.33	3.62-	21.11
10	11.24	5.52-	19.69	4.31-	22.53
11	12.36	6.33-	21.04	5.02-	23.92
12	13.48	7.17-	22.37	5.75-	25.30
13	14.61	8.01-	23.68	6.51-	26.66
14	15.73	8.88-	24.98	7.29-	28.00
15	16.85	9.75-	26.27	8.08-	29.32
16	17.98	10.64-	27.55	8.89-	30.63
17	19.10	11.54-	28.81	9.71-	31.93
18	20.22	12.45-	30.07	10.55-	33.21
19	21.35	13.37-	31.31	11.39-	34.48
20	22.47	14.30-	32.55	12.26-	35.74
21	23.60	15.24-	33.78	13.13-	36.99
22	24.72	16.19-	35.00	14.01-	38.22
23	25.84	17.14-	36.21	14.91-	39.45
24	26.97	18.10-	37.42	15.81-	40.67
25	28.09	19.07-	38.62	16.72-	41.87
26	29.21	20.05-	39.81	17.65-	43.07
27	30.34	21.03-	40.99	18.58-	44.27
28	31.46	22.03-	42.17	19.52-	45.45
29	32.58	23.02-	43.34	20.47-	46.62
30	33.71	24.03-	44.51	21.42-	47.79
31	34.83	25.04-	45.67	22.39-	48.95
32	35.96	26.05-	46.82	23.36-	50.10
33	37.08	27.07-	47.97	24.34-	51.24
34	38.20	28.10-	49.11	25.32-	52.38
35	39.33	29.13-	50.25	26.32-	53.51
36	40.45	30.17-	51.38	27.32-	54.63
37	41.57	31.21-	52.51	28.33-	55.75
38	42.70	32.26-	53.63	29.34-	56.85
39	43.82	33.32-	54.75	30.36-	57.96
40	44.94	34.38-	55.86	31.39-	59.05
41	46.07	35.44-	56.96	32.43-	60.14
42	47.19	36.51-	58.06	33.47-	61.22
43	48.31	37.59-	59.16	34.52-	62.30
44	49.44	38.67-	60.25	35.57-	63.36
45	50.56	39.75-	61.33	36.64-	64.43
46	51.69	40.84-	62.41	37.70-	65.48
47	52.81	41.94-	63.49	38.78-	66.53
48	53.93	43.04-	64.56	39.86-	67.57
49	55.06	44.14-	65.62	40.95-	68.61
50	56.18	45.25-	66.68	42.04-	69.64
51	57.30	46.37-	67.74	43.15-	70.66
52	58.43	47.49-	68.79	44.25-	71.67
53	59.55	48.62-	69.83	45.37-	72.68
54	60.67	49.75-	70.87	46.49-	73.68
55	61.80	50.89-	71.90	47.62-	74.68
56	62.92	52.03-	72.93	48.76-	75.66
57	64.04	53.18-	73.95	49.90-	76.64
58	65.17	54.33-	74.96	51.05-	77.61
59	66.29	55.49-	75.97	52.21-	78.58
60	67.42	56.66-	76.98	53.38-	79.53
61	68.54	57.83-	77.97	54.55-	80.48
62	69.66	59.01-	78.97	55.73-	81.42
63	70.79	60.19-	79.95	56.93-	82.35
64	71.91	61.38-	80.93	58.13-	83.28
65	73.03	62.58-	81.90	59.33-	84.19
66	74.16	63.79-	82.86	60.55-	85.09
67	75.28	65.00-	83.81	61.78-	85.99
68	76.40	66.22-	84.76	63.01-	86.87
69	77.53	67.45-	85.70	64.26-	87.74
70	78.65	68.69-	86.63	65.52-	88.61
71	79.78	69.93-	87.55	66.79-	89.45
72	80.90	71.19-	88.46	68.07-	90.29
73	82.02	72.45-	89.36	69.37-	91.11
74	83.15	73.73-	90.25	70.68-	91.92
75	84.27	75.02-	91.12	72.00-	92.71
76	85.39	76.32-	91.99	73.34-	93.49
77	86.52	77.63-	92.83	74.70-	94.25
78	87.64	78.96-	93.67	76.08-	94.98
79	88.76	80.31-	94.48	77.47-	95.69
80	89.89	81.67-	95.27	78.89-	96.38
81	91.01	83.05-	96.04	80.34-	97.04
82	92.13	84.46-	96.78	81.82-	97.66
83	93.26	85.90-	97.49	83.34-	98.24
84	94.38	87.37-	98.15	84.90-	98.77
85	95.51	88.89-	98.76	86.52-	99.23
86	96.63	90.46-	99.30	88.21-	99.62
87	97.75	92.12-	99.73	90.00-	99.88
88	98.88	93.90-	99.97	91.95-	99.99
89	100.00	95.94-	100.00	94.22-	100.00

$N = 90$

x	$100p_x$	95% $100p_l$	95% $100p_u$	99% $100p_l$	99% $100p_u$
0	0.00	0.00-	4.02	0.00-	5.72
1	1.11	0.03-	6.04	0.01-	7.97
2	2.22	0.27-	7.80	0.12-	9.90
3	3.33	0.69-	9.43	0.38-	11.67
4	4.44	1.22-	10.99	0.76-	13.34
5	5.56	1.83-	12.49	1.22-	14.94
6	6.67	2.49-	13.95	1.74-	16.48
7	7.78	3.18-	15.37	2.32-	17.99
8	8.89	3.92-	16.77	2.93-	19.45

N = number of trials, x = number of successes, etc., $100\,p_x = 100\,x/N$

N = 90 (continued)

x	$100p_x$	100(1 − 2α) limits 95% $100p_l$	95% $100p_r$	99% $100p_l$	99% $100p_r$
9	10.00	4.68	18.14	3.58	20.89
10	11.11	5.46	19.49	4.26	22.29
11	12.22	6.26	20.82	4.96	23.68
12	13.33	7.08	22.13	5.69	25.04
13	14.44	7.92	23.43	6.44	26.38
14	15.56	8.77	24.72	7.20	27.71
15	16.67	9.64	26.00	7.98	29.02
16	17.78	10.52	27.26	8.78	30.32
17	18.89	11.41	28.51	9.60	31.60
18	20.00	12.31	29.75	10.42	32.87
19	21.11	13.22	30.99	11.26	34.13
20	22.22	14.13	32.21	12.11	35.38
21	23.33	15.06	33.43	12.97	36.61
22	24.44	16.00	34.64	13.85	37.84
23	25.56	16.94	35.84	14.73	39.05
24	26.67	17.89	37.03	15.62	40.26
25	27.78	18.85	38.22	16.53	41.46
26	28.89	19.82	39.40	17.44	42.65
27	30.00	20.79	40.57	18.36	43.83
28	31.11	21.77	41.74	19.28	45.00
29	32.22	22.75	42.90	20.22	46.16
30	33.33	23.74	44.05	21.16	47.32
31	34.44	24.74	45.20	22.12	48.47
32	35.56	25.74	46.35	23.08	49.61
33	36.67	26.75	47.49	24.04	50.74
34	37.78	27.77	48.62	25.02	51.87
35	38.89	28.79	49.74	26.00	52.99
36	40.00	29.81	50.87	26.99	54.10
37	41.11	30.84	51.98	27.98	55.21
38	42.22	31.88	53.09	28.98	56.31
39	43.33	32.92	54.20	29.99	57.40
40	44.44	33.96	55.30	31.01	58.49
41	45.56	35.02	56.40	32.03	59.57
42	46.67	36.07	57.49	33.06	60.64
43	47.78	37.13	58.57	34.09	61.71
44	48.89	38.20	59.65	35.13	62.77
45	50.00	39.27	60.73	36.18	63.82
46	51.11	40.35	61.80	37.23	64.87
47	52.22	41.43	62.87	38.29	65.91
48	53.33	42.51	63.93	39.36	66.94
49	54.44	43.60	64.98	40.43	67.97
50	55.56	44.70	66.04	41.51	68.99
51	56.67	45.80	67.08	42.60	70.01
52	57.78	46.91	68.12	43.69	71.02
53	58.89	48.02	69.16	44.79	72.02
54	60.00	49.13	70.19	45.90	73.01
55	61.11	50.26	71.21	47.01	74.00
56	62.22	51.38	72.23	48.13	74.98
57	63.33	52.51	73.25	49.26	75.96
58	64.44	53.65	74.26	50.39	76.92
59	65.56	54.80	75.26	51.53	77.88
60	66.67	55.95	76.26	52.68	78.84
61	67.78	57.10	77.25	53.84	79.78
62	68.89	58.26	78.23	55.00	80.72
63	70.00	59.43	79.21	56.17	81.64
64	71.11	60.60	80.18	57.35	82.56
65	72.22	61.78	81.15	58.54	83.47
66	73.33	62.97	82.11	59.74	84.38
67	74.44	64.16	83.06	60.95	85.27
68	75.56	65.36	84.00	62.16	86.15
69	76.67	66.57	84.94	63.39	87.03
70	77.78	67.79	85.87	64.62	87.89
71	78.89	69.01	86.78	65.87	88.74
72	80.00	70.25	87.69	67.13	89.58
73	81.11	71.49	88.59	68.40	90.40
74	82.22	72.74	89.48	69.68	91.22
75	83.33	74.00	90.36	70.98	92.02
76	84.44	75.28	91.23	72.29	92.80
77	85.56	76.57	92.08	73.62	93.56
78	86.67	77.87	92.92	74.96	94.31
79	87.78	79.18	93.74	76.32	95.04
80	88.89	80.51	94.54	77.71	95.74
81	90.00	81.86	95.32	79.11	96.42
82	91.11	83.23	96.08	80.55	97.07
83	92.22	84.63	96.82	82.01	97.68
84	93.33	86.05	97.51	83.52	98.26
85	94.44	87.51	98.17	85.06	98.78
86	95.56	89.01	98.78	86.66	99.24
87	96.67	90.57	99.31	88.33	99.62
88	97.78	92.20	99.73	90.10	99.88
89	98.89	93.96	99.97	92.03	99.99
90	100.00	95.98	100.00	94.28	100.00

N = 91

x	$100p_x$	95% $100p_l$	95% $100p_r$	99% $100p_l$	99% $100p_r$
0	0.00	0.00	3.97	0.00	5.66
1	1.10	0.03	5.97	0.01	7.88
2	2.20	0.27	7.71	0.11	9.79
3	3.30	0.69	9.33	0.38	11.55
4	4.40	1.21	10.87	0.75	13.20
5	5.49	1.81	12.36	1.20	14.78
6	6.59	2.46	13.80	1.72	16.31
7	7.69	3.15	15.21	2.29	17.80
8	8.79	3.87	16.59	2.90	19.25
9	9.89	4.62	17.95	3.54	20.67
10	10.99	5.40	19.28	4.21	22.06
11	12.09	6.19	20.60	4.91	23.43
12	13.19	7.00	21.90	5.62	24.78
13	14.29	7.83	23.19	6.36	26.12

N = 91 (continued)

x	$100p_x$	95% $100p_l$	95% $100p_r$	99% $100p_l$	99% $100p_r$
14	15.38	8.67	24.46	7.12	27.43
15	16.48	9.53	25.73	7.89	28.73
16	17.58	10.40	26.98	8.68	30.01
17	18.68	11.28	28.22	9.49	31.28
18	19.78	12.17	29.45	10.30	32.54
19	20.88	13.06	30.67	11.13	33.79
20	21.98	13.97	31.88	11.97	35.02
21	23.08	14.89	33.09	12.82	36.25
22	24.18	15.81	34.28	13.69	37.46
23	25.27	16.75	35.47	14.56	38.66
24	26.37	17.69	36.65	15.44	39.86
25	27.47	18.63	37.83	16.33	41.05
26	28.57	19.59	39.00	17.23	42.22
27	29.67	20.55	40.16	18.14	43.39
28	30.77	21.51	41.32	19.06	44.56
29	31.87	22.49	42.47	19.98	45.71
30	32.97	23.47	43.61	20.91	46.85
31	34.07	24.45	44.75	21.85	47.99
32	35.16	25.44	45.88	22.80	49.12
33	36.26	26.44	47.01	23.76	50.25
34	37.36	27.44	48.13	24.72	51.37
35	38.46	28.45	49.25	25.69	52.48
36	39.56	29.46	50.36	26.66	53.58
37	40.66	30.48	51.47	27.65	54.68
38	41.76	31.50	52.57	28.63	55.77
39	42.86	32.53	53.66	29.63	56.85
40	43.96	33.56	54.75	30.63	57.93
41	45.05	34.60	55.84	31.64	59.00
42	46.15	35.64	56.92	32.65	60.07
43	47.25	36.69	58.00	33.68	61.12
44	48.35	37.74	59.07	34.70	62.18
45	49.45	38.80	60.14	35.74	63.22
46	50.55	39.86	61.20	36.78	64.26
47	51.65	40.93	62.26	37.82	65.30
48	52.75	42.00	63.31	38.88	66.32
49	53.85	43.08	64.36	39.93	67.35
50	54.95	44.16	65.40	41.00	68.36
51	56.04	45.25	66.44	42.07	69.37
52	57.14	46.34	67.47	43.15	70.37
53	58.24	47.43	68.50	44.23	71.37
54	59.34	48.53	69.52	45.32	72.35
55	60.44	49.64	70.54	46.42	73.34
56	61.54	50.75	71.55	47.52	74.31
57	62.64	51.87	72.56	48.63	75.28
58	63.74	52.99	73.56	49.75	76.24
59	64.84	54.12	74.56	50.88	77.20
60	65.93	55.25	75.55	52.01	78.15
61	67.03	56.39	76.53	53.15	79.09
62	68.13	57.53	77.51	54.29	80.02
63	69.23	58.68	78.49	55.44	80.94
64	70.33	59.84	79.45	56.61	81.86
65	71.43	61.00	80.41	57.78	82.77
66	72.53	62.17	81.37	58.95	83.67
67	73.63	63.35	82.31	60.14	84.56
68	74.73	64.53	83.25	61.34	85.44
69	75.82	65.72	84.19	62.54	86.31
70	76.92	66.91	85.11	63.75	87.18
71	78.02	68.12	86.03	64.98	88.03
72	79.12	69.33	86.94	66.21	88.87
73	80.22	70.55	87.83	67.46	89.70
74	81.32	71.78	88.72	68.72	90.51
75	82.42	73.02	89.60	69.99	91.32
76	83.52	74.27	90.47	71.27	92.11
77	84.62	75.54	91.33	72.57	92.88
78	85.71	76.81	92.17	73.88	93.64
79	86.81	78.10	93.00	75.22	94.38
80	87.91	79.40	93.81	76.57	95.09
81	89.01	80.72	94.60	77.94	95.79
82	90.11	82.05	95.38	79.33	96.46
83	91.21	83.41	96.13	80.75	97.10
84	92.31	84.79	96.85	82.20	97.71
85	93.41	86.20	97.54	83.69	98.28
86	94.51	87.64	98.19	85.22	98.80
87	95.60	89.13	98.79	86.80	99.25
88	96.70	90.67	99.31	88.45	99.62
89	97.80	92.29	99.73	90.21	99.89
90	98.90	94.03	99.97	92.12	99.99
91	100.00	96.03	100.00	94.34	100.00

N = 92

x	$100p_x$	95% $100p_l$	95% $100p_r$	99% $100p_l$	99% $100p_r$
0	0.00	0.00	3.93	0.00	5.60
1	1.09	0.03	5.91	0.01	7.80
2	2.17	0.26	7.63	0.11	9.69
3	3.26	0.68	9.24	0.37	11.43
4	4.35	1.20	10.76	0.74	13.06
5	5.43	1.79	12.23	1.19	14.63
6	6.52	2.43	13.66	1.70	16.15
7	7.61	3.11	15.05	2.27	17.62
8	8.70	3.83	16.42	2.87	19.05
9	9.78	4.57	17.76	3.50	20.46
10	10.87	5.34	19.08	4.16	21.84
11	11.96	6.12	20.39	4.85	23.20
12	13.04	6.93	21.68	5.56	24.53
13	14.13	7.74	22.95	6.29	25.85
14	15.22	8.58	24.21	7.04	27.15
15	16.30	9.42	25.46	7.80	28.44
16	17.39	10.28	26.70	8.58	29.71
17	18.48	11.15	27.93	9.38	30.97

N = 92 (continued)

x	$100p_x$	95% $100p_l$	95% $100p_r$	99% $100p_l$	99% $100p_r$
18	19.57	12.03	29.15	10.18	32.22
19	20.65	12.92	30.36	11.00	33.45
20	21.74	13.81	31.56	11.83	34.67
21	22.83	14.72	32.75	12.68	35.89
22	23.91	15.63	33.94	13.53	37.09
23	25.00	16.55	35.11	14.39	38.28
24	26.09	17.48	36.29	15.26	39.47
25	27.17	18.42	37.45	16.14	40.64
26	28.26	19.36	38.61	17.03	41.81
27	29.35	20.31	39.76	17.93	42.97
28	30.43	21.27	40.90	18.83	44.12
29	31.52	22.23	42.04	19.75	45.27
30	32.61	23.20	43.18	20.67	46.40
31	33.70	24.17	44.30	21.60	47.53
32	34.78	25.15	45.43	22.53	48.65
33	35.87	26.13	46.54	23.48	49.77
34	36.96	27.12	47.66	24.43	50.87
35	38.04	28.12	48.76	25.38	51.98
36	39.13	29.12	49.86	26.35	53.07
37	40.22	30.12	50.96	27.32	54.16
38	41.30	31.13	52.05	28.29	55.24
39	42.39	32.15	53.14	29.28	56.32
40	43.48	33.17	54.22	30.27	57.38
41	44.57	34.19	55.30	31.26	58.45
42	45.65	35.22	56.37	32.26	59.50
43	46.74	36.26	57.44	33.27	60.55
44	47.83	37.30	58.50	34.28	61.60
45	48.91	38.34	59.56	35.30	62.64
46	50.00	39.39	60.61	36.33	63.67
47	51.09	40.44	61.66	37.36	64.70
48	52.17	41.50	62.70	38.40	65.72
49	53.26	42.56	63.74	39.45	66.73
50	54.35	43.63	64.78	40.50	67.74
51	55.43	44.70	65.81	41.55	68.74
52	56.52	45.78	66.83	42.62	69.73
53	57.61	46.86	67.85	43.68	70.72
54	58.70	47.95	68.87	44.76	71.71
55	59.78	49.04	69.88	45.84	72.68
56	60.87	50.14	70.88	46.93	73.65
57	61.96	51.24	71.88	48.02	74.62
58	63.04	52.34	72.88	49.13	75.57
59	64.13	53.46	73.87	50.23	76.52
60	65.22	54.57	74.85	51.35	77.47
61	66.30	55.70	75.83	52.47	78.40
62	67.39	56.82	76.80	53.60	79.33
63	68.48	57.96	77.77	54.73	80.25
64	69.57	59.10	78.73	55.88	81.17
65	70.65	60.24	79.69	57.03	82.07
66	71.74	61.39	80.64	58.19	82.97
67	72.83	62.55	81.58	59.36	83.86
68	73.91	63.71	82.52	60.53	84.74
69	75.00	64.89	83.45	61.72	85.61
70	76.09	66.06	84.37	62.91	86.47
71	77.17	67.25	85.28	64.11	87.32
72	78.26	68.44	86.19	65.33	88.17
73	79.35	69.64	87.08	66.55	89.00
74	80.43	70.85	87.97	67.78	89.82
75	81.52	72.07	88.85	69.03	90.62
76	82.61	73.30	89.72	70.29	91.42
77	83.70	74.54	90.58	71.56	92.20
78	84.78	75.79	91.42	72.85	92.96
79	85.87	77.05	92.26	74.15	93.71
80	86.96	78.32	93.07	75.47	94.44
81	88.04	79.61	93.88	76.80	95.15
82	89.13	80.92	94.66	78.16	95.84
83	90.22	82.24	95.43	79.54	96.50
84	91.30	83.58	96.17	80.95	97.13
85	92.39	84.95	96.89	82.38	97.73
86	93.48	86.34	97.57	83.85	98.30
87	94.57	87.77	98.21	85.37	98.81
88	95.65	89.24	98.80	86.94	99.26
89	96.74	90.76	99.32	88.57	99.63
90	97.83	92.37	99.74	90.31	99.89
91	98.91	94.09	99.97	92.20	99.99
92	100.00	96.07	100.00	94.40	100.00

N = 93

x	$100p_x$	95% $100p_l$	95% $100p_r$	99% $100p_l$	99% $100p_r$
0	0.00	0.00	3.89	0.00	5.54
1	1.08	0.03	5.85	0.01	7.72
2	2.15	0.26	7.55	0.11	9.59
3	3.23	0.67	9.14	0.37	11.31
4	4.30	1.18	10.65	0.73	12.93
5	5.38	1.77	12.10	1.18	14.48
6	6.45	2.41	13.52	1.68	15.98
7	7.53	3.08	14.90	2.24	17.44
8	8.60	3.79	16.25	2.83	18.86
9	9.68	4.52	17.58	3.46	20.25
10	10.75	5.28	18.89	4.12	21.62
11	11.83	6.05	20.18	4.80	22.96
12	12.90	6.85	21.45	5.50	24.29
13	13.98	7.66	22.72	6.22	25.59
14	15.05	8.48	23.97	6.96	26.88
15	16.13	9.32	25.20	7.72	28.16
16	17.20	10.17	26.43	8.49	29.42
17	18.28	11.02	27.65	9.27	30.66
18	19.35	11.89	28.85	10.07	31.90
19	20.43	12.77	30.05	10.88	33.12
20	21.51	13.66	31.24	11.70	34.33

N = 93 (continued)

x	$100p_x$	95% $100p_l$	95% $100p_r$	99% $100p_l$	99% $100p_r$
21	22.58	14.55	32.42	12.53	35.54
22	23.66	15.46	33.60	13.37	36.73
23	24.73	16.37	34.76	14.23	37.91
24	25.81	17.29	35.92	15.09	39.08
25	26.88	18.21	37.08	15.96	40.25
26	27.96	19.14	38.22	16.84	41.41
27	29.03	20.08	39.36	17.72	42.56
28	30.11	21.03	40.50	18.62	43.70
29	31.18	21.98	41.63	19.52	44.83
30	32.26	22.93	42.75	20.43	45.96
31	33.33	23.89	43.87	21.35	47.08
32	34.41	24.86	44.98	22.27	48.19
33	35.48	25.83	46.09	23.20	49.29
34	36.56	26.81	47.19	24.14	50.39
35	37.63	27.79	48.28	25.09	51.48
36	38.71	28.78	49.38	26.04	52.57
37	39.78	29.78	50.46	27.00	53.65
38	40.86	30.77	51.54	27.96	54.72
39	41.94	31.78	52.62	28.93	55.79
40	43.01	32.78	53.69	29.91	56.85
41	44.09	33.80	54.76	30.89	57.90
42	45.16	34.81	55.83	31.88	58.95
43	46.24	35.84	56.88	32.87	59.99
44	47.31	36.86	57.94	33.88	61.03
45	48.39	37.89	58.99	34.88	62.06
46	49.46	38.93	60.03	35.90	63.09
47	50.54	39.97	61.07	36.91	64.10
48	51.61	41.01	62.11	37.94	65.12
49	52.69	42.06	63.14	38.97	66.12
50	53.76	43.12	64.16	40.01	67.13
51	54.84	44.17	65.19	41.05	68.12
52	55.91	45.24	66.20	42.10	69.11
53	56.99	46.31	67.22	43.15	70.09
54	58.06	47.38	68.22	44.21	71.07
55	59.14	48.46	69.23	45.28	72.04
56	60.22	49.54	70.22	46.35	73.00
57	61.29	50.62	71.22	47.43	73.96
58	62.37	51.72	72.21	48.52	74.91
59	63.44	52.81	73.19	49.61	75.86
60	64.52	53.91	74.17	50.71	76.80
61	65.59	55.02	75.14	51.81	77.73
62	66.67	56.13	76.11	52.92	78.65
63	67.74	57.25	77.07	54.04	79.57
64	68.82	58.37	78.02	55.17	80.48
65	69.89	59.50	78.97	56.30	81.38
66	70.97	60.64	79.92	57.44	82.28
67	72.04	61.78	80.86	58.59	83.16
68	73.12	62.92	81.79	59.75	84.04
69	74.19	64.08	82.71	60.92	84.91
70	75.27	65.24	83.63	62.09	85.77
71	76.34	66.40	84.54	63.27	86.63
72	77.42	67.58	85.45	64.46	87.47
73	78.49	68.76	86.34	65.67	88.30
74	79.57	69.95	87.23	66.88	89.12
75	80.65	71.15	88.11	68.10	89.93
76	81.72	72.35	88.98	69.34	90.73
77	82.80	73.57	89.83	70.58	91.51
78	83.87	74.80	90.68	71.84	92.28
79	84.95	76.03	91.52	73.12	93.04
80	86.02	77.28	92.34	74.41	93.78
81	87.10	78.55	93.15	75.71	94.50
82	88.17	79.82	93.95	77.04	95.20
83	89.25	81.11	94.72	78.38	95.88
84	90.32	82.42	95.48	79.75	96.54
85	91.40	83.75	96.21	81.14	97.17
86	92.47	85.10	96.92	82.56	97.76
87	93.55	86.48	97.59	84.02	98.32
88	94.62	87.90	98.23	85.52	98.82
89	95.70	89.35	98.82	87.07	99.27
90	96.77	90.86	99.33	88.69	99.63
91	97.85	92.45	99.74	90.41	99.89
92	98.92	94.15	99.97	92.28	99.99
93	100.00	96.11	100.00	94.46	100.00

N = 94

x	$100p_x$	95% $100p_l$	95% $100p_r$	99% $100p_l$	99% $100p_r$
0	0.00	0.00	3.85	0.00	5.48
1	1.06	0.03	5.79	0.01	7.64
2	2.13	0.26	7.48	0.11	9.49
3	3.19	0.66	9.04	0.36	11.19
4	4.26	1.17	10.54	0.72	12.80
5	5.32	1.75	11.98	1.17	14.33
6	6.38	2.38	13.38	1.67	15.82
7	7.45	3.05	14.74	2.22	17.26
8	8.51	3.75	16.08	2.80	18.67
9	9.57	4.47	17.40	3.42	20.05
10	10.64	5.22	18.70	4.07	21.40
11	11.70	5.99	19.97	4.74	22.74
12	12.77	6.77	21.24	5.44	24.05
13	13.83	7.57	22.49	6.15	25.34
14	14.89	8.39	23.72	6.88	26.62
15	15.96	9.22	24.95	7.63	27.88
16	17.02	10.05	26.16	8.39	29.13
17	18.09	10.90	27.37	9.17	30.36
18	19.15	11.76	28.56	9.96	31.59
19	20.21	12.63	29.75	10.76	32.80
20	21.28	13.51	30.93	11.57	34.00
21	22.34	14.39	32.10	12.39	35.19
22	23.40	15.29	33.26	13.22	36.37

$N=$ number of trials, $x=$ number of successes, etc., $100\,p_x = 100\,x/N$

$N=94$ (continued)

x	$100p_x$	100(1 − 2α) limits 95% $100p_l$–$100p_r$	100(1 − 2α) limits 99% $100p_l$–$100p_r$
23	24.47	16.19–34.42	14.07–37.54
24	25.53	17.09–35.57	14.92–38.71
25	26.60	18.01–36.71	15.78–39.86
26	27.66	18.93–37.85	16.65–41.01
27	28.72	19.86–38.98	17.52–42.15
28	29.79	20.79–40.10	18.41–43.28
29	30.85	21.73–41.22	19.30–44.40
30	31.91	22.67–42.33	20.20–45.52
31	32.98	23.62–43.44	21.10–46.63
32	34.04	24.58–44.54	22.02–47.73
33	35.11	25.54–45.64	22.94–48.83
34	36.17	26.51–46.73	23.86–49.92
35	37.23	27.48–47.82	24.80–51.00
36	38.30	28.46–48.90	25.74–52.08
37	39.36	29.44–49.98	26.68–53.15
38	40.43	30.42–51.05	27.64–54.21
39	41.49	31.41–52.12	28.59–55.27
40	42.55	32.41–53.18	29.56–56.32
41	43.62	33.41–54.24	30.53–57.37
42	44.68	34.41–55.29	31.51–58.41
43	45.74	35.42–56.34	32.49–59.44
44	46.81	36.44–57.39	33.48–60.47
45	47.87	37.46–58.43	34.47–61.50
46	48.94	38.48–59.46	35.47–62.51
47	50.00	39.51–60.49	36.48–63.52
48	51.06	40.54–61.52	37.49–64.53
49	52.13	41.57–62.54	38.50–65.53
50	53.19	42.61–63.56	39.53–66.52
51	54.26	43.66–64.58	40.56–67.51
52	55.32	44.71–65.59	41.59–68.49
53	56.38	45.76–66.59	42.63–69.47
54	57.45	46.82–67.59	43.68–70.44
55	58.51	47.88–68.59	44.73–71.41
56	59.57	48.95–69.58	45.79–72.36
57	60.64	50.02–70.56	46.85–73.32
58	61.70	51.10–71.54	47.92–74.26
59	62.77	52.18–72.52	49.00–75.20
60	63.83	53.27–73.49	50.08–76.14
61	64.89	54.36–74.46	51.17–77.06
62	65.96	55.46–75.42	52.27–77.98
63	67.02	56.56–76.38	53.37–78.90
64	68.09	57.67–77.33	54.48–79.80
65	69.15	58.78–78.27	55.60–80.70
66	70.21	59.90–79.21	56.72–81.59
67	71.28	61.02–80.14	57.85–82.48
68	72.34	62.15–81.07	58.99–83.35
69	73.40	63.29–81.99	60.14–84.22
70	74.47	64.43–82.91	61.29–85.08
71	75.53	65.58–83.81	62.46–85.93
72	76.60	66.74–84.71	63.63–86.78
73	77.66	67.90–85.61	64.81–87.61
74	78.72	69.07–86.49	66.00–88.43
75	79.79	70.25–87.37	67.20–89.24
76	80.85	71.44–88.24	68.41–90.04
77	81.91	72.63–89.10	69.64–90.83
78	82.98	73.84–89.95	70.87–91.61
79	84.04	75.05–90.78	72.12–92.37
80	85.11	76.28–91.61	73.38–93.12
81	86.17	77.51–92.43	74.66–93.85
82	87.23	78.76–93.23	75.95–94.56
83	88.30	80.03–94.01	77.26–95.26
84	89.36	81.30–94.78	78.60–95.93
85	90.43	82.60–95.53	79.95–96.58
86	91.49	83.92–96.25	81.33–97.20
87	92.55	85.26–96.95	82.74–97.78
88	93.62	86.62–97.62	84.18–98.33
89	94.68	88.02–98.25	85.67–98.83
90	95.74	89.46–98.83	87.20–99.28
91	96.81	90.96–99.34	88.81–99.64
92	97.87	92.52–99.74	90.51–99.89
93	98.94	94.21–99.97	92.36–99.99
94	100.00	96.15–100.00	94.52–100.00

$N=95$

x	$100p_x$	95% $100p_l$–$100p_r$	99% $100p_l$–$100p_r$
0	0.00	0.00–3.81	0.00–5.42
1	1.05	0.03–5.73	0.01–7.56
2	2.11	0.26–7.40	0.11–9.40
3	3.16	0.66–8.95	0.36–11.08
4	4.21	1.16–10.43	0.72–12.67
5	5.26	1.73–11.86	1.15–14.19
6	6.32	2.35–13.24	1.65–15.66
7	7.37	3.01–14.59	2.19–17.09
8	8.42	3.71–15.92	2.77–18.49
9	9.47	4.42–17.22	3.39–19.85
10	10.53	5.16–18.51	4.03–21.19
11	11.58	5.92–19.77	4.69–22.51
12	12.63	6.70–21.03	5.38–23.81
13	13.68	7.49–22.26	6.08–25.09
14	14.74	8.30–23.49	6.81–26.36
15	15.79	9.12–24.70	7.55–27.61
16	16.84	9.94–25.90	8.30–28.84
17	17.89	10.78–27.10	9.07–30.07
18	18.95	11.63–28.28	9.85–31.28
19	20.00	12.49–29.46	10.64–32.48
20	21.05	13.36–30.62	11.44–33.67
21	22.11	14.23–31.78	12.25–34.85
22	23.16	15.12–32.94	13.08–36.02
23	24.21	16.01–34.08	13.91–37.18

$N=95$ (continued)

x	$100p_x$	95% $100p_l$–$100p_r$	99% $100p_l$–$100p_r$
24	25.26	16.91–35.22	14.75–38.34
25	26.32	17.81–36.35	15.60–39.48
26	27.37	18.72–37.48	16.46–40.62
27	28.42	19.64–38.60	17.33–41.75
28	29.47	20.56–39.71	18.20–42.87
29	30.53	21.49–40.82	19.08–43.98
30	31.58	22.42–41.92	19.97–45.09
31	32.63	23.36–43.02	20.86–46.19
32	33.68	24.31–44.11	21.77–47.28
33	34.74	25.26–45.20	22.68–48.37
34	35.79	26.21–46.28	23.59–49.45
35	36.84	27.17–47.36	24.51–50.53
36	37.89	28.14–48.43	25.44–51.59
37	38.95	29.11–49.50	26.38–52.66
38	40.00	30.08–50.56	27.32–53.71
39	41.05	31.06–51.62	28.27–54.76
40	42.11	32.04–52.67	29.22–55.81
41	43.16	33.03–53.72	30.18–56.84
42	44.21	34.02–54.77	31.14–57.88
43	45.26	35.02–55.81	32.11–58.90
44	46.32	36.02–56.85	33.09–59.92
45	47.37	37.03–57.88	34.07–60.94
46	48.42	38.04–58.90	35.06–61.95
47	49.47	39.05–59.93	36.05–62.95
48	50.53	40.07–60.95	37.05–63.95
49	51.58	41.10–61.96	38.05–64.94
50	52.63	42.12–62.97	39.06–65.93
51	53.68	43.15–63.98	40.08–66.91
52	54.74	44.19–64.98	41.10–67.89
53	55.79	45.23–65.98	42.12–68.86
54	56.84	46.28–66.97	43.16–69.82
55	57.89	47.33–67.96	44.19–70.78
56	58.95	48.38–68.94	45.24–71.73
57	60.00	49.44–69.92	46.29–72.68
58	61.05	50.50–70.89	47.34–73.62
59	62.11	51.57–71.86	48.41–74.56
60	63.16	52.64–72.83	49.47–75.49
61	64.21	53.72–73.79	50.55–76.41
62	65.26	54.80–74.74	51.63–77.32
63	66.32	55.89–75.69	52.72–78.23
64	67.37	56.98–76.64	53.81–79.14
65	68.42	58.08–77.58	54.91–80.03
66	69.47	59.18–78.51	56.02–80.92
67	70.53	60.29–79.44	57.13–81.80
68	71.58	61.40–80.36	58.25–82.67
69	72.63	62.52–81.28	59.38–83.54
70	73.68	63.65–82.19	60.52–84.40
71	74.74	64.78–83.09	61.66–85.25
72	75.79	65.92–83.99	62.82–86.09
73	76.84	67.06–84.88	63.98–86.92
74	77.89	68.22–85.77	65.15–87.75
75	78.95	69.38–86.64	66.33–88.56
76	80.00	70.54–87.51	67.52–89.36
77	81.05	71.72–88.37	68.72–90.15
78	82.11	72.90–89.22	69.93–90.93
79	83.16	74.10–90.06	71.16–91.70
80	84.21	75.30–90.88	72.39–92.45
81	85.26	76.51–91.70	73.64–93.19
82	86.32	77.74–92.51	74.91–93.92
83	87.37	78.97–93.30	76.19–94.62
84	88.42	80.23–94.08	77.49–95.31
85	89.47	81.49–94.84	78.81–95.97
86	90.53	82.78–95.58	80.15–96.61
87	91.58	84.08–96.29	81.51–97.23
88	92.63	85.41–96.99	82.91–97.81
89	93.68	86.76–97.65	84.34–98.35
90	94.74	88.14–98.27	85.81–98.85
91	95.79	89.57–98.84	87.33–99.28
92	96.84	91.05–99.34	88.92–99.64
93	97.89	92.60–99.74	90.60–99.89
94	98.95	94.27–99.97	92.44–99.99
95	100.00	96.19–100.00	94.58–100.00

$N=96$

x	$100p_x$	95% $100p_l$–$100p_r$	99% $100p_l$–$100p_r$
0	0.00	0.00–3.77	0.00–5.37
1	1.04	0.03–5.67	0.01–7.49
2	2.08	0.25–7.32	0.11–9.30
3	3.13	0.65–8.86	0.36–10.97
4	4.17	1.15–10.33	0.71–12.54
5	5.21	1.71–11.74	1.14–14.05
6	6.25	2.33–13.11	1.63–15.51
7	7.29	2.98–14.45	2.17–16.92
8	8.33	3.67–15.76	2.74–18.30
9	9.38	4.38–17.05	3.35–19.66
10	10.42	5.11–18.32	3.98–20.99
11	11.46	5.86–19.58	4.64–22.29
12	12.50	6.63–20.82	5.32–23.58
13	13.54	7.41–22.04	6.02–24.85
14	14.58	8.21–23.26	6.73–26.10
15	15.63	9.02–24.46	7.47–27.34
16	16.67	9.84–25.65	8.21–28.57
17	17.71	10.67–26.83	8.97–29.78
18	18.75	11.51–28.00	9.74–30.98
19	19.79	12.36–29.17	10.52–32.17
20	20.83	13.21–30.33	11.32–33.35
21	21.88	14.08–31.47	12.12–34.52
22	22.92	14.95–32.62	12.93–35.68
23	23.96	15.83–33.75	13.76–36.83

$N=96$ (continued)

x	$100p_x$	95% $100p_l$–$100p_r$	99% $100p_l$–$100p_r$
24	25.00	16.72–34.88	14.59–37.98
25	26.04	17.62–36.00	15.43–39.11
26	27.08	18.52–37.11	16.28–40.24
27	28.13	19.42–38.22	17.13–41.36
28	29.17	20.33–39.33	18.00–42.47
29	30.21	21.25–40.43	18.87–43.57
30	31.25	22.18–41.52	19.75–44.67
31	32.29	23.10–42.61	20.63–45.76
32	33.33	24.04–43.69	21.52–46.85
33	34.38	24.98–44.77	22.42–47.92
34	35.42	25.92–45.84	23.33–48.99
35	36.46	26.87–46.91	24.24–50.06
36	37.50	27.82–47.97	25.16–51.12
37	38.54	28.78–49.03	26.08–52.17
38	39.58	29.75–50.08	27.01–53.22
39	40.63	30.71–51.13	27.94–54.26
40	41.67	31.68–52.18	28.88–55.30
41	42.71	32.66–53.22	29.83–56.33
42	43.75	33.64–54.25	30.78–57.35
43	44.79	34.63–55.29	31.74–58.37
44	45.83	35.62–56.31	32.71–59.38
45	46.88	36.61–57.34	33.68–60.39
46	47.92	37.61–58.36	34.65–61.39
47	48.96	38.61–59.37	35.63–62.39
48	50.00	39.62–60.38	36.62–63.38
49	51.04	40.63–61.39	37.61–64.37
50	52.08	41.64–62.39	38.61–65.35
51	53.13	42.66–63.39	39.61–66.32
52	54.17	43.69–64.38	40.62–67.29
53	55.21	44.71–65.37	41.63–68.26
54	56.25	45.75–66.36	42.65–69.22
55	57.29	46.78–67.34	43.67–70.17
56	58.33	47.82–68.32	44.70–71.12
57	59.38	48.87–69.29	45.74–72.06
58	60.42	49.92–70.25	46.78–72.99
59	61.46	50.97–71.22	47.83–73.92
60	62.50	52.03–72.18	48.88–74.84
61	63.54	53.09–73.13	49.94–75.76
62	64.58	54.16–74.08	51.01–76.67
63	65.63	55.23–75.02	52.08–77.58
64	66.67	56.31–75.96	53.15–78.48
65	67.71	57.39–76.90	54.24–79.37
66	68.75	58.48–77.82	55.33–80.25
67	69.79	59.57–78.75	56.43–81.13
68	70.83	60.67–79.67	57.53–82.00
69	71.88	61.78–80.58	58.64–82.87
70	72.92	62.89–81.48	59.76–83.72
71	73.96	64.00–82.38	60.89–84.57
72	75.00	65.12–83.28	62.02–85.41
73	76.04	66.25–84.17	63.17–86.24
74	77.08	67.38–85.05	64.32–87.07
75	78.13	68.53–85.92	65.48–87.88
76	79.17	69.67–86.79	66.65–88.68
77	80.21	70.83–87.64	67.83–89.48
78	81.25	72.00–88.49	69.02–90.26
79	82.29	73.17–89.33	70.22–91.03
80	83.33	74.35–90.16	71.43–91.79
81	84.38	75.54–90.98	72.66–92.53
82	85.42	76.74–91.79	73.90–93.27
83	86.46	77.96–92.59	75.15–93.98
84	87.50	79.18–93.37	76.42–94.68
85	88.54	80.42–94.14	77.71–95.36
86	89.58	81.68–94.89	79.01–96.02
87	90.63	82.95–95.62	80.34–96.65
88	91.67	84.24–96.33	81.70–97.26
89	92.71	85.55–97.02	83.08–97.83
90	93.75	86.89–97.67	84.49–98.37
91	94.79	88.26–98.29	85.95–98.86
92	95.83	89.67–98.85	87.46–99.29
93	96.88	91.14–99.35	89.03–99.64
94	97.92	92.68–99.75	90.70–99.89
95	98.96	94.33–99.97	92.51–99.99
96	100.00	96.23–100.00	94.63–100.00

$N=97$

x	$100p_x$	95% $100p_l$–$100p_r$	99% $100p_l$–$100p_r$
0	0.00	0.00–3.73	0.00–5.32
1	1.03	0.03–5.61	0.01–7.41
2	2.06	0.25–7.25	0.11–9.21
3	3.09	0.64–8.77	0.35–10.86
4	4.12	1.13–10.22	0.70–12.42
5	5.15	1.69–11.62	1.13–13.91
6	6.19	2.30–12.98	1.61–15.35
7	7.22	2.95–14.30	2.15–16.76
8	8.25	3.63–15.61	2.71–18.13
9	9.28	4.33–16.88	3.31–19.47
10	10.31	5.06–18.14	3.94–20.78
11	11.34	5.80–19.39	4.59–22.08
12	12.37	6.56–20.61	5.26–23.35
13	13.40	7.33–21.83	5.95–24.61
14	14.43	8.12–23.03	6.66–25.85
15	15.46	8.92–24.22	7.39–27.08
16	16.49	9.73–25.40	8.12–28.29
17	17.53	10.55–26.57	8.87–29.50
18	18.56	11.38–27.73	9.63–30.69
19	19.59	12.22–28.89	10.41–31.87
20	20.62	13.07–30.03	11.19–33.03
21	21.65	13.93–31.17	11.99–34.19
22	22.68	14.79–32.30	12.79–35.34

$N=97$ (continued)

x	$100p_x$	95% $100p_l$–$100p_r$	99% $100p_l$–$100p_r$
23	23.71	15.66–33.42	13.61–36.49
24	24.74	16.54–34.54	14.43–37.62
25	25.77	17.42–35.65	15.26–38.74
26	26.80	18.32–36.76	16.10–39.86
27	27.84	19.21–37.86	16.94–40.97
28	28.87	20.11–38.95	17.80–42.07
29	29.90	21.02–40.04	18.66–43.17
30	30.93	21.93–41.12	19.53–44.26
31	31.96	22.85–42.20	20.40–45.34
32	32.99	23.78–43.27	21.28–46.41
33	34.02	24.70–44.34	22.17–47.48
34	35.05	25.64–45.41	23.07–48.55
35	36.08	26.58–46.46	23.97–49.60
36	37.11	27.52–47.52	24.87–50.65
37	38.14	28.47–48.57	25.79–51.70
38	39.18	29.42–49.61	26.71–52.74
39	40.21	30.37–50.65	27.63–53.77
40	41.24	31.33–51.69	28.56–54.80
41	42.27	32.30–52.72	29.49–55.82
42	43.30	33.27–53.75	30.44–56.84
43	44.33	34.24–54.77	31.38–57.85
44	45.36	35.22–55.79	32.33–58.85
45	46.39	36.20–56.81	33.29–59.86
46	47.42	37.19–57.82	34.26–60.85
47	48.45	38.18–58.82	35.22–61.84
48	49.48	39.17–59.83	36.20–62.82
49	50.52	40.17–60.83	37.18–63.80
50	51.55	41.18–61.82	38.16–64.78
51	52.58	42.18–62.81	39.15–65.74
52	53.61	43.19–63.80	40.14–66.71
53	54.64	44.21–64.78	41.15–67.67
54	55.67	45.23–65.76	42.15–68.62
55	56.70	46.25–66.73	43.16–69.56
56	57.73	47.28–67.70	44.18–70.51
57	58.76	48.31–68.67	45.20–71.44
58	59.79	49.35–69.63	46.23–72.37
59	60.82	50.39–70.58	47.26–73.29
60	61.86	51.43–71.53	48.30–74.21
61	62.89	52.48–72.48	49.35–75.13
62	63.92	53.54–73.42	50.40–76.03
63	64.95	54.59–74.36	51.45–76.93
64	65.98	55.66–75.30	52.52–77.83
65	67.01	56.73–76.22	53.59–78.72
66	68.04	57.80–77.15	54.66–79.60
67	69.07	58.88–78.07	55.74–80.47
68	70.10	59.96–78.98	56.83–81.34
69	71.13	61.05–79.89	57.93–82.20
70	72.16	62.14–80.79	59.03–83.06
71	73.20	63.24–81.68	60.14–83.90
72	74.23	64.35–82.58	61.26–84.74
73	75.26	65.46–83.46	62.38–85.57
74	76.29	66.58–84.34	63.51–86.39
75	77.32	67.70–85.21	64.66–87.21
76	78.35	68.83–86.07	65.81–88.01
77	79.38	69.97–86.93	66.97–88.81
78	80.41	71.11–87.78	68.13–89.59
79	81.44	72.27–88.62	69.31–90.37
80	82.47	73.43–89.45	70.50–91.13
81	83.51	74.60–90.27	71.71–91.88
82	84.54	75.78–91.08	72.92–92.61
83	85.57	76.97–91.88	74.15–93.34
84	86.60	78.17–92.67	75.39–94.05
85	87.63	79.39–93.44	76.65–94.74
86	88.66	80.61–94.20	77.92–95.41
87	89.69	81.86–94.94	79.22–96.06
88	90.72	83.12–95.67	80.53–96.69
89	91.75	84.39–96.37	81.87–97.29
90	92.78	85.70–97.05	83.24–97.85
91	93.81	87.02–97.70	84.65–98.39
92	94.85	88.38–98.31	86.09–98.87
93	95.88	89.78–98.87	87.58–99.30
94	96.91	91.23–99.36	89.14–99.65
95	97.94	92.75–99.75	90.79–99.89
96	98.97	94.39–99.97	92.59–99.99
97	100.00	96.27–100.00	94.68–100.00

$N=98$

x	$100p_x$	95% $100p_l$–$100p_r$	99% $100p_l$–$100p_r$
0	0.00	0.00–3.69	0.00–5.26
1	1.02	0.03–5.55	0.01–7.34
2	2.04	0.25–7.18	0.11–9.12
3	3.06	0.64–8.69	0.35–10.75
4	4.08	1.12–10.12	0.69–12.30
5	5.10	1.68–11.51	1.12–13.78
6	6.12	2.28–12.85	1.60–15.21
7	7.14	2.92–14.16	2.12–16.60
8	8.16	3.59–15.45	2.69–17.95
9	9.18	4.29–16.72	3.28–19.28
10	10.20	5.00–17.97	3.90–20.58
11	11.22	5.74–19.20	4.54–21.87
12	12.24	6.49–20.41	5.21–23.13
13	13.27	7.26–21.62	5.89–24.38
14	14.29	8.04–22.81	6.59–25.61
15	15.31	8.83–23.99	7.31–26.82
16	16.33	9.63–25.16	8.04–28.03
17	17.35	10.44–26.31	8.78–29.22
18	18.37	11.26–27.47	9.53–30.40
19	19.39	12.10–28.61	10.30–31.57
20	20.41	12.93–29.74	11.07–32.73

N = number of trials, x = number of successes, etc., $100p_x = 100x/N$

N = 98 (continued)

x	$100p_x$	95% $100p_l$ – $100p_r$	99% $100p_l$ – $100p_r$
21	21.43	13.78– 30.87	11.86– 33.87
22	22.45	14.64– 31.99	12.65– 35.01
23	23.47	15.50– 33.11	13.46– 36.15
24	24.49	16.36– 34.21	14.27– 37.27
25	25.51	17.24– 35.31	15.09– 38.38
26	26.53	18.12– 36.41	15.92– 39.49
27	27.55	19.01– 37.50	16.76– 40.59
28	28.57	19.90– 38.58	17.60– 41.69
29	29.59	20.79– 39.66	18.46– 42.77
30	30.61	21.70– 40.74	19.31– 43.85
31	31.63	22.61– 41.80	20.18– 44.92
32	32.65	23.52– 42.87	21.05– 45.99
33	33.67	24.44– 43.93	21.93– 47.05
34	34.69	25.36– 44.98	22.81– 48.11
35	35.71	26.29– 46.03	23.70– 49.15
36	36.73	27.22– 47.07	24.60– 50.20
37	37.76	28.16– 48.12	25.50– 51.23
38	38.78	29.10– 49.15	26.41– 52.26
39	39.80	30.04– 50.18	27.32– 53.29
40	40.82	30.99– 51.21	28.24– 54.31
41	41.84	31.95– 52.23	29.17– 55.32
42	42.86	32.90– 53.25	30.10– 56.33
43	43.88	33.87– 54.27	31.03– 57.34
44	44.90	34.83– 55.28	31.97– 58.33
45	45.92	35.80– 56.29	32.92– 59.33
46	46.94	36.78– 57.29	33.87– 60.31
47	47.96	37.76– 58.29	34.82– 61.30
48	48.98	38.74– 59.28	35.79– 62.27
49	50.00	39.73– 60.27	36.75– 63.25
50	51.02	40.72– 61.26	37.73– 64.21
51	52.04	41.71– 62.24	38.70– 65.18
52	53.06	42.71– 63.22	39.69– 66.13
53	54.08	43.71– 64.20	40.67– 67.08
54	55.10	44.72– 65.17	41.67– 68.03
55	56.12	45.73– 66.13	42.66– 68.97
56	57.14	46.75– 67.10	43.67– 69.90
57	58.16	47.77– 68.05	44.68– 70.83
58	59.18	48.79– 69.01	45.69– 71.76
59	60.20	49.82– 69.96	46.71– 72.68
60	61.22	50.85– 70.90	47.74– 73.59
61	62.24	51.88– 71.84	48.77– 74.50
62	63.27	52.93– 72.78	49.80– 75.40
63	64.29	53.97– 73.71	50.85– 76.30
64	65.31	55.02– 74.64	51.89– 77.19
65	66.33	56.07– 75.56	52.95– 78.07
66	67.35	57.13– 76.48	54.01– 78.95
67	68.37	58.20– 77.39	55.08– 79.82
68	69.39	59.26– 78.30	56.15– 80.69
69	70.41	60.34– 79.21	57.23– 81.54
70	71.43	61.42– 80.10	58.31– 82.40
71	72.45	62.50– 80.99	59.41– 83.24
72	73.47	63.59– 81.88	60.51– 84.08
73	74.49	64.69– 82.76	61.62– 84.91
74	75.51	65.79– 83.64	62.73– 85.73
75	76.53	66.89– 84.50	63.85– 86.54
76	77.55	68.01– 85.36	64.99– 87.35
77	78.57	69.13– 86.22	66.13– 88.14
78	79.59	70.26– 87.07	67.27– 88.93
79	80.61	71.39– 87.90	68.43– 89.70
80	81.63	72.53– 88.74	69.60– 90.47
81	82.65	73.69– 89.56	70.78– 91.22
82	83.67	74.84– 90.37	71.97– 91.96
83	84.69	76.01– 91.17	73.18– 92.69
84	85.71	77.19– 91.96	74.39– 93.41
85	86.73	78.38– 92.74	75.62– 94.11
86	87.76	79.59– 93.51	76.87– 94.79
87	88.78	80.80– 94.26	78.13– 95.46
88	89.80	82.03– 95.00	79.42– 96.10
89	90.82	83.28– 95.71	80.72– 96.72
90	91.84	84.55– 96.41	82.05– 97.31
91	92.86	85.84– 97.08	83.40– 97.88

N = 98 (continued)

x	$100p_x$	95% $100p_l$ – $100p_r$	99% $100p_l$ – $100p_r$
92	93.88	87.15– 97.72	84.79– 98.40
93	94.90	88.49– 98.32	86.22– 98.88
94	95.92	89.88– 98.88	87.70– 99.31
95	96.94	91.31– 99.36	89.25– 99.65
96	97.96	92.82– 99.75	90.88– 99.89
97	98.98	94.45– 99.97	92.66– 99.99
98	100.00	96.31–100.00	94.74–100.00

N = 99

x	$100p_x$	95% $100p_l$ – $100p_r$	99% $100p_l$ – $100p_r$
0	0.00	0.00– 3.66	0.00– 5.21
1	1.01	0.03– 5.50	0.01– 7.27
2	2.02	0.25– 7.11	0.11– 9.03
3	3.03	0.63– 8.60	0.34– 10.65
4	4.04	1.11– 10.02	0.69– 12.18
5	5.05	1.66– 11.39	1.11– 13.64
6	6.06	2.26– 12.73	1.58– 15.06
7	7.07	2.89– 14.03	2.10– 16.44
8	8.08	3.55– 15.30	2.66– 17.78
9	9.09	4.24– 16.56	3.25– 19.10
10	10.10	4.95– 17.79	3.86– 20.39
11	11.11	5.68– 19.01	4.50– 21.66
12	12.12	6.42– 20.22	5.15– 22.91
13	13.13	7.18– 21.41	5.83– 24.15
14	14.14	7.95– 22.59	6.52– 25.36
15	15.15	8.74– 23.76	7.23– 26.57
16	16.16	9.53– 24.91	7.95– 27.76
17	17.17	10.33– 26.06	8.69– 28.94
18	18.18	11.15– 27.20	9.43– 30.11
19	19.19	11.97– 28.34	10.19– 31.27
20	20.20	12.80– 29.46	10.96– 32.42
21	21.21	13.64– 30.58	11.73– 33.56
22	22.22	14.48– 31.69	12.52– 34.69
23	23.23	15.33– 32.79	13.32– 35.81
24	24.24	16.19– 33.89	14.12– 36.93
25	25.25	17.06– 34.98	14.93– 38.03
26	26.26	17.93– 36.07	15.75– 39.13
27	27.27	18.80– 37.15	16.58– 40.22
28	28.28	19.69– 38.22	17.42– 41.31
29	29.29	20.57– 39.29	18.26– 42.38
30	30.30	21.47– 40.36	19.11– 43.45
31	31.31	22.36– 41.41	19.96– 44.52
32	32.32	23.27– 42.47	20.82– 45.57
33	33.33	24.18– 43.52	21.69– 46.63
34	34.34	25.09– 44.56	22.56– 47.67
35	35.35	26.01– 45.60	23.44– 48.71
36	36.36	26.93– 46.64	24.33– 49.75
37	37.37	27.85– 47.67	25.22– 50.77
38	38.38	28.78– 48.70	26.12– 51.80
39	39.39	29.72– 49.72	27.02– 52.81
40	40.40	30.66– 50.74	27.93– 53.83
41	41.41	31.60– 51.76	28.84– 54.83
42	42.42	32.55– 52.77	29.76– 55.83
43	43.43	33.50– 53.77	30.69– 56.83
44	44.44	34.45– 54.78	31.62– 57.82
45	45.45	35.41– 55.77	32.55– 58.81
46	46.46	36.38– 56.77	33.49– 59.79
47	47.47	37.34– 57.76	34.44– 60.76
48	48.48	38.32– 58.75	35.39– 61.73
49	49.49	39.29– 59.73	36.34– 62.70
50	50.51	40.27– 60.71	37.30– 63.66
51	51.52	41.25– 61.68	38.27– 64.61
52	52.53	42.24– 62.66	39.24– 65.56
53	53.54	43.23– 63.62	40.21– 66.51
54	54.55	44.23– 64.59	41.19– 67.45
55	55.56	45.22– 65.55	42.18– 68.38
56	56.57	46.23– 66.50	43.17– 69.31
57	57.58	47.23– 67.45	44.17– 70.24
58	58.59	48.24– 68.40	45.17– 71.16
59	59.60	49.26– 69.34	46.17– 72.07
60	60.61	50.28– 70.28	47.19– 72.98
61	61.62	51.30– 71.22	48.20– 73.88

N = 99 (continued)

x	$100p_x$	95% $100p_l$ – $100p_r$	99% $100p_l$ – $100p_r$
62	62.63	52.33– 72.15	49.23– 74.78
63	63.64	53.36– 73.07	50.25– 75.67
64	64.65	54.40– 73.99	51.29– 76.56
65	65.66	55.44– 74.91	52.33– 77.44
66	66.67	56.48– 75.82	53.37– 78.31
67	67.68	57.53– 76.73	54.43– 79.18
68	68.69	58.59– 77.64	55.48– 80.04
69	69.70	59.64– 78.53	56.55– 80.89
70	70.71	60.71– 79.43	57.62– 81.74
71	71.72	61.78– 80.31	58.69– 82.58
72	72.73	62.85– 81.20	59.78– 83.42
73	73.74	63.93– 82.07	60.87– 84.25
74	74.75	65.02– 82.94	61.97– 85.07
75	75.76	66.11– 83.81	63.07– 85.88
76	76.77	67.21– 84.67	64.19– 86.68
77	77.78	68.31– 85.52	65.31– 87.48
78	78.79	69.42– 86.36	66.44– 88.27
79	79.80	70.54– 87.20	67.58– 89.04
80	80.81	71.66– 88.03	68.73– 89.81
81	81.82	72.80– 88.85	69.89– 90.57
82	82.83	73.94– 89.67	71.06– 91.31
83	83.84	75.09– 90.47	72.24– 92.05
84	84.85	76.24– 91.26	73.43– 92.77
85	85.86	77.41– 92.05	74.64– 93.48
86	86.87	78.59– 92.82	75.85– 94.17
87	87.88	79.78– 93.58	77.09– 94.85
88	88.89	80.99– 94.32	78.34– 95.50
89	89.90	82.21– 95.05	79.61– 96.14
90	90.91	83.44– 95.76	80.90– 96.75
91	91.92	84.70– 96.45	82.22– 97.34
92	92.93	85.97– 97.11	83.56– 97.90
93	93.94	87.27– 97.74	84.94– 98.42
94	94.95	88.61– 98.34	86.36– 98.89
95	95.96	89.98– 98.89	87.82– 99.31
96	96.97	91.40– 99.37	89.35– 99.66
97	97.98	92.89– 99.75	90.97– 99.89
98	98.99	94.50– 99.97	92.73– 99.99
99	100.00	96.34–100.00	94.79–100.00

N = 100

x	$100p_x$	95% $100p_l$ – $100p_r$	99% $100p_l$ – $100p_r$
0	0.00	0.00– 3.62	0.00– 5.16
1	1.00	0.03– 5.45	0.01– 7.20
2	2.00	0.24– 7.04	0.10– 8.94
3	3.00	0.62– 8.52	0.34– 10.55
4	4.00	1.10– 9.93	0.68– 12.06
5	5.00	1.64– 11.28	1.09– 13.51
6	6.00	2.23– 12.60	1.56– 14.92
7	7.00	2.86– 13.89	2.08– 16.28
8	8.00	3.52– 15.16	2.63– 17.61
9	9.00	4.20– 16.40	3.21– 18.92
10	10.00	4.90– 17.62	3.82– 20.20
11	11.00	5.62– 18.83	4.45– 21.45
12	12.00	6.36– 20.02	5.10– 22.70
13	13.00	7.11– 21.20	5.77– 23.92
14	14.00	7.87– 22.37	6.45– 25.13
15	15.00	8.65– 23.53	7.15– 26.32
16	16.00	9.43– 24.68	7.87– 27.51
17	17.00	10.23– 25.82	8.59– 28.68
18	18.00	11.03– 26.95	9.33– 29.84
19	19.00	11.84– 28.07	10.08– 30.98
20	20.00	12.67– 29.18	10.84– 32.12
21	21.00	13.49– 30.29	11.61– 33.25
22	22.00	14.33– 31.39	12.39– 34.37
23	23.00	15.17– 32.49	13.18– 35.49
24	24.00	16.02– 33.57	13.97– 36.59
25	25.00	16.88– 34.66	14.77– 37.69
26	26.00	17.74– 35.73	15.59– 38.77
27	27.00	18.61– 36.80	16.40– 39.86
28	28.00	19.48– 37.87	17.23– 40.93
29	29.00	20.36– 38.93	18.06– 42.00

N = 100 (continued)

x	$100p_x$	95% $100p_l$ – $100p_r$	99% $100p_l$ – $100p_r$
30	30.00	21.24– 39.98	18.90– 43.06
31	31.00	22.13– 41.03	19.75– 44.12
32	32.00	23.02– 42.08	20.60– 45.17
33	33.00	23.92– 43.12	21.46– 46.21
34	34.00	24.82– 44.15	22.32– 47.25
35	35.00	25.73– 45.18	23.19– 48.28
36	36.00	26.64– 46.21	24.07– 49.30
37	37.00	27.56– 47.24	24.95– 50.32
38	38.00	28.48– 48.25	25.84– 51.34
39	39.00	29.40– 49.27	26.73– 52.35
40	40.00	30.33– 50.28	27.63– 53.35
41	41.00	31.26– 51.29	28.53– 54.35
42	42.00	32.20– 52.29	29.44– 55.35
43	43.00	33.14– 53.29	30.35– 56.33
44	44.00	34.08– 54.28	31.27– 57.32
45	45.00	35.03– 55.27	32.19– 58.30
46	46.00	35.98– 56.26	33.12– 59.27
47	47.00	36.94– 57.24	34.06– 60.24
48	48.00	37.90– 58.22	34.99– 61.20
49	49.00	38.86– 59.20	35.94– 62.16
50	50.00	39.83– 60.17	36.89– 63.11
51	51.00	40.80– 61.14	37.84– 64.06
52	52.00	41.78– 62.10	38.80– 65.01
53	53.00	42.76– 63.06	39.76– 65.94
54	54.00	43.74– 64.02	40.73– 66.88
55	55.00	44.73– 64.97	41.70– 67.81
56	56.00	45.72– 65.92	42.68– 68.73
57	57.00	46.71– 66.86	43.67– 69.65
58	58.00	47.71– 67.80	44.65– 70.56
59	59.00	48.71– 68.74	45.65– 71.47
60	60.00	49.72– 69.67	46.65– 72.37
61	61.00	50.73– 70.60	47.65– 73.27
62	62.00	51.75– 71.52	48.66– 74.16
63	63.00	52.76– 72.44	49.68– 75.05
64	64.00	53.79– 73.36	50.70– 75.93
65	65.00	54.82– 74.27	51.72– 76.81
66	66.00	55.85– 75.18	52.75– 77.68
67	67.00	56.88– 76.08	53.79– 78.54
68	68.00	57.92– 76.98	54.83– 79.40
69	69.00	58.97– 77.87	55.88– 80.25
70	70.00	60.02– 78.76	56.94– 81.10
71	71.00	61.07– 79.64	58.00– 81.94
72	72.00	62.13– 80.52	59.07– 82.77
73	73.00	63.20– 81.39	60.14– 83.60
74	74.00	64.27– 82.26	61.23– 84.41
75	75.00	65.34– 83.12	62.31– 85.23
76	76.00	66.43– 83.98	63.41– 86.03
77	77.00	67.51– 84.83	64.51– 86.82
78	78.00	68.61– 85.67	65.63– 87.61
79	79.00	69.71– 86.51	66.75– 88.39
80	80.00	70.82– 87.33	67.88– 89.16
81	81.00	71.93– 88.16	69.02– 89.92
82	82.00	73.05– 88.97	70.16– 90.67
83	83.00	74.18– 89.77	71.32– 91.41
84	84.00	75.32– 90.57	72.49– 92.13
85	85.00	76.47– 91.35	73.68– 92.85
86	86.00	77.63– 92.13	74.87– 93.55
87	87.00	78.80– 92.89	76.08– 94.23
88	88.00	79.98– 93.64	77.30– 94.90
89	89.00	81.17– 94.38	78.55– 95.55
90	90.00	82.38– 95.10	79.80– 96.18
91	91.00	83.60– 95.80	81.08– 96.79
92	92.00	84.84– 96.48	82.39– 97.37
93	93.00	86.11– 97.14	83.72– 97.92
94	94.00	87.40– 97.77	85.08– 98.44
95	95.00	88.72– 98.36	86.49– 98.91
96	96.00	90.07– 98.90	87.94– 99.32
97	97.00	91.48– 99.38	89.45– 99.66
98	98.00	92.96– 99.76	91.06– 99.90
99	99.00	94.55– 99.97	92.80– 99.99
100	100.00	96.38–100.00	94.84–100.00

$N=$ number of trials, $x=$ number of successes, etc., $100\,p_x = 100\,x/N$

Values in *italics* are exact, all others have been calculated from FREEMAN and TUKEY's approximation. For interpolation see page 186

x	$N=105$	100 (1 − 2 α) limits		$N=110$	100 (1 − 2 α) limits		$N=120$	100 (1 − 2 α) limits		$N=130$	100 (1 − 2 α) limits	
	$100\,p_x$	95% $100\,p_l$ $100\,p_r$	99% $100\,p_l$ $100\,p_r$	$100\,p_x$	95% $100\,p_l$ $100\,p_r$	99% $100\,p_l$ $100\,p_r$	$100\,p_x$	95% $100\,p_l$ $100\,p_r$	99% $100\,p_l$ $100\,p_r$	$100\,p_x$	95% $100\,p_l$ $100\,p_r$	99% $100\,p_l$ $100\,p_r$
0	*0.00*	*0.00- 3.45*	*0.00- 4.92*	*0.00*	*0.00- 3.30*	*0.00- 4.70*	*0.00*	*0.00- 3.03*	*0.00- 4.32*	*0.00*	*0.00- 2.80*	*0.00- 3.99*
1	*0.95*	*0.02- 5.19*	*0.00- 6.86*	*0.91*	*0.02- 4.96*	*0.00- 6.56*	*0.83*	*0.02- 4.56*	*0.00- 6.03*	*0.77*	*0.02- 4.21*	*0.00- 5.58*
2	*1.90*	*0.23- 6.71*	*0.10- 8.53*	*1.82*	*0.22- 6.41*	*0.09- 8.16*	*1.67*	*0.20- 5.89*	*0.09- 7.50*	*1.54*	*0.19- 5.45*	*0.08- 6.94*
3	*2.86*	*0.59- 8.12*	*0.32-10.07*	*2.73*	*0.57- 7.76*	*0.31- 9.62*	*2.50*	*0.52- 7.13*	*0.28- 8.85*	*2.31*	*0.48- 6.60*	*0.26- 8.19*
4	*3.81*	*1.05- 9.47*	*0.65-11.51*	*3.64*	*1.00- 9.05*	*0.62-11.01*	*3.33*	*0.92- 8.31*	*0.57-10.13*	*3.08*	*0.84- 7.69*	*0.52- 9.37*
5	4.76	1.53-10.84	0.88-12.78	4.55	1.46-10.37	0.84-12.23	4.17	1.34- 9.53	0.77-11.24	3.85	1.23- 8.81	0.71-10.41
6	5.71	2.10-12.10	1.33-14.13	5.45	2.00-11.56	1.26-13.51	5.00	1.83-10.63	1.16-12.43	4.62	1.69- 9.84	1.06-11.50
7	6.67	2.70-13.32	1.81-15.43	6.36	2.58-12.74	1.73-14.76	5.83	2.36-11.71	1.58-13.58	5.38	2.17-10.84	1.46-12.57
8	7.62	3.33-14.53	2.34-16.71	7.27	3.18-13.89	2.23-15.98	6.67	2.91-12.77	2.04-14.71	6.15	2.68-11.82	1.88-13.62
9	8.57	3.99-15.71	2.90-17.96	8.18	3.80-15.02	2.76-17.18	7.50	3.48-13.81	2.52-15.81	6.92	3.20-12.79	2.32-14.64
10	9.52	4.66-16.87	3.48-19.19	9.09	4.44-16.14	3.31-18.36	8.33	4.06-14.84	3.03-16.90	7.69	3.74-13.74	2.79-15.65
11	10.48	5.35-18.03	4.08-20.40	10.00	5.10-17.24	3.89-19.52	9.17	4.66-15.86	3.55-17.97	8.46	4.30-14.68	3.27-16.65
12	11.43	6.05-19.16	4.70-21.59	10.91	5.77-18.33	4.48-20.66	10.00	5.28-16.86	4.09-19.02	9.23	4.86-15.61	3.77-17.62
13	12.38	6.77-20.29	5.34-22.76	11.82	6.45-19.41	5.09-21.79	10.83	5.90-17.86	4.65-20.06	10.00	5.43-16.53	4.28-18.59
14	13.33	7.50-21.41	6.00-23.92	12.73	7.15-20.48	5.71-22.90	11.67	6.53-18.84	5.22-21.09	10.77	6.02-17.45	4.80-19.55
15	14.29	8.24-22.51	6.67-25.07	13.64	7.85-21.54	6.35-24.00	12.50	7.18-19.82	5.80-22.11	11.54	6.61-18.35	5.34-20.49
16	15.24	8.99-23.61	7.35-26.21	14.55	8.57-22.59	7.00-25.09	13.33	7.83-20.79	6.39-23.12	12.31	7.21-19.25	5.88-21.43
17	16.19	9.75-24.69	8.04-27.33	15.45	9.29-23.63	7.66-26.17	14.17	8.49-21.75	6.99-24.11	13.08	7.82-20.15	6.43-22.36
18	17.14	10.51-25.77	8.75-28.45	16.36	10.02-24.66	8.33-27.24	15.00	9.16-22.70	7.61-25.10	13.85	8.43-21.03	7.00-23.28
19	18.10	11.29-26.85	9.47-29.55	17.27	10.76-25.69	9.01-28.30	15.83	9.83-23.65	8.23-26.08	14.62	9.05-21.91	7.57-24.19
20	19.05	12.07-27.91	10.19-30.65	18.18	11.50-26.71	9.70-29.35	16.67	10.51-24.59	8.86-27.06	15.38	9.68-22.79	8.14-25.10
21	20.00	12.86-28.97	10.93-31.74	19.09	12.25-27.73	10.40-30.39	17.50	11.20-25.53	9.49-28.02	16.15	10.31-23.66	8.73-25.99
22	20.95	13.66-30.02	11.67-32.82	20.00	13.01-28.73	11.11-31.43	18.33	11.89-26.46	10.14-28.98	16.92	10.94-24.52	9.32-26.89
23	21.90	14.46-31.07	12.42-33.89	20.91	13.78-29.74	11.83-32.46	19.17	12.58-27.39	10.79-29.93	17.69	11.58-25.39	9.92-27.77
24	22.86	15.27-32.11	13.18-34.95	21.82	14.55-30.74	12.55-33.48	20.00	13.29-28.31	11.44-30.88	18.46	12.23-26.24	10.52-28.65
25	23.81	16.09-33.14	13.95-36.01	22.73	15.32-31.73	13.28-34.49	20.83	13.99-29.23	12.11-31.82	19.23	12.88-27.09	11.13-29.53
26	24.76	16.91-34.17	14.73-37.05	23.64	16.10-32.73	14.01-35.50	21.67	14.70-30.14	12.78-32.76	20.00	13.53-27.94	11.74-30.40
27	25.71	17.73-35.20	15.51-38.10	24.55	16.89-33.70	14.76-36.50	22.50	15.42-31.05	13.45-33.68	20.77	14.19-28.79	12.36-31.27
28	26.67	18.56-36.22	16.30-39.13	25.45	17.68-34.68	15.51-37.50	23.33	16.14-31.96	14.13-34.61	21.54	14.85-29.63	12.99-32.13
29	27.62	19.40-37.23	17.09-40.16	26.36	18.47-35.65	16.26-38.49	24.17	16.86-32.86	14.82-35.53	22.31	15.51-30.47	13.62-32.98
30	28.57	20.24-38.24	17.89-41.19	27.27	19.27-36.62	17.02-39.47	25.00	17.59-33.75	15.51-36.44	23.08	16.18-31.30	14.25-33.84
31	29.52	21.08-39.25	18.70-42.20	28.18	20.08-37.59	17.79-40.45	25.83	18.32-34.65	16.21-37.35	23.85	16.85-32.13	14.89-34.68
32	30.48	21.93-40.25	19.52-43.22	29.09	20.88-38.55	18.56-41.43	26.67	19.06-35.54	16.91-38.25	24.62	17.53-32.96	15.53-35.53
33	31.43	22.79-41.25	20.33-44.22	30.00	21.69-39.50	19.34-42.39	27.50	19.80-36.42	17.62-39.15	25.38	18.20-33.79	16.18-36.37
34	32.38	23.65-42.24	21.16-45.22	30.91	22.51-40.46	20.12-43.36	28.33	20.54-37.31	18.33-40.05	26.15	18.88-34.61	16.83-37.20
35	33.33	24.51-43.23	21.99-46.22	31.82	23.33-41.41	20.91-44.32	29.17	21.28-38.19	19.04-40.94	26.92	19.57-35.43	17.48-38.03
36	34.29	25.38-44.21	22.82-47.21	32.73	24.15-42.35	21.70-45.27	30.00	22.03-39.06	19.76-41.83	27.69	20.25-36.24	18.14-38.86
37	35.24	26.25-45.19	23.66-48.20	33.64	24.98-43.30	22.50-46.22	30.83	22.78-39.94	20.48-42.71	28.46	20.94-37.06	18.80-39.69
38	36.19	27.12-46.17	24.51-49.18	34.55	25.81-44.23	23.30-47.16	31.67	23.54-40.81	21.21-43.59	29.23	21.64-37.87	19.47-40.51
39	37.14	28.00-47.14	25.36-50.15	35.45	26.64-45.17	24.11-48.10	32.50	24.30-41.68	21.94-44.46	30.00	22.33-38.68	20.13-41.33
40	38.10	28.88-48.11	26.22-51.12	36.36	27.48-46.10	24.92-49.04	33.33	25.06-42.54	22.68-45.33	30.77	23.03-39.48	20.81-42.14
41	39.05	29.77-49.08	27.08-52.09	37.27	28.32-47.03	25.74-49.97	34.17	25.82-43.40	23.42-46.20	31.54	23.73-40.29	21.48-42.95
42	40.00	30.66-50.04	27.94-53.05	38.18	29.17-47.96	26.56-50.90	35.00	26.59-44.26	24.16-47.06	32.31	24.43-41.09	22.16-43.76
43	40.95	31.55-51.00	28.81-54.01	39.09	30.01-48.88	27.38-51.82	35.83	27.36-45.12	24.90-47.92	33.08	25.14-41.89	22.84-44.56
44	41.90	32.45-51.96	29.69-54.96	40.00	30.87-49.80	28.21-52.74	36.67	28.13-45.97	25.65-48.78	33.85	25.84-42.68	23.53-45.37
45	42.86	33.35-52.91	30.57-55.91	40.91	31.72-50.71	29.04-53.65	37.50	28.90-46.82	26.41-49.63	34.62	26.55-43.48	24.22-46.17
46	43.81	34.25-53.86	31.45-56.85	41.82	32.58-51.63	29.88-54.56	38.33	29.68-47.67	27.17-50.48	35.38	27.26-44.27	24.91-46.96
47	44.76	35.16-54.80	32.34-57.79	42.73	33.44-52.54	30.72-55.47	39.17	30.46-48.52	27.93-51.33	36.15	27.98-45.06	25.60-47.75
48	45.71	36.07-55.74	33.23-58.72	43.64	34.30-53.44	31.57-56.37	40.00	31.25-49.36	28.69-52.17	36.92	28.69-45.84	26.30-48.54
49	46.67	36.98-56.68	34.13-59.65	44.55	35.17-54.35	32.42-57.27	40.83	32.03-50.20	29.46-53.01	37.69	29.41-46.63	27.00-49.33
50	47.62	37.90-57.62	35.04-60.57	45.45	36.04-55.25	33.27-58.16	41.67	32.82-51.04	30.23-53.85	38.46	30.13-47.41	27.70-50.12
51	48.57	38.82-58.55	35.94-61.49	46.36	36.91-56.14	34.13-59.05	42.50	33.61-51.87	31.00-54.68	39.23	30.86-48.19	28.41-50.90
52	49.52	39.74-59.48	36.85-62.41	47.27	37.79-57.04	34.99-59.94	43.33	34.40-52.71	31.78-55.51	40.00	31.58-48.97	29.12-51.68
53	50.48	40.52-60.26	37.59-63.15	48.18	38.67-57.93	35.86-60.82	44.17	35.20-53.54	32.56-56.34	40.77	32.31-49.75	29.83-52.45
54	51.43	41.45-61.18	38.51-64.06	49.09	39.55-58.82	36.73-61.70	45.00	36.00-54.36	33.35-57.16	41.54	33.04-50.52	30.54-53.22
55	52.38	42.38-62.10	39.43-64.96	50.00	40.36-59.64	37.51-62.49	45.83	36.80-55.19	34.13-57.98	42.31	33.77-51.30	31.26-53.99
56	53.33	43.32-63.02	40.35-65.87	50.91	41.18-60.45	38.30-63.27	46.67	37.60-56.01	34.92-58.79	43.08	34.51-52.07	31.98-54.76
57	54.29	44.26-63.93	41.28-66.77	51.82	42.07-61.33	39.18-64.14	47.50	38.41-56.83	35.72-59.61	43.85	35.24-52.83	32.70-55.53
58	55.24	45.20-64.84	42.21-67.66	52.73	42.96-62.21	40.06-65.01	48.33	39.22-57.65	36.52-60.42	44.62	35.98-53.60	33.43-56.29
59	56.19	46.14-65.75	43.15-68.55	53.64	43.86-63.09	40.95-65.87	49.17	40.03-58.47	37.32-61.23	45.38	36.72-54.36	34.16-57.05
60	57.14	47.09-66.65	44.09-69.43	54.55	44.75-63.96	41.84-66.73	50.00	40.78-59.22	38.04-61.96	46.15	37.46-55.13	34.89-57.81
61	58.10	48.04-67.55	45.04-70.31	55.45	45.65-64.83	42.73-67.58	50.83	41.53-59.97	38.77-62.68	46.92	38.21-55.89	35.62-58.56
62	59.05	49.00-68.45	45.99-71.19	56.36	46.56-65.70	43.63-68.43	51.67	42.35-60.78	39.58-63.48	47.69	38.95-56.64	36.36-59.31
63	60.00	49.96-69.34	46.95-72.06	57.27	47.46-66.56	44.53-69.28	52.50	43.17-61.59	40.39-64.28	48.46	39.70-57.40	37.10-60.06
64	60.95	50.92-70.23	47.91-72.92	58.18	48.37-67.42	45.44-70.12	53.33	43.99-62.40	41.21-65.08	49.23	40.45-58.15	37.84-60.81
65	61.90	51.89-71.12	48.88-73.78	59.09	49.29-68.28	46.35-70.96	54.17	44.81-63.20	42.02-65.87	50.00	41.14-58.86	38.51-61.51
66	62.86	52.86-72.00	49.85-74.64	60.00	50.20-69.13	47.26-71.79	55.00	45.64-64.00	42.84-66.65	50.77	41.85-59.55	39.19-62.16
67	63.81	53.83-72.88	50.82-75.49	60.91	51.12-69.99	48.18-72.62	55.83	46.46-64.80	43.66-67.44	51.54	42.60-60.30	39.94-62.90
68	64.76	54.81-73.75	51.80-76.34	61.82	52.04-70.83	49.10-73.44	56.67	47.29-65.60	44.49-68.22	52.31	43.36-61.05	40.69-63.64
69	65.71	55.79-74.62	52.79-77.18	62.73	52.97-71.68	50.03-74.26	57.50	48.13-66.39	45.32-69.00	53.08	44.11-61.79	41.44-64.38
70	66.67	56.77-75.49	53.78-78.01	63.64	53.90-72.52	50.96-75.08	58.33	48.96-67.18	46.15-69.77	53.85	44.87-62.54	42.19-65.11
71	67.62	57.76-76.35	54.78-78.84	64.55	54.83-73.36	51.90-75.89	59.17	49.80-67.97	46.99-70.54	54.62	45.64-63.28	42.95-65.84
72	68.57	58.75-77.21	55.78-79.67	65.45	55.77-74.19	52.84-76.70	60.00	50.64-68.75	47.83-71.31	55.38	46.40-64.02	43.71-66.57
73	69.52	59.75-78.07	56.78-80.48	66.36	56.70-75.02	53.78-77.50	60.83	51.48-69.54	48.67-72.07	56.15	47.17-64.76	44.47-67.30
74	70.48	60.75-78.92	57.80-81.30	67.27	57.65-75.85	54.73-78.30	61.67	52.33-70.32	49.52-72.83	56.92	47.93-65.49	45.24-68.02
75	71.43	61.76-79.76	58.81-82.11	68.18	58.59-76.67	55.68-79.09	62.50	53.18-71.10	50.37-73.59	57.69	48.70-66.23	46.01-68.74
76	72.38	62.77-80.60	59.84-82.91	69.09	59.54-77.49	56.64-79.88	63.33	54.03-71.87	51.22-74.35	58.46	49.48-66.96	46.78-69.46
77	73.33	63.78-81.44	60.87-83.70	70.00	60.50-78.31	57.61-80.66	64.17	54.88-72.64	52.08-75.10	59.23	50.25-67.69	47.55-70.17
78	74.29	64.80-82.27	61.90-84.49	70.91	61.45-79.12	58.57-81.44	65.00	55.74-73.41	52.94-75.84	60.00	51.03-68.42	48.32-70.88
79	75.24	65.83-83.09	62.95-85.27	71.82	62.41-79.92	59.55-82.21	65.83	56.60-74.18	53.80-76.58	60.77	51.81-69.14	49.10-71.59
80	76.19	66.86-83.91	63.99-86.05	72.73	63.38-80.73	60.53-82.98	66.67	57.46-74.94	54.67-77.32	61.54	52.59-69.87	49.88-72.30
81	77.14	67.89-84.73	65.05-86.82	73.64	64.35-81.53	61.51-83.74	67.50	58.32-75.70	55.54-78.06	62.31	53.37-70.59	50.67-73.00
82	78.10	68.93-85.54	66.11-87.58	74.55	65.32-82.32	62.50-84.49	68.33	59.19-76.46	56.41-78.79	63.08	54.16-71.31	51.46-73.70
83	79.05	69.98-86.34	67.18-88.33	75.45	66.30-83.11	63.50-85.24	69.17	60.06-77.22	57.29-79.52	63.85	54.94-72.02	52.25-74.40
84	80.00	71.03-87.14	68.26-89.07	76.36	67.27-83.90	64.50-85.99	70.00	60.94-77.97	58.17-80.24	64.62	55.73-72.74	53.04-75.09
85	80.95	72.09-87.93	69.35-89.81	77.27	68.27-84.68	65.51-86.72	70.83	61.81-78.72	59.06-80.96	65.38	56.52-73.45	53.83-75.78
86	81.90	73.15-88.71	70.45-90.53	78.18	69.26-85.45	66.52-87.45	71.67	62.69-79.46	59.95-81.67	66.15	57.32-74.16	54.63-76.47
87	82.86	74.23-89.49	71.55-91.25	79.09	70.26-86.22	67.54-88.17	72.50	63.58-80.20	60.85-82.38	66.92	58.11-74.86	55.44-77.16
88	83.81	75.31-90.25	72.67-91.96	80.00	71.27-86.99	68.57-88.89	73.33	64.46-80.94	61.75-83.09	67.69	58.91-75.57	56.24-77.84
89	84.76	76.39-91.01	73.79-92.65	80.91	72.27-87.75	69.61-89.60	74.17	65.35-81.68	62.65-83.79	68.46	59.71-76.27	57.05-78.52
90	85.71	77.49-91.76	74.93-93.33	81.82	73.29-88.50	70.65-90.30	75.00	66.25-82.41	63.56-84.49	69.23	60.52-76.97	57.86-79.19
91	86.67	78.59-92.50	76.08-94.00	82.73	74.31-89.24	71.70-90.99	75.83	67.14-83.14	64.47-85.18	70.00	61.32-77.67	58.67-79.87
92	87.62	79.71-93.23	77.24-94.66	83.64	75.34-89.98	72.76-91.67	76.67	68.04-83.86	65.39-85.87	70.77	62.13-78.36	59.49-80.53
93	88.57	80.84-93.95	78.41-95.30	84.55	76.37-90.71	73.83-92.34	77.50	68.95-84.58	66.32-86.55	71.54	62.94-79.06	60.31-81.20
94	89.52	81.97-94.65	79.60-95.92	85.45	77.41-91.43	74.91-93.00	78.33	69.86-85.30	67.24-87.22	72.31	63.76-79.75	61.14-81.86
95	90.48	83.13-95.34	80.81-96.52	86.36	78.46-92.15	76.00-93.65	79.17	70.77-86.01	68.18-87.89	73.08	64.57-80.43	61.97-82.52
96	91.43	84.29-96.01	82.04-97.10	87.27	79.52-92.85	77.10-94.29	80.00	71.69-86.71	69.12-88.56	73.85	65.39-81.12	62.80-83.17
97	92.38	85.47-96.67	83.29-97.66	88.18	80.59-93.55	78.21-94.91	80.83	72.61-87.42	70.07-89.21	74.62	66.21-81.80	63.63-83.82
98	93.33	86.68-97.30	84.57-98.19	89.09	81.67-94.23	79.34-95.52	81.67	73.54-88.11	71.02-89.86	75.38	67.04-82.47	64.47-84.47
99	94.29	87.90-97.90	85.87-98.67	90.00	82.76-94.90	80.48-96.11	82.50	74.47-88.80	71.98-90.51	76.15	67.87-83.15	65.32-85.11
100	95.24	89.16-98.47	87.22-99.12	90.91	83.86-95.56	81.64-96.69	83.33	75.41-89.49	72.94-91.14	76.92	68.70-83.82	66.16-85.75

N = number of trials, x = number of successes, etc., $100\,p_x = 100\,x/N$

Values in *italics* are exact, all others have been calculated from Freeman and Tukey's approximation. For interpolation see page 186

x	N = 140			N = 150			N = 160			N = 170		
	$100p_x$	100 (1 − 2α) limits 95 % $100p_l$ $100p_r$	99 % $100p_l$ $100p_r$	$100p_x$	95 % $100p_l$ $100p_r$	99 % $100p_l$ $100p_r$	$100p_x$	95 % $100p_l$ $100p_r$	99 % $100p_l$ $100p_r$	$100p_x$	95 % $100p_l$ $100p_r$	99 % $100p_l$ $100p_r$
0	0.00	0.00– 2.60	0.00– 3.71	0.00	0.00– 2.43	0.00– 3.47	0.00	0.00– 2.28	0.00– 3.26	0.00	0.00– 2.15	0.00– 3.07
1	0.71	0.02– 3.92	0.00– 5.19	0.67	0.02– 3.66	0.00– 4.85	0.63	0.02– 3.43	0.00– 4.55	0.59	0.01– 3.23	0.00– 4.29
2	1.43	0.17– 5.07	0.07– 6.45	1.33	0.16– 4.73	0.07– 6.03	1.25	0.15– 4.44	0.07– 5.67	1.18	0.14– 4.19	0.06– 5.34
3	2.14	0.45– 6.13	0.24– 7.62	2.00	0.42– 5.73	0.23– 7.13	1.88	0.39– 5.38	0.21– 6.69	1.76	0.37– 5.07	0.20– 6.31
4	2.86	0.78– 7.15	0.49– 8.72	2.67	0.73– 6.69	0.45– 8.16	2.50	0.69– 6.28	0.42– 7.66	2.35	0.64– 5.91	0.40– 7.22
5	3.57	1.14– 8.20	0.66– 9.68	3.33	1.07– 7.66	0.61– 9.06	3.13	1.00– 7.20	0.57– 8.51	2.94	0.94– 6.78	0.54– 8.02
6	4.29	1.57– 9.15	0.99–10.71	4.00	1.46– 8.56	0.92–10.02	3.75	1.37– 8.03	0.86– 9.41	3.53	1.29– 7.57	0.81– 8.87
7	5.00	2.02–10.08	1.35–11.71	4.67	1.88– 9.43	1.26–10.95	4.38	1.76– 8.85	1.18–10.29	4.12	1.66– 8.34	1.11– 9.70
8	5.71	2.48–11.00	1.74–12.68	5.33	2.32–10.28	1.62–11.86	5.00	2.17– 9.66	1.52–11.14	4.71	2.04– 9.10	1.43–10.51
9	6.43	2.97–11.90	2.15–13.64	6.00	2.77–11.13	2.00–12.76	5.63	2.59–10.45	1.88–11.99	5.29	2.44– 9.85	1.76–11.30
10	7.14	3.47–12.79	2.58–14.58	6.67	3.23–11.96	2.41–13.64	6.25	3.03–11.23	2.25–12.82	5.88	2.85–10.59	2.12–12.09
11	7.86	3.98–13.67	3.03–15.50	7.33	3.71–12.78	2.82–14.51	6.88	3.47–12.01	2.64–13.63	6.47	3.27–11.32	2.48–12.86
12	8.57	4.50–14.53	3.49–16.42	8.00	4.20–13.60	3.25–15.37	7.50	3.93–12.77	3.04–14.44	7.06	3.70–12.04	2.86–13.62
13	9.29	5.04–15.39	3.96–17.32	8.67	4.69–14.40	3.69–16.21	8.13	4.39–13.53	3.45–15.24	7.65	4.13–12.75	3.24–14.37
14	10.00	5.58–16.25	4.45–18.21	9.33	5.20–15.20	4.14–17.05	8.75	4.87–14.28	3.87–16.03	8.24	4.57–13.46	3.64–15.12
15	10.71	6.13–17.09	4.94–19.10	10.00	5.71–15.99	4.60–17.88	9.38	5.34–15.02	4.30–16.81	8.82	5.02–14.17	4.04–15.85
16	11.43	6.68–17.93	5.44–19.97	10.67	6.23–16.78	5.07–18.70	10.00	5.83–15.76	4.74–17.58	9.41	5.48–14.86	4.45–16.58
17	12.14	7.24–18.76	5.96–20.84	11.33	6.75–17.56	5.54–19.51	10.63	6.32–16.50	5.19–18.34	10.00	5.94–15.56	4.87–17.31
18	12.86	7.81–19.59	6.48–21.70	12.00	7.28–18.33	6.03–20.32	11.25	6.81–17.23	5.64–19.10	10.59	6.40–16.25	5.30–18.03
19	13.57	8.38–20.41	7.00–22.55	12.67	7.81–19.10	6.52–21.12	11.88	7.31–17.95	6.10–19.86	11.18	6.87–16.93	5.73–18.74
20	14.29	8.96–21.23	7.54–23.40	13.33	8.35–19.87	7.02–21.91	12.50	7.81–18.67	6.56–20.61	11.76	7.34–17.61	6.16–19.45
21	15.00	9.55–22.04	8.08–24.24	14.00	8.89–20.63	7.52–22.70	13.13	8.32–19.39	7.03–21.35	12.35	7.82–18.29	6.60–20.15
22	15.71	10.13–22.85	8.62–25.07	14.67	9.44–21.39	8.03–23.49	13.75	8.83–20.10	7.50–22.09	12.94	8.30–18.96	7.05–20.85
23	16.43	10.73–23.65	9.18–25.90	15.33	9.99–22.14	8.54–24.27	14.38	9.35–20.81	7.98–22.82	13.53	8.78–19.63	7.50–21.54
24	17.14	11.32–24.45	9.73–26.73	16.00	10.55–22.89	9.06–25.04	15.00	9.87–21.52	8.47–23.55	14.12	9.27–20.30	7.95–22.23
25	17.86	11.92–25.25	10.30–27.55	16.67	11.10–23.64	9.58–25.81	15.63	10.39–22.22	8.96–24.28	14.71	9.76–20.96	8.41–22.92
26	18.57	12.53–26.04	10.86–28.36	17.33	11.67–24.38	10.11–26.57	16.25	10.91–22.92	9.45–25.00	15.29	10.25–21.62	8.87–23.60
27	19.29	13.14–26.83	11.43–29.17	18.00	12.23–25.12	10.64–27.34	16.88	11.44–23.62	9.94–25.72	15.88	10.75–22.28	9.34–24.28
28	20.00	13.75–27.62	12.01–29.98	18.67	12.80–25.86	11.17–28.09	17.50	11.97–24.31	10.44–26.43	16.47	11.25–22.94	9.80–24.96
29	20.71	14.36–28.40	12.59–30.78	19.33	13.37–26.59	11.71–28.85	18.13	12.51–25.00	10.95–27.14	17.06	11.75–23.59	10.28–25.63
30	21.43	14.98–29.18	13.18–31.58	20.00	13.94–27.33	12.25–29.60	18.75	13.04–25.69	11.45–27.85	17.65	12.25–24.24	10.75–26.30
31	22.14	15.60–29.96	13.77–32.37	20.67	14.52–28.06	12.80–30.34	19.38	13.58–26.38	11.96–28.56	18.24	12.76–24.89	11.23–26.97
32	22.86	16.22–30.73	14.36–33.16	21.33	15.10–28.78	13.35–31.09	20.00	14.12–27.07	12.48–29.26	18.82	13.27–25.54	11.71–27.63
33	23.57	16.85–31.50	14.95–33.95	22.00	15.68–29.51	13.90–31.83	20.63	14.67–27.75	12.99–29.96	19.41	13.78–26.19	12.19–28.29
34	24.29	17.48–32.27	15.55–34.73	22.67	16.27–30.23	14.46–32.56	21.25	15.21–28.43	13.51–30.65	20.00	14.29–26.83	12.68–28.95
35	25.00	18.11–33.04	16.16–35.51	23.33	16.85–30.95	15.02–33.30	21.88	15.76–29.11	14.03–31.34	20.59	14.80–27.47	13.17–29.61
36	25.71	18.74–33.80	16.76–36.29	24.00	17.44–31.67	15.58–34.03	22.50	16.31–29.78	14.56–32.03	21.18	15.32–28.11	13.66–30.26
37	26.43	19.38–34.56	17.37–37.06	24.67	18.03–32.38	16.15–34.76	23.13	16.86–30.46	15.09–32.72	21.76	15.84–28.75	14.16–30.91
38	27.14	20.02–35.32	17.99–37.83	25.33	18.63–33.09	16.72–35.48	23.75	17.42–31.13	15.62–33.41	22.35	16.36–29.38	14.65–31.56
39	27.86	20.66–36.08	18.60–38.60	26.00	19.22–33.81	17.29–36.21	24.38	17.97–31.80	16.15–34.09	22.94	16.88–30.02	15.15–32.21
40	28.57	21.30–36.83	19.22–39.36	26.67	19.82–34.51	17.86–36.93	25.00	18.53–32.47	16.69–34.77	23.53	17.40–30.65	15.65–32.85
41	29.29	21.95–37.59	19.85–40.12	27.33	20.42–35.22	18.44–37.64	25.63	19.09–33.13	17.22–35.45	24.12	17.92–31.28	16.16–33.49
42	30.00	22.60–38.34	20.47–40.88	28.00	21.02–35.93	19.02–38.36	26.25	19.65–33.80	17.76–36.12	24.71	18.45–31.91	16.66–34.13
43	30.71	23.25–39.08	21.10–41.64	28.67	21.63–36.63	19.60–39.07	26.88	20.22–34.46	18.31–36.80	25.29	18.98–32.54	17.17–34.77
44	31.43	23.90–39.83	21.73–42.39	29.33	22.23–37.33	20.19–39.78	27.50	20.78–35.12	18.85–37.47	25.88	19.51–33.16	17.68–35.41
45	32.14	24.56–40.57	22.36–43.14	30.00	22.84–38.03	20.77–40.49	28.13	21.35–35.78	19.40–38.14	26.47	20.04–33.79	18.19–36.04
46	32.86	25.21–41.31	23.00–43.89	30.67	23.45–38.73	21.36–41.19	28.75	21.92–36.44	19.95–38.80	27.06	20.57–34.41	18.71–36.67
47	33.57	25.87–42.05	23.64–44.64	31.33	24.06–39.42	21.95–41.90	29.38	22.49–37.10	20.50–39.47	27.65	21.11–35.03	19.22–37.30
48	34.29	26.53–42.79	24.28–45.38	32.00	24.67–40.12	22.55–42.60	30.00	23.06–37.75	21.05–40.13	28.24	21.64–35.65	19.74–37.93
49	35.00	27.19–43.53	24.92–46.12	32.67	25.29–40.81	23.15–43.29	30.63	23.63–38.41	21.61–40.79	28.82	22.18–36.27	20.26–38.56
50	35.71	27.86–44.26	25.57–46.86	33.33	25.90–41.50	23.74–43.99	31.25	24.21–39.06	22.16–41.45	29.41	22.72–36.89	20.78–39.18
51	36.43	28.52–44.99	26.22–47.59	34.00	26.52–42.19	24.34–44.68	31.88	24.78–39.71	22.72–42.11	30.00	23.26–37.51	21.30–39.81
52	37.14	29.19–45.73	26.87–48.33	34.67	27.14–42.88	24.95–45.38	32.50	25.36–40.36	23.28–42.76	30.59	23.80–38.12	21.83–40.43
53	37.86	29.86–46.45	27.52–49.06	35.33	27.76–43.56	25.55–46.07	33.13	25.94–41.01	23.85–43.41	31.18	24.34–38.73	22.35–41.05
54	38.57	30.53–47.18	28.18–49.78	36.00	28.39–44.25	26.16–46.75	33.75	26.52–41.65	24.41–44.07	31.76	24.89–39.35	22.88–41.67
55	39.29	31.21–47.91	28.84–50.51	36.67	29.01–44.93	26.77–47.44	34.38	27.10–42.30	24.98–44.71	32.35	25.43–39.96	23.41–42.28
56	40.00	31.88–48.63	29.50–51.23	37.33	29.64–45.61	27.38–48.12	35.00	27.69–42.94	25.55–45.36	32.94	25.98–40.57	23.94–42.90
57	40.71	32.56–49.35	30.16–51.95	38.00	30.26–46.29	27.99–48.80	35.63	28.27–43.59	26.12–46.01	33.53	26.52–41.17	24.48–43.51
58	41.43	33.24–50.07	30.83–52.67	38.67	30.89–46.97	28.61–49.48	36.25	28.86–44.23	26.69–46.65	34.12	27.07–41.78	25.01–44.12
59	42.14	33.92–50.79	31.50–53.39	39.33	31.52–47.65	29.23–50.16	36.88	29.44–44.87	27.26–47.29	34.71	27.62–42.39	25.55–44.73
60	42.86	34.60–51.50	32.17–54.10	40.00	32.16–48.32	29.85–50.84	37.50	30.03–45.50	27.84–47.93	35.29	28.17–42.99	26.09–45.34
61	43.57	35.29–52.22	32.84–54.82	40.67	32.79–48.99	30.47–51.51	38.13	30.62–46.14	28.42–48.57	35.88	28.73–43.60	26.63–45.95
62	44.29	35.97–52.93	33.51–55.53	41.33	33.42–49.67	31.08–52.18	38.75	31.21–46.78	28.99–49.21	36.47	29.28–44.20	27.17–46.55
63	45.00	36.66–53.64	34.19–56.23	42.00	34.06–50.34	31.71–52.85	39.38	31.81–47.41	29.58–49.85	37.06	29.83–44.80	27.71–47.16
64	45.71	37.35–54.35	34.87–56.94	42.67	34.70–51.01	32.34–53.52	40.00	32.40–48.04	30.16–50.48	37.65	30.39–45.40	28.25–47.76
65	46.43	38.04–55.06	35.55–57.64	43.33	35.34–51.68	32.97–54.19	40.63	33.00–48.68	30.74–51.11	38.24	30.95–46.00	28.80–48.36
66	47.14	38.74–55.77	36.24–58.34	44.00	35.98–52.34	33.60–54.85	41.25	33.59–49.31	31.33–51.74	38.82	31.51–46.60	29.35–48.96
67	47.86	39.43–56.47	36.92–59.04	44.67	36.62–53.01	34.23–55.51	41.88	34.19–49.94	31.92–52.37	39.41	32.06–47.20	29.89–49.56
68	48.57	40.13–57.17	37.61–59.74	45.33	37.27–53.67	34.87–56.17	42.50	34.79–50.56	32.50–53.00	40.00	32.62–47.79	30.44–50.15
69	49.29	40.82–57.87	38.30–60.44	46.00	37.91–54.33	35.51–56.83	43.13	35.39–51.19	33.10–53.62	40.59	33.19–48.39	30.99–50.75
70	50.00	41.47–58.53	38.93–61.07	46.67	38.56–54.99	36.14–57.49	43.75	35.99–51.82	33.69–54.25	41.18	33.75–48.98	31.55–51.34
71	50.71	42.13–59.18	39.56–61.70	47.33	39.21–55.65	36.78–58.14	44.38	36.59–52.44	34.28–54.87	41.76	34.31–49.57	32.10–51.94
72	51.43	42.83–59.87	40.26–62.39	48.00	39.86–56.31	37.43–58.80	45.00	37.20–53.06	34.88–55.49	42.35	34.88–50.17	32.66–52.53
73	52.14	43.53–60.57	40.96–63.08	48.67	40.51–56.97	38.07–59.45	45.63	37.80–53.69	35.47–56.11	42.94	35.44–50.76	33.21–53.12
74	52.86	44.23–61.26	41.66–63.76	49.33	41.16–57.62	38.72–60.10	46.25	38.41–54.31	36.07–56.73	43.53	36.01–51.35	33.77–53.71
75	53.57	44.94–61.96	42.36–64.45	50.00	41.76–58.24	39.30–60.70	46.88	39.02–54.93	36.67–57.34	44.12	36.58–51.93	34.33–54.29
76	54.29	45.65–62.65	43.06–65.13	50.67	42.38–58.84	39.90–61.28	47.50	39.63–55.55	37.28–57.96	44.71	37.15–52.52	34.89–54.88
77	55.00	46.36–63.34	43.77–65.81	51.33	43.03–59.49	40.55–61.93	48.13	40.24–56.16	37.88–58.56	45.29	37.72–53.11	35.46–55.46
78	55.71	47.07–64.03	44.47–66.49	52.00	43.69–60.14	41.20–62.57	48.75	40.85–56.78	38.48–59.18	45.88	38.29–53.69	36.02–56.05
79	56.43	47.78–64.71	45.18–67.16	52.67	44.35–60.79	41.86–63.22	49.38	41.46–57.39	39.09–59.79	46.47	38.86–54.28	36.59–56.63
80	57.14	48.50–65.40	45.90–67.83	53.33	45.01–61.44	42.51–63.86	50.00	42.03–57.97	39.65–60.35	47.06	39.43–54.86	37.15–57.21
81	57.86	49.21–66.08	46.61–68.50	54.00	45.67–62.09	43.17–64.49	50.63	42.61–58.54	40.21–60.91	47.65	40.01–55.44	37.72–57.79
82	58.57	49.93–66.76	47.33–69.17	54.67	46.33–62.73	43.83–65.13	51.25	43.22–59.15	40.82–61.52	48.24	40.58–56.02	38.29–58.36
83	59.29	50.65–67.44	48.05–69.84	55.33	46.99–63.38	44.49–65.77	51.88	43.84–59.76	41.44–62.12	48.82	41.16–56.60	38.86–58.94
84	60.00	51.37–68.12	48.77–70.50	56.00	47.66–64.02	45.15–66.40	52.50	44.45–60.37	42.04–62.72	49.41	41.73–57.18	39.43–59.51
85	60.71	52.09–68.79	49.49–71.16	56.67	48.32–64.66	45.81–67.03	53.13	45.07–60.98	42.66–63.33	50.00	42.27–57.73	39.96–60.04
86	61.43	52.82–69.47	50.22–71.82	57.33	48.99–65.30	46.48–67.66	53.75	45.69–61.59	43.27–63.93	50.59	42.82–58.27	40.49–60.57
87	62.14	53.55–70.14	50.94–72.48	58.00	49.66–65.94	47.15–68.29	54.38	46.31–62.20	43.89–64.53	51.18	43.40–58.84	41.06–61.14
88	62.86	54.27–70.81	51.67–73.13	58.67	50.33–66.58	47.82–68.92	55.00	46.94–62.80	44.51–65.12	51.76	43.98–59.42	41.64–61.71
89	63.57	55.01–71.48	52.41–73.78	59.33	51.01–67.21	48.49–69.53	55.63	47.56–63.41	45.13–65.72	52.35	44.56–59.99	42.21–62.28
90	64.29	55.74–72.14	53.14–74.43	60.00	51.68–67.84	49.16–70.15	56.25	48.18–64.01	45.75–66.31	52.94	45.14–60.57	42.79–62.85
91	65.00	56.47–72.81	53.88–75.08	60.67	52.35–68.48	49.84–70.77	56.88	48.81–64.61	46.38–66.90	53.53	45.72–61.14	43.37–63.41
92	65.71	57.21–73.47	54.62–75.72	61.33	53.03–69.11	50.52–71.39	57.50	49.44–65.21	47.00–67.50	54.12	46.31–61.71	43.95–63.98
93	66.43	57.95–74.13	55.36–76.36	62.00	53.71–69.74	51.20–72.01	58.13	50.06–65.81	47.63–68.08	54.71	46.89–62.28	44.54–64.54
94	67.14	58.69–74.79	56.11–77.00	62.67	54.39–70.36	51.88–72.62	58.75	50.69–66.41	48.26–68.67	55.29	47.48–62.85	45.12–65.11
95	67.86	59.43–75.44	56.86–77.64	63.33	55.07–70.99	52.56–73.23	59.38	51.32–67.00	48.89–69.26	55.88	48.07–63.42	45.71–65.67
96	68.57	60.17–76.10	57.61–78.27	64.00	55.75–71.61	53.25–73.84	60.00	51.96–67.60	49.52–69.84	56.47	48.65–63.99	46.29–66.23
97	69.29	60.92–76.75	58.36–78.90	64.67	56.44–72.24	53.93–74.45	60.63	52.59–68.19	50.15–70.42	57.06	49.24–64.56	46.88–66.79
98	70.00	61.66–77.40	59.12–79.53	65.33	57.12–72.86	54.62–75.05	61.25	53.22–68.79	50.79–71.01	57.65	49.83–65.12	47.47–67.34
99	70.71	62.41–78.05	59.88–80.15	66.00	57.81–73.48	55.32–75.66	61.88	53.86–69.38	51.43–71.58	58.24	50.43–65.69	48.06–67.90
100	71.43	63.17–78.70	60.64–80.78	66.67	58.50–74.10	56.01–76.26	62.50	54.50–69.97	52.07–72.16	58.82	51.02–66.25	48.66–68.45

$N=$ number of trials, $x=$ number of successes, etc., $100\,p_x = 100\,x/N$

Values in *italics* are exact, all others have been calculated from FREEMAN and TUKEY's approximation. For interpolation see page 186

x	N = 180: $100p_x$	N = 180: 100 (1 − 2α) limits 95 % $100p_l$ – $100p_r$	N = 180: 100 (1 − 2α) limits 99 % $100p_l$ – $100p_r$	N = 190: $100p_x$	N = 190: 100 (1 − 2α) limits 95 % $100p_l$ – $100p_r$	N = 190: 100 (1 − 2α) limits 99 % $100p_l$ – $100p_r$
0	*0.00*	*0.00– 2.03*	*0.00– 2.90*	*0.00*	*0.00– 1.92*	*0.00– 2.75*
1	*0.56*	*0.01– 3.06*	*0.00– 4.06*	*0.53*	*0.01– 2.90*	*0.00– 3.85*
2	*1.11*	*0.14– 3.96*	*0.06– 5.05*	*1.05*	*0.13– 3.75*	*0.05– 4.79*
3	*1.67*	*0.35– 4.79*	*0.19– 5.97*	*1.58*	*0.33– 4.54*	*0.18– 5.66*
4	*2.22*	*0.61– 5.59*	*0.38– 6.83*	*2.11*	*0.58– 5.30*	*0.36– 6.48*
5	2.78	0.89– 6.41	0.51– 7.58	2.63	0.84– 6.08	0.48– 7.19
6	3.33	1.21– 7.16	0.76– 8.39	3.16	1.15– 6.79	0.72– 7.96
7	3.89	1.56– 7.89	1.04– 9.17	3.68	1.48– 7.48	0.99– 8.70
8	4.44	1.92– 8.61	1.35– 9.94	4.21	1.82– 8.17	1.27– 9.43
9	5.00	2.30– 9.32	1.66–10.69	4.74	2.18– 8.84	1.57–10.15
10	5.56	2.69–10.01	2.00–11.44	5.26	2.54– 9.50	1.89–10.85
11	6.11	3.08–10.71	2.34–12.17	5.79	2.92–10.15	2.21–11.54
12	6.67	3.49–11.39	2.69–12.89	6.32	3.30–10.80	2.55–12.23
13	7.22	3.90–12.06	3.06–13.60	6.84	3.69–11.45	2.89–12.91
14	7.78	4.31–12.74	3.43–14.31	7.37	4.08–12.08	3.25–13.58
15	8.33	4.74–13.40	3.81–15.00	7.89	4.48–12.71	3.61–14.24
16	8.89	5.17–14.06	4.20–15.70	8.42	4.89–13.34	3.97–14.90
17	9.44	5.60–14.72	4.59–16.38	8.95	5.30–13.97	4.35–15.55
18	10.00	6.04–15.37	4.99–17.06	9.47	5.71–14.58	4.72–16.20
19	10.56	6.48–16.02	5.40–17.74	10.00	6.13–15.20	5.11–16.84
20	11.11	6.93–16.66	5.81–18.41	10.53	6.55–15.81	5.49–17.48
21	11.67	7.38–17.30	6.22–19.08	11.05	6.98–16.42	5.89–18.11
22	12.22	7.83–17.94	6.64–19.74	11.58	7.41–17.03	6.28–18.74
23	12.78	8.28–18.58	7.07–20.40	12.11	7.84–17.63	6.68–19.37
24	13.33	8.74–19.21	7.49–21.05	12.63	8.27–18.23	7.09–19.99
25	13.89	9.20–19.84	7.92–21.70	13.16	8.71–18.83	7.49–20.61
26	14.44	9.67–20.47	8.36–22.35	13.68	9.15–19.43	7.90–21.22
27	15.00	10.14–21.09	8.80–22.99	14.21	9.59–20.02	8.32–21.84
28	15.56	10.61–21.71	9.24–23.64	14.74	10.03–20.61	8.73–22.45
29	16.11	11.08–22.33	9.68–24.27	15.26	10.48–21.20	9.15–23.05
30	16.67	11.55–22.95	10.13–24.91	15.79	10.93–21.79	9.58–23.66
31	17.22	12.03–23.57	10.58–25.54	16.32	11.38–22.37	10.00–24.26
32	17.78	12.51–24.18	11.03–26.17	16.84	11.83–22.95	10.43–24.86
33	18.33	12.99–24.79	11.49–26.80	17.37	12.28–23.54	10.86–25.46
34	18.89	13.47–25.40	11.95–27.43	17.89	12.74–24.12	11.29–26.05
35	19.44	13.95–26.01	12.41–28.05	18.42	13.20–24.69	11.73–26.65
36	20.00	14.44–26.62	12.87–28.67	18.95	13.65–25.27	12.16–27.24
37	20.56	14.93–27.22	13.33–29.29	19.47	14.12–25.85	12.60–27.83
38	21.11	15.42–27.82	13.80–29.90	20.00	14.58–26.42	13.04–28.41
39	21.67	15.91–28.42	14.27–30.52	20.53	15.04–26.99	13.49–29.00
40	22.22	16.40–29.02	14.74–31.13	21.05	15.51–27.56	13.93–29.58
41	22.78	16.89–29.62	15.21–31.74	21.58	15.97–28.13	14.38–30.16
42	23.33	17.39–30.22	15.69–32.35	22.11	16.44–28.70	14.83–30.74
43	23.89	17.89–30.81	16.17–32.96	22.63	16.91–29.26	15.28–31.32
44	24.44	18.38–31.41	16.65–33.56	23.16	17.38–29.83	15.73–31.89
45	25.00	18.88–32.00	17.13–34.16	23.68	17.85–30.39	16.18–32.47
46	25.56	19.39–32.59	17.61–34.76	24.21	18.33–30.96	16.64–33.04
47	26.11	19.89–33.18	18.10–35.36	24.74	18.80–31.52	17.09–33.61
48	26.67	20.39–33.77	18.58–35.96	25.26	19.28–32.08	17.55–34.18
49	27.22	20.90–34.36	19.07–36.56	25.79	19.75–32.64	18.01–34.75
50	27.78	21.40–34.94	19.56–37.15	26.32	20.23–33.19	18.48–35.32
51	28.33	21.91–35.53	20.05–37.74	26.84	20.71–33.75	18.94–35.88
52	28.89	22.42–36.11	20.54–38.33	27.37	21.19–34.31	19.40–36.44
53	29.44	22.93–36.70	21.04–38.92	27.89	21.67–34.86	19.87–37.01
54	30.00	23.44–37.28	21.53–39.51	28.42	22.16–35.41	20.34–37.57
55	30.56	23.95–37.86	22.03–40.10	28.95	22.64–35.97	20.81–38.13
56	31.11	24.47–38.44	22.53–40.68	29.47	23.13–36.52	21.28–38.68
57	31.67	24.98–39.02	23.03–41.27	30.00	23.61–37.07	21.75–39.24
58	32.22	25.50–39.59	23.53–41.85	30.53	24.10–37.62	22.22–39.80
59	32.78	26.02–40.17	24.04–42.43	31.05	24.59–38.17	22.70–40.35
60	33.33	26.53–40.74	24.54–43.01	31.58	25.07–38.71	23.17–40.90
61	33.89	27.05–41.32	25.05–43.59	32.11	25.56–39.26	23.65–41.45
62	34.44	27.57–41.89	25.56–44.16	32.63	26.05–39.81	24.13–42.00
63	35.00	28.09–42.46	26.07–44.74	33.16	26.55–40.35	24.61–42.55
64	35.56	28.62–43.03	26.58–45.31	33.68	27.04–40.89	25.09–43.10
65	36.11	29.14–43.60	27.09–45.89	34.21	27.53–41.44	25.57–43.65
66	36.67	29.66–44.17	27.60–46.46	34.74	28.03–41.98	26.05–44.19
67	37.22	30.19–44.74	28.11–47.03	35.26	28.52–42.52	26.54–44.74
68	37.78	30.72–45.30	28.63–47.60	35.79	29.02–43.06	27.02–45.28
69	38.33	31.24–45.87	29.15–48.16	36.32	29.52–43.60	27.51–45.82
70	38.89	31.77–46.44	29.67–48.73	36.84	30.01–44.14	28.00–46.36
71	39.44	32.30–47.00	30.18–49.29	37.37	30.51–44.68	28.49–46.90
72	40.00	32.83–47.56	30.71–49.86	37.89	31.01–45.21	28.98–47.44
73	40.56	33.36–48.12	31.23–50.42	38.42	31.51–45.75	29.47–47.98
74	41.11	33.89–48.68	31.75–50.98	38.95	32.01–46.28	29.96–48.52
75	41.67	34.43–49.25	32.28–51.54	39.47	32.52–46.82	30.45–49.05
76	42.22	34.96–49.80	32.80–52.10	40.00	33.02–47.35	30.95–49.59
77	42.78	35.50–50.36	33.33–52.66	40.53	33.52–47.88	31.44–50.12
78	43.33	36.03–50.92	33.86–53.21	41.05	34.03–48.41	31.94–50.65
79	43.89	36.57–51.48	34.39–53.77	41.58	34.53–48.95	32.44–51.18
80	44.44	37.11–52.03	34.92–54.32	42.11	35.04–49.48	32.94–51.71
81	45.00	37.64–52.59	35.45–54.88	42.63	35.55–50.01	33.44–52.24
82	45.56	38.18–53.14	35.98–55.43	43.16	36.06–50.53	33.94–52.77
83	46.11	38.72–53.69	36.51–55.98	43.68	36.56–51.06	34.44–53.29
84	46.67	39.26–54.25	37.05–56.53	44.21	37.07–51.59	34.94–53.82
85	47.22	39.81–54.80	37.59–57.08	44.74	37.58–52.11	35.45–54.34
86	47.78	40.35–55.35	38.12–57.62	45.26	38.10–52.64	35.95–54.87
87	48.33	40.89–55.90	38.66–58.17	45.79	38.61–53.16	36.46–55.39
88	48.89	41.44–56.44	39.20–58.71	46.32	39.12–53.69	36.96–55.91
89	49.44	41.98–56.99	39.74–59.26	46.84	39.63–54.21	37.47–56.43
90	50.00	42.49–57.51	40.24–59.76	47.37	40.15–54.73	37.98–56.95
91	50.56	43.01–58.02	40.74–60.26	47.89	40.66–55.25	38.49–57.47
92	51.11	43.56–58.56	41.29–60.80	48.42	41.18–55.78	39.00–57.99
93	51.67	44.10–59.11	41.83–61.34	48.95	41.70–56.29	39.52–58.51
94	52.22	44.65–59.65	42.38–61.88	49.47	42.21–56.81	40.03–59.02
95	52.78	45.20–60.19	42.92–62.41	50.00	42.70–57.30	40.50–59.50
96	53.33	45.75–60.74	43.47–62.95	50.53	43.19–57.79	40.98–59.97
97	53.89	46.31–61.28	44.02–63.49	51.05	43.71–58.30	41.49–60.48
98	54.44	46.86–61.82	44.57–64.02	51.58	44.22–58.82	42.01–61.00
99	55.00	47.41–62.36	45.12–64.55	52.11	44.75–59.34	42.53–61.51
100	55.56	47.97–62.89	45.68–65.08	52.63	45.27–59.85	43.05–62.02

x	N = 200: $100p_x$	N = 200: 100 (1 − 2α) limits 95 % $100p_l$ – $100p_r$	N = 200: 100 (1 − 2α) limits 99 % $100p_l$ – $100p_r$	N = 250: $100p_x$	N = 250: 100 (1 − 2α) limits 95 % $100p_l$ – $100p_r$	N = 250: 100 (1 − 2α) limits 99 % $100p_l$ – $100p_r$
0	*0.00*	*0.00– 1.83*	*0.00– 2.61*	*0.00*	*0.00– 1.46*	*0.00– 2.10*
1	*0.50*	*0.01– 2.75*	*0.00– 3.66*	*0.40*	*0.01– 2.21*	*0.00– 2.93*
2	*1.00*	*0.12– 3.57*	*0.05– 4.55*	*0.80*	*0.10– 2.86*	*0.04– 3.66*
3	*1.50*	*0.31– 4.32*	*0.17– 5.38*	*1.20*	*0.25– 3.47*	*0.14– 4.32*
4	*2.00*	*0.55– 5.04*	*0.34– 6.16*	*1.60*	*0.44– 4.05*	*0.27– 4.95*
5	2.50	0.80– 5.78	0.46– 6.84	2.00	0.64– 4.64	0.36– 5.49
6	3.00	1.09– 6.46	0.69– 7.57	2.40	0.87– 5.18	0.55– 6.08
7	3.50	1.40– 7.12	0.94– 8.28	2.80	1.12– 5.71	0.75– 6.65
8	4.00	1.73– 7.76	1.21– 8.97	3.20	1.38– 6.24	0.96– 7.21
9	4.50	2.07– 8.40	1.49– 9.65	3.60	1.65– 6.75	1.19– 7.76
10	5.00	2.41– 9.03	1.79– 10.32	4.00	1.93– 7.26	1.43– 8.30
11	5.50	2.77– 9.66	2.10– 10.98	4.40	2.21– 7.76	1.67– 8.84
12	6.00	3.13– 10.28	2.42– 11.64	4.80	2.50– 8.26	1.93– 9.36
13	6.50	3.50– 10.89	2.75– 12.28	5.20	2.79– 8.75	2.19– 9.88
14	7.00	3.88– 11.49	3.08– 12.92	5.60	3.09– 9.24	2.45– 10.40
15	7.50	4.26– 12.09	3.42– 13.55	6.00	3.39– 9.72	2.72– 10.91
16	8.00	4.64– 12.69	3.77– 14.18	6.40	3.70– 10.21	3.00– 11.42
17	8.50	5.03– 13.29	4.12– 14.80	6.80	4.01– 10.68	3.28– 11.92
18	9.00	5.42– 13.88	4.48– 15.42	7.20	4.32– 11.16	3.57– 12.42
19	9.50	5.82– 14.46	4.84– 16.03	7.60	4.64– 11.63	3.85– 12.91
20	10.00	6.22– 15.04	5.21– 16.63	8.00	4.96– 12.10	4.15– 13.40
21	10.50	6.62– 15.62	5.58– 17.24	8.40	5.28– 12.57	4.44– 13.89
22	11.00	7.03– 16.20	5.96– 17.84	8.80	5.60– 13.04	4.74– 14.38
23	11.50	7.44– 16.78	6.34– 18.44	9.20	5.92– 13.50	5.04– 14.86
24	12.00	7.85– 17.35	6.72– 19.03	9.60	6.25– 13.96	5.34– 15.34
25	12.50	8.26– 17.92	7.11– 19.62	10.00	6.58– 14.42	5.65– 15.82
26	13.00	8.68– 18.49	7.50– 20.21	10.40	6.91– 14.88	5.96– 16.30
27	13.50	9.10– 19.05	7.89– 20.79	10.80	7.24– 15.34	6.27– 16.77
28	14.00	9.52– 19.61	8.28– 21.37	11.20	7.58– 15.80	6.58– 17.24
29	14.50	9.94– 20.18	8.68– 21.95	11.60	7.91– 16.25	6.90– 17.71
30	15.00	10.37– 20.73	9.08– 22.53	12.00	8.25– 16.70	7.21– 18.18
31	15.50	10.79– 21.29	9.48– 23.10	12.40	8.59– 17.15	7.53– 18.65
32	16.00	11.22– 21.85	9.89– 23.67	12.80	8.93– 17.60	7.85– 19.11
33	16.50	11.65– 22.40	10.30– 24.24	13.20	9.27– 18.05	8.17– 19.57
34	17.00	12.08– 22.95	10.70– 24.81	13.60	9.61– 18.50	8.50– 20.03
35	17.50	12.52– 23.51	11.12– 25.38	14.00	9.96– 18.94	8.82– 20.49
36	18.00	12.95– 24.05	11.53– 25.94	14.40	10.30– 19.39	9.15– 20.95
37	18.50	13.39– 24.60	11.95– 26.50	14.80	10.65– 19.83	9.48– 21.41
38	19.00	13.83– 25.15	12.36– 27.06	15.20	11.00– 20.27	9.81– 21.86
39	19.50	14.27– 25.69	12.78– 27.62	15.60	11.34– 20.72	10.14– 22.32
40	20.00	14.71– 26.24	13.20– 28.18	16.00	11.69– 21.16	10.47– 22.77
41	20.50	15.15– 26.78	13.63– 28.73	16.40	12.04– 21.60	10.81– 23.22
42	21.00	15.59– 27.32	14.05– 29.28	16.80	12.40– 22.04	11.14– 23.67
43	21.50	16.04– 27.86	14.48– 29.84	17.20	12.75– 22.47	11.48– 24.12
44	22.00	16.48– 28.40	14.91– 30.39	17.60	13.10– 22.91	11.82– 24.57
45	22.50	16.93– 28.94	15.34– 30.93	18.00	13.45– 23.35	12.16– 25.01
46	23.00	17.38– 29.47	15.77– 31.48	18.40	13.81– 23.78	12.50– 25.46
47	23.50	17.83– 30.01	16.20– 32.03	18.80	14.17– 24.22	12.84– 25.90
48	24.00	18.28– 30.54	16.63– 32.57	19.20	14.52– 24.65	13.18– 26.35
49	24.50	18.73– 31.08	17.07– 33.11	19.60	14.88– 25.08	13.52– 26.79
50	25.00	19.18– 31.61	17.51– 33.65	20.00	15.24– 25.51	13.87– 27.23
60	30.00	23.77– 36.88	21.95– 38.99	24.00	18.86– 29.80	17.36– 31.59
70	35.00	28.44– 42.06	26.51– 44.21	28.00	22.55– 34.01	20.94– 35.87
80	40.00	33.19– 47.16	31.17– 49.33	32.00	26.29– 38.18	24.60– 40.08
90	45.00	38.02– 52.18	35.93– 54.36	36.00	30.07– 42.30	28.31– 44.23
100	50.00	42.89– 57.11	40.74– 59.26	40.00	33.91– 46.37	32.08– 48.31
110	55.00	47.82– 61.98	45.64– 64.07	44.00	37.78– 50.40	35.91– 52.35
120	60.00	52.84– 66.81	50.67– 68.83	48.00	41.70– 54.39	39.80– 56.33
130	65.00	57.94– 71.56	55.79– 73.49	52.00	45.61– 58.30	43.67– 60.20
140	70.00	63.12– 76.23	61.01– 78.05	56.00	49.60– 62.22	47.65– 64.09
150	75.00	68.39– 80.82	66.35– 82.49	60.00	53.63– 66.09	51.69– 67.92
160	80.00	73.76– 85.29	71.82– 86.80	64.00	57.70– 69.93	55.77– 71.69
170	85.00	79.27– 89.63	77.47– 90.92	68.00	61.82– 73.71	59.92– 75.40
180	90.00	84.96– 93.78	83.37– 94.79	72.00	65.99– 77.45	64.13– 79.06
190	95.00	90.97– 97.59	89.68– 98.21	76.00	70.20– 81.14	68.41– 82.64
200	*100.00*	*98.17–100.00*	*97.39–100.00*	80.00	74.49– 84.76	72.77– 86.13
210				84.00	78.84– 88.31	77.23– 89.53
220				88.00	83.30– 91.75	81.82– 92.79
230				92.00	87.90– 95.04	86.60– 95.85
240				96.00	92.74– 98.07	91.70– 98.57
250				*100.00*	*98.54–100.00*	*97.90–100.00*

N= number of trials, x = number of successes, etc., $100\,p_x = 100\,x/N$

Values in *italics* are exact, all others have been calculated from FREEMAN and TUKEY's approximation. For interpolation see page 186

x	N = 300					N = 400					N = 500					N = 600				
		100 (1 − 2α) limits					100 (1 − 2α) limits					100 (1 − 2α) limits					100 (1 − 2α) limits			
		95%		99%			95%		99%			95%		99%			95%		99%	
	$100\,p_x$	$100\,p_l$	$100\,p_r$	$100\,p_l$	$100\,p_r$	$100\,p_x$	$100\,p_l$	$100\,p_r$	$100\,p_l$	$100\,p_r$	$100\,p_x$	$100\,p_l$	$100\,p_r$	$100\,p_l$	$100\,p_r$	$100\,p_x$	$100\,p_l$	$100\,p_r$	$100\,p_l$	$100\,p_r$
0	*0.00*	*0.00*	*1.22*	*0.00*	*1.75*	*0.00*	*0.00*	*0.92*	*0.00*	*1.32*	*0.00*	*0.00*	*0.74*	*0.00*	*1.05*	*0.00*	*0.00*	*0.61*	*0.00*	*0.88*
1	*0.33*	*0.01*	*1.84*	*0.00*	*2.45*	*0.25*	*0.01*	*1.38*	*0.00*	*1.84*	*0.20*	*0.01*	*1.11*	*0.00*	*1.48*	*0.17*	*0.00*	*0.93*	*0.00*	*1.23*
2	*0.67*	*0.08*	*2.39*	*0.03*	*3.05*	*0.50*	*0.06*	*1.79*	*0.03*	*2.30*	*0.40*	*0.05*	*1.44*	*0.02*	*1.84*	*0.33*	*0.04*	*1.20*	*0.02*	*1.54*
3	*1.00*	*0.21*	*2.89*	*0.11*	*3.61*	*0.75*	*0.16*	*2.18*	*0.08*	*2.72*	*0.60*	*0.12*	*1.74*	*0.07*	*2.18*	*0.50*	*0.10*	*1.45*	*0.06*	*1.82*
4	*1.33*	*0.36*	*3.38*	*0.23*	*4.14*	*1.00*	*0.27*	*2.54*	*0.17*	*3.11*	*0.80*	*0.22*	*2.04*	*0.14*	*2.50*	*0.67*	*0.18*	*1.70*	*0.11*	*2.08*
5	1.67	0.53	3.88	0.30	4.59	1.25	0.40	2.92	0.23	3.46	1.00	0.32	2.34	0.18	2.77	0.83	0.26	1.95	0.15	2.31
6	2.00	0.73	4.33	0.45	5.08	1.50	0.54	3.26	0.34	3.83	1.20	0.43	2.61	0.27	3.07	1.00	0.36	2.18	0.23	2.56
7	2.33	0.93	4.77	0.62	5.56	1.75	0.70	3.59	0.46	4.19	1.40	0.56	2.88	0.37	3.36	1.17	0.46	2.40	0.31	2.80
8	2.67	1.15	5.21	0.80	6.03	2.00	0.86	3.92	0.60	4.54	1.60	0.69	3.14	0.48	3.64	1.33	0.57	2.62	0.40	3.04
9	3.00	1.37	5.64	0.99	6.49	2.25	1.03	4.25	0.74	4.89	1.80	0.82	3.40	0.59	3.92	1.50	0.68	2.84	0.49	3.27
10	3.33	1.60	6.07	1.19	6.94	2.50	1.20	4.57	0.89	5.23	2.00	0.96	3.66	0.71	4.20	1.67	0.80	3.06	0.59	3.50
11	3.67	1.84	6.49	1.39	7.39	2.75	1.37	4.88	1.04	5.57	2.20	1.10	3.92	0.83	4.47	1.83	0.91	3.27	0.69	3.73
12	4.00	2.08	6.90	1.60	7.83	3.00	1.55	5.20	1.20	5.90	2.40	1.24	4.17	0.96	4.74	2.00	1.03	3.48	0.79	3.95
13	4.33	2.32	7.32	1.82	8.27	3.25	1.74	5.51	1.36	6.23	2.60	1.39	4.42	1.08	5.00	2.17	1.15	3.69	0.90	4.18
14	4.67	2.57	7.73	2.04	8.70	3.50	1.92	5.82	1.52	6.56	2.80	1.54	4.67	1.22	5.26	2.33	1.28	3.89	1.01	4.39
15	5.00	2.82	8.13	2.26	9.13	3.75	2.11	6.12	1.69	6.88	3.00	1.69	4.91	1.35	5.52	2.50	1.40	4.10	1.12	4.61
16	5.33	3.08	8.53	2.49	9.55	4.00	2.30	6.43	1.86	7.20	3.20	1.84	5.16	1.49	5.78	2.67	1.53	4.30	1.24	4.83
17	5.67	3.33	8.94	2.72	9.98	4.25	2.49	6.73	2.03	7.52	3.40	1.99	5.40	1.62	6.04	2.83	1.66	4.51	1.35	5.04
18	6.00	3.59	9.33	2.96	10.39	4.50	2.69	7.03	2.21	7.84	3.60	2.14	5.64	1.76	6.29	3.00	1.78	4.71	1.47	5.26
19	6.33	3.85	9.73	3.20	10.81	4.75	2.88	7.33	2.39	8.15	3.80	2.30	5.88	1.91	6.55	3.17	1.91	4.91	1.59	5.47
20	6.67	4.12	10.12	3.44	11.22	5.00	3.08	7.63	2.57	8.47	4.00	2.46	6.12	2.05	6.80	3.33	2.05	5.11	1.71	5.68
21	7.00	4.38	10.52	3.69	11.63	5.25	3.28	7.93	2.75	8.78	4.20	2.62	6.36	2.20	7.05	3.50	2.18	5.31	1.83	5.89
22	7.33	4.65	10.91	3.93	12.04	5.50	3.48	8.22	2.94	9.09	4.40	2.78	6.60	2.34	7.30	3.67	2.31	5.51	1.95	6.09
23	7.67	4.92	11.30	4.18	12.45	5.75	3.68	8.51	3.12	9.39	4.60	2.94	6.83	2.49	7.54	3.83	2.44	5.70	2.07	6.30
24	8.00	5.19	11.68	4.43	12.85	6.00	3.88	8.81	3.31	9.70	4.80	3.10	7.07	2.64	7.79	4.00	2.58	5.90	2.19	6.51
25	8.33	5.47	12.07	4.69	13.25	6.25	4.08	9.10	3.50	10.00	5.00	3.26	7.30	2.79	8.03	4.17	2.71	6.10	2.32	6.71
26	8.67	5.74	12.45	4.94	13.65	6.50	4.29	9.39	3.69	10.31	5.20	3.42	7.54	2.94	8.28	4.33	2.85	6.29	2.45	6.92
27	9.00	6.02	12.84	5.20	14.05	6.75	4.49	9.68	3.88	10.61	5.40	3.59	7.77	3.09	8.52	4.50	2.99	6.49	2.57	7.12
28	9.33	6.29	13.22	5.46	14.45	7.00	4.70	9.97	4.07	10.91	5.60	3.75	8.00	3.25	8.76	4.67	3.12	6.68	2.70	7.32
29	9.67	6.57	13.60	5.72	14.84	7.25	4.91	10.26	4.27	11.21	5.80	3.92	8.23	3.40	9.01	4.83	3.26	6.88	2.83	7.53
30	10.00	6.85	13.98	5.98	15.24	7.50	5.12	10.54	4.46	11.51	6.00	4.08	8.46	3.56	9.25	5.00	3.40	7.07	2.96	7.73
31	10.33	7.13	14.36	6.25	15.63	7.75	5.33	10.83	4.66	11.81	6.20	4.25	8.69	3.71	9.49	5.17	3.54	7.26	3.09	7.93
32	10.67	7.41	14.74	6.51	16.02	8.00	5.54	11.12	4.85	12.10	6.40	4.42	8.92	3.87	9.72	5.33	3.68	7.45	3.22	8.13
33	11.00	7.70	15.11	6.78	16.41	8.25	5.75	11.40	5.05	12.40	6.60	4.59	9.15	4.03	9.96	5.50	3.82	7.64	3.35	8.33
34	11.33	7.98	15.49	7.05	16.80	8.50	5.96	11.69	5.25	12.69	6.80	4.76	9.38	4.19	10.20	5.67	3.96	7.84	3.48	8.52
35	11.67	8.27	15.86	7.32	17.18	8.75	6.17	11.97	5.45	12.99	7.00	4.92	9.61	4.35	10.44	5.83	4.10	8.03	3.61	8.72
36	12.00	8.55	16.24	7.59	17.57	9.00	6.38	12.25	5.65	13.28	7.20	5.09	9.84	4.51	10.67	6.00	4.24	8.22	3.75	8.92
37	12.33	8.84	16.61	7.86	17.95	9.25	6.60	12.53	5.86	13.57	7.40	5.26	10.06	4.67	10.91	6.17	4.38	8.41	3.88	9.12
38	12.67	9.13	16.98	8.13	18.34	9.50	6.81	12.82	6.06	13.86	7.60	5.43	10.29	4.83	11.14	6.33	4.52	8.60	4.01	9.31
39	13.00	9.42	17.35	8.41	18.72	9.75	7.03	13.10	6.26	14.15	7.80	5.61	10.52	4.99	11.38	6.50	4.66	8.79	4.15	9.51
40	13.33	9.71	17.72	8.68	19.10	10.00	7.24	13.38	6.47	14.44	8.00	5.78	10.74	5.15	11.61	6.67	4.81	8.97	4.28	9.71
41	13.67	10.00	18.09	8.96	19.48	10.25	7.46	13.66	6.67	14.73	8.20	5.95	10.97	5.32	11.84	6.83	4.95	9.16	4.42	9.90
42	14.00	10.29	18.46	9.23	19.86	10.50	7.68	13.94	6.88	15.02	8.40	6.12	11.19	5.48	12.08	7.00	5.09	9.35	4.55	10.10
43	14.33	10.58	18.83	9.51	20.24	10.75	7.89	14.21	7.08	15.31	8.60	6.30	11.42	5.64	12.31	7.17	5.24	9.54	4.69	10.29
44	14.67	10.87	19.20	9.79	20.62	11.00	8.11	14.49	7.29	15.59	8.80	6.47	11.64	5.81	12.54	7.33	5.38	9.73	4.83	10.48
45	15.00	11.16	19.56	10.07	20.99	11.25	8.33	14.77	7.50	15.88	9.00	6.64	11.86	5.97	12.77	7.50	5.52	9.91	4.96	10.68
46	15.33	11.46	19.93	10.35	21.37	11.50	8.55	15.05	7.71	16.17	9.20	6.82	12.09	6.14	13.00	7.67	5.67	10.10	5.10	10.87
47	15.67	11.75	20.29	10.63	21.74	11.75	8.77	15.33	7.92	16.45	9.40	6.99	12.31	6.31	13.23	7.83	5.81	10.29	5.24	11.06
48	16.00	12.05	20.66	10.92	22.12	12.00	8.99	15.60	8.13	16.74	9.60	7.17	12.53	6.47	13.46	8.00	5.96	10.47	5.38	11.26
49	16.33	12.34	21.02	11.20	22.49	12.25	9.21	15.88	8.34	17.02	9.80	7.34	12.76	6.64	13.69	8.17	6.10	10.66	5.52	11.45
50	16.67	12.64	21.39	11.48	22.86	12.50	9.43	16.15	8.55	17.30	10.00	7.52	12.98	6.81	13.92	8.33	6.25	10.84	5.66	11.64
60	20.00	15.63	24.99	14.37	26.55	15.00	11.65	18.89	10.68	20.11	12.00	9.29	15.18	8.50	16.18	10.00	7.72	12.69	7.06	13.54
70	23.33	18.68	28.55	17.32	30.16	17.50	13.91	21.59	12.86	22.87	14.00	11.08	17.36	10.23	18.42	11.67	9.21	14.51	8.50	15.41
80	26.67	21.76	32.06	20.32	33.73	20.00	16.20	24.27	15.08	25.60	16.00	12.90	19.52	11.99	20.62	13.33	10.72	16.32	9.95	17.26
90	30.00	24.89	35.54	23.37	37.25	22.50	18.51	26.92	17.33	28.30	18.00	14.74	21.66	13.77	22.80	15.00	12.24	18.12	11.43	19.09
100	33.33	28.04	38.99	26.46	40.73	25.00	20.84	29.55	19.61	30.96	20.00	16.59	23.78	15.58	24.97	16.67	13.78	19.90	12.92	20.91
110	36.67	31.22	42.40	29.59	44.17	27.50	23.19	32.16	21.91	33.61	22.00	18.45	25.90	17.40	27.11	18.33	15.32	21.67	14.43	22.71
120	40.00	34.44	45.79	32.76	47.57	30.00	25.56	34.76	24.23	36.23	24.00	20.33	28.00	19.23	29.24	20.00	16.87	23.43	15.95	24.51
130	43.33	37.67	49.15	35.97	50.93	32.50	27.94	37.34	26.57	38.83	26.00	22.21	30.08	21.08	31.35	21.67	18.44	25.19	17.47	26.28
140	46.67	40.94	52.49	39.20	54.27	35.00	30.34	39.90	28.94	41.41	28.00	24.11	32.16	22.95	33.45	23.33	20.01	26.93	19.01	28.05
150	50.00	44.21	55.79	42.45	57.55	37.50	32.75	42.45	31.32	43.98	30.00	26.02	34.23	24.82	35.54	25.00	21.59	28.67	20.56	29.81
160	53.33	47.51	59.06	45.73	60.80	40.00	35.18	44.99	33.72	46.52	32.00	27.94	36.29	26.71	37.62	26.67	23.17	30.40	22.12	31.56
170	56.67	50.85	62.33	49.07	64.03	42.50	37.62	47.51	36.14	49.05	34.00	29.86	38.34	28.61	39.68	28.33	24.76	32.13	23.69	33.31
180	60.00	54.21	65.56	52.43	67.24	45.00	40.07	50.03	38.57	51.57	36.00	31.80	40.38	30.52	41.74	30.00	26.36	33.84	25.26	35.04
190	63.33	57.60	68.78	55.83	70.41	47.50	42.53	52.52	41.02	54.06	38.00	33.74	42.42	32.45	43.78	31.67	27.97	35.56	26.85	36.77
200	66.67	61.01	71.96	59.27	73.54	50.00	45.00	55.00	43.47	56.53	40.00	35.69	44.45	34.38	45.82	33.33	29.58	37.27	28.44	38.49
210	70.00	64.46	75.11	62.75	76.63	52.50	47.48	57.47	45.94	58.98	42.00	37.64	46.47	36.32	47.84	35.00	31.19	38.97	30.03	40.20
220	73.33	67.94	78.24	66.27	79.68	55.00	49.97	59.93	48.43	61.43	44.00	39.61	48.48	38.27	49.86	36.67	32.81	40.67	31.64	41.90
230	76.67	71.45	81.32	69.84	82.68	57.50	52.49	62.38	50.95	63.86	46.00	41.58	50.48	40.23	51.86	38.33	34.43	42.36	33.25	43.60
240	80.00	75.01	84.37	73.45	85.63	60.00	55.01	64.82	53.48	66.28	48.00	43.56	52.48	42.20	53.86	40.00	36.06	44.05	34.86	45.30
250	83.33	78.61	87.36	77.14	88.52	62.50	57.55	67.25	56.02	68.68	50.00	45.54	54.46	44.17	55.83	41.67	37.70	45.73	36.49	46.98
260	86.67	82.28	90.29	80.90	91.32	65.00	60.10	69.66	58.59	71.06	52.00	47.52	56.44	46.14	57.80	43.33	39.34	47.41	38.11	48.66
270	90.00	86.02	93.15	84.76	94.02	67.50	62.66	72.06	61.17	73.43	54.00	49.52	58.42	48.14	59.77	45.00	40.98	49.08	39.75	50.34
280	93.33	89.88	95.88	88.78	96.56	70.00	65.24	74.44	63.77	75.77	56.00	51.52	60.39	50.14	61.73	46.67	42.63	50.75	41.39	52.01
290	96.67	93.93	98.40	93.06	98.81	72.50	67.84	76.81	66.39	78.09	58.00	53.53	62.36	52.16	63.68	48.33	44.28	52.42	43.03	53.67
300	*100.00*	*98.78*	*100.00*	*98.25*	*100.00*	75.00	70.45	79.16	69.04	80.39	60.00	55.55	64.31	54.18	65.62	50.00	45.93	54.07	44.68	55.32
310						77.50	73.08	81.49	71.70	82.67	62.00	57.58	66.26	56.22	67.55	51.67	47.58	55.72	46.33	56.97
320						80.00	75.73	83.80	74.40	84.92	64.00	59.62	68.20	58.26	69.48	53.33	49.25	57.37	47.99	58.61
330						82.50	78.41	86.09	77.13	87.14	66.00	61.66	70.14	60.32	71.39	55.00	50.92	59.02	49.66	60.25
340						85.00	81.11	88.35	79.89	89.32	68.00	63.71	72.06	62.38	73.29	56.67	52.59	60.66	51.34	61.89
350						87.50	83.85	90.57	82.70	91.45	70.00	65.77	73.98	64.46	75.18	58.33	54.27	62.30	53.02	63.51
360						90.00	86.62	92.76	85.56	93.53	72.00	67.84	75.89	66.55	77.05	60.00	55.95	63.94	54.70	65.14
370						92.50	89.46	94.88	88.49	95.54	74.00	69.92	77.79	68.65	78.92	61.67	57.64	65.57	56.40	66.75
380						95.00	92.37	96.92	91.53	97.43	76.00	72.00	79.67	70.76	80.77	63.33	59.33	67.19	58.10	68.36
390						97.50	95.43	98.80	94.77	99.11	78.00	74.10	81.55	72.89	82.60	65.00	61.03	68.81	59.80	69.97
400						*100.00*	*99.08*	*100.00*	*98.68*	*100.00*	80.00	76.22	83.41	75.03	84.42	66.67	62.73	70.42	61.51	71.56
410											82.00	78.34	85.26	77.20	86.23	68.33	64.44	72.03	63.23	73.15
420											84.00	80.48	87.10	79.38	88.01	70.00	66.16	73.64	64.96	74.74
430											86.00	82.64	88.92	81.58	89.77	71.67	67.87	75.24	66.69	76.31
440											88.00	84.82	90.71	83.82	91.50	73.33	69.60	76.83	68.44	77.88
450											90.00	87.02	92.48	86.08	93.19	75.00	71.33	78.41	70.19	79.44
460											92.00	89.26	94.22	88.39	94.85	76.67	73.07	79.99	71.95	80.99
470											94.00	91.54	95.92	90.75	96.44	78.33	74.81	81.56	73.72	82.53
480											96.00	93.88	97.54	93.20	97.95	80.00	76.57	83.13	75.49	84.05
490											98.00	96.34	99.04	95.80	99.29	81.67	78.33	84.68	77.29	85.57
500											*100.00*	*99.26*	*100.00*	*98.95*	*100.00*	83.33	80.10	86.22	79.09	87.08
510																85.00	81.88	87.76	80.91	88.57
520																86.67	83.68	89.28	82.74	90.05
530																88.33	85.49	90.79	84.59	91.50
540																90.00	87.31	92.28	86.46	92.94
550																91.67	89.16	93.75	88.36	94.34

Confidence Limits* for p $N=700-1000$

N = number of trials, x = number of successes, etc., $100\ p_x = 100\ x/N$

Values in *italics* are exact, all others have been calculated from FREEMAN and TUKEY's approximation. For interpolation see page 186

x	$N=700$ $100p_x$	$N=700$ $100(1-2\alpha)$ limits 95% $100p_l$ $100p_r$	$N=700$ 99% $100p_l$ $100p_r$	$N=800$ $100p_x$	$N=800$ 95% $100p_l$ $100p_r$	$N=800$ 99% $100p_l$ $100p_r$	$N=900$ $100p_x$	$N=900$ 95% $100p_l$ $100p_r$	$N=900$ 99% $100p_l$ $100p_r$	$N=1000$ $100p_x$	$N=1000$ 95% $100p_l$ $100p_r$	$N=1000$ 99% $100p_l$ $100p_r$
0	*0.00*	*0.00–0.53*	*0.00–0.75*	*0.00*	*0.00–0.46*	*0.00–0.66*	*0.00*	*0.00–0.41*	*0.00–0.59*	*0.00*	*0.00–0.37*	*0.00–0.53*
1	*0.14*	*0.00–0.79*	*0.00–1.06*	*0.13*	*0.00–0.69*	*0.00–0.93*	*0.11*	*0.00–0.62*	*0.00–0.82*	*0.10*	*0.00–0.56*	*0.00–0.74*
2	*0.29*	*0.03–1.03*	*0.01–1.32*	*0.25*	*0.03–0.90*	*0.01–1.15*	*0.22*	*0.03–0.80*	*0.01–1.03*	*0.20*	*0.02–0.72*	*0.01–0.92*
3	*0.43*	*0.09–1.25*	*0.05–1.56*	*0.38*	*0.08–1.09*	*0.04–1.37*	*0.33*	*0.07–0.97*	*0.04–1.21*	*0.30*	*0.06–0.87*	*0.03–1.09*
4	*0.57*	*0.16–1.46*	*0.10–1.79*	*0.50*	*0.14–1.28*	*0.08–1.57*	*0.44*	*0.12–1.13*	*0.07–1.39*	*0.40*	*0.11–1.02*	*0.07–1.25*
5	0.71	0.23–1.67	0.13–1.98	0.63	0.20–1.46	0.11–1.74	0.56	0.18–1.30	0.10–1.54	0.50	0.16–1.17	0.09–1.39
6	0.86	0.31–1.87	0.19–2.20	0.75	0.27–1.64	0.17–1.92	0.67	0.24–1.45	0.15–1.71	0.60	0.22–1.31	0.14–1.54
7	1.00	0.40–2.06	0.26–2.40	0.88	0.35–1.80	0.23–2.11	0.78	0.31–1.60	0.21–1.87	0.70	0.28–1.44	0.18–1.69
8	1.14	0.49–2.25	0.34–2.61	1.00	0.43–1.97	0.30–2.28	0.89	0.38–1.75	0.26–2.03	0.80	0.34–1.58	0.24–1.83
9	1.29	0.59–2.44	0.42–2.81	1.13	0.51–2.13	0.37–2.46	1.00	0.45–1.90	0.33–2.19	0.90	0.41–1.71	0.29–1.97
10	1.43	0.68–2.62	0.50–3.01	1.25	0.60–2.30	0.44–2.63	1.11	0.53–2.04	0.39–2.34	1.00	0.48–1.84	0.35–2.11
11	1.57	0.78–2.80	0.59–3.20	1.38	0.68–2.46	0.52–2.80	1.22	0.61–2.18	0.46–2.49	1.10	0.55–1.97	0.41–2.25
12	1.71	0.89–2.98	0.68–3.39	1.50	0.77–2.61	0.60–2.97	1.33	0.69–2.32	0.53–2.64	1.20	0.62–2.09	0.48–2.38
13	1.86	0.99–3.16	0.77–3.58	1.63	0.87–2.77	0.68–3.14	1.44	0.77–2.46	0.60–2.79	1.30	0.69–2.22	0.54–2.51
14	2.00	1.09–3.34	0.87–3.77	1.75	0.96–2.93	0.76–3.30	1.56	0.85–2.60	0.67–2.94	1.40	0.77–2.34	0.60–2.65
15	2.14	1.20–3.52	0.96–3.96	1.88	1.05–3.08	0.84–3.47	1.67	0.93–2.74	0.75–3.09	1.50	0.84–2.47	0.67–2.78
16	2.29	1.31–3.69	1.06–4.15	2.00	1.14–3.23	0.92–3.63	1.78	1.02–2.88	0.82–3.23	1.60	0.92–2.59	0.74–2.91
17	2.43	1.42–3.87	1.16–4.33	2.13	1.24–3.39	1.01–3.79	1.89	1.10–3.01	0.90–3.37	1.70	0.99–2.71	0.81–3.04
18	2.57	1.53–4.04	1.26–4.51	2.25	1.34–3.54	1.10–3.95	2.00	1.19–3.15	0.98–3.52	1.80	1.07–2.84	0.88–3.17
19	2.71	1.64–4.21	1.36–4.69	2.38	1.43–3.69	1.19–4.11	2.11	1.27–3.28	1.05–3.66	1.90	1.15–2.96	0.95–3.30
20	2.86	1.75–4.39	1.46–4.87	2.50	1.53–3.84	1.28–4.27	2.22	1.36–3.42	1.13–3.80	2.00	1.22–3.08	1.02–3.42
21	3.00	1.86–4.56	1.56–5.05	2.63	1.63–3.99	1.37–4.43	2.33	1.45–3.55	1.21–3.94	2.10	1.30–3.20	1.09–3.55
22	3.14	1.98–4.73	1.67–5.23	2.75	1.73–4.14	1.46–4.58	2.44	1.54–3.68	1.29–4.08	2.20	1.38–3.32	1.16–3.67
23	3.29	2.09–4.90	1.77–5.41	2.88	1.83–4.29	1.55–4.74	2.56	1.63–3.82	1.38–4.22	2.30	1.46–3.44	1.24–3.80
24	3.43	2.21–5.07	1.88–5.59	3.00	1.93–4.44	1.64–4.90	2.67	1.71–3.95	1.46–4.36	2.40	1.54–3.55	1.31–3.92
25	3.57	2.32–5.23	1.99–5.76	3.13	2.03–4.58	1.74–5.05	2.78	1.80–4.08	1.54–4.49	2.50	1.62–3.67	1.39–4.05
26	3.71	2.44–5.40	2.09–5.94	3.25	2.13–4.73	1.83–5.20	2.89	1.89–4.21	1.62–4.63	2.60	1.70–3.79	1.46–4.17
27	3.86	2.56–5.57	2.20–6.11	3.38	2.23–4.88	1.92–5.36	3.00	1.99–4.34	1.71–4.77	2.70	1.79–3.91	1.54–4.29
28	4.00	2.67–5.74	2.31–6.29	3.50	2.34–5.02	2.02–5.51	3.11	2.08–4.47	1.79–4.90	2.80	1.87–4.03	1.61–4.42
29	4.14	2.79–5.90	2.42–6.46	3.63	2.44–5.17	2.12–5.66	3.22	2.17–4.60	1.88–5.04	2.90	1.95–4.14	1.69–4.54
30	4.29	2.91–6.07	2.53–6.64	3.75	2.54–5.32	2.21–5.81	3.33	2.26–4.73	1.96–5.17	3.00	2.03–4.26	1.77–4.66
31	4.43	3.03–6.23	2.64–6.81	3.88	2.65–5.46	2.31–5.97	3.44	2.35–4.86	2.05–5.31	3.10	2.12–4.38	1.84–4.78
32	4.57	3.15–6.40	2.75–6.98	4.00	2.75–5.61	2.41–6.12	3.56	2.44–4.99	2.14–5.44	3.20	2.20–4.49	1.92–4.90
33	4.71	3.27–6.56	2.87–7.15	4.13	2.86–5.75	2.50–6.27	3.67	2.54–5.12	2.22–5.58	3.30	2.28–4.61	2.00–5.02
34	4.86	3.39–6.73	2.98–7.32	4.25	2.96–5.89	2.60–6.42	3.78	2.63–5.24	2.31–5.71	3.40	2.37–4.72	2.08–5.14
35	5.00	3.51–6.89	3.09–7.49	4.38	3.07–6.04	2.70–6.57	3.89	2.72–5.37	2.40–5.84	3.50	2.45–4.84	2.16–5.26
36	5.14	3.63–7.05	3.21–7.66	4.50	3.17–6.18	2.80–6.72	4.00	2.82–5.50	2.49–5.98	3.60	2.53–4.95	2.24–5.38
37	5.29	3.75–7.22	3.32–7.83	4.63	3.28–6.32	2.90–6.86	4.11	2.91–5.63	2.58–6.11	3.70	2.62–5.07	2.32–5.50
38	5.43	3.87–7.38	3.43–8.00	4.75	3.38–6.47	3.00–7.01	4.22	3.00–5.75	2.66–6.24	3.80	2.70–5.18	2.40–5.62
39	5.57	3.99–7.54	3.55–8.17	4.88	3.49–6.61	3.10–7.16	4.33	3.10–5.88	2.75–6.37	3.90	2.79–5.30	2.48–5.74
40	5.71	4.11–7.71	3.66–8.34	5.00	3.60–6.75	3.20–7.31	4.44	3.19–6.01	2.84–6.50	4.00	2.87–5.41	2.56–5.86
41	5.86	4.24–7.87	3.78–8.51	5.13	3.70–6.89	3.30–7.46	4.56	3.29–6.13	2.93–6.64	4.10	2.96–5.53	2.64–5.98
42	6.00	4.36–8.03	3.90–8.67	5.25	3.81–7.04	3.40–7.60	4.67	3.38–6.26	3.02–6.77	4.20	3.04–5.64	2.72–6.10
43	6.14	4.48–8.19	4.01–8.84	5.38	3.92–7.18	3.51–7.75	4.78	3.48–6.39	3.11–6.90	4.30	3.13–5.75	2.80–6.21
44	6.29	4.60–8.35	4.13–9.01	5.50	4.02–7.32	3.61–7.90	4.89	3.57–6.51	3.20–7.03	4.40	3.21–5.87	2.88–6.33
45	6.43	4.73–8.51	4.25–9.17	5.63	4.13–7.46	3.71–8.04	5.00	3.67–6.64	3.29–7.16	4.50	3.30–5.98	2.96–6.45
46	6.57	4.85–8.67	4.36–9.34	5.75	4.24–7.60	3.81–8.19	5.11	3.77–6.76	3.39–7.29	4.60	3.39–6.09	3.04–6.57
47	6.71	4.98–8.83	4.48–9.51	5.88	4.35–7.74	3.92–8.33	5.22	3.86–6.89	3.48–7.42	4.70	3.47–6.20	3.13–6.68
48	6.86	5.10–8.99	4.60–9.67	6.00	4.46–7.88	4.02–8.48	5.33	3.96–7.01	3.57–7.55	4.80	3.56–6.32	3.21–6.80
49	7.00	5.22–9.15	4.72–9.84	6.13	4.57–8.02	4.12–8.62	5.44	4.05–7.14	3.66–7.68	4.90	3.65–6.43	3.29–6.92
50	7.14	5.35–9.31	4.84–10.00	6.25	4.67–8.16	4.23–8.77	5.56	4.15–7.26	3.75–7.80	5.00	3.73–6.54	3.37–7.03
60	8.57	6.61–10.90	6.04–11.64	7.50	5.77–9.55	5.28–10.20	6.67	5.13–8.50	4.68–9.08	6.00	4.61–7.66	4.21–8.19
70	10.00	7.88–12.47	7.27–13.25	8.75	6.89–10.93	6.34–11.62	7.78	6.11–9.73	5.63–10.35	7.00	5.50–8.76	5.06–9.32
80	11.43	9.17–14.03	8.51–14.84	10.00	8.01–12.29	7.43–13.02	8.89	7.11–10.94	6.59–11.59	8.00	6.40–9.86	5.93–10.45
90	12.86	10.47–15.57	9.77–16.42	11.25	9.15–13.65	8.53–14.41	10.00	8.12–12.15	7.57–12.83	9.00	7.30–10.95	6.80–11.57
100	14.29	11.78–17.10	11.04–17.99	12.50	10.29–15.00	9.64–15.78	11.11	9.13–13.35	8.55–14.06	10.00	8.21–12.03	7.69–12.67
110	15.71	13.10–18.63	12.32–19.54	13.75	11.44–16.34	10.76–17.15	12.22	10.15–14.54	9.54–15.28	11.00	9.13–13.11	8.58–13.77
120	17.14	14.43–20.15	13.62–21.09	15.00	12.60–17.67	11.89–18.51	13.33	11.18–15.73	10.54–16.49	12.00	10.05–14.18	9.47–14.87
130	18.57	15.76–21.66	14.92–22.62	16.25	13.76–19.00	13.02–19.86	14.44	12.21–16.92	11.55–17.69	13.00	10.98–15.25	10.38–15.95
140	20.00	17.10–23.16	16.23–24.15	17.50	14.93–20.32	14.16–21.20	15.56	13.25–18.09	12.56–18.89	14.00	11.91–16.31	11.29–17.03
150	21.43	18.45–24.66	17.55–25.67	18.75	16.11–21.63	15.31–22.54	16.67	14.29–19.27	13.58–20.08	15.00	12.84–17.37	12.20–18.11
160	22.86	19.80–26.15	18.88–27.18	20.00	17.28–22.95	16.47–23.87	17.78	15.34–20.44	14.60–21.27	16.00	13.78–18.42	13.12–19.18
170	24.29	21.16–27.64	20.21–28.69	21.25	18.47–24.25	17.63–25.19	18.89	16.38–21.60	15.63–22.46	17.00	14.72–19.48	14.04–20.25
180	25.71	22.52–29.12	21.55–30.19	22.50	19.65–25.56	18.80–26.51	20.00	17.44–22.77	16.66–23.63	18.00	15.67–20.53	14.97–21.32
190	27.14	23.88–30.60	22.90–31.68	23.75	20.84–26.86	19.97–27.83	21.11	18.49–23.93	17.70–24.81	19.00	16.61–21.57	15.90–22.38
200	28.57	25.25–32.08	24.25–33.17	25.00	22.04–28.15	21.14–29.14	22.22	19.55–25.08	18.74–25.98	20.00	17.56–22.64	16.83–23.44
210	30.00	26.63–33.55	25.61–34.65	26.25	23.23–29.45	22.32–30.44	23.33	20.61–26.24	19.79–27.15	21.00	18.52–23.66	17.77–24.49
220	31.43	28.01–35.01	26.97–36.13	27.50	24.44–30.74	23.51–31.75	24.44	21.67–27.39	20.83–28.31	22.00	19.47–24.70	18.71–25.54
230	32.86	29.39–36.48	28.34–37.60	28.75	25.64–32.03	24.70–33.05	25.56	22.74–28.54	21.88–29.47	23.00	20.43–25.74	19.65–26.59
240	34.29	30.78–37.94	29.71–39.07	30.00	26.85–33.31	25.89–34.34	26.67	23.81–29.69	22.94–30.63	24.00	21.39–26.77	20.59–27.64
250	35.71	32.17–39.39	31.09–40.53	31.25	28.05–34.59	27.08–35.63	27.78	24.88–30.83	24.00–31.78	25.00	22.35–27.81	21.54–28.68
260	37.14	33.56–40.84	32.47–41.99	32.50	29.27–35.87	28.28–36.92	28.89	25.95–31.97	25.06–32.93	26.00	23.31–28.84	22.49–29.72
270	38.57	34.96–42.29	33.85–43.44	33.75	30.48–37.15	29.48–38.20	30.00	27.02–33.11	26.12–34.08	27.00	24.27–29.87	23.44–30.76
280	40.00	36.36–43.74	35.24–44.89	35.00	31.70–38.42	30.69–39.48	31.11	28.10–34.25	27.18–35.23	28.00	25.24–30.90	24.40–31.80
290	41.43	37.76–45.18	36.63–46.34	36.25	32.92–39.69	31.90–40.76	32.22	29.18–35.39	28.25–36.37	29.00	26.21–31.92	25.36–32.83
300	42.86	39.16–46.62	38.03–47.78	37.50	34.14–40.96	33.11–42.03	33.33	30.26–36.52	29.32–37.51	30.00	27.18–32.95	26.31–33.87
310	44.29	40.57–48.06	39.43–49.22	38.75	35.36–42.23	34.33–43.30	34.44	31.34–37.65	30.40–38.65	31.00	28.15–33.97	27.28–34.90
320	45.71	41.99–49.49	40.84–50.65	40.00	36.59–43.49	35.55–44.57	35.56	32.43–38.78	31.47–39.79	32.00	29.12–34.99	28.24–35.92
330	47.14	43.40–50.92	42.25–52.08	41.25	37.82–44.75	36.77–45.84	36.67	33.52–39.91	32.55–40.92	33.00	30.09–36.01	29.20–36.95
340	48.57	44.82–52.35	43.66–53.51	42.50	39.05–46.01	37.99–47.10	37.78	34.60–41.04	33.63–42.05	34.00	31.07–37.03	30.17–37.97
350	50.00	46.24–53.76	45.07–54.93	43.75	40.28–47.27	39.22–48.36	38.89	35.69–42.16	34.71–43.18	35.00	32.05–38.05	31.14–39.00
360	51.43	47.65–55.18	46.49–56.34	45.00	41.52–48.52	40.45–49.61	40.00	36.79–43.29	35.80–44.30	36.00	33.02–39.06	32.11–40.02
370	52.86	49.08–56.60	47.92–57.75	46.25	42.76–49.78	41.68–50.87	41.11	37.88–44.41	36.89–45.43	37.00	34.00–40.08	33.09–41.03
380	54.29	50.51–58.01	49.35–59.16	47.50	44.00–51.03	42.92–52.12	42.22	38.97–45.53	37.98–46.55	38.00	34.98–41.09	34.06–42.05
390	55.71	51.94–59.43	50.78–60.57	48.75	45.24–52.28	44.16–53.36	43.33	40.07–46.64	39.07–47.67	39.00	35.97–42.10	35.04–43.07
400	57.14	53.38–60.84	52.22–61.97	50.00	46.49–53.51	45.39–54.61	44.44	41.17–47.76	40.16–48.79	40.00	36.95–43.11	36.01–44.08
410	58.57	54.82–62.24	53.66–63.37	51.25	47.72–54.76	46.64–55.84	45.56	42.27–48.88	41.26–49.90	41.00	37.94–44.12	36.99–45.09
420	60.00	56.26–63.64	55.11–64.76	52.50	48.97–56.00	47.88–57.08	46.67	43.37–49.99	42.36–51.02	42.00	38.92–45.13	37.98–46.10
430	61.43	57.71–65.04	56.56–66.15	53.75	50.22–57.24	49.13–58.32	47.78	44.48–51.10	43.46–52.13	43.00	39.91–46.14	38.96–47.11
440	62.86	59.16–66.44	58.01–67.53	55.00	51.48–58.48	50.39–59.55	48.89	45.58–52.21	44.56–53.24	44.00	40.90–47.14	39.95–48.11
450	64.29	60.61–67.83	59.47–68.91	56.25	52.73–59.72	51.64–60.78	50.00	46.69–53.31	45.66–54.34	45.00	41.89–48.15	40.93–49.12
460	65.71	62.06–69.22	60.93–70.29	57.50	53.99–60.95	52.90–62.01	51.11	47.79–54.42	46.76–55.44	46.00	42.88–49.15	41.92–50.12
470	67.14	63.52–70.61	62.40–71.66	58.75	55.25–62.18	54.16–63.23	52.22	48.90–55.52	47.87–56.54	47.00	43.87–50.15	42.91–51.12
480	68.57	64.99–71.99	63.87–73.03	60.00	56.51–63.41	55.43–64.45	53.33	50.01–56.63	48.98–57.64	48.00	44.87–51.15	43.90–52.12
490	70.00	66.45–73.37	65.35–74.39	61.25	57.77–64.64	56.70–65.67	54.44	51.12–57.73	50.10–58.74	49.00	45.86–52.15	44.90–53.12
500	71.43	67.92–74.75	66.83–75.75	62.50	59.04–65.86	57.97–66.89	55.56	52.24–58.83	51.21–59.84	50.00	46.85–53.15	45.88–54.12
510	72.86	69.40–76.12	68.32–77.10	63.75	60.31–67.08	59.24–68.10	56.67	53.36–59.93	52.33–60.93	51.00	47.85–54.14	46.88–55.10
520	74.29	70.88–77.48	69.81–78.45	65.00	61.58–68.30	60.52–69.31	57.78	54.47–61.03	53.45–62.02	52.00	48.85–55.13	47.88–56.10
530	75.71	72.36–78.84	71.31–79.79	66.25	62.85–69.52	61.80–70.52	58.89	55.59–62.12	54.57–63.11	53.00	49.85–56.13	48.88–57.09
540	77.14	73.85–80.20	72.82–81.12	67.50	64.13–70.73	63.08–71.72	60.00	56.71–63.21	55.70–64.20	54.00	50.85–57.12	49.88–58.08
550	78.57	75.34–81.55	74.33–82.45	68.75	65.41–71.95	64.37–72.92	61.11	57.84–64.31	56.82–65.29	55.00	51.85–58.11	50.88–59.07

Confidence Limits* for Np (sign test, etc.)

N = number of trials

Confidence limits for binomial distributions: Prob $[x_l < Np < x_r] \geqq 1 - 2\alpha$; for quantiles of continuous distributions: Prob $[(x_l + 1) < Np < x_r] \geqq 1 - 2\alpha$

The lack of a significant limit on one side is indicated by a period, on both sides by a single dash

p =	0.05		0.10		0.15		0.20		0.25	
2α =	0.05	0.01	0.05	0.01	0.05	0.01	0.05	0.01	0.05	0.01
N	x_l x_r	x_l x_r	x_l x_r	x_l x_r	x_l x_r	x_l x_r	x_l x_r	x_l x_r	x_l x_r	x_l x_r
5	•– 2	•– 3	•– 3	•– 4	•– 4	•– 4	•– 4	•– 5	•– 4	•– 5
6	•– 3	•– 3	•– 3	•– 4	•– 4	•– 5	•– 4	•– 5	•– 5	•– 5
7	•– 3	•– 3	•– 4	•– 4	•– 4	•– 5	•– 5	•– 5	•– 5	•– 6
8	•– 3	•– 4	•– 4	•– 5	•– 4	•– 5	•– 5	•– 6	•– 6	•– 6
9	•– 3	•– 4	•– 4	•– 5	•– 5	•– 6	•– 5	•– 6	•– 6	•– 7
10	•– 3	•– 4	•– 4	•– 5	•– 5	•– 6	•– 6	•– 7	•– 6	•– 7
11	•– 3	•– 4	•– 4	•– 5	•– 5	•– 6	•– 6	•– 7	•– 7	•– 8
12	•– 3	•– 4	•– 5	•– 5	•– 5	•– 6	•– 6	•– 7	•– 7	•– 8
13	•– 3	•– 4	•– 5	•– 6	•– 6	•– 7	•– 7	•– 8	0– 7	•– 9
14	•– 4	•– 4	•– 5	•– 6	•– 6	•– 7	•– 7	•– 8	0– 8	•– 9
15	•– 4	•– 5	•– 5	•– 6	•– 6	•– 7	•– 7	•– 8	0– 8	•– 9
16	•– 4	•– 5	•– 5	•– 6	•– 6	•– 8	•– 8	•– 9	0– 9	•–10
17	•– 4	•– 5	•– 5	•– 6	•– 7	•– 8	0– 8	•– 9	0– 9	•–10
18	•– 4	•– 5	•– 6	•– 7	•– 7	•– 8	0– 8	•– 9	0– 9	•–11
19	•– 4	•– 5	•– 6	•– 7	•– 7	•– 8	0– 8	•–10	0–10	0–11
20	•– 4	•– 5	•– 6	•– 7	•– 7	•– 9	0– 9	•–10	1–10	0–11
21	•– 4	•– 5	•– 6	•– 7	•– 8	•– 9	0– 9	•–10	1–10	0–12
22	•– 4	•– 5	•– 6	•– 7	•– 8	•– 9	0– 9	•–11	1–11	0–12
23	•– 5	•– 5	•– 6	•– 8	0– 8	•– 9	0–10	•–11	1–11	0–12
24	•– 5	•– 6	•– 7	•– 8	0– 8	•–10	0–10	0–11	1–11	0–13
25	•– 5	•– 6	•– 7	•– 8	0– 9	•–10	0–10	0–12	1–12	0–13
26	•– 5	•– 6	•– 7	•– 8	0– 9	•–10	1–10	0–12	1–12	0–14
27	•– 5	•– 6	•– 7	•– 8	0– 9	•–10	1–11	0–12	2–12	1–14
28	•– 5	•– 6	•– 7	•– 8	0– 9	•–11	1–11	0–12	2–13	1–14
29	•– 5	•– 6	•– 7	•– 9	0– 9	•–11	1–11	0–13	2–13	1–15
30	•– 5	•– 6	•– 8	•– 9	0–10	•–11	1–12	0–13	2–13	1–15
31	•– 5	•– 6	•– 8	•– 9	0–10	•–11	1–12	0–13	2–14	1–15
32	•– 5	•– 6	•– 8	•– 9	0–10	•–12	1–12	0–14	2–14	1–16
33	•– 5	•– 7	•– 8	•– 9	0–10	0–12	1–12	0–14	3–14	1–16
34	•– 6	•– 7	•– 8	•–10	0–10	0–12	2–13	1–14	3–15	2–16
35	•– 6	•– 7	•– 8	•–10	1–11	0–12	2–13	1–15	3–15	2–17
36	•– 6	•– 7	0– 8	•–10	1–11	0–12	2–13	1–15	3–15	2–17
37	•– 6	•– 7	0– 9	•–10	1–11	0–13	2–13	1–15	3–16	2–17
38	•– 6	•– 7	0– 9	•–10	1–11	0–13	2–14	1–15	4–16	2–18
39	•– 6	•– 7	0– 9	•–10	1–11	0–13	2–14	1–16	4–16	2–18
40	•– 6	•– 7	0– 9	•–11	1–12	0–13	2–14	1–16	4–17	3–18
41	•– 6	•– 7	0– 9	•–11	1–12	0–14	3–14	1–16	4–17	3–19
42	•– 6	•– 7	0– 9	•–11	1–12	0–14	3–15	1–17	4–17	3–19
43	•– 6	•– 8	0– 9	•–11	1–12	0–14	3–15	2–17	4–18	3–19
44	•– 6	•– 8	0–10	•–11	1–13	0–14	3–15	2–17	5–18	3–20
45	•– 6	•– 8	0–10	•–11	1–13	0–14	3–15	2–17	5–18	3–20
46	•– 7	•– 8	0–10	•–11	2–13	0–15	3–16	2–18	5–18	4–20
47	•– 7	•– 8	0–10	•–12	2–13	1–15	3–16	2–18	5–19	4–21
48	•– 7	•– 8	0–10	•–12	2–13	1–15	4–16	2–18	5–19	4–21
49	•– 7	•– 8	0–10	•–12	2–14	1–15	4–17	2–18	6–19	4–21
50	•– 7	•– 8	0–10	•–12	2–14	1–16	4–17	2–19	6–20	4–22
51	•– 7	•– 8	0–11	0–12	2–14	1–16	4–17	3–19	6–20	4–22
52	•– 7	•– 8	0–11	0–12	2–14	1–16	4–17	3–19	6–20	5–22
53	•– 7	•– 8	0–11	0–13	2–14	1–16	4–18	3–20	6–21	5–23
54	•– 7	•– 9	1–11	0–13	2–15	1–16	4–18	3–20	7–21	5–23
55	•– 7	•– 9	1–11	0–13	2–15	1–17	5–18	3–20	7–21	5–23
56	•– 7	•– 9	1–11	0–13	3–15	1–17	5–18	3–20	7–22	5–24
57	•– 7	•– 9	1–11	0–13	3–15	1–17	5–19	3–21	7–22	5–24
58	•– 8	•– 9	1–12	0–13	3–15	1–17	5–19	3–21	7–22	6–24
59	•– 8	•– 9	1–12	0–13	3–16	2–17	5–19	4–21	8–22	6–25
60	•– 8	•– 9	1–12	0–14	3–16	2–18	5–19	4–21	8–23	6–25
61	•– 8	•– 9	1–12	0–14	3–16	2–18	5–20	4–22	8–23	6–25
62	•– 8	•– 9	1–12	0–14	3–16	2–18	6–20	4–22	8–23	6–26
63	•– 8	•– 9	1–12	0–14	3–16	2–18	6–20	4–22	8–24	6–26
64	•– 8	•– 9	1–12	0–14	3–16	2–19	6–20	4–23	8–24	7–26
65	•– 8	•– 9	1–13	0–14	3–17	2–19	6–21	4–23	9–24	7–27
66	•– 8	•–10	1–13	0–15	4–17	2–19	6–21	5–23	9–25	7–27
67	•– 8	•–10	1–13	0–15	4–17	2–19	6–21	5–23	9–25	7–27
68	•– 8	•–10	1–13	0–15	4–17	2–19	6–21	5–24	9–25	7–28
69	•– 8	•–10	1–13	0–15	4–17	2–20	7–22	5–24	9–26	8–28
70	•– 8	•–10	2–13	0–15	4–18	3–20	7–22	5–24	10–26	8–28
71	•– 9	•–10	2–13	0–15	4–18	3–20	7–22	5–24	10–26	8–29
72	0– 9	•–10	2–14	1–15	4–18	3–20	7–22	5–25	10–26	8–29
73	0– 9	•–10	2–14	1–16	4–18	3–20	7–23	5–25	10–27	8–29
74	0– 9	•–10	2–14	1–16	4–18	3–21	7–23	6–25	10–27	8–29
75	0– 9	•–10	2–14	1–16	5–19	3–21	8–23	6–25	11–27	9–30
76	0– 9	•–10	2–14	1–16	5–19	3–21	8–23	6–26	11–28	9–30
77	0– 9	•–10	2–14	1–16	5–19	3–21	8–24	6–26	11–28	9–30
78	0– 9	•–11	2–14	1–16	5–19	3–21	8–24	6–26	11–28	9–31
79	0– 9	•–11	2–14	1–16	5–19	3–22	8–24	6–26	11–28	9–31
80	0– 9	•–11	2–15	1–17	5–20	4–22	8–24	6–27	12–29	10–31
81	0– 9	•–11	2–15	1–17	5–20	4–22	8–25	7–27	12–29	10–32
82	0– 9	•–11	2–15	1–17	5–20	4–22	9–25	7–27	12–29	10–32
83	0– 9	•–11	2–15	1–17	5–20	4–22	9–25	7–27	12–30	10–32
84	0– 9	•–11	2–15	1–17	6–20	4–23	9–25	7–28	12–30	10–33
85	0–10	•–11	3–15	1–17	6–20	4–23	9–25	7–28	13–30	11–33
86	0–10	•–11	3–15	1–17	6–21	4–23	9–26	7–28	13–31	11–33
87	0–10	•–11	3–16	1–18	6–21	4–23	9–26	7–28	13–31	11–34
88	0–10	•–11	3–16	1–18	6–21	4–23	10–26	8–29	13–31	11–34
89	0–10	•–11	3–16	1–18	6–21	4–24	10–26	8–29	14–31	11–34
90	0–10	•–12	3–16	2–18	6–21	5–24	10–27	8–29	14–32	11–34
91	0–10	•–12	3–16	2–18	6–22	5–24	10–27	8–30	14–32	12–35
92	0–10	•–12	3–16	2–18	6–22	5–24	10–27	8–30	14–32	12–35
93	0–10	•–12	3–16	2–18	7–22	5–24	10–27	8–30	14–33	12–35
94	0–10	•–12	3–16	2–19	7–22	5–25	11–28	8–30	15–33	12–36
95	0–10	•–12	3–17	2–19	7–22	5–25	11–28	9–31	15–33	12–36
96	0–10	•–12	3–17	2–19	7–23	5–25	11–28	9–31	15–34	13–36
97	0–10	•–12	3–17	2–19	7–23	5–25	11–28	9–31	15–34	13–37
98	0–11	•–12	3–17	2–19	7–23	5–25	11–29	9–31	15–34	13–37
99	0–11	•–12	3–17	2–19	7–23	5–26	11–29	9–32	16–34	13–37
100	0–11	•–12	4–17	2–19	7–23	6–26	11–29	9–32	16–35	13–38

p =	0.30		0.35		0.40		0.45		0.50	
2α =	0.05	0.01	0.05	0.01	0.05	0.01	0.05	0.01	0.05	0.01
N	x_l x_r	x_l x_r	x_l x_r	x_l x_r	x_l x_r	x_l x_r	x_l x_r	x_l x_r	x_l x_r	x_l x_r
5	•– 5	•– 5	•– 5	—	•– 5	—	•– 5	—	—	—
6	•– 5	•– 6	•– 5	•– 6	•– 6	•– 6	•– 6	—	0– 6	—
7	•– 6	•– 6	•– 6	•– 7	•– 6	•– 7	0– 7	•– 7	0– 7	—
8	•– 6	•– 7	•– 7	•– 7	0– 7	•– 8	0– 7	•– 8	0– 8	0– 8
9	•– 7	•– 7	0– 7	•– 8	0– 8	•– 8	0– 8	0– 9	1– 8	0– 9
10	•– 7	•– 8	0– 8	•– 8	0– 8	•– 9	1– 9	0– 9	1– 9	0–10
11	0– 7	•– 8	0– 8	•– 9	0– 9	0–10	1– 9	0–10	1–10	0–11
12	0– 8	•– 9	0– 9	•–10	1– 9	0–10	1–10	0–11	2–10	1–11
13	0– 8	•– 9	0– 9	0–10	1–10	0–11	1–10	1–11	2–11	1–12
14	0– 9	•–10	1– 9	0–11	1–10	0–11	2–11	1–12	2–12	1–13
15	0– 9	0–10	1–10	0–11	1–11	0–12	2–12	1–13	3–12	2–13
16	0–10	0–11	1–10	0–12	2–11	1–12	2–12	1–13	3–13	2–14
17	1–10	0–11	1–11	0–12	2–12	1–13	3–13	2–14	4–13	2–15
18	1–10	0–12	2–11	1–13	2–12	1–14	3–13	2–14	4–14	3–15
19	1–11	0–12	2–12	1–13	3–13	1–14	3–14	2–15	4–15	3–16
20	1–11	0–13	2–12	1–14	3–13	2–15	4–14	3–16	5–15	3–17
21	1–12	0–13	2–13	1–14	3–14	2–15	4–15	3–16	5–16	4–17
22	2–12	1–13	3–13	1–15	3–14	2–16	4–15	3–17	5–17	4–18
23	2–12	1–14	3–14	2–15	4–15	2–16	5–16	3–17	6–17	4–19
24	2–13	1–14	3–14	2–16	4–15	3–17	5–17	4–18	6–18	5–19
25	2–13	1–15	3–15	2–16	4–16	3–17	5–17	4–19	7–18	5–20
26	2–14	1–15	4–15	2–17	5–16	3–18	6–18	4–19	7–19	6–20
27	3–14	1–15	4–15	2–17	5–17	4–18	6–18	5–20	7–20	6–21
28	3–14	2–16	4–16	3–17	5–17	4–19	7–19	5–20	8–20	6–22
29	3–15	2–16	4–16	3–18	6–18	4–19	7–19	5–21	8–21	7–22
30	3–15	2–17	5–17	3–18	6–18	4–20	7–20	6–22	9–21	7–23
31	4–15	2–17	5–17	3–19	6–19	5–21	8–20	6–22	9–22	7–24
32	4–16	2–18	5–18	4–19	7–19	5–21	8–21	6–23	9–23	8–24
33	4–16	3–18	5–18	4–20	7–20	5–22	8–21	7–23	10–23	8–25
34	4–17	3–18	6–18	4–20	7–20	6–22	9–22	7–24	10–24	9–25
35	4–17	3–19	6–19	4–21	7–21	6–23	9–23	7–24	11–24	9–26
36	5–17	3–19	6–19	5–21	8–21	6–23	9–23	8–25	11–25	9–27
37	5–18	3–20	6–20	5–22	8–22	6–24	10–24	8–25	12–25	10–27
38	5–18	4–20	7–20	5–22	8–22	7–24	10–24	8–26	12–26	10–28
39	5–18	4–20	7–21	5–23	9–23	7–25	11–25	9–27	12–27	11–28
40	6–19	4–21	7–21	6–23	9–23	7–25	11–25	9–27	13–27	11–29
41	6–19	4–21	8–21	6–23	9–24	8–26	11–26	9–28	13–28	11–30
42	6–20	4–22	8–22	6–24	10–24	8–26	12–26	10–28	14–28	12–30
43	6–20	5–22	8–22	6–24	10–25	8–27	12–27	10–29	14–29	12–31
44	6–20	5–22	8–23	7–25	10–25	9–27	12–27	10–29	15–29	13–31
45	7–21	5–23	9–23	7–25	11–25	9–28	13–28	11–30	15–30	13–32
46	7–21	5–23	9–24	7–26	11–26	9–28	13–28	11–30	15–31	13–33
47	7–21	5–23	9–24	7–26	11–26	9–29	14–29	12–31	16–31	14–33
48	7–22	6–24	10–24	8–27	12–27	10–29	14–29	12–31	16–32	14–34
49	8–22	6–24	10–25	8–27	12–27	10–30	14–30	12–32	17–32	15–34
50	8–23	6–25	10–25	8–27	12–28	10–30	15–30	13–33	17–33	15–35
51	8–23	6–25	10–26	8–28	13–28	11–31	15–31	13–33	18–33	15–36
52	8–23	7–25	11–26	9–28	13–29	11–31	15–31	13–34	18–34	16–36
53	9–24	7–26	11–26	9–29	13–29	11–31	16–32	14–34	18–35	16–37
54	9–24	7–26	11–27	9–29	14–30	12–32	16–32	14–35	19–35	17–37
55	9–24	7–27	11–27	10–30	14–30	12–32	17–33	14–35	19–36	17–38
56	9–25	7–27	12–28	10–30	14–31	12–33	17–34	15–36	20–36	17–39
57	10–25	8–27	12–28	10–30	15–31	13–33	17–34	15–36	20–37	18–39
58	10–25	8–28	12–29	10–31	15–32	13–34	18–35	16–37	21–37	18–40
59	10–26	8–28	13–29	11–31	15–32	13–34	18–35	16–37	21–38	19–40
60	10–26	8–28	13–29	11–32	16–32	13–35	19–36	16–38	21–39	19–41
61	11–26	9–29	13–30	11–32	16–33	14–35	19–36	17–38	22–39	20–41
62	11–27	9–29	14–30	11–33	16–33	14–36	19–37	17–39	22–40	20–42
63	11–27	9–30	14–31	12–33	17–34	14–36	20–37	17–40	23–40	20–43
64	11–28	9–30	14–31	12–33	17–34	15–37	20–38	18–40	23–41	21–43
65	11–28	9–30	14–31	12–34	17–35	15–37	20–38	18–41	24–41	21–44
66	12–28	10–31	15–32	12–34	18–35	15–38	21–39	18–41	24–42	22–44
67	12–29	10–31	15–32	13–35	18–36	16–38	21–39	19–42	25–42	22–45
68	12–29	10–31	15–33	13–35	18–36	16–39	22–40	19–42	25–43	22–46
69	12–29	10–32	16–33	13–36	19–37	16–39	22–40	20–43	25–44	23–46
70	13–30	11–32	16–33	14–36	19–37	17–40	22–41	20–43	26–44	23–47
71	13–30	11–33	16–34	14–36	19–38	17–40	23–41	20–44	26–45	24–47
72	13–30	11–33	16–34	14–37	20–38	17–41	23–42	21–44	27–45	24–48
73	13–31	11–33	17–35	14–37	20–38	18–41	24–42	21–45	27–46	25–48
74	14–31	12–34	17–35	15–38	20–39	18–42	24–43	21–45	28–46	25–49
75	14–31	12–34	17–35	15–38	21–39	18–42	24–43	22–46	28–47	25–50
76	14–32	12–34	18–36	15–39	21–40	19–43	25–44	22–46	28–48	26–50
77	14–32	12–35	18–36	16–39	21–40	19–43	25–44	23–47	29–48	26–51
78	15–32	12–35	18–37	16–39	22–41	19–43	26–45	23–47	29–49	27–51
79	15–33	13–35	19–37	16–40	22–41	20–44	26–45	23–48	30–49	27–52
80	15–33	13–36	19–37	16–40	23–42	20–44	26–46	24–48	30–50	28–52
81	15–34	13–36	19–38	17–41	23–42	20–45	27–46	24–49	31–50	28–53
82	16–34	13–37	19–38	17–41	23–43	21–45	27–47	24–50	31–51	28–54
83	16–34	14–37	20–39	17–41	24–43	21–46	28–47	25–50	32–51	29–54
84	16–35	14–37	20–39	17–42	24–43	21–46	28–48	25–51	32–52	29–55
85	16–35	14–38	20–39	18–42	24–44	22–47	28–48	26–51	32–53	30–55
86	17–35	14–38	21–40	18–43	25–44	22–47	29–49	26–52	33–53	30–56
87	17–36	15–38	21–40	18–43	25–45	22–48	29–49	26–52	33–54	31–56
88	17–36	15–39	21–41	19–44	25–45	23–48	30–50	27–53	34–54	31–57
89	17–36	15–39	21–41	19–44	26–46	23–49	30–50	27–53	34–55	31–58
90	18–37	15–40	22–41	19–44	26–46	23–49	30–51	27–54	35–55	32–58
91	18–37	15–40	22–42	19–45	26–47	24–50	31–51	28–54	35–56	32–59
92	18–37	16–40	22–42	20–45	27–47	24–50	31–52	28–55	36–56	33–59
93	18–38	16–41	23–43	20–46	27–48	24–50	32–52	29–55	36–57	33–60
94	19–38	16–41	23–43	20–46	27–48	25–51	32–53	29–56	37–57	34–60
95	19–38	16–41	23–43	21–46	28–48	25–51	32–53	29–56	37–58	34–61
96	19–39	17–42	24–44	21–47	28–49	25–52	33–54	30–57	37–59	34–62
97	19–39	17–42	24–44	21–47	28–49	26–52	33–54	30–57	38–59	35–62
98	20–39	17–42	24–45	21–48	29–50	26–53	34–55	31–58	38–60	35–63
99	20–40	17–43	25–45	22–48	29–50	26–53	34–55	31–58	39–60	36–63
100	20–40	18–43	25–45	22–49	30–51	27–54	34–56	31–59	39–61	36–64

Confidence Limits* for Np ($p = 0.5$, $N = 6 - 500$) (sign test, etc.)

N = number of trials. See also page 104

N	$2\alpha = 0.05$	$2\alpha = 0.01$	N	$2\alpha = 0.05$	$2\alpha = 0.01$	N	$2\alpha = 0.05$	$2\alpha = 0.01$	N	$2\alpha = 0.05$	$2\alpha = 0.01$	N	$2\alpha = 0.05$	$2\alpha = 0.01$
	x_l x_r	x_l x_r		x_l x_r	x_l x_r		x_l x_r	x_l x_r		x_l x_r	x_l x_r		x_l x_r	x_l x_r
0	–	–	**100**	39- 61	36- 64	**200**	85-115	81-119	**300**	132-168	127-173	**400**	179-221	173-227
1	–	–	101	40- 61	37- 64	201	86-115	81-120	301	132-169	127-174	401	180-221	174-227
2	–	–	102	40- 62	37- 65	202	86-116	82-120	302	133-169	128-174	402	180-222	174-228
3	–	–	103	41- 62	37- 66	203	87-116	82-121	303	133-170	128-175	403	181-222	175-228
4	–	–	104	41- 63	38- 66	204	87-117	83-121	304	134-170	129-175	404	181-223	175-229
5	–	–	**105**	41- 64	38- 67	**205**	87-118	83-122	**305**	134-171	129-176	**405**	182-223	176-229
6	0- 6	–	106	42- 64	39- 67	206	88-118	84-122	306	135-171	129-177	406	182-224	176-230
7	0- 7	–	107	42- 65	39- 68	207	88-119	84-123	307	135-172	130-177	407	183-224	177-230
8	0- 8	0- 8	108	43- 65	40- 68	208	89-119	84-124	308	136-172	130-178	408	183-225	177-231
9	1- 8	0- 9	109	43- 66	40- 69	209	89-120	85-124	309	136-173	131-178	409	184-225	177-232
10	1- 9	0-10	**110**	44- 66	41- 69	**210**	90-120	85-125	**310**	137-173	131-179	**410**	184-226	178-232
11	1-10	0-11	111	44- 67	41- 70	211	90-121	86-125	311	137-174	132-179	411	185-226	178-233
12	2-10	1-11	112	45- 67	42- 71	212	91-121	86-126	312	138-174	132-180	412	185-227	179-233
13	2-11	1-12	113	45- 68	42- 71	213	91-122	87-126	313	138-175	133-180	413	186-227	179-234
14	2-12	1-13	114	46- 68	43- 72	214	92-122	87-127	314	139-175	133-181	414	186-228	180-234
15	3-12	2-13	**115**	46- 69	43- 72	**215**	92-123	88-127	**315**	139-176	134-181	**415**	187-228	180-235
16	3-13	2-14	116	46- 70	43- 73	216	93-123	88-128	316	140-176	134-182	416	187-229	181-235
17	4-13	2-15	117	47- 70	44- 73	217	93-124	89-128	317	140-177	135-182	417	187-230	181-236
18	4-14	3-15	118	47- 71	44- 74	218	94-124	89-129	318	141-177	135-183	418	188-230	182-236
19	4-15	3-16	119	48- 71	45- 75	219	94-125	89-130	319	141-178	135-184	419	188-231	182-237
20	5-15	3-17	**120**	48- 72	45- 75	**220**	94-126	90-130	**320**	141-179	136-184	**420**	189-231	183-237
21	5-16	4-17	121	49- 72	45- 76	221	95-126	90-131	321	142-179	136-185	421	189-232	183-238
22	5-17	4-18	122	49- 73	46- 76	222	95-127	91-131	322	142-180	137-185	422	190-232	184-238
23	6-17	4-19	123	50- 73	46- 77	223	96-127	91-132	323	143-180	137-186	423	190-233	184-239
24	6-18	5-19	124	50- 74	47- 77	224	96-128	92-132	324	143-181	138-186	424	191-233	184-240
25	7-18	5-20	**125**	51- 74	47- 78	**225**	97-128	92-133	**325**	144-181	138-187	**425**	191-234	185-240
26	7-19	6-20	126	51- 75	48- 78	226	97-129	93-133	326	144-182	139-187	426	192-234	185-241
27	7-20	6-21	127	51- 76	48- 79	227	98-129	93-134	327	145-182	139-188	427	192-235	186-241
28	8-20	6-22	128	52- 76	48- 80	228	98-130	94-134	328	145-183	140-188	428	193-235	186-242
29	8-21	7-22	129	52- 77	49- 80	229	99-130	94-135	329	146-183	140-189	429	193-236	187-242
30	9-21	7-23	**130**	53- 77	49- 81	**230**	99-131	94-136	**330**	146-184	141-189	**430**	194-236	187-243
31	9-22	7-24	131	53- 78	50- 81	231	100-131	95-136	331	147-184	141-190	431	194-237	188-243
32	9-23	8-24	132	54- 78	50- 82	232	100-132	95-137	332	147-185	142-190	432	195-237	188-244
33	10-23	8-25	133	54- 79	51- 82	233	101-132	96-137	333	148-185	142-191	433	195-238	189-244
34	10-24	9-25	134	55- 79	51- 83	234	101-133	96-138	334	148-186	142-192	434	196-238	189-245
35	11-24	9-26	**135**	55- 80	52- 83	**235**	101-134	97-138	**335**	149-186	143-192	**435**	196-239	190-245
36	11-25	9-27	136	56- 80	52- 84	236	102-134	97-139	336	149-187	143-193	436	197-239	190-246
37	12-25	10-27	137	56- 81	52- 85	237	102-135	98-139	337	150-187	144-193	437	197-240	191-246
38	12-26	10-28	138	56- 82	53- 85	238	103-135	98-140	338	150-188	144-194	438	197-241	191-247
39	12-27	11-28	139	57- 82	53- 86	239	103-136	99-140	339	150-189	145-194	439	198-241	192-247
40	13-27	11-29	**140**	57- 83	54- 86	**240**	104-136	99-141	**340**	151-189	145-195	**440**	198-242	192-248
41	13-28	11-30	141	58- 83	54- 87	241	104-137	100-141	341	151-190	146-195	441	199-242	192-249
42	14-28	12-30	142	58- 84	55- 87	242	105-137	100-142	342	152-190	146-196	442	199-243	193-249
43	14-29	12-31	143	59- 84	55- 88	243	105-138	100-143	343	152-191	147-196	443	200-243	193-250
44	15-29	13-31	144	59- 85	56- 88	244	106-138	101-143	344	153-191	147-197	444	200-244	194-250
45	15-30	13-32	**145**	60- 85	56- 89	**245**	106-139	101-144	**345**	153-192	148-197	**445**	201-244	194-251
46	15-31	13-33	146	60- 86	56- 90	246	107-139	102-144	346	154-192	148-198	446	201-245	195-251
47	16-31	14-33	147	61- 86	57- 90	247	107-140	102-145	347	154-193	149-198	447	202-245	195-252
48	16-32	14-34	148	61- 87	57- 91	248	108-140	103-145	348	155-193	149-199	448	202-246	196-252
49	17-32	15-34	149	62- 87	58- 91	249	108-141	103-146	349	155-194	149-200	449	203-246	196-253
50	17-33	15-35	**150**	62- 88	58- 92	**250**	109-141	104-146	**350**	156-194	150-200	**450**	203-247	197-253
51	18-33	15-36	151	62- 89	59- 92	251	109-142	104-147	351	156-195	150-201	451	204-247	197-254
52	18-34	16-36	152	63- 89	59- 93	252	109-143	105-147	352	157-195	151-201	452	204-248	198-254
53	18-35	16-37	153	63- 90	60- 93	253	110-143	105-148	353	157-196	151-202	453	205-248	198-255
54	19-35	17-37	154	64- 90	60- 94	254	110-144	105-149	354	158-196	152-202	454	205-249	199-255
55	19-36	17-38	**155**	64- 91	60- 95	**255**	111-144	106-149	**355**	158-197	152-203	**455**	206-249	199-256
56	20-36	17-39	156	65- 91	61- 95	256	111-145	106-150	356	159-197	153-203	456	206-250	199-257
57	20-37	18-39	157	65- 92	61- 96	257	112-145	107-150	357	159-198	153-204	457	207-250	200-257
58	21-37	18-40	158	66- 92	62- 96	258	112-146	107-151	358	159-199	154-204	458	207-251	200-258
59	21-38	19-40	159	66- 93	62- 97	259	113-146	108-151	359	160-199	154-205	459	208-251	201-258
60	21-39	19-41	**160**	67- 93	63- 97	**260**	113-147	108-152	**360**	160-200	155-205	**460**	208-252	201-259
61	22-39	20-41	161	67- 94	63- 98	261	114-147	109-152	361	161-200	155-206	461	208-253	202-259
62	22-40	20-42	162	68- 94	64- 98	262	114-148	109-153	362	161-201	155-207	462	209-253	202-260
63	23-40	20-43	163	68- 95	64- 99	263	115-148	110-153	363	162-201	156-207	463	209-254	203-260
64	23-41	21-43	164	68- 96	65- 99	264	115-149	110-154	364	162-202	156-208	464	210-254	203-261
65	24-41	21-44	**165**	69- 96	65-100	**265**	116-149	111-154	**365**	163-202	157-208	**465**	210-255	204-261
66	24-42	22-44	166	69- 97	65-101	266	116-150	111-155	366	163-203	157-209	466	211-255	204-262
67	25-42	22-45	167	70- 97	66-101	267	116-151	111-156	367	164-203	158-209	467	211-256	205-262
68	25-43	22-46	168	70- 98	66-102	268	117-151	112-156	368	164-204	158-210	468	212-256	205-263
69	25-44	23-46	169	71- 98	67-102	269	117-152	112-157	369	165-204	159-210	469	212-257	206-263
70	26-44	23-47	**170**	71- 99	67-103	**270**	118-152	113-157	**370**	165-205	159-211	**470**	213-257	206-264
71	26-45	24-47	171	72- 99	68-103	271	118-153	113-158	371	166-205	160-211	471	213-258	207-264
72	27-45	24-48	172	72-100	68-104	272	119-153	114-158	372	166-206	160-212	472	214-258	207-265
73	27-46	25-48	173	73-100	69-104	273	119-154	114-159	373	167-206	161-212	473	214-259	207-266
74	28-46	25-49	174	73-101	69-105	274	120-154	115-159	374	167-207	161-213	474	215-259	208-266
75	28-47	25-50	**175**	74-101	69-106	**275**	120-155	115-160	**375**	168-207	162-213	**475**	215-260	208-267
76	28-48	26-50	176	74-102	70-106	276	121-155	116-160	376	168-208	162-214	476	216-260	209-267
77	29-48	26-51	177	74-103	70-107	277	121-156	116-161	377	168-209	162-215	477	216-261	209-268
78	29-49	27-51	178	75-103	71-107	278	122-156	117-161	378	169-209	163-215	478	217-261	210-268
79	30-49	27-52	179	75-104	71-108	279	122-157	117-162	379	169-210	163-216	479	217-262	210-269
80	30-50	28-52	**180**	76-104	72-108	**280**	123-157	117-163	**380**	170-210	164-216	**480**	218-262	211-269
81	31-50	28-53	181	76-105	72-109	281	123-158	118-163	381	170-211	164-217	481	218-263	211-270
82	31-51	28-54	182	77-105	73-109	282	124-158	118-164	382	171-211	165-217	482	218-264	212-270
83	32-51	29-54	183	77-106	73-110	283	124-159	119-164	383	171-212	165-218	483	219-264	212-271
84	32-52	29-55	184	78-106	74-110	284	124-160	119-165	384	172-212	166-218	484	219-265	213-271
85	32-53	30-55	**185**	78-107	74-111	**285**	125-160	120-165	**385**	172-213	166-219	**485**	220-265	213-272
86	33-53	30-56	186	79-107	74-112	286	125-161	120-166	386	173-213	167-219	486	220-266	214-272
87	33-54	31-56	187	79-108	75-112	287	126-161	121-166	387	173-214	167-220	487	221-266	214-273
88	34-54	31-57	188	80-108	75-113	288	126-162	121-167	388	174-214	168-220	488	221-267	215-273
89	34-55	31-58	189	80-109	76-113	289	127-162	122-167	389	174-215	168-221	489	222-267	215-274
90	35-55	32-58	**190**	80-110	76-114	**290**	127-163	122-168	**390**	175-215	169-221	**490**	222-268	215-275
91	35-56	32-59	191	81-110	77-114	291	128-163	123-168	391	175-216	169-222	491	223-268	216-275
92	36-56	33-59	192	81-111	77-115	292	128-164	123-169	392	176-216	170-222	492	223-269	216-276
93	36-57	33-60	193	82-111	78-115	293	129-164	123-170	393	176-217	170-223	493	224-269	217-276
94	37-57	34-60	194	82-112	78-116	294	129-165	124-170	394	177-217	170-224	494	224-270	217-277
95	37-58	34-61	**195**	83-112	79-116	**295**	130-165	124-171	**395**	177-218	171-224	**495**	225-270	218-277
96	37-59	34-62	196	83-113	79-117	296	130-166	125-171	396	177-219	171-225	496	225-271	218-278
97	38-59	35-62	197	84-113	79-118	297	131-166	125-172	397	178-219	172-225	497	226-271	219-278
98	38-60	35-63	198	84-114	80-118	298	131-167	126-172	398	178-220	172-226	498	226-272	219-279
99	39-60	36-63	199	85-114	80-119	299	132-167	126-173	399	179-220	173-226	499	227-272	220-279
100	39-61	36-64	**200**	85-115	81-119	**300**	132-168	127-173	**400**	179-221	173-227	**500**	227-273	220-280

Confidence Limits* for Np ($p=0.5$, $N=500-1000$) (sign test, etc.)

N = number of trials. See also page 104

N	$2\alpha=0.05$	$2\alpha=0.01$	N	$2\alpha=0.05$	$2\alpha=0.01$	N	$2\alpha=0.05$	$2\alpha=0.01$	N	$2\alpha=0.05$	$2\alpha=0.01$	N	$2\alpha=0.05$	$2\alpha=0.01$
	x_l x_r	x_l x_r		x_l x_r	x_l x_r		x_l x_r	x_l x_r		x_l x_r	x_l x_r		x_l x_r	x_l x_r
500	227–273	220–280	**600**	275–325	267–333	**700**	323–377	315–385	**800**	371–429	363–437	**900**	420–480	410–490
501	228–273	221–280	601	275–326	268–333	701	324–377	315–386	801	372–429	363–438	901	420–481	411–490
502	228–274	221–281	602	276–326	268–334	702	324–378	316–386	802	372–430	364–438	902	421–481	411–491
503	229–274	222–281	603	276–327	269–334	703	325–378	316–387	803	373–430	364–439	903	421–482	412–491
504	229–275	222–282	604	277–327	269–335	704	325–379	317–387	804	373–431	364–440	904	422–482	412–492
505	229–276	223–282	**605**	277–328	270–335	**705**	325–380	317–388	**805**	374–431	365–440	**905**	422–483	413–492
506	230–276	223–283	606	278–328	270–336	706	326–380	318–388	806	374–432	365–441	906	423–483	413–493
507	230–277	224–283	607	278–329	271–336	707	326–381	318–389	807	375–432	366–441	907	423–484	414–493
508	231–277	224–284	608	279–329	271–337	708	327–381	319–389	808	375–433	366–442	908	423–485	414–494
509	231–278	224–285	609	279–330	272–337	709	327–382	319–390	809	376–433	367–442	909	424–485	415–494
510	232–278	225–285	**610**	280–330	272–338	**710**	328–382	320–390	**810**	376–434	367–443	**910**	424–486	415–495
511	232–279	225–286	611	280–331	273–338	711	328–383	320–391	811	377–434	368–443	911	425–486	416–495
512	233–279	226–286	612	281–331	273–339	712	329–383	321–391	812	377–435	368–444	912	425–487	416–496
513	233–280	226–287	613	281–332	274–339	713	329–384	321–392	813	378–435	369–444	913	426–487	417–496
514	234–280	227–287	614	282–332	274–340	714	330–384	322–392	814	378–436	369–445	914	426–488	417–497
515	234–281	227–288	**615**	282–333	275–340	**715**	330–385	322–393	**815**	379–436	370–445	**915**	427–488	418–497
516	235–281	228–288	616	283–333	275–341	716	331–385	323–393	816	379–437	370–446	916	427–489	418–498
517	235–282	228–289	617	283–334	276–341	717	331–386	323–394	817	379–438	371–446	917	428–489	418–499
518	236–282	229–289	618	284–334	276–342	718	332–386	323–395	818	380–438	371–447	918	428–490	419–499
519	236–283	229–290	619	284–335	276–343	719	332–387	324–395	819	380–439	372–447	919	429–490	419–500
520	237–283	230–290	**620**	285–335	277–343	**720**	333–387	324–396	**820**	381–439	372–448	**920**	429–491	420–500
521	237–284	230–291	621	285–336	277–344	721	333–388	325–396	821	381–440	373–448	921	430–491	420–501
522	238–284	231–291	622	286–336	278–344	722	334–388	325–397	822	382–440	373–449	922	430–492	421–501
523	238–285	231–292	623	286–337	278–345	723	334–389	326–397	823	382–441	374–449	923	431–492	421–502
524	239–285	232–292	624	287–337	279–345	724	335–389	326–398	824	383–441	374–450	924	431–493	422–502
525	239–286	232–293	**625**	287–338	279–346	**725**	335–390	327–398	**825**	383–442	375–450	**925**	432–493	422–503
526	240–286	232–294	626	287–339	280–346	726	336–390	327–399	826	384–442	375–451	926	432–494	423–503
527	240–287	233–294	627	288–339	280–347	727	336–391	328–399	827	384–443	375–452	927	433–494	423–504
528	240–288	233–295	628	288–340	281–347	728	337–391	328–400	828	385–443	376–452	928	433–495	424–504
529	241–288	234–295	629	289–340	281–348	729	337–392	329–400	829	385–444	376–453	929	434–495	424–505
530	241–289	234–296	**630**	289–341	282–348	**730**	338–392	329–401	**830**	386–444	377–453	**930**	434–496	425–505
531	242–289	235–296	631	290–341	282–349	731	338–393	330–401	831	386–445	377–454	931	435–496	425–506
532	242–290	235–297	632	290–342	283–349	732	338–394	330–402	832	387–445	378–454	932	435–497	426–506
533	243–290	236–297	633	291–342	283–350	733	339–394	331–402	833	387–446	378–455	933	436–497	426–507
534	243–291	236–298	634	291–343	284–350	734	339–395	331–403	834	388–446	379–455	934	436–498	427–507
535	244–291	237–298	**635**	292–343	284–351	**735**	340–395	332–403	**835**	388–447	379–456	**935**	437–498	427–508
536	244–292	237–299	636	292–344	285–351	736	340–396	332–404	836	389–447	380–456	936	437–499	428–508
537	245–292	238–299	637	293–344	285–352	737	341–396	333–404	837	389–448	380–457	937	438–499	428–509
538	245–293	238–300	638	293–345	285–353	738	341–397	333–405	838	390–448	381–457	938	438–500	429–509
539	246–293	239–300	639	294–345	286–353	739	342–397	333–406	839	390–449	381–458	939	438–501	429–510
540	246–294	239–301	**640**	294–346	286–354	**740**	342–398	334–406	**840**	391–449	382–458	**940**	439–501	430–510
541	247–294	240–301	641	295–346	287–354	741	343–398	334–407	841	391–450	382–459	941	439–502	430–511
542	247–295	240–302	642	295–347	287–355	742	343–399	335–407	842	392–450	383–459	942	440–502	430–512
543	248–295	240–303	643	296–347	288–355	743	344–399	335–408	843	392–451	383–460	943	440–503	431–512
544	248–296	241–303	644	296–348	288–356	744	344–400	336–408	844	393–451	384–460	944	441–503	431–513
545	249–296	241–304	**645**	297–348	289–356	**745**	345–400	336–409	**845**	393–452	384–461	**945**	441–504	432–513
546	249–297	242–304	646	297–349	289–357	746	345–401	337–409	846	393–453	385–461	946	442–504	432–514
547	250–297	242–305	647	298–349	290–357	747	346–401	337–410	847	394–453	385–462	947	442–505	433–514
548	250–298	243–305	648	298–350	290–358	748	346–402	338–410	848	394–454	385–463	948	443–505	433–515
549	251–298	243–306	649	299–350	291–358	749	347–402	338–411	849	395–454	386–463	949	443–506	434–515
550	251–299	244–306	**650**	299–351	291–359	**750**	347–403	339–411	**850**	395–455	386–464	**950**	444–506	434–516
551	251–300	244–307	651	299–352	292–359	751	348–403	339–412	851	396–455	387–464	951	444–507	435–516
552	252–300	245–307	652	300–352	292–360	752	348–404	340–412	852	396–456	387–465	952	445–507	435–517
553	252–301	245–308	653	300–353	293–360	753	349–404	340–413	853	397–456	388–465	953	445–508	436–517
554	253–301	246–308	654	301–353	293–361	754	349–405	341–413	854	397–457	388–466	954	446–508	436–518
555	253–302	246–309	**655**	301–354	294–361	**755**	350–405	341–414	**855**	398–457	389–466	**955**	446–509	437–518
556	254–302	247–309	656	302–354	294–362	756	350–406	342–414	856	398–458	389–467	956	447–509	437–519
557	254–303	247–310	657	302–355	294–363	757	351–406	342–415	857	399–458	390–467	957	447–510	438–519
558	255–303	248–310	658	303–355	295–363	758	351–407	343–415	858	399–459	390–468	958	448–510	438–520
559	255–304	248–311	659	303–356	295–364	759	352–407	343–416	859	400–459	391–468	959	448–511	439–520
560	256–304	249–311	**660**	304–356	296–364	**760**	352–408	343–417	**860**	400–460	391–469	**960**	449–511	439–521
561	256–305	249–312	661	304–357	296–365	761	352–409	344–417	861	401–460	392–469	961	449–512	440–521
562	257–305	249–313	662	305–357	297–365	762	353–409	344–418	862	401–461	392–470	962	450–512	440–522
563	257–306	250–313	663	305–358	297–366	763	353–410	345–418	863	402–461	393–470	963	450–513	441–522
564	258–306	250–314	664	306–358	298–366	764	354–410	345–419	864	402–462	393–471	964	451–513	441–523
565	258–307	251–314	**665**	306–359	298–367	**765**	354–411	346–419	**865**	403–462	394–471	**965**	451–514	441–524
566	259–307	251–315	666	307–359	299–367	766	355–411	346–420	866	403–463	394–472	966	452–514	442–524
567	259–308	252–315	667	307–360	299–368	767	355–412	347–420	867	404–463	395–472	967	452–515	442–525
568	260–308	252–316	668	308–360	300–368	768	356–412	347–421	868	404–464	395–473	968	453–515	443–525
569	260–309	253–316	669	308–361	300–369	769	356–413	348–421	869	405–464	396–473	969	453–516	443–526
570	261–309	253–317	**670**	309–361	301–369	**770**	357–413	348–422	**870**	405–465	396–474	**970**	453–517	444–526
571	261–310	254–317	671	309–362	301–370	771	357–414	349–422	871	406–465	396–475	971	454–517	444–527
572	262–310	254–318	672	310–362	302–370	772	358–414	349–423	872	406–466	397–475	972	454–518	445–527
573	262–311	255–318	673	310–363	302–371	773	358–415	350–423	873	407–466	397–476	973	455–518	445–528
574	263–311	255–319	674	311–363	303–371	774	359–415	350–424	874	407–467	398–476	974	455–519	446–528
575	263–312	256–319	**675**	311–364	303–372	**775**	359–416	351–424	**875**	408–467	398–477	**975**	456–519	446–529
576	263–313	256–320	676	312–364	304–372	776	360–416	351–425	876	408–468	399–477	976	456–520	447–529
577	264–313	257–320	677	312–365	304–373	777	360–417	352–425	877	408–469	399–478	977	457–520	447–530
578	264–314	257–321	678	312–366	304–374	778	361–417	352–426	878	409–469	400–478	978	457–521	448–530
579	265–314	258–321	679	313–366	305–374	779	361–418	353–426	879	409–470	400–479	979	458–521	448–531
580	265–315	258–322	**680**	313–367	305–375	**780**	362–418	353–427	**880**	410–470	401–479	**980**	458–522	449–531
581	266–315	258–323	681	314–367	306–375	781	362–419	354–427	881	410–471	401–480	981	459–522	449–532
582	266–316	259–323	682	314–368	306–376	782	363–419	354–428	882	411–471	402–480	982	459–523	450–532
583	267–316	259–324	683	315–368	307–376	783	363–420	354–429	883	411–472	402–481	983	460–523	450–533
584	267–317	260–324	684	315–369	307–377	784	364–420	355–429	884	412–472	403–481	984	460–524	451–533
585	268–317	260–325	**685**	316–369	308–377	**785**	364–421	355–430	**885**	412–473	403–482	**985**	461–524	451–534
586	268–318	261–325	686	316–370	308–378	786	365–421	356–430	886	413–473	404–482	986	461–525	452–534
587	269–318	261–326	687	317–370	309–378	787	365–422	356–431	887	413–474	404–483	987	462–525	452–535
588	269–319	262–326	688	317–371	309–379	788	365–423	357–431	888	414–474	405–483	988	462–526	453–535
589	270–319	262–327	689	318–371	310–379	789	366–423	357–432	889	414–475	405–484	989	463–526	453–536
590	270–320	263–327	**690**	318–372	310–380	**790**	366–424	358–432	**890**	415–475	406–484	**990**	463–527	453–537
591	271–320	263–328	691	319–372	311–380	791	367–424	358–433	891	415–476	406–485	991	464–527	454–537
592	271–321	264–328	692	319–373	311–381	792	367–425	359–433	892	416–476	407–485	992	464–528	454–538
593	272–321	264–329	693	320–373	312–381	793	368–425	359–434	893	416–477	407–486	993	465–528	455–538
594	272–322	265–329	694	320–374	312–382	794	368–426	360–434	894	417–477	407–487	994	465–529	455–539
595	273–322	265–330	**695**	321–374	313–382	**795**	369–426	360–435	**895**	417–478	408–487	**995**	466–529	456–539
596	273–323	266–330	696	321–375	313–383	796	369–427	361–435	896	418–478	408–488	996	466–530	456–540
597	274–323	266–331	697	322–375	313–384	797	370–427	361–436	897	418–479	409–488	997	467–530	457–540
598	274–324	267–331	698	322–376	314–384	798	370–428	362–436	898	419–479	409–489	998	467–531	457–541
599	275–324	267–332	699	323–376	314–385	799	371–428	362–437	899	419–480	410–489	999	468–531	458–541
600	275–325	267–333	**700**	323–377	315–385	**800**	371–429	363–437	**900**	420–480	410–490	**1000**	468–532	458–542

Values from 0 to 100 are exact, all others have been calculated from FREEMAN and TUKEY's approximation (cf. page 189)

x	0	1 10 100	2 20 200	3 30 300	4 40 400	5 50 500	6 60 600	7 70 700	8 80 800	9 90 900
	λ_l λ_r	λ_l λ_r	λ_l λ_r	λ_l λ_r	λ_l λ_r	λ_l λ_r	λ_l λ_r	λ_l λ_r	λ_l λ_r	λ_l λ_r
0	0 –3.6889	0.0253–5.5716	0.2422–7.2247	0.6187–8.7673	1.0899–10.242	1.6235–11.669	2.2019–13.060	2.8144–14.423	3.4539–15.764	4.1154–17.085
10	4.7954–18.391	5.4913–19.683	6.2008–20.962	6.9223–22.231	7.6542–23.490	8.3957–24.741	9.1459–25.983	9.9037–27.219	10.668–28.448	11.440–29.671
20	12.217–30.889	13.000–32.101	13.788–33.309	14.581–34.512	15.378–35.711	16.178–36.905	16.983–38.097	17.793–39.284	18.606–40.468	19.422–41.649
30	20.241–42.827	21.063–44.002	21.888–45.175	22.715–46.345	23.545–47.512	24.378–48.677	25.213–49.840	26.050–51.000	26.890–52.158	27.732–53.315
40	28.575–54.469	29.421–55.622	30.269–56.772	31.119–57.921	31.970–59.068	32.823–60.214	33.678–61.358	34.534–62.501	35.392–63.642	36.251–64.781
50	37.112–65.919	37.973–67.056	38.837–68.192	39.701–69.326	40.567–70.459	41.433–71.591	42.301–72.721	43.171–73.851	44.041–74.979	44.912–76.106
60	45.785–77.232	46.658–78.357	47.533–79.482	48.409–80.605	49.286–81.727	50.164–82.848	51.042–83.969	51.922–85.088	52.803–86.207	53.685–87.324
70	54.567–88.441	55.451–89.557	56.335–90.673	57.220–91.787	58.106–92.901	58.993–94.014	59.880–95.126	60.768–96.237	61.657–97.348	62.547–98.458
80	63.437–99.567	64.328–100.68	65.219–101.79	66.111–102.90	67.003–104.00	67.897–105.11	68.790–106.21	69.684–107.32	70.579–108.42	71.474–109.53
90	72.370–110.63	73.267–111.73	74.164–112.83	75.061–113.94	75.959–115.04	76.858–116.14	77.757–117.24	78.657–118.34	79.557–119.44	80.458–120.53
100	81.36–121.66	90.40–132.61	99.49–143.52	108.61–154.39	117.77–165.23	126.96–176.04	136.17–186.83	145.41–197.59	154.66–208.33	163.94–219.05
200	173.24–229.75	182.56–240.43	191.89–251.10	201.24–261.75	210.60–272.39	219.97–283.01	229.36–293.62	238.75–304.23	248.16–314.82	257.58–325.39
300	267.01–335.96	276.45–346.52	285.90–357.08	295.36–367.62	304.82–378.15	314.29–388.68	323.77–399.20	333.26–409.71	342.75–420.22	352.25–430.72
400	361.76–441.21	371.27–451.69	380.79–462.18	390.32–472.65	399.85–483.12	409.38–493.58	418.92–504.04	428.47–514.50	438.02–524.95	447.57–535.39
500	457.13–545.83	466.70–556.27	476.27–566.70	485.84–577.12	495.41–587.55	505.00–597.97	514.58–608.38	524.17–618.79	533.76–629.20	543.35–639.61
600	552.95–650.01	562.55–660.41	572.16–670.80	581.77–681.19	591.38–691.58	600.99–701.97	610.61–712.35	620.23–722.73	629.85–733.11	639.48–743.48
700	649.10–753.85	658.74–764.22	668.37–774.59	678.01–784.95	687.64–795.31	697.28–805.67	706.93–816.03	716.57–826.38	726.22–836.73	735.87–847.08
800	745.52–857.43	755.18–867.78	764.84–878.12	774.49–888.46	784.16–898.80	793.82–909.14	803.48–919.47	813.15–929.80	822.82–940.14	832.49–950.46
900	842.16–960.79	851.84–971.12	861.51–981.44	871.19–991.76	880.87–1002.1	890.55–1012.5	900.23–1022.8	909.92–1033.1	919.60–1043.4	929.29–1053.7
1000	938.98–1064.0	948.67–1074.3	958.36–1084.6	968.06–1094.9	977.75–1105.2	987.45–1115.6	997.15–1125.8	1006.8–1136.1	1016.5–1146.4	1026.2–1156.7
1100	1035.9–1167.0	1045.6–1177.3	1055.3–1187.6	1065.0–1197.9	1074.7–1208.2	1084.4–1218.5	1094.2–1228.8	1103.9–1239.1	1113.6–1249.4	1123.3–1259.6
1200	1133.0–1269.9	1142.7–1280.2	1152.5–1290.5	1162.2–1300.8	1171.9–1311.1	1181.6–1321.3	1191.3–1331.6	1201.1–1341.9	1210.8–1352.2	1220.5–1362.4
1300	1230.2–1372.7	1240.0–1383.0	1249.7–1393.2	1259.4–1403.5	1269.2–1413.8	1278.9–1424.0	1288.6–1434.3	1298.4–1444.6	1308.1–1454.8	1317.8–1465.1
1400	1327.6–1475.4	1337.3–1485.6	1347.1–1495.9	1356.8–1506.1	1366.5–1516.4	1376.3–1526.7	1386.0–1536.9	1395.8–1547.2	1405.5–1557.4	1415.3–1567.7
1500	1425.0–1577.9	1434.8–1588.2	1444.5–1598.4	1454.3–1608.7	1464.0–1618.9	1473.8–1629.2	1483.5–1639.4	1493.3–1649.7	1503.0–1659.9	1512.8–1670.2
1600	1522.5–1680.4	1532.3–1690.7	1542.0–1700.9	1551.8–1711.2	1561.5–1721.4	1571.3–1731.7	1581.1–1741.9	1590.8–1752.1	1600.6–1762.4	1610.3–1772.6
1700	1620.1–1782.8	1629.9–1793.1	1639.6–1803.3	1649.4–1813.6	1659.2–1823.8	1668.9–1834.0	1678.7–1844.3	1688.5–1854.5	1698.2–1864.7	1708.0–1875.0
1800	1717.8–1885.2	1727.5–1895.4	1737.3–1905.6	1747.1–1915.9	1756.8–1926.1	1766.6–1936.3	1776.4–1946.6	1786.2–1956.8	1795.9–1967.0	1805.7–1977.2
1900	1815.5–1987.5	1825.3–1997.7	1835.0–2007.9	1844.8–2018.1	1854.6–2028.4	1864.4–2038.6	1874.1–2048.8	1883.9–2059.0	1893.7–2069.3	1903.5–2079.5
2000	1913.3–2089.7	1923.0–2099.9	1932.8–2110.1	1942.6–2120.3	1952.4–2130.6	1962.2–2140.8	1972.0–2151.0	1981.7–2161.2	1991.5–2171.4	2001.3–2181.6
2100	2011.1–2191.8	2020.9–2202.1	2030.7–2212.3	2040.5–2222.5	2050.2–2232.7	2060.0–2242.9	2069.8–2253.1	2079.6–2263.3	2089.4–2273.5	2099.2–2283.7
2200	2109.0–2294.0	2118.8–2304.2	2128.6–2314.4	2138.4–2324.6	2148.2–2334.8	2157.9–2345.0	2167.7–2355.2	2177.5–2365.4	2187.3–2375.6	2197.1–2385.8
2300	2206.9–2396.0	2216.7–2406.2	2226.5–2416.4	2236.3–2426.6	2246.1–2436.8	2255.9–2447.0	2265.7–2457.2	2275.5–2467.4	2285.3–2477.6	2295.1–2487.8
2400	2304.9–2498.0	2314.7–2508.2	2324.5–2518.4	2334.3–2528.6	2344.1–2538.8	2353.9–2549.0	2363.7–2559.2	2373.5–2569.4	2383.3–2579.6	2393.1–2589.8
2500	2402.9–2600.0	2412.7–2610.2	2422.5–2620.4	2432.3–2630.6	2442.1–2640.8	2451.9–2651.0	2461.7–2661.2	2471.6–2671.4	2481.4–2681.6	2491.2–2691.8
2600	2501.0–2702.0	2510.8–2712.2	2520.6–2722.3	2530.4–2732.5	2540.2–2742.7	2550.0–2752.9	2559.8–2763.1	2569.6–2773.3	2579.5–2783.5	2589.3–2793.7
2700	2599.1–2803.9	2608.9–2814.1	2618.7–2824.2	2628.5–2834.4	2638.3–2844.6	2648.1–2854.8	2657.9–2865.0	2667.8–2875.2	2677.6–2885.4	2687.4–2895.6
2800	2697.2–2905.7	2707.0–2915.9	2716.8–2926.1	2726.6–2936.3	2736.5–2946.5	2746.3–2956.7	2756.1–2966.8	2765.9–2977.0	2775.7–2987.2	2785.6–2997.4
2900	2795.4–3007.6	2805.2–3017.8	2815.0–3027.9	2824.8–3038.1	2834.6–3048.3	2844.5–3058.5	2854.3–3068.7	2864.1–3078.8	2873.9–3089.0	2883.7–3099.2
3000	2893.6–3109.4	2903.4–3119.6	2913.2–3129.7	2923.0–3139.9	2932.9–3150.1	2942.7–3160.3	2952.5–3170.4	2962.3–3180.6	2972.1–3190.8	2982.0–3201.0
3100	2991.8–3211.1	3001.6–3221.3	3011.4–3231.5	3021.3–3241.7	3031.1–3251.9	3040.9–3262.0	3050.7–3272.2	3060.6–3282.4	3070.4–3292.5	3080.2–3302.7
3200	3090.0–3312.9	3099.9–3323.1	3109.7–3333.2	3119.5–3343.4	3129.4–3353.6	3139.2–3363.8	3149.0–3373.9	3158.8–3384.1	3168.7–3394.3	3178.5–3404.4
3300	3188.3–3414.6	3198.2–3424.8	3208.0–3435.0	3217.8–3445.1	3227.6–3455.3	3237.5–3465.5	3247.3–3475.6	3257.1–3485.8	3267.0–3496.0	3276.8–3506.1
3400	3286.6–3516.3	3296.5–3526.5	3306.3–3536.6	3316.1–3546.8	3326.0–3557.0	3335.8–3567.1	3345.6–3577.3	3355.5–3587.5	3365.3–3597.6	3375.1–3607.8
3500	3385.0–3618.0	3394.8–3628.1	3404.6–3638.3	3414.5–3648.5	3424.3–3658.6	3434.1–3668.8	3444.0–3679.0	3453.8–3689.1	3463.6–3699.3	3473.5–3709.5
3600	3483.3–3719.6	3493.2–3729.8	3503.0–3739.9	3512.8–3750.1	3522.7–3760.3	3532.5–3770.4	3542.3–3780.6	3552.2–3790.8	3562.0–3800.9	3571.9–3811.1
3700	3581.7–3821.2	3591.5–3831.4	3601.4–3841.6	3611.2–3851.7	3621.1–3861.9	3630.9–3872.0	3640.7–3882.2	3650.6–3892.4	3660.4–3902.5	3670.3–3912.7
3800	3680.1–3922.8	3689.9–3933.0	3699.8–3943.2	3709.6–3953.3	3719.5–3963.5	3729.3–3973.6	3739.1–3983.8	3749.0–3993.9	3758.8–4004.1	3768.7–4014.3
3900	3778.5–4024.4	3788.4–4034.6	3798.2–4044.7	3808.0–4054.9	3817.9–4065.0	3827.7–4075.2	3837.6–4085.4	3847.4–4095.5	3857.3–4105.7	3867.1–4115.8
4000	3877.0–4126.0	3886.8–4136.1	3896.6–4146.3	3906.5–4156.4	3916.3–4166.6	3926.2–4176.8	3936.0–4186.9	3945.9–4197.1	3955.7–4207.2	3965.6–4217.4
4100	3975.4–4227.5	3985.3–4237.7	3995.1–4247.8	4005.0–4258.0	4014.8–4268.1	4024.7–4278.3	4034.5–4288.4	4044.3–4298.6	4054.2–4308.7	4064.0–4318.9
4200	4073.9–4329.0	4083.7–4339.2	4093.6–4349.3	4103.4–4359.5	4113.3–4369.6	4123.1–4379.8	4133.0–4389.9	4142.8–4400.1	4152.7–4410.2	4162.5–4420.4
4300	4172.4–4430.5	4182.2–4440.7	4192.1–4450.8	4201.9–4461.0	4211.8–4471.1	4221.6–4481.3	4231.5–4491.4	4241.4–4501.6	4251.2–4511.7	4261.1–4521.9
4400	4270.9–4532.0	4280.8–4542.2	4290.6–4552.3	4300.5–4562.5	4310.3–4572.6	4320.2–4582.8	4330.0–4592.9	4339.9–4603.1	4349.7–4613.2	4359.6–4623.4
4500	4369.4–4633.5	4379.3–4643.6	4389.1–4653.8	4399.0–4663.9	4408.9–4674.1	4418.7–4684.2	4428.6–4694.4	4438.4–4704.5	4448.3–4714.7	4458.1–4724.8
4600	4468.0–4735.0	4477.8–4745.1	4487.7–4755.2	4497.6–4765.4	4507.4–4775.5	4517.3–4785.7	4527.1–4795.8	4537.0–4806.0	4546.8–4816.1	4556.7–4826.2
4700	4566.5–4836.4	4576.4–4846.5	4586.3–4856.7	4596.1–4866.8	4606.0–4877.0	4615.8–4887.1	4625.7–4897.2	4635.6–4907.4	4645.4–4917.5	4655.3–4927.7
4800	4665.1–4937.8	4675.0–4948.0	4684.8–4958.1	4694.7–4968.2	4704.6–4978.4	4714.4–4988.5	4724.3–4998.7	4734.1–5008.8	4744.0–5018.9	4753.9–5029.1
4900	4763.7–5039.2	4773.6–5049.4	4783.4–5059.5	4793.3–5069.6	4803.2–5079.8	4813.0–5089.9	4822.9–5100.1	4832.7–5110.2	4842.6–5120.3	4852.5–5130.5
5000	4862.3–5140.6	4960.9–5242.0	5059.6–5343.4	5158.2–5444.7	5256.9–5546.0	5355.6–5647.4	5454.2–5748.7	5552.9–5850.0	5651.6–5951.3	5750.4–6052.6
6000	5849.1–6153.8	5947.8–6255.1	6046.6–6356.3	6145.3–6457.6	6244.1–6558.8	6342.9–6660.0	6441.7–6761.3	6540.5–6862.4	6639.3–6963.6	6738.1–7064.8
7000	6836.9–7166.0	6935.8–7267.2	7034.6–7368.3	7133.5–7469.5	7232.3–7570.6	7331.2–7671.8	7430.0–7772.9	7528.9–7874.0	7627.8–7975.1	7726.7–8076.2
8000	7825.6–8177.3	7924.5–8278.4	8023.4–8379.5	8122.4–8480.6	8221.3–8581.6	8320.2–8682.7	8419.2–8783.8	8518.1–8884.8	8617.1–8985.9	8716.0–9086.9
9000	8815.0–9188.0	8913.9–9289.0	9012.9–9390.0	9111.9–9491.0	9210.9–9592.0	9309.9–9693.0	9408.9–9794.1	9507.9–9895.0	9606.9–9996.0	9705.9–10097
10000	9804.9–10198	9903.9–10299	10003–10400	10102–10501	10201–10602	10300–10703	10399–10804	10498–10905	10597–11006	10696–11107
11000	10795–11208	10894–11309	10993–11410	11092–11511	11191–11612	11290–11713	11389–11814	11488–11914	11588–12015	11687–12116
12000	11786–12217	11885–12318	11984–12419	12083–12520	12182–12621	12281–12722	12380–12822	12480–12923	12579–13024	12678–13125
13000	12777–13226	12876–13327	12975–13428	13074–13528	13174–13629	13273–13730	13372–13831	13471–13932	13570–14033	13669–14134
14000	13769–14234	13868–14335	13967–14436	14066–14537	14165–14638	14264–14738	14364–14839	14463–14940	14562–15041	14661–15142
15000	14760–15243	14860–15343	14959–15444	15058–15545	15157–15646	15256–15746	15356–15847	15455–15948	15554–16049	15653–16150
16000	15753–16250	15852–16351	15951–16452	16050–16553	16149–16653	16249–16754	16348–16855	16447–16956	16546–17057	16646–17157
17000	16745–17258	16844–17359	16943–17460	17043–17560	17142–17661	17241–17762	17340–17862	17440–17963	17539–18064	17638–18165
18000	17738–18265	17837–18366	17936–18467	18035–18568	18135–18668	18234–18769	18333–18870	18432–18970	18532–19071	18631–19172
19000	18730–19273	18830–19373	18929–19474	19028–19575	19127–19675	19227–19778	19326–19877	19425–19978	19525–20078	19624–20179
20000	19723–20280	19823–20380	19922–20481	20021–20582	20121–20682	20220–20783	20319–20884	20418–20984	20518–21085	20617–21186
21000	20716–21286	20816–21387	20915–21488	21014–21589	21114–21689	21213–21790	21312–21891	21412–21991	21511–22092	21610–22193
22000	21710–22293	21809–22394	21908–22494	22008–22595	22107–22696	22206–22796	22306–22897	22405–22998	22505–23098	22604–23199
23000	22703–23300	22803–23400	22902–23501	23001–23602	23101–23702	23200–23803	23299–23904	23399–24004	23498–24105	23597–24205
24000	23697–24306	23796–24407	23896–24507	23995–24608	24094–24709	24194–24809	24293–24910	24392–25010	24492–25111	24591–25212
25000	24691–25312	24790–25413	24889–25514	24989–25614	25088–25715	25187–25815	25287–25916	25386–26017	25486–26117	25585–26218
26000	25684–26318	25784–26419	25883–26520	25983–26620	26082–26721	26181–26822	26281–26922	26380–27023	26480–27123	26579–27224
27000	26678–27325	26778–27425	26877–27526	26977–27626	27076–27727	27175–27827	27275–27928	27374–28029	27474–28129	27573–28230
28000	27673–28330	27772–28431	27871–28532	27971–28632	28070–28733	28170–28833	28269–28934	28368–29035	28468–29135	28567–29236
29000	28667–29336	28766–29437	28866–29537	28965–29638	29064–29739	29164–29839	29263–29940	29363–30040	29462–30141	29562–30241
30000	29661–30342	29760–30443	29860–30543	29959–30644	30059–30744	30158–30845	30258–30945	30357–31046	30456–31146	30556–31247
31000	30655–31348	30755–31448	30854–31549	30954–31649	31053–31750	31153–31850	31252–31951	31352–32051	31451–32152	31550–32253
32000	31650–32353	31749–32454	31849–32554	31948–32655	32048–32755	32147–32856	32247–32956	32346–33057	32446–33157	32545–33258
33000	32644–33359	32744–33459	32843–33560	32943–33660	33042–33761	33142–33861	33241–33962	33341–34062	33440–34163	33540–34263
34000	33639–34364	33739–34464	33838–34565	33937–34665	34037–34766	34136–34867	34236–34967	34335–35068	34435–35168	34534–35269
35000	34634–35369	34733–35470	34833–35570	34932–35671	35032–35771	35131–35872	35231–35972	35330–36073	35430–36173	35529–36274
36000	35629–36374	35728–36475	35828–36575	35927–36676	36027–36776	36126–36877	36226–36977	36325–37078	36424–37178	36524–37279
37000	36623–37379	36723–37480	36822–37580	36922–37681	37021–37781	37121–37882	37220–37983	37320–38083	37419–38184	37519–38284
38000	37618–38385	37718–38485	37817–38586	37917–38686	38016–38787	38116–38887	38215–38988	38315–39088	38414–39189	38514–39289
39000	38613–39390	38713–39490	38812–39591	38912–39691	39011–39792	39111–39892	39210–39992	39310–40093	39409–40193	39509–40294
40000	39608–40394	39708–40495	39807–40595	39907–40696	40007–40796	40106–40897	40206–40997	40305–41098	40405–41198	40504–41299
41000	40604–41399	40703–41500	40803–41600	40902–41701	41002–41801	41101–41902	41201–42002	41300–42103	41400–42203	41499–42304
42000	41599–42404	41698–42505	41798–42605	41897–42706	41997–42806	42096–42907	42196–43007	42295–43107	42395–43208	42495–43308
43000	42594–43409	42694–43509	42793–43610	42893–43710	42992–43811	43092–43911	43191–44012	43291–44112	43390–44213	43490–44313
44000	43589–44414	43689–44514	43788–44615	43888–44715	43987–44815	44087–44916	44187–45016	44286–45117	44386–45217	44485–45318

Values from 0 to 100 are exact, all others have been calculated from FREEMAN and TUKEY's approximation (cf. page 189)

x	0	1 10 100	2 20 200	3 30 300	4 40 400	5 50 500	6 60 600	7 70 700	8 80 800	9 90 900
	λ_l λ_r	λ_l λ_r	λ_l λ_r	λ_l λ_r	λ_l λ_r	λ_l λ_r	λ_l λ_r	λ_l λ_r	λ_l λ_r	λ_l λ_r
0	0 –5.2983	0.0050–7.4301	0.1035–9.2738	0.3379–10.978	0.6722–12.595	1.0779–14.150	1.5369–15.660	2.0374–17.134	2.5711–18.579	3.1325–19.999
10	3.7172–21.398	4.3216–22.780	4.9434–24.145	5.5807–25.497	6.2316–26.836	6.8946–28.164	7.5680–29.482	8.2518–30.791	8.9453–32.091	9.6470–33.383
20	10.355–34.668	11.072–35.947	11.795–37.219	12.525–38.485	13.260–39.745	14.000–41.001	14.745–42.251	15.495–43.497	16.244–44.739	17.003–45.976
30	17.767–47.210	18.535–48.439	19.306–49.666	20.080–50.888	20.858–52.108	21.638–53.324	22.422–54.538	23.208–55.748	23.997–56.956	24.789–58.161
40	25.583–59.363	26.381–60.564	27.181–61.761	27.983–62.957	28.788–64.150	29.596–65.341	30.406–66.530	31.218–67.717	32.032–68.902	32.848–70.085
50	33.666–71.267	34.485–72.446	35.306–73.624	36.129–74.800	36.953–75.975	37.779–77.148	38.605–78.319	39.434–79.489	40.263–80.657	41.094–81.825
60	41.926–82.990	42.759–84.155	43.594–85.317	44.430–86.479	45.267–87.640	46.106–88.799	46.946–89.957	47.787–91.114	48.630–92.269	49.475–93.424
70	50.320–94.577	51.167–95.730	52.015–96.881	52.865–98.031	53.716–99.180	54.567–100.33	55.420–101.48	56.275–102.63	57.130–103.77	57.986–104.92
80	58.844–106.06	59.701–107.20	60.559–108.34	61.419–109.49	62.279–110.63	63.140–111.77	64.001–112.90	64.863–114.04	65.725–115.18	66.587–116.31
90	67.451–117.45	68.314–118.59	69.179–119.72	70.043–120.85	70.909–121.98	71.775–123.12	72.641–124.25	73.508–125.38	74.375–126.51	75.244–127.64
100	75.90–128.55	84.64–139.80	93.44–150.99	102.29–162.14	111.18–173.24	120.11–184.31	129.08–195.34	138.07–206.34	147.10–217.31	156.15–228.26
200	165.23–239.18	174.33–250.07	183.45–260.95	192.59–271.81	201.75–282.65	210.93–293.47	220.12–304.27	229.33–315.06	238.56–325.84	247.79–336.60
300	257.04–347.35	266.31–358.08	275.58–368.81	284.87–379.52	294.16–390.22	303.47–400.92	312.79–411.60	322.11–422.27	331.45–432.94	340.79–443.59
400	350.14–454.24	359.50–464.88	368.87–475.51	378.25–486.13	387.63–496.75	397.02–507.36	406.41–517.96	415.82–528.56	425.23–539.15	434.64–549.74
500	444.06–560.31	453.49–570.89	462.92–581.45	472.36–592.01	481.80–602.57	491.25–613.12	500.70–623.67	510.16–634.21	519.62–644.75	529.09–655.28
600	538.56–665.81	548.04–676.33	557.52–686.85	567.01–697.36	576.49–707.87	585.99–718.38	595.48–728.88	604.99–739.38	614.49–749.88	624.00–760.37
700	633.51–770.86	643.02–781.34	652.54–791.82	662.06–802.30	671.59–812.78	681.12–823.25	690.65–833.72	700.18–844.18	709.72–854.64	719.26–865.10
800	728.80–875.56	738.35–886.01	747.90–896.46	757.45–906.91	767.00–917.36	776.56–927.80	786.12–938.24	795.68–948.68	805.25–959.11	814.81–969.55
900	824.38–979.98	833.96–990.40	843.53–1000.9	853.11–1011.3	862.69–1021.7	872.27–1032.1	881.85–1042.6	891.43–1053.0	901.02–1063.4	910.61–1073.8
1000	920.20–1084.2	929.80–1094.6	939.39–1105.0	948.99–1115.4	958.59–1125.8	968.19–1136.2	977.80–1146.6	987.40–1157.0	997.01–1167.4	1006.6–1177.8
1100	1016.2–1188.2	1025.8–1198.6	1035.4–1209.0	1045.0–1219.3	1054.6–1229.7	1064.3–1240.1	1073.9–1250.5	1083.5–1260.9	1093.1–1271.2	1102.8–1281.6
1200	1112.4–1292.0	1122.0–1302.3	1131.6–1312.7	1141.3–1323.1	1150.9–1333.4	1160.5–1343.8	1170.2–1354.2	1179.8–1364.5	1189.5–1374.9	1199.1–1385.3
1300	1208.7–1395.6	1218.4–1406.0	1228.0–1416.3	1237.7–1426.7	1247.3–1437.0	1257.0–1447.4	1266.6–1457.7	1276.3–1468.1	1285.9–1478.4	1295.6–1488.8
1400	1305.2–1499.1	1314.9–1509.5	1324.5–1519.8	1334.2–1530.1	1343.9–1540.5	1353.5–1550.8	1363.2–1561.2	1372.9–1571.5	1382.5–1581.8	1392.2–1592.2
1500	1401.9–1602.5	1411.5–1612.8	1421.2–1623.2	1430.9–1633.5	1440.5–1643.8	1450.2–1654.1	1459.9–1664.5	1469.6–1674.8	1479.2–1685.1	1488.9–1695.4
1600	1498.6–1705.8	1508.3–1716.1	1517.9–1726.4	1527.6–1736.7	1537.3–1747.0	1547.0–1757.4	1556.7–1767.7	1566.4–1778.0	1576.0–1788.3	1585.7–1798.6
1700	1595.4–1808.9	1605.1–1819.3	1614.8–1829.6	1624.5–1839.9	1634.2–1850.2	1643.9–1860.5	1653.6–1870.8	1663.2–1881.1	1672.9–1891.4	1682.6–1901.7
1800	1692.3–1912.0	1702.0–1922.3	1711.7–1932.6	1721.4–1942.9	1731.1–1953.2	1740.8–1963.5	1750.5–1973.8	1760.2–1984.1	1769.9–1994.4	1779.6–2004.7
1900	1789.3–2015.0	1799.0–2025.3	1808.7–2035.6	1818.5–2045.9	1828.2–2056.2	1837.9–2066.5	1847.6–2076.8	1857.3–2087.1	1867.0–2097.3	1876.7–2107.6
2000	1886.4–2117.9	1896.1–2128.2	1905.8–2138.5	1915.6–2148.8	1925.3–2159.1	1935.0–2169.4	1944.7–2179.6	1954.4–2189.9	1964.1–2200.2	1973.9–2210.5
2100	1983.6–2220.8	1993.3–2231.1	2003.0–2241.3	2012.7–2251.6	2022.5–2261.9	2032.2–2272.2	2041.9–2282.4	2051.6–2292.7	2061.3–2303.0	2071.1–2313.3
2200	2080.8–2323.5	2090.5–2333.8	2100.2–2344.1	2110.0–2354.4	2119.7–2364.6	2129.4–2374.9	2139.2–2385.2	2148.9–2395.5	2158.6–2405.7	2168.4–2416.0
2300	2178.1–2426.3	2187.8–2436.5	2197.5–2446.8	2207.3–2457.1	2217.0–2467.3	2226.7–2477.6	2236.5–2487.9	2246.2–2498.1	2256.0–2508.4	2265.7–2518.7
2400	2275.4–2528.9	2285.2–2539.2	2294.9–2549.4	2304.6–2559.7	2314.4–2570.0	2324.1–2580.2	2333.9–2590.5	2343.6–2600.7	2353.3–2611.0	2363.1–2621.3
2500	2372.8–2631.5	2382.6–2641.8	2392.3–2652.0	2402.1–2662.3	2411.8–2672.5	2421.5–2682.8	2431.3–2693.1	2441.0–2703.3	2450.8–2713.6	2460.5–2723.8
2600	2470.3–2734.1	2480.0–2744.3	2489.8–2754.6	2499.5–2764.8	2509.3–2775.1	2519.0–2785.3	2528.8–2795.6	2538.5–2805.8	2548.3–2816.1	2558.0–2826.3
2700	2567.8–2836.6	2577.5–2846.8	2587.3–2857.1	2597.0–2867.3	2606.8–2877.6	2616.5–2887.8	2626.3–2898.1	2636.0–2908.3	2645.8–2918.5	2655.6–2928.8
2800	2665.3–2939.0	2675.1–2949.3	2684.8–2959.5	2694.6–2969.8	2704.3–2980.0	2714.1–2990.2	2723.9–3000.5	2733.6–3010.7	2743.4–3021.0	2753.1–3031.2
2900	2762.9–3041.4	2772.7–3051.7	2782.4–3061.9	2792.2–3072.2	2801.9–3082.4	2811.7–3092.6	2821.5–3102.9	2831.2–3113.1	2841.0–3123.3	2850.8–3133.6
3000	2860.5–3143.8	2870.3–3154.0	2880.1–3164.3	2889.8–3174.5	2899.6–3184.7	2909.4–3195.0	2919.1–3205.2	2928.9–3215.4	2938.7–3225.7	2948.4–3235.9
3100	2958.2–3246.1	2968.0–3256.4	2977.7–3266.6	2987.5–3276.8	2997.3–3287.1	3007.0–3297.3	3016.8–3307.5	3026.6–3317.8	3036.4–3328.0	3046.1–3338.2
3200	3055.9–3348.4	3065.7–3358.7	3075.4–3368.9	3085.2–3379.1	3095.0–3389.3	3104.8–3399.6	3114.5–3409.8	3124.3–3420.0	3134.1–3430.2	3143.9–3440.5
3300	3153.6–3450.7	3163.4–3460.9	3173.2–3471.1	3183.0–3481.4	3192.7–3491.6	3202.5–3501.8	3212.3–3512.0	3222.1–3522.3	3231.9–3532.5	3241.6–3542.7
3400	3251.4–3552.9	3261.2–3563.1	3271.0–3573.4	3280.8–3583.6	3290.5–3593.8	3300.3–3604.0	3310.1–3614.2	3319.9–3624.5	3329.7–3634.7	3339.4–3644.9
3500	3349.2–3655.1	3359.0–3665.3	3368.8–3675.5	3378.6–3685.8	3388.4–3696.0	3398.1–3706.2	3407.9–3716.4	3417.7–3726.6	3427.5–3736.8	3437.3–3747.1
3600	3447.1–3757.3	3456.8–3767.5	3466.6–3777.7	3476.4–3787.9	3486.2–3798.1	3496.0–3808.3	3505.8–3818.6	3515.6–3828.8	3525.4–3839.0	3535.1–3849.2
3700	3544.9–3859.4	3554.7–3869.6	3564.5–3879.8	3574.3–3890.0	3584.1–3900.3	3593.9–3910.5	3603.7–3920.7	3613.5–3930.9	3623.2–3941.1	3633.0–3951.3
3800	3642.8–3961.5	3652.6–3971.7	3662.4–3981.9	3672.2–3992.1	3682.0–4002.3	3691.8–4012.6	3701.6–4022.8	3711.4–4033.0	3721.2–4043.2	3731.0–4053.4
3900	3740.8–4063.6	3750.5–4073.8	3760.3–4084.0	3770.1–4094.2	3779.9–4104.4	3789.7–4114.6	3799.5–4124.8	3809.3–4135.0	3819.1–4145.2	3828.9–4155.4
4000	3838.7–4165.6	3848.5–4175.8	3858.3–4186.0	3868.1–4196.2	3877.9–4206.4	3887.7–4216.6	3897.5–4226.9	3907.3–4237.1	3917.1–4247.3	3926.9–4257.5
4100	3936.7–4267.7	3946.5–4277.9	3956.3–4288.1	3966.1–4298.3	3975.9–4308.5	3985.7–4318.7	3995.5–4328.9	4005.3–4339.1	4015.1–4349.3	4024.9–4359.5
4200	4034.7–4369.7	4044.5–4379.9	4054.3–4390.1	4064.1–4400.3	4073.9–4410.4	4083.7–4420.6	4093.5–4430.8	4103.3–4441.0	4113.1–4451.2	4122.9–4461.4
4300	4132.7–4471.6	4142.5–4481.8	4152.3–4492.0	4162.1–4502.2	4171.9–4512.4	4181.7–4522.6	4191.5–4532.8	4201.3–4543.0	4211.1–4553.2	4220.9–4563.4
4400	4230.8–4573.6	4240.6–4583.8	4250.4–4594.0	4260.2–4604.2	4270.0–4614.4	4279.8–4624.6	4289.6–4634.7	4299.4–4644.9	4309.2–4655.1	4319.0–4665.3
4500	4328.8–4675.5	4338.6–4685.7	4348.4–4695.9	4358.2–4706.1	4368.1–4716.3	4377.9–4726.5	4387.7–4736.7	4397.5–4746.9	4407.3–4757.0	4417.1–4767.2
4600	4426.9–4777.4	4436.7–4787.6	4446.5–4797.8	4456.3–4808.0	4466.2–4818.2	4476.0–4828.4	4485.8–4838.6	4495.6–4848.7	4505.4–4858.9	4515.2–4869.1
4700	4525.0–4879.3	4534.8–4889.5	4544.6–4899.7	4554.5–4909.9	4564.3–4920.1	4574.1–4930.2	4583.9–4940.4	4593.7–4950.6	4603.5–4960.8	4613.3–4971.0
4800	4623.2–4981.2	4633.0–4991.4	4642.8–5001.6	4652.6–5011.7	4662.4–5021.9	4672.2–5032.1	4682.0–5042.3	4691.9–5052.5	4701.7–5062.7	4711.5–5072.8
4900	4721.3–5083.0	4731.1–5093.2	4740.9–5103.4	4750.8–5113.6	4760.6–5123.8	4770.4–5134.0	4780.2–5144.1	4790.0–5154.3	4799.8–5164.5	4809.7–5174.7
5000	4819.5–5184.9	4917.7–5286.7	5015.9–5388.5	5114.1–5490.2	5212.3–5592.0	5310.6–5693.7	5408.9–5795.5	5507.1–5897.2	5605.4–5998.9	5703.8–6100.6
6000	5802.1–6202.2	5900.4–6303.9	5998.8–6405.5	6097.2–6507.2	6195.5–6608.8	6293.9–6710.4	6392.4–6812.0	6490.8–6913.6	6589.2–7015.1	6687.6–7116.7
7000	6786.1–7218.2	6884.6–7319.8	6983.0–7421.3	7081.5–7522.8	7180.0–7624.3	7278.5–7725.8	7377.1–7827.3	7475.6–7928.7	7574.1–8030.2	7672.7–8131.7
8000	7771.2–8233.1	7869.8–8334.5	7968.4–8436.0	8066.9–8537.4	8165.5–8638.8	8264.1–8740.2	8362.7–8841.6	8461.4–8943.0	8560.0–9044.4	8658.6–9145.7
9000	8757.2–9247.1	8855.9–9348.4	8954.5–9449.8	9053.2–9551.1	9151.9–9652.5	9250.6–9753.8	9349.2–9855.1	9447.9–9956.4	9546.6–10058	9645.3–10159
10000	9744.0–10261	9842.7–10362	9941.5–10463	10040–10565	10138–10666	10237–10767	10336–10868	10435–10970	10533–11071	10632–11172
11000	10731–11273	10830–11375	10929–11476	11027–11577	11126–11678	11225–11779	11324–11881	11423–11982	11521–12083	11620–12184
12000	11719–12285	11818–12387	11917–12488	12015–12589	12114–12690	12213–12791	12312–12892	12411–12993	12510–13095	12609–13196
13000	12707–13297	12806–13398	12905–13499	13004–13600	13103–13701	13202–13802	13301–13904	13400–14005	13499–14106	13597–14207
14000	13696–14308	13795–14409	13894–14510	13993–14611	14092–14712	14191–14813	14290–14914	14389–15015	14488–15117	14587–15218
15000	14686–15319	14785–15420	14884–15521	14983–15622	15082–15723	15180–15824	15279–15925	15378–16026	15477–16127	15576–16228
16000	15675–16329	15774–16430	15873–16531	15972–16632	16071–16733	16170–16834	16269–16935	16368–17036	16467–17137	16566–17238
17000	16665–17339	16764–17440	16863–17541	16962–17642	17061–17743	17160–17844	17259–17945	17358–18046	17458–18147	17557–18248
18000	17656–18349	17755–18450	17854–18551	17953–18652	18052–18753	18151–18854	18250–18954	18349–19055	18448–19156	18547–19257
19000	18646–19358	18745–19459	18844–19560	18943–19661	19042–19762	19141–19863	19241–19964	19340–20065	19439–20166	19538–20267
20000	19637–20367	19736–20468	19835–20569	19934–20670	20033–20771	20132–20872	20231–20973	20331–21074	20430–21175	20529–21276
21000	20628–21376	20727–21477	20826–21578	20925–21679	21024–21780	21123–21881	21223–21982	21322–22083	21421–22183	21520–22284
22000	21619–22385	21718–22486	21817–22587	21917–22688	22016–22789	22115–22890	22214–22990	22313–23091	22412–23192	22511–23293
23000	22611–23394	22710–23495	22809–23596	22908–23696	23007–23797	23106–23898	23205–23999	23305–24100	23404–24201	23503–24301
24000	23602–24401	23701–24503	23800–24604	23900–24705	23999–24806	24098–24906	24197–25007	24296–25108	24396–25209	24495–25310
25000	24594–25410	24693–25511	24792–25612	24891–25713	24991–25814	25090–25914	25189–26015	25288–26116	25387–26217	25487–26318
26000	25586–26419	25685–26519	25784–26620	25883–26721	25983–26822	26082–26922	26181–27023	26280–27124	26379–27225	26479–27326
27000	26578–27426	26677–27527	26776–27628	26876–27729	26975–27830	27074–27930	27173–28031	27272–28132	27372–28233	27471–28333
28000	27570–28434	27669–28535	27769–28636	27868–28736	27967–28837	28066–28938	28166–29039	28265–29140	28364–29240	28463–29341
29000	28563–29442	28662–29543	28761–29643	28860–29744	28960–29845	29059–29946	29158–30046	29257–30147	29357–30248	29456–30349
30000	29555–30449	29654–30550	29754–30651	29853–30752	29952–30852	30051–30953	30151–31054	30250–31154	30349–31255	30448–31356
31000	30548–31457	30647–31556	30746–31658	30845–31759	30945–31860	31044–31960	31143–32061	31243–32162	31342–32263	31441–32363
32000	31540–32464	31640–32565	31739–32665	31838–32766	31938–32867	32037–32968	32136–33068	32235–33169	32335–33270	32434–33370
33000	32533–33471	32633–33572	32732–33672	32831–33773	32930–33874	33030–33975	33129–34075	33228–34176	33328–34277	33427–34377
34000	33526–34478	33626–34579	33725–34680	33824–34780	33923–34881	34023–34982	34122–35082	34221–35183	34321–35284	34420–35384
35000	34519–35485	34619–35586	34718–35686	34817–35787	34917–35888	35016–35988	35115–36089	35214–36190	35314–36291	35413–36391
36000	35512–36492	35612–36593	35711–36693	35810–36794	35910–36895	36009–36995	36108–37096	36208–37197	36307–37297	36406–37398
37000	36506–37499	36605–37599	36704–37700	36804–37801	36903–37901	37002–38002	37102–38103	37201–38203	37300–38304	37400–38405
38000	37499–38505	37598–38606	37698–38707	37797–38807	37896–38908	37996–39009	38095–39109	38194–39210	38294–39311	38393–39411
39000	38492–39512	38592–39612	38691–39713	38791–39814	38890–39914	38989–40015	39089–40116	39188–40216	39287–40317	39387–40418
40000	39486–40518	39585–40619	39685–40720	39784–40820	39883–40921	39983–41022	40082–41122	40182–41223	40281–41323	40380–41424
41000	40480–41525	40579–41625	40678–41726	40778–41827	40877–41927	40976–42028	41076–42129	41175–42229	41275–42330	41374–42430
42000	41473–42531	41573–42632	41672–42732	41771–42833	41871–42934	41970–43034	42070–43135	42169–43235	42268–43336	42368–43437
43000	42467–43537	42566–43638	42666–43739	42765–43839	42865–43940	42964–44040	43063–44141	43163–44242	43262–44342	43361–44443
44000	43461–44543	43560–44644	43660–44745	43759–44845	43858–44946	43958–45047	44057–45147	44157–45248	44256–45348	44355–45449

Significance Limits* for the Fourfold Table Test

x_1	$N_1 - x_1$	N_1
x_2	$N_2 - x_2$	N_2
X	$N - X$	N

$N = N_1 + N_2$, $X = x_1 + x_2$, $N_1 \leqq N_2$, $x_1 \leqq N_1 - x_1$

For explanation see page 123

N_1	x_1	2 α = 0.20	2 α = 0.10	2 α = 0.05	2 α = 0.02	2 α = 0.01	2 α = 0.002
$N = 8$							
4	0	•- 3	•- 4	•- 4	-	-	-
	1	•- 5	-	-	-	-	-
	2	-	-	-	-	-	-
$N = 9$							
4	0	•- 4	•- 4	•- 5	•- 5	-	-
	1	•- 6	•- 6	-	-	-	-
	2	-	-	-	-	-	-
$N = 10$							
4	0	•- 4	•- 5	•- 5	•- 6	•- 6	-
	1	•- 7	•- 7	-	-	-	-
	2	-	-	-	-	-	-
5	0	•- 3	•- 4	•- 4	•- 5	•- 5	-
	1	•- 6	•- 6	•- 6	-	-	-
	2	•- 7	-	-	-	-	-
$N = 11$							
4	0	•- 5	•- 5	•- 6	•- 7	•- 7	-
	1	•- 7	•- 8	•- 8	-	-	-
	2	-	-	-	-	-	-
5	0	•- 4	•- 4	•- 5	•- 6	•- 6	-
	1	•- 6	•- 7	•- 7	-	-	-
	2	•- 8	-	-	-	-	-
$N = 12$							
4	0	•- 5	•- 6	•- 7	•- 8	•- 8	-
	1	•- 8	•- 9	•- 9	-	-	-
	2	2-10	-	-	-	-	-
5	0	•- 4	•- 5	•- 6	•- 6	•- 7	-
	1	•- 7	•- 7	•- 8	-	-	-
	2	•- 9	•- 9	-	-	-	-
6	0	•- 3	•- 4	•- 5	•- 5	•- 6	-
	1	•- 6	•- 6	•- 7	•- 7	-	-
	2	•- 8	•- 8	-	-	-	-
	3	3- 9	-	-	-	-	-
$N = 13$							
4	0	•- 5	•- 6	•- 7	•- 8	•- 9	-
	1	•- 9	•-10	•-10	-	-	-
	2	2-11	-	-	-	-	-
5	0	•- 4	•- 5	•- 6	•- 7	•- 7	•- 8
	1	•- 7	•- 8	•- 9	•- 9	-	-
	2	•-10	•-10	-	-	-	-
6	0	•- 4	•- 4	•- 5	•- 6	•- 6	•- 7
	1	•- 6	•- 7	•- 8	•- 8	•- 8	-
	2	•- 8	•- 9	•- 9	-	-	-
	3	3-10	-	-	-	-	-
$N = 14$							
4	0	•- 6	•- 7	•- 8	•- 9	•- 9	•-10
	1	•- 9	•-10	•-11	-	-	-
	2	2-12	-	-	-	-	-
5	0	•- 5	•- 6	•- 7	•- 8	•- 8	•- 9
	1	•- 8	•- 9	•- 9	•-10	•-10	-
	2	•-10	•-11	-	-	-	-
6	0	•- 4	•- 5	•- 6	•- 6	•- 7	•- 8
	1	•- 7	•- 8	•- 8	•- 9	•- 9	-
	2	•- 9	•-10	•-10	-	-	-
	3	3-11	-	-	-	-	-
7	0	•- 3	•- 4	•- 5	•- 6	•- 6	•- 7
	1	•- 6	•- 7	•- 7	•- 8	•- 8	-
	2	•- 8	•- 9	•- 9	-	-	-
	3	3-10	•-10	-	-	-	-
$N = 15$							
4	0	•- 6	•- 8	•- 9	•-10	•-10	•-11
	1	•-10	•-11	•-12	•-12	-	-
	2	2-13	-	-	-	-	-
5	0	•- 5	•- 6	•- 7	•- 8	•- 9	•-10
	1	•- 9	•- 9	•-10	•-11	•-11	-
	2	2-11	•-12	•-12	-	-	-
6	0	•- 4	•- 5	•- 6	•- 7	•- 8	•- 9
	1	•- 7	•- 8	•- 9	•-10	•-10	-
	2	•-10	•-10	•-11	-	-	-
	3	3-12	3-12	-	-	-	-
7	0	•- 4	•- 5	•- 5	•- 6	•- 7	•- 8
	1	•- 6	•- 7	•- 8	•- 8	•- 9	-
	2	•- 9	•- 9	•-10	•-10	-	-
	3	3-11	•-11	-	-	-	-
$N = 16$							
4	0	•- 7	•- 8	•- 9	•-10	•-11	•-12
	1	•-11	•-12	•-13	•-13	-	-
	2	2-14	-	-	-	-	-
5	0	•- 6	•- 7	•- 8	•- 9	•- 9	•-11
	1	•- 9	•-10	•-11	•-12	•-12	-
	2	2-12	•-13	•-13	-	-	-
$N = 16$ (continued)							
6	0	•- 5	•- 6	•- 7	•- 8	•- 8	•- 9
	1	•- 8	•- 9	•- 9	•-10	•-11	-
	2	•-10	•-11	•-12	•-12	-	-
	3	3-13	3-13	-	-	-	-
7	0	•- 4	•- 5	•- 6	•- 7	•- 7	•- 8
	1	•- 7	•- 8	•- 8	•- 9	•-10	•-10
	2	•- 9	•-10	•-10	•-11	•-11	-
	3	3-11	•-12	•-12	-	-	-
8	0	•- 3	•- 4	•- 5	•- 6	•- 6	•- 7
	1	•- 6	•- 7	•- 7	•- 8	•- 9	•- 9
	2	•- 8	•- 9	•- 9	•-10	•-10	-
	3	•-10	•-11	•-11	-	-	-
	4	4-12	4-12	-	-	-	-
$N = 17$							
4	0	•- 7	•- 9	•-10	•-11	•-12	•-13
	1	•-11	•-13	•-13	•-14	-	-
	2	2-15	2-15	-	-	-	-
5	0	•- 6	•- 7	•- 8	•- 9	•-10	•-11
	1	•-10	•-11	•-12	•-12	•-13	-
	2	2-13	•-14	•-14	-	-	-
6	0	•- 5	•- 6	•- 7	• 8	•- 9	•-10
	1	•- 8	•- 9	•-10	•-11	•-12	•-12
	2	•-11	•-12	•-13	•-13	-	-
	3	4-13	3-14	-	-	-	-
7	0	•- 4	•- 5	•- 6	•- 7	•- 8	•- 9
	1	•- 7	•- 8	•- 9	•-10	•-10	•-11
	2	•-10	•-11	•-11	•-12	•-12	-
	3	3-12	•-13	•-13	-	-	-
8	0	•- 4	•- 5	•- 5	•- 6	•- 7	•- 8
	1	•- 6	•- 7	•- 8	•- 9	•- 9	•-10
	2	•- 9	•- 9	•-10	•-11	•-11	-
	3	3-11	•-11	•-12	•-12	-	-
	4	4-13	4-13	-	-	-	-
$N = 18$							
4	0	•- 8	•- 9	•-10	•-12	•-12	•-14
	1	•-12	•-13	•-14	•-15	•-15	-
	2	2-16	2-16	-	-	-	-
5	0	•- 6	•- 8	•- 9	•-10	•-11	•-12
	1	•-10	•-11	•-12	•-13	•-14	-
	2	2-13	•-14	•-15	-	-	-
6	0	•- 5	•- 6	•- 7	•- 9	•- 9	•-11
	1	•- 9	•-10	•-11	•-12	•-12	•-13
	2	2-12	•-13	•-13	•-14	•-14	-
	3	4-14	3-15	3-15	-	-	-
7	0	•- 5	•- 6	•- 6	•- 8	•- 8	•-10
	1	•- 8	•- 9	•- 9	•-10	•-11	•-12
	2	•-10	•-11	•-12	•-13	•-13	-
	3	3-13	3-13	•-14	-	-	-
8	0	•- 4	•- 5	•- 6	•- 7	•- 7	•- 9
	1	•- 7	•- 8	•- 8	•- 9	•-10	•-11
	2	•- 9	•-10	•-11	•-11	•-12	-
	3	3-11	•-12	•-13	•-13	-	-
	4	5-13	4-14	4-14	-	-	-
9	0	•- 4	•- 4	•- 5	•- 6	•- 6	•- 8
	1	•- 6	•- 7	•- 7	•- 8	•- 9	•-10
	2	•- 8	•- 9	•-10	•-10	•-11	-
	3	•-10	•-11	•-11	•-12	•-12	-
	4	4-12	4-13	•-13	-	-	-
$N = 19$							
4	0	•- 8	•-10	•-11	•-12	•-13	•-15
	1	•-13	•-14	•-15	•-16	•-16	-
	2	3-16	2-17	-	-	-	-
5	0	•- 7	•- 8	•- 9	•-11	•-11	•-13
	1	•-11	•-12	•-13	•-14	•-15	-
	2	2-14	•-15	•-16	-	-	-
6	0	•- 6	•- 7	•- 8	•- 9	•-10	•-12
	1	•- 9	•-10	•-11	•-12	•-13	•-14
	2	2-12	•-13	•-14	•-15	•-15	-
	3	4-15	3-16	3-16	-	-	-
7	0	•- 5	•- 6	•- 7	•- 8	•- 9	•-10
	1	•- 8	•- 9	•-10	•-11	•-12	•-13
	2	•-11	•-12	•-13	•-13	•-14	-
	3	3-13	3-14	•-15	•-15	-	-
8	0	•- 4	•- 5	•- 6	•- 7	•- 8	•- 9
	1	•- 7	•- 8	•- 9	•-10	•-10	•-12
	2	•-10	•-11	•-11	•-12	•-13	-
	3	3-12	•-13	•-13	•-14	•-14	-
	4	5-14	4-15	4-15	-	-	-
9	0	•- 4	•- 5	•- 5	•- 6	•- 7	•- 8
	1	•- 6	•- 7	•- 8	•- 9	•- 9	•-10
	2	•- 9	•-10	•-10	•-11	•-11	•-12
	3	3-11	•-12	•-12	•-13	•-13	-
	4	4-13	4-13	•-14	-	-	-
$N = 20$							
4	0	•- 9	•-10	•-12	•-13	•-14	•-16
	1	•-14	•-15	•-16	•-17	•-17	-
	2	3-17	2-18	-	-	-	-
$N = 20$ (continued)							
5	0	•- 7	•- 9	•-10	•-11	•-12	•-14
	1	•-11	•-13	•-14	•-15	•-15	-
	2	2-15	•-16	•-17	•-17	-	-
6	0	•- 6	•- 7	•- 8	•-10	•-11	•-12
	1	•-10	•-11	•-12	•-13	•-14	•-15
	2	2-13	•-14	•-15	•-16	•-16	-
	3	4-16	3-17	3-17	-	-	-
7	0	•- 5	•- 6	•- 7	•- 9	•- 9	•-11
	1	•- 9	•-10	•-11	•-12	•-12	•-14
	2	•-12	•-13	•-13	•-14	•-15	-
	3	3-14	3-15	•-16	•-16	-	-
8	0	•- 5	•- 6	•- 6	•- 8	•- 8	•-10
	1	•- 8	•- 9	•- 9	•-10	•-11	•-12
	2	•-10	•-11	•-12	•-13	•-13	•-14
	3	3-13	3-14	•-14	•-15	•-15	-
	4	5-15	4-16	4-16	-	-	-
9	0	•- 4	•- 5	•- 6	•- 7	•- 7	•- 9
	1	•- 7	•- 8	•- 8	•- 9	•-10	•-11
	2	•- 9	•-10	•-11	•-12	•-12	•-13
	3	3-11	•-12	•-13	•-14	•-14	-
	4	5-14	4-14	•-15	•-15	-	-
10	0	•- 4	•- 4	•- 5	•- 6	•- 7	•- 8
	1	• 6	•- 7	•- 8	•- 8	•- 9	•-10
	2	•- 8	•- 9	•-10	•-11	•-11	•-12
	3	•-10	•-11	•-12	•-12	•-13	-
	4	4-12	4-13	•-14	•-14	-	-
	5	6-14	5-15	5-15	-	-	-
$N = 21$							
4	0	•- 9	•-11	•-12	•-14	•-15	•-16
	1	•-14	•-16	•-17	•-18	•-18	-
	2	3-18	2-19	-	-	-	-
5	0	•- 7	•- 9	•-10	•-12	•-13	•-15
	1	•-12	•-13	•-15	•-16	•-16	•-17
	2	2-16	2-17	•-18	•-18	-	-
6	0	•- 6	•- 8	•- 9	•-10	•-11	•-13
	1	•-10	•-12	•-13	•-14	•-15	•-16
	2	2-14	•-15	•-16	•-17	•-17	-
	3	4-17	3-18	3-18	-	-	-
7	0	•- 5	•- 7	•- 8	•- 9	•-10	•-12
	1	•- 9	•-10	•-11	•-12	•-13	•-14
	2	•-12	•-13	•-14	•-15	•-16	-
	3	4-15	3-16	•-17	•-17	-	-
8	0	•- 5	•- 6	•- 7	•- 8	•- 9	•-10
	1	•- 8	•- 9	•-10	•-11	•-12	•-13
	2	•-11	•-12	•-13	•-14	•-14	•-15
	3	3-13	3-14	•-15	•-16	•-16	-
	4	5-16	5-16	4-17	-	-	-
9	0	•- 4	•- 5	•- 6	•- 7	•- 8	•- 9
	1	•- 7	•- 8	•- 9	•-10	•-11	•-12
	2	•-10	•-11	•-11	•-12	•-13	•-14
	3	3-12	•-13	•-14	•-14	•-15	-
	4	5-14	4-15	4-16	•-16	-	-
10	0	•- 4	•- 5	•- 5	•- 6	•- 7	•- 8
	1	•- 6	•- 7	•- 8	•- 9	•-10	•-11
	2	•- 9	•-10	•-10	•-11	•-12	•-13
	3	3-11	•-12	•-12	•-13	•-14	-
	4	4-13	4-14	•-14	•-15	•-15	-
	5	6-15	5-16	5-16	-	-	-
$N = 22$							
4	0	•- 9	•-11	•-13	•-14	•-15	•-17
	1	•-15	•-16	•-17	•-18	•-19	-
	2	3-19	2-20	-	-	-	-
5	0	•- 8	•- 9	•-11	•-12	•-13	•-15
	1	•-13	•-14	•-15	•-16	•-17	•-18
	2	2-17	2-18	•-18	•-19	-	-
6	0	•- 7	•- 8	•- 9	•-11	•-12	•-14
	1	•-11	•-12	•-13	•-15	•-15	•-17
	2	2-14	•-16	•-17	•-17	•-18	-
	3	4-18	4-18	3-19	-	-	-
7	0	•- 6	•- 7	•- 8	•-10	•-10	•-12
	1	•-10	•-11	•-12	•-13	•-14	•-15
	2	2-13	•-14	•-15	•-16	•-16	•-17
	3	4-16	3-17	3-17	•-18	•-18	-
8	0	•- 5	•- 6	•- 7	•- 8	•- 9	•-11
	1	•- 8	•-10	•-11	•-12	•-12	•-14
	2	•-11	•-12	•-13	•-14	•-15	•-16
	3	3-14	3-15	•-16	•-17	•-17	-
	4	6-16	5-17	4-18	4-18	-	-
9	0	•- 4	•- 5	•- 6	•- 8	•- 8	•-10
	1	•- 8	•- 9	•- 9	•-11	•-11	•-13
	2	•-10	•-11	•-12	•-13	•-14	•-15
	3	3-13	•-14	•-14	•-15	•-16	-
	4	5-15	4-16	4-16	•-17	•-17	-
10	0	•- 4	•- 5	•- 6	•- 7	•- 7	•- 9
	1	•- 7	•- 8	•- 9	•-10	•-10	•-11
	2	•- 9	•-10	•-11	•-12	•-12	•-14
	3	3-11	•-12	•-13	•-14	•-14	•-15
	4	4-14	4-14	•-15	•-16	•-16	-
	5	6-16	6-16	5-17	5-17	-	-
11	0	•- 4	•- 4	•- 5	•- 6	•- 7	•- 8

Significance Limits* for the Fourfold Table Test

x_1	$N_1 - x_1$	N_1
x_2	$N_2 - x_2$	N_2
X	$N - X$	N

$N = N_1 + N_2$, $X = x_1 + x_2$, $N_1 \leqq N_2$, $x_1 \leqq N_1 - x_1$

For explanation see page 123

N = 22 (continued)

N_1	x_1	2α = 0.20	2α = 0.10	2α = 0.05	2α = 0.02	2α = 0.01	2α = 0.002
11	1	•-6	•-7	•-8	•-9	•-9	•-10
	2	•-8	•-9	•-10	•-11	•-11	•-12
	3	•-10	•-11	•-12	•-13	•-13	•-14
	4	4-12	4-13	•-14	•-15	•-15	–
	5	6-14	5-15	5-16	•-16	–	–

N = 23

N_1	x_1	2α = 0.20	2α = 0.10	2α = 0.05	2α = 0.02	2α = 0.01	2α = 0.002
4	0	•-10	•-12	•-13	•-15	•-16	•-18
	1	•-16	•-17	•-18	•-19	•-20	–
	2	3-20	2-21	2-21	–	–	–
5	0	•-8	•-10	•-11	•-13	•-14	•-16
	1	•-13	•-15	•-16	•-17	•-18	•-19
	2	2-17	2-18	•-19	•-20	–	–
6	0	•-7	•-8	•-10	•-11	•-12	•-14
	1	•-11	•-13	•-14	•-15	•-16	•-18
	2	2-15	•-16	•-17	•-18	•-19	–
	3	5-18	4-19	3-20	–	–	–
7	0	•-6	•-7	•-9	•-10	•-11	•-13
	1	•-10	•-11	•-12	•-14	•-14	•-16
	2	2-13	•-15	•-16	•-17	•-17	•-18
	3	4-16	3-17	3-18	•-19	•-19	–
8	0	•-5	•-6	•-8	•-9	•-10	•-12
	1	•-9	•-10	•-11	•-12	•-13	•-15
	2	•-12	•-13	•-14	•-15	•-16	•-17
	3	3-15	3-16	•-17	•-17	•-18	–
	4	6-17	5-18	4-19	4-19	–	–
9	0	•-5	•-6	•-7	•-8	•-9	•-10
	1	•-8	•-9	•-10	•-11	•-12	•-13
	2	•-11	•-12	•-13	•-14	•-14	•-16
	3	3-13	3-14	•-15	•-16	•-16	•-17
	4	5-16	4-17	4-17	•-18	•-18	–
10	0	•-4	•-5	•-6	•-7	•-8	•-9
	1	•-7	•-8	•-9	•-10	•-11	•-12
	2	•-10	•-11	•-12	•-13	•-13	•-14
	3	3-12	•-13	•-14	•-15	•-15	•-16
	4	5-14	4-15	4-16	•-17	•-17	–
	5	7-16	6-17	5-18	5-18	–	–
11	0	•-4	•-5	•-5	•-6	•-7	•-9
	1	•-6	•-7	•-8	•-9	•-10	•-11
	2	•-9	•-10	•-11	•-11	•-12	•-13
	3	3-11	•-12	•-13	•-14	•-14	•-15
	4	4-13	4-14	•-15	•-15	•-16	–
	5	6-15	5-16	5-16	•-17	•-17	–

N = 24

N_1	x_1	2α = 0.20	2α = 0.10	2α = 0.05	2α = 0.02	2α = 0.01	2α = 0.002
4	0	•-10	•-12	•-14	•-16	•-17	•-19
	1	•-16	•-18	•-19	•-20	•-21	–
	2	3-21	2-22	2-22	–	–	–
5	0	•-9	•-10	•-12	•-14	•-15	•-17
	1	•-14	•-15	•-17	•-18	•-19	•-20
	2	3-18	2-19	•-20	•-21	•-21	–
6	0	•-7	•-9	•-10	•-12	•-13	•-15
	1	•-12	•-13	•-15	•-16	•-17	•-18
	2	2-16	•-17	•-18	•-19	•-20	–
	3	5-19	4-20	3-21	3-21	–	–
7	0	•-6	•-8	•-9	•-10	•-11	•-13
	1	•-10	•-12	•-13	•-14	•-15	•-17
	2	2-14	•-15	•-16	•-17	•-18	•-19
	3	4-17	3-18	3-19	•-20	•-20	–
8	0	•-6	•-7	•-8	•-9	•-10	•-12
	1	•-9	•-11	•-12	•-13	•-14	•-15
	2	•-12	•-14	•-15	•-16	•-16	•-18
	3	4-15	3-16	•-17	•-18	•-19	–
	4	6-18	5-19	4-20	4-20	–	–
9	0	•-5	•-6	•-7	•-8	•-9	•-11
	1	•-8	•-9	•-10	•-12	•-12	•-14
	2	•-11	•-12	•-13	•-14	•-15	•-16
	3	3-14	3-15	•-16	•-17	•-17	•-18
	4	5-16	5-17	4-18	•-19	•-19	–
10	0	•-4	•-5	•-6	•-7	•-8	•-10
	1	•-7	•-9	•-9	•-11	•-11	•-13
	2	•-10	•-11	•-12	•-13	•-14	•-15
	3	3-13	•-14	•-14	•-15	•-16	•-17
	4	5-15	4-16	4-17	•-17	•-18	–
	5	7-17	6-18	5-19	5-19	–	–
11	0	•-4	•-5	•-6	•-7	•-7	•-9
	1	•-7	•-8	•-9	•-10	•-10	•-12
	2	•-9	•-10	•-11	•-12	•-13	•-14
	3	3-12	•-12	•-13	•-14	•-15	•-16
	4	4-14	4-15	•-15	•-16	•-17	•-17
	5	6-16	6-17	5-17	•-18	•-18	–
12	0	•-4	•-4	•-5	•-6	•-7	•-8
	1	•-6	•-7	•-8	•-9	•-9	•-11
	2	•-8	•-9	•-10	•-11	•-12	•-13
	3	•-11	•-11	•-12	•-13	•-14	•-15
	4	4-13	4-13	•-14	•-15	•-15	•-16
	5	6-15	5-15	5-16	•-17	•-17	–
	6	8-16	7-17	6-18	6-18	–	–

N = 25

N_1	x_1	2α = 0.20	2α = 0.10	2α = 0.05	2α = 0.02	2α = 0.01	2α = 0.002
4	0	•-11	•-13	•-15	•-16	•-18	•-20
	1	•-17	•-19	•-20	•-21	•-22	–
	2	3-22	2-23	2-23	–	–	–
5	0	•-9	•-11	•-12	•-14	•-15	•-18
	1	•-14	•-16	•-17	•-19	•-20	•-21
	2	3-19	2-20	•-21	•-22	•-22	–
6	0	•-8	•-9	•-11	•-12	•-14	•-16
	1	•-12	•-14	•-15	•-17	•-18	•-19
	2	2-16	•-18	•-19	•-20	•-21	–
	3	5-20	4-21	3-22	3-22	–	–
7	0	•-7	•-8	•-9	•-11	•-12	•-14
	1	•-11	•-12	•-14	•-15	•-16	•-18
	2	2-15	•-16	•-17	•-18	•-19	•-20
	3	4-18	3-19	3-20	•-21	•-21	–
8	0	•-6	•-7	•-8	•-10	•-11	•-13
	1	•-10	•-11	•-12	•-13	•-14	•-16
	2	2-13	•-14	•-15	•-16	•-17	•-19
	3	4-16	3-17	3-18	•-19	•-20	–
	4	6-19	5-20	5-20	4-21	–	–
9	0	•-5	•-6	•-7	•-9	•-10	•-11
	1	•-9	•-10	•-11	•-12	•-13	•-15
	2	•-12	•-13	•-14	•-15	•-16	•-17
	3	3-14	3-16	•-17	•-17	•-18	•-19
	4	6-17	5-18	4-19	4-20	•-20	–
10	0	•-5	•-6	•-7	•-8	•-9	•-10
	1	•-8	•-9	•-10	•-11	•-12	•-13
	2	•-11	•-12	•-13	•-14	•-14	•-16
	3	3-13	•-14	•-15	•-16	•-17	•-18
	4	5-16	4-17	4-17	•-18	•-19	–
	5	7-18	6-19	6-19	5-20	5-20	–
11	0	•-4	•-5	•-6	•-7	•-8	•-9
	1	•-7	•-8	•-9	•-10	•-11	•-12
	2	•-10	•-11	•-12	•-13	•-13	•-15
	3	3-12	•-13	•-14	•-15	•-15	•-17
	4	5-14	4-15	•-16	•-17	•-17	•-18
	5	6-16	6-17	5-18	5-19	•-19	–
12	0	•-4	•-5	•-5	•-6	•-7	•-9
	1	•-6	•-7	•-8	•-9	•-10	•-11
	2	•-9	•-10	•-11	•-12	•-12	•-14
	3	3-11	•-12	•-13	•-14	•-14	•-15
	4	4-13	4-14	•-15	•-16	•-16	•-17
	5	6-15	5-16	5-17	•-17	•-18	–
	6	8-17	7-18	6-19	6-19	–	–

N = 26

N_1	x_1	2α = 0.20	2α = 0.10	2α = 0.05	2α = 0.02	2α = 0.01	2α = 0.002
4	0	•-11	•-13	•-15	•-17	•-18	•-21
	1	•-18	•-19	•-21	•-22	•-23	–
	2	4-22	2-24	2-24	–	–	–
5	0	•-9	•-11	•-13	•-15	•-16	•-18
	1	•-15	•-17	•-18	•-20	•-20	•-22
	2	3-20	2-21	•-22	•-23	•-23	–
6	0	•-8	•-10	•-11	•-13	•-14	•-16
	1	•-13	•-15	•-16	•-17	•-18	•-20
	2	2-17	2-19	•-20	•-21	•-21	–
	3	5-21	4-22	3-23	3-23	–	–
7	0	•-7	•-8	•-10	•-11	•-13	•-15
	1	•-11	•-13	•-14	•-16	•-17	•-18
	2	2-15	•-17	•-18	•-19	•-20	•-21
	3	4-19	4-20	3-21	•-22	•-22	–
8	0	•-6	•-7	•-9	•-10	•-11	•-13
	1	•-10	•-11	•-13	•-14	•-15	•-17
	2	2-14	•-15	•-16	•-17	•-18	•-19
	3	4-17	3-18	3-19	•-20	•-20	•-21
	4	6-20	5-21	5-21	4-22	4-22	–
9	0	•-5	•-7	•-8	•-9	•-10	•-12
	1	•-9	•-10	•-11	•-13	•-14	•-15
	2	•-12	•-13	•-15	•-16	•-16	•-18
	3	3-15	3-16	•-17	•-18	•-19	•-20
	4	6-18	5-19	4-20	4-20	•-21	–
10	0	•-5	•-6	•-7	•-8	•-9	•-11
	1	•-8	•-9	•-10	•-12	•-12	•-14
	2	•-11	•-12	•-13	•-14	•-15	•-17
	3	3-14	3-15	•-16	•-17	•-17	•-19
	4	5-16	4-17	4-18	•-19	•-20	•-20
	5	7-19	6-20	6-20	5-21	5-21	–
11	0	•-4	•-5	•-6	•-7	•-8	•-10
	1	•-7	•-8	•-9	•-11	•-11	•-13
	2	•-10	•-11	•-12	•-13	•-14	•-15
	3	3-13	•-14	•-15	•-16	•-16	•-17
	4	5-15	4-16	4-17	•-18	•-18	•-19
	5	7-17	6-18	5-19	5-20	•-20	–
12	0	•-4	•-5	•-6	•-7	•-8	•-9
	1	•-7	•-8	•-9	•-10	•-10	•-12
	2	•-9	•-10	•-11	•-12	•-13	•-14
	3	3-12	•-13	•-13	•-14	•-15	•-16
	4	4-14	4-15	•-16	•-16	•-17	•-18
	5	6-16	5-17	5-18	•-18	•-19	–
	6	8-18	7-19	7-19	6-20	6-20	–
13	0	•-4	•-4	•-5	•-6	•-7	•-8
	1	•-6	•-7	•-8	•-9	•-10	•-11
	2	•-9	•-9	•-10	•-11	•-12	•-13
	3	•-11	•-12	•-12	•-13	•-14	•-15
	4	4-13	4-14	•-14	•-15	•-16	•-17
	5	6-15	5-16	5-16	•-17	•-18	•-18
	6	7-17	7-17	6-18	6-19	•-19	–

N = 27

N_1	x_1	2α = 0.20	2α = 0.10	2α = 0.05	2α = 0.02	2α = 0.01	2α = 0.002
4	0	•-12	•-14	•-16	•-18	•-19	•-21
	1	•-18	•-20	•-21	•-23	•-24	–
	2	4-23	3-24	2-25	–	–	–
5	0	•-10	•-12	•-13	•-15	•-17	•-19
	1	•-16	•-17	•-19	•-20	•-21	•-23
	2	3-20	2-22	•-23	•-24	•-24	–
6	0	•-8	•-10	•-12	•-14	•-15	•-17
	1	•-13	•-15	•-17	•-18	•-19	•-21
	2	2-18	2-19	•-20	•-22	•-22	•-23
	3	5-22	4-23	4-23	3-24	–	–
7	0	•-7	•-9	•-10	•-12	•-13	•-15
	1	•-12	•-13	•-15	•-16	•-17	•-19
	2	2-16	•-17	•-18	•-20	•-20	•-22
	3	5-19	4-20	3-21	•-22	•-23	–
8	0	•-6	•-8	•-9	•-11	•-12	•-14
	1	•-10	•-12	•-13	•-15	•-16	•-17
	2	2-14	•-15	•-17	•-18	•-19	•-20
	3	4-17	3-19	3-20	•-21	•-21	•-22
	4	7-20	6-21	5-22	4-23	4-23	–
9	0	•-6	•-7	•-8	•-10	•-11	•-13
	1	•-9	•-11	•-12	•-13	•-14	•-16
	2	•-13	•-14	•-15	•-16	•-17	•-19
	3	4-16	3-17	•-18	•-19	•-20	•-21
	4	6-18	5-20	4-20	4-21	•-22	–
10	0	•-5	•-6	•-7	•-9	•-10	•-11
	1	•-8	•-10	•-11	•-12	•-13	•-15
	2	•-11	•-13	•-14	•-15	•-16	•-17
	3	3-14	3-15	•-16	•-18	•-18	•-19
	4	5-17	5-18	4-19	•-20	•-20	•-21
	5	8-19	7-20	6-21	5-22	5-22	–
11	0	•-5	•-6	•-7	•-8	•-9	•-10
	1	•-8	•-9	•-10	•-11	•-12	•-14
	2	•-10	•-12	•-13	•-14	•-15	•-16
	3	3-13	•-14	•-15	•-16	•-17	•-18
	4	5-16	4-17	4-17	•-18	•-19	•-20
	5	7-18	6-19	5-20	5-20	•-21	–
12	0	•-4	•-5	•-6	•-7	•-8	•-10
	1	•-7	•-8	•-9	•-10	•-11	•-12
	2	•-10	•-11	•-12	•-13	•-13	•-15
	3	3-12	•-13	•-14	•-15	•-16	•-17
	4	4-14	4-15	•-16	•-17	•-18	•-19
	5	6-17	6-17	5-18	5-19	•-20	•-20
	6	8-19	8-19	7-20	6-21	6-21	–
13	0	•-4	•-5	•-5	•-7	•-7	•-9
	1	•-6	•-7	•-8	•-9	•-10	•-12
	2	•-9	•-10	•-11	•-12	•-12	•-14
	3	3-11	•-12	•-13	•-14	•-15	•-16
	4	4-13	4-14	•-15	•-16	•-17	•-18
	5	6-15	5-16	5-17	•-18	•-18	•-19
	6	8-17	7-18	6-19	6-20	•-20	–

N = 28

N_1	x_1	2α = 0.20	2α = 0.10	2α = 0.05	2α = 0.02	2α = 0.01	2α = 0.002
4	0	•-12	•-14	•-16	•-19	•-20	•-22
	1	•-19	•-21	•-22	•-24	•-24	–
	2	4-24	3-25	2-26	–	–	–
5	0	•-10	•-12	•-14	•-16	•-17	•-20
	1	•-16	•-18	•-20	•-21	•-22	•-24
	2	3-21	2-23	•-24	•-25	•-25	–
6	0	•-9	•-10	•-12	•-14	•-15	•-18
	1	•-14	•-16	•-17	•-19	•-20	•-22
	2	2-18	2-20	•-21	•-22	•-23	•-24
	3	6-22	4-24	4-24	3-25	–	–
7	0	•-7	•-9	•-11	•-12	•-14	•-16
	1	•-12	•-14	•-15	•-17	•-18	•-20
	2	2-16	•-18	•-19	•-20	•-21	•-23
	3	5-20	4-21	3-22	•-23	•-24	–
8	0	•-7	•-8	•-9	•-11	•-12	•-14
	1	•-11	•-12	•-14	•-15	•-16	•-18
	2	2-15	•-16	•-17	•-19	•-19	•-21
	3	4-18	3-19	3-20	•-21	•-22	•-23
	4	7-21	6-22	5-23	4-24	4-24	–
9	0	•-6	•-7	•-8	•-10	•-11	•-13
	1	•-10	•-11	•-12	•-14	•-15	•-17
	2	2-13	•-15	•-16	•-17	•-18	•-19
	3	4-16	3-18	•-19	•-20	•-20	•-22
	4	6-19	5-20	4-21	4-22	•-23	–
10	0	•-5	•-6	•-8	•-9	•-10	•-12
	1	•-9	•-10	•-11	•-13	•-14	•-15
	2	•-12	•-13	•-14	•-16	•-16	•-18
	3	3-15	3-16	•-17	•-18	•-19	•-20
	4	6-18	5-19	4-20	•-21	•-21	•-22
	5	8-20	7-21	6-22	5-23	5-23	–
11	0	•-5	•-6	•-7	•-8	•-9	•-11
	1	•-8	•-9	•-10	•-12	•-12	•-14
	2	•-11	•-12	•-13	•-14	•-15	•-17
	3	3-14	•-15	•-16	•-17	•-18	•-19
	4	5-16	4-17	4-18	•-19	•-20	•-21
	5	7-19	6-20	6-20	5-21	5-22	–
12	0	•-4	•-5	•-6	•-7	•-8	•-10
	1	•-7	•-8	•-9	•-11	•-11	•-13
	2	•-10	•-11	•-12	•-13	•-14	•-16
	3	3-13	•-14	•-15	•-16	•-16	•-18
	4	5-15	4-16	4-17	•-18	•-18	•-20
	5	7-17	6-18	5-19	5-20	•-20	•-21

Significance Limits* for the Fourfold Table Test

x_1	$N_1 - x_1$	N_1
x_2	$N_2 - x_2$	N_2
X	$N - X$	N

$N = N_1 + N_2$, $X = x_1 + x_2$, $N_1 \leqq N_2$, $x_1 \leqq N_1 - x_1$

For explanation see page 123

N_1	x_1	$2\alpha =$ 0.20	$2\alpha =$ 0.10	$2\alpha =$ 0.05	$2\alpha =$ 0.02	$2\alpha =$ 0.01	$2\alpha =$ 0.002
$N = 28$ (continued)							
	6	9–19	8–20	7–21	6–22	6–22	–
13	0	•–4	•–5	•–6	•–7	•–8	•–9
	1	•–7	•–8	•–9	•–10	•–11	•–12
	2	•–9	•–10	•–11	•–12	•–13	•–14
	3	3–12	•–13	•–14	•–15	•–15	•–17
	4	4–14	4–15	•–16	•–17	•–17	•–18
	5	6–16	5–17	5–18	•–19	•–19	•–20
	6	8–18	7–19	7–20	6–20	6–21	–
14	0	•–4	•–4	•–5	•–6	•–7	•–8
	1	•–6	•–7	•–8	•–9	•–10	•–11
	2	•–9	•–10	•–10	•–11	•–12	•–13
	3	•–11	•–12	•–13	•–14	•–14	•–15
	4	4–13	4–14	•–15	•–16	•–16	•–17
	5	6–15	5–16	5–17	•–17	•–18	•–19
	6	7–17	7–18	6–18	6–19	•–20	•–20
	7	9–19	8–20	8–20	7–21	7–21	–
$N = 29$							
4	0	•–13	•–15	•–17	•–19	•–21	•–23
	1	•–20	•–22	•–23	•–25	•–25	–
	2	4–25	3–26	2–27	–	–	–
5	0	•–10	•–13	•–15	•–17	•–18	•–21
	1	•–17	•–19	•–20	•–22	•–23	•–25
	2	3–22	2–23	2–24	•–26	•–26	–
6	0	•–9	•–11	•–13	•–15	•–16	•–18
	1	•–14	•–16	•–18	•–20	•–21	•–22
	2	3–19	2–21	•–22	•–23	•–24	•–25
	3	6–23	5–24	4–25	3–26	–	–
7	0	•–8	•–9	•–11	•–13	•–14	•–17
	1	•–13	•–14	•–16	•–18	•–19	•–21
	2	2–17	•–19	•–20	•–21	•–22	•–23
	3	5–21	4–22	3–23	3–24	•–25	–
8	0	•–7	•–8	•–10	•–12	•–13	•–15
	1	•–11	•–13	•–14	•–16	•–17	•–19
	2	2–15	•–17	•–18	•–19	•–20	•–22
	3	4–19	3–20	3–21	•–22	•–23	•–24
	4	7–22	6–23	5–24	4–25	4–25	–
9	0	•–6	•–7	•–9	•–10	•–11	•–14
	1	•–10	•–12	•–13	•–14	•–15	•–17
	2	2–14	•–15	•–16	•–18	•–19	•–20
	3	4–17	3–18	3–19	•–21	•–21	•–23
	4	6–20	5–21	5–22	4–23	•–24	–
10	0	•–5	•–7	•–8	•–9	•–10	•–12
	1	•–9	•–11	•–12	•–13	•–14	•–16
	2	•–12	•–14	•–15	•–16	•–17	•–19
	3	3–15	3–17	•–18	•–19	•–20	•–21
	4	6–18	5–19	4–20	4–21	•–22	•–23
	5	8–21	7–22	6–23	5–24	5–24	–
11	0	•–5	•–6	•–7	•–9	•–9	•–11
	1	•–8	•–10	•–11	•–12	•–13	•–15
	2	•–11	•–13	•–14	•–15	•–16	•–17
	3	3–14	3–15	•–16	•–18	•–18	•–20
	4	5–17	4–18	4–19	•–20	•–21	•–22
	5	7–19	6–20	6–21	5–22	5–23	•–23
12	0	•–5	•–6	•–7	•–8	•–9	•–10
	1	•–8	•–9	•–10	•–11	•–12	•–14
	2	•–10	•–12	•–13	•–14	•–15	•–16
	3	3–13	•–14	•–15	•–16	•–17	•–18
	4	5–15	4–17	4–18	•–19	•–19	•–20
	5	7–18	6–19	5–20	5–21	•–21	•–22
	6	9–20	8–21	7–22	6–23	6–23	–
13	0	•–4	•–5	•–6	•–7	•–8	•–10
	1	•–7	•–8	•–9	•–10	•–11	•–13
	2	•–10	•–11	•–12	•–13	•–14	•–15
	3	3–12	•–13	•–14	•–15	•–16	•–17
	4	4–14	4–15	•–16	•–17	•–18	•–19
	5	6–17	6–18	5–18	•–19	•–20	•–21
	6	8–19	7–20	7–20	6–21	6–22	–
14	0	•–4	•–5	•–6	•–7	•–7	•–9
	1	•–6	•–7	•–8	•–9	•–10	•–12
	2	•–9	•–10	•–11	•–12	•–13	•–14
	3	3–11	•–12	•–13	•–14	•–15	•–16
	4	4–13	4–14	•–15	•–16	•–17	•–18
	5	6–15	5–16	5–17	•–18	•–19	•–20
	6	8–17	7–18	6–19	6–20	•–20	•–21
	7	10–19	9–20	8–21	7–22	7–22	–
$N = 30$							
4	0	•–13	•–15	•–18	•–20	•–21	•–24
	1	•–20	•–22	•–24	•–25	•–26	•–27
	2	4–26	3–27	2–28	–	–	–
5	0	•–11	•–13	•–15	•–17	•–19	•–21
	1	•–17	•–19	•–21	•–23	•–24	•–25
	2	3–23	2–24	2–25	•–26	•–27	–
6	0	•–9	•–11	•–13	•–15	•–17	•–19
	1	•–15	•–17	•–19	•–20	•–21	•–23
	2	3–20	2–21	•–23	•–24	•–25	•–26
	3	6–24	5–25	4–26	3–27	3–27	–
7	0	•–8	•–10	•–11	•–13	•–15	•–17
	1	•–13	•–15	•–17	•–18	•–19	•–21
	2	2–18	2–19	•–21	•–22	•–23	•–24
	3	5–21	4–23	3–24	3–25	•–26	–
8	0	•–7	•–9	•–10	•–12	•–13	•–16
	1	•–12	•–13	•–15	•–16	•–18	•–20

N_1	x_1	$2\alpha =$ 0.20	$2\alpha =$ 0.10	$2\alpha =$ 0.05	$2\alpha =$ 0.02	$2\alpha =$ 0.01	$2\alpha =$ 0.002
$N = 30$ (continued)							
	2	2–16	•–17	•–19	•–20	•–21	•–23
	3	4–19	4–21	3–22	•–23	•–24	•–25
	4	7–23	6–24	5–25	4–26	4–26	–
9	0	•–6	•–8	•–9	•–11	•–12	•–14
	1	•–10	•–12	•–13	•–15	•–16	•–18
	2	2–14	•–16	•–17	•–18	•–19	•–21
	3	4–17	3–19	3–20	•–21	•–22	•–23
	4	7–21	6–22	5–23	4–24	4–24	•–25
10	0	•–6	•–7	•–8	•–10	•–11	•–13
	1	•–9	•–11	•–12	•–14	•–15	•–17
	2	•–13	•–14	•–16	•–17	•–18	•–19
	3	4–16	3–17	•–18	•–20	•–20	•–22
	4	6–19	5–20	4–21	4–22	•–23	•–24
	5	8–22	7–23	6–24	6–24	5–25	–
11	0	•–5	•–6	•–7	•–9	•–10	•–12
	1	•–9	•–10	•–11	•–13	•–13	•–15
	2	•–12	•–13	•–14	•–16	•–16	•–18
	3	3–15	3–16	•–17	•–18	•–19	•–20
	4	5–17	5–19	4–20	•–21	•–21	•–23
	5	8–20	7–21	6–22	5–23	5–23	•–24
12	0	•–5	•–6	•–7	•–8	•–9	•–11
	1	•–8	•–9	•–10	•–12	•–12	•–14
	2	•–11	•–12	•–13	•–14	•–15	•–17
	3	3–13	•–15	•–16	•–17	•–18	•–19
	4	5–16	4–17	4–18	•–19	•–20	•–21
	5	7–18	6–20	5–20	5–21	•–22	•–23
	6	9–21	8–22	7–23	7–23	6–24	–
13	0	•–4	•–5	•–6	•–7	•–8	•–10
	1	•–7	•–8	•–9	•–11	•–11	•–13
	2	•–10	•–11	•–12	•–13	•–14	•–16
	3	3–12	•–14	•–15	•–16	•–17	•–18
	4	5–15	4–16	•–17	•–18	•–19	•–20
	5	6–17	6–18	5–19	5–20	•–21	•–22
	6	9–19	8–20	7–21	6–22	6–23	•–23
14	0	•–4	•–5	•–6	•–7	•–8	•–9
	1	•–7	•–8	•–9	•–10	•–11	•–12
	2	•–9	•–10	•–11	•–12	•–13	•–15
	3	3–12	•–13	•–14	•–15	•–15	•–17
	4	4–14	4–15	•–16	•–17	•–18	•–19
	5	6–16	5–17	5–18	•–19	•–19	•–21
	6	8–18	7–19	6–20	6–21	•–21	•–22
	7	10–20	9–21	8–22	8–22	7–23	–
15	0	•–4	•–4	•–5	•–6	•–7	•–9
	1	•–6	•–7	•–8	•–9	•–10	•–11
	2	•–9	•–10	•–11	•–12	•–12	•–14
	3	•–11	•–12	•–13	•–14	•–14	•–16
	4	4–13	4–14	•–15	•–16	•–16	•–18
	5	6–15	5–16	5–17	•–18	•–18	•–19
	6	7–17	7–18	6–19	6–20	•–20	•–21
	7	9–19	8–20	8–21	7–21	7–22	–
$N = 31$							
4	0	•–13	•–16	•–18	•–21	•–22	•–25
	1	•–21	•–23	•–25	•–26	•–27	•–28
	2	4–27	3–28	2–29	–	–	–
5	0	•–11	•–14	•–16	•–18	•–19	•–22
	1	•–18	•–20	•–22	•–23	•–25	•–26
	2	3–23	2–25	2–26	•–27	•–28	–
6	0	•–10	•–12	•–14	•–16	•–17	•–20
	1	•–15	•–18	•–19	•–21	•–22	•–24
	2	3–20	2–22	•–24	•–25	•–26	•–27
	3	6–25	5–26	4–27	3–28	3–28	–
7	0	•–8	•–10	•–12	•–14	•–15	•–18
	1	•–14	•–16	•–17	•–19	•–20	•–22
	2	2–18	2–20	•–21	•–23	•–24	•–25
	3	5–22	4–24	3–25	3–26	•–27	–
8	0	•–7	•–9	•–11	•–12	•–14	•–16
	1	•–12	•–14	•–15	•–17	•–18	•–20
	2	2–16	•–18	•–19	•–21	•–22	•–23
	3	5–20	4–21	3–23	•–24	•–25	•–26
	4	8–23	6–25	5–26	5–26	4–27	–
9	0	•–7	•–8	•–9	•–11	•–12	•–15
	1	•–11	•–12	•–14	•–16	•–17	•–19
	2	2–15	•–16	•–18	•–19	•–20	•–22
	3	4–18	3–20	3–21	•–22	•–23	•–24
	4	7–21	6–23	5–24	4–25	4–25	•–26
10	0	•–6	•–7	•–9	•–10	•–11	•–13
	1	•–10	•–11	•–13	•–14	•–15	•–17
	2	2–13	•–15	•–16	•–17	•–18	•–20
	3	4–17	3–18	•–19	•–20	•–21	•–23
	4	6–20	5–21	4–22	4–23	•–24	•–25
	5	9–22	8–23	7–24	6–25	5–26	–
11	0	•–5	•–7	•–8	•–9	•–10	•–12
	1	•–9	•–10	•–12	•–13	•–14	•–16
	2	•–12	•–14	•–15	•–16	•–17	•–19
	3	3–15	3–17	•–18	•–19	•–20	•–21
	4	6–18	5–19	4–20	•–21	•–22	•–23
	5	8–21	7–22	6–23	5–24	5–24	•–25
12	0	•–5	•–6	•–7	•–8	•–9	•–11
	1	•–8	•–9	•–11	•–12	•–13	•–15
	2	•–11	•–12	•–14	•–15	•–16	•–18
	3	3–14	3–15	•–16	•–18	•–18	•–20
	4	5–17	4–18	4–19	•–20	•–21	•–22
	5	7–19	6–20	6–21	5–22	5–23	•–24
	6	9–22	8–23	8–23	7–24	6–25	–

N_1	x_1	$2\alpha =$ 0.20	$2\alpha =$ 0.10	$2\alpha =$ 0.05	$2\alpha =$ 0.02	$2\alpha =$ 0.01	$2\alpha =$ 0.002
$N = 31$ (continued)							
13	0	•–4	•–6	•–7	•–8	•–9	•–10
	1	•–8	•–9	•–10	•–11	•–12	•–14
	2	•–10	•–12	•–13	•–14	•–15	•–16
	3	3–13	•–14	•–15	•–16	•–17	•–19
	4	5–15	4–17	4–18	•–19	•–19	•–21
	5	7–18	6–19	5–20	5–21	•–21	•–23
	6	9–20	8–21	7–22	6–23	6–23	•–24
14	0	•–4	•–5	•–6	•–7	•–8	•–10
	1	•–7	•–8	•–9	•–10	•–11	•–13
	2	•–10	•–11	•–12	•–13	•–14	•–15
	3	3–12	•–13	•–14	•–15	•–16	•–17
	4	4–14	4–15	•–16	•–17	•–18	•–20
	5	6–17	5–18	5–19	•–20	•–20	•–21
	6	8–19	7–20	7–21	6–21	6–22	•–23
	7	10–21	9–22	8–23	8–23	7–24	–
15	0	•–4	•–5	•–6	•–7	•–7	•–9
	1	•–6	•–8	•–8	•–10	•–10	•–12
	2	•–9	•–10	•–11	•–12	•–13	•–14
	3	•–11	•–12	•–13	•–14	•–15	•–16
	4	4–13	4–14	•–15	•–16	•–17	•–18
	5	6–16	5–17	5–17	•–18	•–19	•–20
	6	8–18	7–19	6–19	6–20	•–21	•–22
	7	9–20	9–21	8–21	7–22	7–23	•–23
$N = 32$							
4	0	•–14	•–17	•–19	•–21	•–23	•–25
	1	•–22	•–24	•–26	•–27	•–28	•–29
	2	4–28	3–29	2–30	–	–	–
5	0	•–12	•–14	•–16	•–18	•–20	•–23
	1	•–18	•–21	•–22	•–24	•–25	•–27
	2	3–24	2–26	2–27	•–28	•–29	–
6	0	•–10	•–12	•–14	•–16	•–18	•–21
	1	•–16	•–18	•–20	•–22	•–23	•–25
	2	3–21	2–23	•–24	•–26	•–27	•–28
	3	6–26	5–27	4–28	3–29	3–29	–
7	0	•–9	•–11	•–12	•–14	•–16	•–19
	1	•–14	•–16	•–18	•–20	•–21	•–23
	2	2–19	2–21	•–22	•–24	•–24	•–26
	3	5–23	4–24	3–26	3–27	•–27	•–28
8	0	•–8	•–9	•–11	•–13	•–14	•–17
	1	•–13	•–14	•–16	•–18	•–19	•–21
	2	2–17	•–18	•–20	•–21	•–22	•–24
	3	5–21	4–22	3–23	•–25	•–25	•–27
	4	8–24	7–25	6–26	5–27	4–28	–
9	0	•–7	•–8	•–10	•–12	•–13	•–15
	1	•–11	•–13	•–14	•–16	•–17	•–19
	2	2–15	•–17	•–18	•–20	•–21	•–23
	3	4–19	3–20	3–21	•–23	•–24	•–25
	4	7–22	6–23	5–24	4–26	4–26	•–27
10	0	•–6	•–8	•–9	•–11	•–12	•–14
	1	•–10	•–12	•–13	•–15	•–16	•–18
	2	2–14	•–15	•–17	•–18	•–19	•–21
	3	4–17	3–19	3–20	•–21	•–22	•–24
	4	6–20	5–22	5–23	4–24	•–24	•–26
	5	9–23	8–24	7–25	6–26	5–27	–
11	0	•–6	•–7	•–8	•–10	•–11	•–13
	1	•–9	•–11	•–12	•–13	•–14	•–17
	2	•–13	•–14	•–15	•–17	•–18	•–19
	3	3–16	3–17	•–18	•–20	•–20	•–22
	4	6–19	5–20	4–21	4–22	•–23	•–24
	5	8–21	7–23	6–23	5–24	5–25	•–26
12	0	•–5	•–6	•–7	•–9	•–10	•–12
	1	•–9	•–10	•–11	•–12	•–13	•–15
	2	•–12	•–13	•–14	•–15	•–16	•–18
	3	3–14	3–16	•–17	•–18	•–19	•–21
	4	5–17	4–18	4–20	•–21	•–21	•–23
	5	7–20	6–21	6–22	5–23	5–24	•–25
	6	10–22	9–23	8–24	7–25	6–26	–
13	0	•–5	•–6	•–7	•–8	•–9	•–11
	1	•–8	•–9	•–10	•–11	•–12	•–14
	2	•–11	•–12	•–13	•–14	•–15	•–17
	3	3–13	•–15	•–16	•–17	•–18	•–19
	4	5–16	4–17	4–18	•–19	•–20	•–21
	5	7–18	6–20	5–21	5–22	•–22	•–23
	6	9–21	8–22	7–23	6–24	6–24	•–25
14	0	•–4	•–5	•–6	•–7	•–8	•–10
	1	•–7	•–8	•–9	•–11	•–11	•–13
	2	•–10	•–11	•–12	•–13	•–14	•–16
	3	3–12	•–14	•–15	•–16	•–17	•–18
	4	5–15	4–16	•–17	•–18	•–19	•–20
	5	6–17	6–18	5–19	5–20	•–21	•–22
	6	8–19	8–20	7–21	6–22	6–23	•–24
	7	10–22	9–23	9–23	8–24	7–25	–
15	0	•–4	•–5	•–6	•–7	•–8	•–9
	1	•–7	•–8	•–9	•–10	•–11	•–12
	2	•–9	•–10	•–11	•–12	•–13	•–15
	3	3–12	•–13	•–14	•–15	•–16	•–17
	4	4–14	4–15	•–16	•–17	•–18	•–19
	5	6–16	5–17	5–18	•–19	•–20	•–21
	6	8–18	7–19	6–20	6–21	•–22	•–23
	7	10–20	9–21	8–22	7–23	7–23	•–24
16	0	•–4	•–5	•–5	•–6	•–7	•–9
	1	•–6	•–7	•–8	•–9	•–10	•–12
	2	•–9	•–10	•–11	•–12	•–12	•–14
	3	•–11	•–12	•–13	•–14	•–15	•–16

x_1	$N_1 - x_1$	N_1
x_2	$N_2 - x_2$	N_2
X	$N - X$	N

$N = N_1 + N_2$, $X = x_1 + x_2$, $N_1 \leq N_2$, $x_1 \leq N_1 - x_1$

For explanation see page 123

N = 32 (continued)

N_1	x_1	$2\alpha=$ 0.20	$2\alpha=$ 0.10	$2\alpha=$ 0.05	$2\alpha=$ 0.02	$2\alpha=$ 0.01	$2\alpha=$ 0.002
16	4	4–13	•–14	•–15	•–16	•–17	•–18
	5	6–15	5–16	5–17	•–18	•–19	•–20
	6	7–17	7–18	6–19	6–20	•–20	•–22
	7	9–19	8–20	8–21	7–22	7–22	•–23
	8	11–21	10–22	9–23	9–23	8–24	–

N = 33

N_1	x_1	$2\alpha=$ 0.20	$2\alpha=$ 0.10	$2\alpha=$ 0.05	$2\alpha=$ 0.02	$2\alpha=$ 0.01	$2\alpha=$ 0.002
4	0	•–14	•–17	•–19	•–22	•–24	•–26
	1	•–22	•–25	•–26	•–28	•–29	•–30
	2	5–28	3–30	2–31	–	–	–
5	0	•–12	•–14	•–17	•–19	•–21	•–24
	1	•–19	•–21	•–23	•–25	•–26	•–28
	2	4–25	2–27	2–28	•–29	•–30	–
6	0	•–10	•–12	•–14	•–17	•–18	•–21
	1	•–17	•–19	•–20	•–22	•–24	•–26
	2	3–22	2–24	•–25	•–27	•–27	•–29
	3	7–26	5–28	4–29	3–30	3–30	–
7	0	•– 9	•–11	•–13	•–15	•–16	•–19
	1	•–15	•–17	•–18	•–20	•–21	•–24
	2	2–19	2–21	•–23	•–24	•–25	•–27
	3	6–24	4–25	4–26	3–28	•–28	•–29
8	0	•– 8	•–10	•–11	•–13	•–15	•–17
	1	•–13	•–15	•–16	•–18	•–19	•–22
	2	2–17	•–19	•–21	•–22	•–23	•–25
	3	5–21	4–23	3–24	•–25	•–26	•–28
	4	8–25	7–26	6–27	5–28	4–29	–
9	0	•– 7	•– 9	•–10	•–12	•–13	•–16
	1	•–12	•–13	•–15	•–17	•–18	•–20
	2	2–16	•–17	•–19	•–20	•–21	•–23
	3	4–19	3–21	3–22	•–24	•–24	•–26
	4	7–23	6–24	5–25	4–26	4–27	•–28
10	0	•– 6	•– 8	•– 9	•–11	•–12	•–14
	1	•–11	•–12	•–14	•–15	•–16	•–19
	2	2–14	•–16	•–17	•–19	•–20	•–22
	3	4–18	3–19	3–20	•–22	•–23	•–24
	4	6–21	5–22	5–23	4–25	•–25	•–27
	5	9–24	8–25	7–26	6–27	5–28	–
11	0	•– 6	•– 7	•– 8	•–10	•–11	•–13
	1	•–10	•–11	•–12	•–14	•–15	•–17
	2	•–13	•–15	•–16	•–17	•–18	•–20
	3	4–16	3–18	•–19	•–20	•–21	•–23
	4	6–19	5–21	4–22	4–23	•–24	•–25
	5	8–22	7–23	6–24	6–25	5–26	•–27
12	0	•– 5	•– 6	•– 8	•– 9	•–10	•–12
	1	•– 9	•–10	•–11	•–13	•–14	•–16
	2	•–12	•–13	•–15	•–16	•–17	•–19
	3	3–15	3–16	•–18	•–19	•–20	•–21
	4	5–18	5–19	4–20	•–21	•–22	•–24
	5	8–20	7–22	6–23	5–24	5–24	•–26
	6	10–23	9–24	8–25	7–26	7–26	6–27
13	0	•– 5	•– 6	•– 7	•– 8	•– 9	•–11
	1	•– 8	•– 9	•–11	•–12	•–13	•–15
	2	•–11	•–12	•–14	•–15	•–16	•–18
	3	3–14	•–15	•–16	•–18	•–18	•–20
	4	5–16	4–18	4–19	•–20	•–21	•–22
	5	7–19	6–20	6–21	5–22	•–23	•–24
	6	9–21	8–23	7–23	7–24	6–25	•–26
14	0	•– 4	•– 5	•– 6	•– 8	•– 9	•–10
	1	•– 8	•– 9	•–10	•–11	•–12	•–14
	2	•–10	•–12	•–13	•–14	•–15	•–16
	3	3–13	•–14	•–15	•–16	•–17	•–19
	4	5–15	4–17	4–18	•–19	•–20	•–21
	5	7–18	6–19	5–20	5–21	•–22	•–23
	6	9–20	8–21	7–22	6–23	6–24	•–25
	7	11–22	10–23	9–24	8–25	8–25	7–26
15	0	•– 4	•– 5	•– 6	•– 7	•– 8	•–10
	1	•– 7	•– 8	•– 9	•–10	•–11	•–13
	2	•–10	•–11	•–12	•–13	•–14	•–15
	3	3–12	•–13	•–14	•–15	•–16	•–18
	4	4–14	4–16	•–17	•–18	•–18	•–20
	5	6–17	5–18	5–19	•–20	•–20	•–22
	6	8–19	7–20	7–21	6–22	6–22	•–24
	7	10–21	9–22	8–23	8–24	7–24	•–25
16	0	•– 4	•– 5	•– 6	•– 7	•– 7	•– 9
	1	•– 7	•– 8	•– 8	•–10	•–10	•–12
	2	•– 9	•–10	•–11	•–12	•–13	•–14
	3	•–11	•–12	•–13	•–14	•–15	•–17
	4	4–13	4–15	•–16	•–17	•–17	•–19
	5	6–16	5–17	5–18	•–19	•–19	•–21
	6	8–18	7–19	6–20	6–21	•–21	•–22
	7	9–20	9–21	8–22	7–22	7–23	•–24
	8	11–22	10–23	10–23	9–24	8–25	8–25

N = 34

N_1	x_1	$2\alpha=$ 0.20	$2\alpha=$ 0.10	$2\alpha=$ 0.05	$2\alpha=$ 0.02	$2\alpha=$ 0.01	$2\alpha=$ 0.002
4	0	•–15	•–18	•–20	•–23	•–24	•–27
	1	•–23	•–25	•–27	•–29	•–30	•–31
	2	5–29	3–31	2–32	–	–	–
5	0	•–12	•–15	•–17	•–20	•–21	•–24
	1	•–20	•–22	•–24	•–26	•–27	•–29
	2	4–26	2–27	2–29	•–30	•–31	–
6	0	•–11	•–13	•–15	•–17	•–19	•–22
	1	•–17	•–19	•–21	•–23	•–24	•–27
	2	3–22	2–24	•–26	•–27	•–28	•–30
	3	7–27	5–29	4–30	3–31	3–31	–

N = 34 (continued)

N_1	x_1	$2\alpha=$ 0.20	$2\alpha=$ 0.10	$2\alpha=$ 0.05	$2\alpha=$ 0.02	$2\alpha=$ 0.01	$2\alpha=$ 0.002
7	0	•– 9	•–11	•–13	•–15	•–17	•–20
	1	•–15	•–17	•–19	•–21	•–22	•–24
	2	2–20	2–22	•–23	•–25	•–26	•–28
	3	6–24	5–26	4–27	3–28	•–29	•–30
8	0	•– 8	•–10	•–12	•–14	•–15	•–18
	1	•–13	•–15	•–17	•–19	•–20	•–22
	2	2–18	2–20	•–21	•–23	•–24	•–26
	3	5–22	4–24	3–25	3–26	•–27	•–29
	4	8–26	7–27	6–28	5–29	4–30	–
9	0	•– 7	•– 9	•–10	•–12	•–14	•–16
	1	•–12	•–14	•–15	•–17	•–18	•–21
	2	2–16	•–18	•–19	•–21	•–22	•–24
	3	4–20	4–22	3–23	•–24	•–25	•–27
	4	7–23	6–25	5–26	4–27	4–28	•–29
10	0	•– 7	•– 8	•– 9	•–11	•–12	•–15
	1	•–11	•–13	•–14	•–16	•–17	•–19
	2	2–15	•–16	•–18	•–19	•–20	•–22
	3	4–18	3–20	3–21	•–23	•–23	•–25
	4	7–21	6–23	5–24	4–25	4–26	•–27
	5	9–25	8–26	7–27	6–28	6–28	5–29
11	0	•– 6	•– 7	•– 9	•–10	•–11	•–14
	1	•–10	•–11	•–13	•–14	•–16	•–18
	2	2–13	•–15	•–16	•–18	•–19	•–21
	3	4–17	3–18	•–19	•–21	•–22	•–24
	4	6–20	5–21	4–22	4–24	•–24	•–26
	5	9–23	7–24	7–25	6–26	5–27	•–28
12	0	•– 5	•– 7	•– 8	•– 9	•–10	•–13
	1	•– 9	•–11	•–12	•–13	•–14	•–16
	2	•–12	•–14	•–15	•–17	•–18	•–19
	3	3–15	3–17	•–18	•–19	•–20	•–22
	4	6–18	5–20	4–21	•–22	•–23	•–24
	5	8–21	7–22	6–23	5–25	5–25	•–26
	6	10–24	9–25	8–26	7–27	7–27	6–28
13	0	•– 5	•– 6	•– 7	•– 9	•–10	•–12
	1	•– 8	•–10	•–11	•–12	•–13	•–15
	2	•–11	•–13	•–14	•–15	•–16	•–18
	3	3–14	3–16	•–17	•–18	•–19	•–21
	4	5–17	4–18	4–19	•–21	•–22	•–23
	5	7–20	6–21	6–22	5–23	5–24	•–25
	6	10–22	8–23	8–24	7–25	6–26	•–27
14	0	•– 5	•– 6	•– 7	•– 8	•– 9	•–11
	1	•– 8	•– 9	•–10	•–11	•–12	•–14
	2	•–11	•–12	•–13	•–14	•–15	•–17
	3	3–13	•–15	•–16	•–17	•–18	•–20
	4	5–16	4–17	4–18	•–19	•–20	•–22
	5	7–18	6–20	5–21	5–22	•–22	•–24
	6	9–21	8–22	7–23	6–24	6–24	•–26
	7	11–23	10–24	9–25	8–26	8–26	7–27
15	0	•– 4	•– 5	•– 6	•– 7	•– 8	•–10
	1	•– 7	•– 8	•– 9	•–11	•–12	•–13
	2	•–10	•–11	•–12	•–13	•–14	•–16
	3	3–12	•–14	•–15	•–16	•–17	•–18
	4	4–15	4–16	•–17	•–18	•–19	•–21
	5	6–17	6–18	5–19	•–20	•–21	•–22
	6	8–19	7–21	7–21	6–22	6–23	•–24
	7	10–22	9–23	9–23	8–24	7–25	•–26
16	0	•– 4	•– 5	•– 6	•– 7	•– 8	•– 9
	1	•– 7	•– 8	•– 9	•–10	•–11	•–12
	2	•– 9	•–10	•–11	•–13	•–13	•–15
	3	3–12	•–13	•–14	•–15	•–16	•–17
	4	4–14	4–15	•–16	•–17	•–18	•–19
	5	6–16	5–17	5–18	•–19	•–20	•–21
	6	8–18	7–19	6–20	6–21	•–22	•–23
	7	10–20	9–21	8–22	7–23	7–24	•–25
	8	12–22	11–23	10–24	9–25	9–25	8–26
17	0	•– 4	•– 5	•– 5	•– 6	•– 7	•– 9
	1	•– 6	•– 7	•– 8	•– 9	•–10	•–12
	2	•– 9	•–10	•–11	•–12	•–13	•–14
	3	•–11	•–12	•–13	•–14	•–15	•–16
	4	4–13	•–14	•–15	•–16	•–17	•–18
	5	6–15	5–16	5–17	•–18	•–19	•–20
	6	7–17	7–18	6–19	6–20	•–21	•–22
	7	9–19	8–20	8–21	7–22	7–23	•–24
	8	11–21	10–22	9–23	9–24	8–24	•–25

N = 35

N_1	x_1	$2\alpha=$ 0.20	$2\alpha=$ 0.10	$2\alpha=$ 0.05	$2\alpha=$ 0.02	$2\alpha=$ 0.01	$2\alpha=$ 0.002
4	0	•–15	•–18	•–21	•–23	•–25	•–28
	1	•–24	•–26	•–28	•–30	•–31	•–32
	2	5–30	3–32	2–33	–	–	–
5	0	•–13	•–15	•–18	•–20	•–22	•–25
	1	•–20	•–23	•–25	•–27	•–28	•–30
	2	4–26	3–28	2–30	•–31	•–32	–
6	0	•–11	•–13	•–15	•–18	•–19	•–23
	1	•–18	•–20	•–22	•–24	•–25	•–27
	2	3–23	2–25	•–27	•–28	•–29	•–31
	3	7–28	6–29	4–31	3–32	3–32	–
7	0	•– 9	•–12	•–14	•–16	•–17	•–20
	1	•–15	•–18	•–19	•–21	•–23	•–25
	2	3–21	2–23	•–24	•–26	•–27	•–29
	3	6–25	5–27	4–28	3–29	•–30	•–31
8	0	•– 8	•–10	•–12	•–14	•–16	•–19
	1	•–14	•–16	•–17	•–19	•–21	•–23
	2	2–18	2–20	•–22	•–24	•–25	•–27
	3	5–23	4–24	3–26	3–27	•–28	•–29
	4	9–26	7–28	6–29	5–30	4–31	–

N = 35 (continued)

N_1	x_1	$2\alpha=$ 0.20	$2\alpha=$ 0.10	$2\alpha=$ 0.05	$2\alpha=$ 0.02	$2\alpha=$ 0.01	$2\alpha=$ 0.002
9	0	•– 7	•– 9	•–11	•–13	•–14	•–17
	1	•–12	•–14	•–16	•–18	•–19	•–21
	2	2–17	•–18	•–20	•–22	•–23	•–25
	3	5–21	4–22	3–24	•–25	•–26	•–28
	4	8–24	6–26	5–27	4–28	4–29	•–30
10	0	•– 7	•– 8	•–10	•–12	•–13	•–16
	1	•–11	•–13	•–14	•–16	•–17	•–20
	2	2–15	•–17	•–18	•–20	•–21	•–23
	3	4–19	3–20	3–22	•–23	•–24	•–26
	4	7–22	6–24	5–25	4–26	4–27	•–28
	5	10–25	8–27	7–28	6–29	6–29	5–30
11	0	•– 6	•– 8	•– 9	•–11	•–12	•–14
	1	•–10	•–12	•–13	•–15	•–16	•–18
	2	2–14	•–15	•–17	•–18	•–20	•–22
	3	4–17	3–19	•–20	•–22	•–23	•–24
	4	6–20	5–22	4–23	4–24	•–25	•–27
	5	9–23	8–25	7–26	6–27	5–28	•–29
12	0	•– 6	•– 7	•– 8	•–10	•–11	•–13
	1	•– 9	•–11	•–12	•–14	•–15	•–17
	2	•–13	•–14	•–16	•–17	•–18	•–20
	3	3–16	3–17	•–19	•–20	•–21	•–23
	4	6–19	5–20	4–21	4–23	•–24	•–25
	5	8–22	7–23	6–24	5–25	5–26	•–27
	6	11–24	9–26	8–27	7–28	7–28	6–29
13	0	•– 5	•– 6	•– 8	•– 9	•–10	•–12
	1	•– 9	•–10	•–11	•–13	•–14	•–16
	2	•–12	•–13	•–14	•–16	•–17	•–19
	3	3–15	3–16	•–17	•–19	•–20	•–21
	4	5–18	4–19	4–20	•–21	•–22	•–24
	5	7–20	6–22	6–23	5–24	5–25	•–26
	6	10–23	9–24	8–25	7–26	6–27	•–28
14	0	•– 5	•– 6	•– 7	•– 8	•– 9	•–11
	1	•– 8	•– 9	•–10	•–12	•–13	•–15
	2	•–11	•–12	•–13	•–15	•–16	•–18
	3	3–14	•–15	•–16	•–18	•–18	•–20
	4	5–16	4–18	4–19	•–20	•–21	•–22
	5	7–19	6–20	5–21	5–22	•–23	•–25
	6	9–21	8–23	7–23	7–25	6–25	•–26
	7	11–24	10–25	9–26	8–27	8–27	7–28
15	0	•– 4	•– 5	•– 6	•– 8	•– 9	•–11
	1	•– 7	•– 9	•–10	•–11	•–12	•–14
	2	•–10	•–11	•–13	•–14	•–15	•–17
	3	3–13	•–14	•–15	•–16	•–17	•–19
	4	5–15	4–17	•–18	•–19	•–20	•–21
	5	6–18	6–19	5–20	5–21	•–22	•–23
	6	8–20	8–21	7–22	6–23	6–24	•–25
	7	11–22	10–23	9–24	8–25	7–26	7–27
16	0	•– 4	•– 5	•– 6	•– 7	•– 8	•–10
	1	•– 7	•– 8	•– 9	•–10	•–11	•–13
	2	•–10	•–11	•–12	•–13	•–14	•–16
	3	3–12	•–13	•–14	•–15	•–16	•–18
	4	4–14	4–16	•–17	•–18	•–19	•–20
	5	6–17	5–18	5–19	•–20	•–21	•–22
	6	8–19	7–20	7–21	6–22	6–23	•–24
	7	10–21	9–22	8–23	8–24	7–25	•–26
	8	12–23	11–24	10–25	9–26	9–26	8–27
17	0	•– 4	•– 5	•– 6	•– 7	•– 7	•– 9
	1	•– 7	•– 8	•– 8	•–10	•–10	•–12
	2	•– 9	•–10	•–11	•–12	•–13	•–15
	3	•–11	•–12	•–13	•–15	•–15	•–17
	4	4–14	4–15	•–16	•–17	•–17	•–19
	5	6–16	5–17	5–18	•–19	•–20	•–21
	6	8–18	7–19	6–20	6–21	•–21	•–23
	7	9–20	9–21	8–22	7–23	7–23	•–24
	8	11–22	10–23	10–24	9–24	8–25	•–26

N = 36

N_1	x_1	$2\alpha=$ 0.20	$2\alpha=$ 0.10	$2\alpha=$ 0.05	$2\alpha=$ 0.02	$2\alpha=$ 0.01	$2\alpha=$ 0.002
4	0	•–16	•–19	•–21	•–24	•–26	•–29
	1	•–24	•–27	•–29	•–31	•–32	•–33
	2	5–31	3–33	2–34	2–34	–	–
5	0	•–13	•–16	•–18	•–21	•–23	•–26
	1	•–21	•–23	•–25	•–27	•–29	•–31
	2	4–27	3–29	2–30	•–32	•–33	–
6	0	•–11	•–14	•–16	•–18	•–20	•–23
	1	•–18	•–20	•–22	•–25	•–26	•–28
	2	3–24	2–26	2–27	•–29	•–30	•–32
	3	7–29	6–30	5–31	3–33	3–33	–
7	0	•–10	•–12	•–14	•–16	•–18	•–21
	1	•–16	•–18	•–20	•–22	•–23	•–26
	2	3–21	2–23	•–25	•–27	•–28	•–30
	3	6–26	5–27	4–29	3–30	3–31	•–32
8	0	•– 9	•–11	•–12	•–15	•–16	•–19
	1	•–14	•–16	•–18	•–20	•–21	•–24
	2	2–19	2–21	•–23	•–24	•–25	•–28
	3	5–23	4–25	3–26	3–28	•–29	•–30
	4	9–27	7–29	6–30	5–31	4–32	–
9	0	•– 8	•– 9	•–11	•–13	•–15	•–17
	1	•–13	•–15	•–16	•–18	•–20	•–22
	2	2–17	•–19	•–21	•–22	•–23	•–26
	3	5–21	4–23	3–24	•–26	•–27	•–29
	4	8–25	7–26	6–28	5–29	4–30	•–31
10	0	•– 7	•– 9	•–10	•–12	•–13	•–16
	1	•–12	•–13	•–15	•–17	•–18	•–20
	2	2–16	•–17	•–19	•–21	•–22	•–24
	3	4–19	3–21	3–22	•–24	•–25	•–27

Significance Limits* for the Fourfold Table Test

$$\begin{array}{ll|l} x_1 & N_1 - x_1 & N_1 \\ x_2 & N_2 - x_2 & N_2 \\ \hline X & N - X & N \end{array} \qquad \begin{array}{l} N = N_1 + N_2 \\ X = x_1 + x_2 \\ N_1 \leq N_2 \\ x_1 \leq N_1 - x_1 \end{array}$$

For explanation see page 123

$N = 36$ (continued)

N_1	x_1	2α = 0.20	2α = 0.10	2α = 0.05	2α = 0.02	2α = 0.01	2α = 0.002
	4	7–23	6–24	5–26	4–27	4–28	•–29
	5	10–26	9–27	8–28	6–30	6–30	5–31
11	0	•– 6	•– 8	•– 9	•–11	•–12	•–15
	1	•–11	•–12	•–14	•–15	•–17	•–19
	2	2–14	•–16	•–17	•–19	•–20	•–22
	3	4–18	3–19	3–21	•–22	•–23	•–25
	4	6–21	5–23	5–24	4–25	•–26	•–28
	5	9–24	8–25	7–27	6–28	5–28	•–30
12	0	•– 6	•– 7	•– 8	•–10	•–11	•–14
	1	•–10	•–11	•–13	•–14	•–15	•–18
	2	•–13	•–15	•–16	•–18	•–19	•–21
	3	4–16	3–18	•–19	•–21	•–22	•–24
	4	6–19	5–21	4–22	4–24	•–24	•–26
	5	8–22	7–24	6–25	5–26	5–27	•–28
	6	11–25	10–26	9–27	8–28	7–29	6–30
13	0	•– 5	•– 7	•– 8	•– 9	•–10	•–13
	1	•– 9	•–10	•–12	•–13	•–14	•–16
	2	•–12	•–14	•–15	•–16	•–17	•–19
	3	3–15	3–17	•–18	•–19	•–20	•–22
	4	5–18	5–19	4–21	•–22	•–23	•–25
	5	8–21	7–22	6–23	5–25	5–25	•–27
	6	10–23	9–25	8–26	7–27	7–27	6–29
14	0	•– 5	•– 6	•– 7	•– 9	•–10	•–12
	1	•– 8	•–10	•–11	•–12	•–13	•–15
	2	•–11	•–13	•–14	•–15	•–16	•–18
	3	3–14	•–16	•–17	•–18	•–19	•–21
	4	5–17	4–18	4–19	•–21	•–22	•–23
	5	7–19	6–21	6–22	5–23	•–24	•–25
	6	9–22	8–23	7–24	7–25	6–26	•–27
	7	12–24	10–26	10–26	9–27	8–28	7–29
15	0	•– 5	•– 6	•– 7	•– 8	•– 9	•–11
	1	•– 8	•– 9	•–10	•–11	•–12	•–14
	2	•–11	•–12	•–13	•–14	•–15	•–17
	3	3–13	•–15	•–16	•–17	•–18	•–20
	4	5–16	4–17	4–18	•–19	•–20	•–22
	5	7–18	6–20	5–21	5–22	•–23	•–24
	6	9–21	8–22	7–23	6–24	6–25	•–26
	7	11–23	10–24	9–25	8–26	8–27	7–28
16	0	•– 4	•– 5	•– 6	•– 7	•– 8	•–10
	1	•– 7	•– 8	•– 9	•–11	•–12	•–13
	2	•–10	•–11	•–12	•–13	•–14	•–16
	3	3–12	•–14	•–15	•–16	•–17	•–19
	4	4–15	4–16	•–17	•–18	•–19	•–21
	5	6–17	6–18	5–19	•–21	•–21	•–23
	6	8–19	7–21	7–22	6–23	6–23	•–25
	7	10–22	9–23	8–24	8–25	7–25	•–26
	8	12–24	11–25	10–26	9–27	9–27	8–28
17	0	•– 4	•– 5	•– 6	•– 7	•– 8	•– 9
	1	•– 7	•– 8	•– 9	•–10	•–11	•–13
	2	•– 9	•–10	•–11	•–13	•–13	•–15
	3	3–12	•–13	•–14	•–15	•–16	•–17
	4	4–14	4–15	•–16	•–17	•–18	•–20
	5	6–16	5–17	5–18	•–19	•–20	•–22
	6	8–18	7–19	6–20	6–21	•–22	•–23
	7	10–20	9–22	8–22	7–23	7–24	•–25
	8	12–22	11–23	10–24	9–25	8–26	8–27
18	0	•– 4	•– 5	•– 5	•– 6	•– 7	•– 9
	1	•– 6	•– 7	•– 8	•– 9	•–10	•–12
	2	•– 9	•–10	•–11	•–12	•–13	•–14
	3	•–11	•–12	•–13	•–14	•–15	•–17
	4	4–13	•–14	•–15	•–16	•–17	•–19
	5	6–15	5–16	5–17	•–18	•–19	•–21
	6	7–17	7–18	6–19	6–20	•–21	•–22
	7	9–19	8–20	8–21	7–22	7–23	•–24
	8	11–21	10–22	9–23	9–24	8–25	•–26
	9	13–23	12–24	11–25	10–26	10–26	9–27

$N = 37$

N_1	x_1	2α = 0.20	2α = 0.10	2α = 0.05	2α = 0.02	2α = 0.01	2α = 0.002
4	0	•–16	•–19	•–22	•–25	•–26	•–30
	1	•–25	•–28	•–30	•–31	•–32	•–34
	2	5–32	4–33	2–35	2–35	–	–
5	0	•–13	•–16	•–19	•–22	•–23	•–27
	1	•–21	•–24	•–26	•–28	•–29	•–32
	2	4–28	3–30	2–31	•–33	•–33	–
6	0	•–11	•–14	•–16	•–19	•–21	•–24
	1	•–19	•–21	•–23	•–25	•–27	•–29
	2	3–24	2–27	2–28	•–30	•–31	•–33
	3	7–30	6–31	5–32	4–33	3–34	–
7	0	•–10	•–12	•–14	•–17	•–18	•–22
	1	•–16	•–19	•–21	•–23	•–24	•–27
	2	3–22	2–24	•–26	•–27	•–28	•–30
	3	6–26	5–28	4–30	3–31	3–32	•–33
8	0	•– 9	•–11	•–13	•–15	•–17	•–20
	1	•–15	•–17	•–19	•–21	•–22	•–25
	2	2–19	2–22	•–23	•–25	•–26	•–28
	3	5–24	4–26	3–27	3–29	•–30	•–31
	4	9–28	8–29	6–31	5–32	5–32	–
9	0	•– 8	•–10	•–12	•–14	•–15	•–18
	1	•–13	•–15	•–17	•–19	•–20	•–23
	2	2–18	•–20	•–21	•–23	•–24	•–26
	3	5–22	4–24	3–25	•–27	•–28	•–29
	4	8–25	7–27	6–28	5–30	4–30	•–32
10	0	•– 7	•– 9	•–10	•–12	•–14	•–17
	1	•–12	•–14	•–15	•–17	•–19	•–21
	2	2–16	•–18	•–19	•–21	•–22	•–25

$N = 37$ (continued)

N_1	x_1	2α = 0.20	2α = 0.10	2α = 0.05	2α = 0.02	2α = 0.01	2α = 0.002
	3	4–20	3–22	3–23	•–25	•–26	•–28
	4	7–23	6–25	5–26	4–28	4–29	•–30
	5	10–27	9–28	8–29	7–30	6–31	5–32
11	0	•– 6	•– 8	•–10	•–11	•–13	•–15
	1	•–11	•–13	•–14	•–16	•–17	•–20
	2	2–15	•–16	•–18	•–20	•–21	•–23
	3	4–18	3–20	3–21	•–23	•–24	•–26
	4	7–22	5–23	5–24	4–26	4–27	•–28
	5	9–25	8–26	7–27	6–29	5–29	•–31
12	0	•– 6	•– 7	•– 9	•–10	•–12	•–14
	1	•–10	•–12	•–13	•–15	•–16	•–18
	2	2–14	•–15	•–17	•–18	•–19	•–21
	3	4–17	3–18	•–20	•–21	•–22	•–24
	4	6–20	5–22	4–23	4–24	•–25	•–27
	5	9–23	7–24	6–26	6–27	5–28	•–29
	6	11–26	10–27	9–28	8–29	7–30	6–31
13	0	•– 5	•– 7	•– 8	•–10	•–11	•–13
	1	•– 9	•–11	•–12	•–14	•–15	•–17
	2	•–13	•–14	•–15	•–17	•–18	•–20
	3	3–16	3–17	•–18	•–20	•–21	•–23
	4	6–19	5–20	4–21	•–23	•–24	•–25
	5	8–21	7–23	6–24	5–25	5–26	•–28
	6	10–24	9–25	8–26	7–28	7–28	6–30
14	0	•– 5	•– 6	•– 7	•– 9	•–10	•–12
	1	•– 9	•–10	•–11	•–13	•–14	•–16
	2	•–12	•–13	•–14	•–16	•–17	•–19
	3	3–15	3–16	•–17	•–19	•–20	•–22
	4	5–17	4–19	4–20	•–21	•–22	•–24
	5	7–20	6–21	6–23	5–24	5–25	•–26
	6	10–23	8–24	8–25	7–26	6–27	•–28
	7	12–25	11–26	10–27	9–28	8–29	7–30
15	0	•– 5	•– 6	•– 7	•– 8	•– 9	•–11
	1	•– 8	•– 9	•–10	•–12	•–13	•–15
	2	•–11	•–12	•–13	•–15	•–16	•–18
	3	3–14	•–15	•–16	•–18	•–18	•–20
	4	5–16	4–18	4–19	•–20	•–21	•–23
	5	7–19	6–20	5–21	5–22	•–23	•–25
	6	9–21	8–22	7–24	6–25	6–25	•–27
	7	11–24	10–25	9–26	8–27	8–27	7–29
16	0	•– 4	•– 5	•– 6	•– 8	•– 9	•–11
	1	•– 7	•– 9	•–10	•–11	•–12	•–14
	2	•–10	•–11	•–13	•–14	•–15	•–17
	3	3–13	•–14	•–15	•–17	•–17	•–19
	4	5–15	4–17	•–18	•–19	•–20	•–21
	5	6–18	6–19	5–20	•–21	•–22	•–24
	6	8–20	7–21	7–22	6–23	6–24	•–25
	7	10–22	9–23	9–24	8–25	7–26	•–27
	8	13–24	11–26	11–26	10–27	9–28	8–29
17	0	•– 4	•– 5	•– 6	•– 7	•– 8	•–10
	1	•– 7	•– 8	•– 9	•–10	•–11	•–13
	2	•–10	•–11	•–12	•–13	•–14	•–16
	3	3–12	•–13	•–14	•–16	•–16	•–18
	4	4–14	4–16	•–17	•–18	•–19	•–20
	5	6–17	5–18	5–19	•–20	•–21	•–22
	6	8 19	7–20	6–21	6–22	•–23	•–24
	7	10–21	9–22	8–23	7–24	7–25	•–26
	8	12–23	11–24	10–25	9–26	9–27	8–28
18	0	•– 4	•– 5	•– 6	•– 7	•– 7	•– 9
	1	• 7	•– 8	•– 9	•–10	•–11	•–12
	2	•– 9	•–10	•–11	•–12	•–13	•–15
	3	•–11	•–12	•–13	•–15	•–15	•–17
	4	4–14	4–15	•–16	•–17	•–18	•–19
	5	6–16	5–17	5–18	•–19	•–20	•–21
	6	8–18	7–19	6–20	6–21	•–22	•–23
	7	9–20	8–21	8–22	7–23	7–24	•–25
	8	11–22	10–23	10–24	9–25	8–25	•–27
	9	13–24	12–25	11–26	10–27	10–27	9–28

$N = 38$

N_1	x_1	2α = 0.20	2α = 0.10	2α = 0.05	2α = 0.02	2α = 0.01	2α = 0.002
4	0	•–16	•–20	•–22	•–25	•–27	•–30
	1	•–26	•–28	•–30	•–32	•–33	•–35
	2	5–33	4–34	3–35	2–36	–	–
5	0	•–14	•–17	•–19	•–22	•–24	•–27
	1	•–22	•–25	•–27	•–29	•–30	•–32
	2	4–29	3–31	2–32	•–34	•–34	–
6	0	•–12	•–14	•–17	•–19	•–21	•–25
	1	•–19	•–22	•–24	•–26	•–27	•–30
	2	3–25	2–27	2–29	•–31	•–32	•–33
	3	8–30	6–32	5–33	4–34	3–35	–
7	0	•–10	•–13	•–15	•–17	•–19	•–22
	1	•–17	•–19	•–21	•–23	•–25	•–28
	2	3–22	2–24	•–26	•–28	•–29	•–31
	3	6–27	5–29	4–30	3–32	3–33	•–34
8	0	•– 9	•–11	•–13	•–16	•–17	•–20
	1	•–15	•–17	•–19	•–21	•–23	•–25
	2	2–20	2–22	•–24	•–26	•–27	•–29
	3	6–25	4–26	4–28	3–30	•–30	•–32
	4	9–29	8–30	7–31	5–33	5–33	4–34
9	0	•– 8	•–10	•–12	•–14	•–16	•–19
	1	•–13	•–16	•–17	•–19	•–21	•–23
	2	2–18	•–20	•–22	•–24	•–25	•–27
	3	5–22	4–24	3–26	3–27	•–28	•–30
	4	8–26	7–28	6–29	5–31	4–31	•–33
10	0	•– 7	•– 9	•–11	•–13	•–14	•–17
	1	•–12	•–14	•–16	•–18	•–19	•–22

$N = 38$ (continued)

N_1	x_1	2α = 0.20	2α = 0.10	2α = 0.05	2α = 0.02	2α = 0.01	2α = 0.002
	2	2–16	•–18	•–20	•–22	•–23	•–25
	3	4–20	4–22	3–24	•–25	•–26	•–28
	4	7–24	6–26	5–27	4–28	4–29	•–31
	5	11–27	9–29	8–30	7–31	6–32	5–33
11	0	•– 7	•– 8	•–10	•–12	•–13	•–16
	1	•–11	•–13	•–14	•–16	•–18	•–20
	2	2–15	•–17	•–18	•–20	•–21	•–24
	3	4–19	3–20	3–22	•–24	•–25	•–27
	4	7–22	6–24	5–25	4–27	4–28	•–29
	5	10–25	8–27	7–28	6–29	6–30	5–32
12	0	•– 6	•– 8	•– 9	•–11	•–12	•–14
	1	•–10	•–12	•–13	•–15	•–16	•–19
	2	2–14	•–16	•–17	•–19	•–20	•–22
	3	4–17	3–19	•–20	•–22	•–23	•–25
	4	6–21	5–22	4–23	4–25	•–26	•–28
	5	9–24	8–25	7–26	6–28	5–28	•–30
	6	11–27	10–28	9–29	8–30	7–31	6–32
13	0	•– 6	•– 7	•– 8	•–10	•–11	•–13
	1	•– 9	•–11	•–12	•–14	•–15	•–17
	2	•–13	•–14	•–16	•–17	•–19	•–21
	3	3–16	3–18	•–19	•–21	•–22	•–24
	4	6–19	5–21	4–22	4–23	•–24	•–26
	5	8–22	7–23	6–25	5–26	5–27	•–28
	6	11–25	9–26	8 27	7–28	7–29	6–30
14	0	•– 5	•– 6	•– 8	•– 9	•–10	•–12
	1	•– 9	•–10	•–11	•–13	•–14	•–16
	2	•–12	•–13	•–15	•–16	•–17	•–19
	3	3–15	3–16	•–18	•–19	•–20	•–22
	4	5–18	4–19	4–21	•–22	•–23	•–25
	5	7–21	7–22	6–23	5–24	5–25	•–27
	6	10–23	9–25	8–26	7–27	6–28	•–29
	7	12–26	11–27	10–28	9–29	8–30	7–31
15	0	•– 5	•– 6	•– 7	•– 9	•–10	•–12
	1	•– 8	•–10	•–11	•–12	•–13	•–15
	2	•–11	•–13	•–14	•–15	•–16	•–18
	3	3–14	•–15	•–17	•–18	•–19	•–21
	4	5–17	4–18	4–19	•–21	•–22	•–23
	5	7–19	6–21	5–22	5–23	•–24	•–26
	6	9–22	8–23	7–24	7–25	6–26	•–28
	7	11–24	10–25	9–26	8–28	8–28	7–29
16	0	•– 4	•– 6	•– 7	•– 8	•– 9	•–11
	1	•– 8	•– 9	•–10	•–11	•–12	•–14
	2	•–10	•–12	•–13	•–14	•–15	•–17
	3	3–13	•–14	•–16	•–17	•–18	•–20
	4	5–16	4–17	4–18	•–20	•–20	•–22
	5	7–18	6–19	5–21	5–22	•–23	•–24
	6	9–21	8–22	7–23	6–24	6–25	•–26
	7	11–23	10–24	9–25	8–26	7–27	7–28
	8	13–25	12–26	11–27	10–28	9–29	8–30
17	0	•– 4	•– 5	•– 6	•– 7	•– 8	•–10
	1	•– 7	•– 8	•– 9	•–11	•–12	•–13
	2	•–10	•–11	•–12	•–13	•–14	•–16
	3	3–12	•–14	•–15	•–16	•–17	•–19
	4	4–15	4–16	•–17	•–18	•–19	•–21
	5	6–17	5–18	5–19	•–21	•–21	•–23
	6	8–19	7–21	7–22	6–23	6–24	•–25
	7	10–22	9–23	8–24	8–25	7–26	•–27
	8	12–24	11–25	10–26	9–27	9–27	8–29
18	0	•– 4	•– 5	•– 6	•– 7	•– 8	•–10
	1	•– 7	•– 8	•– 9	•–10	•–11	•–13
	2	•– 9	•–10	•–11	•–13	•–14	•–15
	3	3–12	•–13	•–14	•–15	•–16	•–18
	4	4–14	4–15	•–16	•–17	•–18	•–20
	5	6 16	5–17	5–18	•–20	•–20	•–22
	6	8–18	7–20	6–21	6–22	•–22	•–24
	7	10–20	9–22	8–23	7–24	7–24	•–26
	8	11–23	11–24	10–25	9–26	8–26	8–27
	9	13–25	12–26	12–26	11–27	10–28	9–29
19	0	•– 4	•– 5	•– 5	•– 6	•– 7	•– 9
	1	•– 6	•– 7	•– 8	•– 9	•–10	•–12
	2	•– 9	•–10	•–11	•–12	•–13	•–14
	3	•–11	•–12	•–13	•–14	•–15	•–17
	4	4–13	•–14	•–15	•–17	•–17	•–19
	5	6–15	5–16	5–17	•–19	•–19	•–21
	6	7–17	7–19	6–20	6–21	•–21	•–23
	7	9–19	8–21	8–21	7–23	7–23	•–24
	8	11–21	10–22	9–23	9–24	8–25	•–26
	9	13–23	12–24	11–25	10–26	10–27	9–28

$N = 39$

N_1	x_1	2α = 0.20	2α = 0.10	2α = 0.05	2α = 0.02	2α = 0.01	2α = 0.002
4	0	•–17	•–20	•–23	•–26	•–28	•–31
	1	•–26	•–29	•–31	•–33	•–34	•–36
	2	5–34	4–35	3–36	2–37	–	–
5	0	•–14	•–17	•–20	•–23	•–25	•–28
	1	•–23	•–25	•–27	•–30	•–31	•–33
	2	4–29	3–31	2–33	•–35	•–35	–
6	0	•–12	•–15	•–17	•–20	•–22	•–25
	1	•–20	•–22	•–24	•–27	•–28	•–31
	2	3–26	2–28	2–30	•–32	•–33	•–34
	3	8–31	6–33	5–34	4–35	3–36	–
7	0	•–11	•–13	•–15	•–18	•–20	•–23
	1	•–17	•–20	•–22	•–24	•–26	•–28
	2	3–23	2–25	•–27	•–29	•–30	•–32
	3	7–28	5–30	4–31	3–33	3–34	•–35
8	0	•– 9	•–12	•–14	•–16	•–18	•–21
	1	•–15	•–18	•–20	•–22	•–23	•–26

Significance Limits* for the Fourfold Table Test

x_1	$N_1 - x_1$	N_1
x_2	$N_2 - x_2$	N_2
X	$N - X$	N

$N = N_1 + N_2$, $X = x_1 + x_2$, $N_1 \leq N_2$, $x_1 \leq N_1 - x_1$

For explanation see page 123

N = 39 (continued)

N_1	x_1	2α = 0.20	2α = 0.10	2α = 0.05	2α = 0.02	2α = 0.01	2α = 0.002
	2	2-21	2-23	•-25	•-26	•-28	•-30
	3	6-25	5-27	4-29	3-30	•-31	•-33
	4	10-29	8-31	7-32	5-34	5-34	4-35
9	0	•- 8	•-10	•-12	•-14	•-16	•-19
	1	•-14	•-16	•-18	•-20	•-21	•-24
	2	2-19	2-21	•-22	•-24	•-26	•-28
	3	5-23	4-25	3-26	3-28	•-29	•-31
	4	8-27	7-29	6-30	5-31	4-32	•-34
10	0	•- 8	•- 9	•-11	•-13	•-15	•-18
	1	•-13	•-15	•-16	•-18	•-20	•-22
	2	2-17	•-19	•-21	•-22	•-24	•-26
	3	5-21	4-23	3-24	•-26	•-27	•-29
	4	8-25	6-26	5-28	4-29	4-30	•-32
	5	11-28	9-30	8-31	7-32	6-33	5-34
11	0	•- 7	•- 9	•-10	•-12	•-13	•-16
	1	•-11	•-13	•-15	•-17	•-18	•-21
	2	2-16	•-17	•-19	•-21	•-22	•-24
	3	4-19	3-21	3-23	•-24	•-25	•-27
	4	7-23	6-24	5-26	4-27	4-28	•-30
	5	10-26	8-28	7-29	6-30	6-31	5-32
12	0	•- 6	•- 8	•- 9	•-11	•-12	•-15
	1	•-11	•-12	•-14	•-16	•-17	•-19
	2	2-14	•-16	•-18	•-19	•-20	•-23
	3	4-18	3-20	3-21	•-23	•-24	•-26
	4	6-21	5-23	5-24	4-26	•-27	•-28
	5	9-24	8-26	7-27	6-28	5-29	•-31
	6	12-27	10-29	9-30	8-31	7-32	6-33
13	0	•- 6	•- 7	•- 9	•-10	•-11	•-14
	1	•-10	•-11	•-13	•-14	•-16	•-18
	2	•-13	•-15	•-16	•-18	•-19	•-21
	3	4-17	3-18	•-20	•-21	•-22	•-24
	4	6-20	5-21	4-23	4-24	•-25	•-27
	5	8-23	7-24	6-25	5-27	5-28	•-29
	6	11-25	10-27	9-28	8-29	7-30	6-31
14	0	•- 5	•- 7	•- 8	•- 9	•-11	•-13
	1	•- 9	•-11	•-12	•-13	•-15	•-17
	2	•-12	•-14	•-15	•-17	•-18	•-20
	3	3-15	3-17	•-18	•-20	•-21	•-23
	4	5-18	5-20	4-21	•-23	•-24	•-25
	5	8-21	7-23	6-24	5-25	5-26	•-28
	6	10-24	9-25	8-26	7-28	6-28	6-30
	7	13-26	11-28	10-29	9-30	8-31	7-32
15	0	•- 5	•- 6	•- 7	•- 9	•-10	•-12
	1	•- 8	•-10	•-11	•-13	•-14	•-16
	2	•-12	•-13	•-14	•-16	•-17	•-19
	3	3-14	3-16	•-17	•-19	•-20	•-22
	4	5-17	4-19	4-20	•-21	•-22	•-24
	5	7-20	6-21	6-22	5-24	•-25	•-26
	6	9-22	8-24	7-25	7-26	6-27	•-28
	7	12-25	11-26	10-27	9-28	8-29	7-30
16	0	•- 5	•- 6	•- 7	•- 8	•- 9	•-11
	1	•- 8	•- 9	•-10	•-12	•-13	•-15
	2	•-11	•-12	•-13	•-15	•-16	•-18
	3	3-14	•-15	•-16	•-18	•-18	•-20
	4	5-16	4-18	4-19	•-20	•-21	•-23
	5	7-19	6-20	5-21	5-22	•-23	•-25
	6	9-21	8-22	7-24	6-25	6-26	•-27
	7	11-24	10-25	9-26	8-27	8-28	7-29
	8	13-26	12-27	11-28	10-29	9-30	8-31
17	0	•- 4	•- 5	•- 6	•- 8	•- 9	•-11
	1	•- 7	•- 9	•-10	•-11	•-12	•-14
	2	•-10	•-11	•-13	•-14	•-15	•-17
	3	3-13	•-14	•-15	•-17	•-17	•-19
	4	4-15	4-17	•-18	•-19	•-20	•-22
	5	6-18	6-19	5-20	•-21	•-22	•-24
	6	8-20	7-21	7-22	6-23	6-24	•-26
	7	10-22	9-23	9-24	8-26	7-26	•-28
	8	12-24	11-26	10-27	10-28	9-28	8-29
18	0	•- 4	•- 5	•- 6	•- 7	•- 8	•-10
	1	•- 7	•- 8	•- 9	•-10	•-11	•-13
	2	•-10	•-11	•-12	•-13	•-14	•-16
	3	3-12	•-13	•-14	•-16	•-16	•-18
	4	4-14	4-16	•-17	•-18	•-19	•-20
	5	6-17	5-18	5-19	•-20	•-21	•-23
	6	8-19	7-20	6-21	6-22	•-23	•-25
	7	10-21	9-22	8-23	7-24	7-25	•-26
	8	12-23	11-24	10-25	9-26	9-27	8-28
	9	14-25	13-26	12-27	11-28	10-29	9-30
19	0	•- 4	•- 5	•- 6	•- 7	•- 8	•- 9
	1	•- 7	•- 8	•- 9	•-10	•-11	•-12
	2	•- 9	•-10	•-11	•-12	•-13	•-15
	3	•-11	•-13	•-14	•-15	•-16	•-17
	4	4-14	4-15	•-16	•-17	•-18	•-19
	5	6-16	5-17	5-18	•-19	•-20	•-21
	6	7-18	7-19	6-20	6-21	•-22	•-23
	7	9-20	8-21	8-22	7-23	7-24	•-25
	8	11-22	10-23	9-24	9-25	8-26	•-27
	9	13-24	12-25	11-26	10-27	10-27	9-29

N = 40

N_1	x_1	2α = 0.20	2α = 0.10	2α = 0.05	2α = 0.02	2α = 0.01	2α = 0.002
4	0	•-17	•-21	•-24	•-27	•-29	•-32
	1	•-27	•-30	•-32	•-34	•-35	•-37
	2	6-34	4-36	3-37	2-38	–	–
5	0	•-14	•-18	•-20	•-23	•-25	•-29
	1	•-23	•-26	•-28	•-30	•-32	•-34
	2	4-30	3-32	2-34	•-35	•-36	–

N = 40 (continued)

N_1	x_1	2α = 0.20	2α = 0.10	2α = 0.05	2α = 0.02	2α = 0.01	2α = 0.002
6	0	•-12	•-15	•-18	•-21	•-22	•-26
	1	•-20	•-23	•-25	•-27	•-29	•-32
	2	4-26	2-29	2-31	•-32	•-33	•-35
	3	8-32	6-34	5-35	4-36	3-37	–
7	0	•-11	•-13	•-16	•-18	•-20	•-24
	1	•-18	•-20	•-22	•-25	•-26	•-29
	2	3-24	2-26	•-28	•-30	•-31	•-33
	3	7-29	5-31	4-32	3-34	3-34	•-36
8	0	•-10	•-12	•-14	•-16	•-18	•-21
	1	•-16	•-18	•-20	•-22	•-24	•-27
	2	3-21	2-23	•-25	•-27	•-28	•-31
	3	6-26	5-28	4-29	3-31	•-32	•-34
	4	10-30	8-32	7-33	6-34	5-35	4-36
9	0	•- 9	•-11	•-13	•-15	•-16	•-20
	1	•-14	•-16	•-18	•-20	•-22	•-25
	2	2-19	2-21	•-23	•-25	•-26	•-29
	3	5-24	4-25	3-27	3-29	•-30	•-32
	4	9-28	7-29	6-31	5-32	4-33	•-35
10	0	•- 8	•-10	•-11	•-13	•-15	•-18
	1	•-13	•-15	•-17	•-19	•-20	•-23
	2	2-17	•-19	•-21	•-23	•-24	•-27
	3	5-22	4-23	3-25	•-27	•-28	•-30
	4	8-25	6-27	5-29	5-30	4-31	•-33
	5	11-29	10-30	8-32	7-33	6-34	5-35
11	0	•- 7	•- 9	•-10	•-12	•-14	•-17
	1	•-12	•-14	•-15	•-17	•-19	•-21
	2	2-16	•-18	•-19	•-21	•-23	•-25
	3	4-20	3-22	3-23	•-25	•-26	•-28
	4	7-23	6-25	5-27	4-28	4-29	•-31
	5	10-27	9-28	8-30	6-31	6-32	5-33
12	0	•- 6	•- 8	•-10	•-11	•-13	•-15
	1	•-11	•-13	•-14	•-16	•-17	•-20
	2	2-15	•-16	•-18	•-20	•-21	•-23
	3	4-18	3-20	3-22	•-23	•-24	•-26
	4	6-22	5-23	5-25	4-26	•-27	•-29
	5	9-25	8-26	7-28	6-29	5-30	•-32
	6	12-28	11-29	9-31	8-32	8-32	6-34
13	0	•- 6	•- 7	•- 9	•-10	•-12	•-14
	1	•-10	•-12	•-13	•-15	•-16	•-19
	2	•-14	•-15	•-17	•-18	•-20	•-22
	3	4-17	3-19	•-20	•-22	•-23	•-25
	4	6-20	5-22	4-23	4-25	•-26	•-28
	5	8-23	7-25	6-26	6-27	5-28	•-30
	6	11-26	10-28	9-29	8-30	7-31	6-32
14	0	•- 5	•- 7	•- 8	•-10	•-11	•-13
	1	•- 9	•-11	•-12	•-14	•-15	•-17
	2	•-13	•-14	•-16	•-17	•-18	•-21
	3	3-16	3-17	•-19	•-20	•-21	•-24
	4	6-19	5-20	4-22	•-23	•-24	•-26
	5	8-22	7-23	6-25	5-26	5-27	•-28
	6	10-24	9-26	8-27	7-28	7-29	6-31
	7	13-27	12-28	10-30	9-31	9-31	7-33
15	0	•- 5	•- 6	•- 8	•- 9	•-10	•-12
	1	•- 9	•-10	•-11	•-13	•-14	•-16
	2	•-12	•-13	•-15	•-16	•-17	•-19
	3	3-15	3-16	•-18	•-19	•-20	•-22
	4	5-18	4-19	4-20	•-22	•-23	•-25
	5	7-20	6-22	6-23	5-24	5-25	•-27
	6	10-23	9-24	8-26	7-27	6-28	•-29
	7	12-26	11-27	10-28	9-29	8-30	7-31
16	0	•- 5	•- 6	•- 7	•- 8	•- 9	•-12
	1	•- 8	•- 9	•-11	•-12	•-13	•-15
	2	•-11	•-12	•-14	•-15	•-16	•-18
	3	3-14	•-15	•-17	•-18	•-19	•-21
	4	5-17	4-18	4-19	•-21	•-22	•-23
	5	7-19	6-21	5-22	5-23	•-24	•-26
	6	9-22	8-23	7-24	6-25	6-26	•-28
	7	11-24	10-25	9-27	8-28	8-28	7-30
	8	14-26	12-28	11-29	10-30	10-30	8-32
17	0	•- 4	•- 6	•- 7	•- 8	•- 9	•-11
	1	•- 8	•- 9	•-10	•-11	•-12	•-14
	2	•-10	•-12	•-13	•-14	•-15	•-17
	3	3-13	•-14	•-16	•-17	•-18	•-20
	4	5-16	4-17	•-18	•-20	•-20	•-22
	5	6-18	6-19	5-21	5-22	•-23	•-24
	6	8-21	8-22	7-23	6-24	6-25	•-27
	7	11-23	10-24	9-25	8-26	7-27	•-28
	8	13-25	12-26	11-27	10-28	9-29	8-30
18	0	•- 4	•- 5	•- 6	•- 7	•- 8	•-10
	1	•- 7	•- 8	•- 9	•-11	•-12	•-14
	2	•-10	•-11	•-12	•-13	•-14	•-16
	3	3-12	•-14	•-15	•-16	•-17	•-19
	4	4-15	4-16	•-17	•-18	•-19	•-21
	5	6-17	5-18	5-20	•-20	•-22	•-23
	6	8-19	7-21	7-22	6-23	6-24	•-25
	7	10-22	9-23	8-24	8-25	7-26	•-27
	8	12-24	11-25	10-26	9-27	9-28	8-29
	9	14-26	13-27	12-28	11-29	10-30	9-31
19	0	•- 4	•- 5	•- 6	•- 7	•- 8	•-10
	1	•- 7	•- 8	•- 9	•-10	•-11	•-13
	2	•- 9	•-10	•-11	•-13	•-14	•-15
	3	3-12	•-13	•-14	•-15	•-16	•-18
	4	4-14	4-15	•-16	•-18	•-18	•-20
	5	6-16	5-17	5-19	•-20	•-21	•-22
	6	8-18	7-20	6-21	6-22	•-23	•-24
	7	9-21	9-22	8-23	7-24	7-25	•-26
	8	11-23	10-24	10-25	9-26	8-26	8-28

N = 40 (continued)

N_1	x_1	2α = 0.20	2α = 0.10	2α = 0.05	2α = 0.02	2α = 0.01	2α = 0.002
	9	13-25	12-26	11-27	11-28	10-28	9-29
20	0	•- 4	•- 5	•- 5	•- 7	•- 7	•- 9
	1	•- 6	•- 7	•- 8	•- 9	•-10	•-12
	2	•- 9	•-10	•-11	•-12	•-13	•-15
	3	•-11	•-12	•-13	•-14	•-15	•-17
	4	4-13	•-14	•-15	•-17	•-17	•-19
	5	6-15	5-17	5-18	•-19	•-20	•-21
	6	7-18	7-19	6-20	•-21	•-22	•-23
	7	9-20	8-21	8-22	7-23	7-23	•-25
	8	11-22	10-23	9-24	9-25	8-25	•-27
	9	13-24	12-25	11-25	10-26	10-27	9-28
	10	15-25	14-26	13-27	12-28	11-29	10-30

N = 41

N_1	x_1	2α = 0.20	2α = 0.10	2α = 0.05	2α = 0.02	2α = 0.01	2α = 0.002
4	0	•-18	•-21	•-24	•-27	•-29	•-33
	1	1-28	•-31	•-33	•-35	•-36	•-38
	2	6-35	4-37	3-38	2-39	–	–
5	0	•-15	•-18	•-21	•-24	•-26	•-30
	1	•-24	•-27	•-29	•-31	•-33	•-35
	2	4-31	3-33	2-35	•-36	•-37	•-38
6	0	•-13	•-16	•-18	•-21	•-23	•-27
	1	•-21	•-23	•-26	•-28	•-30	•-32
	2	4-27	2-30	2-31	•-33	•-34	•-36
	3	8-33	6-35	5-36	4-37	3-38	–
7	0	•-11	•-14	•-16	•-19	•-21	•-24
	1	•-18	•-21	•-23	•-25	•-27	•-30
	2	3-24	2-26	•-28	•-30	•-32	•-34
	3	7-29	5-31	4-33	3-34	3-35	•-37
8	0	•-10	•-12	•-14	•-17	•-19	•-22
	1	•-16	•-19	•-21	•-23	•-25	•-28
	2	3-22	2-24	•-26	•-28	•-29	•-32
	3	6-27	5-29	4-30	3-32	•-33	•-35
	4	10-31	8-33	7-34	6-35	5-36	4-37
9	0	•- 9	•-11	•-13	•-15	•-17	•-20
	1	•-15	•-17	•-19	•-21	•-23	•-25
	2	2-20	2-22	•-24	•-26	•-27	•-29
	3	5-24	4-26	3-28	3-30	•-31	•-33
	4	9-28	7-30	6-32	5-33	4-34	•-35
10	0	•- 8	•-10	•-12	•-14	•-15	•-19
	1	•-13	•-15	•-17	•-19	•-21	•-24
	2	2-18	•-20	•-22	•-24	•-25	•-27
	3	5-22	4-24	3-26	•-27	•-29	•-31
	4	8-26	7-28	6-29	5-31	4-32	•-34
	5	11-30	10-31	8-33	7-34	6-35	5-36
11	0	•- 7	•- 9	•-11	•-13	•-14	•-17
	1	•-12	•-14	•-16	•-18	•-19	•-22
	2	2-16	•-18	•-20	•-22	•-23	•-26
	3	4-20	3-22	3-24	•-26	•-27	•-29
	4	7-24	6-26	5-27	4-29	4-30	•-32
	5	10-27	9-29	8-30	7-32	6-33	5-34
12	0	•- 7	•- 8	•-10	•-12	•-13	•-16
	1	•-11	•-13	•-15	•-16	•-18	•-20
	2	2-15	•-17	•-19	•-20	•-22	•-24
	3	4-19	3-21	3-22	•-24	•-25	•-27
	4	7-22	5-24	5-25	4-27	4-28	•-30
	5	9-26	8-27	7-28	6-30	5-31	•-32
	6	12-29	11-30	10-31	8-33	8-33	6-35
13	0	•- 6	•- 8	•- 9	•-11	•-12	•-15
	1	•-10	•-12	•-13	•-15	•-17	•-19
	2	2-14	•-16	•-17	•-19	•-20	•-23
	3	4-17	3-19	•-21	•-22	•-23	•-26
	4	6-21	5-22	4-24	4-25	•-26	•-28
	5	9-24	7-25	7-27	6-28	5-29	•-31
	6	11-27	10-28	9-29	8-31	7-32	6-33
14	0	•- 6	•- 7	•- 8	•-10	•-11	•-14
	1	•-10	•-11	•-13	•-14	•-15	•-18
	2	•-13	•-15	•-16	•-18	•-19	•-20
	3	3-16	3-18	•-19	•-21	•-22	•-24
	4	6-19	5-21	4-22	4-24	•-25	•-27
	5	8-22	7-24	6-25	5-27	5-28	•-29
	6	11-25	9-27	8-28	7-29	7-30	6-31
	7	13-28	12-29	11-30	10-31	9-32	7-34
15	0	•- 5	•- 7	•- 8	•- 9	•-10	•-13
	1	•- 9	•-10	•-12	•-13	•-14	•-17
	2	•-12	•-14	•-15	•-17	•-18	•-20
	3	3-15	3-17	•-18	•-20	•-21	•-23
	4	5-18	4-20	4-21	•-23	•-23	•-25
	5	7-21	7-22	6-24	5-25	5-26	•-28
	6	10-24	9-25	8-26	7-28	6-28	•-30
	7	12-26	11-28	10-29	9-30	8-31	7-32
16	0	•- 5	•- 6	•- 7	•- 9	•-10	•-12
	1	•- 8	•-10	•-11	•-12	•-14	•-16
	2	•-11	•-13	•-14	•-16	•-17	•-19
	3	3-14	•-16	•-17	•-19	•-20	•-22
	4	5-17	4-19	4-20	•-21	•-22	•-24
	5	7-20	6-21	5-22	5-24	•-25	•-26
	6	9-22	8-24	7-25	7-26	6-27	•-29
	7	11-25	10-26	9-27	8-28	8-29	7-31
	8	14-27	13-28	12-29	10-31	10-31	9-32
17	0	•- 5	•- 6	•- 7	•- 8	•- 9	•-11
	1	•- 8	•- 9	•-10	•-12	•-13	•-15
	2	•-11	•-12	•-13	•-15	•-16	•-18
	3	3-13	•-15	•-16	•-18	•-18	•-20
	4	5-16	4-17	4-19	•-20	•-21	•-23
	5	7-19	6-20	5-21	5-23	•-23	•-25
	6	9-21	8-22	7-24	6-25	6-26	•-27

Significance Limits* for the Fourfold Table Test

x_1	$N_1 - x_1$	N_1
x_2	$N_2 - x_2$	N_2
X	$N - X$	N

$N = N_1 + N_2$, $X = x_1 + x_2$, $N_1 \leqq N_2$, $x_1 \leqq N_1 - x_1$

For explanation see page 123

N = 41 (continued)

N_1	x_1	$2\alpha=0.20$	$2\alpha=0.10$	$2\alpha=0.05$	$2\alpha=0.02$	$2\alpha=0.01$	$2\alpha=0.002$
	7	11-23	10-25	9-26	8-27	7-28	7-29
	8	13-26	12-27	11-28	10-29	9-30	8-31
18	0	•-4	•-5	•-6	•-8	•-9	•-11
	1	•-7	•-9	•-10	•-11	•-12	•-14
	2	•-10	•-11	•-13	•-14	•-15	•-17
	3	3-13	•-14	•-15	•-17	•-17	•-19
	4	4-15	4-17	•-18	•-19	•-20	•-22
	5	6-18	6-19	5-20	•-21	•-22	•-24
	6	8-20	7-21	7-22	6-24	6-24	•-26
	7	10-22	9-23	8-25	8-26	7-26	•-28
	8	12-24	11-26	10-27	9-28	9-28	8-30
	9	14-27	13-28	12-29	11-30	11-30	9-32
19	0	•-4	•-5	•-6	•-7	•-8	•-10
	1	•-7	•-8	•-9	•-10	•-11	•-13
	2	•-10	•-11	•-12	•-13	•-14	•-16
	3	3-12	•-13	•-14	•-16	•-17	•-18
	4	4-14	4-16	•-17	•-18	•-19	•-21
	5	6-17	5-18	5-19	•-20	•-21	•-23
	6	8-19	7-20	6-21	6-22	•-23	•-25
	7	10-21	9-22	8-23	7-25	7-25	•-27
	8	12-23	11-24	10-25	9-27	8-27	8-29
	9	14-25	13-26	12-27	11-28	10-29	9-30
20	0	•-4	•-5	•-6	•-7	•-8	•-9
	1	•-7	•-8	•-9	•-10	•-11	•-12
	2	•-9	•-10	•-11	•-12	•-13	•-15
	3	•-11	•-13	•-14	•-15	•-16	•-17
	4	4-14	4-15	•-16	•-17	•-18	•-20
	5	6-16	5-17	5-18	•-19	•-20	•-22
	6	7-18	7-19	6-20	6-21	•-22	•-24
	7	9-20	8-21	8-22	7-23	7-24	•-26
	8	11-22	10-23	9-24	9-25	8-26	•-27
	9	13-24	12-25	11-26	10-27	10-28	9-29
	10	15-26	14-27	13-28	12-29	11-30	10-31

N = 42

N_1	x_1	$2\alpha=0.20$	$2\alpha=0.10$	$2\alpha=0.05$	$2\alpha=0.02$	$2\alpha=0.01$	$2\alpha=0.002$
4	0	•-18	•-22	•-25	•-28	•-30	•-34
	1	1-28	•-31	•-34	•-36	•-37	•-39
	2	6-36	4-38	3-39	2-40	–	–
5	0	•-15	•-18	•-21	•-25	•-27	•-30
	1	•-24	•-27	•-30	•-32	•-34	•-36
	2	5-32	3-34	2-36	•-37	•-38	•-39
6	0	•-13	•-16	•-19	•-22	•-24	•-27
	1	•-21	•-24	•-26	•-29	•-30	•-33
	2	4-28	3-30	2-32	•-34	•-35	•-37
	3	8-34	7-35	5-37	4-38	3-39	–
7	0	•-11	•-14	•-16	•-19	•-21	•-25
	1	•-19	•-21	•-23	•-26	•-28	•-31
	2	3-25	2-27	2-29	•-31	•-32	•-35
	3	7-30	6-32	4-34	3-35	3-36	•-38
8	0	•-10	•-12	•-15	•-17	•-19	•-23
	1	•-17	•-19	•-21	•-24	•-25	•-28
	2	3-22	2-25	•-26	•-29	•-30	•-32
	3	6-27	5-29	4-31	3-33	3-34	•-36
	4	10-32	9-33	7-35	6-36	5-37	4-38
9	0	•-9	•-11	•-13	•-16	•-17	•-21
	1	•-15	•-17	•-19	•-22	•-23	•-26
	2	2-20	2-22	•-24	•-26	•-28	•-30
	3	5-25	4-27	3-29	3-30	•-32	•-34
	4	9-29	8-31	6-32	5-34	4-35	•-36
10	0	•-8	•-10	•-12	•-14	•-16	•-19
	1	•-14	•-16	•-18	•-20	•-21	•-24
	2	2-18	•-20	•-22	•-24	•-26	•-28
	3	5-23	4-25	3-26	•-28	•-29	•-32
	4	8-27	7-29	6-30	5-32	4-33	•-34
	5	12-30	10-32	9-33	7-35	7-35	5-37
11	0	•-7	•-9	•-11	•-13	•-15	•-18
	1	•-12	•-14	•-16	•-18	•-20	•-22
	2	2-17	•-19	•-21	•-23	•-24	•-26
	3	4-21	4-23	3-24	•-26	•-27	•-30
	4	7-25	6-26	5-28	4-30	4-31	•-33
	5	10-28	9-30	8-31	7-33	6-34	5-35
12	0	•-7	•-8	•-10	•-12	•-13	•-16
	1	•-11	•-13	•-15	•-17	•-18	•-21
	2	2-15	•-17	•-19	•-21	•-22	•-25
	3	4-19	3-21	3-23	•-25	•-26	•-28
	4	7-23	6-25	5-26	4-28	4-29	•-31
	5	10-26	8-28	7-29	6-31	6-32	5-33
	6	13-29	11-31	10-32	9-33	8-34	6-36
13	0	•-6	•-8	•-9	•-11	•-12	•-15
	1	•-11	•-12	•-14	•-16	•-17	•-20
	2	2-14	•-16	•-18	•-20	•-21	•-23
	3	4-18	3-20	3-21	•-23	•-24	•-26
	4	6-21	5-23	4-24	4-26	•-27	•-29
	5	9-24	8-26	7-27	6-29	5-30	•-32
	6	12-27	10-29	9-30	8-32	7-32	6-34
14	0	•-6	•-7	•-9	•-10	•-12	•-14
	1	•-10	•-11	•-13	•-15	•-16	•-18
	2	•-13	•-15	•-17	•-18	•-19	•-22
	3	4-17	3-18	•-20	•-22	•-23	•-25
	4	6-20	5-22	4-23	4-25	•-26	•-28
	5	8-23	7-24	6-26	5-27	5-28	•-30
	6	11-26	9-27	8-29	7-30	7-31	6-32
	7	13-29	12-30	11-31	10-32	9-33	8-34
15	0	•-5	•-7	•-8	•-10	•-11	•-13
	1	•-9	•-11	•-12	•-14	•-15	•-17

N = 42 (continued)

N_1	x_1	$2\alpha=0.20$	$2\alpha=0.10$	$2\alpha=0.05$	$2\alpha=0.02$	$2\alpha=0.01$	$2\alpha=0.002$
	2	•-12	•-14	•-15	•-17	•-18	•-21
	3	3-16	3-17	•-19	•-20	•-21	•-23
	4	5-19	5-20	4-22	•-23	•-24	•-26
	5	8-21	7-23	6-24	5-26	5-27	•-29
	6	10-24	9-26	8-27	7-28	6-29	6-31
	7	13-27	11-28	10-29	9-31	8-31	7-33
16	0	•-5	•-6	•-7	•-9	•-10	•-12
	1	•-9	•-10	•-11	•-13	•-14	•-16
	2	•-12	•-13	•-15	•-16	•-17	•-19
	3	3-15	3-16	•-18	•-19	•-20	•-22
	4	5-17	4-19	4-20	•-22	•-23	•-25
	5	7-20	6-22	6-23	5-24	•-25	•-27
	6	9-23	8-24	8-26	7-27	6-28	•-29
	7	12-25	11-27	10-28	9-29	8-30	7-31
	8	14-28	13-29	12-30	11-31	10-32	9-33
17	0	•-5	•-6	•-7	•-8	•-9	•-12
	1	•-8	•-9	•-11	•-12	•-13	•-15
	2	•-11	•-12	•-14	•-15	•-16	•-18
	3	3-14	•-15	•-17	•-18	•-19	•-21
	4	5-16	4-18	4-19	•-21	•-22	•-24
	5	7-19	6-21	5-22	5-23	•-24	•-26
	6	9-22	8-23	7-24	6-26	6-26	•-28
	7	11-24	10-25	9-27	8-28	8-29	7-30
	8	13-26	12-28	11-29	10-30	9-31	8-32
18	0	•-4	•-5	•-7	•-8	•-9	•-11
	1	•-8	•-9	•-10	•-11	•-12	•-14
	2	•-10	•-12	•-13	•-14	•-15	•-17
	3	3-13	•-14	•-16	•-17	•-18	•-20
	4	5-16	4-17	•-18	•-20	•-20	•-22
	5	6-18	6-19	5-21	•-22	•-23	•-25
	6	8-20	7-22	7-23	6-24	6-25	•-27
	7	10-23	9-24	9-25	8-26	7-27	•-29
	8	13-25	11-26	11-27	10-29	9-29	8-31
	9	15-27	14-28	13-29	11-31	11-31	10-32
19	0	•-4	•-5	•-6	•-7	•-8	•-10
	1	•-7	•-8	•-9	•-11	•-12	•-14
	2	•-10	•-11	•-12	•-14	•-14	•-16
	3	3-12	•-14	•-15	•-16	•-17	•-19
	4	4-15	4-16	•-17	•-19	•-19	•-21
	5	6-17	5-18	5-20	•-21	•-22	•-23
	6	8-19	7-21	7-22	6-23	•-24	•-26
	7	10-22	9-23	8-24	7-25	7-26	•-27
	8	12-24	11-25	10-26	9-27	9-28	8-29
	9	14-26	13-27	12-28	11-29	10-30	9-31
20	0	•-4	•-5	•-6	•-7	•-8	•-10
	1	•-7	•-8	•-9	•-10	•-11	•-13
	2	•-9	•-10	•-12	•-13	•-14	•-16
	3	3-12	•-13	•-14	•-15	•-16	•-18
	4	4-14	4-15	•-16	•-18	•-18	•-20
	5	6-16	5-18	5-19	•-20	•-21	•-22
	6	8-18	7-20	6-21	6-22	•-23	•-24
	7	9-21	9-22	8-23	7-24	7-25	•-26
	8	11-23	10-24	10-25	9-26	8-27	•-28
	9	13-25	12-26	11-27	10-28	10-29	9-30
	10	15-27	14-28	13-29	12-30	12-30	11-31
21	0	•-4	•-5	•-5	•-7	•-7	•-9
	1	•-6	•-7	•-8	•-10	•-10	•-12
	2	•-9	•-10	•-11	•-12	•-13	•-15
	3	•-11	•-12	•-13	•-15	•-15	•-17
	4	4-13	•-15	•-16	•-17	•-18	•-19
	5	6-15	5-17	5-18	•-19	•-20	•-21
	6	7-18	7-19	6-20	•-21	•-22	•-23
	7	9-20	8-21	8-22	7-23	7-24	•-25
	8	11-22	10-23	9-24	8-25	8-26	•-27
	9	13-24	12-25	11-26	10-27	10-27	9-29
	10	15-26	13-27	13-28	12-29	11-29	10-30

N = 43

N_1	x_1	$2\alpha=0.20$	$2\alpha=0.10$	$2\alpha=0.05$	$2\alpha=0.02$	$2\alpha=0.01$	$2\alpha=0.002$
4	0	•-19	•-22	•-25	•-29	•-31	•-35
	1	1-29	•-32	•-34	•-37	•-38	•-40
	2	6-37	4-39	3-40	2-41	–	–
5	0	•-16	•-19	•-22	•-25	•-27	•-31
	1	•-25	•-28	•-30	•-33	•-34	•-37
	2	5-32	3-35	2-36	•-38	•-39	•-40
6	0	•-13	•-16	•-19	•-22	•-24	•-28
	1	•-22	•-25	•-27	•-30	•-31	•-34
	2	4-28	3-31	2-33	•-35	•-36	•-38
	3	9-34	7-36	5-38	4-39	3-40	–
7	0	•-12	•-14	•-17	•-20	•-22	•-25
	1	•-19	•-22	•-24	•-27	•-28	•-31
	2	3-25	2-28	2-30	•-32	•-33	•-36
	3	7-31	6-33	5-35	3-36	3-37	•-39
8	0	•-10	•-13	•-15	•-18	•-20	•-23
	1	•-17	•-20	•-22	•-24	•-26	•-29
	2	3-23	2-25	•-27	•-29	•-31	•-33
	3	6-28	5-30	4-32	3-34	3-35	•-37
	4	11-32	9-34	7-36	6-37	5-38	4-39
9	0	•-9	•-11	•-14	•-16	•-18	•-21
	1	•-15	•-18	•-20	•-22	•-24	•-27
	2	2-21	2-23	•-25	•-27	•-28	•-31
	3	6-25	4-27	4-29	3-31	•-32	•-34
	4	9-30	8-32	6-33	5-35	5-36	•-37
10	0	•-8	•-10	•-12	•-15	•-16	•-20
	1	•-14	•-16	•-18	•-20	•-22	•-25
	2	2-19	2-21	•-23	•-25	•-26	•-29
	3	5-23	4-25	3-27	3-29	•-30	•-32

N = 43 (continued)

N_1	x_1	$2\alpha=0.20$	$2\alpha=0.10$	$2\alpha=0.05$	$2\alpha=0.02$	$2\alpha=0.01$	$2\alpha=0.002$
	4	8-27	7-29	6-31	5-32	4-33	•-35
	5	12-31	10-33	9-34	7-36	7-36	5-38
11	0	•-8	•-9	•-11	•-13	•-15	•-18
	1	•-13	•-15	•-17	•-19	•-20	•-23
	2	2-17	•-19	•-21	•-23	•-24	•-27
	3	5-21	4-23	3-25	•-27	•-28	•-30
	4	8-25	6-27	5-29	4-30	4-31	•-33
	5	11-29	9-31	8-32	7-33	6-34	5-36
12	0	•-7	•-9	•-10	•-12	•-14	•-17
	1	•-12	•-14	•-15	•-17	•-19	•-22
	2	2-16	•-18	•-20	•-21	•-23	•-25
	3	4-20	3-22	3-23	•-25	•-26	•-29
	4	7-23	6-25	5-27	4-28	4-30	•-32
	5	10-27	8-29	7-30	6-31	6-32	5-34
	6	13-30	11-32	10-33	9-34	8-35	7-36
13	0	•-6	•-8	•-10	•-11	•-13	•-16
	1	•-11	•-13	•-14	•-16	•-17	•-20
	2	2-15	•-17	•-18	•-20	•-21	•-24
	3	4-18	3-20	3-22	•-24	•-25	•-27
	4	6-22	5-24	5-25	4-27	•-28	•-30
	5	9-25	8-27	7-28	6-30	5-31	•-32
	6	12-28	10-30	9-31	8-32	7-33	6-35
14	0	•-6	•-7	•-9	•-11	•-12	•-14
	1	•-10	•-12	•-13	•-15	•-16	•-19
	2	•-14	•-15	•-17	•-19	•-20	•-22
	3	4-17	3-19	•-20	•-22	•-23	•-26
	4	6-20	5-22	4-24	4-25	•-26	•-28
	5	8-23	7-25	6-26	5-28	5-29	•-31
	6	11-26	10-28	9-29	8-31	7-32	6-33
	7	14-29	12-31	11-32	10-33	9-34	8-35
15	0	•-6	•-7	•-8	•-10	•-11	•-14
	1	•-9	•-11	•-12	•-14	•-15	•-18
	2	•-13	•-14	•-16	•-18	•-19	•-21
	3	3-16	3-18	•-19	•-21	•-22	•-24
	4	6-19	5-21	4-22	•-24	•-25	•-27
	5	8-22	7-24	6-25	5-26	5-27	•-29
	6	10-25	9-26	8-28	7-29	7-30	6-32
	7	13-28	11-29	10-30	9-31	9-32	7-34
16	0	•-5	•-6	•-8	•-9	•-10	•-13
	1	•-9	•-10	•-12	•-13	•-14	•-17
	2	•-12	•-14	•-15	•-17	•-18	•-20
	3	3-15	3-17	•-18	•-20	•-21	•-23
	4	5-18	4-20	4-21	•-22	•-23	•-25
	5	7-21	6-22	6-24	5-25	5-26	•-28
	6	10-23	9-25	8-26	7-28	6-28	•-30
	7	12-26	11-27	10-29	9-30	8-31	7-32
	8	14-29	13-30	12-31	11-32	10-33	9-34
17	0	•-5	•-6	•-7	•-9	•-10	•-12
	1	•-8	•-10	•-11	•-12	•-13	•-16
	2	•-11	•-13	•-14	•-16	•-17	•-19
	3	3-14	•-16	•-17	•-18	•-20	•-22
	4	5-17	4-18	4-20	•-21	•-22	•-24
	5	7-20	6-21	5-22	5-24	•-25	•-27
	6	9-22	8-24	7-25	6-26	6-27	•-29
	7	11-25	10-26	9-27	8-28	8-29	7-31
	8	14-27	12-28	11-29	10-31	10-31	8-33
18	0	•-5	•-6	•-7	•-8	•-9	•-11
	1	•-8	•-9	•-10	•-12	•-13	•-15
	2	•-11	•-12	•-13	•-15	•-16	•-18
	3	3-13	•-15	•-16	•-17	•-18	•-20
	4	5-16	4-17	4-19	•-20	•-21	•-23
	5	7-19	6-20	5-21	5-23	•-23	•-25
	6	9-21	8-22	7-24	6-25	6-26	•-27
	7	11-23	10-25	9-26	8-27	7-28	7-30
	8	13-26	12-27	11-28	10-29	9-30	8-31
	9	15-28	14-29	13-30	12-31	11-32	10-33
19	0	•-4	•-5	•-6	•-8	•-9	•-11
	1	•-7	•-9	•-10	•-11	•-12	•-14
	2	•-10	•-11	•-13	•-14	•-15	•-17
	3	3-13	•-14	•-15	•-17	•-18	•-19
	4	4-15	4-17	•-18	•-19	•-20	•-22
	5	6-18	5-19	5-20	•-21	•-22	•-24
	6	8-20	7-21	7-22	6-24	6-25	•-26
	7	10-22	9-24	8-25	8-26	7-27	•-28
	8	12-24	11-26	10-27	9-28	9-29	8-30
	9	14-27	13-28	12-29	11-30	11-31	9-32
20	0	•-4	•-5	•-6	•-7	•-8	•-10
	1	•-7	•-8	•-9	•-10	•-11	•-13
	2	•-10	•-11	•-12	•-13	•-14	•-16
	3	3-12	•-13	•-14	•-16	•-17	•-18
	4	4-14	4-16	•-17	•-18	•-19	•-21
	5	6-17	5-18	5-19	•-20	•-21	•-23
	6	8-19	7-20	6-21	6-23	•-23	•-25
	7	10-21	9-22	8-23	7-25	7-25	•-27
	8	12-23	11-25	10-26	9-27	8-27	8-29
	9	14-25	12-27	12-28	11-29	10-29	9-31
	10	16-27	14-29	13-30	12-31	12-31	11-32
21	0	•-4	•-5	•-6	•-7	•-8	•-9
	1	•-7	•-8	•-9	•-10	•-11	•-13
	2	•-9	•-10	•-11	•-12	•-13	•-15
	3	•-11	•-13	•-14	•-15	•-16	•-18
	4	4-14	4-15	•-16	•-17	•-18	•-20
	5	6-16	5-17	5-18	•-19	•-20	•-22
	6	7-18	7-19	6-20	6-22	•-22	•-24
	7	9-20	8-21	8-22	7-24	7-24	•-26
	8	11-22	10-23	9-24	9-26	8-26	•-28
	9	13-24	12-25	11-26	10-27	10-28	9-29
	10	15-26	14-27	13-28	12-29	11-30	10-31

$$\begin{array}{cc|c} x_1 & N_1-x_1 & N_1 \\ x_2 & N_2-x_2 & N_2 \\ \hline X & N-X & N \end{array} \left.\right\} \quad \begin{array}{l} N=N_1+N_2 \\ X=x_1+x_2 \\ N_1 \leq N_2 \\ x_1 \leq N_1-x_1 \end{array} \left.\right\}$$

For explanation see page 123

N_1	x_1	$2\alpha=$ 0.20	$2\alpha=$ 0.10	$2\alpha=$ 0.05	$2\alpha=$ 0.02	$2\alpha=$ 0.01	$2\alpha=$ 0.002
				$N=44$			
4	0	•–19	•–23	•–26	•–30	•–32	•–35
	1	1–30	•–33	•–35	•–37	•–39	•–41
	2	6–38	4–40	3–41	2–42	–	–
5	0	•–16	•–19	•–22	•–26	•–28	•–32
	1	•–25	•–29	•–31	•–34	•–35	•–38
	2	5–33	3–36	2–37	•–39	•–40	•–41
6	0	•–14	•–17	•–20	•–23	•–25	•–29
	1	•–22	•–25	•–28	•–30	•–32	•–35
	2	4–29	3–32	2–34	•–36	•–37	•–39
	3	9–35	7–37	5–39	4–40	3–41	–
7	0	•–12	•–15	•–17	•–20	•–22	•–26
	1	•–20	•–22	•–25	•–27	•–29	•–32
	2	3–26	2–28	2–31	•–33	•–34	•–36
	3	7–32	6–34	5–35	4–37	3–38	•–40
8	0	•–11	•–13	•–15	•–18	•–20	•–24
	1	•–17	•–20	•–22	•–25	•–26	•–30
	2	3–23	2–26	•–28	•–30	•–31	•–34
	3	6–28	5–31	4–32	3–34	3–35	•–37
	4	11–33	9–35	7–37	6–38	5–39	4–40
9	0	•– 9	•–12	•–14	•–16	•–18	•–22
	1	•–16	•–18	•–20	•–23	•–24	•–27
	2	2–21	2–23	•–25	•–28	•–29	•–32
	3	6–26	4–28	4–30	3–32	•–33	•–35
	4	9–30	8–32	7–34	5–36	5–36	4–38
10	0	•– 9	•–11	•–13	•–15	•–17	•–20
	1	•–14	•–16	•–18	•–21	•–22	•–25
	2	2–19	2–21	•–23	•–26	•–27	•–30
	3	5–24	4–26	3–28	3–30	•–31	•–33
	4	8–28	7–30	6–32	5–33	4–34	•–36
	5	12–32	10–34	9–35	8–36	7–37	5–39
11	0	•– 8	•–10	•–12	•–14	•–15	•–19
	1	•–13	•–15	•–17	•–19	•–21	•–24
	2	2–18	•–20	•–22	•–24	•–25	•–28
	3	5–22	4–24	3–26	•–28	•–29	•–31
	4	8–26	6–28	5–29	4–31	4–32	•–34
	5	11–30	9–31	8–33	7–34	6–35	5–37
12	0	•– 7	•– 9	•–11	•–13	•–14	•–17
	1	•–12	•–14	•–16	•–18	•–19	•–22
	2	2–16	•–18	•–20	•–22	•–23	•–26
	3	4–20	3–22	3–24	•–26	•–27	•–29
	4	7–24	6–26	5–27	4–29	4–30	•–32
	5	10–27	9–29	8–31	6–32	6–33	5–35
	6	13–31	12–32	10–34	9–35	8–36	7–37
13	0	•– 7	•– 8	•–10	•–12	•–13	•–16
	1	•–11	•–13	•–15	•–17	•–18	•–21
	2	2–15	•–17	•–19	•–21	•–22	•–24
	3	4–19	3–21	3–22	•–24	•–25	•–28
	4	6–22	5–24	5–26	4–27	•–29	•–31
	5	9–26	8–27	7–29	6–30	5–31	•–33
	6	12–29	11–30	9–32	8–33	8–34	6–36
14	0	•– 6	•– 8	•– 9	•–11	•–12	•–15
	1	•–10	•–12	•–14	•–15	•–17	•–19
	2	2–14	•–16	•–17	•–19	•–20	•–23
	3	4–18	3–19	•–21	•–23	•–24	•–26
	4	6–21	5–23	4–24	4–26	•–27	•–29
	5	9–24	7–26	6–27	6–29	5–30	•–32
	6	11–27	10–29	9–30	8–31	7–32	6–34
	7	14–30	13–31	11–33	10–34	9–35	8–36
15	0	•– 6	•– 7	•– 8	•–10	•–11	•–14
	1	•–10	•–11	•–13	•–14	•–16	•–18
	2	•–13	•–15	•–16	•–18	•–19	•–22
	3	3–16	3–18	•–20	•–21	•–22	•–25
	4	6–20	5–21	4–23	•–24	•–25	•–28
	5	8–23	7–24	6–26	5–27	5–28	•–30
	6	10–25	9–27	8–28	7–30	7–31	6–32
	7	13–28	12–30	11–31	9–32	9–33	7–35
16	0	•– 5	•– 7	•– 8	•– 9	•–11	•–13
	1	•– 9	•–10	•–12	•–14	•–15	•–17
	2	•–12	•–14	•–15	•–17	•–18	•–20
	3	3–15	3–17	•–18	•–20	•–21	•–23
	4	5–18	4–20	4–21	•–23	•–24	•–26
	5	8–21	7–23	6–24	5–26	5–27	•–29
	6	10–24	9–26	8–27	7–28	6–29	•–31
	7	12–27	11–28	10–29	9–31	8–32	7–33
	8	15–29	13–31	12–32	11–33	10–34	9–35
17	0	•– 5	•– 6	•– 7	•– 9	•–10	•–12
	1	•– 8	•–10	•–11	•–13	•–14	•–16
	2	•–12	•–13	•–14	•–16	•–17	•–19
	3	3–15	•–16	•–17	•–19	•–20	•–22
	4	5–17	4–19	4–20	•–22	•–23	•–25
	5	7–20	6–22	5–23	5–24	•–25	•–27
	6	9–23	8–24	7–25	7–27	6–28	•–30
	7	12–25	10–27	9–28	8–29	8–30	7–32
	8	14–28	13–29	12–30	10–31	10–32	9–34
18	0	•– 5	•– 6	•– 7	•– 8	•– 9	•–12
	1	•– 8	•– 9	•–10	•–12	•–13	•–15
	2	•–11	•–12	•–14	•–15	•–16	•–18
	3	3–14	•–15	•–16	•–18	•–19	•–21
	4	5–16	4–18	4–19	•–21	•–22	•–24
	5	7–19	6–20	5–22	5–23	•–24	•–26
	6	9–21	8–23	7–24	6–26	6–26	•–28
	7	11–24	10–25	9–27	8–28	8–29	7–30
	8	13–26	12–28	11–29	10–30	9–31	8–32
	9	15–29	14–30	13–31	12–32	11–33	10–34
19	0	•– 4	•– 5	•– 7	•– 8	•– 9	•–11
	1	•– 8	•– 9	•–10	•–11	•–12	•–14
				$N=44$ (continued)			
	2	•–10	•–12	•–13	•–14	•–15	•–17
	3	3–13	•–14	•–16	•–17	•–18	•–20
	4	5–16	4–17	•–18	•–20	•–21	•–22
	5	6–18	6–19	5–21	•–22	•–23	•–25
	6	8–20	7–22	7–23	6–24	6–25	•–27
	7	10–23	9–24	9–25	8–27	7–27	•–29
	8	12–25	11–26	10–27	9–29	9–29	8–31
	9	15–27	13–29	12–30	11–31	11–31	10–33
20	0	•– 4	•– 5	•– 6	•– 7	•– 8	•–10
	1	•– 7	•– 8	•– 9	•–11	•–12	•–14
	2	•–10	•–11	•–12	•–14	•–14	•–16
	3	3–12	•–14	•–15	•–16	•–17	•–19
	4	4–15	4–16	•–17	•–19	•–20	•–21
	5	6–17	5–18	5–20	•–21	•–22	•–24
	6	8–19	7–21	6–22	6–23	•–24	•–26
	7	10–22	9–23	8–24	7–25	7–26	•–28
	8	12–24	11–25	10–26	9–27	9–28	8–30
	9	14–26	13–27	12–28	11–29	10–30	9–31
	10	16–28	15–29	14–30	13–31	12–32	11–33
21	0	•– 4	•– 5	•– 6	•– 7	•– 8	•–10
	1	•– 7	•– 8	•– 9	•–10	•–11	•–13
	2	•– 9	•–10	•–12	•–13	•–14	•–16
	3	•–12	•–13	•–14	•–15	•–16	•–18
	4	4–14	4–15	•–16	•–18	•–19	•–20
	5	6–16	5–18	5–19	•–20	•–21	•–23
	6	8–18	7–20	6–21	6–22	•–23	•–25
	7	9–21	9–22	8–23	7–24	7–25	•–27
	8	11–23	10–24	10–25	9–26	8–27	•–28
	9	13–25	12–26	11–27	10–28	10–29	9–30
	10	15–27	14–28	13–29	12–30	12–31	10–32
22	0	•– 4	•– 5	•– 5	•– 7	•– 7	•– 9
	1	•– 6	•– 7	•– 8	•–10	•–10	•–12
	2	•– 9	•–10	•–11	•–12	•–13	•–15
	3	•–11	•–12	•–13	•–15	•–15	•–17
	4	4–13	•–15	•–16	•–17	•–18	•–19
	5	6–16	5–17	5–18	•–19	•–20	•–22
	6	7–18	7–19	6–20	•–21	•–22	•–24
	7	9–20	8–21	8–22	7–23	7–24	•–25
	8	11–22	10–23	9–24	8–25	8–26	•–27
	9	13–24	12–25	11–26	10–27	10–28	9–29
	10	14–26	13–27	13–28	12–29	11–29	10–31
	11	16–28	15–29	14–30	13–31	13–31	12–32
				$N=45$			
4	0	•–20	•–23	•–27	•–30	•–32	•–36
	1	1–31	•–34	•–36	•–38	•–40	•–42
	2	6–39	4–41	3–42	2–43	–	–
5	0	•–16	•–20	•–23	•–26	•–29	•–33
	1	•–26	•–29	•–32	•–34	•–36	•–39
	2	5–34	3–36	2–38	•–40	•–41	•–42
6	0	•–14	•–17	•–20	•–23	•–25	•–29
	1	•–23	•–26	•–28	•–31	•–33	•–36
	2	4–30	3–32	2–34	•–37	•–38	•–40
	3	9–36	7–38	6–39	4–41	3–42	–
7	0	•–12	•–15	•–18	•–21	•–23	•–27
	1	•–20	•–23	•–25	•–28	•–30	•–33
	2	3–26	2–29	2–31	•–33	•–35	•–37
	3	8–32	6–34	5–36	4–38	3–39	•–41
8	0	•–11	•–13	•–16	•–19	•–21	•–24
	1	•–18	•–20	•–23	•–25	•–27	•–30
	2	3–24	2–26	•–28	•–31	•–32	•–35
	3	7–29	5–31	4–33	3–35	3–36	•–38
	4	11–34	9–36	8–37	6–39	5–40	4–41
9	0	•–10	•–12	•–14	•–17	•–19	•–22
	1	•–16	•–19	•–21	•–23	•–25	•–28
	2	3–22	2–24	•–26	•–28	•–30	•–33
	3	6–27	5–29	4–31	3–33	•–34	•–36
	4	10–31	8–33	7–35	5–36	5–37	4–39
10	0	•– 9	•–11	•–13	•–15	•–17	•–21
	1	•–15	•–17	•–19	•–21	•–23	•–26
	2	2–20	2–22	•–24	•–26	•–28	•–30
	3	5–24	4–26	3–28	3–30	•–32	•–34
	4	9–29	7–31	6–32	5–34	4–35	•–37
	5	12–33	11–34	9–36	8–37	7–38	5–40
11	0	•– 8	•–10	•–12	•–14	•–16	•–19
	1	•–13	•–15	•–17	•–20	•–21	•–24
	2	2–18	•–20	•–22	•–24	•–26	•–28
	3	5–22	4–24	3–26	•–28	•–30	•–32
	4	8–26	7–28	6–30	5–32	4–33	•–35
	5	11–30	10–32	8–34	7–35	6–36	5–38
12	0	•– 7	•– 9	•–11	•–13	•–14	•–18
	1	•–12	•–14	•–16	•–18	•–20	•–23
	2	2–17	•–19	•–20	•–23	•–24	•–27
	3	4–21	3–23	3–24	•–26	•–28	•–30
	4	7–24	6–26	5–28	4–30	4–31	•–33
	5	10–28	9–30	8–31	7–33	6–34	5–36
	6	13–32	12–33	10–35	9–36	8–37	7–38
13	0	•– 7	•– 8	•–10	•–12	•–13	•–16
	1	•–11	•–13	•–15	•–17	•–18	•–21
	2	2–15	•–17	•–19	•–21	•–22	•–25
	3	4–19	3–21	3–23	•–25	•–26	•–28
	4	7–23	6–25	5–26	4–28	4–29	•–31
	5	9–26	8–28	7–30	6–31	5–32	•–34
	6	12–29	11–31	10–33	8–34	8–35	6–37
14	0	•– 6	•– 8	•– 9	•–11	•–12	•–15
	1	•–11	•–12	•–14	•–16	•–17	•–20
				$N=45$ (continued)			
	2	2–14	•–16	•–18	•–20	•–21	•–24
	3	4–18	3–20	•–21	•–23	•–24	•–27
	4	6–21	5–23	4–25	4–26	•–28	•–30
	5	9–25	8–26	7–28	6–29	5–30	•–32
	6	11–28	10–29	9–31	8–32	7–33	6–35
	7	14–31	13–32	12–33	10–35	9–36	8–37
15	0	•– 6	•– 7	•– 9	•–10	•–12	•–14
	1	•–10	•–11	•–13	•–15	•–16	•–19
	2	•–13	•–15	•–17	•–18	•–20	•–22
	3	3–17	3–19	•–20	•–22	•–23	•–25
	4	6–20	5–22	4–23	4–25	•–26	•–28
	5	8–23	7–25	6–26	5–28	5–29	•–31
	6	11–26	9–28	8–29	7–30	7–31	6–33
	7	13–29	12–30	11–32	10–33	9–34	8–35
16	0	•– 5	•– 7	•– 8	•–10	•–11	•–13
	1	•– 9	•–11	•–12	•–14	•–15	•–18
	2	•–13	•–14	•–16	•–17	•–19	•–21
	3	3–16	3–17	•–19	•–21	•–22	•–24
	4	5–19	5–20	4–22	•–24	•–25	•–27
	5	8–22	7–23	6–25	5–26	5–27	•–29
	6	10–25	9–26	8–27	7–29	6–30	6–32
	7	13–27	11–29	10–30	9–31	8–32	7–34
	8	15–30	14–31	12–33	11–34	10–35	9–36
17	0	•– 5	•– 6	•– 8	•– 9	•–10	•–13
	1	•– 9	•–10	•–11	•–13	•–14	•–17
	2	•–12	•–13	•–15	•–16	•–18	•–20
	3	3–15	3–16	•–18	•–19	•–21	•–23
	4	5–18	4–19	4–21	•–22	•–23	•–25
	5	7–21	6–22	6–23	5–25	•–26	•–28
	6	9–23	8–25	8–26	7–28	6–28	•–30
	7	12–26	11–27	10–29	9–30	8–31	7–32
	8	14–28	13–30	12–31	11–32	10–33	9–34
18	0	•– 5	•– 6	•– 7	•– 9	•–10	•–12
	1	•– 8	•–10	•–11	•–12	•–13	•–16
	2	•–11	•–13	•–14	•–15	•–17	•–19
	3	3–14	•–16	•–17	•–18	•–19	•–22
	4	5–17	4–18	4–20	•–21	•–22	•–24
	5	7–19	6–21	5–22	5–24	•–25	•–27
	6	9–22	8–23	7–25	6–26	6–27	•–29
	7	11–25	10–26	9–27	8–29	8–29	7–31
	8	13–27	12–28	11–29	10–31	9–32	8–33
	9	16–29	14–31	13–32	12–33	11–34	10–35
19	0	•– 5	•– 6	•– 7	•– 8	•– 9	•–11
	1	•– 8	•– 9	•–10	•–12	•–13	•–15
	2	•–11	•–12	•–13	•–15	•–16	•–18
	3	3–13	•–15	•–16	•–17	•–18	•–21
	4	5–16	4–17	•–19	•–20	•–21	•–23
	5	7–18	6–20	5–21	5–23	•–24	•–25
	6	8–21	8–22	7–24	6–25	6–26	•–28
	7	11–23	10–25	9–26	8–27	7–28	•–30
	8	13–26	12–27	11–28	10–29	9–30	8–32
	9	15–28	14–29	13–30	12–31	11–32	10–34
20	0	•– 4	•– 5	•– 6	•– 8	•– 9	•–11
	1	•– 7	•– 8	•–10	•–11	•–12	•–14
	2	•–10	•–11	•–12	•–14	•–15	•–17
	3	3–13	•–14	•–15	•–17	•–18	•–20
	4	4–15	4–16	•–18	•–19	•–20	•–22
	5	6–18	5–19	5–20	•–21	•–22	•–24
	6	8–20	7–21	7–22	6–24	6–25	•–26
	7	10–22	9–24	8–25	8–26	7–27	•–28
	8	12–24	11–26	10–27	9–28	9–29	8–30
	9	14–27	13–28	12–29	11–30	10–31	9–32
	10	16–29	15–30	14–31	13–32	12–33	11–34
21	0	•– 4	•– 5	•– 6	•– 7	•– 8	•–10
	1	•– 7	•– 8	•– 9	•–10	•–11	•–13
	2	•–10	•–11	•–12	•–13	•–14	•–16
	3	3–12	•–13	•–14	•–16	•–17	•–19
	4	4–14	4–16	•–17	•–18	•–19	•–21
	5	6–17	5–18	5–19	•–20	•–21	•–23
	6	8–19	7–20	6–21	6–23	•–24	•–25
	7	10–21	9–22	8–24	7–25	7–26	•–27
	8	12–23	11–25	10–26	9–27	8–28	8–29
	9	13–25	12–27	12–28	11–29	10–30	9–31
	10	15–28	14–29	13–30	12–31	12–31	11–33
22	0	•– 4	•– 5	•– 6	•– 7	•– 8	•– 9
	1	•– 7	•– 8	•– 9	•–10	•–11	•–13
	2	•– 9	•–10	•–11	•–13	•–13	•–15
	3	•–11	•–13	•–14	•–15	•–16	•–18
	4	4–14	4–15	•–16	•–17	•–18	•–20
	5	6–16	5–17	5–18	•–20	•–20	•–22
	6	7–18	7–19	6–20	6–22	•–23	•–24
	7	9–20	8–21	8–23	7–24	7–25	•–26
	8	11–22	10–24	9–25	9–26	8–27	•–28
	9	13–24	12–26	11–27	10–28	10–28	9–30
	10	15–26	14–27	13–28	12–30	11–30	10–32
	11	17–28	16–29	15–30	14–31	13–32	12–33
				$N=46$			
4	0	•–20	•–24	•–27	•–31	•–33	•–37
	1	1–31	•–34	•–37	•–39	•–40	•–43
	2	6–40	4–42	3–43	2–44	–	–
5	0	•–17	•–20	•–23	•–27	•–29	•–33
	1	•–27	•–30	•–32	•–35	•–37	•–40
	2	5–35	3–37	2–39	2–41	•–42	•–43
6	0	•–14	•–18	•–20	•–24	•–26	•–30
	1	•–23	•–26	•–29	•–32	•–33	•–36
	2	4–30	3–33	2–35	•–37	•–39	•–41

x_1	$N_1 - x_1$	N_1
x_2	$N_2 - x_2$	N_2
X	$N - X$	N

$N = N_1 + N_2$, $X = x_1 + x_2$, $N_1 \leq N_2$, $x_1 \leq N_1 - x_1$

For explanation see page 123

N = 46 (continued)

N_1	x_1	2α = 0.20	2α = 0.10	2α = 0.05	2α = 0.02	2α = 0.01	2α = 0.002
	3	9-37	7-39	6-40	4-42	4-42	–
7	0	•-13	•-15	•-18	•-21	•-23	•-27
	1	•-20	•-23	•-26	•-29	•-30	•-34
	2	3-27	2-30	2-32	•-34	•-36	•-38
	3	8-33	6-35	5-37	4-39	3-40	•-42
8	0	•-11	•-14	•-16	•-19	•-21	•-25
	1	•-18	•-21	•-23	•-26	•-28	•-31
	2	3-24	2-27	•-29	•-31	•-33	•-36
	3	7-30	5-32	4-34	3-36	3-37	•-39
	4	11-35	9-37	8-38	6-40	5-41	4-42
9	0	•-10	•-12	•-15	•-17	•-19	•-23
	1	•-16	•-19	•-21	•-24	•-25	•-29
	2	3-22	2-25	•-27	•-29	•-30	•-33
	3	6-27	5-29	4-31	3-33	•-35	•-37
	4	10-32	8-34	7-35	6-37	5-38	4-40
10	0	•-9	•-11	•-13	•-16	•-17	•-21
	1	•-15	•-17	•-19	•-22	•-23	•-27
	2	2-20	2-22	•-24	•-27	•-28	•-31
	3	5-25	4-27	3-29	3-31	•-32	•-35
	4	9-29	7-31	6-33	5-35	4-36	•-38
	5	13-33	11-35	9-37	8-38	7-39	6-40
11	0	•-8	•-10	•-12	•-14	•-16	•-19
	1	•-14	•-16	•-18	•-20	•-22	•-25
	2	2-18	•-21	•-23	•-25	•-26	•-29
	3	5-23	4-25	3-27	•-29	•-30	•-33
	4	8-27	7-29	6-31	5-33	4-34	•-36
	5	11-31	10-33	9-34	7-36	6-37	5-39
12	0	•-8	•-9	•-11	•-13	•-15	•-18
	1	•-13	•-15	•-16	•-19	•-20	•-23
	2	2-17	•-19	•-21	•-23	•-25	•-27
	3	4-21	4-23	3-25	•-27	•-28	•-31
	4	7-25	6-27	5-29	4-31	4-32	•-34
	5	10-29	9-31	8-32	7-34	6-35	5-37
	6	14-32	12-34	11-35	9-37	8-38	7-39
13	0	•-7	•-9	•-10	•-12	•-14	•-17
	1	•-12	•-14	•-15	•-17	•-19	•-22
	2	2-16	•-18	•-20	•-22	•-23	•-26
	3	4-20	3-22	3-23	•-25	•-27	•-29
	4	7-23	6-25	5-27	4-29	4-30	•-32
	5	10-27	8-29	7-30	6-32	6-33	5-35
	6	13-30	11-32	10-33	9-35	8-36	6-37
14	0	•-6	•-8	•-10	•-11	•-13	•-16
	1	•-11	•-13	•-14	•-16	•-18	•-20
	2	2-15	•-17	•-18	•-20	•-22	•-24
	3	4-18	3-20	3-22	•-24	•-25	•-27
	4	6-22	5-24	5-25	4-27	•-28	•-30
	5	9-25	8-27	7-28	6-30	5-31	•-33
	6	12-28	10-30	9-31	8-33	7-34	6-36
	7	15-31	13-33	12-34	10-36	10-36	8-38
15	0	•-6	•-7	•-9	•-11	•-12	•-15
	1	•-10	•-12	•-13	•-15	•-16	•-19
	2	•-14	•-16	•-17	•-19	•-20	•-23
	3	4-17	3-19	•-21	•-22	•-24	•-26
	4	6-20	5-22	4-24	4-26	•-27	•-29
	5	8-24	7-25	6-27	5-28	5-30	•-32
	6	11-27	10-28	9-30	8-31	7-32	6-34
	7	14-30	12-31	11-32	10-34	9-35	8-36
16	0	•-6	•-7	•-8	•-10	•-11	•-14
	1	•-9	•-11	•-12	•-14	•-15	•-18
	2	•-13	•-15	•-16	•-18	•-19	•-22
	3	3-16	3-18	•-19	•-21	•-22	•-25
	4	6-19	5-21	4-22	•-24	•-25	•-27
	5	8-22	7-24	6-25	5-27	5-28	•-30
	6	10-25	9-27	8-28	7-30	7-31	6-32
	7	13-28	11-29	10-31	9-32	9-33	7-35
	8	15-31	14-32	13-33	11-35	11-35	9-37
17	0	•-5	•-7	•-8	•-9	•-10	•-13
	1	•-9	•-10	•-12	•-13	•-15	•-17
	2	•-12	•-14	•-15	•-17	•-18	•-20
	3	3-15	3-17	•-18	•-20	•-21	•-23
	4	5-18	4-20	4-21	•-23	•-24	•-26
	5	7-21	6-23	6-24	5-26	5-27	•-29
	6	10-24	9-25	8-27	7-28	6-29	•-31
	7	12-26	11-28	10-29	9-31	8-32	7-33
	8	14-29	13-30	12-32	11-33	10-34	9-35
18	0	•-5	•-6	•-7	•-9	•-10	•-12
	1	•-8	•-10	•-11	•-13	•-14	•-16
	2	•-11	•-13	•-14	•-16	•-17	•-19
	3	3-14	•-16	•-17	•-19	•-20	•-22
	4	5-17	4-19	4-20	•-22	•-23	•-25
	5	7-20	6-21	5-23	5-24	•-25	•-27
	6	9-23	8-24	7-25	6-27	6-28	•-30
	7	11-25	10-27	9-28	8-29	8-30	7-32
	8	14-28	12-29	11-30	10-31	10-32	8-34
	9	16-30	15-31	14-32	12-34	12-34	10-36
19	0	•-5	•-6	•-7	•-8	•-9	•-11
	1	•-8	•-9	•-10	•-12	•-13	•-15
	2	•-11	•-12	•-14	•-15	•-16	•-18
	3	3-14	•-15	•-16	•-18	•-19	•-21
	4	5-16	4-18	4-19	•-21	•-22	•-24
	5	7-19	6-20	5-22	5-23	•-24	•-26
	6	9-21	8-23	7-24	6-26	6-26	•-28
	7	11-24	10-25	9-26	8-28	7-29	7-30
	8	13-26	12-28	11-29	10-30	9-31	8-32
	9	15-29	14-30	13-31	12-32	11-33	10-34
20	0	•-4	•-5	•-6	•-8	•-9	•-11

N = 46 (continued)

N_1	x_1	2α = 0.20	2α = 0.10	2α = 0.05	2α = 0.02	2α = 0.01	2α = 0.002
	1	•-7	•-9	•-10	•-11	•-12	•-14
	2	•-10	•-12	•-13	•-14	•-15	•-17
	3	3-13	•-14	•-16	•-17	•-18	•-20
	4	4-15	4-17	•-18	•-20	•-21	•-23
	5	6-18	6-19	5-21	•-22	•-23	•-25
	6	8-20	7-22	7-23	6-24	6-25	•-27
	7	10-23	9-24	8-25	8-27	7-27	•-29
	8	12-25	11-26	10-27	9-29	9-30	8-31
	9	14-27	13-29	12-30	11-31	11-32	9-33
	10	17-29	15-31	14-32	13-33	12-34	11-35
21	0	•-4	•-5	•-6	•-7	•-8	•-10
	1	•-7	•-8	•-9	•-11	•-12	•-14
	2	•-10	•-11	•-12	•-14	•-15	•-17
	3	3-12	•-14	•-15	•-16	•-17	•-19
	4	4-15	4-16	•-17	•-19	•-20	•-22
	5	6-17	5-18	5-20	•-21	•-22	•-24
	6	8-19	7-21	6-22	6-23	•-24	•-26
	7	10-22	9-23	8-24	7-25	7-26	•-28
	8	12-24	11-25	10-26	9-28	9-28	8-30
	9	14-26	13-27	12-28	11-30	10-30	9-32
	10	16-28	15-29	14-30	13-32	12-32	11-34
22	0	•-4	•-5	•-6	•-7	•-8	•-10
	1	•-7	•-8	•-9	•-10	•-11	•-13
	2	•-9	•-10	•-12	•-13	•-14	•-16
	3	•-12	•-13	•-14	•-15	•-16	•-18
	4	4-14	4-15	•-16	•-18	•-19	•-21
	5	6-16	5-18	5-19	•-20	•-21	•-23
	6	8-19	7-20	6-21	6-22	•-23	•-25
	7	9-21	8-22	8-23	7-24	7-25	•-27
	8	11-23	10-24	10-25	9-26	8-27	•-29
	9	13-25	12-26	11-27	10-28	10-29	9-31
	10	15-27	14-28	13-29	12-30	11-31	10-32
	11	17-29	16-30	15-31	14-32	13-33	12-34
23	0	•-4	•-5	•-5	•-7	•-7	•-9
	1	•-6	•-7	•-8	•-10	•-10	•-12
	2	•-9	•-10	•-11	•-12	•-13	•-15
	3	•-11	•-12	•-13	•-15	•-16	•-17
	4	4-13	•-15	•-16	•-17	•-18	•-20
	5	6-16	5-17	5-18	•-19	•-20	•-22
	6	7-18	7-19	6-20	•-21	•-22	•-24
	7	9-20	8-21	8-22	7-23	7-24	•-26
	8	11-22	10-23	9-24	8-25	8-26	•-28
	9	13-24	12-25	11-26	10-27	10-28	9-29
	10	14-26	13-27	13-28	12-29	11-30	10-31
	11	16-28	15-29	14-30	13-31	13-32	12-33

N = 47

N_1	x_1	2α = 0.20	2α = 0.10	2α = 0.05	2α = 0.02	2α = 0.01	2α = 0.002
4	0	•-20	•-24	•-28	•-32	•-34	•-38
	1	1-32	•-35	•-38	•-40	•-41	•-43
	2	7-40	4-43	3-44	2-45	–	–
5	0	•-17	•-21	•-24	•-28	•-30	•-34
	1	•-27	•-31	•-33	•-36	•-38	•-40
	2	5-35	3-38	2-40	2-42	•-43	•-44
6	0	•-15	•-18	•-21	•-24	•-27	•-31
	1	•-24	•-27	•-29	•-32	•-34	•-37
	2	4-31	3-34	2-36	•-38	•-40	•-42
	3	9-38	7-40	6-41	4-43	4-43	–
7	0	•-13	•-16	•-18	•-22	•-24	•-28
	1	•-21	•-24	•-26	•-29	•-31	•-34
	2	4-28	2-30	2-33	•-35	•-36	•-39
	3	8-34	6-36	5-38	4-40	3-41	•-42
8	0	•-11	•-14	•-17	•-19	•-21	•-26
	1	•-19	•-21	•-24	•-27	•-28	•-32
	2	3-25	2-28	•-30	•-32	•-34	•-36
	3	7-30	5-33	4-35	3-37	3-38	•-40
	4	11-36	9-38	8-39	6-41	5-42	4-43
9	0	•-10	•-13	•-15	•-18	•-20	•-23
	1	•-17	•-19	•-22	•-24	•-26	•-29
	2	3-23	2-25	•-27	•-30	•-31	•-34
	3	6-28	5-30	4-32	3-34	•-35	•-38
	4	10-32	8-35	7-36	6-38	5-39	4-41
10	0	•-9	•-11	•-14	•-16	•-18	•-22
	1	•-15	•-18	•-20	•-22	•-24	•-27
	2	2-21	2-23	•-25	•-27	•-29	•-32
	3	5-25	4-28	3-30	3-32	•-33	•-36
	4	9-30	7-32	6-34	5-36	4-37	•-39
	5	13-34	11-36	10-37	8-39	7-40	6-41
11	0	•-8	•-10	•-12	•-15	•-16	•-20
	1	•-14	•-16	•-18	•-21	•-22	•-25
	2	2-19	•-21	•-23	•-25	•-27	•-30
	3	5-23	4-26	3-27	•-30	•-31	•-34
	4	8-28	7-30	6-31	5-33	4-35	•-37
	5	12-32	10-33	9-35	7-37	7-38	5-39
12	0	•-8	•-10	•-11	•-14	•-15	•-18
	1	•-13	•-15	•-17	•-19	•-21	•-24
	2	2-17	•-20	•-21	•-24	•-25	•-28
	3	5-22	4-24	3-26	•-28	•-29	•-32
	4	7-26	6-28	5-29	4-31	4-32	•-35
	5	11-29	9-31	8-33	7-35	6-36	5-38
	6	14-33	12-35	11-36	9-38	9-38	7-40
13	0	•-7	•-9	•-11	•-13	•-14	•-17
	1	•-12	•-14	•-16	•-18	•-19	•-22
	2	2-16	•-18	•-20	•-22	•-23	•-26
	3	4-20	3-22	3-24	•-26	•-27	•-30
	4	7-24	6-26	5-28	4-29	4-31	•-33
	5	10-27	8-29	7-31	6-33	6-34	5-36

N = 47 (continued)

N_1	x_1	2α = 0.20	2α = 0.10	2α = 0.05	2α = 0.02	2α = 0.01	2α = 0.002
	6	13-31	11-33	10-34	9-36	8-37	7-38
14	0	•-7	•-8	•-10	•-12	•-13	•-16
	1	•-11	•-13	•-15	•-17	•-18	•-21
	2	2-15	•-17	•-19	•-21	•-22	•-25
	3	4-19	3-21	3-22	•-24	•-26	•-28
	4	6-22	5-24	5-26	4-28	•-29	•-31
	5	9-26	8-28	7-29	6-31	5-32	•-34
	6	12-29	11-31	9-32	8-34	7-35	6-37
	7	15-32	13-34	12-35	11-36	10-37	8-39
15	0	•-6	•-8	•-9	•-11	•-12	•-15
	1	•-10	•-12	•-14	•-16	•-17	•-20
	2	2-14	•-16	•-18	•-19	•-21	•-23
	3	4-18	3-19	•-21	•-23	•-24	•-27
	4	6-21	5-23	4-24	4-26	•-27	•-30
	5	9-24	7-26	6-27	6-29	5-30	•-32
	6	11-27	10-29	9-30	8-32	7-33	6-35
	7	14-30	12-32	11-33	10-35	9-35	8-37
16	0	•-6	•-7	•-9	•-10	•-11	•-14
	1	•-10	•-11	•-13	•-15	•-16	•-18
	2	•-13	•-15	•-16	•-18	•-20	•-22
	3	3-17	3-18	•-20	•-22	•-23	•-25
	4	6-20	5-21	4-23	•-25	•-26	•-28
	5	8-23	7-24	6-26	5-28	5-29	•-31
	6	10-26	9-27	8-29	7-30	7-31	6-33
	7	13-29	12-30	11-31	9-33	9-34	7-36
	8	16-31	14-33	13-34	12-35	11-36	9-38
17	0	•-5	•-7	•-8	•-10	•-11	•-13
	1	•-9	•-11	•-12	•-14	•-15	•-17
	2	•-12	•-14	•-16	•-17	•-18	•-21
	3	3-16	3-17	•-19	•-20	•-22	•-24
	4	5-19	4-20	4-22	•-23	•-25	•-27
	5	8-21	7-23	6-25	5-26	5-27	•-29
	6	10-24	9-26	8-27	7-29	6-30	•-32
	7	12-27	11-29	10-30	9-31	8-32	7-34
	8	15-30	13-31	12-32	11-34	10-35	9-36
18	0	•-5	•-6	•-7	•-9	•-10	•-12
	1	•-9	•-10	•-11	•-13	•-14	•-16
	2	•-12	•-13	•-15	•-16	•-17	•-20
	3	3-15	•-16	•-18	•-19	•-20	•-23
	4	5-18	4-19	4-21	•-22	•-23	•-25
	5	7-20	6-22	6-23	5-25	•-26	•-28
	6	9-23	8-25	7-26	7-27	6-28	•-30
	7	12-26	10-27	9-28	8-30	8-31	7-33
	8	14-28	13-30	12-31	10-32	10-33	9-35
	9	16-31	15-32	14-33	13-34	12-35	10-37
19	0	•-5	•-6	•-7	•-8	•-10	•-12
	1	•-8	•-9	•-11	•-12	•-13	•-16
	2	•-11	•-13	•-14	•-15	•-17	•-19
	3	3-14	•-15	•-17	•-18	•-19	•-22
	4	5-17	4-18	4-20	•-21	•-22	•-24
	5	7-19	6-21	5-22	5-24	•-25	•-27
	6	9-22	8-23	7-25	6-26	6-27	•-29
	7	11-24	10-26	9-27	8-29	8-29	7-31
	8	13-27	12-28	11-29	10-31	9-32	8-33
	9	15-29	14-31	13-32	12-33	11-34	10-35
20	0	•-4	•-6	•-7	•-8	•-9	•-11
	1	•-8	•-9	•-10	•-12	•-13	•-15
	2	•-11	•-12	•-13	•-15	•-16	•-18
	3	3-13	•-15	•-16	•-17	•-18	•-21
	4	5-16	4-17	•-19	•-20	•-21	•-23
	5	6-18	6-20	5-21	•-23	•-24	•-26
	6	8-21	7-22	7-24	6-25	6-26	•-28
	7	10-23	9-25	9-26	8-27	7-28	•-30
	8	13-26	11-27	11-28	10-29	9-30	8-32
	9	15-28	13-29	12-30	11-32	11-32	10-34
	10	17-30	16-31	15-32	13-34	13-34	11-36
21	0	•-4	•-5	•-6	•-8	•-8	•-11
	1	•-7	•-8	•-10	•-11	•-12	•-14
	2	•-10	•-11	•-12	•-14	•-15	•-17
	3	3-13	•-14	•-15	•-17	•-18	•-20
	4	4-15	4-16	•-18	•-19	•-20	•-22
	5	6-17	5-19	5-20	•-22	•-22	•-24
	6	8-20	7-21	7-22	6-24	•-25	•-27
	7	10-22	9-24	8-25	7-26	7-27	•-29
	8	12-24	11-26	10-27	9-28	9-29	8-31
	9	14-27	13-28	12-29	11-30	10-31	9-33
	10	16-29	15-30	14-31	13-32	12-33	11-34
22	0	•-4	•-5	•-6	•-7	•-8	•-10
	1	•-7	•-8	•-9	•-10	•-11	•-13
	2	•-10	•-11	•-12	•-13	•-14	•-16
	3	3-12	•-13	•-14	•-16	•-17	•-19
	4	4-14	4-16	•-17	•-18	•-19	•-21
	5	6-17	5-18	5-19	•-21	•-21	•-23
	6	8-19	7-20	6-21	6-23	•-24	•-25
	7	10-21	9-23	8-24	7-25	7-26	•-28
	8	11-23	10-25	10-26	9-27	8-28	•-29
	9	13-25	12-27	11-28	11-29	10-30	9-31
	10	15-28	14-29	13-30	12-31	12-32	11-33
	11	17-30	16-31	15-32	14-33	13-34	12-35
23	0	•-4	•-5	•-6	•-7	•-8	•-9
	1	•-7	•-8	•-9	•-10	•-11	•-13
	2	•-9	•-10	•-11	•-13	•-13	•-15
	3	•-11	•-13	•-14	•-15	•-16	•-18
	4	4-14	4-15	•-16	•-17	•-18	•-20
	5	6-16	5-17	5-18	•-20	•-21	•-22
	6	7-18	7-19	6-21	6-22	•-23	•-24
	7	9-20	8-22	8-23	7-24	7-25	•-26
	8	11-22	10-24	9-25	9-26	8-27	•-28

Significance Limits* for the Fourfold Table Test

$$\begin{array}{cc|c} x_1 & N_1-x_1 & N_1 \\ x_2 & N_2-x_2 & N_2 \\ \hline X & N-X & N \end{array} \quad \left\} \begin{array}{l} N = N_1+N_2 \\ X = x_1+x_2 \\ N_1 \leqq N_2 \\ x_1 \leqq N_1-x_1 \end{array} \right\}$$

For explanation see page 123

N_1	x_1	$2\alpha =$ 0.20	$2\alpha =$ 0.10	$2\alpha =$ 0.05	$2\alpha =$ 0.02	$2\alpha =$ 0.01	$2\alpha =$ 0.002
$N = 47$ (continued)							
23	9	13–24	12–26	11–27	10–28	10–29	9–30
	10	15–26	14–28	13–29	12–30	11–31	10–32
	11	17–28	16–30	15–31	14–32	13–32	12–34
$N = 48$							
4	0	•–21	•–25	•–28	•–32	•–35	•–39
	1	1–33	•–36	•–38	•–41	•–42	•–44
	2	7–41	5–43	3–45	2–46	–	–
5	0	•–17	•–21	•–24	•–28	•–31	•–35
	1	•–28	•–31	•–34	•–37	•–38	•–41
	2	5–36	4–39	2–41	2–43	•–44	•–45
6	0	•–15	•–18	•–21	•–25	•–27	•–32
	1	•–24	•–27	•–30	•–33	•–35	•–38
	2	4–32	3–35	2–37	•–39	•–40	•–43
	3	10–38	8–40	6–42	4–44	4–44	–
7	0	•–13	•–16	•–19	•–22	•–24	•–29
	1	•–21	•–24	•–27	•–30	•–32	•–35
	2	4–28	2–31	2–33	•–36	•–37	•–40
	3	8–34	6–37	5–39	4–41	3–42	•–43
8	0	•–12	•–14	•–17	•–20	•–22	•–26
	1	•–19	•–22	•–24	•–27	•–29	•–33
	2	3–25	2–28	2–30	•–33	•–34	•–37
	3	7–31	6–34	4–36	3–38	3–39	•–41
	4	12–36	10–38	8–40	6–42	6–42	4–44
9	0	•–10	•–13	•–15	•–18	•–20	•–24
	1	•–17	•–20	•–22	•–25	•–27	•–30
	2	3–23	2–26	•–28	•–30	•–32	•–35
	3	6–28	5–31	4–33	3–35	3–36	•–39
	4	10–33	9–35	7–37	6–39	5–40	4–42
10	0	•– 9	•–12	•–14	•–16	•–18	•–22
	1	•–16	•–18	•–20	•–23	•–25	•–28
	2	2–21	2–23	•–26	•–28	•–30	•–33
	3	6–26	4–28	4–30	3–32	•–34	•–36
	4	9–31	8–33	6–34	5–36	5–38	•–40
	5	13–35	11–37	10–38	8–40	7–41	6–42
11	0	•– 9	•–11	•–13	•–15	•–17	•–20
	1	•–14	•–17	•–19	•–21	•–23	•–26
	2	2–19	2–22	•–24	•–26	•–28	•–30
	3	5–24	4–26	3–28	3–30	•–32	•–34
	4	8–28	7–30	6–32	5–34	4–35	•–38
	5	12–32	10–34	9–36	7–37	7–39	5–40
12	0	•– 8	•–10	•–12	•–14	•–16	•–19
	1	•–13	•–15	•–17	•–20	•–21	•–24
	2	2–18	•–20	•–22	•–24	•–26	•–29
	3	5–22	4–24	3–26	•–28	•–30	•–32
	4	8–26	6–28	5–30	4–32	4–33	•–36
	5	11–30	9–32	8–34	7–35	6–36	5–38
	6	14–34	13–35	11–37	10–38	9–39	7–41
13	0	•– 7	•– 9	•–11	•–13	•–14	•–18
	1	•–12	•–14	•–16	•–18	•–20	•–23
	2	2–17	•–19	•–20	•–23	•–24	•–27
	3	4–21	3–23	3–24	•–26	•–28	•–30
	4	7–24	6–26	5–28	4–30	4–31	•–34
	5	10–28	9–30	7–32	6–33	6–34	5–37
	6	13–32	12–33	10–35	9–36	8–37	7–39
14	0	•– 7	•– 8	•–10	•–12	•–13	•–16
	1	•–11	•–13	•–15	•–17	•–18	•–21
	2	2–15	•–17	•–19	•–21	•–23	•–25
	3	4–19	3–21	3–23	•–25	•–26	•–29
	4	7–23	5–25	5–26	4–28	•–30	•–32
	5	9–26	8–28	7–30	6–31	5–33	•–35
	6	12–30	11–31	10–33	8–34	8–35	6–37
	7	15–33	14–34	12–36	11–37	10–38	8–40
15	0	•– 6	•– 8	•– 9	•–11	•–13	•–15
	1	•–11	•–12	•–14	•–16	•–17	•–20
	2	2–14	•–16	•–18	•–20	•–21	•–24
	3	4–18	3–20	•–22	•–23	•–25	•–27
	4	6–21	5–23	4–25	4–27	•–28	•–30
	5	9–25	7–27	7–28	6–30	5–31	•–33
	6	11–28	10–30	9–31	8–33	7–34	6–36
	7	14–31	13–33	11–34	10–35	9–36	8–38
16	0	•– 6	•– 7	•– 9	•–10	•–12	•–14
	1	•–10	•–12	•–13	•–15	•–16	•–19
	2	•–14	•–15	•–17	•–19	•–20	•–23
	3	3–17	3–19	•–20	•–22	•–23	•–26
	4	6–20	5–22	4–24	4–25	•–26	•–29
	5	8–23	7–25	6–27	5–28	5–29	•–32
	6	11–26	9–28	8–29	7–31	7–32	6–34
	7	13–29	12–31	11–32	10–34	9–35	7–36
	8	16–32	14–34	13–35	12–36	11–37	9–39
17	0	•– 5	•– 7	•– 8	•–10	•–11	•–14
	1	•– 9	•–11	•–12	•–14	•–15	•–18
	2	•–13	•–14	•–16	•–18	•–19	•–21
	3	3–16	3–18	•–19	•–21	•–22	•–25
	4	5–19	5–21	4–22	•–24	•–25	•–27
	5	8–22	7–24	6–25	5–27	5–28	•–30
	6	10–25	9–27	8–28	7–30	6–31	•–33
	7	12–28	11–29	10–31	9–32	8–33	7–35
	8	15–30	14–32	12–33	11–34	10–35	9–37
18	0	•– 5	•– 6	•– 8	•– 9	•–10	•–13
	1	•– 9	•–10	•–12	•–13	•–14	•–17
	2	•–12	•–14	•–15	•–17	•–18	•–20
	3	3–15	3–17	•–18	•–20	•–21	•–23
	4	5–18	4–20	4–21	•–22	•–24	•–26
	5	7–21	6–22	6–24	5–25	•–27	•–29

N_1	x_1	$2\alpha =$ 0.20	$2\alpha =$ 0.10	$2\alpha =$ 0.05	$2\alpha =$ 0.02	$2\alpha =$ 0.01	$2\alpha =$ 0.002
$N = 48$ (continued)							
	6	9–24	8–25	8–27	7–28	6–29	•–31
	7	12–26	11–28	10–29	9–31	8–32	7–33
	8	14–29	13–30	12–32	11–33	10–34	9–35
	9	17–31	15–33	14–34	13–35	12–36	11–37
19	0	•– 5	•– 6	•– 7	•– 9	•–10	•–12
	1	•– 8	•–10	•–11	•–13	•–14	•–16
	2	•–11	•–13	•–14	•–16	•–17	•–19
	3	3–14	•–16	•–17	•–19	•–20	•–22
	4	5–17	4–19	4–20	•–22	•–23	•–25
	5	7–20	6–21	5–23	5–24	•–25	•–27
	6	9–22	8–24	7–25	6–27	6–28	•–30
	7	11–25	10–26	9–28	8–29	8–30	7–32
	8	13–27	12–29	11–30	10–32	9–32	8–34
	9	16–30	14–31	13–32	12–34	11–35	10–36
20	0	•– 5	•– 6	•– 7	•– 8	•– 9	•–11
	1	•– 8	•– 9	•–10	•–12	•–13	•–15
	2	•–11	•–12	•–13	•–15	•–16	•–18
	3	3–14	•–15	•–16	•–18	•–19	•–21
	4	5–16	4–18	4–19	•–21	•–22	•–24
	5	7–19	6–20	5–22	5–23	•–24	•–26
	6	9–21	8–23	7–24	6–26	6–27	•–28
	7	11–24	10–25	9–26	8–28	7–29	•–31
	8	13–26	12–28	11–29	10–30	9–31	8–33
	9	15–28	14–30	13–31	12–32	11–33	10–35
	10	17–31	16–32	15–33	14–34	13–35	11–37
21	0	•– 4	•– 5	•– 6	•– 8	•– 9	•–11
	1	•– 7	•– 9	•–10	•–11	•–12	•–14
	2	•–10	•–12	•–13	•–14	•–15	•–17
	3	3–13	•–14	•–16	•–17	•–18	•–20
	4	4–15	4–17	•–18	•–20	•–21	•–23
	5	6–18	6–19	5–21	•–22	•–23	•–25
	6	8–20	7–22	7–23	6–24	6–25	•–27
	7	10–23	9–24	8–25	8–27	7–28	•–29
	8	12–25	11–26	10–28	9–29	9–30	8–31
	9	14–27	13–29	12–30	11–31	10–32	9–33
	10	16–29	15–31	14–32	13–33	12–34	11–35
22	0	•– 4	•– 5	•– 6	•– 7	•– 8	•–10
	1	•– 7	•– 8	•– 9	•–11	•–12	•–14
	2	•–10	•–11	•–12	•–14	•–15	•–17
	3	3–12	•–14	•–15	•–16	•–17	•–19
	4	4–15	4–16	•–17	•–19	•–20	•–22
	5	6–17	5–18	5–20	•–21	•–22	•–24
	6	8–19	7–21	6–22	6–23	•–24	•–26
	7	10–22	9–23	8–24	7–26	7–26	•–28
	8	12–24	11–25	10–26	9–28	8–29	8–30
	9	14–26	13–27	12–28	11–30	10–31	9–32
	10	16–28	14–29	14–31	13–32	12–32	11–34
	11	18–30	16–32	15–33	14–34	14–34	12–36
23	0	•– 4	•– 5	•– 6	•– 7	•– 8	•–10
	1	•– 7	•– 8	•– 9	•–10	•–11	•–13
	2	•– 9	•–10	•–12	•–13	•–14	•–16
	3	•–12	•–13	•–14	•–15	•–16	•–18
	4	4–14	4–15	•–17	•–18	•–19	•–21
	5	6–16	5–18	5–19	•–20	•–21	•–23
	6	8–19	7–20	6–21	6–22	•–23	•–25
	7	9–21	8–22	8–23	7–24	7–25	•–27
	8	11–23	10–24	9–25	9–27	8–27	•–29
	9	13–25	12–26	11–27	10–29	10–29	9–31
	10	15–27	14–28	13–29	12–30	11–31	10–33
	11	17–29	16–30	15–31	14–32	13–33	12–34
24	0	•– 4	•– 5	•– 5	•– 7	•– 7	•– 9
	1	•– 6	•– 7	•– 8	•–10	•–11	•–12
	2	•– 9	•–10	•–11	•–12	•–13	•–15
	3	•–11	•–12	•–13	•–15	•–16	•–18
	4	4–13	•–15	•–16	•–17	•–18	•–20
	5	6–16	5–17	5–18	•–19	•–20	•–22
	6	7–18	7–19	6–20	•–21	•–22	•–24
	7	9–20	8–21	8–22	7–23	7–24	•–26
	8	11–22	10–23	9–24	8–25	8–26	•–28
	9	13–24	12–25	11–26	10–27	9–28	9–30
	10	14–26	13–27	13–28	12–29	11–30	10–32
	11	16–28	15–29	14–30	13–31	13–32	12–33
	12	18–30	17–31	16–32	15–33	14–34	13–35
$N = 49$							
4	0	•–21	•–26	•–29	•–33	•–35	•–39
	1	1–33	•–37	•–39	•–42	•–43	•–45
	2	7–42	5–44	3–46	2–47	–	–
5	0	•–18	•–22	•–25	•–29	•–31	•–36
	1	•–28	•–32	•–35	•–38	•–39	•–42
	2	5–37	4–40	3–42	2–43	•–45	•–46
6	0	•–15	•–19	•–22	•–25	•–28	•–32
	1	•–25	•–28	•–31	•–34	•–36	•–39
	2	4–32	3–35	2–38	•–40	•–41	•–43
	3	10–39	8–41	6–43	5–44	4–45	–
7	0	•–13	•–16	•–19	•–23	•–25	•–29
	1	•–22	•–25	•–28	•–31	•–32	•–36
	2	4–29	3–32	2–34	•–37	•–38	•–41
	3	8–35	6–38	5–39	4–41	3–42	•–44
8	0	•–12	•–15	•–17	•–20	•–22	•–27
	1	•–19	•–22	•–25	•–28	•–30	•–33
	2	3–26	2–29	2–31	•–34	•–35	•–38
	3	7–32	6–34	4–36	3–38	3–40	•–42
	4	12–37	10–39	8–41	7–42	6–43	4–45
9	0	•–11	•–13	•–16	•–18	•–20	•–24
	1	•–18	•–20	•–23	•–25	•–27	•–31

N_1	x_1	$2\alpha =$ 0.20	$2\alpha =$ 0.10	$2\alpha =$ 0.05	$2\alpha =$ 0.02	$2\alpha =$ 0.01	$2\alpha =$ 0.002
$N = 49$ (continued)							
	2	3–24	2–26	•–28	•–31	•–33	•–36
	3	6–29	5–31	4–33	3–36	3–37	•–39
	4	11–34	9–36	7–38	6–40	5–41	4–43
10	0	•–10	•–12	•–14	•–17	•–19	•–23
	1	•–16	•–18	•–21	•–23	•–25	•–29
	2	2–21	2–24	•–26	•–29	•–30	•–33
	3	6–26	4–29	4–31	3–33	•–35	•–37
	4	9–31	8–33	7–35	5–37	5–38	4–40
	5	13–36	11–38	10–39	8–41	7–42	6–43
11	0	•– 9	•–11	•–13	•–15	•–17	•–21
	1	•–15	•–17	•–19	•–22	•–23	•–27
	2	2–20	2–22	•–24	•–27	•–28	•–31
	3	5–24	4–27	3–29	3–31	•–32	•–35
	4	9–29	7–31	6–33	5–35	4–36	•–38
	5	12–33	10–35	9–37	8–38	7–39	5–41
12	0	•– 8	•–10	•–12	•–14	•–16	•–19
	1	•–13	•–16	•–18	•–20	•–22	•–25
	2	2–18	•–20	•–22	•–25	•–26	•–29
	3	5–23	4–25	3–27	•–29	•–30	•–33
	4	8–27	6–29	5–31	4–33	4–34	•–36
	5	11–31	9–33	8–34	7–36	6–37	5–39
	6	15–34	13–36	11–38	10–39	9–40	7–42
13	0	•– 7	•– 9	•–11	•–13	•–15	•–18
	1	•–12	•–15	•–16	•–19	•–20	•–23
	2	2–17	•–19	•–21	•–23	•–25	•–28
	3	4–21	3–23	3–25	•–27	•–28	•–31
	4	7–25	6–27	5–29	4–31	4–32	•–34
	5	10–29	9–31	8–32	6–34	6–35	5–37
	6	13–32	12–34	10–36	9–37	8–38	7–40
14	0	•– 7	•– 9	•–10	•–12	•–14	•–17
	1	•–12	•–14	•–15	•–17	•–19	•–22
	2	2–16	•–18	•–20	•–22	•–23	•–26
	3	4–20	3–22	3–23	•–25	•–27	•–29
	4	7–23	6–25	5–27	4–29	4–30	•–33
	5	9–27	8–29	7–30	6–32	5–33	•–36
	6	12–30	11–32	10–34	8–35	8–36	6–38
	7	16–33	14–35	12–37	11–38	10–39	8–41
15	0	•– 6	•– 8	•–10	•–11	•–13	•–16
	1	•–11	•–13	•–14	•–16	•–18	•–21
	2	2–15	•–17	•–18	•–20	•–22	•–24
	3	4–18	3–20	3–22	•–24	•–25	•–28
	4	6–22	5–24	4–25	4–27	•–29	•–31
	5	9–25	8–27	7–29	6–30	5–32	•–34
	6	12–28	10–30	9–32	8–33	7–34	6–36
	7	14–32	13–33	12–35	10–36	9–37	8–39
16	0	•– 6	•– 7	•– 9	•–11	•–12	•–15
	1	•–10	•–12	•–13	•–15	•–17	•–19
	2	•–14	•–16	•–17	•–19	•–20	•–23
	3	4–17	3–19	•–21	•–23	•–24	•–26
	4	6–21	5–22	4–24	4–26	•–27	•–29
	5	8–24	7–26	6–27	5–29	5–30	•–32
	6	11–27	10–29	9–30	7–32	7–33	6–35
	7	14–30	12–31	11–33	10–34	9–35	8–37
	8	16–33	15–34	13–36	12–37	11–38	10–39
17	0	•– 6	•– 7	•– 8	•–10	•–11	•–14
	1	•–10	•–11	•–13	•–14	•–16	•–18
	2	•–13	•–15	•–16	•–18	•–19	•–22
	3	3–16	3–18	•–20	•–21	•–23	•–25
	4	6–19	5–21	4–23	•–25	•–26	•–28
	5	8–22	7–24	6–26	5–27	5–29	•–31
	6	10–25	9–27	8–29	7–30	7–31	6–33
	7	13–28	11–30	10–31	9–33	8–34	7–36
	8	15–31	14–33	13–34	11–35	11–36	9–38
18	0	•– 5	•– 7	•– 8	•– 9	•–11	•–13
	1	•– 9	•–10	•–12	•–14	•–15	•–17
	2	•–12	•–14	•–15	•–17	•–18	•–21
	3	3–15	3–17	•–19	•–20	•–21	•–24
	4	5–18	4–20	4–22	•–23	•–24	•–27
	5	7–21	6–23	6–24	5–26	5–27	•–29
	6	10–24	9–26	8–27	7–29	6–30	•–32
	7	12–27	11–28	10–30	9–31	8–32	7–34
	8	14–29	13–31	12–32	11–34	10–35	9–36
	9	17–32	16–33	14–35	13–36	12–37	11–38
19	0	•– 5	•– 6	•– 7	•– 9	•–10	•–12
	1	•– 8	•–10	•–11	•–13	•–14	•–16
	2	•–12	•–13	•–15	•–16	•–17	•–20
	3	3–15	•–16	•–18	•–19	•–20	•–23
	4	5–17	4–19	4–20	•–22	•–23	•–25
	5	7–20	6–22	5–23	5–25	•–26	•–28
	6	9–23	8–24	7–26	6–27	6–28	•–30
	7	11–25	10–27	9–28	8–30	8–31	7–33
	8	14–28	12–30	11–31	10–32	10–33	8–35
	9	16–30	15–32	14–33	12–34	12–35	10–37
20	0	•– 5	•– 6	•– 7	•– 8	•– 9	•–12
	1	•– 8	•– 9	•–11	•–12	•–13	•–16
	2	•–11	•–12	•–14	•–15	•–16	•–19
	3	3–14	•–15	•–17	•–18	•–19	•–22
	4	5–17	4–18	4–19	•–21	•–22	•–24
	5	7–19	6–21	5–22	5–24	•–25	•–27
	6	9–22	8–23	7–25	6–26	6–27	•–29
	7	11–24	10–26	9–27	8–29	7–29	7–31
	8	13–27	12–28	11–29	10–31	9–32	8–33
	9	15–29	14–31	13–32	12–33	11–34	10–35
	10	18–31	16–33	15–34	14–35	13–36	12–37
21	0	•– 4	•– 6	•– 7	•– 8	•– 9	•–11
	1	•– 8	•– 9	•–10	•–12	•–13	•–15
	2	•–10	•–12	•–13	•–15	•–16	•–18

x_1	$N_1 - x_1$	N_1
x_2	$N_2 - x_2$	N_2
X	$N - X$	N

$N = N_1 + N_2$, $X = x_1 + x_2$, $N_1 \leq N_2$, $x_1 \leq N_1 - x_1$

For explanation see page 123

N_1	x_1	$2\alpha=$ 0.20	$2\alpha=$ 0.10	$2\alpha=$ 0.05	$2\alpha=$ 0.02	$2\alpha=$ 0.01	$2\alpha=$ 0.002
		$N = 49$ (continued)					
	3	3–13	•–15	•–16	•–17	•–18	•–21
	4	5–16	4–17	•–19	•–20	•–21	•–23
	5	6–18	6–20	5–21	•–23	•–24	•–26
	6	8–21	7–22	7–24	6–25	6–26	•–28
	7	10–23	9–25	9–26	8–27	7–28	•–30
	8	12–26	11–27	10–28	9–30	9–30	8–32
	9	15–28	13–29	12–30	11–32	11–33	9–34
	10	17–30	15–31	14–33	13–34	13–35	11–36
22	0	•– 4	•– 5	•– 6	•– 8	•– 8	•–11
	1	•– 7	•– 8	•–10	•–11	•–12	•–14
	2	•–10	•–11	•–12	•–14	•–15	•–17
	3	3–13	•–14	•–15	•–17	•–18	•–20
	4	4–15	4–16	•–18	•–19	•–20	•–22
	5	6–17	5–19	5–20	•–22	•–23	•–25
	6	8–20	7–21	6–22	6–24	•–25	•–27
	7	10–22	9–24	8–25	7–26	7–27	•–29
	8	12–24	11–26	10–27	9–28	9–29	8–31
	9	14–27	13–28	12–29	11–30	10–31	9–33
	10	16–29	15–30	14–31	13–32	12–33	11–35
	11	18–31	17–32	16–33	15–34	14–35	12–37
23	0	•– 4	•– 5	•– 6	•– 7	•– 8	•–10
	1	•– 7	•– 8	•– 9	•–10	•–11	•–13
	2	•–10	•–11	•–12	•–13	•–14	•–16
	3	3–12	•–13	•–14	•–16	•–17	•–19
	4	4–14	4–16	•–17	•–18	•–19	•–21
	5	6–17	5–18	5–19	•–21	•–22	•–24
	6	8–19	7–20	6–22	6–23	•–24	•–26
	7	10–21	9–23	8–24	7–25	7–26	•–28
	8	11–23	10–25	10–26	9–27	8–28	•–30
	9	13–26	12–27	11–28	10–29	10–30	9–32
	10	15–28	14–29	13–30	12–31	12–32	10–33
	11	17–30	16–31	15–32	14–33	13–34	12–35
24	0	•– 4	•– 5	•– 6	•– 7	•– 8	•– 9
	1	•– 7	•– 8	•– 9	•–10	•–11	•–13
	2	•– 9	•–10	•–11	•–13	•–14	•–15
	3	•–11	•–13	•–14	•–15	•–16	•–18
	4	4–14	•–15	•–16	•–18	•–18	•–20
	5	6–16	5–17	5–18	•–20	•–21	•–23
	6	7–18	7–19	6–21	6–22	•–23	•–25
	7	9–20	8–22	8–23	7–24	7–25	•–27
	8	11–22	10–24	9–25	9–26	8–27	•–29
	9	13–24	12–26	11–27	10–28	10–29	9–30
	10	15–27	14–28	13–29	12–30	11–31	10–32
	11	17–29	15–30	15–31	14–32	13–33	12–34
	12	19–30	17–32	16–33	15–34	15–34	13–36
		$N = 50$					
4	0	•–22	•–26	•–30	•–34	•–36	•–40
	1	1–34	•–37	•–40	•–43	•–44	•–46
	2	7–43	5–45	3–47	2–48	2–48	–
5	0	•–18	•–22	•–26	•–29	•–32	•–36
	1	•–29	•–33	•–35	•–38	•–40	•–43
	2	5–38	4–40	3–42	2–44	•–45	•–47
6	0	•–16	•–19	•–22	•–26	•–28	•–33
	1	•–25	•–29	•–31	•–34	•–36	•–40
	2	4–33	3–36	2–38	•–41	•–42	•–44
	3	10–40	8–42	6–44	5–45	4–46	–
7	0	•–14	•–17	•–20	•–23	•–25	•–30
	1	•–22	•–25	•–28	•–31	•–33	•–37
	2	4–29	3–32	2–35	•–37	•–39	•–42
	3	9–36	7–38	5–40	4–42	3–43	•–45
8	0	•–12	•–15	•–18	•–21	•–23	•–27
	1	•–20	•–23	•–25	•–28	•–30	•–34
	2	3–26	2–29	2–32	•–34	•–36	•–39
	3	7–32	6–35	5–37	3–39	3–40	•–43
	4	12–38	10–40	8–42	7–43	6–44	4–46
9	0	•–11	•–13	•–16	•–19	•–21	•–25
	1	•–18	•–21	•–23	•–26	•–28	•–31
	2	3–24	2–27	•–29	•–32	•–33	•–36
	3	7–30	5–32	4–34	3–36	3–38	•–40
	4	11–35	9–37	7–39	6–41	5–42	4–44
10	0	•–10	•–12	•–14	•–17	•–19	•–23
	1	•–16	•–19	•–21	•–24	•–26	•–29
	2	3–22	2–24	•–27	•–29	•–31	•–34
	3	6–27	5–30	4–32	3–34	•–35	•–38
	4	10–32	8–34	7–36	5–38	5–39	4–41
	5	14–36	12–38	10–40	8–42	8–42	6–44
11	0	•– 9	•–11	•–13	•–16	•–18	•–21
	1	•–15	•–17	•–19	•–22	•–24	•–27
	2	2–20	2–23	•–25	•–27	•–29	•–32
	3	5–25	4–27	3–29	3–32	•–33	•–36
	4	9–29	7–32	6–34	5–36	4–37	•–39
	5	12–34	11–36	9–37	8–39	7–40	5–42
12	0	•– 8	•–10	•–12	•–15	•–16	•–20
	1	•–14	•–16	•–18	•–20	•–22	•–25
	2	2–19	•–21	•–23	•–25	•–27	•–30
	3	5–23	4–25	3–27	•–30	•–31	•–34
	4	8–27	7–29	6–31	5–33	4–35	•–37
	5	11–31	10–33	8–35	7–37	6–38	5–40
	6	15–35	13–37	12–38	10–40	9–41	7–43
13	0	•– 8	•– 9	•–11	•–14	•–15	•–18
	1	•–13	•–15	•–17	•–19	•–21	•–24
	2	2–17	•–19	•–21	•–24	•–25	•–28
	3	4–21	4–24	3–26	•–28	•–29	•–32
	4	7–25	6–28	5–29	4–31	4–33	•–35
	5	10–29	9–31	8–33	7–35	6–36	5–38

N_1	x_1	$2\alpha=$ 0.20	$2\alpha=$ 0.10	$2\alpha=$ 0.05	$2\alpha=$ 0.02	$2\alpha=$ 0.01	$2\alpha=$ 0.002
		$N = 50$ (continued)					
	6	14–33	12–35	11–36	9–38	8–39	7–41
14	0	•– 7	•– 9	•–10	•–13	•–14	•–17
	1	•–12	•–14	•–16	•–18	•–19	•–22
	2	2–16	•–18	•–20	•–22	•–24	•–27
	3	4–20	3–22	3–24	•–26	•–27	•–30
	4	7–24	6–26	5–28	4–30	4–31	•–33
	5	10–27	8–29	7–31	6–33	6–34	5–36
	6	13–31	11–33	10–34	9–36	8–37	6–39
	7	16–34	14–36	13–37	11–39	10–40	9–41
15	0	•– 7	•– 8	•–10	•–12	•–13	•–16
	1	•–11	•–13	•–15	•–17	•–18	•–21
	2	2–15	•–17	•–19	•–21	•–22	•–25
	3	4–19	3–21	3–23	•–25	•–26	•–29
	4	6–22	5–24	5–26	4–28	•–29	•–32
	5	9–26	8–28	7–29	6–31	5–32	•–35
	6	12–29	10–31	9–32	8–34	7–35	6–37
	7	15–32	13–34	12–35	10–37	10–38	8–40
16	0	•– 6	•– 8	•– 9	•–11	•–12	•–15
	1	•–10	•–12	•–14	•–16	•–17	•–20
	2	2–14	•–16	•–18	•–20	•–21	•–24
	3	4–18	3–20	•–21	•–23	•–24	•–27
	4	6–21	5–23	4–25	4–26	•–28	•–30
	5	8–24	7–26	6–28	6–30	5–31	•–33
	6	11–27	10–29	9–31	8–32	7–34	6–36
	7	14–30	12–32	11–34	10–35	9–36	8–38
	8	17–33	15–35	14–36	12–38	11–39	10–40
17	0	•– 6	•– 7	•– 9	•–10	•–12	•–14
	1	•–10	•–11	•–13	•–15	•–16	•–19
	2	•–13	•–15	•–17	•–18	•–20	•–22
	3	3–17	3–18	•–20	•–22	•–23	•–26
	4	6–20	5–22	4–23	•–25	•–26	•–29
	5	8–23	7–25	6–26	5–28	5–29	•–31
	6	10–26	9–28	8–29	7–31	7–32	6–34
	7	13–29	12–31	10–32	9–33	9–35	7–36
	8	16–32	14–33	13–35	12–36	11–37	9–39
18	0	•– 5	•– 7	•– 8	•–10	•–11	•–13
	1	•– 9	•–11	•–12	•–14	•–15	•–18
	2	•–13	•–14	•–16	•–17	•–19	•–21
	3	3–16	3–17	•–19	•–21	•–22	•–24
	4	5–19	4–21	4–22	•–24	•–25	•–27
	5	8–22	7–23	6–25	5–27	5–28	•–30
	6	10–25	9–26	8–28	7–29	6–30	•–33
	7	12–27	11–29	10–30	9–32	8–33	7–35
	8	15–30	13–32	12–33	11–34	10–35	9–37
	9	17–33	16–34	15–35	13–37	12–38	11–39
19	0	•– 5	•– 6	•– 8	•– 9	•–10	•–13
	1	•– 9	•–10	•–11	•–13	•–14	•–17
	2	•–12	•–13	•–15	•–17	•–18	•–20
	3	3–15	3–17	•–18	•–20	•–21	•–23
	4	5–18	4–19	4–21	•–23	•–24	•–26
	5	7–21	6–22	6–24	5–25	•–26	•–29
	6	9–23	8–25	7–26	7–28	6–29	•–31
	7	12–26	10–28	9–29	8–31	8–32	7–33
	8	14–29	13–30	12–31	10–33	10–34	9–36
	9	16–31	15–33	14–34	13–35	12–36	10–38
20	0	•– 5	•– 6	•– 7	•– 9	•–10	•–12
	1	•– 8	•–10	•–11	•–12	•–14	•–16
	2	•–11	•–13	•–14	•–16	•–17	•–19
	3	3–14	•–16	•–17	•–19	•–20	•–22
	4	5–17	4–19	4–20	•–22	•–23	•–25
	5	7–20	6–21	5–23	5–24	•–25	•–27
	6	9–22	8–24	7–25	6–27	6–28	•–30
	7	11–25	10–26	9–28	8–29	8–30	7–32
	8	13–27	12–29	11–30	10–32	9–32	8–34
	9	16–30	14–31	13–32	12–34	11–35	10–36
	10	18–32	16–34	15–35	14–36	13–37	12–38
21	0	•– 5	•– 6	•– 7	•– 8	•– 9	•–11
	1	•– 8	•– 9	•–10	•–12	•–13	•–15
	2	•–11	•–12	•–13	•–15	•–16	•–18
	3	3–13	•–15	•–16	•–18	•–19	•–21
	4	5–16	4–18	•–19	•–21	•–22	•–24
	5	7–19	6–20	5–22	5–23	•–24	•–26
	6	8–21	8–23	7–24	6–26	6–27	•–29
	7	11–24	9–25	9–26	8–28	7–29	•–31
	8	13–26	12–28	11–29	10–30	9–31	8–33
	9	15–28	14–30	13–31	11–32	11–33	10–35
	10	17–31	16–32	15–33	13–35	13–35	11–37
22	0	•– 4	•– 5	•– 6	•– 8	•– 9	•–11
	1	•– 7	•– 9	•–10	•–11	•–12	•–14
	2	•–10	•–12	•–13	•–14	•–15	•–17
	3	3–13	•–14	•–16	•–17	•–18	•–20
	4	4–15	4–17	•–18	•–20	•–21	•–23
	5	6–18	5–19	5–21	•–22	•–23	•–25
	6	8–20	7–22	7–23	6–24	6–25	•–27
	7	10–23	9–24	8–25	8–27	7–28	•–30
	8	12–25	11–26	10–28	9–29	9–30	8–32
	9	14–27	13–29	12–30	11–31	10–32	9–34
	10	16–29	15–31	14–32	13–33	12–34	11–36
	11	18–32	17–33	16–34	15–35	14–36	13–37
23	0	•– 4	•– 5	•– 6	•– 7	•– 8	•–10
	1	•– 7	•– 8	•– 9	•–11	•–12	•–14
	2	•–10	•–11	•–12	•–14	•–15	•–17
	3	3–12	•–14	•–15	•–16	•–17	•–19
	4	4–15	4–16	•–17	•–19	•–20	•–22
	5	6–17	5–18	5–20	•–21	•–22	•–24
	6	8–19	7–21	6–22	6–23	•–24	•–26
	7	10–22	9–23	8–24	7–26	7–27	•–28
	8	12–24	11–25	10–26	9–28	8–29	8–30

N_1	x_1	$2\alpha=$ 0.20	$2\alpha=$ 0.10	$2\alpha=$ 0.05	$2\alpha=$ 0.02	$2\alpha=$ 0.01	$2\alpha=$ 0.002
		$N = 50$ (continued)					
	9	14–26	12–27	12–29	11–30	10–31	9–32
	10	16–28	14–30	13–31	12–32	12–33	11–34
	11	18–30	16–32	15–33	14–34	14–35	12–36
24	0	•– 4	•– 5	•– 6	•– 7	•– 8	•–10
	1	•– 7	•– 8	•– 9	•–10	•–11	•–13
	2	•– 9	•–10	•–12	•–13	•–14	•–16
	3	•–12	•–13	•–14	•–16	•–16	•–18
	4	4–14	4–15	•–17	•–18	•–19	•–21
	5	6–16	5–18	5–19	•–20	•–21	•–23
	6	8–19	7–20	6–21	6–22	•–23	•–25
	7	9–21	8–22	8–23	7–25	7–26	•–27
	8	11–23	10–24	9–25	9–27	8–28	•–29
	9	13–25	12–26	11–27	10–29	10–30	9–31
	10	15–27	14–28	13–29	12–31	11–31	10–33
	11	17–29	16–30	15–31	14–33	13–33	12–35
	12	19–31	18–32	17–33	16–34	15–35	13–37
25	0	•– 4	•– 5	•– 6	•– 7	•– 7	•– 9
	1	•– 6	•– 7	•– 8	•–10	•–11	•–12
	2	•– 9	•–10	•–11	•–12	•–13	•–15
	3	•–11	•–12	•–14	•–15	•–16	•–18
	4	4–13	•–15	•–16	•–17	•–18	•–20
	5	6–16	5–17	•–18	•–19	•–20	•–22
	6	7–18	7–19	6–20	•–22	•–22	•–24
	7	9–20	8–21	8–22	7–24	7–25	•–26
	8	11–22	10–23	9–24	8–26	8–27	•–28
	9	13–24	12–25	11–26	10–28	9–28	9–30
	10	14–26	13–27	12–28	12–30	11–30	10–32
	11	16–28	15–29	14–30	13–31	13–32	12–34
	12	18–30	17–31	16–32	15–33	14–34	13–35
		$N = 52$					
4	0	•–23	•–27	•–31	•–35	•–38	•–42
	1	1–35	•–39	•–42	•–44	•–46	•–48
	2	7–45	5–47	3–49	2–50	2–50	–
5	0	•–19	•–23	•–27	•–31	•–33	•–38
	1	1–30	•–34	•–37	•–40	•–42	•–45
	2	6–39	4–42	3–44	2–46	•–47	•–49
6	0	•–16	•–20	•–23	•–27	•–29	•–34
	1	•–26	•–30	•–33	•–36	•–38	•–41
	2	5–34	3–38	2–40	•–42	•–44	•–46
	3	10–42	8–44	6–46	5–47	4–48	3–49
7	0	•–14	•–18	•–21	•–24	•–26	•–31
	1	•–23	•–26	•–29	•–32	•–34	•–38
	2	4–31	3–34	2–36	•–39	•–40	•–43
	3	9–37	7–40	5–42	4–44	3–45	•–47
8	0	•–13	•–16	•–18	•–22	•–24	•–28
	1	•–21	•–24	•–26	•–30	•–32	•–35
	2	3–28	2–31	2–33	•–36	•–37	•–41
	3	8–34	6–36	5–39	4–41	3–42	•–45
	4	13–39	10–42	9–43	7–45	6–46	4–48
9	0	•–11	•–14	•–17	•–20	•–22	•–26
	1	•–19	•–22	•–24	•–27	•–29	•–33
	2	3–25	2–28	•–30	•–33	•–35	•–38
	3	7–31	5–33	4–36	3–38	3–39	•–42
	4	11 36	9–38	8–40	6–42	5–43	4–45
10	0	•–10	•–13	•–15	•–18	•–20	•–24
	1	•–17	•–20	•–22	•–25	•–27	•–30
	2	3–23	2–26	•–28	•–30	•–32	•–35
	3	6–28	5–31	4–33	3–35	•–37	•–40
	4	10–33	8–35	7–37	6–39	5–41	4–43
	5	14–38	12–40	10–42	9–43	8–44	6–46
11	0	•– 9	•–12	•–14	•–16	•–18	•–22
	1	•–16	•–18	•–20	•–23	•–25	•–28
	2	2–21	2–24	•–26	•–28	•–30	•–33
	3	5–26	4–28	3–31	3–33	•–34	•–37
	4	9–31	7–33	6–35	5–37	4–38	•–41
	5	13–35	11–37	9–39	8–41	7–42	6–44
12	0	•– 9	•–11	•–13	•–15	•–17	•–21
	1	•–14	•–17	•–19	•–21	•–23	•–27
	2	2–19	2–22	•–24	•–26	•–28	•–31
	3	5–24	4–26	3–28	3–31	•–32	•–35
	4	8–28	7–31	6–33	5–35	4–36	•–39
	5	12–33	10–35	9–36	7–38	7–40	5–42
	6	15–37	14–38	12–40	10–42	9–43	7–45
13	0	•– 8	•–10	•–12	•–14	•–16	•–19
	1	•–13	•–15	•–17	•–20	•–21	•–25
	2	2–18	•–20	•–22	•–25	•–26	•–29
	3	5–22	4–25	3–27	•–29	•–30	•–33
	4	8–26	6–29	5–31	4–33	4–34	•–37
	5	11–30	9–33	8–34	7–36	6–37	5–40
	6	14–34	12–36	11–38	10–40	9–41	7–43
14	0	•– 7	•– 9	•–11	•–13	•–15	•–18
	1	•–12	•–14	•–16	•–19	•–20	•–23
	2	2–17	•–19	•–21	•–23	•–25	•–28
	3	4–21	3–23	3–25	•–27	•–29	•–31
	4	7–25	6–27	5–29	4–31	4–32	•–35
	5	10–29	9–31	7–32	6–34	6–36	5–38
	6	13–32	12–34	10–36	9–37	8–39	7–41
	7	16–36	15–37	13–39	12–40	11–41	9–43
15	0	•– 7	•– 9	•–10	•–12	•–14	•–17
	1	•–12	•–13	•–15	•–17	•–19	•–22
	2	2–16	•–18	•–20	•–22	•–23	•–26
	3	4–20	3–22	3–23	•–26	•–27	•–30
	4	7–23	5–25	5–27	4–29	•–30	•–33
	5	9–27	8–29	7–31	6–32	5–34	•–36
	6	12–30	11–32	10–34	8–36	8–37	6–39

x_1	$N_1 - x_1$	N_1
x_2	$N_2 - x_2$	N_2
X	$N - X$	N

$N = N_1 + N_2$, $X = x_1 + x_2$, $N_1 \leq N_2$, $x_1 \leq N_1 - x_1$

For explanation see page 123

N = 52 (continued)

N_1	x_1	2α = 0.20	2α = 0.10	2α = 0.05	2α = 0.02	2α = 0.01	2α = 0.002
	7	15-34	14-35	12-37	11-38	10-39	8-41
16	0	•-6	•-8	•-10	•-11	•-13	•-16
	1	•-11	•-13	•-14	•-16	•-18	•-21
	2	2-15	•-17	•-18	•-20	•-22	•-25
	3	4-18	3-20	•-22	•-24	•-26	•-28
	4	6-22	5-24	4-26	4-28	•-29	•-31
	5	9-25	8-27	7-29	6-31	5-32	•-34
	6	11-29	10-30	9-32	8-34	7-35	6-37
	7	14-32	13-33	12-35	10-37	9-38	8-40
	8	17-35	16-36	14-38	13-39	12-40	10-42
17	0	•-6	•-8	•-9	•-11	•-12	•-15
	1	•-10	•-12	•-13	•-15	•-17	•-20
	2	•-14	•-16	•-17	•-19	•-21	•-23
	3	4-17	3-19	•-21	•-23	•-24	•-27
	4	6-21	5-23	4-24	4-26	•-27	•-30
	5	8-24	7-26	6-27	5-29	5-30	•-33
	6	11-27	10-29	8-30	7-32	7-33	6-36
	7	13-30	12-32	11-33	10-35	9-36	8-38
	8	16-33	15-35	13-36	12-38	11-39	10-40
18	0	•-6	•-7	•-8	•-10	•-11	•-14
	1	•-10	•-11	•-13	•-15	•-16	•-19
	2	•-13	•-15	•-16	•-18	•-20	•-22
	3	3-16	3-18	•-20	•-22	•-23	•-26
	4	6-20	5-21	4-23	•-25	•-26	•-29
	5	8-23	7-24	6-26	5-28	5-29	•-31
	6	10-26	9-27	8-29	7-31	7-32	6-34
	7	13-28	11-30	10-32	9-33	8-34	7-36
	8	15-31	14-33	13-34	11-36	11-37	9-39
	9	18-34	16-36	15-37	14-38	13-39	11-41
19	0	•-5	•-7	•-8	•-10	•-11	•-13
	1	•-9	•-11	•-12	•-14	•-15	•-18
	2	•-12	•-14	•-16	•-17	•-19	•-21
	3	3-16	3-17	•-19	•-21	•-22	•-24
	4	5-19	4-20	4-22	•-24	•-25	•-27
	5	7-22	6-23	6-25	5-27	5-28	•-30
	6	10-24	9-26	8-28	7-29	6-30	•-33
	7	12-27	11-29	10-30	9-32	8-33	7-35
	8	14-30	13-31	12-33	11-34	10-35	9-37
	9	17-32	16-34	14-35	13-37	12-38	11-39
20	0	•-5	•-6	•-8	•-9	•-10	•-13
	1	•-9	•-10	•-11	•-13	•-14	•-17
	2	•-12	•-13	•-15	•-16	•-18	•-20
	3	3-15	•-16	•-18	•-20	•-21	•-23
	4	5-18	4-19	4-21	•-23	•-24	•-26
	5	7-20	6-22	5-24	5-25	•-26	•-29
	6	9-23	8-25	7-26	7-28	6-29	•-31
	7	11-26	10-27	9-29	8-30	8-32	7-34
	8	14-28	12-30	11-31	10-33	10-34	8-36
	9	16-31	15-33	14-34	12-35	12-36	10-38
	10	19-33	17-35	16-36	15-37	14-38	12-40
21	0	•-5	•-6	•-7	•-9	•-10	•-12
	1	•-8	•-10	•-11	•-12	•-13	•-16
	2	•-11	•-13	•-14	•-16	•-17	•-19
	3	3-14	•-16	•-17	•-19	•-20	•-22
	4	5-17	4-18	4-20	•-21	•-23	•-25
	5	7-20	6-21	5-23	5-24	•-25	•-27
	6	9-22	8-24	7-25	6-27	6-28	•-30
	7	11-25	10-26	9-28	8-29	7-30	7-32
	8	13-27	12-29	11-30	10-32	9-33	8-34
	9	15-30	14-31	13-32	12-34	11-35	10-36
	10	18-32	16-33	15-35	14-36	13-37	12-38
22	0	•-5	•-6	•-7	•-8	•-9	•-11
	1	•-8	•-9	•-10	•-12	•-13	•-15
	2	•-11	•-12	•-13	•-15	•-16	•-18
	3	3-13	•-15	•-16	•-18	•-19	•-21
	4	5-16	4-18	•-19	•-21	•-22	•-24
	5	6-19	6-20	5-22	•-23	•-24	•-26
	6	8-21	7-23	7-24	6-26	6-27	•-29
	7	10-24	9-25	9-26	8-28	7-29	•-31
	8	13-26	11-27	10-29	10-30	9-31	8-33
	9	15-28	13-30	12-31	11-32	11-33	10-35
	10	17-31	16-32	14-33	13-35	13-35	11-37
	11	19-33	18-34	17-35	15-37	15-37	13-39
23	0	•-4	•-5	•-6	•-8	•-9	•-11
	1	•-7	•-9	•-10	•-11	•-12	•-14
	2	•-10	•-12	•-13	•-14	•-15	•-17
	3	3-13	•-14	•-15	•-17	•-18	•-20
	4	4-15	4-17	•-18	•-20	•-21	•-23
	5	6-18	5-19	5-21	•-22	•-23	•-25
	6	8-20	7-22	7-23	6-24	6-26	•-28
	7	10-23	9-24	8-25	7-27	7-28	•-30
	8	12-25	11-26	10-28	9-29	9-30	8-32
	9	14-27	13-29	12-30	11-31	10-32	9-34
	10	16-29	15-31	14-32	13-33	12-34	11-36
	11	18-32	17-33	16-34	15-35	14-36	13-38
24	0	•-4	•-5	•-6	•-7	•-8	•-10
	1	•-7	•-8	•-9	•-11	•-12	•-14
	2	•-10	•-11	•-12	•-14	•-15	•-17
	3	3-12	•-14	•-15	•-16	•-17	•-19
	4	4-15	4-16	•-17	•-19	•-20	•-22
	5	6-17	5-18	5-20	•-21	•-22	•-24
	6	8-19	7-21	6-22	6-23	•-24	•-26
	7	10-22	9-23	8-24	7-26	7-27	•-29
	8	12-24	11-25	10-27	9-28	8-29	8-31
	9	13-26	12-27	12-29	11-30	10-31	9-33
	10	15-28	14-30	13-31	12-32	12-33	11-35
	11	18-30	16-32	15-33	14-34	13-35	12-36
	12	20-32	18-34	17-35	16-36	15-37	14-38

N = 52 (continued)

N_1	x_1	2α = 0.20	2α = 0.10	2α = 0.05	2α = 0.02	2α = 0.01	2α = 0.002
25	0	•-4	•-5	•-6	•-7	•-8	•-10
	1	•-7	•-8	•-9	•-10	•-11	•-13
	2	•-9	•-11	•-12	•-13	•-14	•-16
	3	•-12	•-13	•-14	•-16	•-17	•-19
	4	4-14	4-15	•-17	•-18	•-19	•-21
	5	6-16	5-18	5-19	•-20	•-21	•-23
	6	7-19	7-20	6-21	6-23	•-24	•-25
	7	9-21	8-22	8-23	7-25	7-26	•-28
	8	11-23	10-24	9-25	9-27	8-28	•-30
	9	13-25	12-26	11-28	10-29	10-30	9-31
	10	15-27	14-28	13-30	12-31	11-32	10-33
	11	17-29	16-30	15-32	14-33	13-34	12-35
	12	19-31	18-32	17-34	15-35	15-35	13-37
26	0	•-4	•-5	•-6	•-7	•-7	•-9
	1	•-6	•-7	•-8	•-10	•-11	•-13
	2	•-9	•-10	•-11	•-12	•-13	•-15
	3	•-11	•-12	•-14	•-15	•-16	•-18
	4	4-13	•-15	•-16	•-17	•-18	•-20
	5	6-16	5-17	•-18	•-20	•-20	•-22
	6	7-18	7-19	6-20	•-22	•-23	•-24
	7	9-20	8-21	8-22	7-24	7-25	•-26
	8	11-22	10-23	9-25	8-26	8-27	•-28
	9	13-24	12-25	11-27	10-28	9-29	9-30
	10	14-26	13-27	12-29	12-30	11-31	10-32
	11	16-28	15-29	14-30	13-32	13-32	11-34
	12	18-30	17-31	16-32	15-34	14-34	13-36
	13	20-32	19-33	18-34	17-35	16-36	15-37

N = 54

N_1	x_1	2α = 0.20	2α = 0.10	2α = 0.05	2α = 0.02	2α = 0.01	2α = 0.002
4	0	•-23	•-28	•-32	•-36	•-39	•-44
	1	1-37	•-40	•-43	•-46	•-48	•-50
	2	7-47	5-49	4-50	2-52	2-52	–
5	0	•-20	•-24	•-28	•-32	•-34	•-39
	1	1-31	•-35	•-38	•-41	•-43	•-47
	2	6-41	4-44	3-46	2-48	•-49	•-51
6	0	•-17	•-21	•-24	•-28	•-31	•-36
	1	•-27	•-31	•-34	•-37	•-39	•-43
	2	5-36	3-39	2-41	•-44	•-46	•-48
	3	11-43	8-46	7-47	5-49	4-50	3-51
7	0	•-15	•-18	•-21	•-25	•-28	•-32
	1	•-24	•-28	•-30	•-34	•-36	•-40
	2	4-32	3-35	2-38	•-40	•-42	•-45
	3	9-39	7-41	6-44	4-46	3-47	•-49
8	0	•-13	•-16	•-19	•-23	•-25	•-30
	1	•-21	•-25	•-28	•-31	•-33	•-37
	2	3-29	2-32	2-34	•-37	•-39	•-42
	3	8-35	6-38	5-40	4-42	3-44	•-46
	4	13-41	11-43	9-45	7-47	6-48	4-50
9	0	•-12	•-15	•-17	•-20	•-23	•-27
	1	•-19	•-22	•-25	•-28	•-30	•-34
	2	3-26	2-29	•-31	•-34	•-36	•-39
	3	7-32	5-35	4-37	3-39	3-41	•-44
	4	12-37	10-40	8-42	6-44	5-45	4-47
10	0	•-11	•-13	•-16	•-19	•-21	•-25
	1	•-18	•-20	•-23	•-26	•-28	•-32
	2	3-24	2-27	•-29	•-32	•-33	•-37
	3	6-29	5-32	4-34	3-37	3-38	•-41
	4	10-34	9-37	7-39	6-41	5-42	4-45
	5	15-39	13-41	11-43	9-45	8-46	6-48
11	0	•-10	•-12	•-14	•-17	•-19	•-23
	1	•-16	•-19	•-21	•-24	•-26	•-30
	2	2-22	2-24	•-27	•-29	•-31	•-35
	3	6-27	4-30	4-32	3-34	•-36	•-39
	4	9-32	8-34	6-36	5-39	5-40	•-42
	5	13-36	11-39	10-40	8-42	7-44	6-46
12	0	•-9	•-11	•-13	•-16	•-18	•-22
	1	•-15	•-17	•-20	•-22	•-24	•-28
	2	2-20	2-23	•-25	•-27	•-29	•-33
	3	5-25	4-27	3-30	3-32	•-34	•-37
	4	9-30	7-32	6-34	5-36	4-38	•-40
	5	12-34	10-36	9-38	8-40	7-41	5-43
	6	16-38	14-40	12-42	11-43	10-44	8-46
13	0	•-8	•-10	•-12	•-15	•-16	•-20
	1	•-14	•-16	•-18	•-21	•-22	•-26
	2	2-19	•-21	•-23	•-26	•-27	•-31
	3	5-23	4-26	3-28	•-30	•-32	•-35
	4	8-28	7-30	6-32	5-34	4-35	•-38
	5	11-32	10-34	8-36	7-38	6-39	5-41
	6	15-36	13-38	11-39	10-41	9-42	7-44
14	0	•-8	•-10	•-11	•-14	•-15	•-19
	1	•-13	•-15	•-17	•-19	•-21	•-24
	2	2-17	•-20	•-22	•-24	•-26	•-29
	3	4-22	4-24	3-26	•-28	•-30	•-33
	4	7-26	6-28	5-30	4-32	4-34	•-36
	5	10-30	9-32	8-34	7-36	6-37	5-39
	6	14-33	12-35	11-37	9-39	8-40	7-42
	7	17-37	15-39	14-40	12-42	11-43	9-45
15	0	•-7	•-9	•-11	•-13	•-14	•-18
	1	•-12	•-14	•-16	•-18	•-20	•-23
	2	2-16	•-18	•-20	•-23	•-24	•-27
	3	4-20	3-23	3-24	•-27	•-28	•-31
	4	7-24	6-26	5-28	4-30	4-32	•-34
	5	10-28	8-30	7-32	6-34	6-35	5-38
	6	13-31	11-33	10-35	9-37	8-38	6-40
	7	16-35	14-37	13-38	11-40	10-41	9-43
16	0	•-7	•-8	•-10	•-12	•-13	•-17

N = 54 (continued)

N_1	x_1	2α = 0.20	2α = 0.10	2α = 0.05	2α = 0.02	2α = 0.01	2α = 0.002
	1	•-11	•-13	•-15	•-17	•-19	•-22
	2	2-15	•-17	•-19	•-21	•-23	•-26
	3	4-19	3-21	3-23	•-25	•-27	•-29
	4	6-23	5-25	5-27	4-29	•-30	•-33
	5	9-26	8-28	7-30	6-32	5-33	•-36
	6	12-30	10-32	9-33	8-35	7-36	6-39
	7	15-33	13-35	12-36	10-38	10-39	8-41
	8	18-36	16-38	15-39	13-41	12-42	10-44
17	0	•-6	•-8	•-9	•-11	•-13	•-16
	1	•-11	•-12	•-14	•-16	•-17	•-20
	2	2-14	•-16	•-18	•-20	•-22	•-24
	3	4-18	3-20	•-22	•-24	•-25	•-28
	4	6-22	5-24	4-25	4-27	•-29	•-31
	5	9-25	7-27	6-29	6-30	5-32	•-34
	6	11-28	10-30	9-32	8-33	7-35	6-37
	7	14-31	12-33	11-35	10-36	9-37	8-40
	8	17-34	15-36	14-37	12-39	11-40	10-42
18	0	•-6	•-7	•-9	•-11	•-12	•-15
	1	•-10	•-12	•-13	•-15	•-17	•-19
	2	•-14	•-15	•-17	•-19	•-20	•-23
	3	3-17	3-19	•-21	•-23	•-24	•-27
	4	6-20	5-22	4-24	4-26	•-27	•-30
	5	8-24	7-25	6-27	5-29	5-30	•-33
	6	11-27	9-29	8-30	7-32	7-33	6-35
	7	13-30	12-31	11-33	9-35	9-36	7-38
	8	16-33	14-34	13-36	12-37	11-38	9-40
	9	19-35	17-37	16-38	14-40	13-41	11-43
19	0	•-6	•-7	•-8	•-10	•-11	•-14
	1	•-9	•-11	•-13	•-14	•-16	•-18
	2	•-13	•-15	•-16	•-18	•-19	•-22
	3	3-16	3-18	•-20	•-21	•-23	•-25
	4	5-19	5-21	4-23	•-25	•-26	•-28
	5	8-22	7-24	6-26	5-28	5-29	•-31
	6	10-25	9-27	8-29	7-30	6-32	•-34
	7	12-28	11-30	10-31	9-33	8-34	7-36
	8	15-31	14-33	12-34	11-36	10-37	9-39
	9	18-34	16-35	15-37	13-38	13-39	11-41
20	0	•-5	•-7	•-8	•-9	•-11	•-13
	1	•-9	•-10	•-12	•-14	•-15	•-17
	2	•-12	•-14	•-15	•-17	•-18	•-21
	3	3-15	3-17	•-19	•-20	•-22	•-24
	4	5-18	4-20	4-22	•-23	•-25	•-27
	5	7-21	6-23	6-25	5-26	5-28	•-30
	6	10-24	8-26	8-27	7-29	6-30	•-33
	7	12-27	11-29	10-30	9-32	8-33	7-35
	8	14-30	13-31	12-33	11-34	10-35	9-37
	9	17-32	15-34	14-35	13-37	12-38	10-39
	10	19-35	18-36	16-38	15-39	14-40	12-42
21	0	•-5	•-6	•-7	•-9	•-10	•-13
	1	•-8	•-10	•-11	•-13	•-14	•-17
	2	•-12	•-13	•-15	•-16	•-18	•-20
	3	3-15	•-16	•-18	•-19	•-21	•-23
	4	5-18	4-19	4-21	•-22	•-24	•-26
	5	7-20	6-22	5-23	5-25	•-26	•-29
	6	9-23	8-25	7-26	6-28	6-29	•-31
	7	11-26	10-27	9-29	8-30	8-31	7-34
	8	14-28	12-30	11-31	10-33	10-34	8-36
	9	16-31	15-32	13-34	12-35	11-36	10-38
	10	18-33	17-35	16-36	14-37	13-38	12-40
22	0	•-5	•-6	•-7	•-9	•-10	•-12
	1	•-8	•-9	•-11	•-12	•-13	•-16
	2	•-11	•-13	•-14	•-16	•-17	•-19
	3	3-14	•-16	•-17	•-19	•-20	•-22
	4	5-17	4-18	4-20	•-21	•-23	•-25
	5	7-19	6-21	5-22	5-24	•-25	•-27
	6	9-22	8-24	7-25	6-27	6-28	•-30
	7	11-25	10-26	9-28	8-29	7-30	7-32
	8	13-27	12-29	11-30	10-32	9-33	8-35
	9	15-29	14-31	13-32	12-34	11-35	10-37
	10	17-32	16-33	15-35	14-36	13-37	11-39
	11	20-34	18-36	17-37	16-38	15-39	13-41
23	0	•-4	•-6	•-7	•-8	•-9	•-11
	1	•-8	•-9	•-10	•-12	•-13	•-15
	2	•-11	•-12	•-13	•-15	•-16	•-18
	3	3-13	•-15	•-16	•-18	•-19	•-21
	4	5-16	4-18	•-19	•-20	•-22	•-24
	5	6-19	6-20	5-21	•-23	•-24	•-26
	6	8-21	7-23	7-24	6-26	6-27	•-29
	7	10-24	9-25	9-26	8-28	7-29	•-31
	8	12-26	11-27	10-29	9-30	9-31	8-33
	9	15-28	13-30	12-31	11-33	11-33	9-35
	10	17-31	15-32	14-33	13-35	12-36	11-37
	11	19-33	18-34	16-35	15-37	14-38	13-39
24	0	•-4	•-5	•-6	•-8	•-9	•-11
	1	•-7	•-9	•-10	•-11	•-12	•-14
	2	•-10	•-11	•-13	•-14	•-15	•-17
	3	3-13	•-14	•-15	•-17	•-18	•-20
	4	4-15	4-17	•-18	•-20	•-21	•-23
	5	6-18	5-19	5-21	•-22	•-23	•-25
	6	8-20	7-22	7-23	6-25	•-26	•-28
	7	10-23	9-24	8-25	7-27	7-28	•-30
	8	12-25	11-26	10-28	9-29	9-30	8-32
	9	14-27	13-29	12-30	11-31	10-32	9-34
	10	16-29	15-31	14-32	13-33	12-34	11-36
	11	18-32	17-33	16-34	15-35	14-36	12-38
	12	20-34	19-35	18-36	17-37	16-38	14-40
25	0	•-4	•-5	•-6	•-7	•-8	•-10
	1	•-7	•-8	•-9	•-11	•-12	•-14

$$\begin{array}{cc|c} x_1 & N_1 - x_1 & N_1 \\ x_2 & N_2 - x_2 & N_2 \\ \hline X & N - X & N \end{array} \quad \left\} \begin{array}{l} N = N_1 + N_2 \\ X = x_1 + x_2 \\ N_1 \leqq N_2 \\ x_1 \leqq N_1 - x_1 \end{array} \right\}$$

For explanation see page 123

N_1	x_1	$2\alpha=$ 0.20	$2\alpha=$ 0.10	$2\alpha=$ 0.05	$2\alpha=$ 0.02	$2\alpha=$ 0.01	$2\alpha=$ 0.002
		$N = 54$ (continued)					
	2	•–10	•–11	•–12	•–14	•–15	•–17
	3	3–12	•–14	•–15	•–16	•–17	•–19
	4	4–15	4–16	•–17	•–19	•–20	•–22
	5	6–17	5–18	5–20	•–21	•–22	•–24
	6	8–19	7–21	6–22	6–24	•–25	•–27
	7	10–22	9–23	8–24	7–26	7–27	•–29
	8	11–24	10–25	10–27	9–28	8–29	•–31
	9	13–26	12–28	11–29	11–30	10–31	9–33
	10	15–28	14–30	13–31	12–32	12–33	10–35
	11	17–30	16–32	15–33	14–34	13–35	12–37
	12	19–32	18–34	17–35	16–36	15–37	14–38
26	0	•– 4	•– 5	•– 6	•– 7	•– 8	•–10
	1	•– 7	•– 8	•– 9	•–10	•–11	•–13
	2	•– 9	•–11	•–12	•–13	•–14	•–16
	3	•–12	•–13	•–14	•–16	•–17	•–19
	4	4–14	4–15	•–17	•–18	•–19	•–21
	5	6–16	5–18	5–19	•–20	•–21	•–23
	6	7–19	7–20	6–21	6–23	•–24	•–26
	7	9–21	8–22	8–23	7–25	7–26	•–28
	8	11–23	10–24	9–26	9–27	8–28	•–30
	9	13–25	12–26	11–28	10–29	10–30	9–32
	10	15–27	14–29	13–30	12–31	11–32	10–34
	11	17–29	16–31	15–32	14–33	13–34	12–35
	12	19–31	17–33	16–34	15–35	15–36	13–37
	13	21–33	19–35	18–36	17–37	16–38	15–39
27	0	•– 4	•– 5	•– 6	•– 7	•– 8	•– 9
	1	•– 6	•– 8	•– 9	•–10	•–11	•–13
	2	•– 9	•–10	•–11	•–12	•–13	•–15
	3	•–11	•–12	•–14	•–15	•–16	•–18
	4	4–14	•–15	•–16	•–17	•–18	•–20
	5	6–16	5–17	•–18	•–20	•–21	•–22
	6	7–18	6–19	6–20	•–22	•–23	•–25
	7	9–20	8–21	7–23	7–24	•–25	•–27
	8	11–22	10–23	9–25	8–26	8–27	•–29
	9	12–24	12–26	11–27	10–28	9–29	9–31
	10	14–26	13–28	12–29	12–30	11–31	10–32
	11	16–28	15–30	14–31	13–32	13–33	11–34
	12	18–30	17–31	16–33	15–34	14–35	13–36
	13	20–32	19–33	18–34	17–36	16–36	15–38
		$N = 56$					
4	0	•–24	•–29	•–33	•–38	•–40	•–45
	1	1–38	•–42	•–45	•–48	•–49	•–52
	2	8–48	5–51	4–52	2–54	2–54	–
5	0	•–20	•–25	•–29	•–33	•–36	•–41
	1	1–33	•–36	•–40	•–43	•–45	•–48
	2	6–42	4–45	3–48	2–50	•–51	•–53
6	0	•–18	•–21	•–25	•–29	•–32	•–37
	1	•–28	•–32	•–35	•–39	•–41	•–45
	2	5–37	3–40	2–43	2–46	•–47	•–50
	3	11–45	9–47	7–49	5–51	4–52	3–53
7	0	•–15	•–19	•–22	•–26	•–29	•–34
	1	•–25	•–29	•–32	•–35	•–37	•–41
	2	4–33	3–36	2–39	•–42	•–44	•–47
	3	10–40	7–43	6–45	4–47	4–49	•–51
8	0	•–14	•–17	•–20	•–23	•–26	•–31
	1	•–22	•–26	•–29	•–32	•–34	•–38
	2	4–30	2–33	2–36	•–39	•–40	•–44
	3	8–36	6–39	5–42	4–44	3–45	•–48
	4	14–42	11–45	9–47	7–49	6–50	5–51
9	0	•–12	•–15	•–18	•–21	•–24	•–28
	1	•–20	•–23	•–26	•–29	•–31	•–35
	2	3–27	2–30	2–33	•–36	•–37	•–41
	3	7–33	6–36	4–38	3–41	3–42	•–45
	4	12–39	10–41	8–43	7–45	6–47	4–49
10	0	•–11	•–14	•–16	•–19	•–22	•–26
	1	•–18	•–21	•–24	•–27	•–29	•–33
	2	3–25	2–28	•–30	•–33	•–35	•–38
	3	7–30	5–33	4–36	3–38	3–40	•–43
	4	11–36	9–38	7–40	6–43	5–44	4–47
	5	15–41	13–43	11–45	9–47	8–48	6–50
11	0	•–10	•–13	•–15	•–18	•–20	•–24
	1	•–17	•–20	•–22	•–25	•–27	•–31
	2	3–23	2–25	•–28	•–31	•–32	•–36
	3	6–28	5–31	4–33	3–36	•–37	•–40
	4	10–33	8–36	7–38	5–40	5–41	4–44
	5	14–38	12–40	10–42	9–44	8–45	6–47
12	0	•– 9	•–12	•–14	•–17	•–18	•–22
	1	•–15	•–18	•–20	•–23	•–25	•–29
	2	2–21	2–24	•–26	•–29	•–30	•–34
	3	5–26	4–29	3–31	3–33	•–35	•–38
	4	9–31	7–33	6–35	5–38	4–39	•–42
	5	13–35	11–37	9–39	8–41	7–43	5–45
	6	17–39	14–42	13–43	11–45	10–46	8–48
13	0	•– 9	•–11	•–13	•–15	•–17	•–21
	1	•–14	•–17	•–19	•–22	•–23	•–27
	2	2–19	•–22	•–24	•–27	•–28	•–32
	3	5–24	4–27	3–29	•–31	•–33	•–36
	4	8–29	7–31	6–33	5–35	4–37	•–40
	5	12–33	10–35	9–37	7–39	6–41	5–43
	6	15–37	13–39	12–41	10–43	9–44	7–46
14	0	•– 8	•–10	•–12	•–14	•–16	•–20
	1	•–13	•–16	•–18	•–20	•–22	•–25
	2	2–18	•–20	•–23	•–25	•–27	•–30
	3	5–23	4–25	3–27	•–29	•–31	•–34
	4	8–27	6–29	5–31	4–33	4–35	•–38

N_1	x_1	$2\alpha=$ 0.20	$2\alpha=$ 0.10	$2\alpha=$ 0.05	$2\alpha=$ 0.02	$2\alpha=$ 0.01	$2\alpha=$ 0.002
		$N = 56$ (continued)					
	5	11–31	9–33	8–35	7–37	6–38	5–41
	6	14–35	12–37	11–39	9–40	9–42	7–44
	7	18–38	16–40	14–42	12–44	11–45	9–47
15	0	•– 7	•– 9	•–11	•–13	•–15	•–18
	1	•–12	•–15	•–17	•–19	•–21	•–24
	2	2–17	•–19	•–21	•–24	•–25	•–28
	3	4–21	3–23	3–25	•–28	•–29	•–32
	4	7–25	6–27	5–29	4–32	4–33	•–36
	5	10–29	9–31	7–33	6–35	6–36	5–39
	6	13–33	11–35	10–37	9–38	8–40	7–42
	7	16–36	15–38	13–40	12–42	11–43	9–45
16	0	•– 7	•– 9	•–10	•–13	•–14	•–17
	1	•–12	•–14	•–16	•–18	•–19	•–23
	2	2–16	•–18	•–20	•–22	•–24	•–27
	3	4–20	3–22	3–24	•–26	•–28	•–31
	4	7–24	6–26	5–28	4–30	4–31	•–34
	5	9–27	8–29	7–31	6–33	5–35	•–37
	6	12–31	11–33	10–35	8–37	8–38	6–40
	7	15–34	14–36	12–38	11–40	10–41	8–43
	8	19–37	17–39	15–41	14–42	12–44	11–45
17	0	•– 7	•– 8	•–10	•–12	•–13	•–16
	1	•–11	•–13	•–15	•–17	•–18	•–21
	2	2–15	•–17	•–19	•–21	•–22	•–25
	3	4–19	3–21	3–23	•–25	•–26	•–29
	4	6–22	5–24	4–26	4–28	•–30	•–33
	5	9–26	8–28	7–30	6–32	5–33	•–36
	6	12–29	10–31	9–33	8–35	7–36	6–38
	7	14–32	13–34	12–36	10–38	9–39	8–41
	8	17–36	16–37	14–39	13–41	12–42	10–44
18	0	•– 6	•– 8	•– 9	•–11	•–12	•–15
	1	•–10	•–12	•–14	•–16	•–17	•–20
	2	2–14	•–16	•–18	•–20	•–21	•–24
	3	4–18	3–20	•–21	•–24	•–25	•–28
	4	6–21	5–23	4–25	4–27	•–28	•–31
	5	8–24	7–26	6–28	5–30	5–31	•–34
	6	11–28	10–30	9–31	7–33	7–34	6–37
	7	14–31	12–33	11–34	10–36	9–37	8–39
	8	16–34	15–36	13–37	12–39	11–40	10–42
	9	19–37	18–38	16–40	15–41	14–42	12–44
19	0	•– 6	•– 7	•– 9	•–10	•–12	•–15
	1	•–10	•–12	•–13	•–15	•–16	•–19
	2	•–13	•–15	•–17	•–19	•–20	•–23
	3	3–17	3–19	•–20	•–22	•–24	•–26
	4	6–20	5–22	4–24	•–26	•–27	•–30
	5	8–23	7–25	6–27	5–29	5–30	•–33
	6	10–26	9–28	8–30	7–32	7–33	6–35
	7	13–29	12–31	10–33	9–34	9–36	7–38
	8	16–32	14–34	13–36	11–37	11–38	9–40
	9	18–35	17–37	15–38	14–40	13–41	11–43
20	0	•– 5	•– 7	•– 8	•–10	•–11	•–14
	1	•– 9	•–11	•–12	•–14	•–16	•–18
	2	•–13	•–14	•–16	•–18	•–19	•–22
	3	3–16	3–18	•–19	•–21	•–23	•–25
	4	5–19	5–21	4–23	•–24	•–26	•–28
	5	8–22	7–24	6–26	5–27	5–29	•–31
	6	10–25	9–27	8–28	7–30	6–31	•–34
	7	12–28	11–30	10–31	9–33	8–34	7–36
	8	15–31	13–32	12–34	11–36	10–37	9–39
	9	17–33	16–35	14–37	13–38	12–39	11–41
	10	20–36	18–38	17–39	15–41	15–41	13–43
21	0	•– 5	•– 6	•– 8	•– 9	•–11	•–13
	1	•– 9	•–10	•–12	•–14	•–15	•–17
	2	•–12	•–14	•–15	•–17	•–18	•–21
	3	3–15	3–17	•–18	•–20	•–22	•–24
	4	5–18	4–20	4–22	•–23	•–25	•–27
	5	7–21	6–23	6–24	5–26	•–27	•–30
	6	9–24	8–26	7–27	7–29	6–30	•–32
	7	12–27	10–28	9–30	8–32	8–33	7–35
	8	14–29	13–31	12–33	10–34	10–35	9–37
	9	16–32	15–34	14–35	13–37	12–38	10–40
	10	19–35	17–36	16–38	15–39	14–40	12–42
22	0	•– 5	•– 6	•– 7	•– 9	•–10	•–12
	1	•– 8	•–10	•–11	•–13	•–14	•–17
	2	•–12	•–13	•–15	•–16	•–17	•–20
	3	3–15	•–16	•–18	•–19	•–21	•–23
	4	5–17	4–19	4–21	•–22	•–24	•–26
	5	7–20	6–22	5–23	5–25	•–26	•–29
	6	9–23	8–25	7–26	6–28	6–29	•–31
	7	11–26	10–27	9–29	8–30	8–31	7–34
	8	13–28	12–30	11–31	10–33	9–34	8–36
	9	16–31	14–32	13–34	12–35	11–36	10–38
	10	18–33	17–35	15–36	14–37	13–38	12–40
	11	20–36	19–37	18–38	16–40	15–41	14–42
23	0	•– 5	•– 6	•– 7	•– 8	•–10	•–12
	1	•– 8	•– 9	•–11	•–12	•–13	•–16
	2	•–11	•–13	•–14	•–16	•–17	•–19
	3	3–14	•–15	•–17	•–19	•–20	•–22
	4	5–17	4–18	4–20	•–21	•–23	•–25
	5	7–19	6–21	5–22	5–24	•–25	•–28
	6	9–22	8–24	7–25	6–27	6–28	•–30
	7	11–24	10–26	9–27	8–29	7–30	•–32
	8	13–27	12–29	11–30	10–32	9–33	8–35
	9	15–29	14–31	13–32	12–34	11–35	10–37
	10	17–32	16–33	15–35	14–36	13–37	11–39
	11	20–34	18–36	17–37	16–38	15–39	13–41
24	0	•– 4	•– 6	•– 7	•– 8	•– 9	•–11
	1	•– 8	•– 9	•–10	•–12	•–13	•–15
	2	•–11	•–12	•–13	•–15	•–16	•–18

N_1	x_1	$2\alpha=$ 0.20	$2\alpha=$ 0.10	$2\alpha=$ 0.05	$2\alpha=$ 0.02	$2\alpha=$ 0.01	$2\alpha=$ 0.002
		$N = 56$ (continued)					
	3	3–13	•–15	•–16	•–18	•–19	•–21
	4	4–16	4–17	•–19	•–20	•–22	•–24
	5	6–18	6–20	5–21	•–23	•–24	•–26
	6	8–21	7–23	7–24	6–26	6–27	•–29
	7	10–23	9–25	8–26	8–28	7–29	•–31
	8	12–26	11–27	10–29	9–30	9–31	8–33
	9	14–28	13–30	12–31	11–33	11–34	9–35
	10	17–31	15–32	14–33	13–35	12–36	11–38
	11	19–33	17–34	16–36	15–37	14–38	13–40
	12	21–35	20–36	18–38	17–39	16–40	15–41
25	0	•– 4	•– 5	•– 6	•– 8	•– 9	•–11
	1	•– 7	•– 9	•–10	•–11	•–12	•–14
	2	•–10	•–11	•–13	•–14	•–15	•–17
	3	3–13	•–14	•–15	•–17	•–18	•–20
	4	4–15	4–17	•–18	•–20	•–21	•–23
	5	6–18	5–19	5–21	•–22	•–23	•–25
	6	8–20	7–22	6–23	6–25	•–26	•–28
	7	10–23	9–24	8–25	7–27	7–28	•–30
	8	12–25	11–26	10–28	9–29	9–30	8–32
	9	14–27	13–29	12–30	11–31	10–32	9–34
	10	16–29	15–31	14–32	13–34	12–34	11–36
	11	18–32	17–33	16–34	14–36	14–36	12–38
	12	20–34	19–35	18–36	16–38	16–38	14–40
26	0	•– 4	•– 5	•– 6	•– 7	•– 8	•–10
	1	•– 7	•– 8	•– 9	•–11	•–12	•–14
	2	•–10	•–11	•–12	•–14	•–15	•–17
	3	3–12	•–14	•–15	•–16	•–17	•–19
	4	4–15	4–16	•–17	•–19	•–20	•–22
	5	6–17	5–18	5–20	•–21	•–22	•–24
	6	8–19	7–21	6–22	6–24	•–25	•–27
	7	10–22	9–23	8–24	7–26	7–27	•–29
	8	11–24	10–25	10–27	9–28	8–29	•–31
	9	13–26	12–28	11–29	10–30	10–31	9–33
	10	15–28	14–30	13–31	12–32	12–33	10–35
	11	17–30	16–32	15–33	14–34	13–35	12–37
	12	19–33	18–34	17–35	16–36	15–37	14–39
	13	21–35	20–36	19–37	18–38	17–39	15–41
27	0	•– 4	•– 5	•– 6	•– 7	•– 8	•–10
	1	•– 7	•– 8	•– 9	•–10	•–11	•–13
	2	•– 9	•–11	•–12	•–13	•–14	•–16
	3	•–12	•–13	•–14	•–16	•–17	•–19
	4	4–14	4–15	•–17	•–18	•–19	•–21
	5	6–16	5–18	5–19	•–20	•–21	•–24
	6	7–19	7–20	6–21	6–23	•–24	•–26
	7	9–21	8–22	8–23	7–25	7–26	•–28
	8	11–23	10–24	9–26	9–27	8–28	•–30
	9	13–25	12–27	11–28	10–29	10–30	9–32
	10	15–27	14–29	13–30	12–31	11–32	10–34
	11	17–29	16–31	15–32	14–33	13–34	12–36
	12	19–31	17–33	16–34	15–35	15–36	13–38
	13	21–33	19–35	18–36	17–37	16–38	15–39
28	0	•– 4	•– 5	•– 6	•– 7	•– 8	•– 9
	1	•– 6	•– 8	•– 9	•–10	•–11	•–13
	2	•– 9	•–10	•–11	•–13	•–13	•–15
	3	•–11	•–13	•–14	•–15	•–16	•–18
	4	4–14	•–15	•–16	•–17	•–18	•–20
	5	6–16	5–17	•–18	•–20	•–21	•–23
	6	7–18	6–19	6–20	•–22	•–23	•–25
	7	9–20	8–21	7–23	7–24	•–25	•–27
	8	11–22	10–24	9–25	8–26	8–27	•–29
	9	12–24	11–26	11–27	10–28	9–29	9–31
	10	14–26	13–28	12–29	11–30	11–31	10–33
	11	16–28	15–30	14–31	13–32	13–33	11–35
	12	18–30	17–32	16–33	15–34	14–35	13–36
	13	20–32	19–34	18–35	17–36	16–37	15–38
	14	22–34	21–35	20–36	18–38	18–38	16–40
		$N = 58$					
4	0	•–25	•–30	•–35	•–39	•–42	•–47
	1	1–39	•–43	•–47	•–49	•–51	•–54
	2	8–50	6–52	4–54	2–56	2–56	–
5	0	•–21	•–26	•–30	•–34	•–37	•–42
	1	1–34	•–38	•–41	•–45	•–47	•–50
	2	6–44	4–47	3–49	2–52	•–53	•–55
6	0	•–18	•–22	•–26	•–30	•–33	•–38
	1	•–29	•–33	•–37	•–40	•–42	•–46
	2	5–38	4–42	2–45	2–47	•–49	•–52
	3	12–46	9–49	7–51	5–53	4–54	3–55
7	0	•–16	•–20	•–23	•–27	•–30	•–35
	1	•–26	•–30	•–33	•–36	•–39	•–43
	2	4–34	3–38	2–40	•–43	•–45	•–48
	3	10–42	8–45	6–47	4–49	4–50	•–53
8	0	•–14	•–17	•–21	•–24	•–27	•–32
	1	•–23	•–27	•–30	•–33	•–35	•–40
	2	4–31	3–34	2–37	•–40	•–42	•–45
	3	9–38	7–41	5–43	4–46	3–47	•–50
	4	14–44	12–46	10–48	8–50	7–51	5–53
9	0	•–13	•–16	•–19	•–22	•–24	•–29
	1	•–21	•–24	•–27	•–30	•–32	•–37
	2	3–28	2–31	2–34	•–37	•–39	•–42
	3	8–34	6–37	5–40	4–42	3–44	•–47
	4	12–40	10–43	8–45	7–47	6–48	4–51
10	0	•–11	•–14	•–17	•–20	•–22	•–27
	1	•–19	•–22	•–25	•–28	•–30	•–34
	2	3–26	2–29	•–31	•–34	•–36	•–40
	3	7–31	5–34	4–37	3–39	3–41	•–44
	4	11–37	9–40	8–42	6–44	5–46	4–48

Significance Limits* for the Fourfold Table Test

x_1	$N_1 - x_1$	N_1
x_2	$N_2 - x_2$	N_2
X	$N - X$	N

$N = N_1 + N_2$, $X = x_1 + x_2$, $N_1 \leqq N_2$, $x_1 \leqq N_1 - x_1$

For explanation see page 123

N_1	x_1	2α = 0.20	2α = 0.10	2α = 0.05	2α = 0.02	2α = 0.01	2α = 0.002
		$N = 58$ (continued)					
	5	16–42	13–45	12–46	10–48	9–49	7–51
11	0	•–10	•–13	•–16	•–19	•–21	•–25
	1	•–17	•–20	•–23	•–26	•–28	•–32
	2	3–23	2–26	•–29	•–32	•–34	•–37
	3	6–29	5–32	4–34	3–37	•–39	•–42
	4	10–34	8–37	7–39	6–41	5–43	4–46
	5	14–39	12–42	10–44	9–46	8–47	6–49
12	0	•–10	•–12	•–14	•–17	•–19	•–23
	1	•–16	•–19	•–21	•–24	•–26	•–30
	2	2–22	2–24	•–27	•–30	•–31	•–35
	3	6–27	4–30	3–32	3–35	•–36	•–40
	4	9–32	8–34	6–37	5–39	4–41	•–43
	5	13–36	11–39	10–41	8–43	7–44	6–47
	6	17–41	15–43	13–45	11–47	10–48	8–50
13	0	•– 9	•–11	•–13	•–16	•–18	•–22
	1	•–15	•–17	•–20	•–22	•–24	•–28
	2	2–20	2–23	•–25	•–28	•–29	•–33
	3	5–25	4–28	3–30	3–32	•–34	•–37
	4	8–30	7–32	6–34	5–37	4–38	•–41
	5	12–34	10–36	9–38	7–41	7–42	5–45
	6	16–38	14–40	12–42	10–44	9–45	8–48
14	0	•– 8	•–10	•–12	•–15	•–17	•–20
	1	•–14	•–16	•–18	•–21	•–23	•–26
	2	2–19	•–21	•–23	•–26	•–28	•–31
	3	5–23	4–26	3–28	•–31	•–32	•–35
	4	8–28	6–30	5–32	4–35	4–36	•–39
	5	11–32	9–34	8–36	7–38	6–40	5–43
	6	15–36	13–38	11–40	10–42	9–43	7–46
	7	18–40	16–42	15–43	13–45	12–46	10–48
15	0	•– 8	•–10	•–12	•–14	•–16	•–19
	1	•–13	•–15	•–17	•–20	•–21	•–25
	2	2–18	•–20	•–22	•–24	•–26	•–30
	3	4–22	4–24	3–26	•–29	•–30	•–34
	4	7–26	6–28	5–30	4–33	4–34	•–37
	5	10–30	9–32	8–34	7–36	6–38	5–41
	6	14–34	12–36	10–38	9–40	8–41	7–44
	7	17–37	15–40	14–41	12–43	11–44	9–46
16	0	•– 7	•– 9	•–11	•–13	•–15	•–18
	1	•–12	•–14	•–16	•–18	•–20	•–23
	2	2–17	•–19	•–21	•–23	•–25	•–28
	3	4–21	3–23	3–25	•–27	•–29	•–32
	4	7–25	6–27	5–29	4–31	4–33	•–35
	5	10–28	8–31	7–32	6–35	6–36	5–39
	6	13–32	11–34	10–36	9–38	8–39	6–42
	7	16–35	14–38	13–39	11–41	10–42	9–45
	8	19–39	17–41	16–42	14–44	13–45	11–47
17	0	•– 7	•– 8	•–10	•–12	•–14	•–17
	1	•–11	•–13	•–15	•–17	•–19	•–22
	2	2–16	•–18	•–20	•–22	•–23	•–27
	3	4–19	3–22	3–24	•–26	•–27	•–30
	4	6–23	5–25	5–27	4–29	•–31	•–34
	5	9–27	8–29	7–31	6–33	5–34	•–37
	6	12–30	10–32	9–34	8–36	7–37	6–40
	7	15–34	13–36	12–37	11–39	10–40	8–43
	8	18–37	16–39	15–40	13–42	12–43	10–45
18	0	•– 6	•– 8	•–10	•–12	•–13	•–16
	1	•–11	•–13	•–14	•–16	•–18	•–21
	2	2–15	•–17	•–19	•–21	•–22	•–25
	3	4–18	3–20	•–22	•–24	•–26	•–29
	4	6–22	5–24	4–26	4–28	•–29	•–32
	5	9–25	7–27	7–29	6–31	5–33	•–35
	6	11–29	10–31	9–32	8–34	7–36	6–38
	7	14–32	13–34	11–36	10–37	9–39	8–41
	8	17–35	15–37	14–39	12–40	11–41	10–44
	9	20–38	18–40	17–41	15–43	14–44	12–46
19	0	•– 6	•– 8	•– 9	•–11	•–12	•–15
	1	•–10	•–12	•–14	•–16	•–17	•–20
	2	•–14	•–16	•–18	•–20	•–21	•–24
	3	4–17	3–19	•–21	•–23	•–25	•–28
	4	6–21	5–23	4–25	4–27	•–28	•–31
	5	8–24	7–26	6–28	5–30	5–31	•–34
	6	11–27	9–29	8–31	7–33	7–34	6–37
	7	13–30	12–32	11–34	10–36	9–37	7–39
	8	16–33	14–35	13–37	12–39	11–40	9–42
	9	19–36	17–38	16–40	14–41	13–42	11–44
20	0	•– 6	•– 7	•– 9	•–10	•–12	•–14
	1	•–10	•–11	•–13	•–15	•–16	•–19
	2	•–13	•–15	•–17	•–19	•–20	•–23
	3	3–17	3–18	•–20	•–22	•–24	•–26
	4	6–20	5–22	4–23	•–25	•–27	•–29
	5	8–23	7–25	6–27	5–29	5–30	•–32
	6	10–26	9–28	8–30	7–31	6–33	6–35
	7	13–29	11–31	10–32	9–34	8–35	7–38
	8	15–32	14–34	13–35	11–37	10–38	9–40
	9	18–35	16–36	15–38	14–40	13–41	11–43
	10	21–37	19–39	17–41	16–42	15–43	13–45
21	0	•– 5	•– 7	•– 8	•–10	•–11	•–14
	1	•– 9	•–11	•–12	•–14	•–15	•–18
	2	•–13	•–14	•–16	•–18	•–19	•–22
	3	3–16	3–18	•–19	•–21	•–22	•–25
	4	5–19	4–21	4–22	•–24	•–26	•–28
	5	7–22	6–24	6–25	5–27	5–29	•–31
	6	10–25	9–27	8–28	7–30	6–31	•–34
	7	12–28	11–30	10–31	9–33	8–34	7–36
	8	15–30	13–32	12–34	11–35	10–37	9–39
	9	17–33	15–35	14–36	13–38	12–39	11–41
	10	20–36	18–38	17–39	15–40	14–41	13–43

N_1	x_1	2α = 0.20	2α = 0.10	2α = 0.05	2α = 0.02	2α = 0.01	2α = 0.002
		$N = 58$ (continued)					
22	0	•– 5	•– 6	•– 8	•– 9	•–10	•–13
	1	•– 9	•–10	•–12	•–13	•–15	•–17
	2	•–12	•–14	•–15	•–17	•–18	•–21
	3	3–15	3–17	•–18	•–20	•–21	•–24
	4	5–18	4–20	4–21	•–23	•–24	•–27
	5	7–21	6–23	5–24	5–26	•–27	•–30
	6	9–24	8–26	7–27	7–29	6–30	•–32
	7	12–26	10–28	9–30	8–32	8–33	7–35
	8	14–29	13–31	11–32	10–34	10–35	8–37
	9	16–32	15–33	14–35	12–37	12–38	10–40
	10	19–34	17–36	16–37	15–39	14–40	12–42
	11	21–37	20–38	18–40	17–41	16–42	14–44
23	0	•– 5	•– 6	•– 7	•– 9	•–10	•–12
	1	•– 8	•–10	•–11	•–13	•–14	•–16
	2	•–11	•–13	•–14	•–16	•–17	•–20
	3	3–14	•–16	•–18	•–19	•–21	•–23
	4	5–17	4–19	4–20	•–22	•–23	•–26
	5	7–20	6–22	5–23	5–25	•–26	•–29
	6	9–23	8–24	7–26	6–28	6–29	•–31
	7	11–25	10–27	9–29	8–30	8–31	7–34
	8	13–28	12–30	11–31	10–33	9–34	8–36
	9	16–30	14–32	13–34	12–35	11–36	10–38
	10	18–33	16–35	15–36	14–37	13–38	12–40
	11	20–35	19–37	17–38	16–40	15–41	14–42
24	0	•– 5	•– 6	•– 7	•– 8	•– 9	•–12
	1	•– 8	•– 9	•–11	•–12	•–13	•–16
	2	•–11	•–12	•–14	•–15	•–17	•–19
	3	3–14	•–15	•–17	•–18	•–20	•–22
	4	5–17	4–18	•–20	•–21	•–22	•–25
	5	7–19	6–21	5–22	5–24	•–25	•–28
	6	9–22	8–23	7–25	6–27	6–28	•–30
	7	11–24	10–26	9–27	8–29	7–30	•–32
	8	13–27	12–28	11–30	10–32	9–33	8–35
	9	15–29	14–31	13–32	11–34	11–35	10–37
	10	17–32	16–33	15–35	13–36	13–37	11–39
	11	19–34	18–36	17–37	15–38	15–39	13–41
	12	22–36	20–38	19–39	18–40	17–41	15–43
25	0	•– 4	•– 6	•– 7	•– 8	•– 9	•–11
	1	•– 8	•– 9	•–10	•–12	•–13	•–15
	2	•–11	•–12	•–13	•–15	•–16	•–18
	3	3–13	•–15	•–16	•–18	•–19	•–21
	4	4–16	4–17	•–19	•–20	•–22	•–24
	5	6–18	6–20	5–21	•–23	•–24	•–26
	6	8–21	7–23	7–24	6–26	6–27	•–29
	7	10–23	9–25	8–26	8–28	7–29	•–31
	8	12–26	11–27	10–29	9–30	9–31	8–33
	9	14–28	13–30	12–31	11–33	10–34	9–36
	10	16–30	15–32	14–33	13–35	12–36	11–38
	11	19–33	17–34	16–36	15–37	14–38	13–40
	12	21–35	19–36	18–38	17–39	16–40	14–42
26	0	•– 4	•– 5	•– 6	•– 8	•– 9	•–11
	1	•– 7	•– 9	•–10	•–11	•–12	•–14
	2	•–10	•–11	•–13	•–14	•–15	•–18
	3	3–13	•–14	•–15	•–17	•–18	•–20
	4	4–15	4–17	•–18	•–20	•–21	•–23
	5	6–18	5–19	5–21	•–22	•–23	•–25
	6	8–20	7–22	6–23	6–25	•–26	•–28
	7	10–22	9–24	8–25	7–27	7–28	•–30
	8	12–25	11–26	10–28	9–29	9–30	8–32
	9	14–27	13–29	12–30	11–31	10–32	9–34
	10	16–29	15–31	14–32	13–34	12–35	11–36
	11	18–32	17–33	16–34	14–36	14–37	12–38
	12	20–34	19–35	18–36	16–38	15–39	14–40
	13	22–36	21–37	20–38	18–40	17–41	16–42
27	0	•– 4	•– 5	•– 6	•– 7	•– 8	•–10
	1	•– 7	•– 8	•– 9	•–11	•–12	•–14
	2	•–10	•–11	•–12	•–14	•–15	•–17
	3	3–12	•–14	•–15	•–16	•–17	•–20
	4	4–15	4–16	•–17	•–19	•–20	•–22
	5	6–17	5–18	5–20	•–21	•–22	•–25
	6	8–19	7–21	6–22	6–24	•–25	•–27
	7	10–22	9–23	8–24	7–26	7–27	•–29
	8	11–24	10–25	10–27	9–28	8–29	•–31
	9	13–26	12–28	11–29	10–30	10–31	9–33
	10	15–28	14–30	13–31	12–32	12–33	10–35
	11	17–30	16–32	15–33	14–35	13–35	12–37
	12	19–33	18–34	17–35	16–37	15–37	14–39
	13	21–35	20–36	19–37	18–38	17–39	15–41
28	0	•– 4	•– 5	•– 6	•– 7	•– 8	•–10
	1	•– 7	•– 8	•– 9	•–10	•–11	•–13
	2	•– 9	•–11	•–12	•–13	•–14	•–16
	3	•–12	•–13	•–14	•–16	•–17	•–19
	4	4–14	4–15	•–17	•–18	•–19	•–21
	5	6–16	5–18	5–19	•–21	•–22	•–24
	6	7–19	7–20	6–21	6–23	•–24	•–26
	7	9–21	8–22	8–24	7–25	7–26	•–28
	8	11–23	10–24	9–26	9–27	8–28	•–30
	9	13–25	12–27	11–28	10–29	10–30	9–32
	10	15–27	14–29	13–30	12–31	11–32	10–34
	11	17–29	15–31	15–32	13–33	13–34	12–36
	12	19–31	17–33	16–34	15–35	15–36	13–38
	13	21–33	19–35	18–36	17–37	16–38	15–40
	14	23–35	21–37	20–38	19–39	18–40	17–41
29	0	•– 4	•– 5	•– 6	•– 7	•– 8	•– 9
	1	•– 6	•– 8	•– 9	•–10	•–11	•–13
	2	•– 9	•–10	•–11	•–13	•–13	•–16
	3	•–11	•–13	•–14	•–15	•–16	•–18
	4	4–14	•–15	•–16	•–17	•–18	•–20
	5	6–16	5–17	•–18	•–20	•–21	•–23

N_1	x_1	2α = 0.20	2α = 0.10	2α = 0.05	2α = 0.02	2α = 0.01	2α = 0.002
		$N = 58$ (continued)					
	6	7–18	6–19	6–21	•–22	•–23	•–25
	7	9–20	8–22	7–23	7–24	•–25	•–27
	8	11–22	10–24	9–25	8–26	8–27	•–29
	9	12–24	11–26	11–27	10–28	9–29	9–31
	10	14–26	13–28	12–29	11–30	11–31	10–33
	11	16–28	15–30	14–31	13–32	13–33	11–35
	12	18–30	17–32	16–33	15–34	14–35	13–37
	13	20–32	19–34	18–35	17–36	16–37	14–38
	14	22–34	20–36	19–37	18–38	18–39	16–40
		$N = 60$					
4	0	•–26	•–31	•–36	•–40	•–43	•–49
	1	1–41	•–45	•–48	•–51	•–53	•–56
	2	8–52	6–54	4–56	3–57	2–58	–
5	0	•–22	•–27	•–31	•–35	•–38	•–44
	1	1–35	•–39	•–43	•–46	•–48	•–52
	2	7–45	4–48	3–51	2–53	•–55	•–57
6	0	•–19	•–23	•–27	•–31	•–34	•–40
	1	•–30	•–34	•–38	•–42	•–44	•–48
	2	5–40	4–43	3–46	2–49	•–51	•–53
	3	12–48	9–51	7–53	5–55	4–56	3–57
7	0	•–16	•–20	•–24	•–28	•–31	•–36
	1	•–27	•–31	•–34	•–38	•–40	•–44
	2	5–35	3–39	2–42	•–45	•–47	•–50
	3	10–43	8–46	6–48	5–51	4–52	•–54
8	0	•–15	•–18	•–21	•–25	•–28	•–33
	1	•–24	•–28	•–31	•–34	•–37	•–41
	2	4–32	3–35	2–38	•–41	•–43	•–47
	3	9–39	7–42	5–45	4–47	3–49	•–52
	4	15–45	12–48	10–50	8–52	7–53	5–55
9	0	•–13	•–16	•–19	•–23	•–25	•–30
	1	•–22	•–25	•–28	•–31	•–34	•–38
	2	3–29	2–32	2–35	•–38	•–40	•–44
	3	8–36	6–39	5–41	4–44	3–46	•–49
	4	13–42	11–44	9–47	7–49	6–50	4–53
10	0	•–12	•–15	•–18	•–21	•–23	•–28
	1	•–20	•–23	•–26	•–29	•–31	•–35
	2	3–26	2–30	•–32	•–35	•–37	•–41
	3	7–33	5–36	4–38	3–41	3–43	•–46
	4	11–38	9–41	8–43	6–46	5–47	4–50
	5	16–44	14–46	12–48	10–50	9–51	7–53
11	0	•–11	•–14	•–16	•–19	•–21	•–26
	1	•–18	•–21	•–24	•–27	•–29	•–33
	2	3–24	2–27	•–30	•–33	•–35	•–39
	3	6–30	5–33	4–35	3–38	3–40	•–43
	4	10–35	9–38	7–40	6–43	5–45	4–47
	5	15–40	13–43	11–45	9–47	8–49	6–51
12	0	•–10	•–12	•–15	•–18	•–20	•–24
	1	•–17	•–19	•–22	•–25	•–27	•–31
	2	3–22	2–25	•–28	•–31	•–33	•–36
	3	6–28	5–31	4–33	3–36	•–38	•–41
	4	9–33	8–36	7–38	5–40	5–42	•–45
	5	13–38	11–40	10–42	8–45	7–46	6–49
	6	18–42	15–45	14–46	12–48	10–50	8–52
13	0	•– 9	•–12	•–14	•–17	•–18	•–23
	1	•–15	•–18	•–20	•–23	•–25	•–29
	2	2–21	2–24	•–26	•–29	•–31	•–34
	3	5–26	4–29	3–31	3–34	•–35	•–39
	4	9–31	7–33	6–36	5–38	4–40	•–43
	5	12–35	11–38	9–40	8–42	7–44	5–46
	6	16–40	14–42	13–44	11–46	10–47	8–49
14	0	•– 9	•–11	•–13	•–15	•–17	•–21
	1	•–14	•–17	•–19	•–22	•–24	•–27
	2	2–19	•–22	•–24	•–27	•–29	•–32
	3	5–24	4–27	3–29	•–32	•–33	•–37
	4	8–29	7–31	6–33	5–36	4–38	•–41
	5	11–33	10–35	8–38	7–40	6–41	5–44
	6	15–37	13–39	12–41	10–44	9–45	7–47
	7	19–41	17–43	15–45	13–47	12–48	10–50
15	0	•– 8	•–10	•–12	•–14	•–16	•–20
	1	•–13	•–16	•–18	•–20	•–22	•–26
	2	2–18	•–21	•–23	•–25	•–27	•–31
	3	5–23	4–25	3–27	•–30	•–32	•–35
	4	8–27	6–29	5–32	4–34	4–36	•–39
	5	11–31	9–33	8–36	7–38	6–39	5–42
	6	14–35	12–37	11–39	9–41	8–43	7–45
	7	18–39	16–41	14–43	12–45	11–46	9–48
16	0	•– 7	•– 9	•–11	•–14	•–15	•–19
	1	•–13	•–15	•–17	•–19	•–21	•–24
	2	2–17	•–19	•–21	•–24	•–26	•–29
	3	4–21	3–24	3–26	•–28	•–30	•–33
	4	7–25	6–28	5–30	4–32	4–34	•–37
	5	10–29	9–32	7–34	6–36	6–37	5–40
	6	13–33	11–35	10–37	9–39	8–41	7–43
	7	16–37	15–39	13–41	11–43	10–44	9–46
	8	20–40	18–42	16–44	14–46	13–47	11–49
17	0	•– 7	•– 9	•–11	•–13	•–14	•–18
	1	•–12	•–14	•–16	•–18	•–20	•–23
	2	2–16	•–18	•–20	•–23	•–24	•–28
	3	4–20	3–22	3–24	•–27	•–28	•–31
	4	7–24	6–26	5–28	4–31	4–32	•–35
	5	9–28	8–30	7–32	6–34	5–36	•–38
	6	12–31	11–34	10–35	8–37	8–39	6–41
	7	15–35	14–37	12–39	11–41	10–42	8–44
	8	19–38	17–40	15–42	13–44	12–45	11–47

x_1	$N_1 - x_1$	N_1	$N = N_1 + N_2$	For explanation see below
x_2	$N_2 - x_2$	N_2	$X = x_1 + x_2$	
X	$N - X$	N	$N_1 \leqq N_2$	
			$x_1 \leqq N_1 - x_1$	

$N = 60$ (continued)

N_1	x_1	2α = 0.20	2α = 0.10	2α = 0.05	2α = 0.02	2α = 0.01	2α = 0.002
18	0	•–7	•–8	•–10	•–12	•–13	•–17
	1	•–11	•–13	•–15	•–17	•–19	•–22
	2	2–15	•–17	•–19	•–21	•–23	•–26
	3	4–19	3–21	3–23	•–25	•–27	•–30
	4	6–23	5–25	4–27	4–29	•–31	•–33
	5	9–26	8–28	7–30	6–32	5–34	•–37
	6	12–30	10–32	9–34	8–36	7–37	6–40
	7	15–33	13–35	12–37	10–39	9–40	8–43
	8	18–36	16–38	14–40	13–42	12–43	10–45
	9	21–39	19–41	17–43	15–45	14–46	12–48
19	0	•–6	•–8	•–9	•–11	•–13	•–16
	1	•–11	•–12	•–14	•–16	•–18	•–21
	2	2–14	•–16	•–18	•–20	•–22	•–25
	3	4–18	3–20	•–22	•–24	•–26	•–29
	4	6–22	5–24	4–26	4–28	•–29	•–32
	5	8–25	7–27	6–29	5–31	5–32	•–35
	6	11–28	10–30	9–32	8–34	7–35	6–38
	7	14–31	12–33	11–35	10–37	9–38	8–41
	8	17–35	15–37	14–38	12–40	11–41	10–43
	9	19–38	18–39	16–41	15–43	14–44	12–46
20	0	•–6	•–7	•–9	•–11	•–12	•–15
	1	•–10	•–12	•–13	•–15	•–17	•–20
	2	•–14	•–16	•–17	•–19	•–21	•–24
	3	3–17	3–19	•–21	•–23	•–24	•–27
	4	6–21	5–23	4–24	4–26	•–28	•–31
	5	8–24	7–26	6–28	5–30	5–31	•–34
	6	11–27	9–29	8–31	7–33	7–34	6–37
	7	13–30	12–32	11–34	9–36	9–37	7–39
	8	16–33	14–35	13–37	12–38	11–40	9–42
	9	18–36	17–38	15–39	14–41	13–42	11–44
	10	21–39	19–41	18–42	16–44	15–45	13–47
21	0	•–6	•–7	•–8	•–10	•–11	•–14
	1	•–10	•–11	•–13	•–15	•–16	•–19
	2	•–13	•–15	•–16	•–18	•–20	•–23
	3	3–16	3–18	•–20	•–22	•–23	•–26
	4	5–20	5–22	4–23	•–25	•–27	•–29
	5	8–23	7–25	6–26	5–28	5–30	•–32
	6	10–26	9–28	8–29	7–31	6–33	•–35
	7	12–29	11–31	10–32	9–34	8–35	7–38
	8	15–32	14–33	12–35	11–37	10–38	9–40
	9	18–34	16–36	15–38	13–39	12–41	11–43
	10	20–37	19–39	17–40	16–42	15–43	13–45
22	0	•–5	•–7	•–8	•–10	•–11	•–14
	1	•–9	•–11	•–12	•–14	•–15	•–18
	2	•–12	•–14	•–16	•–18	•–19	•–22
	3	3–16	3–17	•–19	•–21	•–22	•–25
	4	5–19	4–21	4–22	•–24	•–25	•–28
	5	7–22	6–24	6–25	5–27	5–28	•–31
	6	10–25	8–26	8–28	7–30	6–31	•–34
	7	12–27	11–29	10–31	9–33	8–34	7–36
	8	14–30	13–32	12–34	11–35	10–37	9–39
	9	17–33	15–35	14–36	13–38	12–39	10–41
	10	19–36	18–37	16–39	15–40	14–41	12–43
	11	22–38	20–40	19–41	17–43	16–44	14–46
23	0	•–5	•–6	•–8	•–9	•–10	•–13
	1	•–9	•–10	•–12	•–13	•–15	•–17
	2	•–12	•–14	•–15	•–17	•–18	•–21
	3	3–15	•–17	•–18	•–20	•–21	•–24
	4	5–18	4–20	4–21	•–23	•–24	•–27
	5	7–21	6–23	5–24	5–26	•–27	•–30
	6	9–24	8–25	7–27	6–29	6–30	•–32
	7	11–26	10–28	9–30	8–31	8–33	7–35
	8	14–29	12–31	11–32	10–34	10–35	8–37
	9	16–32	15–33	13–35	12–36	11–38	10–40
	10	18–34	17–36	16–37	14–39	13–40	12–42
	11	21–37	19–38	18–40	17–41	16–42	14–44
24	0	•–5	•–6	•–7	•–9	•–10	•–12
	1	•–8	•–10	•–11	•–13	•–14	•–16
	2	•–11	•–13	•–14	•–16	•–17	•–20
	3	3–14	•–16	•–17	•–19	•–20	•–23
	4	5–17	4–19	4–20	•–22	•–23	•–26
	5	7–20	6–22	5–23	5–25	•–26	•–29
	6	9–23	8–24	7–26	6–28	6–29	•–31
	7	11–25	10–27	9–28	8–30	7–31	7–34
	8	13–28	12–30	11–31	10–33	9–34	8–36
	9	15–30	14–32	13–33	12–35	11–36	10–38
	10	18–33	16–34	15–36	14–37	13–39	12–41
	11	20–35	18–37	17–38	16–40	15–41	13–43
	12	22–38	21–39	19–41	18–42	17–43	15–45
25	0	•–5	•–6	•–7	•–8	•–9	•–12
	1	•–8	•–9	•–11	•–12	•–13	•–16
	2	•–11	•–12	•–14	•–15	•–17	•–19
	3	3–14	•–15	•–17	•–18	•–20	•–22
	4	5–16	4–18	•–20	•–21	•–22	•–25
	5	7–19	6–21	5–22	5–24	•–25	•–28
	6	8–22	8–23	7–25	6–27	6–28	•–30
	7	11–24	9–26	9–27	8–29	7–30	•–32
	8	13–27	11–28	11–30	10–31	9–33	8–35
	9	15–29	14–31	12–32	11–34	11–35	10–37
	10	17–32	16–33	14–35	13–36	13–37	11–39
	11	19–34	18–36	17–37	15–38	14–39	13–41
	12	21–36	20–38	19–39	17–41	16–41	15–43
26	0	•–4	•–6	•–7	•–8	•–9	•–11
	1	•–8	•–9	•–10	•–12	•–13	•–15
	2	•–10	•–12	•–13	•–15	•–16	•–18
	3	3–13	•–15	•–16	•–18	•–19	•–21
	4	4–16	4–17	•–19	•–20	•–22	•–24
	5	6–18	6–20	5–21	•–23	•–24	•–27
	6	8–21	7–22	7–24	6–26	6–27	•–29
	7	10–23	9–25	8–26	8–28	7–29	•–31
	8	12–26	11–27	10–29	9–30	9–31	8–34
	9	14–28	13–30	12–31	11–33	10–34	9–36
	10	16–30	15–32	14–33	13–35	12–36	11–38
	11	18–33	17–34	16–36	15–37	14–38	13–40
	12	21–35	19–36	18–38	17–39	16–40	14–42
	13	23–37	21–39	20–40	19–41	18–42	16–44
27	0	•–4	•–5	•–6	•–8	•–9	•–11
	1	•–7	•–9	•–10	•–11	•–12	•–14
	2	•–10	•–11	•–13	•–14	•–15	•–18
	3	3–13	•–14	•–15	•–17	•–18	•–20
	4	4–15	4–17	•–18	•–20	•–21	•–23
	5	6–18	5–19	5–21	•–22	•–23	•–26
	6	8–20	7–22	6–23	6–25	•–26	•–28
	7	10–22	9–24	8–25	7–27	7–28	•–30
	8	12–25	11–26	10–28	9–29	8–30	8–32
	9	14–27	13–29	12–30	11–32	10–33	9–35
	10	16–29	15–31	14–32	12–34	12–35	11–37
	11	18–32	16–33	15–34	14–36	14–37	12–39
	12	20–34	19–35	17–36	16–38	15–39	14–41
	13	22–36	21–37	19–39	18–40	17–41	16–42
28	0	•–4	•–5	•–6	•–7	•–8	•–10
	1	•–7	•–8	•–9	•–11	•–12	•–14
	2	•–10	•–11	•–12	•–14	•–15	•–17
	3	3–12	•–14	•–15	•–16	•–17	•–20
	4	4–15	4–16	•–17	•–19	•–20	•–22
	5	6–17	5–18	5–20	•–21	•–22	•–25
	6	8–19	7–21	6–22	6–24	•–25	•–27
	7	9–22	9–23	8–24	7–26	7–27	•–29
	8	11–24	10–25	10–27	9–28	8–29	•–31
	9	13–26	12–28	11–29	10–30	10–31	9–33
	10	15–28	14–30	13–31	12–33	11–34	10–35
	11	17–30	16–32	15–33	14–35	13–36	12–37
	12	19–33	18–34	17–35	16–37	15–38	14–39
	13	21–35	20–36	19–37	18–39	17–40	15–41
	14	23–37	22–38	21 39	19–41	19–41	17–43
29	0	•–4	•–5	•–6	•–7	•–8	•–10
	1	•–7	•–8	•–9	•–10	•–11	•–13
	2	•–9	•–11	•–12	•–13	•–14	•–16
	3	•–12	•–13	•–14	•–16	•–17	•–19
	4	4–14	4–15	•–17	•–18	•–19	•–21
	5	6–16	5–18	5–19	•–21	•–22	•–24
	6	7–19	7–20	6–21	6–23	•–24	•–26
	7	9–21	8–22	8–24	7–25	7–26	•–28
	8	11–23	10–25	9–26	9–27	8–28	•–30
	9	13–25	12–27	11–28	10–29	10–30	9–32
	10	15–27	14–29	13–30	12–31	11–32	10–34
	11	17–29	15–31	14–32	13–34	13–34	12–36
	12	19–31	17–33	16–34	15–35	14–36	13–38
	13	20–34	19–35	18–36	17–37	16–38	15–40
	14	22–36	21–37	20–38	19–39	18–40	17–42
30	0	•–4	•–5	•–6	•–7	•–8	•–9
	1	•–6	•–8	•–9	•–10	•–11	•–13
	2	•–9	•–10	•–11	•–13	•–14	•–16
	3	•–11	•–13	•–14	•–15	•–16	•–18
	4	4–14	•–15	•–16	•–18	•–19	•–21
	5	6–16	5–17	•–18	•–20	•–21	•–23
	6	7–18	6–19	6–21	•–22	•–23	•–25
	7	9–20	8–22	7–23	7–24	•–25	•–27
	8	11–22	10–24	9–25	8–26	8–27	•–29
	9	12–24	11–26	11–27	10–28	9–29	9–31
	10	14–26	13–28	12–29	11–30	11–31	10–33
	11	16–28	15–30	14–31	13–32	12–33	11–35
	12	18–30	17–32	16–33	15–34	14–35	13–37
	13	20–32	19–34	18–35	16–36	16–37	14–39
	14	22–34	20–36	19–37	18–38	17–39	16–41
	15	24–36	22–38	21–39	20–40	19–41	18–42

Explanation of the tables on pages 109–123 (see also page 191)

Any statistical test can be put in the form of a fourfold table

x_1	$(N_1 - x_1)$	N_1
x_2	$(N_2 - x_2)$	N_2

which is so arranged that $N_1 \leqq N_2$ and $x_1 \leqq (N_1 - x_1)$. The sum of $N_1 + N_2 = N$, of $x_1 + x_2 = X$. N and N_1 are looked for in the table, where against x_1 will be found the limits X_l and X_r for any desired significance. Putting $x_1/N_1 = p_1$ and $x_2/N_2 = p_2$, then if $X \leqq X_l$, the significance limit when testing for

$p_1 > p_2$ is $P_l \leqq \alpha$
and for $p_1 \neq p_2$ is $2P_l \leqq 2\alpha$

If $X \geqq X_r$, the significance limit when testing for

$p_1 < p_2$ is $P_r \leqq \alpha$
and for $p_1 \neq p_2$ is $2P_r \leqq 2\alpha$

If X lies between X_l and X_r, the null hypothesis $p_1 = p_2$ cannot be rejected.

Prob $[T_l < \boldsymbol{T} < T_r] \geqq 1 - 2\alpha$. For explanation see page 192. The italic values are 'exact' limits[1], the others approximate limits[2]
The limits for $N_1 = N_2$ are in bold figures

$2\alpha = 0.10$

N_2 \ N_1	4	5	6	7	8	9	10	11	12	13	14	15	16	17	18	19	20	21	22	23	24	25
	T_l–T_r	T_l–T_r	T_l–T_r	T_l–T_r	T_l–T_r	T_l–T_r	T_l–T_r	T_l–T_r	T_l–T_r	T_l–T_r	T_l–T_r	T_l–T_r	T_l–T_r	T_l–T_r	T_l–T_r	T_l–T_r	T_l–T_r	T_l–T_r	T_l–T_r	T_l–T_r	T_l–T_r	T_l–T_r
4	**11–25**	*17–33*	*24–42*	*32–52*	*41–63*	*51–75*	*62–88*	*74–102*	*87–117*	*101–133*	*116–150*	*132–168*	*150–186*	*168–206*	*187–227*	*207–249*	*228–272*	*250–296*	*273–321*	*297–347*	*322–374*	*348–402*
5	*12–28*	**19–36**	*26–46*	*34–57*	*44–68*	*54–81*	*66–94*	*78–109*	*91–125*	*106–141*	*121–159*	*138–177*	*155–197*	*173–218*	*193–239*	*213–262*	*235–285*	*257–310*	*281–335*	*305–362*	*330–390*	*357–418*
6	*13–31*	*20–40*	**28–50**	*36–62*	*46–74*	*57–87*	*69–101*	*82–116*	*95–133*	*110–150*	*126–168*	*143–187*	*161–207*	*179–229*	*199–251*	*220–274*	*242–298*	*265–323*	*289–349*	*313–377*	*339–405*	*366–434*
7	*14–34*	*21–44*	*29–55*	**39–66**	*49–79*	*60–93*	*72–108*	*85–124*	*99–141*	*115–158*	*131–177*	*148–197*	*166–218*	*186–239*	*206–262*	*227–286*	*249–311*	*272–337*	*297–363*	*322–391*	*348–420*	*375–450*
8	*15–37*	*23–47*	*31–59*	*41–71*	**51–85**	*63–99*	*75–115*	*89–131*	*104–148*	*119–167*	*136–186*	*153–207*	*172–228*	*192–250*	*212–274*	*234–298*	*257–323*	*280–350*	*305–377*	*330–406*	*357–435*	*385–465*
9	*16–40*	*24–51*	*33–63*	*43–76*	*54–90*	**66–105**	*79–121*	*93–138*	*108–156*	*124–178*	*141–195*	*159–216*	*178–238*	*198–261*	*219–285*	*241–310*	*264–336*	*288–363*	*313–391*	*339–420*	366–450	394–481
10	*17–43*	*26–54*	*35–67*	*45–81*	*56–96*	*69–111*	**82–128**	*97–145*	*112–164*	*128–184*	*146–204*	*164–226*	*184–248*	*204–272*	*226–297*	*248–322*	*272–348*	*296–376*	321–405	348–434	375–465	403–497
11	*18–46*	*27–58*	*37–71*	*47–86*	*59–101*	*72–117*	*86–134*	**100–153**	*116–172*	*133–192*	*151–213*	*170–235*	*190–258*	*210–283*	*232–308*	*255–334*	279–361	304–389	329–419	356–449	384–480	413–512
12	*19–49*	*28–62*	*38–76*	*49–91*	*62–106*	*75–123*	*89–141*	*104–160*	**120–180**	*138–200*	*156–222*	*175–245*	*196–268*	*217–293*	239–319	262–346	286–374	312–402	338–432	365–463	393–495	423–527
13	*20–52*	*30–65*	*40–80*	*52–95*	*64–112*	*78–129*	*92–148*	*108–167*	*125–187*	**142–209**	*161–231*	*181–254*	*201–279*	223–304	245–331	269–358	294–386	320–415	346–446	374–477	403–509	433–542
14	*21–55*	*31–69*	*42–84*	*54–100*	*67–117*	*81–135*	*96–154*	*112–174*	*129–195*	*147–217*	**166–240**	186–264	207–289	229–315	252–342	276–370	301–399	328–428	355–459	383–491	412–524	442–558
15	*22–58*	*33–72*	*44–88*	*56–105*	*69–123*	*84–141*	*99–161*	*116–181*	*133–203*	*152–225*	171–249	**191–274**	213–299	235–326	259–353	284–381	309–411	336–441	363–473	392–505	422–538	452–573
16	*24–60*	*34–76*	*46–92*	*58–110*	*72–128*	*87–147*	*103–167*	*120–188*	*138–210*	*156–234*	176–258	197–283	**219–309**	242–336	266–364	291–393	317–423	344–454	372–486	401–519	431–553	462–588
17	*25–63*	*35–80*	*47–97*	*61–114*	*75–133*	*90–153*	*106–174*	*123–196*	*142–218*	161–242	181–267	202–293	225–319	**248–347**	273–375	298–405	325–435	352–467	380–500	410–533	440–568	472–603
18	*26–66*	*37–83*	*49–101*	*63–119*	*77–139*	*93–159*	*110–180*	*127–203*	146–226	165–251	186–276	208–302	231–329	255–357	**280–386**	305–417	332–448	360–480	389–513	419–547	450–582	482–618
19	*27–69*	*38–87*	*51–105*	*65–124*	*80–144*	*96–165*	*113–187*	*131–210*	150–234	170–259	191–285	214–311	237–339	261–368	286–398	**313–428**	340–460	368–493	398–526	428–561	459–597	492–633
20	*28–72*	*40–90*	*53–109*	*67–129*	*83–149*	*99–171*	*117–193*	135–217	154–242	175–267	196–294	219–321	243–349	268–378	293–409	320–440	**348–472**	376–506	406–540	437–575	469–611	501–649
21	*29–75*	*41–94*	*55–113*	*69–134*	*85–155*	*102–177*	*120–200*	139–224	159–249	180–275	202–302	225–330	249–359	274–389	300–420	327–452	355–485	**385–518**	415–553	446–589	478–626	511–664
22	*30–78*	*43–97*	*57–117*	*72–138*	*88–160*	*105–183*	123–207	142–232	163–257	184–284	207–311	230–340	255–369	280–400	307–431	335–463	363–497	393–531	**423–567**	455–603	488–640	521–679
23	*31–81*	*44–101*	*58–122*	*74–143*	*90–166*	*108–189*	127–213	146–239	167–265	189–292	212–320	236–349	261–379	287–410	314–442	342–475	371–509	401–544	432–580	**464–617**	497–655	531–694
24	*32–84*	*45–105*	*60–126*	*76–148*	*93–171*	111–195	130–220	150–246	171–273	194–300	217–329	242–358	267–389	293–421	321–453	349–487	379–521	409–557	441–593	473–631	**507–669**	541–709
25	*33–87*	*47–108*	*62–130*	*78–153*	*96–176*	114–201	133–227	154–253	176–280	199–308	222–338	247–368	273–399	300–431	328–464	357–498	386–534	417–570	449–607	482–645	516–684	**551–724**
26	*34–90*	*48–112*	*64–134*	*81–157*	*98–182*	117–207	137–233	158–260	180–288	203–317	227–347	253–377	279–409	306–442	335–475	364–510	394–546	426–582	458–620	491–659	526–698	561–739
27	*35–93*	*50–115*	*66–138*	*83–162*	*101–187*	120–213	140–240	162–267	184–296	208–325	233–355	258–387	285–419	313–452	342–486	371–522	402–558	434–595	467–633	500–673	535–713	571–754
28	*36–96*	*51–119*	*67–143*	*85–167*	103–193	123–219	144–246	166–274	189–303	213–333	238–364	264–396	291–429	319–463	348–498	379–533	410–570	442–608	475–647	510–686	545–727	581–769
29	*37–99*	*53–122*	*69–147*	*87–172*	106–198	126–225	147–253	170–281	193–311	218–341	243–373	270–405	297–439	326–473	355–509	386–545	418–582	450–621	484–660	519–700	554–742	591–784
30	*38–102*	*54–126*	*71–151*	*89–177*	109–203	129–231	151–259	174–288	197–319	222–350	248–382	275–415	303–449	332–484	362–520	393–557	425–595	459–633	493–673	528–714	564–756	601–799
31	*39–105*	*55–130*	*73–155*	*92–181*	111–209	132–237	154–266	178–295	202–326	227–358	253–391	281–424	309–459	339–494	369–531	401–568	433–607	467–646	501–687	537–728	574–770	611–814
32	*40–108*	*57–133*	*75–159*	*94–186*	114–214	135–243	158–272	181–303	206–334	232–366	259–399	286–434	315–469	345–505	376–542	408–580	441–619	475–659	510–700	546–742	583–785	621–829
33	*41–111*	*58–137*	*77–163*	*96–191*	117–219	138–249	161–279	185–310	210–342	237–374	264–408	292–443	321–479	352–515	383–553	415–592	449–631	483–672	519–713	555–756	593–799	631–844
34	*42–114*	*60–140*	*78–168*	98–196	119–225	141–255	165–285	189–317	215–349	241–383	269–417	298–452	327–489	358–526	390–564	423–603	457–643	492–684	527–727	564–770	602–814	641–859
35	*43–117*	*61–144*	80–172	100–201	122–230	144–261	168–292	193–324	219–357	246–391	274–426	303–462	333–499	365–536	397–575	430–615	464–656	500–697	536–740	574–783	612–828	651–874
36	*44–120*	62–148	82–176	102–206	124–236	148–266	172–298	197–331	223–365	251–399	279–435	309–471	340–508	371–547	404–586	438–626	472–668	508–710	545–753	583–797	621–843	661–889
37	45–123	64–151	84–180	105–210	127–241	151–272	175–305	201–338	228–372	256–407	285–443	315–480	346–518	378–557	411–597	445–638	480–680	516–723	554–766	592–811	631–857	671–904
38	46–126	65–155	85–185	107–215	130–246	154–278	179–311	205–345	232–380	260–416	290–452	320–490	352–528	384–568	418–608	452–650	488–692	525–735	562–780	601–825	641–871	681–919
39	47–129	67–158	87–189	109–220	132–252	157–284	182–318	209–352	236–388	265–424	295–461	326–499	358–538	391–578	425–619	460–661	496–704	533–748	571–793	610–839	650–886	691–934
40	48–132	68–162	89–193	111–225	135–257	160–290	186–324	213–359	241–395	270–432	300–470	331–509	364–548	397–589	432–630	467–673	504–716	541–761	580–806	619–853	660–900	702–948
41	49–135	69–166	91–197	114–229	138–262	163–296	189–331	217–366	245–403	275–440	305–479	337–518	370–558	404–599	439–641	474–685	511–729	549–774	588–820	628–867	669–915	712–963
42	50–138	71–169	93–201	116–234	140–268	166–302	193–337	221–373	249–411	279–449	311–487	343–527	376–568	410–610	446–652	482–696	519–741	558–786	597–833	638–880	679–929	722–978
43	51–141	72–173	95–205	118–239	143–273	169–308	196–344	224–381	254–418	284–457	316–496	348–537	382–578	417–620	452–664	489–708	527–753	566–799	606–846	647–894	689–943	732–993
44	52–144	74–176	96–210	120–244	146–278	172–314	200–350	228–388	258–426	289–465	321–505	354–546	388–588	423–631	459–675	497–719	535–765	574–812	615–859	656–908	698–958	742–1008
45	53–147	75–180	98–214	123–248	148–284	175–320	203–357	232–395	262–434	294–473	326–514	360–555	394–598	430–641	466–686	504–731	543–777	583–824	623–873	665–922	708–972	752–1023
46	55–149	77–183	100–218	125–253	151–289	178–326	207–363	236–402	267–441	299–481	331–523	365–565	400–608	436–652	473–697	511–743	551–789	591–837	632–886	674–936	718–986	762–1038
47	56–152	78–187	102–222	127–258	154–294	181–332	210–370	240–409	271–449	303–490	337–531	371–574	406–618	443–662	480–708	519–754	558–802	599–850	641–899	683–950	727–1001	772–1053
48	57–155	79–191	104–226	129–263	156–300	184–338	214–376	244–416	275–457	308–498	342–540	377–583	412–628	449–673	487–719	526–766	566–814	607–863	649–913	693–963	737–1015	782–1068
49	58–158	81–194	106–230	132–267	159–305	187–344	217–383	248–423	280–464	313–506	347–549	382–593	418–638	456–683	494–730	534–777	574–826	616–875	658–926	702–977	746–1030	792–1083
50	59–161	82–198	107–235	134–272	162–310	190–350	221–387	252–430	284–472	318–514	352–558	388–602	425–647	462–694	501–741	541–789	582–838	624–888	667–939	711–991	756–1044	802–1098

[1] Based on the exact limits for $W = 2U$ in WABEKE and VAN EEDEN, *Handleiding voor de toets van Wilcoxon*, Report S 176 (M 65), Mathematisch Centrum, Statistische Afdeling (Prof. D. VAN DANTZIG), Amsterdam, 1955, by kind permission of the authors and publishers.

[2] Based on the normal approximation with empirical continuity correction.

Prob $[T_l < \boldsymbol{T} < T_r] \geqq 1 - 2\alpha$. For explanation see page 192. The italic values are 'exact' limits [1], the others approximate limits [2]
The limits for $N_1 = N_2$ are in bold figures

$2\alpha = 0.05$

Each cell gives T_l–T_r.

N_2 \ N_1	4	5	6	7	8	9	10	11	12	13	14	15	16	17	18	19	20	21	22	23	24	25
4	**10–26**	16–34	23–43	31–53	40–64	49–77	60–90	72–104	85–119	99–135	114–152	130–170	147–189	164–210	183–231	203–253	224–276	246–300	269–325	293–351	317–379	343–407
5	11–29	**17–38**	24–48	33–58	42–70	52–83	63–97	75–112	89–127	103–144	118–162	134–181	151–201	170–221	189–243	209–266	230–290	253–314	276–340	300–367	325–395	352–423
6	12–32	18–42	**26–52**	34–64	44–76	55–89	66–104	79–119	92–136	107–153	122–172	139–191	157–211	175–233	195–255	215–279	237–303	260–328	283–355	308–382	333–411	360–440
7	13–35	20–45	27–57	**36–69**	46–82	57–96	69–111	82–127	96–144	111–162	127–181	144–201	162–222	181–244	201–267	222–291	244–316	267–342	291–369	316–397	342–426	369–456
8	14–38	21–49	29–61	38–74	**49–87**	60–102	72–118	85–135	100–152	115–171	131–191	149–211	167–233	187–255	207–279	228–304	251–329	274–356	298–384	324–412	350–442	378–472
9	14–42	22–53	31–65	40–79	51–93	**62–109**	75–125	89–142	104–160	119–180	136–200	154–221	173–243	192–267	213–291	235–316	258–342	281–370	306–398	332–427	359–457	387–488
10	15–45	23–57	32–70	42–84	53–99	65–115	**78–132**	92–150	107–169	124–188	141–209	159–231	178–254	198–278	219–303	242–328	265–355	289–383	314–412	340–442	368–472	396–504
11	16–48	24–61	34–74	44–89	55–105	68–121	81–139	**96–157**	111–177	128–197	145–219	164–241	183–265	204–289	226–314	248–341	272–368	296–397	322–426	349–456	376–488	405–520
12	17–51	26–64	35–79	46–94	58–110	71–127	84–146	99–165	**115–185**	132–206	150–228	169–251	189–275	210–300	232–326	255–353	279–381	304–410	330–440	357–471	385–503	414–536
13	18–54	27–68	37–83	48–99	60–116	73–134	88–152	103–172	119–193	**136–215**	155–237	174–261	195–285	216–311	239–337	262–365	286–394	312–423	338–454	365–486	394–518	423–552
14	19–57	28–72	38–88	50–104	62–122	76–140	91–159	106–180	123–201	141–223	**160–246**	179–271	200–296	222–322	245–349	269–377	293–407	319–437	346–468	374–500	403–533	433–567
15	20–60	29–76	40–92	52–109	65–127	79–146	94–166	110–187	127–209	145–232	164–256	**184–281**	206–306	228–333	251–361	275–390	301–419	327–450	354–482	382–515	412–548	442–583
16	21–63	30–80	42–96	54–114	67–133	82–152	97–173	113–195	131–217	150–240	169–265	190–290	**211–317**	234–344	258–372	282–402	308–432	335–463	362–496	391–529	421–563	451–599
17	21–67	32–83	43–101	56–119	70–138	84–159	100–180	117–202	135–225	154–249	174–274	195–300	217–327	**240–355**	264–384	289–414	315–445	342–477	370–510	399–544	429–579	461–614
18	22–70	33–87	45–105	58–124	72–144	87–165	103–187	121–209	139–233	159–257	179–283	200–310	223–337	246–366	**271–395**	296–426	322–458	350–490	378–524	408–558	438–594	470–630
19	23–73	34–91	46–110	60–129	74–150	90–171	107–193	124–217	143–241	163–266	184–292	205–320	228–348	252–377	277–407	**303–438**	330–470	358–503	387–537	416–573	447–609	479–646
20	24–76	35–95	48–114	62–134	77–155	93–177	110–200	128–224	147–249	167–275	188–302	211–329	234–358	258–388	283–419	310–450	**337–483**	365–517	395–551	425–587	456–624	489–661
21	25–79	37–98	50–118	64–139	79–161	95–184	113–207	131–232	151–257	172–283	193–311	216–339	240–368	264–399	290–430	317–462	344–496	**373–530**	403–565	434–601	465–639	498–677
22	26–82	38–102	51–123	66–144	81–167	98–190	116–214	135–239	155–265	176–292	198–320	221–349	245–379	270–410	296–442	324–474	352–508	381–543	**411–579**	442–616	474–654	508–692
23	27–85	39–106	53–127	68–149	84–172	101–196	119–221	139–246	159–273	180–301	203–329	226–359	251–389	276–421	303–453	330–487	359–521	389–556	419–593	**451–630**	483–669	517–708
24	27–89	40–110	54–132	70–154	86–178	104–202	123–227	142–254	163–281	185–309	208–338	232–368	257–399	282–432	309–465	337–499	366–534	396–570	427–607	459–645	**492–684**	527–723
25	28–92	42–113	56–136	72–159	89–183	107–208	126–234	146–261	167–289	189–318	213–347	237–378	262–410	289–442	316–476	344–511	374–546	404–583	436–620	468–659	502–698	**536–739**
26	29–95	43–117	58–140	74–164	91–189	109–215	129–241	150–268	171–297	194–326	217–357	242–388	268–420	295–453	322–488	351–523	381–559	412–596	444–634	477–673	511–713	545–755
27	30–98	44–121	59–145	76–169	93–195	112–221	132–248	153–276	175–305	198–335	222–366	247–398	273–431	301–464	329–499	358–535	388–572	420–609	452–648	485–688	520–728	555–770
28	31–101	45–125	61–149	78–174	96–200	115–227	135–255	157–283	179–313	203–343	227–375	253–407	279–441	307–475	335–511	365–547	396–584	427–623	460–662	494–702	529–743	564–786
29	32–104	47–128	63–153	80–179	98–206	118–233	139–261	160–291	183–321	207–352	232–384	258–417	285–451	313–486	342–522	372–559	403–597	435–636	468–676	503–716	538–758	574–801
30	33–107	48–132	64–158	82–184	101–211	121–239	142–268	164–298	187–329	211–361	237–393	263–427	291–461	319–497	348–534	379–571	411–609	443–649	477–689	511–731	547–773	584–816
31	34–110	49–136	66–162	84–189	103–217	123–246	145–275	167–306	191–337	216–369	242–402	268–437	296–472	325–508	355–545	386–583	418–622	451–662	485–703	520–745	556–788	593–832
32	34–114	50–140	67–167	86–194	106–222	126–252	148–282	171–313	195–345	220–378	246–412	274–446	302–482	331–519	362–556	393–595	425–635	459–675	493–717	529–759	565–803	603–847
33	35–117	52–143	69–171	88–199	108–228	129–258	151–289	175–320	199–353	225–386	251–421	279–456	308–492	337–530	368–568	400–607	433–647	467–688	501–731	537–774	574–818	612–863
34	36–120	53–147	71–175	90–204	110–234	132–264	155–295	178–328	203–361	229–395	256–430	284–466	313–503	343–541	375–579	407–619	440–660	474–702	510–744	546–788	583–833	622–878
35	37–123	54–151	72–180	92–209	113–239	135–270	158–302	182–335	207–369	234–403	261–439	289–476	319–513	350–551	381–591	414–631	447–673	482–715	518–758	555–802	592–848	631–894
36	38–126	55–155	74–184	94–214	115–245	137–277	161–309	185–343	211–377	238–412	266–448	295–485	325–523	356–562	388–602	421–643	455–685	490–728	526–772	563–817	602–862	641–909
37	39–129	57–158	76–188	96–219	117–251	140–283	164–316	189–350	215–385	242–421	271–457	300–495	330–534	362–573	394–614	428–655	462–698	498–741	534–786	572–831	611–877	650–925
38	40–132	58–162	77–193	98–224	120–256	143–289	167–323	193–357	219–393	247–429	275–467	305–505	336–544	368–584	401–625	435–667	470–710	506–754	543–799	581–845	620–892	660–940
39	41–135	59–166	79–197	100–229	122–262	146–295	170–330	196–365	223–401	251–438	280–476	311–514	342–554	374–595	407–637	442–679	477–723	514–767	551–813	589–860	629–907	670–955
40	41–139	60–170	80–202	102–234	125–267	149–301	174–336	200–372	227–409	256–446	285–485	316–524	347–565	380–606	414–648	449–691	485–735	521–781	559–827	598–874	638–922	679–971
41	42–142	61–174	82–206	104–239	127–273	151–308	177–343	204–379	231–417	260–455	290–494	321–534	353–575	386–617	420–660	456–703	492–748	529–794	568–840	607–888	647–937	689–986
42	43–145	63–177	84–210	106–244	129–279	154–314	180–350	207–387	235–425	265–463	295–503	326–544	359–585	392–628	427–671	463–715	499–761	537–807	576–854	616–902	656–952	698–1002
43	44–148	64–181	85–215	108–249	132–284	157–320	183–357	211–394	239–433	269–472	300–512	332–553	365–595	399–638	434–682	470–727	507–773	545–820	584–868	624–917	666–966	708–1017
44	45–151	65–185	87–219	110–254	134–290	160–326	186–364	214–402	243–441	273–481	305–521	337–563	370–606	405–649	440–694	477–739	514–786	553–833	592–882	633–931	675–981	717–1033
45	46–154	66–189	88–224	112–259	137–295	163–332	190–370	218–409	247–449	278–489	309–531	342–573	376–616	411–660	447–705	484–751	522–798	561–846	601–895	642–945	684–996	727–1048
46	47–157	68–192	90–228	114–264	139–301	165–339	193–377	222–416	251–457	282–498	314–540	347–583	382–626	417–671	453–717	491–763	529–811	568–860	609–909	651–959	693–1011	737–1063
47	48–160	69–196	92–232	116–269	141–307	168–345	196–384	225–424	255–465	287–506	319–549	353–592	387–637	423–682	460–728	498–775	536–824	576–873	617–923	659–974	702–1026	746–1079
48	48–164	70–200	93–237	118–274	144–312	171–351	199–391	229–431	259–473	291–515	324–558	358–602	393–647	429–693	466–740	505–787	544–836	584–886	626–936	668–988	711–1041	756–1094
49	49–167	71–204	95–241	120–279	146–318	174–357	202–398	232–439	263–481	296–523	329–567	363–612	399–657	435–704	473–751	512–799	551–849	592–899	634–950	677–1002	721–1055	766–1109
50	50–170	73–207	97–245	122–284	149–323	177–363	206–404	236–446	267–489	300–532	334–576	369–621	405–667	441–715	480–762	519–811	559–861	600–912	642–964	685–1017	730–1070	775–1125

[1] Based on the exact limits for $W = 2U$ in WABEKE and VAN EEDEN, *Handleiding voor de toets van Wilcoxon*, Report S 176 (M 65), Mathematisch Centrum, Statistische Afdeling (Prof. D. VAN DANTZIG), Amsterdam, 1955, by kind permission of the authors and publishers.

[2] Based on the normal approximation with empirical continuity correction.

Prob $[T_l < T < T_r] \geqq 1 - 2\alpha$. For explanation see page 192. The italic values are 'exact' limits [1], the others approximate limits [2]
The limits for $N_1 = N_2$ are in bold figures

$2\alpha = 0.02$

Each cell gives T_l–T_r.

N_2 \ N_1	4	5	6	7	8	9	10	11	12	13	14	15	16	17	18	19	20	21	22	23	24	25
4	—	15–35	22–44	29–55	38–66	48–78	58–92	70–106	83–121	96–138	111–155	127–173	143–193	161–213	180–234	199–257	220–280	242–304	264–330	288–356	313–383	338–412
5	10–30	**16–39**	23–49	31–60	40–72	50–85	61–99	73–114	86–130	100–147	115–165	131–184	148–204	166–225	185–247	205–270	226–294	248–319	271–345	295–372	320–400	346–429
6	11–33	17–43	**24–54**	32–66	42–78	52–92	63–107	75–123	89–139	103–157	118–176	135–195	152–216	171–237	190–260	210–284	232–308	254–334	277–361	302–388	327–417	354–446
7	11–37	18–47	25–59	**34–71**	43–85	54–99	66–114	78–131	92–148	107–166	122–186	139–206	157–227	176–249	195–273	216–297	238–322	261–348	284–376	309–404	335–433	361–464
8	12–40	19–51	27–63	35–77	**45–91**	56–106	68–122	81–139	95–157	111–175	127–195	144–216	162–238	181–261	201–285	222–310	244–336	267–363	291–391	316–420	342–450	370–480
9	13–43	20–55	28–68	37–82	47–97	**59–112**	71–129	84–147	99–165	114–185	131–205	148–227	167–249	186–273	207–297	228–323	250–350	274–377	298–406	324–435	350–466	378–497
10	13–47	21–59	29–73	39–87	49–103	61–119	**74–136**	88–154	102–174	118–194	135–215	153–237	172–260	191–285	212–310	234–336	257–363	281–391	306–420	331–451	358–482	386–514
11	14–50	22–63	30–78	40–93	51–109	63–126	77–143	**91–162**	106–182	122–203	139–225	157–248	177–271	197–296	218–322	240–349	263–377	288–405	313–435	339–466	366–498	394–531
12	15–53	23–67	32–82	42–98	53–115	66–132	79–151	94–170	**109–191**	126–212	143–235	162–258	182–282	202–308	224–334	246–362	270–390	295–419	320–450	347–481	374–514	403–547
13	15–57	24–71	33–87	44–103	56–120	68–139	82–158	97–178	113–199	**130–221**	148–244	167–268	187–293	208–319	230–346	253–374	276–404	301–434	327–465	354–497	382–530	411–564
14	16–60	25–75	34–92	45–109	58–126	71–145	85–165	100–186	116–208	134–230	**152–254**	171–279	192–304	213–331	235–359	259–387	283–417	308–448	335–479	362–512	391–545	420–580
15	17–63	26–79	36–96	47–114	60–132	73–152	88–172	103–194	120–216	138–239	156–264	**176–289**	197–315	218–343	241–371	265–400	290–430	315–462	342–494	370–527	399–561	429–596
16	17–67	27–83	37–101	49–119	62–138	76–158	91–179	107–201	124–224	142–248	161–273	181–299	**202–326**	224–354	247–383	271–413	296–444	323–475	350–508	378–542	407–577	437–613
17	18–70	28–87	39–105	51–124	64–144	78–165	93–187	110–209	127–233	146–257	165–283	185–310	207–337	**229–366**	253–395	278–425	303–457	330–489	357–523	386–557	416–592	446–629
18	19–73	29–91	40–110	52–130	66–150	81–171	96–194	113–217	131–241	150–266	169–293	190–320	212–348	235–377	**259–407**	284–438	310–470	337–503	365–537	394–572	424–608	455–645
19	19–77	30–95	41–115	54–135	68–156	83–178	99–201	116–225	134–250	154–275	174–302	195–330	217–359	241–388	265–419	**290–451**	317–483	344–517	373–551	402–587	432–624	464–661
20	20–80	31–99	43–119	56–140	70–162	85–185	102–208	119–233	138–258	157–285	178–312	200–340	222–370	246–400	271–431	297–463	**323–497**	351–531	380–566	410–602	441–639	473–677
21	21–83	32–103	44–124	58–145	72–168	88–191	105–215	123–240	142–266	161–294	182–322	204–351	228–380	252–411	277–443	303–476	330–510	**359–544**	388–580	418–617	449–655	482–693
22	21–87	33–107	45–129	59–151	74–174	90–198	108–222	126–248	145–275	165–303	187–331	209–361	233–391	257–423	283–455	310–488	337–523	366–558	**395–595**	426–632	458–670	490–710
23	22–90	34–111	47–133	61–156	76–180	93–204	110–230	129–256	149–283	169–312	191–341	214–371	238–402	263–434	289–467	316–501	344–536	373–572	403–609	**434–647**	466–686	499–726
24	23–93	35–115	48–138	63–161	78–186	95–211	113–237	132–264	152–292	173–321	196–350	219–381	243–413	269–445	295–479	322–514	351–549	380–586	411–623	442–662	**475–701**	508–742
25	23–97	36–119	50–142	64–167	81–191	98–217	116–244	135–272	156–300	177–330	200–360	224–391	248–424	274–457	301–491	329–526	358–562	388–599	418–638	450–677	483–717	**517–758**
26	24–100	37–123	51–147	66–172	83–197	100–224	119–251	138–280	159–309	181–339	204–370	229–401	254–434	280–468	307–503	335–539	365–575	395–613	426–652	458–692	492–732	526–774
27	25–103	38–127	52–152	68–177	85–203	103–230	121–259	142–287	163–317	185–348	209–379	233–412	259–445	285–480	313–515	342–551	371–589	402–627	434–666	466–707	500–748	535–790
28	26–106	39–131	54–156	70–182	87–209	105–237	124–266	145–295	167–325	189–357	213–389	238–422	264–456	291–491	319–527	348–564	378–602	409–641	441–681	475–721	509–763	544–806
29	26–110	40–135	55–161	71–188	89–215	108–243	127–273	148–303	170–334	193–366	218–398	243–432	269–467	297–502	325–539	355–576	385–615	417–654	449–695	483–736	517–779	553–822
30	27–113	41–139	56–166	73–193	91–221	110–250	130–280	151–311	174–342	198–374	222–408	248–442	275–477	302–514	331–551	361–589	392–628	424–668	457–709	491–751	526–794	562–838
31	28–116	42–143	58–170	75–198	93–227	112–257	133–287	155–318	178–350	202–383	227–417	253–452	280–488	308–525	337–563	368–601	399–641	431–682	465–723	499–766	534–810	571–854
32	28–120	43–147	59–175	77–203	95–233	115–263	136–294	158–326	181–359	206–392	231–427	258–462	285–499	314–536	343–575	374–614	406–654	439–695	472–738	507–781	543–825	580–870
33	29–123	44–151	61–179	78–209	97–239	117–270	139–301	161–334	185–367	210–401	235–437	262–473	290–510	319–548	349–587	381–626	413–667	446–709	480–752	515–796	552–840	589–886
34	30–126	45–155	62–184	79–215	99–245	120–276	141–309	164–342	189–375	214–410	240–446	267–483	296–520	325–559	356–598	387–639	420–680	453–723	488–766	523–811	560–856	598–902
35	30–130	46–159	63–189	81–220	101–251	122–283	144–316	168–349	192–384	218–419	244–456	272–493	301–531	331–570	362–610	394–651	427–693	461–736	496–780	532–825	569–871	607–918
36	31–133	47–163	65–193	83–225	103–257	125–289	147–323	171–357	196–392	222–428	249–465	277–503	306–542	336–582	368–622	400–664	433–707	468–750	503–795	540–840	577–887	616–934
37	32–136	48–167	66–198	84–231	105–263	127–296	150–330	174–365	199–401	226–437	253–475	282–513	311–553	342–593	374–634	407–676	440–720	475–764	511–809	548–855	586–902	625–950
38	32–140	49–171	67–203	86–236	107–269	129–303	153–337	177–373	203–409	230–446	258–484	287–523	317–563	348–604	380–646	413–689	447–733	483–777	519–823	556–870	595–917	634–966
39	33–143	50–175	69–207	88–241	109–275	132–309	156–344	181–380	207–417	234–455	262–494	292–533	322–574	353–616	386–658	420–701	454–746	490–791	527–837	564–885	603–933	643–982
40	34–146	51–179	70–212	90–246	111–281	134–316	159–351	184–388	210–426	238–464	267–503	296–544	327–585	359–627	392–670	426–714	461–759	497–805	534–852	573–899	612–948	652–998
41	34–150	52–183	72–216	91–252	113–287	137–322	161–359	187–396	214–434	242–473	271–513	301–554	333–595	365–638	398–682	433–726	468–772	505–818	542–866	581–914	620–964	661–1014
42	35–153	53–187	73–221	93–257	116–292	139–329	164–366	190–404	218–442	246–482	276–522	306–564	338–606	371–649	404–694	439–739	475–785	512–832	550–880	589–929	629–979	670–1030
43	35–157	54–191	74–226	95–262	118–298	142–335	167–373	194–411	221–451	250–491	280–532	311–574	343–617	376–661	410–706	446–751	482–798	519–846	558–894	597–944	638–994	679–1046
44	36–160	55–195	76–230	97–267	120–304	144–342	170–380	197–419	225–459	254–500	284–542	316–584	348–628	382–672	416–718	452–764	489–811	527–859	565–909	605–959	646–1010	688–1062
45	37–163	56–199	77–235	98–273	122–310	147–348	173–387	200–427	229–467	258–509	289–551	321–594	354–638	388–683	423–729	459–776	496–824	534–873	573–923	614–973	655–1025	697–1078
46	37–167	57–203	78–240	100–278	124–316	149–355	176–394	203–435	232–476	262–518	293–561	326–604	359–649	393–695	429–741	465–789	503–837	541–887	581–937	622–988	663–1041	706–1094
47	38–170	58–207	80–244	102–283	126–322	152–361	179–401	207–442	236–484	266–527	298–570	330–615	364–660	399–706	435–753	472–801	510–850	549–900	589–951	630–1003	672–1056	715–1110
48	39–173	59–211	81–249	103–289	128–328	154–368	181–409	210–450	240–492	270–536	302–580	335–625	369–671	405–717	441–765	478–814	517–863	556–914	597–965	638–1018	681–1071	724–1126
49	39–177	60–215	82–254	105–294	130–334	157–374	184–416	213–458	243–501	274–545	307–589	340–635	375–681	410–729	447–777	485–826	524–876	563–928	604–980	646–1033	689–1087	733–1142
50	40–180	61–219	84–258	107–299	132–340	159–381	187–423	216–466	247–509	279–553	311–599	345–645	380–692	416–740	453–789	491–839	531–889	571–941	612–994	655–1047	698–1102	743–1157

[1] Based on the exact limits for $W = 2U$ in WABEKE and VAN EEDEN, *Handleiding voor de toets van Wilcoxon*, Report S 176 (M 65), Mathematisch Centrum, Statistische Afdeling (Prof. D. VAN DANTZIG), Amsterdam, 1955, by kind permission of the authors and publishers.

[2] Based on the normal approximation with empirical continuity correction.

Prob $[T_l < T < T_r] \geq 1 - 2\alpha$. For explanation see page 192. The italic values are 'exact' limits[1], the others approximate limits[2]
The limits for $N_1 = N_2$ are in bold figures

$2\alpha = 0.01$

N_2 \ N_1	4	5	6	7	8	9	10	11	12	13	14	15	16	17	18	19	20	21	22	23	24	25
	T_l T_r	T_l T_r	T_l T_r	T_l T_r	T_l T_r	T_l T_r	T_l T_r	T_l T_r	T_l T_r	T_l T_r	T_l T_r	T_l T_r	T_l T_r	T_l T_r	T_l T_r	T_l T_r	T_l T_r	T_l T_r	T_l T_r	T_l T_r	T_l T_r	T_l T_r
4	—	—	21–45	28–56	37–67	46–80	57–93	68–108	81–123	94–140	109–157	125–175	141–195	159–215	177–237	197–259	218–282	239–307	262–332	285–359	310–386	335–415
5	—	**15–40**	22–50	29–62	38–74	48–87	59–101	71–116	84–132	98–149	112–168	128–187	145–207	163–228	182–250	202–273	223–297	245–322	267–349	291–376	316–404	342–433
6	10–34	16–44	**23–55**	31–67	40–80	50–94	61–109	73–125	87–141	101–159	116–178	132–198	149–219	168–240	187–263	207–287	228–312	250–338	274–364	298–392	323–421	349–451
7	10–38	16–49	24–60	**32–73**	42–86	52–101	64–116	76–133	90–150	104–169	120–188	136–209	154–230	172–253	192–276	212–301	234–326	256–353	280–380	305–408	330–438	357–468
8	11–41	17–53	25–65	34–78	**43–93**	54–108	66–124	79–141	93–159	108–178	123–199	140–220	158–242	177–265	197–289	218–314	240–340	263–367	287–395	311–425	337–455	364–486
9	11–45	18–57	26–70	35–84	45–99	**56–115**	68–132	82–149	96–168	111–188	127–209	144–231	163–253	182–277	202–302	223–328	246–354	269–382	293–411	319–440	345–471	372–503
10	12–48	19–61	27–75	37–89	47–105	58–122	**71–139**	84–158	99–177	115–197	131–219	149–241	167–265	187–289	208–314	229–341	252–368	275–397	300–426	326–456	352–488	380–520
11	12–52	20–65	28–80	38–95	49–111	61–128	73–147	**87–166**	102–186	118–207	135–229	153–252	172–276	192–301	213–327	235–354	258–382	282–411	307–441	333–472	360–504	388–537
12	13–55	21–69	30–84	40–100	51–117	63–135	76–154	90–174	**105–195**	122–216	139–239	157–263	177–287	197–313	218–340	241–367	264–396	289–425	314–456	340–488	368–520	396–554
13	13–59	22–73	31–89	41–106	53–123	65–142	79–161	93–182	109–203	**125–226**	143–249	162–273	181–299	202–325	224–352	247–380	271–409	295–440	321–471	348–503	376–536	404–571
14	14–62	22–78	32–94	43–111	54–130	67–149	81–169	96–190	112–212	129–235	**147–259**	166–284	186–310	208–336	230–364	253–393	277–423	302–454	328–486	355–519	383–553	413–587
15	15–65	23–82	33–99	44–117	56–136	69–156	84–176	99–198	115–221	133–244	151–269	**171–294**	191–321	213–348	235–377	259–406	283–437	309–468	335–501	363–534	391–569	421–604
16	15–69	24–86	34–104	46–122	58–142	72–162	86–184	102–206	119–229	136–254	155–279	175–305	**196–332**	218–360	241–389	265–419	290–450	315–483	342–516	370–550	399–585	429–621
17	16–72	25–90	36–108	47–128	60–148	74–169	89–191	105–214	122–238	140–263	160–288	180–315	201–343	**223–372**	246–402	271–432	296–464	322–497	350–530	378–565	407–601	437–638
18	16–76	26–94	37–113	49–133	62–154	76–176	92–198	108–222	125–247	144–272	164–298	184–326	206–354	228–384	**252–414**	277–445	302–478	329–511	357–545	385–581	415–617	446–654
19	17–79	27–98	38–118	50–139	64–160	78–183	94–206	111–230	129–255	148–281	168–308	189–336	211–365	234–395	258–426	**283–458**	309–491	336–525	364–560	393–596	423–633	454–671
20	18–82	28–102	39–123	52–144	66–166	81–189	97–213	114–238	132–264	152–290	172–318	193–347	216–376	239–407	263–439	289–471	**315–505**	343–539	371–575	401–611	431–649	463–687
21	18–86	29–106	40–128	53–150	68–172	83–196	99–221	117–246	136–272	155–300	176–328	198–357	220–388	244–419	269–451	295–484	322–518	**350–553**	378–590	408–627	439–665	471–704
22	19–89	29–111	42–132	55–155	70–178	85–203	102–228	120–254	139–281	159–309	180–338	202–368	225–399	250–430	275–463	301–497	328–532	356–568	**386–604**	416–642	447–681	480–720
23	19–93	30–115	43–137	57–160	71–185	88–209	105–235	123–262	142–290	163–318	184–348	207–378	230–410	255–442	280–476	307–510	335–545	363–582	393–619	**424–657**	455–697	488–737
24	20–96	31–119	44–142	58–166	73–191	90–216	107–243	126–270	146–298	167–327	188–358	211–389	235–421	260–454	286–488	313–523	341–559	370–596	400–634	431–673	**464–712**	497–753
25	20–100	32–123	45–147	60–171	75–197	92–223	110–250	129–278	149–307	170–337	193–367	216–399	240–432	265–466	292–500	319–536	348–572	377–610	408–648	439–688	472–728	**505–770**
26	21–103	33–127	46–152	61–177	77–203	94–230	113–257	132–286	152–316	174–346	197–377	220–410	245–443	271–477	298–512	325–549	354–586	384–624	415–663	447–703	480–744	514–786
27	22–106	34–131	48–156	63–182	79–209	97–236	115–265	135–294	156–324	178–355	201–387	225–420	250–454	276–489	303–525	332–561	361–599	391–638	422–678	455–718	488–760	522–803
28	22–110	35–135	49–161	64–188	81–215	99–243	118–272	138–302	159–333	182–364	205–397	229–431	255–465	281–501	309–537	338–574	367–613	398–652	430–692	462–734	496–776	531–819
29	23–113	36–139	50–166	66–193	83–221	101–250	120–280	141–310	163–341	185–374	209–407	234–441	260–476	287–512	315–549	344–587	374–626	405–666	437–707	470–749	504–792	540–835
30	23–117	37–143	51–171	68–198	85–227	103–257	123–287	144–318	166–350	189–383	213–417	239–451	265–487	292–524	321–561	350–600	380–640	412–680	444–722	478–764	513–807	548–852
31	24–120	37–148	53–175	69–204	87–233	106–263	126–294	147–326	169–359	193–392	217–427	243–462	270–498	298–535	326–574	356–613	387–653	419–694	452–736	486–779	521–823	557–868
32	24–124	38–152	54–180	71–209	89–239	108–270	128–302	150–334	173–367	197–401	222–436	248–472	275–509	303–547	332–586	362–626	394–666	426–708	459–751	494–794	529–839	565–885
33	25–127	39–156	55–185	72–215	90–246	110–277	131–309	153–342	176–376	200–411	226–446	252–483	280–520	308–559	338–598	368–639	400–680	433–722	467–765	501–810	537–855	574–901
34	26–130	40–160	56–190	73–221	92–252	112–284	134–316	156–350	180–384	204–420	230–456	257–493	285–531	314–570	344–610	375–651	407–693	440–736	474–780	509–825	545–871	583–917
35	26–134	41–164	57–195	75–226	94–258	114–291	136–324	159–358	183–393	208–429	234–466	261–504	290–542	319–582	349–623	381–664	413–707	447–750	481–795	517–840	554–886	591–934
36	27–137	42–168	58–200	76–232	96–264	117–297	139–331	162–366	186–402	212–438	238–476	266–514	295–553	324–594	355–635	387–677	420–720	454–764	489–809	525–855	562–902	600–950
37	28–140	43–172	60–204	78–237	98–270	119–304	141–339	165–374	190–410	216–447	242–486	270–525	300–564	330–605	361–647	393–690	426–734	461–778	496–824	533–870	570–918	608–967
38	28–144	44–176	61–209	79–243	100–276	121–311	144–346	168–382	193–419	219–457	247–495	275–535	305–575	335–617	367–659	399–703	433–747	468–792	504–838	540–886	578–934	617–983
39	29–147	45–180	62–214	81–248	102–282	123–318	147–353	171–390	197–427	223–466	251–505	280–545	310–586	340–629	372–672	406–715	440–760	475–806	511–853	548–901	587–949	626–999
40	29–151	46–184	63–219	82–254	103–289	126–324	149–361	174–398	200–436	227–475	255–515	284–556	314–598	346–640	378–684	412–728	446–774	482–820	518–868	556–916	595–965	634–1016
41	30–154	46–189	65–223	84–259	105–295	128–331	152–368	177–406	203–445	231–484	259–525	289–566	319–609	351–652	384–696	418–741	453–787	489–834	526–882	564–931	603–981	643–1032
42	31–157	47–193	66–228	85–265	107–301	130–338	155–375	180–414	207–453	234–494	263–535	293–577	324–620	357–663	390–708	424–754	459–801	496–848	533–897	572–946	611–997	652–1048
43	31–161	48–197	67–233	87–270	109–307	133–344	157–383	183–422	210–462	238–503	268–544	298–587	329–631	362–675	396–720	430–767	466–814	503–862	541–911	580–961	620–1012	660–1065
44	32–164	49–201	68–238	88–276	111–313	135–351	160–390	186–430	214–470	242–512	272–554	303–597	334–642	367–687	401–733	437–779	473–827	510–876	548–926	587–977	628–1028	669–1081
45	32–168	50–205	69–243	90–281	113–319	137–358	162–398	189–438	217–479	246–521	276–564	307–608	339–653	373–698	407–745	443–792	479–841	517–890	556–940	595–992	636–1044	678–1097
46	33–171	51–209	71–247	91–287	115–325	139–365	165–405	192–446	220–488	250–530	280–574	312–618	344–664	378–710	413–757	449–805	486–854	524–904	563–955	603–1007	644–1060	687–1113
47	34–174	52–213	72–252	93–292	117–331	142–371	168–412	195–454	224–496	253–540	284–584	316–629	349–675	384–721	419–769	455–818	493–867	531–918	570–970	611–1022	653–1075	695–1130
48	34–178	53–217	73–257	95–297	118–338	144–378	170–420	198–462	227–505	257–549	289–593	321–639	354–686	389–733	425–781	461–831	499–881	538–932	578–984	619–1037	661–1091	704–1146
49	35–181	54–221	74–262	96–303	120–344	146–385	173–427	201–470	231–513	261–558	293–603	325–650	359–697	394–745	430–794	468–843	506–894	545–946	585–999	627–1052	669–1107	713–1162
50	36–184	55–225	76–266	98–308	122–350	148–392	176–434	204–478	234–522	265–567	297–613	330–660	364–708	400–756	436–806	474–856	512–908	552–960	593–1013	635–1067	677–1123	721–1179

[1] The lower exact limits are based on data kindly supplied by Prof. C. WHITE, Department of Public Health, Yale Universtiy, New Haven, Connecticut, and published in part in *Biometrics*, **8**, 33 (1952).

[2] Based on the normal approximation with empirical continuity correction.

Distribution-Free Tolerance Limits*

(Values in *italics* are approximate)

The table gives the minimum size N of the sample for which it can be assumed with a confidence probability of β_t that $100\,\beta_p$% of the *values* in the population

($k = 0$) lie either above the lowest or below the highest value of the sample;

($k = 1$) lie between the lowest and highest values of the sample;

($k = 2$) lie between the second lowest and second highest values of the sample, etc.

Example: How large must a sample be if, with a confidence probability of $\beta_t = 0.99$, $100\,\beta_p = 95\%$ of the values in the population

(a) are to lie either above the lowest or below the highest value of the sample? With $k = 0$ the table gives $N = 90$;

(b) are to lie between the fifth lowest and fifth highest values of the sample? With $k = 5$ the table gives $N = 371$.

k \ β_p	0.999	0.990	0.950	0.90	0.80	0.70	0.60	0.50	0.40	0.30
$\beta_t = 0.999$										
0	6905	688	135	66	31	20	14	10	8	6
1	9230	919	181	88	42	27	19	14	11	9
2	13058	1301	256	126	60	38	27	21	16	13
3	16450	1640	324	159	77	49	35	27	21	17
4	19620	1957	387	190	92	59	43	33	26	21
5	22651	2260	447	220	107	69	50	38	30	25
6	25583	2552	505	249	121	78	57	44	35	28
7		2838	562	277	135	87	63	49	39	32
8		*3116*	617	305	148	96	70	54	43	35
9		*3390*	672	332	162	105	76	59	47	39
10		*3661*	*725*	359	175	113	83	64	51	42
$\beta_t = 0.990$										
0	4603	459	90	44	21	13	10	7	6	4
1	6636	661	130	64	31	20	14	10	8	6
2	10042	1001	197	97	46	30	21	16	13	10
3	13105	1307	259	128	62	40	29	22	18	14
4	15996	1596	316	156	76	49	36	28	22	18
5	18779	1874	371	184	90	58	42	33	26	21
6	21486	2145	425	210	103	67	49	38	30	25
7		2409	478	237	116	75	55	43	34	28
8		*2668*	530	262	128	83	61	47	38	31
9		*2924*	581	288	141	92	67	52	42	35
10		*3178*	*630*	313	153	100	73	57	46	38
$\beta_t = 0.980$										
0	3911	390	77	38	18	11	8	6	5	4
1	5832	581	115	56	27	17	12	9	7	6
2	9081	906	179	88	43	27	19	15	12	9
3	12024	1200	238	117	57	37	27	21	16	13
4	14813	1478	293	145	71	46	34	26	21	17
5	17506	1747	347	172	84	55	40	31	25	20
6	20131	2010	399	198	97	63	46	36	29	24
7		2267	450	223	109	71	52	40	33	27
8			501	248	122	79	58	45	37	30
9			551	273	134	87	64	50	40	33
10				297	146	95	70	55	44	37
$\beta_t = 0.950$										
0	2995	299	59	29	14	9	6	5	4	3
1	4742	473	93	45	22	14	10	7	6	5
2	7751	773	153	75	36	23	17	13	10	8
3	10511	1049	208	103	50	33	24	18	15	12
4	13146	1313	261	129	63	41	30	24	19	16
5	15703	1568	312	154	76	50	36	28	23	19
6	18205	1818	362	179	88	58	42	33	27	22
7		2064	410	204	100	65	48	38	30	25
8		*2305*	459	228	112	73	54	42	34	28
9		*2545*	507	252	124	81	60	47	38	32
10		*2783*	*553*	275	135	89	65	51	42	35
$\beta_t = 0.900$										
0	2302	230	45	22	11	7	5	4	3	2
1	3889	388	77	38	18	12	8	6	5	4
2	6679	666	132	65	32	20	14	11	9	7
3	9273	926	184	91	45	29	21	17	13	11
4	11770	1176	234	116	57	38	28	21	17	14
5	14204	1419	283	140	69	45	33	26	21	18
6	16596	1658	330	164	81	53	39	31	25	21
7		1894	377	188	92	61	45	35	29	24
8		*2126*	424	211	104	68	50	40	32	27
9		*2347*	470	234	115	76	56	44	36	30
10		*2586*	*514*	256	127	83	61	48	40	33

* Reproduction only by permission of the publishers of these *Scientific Tables*.

Wilcoxon Test for Pair Differences[1]

n = number of pairs. For explanation see page 192

n	$2\alpha \leq 0.10$	$2\alpha \leq 0.05$	$2\alpha \leq 0.02$	$2\alpha \leq 0.01$
5	0– 15	–	–	–
6	2– 19	0– 21	–	–
7	3– 25	2– 26	0– 28	–
8	5– 31	3– 33	1– 35	0– 36
9	8– 37	5– 40	3– 42	1– 44
10	10– 45	8– 47	5– 50	3– 52
11	13– 53	10– 56	7– 59	5– 61
12	17– 61	13– 65	9– 69	7– 71
13	21– 70	17– 74	12– 79	9– 82
14	25– 80	21– 84	15– 90	12– 93
15	30– 90	25– 95	19–101	15–105
16	35–101	29–107	23–113	19–117
17	41–112	34–119	28–125	23–130
18	47–124	40–131	32–139	27–144
19	53–137	46–144	37–153	32–158
20	60–150	52–158	43–167	37–173
21	67–164	58–173	49–182	42–189
22	75–178	66–187	55–198	48–205
23	83–193	73–203	62–214	54–222
24	91–209	81–219	69–231	61–239
25	100–225	89–236	76–249	68–257

Poisson Distribution

Significance limits* for x when λ is given. For explanation see page 189

λ	$2\alpha \leq 0.05$	$2\alpha \leq 0.01$	λ	$2\alpha \leq 0.05$	$2\alpha \leq 0.01$
0	–	–	50	36– 65	32– 70
1	•– 4	•– 5	51	36– 66	33– 71
2	•– 6	•– 7	52	37– 68	33– 72
3	•– 8	•– 9	53	38– 69	34– 74
4	0– 9	•–11	54	39– 70	35– 75
5	0–11	•–13	55	40– 71	36– 76
6	1–12	0–14	56	41– 72	37– 77
7	1–14	0–16	57	42– 73	38– 78
8	2–15	1–17	58	43– 74	38– 80
9	3–16	1–19	59	43– 76	39– 81
10	3–18	2–20	60	44– 77	40– 82
11	4–19	3–21	61	45– 78	41– 83
12	5–20	3–23	62	46– 79	42– 84
13	5–21	4–24	63	47– 80	43– 85
14	6–23	4–25	64	48– 81	43– 86
15	7–24	5–27	65	49– 82	44– 88
16	8–25	6–28	66	50– 83	45– 89
17	8–27	6–29	67	50– 84	46– 90
18	9–28	7–31	68	51– 86	47– 91
19	10–29	8–32	69	52– 87	48– 92
20	11–30	9–33	70	53– 88	48– 93
21	12–31	9–35	71	54– 89	49– 95
22	12–33	10–36	72	55– 90	50– 96
23	13–34	11–37	73	56– 91	51– 97
24	14–35	11–39	74	57– 92	52– 98
25	15–36	12–40	75	58– 93	53– 99
26	16–37	13–41	76	58– 95	54–101
27	16–39	14–42	77	59– 96	54–102
28	17–40	14–44	78	60– 97	55–103
29	18–41	15–45	79	61– 98	56–104
30	19–42	16–46	80	62– 99	57–105
31	20–43	17–47	81	63–100	58–106
32	20–45	17–48	82	64–101	59–107
33	21–46	18–50	83	65–102	60–109
34	22–47	19–51	84	66–103	60–110
35	23–48	20–52	85	66–105	61–111
36	24–49	21–53	86	67–106	62–112
37	25–50	21–55	87	68–107	63–113
38	25–52	22–56	88	69–108	64–114
39	26–53	23–57	89	70–109	65–115
40	27–54	24–58	90	71–110	66–117
41	28–55	24–59	91	72–111	66–118
42	29–56	25–61	92	73–112	67–119
43	30–57	26–62	93	74–113	68–120
44	30–58	27–63	94	74–114	69–121
45	31–60	28–64	95	75–116	70–122
46	32–61	29–65	96	76–117	71–123
47	33–62	29–67	97	77–118	72–125
48	34–63	30–68	98	78–119	72–126
49	35–64	31–69	99	79–120	73–127
50	36–65	32–70	100	80–121	74–128

[1] Values (rounded off outwards) are from TUKEY, J.W., *Memorandum Report 17*, Statistical Research Group, Princeton University, 1949. Reprinted by kind permission of the author.

Geigy
Medomin®
Capsules
Each capsule or tablet contains
200 mg cycloheptenylethyl
barbituric acid (Heptabarbitone)
sound sleep

Runs: Significance Limits[1] for the Total Number *I*

For explanation see below

The lack of a significant limit on one side is indicated by a period, on both sides by a single dash

$N_1 = N_2 = \frac{1}{2}N \leqq 100$

$\frac{1}{2}N$	$2\alpha=0.10$	$2\alpha=0.05$	$2\alpha=0.02$	$2\alpha=0.01$
4	2- 8	–	–	–
5	3- 9	2- 10	2- 10	–
6	3- 11	3- 11	2- 12	2- 12
7	4- 12	3- 13	3- 13	3- 13
8	5- 13	4- 14	4- 14	3- 15
9	6- 14	5- 15	4- 16	4- 16
10	6- 16	6- 16	5- 17	5- 17
11	7- 17	7- 17	6- 18	5- 19
12	8- 18	7- 19	7- 19	6- 20
13	9- 19	8- 20	7- 21	7- 21
14	10- 20	9- 21	8- 22	7- 23
15	11- 21	10- 22	9- 23	8- 24
16	11- 23	11- 23	10- 24	9- 25
17	12- 24	11- 25	10- 26	10- 26
18	13- 25	12- 26	11- 27	11- 27
19	14- 26	13- 27	12- 28	11- 29
20	15- 27	14- 28	13- 29	12- 30
21	16- 28	15- 29	14- 30	13- 31
22	17- 29	16- 30	14- 32	14- 32
23	17- 31	16- 32	15- 33	14- 34
24	18- 32	17- 33	16- 34	15- 35
25	19- 33	18- 34	17- 35	16- 36
26	20- 34	19- 35	18- 36	17- 37
27	21- 35	20- 36	19- 37	18- 38
28	22- 36	21- 37	19- 39	18- 40
29	23- 37	22- 38	20- 40	19- 41
30	24- 38	22- 40	21- 41	20- 42
31	25- 39	23- 41	22- 42	21- 43
32	25- 41	24- 42	23- 43	22- 44
33	26- 42	25- 43	24- 44	23- 45
34	27- 43	26- 44	24- 46	23- 47
35	28- 44	27- 45	25- 47	24- 48
36	29- 45	28- 46	26- 48	25- 49
37	30- 46	29- 47	27- 49	26- 50
38	31- 47	30- 48	28- 50	27- 51
39	32- 48	30- 50	29- 51	28- 52
40	33- 49	31- 51	30- 52	29- 53
41	34- 50	32- 52	31- 53	29- 55
42	35- 51	33- 53	31- 54	30- 56
43	35- 53	34- 54	32- 56	31- 57
44	36- 54	35- 55	33- 57	32- 58
45	37- 55	36- 56	34- 58	33- 59
46	38- 56	37- 57	35- 59	34- 60
47	39- 57	38- 58	36- 60	35- 61
48	40- 58	38- 60	37- 61	36- 63
49	41- 59	39- 61	38- 62	36- 64
50	42- 60	40- 62	38- 64	37- 65
51	43- 61	41- 63	39- 65	38- 66
52	44- 62	42- 64	40- 66	39- 67
53	45- 63	43- 65	41- 67	40- 68
54	45- 65	44- 66	42- 68	41- 69
55	46- 66	45- 67	43- 69	42- 70
56	47- 67	46- 68	44- 70	42- 72
57	48- 68	47- 69	45- 71	43- 73
58	49- 69	47- 71	46- 72	44- 74
59	50- 70	48- 72	46- 74	45- 75
60	51- 71	49- 73	47- 75	46- 76
61	52- 72	50- 74	48- 76	47- 77
62	53- 73	51- 75	49- 77	48- 78
63	54- 74	52- 76	50- 78	49- 79
64	55- 75	53- 77	51- 79	49- 81
65	56- 76	54- 78	52- 80	50- 82
66	57- 77	55- 79	53- 81	51- 83
67	58- 78	56- 80	54- 82	52- 84
68	58- 80	57- 81	54- 84	53- 85
69	59- 81	58- 82	55- 85	54- 86
70	60- 82	58- 84	56- 86	55- 87
71	61- 83	59- 85	57- 87	56- 88
72	62- 84	60- 86	58- 88	57- 89
73	63- 85	61- 87	59- 89	57- 91
74	64- 86	62- 88	60- 90	58- 92
75	65- 87	63- 89	61- 91	59- 93
76	66- 88	64- 90	62- 92	60- 94
77	67- 89	65- 91	63- 93	61- 95
78	68- 90	66- 92	64- 94	62- 96
79	69- 91	67- 93	64- 96	63- 97
80	70- 92	68- 94	65- 97	64- 98
81	71- 93	69- 95	66- 98	65- 99
82	71- 95	69- 97	67- 99	66-100
83	72- 96	70- 98	68-100	66-102
84	73- 97	71- 99	69-101	67-103
85	74- 98	72-100	70-102	68-104
86	75- 99	73-101	71-103	69-105
87	76-100	74-102	72-104	70-106
88	77-101	75-103	73-105	71-107
89	78-102	76-104	74-106	72-108
90	79-103	77-105	74-108	73-109
91	80-104	78-106	75-109	74-110
92	81-105	79-107	76-110	75-111
93	82-106	80-108	77-111	75-113
94	83-107	81-109	78-112	76-114
95	84-108	82-110	79-113	77-115
96	85-109	82-112	80-114	78-116
97	86-110	83-113	81-115	79-117
98	87-111	84-114	82-116	80-118
99	87-113	85-115	83-117	81-119
100	88-114	86-116	84-118	82-120

$N_1 < N_2, N_2 \leqq 20$

N_2	$2\alpha=$ 0.10	$2\alpha=$ 0.05	$2\alpha=$ 0.02	$2\alpha=$ 0.01
$N_1 = 2$				
2	–	–	–	–
3	–	–	–	–
4	–	–	–	–
5	–	–	–	–
6	–	–	–	–
7	–	–	–	–
8	2- •	–	–	–
9	2- •	–	–	–
10	2- •	–	–	–
11	2- •	–	–	–
12	2- •	2- •	–	–
13	2- •	2- •	–	–
14	2- •	2- •	–	–
15	2- •	2- •	–	–
16	2- •	2- •	–	–
17	2- •	2- •	–	–
18	2- •	2- •	–	–
19	2- •	2- •	2- •	–
20	2- •	2- •	2- •	–
$N_1 = 3$				
3	–	–	–	–
4	•- 7	–	–	–
5	2- •	–	–	–
6	2- •	2- •	–	–
7	2- •	2- •	–	–
8	2- •	2- •	–	–
9	2- •	2- •	2- •	–
10	3- •	2- •	2- •	–
11	3- •	2- •	2- •	–
12	3- •	2- •	2- •	2- •
13	3- •	2- •	2- •	2- •
14	3- •	2- •	2- •	2- •
15	3- •	3- •	2- •	2- •
16	3- •	3- •	2- •	2- •
17	3- •	3- •	2- •	2- •
18	3- •	3- •	2- •	2- •
19	3- •	3- •	2- •	2- •
20	3- •	3- •	2- •	2- •
$N_1 = 4$				
4	2- 8	–	–	–
5	2- 9	2- 9	•- 9	–
6	3- 9	2- 9	2- •	–
7	3- 9	2- •	2- •	–
8	3- •	3- •	2- •	2- •
9	3- •	3- •	2- •	2- •
10	3- •	3- •	2- •	2- •
11	3- •	3- •	2- •	2- •
12	4- •	3- •	3- •	2- •
13	4- •	3- •	3- •	2- •
14	4- •	3- •	3- •	2- •
15	4- •	3- •	3- •	3- •
16	4- •	4- •	3- •	3- •
17	4- •	4- •	3- •	3- •
18	4- •	4- •	3- •	3- •
19	4- •	4- •	3- •	3- •
20	4- •	4- •	3- •	3- •
$N_1 = 5$				
5	3- 9	2-10	2-10	–
6	3-10	3-10	2-11	2- •
7	3-10	3-11	2-11	2-11
8	3-11	3-11	2- •	2- •
9	4-11	3- •	3- •	2- •
10	4-11	3- •	3- •	3- •
11	4- •	4- •	3- •	3- •
12	4- •	4- •	3- •	3- •
13	4- •	4- •	3- •	3- •
14	5- •	4- •	3- •	3- •
15	5- •	4- •	4- •	3- •
16	5- •	4- •	4- •	3- •
17	5- •	4- •	4- •	3- •
18	5- •	5- •	4- •	4- •
19	5- •	5- •	4- •	4- •
20	5- •	5- •	4- •	4- •
$N_1 = 6$				
6	3-11	3-11	2-12	2-12
7	4-11	3-12	3-12	2-13
8	4-12	3-12	3-13	3-13
9	4-12	4-13	3-13	3- •
10	5-12	4-13	3- •	3- •
11	5-13	4-13	4- •	3- •
12	5-13	4-13	4- •	3- •
13	5-13	5- •	4- •	3- •
14	5-13	5- •	4- •	4- •
15	6- •	5- •	4- •	4- •
16	6- •	5- •	4- •	4- •
17	6- •	5- •	5- •	4- •
18	6- •	5- •	5- •	4- •
19	6- •	6- •	5- •	4- •
20	6- •	6- •	5- •	4- •
$N_1 = 7$				
7	4-12	3-13	3-13	3-13
8	4-13	4-13	3-14	3-14
9	5-13	4-14	4-14	3-15
10	5-13	5-14	4-15	3-15
11	5-14	5-14	4-15	4-15
12	6-14	5-14	4-15	4- •
13	6-14	5-15	5- •	4- •
14	6-14	5-15	5- •	4- •
15	6-15	6-15	5- •	4- •
16	6-15	6- •	5- •	5- •
17	7-15	6- •	5- •	5- •
18	7-15	6- •	5- •	5- •
19	7-15	6- •	6- •	5- •
20	7-15	6- •	6- •	5- •
$N_1 = 8$				
8	5-13	4-14	4-14	3-15
9	5-14	5-14	4-15	3-15
10	6-14	5-15	4-15	4-16
11	6-15	5-15	5-16	4-16
12	6-15	6-16	5-16	4-17
13	6-15	6-16	5-17	5-17
14	7-16	6-16	5-17	5-17
15	7-16	6-16	5-17	5- •
16	7-16	6-17	6-17	5- •
17	7-16	7-17	6- •	5- •
18	8-16	7-17	6- •	6- •
19	8-16	7-17	6- •	6- •
20	8-17	7-17	6- •	6- •
$N_1 = 9$				
9	6-14	5-15	4-16	4-16
10	6-15	5-16	5-16	4-17
11	6-15	6-16	5-17	5-17
12	7-16	6-16	5-17	5-18
13	7-16	6-17	6-18	5-18
14	7-17	7-17	6-18	5-18
15	8-17	7-18	6-18	6-19
16	8-17	7-18	6-18	6-19
17	8-17	7-18	7-19	6-19
18	8-18	8-18	7-19	6- •
19	8-18	8-18	7-19	6- •
20	9-18	8-18	7-19	7- •
$N_1 = 10$				
10	6-16	6-16	5-17	5-17
11	7-16	6-17	5-18	5-18
12	7-17	7-17	6-18	5-19
13	8-17	7-18	6-19	5-19
14	8-17	7-18	6-19	6-19
15	8-18	7-18	7-19	6-20
16	8-18	8-19	7-20	6-20
17	9-18	8-19	7-20	7-20
18	9-19	8-19	7-20	7-21
19	9-19	8-20	8-20	7-21
20	9-19	9-20	8-20	7-21
$N_1 = 11$				
11	7-17	7-17	6-18	5-19
12	8-17	7-18	6-19	6-19
13	8-18	7-19	6-19	6-20
14	8-18	8-19	7-20	6-20
15	9-19	8-19	7-20	7-21
16	9-19	8-20	7-21	7-21
17	9-19	9-20	8-21	7-22
18	10-20	9-20	8-21	7-22
19	10-20	9-21	8-22	8-22
20	10-20	9-21	8-22	8-22
$N_1 = 12$				
12	8-18	7-19	7-19	6-20
13	9-18	8-19	7-20	6-21
14	9-19	8-20	7-21	7-21
15	9-19	8-20	8-21	7-22
16	10-20	9-21	8-22	7-22
17	10-20	9-21	8-22	8-22
18	10-21	9-21	8-22	8-23
19	10-21	10-22	9-23	8-23
20	11-21	10-22	9-23	8-23
$N_1 = 13$				
13	9-19	8-20	7-21	7-21
14	9-20	9-20	8-21	7-22
15	10-20	9-21	8-22	7-22
16	10-21	9-21	8-22	8-23
17	10-21	10-22	9-23	8-23
18	11-21	10-22	9-23	8-24
19	11-22	10-23	9-24	9-24
20	11-22	10-23	10-24	9-24
$N_1 = 14$				
14	10-20	9-21	8-22	7-23
15	10-21	9-22	8-23	8-23
16	11-21	10-22	9-23	8-24
17	11-22	10-23	9-24	8-24
18	11-22	10-23	9-24	9-25
19	12-23	11-23	10-24	9-25
20	12-23	11-24	10-25	9-25
$N_1 = 15$				
15	11-21	10-22	9-23	8-24
16	11-22	10-23	9-24	9-24
17	11-22	11-23	10-24	9-25
18	12-23	11-24	10-25	9-25
19	12-23	11-24	10-25	10-26
20	12-24	12-25	11-26	10-26
$N_1 = 16$				
16	11-23	11-23	10-24	9-25
17	12-23	11-24	10-25	9-26
18	12-24	11-25	10-26	10-26
19	13-24	12-25	11-26	10-27
20	13-25	12-25	11-26	10-27
$N_1 = 17$				
17	12-24	11-25	10-26	10-26
18	13-24	12-25	11-26	10-27
19	13-25	12-26	11-27	10-27
20	13-25	13-26	11-27	11-28
$N_1 = 18$				
18	13-25	12-26	11-27	11-27
19	14-25	13-26	12-27	11-28
20	14-26	13-27	12-28	11-29
$N_1 = 19$				
19	14-26	13-27	12-28	11-29
20	14-27	13-27	12-29	12-29

Explanation (see also pages 194 and 195)

(Time)	1	2	3	4	5	6	7	8	9	10
Series (I)	A	B	A	A	A	B	B	A	B	A
Series (II)	A	B	A	B	A	A	B	A	B	A
Series (III)	A	A	A	A	A	A	B	B	B	B

Each of the series (I), (II), (III) has a size $N = 10$ and contains $N_1 = 4$ B's and $N_2 = 6$ A's (provided that $N = N_1 + N_2 < 40$, the smaller number is denoted by N_1). In these series the underscored letters in each case form a run. The total number of runs I is 7 in series (I), 9 in series (II), 2 in series (III).

The table gives the significance limits for the estimate I (total | N_1, N_2) of the expectation $\mathcal{I}$ (total) under the condition (N_1, N_2).

(a) If the left limit is *attained* or *exceeded*, then I is significantly less than $\mathcal{I}$ (significance probability α) or I differs significantly from $\mathcal{I}$ (significance probability 2α).

(b) If the right limit is *attained* or *exceeded*, then I is significantly greater than $\mathcal{I}$ (significance probability α) or I differs significantly from $\mathcal{I}$ (significance probability 2α).

(c) If I lies between the limits and *attains neither*, then the null hypothesis cannot be rejected.

[1] Values from SWED and EISENHART, *Ann. math. Statist.*, **14**, 66 (1943). Reprinted by kind permission of the authors and publishers.

The table[1] gives the probability α that for the size of sample given in the table the longest run above or below the median will attain or exceed the length l. The choice of which side of the median is to be tested must be made beforehand.

Example: Size of sample = 28. Longest run above = 4. Result: $0.50 < \alpha < 0.90$.

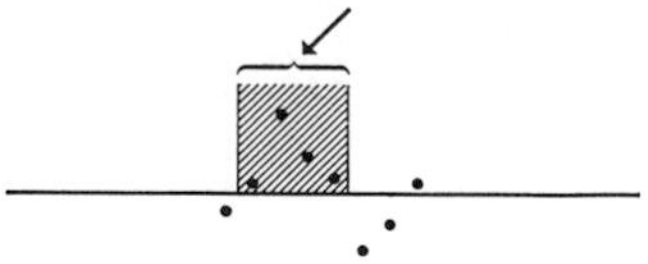

l	$\alpha \leqq 0.01$	$\alpha \leqq 0.10$	$\alpha \leqq 0.50$	$\alpha \leqq 0.90$	$\alpha \leqq 0.99$
1	2	2	2	2	2
2	4	4	6	8	12
3	6	6	12	22	38
4	8	10	22	54	100
5	10	16	46	116	230
6	14	26	92	260	490
7	18	44	182	530	1 044
8	26	78	360	1 104	2 140
9	38	142	714	2 240	4 370
10	56	256	1 424	4 530	8 980
11	86	480	2 850	9 190	18 240
12	140	930	5 680	18 540	37 200
13	234	1 838	11 330	37 600	75 500
14	410	3 630	22 700	75 700	151 700
15	748	7 160	45 300	151 700	303 000
16	1 446	14 190	90 600	303 000	607 000
17	2 830	28 100	181 200	607 000	1 214 000
18	5 530	56 100	362 000	1 214 000	2 430 000
19	10 860	117 300	725 000	2 430 000	4 850 000
20	21 500	235 000	1 450 000	4 850 000	9 710 000

The table[1] gives the probability α that for the size of sample given in the table the *shorter* of the two runs that are respectively the longest above and the longest below the median will attain or exceed the length l.

Example: Size of sample = 28. Longest run above = 4, below = 9. Result: $0.10 < \alpha < 0.50$.

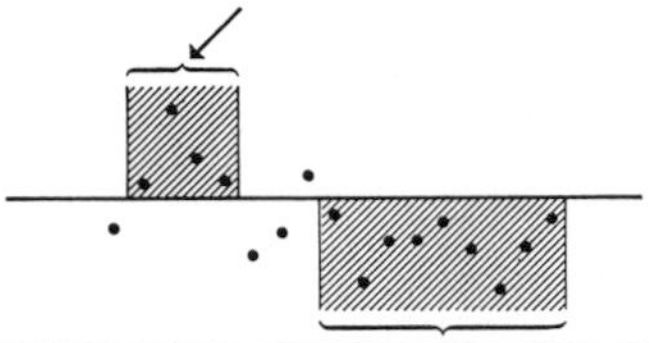

l	$\alpha \leqq 0.01$	$\alpha \leqq 0.10$	$\alpha \leqq 0.50$	$\alpha \leqq 0.90$	$\alpha \leqq 0.99$
1	2	2	2	2	2
2	4	4	6	10	14
3	6	8	14	26	44
4	8	14	30	68	116
5	12	26	68	152	252
6	20	50	140	322	552
7	34	98	290	676	1 164
8	62	194	596	1 390	2 390
9	116	390	1 208	2 830	4 930
10	216	782	2 440	5 650	10 140
11	446	1 182	4 910	11 750	20 700
12	884	2 360	9 840	23 800	42 500
13	1 762	4 720	19 890	48 600	86 700
14	3 510	9 450	39 900	98 600	174 200
15	6 990	18 900	80 500	197 300	348 000
16	13 930	37 800	161 300	395 000	697 000
17	27 900	75 600	323 000	789 000	1 394 000
18	55 500	151 200	645 000	1 578 000	2 790 000
19	111 000	302 000	1 290 000	3 160 000	5 570 000
20	222 000	605 000	2 580 000	6 310 000	11 150 000

The table[1] gives the probability α that for the size of sample given in the table the *longer* of the two runs that are respectively the longest above and the longest below the median will attain or exceed the length l.

Example: Size of sample = 28. Longest run above = 4, below = 9. Result: $\alpha < 0.01$.

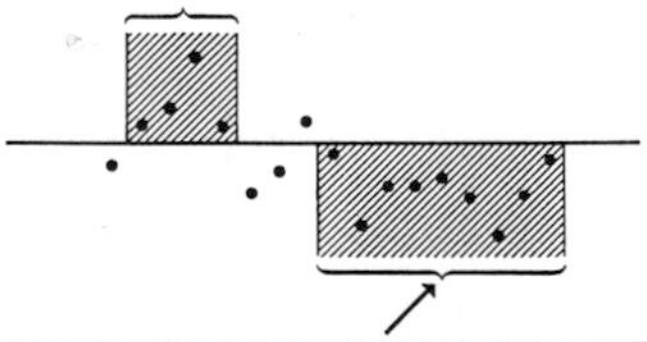

l	$\alpha \leqq 0.01$	$\alpha \leqq 0.10$	$\alpha \leqq 0.50$	$\alpha \leqq 0.90$	$\alpha \leqq 0.99$
1	2	2	2	2	2
2	4	4	4	8	10
3	6	6	8	16	28
4	8	8	16	36	64
5	10	14	30	76	136
6	12	20	58	152	282
7	16	32	106	296	568
8	22	52	200	580	1 150
9	32	86	388	1 174	2 310
10	42	150	758	2 350	4 640
11	62	262	1 488	4 720	9 330
12	94	500	2 920	9 460	18 730
13	156	962	5 860	10 660	37 700
14	256	1 876	11 250	21 300	75 700
15	418	3 670	22 600	42 600	151 600
16	766	7 330	45 200	85 300	303 000
17	1 472	14 090	90 100	170 500	606 000
18	2 860	27 900	180 300	341 000	1 213 000
19	5 570	55 500	361 000	682 000	2 430 000
20	10 860	111 100	721 000	1 364 000	4 850 000

The table[1] gives the probability α that for the size of sample given in the table the *shorter* of the two runs that are respectively the longest run above and the longest run below a maximal cut will attain or exceed the length l. The maximal cut is so made that this particular run is maximalized.

Example: Size of sample = 28. Longest run above the maximal cut = 8, below = 9. Result: $\alpha < 0.01$.

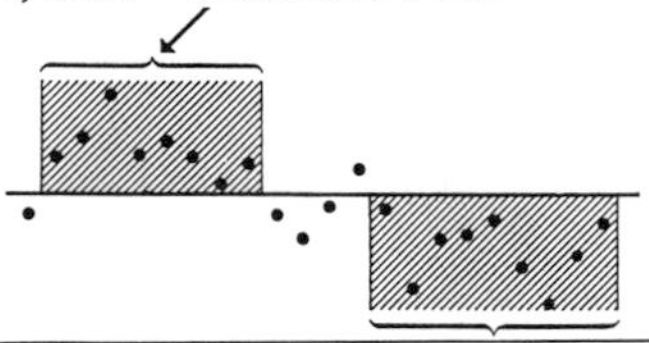

l	$\alpha \leqq 0.01$	$\alpha \leqq 0.10$	$\alpha \leqq 0.50$	$\alpha \leqq 0.90$	$\alpha \leqq 0.99$
1	2	2	2	2	2
2	4	4	6	8	12
3	6	8	12	22	34
4	8	12	22	48	76
5	12	18	46	96	162
6	16	34	86	192	380
7	24	58	166	382	668
8	38	108	324	760	1 342
9	66	204	638	1 518	2 690
10	118	400	1 266	3 030	5 410
11	228	790	2 530	6 070	10 870
12	444	1 568	5 050	12 130	21 500
13	878	3 130	10 070	24 300	43 100
14	1 750	6 220	20 100	48 500	86 200
15	3 480	12 490	40 300	97 000	172 300
16	6 790	25 000	80 600	194 100	345 000
17	13 860	49 900	161 100	388 000	689 000
18	27 700	99 900	322 000	776 000	1 379 000
19	55 400	199 800	644 000	1 553 000	2 760 000
20	110 800	400 000	1 289 000	3 110 000	5 510 000

The table[2,3] gives the probability α that for the size of sample given in the table at least one run up or down of length l or longer will occur.

Example: Size of sample = 28. Up-run to be tested = 5. Result: $0.05 < \alpha < 0.10$.

l	$\alpha \leqq 0.01$	$\alpha \leqq 0.05$	$\alpha \leqq 0.10$	$\alpha \leqq 0.90$	$\alpha \leqq 0.95$	$\alpha \leqq 0.99$
2	—	—	—	7	8	12
3	—	—	4	32	40	61
4	—	7	11	162	210	321
5	9	26	48	964	1 253	1 923
6	34	153	309	6 637	8 633	13 268
7	234	1 170	2 396	52 229	67 950	104 452
8	2 034	10 348	21 248	464 209	603 947	928 410
9	20 067	102 382	210 291	4 595 600	5 979 012	9 191 191
10	218 833	1 116 808	2 294 003	50 133 734	65 225 489	100 267 459

Illustration of up- and down-runs:

Time sequence:	1	2	3	4	5	6
Values:	1.14	1.17	1.20	1.19	1.21	1.16
	up			down	up	down
Length l:	3			1	1	1

[1] Values from OLMSTEAD, P. S., *Runs Determined in a Sample by an Arbitrary Cut*, Bell Telephone System Technical Publications, Monograph 2937, New York, 1958.

[2] Values of l from 2 to 5 from OLMSTEAD, P. S., *Distribution of Sample Arrangements for Runs Up and Down*, Bell Telephone System Technical Publications, Monograph 2289, New York, 1946, and *Ann. math. Statist.*, **17**, 24 (1946). Reprinted by kind permission of the author, publishers and Bell Telephone Laboratories, Inc., New York.

[3] Values of l from 6 to 10 calculated with POISSON approximation by the editors of these *Scientific Tables*.

72137	73850	32733	35321	80647	39713	61060	57865	88049	20557	43375	50914	83628	73935	72502	48174	62551	96122	22375	96488
04254	60099	50584	10961	57642	19101	30613	01549	96531	83936	45842	78222	88481	44933	12839	20750	47116	58973	99018	22769
48083	50731	81250	57995	41467	29834	08059	22945	72193	36077	82577	16210	76092	87730	90049	02115	37096	20505	91937	69776
16602	26772	89693	92558	38394	84119	68486	17622	30953	78267	31568	58297	88922	50436	86135	42726	54307	29170	13045	65527
29910	55480	47184	79775	09779	08718	45822	17643	63252	00232	98059	07255	90786	95246	15280	61692	45137	17539	31799	64780
77708	83761	89238	86521	82711	79266	47763	26173	36183	65869	64355	91271	49295	98354	28005	69792	01480	51557	70726	35862
90715	65115	12870	89922	24926	44062	94896	97561	96490	35454	51623	98381	11055	32951	28363	16451	67912	66404	76254	75495
79666	48119	38525	82189	34921	49838	47558	92343	47408	99542	44247	12762	54488	74321	36224	95619	16238	25374	13653	25345
53294	49761	76235	55814	29900	03796	73326	94291	10739	36087	32326	52225	72447	77804	57045	27552	72387	34001	83792	66764
44422	78305	76369	20601	39701	80769	17322	78280	42376	64899	62390	68375	42921	28545	33167	85710	11035	40171	04840	69848
12601	54432	65017	91131	50515	97477	80691	31834	32401	11994	97820	06653	27477	61364	22681	02280	53815	47479	44017	37563
65664	73669	24910	25458	23699	86413	19985	49355	24358	02915	81553	92012	50435	73814	96290	86827	81430	45597	82296	28947
18363	66515	23098	22384	87756	66396	63646	50963	99099	62895	09202	48494	95974	33534	94657	71126	71770	16092	03942	90111
00491	53688	72033	68063	86104	90576	04119	65531	30304	39202	82110	82254	03669	03281	11613	36336	98297	48100	71594	52667
02878	83197	94318	47901	85252	91124	32939	75043	40325	53252	18175	09457	83810	46392	02705	85591	33192	65127	80852	42030
79920	22780	43100	83886	26378	66010	00020	80666	66861	17820	50756	80608	35695	72641	26306	76298	32532	22644	96853	18610
97556	54260	42361	12741	56996	48177	85725	36668	45531	85245	12710	60264	74650	92126	08152	32147	17457	56298	48964	64733
79435	52143	12322	12254	04314	98550	58315	78036	24355	85822	44424	88508	66190	74060	93206	92840	44833	81146	64060	62975
93903	78220	09178	33676	58996	78675	11648	96220	54127	24804	24720	66501	74157	42246	41688	72835	87258	89384	11251	34329
04758	50961	90230	72006	24268	77817	10524	60304	79352	31942	85419	93017	28087	78323	77109	56832	78400	24190	37978	85863
53841	28758	93442	42983	25254	96336	16570	89358	36619	72838	10933	99964	13468	17211	48046	51122	92668	96750	11139	06275
07626	78473	17708	59059	33584	52451	11575	55992	83228	38546	49559	71671	53603	24491	57570	90789	32932	67449	05115	45941
40645	27008	16341	05870	42604	79286	08720	13175	89573	38051	39391	92039	71664	40219	97707	93975	66981	19556	24605	52169
82666	14127	94390	07069	39152	10357	94612	56748	75428	28101	38543	54214	48928	32818	51963	87353	15094	29529	87305	01361
60147	99378	58310	34655	48242	58656	30544	01860	08322	70476	44242	54227	28598	64422	29361	20359	48577	05971	92373	22765
61557	43927	11643	65522	76713	95782	34956	67384	47654	64999	11468	74149	81386	94127	67342	38010	92522	57728	39432	27914
71522	16545	68464	62540	76143	06328	94718	58404	84099	73641	52165	54336	89196	40042	37889	06003	58033	59082	94988	62152
05366	66273	49518	25413	20346	22719	18255	47685	78475	67421	83093	77038	55399	67893	89597	85630	08059	35757	49479	63531
72668	62720	08971	97908	15905	86615	97559	68107	10649	30976	66455	90708	08450	50120	17795	55604	51222	17900	55553	02980
51497	78491	83680	08319	51223	19735	72708	82599	28127	29660	30790	65154	19582	20942	81439	83917	90452	64753	99645	19799
66170	68781	91423	86645	02925	51327	41022	76893	29200	82747	97297	74420	18783	93471	89055	56413	77817	10655	52915	68198
23361	60672	52451	03774	06365	94880	70978	57385	70532	46978	87390	53319	90155	03154	20301	47831	86786	11284	49160	79852
53608	59661	70966	24937	56559	98856	19207	41684	20288	19783	82215	35810	39852	43795	21530	96315	55657	76473	08217	46810
24079	01177	02666	35515	24819	73382	50172	23114	28745	12249	35844	63265	26451	06986	08707	99251	06260	74779	96285	31998
50495	87947	20592	91917	59595	55083	43112	94833	72864	58785	53473	06308	56778	30474	57277	23425	27092	47759	18422	56074
93550	48308	20282	92711	74402	51335	64031	41740	69680	69373	73674	97914	77989	47280	71804	74587	70563	77813	50242	60398
16269	03381	09798	89487	33632	47073	92357	38870	73784	95662	83923	90790	49474	11901	30322	80254	99608	17019	17892	76813
32868	72831	55156	90166	91599	09471	79945	42580	86605	97758	08206	54536	41327	01170	21745	71318	07978	35440	26128	10545
80722	21328	19977	82161	29385	62151	48030	05125	70866	72154	86385	39490	57482	32921	33795	43155	30432	48384	85430	51828
67362	87389	09559	98456	70498	40173	80016	81500	48061	25583	74101	87573	01556	89183	64830	16779	35724	82103	61658	20296
83452	92994	85019	57720	36951	03383	34265	65728	89776	04006	06089	84076	12445	47416	83620	59151	97420	23689	74515	55211
51168	41624	94768	53124	95920	04777	82534	76335	21108	42302	79496	21054	80132	67719	72662	58360	57384	65406	63918	17046
83805	28803	63272	65480	08764	16379	72055	61146	82780	89411	53131	57879	39099	42715	24830	60045	23250	39847	46616	17817
59782	50488	77081	10186	86577	28581	26999	96294	20431	30114	23035	30380	76272	60343	57573	42492	47962	21439	54664	97968
09627	26695	79373	09119	79765	99918	01628	47335	17893	53176	07436	14799	78197	48601	97557	83918	20530	61565	69344	71964
20160	50603	71684	34875	60617	77991	66322	27390	73834	73494	21527	93579	20949	85666	25102	64733	93872	72698	87520	43340
04375	15463	49139	17369	71179	77472	96239	18521	67354	41883	58939	36222	43935	36272	47817	90287	91434	86453	84477	03559
67163	48629	25607	27003	09721	70206	10497	83617	39176	45062	63903	33862	14903	38996	60027	41702	78189	28598	12707	91191
49380	42273	93835	32621	60848	67721	69712	33438	85908	58620	50646	47857	96024	58568	67614	44370	40276	85964	71604	05691
56013	02278	53110	33235	62949	53799	51375	42451	76889	68096	80657	91046	95340	70209	23825	46031	45306	64476	31460	61553
46596	51960	02957	56574	18672	02994	39960	02489	53079	72789	22562	39359	38220	13972	86115	17196	24569	26820	66299	50962
52928	66296	15570	31407	54988	78749	16135	82797	31296	93268	10104	95616	82618	85756	51156	74037	12501	94162	42006	99213
09403	50848	71088	31308	35677	49046	10870	72107	11550	61175	33345	56717	07896	74085	59886	03051	78702	13402	74318	20992
30328	72163	66728	81091	52307	78952	60261	11207	73065	48286	57057	49472	95241	84360	13960	95736	43637	60399	19080	72417
78707	57821	28410	64908	30432	78760	36880	02564	96978	62332	77321	92228	53849	26578	39954	86726	91039	13884	25376	60187
73597	94657	72927	46459	61325	50908	25601	30038	78786	65197	65283	18169	72967	53031	47906	99501	27753	69946	66875	31598
07446	66408	19958	65159	11338	39231	72802	70630	87336	16385	32784	38073	87910	89260	66444	15979	83469	76952	50065	89540
47870	55448	14158	83451	58729	42430	42234	04905	83274	22459	75032	93544	10482	34277	40177	01081	57788	08612	39886	33050
84269	35324	35508	49481	56478	30246	41771	61398	98154	61644	12405	45037	68034	98561	46747	30655	41878	93610	51745	97527
52704	71441	50581	65679	37597	17182	60733	11765	09293	70076	40751	95846	80277	92450	60888	18689	45966	25837	70906	62841
19020	09999	08316	32781	89731	52148	09111	64205	77930	32391	69076	13459	59896	78185	60268	03650	36814	88460	34049	19544
19442	94873	36976	30366	65815	66895	27222	17378	59359	00055	66780	54939	78369	04163	77673	73342	78915	20537	06126	92480
39523	74227	51895	39733	29426	76685	93548	87546	07687	47338	12240	32277	23015	54261	95020	77705	81682	96907	37411	90717
01201	85057	93409	81200	21176	78459	18960	85182	02245	11566	52527	62992	55171	85448	12545	75992	08790	88992	69756	46722
51725	60273	84903	84374	31438	36959	83719	40702	79038	68639	63329	93821	58095	62204	69319	00672	96037	78680	98734	92743
91045	72642	42684	32419	12825	58785	84563	62071	17799	96994	41635	52830	19700	98193	37600	70617	58959	45486	58338	12464
54896	95603	17290	91508	95605	82514	32257	15699	02654	83110	44278	95523	12666	87597	23190	26243	36690	75829	71060	91605
92324	88115	77848	38006	45600	02181	79261	49705	31491	25318	52586	72494	66685	05344	71633	68536	18786	28575	00455	93825
88397	78035	06366	37342	62070	74459	62026	13032	14048	16304	11959	78684	72590	47283	45445	35611	98354	53680	45747	87442
52118	65337	13461	18438	16099	57330	05018	92605	10316	07351	78020	86361	30286	06434	50229	09070	44848	09996	77753	49227
37202	05623	23595	79677	59772	37141	63390	48093	02366	05407	08325	52046	87494	95585	25547	53500	45047	08406	66984	71128
71637	80269	83299	89743	94628	26784	17792	09214	53781	90102	25774	92525	32301	25923	76556	13274	39776	97027	56919	88547
35790	19603	31212	34419	34728	47391	93272	09887	34196	98251	62453	37703	70711	37921	54989	17828	60976	57662	61757	71249
99087	72525	34402	50115	09825	54728	37514	24437	01316	04770	06534	17768	36086	05468	41631	95632	78154	38634	47463	99728
89768	36608	49108	92337	79809	81934	06370	18703	90858	55130	40869	88243	37403	42231	17073	49097	54147	03656	14735	78351
83816	00718	94663	39629	27812	28250	44983	33834	54280	67850	96025	96117	00768	14821	69029	25453	48798	15486	73835	51776
00806	20667	81224	24296	39967	60239	89494	34431	44890	59892	79682	20308	82510	53609	13258	89631	80497	49167	81559	47202
65733	03902	29140	05414	62087	65727	54430	52632	94126	95597	48338	67645	44676	14730	22642	21919	21050	87791	76192	56686
60671	23190	47433	86979	45281	69750	96999	42104	34377	63309	82181	00278	28209	95629	75818	09043	48564	87355	27209	09827
45326	86280	74876	51858	03263	10215	87947	09427	32380	43636	58578	07761	28456	46570	11623	50417	37763	30136	58254	71090
54419	65493	88741	89069	10789	00973	30238	46126	85306	37114	22718	50584	92291	56575	24075	43889	40909	18741	86154	20843
72845	68939	06483	40835	16564	75047	22938	13073	32066	43098	75738	94910	15403	89151	73322	18370	90586	46115	87375	79147
01828	48113	60005	87083	90000	22346	89182	27750	63314	87302	49472	24885	79506	60638	07132	00908	92035	75518	30878	14979
89871	81320	05251	25930	37320	11895	16187	03303	40287	52435	23926	92544	54099	31497	03863	22864	72620	74169	25311	80669
74883	93005	77888	64673	19302	54669	21526	07401	30925	46148	20138	33874	56715	38424	38273	11361	15203	64912	62494	31231
25493	56247	46907	25634	84761	76421	42907	95158	27146	37012	43361	03173	97911	71313	44256	66609	42504	76799	46790	28464
28278	93841	13134	25129	65536	19838	21479	48265	01674	47274	56350	37512	14883	99673	62298	33948	32456	28675	04242	20735
44834	89816	52509	85192	32114	83770	90076	70233	76730	25043	16686	54737	57431	01786	20803	69465	37970	05673	49516	98035
23329	74767	85661	54449	76606	02131	93202	25355	93941	84434	22384	13240	93617	51549	28532	57150	77261	62643	74966	08777
33176	16108	98145	27652	76918	41000	46059	72208	90475	10341	39703	83224	37858	61657	04184	15597	29448	01922	05709	77900
44597	28074	92908	22392	38034	83739	32876	98604	75652	95680	51386	48724	76069	94867	93570	20306	31712	96238	57864	86267
81456	81110	94771	13664	07478	80992	58485	18882	13238	59865	55644	05528	49935	58972	43340	94718	97397	92197	57257	73187
91503	59589	22803	18122	17790	00236	93750	20468	92189	66781	06210	18208	13973	57905	66878	55721	67437	61709	88182	92769
63651	64109	13207	68346	42140	00052	04099	48767	23355	42505	34539	51129	48580	59386	62209	29754	77409	48146	50411	50511
30709	25869	68851	65221	69392	35106	36393	27129	17326	86452	69952	68433	72332	62502	76323	38379	07293	76788	84281	58581
50664	89487	41973	98456	51147	51327	26590	94684	58103	96936	71276	30275	22753	46046	67196	65135	54879	71903	23541	92400
80089	83750	36605	85343	26090	28447	33179	69730	09683	08770	50381	43130	88108	64709	15191	68718	38375	46747	19860	76129
19293	91304	37043	82077	42231	31534	54358	52939	26655	72687	26616	09608	59223	74533	64986	49667	78039	61030	46122	54941
97754	28401	62553	98641	48553	35996	08033	91811	70471	81538	20017	19613	81103	37642	41866	96777	08667	74544	92903	58427
47923	38366	81939	61526	27691	13988	21630	00957	50599	91260	72832	89364	14158	71740	91289	61204	91185	23485	18424	65084

[1] From LINDER, A., *Planen und Auswerten von Versuchen*, Birkhäuser, Basle, 1959, pages 177 et seq. Reprinted by kind permission of the author and publishers.

I. Symbols

$a \to b$	a tending toward b
∞	Infinity
lim	Limiting value
$a \sim b$	a approximately equal to b
$a \approx b$	a very nearly equal to b
$a = b$	a equal to b [cf. (**1**) below]
$a \equiv b$	a identical with b (for formulae only)
$a > b$	a greater than b } Cf. (**2**) and (**3**) below
$a < b$	a smaller than b } Cf. (**2**) and (**3**) below
$a \gg b$	a much greater than b
$a \ll b$	a much smaller than b
$a \neq b$, $a \lessgtr b$	a not equal to b
$b < a < c$	a greater than b and smaller than c
$a \geqq b$, $a \geq b$	a equal to or greater than b, i.e., a at least as great as b
$a \leqq b$, $a \leq b$	a equal to or smaller than b, i.e., a at most as great as b
$b \leqq a \leqq c$	a lying between b and c
$\lvert a \rvert$	Absolute value of a; this is always positive, for example $\lvert -5 \rvert = 5$
$+$	Addition sign, plus, positive
$-$	Subtraction sign, minus, negative
$\times$ or $\cdot$	Multiplication sign, times (the period sign is not used in these *Tables*)
: or $\div$	Division sign, divided by (the sign $\div$ is not used in these *Tables*)
$a + b = c$	$a + b$, read as 'a plus b', denotes the sum of a and b. The result of the addition, c, is also known as the sum
$\sum_1^k x_i$	Sum of all values $x_1, x_2, x_3, \ldots$, i.e., of all values x_i, from $i = 1$ to $i = k$ inclusive, or $\sum_1^k x_i = x_1 + x_2 + x_3 + \cdots + x_k$ (the limits of the summation above and below the sign Σ are usually omitted if there is no possibility of confusion)
$\int$	Indefinite integral
$\int_a^b$	Definite integral, or integral between $x = a$ and $x = b$
$a - b = c$	$a - b$, read as 'a minus b', denotes subtraction of b from a. a is the minuend, b the subtrahend; $a - b$, or c, is the difference. Subtraction is the opposite of addition
$a \times b = c$, $a\,b = c$, $a \cdot b = c$	$a \times b$, read as 'a times b', denotes multiplication of a by b. a and b are the multiplicands or factors; $a \times b$, or c, is the product. For the sake of clarity the period sign is not used in these *Tables*
$a : b = c$	$a : b$, read as 'a divided by b', denotes division. a is the dividend, b the divisor; $a : b$, or c, is the quotient. Division is the opposite of multiplication and can also be represented by the fraction $\frac{a}{b}$ or a/b. In fractions, a is the numerator (= dividend), b the denominator (= divisor)
$a^b = c$	a^b, read as 'a to the power b', is known as involution. a is the base, b the exponent; a^b, or c, is the bth power of a. In the special case of $a^2 = c$, a^2 or c is the square of a; in that of $a^3 = c$, a^3 or c is the cube of a
$\sqrt[b]{a} = c$	$\sqrt[b]{a}$, is the bth root of a, b being known as the root exponent. In the special case of $\sqrt[2]{a} = c$, $\sqrt[2]{a}$ or c is known as the square root of a, and the root exponent is usually omitted, i.e., $\sqrt[2]{a} = \sqrt{a}$. In the special case of $\sqrt[3]{a} = c$, $\sqrt[3]{a}$ or c is known as the cube root of a. Extraction of a root is the opposite of involution. See also 'Logarithms', page 134
log, ln	See 'Logarithms', page 134
e	Base of natural (napierian) logarithms $= 2.718\,281\,828\,4\ldots$
π	Ratio of the circumference of a circle to its diameter $= 3.141\,592\,653\,5\ldots$
sin, cos, tan, tg	See page 138
arc sin	See page 139

II. Numbers

The *natural numbers* consist of all positive whole numbers (positive integers). Zero* and negative numbers are not natural numbers.

The *rational numbers* consist of all positive and negative integers, the fractions formed from them, and zero.

The *irrational numbers* are incommensurable quantities that cannot be expressed as quotients either of integers or of rational fractions. Examples are $\sqrt{2}$ and $\sqrt{5}$. π and e are also irrational numbers.

The *real numbers* consist of all rational and irrational numbers. The fundamental laws of real numbers are the following:

1. The four fundamental operations

Addition, subtraction, multiplication and division (except division by zero) can always and without ambiguity be carried out with real numbers.

2. The order of numbers

Between any two real numbers a and b there can exist *only one* of the three relationships

$a = b$ or $a > b$ or $a < b$

where

$$a = b \quad \text{when} \quad a - b = 0 \qquad (1)$$

$$a > b \quad \text{when} \quad a - b > 0 \qquad (2)$$

$$a < b \quad \text{when} \quad a - b < 0 \qquad (3)$$

Examples of inequalities (**2**) and (**3**) are

$$\cdots > 10 > 9 > \cdots > 1 > 0 > -1 > \cdots > -10 > \cdots$$

$$\cdots < -10 < -9 < \cdots < -1 < 0 < 1 < \cdots < 10 < \cdots$$

3. The commutative law

$$a + b = b + a \qquad (4)$$

$$a\,b = b\,a \qquad (5)$$

4. The associative law

$$(a + b) + c = a + (b + c) \qquad (6)$$

$$(a\,b)\,c = a\,(b\,c) \qquad (7)$$

5. The distributive law

$$a\,(b + c) = a\,b + a\,c \qquad (8)$$

III. Calculations with zero and infinity

$$a - a = 0 \qquad (9)$$

$$\lvert 0 \rvert = 0 \qquad (10)$$

$$0 \times a = 0 \qquad (11)$$

* Some mathematicians regard zero also as a natural number.

$$\frac{a}{\infty} = 0 \quad (a \neq \infty) \qquad (12)$$

$$\frac{0}{a} = 0 \quad (a \neq 0) \qquad (13)$$

$$\frac{a}{0} \quad \text{not defined} \qquad (14)$$

$$0^a = 0 \quad (a > 0) \qquad (15)$$

$$a^0 = 1 \quad (a \neq 0) \qquad (16)$$

$$\lim_{(n \to \infty)} a^n = \begin{cases} \infty & \text{for } a > 1 \\ 1 & \text{for } a = 1 \\ 0 & \text{for } -1 < a < 1 \text{ and } a \neq 0 \\ \text{nonconvergent} & \text{for } a \leqq -1 \end{cases} \qquad (17)$$

$$\log_c 0 = -\infty \quad (c > 1) \qquad (18)$$

$$\log_c \infty = +\infty \quad (c > 1) \qquad (19)$$

$$\log_c 1 = 0 \qquad (20)$$

$$0! = 1 \qquad (21)$$

$$\binom{n}{0} = 1 \qquad (22)$$

IV. Addition, subtraction, multiplication, division

1. Algebraic signs

If a, b, c are positive numbers, then

$$a \pm b = a \mp (-b) \qquad (23)$$

$$a(-b) = (-a)b = -(ab) = -c \qquad (24)$$

$$(-a)(-b) = +ab = +c \qquad (25)$$

$$\frac{-b}{a} = \frac{b}{-a} = -\frac{b}{a} = -c \qquad (26)$$

$$\frac{-b}{-a} = +\frac{b}{a} = +c \qquad (27)$$

2. Brackets

$$a - b - c - d - \cdots = a - (b + c + d + \cdots) \qquad (28)$$

$$\pm ab \pm ac \pm ad \pm \cdots = a(\pm b \pm c \pm d \pm \cdots) = \pm a(b + c + d + \cdots) \qquad (29)$$

3. Conversion of divisions into multiplications

$$\frac{b}{a} = \frac{1}{a} \times b \qquad (30)$$

For values of $1/a$ for numbers from 1 to 999 see page 18. Equation **(30)** is particularly useful in mechanical calculation with a constant divisor.

4. Conversion of multiplications and divisions into additions

If b is an integer (or can be converted into an integer), then

$$\left.\begin{aligned} ab &= a + a + a + \cdots \\ \frac{b}{a} &= \frac{1}{a} + \frac{1}{a} + \frac{1}{a} + \cdots \end{aligned}\right\} b \text{ components} \qquad (31)$$

Equation **(31)** is particularly useful in the mechanical tabulation of linear functions.

5. Fractions

$$\frac{a}{a} = 1 \quad (a \neq 0) \qquad (32)$$

$$\frac{ma}{mb} = \frac{a}{b} \quad (m \neq 0) \qquad (33)$$

$$\frac{a}{b} + \frac{c}{b} = \frac{a + c}{b} \quad \text{(can also be used from right to left)} \qquad (34)$$

$$\frac{a}{b} + \frac{c}{d} = \frac{ad + bc}{bd} \quad \text{(can also be used from right to left)} \qquad (35)$$

$$\frac{a}{b} \times \frac{c}{d} = \frac{a}{d} \times \frac{c}{b} = \frac{ac}{bd} \qquad (36)$$

$$\frac{a}{b} : \frac{c}{d} = \frac{a}{b} \times \frac{d}{c} = \frac{a}{c} \times \frac{d}{b} = \frac{a}{c} : \frac{b}{d} \qquad (37)$$

6. Proportions

The equation

$$a : b = c : d \qquad (38)$$

read as 'a is to b as c is to d', is known as a proportion. a and d are the extremes, b and c the means of the proportion. The product of the extremes equals the product of the means:

$$ad = bc \qquad (39)$$

If a constant proportion is of the type expressed by

$$a : b = b : c \qquad (40)$$

then in accordance with equation **(39)**, $ac = b^2$, that is, $b = \sqrt{ac}$ **(41)**

b is known as the mean proportional between a and c, or the geometric mean of a and c. c is known as the third proportional to a and b.

A special case of proportions of type **(40)** is the so-called 'golden section' (extreme and mean ratio)

$$\left.\begin{aligned} &\frac{a}{b} = \frac{b}{a - b}, \text{ that is} \\ &b = \frac{a(\sqrt{5} - 1)}{2} = 0.618034\,a \quad \text{or} \quad \frac{a}{b} = 1.618034 \end{aligned}\right\} \qquad (42)$$

Another special case is that of the so-called 'normal' format, expressed by

$$\left.\begin{aligned} &\frac{a}{b} = \frac{b}{a/2}, \text{ that is} \\ &b = a/\sqrt{2} = 0.707107\,a \quad \text{or} \quad \frac{a}{b} = 1.414214 \end{aligned}\right\} \qquad (43)$$

If the individual values of two related variables x, y are such that

$$\frac{y_1}{x_1} = \frac{y_2}{x_2} = \frac{y_3}{x_3} = \cdots = k \qquad (44)$$

then

$$y = kx \qquad (45)$$

read as 'y is proportional to x in the ratio k'. k is known as the proportionality constant. As x increases, y increases in proportion when k is positive, decreases when k is negative. The graphical representation of a proportional relationship on rectangular coordinates results in a straight line, whence the expression linear relationship. On the other hand, a linear relationship between x and y does not necessarily mean that they are proportional to one another since there are many straight lines that do not correspond to equation **(45)**. For example, $y = a + kx$ is *not* a proportional relationship between x and y. In this case $(y - a)$ is proportional to x.

If the individual values of two related variables x, y are such that

$$\left.\begin{aligned} &\frac{y_1}{1/x_1} = \frac{y_2}{1/x_2} = \frac{y_3}{1/x_3} = \cdots = k \\ &\text{that is} \\ &y_1 x_1 = y_2 x_2 = y_3 x_3 = \cdots = k \end{aligned}\right\} \qquad (46)$$

then

$$y = \frac{k}{x} \qquad (47)$$

read as 'y is inversely proportional to x in the ratio k'. The graphical representation of an inversely proportional relationship on rectangular coordinates results in a hyperbola. Such a relationship is therefore a nonlinear one.

V. Powers and roots

1. Powers with integral exponents

If a and b are any real numbers, m and r positive integers, then

$$0^m = 0 \quad (m > 0) \qquad (15)$$

$a^0 = 1 \quad (a \neq 0)$ **(16)**

$$\lim_{(m \to \infty)} a^m = \begin{cases} \infty & \text{for } a > 1 \\ 1 & \text{for } a = 1 \\ 0 & \text{for } -1 < a < 1 \text{ and } a \neq 0 \\ \text{nonconvergent for } a \leqq -1 \end{cases} \quad \textbf{(17)}$$

$a \times a \times a \times \cdots (m \text{ factors}) = a^m$ **(48)**

$\frac{1}{a} \times \frac{1}{a} \times \frac{1}{a} \times \cdots (m \text{ factors}) = \frac{1}{a^m} = a^{-m} \quad (a \neq 0)$ **(49)**

$a^m \times b^m = (a\,b)^m$ **(50)**

$\frac{a^m}{b^m} = \left(\frac{a}{b}\right)^m = a^m\,b^{-m} \quad (b \neq 0)$ **(51)**

$a^m \times a^r = a^{m+r}$ **(52)**

$\frac{a^m}{a^r} = a^m\,a^{-r} = a^{m-r} \quad (a \neq 0)$ **(53)**

$(a^m)^r = (a^r)^m = a^{mr}$ **(54)**

Algebraic signs: If in equations **(48)** to **(54)** R is the resulting *absolute value* of the base, c the absolute value of the power, $2\,m$ or $2m - 1$ the resulting even or uneven exponent, then

$(\pm R)^{2m} = +c$ **(55)**

$(\pm R)^{2m-1} = \pm c$ **(56)**

2. Extraction of roots with integral exponents

If a and b are any real numbers, n and s positive integers but not zero, then

$\sqrt[n]{a} = a^{\frac{1}{n}}$ **(57)**

$\frac{1}{\sqrt[n]{a}} = a^{-\frac{1}{n}} \quad (a \neq 0)$ **(58)**

$\sqrt[n]{a\,b} = \sqrt[n]{a}\,\sqrt[n]{b} = (a\,b)^{\frac{1}{n}}$ **(59)**

$\sqrt[n]{\frac{a}{b}} = \frac{\sqrt[n]{a}}{\sqrt[n]{b}} = \left(\frac{a}{b}\right)^{\frac{1}{n}} \quad (b \neq 0)$ **(60)**

$\sqrt[s]{\sqrt[n]{a}} = \sqrt[n]{\sqrt[s]{a}} = a^{\frac{1}{ns}}$ **(61)**

Algebraic signs: If in equations **(57)** to **(61)** R is the resulting *absolute value* of the base, c the absolute value of the power, $2n$ or $2n - 1$ the resulting even or uneven exponent, then

$\sqrt[2n]{(+R)} = (+R)^{\frac{1}{2n}} = +c$ **(62)**

$\sqrt[2n]{(-R)} = (-R)^{\frac{1}{2n}}$ has no real solution **(63)**

$\sqrt[2n-1]{(\pm R)} = (\pm R)^{\frac{1}{2n-1}} = \pm c$ **(64)**

3. Mixed powers and roots

If a and b are any real numbers, m and r positive integers, k, n and s likewise positive integers but not zero, then

$\sqrt[n]{a^m} = a^{\frac{m}{n}}$ **(65)**

$\frac{1}{\sqrt[n]{a^m}} = a^{-\frac{m}{n}} \quad (a \neq 0)$ **(66)**

$\sqrt[kn]{a^{km}} = \sqrt[n]{a^m} = a^{\frac{m}{n}}$ **(67)**

If in equation **(67)** a is negative it is important that all other necessary conversion operations on the exponent should be performed *before* reduction is carried out. If the resulting numerator in the exponent is even, then a negative a is made positive and reduction carried out.

$\sqrt[n]{(a\,b)^m} = \sqrt[n]{a^m} \times \sqrt[n]{b^m} = (a\,b)^{\frac{m}{n}}$ **(68)**

$\frac{\sqrt[n]{a^m}}{\sqrt[n]{b^m}} = \sqrt[n]{\left(\frac{a}{b}\right)^m} = \left(\frac{a}{b}\right)^{\frac{m}{n}} \quad (b \neq 0)$ **(69)**

$\sqrt[n]{a} \times \sqrt[s]{a} = a^{\frac{1}{n}+\frac{1}{s}} = a^{\frac{n+s}{ns}} = \sqrt[ns]{a^{n+s}}$ **(70)**

$\sqrt[n]{a^m} \times \sqrt[s]{a^r} = a^{\frac{m}{n}+\frac{r}{s}} = a^{\frac{ms+nr}{ns}} = \sqrt[ns]{a^{ms+nr}}$ **(71)**

$\left(a^{\frac{m}{n}}\right)^{\frac{r}{s}} = \left(a^{\frac{r}{s}}\right)^{\frac{m}{n}} = a^{\frac{mr}{ns}}$ **(72)**

Algebraic signs: If in equations **(65)** to **(72)** R is the resulting *absolute value* of the base, c the absolute value of the power, $2m$, $2n$, or $2m - 1$, $2n - 1$ respectively the resulting even or uneven numerator and denominator of the exponent, then

$\sqrt[2n]{(\pm R)^{2m}} = (\pm R)^{\frac{2m}{2n}} = (+R)^{\frac{2m}{2n}} = +c$ **(73)**

(always to be used in any reduction of an exponent)

$\sqrt[2n]{(+R)^{2m-1}} = (+R)^{\frac{2m-1}{2n}} = +c$ **(74)**

$\sqrt[2n]{(-R)^{2m-1}} = (-R)^{\frac{2m-1}{2n}}$ has no real solution **(75)**

$\sqrt[2n-1]{(\pm R)^{2m}} = (\pm R)^{\frac{2m}{2n-1}} = +c$ **(76)**

$\sqrt[2n-1]{(\pm R)^{2m-1}} = (\pm R)^{\frac{2m-1}{2n-1}} = \pm c$ **(77)**

VI. Logarithms

In accordance with the equation

$a = c^{\log_c a}$ **(78)**

(a = number or antilogarithm, c = base, $\log_c a$ = logarithm of a to the base c)

the logarithm of a to the base c is defined as the exponent of the power of the base c which equals the number a. The usual bases are 10 (common or briggsian logarithms) and $e = 2.718\,281\,828\,5$ (natural, napierian or hyperbolic logarithms). In these *Tables* the symbol log is used for common logarithms and the symbol ln for natural logarithms. The relation between the two is given by

$\ln a = \frac{\log a}{\log e} = 2.302\,585\,093\,0 \log a = \ln 10 \times \log a$ **(79)**

$\log a = \frac{\ln a}{\ln 10} = 0.434\,294\,481\,9 \ln a = \log e \times \ln a$ **(80)**

In general the relation is expressed by

$\log_c a = \frac{\log_{10} a}{\log_{10} c}$ **(81)**

Example: It is required to find the logarithm of 20 to the base 2. From equation **(81)**

$$\log_2 20 = \frac{\log_{10} 20}{\log_{10} 2} = \frac{1.301\,030\,0}{0.301\,030\,0} = 4.321\,928$$

The use of logarithms reduces multiplication, division, raising to powers and the extraction of roots to addition, subtraction, multiplication and division respectively.

For common logarithms equation **(78)** gives

$a = 10^{\log a}$ and $b = 10^{\log b}$

so that according to equation **(52)**

$a \times b = 10^{\log a} \times 10^{\log b} = 10^{\log a + \log b}$

that is $\log (a \times b) = \log a + \log b$

whence $(a \times b) = \text{antilog}\,(\log a + \log b)$

All the principles of logarithmic calculation can be deduced from section V in an analogous manner. The most important are:

$\log (a \times b) = \log a + \log b$ **(82)**

$\log \left(\frac{a}{b}\right) = \log a - \log b$ **(83)**

$$\log a^b \quad = b \log a \tag{84}$$

$$\log \sqrt[b]{a} \quad = \frac{\log a}{b} \tag{85}$$

Since by definition there are only logarithms of positive numbers, logarithmic calculation is made without regard to the algebraic sign of a, b, ... and the result assigned the appropriate sign according to the rules already given.

A logarithmic calculation falls into three parts:

1. Finding the logarithms
2. Operating with them according to the above rules
3. Finding the antilogarithms.

1. Finding the logarithm

The number of which the logarithm is required is first converted into a product as follows:

$$a = 10^x \times \frac{a}{10^x} = K' \times M' \tag{86}$$

x is determined for $|a| \geqq 1$ by counting the number b of places to the left of the decimal point, for $|a| < 1$ by counting the number b of ciphers to the right of the decimal point, so that

$$x = b - 1 \quad \text{when} \quad |a| \geqq 1 \tag{87}$$

and

$$x = -b - 1 \quad \text{when} \quad |a| < 1 \tag{88}$$

Examples:

a	b	x	K'	$K' \times M'$
1 566.3	4	3	10^3	$10^3 \times 1.566\,3$
1.2	1	0	10^0	$10^0 \times 1.2$
0.12	0	−1	10^{-1}	$10^{-1} \times 1.2$
0.000 34	−3	−4	10^{-4}	$10^{-4} \times 3.4$

In accordance with equation (**82**)

$$\log a = \log(K' \times M') = \log K' + \log M' = K + M \tag{89}$$

K is known as the characteristic, M as the mantissa of the logarithm of a.

The characteristic K is the positive or negative exponent x of K' in equation (**86**). The mantissa M must be looked for in a table of logarithms. For this purpose M' is first rounded off so that it contains the same number of figures as the logarithms in the table used. In the following examples four-figure logarithms are used:

For $M' < 1.1$, round off M' to 5 significant places

For $M' \geqq 1.1$, round off M' to 4 significant places

Example:

$\log 1.099\,3 = ?$ $\quad \log 1.566\,3 \approx \log 1.566 = ?$

From the table on page 10:

x	$\log x$		Proportional parts	
↓→	6	9	3	6
109		0410	1	
15	1931			17

$\log 1.099\,3 = 0.041\,0 + 0.000\,1 = 0.041\,1$

$\log 1.566 \quad = 0.193\,1 + 0.001\,7 = 0.194\,8$

Further examples:

(a) $\log 3048 \quad = \log(10^3 \times 3.048)$
$\quad = 3 + 0.482\,9 + 0.001\,1 = 3.484\,0$

(b) $\log 0.213\,0 \quad = \log(10^{-1} \times 2.130)$
$\quad = -1 + 0.328\,4 + 0 = 0.328\,4 - 1$

(c) $\log 1/3048 \quad = \log(10^{-3} \times 3.048^{-1})$
$\quad = -3 - (0.482\,9 + 0.001\,1) = -0.484\,0 - 3$

(d) $\log 1/0.213\,0 = \log(10^1 \times 2.13^{-1})$
$\quad = 1 - 0.328\,4 = 0.671\,6$

In example (c) the mantissa as well as the characteristic is negative. A negative mantissa must be converted into a positive one by adding 1 to the mantissa and subtracting 1 from the characteristic. For example:

$$-0.484\,0 - 3 = \underbrace{-0.484\,0 + 1}_{= 0.516\,0} \underbrace{-3 - 1}_{-4}$$

2. Operating with logarithms

This is done in accordance with equations (**82**) to (**85**) and the following rules:

1. Calculations are so made that no negative mantissa arises.
2. In extracting the roots of fractions, the difference between the root exponent and the characteristic is subtracted from the characteristic and added to the mantissa (examples e and f).
3. When the logarithmic calculation is complete, positive and negative characteristics are added together. The resulting characteristic x gives the number b of places to the left of the decimal point (when $x \geqq 0$) or the number b of ciphers to the right of the decimal point (when $x < 0$), as follows:

$$b = x + 1 \qquad \text{when } x \geqq 0 \tag{90}$$

$$b = -(x + 1) \quad \text{when } x < 0 \tag{91}$$

Examples:

(a) $\log(3048 \times 0.213\,0) \quad = \begin{array}{r} 3.484\,0 \\ +0.328\,4 - 1 \\ \hline 3.812\,4 - 1 \end{array} = 2.812\,4$

(b) $\log(0.213\,0 : 3048) \quad = \begin{array}{r} 0.328\,4 - 1 \\ +0.516\,0 - 4 \\ \hline 0.844\,4 - 5 \end{array} = 0.844\,4 - 5$

(c) $\log(0.213\,0 : 0.000\,328\,1) = \begin{array}{r} 0.328\,4 - 1 \\ -(0.516\,0 - 4) \end{array}$
$\quad = \begin{array}{r} 1.328\,4 - 2 \\ -0.516\,0 + 4 \\ \hline 0.812\,4 + 2 \end{array} = 2.812\,4$

(d) $\log(0.213\,0^5) \quad = 5 \log 0.213\,0 = 5 \times (0.328\,4 - 1)$
$\quad = 1.642\,0 - 5 \quad = 0.642\,0 - 4$

(e) $\log(\sqrt[6]{0.213\,0}) = \dfrac{\log 0.213\,0}{6} = \dfrac{0.328\,4 - 1}{6} = \dfrac{5.328\,4 - 6}{6}$
$\quad = 0.888\,1 - 1$

(f) $\log(\sqrt[1.5]{0.213\,0}) = \dfrac{\log 0.213\,0}{1.5} = \dfrac{0.328\,4 - 1}{1.5} = \dfrac{0.8284 - 1.5}{1.5}$
$\quad = 0.552\,3 - 1$

3. Finding the antilogarithm

The antilogarithm corresponding to a mantissa is looked for in a table of antilogarithms (see page 11) in the same way as a logarithm is looked for in a table of logarithms. (Care should be taken not to confuse the two tables.) The position of the decimal point is determined by means of equations (**90**) and (**91**).

Examples: antilog $2.812\,4 \quad = 649.2$

antilog $(0.888\,1 - 1) = 0.772\,9$

antilog $(0.642\,0 - 4) = 0.000\,438\,5$

VII. Factorials and binomial coefficients

1. $n^{(r)}$

For a positive integer r and any real number n the symbol $n^{(r)}$ represents the product

$$n^{(r)} = n(n-1)(n-2)\cdots(n-r+1) \tag{92}$$

where

$$n^{(0)} = 1 \tag{93}$$

by definition.

Examples:

(a) $10^{(4)} = ?$

In this case, $(n - r + 1) = 10 - 4 + 1 = 7$, so that $10^{(4)} = 10 \times 9 \times 8 \times 7 = 5040$

(b) $4^{(5)} = ?$

In this case, $(n - r + 1) = 4 - 5 + 1 = 0$, so that $4^{(5)} = 4 \times 3 \times 2 \times 1 \times 0 = 0$

From example (b) it can be seen that

$$n^{(r)} = 0 \qquad (94)$$

when $r > n$ and n is a positive integer.

2. Factorials

The factorial of a positive integer n, symbol $n!$, is defined as

$$n! = n(n-1)(n-2)\cdots 3 \times 2 \times 1 \qquad (95)$$

where

$$0! = 1 \qquad (96)$$

by definition.

For positive integers n, the factorial $n!$ can be expressed as $n^{(n)}$, in which case equation (**92**) can be written

$$n^{(r)} = \frac{n!}{(n-r)!} \qquad (97)$$

Equations (**93**) and (**94**) remain valid.

Logarithms of the factorials of numbers n from 1 to 999 and of their reciprocals are given on pages 26 and 27. For the factorials of numbers $n \geqq 1000$ the STIRLING approximation is used:

$$\underset{(n \to \infty)}{n!} \to n^n e^{-n} \sqrt{2 \pi n} \qquad (98)$$

or

$$\log n! \to 0.5 \times [2n(\log n - 0.434\,294\,481\,9) + \log n + 0.798\,178] \qquad (99)$$

3. Binomial coefficients

In its general form the binomial coefficient $\binom{n}{r}$ or $C(n, r)$ is defined as

$$\binom{n}{r} = \frac{n^{(r)}}{r!} \qquad (100)$$

For $n^{(r)}$ and $r!$ see subsections 1 and 2 above.

When n is a positive integer equations (**97**) and (**100**) give

$$\binom{n}{r} = \frac{n!}{r!(n-r)!} \qquad (101)$$

From equations (**93**), (**94**) and (**96**) it follows that

$$\binom{n}{0} = 1 \qquad (102)$$

$$\binom{0}{0} = 1 \qquad (103)$$

$$\binom{n}{r} = 0 \quad \text{when } r > n \text{ and } n \text{ is a positive integer.} \qquad (104)$$

It is also clear that

$$\binom{n}{n} = 1 \qquad (105)$$

Example: For $n = 9$ and $n = 10$ all the coefficients for values of r between zero and n are tabulated:

	r	0	1	2	3	4	5	6	7	8	9	
n =	9	1	9	36	84	126	126	84	36	9	1	
n =	10	1	10	45	120	210	252	210	120	45	10	1
	r	0	1	2	3	4	5	6	7	8	9	10

($n/2$ falls between 4 and 5 for $n = 9$; at $r = 5$ for $n = 10$.)

It will be seen that as r increases, the values of $\binom{n}{r}$ increase up to $n/2$ and then decrease again in symmetrical fashion:

$$\binom{n}{r} = \binom{n}{n-r} \qquad (106)$$

For uneven numbers n, the median falls between the two highest values of the series, for even numbers n it is at the highest value.

Binomial coefficients for n from zero to 39 and for r from zero to 15 are given on page 25. Logarithms of the binomial coefficients for n from 2 to 100 and for r from zero to $n/2$ are given on pages 70–77. For $101 \leqq n \leqq 999$ the binomial coefficients are calculated from equation (**101**) using the logarithms of factorials and their reciprocals given on pages 26 and 27.

VIII. Series

The sum $a_1 + a_2 + a_3 + \cdots + a_n$ of a sequence of numbers $a_1, a_2, a_3, \ldots a_n$ formed according to some fixed rule or law is known as a series.

1. Arithmetic series of the 1st order

This is a series in which the difference d between successive terms is constant:

$$a_2 - a_1 = a_3 - a_2$$

The individual terms are therefore

$$\left.\begin{matrix} a_1 & a_2 & a_3 & \ldots & a_n \\ a_1 & (a_1 + d) & (a_1 + 2d) & \ldots & a_1 + (n-1)d \end{matrix}\right\} \qquad (107)$$

The sum of the first n terms is

$$S = \frac{n(a_1 + a_n)}{2} \qquad (108)$$

A special case of (**108**) is the sum of the natural sequence of numbers $1, 2, 3, \ldots, n$

$$1 + 2 + 3 + \cdots + n = \frac{n(n+1)}{2} \qquad (109)$$

Example: The sum of all numbers from 1 to 81 is

$(81 \times 82) / 2 = 3321$

2. Geometric series

A geometric series is one in which there is a constant ratio q between successive terms

$$\left.\begin{matrix} a_1 & a_2 & a_3 & \ldots & a_n \\ a_1 & a_1 q & a_1 q^2 & \ldots & a_1 q^{n-1} \end{matrix}\right\} \qquad (110)$$

The sum of the first n terms is

$$S = a_1 \frac{1 - q^n}{1 - q} = a_1 \frac{q^n - 1}{q - 1} \quad (q \neq 1) \qquad (111)$$

When $-1 < q < 1$, $q^\infty = 0$ in accordance with (**17**), and (**111**) becomes

$$S_\infty = \frac{a_1}{1 - q} \quad (-1 < q < 1) \qquad (112)$$

With the aid of equation (**112**) infinite periodic decimal fractions, for example, can be converted into true fractions.

Examples:

(a) $0.3333\dot{3} = \frac{3}{10} + \frac{3}{100} + \frac{3}{1000} \cdots$

$q = \frac{1}{10} \qquad a_1 = \frac{3}{10}$

$0.3333\dot{3} = \frac{3}{10} \Big/ \frac{9}{10} = \frac{3}{9} = \frac{1}{3}$

(b) $0.0333\dot{3} = \frac{3}{100} + \frac{3}{1000} + \cdots$

$q = \frac{1}{10} \quad a_1 = \frac{3}{100}$

$$0.033\,3\dot{3} = \frac{3}{100} \bigg/ \frac{9}{10} = \frac{3}{90} = \frac{1}{30}$$

$$\text{(c) } 0.233\,3\dot{3} = \frac{2}{10} + \frac{3}{100} + \frac{3}{1000} + \cdots$$

The infinite series begins with 3/100, whence $q = 1/10$, $a_1 = 3/100$, etc., as in the previous example. There remains 2/10 to be added to it.

$$0.233\,3\dot{3} = \frac{2}{10} + \frac{1}{30} = \frac{60+10}{300} = \frac{7}{30}$$

$$\text{(d) } 0.123\,123\,\dot{1}\dot{2}\dot{3} = \frac{123}{1000} + \frac{123}{1\,000\,000} + \cdots$$

$$q = \frac{1}{1000} \quad a_1 = \frac{123}{1000}$$

$$0.123\,\dot{1}\dot{2}\dot{3} = \frac{123}{1000} \bigg/ \frac{999}{1000} = \frac{123}{999} = \frac{41}{333}$$

3. Binomial series for positive integers n

$$\left.\begin{aligned}(a+b)^n &= \binom{n}{0} a^n b^0 + \binom{n}{1} a^{n-1} b^1 + \binom{n}{2} a^{n-2} b^2 \\ &\quad + \binom{n}{3} a^{n-3} b^3 + \cdots + \binom{n}{n} a^0 b^n\end{aligned}\right\} \quad \textbf{(113)}$$

Algebraic signs: When b is negative, all terms in which the exponent of b is uneven are negative.

Examples: $(a+b)^2 = a^2 + 2ab + b^2$

$(a+b)^3 = a^3 + 3a^2 b + 3ab^2 + b^3$ etc.

IX. Means

For n positive variates $x_1, x_2, \ldots, x_n$

(a) the arithmetic mean $m_a = \dfrac{x_1 + x_2 + \cdots + x_n}{n} = \dfrac{\sum_1^n x_i}{n}$ **(114)**

(b) the geometric mean $m_g = \sqrt[n]{x_1 \times x_2 \times \cdots \times x_n}$ **(115)**

(c) the harmonic mean $m_h = 1 : \dfrac{1}{n}\left(\dfrac{1}{x_1} + \dfrac{1}{x_2} + \cdots + \dfrac{1}{x_n}\right)$ **(116)**

When $n = 2$, then

$$m_a = \frac{x_1 + x_2}{2} \quad \textbf{(117)}$$

$$m_g = \sqrt{x_1 x_2} \quad \textbf{(118)}$$

$$m_h = \frac{2 x_1 x_2}{x_1 + x_2} \quad \textbf{(119)}$$

CAUCHY's principle: $m_a \geqq m_g \geqq m_h$ **(120)**

where the equality signs are valid only when

$x_1 = x_2 = \cdots = x_n$

X. Solutions of equations

Solutions of equations exist only when all the denominators differ from zero.

Required is x:

$$ax \pm b = 0; \quad x = \mp \frac{b}{a} \quad \textbf{(121)}$$

$$\frac{a}{x} \pm b = 0; \quad x = \mp \frac{a}{b} \quad \textbf{(122)}$$

1. Simplification of equations of higher degree

$$(ax \pm b)^m \pm c = 0; \quad x = \frac{\sqrt[m]{\mp c} \mp b}{a} \quad \textbf{(123)}$$

$$\sqrt[n]{ax \pm b} \pm c = 0; \quad x = \frac{(\mp c)^n \mp b}{a} \quad \textbf{(124)}$$

2. Equations of the first degree with two unknowns

x and y are required:

$a_1 x + b_1 y + c_1 = 0$

$a_2 x + b_2 y + c_2 = 0$

$$\left.\begin{aligned} x &= \frac{b_1 c_2 - b_2 c_1}{a_1 b_2 - a_2 b_1} \\ y &= -\frac{a_1 x + c_1}{b_1} = -\frac{a_2 x + c_2}{b_2}\end{aligned}\right\} \quad \textbf{(125)}$$

3. Equations of the first degree with three unknowns

x, y, z are required:

$a_1 x + b_1 y + c_1 z + d_1 = 0$

$a_2 x + b_2 y + c_2 z + d_2 = 0$

$a_3 x + b_3 y + c_3 z + d_3 = 0$

Let

$$\left.\begin{aligned} A &= c_2 a_1 - c_1 a_2 \\ B &= c_2 b_1 - c_1 b_2 \\ C &= c_2 d_1 - c_1 d_2 \\ D &= c_2 a_3 - c_3 a_2 \\ E &= c_2 b_3 - c_3 b_2 \\ F &= c_2 d_3 - c_3 d_2 \end{aligned}\right\} \quad \textbf{(126)}$$

then

$$x = \frac{BF - CE}{AE - BD}$$

$$y = -\frac{C + Ax}{B} = -\frac{F + Dx}{E}$$

$$z = -\frac{a_1 x + b_1 y + d_1}{c_1} = -\frac{a_2 x + b_2 y + d_2}{c_2} = -\frac{a_3 x + b_3 y + d_3}{c_3}$$

4. Quadratic equations with one unknown

$ax^2 + bx + c = 0$

$$x_{(1,2)} = \frac{-b \pm \sqrt{b^2 - 4ac}}{2a} = \frac{-b}{2a} \pm \sqrt{\left(\frac{b}{2a}\right)^2 - \frac{c}{a}} \quad \textbf{(127)}$$

The magnitude $D = b^2 - 4ac$ is known as the discriminant of the equation. When

$D > 0$ there are two real solutions

$D = 0$ there is only one real solution

$D < 0$ there is no real solution

5. Exponential equations in common use

$x = 1 - e^{-\lambda}$; $x = 1 - \text{antilog}\,(-0.434\,294\,481\,9\,\lambda)$ **(128)**

$a = 1 - e^{-z}$; $z = -2.302\,585\,093\,0 \log(1-a)$ $[0 \leqq a \leqq 1]$ **(129)**

If in equation (**129**)

$$z = \frac{ax^b \pm c}{d}, \text{ then } \log x = \frac{\log\left(\dfrac{dz \mp c}{a}\right)}{b} \quad \textbf{(130)}$$

(when $b = 1$ the log sign disappears on both sides)

$$z = \frac{ab^x \pm c}{d}, \text{ then } \quad x = \frac{\log\left(\dfrac{dz \mp c}{a}\right)}{\log b} \quad (b \neq 1) \quad \textbf{(131)}$$

$$z = \frac{d}{ax^b \pm c}, \text{ then } \log x = \frac{\log\left(\dfrac{d/z \mp c}{a}\right)}{b} \quad \textbf{(132)}$$

(when $b = 1$ the log sign disappears on both sides)

$$z = \frac{d}{ab^x \pm c}\,, \text{ then } x = \frac{\log\left(\frac{d/z \mp c}{a}\right)}{\log b} \qquad (b \neq 1) \qquad \textbf{(133)}$$

Equations (**130**) to (**133**) have no solution when

$(dz \mp c) < 0$ or $(d/z \mp c) < 0$

This is true for equations (**130**) and (**132**), however, only when $b \neq 1$.

The following table gives z values [solutions of equation (**129**)] for various numbers a in common use:

a	$1-a$	$\log(1-a)$	$z = -\ln 10 \times \log(1-a)$ $= -\ln(1-a)$
0.999	0.001	− 3	6.907 755 279
0.995	0.005	0.698 970 004 3 − 3	5.298 317 367
0.99	0.01	− 2	4.605 170 186
0.975	0.025	0.397 940 008 7 − 2	3.688 879 453
0.95	0.05	0.698 970 004 3 − 2	2.995 732 274
0.90	0.10	− 1	2.302 585 093
0.85	0.15	0.176 091 259 1 − 1	1.897 119 985
0.80	0.20	0.301 029 995 7 − 1	1.609 437 912
0.75	0.25	0.397 940 008 7 − 1	1.386 294 361
0.70	0.30	0.477 121 254 7 − 1	1.203 972 804
0.65	0.35	0.544 068 044 4 − 1	1.049 822 124
0.60	0.40	0.602 059 991 3 − 1	0.916 290 731 9
0.55	0.45	0.653 212 513 8 − 1	0.798 507 696 2
0.50	0.50	0.698 970 004 3 − 1	0.693 147 180 4
0.45	0.55	0.740 362 689 5 − 1	0.597 837 000 7
0.40	0.60	0.778 151 250 4 − 1	0.510 825 623 7
0.35	0.65	0.812 913 356 6 − 1	0.430 782 916 2
0.30	0.70	0.845 098 040 0 − 1	0.356 674 944 0
0.25	0.75	0.875 061 263 4 − 1	0.287 682 072 4
0.20	0.80	0.903 089 987 0 − 1	0.223 143 551 5
0.15	0.85	0.929 418 925 7 − 1	0.162 518 929 5
0.10	0.90	0.954 242 509 4 − 1	0.105 360 515 7
0.05	0.95	0.977 723 605 3 − 1	0.051 293 294 39
0.025	0.975	0.989 004 615 7 − 1	0.025 317 807 98
0.01	0.99	0.995 635 194 6 − 1	0.010 050 335 85
0.005	0.995	0.997 823 080 7 − 1	0.005 012 541 823
0.001	0.999	0.999 565 488 2 − 1	0.001 000 500 333

XI. Rectangular coordinate system

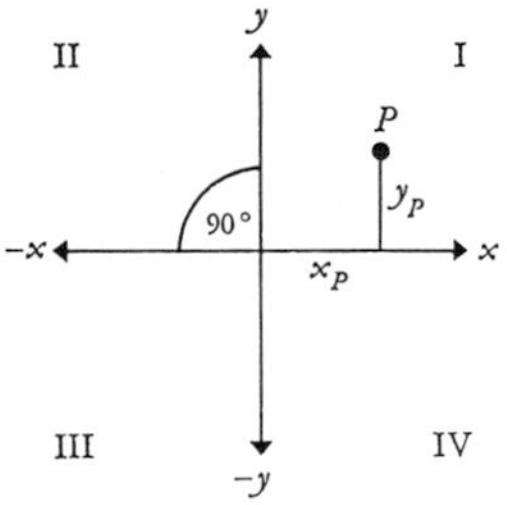

x axis = abscissa axis

y axis = ordinate axis

I, II, III, IV = quadrants

x_P and y_P = coordinates of the point P

x_P = abscissa of the point P

y_P = ordinate of the point P

Signs of the coordinates of points in each of the 4 quadrants

Quadrant	x	y
I	+	+
II	−	+
III	−	−
IV	+	−

XII. Angles, trigonometric functions, inverse trigonometric functions

1. Positive and negative angles

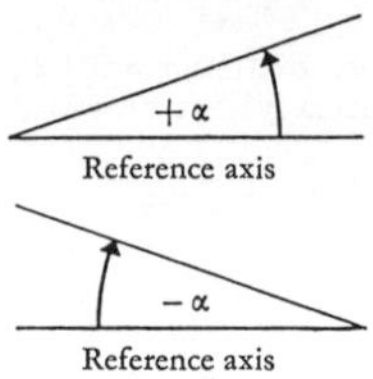

Rotation in an *anti*clockwise direction is defined as positive rotation, rotation in a clockwise direction as negative rotation. Similarly an angle measured by positive rotation is a positive angle, one measured by negative rotation a negative angle.

By angle of inclination of a straight line a is usually meant the *acute* angle between the straight line and the x axis.

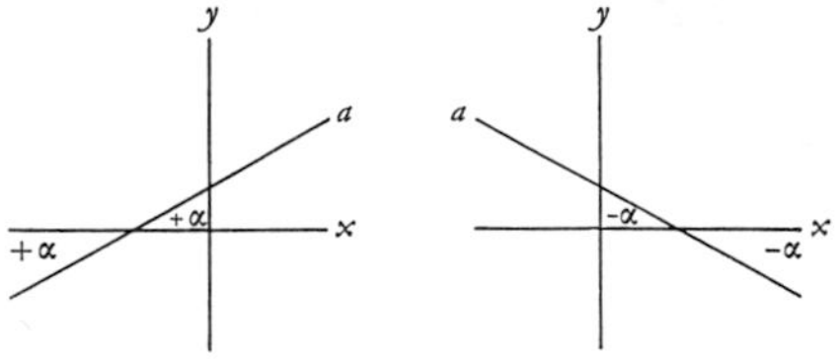

2. Angle units (see also under 'Units of Measurement', page 207)

The basis of all angle units is the circumference of a circle drawn with its centre at the point of intersection of the lines forming the angle. This is divided into 360 equal parts (degrees, the unit normally used) or into 400 equal parts (grades), or measured in terms of its own radius (arc, circular or radian measure). Since the circumference of a circle is 2π times its radius, angles are often expressed as fractions or multiples of π. The arc measure of the angle α is designated arcus α (arc α).

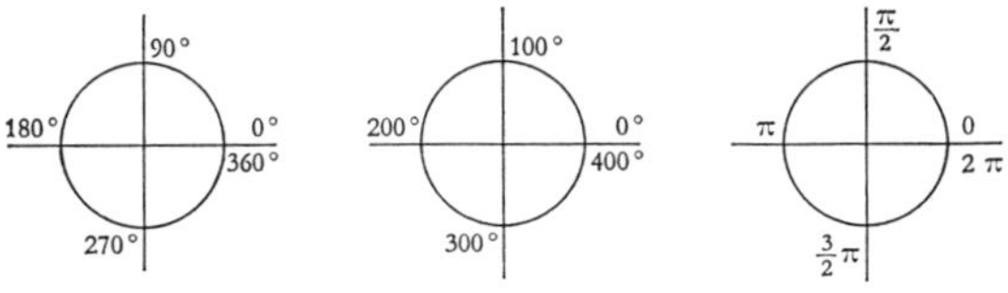

Degrees Grades Arc measure

Degrees	0°	1°	30°	57°17′45″	60°	90°	180°	270°	360°
Arc measure	0	0.017 45	$\frac{\pi}{6}$	1	$\frac{\pi}{3}$	$\frac{\pi}{2}$	π	$\frac{3}{2}\pi$	2π

3. Trigonometric functions (other than secant and cosecant)

The definitions are based on the right triangle and are valid only for acute angles between 0 and 90°:

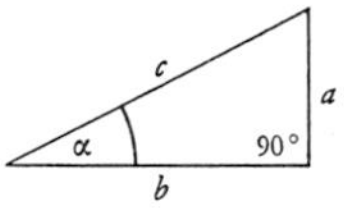

$$\left.\begin{aligned} &\text{sine } \alpha &&= \sin\alpha = \frac{a}{c} \\ &\text{cosine } \alpha &&= \cos\alpha = \frac{b}{c} \\ &\text{tangent } \alpha &&= \tan\alpha = \frac{a}{b} \\ &\text{cotangent } \alpha &&= \cot\alpha = \frac{b}{a} \end{aligned}\right\} \qquad \textbf{(134)}$$

(the tangent is also sometimes abbreviated to tg, the cotangent to ctg or ctn)

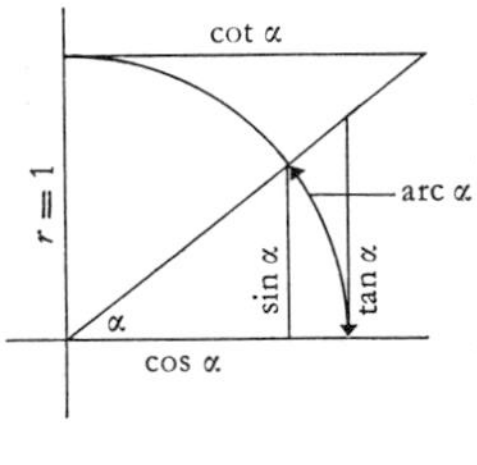

Representation of trigonometric functions on the unit circle (circle with radius = 1)

Algebraic signs of trigonometric functions in the 4 quadrants

Function	Quadrant I	II	III	IV	
sin	+	+	−	−	**(135)**
cos	+	−	−	+	
tan	+	−	+	−	
cot	+	−	+	−	

Ranges of trigonometric functions in the 4 quadrants

Function	Quadrant I	II	III	IV	
sin	0 to 1	1 to 0	0 to −1	−1 to 0	**(136)**
cos	1 to 0	0 to −1	−1 to 0	0 to 1	
tan	0 to ∞	−∞ to 0	0 to ∞	−∞ to 0	
cot	∞ to 0	0 to −∞	∞ to 0	0 to −∞	

Behaviour of trigonometric functions

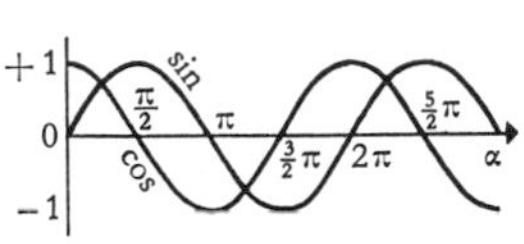

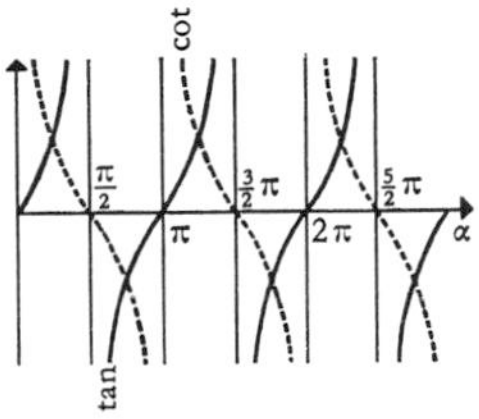

Functions of negative angles

$$\left.\begin{aligned} \sin(-\alpha) &= -\sin\alpha \\ \cos(-\alpha) &= +\cos\alpha \\ \tan(-\alpha) &= -\tan\alpha \\ \cot(-\alpha) &= -\cot\alpha \end{aligned}\right\} \quad \textbf{(137)}$$

Conversion of the functions of obtuse angles into those of acute angles

	90° ± α	180° ± α	270° ± α	n* (360°) ± α	
sin	+ cos α	∓ sin α	− cos α	± sin α	**(138)**
cos	∓ sin α	− cos α	± sin α	+ cos α	
tan	∓ cot α	± tan α	∓ cot α	± tan α	
cot	∓ tan α	± cot α	∓ tan α	± cot α	

* *n* = positive integer.

Example: sin 125° = cos 35°

Relationships between trigonometric functions

Function	sin α	cos α	tan α	cot α	
sin α	$\sin\alpha$	$\pm\sqrt{1-\cos^2\alpha}$	$\dfrac{\tan\alpha}{\pm\sqrt{1+\tan^2\alpha}}$	$\dfrac{1}{\pm\sqrt{1+\cot^2\alpha}}$	
cos α	$\pm\sqrt{1-\sin^2\alpha}$	$\cos\alpha$	$\dfrac{1}{\pm\sqrt{1+\tan^2\alpha}}$	$\dfrac{\cot\alpha}{\pm\sqrt{1+\cot^2\alpha}}$	**(139)**
tan α	$\dfrac{\sin\alpha}{\pm\sqrt{1-\sin^2\alpha}}$	$\dfrac{\pm\sqrt{1-\cos^2\alpha}}{\cos\alpha}$	$\tan\alpha$	$\dfrac{1}{\cot\alpha}$	
cot α	$\dfrac{\pm\sqrt{1-\sin^2\alpha}}{\sin\alpha}$	$\dfrac{\cos\alpha}{\pm\sqrt{1-\cos^2\alpha}}$	$\dfrac{1}{\tan\alpha}$	$\cot\alpha$	

Algebraic sign of the square root: This is determined by the quadrant into which the angle falls. For algebraic signs in the quadrants see (**135**).

Functions of half the angle and of twice the angle

$$\left.\begin{aligned} \sin\frac{\alpha}{2} &= \pm\tfrac{1}{2}\left(\underset{+}{\sqrt{1+\sin\alpha}} - \underset{+}{\sqrt{1-\sin\alpha}}\right) \\ &= \pm\sqrt{\frac{1-\cos\alpha}{2}} \end{aligned}\right\} \quad \textbf{(140)}$$

$$\cos\frac{\alpha}{2} = \pm\sqrt{\frac{1+\cos\alpha}{2}} \quad \textbf{(141)}$$

$$\left.\begin{aligned} \tan\frac{\alpha}{2} &= \frac{-1\pm\sqrt{1+\tan^2\alpha}}{\tan\alpha} = \frac{1-\cos\alpha}{\sin\alpha} \\ &= \frac{\sin\alpha}{1+\cos\alpha} = \pm\sqrt{\frac{1-\cos\alpha}{1+\sin\alpha}} \end{aligned}\right\} \quad \textbf{(142)}$$

$$\sin 2\alpha = 2\sin\alpha\cos\alpha \quad \textbf{(143)}$$

$$\cos 2\alpha = 2\cos^2\alpha - 1 = 1 - 2\sin^2\alpha = \cos^2\alpha - \sin^2\alpha \quad \textbf{(144)}$$

$$\tan 2\alpha = \frac{2\tan\alpha}{1-\tan^2\alpha} \quad \textbf{(145)}$$

Algebraic signs: ± indicates that the algebraic sign is determined by the quadrant into which the *required* angle falls. For algebraic signs in the quadrants see (**135**).

Relationships between the functions of two angles

$$\sin(\alpha\pm\beta) = \sin\alpha\cos\beta \pm \cos\alpha\sin\beta \quad \textbf{(146)}$$

$$\cos(\alpha\pm\beta) = \cos\alpha\cos\beta \mp \sin\alpha\sin\beta \quad \textbf{(147)}$$

$$\mathrm{tg}(\alpha\pm\beta) = \frac{\mathrm{tg}\,\alpha \pm \mathrm{tg}\,\beta}{1 \mp \mathrm{tg}\,\alpha\,\mathrm{tg}\,\beta} = \frac{\sin(\alpha\pm\beta)}{\cos(\alpha\pm\beta)} \quad \textbf{(148)}$$

$$\sin\alpha + \sin\beta = 2\sin\left(\frac{\alpha+\beta}{2}\right)\cos\left(\frac{\alpha-\beta}{2}\right) \quad \textbf{(149)}$$

$$\sin\alpha - \sin\beta = 2\cos\left(\frac{\alpha+\beta}{2}\right)\sin\left(\frac{\alpha-\beta}{2}\right) \quad \textbf{(150)}$$

$$\cos\alpha + \cos\beta = 2\cos\left(\frac{\alpha+\beta}{2}\right)\cos\left(\frac{\alpha-\beta}{2}\right) \quad \textbf{(151)}$$

$$\cos\alpha - \cos\beta = -2\sin\left(\frac{\alpha+\beta}{2}\right)\sin\left(\frac{\alpha-\beta}{2}\right) \quad \textbf{(152)}$$

$$\tan\alpha \pm \tan\beta = \frac{\sin(\alpha\pm\beta)}{\cos\alpha\cos\beta} \quad \textbf{(153)}$$

$$\sin\alpha\sin\beta = \tfrac{1}{2}\cos(\alpha-\beta) - \tfrac{1}{2}\cos(\alpha+\beta) \quad \textbf{(154)}$$

$$\cos\alpha\cos\beta = \tfrac{1}{2}\cos(\alpha-\beta) + \tfrac{1}{2}\cos(\alpha+\beta) \quad \textbf{(155)}$$

$$\sin\alpha\cos\beta = \tfrac{1}{2}\sin(\alpha+\beta) + \tfrac{1}{2}\sin(\alpha-\beta) \quad \textbf{(156)}$$

4. Inverse trigonometric functions

These are also known as arc or cyclometric functions. Only the inverse sine (arc-sine) function will be described here, since this is used for the stabilization of the variance of binomial distributions (see page 187).

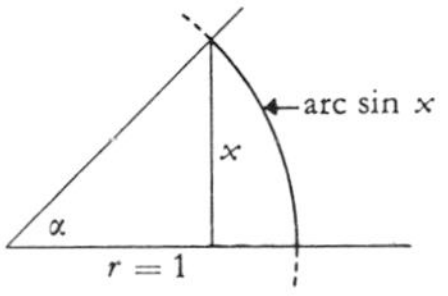

Arc sine x, abbreviated to $\sin^{-1} x$ or arc sin x, is the arc or degree measure of the angle with sine $= x$. An arc-sine table in arc measure for the range $0 \leq x \leq 1$ is given on page 69. If the value of an arc sine in degrees is required, the value given in this table must be multiplied by $180/\pi = 57.295\,779\,513$.

Behaviour of the function arc sin x in the range $0 \leq x \leq 1$

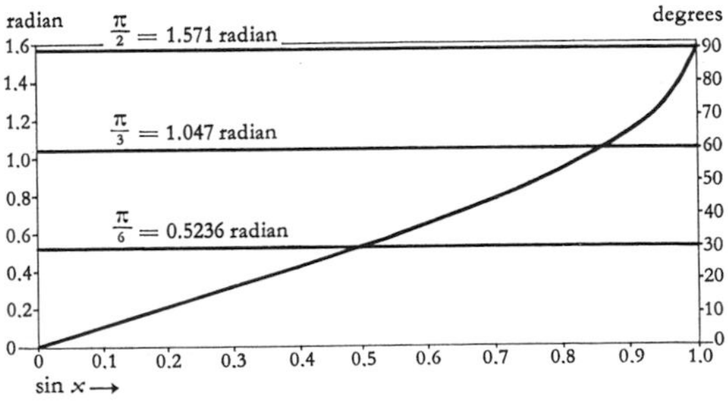

XIII. Hyperbolic functions

These derive their name from their geometric representation in relation to a rectangular hyperbola in a manner similar to that in which the trigonometric functions are related to a circle. Here only the hyperbolic tangent ($\tanh z$) and the corresponding inverse function ($\tanh^{-1} r$) will be dealt with, since these functions are required for the transformation of the correlation coefficient r (see page 180). They are defined as follows:

$$\tanh z = r = \frac{e^{2z} - 1}{e^{2z} + 1} \qquad \textbf{(157)}$$

$$\tanh^{-1} r = z = {}^1/_2 \ln \frac{1+r}{1-r} = 1.151\,292\,55 \log_{10} \frac{1+r}{1-r} \qquad \textbf{(158)}$$

Only the following two relationships are required:

$$\tanh(-z) = -\tanh z \qquad \textbf{(159)}$$

$$\tanh^{-1}(-r) = -\tanh^{-1} r \qquad \textbf{(160)}$$

The range of variation of $\tanh z$ is -1 to $+1$ for values of z from $-\infty$ to $+\infty$.

Behaviour of the function $\tanh z$ in the range $-3.2 \leqq z \leqq +3.2$

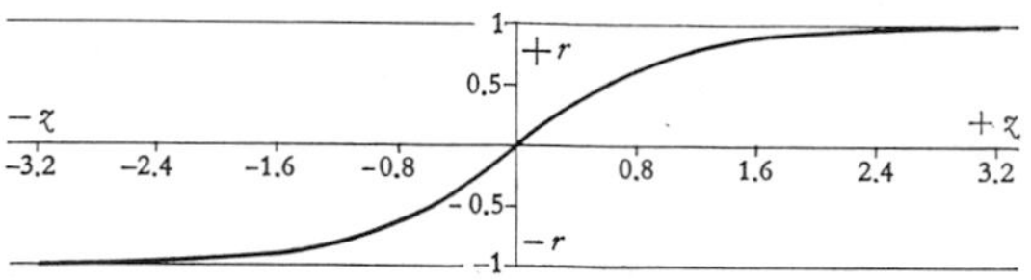

Tables of $\tanh z$ are given on pages 64 and 65, of $\tanh^{-1} r$ on page 62.

XIV. Geometric calculations

1. Right triangle ABC

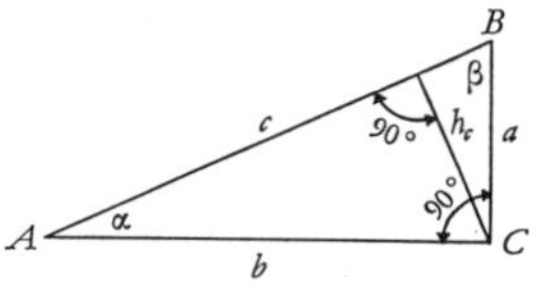

a = perpendicular, b = base (sides)
c = hypotenuse
h_c = altitude above hypotenuse

Given	Required	Solution	
β	α	$= 90° - \beta$	**(161)**
a, b	α	$\tan \alpha = \frac{a}{b}$	**(162)**
	c	$= \frac{a}{\sin \alpha}$	**(163)**
		$= \frac{b}{\cos \alpha}$	**(164)**
		$= \underset{+}{\sqrt{a^2 + b^2}}$	**(165)**
	h_c	$= a \cos \alpha$	**(166)**
		$= b \sin \alpha$	**(167)**
		$= \frac{a\,b}{c}$	**(168)**
	Area A	$= \frac{a\,b}{2}$	**(169)**
a, c	α	$\sin \alpha = \frac{a}{c}$	**(170)**
	b	$= c \cos \alpha$	**(171)**
		$= \underset{+}{\sqrt{c^2 - a^2}}$	**(172)**
	h_c	$= a \cos \alpha$	**(173)**

Given	Required	Solution	
a, c	Area A	$\frac{a\,c \cos \alpha}{2}$	**(174)**
b, c	α	$\cos \alpha = \frac{b}{c}$	**(175)**
	a	$= c \sin \alpha$	**(176)**
		$= \underset{+}{\sqrt{c^2 - b^2}}$	**(177)**
	h_c	$= b \sin \alpha$	**(178)**
	Area A	$= \frac{b\,c \sin \alpha}{2}$	**(179)**
a, α	b	$= \frac{a}{\tan \alpha}$	**(180)**
	c	$= \frac{a}{\sin \alpha}$	**(181)**
	h_c	$= a \cos \alpha$	**(182)**
	Area A	$= \frac{a^2}{2 \tan \alpha}$	**(183)**
c, α	a	$= c \sin \alpha$	**(184)**
	b	$= c \cos \alpha$	**(185)**
	h_c	$= \frac{c \sin 2\alpha}{2}$	**(186)**
	Area A	$= \frac{c^2 \sin 2\alpha}{4}$	**(187)**
c, h_c	α	$\sin 2\alpha = \frac{2 h_c}{c}$	**(188)**
	a	$= \frac{h_c}{\cos \alpha}$	**(189)**
	b	$= \frac{h_c}{\sin \alpha}$	**(190)**
	Area A	$= \frac{c\,h_c}{2}$	**(191)**

2. Obtuse triangle

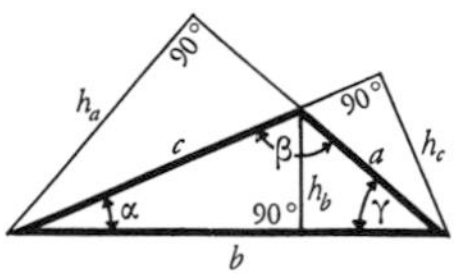

All the sides are of equal value in the obtuse triangle, and permutation of a, b, c, etc. in a cyclic fashion results in different formulae which are equally valid. When one of the symbols in any formula in a group is permuted, the symbols in all the other formulae of the group must be permuted in accordance with the following scheme:

Permutation by one step	Permutation by two steps	
$a \to b$	$a \to c$	
$b \to c$	$b \to a$	
$c \to a$	$c \to b$	
$\alpha \to \beta$	$\alpha \to \gamma$	**(192)**
$\beta \to \gamma$	$\beta \to \alpha$	
$\gamma \to \alpha$	$\gamma \to \beta$	
$h_a \to h_b$	$h_a \to h_c$	

Altitudes and areas

$$h_a = b \sin\gamma \quad \textbf{(193)}$$

$$= c \sin\beta \quad \textbf{(194)}$$

$$= a\,\frac{\sin\beta \sin\gamma}{\sin\alpha} \quad \textbf{(195)}$$

$$\text{Area } A = \frac{a\,h_a}{2} \quad \textbf{(196)}$$

Given	Required	Solution	
$\beta + \gamma$	α	$= 180° - (\beta + \gamma)$	**(197)**
$\sin\alpha$		$\sin(\beta+\gamma) = \sin\alpha$	**(198)**
$\cos\alpha$		$\cos(\beta+\gamma) = -\cos\alpha$	**(198)**
$\tan\alpha$		$\tan(\beta+\gamma) = -\tan\alpha$	**(198)**
a, b, c	α	$\cos\alpha = \dfrac{b^2 + c^2 - a^2}{2bc}$	**(199)**
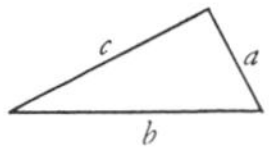	h_a	$= b \sin\gamma$	**(200)**
		$= \dfrac{2A}{a}$	**(201)**
	Area A	$= \dfrac{bc\sin\alpha}{2}$	**(202)**
		$= \underset{+}{\sqrt{s(s-a)(s-b)(s-c)}}$	**(203)**
		where $s = \dfrac{a+b+c}{2}$	
a, b, γ	α	$\tan\alpha = \dfrac{a\sin\gamma}{b - a\cos\gamma}$	**(204)**
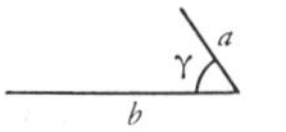	c	$= \dfrac{a\sin\gamma}{\sin\alpha}$	**(205)**
		$= \underset{+}{\sqrt{a^2 + b^2 - 2ab\cos\gamma}}$	**(206)**
	h_a	$= b\sin\gamma$	**(207)**
	h_b	$= a\sin\gamma$	**(208)**
	Area A	$= \dfrac{ab\sin\gamma}{2}$	**(209)**
a, b, α	β	$\sin\beta = \dfrac{b\sin\alpha}{a}$	**(210)**
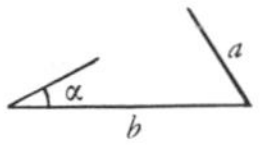	c	$= \dfrac{a\sin\gamma}{\sin\alpha}$	**(211)**
		$= b\cos\alpha \pm \sqrt{a^2 - b^2\sin^2\alpha}$	**(212)**
	h_a	$= b\sin\gamma$	**(213)**
	h_b	$= a\sin\gamma$	**(214)**
	h_c	$= b\sin\alpha$	**(215)**
	Area A	$= \dfrac{b}{2}\sin\alpha \times \left(b\cos\alpha \pm \sqrt{a^2 - b^2\sin^2\alpha}\right)$	**(216)**
a, b, β	α	$\sin\alpha = \dfrac{a\sin\beta}{b}$	**(217)**
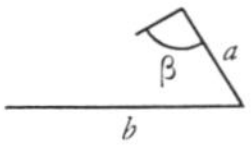	c	$= \dfrac{b\sin\gamma}{\sin\beta}$	**(218)**
	h_a	$= b\sin\gamma$	**(219)**
	h_b	$= a\sin\gamma$	**(220)**

Given	Required	Solution	
a, b, β	h_c	$= a\sin\beta$	**(221)**
	Area A	$= \dfrac{a}{2}\sin\beta \times \left(a\cos\beta \pm \sqrt{b^2 - a^2\sin^2\beta}\right)$	**(222)**

Note that in the above group of equations (given two sides and the angle they enclose), the following conditions hold:

	Equations **(210)** – **(216)**	Equations **(217)** – **(222)**
Solution is only possible when	$b\sin\alpha \leqq a$	$a\sin\beta \leqq b$
If	$b\sin\alpha = a$	$a\sin\beta = b$
then	$\beta = 90°$	$\alpha = 90°$
If	$b\sin\alpha < a$ and $a < b$	$a\sin\beta < b$ and $b < a$
two solutions are possible:	β_1 and $\beta_2 = 180° - \beta_1$	α_1 and $\alpha_2 = 180° - \alpha_1$
If	$b\sin\alpha < a$ and $a \geqq b$	$a\sin\beta < a$ and $b \geqq a$
no solution is possible.		

Given	Required	Solution	
a, β, γ	b	$= \dfrac{a\sin\beta}{\sin(\beta+\gamma)}$	**(223)**
	c	$= \dfrac{a\sin\gamma}{\sin(\beta+\gamma)}$	**(224)**
(Note that if two angles are given, the third is also given)	h_a	$= \dfrac{a\sin\beta\sin\gamma}{\sin(\beta+\gamma)}$	**(225)**
	h_b	$= a\sin\gamma$	**(226)**
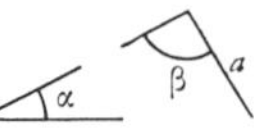	h_c	$= a\sin\beta$	**(227)**
$\gamma = 180° - (\alpha + \beta)$	Area A	$= \dfrac{a^2}{2} \times \dfrac{\sin\beta\sin\gamma}{\sin(\beta+\gamma)}$	**(228)**

3. Quadrilateral

In general the area of any quadrilateral can be calculated from the diagonals and the angle θ (or $\theta' = 180° - \theta$) enclosed by them:

Any quadrilateral

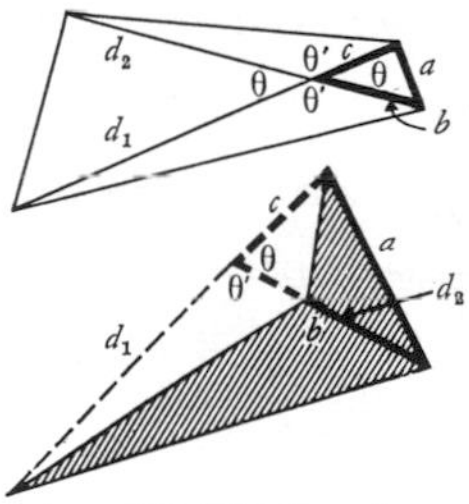

Area of shaded part $= A$

$\sin\theta = \sin\theta'$

$$= \frac{2}{bc}\sqrt{s(s-a)(s-b)(s-c)} \quad \textbf{(229)}$$

where $s = \frac{1}{2}(a + b + c)$ is half the circumference of the triangle bounded by the two diagonals and the side a. Any triangle can be chosen, but the sides indicated by b, c must *enclose* the angle θ or θ'.

$$\text{Area } A = \frac{d_1 d_2 \sin\theta}{2} \quad \textbf{(230)}$$

Square

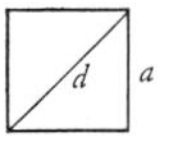

$$d = a\sqrt{2} = 1.414214\,a \quad \textbf{(231)}$$

$$\text{Area } A = a^2 \quad \textbf{(232)}$$

Rectangle

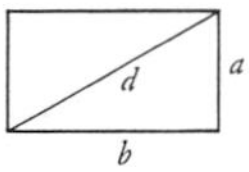

$$d = \sqrt{a^2 + b^2} \quad \textbf{(233)}$$

$$\text{Area } A = ab \quad \textbf{(234)}$$

Parallelogram

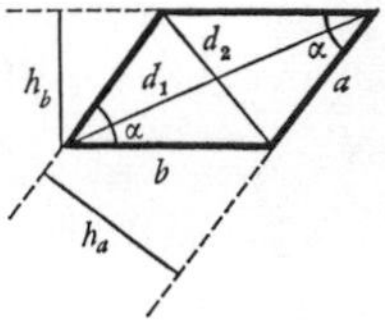

$$d_1, d_2 = \sqrt{a^2 + b^2 \pm 2ab\cos\alpha} \quad (235)$$

$$= \sqrt{a^2 + b^2 \pm 2a\sqrt{b^2 - h_a^2}} \quad (236)$$

$$h_a = b\sin\alpha \quad (237)$$

$$h_b = a\sin\alpha \quad (238)$$

$$\text{Area } A = a\,h_a = b\,h_b = a\,b\sin\alpha \quad (239)$$

Trapezoid

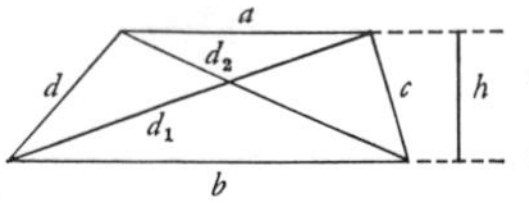

a, b are parallel, c, d nonparallel sides; d_1 = diagonal drawn between the points of intersection of d with b and a with c.

$$d_1 = \sqrt{ab + \frac{ac^2 - bd^2}{a - b}} \quad (240)$$

$$d_2 = \sqrt{ab + \frac{ad^2 - bc^2}{a - b}} \quad (241)$$

$$h = \frac{2}{a - b} \times \sqrt{s(s-a+b)(s-c)(s-d)} \quad (242)$$

where $s = \frac{1}{2}(a - b + c + d)$

$$\text{Area } A = \frac{(a + b)\,h}{2} \quad (243)$$

4. Circle

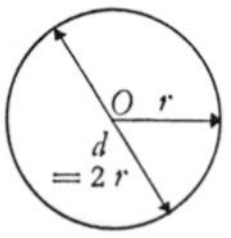

$$\left.\begin{aligned}\text{Circumference } c &= 2\pi r \\ &= 6.283\,185\,3\,r \\ &= 3.141\,592\,65\,d\end{aligned}\right\} \quad (244)$$

$$\left.\begin{aligned}\text{Area } A &= \pi r^2 = 3.141\,592\,65\,r^2 \\ &= 0.785\,398\,16\,d^2\end{aligned}\right\} \quad (245)$$

Sector

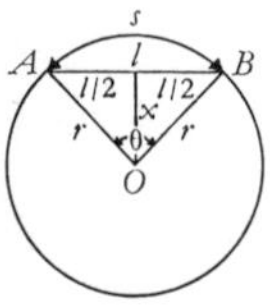

Angle θ between the radii r

$$\cos\theta = 1 - \frac{l^2}{2r^2} \quad (246)$$

or

$$\theta = 180° - 2\arcsin(x/r) \quad (247)$$

Length of a chord

$$l = 2r\sin\frac{\theta}{2} \quad (248)$$

Length of an arc s

$$s = \frac{\pi r\theta}{180} = 0.017\,453\,293\,r\,\theta \quad (249)$$

Area of a sector

$$A_{Se} = \frac{\pi r^2\theta}{360} = 0.008\,726\,646\,3\,r^2\theta \quad (250)$$

Area of a triangle OAB

$$A_\triangle = \frac{r^2\sin\theta}{2} \quad (251)$$

Area of a segment AsB

$$\left.\begin{aligned}A_{Sg} &= \frac{\pi r^2\theta}{360} - \frac{r^2\sin\theta}{2} \\ &= 0.008\,726\,646\,3\,r^2 \times \\ &\quad (\theta - 57.295\,779\,5\sin\theta)\end{aligned}\right\} \quad (252)$$

Annulus

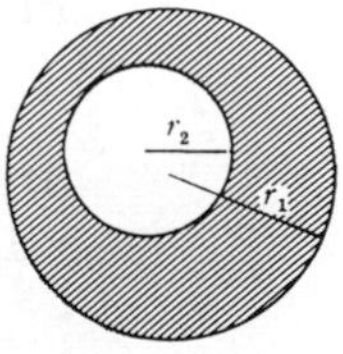

(The two circles bounding an annulus need not be concentric.)

Area of shaded part

$$\left.\begin{aligned}A &= \pi(r_1 + r_2)(r_1 - r_2)\ [r_1 \geq r_2] \\ &= 3.141\,592\,65\,(r_1 + r_2)(r_1 - r_2)\end{aligned}\right. \quad (253)$$

Annular segment (concentric)

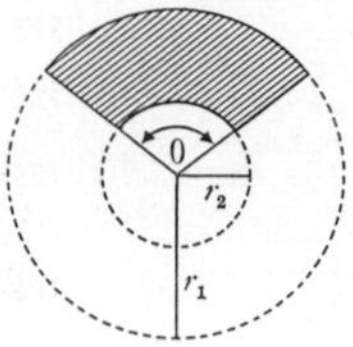

Area of shaded part

$$\left.\begin{aligned}A &= \frac{\pi\theta}{360}(r_1 + r_2)(r_1 - r_2)\ [r_1 \geq r_2] \\ \frac{\pi}{360} &= 0.008\,726\,646\,26\end{aligned}\right\} \quad (254)$$

For the angle θ see equations (**246**) and (**247**).

5. Ellipse

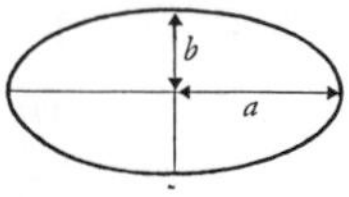

$$\left.\begin{aligned}\text{Circumference} &\sim 2\pi\sqrt{\frac{a^2 + b^2}{2}} \\ &\sim 4.443\sqrt{a^2 + b^2}\end{aligned}\right\} \quad (255)$$

$$\text{Area } A = \pi\,a\,b = 3.141\,592\,65\,a\,b \quad (256)$$

XV. Solid geometry

1. Rectangular parallelepiped (all edges at right angles to the adjacent ones)

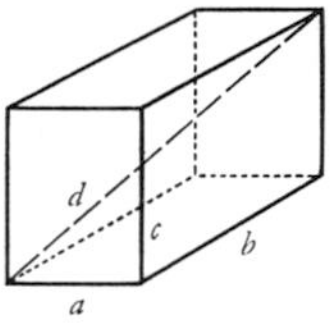

Surface area

$$A = 2(ab + bc + ca) \quad (257)$$

Internal diagonal

$$d = \sqrt{a^2 + b^2 + c^2} \quad (258)$$

Volume

$$V = abc \quad (259)$$

In the case of the cube, equations (**257**) to (**259**) become

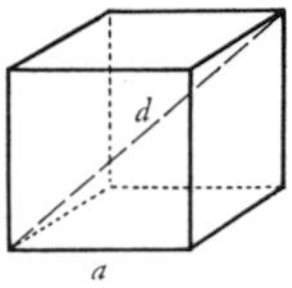

$$A = 6a^2 \quad (260)$$

$$d = a\sqrt{3} = 1.732\,051\,a \quad (261)$$

$$V = a^3 \quad (262)$$

2. Pyramid (any base)

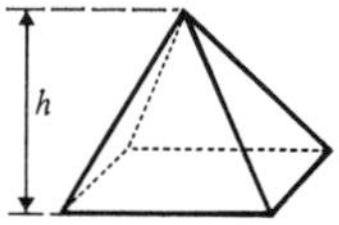

Volume

$$V = \frac{h}{3}A_B \quad (263)$$

(A_B = area of base)

3. Right circular cylinder

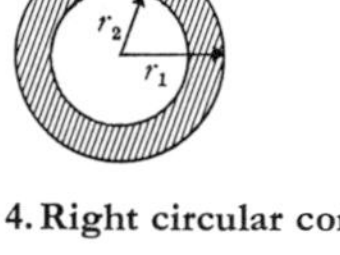

Area of convex surface

$$A_C = 2\pi rh = 6.283\,185\,3\,rh \quad (264)$$

Total surface area

$$\begin{aligned}A &= 2\pi r(r + h) \\ &= 6.283\,185\,3\,r(r + h)\end{aligned} \quad (265)$$

Volume

$$V = \pi r^2 h = 3.141\,592\,65\,r^2 h \quad (266)$$

Hollow cylinder

Internal volume

$$\begin{aligned}V_I &= \pi(r_1^2 - r_2^2)\,h\ [r_1 \geq r_2] \\ &= 3.141\,592\,65\,(r_1^2 - r_2^2)\,h\end{aligned} \quad (267)$$

4. Right circular cone

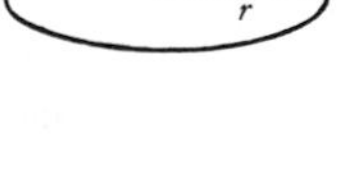

Area of convex surface

$$A_C = \pi r l = 3.141\,592\,65\,r\,l \quad (268)$$

$\left(l = \text{slant height} = \sqrt{r^2 + h^2}\right)$

Total surface area

$$\begin{aligned}A &= \pi r(r + l) \\ &= 3.141\,592\,65\,r(r + l)\end{aligned} \quad (269)$$

Volume

$$V = \frac{1}{3}\pi r^2 h = 1.047\,197\,55\,r^2 h \quad (270)$$

Truncated cone (right circular, plane surfaces parallel)

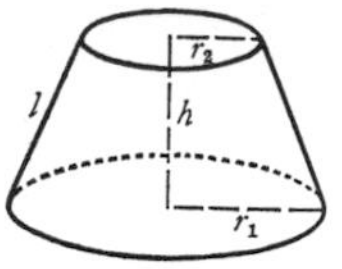

Area of convex surface

$$A_C = \pi l (r_1 + r_2) = 3.141\,592\,65\, l (r_1 + r_2) \quad (271)$$

Total surface area

$$A = \pi \left[r_1 (r_1 + l) + r_2 (r_2 + l) \right] \quad (272)$$

Volume

$$V = \frac{\pi h}{3} (r_1^2 + r_1 r_2 + r_2^2) = 1.047\,197\,55\, h (r_1^2 + r_1 r_2 + r_2^2) \quad (273)$$

5. Sphere

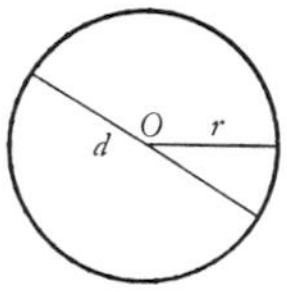

Surface area

$$A = 4 \pi r^2 = \pi d^2 = 12.566\,370\,6\, r^2 = 3.141\,592\,65\, d^2 \quad (274)$$

Volume

$$V = \frac{4 \pi r^3}{3} = \frac{\pi d^3}{6} = 4.188\,790\,20\, r^3 = 0.523\,598\,78\, d^3 \quad (275)$$

Segment of a sphere (cut by a single plane)

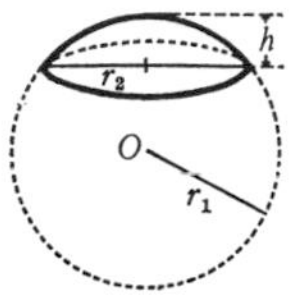

Area of convex surface

$$A_C = \pi (r_2^2 + h^2) = 2 \pi r_1 h \quad (276)$$

Total surface area

$$A - \pi (2 r_2^2 + h^2) \quad (277)$$

Volume

$$V = \frac{\pi h}{6} (3 r_2^2 + h^2) = \frac{\pi h^2}{3} (3 r_1 - h) \quad (278)$$

($\pi = 3.141\,592\,65$; $\pi/6 = 0.523\,598\,78$; $\pi/3 = 1.047\,197\,55$)

Segment of a sphere (between two parallel planes)

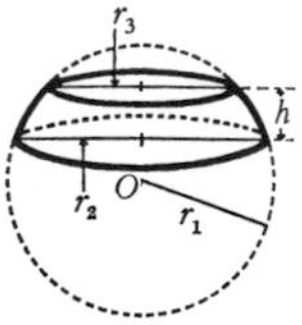

Area of convex surface

$$A_C = 2 \pi r_1 h = 6.283\,185\,3\, r_1 h \quad (279)$$

Total surface area

$$A = \pi (r_2^2 + 2 r_1 h + r_3^2) \quad (280)$$

Volume

$$V = \frac{\pi h}{6} (3 r_2^2 + 3 r_3^2 + h^2) = 0.523\,598\,78\, h (3 r_2^2 + 3 r_3^2 + h^2) \quad (281)$$

Wedge segment of a sphere

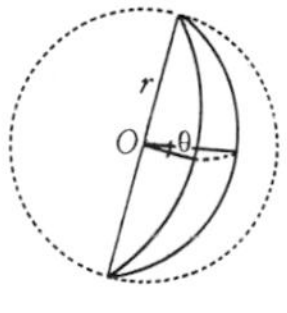

Volume

$$V = \frac{\pi r^3 \theta}{270} = 0.011\,635\,528\, r^3 \theta \quad (282)$$

[for θ (= angle between the two planes passing through the centre of the sphere) see **(246)** and **(247)**]

6. Bodies of the same shape

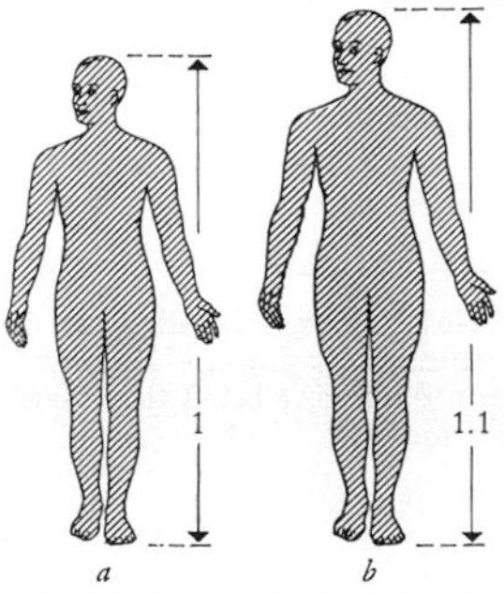

Bodies of the same shape, i.e., those in which *all corresponding linear measurements bear the same ratio* $a:b$*, have surface areas in the ratio $a^2:b^2$ and weights and volumes in the ratio $a^3:b^3$. **(283)**

All linear dimensions of body b are 10% greater than those of body a; b has 21% more surface area and 33% more weight.

* Note that this is usually not true of human bodies of different *heights*.

XVI. Formulae of analytical geometry

1. Transformation of rectangular coordinates

The new coordinates are indicated by C, the transformed variables by X, Y, the old coordinates and variables by c, x, y. For the sake of simplicity the transformation is illustrated in the first quadrant (see section XI, page 138) but the equations are valid for all quadrants.

(*a*) Translation of coordinate axes

The origin is translated from O to O', i.e., a distance a in the direction x and a distance b in the direction y.

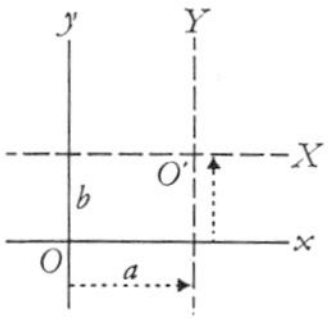

Transformation $c \to C$

$$X = x - a \qquad Y = y - b \quad (284)$$

Transformation $C \to c$

$$x = a + X \qquad y = b + Y \quad (285)$$

(*b*) Alteration of linear scale

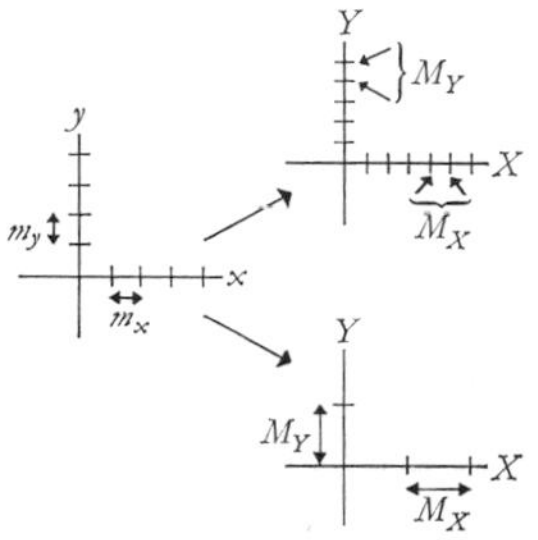

Transformation $c \to C$

$$X = \frac{M_X}{m_x} x \qquad Y = \frac{M_Y}{m_y} y \quad (286)$$

Transformation $C \to c$

$$x = \frac{m_x}{M_X} X \qquad y = \frac{m_y}{M_Y} Y \quad (287)$$

(*c*) Translation of axes and alteration of linear scale

Transformation $c \to C$

$$X = \frac{M_X}{m_x} (x - a) \qquad Y = \frac{M_Y}{m_y} (y - b) \quad (288)$$

Transformation $C \to c$

$$x = a + \frac{m_x}{M_X} X \qquad y = b + \frac{m_y}{M_Y} Y \quad (289)$$

(*d*) Rotation of coordinate axes

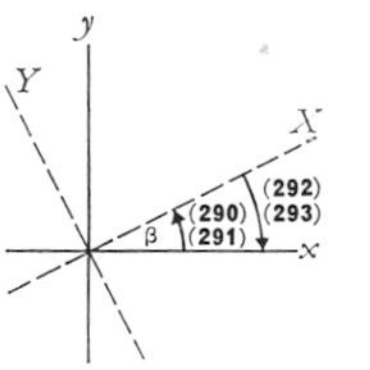

Transformation $c \to C$

$$X = x \cos \beta + y \sin \beta \qquad Y = y \cos \beta - x \sin \beta \quad (290)$$

or

$$X = \frac{1}{\sqrt{1 + \tan^2 \beta}} (x + y \tan \beta) \qquad Y = \frac{1}{\sqrt{1 + \tan^2 \beta}} (y - x \tan \beta) \quad (291)$$

Transformation $C \to c$

$$x = X \cos \beta - Y \sin \beta \qquad y = X \sin \beta + Y \cos \beta \quad (292)$$

or

$$x = \frac{1}{\sqrt{1 + \tan^2 \beta}} (X - Y \tan \beta) \qquad y = \frac{1}{\sqrt{1 + \tan^2 \beta}} (Y + X \tan \beta) \quad (293)$$

(*e*) Rotation and translation of the coordinate axes

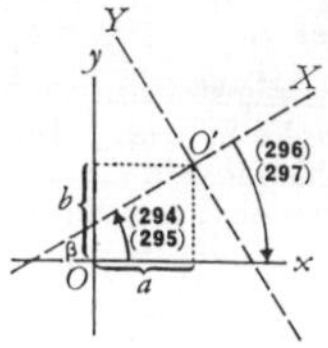

Transformation $c \rightarrow C$

$$\left.\begin{aligned} X &= (x-a)\cos\beta + (y-b)\sin\beta \\ Y &= (y-b)\cos\beta - (x-a)\sin\beta \end{aligned}\right\} \quad \textbf{(294)}$$

or

$$\left.\begin{aligned} X &= \frac{x-a+(y-b)\tan\beta}{\sqrt{1+\tan^2\beta}} \\ Y &= \frac{y-b-(x-a)\tan\beta}{\sqrt{1+\tan^2\beta}} \end{aligned}\right\} \quad \textbf{(295)}$$

Transformation $C \rightarrow c$

$$\left.\begin{aligned} x &= a + X\cos\beta - Y\sin\beta \\ y &= b + Y\cos\beta + X\sin\beta \end{aligned}\right\} \quad \textbf{(296)}$$

or

$$\left.\begin{aligned} x &= a + \frac{X - Y\tan\beta}{\sqrt{1+\tan^2\beta}} \\ y &= b + \frac{Y + X\tan\beta}{\sqrt{1+\tan^2\beta}} \end{aligned}\right\} \quad \textbf{(297)}$$

2. Straight line

General equation

$$Ax + By + C = 0 \quad \textbf{(298)}$$

Equation of slope

$$y = a + bx \quad \text{or} \quad x = \frac{y-a}{b} \quad \textbf{(299)}$$

a = intercept with y axis, b = tangent of the angle of slope β. Note that $b = \tan\beta$ is valid only when the same unit is used for both coordinate axes.

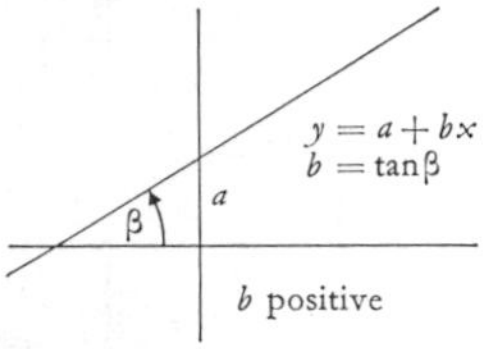

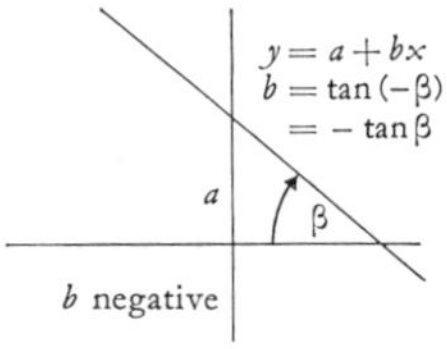

Special cases

$x = a$ is the equation of a line parallel to the y axis **(300)**

$y = c$ is the equation of a line parallel to the x axis **(301)**

A straight line is at right angles to another straight line with slope b when its slope is $-1/b$. **(302)**

Straight line through two points with coordinates x_1, y_1; x_2, y_2

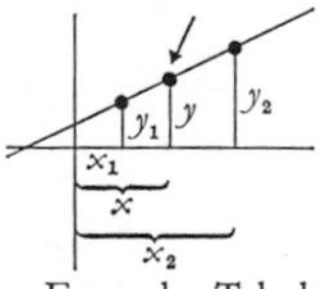

$$y = y_1 + \frac{y_2 - y_1}{x_2 - x_1}(x - x_1) \quad \textbf{(303)}$$

This formula is used for linear interpolation.

Example: Tabulated values

	x	y
	110	83.83
	120	95.66

Required: the y value for $x = 116$

Solution: $y = 83.83 + \dfrac{95.66 - 83.83}{120 - 110}(116 - 110) = 90.93$

Straight line with slope b through a point x_1, y_1

$$y = y_1 + b(x - x_1) \quad \textbf{(304)}$$

Straight line through the origin and a point x_1, y_1

$$y = \frac{y_1}{x_1}x \quad \textbf{(305)}$$

Length p of the straight line parallel to the y axis between a point x_1, y_1 and the straight line $y = a + bx$

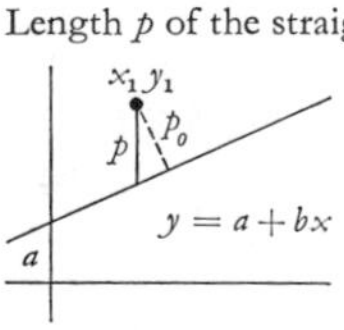

$$p = y_1 - a - bx_1 \quad \textbf{(306)}$$

Shortest (orthogonal) distance p_0 between a point and the straight line $y = a + bx$

$$p_0 = \frac{y_1 - a - bx_1}{\sqrt{1 + b^2}} \quad \textbf{(307)}$$

Distance p_x parallel to the x axis at a height y_p between two straight lines $y = a_1 + b_1x$ and $y = a_2 + b_2x$

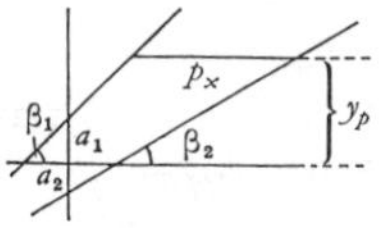

$$p_x = \left| \frac{y_p - a_1}{b_1} - \frac{y_p - a_2}{b_2} \right| \quad \textbf{(308)}$$

Distance p_x parallel to the x axis between two parallel lines $y = a_1 + bx$ and $y = a_2 + bx$ [special case of **(308)** with $b_1 = b_2$]

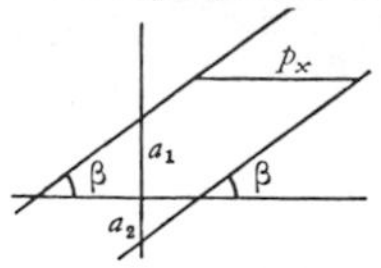

$$p_x = \left| \frac{a_1 - a_2}{b} \right| \quad \textbf{(309)}$$

Coordinates of the intersection of two straight lines $y = a_1 + b_1x$ and $y = a_2 + b_2x$

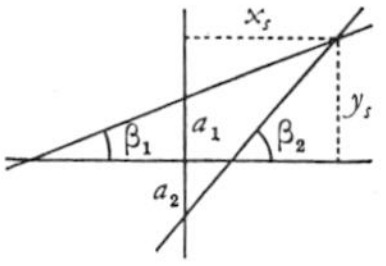

$$\left.\begin{aligned} x_s &= \frac{a_2 - a_1}{b_1 - b_2} \\ y_s &= \frac{b_1a_2 - b_2a_1}{b_1 - b_2} \end{aligned}\right\} \quad \textbf{(310)}$$

Angle θ between two straight lines with slopes b_1 and b_2

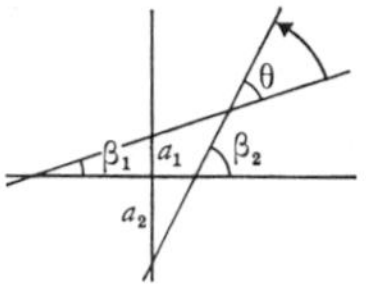

$$\tan\theta = \frac{b_1 - b_2}{b_1b_2 + 1} \quad \textbf{(311)}$$

The angle θ is the positive angle through which the first straight line must be rotated in order that it shall coincide with the second straight line. Note that equation **(311)** is valid only when the same unit is used for both coordinate axes.

3. Ellipse

Standard equation in rectangular coordinates (the principal axes):

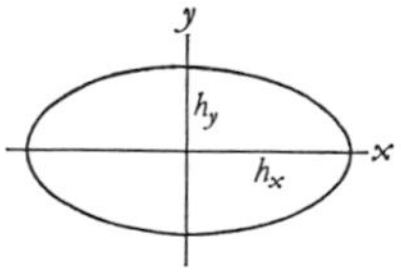

$$\frac{x^2}{a^2} + \frac{y^2}{b^2} = c^2 \quad \textbf{(312)}$$

a and b determine the relation between the two semi-axes and thus the shape of the ellipse.

If h_x is the semi-major, h_y the semi-minor axis, equation **(312)** becomes

$$\frac{x^2}{h_x^2} + \frac{y^2}{h_y^2} = 1 \quad \left\{ \begin{aligned} h_x^2 &= c^2a^2 \\ h_y^2 &= c^2b^2 \end{aligned} \right. \quad \textbf{(313)}$$

The focal width F_1F_2 is given by

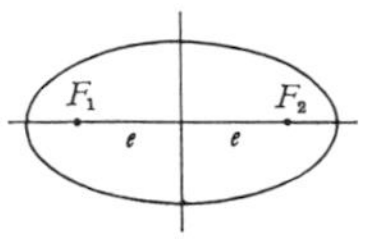

$$2e = 2\sqrt{h_x^2 - h_y^2} \quad \textbf{(314)}$$

e is known as the linear eccentricity.

If s is the sum of the distances from a point P on the curve to the foci F_1 and F_2, then

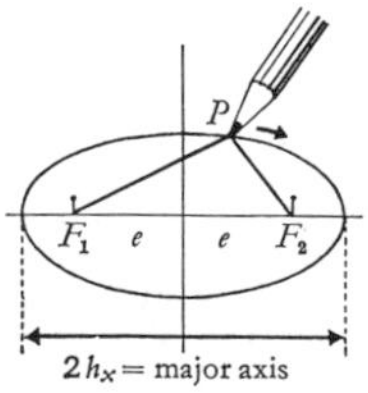

$$s = 2h_x = \text{major axis} \quad \textbf{(315)}$$

Any desired ellipse may therefore be drawn by means of a thread of length $2h_x$ attached to the foci, e being determined from equation **(314)**.

For area and circumference of the ellipse see equations (**255**) and (**256**) on page 142.

Contents (pages 146–196)

Foreword 146

1. Introductory definitions 146

2. Population and sample 146

3. Variable and event 147

4. Frequency, probability, compound events 147

5. Discrete probability distribution 148

6. Continuous probability distribution 151

7. Estimates 153
- A. Expectation and bias 153
- B. Consistency 153
- C. Efficiency 153
- D. Sufficient estimates 154

8. Confidence limits and tolerance limits 154
- A. Confidence limits for continuous and discrete distributions 154
- B. Tolerance limits for continuous distributions 155
- C. Distribution-free confidence and tolerance limits 155

9. Statistical significance tests 156
- A. Introduction 156
- B. Significance limits 156
- C. Significance tests 157

10. Parameters 159
- A. Mean and variance of the population 159
- B. Transformations 159
- C. Estimates of μ and σ based on ungrouped samples 159
- D. Estimates of μ and σ based on grouped samples 160
- E. Quantiles of continuous distributions 160
- F. Distribution-free confidence limits for the quantiles of continuous distributions 161
- G. Relations between mode, median and mean 161
- H. The sign test 161

11. The normal distribution 161
- A. Definition and characteristics 161
- B. The standardized normal distribution 162
- C. Tables of the standardized normal distribution 162
- D. Conversion of a normal distribution into the standardized form and vice versa 162
- E. The probit transformation 163
- F. Fitting of normal curves to samples 163
- G. Standard deviations of the quantiles of samples from normally distributed populations 165
- H. The logarithmic-normal (lognormal) distribution 165
- I. The addition theorem for the normal distribution 166
- J. The central limit theorem 166

12. Distributions closely allied to the normal distribution 166
- A. The Student distribution 166
- B. The χ^2 distribution 166
- C. The F-distribution (variance-ratio distribution) 168

13. The normally distributed population: Confidence and tolerance intervals 169
- A. Confidence intervals for the mean μ 169
- B. Tolerance intervals 169
- C. Confidence intervals for the standard deviation σ 169

14. The normally distributed population: Extreme range and extreme deviations 170
- A. The extreme range 170
- B. Testing extreme ranges and extreme deviations 170

15. The normally distributed population: Comparison of a sample with the hypothetical population 171
- A. Comparison of the sample and population standard deviations s and σ (or of the variances s^2 and σ^2) 171
- B. Comparison of the sample and population means $\bar{x}$ and μ 171

16. The normally distributed population: Comparison of two samples 172
- A. Comparison of variances 172
- B. Comparison of means when $\sigma_1^2 = \sigma_2^2$ 172
- C. Comparison of means when $\sigma_1^2 \neq \sigma_2^2$ 173
- D. Testing pair differences 173
- E. Tests for two samples using the extreme range 173

17. The normally distributed population: Testing several samples 173
- A. Testing variances 173
- B. Testing means: simple analysis of variance 173

18. The normally distributed population: Regressions of the first kind 174
- A. Estimation of the parameters of the regression line Y 174
- B. Testing the linearity of the regression function 176
- C. Testing the regression coefficient against zero 177
- D. Testing the difference between estimate and hypothetical value 177
- E. Confidence and tolerance limits 177
- F. Estimation of x when y is given 177
- G. Comparison of two regression lines of the first kind 178

19. The bivariate normal distribution: Regressions of the second kind 179
- A. The correlation coefficient 179
- B. SPEARMAN's coefficient of rank correlation 181
- C. Significance tests 181
- D. Confidence and tolerance limits 182

20. The binomial distribution 183
- A. General 183
- B. Parameters 184
- C. Cumulative probabilities 184
- D. The binomial and the normal distribution 185
- E. The binomial and the POISSON distribution 186
- F. Confidence limits and significance limits 186
- G. Miscellaneous 187

21. The Poisson distribution 187
- A. General 187
- B. The addition theorem for the POISSON distribution 188
- C. Parameters and their estimates 188
- D. Transformations 188
- E. Confidence limits and significance limits 189

22. The hypergeometric distribution 189
- A. General 189
- B. Parameters 191
- C. The hypergeometric distribution and other distributions 191
- D. Significance limits (fourfold table test) 191

23. Testing frequencies 191
- A. Samples from binomially distributed populations 191
- B. Samples from multinomially distributed populations 192
- C. Samples from POISSON distributions 192

24. Rank tests 192
- A. Ranking 192
- B. The WILCOXON test for two samples 192
- C. The WILCOXON test for pair differences 192
- D. HALDANE's test for chance order in series 193
- E. The maximum test for pair differences 193

25. Testing for non-randomness 193
- A. The mean-square successive difference 193
- B. Serial correlation 193
- C. Runs up and down 194
- D. Runs above and/or below the median 194
- E. Runs in samples from binomially distributed populations in which the probabilities p and q are unknown 194
- F. The WALD-WOLFOWITZ test 195
- G. Runs in samples from binomially distributed populations in which the probabilities p and q are known. 195
- H. Runs in samples from multinomially distributed populations 195

26. Sequential analysis 196

References 196

(For references see page 196; for index see pages 197 and 198)

In the limited space here available it is impossible to give more than a brief explanation of the statistical tables on pages 10–131. The following description is therefore limited to those fundamentals the non-mathematician requires to enable him to solve simple statistical problems.

The calculation of probabilities by statistical methods is an essential step in the proper interpretation of experimental results that comply with certain basic laws but are at the same time subject to modification by unknown factors, in other words, to so-called 'chance' variation. This holds not only for the empirical sciences, the exact as well as the biological, but in a wider sense also for the abstract sciences:

On peut même dire à parler en rigueur, que presque toutes nos connaissances ne sont que probables; et dans le petit nombre des choses que nous pouvons savoir avec certitude, dans les sciences mathématiques elles-mêmes, les principaux moyens de parvenir à la vérité, l'induction et l'analogie, se fondent sur les probabilités... (LAPLACE, 1820)[1].

One reason for the physician's frequent mistrust of statistical methods is epitomized in the well-known allegation that 'you can prove anything with statistics'. Some prejudice against mathematics is also understandable in a profession in which intuitive reasoning is generally preferred. These are sentiments without any logical basis. Statistics is one of the most vigorous branches of mathematics, and its techniques for the disciplined assessment of observational data can be readily mastered. Furthermore, it should not be forgotten that every medical diagnosis represents the result of an intentional or unintentional calculation of probabilities.

This critical attitude towards statistics has its origin in their improper use as well as in their false interpretation. The statistical method is no more than another scientific method and cannot by its nature provide proof or disproof. On the other hand it constitutes the only method of subjecting values liable to chance variation (stochastic variables) to fixed and reproducible criteria based on logical mathematical considerations. The converse of the saying quoted is therefore much nearer the truth, namely that *no scientific investigation is capable of proving anything without the aid of statistics*. Human judgement is influenced to a very large extent by the subconscious wish and by the deep-rooted tendency – even in the worst of pessimists – to overrate one's own chances. The most careful investigator can be led astray by these psychological factors if he fails to arm himself against them with an adequate measure of self-control:

Le sentiment par lequel l'homme s'est placé longtemps au centre de l'univers en se considérant comme l'objet spécial des soins de la nature, porte chaque individu à se faire le centre d'une sphère plus ou moins étendue, et à croire que le hasard a pour lui des préférences. Soutenus par cette opinion, les joueurs exposent souvent des sommes considérables à des jeux dont ils savent que les chances leur sont contraires. Dans la conduite de la vie, une semblable opinion peut quelquefois avoir des avantages; mais le plus souvent elle conduit à des entreprises funestes. Ici, comme en tout, les illusions sont dangereuses et la vérité seule est généralement utile.

Un des grands avantages du Calcul des Probabilités est d'apprendre à se défier des premiers aperçus. Comme on reconnaît qu'ils trompent souvent lorsqu'on peut les soumettre au calcul, on doit en conclure que sur d'autres objets il ne faut s'y livrer qu'avec une circonspection extrême (LAPLACE, 1820)[1].

'The wish' as 'father to the thought' may be an indispensable stimulus to research, but it has also been responsible – in the guise of 'our experience' or 'our opinion' backed by a few percentages – for much misunderstanding. One need only reflect on the wealth of new treatments and new drugs which after an enthusiastic reception have been allowed to fall quietly into oblivion.

Many a research worker in the past could have spared himself much wasted time and effort had he submitted his observations and hypotheses to statistical test before publication. Recognition of this fact has clearly become general during the last decades, and close links have now been established between clinical medicine and statistics.

The growing use of statistical methods, however, is not without its own dangers. The general tendency is to overrate any new research tool, particularly when it is unfamiliar and complicated in operation. Too much uncritical dependence is placed on the results obtained; the limitations of the method may not be clearly recognized and the experimental data may be inadequately checked. Statistical methods obviously allow of no such dispensation. On the other hand, the beginner will find that with increasing experience statistical ways of thinking will not only render him more circumspect but give him a deeper insight.

1. Introductory definitions*

An experiment subject to chance factors may be compared to an operation such as the drawing of numbers in a lottery. Imagine a box containing balls bearing the numbers 0, 1, 2, . . ., 9. These are thoroughly mixed before the draw is commenced. The player drawing the balls is supposed to have no influence on the selection.

Using this analogy, we designate

– the mixing of the balls as the *randomization* of the experimental material; **(316)**

– the numbers 0, 1, 2, . . ., 9 distinguishing the balls as *variables* or *attributes*; **(317)**

– the aggregate number of balls in the box as the *parent population*; **(318)**

– a draw as a *trial*; **(319)**

– N trials as *random sampling*; **(320)**

– the result of the trial represented by the drawing of the number 5 as the *random event* 5; **(321)**

– the result of N trials as a *random sample* of size N, or briefly as a sample N; **(322)**

– the succession of events as a *random sequence* (in the numbered balls analogy it is the random series of numbers, or *random numbers*); **(323)**

– the relative frequency of the variate values in the population as the *probabilities* with which these values will be drawn; **(324)**

– the relative frequency of the variate values in the sample as *estimate* of their probability; **(325)**

– the distribution of the probabilities of the different variate values as probability distribution, or briefly as *distribution*. **(326)**

Some of these definitions will be discussed in more detail later in this chapter.

2. Population and sample

A population is finite or infinite when the trials (draws) can be repeated a finite or infinite number of times. **(327)**

A finite population, such as a finite number of balls in a box, can be converted into an effectively infinite one by putting the balls back into the box after each draw. Such an operation is known as *sampling with replacement*. **(328)**

From an infinite population an infinite number of samples can be taken, for example all of the same size N. The totality of such samples of size N is known as the *sampling population* N and their probability distribution as the *sampling distribution* N. **(329)**

An infinite sampling population can also be taken from a finite population in a manner similar to that in (**328**), i.e., by returning the whole of the first sample to the box, drawing a second sample of the same size, returning this sample also to the box, and so on. *All sampling populations can therefore be regarded as infinite*. This is one of the fundamental concepts of mathematical statistics. **(330)**

Quantities such as mean value and variance which relate to the population are known as *parameters*, their counterparts in the sample as *statistics*. **(331)**

Symbols relating to the population are here printed in bold type whenever it is necessary to distinguish them from symbols relating to samples. Exceptions are the symbols for mean value and variance: these are respectively μ and σ^2 for the population and $\bar{x}$ and s^2 for the sample. **(332)**

* The mathematician will appreciate that this presentation is more readily understandable by non-mathematicians than a strictly mathematical one.

3. Variable and event

Variables are accumulated (possible) events in the box, events variables which have been drawn from the box. Where no possibility of confusion exists, the word 'event' is therefore here also used for 'variable', for example in the expression 'population of red and black events'. **(333)**

If A is an event, then the non-occurrence of A is its *complementary event*, designated here as non-A. Examples are success or failure, alive or dead, 6 or non-6 in die throwing, etc. **(334)**

The complementary event non-A is often an event B. For example, a girl can be born instead of a boy. Such events are known as *mutually exclusive events*, denoted by A or B, or by A, B. A and non-A in **(334)** are therefore by definition mutually exclusive events. **(335)**

Simultaneously occurring events can be treated as *successive* events. Whether the events $A, B, C, \ldots$ occur simultaneously or successively, they are denoted by A and B and C and ..., or by $ABC \ldots$ **(336)**

Simultaneous or successive events can together form *an* event. For example, if two sixes are obtained by throwing two dice simultaneously or a single die twice, then the sum 12 is a *combined event*. **(337)**

If the occurrence (or non-occurrence) of an event A is restricted by the condition that an event B has occurred [or occurs simultaneously, cf. **(336)**], then event A is known as a *conditioned event*, denoted by $A \mid B$ and read as event A under the condition B. B can represent several conditions. **(338)**

Qualitative variables can be denoted by numbers, for example 1 for success, 0 for failure. **(339)**

If the events are already numbers they are here denoted by x provided that other symbols are not in general use, as in the case of some sampling distributions. **(340)**

If x (within a finite interval) takes only a finite number of values it is known as a *discontinuous random variable* or *variate*. In this case x changes by *discrete* amounts. Examples are 0, 1, 2, 3, ... successes, 25, 26, 27, ... respirations, etc. **(341)**

If the numbers 1, 2, 3, ... denote the smallest, second smallest, third smallest value, etc., the series is known as an ordered (by magnitude) or *ranked* series. In such a series the *exact* magnitudes determining the ranks of the smallest, second smallest, etc., may be unknown. *Example 1:* a group of persons can be arranged in order of height without their exact heights being known. **(342)**

If x can take all possible values in some interval it is known as a *continuous random variable* or *variate*. In this case x changes *continuously*. Examples of continuous variates are length, area, volume, weight, temperature, time and concentration, i.e., variables that can be *measured*. **(343)**

In practice, continuous variates do not exist since all measured values are rounded values. For example, when the smallest interval a balance can measure is a milligramme, any weight measured will be rounded off to the nearest milligramme. In this case x changes by discrete intervals of one milligramme. Such a variable is often called a *'granulated'* (or *'atomic'*) *variable*. 'Granulated' variables are actually continuous variables that have been converted into discrete variables by rounding off. **(344)**

In the case of discrete variables the same value may occur two or more times in a sample from two or more tests. This is an almost impossible event in the case of continuous variables [cf. **(352)**], but occurs all the more often the more 'coarsely granulated' they are. Cf. **(344)**. **(345)**

If two or more identical values occur in a sample of a 'granulated' variable they are known as *ties* or tied values. Cf. **(344)** and **(345)**. **(346)**

4. Frequency, probability, compound events

If in a group of N individuals there are x females and $N-x$ males, then x and $N-x$ are the *absolute* and x/N and $(N-x)/N$ the *relative frequencies* of females and males in the group. Here the expression frequency will be used to mean the relative frequency. **(347)**

The relative frequency multiplied by 100 is known as the *percentage frequency*. *Example 2:* In 81 operations there are 3 fatalities. The percentage frequency is then $(3/81) \times 100 = 3.7\%$. **(348)**

The percentage frequencies for values of N between 2 and 100 and for any values of $x \leq N$ are given in the column $100\,p_x$ (column 2) of the tables on pages 85–98. For the above example see page 93, $N = 81$, $x = 3$.

The following symbols are used here for probability:

'Probability' in general .... Prob

Probabilities of mutually exclusive events ..... $\dot{\boldsymbol{P}}$

Probabilities of two complementary events.... $\boldsymbol{p}$ and $\boldsymbol{q}$ **(349)**

In a later section the symbols α and $\boldsymbol{P}$ will also be used [cf. **(378)** and **(379)**].

In **(324)** *probability* was defined as the *relative frequency of a variable* [or of an event, cf. **(333)**] *in the population*. Propositions **(350)**–**(355)** follow directly from this definition:

Every probability is a number between zero and one: **(350)**

$0 \leq \text{Prob} \leq 1$

An impossible event has a probability of zero, a certain event a probability of one. **(351)**

The converse of **(351)** *is not valid:*

An event with a probability of zero is an *almost* impossible event, an event with a probability of one an *almost* certain event. *Example 3:* A box contains all the positive integers 1, 2, 3, ..., ∞. The probability of drawing, say, the number 1969 is $1/\infty = 0$. Nevertheless the possibility exists of drawing this number since it is present in the population. **(352)**

The sum of the probabilities of *all* mutually exclusive events $E_0, E_1, \ldots, E_N$ in a single population is equal to one:

$$\text{Prob}\,(E_0 \text{ or } E_1 \text{ or} \ldots E_N) = \dot{\boldsymbol{P}}_0 + \dot{\boldsymbol{P}}_1 + \ldots + \dot{\boldsymbol{P}}_N = 1$$ **(353)**

where the total of all mutually exclusive events is $N+1$, and [cf. **(335)**]

$$\text{Prob}\,(E \text{ or non-}E) = \boldsymbol{p} + \boldsymbol{q} = 1$$

It follows from **(353)** that a population with many mutually exclusive events can be converted in various ways into one with two complementary events. **(354)**

For example:

$$\text{Prob}\left[\underbrace{(E_0 \text{ or } E_1)}_{=E} \text{ or } \underbrace{(E_2 \text{ or} \ldots E_N)}_{=\text{non-}E}\right] = \underbrace{(\dot{\boldsymbol{P}}_0 + \dot{\boldsymbol{P}}_1)}_{=\boldsymbol{p}} + \underbrace{(\dot{\boldsymbol{P}}_2 + \cdots + \dot{\boldsymbol{P}}_N)}_{=\boldsymbol{q}}$$

where the total number of mutually exclusive events is $N+1$.

Example 4 [of **(354)**]. With a true die the probability of throwing any one number is 1/6. The probability of throwing a 6 is 1/6, of throwing a non-6 (1 or 2 or ... 5) 5/6. The probability of throwing an even number (2 or 4 or 6) is $1/6 + 1/6 + 1/6 = 1/2$, of throwing an odd number likewise 1/2.

From **(353)** it follows that:

Of the mutually exclusive events $A, B, \ldots$, the probability that either the event A or the event B will occur is equal to the sum of their probabilities, *provided that the events are from one and the same population.* **(355)**

$$\text{Prob}\,(A \text{ or } B \text{ or} \ldots) = \dot{\boldsymbol{P}}_A + \dot{\boldsymbol{P}}_B + \cdots$$

Example 5 [of **(355)**]. *Correct application.* Assuming that the probability of an 85-year-old person dying of pneumonia is 0.2 and of dying of cancer also 0.2, then the probability that he will die either of pneumonia or cancer is $0.2 + 0.2 = 0.4$.

Example 6 [of **(355)**]. *Incorrect application.* Assuming that the mortality of 85-year-olds is 0.5 and that of 86-year-olds 0.6, then the statement that there is a 1.1 probability of an 85-year-old dying either at 85 or at 86 is false. Here the error is already indicated by the probability figure of 1.1, which according to (**350**) is an impossibility, but it might well have been overlooked had the figure been 0.4, as in example 5. The error arises from the fact that mutually exclusive events from *different* populations, that of the 85-year-olds and that of the 86-year-olds, have been added together.

The probability of two simultaneous or successive events A and B is equal to the probability of the event A multiplied by the probability of the event B under the condition A, or to the probability of the event B multiplied by the probability of the event A under the condition B. On conditioned events see (**338**). (**356**)

$$\text{Prob}(A \text{ and } B) = \text{Prob}(A) \times \text{Prob}(B \mid A) = \text{Prob}(B) \times \text{Prob}(A \mid B)$$

Example 7 [of (**356**)]. A box contains N balls, x red and $N - x$ white. A sample consisting of two balls is drawn *without replacement.* What is the probability of drawing (*a*) two red balls, (*b*) a red and then a white ball, (*c*) a red and a white ball in any order?

(*a*) The probability of a red ball at the first draw is x/N. The conditioned probability of a red ball at the second draw (when there is one red ball less in the box) is $(x - 1)/(N - 1)$. The probability of drawing two red balls is therefore

$$\text{Prob (red, red)} = \frac{x}{N} \times \frac{x-1}{N-1}$$

(*b*) $$\text{Prob (red, white)} = \frac{x}{N} \times \frac{N-x}{N-1} = \frac{N-x}{N} \times \frac{x}{N-1} = \text{Prob (white, red)}$$

(*c*) Prob (red and white) or Prob (white and red)
$= \text{Prob (red, white)} + \text{Prob (white, red)}$
$= 2x(N - x)/N(N - 1)$

Example 8 [of (**356**)]. From the same box as in example 7 a sample of the same size is taken, but *with replacement.* In this case the probabilities are as follows:

(*a*) The probability of a red ball at the first draw remains x/N. Since this ball is replaced in the box, the probability of a red ball at the second draw is the same:

$$\text{Prob (red, red)} = \frac{x}{N} \times \frac{x}{N}$$

(*b*) $$\text{Prob (red, white)} = \frac{x}{N} \times \frac{N-x}{N} = \frac{N-x}{N} \times \frac{x}{N} = \text{Prob (white, red)}$$

(*c*) Prob (red and white) or Prob (white and red)
$= \text{Prob (red, white)} + \text{Prob (white, red)}$
$= 2x(N - x)/N^2$

From example 7 it will be seen that the probabilities change with each draw, i.e., each successive draw is *dependent* on the previous one. The corresponding statistical expressions are *dependent trials* and *dependent events.* In example 8 the second draw is unaffected by the previous one, in which case the trials and events are *independent.*

In other words, in the collection of samples from *finite* populations (no replacement), the trials and events are *dependent* on one another; in the collection of samples from *infinite* populations (replacement), they are *independent* of one another. (**357**)

Two simultaneous or successive events are known as stochastically *dependent* events when in (**356**) the conditioned and the absolute probability of an event are *not the same*, i.e., when (**358**)

$$\text{Prob}(A \mid B) \neq \text{Prob}(A), \text{ or } \text{Prob}(B \mid A) \neq \text{Prob}(B).$$

Two simultaneous or successive events are known as stochastically *independent* events when in (**356**) the conditioned and the absolute probability of an event are *the same*, i.e., when (**359**)

$$\text{Prob}(A \mid B) = \text{Prob}(A), \text{ or } \text{Prob}(B \mid A) = \text{Prob}(B).$$

From (**356**) and (**359**) it follows that the two events A and B are stochastically independent of one another when the probability of their simultaneous or successive occurrence is equal to the product of their probabilities: (**360**)

If $\text{Prob}(A \text{ and } B) = \text{Prob}(A) \times \text{Prob}(B)$
then A *and* B *are stochastically independent of one another.*

In (**358**)–(**360**) the expressions 'dependent' and 'independent' are coupled with the qualification 'stochastic'. This is a precautionary measure of the statistician. *In* (**358**)–(**360**) *a factual conclusion is reached on the basis of a mathematical result.* If such conclusions lie wholly within the domain of the probability calculation the expressions 'dependent' and 'independent' are completely valid, as in examples 7 and 8 under (**356**). However, if they are extended beyond the mathematical domain into those of physics, chemistry, physiology, etc., then the qualification 'stochastic' is necessary since the conceptions 'dependent' and 'independent' do not necessarily imply a *causal* connection. Stochastically independent events can very well be dependent on one another in reality. *The conclusion 'independent' implies only actual independence of the events.* It can be accepted if it is not incompatible with the physical circumstances. *On the other hand it can be regarded as proof* if independence were *presumable* from the physical circumstances and the mathematical treatment led to the *same* result. For this reason the converse of (**360**) should also be noted: (**361**)

If A and B are events independent of one another, then the probability of their simultaneous or successive occurrence is equal to the product of their probabilities: (**362**)

$\text{Prob}(A \text{ and } B) = \text{Prob}(A) \times \text{Prob}(B)$
(*when* A and B are independent of one another).

Example 9 [of (**362**)]. A box contains the events '+' and '−' in equal numbers, so that the probabilities are 1/2. Samples are collected with replacement, so that in accordance with (**357**) the events are independent of one another. What is the probability of drawing a '+' 5, 6 or 7 times in succession? The respective probabilities are $(1/2)^5$, $(1/2)^6$, $(1/2)^7$, or 0.031 25, 0.015 625, 0.007 812 5.

Example 10 [of (**362**)]. An infinite population contains the events A and B with the probabilities $\boldsymbol{p}$ and $\boldsymbol{q}$ respectively. What are the probabilities of the events AA, AB, BA, BB in two draws?

Event	Probability		
AA	$\boldsymbol{p} \times \boldsymbol{p}$	$= \boldsymbol{p}^2$	$= \boldsymbol{p}^2 + 2\boldsymbol{pq} + \boldsymbol{q}^2 = (\boldsymbol{p} + \boldsymbol{q})^2$
AB	$\boldsymbol{p} \times \boldsymbol{q}$	$= 2\boldsymbol{pq}$	$= 1^2 = 1$, as it should be according to (**353**)
BA	$\boldsymbol{q} \times \boldsymbol{p}$		
BB	$\boldsymbol{q} \times \boldsymbol{q}$	$= \boldsymbol{q}^2$	

In the expression $\boldsymbol{p}^2 + 2\boldsymbol{pq} + \boldsymbol{q}^2$ the individual terms represent the *probability distribution* for the events two As, one A, and no As (provided that no importance is attached to the order in the event one A). A *sampling distribution* [cf. (**329**)] is thus obtained for samples of size 2 from an infinite population, the complementary variables A or B, and the probabilities $\boldsymbol{p}$ and $\boldsymbol{q}$. From this example it will be seen intuitively how samples with 3, 4, ... draws can be dealt with: the sampling distributions can be written in accordance with (**113**) as developments of $(\boldsymbol{p} + \boldsymbol{q})^3$, $(\boldsymbol{p} + \boldsymbol{q})^4$, ... Cf. Binomial distribution, page 183.

5. Discrete probability distribution

Example 10 under (**362**) demonstrated a simple sampling distribution of practical importance that will be further discussed later in this chapter. At this point, discussion will be limited to a few conceptions related to such a distribution.

Given an infinite population with the events $x = 0, 1, 2, \ldots, 10$ and the probabilities $\dot{\boldsymbol{P}}_x$, then:

x	$\dot{\boldsymbol{P}}_x = f(x)$	$\sum_{k=0}^{k=x} \dot{\boldsymbol{P}}_k = F(x)$
0	0.001 0	0.001 0 $= \dot{\boldsymbol{P}}_0$
1	0.009 8	0.010 8 $= \dot{\boldsymbol{P}}_0 + \dot{\boldsymbol{P}}_1$
2	0.043 9	0.054 7 $= \dot{\boldsymbol{P}}_0 + \dot{\boldsymbol{P}}_1 + \dot{\boldsymbol{P}}_2$
3	0.117 2	0.171 9 $= \dot{\boldsymbol{P}}_0 + \dot{\boldsymbol{P}}_1 + \dot{\boldsymbol{P}}_2 + \dot{\boldsymbol{P}}_3$
4	0.205 1	0.377 0 etc.
5	0.246 0	0.623 0
6	0.205 1	0.828 1
7	0.117 2	0.945 3
8	0.043 9	0.989 2
9	0.009 8	0.999 0
10	0.001 0	1.000 0

The column $\dot{\boldsymbol{P}}_x = f(x)$ gives the probabilities for the events $x = 0$, $x = 1$, $x = 2$, etc.:

According to **(326)** this is the *probability distribution* for the events $x = 0$, $x = 1$, $x = 2$, etc., denoted by $f(x)$. **(363)**

In column $\sum_{k=0}^{k=x} \dot{\boldsymbol{P}}_k = F(x)$ the probabilities $\dot{\boldsymbol{P}}_x$ are continuously summed, thus giving the probabilities for $x = 0$, $x = 0$ or 1, $x = 0$ or 1 or 2, etc. This is the *cumulative probability distribution* of x, denoted by $F(x)$. **(364)**

These data may be represented graphically:

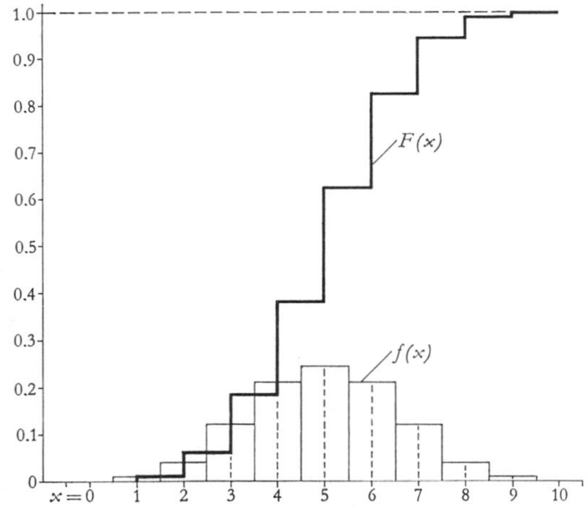

Fig. 1. Abscissae: x; ordinates: probabilities $f(x)$ and $F(x)$.

Since x is a discrete variable [cf. **(341)**] the distributions $f(x)$ and $F(x)$ give stepped curves. It follows that:

A discrete random variable has a discrete probability distribution. **(365)**

The probabilities are dependent on x, i.e., *for every value of x there is a definite probability: $f(x)$ and $F(x)$ are functions of x*, whence the use of the symbols f and F (the Greek letters φ and Φ are also frequently used). The pattern of probabilities can be expressed by a mathematical formula or in some other appropriate manner. **(366)**

In Figure 1 the probabilities $f(x)$ and $F(x)$ are shown as stepped lines in order to emphasize the similarity between discrete and continuous distributions (cf. Fig. 8). In fact, such a stepped curve could represent a *'granulated'* distribution [cf. **(344)**] in which the values of x have been rounded off to whole numbers. In this case all events between 4.5 and 5.5, for example, would be assigned to event 5. For this reason, another method is preferred here for representing discrete distributions which shows clearly that the events x are *discrete:*

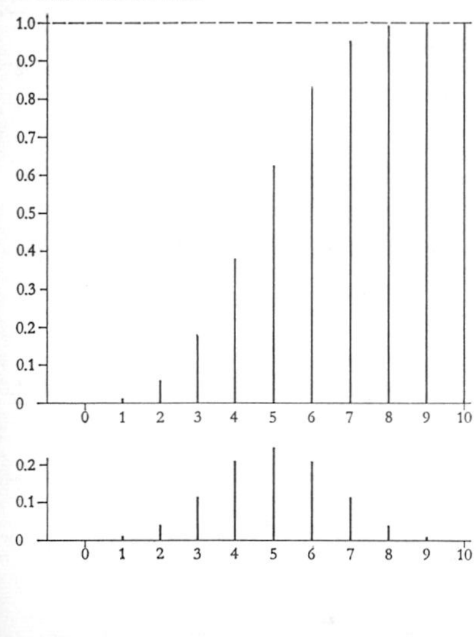

Fig. 2

In the cumulative distribution $F(x)$ representing the probabilities of the events $x = 0$, $x = 0$ or 1, $x = 0$ or 1 or 2, etc., the expression $x = 0, 1$ will in future be used in place of $x = 0$ or 1. Prob $(x = 0, 1)$ can also be written as Prob $(x \leqq 1)$. From **(364)** another notation is Prob $(x < 2, 3, \ldots, N)$, equivalent to Prob $(x < 2)$.

In general, the following expressions are valid for such discrete distributions: **(367)**

$$\text{Prob}\,(x < k+1) = \text{Prob}\,(x \leqq k), \quad \text{or}$$
$$\text{Prob}\,(x < k) = \text{Prob}\,(x \leqq k-1)$$
$$\text{and Prob}\,(x > k-1) = \text{Prob}\,(x \geqq k), \quad \text{or}$$
$$\text{Prob}\,(x > k) = \text{Prob}\,(x \geqq k+1)$$

With increasing values of k, the distribution $F(x)$ thus produces continuously the probabilities for $x \leqq k$ or $x < k+1$. **(368)**

Conversely, with decreasing values of k the cumulative distribution $\sum_{x=k}^{N} \dot{\boldsymbol{P}}_x$ from N in the direction of zero produces continuously the probabilities for $x \geqq k$ or $x > k-1$. **(369)**

For discrete distributions in general the following should be noted:

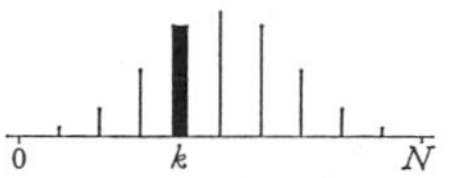

$$\text{Prob}\,(x = k) = \dot{\boldsymbol{P}}_k = f(k) \qquad \textbf{(370)}$$

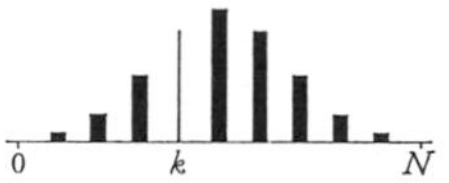

$$\text{Prob}\,(x \neq k) = 1 - \dot{\boldsymbol{P}}_k = 1 - f(k) \qquad \textbf{(371)}$$

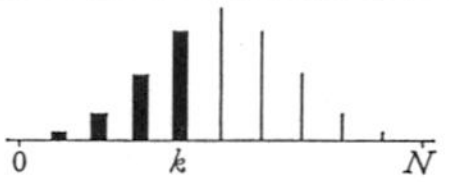

$$\text{Prob}\,(x \leqq k) = \text{Prob}\,(x < k+1) \qquad \textbf{(372)}$$

$= \sum_{0}^{k} \dot{\boldsymbol{P}}_x$, best formula if $k \leqq N/2$ (a)

$= 1 - \sum_{k+1}^{N} \dot{\boldsymbol{P}}_x$, best formula if $k \geqq N/2$ (b)

$= F(x)$, best formula if $F(x)$ is given (c)

$= 1 - \sum_{k+1}^{N} \dot{\boldsymbol{P}}_x$, best formula if $\sum_{x}^{N} \dot{\boldsymbol{P}}_x$ is given (d)

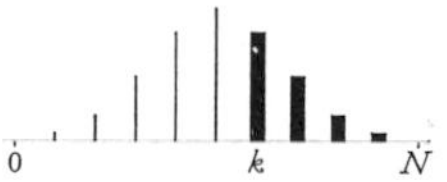

$$\text{Prob}\,(x \geqq k) = \text{Prob}\,(x > k-1) \qquad \textbf{(373)}$$

$= 1 - \sum_{0}^{k-1} \dot{\boldsymbol{P}}_x$, best formula if $k \leqq N/2$ (a)

$= \sum_{k}^{N} \dot{\boldsymbol{P}}_x$, best formula if $k \geqq N/2$ (b)

$= 1 - F(k-1)$, best formula if $F(x)$ is given (c)

$= \sum_{k}^{N} \dot{\boldsymbol{P}}_x$, best formula if $\sum_{x}^{N} \dot{\boldsymbol{P}}_x$ is given (d)

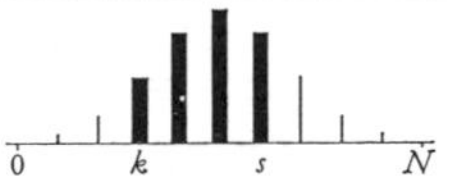

$$\text{Prob}\,(k \leqq x \leqq s) = \text{Prob}\,(x = k, l, \ldots, s)$$
$$= \text{Prob}\,(k-1 < x < s+1) \qquad \textbf{(374)}$$

$= \sum_{k}^{s} \dot{\boldsymbol{P}}_x$, best formula if $s - k \leqq N/2$ (a)

$= 1 - \sum_{0}^{k-1} \dot{\boldsymbol{P}}_x - \sum_{s+1}^{N} \dot{\boldsymbol{P}}_x$, best formula if $s - k \geqq N/2$ (b)

$= F(s) - F(k-1)$, best formula if $F(x)$ is given (c)

$= \sum_{k}^{N} \dot{\boldsymbol{P}}_x - \sum_{s+1}^{N} \dot{\boldsymbol{P}}_x$, best formula if $\sum_{x}^{N} \dot{\boldsymbol{P}}_x$ is given (d)

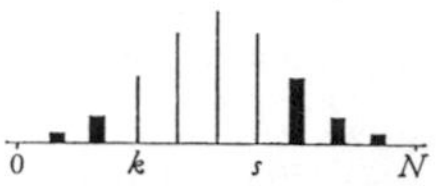

$$\text{Prob}\,(x \leqq k-1) + \text{Prob}\,(x \geqq s+1) = \text{Prob}\,(x < k) + \text{Prob}\,(x > s) \qquad \textbf{(375)}$$

$$= 1 - \sum_{k}^{s} \dot{\boldsymbol{P}}_x, \text{ best formula if } s - k \leqq N/2 \qquad \text{(a)}$$

$$= \sum_{0}^{k-1} \dot{\boldsymbol{P}}_x + \sum_{s+1}^{N} \dot{\boldsymbol{P}}_x, \text{ best formula if } s - k \geqq N/2 \qquad \text{(b)}$$

$$= 1 - F(s) + F(k-1), \text{ best formula if } F(x) \text{ is given} \qquad \text{(c)}$$

$$= 1 - \sum_{k}^{N} \dot{\boldsymbol{P}}_x + \sum_{s+1}^{N} \dot{\boldsymbol{P}}_x, \text{ best formula if } \sum_{x}^{N} \dot{\boldsymbol{P}}_x \text{ is given} \qquad \text{(d)}$$

In **(370)**–**(375)** the best formulae for use in each particular case are indicated. As a rule, the user must calculate $\dot{\boldsymbol{P}}_x$ himself and then proceed with the formulae (a) or (b). The editors know of extensive tabulations of $\sum_x^{\infty} \dot{\boldsymbol{P}}_x$ only for the POISSON distribution[2], of $\sum_x^{N} \dot{\boldsymbol{P}}_x$ only for the binomial distribution[3,4], of $\sum_0^{x} \dot{\boldsymbol{P}}_x \mid N, n, k$ only for the hypergeometric probability distribution[5]. Some publications[2,3,5] include also tabulated values of $f(x)$.

Example 11. Using the formulae (a) or (b) in **(370)**–**(375)**, the probabilities for $k = 2$ and $s = 8$ are calculated from the values of $f(x)$ given in the table on page 148.

(370): $\text{Prob}\,(x = 2) = \dot{\boldsymbol{P}}_2 = 0.0439$

(371): $\text{Prob}\,(x \neq 2) = 1 - \dot{\boldsymbol{P}}_2 = 0.9561$

(372): $\text{Prob}\,(x \leqq 2) = \dot{\boldsymbol{P}}_0 + \dot{\boldsymbol{P}}_1 + \dot{\boldsymbol{P}}_2 = 0.0547$
[by formula (a), since $k < N/2$]

(373): $\text{Prob}\,(x \geqq 2) = 1 - (\dot{\boldsymbol{P}}_0 + \dot{\boldsymbol{P}}_1) = 0.9892$
[by formula (a), since $k < N/2$]

(374): $\text{Prob}\,(2 \leqq x \leqq 8) = \text{Prob}\,(x = 2, 3, \ldots, 8)$
$= 1 - (\dot{\boldsymbol{P}}_0 + \dot{\boldsymbol{P}}_1) - (\dot{\boldsymbol{P}}_9 + \dot{\boldsymbol{P}}_{10}) = 0.9784$
[by formula (b), since $s - k > N/2$]

(375): $\text{Prob}\,(x \neq 2, 3, \ldots, 8) = (\dot{\boldsymbol{P}}_0 + \dot{\boldsymbol{P}}_1) + (\dot{\boldsymbol{P}}_9 + \dot{\boldsymbol{P}}_{10}) = 0.0216$
[by formula (b), since $s - k > N/2$]

Example 12. What is the probability of the event 'x at least equal to 1'? This is the same as saying 'x equal to 1 or more' (cf. page 132), and calculation using **(373a)** gives

$\text{Prob}\,(x \geqq 1) = 1 - \dot{\boldsymbol{P}}_0 = 0.9990$

Example 13

Confidence intervals* and significance limits
(Cf. also sections 8 and 9, pages 154–159)

A. One-sided significance limits

Given α, where $0 < \alpha \leqq 0.5$, determine x_l and x_r in such a way that

$$\text{Prob}\,(x \leqq x_l) = \boldsymbol{P}_l = \sum_{0}^{x_l} \dot{\boldsymbol{P}}_x \leqq \alpha \quad \text{and} \quad \text{Prob}\,(x \leqq x_l + 1) = \sum_{0}^{x_l+1} \dot{\boldsymbol{P}}_x > \alpha \qquad \textbf{(376)}$$

$$\text{Prob}\,(x \geqq x_r) = \boldsymbol{P}_r = \sum_{x_r}^{N} \dot{\boldsymbol{P}}_x \leqq \alpha \quad \text{and} \quad \text{Prob}\,(x \geqq x_r - 1) = \sum_{x_r-1}^{N} \dot{\boldsymbol{P}}_x > \alpha \qquad \textbf{(377)}$$

For $\alpha = 0.10$, $x_l = 2$ and $x_r = 8$; for $\alpha = 0.025$, $x_l = 1$ and $x_r = 9$.

The following definitions follow from the above example:

α is the *postulated* or *nominal one-sided significance probability* **(378)**

$\boldsymbol{P}$ is the *actual one-sided significance probability*, $\boldsymbol{P}_l$ being the *left* (*lower*) and $\boldsymbol{P}_r$ the *right* (*upper*) level, with $\boldsymbol{P}_l$ and $\boldsymbol{P}_r \leqq \alpha$ **(379)**

x_l is the *left* (*lower*) and x_r the *right* (*upper*) significance limit **(380)**

* Also known as 'tolerance intervals'. Cf. section 8, page 154.

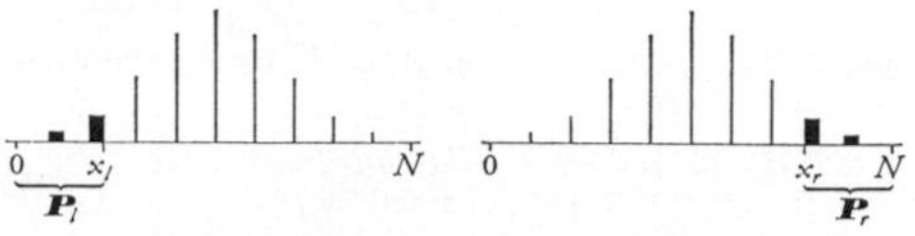

Fig. 3. One-sided significance limits of discrete distributions.

It should be noted that

– if x *attains or exceeds* (to the left) the *left* (lower) significance limit x_l, then in a *one-tailed* test
$\text{Prob}\,(x \leqq x_l) \leqq \alpha = \text{Prob}\,(x < x_{l+1})$ **(381)**

– if x *attains or exceeds* (to the right) the *right* (upper) significance limit x_r, then in a *one-tailed* test
$\text{Prob}\,(x \geqq x_r) \geqq \alpha = \text{Prob}\,(x > x_{r-1})$ **(382)**

– rules **(381)** and **(382)** are valid for *all* significance limits of *discrete* distributions tabulated in these *Tables*. Elsewhere, significance limits of discrete distributions may be found which must be exceeded in an *outward* direction if, for example, they are to satisfy the rule $\boldsymbol{P}_l \leqq \alpha$. **(383)**

– as a rule the *actual* significance probability $\boldsymbol{P}$ in *discrete* distributions is *smaller* than the *nominal* α, for small values of N often considerably smaller. With increasing values of N this difference decreases rapidly. (In example 13 with $\alpha = 0.10$ or 0.025, the corresponding values of $\boldsymbol{P}$ are 0.0547 or 0.0108. In this case the actual significance probability amounts to only about 50% of the nominal.) **(384)**

The following definitions should also be noted:

The range between $x_l + 1$ and N or between zero and $x_r - 1$ is the *one-sided confidence interval.* **(385)**

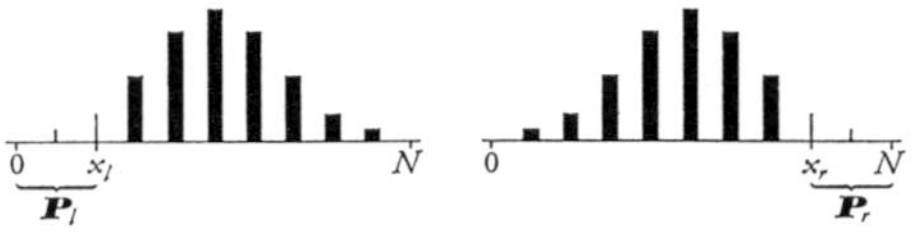

Fig. 4. One-sided confidence intervals for discrete distributions.

x_l or x_r is the *one-sided confidence limit* when the other limit lies at N or zero. **(386)**

The probabilities $1 - \boldsymbol{P}_l \geqq 1 - \alpha$ and $1 - \boldsymbol{P}_r \geqq 1 - \alpha$ are the *one-sided confidence probabilities:*

$$\text{Prob}\,(x_l < x \leqq N) = 1 - \boldsymbol{P}_l = 1 - \sum_{0}^{x_l} \dot{\boldsymbol{P}}_x \geqq 1 - \alpha \qquad \textbf{(387)}$$

$$\text{Prob}\,(0 \leqq x < x_r) = 1 - \boldsymbol{P}_r = 1 - \sum_{x_r}^{N} \dot{\boldsymbol{P}}_x \geqq 1 - \alpha \qquad \textbf{(388)}$$

From **(380)** and **(386)** it will be seen that significance limits and confidence intervals are determined mathematically according to the same principles. **(389)**

B. Two-sided significance limits

If a left and a right significance limit are determined jointly for a discrete distribution according to rules **(376)** and **(377)**, then for the two together $\boldsymbol{P}_l + \boldsymbol{P}_r \leqq 2\alpha$. **(390)**

In this case the following definitions apply:

2α is the *postulated* or *nominal two-sided significance probability*. **(391)**

$\boldsymbol{P}_l + \boldsymbol{P}_r$ is the *actual two-sided significance probability* [note also **(384)**], where $\boldsymbol{P}_l = \boldsymbol{P}_r$ in symmetrical distributions and $\boldsymbol{P}_l \neq \boldsymbol{P}_r$ in unsymmetrical distributions, although both satisfy rules **(376)** and **(377)** (cf. Fig. 5). **(392)**

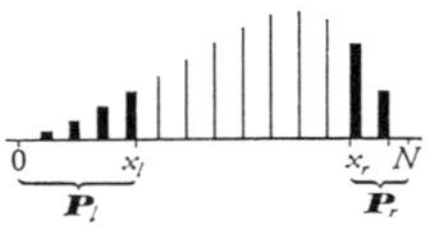

Fig. 5. Two-sided significance limits for discrete (unsymmetrical) distributions.

x_l and x_r together are the *two-sided* significance limits (with symmetrical probability), or briefly *significance limits.* **(393)**

It should be noted that

when x *attains or exceeds* (outwards) *one of the two* significance limits x_l or x_r, then in a *two-sided* test
$\text{Prob}(x \leqq x_l) + \text{Prob}(x \geqq x_r) \leqq 2\alpha =$
$\text{Prob}(x < x_{l+1}) + \text{Prob}(x > x_{r-1})$ **(394)**

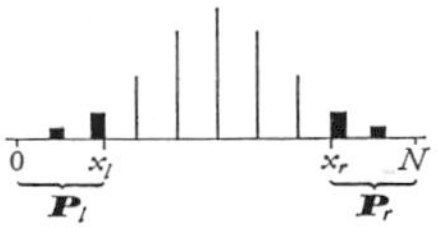

Fig. 6. Two-sided significance limits for discrete (symmetrical) distributions.

The following definitions should also be noted:

The range between $x_l + 1$ and $x_r - 1$ is the two-sided confidence interval, or briefly *confidence interval.* **(395)**

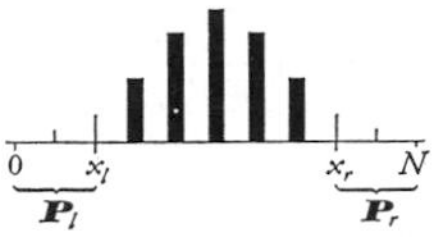

Fig. 7. Two-sided confidence interval for discrete distributions.

x_l and x_r are the two-sided confidence limits, or briefly *confidence limits*, whereby it should again be noted that significance limits and confidence intervals are determined mathematically according to the same principles. **(396)**

The probability $1 - \boldsymbol{P}_l - \boldsymbol{P}_r \geqq 1 - 2\alpha$ is the actual two-sided confidence probability, or briefly *confidence probability:*

$$\text{Prob}(x_l < x < x_r) = 1 - \boldsymbol{P}_l - \boldsymbol{P}_r$$
$$= 1 - \sum_{0}^{x_l} \dot{\boldsymbol{P}}_x - \sum_{x_r}^{N} \dot{\boldsymbol{P}}_x \geqq 1 - 2\alpha \qquad \textbf{(397)}$$

6. Continuous probability distribution

A comparison of Figures 1 and 8 reveals the similarity between discrete and continuous distributions. When the distribution shown at the beginning of the previous section (page 148) is worked out for increasing values of N, the steps in the $f(x)$ and $F(x)$ curves will become smaller and smaller until finally, with infinite N, a continuous curve such as that shown in Figure 8 is obtained. This will be further discussed later.

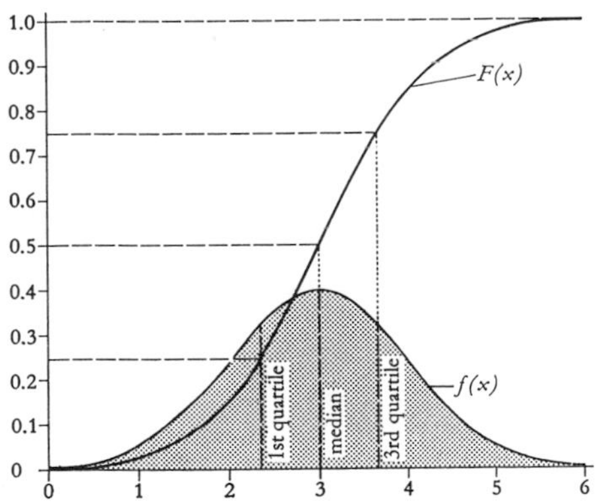

Fig. 8. Abscissae: x; ordinates: probability density function $f(x)$ and probability $F(x)$.

In probability distributions such as those of Figure 8, x is a *continuous* random variable [cf. **(343)**]; there is an infinite number of events x, so that

$$\text{Prob}(x = k) = 1/\infty = 0 \qquad \textbf{(398)}$$

and

$$\text{Prob}(x \leqq k) = \text{Prob}(x < k) + \text{Prob}(x = k) = \text{Prob}(x < k) + 0$$

In practice therefore the following should be noted:

For *continuous* distributions (with an error of zero magnitude)
$\text{Prob}(x \leqq k)$ can be written as $\text{Prob}(x < k)$
$\text{Prob}(x \geqq k)$ can be written as $\text{Prob}(x > k)$ **(399)**

In discrete distributions the individual probability $\text{Prob}(x = k)$ can be read from $f(x)$ but this no longer applies in continuous distributions:

In a continuous distribution, $f(x)$ is the *probability density function* at the point x. **(400)**

The cumulative probability distribution $F(x)$ has the same significance in continuous distributions, however, as in discrete distributions: it represents the probabilities of the events $x \leqq k$. In contrast to the case with discrete distributions, the latter are equivalent to the events $x < k$ [cf. **(399)**]. **(401)**

In discrete distributions, $F(x)$ is the *sum* of the individual probabilities [cf. **(372)**]. In continuous distributions, $F(x)$ is an *integral:*

$$F(x) = \int_{-\infty}^{x} f(x)\,dx \qquad \textbf{(402)}$$

i.e., $F(x)$ corresponds to the area between the abscissa and the curve $f(x)$ from $-\infty$ to x:

Fig. 9

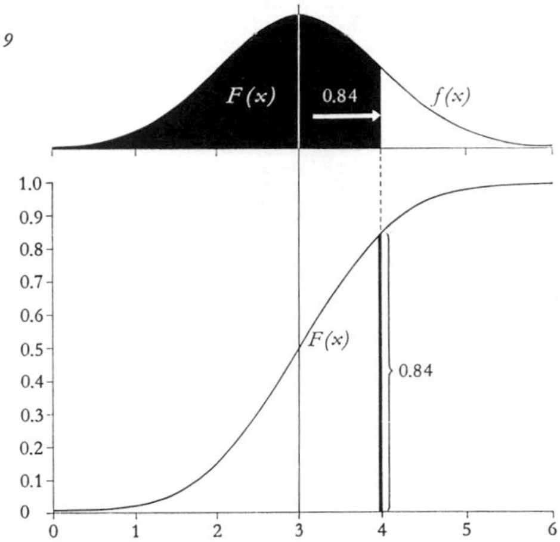

The total area between the abscissa and the curve $f(x)$ from $-\infty$ to $+\infty$ amounts to unity [cf. **(353)**]:
$F(\infty) = 1;\ F(-\infty) = 0$ **(403)**

Fig. 10

For continuous distributions the equations analogous to **(370)**–**(375)** are the following:

$\text{Prob}(x = k) = 0$, cf. **(352)** and **(398)**

$\text{Prob}(x \neq k) = 1$, cf. **(352)** **(404)**

$$\text{Prob}(x \leqq k) = \text{Prob}(x < k) \qquad \textbf{(405)}$$

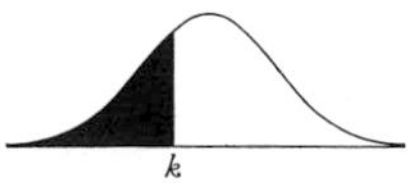

$$= \int_{-\infty}^{k} f(x)\,dx = F(k) \qquad \text{(a)}$$
$$= 1 - \int_{k}^{\infty} f(x)\,dx \qquad \text{(b)}$$

$$\text{Prob}(x \geqq k) = \text{Prob}(x > k) \qquad \textbf{(406)}$$

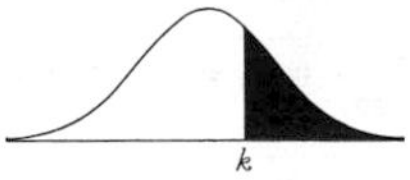

$$= 1 - \int_{-\infty}^{k} f(x)\,dx = 1 - F(k) \qquad \text{(a)}$$
$$= \int_{k}^{\infty} f(x)\,dx \qquad \text{(b)}$$

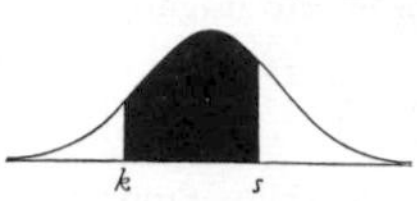

$$\text{Prob}\,(k \leqq x \leqq s) = \int_{-\infty}^{s} f(x)\,dx - \int_{-\infty}^{k} f(x)\,dx = F(s) - F(k) \quad \textbf{(407a)}$$

$$= 1 - \int_{-\infty}^{k} f(x)\,dx - \int_{s}^{\infty} f(x)\,dx \quad \text{(b)}$$

$$= \int_{k}^{s} f(x)\,dx \quad \text{(c)}$$

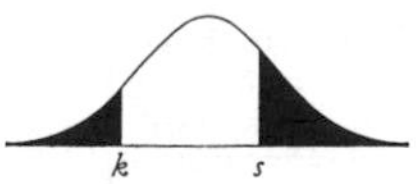

$$\text{Prob}\,(x < k) + \text{Prob}\,(x > s) = 1 - \int_{-\infty}^{s} f(x)\,dx + \int_{-\infty}^{k} f(x)\,dx = 1 - F(s) + F(k) \quad \textbf{(408a)}$$

$$= \int_{-\infty}^{k} f(x)\,dx + \int_{s}^{\infty} f(x)\,dx \quad \text{(b)}$$

$$= 1 - \int_{k}^{s} f(x)\,dx \quad \text{(c)}$$

In equations **(405)**–**(408)**, comparison with **(399)** shows for example that Prob $(k \leqq x \leqq s)$ is the same as Prob $(k < x \leqq s)$, Prob $(k \leqq x < s)$ and Prob $(k < x < s)$.

The numerical values of the various integrals in **(405)**–**(408)** for the most important distributions will be found in the statistical tables on pages 28 onward. They will be discussed further under the headings of the individual distributions later in this chapter. In the examples below in which probabilities in the normal distribution are calculated, the abscissae x are designated deviations c. In the table on page 28, $F(c)$ values are tabulated on the right (deviation→ integral), i.e., *the probabilities $F(c)$ for given deviations c*. On the left (integral→ deviation) are deviations c for given probabilities, so that here the deviation c is a function of $F(c)$, known as the quantile c (cf. section 10 E, page 160). Such a function is known as an *inverse function*. Tables of inverse functions are useful but not absolutely necessary. The values required can also be obtained from tables of basic functions by interpolation.

Example 14. The probabilities for $k = -1.65$ and $s = 1.96$ are calculated for the normal distribution using the form (a) of equations **(405)** to **(408)**.

The right-hand side of the table on page 28 gives $F(-1.65) = 0.049\,47$ and $F(1.96) = 0.975\,00$, so that

(405): Prob $(c \leqq -1.65) = 0.049\,47$

(406): Prob $(c \geqq -1.65) = 1 - 0.049\,47 = 0.950\,53$

(407): Prob $(-1.65 \leqq c \leqq 1.96) = 0.975\,00 - 0.049\,47 = 0.925\,53$

(408): Prob $(c \neq -1.65$ to $1.96) = 1 - 0.975\,00 + 0.049\,47 = 0.074\,47$

Example 15. Given the probabilities $F(c) = 0.001$ and 0.995 it is required to find the corresponding deviations c. The left-hand side of the table on page 28 gives $c = -3.090\,2$ and $2.575\,8$. The corresponding values taken from the right-hand side without interpolation are 3.09 and 2.58.

Example 16

Confidence intervals* and significance limits
(Cf. also sections 8 and 9, pages 154–159)

A. One-sided significance limits

Given α, where $0 < \alpha \leqq 0.5$, determine x_l and x_r in such a way that

$$\text{Prob}\,(x < x_l) = \boldsymbol{P}_l = \int_{-\infty}^{x_l} f(x)\,dx = F(x_l) = \alpha \quad \textbf{(409)}$$

$$\text{Prob}\,(x > x_r) = \boldsymbol{P}_r = \int_{x_r}^{\infty} f(x)\,dx = 1 - \int_{-\infty}^{x_r} f(x)\,dx = 1 - F(x_r) = \alpha \quad \textbf{(410)}$$

From **(410)** it follows that $F(x_r) = 1 - \alpha$ **(411)**

For the normal distribution, the table on page 28, left-hand side, gives for $\alpha = 0.025$, $x_l = -1.96$ and $x_r = 1.96$.

The definitions of the symbols α, $\boldsymbol{P}_l$, $\boldsymbol{P}_r$, x_l and x_r in **(409)** and **(410)** are the same as in **(378)**, **(379)** and **(380)**.

* Also known as 'tolerance intervals'. Cf. section 8, page 154.

It will be noted, however, that in contrast to discrete distributions [cf. **(384)**], the actual and nominal significance probabilities in continuous distributions are of the same magnitude. In continuous distributions therefore, the simple expression 'significance probability' is used, the symbols $\boldsymbol{P}$ and α becoming synonymous. **(412)**

As in the case of discrete distributions it follows that:

If x *attains or exceeds* (to the left) the *left* (lower) significance limit x_l, then in a *one-tailed* test
Prob $(x \leqq x_l) \leqq \alpha =$ Prob $(x < x_l)$ **(413)**

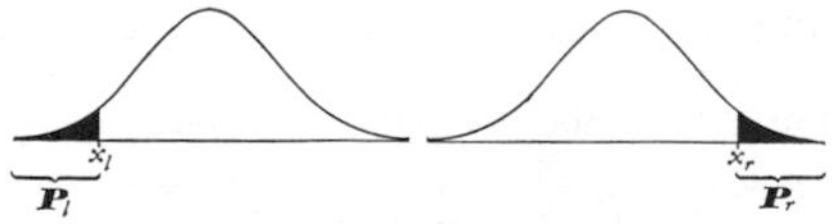

Fig. 11. One-sided significance limits for continuous distributions.

If x *attains or exceeds* (to the right) the *right* (upper) significance limit x_r, then in a *one-tailed* test
Prob $(x \geqq x_r) \leqq \alpha =$ Prob $(x > x_r)$ **(414)**

The following definitions should also be noted:

The range between x_l and ∞ or between $-\infty$ and x_r is the *one-sided confidence interval.* **(415)**

Fig. 12. One-sided confidence intervals for continuous distributions.

x_l and x_r are the *one-sided confidence limits* when the other limit lies at ∞ and $-\infty$ respectively. Again, significance limits and confidence intervals for continuous distributions are determined according to the same mathematical principles. **(416)**

B. Two-sided significance limits

When a left and a right significance limit are jointly determined for a continuous distribution according to rules **(409)** and **(410)**, then for the two together $\boldsymbol{P}_l + \boldsymbol{P}_r = 2\,\boldsymbol{P} = 2\alpha$. **(417)**

In this case

$2\,\boldsymbol{P} = 2\alpha$ is the *two-sided significance level.* **(418)**

x_l and x_r together are the *two-sided* significance limits, or briefly the *significance limits.* **(419)**

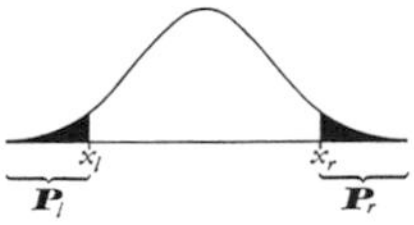

Fig. 13. Two-sided significance limits for continuous distributions.

It should be noted:

If x *attains or exceeds* (outwards) *one of the two* significance limits x_l or x_r, then in a *two-tailed* test
Prob $(x \leqq x_l)$ + Prob $(x \geqq x_r) \leqq 2\alpha =$
Prob $(x < x_l)$ + Prob $(x > x_r)$ **(420)**

The following definitions should also be noted:

The range between x_l and x_r is the *two-sided* confidence interval, or briefly the *confidence interval.* **(421)**

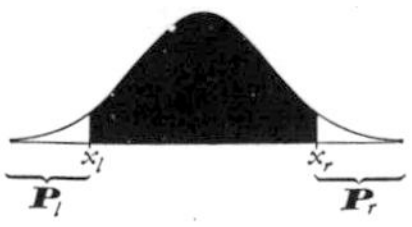

Fig. 14. Two-sided confidence interval for continuous distributions.

x_l and x_r are the *two-sided* confidence limits (with symmetrical probability), or briefly the *confidence limits*. **(422)**

The probability $1-2\boldsymbol{P}=1-2\alpha$ is the two-sided confidence probability, or briefly the *confidence probability:* **(423)**

$$\begin{aligned}\text{Prob}\,(x_l \leqq x \leqq x_r) &= 1-2\boldsymbol{P}\\ &= 1-\int_{-\infty}^{x_l} f(x)\,dx-\int_{x_r}^{\infty} f(x)\,dx=\int_{x_l}^{x_r} f(x)\,dx\\ &= \int_{-\infty}^{x_r} f(x)\,dx-\int_{-\infty}^{x_l} f(x)\,dx=F(x_r)-F(x_l)=1-2\alpha\end{aligned}$$

7. Estimates

The variables of a population are usually known but not always the type of distribution and rarely the parameters, so that the distribution or its parameters must be estimated on the basis of samples. Estimates can be calculated from a sample using the same rules as for calculating the corresponding parameter of the population. This method of estimating is frequently used but it is not the only one and does not always give the best estimates. A general discussion of methods of estimation, such as the *maximum-likelihood method* of R.A. FISHER, would not be appropriate here since their understanding requires a knowledge of higher mathematics*. It is also unnecessary in practice since for the commonest cases a recognized estimating formula can be used.

7A. Expectation and bias

It is assumed that an estimate of some parameter P from a sample of size N is required.

Experience has shown that when a number of similar estimates are made from samples of the *same* size the mean of these estimates approaches closer and closer to a definite value – the *expected value* or *expectation* of the estimate – when the number of samples is increased toward infinity (cf. Fig. 15). **(424)**

This convergence, however, is not a convergence in the usual mathematical sense but a *convergence in probability* or *stochastic convergence*, i.e., *'the probability that...' converges toward unity or zero* [cf. (**427**)].

When the expectation of an estimate is equal to the parameter, the estimate is said to be *unbiased*. When this is not the case, the estimate has *bias*. **(425)**

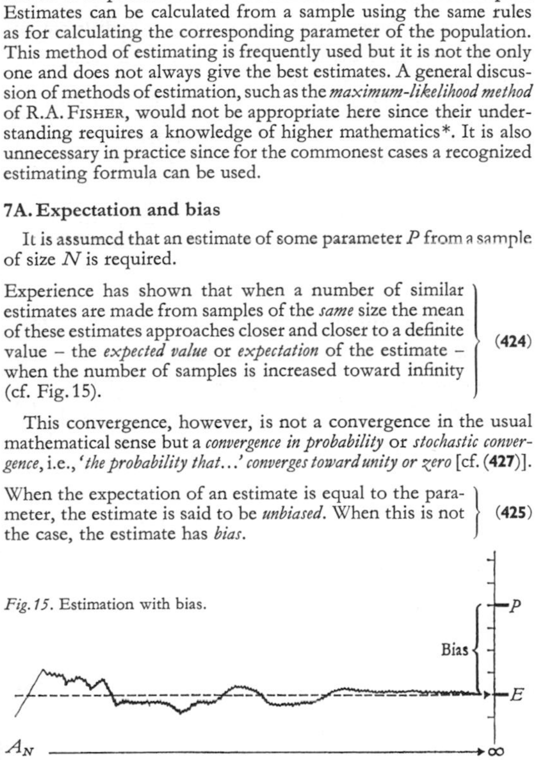

Fig. 15. Estimation with bias.

Broken line = Expected value E of an estimate from samples of size N
Full line = Estimate
P = Parameter
A_N = Number of samples of size N

The bias can be dependent on the size of the sample. As a rule it is larger with small samples and tends toward zero when the sample size N approaches infinity. Such estimates are known as *asymptotically unbiased* estimates (cf. Fig. 16). **(426)**

Broken line = Expected value E of an estimate from samples of size N
Full line = Estimate
P = Parameter

Fig. 16. Asymptotically unbiased estimation.

* 'Higher' from the standpoint of the non-mathematician.

The bias described above is a mathematical one, that is, one inherent in the estimation. If the magnitude of this 'internal' bias is known, it can be eliminated by appropriate corrections*. An estimate can also have a non-mathematical, 'external' bias, however, due to errors of measurement or judgment, to nonrandom collection of samples, or to both these causes. Such a bias is more dangerous than a mathematical one since only in rare cases can it be eliminated by recognition of its extent and direction. External bias can be avoided only by careful experimental design. For further information the reader is referred to the literature.

When estimates are made in order to determine the *difference between samples*, the results will *not* be subject to a bias in those cases in which the samples being compared are subject to *the same* bias, e.g., when the samples are collected under identical conditions. To this must be added the obvious mathematical condition that *all estimates to be compared are calculated according to the same rule.*

7B. Consistency

As in (**424**), experience has shown that with increasing sample size, estimates also usually tend toward a definite value, the expected value in *infinitely large* samples:

(427)

(a) If with increasing sample size N a parameter remains *constant*, then Prob (| estimate minus expectation | $< \varepsilon) \to 1$ $(\varepsilon > 0)$, as the sample size $N \to \infty$

(b) (a) is also valid for parameters that with increasing sample size N increase in proportion to N, N^2, etc. when the absolute value of the difference between estimate and expected value is divided by N, N^2, etc.

(**427**) is interpreted as follows: The probability that the absolute difference between estimate and expectation will not exceed any chosen small number ε tends toward unity as the sample size N tends toward infinity. This is the so-called (weak) *law of large numbers*.

Estimates that satisfy (**427**), i.e., follow the law of large numbers, are known as *consistent estimates*.

7C. Efficiency

Estimates are the result of calculations based on random events and are therefore themselves *random variables* that fluctuate from sample to sample around their expected value within a range dependent on the sample size; in other words, they exhibit *variance*. It is apparent that the accuracy of the estimate will increase or decrease with the range of this fluctuation, i.e., with the magnitude of the standard deviation or of its square, the variance:

The estimate with the *lowest* variance is known as the *most efficient estimate*. The variance of the most efficient estimate, provided that one exists for the parameter concerned, may be calculated by means of the RAO-CRAMÉR Inequality[6,7], for details of which the reader is referred to the original publications.

Here the *most efficient estimate* is defined as that unbiased estimate of a parameter with variance equal to the lower bound of RAO-CRAMÉR. This will be assigned an efficiency of 100%. **(428)**

Estimates fulfilling condition (**428**) for every size of sample are rare. However, there are estimates that meet this condition when the sample size tends toward infinity. Such estimates are known as *asymptotically most efficient estimates* (with an asymptotic efficiency of 100%). **(429)**

Asymptotically most efficient estimates of (**429**) are suitable for χ^2 tests, others not. **(430)**

(**430**) must be qualified to the extent that such estimates do not always exist. In this case, the asymptotically most efficient estimate should be selected from those known, and this one used for χ^2 tests even though its asymptotic efficiency according to (**429**) does not amount to 100%. **(431)**

As a rule, the standard deviation of an estimate decreases either absolutely or relatively (to the magnitude of the estimate) as the sample size increases (cf. Fig. 17):

(432)

(a) If a parameter remains *constant* with increasing sample size, the standard deviation of its estimate shows stochastic convergence toward zero of the order of $1/\sqrt{N}$ with increasing sample size N.

* Corrections are not always possible when N is finite.

(a) is also valid for parameters that with increasing sample size N *increase* in proportion to N, N^2, etc. when the parameter, the estimate and its standard deviation are divided by N, N^2, etc. (b) **(432)**

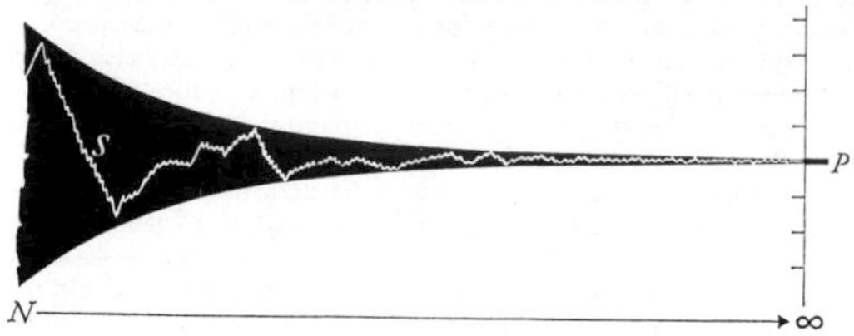

Standard deviation
S Estimate
P Parameter

Fig. 17

If the efficiency of the estimate A is 100%, that of the estimate B for the same parameter 75%, then the sample size when using method B must be 100/75 times larger (⅓ as large again) than when using method A if the same degree of precision is to be obtained [provided that (**432**) applies]. **(433)**

Thus by increasing the size of the sample a less efficient estimate can be given the same precision as a more efficient one,

or conversely, for a given degree of precision the sample size can be smaller when a more efficient method of estimation is used (cf. Fig. 18). **(434)**

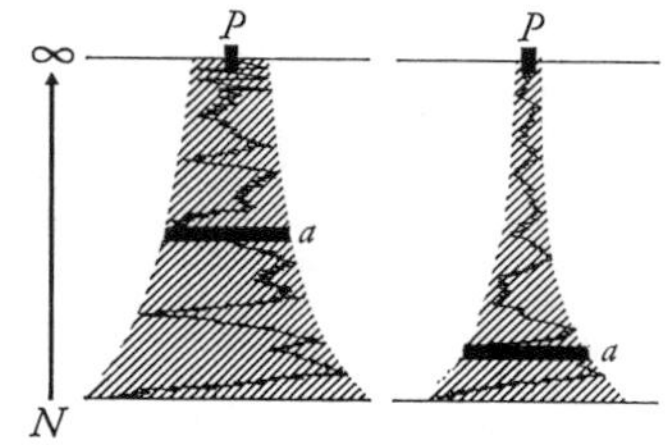

Fig. 18. a = precision of the estimate.

The question arises of which method to use in estimating a parameter when several formulae are available: that which yields the most efficient estimate but is more complicated, or a simpler but less efficient method? Theoretically, only the most efficient method should be used; in practice, however, the niceties of mathematical usage must be tempered by other considerations.

The most efficient of the known estimates of a parameter should be used

- when tests are expensive in comparison with simple counting [cf. (**434**)],
- when the tests cannot be repeated,
- when χ^2 tests are planned,
- when the result must be as exact and informative as possible,
- when the most efficient estimate has been used in similar studies by other investigators (thus offering the possibility of comparisons and significance tests). **(435)**

Where none of the reasons given in (**435**) apply, a less efficient but rapid method of estimating should be used

- when simple counting is more costly than the tests [cf. (**434**)],
- when the precision of the method suffices for the purpose in mind,
- when the object is simply a rapid preliminary check of the results,
- when the investigations are of a routine nature,
- when it is necessary to check more efficient estimates in the calculation of which there is a high possibility of error. **(436)**

7D. Sufficient estimates

An estimate or combination of estimates that in any given case yields *all the information* it is possible to obtain is known as a *sufficient estimate.* **(437)**

Information may be imagined (more or less) as the reciprocal of the variance. **(438)**

In conclusion it should be noted that as in the case of bias, the variance of an estimate is dependent on the experimental conditions and can be reduced by suitable planning of the investigation.

The designations 'consistent', 'efficient' and 'sufficient' are due to R. A. Fisher. However, Fisher reserves the term 'efficient' for those estimates described here as suitable for χ^2 tests [cf. (**430**) and (**431**)].

8. Confidence limits and tolerance limits

8A. Confidence limits for continuous and discrete distributions

In this subsection it is assumed that the reader is familiar with examples 13 and 16, pages 150 and 152.

The estimation of a parameter alone does not yield a great deal of information. In a continuous distribution, for example, as (**398**) shows, the probability that the estimate [x in (**398**)] and parameter [k in (**398**)] agree is equal to zero. More information is provided by calculating from the sample the two values x_l and x_r that with a *high probability* enclose the parameter between them. Such limits are known as *confidence limits.* The associated terminology and mathematical definitions are given in examples 13 and 16 (pages 150 and 152).

The confidence limits used here are characterized as follows:

They are identical with the confidence limits of J. Neyman[8]. **(439)**

The parameter to which they relate is a *constant.* **(440)**

They are *estimates* and therefore *random variables.* Moreover, the *position of the limits* as well as the *width of the confidence interval* is a random variable (cf. Fig. 19). **(441)**

Fig. 19. 95% confidence intervals for the parameter p of a binomially distributed population, calculated from 20 samples of size 40.

For a given sample size, *more efficient* estimates result in a *narrower* confidence interval than less efficient ones. **(442)**

In analogy with (**432**), the confidence interval becomes absolutely or relatively (to the magnitude of the estimate) narrower with increasing sample size.

When a parameter remains *constant* with increasing sample size N, the confidence limits show stochastic convergence of the order of $1/\sqrt{N}$ toward the parameter and the width of the confidence interval shows stochastic convergence toward zero (cf. Fig. 20). (a)

When the parameter is divided by N, N^2, etc. and its confidence limits by N, N^2, etc., (a) is also valid for parameters that with increasing sample size N *increase* in proportion to N, N^2, etc. (b) **(443)**

Confidence limits are to be interpreted as follows [see also (**456**)]: When very many (infinitely many) samples *of the same size* are taken *from the same stable population* and the confidence limits calculated for each, then these limits

(*one-sided confidence intervals*)

- will enclose the true value of the parameter on the average in $\geqq 100\,(1-\alpha)\%$ of cases* (a)

or (an equally valid interpretation)

- will *not* enclose the true value of the parameter on the average in $\leqq 100\,\alpha\%$ of cases* (b) **(444)**

* The 'greater than' and 'smaller than' signs apply to discrete distributions, the 'equals' sign to continuous distributions.

(*two-sided confidence intervals*)

– will enclose the true value of the parameter on the average in $\geqq 100(1-2\alpha)\%$ of cases* (c)

or (an equally valid interpretation)

– will *not* enclose the true value of the parameter on the average in $\leqq 100(2\alpha)\%$ of cases*. Further, in an average of $\leqq 100\alpha\%$ of cases*, x_l (the lower limit) will lie *above* the parameter; and in an average of $\leqq 100\alpha\%$ of cases*, x_r (the upper limit) will lie *below* the parameter. (d) **(444)**

As a rule, the confidence probability 0.95 (more rarely 0.99) is used in medical and biological studies, i.e., α (one-sided intervals) or 2α (two-sided intervals) is equal to 0.05 (more rarely 0.01). **(445)**

Formulae for the calculation of confidence intervals for various parameters will be given later for individual cases.

When the object of a statistical test is the estimation of a parameter, the corresponding confidence limits should always be determined as well. When these are known, an estimate (the result of a series of investigations) gives trustworthy information; without confidence limits it gives no such information. The statistical tables given in this book permit the calculation of confidence limits with *little* or *no* additional calculation.

Fiducial limits. This concept, introduced by R. A. Fisher, strictly speaking has a sense different to that of the *confidence limits* of J. Neyman. *Fiducial limits* can be precisely determined only for certain continuous distributions. For discrete distributions they can be determined approximately, but then only when the sample size is large. *Confidence limits* are not subject to these limitations and their use is therefore preferred here.

8B. Tolerance limits for continuous distributions

Limits for a percentage of a population are known as tolerance limits. **(446)**

The percentage of the population is expressed as $100\beta_p\%$, the confidence probabilities associated with tolerance limits as β_t. **(447)**

(**441**) and (**442**) are also valid for tolerance limits. **(448)**

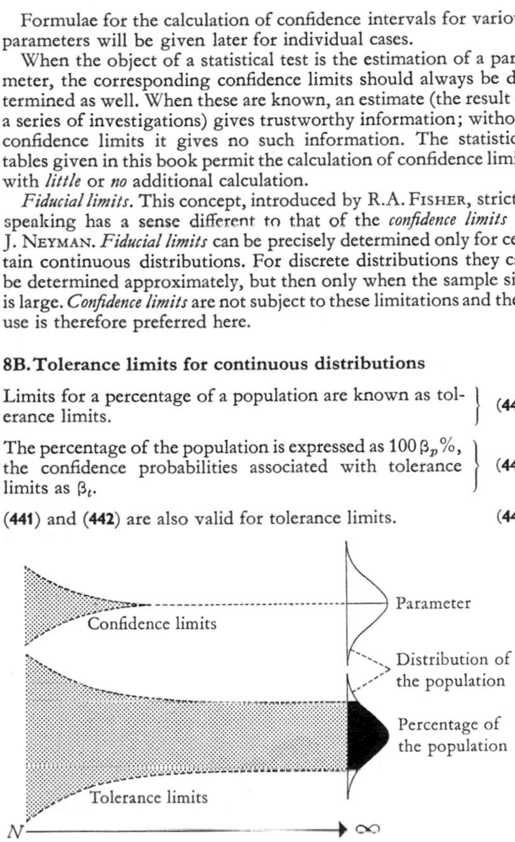

Fig. 20. Convergence of confidence and tolerance limits.

In analogy with (**443**), tolerance limits also converge stochastically with increasing sample size, *but not toward one but toward two* limiting parameters, namely those corresponding to the quantiles of the population between which lies the percentage of the population to which the tolerance limits relate. The tolerance interval between these limits thus tends *not toward zero* but toward a *positive whole number* (cf. Fig. 20). **(449)**

Like confidence limits, tolerance limits can be one- or two-sided. The following statements refer to two-sided tolerance limits in which

$$\beta_p = 1 - 2\alpha, \text{ and } \alpha\,(\text{left}) = \alpha\,(\text{right}) = \int_{-\infty}^{x_l} f(x)\,dx = \int_{x_r}^{\infty} f(x)\,dx.$$

Tolerance limits with confidence probability β_t must be distinguished from those without. They are interpreted as follows [note also (**456**)]:

* The 'greater than' and 'smaller than' signs apply to discrete distributions, the 'equals' sign to continuous distributions.

Sample tolerance limits without confidence probability. When very many (infinitely many) samples of the *same size* are taken from the *same stable population* and the tolerance limits calculated each time, then these limits

– will enclose *on the average* $100\beta_p\%$ of the population (a)

or (an equally valid interpretation)

– will *not* enclose on the average $100(1-\beta_p)\%$ of the population, whereby on the average $100\alpha\%$ of the population will lie *below* the left (lower) limit and $100\alpha\%$ *above* the right (upper) limit. (b) **(450)**

Sample tolerance limits with confidence probability β_t. When very many (infinitely many) samples of the *same size* are taken from the *same stable population* and the tolerance limits calculated each time, then these limits will include *at least* $100\beta_p\%$ of the population in an average of $100\beta_t\%$ of cases. **(451)**

The tolerance factors for tolerance intervals without confidence probability [interpretation (**450**)] given in the left-hand table on page 44 are valid for *normally distributed* populations. These tolerance intervals are identical with the confidence limits for the difference between the mean of a sample and a later single observation[9]. **(452)**

Tolerance intervals *with* confidence probability [interpretation (**451**)] are wider than those *without*, as would be expected. With increasing sample size, however, both intervals converge toward the limiting interval of (**499**). **(453)**

Formulae for the calculation of tolerance intervals for normally distributed populations are given in section 13B, page 169.

Of particular importance in medical and biological studies are tolerance limits for the determination of *normal ranges*. Up to the present these have rarely been calculated precisely according to the rules for tolerance limits*. However, with the aid of the tables given in this book, their exact calculation will involve additional calculation only in a minimum number of cases.

Normal ranges should therefore be determined in accordance with the rules for tolerance limits, and

– in general, as tolerance intervals *without* confidence probability [interpretation (**450**)] for $100\beta_p\% = 95\%$ of the population [cf. (**452**)] (a)

– in special cases (usually industrial, where for example the wastage must be kept as low as possible), as tolerance intervals *with* confidence probability β_t [interpretation (**451**)] (b) **(454)**

In the above text the word 'normal' has been used – in 'normally distributed' and 'normal range' – in two different senses:

In 'normally distributed', the expression is used in its conventional sense and has no deeper significance. The normal distribution is so named because it is frequently encountered and important, although it is not the only distribution that has these attributes.

In 'normal range', the expression is used deliberately to denote that range which embraces the 'normals' of a population. In medical and biological studies this range is conventionally the 95% tolerance interval without confidence probability [cf. (**450**)]. **(455)**

8C. Distribution-free confidence and tolerance limits

(Cf. also section 10F, page 161)

Statements (**444**), (**450**) and (**451**) are correct only when the sample in fact originates from the population for whose parameter or percentage the limits were calculated. The formulae for calculating these limits are specific for the individual types of population. **(456)**

If the type of distribution of a population is unknown, as is often the case, it is pointless – particularly with *small* samples – to calculate confidence and tolerance limits on the basis of *assumptions* concerning the distribution that are not justified by experience, the experimental conditions, and so on.

* With large samples this is in any case pointless.

In such cases the so-called *distribution-free* confidence and tolerance limits are used, provided that these are available for the case concerned. Statements (**444**), (**450**) and (**451**) are then valid *without any stipulation as to the distribution* of the population*, i.e., they are valid for *all* populations with the sole provision that these are *continuous*. (**457**)

Distribution-free confidence and tolerance limits are *wider* than those calculated for populations of a specific type. This is understandable in view of the fact that they must satisfy (**444**), (**450**) and (**451**) for populations of widely differing kinds.

Distribution-free confidence limits for quantiles (median, quartile, percentile, etc.) of small samples (up to $N = 100$) of continuous populations can be read off *without* calculation from the tables on pages 104 et seq. An introduction to the calculation of distribution-free confidence and tolerance limits will be found, together with formulae, in sections 10F (page 161) and 20F (page 186).

The table of distribution-free tolerance limits on page 128 can be used to solve problems of the following type without the need of calculation: At the start of a series of tests it is often necessary to decide the size of the sample to be taken *when it is impossible to know the form of the population distribution*. On the one hand the sample must be large enough to be reasonably representative of the population, on the other hand not unnecessarily large and wasteful. The answer is provided by distribution-free tolerance limits and for most purposes these can be read off directly from the table mentioned. For example, if the two extreme values of the sample are to include 90% of the population with the high probability of 0.999, then the table gives a sample size of 88. In other words, if a sample of size 88 is taken, then with a probability of 0.999, 90% of the population will lie between the 1st and 88th values of the sample.

9. Statistical significance tests

9A. Introduction

With a 'true' die the probability of throwing the number 1, 2, ..., 6 is by definition exactly 1/6, and the probability of throwing an even number is exactly ½. In accordance with (**331**), the probability ½ is a parameter of the population of events 'even number' and 'uneven number' produced by throwing the die.

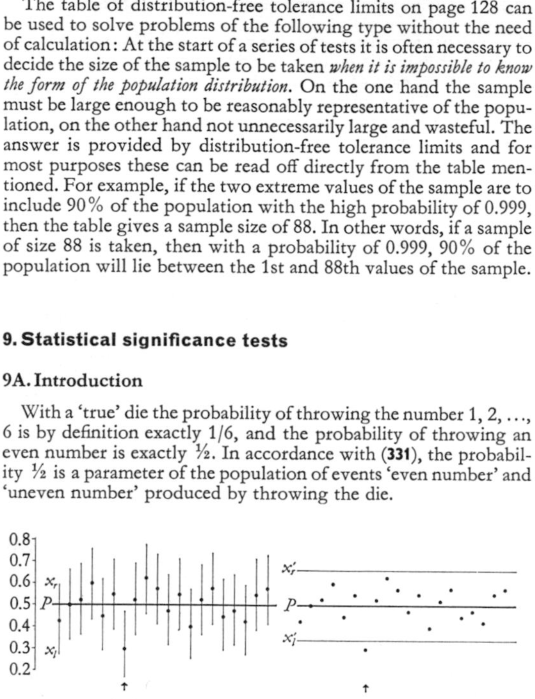

Fig. 21. 95% confidence limits (left) and corresponding 5% significance limits (right) for a given sample size (cf. legend of Fig. 19). The points are estimates p of the probability $\boldsymbol{p} = ½$ (shown here as the parameter P).

Such a die can be used to check statement (**444**d). 20 samples of 40 throws each are made and in each sample the uneven numbers thrown used to determine the 95% confidence limits given in Figure 21 (left) for the parameter ½. In accordance with (**444**d), one of the 20 confidence intervals does not include the parameter (note arrow).

Supposing now that these confidence limits had been obtained not with samples consisting of *twenty throws of a known die* but with separate samples from *each of twenty unknown dice*. The suspicion would immediately arise that 'something was wrong' with that die for which the confidence interval did not include the parameter ½. Only one sample has been thrown with this die, and in this first solitary sample a rare event occurs that according to (**444**d) should only occur in the long run in 5% of cases**. The suspected die is therefore declared to be loaded, but with the reservation that this assertion may err with a significance probability of 0.05.

This is the principle on which, mutatis mutandis, all statistical tests are based.

* Hence the expression 'distribution-free'.

** Further consideration will show that such an occurrence is possible, although with a much lower probability, since (**444**d) gives no indication *when* a rare event has to occur in a series of tests. *With random events no such forecast can be made when the tests are independent.*

9B. Significance limits

The example given above demonstrates that significance tests can be performed with the aid of confidence limits:

In a significance test based on *confidence or tolerance limits*, 1 or 2 *randomly variable limiting values* are compared with a known or hypothetical *fixed parameter value* (cf. Fig. 21, left). (**458**)

Many significance tests are performed with the aid of significance limits:

In a significance test based on *significance limits* in the usual sense, 1 or 2 *constant limiting values* are compared with a *randomly variable test statistic* (cf. Fig. 21, right). (**459**)

It is *immaterial* whether significance tests are made on the basis of confidence and tolerance limits or on the basis of significance limits in the usual sense: the result is the same (cf. Fig. 21, left and right). With both methods it is valid to deduce a significant difference [cf. (**381**), (**382**), (**394**), (**413**), (**414**) and (**420**)] *when the test statistic lies at or outside the limits*. (**460**)

Confidence limits, tolerance limits and significance limits are intimately bound up with one another: (**461**)

- either they differ from one another merely symbolically and are numerically identical (a)
- or they differ in respect of formula and numerical value, with the formulae mutually interconvertible. (b)

Example 17 [of (**461** a)]. In the binomial distribution

↑ $\boldsymbol{p}_l < p < \boldsymbol{p}_r$	are significance limits for p
↓ $p_l < \boldsymbol{p} < p_r$	are confidence limits for $\boldsymbol{p}$

where $\boldsymbol{p}$ are constants and p random variables. When $p = \boldsymbol{p}$, then $\boldsymbol{p}_l = p_l$ and $\boldsymbol{p}_r = p_r$ (for the same sample size).

Example 18 [of (**461** b)]. $\bar{x}$ is the mean, $s_{\bar{x}}$ the estimated standard deviation of the mean of a sample from a normally distributed population. μ_1 is the mean of the hypothetical population, t the significance limit (corresponding to the sample size and desired significance probability) of the Student distribution (see section 12A, page 166). Then

↑ $\bar{x} - t s_{\bar{x}} < \mu_1 < \bar{x} + t s_{\bar{x}}$	are confidence limits for μ_1
$-t s_{\bar{x}} < \bar{x} - \mu_1 < +t s_{\bar{x}}$	are neither confidence limits nor significance limits in the usual sense (like the test statistic, the limits are random variables)
↓ $-t < \dfrac{\bar{x} - \mu_1}{s_{\bar{x}}} < +t$	are significance limits for $\dfrac{\bar{x} - \mu_1}{s_{\bar{x}}}$

All three formulae are suitable for testing the null hypothesis $\mu_0 = \mu_1$ [see (**466**)]. This is done by replacing μ_1 by the hypothetical comparison parameter μ_0 and noting the position of the latter with regard to the limits. The simplest formula (for beginners) is the first, the second allows the quickest calculation, while the third is that most commonly used.

When the simple term 'limits' is used here in connection with significance tests [cf. (**460**) and (**461**) and their examples], then those limits are meant which conform with rules (**376**) and (**377**) or (**409**) and (**410**), depending on the population under consideration.

All limits suitable for significance tests converge absolutely or relatively with increasing sample size or with increasing numbers of samples of the same size [when (**432**) holds]. The statements in (**443**) and (**449**) concerning confidence and tolerance limits are valid for all such limits. (**462**)

It follows from (**462**) that:

(**463**)

- With increasing sample size, any difference existing can be demonstrated more and more significantly. (a)
- With increasing sample size, smaller and smaller differences can be demonstrated for any given significance probability. (b)

When there is a real difference – shown by small samples to be significant – between a real and a hypothetical population, then with increasing sample size the assumption that the real population *differs* from the hypothetical will be *confirmed* (usually) with increasing significance (cf. Fig. 22a). (c)

When there is a real difference that *cannot* be shown with small samples to be significant between a real and a hypothetical population, then with increasing sample size the assumption that the real population is *the same* as the hypothetical will be *controverted* (as a rule) (cf. Fig. 22b). (d) **(463)**

When there is in fact *no* difference between a real and a hypothetical population, then it *may* be possible to demonstrate this with some certainty with very large samples (with complete certainty only with infinitely large samples). (e)

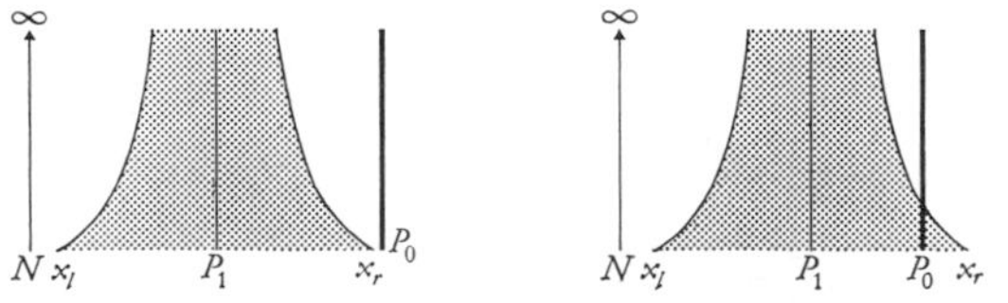

a [cf. (**463**c)] b [cf. (**463**d)]

Fig. 22 a and b. P_0 is the hypothetical parameter, P_1 that to be tested; x_l and x_r are the confidence limits of P_1 converging with increasing sample size.

9 C. Significance tests

General

All statistical tests are based on the fundamental principle of comparing an *unknown population* from which the sample originates with a *known or hypothetical population*. **(464)**

All statistical tests confirm with precise significance probability only differences between the populations compared, *not* their identity [cf. also (**463**)]. **(465)**

The hypothesis H_0 that 2 populations are identical is known as the *null hypothesis*. As implied in (**465**), it is usually postulated in order to be *disproved*. **(466)**

The expression null hypothesis is derived from the postulated identity of the population P_1 from which the sample originates with the hypothetical population P_0, whence $P_1 = P_0$, so that $P_1 - P_0 = 0$ (null).

When a statistical test* 'demonstrates' a difference between two populations with a significance probability α or 2α [cf. (**460**)], then if α is sufficiently small, the null hypothesis may be regarded as provisionally disproved, and the alternative hypothesis – that the populations are different – is provisionally accepted. The probability of making an *error of the first kind* in this decision, i.e., of rejecting the null hypothesis when it is true, in other words of determining a difference where none exists, is α or 2α. **(467)**

The probability of making an *error of the second kind*, i.e., of accepting the null hypothesis when it is untrue, in other words of not determining a difference where one exists, is β. The probabilities α and β are closely related: as α decreases β increases, and vice versa (note, however, that β is *not* $1-\alpha$ or $1-2\alpha$; the reader is referred to more advanced statistical treatises for a detailed discussion of this relationship). **(468)**

With increasing sample size it can be arranged that the probabilities of making an error of the first or second kind both decrease. **(469)**

Remarks on (**467**) and (**468**): When it is important to avoid making an error of the first kind, i.e., when it is necessary to be quite certain that a difference exists before accepting it, then a small value of α or 2α is chosen, say between 10^{-2} and 10^{-6} or less, according to the risk it is permissible to take.

* In the subsequent text the word 'test' is used to mean 'statistical test'.

On the other hand, in a series of experiments designed to *uncover* a difference, larger values of α or 2α are chosen, say between 0.2 and 0.05. In any later and more elaborate experiments the significance probability can always be reduced in order to increase the certainty of a difference already disclosed. However, even though a difference has a significance probability in large samples of only 0.1 it is permissible in some circumstances (for example, with drugs that are life-saving) to reject the null hypothesis. The physician would willingly take the risk that in one case out of ten he has failed to administer a better drug. The tendency in medical and biological investigations is to use *too small* a significance probability.

Power of a test

The probability $1-\beta$, i.e., the probability of disclosing a difference when one actually exists, is known as the *power* of a test. **(470)**

From (**469**) it follows that the power of a test can be increased (usually) by increasing the sample size. **(471)**

The *more* that is *known* about the populations being compared, the *more powerful* are the tests which can (but need not) be carried out on the basis of this knowledge. (Less powerful tests can be used in such cases if they are adequate to meet the purpose in hand.) **(472)**

Remarks on (**472**): A useful analogy is that of the police searching for a criminal: the more that is known about him, the more effective (more powerful) will the search (the test) be.

The *relative* power of different tests having the same object can *only* be decided by their use on *known* populations. **(473)**

Remarks on (**473**): The relative power of a test (previously calculated on the basis of some specific situation) is thus useless as a criterion in any situation in which the populations to be compared are unknown. In such cases care should be taken not to confuse known facts with *assumptions*. The results of statistical tests based on assumptions may not be reliable (see also below).

Interpretations [cf. also (**476**)]

When the purpose of a series of experiments is to demonstrate the *identity* of two populations, then the *failure* of an appropriate test to establish a significant difference justifies acceptance of the null hypothesis as long as it is not controverted by further experimentation. **(474)**

Remarks on (**474**): It is a common mistake to consider the identity of two populations as proven when no significant difference can be shown [cf. also (**463**d and e) and Fig. 22b].

When the purpose of a series of experiments is to demonstrate a *difference* between two populations, then the *failure* of an appropriate test to establish a significant difference justifies the interpretation: 'On the basis of the present sample a difference cannot (with the significance probability used) be statistically guaranteed.' **(475)**

Remarks on (**475**): The interpretation: 'There is *no* difference' would be incorrect [cf. also (**463**d and e) and Fig. 22b].

One-tailed and two-tailed tests

When from previous experience or on theoretical grounds the nature of an assumend difference in magnitude between two parameters is known or thought to be known, then a *one-tailed* test should be made after deciding on the assumed nature of the difference in magnitude ($A < B$ or $A > B$) and on the significance probability α, conventionally 0.05 or 0.01* [cf. remarks on (**468**)]. The one-tailed test checks only one of the limits, either the left or the right, in accordance with the prearranged direction of the test, whence its name. One-tailed tests are more sensitive (more powerful) than two-tailed tests as far as the disclosure of a difference is concerned. However, they are justified only when the nature of the assumed difference in magnitude is *a priori* fairly certain for reasons other than those connected with the sample. For the interpretation of one-tailed tests see (**476**).

* When α or 2α serves as a criterion of *decision* (rejection or acceptance of the null hypothesis), then the decision as to its magnitude must be made *independently* of the sample being tested, that is to say, if the investigator is in direct contact with the sample then *before* it is taken, if he is not in direct contact with it then *before* starting the statistical analysis.

Interpretation of one-tailed tests*

Required significance	Test statistic: Hypothetical	Test statistic: Test	Interpretation and (in brackets) significance: One-tailed	Two-tailed
α	$x < x_l$	$x \leqq x_l$	$x < x_l \ (\leqq \alpha)$	None
		$x > x_l$	**(475)**	
α	$x > x_r$	$x \geqq x_r$	$x > x_r \ (\leqq \alpha)$	None
		$x < x_r$	**(475)**	

Interpretation of two-tailed tests*

2α	Uncertain	$x \leqq x_l$	$x < x_l \ (\leqq 2\alpha)$	Not equal (2α)
		$x \geqq x_r$	$x > x_r \ (\leqq 2\alpha)$	
		$x_l < x < x_r$	**(475)** or **(474)**	

(476)

In general, however, particularly at the start of an investigation, there will be considerable doubt as to which of the populations is the smaller and which the larger, even if they can be distinguished at all. In this case a *two-tailed test* should be made. If no definite choice between a one- or a two-tailed test was made before sampling then no alternative to the latter test remains. The significance probability is 2α, conventionally 0.05 or 0.01**, i.e., $\alpha = 0.025$ or 0.005 [cf. remarks on **(467)** and **(468)**]. Note that even when the two-tailed test is interpreted as a one-tailed test, the significance probability of this interpretation is still 2α.

It should also be noted that the interpretation referred to here relates to the *test statistic*. The *real* interpretation based on this may be different. **(476)** is merely a summarized form of **(381)**, **(382)**, **(392)**, **(413)**, **(414)**, **(420)**, **(474)** and **(475)**.

Conditions requiring fulfilment

It follows from **(472)** that in a situation in which several tests are available the one chosen will usually be that with the greatest power. According to **(473)**, however, the choice is only possible when the form of the populations to be compared is known. The form may be known from *previous experience* or from *theoretical considerations* (game of chance, central limit theorem), or may be deduced from the sample itself when this is very large. When the sample is small, however, particularly in complex biological, medical or psychological studies, the form of the population is often unknown. In such cases, *assumptions* concerning the form are only too often made simply for the purpose of being able to apply a 'more powerful' test [which in actual fact it may not be; cf. **(473)**]. For the following reasons this should be avoided as far as possible:

In regard to the *reliability* of a statistical test result, it is wiser to risk losing a little of the information contained in the sample and to use a test contingent on fewer conditions and involving fewer assumptions or even none at all. A possibly more powerful test would require assumptions to be made that may result in illusory information not contained in the sample. **(477)**

When the conditions on which a test is based are not, or only partly, fulfilled, then the probabilities of making an error of the first or second kind are modified in a manner difficult to estimate. The one certainty is that the probabilities *valid* when the conditions are *fulfilled* are *no longer precise* or may be misleading when the conditions are not, or only partly, fulfilled. **(478)**

First of all therefore, in situations where several tests are available, care should be taken to choose a test in which (if possible) all the conditions it involves are *actually* fulfilled in the case under consideration. **(479)**

Situations are often encountered in which a choice according to **(479)** is impossible because in none of the available tests (sometimes there is only one) can all the conditions be fulfilled. In such a case the test result should be interpreted with a degree of *caution* depending on the effects the non-fulfillment of the conditions could have in the case concerned. It is advisable to *specify the conditions which cannot be fulfilled*, for example as follows: 'On condition that both samples originate from the same normally distributed population, there exists...' **(480)**

* For discrete distributions $x < x_l + 1$ and $x > x_r - 1$ are used.
** See page 157, right-hand column, footnote.

It has already been stressed that the form of the population has an important bearing on the validity of many tests. In **(477)**–**(480)**, however, conditions for tests are mentioned in a quite general sense. The number of conditions and their 'severity' varies from test to test: obviously as many as possible should be fulfilled and not only those concerned with the form of the population. One condition which is fundamental to *all* tests is the following:

All statistical tests require that the samples should be *random* samples, that is to say, that they should be drawn by means of an operation fundamentally similar to that described in section 1, page 146. **(481)**

While this stipulation **(481)** is probably the most important condition in the whole field of statistics it is a very difficult one to fulfil completely in practice, especially in medical and biological studies. When an investigation has reached the stage of statistical testing, any nonrandom samples can probably be discarded provided that testing for nonrandomness is possible in the case concerned. Although this guards against making an erroneous decision, both time and money will have been wasted. For this reason it is advisable – *before* starting the investigation – to take all possible measures to ensure (maximum) randomness of sampling.

When as in **(479)** there are several permissible tests, no generally valid rules can be laid down as to how the choice should be made. Usually the first tests adopted will be those involving the least amount of calculation. If these do not give the postulated level of significance, they will be followed by more powerful tests from among those permissible. Such a procedure is in order* provided that it does not result in the mistake of assuming that a significance is doubly (or more than doubly) guaranteed when two (or more) tests give a significant result. The reason for this is that between many tests there exist correlations not always apparent even to the statistician: to some extent they test in the same manner but with different degrees of acuity. An analogy is provided by the viewing of an object under the microscope at three different magnifications: one is unlikely to fall into the error of assuming that its existence is triply confirmed. Similar but less easily recognizable relationships hold for tests between which there are correlations.

Example 19. Given the sample (in chronological order)

1 hour
– 0.7 hour
0.5 hour
1.1 hour
3 hours
1.2 hour
1.4 hour

Mean $\bar{x} = 1.07$ hour
Median $M = 1.1$ hour

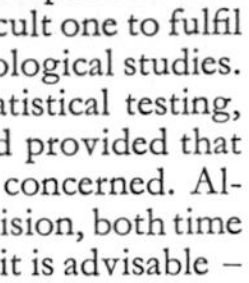

Fig. 23

representing the differences between pairs of observations on the same subject, for example after the administration of two barbiturates. The question is whether these differences differ significantly from zero ($2\alpha = 0.05$).

In such a case the following 7 tests are available (these are all given in the statistical tables preceding this chapter with the exception of the maximum test, for which the significance limits can be memorized):

Test	Stipulation regarding form of population	Calculation involved
1 Student (*t*-test).....	Normally distributed	Among these tests the most
2 Lord............	Normally distributed	About ¼ of that in 1
3 Midrange (Walsh) .	Normally distributed	Less than in 2
4 Walsh	Symmetrical	About the same as in 2
5 Sign.............	None	None
6 Maximum (Walter)	None	Arrangement only
7 Wilcoxon	None	About the same as in 2

If it is known that the sample is from a normally distributed population, then *all* of these tests can be tried. In this case the

* The editors know of no precise indications in this respect.

most powerful is the Student test, followed by the LORD and midrange tests, which are only slightly less powerful with samples of this small size. For normally distributed populations the WILCOXON test is also little inferior to the Student test.

If nothing is known of the form of the population, then tests 5, 6 and 7 must be used, in accordance with (**479**). In the event of failure of all these only the interpretation given in (**475**) remains.

In the above example the tests yield the following significances:

Test	Significance
Student	$0.025 \leqslant 2\alpha < 0.05$
LORD	$0.05 \quad < 2\alpha < 0.1$
Midrange	$0.05 \quad < 2\alpha < 0.1$
WALSH	–
Sign	$0.05 \quad < 2\alpha$
Maximum	$0.05 \quad < 2\alpha \leqslant 0.1$
WILCOXON	$2\alpha < 0.05$

The Student, midrange and WILCOXON tests yield the desired significance while the others more or less fail. This reflects the fact that when two samples are to be tested with respect to a difference in location between their populations, then as a rule for normally distributed populations it is the Student test, for populations of doubtful form the WILCOXON test that is the most powerful (of the available tests as given in the table above).

As stated in (**481**), all tests are conditional upon the samples being random samples. However, a test of the randomness of this sample made on the basis of runs on the median indicates marked nonrandomness with $\alpha \leqq 0.01$. In spite of the obvious significance, the result of the Student and WILCOXON tests is therefore merely accepted as evidence of a possible difference requiring closer investigation by further experiment.

Common sense in statistical testing

Division of the sample values in example 19 above by 10 leaves the significances resulting from the tests unchanged. This would result in a statistically 'guaranteed' difference in the action of the two barbiturates of 6 minutes on the average – in practice a meaningless difference. This illustrates the importance of looking at the *real* meaning of statistically 'guaranteed' differences before drawing conclusions from them.

It often happens that a significance probability is *almost* but not quite reached, 0.054 or 0.06 say, instead of the required 0.05. The line drawn in marking decisions must of course be a hard and fast one, but nevertheless in a case such as this the 'common-sense' course is to investigate further. However, if the results again yield not the postulated significance but one only slightly in excess of it, then the statement that 'in spite of two series of investigations no significant difference could be shown' is *untrue*. In actual fact both series point clearly in the direction of an existing difference. The only proper course in such circumstances – if changing the experimental conditions does not succeed in reducing the variance – is to carry out a *more extensive* series of investigations with the same significance probability [cf. (**463**b) and Fig. 22b, page 157].

10. Parameters

Means, variances and quantiles are dealt with only in a general manner in this section. Special formulae for calculating means and variances of various distributions are given in the sections dealing with these distributions.

10A. Mean and variance of the population

μ_x is the *mean*, σ_x^2 the *variance* of a distribution. In this text the index x will be omitted when there is no danger of confusion arising. The variance is also known as the mean-square deviation. (**482**)

The square root of the variance is known as the *standard deviation* (σ). (**483**)

The variance and standard deviation *of the mean* are expressed respectively by σ^2/N and $\sigma/\sqrt{N}$ and given the symbols $\sigma_{\bar{x}}^2$ and $\sigma_{\bar{x}}$. (**484**)

The quotient σ/μ is known as the coefficient of variance V. It is therefore the standard deviation with the mean expressed as unity. V has meaning only for *positive* values of x. (**485**)

The standard deviation is a measure of the variance. The smaller it is, the steeper the curve of the distribution, the larger it is, the flatter the curve (cf. Fig. 25). This relationship is the basis of the CHEBYSHEF Inequality:

$$\text{Prob}\,(\,|\,x - \mu\,| \geqq k\,\sigma) \leqq 1/k^2 = 2\alpha \quad (k > 1)$$

For $1/k^2 = 2\alpha = 0.05$ and 0.01, k is respectively ~ 4.5 and 10. This inequality is valid for *any* population. (**486**)

10B. Transformations

If the variable x is subject to a constant increment a, then

$$X = x \pm a$$

so that

$$\mu_X = \mu_x \pm a \qquad \sigma_X^2 = \sigma_x^2 \qquad \text{(a)}$$

The inverse transformation is

$$\mu_x = \mu_X \mp a \qquad \sigma_x^2 = \sigma_X^2 \qquad \text{(b)}$$

(**487**)

The variance is *unaffected* by a lateral displacement, i.e., it is translation-invariant.

If the variable x is increased or decreased by a constant factor a, then

$$X = a\,x$$

so that

$$\mu_X = a\,\mu_x \qquad \sigma_X^2 = a^2\,\sigma_x^2 \qquad \text{(a)}$$

The inverse transformation is

$$\mu_x = \mu_X/a \qquad \sigma_x^2 = \sigma_X^2/a^2 \qquad \text{(b)}$$

(**488**)

(**487**) and (**488**) are also valid for the estimates $\bar{x}$, $\bar{X}$ and s_x, s_X of μ_x, μ_X and σ_x, σ_X, the calculation of which they often render easier.

Example 20

(*a*) Given

$x = 145 \quad 145.5 \quad 147 \quad 147.3$ Then with $X = x - 145$
$X = 0 \quad 0.5 \quad 2 \quad 2.3$ from which values $\bar{X}$ and s_X^2 are calculated, when

$\bar{x} = \bar{X} + 145 = 1.2 + 145 = 146.2$ [$\bar{X}$ from (**491**)]
$s_x^2 = s_X^2 = 1.26$ [s_X^2 from (**493**)]

(*b*) Given

$x = 0.00325 \quad 0.00160 \quad 0.00320$ Then with $X = 10^5\,x$
$X = 325 \quad 160 \quad 320$ from which values $\bar{X}$ and s_X^2 are calculated, when

$\bar{x} = \bar{X}/10^5 = 268.\dot{3} \times 10^{-5} = 0.00268\dot{3}$ [$\bar{X}$ from (**491**)]
$s_x^2 = s_X^2/10^{10} = 8808.\dot{3} \times 10^{-10} = 8.808\dot{3} \times 10^{-7}$ [s_X^2 from (**492**)]

A variable x whose distribution has

mean $= 0$
and variance $= 1$

is known as a *standardized* variable, or variable in *standard measure*. (**489**)

If a variable x has the mean μ and the variance σ^2, then the variable

$$X = \frac{x - \mu}{\sigma} \qquad \text{(a)}$$

is in standard measure.

From the standardized variable X the original variable

$$x = \sigma\,X + \mu \qquad \text{(b)}$$

is obtained. (**490**)

(**489**) and (**490**) are in common use in statistics.

10C. Estimates of μ and σ based on ungrouped samples

The *most efficient*, *unbiased* estimate of the mean μ based on a sample from a normal population with the values $x_1, x_2, \ldots, x_N$ is

$$\bar{x} = \frac{x_1 + x_2 + \cdots + x_N}{N} = \frac{\Sigma x}{N} \qquad (491)$$

($\bar{x}$ is read as 'x bar'.)

The *most efficient, unbiased* estimate s^2 of the variance σ^2 is

(*a*) when μ is known

$$s^2 = \frac{\Sigma (x - \mu)^2}{N} = \frac{S'_x}{N}; \text{ for } S'_x \text{ see (493a and b)} \quad \text{(a)}$$

(*b*) when μ is unknown

$$s^2 = \frac{\Sigma (x - \bar{x})^2}{N-1} = \frac{S_x}{N-1}; \text{ for } S_x \text{ see (493)} \quad \text{(b)} \qquad (492)$$

The calculation of S_x (this symbol should be noted) is facilitated by the use of the following sums:

$$\left.\begin{aligned} S_x &= \Sigma (x - \bar{x})^2 \\ &= \Sigma x^2 - N\bar{x}^2 \end{aligned}\right\} \text{ for } S'_x \text{ write } \mu \text{ instead of } \bar{x} \quad \begin{matrix}\text{(a)}\\ \text{(b)}\end{matrix}$$

$$= \Sigma x^2 - \bar{x}\,\Sigma x \quad \text{(c)} \qquad (493)$$

$$= \Sigma x^2 - (\Sigma x)^2/N \quad \text{(d)}$$

$$[= s^2 (N-1)] \quad \text{(e)}$$

The most efficient *asymptotically* unbiased estimate of σ is s. In practice the bias of s can usually be neglected. Correction factors for eliminating this bias in samples from normally distributed populations are given on page 47. **(494)**

The most efficient unbiased estimate of $\sigma_{\bar{x}}^2$ is $s_{\bar{x}}^2 = s^2/N$, the most efficient asymptotically unbiased estimate of $\sigma_{\bar{x}}$ is $s_{\bar{x}} = s/\sqrt{N}$. Cf. also (**494**). **(495)**

Other estimates of σ will be dealt with later.

Example 21 [of (**491**)–(**495**)]. Given the sample of example 19, page 158,

then according to formula (**491**) $\bar{x} = 7.5/7 = 1.0714$

(**493**) $S_x = 15.35 - 8.0357 = 7.3143$

(**492**) $s^2 = 7.3143/6 = 1.2190$

(**494**) $s = \sqrt{1.2190} = 1.1041$

(**495**) $s_{\bar{x}} = 1.1041/\sqrt{7} = 0.4173$

The results should finally be rounded off to a few decimal places in order not to imply an accuracy the estimates do not possess.

10D. Estimates of μ and σ^2 based on grouped samples

Given the classes $x_1, x_2, \ldots, x_n$ with the same class width for all classes $d = x_{i+1} - x_i$ and the frequencies $f_1, f_2, \ldots, f_n$ ($N = \Sigma f_i$), a provisional mean $\bar{x}'$ is chosen falling in one class. The classes are now numbered. $\bar{x}'$ receives the number $z = 0$, the classes downwards receive the numbers $z = -1, -2, \ldots$, the classes upwards the numbers $z = 1, 2, \ldots$

Classes … $(\bar{x}' - 2)$ $(\bar{x}' - 1)$ $\bar{x}'$ $(\bar{x}' + 1)$ $(\bar{x}' + 2)$ …

z … -2 -1 0 1 2 …

Then

$$\bar{x} = \bar{x}' + d\,\frac{\Sigma f z}{N} \qquad (496)$$

$$s^2 = \frac{d^2}{N-1}\left(\Sigma (f z^2) - \frac{(\Sigma f z)^2}{N}\right) \qquad (497)$$

SHEPPARD's *correction*

In the grouping of the individual values into classes a small error arises as a result of the random choice of the individual values. This introduces a small error into the estimate of the variance that can be corrected by subtraction of $k = 0.08\dot{3}$ (i.e., of 1/12) from the variance estimated in class units. This correction (SHEPPARD's correction) can be dispensed with in the testing of differences for significance but is otherwise to be recommended.

$$\text{SHEPPARD's correction: } s^2_{\text{corr.}} = s^2 - \frac{d^2}{12} \qquad (498)$$

Example 22. Diameter of erythrocytes. Class width $d = 0.4$ µm.

Class	Frequency f	Deviation z	Frequency × deviation fz	Frequency × square of deviation $fz^2 = fz \cdot z$
5.6	5	− 4	− 20	80
6.0	78	− 3	− 234	702
6.4	144	− 2	− 288	576
6.8	479	− 1	− 479	479
$7.2 = \bar{x}'$	542	0	0	0
7.6	358	+ 1	+ 358	358
8.0	279	+ 2	+ 558	1114
8.4	99	+ 3	+ 297	891
8.8	15	+ 4	+ 60	240
9.2	1	+ 5	+ 5	25
	$\Sigma(f) = N = 2000$		$\Sigma(fz) = 257$	$\Sigma(fz^2) = 4467$

$$\bar{x} = 7.2 + 0.4\,\frac{257}{2000} = 7.251 \text{ µm}$$

$$s^2 = 0.4^2\,\frac{4467 - 33.0}{1999} = 0.4^2 \times 2.218;$$

$s = 0.4\sqrt{2.218} = 0.596$ µm without SHEPPARD's correction

$s^2 = 0.4^2 (2.218 - 0.0833) = 0.4^2 (2.135)$;

$s = 0.4\sqrt{2.135} = 0.584$ µm with SHEPPARD's correction

10E. Quantiles of continuous distributions

Definition: In $p = F(x)$, x is known as the *quantile* (p), here given the symbol $Q(p)$ or x_p. Quantiles are thus the *inverse function* of $F(x)$; they are so-called parameters of position. The quantile has also been given the name fractile. On $F(x)$ see also (**401**) and (**402**).

The quantiles most commonly used are given special names: **(499)**

Quantile	Probability p
Quartile	$0.25 \times n$ ($n = 1, 2, 3, 4$)
Median	0.5 (= 2nd quartile)
Decile	$0.1 \times n$ ($n = 1, 2, \ldots, 10$)
Percentile	$0.01 \times n$ ($n = 1, 2, \ldots, 100$)

Interpretation of a quantile (p) of a continuous population:
$100p$% of the population lie below the quantile
$100(1-p)$% of the population lie above the quantile. **(500)**

Example 23. See Figure 8 (quartiles and median of a normal distribution), page 151.

Estimation

(*a*) *Ungrouped samples.* The quantile $\boldsymbol{Q}(p)$ of a population is estimated by calculating the corresponding quantile $Q(p)$ of a sample taken from it. The sample values x are arranged in order of magnitude [cf. (**342**)] and numbered serially, the smallest value receiving the number 1. These *order numbers* are known as the *ranks* of the sample values x, so that

$$x_1 < x_2 < x_3 < \cdots < x_N$$

The quantile $Q(p)$ thus corresponds to the sample value with the rank $O(p)$:

$$O(p) = Np + 0.5 \left(\text{for } \frac{1}{N} \leq p \leq \frac{N-1}{N}\right) \qquad (501\text{a})$$

If $O(p)$ is a whole number, the quantile $Q(p)$ *coincides with* the sample value; if $O(p)$ is a fraction, the quantile (p) *lies between* the sample values with ranks adjacent to $O(p)$, i.e., between x_i and x_{i+1}. There would be little point in interpolating between these two values.

If the sequence of ordered sample values contains ties [cf. (**346**)] and $O(p)$ falls on or between the ranks of tied values, then $Q(p)$ is given the magnitude of these tied values provided that the number of such ties is small compared with the sample size. In samples with very many ties (few classes and high frequencies) there is no point in determining quantiles in accordance with (**501** a).

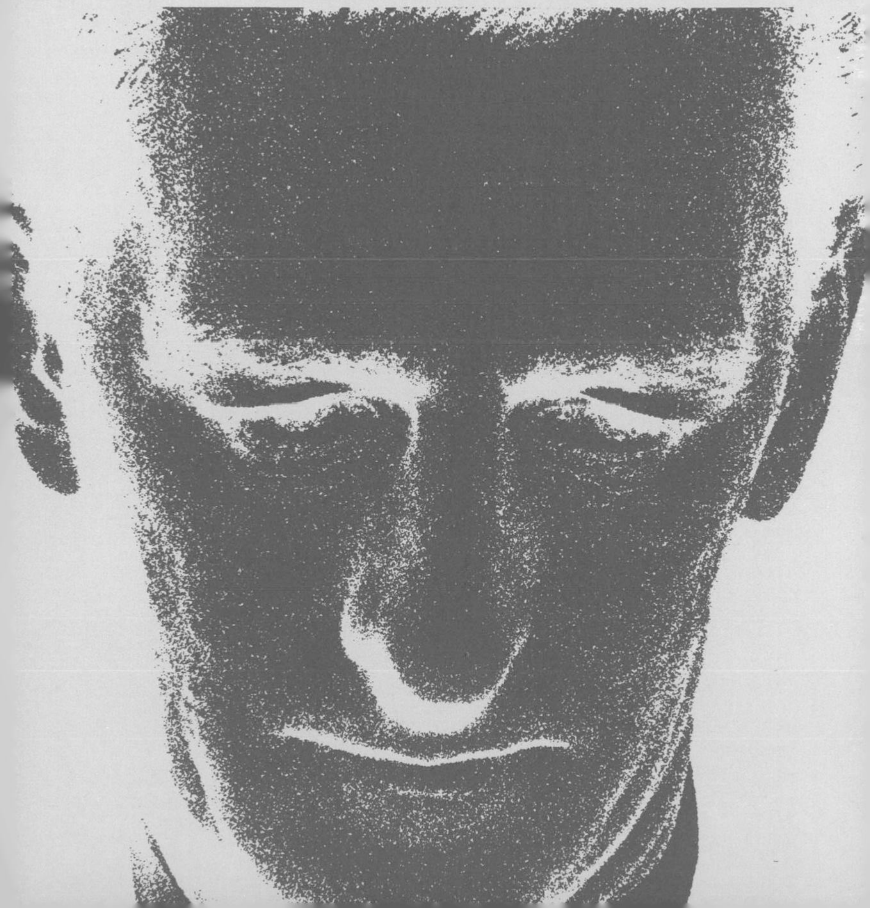

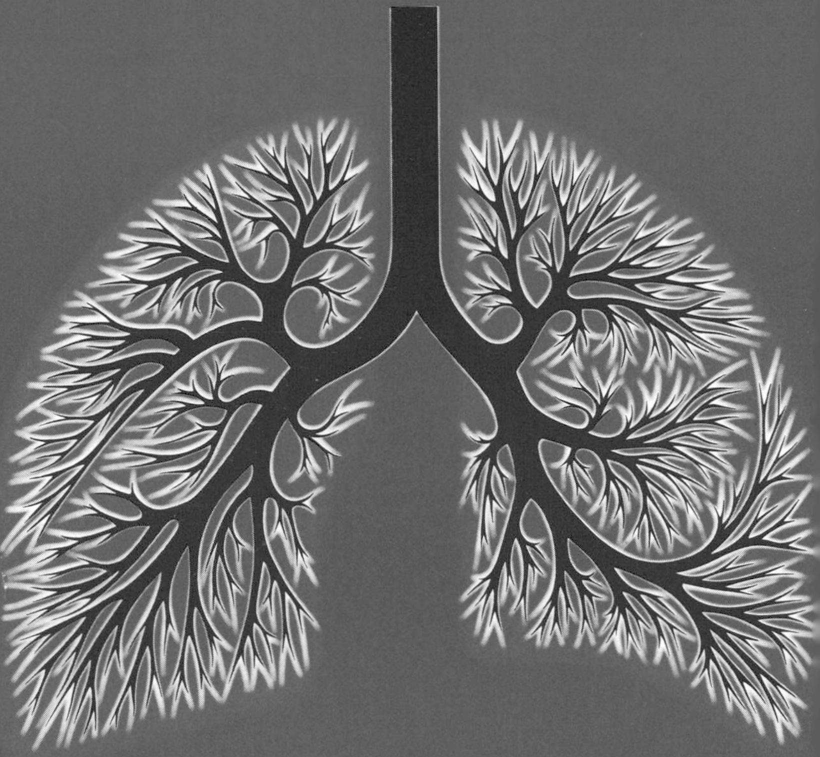

Example 24. Given the ranked sample

x:	1.75	1.76	1.76	1.77	1.78	1.79	1.80	1.81	1.82	1.84	1.86
O:	1	2	3	4	5	6	7	8	9	10	11

x:	1.86	1.93	1.95	2.00	2.07	2.18	2.35	2.68	3.56	4.41
O:	12	13	14	15	16	17	18	19	20	21

it is required to find the 1st quartile, median and percentile (0.7). In accordance with (**501** a)

$O(0.25) = 0.25 \times 21 + 0.5 = 5.75$
[$Q(0.25)$ lies between 1.78 and 1.79]

$O(0.5) = 0.5 \times 21 + 0.5 = 11$
[$Q(0.5) = 1.86$ (note the tie)]

$O(0.7) = 0.7 \times 21 + 0.5 = 15.2$
[$Q(0.7)$ lies between 2.00 and 2.07]

(*b*) *Grouped samples.* Given are the ranked classes $x_1, x_2, \dots x_i, \dots x_n$, with class width $d = x_{i+1} - x_i$, and class frequencies $f_1, f_2, \dots f_i, \dots f_n$, where $f_1 + f_2 + \dots + f_n = N$, the sample size.

The cumulative frequencies are written as follows: $f_1 = F(1)$, $f_1 + f_2 = F(2)$, $f_1 + f_2 + f_3 = F(3)$, up to $f_1 + f_2 + \dots + f_n = F(i)$. Np is now compared with $F(i)$:

If $Np = F(i)$, then $Q(p) = x_i + \frac{1}{2} d$.

If Np lies between $F(i)$ and $F(i+1)$, then $Q(p)$ lies between $x_i + \frac{1}{2} d$ and $x_{i+1} + \frac{1}{2} d$. (**501** b)

10F. Distribution-free confidence limits for quantiles of continuous distributions

(Cf. also section 8C, page 155)

Apart from their importance as the inverse function of $F(x)$, quantiles are useful in practice for two reasons: on the one hand their estimates $Q(p)$ can be obtained with a minimum of calculation*; on the other hand, exact confidence limits can be constructed for the parameter $\mathbf{Q}(p)$ with no knowledge at all of the form of the distribution from which the sample is drawn. The mathematical definition and method of calculating distribution-free confidence limits for quantiles are given in section 20F (c), page 187.

The ranks $O(p)$ for distribution-free confidence limits for quantiles with various values of $p \leq 0.5$ and samples of size up to $N = 100$ can be read directly from the table on page 104. The ranks $O(p)$ for the median and sample sizes up to $N = 1000$ are given in the tables on pages 105 and 106.

The procedure is as follows: The limits x_l and x_r corresponding to the sample size N and the probability $p \leq 0.5$ are looked for in the table. If $p > 0.5$ it is subtracted from 1, giving $p' = (1 - p) < 0.5$. For p' the limits x_l and x_r, symbolized by x_l' and x_r', are looked for in the same way. The ranks $O(p)$ that fix the confidence limits in the sample are then

for $p \leq 0.5$: $O(p)_l = x_l + 1$ and $O(p)_r = x_r$
for $p > 0.5$: $O(p)_l = N - x_r' + 1$ and $O(p)_r = N - x_l'$ (**502**)

Example 25. For the sample in example 24 the 95% confidence limits are as follows:

Quantile	Ranks	95% confidence limits
1st quartile.....	$1 + 1 = 2$ and 10	$1.76 < \mathbf{Q}(p) < 1.84$
Median........	$5 + 1 = 6$ and 16	$1.79 < \mathbf{Q}(p) < 2.07$
Percentile (0.7) .	$21 - 12 + 1 = 10$ and $21 - 1 = 20$	$1.84 < \mathbf{Q}(p) < 3.56$

10G. Relations between mode, median and mean of continuous distributions

The abscissa x of the maximum value of the density function $f(x)$ is known as the *mode*. (**503**)

In practice the mode is of little importance. On $f(x)$ see (**400**).

In one-peaked *symmetrical* distributions the *mode, median and mean are coincident*, but not in unsymmetrical distributions (cf. Fig. 31, page 165). The relationship between the three parameters is expressed by

Median $\sim \frac{2}{3}$ mean $+ \frac{1}{3}$ mode (**504**)

* In the case of large samples the time saved here will be offset by that lost in ranking the sample.

Of main importance in practice is the *identity* of the *median* and the *mean* in *symmetrical* distributions: the distribution-free confidence limits for the median are valid also for the mean. It follows that:

If the population mean $\bar{x}$ of a sample coincides with either of the distribution-free confidence limits for the population median or lies outside them, then with a significance probability $\leq 2\alpha$, the sample *does not* originate from a symmetrical distribution. (**505**)

This is the basis of the sign test, which is easily carried out and also independent of the form of the population.

10H. The sign test

(*a*) *Testing a sample for symmetry.* $\bar{x}$ is calculated, and the sample values, including $\bar{x}$, are ranked. The number $N(-)$ of samples smaller than $\bar{x}$ is then counted, and the levels x_l and x_r corresponding to the sample size N and the significance probability 2α looked for in the table on pages 105 and 106. If the number $N(-)$ coincides with either of these levels or lies outside them, then interpretation (**505**) applies.

Example 26. In example 24 in section 10E, $\bar{x} = 2.130$, $N(-) = 16$. For $N = 21$ and $2\alpha = 0.05$, the table on page 105 gives the levels 5–16. With a significance probability of 0.05, the sample *does not* originate from a symmetrical distribution.

(*b*) *Testing of pair differences (differences between pairs of observations).* In such cases the null hypothesis is that the differences do not on the average differ from zero, or rather that the numbers of differences respectively smaller than and larger than zero are the same. The median is therefore zero. As in (*a*) above, the number $N(-)$ of differences which are smaller than zero, i.e., negative, is counted; in other words, the number $N(-)$ of *minus signs* is counted. The further procedure is as in (*a*).

Example 27. Of 500 pair differences, 210 are negative. Do these 500 differences differ on the average from zero ($2\alpha = 0.05$)? For $2\alpha = 0.05$ and $N = 500$ the table on page 105 gives the levels 227 to 273, so that the difference from zero is confirmed with the desired significance.

Note that if in (*a*) above $\bar{x}$ *coincides* with one of the sample values (or in the case of ties, with 2, 3, ... sample values), or if in (*b*) above 1, 2, ... of the pair differences are equal to zero, then the sample size with which the table is entered must be reduced by 1, 2, ... More powerful, but involving somewhat more calculation, is the Wilcoxon test for pair differences. For *small* samples a desired significance can be more easily reached with this test than with the sign test. Cf. also example 19 on page 158. For samples of over 50 there is no longer much difference between the two tests (as far as power is concerned; in the Wilcoxon test the amount of calculation involved increases rapidly with increasing sample size). Pair differences can also be examined by sequential analysis (cf. section 26, page 196).

11. The normal distribution

[Cf. also section 6, page 151. For the meaning of 'normal' see (**455**)]

11A. Definition and characteristics

The normal distribution is a *continuous* distribution, the probability density function for which is defined by

$$f(x) = \frac{1}{\sigma\sqrt{2\pi}} e^{-\frac{1}{2}\left(\frac{x-\mu}{\sigma}\right)^2} \qquad (506)$$

(μ = mean, σ = standard deviation; for π and e see page 132)

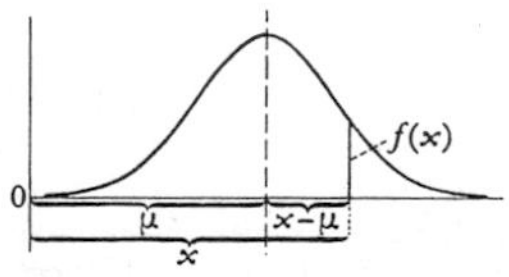

Fig. 24

The curve of the probability density function is *symmetrical* and bell-shaped, that of the cumulative probability distribution $F(x)$ is sigmoid (cf. Figs. 8 and 9). The range of variation of the variable x is from $-\infty$ to ∞. The normal distribution is often criticized on this score since it implies, for example, that the existence of human beings 9 feet tall or more should be 'possible' *. However, the word 'possible' is here inappropriate. 'Almost impossible' would be better, since the probability of extreme deviations from the mean decreases rapidly in the normal distribution.

If Prob ($|x - \mu| \geqq k\sigma$) $\leqq 2\alpha$, 2α changes with increasing k as follows[10]: **(507)**

k	2α	k	2α
1	3.173105×10^{-1}	6	1.973175×10^{-9}
2	4.550026×10^{-2}	7	2.559625×10^{-12}
3	2.699796×10^{-3}	8	1.244192×10^{-15}
4	6.334248×10^{-5}	9	2.257177×10^{-19}
5	5.733031×10^{-7}	10	1.523971×10^{-23}

Remarks on (**507**): In accordance with the CHEBYSHEF Inequality [cf. (**486**)], the probability that in *any* distribution the variable x falls outside the limit $\mu \pm 3\sigma$, for example, is less than 1/9; as (**507**) shows, however, in the normal distribution it is only $\sim 3/1000$. On the other hand, these much closer limits are valid *only* when the population is *in fact* normal. The inverse deduction should therefore also be noted, namely that should a distribution for which the 3σ limits are regarded as adequate *not* be normal, then the probability that the variable x falls outside these limits is *not* 3/1000 but may be as large as 1/9. This is an excellent illustration of (**478**).

As with all symmetrical distributions, the mode, median and mean of the normal distribution are coincident. Their ordinate is the axis of symmetry of the curve of the probability density function [cf. Fig. 24 and (**504**)]. The most important consequences in practice are the following:

With a significance probability $\leqq 2\alpha$, a sample that fails to pass the test for symmetry *does not* originate from a normally distributed population. **(508)**

If a *fairly small* sample passes the symmetry test [cf. also (**474**)], then the population from which it is drawn may still not be normal**. However, in significance tests (cf. page 158, 'Conditions requiring fulfilment') the stipulation of normality may be regarded as *almost* fulfilled. **(509)**

For *small* samples the sign test used for testing symmetry is relatively insensitive, that is, it will disclose an actual lack of symmetry in a population much more rarely with small samples than with large ones. For this reason (**509**) is valid only for *fairly small* samples. For small samples therefore, significance tests should be used – provided they are available – in which there are no conditions regarding symmetry or normality.

As (**506**) shows, the normal distribution is *fully* characterized by the two parameters μ and σ. The mean determines the *position* of the distribution with respect to the x axis, the standard deviation the *shape* of the curve: the larger σ is, the flatter the curve (cf. Fig. 25).

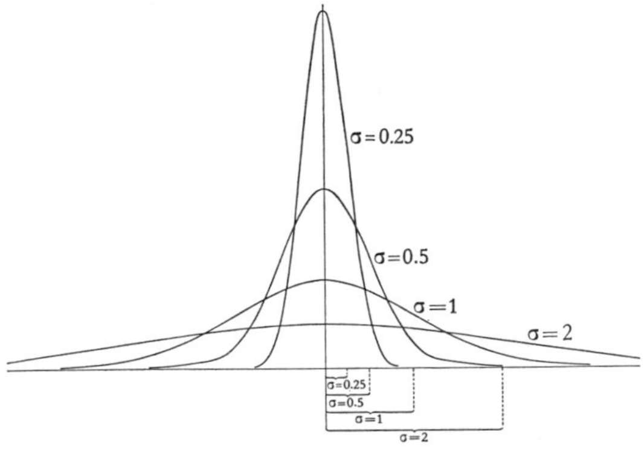

Fig. 25. Normal distributions with various standard deviations.

Since μ and σ can have any values, the number of possible normally distributed populations is infinite. If these are standardized according to (**490** a), they are *all* transformed into *single* standardized normal distributions.

11B. The standardized normal distribution

If the quotient $(x - \mu)/\sigma$ in (**490** a) is denoted by c, then (**506**) becomes the *standardized normal distribution* (with *zero mean* and *unit standard deviation*):

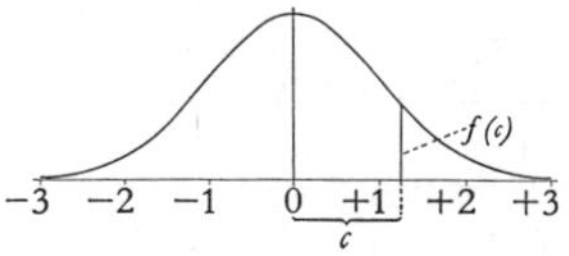

$$f(c) = \frac{1}{\sqrt{2\pi}}\, e^{-c^2/2} \quad \textbf{(510)}$$

Fig. 26. Standardized normal distribution.

The symmetry of the distribution gives rise to the following relationships:

Probability density function

$$f(0) = \max f(c) = 0.398942 \quad \textbf{(511)}$$

$$f(-c) = f(c) \quad \textbf{(512)}$$

Probabilities

$$F(0) = \text{Prob}\,(c < 0) = \text{Prob}\,(c > 0) = \tfrac{1}{2} \quad \textbf{(513)}$$

$$\left.\begin{aligned} \text{Prob}\,(c < -k) &= \text{Prob}\,(c > k) && \text{(a)} \\ &= F(-k) = 1 - F(k) && \text{(b)} \end{aligned}\right\} \quad \textbf{(514)}$$

$$\text{Prob}\,(-k \leqq c \leqq 0) = \text{Prob}\,(0 \leqq c \leqq k) \quad \textbf{(515)}$$

Quantiles

$$Q(\tfrac{1}{2}) = 0 \quad \textbf{(516)}$$

$$Q(p) = -Q(1 - p) \quad \textbf{(517)}$$

11C. Tables of the standardized normal distribution (pages 28–31)

Page	Table relates to	Left-hand side	Right-hand side
28	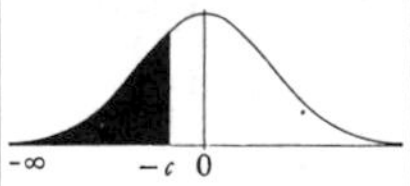	Inverse function of the integral → = Quantile $Q(p)$ = $c(p)$ Argument p	$\int_{-\infty}^{c} f(c)\,dc = F(c) = p(c)$ Argument c
29	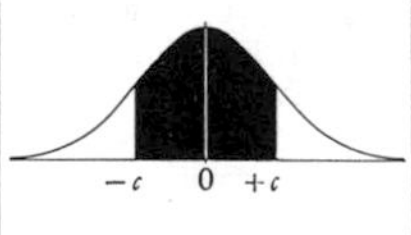	Inverse function of the integral → = $c(p')$ Argument p'	$\int_{-c}^{c} f(c)\,dc = p'(c)$ Argument c
30	Left-hand side 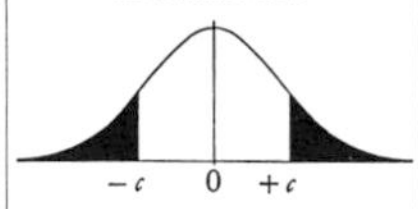	$1 - \int_{-c}^{c} f(c)\,dc = 2P$ Argument c *	
	Right-hand side 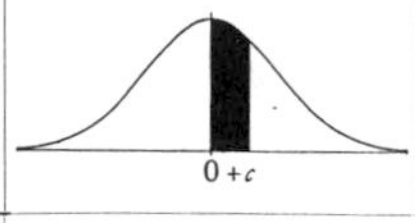		$\int_{0}^{c} f(c)\,dc = \int_{-c}^{0} f(c)\,dc$ Argument c
31	Upper: ordinate $f(c)$, argument c. Cf. Fig. 26. Lower: inverse function of $1 - \int_{-c}^{c} f(c)\,dc$		

* For inverse function see page 31.

11D. Conversion of a normal distribution into the standardized form and vice versa

(Cf. also section 10B, page 159)

The statement 'normal distribution with mean μ and standard deviation σ' is here abbreviated to 'normal distribution (μ; σ)'. **(518)**

* Although they may appear illogical, limits according to probability are more logical than absolute limits. The statement, for instance, that there is an *absolute* limit to the height of the human body at, say, 8′ 3″, would manifestly be untenable.

** Symmetrical distributions that are not normal also exist.

The normal distribution (μ; σ) of the variable x is converted into the standardized normal distribution (0; 1) of the variable c (and vice versa) by substituting X of (**490**) by c. (**519**)

In this conversion the probabilities of the converted values remain *unchanged*, so that

$$\text{Prob}\,(x < x_k) = \text{Prob}\,(c < c_k) \qquad (\mathbf{520})$$

Example 28. Given the normal distribution (174; 7), how large are the probabilities of the events $x < 160$, $x > 181$, $162 \leqq x \leqq 179$?

From (**520**)

$$\frac{160-174}{7} = -2, \qquad \frac{181-174}{7} = 1,$$

$$\frac{162-174}{7} \sim -1.71, \qquad \frac{179-174}{7} \sim 0.71$$

whence

Prob $(c < -2) = F(-2) = 0.02275$ (from the right-hand table on page 28)

Prob $(c > 1) =$ Prob $(c < -1)$ [cf. (**514**a)] $= 0.15866$ (from the same table)

Prob $(-1.71 \leqq c \leqq 0.71)$: Prob $(-1.71 \leqq c \leqq 0)$, from (**515**),
$=$ Prob $(0 \leqq c \leqq 1.71)$, whence the total probability,
Prob $(-1.71 \leqq c \leqq 0.71)$
$=$ Prob $(0 \leqq c \leqq 1.71)$ + Prob $(0 \leqq c \leqq 0.71)$
$= 0.45637 + 0.26115 = 0.71752$ (from the right-hand table on page 30).

Example 29. Given the normal distribution of example 28, it is required to find

(*a*) the one-sided confidence limit x_l for $1 - \alpha_l = 0.95$
(*b*) the one-sided confidence limit x_r for $1 - \alpha_r = 0.99$
(*c*) the two-sided confidence limits x_l and x_r for $1 - 2\alpha = 0.95$.

Solution:

All confidence limits or significance limits are quantiles (α):

(*a*) c_l is the quantile (α_l), where $\alpha_l = 1 - 0.95 = 0.05$. From the left-hand table on page 28, $c_l = -1.6449$, whence $x_l = -1.6449 \times 7 + 174 = 162.4857$.

(*b*) c_r is the quantile $(1 - \alpha_r) = Q(0.99)$. From the left-hand table on page 28, $c_r = 2.3263$, whence $x_r = 2.3263 \times 7 + 174 = 190.2841$.

(*c*) α is here $(1 - 0.95)/2 = 0.025$. Since according to (**517**) the quantile (0.025) is numerically equal to the quantile $(1 - 0.025)$, only the former need be looked for in the left-hand table on page 28. This gives $c = -1.960$, whence $x_l = -1.960 \times 7 + 174 = 160.28$, and $x_r = 1.960 \times 7 + 174 = 187.72$. Even simpler to obtain are the two-sided limits, namely from the left-hand table on page 29, using the deviation c, which can be read off directly by entering with the probability $1 - 2\alpha$.

In connection with examples 28 and 29 it should be noted that, in practice, calculations are made with only as many decimal places as are required. However, it is advisable for beginners to complete the calculation with the full number of decimal places and then round off the result to the required number.

11E. The probit transformation

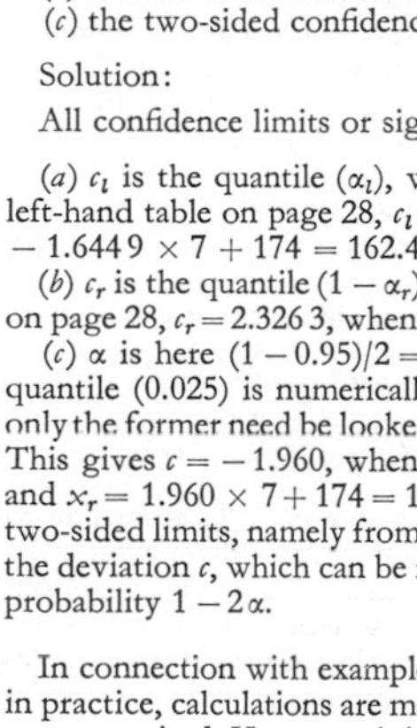

Fig. 27a

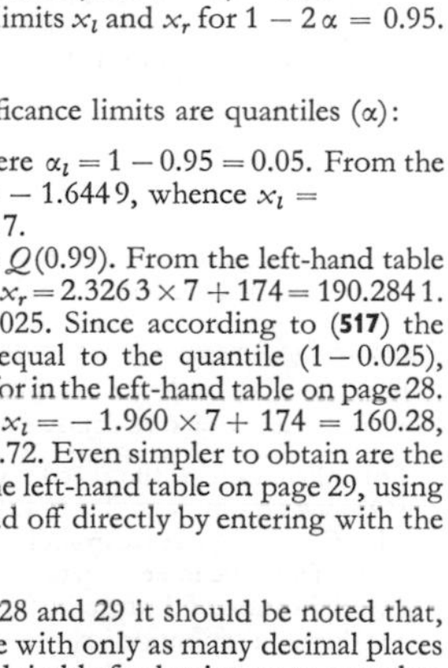

Fig. 27b

The standardized variable $(x - \mu)/\sigma$ can be broken down in accordance with (**34**) into the fractions $-\mu/\sigma$ and x/σ. If $-\mu/\sigma = a$ and $1/\sigma = b$, then

$$c = a + bx, \text{ where } a = -b\mu \text{ and } b = 1/\sigma \qquad (\mathbf{521})$$

In accordance with (**299**), the curve of (**521**) is a *straight line* (cf. Fig. 27a).

The straight line of (**521**) passes through the point (μ; 0). When μ and σ are known its construction therefore only requires *one* other point to be calculated from (**521**). (**522**)

If the straight line in Fig. 27b is displaced 5 units in the direction of the ordinate axis, then

$$c + 5 = \text{probit}^{11} = a + bx = 5 + b(x - \mu), \text{ whence } a = 5 - b\mu \text{ and } b = 1/\sigma \qquad (\mathbf{523})$$

The straight line of (**523**) passes through the point (μ; 5). When μ and σ are known its construction therefore only requires *one* other point to be calculated from (**523**). (**524**)

Since deviations of more than 5 σ are rare, the displacement of (**521**)–(**523**) means that in practice the majority of probit calculations can be carried out in the upper right quadrant (i.e., $c + 5 > 0$).

If the corresponding $F(c)$ values, which in accordance with (**520**) have the same magnitude as the $F(x)$ values, are now inscribed on the ordinate axis alongside the c or $(c + 5)$ scale it will be seen at once that the sigmoid curve can be transformed in this way into a straight line. The following therefore apply to probit calculations on samples:

If the ordinate and abscissa scales are linear scales (cf. the extreme left-hand scale in Fig. 28) and if now in place of $F(x_p)$ the quantiles c_p or probits $c_p + 5$ are plotted in the ordinate direction and x_p in the abscissa direction, then with increasing sample size the points $[x_p;\ c_p]$ or $[x_p;$ probit$]$ will converge stochastically toward the straight line (**521**) or (**523**) provided that the random variable x is normally distributed. (**525**)

If the abscissa axis is divided linearly and the ordinate axis in percentiles $c(0.01 \times n)$ or probits $(0.01 \times n)$, where $n = 1, 2, \ldots, 100$, and if the probabilities $F(c)$ or percentages $100F(c)\%$ corresponding to the latter are entered on the ordinate scale (cf. Fig. 28, right-hand vertical scale) and $F(x_p)$ or $100F(x_p)\%$ is plotted in the ordinate direction and x_p in the abscissa direction, then with increasing sample size the points $[x_p;\ F(x_p)]$ or $[x_p;\ 100F(x_p)\%]$ will converge stochastically toward a straight line provided that the random variable x is normally distributed. (**526**)

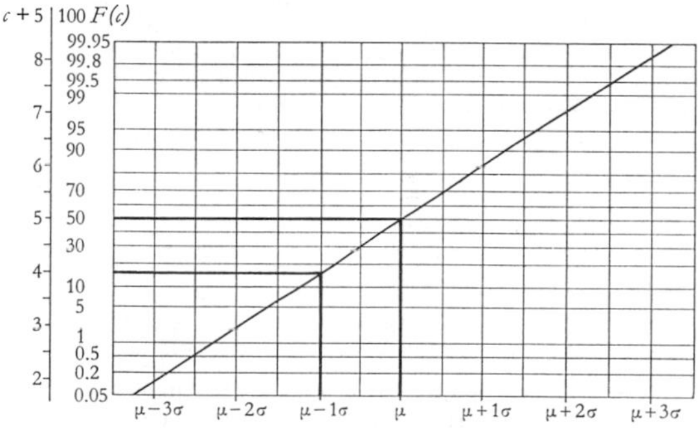

Fig. 28. Probit scale ($= c + 5$) and scale of probability paper.

The operations of (**526**) are carried out on probability paper, those of (**525**) by means of the probit transformation. Here only the latter method, of which further examples are given in later sections, will be used. Tables of probits are given on pages 54 and 55. For descriptions of the *maximum likelihood* method of estimating probit regression lines in those cases where the latter must be used, i.e., when μ and σ cannot be estimated from (**491**) and (**492**), the reader is referred to the literature[12].

11F. Fitting of normal curves to samples

Normal curves *fitted* to the sample are required when it is desired either to make a test of non-normality (either by eye or exactly) or to illustrate this condition. The above-mentioned exact tests for non-normality are more powerful than, for example, the equally exact symmetry test, since the *whole* of the empirical curve of the sample is compared with the normal curve fitted to it, with the result that these tests utilize *all* the information that can be extracted from the sample. For this reason such tests are known as tests of *goodness of fit*. If the test is to be carried out exactly, which here amounts to a χ^2 test, two conditions must be met: the sample must be grouped, and the parameters μ and σ must be estimated by means of $\bar{x}$ and s in accordance with (**491**) and (**492**) [cf. the remarks on these equations and also (**430**)]. *In equations used in testing for goodness of fit, μ and σ are replaced by $\bar{x}$ and s.*

(a) Ungrouped samples

With ungrouped samples, empirical and fitted probit values can be compared only by eye. From (**499**) and (**501** a) it follows that

$$p_i = F(x_i) = \frac{O_i - 0.5}{N} \qquad \textbf{(527)}$$

(O_i = rank of the individual sample value x_i; cf. section 10E, page 160)

The empirical and fitted probits can then be calculated from (**527**) in conjunction with (**523**)–(**525**).

Example 30. Given is the sample of example 24, section 10E, page 161. The mean $\bar{x}$ is 2.130, and the standard deviation s is 0.6713. The $F(x_i)$ values are first calculated according to (**527**): $F(x_1) = 0.5/21$, $F(x_2) = 1.5/21$, etc. [equation (**31**) is used here: $0.5/21 + 1/21 + \cdots$]. By multiplying by 100, these values are converted into percentages, which are then used in the table on pages 54 and 55 to obtain the probits. For $x_1, x_2, \ldots$ this gives the empirical probits 3.0, 3.5, 3.8, 4.0, etc. These values are plotted on millimetre paper in accordance with (**525**) to give the result shown in Figure 29.

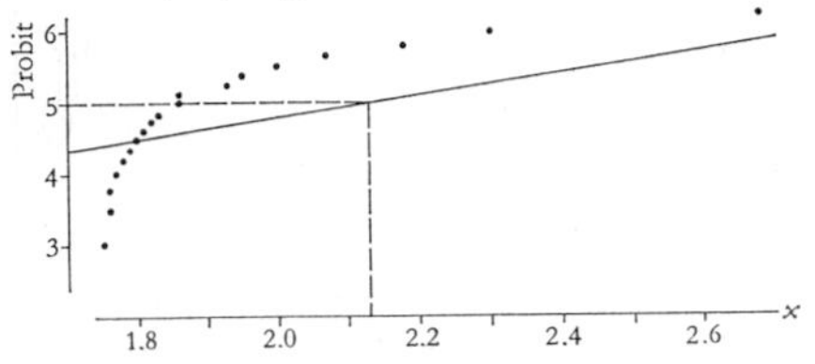

Fig. 29. Empirical probits and fitted probit line for the ungrouped sample of example 24, section 10E, page 161.

It will at once be seen that the points plotted deviate systematically from a straight line, indicating that it is very unlikely that the sample originates from a normally distributed population (as indeed was already clear from the result of the symmetry test of section 10H, page 161). If the sample had originated from a normal population, the points would have been distributed stochastically around the fitted probit line calculated in accordance with (**523**) and (**524**) from $\bar{x}$ and s in place of μ and σ.

(b) Grouped samples

In this case

$$f(x_i) = \frac{Nd}{\sigma} f(c_i), \quad c_i = \frac{x_i - \mu}{\sigma} \qquad \textbf{(528)}$$

$$F(x_i + \tfrac{1}{2} d) = \Big(\sum_{1}^{i} f_i\Big) / N \qquad \textbf{(529)}$$

(i = ranks of the classes x, $d = x_{i+1} - x_i$ = class width, f_i = frequency of the class i)

If both the fitted probability density *and* the cumulative distribution are to be calculated, then $x_i + \frac{1}{2} d$ is also used in (**528**) and the calculated ordinates plotted against $x_i + \frac{1}{2} d$, that is to say, at the *upper* limit of the class i. (**528**) gives the ordinates for the *middle* of the classes.

Example 31. Given is the sample of example 22, section 10D, page 160, with $\bar{x} = 7.251$, $s = 0.584$.

Table 1

$x + \frac{1}{2} d$	$x + \frac{1}{2} d - \bar{x}$	$(x + \frac{1}{2} d - \bar{x})/s = c$	$f(c)$	$f(c) \times Nd/s = f(x + \frac{1}{2} d)$
5.4	−1.851	−3.17	0.00262	3.6
5.8	−1.451	−2.48	0.01842	25.2
6.2	−1.051	−1.80	0.07895	108.2
6.6	−0.651	−1.11	0.21546	295.2
7.0	−0.251	−0.429	0.36387	498.5
7.4	0.149	0.255	0.38618	529.0
7.8	0.549	0.939	0.25671	351.7
8.2	0.949	1.62	0.10741	147.1
8.6	1.349	2.31	0.02768	37.9
9.0	1.749	2.99	0.00457	6.3
9.4	2.149	3.68	0.00046	0.6

Calculation of the fitted probability density

The calculation is made as follows: The differences $x_i + \frac{1}{2} d - \bar{x}$ are multiplied by $1/s$ to obtain the fitted c_i values [this can also be carried out as a simple addition by using equation (**31**)]. For these deviations c, the corresponding ordinates $f(c)$ are obtained from the upper table on page 31 [in this connection see also (**512**)]. Multiplication of these ordinates by Nd/s gives the required ordinates $f(x_i + \frac{1}{2} d)$. (Cf. Fig. 30, left.)

Calculation of the empirical probits

The values of $F(x_i + \frac{1}{2} d)$ are calculated from (**529**), multiplied by 100, and the table on pages 54 and 55 entered to obtain the corresponding probits. The latter are plotted against $x_i + \frac{1}{2} d$ as ordinates, giving the points of Figure 30, right.

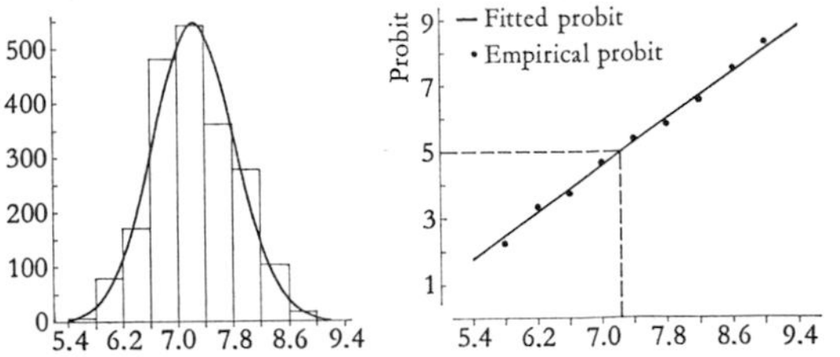

Fig. 30. Fitted probability density, empirical probits and fitted probit line for the sample of example 22 in section 10D, page 160.

Calculation of the fitted probit line

The probit line is constructed according to (**524**). In this example it first passes through the point (7.25; 5). If the value $x = 5.4$, say, is taken as the abscissa of the other necessary point, then from (**523**) the corresponding probit is $5 + 1.712\ (5.4 - 7.25) = 1.8$. When a straight line is drawn between these two points it is seen that the empirical probits all lie very close to it. The immediate impression given by Figure 30, right, is hardly such as to raise doubts that the population from which the sample is taken is other than a normally distributed one. That this impression is misleading, however, is demonstrated below.

Note that when the probability density is calculated as shown above, the two points required for the construction of the fitted probit line can be obtained by taking two remotely separated values from the column headed c of Table 1 and increasing them by 5.

Exact testing for non-normality by the χ^2 test

In this case the test is carried out by means of the c transformation, without probits, as follows (cf. Table 2 on page 165):

1. For calculation of the fitted c values for $x_i + \frac{1}{2} d$ according to (**521**) see column c of Table 1, which contains these values.
2. The $F(c)$ values corresponding to these fitted c values are obtained from the table on page 28. These are the fitted $F(c)$ values.
3. Multiplication of the fitted $F(c)$ values by the sample size N gives the fitted distribution of the cumulative absolute frequencies $H(x_i + \frac{1}{2} d)$.
4. From the differences $H(x_{i+1} + \frac{1}{2} d) - H(x_i + \frac{1}{2} d)$, the fitted absolute class frequencies f_i' are obtained.
5. From these the values of $(f_i - f_i')^2 / f_i' = \chi_i^2$ are calculated.
6. The sum of all the χ_i^2 values is the required test statistic χ^2 with degrees of freedom $\nu = n - 2 - 1$, where n = number of classes.

The significance probability 2α of the χ^2 value obtained (cf. the table on page 36) is considerably smaller than 0.0005. Hence the population from which the sample originates is definitely not normally distributed, a result completely contrary to the impression gained by eye from the empirical probits (above).

Note that in the above calculation the sequence of the signs of the differences $f_i - f_i'$ should be looked at closely. The occurrence of pluses and minuses should vary randomly. If any systematic trend is detected, HALDANE's test (page 193) should be carried out, if there are systematic cycles, a test of randomness of runs (page 194) provided there are enough classes. The reason for this is that if the χ^2 test gives no significant result when the number of classes is large – as in the above example – then it can be assumed with reasonable certainty that the population is normally distributed *provided that there is random variation of the plus and minus runs.* If the latter is not the case then the χ^2 test needs supplementation. The test is also conditional on the classes being *independent* of one another. This is doubtful if the signs follow any systematic cycle.

Table 2

$x+\frac{1}{2}d$	$F(c)$	$F(c)\times N = H(x+\frac{1}{2}d)$	$H(x_{i+1}+\frac{1}{2}d)$ minus $H(x_i+\frac{1}{2}d) = f_i'$	f_i [cf. (**501**b)]	$(f_i-f_i')^2/f_i' - \chi_i^2$
5.4	0.000 76	1.5	$\left.\begin{matrix}1.5^* \\ 11.6\end{matrix}\right\} = 13.1$	5	5.01
5.8	0.006 57	13.1	58.8	78	6.27
6.2	0.035 93	71.9	195.1	144	13.38
6.6	0.133 50	267.0	400.2	479	15.52
7.0	0.333 60	667.2	537.9	542	0.03
7.4	0.602 57	1205.1	447.7	358	17.97
7.8	0.826 39	1652.8	242.0	279	5.66
8.2	0.947 38	1894.8	84.3	99	2.56
8.6	0.989 56	1979.1	18.1	15	0.53
9.0	0.998 61	1997.2	2.8	1	1.16
9.4	—*	—*	2000.0	2000	$\chi^2=68.09$ $\nu=10-2-1$ $=7$

* The large deviation 3.68 for the value $x=9.4$ is not given in these tables. This is unimportant, however, since as shown by column 4 of this table the differences for the extreme classes are given by H (lowest class) minus 0 and N minus H (highest class).

11G. Standard deviations of the quantiles of samples from normally distributed populations

The formulae given here are only *asymptotically* correct and should therefore only be used for *large* samples (the more extreme the position of the quantile the larger the sample should be), so that in practice they are seldom applicable. When confidence limits for the quantiles of small and medium samples are required it is better to use the procedure given in section 10F, page 161 (distribution-free confidence limits) and *not* calculate them by means of the standard deviations defined in the formulae given here.

(Asymptotic)

$$\text{Standard deviation of } x_p = \sigma_{x_p} = \frac{1}{f(x_p)}\sqrt{\frac{p(1-p)}{N}} \tag{530}$$

From (**530**) and (**506**) it follows that

$$\left.\begin{matrix}\text{Standard}\\ \text{deviation of}\\ \text{the median}\end{matrix}\right\} x_{0.5} = \sigma_{x_{0.5}} = \sigma\sqrt{\frac{\pi}{2N}} = 1.253\,3\,\sigma\sqrt{\frac{1}{N}} \tag{531}$$

In a normal distribution the median is identical with the mean μ. The median of a sample is therefore also an estimate of μ. The relative asymptotic efficiency of this estimate according to (**433**), (**484**) and (**531**) is

$$\frac{\sigma/\sqrt{N}}{\sigma\sqrt{\pi/2N}} = \sqrt{\frac{2}{\pi}} \sim 0.8$$

that is to say, about 80% of the efficiency of the estimate of μ made from $\bar{x}$ according to (**491**).

11H. The logarithmic-normal (lognormal) distribution

The probability density function of this distribution is

$$\left.\begin{aligned} f(x) &= \frac{0.434\,3}{x\times\sigma_{\log x}}\times f(c),\\ c &= \frac{\log x-\mu_{\log x}}{\sigma_{\log x}}, \quad (0<x<\infty)\end{aligned}\right\} \tag{532}$$

The estimates of $\mu_{\log x}$ and $\sigma_{\log x}$ are $\bar{x}_{\log x}$ and $s_{\log x}$, calculated according to (**491**) and (**492**a and b) by substituting $\log x$ for x and $(\log x)^2$ for x^2.

The logarithmic-normal distribution is unsymmetrical (cf. Fig. 31a) and has the following characteristics:

$$\text{Mode} = \text{antilog}\,(\mu_{\log x} - 2.302\,6\,\sigma^2_{\log x}) \tag{533}$$

$$\text{Median} = \text{antilog}\,\mu_{\log x} \tag{534}$$

$$\text{Mean} = \text{antilog}\,(\mu_{\log x} + 1.151\,3\,\sigma^2_{\log x}) \tag{535}$$

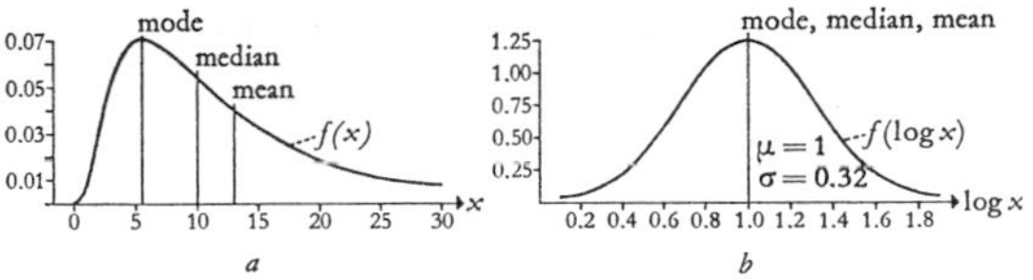

Fig. 31. a Lognormal distribution. *b* Transformation of *a*.

If x is plotted on a logarithmic abscissa scale (or $\log x$ on a linear abscissa scale) the unsymmetrical distribution (**532**) is transformed into the symmetrical normal distribution

$$\left.\begin{aligned} f(\log x) &= \frac{1}{\sigma_{\log x}}\times f(c),\\ c &= \frac{\log x-\mu_{\log x}}{\sigma_{\log x}}, \quad (0<x<\infty)\end{aligned}\right\} \tag{536}$$

[for $\mu_{\log x}$ and $\sigma_{\log x}$ see (**532**)]

From (**532**) and (**536**) it follows that

$$f(x) = \frac{0.434\,3}{x}\times f(\log x) \tag{537}$$

The probability density function of the transformed variables is thus not of the same magnitude as that of the original variables. In Figure 31 note the unequal ordinate scales. The situation is different with the cumulative distribution*, where

$$F(x_p) = F(\log x_p) = p \tag{538}$$

Similarly for the quantiles

$$x_p = \text{antilog}\,(\log x_p) \tag{539}$$

and for ungrouped samples

$$O\,(x_p) = O\,(\log x_p) \tag{540}$$

(O = ranks of the individual sample values, cf. section 10E, page 160)

From (**536**) and (**538**)–(**540**) it follows that [for (**541**)–(**543**)]:

If an unsymmetrical continuous distribution can be converted into a normal distribution by transformation of the individual values in the manner described in (**536**), then this distribution is a lognormal distribution. (**541**)

If the transformation in (**536**) yields samples from a normally distributed population [cf. (**508**) and section 11F, page 163], then any *tests* valid for the latter may be applied to these samples. *The results of these tests will also be valid for the untransformed samples.* (**542**)

For the estimation of the quantiles and their confidence limits in *ungrouped* samples from lognormal populations whose individual values have *not* been transformed, the procedures described in sections 10E and 10F on pages 160–161 are applicable *without modification.* (**543**)

For *grouped* samples the following should be noted: the transformation $x\to\log x$ may be carried out only with the *individual values*. If a sample is grouped into classes it must first be rearranged into an ungrouped sample. The logarithms of the individual values are then obtained, when these may be re-formed into a grouped sample, but with *equidistant logarithmic* class limits. If a grouped sample cannot be rearranged because the individual values were not noted, then a logarithmic transformation is *no longer possible*. In taking samples, the individual values should therefore always be noted before they are grouped. (**544**)

In natural processes many random variables are lognormally distributed. In all cases where the reaction of a body to a given stimulus is proportional to the intensity of the stimulus and to the

* The quantiles of a transformed variable are given by the transformed quantiles of the original variable provided that the transformation was made with an *increasing* function [$f(\log x)$ is an increasing function of x].

size of the body, the form of the distribution is lognormal. In practice, this applies particularly to toxicological and other similar biological studies, where logarithmic transformation of the variable x (dose) is a matter of routine.

11I. The addition theorem for the normal distribution

If $x_1, x_2, \ldots, x_k$ are stochastically independent, normally distributed variables with mean values $\mu_1, \mu_2, \ldots, \mu_k$ and variances $\sigma_1^2, \sigma_2^2, \ldots, \sigma_k^2$, then the variable

$$x = x_1 \pm x_2 \pm \cdots \pm x_k$$

is also normally distributed with mean **(545)**

$$\mu = \mu_1 \pm \mu_2 \pm \cdots \pm \mu_k$$

and variance

$$\sigma^2 = \sigma_1^2 + \sigma_2^2 + \cdots + \sigma_k^2$$

In (**545**) it should be noted that the variances are also *additive* when the mean μ is obtained from *differences*.

11J. The central limit theorem

The importance of the normal distribution lies in the fact that under fairly general conditions, the sum of k stochastically independent variables *of any sort* converges stochastically with increasing k toward a normal distribution with mean **(546)**

$$\mu = \mu_1 + \mu_2 + \cdots + \mu_k$$

and variance

$$\sigma^2 = \sigma_1^2 + \sigma_2^2 + \cdots + \sigma_k^2$$

From (**545**) the sum of normally distributed variables is *always* normally distributed, even when k is small. (**546**) is valid for variables distributed in *any* form, however, only when k approaches infinity. In practice, the expression 'infinity' is interpreted liberally. Thus, if for example in (**546**) the distributions all have the *same*, not too unsymmetrical form, then practically speaking their sum is normally distributed even when k is fairly small (50, 100, 200, ...). In other words, there will be a negligible error if the sample distributions are treated as normal.

In this publication, the statistical tables relating to sample distributions are so arranged that samples exceeding the tabulated sizes can for practical purposes be regarded as normally distributed. **(547)**

With *one* exception, *all* the sample distributions dealt with in this chapter converge toward the normal distribution in accordance with (**546**). The exception is the distribution of the extreme range (and of course that of the extreme deviations).

12. Distributions closely allied to the normal distribution

12A. The Student distribution

If in the standardized *normal* deviation $c = (x - \mu)/\sigma$ the standard deviation σ has to be replaced by its estimate s because σ is unknown and thus has to be estimated from the sample, then the standardized variable

$$t_\nu = \frac{x - \mu}{s_\nu} \quad (s_\nu \text{ independent of } x) \qquad \textbf{(548)}$$

has a probability density function

$$f(t \mid \nu) = \frac{\Gamma\left(\frac{\nu+1}{2}\right)}{\Gamma(\nu/2)\sqrt{\nu\pi}} \left(1 + \frac{t^2}{\nu}\right)^{-(\nu+1)/2} \qquad \textbf{(549)}$$

where $\Gamma(x/2) = \begin{cases} (x/2-1)(x/2-2)\ldots 3 \times 2 \times 1 & \text{when } x \text{ is even} \\ (x/2-1)(x/2-2)\ldots 3/2 \times 1/2 \times \sqrt{\pi} & \text{when } x \text{ is odd} \end{cases}$

(ν is the number of *degrees of freedom* of t)

The Student distribution is independent of μ and σ; its form is determined only by the number of degrees of freedom ν. The determination of the degrees of freedom will be described later for various individual cases.

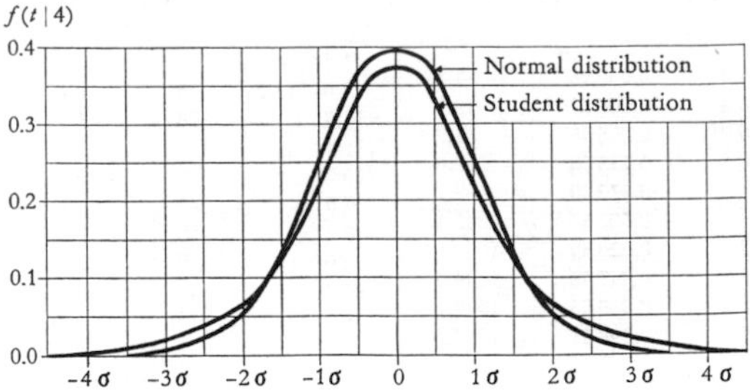

Fig. 32. Probability density of the normal distribution and of the Student distribution with degrees of freedom $\nu = 4$.

The Student distribution (or t-distribution) is very similar to the normal distribution and converges toward it rapidly with increasing degrees of freedom. Its range of variation is from minus infinity to infinity. It is continuous, *symmetrical* and bell-shaped, but in contrast to the normal distribution has more probability concentrated in the tails and less in the central part.

Equations (**512**)–(**517**) for the standardized normal distribution derived from the symmetry are also valid for the Student distribution when c is replaced by t. **(550)**

Tables

In the tables on pages 32–35 the exact deviations t_0 for degrees of freedom ν between 1 and 200 are given for the following integrals: **(551)**

$$P \text{ (of the table)} = \int_{t_0}^{\infty} f(t)\,dt = \text{Prob}\,(t > t_0) \qquad \text{(a)}$$

$$2P \text{ (of the table)} = \int_{-\infty}^{-t_0} f(t)\,dt + \int_{t_0}^{\infty} f(t)\,dt = \text{Prob}\,(t < t_0) + \text{Prob}\,(t > t_0) \qquad \text{(b)}$$

In *one-tailed* tests (confidence limits) $\alpha = P$, in *two-tailed* tests (confidence limits) $2\alpha = 2P$. (c)

In accordance with (**405** b), the cumulative distribution $F(t) = \text{Prob}\,(t \leqq t_0)$ is (d)

$$F(t_0) = 1 - \text{Prob}\,(t > t_0) = 1 - P = 1 - \textbf{(551 a)}$$

In the table on page 42 the exact deviations t_0^2 for degrees of freedom between 1 and 200 are given for the following integral: **(552)**

$$P_r = \int_{t_0^2}^{\infty} f(t^2)\,dt^2 = \text{Prob}\,(t^2 > t_0^2) = 2\,\text{Prob}\,(t > t_0) \qquad \text{(a)}$$

$$\tfrac{1}{2} P_r = \tfrac{1}{2}\,\textbf{(552 a)} \qquad \text{(b)}$$

For *one-tailed* tests $\alpha = \frac{1}{2} P$, for *two-tailed* tests $2\alpha = P$. (c)

For the relationship between the Student and F-distributions see (**575**).

12B. The χ^2 distribution

If $x_1, x_2, \ldots$ are stochastically independent observations from the *same normally distributed* population with mean μ and standard deviation σ, then the sum

$$\chi_\nu^2 = c_1^2 + c_2^2 + \cdots + c_i^2 + \cdots + c_\nu^2 = \sum_1^\nu c_i^2 \qquad \textbf{(553)}$$

of the squares of the standardized deviations

$$c_i^2 = \left(\frac{x_i - \mu}{\sigma}\right)^2$$

has the probability density function

$$f(\chi^2 \mid \nu) = \frac{1}{2^{\nu/2}\,\Gamma(\nu/2)}\, e^{-\chi^2/2} (\chi^2)^{(\nu-2)/2}; \quad (0 \leqq \chi^2 < \infty) \qquad \textbf{(554)}$$

[ν is the number of degrees of freedom of χ^2; for Γ see (**549**)]

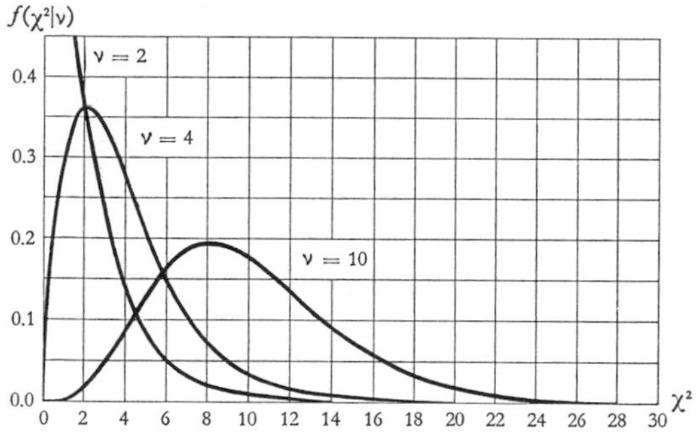

Fig. 33. Probability density functions of the χ^2 distribution with $\nu = 2, 4, 10$.

The χ^2 distribution is a continuous, *unsymmetrical* distribution which like the Student distribution – but more slowly – converges toward the normal distribution with increasing degrees of freedom (see Fig. 33). Its range of variation is from zero to infinity, its form dependent only on the degrees of freedom. The determination of the latter will be described later for various individual cases [see also (**566**) and (**569**)].

Parameters

Mode $= \nu - 2$ (a)
Mean $\mu = \nu$ (b)
Variance $\sigma^2 = 2\nu$ (c) (**555**)

Stochastic convergence when $\nu \to \infty$:

$\chi^2/\nu \to 1$ (a)

χ^2 distribution $\to$ Normal distribution $(\nu; \sqrt{2\nu})$; fairly slowly (b)

$\sqrt{2\chi^2}$ distribution $\to$ Normal distribution $(\sqrt{2\nu - 1}; 1)$*; faster than (b) (c) (**556**)

Approximations for quantiles

More centrally positioned quantiles [in accordance with (**556**c)]:

$$\chi^2_p \sim \tfrac{1}{2}(c_p + \sqrt{2\nu - 1})^2; \ \nu > 30 \quad \text{(a)}$$

More extreme quantiles [13]:

$$\chi^2_p \approx \nu\left(1 - \frac{2}{9\nu} + c_p\sqrt{\frac{2}{9\nu}}\right)^3; \ \nu > 30 \quad \text{(b)}$$

(**557**)

For calculation of the quantiles 0.005, 0.025, 0.975 and 0.995 from the confidence limits for λ of the Poisson distribution see (**563**).

Example 32 [of (**557**)]. Comparison between (a) and (b): The quantile $\chi^2_{0.975;\,\nu=50}$ is required.

(a) $\chi^2_p \sim \tfrac{1}{2}(1.96 + \sqrt{100 - 1})^2 = 70.922$

(b) $\chi^2_p \approx 50\left(1 - \dfrac{2}{450} + 1.96\sqrt{\dfrac{2}{450}}\right)^3 = 71.424$

The exact value is 71.420.

Tables

In the tables on pages 36–39 the exact deviations χ^2_0 for degrees of freedom ν between 1 and 200 are given for the following integrals:

$1 \int_r$ (of the table) $= \int_{\chi^2_0}^{\infty} f(\chi^2)\, d\chi^2 = \text{Prob}(\chi^2 > \chi^2_0)$ (a)

$\tfrac{1}{2} \int_r$ (of the table) $= \tfrac{1}{2}$ (**558**a) (b)

$1 \int_l$ (of the table) $= \int_0^{\chi^2_0} f(\chi^2)\, d\chi^2 = \text{Prob}(\chi^2 < \chi^2_0) = F(\chi^2_0)$ (c)

$\tfrac{1}{2} \int_l$ (of the table) $= \tfrac{1}{2}$ (**558**c) (d)

For *one-tailed* χ^2 tests $\alpha = \tfrac{1}{2} \int_r$
For *two-tailed* χ^2 tests $2\alpha = 1 \int_r$ (e)

With *one-sided* confidence limits for σ:
for *upper* limits $\alpha = 1 \int_r$
for *lower* limits $\alpha = 1 \int_l$
With *two-sided* confidence limits for σ:
for the *upper* limit $\alpha = \tfrac{1}{2} \int_r$
for the *lower* limit $\alpha = \tfrac{1}{2} \int_l$ } $\alpha < 0.5$ (f)

(**558**)

The useful square root $\sqrt{\nu/\chi^2_\nu}$ for degrees of freedom between 1 and 200 is given on page 47 (*confidence factors for* σ) for the following quantiles

χ^2_p	Column $1-2\alpha$	χ^2_p	Column $1-2\alpha$
0.05 and 0.95	0.90	0.01 and 0.99	0.98
0.025 and 0.975	0.95	0.005 and 0.995	0.99

(**559**)

Relationships with other distributions

Normal distribution:

When $\nu = 1$, then $\chi^2_p = c^2_{(1+p)/2}$, that is
$\text{Prob}(\chi^2 < \chi^2_0) = 2\,\text{Prob}(0 < c_0)$ (**560**)

F-Distribution: see (**576**) and (**577**).

Poisson distribution:

The probability that a Poisson variable with mean $\chi^2_0/2$ takes the value x is $\dfrac{e^{-\chi^2_0/2}(\chi^2_0/2)^x}{x!}$ (**561**)

This distribution is shown very clearly in Figure 44, page 185, with $\lambda = \chi^2_0/2$, $x = \nu/2$.

It can be shown that if ν is even

$$\text{Prob}(\chi^2 > \chi^2_0 \mid \nu = 2k) = \sum_0^{k-1} \frac{e^{-\chi^2_0/2}(\chi^2_0/2)^x}{x!} \quad \textbf{(562)}$$

For even numbers of degrees of freedom ν the following quantiles can be calculated on the basis of (**562**) from the confidence limits for λ of the Poisson distribution, pages 107 and 108:

Prob $(\chi^2 \leq \chi^2_p) = p$	Argument (table on pp. 107 and 108)	Page	χ^2_p equals	
0.005	$x = \nu/2$	108	$2\lambda_l$	ν an even number
0.025	$x = \nu/2$	107	$2\lambda_l$	
0.975	$x = (\nu/2) - 1$	107	$2\lambda_r$	
0.995	$x = (\nu/2) - 1$	108	$2\lambda_r$	

(**563**)

Example 33 [of (**563**)]. Required	Solution
$\chi^2_{0.025,\ \nu=260}$	$x = 130$; $\lambda_l = 108.61$; $\chi^2_p = 217.22$
$\chi^2_{0.975,\ \nu=260}$	$x = 129$; $\lambda_r = 153.30$; $\chi^2_p = 306.60$

The value $\lambda_r = 153.30$ has been interpolated linearly:

$154.39 - {}^1/_{10}(154.39 - 143.52) = 153.303$

$\lambda_{130} - {}^1/_{10}(\lambda_{130} - \lambda_{120}) \sim \lambda_{129}$

The addition theorem for the χ^2 *distribution*

In equation (**553**) the sum can be broken up into any number of parts, for example

$$\chi^2 = \underbrace{c_1^2 + c_2^2}_{=\chi_1^2(\nu=2)} + \underbrace{c_3^2 + c_4^2 + c_5^2 + c_6^2}_{=\chi_2^2(\nu=4)} + \underbrace{c_7^2 + \cdots}_{=\chi_3^2(\nu=\ldots)} \quad \text{etc.}$$

It follows that:

If $\chi_1^2, \chi_2^2, \ldots, \chi_n^2$ are stochastically independent and the χ^2 distributions have the degrees of freedom $\nu_1, \nu_2, \ldots, \nu_n$ respectively, then the sum $\chi^2 = \chi_1^2 + \chi_2^2 + \cdots + \chi_n^2$ likewise has a χ^2 distribution with $\nu = \nu_1 + \nu_2 + \cdots + \nu_n$ degrees of freedom. (**564**)

* According to R. A. Fisher.

There is also a division theorem for χ^2 on which the analysis of regression and variance is based. For further details the reader is referred to the literature.

χ^2 and sample variance

In accordance with (**553**), $\chi^2 = [\Sigma(x-\mu)^2]/\sigma^2$. If μ is replaced by $\bar{x}$, then from (**493**c), $\Sigma(x-\bar{x})^2 = (N-1)s^2$. If now $N-1$ is replaced by ν, then νs^2 is eventually obtained in place of $\Sigma(x-\mu)^2$. Intuitively it is surmised that

$$\chi_\nu^2 = \frac{\nu s_\nu^2}{\sigma^2}, \text{ where } \nu = \text{degrees of freedom of } s^2 \qquad (\mathbf{565})$$

and this is a good guess. It should be noted that (**565**) is a second definition of χ^2 equivalent to (**553**) but valid *only* for *normally* distributed populations.

An important asymptotic property of χ^2

Given is a sample divided into n classes from a population *of any form*. If f_i is the observed frequency of the class i, where $f_1+f_2+\cdots+f_i+\cdots+f_n = N$, then f_i is known as the *empirical* (absolute) *frequency*. If p_i is the *given* or a *hypothetical* probability that the variable x will fall in the class i, where $p_1+p_2+\cdots+p_i+\cdots+p_n = 1$, then Np_i is known as the *given* or the *hypothetical* (absolute) *frequency*. The empirical frequencies in the individual classes are random variables. In this case

$$\sum_1^n \frac{(f_i - Np_i)^2}{Np_i} \to \chi_\nu^2; \text{ where } \nu = n-1$$

when $\nu \to \infty$. (**566**)

(**566**) was discovered by K. Pearson. The fact that it is exactly valid only when $\nu \to \infty$ is of little consequence in practice but gives rise to certain restrictions:

In tests for goodness of fit based on (**566**), the *samples* as a whole should *not* be *too small*, the *hypothetical* (absolute) *frequencies in the individual classes not below* $Np_i = 4$. If they are less than this, they should be increased to the required level by combining 2, 3, ... neighbouring classes. This is necessary, however, only when the number of classes is small. If ν is greater than (about) 8 and the sample size over 40, then it is permissible for Np_i in isolated classes to be as low as 1. (**567**)

As a rule the hypothetical frequencies are not given:

Theoretical (absolute) frequencies Np_i which have been calculated on the basis of *estimated* parameters are known as *fitted frequencies*; the theoretical distribution corresponding to them is known as the *fitted distribution*. (**568**)

(**569**)

(a) If k parameters must be estimated in the calculation of fitted frequencies, then the number of degrees of freedom for χ^2 defined by (**566**) is $\nu = n-1-k$, where n = number of classes.

(b) If m samples each grouped into n classes (in an $m \times n$ contingency table) are submitted to a χ^2 test based on (**566**), then the number of degrees of freedom for χ^2 is $\nu = (n-1)(m-1)$.

(c) In the special case, frequently encountered, of the 2×2 table, $\nu = 1$.

For an example of a χ^2 test with estimation of parameters see section 11F (b), page 164. Another χ^2 test is described in section 23, page 191, in which further tests for frequency are dealt with.

In conclusion it should be noted that definitions (**553**) and (**565**) differ *fundamentally* from definition (**566**) in spite of the fact that the formulae are very similar: (**553**) and (**565**) are valid only for *normally distributed* populations, (**566**) is valid for populations of *any* form; in (**553**) and (**565**), $\bar{x}$ and s are *continuous* variables, while in (**566**), f_i is a *discrete* variable.

When χ^2 tests are carried out with the aid of fitted distributions, care must be taken that the estimates made satisfy condition (**430**) or (**431**).

12C. The F-distribution (variance-ratio distribution)

In the expression F-distribution, the letter F symbolizes *not* a cumulative distribution but the name of R. A. Fisher, the discoverer of the z-distribution, which is equivalent to the F-distribution[14].

If s_1^2 and s_2^2 are two stochastically independent estimates of the variance σ^2 of the *same normally distributed* population, then in accordance with (**565**)

$$s_1^2 = \sigma^2 \frac{\chi_1^2}{\nu_1} \text{ and } s_2^2 = \sigma^2 \frac{\chi_2^2}{\nu_2}$$

It follows that the quotient

$$F = \frac{s_1^2}{s_2^2} = \frac{\chi_1^2/\nu_1}{\chi_2^2/\nu_2}; \; 0 \leq F < \infty \qquad (\mathbf{570})$$

(ν_1 and ν_2 are the degrees of freedom of s_1 and s_2 respectively)

has the probability density function

$$f(F) = \frac{\Gamma\left(\frac{\nu_1+\nu_2}{2}\right)}{\Gamma\left(\frac{\nu_1}{2}\right)\Gamma\left(\frac{\nu_2}{2}\right)} \nu_1^{\frac{\nu_1}{2}} \nu_2^{\frac{\nu_2}{2}} \frac{F^{\frac{\nu_1-2}{2}}}{(\nu_2+\nu_1 F)^{\frac{\nu_1+\nu_2}{2}}}; \; 0 \leq F < \infty \qquad (\mathbf{571})$$

[for Γ see (**549**)]

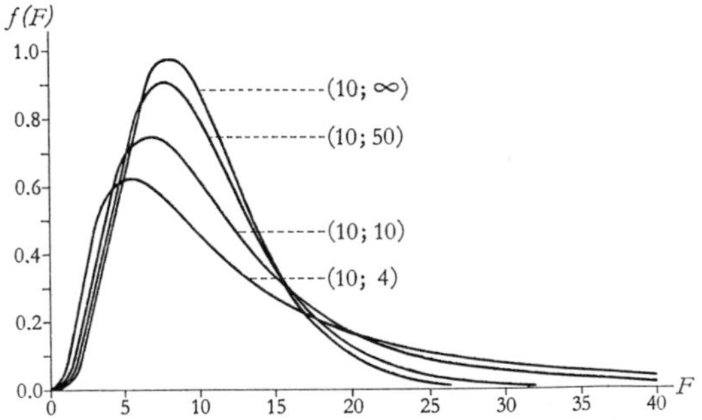

Fig. 34. Probability density functions of the F-distribution with various degrees of freedom (ν_1; ν_2).

The F-distribution is a continuous *unsymmetrical* distribution with a range of variation from zero to infinity.

Parameters

$$\text{Mean} \quad \mu = \nu_2/(\nu_2-2); \; \nu_2 > 2 \qquad \text{(a)}$$

$$\text{Variance } \sigma^2 = \left(\frac{\nu_2}{\nu_2-2}\right)^2 \times \frac{2(\nu_1+\nu_2-2)}{\nu_1(\nu_2-4)}; \; \nu_2 > 4 \qquad \text{(b)} \qquad (\mathbf{572})$$

Interchange of ν_1 and ν_2

$$F_0(p; \nu_1; \nu_2) = 1/[F_0(1-p; \nu_2; \nu_1)] \qquad (\mathbf{573})$$

In (**573**), p can be Prob $(F > F_0)$ just as well as Prob $(F < F_0)$.

Tables

The values of F_0 given on pages 40 and 41 satisfy the following equation:

$$P \text{ (of the table)} = P_r = \int_{F_0}^{\infty} f(F)\,dF = \text{Prob}\,(F > F_0) \qquad \text{(a)}$$

In one-tailed tests $\alpha = P$, in two-tailed tests $2\alpha = 2P$ (b) (**574**)

On the t^2 table of page 42 see (**575**) and (**552**). (c)

Relationships to other distributions

Student distribution:

$$\text{Prob}\,[(F > F_0) \mid 1; \nu_2] = \text{Prob}\,(t^2 > t_0^2 \mid \nu_2) = 2\,\text{Prob}\,(t > t_0 \mid \nu_2) \qquad (\mathbf{575})$$

For $F(1; \nu_2)$ with ν_2 values between 1 and 200, the more comprehensive t^2 table on page 42 should therefore be used. For explanation see (**552**).

χ^2 distribution:

When F_p and χ_p^2 denote quantiles

$$F_p(\nu_1; \infty) = \frac{\chi^2_{p,\,\nu_1}}{\nu_1} \quad \text{(a)}$$

$$F_p(\infty; \nu_2) = \frac{\nu_2}{\chi^2_{1-p,\,\nu_2}} \quad \text{(b)} \qquad \textbf{(576)}$$

From (**576**) and (**556**a) it follows that

$$\left.\begin{aligned} &F(\nu_1; \infty) \to 1, \text{ when } \nu_1 \to \infty \\ &F(\infty; \nu_2) \to 1, \text{ when } \nu_2 \to \infty \end{aligned}\right\} \text{that is, } F(\infty; \infty) = 1 \qquad \textbf{(577)}$$

Binomial distribution:

$$\text{Prob}\left[F(\nu_1; \nu_2) < \frac{N-x}{x+1} \times \frac{p}{1-p}\right] = \sum_{x+1}^{N} \binom{N}{k} p^k (1-p)^{N-k}$$

$$\left.\begin{aligned} \text{where } N &= \frac{\nu_1 + \nu_2}{2} - 1 \\ x &= \frac{\nu_1}{2} - 1 \end{aligned}\right\} \nu_1 \text{ and } \nu_2 \text{ are even numbers} \qquad \textbf{(578)}$$

On the basis of (**578**) the following quantiles F_0 can be calculated from the confidence limits for p of the binomial distribution (pages 85–98):

Prob ($F<F_0$)	Arguments (pages 85–98) Column	N	x	p	Quantile F_0
0.005	99 %	$\frac{\nu_1+\nu_2}{2} - 1$	$\frac{\nu_1}{2} - 1$	p_l	$\frac{\nu_2}{\nu_1} \times \frac{p}{1-p}$
0.025	95 %			p_l	
0.975	95 %			p_r	
0.995	99 %			p_r	

(579)

Example 34. $F_{0.995}(152; 36)$ is required. We have $N = 93$; $x = 75$; $p_r = 0.8993$ (from page 96); $p/(1-p) = 8.93049$; $\nu_2/\nu_1 = 0.236842$; $F_{0.995}(152; 36) = 2.12$.

13. The normally distributed population: Confidence and tolerance intervals

(Cf. also section 8, page 154)

13A. Confidence intervals for the mean μ

One-sided confidence interval with *single upper* limit

$$\text{Prob}(-\infty < \mu < \bar{x} + k \times Sd) = 1 - \alpha \quad \text{(a)}$$
[cf. also (**580**d)]

One-sided confidence interval with *single lower* limit

$$\text{Prob}(\bar{x} - k \times Sd < \mu < \infty) = 1 - \alpha \quad \text{(b)}$$
[cf. also (**580**d)]

Two-sided confidence interval with symmetrical limits

$$\text{Prob}(\bar{x} - k \times Sd < \mu < \bar{x} + k \times Sd) = 1 - 2\alpha \quad \text{(c)}$$
[cf. also (**580**d)]

Factors $k \times Sd$ for (**580** a, b, c) (d)

Equations	Degrees of freedom ν of s	k	Sd	Page (c, t or k)
(a) and (b)	>200	$\lvert c_\alpha \rvert / \sqrt{N}$	σ or s	28
(a) and (b)	≤ 200	$t_{\nu,\alpha}/\sqrt{N}$	s_ν	32–35
(c)	>200	k_2 or $\lvert c_\alpha \rvert / \sqrt{N}$	σ or s	k_2: 43; c: 28
(c)	≤ 200	k_2 or $t_{\nu,2\alpha}/\sqrt{N}$	s_ν	k_2: 43; t: 32–35

(580)

In the table on page 43 (for k_2) the number of degrees of freedom $\nu = N-1$ is contained in the argument N. In this table the transition from t to c takes place at $N = 201$.

13B. Tolerance intervals

Tolerance intervals without confidence probability

One-sided tolerance interval with *single upper* limit

$$\text{Prob}(-\infty < x < m + k \times Sd) = 1 - \alpha = \beta_p; \quad \text{(a)}$$
[cf. also (**581**d)]

One-sided tolerance interval with *single lower* limit

$$\text{Prob}(m - k \times Sd < x < \infty) = 1 - \alpha = \beta_p; \quad \text{(b)}$$
[cf. also (**581**d)]

Two-sided tolerance interval with symmetrical limits

$$\text{Prob}(m - k \times Sd < x < m + k \times Sd) = 1 - 2\alpha = \beta_p \quad \text{(c)}$$
[cf. also (**581** d)]

m, k and Sd for (**581**a, b, c) (d)

Equations	Degrees of freedom ν of s	Known parameters or estimates	m	k	Sd	Page (c, t, k)
(a) and (b)	>200	μ, σ or $\bar{x}$, s	μ or $\bar{x}$	$\lvert c_\alpha \rvert$	σ or s	28
(a) and (b)	$\leqq 100$	$\bar{x}$, σ	$\bar{x}$	k_3*	σ	44, col. 1
(a) and (b)	$\leqq 100$	μ, s	μ	$t_{\nu,\alpha}$	s	32–35
(a) and (b)	$\leqq 100$	$\bar{x}$, s	$\bar{x}$	k_4*	s	44, col. 2
(c)	>200	μ, σ or $\bar{x}$, s	μ or $\bar{x}$	$\lvert c_\alpha \rvert$	σ or s	28
(c)	$\leqq 100$	$\bar{x}$, σ	$\bar{x}$	k_3	σ	44, col. 1
(c)	$\leqq 100$	μ, s	μ	$t_{\nu,2\alpha}$	s	32–35
(c)	$\leqq 100$	$\bar{x}$, s	$\bar{x}$	k_4	s	44, col. 2

* β_p in the table is selected as follows: β_p (required) = $1 - 2\alpha$; α is given.

(581)

Tolerance intervals with confidence probability β_t

Equations (**581**a, b, c) are applicable with the following complementary equation [example of (**581** d)]:

$$\text{Prob}\,[\text{Prob}(m - k \times Sd < x < m + k \times Sd) \geqq 1 - 2\alpha] = \beta_t$$

m, k and Sd for (**581**a, b, c)

Equations	Degrees of freedom ν of s	Known parameters or estimates	m	k	Sd	Page (c, t, k)
(a) and (b)	$\leqq 100$	$\bar{x}$, σ	$\bar{x}$	k_5*	σ	44, col. 3
(a) and (b)	$\leqq 100$	μ, s	μ	k_6*	s	44, col. 4
(a) and (b)	$\leqq 1000$	$\bar{x}$, s	$\bar{x}$	k_7	s	45–46
(c)	≤ 100	$\bar{x}$, σ	$\bar{x}$	k_5	σ	44, col. 3
(c)	$\leqq 100$	μ, s	μ	k_6	s	44, col. 4
(c)	$\leqq 1000$	$\bar{x}$, s	$\bar{x}$	k_7	s	45–46

* β_p in the table is selected as follows: $\beta_p = 1 - 2\alpha$; α is given.

(582)

The following equations are valid for the confidence and tolerance factors

$$k_2 = t_{2\alpha,\,N-1} \times 1/\sqrt{N} \text{ for } N \leq 201 \quad \text{(a)}$$

$$= \lvert c_\alpha \rvert \times 1/\sqrt{N} \text{ for } N > 201 \quad \text{(b)}$$

$$k_3 = \lvert c_\alpha \rvert \times \sqrt{1 + 1/N} \quad \text{(c)}$$

$$k_4 = t_{2\alpha,\,N-1} \times \sqrt{1 + 1/N} \quad \text{(d)}$$

$$k_5 \quad \text{solution of } \int_{c'-k_5}^{c'+k_5} f(c)\,dc = \beta_p; \; (c' = c_{\beta_t}) \quad \text{(e)}$$

$$k_6 = \lvert c_{\alpha_p} \rvert \times \sqrt{(N-1)/\chi^2_{1-\beta_t,\,N-1}} \quad \text{(f)}$$

k_7 cf. EISENHART et al.[15], pages 108–109.

(583)

13C. Confidence intervals for the standard deviation σ

From (**565**) it follows that

$$\text{Prob}(k_l\, s_\nu < \sigma < k_r\, s_\nu) = 1 - 2\alpha$$

$$\text{where } k_l = \sqrt{\nu/\chi^2_{\nu,\,1-\alpha}} \text{ and } k_r = \sqrt{\nu/\chi^2_{\nu,\,\alpha}} \qquad \textbf{(584)}$$

Values of k_l and k_r for degrees of freedom between 1 and 100 are given in the left-hand table on page 47.

14. The normally distributed population: Extreme range and extreme deviations

14A. The extreme range

Definition

If x_1 is the lowest and x_n the highest value of a sample of size n, then $(x_n - x_1)$ is the extreme range w_n of this sample. **(585)**

The standardized extreme range of a sample of size n from a population with standard deviation σ is

$$W_n = \frac{w_n}{\sigma} = \frac{x_n - x_1}{\sigma} \quad \textbf{(586)}$$

The mean extreme range of m samples of size n from one and the same population is

$$\overline{w}_{m,n} = \frac{\sum_1^m w_n}{m} = \frac{\sum_1^m (x_n - x_1)}{m} \quad \textbf{(587)}$$

and the standardized mean extreme range is

$$\overline{W}_{m,n} = \frac{\overline{w}_{m,n}}{\sigma} = \frac{\sum_1^m w_n}{m\sigma} = \frac{\sum_1^m (x_n - x_1)}{m\sigma} \quad \textbf{(588)}$$

Since the extreme range w_n is merely a special case of the mean extreme range $\overline{w}_{m,n}$ with $m = 1$, only the mean extreme range will be referred to in the text that follows.

Mean extreme range as a multiple of σ

The expected value $\boldsymbol{W}_n$ of the extreme range of random samples of size n from a normally distributed population with unit standard deviation satisfies the relation

$$\overline{W}_{m,n} \underset{m \to \infty}{\longrightarrow} \boldsymbol{W}_n \quad \textbf{(589)}$$

The upper right-hand table on page 47 gives values of $\boldsymbol{W}_n$ for the standardized normal distribution as multiples of σ[16]. (Many authors use the symbol d_n in place of $\boldsymbol{W}_n$.)

σ as a fraction of the mean extreme range

The quotient

$$\frac{\overline{w}_{m,n}}{\boldsymbol{W}_n} = \overline{w}_{m,n} \times \boldsymbol{A}_n \quad \textbf{(590)}$$

gives an unbiased estimate of σ. Values of this quotient are given in the lower right-hand table on page 47.

The relative efficiency of **(590)** compared with that of the estimate s [s^2 from (**492** a)] when $m = 1$ is[17]

n	2	3	4	5	6	10	15	20	50	100	∞
Efficiency	1.00	0.99	0.98	0.96	0.93	0.85	0.77	0.70	0.49	0.34	0

For sample sizes between 2 and 10 there is thus little difference between the two estimates. Within this range (**590**) is useful as a *rapid method of estimating* σ but *it should not be used in place of s in a standard t test.*

For larger samples the extreme range of σ can likewise be accurately estimated, namely by dividing the sample into a number m of *independent* subgroups of the same size between 2 and 10 and determining their extreme ranges. In accordance with (**588**), the mean of these ranges is then the mean extreme range. However, such a subdivision must be effected by a *random selection* among the available sample values. If there is no natural method of doing this (such as using the order in time of obtaining the sample values), random numbers may be used, but the time needed to carry out the subdivision will tend to nullify the advantages of the more rapid calculation.

Example 35. A sample of size 24, $x_1, x_2, \ldots, x_{24}$, can be subdivided into 12 groups of 2, 8 groups of 3, 6 groups of 4, or 3 groups of 8:

Groups of 2: $x_1 - x_2, x_3 - x_4, \ldots, x_{23} - x_{24}$

Groups of 3: $x_1 - x_3, x_4 - x_6, \ldots, x_{22} - x_{24}$

Overlapping groups must of course be avoided, for example $x_1 - x_2, x_2 - x_3, \ldots$, since these would obviously no longer be independent.

$\sigma_{\bar{x}}$ as a fraction of the mean extreme range

The quotient

$$\frac{\overline{w}_{m,n}}{\boldsymbol{W}_n \sqrt{mn}} = \overline{w}_{m,n} \times \boldsymbol{A}_{m,n} \quad \textbf{(591)}$$

where mn = sample size N, gives an unbiased estimate of the standard deviation $\sigma_{\bar{x}}$ of the estimate $\bar{x}$. Values of the factor

$\boldsymbol{A}_{m,n} = 1/(\boldsymbol{W}_n \times \sqrt{mn})$

are given in the table on page 48.

Example 36 (section 14A). Given is the sample 3.00, 1.56, 1.34, 2.08, 2.10, 2.67. The estimates of σ and $\sigma_{\bar{x}}$ on the basis of the extreme range or mean extreme range are

(a) 1 extreme range

1.34 − 3.00: range = 1.66 $\quad \sigma' = 1.66 \times 0.39457 = 0.655$; $\sigma'_{\bar{x}} = 1.66 \times 0.16108 = 0.267$

(b) 2 extreme ranges

1.34 − 3.00, 2.08 − 2.67: mean range = 1.125 $\quad \sigma' = 1.125 \times 0.59082 = 0.665$; $\sigma'_{\bar{x}} = 1.125 \times 0.24120 = 0.271$

(c) 3 extreme ranges

1.56 − 3.00, 1.34 − 2.08, 2.10 − 2.67: mean range = $0.91\dot{6}$ $\quad \sigma' = 0.91\dot{6} \times 0.88623 = 0.812$; $\sigma'_{\bar{x}} = 0.91\dot{6} \times 0.36180 = 0.332$

For comparison, σ can be estimated using (**492** b) with the result $s = 0.63257$. In order to correct the bias of this estimate it must be multiplied by the factor $k_s = 1.0509$ (see the left-hand table on page 47, column k_s), giving the result $s = 0.665$ and $s_{\bar{x}} = 0.271$.

All the above estimates may be regarded as equally valid. Although the agreement between s and the estimates (a) and (b) is striking, this does not mean that estimate (c) is not as good. A further sample from the same population could result in estimates nearer to (c).

14B. Testing extreme ranges and extreme deviations

The 'studentized' extreme range (table on page 51, sample size 2–20)

In the test quotients

$$\frac{x_N - x_1}{s_\nu} \quad \textbf{(592)}$$

(ν = degrees of freedom of s; $x_1 < x_2 < \cdots < x_N$)

s is an estimate calculated from a sample *different* from and *independent* of the sample to be tested but originating from the *same* population. If the test quotient attains or exceeds the level in the table corresponding to the degrees of freedom ν_s and the sample size N, then the extreme range in question is *too large* (significance probability α).

If σ is known, the levels at $\nu = \infty$ should be used. If the sample size exceeds the range of the table, testing should be carried out according to (**596** d) for sample sizes between 21 and 25 and according to (**595**) for still larger samples, *if it is desired to test extreme values.*

The 'studentized' extreme deviation (table on page 52, sample size 3–9)

In the test quotients

$$\frac{x_N - \bar{x}}{s_\nu} \text{ or } \frac{\bar{x} - x_1}{s_\nu} \quad \textbf{(593)}$$

(ν = degrees of freedom of s; $x_1 < x_2 < \cdots < x_N$)

s has the same meaning as in (**592**). If σ is known, the levels at $\nu = \infty$ should be used. If the test quotient attains or exceeds the level in the table corresponding to the degrees of freedom ν_s and the sample size N, then the extreme range in question is *too large* (significance probability α).

If the sample size exceeds the range of the table, testing should be carried out according to (**596** c and d) for sample sizes between 10 and 25 and according to (**595**) for still larger samples.

The standardized extreme deviation (upper table on page 52)

We have

$$\left.\begin{aligned} &\text{Prob}\,(c \leqq c_e) = \left[\int_{-\infty}^{c_e} f(c)\,dc\right]^N; \text{ for } c_e \text{ see } (\textbf{595}) && \text{(a)} \\ &\text{Prob}\,(-c_e \leqq c \leqq c_e) = \left[\int_{-c_e}^{c_e} f(c)\,dc\right]^N && \text{(b)} \end{aligned}\right\} (\textbf{594})^*$$

(c_e = standardized extreme deviation; N = sample size)

(**594**a) gives the probability that no deviation from the mean μ is greater than c_e; (**594**b) gives the probability that no deviation from the mean μ is greater than c_e *in absolute value.* In accordance with (**408**b), the corresponding significance probabilities are 1 – (**594**). The table on page 52 gives the probabilities 1 – (**594**a).

In the test quotients

$$\frac{x_N - \mu}{\sigma} \text{ or } \frac{\mu - x_1}{\sigma} = c_e \qquad (\textbf{595})$$

the symbols have the customary meaning. For sample sizes over 25, μ and σ can be replaced by $\bar{x}$ and s. For smaller samples (**593**) should be used.

Testing extreme values of a sample on the basis of their own attributes[18] (upper left-hand table on page 53, sample size 3–25)

When no independent information on the standard deviation of the population is available, extreme deviations in samples up to a size of 25 can be tested by means of the following quotients:

Sample size N	Quotient		Sample size N	Quotient	
3– 7	$\frac{x_N - x_{N-1}}{x_N - x_1}$	(a)	11–13	$\frac{x_N - x_{N-2}}{x_N - x_2}$	(c)
8–10	$\frac{x_N - x_{N-1}}{x_N - x_2}$	(b)	14–25	$\frac{x_N - x_{N-2}}{x_N - x_3}$	(d)

(**596**)

where $x_1 < x_2 < \cdots < x_N$, when a right-hand extreme value is tested,
$x_N < x_{N-1} < \cdots < x_1$, when a left-hand extreme value is tested.

With samples of over 25, (**595**) should be used with μ and σ replaced by $\bar{x}$ and s.

General considerations in testing extreme values

It is common for extreme values to be ignored, often without comment by the author and without their first being tested statistically. Occasionally they are even eliminated *before* the experimental data are put into the hands of the statistician. This is clearly undesirable, for in some situations extreme values are often the most informative ones in the sample.

If an extreme value is found to be significantly too large after proper statistical testing in accordance with (**593**), (**595**) or (**596**), its rejection is actually justifiable only when a check on the experiment reveals a causal circumstance accounting for its existence. Examples would be an error made in measurements or calculations, the unwitting inclusion of a sick person among healthy persons being investigated, and so on. In such cases the extreme values originate from *other* populations and *ought to be rejected.*

If, however, there is a high degree of probability that the extreme value originates from the same population, the following considerations apply: The smaller the sample the more unlikely it is to contain extreme values of the population. A small sample containing an extreme value can give a completely false picture of the population it represents. In such cases the extreme value *may be ignored.* However, it is advisable to use a small significance probability, at least with larger samples.

A third important consideration to be borne in mind in judging extreme values is that the validity of the tests described above is conditional on the population being *normally distributed.* If this is not the case, the tests are practically *worthless* since they are very peculiarly dependent on this condition of normality.

* This formula is derived from (**362**) and (**405** a) or (**407** c).

Special considerations in testing extreme values

If testing in accordance with (**592**) results in the postulated significance, then at least one of the two extreme values, left or right (*or* possibly the *whole* sample, depending on the situation) must be rejected since they do not originate from that population from which the sample with the calculated s was taken.

It is permissible to test extreme values more than once in the same sample. In this case the sample size must be reduced by one after each rejection before a new test is made. The resulting level of significance α_{res} for the total number k of significant tests then has the *very approximate* order of magnitude

$$\alpha_{res} \sim 1 - (1 - \alpha_1)(1 - \alpha_2)\ldots(1 - \alpha_k)$$

Example 37. The sample of example 24, page 160, is to be tested using (**596** d).

1st test ($N = 21$)

Right-hand extreme deviate $\dfrac{4.41 - 2.68}{4.41 - 1.76} = 0.653$; deviate is too large ($\alpha \ll 0.005$)

2nd test ($N = 20$)

Right-hand extreme deviate $\dfrac{3.56 - 2.35}{3.56 - 1.76} = 0.672$; deviate is too large ($\alpha \ll 0.005$)

Only the *5th test* gives no further significant deviation.

After two deletions $\alpha_{res} \sim 1 - (\gg 0.995)(\gg 0.995) < 0.01$, if the sample were from a normally distributed population. This is not the case (cf. section 10H, page 161), so that the extreme values may on no account be rejected.

15. The normally distributed population: Comparison of a sample with the hypothetical population

15A. Comparison of the sample and population standard deviations s and σ (or of the variances s^2 and σ^2)

The confidence limits for σ are obtained from (**584**), those for σ^2 analogously by replacing s by s^2 and k by k^2. The hypothetical σ or σ^2 is then compared with these limits and the result interpreted in accordance with (**476**).

15B. Comparison of the sample and population means $\bar{x}$ and μ

Comparison of the estimate $\bar{x}$ with the hypothetical mean is made by means of the test quotients given in (**598**)–(**602**), the numerical value of the quotient being compared with the limit given:

If the test quotient is *smaller* than the limit, then the result is interpreted in accordance with (**474**) or (**475**). If it attains or exceeds the limit, then

	Significance in brackets	
	One-tailed test	Two-tailed test
When $\bar{x} - \mu < 0$	$\bar{x} < \mu\,(\alpha)$	$\bar{x} \neq \mu\,(2\alpha)$
When $\bar{x} - \mu > 0$	$\bar{x} > \mu\,(\alpha)$	

(**597**)

The c-test (normal distribution)

Applicability: When σ is known or when the degrees of freedom of $s = N - 1 > 200$

Test quotient	Significance limit	
$\frac{\lvert\bar{x} - \mu\rvert\sqrt{N}}{\sigma}$; or $\frac{\lvert\bar{x} - \mu\rvert\sqrt{N}}{s_{N-1}}$; $N > 201$	$\lvert c_\alpha\rvert$, page 28	(a)
$\frac{(\bar{x} - \mu)^2 N}{\sigma^2}$; or $\frac{(\bar{x} - \mu)^2 N}{s_{N-1}^2}$; $N > 201$	$\chi^2_{\nu=1}$, page 36; $\alpha = \frac{1}{2}\int_r$, $2\alpha = 1\int_r$	(b)
$\frac{\lvert\bar{x} - \mu\rvert}{s_{N-1}}$; $N > 201$	$c/\sqrt{N}$ = confidence factor k_2, page 43	(c)

(**598**)

The t-test (Student distribution)

Applicability: When σ is unknown and the degrees of freedom of $s = N - 1 \leq 200$

Test quotient	Significance limit		
$\dfrac{\lvert \bar{x} - \mu \rvert \sqrt{N}}{s_{N-1}}$; $N \leq 201$	t_{N-1}, pages 32–35; $\alpha = P$, $2\alpha = 2P$	(a)	(599)
$\dfrac{(\bar{x} - \mu)^2 N}{s^2_{N-1}}$; $N \leq 201$	t^2_{N-1}, page 42; $\alpha = \tfrac{1}{2} P$, $2\alpha = P$; cf. (552)	(b)	
$\dfrac{\lvert \bar{x} - \mu \rvert}{s_{N-1}}$; $N \leq 201$	$t_{N-1}/\sqrt{N}$ = confidence factor k_2, page 43	(c)	

LORD's test based on the extreme range[19]

Applicability: Samples of size $N \leq 20$ (a) and $N > 20$ (b)

Test quotient	Significance limit		
$\dfrac{\lvert \bar{x} - \mu \rvert}{\bar{x}_N - x_1}$; $N \leq 20$; $x_1 < x_2 < \cdots < x_N$	Page 53, middle left-hand table	(a)	(600)
$\dfrac{\lvert \bar{x} - \mu \rvert m}{[\Sigma (x_n - x_1)] \boldsymbol{A}_{m,n}}$; $m \times n = N$	Page 49; $\boldsymbol{A}_{m,n}$ page 48	(b)	

m = number of subgroups of size n (cf. section 14 A, page 170) in which $x_1 < x_2 < \cdots < x_n$

The midrange test based on the extreme range[20]

Applicability: Samples of size $N \leq 10$

Test quotient	Significance limit	
$\dfrac{\lvert x_N + x_1 - 2\mu \rvert}{x_N - x_1}$; $N \leq 10$	Page 53, upper right-hand table	(601)

WALSH test[20, 21]

Applicability: Samples of size $4 \leq N \leq 14$ from *any symmetrical* population

Test quotient	Significance limit	
Page 53, lower right-hand table	Page 53, lower right-hand table	(602)

Note that while the use of (**598**b) and (**599**b) involves the squaring of $(\bar{x} - \mu)$ it obviates extracting the square root of s^2 (provided s is not required). The use of (**598**c) and (**599**c) avoids the multiplication by $\sqrt{N}$, with the further advantage that the transition from t to c in using the table on page 43 is quite 'automatic'.

(**600**)–(**602**) are straightforward *rapid tests* [especially (**601**)] in which even $\bar{x}$ does not need to be calculated. Within the tabulated range their power is practically the same as that of (**599**). The WALSH test is suitable not only for normal but also for *any* other symmetrical distribution. In this case, the significance probability for N up to 8 is somewhat higher than that in the table. For $N > 8$ the values in the table are exact.

When a calculating machine is not available, multiplication is faster than division. In this event, the significance limit should be multiplied by the divisor of the test quotient in order to obtain the limit for the dividend.

Example 38. When t is the limit for $\dfrac{\lvert x - \mu \rvert \sqrt{N}}{s}$, then ts is the limit for $\lvert x - \mu \rvert \sqrt{N}$.

16. The normally distributed population: Comparison of two samples

In comparing two samples, the following hypotheses concerning the parameters of the original populations must be taken into consideration:

$$\sigma_1^2 = \sigma_2^2 \quad \begin{cases} \mu_1 = \mu_2 & \text{(a)} \\ \mu_1 \neq \mu_2 & \text{(b)} \end{cases} \qquad \textbf{(603)}$$

$$\sigma_1^2 \neq \sigma_2^2 \quad \begin{cases} \mu_1 = \mu_2 & \text{(a)} \\ \mu_1 \neq \mu_2 & \text{(b)} \end{cases} \qquad \textbf{(604)}$$

16A. Comparison of variances

The test quotient for the hypothesis $(\sigma_1^2 = \sigma_2^2)$ (**603**) is (**570**), in which the *larger of the two sample variances must always be made the numerator*. This means that renumbering of the variances with respect to the *indices of the table* is necessary when s_1^2 (from sample 1) is smaller than s_2^2. *The number of degrees of freedom* ν_1 *in the tables on pages 40 and 41 is always that of the numerator of* (**570**). (**605**)

s_1^2 and s_2^2 must be calculated from (**492**). Their degrees of freedom are $\nu_1 = N_1 - 1$ and $\nu_2 = N_2 - 1$.

If the test quotient is *smaller* than the significance limit F in the table on pages 40 and 41, then in accordance with (**474**) it can be assumed that $\sigma_1^2 = \sigma_2^2$. In this case the means are tested by the procedure given in section 16B below. If the test quotient *attains* or *exceeds* the significance limit F, then $\sigma_1^2 > \sigma_2^2$ (significance probability $\alpha = P$) or $\sigma_1^2 \neq \sigma_2^2$ (significance probability $2\alpha = 2P$). The means are tested by the procedure given in section 16C, page 173.

16B. Comparison of means when $\sigma_1^2 = \sigma_2^2$

The following symbols are used here:

$$\lvert \bar{x}_1 - \bar{x}_2 \rvert = d \text{ and } \lvert \mu_1 - \mu_2 \rvert = \boldsymbol{d} \qquad \textbf{(606)}$$

The estimate of the common standard deviation $\sigma = \sigma_1 = \sigma_2$ is

$$\left.\begin{aligned} s &= \sqrt{\frac{S_1 + S_2}{N_1 + N_2 - 2}}; \; S_1 \text{ and } S_2 \text{ from } \textbf{(493)} \\ \nu_s &= \nu_1 + \nu_2 = N_1 + N_2 - 2 \end{aligned}\right\} \qquad \textbf{(607)}$$

The estimate of the standard deviation of the difference $\boldsymbol{d}$ is

$$s_d = s \sqrt{\frac{1}{N_1} + \frac{1}{N_2}}; \; s \text{ from } \textbf{(607)}; \; \nu_{s_d} = N_1 + N_2 - 2 \qquad \textbf{(608)}$$

If σ is known, s is replaced by σ in (**608**). If $N_1 = 1$, then $s_d = s\sqrt{1 + 1/N_2}$, $\nu = N_2 - 1$; cf. also (**452**) and (**583**c and e).

The test quotients for the hypotheses $(\mu_1 = \mu_2 \mid \sigma_1^2 = \sigma_2^2)$ are

if σ is known or $\nu > 200$

d/σ_d or d/s_d; limit $\lvert c_\alpha \rvert$, page 28 (a)

when $\nu \leq 200$

d/s_d; limit t_ν, pages 32–35; $\alpha = P$, $2\alpha = 2P$ (b) (**609**)

or

d^2/s_d^2; limit t_ν^2 $[= F(1; \nu)]$, page 42; $\alpha = \tfrac{1}{2} P$, $2\alpha = P$ (c)

If the test quotient *attains* or *exceeds* the significance limit, then this is considered as evidence that $\mu_1 \neq \mu_2$. In this case it is often desirable to test the hypothesis $(\mu_1 - \mu_2 = \boldsymbol{d} \mid \sigma_1^2 = \sigma_2^2)$:

The test quotients are obtained by replacing d in (**609**) by $\lvert d - \boldsymbol{d} \rvert$. If the quotient exceeds the significance limit, then this is considered as evidence that $\mu_1 - \mu_2 \neq \boldsymbol{d}$. (**610**)

The confidence limits for $\boldsymbol{d}$ are

two-sided

$\text{Prob}\,(d - t_{\nu,\alpha} \times s_d \leq \boldsymbol{d} \leq d + t_{\nu,\alpha} \times s_d) = 1 - 2\alpha$ (a)

one-sided with a single upper limit (**611**)

$\text{Prob}\,(\boldsymbol{d} \leq d + t_{\nu,\alpha} \times s_d) = 1 - \alpha$ (b)

If the test quotient in (**609**) is *smaller* than the significance limit, then it may be assumed in accordance with (**474**) that $\mu_1 = \mu_2$. Since also $\sigma_1^2 = \sigma_2^2$, the conclusion may be drawn that the two samples 1 and 2 originated from the same population with mean μ and variance σ^2. Estimates of these parameters are

$$\bar{x} = \frac{\sum_1^{N_1} x_1 + \sum_1^{N_2} x_2}{N_1 + N_2} = \frac{N_1 \bar{x}_1 + N_2 \bar{x}_2}{N_1 + N_2} \qquad \textbf{(612)}$$

$$\left.\begin{aligned} s^2 &= \frac{S_1 + S_2 + \dfrac{\left(\sum_1^{N_1} x_1\right)^2}{N_1} + \dfrac{\left(\sum_1^{N_2} x_2\right)^2}{N_2} - \dfrac{\left(\sum_1^{N_1} x_1 + \sum_1^{N_2} x_2\right)^2}{N_1 + N_2}}{N_1 + N_2 - 1} \\ &= \frac{\nu_1 s_1^2 + \nu_2 s_2^2 + N_1 \bar{x}_1^2 + N_2 \bar{x}_2^2 - \dfrac{(N_1 \bar{x}_1 + N_2 \bar{x}_2)^2}{N_1 + N_2}}{N_1 + N_2 - 1} \end{aligned}\right\} \qquad \textbf{(613)}$$

where $\nu_s = N_1 + N_2 - 1$; S_1 and S_2 from (**493**).

16C. Comparison of means when $\sigma_1^2 \neq \sigma_2^2$

If σ_1 and σ_2 are known, or $N_1 + N_2 > 200$, then

$$\sigma_{\boldsymbol{d}} = \sqrt{\frac{\sigma_1^2}{N_1} + \frac{\sigma_2^2}{N_2}} \quad \text{and} \quad s_d = \sqrt{\frac{s_1^2}{N_1} + \frac{s_2^2}{N_2}} \qquad \textbf{(614)}$$

and the test quotients

$$\frac{d}{\sigma_{\boldsymbol{d}}} \text{ and } \frac{d}{s_d} \text{ or } \frac{|d - \boldsymbol{d}|}{\sigma_{\boldsymbol{d}}} \text{ and } \frac{|d - \boldsymbol{d}|}{s_d} \qquad \textbf{(615)}$$

have the same limits as (**609**a).

If σ_1 and σ_2 are unknown, then the test quotients

$$\frac{d}{s_d} \text{ and } \frac{|d - \boldsymbol{d}|}{s_d} \qquad \textbf{(616)}$$

have the same limits as (**609**b)[53], where

$$s_d = \sqrt{\frac{s_1^2}{N_1} + \frac{s_2^2}{N_2}} \qquad \text{(a)}$$

$$\nu = \frac{1}{k^2/\nu_1 + (1-k)^2/\nu_2} \qquad \text{(b)} \qquad \textbf{(617)}$$

(ν_1 and ν_2 are degrees of freedom of s_1 and s_2 respectively)

$$k = \frac{N_2 s_1^2}{N_2 s_1^2 + N_1 s_2^2} \qquad \text{(c)}$$

16D. Testing pair differences

When two analytical methods can be tried out on the same substrate, or two methods of treatment on the same individual, then the *power of a test is considerably greater* if in place of the difference between *two* means, *one* mean calculated from the sum of the pair differences is tested.

Let A and B be the methods to be compared, $A_i - B_i = d_i$ the difference between the results given by these methods with the object i, N the total number of objects. A sample of size N of all pair differences d_i is thus obtained and can be tested in accordance with (**598**)–(**602**), usually with a hypothetical mean $\mu = 0$. Other even simpler methods of testing pair differences are the sign test (see section 10H, page 161), the WILCOXON test, and in certain cases appropriate sequential analysis (cf. section 26, page 196).

Methods 16A, B, C, E and 17A, B cannot be used in the case of 16D because of the non-independent nature of the samples.

16E. Tests for two samples using the extreme range[19]

(*a*) *Two samples of the same size* $N' = N'' = N \leq 20$:

$x'_N - x'_1$ and $x''_N - x''_1$ are the extreme ranges of these samples; the test quotient is then

$$\frac{|\bar{x}' - \bar{x}''|}{x'_N - x'_1 + x''_N - x''_1} \qquad \textbf{(618)}$$

(for limit see page 53, bottom left-hand table)

(*b*) *Two samples of unequal size*, or of the same size but larger than in (a):

The samples are divided respectively into m' and m'' random subgroups of the same size n (cf. section 14A, page 170). The sum of all the extreme ranges of these subgroups from both samples is denoted by S_E. The test quotient is then

$$\frac{|\bar{x}' - \bar{x}''|\sqrt{m'm''}}{S_E \times \boldsymbol{A}_{m,n}}; \quad (m = m' + m''; \text{ for limit see page 49, for } \boldsymbol{A}_{m,n} \text{ page 48}) \qquad \textbf{(619)}$$

17. The normally distributed population: Testing several samples

Given are n samples of sizes

$$N_1, N_2, \ldots, N_i, \ldots, N_n, \text{ where } \sum_1^n N_i = N \qquad \text{(a)}$$

The sums of the individual values x are

$$\sum_1^{N_1} x_1, \sum_1^{N_2} x_2, \ldots, \sum_1^{N_i} x_i, \ldots, \sum_1^{N_n} x_n, \text{ where } \sum_1^n \sum_1^{N_i} x_i = \sum_1^N x \qquad \text{(b)}$$

The sums of the individual squares x^2 are

$$\sum_1^{N_1} x_1^2, \sum_1^{N_2} x_2^2, \ldots, \sum_1^{N_i} x_i^2, \ldots, \sum_1^{N_n} x_n^2, \text{ where } \sum_1^n \sum_1^{N_i} x_i^2 = \sum_1^N x^2 \qquad \text{(c)}$$

The sums of squares calculated in accordance with (**493**) are

$$S_1, S_2, \ldots, S_i, \ldots, S_n, \text{ where } \sum_1^n S_i = S \qquad \text{(d)}$$

The degrees of freedom are

$$N_1 - 1, N_2 - 1, \ldots, N_i - 1, \ldots, N_n - 1,$$

(symbolized by $\nu_1, \nu_2, \ldots, \nu_i, \ldots, \nu_n$)

$$\text{where } \sum_1^n (N_i - 1) = N - n = \nu = \sum_1^n \nu_i \qquad \text{(e)} \qquad \textbf{(620)}$$

The means $\bar{x}_1, \bar{x}_2, \ldots, \bar{x}_i, \ldots, \bar{x}_n$ are defined by (**491**) (f)

and the variances $s_1^2, s_2^2, \ldots, s_i^2, \ldots, s_n^2$ by (**492**) (g)

17A. Testing variances

The hypothesis $\sigma_1^2 = \sigma_2^2 = \cdots = \sigma_i^2 = \cdots = \sigma_n^2$ is tested by means of BARTLETT's test[22].

An estimate of the common variance σ^2 is

$$s^2 = S/\nu, \quad \text{where } \nu_s = N - n \quad S, \nu \text{ and } N \text{ from } (\textbf{620}\text{d, e and a}) \qquad \textbf{(621)}$$

The test statistic for s^2 is

$$2.3026\,(\nu \log s^2 - \sum_1^n \nu_i \log s_i^2)/k; \qquad \text{(a)}$$

s^2 from (**621**), ν, ν_i and s_i^2 from (**620**e and g)

where

$$k = 1 + \left(\sum_1^n \frac{1}{\nu_i} - \frac{1}{\nu}\right)/3(n-1); \ \nu \text{ and } \nu_i \text{ from } (\textbf{620}\text{e}) \qquad \text{(b)} \qquad \textbf{(622)}$$

When $\nu_1 = \nu_2 = \cdots = \nu_i = \cdots = \nu_n = \nu_0$, (**622**a and b) become

$$2.3026\,\nu\,[\log s^2 - (1/n) \sum_1^n \log s_i^2]/k; \text{ see (a)} \qquad \text{(c)}$$

and

$$k = 1 + (n+1)/3\nu; \text{ see (b)} \qquad \text{(d)}$$

The significance limit for the test statistics (**622**a) and (**622**c) is found from the χ^2 distribution with degrees of freedom $\nu = n - 1$ (tables on pages 36–39, $2\alpha = 1\int_r$). If the test statistic *attains* or *exceeds* the significance limit, then we may suspect that populations with discrepant variances are among those being compared. If the test statistic is *smaller* than the limit, then in accordance with (**474**) it can be assumed that all the populations have the same variance. In this case the means can be further tested as described in section 17B below.

17B. Testing means: Simple analysis of variance

In testing the hypothesis $\mu_1 = \mu_2 = \cdots = \mu_i = \cdots = \mu_n$ the following tabulation is first made [cf. also (**620**)]:

	Sums of squares	Degrees of freedom	Variance
Variance between the samples....	S_2	$n - 1$	$s_2^2 = S_2/(n-1)$
Variances within the samples....	S_1	$N - n$	$s_1^2 = S_1/(N-n)$
Total..........	S_T	$N - 1$	$s_T^2 = S_T/(N-1)$

(623)

$$\text{where } S_2 = \sum_1^n N_i(\bar{x}_i - \bar{x})^2 = \sum_1^n \left(\sum_1^{N_i} x_i\right)^2 / N_i - \left(\sum_1^N x\right)^2 / N \qquad \text{(a)}$$

$$S_1 = S \,[\text{from } (\textbf{620}\text{d})] = S_T - S_2 \qquad \text{(b)}$$

$$S_T = S_1 + S_2 = \sum_1^N x^2 - \left(\sum_1^N x\right)^2 / N \qquad \text{(c)} \qquad \textbf{(624)}$$

$$\text{and } \bar{x} = \left(\sum_1^N x\right) / N \qquad \text{(d)}$$

In (**624**) a check is made by means of the two identities in (a), (b) and (c).

In (**623**), s_2^2 represents the dispersion of the sample means $\bar{x}_i$ around the common mean $\bar{x}$, s_1^2 the dispersion of the individual values around the sample means. If all the samples originate from the same population, so that $\mu_1 = \mu_2 = \cdots = \mu_i = \cdots = \mu_n = \mu$ (the hypothesis in the light of which the variances have been tested), then the variances s_2^2 and s_1^2 should be approximately of the same magnitude. If they are not, then among the samples are some with discrepant means, in which case s_2^2 must be greater than s_1^2. The necessity of carrying out the appropriate F test is thus avoided when $s_2^2 \leqq s_1^2$.

The test quotient is s_2^2/s_1^2, limit F, pages 40–41; $\alpha = P$ with $s_2^2 > s_1^2$. **(625)**

If the test quotient is smaller than the significance limit, then in accordance with **(474)** it can be assumed that all the samples originate from the same population. The estimates of their mean μ and variance σ^2 are

$\bar{x} =$ (**624**d); $s^2 =$ (**621**), with $\nu = N - n$ **(626)**

with confidence and tolerance intervals constructed as described in **(580)**–**(584)**.

If the test quotient attains or exceeds the significance limit F, then among the means there must be some of discrepant magnitude. Various methods of analysing this situation have been proposed[23]. Here that of DUNCAN[23] will be used.

The method is dependent on *all samples having the same size* N_0. The standard deviation of a mean $\bar{x}_i$ is first calculated

$$s_{\bar{x}_i} = \sqrt{s^2/N_0};\ s^2 \text{ from } (\mathbf{621}) \qquad (\mathbf{627})$$
$$\nu_{s\bar{x}_i} = N - n$$

The means $\bar{x}_i$ are now ranked

$$\bar{x}_1 < \bar{x}_2 < \cdots < \bar{x}_i < \cdots < \bar{x}_n;\quad 1, 2, \ldots, i, \ldots, n = \text{ranks } O \qquad (\mathbf{628})$$

and the n extreme ranges W_i corresponding to the degrees of freedom $\nu_{s\bar{x}_i}$ and the ranks $O = 2, 3, \ldots, n$ looked for in the table on page 50. Multiplication of these by the standard deviation of a mean $s_{\bar{x}_i}$ [cf. **(627)**] gives the extreme ranges of the means $W_{\bar{x}_i}$. Subtraction of these from the means $\bar{x}_i$ gives the 'localized extreme ranges' $\bar{x}_i - W_{\bar{x}_i}$. The following conclusions can now be drawn:

The means falling in a 'localized extreme range' $\bar{x}_i - W_{\bar{x}_i}$ cannot be distinguished from each other significantly. **(629)**

The means not distinguishable in **(629)** are underscored in the order of **(628)**, with the result that

two means *not* underscored with a common line differ from one another significantly (significance probability α of the table). **(630)**

Example 39. Given are 7 samples with the means $\bar{x}_i$ shown below. $N_0 = 5$, $N = 35$, $s_\nu = 0.099$, $\nu_s = 28$. Significance probability $= 0.05$.

From **(627)** the estimated standard deviation of a mean is $s_{\bar{x}_i} = \sqrt{0.099/5} \approx 0.1407$. The extreme ranges W_i and $W_{\bar{x}_i} = W_i \times s_{\bar{x}_i}$ are given in the table below. The differences $\bar{x}_i - W_{\bar{x}_i}$ are then calculated up to the point where the corresponding underscoring reaches or passes the lowest mean.

O	1	2	3	4	5	6	7
$\bar{x}$	1.34	1.36	1.48	1.62	1.74	1.88	2.04
W_i		2.90	3.04	3.13	3.20	3.26	3.30
$W_{\bar{x}_i}$		0.408	0.428	0.440	0.450	0.459	0.464
$\bar{x}_i - W_{\bar{x}_i}$					1.290	1.421	1.576
(629)	1.34	1.36	1.48	1.62	1.74	1.88	2.04

The final result is given by **(630)**: 2.04 > 1.34 to 1.48; 1.88 > 1.34 to 1.36.

18. The normally distributed population: Regressions of the first kind

Discussion will be limited here to *linear* regression functions. The functional relationships between two or more variables are often more or less obscured by random influences. Thus the effect of a dose of a drug, for example, will change in a certain way as the dose is increased. The effect will never be an exact function of the dosage, however, and even in the same subject will fluctuate around a curve – the *regression function* – in a random manner. Using statistical methods it is possible to estimate the parameters of the regression function and the required variances.

Although in the above example the dose is *not* a random variable, the effect it brings about is a random variable. In this case the regression is one of the *first kind*. In cases where *both* variables are random variables the regression is one of the *second kind*. A regression of the second kind can be treated as a regression of the first kind when the range of variation of the dependent variable as well as the points at which it is measured are arbitrarily decided beforehand.

In regressions of the first kind there is a *single* regression line, that of y on x, which is used for calculations in both directions – from y to x as well as from x to y. Cf. also section 19, page 179.

18A. Estimation of the parameters of the regression line Y [cf. also (298)–(311)]

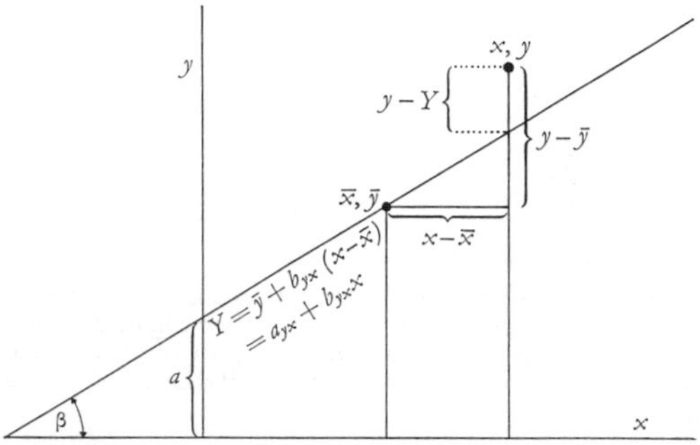

Fig. 35. Linear regression, ungrouped sample.

Ungrouped samples, two variables

Given are n pairs of observations x, y. x is the *independent, non-random* variable, y the *dependent, random* variable.

Estimate Y of the regression line $\mathbf{Y}$

$$Y = \bar{y} + b_{yx}(x - \bar{x}) \quad \text{(a)}$$
$$= a_{yx} + b_{yx}x \quad \text{(b)} \qquad (\mathbf{631})$$

where $a_{yx} = \bar{y} - b_{yx}\bar{x}$, with $\bar{y}$ and $\bar{x}$ calculated from **(491)**, b_{yx} from **(632)**.

Estimate b_{yx} of the regression coefficient $\boldsymbol{b}_{yx}$

$$b_{yx} = \frac{s_{xy}}{s_x^2} = \frac{S_{xy}}{S_x} \qquad (\mathbf{632})$$

with s_x^2 and S_x from **(492)** and **(493)**. For s_{xy} see **(633)**. b_{yx} is the tangent of the angle of inclination β_{yx} of the regression line Y. Cf. also **(299)**.

Estimate s_{xy} of the covariance σ_{xy}

$$s_{xy} = \frac{\Sigma(x - \bar{x})(y - \bar{y})}{n - 1} = \frac{S_{xy}}{n - 1} \qquad (\mathbf{633})$$

For S_{xy} see **(634)**.

The calculation of S_{xy} is facilitated by the use of the following sums:

$$S_{xy} = \Sigma(x - \bar{x})(y - \bar{y}) \quad \text{(a)}$$
$$= \Sigma xy - \bar{x}\Sigma y \quad \text{(b)}$$
$$= \Sigma xy - \bar{y}\Sigma x \quad \text{(c)} \qquad (\mathbf{634})$$
$$= \Sigma xy - \Sigma x \Sigma y/n \quad \text{(d)}$$
$$[= s_{xy}(n - 1)] \quad \text{(e)}$$

Estimate $s^2_{y\cdot x}$ of the residual variance $\sigma^2_{y\cdot x}$

$$s^2_{y\cdot x} = \frac{\Sigma(Y-y)^2}{n-2} = \frac{S_{y\cdot x}}{n-2} \quad \text{(a)}$$
$$= s^2_y(1-r^2)\frac{n-1}{n-2} \quad \text{(b)} \qquad \textbf{(635)}$$

For $S_{y\cdot x}$ and r^2 see **(636)** and **(704)**.

$\sigma^2_{y\cdot x}$ is the variance of y when x is fixed. It is *smaller* than the variance σ^2_y. In very rare cases (with very small correlation or regression coefficients) we can have

$$(1-r^2)\frac{n-1}{n-2} > 1, \text{ in which case } s^2_{y\cdot x} > s^2_y$$

Formula **(635b)** belongs properly in section 19, page 179, but has been included here for the reader's convenience.

If r is known, values of $1-r^2$ and of its square root can be taken from the table on page 59. Values of $(n-1)/(n-2)$ and of its square root for n between 1 and 250 are given in the table on page 60.

$$S_{y\cdot x} = S_y - b_{yx}S_{xy} \quad \text{(a)}$$
$$= S_y - b^2_{yx}S_x \quad \text{(b)} \qquad \textbf{(636)}$$
$$= S_y(1-r^2) \quad \text{(c)}$$

S_y and S_x from **(439)**; S_{xy} from **(634)**; b_{yx} from **(632)**; r^2 from **(704)**. The remarks above on **(635b)** apply also to **(636c)**.

Estimate $s^2_{b_{yx}}$ of the variance $\sigma^2_{b_{yx}}$

$$s^2_{b_{yx}} = s^2_{y\cdot x}/S_x \quad \text{(a)}$$
$$= (s^2_y/s^2_x) \times \frac{1-r^2}{n-2} = (S_y/S_x) \times \frac{1-r^2}{n-2} \quad \text{(b)} \qquad \textbf{(637)}$$

s^2_y and s^2_x from **(492)**; S_y and S_x from **(493)**; $s^2_{y\cdot x}$ from **(635)**; r^2 from **(704)**. The remarks above on **(635b)** apply also to **(637b)**.

Estimate $s^2_{Y|x}$ of the variance $\sigma^2_{Y|x}$ about the regression line $\mathbf{Y}$ for a given value of x

$$s^2_{Y|x} = s^2_{y\cdot x}\,[1/n + (x-\bar{x})^2/S_x] \quad \text{(a)}$$
$$= s^2_{b_{yx}}[S_x/n + (x-\bar{x})^2] \quad \text{(b)} \qquad \nu = n-2 \qquad \textbf{(638)}$$

S_x from **(493)**; $s^2_{y\cdot x}$ from **(635)**; $s^2_{b_{yx}}$ from **(637)**.

Special cases of **(638)** are:

Estimate $s^2_{\bar{y}}$ of the variance $\sigma^2_{\bar{y}}$ of the mean $\bar{y}$

$$s^2_{\bar{y}} = s^2_{y\cdot x}/n;\ \nu = n-2 \qquad \textbf{(639)}$$

Estimate $s^2_{a_{yx}}$ of the variance $\sigma^2_{a_{yx}}$ of the intercept a

$$s^2_{a_{yx}} = s^2_{y\cdot x}(1/n + \bar{x}^2/S_x) \quad \text{(a)}$$
$$= s^2_{b_{yx}}(\Sigma x^2)/n \quad \text{(b)} \qquad \nu = n-2 \qquad \textbf{(640)}$$

$s^2_{b_{yx}}$ from **(637)**.

Example 40. Given is the sample

x	y	x	y	x	y
5.8	2.19	7.0	4.62	8.2	6.58
6.2	3.27	7.4	5.32	8.6	7.41
6.6	3.79	7.8	5.85	9.0	8.29

The y values in this example correspond to the empirical probits of example 31 in section 11F, page 163.

It follows that

$\bar{x}$ = 7.4 from **(491)**
S_x = 9.6 from **(493)**
$\bar{y}$ = 47.32/9 = 5.25$\dot{7}$ from **(491)**
S_y = 280.651 − 248.798 = 31.853 from **(493)**
s^2_y = $S_y/8$ = 3.981625; s_y = 1.9954 from **(492b)**
S_{xy} = 367.620 − 350.168 = 17.452 from **(634)**
b_{yx} = 17.452/9.6 = 1.81791$\dot{6}$ from **(632)**
$S_{y\cdot x}$ = 31.8530 − 31.7263 = 0.1267 from **(636a or b)**
$s^2_{y\cdot x}$ = 0.1267/7 = 0.0181; $s_{y\cdot x}$ = 0.13454 from **(635a)**
$s^2_{b_{yx}}$ = 0.0181/9.6 = 0.00188542; $s_{b_{yx}}$ = 0.043421 from **(637a)**
$s^2_{\bar{y}}$ = 0.0181/9 = 0.0020$\dot{1}$; $s_{\bar{y}}$ = 0.044843 from **(639)**

$s^2_{a_{yx}}$ = 0.0181 $\left(0.\dot{1} + \frac{(7.4)^2}{9.6}\right)$ = 0.105257; $s_{a_{yx}}$ = 0.32443 from **(640a)**

Y = 5.25$\dot{7}$ + 1.81791$\dot{6}$ (x − 7.4) from **(631a)**
= − 8.1948 + 1.8179 x from **(631b)**

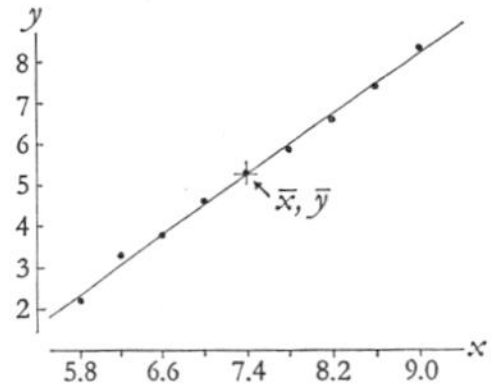

Fig. 36. Probit line of example 40.

A comparison of Figure 36 with Figure 30 (page 164) shows that the two probit lines – obtained by basically different methods – are hardly distinguishable by eye. The slope of the line of Figure 30 is 1/0.584 = 1.7123. As will be shown in section 18D, page 177, this differs significantly from the slope 1.8179 of Figure 36.

Grouped samples, two variables

Given are 1, 2, ..., i, ..., k points of measurement (columns) x_i with $m_1, m_2, \ldots, m_i, \ldots, m_k$ observations y_{ij}. x is the *independent, non-random* variable, y the *dependent, random* variable.

x	1	2	... i	... k		
y	11	21	... i1	... k1		
	12	22	... i2	... k2		
	⋮	⋮	⋮	⋮		
	1j	2j	ij	kj		
	⋮	⋮	⋮	⋮		
	1 m_1	2 m_2	$i\,m_i$	$k\,m_k$		
	$\sum_{j=1}^{m_1} y_{1j}$	$\sum_{j=1}^{m_2} y_{2j}$	$\sum_{j=1}^{m_i} y_{ij}$	$\sum_{j=1}^{m_k} y_{kj}$		
	Overall sum Σy; column sum Σy_i				(a; b)	**(641)**
	$\frac{(\sum_{j=1}^{m_1} y_{1j})^2}{m_1}$	$\frac{(\sum_{j=1}^{m_2} y_{2j})^2}{m_2}$	... $\frac{(\sum_{j=1}^{m_i} y_{ij})^2}{m_i}$	... $\frac{(\sum_{j=1}^{m_k} y_{kj})^2}{m_k}$		
	Overall sum $\Sigma(\Sigma y_i)^2/m_i$				(c)	
xy	$x_1\sum_{j=1}^{m_1} y_{1j}$	$x_2\sum_{j=1}^{m_2} y_{2j}$	... $x_i\sum_{j=1}^{m_i} y_{ij}$	... $x_k\sum_{j=1}^{m_k} y_{kj}$		
	Overall sum Σxy				(d)	
y^2	$(11)^2$	$(21)^2$	... $(i1)^2$	... $(k1)^2$		
	$(12)^2$	$(22)^2$	... $(i2)^2$	... $(k2)^2$		
	⋮	⋮	⋮	⋮		
	$(1j)^2$	$(2j)^2$	... $(ij)^2$	... $(kj)^2$		
	⋮	⋮	⋮	⋮		
	$(1\,m_1)^2$	$(2\,m_2)^2$	... $(i\,m_i)^2$	... $(k\,m_k)^2$		
	$\sum_{j=1}^{m_1} y^2_{1j}$	$\sum_{j=1}^{m_2} y^2_{2j}$	... $\sum_{j=1}^{m_i} y^2_{ij}$	... $\sum_{j=1}^{m_k} y^2_{kj}$		
	Overall sum Σy^2; column sum Σy^2_i				(e; f)	
x	$m_1 x_1$	$m_2 x_2$	... $m_i x_i$	... $m_k x_k$		
	Overall sum Σx				(g)	
	$m_1 x^2_1$	$m_2 x^2_2$	... $m_i x^2_i$	... $m_k x^2_k$		
	Overall sum Σx^2				(h)	
$n = m_1$	$+ m_2 + \cdots + m_i + \cdots + m_k$				(i)	

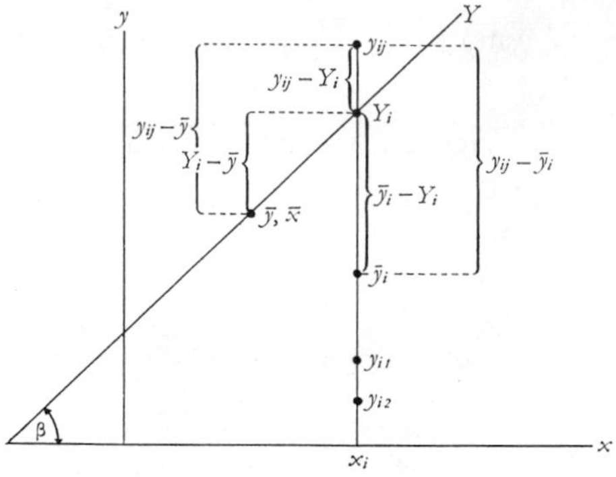

Fig. 37. Linear regression, grouped sample.

(**641**) allows the following to be calculated:

Column means

$$\bar{y}_i = (\Sigma y_i)/m_i = (\mathbf{641}\,\mathrm{b})m_i \qquad (\mathbf{642})$$

Sums of the squares of the deviations of the individual column values from the column means

$$Sy_i = \Sigma y_i^2 - (\Sigma y_i)^2/m_i = (\mathbf{641}\,\mathrm{f}) - (\mathbf{641}\,\mathrm{b})^2/m_i \qquad (\mathbf{643})$$

Overall mean

$$\bar{y} = (\Sigma y)/n = (\mathbf{641}\,\mathrm{a})/(\mathbf{641}\,\mathrm{i}) \qquad (\mathbf{644})$$

Mean of the independent variables

$$\bar{x} = (\Sigma x)/n = (\mathbf{641}\,\mathrm{g})/(\mathbf{641}\,\mathrm{i}) \qquad (\mathbf{645})$$

Sums of the squares of the deviations of x from $\bar{x}$

$$S_x = \Sigma x^2 - (\Sigma x)^2/n = (\mathbf{641}\,\mathrm{h}) - (\mathbf{641}\,\mathrm{g})^2/(\mathbf{641}\,\mathrm{i}) \qquad (\mathbf{646})$$

Sums of products

$$S_{xy} = \Sigma xy - \Sigma x\,\Sigma y/n = (\mathbf{641}\,\mathrm{d}) - (\mathbf{641}\,\mathrm{g})\,(\mathbf{641}\,\mathrm{a})/(\mathbf{641}\,\mathrm{i}) \qquad (\mathbf{647})$$

Regression coefficient

$$b_{yx} = S_{xy}/S_x = (\mathbf{647})/(\mathbf{646}) \qquad (\mathbf{648})$$

Sums of the squares for variation within columns

$$\left.\begin{aligned} S_1 &= \sum_1^k Sy_i = \sum_1^k (\mathbf{643}) \\ &\left[= \sum_{i=1}^{k}\sum_{j=1}^{m_i} (y_{ij} - \bar{y}_i)^2\right] \end{aligned}\right\} \qquad (\mathbf{649})$$

Sums of the squares of the deviations of the column means from the regression line Y

$$\left.\begin{aligned} S_2 &= \Sigma(\Sigma y_i)^2/m_i - (\Sigma y)^2/n - S_3 \\ &= (\mathbf{641}\,\mathrm{c}) - (\mathbf{641}\,\mathrm{a})^2/(\mathbf{641}\,\mathrm{i}) - (\mathbf{651}) \\ &\left[= \sum_{i=1}^{k} m_i\,(\bar{y}_i - Y_i)^2\right] \end{aligned}\right\} \qquad (\mathbf{650})$$

S_3 from (**651**)

Sums of the squares of the deviations of the regression line from the overall mean

$$\left.\begin{aligned} S_3 &= b_{yx}S_{xy} = b_{yx}^2 S_x = S_{xy}^2/S_x = (\mathbf{648})\,(\mathbf{647}) = (\mathbf{648})^2\,(\mathbf{646}) \\ &\left[= \sum_{i=1}^{k} m_i\,(Y_i - \bar{y})^2\right] \end{aligned}\right\} \qquad (\mathbf{651})$$

Sums of the squares of the deviations of the individual values from the overall mean

$$\left.\begin{aligned} S_y &= \Sigma y^2 - (\Sigma y)^2/n = (\mathbf{641}\,\mathrm{e}) - (\mathbf{641}\,\mathrm{a})^2/(\mathbf{641}\,\mathrm{i}) \\ &[= \Sigma\,(y_{ij} - \bar{y})^2] \end{aligned}\right\} \qquad (\mathbf{652})$$

Check:

$$S_1 + S_2 + S_3 = S_y \qquad (\mathbf{653})$$

Sums of the squares of the residual variations

$$S_{y\cdot x} = S_1 + S_2 = S_y - S_3 = (\mathbf{649}) + (\mathbf{650}) = (\mathbf{652}) - (\mathbf{651}) \qquad (\mathbf{654})$$

Estimated variances

$$s_1^2 = S_1/(n-k) = (\mathbf{649})/(n-k);\ \nu = n-k \qquad (\mathbf{655})$$

$$s_2^2 = S_2/(k-2) = (\mathbf{650})/(k-2);\ \nu = k-2 \qquad (\mathbf{656})$$

$$s_3^2 = S_3 = (\mathbf{651});\ \nu = 1 \qquad (\mathbf{657})$$

$$s_y^2 = S_y/(n-1) = (\mathbf{652})/(n-1);\ \nu = n-1 \qquad (\mathbf{658})$$

$$s_{y\cdot x}^2 = S_{y\cdot x}/(n-2) = (\mathbf{654})/(n-2);\ \nu = n-2 \qquad (\mathbf{659})$$

The equation of the regression line Y and the estimated variances $s_{b_{yx}}^2, s_{Y|x}^2, s_{\bar{y}}^2, s_{a_{yx}}^2$ are obtained from (**631**), (**637**), (**638**), (**639**) and (**640**) by replacing b_{yx} by (**648**), $s_{y\cdot x}^2$ by (**659**) and S_x by (**646**).

Example 41. Given is the sample

x	7	8	9
y	1.0 1.4 2.0 2.2	2.0 2.5 2.8 3.1 3.7 4.0	2.9 3.2 3.4 3.9 4.4
$\bar{y}_i$	6.6/4 = 1.65	18.1/6 = 3.01$\dot{6}$	17.8/5 = 3.56 from (**642**)
Sy_i	11.8 − 10.89 = 0.91	57.39 = 54.601$\dot{6}$ = 2.788$\dot{3}$	64.78 − 63.368 = 1.412 from (**643**)

$n = 15$ from (**641** i)
$\bar{y} = 42.5/15 = 2.8\dot{3}$ from (**644**); $\bar{x} = (28 + 48 + 45)/15 = 8.0\dot{6}$ from (**645**)
$S_x = (196 + 384 + 405) - (28 + 48 + 45)^2/15 = 8.9\dot{3}$ from (**646**)
$S_{xy} = 46.2 + 144.8 + 160.2 - 8.06 \times 42.5 = 8.3\dot{6}$ from (**647**)
$b_{yx} = 8.3\dot{6}/8.9\dot{3} = 0.936567164$ from (**648**)
$S_1 = 0.91 + 2.788\dot{3} + 1.412 = 5.110\dot{3}$ from (**649**)
$S_2 = 6.6^2/4 + 18.1^2/6 + 17.8^2/5 - 42.5^2/15 - S_3 = 0.607054728$ from (**650**)
$S_3 = 0.936567164 \times 8.3\dot{6} = 7.835945272$ from (**651**)
$S_y = 133.97 - 42.5^2/15 = 13.55\dot{3}$ from (**652**)

Check: $5.110\dot{3} + 0.607054728 + 7.835945272 = 13.55\dot{3}$ from (**653**)
$S_{x\cdot y} = 5.110\dot{3} + 0.607055 = 5.717388$ from (**654**)
$s_{y\cdot x}^2 = 5.717388/13 = 0.439799$; $s_{y\cdot x} = 0.663173$ from (**659**)
$s_{b_{yx}}^2 = 0.439799/8.9\dot{3} = 0.0492312$; $s_{b_{yx}} = 0.221881$ from (**637** a)
$Y = 2.8\dot{3} + 0.936567(x - 8.0\dot{6}) = -4.72164 + 0.936567\,x$ from (**631**)
$s_1^2 = S_1/12 = 0.425861$ from (**655**); $s_2^2 = S_2/1$ from (**656**); $s_3^2 = S_3$ from (**657**)

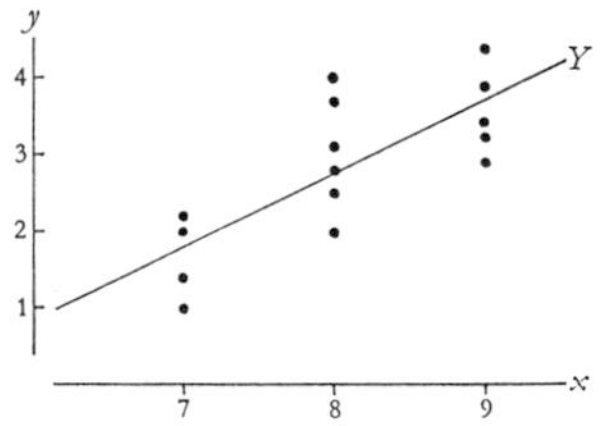

Fig. 38. Regression line of example 41.

18B. Testing the linearity of the regression function

With *ungrouped* samples, general departure from linearity of the regression function can be tested only by eye. The deviations $Y_i - y_i$ should give an impression of randomness and not show any systematic trend (cf. for example Fig. 29 [systematic deviations] with Fig. 30, right [apparently random deviations], on page 164).

With *grouped* samples an exact test is possible, namely by comparing the variance of the column means about the regression line with the variance within the columns.

Test quotient:

$$s_2^2/s_1^2 = (\mathbf{656})/(\mathbf{655});\ \text{significance limit } F \begin{cases} \nu_2 = k-2 \\ \nu_1 = n-k \end{cases} \qquad (\mathbf{660})$$

($2P = 2\alpha$, table on pages 40 and 41 [ν_1 of the table $= \nu_2$ of the test quotient])

If the test quotient *attains* or *exceeds* the significance limit, then the regression function is quite possibly nonlinear (significance probability $2\alpha = 2P$). If the test quotient is *smaller* than the significance limit, then in accordance with **(474)** it can be assumed that the regression is linear. Extrapolation of this interpretation beyond the range of variation of x in the samples should only be done with the greatest caution.

Example 42. In example 41, $s_1^2 = 0.425861$ and $s_2^2 = 0.607055$. From **(660)** the value of the test quotient is 1.43, that of the significance limit $F(1; 12)$ for $P = 0.05$ is 4.75. The statistical test therefore does not disprove the linearity of the regression function.

18C. Testing the regression coefficient against zero

If the linearity of the regression function is not disproved by the test **(660)**, the next step is to test the regression coefficient against zero, that is, to test the hypothesis $\boldsymbol{b}_{yx} = 0$. In other words, the estimate of the regression coefficient is tested for a significant difference from zero.

Test statistics:

$b_{yx}/s_{b_{yx}}$; significance limit t; $2P = 2\alpha$, $\nu = n - 2$, pages 32-35 **(661)**

b_{yx} from **(632)** or **(648)**, $s_{b_{yx}} = \sqrt{(\mathbf{637}\,a)}$

or

$b_{yx}^2/s_{b_{yx}}^2 = b\,S_{xy}/s_{y\cdot x}^2$; significance limit t^2; $P = 2\alpha$, $\nu = n - 2$, page 42 (a)

or **(662)**

$b\,S_{xy} - t_{2\alpha}^2\, s_{y\cdot x}^2$; significance limit null; t^2 as in **(662**a) (b)

[With ungrouped samples, $b\,S_{xy}$ is obtained from **(632)** and **(634)**, with grouped samples from **(651)**. $s_{y\cdot x}^2$ is obtained from **(635)** or **(659)**]

or

if the correlation coefficient r has been calculated (cf. section 19A, page 179), then

when $\boldsymbol{r} = 0$, it follows that $\boldsymbol{b}_{yx}$ (and $\boldsymbol{b}_{xy}$) $= 0$ **(663)**

and vice versa. The hypothesis $\boldsymbol{b}_{yx} = 0$ can be tested using r. Significance limit for $|r|$, see page 61; $\nu = n - 2$.

If any of the test statistics in **(661)**–**(663)** attains or exceeds the corresponding significance limit, then b_{yx} differs significantly from zero. The above tests are special cases of **(664**a) for $\boldsymbol{b}_{yx} = 0$.

18D. Testing the difference between estimate and hypothetical value

All the differences specified are *normally distributed.* For degrees of freedom over 200, the deviation $|c_\alpha|$ of the normal distribution (page 28) is therefore adopted as significance limit, for degrees of freedom up to 200 the deviation $t_{P=\alpha}$ or $t_{2P=2\alpha}$ of the Student distribution [χ^2 or t^2 can of course also be used; cf. **(598**b) and **(599**b)].

Test quotients (absolute values should be used)

$(b_{yx} - \boldsymbol{b}_{yx})/s_{b_{yx}}$; $\nu = n - 2$; $s_{b_{yx}} = \sqrt{(\mathbf{637})}$ (a)

$(Y\,|\,x - \boldsymbol{Y}\,|\,x)/s_{Y|x}$; $\nu = n - 2$; $s_{Y|x} = \sqrt{(\mathbf{638})}$ (b)

$(\bar{y} - \mu_y)/s_{\bar{y}}$; $\nu = n - 2$; $s_{\bar{y}} = \sqrt{(\mathbf{639})}$ (c) **(664)**

$(a_{yx} - \boldsymbol{a}_{yx})/s_{a_{yx}}$; $\nu = n - 2$; $s_{a_{yx}} = \sqrt{(\mathbf{640})}$ (d)

Example 43 [of **(664**a)]. Comparison between the regression coefficients of examples 31 (page 164) and 40 (page 175), which have the values 1.7123 and 1.8179 respectively. Since the former was not calculated from **(632)**, it will be considered here as a hypothetical value. The test quotient has the value

$$\frac{1.8179 - 1.7123}{0.04342} = 2.432; \quad \nu = 7$$

The corresponding significance limit $t_{2\alpha=0.05}$, page 32, is 2.3646. The two regression coefficients, and therefore the regression lines, thus differ significantly.

18E. Confidence and tolerance limits

Here only the formulae for the two-sided limits will be given, and these in the form of 'estimate $\pm G$' (estimate minus G = lower limit, estimate plus G = upper limit). The parameters are intended to be included between these two limits.

Confidence limits

For $\boldsymbol{b}_{yx}$: $b_{yx} \pm t_{2\alpha}\, s_{b_{yx}}$; $\nu = n - 2 \leq 200$; $b_{yx} \pm |c_\alpha|\, s_{b_{yx}}$; $\nu = n - 2 > 200$; $s_{b_{yx}} = \sqrt{(\mathbf{637})}$ **(665)**

For $\boldsymbol{Y}\,|\,x$: $\bar{y} + b_{yx}(x - \bar{x}) \pm t_{2\alpha}\, s_{Y|x}$; $\nu = n - 2 \leq 200$; $\pm |c_\alpha|\, s_{Y|x}$; $\nu = n - 2 > 200$; $s_{Y|x} = \sqrt{(\mathbf{638})}$ **(666)**

For μ_y: $\bar{y} \pm t_{2\alpha}\, s_{\bar{y}}$; $\nu = n - 2 \leq 200$; $\bar{y} \pm |c_\alpha|\, s_{\bar{y}}$; $\nu = n - 2 > 200$; $s_{\bar{y}} = \sqrt{(\mathbf{639})}$ **(667)**

For $\boldsymbol{a}_{yx}$: $a_{yx} \pm t_{2\alpha}\, s_{a_{yx}}$; $\nu = n - 2 \leq 200$; $a_{yx} \pm |c_\alpha|\, s_{a_{yx}}$; $\nu = n - 2 > 200$; $s_{a_{yx}} = \sqrt{(\mathbf{640})}$ **(668)**

(666) is a hyperbola (cf. Fig. 39).

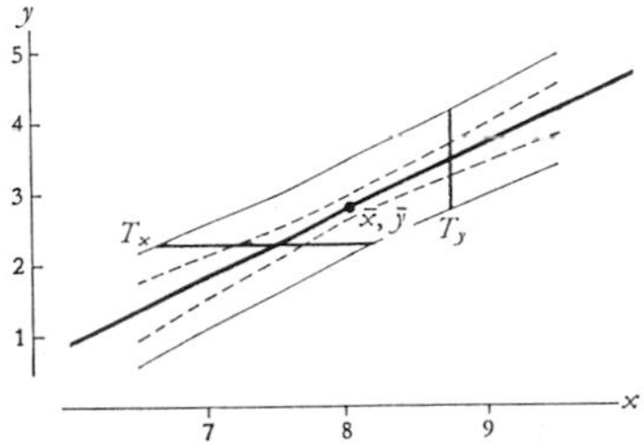

Fig. 39. Confidence and tolerance limits for the regression of Figure 38. - - - Confidence limits for $\boldsymbol{Y}$. ——— Tolerance limits for $\boldsymbol{Y}$. T_y Tolerance interval for $Y\,|\,x$. T_x Tolerance interval for $X\,|\,y$.

Tolerance limits for $\boldsymbol{Y}\,|\,x$

$= \bar{y} + b_{yx}(x - \bar{x}) \pm t_{2\alpha}\, s_T$; $\nu_t = n - 2$; b_{yx} from **(632)** or **(648)** **(669)**

where

$s_T = s_{y\cdot x}\sqrt{1 + 1/n + (x - \bar{x})^2/S_x}$; $\nu = n - 2$ (a)

$= s_{b_{yx}}\sqrt{(1 + 1/n)\, S_x + (x - \bar{x})^2}$; $\nu = n - 2$ (b) **(670)**

S_x from **(493)** or **(646)**; $s_{y\cdot x} = \sqrt{(\mathbf{635})}$ or $\sqrt{(\mathbf{659})}$; $s_{b_{yx}} = \sqrt{(\mathbf{637}\,a)}$; $\bar{x}$ = **(491)** or **(645)**

18F. Estimation of x when y is given

$$x\,|\,y = \bar{x} + \frac{y - \bar{y}}{b_{yx}} \qquad \textbf{(671)}$$

Confidence limits for the expected value of x, *given* y [solution from **(666)** for x]

$$\bar{x} + \frac{y - \bar{y}}{b_{yx}(1 - k^2)} \pm \pm \frac{k}{b_{yx}(1 - k^2)}\sqrt{(1/n)\, b_{yx}^2 (1 - k^2)\, S_x + (y - \bar{y})^2} \qquad \textbf{(672)}$$

where for ungrouped samples b_{yx} and S_x are obtained from **(632)** and **(493)**, for grouped samples from **(648)** and **(646)**

$$k^2 = \frac{t_{2\alpha}^2\, s_{b_{yx}}^2}{b_{yx}^2}; \quad \nu_t = n - 2 \qquad \textbf{(673)}$$

where $s_{b_{yx}}^2$ = **(637)**.

If $k^2 \leq 0.05$, then $1 - k^2$ can be taken as 1 in **(672)**.

Tolerance limits for $x\,|\,y$ [solution from **(669)** for x]

(672) is used, but with $(1 + 1/n)$ in place of $1/n$ in the term under the root. **(674)**

Example 44. In example 40, it is required to calculate x for $y = 5$ and the corresponding confidence and tolerance limits $x\,|\,y = 5$.

$$x = 7.4 + \frac{5 - 5.25\dot{7}}{1.81791\dot{6}} = 7.2582 \text{ from } \textbf{(671)}$$

Confidence limits: k^2 is first calculated from (**673**), giving

$$k^2 = \frac{2.3646^2 \times 0.00188542}{1.817916} = 0.003190;\ k = 0.05648$$

k^2 is less than 0.05, so that $1 - k^2$ can be taken as 1 in (**672**). For purposes of comparison, however, (**672**) is calculated with both values:

	Confidence limits	Tolerance limits
$1 - k^2 = 1$	7.2582 ± 0.0589 $= 7.1993$ to 7.3171	7.2582 ± 0.5534 $= 6.7048$ to 7.8116
$1 - k^2 = 0.996810$	7.2577 ± 0.0590 $= 7.1987$ to 7.3167 from (**672**)	7.2577 ± 0.5545 $= 6.7032$ to 7.8122 from (**674**)

18G. Comparison of two regression lines of the first kind

Given are the following ungrouped and grouped samples

$(x, y)_1$	and $(x, y)_2$	
with n_1	and n_2	pairs of observations
$\bar{x}_1$	and $\bar{x}_2$	from (**491**) or (**645**)
$\bar{y}_1$	and $\bar{y}_2$	from (**491**) or (**644**)
S_{x_1}	and S_{x_2}	from (**493**) or (**646**)
S_{y_1}	and S_{y_2}	from (**493**) or (**652**)
$(S_{xy})_1$	and $(S_{xy})_2$	from (**634**) or (**647**)
$(S_{y\cdot x})_1$	and $(S_{y\cdot x})_2$	from (**636**) or (**654**)
$(s^2_{y\cdot x})_1$	and $(s^2_{y\cdot x})_2$	from (**635**) or (**659**)
$(b_{yx})_1 = b_1$	and $(b_{yx})_2 = b_2$	from (**632**) or (**648**)
Y_1	and Y_2	from (**631**)

In analogy with section 16 (page 172), the following hypotheses must be considered in comparing two linear regressions:

$$(\sigma^2_{y\cdot x})_1 = (\sigma^2_{y\cdot x})_2 \begin{cases} \boldsymbol{b}_1 = \boldsymbol{b}_2 \begin{cases} \boldsymbol{Y}_1 = \boldsymbol{Y}_2 & \text{(a c)} \\ \boldsymbol{Y}_1 \neq \boldsymbol{Y}_2 & \text{(a d)} \end{cases} & \text{(a)} \\ \boldsymbol{b}_1 \neq \boldsymbol{b}_2 & \text{(b)} \end{cases} \quad \textbf{(675)}$$

$$(\sigma^2_{y\cdot x})_1 \neq (\sigma^2_{y\cdot x})_2 \begin{cases} \boldsymbol{b}_1 = \boldsymbol{b}_2 \begin{cases} \boldsymbol{Y}_1 = \boldsymbol{Y}_2 & \text{(a c)} \\ \boldsymbol{Y}_1 \neq \boldsymbol{Y}_2 & \text{(a d)} \end{cases} & \text{(a)} \\ \boldsymbol{b}_1 \neq \boldsymbol{b}_2 & \text{(b)} \end{cases} \quad \textbf{(676)}$$

The hypothesis $(\sigma^2_{y\cdot x})_1 = (\sigma^2_{y\cdot x})_2$ is tested by means of the quotient

$$\frac{(s^2_{y\cdot x})_1}{(s^2_{y\cdot x})_2};\ \begin{cases} \text{significance limit } F; \\ 2P = 2\alpha; \end{cases} \begin{cases} \nu_1 = n_1 - 2 \\ \nu_2 = n_2 - 2 \end{cases};\ \text{pages 40 and 41} \quad \textbf{(677)}$$

where the *greater* of the variances is given the index 1.

If the test quotient (**677**) is *smaller* than the significance limit, then (**678**)–(**693**) are valid; if the quotient attains or exceeds the significance limit, then (**694**)–(**701**) are valid.

If the test quotient (**677**) is *smaller* than the significance limit, then it is reasonable to assume that $(\sigma^2_{y\cdot x})_1 = (\sigma^2_{y\cdot x})_2$. The common variance $\bar{\sigma}^2_{y\cdot x}$ of the two regression lines can then be estimated under the condition of (**675**) as

$$\bar{s}^2_{y\cdot x} = \frac{(S_{y\cdot x})_1 + (S_{y\cdot x})_2}{n_1 + n_2 - 4};\ \nu = n_1 + n_2 - 4 \quad \textbf{(678)}$$

(**678**) is used to test the hypothesis (**675** a), i.e., $b_1 = b_2$. The test quotient for the difference between the two regression coefficients under the conditions of (**675**) is

$$\frac{b_1 - b_2}{s_{Db}};\ \text{significance limit } t;\ 2P = 2\alpha;\ \nu_t = n_1 + n_2 - 4 \quad \textbf{(679)}$$

$$\text{where } s^2_{D_b} = \textbf{(678)} \times \left(\frac{1}{S_{x_1}} + \frac{1}{S_{x_2}}\right) \quad \textbf{(680)}$$

If the test quotient (**679**) is *smaller* than the significance limit, then (**681**)–(**693**) are valid. If the quotient *attains* or *exceeds* the significance limit, then the regression lines are not parallel, i.e., $b_1 \neq b_2$. In other words,

if the test quotient (**679**) is *smaller* than the significance limit, then the two regression lines may be regarded as *parallel*. (**681**)

The estimate of the common residual variance $\bar{\sigma}^2_{y\cdot x}$ when the conditions of (**675** a) are fulfilled is

$$\bar{s}^2_{y\cdot x} \approx \textbf{(678)};\ \nu = n_1 + n_2 - 4$$
$$= \frac{(S_{y\cdot x})_1 + (S_{y\cdot x})_2 + \dfrac{(b_1 - b_2)^2}{1/S_{x_1} + 1/S_{x_2}}}{n_1 + n_2 - 3};\ \nu = n_1 + n_2 - 3 \quad \textbf{(682)}$$

The estimate $\bar{b}_{yx}$ of the common regression coefficient $\boldsymbol{b}_{yx}$ when the conditions of (**675** a) are fulfilled is

$$\bar{b}_{yx} = \frac{(S_{xy})_1 + (S_{xy})_2}{S_{x_1} + S_{x_2}} \quad \textbf{(683)}$$

The estimate $s^2_{\bar{b}_{yx}}$ of the variance $\sigma^2_{\bar{b}_{yx}}$ of the common regression coefficient when the conditions of (**675** a) are fulfilled is

$$s^2_{\bar{b}_{yx}} \approx \frac{\textbf{(678)}}{S_{x_1} + S_{x_2}};\ \nu = n_1 + n_2 - 4 \quad \text{(a)}$$
$$= \frac{\textbf{(682)}}{S_{x_1} + S_{x_2}};\ \nu = n_1 + n_2 - 3 \quad \text{(b)} \qquad \textbf{(684)}$$

The two lines may be considered as *identical* [hypothesis (**675** a c)] when the test quotient

$$\frac{\hat{b} - \bar{b}}{s_{\hat{b}-\bar{b}}};\ \begin{cases} \nu = n_1 + n_2 - 4, \text{ when } s_{\hat{b}-\bar{b}} = \sqrt{\textbf{(687 a)}} & \bar{b} = \textbf{(686)} \\ \nu = n_1 + n_2 - 3, \text{ when } s_{\hat{b}-\bar{b}} = \sqrt{\textbf{(687 b)}} & \bar{b} = \textbf{(683)} \end{cases} \quad \textbf{(685)}$$

is *smaller* than the significance limit t ($2P = 2\alpha$, pages 32–35).

$$\hat{b} = \frac{\bar{y}_1 - \bar{y}_2}{\bar{x}_1 - \bar{x}_2} \quad \textbf{(686)}$$

$$\left.\begin{aligned} s^2_{\hat{b}-\bar{b}} &\approx \textbf{(678)} \times K \\ &= \textbf{(682)} \times K \end{aligned}\right\} \text{ where } K = \textbf{(688)} \quad \begin{matrix}\text{(a)} \\ \text{(b)}\end{matrix} \quad \textbf{(687)}$$

$$K = \frac{1}{(\bar{x}_1 - \bar{x}_2)^2}\left(\frac{1}{n_1} + \frac{1}{n_2}\right) + \frac{1}{S_{x_1} + S_{x_2}} \quad \textbf{(688)}$$

The two parallel regression lines do not coincide [hypothesis (**675** a d)] when the test quotient (**685**) *attains* or *exceeds* the significance limit. In this case the vertical and horizontal distances p_y and p_x are often of interest.

The *vertical distance* p_y and its confidence limits, when the conditions of (**675** a d) are fulfilled, are

$$p_y = |\bar{y}_1 - \bar{y}_2 - \bar{b}_{yx}(\bar{x}_1 - \bar{x}_2)|;\ \bar{b}_{yx} = \textbf{(683)} \quad \textbf{(689)}$$

Confidence limits for $\boldsymbol{p}_{Y|x}$

$$\approx \textbf{(689)} \pm t_{2\alpha}\sqrt{\textbf{(684a)} \times [(1/n_1 + 1/n_2)(S_{x_1} + S_{x_2}) + (\bar{x}_1 - \bar{x}_2)^2]} \quad \text{(a)}$$
where $\nu_t = n_1 + n_2 - 4$
$$= \textbf{(689)} \pm t_{2\alpha}\sqrt{\textbf{(684b)} \times [(1/n_1 + 1/n_2)(S_{x_1} + S_{x_2}) + (\bar{x}_1 - \bar{x}_2)^2]} \quad \text{(b)}$$
where $\nu_t = n_1 + n_2 - 3$ **(690)**

The *horizontal distance* p_x and its confidence limits, when the conditions of (**675** a d) are fulfilled, are

$$p_x = \left|\bar{x}_1 - \bar{x}_2 - \frac{\bar{y}_1 - \bar{y}_2}{\bar{b}_{yx}}\right|;\ \bar{b}_{yx} \text{ from } \textbf{(683)} \quad \textbf{(691)}$$

Confidence limits for $\boldsymbol{p}_x$

$$\approx \text{or} = \left|\bar{x}_1 - \bar{x}_2 - \frac{\bar{y}_1 - \bar{y}_2}{\bar{b}_{yx}(1 - k^2)}\right| \pm \frac{k}{\bar{b}_{yx}(1 - k^2)} \times \sqrt{\left(\frac{1}{n_1} + \frac{1}{n_2}\right)\left(\bar{b}_{yx}\right)^2\left(1 - k^2\right)\left(S_{x_1} + S_{x_2}\right) + \left(\bar{y}_1 - \bar{y}_2\right)^2} \quad \textbf{(692)}$$

where $\bar{b}_{yx} = \textbf{(683)}$ and either $k = k_1 = \textbf{(693}\,\text{a)}$ or $k = k_2 = \textbf{(693}\,\text{b)}$. The approximation sign is for $k = k_1$, the equality sign for $k = k_2$.

$$\left.\begin{matrix} k_1^2 \\ k_2^2 \end{matrix}\right\} = \frac{t^2_{2\alpha}\, s^2_{\bar{b}_{yx}}}{(\bar{b}_{yx})^2};\ \begin{cases} s^2_{\bar{b}_{yx}} = \textbf{684}\text{a};\ \nu_t = n_1 + n_2 - 4 & \text{(a)} \\ s^2_{\bar{b}_{yx}} = \textbf{684}\text{b};\ \nu_t = n_1 + n_2 - 3 & \text{(b)} \end{cases} \quad \textbf{(693)}$$

When $k \leq 0.05$, the term $1 - k^2$ in (**692**) can be taken as 1.

If the test quotient (**677**) *attains* or *exceeds* the significance limit, then hypothesis (**676**) is valid, that is to say, $(\sigma^2_{y\cdot x})_1 \neq (\sigma^2_{y\cdot x})_2$.

Hypothesis (**676**a), that $b_1 = b_2$, is then tested by means of the quotient (**679**), where

$$\left.\begin{aligned} &s^2_{D_b} = \frac{(s^2_{y\cdot x})_1}{S_{x_1}} + \frac{(s^2_{y\cdot x})_2}{S_{x_2}} && \text{(a)} \\ &\text{Degrees of freedom } \nu_t = (\mathbf{617}\text{b}) \\ &\text{with } k = \frac{(s^2_{y\cdot x})_1 S_{x_2}}{(s^2_{y\cdot x})_1 S_{x_2} + (s^2_{y\cdot x})_2 S_{x_1}} && \text{(b)} \end{aligned}\right\} \quad (\mathbf{694})$$

Significance limit $t_{2\alpha}$, with ν_t from (**617**b) and k from (**694**b).

If the test quotient (**679**) fitted to (**694**) is *smaller* than the significance limit, then it can be assumed that $b_1 = b_2$. The common regression coefficient is then

$$\bar{b}_{yx} = \frac{\dfrac{(S_{xy})_1}{(s^2_{y\cdot x})_1} + \dfrac{(S_{xy})_2}{(s^2_{y\cdot x})_2}}{\dfrac{S_{x_1}}{(s^2_{y\cdot x})_1} + \dfrac{S_{x_2}}{(s^2_{y\cdot x})_2}} \quad (\mathbf{695})$$

with the estimated variance

$$s^2_{\bar{b}yx} = \frac{1}{\dfrac{S_{x_1}}{(s^2_{y\cdot x})_1} + \dfrac{S_{x_2}}{(s^2_{y\cdot x})_2}} \quad (\mathbf{696})$$

Provided that the sample sizes n_1 and n_2 are *large*, the hypothesis (**676**a c) that the two parallel regression lines are *identical* can be tested approximately by means of the quotient (**685**), where

$$\hat{b} = (\mathbf{686})$$

$$s^2_{\bar{b}-\bar{b}} = \frac{1}{(\bar{x}_1 - \bar{x}_2)^2}\left[\frac{(s^2_{y\cdot x})_1}{n_1} + \frac{(s^2_{y\cdot x})_2}{n_2} + (\mathbf{696})\right] \quad (\mathbf{697})$$

Significance limit $|c_\alpha|$, page 28.

If the test quotient (**685**) fitted to (**697**) *attains* or *exceeds* the significance limit, then the two parallel regression lines probably do *not* coincide. In this case, when the conditions of (**676**a d) are fulfilled,

the *vertical* distance is

$$p_y = (\mathbf{689});\ \text{where } \bar{b}_{yx} = (\mathbf{695}) \quad (\mathbf{698})$$

with confidence limits

$$\approx (\mathbf{698}) \pm |c_\alpha| \times \sqrt{\frac{(s^2_{y\cdot x})_1}{n_1} + \frac{(s^2_{y\cdot x})_2}{n_2} + (\bar{x}_1 - \bar{x}_2)^2 \times (\mathbf{696})} \quad (\mathbf{699})$$

the *horizontal* distance is

$$p_x = (\mathbf{691});\ \text{where } \bar{b}_{yx} = (\mathbf{695}) \quad (\mathbf{700})$$

with confidence limits

$$\left.\begin{aligned} &\approx \left| x_1 - x_2 - \frac{\bar{y}_1 - \bar{y}_2}{\bar{b}_{yx}(1-k^2)} \right| \pm \frac{k}{\bar{b}_{yx}(1-k^2)} \times \\ &\times \sqrt{\left[\frac{(s^2_{y\cdot x})_1}{n_1} + \frac{(s^2_{y\cdot x})_2}{n_2}\right] \frac{(\bar{b}_{yx})^2(1-k^2)}{(\mathbf{696})} + (\bar{y}_1 - \bar{y}_2)^2} \end{aligned}\right\} \quad (\mathbf{701})$$

$\Big[k^2 = \dfrac{c^2_\alpha \times (\mathbf{696})}{(\bar{b}_{yx})^2}$; c_α, page 28; $c^2_\alpha = \chi^2$, $\nu = 1$, $1\int_r = 2\alpha$, page 36;

$\bar{b}_{yx} = (\mathbf{695})\Big]$

When $k \leq 0.05$, the term $1 - k^2$ in (**701**) can be taken as 1.

Probit and logit regressions

With appropriate modifications, many of the formulae given in section 18 can be applied to probit and logit regressions. For further details the reader is referred to the literature.

Probit regression[11,12,24], tables on pages 54 and 55

Logit regression[25], tables on pages 56 and 57

19. The bivariate normal distribution: Regressions of the second kind

(Cf. introduction to section 18, page 174)

Given are n pairs of observations x, y. Both x and y are *random*, normally distributed variables.

Regressions of the second kind are distinguished from those of the first kind by the existence of *two* regression lines

$$\left.\begin{aligned} Y &= \bar{y} + b_{yx}(x - \bar{x}) && \text{(a)} \\ X &= \bar{x} + b_{xy}(y - \bar{y}) && \text{(b)} \end{aligned}\right\} \quad (\mathbf{702})$$

In regressions of the first kind, inferences both from x to y and from y to x are made on the basis of (**702**a) = (**631**), while in regressions of the second kind they are made from x to y on the basis of (**702**a) and from y to x on the basis of (**702**b).

Estimates of the parameters of (**702**) and their variances are made by means of the appropriate formulae in section 18. In estimating the parameters of (**702**b), x and y in these formulae must be transposed.

19A. The correlation coefficient

A further parameter of regressions of the second kind is the correlation coefficient r, a measure of the stochastic dependence of the two variables x and y. Its value can lie between -1 and $+1$. If it amounts to either -1 or $+1$, the two variables are totally dependent upon one another, and the two regression lines Y and X coincide. If its value is zero, the variables are independent of one another, and the two regression lines Y and X are at right angles to one another and parallel to the coordinate axes. The remarks in (**361**) apply here too to the expressions 'dependent' and 'independent', so that a realistic interpretation of the correlation coefficient is often difficult or even impossible.

When the correlation coefficient is less than, equal to, or greater than zero, the two regression coefficients b_{yx} and b_{xy} are likewise less than, equal to, or greater than zero. (**703**)

The following relationships are valid for the correlation coefficient

$$\left.\begin{aligned} &\mathbf{r} = \frac{\sigma_{xy}}{\sigma_x \sigma_y} && \text{(a)} \\ &\text{and for its estimate} \\ &r = \frac{s_{xy}}{s_x s_y} = \frac{S_{xy}}{\sqrt{S_x S_y}};\ S_x \text{ and } S_y \text{ from } (\mathbf{493}),\ S_{xy} \text{ from } (\mathbf{634}) && \text{(b)} \end{aligned}\right\} \quad (\mathbf{704})$$

The square of the correlation coefficient r^2 is also known as the coefficient (or index) of determination.

From (**704**) it follows that

$$r = \sqrt{\frac{s_{xy}}{s^2_x} \times \frac{s_{xy}}{s^2_y}} = \sqrt{b_{yx} \times b_{xy}} \quad (\mathbf{705})$$

From (**115**) it therefore follows that the correlation coefficient is also the *geometrical mean* of the two regression coefficients b_{yx} and b_{xy}.

Under the hypothesis $\mathbf{r} = 0$ when $n \to \infty$, the correlation coefficient is asymptotically related to the Student distribution. On the other hand,

$$\frac{r\sqrt{(n-2)}}{\sqrt{(1-r^2)}} \quad (\mathbf{706})$$

has a distribution of exact Student type with $\nu = n - 2$ degrees of freedom.

The hypothesis can therefore be tested by means of the quotient

$$\frac{r\sqrt{(n-2)}}{\sqrt{(1-r^2)}};\ \text{significance limit} \left\{\begin{aligned} &t_{2\alpha} && \text{for } n \leq 202 && \text{(a)} \\ &|c_\alpha| && \text{for } n > 202 && \text{(b)} \end{aligned}\right\} \quad (\mathbf{707})$$

where $\nu = n - 2$

(**706**) does not need to be calculated for $\nu \leq 200$ since the significance limits for r can be taken directly from the table on page 61. They are based on the following formula identical with (**707**a):

$$|r| = \frac{t_{2\alpha}}{\sqrt{\nu + t^2_{2\alpha}}};\ \nu_t = n - 2 \quad (\mathbf{708})$$

If the test statistics from (**706**) or (**708**) are *smaller* than the corresponding significance limits, then it can be assumed that the correlation coefficient, and in accordance with (**703**) also the two regression coefficients b_{yx} and b_{xy}, do *not* differ significantly from zero.

If the test statistics from **(706)** or **(708)** *attain* or *exceed* the corresponding significance limits, then the correlation coefficient and the two regression coefficients *differ* significantly from zero. If $r \neq 0$, then the distribution of the sample correlation coefficient r is complicated in form. However, its distribution can be approximately normalized by means of R. A. Fisher's z-transformation, as follows:

$$z = \tanh^{-1} r = \tfrac{1}{2} \ln \frac{1+r}{1-r} \qquad \text{(a)}$$

and

$$r = \tanh z = \frac{e^{2z}-1}{e^{2z}+1} \qquad \text{(b)} \qquad \textbf{(709)}$$

Cf. also Hyperbolic functions, page 140. Tables for **(709** a) are to be found on page 62 and for **(709** b) on pages 64 and 65.

The variance of z (2 variables x, y) is

$$\sigma_z^2 = \frac{1}{n-3}; \text{ cf. also page 62} \qquad \textbf{(710)}$$

The expectation $\boldsymbol{z}$ of z is

$$\boldsymbol{z} \approx \tanh^{-1} \boldsymbol{r} \qquad \text{(a)}$$

$$= \frac{\boldsymbol{r}}{2(n-1)} + \tanh^{-1} \boldsymbol{r} \qquad \text{(b)} \qquad \textbf{(711)}$$

(711 b) can as a rule be neglected (see below).

The following is derived from **(709)**–**(711)**:

Testing the difference between an estimate r and a hypothetical correlation coefficient $\boldsymbol{r}$

Test quotient

$$\frac{|z-\boldsymbol{z}|}{\sigma_z} = |z-\boldsymbol{z}| \sqrt{n-3}; \; z \text{ and } \boldsymbol{z} \text{ from } \textbf{(709}\text{a) and } \textbf{(711}\text{a)} \qquad \textbf{(712)}$$

Significance limit $|c_\alpha|$, page 28, or $c_{2\alpha}$, page 31, lower table.

If the test quotient **(712)** is *smaller* than the significance limit, then there is no evidence that the population correlation coefficient differs from $\boldsymbol{r}$.

Confidence limits for $\boldsymbol{r}$

$$\text{Prob}\left[\tanh\left(z - \frac{|c_\alpha|}{\sqrt{n-3}}\right) \leq \boldsymbol{r} \leq \tanh\left(z + \frac{|c_\alpha|}{\sqrt{n-3}}\right)\right] \approx 1 - 2\alpha \qquad \textbf{(713)}$$

Values for $\frac{|c_\alpha|}{\sqrt{n-3}}$ for $1-2\alpha = 0.95$ and 0.99 are given on page 63.

Comparison of two correlation coefficients $\boldsymbol{r}_1$ *and* $\boldsymbol{r}_2$

Testing the hypothesis $\boldsymbol{r}_1 = \boldsymbol{r}_2$ on the basis of the estimates r_1 and r_2 is effected by means of the following quotient:

$$\frac{|z_1 - z_2|}{\sqrt{\dfrac{1}{n_1-3} + \dfrac{1}{n_2-3}}}; \text{ significance limit } |c_\alpha|, \text{ page 28, or } c_{2\alpha}, \text{ page 31} \qquad \textbf{(714)}$$

If the test quotient **(714)** is *smaller* than the significance limit, then it can be assumed that $\boldsymbol{r}_1 = \boldsymbol{r}_2$. The estimate of the common correlation coefficient is then

$$\bar{r} = \tanh \bar{z} = \tanh \frac{(n_1-3)z_1 + (n_2-3)z_2}{n_1+n_2-6} \qquad \textbf{(715)}$$

$$\text{and } \sigma_{\bar{z}}^2 = \frac{1}{n_1+n_2-6} \qquad \textbf{(716)}$$

The confidence limits for the common correlation coefficient are

$$\text{Prob}\left[\tanh(\bar{z} - |c_\alpha| \sigma_{\bar{z}}) \leq \bar{\boldsymbol{r}} \leq \tanh(\bar{z} + |c_\alpha| \sigma_{\bar{z}})\right] = 1 - 2\alpha; \text{ where } \sigma_{\bar{z}} = \sqrt{\textbf{(716)}} \qquad \textbf{(717)}$$

Comparison of several correlation coefficients

Given are k estimates $r_1, r_2, \ldots, r_i, \ldots, r_k$ from k bivariate samples of sizes $n_1, n_2, \ldots, n_i, \ldots, n_k$ respectively.

Testing the hypothesis $\boldsymbol{r}_1 = \boldsymbol{r}_2 = \cdots = \boldsymbol{r}_k = \boldsymbol{r}$, where $\boldsymbol{r}$ is a hypothetical value, is effected by means of the test statistic

$$\sum_1^k (n_i-3)(z_i - \boldsymbol{z})^2; \text{ significance limit } \chi^2; \; 1\!\int_r = 2\alpha; \; \nu_{\chi^2} = k; \text{ pages 36–39} \qquad \textbf{(718)}$$

z_i and $\boldsymbol{z}$ from **(709** a) and **(711** a).

If the hypothetical value is unknown, then its estimate is

$$\bar{z} = \frac{\sum_1^k (n_i-3) z_i}{\sum_1^k (n_i-3)} \qquad \textbf{(719)}$$

with variance

$$\sigma_{\bar{z}}^2 = \frac{1}{\sum_1^k (n_i-3)} \qquad \textbf{(720)}$$

Testing the hypothesis $\boldsymbol{r}_1 = \boldsymbol{r}_2 = \cdots = \boldsymbol{r}_k = \bar{\boldsymbol{r}}$ is then effected by means of the test statistic

$$\sum_1^k (n_i-3)(z_i - \bar{z})^2; \text{ significance limit } \chi^2; \; 1\!\int_r = 2\alpha; \; \nu_{\chi^2} = k-1; \text{ pages 36–39} \qquad \textbf{(721)}$$

If the test statistic **(721)** is *smaller* than the significance limit, then it can be assumed that $\boldsymbol{r}_1 = \boldsymbol{r}_2 = \cdots = \boldsymbol{r}_k = \bar{\boldsymbol{r}}$. The estimate $\bar{r}$ of the common correlation coefficient $\bar{\boldsymbol{r}}$ is then approximately

$$\bar{r} \approx \tanh(\bar{z} - a \tanh \bar{z}) \qquad \textbf{(722)}$$

where $\bar{z}$ is from **(719)** and

$$a = \frac{\sum_1^k \left(\dfrac{n_i-3}{n_i-1}\right)}{2\sum_1^k (n_i-3)} \qquad \textbf{(723)}$$

The *confidence limits* for the common correlation coefficient $\bar{\boldsymbol{r}}$ are then approximately

$$\text{Prob}\left[\tanh(\bar{z} - a \tanh \bar{z} - |c_\alpha| \sigma_{\bar{z}}) \leq \bar{\boldsymbol{r}} \leq \tanh(\bar{z} - a \tanh \bar{z} + |c_\alpha| \sigma_{\bar{z}})\right] \approx 1 - 2\alpha \qquad \textbf{(724)}$$

$\bar{z}$ from **(719)**, a from **(723)**, $\sigma_{\bar{z}} = \sqrt{\textbf{(720)}}$, and significance limit $|c_\alpha|$, page 28.

Examples, section 19A

Example 45. Given are $r = 0.3223$, $n = 34$. Does r differ from zero ($2\alpha = 0.05$)? Since $\nu = 32$ and the corresponding limit (page 61) is 0.3388, the hypothesis $r = 0$ cannot be rejected.

Example 46. Given are $r = 0.613$, $n = 42$. Required are the 95% confidence limits for $\boldsymbol{r}$:

$$z = 0.71371 \text{ (page 62)}$$

$$c_\alpha \sigma_z = 0.31385 \text{ (page 63)}$$

$$z \pm c_\alpha \sigma_z = 0.400 \text{ to } 1.027$$

whence $\text{Prob}(\underbrace{0.380}_{\text{page 64}} \leq \boldsymbol{r} \leq \underbrace{0.773}_{\text{page 64}}) = 0.95$

Example 47

Given are		whence are obtained		
r_i	n_i	z_i	$n_i - 3$	$n_i - 1$
0.555	12	0.62558	9	11
0.590	20	0.67767	17	19
0.670	15	0.81074	12	14
0.621	9	0.72663	6	8
0.733	26	0.93518	23	25
0.800	13	1.09861	10	12
		page 62		

$\bar{z} = 63.73451/77 = 0.828$ [from **(719)**]; $\tanh \bar{z} = \underbrace{0.6794}_{\text{page 64}}$

$\chi^2 = 1.815$; $\nu = 6 - 1 = 5$ [from **(721)**]

The 0.05 significance limit for χ^2, $\nu = 5$, is 11.07 (page 36), whence it follows that the hypothesis $\boldsymbol{r}_1 = \boldsymbol{r}_2 = \cdots = \boldsymbol{r}_k = \bar{\boldsymbol{r}}$ cannot be rejected.

$a = 5.0734/154 = 0.0329$ [from **(723)**]

$\bar{r} = \tanh(0.828 - 0.0329 \times 0.6794) = \tanh 0.806 = \underbrace{0.667}_{\text{page 64}}$ [from **(722)**]

$\sigma_{\bar{z}}^2 = 1/77 = 0.012\,987$; $\sigma_{\bar{z}} = 0.113\,96$ [from (**720**)]

For $2\alpha = 0.05$, $|c_\alpha| = 1.96$ (page 28). It follows that $|c_\alpha|\,\sigma_{\bar{z}} = 0.223$ and that the 95% confidence limits for $\boldsymbol{r}$ are

$$\underbrace{\tanh(0.806 - 0.223)}_{\substack{= 0.525 \\ \text{(page 64)}}} \leq \boldsymbol{r} \leq \underbrace{\tanh(0.806 + 0.223)}_{\substack{= 0.774 \\ \text{(page 64)}}} \quad \text{[from (724)]}$$

19B. Spearman coefficient of rank correlation

(The SPEARMAN coefficient is introduced at this point because of its suitability for estimating the correlation coefficient r discussed in section 19A.)

If the bivariate sample x, y originates from *any continuous* distribution and its values have been not measured but *ranked* [cf. (**342**)], then the interdependence of y and x can be assessed by means of the SPEARMAN coefficient of rank correlation $\boldsymbol{R}$. There is another correlation coefficient, τ, due to KENDALL[26] with some advantages and some disadvantages (cf. VAN DER WAERDEN[27]).

The SPEARMAN coefficient can be calculated for ranked samples from distributions of any form. When the distribution is a bivariate normal one, the interpretation of this coefficient corresponds to that of the correlation coefficient r (see below). How it should be interpreted for other distributions is not clear.

Given are n pairs of observations $(x, y)_i$. The pairs are first separated to form two samples x_i and y_i. The x and y values are then ranked by magnitude, so that for example x_{i5} is the fifth smallest of all x values, y_{i3} the third smallest of all y values. The original pairs of observations are now re-formed, giving for example $(x_5, y_3)_i$. The rank numbers (order numbers), in this case 5 and 3, are given the symbol O as before. The difference between the rank numbers of each pair of observations is now calculated and squared:

$$D_i^2 = (O_{x_i} - O_{y_i})^2 \qquad (725)$$

For the pair $(x_5, y_3)_i$ for example, $D_i^2 = (5 - 3)^2 = 4$.

The estimate of the SPEARMAN coefficient $\boldsymbol{R}$ is then

$$R = 1 - \frac{6 \sum_1^n D_i^2}{n^3 - n} \qquad (726)$$

Values of the factor $6/(n^3 - n)$ are given in the table on page 68.

(**726**) is exactly valid only when no ties [cf. (**346**)] occur. However, when the number of ties is small it can still be used. For the procedure when there is a large number of ties see KENDALL[26].

The testing of R against zero is made with the significance limits given in the tables on pages 66 and 67. It is not necessary to calculate R, but only ΣD^2:

If the sum ΣD^2 *attains* or *falls outside* the significance limits, then R differs significantly from zero. (a)

If ΣD^2 *falls inside* the significance limits, R does not differ from zero. (b) (**727**)

The calculation of R is therefore proceeded with only in the case of (**727** a).

The exact significance limits in the tables are from KENDALL[26]. For higher values of n the limits have been calculated approximately from the normal distribution as follows:

Significance limits for ΣD^2

$$\sim \frac{n^3 - n}{6}\left(1 \pm \frac{|c_\alpha|}{\sqrt{n-1}}\right) \qquad \text{(a)}$$

Significance limits for $|R|$ (**728**)

$$\sim \pm \frac{|c_\alpha|}{\sqrt{n-1}} \qquad \text{(b)}$$

whereby the user remains on the safe side[27].

If the ranked samples originate from *normally distributed* populations, then according to K. PEARSON $\boldsymbol{r}$ and $\boldsymbol{R}$ have the following relationship

$$\boldsymbol{r} \cong 2 \sin \frac{\pi}{6} \boldsymbol{R} \qquad (729)$$

For estimates, (**729**) is only approximately valid. A table for calculating r from R is given on page 68.

Example 48. Given is the sample of example 49, section 19D. This sample has 4 ties with x and 6 with y, an acceptable number with a sample size $n = 20$. The pairs of observations and corresponding ranks O_x and O_y are

x	O_x	y	O_y	D^2	x	O_x	y	O_y	D^2
2.6	1	2.3	1	0	6.0	11	5.2	8	9
3.0	2.5	3.5	3.5	1	6.5	12.5	6.0	12.5	0
3.0	2.5	4.0	5	6.25	6.5	12.5	8.0	19	42.25
3.5	4	3.5	3.5	0.25	7.0	14.5	6.0	12.5	4
3.8	5	4.5	6.5	2.25	7.0	14.5	7.0	15.5	1
4.2	6	2.7	2	16	7.5	16	7.7	17	1
4.5	7	5.5	9	4	8.0	18	6.5	14	16
4.7	8	5.7	10.5	6.25	8.0	18	7.0	15.5	6.25
5.5	9	4.5	6.5	6.25	8.0	18	8.0	19	1
5.7	10	5.7	10.5	0.25	10.0	20	8.0	19	1

$\Sigma D^2 = 124$, a sum which lies far outside the 0.001 limit of the table on page 66. R therefore differs from zero, and calculation is proceeded with in accordance with (**726**). From the upper table on page 68, the factor $6/(20^3 - 20) = 10^{-4} \times 7.518\,80$, whence it follows that $R = 1 - (10^{-4} \times 7.518\,80 \times 124) = 0.906\,767 \sim 0.907$. Assuming that the sample originates from a normally distributed population, $r \sim 0.915$ from (**729**) (lower table, page 68). The estimate of r from (**704**) is 0.881.

19C. Significance tests

(For significance tests with correlation coefficients see section 19A, page 179.)

Comparisons between estimates and hypothetical values are made by means of the following test quotients:

Estimate	Hypothetical value	Test quotient
b_{yx}	0	(**706**)–(**708**) on the basis of (**703**)
b_{xy}	0	(**706**)–(**708**) on the basis of (**703**)
b_{yx}	$\boldsymbol{b}_{yx}$	(**664** a)
b_{xy}	$\boldsymbol{b}_{xy}$	(**664** a)*
$Y\|x$	$\boldsymbol{Y}\|x$	(**664** b)
$X\|y$	$\boldsymbol{X}\|y$	(**664** b)*
$\bar{y}$	μ_y	(**664** c)
$\bar{x}$	μ_x	(**664** c)*
a_{yx}	$\boldsymbol{a}_{yx}$	(**664** d)
a_{xy}	$\boldsymbol{a}_{xy}$	(**664** d)*

* With x and y transposed.

(**730**)

It will be seen that for comparisons of a *single* estimate with a *hypothetical* value the appropriate formulae for a regression of the first kind are valid also for a regression of the second kind. However, when two estimates from two different *samples* [as for example with $(b_{yx})_1 - (b_{yx})_2$] are to be compared, then the formulae for a regression of the first kind are no longer valid, although for *high values* of n they are approximately so.

Comparison of μ_y with μ_x, that is to say, testing the hypothesis $\mu_y = \mu_x$, is made by means of the test quotient

$$\frac{(\bar{y} - \bar{x})\sqrt{n}}{\sqrt{s_y^2 + s_x^2 - 2 s_{xy}}}; \quad \text{significance limit } t;\ 2P = 2\alpha;\ \nu = n - 1; \text{ pages 32–35} \qquad (731)$$

s_y^2 and s_x^2 from (**492**), s_{xy} from (**633**)

Simultaneous comparison of $\bar{y}$ with μ_y *and* of $\bar{x}$ with μ_x, that is to say, testing the hypothesis $\bar{y} = \mu_y \mid \bar{x} = \mu_x$, is made by means of the test statistic

$$\frac{n(n-2)}{2(1-r^2)} \times \left[\frac{(\bar{x} - \mu_x)^2}{S_x} + \frac{(\bar{y} - \mu_y)^2}{S_y} - \frac{2 S_{xy}(\bar{x} - \mu_x)(\bar{y} - \mu_y)}{S_x S_y}\right] \qquad (732)$$

Significance limit F; $P = \alpha$; $\nu_1 = 2$, $\nu_2 = n - 2$; pages 40 and 41

S_x and S_y are from (**493**), S_{xy} from (**634**), r from (**704**). Calculation is facilitated by using the relationship

$$r^2 = \frac{S_{xy}}{S_x S_y} \times S_{xy}$$

Comparison of a bivariate sample having means $\bar{y}$ and $\bar{x}$ with an *independent* pair of observations x, y, that is to say, testing the hypothesis that (x, y) come from the same (normal) population $(\bar{x}, \bar{y})$, is made by means of the test statistic

$$\left.\begin{aligned} &\frac{n(n-2)}{2(n+1)(1-r^2)} \times \\ &\times \left[\frac{(x-\bar{x})^2}{S_x} + \frac{(y-\bar{y})^2}{S_y} - \frac{2 S_{xy}(x-\bar{x})(y-\bar{y})}{S_x S_y}\right] \end{aligned}\right\} \quad (\mathbf{733})$$

Significance limits, degrees of freedom, etc. are all as in (**732**). (**733**) is a special case of (**734**) with $n_1 = 1$.

Simultaneous comparison of the means of *two* bivariate samples $(x, y)_1$ and $(x, y)_2$, that is to say, testing the hypothesis $(\mu_{y_1} = \mu_{y_2} \mid \mu_{x_1} = \mu_{x_2})$, is made by means of the following test statistic *when* $\sigma^2_{y_1} = \sigma^2_{y_2}$, $\sigma^2_{x_1} = \sigma^2_{x_2}$,

$$\left.\begin{aligned} &\frac{n_1 n_2 (n_1 + n_2 - 3)}{2(n_1 + n_2)(1 - r^2)} \times \left\{\frac{(\bar{x}_1 - \bar{x}_2)^2}{S_{x_1} + S_{x_2}} + \right. \\ &\left. + \frac{(\bar{y}_1 - \bar{y}_2)^2}{S_{y_1} + S_{y_2}} - \frac{2[(S_{xy})_1 + (S_{xy})_2](\bar{x}_1 - \bar{x}_2)(\bar{y}_1 - \bar{y}_2)}{(S_{x_1} + S_{x_2})(S_{y_1} + S_{y_2})}\right\} \end{aligned}\right\} \quad (\mathbf{734})$$

where

$$r^2 = \frac{[(S_{xy})_1 + (S_{xy})_2]^2}{(S_{x_1} + S_{x_2})(S_{y_1} + S_{y_2})}\text{; for calculation cf. } (\mathbf{732}) \qquad (\mathbf{735})$$

Significance limit F; $P = \alpha$; $\nu_1 = 2$, $\nu_2 = n_1 + n_2 - 3$; pages 40 and 41. Otherwise as in (**732**).

Approximate tests, preliminary to (**734**), can be made as follows:

Testing the hypothesis $\sigma^2_{x_1} = \sigma^2_{x_2}$ and $\sigma^2_{y_1} = \sigma^2_{y_2}$ from (**605**)

Testing the hypothesis $\boldsymbol{r}_1 = \boldsymbol{r}_2$ from (**714**)

For further discussion of tests of the above hypotheses see Pearson and Wilks[28].

19D. Confidence and tolerance limits

100 $(1-\alpha)$% confidence and tolerance limits are calculated by means of the formulae below on the basis of the estimates $\bar{x}$, $\bar{y}$, S_x, S_y, S_{xy} of a two-dimensional sample. b_{yx} and $s_{b_{yx}}$ are obtained from (**632**) and (**637**), b_{xy} and $s_{b_{xy}}$ likewise but with x and y transposed. Degrees of freedom of F: $\nu_1 = 2$, $\nu_2 = n - 2$; $1 - \alpha = 1 - P$; pages 40–41.

Confidence limits

$$\left.\begin{aligned} &\mu_y \mid \mu_x = \bar{y} + b_{yx}(\mu_x - \bar{x}) \pm s_{b_{yx}} \sqrt{2FS_x/n - (n-2)(\mu_x - \bar{x})^2} \quad \text{(a)} \\ &\mu_x \mid \mu_y = \bar{x} + b_{xy}(\mu_y - \bar{y}) \pm s_{b_{xy}} \sqrt{2FS_y/n - (n-2)(\mu_y - \bar{y})^2} \quad \text{(b)} \end{aligned}\right\} \quad (\mathbf{736})$$

(**736** a) and (**736** b) are identical *confidence ellipses.*

Tolerance limits

$$\left.\begin{aligned} &\left.\begin{aligned} &\boldsymbol{Y} \mid x = \bar{y} + b_{yx}(x - \bar{x}) \pm \\ &\qquad \pm s_{b_{yx}} \sqrt{2(n+1)FS_x/n - (n-2)(x-\bar{x})^2} \end{aligned}\right\} \text{(a)} \\ &\left.\begin{aligned} &\boldsymbol{X} \mid y = \bar{x} + b_{xy}(y - \bar{y}) \pm \\ &\qquad \pm s_{b_{xy}} \sqrt{2(n+1)FS_y/n - (n-2)(y-\bar{y})^2} \end{aligned}\right\} \text{(b)} \end{aligned}\right\} \quad (\mathbf{737})$$

(**737** a) and (**737** b) are identical *tolerance ellipses* (see below).

The *slopes* of the main axes X_0, Y_0 of the ellipses defined by (**736**) and (**737**) respectively, the so-called *orthogonal* regression coefficients, are

$$b_0, -\frac{1}{b_0} = \frac{S_y - S_x}{2 S_{xy}} \pm \sqrt{1 + \left(\frac{S_y - S_x}{2 S_{xy}}\right)^2} \qquad (\mathbf{738})$$

The lengths of the *semi-axes* of the ellipses of (**736**) and (**737**) are

$$l_1, l_2 = \sqrt{k}\sqrt{S_x + S_y \pm \sqrt{(S_x + S_y)^2 - 4(S_x S_y - S_{xy}^2)}} \qquad (\mathbf{739})$$

where

$$k \left\{\begin{aligned} &= F/n(n-2) \text{ for confidence ellipse } (\mathbf{736}) && \text{(a)} \\ &= F(n+1)/n(n-2) \text{ for tolerance ellipse } (\mathbf{737}) && \text{(b)} \end{aligned}\right\} \quad (\mathbf{740})$$

Construction of ellipses

Rapid method: Calculation from (**738**) and (**739**) and construction from (**315**).

Exact method: From (**736**) or (**737** a) and/or (**737** b) in conjunction with (**738**) and (**739**), according to the accuracy required.

The equations of tangents to the confidence or tolerance ellipses parallel to the coordinate axes are:

$$\left.\begin{aligned} &\left.\begin{aligned} &\text{Horizontal tangents: } y = \bar{y} \pm \sqrt{k S_y} \\ &\text{Abscissae of the points of contact: } x = \bar{x} \pm b_{xy}\sqrt{k S_y} \end{aligned}\right\} \text{(a)} \\ &\left.\begin{aligned} &\text{Vertical tangents: } x = \bar{x} \pm \sqrt{k S_x} \\ &\text{Ordinates of the points of contact: } y = \bar{y} \pm b_{yx}\sqrt{k S_x} \end{aligned}\right\} \text{(b)} \end{aligned}\right\} \quad (\mathbf{741})$$

where

$$k \left\{\begin{aligned} &= 2F/n(n-2) \text{ for confidence ellipse } (\mathbf{736}) && \text{(a)} \\ &= 2F(n+1)/n(n-2) \text{ for tolerance ellipse } (\mathbf{737}) && \text{(b)} \end{aligned}\right\} \quad (\mathbf{742})$$

The lengths of the sides of the rectangle formed by these tangents which circumscribes the ellipse are:

$$\left.\begin{aligned} &\text{Horizontal sides} \\ &l_h = 2\sqrt{k S_x} && \text{(a)} \\ &\text{Vertical sides} \\ &l_v = 2\sqrt{k S_y} && \text{(b)} \end{aligned}\right\} \quad (\mathbf{743})$$

where $k =$ (**742**)

Example 49. Given is the bivariate sample (Figs. 40 and 41)

x	y	x	y	x	y	x	y
2.6	2.3	4.2	2.7	6.0	5.2	7.5	7.7
3.0	3.5	4.5	5.5	6.5	6.0	8.0	6.5
3.0	4.0	4.7	5.7	6.5	8.0	8.0	7.0
3.5	3.5	5.5	4.5	7.0	6.0	8.0	8.0
3.8	4.5	5.7	5.7	7.0	7.0	10.0	8.0

(a) The parameters are estimated.

(b) Using the formulae for the regression lines Y and X, for the orthogonal regression lines Y_0 and X_0, for the tolerance ellipse for $\boldsymbol{Y} \mid x$ or $\boldsymbol{X} \mid y$, and for the horizontal and vertical tangents to the latter, the lengths of the sides of the rectangle formed by the tangents and the lengths of the semi-axes of the ellipse are calculated.

(c) For purposes of comparison, the tolerance limits for $\boldsymbol{Y} \mid x$ and $\boldsymbol{X} \mid y$ are calculated using the appropriate formulae for a regression of the first kind.

(d) A comparison is made of the tolerance limits for $\boldsymbol{Y} \mid x$ and $\boldsymbol{X} \mid y$ of regressions of the second and first kind with $x = \bar{x}$ and $y = \bar{y}$.

(e) $\bar{x}$ and $\bar{y}$ are compared.

(a) Estimates of parameters

$\bar{x} = 115.0/20 = 5.75$	$\bar{y} = 111.3/20 = 5.565$
$S_x = 740.92 - 5.75 \times 115 = 79.67$	$S_y = 679.39 - 5.565 \times 111.3 = 60.0055$
$s_x^2 = 79.67/19 = 4.193158$	$s_y^2 = 60.0055/19 = 3.158184$
$s_x = 2.04772$	$s_y = 1.77713$

$S_{xy} = 700.90 - 5.75 \times 111.3 = 60.925$ from (**634**)

$s_{xy} = 60.925/19 = 3.206579$

$r^2 = 60.925^2 (79.67 \times 60.0055) = 0.776435170 =$ (**704** b)^2

$1 - r^2 = 0.223564830$

$r = 0.881155$

$b_{yx} = 60.925/79.67 = 0.7647170$ from (**632**)

$b_{xy} = 60.925/60.0055 = 1.0153236$ from (**632**)*

* With x and y transposed.

$b_0, -\frac{1}{b_0}$ $= (60.0055 - 79.67)/(2 \times 60.925)$
$\pm\sqrt{1 + (-0.161382848)^2} = 0.85156$ and
-1.17432 from (**738**)

$S_{y \cdot x} = 60.0055 \times 0.223564483 = 13.4151194$ from (**636** c)

$s^2_{y \cdot x} = 13.4151194/18 = 0.745284411$ from (**635** a)

$s^2_{b_{yx}} = 0.745284411/79.67 = 0.009354643$ from (**637** a)

$s_{b_{yx}} = 0.0967224$

$S_{x \cdot y} = 79.67 \times 0.223564483 = 17.8114100$ from (**636** c)*

$s^2_{x \cdot y} = 17.8114100/18 = 0.989522777$ from (**635** a)*

$s^2_{b_{xy}} = 0.989522777/60.0055 = 0.01649053$ from (**637** a)*

$s_{b_{xy}} = 0.128416$

(b) Formulae

Regression lines

$Y = 5.565 + 0.7647(x - 5.75) = 1.1679 + 0.7647\,x$ from (**702** a)

$X = 5.75 + 1.0153(y - 5.565) = 0.0997 + 1.0153\,y$ from (**702** b)

$X_0;\ y = \bar{y} + b_0(x - \bar{x}) = 0.6685 + 0.8516\,x$

$Y_0;\ y = \bar{y} - \frac{1}{b_0}(x - \bar{x}) = 12.317 - 1.1743\,x$

Tolerance ellipse $[F_{0.05}(2; 18) = 3.55$; page 40]

Tolerance limits for $\boldsymbol{Y} \mid x$

$= 5.565 + 0.7647(x - 5.75) \pm 0.09672 \times \sqrt{593.94 - 18(x - 5.75)^2}$ from (**737** a)

Tolerance limits for $\boldsymbol{X} \mid y$

$= 5.75 + 1.0153(y - 5.565) \pm 0.12842 \times \sqrt{447.34 - 18(y - 5.565)^2}$ from (**737** b)

Horizontal tangents y and abscissae of the points of contact

$y = 5.565 \pm 4.99 = 0.58$ and 10.55
$x = 5.75 \pm 5.06 = 0.69$ and 10.81
} from (**741** a) and (**742** b)

Vertical tangents x and ordinates of the points of contact

$x = 5.75 \pm 5.74 = 0.01$ and 11.49
$y = 5.565 \pm 4.39 = 1.18$ and 9.96
} from (**741** b) and (**742** b)

Lengths of the sides of the resulting rectangle

Horizontal sides $l_h = 11.48$
Vertical sides $l_v = 9.98$
} from (**743**) and (**742** b)

Lengths of the semi axes of the ellipse

$= \sqrt{\frac{3.55 \times 21}{20 \times 18}} \times \sqrt{79.67 + 60.0055 \pm \sqrt{139.6755^2 - 4(4780.6382 - 60.925^2)}}$
$= 7.38$ and 1.83 from (**739**) and (**740** b)

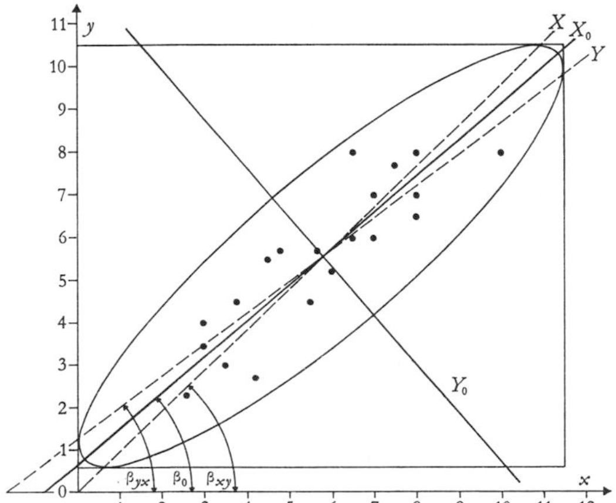

Fig. 40. Tolerance ellipse, example 49.

* With x and y transposed.

(c) Tolerance limits for $\boldsymbol{Y} \mid x$ and $\boldsymbol{X} \mid y$ calculated from the formulae for a regression of the first kind ($t_{2\alpha = 0.05,\, \nu = 18} = 2.1009$, page 32)

$\boldsymbol{Y} \mid x = 5.565 + 0.7647(x - 5.75) \pm 0.2032 \times \sqrt{83.6535 + (x - 5.75)^2}$ from (**669**)

$\boldsymbol{X} \mid y = 5.75 + 1.4070(y - 5.565) \pm 0.3739 \times \sqrt{45.4659 + (y - 5.565)^2}$ from (**674**)

(d) Tolerance limits for $\boldsymbol{Y} \mid x$ and $\boldsymbol{X} \mid y$, with $x = \bar{x}$ and $y = \bar{y}$, calculated from the formulae for

	Regression of second kind	Regression of first kind
$Y \mid \bar{x}$	5.565 ± 2.3572 from (**737** a)	5.565 ± 1.8585 from (**669**)
$X \mid \bar{y}$	5.75 ± 2.7161 from (**737** b)	5.75 ± 2.5213 from (**674**)

(e) Comparison of $\bar{x}$ and $\bar{y}$ ($t_{2\alpha = 0.05,\, \nu = 19} \sim 2.09$)

$$\frac{5.75 - 5.565}{\sqrt{4.1932 + 3.1582 - 2 \times 3.2066}} = 0.191 \text{ from } (\mathbf{731})$$

The test statistic is smaller than the significance limit, so that the hypothesis $\bar{x} = \bar{y}$ cannot be rejected.

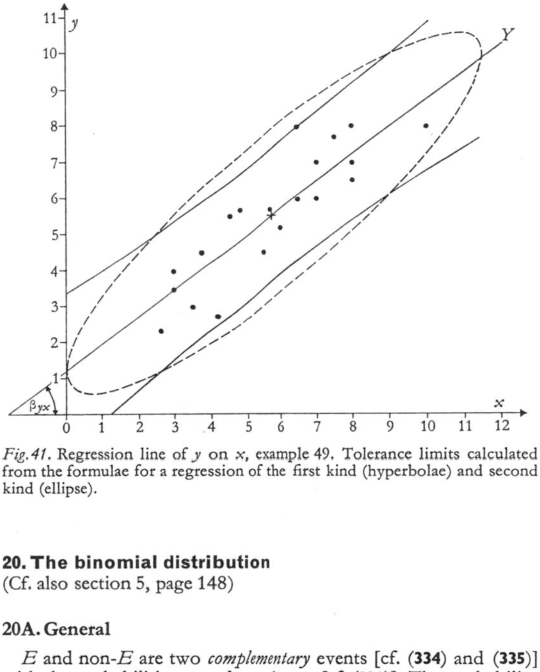

Fig. 41. Regression line of y on x, example 49. Tolerance limits calculated from the formulae for a regression of the first kind (hyperbolae) and second kind (ellipse).

20. The binomial distribution

(Cf. also section 5, page 148)

20A. General

E and non-E are two *complementary* events [cf. (**334**) and (**335**)] with the probabilities $\boldsymbol{p}$ and $\boldsymbol{q} = 1 - \boldsymbol{p}$ [cf. (**339**)]. The probability that in N *independent* trials [cf. (**328**), (**357**), and example 10, page 148] the event E will occur exactly $x = 0, 1, 2, \ldots, N$ times is

$$\left.\begin{aligned} f(x) &= \dot{\boldsymbol{P}}_x = \binom{N}{x} \boldsymbol{p}^x \boldsymbol{q}^{N-x} \\ \dot{\boldsymbol{P}}_0 &= \binom{N}{0} \boldsymbol{p}^0 \boldsymbol{q}^N = \boldsymbol{q}^N \\ \dot{\boldsymbol{P}}_1 &= \binom{N}{1} \boldsymbol{p}^1 \boldsymbol{q}^{N-1}; \ldots \\ \dot{\boldsymbol{P}}_N &= \binom{N}{N} \boldsymbol{p}^N \boldsymbol{q}^0 = \boldsymbol{p}^N \end{aligned}\right\} \quad (\mathbf{744})$$

where $0 \leq \boldsymbol{p} \leq 1$ and $\boldsymbol{q} = 1 - \boldsymbol{p}$

The individual probabilities $\dot{\boldsymbol{P}}_x$ of (**744**) correspond to the terms of the binomial series developed from $(q + p)^N$ [cf. (**113**)]. On the binomial coefficient $\binom{N}{x}$ cf. (**100**)–(**106**), page 136.

From (**744**) follow the recursion formulae

$$\dot{\boldsymbol{P}}_{x+1} = \dot{\boldsymbol{P}}_x \times \frac{\boldsymbol{p}}{\boldsymbol{q}} \times \frac{N-x}{x+1} \qquad \text{(a)}$$
$$\dot{\boldsymbol{P}}_{x-1} = \dot{\boldsymbol{P}}_x \times \frac{\boldsymbol{q}}{\boldsymbol{p}} \times \frac{x}{N-x+1} \qquad \text{(b)} \qquad \textbf{(745)}$$

Example 50. Calculate all the individual probabilities $\dot{\boldsymbol{P}}_x$ for $\boldsymbol{p} = 0.3$ and $N = 7$.

Calculations are made from (**745** a) starting from $x = 0$. $\boldsymbol{p}/\boldsymbol{q} = 3/7$.

$$\dot{\boldsymbol{P}}_0 = \left(\frac{7}{10}\right)^7 = 0.0823543$$

$$\dot{\boldsymbol{P}}_1 = \dot{\boldsymbol{P}}_0 \times \frac{3}{7} \times \frac{7}{1} = \dot{\boldsymbol{P}}_0 \times \frac{21}{7} = 0.2470629$$

$$\dot{\boldsymbol{P}}_2 = \dot{\boldsymbol{P}}_1 \times \frac{3}{7} \times \frac{6}{2} = \dot{\boldsymbol{P}}_1 \times \frac{18}{14} = 0.3176523$$

$$\dot{\boldsymbol{P}}_3 = \dot{\boldsymbol{P}}_2 \times \frac{3}{7} \times \frac{5}{3} = \dot{\boldsymbol{P}}_2 \times \frac{15}{21} = 0.2268945$$

A study of the series 21/7, 18/14, 15/21 at once reveals the regular manner in which the numerators and denominators of the recursion factors decrease and increase respectively. The further factors for calculating $\dot{\boldsymbol{P}}_4, \dot{\boldsymbol{P}}_5, \ldots$ can therefore be assumed to be 12/28, 9/35, 6/42 and 3/49, giving

$$\dot{\boldsymbol{P}}_4 = 0.0972405$$
$$\dot{\boldsymbol{P}}_5 = 0.0250047$$
$$\dot{\boldsymbol{P}}_6 = 0.0035721$$
$$\dot{\boldsymbol{P}}_7 = 0.0002187$$

Check: $\sum_0^N \dot{\boldsymbol{P}}_x = 1$

The individual probabilities for $N = 1, 2, \ldots, 99, 100$ and $\boldsymbol{p} = 0.01, 0.02, \ldots, 0.49, 0.50$ can be obtained in a different manner using the tables on pages 70–77 (logarithms of binomial coefficients) and 78–84 (logarithms of powers of $\boldsymbol{p}$ and $\boldsymbol{q}$).

Example 51. Calculate $\dot{\boldsymbol{P}}_1$ for $\boldsymbol{p} = 0.3$ and $N = 7$.

$\log \binom{7}{1} = 0.84510$ (page 70)

$\log \boldsymbol{p}^1 = 0.47712 - 1$ (page 82)

$\log \boldsymbol{q}^6 = 0.07059 - 1$ (page 82)

$\log \dot{\boldsymbol{P}}_1 = 1.39281 - 2 = 0.3928 - 1$

$\dot{\boldsymbol{P}}_1 = 0.2471$ (page 11)

For binomial coefficients with $N > 100$ see under 'Binomial Coefficients', page 136. For calculating powers of $\boldsymbol{p}$ and $\boldsymbol{q}$, logarithms with 7 or more places should be used*.

The binomial distribution is a *discrete* distribution. It is *symmetrical* when $\boldsymbol{p} = 0.5$, *asymmetrical* when $\boldsymbol{p} \neq 0.5$.

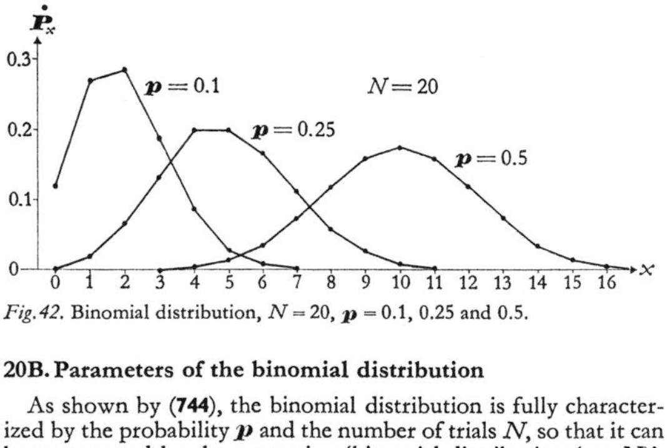

Fig. 42. Binomial distribution, $N = 20$, $\boldsymbol{p} = 0.1$, 0.25 and 0.5.

20B. Parameters of the binomial distribution

As shown by (**744**), the binomial distribution is fully characterized by the probability $\boldsymbol{p}$ and the number of trials N, so that it can be represented by the expression 'binomial distribution ($\boldsymbol{p}$; N)'. Its mean and variance are respectively

$$\mu_x = N\boldsymbol{p} = \text{expectation of } \textbf{(749)} \qquad \textbf{(746)}$$

* Tables of $f(x)$ and the cumulative distribution $\sum_x^N f(x)$ for $N = 2, 3, \ldots, 49$ and $\boldsymbol{p} = 0.01, 0.02, \ldots, 0.5$ are to be found in the literature [3, 4].

$$\sigma_x^2 = N\boldsymbol{p}\boldsymbol{q} = \boldsymbol{q}\mu_x = \text{expectation of } \textbf{(750)} \times \frac{N}{N-1} \qquad \textbf{(747)}$$

For any given sample size N (N trials) the variance of the binomial distribution is greatest when $\boldsymbol{p} = 0.5$, least when $\boldsymbol{p} = 0$ or $\boldsymbol{q} = 0$.

The best estimate of $\boldsymbol{p}$ from a sample of size N in which the event E occurs x times is

$$p = x/N \qquad \textbf{(748)}$$

The following are derived from (**746**)–(**748**):

Estimate of μ_x

$$\bar{x} = Np = x \qquad \textbf{(749)}$$

Estimate of σ_x^2

$$s_x^2 = Npq = \frac{x(N-x)}{N} \qquad \textbf{(750)}$$

The mean and variance of the *relative* frequency x/N are

$$\mu_{x/N} = \boldsymbol{p} = \text{expectation of } \textbf{(748)} \qquad \textbf{(751)}$$

$$\sigma_{x/N}^2 = \frac{\boldsymbol{p}\boldsymbol{q}}{N} = \text{expectation of } \textbf{(753)} \times \frac{N}{N-1} \qquad \textbf{(752)}$$

The corresponding estimates are

for the mean = (**748**)

$$\text{for the variance: } s_p^2 = \frac{pq}{N} = \frac{x(N-x)}{N^3} = \frac{1}{N^2} s_x^2 \qquad \textbf{(753)}$$

Example 52. In 64 trials the event x occurs 6 times. Estimate $\boldsymbol{p}$, s_x^2 and s_p^2.

$p = 6/64 = 0.09375$ from (**748**)

$s_x^2 = 0.09375 \times 58 = 5.4375$ from (**750**)

$s_p^2 = 5.4375/64^2 = 0.001327515$ from (**753**)

20C. Cumulative probabilities of the binomial distribution

The calculation of cumulative probabilities in discrete distributions has been dealt with fully in section 5 (page 149). Here some practical applications are indicated.

Let $\boldsymbol{p}$ be the probability of the event E, $\boldsymbol{q}$ that of the event non-E. $\dot{\boldsymbol{P}}_x$ is defined in (**744**).

The probability that the event E

- will occur exactly $x = k$ times is given by (**370**) (a)
- will *not* occur exactly $x = k$ times is given by (**371**) (b)
- will occur *at the most* or *less* than $x = k$ times is given by (**372**) (c)
- will occur *at least* or *more* than $x = k$ times is given by (**373**) (d)
- will occur at least $x = k$ times *but at the most* $x = s$ times ($k < s$) is given by (**374**) (e)
- will occur *less* than $x = k$ times *or more* than $x = s$ times ($k < s$) is given by (**375**) (f)

(754)

Examples of the calculation of probabilities of this kind are given in section 5, page 150. The following is an additional example.

Example 53. Let $\boldsymbol{p}$ be the probability of the occurrence of an event E in a population. What size N must a sample have if the probability that the event E occurs *at least once* is $\mathfrak{p}^*$?

From (**754** d) and (**373**) it follows that

$$\text{Prob}(x \geqq 1) = \sum_1^N \dot{\boldsymbol{P}}_x \qquad \text{(from } \textbf{373}\text{b)}$$
$$= 1 - \dot{\boldsymbol{P}}_0 \qquad \text{(from } \textbf{373}\text{a)}$$

In accordance with (**744**), $\dot{\boldsymbol{P}}_0 = \boldsymbol{q}^N$, whence

$$\mathfrak{p}^* = 1 - \boldsymbol{q}^N$$

$$\text{that is, } N \sim \frac{\log(1-\mathfrak{p}^*)}{\log \boldsymbol{q}} = \frac{\log(1-\mathfrak{p}^*)}{\log(1-\boldsymbol{p})} \qquad \textbf{(755)}$$

Application. Let the probability of throwing a six with a die be 1/6. How many throws must be made in order to throw a six at least once with a probability $\mathfrak{p}^* \geqq 0.99$?

From **(755)**

$$N = \frac{\log(1-0.99)}{\log(1-1/6)} = \frac{\log 0.01}{\log 5/6} \sim \frac{-2}{-0.0792} = 25.\dot{2}\dot{5}$$

It follows that 26 throws must be made in order that, with a probability $\mathfrak{p}^* \geqq 0.99$, at least one six will be thrown (with 25 throws $\mathfrak{p}^*$ would be a little under 0.99).

20D. The binomial and the normal distribution

As shown by Figure 42, with $\boldsymbol{p} = ½$, the binomial distribution closely resembles the normal distribution even with *fairly small* samples. This is not the case with more extreme values of $\boldsymbol{p}$ (cf. $\boldsymbol{p} = 0.1$). As shown by Figure 43, however, with increasing sample size the binomial distribution approximates to the normal distribution even with more extreme values of $\boldsymbol{p}$. In other words:

With increasing sample size N the binomial distribution $(\boldsymbol{p}, N)$ tends toward the normal distribution $(N\boldsymbol{p}, \sqrt{N\boldsymbol{p}\boldsymbol{q}})$. The closer $\boldsymbol{p}$ lies to 0.5, the greater is this tendency:

$$\binom{N}{x} \boldsymbol{p}^x \boldsymbol{q}^{N-x} \rightarrow \frac{1}{\sqrt{2\pi N\boldsymbol{p}\boldsymbol{q}}} e^{-(x-N\boldsymbol{p})^2/2N\boldsymbol{p}\boldsymbol{q}} \qquad \textbf{(756)}$$

as $N \rightarrow \infty$

With large sample sizes N, in accordance with the definitions

$$\text{Prob}\,(x \leqq x_{\mathfrak{p}}) = \sum_0^{x_{\mathfrak{p}}} \dot{\boldsymbol{P}}_x = \mathfrak{p}$$

$$\text{Prob}\,(c \leqq c_{\mathfrak{p}}) = \int_{-\infty}^{c_{\mathfrak{p}}} \text{of the standardized normal distribution}$$

it follows from **(756)** that

$$\text{Prob}\,(x \leqq x_{\mathfrak{p}}) \sim \text{Prob}\,(c \leqq c_{\mathfrak{p}}) \qquad \textbf{(757)}$$

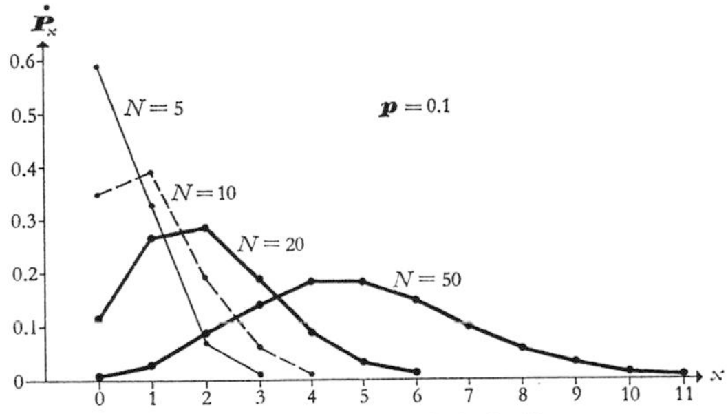

Fig. 43. Binomial distribution, $\boldsymbol{p} = 0.1$, $N = 5, 10, 20, 50$.

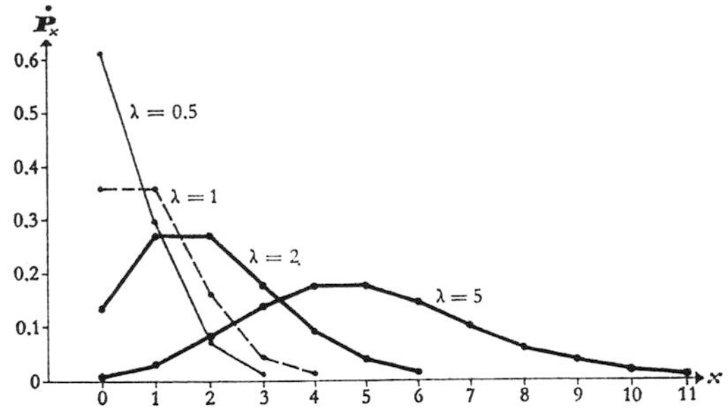

Fig. 44. Poisson distribution, $\lambda = 0.5, 1, 2, 5$.

where

$$c_{\mathfrak{p}} = \frac{x_{\mathfrak{p}} - N\boldsymbol{p}}{\sqrt{N\boldsymbol{p}\boldsymbol{q}}}\,; \text{ (for } c \text{ see page 28, right-hand table)} \qquad \textbf{(758)}$$

or

$$x_{\mathfrak{p}} = N\boldsymbol{p} + c_{\mathfrak{p}}\sqrt{N\boldsymbol{p}\boldsymbol{q}}\,; \text{ (for } c \text{ see page 28, left-hand table)} \qquad \textbf{(759)}$$

With smaller samples, the transformations **(757)** and **(758)** can be improved by using the so-called correction for continuity. In this case, $x + ½$ is used in place of x, whence

$$c_{\mathfrak{p}} = \frac{x_{\mathfrak{p}} + ½ - N\boldsymbol{p}}{\sqrt{N\boldsymbol{p}\boldsymbol{q}}}\,; \text{ (for } c \text{ see page 28, right-hand table)} \qquad \textbf{(760)}$$

$$x_{\mathfrak{p}} = N\boldsymbol{p} - ½ + c_{\mathfrak{p}}\sqrt{N\boldsymbol{p}\boldsymbol{q}}\,; \text{ (for } c \text{ see page 28, left-hand table)} \qquad \textbf{(761)}$$

From the definitions

$$\text{Prob}\,(x \geqq x_{\mathfrak{p}^*}) = 1 - \text{Prob}\,(x \leqq x_{\mathfrak{p}^*} - 1) = \mathfrak{p}^*$$

$$\text{Prob}\,(c \leqq c_{1-\mathfrak{p}^*}) = \int_{-\infty}^{c_{1-\mathfrak{p}^*}} = 1 - \mathfrak{p}^*$$

it follows from **(760)** and **(761)** that

$$c_{1-\mathfrak{p}^*} = \frac{x_{\mathfrak{p}^*} - ½ - N\boldsymbol{p}}{\sqrt{N\boldsymbol{p}\boldsymbol{q}}}\,; \text{ (for } c \text{ see page 28, right-hand table)} \qquad \textbf{(762)}$$

$$x_{\mathfrak{p}^*} = N\boldsymbol{p} + ½ + c_{1-\mathfrak{p}^*}\sqrt{N\boldsymbol{p}\boldsymbol{q}}\,; \text{ (for } c \text{ see page 28, left-hand table)} \qquad \textbf{(763)}$$

Example 54. Given the binomial distribution $(\boldsymbol{p} = 0.1, N = 40)$, calculate the probabilities $\text{Prob}\,(x \leqq 3) = \mathfrak{p}$ and $\text{Prob}\,(x \geqq 6) = \mathfrak{p}^*$ using the approximate formulae **(760)**–**(763)**.

$$c_{\mathfrak{p}} = \frac{3.5 - 4}{\sqrt{3.6}} = -0.264 \text{ [from (760)]}$$

$\mathfrak{p} = 0.396$ (by linear interpolation in right-hand table, page 28)

$$c_{1-\mathfrak{p}^*} = \frac{5.5 - 4}{\sqrt{3.6}} = 0.791 \text{ [from (761)]}$$

$1 - \mathfrak{p}^* = 0.786$

$\mathfrak{p}^* = 0.214$

The exact values of $\mathfrak{p}$ and $\mathfrak{p}^*$, rounded off to 3 decimal places, are 0.423 and 0.206.

Example 55. For the binomial distribution of example 54, calculate $x_{\mathfrak{p}}$ for $\mathfrak{p} = 0.1$ and $x_{\mathfrak{p}^*}$ for $\mathfrak{p}^* = 0.05$ using the approximate formulae **(760)**–**(763)**.

$c_{\mathfrak{p}} = -1.2816$, $c_{1-\mathfrak{p}^*} = 1.6449$ } page 28, left-hand table

whence

$$x_{\mathfrak{p}} = 3.5 - 1.2816\sqrt{3.6} = 1.07 \text{ [from (761)]}$$

$$x_{\mathfrak{p}^*} = 4.5 + 1.6449\sqrt{3.6} = 7.62 \text{ [from (763)]}$$

Since x must be a whole number, this gives the results $x_{\mathfrak{p}} = 1$ and $x_{\mathfrak{p}^*} = 8$, which agree with the nearest exact values.

A further and, if $\boldsymbol{p} < \boldsymbol{q}$, rather better approximation[29] is

$$c_{\mathfrak{p}} = 2\left[\sqrt{(x_{\mathfrak{p}} + 1)\,\boldsymbol{q}} - \sqrt{(N - x_{\mathfrak{p}})\,\boldsymbol{p}}\right] \qquad \textbf{(764)}$$

$$x_{\mathfrak{p}} = \boldsymbol{p}\left(N + 1 - \frac{c^2}{4}\right) + \frac{c^2}{4}\boldsymbol{q} - 1 + c\sqrt{\boldsymbol{p}\boldsymbol{q}\left(N + 1 - \frac{c^2}{4}\right)} \qquad \textbf{(765)}$$

where in **(765)** $c = c_{\mathfrak{p}}$

$$c_{1-\mathfrak{p}^*} = 2\left[\sqrt{x_{\mathfrak{p}^*}\boldsymbol{q}} - \sqrt{(N - x_{\mathfrak{p}^*} + 1)\,\boldsymbol{p}}\right] \qquad \textbf{(766)}$$

$$x_{\mathfrak{p}^*} = \boldsymbol{p}\left(N + 1 - \frac{c^2}{4}\right) + \frac{c^2}{4}\boldsymbol{q} + c\sqrt{\boldsymbol{p}\boldsymbol{q}\left(N + 1 - \frac{c^2}{4}\right)} \qquad \textbf{(767)}$$

where in **(767)** $c = c_{1-\mathfrak{p}^*}$

The meaning of the symbols in **(764)**–**(767)** is the same as that in **(760)**–**(763)**.

Example 56. Calculate examples 54 and 55 in accordance with **(764)**–**(767)**.

$c_{\mathfrak{p}} = 2\left(\sqrt{4 \times 0.9} - \sqrt{37 \times 0.1}\right) = -0.052$

$\mathfrak{p} = 0.479$

$c_{1-\mathfrak{p}^*} = 2\left(\sqrt{6 \times 0.9} - \sqrt{35 \times 0.1}\right) = 0.906$

$\mathfrak{p}^* = 1 - 0.817 = 0.183$

$x_{\mathfrak{p}} = 0.979$

$x_{\mathfrak{p}^*} = 8.00$

20E. The binomial and the Poisson distribution

As shown by Figure 43, with small values of p the binomial distribution closely resembles the Poisson distribution. The following rule of thumb should be noted:

$$\binom{N}{x} p^x q^{N-x} \approx \frac{e^{-\lambda}\lambda^x}{x!}, \text{ where } \lambda = Np \quad \text{if} \quad \frac{Npq}{Np} \approx 1 \qquad (768)$$

20F. Confidence limits and significance limits

(*a*) *Confidence limits for* p, tables on pages 85–103 (or significance limits for $p = x/N$, cf. example 17, page 156)

In N trials, the event E occurs $x = k$ times. According to Clopper and Pearson[30], the confidence limits satisfying the equation

$$\text{Prob}\,(p_l < p < p_r \mid x = k, N) = 1 - 2\alpha;\ \alpha < 0.5$$

are the solutions of

$$\sum_{x=k}^{N} \binom{N}{x} p_l^x (1-p_l)^{N-x} = \alpha \text{ for } p_l \qquad \text{(a)}$$

and

$$\sum_{x=0}^{k} \binom{N}{x} p_r^x (1-p_r)^{N-x} = \alpha \text{ for } p_r \qquad \text{(b)} \qquad (769)$$

For $x = 0$ and $x = N$, only *one-sided* $1-\alpha$ limits are possible:

for $x = 0$

$$0 \text{ and } p_r = 1 - \text{antilog}\left(\frac{\log \alpha}{N}\right) \qquad \text{(a)}$$

for $x = N$

$$p_l = \text{antilog}\left(\frac{\log \alpha}{N}\right) \text{ and } N \qquad \text{(b)} \qquad (770)$$

For $x = 0$ and $x = N$, the confidence limits for p given in the tables on pages 85–103 thus correspond not to $1 - 2\alpha$, but to $1 - \alpha$ limits.

For $0 < x < N$ an exact solution of (**769**) is possible only by means of an iterative process. The tables on pages 85–98 were calculated in this way by computer.

Approximate solutions are

$$p_l, p_r = \frac{x \mp \tfrac{1}{2} + \dfrac{c^2}{2} \mp |c| \sqrt{(x \mp \tfrac{1}{2})\left(1 - \dfrac{x \mp \tfrac{1}{2}}{N}\right) + \dfrac{c^2}{4}}}{N + c^2} \qquad (771)$$

where $c = c_\alpha$, page 28, left-hand table,

or, if $x \leqq N/2$

$$p_l, p_r = (A - B) \mp \sqrt{B\,[2 - (A - B) - A]}$$

where

$$A_{p_l}, A_{p_r} = \frac{x + \tfrac{1}{2} \mp \tfrac{1}{2} + \dfrac{c^2}{4}}{N+1}$$

$$B_{p_l}, B_{p_r} = \frac{c^2}{2}\left(\frac{x + \tfrac{1}{2} \mp \tfrac{1}{2}}{(N+1)^2}\right) \qquad (772)$$

where $c = c_\alpha$, page 28, left-hand table.

With larger samples, $\mp \tfrac{1}{2}$ in (**771**) and (**772**) can be ignored. (**771**) is the solution of (**760**) and (**762**) for p, (**772**) that of (**764**) and (**766**). The tables on pages 99–103 were calculated from (**772**) (for $x > 4$). In practice, (**771**) and (**772**) will seldom be required since the range of the tables is sufficient for most cases.

Figure 45 shows the confidence intervals for p for all possible values of x for sample sizes $N = 30$ and $N = 10$.

Interpolation and extrapolation for limits not contained in the tables on pages 99–103 are carried out as follows (the examples are all for 95% limits):

Four different situations will be considered, of which (1) can be combined with (2), (3) or (4). In the latter case, calculation should begin with (1) and be continued with (2) or (3) or (4) as the case may be.

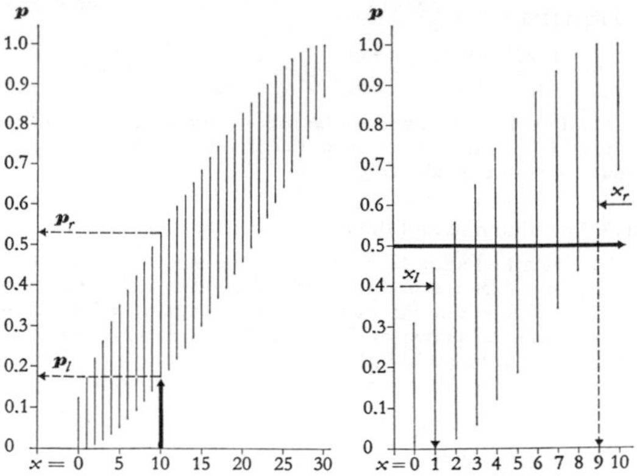

Fig. 45. Binomial distribution. Confidence limits for p; $N = 30$ and $N = 10$.

(1) x or $100\,p_x$ $(= 100\,x/N)$ lies *above* the tabulated values in an N column.

$N - x = x'$, or $100 - 100\,p_x = 100\,p'_x$, is first calculated and the corresponding limits $100\,p'_l$ and $100\,p'_r$ looked for in the table. The required limits are:

$$\text{Lower } p_l = 100 - 100\,p'_r$$
$$\text{Upper } p_r = 100 - 100\,p'_l \qquad (773)$$

Example 57. $N = 150$, $x = 125$. $x' = 150 - 125 = 25$, or $100\,p'_x = 100 - 83.33 = 16.67$. For this the table gives $100\,p'_l = 11.10$ and $100\,p'_r = 23.64$, whence from (**773**) the required limits are 76.36 – 88.90.

(2) x or $100\,p_x$ $(= 100\,x/N)$ lies between two values in an N column. $100\,p_x$ lies between $100\,p'_x$ and $100\,p''_x$ $(p'_x < p''_x)$.

The limits $100\,p'_l$ and $100\,p'_r$ for $100\,p'_x$ and the limits $100\,p''_l$ and $100\,p''_r$ for $100\,p''_x$ are looked for in the table:

$100\,p''_x$	$100\,p''_l$	$100\,p''_r$
$100\,p'_x$	$100\,p'_l$	$100\,p'_r$
$(100\,p''_x - 100\,p'_x)$	$(100\,p''_l - 100\,p'_l) = B_l$	$(100\,p''_r - 100\,p'_r) = B_r$

If the quotient $\dfrac{100\,p_x - 100\,p'_x}{100\,p''_x - 100\,p'_x} = A$

then the required limits are

$$100\,p_l = 100\,p'_l + (A \times B_l)$$
$$100\,p_r = 100\,p'_r + (A \times B_r) \qquad (774)$$

Example 58. $N = 500$, $x = 427$, $100\,p_x = 85.40$

$100\,p''_x = 86.00$	$100\,p''_l = 82.64$	$100\,p''_r = 88.92$
$100\,p'_x = 84.00$	$100\,p'_l = 80.48$	$100\,p'_r = 87.10$
Difference 2.00	2.16	1.82

$$100\,p_x - 100\,p'_x = 85.40 - 84.00 = 1.40$$
$$A = 1.40 / 2.00 = 0.70$$

$$100\,p_l = 80.48 + (0.7 \times 2.16) = 81.99 = \underline{82.0}$$
$$100\,p_r = 87.10 + (0.7 \times 1.82) = 88.37 = \underline{88.4}$$

(3) N lies between N_1 and N_2 $(N_1 < N_2)$. For $100\,p_x$ $(= 100\,x/N)$ interpolation is made in column N_1 to give the limits $100\,p_l^*$ and $100\,p_r^*$, in column N_2 to give the limits $100\,p_l^{**}$ and $100\,p_r^{**}$, in accordance with (**774**). The required limits are then

$$100\,p_l = 100\,p_l^* + \frac{N - N_1}{N_2 - N_1}(100\,p_l^{**} - 100\,p_l^*)$$

$$100\,p_r = 100\,p_r^* + \frac{N - N_1}{N_2 - N_1}(100\,p_r^{**} - 100\,p_r^*) \qquad (775)$$

Example 59. $N = 270$, $x = 22$, $100\,p_x = 8.15$. $N = 270$ lies between $N_1 = 250$ and $N_2 = 300$. The interpolated limits for $100\,p_x = 8.15$ in accordance with (**774**) are in column

$N_2 = 300$	$100\,p_l^{**} = 5.32$	$100\,p_r^{**} = 11.86$
$N_1 = 250$	$100\,p_l^* = 5.08$	$100\,p_r^* = 12.28$
Difference 50	0.24	– 0.42

$$\frac{N - N_1}{N_2 - N_1} = \frac{20}{50} = 0.4$$

$$100\,p_l = 5.08 + (0.4 \times 0.24) = 5.18 = \underline{5.2}$$
$$100\,p_r = 12.28 - (0.4 \times 0.42) = 12.11 = \underline{12.1}$$

(4) N lies above 1000. For $100\,p_x\ (=100\,x/N)$ the limits $100\,p_l'$ and $100\,p_r'$ are looked for in the column $N = 1000$. Then

$$\left.\begin{aligned} 100\,p_x - 100\,p_l' &= A \\ 100\,p_r' - 100\,p_x &= B \\ \text{and } 100\,p_l &= 100\,p_x - A\sqrt{1000/N} \\ 100\,p_r &= 100\,p_x + B\sqrt{1000/N} \end{aligned}\right\} \quad \textbf{(776)}$$

Example 60. Given are $N = 3000$ and $x = 69$, $100\,p_x = 2.30$. For $100\,p_x = 2.30$, column $N = 1000$ gives the limits $100\,p_l' = 1.46$ and $100\,p_r' = 3.44$.

$$A = 2.30 - 1.46 = 0.84$$
$$B = 3.44 - 2.30 = 1.14$$
$$\sqrt{1000/3000} = \sqrt{1/3} \sim 0.577$$
$$100\,p_l = 2.3 - (0.84 \times 0.577) = 1.82 = \underline{1.8}$$
$$100\,p_r = 2.3 + (1.14 \times 0.577) = 2.96 = \underline{3.0}$$

(*b*) *Significance limits for* x, tables on pages 104–106 (or confidence limits for $N\boldsymbol{p}$)

It is assumed that the probability $\boldsymbol{p}$ is known (either on theoretical grounds or from large samples). In a sample *possibly* originating from this population the event E occurs x times. The significance limits for x are in accordance with the conditions (**376**) and (**377**).

The table on page 104 gives limits of this nature for samples of size up to $N = 100$ and for $\boldsymbol{p} = 0.05;\ 0.1;\ \ldots;\ 0.45;\ 0.5$, that on pages 105 and 106 for samples of size up to $N = 1000$ and $\boldsymbol{p} = 0.5$.

As shown in Figure 45, right, the significance limits for x can be obtained from the confidence limits for $\boldsymbol{p}$ without calculation.

Example 61. Required are the 95% confidence limits for x for a sample of size $N = 10$ and a given $\boldsymbol{p} = 0.5$.

As shown by Figure 45, right, the *lower* limit x_l is fixed by that confidence interval for $\boldsymbol{p}$ whose *upper* limit p_r lies *closest* to the given $\boldsymbol{p}$ *without exceeding it*. (a)

The *upper* limit x_r is fixed by that confidence interval for $\boldsymbol{p}$ whose *lower* limit p_l lies *closest* to the given $\boldsymbol{p}$ *without falling below it*. (b) **(777)**

In the table on page 85, $p_r = 44.50$ is in accordance with (**777**a) and $p_l = 55.50$ in accordance with (**777**b). The required limits for x are therefore $x_l = 1$ and $x_r = 9$.

According to WILKS[31], the above significance limits correspond to the *distribution-free confidence limits for quantiles* $Q\,(p)$ (cf. section 10F, page 161) when x_l is replaced by $x_l + 1$ and when p in the table is so chosen that it is of the same magnitude as p in $Q\,(p)$.

In this connection it should be noted [cf. (**383**)] that the postulated significance probability is reached when x *attains* or exceeds in an outward direction from $N\boldsymbol{p}$ the limits x_l or x_r.

Example 62. The hypothetical probability $\boldsymbol{p}$ is 0.05. In 48 trials the event E occurs 7 times. Does this sample originate from the hypothetical population? For $2\alpha = 0.05$, the table on page 104 gives as upper level $x = 7$, so that:

(one-tailed test) the sample originates from a population with $\boldsymbol{p} > 0.05$ $(\alpha = 0.025)$
(two-tailed test) the sample originates from a population with $\boldsymbol{p} \neq 0.05$ $(2\alpha = 0.05)$

On the basis of (**760**) and (**762**) or of (**764**) and (**766**) the following approximations are suitable for calculating the significance limits for x:

$$x_l,\, x_r = N\boldsymbol{p} \mp \left(\tfrac{1}{2} + |c_\alpha|\sqrt{N\boldsymbol{p}\boldsymbol{q}}\right) \quad \textbf{(778)}$$

(c_α, page 28, left-hand table)

or, if $\boldsymbol{p} < \boldsymbol{q}$

$$\left.\begin{aligned} x_l + 1,\, x_r &= \boldsymbol{p}\left(N + 1 - \frac{c^2}{4}\right) + \\ &+ \frac{c^2}{4}\,\boldsymbol{q} \mp |c|\sqrt{\boldsymbol{p}\boldsymbol{q}\left(N + 1 - \frac{c^2}{4}\right)} \end{aligned}\right\} \quad \textbf{(779)}$$

($c = c_\alpha$, page 28, left-hand table)

(*c*) *Distribution-free tolerance limits for continuous distributions*, table on page 128 (cf. also sections 8C, page 155, and 10F, page 161)

The values of the sample sizes N in this table have been calculated by an iterative process based on a formula of WILKS[31], so that

$$\sum_{N-2k+1}^{N} \binom{N}{x} \beta_p^x (1 - \beta_p)^{N-x} \leqq 1 - \beta_t \quad \textbf{(780)}$$

The rounded-off values are based on the approximations[32]

$$\left.\begin{aligned} &N \sim 1.03\,x + 4.74\,\chi^2 - 1 \quad \text{for } \beta_p = 0.90 \\ &N \sim 1.01\,x + 9.75\,\chi^2 - 1 \quad \text{for } \beta_p = 0.95 \\ &N \sim 1.00\,x + 49.75\,\chi^2 - 1 \quad \text{for } \beta_p = 0.99 \end{aligned}\right\} \quad \textbf{(781)}$$

where χ^2 is so chosen that $1\int_r$ of the table on pages 36–39 equals $1 - \beta_t$ for $\nu = 4\,x$.

The approximation to N obtained from (**781**) is very close to (**780**).

20G. Binomial distribution: Miscellaneous

(*a*) *Arc-sine transformation*, table on page 69 (cf. also 'Inverse trigonometric functions', page 139)

According to FREEMAN and TUKEY[29], the best transformation $x \rightarrow X$ for stabilizing the variance of the binomial distribution when $N\boldsymbol{p} \geqq 1$ is in most cases

$$X = \arcsin\sqrt{\frac{x}{N+1}} + \arcsin\sqrt{\frac{x+1}{N+1}}$$

with a variance within $\pm$ 6% of **(782)**

$$s_X^2 = \frac{1}{N + \tfrac{1}{2}}\ \begin{pmatrix}\text{angle in}\\ \text{radians}\end{pmatrix} \text{ or } \frac{821}{N + \tfrac{1}{2}}\ \begin{pmatrix}\text{angle in}\\ \text{degrees}\end{pmatrix}$$

The mean $\bar{X}$ of the values thus transformed is approximately $2 \arcsin\sqrt{\boldsymbol{p}}$.

This transformation can be used in variance analysis and other operations.

(*b*) With a given $\boldsymbol{p}$, how large must the sample size N be for the event E to occur at least x times with a probability $\mathfrak{p}^*$? The solution of this problem for $x = 1$ is given in (**755**).

The simplest approximate solution for $x > 1$, on the basis of (**766**), is (when $\boldsymbol{p} < \boldsymbol{q}$)

$$N \sim \frac{1}{\boldsymbol{p}}\left(\frac{c^2}{4} + x + c\sqrt{x\boldsymbol{q}}\right) - 1 \quad \textbf{(783)}$$

where $c = c_{\mathfrak{p}^*}$

21. The Poisson distribution

21A. General

E is a random event occurring over a long period of observation† an infinite number of times but in a relatively short time† (in general the *observation unit* t) only rarely. The probability that in an observation unit t the event will occur 0, 1, 2, ..., x times is then

$$f(x) = \dot{\boldsymbol{P}}_x = \frac{e^{-\lambda}\lambda^x}{x!} = \underbrace{\frac{e^{-\lambda}\lambda^0}{0!}}_{=\,e^{-\lambda}},\ \frac{e^{-\lambda}\lambda^1}{1!},\ \frac{e^{-\lambda}\lambda^2}{2!} \cdots \quad \textbf{(784)}$$

e = base of natural logarithms; t = observation unit; for λ see (**787**), page 188.

The POISSON distribution is a discrete asymmetrical distribution in which, with increasing x, the individual probabilities decrease in a regular manner when $\lambda < 1$, and first increase but then decrease when $\lambda > 1$. Cf. Figure 44, page 185.

As shown by (**784**), the POISSON distribution is characterized completely by the parameter λ. For this reason it will be written here as POISSON distribution (λ).

Tables of $f(x)$ and the cumulative distribution $\sum_k^\infty \dot{\boldsymbol{P}}_x$ are given by MOLINA[2].

The simplest calculation of several successive individual probabilities is from the recursion formula

$$\dot{\boldsymbol{P}}_{x+1} = \dot{\boldsymbol{P}}_x \times \frac{\lambda}{x+1} \quad \textbf{(785)}$$

† Time has been chosen as an example. The same argument would apply, for instance, to surfaces and volumes.

Example 63. For the Poisson distribution ($\lambda = 1$) calculate the individual probabilities for x from 0 to 5.

$$\boldsymbol{P}_0 = 1/e = 0.367879 \qquad \boldsymbol{P}_3 = \boldsymbol{P}_2 \times 1/3 = 0.061313$$
$$\boldsymbol{P}_1 = \boldsymbol{P}_0 \times 1 = 0.367879 \qquad \boldsymbol{P}_4 = \boldsymbol{P}_3 \times 1/4 = 0.015328$$
$$\boldsymbol{P}_2 = \boldsymbol{P}_1 \times 1/2 = 0.183940 \qquad \boldsymbol{P}_5 = \boldsymbol{P}_4 \times 1/5 = 0.003066$$

Calculation of the *cumulative probabilities* is carried out according to the procedure given in section 5, page 148, with N replaced by infinity. It should also be noted that in the Poisson distribution the probability Prob ($x \geqq k$) can be calculated only from the probability Prob ($x \leqq k - 1$), i.e.,

$$\text{Prob}\,(x \geqq k) = 1 - \text{Prob}\,(x \leqq k - 1)$$

Example 64. How large must λ be for the event E to occur at least once during the observation unit t with a probability p^*? (This is an unusual problem in the Poisson distribution but sometimes occurs when the latter is used as an approximation to other distributions.)

The solution is obtained by using equation (**129**) on page 137. Here the numerical values for various probabilities p^* can also be found. For $p^* = 0.999$, λ for example is 6.9.

21B. The addition theorem for the Poisson distribution

If $x_{t_1}, x_{t_2}, \ldots, x_{t_k}$ are stochastically independent† random variables with Poisson distributions $(\lambda_{t_1}), (\lambda_{t_2}), \ldots, (\lambda_{t_k})$ respectively, then their sum $x = x_{t_1} + x_{t_2} + \cdots + x_{t_k}$ is likewise a Poisson distribution (λ) with $\lambda = \lambda_{t_1} + \lambda_{t_2} + \cdots + \lambda_{t_k}$. **(786)**

21C. Parameters and their estimates

The mean of the Poisson distribution is

$$\mu_{x_t} = \lambda_t = \text{expectation of } x_t \qquad \text{(a)}$$

and the variance **(787)**

$$\sigma^2_{x_t} = \lambda_t = \text{expectation of } x_t \qquad \text{(b)}$$

where t = observation unit to which x and λ_t relate.

If a Poisson distribution with observation unit t is used to calculate another Poisson distribution with observation unit kt, then the mean and variance of the latter are

$$\mu_{x_{kt}}, \sigma^2_{x_{kt}} = k\lambda_t;\ (k > 0) \qquad \textbf{(788)}$$

The equal magnitude of mean and variance in the Poisson distribution results in the following rule of thumb:

If the ratio of mean to variance in a *discrete* distribution is approximately unity (say between 10/9 and 9/10), then a Poisson distribution is likely to approximate to it provided that the variable x can assume high (theoretically, infinitely high) values. **(789)**

Unbiased estimates of λ_t based on n *equal* observation units t are

$$\bar{x}_t = \frac{\Sigma x_t}{n} = \frac{\Sigma x_i f_i}{n} \qquad \text{(a)}$$

or **(790)**

$$s_t^2 = \frac{\Sigma x_t^2 - (\Sigma x_t)^2/n}{n-1} = \frac{\Sigma x_i^2 f_i - (\Sigma x_i f_i)^2/n}{n-1} = \frac{S_t}{n-1} \qquad \text{(b)}$$

$\bar{x}_t$ is the *better* (more efficient) estimate. Since it is also more quickly calculated it is the one usually used. With higher values of n (say $n > 5$), however, the additional calculation of $(n-1)\,s^2$ [the numerator in (**790**b)] offers the advantage of being able to test whether the ratio $s^2/\bar{x}$ differs significantly from 1. The test quotient is

$$\frac{(n-1)\,s_t^2}{\bar{x}_t} = \frac{S_t}{\bar{x}_t} \qquad \textbf{(791)}$$

Significance limit χ^2 with $\nu = n - 1$, $2\alpha = 1 \int_r$, pages 36–39

If the test quotient (**791**) attains or exceeds the significance limit, then the sample probably does not originate from a Poisson distribution. This leads to the following rule of thumb:

When (**791**) is significant, the sample could originate from a binomial distribution when $s^2 < \bar{x}$, from a binomial distribution with negative index when $s^2 > \bar{x}$. Cf. also Bliss[33]. **(792)**

† For example, the observation units $t_1, t_2, \ldots, t_k$ must not overlap.

Example 65. In 60 minutes 12 events are observed. $\lambda_{60\,\text{min}} \sim 12/1 = 12$. In accordance with (**788**), the estimate of $\lambda_{1\,\text{min}}$ is then $12/60 \sim 1/5$.

Example 66. In 60 minutes 12 events are observed, in 30 minutes 8. In accordance with (**786**), $\lambda_{90\,\text{min}} \sim 12 + 8 = 20$, $\lambda_{1\,\text{min}} \sim 20/90$.

Example 67. In 100 observation periods of 1 minute each the event E is observed x_i times in f_i observation periods, as follows:

x_i	f_i	$x_i f_i$	$x_i^2 f_i$	
0	5	0	0	
1	30	30	30	$\bar{x}_t = 2.36$ from (**790**a)
2	24	48	96	
3	20	60	180	$S_t = 778 - 556.96$
4	12	48	192	$= 221.04$ from (**790**b)
5	4	20	100	
6	5	30	180	$\chi^2 = 93.661$,
7	0			$\nu = 99$ from (**791**)
8	0			
	$n = 100$	$\Sigma x = 236$ $= \lambda_{100\,\text{min}}$	$\Sigma x^2 = 778$	

In this case χ^2 lies far inside the significance limit of 0.05 ($0.30 < \alpha < 0.35$), so that the distribution *could* be a Poisson distribution. A *more efficient* test is provided by calculation of the *fitted* Poisson distribution in accordance with (**784**) with $\lambda = 2.36$, multiplication of the value obtained by n and then testing with χ^2 in accordance with (**566**) with degrees of freedom $\nu = k - 2$ from (**569**a), where k = number of classes i.

21D. Transformations

As shown by Figure 44 (page 185), with increasing λ the shape of the Poisson distribution gradually (and fairly rapidly) approaches that of the normal distribution.

$$\frac{e^{-\lambda}\lambda^x}{x!} \to \frac{1}{\sqrt{2\pi\lambda}}\, e^{-\frac{(x-\lambda)^2}{2\lambda}} \qquad \textbf{(793)}$$

as $\lambda \to \infty$.

The corresponding transformations are analogous to the transformations of the binomial distribution to the normal distribution using (**760**)–(**763**), with Np replaced by λ.

The following approximations are better[29]:

$$c_p = 2\left(\sqrt{x_p + 1} - \sqrt{\lambda}\right) \qquad \textbf{(794)}$$
$$x_p = \lambda + c_p\sqrt{\lambda} + \frac{c^2}{4} - 1 \qquad \textbf{(795)}$$
$$c_{1-p^*} = 2\left(\sqrt{x_{p^*}} - \sqrt{\lambda}\right) \qquad \textbf{(796)}$$
$$x_{p^*} = \lambda + c_{1-p^*}\sqrt{\lambda} + \frac{c^2}{4} \qquad \textbf{(797)}$$

$\lambda \geqq 1$

Example 68. Calculate x_p and x_{p^*} for $p = p^* = 0.025$ of the Poisson distribution ($\lambda = 99$).

$$x_p = 99 - 1.96\sqrt{99} + \frac{1.96^2}{4} - 1 = 79.46 \text{ from } \textbf{(795)}$$

$$x_{p^*} = 99 + 1.96\sqrt{99} + \frac{1.96^2}{4} = 119.46 \text{ from } \textbf{(797)}$$

Since x can have only discrete values, these results are rounded off to give 79 and 119. The exact values are 79 and 120. In this connection it should be noted that in such cases it is better to be on the safe side and round off outwards:

In order more adequately to meet the requirements Prob ($x \leqq x_p$) $\leqq p$ and Prob ($x \geqq x_{p^*}$) $\leqq p^*$, x_p should always be rounded off downwards, x_{p^*} always upwards. This also applies to approximations to other discrete distributions. **(798)**

If rule (**798**) had been adhered to in example 68, the correct result would have been obtained. However, this is not necessarily always the case when (**798**) is adhered to.

The following transformation[29] is suitable for stabilizing the variance:

$$\left.\begin{aligned} &X = \sqrt{x} + \sqrt{x+1} \\ &\text{with variance } \sigma_X^2 \sim 1 \\ &\text{and mean } \quad \bar{X} \sim \sqrt{4\lambda + 1} \end{aligned}\right\} \quad (799)$$

The relationship between the Poisson and χ^2 distributions is given in (**561**) and (**562**), whence the following procedure for determining the *exact* values of x_p and x_{p^*}:

(a) x_p is required. The value $\chi^2 \leqq 2\lambda$ is looked for in the column $1\int_l = 1 - p$ of the χ^2 table on pages 36–39. From the degrees of freedom ν of this χ^2 it follows that

$$\left.\begin{aligned} x_p &= \frac{\nu}{2} - 1 \text{ when } \nu \text{ is even} \\ &= \frac{\nu}{2} - 1.5 \text{ when } \nu \text{ is odd} \end{aligned}\right\} \quad (800)$$

(b) x_{p^*} is required. The value $\chi^2 \geqq 2\lambda$ is looked for in the column $1\int_l = p^*$ of the χ^2 table on pages 36–39. From the degrees of freedom ν of this χ^2 it follows that

$$\left.\begin{aligned} x_{p^*} &= \frac{\nu}{2} \text{ when } \nu \text{ is even} \\ &= \frac{\nu}{2} + 0.5 \text{ when } \nu \text{ is odd} \end{aligned}\right\} \quad (801)$$

Example 69. Required are the $(1-2\alpha)$ limits for x when $\lambda = 32$ and $\alpha = 0.0005$. The left limit is obtained from (**800**) and is $\chi^2_{0.9995} = 63.582 \leqq 64$ with $\nu = 31$. $x_l = 31/2 - 1.5 = 14$. The right limit is obtained from (**801**) and is $\chi^2_{0.0005} = 64.526 \geqq 64$ with $\nu = 106$. $x_r = 106/2 = 53$.

21E. Confidence limits and significance limits

(*a*) *Confidence limits for* λ (tables on pages 107 and 108)

In analogy with the binomial distribution, confidence limits for λ are solutions of the equations

$$\sum_{k=x}^{k=\infty} \frac{e^{-\lambda_l}\lambda_l^k}{k!} = \alpha \quad \text{and} \quad \sum_{k=0}^{k=x} \frac{e^{-\lambda_r}\lambda_r^k}{k!} = \alpha;\ \alpha < 0.5 \qquad \text{(a)} \quad \text{(b)} \quad (802)$$

for λ_l and λ_r.

For $x = 0$ there is only one $(1-\alpha)$ confidence interval with the solution $\lambda_r = z$ [equation (**129**), page 137]. The left limit λ_l is zero.

For $x > 0$ only iterative solutions are possible. The tables on pages 107 and 108 were calculated in this way by computer for values of λ up to 100. For values of $x > 100$ the formulae (**804**) were used (from Freeman and Tukey's approximation[29]).

Fig. 46. Poisson distribution, confidence limits for λ.

For significance probabilities other than those in the tables on pages 107 and 108, *exact* limits for x up to 100 (or 99) can be calculated from the χ^2 table on pages 36–39 as follows:

Given x and α, then

$$\left.\begin{aligned} &\tfrac{1}{2}\,[\chi^2_{\alpha,\ \nu=2x}] = \lambda_l && \text{(a)} \\ &\tfrac{1}{2}\,[\chi^2_{1-\alpha,\ \nu=2(x+1)}] = \lambda_r && \text{(b)} \end{aligned}\right\} \quad (803)$$

where χ^2_α and $\chi^2_{1-\alpha}$ denote the α and $1-\alpha$ quantiles; α and $1-\alpha$ are to be found under $1\int_l$.

Example 70. Required are the $(1-2\alpha)$ limits for λ when $x = 98$ and $\alpha = 0.05$. For λ_l the table is entered at $\nu = 2 \times 98 = 196$ and $1\int_l = 0.05$, giving $\chi^2_l = 164.10$. $\lambda_l = 164.10/2 = 82.05$. For λ_r the table is entered at $\nu = 2\,(98+1) = 198$ and $1\int_l = 0.95$, giving $\chi^2_r = 231.829$. $\lambda_r = 231.829/2 = 115.915$.

For higher values of x, very good approximations are obtained from (**794**) and (**796**):

$$\lambda_l, \lambda_r = \left(\frac{|c_\alpha|}{2} \mp \sqrt{x + \tfrac{1}{2} \mp \tfrac{1}{2}}\right)^2 \qquad (804)$$

Example 71. Required are the $(1-2\alpha)$ confidence limits for λ when $x = 99$ and $\alpha = 0.025$.

$$\lambda_l = \left(\frac{1.96}{2} - \sqrt{99 + \tfrac{1}{2} - \tfrac{1}{2}}\right)^2 = 80.459$$

$$\lambda_r = \left(\frac{1.96}{2} + \sqrt{99 + \tfrac{1}{2} + \tfrac{1}{2}}\right)^2 = 120.56$$

The exact values are 80.458 and 120.53.

Example 72. In 12 minutes 24 events are observed. Calculate the 95% limits for $\lambda_{12\,\text{min}}, \lambda_{1\,\text{min}}, \lambda_{1\,\text{h}}$. For $x = 24$ in the table on page 107 the limits 15.378 and 35.711 are given. In accordance with (**788**) these give the following further limits

for $\lambda_{1\,\text{min}}$ = 15.378/12 and 35.711/12 = 1.2815 and 2.9759
for $\lambda_{1\,\text{h}}$ = 15.378 × 5 and 35.711 × 5 = 76.890 and 178.56

The estimate of the limits for λ_{kt} must always be made on the basis of the number of events x observed during the observation unit t, and *not* on the basis of this number multiplied by k. The following calculation in the case of example 72 would be wrong:

$x_{1\,\text{min}}$ = 24/12 = 2; limits 0.2422 – 7.2247
or $x_{1\,\text{h}}$ = 24 × 5 = 120; limits 99.49 – 143.52

(*b*) *Significance limits for* x *when* λ *is given* (table on page 128)

These limits meet the condition (**390**) with N replaced by ∞. They can be obtained without calculation from the confidence limits for λ, as shown in Figure 46, right. The procedure is exactly analogous to that for determining the corresponding limits for the binomial distribution. For $\alpha \neq 0.025$ or 0.005, the left limit is obtained from (**800**), the right limit from (**801**). Cf. example 69 on this page. For $n > 100$ (or 99), approximations are obtained from (**795**) and (**797**).

22. The hypergeometric distribution

22A. General

Given are N balls, of which X are white and $N - X$ red. The probability of drawing exactly x_1 white balls in N_1 draws is then

$$\left.\begin{aligned} f(x_1 \mid X, N, N_1) &= \frac{\binom{X}{x_1}\binom{N-X}{N_1-x_1}}{\binom{N}{N_1}} && \text{(a)} \\ &= \frac{N_1!\,(N-N_1)!\,X!\,(N-X)!}{N!\,x_1!\,(N_1-x_1)!\,(X-x_1)!\,(N-X-N_1+x_1)!} && \text{(b)} \end{aligned}\right\} \quad (805)$$

$f(x_1 \mid X, N, N_1)$ is known as the hypergeometric distribution of x_1 (X, N, N_1 constant).

The corresponding fourfold table (cf. section 22D, page 191) is

$$\left.\begin{array}{llc|c} \text{White } x_1 & N_1 - x_1 & & N_1 \\ \text{Red } X - x_1 & N - X - N_1 + x_1 & & N - N_1 \\ \hline \quad X & N - X & & N \end{array} = \begin{array}{cc|c} x_1 & N_1 - x_1 & N_1 \\ x_2 & N_2 - x_2 & N_2 \\ \hline X & N - X & N \end{array}\right\} \quad (806)$$

For $N \leqq 100$ the calculation of (**805**) is best made from (a) by means of the tables on pages 70–77 (cf. explanation on page 77), for $N > 100$ from (b) by means of the tables on pages 26 and 27. The calculation can also be made with the aid of the recursion formulae

$$f(x_1 + 1 \mid X) = [f(x_1 \mid X)] \times \frac{(N_1 - x_1)(X - x_1)}{(x_1 + 1)(N - X - N_1 + x_1 + 1)} \qquad (807)$$

and

$$f(x_1 \mid X + 1) = [f(x_1 \mid X)] \times \frac{(N - X - N_1 + x_1)(X + 1)}{(N - X)(X + 1 - x_1)} \qquad (808)$$

Hypergeometric distribution, $N = 20$, $N_1 = 5$, individual probabilities Prob $(x_1 = k_1 \mid X = K)$

x_1	$X=K$																				
	0	1	2	3	4	5	6	7	8	9	10	11	12	13	14	15	16	17	18	19	20
0	1	0.75	0.5526	0.3991	0.2817	0.1937	0.1291	0.0830	0.0511	0.0298	0.0163	0.0081	0.0036	0.0014	0.0004	0.0001					
1		0.25	0.3947	0.4605	0.4696	0.4402	0.3874	0.3228	0.2554	0.1916	0.1354	0.0894	0.0542	0.0293	0.0135	0.0048	0.0010				
2			0.0526	0.1316	0.2167	0.2935	0.3522	0.3874	0.3973	0.3831	0.3483	0.2980	0.2384	0.1761	0.1174	0.0677	0.0310	0.0088			
3				0.0088	0.0310	0.0677	0.1174	0.1761	0.2384	0.2980	0.3483	0.3831	0.3973	0.3874	0.3522	0.2935	0.2167	0.1316	0.0526		
4					0.0010	0.0048	0.0135	0.0293	0.0542	0.0894	0.1354	0.1916	0.2554	0.3228	0.3874	0.4402	0.4696	0.4605	0.3947	0.25	
5						0.0001	0.0004	0.0014	0.0036	0.0081	0.0163	0.0298	0.0511	0.0830	0.1291	0.1937	0.2817	0.3991	0.5526	0.75	1

Hypergeometric distribution, $N = 20$, $N_1 = 5$, cumulative probabilities Prob $(x_1 \leqq k_1 \mid X = K)$

x_1	$X=K$																				
	0	1	2	3	4	5	6	7	8	9	10	11	12	13	14	15	16	17	18	19	20
0	1	0.75	0.5526	0.3991	0.2817	0.1937	0.1291	0.0830	0.0511	0.0298	0.0163	0.0081	0.0036	0.0011	0.0004	0.0001					
1		1	0.9474	0.8596	0.7513	0.6339	0.5165	0.4058	0.3065	0.2214	0.1517	0.0975	0.0578	0.0307	0.0139	0.0049	0.0010				
2			1	0.9912	0.9680	0.9274	0.8687	0.7932	0.7038	0.6045	0.5000	0.3955	0.2962	0.2068	0.1313	0.0726	0.0320	0.0088			
3				1	0.9990	0.9951	0.9861	0.9693	0.9422	0.9025	0.8483	0.7786	0.6935	0.5942	0.4835	0.3661	0.2487	0.1404	0.0526		
4					1	0.9999	0.9996	0.9986	0.9964	0.9919	0.9837	0.9702	0.9489	0.9170	0.8709	0.8063	0.7183	0.6009	0.4474	0.25	
5						1	1	1	1	1	1	1	1	1	1	1	1	1	1	1	1

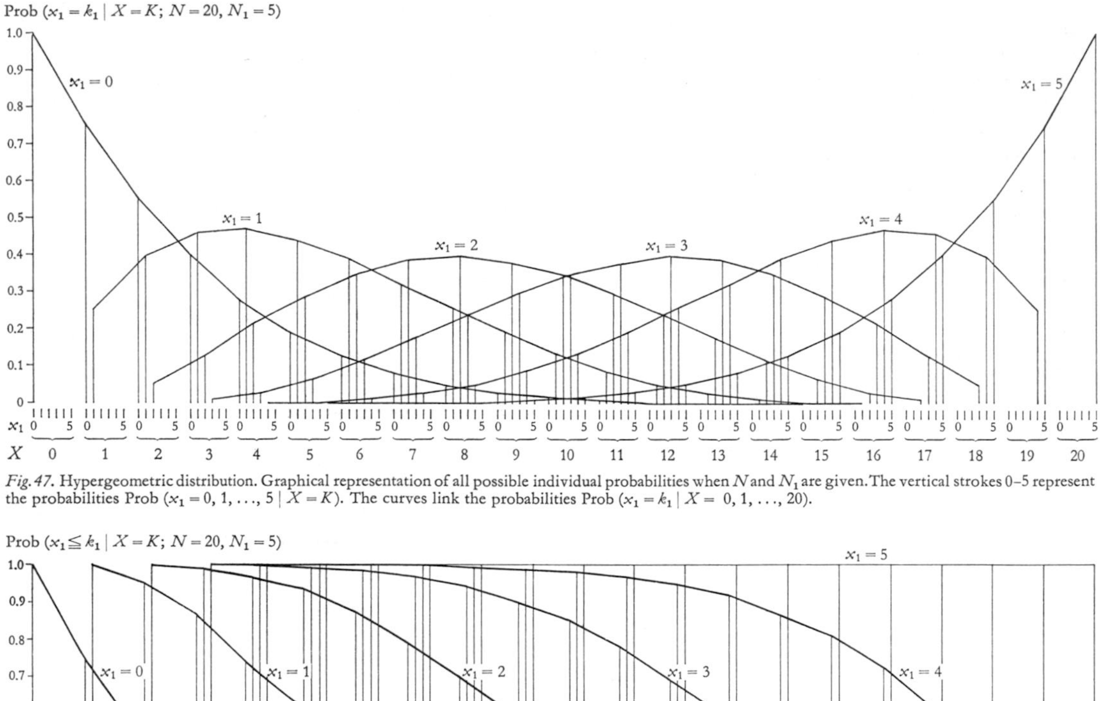

Fig. 47. Hypergeometric distribution. Graphical representation of all possible individual probabilities when N and N_1 are given. The vertical strokes 0–5 represent the probabilities Prob $(x_1 = 0, 1, \ldots, 5 \mid X = K)$. The curves link the probabilities Prob $(x_1 = k_1 \mid X = 0, 1, \ldots, 20)$.

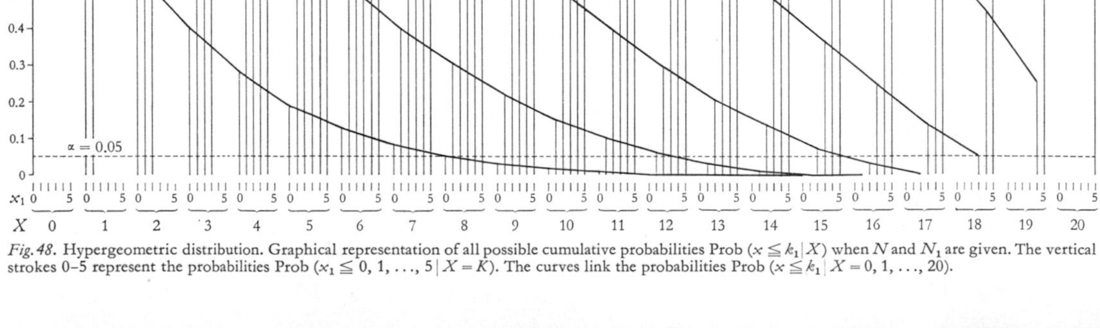

Fig. 48. Hypergeometric distribution. Graphical representation of all possible cumulative probabilities Prob $(x \leqq k_1 \mid X)$ when N and N_1 are given. The vertical strokes 0–5 represent the probabilities Prob $(x_1 \leqq 0, 1, \ldots, 5 \mid X = K)$. The curves link the probabilities Prob $(x \leqq k_1 \mid X = 0, 1, \ldots, 20)$.

All the probabilities $f(x_1 \mid X, N=20, N_1=5)$ and cumulative probabilities $F(x_1 \mid X)$ are given in the tables on page 190, where the same probabilities are shown graphically in Figures 47 and 48.

A check on calculations of this kind is provided by

$$\left.\begin{aligned} &\sum_{x_1=0}^{x_1=N_1} \text{Prob}\,(x_1 \mid X=K) = 1 && \text{(a)} \\ &\sum_{X=0}^{X=N-N_1+k_1} \text{Prob}\,(x_1=k_1 \mid X) = \frac{N+1}{N_1+1} && \text{(b)} \end{aligned}\right\} \quad \textbf{(809)}$$

Figure 47 clearly demonstrates the symmetry of the relationship

$$\left.\begin{aligned} &\text{Prob}\,(x_1=k_1 \mid X=K) = \text{Prob}\,(x_1=N_1-k_1 \mid X=N-K) \\ &\text{whence} \\ &\text{Prob}\,(x_1 \leqq k_1 \mid X=K) = \text{Prob}\,(x_1 \geqq N_1-k_1 \mid X=N-k) \end{aligned}\right\} \quad \textbf{(810)}$$

22B. Parameters

The mean of x when X, N and N_1 are given is (putting $X/N=\boldsymbol{p}$)

$$\mu_x = N_1\boldsymbol{p} \qquad \textbf{(811)}$$

and the variance is

$$\sigma_x^2 = N_1\boldsymbol{p}\boldsymbol{q}\left(\frac{N-N_1}{N-1}\right) \qquad \textbf{(812)}$$

$$X/N=\boldsymbol{p},\quad \boldsymbol{q}=1-\boldsymbol{p}$$

The variance of the hypergeometric distribution $(N, N_1, \boldsymbol{p})$ is thus *smaller* than that of the binomial distribution $(\boldsymbol{p}; N_1)$ by the factor $(N-N_1)/(N-1)$.

22C. The hypergeometric distribution and other distributions

When $\boldsymbol{p} < 0.1$ and N is fairly large (say over 60) the hypergeometric distribution $(N, N_1, \boldsymbol{p})$ approximates to the binomial distribution $(\boldsymbol{p}; N_1)$. In this connection it is advisable in significance tests to remain on the safe side. **(813)**

When $N_1/N < 0.1$ and N is fairly large the Poisson distribution $(\lambda = N_1\boldsymbol{p})$ is a good approximation. **(814)**

When $N_1\boldsymbol{p} \geqq 4$ (about), the normal distribution [(**811**), $\sqrt{(\mathbf{812})}$] is a good approximation, whence **(815)**

$$\left.\begin{aligned} c_p &= \frac{x_1 + \tfrac{1}{2} - (\mathbf{811})}{\sqrt{(\mathbf{812})}} && \text{(a)} \\ c_{1-p^*} &= \frac{x_1 - \tfrac{1}{2} - (\mathbf{811})}{\sqrt{(\mathbf{812})}} && \text{(b)} \end{aligned}\right\} \quad \textbf{(816)}$$

where $+\tfrac{1}{2}$ or $-\tfrac{1}{2}$ can be neglected when N is large.

22D. Significance limits (fourfold table test)

(Cf. remarks on page 123)

The significance limits given in the table on pages 109–123 meet the conditions (when N and N_1 are given)

$$\left.\begin{aligned} &\left.\begin{aligned} &\text{Prob}\,(x_1 \geqq k_1 \mid X_l) \leqq \alpha \\ &\text{Prob}\,(x_1 \geqq k_1 \mid X_l+1) > \alpha \end{aligned}\right\} \text{(a)} \\ &\text{and} \\ &\left.\begin{aligned} &\text{Prob}\,(x_1 \leqq k_1 \mid X_r) \leqq \alpha \\ &\text{Prob}\,(x_1 \leqq k_1 \mid X_r-1) > \alpha \end{aligned}\right\} \text{(b)} \end{aligned}\right\} \quad \textbf{(817)}$$

This form of presentation is preferred since it is also convenient in situations in which X is unknown (these do *not* correspond to the situation described at the start of section 22A, page 189).

The procedure for finding the upper level (**817** b) for $\alpha = 0.05$ is indicated in Figure 48 (horizontal broken line).

With large values of N, (**817**) can be satisfied approximately on the basis of (**816**) as follows[34]:

$$X_l, X_r = \frac{N}{2k}\left(k + 2x_1 - N_1 - 1 \mp \sqrt{k^2 - \frac{2k}{N_1}\left[(x_1 \mp \tfrac{1}{2})^2 + (N_1 - x_1 \pm \tfrac{1}{2})^2\right] + (2x_1 - N_1 \mp 1)^2}\right) \qquad \text{(a)}$$

or without continuity correction

$$X_l, X_r = \frac{N}{2k}\left(k + 2x_1 - N_1 \mp \sqrt{k^2 - \frac{2k}{N_1}\left[x_1^2 + (N_1 - x_1)^2\right] + (2x_1 - N_1)^2}\right) \qquad \text{(b)} \qquad \textbf{(818)}$$

where in (a) and (b) $k = N_1 + (1 - N_1/N)\,c_\alpha^2$. $\;c_\alpha^2 = \chi_{2\alpha}^2$ for $\nu = 1$; $2\alpha = 1\int_r$, page 36

When $N > 60$, $N_1\boldsymbol{p} \geqq 4$, $N_2\boldsymbol{p} \geqq 4$ (about), the $(1-2\alpha)$ significance limits for x_1 with X given can be obtained approximately as follows:

$$x_l, x_r = N_1\boldsymbol{p} \mp \left[\tfrac{1}{2} + |c_\alpha| \sqrt{N_1\boldsymbol{p}\boldsymbol{q}\,(N-N_1)/(N-1)}\right] \qquad \textbf{(819)}$$

For $\boldsymbol{p}$ and $\boldsymbol{q}$ see (**811**).

23. Testing frequencies

23A. Samples from binomially distributed populations

(*a*) Given *2 samples* of sizes N_1 and N_2 in which the event E occurs x_1 and x_2 times respectively. If $N_1 + N_2 \leqq 60$ proceed as given on page 123. If $N_1 + N_2 > 60$ proceed as in (*b*) below. **(820)**

(*b*) Given *several* (*m*) *samples* of sizes $N_1, N_2, \ldots, N_i, \ldots, N_m$ in which the event E occurs $x_1, x_2, \ldots, x_i, \ldots, x_m$ times respectively. The following are calculated:

$$p_i = \frac{x_i}{N_i};\quad q_i = 1 - p_i;\quad \bar{p} = (\Sigma x_i)/(\Sigma N_i);\quad \bar{q} = 1 - \bar{p}$$

The x_i values are now transformed as follows in accordance with (**764**) and (**766**):

$$\left.\begin{aligned} &c_i = 2\left(\sqrt{(x_i+1)\,\bar{q}} - \sqrt{(N_i - x_i)\,\bar{p}}\right), \text{ when } p_i < \bar{p} \\ &\text{or} \\ &c_i = 2\left(\sqrt{x_i\,\bar{q}} - \sqrt{(N_i - x_i + 1)\,\bar{p}}\right), \text{ when } p_i > \bar{p} \end{aligned}\right\} \quad \textbf{(821)}$$

A comparison of the transformed data can be made by two methods:

I. Comparison on the basis of the extreme range (rapid test)

The difference between the highest and lowest values of c_i is the extreme range m, c_i being obtained from (**821**). **(822)**

Significance limits for the extreme range m are given in the table on page 51 at $N_1 = m$ and $\nu = \infty$. For $m = 2$, that is to say, for comparing two samples, these limits are 2.772 $(2\alpha = 0.05)$ and 3.643 $(2\alpha = 0.01)$. If the extreme range m *attains* or *exceeds* the significance limit, then the following interpretations may be made:

$$\left.\begin{aligned} &\text{For } m = 2 \text{ (2 samples)} \\ &\text{one-tailed test: } \begin{cases} \boldsymbol{p}_1 < \boldsymbol{p}_2, \text{ if } p_1 - p_2 < 0 \ (\alpha) \\ \boldsymbol{p}_1 > \boldsymbol{p}_2, \text{ if } p_1 - p_2 > 0 \ (\alpha) \end{cases} \\ &\text{two-tailed test: } \boldsymbol{p}_1 \neq \boldsymbol{p}_2 \qquad (2\alpha) \end{aligned}\right\} \quad \textbf{(823)}$$

For $m > 2$ (more than 2 samples)

two-tailed test: the samples do not all originate from the same population. **(824)**

When $m = 2$ (2 samples), this test has the same power as the following χ^2 test. The range test is *not* recommended when $m > 10$.

II. Comparison on the basis of χ^2

The squares of the c_i values are summed. Then the significance limit for the test statistic

$$\Sigma\, c_i^2$$

is found from χ^2, pages 36–39, with degrees of freedom $\nu = m - 1$ (cf. section 12B, page 166). **(825)**

If the test statistic *attains* or *exceeds* the significance limit, then interpretation (**823**) is valid with $2\alpha = 1\int_r$ and $\alpha = \tfrac{1}{2}\int_r$. The χ^2 test can be applied with any number m of samples. When $m > 2$ it is *more powerful* than the test based on the extreme range.

23B. Samples from multinomially distributed populations

Given are m samples of sizes $N_1, N_2, \ldots, N_i, \ldots, N_m$, in which the events $E_1, E_2, \ldots, E_j, \ldots, E_n$ occur $x_{1j}, x_{2j}, \ldots, x_{ij}, \ldots, x_{mn}$ times respectively, and

$$\sum_{j=1}^{n} x_{ij} = N_i, \ \sum_{i=1}^{m} x_{ij} = X_j \text{ and } \sum_{j=1}^{n} X_j = \sum_{i=1}^{m} N_i = N:$$

$$\begin{array}{cccccccc|c} x_{11} & x_{12} & \ldots & x_{1j} & \ldots & x_{1n} & & & N_1 \\ x_{21} & x_{22} & \ldots & x_{2j} & \ldots & x_{2n} & & & N_2 \\ \vdots & \vdots & & \vdots & & \vdots & & & \vdots \\ x_{i1} & x_{i2} & \ldots & x_{ij} & \ldots & x_{in} & & & N_i \\ \vdots & \vdots & & \vdots & & \vdots & & & \vdots \\ x_{m1} & x_{m2} & \ldots & x_{mj} & \ldots & x_{mn} & & & N_m \\ \hline X_1 & X_2 & & X_j & & X_n & & & N \end{array} \qquad (826)$$

The expected values $E_{ij} = N_i X_j / N$ of x_{ij} on the assumption of constant probabilities and independence are now calculated. The expected value of x_{11} (event 1 in sample 1), for example, is $N_1 X_1 / N$. With these expected values the following quotient is calculated for each observation x_{ij}:

$$\frac{(x_{ij} - E_{ij})^2}{E_{ij}} \quad \text{or} \quad \frac{x_{ij}^2}{X_j N_i} - 1 \qquad \text{(a)} \quad \text{(b)} \qquad (827)$$

and the values summed. The significance limit for the sum

$$\sum_1^n \sum_1^m \text{(827a)} \quad \text{or} \quad N \sum_1^n \sum_1^m \text{(827b)} \qquad (828)$$

is found from χ^2, pages 36–39, with degrees of freedom $\nu = (n-1)(m-1)$ and $2\alpha = 1 \int_r$. If the test statistic **(828)** *attains* or *exceeds* the significance limit, then interpretation **(825)** is valid.

23C. Samples from Poisson distributions

(a) 2 samples from two observation units of equal magnitude $t_1 = t_2 = t$

Given are 2 samples with the *same* observation unit $t_1 = t_2 = t$, in which the event E occurs x_1 and x_2 times respectively.

The sums $x_1 + x_2 = N$ are calculated. The significance limits for x_1 and x_2 are then x_l and x_r of the table on pages 105 and 106 for $N = x_1 + x_2$. If x_1 and x_2 *attain* or *exceed* these limits (in an outward direction from ½ N), then the following interpretations may be made:

$$\left.\begin{array}{ll} \text{one-tailed test:} & \begin{cases} \lambda_1 < \lambda_2, \text{ if } x_1 \leqq x_l \text{ (significance } \alpha) \\ \lambda_1 > \lambda_2, \text{ if } x_1 \geqq x_r \text{ (significance } \alpha) \end{cases} \\ \text{two-tailed test:} & \lambda_1 \neq \lambda_2, \text{ if } x_1 \text{ and } x_2 \text{ attain or exceed (outwards) the levels } x_l \text{ and } x_r \text{ (significance } 2\alpha) \end{array}\right\} \quad (829)$$

For samples with $x_1 + x_2 > 1000$ or $t_1 \neq t_2$ see *(b)* below.

(b) Several samples from any number of observation units t_i

Given are m samples from any number of observation units $t_1, t_2, \ldots, t_i, \ldots, t_m$ in which the event E occurs $x_1, x_2, \ldots, x_i, \ldots, x_m$ times. The following are calculated:

$$\lambda_i^* = \frac{x_i}{t_i} \text{ and } \bar{\lambda} = (\Sigma\, x_i)/(\Sigma\, t_i)$$

and the x_i values transformed into c_i values as follows in accordance with **(794)** and **(796)**:

$$\left.\begin{array}{l} c_i = 2\left(\sqrt{x_i + 1} - \sqrt{t_i \bar{\lambda}}\right), \text{ if } \lambda_i^* < \bar{\lambda} \\ c_i = 2\left(\sqrt{x_i} - \sqrt{t_i \bar{\lambda}}\right), \text{ if } \lambda_i^* > \bar{\lambda} \end{array}\right\} \quad (830)$$

Comparison of these transformed data and their interpretations are as in section 23 A (b), I and II, with $\bar{\lambda}$ and λ_i^* in place of $\bar{p}$ and p_i.

(c) Confidence limits for the increase in frequency of a rare event[35]

Given are two samples of sizes N_1 and N_2 in which the fairly *rare* event E occurs with a relative frequency of $p_1 = x_1/N_1$ and $p_2 = x_2/N_2$ respectively. *The samples should be so numbered that* $p_1 < p_2$. The estimate of the proportionate *increase* in relative frequency from sample 1 to sample 2 is then

$$Proc_{1\to 2} = \frac{p_2 - p_1}{p_1} \qquad (831)$$

with the $(1 - 2\alpha)$ confidence limits for $\boldsymbol{Proc}_{1\to 2}$

$$k\left(\frac{1}{p_r} - 1\right) - 1 < \boldsymbol{Proc}_{1\to 2} < k\left(\frac{1}{p_l} - 1\right) - 1 \qquad (832)$$

where $k = N_1/N_2$ and p_r and p_l are obtained from the table of confidence limits for $\boldsymbol{p}$ of the binomial distribution on pages 85 to 103 for $N = x_1 + x_2$ and $x = x_1$. **(831)** and **(832)** are converted to percentages by multiplying by 100. **(832)** can also be calculated in this way when only the *ratio* N_1/N_2 and the absolute numbers x_1 and x_2 are known. *Interpretation:* When the left limit of **(832)** $\leqq$ zero, then no increase in frequency has occurred.

24. Rank tests

24A. Ranking

(a) By magnitude (continuous distributions). Given are two samples 1 and 2 with the x_1 values 1.06, 1.53, 1.68, 1.68, 1.69, 1.69 and the x_2 values 1.30, 1.55, 1.69, 1.80. These values are ranked as follows:

											(833)
x_1	1.06		1.53		1.68	1.68		1.69	1.69		
x_2		1.30		1.55			1.69			1.80	
$O_{1,2}$	1	2	3	4	5	6	8	8	8	10	
							$= (7 + 8 + 9)/3$				

With ties [cf. **(346)**], the procedure is as in **(833)**: tied values *within* a sample receive *successive* rank numbers, those *between* the samples the *mean* of the two rank numbers at the position concerned. **(834)**

In the above example, the rank numbers O_1 of the x_1 values are $O_1 = 1, 3, 5, 6, 8$ and 8, and their sum $T_1 = \Sigma O_1 = 31$. **(835)**

With *paired observations*, the n pair differences d_i are calculated as in section 16 D, page 173, with all d_i values equal to zero ignored and N reduced accordingly. The *absolute values* of these differences are then ranked and either the rank numbers of all negative differences summed to give T_- or those of all positive differences summed to give T_+. **(836)**

(b) By order in a series (discrete distributions). If in a series of N trials the event E occurs once each in the 2nd, 3rd, 8th and 13th trials, in all N_1 times (for example 4 times), then $O_E = 2, 3, 8$ and 13 respectively and the sum of the O_E numbers $= T_E = 26$. **(837)**

24B. The Wilcoxon test for two samples[36, 37]

Given are two samples from *continuous* distributions of *any* form with means μ_1 and μ_2 respectively. These are so numbered that $N_1 \leqq 25$ and $N_2 \leqq 50$. The x_1 values are now ranked as in **(833)** and **(834)** to give the sum T_1 of **(835)**.

The significance limits for T_1 are given in the tables on pages 124–127. If T_1 *attains* the significance levels or *exceeds them in the outward direction* from its expected value, then this may be regarded as evidence that

$$\left.\begin{array}{ll} \text{one-tailed test:} & \begin{cases} \mu_1 < \mu_2, \text{ if } T_1 \leqq T_l \ (\leqq \alpha) \\ \mu_1 > \mu_2, \text{ if } T_1 \geqq T_r \ (\leqq \alpha) \end{cases} \\ \text{two-tailed test:} & \mu_1 \neq \mu_2, \text{ if } T_1 \leqq T_l \text{ or } T_1 \geqq T_r \ (\leqq 2\alpha) \end{array}\right\} \quad (838)$$

Cf. also section 9 C, page 157.

Under the null hypothesis, the expectation $\boldsymbol{T}_1$ of the estimate T_1 is

$$\left.\begin{array}{lr} \boldsymbol{T}_1 = N_1 (N_1 + N_2 + 1)/2 \quad \text{or} & \text{(a)} \\ 6\, \boldsymbol{T}_1 = 3\, N_1 (N_1 + N_2 + 1) & \text{(b)} \end{array}\right\} \quad (839)$$

$$\left.\begin{array}{lr} \text{and the variance } \sigma_{T_1}^2 = N_2 \boldsymbol{T}_1 / 6 \quad \text{or} & \text{(a)} \\ \sigma_{6T_1}^2 = 6\, N_2 \boldsymbol{T}_1 & \text{(b)} \end{array}\right\} \quad (840)$$

For samples outside the scope of the tables the following test quotient can be used

$$(T_1 - \boldsymbol{T}_1) / \sqrt{\sigma_{T_1}^2} \text{ or } (6\, T_1 - 6\, \boldsymbol{T}_1) / \sqrt{\sigma_{6T_1}^2} \qquad \text{(a)} \quad \text{(b)} \qquad (841)$$

Significance limit c_α, page 28.

24C. The Wilcoxon test for pair differences[37]

(Cf. section 9 C, page 158)

The sum T_- is calculated in accordance with **(836)**. The number of ranked pair differences is denoted by n (all zero values are ignored).

Significance limits for the sum T_- are given in the table on page 128. If the differences have been calculated as $d_i = x_{1i} - x_{2i}$ and the sum T_- *attains* the significance limits or *exceeds them in the outward direction* from the expected value of T_-, then it follows that

one-tailed test: $\mu_1 > \mu_2$, when $T_- \leqq T_l\ (\leqq \alpha)$; $\mu_1 < \mu_2$, when $T_- \geqq T_r\ (\leqq \alpha)$

two-tailed test: $\mu_1 \neq \mu_2$, when $T_- \leqq T_l$ or $T_- \geqq T_r$ $(\leqq 2\alpha)$ **(842)**

Under the null hypothesis, the expectation $\boldsymbol{T}_-$ of the estimate T_- is

$$\boldsymbol{T}_- = n(n+1)/4 \qquad \textbf{(843)}$$

and the variance is

$$\sigma^2_{T_-} = (2n+1)\,\boldsymbol{T}/6 \qquad \textbf{(844)}$$

For samples outside the scope of the tables the following test quotient can be used:

$$(T_- - \boldsymbol{T}_-)\,/\sqrt{\sigma^2_{T_-}} \qquad \textbf{(845)}$$

Significance limit c_α, page 28.

24D. Haldane's test for chance order in series[38]

The WILCOXON test can also be used for testing exactly for the possibility that an event E is affected by the order in which it occurs. Examples of this situation are the possibility that the later children of *one* mother may be more liable to a certain disease, the question whether the mortality in, or success of, a particular operation in the *same* hospital is increasing or decreasing, and so on. The test was developed by HALDANE for such problems independently of WILCOXON.

(*a*) *Investigation of a series.* T_E is calculated as in (**837**). N_1 is the number of trials (births, operations, etc.) in which the event E has occurred. N_2 is $N - N_1$, where N is the total number of trials in the series being investigated.

The significance limits for T_E are the same as those in section 24B; the interpretation, however, is completely different. *One-tailed test:* If T_E attains or exceeds the *left* limit, then the frequency *decreases* with increasing lateness in the series; if it attains or exceeds the *right* limit, the frequency increases. *Two-tailed test:* The order has an influence on the frequency. **(846)**

If all the events in the series cannot be specified, the following sequence, for example, may arise:

Trial	2	3	4	5	6	7	8	9	10	11	12	
	+	+	?	−	+	?	+	−	+	?	+	**(847)**
O_E				5				9				
$O_?$			4			7				11		

and the tables on pages 124–127 can no longer be used. In such cases the test criterion (**841** b) is used, with

$$6\,T_E = 6\,\Sigma\,O_E \quad (a)$$
$$6\,\boldsymbol{T}_E = 6\,N_1 A/N \quad (b)$$
$$\sigma^2_{6T_E} = 36\,N_1 N_2 (NB - A^2)/N^2(N-1) \quad (c) \qquad \textbf{(848)}$$
$$A = N(N+1)/2 - \Sigma\,O_? \quad (d)$$
$$B = N[1 + N(2N+3)]/6 - \Sigma\,O_?^2 \quad (e)$$

If all the events are specified but the sample exceeds the scope of the table, then equations (**839** b) and (**840** b) can be used in conjunction with (**841** b).

(*b*) *Investigation of several series as samples from the same population.* The successive offspring of 1, 2, 3, ..., *i*, ..., *m* mothers, for example, are to be investigated in respect of a childhood disease that appears to be commoner among later births.

The test criterion (**841** b) is used, with

$$6\,T = \Sigma\,6\,T_i$$
$$6\,\boldsymbol{T} = \Sigma\,6\,\boldsymbol{T}_i \qquad \textbf{(849)}$$
$$\sigma^2_{6T} = \Sigma\,\sigma^2_{6T_i}$$

$6\,\boldsymbol{T}_i$ and $\sigma^2_{6T_i}$ are calculated from (**839** b) and (**840** b) or from (**848** b) and (**848** c) respectively, according to whether all the events in the series *i* are specified or not.

24E. The maximum test for pair differences[21,39]

(This name was proposed by E. WALTER. The test is described here since it is also useful for assessing series, though by a method different to that of the WILCOXON test.)

With paired observations from *continuous* populations of *any* form the pair differences d_i are calculated as in section 16D, page 173. All zero values of d_i are excluded and the remainder arranged in the order of their *absolute magnitudes*. If two differences of equal absolute magnitude but opposite sign appear, then in order to be on the safe side these are so arranged that any runs of the same sign are as small as possible. The k differences with the highest absolute magnitude and the *same* sign are then counted.

The significance probability for a difference between the two series of measurements (two-tailed test) is then $2\,\alpha = (\tfrac{1}{2})^{k-1}$, that is, **(850)**

$k =$	$2\,\alpha =$	$\alpha =$
5	$0.0625 \sim 0.1$	$0.03125 \sim 0.05$
6	$0.03125 \sim 0.05$	$0.015625 \sim 0.02$
8	$0.0078125 \sim 0.01$	$0.00390625 \sim 0.005$
11	$0.0009725 \sim 0.001$	$0.00048625 \sim 0.0005$

Example 73. The series +3.2, +2.0, +1.0, +1.0, +0.7, +0.5, −0.3, +0.3 (note the awkward position of −0.3) results in a significance probability of $2\alpha \sim 0.05$.

25. Testing for non-randomness

All statistical tests for non-randomness depend on the *chronological* order in which the values $x_1, x_2, \ldots, x_N$ occur in the series of tries 1, 2, ..., N. Here the indices 1, 2, ..., i, ..., N denote *not the rank but the chronological order.*

25A. The mean-square successive difference[40]

The mean-square successive difference δ^2 is defined as

$$\delta^2 = \frac{1}{N-1}\sum_{1}^{N-1}(x_{i+1} - x_i)^2;\ N = \text{size of the sample} \qquad \textbf{(851)}$$

If the sample originates from a normally distributed population, then

$$\text{Expectation of } \delta^2 = 2\,\sigma^2 \qquad \textbf{(852)}$$

$\delta^2/2$ is thus an unbiased estimate of σ^2 with

$$\text{Efficiency} = 2/3\,[1 + 1/(3N-4)] \qquad \textbf{(853)}$$

For $N = 2$, the efficiency is therefore unity; for $N \to \infty$ (asymptotically) it is ⅔.

Since the mean-square successive difference is calculated on the basis of the successive differences $x_{i+1} - x_i$, it is *less sensitive* to *long-term* displacements of the mean and *more sensitive* to rapid *cyclic* influences on the mean than the estimate s^2, which is calculated on the basis of the differences $x_i - \bar{x}$.

$$\text{The ratio } \eta = \frac{\delta^2}{s^2} = \frac{\sum_{1}^{N-1}(x_{i+1} - x_i)^2}{\sum_{1}^{N}(x_i - \bar{x})^2} \qquad \textbf{(854)}$$

is therefore an indication of a possible non-random influence on the mean of a *normally distributed* population.

Significance limits for η are given in the left-hand table on page 58. *Interpretation:* If η attains or exceeds the *left* limit, then the mean of the population is affected* by *non-random* long-term factors; if it attains or exceeds the *right* limit, the population mean is affected* by *short-term cyclic* factors (significance α). **(855)**

The approximate limits ($N > 60$) in the table on page 58 have been calculated from

$$\eta_l, \eta_r = 2 \mp 2\,|\,c_\alpha\,|\sqrt{\frac{N-2}{(N-1)(N+1)}} \qquad \textbf{(856)}$$

with empirical correction at the transition from exact to approximate values.

25B. Serial correlation[41]

Given is the sample $x_1, x_2, \ldots, x_N$. Serial correlation is defined as the correlation between the pairs of observations x_i and x_{i+h}. h is

* The effect can be linear or nonlinear.

known as the lag. For $i+h>N$, $x_{i+h}=x_{i+h-N}$ in the *cyclic* definition. For further details the reader is referred to the literature[41, 42].

With the cyclic definition, serial correlation is a sensitive instrument for revealing periodic influences on a population (or sample when the population is stable).

A measure of the serial correlation with lag h is the serial correlation coefficient $\boldsymbol{R}_h$. Its estimate is

$$R_h = \frac{\Sigma x_i x_{i+h} - \bar{x}\,\Sigma x_i}{\Sigma (x_i - \bar{x})^2} \qquad \textbf{(857)}$$

As with other correlation coefficients, its value lies between -1 and $+1$.

The right-hand table on page 58 gives the significance limits for $R_h = 0$ (when $h = 1$) on the assumption that the samples are random samples from a normally distributed population. The approximate limits ($N > 75$) have been calculated from

$$R_l, R_r = \frac{-1 \mp |c_\alpha| \sqrt{N-2}}{N-1} \qquad \textbf{(858)}$$

(N = number of values x_i included in the calculation)

with empirical correction at the transition from exact to approximate values. With this approximation the user remains on the safe side.

For lags other than 1 the same levels can be used, provided that h and N do not possess a common factor. The latter is always the case when N is a prime number. In practice these conditions can be met by deleting one or more individual sample values.

25C. Runs up and down[43, 44]

If $x_1, x_2, \ldots, x_i, \ldots, x_N$ are individual sample values from a *continuous* population of *any* form, then a run up of length 1 is defined as the sequence $x_i \rightarrow x_{i+1}$ when $x_{i+1} - x_i > 0$. For runs down, $x_{i+1} - x_i < 0$. A sequence of three runs up of length 1 is called a run up of length 3, and so on.

If the sample is a random one not subject to cyclic or constant non-random influences, then the runs up and down should present a random picture, that is to say, there should be no regular runs and not too many long ones or too few short ones.

Runs up and down can be tested by means of the table at the foot of page 130. Thus a run of length 5 in a sample of size $N = 9$, for example, is not likely to be random ($\alpha = 0.01$). In the same way, a sample of size $N = 12$ is not likely to be a random sample when no run of length 2 is present (significance probability $1 - 0.99 = 0.01$).

The number $I\,(l\,|\,N)$ of runs up and down of length l and the number $I\,(l+|\,N)$ of runs of length l and *longer* can be regarded as normally distributed from $N = 20$ onwards. This can be tested by means of the quotient

$(I - \boldsymbol{I}) / \sqrt{\sigma_I^2}$; significance level $|c_\alpha|$, page 28 **(859)**

The expected value $\boldsymbol{I}$ and the variance σ_I^2 are functions of N; appropriate formulae are to be found in the literature[43]. To some extent their calculation is a tedious operation. The two tables (**860**) and (**861**) above give values up to the length usually found in practice; they also show clearly how σ^2 for greater lengths converges rapidly toward the expected value $\boldsymbol{I}$. It follows from (**789**) that the distribution of runs up and down very closely approximates, for runs of greater length, to a Poisson distribution (or to approximations to a Poisson distribution) with $\lambda = \boldsymbol{I}$.

25D. Runs above and/or below the median[45]

Runs above and/or below the median can be tested by means of the table on page 130, where a brief explanation of the method will be found.

25E. Runs in samples from binomially distributed populations in which the probabilities p and q are unknown

The definition is as follows:

(Time)	1	2	3	4	5	6	7	8	9	10
Series (I)	*A*	*B*	*A*	*A*	*A*	*B*	*B*	*A*	*B*	*A*
Series (II)	*A*	*B*	*A*	*B*	*A*	*A*	*B*	*A*	*B*	*A*
Series (III)	*A*	*A*	*A*	*A*	*A*	*A*	*B*	*B*	*B*	*B*

Each of the series (I), (II), (III) has a size $N = 10$ and contains $N_1 = 4$ B's and $N_2 = 6$ A's (provided that $N = N_1 + N_2 < 40$, the smaller number is denoted by N_1). In these series the underscored

Expected value $\boldsymbol{I}\,(l\,|\,N)$ and variance of runs up and down of length l

(860)

Length	Expected value $\boldsymbol{I}\,(l\,\vert\,N)$: Exact $\boldsymbol{I}\,(l\,\vert\,N) = a\,N - b$		Asymptotic $\boldsymbol{I}\,(l\,\vert\,N \rightarrow \boldsymbol{I}\,(1+\vert\,N) \times c$ $(N \rightarrow \infty)$	Variance $\sigma_I^2 - d \times \boldsymbol{I}\,(l\,\vert\,N) + e$		Remarks
l	a	b	c	d	e	Note
1	$4.1\dot{6} \times 10^{-1}$	$-8.\dot{3} \times 10^{-2}$	6.25×10^{-1}	$1.01\dot{6}$	$-0.397\dot{2}$	– for b and e
2	$1.8\dot{3} \times 10^{-1}$	$2.\dot{3} \times 10^{-1}$	2.75×10^{-1}	0.614550	-0.01943342	– for e
3	$5.2\dot{7} \times 10^{-2}$	$1.30\dot{5} \times 10^{-1}$	$7.91\dot{6} \times 10^{-2}$	0.794215	0.00678218	
4	$1.15079365 \times 10^{-2}$	$4.12698413 \times 10^{-2}$	$1.72619048 \times 10^{-2}$	0.935800	0.00083924	
5	$2.03373016 \times 10^{-3}$	$9.47420634 \times 10^{-3}$	$3.05059524 \times 10^{-3}$	0.985361	0.00004629	
6	$3.03130511 \times 10^{-4}$	$1.73059965 \times 10^{-3}$	$4.54695767 \times 10^{-4}$	0.997338	0.00000156	
7	$3.91313933 \times 10^{-5}$	$2.63999118 \times 10^{-4}$	$5.86970899 \times 10^{-5}$	0.999595	0.00000004	
8	$4.45927529 \times 10^{-6}$	$3.46721180 \times 10^{-5}$	$6.68891294 \times 10^{-6}$	0.999947	0.00000000	
9	$4.55113302 \times 10^{-7}$	$4.00416199 \times 10^{-6}$	$6.82669953 \times 10^{-7}$	0.999994	0.00000000	
10	$4.20746948 \times 10^{-8}$	$4.13038607 \times 10^{-7}$	$6.31120422 \times 10^{-8}$	0.999999	0.00000000	

Expected value $\boldsymbol{I}\,(l+|\,N)$ and variance of runs up and down of length l and longer

(861)

Length	Expected value $\boldsymbol{I}\,(l+\vert\,N)$: Exact $\boldsymbol{I}\,(l+\vert\,N) = a\,N - b$		Asymptotic $\boldsymbol{I}\,(l+\vert\,N) \rightarrow \boldsymbol{I}\,(1+\vert\,N) \times c$ $(N \rightarrow \infty)$	Variance $\sigma_I^2 = d \times \boldsymbol{I}\,(l+\vert\,N) + e$		Remarks
$l+$	a	b	c	d	e	Note
1	$6.\dot{6} \times 10^{-1}$	$3.\dot{3} \times 10^{-1}$	1	$0.2\dot{6}$	$-0.2\dot{3}$	– for e
2	$2.\dot{5} \times 10^{-1}$	$4.1\dot{6} \times 10^{-1}$	3.75×10^{-1}	$0.31\dot{6}$	$0.07\dot{2}$	
3	$6.\dot{6} \times 10^{-2}$	$1.8\dot{3} \times 10^{-1}$	1×10^{-1}	0.710847	0.01729497	
4	$1.3\dot{8} \times 10^{-2}$	$5.2\dot{7} \times 10^{-2}$	$2.08\dot{3} \times 10^{-2}$	0.917857	0.00147817	
5	$\dot{2}.\dot{3}\dot{8}09\dot{5} \times 10^{-3}$	$1.15079365 \times 10^{-2}$	$3.57142857 \times 10^{-3}$	0.982145	0.00007053	
6	$3.47\dot{2} \times 10^{-4}$	$2.03373016 \times 10^{-3}$	$5.208\dot{3} \times 10^{-4}$	0.996871	0.00000220	
7	$4.40917108 \times 10^{-5}$	$3.03130511 \times 10^{-4}$	$6.61375661 \times 10^{-5}$	0.999535	0.00000005	
8	$4.96031746 \times 10^{-6}$	$3.91313933 \times 10^{-5}$	$7.44047619 \times 10^{-6}$	0.999940	0.00000000	
9	$5.01042167 \times 10^{-7}$	$4.45927529 \times 10^{-6}$	$7.51563251 \times 10^{-7}$	0.999993	0.00000000	
10	$4.59288653 \times 10^{-8}$	$4.55113302 \times 10^{-7}$	$6.88932980 \times 10^{-8}$	0.999999	0.00000000	
11	$3.85417052 \times 10^{-9}$	$4.20746948 \times 10^{-8}$	$5.78125578 \times 10^{-9}$	0.999999	0.00000000	

letters in each case form a run. The total number of runs I is 7 in series (I), 9 in series (II), 2 in series (III).

The table on page 129 gives the significance limits for the estimate I (total | N_1, N_2) of the expectation $\boldsymbol{I}$ (total | N_1, N_2) of the total number of all runs of events 1 and 2.

(a) If the left limit is *attained* or *exceeded*, then
I is significantly less than $\boldsymbol{I}$ (significance probability α) or
I differs significantly from $\boldsymbol{I}$ (significance probability 2α).

(b) If the right limit is *attained* or *exceeded*, then
I is significantly greater than $\boldsymbol{I}$ (significance probability α) or
I differs significantly from $\boldsymbol{I}$ (significance probability 2α).

(c) If I lies between the limits and *attains neither*, then the null hypothesis cannot be rejected.

For N_1 and N_2 values outside the scope of the table, the test quotient (**859**) can be used in conjunction with (**868**a) and (**848**b).

Expected values and variances

– for the number of runs of length l of the event 1 that has occurred a total of N_1 times (N_2 = number of events 2; $N = N_1 + N_2$)

$$\boldsymbol{I}_1(l \mid N_1, N_2) = N_2(N_2+1)\frac{N_1!\,(N-l-1)!}{N!\,(N_1-l)!} \quad \text{(a)}$$
$$\sigma^2 = \boldsymbol{I}\left[1-\boldsymbol{I}+N_2(N_2-1)\frac{(N-2l-2)!\,(N_1-l)!}{(N-l-1)!\,(N_1-2l)!}\right] \quad \text{(b)}$$
(**862**)[46]

and asymptotically for higher values of N

$$\boldsymbol{I}_1(l \mid N_1, N_2) = Np^lq^2 \quad \text{(a)}$$
$$\sigma^2 = \boldsymbol{I}\left\{1-\frac{\boldsymbol{I}}{N}\left[\frac{l^2}{p}+\frac{2}{q}-(l+1)^2\right]\right\} \quad \text{(b)}$$
$p = N_1/N$, $q = 1-p$ (**863**)[46]

– for the number of runs of length l and *longer* of the event 1

$$\boldsymbol{I}_1(l+ \mid N_1, N_2) = (N_2+1)\frac{N_1!\,(N-l)!}{N!\,(N_1-l)!} \quad \text{(a)}$$
$$\sigma^2 = \boldsymbol{I}\left[1-\boldsymbol{I}+N_2\frac{(N-2l)!\,(N_1-l)!}{(N-l)!\,(N_1-2l)!}\right] \quad \text{(b)}$$
(**864**)[46]

and asymptotically

$$\boldsymbol{I}_1(l+ \mid N_1, N_2) = Np^lq \quad \text{(a)}$$
$$\sigma^2 = \boldsymbol{I}\left\{1-\frac{\boldsymbol{I}}{N}\left[\frac{l^2q}{p}+\frac{1}{q}\right]\right\} \quad \text{(b)}$$
p and q as in (**863**) (**865**)[46]

– for the total number of all runs of the event 1

$$\boldsymbol{I}_1(\text{total} \mid N_1, N_2) = \boldsymbol{I}_1(1+ \mid N_1, N_2) = \frac{N_1(N_2+1)}{N} \quad \text{(a)}$$
$$\sigma^2 = \frac{\boldsymbol{I}(\boldsymbol{I}-1)}{N-1} \quad \text{(b)}$$
(**866**)[47]

and asymptotically

$$\boldsymbol{I}_1(\text{total} \mid N_1, N_2) = \boldsymbol{I}(1+ \mid N_1, N_2) = Npq \quad \text{(a)}$$
$$\sigma^2 = \boldsymbol{I}^2/N \quad \text{(b)}$$
p and q as in (**863**) (**867**)[46]

– for the total number of all runs of events 1 and 2

$$\boldsymbol{I}_{1+2}(\text{total} \mid N_1, N_2) = \frac{2N_1N_2}{N}+1 \quad \text{(a)}$$
$$\sigma^2 = \frac{(\boldsymbol{I}-1)(\boldsymbol{I}-2)}{N-1} \quad \text{(b)}$$
(**868**)[48]

and asymptotically

$$\boldsymbol{I}_{1+2}(\text{total} \mid N_1, N_2) = 2Npq \quad \text{(a)}$$
$$\sigma^2 = \boldsymbol{I}^2/N \quad \text{(b)}$$
p and q as in (**863**) (**869**)[48]

The total number of all runs of the event 1 can be tested exactly (within the scope of the tables on pages 109–123) by means of the fourfold table test[47]:

I_1	$N_1 - I_1$	N_1
$N_2 + 1 - I_1$	$I_1 - 1$	N_2
$N_2 + 1$	$N_1 - 1$	N

(**870**)

25F. The Wald-Wolfowitz test[48]

Given are two samples from *continuous* populations of *any* form. These are ranked as in (**833**) and the total number of all runs (a run being defined as the occurrence of *successive* rank numbers in a sample) counted. Testing is carried out by means of the table on page 129 (cf. section 25E) or, for samples outside the scope of this table, by means of the test quotient (**859**) in conjunction with (**868**a and b) or (**869**a and b).

Example 74. Ranking and determination of runs (1, 2, ... is here a rank order):

Sample 1	1.55	1.58	1.70		1.92			2.20	2.21		
Sample 2				1.91		1.93	2.00			2.30	2.40
$O_{1,2}$	1	2	3	4	5	6	7	8	9	10	11
Run 1 and 2		1		1	1	1		1		1	

Total runs: 6, $N = 11$, $N_1 = 6$, $N_2 = 5$

If the total number of runs *attains* or *passes* the *left* limit (only this limit can be used in this test), then the samples do not originate from the same population (significance probability 2α).

25G. Runs in samples from binomially distributed populations in which the probabilities $\boldsymbol{p}$ and $\boldsymbol{q}$ are known

Expected values and variances

– for the number of runs of length l of the event 1 the probability of whose occurrence is $\boldsymbol{p}$ ($\boldsymbol{q} = 1 - \boldsymbol{p}$)

$$\boldsymbol{I}_1(l = N \mid N, \boldsymbol{p}) = \boldsymbol{p}^N \quad \text{(a)[49]}$$
$$\sigma^2 = \boldsymbol{I}(1-\boldsymbol{I}) \quad \text{(b)[50]}$$
$$\boldsymbol{I}_1(l \le N-1 \mid N, \boldsymbol{p}) = \boldsymbol{p}^l\boldsymbol{q}[(N-l-1)\boldsymbol{q}+2] \quad \text{(c)[49]}$$
$$\sigma^2 = \boldsymbol{I}(1-\boldsymbol{I}) + \varphi(N, l) \quad \text{(d)[50]}$$
where
$$\varphi(N,l) = 0;\ 2l \ge N \quad \text{(e)[50]}$$
$$\varphi(N,l) = \boldsymbol{p}^{2l}\boldsymbol{q}^2[6+6(N-2l-2)\boldsymbol{q} + (N-2l-2) \times (N-2l-3)\boldsymbol{q}^2];\quad 2 \le 2l \le N-2 \quad \text{(f)[50]}$$
$$\varphi\left(N, \frac{N-1}{2}\right) = 2\boldsymbol{p}^{N-1}\boldsymbol{q};\ N \text{ odd} \quad \text{(g)[50]}$$
(**871**)

and asymptotically when $N - l \to \infty$

$$\boldsymbol{I}_1(l \mid N, \boldsymbol{p}) = N\boldsymbol{p}^l\boldsymbol{q}^2 \quad \text{(a)[49]}$$
$$\sigma^2 = \boldsymbol{I}\left\{1-\boldsymbol{p}^l\boldsymbol{q}^2\left[2\left(l-\frac{\boldsymbol{p}}{\boldsymbol{q}}\right)+1\right]\right\} \quad \text{(b)[46]}$$
(**872**)

– for the number of runs of length l and *longer*

$$\boldsymbol{I}_1(l+ \mid N, \boldsymbol{p}) = \boldsymbol{p}^l[(N-l)\boldsymbol{q}+1] \quad \text{(a)[49]}$$
$$\sigma^2 = \boldsymbol{I}(1-\boldsymbol{I}) + \psi(N,l) \quad \text{(b)[50]}$$
where
$$\psi(N,l) = 0;\ 2l \ge N \quad \text{(c)[50]}$$
$$\psi(N,l) = \boldsymbol{p}^{2l}\boldsymbol{q}(N-2l)[2+(N-2l-1)\boldsymbol{q}];\quad 2 \le 2l \le N \quad \text{(d)[50]}$$
(**873**)

and asymptotically when $N - l \to \infty$

$$\boldsymbol{I}_1(l+ \mid N, \boldsymbol{p}) = N\boldsymbol{p}^l\boldsymbol{q} \quad \text{(a)[49]}$$
$$\sigma^2 = \boldsymbol{I}[1-\boldsymbol{p}^l\boldsymbol{q}(2l+1)] \quad \text{(b)[46]}$$
(**874**)

– for the total number of runs of the event 1

$$\boldsymbol{I}_1(\text{total} \mid N, \boldsymbol{p}) = \boldsymbol{p}[(N-1)\boldsymbol{q}+1] \quad \text{(a)[49]}$$
$$\sigma^2 = \boldsymbol{I}(1-\boldsymbol{I}) + (N-2)\boldsymbol{p}^2\boldsymbol{q}[(N-3)\boldsymbol{q}+2] \quad \text{(b)[46]}$$
(**875**)

and asymptotically

$$\boldsymbol{I}_1(\text{total} \mid N, \boldsymbol{p}) = N\boldsymbol{p}\boldsymbol{q} \quad \text{(a)}$$
$$\sigma^2 = \boldsymbol{I}(1-3\boldsymbol{p}\boldsymbol{q}) \quad \text{(b)}$$
(**876**)[49]

– for the total number of runs of events 1 and 2

$$\boldsymbol{I}_{1+2}(\text{total} \mid N, \boldsymbol{p}) = 2(N-1)\boldsymbol{p}\boldsymbol{q}+1 \quad \text{(a)}$$
$$\sigma^2 = 2\boldsymbol{p}\boldsymbol{q}\{2[N-(3N-5)\boldsymbol{p}\boldsymbol{q}]-3\} \quad \text{(b)}$$
(**877**)[49]

and asymptotically

$$\boldsymbol{I}_{1+2}(\text{total} \mid N, \boldsymbol{p}) = 2N\boldsymbol{p}\boldsymbol{q} \quad \text{(a)}$$
$$\sigma^2 = \boldsymbol{I}(2-3\boldsymbol{p}\boldsymbol{q}) \quad \text{(b)}$$
(**878**)[49]

25H. Runs in samples from multinomially distributed populations

(*a*) *The probabilities* $\boldsymbol{p}_1, \boldsymbol{p}_2, \ldots, \boldsymbol{p}_i, \ldots, \boldsymbol{p}_k$ *are unknown*

Expected values and variances

– for the total number of runs of the event i that has occurred a total of N_i times

$$\left.\begin{aligned} \boldsymbol{I}_i\,(\text{total} \mid N_i, N) &= \frac{N_i\,(N - N_i + 1)}{N} && \text{(a)} \\ \sigma^2 &= \frac{\boldsymbol{I}\,(\boldsymbol{I} - 1)}{N - 1} && \text{(b)} \end{aligned}\right\} \mathbf{(879)}^{46}$$

and asymptotically

$$\left.\begin{aligned} \boldsymbol{I}_i\,(\text{total} \mid N_i, N) &= N p_i\,(1 - p_i) \\ \sigma^2 &= \boldsymbol{I}^2/N \end{aligned}\right\} p_i = \frac{N_i}{N} \qquad \begin{aligned} &\text{(a)} \\ &\text{(b)} \end{aligned} \Big\} \mathbf{(880)}^{46}$$

– for the total number of runs of all events

asymptotically

$$\left.\begin{aligned} \boldsymbol{I}\,(\text{total}, N) &= N(1 - \sum_{1}^{k} p_i^2) \\ \sigma^2 &= N[\Sigma p_i^2 - 2\Sigma p_i^3 + (\Sigma p_i^2)^2] \end{aligned}\right\} p_i \text{ as in } \mathbf{(880)} \qquad \begin{aligned} &\text{(a)} \\ &\text{(b)} \end{aligned} \Big\} \mathbf{(881)}^{46}$$

When $N_1 = N_2 = \cdots = N_k = N_0$, **(881)** becomes

$$\left.\begin{aligned} \boldsymbol{I}\,(\text{total}) &= N(1 - p) \\ \sigma^2 &= p\,\boldsymbol{I} \end{aligned}\right\} p = 1/k;\ N = k N_0 \qquad \begin{aligned} &\text{(a)} \\ &\text{(b)} \end{aligned} \Big\} \mathbf{(882)}$$

(b) The probabilities $\boldsymbol{p}_i$ are known

$\boldsymbol{p}_i$ is the probability that the event i will occur.

Expected values and variances

– for the total number of runs of the event i

$$\left.\begin{aligned} \boldsymbol{I}_i\,(\text{total} \mid N, \boldsymbol{p}_i) &= \boldsymbol{p}_i\,[(N-1)(1 - \boldsymbol{p}_i) + 1] && \text{(a)} \\ \sigma^2 &= N\boldsymbol{p}_i\,(1 - 4\boldsymbol{p}_i + 6\boldsymbol{p}_i^2 - 3\boldsymbol{p}_i^3) + \\ &\quad + \boldsymbol{p}_i^2\,(3 - 8\boldsymbol{p}_i + 5\boldsymbol{p}_i^2) && \text{(b)} \end{aligned}\right\} \mathbf{(883)}^{46}$$

[Formula **(883)** is identical with **(875)** when, in the latter, $\boldsymbol{p}$ is replaced by $\boldsymbol{p}_i$]

and asymptotically

$$\left.\begin{aligned} \boldsymbol{I}_i\,(\text{total} \mid N, \boldsymbol{p}_i) &= N\boldsymbol{p}_i\,(1 - \boldsymbol{p}_i) && \text{(a)} \\ \sigma^2 &= \boldsymbol{I}\,[1 - 3\boldsymbol{p}_i\,(1 - \boldsymbol{p}_i)] && \text{(b)} \end{aligned}\right\} \mathbf{(884)}^{46}$$

– for the total number of runs of all events

asymptotically

$$\left.\begin{aligned} \boldsymbol{I}\,(\text{total}) &= N(1 - \Sigma\boldsymbol{p}_i^2) && \text{(a)} \\ \sigma^2 &= N[\Sigma\boldsymbol{p}_i^2 + 2\Sigma\boldsymbol{p}_i^3 - 3(\Sigma\boldsymbol{p}_i^2)^2] && \text{(b)} \end{aligned}\right\} \mathbf{(885)}^{46}$$

When $\boldsymbol{p}_1 = \boldsymbol{p}_2 = \cdots \boldsymbol{p}_k = \boldsymbol{p} = 1/k$, **(885)** becomes

$$\left.\begin{aligned} \boldsymbol{I}\,(\text{total}) &= N(1 - \boldsymbol{p}) && \text{(a)} \\ \sigma^2 &= \boldsymbol{p}\,\boldsymbol{I} && \text{(b)} \end{aligned}\right\} \mathbf{(886)}^{46}$$

26. Sequential analysis

Sequential analysis is one of the more recently developed statistical methods, and its use in medical trials is increasing[51]. It is illustrated here by two charts[52] that enable a comparison to be made, for example between two drugs, without calculation.

Example 75. The effect on patients of drug A is to be compared with that of drug B. Two patients are selected, the toss of a coin deciding which one is to receive drug A and which drug B. They should receive the drugs *simultaneously or in quick succession.* The result is given one of the three ratings

Drug A better Drug B better No difference

If drug A is better, a cross is made in the square immediately *above* the black square in the charts (Figs. 49 and 50). If drug B is better, a

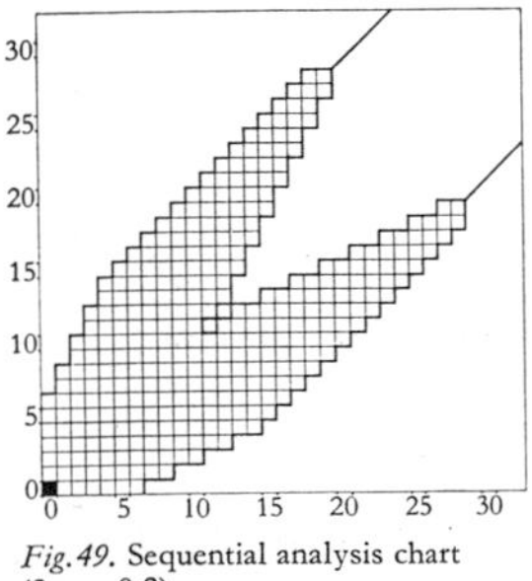

Fig. 49. Sequential analysis chart ($2\alpha \sim 0.2$).

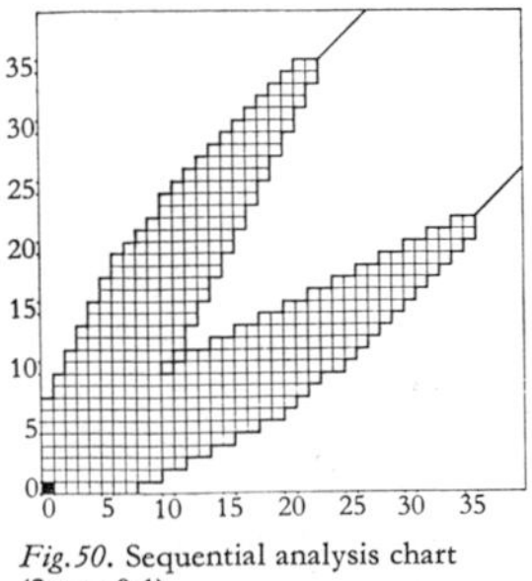

Fig. 50. Sequential analysis chart ($2\alpha \sim 0.1$).

cross is made in the square immediately *to the right* of the black square. If there is no difference, no entry is made in the charts. A second test is then made in exactly the same way with two different patients and the result entered in the square above or to the right of that marked in the first test, and so on for successive tests. As soon as a barrier is overstepped one of the following decisions can be made:

(a) upper barrier overstepped:	drug A is better
(b) lower barrier overstepped:	drug B is better
(c) middle barrier overstepped:	no difference demonstrated

The significance probability for (a) and (b) combined is 2α.

References

1 Laplace, P.-S., *Théorie analytique des probabilités*, 3rd ed., Gauthier-Villars, Paris, 1820.
2 Molina, E.C., *Poisson's Exponential Binomial Limit*, Van Nostrand, Princeton, 1942.
3 Pearson, K., *Tables of the Incomplete Beta-Function*, Cambridge University Press, Cambridge, 1934; *Tables of the Binomial Probability Distribution*, National Bureau of Standards, Applied Mathematics Series 6, Washington, 1949.
4 Harvard University Computation Laboratory, *Tables of the Cumulative Binomial Probability Distribution*, Cambridge, Mass., 1955.
5 Lieberman and Owen, *Tables of the Hypergeometric Probability Distribution*, Stanford University Press, Stanford, Calif., 1961.
6 Rao, C.R., *Bull. Calcutta math. Soc.*, **37**, 81 (1945).
7 Cramér, H., *Mathematical Methods of Statistics*, Princeton University Press, Princeton, 1946.
8 Neyman, J., *Ann. math. Statist.*, **6**, 111 (1935); Neyman, J., *Phil. Trans. A*, **236**, 333 (1937); Neyman, J., *Biometrika*, **32**, 128 (1941/42).
9 Proschan, F., *J. Amer. statist. Ass.*, **48**, 550 (1953).
10 *Tables of Normal Probability Functions*, National Bureau of Standards, Applied Mathematics Series 23, Washington, 1953.
11 Bliss, C.I., *Ann. appl. Biol.*, **22**, 134 (1935).
12 Finney, D.J., *Probit Analysis*, 2nd ed., Cambridge University Press, Cambridge, 1952; Fisher and Yates, *Statistical Tables for Biological, Agricultural and Medical Research*, 4th ed., Oliver & Boyd, Edinburgh, 1953; Pearson and Hartley (Eds.), *Biometrika Tables for Statisticians*, vol. 1, Cambridge University Press, Cambridge, 1954.
13 Wilson and Hilferty, *Proc. nat. Acad. Sci. (Wash.)*, **17**, 684 (1931).
14 Fisher, R.A., On a distribution yielding the error functions of several well-known statistics, *Proceedings of the International Mathematical Congress*, vol. 2, Toronto, 1924, page 805.
15 Eisenhart et al. (Eds.), *Selected Techniques of Statistical Analysis for Scientific and Industrial Research and Production and Management Engineering*, McGraw-Hill, New York, 1947, page 108.
16 Cf. Tippett, L.H.C., *Biometrika*, **17**, 364 (1925).
17 Davies and Pearson, suppl. to *J. roy. statist. Soc.*, **1**, 76 (1934).
18 Dixon, W.J., *Ann. math. Statist.*, **21**, 488 (1950); Dixon, W.J., *Ann. math. Statist.*, **22**, 68 (1951); Dixon, W.J., *Biometrics*, **9**, 74 (1953).
19 Lord, E., *Biometrika*, **34**, 41 (1947).
20 Walsh, J.E., *Ann. math. Statist.*, **20**, 257 (1949).
21 Walsh, J.E., *J. Amer. statist. Ass.*, **44**, 342 (1949).
22 Bartlett, M.S., *Proc. roy. Soc. A*, **160**, 268 (1937).
23 Duncan, D.B., *Biometrics*, **11**, 1 (1955).
24 Bliss, C.I., *Biometrics*, **1**, 57 (1945).
25 Berkson, J., *Biometrics*, **7**, 327 (1951); Berkson, J., *J. Amer. statist. Ass.*, **48**, 565 (1953).
26 Kendall, M.G., *Rank Correlation Methods*, 2nd ed., Griffin, London, 1955.
27 van der Waerden, B.L., *Mathematische Statistik*, Springer, Berlin, 1957.
28 Pearson and Wilks, *Biometrika*, **25**, 353 (1933).
29 Freeman and Tukey, *Ann. math. Statist.*, **21**, 607 (1950).
30 Clopper and Pearson, *Biometrika*, **26**, 404 (1934).
31 Wilks, S.S., *Bull. Amer. math. Soc.*, **54**, 6 (1948).
32 Scheffé and Tukey, *Memorandum Report 28*, Statistical Research Group, Princeton University, 1949.
33 Bliss, C.I., *Biometrics*, **9**, 176 (1953).
34 Katz, L., *J. Amer. statist. Ass.*, **48**, 256 (1953).
35 Bross, I., *Biometrics*, **10**, 245 (1954).
36 Wilcoxon, F., *Biometrics*, **1**, 80 (1945).
37 Wilcoxon, F., *Biometrics*, **3**, 119 (1947).
38 Haldane and Smith, *Ann. Eugen. (Lond.)*, **14**, 117 (1947–1949).
39 Walter, E., *Mittbl. math. Statist.*, **6**, 92 and 170 (1954); Walter, E., *Metrika*, **1**, 81 (1958).
40 Neumann et al., *Ann. math. Statist.*, **12**, 153 (1941).
41 Anderson, R.L., *Ann. math. Statist.*, **13**, 1 (1942); Wald and Wolfowitz, *Ann. math. Statist.*, **14**, 378 (1943).
42 Bennett and Franklin, *Statistical Analysis in Chemistry and the Chemical Industry*, Wiley, New York, 1954.
43 Levene and Wolfowitz, *Ann. math. Statist.*, **15**, 58 (1944).
44 Wolfowitz, J., *Ann. math. Statist.*, **15**, 163 (1944); Olmstead, P.S., *Ann. math. Statist.*, **17**, 24 (1946).
45 Olmstead, P.S., *Runs Determined in a Sample by an Arbitrary Cut*, Bell Telephone System, Technical Publications, Monograph 2937, New York, 1958.
46 Mood, A.M., *Ann. math. Statist.*, **11**, 367 (1940).
47 Stevens, W.L., *Ann. Eugen. (Lond.)*, **9**, 10 (1939).
48 Wald and Wolfowitz, *Ann. math. Statist.*, **11**, 147 (1940).
49 von Bortkiewicz, L., *Die Iterationen*, Springer, Berlin, 1917.
50 Geppert, M.P., Tübingen, personal communication, 1965.
51 Armitage, P., *Sequential Medical Trials*, Blackwell, Oxford, 1960.
52 Bross, I., *Biometrics*, **8**, 188 (1952).
53 Welch, B.L., *Biometrika*, **36**, 293 (1949).

Index (pages 28–131 and 146–196; page numbers are in roman type, proposition numbers in **bold** type)

Addition theorem for χ^2 distribution **564**
– for normal distribution **545**
– for POISSON distribution **786**
Approximations and transformations
– *by binomial distribution*, of F-distribution **578, 579**
– – of hypergeometric distribution **813**
– *by χ^2 distribution*, of F-distribution **576**
– – of hypergeometric distribution **818, 826–828**
– – of multinomial distributions **826–828**
– – of POISSON distribution **800, 801, 803**
– – of distribution-free tolerance limits **781**
– *by normal distribution*, of binomial distribution **756–767, 771, 772, 778, 779, 821**
– – of χ^2 distribution **556, 557**
– – of mean-square successive difference ... **856**
– – of hypergeometric distribution.... **816, 819**
– – of runs **859**
– – of correlation coefficient r **706–724**
– – of serial correlation coefficient R_h **858**
– – of SPEARMAN correlation coefficient R .. **728**
– – of POISSON distribution **793–797, 804**
– *by Poisson distribution*, of binomial distn.... **768**
– – of hypergeometric distribution **814**
– – of χ^2 distribution **561–563**
– *by Student distribution*, of F-distribution ... **575**
Arc-sine transformation of binomial distn. 69, **782**
– of POISSON distribution **799**
Asymptotically unbiased estimates **426**
– most efficient estimate **429–431**
Atomic variables **344–366**
Attributes, definition **317**

BARTLETT's test **621, 622**
Bias and expectation of estimates 153
Bias due to non-random sampling 153
Binomial coefficients, tables 70–77
Binomial distribution .... 183 sq.
– arc-sine transformation **782**
– confidence and significance limits.... 186, 187
– parameters 184
– and hypergeometric distribution **813**
– and normal distribution 185
– and POISSON distribution 186
– samples, frequency testing 191
– – runs in 194, 195
– tables 69–105

c-test **598**
Central limit theorem 166
Chance order, test for 193
CHEBYSHEF inequality **486, 507**
Chi-squared (χ^2) distribution .... 166 sq.
– addition theorem **564**
– asymptotic property **566–569**
– fitted **568**
– parameters **555**
– probability density function **554**
– and normal distribution **560**
– and POISSON distribution **561–563**
– and variance of samples **565**
– tables 36–39
Chi-squared tests. See under Tests
Coefficient of correlation r. See Correlation
– of determination 179
– of rank correlation, SPEARMAN 181
– of variance **485**
Confidence ellipse of regressions of 2nd kind. **736**
Confidence limits (factors, intervals, levels) 154, 155
– – definitions **439**
– – convergence **443**
– – interpretation **444**
– – for binomial distributions .. 85–106, 186, 187
– – for continuous distributions, one-sided . **416**
– – – two-sided **422**
– – for discrete distributions, one-sided **386**
– – – two-sided **396**
– – for correlation coefficient r 180
– – distribution-free 155, 156
– – for λ of POISSON distribution .. 108, 109, 189
– – for mean of normal distributions 43, 169, **580**
– – for quantiles of binomial distributions .. 187
– – for quantiles of continuous distn. .. 161, 187
– – for regressions of first kind 177
– – for regressions of second kind 182
– – for standard deviation of normal distributions **584**
Confidence probabilities **387, 388, 397, 423**
Consistency of estimates 153
Continuous probability distributions .... 151 sq.
– random variables **343**
Convergence, in probability 153
Convergence, stochastic 153
– of confidence limits **443**
– of estimates 153
– of significance limits **462**
– of standard deviation **432**
– of tolerance limits **449**
Correlation, serial 193, 194
– coefficient r .... 179 sq.
– – and regression coefficient **705**
– – and SPEARMAN coefficient R 68, **729**
– – z-transformation of 180
– – SPEARMAN 66–68, 181
– – tables 59–65
Covariance **633, 634, 647, 678, 682**
Cumulative probability distribution ... **364, 368, 401–403**

Deciles **499**
Degrees of freedom for χ^2 distribution **569**
– for Student distribution **549**
Dependent events and tries **337, 356–362**
– variables 179
Differences, statistically significant, meaning . 159
Discrete probability distributions .... 148 sq.
– random variables **341**
Distributions, definition **326**
– assumptions as to form of 158
– closely allied to normal distribution ... 166 sq.
– continuous .... 151 sq.
– – quantiles 160, 161
– – tolerance limits 155
– discrete .... 148 sq.
– – tolerance limits 155
– See also Binomial, Chi-squared, Normal, etc.
DUNCAN's test **627–630**

Efficiency of estimates 153, 154
Ellipses, confidence and tolerance **736, 737**
Errors of first kind **467**
– of second kind **468**
Estimates .... 153 sq.
– consistency of 153
– convergence of 153
– efficiency of 153, 154
– symbols **332**
– test of difference from hypothetical value .. 177
– asymptotically most efficient **429–431**
– asymptotically unbiased **426**
– of correlation coefficient r **704**
– of covariance **633, 647, 678, 682**
– exhaustive **437**
– of mean λ (POISSON distribution) **790**
– of parameters of regression line Y ..... 174 sq.
– of probability p (binomial distribution) ... **748**
– of quantiles **501**
– rapid **436**
– – of σ (normal distribution) 170
– of regression coefficients ... **632, 648, 683, 695**
– of regression functions **631, 702**
– of sample means **491**
– of serial correlation coefficient **857**
– of SPEARMAN correlation coefficient **726**
– sufficient 154
– of variance of correlation coefficients . **707, 710, 716, 720**
– of variance of mean in regressions **639**
– of variance of sample means **495**
– of variance between samples **624**a
– of variance within samples **624**b, **655**
– of variance of regression coefficients **637, 684, 696**
– of variance of regression lines **638**
– of residual variance of regressions **635, 659, 678, 682**
Events, definitions 147
– certain **351**
– almost certain **352**
– complementary **334, 354**
– compound **338**
– conditional **337, 356–362**
– exclusive **334, 335, 353–355**
– impossible **345, 351**
– random **321**
– simultaneous **336, 356–362**
– stochastically dependent and independent . 148
– successive **336, 337, 356–362**
Exhaustive estimates **437**
Expectation (expected value) of estimates ... **424**
– and bias of estimates 153
– and variance of runs 194
Extreme deviations of normal distributions 170 sq.
– tables 47, 52, 53
Extreme deviations, standardized 171
– 'studentized' 170
Extreme range of normal distributions ... 170 sq.
– tables 47–53
– 'studentized' 170
– tests for two samples using 173
– variance as fraction of 170

F-distribution 168, 169
– tables 40, 41
F-test **605**
FISHER transformation (z-transformation) ... 180
Fitted distributions **568**
– frequencies **568**
– probability density, calculation 164
– probit line, calculation 164
Fitting of normal curves to samples ..... 163 sq.
Fourfold table test 109–123, 191, **870**
Fractiles. See Quantiles
Freedom, degrees of. See Degrees of freedom
Frequency, definitions **347–349**
– confidence limits for **769–776**
– confidence limits for increase of **831, 832**
– testing of 191, 192
– of classes in χ^2 tests **567**
– fitted **568**

'Granulated' variables **344–346**

HALDANE's test 193
Hypergeometric distribution .... 77, 189 sq.
– significance limits, fourfold table test . 109–123

Independent events and tries **357, 359–362**
– variables 179
Index of determination r^2 179
Infinite populations **327, 328**

Law of large numbers 153
Logarithmic-normal distribution 165
Logit regression 179
– tables 56, 57
Lognormal distribution 165
LORD test 158, 159, **600**

Maximum-likelihood method for probit lines 163
Maximum test for pair differences .. 158, 159, 193
Mean, relation between mode, median and .. **504**
– estimates of, based on grouped samples ... 160
– – based on ungrouped samples 159
– of binomial distribution **746**
– of χ^2 distribution **555**
– of F-distribution **572**
– of hypergeometric distribution **811**
– of lognormal distribution **535**
– of normal distribution ... 161 sq., 169, 171 sq.
– of POISSON distribution **787**
– of the population 159
– of runs **860–886**
– of samples. See under Estimates
– of standardized normal distribution 162
Mean-square successive difference 58, 193
Median, definition **499**
– relation to mean and mode **504**
– runs around 194
– of lognormal distributions **534**
– of normal distributions 162
– – distribution-free confidence limits for .. 161
Midrange test 158, 159, **601**
Mode, definition **503**
– relation to mean and median **504**
– of χ^2 distribution **555**
– of lognormal distribution **533**
– of normal distribution **163**
Multinomial distributions, samples, frequency 192
– – runs in 195, 196

Non-randomness tests .... 193 sq.
'Normal' **455**
Normal distribution .... 161 sq., 169 sq.
– addition theorem **545**
– and binomial distribution 185
– and χ^2 distribution **560**
– and hypergeometric distribution **815, 816**
– and POISSON distribution 186
– closely allied distributions .... 166 sq.
– confidence and tolerance intervals 43–46, 169 sq.
– curves, fitting to samples .... 163 sq.
– extreme range and extreme deviations 170, 171
– probability density function **506**
– probit transformation 163, 164

Normal quantiles, standard deviation 165
– regressions, first kind 174 sq.
– – second kind 179 sq.
– samples, and hypothetical population. 171, 172
– – comparison of two 172, 173
– distn., samples, testing of several 173, 174
– – quantiles, standard deviations 165
– bivariate 179 sq.
– logarithmic 165
– standardized 162, 163
– – tables 29–31, 43–55, 58–65, 162
Normal range **454, 455**
Null hypothesis 157

Orthogonal regression coefficient **738**

Pair differences, tests of .. 158, 161, 173, 192, 196
Parameters 159 sq.
– See also Mean, Mode, Quantiles, Variance
Percentiles **499**
Poisson distribution 187 sq.
– addition theorem **786**
– arc-sine transformation **799**
– and binomial distribution 186
– and χ^2 distribution **561–563**
– confidence limits, tables 107, 108
– confidence limits and significance limits 189
– parameters 188
– and hypergeometric distribution **814**
– samples, frequency testing 192
– significance limits, table 128
– transformations 188, 189
Populations, definition **318**
– infinite **327, 328**
– normally distributed. See Normal distribution
– unknown and hypothetical **464–466**
– See also Distributions
Power of significance tests 157
Probability, definitions **324, 350–423**
– symbols **349**
– continuous distribution 151 sq.
– cumulative, of binomial distribution . 184, 185
– discrete distribution 148 sq.
– individual, of binomial distribution **744**
– – of hypergeometric distribution **805**
– – of Poisson distribution **784**
Probability density function, definition **400**
– of χ^2 distribution **554**
– of F-distribution **571**
– of lognormal distribution **532**
– of normal distribution **506**
– of standardized normal distribution **510**
– of Student distribution **549**
– of t-distribution **549**
Probits, empirical, calculation 164
Probit line, fitted, calculation 164
– regression 179
– transformation 163, 164
– – tables 54, 55

Quantiles of continuous distributions .. 160, 161
– distribution-free confidence limits 104, 161, 187
– of samples, standard deviations 165
Quartiles **499**

Random events **321**
– numbers, table 131
– variables. See under Variables
Ranks, definition **342**
Rank correlation coefficient 181
– tests 192, 193
Ranking of samples 192, **342, 501**
Recursion formulae, for binomial distribution **745**
– for hypergeometric distribution **807, 808**
– for Poisson distribution **785**
Regressions of 1st kind 174 sq.
– of 2nd kind 179 sq.
– logit and probit 179
Regression coefficient, testing against zero .. 177
– orthogonal **738**
Regression functions 174
– testing for linearity 176, 177
Regression lines, 1st kind, comparison . 178, 179
– – estimates of parameters 174 sq.
– – estimates of x, given y 177, 178
– – parallel **689–692, 698–701**
Root-mean-square deviation. See Variance
Runs, above and/or below the median 194
– up and down 194
– in samples from binomial distributions 194, 195
– in samples from multinomial distributions . 195
– fourfold table test for 195
– length of 131
– significance limits for total 130

Samples, definition **322**
– distributions, populations and **329**
– fitting normal curves to 163 sq.
– ranking of 192, **342, 501**
– from binomial distributions, frequency test 191
– – size for given probability 187
– grouped, estimates of mean and variance .. 160
– – fitting normal curves to 164
– – and lognormal distribution **544**
– from normal distributions, standard deviations of quantiles 165
– from normal distributions, and hypothetical population 171, 172
– – tests for several 173, 174
– – tests for two, using extreme range 173
– from multinomial and Poisson distributions, frequency tests 192
– ungrouped, mean and variance estimates 159, 160
– – fitting normal curves to 164
– – and lognormal distribution **543**
Sampling, from finite and infinite populations **357**
– random **320**
– with replacement **328**
Sequences, random **323**
– – testing of 193 sq.
– ranked **342**, 192
– – testing of 192, 193
Sequential analysis 196
Serial correlation 58, 193, 194
Sheppard's correction **498**
Sign test 158, 159, 161
– tables 104–106
Significance limits 152, 156, 157
– convergence **462**
– of binomial distributions 186, 187
– of continuous distributions, one-sided **409, 410**
– – two-sided **417**
– of discrete distributions, one-sided **376, 377**
– – two-sided **390**
– of hypergeometrical distributions 109–123, 191
– of normal distribution 58, 61
– of Poisson distributions 189
– in Wilcoxon test 124–128, 193
– for runs, table 129
Significance probability (α, 2α) **376–379, 384, 390, 391, 409–412, 417–420**
– See also under Tests
Spearman correlation coefficient 181
Standard deviation. See under Variance
Standardized extreme deviation **594**
– extreme range **586, 588**
– normal distribution 162, 163
– variables **489**
Statistically significant differences, meaning . 159
Stochastic convergence of estimates 153
– dependence of events **358, 361**
– independence of events **359, 361**
Student distribution 166
– tables 32–35, 42, 165
– test (t-test) 158, 159, **599**
'Studentized' extreme deviation 170
– extreme range 170
Sums of squares **493, 634, 636, 643–654**
Symmetry of normal distribution 161
– of samples 162

t-distribution (Student) 166
t-test (Student) 158, 159, **599**
Test, Bartlett's **621, 622**
– c- **598**
– chi-squared (χ^2) **558, 565–569, 584, 721, 791, 825–828**
– – for normal distribution 163–165
– – for Poisson distribution 188
– for chronological order effect 193
– of correlation coefficient r 179, 180
– of serial correlation coefficient **857, 858**
– of Spearman correlation coefficient 181
– Duncan's **627–630**
– of extreme values 170, 171
– F- **605**
– fourfold table 191, **870**
– of frequencies 191, 192
– for goodness of fit **566, 567**
– Haldane's 193
– Lord 158, 159, **600**
– maximum 158, 159, 193
– midrange 158, 159, **601**
– for non-randomness 193 sq.
– one-tailed and two-tailed 157, 158
– of pair differences 158, 161, 173, 192, 196
– of ranks 192, 193
– rapid (normal distribution) 172

Test, of regressions of first kind 177
– of regressions of second kind 181
– for linearity of regression functions .. 176, 177
– of runs 194
– of chance order in series 193
– of samples, from binomial populations 191
– – from multinomial populations 192
– – from normal populations 173
– – from Poisson populations 192
– sign 158, 159, 161
– significance 156 sq.
– – for correlation coefficients 180
– – for regressions of second kind 181, 182
– for symmetry 162
– t- (Student) 158, 159, **599**
– for two samples using the extreme range .. 173
– two-by-two (fourfold) table 191, **870**
– of variances 173
– Wald-Wolfowitz 195
– Walsh 158, 159, **602**
– Wilcoxon, for pair differences 158, 192
– – for two samples 192
Ties **346**
– ranking of **834**
Tolerance ellipse of regressions of 2nd kind . **737**
– limits (factors, intervals) 154, 155
– – convergence of **449**
– – distribution-free 128, 155, 156, 187
– – of continuous distributions 152
– – of discrete distributions 150
– – of normal distributions 44–46, 169
– – of regressions of first kind **669, 670, 674**
– – of regressions of second kind **737**
Transformations 159
– arc-sine. See Arc-sine transformation
– z-, of correlation coefficient 180
– See also under Approximations
Tries **319**
Two-by-two (fourfold) table test 191

Unbiased estimates of standard deviation 170

Variables, definition **317**
– and events 147
– 'atomic' or 'granulated' **344–346**
– continuous **343**
– dependent and independent 179
– discrete **341**
– random **339–346**
– standardized **489**
Variance (and standard deviation) 153 sq., 161, 162
– analysis of (normal distribution) 173, 174
– Bartlett's test for **621, 622**
– and χ^2 distribution **565**
– confidence limits for **565, 584**
– convergence of **432**
– coefficient of **485**
– estimates of, based on grouped samples 160
– – based on ungrouped samples 159
– – unbiased **494**, 170
– and extreme range 170
– F-test for **605**
– and mean-square successive difference **852, 853**
– and probit line 164
– and Chebyshef inequality **486**
– of binomial distribution 184
– of χ^2 distribution **555**
– of F-distribution **572**
– of hypergeometric distribution **812**
– of the mean **484, 495**
– of normal distribution 161, 171, 172, 173
– – confidence intervals for 169
– of Poisson distribution **787–789**
– of the population 159
– of rank sums (Wilcoxon) 192, 193
– in regressions 174, 175
– of runs 194
– of samples 159
– – and χ^2 distribution **565**
Variation, coefficient of **485**

Wald-Wolfowitz test 195
Walsh test 158, 159, **602**
Wilcoxon tests 158, 192, 193
– tables 124–128

z-distribution 168
z-transformation (of correlation coefficient) . 180

Symbols – Abbreviations

(Combinations and multiples of symbols like cm, m^3, km h^{-1}, etc. are not included)

Symbol		Page
′	(sexagesimal) minute	207
″	(sexagesimal) second	207
°	degree	207
□°	square degree	207
∟	right angle	207
A		
a	are	203
a	atto- (10^{-18})	9
a	year (astronomy)	206
amu	atomic mass unit (old)	227
ap, apoth	apothecaries' (measures)	205
asb	apostilb	223
at	technical atmosphere	212
atm	physical atmosphere	212
av, avdp	avoirdupois (measures)	205
A	ampere	215, 216
AU	astronomical unit	200
Å	ångström	200, 202
B		
b	barn	202, 203
bar	bar	211
bbl	barrel	204
bu	bushel	203, 204
$B.t.u._{IT}$, Btu	British thermal unit	213
C		
c	centesimal minute	207
c	centi- (10^{-2})	9
c, c/s	cycle per second	208
cal_{15}	15° calorie	213
cal_{IT}	Int. Steam Table calorie	213
$cal_{thermochem}$	thermochemical calorie	213
cc	centesimal second	207
cd	candela	223
ch	chain	200
ch	metric horsepower	213
cm^{-1}	reciprocal centimetre	213
cwt	hundredweight	205
C	coulomb	216
°C	degree Celsius (Centigrade)	208
Ci	curie	217
D		
d	deci- (10^{-1})	9
d	day	205
da, dk	deca- (10^{1})	9
db	decibel	225
dr	dram, drachm	205
dry pt	dry pint	204
dry qt	dry quart	204
dwt	pennyweight	205
dyn	dyne	211
E		
emu	electromagnetic unit	215
erg	erg	212, 213
esu	electrostatic unit	215
eV	electron volt	213
Eq	gramme-equivalent	226
F		
f	femto- (10^{-15})	9
fath	fathom	200
fl dr	fluid dram (fluid drachm)	204
fl oz	fluid ounce	204
ft	foot	200
ftH_2O	foot of water	212
fur	furlong	200
F	farad	216
°F	degree Fahrenheit	209
G		
g	grade	207
g	gramme	204, 213
gal	gallon	203
gf	gramme-force	211
gi	gill	204
gr	grain	204
grf	grain-force	211
G	giga- (10^{9})	9
Gal	galileo	210
Gb	gilbert	216
Gs	gauss	216
γ (μg)	gamma* (microgramme)	204
H		
h	hecto- (10^{2})	9
h	hour	205
hp	horsepower	214
H	henry	216
Hz	hertz (cycle per second)	208
I		
in	inch	200
inHg	inch of mercury	212
inH_2O	inch of water	212
J		
J	joule	212, 213, 216
K		
k	kilo- (10^{3})	9
kgf	kilogramme-force	211
kn	knot	200
K	kelvin	208, 213
L		
l	litre	203
lb	pound	204
lbf	pound-force	211
li	link	200
liq.pt	liquid pint	204
liq.qt	liquid quart	204
lm	lumen	222
lx	lux	223
l.y.	light year	201
L	lambert	223
M		
m	milli- (10^{-3})	9
m	metre	200
mi	mile	200
min	minute	205
min	minim	204
mmHg	millimetre of mercury	212
mmH_2O	millimetre of water	212
mol	mole	226
M	mega- (10^{6})	9
Mx	maxwell	216
μ	micro- (10^{-6})	9
μ (μm)	micron* (micrometre)	200
N		
n	nano- (10^{-9})	9
n mile	nautical mile	200
N	newton	211, 216
O		
osm	osmole	271
oz	ounce	205
Oe	oersted	216
Ω	ohm	215, 216
Ω^{-1}	mho (reciprocal ohm)	216
P		
p	pico- (10^{-12})	9
p	pond	211
pc	parsec	201
pdl	poundal	211
phon	phon	225
phot	phot	223
pk	peck	204
pt	pint	204
P	poise	214
PS	metric horsepower	214
Q		
qr	quarter	205
qt	quart	205
R		
r	revolution	208
r	roentgen (old)	218
rad	radian	207
rd	rad	218
rd	rod	200
rem	rem	221
R	roentgen	218
°R	degree Rankine	208
Ry	rydberg	213
S		
s	second	205
s	scruple	205
s^{-1}	reciprocal second	208, 213
sb	stilb	223
sh cwt	short hundredweight	205
sh tn	short ton	205
sone	sone	225
sr	steradian	207
st	stere	203
St	stokes	214
T		
t	metric ton	204
t, tr	troy (measures)	205
ton	ton	205
tonf	ton-force	211
T	tera- (10^{12})	9
T	tesla	216
torr	torr	212
U		
u	atomic mass unit	213, 226
V		
V	volt	215, 216
W		
W	watt	214, 216
Wb	weber	216
X		
XU	X-unit	201
Y		
yd	yard	200

* This name and symbol should no longer be used

CGS	centimetre-gramme-second (system of units)
CIPM	Comité International des Poids et Mesures
IAU	International Astronomical Union
ICRU	International Commission on Radiological Units and Measurements
IEC	International Electrotechnical Commission
IPTS-68	International Practical Temperature Scale of 1968
ISO	International Organization for Standardization
IT	International Steam Table
IUPAC	International Union of Pure and Applied Chemistry
IUPAP	International Union of Pure and Applied Physics
MKS	metre-kilogramme-second (system of units)
MKSA	metre-kilogramme-second-ampere (system of units)
RBE	relative biological effectiveness
SAT	Stepped Atomic Time
SI	International System of Units
UT	Universal Time
UTC	Coordinated Universal Time

Length (l)

Dimension = L

Coherent units

International System of Units: metre (m)
CGS system: centimetre (cm)
ft-lb-s system: foot (ft)

International System of Units (SI units)[1]

The base (or 'basic') unit of length is the metre** (m). This was redefined[1a] in 1960 as a multiple of the vacuum wave length λ (^{86}Kr) of the orange-red spectral line of the atom of krypton-86, as follows: The metre is the length equal to $1\,650\,763.7\mathbf{3}$ wave lengths in vacuum of the radiation corresponding to the transition between the levels $2p_{10}$ and $5d_5$ of the krypton-86 atom. The re-defined metre is therefore based on a natural quantity, namely the energy difference between two electron terms of an unperturbed atom. It follows that

$$\lambda\,(^{86}\mathrm{Kr}) = 6.057\,802\,21 \times 10^{-7} \text{ metre}$$

For the history of the metre as a unit see the literature[2].

Secondary standards[3]

(a) Vacuum wave lengths of the krypton nuclide ^{86}Kr

$2p_9 - 5d_4'$: $6.458\,072\,0 \times 10^{-7}$ m
$2p_8 - 5d_4$: $6.422\,800\,6 \times 10^{-7}$ m
$1s_3 - 3p_{10}$: $5.651\,128\,6 \times 10^{-7}$ m
$1s_4 - 3p_8$: $4.503\,616\,2 \times 10^{-7}$ m

(b) Vacuum wave lengths of the mercury nuclide ^{198}Hg

$6^1P_1 - 6^1D_2$: $5.792\,268\,3 \times 10^{-7}$ m
$6^1P_1 - 6^3D_2$: $5.771\,198\,3 \times 10^{-7}$ m
$6^3P_2 - 7^3S_1$: $5.462\,270\,5 \times 10^{-7}$ m
$6^3P_1 - 7^3S_1$: $4.359\,562\,4 \times 10^{-7}$ m

(c) Vacuum wave lengths of the cadmium nuclide ^{114}Cd

$5^1P_1 - 5^1D_2$: $6.440\,248\,0 \times 10^{-7}$ m
$5^3P_2 - 6^3S_1$: $5.087\,237\,9 \times 10^{-7}$ m
$5^3P_1 - 6^3S_1$: $4.801\,252\,1 \times 10^{-7}$ m
$5^3P_0 - 6^3S_1$: $4.679\,458\,1 \times 10^{-7}$ m

Conversion of metric units of length

		1 **A** unit = b **B** units (b in the table)						
A		**B**						
Name	Symbol	nm	µm	mm	cm	dm	m	km
ångström	Å	10^{-1}	10^{-4}	10^{-7}	10^{-8}	10^{-9}	10^{-10}	10^{-13}
nanometre (millimicron†)	nm (mµ†)	1	10^{-3}	10^{-6}	10^{-7}	10^{-8}	10^{-9}	10^{-12}
micrometre (micron†)	µm (µ†)	10^{3}	1	10^{-3}	10^{-4}	10^{-5}	10^{-6}	10^{-9}
millimetre	mm	10^{6}	10^{3}	1	10^{-1}	10^{-2}	10^{-3}	10^{-6}
centimetre	cm	10^{7}	10^{4}	10	1	10^{-1}	10^{-2}	10^{-5}
decimetre	dm	10^{8}	10^{5}	10^{2}	10	1	10^{-1}	10^{-4}
metre	m	10^{9}	10^{6}	10^{3}	10^{2}	10	1	10^{-3}
decametre	dam	10^{10}	10^{7}	10^{4}	10^{3}	10^{2}	10	10^{-2}
hectometre	hm	10^{11}	10^{8}	10^{5}	10^{4}	10^{3}	10^{2}	10^{-1}
kilometre	km	10^{12}	10^{9}	10^{6}	10^{5}	10^{4}	10^{3}	1

† In accordance with a resolution of the 13th General Conference of Weights and Measures (1967), these names and symbols, formerly in common use, should no longer be used.

Anglo-Saxon systems of measurement

The primary standard of length in the Anglo-Saxon systems of measurement is the *yard* (yd), though the coherent length unit in the ft-lb-s system is the foot (ft) = ⅓ yard. Recently the yard has been defined in terms of the metre as follows[4]:

$$1 \text{ yard} = 0.914\mathbf{4} \text{ m} = 1.509\,458\,3_5 \times 10^6\, \lambda\,(^{86}\mathrm{Kr})$$

This newly defined 'unified' yard† lies between the former imperial yard of the United Kingdom[5] and the former US yard[6]:

$$1 \text{ imperial yard} = 0.914\,398\,41 \text{ m} < 1 \text{ unified yard} < 1 \text{ US yard} = (3\mathbf{6}/39.3\mathbf{7}) \text{ m} = 0.914\,401\,83 \text{ m}^{\dagger\dagger}$$

Conversion of Anglo-Saxon units of length

		1 **A** unit = b **B** units (b in the table)		
A		**B**		
Name	Symbol	yd	ft	m
mil	–	1/36 000	1/12 000	$2.5\mathbf{4} \times 10^{-5}$
point (printers') (US)†	–	–	–	3.515×10^{-4}
line (button) (US)	–	1/1440	1/480	$6.3\mathbf{5} \times 10^{-4}$
inch	in	1/36	1/12	$2.5\mathbf{4} \times 10^{-2}$
hand (US)	–	1/9	1/3	$1.01\mathbf{6} \times 10^{-1}$
link	li ††	22/100	66/100	$2.011\,6\mathbf{8} \times 10^{-1}$
span (US)	–	1/4	3/4	$2.28\mathbf{6} \times 10^{-1}$
foot	ft	1/3	1	$3.04\mathbf{8} \times 10^{-1}$
yard	yd	1	3	$9.14\mathbf{4} \times 10^{-1}$
fathom	fath ††	2	6	$1.828\,\mathbf{8}$
rod (pole, perch)	rd ††	11/2	33/2	$5.029\,\mathbf{2}$
chain	ch ††	22	66	$2.011\,6\mathbf{8} \times 10$
furlong	fur. ††	220	660	$2.011\,6\mathbf{8} \times 10^{2}$
(statute) mile	mile †††	1760	5280	$1.609\,\mathbf{344} \times 10^{3}$

† Definition: 1 point (printers') (US) = 0.013 837 in.
†† Symbols in use only in USA.
††† Symbol in USA: mi.

Nautical and geodetic units of length

The *nautical mile* is defined as the length of the mean minute of arc on the meridian of the earth (mean minute of latitude). When the values of the terrestrial polar and equatorial radii derived from the international terrestrial geoid[7] are used

$$1 \text{ nautical mile} = \frac{\text{quadrant of meridian } Q_{\delta}^{\mathrm{Me}}}{90 \times 60} = 1852.276 \text{ m}$$

In 1928 the International Hydrographic Conference in Monaco proposed the following international unified definition[8]:

$$1 \text{ international nautical mile} = 185\mathbf{2} \text{ m}$$

This value was accepted by all maritime nations (by USA in 1954[9]) with the exception of the United Kingdom, where the nautical mile is based on the knot:

$$1 \text{ Admiralty knot} = \frac{1 \text{ nautical mile}}{\text{hour}} = 608\mathbf{0} \text{ imperial feet per hour}$$

whence

$$1 \text{ imperial nautical mile (n mile)} = 1853.181 \text{ m}$$

The *geographical mile* (not to be confused with the land, or statute, mile) is now based on the equatorial quadrant Q_{δ}^{E} ($\triangleq$ 4 minutes of arc on the equator). When the value of the terrestrial equatorial radius derived from the international terrestrial geoid[7] is used

$$1 \text{ geographical mile} = 4 \times \frac{\text{equatorial quadrant } Q_{\delta}^{\mathrm{E}}}{90 \times 60} = 7421.591 \text{ metres}$$

Astronomical units of length

In astronomy the unit of length is the *astronomical unit* (AU). This is based on a definition requiring some preliminary explanation. With the ephemeris day (d) of 86 400 ephemeris seconds (s) as time unit and the mass of the sun ($M_\odot$) as mass unit the undisturbed elliptical ('KEPLER') path of a planet is characterized by

n the sideral mean daily motion (angular velocity) in rad/d
$\bar{m}$ the mass in $M_\odot$
a the semi-major axis in AU
k the GAUSS gravitational constant in $(\mathrm{AU})^{3/2}$ rad d^{-1} $M_\odot^{-1/2}$

* This chapter (pages 200–227) has been compiled in collaboration with G. BECKER, W. FRITZ, J. HOPPE-BLANK, W. HÜBNER, U. STILLE, H.-M. WEISS, Braunschweig, and S. BÖHME, Heidelberg.
** In the USA, 'meter'.

† Formerly also called 'international yard' in English-speaking countries.
†† In the US Coast and Geodetic Survey the foot legally defined in 1866 and 1893[6] (US Survey Foot = $\mathbf{12}/39.3\mathbf{7}$ m ≈ 0.304 800 609 m) retains its validity, for instance for the basic geodetic survey networks of the United States (see National Bureau of Standards[4]).

The AU is then defined as that unit in which the quantity a is measured in KEPLER's Third Law $n^2 a^3 = k^2 (1 + \overline{m})$ (as equation between numerical values) with the conventionally agreed numerical value $k = na^{3/2} = 0.017\,202\,098\,95$ for the GAUSS gravitational constant, measured in $(\text{AU})^{3/2}$ rad d^{-1} $\text{M}_\odot^{-1/2}$. The AU is thus a derived unit determined by the units chosen for time and mass and the fixed value of the GAUSS constant k. It can be described as the radius of the circular path round the sun followed by a body of negligible mass in the time $P_0 = (2\,\pi/k)$ d $= 365.256\,898\,3...$ d, i.e., with the uniform angular velocity $360°/P_0 = k\,180°/(\pi\text{ d}) = 0.985\,607\,668\,6...°/\text{d}$[9a,10]. The AU can be taken as nearly equal to the semi-major axis of the earth's path (establishing this agreement was the reason for GAUSS's measurement of k). When the disturbing effects of the other planets are taken into account the value is 1.000 000 2 AU.

It is still necessary to express the AU as a multiple A of the metre or some other reference length. The former is obtained directly from radar measurements (up to now mainly of the planet Venus, whose distance is known from the ephemerides); determination of the solar parallax $\pi_\odot$ measures the relationship of the AU to the equatorial radius a_e of the earth. The 'IAU System of Astronomical Constants' was laid down by the 12th General Assembly of the International Astronomical Union in 1964[10] by assigning conventionally agreed values to the 'defining' and 'primary' constants. In this system

$$1\text{ AU} = A\text{ m} = 149\,600 \times 10^6\text{ m}$$
$$\pi_\odot = \arcsin (a_e/A\text{ m}) = 8.794\,05'', \text{ with } a_e = 6\,378\,160\text{ m}$$

Since radar measurements are measurements of time differences the time τ_A taken by light to travel 1 AU is also given; in the same system it is

$$\tau_A = (A\text{ m})/c = 499.012\text{ s, with } c = 299\,792.5 \times 10^3\text{ m s}^{-1}$$ [10,11]

In stellar astronomy the distances involved are far greater than those of the solar system ($> 2 \times 10^5$ AU), and more appropriate length units have been introduced, namely the parsec, light year and distance modulus.

The *parsec* (pc) is defined as that distance at which 1 AU subtends an angle p of 1″. The angle p (measured in seconds of arc) is known as the annual parallax of the object, so that the parsec so defined is the distance of a fixed star with parallax $p = 1''$ (whence parsec from parallax and second). Since $p < 0.8''$ for all stellar parallaxes, parallax and distance are related as follows:

$$\pi\, r\, p/648\,000'' = 1\text{ AU}$$
whence $r = 648\,000''/(\pi p)$ AU
and $r = 1/p$ pc by definition

It follows that $1\text{ pc} = 648\,000/\pi\text{ AU} = 206\,264.8\text{ AU}$
and $1\text{ pc} = 648\,000/\pi\ A\text{ m} = 3.085\,72 \times 10^{13}\text{ km}$

The larger units usually employed are

$$1\text{ kpc} = 10^3\text{ pc};\ 1\text{ Mpc} = 10^6\text{ pc}$$

The *light year* (l.y.) is the distance travelled by light in one tropical year. When the values of the IAU System of Astronomical Constants[10] for the velocity of light and the number of ephemeris seconds in 1 tropical year are used

$$1\text{ l.y.} = 299\,792\,500\text{ m s}^{-1} \times 31\,556\,925.974\,7\text{ s} = 9.460\,529\,73 \times 10^{12}\text{ km}$$

For objects whose parallax cannot be (more or less) directly measured, the *distance modulus* is used as indirect measure of distance. If m is the apparent (i.e., measured) brightness in magnitudes (^{m} or mag.) of an object at distance r pc, M its absolute brightness at the standard distance of 10 pc, then the distance modulus is defined as the quantity $m - M$. According to the $1/r^2$ law governing the propagation of light in an absorption-free space

$$m - M = 5 \log_{10} (r/\text{pc}) - 5 = -5 - 5 \log_{10} (p/'')$$

For $m - M = -5^m, 0^m, +5^m, +10^m, \ldots +25^m$ the corresponding distances are $r = 1, 10, 100, 1000, \ldots 10^6$ pc.

If M can be determined from the physical structure of the object, r or p can be obtained from

$$\log_{10} (r/\text{pc}) = 0.2\,(m - M + 5) = -\log_{10} (p/'')$$

Conversion of astronomical units of length†

1 **A** unit = b **B** units (b in the table)				
A		**B**		
Name	Symbol	AU	pc	l.y.
astronomica unit	AU	1	$4.848\,14 \times 10^{-6}$	$1.581\,31 \times 10^{-5}$
parsec	pc	$2.062\,648 \times 10^5$	1	3.261 68
light year	l.y.	$6.323\,88 \times 10^4$	$3.065\,91 \times 10^{-1}$	1

† Based on the values of the solar parallax and terrestrial equatorial radius laid down by the International Astronomical Union in 1964[10].

Spectrometric units of length

X-Unit

The customary *wave-length unit in X-ray spectrometry* is the X-unit (XU), related by SIEGBAHN[12] to the lattice constant of calcite, i.e., the interval $d_{211}^{18°}$ ($CaCO_3$) between the (211) levels of the crystal at 18 °C, and defined as

$$1\text{ XU} = [1/3029.45\ d_{211}^{18°}\ (CaCO_3)]$$

The very great accuracy necessary in X-ray wave-length measurements (relative uncertainty $\approx 10^{-6}$) is no longer met by SIEGBAHN's definition of the X-unit since the natural imperfections of the calcite crystal (impurities, lattice defects, mosaic- or superstructure, surface effects, etc.) render it an unsatisfactory primary standard.

Today no value for the conversion factor Λ between X-unit and metre ($\Lambda = 1\text{ XU}/10^{-13}\text{ m} = 1\text{ XU}/1\text{ mÅ}$ [for Å see below]) can be given with the degree of certainty called for in X-ray spectrometry and lattice-constant measurements (e.g., $3\,s < 10^{-5}$)*.

Measurements 'in XU' are now mostly based on tabulated wave lengths of X-ray lines in XU[15,16], namely in the 'long-wave' region on λ (CuKα_1) = 1537.396 XU (or 1537.40 XU), in the 'short-wave' region on λ (MoKα_1) = 707.831 XU. In 1958 the suggestion was made to base the XU on one or several X-ray wave lengths, using a well-defined point on the line profile as reference point, in other words to replace the *calcite standard* by a *wave-length standard*[17].

In 1962, 1963 and 1965 COHEN and DUMOND[18,19] published a series of values of Λ determined *experimentally* by various direct and indirect methods of other workers. In a later discussion of these results, which in the meantime had been corrected and adjusted in accordance with the new X-ray wave-length tables of BEARDEN[25] (Λ between 1.002 00 and 1.002 09), DUMOND[20] in 1966 derived a new value of $\Lambda = 1.002\,064$ ($3\,s = 28 \times 10^{-6}$), an 'experimental' mean based on the values for constants resulting from the 1963 adjustment[19] (see page 228). Earlier, in 1965, a *special re-evaluation of the atomic constants* by COHEN and DUMOND[19] led to a value of $\Lambda = 1.002\,080$ ($3\,s = 18 \times 10^{-6}$) based on λ (WKα_1) = 208.577 0 XU.

In 1964 BEARDEN et al.[21] published the results of very precise determinations (relatively to each other) of 5 standard red wave lengths (CrKα_2, CuKα_1, MoKα_1, AgKα_1, WKα_1), and in 1965 there appeared some experimental values for Λ determined from the product $N_A \Lambda^3$ measured on carefully selected crystals[22]. The former led to the value of 2.171 945 for the ratio λ(CuKα_1)/λ(MoKα_1) (relative probable error $\pm\, 1 \times 10^{-6}$), a value about 20 parts per million smaller than the existing tabulated values[15,16], so that taking λ(MoKα_1) = 707.831 XU as a 'working standard' means that λ(CuKα_1) must be reduced to 1537.370 XU while the standard wave length λ(WKα_1) becomes 208.577 0 XU. From the experimental $N_A \Lambda^3$ values, together with Λ determinations by other workers, BEARDEN[23] – using values for the AVOGADRO constant N_A from the set of constants from the 1963 re-evaluation (see page 228) – derived the following mean values for the conversion factor Λ (relative probable error $\pm\, 5 \times 10^{-6}$):

$\Lambda = 1.002\,076$ based on λ(MoKα_1) = 707.831 XU or λ(CuKα_1) = 1537.370 XU

$= 1.002\,056$ based on λ(CuKα_1) = 1537.400 XU or λ(MoKα_1) = 707.845 XU

At the same time BEARDEN[24] suggested that SIEGBAHN's definition of the XU should be replaced by a new scale of X-ray wave lengths whose unit should be denoted provisionally by Å and de-

* Some authorities[14] still use the value[13] 1 XU = (1.002 02 ± 0.000 03) mÅ agreed on in 1942 between SIEGBAHN, the X-Ray Analysis Group of the Institute of Physics (UK) and the American Society for X-Ray and Electron Diffraction.

fined by adopting an exact value of the wave length of the peak of the $WK\alpha_1$ line, namely $\lambda(WK\alpha_1) = 0.209010\mathbf{0}$ Å. This defining value had been derived by Bearden in 1964 from the value of $\lambda(WK\alpha_1) = 208.5770$ XU $= 208.5770 \times \Lambda$ mÅ and his experimentally determined value $\Lambda = 1.002076$ based on the 'working standard' wave length $\lambda(MoK\alpha_1)$; this means that the new X-ray wave-length unit also satisfies the relationship 1 mÅ $= (1.002076 \pm 5 \times 10^{-6})^{-1}$ XU. According to Bearden, 1 Å is identical with 1 Å (within a relative probable error of $\pm 5 \times 10^{-6}$).

Subsequently Bearden, in conjunction with six collaborators, prepared a new table[25] of some 2700 wave lengths of X-ray fluorescence lines of the K-, L-, M-, N- and O-series (given as maximum of the line profile) and X-ray absorption edges in his proposed Å unit; this includes in an appendix a table of the wave lengths in XU based on $\lambda(WK\alpha_1) = 208.5770$ XU.

In 1967 Bearden's wave-length table was re-published[26] with the following changes: 1. The new X-ray wave-length unit defined by the value $\lambda(WK\alpha_1) = 0.209010\mathbf{0}$ is given the symbol Å* [1 Å* $= (1 \pm 5 \times 10^{-6})$Å]. 2. As 'working standard' the wave length λ $(CuK\alpha_1) = 1537.400$ XU is given, with a resulting experimental Λ value of 1.002056. 3. The wave lengths are given in Å* only (the appendix with values in XU is omitted). 4. The wave lengths of the 4 secondary standard lines are given in Å* only: $\lambda(AgK\alpha_1) = 0.5594075$ Å*, $\lambda(MoK\alpha_1) = 0.709300$ Å*, $\lambda(CuK\alpha_1) = 1.540562$ Å*, $\lambda(CrK\alpha_2) = 2.393606$ Å* [relative probable error compared to the primary standard wave length $\lambda(WK\alpha_1) = 0.209010\mathbf{0}$ Å*: $\pm$ 1.1 – 1.3 $\times 10^{-6}$].

When using Bearden's tables it should be noted that in the original publication[25] the Λ value 1.002076 was based on a *$MoK\alpha_1$ X-unit*, i.e., it was derived from the value $\lambda(MoK\alpha_1) = 707.831$ XU [or $\lambda(CuK\alpha_1) = 1537.3700$ XU or $\lambda(WK\alpha_1) = 208.5770$ XU], whereas in the later publication[26] the Λ value 1.002056 is based on a 20 parts per million smaller *$CuK\alpha_1$ X-unit* derived from the value $\lambda(CuK\alpha_1) = 1537.400$ XU′ [or $\lambda(MoK\alpha_1) = 707.845$ XU′ or $\lambda(WK\alpha_1) = 208.5810$ XU′].

The relationship 1 Å* $= (1 \pm 5 \times 10^{-6})$ Å given by Bearden for his new X-ray wave-length unit will remain valid only as long as 1. the relevant 'working standard' wave length [$\lambda(MoK\alpha_1)$ for the original tables[25] and $\lambda(CuK\alpha_1)$ for the later publication[26]] and the wave-length ratios $\lambda(CuK\alpha_1)/\lambda(MoK\alpha_1) = 2.171945$ and $\lambda(CuK\alpha_1)/\lambda(WK\alpha_1) = 7.370757$ (relative probable errors $\pm 1.0 \times 10^{-6}$ and $\pm 1.1 \times 10^{-6}$) are adhered to, and 2. doubt is not thrown on the Λ value (1.002076 or 1.002056) based on the relevant 'working standard' wave length by new experimental results, whether these are direct or indirect determinations of Λ or new values for the atomic constants involved, in particular the Avogadro constant N_A. The second of these conditions could be avoided if, instead of introducing a new wave-length unit such as Bearden proposes, the now practically defunct Siegbahn definition of the X-unit were replaced by a new one based for instance on the $WK\alpha_1$ line: 1 XU $= \lambda(WK\alpha_1)/208.5770$ or $\lambda(WK\alpha_1)/208.5810$. Up to now the international bodies concerned have been unable to agree on a new definition of the X-unit.

Tables of the atomic energy differences (in eV and Ry; see page 213) between two levels together with the wave lengths (in mÅ*) corresponding to the energy differences are to be found in Bearden and Burr's tables of atomic energy levels[27]. Some examples of energy differences are also given in the tables of energy levels published by these authors in *Reviews of Modern Physics*[28].

The ångström

The ångström (Å) is widely used as a *unit of length in atomic and molecular spectrometry*, especially in the visible and ultraviolet spectral range. Following the new definition of the metre by the 11th General Conference on Weights and Measures[1] in 1960, the International Astronomical Union in 1961 replaced its 1907 definition[29] of the ångström based on the wave length of cadmium as primary standard by the relationship[30]

1 ångström $= 10^{-10}$ metre

Ångström is thus now no more than a special name for 10^{-10} m.

References

1 For a summary see *The International System (SI) Units*, BS 3763: 1964, British Standards Institution, London, 1964.

1a Conférence Générale des Poids et Mesures, *Comptes rendus des séances de la 11e Conférence générale des Poids et Mesures*, Paris 1960, Gauthier-Villars, Paris, 1961, pages 51 and 85.

2 Barrell, H., *Contemp. Phys.*, 3, 415 (1961/62); Stille, U., *Z. angew. Phys.*, **11**, 316 (1959); Stille, U., *Messen und Rechnen in der Physik*, 2nd ed., Vieweg, Braunschweig, 1961; Engelhard and Vieweg, *Z. angew. Phys.*, **13**, 580 (1961); Clusius, K., *Experientia (Basel)*, **19**, 169 (1963).

3 Comité International des Poids et Mesures, *Proc.-Verb. Com. int. Poids Mes.*, **31**, 26 (1963).

4 National Bureau of Standards, *Nat. Bur. Stand., Techn. News Bull.*, **43**, 1 (1959); National Physical Laboratory, *Nature*, **183**, 80 (1959); Howlett, L. E., for National Research Council, *Canad. J. Phys.*, **37**, 84 (1959); United States of America, *U.S. Federal Register*, Document 59-5442, filed June 30, 1959; Great Britain, *Weights and Measures Act, 1963:* 11 Eliz. 2, Ch. 31, H. M. S. O., London, 1963.

5 Great Britain, *Weights and Measures Act, 1878:* 41 & 42 Vict., Ch. 49, H. M. S. O., London; National Physical Laboratory, *Units and Standards of Measurement Employed at the National Physical Laboratory*, Part 1: Length, Mass, Time etc., 1st ed., H.M.S.O., London, 1951, page 4, and 3rd ed., H.M.S.O., London, 1962, page 3; British Standards Institution, *Conversion Factors and Tables*, B. S. 350: Part 1: 1959, page 9; Part 2: 1962; Part 2, Supplement: 1967.

6 United States of America, *U.S. Code of Federal Regulations*, 1946, Title 15, Ch. 6: Metric System, Sec. 204 – Metric System authorized (1866), Sec. 205 – Authorized Tables (1866), Revised Statutes, Sec. 3570; U.S. Coast and Geodetic Survey, Treasury Department, Bulletin No. 26: *Fundamental Standards of Length and Mass*, approved for publication April 5, 1893 (Mendenhall Order); U.S. Coast and Geodetic Survey, Treasury Department, *Report for 1893*, Appendix No. 6 (1894); Judson, L. V., *Weights and Measures Standards of the United States, A Brief History*, National Bureau of Standards, Miscellaneous Publications No. 247, U. S. Government Printing Office, Washington, 1963.

7 International Union of Geodesy and Geophysics, *Bull. géod. int.*, **1925**, 157, 540 and 552.

8 International Hydrographic Bureau, *Abridged Manual of the Symbols and Abbreviations Used on Charts*, Special Publication 22, Monaco, 1928; also in *Hydrogr. Rev.*, **5**, 227 (1928).

9 National Bureau of Standards, Adoption of International Nautical Mile, *Nat. Bur. Stand., Techn. News Bull.*, **38**, 122 (1954).

9a Bureau des Longitudes, *Annuaire pour l'an 1954*, Gauthier-Villars, Paris, 1953, page 189; *Annuaire pour l'an 1968*, Gauthier-Villars, Paris, 1968, pages 385 and 390.

10 International Astronomical Union, *Trans. int. astron. Un.*, **XII B**, 593 (1964).

11 *c* value of the International Scientific Radio Union and International Union of Geodesy and Geophysics, *Bull. géod.* (NS), No. 47, 66, 91 (1958).

12 Siegbahn, M., *Ann. Phys.*, 4th Series, **59**, 56 (1919); *Ark. Mat. Astron. Fys.*, **14**, No. 9 (1920); *Spektroskopie der Röntgenstrahlen*, 2nd ed., Springer, Berlin, 1931, pages 42 sq.

13 Cf. Bragg, W. L., *J. sci. Instrum.*, **24**, 27 (1947); *Acta Cryst.*, **1**, 46 (1948); Wood, E. A., *Phys. Rev.*, 2nd Series, **72**, 436 (1947).

14 Cf. Lonsdale, K., in International Union of Crystallography, *International Tables for X-Ray Crystallography*, vol. 3, Physical and Chemical Tables, Kynoch Press, Birmingham, 1962, pages 41 and 59.

15 Cauchois and Hulubei, *Longueurs d'onde des émissions X et des discontinuités d'absorption X*, Hermann, Paris, 1947.

16 Sandström, A. E., in Flügge, S. (Ed.), *Handbuch der Physik*, vol. 30, Springer, Berlin, 1957, pages 78 sq.

17 Cf. Merrill and DuMond, *Phys. Rev.*, 2nd Series, **110**, 79 (1958); DuMond, J. W. M., *Proc. Nat. Acad. Sci.*, **45**, 1052 (1959).

18 Cohen, E. R., *Bull. Amer. Phys. Soc.*, 2nd Series, **7**, 305 (1962); Cohen and DuMond, in Johnson, W. (Ed.), *Nuclidic Masses*, Proceedings of the 2nd International Conference on Nuclidic Masses, Vienna 1963, Springer, Vienna, 1965, page 152.

19 Cohen and DuMond, *Rev. mod. Phys.*, **37**, 537 (1965).

20 DuMond, J. W. M., *Z. Naturforsch.*, **21a**, 70 (1966).

21 Bearden et al., *Phys. Rev.*, 2nd Series, **135A**, 899 (1964).

22 Henins and Bearden, *Phys. Rev.*, 2nd Series, **135A**, 890 (1964); Henins, I., *J. Res. Nat. Bur. Stand.*, **68A**, 529 (1964).

23 Bearden, J. A., *Phys. Rev.*, 2nd Series, **137B**, 181 (1965).

24 Bearden, J. A., *Phys. Rev.*, 2nd Series, **137B**, 455 (1965); Deslattes et al., *Metrologia*, **2**, 104 (1966).

25 Bearden, J. A., *X-Ray Wavelengths*, U. S. Atomic Energy Commission, Division of Technical Information Extension, NYO-10586, Oak Ridge, Tenn., 1964 (Clearinghouse for Federal Scientific and Technical Information of the U.S. Department of Commerce, Springfield, Va.).

26 Bearden, J. A., *Rev. mod. Phys.*, **39**, 78 (1967).

27 Bearden and Burr, *Atomic Energy Levels*, U. S. Atomic Energy Commission, Division of Technical Information Extension, NYO-2543-1, Oak Ridge, Tenn., 1965 (Clearinghouse for Federal Scientific and Technical Information of the U.S. Department of Commerce, Springfield, Va.).

28 Bearden and Burr, *Rev. mod. Phys.*, **39**, 125 (1967).

29 International Union for Co-operation in Solar Research, *Trans. int. Un. Coop. Sol. Res.*, **2**, 20 (1908).

30 International Astronomical Union, *Trans. int. astron. Un.*, **XI B**, 88 (1962).

Area (*A* or *S*)

Dimension $= L^2$

Coherent units

International System of Units: square metre (m²)
CGS system: square centimetre (cm²)
ft-lb-s system: square foot (ft²)

The units of length on which the units of area are based are described on page 200.

The International Union of Pure and Applied Physics (IUPAP), at its 10th General Assembly in 1960, recommended the name barn (b) for 10^{-24} cm², a quantity in common use in atomic and nuclear physics as unit of nuclear cross section[1].

Conversion of metric units of area

		1 **A** unit = *b* **B** units (*b* in the table)					
A		**B**					
Name	Symbol	μm^2	mm^2	cm^2	dm^2	m^2	km^2
barn	b	10^{-16}	10^{-22}	10^{-24}	10^{-26}	10^{-28}	10^{-34}
square micrometre	μm^2	1	10^{-6}	10^{-8}	10^{-10}	10^{-12}	10^{-18}
square millimetre	mm^2	10^{6}	1	10^{-2}	10^{-4}	10^{-6}	10^{-12}
square centimetre	cm^2	10^{8}	10^{2}	1	10^{-2}	10^{-4}	10^{-10}
square decimetre	dm^2	10^{10}	10^{4}	10^{2}	1	10^{-2}	10^{-8}
square metre	m^2	10^{12}	10^{6}	10^{4}	10^{2}	1	10^{-6}
square decametre (are)	dam^2 (a)	10^{14}	10^{8}	10^{6}	10^{4}	10^{2}	10^{-4}
square hectometre (hectare)	hm^2 (ha)	10^{16}	10^{10}	10^{8}	10^{6}	10^{4}	10^{-2}
square kilometre	km^2	10^{18}	10^{12}	10^{10}	10^{8}	10^{6}	1

Conversion of Anglo-Saxon units of area

		1 **A** unit = *b* **B** units (*b* in the table)		
A		**B**		
Name	Symbol	yd^2	ft^2	m^2
circular mil*	–	$\pi/(5184\times10^{6})$	$\pi/(576\times10^{6})$	$1.612\mathbf{9}\,\pi \times 10^{-10}$
square inch	in^2	1/1296	1/144	$6.451\,\mathbf{6} \times 10^{-4}$
circular inch	–	$\pi/5184$	$\pi/576$	$1.612\mathbf{9}\,\pi \times 10^{-4}$
square link	li^2**	$484/10^4$	$4356/10^4$	$4.046\,86 \times 10^{-2}$
square foot	ft^2	1/9	1	$9.290\,30\mathbf{4} \times 10^{-2}$
square yard	yd^2	1	9	$8.361\,273\,\mathbf{6} \times 10^{-1}$
square rod***	rd^2**	121/4	1089/4	$2.529\,29 \times 10$
square chain	ch^2**	484	4356	$4.046\,86 \times 10^{2}$
rood (UK)	–	1210	10 890	$1.011\,71 \times 10^{3}$
acre	–	4840	43 560	$4.046\,86 \times 10^{3}$
square mile	$mile^2$†	3 097 600	27 878 400	$2.589\,99 \times 10^{6}$

* The circular mil is defined as the area of a circle of 0.001 inch diameter:
1 circular mil = 10^{-6} circular inch = $(\pi/4) \times 10^{-6}$ in^2.
** Symbols in use onyl in USA.
*** Also known as square perch or square pole.
† Symbol in USA: mi^2.

Reference

[1] International Union of Pure and Applied Physics, *Report of the 10th General Assembly*, Ottawa, 1960, pages 7 and 24; International Union of Pure and Applied Physics, *Symbols, Units and Nomenclature in Physics*, Document U.I.P. 11 (S.U.N. 65-3), 1965, page 25.

Volume (V)

Dimension = L^3

Coherent units

International System of Units: cubic metre (m^3)
CGS system: cubic centimetre (cm^3)
ft-lb-s system: cubic foot (ft^3)

The units of length on which the units of volume are based are described on page 200.

Conversion of metric units of volume

		1 **A** unit = *b* **B** units (*b* in the table)					
A		**B**					
Name	Symbol	nm^3	μm^3	mm^3	cm^3	dm^3	m^3
cubic nanometre	nm^3	1	10^{-9}	10^{-18}	10^{-21}	10^{-24}	10^{-27}
cubic micrometre	μm^3	10^{9}	1	10^{-9}	10^{-12}	10^{-15}	10^{-18}
cubic millimetre	mm^3	10^{18}	10^{9}	1	10^{-3}	10^{-6}	10^{-9}
cubic centimetre	cm^3	10^{21}	10^{12}	10^{3}	1	10^{-3}	10^{-6}
cubic decimetre	dm^3	10^{24}	10^{15}	10^{6}	10^{3}	1	10^{-3}
cubic metre (stere*)	m^3 (st)	10^{27}	10^{18}	10^{9}	10^{6}	10^{3}	1
cubic kilometre	km^3	10^{36}	10^{27}	10^{18}	10^{15}	10^{12}	10^{9}

* Name mainly in use in French-speaking countries.

Noncoherent unit

Up to 1964 the *litre* (l) was defined as the volume of 1 kg of pure, air-free water at its maximum density (≈3.98 °C) under normal atmospheric pressure (1 atm = 76**0** torr)[1]. In 1950 the International Committee of Weights and Measures[2] gave 1 litre = 1.000028 cubic decimetre (relative uncertainty ≈ ± 3 × 10^{-6}) as the best conversion factor between the litre so defined and the cubic decimetre.

In 1964 the 12th General Conference of Weights and Measures[3] abolished the old litre definition of the 3rd General Conference in 1901 and agreed that the name 'litre' should be used as synonym for cubic decimetre with the express recommendation that the results of very precise volume determinations should be given not in litres but in the SI-unit cubic metre or its decimal multiples or submultiples: 1 l = 1 dm^3.

Conversion of decimal submultiples and multiples of the litre

		1 **A** unit = *b* **B** units (*b* in the table)			
A		**B**			
Name	Symbol	µl	ml	l	m^3
microlitre (= 1 mm^3)	µl	1	10^{-3}	10^{-6}	10^{-9}
millilitre (= 1 cm^3)	ml	10^{3}	1	10^{-3}	10^{-6}
decilitre (= 0.1 dm^3)	dl	10^{5}	10^{2}	10^{-1}	10^{-4}
litre (= 1 dm^3)	l	10^{6}	10^{3}	1	10^{-3}
hectolitre (= 0.1 m^3)	hl	10^{8}	10^{5}	10^{2}	10^{-1}

Anglo-Saxon units of volume[4]

In the United Kingdom the *commercial* units of volume both for fluids and dry substances are the gallon (gal) and units derived from it. The gallon is the volume of a quantity of water of a specified mass when weighed under the conditions laid down[5]; this definition results in the following relationships:

1 gal(UK) = 277.42 in^3
= 4.546 09 dm^3

In the United States the gallon (gal) and the units of volume derived from it are legal measures only for fluids. The gallon is there defined[6,7] as

1 gal(US) = 23**1** in^3
= 3.785 411 78**4** dm^3

whence the relationships

1 gal(US) = 0.832 674 gal(UK)
1 gal(UK) = 1.200 950 gal(US)

In the United States the units of volume for dry substances are the bushel (bu) and units derived from it. The bushel (bu) is defined as follows:

1 bu(US) = 2150.4**2** in^3
= 35.239 070 166 8**8** dm^3

This unit is related to the bushel used in the United Kingdom, defined as 1 bushel (UK) = 8 gal(UK), as follows:

1 bu(US) = 0.968 939 bushel(UK)
1 bushel(UK) = 1.032 057 bu(US)

Conversion of Anglo-Saxon units of volume

		1 **A** unit = *b* **B** units (*b* in the table)		
A		**B**		
Name	Symbol	yd^3	ft^3	m^3
cubic inch	in^3	1/46 656	1/1728	$1.638\,706\,\mathbf{4} \times 10^{-5}$
board foot (timber)	fbm	1/324	1/12	$2.359\,74 \times 10^{-3}$
cubic foot	ft^3	1/27	1	$2.831\,68 \times 10^{-2}$
cubic yard	yd^3	1	27	$7.645\,55 \times 10^{-1}$
cord (timber)	cd	128/27	128	3.624 56

Conversion of United Kingdom units of volume (UK units)

		1 **A** unit = *b* **B** units (*b* in the table)		
A		**B**		
Name	Symbol	gal	in³	l = dm³
minim	min	1/76 800	$3.612\,23 \times 10^{-3}$	$5.919\,39 \times 10^{-5}$
fluid drachm. (= 60 min)	fl dr	1/1280	$2.167\,34 \times 10^{-1}$	$3.551\,63 \times 10^{-3}$
fluid ounce .. (= 480 min)	fl oz	1/160	1.733 87	$2.841\,31 \times 10^{-2}$
gill	–	1/32	8.669 36	$1.420\,65 \times 10^{-1}$
pint	–	1/8	$3.467\,74 \times 10$	$5.682\,61 \times 10^{-1}$
quart	–	1/4	$6.935\,49 \times 10$	1.136 52
gallon	gal	1	$2.774\,20 \times 10^{2}$	4.546 09
peck	–	2	$5.548\,39 \times 10^{2}$	9.092 18
bushel	–	8	$2.219\,35 \times 10^{3}$	$3.636\,87 \times 10$
quarter ..... (volume)	–	64	$1.775\,49 \times 10^{4}$	$2.909\,50 \times 10^{2}$
chaldron	–	288	$7.989\,68 \times 10^{4}$	$1.309\,27 \times 10^{3}$

Conversion of United States units of volume (US units)

For fluids (liquid measure)

		1 **A** unit = *b* **B** units (*b* in the table)		
A		**B**		
Name	Symbol	gal	in³	l = dm³
minim	min	1/61 440	$3.759\,77 \times 10^{-3}$	$6.161\,15 \times 10^{-5}$
fluid dram ..	fl dr	1/1024	$2.255\,86 \times 10^{-1}$	$3.696\,69 \times 10^{-3}$
fluid ounce ..	fl oz	1/128	1.804 69	$2.957\,35 \times 10^{-2}$
gill	gi	1/32	7.218 **75**	$1.182\,94 \times 10^{-1}$
liquid pint ..	liq pt	1/8	$2.887\,\mathbf{5} \times 10$	$4.731\,76 \times 10^{-1}$
liquid quart .	liq qt	1/4	$5.77\mathbf{5} \times 10$	$9.463\,53 \times 10^{-1}$
gallon	gal	1	2.31×10^{2}	3.785 41
barrel (petroleum)[7,8]		42	$9.70\mathbf{2} \times 10^{3}$	$1.589\,87 \times 10^{2}$

For dry substances (dry measure)

		1 **A** unit = *b* **B** units (*b* in the table)		
A		**B**		
Name	Symbol	bu	in³	l = dm³
dry pint	dry pt	1/64	$3.360\,03 \times 10$	$5.506\,10 \times 10^{-1}$
dry quart ...	dry qt	1/32	$6.720\,06 \times 10$	1.101 22
peck	pk	1/4	$5.376\,\mathbf{05} \times 10^{2}$	8.809 77
bushel*	bu	1	$2.150\,\mathbf{42} \times 10^{3}$	$3.523\,91 \times 10$
barrel**	bbl	105/32†	$7.05\mathbf{6} \times 10^{3}$	$1.156\,27 \times 10^{2}$

* So-called stricken or struck bushel. There is also a heaped bushel of 2747.7**15** in³ ≈ 45.027 l for apples and a heaped bushel = 1¼ stricken bushels = 44.049 l[6,7].
** For fruit and other products except cranberries this barrel = 705**6** in³; for cranberries the barrel = 582**6** in³ ≈ 95.471 l[6,7].
† This fraction is approximate. Precise calculation based on the cubic inch definitions of bushel and barrel gives 1 bbl = (705**6**/2150.4**2**) bu.

References

1 Conférence Générale des Poids et Mesures, *Comptes rendus des séances de la 3e Conférence générale des Poids et Mesures*, Paris 1901, Gauthier-Villars, Paris, 1901, page 37.

2 Comité International des Poids et Mesures, *Proc.-Verb. Com. int. Poids Mes.*, **22**, 77 and 94 (1950).

3 Conférence Générale des Poids et Mesures, *Comptes rendus des séances de la 12e Conférence générale des Poids et Mesures*, Paris 1964, Gauthier-Villars, Paris, 1964, page 93.

4 Skinner, F. G., *Weights and Measures: Their Ancient Origins and Their Development in Great Britain up to AD 1855*, H.M.S.O., London, 1967; Kaye and Laby, *Tables of Physical and Chemical Constants and Some Mathematical Functions*, 13th ed., Longmans, London, 1966; Stille, U., *Messen und Rechnen in der Physik*, 2nd ed., Vieweg, Braunschweig, 1961.

5 Great Britain, *Weights and Measures Act, 1963:* 11 Eliz. 2, Ch. 31, H.M.S.O., London, 1963; *Weights and Measures Act, 1878:* 41 & 42 Vict., Ch. 49, H.M.S.O., London; National Physical Laboratory, *Units and Standards of Measurement Employed at the National Physical Laboratory*, Part 1: Length, Mass, Time etc., 1st ed., H.M.S.O., London, 1951, page 4, and 3rd ed., H.M.S.O., London, 1962, page 3; British Standards Institution, *Conversion Factors and Tables*, B.S. 350: Part 1: 1959, page 14.

6 United States of America, *U.S. Code of Federal Regulations*, 1946, Title 15, Ch. 6: Metric System, Sec. 204 – Metric System authorized (1866), Sec. 205 – Authorized Tables (1866), Revised Statutes, Sec. 3570; U.S. Coast and Geodetic Survey, Treasury Department, Bulletin No. 26: *Fundamental Standards of Length and Mass*, approved for publication April 5, 1893 (Mendenhall Order); U.S. Coast and Geodetic Survey, Treasury Department, *Report for 1893*, Appendix No. 6 (1894); Judson, L. V., *Weights and Measures Standards of the United States, A Brief History*, National Bureau of Standards, Miscellaneous Publications No. 247, U.S. Government Printing Office, Washington, 1963.

7 Judson, L. V., *Units of Weight and Measure (United States Customary and Metric), Definitions and Tables of Equivalents*, National Bureau of Standards, Miscellaneous Publications No. 233, U.S. Government Printing Office, Washington, 1960.

8 International Organization for Standardization, *Basic Quantities and Units of the SI*, ISO Recommendation R 31, Part 1, 2nd ed., December 1965.

Mass (*m*)

Dimension = M

Coherent units

International System of Units: kilogramme (kg)
CGS system: gramme (g)
ft-lb-s system: pound (lb)

International System of Units

The base unit of mass is the kilogramme (kg)*. It is equal to the mass of the international prototype of the kilogramme, a platinum-iridium cylinder preserved at the International Bureau of Weights and Measures in Sèvres (France)[1].

Conversion of metric units of mass

		1 **A** unit = *b* **B** units (*b* in the table)							
A		**B**							
Name	Symbol	ag	fg	pg	ng	µg	mg	g	kg
attogramme ..	ag	1	10^{-3}	10^{-6}	10^{-9}	10^{-12}	10^{-15}	10^{-18}	10^{-21}
femtogramme	fg	10^{3}	1	10^{-3}	10^{-6}	10^{-9}	10^{-12}	10^{-15}	10^{-18}
picogramme ..	pg	10^{6}	10^{3}	1	10^{-3}	10^{-6}	10^{-9}	10^{-12}	10^{-15}
nanogramme .	ng	10^{9}	10^{6}	10^{3}	1	10^{-3}	10^{-6}	10^{-9}	10^{-12}
microgramme*	µg	10^{12}	10^{9}	10^{6}	10^{3}	1	10^{-3}	10^{-6}	10^{-9}
milligramme .	mg	10^{15}	10^{12}	10^{9}	10^{6}	10^{3}	1	10^{-3}	10^{-6}
gramme	g	10^{18}	10^{15}	10^{12}	10^{9}	10^{6}	10^{3}	1	10^{-3}
kilogramme ..	kg	10^{21}	10^{18}	10^{15}	10^{12}	10^{9}	10^{6}	10^{3}	1
metric ton (tonne)	t	10^{24}	10^{21}	10^{18}	10^{15}	10^{12}	10^{9}	10^{6}	10^{3}

* Formerly also known as the gamma (γ), a name that should no longer be used.

Technical unit of mass

In the so-called 'technical system of measurement', the still widely used metre-kilopond-second system (m-kp-s system; on the kilopond see under 'Force', page 211) the coherent derived unit of mass, the so-called 'technical mass unit', is 1 m^{-1} kp s^{2} = 9.806 **65** kg. This unit has been little used and with the rapidly increasing popularity of the SI units it will cease to have any importance. In technology the physical quantity mass (*m*) is usually replaced by the quotient weight/acceleration due to gravity (G/g) (see under 'Force', page 211), the unit of which is 1 kp/9.806 **65** m s^{-2}, equal to the kilogramme of the MKS system.

International unit for precious stones

1 metric carat = 0.000 2 kg = 0.2 g = 200 mg[2]

Anglo-Saxon units of mass

In the Anglo-Saxon countries, in addition to the metric units employed in scientific work, three groups of mass units are in simultaneous use: the *avoirdupois* units of commerce and industry, the *troy* units for precious metals and coins, and the *apothecaries'* units. Common to all three groups is the grain (gr), defined as the 7000th part of the avoirdupois pound (lb avdp or lb av).

The avoirdupois pound has for some years been related[3] to the kilogramme by a precise numerical factor:

1 pound (lb) = 0.453 592 **37** kg

* In the USA, usually 'kilogram'.

This new 'unified' pound, sometimes called the international pound, is divisible by 7; it is somewhat larger than the former imperial pound of the United Kingdom[4] and somewhat smaller than the earlier avoirdupois pound of the United States[5]:

1 imperial pound = 0.453 592 338 kg < 1 unified pound
< 1 U.S. pound avoirdupois = 0.453 592 427 **7** kg

In the United Kingdom the troy pound (lb t) is no longer a statutory unit; however, a number of its subsidiary units still have legal standing for precious metals. In the United States, on the other hand, the troy pound (lb t[US]) is the statutory unit for coins:

1 U.S. pound troy [lb t(US)]
= 576**0**/700**0** U.S. pound avoirdupois [lb avdp(US)]

Conversion of Anglo-Saxon units of mass

Avoirdupois units

A		1 **A** unit = *b* **B** units (*b* in the table) B		
Name	Symbol	gr	lb	kg
grain (UK, US) ...	gr	1	1/7000	$6.479\,89\mathbf{1} \times 10^{-5}$
dram (UK, US) ...	dr	875/32	1/256	$1.771\,85 \times 10^{-3}$
ounce (UK, US)...	oz	875/2	1/16	$2.834\,95 \times 10^{-2}$
pound (UK, US) ..	lb	7×10^3	1	$4.535\,923\,\mathbf{7} \times 10^{-1}$
stone (UK)	–	$9.\mathbf{8} \times 10^4$	14	6.350 29
quarter (UK)	qr	$1.\mathbf{96} \times 10^4$	28	$1.270\,06 \times 10$
cental (UK)	–	7×10^5	100	$4.535\,92 \times 10$
short hundredweight (US)	sh cwt			
hundredweight (UK)	cwt	$7.\mathbf{84} \times 10^5$	112	$5.080\,23 \times 10$
long hundredweight (US)	–			
(short) ton (US)...	sh tn	$1.\mathbf{4} \times 10^7$	2000	$9.071\,85 \times 10^2$
ton (UK).........	ton	$1.56\mathbf{8} \times 10^7$	2240	$1.016\,05 \times 10^3$
long ton (US).....	–			

Troy units

A		1 **A** unit = *b* **B** units (*b* in the table) B		
Name	Symbol	gr	lb	g
pennyweight......	dwt	24	3/875	1.555 17
troy ounce	oz tr*	480	12/175	$3.110\,35 \times 10$
troy pound (US) ..	lb t	5760	144/175	$3.732\,42 \times 10^2$

* In the United States: oz t.

Apothecaries' units

A		1 **A** unit = *b* **B** units (*b* in the table) B		
Name	Symbol	gr	lb	g
scruple (UK)	s apoth*	20	1/350	1.295 98
apothecaries' scruple (US).............				
drachm (UK)	dr apoth*	60	3/350	3.887 93
apothecaries' dram (US).............				
apothecaries' ounce (UK, US)	oz apoth*	480	12/175	$3.110\,35 \times 10$
apothecaries' pound (US).............	lb apoth*	5760	144/175	$3.732\,42 \times 10^2$

* In the United States, ap instead of apoth.

References

[1] Conférence Générale des Poids et Mesures, *Comptes rendus des séances de la 3e Conférence générale des Poids et Mesures*, Paris 1901, Gauthier-Villars, Paris, 1901, pages 62 and 68.

[2] Conférence Générale des Poids et Mesures, *Comptes rendus des séances de la 4e Conférence générale des Poids et Mesures*, Paris 1907, Gauthier-Villars, Paris, 1907, page 89.

[3] National Bureau of Standards, *Nat. Bur. Stand., Techn. News Bull.*, **43**, 1 (1959); National Physical Laboratory, *Nature*, **183**, 80 (1959); Howlett, L.E., for National Research Council, *Canad. J. Phys.*, **37**, 84 (1959); United States of America, *U.S. Federal Register*, Document 59-5442, filed June 30, 1959; Great Britain, *Weights and Measures Act, 1963:* 11 Eliz. 2, Ch. 31, H.M.S.O., London, 1963.

[4] Great Britain, *Weights and Measures Act, 1878:* 41 & 42 Vict., Ch. 49, H.M.S.O., London; National Physical Laboratory, *Units and Standards of Measurement Employed at the National Physical Laboratory*, Part I: Length, Mass, Time etc., 1st ed., H.M.S.O., London, 1951, page 4, and 3rd ed., H.M.S.O., London, 1962, page 3; British Standards Institution, *Conversion Factors and Tables*, B.S. 350: Part 1: 1959, page 9.

[5] United States of America, *U.S. Code of Federal Regulations*, 1946, Title 15, Ch. 6: Metric System, Sec. 204 – Metric System authorized (1866), Sec. 205 – Authorized Tables (1866), Revised Statutes, Sec. 3570; U.S. Coast and Geodetic Survey, Treasury Department, Bulletin No. 26: *Fundamental Standards of Length and Mass*, approved for publication April 5, 1893 (Mendenhall Order); U.S. Coast and Geodetic Survey, Treasury Department, *Report for 1893*, Appendix No. 6 (1894); Judson, L.V., *Weights and Measures Standards of the United States, A Brief History*, National Bureau of Standards, Miscellaneous Publications No. 247, U.S. Government Printing Office, Washington, 1963; Judson, L.V., *Units of Weight and Measure (United States Customary and Metric), Definitions and Tables of Equivalents*, National Bureau of Standards, Miscellaneous Publications No. 233, U.S. Government Printing Office, Washington, 1960; International Organization for Standardization, *Basic Quantities and Units of the SI*, ISO Recommendation R 31, Part 1, 2nd ed., December 1965.

Time (t)

Dimension = T

Base unit: second (s)
(in all systems of measurement)

Time scales can be derived from all periodic natural phenomena (axial rotation of the earth, revolution of the planets and moon, transitions in atoms and molecules). The second of the International System of Units (SI units) is now (since October 1967) linked to an atomic frequency: it is defined as the duration of 9 192 631 77**0** periods of the radiation corresponding to the transition between the two hyperfine levels of the ground state of the caesium-133 atom[1]. Previously the second was based on Ephemeris Time (see below). For everyday time measurements a time scale derived from the axial rotation of the earth is used. For historical data on the second and on the 'atomic clock' see the literature[2].

Units of time derived from the earth's rotation • Universal Time

The *apparent solar day* is the time elapsing between two successive passages of the sun through the meridian of the observer. Owing to the inclination of the ecliptic and the fact that the earth moves around the sun not in a circular but in an elliptical path the apparent solar day differs from the *mean solar day* d by a varying amount (up to about 30 seconds). The mean solar day is derived from the movement of a 'mean sun' assumed to move with uniform speed along the celestial equator in such a way that its passage through the vernal equinox (one of the intersections of the celestial equator and the ecliptic) coincides with that of the true sun. The difference between apparent and mean solar time, known as the equation of time, varies in the course of the year between about +15 and −16 minutes. The mean solar day is the time elapsing between two successive passages of the mean sun through the meridian of the observer. These passages define the time 12 noon of mean solar time (mean local time).

The mean solar day (d) is divided into 24 hours (h) each of 60 minutes (min) each of 60 seconds (s). This second of mean solar time is also the time unit of a special mean solar time known as *Universal Time* (UT) (see below).

In practice the length of the mean solar day and thus that of the second of Universal Time are obtained from the stellar day d*, the time elapsing between two successive passages of the vernal equinox through the meridian of the observer. Since the position of the vernal equinox varies as a result of the *general precession* of the earth the stellar day is about 9 ms shorter than the time taken by the earth to complete a 360° revolution with respect to the fixed stars.

d and d* are related by

$$d = d^*(1 + 1/n)$$

where n is the number of mean solar days in the tropical year.

The stellar day (d*) is divided into 24 stellar hours (h*) each of 60 stellar minutes (min*) each of 60 stellar seconds (s*).

On the *Universal Time* scale the time 12 noon UT is defined by the passages of the mean sun through the zero meridian (Greenwich). Statutory local time scales in use in particular countries are *zonal time* scales (15° difference of longitude $\approx$ 1 h), for example Central European Time (CET) = Universal Time + 1 h. For the differences between the various local times see the yearbooks issued by the Bureau des Longitudes[3].

Times on a particular time scale are often given with the symbols h, m (instead of min) and s raised, for example $2^h25^m3^s$ CET. In astronomy a particular point in time is known as an epoch.

Variations in the polar altitude of the earth and the seasonal variations in the earth's rotation (the latter in a pattern remaining roughly constant from year to year) result in changes in the length of the mean solar day that can be calculated. This has made it possible to define a more uniform scale of Universal Time known as UT 2. Up to 1956 the second of UT 2 was in use for very precise time measurements, but this practice has since been abandoned because the gradual slowing of the earth's rotational speed causes the second of UT 2 to increase by about 2×10^{-10} s per year. Moreover, irregular variations in the earth's rotation may result in fairly rapid changes in the UT second of, for instance, 10^{-8} s during the course of the year.

Multiples of the mean solar day and UT second

Calendar ordinary year = **365** mean solar days = 31 536 0**00** UT seconds

Calendar leap year = 36**6** mean solar days = 31 622 4**00** UT seconds

Mean Julian year (a_{jul}) = (3 calendar ordinary years + 1 calendar leap year)/4 = 365.2**5** mean solar days = 31 557 6**00** UT seconds

Mean Gregorian year (a_{greg}) = (400 a_{jul} − 3 d)/ 400 = 365.242**5** mean solar days = 31 556 95**2** UT seconds

The definitions of the mean Julian and Gregorian years are chosen in such a way that their lengths approximate to that of the tropical year (ca. 365.2422 mean solar days). This figure is not constant but varies not only as a result of changes in the earth's rotation but also because the length of the tropical year itself is variable.

The zero point of the Universal Time scale is January 1 of the year 1 B.C. at 0^h UT, so that the number of the year indicates the number of complete calendar years that have since elapsed. It should be noted that only one calendar year separates 1 B.C. 0^h UT and 1 A.D. 0^h UT.

Up to 1581 each year exactly divisible by 4 was a leap year, as were the years 1, 5, 9, etc. B.C. This constituted the so-called Julian Calendar, introduced by JULIUS CAESAR in 45 B.C. Owing to the fact that the Julian year is some 11 minutes longer than the tropical year (based on the earth's orbital motion) the Julian Calendar showed earlier and earlier dates for natural events like the seasons. The growing discrepancy was finally rectified by the calendar reform introduced by Pope GREGORY XIII's bull of February 24 1582. Under this reform, 10 days were to be dropped from the calendar of the year 1582, October 5–14 inclusive, in order to restore the vernal equinox to March 21. France adopted the reform the same year, dropping the days from December 10 to 19 1582. In England, the Gregorian Calendar was not adopted until 1752, when 11 days, September 3–13, had to be dropped. In order to keep the Gregorian Calendar in step with the tropical years, the reform also laid down that three out of every four century years were to be ordinary years instead of leap years, i.e., that only those century years divisible by 400 were to be leap years. The mean Gregorian year is therefore 0.4 min longer than the tropical year.

Units of time derived from the orbital movement of the earth • Ephemeris Time

The following time intervals are derived from the revolution of the earth around the sun:

The *sidereal year* (a_{sid}) is the time taken by the earth to complete one 360° revolution around the sun, as related to the system of fixed stars. Since it cannot be measured directly the sidereal year is not used in time measurements.

The *anomalistic year* (a_{anom}) is the time elapsing between two successive passages of the earth through the perihelion.

The *astronomical year* (a_{astr}), also known as Bessel's year or annus fictus, is the time during which the right ascension of the (fictitious) mean sun increases by 360°; it differs only slightly from the tropical year.

The *tropical year* (a_{trop}), of great importance in time measurements, is the time elapsing between two successive passages of the true sun through the mean vernal equinox. Owing to the general precession of the earth the vernal equinox moves once round the ecliptic in about 26000 years. In addition to this movement, the vernal equinox is subject to a slight 'secular' acceleration as well as to periodic fluctuations. The fictitious *mean* vernal equinox is not subject to these periodic fluctuations. As a result of the general precession of the earth the tropical year is 20.4 min shorter than the sidereal year, and because of the secular acceleration of the vernal equinox each tropical year is about 5.3 ms shorter than the preceding one. The tropical year remains in phase with the seasons of the earth.

In order to construct calendars the approximate tropical year up to 1581 was calculated from the mean Julian year based on the mean solar day (a_{trop} is 11.2 min shorter) and for 1583 and subsequently from the mean Gregorian year likewise based on the mean solar day (a_{trop} is 0.4 min shorter). The tropical year is also 20.4 min shorter than the sidereal year and 25.1 min shorter than the anomalistic year.

The tropical year at a particular epoch is equal to $360°/(dL/dt)$, where L is the mean longitude of the sun, or angle subtended at the earth by the positions of the mean sun and the mean vernal equinox at that epoch. Owing to the secular acceleration of the vernal equinox the angular velocity dL/dt is a function of time. Of special importance is the length of the tropical year at the epoch 1900, January 0, 12 noon Ephemeris Time, which is December 31

Conversion of units of time

			1 **A** unit = *b* **B** units (*b* in the table)				
	A (Universal Time)		**B** (Universal Time)				
	Name	Symbol	s	min	h	d	Symbol
	second	s	1	$1.\dot{6} \times 10^{-2}$	$2.\dot{7} \times 10^{-4}$	$1.15\dot{7}\,4\dot{0} \times 10^{-5}$	s
Mean solar time	minute	min	$\mathbf{6} \times 10$	1	$1.\dot{6} \times 10^{-2}$	$6.9\dot{4} \times 10^{-4}$	min
Mean solar time	hour	h	$3.\mathbf{6} \times 10^3$	$\mathbf{6} \times 10$	1	$4.1\dot{6} \times 10^{-2}$	h
Mean solar time	day	d	$8.6\mathbf{4} \times 10^4$	$1.4\mathbf{4} \times 10^3$	$2.\mathbf{4} \times 10$	1	d
Mean solar time	month, 28 days		$2.419\,\mathbf{2} \times 10^6$	$4.03\mathbf{2} \times 10^4$	$6.7\mathbf{2} \times 10^2$	$2.\mathbf{8} \times 10$	month 28 d
Mean solar time	month, 29 days		$2.505\,\mathbf{6} \times 10^6$	$4.17\mathbf{6} \times 10^4$	$6.9\mathbf{6} \times 10^2$	$2.\mathbf{9} \times 10$	month 29 d
Mean solar time	month, 30 days		$2.59\mathbf{2} \times 10^6$	$4.3\mathbf{2} \times 10^4$	$7.\mathbf{2} \times 10^2$	$\mathbf{3} \times 10$	month 30 d
Mean solar time	month, 31 days		$2.678\,\mathbf{4} \times 10^6$	$4.46\mathbf{4} \times 10^4$	$7.4\mathbf{4} \times 10^2$	$3.\mathbf{1} \times 10$	month 31 d
Mean solar time	year, 365 days	a_{365}	$3.153\,\mathbf{6} \times 10^7$	$5.25\mathbf{6} \times 10^5$	$8.7\mathbf{6} \times 10^3$	$3.6\mathbf{5} \times 10^2$	a_{365}
Mean solar time	year, 366 days	a_{366}	$3.162\,2\mathbf{4} \times 10^7$	$5.270\,\mathbf{4} \times 10^5$	$8.78\mathbf{4} \times 10^3$	$3.6\mathbf{6} \times 10^2$	a_{366}
Stellar time	stellar second[8]	s*	$9.972\,696 \times 10^{-1}$	$1.662\,116 \times 10^{-2}$	$2.770\,193 \times 10^{-4}$	$1.154\,247 \times 10^{-5}$	s*
Stellar time	stellar minute[8]	min*	$5.983\,617 \times 10$	$9.972\,696 \times 10^{-1}$	$1.662\,116 \times 10^{-2}$	$6.925\,483 \times 10^{-4}$	min*
Stellar time	stellar hour[8]	h*	$3.590\,170 \times 10^3$	$5.983\,617 \times 10$	$9.972\,696 \times 10^{-1}$	$4.155\,290 \times 10^{-2}$	h*
Stellar time	stellar day[8]	d*	$8.616\,409 \times 10^4$	$1.436\,068 \times 10^3$	$2.393\,447 \times 10$	$9.972\,696 \times 10^{-1}$	d*
Calendar years	julian year	a_{jul}	$3.155\,7\mathbf{6} \times 10^7$	$5.259\,\mathbf{6} \times 10^5$	$8.76\mathbf{6} \times 10^3$	$3.652\,\mathbf{5} \times 10^2$	a_{jul}
Calendar years	gregorian year	a_{greg}	$3.155\,695\,\mathbf{2} \times 10^7$	$5.259\,49\mathbf{2} \times 10^5$	$8.765\,8\mathbf{2} \times 10^3$	$3.652\,42\mathbf{5} \times 10^2$	a_{greg}
	A (Ephemeris Time)		**B** (Ephemeris Time)				
At time 1900.0	sidereal year[8]	a_{sid}	$3.155\,814\,97 \times 10^7$	$5.259\,691\,62 \times 10^5$	$8.766\,152\,71 \times 10^3$	$3.652\,563\,63 \times 10^2$	a_{sid}
At time 1900.0	tropical year[8]	a_{trop}	$3.155\,692\,60 \times 10^7$	$5.259\,487\,66 \times 10^5$	$8.765\,812\,77 \times 10^3$	$3.652\,421\,99 \times 10^2$	a_{trop}
At time 1900.0	anomalistic year[8]	a_{anom}	$3.155\,843\,30 \times 10^7$	$5.259\,738\,83 \times 10^5$	$8.766\,231\,38 \times 10^3$	$3.652\,596\,41 \times 10^2$	a_{anom}

1899, 12 noon plus ca. 4.5s Universal Time. At this time the mean longitude of the sun was 279° 41′ 48.04″. The ephemeris second is derived from the length of the tropical year at this particular time.

Because of the fluctuations in the length of the second of Universal Time due to the rotational irregularities of the earth the International Committee of Weights and Measures[4] in 1956 had defined the second as basic unit of the International System of Units (SI units) for use in time and frequency measurements in science and technology as the 31 556 925.9747th part of the tropical year at the epoch 1900, January 0, 12 noon Ephemeris Time. This fraction had been so chosen that the length of the second defined in this way (*ephemeris second*) was identical with the mean second of Universal Time between 1680 and 1895. Measurements of the longitude L of the sun made during this period and related to Universal Time (comparison of the axial and orbital movements of the earth) have been evaluated by Newcomb. For astronomical use the ephemeris second has formed the basis of the very uniform *Ephemeris Time* scale. At the beginning of this century, times on the Ephemeris Time and Universal Time scales still almost coincided, whereas by 1967 they differed by about 37 s as a result of the slowing of the earth's rotation in the period of about 200 years since the time on which the ephemeris second is based. At present the second of Universal Time is about 3×10^{-8} s longer than the ephemeris second.

Since the mean longitude L of the sun cannot be measured with sufficient accuracy Ephemeris Time is actually determined from the motion of the moon. This is possible since lunar theory has now developed to the point where the variable relationship between the moon's orbital and the earth's axial rotational frequencies is well known.

Comparison of Ephemeris Time with Atomic Time[6] commenced in 1954 and led up to the present definition of the second (see above) based on the period of the hyperfine structure transition frequency of the atom of caesium-133.

Multiples of the ephemeris second are analogous to those of the second of Universal Time, e.g., ephemeris day = 86 400 ephemeris seconds. Occasionally the older designation *mean day* (not to be confused with the mean solar day) is used for ephemeris day. It is also sometimes stated that the mean day equals 86 400 seconds of the mean solar day (i.e., seconds of Universal Time) at the time 1900.0. This is, however, incorrect. The mean day is Newcomb's calculated mean value of the mean solar day during the period 1680–1895.

Units of time derived from atomic transitions · Atomic Time

Atomic Time is based on the frequencies corresponding to hyperfine structure transitions in the atoms of the caesium, hydrogen and thallium nuclides ^{133}Cs, ^{1}H and ^{205}Tl; in the classical interpretation such transitions are due to the precession of the electrons of the outer shell (photoelectrons) in the magnetic field of the nucleus. The hydrogen frequency is measured in the *hydrogen maser* and the caesium and thallium frequencies in an *atomic beam resonance apparatus*. To obtain time intervals and time scales the periods of the atomic frequencies must be counted continuously. A typical instrument for this purpose is variously known as a caesium beam apparatus, caesium atomic clock or caesium time and frequency standard.

In the best of present instruments the relative frequency deviation from the natural frequency of the undisturbed atomic transition – after correction for all known disturbing effects – is only about 10^{-12}. This corresponds to a time difference between two atomic clocks of 1 s in 30 000 years.

Since the ephemeris second is known only to an accuracy of 10^{-9} s and is thus inadequate for precise time and frequency measurements the International Committee of Weights and Measures had declared (on the authority of the 12th General Conference[7]) that precise time and frequency measurements could provisionally be made on the basis of a frequency value of 9 192 631 770 Hz for the hyperfine structure transition of the ^{133}Cs atom. The 13th General Conference of Weights and Measures[1] in October 1967 adopted this relationship as the basis for the *new definition* of the SI second, and the ephemeris second continues to be used only in astronomy.

Standard frequency and time-signal transmitters transmit time signals by various systems. Thus UTC (Coordinated Universal Time) signals are transmitted partly with the aid of a time scale derived from atomic clocks that agrees approximately with Universal Time 2 and remains unchanged in each case for one calendar year. When the deviation from Universal Time exceeds 0.1 s the UTC signals are adjusted. Other transmitters send out SAT (Stepped Atomic Time) signals whose time unit is the atomic second. Here too the time signals are adjusted only when the deviation from Universal Time exceeds 0.1 s.

References

1 Conférence Générale des Poids et Mesures, *Comptes rendus des séances de la 13e Conférence générale des Poids et Mesures*, Paris 1967/1968, Bureau International des Poids et Mesures, Sèvres, 1969, pages 60 and 103.

2 Essen, L., *Free Bodily Vibrations of the Terrestrial Planets*, in vol. 11 *of* Beer, A. (Ed.), *Vistas in Astronomy*, Pergamon Press, London, 1969; Beehler et al., *Metrologia*, **1**, 114 (1965); McNish, A.G., *Internat. Sci. Techn.*, No. 47, 58 (1965); Stille, U., *Messen und Rechnen in der Physik*, 2nd ed., Vieweg, Braunschweig, 1961; Becker, G., *Physikalisch-Technische Bundesanstalt Braunschweig, Mitteilungen*, **76**, 315 and 415 (1966); Becker, G., *Naturwiss.*, **54**, 330 (1967).

3 Bureau des Longitudes, *Annuaire pour l'an 1967*, Gauthier-Villars, Paris, 1967, page 270.

4 Comité International des Poids et Mesures, *Proc.-Verb. Com. int. Poids Mes.*, **25**, 77 (1957).

5 Conférence Générale des Poids et Mesures, *Comptes rendus des séances de la 11e Conférence générale des Poids et Mesures*, Paris 1960, Gauthier-Villars, Paris, 1961, page 86.

6 Nicholson and Sadler, *Nature*, **210**, 187 (1966).

7 Conférence Générale des Poids et Mesures, *Comptes rendus des séances de la 12e Conférence générale des Poids et Mesures*, Paris 1964, Gauthier-Villars, Paris, 1964, page 93.

8 Values from or calculated from Bureau des Longitudes, *Annuaire pour l'an 1966*, Gauthier-Villars, Paris, 1965.

Angle ($\alpha, \beta, \gamma, \vartheta, \varphi$)

Dimension = L°

Plane angles

SI unit: radian (rad) = 1 m/m

The plane angle φ between two straight lines a and b is defined as the ratio of the arc s to the radius r of a circle whose centre lies at the point of intersection of the lines.

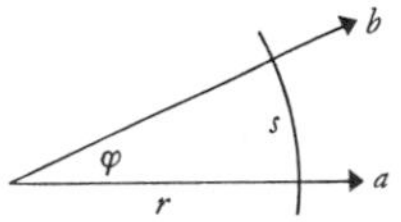

$$\varphi = \frac{s}{r}$$

Since the angle φ is the ratio of two lengths it is a dimensionless quantity.

The radian is defined as the angle between two radii of a circle which cut off on the circumference an arc equal in length to the radius. The right angle, symbol ∟, is equal to $(\pi/2)$ rad; the degree, symbol °, is equal to $(\pi/180)$ rad; the grade (German *Gon*), symbol g, is equal to $(\pi/200)$ rad. There is no special designation for the whole circular angle $2\,\pi$ rad = 4∟ = 360° = 400g; in the conversion table below it is indicated by 'whole', with the symbol $2\,\pi$ rad.

The subdivision of the unit of angle is sexagesimal in the case of the degree:

1 degree (°) = 60 minutes (′) = 60 × 60 seconds (″)

The grade is subdivided centesimally:

1 grade (g) = 100 centesimal minutes (c) = 100 × 100 centesimal seconds (cc)

The radian, right angle and whole circular angle are subdivided decimally without special designation.

Solid angles (Ω)

SI unit: steradian (sr) = 1 m^2/m^2

The solid angle Ω is defined as the ratio F/r^2, where F is that part of the surface of a sphere of radius r cut out by a cone whose apex coincides with the centre of the sphere.

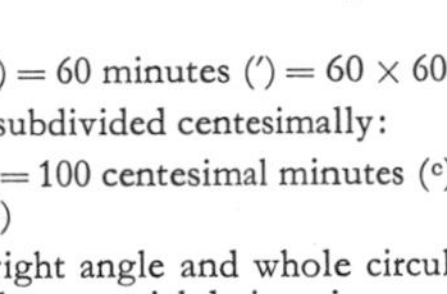

$$\Omega = \frac{F}{r^2}$$

Since the solid angle is the ratio of two areas it is likewise a dimensionless quantity. When the apical angle of the cone is $2\,\varphi$ the following relation holds:

$$\Omega = 2\,\pi\,(1 - \cos\varphi)$$

The steradian (sr) is defined as the solid angle subtended at the centre of a sphere of unit radius by a cap of unit area on the surface of the sphere. The *square degree* [symbol: □° or $(°)^2$] is defined by $(\pi/180)^2$ sr, the *square grade* [symbol: $(^g)^2$] by $(\pi/200)^2$ sr.

Conversion of plane angles

		1 **A** unit = b **B** units (b in the table)		
A		**B**		
Name	Symbol	°	g	rad
degree......	°	1	$1.\dot{1}$	$1.745\,32\dot{8}\times10^{-2}$
minute.....	′	$1.\dot{6}\times10^{-2}$	$1.85\dot{1}\,\dot{8}\dot{5}\times10^{-2}$	$2.908\,882\times10^{-4}$
second.....	″	$2.\dot{7}\times10^{-4}$	$3.086\,420\times10^{-4}$	$4.848\,137\times10^{-6}$
grade.......	g	$\mathbf{9}\times10^{-1}$	1	$1.570\,796\times10^{-2}$
centesimal minute...	c	$\mathbf{9}\times10^{-3}$	10^{-2}	$1.570\,796\times10^{-4}$
centesimal second...	cc	$\mathbf{9}\times10^{-5}$	10^{-4}	$1.570\,796\times10^{-6}$
radian......	rad	$5.729\,579\times10$	$6.366\,198\times10$	1
right angle..	∟	$\mathbf{9}\times10$	10^{2}	1.570 796
whole......	2π rad	$3.\mathbf{6}\times10^{2}$	$\mathbf{4}\times10^{2}$	6.283 185

Conversion of solid angles

		1 **A** unit = b **B** units (b in the table)		
A		**B**		
Name	Symbol	□°	$(^{g})^2$	sr
square degree..	□° $(^\circ)^2$	1	1.234 568	$3.046\,174\times10^{-4}$
square grade...	$(^{g})^2$	$8.\mathbf{1}\times10^{-1}$	1	$2.467\,401\times10^{-4}$
steradian......	sr	$3.282\,806\times10^{3}$	$4.052\,847\times10^{3}$	1

Frequency (ν or $f = 1/T$; T = period)

Dimension = T^{-1}

SI unit: hertz (Hz) = 1 s^{-1}

In Anglo-Saxon usage the reciprocal second as frequency unit is sometimes designated cycle per second (c/s), often wrongly shortened to cycle (c). 1 kilohertz (kHz; kilocycle per second, kc/s) = 1000 Hz.

Angular frequency (pulsatance) $\omega = 2\pi f$ should not be expressed in hertz (Hz) but in reciprocal seconds (s^{-1}). 1 reciprocal millisecond (ms^{-1}) = 1000 s^{-1}.

Frequency of rotation (n)

Dimension = T^{-1}

SI unit: reciprocal second (s^{-1})

Other units

Revolution/second (r s^{-1}) = 1 s^{-1}; revolution/minute (r min^{-1}) = $1.\dot{6}\times10^{-2}$ s^{-1}; revolution/hour (r h^{-1}) = $2.\dot{7}\times10^{-4}$ s^{-1}; revolution/day (r d^{-1}) = $1.5\dot{7}4\dot{0}\times10^{-5}$ s^{-1}

Temperature

Dimension = Θ

The concepts *temperature* and *heat* (quantity of heat) are rigorously differentiated in physics. The same quantity of heat can be distributed over a larger or smaller amount of the same material, which will have a lower temperature in the former case than in the latter.

Heat is a form of energy (see 'Energy', page 212), while the temperature of a body is a measure of the average kinetic energy per degree of freedom of the constituent molecules. Since it is related to the average movement of the latter, the concept of temperature can be applied only to bodies consisting of a large number of molecules. This simple relationship no longer applies at very low temperatures.

Thermodynamic temperature (T) and temperature scales

The only term for temperature that allows clear and consistent expression of all the states, processes and laws of thermodynamics is the thermodynamic temperature T, whether this is introduced by way of relationships between quantities of classical thermodynamics (for instance, the amounts of heat and work in a CARNOT cycle or the behaviour of ideal gases) or statistically defined (either kinetically, starting from the energy distribution of the molecules of a system or from the characteristic parameter $\Theta = kT$ of the GIBBS canonical distribution in statistical mechanics)[1]. In a CARNOT cycle operating between two temperatures T_1 and $T_2 < T_1$ the amounts of heat Q_1 and Q_2 absorbed or liberated are proportional to the corresponding temperatures: $Q_1/Q_2 = T_1/T_2$. According to the Second Law of Thermodynamics the thermodynamic temperature T has a lowest value below which it cannot fall and which can be given the value zero: the 'absolute zero' of thermodynamics. In a CARNOT cycle operating between a finite temperature T_1 and the absolute zero (a special case in physics) the efficiency (η = work done, ΔA, divided by the amount of heat removed, ΔQ) attains the value 1.

International System of Units

The base unit of thermodynamic temperature is the kelvin (K), defined[2,3] as the fraction 1/273.1**6** of the thermodynamic temperature T_{tr} of the triple point of water (the point at which the solid, liquid and gaseous phases of pure water are in equilibrium). The same name kelvin (K) is also used to express an interval or a difference of thermodynamic temperature $\Delta T = T_1 - T_2$*.

This definition is also the basis of the thermodynamic Kelvin scale, starting at the absolute zero T = **0** K, introduced by Lord KELVIN in 1848; as a linear scale this can be constructed from any variable quantity bearing a linear relationship to the thermodynamic temperature T. Such a simple relationship relates the energy of ideal gases to a function of temperature expressed by the equation of state $T = pV_{m0}/R$ (where p = gas pressure, V_{m0} = molar volume of an ideal gas, R = molar gas constant (see under 'Physical Constants', page 228) and can be determined experimentally by means of a gas thermometer.

Anglo-Saxon unit of thermodynamic temperature

Also occasionally used as unit of thermodynamic temperature is the degree Rankine (°R), defined as **5/9** of the kelvin[4]. The thermodynamic Rankine scale starts at the absolute zero T = **0** °R, and can likewise be realized by gas thermometry.

When expressing temperature interval $\Delta T = T_1 - T_2$ the degree Rankine is usually written degR.

Celsius temperature (t) and temperature scale

The Celsius temperature t assigned to a system is defined as the difference between the corresponding thermodynamic temperature T of the system and a special thermodynamic temperature $T_{0,C}$ the value of which has no special physical significance but is arbitrarily chosen and conventionally fixed[4,5,*]: $t = T - T_{0,C}$. The zero point defining Celsius temperature is the temperature $T_{0,C}$ = 273.1**5** K lying 0.0**1** K below the triple point of water.

To express Celsius temperatures the base SI unit kelvin is designated simply degree Celsius (°C). The thermodynamic Celsius scale is subdivided into the same intervals as the thermodynamic Kelvin scale but has a zero point displaced by 273.1**5** K. The Celsius temperature t_0 = **0** °C expresses the same temperature as the thermodynamic temperature $T_{0,C}$ = 273.1**5** K. The degree Celsius (°C) or the kelvin (K), as names and symbols for the same unit, may be used to express an interval or a difference of Celsius temperature $\Delta t = t_1 - t_2$ equal to an interval or difference of thermodynamic temperature $\Delta T = T_1 - T_2$.

Fahrenheit temperature (ϑ) and temperature scale

In English-speaking countries Fahrenheit temperature ϑ also continues in use for the time being. The Fahrenheit temperature assigned to a system is defined as the difference between the corresponding thermodynamic temperature T of the system and a special temperature $T_{0,F}$ established by convention and without special physical significance[4]: $\vartheta = T - T_{0,F}$. The zero point defining Fahrenheit temperature is the temperature $T_{0,F}$ = 459.6**7** °R lying 32.01**8** °R below the triple point of water.

To express Fahrenheit temperatures the degree Rankine is designated simply degree Fahrenheit (°F). The thermodynamic Fahrenheit scale is subdivided into the same intervals as the thermodynamic Rankine scale but has a zero point displaced by 459.6**7** degR. The Fahrenheit temperature ϑ_0 = **0** °F expresses the same temperature as the thermodynamic temperature $T_{0,F}$ = 459.6**7** °R.

* The 13th General Conference of Weights and Measures[3] in October 1967 abrogated the names and symbols previously used – including the degree Kelvin (°K) and degree (deg, for temperature interval or difference) – but agreed that the formulations resulting from the earlier usage should be admitted for the time being. In this chapter on 'Units of Measurement' the text conforms with the new definition of the kelvin (K) but in other chapters of these *Scientific Tables* the old usage is followed.

When expressing a temperature interval or difference $\Delta\vartheta = \vartheta_1 - \vartheta_2$ the degree Fahrenheit is usually written degF (= degR).

Conversion of temperature units and values

(a) Between temperature interval units:

$$1 \text{ degR} = 1 \text{ degF} = \frac{5}{9}\text{K} = \frac{5}{9}{}^\circ\text{C}$$

$$1 \text{ K} = 1\,{}^\circ\text{C} = \frac{9}{5}\text{degR} = \frac{9}{5}\text{degF}$$

(b) For temperature values on the four thermodynamic scales ($T = T_K \text{K} = T_R\,{}^\circ\text{R};\ t = t_C\,{}^\circ\text{C};\ \vartheta = \vartheta_F\,{}^\circ\text{F}$):

$$T_K = \frac{5}{9}T_R = t_C + 273.15 = \frac{5}{9}(\vartheta_F + 459.67)$$

$$T_R = \frac{9}{5}T_K = \vartheta_F + 459.67 = \frac{9}{5}t_C + 491.67$$

$$t_C = T_K - 273.15 = \frac{5}{9}(T_R - 491.67) = \frac{5}{9}(\vartheta_F - 32)$$

$$\vartheta_F = T_R - 459.67 = \frac{9}{5}T_K - 459.67 = \frac{9}{5}t_C + 32$$

Fundamental points of the thermodynamic temperature scales

Unit	Symbol	Temperature value at absolute zero	triple point of water*
kelvin	K	0	273.16
degree Celsius	°C	−273.15	0.01
degree Rankine	°R	0	491.688
degree Fahrenheit	°F	−459.67	32.018

* Temperature at which the solid, liquid and gaseous phases of water are in equilibrium.

Up to 1954 the thermodynamic scales were based on the interval between the melting point of ice (ice point) and the condensing point of steam (steam point), two fixed points assigned the values 273.15 K and 373.15 K. The new definition of the scale by the triple point of water and the absolute zero, which is very near to the old definition, means that the temperatures of the ice and steam point are now values that must be determined experimentally.

International Practical Temperature Scale of 1968 (IPTS-68)

The IPTS-68 was adopted by the International Committee of Weights and Measures[5] in 1968 under the powers conferred on it by Resolution 8 of the 13th General Conference of Weights and Measures[3] in 1967.

The IPTS-68 is based on the assigned values of the temperatures (columns 2 and 3 of the table below) of a number of reproducible equilibrium states (defining fixed points; column 1 of the table) and on standard instruments calibrated at these temperatures. Interpolation between the fixed point temperatures is effected by means of formulae establishing the relationship between the readings of the standard instruments and the temperature values.

Values of the thermodynamic temperature T and of the Celsius temperature t measured on the IPTS-68 are indicated by adding the subscript '68' to the symbol: T_{68}, t_{68}. Values of T_{68} and t_{68} are expressed in kelvin (K) and degree Celsius (°C) respectively, as in the case of T and t.

The defining fixed points are established by realizing specified equilibrium states between phases of pure substances. The standard instruments and interpolation formulae are as follows: in the range $13.81\text{ K} \leqq T_{68} \leqq 730.89\text{ K}$ (freezing point of antimony as a secondary reference point) the platinum resistance thermometer; in the range $730.89\text{ K} \leqq T_{68} \leqq 1337.58\text{ K}$ the platinum–10% rhodium/platinum thermocouple; in the range above 1337.58 K the PLANCK law for radiation in terms of spectral concentration of radiance $L_{e\lambda}$ (see page 222), with 1337.58 K as reference temperature and the value 0.014 388 m K for the 2nd PLANCK radiation constant c_2 (see page 228).

The IPTS-68 has been chosen in such a way that temperature measured on it closely approximates to thermodynamic temperature: $T_{68} = T + \Delta T_{68} \approx T$ and $t_{68} = t + \Delta t_{68} \approx t$. The difference is within the present limits of accuracy of measurement (see column 4 of the table). At the triple point of water both temperature values are exactly equal by definition.

Defining fixed points of the IPTS-68, values assigned to T_{68} and t_{68}, and estimated uncertainties $\Delta T_{68} = \Delta t_{68}$

Defining fixed point (equilibrium state*)	Assigned value T_{68} in K	t_{68} in °C	$\Delta T_{68} = \Delta t_{68}$
Triple point of equilibrium hydrogen	13.81	− 259.34	± 0.01 K
25/76 standard atmosphere point of equilibrium hydrogen	17.042	− 256.108	± 0.01 K
Boiling point of equilibrium hydrogen	20.28	− 252.87	± 0.01 K
Boiling point of neon	27.102	− 246.048	± 0.01 K
Triple point of oxygen	54.361	− 218.789	± 0.01 K
Boiling point of oxygen	90.188	− 182.962	± 0.01 K
Triple point of water***	273.16	0.01	(exact by definition)
Boiling point of water** ***	373.15	100	± 0.005 K
Freezing point of zinc	692.73	419.58	± 0.03 K
Freezing point of silver	1235.08	961.93	± 0.2 K
Freezing point of gold	1337.58	1064.43	± 0.2 K

* Except for the triple points and one equilibrium hydrogen point (17.042 K), assigned temperature values are for equilibrium states at a pressure of one standard atmosphere ($p_0 = 101\,325\text{ N m}^{-2}$).
** The equilibrium state between the solid and liquid phases of tin (freezing point of tin) has the assigned value of $T_{68} = 505.118\,1$ K or $t_{68} = 231.968\,1$ °C (with $\Delta T_{68} = \Delta t_{68} = \pm 0.015$ K) and may be used as an alternative to the boiling point of water.
*** The water used should have the isotopic composition of ocean water.

Practical scales of temperature (outside the IPTS-68 range) for use over the range 0.2 K–5.2 K[5]

Temperatures can be derived from measured vapour pressures of ^{4}He and ^{3}He. The upper limits for use are set by the critical points of the gases (5.2 K for ^{4}He and 3.3 K for ^{3}He) and the lower limits by the minimum vapour pressure capable of practical measurement. On these scales – the '1958 ^{4}He Scale' and the '1962 ^{3}He Scale' – temperature values are denoted by adding the subscript '58' or '62' to the symbol T: T_{58}, T_{62}.

The '1958 ^{4}He Scale', recommended by the International Committee of Weights and Measures in 1958, is defined by a table of ^{4}He vapour pressures versus temperature[6]. The '1962 ^{3}He Scale', recommended by the International Committee of Weights and Measures in 1962, is defined by an equation giving the vapour pressure of ^{3}He as a function of temperature[7]. In the range between 0.9 K and the critical temperature of ^{3}He the temperatures T_{58} and T_{62} are believed to be in agreement to within 0.000 3 K.

References

[1] Cf. DE BOER, J., *Metrologia*, **1**, 158 (1965).
[2] Conférence Générale des Poids et Mesures, *Comptes rendus des séances de la 10e Conférence générale des Poids et Mesures*, Paris 1954, Gauthier-Villars, Paris, 1955, page 79.
[3] Conférence Générale des Poids et Mesures, *Comptes rendus des séances de la 13e Conférence générale des Poids et Mesures*, Paris 1967/1968, Bureau International des Poids et Mesures, Sèvres, 1969: Résolutions 3, 4 and 8, pages 18, 19, 60, 62, 70, 104, 105, A1.
[4] International Organization for Standardization, *Quantities and Units of Heat*, ISO Recommendation R31, Part IV, December 1960; British Standards Institution, *Conversion Factors and Tables*, B.S. 350: Part 1: 1959, page 26.
[5] Comité International des Poids et Mesures, *Proc.-Verb. Com. int. Poids Mes.*, (2), **36** (in press); Comité Consultatif de Thermométrie, 8e session, Washington and Ottawa 1967, page A1; also in *Metrologia* **5**, 35 (1969); National Physical Laboratory, *The International Practical Temperature Scale of 1968*, H.M.S.O., London, 1969; BARBER, C.R., *Nature*, **222**, 929 (1969).
[6] Comité International des Poids et Mesures and Comité Consultatif de Thermométrie, *Proc.-Verb. Com. int. Poids Mes.*, (2) **26-A**, 73 and T 192 (1959); *Nat. Bur. Stand. J. Res.*, **64A**, 1 (1960).
[7] Comité International des Poids et Mesures, *Proc.-Verb. Com. int. Poids Mes.*, (2) **30**, 25, 124 (1962); Comité Consultatif de Thermométrie, 6e session, Paris 1962, page T 183; *Nat. Bur. Stand. J. Res.* **68A**, 547, 559, 567 and 579 (1964).

Density ($\varrho = m/V$)

Dimension = $L^{-3}M$

Coherent units

International System of Units: kilogramme/cubic metre (kg m^{-3})
CGS system: gramme/cubic centimetre (g cm^{-3})
ft-lb-s system: pound per cubic foot (lb ft^{-3})

The *density* (ϱ) of a substance is the ratio of its mass to its volume. Density is dependent on both temperature and pressure, so that these must be specified when density values are given.

The *standard density* of a substance is its density at standard temperature and pressure (0 °C and 760 torr).

Important density constants are the maximum density of air-free water[1] at 760 torr (i.e., at ≈ 4 °C): $\varrho_{max}(H_2O) = 0.999972$ kg dm^{-3} and the standard density of mercury: $\varrho_n(Hg) = 13.59508$ kg dm^{-3} [2].

The product of the density ϱ and the (local) acceleration due to gravity g is the specific weight ($\gamma = \varrho\, g$) of the substance. Specific weight is thus dependent not only on thermodynamic variables but also on the acceleration due to gravity, so that unlike density it is not in fact a *specific* property of a substance.

The *relative density* (d) of a substance is the ratio of its density to that of a reference substance. As the ratio of two quantities with the same dimensions it is a dimensionless quantity. Relative density is still often given the name 'specific gravity', but this is a term open to the same objection as specific weight. The usual reference density for liquids and solids is the maximum density of water, for gases the standard density of dry air free of carbon dioxide ($\varrho_n = 1.2928 \times 10^{-0}$ kg dm^{-3})[3].

Since the maximum density of water is very nearly equal to 1 kg dm^{-3} relative, density in practice can usually be equated numerically with density expressed in kg dm^{-3}. Since relative density is the ratio of two densities, two particular temperatures must be specified. Thus the relative density of a substance at 20 °C/4 °C is the ratio

$$\frac{\text{density of the substance at 20 °C}}{\text{density of water at 4 °C}}$$

written as d_4^{20}.

Conversion of metric units of density

		1 **A** unit = b **B** units (b in the table)	
A		**B**	
Name	Symbol	mg mm^{-3} g cm^{-3} kg dm^{-3}	mg cm^{-3} g dm^{-3} kg m^{-3}
microgramme per cubic centimetre … or millilitre …	µg cm^{-3} µg ml^{-1}	10^{-6}	10^{-3}
milligramme per cubic decimetre … or litre …	mg dm^{-3} mg l^{-1}		
milligramme per cubic centimetre … or millilitre …	mg cm^{-3} mg ml^{-1}	10^{-3}	1
gramme per cubic decimetre … or litre …	g dm^{-3} g l^{-1}		
kilogramme per cubic metre . .	kg m^{-3}		
picogramme per cubic micrometre …	pg µm^{-3}	1	10^3
milligramme per cubic millimetre … or microlitre …	mg mm^{-3} mg µl^{-1}		
gramme per cubic centimetre … or millilitre …	g cm^{-3} g ml^{-1}		
kilogramme per cubic decimetre … or litre …	kg dm^{-3} kg l^{-1}		

Conversion of Anglo-Saxon units of density

		1 **A** unit = b **B** units (b in the table)	
A		**B**	
Name	Symbol	lb ft^{-3}	kg m^{-3}
pound per cubic foot . . .	lb ft^{-3}	1	$1.601\,85 \times 10$
pound per gallon (UK) .	lb gal(UK)$^{-1}$	6.228 83	$9.977\,64 \times 10$
pound per gallon (US) .	lb gal(US)$^{-1}$	172**8**/231	$1.198\,26 \times 10^2$

References

[1] Comité International des Poids et Mesures, *Proc.-Verb. Com. int. Poids Mes.* (2), **22**, 77 (1950); Stille, U., *Messen und Rechnen in der Physik*, 2nd ed., Vieweg, Braunschweig, 1961, page 286.

[2] Cook and Stone, *Phil. Trans. Roy. Soc.*, **250A**, 279 (1957); Cook, A. H., *Phil. Trans. Roy. Soc.*, **254A**, 125 (1961); Beattie et al., *Proc. Amer. Acad. Arts Sci.*, **74**, 371 (1941).

[3] Otto and Thomas, in Hausen, H. (Ed.), *Landolt-Börnstein, Physikalisch-chemische Tabellen*, 6th ed., vol. 4, part 4, section a, Springer, Berlin, 1967, page 174; Din, F., *Thermodynamic Functions of Gases*, vol. 2, Butterworth, London, 1956.

Linear velocity (u or $v = ds/dt$; s = distance)

Dimension = LT^{-1}

Coherent units

International System of Units: metre per second (m s^{-1})
CGS system: centimetre per second (cm s^{-1})
ft-lb-s system: foot per second (ft s^{-1})

Conversion of metric units of velocity

		1 **A** unit = b **B** units (b in the table)		
A		**B**		
Name	Symbol	m min^{-1}	km h^{-1}	m s^{-1}
centimetre per second	cm s^{-1}	$\mathbf{6}\times10^{-1}$	$\mathbf{3.6}\times10^{-2}$	10^{-2}
metre per minute	m min^{-1}	1	$\mathbf{6}\times10^{-2}$	$1.\dot{6}\times10^{-2}$
kilometre per hour	km h^{-1}	$1.\dot{6}\times10$	1	$2.\dot{7}\times10^{-1}$
metre per second	m s^{-1}	$\mathbf{6}\times10$	**3.6**	1
kilometre per second	km s^{-1}	$\mathbf{6}\times10^4$	$\mathbf{3.6}\times10^3$	10^3

Conversion of Anglo-Saxon units of velocity

		1 **A** unit = b **B** units (b in the table)		
A		**B**		
Name	Symbol	ft s^{-1}	mile h^{-1}	m s^{-1}
foot per minute .	ft min^{-1}	$1.\dot{6}\times10^{-2}$	$1.\dot{1}3\dot{6}\times10^{-2}$	$5.0\mathbf{8}\times10^{-3}$
foot per second .	ft s^{-1}	1	$6.\dot{8}\dot{1}\times10^{-1}$	$3.04\mathbf{8}\times10^{-1}$
mile per hour	mile h^{-1}	$1.4\dot{6}$	1	$4.470\,\mathbf{4}\times10^{-1}$
knot, nautical mile per hour . .	kn = n mile/h	1.687 81	1.150 78	$5.1\dot{4}\times10^{-1}$
knot (UK), nautical mile (UK) per hour . .	kn (UK) = n mile (UK)/h	1.688 89	$1.\dot{1}\dot{5}$	$5.147\,72\times10^{-1}$
mile per second .	mile s^{-1}	$5.2\mathbf{8}\times10^3$	$3.\mathbf{6}\times10^3$	$1.609\,34\mathbf{4}\times10^3$

Angular velocity ($\omega = d\varphi/dt$)

Dimension = L° T^{-1}

SI unit: radian per second (rad s^{-1})

Conversion of units of angular velocity

		1 **A** unit = b **B** units (b in the table)		
A		**B**		
Name	Symbol	^{g} s^{-1}	° s^{-1}	rad s^{-1}
grade per minute . .	^{g} min^{-1}	$1.\dot{6}\times10^{-2}$	$\mathbf{1.5}\times10^{-2}$	$2.617\,99\times10^{-4}$
degree per minute . .	° min^{-1}	$1.\dot{8}5\dot{1}\times10^{-2}$	$1.\dot{6}\times10^{-2}$	$2.908\,88\times10^{-4}$
grade per second . .	^{g} s^{-1}	1	$\mathbf{9}\times10^{-1}$	$1.570\,80\times10^{-2}$
radian per minute . .	rad min^{-1}	1.061 03	$9.549\,30\times10^{-1}$	$1.\dot{6}\times10^{-2}$
degree per second . .	° s^{-1}	$1.\dot{1}$	1	$1.745\,33\times10^{-2}$
radian per second . .	rad s^{-1} . .	$6.366\,20\times10$	$5.729\,58\times10$	1

Acceleration ($a = dv/dt$)

Dimension = LT^{-2}

Coherent units

International System of Units: metre per second squared (m s^{-2})
CGS system: centimetre per second squared (cm s^{-2})
= galileo (Gal) (for acceleration due to gravity)
ft-lb-s system: foot per second squared (ft s^{-2})

The internationally accepted value[1] of the normal acceleration due to gravity (see also page 230) is

$$g_n = 9.806\,\mathbf{65}\ \mathrm{m\ s^{-2}} = 980.66\mathbf{5}\ \mathrm{Gal\ (cm\ s^{-2})} \approx 32.174\,05\ \mathrm{ft\ s^{-2}}$$

Conversion of metric units of acceleration

		1 **A** unit = *b* **B** units (*b* in the table)		
A		**B**		
Name	Symbol	Gal = cm s⁻²	km h⁻¹ s⁻¹	m s⁻²
galileo	Gal	} 1	3.**6** × 10⁻²	10⁻²
centimetre per second squared	cm s⁻²			
kilometre per hour per second	km h⁻¹ s⁻¹	$2.\dot{7} \times 10$	1	$2.\dot{7} \times 10^{-1}$
metre per second squared	m s⁻²	10²	3.**6**	1

Conversion of Anglo-Saxon units of acceleration

		1 **A** unit = *b* **B** units (*b* in the table)		
A		**B**		
Name	Symbol	ft s⁻²	mile h⁻¹ s⁻¹	m s⁻²
foot per second squared	ft s⁻²	1	$6.\dot{8}\dot{1} \times 10^{-1}$	3.04**8** × 10⁻¹
mile per hour per second	mile h⁻¹ s⁻¹	$1.4\dot{6}$	1	4.470 **4** × 10⁻¹

Reference

[1] Conférence Générale des Poids et Mesures, *Comptes rendus des séances de la 3e Conférence générale des Poids et Mesures*, Paris 1901, Gauthier-Villars, Paris, 1901, page 70.

Force (F) (= mass × acceleration)

Dimension = L M T⁻²

Coherent units

International System of Units: newton (N) = m kg s⁻² = 10⁵ dyn
CGS system: dyne (dyn) = cm g s⁻² = 10⁻⁵ N
ft-lb-s system: poundal (pdl) = ft lb s⁻² = 0.138 254 954 37**6** N

Noncoherent 'technical' units of force

In technology many units of force are still in use in which the mass unit (kilogramme, pound, etc.) is multiplied not by the coherent unit of acceleration (1 m s⁻², 1 ft s⁻², etc.) but by the standard acceleration due to gravity g_n = 9.806 **65** m s⁻². There is no international uniformity in the nomenclature of these 'technical' units of force. In English- and French-speaking countries the word '-force' is added to the name of the unit of mass and the letter 'f' to the symbol – for example, pound-force (lbf), kilogramme-force (kgf). In some countries 'technical' units of force formed from the gramme and its decimal multiples or parts are known as the pond (p), kilopond (kp), millipond (mp), etc., while in Switzerland the names 'Gramm-Kraft' (gf), 'Kilogramm-Kraft' (kgf), 'Milligramm-Kraft' (mgf), etc. are used. In Germany, in order to avoid the ambiguity in the meaning of the word 'weight' (used for both mass m and force $G = m\,g$, g being the local acceleration due to gravity), it has been suggested[1] that the term should be abandoned and the expressions 'mass' and 'weight-force' used as appropriate. Thus a body whose mass on the balance is m = 65 kg exerts a weight-force on the balance of $G = m\,g = (g/g_n) \times 65$ kp ≈ 65 kp.

The 'technical' units of force are in themselves superfluous and will in due course cease to be used. In scientific work they should in any case be avoided. In some countries, particularly France, they are no longer statutory units.

Reference

[1] Deutscher Normenausschuß, *Masse, Gewicht, Gewichtskraft, Fallbeschleunigung: Begriffe*, DIN 1305, June 1968, Beuth-Vertrieb, Berlin, 1968.

Angular acceleration ($\alpha = \mathrm{d}\omega/\mathrm{d}t = \mathrm{d}^2\varphi/\mathrm{d}t^2$)

Dimension = L⁰ T⁻²

SI unit: radian per second squared (rad s⁻²)

Conversion of units of angular acceleration

		1 **A** unit = *b* **B** units (*b* in the table)		
A		**B**		
Name	Symbol	ᵍ s⁻²	° s⁻²	rad s⁻²
grade per second squared	ᵍ s⁻²	1	**9** × 10⁻¹	1.570 80 × 10⁻²
degree per second squared	° s⁻²	$1.\dot{1}$	1	1.745 33 × 10⁻²
radian per second squared	rad s⁻²	6.366 20 × 10	5.729 58 × 10	1

Conversion of noncoherent units of force (g_n = standard acceleration due to gravity = 9.806 **65** m s⁻² = 32.174 048 ft s⁻²)

			1 **A** unit = *b* **B** units (*b* in the table)	
A			**B**	
Name	Symbol	Definition	pdl	N
grain-force	grf	g_n × (1 gr)	4.596 29 × 10⁻³	6.354 60 × 10⁻⁴
pond .... gramme-force	p gf	} g_n × (1 g)	7.093 16 × 10⁻²	9.806 **65** × 10⁻³
pound-force	lbf	g_n × (1 lb)	3.217 40 × 10	4.448 22
kilopond .... kilogramme-force	kp kgf	} g_n × (1 kg)	7.093 16 × 10	9.806 **65**
short ton-force	sh tnf	g_n × (1 sh tn)	6.434 81 × 10⁴	8.896 44 × 10³
ton-force (UK)............ long ton-force (US)............ }	tonf	} g_n × (1 ton)	7.206 99 × 10⁴	9.964 02 × 10³

Pressure (p) (= force/area)

Dimension = L⁻¹ M T⁻²

Coherent units

International System of Units: newton per square metre (N m⁻²) = m⁻¹ kg s⁻² = 10 dyn cm⁻²
CGS system: dyne per square centimetre (dyn cm⁻²) = cm⁻¹ g s⁻² = 0.1 N m⁻²
ft-lb-s system: poundal per square foot (pdl ft⁻²) = ft⁻¹ lb s⁻² = 1.488 163 943 N m⁻²

Noncoherent metric units of pressure

The 10⁶ multiple of the dyn cm⁻² is known as the *bar* (bar).

1 bar = 10³ millibar (mbar) = 10⁵ N m⁻² = 10⁶ dyn cm⁻²
= 10⁶ microbar (μbar)

The millibar is now the internationally accepted unit of pressure in meteorology*; the microbar is used in acoustics for sound pressure data.

* In meteorology the millibar is widely, but wrongly, denoted by the symbol mb, the recognized symbol for millibarn (see page 202).

Conversion of metric units of pressure

A		1 **A** unit = b **B** units (b in the table) B			
Name	Symbol	dyn cm^{-2} = μbar	N m^{-2}	mbar	bar
dyne per square centimetre ...... microbar	dyn cm^{-2} μbar	1	10^{-1}	10^{-3}	10^{-6}
newton per square metre	N m^{-2}	10	1	10^{-2}	10^{-5}
millibar	mbar	10^3	10^2	1	10^{-3}
bar	bar	10^6	10^5	10^3	1

Noncoherent 'technical' units of pressure

These are derived from the 'technical' units of force and the units of area. The *technical atmosphere* (at) is widely used:

$$1 \text{ at} = 10^4 \text{ kilopond/square metre (kp m}^{-2}) = 1 \text{ kilopond/square centimetre (kp cm}^{-2}) = 9.806\,\mathbf{65} \times 10^4 \text{ N m}^{-2} = \frac{9.806\,\mathbf{65} \times 10^4}{1.013\,\mathbf{25} \times 10^5} \text{ atm} = 0.967\,841\,105 \text{ atm}$$

Noncoherent special units of pressure

Standard physical atmosphere (atm). Defined in connection with the International Practical Scale of Temperature of 1948[1] as

$$1 \text{ atm} = 101\,\mathbf{325} \text{ N m}^{-2} = 1\,013\,25\mathbf{0} \text{ dyn cm}^{-2}$$

Torr (torr). Defined as
$1 \text{ torr} = 1 \text{ atm}/76\mathbf{0} = 133.322\,368 \text{ N m}^{-2} = 1333.223\,68 \text{ dyn cm}^{-2}$

*Millimetre of water** (mm water). Defined as the pressure exerted by a column of water 1 mm in height at its maximum density (0.999 972 g cm^{-3}) at standard pressure (760 torr) under the standard acceleration due to gravity g_n:

$$1 \text{ mm water} = 0.1 \text{ cm} \times 0.999\,972 \text{ g cm}^{-3} \times 980.66\mathbf{5} \text{ cm s}^{-2} = 9.806\,375\,41 \text{ N m}^{-2} = 98.063\,754\,1 \text{ dyn cm}^{-2}$$

*Conventional millimetre of water** (mmH_2O). Defined as the pressure exerted by a column of liquid 1 mm in height with a density of 1 g cm^{-3} under the standard acceleration due to gravity g_n:

$$1 \text{ mmH}_2\text{O} = 0.1 \text{ cm} \times 1 \text{ g cm}^{-3} \times 980.66\mathbf{5} \text{ cm s}^{-2} = 9.806\,6\mathbf{5} \text{ N m}^{-2} = 98.066\,\mathbf{5} \text{ dyn cm}^{-2} = 1 \text{ kp m}^{-2}$$

In practice this definition is based on a column of water 1 mm in height at 4 °C at standard pressure.

*Conventional millimetre of mercury** (mmHg). In accordance with the International Barometric Conventions of the World Meteorological Organization[2] this is defined as the pressure exerted by a column of liquid 1 mm in height with a density of 13.595 **1** g cm^{-3} under the standard acceleration due to gravity g_n:

$$1 \text{ mmHg} = 0.1 \text{ cm} \times 13.595\,\mathbf{1} \text{ g cm}^{-3} \times 980.66\mathbf{5} \text{ cm s}^{-2} = 133.322\,387 \text{ N m}^{-2} = 1\,333.223\,87 \text{ dyn cm}^{-2} = 1.000\,000\,14 \text{ torr}$$

In practice this definition is based with adequate accuracy on a column of mercury 1 mm in height at 0 °C at standard pressure (1 atm = 101 3**25** N m^{-2}).

The noncoherent Anglo-Saxon units of pressure, conventional inch of water (inH_2O), conventional foot of water (ftH_2O) and conventional inch of mercury (inHg), are defined by the formulae given for conventional millimetre of water and conventional millimetre of mercury by replacing the metric length unit (0.1 cm) by 1 inch or 1 foot.

For very precise measurements the unit torr is now preferred to the mmHg since unlike the latter the torr is independent of material constants.

Standard pressure in both physics and meteorology is 101 3**25** N m^{-2} = 1 atm = 76**0** torr. It is roughly the mean atmospheric pressure at sea level under the standard acceleration due to gravity.

* The names of these units of pressure actually signify the height h at which the barometer liquid with density ϱ under the acceleration due to gravity g exerts the pressure $p = g\,h\,\varrho$.

Conversion of noncoherent units of pressure

A		1 **A** unit = b **B** units (b in the table) B		
Name	Symbol	atm	pdl ft^{-2}	N m^{-2}
millimetre of water	mm water	$9.678\,14 \times 10^{-5}$	6.589 58	9.806 38
kilopond per square metre .... kilogramme-force per square metre	kp m^{-2} kgf m^{-2}	$9.678\,41 \times 10^{-5}$	6.589 76	9.806 **65**
pound-force per square foot	lbf ft^{-2}	$4.725\,41 \times 10^{-4}$	$3.217\,40 \times 10$	$4.788\,03 \times 10$
torr	torr	$1.315\,79 \times 10^{-3}$	$8.958\,85 \times 10$	$1.333\,22 \times 10^2$
conventional inch of water........................	inH_2O	$2.458\,32 \times 10^{-3}$	$1.673\,80 \times 10^2$	$2.490\,89 \times 10^2$
conventional foot of water........................	ftH_2O	$2.949\,98 \times 10^{-2}$	$2.008\,56 \times 10^3$	$2.989\,07 \times 10^3$
conventional inch of mercury	inHg	$3.342\,11 \times 10^{-2}$	$2.275\,55 \times 10^3$	$3.386\,39 \times 10^3$
pound-force per square inch	lbf in^{-2}	$6.804\,60 \times 10^{-2}$	$4.633\,06 \times 10^3$	$6.894\,76 \times 10^3$
technical atmosphere	at	$9.678\,41 \times 10^{-1}$	$6.589\,76 \times 10^4$	$9.806\,\mathbf{65} \times 10^4$
physical atmosphere	atm	1	$6.808\,73 \times 10^4$	$1.013\,\mathbf{25} \times 10^5$
ton-force per square foot	tonf ft^{-2}	1.058 49	$7.206\,99 \times 10^4$	$1.072\,52 \times 10^5$

References

[1] Conférence Générale des Poids et Mesures, *Comptes rendus des séances de la 9e Conférence générale des Poids et Mesures*, Paris 1948, Gauthier-Villars, Paris, 1949, pages 57 and 89; *Comptes rendus des séances de la 10e Conférence générale des Poids et Mesures*, Paris 1954, Gauthier-Villars, Paris, 1955, page 79.

[2] World Meteorological Organization, *International Barometric Conventions*, in British Standards Institution, *Barometer Conventions and Tables*, B.S. 2520: 1954, and in Stille, U., *Messen und Rechnen in der Physik*, 2nd ed., Vieweg, Braunschweig, 1961.

Energy, Work, Amount of heat

Dimension = $L^2 M T^{-2}$

Coherent units

International System of Units: joule (J) = newton × metre = m^2 kg s^{-2} = 10^7 erg = watt second (Ws) (for W see under 'Power', page 214)
CGS system: erg (erg) = dyne × centimetre = cm^2 g s^{-2} = 10^{-7} J
ft-lb-s system: foot poundal (ft pdl) = ft^2 lb s^{-2} = 0.042 140 110 1 J

Symbols

Energy = E, W
Potential energy = E_p, V, Φ
Kinetic energy = E_K, T, K
Work = W, A
Amount of heat = Q
Radiant energy = Q, Q_e, W (see also page 222)

Energy, *work* and *amount of heat* are physical quantities with the same dimensions and ideally should be measured in a common unit. In the International System of Units this simplification has

Conversion of noncoherent units of energy

A		1 **A** unit = b **B** units (b in the table) **B**		
Name	Symbol	kWh	ft pdl	J
foot pound-force	ft lbf	$3.766\,16 \times 10^{-7}$	$3.217\,40 \times 10$	$1.355\,82$
thermochemical calorie	$cal_{thermochem}$	1.162×10^{-6}	$9.928\,78 \times 10$	$4.18\mathbf{4}$
15° calorie	cal_{15}	$1.162\,6 \times 10^{-6}$	$9.932\,34 \times 10$	$4.185\,5$
International Steam Table calorie	cal_{IT}	$1.16\mathbf{3} \times 10^{-6}$	$9.935\,43 \times 10$	$4.186\,\mathbf{8}$
kilopond metre, kilogramme-force mètre	kp m = kgf m	$2.724\,07 \times 10^{-6}$	$2.327\,15 \times 10^{2}$	$9.806\,6\mathbf{5}$
litre atmosphere	l atm	$2.814\,58 \times 10^{-5}$	$2.404\,48 \times 10^{3}$	$1.013\,2\mathbf{5} \times 10^{2}$
British thermal unit	Btu	$2.930\,71 \times 10^{-4}$	$2.503\,69 \times 10^{4}$	$1.055\,06 \times 10^{3}$
horsepower-hour	hph	$7.457\,00 \times 10^{-1}$	$6.370\,46 \times 10^{7}$	$2.684\,52 \times 10^{6}$
metric horsepower-hour	ch or PSh	$7.354\,987\,\mathbf{5} \times 10^{-1}$	$6.283\,31 \times 10^{7}$	$2.647\,80 \times 10^{6}$
kilowatt hour	kWh	1	$8.542\,93 \times 10^{7}$	$3.\mathbf{6} \times 10^{6}$

Conversion of units of energy used in atomic physics [2,7]

A			1 **A** unit equals or corresponds to b **B** units (b in the table) **B**		
Name	Identifying formula	Symbol	g	J	erg
gramme	$\triangleq E(g) = c^2 \times (1 g)$	g	1	$8.987\,554 \times 10^{13}$	$8.987\,554 \times 10^{20}$
joule		J	$1.112\,6 \times 10^{-14}$	1	1×10^{7}
erg		erg	$1.112\,6 \times 10^{-21}$	1×10^{-7}	1
atomic mass unit	$\triangleq E(u) = c^2 \times (1 u)$	u	$1.660\,4 \times 10^{-24}$	$1.492\,32 \times 10^{-10}$	$1.492\,32 \times 10^{-3}$
rydberg	$h c R_\infty$	Ry	$2.425\,3 \times 10^{-32}$	$2.179\,71 \times 10^{-18}$	$2.179\,71 \times 10^{-11}$
electronvolt	$e \times (1 V)$	eV	$1.782\,6 \times 10^{-33}$	$1.602\,10 \times 10^{-19}$	$1.602\,10 \times 10^{-12}$
centimetre^{-1}	$\triangleq E(cm^{-1}) = hc \times (1 cm^{-1})$	cm^{-1}	$2.210\,1 \times 10^{-37}$	$1.986\,30 \times 10^{-23}$	$1.986\,30 \times 10^{-16}$
kelvin	$\triangleq E(K) = k \times (1 K)$	K	$1.536\,1 \times 10^{-37}$	$1.380\,54 \times 10^{-23}$	$1.380\,54 \times 10^{-16}$
second^{-1}	$\triangleq E(s^{-1}) = h \times (s^{-1})$	s^{-1}	$7.372\,0 \times 10^{-48}$	$6.625\,59 \times 10^{-34}$	$6.625\,59 \times 10^{-27}$
Name	Identifying formula	Symbol	u	Ry	eV
gramme	$\triangleq E(g) = c^2 \times (1 g)$	g	$6.022\,5 \times 10^{23}$	$4.123\,3 \times 10^{31}$	$5.609\,85 \times 10^{32}$
joule		J	$6.701\,0 \times 10^{9}$	$4.587\,8 \times 10^{17}$	$6.241\,81 \times 10^{18}$
erg		erg	$6.701\,0 \times 10^{2}$	$4.587\,8 \times 10^{10}$	$6.241\,81 \times 10^{11}$
atomic mass unit	$\triangleq E(u) = c^2 \times (1 u)$	u	1	$6.846\,4 \times 10^{7}$	$9.314\,78 \times 10^{8}$
rydberg	$h c R_\infty$	Ry	$1.460\,6 \times 10^{-8}$	1	$1.360\,54 \times 10$
electronvolt	$e \times (1 V)$	eV	$1.073\,6 \times 10^{-9}$	$7.350\,0 \times 10^{-2}$	1
centimetre^{-1}	$\triangleq E(cm^{-1}) = hc \times (1 cm^{-1})$	cm^{-1}	$1.331\,0 \times 10^{-13}$	$9.112\,7 \times 10^{-6}$	$1.239\,81 \times 10^{-4}$
kelvin	$\triangleq E(K) = k \times (1 K)$	K	$9.250\,9 \times 10^{-14}$	$6.333\,6 \times 10^{-6}$	$8.617\,06 \times 10^{-5}$
second^{-1}	$\triangleq E(s^{-1}) = h \times (s^{-1})$	s^{-1}	$4.439\,8 \times 10^{-24}$	$3.039\,7 \times 10^{-16}$	$4.135\,56 \times 10^{-15}$
Name	Identifying formula	Symbol	cm^{-1}	K	s^{-1}
gramme	$\triangleq E(g) = c^2 \times (1 g)$	g	$4.524\,8 \times 10^{36}$	$6.510\,2 \times 10^{36}$	$1.356\,5 \times 10^{47}$
joule		J	$5.034\,5 \times 10^{22}$	$7.243\,5 \times 10^{22}$	$1.509\,3 \times 10^{33}$
erg		erg	$5.034\,5 \times 10^{15}$	$7.243\,5 \times 10^{15}$	$1.509\,3 \times 10^{26}$
atomic mass unit	$\triangleq E(u) - c^2 \times (1 u)$	u	$7.513\,1 \times 10^{12}$	$1.081\,0 \times 10^{13}$	$2.252\,4 \times 10^{23}$
rydberg	$h c R_\infty$	Ry	$1.097\,4 \times 10^{5}$	$1.578\,9 \times 10^{5}$	$3.289\,8 \times 10^{15}$
electronvolt	$e \times (1 V)$	eV	$8.065\,7 \times 10^{3}$	$1.160\,5 \times 10^{4}$	$2.418\,0 \times 10^{14}$
centimetre^{-1}	$\triangleq E(cm^{-1}) = hc \times (1 cm^{-1})$	cm^{-1}	1	$1.438\,8$	$2.997\,9 \times 10^{10}$
kelvin	$\triangleq E(K) = k \times (1 K)$	K	$6.950\,3 \times 10^{-1}$	1	$2.083\,6 \times 10^{10}$
second^{-1}	$\triangleq E(s^{-1}) = h \times (s^{-1})$	s^{-1}	$3.335\,6 \times 10^{-11}$	$4.799\,3 \times 10^{-11}$	1

now been achieved, and many of the present noncoherent 'mechanical', 'electrical' and 'caloric' units will eventually be of historical interest only. This is likely to take a long time, however, since the traditional units of this kind, for instance the calorie, are deeply rooted in technical as well as everyday usage. In scientific work, amount of heat should now be expressed only in joules. Where 'caloric' units are still used, however, they should at least be limited to those exactly convertible into joules[7].

Noncoherent units of energy

Foot pound-force = ft × lbf (for lbf see under 'Force', page 211).

Thermochemical calorie ($cal_{thermochem}$). Newly defined[2,3,4] in 1948 as 1 $cal_{thermochem}$ = 4.18**4** J.

15° Calorie (cal_{15}), also known as *gramme-calorie*. This is defined as the amount of heat required to warm 1 g of water from 14.5 °C to 15.5 °C at a pressure of 1 standard atmosphere. This unit is thus dependent on the specific heat of water at 15 °C at the pressure p_n = 1 atm. The values for the specific heat capacity of water between 0 and 100 °C agreed upon in 1950 by the International Committee of Weights and Measures[5] are given in joules and 15° calories on page 230 (relative uncertainty ≈ 0.01%). – 15° kilocalorie ($kcal_{15}$) = 1000 cal_{15}.

International Steam Table calorie (cal_{IT}). In 1956 the 5th International Conference on Properties of Steam[2,3,6] redefined the International Steam Table calorie as 1 cal_{IT} = 4.186**8** J.

Kilopond metre (kp m) or *kilogramme-force mètre* (kgf m). (For kp and kgf see under 'Force', page 211.)

Litre atmosphere (new) = l × atm = 1 dm³ × atm = 101.32**5** J. The old litre atmosphere based on the earlier definition of the litre abandoned in 1964 (see page 203) was equal to 1.000 02**8** dm³ atm = 101.327 8 ... J.

British thermal unit ($B.t.u._{IT}$ = Btu). Like the Steam Table calorie this was redefined in 1956[2,3,6] (for lb see under 'Mass', page 204):

$$1 \text{ Btu} = 4.186\mathbf{8}\ \frac{\text{degF}}{\text{K}} \times \frac{\text{lb}}{\text{g}}\ \text{J} = 2.32\mathbf{6}\ \frac{\text{lb}}{\text{g}}\ \text{J}$$

Horsepower-hour (hph) = hp × h; 1 hp = **550** ft lbf s^{-1} (for lbf see under 'Force', page 211).

Metric horsepower-hour (French ch h, German PSh) = ch (or PS) × h; 1 ch (or PS) = **75** m kp s^{-1} (for kp see under 'Force', page 211).

Kilowatt hour (kWh) = kW × h; 1 W = 1 J s^{-1}.

Units of energy and energy equivalents in atomic and nuclear physics

The units of energy used in atomic and nuclear physics contain one or more physical constants as factors, namely the velocity of light in vacuum c, elementary charge e, PLANCK constant h, AVOGADRO constant N_A, BOLTZMANN constant k and RYDBERG constant R_∞. These constants are used to define the energy units rydberg (Ry) and electronvolt (eV) as well as the following energy equivalents (treated as energy units because they are proportional to energy): gramme [g ~ E(g)], atomic mass unit [u ~ E(u)], centimetre^{-1} [cm^{-1} ~ E(cm^{-1})], kelvin [K ~ E(K)] and second^{-1} [s^{-1} ~ E(s^{-1})]. The relationships of these energy units to those used in macrophysics (joule and erg) depend numerically on the results of determinations of the atomic constants. For the physical constants and other units and measures of energy in atomic and nuclear physics see the table on pages 228 and 229.

References

1 Conférence Générale des Poids et Mesures, *Comptes rendus des séances de la 9e Conférence générale des Poids et Mesures*, Paris 1948, Gauthier-Villars, Paris, 1949, pages 55 and 63.
2 Stille, U., *Messen und Rechnen in der Physik*, 2nd ed., Vieweg, Braunschweig, 1961.
3 International Organization for Standardization, *Quantities and Units of Mechanics*, ISO Recommendation R31, part III, December 1960.
4 Rossini, F. D., *Nat. Bur. Stand. J. Res.*, **6**, 1 (1931); Wagman et al., *Nat. Bur. Stand. J. Res.*, **34**, 143 (1945).
5 Comité International des Poids et Mesures, *Proc.-Verb. Com. int. Poids Mes.*, **22**, 79 (1950).
6 Schmidt, E., *Brennstoff, Wärme, Kraft*, **9**, 432 (1957).
7 Cohen and DuMond, *Rev. mod. Phys.*, **37**, 537 (1965); International Union of Pure and Applied Physics, *Symbols, Units and Nomenclature in Physics*, Document U.I.P. 11 (S.U.N. 65-3), 1965, page 30.

Power (P) (= energy/time = force × velocity)

Dimension = $L^2 M T^{-3}$

Coherent units

International System of Units: watt (W) = joule per second = newton × metre per second = m^2 kg s^{-3} = 10^7 erg s^{-1}.
CGS system: erg per second (erg s^{-1}) = dyne × centimetre per second = cm^2 g s^{-3} = 10^{-7} W
ft-lb-s system: foot poundal per second (ft pdl s^{-1}) = ft^2 lb s^{-3} = 0.042 140 110 1 W

Conversion of noncoherent units of power

The units of power related to the second (e.g., cal$_{IT}$ s^{-1}) are converted into ft pdl s^{-1} or watt (= J s^{-1}) by means of the factors given for the conversion of the noncoherent units of energy (page 212).

1 **A** unit = b **B** units (b in the table)			
A		**B**	
Name	Symbol	ft pdl s^{-1}	W = J s^{-1}
International Steam Table calorie per hour	cal$_{IT}$ h^{-1}	2.759 84 × 10^{-2}	1.163 × 10^{-3}
British thermal unit per hour	Btu h^{-1}	6.954 68	2.930 71 × 10^{-1}
horsepower*............	hp	1.769 57 × 10^4	7.457 00 × 10^2
metric horsepower*......	ch or PS	1.745 37 × 10^4	7.354 9875 × 10^2

* 1 ch or PS = **75** m kp s^{-1}; 1 hp = 55**0** ft lbf s^{-1}.

Action (= energy × time)

Dimension = $L^2 M T^{-1}$

Coherent units

International System of Units: joule × second (J s) = newton × metre × second = m^2 kg s^{-1} = 10^7 erg s
CGS system: erg × second (erg s) = dyne × centimetre × second = cm^2 g s^{-1} = 10^{-7} J s
ft-lb-s system: foot poundal second (ft pdl s) = ft^2 lb s^{-1} = 0.042 140 110 1 J s

Entropy (S)

Dimension = $L^2 M T^{-2} \Theta^{-1}$

Coherent units

International System of Units: joule per kelvin (J K^{-1}) = 10^7 erg K^{-1}

Noncoherent units

erg per kelvin (erg K^{-1}) = 10^{-7} J K^{-1}
foot poundal per degree Fahrenheit (ft pdl degF^{-1}) = ft^2 lb s^{-2} degF^{-1} = 0.075 852 198 2 J K^{-1}

Viscosity

Dynamic viscosity (η)

Dimension = $L^{-1} M T^{-1}$

Dynamic viscosity is the property of a fluid (liquid or gas) of offering resistance ('internal friction') to the non-accelerated displacement of two adjacent layers.

Coherent units

International System of Units: newton × second per square metre (N s m^{-2}) = m^{-1} kg s^{-1} = 0.671 969 pdl s ft^{-2}

CGS system: poise (P) = dyne × second per square centimetre (dyn s cm^{-2}) = cm^{-1} g s^{-1} = 10^{-1} N s m^{-2}
ft-lb-s system: poundal second per square foot (pdl s ft^{-2}) = ft^{-1} lb s^{-1} = 1.488 16 N s m^{-2}

Conversion of metric units of dynamic viscosity

		1 **A** unit = b **B** units (b in the table)				
A		**B**				
Name	Symbol	µP	mP	cP	P	N s m^{-2}
micropoise ...	µP	1	10^{-3}	10^{-4}	10^{-6}	10^{-7}
millipoise	mP	10^3	1	10^{-1}	10^{-3}	10^{-4}
centipoise	cP	10^4	10	1	10^{-2}	10^{-3}
poise	P	10^6	10^3	10^2	1	10^{-1}
newton × second per square metre	N s m^{-2}	10^7	10^4	10^3	10	1

Kinematic viscosity (ν) (= viscosity/density)

Dimension = $L^2 T^{-1}$

Maxwell's kinematic viscosity is the ratio of the dynamic viscosity η and the density ϱ, so that strictly speaking the term viscosity is here a misnomer. ν occurs in many flow processes, particularly when using models, as determinative magnitude (for instance in Reynold's number $Re = lu/\nu$).

Coherent units

International System of Units: square metre per second (m^2 s^{-1}) = 10.763 9 ft^2 s^{-1} = 360**0** m^2 h^{-1}
CGS system: stokes (St) = square centimetre per second (cm^2 s^{-1}) = 10^{-4} m^2 s^{-1}
ft-lb-s system: square foot per second (ft^2 s^{-1}) = 9.290 30 × 10^{-2} m^2 s^{-1} = 334.451 m^2 h^{-1}

Other unit

square metre per hour (m^2 h^{-1}) = $2.\dot{7}$ × 10^{-4} m^2 s^{-1} = $2.\dot{7}$ St

Viscosity of solutions

The ratio of the viscosity of a solution η to the viscosity of the solvent η_0 is known as the *viscosity ratio* (formerly called relative viscosity) (η/η_0). The quotient $(\eta - \eta_0)/\eta_0$ is the *viscosity increment*. In dilute solutions a further important magnitude is the *viscosity number* (formerly called reduced viscosity) (I_s), dimension $L^3 M^{-1}$, defined as $I_s = (1/c) \times (\eta - \eta_0)/\eta_0$, where c is the mass concentration of the solution. The limiting value

$$I_0 = \lim_{\substack{c \to 0 \\ \tau \to 0}} \frac{1}{c} \times \frac{\eta - \eta_0}{\eta_0}$$

is the *limiting viscosity number* (formerly called intrinsic viscosity) (I_0) (τ = shear stress).

Coherent units for I_s and I_0

International System of Units: cubic metre per kilogramme (m^3 kg^{-1}) = 16.018 5 ft^3 lb^{-1}
CGS system: cubic centimetre per gramme (cm^3 g^{-1}) = 10^{-3} m^3 kg^{-1}
ft-lb-s system: cubic foot per pound (ft^3 lb^{-1}) = 0.062 428 0 m^3 kg^{-1}

Surface tension (σ)

Dimension = $\mathsf{M\,T^{-2}}$

Coherent units

International System of Units: newton per metre (N m^{-1})
= joule per square metre (J m^{-2}) = kg s^{-2}
CGS system: dyne per centimetre (dyn cm^{-1})
= erg per square centimetre (erg cm^{-2}) = g s^{-2} = 10^{-3} N m^{-1}

Thermal conductivity (λ)

Dimension = $\mathsf{L\,M\,T^{-3}\,\Theta^{-1}}$

Coherent unit

International System of Units: watt per (metre × kelvin)
(W m^{-1} K^{-1}) = 1 m kg s^{-3} K^{-1}
= 2.388 46 × 10^{-3} cal$_{\mathrm{IT}}$ cm^{-1} s^{-1} K^{-1}
= 0.859 845 kcal$_{\mathrm{IT}}$ m^{-1} h^{-1} K^{-1}
= 1.604 97 × 10^{-4} Btu ft^{-1} s^{-1} degF^{-1}

Other unit

erg per (second × centimetre × kelvin) (erg s^{-1} cm^{-1} K^{-1})
= 1 cm g s^{-3} K^{-1} = 10^{-5} W m^{-1} K^{-1}
= 2.388 46 × 10^{-8} cal$_{\mathrm{IT}}$ cm^{-1} s^{-1} K^{-1}
= 8.598 45 × 10^{-6} kcal$_{\mathrm{IT}}$ m^{-1} h^{-1} K^{-1}
= 1.604 97 × 10^{-9} Btu ft^{-1} s^{-1} degF^{-1}

Other units with 1 cal$_{\mathrm{IT}}$ = 4.186**8** J

calorie per (centimetre × second × kelvin) (cal$_{\mathrm{IT}}$ cm^{-1} s^{-1} K^{-1})
= 418.6**8** W m^{-1} K^{-1} = 36**0** kcal$_{\mathrm{IT}}$ m^{-1} h^{-1} K^{-1}
= 0.067 196 9 Btu ft^{-1} s^{-1} degF^{-1}
kilocalorie per (metre × hour × kelvin) (kcal$_{\mathrm{IT}}$ m^{-1} h^{-1} K^{-1})
= 1.16**3** W m^{-1} K^{-1} = $2.\dot{7}$ × 10^{-3} cal$_{\mathrm{IT}}$ cm^{-1} s^{-1} K^{-1}

Anglo-Saxon units with 1 Btu = 232**6** $\frac{\text{lb}}{\text{kg}}$ J = 1055.056 J

British thermal unit per foot second degree Fahrenheit
(Btu ft^{-1} s^{-1} degF^{-1}) = 6230.64 W m^{-1} K^{-1}
= 36**00** Btu ft^{-1} h^{-1} degF^{-1} = 43 2**00** Btu in ft^{-2} h^{-1} degF^{-1}
= 14.881 6 cal$_{\mathrm{IT}}$ cm^{-1} s^{-1} K^{-1}
British thermal unit per foot hour degree Fahrenheit
(Btu ft^{-1} h^{-1} degF^{-1}) = 1.730 73 W m^{-1} K^{-1}
= $2.\dot{7}$ × 10^{-4} Btu ft^{-1} s^{-1} degF^{-1} = **12** Btu in ft^{-2} h^{-1} degF^{-1}
= 1.488 16 kcal$_{\mathrm{IT}}$ m^{-1} h^{-1} K^{-1}
British thermal unit inch per square foot hour degree Fahrenheit
(Btu in ft^{-2} h^{-1} degF^{-1}) = 0.144 228 W m^{-1} K^{-1}
= 2.314 81 × 10^{-5} Btu ft^{-1} s^{-1} degF^{-1}
= $0.08\dot{3}$ Btu ft^{-1} h^{-1} degF^{-1} = 0.124 014 kcal$_{\mathrm{IT}}$ m^{-1} h^{-1} K^{-1}

(Surface) coefficient of heat transfer (α)
(Over-all) coefficient of heat transfer (K)

Dimension = $\mathsf{M\,T^{-3}\,\Theta^{-1}}$

Coherent unit

SI: watt per (square metre × kelvin) (W m^{-2} K^{-1})
= 1 kg s^{-3} K^{-1} = 2.388 46 × 10^{-5} cal$_{\mathrm{IT}}$ cm^{-2} s^{-1} K^{-1}
= 0.859 845 kcal$_{\mathrm{IT}}$ m^{-2} h^{-1} K^{-1}
= 4.891 95 × 10^{-5} Btu ft^{-2} s^{-1} degF^{-1}

Other unit

erg per (square centimetre × second × kelvin)
(erg cm^{-2} s^{-1} K^{-1}) = 1 g s^{-3} K^{-1} = 10^{-3} W m^{-2} K^{-1}
= 2.388 46 × 10^{-8} cal$_{\mathrm{IT}}$ cm^{-2} s^{-1} K^{-1}
= 8.598 45 × 10^{-4} kcal$_{\mathrm{IT}}$ m^{-2} h^{-1} K^{-1}
= 4.891 95 × 10^{-8} Btu ft^{-2} s^{-1} degF^{-1}

Other units with 1 cal$_{\mathrm{IT}}$ = 4.186**8** J

calorie per (square centimetre × second × kelvin)
(cal$_{\mathrm{IT}}$ cm^{-2} s^{-1} K^{-1}) = 41 86**8** W m^{-2} K^{-1}
= 36 0**00** kcal$_{\mathrm{IT}}$ m^{-2} h^{-1} K^{-1} = 2.048 16 Btu ft^{-2} s^{-1} degF^{-1}
kilocalorie per (square metre × hour × kelvin)
(kcal$_{\mathrm{IT}}$ m^{-2} h^{-1} K^{-1}) = 1.16**3** W m^{-2} K^{-1}
= $2.\dot{7}$ × 10^{-5} cal$_{\mathrm{IT}}$ cm^{-2} s^{-1} K^{-1}

Anglo-Saxon units with 1 Btu = 232**6** $\frac{\text{lb}}{\text{kg}}$ J = 1055.056 J

British thermal unit per square foot second degree Fahrenheit
(Btu ft^{-2} s^{-1} degF^{-1}) = 20 441.7 W m^{-2} K^{-1}
= 36**00** Btu ft^{-2} h^{-1} degF^{-1} = 0.488 243 cal$_{\mathrm{IT}}$ cm^{-2} s^{-1} K^{-1}
= 17 576.7 kcal$_{\mathrm{IT}}$ m^{-2} h^{-1} K^{-1}
British thermal unit per square foot hour degree Fahrenheit
(Btu ft^{-2} h^{-1} degF^{-1}) = 5.678 26 W m^{-2} K^{-1}
= $2.\dot{7}$ × 10^{-4} Btu ft^{-2} s^{-1} degF^{-1} = 4.882 43 kcal$_{\mathrm{IT}}$ m^{-2} h^{-1} K^{-1}

Electricity and magnetism (for references see page 217)

International System of Units (SI units)

The base electrical unit is that of electric current, the ampere (A), defined[7] as that constant current which, if maintained in two straight parallel conductors of infinite length, of negligible circular cross-section, and placed one metre apart in vacuum, would produce between these conductors a force equal to 2×10^{-7} newton per metre of length.

This theoretical definition is realized experimentally in so-called 'absolute ampere measurements' by determining the force between arrangements of conductors carrying current. The ampere is 'maintained' in various national institutes as the ratio volt/ohm in the form of standard cells and resistors. In scalar terms the law of force valid for the length l of the pair of conductors a distance d apart and carrying electric currents of intensity I_1 and I_2 is given by $F/l = \mu_0 I_1 I_2/(2\pi d)$; inserting the data contained in the definition of the ampere gives for the magnetic field constant $\mu_0 = 4\pi \times 10^{-7}$ N/A^2, i.e., the relation[2] 1 A = $(4\pi \times 10^{-7}\ \mathrm{N}/\mu_0)^{1/2}$ is equivalent to the definition given for the ampere by the General Conference of Weights and Measures[7].

Electrodynamics is now generally described by means of the field theory (as recommended by the IUPAP[3], IEC[4], ISO[5], etc.). In so doing it is customary to use a four-dimensional system of quantities (general symbol X), for example length, mass, time, intensity of electric current as four base quantities, dimensional system LMTI. The equations with four base quantities involve explicitly two field constants, the electric field constant ε_0 and the magnetic field constant μ_0, linked by the velocity of light in vacuum c (c = 2.997 925 × 10^8 m s^{-1} = ζ cm s^{-1}; $3s = \pm 3 \times 10^2$ m s^{-1}): $\mu_0 = 4\pi \times 10^{-7}$ H m^{-1} = 1.256 637 ... × 10^{-6} H m^{-1}, and $\varepsilon_0 = 1/(\mu_0 c^2)$ = 8.854 19 × 10^{-12} F m^{-1}.

This system has now largely displaced the three-dimensional systems derived from three base quantities (e.g., length, mass, time; dimensional system LMT) used almost exclusively in the 19th century. The latter can be subdivided into 'electrical' and 'magnetic' variants, namely those with an 'electromagnetic' (general symbol X_{m}) and an 'electrostatic' (general symbol X_{e}) three-dimensional definition of quantities. These variants, and the four-dimensional system, use different dimensions. ε_0 and μ_0 do not appear in the equations of the three-dimensional systems, where only c occurs.

A coherent system of units appropriate to the four-dimensional system X is the International System of Units (SI) or, more precisely, the sub-system (MKSA system) derived from the SI units m, kg, s, A. A coherent system of units appropriate to the three-dimensional quantities is the CGS system, with the 'electromagnetic' CGS units (emu) for the quantities X_{m} with electromagnetic definitions and the 'electrostatic' CGS units (esu) for the quantities X_{e} with electrostatic definitions as its two sub-systems.

Apart from the dimensional difference between the three- and four-dimensional systems there is also the alternative between geometrically 'rationalized' and 'non-rationalized' versions. The conversion factors in the table on page 216 are based on *rationalized* versions of the *four-dimensional quantities* X and on *non-rationalized* versions of the *three-dimensional quantities* X_{m} and X_{e}.

The dimensional difference between the SI units and the emu and esu implies that they are not interconvertible simply by the use of *numerical* factors (b or b'); a possible means of expressing the relationship between the two for a particular electrical or magnetic quantity is: 1 SI unit = b^{-1} (X/X_{m}) emu = b'^{-1} (X/X_{e}) esu. (On the quotients X/X_{m} and X/X_{e} and the formulae defining the three- and four-dimensional quantities see for example STILLE[2].) For this reason the table on page 216 lists all the conversion factors of practical interest relating the *numerical values* of the non-rationalized three-dimensional quantities X_{m} and X_{e}, measured in their emu and esu respectively, to the *numerical value* of the corresponding rationalized four-dimensional quantity X measured in its SI unit:

$$\frac{X}{\text{SI unit}} = b\,\frac{X_{\mathrm{m}}}{\text{emu}} = b'\,\frac{X_{\mathrm{e}}}{\text{esu}}$$

Quantity (symbol)	Dimension in LMTI	SI Unit		Numerical value of X in SI unit $= b \times$ numerical value of X_m in emu $= b' \times$ numerical value of X_e in esu			
				CGS system			
				electromagnetic (X_m/emu)		electrostatic (X_e/esu)	
		Name	Symbol	emu	b *	esu	b' *
Electric potential difference (U)	$L^2MT^{-3}I^{-1}$	volt	V	$cm^{3/2} g^{1/2} s^{-2}$	10^{-8}	$cm^{1/2} g^{1/2} s^{-1}$	$\zeta \times 10^{-8}$
Electric current (I)	I	ampere	A	$cm^{1/2} g^{1/2} s^{-1}$	10	$cm^{3/2} g^{1/2} s^{-2}$	$10/\zeta$
Electric current density ($\boldsymbol{j}$ or $\boldsymbol{S}$)	$L^{-2}I$	ampere per square metre	$A\,m^{-2}$	$cm^{-3/2} g^{1/2} s^{-1}$	10^5	$cm^{-1/2} g^{1/2} s^{-2}$	$10^5/\zeta$
Electric linear current density (A or α)	$L^{-1}I$	ampere/metre	$A\,m^{-1}$	$cm^{-1/2} g^{1/2} s^{-1}$	10^3	$cm^{1/2} g^{1/2} s^{-2}$	$10^3/\zeta$
Electric field strength ($\boldsymbol{E}$)	$LMT^{-3}I^{-1}$	volt per metre	$V\,m^{-1}$	$cm^{1/2} g^{1/2} s^{-2}$	10^{-6}	$cm^{-1/2} g^{1/2} s^{-1}$	$\zeta \times 10^{-6}$
Electric flux density, displacement ($\boldsymbol{D}$)	$L^{-2}TI$	coulomb per square metre	$C\,m^{-2}$	$cm^{-3/2} g^{1/2}$	$10^5/4\pi$	$cm^{-1/2} g^{1/2} s^{-1}$	$10^5/(4\pi\zeta)$
Electric (displacement) flux (Ψ)	TI	coulomb	C(=A s)	$cm^{1/2} g^{1/2}$	$10/4\pi$	$cm^{3/2} g^{1/2} s^{-1}$	$10/(4\pi\zeta)$
Electric polarization ($\boldsymbol{P}$)	$L^{-2}TI$	coulomb per square metre	$C\,m^{-2}$	$cm^{-3/2} g^{1/2}$	10^5	$cm^{-1/2} g^{1/2} s^{-1}$	$10^5/\zeta$
Electric dipole moment ($\boldsymbol{p}$)	LTI	coulomb × metre	C m	$cm^{3/2} g^{1/2}$	10^{-1}	$cm^{5/2} g^{1/2} s^{-1}$	$10^{-1}/\zeta$
Electric polarizability (α_e)	$M^{-1}T^4I^2$	farad × square metre	$F\,m^2$	$cm\,s^2$	10^5	cm^3	$10^5/\zeta^2$
Electric susceptibility (χ_e or χ)	$L^0M^0T^0I^0$	1	1	1	4π	1	4π
Electric charge (Q)	TI	coulomb	C(=A s)	$cm^{1/2} g^{1/2}$	10	$cm^{3/2} g^{1/2} s^{-1}$	$10/\zeta$
Volume density of electric charge, charge density (ϱ or η)	$L^{-3}TI$	coulomb per cubic metre	$C\,m^{-3}$	$cm^{-5/2} g^{1/2}$	10^7	$cm^{-3/2} g^{1/2} s^{-1}$	$10^7/\zeta$
Surface density of electric charge (σ)	$L^{-2}TI$	coulomb per square metre	$C\,m^{-2}$	$cm^{-3/2} g^{1/2}$	10^5	$cm^{-1/2} g^{1/2} s^{-1}$	$10^5/\zeta$
Capacitance (C)	$L^{-2}M^{-1}T^4I^2$	farad	$F(=A\,s\,V^{-1})$	$cm^{-1} s^2$	10^9	cm	$10^9/\zeta^2$
Electric resistance (R) (to direct current)	$L^2MT^{-3}I^{-2}$	ohm	$\Omega(=V\,A^{-1})$	$cm\,s^{-1}$	10^{-9}	$cm^{-1} s$	$\zeta^2 \times 10^{-9}$
Electric conductance (G) (to direct current)	$L^{-2}M^{-1}T^3I^2$	reciprocal ohm**	$A\,V^{-1}$	$cm^{-1} s$	10^9	$cm\,s^{-1}$	$10^9/\zeta^2$
Electric resistivity (ϱ)	$L^3MT^{-3}I^{-2}$	ohm × metre	Ω m	$cm^2 s^{-1}$	10^{-11}	s	$\zeta^2 \times 10^{-11}$
Electric conductivity (γ or σ)	$L^{-3}M^{-1}T^3I^2$	reciprocal ohm** per metre	$A\,V^{-1} m^{-1}$	$cm^{-2} s$	10^{11}	s^{-1}	$10^{11}/\zeta^2$
Magnetic potential difference (V)	I	ampere	A	$cm^{1/2} g^{1/2} s^{-1}$ (gilbert, Gb)	$10/4\pi$	$cm^{3/2} g^{1/2} s^{-2}$	$10/(4\pi\zeta)$
Magnetic field strength ($\boldsymbol{H}$)	$L^{-1}I$	ampere per metre	$A\,m^{-1}$	$cm^{-1/2} g^{1/2} s^{-1}$ (oersted, Oe)†	$10^3/4\pi$	$cm^{1/2} g^{1/2} s^{-2}$	$10^3/(4\pi\zeta)$
Magnetic vector potential ($\boldsymbol{A}$)	$LMT^{-2}I^{-1}$	weber per metre	$Wb\,m^{-1}$	$cm^{1/2} g^{1/2} s^{-1}$	10^{-6}	$cm^{-1/2} g^{1/2}$	$\zeta \times 10^{-6}$
Magnetic flux density ($\boldsymbol{B}$) (magnetic induction)	$MT^{-2}I^{-1}$	tesla	$T(=Wb\,m^{-2})$	$cm^{-1/2} g^{1/2} s^{-1}$ (gauss, Gs)†	10^{-4}	$cm^{-3/2} g^{1/2}$	$\zeta \times 10^{-4}$
Magnetic flux (Φ)	$L^2MT^{-2}I^{-1}$	weber	Wb	$cm^{3/2} g^{1/2} s^{-1}$ (maxwell, Mx)	10^{-8}	$cm^{1/2} g^{1/2}$	$\zeta \times 10^{-8}$
Magnetization ($\boldsymbol{M}$ or $\boldsymbol{H}_i$)	$L^{-1}I$	ampere per metre	$A\,m^{-1}$	$cm^{-1/2} g^{1/2} s^{-1}$	10^3	$cm^{1/2} g^{1/2} s^{-2}$	$10^3/\zeta$
(Electro)magnetic moment ($\boldsymbol{m}$ or $\boldsymbol{\mu}$)	L^2I	ampere × square metre	$A\,m^2$	$cm^{5/2} g^{1/2} s^{-1}$	10^{-3}	$cm^{7/2} g^{1/2} s^{-2}$	$10^{-3}/\zeta$
Magnetic susceptibility (χ_m or κ)	$L^0M^0T^0I^0$	1	1	1	4π	1	4π
Magnetic polarization ($\boldsymbol{J}$ or $\boldsymbol{B}_i$)	$MT^{-2}I^{-1}$	tesla	$T(=Wb\,m^{-2})$	$cm^{-1/2} g^{1/2} s^{-1}$	$4\pi \times 10^{-4}$	$cm^{-3/2} g^{1/2}$	$4\pi\zeta \times 10^{-4}$
Magnetic dipole moment ($\boldsymbol{p}_m$)	$L^3MT^{-2}I^{-1}$	weber × metre	Wb m	$cm^{5/2} g^{1/2} s^{-1}$	$4\pi \times 10^{-10}$	$cm^{3/2} g^{1/2}$	$4\pi\zeta \times 10^{-10}$
(Coulomb's) magnetic pole strength (m)	$L^2MT^{-2}I^{-1}$	weber	Wb (= V s)	$cm^{3/2} g^{1/2} s^{-1}$	$4\pi \times 10^{-8}$	$cm^{1/2} g^{1/2}$	$4\pi\zeta \times 10^{-8}$
Self inductance (L)	$L^2MT^{-2}I^{-2}$	henry	$H(=V\,s\,A^{-1})$	cm	10^{-9}	$cm^{-1} s^2$	$\zeta^2 \times 10^{-9}$
Permeance (Λ)	$L^2MT^{-2}I^{-2}$	henry	$H(=V\,s\,A^{-1})$	cm	$4\pi \times 10^{-9}$	$cm^{-1} s^2$	$4\pi\zeta^2 \times 10^{-9}$
De-electrification or demagnetization factor (N)	$L^0M^0T^0I^0$	1	1	1	$1/4\pi$	1	$1/4\pi$
Electric or magnetic force ($\boldsymbol{F}$)††	LMT^{-2}	newton	$N(=J\,m^{-1})$	$cm\,g\,s^{-2}$ = dyn	10^{-5}	$cm\,g\,s^{-2}$ = dyn	10^{-5}
Electric or magnetic energy (W)††	L^2MT^{-2}	joule	J(=VA s)	$cm^2 g\,s^{-2}$ = erg	10^{-7}	$cm^2 g\,s^{-2}$ = erg	10^{-7}
Electric or magnetic energy density (w)††	$L^{-1}MT^{-2}$	joule per cubic metre	$J\,m^{-3}$	$cm^{-1} g\,s^{-2}$	10^{-1}	$cm^{-1} g\,s^{-2}$	10^{-1}
Electric or magnetic power (P)††	L^2MT^{-3}	watt	W(=V A)	$cm^2 g\,s^{-3}$	10^{-7}	$cm^2 g\,s^{-3}$	10^{-7}
Poynting vector ($\boldsymbol{S}$) (surface density of power in an electromagnetic wave)	MT^{-3}	watt per square metre	$W\,m^{-2}$	$g\,s^{-3}$	10^{-3}	$g\,s^{-3}$	10^{-3}

* $\zeta = 2.997\,925 \times 10^{10}$ ($3s = \pm 3 \times 10^2$ m s^{-1})
$1/\zeta = 3.335\,640 \times 10^{-11}$
$\zeta^2 = 8.987\,55 \times 10^{20}$
$1/\zeta^2 = 1.112\,650 \times 10^{-21}$
$4\pi = 1.256\,637 \times 10$

$1/4\pi = 7.957\,75 \times 10^{-2}$
$4\pi\zeta = 3.767\,304 \times 10^{11}$
$1/4\pi\zeta = 2.654\,418 \times 10^{-12}$
$4\pi\zeta^2 = 1.129\,409 \times 10^{22}$
$1/4\pi\zeta^2 = 8.854\,19 \times 10^{-23}$

** Often called 'mho'. The name siemens, adopted by the IEC in 1935, will come up for approval as name of the SI unit of conductance at the next General Conference of Weights and Measures.
† The names oersted and gauss are often interchanged.
†† See also under 'Force', 'Energy' and 'Power', pages 211–214.

(For references see page 221)

References (text on page 215)

1 Conférence Générale des Poids et Mesures, *Comptes rendus des séances de la 9e Conférence Générale des Poids et Mesures*, Paris 1948, Gauthier-Villars, Paris, 1949, page 49.

2 HVISTENDAHL, H. S., *Engineering Units and Physical Quantities*, Macmillan, London, 1964, chapter 5; STILLE, U., *Messen und Rechnen in der Physik*, 2nd ed., Vieweg, Braunschweig, 1961; STILLE, U., in EBERT, H. (Ed.), *Physikalisches Taschenbuch*, 4th ed., Vieweg, Braunschweig, 1967, section 111.2.

3 International Union of Pure and Applied Physics, *Symbols, Units and Nomenclature in Physics*, Document U.I.P. 11 (S.U.N. 65-3), 1965.

4 International Electrotechnical Commission, *Letter Symbols to be Used in Electrical Technology*, Publication 27, 4th ed., Geneva, 1966.

5 International Organization for Standardization, *Quantities and Units of Electricity and Magnetism*, ISO Recommendation R31, part 5, November 1965.

Radioactivity

1. Basic concepts

The term *nuclide* indicates a species of atom having specified numbers of protons and neutrons in its nucleus. Nuclides of one and the same chemical element, i.e., nuclides with the same number of protons and differing only in the number of neutrons, are known as *isotopes* of the element concerned. In some nuclides various energy states of the nucleus with finite lifetimes are possible. These states are called *isomers* of the nuclide. Isomeric *nuclides* have the same numbers of protons and neutrons and differ only in their energy content and thus their lifetime.

The nature of a nuclide is indicated unambiguously by the chemical symbol of the element and the number of nucleons (sum of the protons and neutrons = mass number) shown as an upper index to the left of the element symbol (e.g., ^{12}C, ^{32}P). Additionally, the number of protons (atomic number) can be given as a lower index on the left. Isomers in an excited, metastable state are indicated by a right upper index 'm' (e.g., $^{99}Tc^{m}$).

2. Radioactivity and law of disintegration

Radioactivity is the property of certain nuclides of spontaneously emitting either particles or gamma rays from the nucleus (nuclear radiation) or X rays from the shell after capture of an electron from the shell by the nucleus (characteristic X radiation). Except for isomeric transitions, this process always results in a change in the nature of the nuclide (radioactive transformation or radioactive disintegration). Nuclides possessing this property are known as radionuclides.

It is impossible to predict the time when an individual atom will disintegrate; the occurrence of disintegrations is statistically distributed, i.e., it is a stochastic process. For a large number of atoms of the same radionuclide disintegration is governed by the empirical law stating that the number $\mathrm{d}N$ of atoms disintegrating in the time $\mathrm{d}t$ is at all times proportional to the number N of atoms not yet disintegrated. The proportionality factor is known as the *decay constant* λ; this is a characteristic constant of the nuclide concerned:

$$-\mathrm{d}N = \lambda N \,\mathrm{d}t$$

If at time zero N_0 atoms of an isolated radionuclide are present the number N_t of atoms not yet disintegrated at any time t is given by

$$N_t = N_0 \,\mathrm{e}^{-\lambda t}$$

In equal time intervals the number of radioactive atoms decreases by the same proportion; the time interval during which the number decreases by half is known as the *half-life* ($T_{1/2}$):

$$T_{1/2} = \frac{\ln 2}{\lambda} = \frac{0.693}{\lambda}$$

The reciprocal of the decay constant λ has the dimension of time and is known as the *mean lifetime* τ. τ is the time during which the number of atoms of a radionuclide falls to the fraction $1/\mathrm{e}$ ($\approx 37\%$) of its original value.

3. Activity

The quantity $-(\mathrm{d}N/\mathrm{d}t) = \lambda N$, i.e., the number of radioactive transformations taking place in a sample during the time $\mathrm{d}t$ divided by this time interval, is called the *activity* A. It is a measure of the 'strength' of the radioactive sample.

The unit of activity in the International System of Units is the reciprocal second (s^{-1})*; the commonly used unit is the curie (Ci):

$$1\ \mathrm{Ci} = 3.7 \times 10^{10}\ \mathrm{s}^{-1}\,**$$

Decimal multiples and submultiples of the curie are

1 megacurie (MCi)	$= 10^{6}$ Ci	$= 3.7 \times 10^{16}\ \mathrm{s}^{-1}$
1 kilocurie (kCi)	$= 10^{3}$ Ci	$= 3.7 \times 10^{13}\ \mathrm{s}^{-1}$
1 millicurie (mCi)	$= 10^{-3}$ Ci	$= 3.7 \times 10^{7}\ \mathrm{s}^{-1}$
1 microcurie (μCi)	$= 10^{-6}$ Ci	$= 3.7 \times 10^{4}\ \mathrm{s}^{-1}$
1 nanocurie (nCi)	$= 10^{-9}$ Ci	$= 3.7 \times 10^{1}\ \mathrm{s}^{-1}$
1 picocurie (pCi)	$= 10^{-12}$ Ci	$= 3.7 \times 10^{-2}\ \mathrm{s}^{-1}$

4. Specific activity

The *specific activity a of a radioactive material* (for instance a radioactive solution) is the activity A of the radionuclide contained in it divided by the mass m of the material:

$$a = \frac{A}{m}$$

The commonly used unit of specific activity is the curie per gramm ($\mathrm{Ci\ g^{-1}}$) or a decimal multiple of it.

The *specific activity of a radionuclide* is obtained by dividing the activity $A = \lambda N$ of the radionuclide by the mass of N of its atoms. This quantity is a characteristic constant of the radionuclide expressing the maximum specific activity attainable (i.e., in the carrier-free state):

$$a = \frac{\lambda N_A}{M} = 1.63 \times 10^{13} \frac{\lambda}{A_r}\ \mathrm{Ci\ g^{-1}}$$

where N_A is the AVOGADRO constant, M the molar mass in gramme per mole (see page 227) of the radionuclide, A_r its relative atomic mass (see page 226) and λ the value of its decay constant in s^{-1}.

Table 1 Reciprocals of the specific activities of some radionuclides [2]

Nuclide	$T_{1/2}$	$1/a$ in g Ci^{-1}
^{24}Na	14.8 h	0.000 000 113
^{131}I	8.06 d	0.000 008 1
^{32}P	14 d	0.000 003 52
^{45}Ca	164 d	0.000 056 6
^{14}C	5570 a	0.187

The *activity concentration* of a radioactive material (liquid or gaseous, at a given temperature and pressure) is the ratio of the activity of the contained radionuclide to the volume of the material. The commonly used unit is the curie per litre ($\mathrm{Ci\ l^{-1}}$) or a decimal multiple of it. A special unit of activity concentration used in balneology for the activity concentration of water containing ^{222}Rn is the eman:

$$1\ \mathrm{eman} = 10^{-10}\ \mathrm{Ci\ l^{-1}}$$

The MACHE unit formerly in common use is equal to 3.64 eman.

Radiation dosimetry

A long discussion on radiological quantities and units ended provisionally in 1962 with the general acceptance of the definitions recommended by the International Commission on Radiological Units and Measurements (ICRU)[3]. These are formulated in accordance with the customary physical principles, and the units have been assimilated into the International System of Units of the Metric Convention. For comprehensive surveys of the physical concepts and quantities in the dosimetry of ionizing radiations as well as of the quantities characterizing radiation sources and radiation fields see the literature[3, 5].

* In English-speaking countries other units in common use are dps (disintegrations per second) and dpm (disintegrations per minute):
1 dpm = 0.016 7 dps = 0.45 pCi; 1 pCi = 0.037 dps = 2.22 dpm.

** The 12th General Conference of Weights and Measures (1964)[7] decided that the curie so defined should be retained as a special unit of activity.

(For references see page 221)

1. Introductory

In accordance with the fundamental GROTTHUS-DRAPER law for radiation of any kind, when matter is traversed by energy-rich radiation only that part of the energy that is absorbed can have an action on the matter. With ionizing radiations this absorption of energy occurs in several stages[6] before it becomes evident biologically. It has been agreed internationally that 'energy imparted to matter' shall be understood to mean only that energy manifested as excitation, ionization or change in the chemical bond energy of the atoms or molecules. This dosimetrically important quantity is defined[3] as follows:

The *energy E_D imparted* by ionizing radiation to the matter in a volume is the difference between the sum E_{in} of the energies (exclusive of rest energies) of all the directly and indirectly ionizing particles which have entered the volume and the sum E_{ex} of the energies (exclusive of rest energies) of all those which have left it, minus the energy equivalent Q of any increase in rest mass that took place in nuclear or elementary particle reactions within the volume:

$$E_D = \sum E_{in} - \sum E_{ex} + \sum Q$$

Whereas there can be no confusion concerning the energy totals E_{in} and E_{ex} it is necessary in the case of Q to be quite clear as to whether the nuclear or elementary particle reaction is exothermic or endothermic, i.e., whether Q is positive or negative. For example, the absorption of a photon in the volume concerned may produce an electron pair (electron + positron), an endothermic process; for this reaction therefore $Q = +2\,m_e c^2$ (m_e is the rest mass of the electron, c the velocity of light) for each interaction.

The *absorbed dose* is the amount of energy E_D imparted to the matter divided by the mass m of the matter (see below). The most important task of dosimetry is to determine this absorbed dose, which is now regarded as the most meaningful quantity to which the observable chemical and biological effects can be related. The absorbed dose is the result of certain physical reactions between radiation and matter, reactions that are in turn dependent on the nature, intensity and spectral energy distribution of the radiation and the atomic composition of the material.

Radiation fields in the body are usually non-uniform in space as well as in time. Thus there may be non-uniform distribution of the absorbed dose at the boundary surfaces of soft tissues or bones, while the pulsed electrons from particle accelerators constitute radiation non-uniform in time. The quantities concerned must therefore be determined for regions of space or intervals of time so small that any further reduction would not appreciably change the values of the quotients measured. This requirement necessitates the use of some limiting procedure, and in the ICRU definitions[3] the quantities are presented as quotients of small differences. As the ICRU Reports[3] point out, the region of space considered also has a lower limit of size, for it must still be large enough to contain many interactions and be traversed by many particles. If it is impossible to find a mass fulfilling both these conditions the dose has to be deduced from multiple measurements involving extrapolation or averaging procedures. The symbol Δ is placed before symbols for quantities concerned in such averaging procedures.

2. Radiation field quantities

A radiation field is a region in vacuum or matter that is traversed by radiation.

2.1 Particle fluence $\Phi = \dfrac{\Delta N}{\Delta a}$

where ΔN is the number of particles* entering a sphere of cross-sectional area Δa.

2.2 Particle flux density or *particle fluence rate* $\varphi = \dfrac{\Delta \Phi}{\Delta t}$

where $\Delta\Phi$ is the particle fluence in time Δt.

2.3 Energy fluence $\Psi = \dfrac{\Delta E\psi}{\Delta a}$

where $\Delta E\psi$ is the sum of the energies, exclusive of rest energies, of all the particles entering a sphere of cross-sectional area Δa.

2.4 Energy flux density or *energy fluence rate* $\psi = \dfrac{\Delta \Psi}{\Delta t}$

where $\Delta\Psi$ is the energy fluence in the time Δt.

3. Interactions

Since the great majority of radiations used in medicine are X rays, gamma rays or electrons discussion will be limited here to the interactions of photons and electrons with matter. Neutron/matter interactions and neutron dosimetry fall outside the scope of the present article.

3.1 When photons collide with atoms or molecules, electrons are liberated (as a result of the photoelectric effect, COMPTON effect and pair production) and absorb some of the energy of the photons.

Mass energy transfer coefficient $\dfrac{\mu_K}{\varrho} = \dfrac{1}{E\varrho} \cdot \dfrac{\Delta E_K}{\Delta l}$

where ΔE_K is the sum of the kinetic energies of the secondary electrons liberated in a layer of thickness Δl and density ϱ, and E is the sum of the energies (excluding rest energies) of the photons incident normally upon the layer.

3.2 When charged particles collide with atoms or molecules, part of their kinetic energy is lost in collisions with atoms or molecules due to ionization, electronic excitation and production of bremsstrahlung.

Mass stopping power $\dfrac{S}{\varrho} = \dfrac{1}{\varrho} \cdot \dfrac{\Delta E}{\Delta l}$

where ΔE is the average amount of energy lost by a charged particle of energy E when traversing a path of length Δl in a layer of density ϱ.

S_e/ϱ = electron mass stopping power

4. Quantities and units of dose

4.1 Absorbed dose and absorbed dose rate

4.1.1 The *absorbed dose** D produced by ionizing radiation in matter is the quotient of ΔE_D by Δm, where ΔE_D is the energy imparted by the radiation to the matter in a volume element and $\Delta m = \varrho \times \Delta V$ is the mass of the matter in that volume element:

$$D = \frac{\Delta E_D}{\Delta m} = \frac{1}{\varrho} \cdot \frac{\Delta E_D}{\Delta V}$$

The expression 'integral absorbed dose' still in common use thus simply means the amount of energy imparted to matter (see under 1. above):

$$E_D = \sum_i (D_i \cdot \Delta m_i)$$

In medical radiology 'matter' could for instance be a single organ or the whole body. The term 'energy imparted to matter' is much to be preferred from the point of view of clarity.

The special *unit of absorbed dose* is the rad (rd):

$$1\ \text{rd} = 0.01\ \text{J kg}^{-1} = 100\ \text{erg g}^{-1} = 2.388 \times 10^{-6}\ \text{cal}_{IT}\ \text{g}^{-1} = 6.242 \times 10^{13}\ \text{eV g}^{-1}$$

4.1.2 The *absorbed dose rate* $\dot{D}$ is the quotient of ΔD by Δt, where ΔD is the increment in absorbed dose in the time Δt:

$$\dot{D} = \frac{\Delta D}{\Delta t}$$

When the conditions are such that there is no variability in time $\dot{D} = D/t$.

Special *units of absorbed dose rate* are rad per second (rd s^{-1}), rad per minute (rd min^{-1}), rad per hour (rd h^{-1}), etc.:

$$1\ \text{rd s}^{-1} = 0.01\ \text{W kg}^{-1}$$

The direct measurement of absorbed dose or absorbed dose rate is possible only by means of calorimetry in phantoms and is very time-consuming. In practical dosimetry indirect methods are used, particularly those based on ionization measurements in air, in which the absorbed dose is obtained by simple calculation.

---

* In this chapter the expression 'particle' is understood to include not only corpuscles like electrons, protons, neutrons, etc. but also photons.

* The designation 'absorbed dose' has been criticized on the grounds that an 'absorbed dose' can be produced only in matter and not in vacuum. For this reason this quantity is known in the German literature as 'energy dose'.

4.2 Exposure and exposure rate

4.2.1 The *exposure* (X) is the quotient of ΔQ by Δm, where ΔQ is the sum of the electrical charges on all the ions of one sign produced in air when all the electrons (negatrons and positrons), liberated by photons in a volume element of air whose mass is Δm, are completely stopped in air:

$$X = \frac{\Delta Q}{\Delta m}$$

The special *unit of exposure* is the roentgen** (R), defined as

1 R = 2.58 × 10^{-4} C kg^{-1} (exactly)

From the definition of the roentgen and the elementary charge $e \approx 1.602 \times 10^{-19}$ C it follows that an exposure of 1 R produces 1.610×10^{12} ion pairs per gramme (2.082×10^{9} ion pairs per cubic centimetre) of air at its normal density of 1.293 mg cm^{-3}.

4.2.1.1 In German-speaking countries a quantity equivalent to exposure, the *equilibrium ion dose* (J_s) is used in medical radiology; this is defined as the ion dose (see paragraph 4.2.3 below) produced by photons at the point of interest when there is secondary electron equilibrium at this point. Equilibrium ion dose is measured by the same methods as exposure and has the same numerical value when expressed in roentgen.

Secondary electron equilibrium exists at a point in matter when the sum of the kinetic energies of the photon-produced secondary electrons entering a volume containing this point is equal to the sum of the kinetic energies of the secondary electrons leaving this volume. This equilibrium can be established in an ionization chamber by enclosing the volume of air by a wall equivalent to air, for instance graphite, of a thickness at least equal to the range of the secondary electrons in this wall. A further condition is that the mean range of the photon-produced secondary electrons is small compared to $1/\mu$ (μ being the linear attenuation coefficient for the photons). Since this second condition is approximately fulfilled only for photons of energies up to about 3 MeV the equilibrium ion dose can be measured only when the photon energy is below this level. The introduction of the ionization chamber must not noticeably disturb the radiation field of the photons.

4.2.2 The *exposure rate* ($\dot{X}$) is the quotient of ΔX by Δt, where ΔX is the increment in exposure in time Δt:

$$\dot{X} = \frac{\Delta X}{\Delta t}$$

When the conditions are such that there is no variability in time $\dot{X} = X/t$.

Special *units of exposure rate* are roentgen per second (R s^{-1}), roentgen per minute (R min^{-1}), roentgen per hour (R h^{-1}), etc.

1 R/s = 2.58 × 10^{-4} A kg^{-1}

Not included in the ICRU Reports[3] but appearing in the appropriate German DIN Standard[4] is the quantity 'ion dose', applicable to all kinds of radiation except neutrons.

4.2.3 The *ion dose* J produced by ionizing radiation in matter is the quotient of ΔQ by Δm_A, where ΔQ is the electric charge of the ions of one sign formed directly or indirectly by the radiation in air in a volume element ΔV, and Δm_A is the mass of the air of density ϱ_A in that volume element:

$$J = \frac{\Delta Q}{\Delta m_A} = \frac{1}{\varrho_A} \cdot \frac{\Delta Q}{\Delta V}$$

The special *unit of ion dose* is likewise the roentgen (see above). From the definition of the roentgen and the elementary charge $e \approx 1.602 \times 10^{-19}$ C it follows that an ion dose of 1 R produces 1.610×10^{12} ion pairs per gramme (2.082×10^{9} ion pairs per cubic centimetre) of air at its normal density of 1.293 mg cm^{-3}.

4.2.4 The *ion dose rate* $\dot{J}$ is the quotient of ΔJ by Δt, where ΔJ is the increment in ion dose in time Δt:

$$\dot{J} = \frac{\Delta J}{\Delta t}$$

When the conditions are such that there is no variability in time $\dot{J} = J/t$.

The special *units of ion dose rate* are roentgen per second (R s^{-1}), roentgen per minute (R min^{-1}), roentgen per hour (R h^{-1}), etc.

** This unit is numerically identical with the old roentgen (r), defined as 1 electrostatic unit of charge per 1.293 mg of air.

Table 2 Conversion of common units of exposure rate and ion dose rate

	mR h^{-1}	μR s^{-1}	R h^{-1}	R min^{-1}	R s^{-1}
1 mR h^{-1} -	1	2.8×10^{-1}	10^{-3}	1.7×10^{-5}	2.8×10^{-7}
1 μR s^{-1} -	3.6	1	3.6×10^{-3}	6×10^{-5}	10^{-6}
1 R h^{-1} -	10^{3}	2.8×10^{2}	1	1.7×10^{-2}	2.8×10^{-4}
1 R min^{-1} -	6×10^{4}	1.7×10^{4}	60	1	1.7×10^{-2}
1 R s^{-1} -	3.6×10^{6}	10^{6}	3.6×10^{3}	60	1

4.2.5 The *cavity ion dose* J_c is the ion dose produced by photon or electron irradiation in an air-filled cavity surrounded by matter of any kind when the Bragg-Gray conditions are fulfilled.

If a cavity within a material A is filled with a material B (for instance air) the *Bragg-Gray conditions* are fulfilled when

(a) the flux density of the first generation of electrons and their energy distribution remain unchanged by the cavity filled with material B,
(b) the energy of the secondary electrons produced by the photons in material B is negligible in comparison with the energy imparted to material B,
(c) the flux density of the electrons of all generations within the material B is uniform throughout.

These conditions can be approximately met if the cavity contains air and its linear dimensions are small compared with $1/\mu$ (μ being the linear attenuation coefficient for the photons) and compared with the mean range of the secondary electrons. The walls of such a cavity ionization chamber must either be very thin or have values for mass energy transfer coefficient μ_K/ϱ and electron mass stopping power S_e/ϱ deviating only slightly from those of the surrounding material A; in other words, the ionization of the air molecules in the cavity by the photons must be due predominantly to the secondary electrons produced in the surrounding material A. In order to reduce boundary layer effects between the material of the wall and the air in the cavity resulting from low-energy delta-electrons the inner side of the wall must be covered with a graphite layer about 1 μm thick. If this is not done the mean cavity ion dose will be dependent on the volume in which the dose is being measured.

5. Conversion of dose quantities

5.1 The absorbed dose D_A for air is obtained from the ion dose J (measured as J_s* or J_c):

$$D_A = U_{iA} \cdot J$$

where U_{iA} = 0.869 rd/R is the ionization constant of air, obtained from the average energy E_i (= 33.7 eV) required for the formation of an ion pair in air, from the elementary charge e and from the relationship 1 V = 1 J/1 C = 2.58 × 10^{-4} rd R^{-1}. Above about 10 keV, U_{iA} remains practically constant over a wide energy range.

5.2 For photon irradiation the absorbed dose D_Z at the point of interest in material Z is obtained from the absorbed dose D_A at the same point with secondary electron equilibrium in air (see paragraph 4.2.1.1 above) in accordance with the relationship

$$D_Z = D_A \cdot (\mu_K/\varrho)_Z / (\mu_K/\varrho)_A$$

where $(\mu_K/\varrho)_Z$ and $(\mu_K/\varrho)_A$ are the mass energy transfer coefficients (see paragraph 3.1, page 218) of the material Z (for instance body tissues) and air respectively for photons of energy E. For a photon spectrum the values $(\bar{\mu}_K/\varrho)_Z$ and $(\bar{\mu}_K/\varrho)_A$ averaged over the spectrum must be used instead.

For the *exposure* X** the conversion equations are as follows:

(a) for photons of uniform energy E:

$$D_Z = f \cdot X, \text{ with } f = U_{iA} \cdot (\mu_K/\varrho)_Z / (\mu_K/\varrho)_A$$

(b) for a photon spectrum:

$$D_Z = \bar{f} \cdot X, \text{ with } \bar{f} = U_{iA} \cdot (\bar{\mu}_K/\varrho)_Z / (\bar{\mu}_K/\varrho)_A$$

Values of the conversion factors f and $\bar{f}$ for air, water, soft tissues and bone are given in Tables 3 and 4.

5.3 For photon and electron irradiation the absorbed dose D_Z at the point of interest in the material Z is obtained from the ab-

* Or exposure X (see paragraph 4.2.1.1).

** Or equilibrium ion dose J_s (see paragraph 4.2.1.1), in which case J_s must replace X in the formulae.

sorbed dose D_A for air measured at the same point *under Bragg-Gray conditions* (see paragraph 4.2.5 above) in accordance with the relationship

$$D_Z = D_A \cdot (\bar{S}_e/\varrho)_Z/(\bar{S}_e/\varrho)_A$$

where $(\bar{S}_e/\varrho)_Z$ and $(\bar{S}_e/\varrho)_A$ are the electron mass stopping powers (see paragraph 3.2, page 218) of the material Z and of air averaged over the electron spectrum. Using the *cavity ion dose* J_c the conversion equation is as follows:

$$D_Z = \bar{g} \cdot J_c, \text{ with } \bar{g} = U_{IA} \cdot (\bar{S}_e/\varrho)_Z/(\bar{S}_e/\varrho)_A$$

Values of the conversion factor $\bar{g}$ for air, water and soft tissues are given in Table 5.

6. Relation of absorbed dose to radiation field

6.1 For photons of uniform energy the energy flux density ψ_{ph} of the photons at the point of interest is related to the absorbed dose rate $\dot{D}$ at the same point when there is secondary electron equilibrium as follows:

$$\dot{D} = (\mu_K/\varrho) \cdot \psi_{ph}$$

Similarly, for the absorbed dose D and the energy fluence Ψ_{ph} of the photons,

$$D = (\mu_K/\varrho) \cdot \Psi_{ph}$$

where μ_K/ϱ is the mass energy transfer coefficient of the material for photons of this energy.

6.2 For electrons of uniform energy the particle flux density φ_e of the electrons at the point of interest is related to the absorbed dose rate $\dot{D}$ at the same point under BRAGG-GRAY conditions as follows:

$$\dot{D} = (S_e/\varrho) \cdot \varphi_e$$

Table 3 Conversion factor $f = D/X$

E in MeV	f in rd R^{-1} for Air	Water*	Soft tissues**	Bone (compact)**
0.010	0.869	0.912	0.925	3.54
0.015	0.869	0.890	0.916	3.97
0.020	0.869	0.877	0.916	4.23
0.030	0.869	0.870	0.910	4.39
0.04	0.869	0.873	0.919	4.14
0.05	0.869	0.893	0.926	3.58
0.06	0.869	0.915	0.929	2.91
0.08	0.869	0.937	0.939	1.91
0.10	0.869	0.942	0.948	1.45
0.15	0.869	0.964	0.956	1.05
0.20	0.869	0.971	0.963	0.979
0.30	0.869	0.964	0.957	0.938
0.4	0.869	0.967	0.954	0.928
0.5	0.869	0.964	0.957	0.925
0.6	0.869	0.964	0.957	0.925
0.8	0.869	0.967	0.956	0.920
1.0	0.869	0.967	0.956	0.922
1.5	0.869	0.966	0.958	0.920
2.0	0.869	0.966	0.954	0.921
3.0	0.869	0.964	0.954	0.928

* From National Bureau of Standards, Report 8681, U.S. Government Printing Office, Washington, 1965.
** From National Bureau of Standards, *Physical Aspects of Irradiation, ICRU Report 10b, 1962*, Handbook 85, U.S. Government Printing Office, Washington, 1964.

Table 5 Conversion factor $\bar{g} = D/J_c$

Radiation: Quantum energy or electron energy	Half-value layer or radionuclide	$\bar{g}$ in rd R^{-1} for Air	Water	Soft tissues
(a) Bremsstrahlung at 400 kV tube potential	4.2 mm Cu	0.87	1.01	1.00
0.66 MeV	^{137}Cs	0.87	1.00	1.00
1.25 MeV	^{60}Co	0.87	0.99	0.99
Bremsstrahlung 15 MeV	–	0.87	0.98	0.97
Bremsstrahlung 30 MeV	–	0.87	0.95	0.94
Bremsstrahlung 45 MeV	–	0.87	0.94	0.93
(b) Electrons				
5 MeV	–	0.87	0.92	0.91
10 MeV	–	0.87	0.88	0.87
20 MeV	–	0.87	0.84	0.83
30 MeV	–	0.87	0.82	0.81
40 MeV	–	0.87	0.81	0.80
50 MeV	–	0.87	0.80	0.79

When calculating the absorbed dose for soft tissues embedded in bone the factor for the latter should be used since the effect of bone has already been allowed for in measurement of the cavity ion dose.
Values (a) from National Bureau of Standards, *Physical Aspects of Irradiation, ICRU Report 10b, 1962*, Handbook 85, U.S. Government Printing Office, Washington, 1964; (b) calculated from BERGER and SELTZER, *Tables of Energy Losses and Ranges of Electrons and Positrons*, NASA SP-3012, National Aeronautics and Space Administration, Washington, 1964, and *Additional Stopping Power and Range Tables for Protons, Mesons and Electrons*, NASA SP-3036, National Aeronautics and Space Administration, Washington, 1966.

Table 4 Conversion factor $\bar{f} = D/X$

Radiation: Tube potential in kV	Filter mm Al	Filter mm Cu	Half-value layer mm Al	Half-value layer mm Cu	$\bar{f}$ in rd R^{-1} for Air	Water	Soft tissues	Bone (compact)
50	1.4	–	1.2	0.03	0.87	0.88	0.93	4.2
100	–	0.2	4.2	0.18	0.87	0.89	0.92	3.6
150	–	0.5	–	0.75	0.87	0.92	0.94	2.3
200	–	1.0	–	1.45	0.87	0.94	0.95	1.6
250	–	1.5	–	2.35	0.87	0.95	0.95	1.4
300	–	3.0	–	3.5	0.87	0.96	0.95	1.2
400	–	3.0	–	4.2	0.87	0.96	0.96	1.1

When calculating the absorbed dose for soft tissues embedded in bone from the measured exposure a value of $\bar{f}$ should be chosen lying between those for soft tissues and bone and depending on the distance of the bone from the point of measurement (cf. National Bureau of Standards, *Physical Aspects of Irradiation, ICRU Report 10b, 1962*, Handbook 85, U.S. Government Printing, Washington, 1964).

Similarly, for the absorbed dose D and the particle fluence Φ_e of the electrons,

$$D = (S_e/\varrho) \cdot \Phi_e$$

where S_e/ϱ is the electron mass stopping power of the material for electrons of this energy.

Since the coefficients μ_K/ϱ and S_e/ϱ are themselves functions of the photon and electron energy respectively the absorbed dose rates for two different particle energies generally differ even when the energy flux density or particle flux density, as the case may be, is the same. In practice, radiation is usually not of uniform energy but has an energy spectrum, in which case mean values of the coefficients over the spectral range must be used.

7. Relative biological effectiveness (RBE)

Radiobiological studies have shown that different kinds of ionizing radiation can produce biological effects of different intensity even when the absorbed dose in the biological material being irradiated, and all other conditions, are the same. The absorbed dose is therefore still not an adequate physical quantity from which all the biological effects can be deduced. This has led to the introduction of the concept of relative biological effectiveness (RBE), with the dimensionless RBE factor ξ defined as

$$\xi = D_0/D$$

where D is the absorbed dose of the radiation under consideration that produces a particular biological effect, and D_0 the absorbed dose of a standard radiation (at present hard filtered 200 kV X rays) that produces the same effect under otherwise identical conditions. The RBE factor is not a constant for a particular kind of radiation since different values are obtained depending on the nature of the irradiation reaction being observed, on the kind of biological system under study, on the stage of development of the object being irradiated, and on the distribution of the absorbed dose in space and time[7]. Since the RBE factor as such is unsuitable for use in the field of radiation protection the ICRU[3] has recommended that the term RBE should be employed in radiobiology only.

8. Dose equivalent and quality factor[3, 8]

In radiation protection the place of the RBE factor ξ is taken by the quality factor* q, and that of the absorbed dose of the standard radiation – which is not used in radiation protection – by the dose equivalent* D_q, defined as follows:

$$D_q = q \cdot D$$

The concept of dose equivalent is intended for use in radiation protection only. The quality factor q is a dimensionless number whose magnitude depends mainly on the nature of the radiation, the particle energy and the conditions under which the irradiation takes place. In practice, agreed conventional values of q are used based on the relative biological effectiveness ξ. The dose equivalent is equal to the absorbed dose produced by a standard radiation with a quality factor $q = 1$ (at present 200 kV X rays); this absorbed dose is considered from the point of view of risk to be the same as the absorbed dose produced by the actual radiation with a quality factor $q \neq 1$.

If a number of different radiations are present simultaneously the total dose equivalent is the sum of the dose equivalents of the individual radiations:

$$D_q = \sum_i D_{qi} = \sum_i (D_i q_i)$$

For dose equivalents the unit rad is given the special name rem (symbol rem):

$$1 \text{ rem} = 1 \text{ rd}$$

The term rem is reserved exclusively for expressing dose equivalents, so that data given in this unit are immediately recognizable as such.

9. Specific gamma ray constant

The specific gamma ray constant Γ of a gamma-emitting radionuclide is the quotient of $l^2 \times \Delta\dot{X}$ by the activity A of the nuclide, where $\Delta\dot{X}$ is the exposure rate at a distance l from a point source of the nuclide and the gamma rays are assumed to undergo no absorption either in the sample or over the distance l:

$$\Gamma = \frac{\dot{X} \cdot l^2}{A}$$

$\dot{X}$ is normally only the exposure rate resulting from gamma radiation and from the annihilation radiation of positron-emitting nuclides. If the X rays due to internal conversion or electron capture are not included this must be clearly stated when giving the specific gamma ray constant.

In the case of radionuclides with short-lived decay products Γ is given for the state of radioactive equilibrium; here $\dot{X}$ is the exposure rate resulting from the gamma rays emitted by all members of the series, A the activity of the parent nuclide. For radium the specific gamma ray constant is related to the mass m_{Ra} of the radium nuclide ^{226}Ra in equilibrium with its decay products and enclosed in a platinum envelope of 0.5 mm thickness:

$$\Gamma_{Ra} = \frac{\dot{X} \cdot l^2}{m}; \text{ numerically } \Gamma_{Ra} = 0.825 \text{ R h}^{-1} \text{ m}^2 \text{ g}^{-1}$$

The special unit of specific gamma ray constant is

$$\frac{\text{roentgen} \times \text{square metre}}{\text{hour} \times \text{curie}} \quad (\text{R h}^{-1} \text{ m}^2 \text{ Ci}^{-1})$$

For ^{226}Ra the unit is

$$\frac{\text{roentgen} \times \text{square metre}}{\text{hour} \times \text{gramme}} \quad (\text{R h}^{-1} \text{ m}^2 \text{ g}^{-1})$$

If the activity A or the mass m_{Ra} of the radium is known the exposure rate at the distance l can therefore be calculated provided absorption of the gamma rays in the source and intervening air is neglected:

$$\dot{X} = \Gamma \frac{A}{l^2} \quad \text{or} \quad \dot{X} = \Gamma_{Ra} \frac{m_{Ra}}{l^2}$$

* The symbol QF used in the ICRU Reports[3], like the symbol DE for dose equivalent, is inconvenient for use in formulae.

Table 6 Specific gamma ray constants of some radionuclides

Γ in R h^{-1} m^2 Ci^{-1}											
^{22}Na	^{24}Na	^{42}K	^{54}Fe	^{58}Co	^{60}Co	^{64}Cu	^{130}I	^{131}I	$^{137}Cs + ^{137}Ba^m$	^{192}Ir	^{198}Au
1.19	1.84	0.14	0.63	0.55	1.31	0.12	1.22	0.22	0.31	0.50	0.23

References

1 Conférence Générale des Poids et Mesures, *Comptes rendus des séances de la 12e Conférence générale des Poids et Mesures*, Paris 1964, Gauthier-Villars, Paris, 1964, page 94.

2 QUIMBY et al., *Radioactive Isotopes in Clinical Practice*, Lea & Febiger, Philadelphia, 1958.

3 National Bureau of Standards, *Radiation Quantities and Units, ICRU Report 10a, 1962*, Handbook 84, U.S. Government Printing Office, Washington, 1962; International Commission on Radiological Units, *Radiation Quantities and Units (1968)*, ICRU Report No. 11, ICRU Publications, Washington, D.C., 1968.

4 Deutscher Normenausschuß, DIN 6809, October 1963; Entwurf DIN 6814, Blatt 3, November 1968.

5 ATTIX and ROESCH (Eds.), *Radiation Dosimetry*, 2nd ed., vol. 1, Academic Press, New York, 1968; National Bureau of Standards, *Physical Aspects of Irradiation, ICRU Report 10b, 1962*, U.S. Government Printing Office, Washington, 1964.

6 United Nations Scientific Committee on the Effects of Atomic Radiation, *Report to the General Assembly, Seventeenth Session, Suppl. No. 16*, United Nations, New York, 1962; DEELEY and WOOD (Eds.), *Modern Trends in Radiotherapy*, vol. 1, Butterworth, London, 1967.

7 Relative Biological Effectiveness Committee, *Health Phys.*, **9**, 357 (1963).

8 BERGER et al., *Strahlentherapie*, **131**, 143 (1966).

Quantity* and definition†	SI Unit: Name	SI Unit: Symbol
Electromagnetic radiation (radiant quantities)		
The **radiant energy** Q_e (or W) is the energy emitted, transferred or received as radiation.	joule	J
The **radiant energy density** w is the radiant energy in an element of volume divided by that element: $w = dQ_e/dV$.	joule per cubic metre	$J\ m^{-3}$
The **radiant flux** or **radiant power** Φ_e is the power emitted, transferred or received as radiation: $\Phi_e = P = dQ_e/dt$.	watt	W
The **spectral concentration of radiant flux**** $\Phi_{e\lambda}$ is a spectral distribution function of radiant flux, i.e., the radiant flux in an infinitesimal wave-length interval divided by the range of that interval: $\Phi_e = \int \Phi_{e\lambda}\, d\lambda$. $\Phi_{e\lambda}$ is often given in watt per nanometre ($1\ W\ nm^{-1} = 10^9\ W\ m^{-1}$).	watt per metre	$W\ m^{-1}$
The **radiant intensity** I_e of a source in a given direction is the radiant flux leaving the source, propagated in an element of solid angle containing the given direction divided by that element of solid angle: $\Phi_e = \int I_e\, d\Omega$.	watt per steradian	$W\ sr^{-1}$
The **radiance** L_e at a point of a surface and in a given direction (ϑ = angle between the direction and the normal to the surface) is the radiant intensity of an element of the surface divided by the area of the orthogonal projection of that element on a plane perpendicular to the given direction: $\Phi_e = \int I_e\, d\Omega = \iint L_e \cos\vartheta\, dA\, d\Omega$.	watt per steradian per square metre	$W\ sr^{-1}\ m^{-2}$
The **radiant exitance** M_e at a point of a surface element is the radiant flux leaving an element of the surface divided by the area of that element: $\Phi_e = \int M_e\, dA$.	watt per square metre	$W\ m^{-2}$
The **irradiance** E_e at a point of a surface is the radiant flux incident on an element of the surface divided by the area of that element: $\Phi_e = \int E_e\, dA$.	watt per square metre	$W\ m^{-2}$
The **radiant exposure** H_e is the time integral of the irradiance: $H_e = \int E_e dt$.	joule per square metre	$J\ m^{-2}$
The (hemispherical) **emissivity** of a thermal radiator ε is the ratio of the radiant exitance of the radiator to that of a black body at the same temperature: $\varepsilon = M_e/M_{e,s}$***.	1	1
The **spectral** (hemispherical) **emissivity** of a thermal radiator $\varepsilon(\lambda)$ is the ratio of the spectral concentration of the radiant exitance of the radiator to that of a black body at the same temperature: $\varepsilon(\lambda) = M_{e\lambda}/M_{e\lambda,s}$†.	1	1
The **directional emissivity** of a thermal radiator $\varepsilon(\vartheta, \varphi)$ is the ratio of the radiance of the radiator in a given direction (ϑ, φ) to that of a black body at the same temperature: $\varepsilon(\vartheta, \varphi) = L_e/L_{e,s} = \int L_{e\lambda}\, d\lambda / \int L_{e\lambda,s}\, d\lambda$.	1	1
The **spectral directional emissivity** of a thermal radiator $\varepsilon(\lambda; \vartheta, \varphi)$ is the ratio of the spectral concentration of radiance in a given direction (ϑ, φ) of the radiator to that of a black body at the same temperature: $\varepsilon(\lambda; \vartheta, \varphi) = L_{e\lambda}/L_{e\lambda,s} < 1$.	1	1
Light (luminous quantities)		
The **luminous flux** Φ_v is the radiant flux evaluated photometrically, i.e., by its action on a selective receptor. The spectral function for evaluating the spectral concentration of radiant flux $\Phi_{e\lambda}$ is the spectral luminous efficacy $K(\lambda)$ or the spectral luminous efficiency $V(\lambda)$: $\Phi_v = \int K(\lambda)\, \Phi_{e\lambda}\, d\lambda = K_{max} \int V(\lambda)\, \Phi_{e\lambda}\, d\lambda$.	lumen	lm = cd sr

* Where there is no risk of confusion between *radiant quantities* and the corresponding *luminous quantities* (i.e., the photometrically evaluated radiant quantities), or where the discussion concerns exclusively one of the two kinds of quantities, the subscripts of the symbols ('e' from 'energy', 'v' from 'visible') are omitted.

** Where there is no risk of confusion with the so-called 'spectral' quantities – for instance $\varepsilon(\lambda)$, $K(\lambda)$, $V(\lambda)$, $\varrho(\lambda)$, $\alpha(\lambda)$, $\tau(\lambda)$ – which though functions of wave length are nevertheless not spectral distribution functions in the sense of differential quotients with respect to wave length, the 'spectral concentration of a' quantity X (i.e., $X_\lambda = dX/d\lambda$) may be designated shortly the 'spectral' quantity X. Thus the 'spectral concentration of radiant flux' ($\Phi_{e\lambda}$) may be abbreviated to 'spectral radiant flux'.

*** $M_{e,s}$ is the unpolarized radiant exitance of a black body at the temperature T: $M_{e,s} = \sigma T^4$ (for the STEFAN-BOLTZMANN constant $\sigma = \pi^2 k^4/60\, \hbar^3 c^2$ see page 228).

† $M_{e\lambda,s}$ is PLANCK's expression for the unpolarized spectral concentration of radiant exitance of a black body at the temperature T: $M_{e\lambda,s} = c_1 \lambda^{-5} [\exp(c_2/\lambda T) - 1]^{-1}$ (for the 1st and 2nd PLANCK radiation constants, $c_1 = 2\pi hc^2$ and $c_2 = hc/k$, see page 228).

Quantity* and definition[1]	SI Unit	
	Name	Symbol
Light (continued)		
The **spectral concentration of luminous flux**** $\Phi_{v\lambda}$ is a spectral distribution function of luminous flux, i.e., the luminous flux in an infinitesimal wave-length interval divided by the range of that interval: $\Phi_v = \int \Phi_{v\lambda}\, d\lambda$. $\Phi_{v\lambda}$ is often given in lumen per nanometre ($1\ lm\, nm^{-1} = 10^9\ lm\, m^{-1}$).	lumen per metre	$lm\ m^{-1}$
The **spectral luminous efficacy** of radiation $K(\lambda)$ is the luminous output of the radiation at a specified wave length λ, i.e., the ratio of the spectral concentration of luminous flux to that of radiant flux: $K(\lambda) = \Phi_{v\lambda}/\Phi_{e\lambda}$. Its maximum value $K_{max} = K$ (555 nm) is 670–680 $lm\ W^{-1}$ for the standard photometric observer.	lumen per watt	$lm\ W^{-1}$
The **spectral luminous efficiency** $V(\lambda)$ is the ratio of the spectral luminous efficacy (at a specified wave length λ) $K(\lambda)$ to the maximum spectral luminous efficacy K_{max}: $V(\lambda) = K(\lambda)/K_{max}$***.	1	1
The **quantity of light** Q_v is the time integral of luminous flux: $Q_v = \int \Phi_v\, dt$. Q_v is often given in lumen hour ($1\ lm\ h = 3600\ lm\ s$).	lumen second	$lm\ s = cd\ sr\ s$
The **luminous intensity** I_v of a light source in a given direction is the luminous flux leaving the light source, propagated in an element of solid angle containing the given direction, divided by that element of solid angle: $\Phi_v = \int I_v\, d\Omega$. The base SI unit of luminous intensity, the *candela*, is defined[3] as the luminous intensity, in the perpendicular direction, of a surface of 1/600 000 square metre of a black body at the temperature of freezing platinum under a pressure of 101 325 newton per square metre.	candela	cd
The **luminance** L_v at a point of a surface and in a given direction (ϑ = angle between the direction and the normal to the surface) is the luminous intensity of an element of the surface divided by the area of the orthogonal projection of that element on a plane perpendicular to the given direction: $\Phi_v = \int I_v\, d\Omega = \iint L_v \cos\vartheta\, dA\, d\Omega$†.	candela per square metre	$cd\ m^{-2}$
The **luminous exitance** M_v†† at a point of a surface is the luminous flux leaving an element of the surface divided by the area of that element: $\Phi_v = \int M_v\, dA$.	lux	$lx = lm\ m^{-2}$ $= cd\ sr\ m^{-2}$
The **illuminance** E_v at a point of a surface is the luminous flux incident on an element of the surface divided by the area of that element: $\Phi_v = \int E_v\, dA$†††.	lux	$lx = lm\ m^{-2}$ $= cd\ sr\ m^{-2}$
The **light exposure** H_v is the time integral of illuminance: $H_v = \int E_v\, dt$.	lux second	$lx\ s$ $= cd\ sr\ m^{-2}\ s$
The **luminous efficacy** η_v of a light source is the luminous flux emitted, Φ_v, divided by the power consumed: $\eta_v = \Phi_v/P_{abs}$.	lumen per watt	$lm\ W^{-1}$

* See footnote *, page 222.
** See footnote **, page 222.
*** The spectral luminous efficiency $V(\lambda)$ is at present given by the following internationally accepted values[2] [λ = numerical value of the wave length of light in nanometre (nm)]:

λ	$V(\lambda)$	λ	$V(\lambda)$	λ	$V(\lambda)$	λ	$V(\lambda)$	λ	$V(\lambda)$	λ	$V(\lambda)$	λ	$V(\lambda)$	λ	$V(\lambda)$	λ	$V(\lambda)$	λ	$V(\lambda)$
400	0.000 4	440	0.023	480	0.139	520	0.710	555	1.000	590	0.757	630	0.265	670	0.032	710	0.0021	750	0.000 12
410	0.001 2	450	0.038	490	0.208	530	0.862	560	0.995	600	0.631	640	0.175	680	0.017	720	0.0010 5	760	0.000 06
420	0.004 0	460	0.060	500	0.323	540	0.954	570	0.952	610	0.503	650	0.107	690	0.008 2	730	0.0005 2		
430	0.011 6	470	0.091	510	0.503	550	0.995	580	0.870	620	0.381	660	0.061	700	0.004 1	740	0.0002 5		

In order to distinguish them from the luminous quantities related to the spectral luminous efficiency for daylight vision $V(\lambda)$ (International Commission on Illumination, 1924), i.e., those related to photopic vision (pure *cone* vision), the luminous quantities related to the spectral luminous efficiency for night vision $V'(\lambda)$ (International Commission on Illumination, 1951), i.e., those related to scotopic vision (pure *rod* vision), are known as 'scotopic quantities'.

† The unit candela per square centimetre ($1\ cd\ cm^{-2} = 10^4\ cd\ m^{-2}$) was formerly also known as the stilb (sb). Other luminance units occasionally used are the apostilb [$1\ asb = (1/10^4\pi)\ sb$], the lambert [$1\ L = (10^4/\pi)\ cd\ m^{-2}$] and the foot lambert ($1\ ftL = \pi^{-1}\ cd\ ft^{-2}$).

†† The (unpolarized) luminous exitance of a black body at the temperature T_{Pt} of freezing platinum

$M_{v,s}(T_{Pt}) = \int_0^\infty M_{e\lambda,s}(T_{Pt})\, K(\lambda)\, d\lambda$ (for $M_{e\lambda,s}$ see footnote †, page 222)

is given by the relationship $\Phi_v = \int I_v\, d\Omega = \int M_v\, dA$ together with the definition of the candela, as follows:

$$M_{v,s}(T_{Pt}) = K_{max}\, c_1 \int_0^\infty V(\lambda)\, \lambda^{-5} [\exp(c_2/\lambda T_{Pt}) - 1]^{-1}\, d\lambda = 6\pi \times 10^{-5}\ lx.$$

††† When used for illuminance the unit lumen per square centimetre ($1\ lm\ cm^{-2} = 10^4\ lm\ m^{-2}$) was formerly also known as the phot (phot). Another unit of illuminance occasionally used is the foot candle or lumen per square foot ($1\ fc = 1\ lm\ ft^{-2}$).

Quantity* and definition[7]	SI Unit	
	Name	Symbol
Light (concluded)		
The **spectral reflectance** $\varrho(\lambda)$ is the ratio of the spectral concentration of the reflected radiant (or luminous) flux to that of the incident radiant (or luminous) flux: $\varrho(\lambda) = \Phi_{\lambda r}/\Phi_\lambda$.	1	1
The **spectral absorptance** $\alpha(\lambda)$ is the ratio of the spectral concentration of the absorbed radiant (or luminous) flux to that of the incident radiant (or luminous) flux: $\alpha(\lambda) = \Phi_{\lambda a}/\Phi_\lambda$**.	1	1
The **spectral transmittance** $\tau(\lambda)$ is the ratio of the spectral concentration of the transmitted radiant (or luminous) flux to that of the incident radiant (or luminous) flux: $\tau(\lambda) = \Phi_{\lambda tr}/\Phi_\lambda$.	1	1
The **reflectance** ϱ, **absorptance** α and **transmittance** τ are the respective ratios of the reflected, absorbed and transmitted radiant (or luminous) flux Φ_r, Φ_a and Φ_{tr} to the incident radiant (or luminous) flux Φ. The following relationships hold for the quantities ϱ, α, τ and $\varrho(\lambda)$, $\alpha(\lambda)$, $\tau(\lambda)$: $\varrho = \int \Phi_\lambda\, \varrho(\lambda)\, d\lambda / \int \Phi_\lambda\, d\lambda = \Phi_r/\Phi$ $\alpha = \int \Phi_\lambda\, \alpha(\lambda)\, d\lambda / \int \Phi_\lambda\, d\lambda = \Phi_a/\Phi$ $\tau = \int \Phi_\lambda\, \tau(\lambda)\, d\lambda / \int \Phi_\lambda\, d\lambda = \Phi_{tr}/\Phi$ $\Phi = \Phi_r + \Phi_a + \Phi_{tr}$ $\varrho + \alpha + \tau = \varrho(\lambda) + \alpha(\lambda) + \tau(\lambda) = 1$	1	1

* See footnote *, page 222.

** For a thermal radiator emitting or absorbing in any direction (ϑ, φ): $\alpha(\lambda; \vartheta, \varphi) = \varepsilon(\lambda; \vartheta, \varphi) = L_{e\lambda}/L_{e\lambda,s} < 1$.

References

[7] International Electrotechnical Commission, *International Lighting Vocabulary*, Draft 3rd ed. and amendments, Geneva, 1966 (unpublished); International Organization for Standardization, *Quantities and Units of Light and Related Electromagnetic Radiations*, Draft ISO Recommendation No. 1778, January 1969 (unpublished).

[2] Comité International des Poids et Mesures, *Proc.-Verb. Com. int. Poids Mes.*, **15**, 65 (1933).

[3] Comité International des Poids et Mesures, *Proc.-Verb. Com. int. Poids Mes.*, **20**, 119 (1946), and **21**, 67 (1948); Conférence Générale des Poids et Mesures, *Comptes rendus des séances de la 9e Conférence générale des Poids et Mesures*, Paris 1948, Gauthier-Villars, Paris, 1949, page 54; *Comptes rendus des séances de la 13e Conférence générale des Poids et Mesures*, Paris 1967/1968, Bureau International des Poids et Mesures, Sèvres, 1969, pages 71 and 104.

Quantity and definition[7]	Dimension	Units	
		SI unit	CGS unit
Acoustics†			
The **sound pressure** p is the alternating pressure due to an acoustical phenomenon and superimposed on the stationary atmospheric pressure. Values not otherwise specified are root mean square values, often called 'effective' values.	$L^{-1}\,M\,T^{-2}$	$N\,m^{-2}$	$dyn\,cm^{-2}$ (= μbar)
The **sound particle velocity** v is the instantaneous velocity of a particle of the medium set in motion by an acoustical phenomenon. Values not otherwise specified are root mean square values, often called 'effective' values.	$L\,T^{-1}$	$m\,s^{-1}$	$cm\,s^{-1}$
The **sound pressure level** L_p is defined[7] as $20 \log_{10}(p/p_0)$ in decibel (dB), where p is the root mean square value of the measured sound pressure, and p_0 is the root mean square value of a reference pressure. For air: $p_0 = 2 \times 10^{-5}\ N\,m^{-2} = 2 \times 10^{-4}\ \mu bar$ is generally used[7].	$L^0\,M^0\,T^0$	dB††	dB††
The **sound energy** W is the mechanical energy radiated as sound.	$L^2\,M\,T^{-2}$	W s	erg
The **sound power** or **sound energy flux** P is the sound energy transferred in a certain time interval divided by the duration of that interval: $P = dW/dt$.	$L^2\,M\,T^{-3}$	W	$erg\,s^{-1}$

† This section (pages 224–226) has been compiled in collaboration with W. Furrer, Zurich.

†† The decibel is not a unit of either the SI or the CGS system.

Quantity and definition[7]	Dimension	Units	
		SI unit	CGS unit
Acoustics (continued)			
The **sound intensity** I for unidirectional sound energy flux is the sound energy flux through an area normal to the direction of propagation divided by that area: $P = \int I dA$.	MT^{-3}	$W\,m^{-2}$	$erg\,s^{-1}\,cm^{-2}$
The **velocity of sound** c is the velocity of propagation of a sound wave. It is a constant depending on the medium and independent of the frequency or intensity of the sound wave. The velocity of sound in air depends mainly on the temperature and is given by $c_{air} = (331.4 + 0.607\,t)\ m\,s^{-1}$, where t is the numerical value of the temperature in degree Celsius. Note: At very high intensities (explosions) the velocity of sound may be higher.	LT^{-1}	$m\,s^{-1}$	$cm\,s^{-1}$

	Dimension	SI unit
The **periodic time** or **period** T is the time taken by a periodic phenomenon in an arbitrarily defined state to return for the first time to that state.	T	s
The **frequency** ν (or f) of a periodic phenomenon is the reciprocal of its periodic time. In acoustical phenomena the subjective impression of the pitch depends on the frequency. *Standard musical pitch* is the frequency for the note A in the treble stave, defined as 440 Hz[2].	T^{-1}	Hz
The **loudness level** L_N (or Λ) of a sound or noise is expressed on the dimensionless phon scale[7]. The loudness level amounts to n phon when it is judged by a normal observer under standardized listening conditions to be as loud as a pure tone of frequency 1000 Hz consisting of a plane progressive sound wave, coming from directly in front of the observer, the sound pressure level of which is $L_p = n$ dB (see above); i.e., $L_N = 20 \log_{10}(p/p_0)_{1\,kHz}$. In principle, therefore, loudness levels can be measured in phon only by a subjective hearing test; objective tests yield only more or less exact approximations.	$L^0 M^0 T^0$	phon*
Loudness N (or S). Owing to the arbitrary definition of the decibel and phon scales, loudness levels on these scales do not immediately correspond to the sensation of loudness but have to be interpreted by the user on the basis of his personal experience of sounds of known phon value. The sone scale provides a means of expressing the subjective sensation of loudness and is defined[7] by the following relationship between loudness N in sone and loudness level L_N in phon:	$L^0 M^0 T^0$	sone*

$$N = 2^{0.1(L_N - 40)} \quad \text{or} \quad \log_{10} N = 0.1(L_N - 40) \cdot \log_{10} 2 \approx 0.03\,(L_N - 40)$$

Corresponding values of L_N and N calculated from this 'loudness function' are as follows:

L_N in phon	N in sone	L_N in phon	N in sone	L_N in phon	N in sone
20	0.25	55	2.83	90	32.0
25	0.35	60	4.00	95	45.3
30	0.50	65	5.66	100	64.0
35	0.70	70	8.00	105	90.5
40	1.00	75	11.3	110	128
45	1.41	80	16.0	115	181
50	2.00	85	22.6	120	256

It should be noted that

1. Loudness in sone cannot be measured directly but must be calculated from the loudness level in phon.
2. A loudness of 1 sone corresponds to a loudness level of 40 phon.
3. A twofold change in loudness corresponds to a loudness level difference of 10 phon.
4. The relationship has been confirmed experimentally only between 20 and 120 phon; outside this range its use must be regarded as an extrapolation.

* Not an SI unit.

Calculation of loudness levels

Loudness levels can also be calculated from noise analyses, the two best-known methods being those of STEVENS[3] and ZWICKER[4]. The precision of these methods, i.e., the agreement of their results with loudness levels measured subjectively in accordance with the ISO recommendations[7], is adequate for many purposes. Values calculated in this way, however, should not be given simply in 'phon' but should bear an indication that they have been arrived at by a particular method.

A modification of STEVENS' method has been introduced for the measurement of aircraft noise[5]. The values so obtained are known as 'perceived noise levels' (PN) and are expressed in decibel. They represent a degree of correlation of objective measurements with subjective sensation not attainable simply by measuring sound pressure levels.

Sound level meters

In view of the complexity of the human ear and the difficult nature of the subjective hearing tests required for the measurement of loudness levels in phon, sound level meters measuring certain weighted sound pressure levels have been standardized[6]. The weighting applied to each sinusoidal component of the sound pressure is given as a function of frequency by three standard reference curves A, B and C. The varying sensitivity of the ear is taken into account by using curve A for low sound pressure levels, curve B for moderate sound pressure levels, and curve C for high sound pressure levels. In each measurement the curve used must be shown, for instance by placing the appropriate letter after the decibel value: 45 dB(A), 95 dB(C). The 'DIN-phon' earlier used in Germany[7] was based on the same principle.

More recent measurements of the frequency response of the ear[8] and studies of the correlation between sound pressure level and loudness level measurements have shown that the use of the curve A gives best agreement with the subjective sensation and that this applies not only to low but also to high sound pressure levels. This is being taken into account by the ISO when standardizing in this field, with the result that the tendency is now for sound levels to be measured and given in dB(A). Sound pressure levels in dB(A) should also be given when loudness levels are measured or calculated in any form (for instance L_N in phon or in phon by STEVENS' method, PN in dB, etc.).

Typical sound levels

The following examples from everyday life illustrate the range of the dB(A) sound level scale:

Source	Sound level in dB(A)
Propeller aircraft at 5 m	130
Pneumatic hammer at 1 m	120
Brass foundry	110
Motor-car horn at 5 m	100
Truck at 5 m	90
Loud radio music	80
Normal conversation at 1 m	70
Motor car at 10 m	60
Quiet stream or river	50
Residential district without traffic	40
Quiet garden	30
Ticking of a watch	20
Limit of audible noise	10
Absolute silence	0

References

1 International Organization for Standardization, *Expression of the Physical and Subjective Magnitudes of Sound or Noise*, ISO Recommendation R 131, September 1959; *Quantities and Units of Acoustics*, ISO Recommendation R 31, Part VII, November 1965.
2 International Organization for Standardization, *Standard Tuning Frequency*, ISO Recommendation R 16, November 1955.
3 STEVENS, S. S., *J. acoust. Soc. Amer.*, **28**, 807 (1956).
4 ZWICKER, E., *Acustica*, **10**, 304 (1960).
5 KRYTER and PEARSONS, *J. acoust. Soc. Amer.*, **35**, 866 (1963).
6 International Electrotechnical Commission, *Recommendations for Sound Level Meters*, Publication 123, and *Precision Sound Level Meters*, Publication 179, Bureau central de la Commission électrotechnique internationale, Geneva, 1961 and 1965.
7 Deutscher Normenausschuß (DNA), *Meßgerät für DIN-Lautstärken*, DIN 5045, May 1963, Beuth-Vertrieb, Berlin, 1963 (superseded by *Präzisionsschallpegelmesser, Allgemeine Anforderungen*, DIN 45633, Blatt 1, July 1967, Beuth-Vertrieb, Berlin, 1967).
8 International Organization for Standardization, *Preferred Frequencies for Acoustical Measurements*, ISO Recommendation R 266, August 1962.

Amount of substance

Amount of substance (n) and amount of equivalent (n_{aeq})

Dimension = N
(Additional*) base unit = mole (mol)

Except in special cases, there is no practicable method of counting the numbers of particles involved in a chemical or physical process. For this reason the IUPAP[1,5] in 1957 introduced the basic quantity *amount of substance n* for use in chemical and molecular physics. The concept of amount of substance is founded on the 'countability' of identical individuals (particles) in an atomic or other discontinuous system[2]. The value of n is proportional to the number of particles N, the proportionality factor being a fundamental constant, the AVOGADRO constant (see also page 228) $N_A = N/n$ (dimension = N^{-1}). The number of particles in a population having the amount of substance $n = 1$ mol is therefore $N = N_A \times 1\ \text{mol} = 6.0222 \times 10^{23}$.

The *base unit of amount of substance* is the *mole** (mol). The primary standard for the mole – as well as for the scale of relative atomic masses A_r and the (unified) atomic mass unit (u) – is the carbon nuclide ^{12}C on which the IUPAC and IUPAP agreed in 1960–61[3,4]. As defined by the IUPAC[6, **], the mole is the amount of substance of a system which contains as many elementary units as there are carbon atoms in 0.012 kg of the pure nuclide carbon-12 (^{12}C). The elementary unit *must be specified* and may be an atom, a molecule, an ion, an electron, a photon, etc., or a *specified* group of such entities.

The concept of amount of substance may be extended to FARADAY's *law of equivalence* and *chemical bonds*. Here use is made of the *amount of equivalent* n_{aeq} (dimension likewise N): $n_{aeq} = z\,n$, where z is the charge number in the case of ions and the number (single, double, etc.) in the case of bonds. The amount of equivalent n_{aeq} is proportional to the electric charge $Q = N z e$ (e = elementary charge; see also page 228) of N ions of charge number z, the proportionality factor again being a fundamental constant, the FARADAY constant F (see also page 228) $= Q/n_{aeq} = e\,N/n = e\,N_A$ (dimension = TIN^{-1}). The *unit of amount of equivalent* is likewise the base unit mole*. The electric charge carried by the amount of equivalent $n_{aeq} = z\,n = 1$ mole of a particular species of ion is therefore $Q = F\,n_{aeq} = F \times 1\ \text{mol} = 9.6487 \times 10^4$ C.

Scale of relative atomic masses (A_r) and the (unified) atomic mass unit (u)

The unified scale of relative atomic masses A_r, with ^{12}C as reference nuclide or primary standard, is defined[3,4] by the assigned value

$$A_r(^{12}C) = 12$$

Using the mass $m(^{12}C)$ of an atom of the nuclide ^{12}C as primary standard, the (unified) atomic mass unit (u) is defined by the relation[3]

$$1\ \text{u} = m(^{12}C)/12$$

The atomic mass of any nuclide X can therefore be written as $m(X) = A_r(X)$ u with

$$1\ \text{u} = 10^{-3}\,(N_A\ \text{mol})^{-1}\ \text{kg} = 1.66053 \times 10^{-27}\ \text{kg}$$

Tables of the relative atomic masses $m(X)$ of the nuclides have been published at the instance of the Commission on Atomic Masses and Related Atomic Constants of the IUPAP[9,10]. These data, together with the 'natural' or 'average' relative abundancies of the stable isotopes of the elements, have formed since 1961 the basis of the tables of 'atomic weights' of the elements issued by the Commission on Atomic Weights of the IUPAC[11].

* Previously the mole, defined as 1 mol = M_r g (M_r = relative molecular mass, or 'molecular weight', of the substance concerned), has been used as an individual (chemical) mass unit[2]. Linked to the mole there is a further individual (electrochemical) mass unit for ions of a chemically homogeneous substance, the gramme-equivalent Eq, defined by 1 Eq = $(1/z)$ mol = (M_r/z) g (the symbol val is also used in place of Eq). The ratio M_r/z is known as the equivalent weight of the ions. These units have now been superseded by the dimensionless quantity *amount of equivalent* ($n_{aeq} = zn$), i.e., the terms amount of equivalent $n_{aeq} = y$ mol and amount of substance $n = (y/z)$ mol of the ions in the new formulation replace the earlier statement of a 'mass y Eq of ions of molecular weight M_r and electrovalency z'.

At the instigation of the IUPAC, IUPAP and ISO, the Advisory Committee on Units in 1967 recommended[8] to the International Committee of Weights and Measures that the International System of Units should be extended to include a seventh base unit, the mole, as base unit of amount of substance. The 13th General Conference of Weights and Measures in 1967 deferred a decision on this proposal. This recommendation was confirmed[8a] by the Advisory Committee on Units in 1969.

Editors' note: In view of the fact that in clinical chemistry the equivalent, milliequivalent, etc., continue for the time being to be used as mass units for ions, the editors have refrained from making corresponding changes in the data given in subsequent chapters of these *Scientific Tables*.

** The same definition of the mole has been agreed upon by the ISO[7] and IUPAP[5], except that the latter has chosen a slightly different wording.

Important quantities representing concentration

Quantity*	Symbol and definition	mol-SI unit**
Molecular concentration of the component i (L^{-3}) .	$C_i = N_i/V$ (in a mixture of volume V)	m^{-3}
Mass concentration of the component i (L^{-3} M) . . .	$\varrho_i = \overline{m}_i/V$ (in a mixture of volume V) ($\overline{m}_i$ = mass of component i)	kg m^{-3}
Molarity of the component i (L^{-3} N)	$c_i = n_i/V$ (amount of substance in mol related to the volume of the mixture or solution)***	mol m^{-3}
Molality of the solute substance i (M^{-1} N)	$m_i = n_i/\overline{m}_0$ (amount of substance in mol related to the mass $\overline{m}_0$ of the solvent)***	mol kg^{-1}
Equivalent concentration of the ion i (L^{-3} N)	$c_{\mathrm{aeq},i} = z_i\, c_i = z_i\, n_i/V$ (in a solution of volume V)***	mol m^{-3}
Ionic strength of a solution (M^{-1} N)	$I = \frac{1}{2}\sum_i z_i^2 m_i = \frac{1}{2}\sum_i z_i^2 n_i/\overline{m}_0$ ($\overline{m}_0$ = mass of solvent)	mol kg^{-1}

* Dimensions in brackets.
** Coherent unit in the International System of Units supplemented by the base unit mole (see above and reference[8]).

*** A solution of molarity $c_i = y$ mol/l is known as 'y-molar' with respect to the component i, a solution of molality $m_i = y$ mol/kg as 'y-molal' with respect to the component i, a solution of equivalent concentration $c_{\mathrm{aeq},i} = y$ mol/l as 'y-normal' with respect to the ions of species i.

Quantities related to amount of substance

Apart from amount of substance n, a number of other quantities with amount of substance as reference quantity (whence, unfortunately, the designation 'molar') are widely used, especially in thermodynamics and statistics. Examples (dimensions in brackets) are molar volume $V_m = V/n$ ($L^3\,N^{-1}$), molar mass $M = m/n$ ($M\,N^{-1}$), molar enthalpy $H_m = H/n$, molar internal energy $U_m = U/n$ (for H_m and U_m: $L^2\,M\,T^{-2}\,N^{-1}$), molar entropy $S_m = S/n$, molar heat capacity $C_m = C/n$, and molar gas constant $R = R'/n$ (for S_m, C_m and R: $L^2\,M\,T^{-2}\,\Theta^{-1}\,N^{-1}$).

In analogy with the quantities related to amount of substance the equivalent conductivity Λ ($L^{-3}\,M^{-1}\,T^3\,I^2\,N^{-1}$) has, for instance, been introduced as the conductivity γ related to the equivalent concentration $c_{\mathrm{aeq}} = n_{\mathrm{aeq}}/V$ (V = volume of the solution): $\Lambda = \gamma/c_{\mathrm{aeq}}$.

Earlier 'physical' (A_{ph}) and 'chemical' (A_{ch}) scales of atomic weights

Before agreement was reached on the unified ^{12}C scale, different relative mass scales[2] were in use in physics and chemistry[2], namely the 'physical scale of atomic weights' based on the oxygen nuclide ^{16}O as primary standard and defined by $A_{\mathrm{ph}}(^{16}O) = \mathbf{16}$, and the 'chemical scale of atomic weights' based on elementary oxygen, i.e., on the 'naturally' occurring mixture of the stable oxygen isotopes ^{16}O, ^{17}O and ^{18}O, the primary standard being a 'mean' oxygen atom $\bar{O}$ with the definition $A_{\mathrm{ch}}(\bar{O}) = \mathbf{16}$.

The abundance ratio of the three stable oxygen isotopes varies according to the source of the element, with the result that there was a scatter of at least 15 parts per million in experimental values of the conversion factor k_A (SMYTHE factor) between the two scales. This circumstance led the Commission on Atomic Weights of the IUPAC[12] to recommend a mean *conventional* value for k_A as follows: $k_A = A_{\mathrm{ph}}/A_{\mathrm{ch}} = \mathrm{mol_{ph}}/\mathrm{mol_{ch}} = 1.000\,275$.

The following relationships hold between the two earlier atomic weight scales [$A_{\mathrm{ph}} = A_r(^{16}O = 16)$ and $A_{\mathrm{ch}} = A_r(\bar{O} = 16)$] and the newer unified scale of relative atomic masses [$A_r(^{12}C) = 12$], and between the three corresponding units of amount of substance mol ($^{16}O = 16$), mol ($\bar{O} = 16$) and mol($^{12}C = 12$):

$$\frac{A_r\,(^{16}O = 16)}{A_r\,(^{12}C = 12)} = \frac{\mathrm{mol}\,(^{16}O = 16)}{\mathrm{mol}\,(^{12}C = 12)} = 1.000\,317\,91^{10}$$

($3\,s = \pm 5 \times 10^{-8}$)

$$\frac{A_r\,(\bar{O} = 16)}{A_r\,(^{12}C = 12)} = \frac{\mathrm{mol}\,(\bar{O} = 16)}{\mathrm{mol}\,(^{12}C = 12)} = \frac{1.000\,318}{k_A} = 1.000\,043$$

($3\,s = \pm 15 \times 10^{-6}$)

Former atomic mass unit (amu)

The former atomic mass unit (amu), based on the oxygen nuclide ^{16}O as primary standard and linked to the physical scale of atomic weights, was defined through the mass $m(^{16}O)$ of an atom of the nuclide ^{16}O:

$$1\ \mathrm{amu} = m(^{16}O)/\mathbf{16}$$

The atomic mass of any nuclide X was therefore written as $m(X) = A_{\mathrm{ph}}(X)$ amu. The relationship between the earlier and the present unified atomic mass unit is given by

$$1\ \mathrm{u} = \frac{A_r\,(^{16}O = 16)}{A_r\,(^{12}C = 12)}\,\mathrm{amu}$$

References

1 International Union of Pure and Applied Physics, *Report of the 9th General Assembly*, Rome, 1957, page 7; also in *Ned. T. Natuurkde*, **23**, 327 (1957), *Nuclear Phys.*, **7**, 299 (1958), and *Phys.Bl.*, **14**, 259 (1958).
2 Cf. STILLE, U., *Rechnen und Messen in der Physik*, 2nd ed., Vieweg, Braunschweig, 1961.
3 International Union of Pure and Applied Physics, *Report of the 10th General Assembly*, Ottawa, 1960, page 24.
4 International Union of Pure and Applied Chemistry, *Comptes rendus de la 20e conférence*, Munich 1959, Butterworth, London, page 202; *Information Bulletin*, No. 10, London, 1959, page 17; *Comptes rendus de la 21e conférence*, Montreal 1961, Butterworth, London, pages 221, 252 and 281.
5 International Union of Pure and Applied Physics, *Symbols, Units and Nomenclature in Physics*, Document U.I.P. 11 (S.U.N. 65-3), 1965, page 25.
6 International Union of Pure and Applied Chemistry, *Comptes rendus de la 22e conférence*, London 1963, Butterworth, London, pages 156 and 178; *Comptes rendus de la 23e conférence*, Paris 1965, Butterworth, London, pages 131 and 149; *Information Bulletin* Number 32, London, 1968, page 27.
7 International Organization for Standardization, *Quantities and Units of Physical Chemistry and Molecular Physics*, Draft ISO Recommendation No. 1777, January 1969 (unpublished).
8 Comité consultatif des unités, 1re session, Paris, 1967, page U17.
8a Comité consultatif des unités, 2e session, Paris 1969 (in press).
9 EVERLING et al., *Nuclear Phys.*, **18**, 529 (1960); KÖNIG et al., *Nuclear Phys.*, **31**, 18 (1962).
10 MATTAUCH et al., *Nuclear Phys.*, **67**, 1 (1965).
11 International Union of Pure and Applied Chemistry, *Comptes rendus de la 21e conférence*, Montreal 1961, Butterworth, London, page 281; *Comptes rendus de la 22e conférence*, London 1963, Butterworth, London, page 196; *Comptes rendus de la 23e conférence*, Paris 1965, Butterworth, London, pages 169, 170 and 173.
12 International Union of Pure and Applied Chemistry, *Comptes rendus de la 17e conférence*, Stockholm 1953, Butterworth, London, page 93; *Comptes rendus de la 18e conférence*, Zurich 1955, Butterworth, London, page 115.

Physical Constants†

	Symbol and formula	Numerical value	CGS system	International System of Units	Noncoherent units
Gravitational constant[1]	G	6.670 ± 0.015	10^{-8} dyn cm^2 g^{-2}	10^{-11} N m^2 kg^{-2}	
Electromagnetic field constants (see also page 215)					
Velocity of light in vacuum[1]	c	2.997 925	10^{10} cm s^{-1}	10^{8} m s^{-1}	
	$1/c$	3.335 640 5	10^{-11} cm^{-1} s	10^{-9} m^{-1} s	
	c^2	8.987 554 3	10^{20} cm^2 s^{-2}	10^{16} m^2 s^{-2}	
	$1/c^2$	1.112 649 7	10^{-21} cm^{-2} s^2	10^{-17} m^{-2} s^2	
Magnetic field constant	$\mu_0 = 4\pi\,10^{-7}$ Hm^{-1}	1.256 637 061		10^{-6} H m^{-1}	
Electric field constant	$\varepsilon_0 = 1/\mu_0 c^2$	8.854 185 3		10^{-12} F m^{-1}	
Impedance of vacuum	$\Gamma_0 = \mu_0 c$	3.767 303 7		10^{2} Ω	
Thermodynamic constants[1-4]					
Molar volume of an ideal gas under standard conditions	V_{m0}	2.241 36	10^4 cm^3 mol^{-1}	10^{-2} m^3 mol^{-1}	
Molar gas constant	$R = p_0 V_{m0}/T_0$	8.314 3	10^7 erg K^{-1} mol^{-1}	J K^{-1} mol^{-1}	
		8.205 6			10 cm^3 atm K^{-1} mol^{-1}
		1.987 2			cal$_{th}$ K^{-1} mol^{-1} §
		1.986 5			cal$_{15}$ K^{-1} mol^{-1}
		1.985 8			cal$_{IT}$ K^{-1} mol^{-1}
Atomic constants[1-4]					
AVOGADRO constant††	N_A	6.022 2	10^{23} mol^{-1}	10^{23} mol^{-1}	
LOSCHMIDT constant†††	$n_L = N_A/V_{m0}$	2.686 8	10^{19} cm^{-3}	10^{25} m^{-3}	
BOLTZMANN entropy constant	$k = R/N_A$	1.380 6	10^{-16} erg K^{-1}	10^{-23} J K^{-1}	
		1.362 6			10^{-22} cm^3 atm K^{-1}
		8.617 1			10^{-5} eV K^{-1}
		3.299 8			10^{-24} cal$_{th}$ K^{-1} §
		3.298 6			10^{-24} cal$_{15}$ K^{-1}
		3.297 6			10^{-24} cal$_{IT}$ K^{-1}
Elementary charge	e	1.602 2		10^{-19} C	
	e^*	4.803 2	10^{-10} esu		
	e^*/c	1.602 2	10^{-20} emu		
FARADAY constant	$F = N_A e$	9.648 7		10^4 C mol^{-1}	
	$F^* = N_A e^*$	2.892 6	10^{14} esu mol^{-1}		
	$F^*/c = N_A e^*/c$	9.648 7	10^{3} emu mol^{-1}		
SOMMERFELD fine-structure constant	α	7.297 35	10^{-3}	10^{-3}	
	$1/\alpha$	1.370 36	10^{2}	10^{2}	
	α^2	5.325 1	10^{-5}	10^{-5}	
PLANCK constant (quantum of action)	$h = 2\pi (e^*)^2/\alpha c$	6.626 2	10^{-27} erg s	10^{-34} J s	
	h/e^*	1.379 52	10^{-17} erg s esu^{-1}		
	$h c/e^*$	} 4.135 71	10^{-7} erg s emu^{-1}		
	h/e			10^{-15} J s C^{-1}	
Quantum-mechanical unit of angular momentum	$\hbar = h/2\pi$	1.054 59	10^{-27} erg s	10^{-34} J s	
1st PLANCK radiation constant	$c_1 = 2\pi h c^2$	3.741 8	10^{-5} erg cm^2 s^{-1}	10^{-16} W m^2	
	$h c^2$	5.955 3	10^{-6} erg cm^2 s^{-1}	10^{-17} W m^2	
2nd PLANCK radiation constant	$c_2 = h c/k$	1.438 8	cm K	10^{-2} m K	
	$c_2/c = h/k$	4.799 4	10^{-11} s K	10^{-11} s K	
Constant of WIEN's displacement law	$b = \lambda_{max} T = c_2/x$; $x = 4.965\,114\,23$	2.897 9	10^{-1} cm K	10^{-3} m K	
STEFAN-BOLTZMANN constant	$\sigma = \pi^2 k^4/60 \hbar^3 c^2$	5.669 6	10^{-5} erg cm^{-2} s^{-1} K^{-4}	10^{-8} W m^{-2} K^{-4}	
BOHR radius (of the first-quantized electron orbit of the hydrogen atom)	$a_0 = \alpha/4\pi R_\infty$	5.291 77	10^{-9} cm	10^{-11} m	

† The data on the physical constants (pages 228 and 229) have been compiled in collaboration with E. R. COHEN, North American Aviation Science Center, Thousand Oaks, Calif., USA. The values given are corrected from a consistent set derived by the Committee on Fundamental Constants of the National Academy of Sciences – National Research Council (USA)[1, 2]. The original set was approved by the International Union of Pure and Applied Physics at the 12th General Assembly in 1963[3] and published in 1965[4]. The numerical values given here correct these data to reflect a change of 20 ppm in the value of the Sommerfeld fine-structure constant. This change has been made necessary by recent measurements of the macroscopic quantum phase coherence in superconductors and on the fine structure in the spectrum of atomic hydrogen.

The quantities elementary charge, FARADAY constant, gyromagnetic ratio and magnetic moment, defined non-rationally in the symmetrical three-dimensional system of quantities, are given the symbols e^*, F^*, γ^* and μ^*; the corresponding quantities defined rationally in the four-dimensional system have the symbols e, F, γ and μ: $e^*/e = F^*/F = (4\pi\varepsilon_0)^{-1/2}$, $\gamma^*/\gamma = \mu^*/\mu = (\mu_0/4\pi)^{1/2}$ (see 'Electricity and Magnetism', page 215).

†† The molar number of molecules (see 'Quantities related to amount of substance', page 227). Formerly known as the LOSCHMIDT constant in German-speaking countries.

††† The number density of molecules of an ideal gas at 0 °C and 760 torr. Formerly known as the AVOGADRO constant in German-speaking countries.

§ cal$_{th}$ is an abbreviation of cal$_{thermochem}$ (see page 213).

	Symbol and formula	Numerical value	CGS system	International System of Units	Noncoherent units
Atomic constants (continued)					
Electron radius	$r_e = \alpha^3/4\pi R_\infty$	2.817 94	10^{-13} cm	10^{-15} m	
THOMSON cross-section	$(8\pi/3)\, r_e^2$	6.652 5	10^{-25} cm²	10^{-29} m²	10^{-1} barn
COMPTON wave length					
of electron	$\lambda_{C,e} = h/m_e c$	2.426 31	10^{-10} cm	10^{-12} m	
	$\lambda_{C,e}/2\pi$	3.861 59	10^{-11} cm	10^{-13} m	
of proton	$\lambda_{C,p} = h/m_p c$	1.321 44	10^{-13} cm	10^{-15} m	
	$\lambda_{C,p}/2\pi$	2.103 14	10^{-14} cm	10^{-16} m	
of neutron	$\lambda_{C,n} = h/m_n c$	1.319 62	10^{-13} cm	10^{-15} m	
	$\lambda_{C,n}/2\pi$	2.100 24	10^{-14} cm	10^{-16} m	
RYDBERG constant					
for an atom with a nucleus of infinite mass	R_∞	1.097 373 1	10^5 cm^{-1}	10^7 m^{-1}	
for ^{1}H atom	$R_H = R_\infty/(1+m_e/m_p)$	1.096 775 8	10^5 cm^{-1}	10^{-7} m^{-1}	
RYDBERG frequency					
for an atom with a nucleus of infinite mass	$R'_\infty = R_\infty c$	3.289 842	10^{15} s^{-1}	10^{15} s^{-1}	
for ^{1}H atom	$R'_H = R_H c$	3.288 052	10^{15} s^{-1}	10^{15} s^{-1}	
Charge to mass ratio for positron	e/m_e	1.758 80		10^{11} C kg^{-1}	
	e^*/m_e	5.272 76	10^{17} esu g^{-1}		
	$e^*/c\, m_e$	1.758 80	10^7 emu g^{-1}		
Charge to mass ratio for proton	e/m_p	9.579 00		10^7 C kg^{-1}	
	e^*/m_p	2.871 72	10^{14} esu g^{-1}		
	$e^*/m_p c$	9.579 00	10^3 emu g^{-1}		
Gyromagnetic ratio of proton	γ_p^* γ_p	} 2.675 19	10^4 s^{-1} emu^{-1}	10^8 s^{-1} T^{-1}	
Effective gyromagnetic ratio of proton in a spherical sample of water (uncorrected for diamagnetism in water sample)	$\gamma_p^{*\prime}$ γ'_p	} 2.675 13	10^4 s^{-1} emu^{-1}	10^8 s^{-1} T^{-1}	
BOHR magneton	$\mu_B^* = \hbar e^*/2 m_e c$ $\mu_B = \hbar e/2 m_e$	} 9.274 1	10^{-21} erg emu^{-1}	10^{-24} J T^{-1}	
Nuclear magneton	$\mu_N^* = (m_e/m_p)\, \mu_B^*$ $\mu_N = (m_e/m_p)\, \mu_B$	} 5.051 0	10^{-24} erg emu^{-1}	10^{-27} J T^{-1}	
Magnetic moment of electron	$\mu_e^* = \mu_B^* (\mu_e^*/\mu_B^*)$ $\mu_e = \mu_B (\mu_e/\mu_B)$	} 9.284 9	10^{-21} erg emu^{-1}	10^{-24} J T^{-1}	
	$\mu_e^*/\mu_B^* = \mu_e/\mu_B = 1+\alpha/2\pi - 0.328\alpha^2/\pi^2$	} 1.001 159 64			
Magnetic moment of proton	$\mu_p^* = \gamma_p^* \hbar/2$ $\mu_p = \gamma_p \hbar/2$	} 1.410 6	10^{-23} erg emu^{-1}	10^{-26} J T^{-1}	
	$\mu_p^*/\mu_B^* = \mu_p/\mu_B$	1.521 033	10^{-3}	10^{-3}	
	$\mu_p^*/\mu_N^* = \mu_p/\mu_N$	2.792 78			
Effective magnetic moment of proton in a spherical sample of water	$\mu_p^{*\prime}/\mu_N^* = \mu'_p/\mu_N$	2.792 71			
ZEEMAN splitting constant	$e^*/4\pi m c^2$ $e/4\pi m c$	} 4.668 6	10^{-5} cm^{-1} emu^{-1}	10 m^{-1} T^{-1}	
Atomic mass constant	$m_u = (1/N_A)$ g mol^{-1}	1.660 53	10^{-24} g	10^{-27} kg	
	$= m(^{12}C)/12$	1			u
Rest mass of electron †	$m_e = 4\pi (e^*)^2 R_\infty/\alpha^3 c^2$	9.109 6	10^{-28} g	10^{-31} kg	
	$= e^2 R_\infty/\varepsilon_0 \alpha^3 c^2$	5.485 93			10^{-4} u
Rest mass of proton †	$m_p = m(^1H) - m_e$	1.672 62	10^{-24} g	10^{-27} kg	
		1.007 276 61			u
Ratio of the rest masses of proton and electron	m_p/m_e	1.836 1	10^3	10^3	
Rest mass of neutron †	$m_n = A_{rn} m_u$	1.674 92	10^{-24} g	10^{-27} kg	
		1.008 665 20			u
Rest mass of ^{1}H atom †	$m(^1H) = A_r(^1H)\, m_u$	1.673 52	10^{-24} g	10^{-27} kg	
		1.007 825 2			u
Reduced mass of electron in ^{1}H atom	$\mu = m_e m_p/m(^1H)$	9.104 6	10^{-28} g	10^{-31} kg	
		5.482 94			10^{-4} u
Energy equivalents ††					
Atomic mass unit	$E(u) = c^2 \times (1\,u)$	1.492 411	10^{-3} erg	10^{-10} J	
		9.314 81			10^8 eV
Electron mass	$E(m_e) = c^2 m_e$	8.187 26	10^{-7} erg	10^{-14} J	
		5.110 04			10^5 eV
Proton mass	$E(m_p) = c^2 m_p$	1.503 27	10^{-3} erg	10^{-10} J	
		9.382 60			10^8 eV
Neutron mass	$E(m_n) = c^2 m_n$	1.505 34	10^{-3} erg	10^{-10} J	
		9.395 53			10^8 eV

† Relative atomic masses (A_r) (formerly 'atomic weights') of electron, proton, neutron and ^{1}H atom = numerical value × power of ten of the appropriate rest mass measured in the atomic mass unit u (dimensionless).

†† For other energy equivalents see page 213.

References

[1] National Academy of Sciences – National Research Council Committee, *Nat. Bur. Stand., Techn. News Bull.*, **47**, 175 (1963).

[2] COHEN and DUMOND, in JOHNSON, W. (Ed.), *Nuclidic Masses*, Proceedings of the 2nd International Conference on Nuclidic Masses, Vienna 1963, Springer, Vienna, 1964, page 152; COHEN and DUMOND, *Rev. mod. Phys.*, **37**, 537 (1965).

[3] International Union of Pure and Applied Physics, *Report of the 11th General Assembly*, Warsaw, 1963, pages 19 and 22.

[4] International Union of Pure and Applied Physics, *Symbols, Units and Nomenclature in Physics*, Document U.I.P.11 (S.U.N.65-3), 1965, page 30.

Standard substances

Mercury

Density under standard conditions[1] (0 °C, 760 torr):
$\varrho_n(\mathrm{Hg}) = 13.595\,08\ \mathrm{kg\ dm^{-3}}$

The mean density of pure mercury at the temperature t_{68} in a barometric column supported by the pressure p being measured is given, with sufficient accuracy over the temperature range from 0 °C to 40 °C and for the pressures relevant to the IPTS-68 (see page 209), by the relation[2]

$$\varrho\left(t_{68}, \frac{p}{2}\right) = \frac{\varrho\,(20\ ^\circ\mathrm{C}, p_0)}{[1 + A(t_{68} - 20\ ^\circ\mathrm{C}) + B(t_{68} - 20\ ^\circ\mathrm{C})^2] \cdot [1 - \varkappa\,(\frac{p}{2} - p_0)]}$$

where $A = 18\,115 \times 10^{-8}\ ^\circ\mathrm{C}^{-1}$; $B = 0.8 \times 10^{-8}\ ^\circ\mathrm{C}^{-2}$; compressibility $\varkappa = 4 \times 10^{-11}\ \mathrm{N^{-1}\ m^2}$; $\varrho\,(20\ ^\circ\mathrm{C}, p_0) = 13\,545.87\ \mathrm{kg/m^3}$.

Relative density with density of water as reference quantity ('specific gravity'):
$d(\mathrm{Hg}) = \varrho_n(\mathrm{Hg})/\varrho_{max}(H_2O) = 13.595\,46$

Water

Maximum density[3] (≈ 3.98 °C, 760 torr, air-free):
$\varrho_{max}(H_2O) = (0.999\,972 \pm 0.000\,003)\ \mathrm{kg\ dm^{-3}}$

Density between 0 and 40 °C in kg dm^{-3} (760 torr, air-saturated)[4]

°C		°C		°C		°C		°C	
0	0.999 840	3	0.999 964	6	0.999 940	9	0.999 781	12	0.999 498
1	0.999 899	4	0.999 972	7	0.999 902	10	0.999 700	13	0.999 378
2	0.999 940	5	0.999 964	8	0.999 849	11	0.999 606	14	0.999 245

°C	0.0	0.1	0.2	0.3	0.4	0.5	0.6	0.7	0.8	0.9
15	0.999 101	085	070	055	039	024	008	*992*	*976*	*960*
16	0.998 944	928	911	895	878	862	845	828	811	793
17	0.998 776	759	741	724	706	688	670	652	634	615
18	0.998 597	578	560	541	522	503	484	465	446	426
19	0.998 407	387	367	347	328	308	287	267	247	226
20	0.998 206	185	164	143	122	101	080	059	037	016
21	0.997 994	972	951	929	907	885	862	840	818	795
22	0.997 772	750	727	704	681	658	634	611	588	564
23	0.997 540	517	493	469	445	421	397	372	348	323
24	0.997 299	274	249	224	199	174	149	124	098	073
25	0.997 048	021	*996*	*970*	*944*	*918*	*892*	*865*	*839*	*813*

°C		°C		°C		°C		°C	
26	0.996 786	29	0.995 948	32	0.995 030	35	0.994 036	38	0.992 969
27	0.996 516	30	0.995 650	33	0.994 707	36	0.993 688	39	0.992 598
28	0.996 236	31	0.995 344	34	0.994 375	37	0.993 333	40	0.992 220

Density of heavy water (100% D_2O, 760 torr, air-free)

°C	kg dm^{-3}	Reference	°C	kg dm^{-3}	Reference
3.8	1.105 30	4a	20	1.105 24	4a
5	1.105 46	4a	25	1.104 34	6
10	1.105 85	4a	30	1.103 12	6
11.23	1.105 93*	5	35	1.101 64	6
15	1.105 74	4a	40	1.099 86	6

* Maximum density.

Specific heat capacity of water between 0 and 100 °C (at 760 torr)[7]

J g^{-1} K^{-1}

°C	0	1	2	3	4	5	6	7	8	9
0	4.2174	4.2138	4.2104	4.2074	4.2048	4.2019	4.1996	4.1974	4.1954	4.1936
10	4.1919	4.1904	4.1890	4.1877	4.1866	4.1855	4.1846	4.1837	4.1829	4.1822
20	4.1816	4.1810	4.1805	4.1801	4.1797	4.1793	4.1790	4.1787	4.1785	4.1783
30	4.1782	4.1781	4.1780	4.1780	4.1779	4.1779	4.1780	4.1780	4.1781	4.1782
40	4.1783	4.1784	4.1786	4.1788	4.1789	4.1792	4.1794	4.1796	4.1799	4.1801
50	4.1804	4.1807	4.1811	4.1814	4.1817	4.1821	4.1825	4.1829	4.1833	4.1837
60	4.1841	4.1846	4.1850	4.1855	4.1860	4.1865	4.1871	4.1876	4.1882	4.1887
70	4.1893	4.1899	4.1905	4.1912	4.1918	4.1925	4.1932	4.1939	4.1946	4.1954
80	4.1961	4.1969	4.1977	4.1985	4.1994	4.2002	4.2011	4.2020	4.2029	4.2039
90	4.2048	4.2058	4.2068	4.2078	4.2089	4.2100	4.2111	4.2122	4.2133	4.2145
100	4.2156									

$\mathrm{cal_{15}\ g^{-1}\ K^{-1}}$ (calculated by the editors from the CIPM values)[7]

°C	0	1	2	3	4	5	6	7	8	9
	1. *0.*	1. *0.*	1. *0.*	1. *0.*	1. *0.*	1. *0.*	1. *0.*	1. *0.*	1. *0.*	1. *0.*
0	007 62	006 76	005 95	005 23	004 54	003 92	003 37	002 84	002 37	001 94
10	001 53	001 17	000 84	000 53	000 26	000 00	*999 78*	*999 57*	*999 38*	*999 21*
20	*999 07*	*998 92*	*998 81*	*998 71*	*998 61*	*998 52*	*998 45*	*998 38*	*998 33*	*998 28*
30	*998 26*	*998 23*	*998 21*	*998 21*	*998 18*	*998 18*	*998 21*	*998 21*	*998 23*	*998 26*
40	*998 28*	*998 30*	*998 35*	*998 40*	*998 42*	*998 49*	*998 54*	*998 59*	*998 66*	*998 71*
50	*998 78*	*998 85*	*998 95*	*999 02*	*999 09*	*999 19*	*999 28*	*999 38*	*999 47*	*999 57*
60	*999 67*	*999 78*	*999 88*	000 00	000 12	000 24	000 38	000 50	000 65	000 76
70	000 91	001 05	001 19	001 36	001 51	001 67	001 84	002 01	002 17	002 37
80	002 53	002 72	002 91	003 11	003 32	003 51	003 73	003 94	004 16	004 40
90	004 61	004 85	005 09	005 33	005 59	005 85	006 12	006 38	006 64	006 93
100	007 19									

For the triple and boiling points of water and melting point of ice see page 209; for the vapour pressure of water see pages 256–258.

Viscosity of water between 0 and 40 °C[8]

Temperature t in °C	Viscosity ratio $\eta_t/\eta_{20\ ^\circ\mathrm{C}}$	Dynamic viscosity η in cP	Kinematic viscosity ν in cSt
0	1.788 5	1.792	1.792
5	1.517 0	1.520	1.520
10	1.304 3	1.306 9	1.307 3
15	1.136 0	1.138 3	1.139 3
20	1.000 0	1.002 0	1.003 8
25	0.888 5	0.890 3	0.892 9
30	0.795 9	0.797 5	0.801 0
35	0.717 9	0.719 3	0.723 6
40	0.651 8	0.653 1	0.658 2

Air

Standard density of dry air free of carbon dioxide (0 °C, 760 torr)[9]:
$\varrho_n(\mathrm{air}) = 1.292\,8 \times 10^{-3}\ \mathrm{kg\ dm^{-3}}$

Standard conditions for air in spectroscopy:
760 torr, 15 °C, 0.03% CO_2, dry

Acceleration due to gravity

Standard acceleration due to gravity[10]:
$g_n = 980.665$ Gal (cm s^{-2})

International gravity formula[11] (based on the international terrestrial ellipsoid):

$$\gamma_0 = (980.632\,272 - 2.586\,145 \cos 2B + 0.002\,878 \cos 4B - 0.000\,004 \cos 6B)\ \mathrm{Gal}$$

where γ_0 = acceleration due to gravity at sea level, B = latitude. This yields the following values for different degrees of latitude (calculated by the editors):

Latitude in °	γ_0 in Gal	γ_0/g_n	g_n/γ_0	Latitude in °	γ_0 in Gal	γ_0/g_n	g_n/γ_0
0	978.0490	0.997 332	1.002 675	45	980.6294	0.999 964	1.000 036
5	0881	372	635	46	7197	1.000 056	0.999 944
10	2043	491	516	47	8098	148	852
15	3940	684	321	48	8998	239	761
20	6517	947	057	49	9894	331	669
25	9694	0.998 271	1.001 732	50	981.0787	422	578
30	979.3378	647	355	51	1673	512	488
31	4165	727	275	52	2554	602	398
32	4968	809	193	53	3427	691	309
33	5785	892	109	54	4291	779	221
34	6614	977	025	55	5146	866	134
35	7456	0.999 062	1.000 938	56	5990	952	048
36	8308	149	851	57	6822	1.001 037	0.998 964
37	9170	237	763	58	7642	121	880
38	980.0041	326	674	59	8448	203	798
39	0920	416	585	60	9239	284	718
40	1805	506	494	65	982.2941	661	342
41	2696	597	403	70	6139	987	017
42	3591	688	312	75	8734	1.002 252	0.997 753
43	4490	780	220	80	983.0647	447	559
44	5391	872	128	85	1818	566	440
				90	2213	607	400

The true acceleration due to gravity is probably about 14 mGal less than the value calculated from the international gravity formula[12].

Several new determinations of the acceleration due to gravity have recently been made[13]. The reference value of the acceleration due to gravity in the Potsdam system has meanwhile been lowered by 14 mGal following the resolutions adopted by the International Association of Geodesy[14] and by the International Committee of Weights and Measures[15] under the powers conferred on it by the 11th General Conference of Weights and Measures[15].

References

1 Cook and Stone, *Phil. Trans. Roy. Soc.*, **250A**, 279 (1957); Cook, A. H., *Phil. Trans. Roy. Soc.*, **254A**, 125 (1961); Beattie et al., *Proc. Amer. Acad. Arts Sci.*, **74**, 371 (1941).

2 Conférence Générale des Poids et Mesures, *Comptes rendus des séances de la 13e Conférence générale des Poids et Mesures*, Paris 1967/1968, Bureau International des Poids et Mesures, Sèvres, 1969, page A8.

3 Comité International des Poids et Mesures, *Proc.-Verb. Com. internat. Poids Mes.* (2), **22**, 77 (1950); Stille, U., *Messen und Rechnen in der Physik*, 2nd ed., Vieweg, Braunschweig, 1961, page 286.

4 Calculated from Tilton and Taylor, *J. Res. Nat. Bur. Stand.*, **18**, 205 (1937).

4a Chang and Chien, *J. Amer. chem. Soc.*, **63**, 1709 (1941).

5 Stokland et al., *Trans. Faraday Soc.*, **35**, 312 (1939).

6 Schrader and Wirtz, *Z. Naturforsch.*, **6a**, 220 (1951).

7 Comité International des Poids et Mesures, *Proc.-Verb. Com. int. Poids Mes.*, **22**, 79 (1950).

8 Weber, W., *Z. angew. Phys.*, **7**, 96 (1955).

9 Otto and Thomas, in Hausen, H. (Ed.), *Landolt-Börnstein, Physikalisch-chemische Tabellen*, 6th ed., vol. 4, part 4, section a, Springer, Berlin, 1967, page 174; Din, F., *Thermodynamic Functions of Gases*, vol. 2, Butterworth, London, 1956.

10 Conférence Générale des Poids et Mesures, *Comptes rendus des séances de la 3e Conférence générale des Poids et Mesures*, Paris 1901, Gauthier-Villars, Paris, 1901, page 70.

Periodic System of the Elements[1]

For each element the following are given: atomic number (*italics*), symbol, atomic weight (relative atomic mass)[2]

Period	Group I	Group II	Group III	Group IV	Group V	Group VI	Group VII	Group VIII
	a b	a b	a b	a b	a b	a b	a b	a b[3]
1	*1.* H 1.00797[4]							*2.* He 4.0026
2	*3.* Li 6.939	*4.* Be 9.0122	*5.* B 10.811[4]	*6.* C 12.01115[4]	*7.* N 14.0067	*8.* O 15.9994[4]	*9.* F 18.9984	*10.* Ne 20.179[5]
3	*11.* Na 22.9898	*12.* Mg 24.305	*13.* Al 26.9815	*14.* Si 28.086[4]	*15.* P 30.9738	*16.* S 32.064[4]	*17.* Cl 35.453[5]	*18.* Ar 39.948
4 (3 d)	*19.* K 39.102	*20.* Ca 40.08	*21.* Sc 44.956	*22.* Ti 47.90	*23.* V 50.942	*24.* Cr 51.996	*25.* Mn 54.9380	*26.* Fe; *27.* Co; *28.* Ni 55.847[5] 58.9332 58.71
	29. Cu 63.546[5]	*30.* Zn 65.37	*31.* Ga 69.72	*32.* Ge 72.59	*33.* As 74.9216	*34.* Se 78.96	*35.* Br 79.904[5]	*36.* Kr 83.80
5 (4 d)	*37.* Rb 85.47	*38.* Sr 87.62	*39.* Y 88.905	*40.* Zr 91.22	*41.* Nb 92.906	*42.* Mo 95.94	*43.* Tc (99)*	*44.* Ru; *45.* Rh; *46.* Pd 101.07 102.905 106.4
	47. Ag 107.868[5]	*48.* Cd 112.40	*49.* In 114.82	*50.* Sn 118.69	*51.* Sb 121.75	*52.* Te 127.60	*53.* I 126.9044	*54.* Xe 131.30
6 (5 d) (4 f)	*55.* Cs 132.905	*56.* Ba 137.34	*57.* La 138.91 4f	*72.* Hf 178.49	*73.* Ta 180.948	*74.* W 183.85	*75.* Re 186.2	*76.* Os; *77.* Ir; *78.* Pt 190.2 192.2 195.09
	79. Au 196.967	*80.* Hg 200.59	*81.* Tl 204.37	*82.* Pb 207.19	*83.* Bi 208.980	*84.* Po (210)*	*85.* At (210)	*86.* Rn (222)
7 (6 d) (5 f)	*87.* Fr (223)	*88.* Ra (226)	*89.* Ac (227) 5f					

Lanthanides (rare-earth elements)

4f	*58.* Ce 140.12	*59.* Pr 140.907	*60.* Nd 144.24	*61.* Pm (147)*	*62.* Sm 150.35	*63.* Eu 151.96	*64.* Gd 157.25	*65.* Tb 158.924	*66.* Dy 162.50	*67.* Ho 164.930	*68.* Er 167.26	*69.* Tm 168.934	*70.* Yb 173.04	*71.* Lu 174.97

Actinides

5f	*90.* Th 232.038	*91.* Pa (231)	*92.* U 238.03	*93.* Np (237)	*94.* Pu (244)	*95.* Am (243)	*96.* Cm (247)	*97.* Bk (247)	*98.* Cf (252)*	*99.* Es (254)	*100.* Fm (257)	*101.* Md (257)	*102.* No (255)	*103.* Lr (256)

[1] Adapted from Eucken, A. (Ed.), *Landolt-Börnstein, Zahlenwerte und Funktionen aus Physik, Chemie, Astronomie, Geophysik und Technik*, vol. 1: *Atom- und Molekularphysik*, Part 1: *Atome und Ionen*, 6th ed., Springer, Berlin, 1950, page 11.

[2] Based on the assigned mass 12 for the carbon isotope ^{12}C and taken from the Table of Atomic Weights 1967 (International Union of Pure and Applied Chemistry, *Comptes rendus de la 24e Conférence, 1967*, Butterworth, London, 1968, page 130 sq.). A value in parentheses is the mass number of the most stable known isotope or, when marked with an asterisk, of the best-known one. See also page 226.

[3] Also known as Group 0.

[4] These atomic weights vary because of natural variations in the relative abundances of their isotopes. The observed ranges are: boron ± 0.003, carbon ± 0.00005, oxygen ± 0.0001, silicon ± 0.001, sulphur ± 0.003, hydrogen ±0.00001.

[5] These atomic weights have the following uncertainty due to experimental error: bromine ± 0.001, chlorine ± 0.001, copper ± 0.001, iron ± 0.003, neon ± 0.003, silver ± 0.001.

[11] Heiskanen, W., *Gerlands Beitr. Geophys.*, **19**, 356 (1928); International Union of Geodesy and Geophysics, *Bull. géod. int.*, No. 27, 238 (1930); Cassinis, G., *Bull. géod. int.*, No. 26, 40 (1930); Cassinis, G., *Bull. géod. int.*, No. 32, 313 (1931); Cassinis et al., *R. Comm. geod. ital.* (NS), No. 13 (1937).

[12] International Association of Geodesy, *Comptes rendus de la XIVe Assemblée générale de l'Union Internationale Géodésique et Géophysique*, Zurich 1967, Institut Géophysique National, Paris, 1968, page 146: Résolution 22.

[13] Cook, A. H., *Metrologia*, **1**, 84 and 184 (1965); Faller, J. E., Thesis, Princeton University, March 1963, and *J. Geophys. Res.*, **70**, 4035 (1965); Hammond and Faller, IEEE, **QE-3**, 597 (1967); News and Views, *Nature*, **214**, 228 (1967); Sakuma et al., *Proc.-Verb. Com. int. Poids Mes.*, (2) **35**, 45 (1967); Sakuma and Chartier, *Proc.-Verb. Com. int. Poids Mes.*, (2) **36** (in press).

[14] Bureau Gravimétrique International, *Bulletin d'Information*, No. 17, Paris, 1967, page 58.

[15] Conférence Générale des Poids et Mesures, *Comptes rendus des séances de la 11e Conférence générale des Poids et Mesures*, Paris 1960, Gauthier-Villars, Paris, 1961, pages 61 and 86: Résolution 11; Comité International des Poids et Mesures, *Proc.-Verb. Com. int. Poids Mes.*, (2) **36** (in press).

Name	Symbol	Atomic number	Atomic weight[1] 1967
Actinium	Ac	89	(227)
Aluminium	Al	13	26.9815
Americium	Am	95	(243)
Antimony	Sb	51	121.75
Argon	Ar	18	39.948
Arsenic	As	33	74.9216
Astatine	At	85	(210)
Barium	Ba	56	137.34
Berkelium	Bk	97	(247)
Beryllium	Be	4	9.0122
Bismuth	Bi	83	208.980
Boron	B	5	10.811[2]
Bromine	Br	35	79.904[3]
Cadmium	Cd	48	112.40
Caesium	Cs	55	132.905
Calcium	Ca	20	40.08
Californium	Cf	98	(252)*
Carbon	C	6	12.01115[2]
Cassiopeium	Cp	See Lutetium	
Cerium	Ce	58	140.12
Chlorine	Cl	17	35.453[3]
Chromium	Cr	24	51.996
Cobalt	Co	27	58.9332
Columbium	Cb	See Niobium	
Copper	Cu	29	63.546[3]
Curium	Cm	96	(247)
Dysprosium	Dy	66	162.50
Einsteinium	Es	99	(254)
Emanation	Em	See Radon	
Erbium	Er	68	167.26
Europium	Eu	63	151.96
Fermium	Fm	100	(257)
Fluorine	F	9	18.9984
Francium	Fr	87	(223)
Gadolinium	Gd	64	157.25
Gallium	Ga	31	69.72
Germanium	Ge	32	72.59
Glucinium	Gl	See Beryllium	
Gold	Au	79	196.967
Hafnium	Hf	72	178.49
Helium	He	2	4.0026
Holmium	Ho	67	164.930
Hydrogen	H	1	1.00797[2]
Illinium	Il	See Promethium	
Indium	In	49	114.82
Iodine	I	53	126.9044
Iridium	Ir	77	192.2
Iron	Fe	26	55.847[3]
Krypton	Kr	36	83.80
Lanthanum	La	57	138.91
Lawrencium	Lr	103	(256)
Lead	Pb	82	207.19
Lithium	Li	3	6.939
Lutetium	Lu	71	174.97
Magnesium	Mg	12	24.305
Manganese	Mn	25	54.9380
Mendelevium	Md	101	(257)
Mercury	Hg	80	200.59

Name	Symbol	Atomic number	Atomic weight[1] 1967
Molybdenum	Mo	42	95.94
Neodymium	Nd	60	144.24
Neon	Ne	10	20.179[3]
Neptunium	Np	93	(237)
Nickel	Ni	28	58.71
Niobium	Nb	41	92.906
Niton	Nt	See Radon	
Nitrogen	N	7	14.0067
Nobelium	No	102	(255)
Osmium	Os	76	190.2
Oxygen	O	8	15.9994[2]
Palladium	Pd	46	106.4
Phosphorus	P	15	30.9738
Platinum	Pt	78	195.09
Plutonium	Pu	94	(244)
Polonium	Po	84	(210)*
Potassium	K	19	39.102
Praseodymium	Pr	59	140.907
Promethium	Pm	61	(147)*
Protactinium	Pa	91	(231)
Radium	Ra	88	(226)
Radon	Rn	86	(222)
Rhenium	Re	75	186.2
Rhodium	Rh	45	102.905
Rubidium	Rb	37	85.47
Ruthenium	Ru	44	101.07
Samarium	Sm	62	150.35
Scandium	Sc	21	44.956
Selenium	Se	34	78.96
Silicon	Si	14	28.086[2]
Silver	Ag	47	107.868[3]
Sodium	Na	11	22.9898
Strontium	Sr	38	87.62
Sulphur	S	16	32.064[2]
Tantalum	Ta	73	180.948
Technetium	Tc	43	(99)*
Tellurium	Te	52	127.60
Terbium	Tb	65	158.924
Thallium	Tl	81	204.37
Thorium	Th	90	232.038
Thulium	Tm	69	168.934
Tin	Sn	50	118.69
Titanium	Ti	22	47.90
Tungsten	W	74	183.85
Uranium	U	92	238.03
Vanadium	V	23	50.942
Wolfram	W	See Tungsten	
Xenon	Xe	54	131.30
Ytterbium	Yb	70	173.04
Yttrium	Y	39	88.905
Zinc	Zn	30	65.37
Zirconium	Zr	40	91.22

[1] See footnote [2], page 231.
[2] See footnote [4], page 231.
[3] See footnote [5], page 231.

Symbol	Name	Atomic number	Atomic weight[1] 1967
Ac	Actinium	89	(227)
Ag	Silver	47	107.868 [3]
Al	Aluminium	13	26.9815
Am	Americium	95	(243)
Ar	Argon	18	39.948
As	Arsenic	33	74.9216
At	Astatine	85	(210)
Au	Gold	79	196.967
B	Boron	5	10.811 [2]
Ba	Barium	56	137.34
Be	Beryllium	4	9.0122
Bi	Bismuth	83	208.980
Bk	Berkelium	97	(247)
Br	Bromine	35	79.904 [3]
C	Carbon	6	12.01115 [2]
Ca	Calcium	20	40.08
Cb	Columbium	See Nb	
Cd	Cadmium	48	112.40
Ce	Cerium	58	140.12
Cf	Californium	98	(252)*
Cl	Chlorine	17	35.453 [3]
Cm	Curium	96	(247)
Co	Cobalt	27	58.9332
Cp	Cassiopeium	See Lu	
Cr	Chromium	24	51.996
Cs	Caesium	55	132.905
Cu	Copper	29	63.546 [3]
Dy	Dysprosium	66	162.50
Em	Emanation	See Rn	
Er	Erbium	68	167.26
Es	Einsteinium	99	(254)
Eu	Europium	63	151.96
F	Fluorine	9	18.9984
Fe	Iron	26	55.847 [3]
Fm	Fermium	100	(257)
Fr	Francium	87	(223)
Ga	Gallium	31	69.72
Gd	Gadolinium	64	157.25
Ge	Germanium	32	72.59
Gl	Glucinium	See Be	
H	Hydrogen	1	1.00797 [2]
He	Helium	2	4.0026
Hf	Hafnium	72	178.49
Hg	Mercury	80	200.59
Ho	Holmium	67	164.930
I	Iodine	53	126.9044
Il	Illinium	See Pm	
In	Indium	49	114.82
Ir	Iridium	77	192.2
K	Potassium	19	39.102
Kr	Krypton	36	83.80
La	Lanthanum	57	138.91
Li	Lithium	3	6.939
Lr	Lawrencium	103	(256)
Lu	Lutetium	71	174.97
Md	Mendelevium	101	(257)
Mg	Magnesium	12	24.305
Mn	Manganese	25	54.9380
Mo	Molybdenum	42	95.94
N	Nitrogen	7	14.0067
Na	Sodium	11	22.9898
Nb	Niobium	41	92.906
Nd	Neodymium	60	144.24
Ne	Neon	10	20.179 [3]
Ni	Nickel	28	58.71
No	Nobelium	102	(255)
Np	Neptunium	93	(237)
Nt	Niton	See Rn	
O	Oxygen	8	15.9994 [2]
Os	Osmium	76	190.2
P	Phosphorus	15	30.9738
Pa	Protactinium	91	(231)
Pb	Lead	82	207.19
Pd	Palladium	46	106.4
Pm	Promethium	61	(147)*
Po	Polonium	84	(210)*
Pr	Praseodymium	59	140.907
Pt	Platinum	78	195.09
Pu	Plutonium	94	(244)
Ra	Radium	88	(226)
Rb	Rubidium	37	85.47
Re	Rhenium	75	186.2
Rh	Rhodium	45	102.905
Rn	Radon	86	(222)
Ru	Ruthenium	44	101.07
S	Sulphur	16	32.064 [2]
Sb	Antimony	51	121.75
Sc	Scandium	21	44.956
Se	Selenium	34	78.96
Si	Silicon	14	28.086 [2]
Sm	Samarium	62	150.35
Sn	Tin	50	118.69
Sr	Strontium	38	87.62
Ta	Tantalum	73	180.948
Tb	Terbium	65	158.924
Tc	Technetium	43	(99)*
Te	Tellurium	52	127.60
Th	Thorium	90	232.038
Ti	Titanium	22	47.90
Tl	Thallium	81	204.37
Tm	Thulium	69	168.934
Tu	Tungsten	See W	
U	Uranium	92	238.03
V	Vanadium	23	50.942
W	Tungsten	74	183.85
Xe	Xenon	54	131.30
Y	Yttrium	39	88.905
Yb	Ytterbium	70	173.04
Zn	Zinc	30	65.37
Zr	Zirconium	40	91.22

[1] See footnote [2], page 231.
[2] See footnote [4], page 231.
[3] See footnote [5], page 231.

Z Atomic number	Symbol	Element English French German	Atomic weight 1967[1] [or mol. wt.]	Valency	Melting point[2] at 760 mm Hg (unless otherwise stated) °C	Boiling point[2] at 760 mm Hg (unless otherwise stated) °C	Density[2] Gases: g/l at 760 mm Hg and 0 °C Others: g/cm³ or specific gravity 20 °/4 °C (unless otherwise stated)		Natural abundance: Earth's crust, hydrosphere, atmosphere[3] %	Natural abundance: Atmosphere (troposphere)[4] vol %	Natural abundance: Universe (atoms per 10^6 Si atoms)[5]	Natural abundance: Human body[6] %	Natural isotopes[7]: Isotope (mass number A)	Natural isotopes[7]: Relative abundance atoms %	Natural isotopes[7]: Mass[8]	Natural isotopes[7]: Mode of decay[9]	Natural isotopes[7]: Energy in MeV and percentage of decay	Natural isotopes[7]: Half-life[10]
1	H $[H_2]$	**Hydrogen**[11] Hydrogène Wasserstoff	1.00797[12] [2.01594]	1	−259.14	−252.5	gas liquid	0.08988 0.070/−252°	0.88	0.00005	4.00×10^{10}	10.0	^{1}H(H) ^{2}H(D) ^{3}H(T)	99.985 0.015 see ref.[13]	1.00783 2.01410 3.016049	 β⁻ no γ	 0.0181 (100%)	 12.26y
2	He	**Helium** Hélium Helium	4.0026	0	−272.2 at 26 atm	−268.6	gas	0.177	4.2×10^{-7}	0.000524	3.08×10^{9}		^{3}He ^{4}He	1.3×10^{-4} (in the atmosphere) ~100	3.01603 4.00260			
3	Li	**Lithium** Lithium Lithium	6.939	1	179	1317	solid liquid	0.534 0.507/200°	0.006		100		^{6}Li ^{7}Li	7.42 92.58	6.01513 7.01601			
4	Be	**Beryllium** Béryllium Beryllium	9.0122	2	1278±5	2970	solid	1.848	5.3×10^{-4}		20		^{9}Be	100	9.01219			
5	B	**Boron** Bore Bor	10.811[12]	3	2300	(sublimes 2550)	crystalline amorphous	2.34 2.37	0.0016		24	$<1.4\times10^{-5}$	^{10}B ^{11}B	19.6 80.4	10.01294 11.00931			
6	C	**Carbon** Carbone Kohlenstoff	12.01115[12]	2, 4	3550 (sublimes > 3500)	4827	amorphous graphite diamond	1.8–2.1 1.9–2.3 3.15–3.53	0.087	CO: 0–trace CO_2: 0.0314	3.5×10^{6}	18.0	^{12}C ^{13}C ^{14}C	98.89 1.11 see ref.[14]	12.00000 13.00335 14.00324	 β⁻ no γ	 0.1567 (100%)	 5.77×10^{3}y
7	N $[N_2]$	**Nitrogen** Azote Stickstoff	14.0067 [28.0134]	3, 5	−209.86	−195.8	gas liquid solid	1.25060 0.808/−195.8° 1.026/−252°	0.030	78.084	6.6×10^{6}	3.0	^{14}N ^{15}N	99.63 0.37	14.00307 15.00011			
8	O $[O_2]$	**Oxygen** Oxygène Sauerstoff	15.9994[12] [31.9988]	2	−218.4	−182.970	gas liquid	1.4290 1.14/−182.96°	49.5	20.9476 (O_2) $2\text{–}7\times10^{-6}$ (O_3)	2.15×10^{7}	65.0	^{16}O ^{17}O ^{18}O	99.759 0.037 0.204	15.99491 16.99913 17.99916			
9	F $[F_2]$	**Fluorine** Fluor Fluor	18.9984 [37.9968]	1	−219.62 (freezing point)	−188.14	gas liquid	1.696 1.108/−188.14°	0.028		1600	2×10^{-2}	^{19}F	100	18.9984			
10	Ne	**Neon** Néon Neon	20.179[15]	0	−248.67	−245.92	gas liquid	0.89990 1.207/−245.92°	5×10^{-7}	0.001818	8.6×10^{6}		^{20}Ne ^{21}Ne ^{22}Ne	90.92 0.257 8.82	19.99244 20.99385 21.99138			
11	Na	**Sodium** Sodium Natrium	22.9898	1	97.81 ±0.03	892	solid	0.971	2.63		4.38×10^{4}	1.5×10^{-1}	^{23}Na	100	22.98977			
12	Mg	**Magnesium** Magnésium Magnesium	24.305	2	651	1107	solid	1.738	1.95		9.12×10^{5}	5×10^{-2}	^{24}Mg ^{25}Mg ^{26}Mg	78.70 10.13 11.17	23.98504 24.98584 25.98259			

13	Al	**Aluminium (Aluminum)** Aluminium Aluminium	26.9815	3	660.1	2467	solid	2.6989	7.57		9.48×10^{4}	1.4×10^{-4}	^{27}Al	100	26.98153			
14	Si	**Silicon** Silicium Silicium	28.086[12]	4	1410	2355	solid	2.33/25°	25.80		1×10^{6}	2×10^{-3}	^{28}Si ^{29}Si ^{30}Si	92.21 4.70 3.09	27.97693 28.97649 29.97376			
15	P	**Phosphorus** Phosphore Phosphor	30.9738	3, 5	yellow 44.1	280	yellow: red: black:	solid 1.82 solid 2.20 solid 2.25–2.69	0.09		1×10^{4}	1.0	^{31}P	100	30.97376			
16	S	**Sulphur (Sulfur)** Soufre Schwefel	32.064[12]	2, 4, 6	rhombic 112.8 mono-clinic 119.0	444.600	rhombic: monoclinic:	solid 2.07 solid 1.957	0.048	0–0.0001 (SO_2)	3.75×10^{5}	2.5×10^{-1}	^{32}S ^{33}S ^{34}S ^{36}S	95.0 0.76 4.22 0.014	31.97207 32.97146 33.96786 35.96709			
17	Cl [Cl_2]	**Chlorine** Chlore Chlor	35.453[15] [70.906]	1, 3, 5, 7	−100.98 (freezing point)	−34.6	gas liquid	3.214 1.56/−33.6°	0.19		8850	1.5×10^{-1}	^{35}Cl ^{37}Cl	75.53 24.47	34.96885 36.96590			
18	Ar	**Argon** Argon Argon	39.948	0	−189.2 (freezing point)	−185.7	gas liquid solid	1.7837 1.402/−185.7° 1.65/−223°	3.6×10^{-4}	0.934	1.5×10^{5}		^{36}Ar ^{38}Ar ^{40}Ar	0.337 0.063 99.60	35.96755 37.96272 39.96238			
19	K	**Potassium** Potassium Kalium	39.102	1	63.65	754	solid	0.862	2.41		3160	2×10^{-1}	^{39}K ^{40}K ^{41}K	93.10 0.0118 6.88	38.96371 39.96401 40.96184	 β^- γ K	 1.32(9%) 1.46 (11%) 1.51 (11%)	 1.3×10^{9}y
20	Ca	**Calcium** Calcium Calcium	40.08	2	842–848	1487	solid	1.55	3.38		4.90×10^{4}	1.5	^{40}Ca ^{42}Ca ^{43}Ca ^{44}Ca ^{46}Ca ^{48}Ca	96.97 0.64 0.145 2.06 0.0033 0.18	39.96259 41.95863 42.95878 43.95549 45.95369 47.95236	 β^-	 0.12	 $>2\times10^{16}$y
21	Sc	**Scandium** Scandium Scandium	44.956	3	1539	2727	solid	2.992	5.1×10^{-4}		28		^{45}Sc	100	44.95592			
22	Ti	**Titanium** Titane Titan	47.90	2, 3, 4	1675	3260	solid	4.54	0.41		2440	$<2\times10^{-5}$	^{46}Ti ^{47}Ti ^{48}Ti ^{49}Ti ^{50}Ti	7.93 7.28 73.94 5.51 5.34	45.95263 46.95176 47.94795 48.94787 49.94479			
23	V	**Vanadium** Vanadium Vanadium (Vanadin)	50.942	2, 3, 4, 5	1890±10	~3000	solid	6.11/18.7°	0.014		220	3×10^{-5}	^{50}V ^{51}V	0.24 99.76	49.94716 50.94398	β^-, K γ	 0.71 1.59	$\approx6\times10^{14}$y

For footnotes see page 247.

Z Atomic number	Symbol	Element: **English** French German *Latin*	Atomic weight 1967[1]	Valency	Melting point[2] at 760 mm Hg (unless otherwise stated) °C	Boiling point[2] at 760 mm Hg (unless otherwise stated) °C	Density[2] Gases: g/l at 760 mm Hg and 0 °C Others: g/cm³ or specific gravity 20 °/4 °C (unless otherwise stated)	Natural abundance: Earth's crust, hydrosphere, atmosphere[3] %	Natural abundance: Atmosphere (troposphere)[4] vol %	Natural abundance: Universe (atoms per 10⁶ Si atoms)[5]	Natural abundance: Human body[6] %	Natural isotopes[7]: Isotope (mass number A)	Natural isotopes: Relative abundance atoms %	Natural isotopes: Mass[8]	Natural isotopes: Mode of decay[9]	Natural isotopes: Energy in MeV and percentage of decay	Natural isotopes: Half-life[10]
24	Cr	**Chromium** Chrome Chrom	51.996	2, 3, 6	1890	2482	solid 7.18–7.20	0.019		7800	$<9 \times 10^{-6}$	^{50}Cr ^{52}Cr ^{53}Cr ^{54}Cr	4.31 83.76 9.55 2.38	49.946 05 51.940 51 52.940 65 53.938 88			
25	Mn	**Manganese** Manganèse Mangan	54.938 0	1, 2, 3, 4, 6, 7	1244±3	2097	solid 7.21–7.44	0.085		6850	3×10^{-5}	^{55}Mn	100	54.938 05			
26	Fe	**Iron** Fer Eisen *Ferrum*	55.847[15]	2, 3, 4, 6	1535	3000	solid 7.874	4.7		6.00×10^{5}	6×10^{-3}	^{54}Fe ^{56}Fe ^{57}Fe ^{58}Fe	5.82 91.66 2.19 0.33	53.939 62 55.934 93 56.935 39 57.933 27			
27	Co	**Cobalt** Cobalt Cobalt	58.933 2	2, 3	1492	2900	solid 8.9	0.003 7		1800	$<4 \times 10^{-6}$	^{59}Co	100	58.933 19			
28	Ni	**Nickel** Nickel Nickel	58.71	0, 1, 2, 3	1453	2732	solid 8.902/25°	0.015		2.74×10^{4}	$<1.4 \times 10^{-5}$	^{58}Ni ^{60}Ni ^{61}Ni ^{62}Ni ^{64}Ni	67.88 26.23 1.19 3.66 1.08	57.935 34 59.930 78 60.931 05 61.928 35 63.927 96			
29	Cu	**Copper** Cuivre Kupfer *Cuprum*	63.546[15]	1, 2	1083	2595	solid 8.96	0.010		212	1.4×10^{-4}	^{63}Cu ^{65}Cu	69.09 30.91	62.929 59 64.927 79			
30	Zn	**Zinc** Zinc Zink	65.37	2	419.505	907	solid 7.133/25°	0.012		486	3.3×10^{-3}	^{64}Zn ^{66}Zn ^{67}Zn ^{68}Zn ^{70}Zn	48.89 27.81 4.11 18.57 0.62	63.929 15 65.926 05 66.927 15 67.924 87 69.925 35			
31	Ga	**Gallium** Gallium Gallium	69.72	2, 3	29.78	2403	solid 5.907	0.001 4		11.4		^{69}Ga ^{71}Ga	60.4 39.6	68.925 68 70.924 84			
32	Ge	**Germanium** Germanium Germanium	72.59	2, 4	937.4	2830	solid 5.323/25°	5.6×10^{-4}		50.5		^{70}Ge ^{72}Ge ^{73}Ge ^{74}Ge ^{76}Ge	20.52 27.43 7.76 36.54 7.76	69.924 28 71.921 74 72.923 36 73.921 15 75.921 36			
33	As	**Arsenic** Arsenic Arsen	74.921 6	3, 5	crystalline 817 at 28 atm (subl. 613)		crystalline 5.73 amorphous 4.73 yellow: solid 1.97	5.5×10^{-4}		4.0	2×10^{-5}	^{75}As	100	74.921 58			

34	Se	**Selenium** Sélénium Selen	78.96	2, 4, 6	grey 217 red 70–180	684.9 ±1.0	grey red	4.79/25° 4.46	8×10^{-5}		67.6		^{74}Se ^{76}Se ^{77}Se ^{78}Se ^{80}Se ^{82}Se	0.87 9.02 7.58 23.52 49.82 9.19	73.92245 75.91923 76.91993 77.91735 79.91651 81.91666			
35	Br	**Bromine** Brome Brom	79.904[15]	1, 3, 5, 7	−7.2	58.78	gas liquid	7.59 3.12	6×10^{-4}		13.4		^{79}Br ^{81}Br	50.54 49.46	78.91835 80.91634			
36	Kr	**Krypton** Krypton Krypton	83.80	0 (2, 4)	−156.6	−152.30 ±0.10	gas	3.733	1.9×10^{-8}	0.000114	51.3		^{78}Kr ^{80}Kr ^{82}Kr ^{83}Kr ^{84}Kr ^{86}Kr	0.35 2.27 11.56 11.55 57.90 17.37	77.92037 79.91639 81.91348 82.91413 83.9115 85.91062			
37	Rb	**Rubidium** Rubidium Rubidium	85.47	1, 2, 3, 4	38.89	688	liquid solid	1.475/39.0° 1.532	0.029		6.5	1.7×10^{-3}	^{85}Rb ^{87}Rb	72.15 27.85	84.91171 86.90918	 β^- no γ	 0.27	 4.7×10^{10}y
38	Sr	**Strontium** Strontium Strontium	87.62	2	769	1384	solid	2.54	0.014		18.9	2×10^{-4}	^{84}Sr ^{86}Sr ^{87}Sr ^{88}Sr	0.56 9.86 7.02 82.56	83.91338 85.90926 86.90889 87.90561			
39	Y	**Yttrium** Yttrium Yttrium	88.905	3	1495±5	2927	solid	4.45	0.0026		8.9		^{89}Y	100	88.90543			
40	Zr	**Zirconium** Zirconium Zirkonium (Zirkon)	91.22	2, 4	1852±2	3578	solid	6.53±0.01 (calc.)	0.021		54.5	3.5×10^{-4}	^{90}Zr ^{91}Zr ^{92}Zr ^{94}Zr ^{96}Zr	51.46 11.23 17.11 17.40 2.80	89.90432 90.90525 91.90459 93.90614 95.9082			
41	Nb (Cb)	**Niobium** Niobium Niob (Columbium)	92.906	2, 3, 4?,5	2468±10	4927	solid	8.57	0.0019		1.00	1.4×10^{-4}	^{93}Nb	100	92.90602			
42	Mo	**Molybdenum** Molybdène Molybdän	95.94	2, 3, 4, 6	2610	5560	solid	10.22	0.0014		2.42	$<7\times10^{-6}$	^{92}Mo ^{94}Mo ^{95}Mo ^{96}Mo ^{97}Mo ^{98}Mo ^{100}Mo	15.84 9.04 15.72 16.53 9.46 23.78 9.13	91.90629 93.90474 94.90572 95.90455 96.90575 97.90551 99.90757			
43	Tc	**Technetium** Technétium Technetium	(99)*	3, 4, 6, 7	2200±50		solid	11.50 (calc.)					$^{92-102}Tc$ $^{104,\ 105}Tc$	artificial element: all very unstable, except ^{97}Tc, ^{98}Tc, ^{99}Tc (half-lives 2.6×10^{6} y, 1.5×10^{6} y, 2.12×10^{5} y)				

For footnotes see page 247.

Z Atomic number	Symbol	Element: **English**, French, German, *Latin*	Atomic weight 1967[1]	Valency	Melting point[2] at 760 mm Hg (unless otherwise stated) °C	Boiling point[2] at 760 mm Hg (unless otherwise stated) °C	Density[2] Gases: g/l at 760 mm Hg and 0 °C Others: g/cm³ or specific gravity 20 °/4 °C (unless otherwise stated)	Natural abundance: Earth's crust, hydrosphere, atmosphere[3] %	Natural abundance: Atmosphere (troposphere)[4] vol %	Natural abundance: Universe (atoms per 10⁶ Si atoms)[5]	Natural abundance: Human body[6] %	Natural isotopes[7]: Isotope (mass number *A*)	Natural isotopes: Relative abundance atoms %	Natural isotopes: Mass[8]	Natural isotopes: Mode of decay[9]	Natural isotopes: Energy in MeV and percentage of decay	Natural isotopes: Half-life[10]
44	Ru	**Ruthenium** Ruthénium Ruthenium	101.07	0, 1, 2, 3, 4, 5, 6, 7, 8	2250	(3900)	solid 12.41	2×10^{-6}		1.49		^{96}Ru	5.51	95.9076			
												^{98}Ru	1.87	97.9055			
												^{99}Ru	12.72	98.90608			
												^{100}Ru	12.62	99.90302			
												^{101}Ru	17.07	100.90412			
												^{102}Ru	31.61	101.90372			
												^{104}Ru	18.58	103.90553			
45	Rh	**Rhodium** Rhodium Rhodium	102.905	2, 3, 4, 5	1960	(3727 ±100)	solid 12.41	1×10^{-7}		0.214		^{103}Rh	100	102.9048			
46	Pd	**Palladium** Palladium Palladium	106.4	2, 3, 4	1552	(2927)	solid 12.02	1×10^{-6}		0.675		^{102}Pd	0.96	101.90494			
												^{104}Pd	10.97	103.90356			
												^{105}Pd	22.23	104.90464			
												^{106}Pd	27.33	105.9032			
												^{108}Pd	26.71	107.90392			
												^{110}Pd	11.81	109.9045			
47	Ag	**Silver** Argent Silber *Argentum*	107.868[15]	1, 2	960.8	2112	solid 10.50	1×10^{-5}		0.26	$<1\times10^{-6}$	^{107}Ag	51.82	106.90497			
												^{109}Ag	48.18	108.9047			
48	Cd	**Cadmium** Cadmium Cadmium	112.40	2	321.03	765	solid 8.65	3×10^{-5}		0.89	4.3×10^{-5}	^{106}Cd	1.22	105.90595			
												^{108}Cd	0.88	107.904			
												^{110}Cd	12.39	109.90297			
												^{111}Cd	12.75	110.90415			
												^{112}Cd	24.07	111.90284			
												^{113}Cd	12.26	112.90461			
												^{114}Cd	28.86	113.90357			
												^{116}Cd	7.58	115.90501			
49	In	**Indium** Indium Indium	114.82	1, 2, 3	156.61	2000±10	solid 7.31	1×10^{-5}		0.11		^{113}In	4.28	112.90428			
												^{115}In	95.72	114.90407	β^-	0.6 (100%)	6×10^{14} y
50	Sn	**Tin** Etain Zinn *Stannum*	118.69	2, 4	231.91	2270	cubic (α) solid 5.750; tetragonal (β) solid 7.31	0.0035		1.33	4.3×10^{-5}	^{112}Sn	0.96	111.90494			
												^{114}Sn	0.66	113.90296			
												^{115}Sn	0.35	114.90353			
												^{116}Sn	14.30	115.90211			
												^{117}Sn	7.61	116.90306			
												^{118}Sn	24.03	117.90179			
												^{119}Sn	8.58	118.90339			
												^{120}Sn	32.85	119.90213			
												^{122}Sn	4.92	121.90341			
												^{124}Sn	5.94	123.90524			

51	Sb	**Antimony** Antimoine Antimon *Stibium*	121.75	3, 5	630.5	1380	solid	6.691	6.5×10^{-5}		0.246	$<1.3\times10^{-4}$	^{121}Sb	57.25	120.90375			
													^{123}Sb	42.75	122.90415			
52	Te	**Tellurium** Tellure Tellur	127.60	2, 4, 6	449.5 ±0.3	989.8 ±3.8	rhombic	6.24	1×10^{-6}		4.67		^{120}Te	0.089	119.90451			
													^{122}Te	2.46	121.9030			
													^{123}Te	0.87	122.90418			
													^{124}Te	4.61	123.90276			
													^{125}Te	6.99	124.90442			
													^{126}Te	18.71	125.90324			
													^{128}Te	31.79	127.90471			
													^{130}Te	32.48	129.9067			
53	I	**Iodine** Iode Jod	126.9044	1, 3, 5, 7	113.5	184.35	gas solid	11.27 4.93	6×10^{-6}	$0–1\times10^{-6}$ (I_2)	0.80	4×10^{-5}	^{127}I	100	126.90435			
54	Xe	**Xenon** Xénon Xenon	131.30	0 (2, 4, 6)	−111.9	−107.1 ±3	gas liquid	5.887 ±0.009 3.52/−109°	2.4×10^{-9}	8.7×10^{-6}	4.0		^{124}Xe	0.096	123.90612			
													^{126}Xe	0.090	125.90417			
													^{128}Xe	1.92	127.90354			
													^{129}Xe	26.44	128.90478			
													^{130}Xe	4.08	129.90351			
													^{131}Xe	21.18	130.90509			
													^{132}Xe	26.89	131.90416			
													^{134}Xe	10.44	133.9054			
													^{136}Xe	8.87	135.90722			
55	Cs	**Caesium** **(Cesium)** Césium Caesium	132.905	1	28.5	690	solid	1.873	6.5×10^{-4}		0.456	$<1.4\times10^{-8}$	^{133}Cs	100	132.90509			
56	Ba	**Barium** Baryum Barium	137.34	2	725	1140	solid	3.5	0.026		3.66	2.3×10^{-5}	^{130}Ba	0.101	129.90625			
													^{132}Ba	0.097	131.90512			
													^{134}Ba	2.42	133.90431			
													^{135}Ba	6.59	134.9057			
													^{136}Ba	7.81	135.90436			
													^{137}Ba	11.32	136.90556			
													^{138}Ba	71.66	137.90501			
57	La	**Lanthanum** Lanthane Lanthan	138.91	3	920	3469	solid	5.93–6.186	0.0017		2.00		^{138}La	0.089	137.90681	β^-	0.205 (30%)	1.1×10^{11} y
																γ	0.54 (15%) 0.81 (30%) 1.43 (70%)	
																K	(70%)	
													^{139}La	99.911	138.90606			
58	Ce	**Cerium** Cérium Cer	140.12	3, 4	795	3468	cubic hexagonal	α 8.23 β 6.66	0.0043		2.26		^{136}Ce	0.193	135.9071			
													^{138}Ce	0.250	137.90572			
													^{140}Ce	88.48	139.90528			
													^{142}Ce	11.07	141.90904	α	1.5	5×10^{15} y

For footnotes see page 247.

Z Atomic number	Symbol	Element English French German	Atomic weight 1967[1]	Valency	Melting point[2] at 760 mm Hg (unless otherwise stated) °C	Boiling point[2] at 760 mm Hg (unless otherwise stated) °C	Density[2] Gases: g/l at 760 mm Hg and 0 °C Others: g/cm³ or specific gravity 20 °/4 °C (unless otherwise stated)		Natural abundance: Earth's crust, hydrosphere, atmosphere[3] %	Natural abundance: Atmosphere (troposphere)[4] vol %	Natural abundance: Universe (atoms per 10^6 Si atoms)[5]	Natural abundance: Human body[6] %	Natural isotopes[7]: Isotope (mass number A)	Natural isotopes: Relative abundance atoms %	Natural isotopes: Mass[8]	Natural isotopes: Mode of decay[9]	Natural isotopes: Energy in MeV and percentage of decay	Natural isotopes: Half-life[10]
59	Pr	**Praseodymium** Praséodyme Praseodym	140.907	3, 4	935	3127	hexagonal cubic	α 6.782 β 6.64	5.2×10^{-4}		0.40		^{141}Pr	100	140.90739			
60	Nd	**Neodymium** Néodyme Neodym	144.24	3	1024	3027	hexagonal cubic	α 7.004 β 6.80	0.0022		1.44		^{142}Nd	27.11	141.90748			
													^{143}Nd	12.17	142.90962			
													^{144}Nd	23.85	143.9099	α	1.8	$\approx5\times10^{15}$ y
													^{145}Nd	8.30	144.91216			
													^{146}Nd	17.22	145.91269			
													^{148}Nd	5.73	147.91648			
													^{150}Nd	5.62	149.92071			
61	Pm	**Promethium** Prométhium Promethium	(147)*	3	1035	2730							^{147}Pm	see ref.[16]	146.91486	β^-	0.225 (100%) 0.10 (10^{-2}%)	2.5 y
62	Sm	**Samarium** Samarium Samarium	150.35	2, 3	1072	1900	rhombohedral	α 7.536 β 7.40	6×10^{-4}		0.664		^{144}Sm	3.09	143.91165			
													^{147}Sm	14.97	146.91462	α	2.24	1.06×10^{11} y
													^{148}Sm	11.24	147.91456	α	2.14	1.2×10^{13} y
													^{149}Sm	13.83	148.91693	α	1.84	$\sim4\times10^{14}$ y
													^{150}Sm	7.44	149.91701			
													^{152}Sm	26.72	151.91949			
													^{154}Sm	22.71	153.92201			
63	Eu	**Europium** Europium Europium	151.96	2, 3	826	1439	solid	5.259	9.9×10^{-5}		0.187		^{151}Eu	47.82	150.91963			
													^{153}Eu	52.18	152.92086			
64	Gd	**Gadolinium** Gadolinium Gadolinium	157.25	3	1312	~3000	hexagonal cubic	α 7.895 β 7.80	5.9×10^{-4}		0.684		^{152}Gd	0.20	151.91953	α	2.15	1.1×10^{14} y
													^{154}Gd	2.15	153.92072			
													^{155}Gd	14.73	154.92259			
													^{156}Gd	20.47	155.9221			
													^{157}Gd	15.68	156.92394			
													^{158}Gd	24.87	157.9241			
													^{160}Gd	21.90	159.92712			
65	Tb	**Terbium** Terbium Terbium	158.924	3, 4	1356	2800	solid	8.272	8.5×10^{-5}		0.0956		^{159}Tb	100	158.92495			
66	Dy	**Dysprosium** Dysprosium Dysprosium	162.50	3	1407	2600	solid	8.536	4.2×10^{-4}		0.556		^{156}Dy	0.052	155.92376			
													^{158}Dy	0.090	157.92396			
													^{160}Dy	2.29	159.92483			
													^{161}Dy	18.88	160.9266			
													^{162}Dy	25.53	161.92647			
													^{163}Dy	24.97	162.92837			
													^{164}Dy	28.18	163.92883			

67	Ho	**Holmium** Holmium Holmium	164.930	3	1461	2600	solid	8.803	1.1×10^{-4}		0.118		^{165}Ho	100	164.9303			
68	Er	**Erbium** Erbium Erbium	167.26	3	1497	2900	solid	9.051	2.3×10^{-4}		0.316		^{162}Er ^{164}Er ^{166}Er ^{167}Er ^{168}Er ^{170}Er	0.136 1.56 33.41 22.94 27.07 14.88	161.92878 163.92929 165.9304 166.93205 167.93238 169.93551			
69	Tm	**Thulium** Thulium Thulium	168.934	2, 3	1545	1727	solid	9.332	1.9×10^{-5}		0.0318		^{169}Tm	100	168.93435			
70	Yb	**Ytterbium** Ytterbium Ytterbium	173.04	2, 3	824±5	1427	cubic	α 6.977 β 6.54	2.5×10^{-4}		0.220		^{168}Yb ^{170}Yb ^{171}Yb ^{172}Yb ^{173}Yb ^{174}Yb ^{176}Yb	0.135 3.03 14.31 21.82 16.13 31.84 12.73	167.9339 169.93488 170.93646 171.93656 172.9383 173.93902 175.94274			
71	Lu (Cp)	**Lutetium** **(Lutecium)** Lutétium Lutetium (Cassiopeium)	174.97	3	1652	3327	solid	9.842	7×10^{-5}		0.050		^{175}Lu ^{176}Lu	97.41 2.59	174.94089 175.94274	 β⁻ γ	 0.42 (100%) 0.0883 (100%) 0.202 (100%) 0.309 (100%)	 2.1×10^{10} y
72	Hf	**Hafnium** Hafnium Hafnium	178.49	4	2150	5400	solid	13.29	4.2×10^{-4}		0.438		^{174}Hf ^{176}Hf ^{177}Hf ^{178}Hf ^{179}Hf ^{180}Hf	0.18 5.20 18.50 27.14 13.75 35.24	173.94026 175.94165 176.94348 177.94387 178.94602 179.94681	α	≈2.5	4.3×10^{15} y
73	Ta	**Tantalum** Tantale Tantal	180.948	2, 3, 4, 5	2996	5425 ±100	solid	16.6	8×10^{-4}		0.065		^{180}Ta ^{181}Ta	0.0123 99.988	179.94752 180.94798			
74	W	**Tungsten** Tungstène Wolfram	183.85	2, 3, 4, 5, 6	3380	5927	solid	19.3	0.0064		0.49		^{180}W ^{182}W ^{183}W ^{184}W ^{186}W	0.14 26.41 14.40 30.64 28.41	179.94698 181.94827 182.95029 183.95099 185.95434			
75	Re	**Rhenium** Rhénium Rhenium	186.2	1, 2, 3, 4, 5, 6, 7	3180	5627 (estimated)	solid	21.02	1×10^{-7}		0.135		^{185}Re ^{187}Re	37.07 62.93	184.95302 186.95737	 β⁻	 ≦0.008	 7×10^{10} y

For footnotes see page 247.

Z Atomic number	Symbol	Element: **English** / French / German / *Latin*	Atomic weight 1967[1]	Valency	Melting point[2] at 760 mm Hg (unless otherwise stated) °C	Boiling point[2] at 760 mm Hg (unless otherwise stated) °C	Density[2] Gases: g/l at 760 mm Hg and 0 °C; Others: g/cm³ or specific gravity 20 °/4 °C (unless otherwise stated)	Natural abundance: Earth's crust, hydrosphere, atmosphere[3] %	Natural abundance: Atmosphere (troposphere)[4] vol %	Natural abundance: Universe (atoms per 10⁶ Si atoms)[5]	Natural abundance: Human body[6] %	Natural isotopes[7]: Isotope (mass number A)	Relative abundance atoms %	Mass[8]	Mode of decay[9]	Energy in MeV and percentage of decay	Half-life[10]
76	Os	**Osmium** Osmium Osmium	190.2	2, 3, 4, 8	3000±10	(5000)	solid 22.57 (heaviest element)	1×10^{-6}		1.00		^{184}Os	0.018	183.95256			
												^{186}Os	1.59	185.95394			
												^{187}Os	1.64	186.95596			
												^{188}Os	13.3	187.95597			
												^{189}Os	16.1	188.95825			
												^{190}Os	26.4	189.9586			
												^{192}Os	41.0	191.96141			
77	Ir	**Iridium** Iridium Iridium	192.2	3, 4	2443	(4527 ±100)	solid 22.42/17°	1×10^{-7}		0.821		^{191}Ir	37.3	190.96085			
												^{193}Ir	62.7	192.96328			
78	Pt	**Platinum** Platine Platin	195.09	1, 2, 3, 4	1769	(3827 ±100)	solid 21.45	5×10^{-7}		1.625		^{190}Pt	0.0127	189.95995	α	3.11	7×10^{11} y
												^{192}Pt	0.78	191.96143	α	~2.6	~10^{15} y
												^{194}Pt	32.9	193.96281			
												^{195}Pt	33.8	194.96482			
												^{196}Pt	25.3	195.96498			
												^{198}Pt	7.21	197.96753			
79	Au	**Gold** Or Gold *Aurum*	196.967	1, 3	1063.0	2966	solid 19.32	5×10^{-7}		0.145	$<1\times10^{-6}$	^{197}Au	100	196.96655			
80	Hg	**Mercury** Mercure Quecksilber *Hydrargyrum*	200.59	1, 2	−38.87	356.58	14.43/−38.87° 13.595/0° 13.546/20°[17]	4×10^{-5}		0.284		^{196}Hg	0.146	195.96582			
												^{198}Hg	10.02	197.96677			
												^{199}Hg	16.84	198.96826			
												^{200}Hg	23.13	199.96834			
												^{201}Hg	13.22	200.97032			
												^{202}Hg	29.80	201.97063			
												^{204}Hg	6.85	203.97348			
81	Tl	**Thallium** Thallium Thallium	204.37	1, 3	303.5	1457±10	solid 11.85	3×10^{-5}		0.108		^{203}Tl	29.50	202.97233			
												^{205}Tl	70.50	204.97446			
												^{206}Tl (Radium E″)		205.97608	β^- no γ	1.51	4.20 min
												^{207}Tl (Actinium C″)		206.97745	β^- γ	1.44 0.89 (≈0.2%)	4.78 min
												^{208}Tl (Thorium C″)		207.98201	β^-	1.80 (50%) 1.52 (21%) 1.28 (25%)	3.1 min
															γ	2.615 (100%) 0.511 (25%) 0.860 (12%) 0.583 (87%) 0.277 (10%)	

													^{210}Tl (Radium C″)		209.990	β− γ	1.96 (100%) 0.297 (100%) 0.783 (100%) 1.1	1.3 min
82	Pb	**Lead** Plomb Blei *Plumbum*	207.19	2, 4	327.5	1744	solid	11.35	0.0018		0.47	1.1×10^{-4}	^{204}Pb	1.48	203.97307	α	2.6	1.4×10^{19} y
													^{206}Pb (Radium G)	23.6	205.97446			
													^{207}Pb	22.6	206.9759			
													^{208}Pb	52.3	207.97664			
													^{210}Pb (Radium D)		209.98418	β− γ	0.015 (85%) 0.061 (15%) 0.047 (85%)	21 y
													^{211}Pb (Actinium B)		210.9888	β− γ	1.39 (80%) 0.56 0.065 0.083 (5%) 0.404 (6%) 0.829 (13%)	36.1 min
													^{212}Pb (Thorium B)		211.99190	β− γ	0.34 (84%) 0.58 (12%) 0.1151 0.1764 0.2383 (80%) 0.3 (4%) 0.4152	10.64 h
													^{214}Pb (Radium B)		213.99976	β− γ (>10)	0.7 (6%) 1.03 0.352 0.053–0.259	26.8 min
83	Bi	**Bismuth** Bismuth Wismut	208.980	3, 5	271.3	1560±5	solid	9.747	2×10^{-5}		0.144		^{209}Bi	100	208.98042			
													^{210}Bi (Radium E)		209.98411	α β− no γ	4.7 (≈10^{-5}%) 1.16	5.00 d
													^{211}Bi (Actinium C)		210.98729	α β− γ	6.617 (83%) 6.273 (17%) 0.06 (0.3%) 0.351 (17%)	2.15 min
													^{212}Bi (Thorium C)		211.99127	α β− γ (>10)	6.049 (25%) 6.088 (10%) 0.085–2.25 (65%) 0.040 (25%) 0.727 0.124–2.2	60.6 min
													^{214}Bi (Radium C)		213.99863	α β− γ (>10)	5.5 (0.04%) 0.4–3.2 (≧99%) 0.609 1.12 1.76 0.45–2.43	19.7 min
													^{215}Bi		215.0019	β−		8 min

For footnotes see page 247.

Z Atomic number	Symbol	Element: **English** French German	Atomic weight 1967[1]	Valency	Melting point[2] at 760 mm Hg (unless otherwise stated) °C	Boiling point[2] at 760 mm Hg (unless otherwise stated) °C	Density[2] Gases: g/l at 760 mm Hg and 0 °C Others: g/cm³ or specific gravity 20 °/4 °C (unless otherwise stated)	Natural abundance: Earth's crust, hydrosphere, atmosphere[3] %	Natural abundance: Atmosphere (troposphere)[4] vol %	Natural abundance: Universe (atoms per 10^6 Si atoms)[5]	Natural abundance: Human body[6] %	Natural isotopes[7]: Isotope (mass number A)	Natural isotopes[7]: Relative abundance atoms %	Natural isotopes[7]: Mass[8]	Natural isotopes[7]: Mode of decay[9]	Natural isotopes[7]: Energy in MeV and percentage of decay	Natural isotopes[7]: Half-life[10]
84	Po	**Polonium**	(210)*	(2, 4, 6)	254	962	solid α 9.32	2.1×10^{-14}				^{210}Po (Radium F)		209.98287	α	5.30	138.40 d
		Polonium													γ	0.79 (1.2×10^{-3}%)	
		Polonium															
												^{211}Po (Actinium C′)		210.98665	α	7.44 (99%)	0.52 s
																6.90 (0.5%)	
																6.57 (0.5%)	
															γ	0.88 (0.5%)	
																0.562 (0.5%)	
												^{212}Po (Thorium C′)		211.98886	α	8.78	0.30 μs
												^{214}Po (Radium C′)		213.99519	α	7.68	164 μs
												^{215}Po (Actinium A)		214.99947	α	7.36 (≧99%)	0.0018 s
															β−	(0.005%)	
												^{216}Po (Thorium A)		216.00192	α	6.78 (99.986%)	0.16 s
															β−	(0.014%)	
												^{218}Po (Radium A)		218.00893	α	6.00 (≧99%)	3.05 min
															β−	(0.02%)	
85	At	**Astatine**	(210)	(1, 3, 5, 7)				3×10^{-24}				^{215}At		214.99866	α	8.00	≈100 μs
		Astatine (Astate)										^{216}At		216.00241	α	7.79	≈300 μs
		Astatin										^{218}At		218.00855	α	6.70	1.35 s
																6.65	
												^{219}At		219.01136	α	6.27	54 s
															β−		
86	Rn	**Radon**	(222)	0	−71	−61.8	gas 9.73	6.2×10^{-16}				^{219}Rn (Actinon)		219.00952	α	6.81 (82%)	4.0 s
		Radon					liquid 4.4/−62°									6.54 (13%)	
		Radon					solid 4									6.41 (5%)	
	(Em)	(Emanation)													γ	0.270 (13%)	
	(Nt)	(Niton)														0.399 (4.8%)	
												^{220}Rn (Thoron)		220.0114	α	6.282 (≧99%)	51.5 s
																5.747 (0.3%)	
															γ	0.542 (≈0.3%)	
												^{222}Rn (Radon)		222.01753	α	4.586 (≧99%)	3.823 d
																4.98 (0.08%)	
																4.83	
															γ	0.51 (≈0.08%)	
87	Fr	**Francium**	(223)	1				1.3×10^{-21}				^{223}Fr (Actinium K)		223.0198	α	5.34 (0.005%)	22 min
		Francium													β−	1.15 (≧99%)	
		Francium													γ	0.049 (40%)	
																0.080 (24%)	
																0.215 (3%)	
																0.31 (0.8%)	

88	Ra	**Radium** Radium Radium	(226)	2	700	<1737	solid	5?	9.5×10^{-11}			1.4×10^{-13}	^{223}Ra (Actinium X)		223.0187	α	5.71 (50%) 5.60 (24%) 5.23 (10%) 5.33–5.87	11.7 d
																γ (>10)	0.155 0.122 0.270 0.338 0.031–0.45	
													^{224}Ra (Thorium X)		224.02022	α	5.68 (95%) 5.44 (5%)	3.64 d
																γ	0.24098 (3.7%) 0.290 (8×10^{-3}%) 0.410 (4×10^{-3}%) 0.650 (9×10^{-3}%)	
													^{226}Ra		226.02536	α	4.78 (95%) 4.59 (4%)	1622 y
																γ	0.187 (4%) 0.260 (0.001%) 0.420 0.64	
													^{228}Ra (Meso-thorium I)		228.03123	β⁻ γ	0.055 ≈0.03	6.7 y
89	Ac	**Actinium** Actinium Actinium	(227)	3	1050	3200 ±300 (estimated)	solid	10.07 (calc.)	6.1×10^{-14}				^{227}Ac		227.02781	α	4.949 (1%) 4.936 4.517–4.866	21.6 y
																β⁻	0.043 (99%)	
																γ (9)	0.009–0.190	
													^{228}Ac (Meso-thorium II)		228.03117	β⁻	1.11 (53%) 0.45–2.18	6.13 h
																γ (>10)	0.057 0.10 0.91 0.08–0.966	
90	Th	**Thorium** Thorium Thorium	232.038	4	~1700	4000	solid	~11.66	0.0011				^{227}Th (Radio-actinium)		227.02777	α	5.976 (24%) 6.036 (23%) 5.755 (2.1%) 5.667–6.007	18.17 d
																γ (>10)	0.050 (14%) 0.061 (9%) 0.236 (11%) 0.029–0.334	
													^{228}Th (Radio-thorium)		228.02875	α	5.421 (71%) 5.338 (28%) 5.137–5.208	1.91 y
																γ	0.085 (1.6%) 0.134 (0.16%) 0.169 (0.13%) 0.205 (0.03%) 0.214 (0.27%)	

For footnotes see page 247.

Z Atomic number	Symbol	Element English French German	Atomic weight 1967[1]	Valency	Melting point[2] at 760 mm Hg (unless otherwise stated) °C	Boiling point[2] at 760 mm Hg (unless otherwise stated) °C	Density[2] Gases: g/l at 760 mm Hg and 0 °C Others: g/cm³ or specific gravity 20°/4°C (unless otherwise stated)	Natural abundance: Earth's crust, hydrosphere, atmosphere[3] %	Natural abundance: Atmosphere (troposphere)[4] vol %	Natural abundance: Universe (atoms per 10^6 Si atoms)[5]	Natural abundance: Human body[6] %	Natural isotopes[7]: Isotope (mass number A)	Relative abundance atoms %	Mass[8]	Mode of decay[9]	Energy in MeV and percentage of decay	Half-life[10]
90	Th	**Thorium** (continued)										^{230}Th (Ionium)		230.03308	α γ	4.682 (76%) 4.615 (24%) 4.240–4.474 0.0677 (0.59%) 0.110 (1×10^{-4}%) 0.144 (0.77%) 0.19 (1.4×10^{-2}%) 0.203 ($\approx5\times10^{-6}$%) 0.235 ($\approx5\times10^{-6}$%) 0.255 (1.7×10^{-2}%)	8×10^4 y
												^{231}Th (Uranium Y)		231.03635	β⁻ γ (>10)	0.30 (78%) 0.084 (11%) 0.256 (13%) 0.017–0.31	25.6 h
												^{232}Th		232.03821	α γ	4.007 (76%) 3.99 (24%) 0.059 (24%)	1.39×10^{10} y
												^{234}Th (Uranium X_1)		234.04357	β⁻ γ	0.192 (65%) 0.10 (35%) 0.092 0.063 0.029	24.10 d
91	Pa	**Protactinium** Protactinium Protactinium	(231)	4, 5	~1230?		solid 15.37	9×10^{-11}				^{231}Pa		231.03594	α γ (>10)	5.001 (24%) 5.017 (23%) 5.046 (10%) 4.938 (22%) 4.666–4.971 0.29 0.027–0.356	3.43×10^4 y
												^{234}Pa (Uranium X_2)			β⁻ γ (>10) IT	0.58 (99%) 2.31 (1%) 0.043 0.23–1.83	1.18 min
												^{234}Pa (Uranium Z)		234.04337	β⁻ γ (>10)	0.23–1.35 0.044 (92%) 0.100 (71%) 0.228 (33%) 0.126–1.85	6.66 h

92	U	**Uranium** Uranium Uran	238.03	3, 4, 5, 6	1132.3 ±0.8	3818	solid	~18.95	2.9×10^{-4}			3×10^{-8}	^{234}U (Uranium II)	0.0057	234.0409	α	4.768	(72%)	2.48×10^{5} y
																	4.717	(28%)	
																γ	0.053		
																	0.118		
													^{235}U (Actino- uranium)	0.720	235.04393	α	4.559	(6.7%)	7.13×10^{8} y
																	4.370	(25%)	
																	4.354	(35%)	
																	4.333	(14%)	
																	4.318	(8%)	
																	4.117	(5.8%)	
																γ	0.074		
																	0.094	(9%)	
																	0.1096	(5%)	
																	0.144	(12%)	
																	0.165	(>4%)	
																	0.185	(55%)	
																	0.203	(>4%)	
																	0.2890		
																	0.367		
																	0.385		
													^{238}U (Uranium I)	99.27	238.05076	α	4.195	(77%)	4.51×10^{9} y
																	4.14	(23%)	
																γ	0.048	(23%)	

1 See footnote 2, page 231.

2 From HAMMOND, C. R., in WEAST et al. (Eds.), *Handbook of Chemistry and Physics*, 49th ed., The Chemical Rubber Co., Cleveland, 1968, page B-97; HAMPEL, C. A. (Ed.), *Rare Metals Handbook*, 2nd ed., Reinhold, London, 1961.

3 Values are total percentages in the lithosphere (outer 10 miles), hydrosphere and atmosphere (from REMY, H., *Lehrbuch der anorganischen Chemie*, 11th ed., vol. 2, Akademische Verlagsgesellschaft, Leipzig, 1961, page 769).

4 Dry atmosphere at sea level. From *Manual of the ICAO Standard Atmosphere*, International Civil Aviation Organization, Montreal, 1964.

5 From SUESS and UREY, *Rev. mod. Phys.*, **28**, 53 (1956).

6 From SCHROEDER, H. A., *J. chron. Dis.*, **18**, 217 (1965); for As from SCHROEDER und BALASSA, *J. chron. Dis.*, **19**, 85 (1966); for Zr from SCHROEDER und BALASSA, *J. chron. Dis.*, **19**, 573 (1966); for Nb from SCHROEDER und BALASSA, *J. chron. Dis.*, **18**, 229 (1965). See also 'Composition of the Body', pages 517–522.

7 From HEATH, R. L., in WEAST et al. (Eds.), *Handbook of Chemistry and Physics*, 49th ed., The Chemical Rubber Co., Cleveland, 1968, page B-4.

8 Unified scale of atomic masses (^{12}C scale; see page 226). Values from KÖNIG et al., *Nucl. Phys.*, **31**, 18 (1962).

9 α = alpha particle (helium nucleus = 2 protons + 2 neutrons), β^- = beta particle (electron), γ = gamma ray, K = orbital electron capture, IT = isomeric transition.

10 y = year, d = day, h = hour, min = minute, s = second.

11 Normal molecular hydrogen is a mixture of *ortho-* and *para*-hydrogen (molecules in which the two nuclei have respectively parallel and anti-parallel spins) in the proportions 3 : 1.

12 See footnote 4, page 231.

13 A disintegration product of ^{14}N in the atmosphere due to the action of cosmic rays. The ratio of ^{1}H to ^{3}H atoms in atmospheric hydrogen is of the order of 10^{14}. Cf. GROSSE et al., *Phys. Rev.*, **93**, 250 (1954).

14 A disintegration product of ^{14}N in the atmosphere due to the action of naturally occurring neutrons.

15 See footnote 5, page 231.

16 A disintegration product of ^{146}Nd due to the action of naturally occurring neutrons.

17 For density of mercury under standard conditions see page 230. For internationally accepted density values for mercury at different temperatures see LINDSAY, R. B., in GRAY, D. E. (Ed.), *American Institute of Physics Handbook*, McGraw-Hill, New York, 1957, pages 2–140.

Atomic number Z	Symbol	Transuranic element[1]	Atomic weight 1967[2]	Valency[3]	Melting point[3] °C	Boiling point[3] °C	Density[3] g/cm³	Isotopes: Isotope (mass number A)	Mass[5]	Mode of decay[6] (radiation)	Energy in MeV[4] (percentage of decay in brackets)	Half-life[7]
93	Np	**Neptunium**	(237)	3, 4, 5, 6	640±1		solid 18.0–20.45	^{237}Np	237.04803	α	4.787 (53%)	2.14×10^{6} y
											4.767 (29%)	
											4.52–4.87	
										γ	0.020	
											0.087 (14%)	
											0.0296 (14%)	
											0.0568 (0.8%)	
											0.143 (0.1%)	
											0.175 (0.3%)	
											0.200	
94	Pu	**Plutonium**	(244)	3, 4, 5, 6	639.5±2	3235±19	solid α19.84/25°	^{244}Pu		α		8.2×10^{7} y
95	Am	**Americium**	(243)	3, 4, 5, 6	>850		solid 11.7	^{243}Am	243.06138	α, γ		7950 y
96	Cm	**Curium**	(247)	3			solid ~7	^{247}Cm		α		1.6×10^{7} y
97	Bk	**Berkelium**	(247)	3, 4				^{247}Bk	247.07018	α, γ		1.4×10^{3} y
98	Cf	**Californium**	(252)*	3				^{252}Cf		α		2.65 y
99	Es	**Einsteinium**	(254)	3				^{254}Es	254.08811	α, γ		270 d
100	Fm	**Fermium**	(257)	3				^{257}Fm		α		80 d
101	Md	**Mendelevium**	(257)	3				^{257}Md		α, K		3.0 h
102	No	**Nobelium**	(255)					^{255}No		α		3.0 min
103	Lr	**Lawrencium**	(256)					^{256}Lr		α		45 s

[1] The transuranic elements have become known as artificially produced elements. However, since they have in the past occurred naturally (or are still, like ^{239}Pu, identifiable in very small amounts in nature) they can be regarded also as naturally occurring elements. In a sense they are elements which as a result of their short half-lives have become extinct.
[2] See footnote [2], page 231.
[3] From HAMMOND, C. R., in WEAST et al. (Eds.), *Handbook of Chemistry and Physics*, 49th ed., The Chemical Rubber Co., Cleveland, 1968, page B-97; HAMPEL, C. A. (Eds.), *Rare Metals Handbook*, 2nd ed., Reinhold, London, 1961.
[4] Values from HEATH, R. L., in WEAST et al. (Eds.), *Handbook of Chemistry and Physics*, 49th ed., The Chemical Rubber Co., Cleveland, 1968, page B-4.
[5] Unified scale of atomic masses (^{12}C scale; see page 226). Values from KÖNIG et al., *Nucl. Phys.*, **31**, 18 (1962).
[6] α = alpha particle (helium nucleus = 2 protons + 2 neutrons), γ = gamma ray, K = orbital electron capture from K shell.
[7] y = year, d = day, h = hour, min = minute, s = second. Values from International Union of Pure and Applied Chemistry, *Comptes rendus de la 24e Conférence, 1967*, Butterworth, London, 1968, page 140.

Electronic Configurations of the Elements[1]

Z = atomic number; E_r = resonance energy (eV); E_i = ionization energy (eV); E_{r_1} = resonance energy of singly-ionized atom (eV)

Z	Element	E_r	E_i	E_{r_1}	*K*	*L*		*M*			*N*				*O*				*P*			*Q*
					1s	2s	2p	3s	3p	3d	4s	4p	4d	4f	5s	5p	5d	5f	6s	6p	6d	7s
1	H	10.19	13.60		1																	
2	He	21.20	24.58	40.8	2																	
3	Li	1.85	5.39	62.2	2	1																
4	Be	5.28	9.32	3.96	2	2																
5	B	4.96	8.30	9.10	2	2	1															
6	C	7.48	11.26	9.29	2	2	2															
7	N	10.3	14.54	11.4	2	2	3															
8	O	9.52	13.61	14.8	2	2	4															
9	F	12.98	17.42	20.42	2	2	5															
10	Ne	16.84	21.56	26.89	2	2	6															
11	Na	2.10	5.14	33.3	2	2	6	1														
12	Mg	4.34	7.64	4.42	2	2	6	2														
13	Al	3.14	5.98	7.42	2	2	6	2	1													
14	Si	4.92	8.15	6.86	2	2	6	2	2													
15	P	6.94	10.95	8.09	2	2	6	2	3													
16	S	6.86	10.36	9.84	2	2	6	2	4													
17	Cl	9.21	13.01	11.56	2	2	6	2	5													
18	Ar	11.53	15.75	13.47	2	2	6	2	6													
19	K	1.61	4.34	20.6	2	2	6	2	6		1											
20	Ca	2.93	6.11	3.12	2	2	6	2	6		2											
21	Sc	2.32	6.56	3.40	2	2	6	2	6	1	2											
22	Ti	1.97	6.83	3.66	2	2	6	2	6	2	2											
23	V	2.24	6.74	4.40	2	2	6	2	6	3	2											
24	Cr	2.89	6.76	6.00	2	2	6	2	6	5	1											
25	Mn	3.07	7.43	4.76	2	2	6	2	6	5	2											
26	Fe	3.21	7.90	5.20	2	2	6	2	6	6	2											
27	Co	3.57	7.86	5.83	2	2	6	2	6	7	2											
28	Ni	3.54	7.63	6.39	2	2	6	2	6	8	2											
29	Cu	3.79	7.72	8.26	2	2	6	2	6	10	1											
30	Zn	4.03	9.39	5.91	2	2	6	2	6	10	2											
31	Ga	3.07	6.00	8.78	2	2	6	2	6	10	2	1										
32	Ge	4.64	8.13	8.06	2	2	6	2	6	10	2	2										
33	As	6.28	9.81	9.14	2	2	6	2	6	10	2	3										
34	Se	6.32	9.75	10.39	2	2	6	2	6	10	2	4										
35	Br	8.32	11.84	12.21	2	2	6	2	6	10	2	5										
36	Kr	10.03	13.99	15.82	2	2	6	2	6	10	2	6										
37	Rb	1.59	4.17	17.8	2	2	6	2	6	10	2	6			1							
38	Sr	2.69	5.69	2.94	2	2	6	2	6	10	2	6			2							
39	Y	1.99	6.57	2.91	2	2	6	2	6	10	2	6	1		2							
40	Zr	2.02	6.95	3.47	2	2	6	2	6	10	2	6	2		2							
41	Nb	2.97	6.77	4.13	2	2	6	2	6	10	2	6	4		1							
42	Mo	3.18	7.18	6.08	2	2	6	2	6	10	2	6	5		1							
43	Tc	2.88	7.45	4.68	2	2	6	2	6	10	2	6	(5)		(2)							
44	Ru	3.26	7.5	6.29	2	2	6	2	6	10	2	6	7		1							
45	Rh	3.35	7.7	4.97	2	2	6	2	6	10	2	6	8		1							
46	Pd	4.22	8.33	8.12	2	2	6	2	6	10	2	6	10									
47	Ag	3.66	7.58	11.1	2	2	6	2	6	10	2	6	10		1							
48	Cd	3.80	8.99	5.47	2	2	6	2	6	10	2	6	10		2							
49	In	3.02	5.78	7.82	2	2	6	2	6	10	2	6	10		2	1						
50	Sn	4.30	7.33	7.30	2	2	6	2	6	10	2	6	10		2	2						
51	Sb	5.36	8.64	9.56	2	2	6	2	6	10	2	6	10		2	3						
52	Te	5.78	9.01	8.82	2	2	6	2	6	10	2	6	10		2	4						
53	I	7.67	10.44	10.04	2	2	6	2	6	10	2	6	10		2	5						
54	Xe	8.44	12.13	11.27	2	2	6	2	6	10	2	6	10		2	6						
55	Cs	1.38	3.89	15.2	2	2	6	2	6	10	2	6	10		2	6			1			
56	Ba	2.24	5.21	2.51	2	2	6	2	6	10	2	6	10		2	6			2			
57	La	1.64	5.61	1.75	2	2	6	2	6	10	2	6	10		2	6	1		2			
58	Ce		6.91	2.72	2	2	6	2	6	10	2	6	10	2	2	6			2			
59	Pr		5.76	2.81	2	2	6	2	6	10	2	6	10	3	2	6			2			
60	Nd		6.31	2.63	2	2	6	2	6	10	2	6	10	4	2	6			2			
61	Pm				2	2	6	2	6	10	2	6	10	5	2	6			2			
62	Sm	1.71	5.6	2.63	2	2	6	2	6	10	2	6	10	6	2	6			2			
63	Eu	1.74	5.67	2.95	2	2	6	2	6	10	2	6	10	7	2	6			2			
64	Gd	1.665	6.16	3.18	2	2	6	2	6	10	2	6	10	7	2	6	1		2			
65	Tb		6.74		2	2	6	2	6	10	2	6	10	8	2	6	1		2			
66	Dy		6.82		2	2	6	2	6	10	2	6	10	9	2	6	1		2			
67	Ho				2	2	6	2	6	10	2	6	10	10	2	6	1		2			
68	Er				2	2	6	2	6	10	2	6	10	11	2	6	1		2			
69	Tm	2.62 ?		2.68	2	2	6	2	6	10	2	6	10	13	2	6			2			
70	Yb	2.23	6.2	3.35	2	2	6	2	6	10	2	6	10	14	2	6			2			
71	Lu	2.16 ?	5.0	3.38	2	2	6	2	6	10	2	6	10	14	2	6	1		2			
72	Hf	2.19	5.5	3.43	2	2	6	2	6	10	2	6	10	14	2	6	2		2			
73	Ta	2.44	6	3.63	2	2	6	2	6	10	2	6	10	14	2	6	3		2			
74	W	2.49	7.98	4.48	2	2	6	2	6	10	2	6	10	14	2	6	4		2			
75	Re	3.57	7.88		2	2	6	2	6	10	2	6	10	14	2	6	5		2			
76	Os	2.80	8.7		2	2	6	2	6	10	2	6	10	14	2	6	6		2			
77	Ir	4.65	9.2		2	2	6	2	6	10	2	6	10	14	2	6	7		2			
78	Pt	4.04	8.97	6.38	2	2	6	2	6	10	2	6	10	14	2	6	9		1			
79	Au	4.63	9.22	7.81	2	2	6	2	6	10	2	6	10	14	2	6	10		1			
80	Hg	4.89	10.43	6.38	2	2	6	2	6	10	2	6	10	14	2	6	10		2			
81	Tl	3.28	6.11	9.38	2	2	6	2	6	10	2	6	10	14	2	6	10		2	1		
82	Pb	4.33	7.42	7.35	2	2	6	2	6	10	2	6	10	14	2	6	10		2	2		
83	Bi	4.04	8.0	8.63	2	2	6	2	6	10	2	6	10	14	2	6	10		2	3		
84	Po		7.25		2	2	6	2	6	10	2	6	10	14	2	6	10		2	4		
85	At				2	2	6	2	6	10	2	6	10	14	2	6	10		2	5		
86	Rn	6.78	10.75		2	2	6	2	6	10	2	6	10	14	2	6	10		2	6		
87	Fr				2	2	6	2	6	10	2	6	10	14	2	6	10		2	6		1
88	Ra	2.57	5.28	2.65	2	2	6	2	6	10	2	6	10	14	2	6	10		2	6		2
89	Ac				2	2	6	2	6	10	2	6	10	14	2	6	10		2	6	1	2
90	Th			2.12	2	2	6	2	6	10	2	6	10	14	2	6	10		2	6	2	2
91	Pa				2	2	6	2	6	10	2	6	10	14	2	6	10	2	2	6	1	2
92	U	1.44	~ 4	3.21	2	2	6	2	6	10	2	6	10	14	2	6	10	3	2	6	1	2
93	Np				2	2	6	2	6	10	2	6	10	14	2	6	10	4	2	6	1	2
94	Pu				2	2	6	2	6	10	2	6	10	14	2	6	10	6	2	6		2
95	Am				2	2	6	2	6	10	2	6	10	14	2	6	10	7	2	6		2
96	Cm				2	2	6	2	6	10	2	6	10	14	2	6	10	7	2	6	1	2
97	Bk				2	2	6	2	6	10	2	6	10	14	2	6	10	8	2	6	1	2
98	Cf				2	2	6	2	6	10	2	6	10	14	2	6	10	10	2	6		2
99	Es				2	2	6	2	6	10	2	6	10	14	2	6	10	11	2	6		2
100	Fm				2	2	6	2	6	10	2	6	10	14	2	6	10	12	2	6		2
101	Md				2	2	6	2	6	10	2	6	10	14	2	6	10	13	2	6		2

[1] From Mavrodineanu and Boiteux, *L'analyse spectrale quantitative par la flamme*, Masson, Paris, 1954. Reproduced by permission of the authors and publishers.

Data for elements 94–101 from Weast et al. (Eds.), *Handbook of Chemistry and Physics*, 49th ed., The Chemical Rubber Co., Cleveland, 1968, page B-2.

Multiples of Atomic Weights of Important Elements

This table is based on the Table of Atomic Weights 1967 (see footnote [2], page 231)

Z	Symbol			0	1	2	3	4	5	6	7	8	9
1	H	Hydrogen	0	0.000 00	1.007 97	2.015 94	3.023 91	4.031 88	5.039 85	6.047 82	7.055 79	8.063 76	9.071 73
			10	10.079 70	11.087 67	12.095 64	13.103 61	14.111 58	15.119 55	16.127 52	17.135 49	18.143 46	19.151 43
			20	20.159 40	21.167 37	22.175 34	23.183 31	24.191 28	25.199 25	26.207 22	27.215 19	28.223 16	29.231 13
			30	30.239 10	31.247 07	32.255 04	33.263 01	34.270 98	35.278 95	36.286 92	37.294 89	38.302 86	39.310 83
			40	40.318 80	41.326 77	42.334 74	43.342 71	44.350 68	45.358 65	46.366 62	47.374 59	48.382 56	49.390 53
			50	50.398 50	51.406 47	52.414 44	53.422 41	54.430 38	55.438 35	56.446 32	57.454 29	58.462 26	59.470 23
			60	60.478 20	61.486 17	62.494 14	63.502 11	64.510 08	65.518 05	66.526 02	67.533 99	68.541 96	69.549 93
			70	70.557 90	71.565 87	72.573 84	73.581 81	74.589 78	75.597 75	76.605 72	77.613 69	78.621 66	79.629 63
			80	80.637 60	81.645 57	82.653 54	83.661 51	84.669 48	85.677 45	86.685 42	87.693 39	88.701 36	89.709 33
			90	90.717 30	91.725 27	92.733 24	93.741 21	94.749 18	95.757 15	96.765 12	97.773 09	98.781 06	99.789 03
			100	100.797 00	101.804 97	102.812 94	103.820 91	104.828 88	105.836 85	106.844 82	107.852 79	108.860 76	109.868 73
			110	110.876 70	111.884 67	112.892 64	113.900 61	114.908 58	115.916 55	116.924 52	117.932 49	118.940 46	119.948 43
			120	120.956 40	121.964 37	122.972 34	123.980 31	124.988 28	125.996 25	127.004 22	128.012 19	129.020 16	130.028 13
			130	131.036 10	132.044 07	133.052 04	134.060 01	135.067 98	136.075 95	137.083 92	138.091 89	139.099 86	140.107 83
			140	141.115 80	142.123 77	143.131 74	144.139 71	145.147 68	146.155 65	147.163 62	148.171 59	149.179 56	150.187 53
			150	151.195 50	152.203 47	153.211 44	154.219 41	155.227 38	156.235 35	157.243 32	158.251 29	159.259 26	160.267 23
			160	161.275 20	162.283 17	163.291 14	164.299 11	165.307 08	166.315 05	167.323 02	168.330 99	169.338 96	170.346 93
			170	171.354 90	172.362 87	173.370 84	174.378 81	175.386 78	176.394 75	177.402 72	178.410 69	179.418 66	180.426 63
			180	181.434 60	182.442 57	183.450 54	184.458 51	185.466 48	186.474 45	187.482 42	188.490 39	189.498 36	190.506 33
			190	191.514 30	192.522 27	193.530 24	194.538 21	195.546 18	196.554 15	197.562 12	198.570 09	199.578 06	200.586 03
6	C	Carbon	0	00.000 00	12.011 15	24.022 30	36.033 45	48.044 60	60.055 75	72.066 90	84.078 05	96.089 20	108.100 35
			10	120.111 50	132.122 65	144.133 80	156.144 95	168.156 10	180.167 25	192.178 40	204.189 55	216.200 70	228.211 85
			20	240.223 00	252.234 15	264.245 30	276.256 45	288.267 60	300.278 75	312.289 90	324.301 05	336.312 20	348.323 35
			30	360.334 50	372.345 65	384.356 80	396.367 95	408.379 10	420.390 25	432.401 40	444.412 55	456.423 70	468.434 85
			40	480.446 00	492.457 15	504.468 30	516.479 45	528.490 60	540.501 75	552.512 90	564.524 05	576.535 20	588.546 35
			50	600.557 50	612.568 65	624.579 80	636.590 95	648.602 10	660.613 25	672.624 40	684.635 55	696.646 70	708.657 85
			60	720.669 00	732.680 15	744.691 30	756.702 45	768.713 60	780.724 75	792.735 90	804.747 05	816.758 20	828.769 35
			70	840.780 50	852.791 65	864.802 80	876.813 95	888.825 10	900.836 25	912.847 40	924.858 55	936.869 70	948.880 85
			80	960.892 00	972.903 15	984.914 30	996.925 45	1008.936 60	1020.947 75	1032.958 90	1044.970 05	1056.981 20	1068.992 35
			90	1081.003 50	1093.014 65	1105.025 80	1117.036 95	1129.048 10	1141.059 25	1153.070 40	1165.081 55	1177.092 70	1189.103 85
7	N	Nitrogen	0	00.000 0	14.006 7	28.013 4	42.020 1	56.026 8	70.033 5	84.040 2	98.046 9	112.053 6	126.060 3
			10	140.067 0	154.073 7	168.080 4	182.087 1	196.093 8	210.100 5	224.107 2	238.113 9	252.120 6	266.127 3
			20	280.134 0	294.140 7	308.147 4	322.154 1	336.160 8	350.167 5	364.174 2	378.180 9	392.187 6	406.194 3
			30	420.201 0	434.207 7	448.214 4	462.221 1	476.227 8	490.234 5	504.241 2	518.247 9	532.254 6	546.261 3
			40	560.268 0	574.274 7	588.281 4	602.288 1	616.294 8	630.301 5	644.308 2	658.314 9	672.321 6	686.328 3
8	O	Oxygen	0	00.000 0	15.999 4	31.998 8	47.998 2	63.997 6	79.997 0	95.996 4	111.995 8	127.995 2	143.994 6
			10	159.994 0	175.993 4	191.992 8	207.992 2	223.991 6	239.991 0	255.990 4	271.989 8	287.989 2	303.988 6
			20	319.988 0	335.987 4	351.986 8	367.986 2	383.985 6	399.985 0	415.984 4	431.983 8	447.983 2	463.982 6
			30	479.982 0	495.981 4	511.980 8	527.980 2	543.979 6	559.979 0	575.978 4	591.977 8	607.977 2	623.976 6
			40	639.976 0	655.975 4	671.974 8	687.974 2	703.973 6	719.973 0	735.972 4	751.971 8	767.971 2	783.970 6
9	F	Fluorine	0	00.000 0	18.998 4	37.996 8	56.995 2	75.993 6	94.992 0	113.990 4	132.988 8	151.987 2	170.985 6
11	Na	Sodium	0	00.000 0	22.989 8	45.979 6	68.969 4	91.959 2	114.949 0	137.938 8	160.928 6	183.918 4	206.908 2
12	Mg	Magnesium	0	00.000	24.305	48.610	72.915	97.220	121.525	145.830	170.135	194.440	218.745
13	Al	Aluminium	0	00.000 0	26.981 5	53.963 0	80.944 5	107.926 0	134.907 5	161.889 0	188.870 5	215.852 0	242.833 5
14	Si	Silicon	0	00.000	28.086	56.172	84.258	112.344	140.430	168.516	196.602	224.688	252.774
15	P	Phosphorus	0	00.000 0	30.973 8	61.947 6	92.921 4	123.895 2	154.869 0	185.842 8	216.816 6	247.790 4	278.764 2
			10	309.738 0	340.711 8	371.685 6	402.659 4	433.633 2	464.607 0	495.580 8	526.554 6	557.528 4	588.502 2
16	S	Sulphur	0	00.000	32.064	64.128	96.192	128.256	160.320	192.384	224.448	256.512	288.576
			10	320.640	352.704	384.768	416.832	448.896	480.960	513.024	545.088	577.152	609.216
17	Cl	Chlorine	0	00.000	35.453	70.906	106.359	141.812	177.265	212.718	248.171	283.624	319.077
19	K	Potassium	0	00.000	39.102	78.204	117.306	156.408	195.510	234.612	273.714	312.816	351.918
20	Ca	Calcium	0	00.00	40.08	80.16	120.24	160.32	200.40	240.48	280.56	320.64	360.72
25	Mn	Manganese	0	00.000	54.938	109.876	164.814	219.752	274.690	329.628	384.566	439.504	494.442
26	Fe	Iron	0	00.000	55.847	111.694	167.541	223.388	279.235	335.082	390.929	446.776	502.623
27	Co	Cobalt	0	00.000 0	58.933 2	117.866 4	176.799 6	235.732 8	294.666 0	353.599 2	412.532 4	471.465 6	530.398 8
29	Cu	Copper	0	00.00	63.546	127.092	190.638	254.184	317.730	381.276	444.822	508.368	571.914
30	Zn	Zinc	0	00.00	65.37	130.74	196.11	261.48	326.85	392.22	457.59	522.96	588.33
33	As	Arsenic	0	00.000 0	74.921 6	149.843 2	224.764 8	299.686 4	374.608 0	449.529 6	524.451 2	599.372 8	674.294 4
35	Br	Bromine	0	00.000	79.904	159.808	239.712	319.616	399.520	479.424	559.328	639.232	719.136
53	I	Iodine	0	000.000 0	126.904 4	253.808 8	380.713 2	507.617 6	634.522 0	761.426 4	888.330 8	1015.235 2	1142.139 6
	H_2O	Water (½H_2O = 9.007 67)	0	00.000 00	18.015 34	36.030 68	54.046 02	72.061 36	90.076 70	108.092 04	126.107 38	144.122 72	162.138 06
			10	180.153 40	198.168 74	216.184 08	234.199 42	252.214 76	270.230 10	288.245 44	306.260 78	324.276 12	342.291 46
	CH_2	Methylene	0	00.000 00	14.027 09	28.054 18	42.081 27	56.108 36	70.135 45	84.162 54	98.189 63	112.216 72	126.243 81
			10	140.270 90	154.297 99	168.325 08	182.352 17	196.379 26	210.406 35	224.433 44	238.460 53	252.487 62	266.514 71
			20	280.541 80	294.568 89	308.595 98	322.623 07	336.650 16	350.677 25	364.704 34	378.731 43	392.758 52	406.785 61
			30	420.812 70	434.839 79	448.866 88	462.893 97	476.921 06	490.948 15	504.975 24	519.002 33	533.029 42	547.056 51
			40	561.083 60	575.110 69	589.137 78	603.164 87	617.191 96	631.219 05	645.246 14	659.273 23	673.300 32	687.327 41
	CH_3	Methyl	0	00.000 00	15.035 06	30.070 12	45.105 18	60.140 24	75.175 30	90.210 36	105.245 42	120.280 48	135.315 54
			10	150.350 60	165.385 66	180.420 72	195.455 78	210.490 84	225.525 90	240.560 96	255.596 02	270.631 08	285.666 14
			20	300.701 20	315.736 26	330.771 32	345.806 38	360.841 44	375.876 50	390.911 56	405.946 62	420.981 68	436.016 74
	NH_4	Ammonium	0	00.000 00	18.038 58	36.077 16	54.115 74	72.154 32	90.192 90	108.231 48	126.270 06	144.308 64	162.347 22
			10	180.385 80	198.424 38	216.462 96	234.501 54	252.540 12	270.578 70	288.617 28	306.655 86	324.694 44	342.733 02

Common chemical conversion factors

For converting		Factor	$\log_{10}$	For converting		Factor	$\log_{10}$
Acetone	into acetoacetic acid	1.758	0.2450	Acetoacetic acid	into acetone	0.5689	0.7550−1
Acetone	into β-hydroxybutyric acid	1.792	0.2533	β-Hydroxybutyric acid	into acetone	0.5579	0.7466−1
Ca	into CaO	1.399	0.1458	CaO	into Ca	0.7147	0.8541−1
Cl	into NaCl	1.648	0.2170	NaCl	into Cl	0.6066	0.7829−1
K	into K_2O	1.205	0.0810	K_2O	into K	0.8302	0.9192−1
Mg	into MgO	1.658	0.2195	MgO	into Mg	0.6032	0.7805−1
Na	into NaCl	2.542	0.4052	NaCl	into Na	0.3934	0.5948−1
Na	into Na_2O	1.348	0.1297	Na_2O	into Na	0.7419	0.8704−1
P	into P_2O_5	2.291	0.3600	P_2O_5	into P	0.4364	0.6399−1
P	into H_3PO_4	3.164	0.5002	H_3PO_4	into P	0.3161	0.4998−1
S	into SO_3	2.497	0.3974	SO_3	into S	0.4005	0.6026−1
S	into H_2SO_4	3.059	0.4857	H_2SO_4	into S	0.3269	0.5144−1
Protein-N	into protein	6.25	0.7959	Protein	into protein-N	0.16	0.2041−1
Ammonia-N	into ammonia	1.216	0.0849	Ammonia	into ammonia-N	0.8224	0.9151−1
Creatine-N	into creatine	3.121	0.4943	Creatine	into creatine-N	0.3204	0.5057−1
Creatinine-N	into creatinine	2.692	0.4301	Creatinine	into creatinine-N	0.3715	0.5700−1
Urea-N	into urea	2.144	0.3312	Urea	into urea-N	0.4665	0.6689−1
Uric acid-N	into uric acid	3.001	0.4772	Uric acid	into uric acid-N	0.3333	0.5228−1
Lipid-P	into phosphatides	23.5	1.3711				
Lipid-P	into lecithin	25	1.3979	Lecithin	into lipid-P	0.040	0.6021−2

Conversion of concentration units

In clinical chemistry, concentration data for fluids should be related to the unit litre, those for solids to the unit kilogramme. The use of ambiguous units like 'g%', 'mg%', 'p.p.m.', etc. should be avoided since they do not make it clear whether the data relate to mass or to volume.

Conversion of mg/100 ml into mmol/l and vice versa

$$\text{mmol/l} = \frac{10 \times \text{mg/100 ml}}{\text{molecular weight}} = \frac{10\,000 \times \text{g/100 ml}}{\text{molecular weight}}$$

$$\text{mg/100 ml} = \frac{\text{mmol} \times \text{molecular weight}}{10}$$

Conversion of ml of gas/100 ml into mmol/l and vice versa
(at 0 °C; 2.24 = millimolar normal volume of an ideal gas)

$$\text{mmol/l} = \frac{\text{ml/100 ml}}{2.24}$$

$$\text{ml/100 ml} = 2.24 \times \text{mmol/l}$$

Conversion of mg/100 ml into mEq/l and vice versa*

$$\text{mEq/l} = \frac{10 \times \text{mg/100 ml} \times \text{valency}}{\text{molecular weight}}$$

$$\text{mg/100 ml} = \frac{\text{mEq/l} \times \text{molecular weight}}{10 \times \text{valency}}$$

* Cf. footnote on page 226.

Temperature variation of molarity and normality of aqueous solutions

The following conversion factors for temperatures deviating from the normal temperature of 20 °C are for 0.1-N solutions and assume a coefficient of expansion for glass of 0.000027[1].

Temperature	Factor
14 °C	1.0010
15 °C	1.0009
16 °C	1.0007
17 °C	1.0006
18 °C	1.0004
19 °C	1.0002
20 °C	1.0000
21 °C	0.9998
22 °C	0.9996
23 °C	0.9994
24 °C	0.9991
25 °C	0.9989
26 °C	0.9986
27 °C	0.9983

Reference

[1] From a more extensive table in Kolthoff, I. M., *Die Maßanalyse*, part 2, Springer, Berlin, 1928, page 30.

The ICAO standard atmosphere is fundamentally defined in terms of an ideal air assumed to be devoid of moisture, water vapour and dust. It is based on accepted *standard values for the sea-level air*, as follows:

Atmospheric pressure $p_0 = 1.0132\mathbf{5} \times 10^5$ N m^{-2} (= 76**0** torr)
Temperature T_0 = 288.1**5** K (= 1**5** °C)
Density ϱ_0 = 1.225**0** kg m^{-3}
Acceleration due to gravity at 45° geographic latitude g_0 = 9.806**65** m s^{-2}

The relative molecular mass M (molecular weight) of air at sea level is calculated from the equation of state of a perfect gas

$$\varrho = \frac{M p}{R T}$$

using the standard values for ϱ_0, p_0, T_0 at sea level and for the molar gas constant R, which is based on the relative atomic mass (atomic weight; see page 226) of the nuclide ^{12}C = **12**.

Molar gas constant R = 8.3143 J K^{-1} mol^{-1}
Relative molecular mass of air at sea level M_0 = 28.9644

Note that for the altitudes tabulated below the mean relative molecular mass of air is assumed to be the same as at sea level (M_0).

Composition of clean, dry atmospheric air near sea level

Gas	Relative molecular mass	vol %	Gas	Relative molecular mass	vol %
N_2	28.0134	78.084	CH_4	16.04303	*0.0002
O_2	31.9988	20.9476	N_2O	44.0128	0.00005
Ar	39.948	0.934	O_3	47.9982	*Summer 0–0.000007
CO_2	44.00995	*0.0314			*Winter 0–0.000002
Ne	20.183	0.001818	SO_2	64.0628	*0–0.0001
He	4.0026	0.000524	NO_2	46.0055	*0–0.000002
Kr	83.80	0.000114	NH_3	17.03061	*0 to traces
Xe	131.30	0.0000087	CO	28.01055	*0 to traces
H_2	2.01594	0.00005	I_2	253.8088	*0–0.000001

* The content of these gases may undergo significant variations from time to time or from place to place relative to the normal indicated for them.

Reference

[1] From the *Manual of the ICAO Standard Atmosphere*, 2nd ed., International Civil Aviation Organization, Montreal, 1964. Reproduced by kind permission of the publishers.

Geometric altitude (m)	Temperature (°C)	Atmospheric pressure mbar	Atmospheric pressure torr	p/p_0	Boiling point of water* (°C)	Density (kg m^{-3})	ϱ/ϱ_0	Velocity of sound (m s^{-1})	Dynamic viscosity (N s m^{-2})	Thermal conductivity (kcal m^{-1} s^{-1} deg^{-1})	Geometric altitude (ft)
-1000	21.501	1.13931+3	8.54554+2	1.12441+0	103.31	1.3470+0	1.0996+0	344.111	1.8206-5	6.1748-6	-3280.8
- 950	21.176	1.13272	8.49610	1.11791	103.15	1.3407	1.0945	343.921	1.8190	6.1687	-3116.8
- 900	20.851	1.12616	8.44689	1.11143	102.98	1.3344	1.0893	343.731	1.8175	6.1626	-2952.8
- 850	20.526	1.11963	8.39792	1.10499	102.81	1.3281	1.0842	343.541	1.8159	6.1566	-2788.7
- 800	20.201	1.11313	8.34917	1.09858	102.65	1.3219	1.0791	343.351	1.8144	6.1505	-2624.7
- 750	19.876	1.10666	8.30066	1.09219	102.48	1.3157	1.0740	343.161	1.8128	6.1444	-2460.6
- 700	19.550	1.10023	8.25237	1.08584	102.32	1.3095	1.0690	342.970	1.8113	6.1383	-2296.6
- 650	19.225	1.09382	8.20432	1.07952	102.15	1.3033	1.0639	342.780	1.8097	6.1323	-2132.5
- 600	18.900	1.08744	8.15649	1.07322	101.99	1.2971	1.0589	342.589	1.8081	6.1262	-1968.5
- 550	18.575	1.08110	8.10889	1.06696	101.83	1.2910	1.0539	342.399	1.8066	6.1201	-1804.5
- 500	18.250	1.07478+3	8.06151+2	1.06073+0	101.66	1.2849+0	1.0489+0	342.208	1.8050-5	6.1140-6	-1640.4
- 450	17.925	1.06849	8.01436	1.05452	101.49	1.2788	1.0439	342.017	1.8035	6.1079	-1476.4
- 400	17.600	1.06224	7.96743	1.04835	101.32	1.2727	1.0390	341.826	1.8019	6.1018	-1312.3
- 350	17.275	1.05601	7.92073	1.04220	101.16	1.2667	1.0340	341.635	1.8003	6.0957	-1148.3
- 300	16.950	1.04981	7.87425	1.03609	100.99	1.2607	1.0291	341.443	1.7988	6.0896	- 984.3
- 250	16.625	1.04365	7.82799	1.03000	100.82	1.2547	1.0242	341.252	1.7972	6.0835	- 820.2
- 200	16.300	1.03751	7.78195	1.02394	100.66	1.2487	1.0193	341.061	1.7956	6.0774	- 656.2
- 150	15.975	1.03140	7.73614	1.01791	100.49	1.2427	1.0145	340.869	1.7941	6.0713	- 492.1
- 100	15.650	1.02532	7.69054	1.01191	100.33	1.2368	1.0096	340.678	1.7925	6.0652	- 328.1
- 50	15.325	1.01927	7.64516	1.00594	100.16	1.2309	1.0048	340.486	1.7909	6.0591	- 164.0
0	15.000	1.01325+3	7.60000+2	1.00000+0	100.00	1.2250+0	1.0000+0	340.294	1.7894-5	6.0530-6	0
50	14.675	1.00726	7.55505	9.94086-1	99.83	1.2191	9.9521-1	340.102	1.7878	6.0469	164.0
100	14.350	1.00129	7.51032	9.88201	99.66	1.2133	9.9044	339.910	1.7862	6.0408	328.1
150	14.025	9.95360+2	7.46581	9.82344	99.50	1.2075	9.8568	339.718	1.7847	6.0347	492.1
200	13.700	9.89454	7.42151	9.76515	99.33	1.2017	9.8094	339.525	1.7831	6.0286	656.2
250	13.375	9.83576	7.37743	9.70714	99.17	1.1959	9.7622	339.333	1.7815	6.0225	820.2
300	13.050	9.77727	7.33356	9.64942	99.00	1.1901	9.7152	339.141	1.7800	6.0164	984.3
350	12.725	9.71906	7.28990	9.59197	98.83	1.1844	9.6683	338.948	1.7784	6.0102	1148.3
400	12.400	9.66114	7.24645	9.53480	98.67	1.1786	9.6216	338.755	1.7768	6.0041	1312.3
450	12.075	9.60349	7.20321	9.47791	98.50	1.1729	9.5751	338.562	1.7752	5.9980	1476.4
500	11.750	9.54612+2	7.16018+2	9.42129-1	98.33	1.1673+0	9.5288-1	338.370	1.7737-5	5.9919-6	1640.4
550	11.425	9.48904	7.11736	9.36495	98.17	1.1616	9.4826	338.177	1.7721	5.9858	1804.5
600	11.100	9.43223	7.07475	9.30889	98.00	1.1560	9.4366	337.983	1.7705	5.9796	1968.5
650	10.775	9.37570	7.03235	9.25309	97.84	1.1504	9.3908	337.790	1.7689	5.9735	2132.5
700	10.450	9.31944	6.99015	9.19757	97.67	1.1448	9.3451	337.597	1.7673	5.9674	2296.6
750	10.126	9.26346	6.94816	9.14232	97.50	1.1392	9.2996	337.403	1.7658	5.9612	2460.6
800	9.801	9.20775	6.90638	9.08734	97.34	1.1337	9.2543	337.210	1.7642	5.9551	2624.7
850	9.476	9.15231	6.86480	9.03263	97.17	1.1281	9.2092	337.016	1.7626	5.9490	2788.7
900	9.151	9.09714	6.82342	8.97818	97.00	1.1226	9.1642	336.822	1.7610	5.9428	2952.8
950	8.826	9.04225	6.78225	8.92401	96.84	1.1171	9.1194	336.629	1.7594	5.9367	3116.8
1000	8.501	8.98762+2	6.74127+2	8.87009-1	96.68	1.1117+0	9.0748-1	336.435	1.7579-5	5.9305-6	3280.8
1050	8.176	8.93327	6.70050	8.81645	96.50	1.1062	9.0303	336.240	1.7563	5.9244	3444.9
1100	7.851	8.87918	6.65993	8.76307	96.34	1.1008	8.9860	336.046	1.7547	5.9182	3608.9
1150	7.526	8.82535	6.61956	8.70995	96.18	1.0954	8.9419	335.852	1.7531	5.9121	3773.0
1200	7.201	8.77180	6.57939	8.65709	96.00	1.0900	8.8979	335.657	1.7515	5.9059	3937.0
1250	6.877	8.71850	6.53941	8.60449	95.84	1.0846	8.8541	335.463	1.7499	5.8998	4101.0
1300	6.552	8.66547	6.49964	8.55215	95.68	1.0793	8.8105	335.268	1.7483	5.8936	4265.1
1350	6.227	8.61270	6.46006	8.50008	95.51	1.0740	8.7670	335.074	1.7467	5.8875	4429.1
1400	5.902	8.56020	6.42068	8.44826	95.34	1.0687	8.7237	334.879	1.7451	5.8813	4593.2
1450	5.577	8.50795	6.38149	8.39669	95.18	1.0634	8.6806	334.684	1.7436	5.8752	4757.2
1500	5.252	8.45596+2	6.34249+2	8.34539-1	95.01	1.0581+0	8.6376-1	334.489	1.7420-5	5.8690-6	4921.3
1550	4.927	8.40423	6.30369	8.29433	94.84	1.0529	8.5948	334.293	1.7404	5.8628	5085.3
1600	4.603	8.35276	6.26509	8.24354	94.68	1.0476	8.5521	334.098	1.7388	5.8567	5249.3
1650	4.278	8.30155	6.22667	8.19299	94.51	1.0424	8.5096	333.903	1.7372	5.8505	5413.4
1700	3.953	8.25059	6.18845	8.14270	94.34	1.0372	8.4673	333.707	1.7356	5.8443	5577.4
1750	3.628	8.19988	6.15042	8.09265	94.17	1.0321	8.4252	333.511	1.7340	5.8382	5741.5
1800	3.303	8.14943	6.11258	8.04286	94.01	1.0269	8.3832	333.316	1.7324	5.8320	5905.5
1850	2.978	8.09923	6.07492	7.99332	93.84	1.0218	8.3413	333.120	1.7308	5.8258	6069.6
1900	2.654	8.04928	6.03746	7.94402	93.68	1.0167	8.2996	332.924	1.7292	5.8197	6233.6
1950	2.329	7.99958	6.00018	7.89498	93.51	1.0116	8.2581	332.728	1.7276	5.8135	6397.6
2000	2.004	7.95014+2	5.96309+2	7.84618-1	93.34	1.0066+0	8.2168-1	332.532	1.7260-5	5.8073-6	6561.7
2050	1.679	7.90094	5.92619	7.79762	93.17	1.0015	8.1756	332.335	1.7244	5.8011	6725.7
2100	1.355	7.85199	5.88947	7.74931	93.01	9.9648-1	8.1345	332.139	1.7228	5.7949	6889.8
2150	1.030	7.80328	5.85294	7.70124	92.84	9.9147	8.0936	331.942	1.7212	5.7887	7053.8
2200	0.705	7.75482	5.81659	7.65341	92.67	9.8648	8.0529	331.746	1.7196	5.7826	7217.8
2250	0.380	7.70661	5.78043	7.60583	92.51	9.8151	8.0124	331.549	1.7180	5.7764	7381.9
2300	0.055	7.65863	5.74445	7.55849	92.34	9.7656	7.9719	331.352	1.7164	5.7702	7545.9
2350	−0.269	7.61091	5.70865	7.51138	92.17	9.7163	7.9317	331.155	1.7147	5.7640	7710.0
2400	−0.594	7.56342	5.67303	7.46452	92.01	9.6672	7.8916	330.958	1.7131	5.7578	7874.0
2450	−0.919	7.51618	5.63760	7.41789	91.84	9.6183	7.8517	330.761	1.7115	5.7516	8038.1

* Interpolated by the editors from the table on page 257.

Geometric altitude (m)	Temperature (°C)	Atmospheric pressure		p/p_0	Boiling point of water* (°C)	Density ($kg\ m^{-3}$)	ϱ/ϱ_0	Velocity of sound ($m\ s^{-1}$)	Dynamic viscosity ($N\ s\ m^{-2}$)	Thermal conductivity ($kcal\ m^{-1}\ s^{-1}\ deg^{-1}$)	Geometric altitude (ft)
		mbar	torr								
2500	− 1.244	7.46917+2	5.60234+2	7.37150−1	91.67	9.5695−1	7.8119−1	330.563	1.7099−5	5.7454−6	8202.1
2550	− 1.568	7.42240	5.56726	7.32534	91.51	9.5210	7.7722	330.366	1.7083	5.7392	8366.1
2600	− 1.893	7.37588	5.53236	7.27942	91.34	9.4726	7.7328	330.168	1.7067	5.7330	8530.2
2650	− 2.218	7.32958	5.49764	7.23374	91.17	9.4245	7.6934	329.971	1.7051	5.7268	8694.2
2700	− 2.543	7.28353	5.46310	7.18829	91.01	9.3765	7.6543	329.773	1.7035	5.7206	8858.3
2750	− 2.867	7.23771	5.42873	7.14307	90.84	9.3287	7.6153	329.575	1.7019	5.7144	9022.3
2800	− 3.192	7.19213	5.39454	7.09808	90.67	9.2811	7.5764	329.377	1.7002	5.7082	9186.4
2850	− 3.517	7.14677	5.36052	7.05332	90.50	9.2337	7.5377	329.179	1.6986	5.7019	9350.4
2900	− 3.841	7.10166	5.32668	7.00879	90.33	9.1864	7.4991	328.980	1.6970	5.6957	9514.4
2950	− 4.166	7.05677	5.29301	6.96449	90.17	9.1394	7.4607	328.782	1.6954	5.6895	9678.5
3000	− 4.491	7.01211+2	5.25952+2	6.92042−1	90.01	9.0925−1	7.4225−1	328.583	1.6938−5	5.6833−6	9842.5
3050	− 4.815	6.96768	5.22619	6.87657	89.84	9.0459	7.3844	328.385	1.6921	5.6771	10006.6
3100	− 5.140	6.92349	5.19304	6.83295	89.67	8.9994	7.3464	328.186	1.6905	5.6709	10170.6
3150	− 5.465	6.87952	5.16006	6.78956	89.50	8.9531	7.3086	327.987	1.6889	5.6646	10334.6
3200	− 5.790	6.83577	5.12725	6.74638	89.34	8.9069	7.2710	327.788	1.6873	5.6584	10498.7
3250	− 6.114	6.79226	5.09461	6.70344	89.16	8.8610	7.2335	327.589	1.6857	5.6522	10662.7
3300	− 6.439	6.74897	5.06214	6.66071	89.00	8.8152	7.1961	327.390	1.6840	5.6460	10826.8
3350	− 6.764	6.70590	5.02984	6.61821	88.83	8.7697	7.1589	327.191	1.6824	5.6397	10990.8
3400	− 7.088	6.66305	4.99770	6.57592	88.67	8.7243	7.1219	326.991	1.6808	5.6335	11154.9
3450	− 7.413	6.62043	4.96573	6.53386	88.50	8.6791	7.0849	326.792	1.6792	5.6273	11318.9
3500	− 7.737	6.57803+2	4.93393+2	6.49201−1	88.33	8.6340−1	7.0482−1	326.592	1.6775−5	5.6210−6	11482.9
3550	− 8.062	6.53586	4.90229	6.45039	88.16	8.5892	7.0116	326.392	1.6759	5.6148	11647.0
3600	− 8.387	6.49390	4.87082	6.40898	87.99	8.5445	6.9751	326.192	1.6743	5.6085	11811.0
3650	− 8.711	6.45216	4.83952	6.36778	87.83	8.5000	6.9388	325.992	1.6726	5.6023	11975.1
3700	− 9.036	6.41064	4.80837	6.32681	87.66	8.4557	6.9026	325.792	1.6710	5.5961	12139.1
3750	− 9.361	6.36933	4.77739	6.28604	87.49	8.4115	6.8666	325.592	1.6694	5.5898	12303.1
3800	− 9.685	6.32824	4.74657	6.24549	87.32	8.3676	6.8307	325.391	1.6677	5.5836	12467.2
3850	−10.010	6.28737	4.71592	6.20515	87.16	8.3238	6.7949	325.191	1.6661	5.5773	12631.2
3900	−10.334	6.24671	4.68542	6.16503	86.99	8.2802	6.7593	324.990	1.6645	5.5711	12795.3
3950	−10.659	6.20627	4.65509	6.12511	86.82	8.2367	6.7239	324.790	1.6628	5.5648	12959.3
4000	−10.984	6.16604+2	4.62491+2	6.08541−1	86.65	8.1935−1	6.6885−1	324.589	1.6612−5	5.5586−6	13123.4
4050	−11.308	6.12602	4.59489	6.04591	86.49	8.1504	6.6534	324.388	1.6596	5.5523	13287.4
4100	−11.633	6.08621	4.56504	6.00663	86.32	8.1075	6.6183	324.187	1.6579	5.5460	13451.4
4150	−11.957	6.04662	4.53533	5.96755	86.15	8.0647	6.5835	323.985	1.6563	5.5398	13615.5
4200	−12.282	6.00723	4.50579	5.92867	85.98	8.0222	6.5487	323.784	1.6546	5.5335	13779.5
4250	−12.607	5.96805	4.47640	5.89001	85.82	7.9798	6.5141	323.582	1.6530	5.5273	13943.6
4300	−12.931	5.92908	4.44717	5.85154	85.65	7.9376	6.4796	323.381	1.6513	5.5210	14107.6
4350	−13.256	5.89031	4.41810	5.81329	85.48	7.8955	6.4453	323.179	1.6497	5.5147	14271.7
4400	−13.580	5.85175	4.38918	5.77523	85.32	7.8536	6.4111	322.977	1.6481	5.5084	14435.7
4450	−13.905	5.81340	4.36041	5.73738	85.14	7.8119	6.3771	322.775	1.6464	5.5022	14599.7
4500	−14.229	5.77525+2	4.33180+2	5.69973−1	84.98	7.7704−1	6.3432−1	322.573	1.6448−5	5.4959−6	14763.8
4550	−14.554	5.73731	4.30333	5.66228	84.81	7.7290	6.3094	322.371	1.6431	5.4896	14927.8
4600	−14.878	5.69957	4.27503	5.62503	84.64	7.6878	6.2758	322.169	1.6415	5.4833	15091.9
4650	−15.203	5.66202	4.24687	5.58798	84.47	7.6468	6.2423	321.966	1.6398	5.4771	15255.9
4700	−15.527	5.62468	4.21886	5.55113	84.30	7.6059	6.2089	321.764	1.6382	5.4708	15419.9
4750	−15.852	5.58755	4.19100	5.51448	84.14	7.5652	6.1757	321.561	1.6365	5.4645	15584.0
4800	−16.176	5.55061	4.16330	5.47802	83.97	7.5247	6.1426	321.358	1.6349	5.4582	15748.0
4850	−16.501	5.51386	4.13574	5.44176	83.80	7.4844	6.1097	321.155	1.6332	5.4519	15912.1
4900	−16.825	5.47732	4.10833	5.40570	83.63	7.4442	6.0769	320.952	1.6316	5.4456	16076.1
4950	−17.150	5.44097	4.08107	5.36982	83.47	7.4041	6.0442	320.749	1.6299	5.4393	16240.2
5000	−17.474	5.40482+2	4.05395+2	5.33415−1	83.29	7.3643−1	6.0117−1	320.545	1.6282−5	5.4331−6	16404.2
5050	−17.799	5.36887	4.02698	5.29866	83.13	7.3246	5.9793	320.342	1.6266	5.4268	16568.2
5100	−18.123	5.33311	4.00016	5.26337	82.96	7.2851	5.9470	320.138	1.6249	5.4205	16732.3
5150	−18.448	5.29754	3.97348	5.22827	82.79	7.2457	5.9149	319.935	1.6233	5.4142	16896.3
5200	−18.772	5.26217	3.94695	5.19335	82.62	7.2065	5.8829	319.731	1.6216	5.4079	17060.4
5250	−19.097	5.22698	3.92056	5.15863	82.45	7.1675	5.8510	319.527	1.6200	5.4016	17224.4
5300	−19.421	5.19199	3.89432	5.12410	82.29	7.1286	5.8192	319.323	1.6183	5.3953	17388.5
5350	−19.746	5.15719	3.86821	5.08975	82.12	7.0899	5.7876	319.118	1.6166	5.3890	17552.5
5400	−20.070	5.12258	3.84225	5.05560	81.95	7.0513	5.7562	318.914	1.6150	5.3826	17716.5
5450	−20.395	5.08816	3.81643	5.02162	81.78	7.0129	5.7248	318.710	1.6133	5.3763	17880.6
5500	−20.719	5.05393+2	3.79076+2	4.98784−1	81.61	6.9747−1	5.6936−1	318.505	1.6116−5	5.3700−6	18044.6
5550	−21.044	5.01988	3.76522	4.95424	81.45	6.9366	5.6625	318.300	1.6100	5.3637	18208.7
5600	−21.368	4.98602	3.73982	4.92082	81.28	6.8987	5.6316	318.095	1.6083	5.3574	18372.7
5650	−21.692	4.95235	3.71456	4.88759	81.11	6.8610	5.6008	317.890	1.6066	5.3511	18536.7
5700	−22.017	4.91886	3.68945	4.85453	80.94	6.8234	5.5701	317.685	1.6050	5.3448	18700.8
5750	−22.341	4.88555	3.66446	4.82166	80.77	6.7859	5.5395	317.480	1.6033	5.3384	18864.8
5800	−22.666	4.85243	3.63962	4.78898	80.60	6.7486	5.5091	317.275	1.6016	5.3321	19028.9
5850	−22.990	4.81949	3.61491	4.75647	80.43	6.7115	5.4788	317.069	1.6000	5.3258	19192.9
5900	−23.314	4.78673	3.59034	4.72414	80.26	6.6746	5.4486	316.863	1.5983	5.3195	19357.0
5950	−23.639	4.75416	3.56591	4.69199	80.09	6.6378	5.4186	316.658	1.5966	5.3131	19521.0
6000	−23.963	4.72176+2	3.54161+2	4.66001−1	79.92	6.6011−1	5.3887−1	316.452	1.5949−5	5.3068−6	19685.0
6050	−24.288	4.68954	3.51745	4.62822	79.76	6.5646	5.3589	316.246	1.5933	5.3005	19849.1
6100	−24.612	4.65750	3.49342	4.59660	79.59	6.5283	5.3292	316.039	1.5916	5.2941	20013.1
6150	−24.936	4.62564	3.46952	4.56516	79.42	6.4921	5.2997	315.833	1.5899	5.2878	20177.2
6200	−25.261	4.59396	3.44576	4.53389	79.25	6.4561	5.2703	315.627	1.5882	5.2815	20341.2
6250	−25.585	4.56246	3.42212	4.50279	79.08	6.4202	5.2410	315.420	1.5865	5.2751	20505.2
6300	−25.909	4.53112	3.39862	4.47187	78.91	6.3845	5.2118	315.213	1.5849	5.2688	20669.3
6350	−26.234	4.49997	3.37525	4.44112	78.75	6.3489	5.1828	315.007	1.5832	5.2624	20833.3
6400	−26.558	4.46899	3.35202	4.41055	78.57	6.3135	5.1539	314.800	1.5815	5.2561	20997.4
6450	−26.882	4.43818	3.32891	4.38014	78.40	6.2782	5.1251	314.593	1.5798	5.2497	21161.4
6500	−27.207	4.40754+2	3.30593+2	4.34991−1	78.24	6.2431−1	5.0964−1	314.385	1.5781−5	5.2434−6	21325.5
6550	−27.531	4.37708	3.28308	4.31984	78.07	6.2081	5.0679	314.178	1.5764	5.2370	21489.5
6600	−27.855	4.34679	3.26036	4.28995	77.90	6.1733	5.0394	313.970	1.5748	5.2307	21653.5
6650	−28.180	4.31667	3.23777	4.26022	77.73	6.1387	5.0111	313.763	1.5731	5.2243	21817.6
6700	−28.504	4.28671	3.21530	4.23066	77.56	6.1041	4.9830	313.555	1.5714	5.2180	21981.6
6750	−28.828	4.25693	3.19296	4.20126	77.39	6.0698	4.9549	313.347	1.5697	5.2116	22145.7
6800	−29.153	4.22732	3.17075	4.17204	77.23	6.0356	4.9270	313.139	1.5680	5.2052	22309.7
6850	−29.477	4.19787	3.14866	4.14297	77.05	6.0015	4.8992	312.931	1.5663	5.1989	22473.8
6900	−29.801	4.16859	3.12670	4.11408	76.88	5.9676	4.8715	312.723	1.5646	5.1925	22637.8
6950	−30.126	4.13947	3.10486	4.08534	76.71	5.9338	4.8439	312.514	1.5629	5.1862	22801.8
7000	−30.450	4.11052+2	3.08315+2	4.05677−1	76.55	5.9002−1	4.8165−1	312.306	1.5612−5	5.1798−6	22965.9
7050	−30.774	4.08174	3.06156	4.02836	76.37	5.8667	4.7891	312.097	1.5595	5.1734	23129.9
7100	−31.099	4.05312	3.04009	4.00012	76.20	5.8334	4.7619	311.888	1.5578	5.1670	23294.0
7150	−31.423	4.02466	3.01874	3.97203	76.03	5.8002	4.7348	311.679	1.5561	5.1607	23458.0
7200	−31.747	3.99636	2.99752	3.94411	75.86	5.7671	4.7079	311.470	1.5544	5.1543	23622.0
7250	−32.071	3.96823	2.97642	3.91634	75.69	5.7342	4.6810	311.261	1.5527	5.1479	23786.1
7300	−32.396	3.94026	2.95544	3.88873	75.52	5.7015	4.6543	311.051	1.5510	5.1415	23950.1
7350	−32.720	3.91245	2.93458	3.86128	75.36	5.6689	4.6277	310.842	1.5493	5.1352	24114.2
7400	−33.044	3.88479	2.91384	3.83399	75.18	5.6364	4.6012	310.632	1.5476	5.1288	24278.2
7450	−33.368	3.85730	2.89321	3.80686	75.02	5.6041	4.5748	310.422	1.5459	5.1224	24442.3

* Interpolated by the editors from the table on page 257.

Geometric altitude (m)	Temperature (°C)	Atmospheric pressure mbar	Atmospheric pressure torr	p/p_0	Boiling point of water* (°C)	Density (kg m⁻³)	ϱ/ϱ_0	Velocity of sound (m s⁻¹)	Dynamic viscosity (N s m⁻²)	Thermal conductivity (kcal m⁻¹ s⁻¹ deg⁻¹)	Geometric altitude (ft)
7500	−33.693	3.82996+2	2.87271+2	3.77988−1	74.84	5.5719−1	4.5485−1	310.212	1.5442−5	5.1160−6	24606.3
7550	−34.017	3.80279	2.85232	3.75306	74.68	5.5399	4.5224	310.002	1.5425	5.1096	24770.3
7600	−34.341	3.77577	2.83206	3.72639	74.51	5.5080	4.4963	309.792	1.5408	5.1032	24934.4
7650	−34.665	3.74890	2.81191	3.69988	74.34	5.4762	4.4704	309.582	1.5391	5.0968	25098.4
7700	−34.989	3.72219	2.79187	3.67352	74.17	5.4446	4.4446	309.371	1.5374	5.0904	25262.5
7750	−35.314	3.69564	2.77196	3.64731	74.00	5.4131	4.4189	309.160	1.5357	5.0840	25426.5
7800	−35.638	3.66924	2.75215	3.62125	73.83	5.3818	4.3933	308.950	1.5340	5.0776	25590.6
7850	−35.962	3.64299	2.73247	3.59535	73.66	5.3506	4.3678	308.739	1.5323	5.0712	25754.6
7900	−36.286	3.61689	2.71289	3.56960	73.49	5.3196	4.3425	308.528	1.5305	5.0648	25918.6
7950	−36.610	3.59095	2.69343	3.54399	73.32	5.2886	4.3173	308.317	1.5288	5.0584	26082.7
8000	−36.935	3.56516+2	2.67409+2	3.51854−1	73.15	5.2579−1	4.2921−1	308.105	1.5271−5	5.0520−6	26246.7
8050	−37.259	3.53952	2.65486	3.49323	72.97	5.2272	4.2671	307.894	1.5254	5.0456	26410.8
8100	−37.583	3.51403	2.63574	3.46807	72.80	5.1967	4.2422	307.682	1.5237	5.0392	26574.8
8150	−37.907	3.48868	2.61673	3.44306	72.63	5.1663	4.2174	307.470	1.5220	5.0328	26738.8
8200	−38.231	3.46349	2.59783	3.41820	72.47	5.1361	4.1927	307.258	1.5202	5.0264	26902.9
8250	−38.555	3.43845	2.57905	3.39348	72.29	5.1060	4.1682	307.046	1.5185	5.0200	27066.9
8300	−38.880	3.41355	2.56037	3.36891	72.12	5.0761	4.1437	306.834	1.5168	5.0135	27231.0
8350	−39.204	3.38880	2.54181	3.34448	71.96	5.0462	4.1194	306.622	1.5151	5.0071	27395.0
8400	−39.528	3.36419	2.52335	3.32020	71.78	5.0165	4.0951	306.409	1.5134	5.0007	27559.1
8450	−39.852	3.33973	2.50500	3.29606	71.62	4.9870	4.0710	306.197	1.5116	4.9943	27723.1
8500	−40.176	3.31541+2	2.48677+2	3.27206−1	71.44	4.9576−1	4.0470−1	305.984	1.5099−5	4.9878−6	27887.1
8600	−40.824	3.26721	2.45061	3.22449	71.11	4.8991	3.9993	305.558	1.5065	4.9750	28215.2
8700	−41.473	3.21958	2.41489	3.17748	70.76	4.8412	3.9520	305.131	1.5030	4.9621	28543.3
8800	−42.121	3.17252	2.37959	3.13103	70.42	4.7838	3.9052	304.704	1.4995	4.9493	28871.4
8900	−42.769	3.12602	2.34470	3.08514	70.08	4.7270	3.8588	304.276	1.4961	4.9364	29199.5
9000	−43.417	3.08007+2	2.31024+2	3.03979−1	69.73	4.6706−1	3.8128−1	303.848	1.4926−5	4.9235−6	29527.6
9100	−44.065	3.03467	2.27619	2.99498	69.39	4.6148	3.7672	303.419	1.4891	4.9106	29855.6
9200	−44.714	2.98981	2.24254	2.95071	69.05	4.5595	3.7220	302.989	1.4856	4.8977	30183.7
9300	−45.362	2.94550	2.20930	2.90698	68.70	4.5047	3.6773	302.559	1.4822	4.8848	30511.8
9400	−46.010	2.90172	2.17647	2.86377	68.37	4.4504	3.6330	302.129	1.4787	4.8719	30839.9
9500	−46.658	2.85846+2	2.14402+2	2.82109−1	68.02	4.3966−1	3.5891−1	301.697	1.4752−5	4.8590−6	31168.0
9600	−47.306	2.81574	2.11198	2.77892	67.68	4.3433	3.5456	301.265	1.4717	4.8460	31496.1
9700	−47.954	2.77353	2.08032	2.73726	67.33	4.2905	3.5025	300.833	1.4682	4.8331	31824.1
9800	−48.602	2.73184	2.04905	2.69612	66.99	4.2382	3.4598	300.400	1.4647	4.8201	32152.2
9900	−49.250	2.69066	2.01816	2.65548	66.65	4.1864	3.4175	299.966	1.4612	4.8072	32480.3
10000	−49.898	2.64999+2	1.98765+2	2.61533−1	66.30	4.1351−1	3.3756−1	299.532	1.4577−5	4.7942−6	32808.4
10100	−50.546	2.60981	1.95752	2.57568	65.96	4.0843	3.3341	299.097	1.4541	4.7813	33136.5
10200	−51.194	2.57013	1.92776	2.53652	65.61	4.0339	3.2930	298.661	1.4506	4.7683	33464.6
10300	−51.842	2.53094	1.89836	2.49785	65.27	3.9840	3.2523	298.225	1.4471	4.7553	33792.7
10400	−52.490	2.49224	1.86934	2.45965	64.92	3.9346	3.2119	297.788	1.4436	4.7423	34120.7
10500	−53.137	2.45402	1.84067	2.42193	64.58	3.8857	3.1720	297.350	1.4400	4.7293	34448.8
10600	−53.785	2.41628	1.81236	2.38468	64.24	3.8372	3.1324	296.912	1.4365	4.7163	34776.9
10700	−54.433	2.37901	1.78441	2.34790	63.89	3.7892	3.0933	296.474	1.4329	4.7033	35105.0
10800	−55.081	2.34221	1.75680	2.31158	63.55	3.7417	3.0545	296.034	1.4294	4.6903	35433.1
10900	−55.729	2.30587	1.72955	2.27572	63.20	3.6946	3.0160	295.594	1.4258	4.6772	35761.2
11000	−56.376	2.26999+2	1.70263+2	2.24031−1	62.85	3.6480−1	2.9780−1	295.154	1.4223−5	4.6642−6	36089.2
11100	−56.500	2.23460	1.67609	2.20538	62.51	3.5932	2.9332	295.069	1.4216	4.6617	36417.3
11200	−56.500	2.19976	1.64996	2.17100	62.16	3.5372	2.8875	295.069	1.4216	4.6617	36745.4
11300	−56.500	2.16547	1.62423	2.13715	61.82	3.4820	2.8425	295.069	1.4216	4.6617	37073.5
11400	−56.500	2.13171	1.59891	2.10383	61.47	3.4277	2.7982	295.069	1.4216	4.6617	37401.6
11500	−56.500	2.09848	1.57399	2.07103	61.14	3.3743	2.7545	295.069	1.4216	4.6617	37729.7
11600	−56.500	2.06576	1.54945	2.03875	60.79	3.3217	2.7116	295.069	1.4216	4.6617	38057.7
11700	−56.500	2.03356	1.52530	2.00697	60.45	3.2699	2.6693	295.069	1.4216	4.6617	38385.8
11800	−56.500	2.00186	1.50152	1.97568	60.11	3.2189	2.6277	295.069	1.4216	4.6617	38713.9
11900	−56.500	1.97066	1.47812	1.94489	59.77	3.1688	2.5868	295.069	1.4216	4.6617	39042.0
12000	−56.500	1.93994+2	1.45508+2	1.91457−1	59.44	3.1194−1	2.5464−1	295.069	1.4216−5	4.6617−6	39370.1
12100	−56.500	1.90970	1.43240	1.88473	59.10	3.0708	2.5067	295.069	1.4216	4.6617	39698.2
12200	−56.500	1.87994	1.41007	1.85536	58.76	3.0229	2.4677	295.069	1.4216	4.6617	40026.2
12300	−56.500	1.85064	1.38809	1.82644	58.42	2.9758	2.4292	295.069	1.4216	4.6617	40354.3
12400	−56.500	1.82180	1.36646	1.79797	58.09	2.9294	2.3914	295.069	1.4216	4.6617	40682.4
12500	−56.500	1.79341	1.34517	1.76995	57.75	2.8838	2.3541	295.069	1.4216	4.6617	41010.5
12600	−56.500	1.76546	1.32420	1.74237	57.42	2.8388	2.3174	295.069	1.4216	4.6617	41338.6
12700	−56.500	1.73795	1.30357	1.71522	57.09	2.7946	2.2813	295.069	1.4216	4.6617	41666.7
12800	−56.500	1.71086	1.28325	1.68849	56.75	2.7510	2.2457	295.069	1.4216	4.6617	41994.8
12900	−56.500	1.68420	1.26326	1.66218	56.42	2.7082	2.2107	295.069	1.4216	4.6617	42322.8
13000	−56.500	1.65796+2	1.24357+2	1.63628−1	56.09	2.6660−1	2.1763−1	295.069	1.4216−5	4.6617−6	42650.9
13100	−56.500	1.63213	1.22420	1.61078	55.76	2.6244	2.1424	295.069	1.4216	4.6617	42979.0
13200	−56.500	1.60670	1.20512	1.58569	55.43	2.5835	2.1090	295.069	1.4216	4.6617	43307.1
13300	−56.500	1.58166	1.18634	1.56098	55.10	2.5433	2.0761	295.069	1.4216	4.6617	43635.2
13400	−56.500	1.55702	1.16786	1.53666	54.77	2.5037	2.0438	295.069	1.4216	4.6617	43963.3
13500	−56.500	1.53276	1.14967	1.51272	54.45	2.4646	2.0120	295.069	1.4216	4.6617	44291.3
13600	−56.500	1.50888	1.13176	1.48915	54.12	2.4262	1.9806	295.069	1.4216	4.6617	44619.4
13700	−56.500	1.48538	1.11412	1.46595	53.80	2.3884	1.9498	295.069	1.4216	4.6617	44947.5
13800	−56.500	1.46224	1.09677	1.44312	53.48	2.3512	1.9194	295.069	1.4216	4.6617	45275.6
13900	−56.500	1.43946	1.07968	1.42063	53.15	2.3146	1.8895	295.069	1.4216	4.6617	45603.7
14000	−56.500	1.41704+2	1.06286+2	1.39851−1	52.83	2.2786−1	1.8600−1	295.069	1.4216−5	4.6617−6	45931.8
14500	−56.500	1.31006	9.82628+1	1.29293	51.22	2.1065	1.7196	295.069	1.4216	4.6617	47572.2
15000	−56.500	1.21118	9.08460	1.19534	49.63	1.9475	1.5898	295.069	1.4216	4.6617	49212.6
15500	−56.500	1.11978	8.39901	1.10513	48.07	1.8006	1.4699	295.069	1.4216	4.6617	50853.0
16000	−56.500	1.03528	7.76525	1.02174	46.51	1.6647	1.3589	295.069	1.4216	4.6617	52493.4
16500	−56.500	9.57175+1	7.17940	9.44658−2	44.98	1.5391	1.2564	295.069	1.4216	4.6617	54133.9
17000	−56.500	8.84971	6.63783	8.73399	43.47	1.4230	1.1616	295.069	1.4216	4.6617	55774.3
17500	−56.500	8.18225	6.13719	8.07525	41.96	1.3157	1.0740	295.069	1.4216	4.6617	57414.7
18000	−56.500	7.56522	5.67438	7.46629	40.41	1.2165	9.9304−2	295.069	1.4216	4.6617	59055.1
18500	−56.500	6.99481	5.24654	6.90334	39.01	1.1247	9.1816	295.069	1.4216	4.6617	60695.5
19000	−56.500	6.46748+1	4.85101+1	6.38291−2	37.56	1.0400−1	8.4894−2	295.069	1.4216−5	4.6617−6	62336.0
19500	−56.500	5.97998	4.48536	5.90179	36.13	9.6157−2	7.8495	295.069	1.4216	4.6617	63976.4
20000	−56.500	5.52930	4.14732	5.45700	34.70	8.8910	7.2579	295.069	1.4216	4.6617	65616.8
21000	−55.569	4.72893	3.54699	4.66709	31.92	7.5715	6.1808	295.703	1.4267	4.6804	68897.6
22000	−54.576	4.04749	3.03587	3.99456	29.19	6.4510	5.2661	296.377	1.4322	4.7004	72178.5
23000	−53.583	3.46686	2.60036	3.42153	26.53	5.5006	4.4903	297.049	1.4376	4.7204	75459.3
24000	−52.590	2.97174	2.22899	2.93288	23.94	4.6938	3.8317	297.720	1.4430	4.7403	78740.2
25000	−51.598	2.54922	1.91207	2.51588	21.42	4.0084	3.2722	298.389	1.4484	4.7602	82021.0
26000	−50.606	2.18837	1.64141	2.15976	18.94	3.4257	2.7965	299.056	1.4538	4.7800	85301.8
27000	−49.614	1.87997	1.41009	1.85539	16.54	2.9298	2.3917	299.722	1.4592	4.7999	88582.7
28000	−48.623	1.61619+1	1.21225+1	1.59506−2	14.18	2.5076−2	2.0470−2	300.386	1.4646−5	4.8197−6	91863.5
29000	−47.632	1.39042	1.04290	1.37224	11.87	2.1478	1.7533	301.048	1.4699	4.8395	95144.4
30000	−46.641	1.19703	8.97846+0	1.18138	9.63	1.8410	1.5029	301.709	1.4753	4.8593	98425.2
31000	−45.650	1.03126	7.73508	1.01777	7.43	1.5792	1.2891	302.368	1.4806	4.8790	101706.0
32000	−44.660	8.89063+0	6.66852	8.77437−3	5.26	1.3555	1.1065	303.025	1.4859	4.8988	104986.9

* Interpolated by the editors from the table on page 257.

Mercury Barometer Correction* (1–40°C, 600–790 mm Hg)

Subtract from the barometer reading the amount Δ_t corresponding to the actual temperature t, *or* multiply the barometer reading by the correction factor f_t. The vapour pressure correction for air fully saturated with water vapour is already included in the conversion tables for gas volumes on pages 260–269 and can be ignored.

The correction factor f_t is calculated from the formula $f_t = 1 - \dfrac{(\beta - \alpha)\,t}{1 + \beta t}$

where

$\beta = 1.818 \times 10^{-4}\,°C^{-1} \approx$ volume expansion coefficient of mercury,
$\alpha = 1.84 \times 10^{-5}\,°C^{-1} \approx$ linear expansion coefficient of brass, or
$\alpha = 8.5 \times 10^{-6}\,°C^{-1} \approx$ linear expansion coefficient of glass of type Standard-Flint, Jena 16III, Corning 8810, etc.

Brass scale

Barometer temperature t = °C	Barometer reading β_t in mm Hg																				Correction factor f_t
	600	610	620	630	640	650	660	670	680	690	700	710	720	730	740	750	760	770	780	790	
	Amount Δ_t in millimetres to be subtracted																				
1	0.10	0.10	0.10	0.10	0.10	0.11	0.11	0.11	0.11	0.11	0.11	0.12	0.12	0.12	0.12	0.12	0.12	0.13	0.13	0.13	0.999 837
2	0.20	0.20	0.20	0.21	0.21	0.21	0.22	0.22	0.22	0.23	0.23	0.23	0.24	0.24	0.24	0.25	0.25	0.25	0.26	0.26	999 673
3	0.29	0.29	0.30	0.30	0.31	0.31	0.32	0.32	0.33	0.33	0.34	0.34	0.35	0.35	0.36	0.36	0.36	0.37	0.37	0.38	999 520
4	0.39	0.40	0.41	0.41	0.42	0.43	0.43	0.44	0.44	0.45	0.46	0.46	0.47	0.48	0.48	0.49	0.50	0.50	0.51	0.52	999 346
5	0.49	0.50	0.51	0.51	0.52	0.53	0.54	0.55	0.55	0.56	0.57	0.58	0.59	0.60	0.60	0.61	0.62	0.63	0.64	0.64	0.999 184
6	0.59	0.60	0.61	0.62	0.63	0.64	0.65	0.66	0.67	0.68	0.69	0.70	0.70	0.71	0.72	0.73	0.74	0.75	0.76	0.77	999 021
7	0.69	0.70	0.71	0.72	0.73	0.74	0.75	0.77	0.78	0.79	0.80	0.81	0.82	0.83	0.85	0.86	0.87	0.88	0.89	0.90	998 858
8	0.78	0.80	0.81	0.82	0.84	0.85	0.86	0.87	0.89	0.90	0.91	0.93	0.94	0.95	0.97	0.98	0.99	1.00	1.02	1.03	998 695
9	0.88	0.90	0.91	0.92	0.94	0.95	0.97	0.98	1.00	1.01	1.03	1.04	1.06	1.07	1.09	1.10	1.12	1.13	1.15	1.16	998 532
10	0.98	0.99	1.01	1.03	1.04	1.06	1.08	1.09	1.11	1.13	1.14	1.16	1.17	1.19	1.21	1.22	1.24	1.26	1.27	1.29	0.998 369
11	1.08	1.09	1.11	1.13	1.15	1.17	1.18	1.20	1.22	1.24	1.26	1.27	1.29	1.31	1.33	1.35	1.36	1.38	1.40	1.42	998 206
12	1.17	1.19	1.21	1.23	1.25	1.27	1.29	1.31	1.33	1.35	1.37	1.39	1.41	1.43	1.45	1.47	1.49	1.51	1.53	1.55	998 044
13	1.27	1.29	1.31	1.33	1.36	1.38	1.40	1.42	1.44	1.46	1.48	1.50	1.53	1.55	1.57	1.59	1.61	1.63	1.65	1.67	997 881
14	1.37	1.39	1.41	1.44	1.46	1.48	1.51	1.53	1.55	1.57	1.60	1.62	1.64	1.67	1.69	1.71	1.73	1.76	1.78	1.80	997 718
15	1.47	1.49	1.52	1.54	1.56	1.59	1.61	1.64	1.66	1.69	1.71	1.74	1.76	1.78	1.81	1.83	1.86	1.88	1.91	1.93	0.997 556
16	1.56	1.59	1.62	1.64	1.67	1.69	1.72	1.75	1.77	1.80	1.82	1.85	1.88	1.90	1.93	1.96	1.98	2.01	2.03	2.06	997 393
17	1.66	1.69	1.72	1.74	1.77	1.80	1.83	1.86	1.88	1.91	1.94	1.97	1.99	2.02	2.05	2.08	2.10	2.13	2.16	2.19	997 231
18	1.76	1.79	1.82	1.85	1.88	1.91	1.94	1.96	1.99	2.02	2.05	2.08	2.11	2.14	2.17	2.20	2.23	2.26	2.29	2.32	997 068
19	1.86	1.89	1.92	1.95	1.98	2.01	2.04	2.07	2.10	2.13	2.17	2.20	2.23	2.26	2.29	2.32	2.35	2.38	2.41	2.44	996 906
20	1.95	1.99	2.02	2.05	2.08	2.12	2.15	2.18	2.21	2.25	2.28	2.31	2.34	2.38	2.41	2.44	2.47	2.51	2.54	2.57	0.996 744
21	2.05	2.08	2.12	2.15	2.19	2.22	2.26	2.29	2.32	2.36	2.39	2.43	2.46	2.50	2.53	2.56	2.60	2.63	2.67	2.70	996 582
22	2.15	2.18	2.22	2.26	2.29	2.33	2.36	2.40	2.43	2.47	2.51	2.54	2.58	2.61	2.65	2.69	2.72	2.76	2.79	2.83	996 420
23	2.25	2.28	2.32	2.36	2.39	2.43	2.47	2.51	2.54	2.58	2.62	2.66	2.69	2.73	2.77	2.81	2.84	2.88	2.92	2.96	996 258
24	2.34	2.38	2.42	2.46	2.50	2.54	2.58	2.62	2.66	2.69	2.73	2.77	2.81	2.85	2.89	2.93	2.97	3.01	3.05	3.08	996 095
25	2.44	2.48	2.52	2.56	2.60	2.64	2.68	2.72	2.76	2.81	2.85	2.89	2.93	2.97	3.01	3.05	3.09	3.13	3.17	3.21	0.995 934
26	2.54	2.58	2.62	2.66	2.71	2.75	2.79	2.83	2.88	2.92	2.96	3.00	3.04	3.09	3.13	3.17	3.21	3.26	3.30	3.34	995 772
27	2.63	2.68	2.72	2.77	2.81	2.85	2.90	2.94	2.99	3.03	3.07	3.12	3.16	3.20	3.25	3.29	3.34	3.38	3.42	3.47	995 610
28	2.73	2.78	2.82	2.87	2.91	2.96	3.00	3.05	3.10	3.14	3.19	3.23	3.28	3.32	3.37	3.41	3.46	3.51	3.55	3.60	995 448
29	2.83	2.88	2.92	2.97	3.02	3.06	3.11	3.16	3.21	3.25	3.30	3.35	3.39	3.44	3.49	3.54	3.58	3.63	3.68	3.72	995 286
30	2.93	2.97	3.02	3.07	3.12	3.17	3.22	3.27	3.32	3.36	3.41	3.46	3.51	3.56	3.61	3.66	3.71	3.75	3.80	3.85	0.995 125
31	3.02	3.07	3.12	3.17	3.22	3.27	3.32	3.37	3.43	3.48	3.53	3.58	3.63	3.68	3.73	3.78	3.83	3.88	3.93	3.98	994 963
32	3.12	3.17	3.22	3.28	3.33	3.38	3.43	3.48	3.54	3.59	3.64	3.69	3.74	3.80	3.85	3.90	3.95	4.00	4.06	4.11	994 801
33	3.22	3.27	3.32	3.38	3.43	3.48	3.54	3.59	3.64	3.70	3.75	3.81	3.86	3.91	3.97	4.02	4.07	4.13	4.18	4.23	994 640
34	3.31	3.37	3.42	3.48	3.53	3.59	3.64	3.70	3.75	3.81	3.86	3.92	3.98	4.03	4.09	4.14	4.20	4.25	4.31	4.36	994 479
35	3.41	3.47	3.52	3.58	3.64	3.69	3.75	3.81	3.86	3.92	3.98	4.03	4.09	4.15	4.21	4.26	4.32	4.38	4.43	4.49	0.994 317
36	3.51	3.56	3.62	3.68	3.74	3.80	3.86	3.92	3.97	4.03	4.09	4.15	4.21	4.27	4.32	4.38	4.44	4.50	4.56	4.62	994 156
37	3.60	3.66	3.72	3.78	3.84	3.90	3.96	4.02	4.08	4.14	4.20	4.26	4.32	4.38	4.44	4.50	4.56	4.62	4.68	4.74	993 995
38	3.70	3.76	3.82	3.89	3.95	4.01	4.07	4.13	4.19	4.26	4.32	4.38	4.44	4.50	4.56	4.63	4.69	4.75	4.81	4.87	993 833
39	3.80	3.86	3.92	3.99	4.05	4.11	4.18	4.24	4.30	4.37	4.43	4.49	4.56	4.62	4.68	4.75	4.81	4.87	4.94	5.00	993 672
40	3.89	3.96	4.02	4.09	4.15	4.22	4.28	4.35	4.41	4.48	4.54	4.61	4.67	4.74	4.80	4.87	4.93	5.00	5.06	5.13	0.993 511

Glass scale

Barometer temperature t = °C	600	610	620	630	640	650	660	670	680	690	700	710	720	730	740	750	760	770	780	790	Correction factor f_t
1	0.10	0.11	0.11	0.11	0.11	0.11	0.11	0.12	0.12	0.12	0.12	0.12	0.12	0.13	0.13	0.13	0.13	0.13	0.13	0.14	0.999 827
2	0.21	0.21	0.21	0.22	0.22	0.22	0.23	0.23	0.24	0.24	0.24	0.25	0.25	0.25	0.26	0.26	0.26	0.27	0.27	0.27	999 654
3	0.31	0.32	0.32	0.33	0.33	0.34	0.34	0.35	0.35	0.36	0.36	0.37	0.37	0.38	0.38	0.39	0.40	0.40	0.41	0.41	999 480
4	0.42	0.42	0.43	0.44	0.44	0.45	0.46	0.46	0.47	0.48	0.49	0.49	0.50	0.51	0.51	0.52	0.53	0.53	0.54	0.55	999 307
5	0.52	0.53	0.54	0.55	0.55	0.56	0.57	0.58	0.59	0.60	0.61	0.61	0.62	0.63	0.64	0.65	0.66	0.67	0.68	0.68	0.999 134
6	0.62	0.63	0.64	0.65	0.66	0.68	0.69	0.70	0.71	0.72	0.73	0.74	0.75	0.76	0.77	0.78	0.79	0.80	0.81	0.82	998 961
7	0.73	0.74	0.75	0.76	0.78	0.79	0.80	0.81	0.82	0.84	0.85	0.86	0.87	0.88	0.90	0.91	0.92	0.93	0.95	0.96	998 788
8	0.83	0.84	0.86	0.87	0.89	0.90	0.91	0.93	0.94	0.95	0.97	0.98	1.00	1.01	1.02	1.04	1.05	1.07	1.08	1.09	998 616
9	0.93	0.95	0.97	0.98	1.00	1.01	1.03	1.04	1.06	1.07	1.09	1.11	1.12	1.14	1.15	1.17	1.18	1.20	1.21	1.23	998 443
10	1.04	1.06	1.07	1.09	1.11	1.12	1.14	1.16	1.18	1.19	1.21	1.23	1.25	1.26	1.28	1.30	1.31	1.33	1.35	1.37	0.998 270
11	1.14	1.16	1.18	1.20	1.22	1.24	1.26	1.27	1.29	1.31	1.33	1.35	1.37	1.39	1.41	1.43	1.45	1.46	1.48	1.50	998 098
12	1.25	1.27	1.29	1.31	1.33	1.35	1.37	1.39	1.41	1.43	1.45	1.47	1.49	1.51	1.54	1.56	1.58	1.60	1.62	1.64	997 925
13	1.35	1.37	1.39	1.42	1.44	1.46	1.48	1.51	1.53	1.55	1.57	1.60	1.62	1.64	1.66	1.69	1.71	1.73	1.75	1.78	997 752
14	1.45	1.48	1.50	1.52	1.55	1.57	1.60	1.62	1.65	1.67	1.69	1.72	1.74	1.77	1.79	1.82	1.84	1.86	1.89	1.91	997 580
15	1.56	1.58	1.61	1.63	1.66	1.68	1.71	1.74	1.76	1.79	1.81	1.84	1.87	1.89	1.92	1.94	1.97	2.00	2.02	2.05	0.997 408
16	1.66	1.69	1.71	1.74	1.77	1.80	1.82	1.85	1.88	1.91	1.94	1.96	1.99	2.02	2.05	2.07	2.10	2.13	2.16	2.18	997 235
17	1.76	1.79	1.82	1.85	1.88	1.91	1.94	1.97	2.00	2.03	2.06	2.09	2.11	2.14	2.17	2.20	2.23	2.26	2.29	2.32	997 063
18	1.87	1.90	1.93	1.96	1.99	2.02	2.05	2.08	2.11	2.15	2.18	2.21	2.24	2.27	2.30	2.33	2.36	2.39	2.43	2.46	996 891
19	1.97	2.00	2.03	2.07	2.10	2.13	2.17	2.20	2.23	2.26	2.30	2.33	2.36	2.40	2.43	2.46	2.49	2.53	2.56	2.59	996 719
20	2.07	2.11	2.14	2.18	2.21	2.24	2.28	2.31	2.35	2.38	2.42	2.45	2.49	2.52	2.56	2.59	2.62	2.66	2.69	2.73	0.996 547
21	2.18	2.21	2.25	2.28	2.32	2.36	2.39	2.43	2.47	2.50	2.54	2.57	2.61	2.65	2.68	2.72	2.76	2.79	2.83	2.86	996 375
22	2.28	2.32	2.35	2.39	2.43	2.47	2.51	2.54	2.58	2.62	2.66	2.70	2.73	2.77	2.81	2.85	2.89	2.92	2.96	3.00	996 203
23	2.38	2.42	2.46	2.50	2.54	2.58	2.62	2.66	2.70	2.74	2.78	2.82	2.86	2.90	2.94	2.98	3.02	3.06	3.10	3.14	996 031
24	2.48	2.53	2.57	2.61	2.65	2.69	2.73	2.77	2.82	2.86	2.90	2.94	2.98	3.02	3.06	3.11	3.15	3.19	3.23	3.27	995 859
25	2.59	2.63	2.67	2.72	2.76	2.80	2.85	2.89	2.93	2.98	3.02	3.06	3.11	3.15	3.19	3.23	3.28	3.32	3.36	3.41	0.995 687
26	2.69	2.74	2.78	2.83	2.87	2.92	2.96	3.00	3.05	3.09	3.14	3.18	3.23	3.27	3.32	3.36	3.41	3.45	3.50	3.54	995 515
27	2.79	2.84	2.89	2.93	2.98	3.03	3.07	3.12	3.17	3.21	3.26	3.31	3.35	3.40	3.45	3.49	3.54	3.59	3.63	3.68	995 344
28	2.90	2.95	2.99	3.04	3.09	3.14	3.19	3.24	3.28	3.33	3.38	3.43	3.48	3.53	3.57	3.62	3.67	3.72	3.77	3.82	995 170
29	3.00	3.05	3.10	3.15	3.20	3.25	3.30	3.35	3.40	3.45	3.50	3.55	3.60	3.65	3.70	3.75	3.80	3.85	3.90	3.95	995 001
30	3.10	3.15	3.21	3.26	3.31	3.36	3.41	3.46	3.52	3.57	3.62	3.67	3.72	3.77	3.83	3.88	3.93	3.98	4.03	4.09	0.994 829
31	3.21	3.26	3.31	3.37	3.42	3.47	3.53	3.58	3.63	3.69	3.74	3.79	3.85	3.90	3.95	4.01	4.06	4.11	4.17	4.22	994 658
32	3.31	3.36	3.42	3.47	3.53	3.58	3.64	3.69	3.75	3.80	3.86	3.91	3.97	4.02	4.08	4.13	4.19	4.25	4.30	4.36	994 487
33	3.41	3.47	3.52	3.58	3.64	3.70	3.75	3.81	3.87	3.92	3.98	4.04	4.09	4.15	4.21	4.26	4.32	4.38	4.43	4.49	994 315
34	3.51	3.57	3.63	3.69	3.75	3.81	3.86	3.92	3.98	4.04	4.10	4.16	4.22	4.27	4.33	4.39	4.45	4.51	4.57	4.63	994 144
35	3.62	3.68	3.74	3.80	3.86	3.92	3.98	4.04	4.10	4.16	4.22	4.28	4.34	4.40	4.46	4.52	4.58	4.64	4.70	4.76	0.993 974
36	3.72	3.78	3.84	3.90	3.97	4.03	4.09	4.15	4.21	4.28	4.34	4.40	4.46	4.52	4.59	4.65	4.71	4.77	4.83	4.90	993 802
37	3.82	3.89	3.95	4.01	4.08	4.14	4.20	4.27	4.33	4.39	4.46	4.52	4.59	4.65	4.71	4.78	4.84	4.90	4.97	5.03	993 631
38	3.92	3.99	4.05	4.12	4.19	4.25	4.32	4.38	4.45	4.51	4.58	4.64	4.71	4.77	4.84	4.91	4.97	5.04	5.10	5.17	993 460
39	4.03	4.09	4.16	4.23	4.30	4.36	4.43	4.50	4.56	4.63	4.70	4.76	4.83	4.90	4.97	5.03	5.10	5.17	5.23	5.30	993 289
40	4.13	4.20	4.27	4.34	4.40	4.47	4.54	4.61	4.68	4.75	4.82	4.89	4.96	5.02	5.09	5.16	5.23	5.30	5.37	5.44	0.993 118

Saturation pressure of water vapour below 0 °C over ice

°C	microbar (µb)[1] 9	8	7	6	5	4	3	2	1	0
-90	0.017	0.021	0.026	0.031	0.038	0.046	0.055	0.067	0.080	0.097
-80	0.116	0.139	0.166	0.198	0.235	0.280	0.332	0.393	0.464	0.547
-70	0.644	0.758	0.889	1.042	1.220	1.425	1.662	1.936	2.252	2.615
-60	3.032	3.511	4.060	4.688	5.406	6.225	7.159	8.223	9.432	10.80
-50	12.36	14.13	16.12	18.38	20.92	23.80	27.03	30.67	34.76	39.35
-40	44.49	50.26	56.71	63.93	71.98	80.97	90.98	102.1	114.5	128.3
-30	143.6	160.6	179.4	200.2	223.3	248.8	276.9	307.9	342.1	379.8

°C	0.001 torr* 9	8	7	6	5	4	3	2	1	0
-90	0.013	0.016	0.019	0.023	0.028	0.034	0.042	0.050	0.060	0.073
-80	0.087	0.104	0.124	0.148	0.176	0.210	0.249	0.294	0.348	0.410
-70	0.483	0.568	0.667	0.782	0.915	1.07	1.25	1.45	1.69	1.96
-60	2.27	2.63	3.05	3.52	4.05	4.67	5.37	6.17	7.07	8.10
-50	9.27	10.60	12.09	13.79	15.69	17.85	20.27	23.00	26.07	29.51
-40	33.37	37.70	42.54	47.95	53.99	60.73	68.24	76.58	85.88	96.23
-30	107.7	120.5	134.6	150.2	167.5	186.6	207.7	230.9	256.6	284.9

°C	millibar (mb)[1] .9	.8	.7	.6	.5	.4	.3	.2	.1	.0
-29	0.384	0.388	0.392	0.396	0.400	0.404	0.408	0.413	0.417	0.421
-28	0.426	0.430	0.435	0.439	0.444	0.448	0.453	0.457	0.462	0.467
-27	0.472	0.477	0.481	0.486	0.491	0.496	0.501	0.507	0.512	0.517
-26	0.522	0.528	0.533	0.538	0.544	0.549	0.555	0.561	0.566	0.572
-25	0.578	0.584	0.590	0.596	0.602	0.608	0.614	0.620	0.626	0.632
-24	0.639	0.645	0.652	0.658	0.665	0.671	0.678	0.685	0.692	0.699
-23	0.706	0.713	0.720	0.727	0.734	0.741	0.749	0.756	0.763	0.771
-22	0.779	0.786	0.794	0.802	0.810	0.818	0.826	0.834	0.842	0.850
-21	0.859	0.867	0.875	0.884	0.893	0.901	0.910	0.919	0.928	0.937
-20	0.946	0.955	0.965	0.974	0.983	0.993	1.002	1.012	1.022	1.032
-19	1.042	1.052	1.062	1.072	1.082	1.092	1.103	1.114	1.124	1.135
-18	1.146	1.157	1.168	1.179	1.190	1.201	1.213	1.225	1.236	1.248
-17	1.260	1.272	1.284	1.296	1.308	1.320	1.333	1.345	1.358	1.371
-16	1.384	1.397	1.410	1.424	1.437	1.451	1.464	1.478	1.492	1.506
-15	1.520	1.534	1.548	1.562	1.577	1.592	1.607	1.622	1.637	1.652
-14	1.667	1.683	1.698	1.714	1.730	1.746	1.762	1.778	1.795	1.811
-13	1.827	1.844	1.861	1.878	1.895	1.913	1.930	1.948	1.966	1.984
-12	2.002	2.020	2.039	2.057	2.076	2.095	2.114	2.133	2.153	2.172
-11	2.191	2.211	2.231	2.251	2.271	2.292	2.313	2.334	2.355	2.376
-10	2.397	2.419	2.440	2.462	2.484	2.506	2.529	2.551	2.574	2.597
- 9	2.620	2.644	2.667	2.691	2.715	2.739	2.763	2.787	2.812	2.837
- 8	2.862	2.888	2.913	2.939	2.965	2.991	3.017	3.043	3.070	3.097
- 7	3.124	3.152	3.180	3.208	3.236	3.264	3.292	3.321	3.350	3.379
- 6	3.409	3.438	3.468	3.499	3.529	3.560	3.591	3.622	3.653	3.685
- 5	3.717	3.748	3.781	3.813	3.846	3.879	3.913	3.947	3.981	4.015
- 4	4.049	4.084	4.119	4.154	4.190	4.226	4.262	4.298	4.335	4.372
- 3	4.409	4.447	4.485	4.523	4.561	4.600	4.638	4.678	4.717	4.757
- 2	4.797	4.838	4.878	4.920	4.961	5.003	5.045	5.087	5.130	5.173
- 1	5.217	5.260	5.305	5.349	5.394	5.439	5.485	5.530	5.577	5.623
0	5.670	5.717	5.764	5.812	5.860	5.909	5.958	6.007	6.057	6.107

°C	torr* .9	.8	.7	.6	.5	.4	.3	.2	.1	.0
-29	0.288	0.291	0.294	0.297	0.300	0.303	0.306	0.310	0.313	0.316
-28	0.319	0.323	0.326	0.329	0.333	0.336	0.340	0.343	0.347	0.350
-27	0.354	0.357	0.361	0.365	0.369	0.372	0.376	0.380	0.384	0.388
-26	0.392	0.396	0.400	0.404	0.408	0.412	0.416	0.421	0.425	0.430
-25	0.433	0.438	0.442	0.447	0.451	0.456	0.460	0.465	0.470	0.474
-24	0.479	0.484	0.489	0.494	0.499	0.504	0.509	0.514	0.519	0.524
-23	0.529	0.534	0.540	0.545	0.551	0.556	0.561	0.567	0.573	0.578
-22	0.584	0.590	0.596	0.601	0.607	0.613	0.619	0.625	0.632	0.638
-21	0.644	0.650	0.657	0.663	0.670	0.676	0.683	0.689	0.696	0.703
-20	0.710	0.717	0.723	0.731	0.738	0.745	0.752	0.759	0.767	0.774
-19	0.782	0.789	0.797	0.804	0.812	0.819	0.827	0.836	0.843	0.851
-18	0.860	0.868	0.876	0.884	0.893	0.901	0.910	0.919	0.927	0.936
-17	0.945	0.954	0.963	0.972	0.981	0.990	1.000	1.009	1.019	1.028
-16	1.038	1.048	1.058	1.068	1.078	1.088	1.098	1.109	1.119	1.130
-15	1.140	1.151	1.161	1.172	1.183	1.194	1.205	1.217	1.228	1.239
-14	1.250	1.262	1.274	1.286	1.298	1.310	1.322	1.334	1.346	1.358
-13	1.370	1.383	1.396	1.409	1.421	1.435	1.448	1.461	1.475	1.488
-12	1.502	1.515	1.529	1.543	1.557	1.571	1.586	1.600	1.615	1.629
-11	1.643	1.658	1.673	1.688	1.703	1.719	1.735	1.751	1.766	1.782
-10	1.798	1.814	1.830	1.847	1.863	1.880	1.897	1.913	1.931	1.948
- 9	1.965	1.983	2.000	2.018	2.036	2.054	2.072	2.090	2.109	2.128
- 8	2.147	2.166	2.185	2.204	2.224	2.243	2.263	2.282	2.303	2.323
- 7	2.343	2.364	2.385	2.406	2.427	2.448	2.469	2.491	2.513	2.534
- 6	2.557	2.579	2.601	2.624	2.647	2.670	2.693	2.717	2.740	2.764
- 5	2.788	2.811	2.836	2.860	2.885	2.909	2.935	2.960	2.986	3.011
- 4	3.037	3.063	3.090	3.116	3.143	3.170	3.197	3.224	3.252	3.279
- 3	3.307	3.336	3.364	3.393	3.421	3.450	3.479	3.509	3.538	3.568
- 2	3.598	3.629	3.659	3.690	3.721	3.753	3.784	3.816	3.848	3.880
- 1	3.913	3.945	3.979	4.012	4.046	4.080	4.114	4.148	4.183	4.218
0	4.253	4.288	4.323	4.359	4.395	4.432	4.469	4.506	4.543	4.581

Saturation pressure of water vapour below 0 °C over water

°C	millibar (mb)[1] .9	.8	.7	.6	.5	.4	.3	.2	.1	.0
-14	1.928	1.944	1.960	1.976	1.992	2.009	2.025	2.042	2.059	2.076
-13	2.093	2.110	2.127	2.144	2.162	2.180	2.197	2.215	2.233	2.252
-12	2.270	2.288	2.307	2.326	2.345	2.364	2.383	2.402	2.421	2.441
-11	2.461	2.480	2.500	2.521	2.541	2.561	2.582	2.602	2.623	2.644
-10	2.666	2.687	2.708	2.730	2.752	2.774	2.796	2.818	2.840	2.863
- 9	2.885	2.908	2.931	2.954	2.978	3.001	3.025	3.049	3.073	3.097
- 8	3.121	3.146	3.171	3.196	3.221	3.246	3.271	3.297	3.323	3.348
- 7	3.375	3.401	3.427	3.454	3.481	3.508	3.535	3.562	3.590	3.618
- 6	3.646	3.674	3.702	3.731	3.759	3.788	3.818	3.847	3.876	3.906
- 5	3.936	3.966	3.997	4.027	4.058	4.089	4.120	4.151	4.183	4.215
- 4	4.247	4.279	4.312	4.344	4.377	4.410	4.444	4.477	4.511	4.545
- 3	4.579	4.614	4.649	4.684	4.719	4.754	4.790	4.826	4.862	4.898
- 2	4.935	4.972	5.009	5.046	5.084	5.121	5.160	5.198	5.236	5.275
- 1	5.314	5.354	5.393	5.433	5.473	5.514	5.554	5.595	5.637	5.678
0	5.720	5.762	5.804	5.847	5.889	5.933	5.976	6.020	6.064	6.108

°C	torr* .9	.8	.7	.6	.5	.4	.3	.2	.1	.0
-14	1.446	1.458	1.470	1.482	1.494	1.507	1.519	1.532	1.544	1.557
-13	1.570	1.582	1.595	1.608	1.622	1.635	1.648	1.662	1.675	1.689
-12	1.703	1.716	1.730	1.744	1.759	1.773	1.787	1.802	1.816	1.831
-11	1.846	1.861	1.876	1.891	1.906	1.921	1.936	1.952	1.968	1.983
-10	1.999	2.015	2.031	2.048	2.064	2.080	2.097	2.114	2.130	2.147
- 9	2.164	2.181	2.199	2.216	2.234	2.251	2.269	2.287	2.305	2.323
- 8	2.341	2.360	2.378	2.397	2.416	2.435	2.454	2.473	2.492	2.512
- 7	2.531	2.551	2.571	2.591	2.611	2.631	2.651	2.672	2.693	2.714
- 6	2.734	2.756	2.777	2.798	2.820	2.842	2.863	2.885	2.908	2.930
- 5	2.952	2.975	2.998	3.021	3.044	3.067	3.090	3.114	3.138	3.161
- 4	3.185	3.210	3.234	3.259	3.283	3.308	3.333	3.358	3.384	3.409
- 3	3.435	3.461	3.487	3.513	3.539	3.566	3.593	3.620	3.647	3.674
- 2	3.701	3.729	3.757	3.785	3.813	3.841	3.870	3.899	3.928	3.957
- 1	3.986	4.016	4.045	4.075	4.105	4.136	4.166	4.197	4.228	4.259
0	4.290	4.322	4.353	4.385	4.417	4.450	4.482	4.515	4.548	4.581

Saturation pressure of water vapour above 100 °C

°C	bar (b)* 0	1	2	3	4	5	6	7	8	9
100	1.0133	1.0499	1.0877	1.1267	1.1667	1.2080	1.2505	1.2940	1.3391	1.3851
110	1.4326	1.4815	1.5315	1.5831	1.6362	1.6905	1.7464	1.8038	1.8628	1.9234
120	1.9854	2.0489	2.1146	2.1816	2.2502	2.3211	2.3933	2.4676	2.5436	2.6216
130	2.7013	2.7830	2.8670	2.9526	3.0408	3.1294	3.2215	3.3173	3.4139	3.5128
140	3.614	3.718	3.823	3.931	4.042	4.155	4.271	4.389	4.510	4.635
150	4.760	4.889	5.022	5.155	5.293	5.434	5.578	5.724	5.873	6.026
160	6.181	6.340	6.502	6.666	6.835	7.008	7.182	7.361	7.544	7.730
170	7.921	8.113	8.311	8.510	8.717	8.925	9.136	9.353	9.573	9.798
180	10.026	10.258	10.495	10.736	10.982	11.231	11.487	11.746	12.009	12.277
190	12.550	12.828	13.107	13.395	13.686	13.984	14.286	14.592	14.905	15.222
200	15.544	15.873	16.206	16.543	16.887	17.237	17.595	17.956	18.322	18.695
210	19.072	19.458	19.850	20.245	20.649	21.055	21.471	21.892	22.321	22.755
220	23.192	23.640	24.095	24.555	25.020	25.495	25.975	26.463	26.958	27.460
230	27.969	28.484	29.007	29.536	30.075	30.621	31.175	31.734	32.303	32.879
240	33.465	34.055	34.656	35.263	35.880	36.505	37.138	37.778	38.429	39.086
250	39.754	40.429	41.114	41.806	42.510	43.220	43.940	44.670	45.409	46.155
260	46.913	47.678	48.454	49.239	50.035	50.840	51.652	52.478	53.311	54.155
270	55.010	55.876	56.750	57.635	58.531	59.436	60.354	61.280	62.221	63.171
280	64.134	65.106	66.088	67.083	68.091	69.112	70.143	71.188	72.244	73.313
290	74.39	75.48	76.59	77.71	78.84	79.99	81.14	82.32	83.49	84.70
300	85.90	87.13	88.37	89.61	90.87	92.14	93.42	94.73	96.06	97.36
310	98.69	100.05	101.43	102.81	104.21	105.63	107.05	108.49	109.95	111.42
320	112.91	114.42	115.94	117.48	119.03	120.59	122.17	123.76	125.38	127.02
330	128.67	130.33	132.02	133.72	135.43	137.16	138.92	140.69	142.48	144.29
340	146.11	147.94	149.80	151.65	153.56	155.47	157.42	159.36	161.34	163.33
350	165.32	167.35	169.39	171.45	173.53	175.63	177.75	179.90	182.09	184.29
360	186.51	188.75	191.02	193.31	195.63	198.01	200.41	202.82	205.26	207.74
370	210.24	212.76	215.33	217.94	220.60	(← critical temperature)				

°C	atmosphere (atm)[2] 0	1	2	3	4	5	6	7	8	9
100	1.0000	1.0362	1.0735	1.1120	1.1514	1.1922	1.2341	1.2771	1.3216	1.3670
110	1.4139	1.4621	1.5115	1.5624	1.6148	1.6684	1.7236	1.7802	1.8384	1.8982
120	1.9594	2.0221	2.0869	2.1531	2.2208	2.2907	2.3620	2.4353	2.5103	2.5873
130	2.6660	2.7466	2.8295	2.9140	3.0010	3.0885	3.1794	3.2739	3.3693	3.4669
140	3.567	3.669	3.773	3.880	3.989	4.101	4.215	4.332	4.451	4.574
150	4.698	4.825	4.956	5.088	5.224	5.363	5.505	5.649	5.796	5.947
160	6.100	6.257	6.417	6.579	6.746	6.916	7.088	7.265	7.445	7.629
170	7.817	8.007	8.202	8.399	8.603	8.808	9.017	9.231	9.448	9.670
180	9.895	10.124	10.358	10.596	10.838	11.084	11.337	11.592	11.852	12.116
190	12.386	12.658	12.936	13.220	13.507	13.801	14.099	14.401	14.710	15.023
200	15.341	15.665	15.994	16.327	16.666	17.012	17.365	17.721	18.082	18.451
210	18.823	19.204	19.590	19.980	20.379	20.780	21.190	21.606	22.029	22.457
220	22.889	23.331	23.780	24.234	24.693	25.162	25.635	26.117	26.605	27.101
230	27.603	28.112	28.628	29.150	29.682	30.221	30.767	31.319	31.881	32.449
240	33.027	33.610	34.203	34.802	35.411	36.028	36.652	37.284	37.926	38.575
250	39.234	39.900	40.576	41.259	41.954	42.655	43.365	44.086	44.815	45.551
260	46.300	47.055	47.820	48.595	49.381	50.175	50.977	51.792	52.614	53.447
270	54.291	55.145	56.008	56.881	57.766	58.659	59.565	60.479	61.407	62.345
280	63.295	64.255	65.224	66.206	67.201	68.208	69.226	70.257	71.299	72.354
290	73.42	74.49	75.59	76.69	77.81	78.94	80.08	81.24	82.40	83.59
300	84.78	85.99	87.21	88.44	89.68	90.94	92.20	93.49	94.80	96.09
310	97.40	98.74	100.10	101.47	102.85	104.25	105.65	107.07	108.51	109.96
320	111.43	112.92	114.42	115.94	117.47	119.01	120.57	122.14	123.74	125.36
330	126.99	128.63	130.29	131.97	133.66	135.37	137.10	138.85	140.62	142.40
340	144.20	146.01	147.84	149.67	151.55	153.44	155.36	157.28	159.23	161.19
350	163.16	165.16	167.17	169.21	171.26	173.33	175.43	177.56	179.71	181.88
360	184.07	186.28	188.52	190.78	193.07	195.42	197.79	200.17	202.58	205.02
370	207.49	209.98	212.51	215.09	217.72	(← critical temperature)				

[1] Values from *Smithsonian Meteorological Tables*, Smithsonian Institution, Washington (D.C.), 1966.

[2] Values from KEYES, F.G., *Int. crit. Tab.*, **3**, 233 (1928).

* Values calculated by the editors of these *Scientific Tables*.

Saturation pressure in torr[1]

°C	.0	.1	.2	.3	.4	.5	.6	.7	.8	.9
0	4.58	4.61	4.65	4.68	4.72	4.75	4.78	4.82	4.85	4.89
1	4.93	4.96	5.00	5.03	5.07	5.11	5.14	5.18	5.22	5.25
2	5.29	5.33	5.37	5.41	5.44	5.48	5.52	5.56	5.60	5.64
3	5.68	5.72	5.76	5.80	5.85	5.89	5.93	5.97	6.01	6.05
4	6.10	6.14	6.18	6.23	6.27	6.32	6.36	6.40	6.45	6.49
5	6.54	6.59	6.63	6.68	6.72	6.77	6.82	6.87	6.91	6.96
6	7.01	7.06	7.11	7.16	7.21	7.26	7.31	7.36	7.41	7.46
7	7.51	7.56	7.61	7.67	7.72	7.77	7.83	7.88	7.93	7.99
8	8.04	8.10	8.15	8.21	8.26	8.32	8.38	8.43	8.49	8.55
9	8.61	8.66	8.72	8.78	8.84	8.90	8.96	9.02	9.08	9.14
10	9.20	9.27	9.33	9.39	9.46	9.52	9.58	9.65	9.71	9.77
11	9.84	9.91	9.97	10.04	10.10	10.17	10.24	10.31	10.38	10.44
12	10.51	10.58	10.65	10.72	10.79	10.87	10.94	11.01	11.08	11.15
13	11.23	11.30	11.38	11.45	11.52	11.60	11.68	11.75	11.83	11.91
14	11.98	12.06	12.14	12.22	12.30	12.38	12.46	12.54	12.62	12.70
15	12.78	12.87	12.95	13.03	13.12	13.20	13.29	13.37	13.46	13.54
16	13.63	13.72	13.81	13.89	13.98	14.07	14.16	14.25	14.34	14.43
17	14.53	14.62	14.71	14.81	14.90	14.99	15.09	15.18	15.28	15.38
18	15.47	15.57	15.67	15.77	15.87	15.97	16.07	16.17	16.27	16.37
19	16.47	16.58	16.68	16.79	16.89	17.00	17.10	17.21	17.32	17.42
20	17.53	17.64	17.75	17.86	17.97	18.08	18.19	18.31	18.42	18.53
21	18.65	18.76	18.88	18.99	19.11	19.23	19.35	19.46	19.58	19.70
22	19.82	19.95	20.07	20.19	20.31	20.44	20.56	20.69	20.81	20.94
23	21.07	21.19	21.32	21.45	21.58	21.71	21.84	21.98	22.11	22.24
24	22.38	22.51	22.65	22.78	22.92	23.06	23.19	23.33	23.47	23.61
25	23.76	23.90	24.04	24.18	24.33	24.47	24.62	24.76	24.91	25.06
26	25.21	25.36	25.51	25.66	25.81	25.96	26.12	26.27	26.43	26.58
27	26.74	26.90	27.05	27.21	27.37	27.53	27.70	27.86	28.02	28.18
28	28.35	28.52	28.68	28.85	29.02	29.19	29.36	29.53	29.70	29.87
29	30.04	30.22	30.39	30.57	30.75	30.92	31.10	31.28	31.46	31.64
30	31.83	32.01	32.19	32.38	32.56	32.75	32.94	33.13	33.32	33.51
31	33.70	33.89	34.08	34.28	34.47	34.67	34.87	35.07	35.26	35.47
32	35.67	35.87	36.07	36.28	36.48	36.69	36.89	37.10	37.31	37.52
33	37.73	37.95	38.16	38.37	38.59	38.81	39.02	39.24	39.46	39.68
34	39.90	40.13	40.35	40.58	40.80	41.03	41.26	41.49	41.72	41.95
35	42.18	42.41	42.65	42.89	43.12	43.36	43.60	43.84	44.08	44.33
36	44.57	44.82	45.06	45.31	45.56	45.81	46.06	46.31	46.56	46.82
37	47.08	47.33	47.59	47.85	48.11	48.37	48.64	48.90	49.17	49.43
38	49.70	49.97	50.24	50.51	50.79	51.06	51.34	51.62	51.89	52.17
39	52.45	52.74	53.02	53.31	53.59	53.88	54.17	54.46	54.75	55.04
40	55.34	55.63	55.93	56.23	56.53	56.83	57.13	57.44	57.74	58.05
41	58.36	58.67	58.98	59.29	59.60	59.92	60.24	60.55	60.87	61.19
42	61.52	61.84	62.17	62.49	62.82	63.15	63.48	63.81	64.15	64.49
43	64.82	65.16	65.50	65.84	66.19	66.53	66.88	67.23	67.58	67.93
44	68.28	68.64	68.99	69.35	69.71	70.07	70.43	70.80	71.16	71.53
45	71.90	72.27	72.64	73.01	73.39	73.77	74.15	74.53	74.91	75.29
46	75.67	76.06	76.45	76.84	77.23	77.63	78.03	78.43	78.82	79.22
47	79.63	80.03	80.44	80.84	81.25	81.67	82.08	82.49	82.91	83.33
48	83.75	84.17	84.60	85.03	85.45	85.88	86.31	86.74	87.18	87.61
49	88.06	88.50	88.94	89.38	89.83	90.28	90.73	91.19	91.64	92.10
50	92.56	93.02	93.48	93.95	94.41	94.88	95.35	95.82	96.29	96.77
51	97.25	97.73	98.21	98.69	99.18	99.67	100.16	100.65	101.14	101.64
52	102.14	102.64	103.14	103.64	104.15	104.66	105.17	105.69	106.21	106.73
53	107.24	107.77	108.29	108.82	109.34	109.88	110.41	110.94	111.48	112.02
54	112.56	113.11	113.66	114.20	114.75	115.31	115.86	116.42	116.98	117.54
55	118.10	118.67	119.24	119.81	120.38	120.96	121.54	122.13	122.70	123.30
56	123.88	124.47	125.07	125.66	126.26	126.86	127.46	128.07	128.67	129.28
57	129.90	130.51	131.13	131.75	132.37	132.99	133.62	134.25	134.88	135.52
58	136.16	136.80	137.44	138.09	138.73	139.38	140.04	140.70	141.35	142.02
59	142.68	143.34	144.01	144.68	145.35	146.03	146.71	147.39	148.08	148.77
60	149.46	150.15	150.84	151.55	152.25	152.95	153.66	154.37	155.08	155.80
61	156.52	157.24	157.96	158.68	159.41	160.15	160.88	161.62	162.36	163.10
62	163.85	164.60	165.35	166.11	166.87	167.62	168.39	169.15	169.92	170.70
63	171.47	172.25	173.04	173.82	174.61	175.40	176.20	176.99	177.79	178.60
64	179.40	180.21	181.02	181.84	182.66	183.48	184.31	185.13	185.96	186.80
65	187.64	188.48	189.32	190.17	191.02	191.87	192.73	193.59	194.45	195.32
66	196.19	197.06	197.94	198.82	199.70	200.59	201.47	202.37	203.27	204.17
67	205.07	205.97	206.88	207.80	208.71	209.63	210.56	211.49	212.42	213.36
68	214.29	215.24	216.18	217.13	218.08	219.03	219.99	220.95	221.91	222.88
69	223.86	224.83	225.81	226.80	227.79	228.78	229.77	230.77	231.77	232.77
70	233.79	234.80	235.81	236.83	237.86	238.89	239.92	240.96	241.99	243.03
71	244.09	245.14	246.19	247.24	248.31	249.37	250.44	251.52	252.59	253.67
72	254.76	255.85	256.94	258.04	259.15	260.25	261.36	262.47	263.59	264.70
73	265.83	266.95	268.09	269.23	270.37	271.51	272.66	273.82	274.98	276.14
74	277.31	278.48	279.65	280.83	282.02	283.20	284.39	285.59	286.79	287.99
75	289.19	290.41	291.62	292.85	294.07	295.30	296.53	297.77	299.01	300.26
76	301.51	302.76	304.03	305.29	306.56	307.83	309.11	310.39	311.67	312.96
77	314.26	315.56	316.86	318.18	319.49	320.81	322.13	323.46	324.79	326.13
78	327.47	328.81	330.16	331.52	332.88	334.24	335.62	336.99	338.36	339.75
79	341.14	342.53	343.93	345.33	346.74	348.15	349.57	350.98	352.42	353.85
80	355.28	356.72	358.17	359.62	361.07	362.53	364.00	365.47	366.95	368.42
81	369.91	371.40	372.89	374.40	375.91	377.42	378.93	380.45	381.98	383.51
82	385.04	386.59	388.13	389.69	391.25	392.81	394.37	395.95	397.53	399.11
83	400.70	402.30	403.89	405.50	407.11	408.72	410.34	411.97	413.61	415.24
84	416.88	418.53	420.18	421.84	423.50	425.17	426.85	428.53	430.21	431.91
85	433.60	435.31	437.02	438.73	440.45	442.18	443.91	445.64	447.38	449.13
86	450.88	452.65	454.41	456.18	457.96	459.74	461.53	463.33	465.13	466.93
87	468.74	470.56	472.38	474.21	476.05	477.89	479.73	481.59	483.45	485.31
88	487.19	489.06	490.95	492.84	494.73	496.63	498.54	500.46	502.38	504.30
89	506.23	508.17	510.11	512.06	514.02	515.98	517.96	519.93	521.91	523.90
90	525.89	527.89	529.90	531.91	533.93	535.96	537.99	540.03	542.08	544.13
91	546.19	548.25	550.32	552.40	554.48	556.58	558.68	560.78	562.89	565.01
92	567.13	569.26	571.40	573.54	575.69	577.85	580.02	582.18	584.37	586.55
93	588.74	590.94	593.14	595.35	597.57	599.79	602.02	604.26	606.51	608.77
94	611.02	613.29	615.57	617.85	620.14	622.43	624.73	627.04	629.36	631.68
95	634.01	636.35	638.69	641.05	643.40	645.77	648.14	650.53	652.91	655.31
96	657.71	660.12	662.54	664.97	667.40	669.84	672.28	674.73	677.20	679.67
97	682.14	684.63	687.12	689.62	692.13	694.64	697.16	699.69	702.23	704.77
98	707.32	709.88	712.45	715.02	717.61	720.19	722.80	725.40	728.02	730.64
99	733.27	735.91	738.55	741.20	743.87	746.54	749.21	751.90	754.59	757.29
100	760.00									

Boiling point in degree Centigrade*

torr	0	1	2	3	4	5	6	7	8	9
0		−17.28	−9.69	−5.03	−1.63	+1.22	3.78	5.99	7.93	9.67
10	11.25	12.70	14.03	15.27	16.43	17.52	18.54	19.51	20.44	21.32
20	22.15	22.96	23.73	24.47	25.18	25.87	26.53	27.18	27.80	28.40
30	28.99	29.55	30.11	30.64	31.17	31.68	32.18	32.66	33.14	33.60
40	34.05	34.50	34.93	35.36	35.78	36.19	36.59	36.98	37.37	37.75
50	38.12	38.49	38.85	39.20	39.55	39.90	40.23	40.57	40.90	41.22
60	41.54	41.85	42.16	42.47	42.77	43.06	43.36	43.65	43.93	44.21
70	44.49	44.77	45.04	45.31	45.57	45.84	46.10	46.35	46.60	46.86
80	47.10	47.35	47.59	47.83	48.07	48.31	48.54	48.77	49.00	49.23
90	49.45	49.67	49.89	50.11	50.32	50.54	50.75	50.96	51.17	51.37
100	51.58	51.78	51.98	52.18	52.38	52.58	52.77	52.96	53.16	53.35
110	53.54	53.72	53.91	54.09	54.28	54.46	54.64	54.81	54.99	55.17
120	55.34	55.52	55.69	55.86	56.03	56.20	56.37	56.53	56.70	56.86
130	57.03	57.19	57.35	57.51	57.67	57.83	57.99	58.14	58.30	58.45
140	58.61	58.76	58.91	59.06	59.21	59.36	59.51	59.65	59.80	59.94
150	60.09	60.23	60.38	60.52	60.66	60.80	60.94	61.08	61.22	61.35
160	61.49	61.63	61.76	61.90	62.03	62.16	62.30	62.43	62.56	62.69
170	62.82	62.95	63.08	63.21	63.33	63.46	63.59	63.71	63.84	63.96
180	64.08	64.21	64.33	64.45	64.57	64.69	64.81	64.93	65.05	65.17
190	65.29	65.41	65.52	65.64	65.76	65.87	65.99	66.10	66.22	66.33
200	66.44	66.56	66.67	66.78	66.89	67.00	67.11	67.22	67.33	67.44
210	67.55	67.66	67.76	67.87	67.98	68.08	68.19	68.30	68.40	68.51
220	68.61	68.71	68.82	68.92	69.02	69.12	69.23	69.33	69.43	69.53
230	69.63	69.73	69.83	69.93	70.03	70.13	70.23	70.32	70.42	70.52
240	70.62	70.71	70.81	70.90	71.00	71.10	71.19	71.28	71.38	71.47
250	71.57	71.66	71.75	71.85	71.94	72.03	72.12	72.21	72.30	72.39
260	72.49	72.58	72.66	72.75	72.84	72.93	73.02	73.11	73.20	73.29
270	73.37	73.46	73.55	73.64	73.72	73.81	73.89	73.98	74.07	74.15
280	74.24	74.32	74.41	74.49	74.57	74.66	74.74	74.82	74.91	74.99
290	75.07	75.15	75.24	75.32	75.40	75.48	75.56	75.64	75.72	75.81
300	75.88	75.97	76.04	76.12	76.20	76.28	76.36	76.44	76.52	76.60
310	76.68	76.75	76.83	76.91	76.99	77.06	77.14	77.22	77.29	77.37
320	77.44	77.52	77.59	77.67	77.75	77.82	77.90	77.97	78.05	78.12
330	78.19	78.27	78.34	78.41	78.49	78.56	78.63	78.71	78.78	78.85
340	78.92	78.99	79.07	79.14	79.21	79.28	79.35	79.42	79.49	79.57
350	79.64	79.71	79.78	79.84	79.91	79.98	80.05	80.12	80.19	80.26
360	80.33	80.40	80.47	80.54	80.60	80.67	80.74	80.81	80.88	80.94
370	81.01	81.08	81.14	81.21	81.28	81.34	81.41	81.48	81.54	81.61
380	81.67	81.74	81.80	81.87	81.94	82.00	82.07	82.13	82.19	82.26
390	82.32	82.39	82.45	82.52	82.58	82.64	82.71	82.77	82.83	82.90
400	82.96	83.02	83.08	83.15	83.21	83.27	83.33	83.40	83.46	83.52
410	83.58	83.64	83.70	83.77	83.83	83.89	83.95	84.01	84.07	84.13
420	84.19	84.25	84.31	84.37	84.43	84.49	84.55	84.61	84.67	84.73
430	84.79	84.85	84.91	84.97	85.02	85.08	85.14	85.20	85.26	85.32
440	85.38	85.43	85.49	85.55	85.61	85.67	85.72	85.78	85.84	85.89
450	85.95	86.01	86.06	86.12	86.18	86.23	86.29	86.35	86.40	86.46
460	86.52	86.57	86.63	86.68	86.74	86.79	86.85	86.90	86.96	87.02
470	87.07	87.13	87.18	87.23	87.29	87.34	87.40	87.45	87.51	87.56
480	87.61	87.67	87.72	87.78	87.83	87.88	87.94	87.99	88.04	88.10
490	88.15	88.20	88.26	88.31	88.36	88.41	88.47	88.52	88.57	88.62
500	88.68	88.73	88.78	88.83	88.89	88.94	88.99	89.04	89.09	89.14
510	89.19	89.25	89.30	89.35	89.40	89.45	89.50	89.55	89.60	89.65
520	89.70	89.75	89.80	89.86	89.91	89.96	90.01	90.06	90.10	90.15
530	90.20	90.25	90.30	90.35	90.40	90.45	90.50	90.55	90.60	90.65
540	90.70	90.75	90.80	90.85	90.89	90.94	90.99	91.04	91.09	91.14
550	91.18	91.23	91.28	91.33	91.38	91.42	91.47	91.52	91.57	91.62
560	91.66	91.71	91.76	91.81	91.85	91.90	91.95	91.99	92.04	92.09
570	92.13	92.18	92.23	92.27	92.32	92.37	92.41	92.46	92.51	92.55
580	92.60	92.64	92.69	92.74	92.78	92.83	92.87	92.92	92.97	93.01
590	93.06	93.10	93.15	93.19	93.24	93.28	93.33	93.37	93.42	93.46
600	93.51	93.55	93.60	93.64	93.69	93.73	93.78	93.82	93.87	93.91
610	93.95	94.00	94.04	94.09	94.13	94.17	94.22	94.26	94.30	94.35
620	94.39	94.44	94.48	94.52	94.57	94.61	94.65	94.70	94.74	94.78
630	94.83	94.87	94.91	94.95	95.00	95.04	95.08	95.13	95.17	95.21
640	95.25	95.30	95.34	95.38	95.42	95.47	95.51	95.55	95.59	95.63
650	95.68	95.72	95.76	95.80	95.84	95.89	95.93	95.97	96.01	96.05
660	96.09	96.13	96.18	96.22	96.26	96.30	96.34	96.38	96.42	96.46
670	96.50	96.55	96.59	96.63	96.67	96.71	96.75	96.79	96.83	96.87
680	96.91	96.95	96.99	97.03	97.07	97.11	97.15	97.19	97.23	97.27
690	97.31	97.35	97.39	97.43	97.47	97.51	97.55	97.59	97.63	97.67
700	97.71	97.75	97.79	97.83	97.87	97.91	97.95	97.99	98.02	98.06
710	98.10	98.14	98.18	98.22	98.26	98.30	98.33	98.37	98.41	98.45
720	98.49	98.53	98.57	98.60	98.64	98.68	98.72	98.76	98.80	98.83
730	98.87	98.91	98.95	98.99	99.02	99.06	99.10	99.14	99.18	99.21
740	99.25	99.29	99.33	99.36	99.40	99.44	99.48	99.51	99.55	99.59
750	99.63	99.66	99.70	99.74	99.77	99.81	99.85	99.89	99.92	99.96
760	100.00	100.03	100.07	100.11	100.14	100.18	100.22	100.25	100.29	100.33
770	100.36	100.40	100.44	100.47	100.51	100.54	100.58	100.62	100.65	100.69
780	100.73	100.76	100.80	100.83	100.87	100.91	100.94	100.98	101.01	101.05
790	101.08	101.12	101.16	101.19	101.23	101.26	101.30	101.33	101.37	101.40
800	101.44	101.47	101.51	101.55	101.58	101.62	101.65	101.69	101.72	101.76
810	101.79	101.83	101.86	101.90	101.93	101.96	102.00	102.03	102.07	102.10
820	102.14	102.17	102.21	102.24	102.28	102.31	102.35	102.38	102.41	102.45
830	102.48	102.52	102.55	102.58	102.62	102.65	102.69	102.72	102.76	102.79
840	102.82	102.86	102.89	102.92	102.96	102.99	103.02	103.06	103.09	103.13
850	103.16	103.19	103.23	103.26	103.29	103.33	103.36	103.40	103.43	103.46
860	103.50	103.53	103.56	103.60	103.63	103.66	103.70	103.73	103.76	103.80
870	103.83	103.86	103.89	103.93	103.96	103.99	104.03	104.06	104.09	104.12
880	104.16	104.19	104.22	104.25	104.29	104.32	104.35	104.38	104.42	104.45
890	104.48	104.51	104.54	104.58	104.61	104.64	104.67	104.70	104.74	104.77
900	104.80	104.83	104.86	104.90	104.93	104.96	104.99	105.02	105.06	105.09
910	105.12	105.15	105.18	105.21	105.25	105.28	105.31	105.34	105.37	105.40
920	105.44	105.47	105.50	105.53	105.56	105.59	105.62	105.66	105.69	105.72
930	105.75	105.78	105.81	105.84	105.87	105.90	105.94	105.97	106.00	106.03
940	106.06	106.09	106.12	106.15	106.18	106.21	106.24	106.28	106.31	106.34
950	106.37	106.40	106.43	106.46	106.49	106.52	106.55	106.58	106.61	106.64
960	106.67	106.70	106.73	106.77	106.80	106.83	106.86	106.89	106.92	106.95
970	106.98	107.01	107.04	107.07	107.10	107.13	107.16	107.19	107.22	107.25
980	107.28	107.31	107.34	107.37	107.40	107.43	107.46	107.49	107.52	107.55
990	107.58	107.61	107.63	107.66	107.69	107.72	107.75	107.78	107.81	107.84
1000	107.87									

[1] Values calculated from *Smithsonian Meteorological Tables*, Smithsonian Institution, Washington (D.C.), 1966.

Saturation pressure in millibar [1]

°C	.0	.1	.2	.3	.4	.5	.6	.7	.8	.9
0	6.11	6.15	6.20	6.24	6.29	6.33	6.38	6.43	6.47	6.52
1	6.57	6.61	6.66	6.71	6.76	6.81	6.86	6.90	6.95	7.00
2	7.05	7.11	7.16	7.21	7.26	7.31	7.36	7.42	7.47	7.52
3	7.58	7.63	7.68	7.74	7.79	7.85	7.90	7.96	8.02	8.07
4	8.13	8.19	8.24	8.30	8.36	8.42	8.48	8.54	8.60	8.66
5	8.72	8.78	8.84	8.90	8.97	9.03	9.09	9.15	9.22	9.28
6	9.35	9.41	9.48	9.54	9.61	9.67	9.74	9.81	9.88	9.94
7	10.01	10.08	10.15	10.22	10.29	10.36	10.43	10.51	10.58	10.65
8	10.72	10.80	10.87	10.94	11.02	11.09	11.17	11.24	11.32	11.40
9	11.47	11.55	11.63	11.71	11.79	11.87	11.95	12.03	12.11	12.19
10	12.27	12.36	12.44	12.52	12.61	12.69	12.78	12.86	12.95	13.03
11	13.12	13.21	13.30	13.38	13.47	13.56	13.65	13.74	13.83	13.93
12	14.02	14.11	14.20	14.30	14.39	14.49	14.58	14.68	14.77	14.87
13	14.97	15.07	15.17	15.27	15.37	15.47	15.57	15.67	15.77	15.87
14	15.98	16.08	16.19	16.29	16.40	16.50	16.61	16.72	16.83	16.94
15	17.04	17.15	17.26	17.38	17.49	17.60	17.71	17.83	17.94	18.06
16	18.17	18.29	18.41	18.52	18.64	18.76	18.88	19.00	19.12	19.25
17	19.37	19.49	19.61	19.74	19.86	19.99	20.12	20.24	20.37	20.50
18	20.63	20.76	20.89	21.02	21.16	21.29	21.42	21.56	21.69	21.83
19	21.96	22.10	22.24	22.38	22.52	22.66	22.80	22.94	23.09	23.23
20	23.37	23.52	23.66	23.81	23.96	24.11	24.26	24.41	24.56	24.71
21	24.86	25.01	25.17	25.32	25.48	25.64	25.79	25.95	26.11	26.27
22	26.43	26.59	26.75	26.92	27.08	27.25	27.41	27.58	27.75	27.92
23	28.09	28.26	28.43	28.60	28.77	28.95	29.12	29.30	29.48	29.65
24	29.83	30.01	30.19	30.37	30.56	30.74	30.92	31.11	31.30	31.48
25	31.67	31.86	32.05	32.24	32.43	32.63	32.82	33.02	33.21	33.41
26	33.61	33.81	34.01	34.21	34.41	34.62	34.82	35.03	35.23	35.44
27	35.65	35.86	36.07	36.28	36.50	36.71	36.92	37.14	37.36	37.58
28	37.80	38.02	38.24	38.46	38.69	38.91	39.14	39.37	39.59	39.82
29	40.06	40.29	40.52	40.76	40.99	41.23	41.47	41.71	41.95	42.19
30	42.43	42.67	42.92	43.17	43.41	43.66	43.91	44.17	44.42	44.67
31	44.93	45.18	45.44	45.70	45.96	46.22	46.49	46.75	47.02	47.28
32	47.55	47.82	48.09	48.36	48.64	48.91	49.19	49.47	49.75	50.03
33	50.31	50.59	50.87	51.16	51.45	51.74	52.03	52.32	52.61	52.90
34	53.20	53.50	53.80	54.10	54.40	54.70	55.00	55.31	55.62	55.93
35	56.24	56.55	56.86	57.18	57.49	57.81	58.13	58.45	58.77	59.10
36	59.42	59.75	60.08	60.41	60.74	61.07	61.41	61.74	62.08	62.42
37	62.76	63.11	63.45	63.80	64.14	64.49	64.84	65.20	65.55	65.91
38	66.26	66.62	66.99	67.35	67.71	68.08	68.45	68.82	69.19	69.56
39	69.93	70.31	70.69	71.07	71.45	71.83	72.22	72.61	72.99	73.39
40	73.78	74.17	74.57	74.97	75.37	75.77	76.17	76.58	76.98	77.39
41	77.80	78.22	78.63	79.05	79.47	79.89	80.31	80.73	81.16	81.59
42	82.02	82.45	82.88	83.32	83.75	84.19	84.64	85.08	85.53	85.97
43	86.42	86.88	87.33	87.79	88.24	88.70	89.17	89.63	90.10	90.56
44	91.03	91.51	91.98	92.46	92.94	93.42	93.90	94.39	94.87	95.36
45	95.86	96.35	96.85	97.34	97.84	98.35	98.85	99.36	99.87	100.38
46	100.89	101.41	101.93	102.45	102.97	103.50	104.03	104.56	105.09	105.62
47	106.16	106.70	107.24	107.78	108.33	108.88	109.43	109.98	110.54	111.10
48	111.66	112.22	112.79	113.36	113.93	114.50	115.07	115.65	116.23	116.81
49	117.40	117.99	118.58	119.17	119.77	120.37	120.97	121.57	122.18	122.79
50	123.40	124.01	124.63	125.25	125.87	126.49	127.12	127.75	128.38	129.01
51	129.65	130.29	130.93	131.58	132.23	132.88	133.53	134.19	134.84	135.51
52	136.17	136.84	137.51	138.18	138.86	139.54	140.22	140.91	141.60	142.29
53	142.98	143.68	144.38	145.08	145.78	146.49	147.20	147.91	148.63	149.35
54	150.07	150.80	151.53	152.26	152.99	153.73	154.47	155.21	155.96	156.71
55	157.46	158.22	158.97	159.74	160.50	161.27	162.04	162.82	163.59	164.38
56	165.16	165.95	166.74	167.53	168.33	169.13	169.93	170.74	171.55	172.36
57	173.18	174.00	174.82	175.65	176.48	177.31	178.15	178.99	179.83	180.68
58	181.53	182.38	183.24	184.10	184.96	185.83	186.70	187.58	188.45	189.34
59	190.22	191.11	192.00	192.89	193.79	194.69	195.60	196.51	197.42	198.34
60	199.26	200.18	201.11	202.05	202.98	203.92	204.86	205.81	206.76	207.71
61	208.67	209.63	210.59	211.56	212.53	213.51	214.49	215.48	216.46	217.45
62	218.45	219.45	220.45	221.46	222.47	223.48	224.50	225.52	226.54	227.58
63	228.61	229.65	230.70	231.74	232.79	233.85	234.91	235.97	237.03	238.11
64	239.18	240.26	241.34	242.43	243.52	244.62	245.72	246.82	247.93	249.04
65	250.16	251.28	252.41	253.54	254.67	255.81	256.95	258.10	259.25	260.40
66	261.56	262.73	263.90	265.07	266.25	267.43	268.61	269.80	271.00	272.20
67	273.40	274.61	275.82	277.04	278.26	279.49	280.72	281.96	283.20	284.45
68	285.70	286.96	288.21	289.48	290.75	292.02	293.30	294.58	295.86	297.15
69	298.45	299.75	301.06	302.37	303.69	305.01	306.34	307.67	309.00	310.34
70	311.69	313.04	314.39	315.75	317.12	318.49	319.87	321.25	322.63	324.02
71	325.42	326.82	328.22	329.63	331.05	332.47	333.89	335.33	336.76	338.20
72	339.65	341.10	342.56	344.03	345.50	346.97	348.45	349.93	351.42	352.91
73	354.41	355.91	357.43	358.94	360.46	361.99	363.52	365.06	366.61	368.15
74	369.71	371.27	372.84	374.41	375.99	377.57	379.16	380.75	382.35	383.95
75	385.56	387.18	388.80	390.43	392.06	393.70	395.34	396.99	398.65	400.31
76	401.98	403.65	405.34	407.02	408.71	410.41	412.11	413.82	415.53	417.25
77	418.98	420.71	422.45	424.20	425.95	427.71	429.47	431.24	433.02	434.80
78	436.59	438.38	440.18	441.99	443.80	445.62	447.45	449.28	451.11	452.96
79	454.81	456.67	458.53	460.40	462.28	464.16	466.05	467.94	469.85	471.76
80	473.67	475.59	477.52	479.45	481.39	483.34	485.29	487.25	489.22	491.19
81	493.17	495.16	497.15	499.16	501.17	503.18	505.20	507.23	509.26	511.30
82	513.35	515.41	517.47	519.54	521.62	523.70	525.79	527.89	529.99	532.10
83	534.22	536.35	538.48	540.62	542.77	544.92	547.08	549.25	551.43	553.61
84	555.80	557.99	560.20	562.41	564.62	566.85	569.08	571.32	573.57	575.83
85	578.09	580.36	582.64	584.93	587.22	589.52	591.83	594.14	596.46	598.79
86	601.13	603.48	605.83	608.19	610.56	612.94	615.32	617.72	620.12	622.52
87	624.94	627.36	629.79	632.23	634.68	637.13	639.59	642.07	644.55	647.03
88	649.53	652.03	654.54	657.06	659.59	662.12	664.66	667.22	669.78	672.34
89	674.92	677.50	680.09	682.69	685.30	687.92	690.55	693.18	695.82	698.47
90	701.13	703.80	706.47	709.16	711.85	714.55	717.26	719.98	722.71	725.45
91	728.19	730.94	733.70	736.47	739.25	742.04	744.84	747.64	750.46	753.28
92	756.11	758.95	761.80	764.66	767.52	770.40	773.29	776.18	779.09	782.00
93	784.92	787.85	790.79	793.74	796.69	799.66	802.63	805.62	808.61	811.62
94	814.63	817.65	820.69	823.73	826.78	829.84	832.91	835.99	839.08	842.17
95	845.28	848.40	851.52	854.66	857.80	860.96	864.12	867.30	870.48	873.68
96	876.88	880.09	883.31	886.55	889.79	893.04	896.30	899.57	902.86	906.15
97	909.45	912.76	916.08	919.42	922.76	926.11	929.47	932.84	936.23	939.62
98	943.02	946.43	949.85	953.28	956.73	960.18	963.65	967.12	970.61	974.10
99	977.61	981.13	984.65	988.19	991.74	995.30	998.87	1002.45	1006.04	1009.64
100	1013.25									

Boiling point in degree Celsius *

mbar	0	1	2	3	4	5	6	7	8	9
0		-16.52	-12.90	-8.35	-5.02	-2.40	-0.21	+1.90	3.78	5.46
10	6.99	8.38	9.67	10.87	11.99	13.04	14.03	14.97	15.86	16.71
20	17.52	18.29	19.04	19.75	20.44	21.10	21.74	22.36	22.96	23.54
30	24.10	24.65	25.18	25.70	26.21	26.70	27.18	27.65	28.10	28.55
40	28.99	29.41	29.83	30.24	30.65	31.04	31.43	31.80	32.18	32.54
50	32.90	33.26	33.60	33.94	34.28	34.61	34.93	35.25	35.57	35.88
60	36.19	36.49	36.79	37.08	37.37	37.66	37.94	38.22	38.49	38.76
70	39.03	39.29	39.55	39.81	40.07	40.32	40.57	40.82	41.06	41.30
80	41.54	41.77	42.01	42.24	42.47	42.69	42.92	43.14	43.36	43.58
90	43.79	44.00	44.22	44.43	44.63	44.84	45.04	45.24	45.44	45.64
100	45.84	46.03	46.23	46.42	46.61	46.79	46.98	47.17	47.35	47.53
110	47.72	47.89	48.07	48.25	48.42	48.60	48.77	48.94	49.11	49.28
120	49.45	49.62	49.78	49.95	50.11	50.27	50.43	50.59	50.75	50.91
130	51.07	51.22	51.38	51.53	51.68	51.83	51.99	52.14	52.28	52.43
140	52.58	52.72	52.87	53.01	53.16	53.30	53.44	53.58	53.72	53.86
150	54.00	54.14	54.28	54.41	54.55	54.68	54.82	54.95	55.08	55.21
160	55.35	55.48	55.61	55.73	55.86	55.99	56.12	56.24	56.37	56.49
170	56.62	56.74	56.87	56.99	57.11	57.23	57.35	57.47	57.59	57.71
180	57.93	57.98	58.07	58.18	58.30	58.42	58.53	58.64	58.76	58.87
190	58.99	59.10	59.21	59.32	59.43	59.54	59.65	59.76	59.87	59.98
200	60.09	60.20	60.31	60.41	60.52	60.63	60.73	60.84	60.94	61.04
210	61.15	61.25	61.36	61.46	61.56	61.66	61.76	61.86	61.97	62.07
220	62.17	62.26	62.36	62.46	62.56	62.66	62.76	62.85	62.95	63.05
230	63.14	63.24	63.33	63.43	63.52	63.62	63.71	63.81	63.90	63.99
240	64.09	64.18	64.27	64.36	64.45	64.54	64.64	64.72	64.82	64.91
250	64.99	65.08	65.17	65.26	65.35	65.44	65.53	65.61	65.70	65.79
260	65.87	65.96	66.05	66.13	66.22	66.30	66.39	66.47	66.56	66.64
270	66.72	66.81	66.89	66.97	67.06	67.14	67.22	67.31	67.39	67.47
280	67.55	67.63	67.71	67.79	67.87	67.95	68.03	68.11	68.19	68.27
290	68.35	68.43	68.51	68.59	68.66	68.74	68.82	68.90	68.97	69.05
300	69.13	69.20	69.28	69.36	69.43	69.51	69.58	69.66	69.73	69.81
310	69.88	69.96	70.03	70.10	70.18	70.25	70.33	70.40	70.47	70.54
320	70.62	70.69	70.76	70.83	70.91	70.98	71.05	71.12	71.19	71.26
330	71.33	71.40	71.47	71.54	71.61	71.68	71.75	71.82	71.89	71.96
340	72.03	72.10	72.17	72.24	72.30	72.37	72.44	72.51	72.58	72.64
350	72.71	72.78	72.84	72.91	72.98	73.05	73.11	73.18	73.24	73.31
360	73.38	73.44	73.51	73.57	73.64	73.70	73.77	73.83	73.90	73.96
370	74.02	74.09	74.15	74.22	74.28	74.34	74.41	74.47	74.53	74.60
380	74.66	74.72	74.78	74.85	74.91	74.97	75.03	75.10	75.16	75.22
390	75.28	75.34	75.40	75.46	75.52	75.58	75.65	75.71	75.77	75.83
400	75.89	75.95	76.01	76.07	76.13	76.19	76.25	76.31	76.36	76.42
410	76.48	76.54	76.60	76.66	76.72	76.77	76.83	76.89	76.95	77.01
420	77.06	77.12	77.18	77.24	77.29	77.35	77.41	77.46	77.52	77.58
430	77.63	77.69	77.75	77.80	77.86	77.92	77.97	78.03	78.08	78.14
440	78.19	78.25	78.30	78.36	78.42	78.47	78.53	78.58	78.64	78.69
450	78.74	78.80	78.85	78.91	78.96	79.01	79.07	79.12	79.18	79.23
460	79.28	79.34	79.39	79.44	79.50	79.55	79.60	79.66	79.71	79.76
470	79.81	79.86	79.92	79.97	80.02	80.07	80.12	80.18	80.23	80.28
480	80.33	80.38	80.44	80.49	80.54	80.59	80.64	80.69	80.74	80.79
490	80.84	80.89	80.94	81.00	81.05	81.09	81.15	81.20	81.25	81.30
500	81.35	81.40	81.45	81.49	81.54	81.59	81.64	81.69	81.74	81.79
510	81.84	81.89	81.94	81.99	82.03	82.08	82.13	82.18	82.23	82.28
520	82.33	82.37	82.42	82.47	82.52	82.57	82.61	82.66	82.71	82.76
530	82.80	82.85	82.90	82.94	82.99	83.04	83.09	83.13	83.18	83.23
540	83.27	83.32	83.37	83.41	83.46	83.51	83.55	83.60	83.65	83.69
550	83.74	83.78	83.83	83.87	83.92	83.97	84.01	84.06	84.10	84.15
560	84.19	84.24	84.28	84.33	84.37	84.42	84.46	84.51	84.55	84.60
570	84.64	84.69	84.73	84.78	84.82	84.86	84.91	84.95	85.00	85.04
580	85.09	85.13	85.17	85.22	85.26	85.31	85.35	85.39	85.44	85.48
590	85.52	85.57	85.61	85.65	85.70	85.74	85.78	85.83	85.87	85.91
600	85.95	86.00	86.04	86.08	86.12	86.17	86.21	86.25	86.29	86.33
610	86.38	86.42	86.46	86.50	86.55	86.59	86.63	86.67	86.71	86.75
620	86.80	86.84	86.88	86.92	86.96	87.00	87.05	87.09	87.13	87.17
630	87.21	87.25	87.29	87.33	87.37	87.41	87.46	87.50	87.54	87.58
640	87.62	87.66	87.70	87.74	87.78	87.82	87.86	87.90	87.94	87.98
650	88.02	88.06	88.10	88.14	88.18	88.22	88.26	88.30	88.34	88.38
660	88.42	88.46	88.50	88.54	88.57	88.61	88.65	88.69	88.73	88.77
670	88.81	88.85	88.89	88.93	88.96	89.00	89.04	89.08	89.12	89.16
680	89.20	89.23	89.27	89.31	89.35	89.39	89.43	89.46	89.50	89.54
690	89.58	89.62	89.66	89.69	89.73	89.77	89.81	89.84	89.88	89.92
700	89.96	90.00	90.03	90.07	90.11	90.14	90.18	90.22	90.26	90.29
710	90.33	90.37	90.41	90.44	90.48	90.52	90.55	90.59	90.63	90.66
720	90.70	90.74	90.77	90.81	90.85	90.88	90.92	90.96	90.99	91.03
730	91.06	91.10	91.14	91.17	91.21	91.25	91.28	91.32	91.35	91.39
740	91.43	91.46	91.50	91.53	91.57	91.61	91.64	91.68	91.71	91.75
750	91.78	91.82	91.85	91.89	91.93	91.96	92.00	92.03	92.07	92.10
760	92.14	92.17	92.21	92.24	92.28	92.31	92.35	92.38	92.41	92.45
770	92.48	92.52	92.55	92.59	92.62	92.66	92.69	92.73	92.76	92.80
780	92.83	92.86	92.90	92.93	92.97	93.00	93.04	93.07	93.10	93.14
790	93.17	93.20	93.24	93.27	93.31	93.34	93.37	93.41	93.44	93.48
800	93.51	93.54	93.58	93.61	93.64	93.68	93.71	93.74	93.78	93.81
810	93.84	93.88	93.91	93.94	93.98	94.01	94.04	94.08	94.11	94.14
820	94.18	94.21	94.24	94.27	94.31	94.34	94.37	94.41	94.44	94.47
830	94.50	94.54	94.57	94.60	94.63	94.67	94.70	94.73	94.76	94.79
840	94.83	94.86	94.89	94.92	94.96	94.99	95.02	95.05	95.09	95.12
850	95.15	95.18	95.21	95.24	95.28	95.31	95.34	95.37	95.40	95.44
860	95.47	95.50	95.53	95.56	95.59	95.62	95.66	95.69	95.72	95.75
870	95.78	95.81	95.85	95.88	95.91	95.94	95.97	96.00	96.03	96.06
880	96.09	96.13	96.16	96.19	96.22	96.25	96.28	96.31	96.34	96.37
890	96.40	96.43	96.47	96.50	96.53	96.56	96.59	96.62	96.65	96.68
900	96.71	96.74	96.77	96.80	96.83	96.86	96.89	96.92	96.95	96.98
910	97.01	97.04	97.07	97.10	97.13	97.16	97.19	97.22	97.25	97.29
920	97.32	97.34	97.37	97.40	97.43	97.46	97.49	97.52	97.55	97.58
930	97.61	97.64	97.67	97.70	97.73	97.76	97.79	97.82	97.85	97.88
940	97.91	97.94	97.97	98.00	98.03	98.06	98.08	98.11	98.14	98.17
950	98.20	98.23	98.26	98.29	98.32	98.35	98.38	98.40	98.43	98.46
960	98.49	98.52	98.55	98.58	98.61	98.64	98.66	98.69	98.72	98.75
970	98.78	98.81	98.84	98.87	98.89	98.92	98.95	98.98	99.01	99.04
980	99.06	99.09	99.12	99.15	99.18	99.21	99.24	99.26	99.29	99.32
990	99.35	99.37	99.40	99.43	99.46	99.49	99.52	99.54	99.57	99.60
1000	99.63									

[1] Values from *Smithsonian Meteorological Tables*, Smithsonian Institution, Washington, D.C., 1966.

The table gives factors for conversion of spirometer values to lung values calculated from the formula

$$f = \frac{(p - p_{t\,H_2O})\,(1 + 37\,\alpha)}{(p - p_{37°\,H_2O})\,(1 + t\,\alpha)}$$

where

p = measured pressure of the spirometer volume (mm Hg)

t = measured temperature of the spirometer volume (°C)

$p_{t\,H_2O}$ and $p_{37°\,H_2O}$ = pressure of water vapour at the measured temperature of the spirometer volume and at 37 °C in the lungs respectively

α = volume coefficient of expansion of air per °C (see page 260)

p / t	490	500	510	520	530	540	550	560	570	580	590	600	610	620	630
0	1.2447	1.2423	1.2400	1.2378	1.2357	1.2337	1.2317	1.2299	1.2281	1.2263	1.2247	1.2231	1.2215	1.2200	1.2186
1	2393	2369	2347	2325	2304	2284	2265	2246	2228	2211	2195	2179	2164	2149	2134
2	2339	2315	2293	2271	2250	2231	2212	2193	2176	2159	2143	2127	2112	2097	2083
3	2284	2261	2239	2217	2197	2177	2159	2141	2123	2107	2091	2075	2060	2046	2032
4	2229	2206	2184	2163	2143	2124	2105	2088	2071	2054	2038	2023	2008	1994	1980
5	1.2174	1.2151	1.2130	1.2109	1.2089	1.2070	1.2052	1.2034	1.2018	1.2001	1.1986	1.1971	1.1956	1.1942	1.1929
6	2118	2096	2075	2054	2035	2016	1998	1981	1964	1948	1933	1918	1904	1890	1877
7	2062	2041	2020	2000	1980	1962	1944	1927	1911	1895	1880	1866	1852	1838	1825
8	2006	1985	1964	1944	1926	1907	1890	1873	1857	1842	1827	1813	1799	1786	1773
9	1949	1928	1908	1889	1870	1853	1836	1819	1803	1788	1774	1760	1746	1733	1720
10	1.1892	1.1872	1.1852	1.1833	1.1815	1.1797	1.1781	1.1764	1.1749	1.1734	1.1720	1.1706	1.1693	1.1680	1.1667
11	1835	1814	1795	1776	1759	1742	1725	1709	1694	1680	1666	1652	1639	1627	1614
12	1777	1757	1738	1720	1702	1685	1669	1654	1639	1625	1611	1598	1585	1573	1561
13	1718	1698	1680	1662	1645	1629	1613	1598	1584	1570	1556	1543	1531	1519	1507
14	1658	1640	1622	1604	1588	1572	1556	1542	1528	1514	1501	1488	1476	1464	1453
15	1.1598	1.1580	1.1562	1.1546	1.1529	1.1514	1.1499	1.1485	1.1471	1.1458	1.1445	1.1433	1.1421	1.1409	1.1398
16	1538	1520	1503	1486	1471	1456	1441	1427	1414	1401	1389	1377	1365	1354	1343
17	1476	1459	1442	1426	1411	1397	1383	1369	1356	1344	1332	1320	1309	1298	1288
18	1414	1397	1381	1366	1351	1337	1323	1310	1298	1286	1274	1263	1252	1242	1232
19	1351	1335	1319	1304	1290	1276	1263	1251	1239	1227	1216	1205	1195	1184	1175
20	1.1287	1.1271	1.1256	1.1242	1.1228	1.1215	1.1203	1.1191	1.1179	1.1168	1.1157	1.1146	1.1136	1.1127	1.1117
21	1221	1207	1193	1179	1166	1153	1141	1129	1118	1108	1097	1087	1078	1068	1059
22	1156	1141	1128	1115	1102	1090	1079	1068	1057	1047	1037	1027	1018	1009	1001
23	1089	1075	1062	1050	1038	1026	1015	1005	0995	0985	0975	0966	0958	0949	0941
24	1020	1008	0995	0983	0972	0961	0951	0941	0931	0922	0913	0905	0896	0888	0881
25	1.0951	1.0939	1.0927	1.0916	1.0906	1.0895	1.0886	1.0876	1.0867	1.0859	1.0850	1.0842	1.0834	1.0827	1.0819
26	0880	0869	0858	0848	0838	0828	0819	0810	0802	0794	0786	0778	0771	0764	0757
27	0808	0798	0788	0778	0769	0760	0752	0744	0736	0728	0721	0714	0707	0701	0694
28	0735	0725	0716	0707	0699	0691	0683	0675	0668	0661	0655	0648	0642	0636	0630
29	0660	0651	0643	0635	0627	0620	0613	0606	0600	0593	0587	0581	0576	0570	0565
30	1.0584	1.0576	1.0568	1.0561	1.0554	1.0548	1.0542	1.0536	1.0530	1.0524	1.0519	1.0514	1.0509	1.0504	1.0499
31	0506	0499	0492	0486	0480	0474	0469	0464	0459	0454	0449	0444	0440	0436	0432
32	0426	0420	0415	0409	0404	0399	0395	0390	0386	0382	0378	0374	0370	0367	0363
33	0345	0340	0335	0331	0327	0323	0319	0315	0312	0309	0305	0302	0299	0296	0293
34	0261	0258	0254	0251	0248	0245	0242	0239	0236	0234	0231	0229	0227	0224	0222
35	1.0176	1.0174	1.0171	1.0169	1.0167	1.0165	1.0163	1.0161	1.0159	1.0157	1.0156	1.0154	1.0153	1.0151	1.0150
36	0089	0088	0087	0086	0084	0083	0082	0081	0081	0080	0079	0078	0077	0076	0076

p / t	640	650	660	670	680	690	700	710	720	730	740	750	760	770	780
0	1.2172	1.2158	1.2145	1.2133	1.2120	1.2109	1.2097	1.2086	1.2075	1.2065	1.2054	1.2045	1.2035	1.2025	1.2016
1	2121	2107	2094	2082	2070	2058	2047	2036	2025	2015	2005	1995	1985	1976	1967
2	2070	2056	2044	2031	2019	2008	1997	1986	1975	1965	1955	1945	1936	1927	1918
3	2018	2005	1993	1981	1969	1957	1946	1936	1925	1915	1905	1896	1886	1877	1869
4	1967	1954	1942	1930	1918	1907	1896	1885	1875	1865	1855	1846	1837	1828	1819
5	1.1916	1.1903	1.1891	1.1879	1.1867	1.1856	1.1846	1.1835	1.1825	1.1815	1.1806	1.1796	1.1787	1.1778	1.1770
6	1864	1852	1840	1828	1817	1806	1795	1785	1775	1765	1756	1746	1738	1729	1721
7	1812	1800	1788	1777	1765	1755	1744	1734	1724	1715	1706	1697	1688	1679	1671
8	1760	1748	1736	1725	1714	1704	1693	1683	1674	1664	1655	1647	1638	1630	1621
9	1708	1696	1685	1674	1663	1652	1642	1633	1623	1614	1605	1596	1588	1580	1572
10	1.1655	1.1644	1.1633	1.1622	1.1611	1.1601	1.1591	1.1582	1.1572	1.1563	1.1554	1.1546	1.1538	1.1530	1.1522
11	1603	1591	1580	1570	1559	1549	1540	1530	1521	1512	1504	1495	1487	1479	1472
12	1549	1538	1528	1517	1507	1497	1488	1479	1470	1461	1453	1444	1437	1429	1421
13	1496	1485	1475	1464	1455	1445	1436	1427	1418	1410	1401	1393	1386	1378	1371
14	1442	1431	1421	1411	1402	1392	1383	1375	1366	1358	1350	1342	1334	1327	1320
15	1.1388	1.1377	1.1367	1.1358	1.1348	1.1339	1.1331	1.1322	1.1314	1.1306	1.1298	1.1290	1.1283	1.1276	1.1269
16	1333	1323	1313	1304	1295	1286	1277	1269	1261	1253	1246	1238	1231	1224	1217
17	1278	1268	1258	1249	1241	1232	1224	1216	1208	1200	1193	1186	1179	1172	1166
18	1222	1212	1203	1194	1186	1178	1170	1162	1154	1147	1140	1133	1126	1120	1113
19	1165	1156	1147	1139	1131	1123	1115	1108	1100	1093	1086	1080	1073	1067	1061
20	1.1108	1.1100	1.1091	1.1083	1.1075	1.1067	1.1060	1.1053	1.1046	1.1039	1.1032	1.1026	1.1020	1.1014	1.1008
21	1051	1042	1034	1026	1019	1011	1004	0997	0991	0984	0978	0972	0966	0960	0954
22	0992	0984	0976	0969	0962	0955	0948	0941	0935	0929	0923	0917	0911	0905	0900
23	0933	0926	0918	0911	0904	0897	0891	0885	0879	0873	0867	0861	0856	0851	0845
24	0873	0866	0859	0852	0846	0839	0833	0827	0822	0816	0810	0805	0800	0795	0790
25	1.0812	1.0806	1.0799	1.0793	1.0787	1.0781	1.0775	1.0769	1.0764	1.0759	1.0753	1.0748	1.0744	1.0739	1.0734
26	0751	0744	0738	0732	0727	0721	0716	0710	0705	0700	0696	0691	0686	0682	0678
27	0688	0682	0677	0671	0666	0661	0656	0651	0646	0642	0637	0633	0629	0625	0621
28	0625	0619	0614	0609	0604	0599	0595	0590	0586	0582	0578	0574	0570	0566	0563
29	0560	0555	0551	0546	0542	0537	0533	0529	0525	0521	0518	0514	0511	0507	0504
30	1.0495	1.0490	1.0486	1.0482	1.0478	1.0474	1.0470	1.0467	1.0463	1.0460	1.0457	1.0453	1.0450	1.0447	1.0444
31	0428	0424	0420	0417	0413	0410	0407	0403	0400	0397	0395	0392	0389	0386	0384
32	0360	0357	0353	0350	0347	0345	0342	0339	0337	0334	0332	0329	0327	0325	0322
33	0291	0288	0285	0283	0280	0278	0276	0274	0272	0270	0268	0266	0264	0262	0260
34	0220	0218	0216	0214	0212	0211	0209	0207	0206	0204	0202	0201	0199	0198	0197
35	1.0148	1.0147	1.0145	1.0144	1.0143	1.0142	1.0141	1.0139	1.0138	1.0137	1.0136	1.0135	1.0134	1.0133	1.0132
36	0075	0074	0073	0073	0072	0072	0071	0070	0070	0069	0069	0068	0068	0067	0067

The following remarks are applicable to any other gas in place of air without appreciable error (see under 'Basis of calculation', below).

Explanation of the tables

mm Hg Values in the uppermost line of each table = observed pressure in mm Hg of the measured gas volume. Under many conditions of measurement this will be the same as the ambient (atmospheric) pressure, i.e., the observed barometric pressure after correction for temperature. Correction for pressure of water vapour under conditions of saturation is also provided for in the table (see under '*sat.*' below).

°C Values in the extreme left-hand column = observed temperature of the measured gas volume.

dry Factor for the reduction of the measured volume of *dry* gas to *normal conditions* (0 °C, 760 mm Hg, dry). Normal gas volumes are indicated by the abbreviation NTP (normal temperature and pressure). American lung specialists have introduced the abbreviation STPD (standard temperature and pressure, dry).

sat. Factor for the reduction of the measured volume of gas *saturated with water vapour* to normal conditions (0 °C, 760 mm Hg, dry). Gases may be assumed to be saturated with water vapour if they are in contact with water. This applies to the air in the lungs and to exhaled air, as also to spirometer air (if not dried). For the pressure of saturated water vapour at various temperatures see pages 256–258.

Use of the tables

A. Reduction of measured gas volumes to normal conditions (NTP)

The measured volume is multiplied by the factor appropriate to the conditions of measurement (temperature, pressure, dry or saturated).

Examples: 1. What is the volume at NTP of 1.6 l of dry gas measured at 25 °C and 712 mm Hg? Required volume at NTP = 1.6 × 0.8581 = 1.3730 l (NTP).

2. What is the volume at NTP of 1.6 l of gas saturated with water vapour and measured at 25 °C and 712 mm Hg? Required volume at NTP = 1.6 × 0.8295 = 1.3272 l (NTP). This is the type of calculation required to convert spirometer values to NTP.

B. Conversion of measured volumes to other conditions

The measured volume is multiplied by the appropriate conversion factor to NTP and the resulting value divided by the conversion factor corresponding to the required conditions (temperature, pressure, dry or moist).

Examples: 1. What will be the volume occupied by 1.6 l of gas measured at 25 °C and 730 mm Hg in contact with water when warmed at constant pressure to 37 °C? Required volume = 1.6 × 0.8512/0.7912 = 1.7213 l. This is the type of calculation required to convert spirometer values to lung values. The expression BTPS (body temperature and pressure, saturated) is frequently used to indicate gas volumes under lung conditions, i.e., 37 °C, atmospheric pressure, saturated with water vapour. For direct conversion factors for spirometer to lung values see page 259.

2. What will be the volume occupied by 1.6 l of dry gas measured at 0 °C and 600 mm Hg after saturation with water vapour, warming to 25 °C and compression to 760 mm Hg? Required volume = 1.6 × 0.7895/0.8873 = 1.4236 l.

Basis of calculation

The conversion factors have been calculated on the basis of the following formulae:

Conversion factor for reduction of *dry* gas volumes to normal $= \dfrac{p}{760\,(1+\alpha\,t)}$, Conversion factor for reduction of *saturated* gas volumes to normal $= \dfrac{p - p_{H_2O}}{760\,(1+\alpha\,t)}$, where

p, t pressure in mm Hg and temperature in °C of the measured gas volume.

p_{H_2O} pressure of saturated water vapour at the temperature t (see pages 256–258).

α volume coefficient of thermal expansion of the gas between 0 and 100 °C at a constant pressure of 760 mm Hg. In these tables the value for air, 0.003670 per °C (REGNAULT, 1842), has been used. Under the same conditions the value for an ideal gas is 0.003661 (= 1/273.**15**), for nitrogen 0.003671, for carbon monoxide 0.003669, for carbon dioxide 0.003723, for acetylene 0.003739. The conversion factors are therefore clearly applicable without sensible error to other gases in addition to air.

Note that in calculating the factors the 4th decimal place has been obtained by rounding off upwards or downwards. Any discrepancies with factors given in other tables (e.g., in the *Handbook of Chemistry and Physics*) are due to the use of other values for the expansion coefficient or conversion factors.

mm Hg	600		601		602		603		604		605		606		607		608		609	
°C	dry	*sat.*	dry	*sat.*	dry	*sat.*	dry	*sat.*	dry	*sat.*	dry	*sat.*	dry	*sat.*	dry	*sat.*	dry	*sat.*	dry	*sat.*
0	0.7895	0.7834	0.7908	0.7848	0.7921	0.7861	0.7934	0.7874	0.7947	0.7887	0.7961	0.7900	0.7974	0.7913	0.7987	0.7927	0.8000	0.7940	0.8013	0.7953
1	7866	7801	7879	7814	7892	7828	7905	7841	7918	7854	7931	7867	7945	7880	7958	7893	7971	7906	7984	7919
2	7837	7768	7850	7781	7863	7794	7876	7807	7889	7820	7903	7833	7916	7846	7929	7859	7942	7873	7955	7886
3	7809	7735	7822	7748	7835	7761	7848	7774	7861	7787	7874	7800	7887	7813	7900	7826	7913	7839	7926	7852
4	7781	7701	7793	7714	7806	7727	7819	7740	7832	7753	7845	7766	7858	7779	7871	7792	7884	7805	7897	7818
5	0.7752	0.7668	0.7765	0.7681	0.7778	0.7694	0.7791	0.7707	0.7804	0.7720	0.7817	0.7733	0.7830	0.7745	0.7843	0.7758	0.7856	0.7771	0.7869	0.7784
6	7725	7634	7738	7647	7750	7660	7763	7673	7776	7686	7789	7699	7802	7712	7815	7724	7828	7737	7841	7750
7	7697	7601	7710	7613	7723	7626	7735	7639	7748	7652	7761	7665	7774	7678	7787	7690	7800	7703	7812	7716
8	7670	7567	7682	7580	7695	7592	7708	7605	7721	7618	7733	7631	7746	7643	7759	7656	7772	7669	7785	7682
9	7642	7533	7655	7545	7668	7558	7681	7571	7693	7584	7706	7596	7719	7609	7731	7622	7744	7635	7757	7647
10	0.7615	0.7498	0.7628	0.7511	0.7641	0.7524	0.7653	0.7536	0.7666	0.7549	0.7679	0.7562	0.7691	0.7575	0.7704	0.7587	0.7717	0.7600	0.7729	0.7613
11	7588	7464	7601	7477	7614	7489	7626	7502	7639	7514	7652	7527	7664	7540	7677	7552	7690	7565	7702	7578
12	7562	7429	7574	7442	7587	7454	7600	7467	7612	7480	7625	7492	7637	7505	7650	7517	7663	7530	7675	7543
13	7535	7394	7548	7407	7560	7419	7573	7432	7585	7444	7598	7457	7611	7470	7623	7482	7636	7495	7648	7507
14	7509	7359	7521	7371	7534	7384	7546	7396	7559	7409	7572	7421	7584	7434	7597	7447	7609	7459	7622	7472
15	0.7483	0.7323	0.7495	0.7336	0.7508	0.7348	0.7520	0.7361	0.7533	0.7373	0.7545	0.7386	0.7558	0.7398	0.7570	0.7411	0.7583	0.7423	0.7595	0.7436
16	7457	7287	7469	7300	7482	7312	7494	7325	7507	7337	7519	7350	7531	7362	7544	7374	7556	7387	7569	7399
17	7431	7251	7443	7264	7456	7276	7468	7288	7481	7301	7493	7313	7505	7325	7518	7338	7530	7350	7543	7363
18	7406	7215	7418	7227	7430	7239	7443	7252	7455	7264	7467	7276	7480	7289	7492	7301	7504	7313	7517	7326
19	7380	7177	7392	7190	7405	7202	7417	7214	7429	7227	7442	7239	7454	7251	7466	7264	7479	7276	7491	7288
20	0.7355	0.7140	0.7367	0.7152	0.7379	0.7164	0.7392	0.7177	0.7404	0.7189	0.7416	0.7201	0.7428	0.7213	0.7441	0.7226	0.7453	0.7238	0.7465	0.7250
21	7330	7102	7342	7114	7354	7126	7366	7139	7379	7151	7391	7163	7403	7175	7415	7188	7428	7200	7440	7212
22	7305	7064	7317	7076	7329	7088	7341	7100	7354	7112	7366	7124	7378	7137	7390	7149	7402	7161	7415	7173
23	7280	7025	7292	7037	7304	7049	7317	7061	7329	7073	7341	7085	7353	7097	7365	7110	7377	7122	7389	7134
24	7256	6985	7268	6997	7280	7009	7292	7021	7304	7033	7316	7046	7328	7058	7340	7070	7352	7082	7364	7094
25	0.7231	0.6945	0.7243	0.6957	0.7255	0.6969	0.7267	0.6981	0.7279	0.6993	0.7292	0.7005	0.7304	0.7017	0.7316	0.7029	0.7328	0.7041	0.7340	0.7053
26	7207	6904	7219	6916	7231	6928	7243	6940	7255	6952	7267	6964	7279	6976	7291	6988	7303	7000	7315	7012
27	7183	6863	7195	6875	7207	6887	7219	6899	7231	6911	7243	6923	7255	6935	7267	6947	7279	6959	7291	6971
28	7159	6821	7171	6833	7183	6845	7195	6857	7207	6869	7219	6880	7231	6892	7243	6904	7255	6916	7266	6928
29	7135	6778	7147	6790	7159	6802	7171	6814	7183	6826	7195	6838	7207	6849	7219	6861	7230	6873	7242	6885
30	0.7112	0.6735	0.7124	0.6746	0.7135	0.6758	0.7147	0.6770	0.7159	0.6782	0.7171	0.6794	0.7183	0.6806	0.7195	0.6817	0.7207	0.6829	0.7218	0.6841
31	7088	6690	7100	6702	7112	6714	7124	6726	7136	6737	7147	6749	7159	6761	7171	6773	7183	6785	7195	6797
32	7065	6645	7077	6657	7089	6669	7100	6680	7112	6692	7124	6704	7136	6716	7147	6728	7159	6739	7171	6751
33	7042	6599	7054	6611	7065	6623	7077	6634	7089	6646	7101	6658	7112	6670	7124	6681	7136	6693	7148	6705
34	7019	6552	7031	6564	7042	6576	7054	6587	7066	6599	7077	6611	7089	6622	7101	6634	7113	6646	7124	6657
35	0.6996	0.6504	0.7008	0.6516	0.7019	0.6528	0.7031	0.6539	0.7043	0.6551	0.7054	0.6563	0.7066	0.6574	0.7078	0.6586	0.7089	0.6598	0.7101	0.6609
36	6973	6455	6985	6467	6997	6479	7008	6490	7020	6502	7032	6514	7043	6525	7055	6537	7066	6548	7078	6560
37	6951	6406	6962	6417	6974	6429	6986	6440	6997	6452	7009	6464	7020	6475	7032	6487	7044	6498	7055	6510
38	6928	6355	6940	6366	6952	6378	6963	6389	6975	6401	6986	6412	6998	6424	7009	6436	7021	6447	7032	6459
39	6906	6303	6918	6314	6929	6326	6941	6337	6952	6349	6964	6360	6975	6372	6987	6383	6998	6395	7010	6406
40	0.6884	0.6249	0.6896	0.6261	0.6907	0.6272	0.6919	0.6284	0.6930	0.6295	0.6942	0.6307	0.6953	0.6318	0.6964	0.6330	0.6976	0.6341	0.6987	0.6353
41	6862	6195	6874	6206	6885	6218	6896	6229	6908	6241	6919	6252	6931	6264	6942	6275	6954	6286	6965	6298
42	6840	6139	6852	6151	6863	6162	6875	6173	6886	6185	6897	6196	6909	6208	6920	6219	6932	6230	6943	6242

mm Hg	610		611		612		613		614		615		616		617		618		619	
°C	dry	sat.	dry	sat.	dry	sat.	dry	sat.	dry	sat.	dry	sat.	dry	sat.	dry	sat.	dry	sat.	dry	sat.
0	0.8026	0.7966	0.8039	0.7979	0.8053	0.7992	0.8066	0.8006	0.8079	0.8019	0.8092	0.8032	0.8105	0.8045	0.8118	0.8058	0.8132	0.8071	0.8145	0.8084
1	7997	7932	8010	7945	8023	7959	8036	7972	8049	7985	8063	7998	8076	8011	8089	8024	8102	8037	8115	8050
2	7968	7899	7981	7912	7994	7925	8007	7938	8020	7951	8033	7964	8046	7977	8059	7990	8072	8003	8085	8016
3	7939	7865	7952	7878	7965	7891	7978	7904	7991	7917	8004	7930	8017	7943	8030	7956	8043	7969	8056	7982
4	7910	7831	7923	7844	7936	7857	7949	7870	7962	7883	7975	7896	7988	7909	8001	7922	8014	7935	8027	7948
5	0.7882	0.7797	0.7895	0.7810	0.7908	0.7823	0.7920	0.7836	0.7933	0.7849	0.7946	0.7862	0.7959	0.7875	0.7972	0.7888	0.7985	0.7901	0.7998	0.7913
6	7853	7763	7866	7776	7879	7789	7892	7802	7905	7815	7918	7827	7931	7840	7944	7853	7956	7866	7969	7879
7	7825	7729	7838	7742	7851	7755	7864	7767	7877	7780	7889	7793	7902	7806	7915	7819	7928	7832	7941	7844
8	7797	7695	7810	7707	7823	7720	7836	7733	7849	7746	7861	7758	7874	7771	7887	7784	7900	7797	7912	7810
9	7770	7660	7782	7673	7795	7686	7808	7698	7821	7711	7833	7724	7846	7736	7859	7749	7872	7762	7884	7775
10	0.7742	0.7625	0.7755	0.7638	0.7768	0.7651	0.7780	0.7663	0.7793	0.7676	0.7806	0.7689	0.7818	0.7701	0.7831	0.7714	0.7844	0.7727	0.7856	0.7740
11	7715	7590	7728	7603	7740	7616	7753	7628	7765	7641	7778	7654	7791	7666	7803	7679	7816	7692	7829	7704
12	7688	7555	7700	7568	7713	7580	7726	7593	7738	7606	7751	7618	7763	7631	7776	7643	7789	7656	7801	7669
13	7661	7520	7673	7532	7686	7545	7698	7557	7711	7570	7724	7583	7736	7595	7749	7608	7761	7620	7774	7633
14	7634	7484	7647	7497	7659	7509	7672	7522	7684	7534	7697	7547	7709	7559	7722	7572	7734	7584	7747	7597
15	0.7608	0.7448	0.7620	0.7461	0.7632	0.7473	0.7645	0.7485	0.7657	0.7498	0.7670	0.7510	0.7682	0.7523	0.7695	0.7535	0.7707	0.7548	0.7720	0.7560
16	7581	7412	7594	7424	7606	7437	7618	7449	7631	7461	7643	7474	7656	7486	7668	7499	7681	7511	7693	7524
17	7555	7375	7567	7387	7580	7400	7592	7412	7605	7425	7617	7437	7629	7449	7642	7462	7654	7474	7666	7486
18	7529	7338	7541	7350	7554	7363	7566	7375	7578	7387	7591	7400	7603	7412	7615	7424	7628	7437	7640	7449
19	7503	7300	7515	7313	7528	7325	7540	7337	7552	7350	7565	7362	7577	7374	7589	7387	7602	7399	7614	7411
20	0.7477	0.7263	0.7490	0.7275	0.7502	0.7287	0.7514	0.7299	0.7527	0.7312	0.7539	0.7324	0.7551	0.7336	0.7563	0.7348	0.7576	0.7361	0.7588	0.7373
21	7452	7224	7464	7236	7476	7249	7489	7261	7501	7273	7513	7285	7525	7297	7538	7310	7550	7322	7562	7334
22	7427	7185	7439	7197	7451	7210	7463	7222	7475	7234	7488	7246	7500	7258	7512	7271	7524	7283	7536	7295
23	7402	7146	7414	7158	7426	7170	7438	7182	7450	7194	7462	7207	7474	7219	7486	7231	7499	7243	7511	7255
24	7377	7106	7389	7118	7401	7130	7413	7142	7425	7154	7437	7166	7449	7179	7461	7191	7473	7203	7485	7215
25	0.7352	0.7065	0.7364	0.7078	0.7376	0.7090	0.7388	0.7102	0.7400	0.7114	0.7412	0.7126	0.7424	0.7138	0.7436	0.7150	0.7448	0.7162	0.7460	0.7174
26	7327	7024	7339	7036	7351	7048	7363	7060	7375	7072	7387	7084	7399	7096	7411	7108	7423	7120	7435	7132
27	7303	6983	7315	6995	7327	7007	7339	7018	7351	7030	7363	7042	7375	7054	7386	7066	7398	7078	7410	7090
28	7278	6940	7290	6952	7302	6964	7314	6976	7326	6988	7338	7000	7350	7012	7362	7024	7374	7036	7386	7048
29	7254	6897	7266	6909	7278	6921	7290	6933	7302	6945	7314	6956	7326	6968	7337	6980	7349	6992	7361	7004
30	0.7230	0.6853	0.7242	0.6865	0.7254	0.6877	0.7266	0.6889	0.7278	0.6900	0.7290	0.6912	0.7301	0.6924	0.7313	0.6936	0.7325	0.6948	0.7337	0.6960
31	7206	6808	7218	6820	7230	6832	7242	6844	7254	6856	7266	6867	7277	6879	7289	6891	7301	6903	7313	6915
32	7183	6763	7195	6775	7206	6786	7218	6798	7230	6810	7242	6822	7253	6833	7265	6845	7277	6857	7289	6869
33	7159	6716	7171	6728	7183	6740	7194	6752	7206	6763	7218	6775	7230	6787	7241	6799	7253	6810	7265	6822
34	7136	6669	7148	6681	7159	6693	7171	6704	7183	6716	7194	6728	7206	6739	7218	6751	7229	6763	7241	6774
35	0.7113	0.6621	0.7124	0.6633	0.7136	0.6644	0.7148	0.6656	0.7159	0.6668	0.7171	0.6679	0.7183	0.6691	0.7194	0.6703	0.7206	0.6714	0.7218	0.6726
36	7090	6572	7101	6583	7113	6595	7125	6607	7136	6618	7148	6630	7159	6641	7171	6653	7183	6665	7194	6676
37	7067	6521	7078	6533	7090	6545	7101	6556	7113	6568	7125	6579	7136	6591	7148	6603	7159	6614	7171	6626
38	7044	6470	7056	6482	7067	6493	7079	6505	7090	6516	7102	6528	7113	6539	7125	6551	7136	6563	7148	6574
39	7021	6418	7033	6429	7044	6441	7056	6452	7067	6464	7079	6475	7090	6487	7102	6498	7113	6510	7125	6521
40	0.6999	0.6364	0.7010	0.6376	0.7022	0.6387	0.7033	0.6399	0.7045	0.6410	0.7056	0.6421	0.7068	0.6433	0.7079	0.6444	0.7091	0.6456	0.7102	0.6467
41	6977	6309	6988	6321	6999	6332	7011	6344	7022	6355	7034	6367	7045	6378	7057	6389	7068	6401	7079	6412
42	6954	6253	6966	6265	6977	6276	6989	6287	7000	6299	7011	6310	7023	6322	7034	6333	7046	6344	7057	6356

	620		621		622		623		624		625		626		627		628		629	
0	0.8158	0.8098	0.8171	0.8111	0.8184	0.8124	0.8197	0.8137	0.8211	0.8150	0.8224	0.8163	0.8237	0.8177	0.8250	0.8190	0.8263	0.8203	0.8276	0.8216
1	8128	8063	8141	8077	8154	8090	8167	8103	8181	8116	8194	8129	8207	8142	8220	8155	8233	8168	8246	8181
2	8098	8029	8112	8042	8125	8055	8138	8068	8151	8082	8164	8095	8177	8108	8190	8121	8203	8134	8216	8147
3	8069	7995	8082	8008	8095	8021	8108	8034	8121	8047	8134	8060	8147	8073	8160	8086	8173	8099	8186	8112
4	8040	7961	8053	7974	8066	7987	8079	8000	8092	8013	8105	8026	8118	8039	8131	8052	8144	8064	8157	8077
5	0.8011	0.7926	0.8024	0.7939	0.8037	0.7952	0.8050	0.7965	0.8063	0.7978	0.8075	0.7991	0.8088	0.8004	0.8101	0.8017	0.8114	0.8030	0.8127	0.8043
6	7982	7892	7995	7905	8008	7918	8021	7930	8034	7943	8047	7956	8059	7969	8072	7982	8085	7995	8098	8008
7	7954	7857	7966	7870	7979	7883	7992	7896	8005	7909	8018	7921	8031	7934	8043	7947	8056	7960	8069	7973
8	7925	7822	7938	7835	7951	7848	7964	7861	7976	7874	7989	7886	8002	7899	8015	7912	8027	7925	8040	7937
9	7897	7787	7910	7800	7923	7813	7935	7826	7948	7838	7961	7851	7973	7864	7986	7877	7999	7889	8012	7902
10	0.7869	0.7752	0.7882	0.7765	0.7894	0.7778	0.7907	0.7790	0.7920	0.7803	0.7933	0.7816	0.7945	0.7828	0.7958	0.7841	0.7971	0.7854	0.7983	0.7866
11	7841	7717	7854	7729	7867	7742	7879	7755	7892	7767	7905	7780	7917	7793	7930	7805	7943	7818	7955	7831
12	7814	7681	7826	7694	7839	7706	7852	7719	7864	7732	7877	7744	7889	7757	7902	7769	7915	7782	7927	7795
13	7786	7645	7799	7658	7812	7670	7824	7683	7837	7696	7849	7708	7862	7721	7874	7733	7887	7746	7899	7758
14	7759	7609	7772	7622	7784	7634	7797	7647	7809	7659	7822	7672	7834	7684	7847	7697	7859	7709	7872	7722
15	0.7732	0.7573	0.7745	0.7585	0.7757	0.7598	0.7770	0.7610	0.7782	0.7623	0.7795	0.7635	0.7807	0.7648	0.7820	0.7660	0.7832	0.7673	0.7844	0.7685
16	7705	7536	7718	7548	7730	7561	7743	7573	7755	7586	7768	7598	7780	7611	7792	7623	7805	7635	7817	7648
17	7679	7499	7691	7511	7704	7524	7716	7536	7728	7548	7741	7561	7753	7573	7766	7586	7778	7598	7790	7610
18	7652	7461	7665	7474	7677	7486	7689	7498	7702	7511	7714	7523	7726	7535	7739	7548	7751	7560	7763	7572
19	7626	7423	7638	7436	7651	7448	7663	7460	7675	7473	7688	7485	7700	7497	7712	7510	7725	7522	7737	7534
20	0.7600	0.7385	0.7612	0.7397	0.7625	0.7410	0.7637	0.7422	0.7649	0.7434	0.7661	0.7446	0.7674	0.7459	0.7686	0.7471	0.7698	0.7483	0.7710	0.7495
21	7574	7346	7586	7359	7599	7371	7611	7383	7623	7395	7635	7407	7647	7420	7660	7432	7672	7444	7684	7456
22	7548	7307	7561	7319	7573	7331	7585	7344	7597	7356	7609	7368	7621	7380	7634	7392	7646	7404	7658	7417
23	7523	7267	7535	7279	7547	7292	7559	7304	7571	7316	7584	7328	7596	7340	7608	7352	7620	7364	7632	7376
24	7498	7227	7510	7239	7522	7251	7534	7263	7546	7275	7558	7287	7570	7299	7582	7312	7594	7324	7606	7336
25	0.7472	0.7186	0.7484	0.7198	0.7496	0.7210	0.7508	0.7222	0.7521	0.7234	0.7533	0.7246	0.7545	0.7258	0.7557	0.7270	0.7569	0.7282	0.7581	0.7294
26	7447	7144	7459	7156	7471	7168	7483	7181	7495	7193	7507	7205	7519	7217	7531	7229	7543	7241	7555	7253
27	7422	7102	7434	7114	7446	7126	7458	7138	7470	7150	7482	7162	7494	7174	7506	7186	7518	7198	7530	7210
28	7398	7059	7410	7071	7422	7083	7434	7095	7445	7107	7457	7119	7469	7131	7481	7143	7493	7155	7505	7167
29	7373	7016	7385	7028	7397	7040	7409	7052	7421	7063	7433	7075	7445	7087	7456	7099	7468	7111	7480	7123
30	0.7349	0.6972	0.7361	0.6983	0.7372	0.6995	0.7384	0.7007	0.7396	0.7019	0.7408	0.7031	0.7420	0.7043	0.7432	0.7055	0.7444	0.7066	0.7455	0.7078
31	7325	6927	7336	6938	7348	6950	7360	6962	7372	6974	7384	6986	7395	6997	7407	7009	7419	7021	7431	7033
32	7301	6881	7312	6892	7324	6904	7336	6916	7348	6928	7359	6939	7371	6951	7383	6963	7395	6975	7406	6987
33	7277	6834	7288	6846	7300	6857	7312	6869	7324	6881	7335	6892	7347	6904	7359	6916	7371	6928	7382	6939
34	7253	6786	7265	6798	7276	6810	7288	6821	7300	6833	7311	6845	7323	6856	7335	6868	7346	6880	7358	6891
35	0.7229	0.6738	0.7241	0.6749	0.7253	0.6761	0.7264	0.6773	0.7276	0.6784	0.7288	0.6796	0.7299	0.6807	0.7311	0.6819	0.7323	0.6831	0.7334	0.6842
36	7206	6688	7217	6700	7229	6711	7241	6723	7252	6734	7264	6746	7276	6758	7287	6769	7299	6781	7310	6793
37	7183	6637	7194	6649	7206	6660	7217	6672	7229	6684	7240	6695	7252	6707	7264	6718	7275	6730	7287	6742
38	7159	6586	7171	6597	7183	6609	7194	6620	7206	6632	7217	6643	7229	6655	7240	6666	7252	6678	7263	6690
39	7136	6533	7148	6544	7159	6556	7171	6567	7182	6579	7194	6590	7206	6602	7217	6613	7229	6625	7240	6636
40	0.7114	0.6479	0.7125	0.6490	0.7137	0.6502	0.7148	0.6513	0.7160	0.6525	0.7171	0.6536	0.7182	0.6548	0.7194	0.6559	0.7205	0.6571	0.7217	0.6582
41	7091	6424	7102	6435	7114	6447	7125	6458	7137	6469	7148	6481	7160	6492	7171	6504	7182	6515	7194	6527
42	7068	6367	7080	6379	7091	6390	7103	6401	7114	6413	7125	6424	7137	6436	7148	6447	7160	6458	7171	6470

mm Hg	630		631		632		633		634		635		636		637		638		639	
°C	dry	sat.	dry	sat.	dry	sat.	dry	sat.	dry	sat.	dry	sat.	dry	sat.	dry	sat.	dry	sat.	dry	sat.
0	0.8289	0.8229	0.8303	0.8242	0.8316	0.8256	0.8329	0.8269	0.8342	0.8282	0.8355	0.8295	0.8368	0.8308	0.8382	0.8321	0.8395	0.8334	0.8408	0.8348
1	8259	8195	8272	8208	8285	8221	8298	8234	8312	8247	8325	8260	8338	8273	8351	8286	8364	8299	8377	8313
2	8229	8160	8242	8173	8255	8186	8268	8199	8281	8212	8294	8225	8307	8238	8321	8251	8334	8264	8347	8277
3	8199	8125	8212	8138	8225	8151	8238	8164	8251	8177	8264	8190	8277	8203	8290	8216	8303	8229	8316	8242
4	8170	8090	8183	8103	8195	8116	8208	8129	8221	8142	8234	8155	8247	8168	8260	8181	8273	8194	8286	8207
5	0.8140	0.8056	0.8153	0.8068	0.8166	0.8081	0.8179	0.8094	0.8192	0.8107	0.8205	0.8120	0.8218	0.8133	0.8231	0.8146	0.8243	0.8159	0.8256	0.8172
6	8111	8021	8124	8033	8137	8046	8149	8059	8162	8072	8175	8085	8188	8098	8201	8111	8214	8124	8227	8136
7	8082	7985	8095	7998	8108	8011	8120	8024	8133	8037	8146	8050	8159	8062	8172	8075	8184	8088	8197	8101
8	8053	7950	8066	7963	8079	7976	8091	7989	8104	8001	8117	8014	8130	8027	8143	8040	8155	8052	8168	8065
9	8024	7915	8037	7928	8050	7940	8063	7953	8075	7966	8088	7978	8101	7991	8114	8004	8126	8017	8139	8029
10	0.7996	0.7879	0.8009	0.7892	0.8021	0.7905	0.8034	0.7917	0.8047	0.7930	0.8059	0.7943	0.8072	0.7955	0.8085	0.7968	0.8098	0.7981	0.8110	0.7993
11	7968	7843	7980	7856	7993	7869	8006	7881	8018	7894	8031	7907	8044	7919	8056	7932	8069	7944	8082	7957
12	7940	7807	7952	7820	7965	7832	7978	7845	7990	7858	8003	7870	8015	7883	8028	7895	8041	7908	8053	7921
13	7912	7771	7925	7784	7937	7796	7950	7809	7962	7821	7975	7834	7987	7846	8000	7859	8012	7871	8025	7884
14	7884	7734	7897	7747	7909	7759	7922	7772	7934	7784	7947	7797	7959	7809	7972	7822	7984	7834	7997	7847
15	0.7857	0.7697	0.7869	0.7710	0.7882	0.7722	0.7894	0.7735	0.7907	0.7747	0.7919	0.7760	0.7932	0.7772	0.7944	0.7785	0.7957	0.7797	0.7969	0.7810
16	7830	7660	7842	7673	7855	7685	7867	7698	7879	7710	7892	7722	7904	7735	7917	7747	7929	7760	7942	7772
17	7803	7623	7815	7635	7827	7647	7840	7660	7852	7672	7865	7685	7877	7697	7889	7709	7902	7722	7914	7734
18	7776	7585	7788	7597	7800	7609	7813	7622	7825	7634	7838	7646	7850	7659	7862	7671	7875	7684	7887	7696
19	7749	7546	7761	7559	7774	7571	7786	7583	7798	7596	7811	7608	7823	7620	7835	7633	7848	7645	7860	7657
20	0.7723	0.7508	0.7735	0.7520	0.7747	0.7532	0.7759	0.7544	0.7772	0.7557	0.7784	0.7569	0.7796	0.7581	0.7808	0.7593	0.7821	0.7606	0.7833	0.7618
21	7696	7468	7709	7481	7721	7493	7733	7505	7745	7517	7757	7530	7770	7542	7782	7554	7794	7566	7806	7578
22	7670	7429	7682	7441	7695	7453	7707	7465	7719	7477	7731	7490	7743	7502	7755	7514	7768	7526	7780	7538
23	7644	7389	7656	7401	7668	7413	7681	7425	7693	7437	7705	7449	7717	7461	7729	7474	7741	7486	7753	7498
24	7618	7348	7631	7360	7643	7372	7655	7384	7667	7396	7679	7408	7691	7420	7703	7432	7715	7445	7727	7457
25	0.7593	0.7307	0.7605	0.7319	0.7617	0.7331	0.7629	0.7343	0.7641	0.7355	0.7653	0.7367	0.7665	0.7379	0.7677	0.7391	0.7689	0.7403	0.7701	0.7415
26	7567	7265	7579	7277	7591	7289	7603	7301	7615	7313	7627	7325	7639	7337	7651	7349	7663	7361	7675	7373
27	7542	7222	7554	7234	7566	7246	7578	7258	7590	7270	7602	7282	7614	7294	7626	7306	7638	7318	7650	7330
28	7517	7179	7529	7191	7541	7203	7553	7215	7565	7226	7577	7238	7589	7250	7601	7262	7612	7274	7624	7286
29	7492	7135	7504	7147	7516	7159	7528	7170	7540	7182	7552	7194	7563	7206	7575	7218	7587	7230	7599	7242
30	0.7467	0.7090	0.7479	0.7102	0.7491	0.7114	0.7503	0.7126	0.7515	0.7138	0.7527	0.7149	0.7538	0.7161	0.7550	0.7173	0.7562	0.7185	0.7574	0.7197
31	7443	7045	7455	7056	7466	7068	7478	7080	7490	7092	7502	7104	7514	7116	7525	7127	7537	7139	7549	7151
32	7418	6998	7430	7010	7442	7022	7454	7034	7465	7045	7477	7057	7489	7069	7501	7081	7512	7093	7524	7104
33	7394	6951	7406	6963	7417	6975	7429	6986	7441	6998	7453	7010	7464	7022	7476	7033	7488	7045	7500	7057
34	7370	6903	7382	6915	7393	6927	7405	6938	7417	6950	7428	6962	7440	6973	7452	6985	7463	6997	7475	7008
35	0.7346	0.6854	0.7358	0.6866	0.7369	0.6877	0.7381	0.6889	0.7393	0.6901	0.7404	0.6912	0.7416	0.6924	0.7428	0.6936	0.7439	0.6947	0.7451	0.6959
36	7322	6804	7334	6816	7345	6827	7357	6839	7369	6851	7380	6862	7392	6874	7403	6886	7415	6897	7427	6909
37	7298	6753	7310	6765	7322	6776	7333	6788	7345	6799	7356	6811	7368	6823	7380	6834	7391	6846	7403	6857
38	7275	6701	7286	6713	7298	6724	7310	6736	7321	6747	7333	6759	7344	6770	7356	6782	7367	6793	7379	6805
39	7252	6648	7263	6659	7275	6671	7286	6682	7298	6694	7309	6705	7321	6717	7332	6729	7344	6740	7355	6752
40	0.7228	0.6594	0.7240	0.6605	0.7251	0.6617	0.7263	0.6628	0.7274	0.6639	0.7286	0.6651	0.7297	0.6662	0.7309	0.6674	0.7320	0.6685	0.7332	0.6697
41	7205	6538	7217	6549	7228	6561	7240	6572	7251	6584	7262	6595	7274	6607	7285	6618	7297	6630	7308	6641
42	7182	6481	7194	6493	7205	6504	7217	6515	7228	6527	7239	6538	7251	6550	7262	6561	7274	6572	7285	6584

mm Hg	640		641		642		643		644		645		646		647		648		649	
0	0.8421	0.8361	0.8434	0.8374	0.8447	0.8387	0.8461	0.8400	0.8474	0.8413	0.8487	0.8427	0.8500	0.8440	0.8513	0.8453	0.8526	0.8466	0.8539	0.8479
1	8390	8326	8403	8339	8416	8352	8430	8365	8443	8378	8456	8391	8469	8404	8482	8417	8495	8431	8508	8444
2	8360	8291	8373	8304	8386	8317	8399	8330	8412	8343	8425	8356	8438	8369	8451	8382	8464	8395	8477	8408
3	8329	8255	8342	8268	8355	8281	8368	8294	8381	8307	8394	8320	8407	8333	8420	8346	8433	8359	8446	8372
4	8299	8220	8312	8233	8325	8246	8338	8259	8351	8272	8364	8285	8377	8298	8390	8311	8403	8324	8416	8337
5	0.8269	0.8185	0.8282	0.8198	0.8295	0.8211	0.8308	0.8224	0.8321	0.8236	0.8334	0.8249	0.8347	0.8262	0.8360	0.8275	0.8373	0.8288	0.8386	0.8301
6	8240	8149	8252	8162	8265	8175	8278	8188	8291	8201	8304	8214	8317	8227	8330	8239	8343	8252	8355	8265
7	8210	8114	8223	8127	8236	8139	8249	8152	8261	8165	8274	8178	8287	8191	8300	8204	8313	8216	8326	8229
8	8181	8078	8194	8091	8206	8104	8219	8116	8232	8129	8245	8142	8258	8155	8270	8168	8283	8180	8296	8193
9	8152	8042	8165	8055	8177	8068	8190	8080	8203	8093	8215	8106	8228	8119	8241	8131	8254	8144	8266	8157
10	0.8123	0.8006	0.8136	0.8019	0.8148	0.8031	0.8161	0.8044	0.8174	0.8057	0.8186	0.8070	0.8199	0.8082	0.8212	0.8095	0.8224	0.8108	0.8237	0.8120
11	8094	7970	8107	7982	8120	7995	8132	8008	8145	8020	8158	8033	8170	8046	8183	8058	8195	8071	8208	8084
12	8066	7933	8078	7946	8091	7958	8104	7971	8116	7984	8129	7996	8141	8009	8154	8021	8167	8034	8179	8047
13	8038	7897	8050	7909	8063	7922	8075	7934	8088	7947	8100	7959	8113	7972	8125	7984	8138	7997	8151	8010
14	8010	7860	8022	7872	8035	7885	8047	7897	8060	7910	8072	7922	8085	7935	8097	7947	8110	7960	8122	7972
15	0.7982	0.7822	0.7994	0.7835	0.8007	0.7847	0.8019	0.7860	0.8032	0.7872	0.8044	0.7885	0.8056	0.7897	0.8069	0.7909	0.8081	0.7922	0.8094	0.7934
16	7954	7785	7966	7797	7979	7809	7991	7822	8004	7834	8016	7847	8029	7859	8041	7872	8053	7884	8066	7896
17	7927	7747	7939	7759	7951	7771	7964	7784	7976	7796	7988	7808	8001	7821	8013	7833	8026	7846	8038	7858
18	7899	7708	7912	7721	7924	7733	7936	7745	7949	7758	7961	7770	7973	7782	7986	7795	7998	7807	8010	7819
19	7872	7669	7884	7682	7897	7694	7909	7706	7921	7719	7934	7731	7946	7743	7958	7756	7971	7768	7983	7780
20	0.7845	0.7630	0.7857	0.7643	0.7870	0.7655	0.7882	0.7667	0.7894	0.7679	0.7907	0.7692	0.7919	0.7704	0.7931	0.7716	0.7943	0.7728	0.7956	0.7741
21	7818	7591	7831	7603	7843	7615	7855	7627	7867	7640	7880	7652	7892	7664	7904	7676	7916	7688	7928	7701
22	7792	7551	7804	7563	7816	7575	7828	7587	7841	7599	7853	7611	7865	7624	7877	7636	7889	7648	7902	7660
23	7766	7510	7778	7522	7790	7534	7802	7546	7814	7558	7826	7571	7838	7583	7850	7595	7863	7607	7875	7619
24	7739	7469	7751	7481	7764	7493	7776	7505	7788	7517	7800	7529	7812	7541	7824	7553	7836	7566	7848	7578
25	0.7713	0.7427	0.7725	0.7439	0.7737	0.7451	0.7750	0.7463	0.7762	0.7475	0.7774	0.7487	0.7786	0.7499	0.7798	0.7511	0.7810	0.7523	0.7822	0.7536
26	7688	7385	7700	7397	7712	7409	7724	7421	7736	7433	7748	7445	7760	7457	7772	7469	7784	7481	7796	7493
27	7662	7342	7674	7354	7686	7366	7698	7378	7710	7390	7722	7402	7734	7414	7746	7426	7758	7438	7770	7449
28	7636	7298	7648	7310	7660	7322	7672	7334	7684	7346	7696	7358	7708	7370	7720	7382	7732	7394	7744	7405
29	7611	7254	7623	7266	7635	7278	7647	7289	7659	7301	7670	7313	7682	7325	7694	7337	7706	7349	7718	7361
30	0.7586	0.7209	0.7598	0.7220	0.7610	0.7232	0.7621	0.7244	0.7633	0.7256	0.7645	0.7268	0.7657	0.7280	0.7669	0.7292	0.7681	0.7303	0.7693	0.7315
31	7561	7163	7573	7175	7584	7186	7596	7198	7608	7210	7620	7222	7632	7234	7644	7245	7655	7257	7667	7269
32	7536	7116	7548	7128	7560	7140	7571	7151	7583	7163	7595	7175	7607	7187	7618	7199	7630	7210	7642	7222
33	7511	7069	7523	7080	7535	7092	7547	7104	7558	7115	7570	7127	7582	7139	7594	7151	7605	7162	7617	7174
34	7487	7020	7499	7032	7510	7044	7522	7055	7534	7067	7545	7079	7557	7090	7569	7102	7580	7114	7592	7125
35	0.7462	0.6971	0.7474	0.6982	0.7486	0.6994	0.7497	0.7006	0.7509	0.7017	0.7521	0.7029	0.7532	0.7041	0.7544	0.7052	0.7556	0.7064	0.7567	0.7076
36	7438	6920	7450	6932	7462	6944	7473	6955	7485	6967	7496	6978	7508	6990	7520	7002	7531	7013	7543	7025
37	7414	6869	7426	6881	7437	6892	7449	6904	7461	6915	7472	6927	7484	6939	7495	6950	7507	6962	7519	6973
38	7390	6817	7402	6828	7413	6840	7425	6851	7437	6863	7448	6874	7460	6886	7471	6897	7483	6909	7494	6920
39	7367	6763	7378	6775	7390	6786	7401	6798	7413	6809	7424	6821	7436	6832	7447	6844	7459	6855	7470	6867
40	0.7343	0.6708	0.7355	0.6720	0.7366	0.6731	0.7378	0.6743	0.7389	0.6754	0.7400	0.6766	0.7412	0.6777	0.7423	0.6789	0.7435	0.6800	0.7446	0.6812
41	7320	6652	7331	6664	7343	6675	7354	6687	7365	6698	7377	6710	7388	6721	7400	6732	7411	6744	7423	6755
42	7296	6595	7308	6607	7319	6618	7331	6629	7342	6641	7353	6652	7365	6664	7376	6675	7388	6686	7399	6698

mm Hg	650		651		652		653		654		655		656		657		658		659	
°C	dry	sat.	dry	sat.	dry	sat.	dry	sat.	dry	sat.	dry	sat.	dry	sat.	dry	sat.	dry	sat.	dry	sat.
0	0.8553	0.8492	0.8566	0.8506	0.8579	0.8519	0.8592	0.8532	0.8605	0.8545	0.8618	0.8558	0.8632	0.8571	0.8645	0.8584	0.8658	0.8598	0.8671	0.8611
1	8521	8457	8534	8470	8548	8483	8561	8496	8574	8509	8587	8522	8600	8535	8613	8549	8626	8562	8639	8575
2	8490	8421	8503	8434	8516	8447	8529	8460	8543	8473	8556	8486	8569	8500	8582	8513	8595	8526	8608	8539
3	8459	8386	8473	8399	8486	8412	8499	8425	8512	8438	8525	8451	8538	8464	8551	8477	8564	8490	8577	8503
4	8429	8350	8442	8363	8455	8376	8468	8389	8481	8402	8494	8415	8507	8428	8520	8441	8533	8454	8546	8466
5	0.8399	0.8314	0.8411	0.8327	0.8424	0.8340	0.8437	0.8353	0.8450	0.8366	0.8463	0.8379	0.8476	0.8392	0.8489	0.8404	0.8502	0.8417	0.8515	0.8430
6	8368	8278	8381	8291	8394	8304	8407	8317	8420	8330	8433	8342	8446	8355	8458	8368	8471	8381	8484	8394
7	8338	8242	8351	8255	8364	8268	8377	8281	8390	8293	8403	8306	8415	8319	8428	8332	8441	8345	8454	8357
8	8309	8206	8321	8219	8334	8231	8347	8244	8360	8257	8373	8270	8385	8283	8398	8295	8411	8308	8424	8321
9	8279	8170	8292	8182	8305	8195	8317	8208	8330	8220	8343	8233	8356	8246	8368	8259	8381	8271	8394	8284
10	0.8250	0.8133	0.8263	0.8146	0.8275	0.8158	0.8288	0.8171	0.8301	0.8184	0.8313	0.8196	0.8326	0.8209	0.8339	0.8222	0.8351	0.8235	0.8364	0.8247
11	8221	8096	8233	8109	8246	8122	8259	8134	8271	8147	8284	8159	8297	8172	8309	8185	8322	8197	8335	8210
12	8192	8059	8204	8072	8217	8085	8230	8097	8242	8110	8255	8122	8267	8135	8280	8148	8293	8160	8305	8173
13	8163	8022	8176	8035	8188	8047	8201	8060	8213	8072	8226	8085	8239	8097	8251	8110	8264	8123	8276	8135
14	8135	7985	8147	7997	8160	8010	8172	8022	8185	8035	8197	8047	8210	8060	8222	8072	8235	8085	8247	8097
15	0.8106	0.7947	0.8119	0.7959	0.8131	0.7972	0.8144	0.7984	0.8156	0.7997	0.8169	0.8009	0.8181	0.8022	0.8194	0.8034	0.8206	0.8047	0.8219	0.8059
16	8078	7909	8091	7921	8103	7934	8116	7946	8128	7959	8140	7971	8153	7983	8165	7996	8178	8008	8190	8021
17	8050	7870	8063	7883	8075	7895	8088	7908	8100	7920	8112	7932	8125	7945	8137	7957	8149	7969	8162	7982
18	8023	7832	8035	7844	8047	7856	8060	7869	8072	7881	8084	7893	8097	7906	8109	7918	8121	7930	8134	7943
19	7995	7792	8007	7805	8020	7817	8032	7829	8044	7842	8057	7854	8069	7866	8081	7879	8094	7891	8106	7903
20	0.7968	0.7753	0.7980	0.7765	0.7992	0.7777	0.8005	0.7790	0.8017	0.7802	0.8029	0.7814	0.8041	0.7826	0.8054	0.7839	0.8066	0.7851	0.8078	0.7863
21	7941	7713	7953	7725	7965	7737	7977	7749	7990	7762	8002	7774	8014	7786	8026	7798	8038	7811	8051	7823
22	7914	7672	7926	7684	7938	7697	7950	7709	7962	7721	7975	7733	7987	7745	7999	7758	8011	7770	8023	7782
23	7887	7631	7899	7643	7911	7656	7923	7668	7935	7680	7948	7692	7960	7704	7972	7716	7984	7728	7996	7740
24	7860	7590	7872	7602	7884	7614	7897	7626	7909	7638	7921	7650	7933	7662	7945	7674	7957	7686	7969	7699
25	0.7834	0.7548	0.7846	0.7560	0.7858	0.7572	0.7870	0.7584	0.7882	0.7596	0.7894	0.7608	0.7906	0.7620	0.7918	0.7632	0.7930	0.7644	0.7942	0.7656
26	7808	7505	7820	7517	7832	7529	7844	7541	7856	7553	7868	7565	7880	7577	7892	7589	7904	7601	7916	7613
27	7782	7461	7794	7473	7806	7485	7817	7497	7829	7509	7841	7521	7853	7533	7865	7545	7877	7557	7889	7569
28	7756	7417	7768	7429	7780	7441	7791	7453	7803	7465	7815	7477	7827	7489	7839	7501	7851	7513	7863	7525
29	7730	7373	7742	7385	7754	7396	7766	7408	7778	7420	7789	7432	7801	7444	7813	7456	7825	7468	7837	7480
30	0.7704	0.7327	0.7716	0.7339	0.7728	0.7351	0.7740	0.7363	0.7752	0.7375	0.7764	0.7386	0.7775	0.7398	0.7787	0.7410	0.7799	0.7422	0.7811	0.7434
31	7679	7281	7691	7293	7703	7305	7714	7316	7726	7328	7738	7340	7750	7352	7762	7364	7774	7375	7785	7387
32	7654	7234	7666	7246	7677	7257	7689	7269	7701	7281	7713	7293	7724	7304	7736	7316	7748	7328	7760	7340
33	7629	7186	7640	7198	7652	7209	7664	7221	7676	7233	7687	7245	7699	7256	7711	7268	7723	7280	7734	7292
34	7604	7137	7616	7149	7627	7160	7639	7172	7651	7184	7662	7196	7674	7207	7686	7219	7697	7231	7709	7242
35	0.7579	0.7087	0.7591	0.7099	0.7602	0.7111	0.7614	0.7122	0.7626	0.7134	0.7637	0.7146	0.7649	0.7157	0.7661	0.7169	0.7672	0.7181	0.7684	0.7192
36	7555	7037	7566	7048	7578	7060	7589	7071	7601	7083	7613	7095	7624	7106	7636	7118	7648	7130	7659	7141
37	7530	6985	7542	6996	7553	7008	7565	7020	7576	7031	7588	7043	7600	7054	7611	7066	7623	7078	7634	7089
38	7506	6932	7517	6944	7529	6955	7541	6967	7552	6978	7564	6990	7575	7001	7587	7013	7598	7024	7610	7036
39	7482	6878	7493	6890	7505	6901	7516	6913	7528	6924	7539	6936	7551	6947	7562	6959	7574	6970	7585	6982
40	0.7458	0.6823	0.7469	0.6835	0.7481	0.6846	0.7492	0.6857	0.7504	0.6869	0.7515	0.6880	0.7527	0.6892	0.7538	0.6903	0.7550	0.6915	0.7561	0.6926
41	7434	6767	7445	6778	7457	6790	7468	6801	7480	6813	7491	6824	7503	6835	7514	6847	7526	6858	7537	6870
42	7410	6709	7422	6721	7433	6732	7445	6743	7456	6755	7467	6766	7479	6778	7490	6789	7502	6800	7513	6812

mm Hg	660		661		662		663		664		665		666		667		668		669	
0	0.8684	0.8624	0.8697	0.8637	0.8711	0.8650	0.8724	0.8663	0.8737	0.8677	0.8750	0.8690	0.8763	0.8703	0.8776	0.8716	0.8789	0.8729	0.8803	0.8742
1	8652	8588	8666	8601	8679	8614	8692	8627	8705	8640	8718	8653	8731	8667	8744	8680	8757	8693	8770	8706
2	8621	8552	8634	8565	8647	8578	8660	8591	8673	8604	8686	8617	8699	8630	8712	8643	8725	8656	8738	8669
3	8590	8516	8603	8529	8616	8542	8629	8555	8642	8568	8655	8581	8668	8594	8681	8607	8694	8620	8707	8633
4	8559	8479	8572	8492	8585	8505	8597	8518	8610	8531	8623	8544	8636	8557	8649	8570	8662	8583	8675	8596
5	0.8528	0.8443	0.8541	0.8456	0.8554	0.8469	0.8566	0.8482	0.8579	0.8495	0.8592	0.8508	0.8605	0.8521	0.8618	0.8534	0.8631	0.8547	0.8644	0.8559
6	8497	8407	8510	8420	8523	8433	8536	8445	8549	8458	8561	8471	8574	8184	8587	8497	8600	8510	8613	8523
7	8467	8370	8480	8383	8492	8396	8505	8409	8518	8422	8531	8434	8544	8447	8556	8460	8569	8473	8582	8486
8	8437	8334	8449	8346	8462	8359	8475	8372	8488	8385	8500	8398	8513	8410	8526	8423	8539	8436	8552	8449
9	8407	8297	8419	8310	8432	8322	8445	8335	8457	8348	8470	8361	8483	8373	8496	8386	8508	8399	8521	8412
10	0.8377	0.8260	0.8389	0.8273	0.8402	0.8285	0.8415	0.8298	0.8428	0.8311	0.8440	0.8323	0.8453	0.8336	0.8466	0.8349	0.8478	0.8361	0.8491	0.8374
11	8347	8223	8360	8235	8373	8248	8385	8261	8398	8273	8410	8286	8423	8299	8436	8311	8448	8324	8461	8337
12	8318	8185	8330	8198	8343	8211	8356	8223	8368	8236	8381	8248	8394	8261	8406	8274	8419	8286	8431	8299
13	8289	8148	8301	8160	8314	8173	8326	8185	8339	8198	8352	8211	8364	8223	8377	8236	8389	8248	8402	8261
14	8260	8110	8272	8122	8285	8135	8297	8147	8310	8160	8322	8172	8335	8185	8347	8197	8360	8210	8372	8222
15	0.8231	0.8072	0.8244	0.8084	0.8256	0.8097	0.8269	0.8109	0.8281	0.8121	0.8293	0.8134	0.8306	0.8146	0.8318	0.8159	0.8331	0.8171	0.8343	0.8184
16	8203	8033	8215	8046	8227	8058	8240	8070	8252	8083	8265	8095	8277	8108	8290	8120	8302	8133	8314	8145
17	8174	7994	8187	8007	8199	8019	8211	8031	8224	8044	8236	8056	8249	8069	8261	8081	8273	8093	8286	8106
18	8146	7955	8158	7967	8171	7980	8183	7992	8195	8004	8208	8017	8220	8029	8232	8041	8245	8054	8257	8066
19	8118	7915	8130	7928	8143	7940	8155	7952	8167	7965	8180	7977	8192	7989	8204	8002	8217	8014	8229	8026
20	0.8090	0.7875	0.8103	0.7888	0.8115	0.7900	0.8127	0.7912	0.8139	0.7924	0.8152	0.7937	0.8164	0.7949	0.8176	0.7961	0.8188	0.7973	0.8201	0.7986
21	8063	7835	8075	7847	8087	7859	8099	7872	8112	7884	8124	7896	8136	7908	8148	7920	8161	7933	8173	7945
22	8035	7794	8048	7806	8060	7818	8072	7831	8084	7843	8096	7855	8108	7867	8121	7879	8133	7891	8145	7904
23	8008	7753	8020	7765	8033	7777	8045	7789	8057	7801	8069	7813	8081	7825	8093	7838	8105	7850	8117	7862
24	7981	7711	7993	7723	8005	7735	8018	7747	8030	7759	8042	7771	8054	7783	8066	7795	8078	7807	8090	7819
25	0.7954	0.7668	0.7966	0.7680	0.7978	0.7692	0.7991	0.7704	0.8003	0.7716	0.8015	0.7728	0.8027	0.7740	0.8039	0.7752	0.8051	0.7765	0.8063	0.7777
26	7928	7625	7940	7637	7952	7649	7964	7661	7976	7673	7988	7685	8000	7697	8012	7709	8024	7721	8036	7733
27	7901	7581	7913	7593	7925	7605	7937	7617	7949	7629	7961	7641	7973	7653	7985	7665	7997	7677	8009	7689
28	7875	7537	7887	7549	7899	7561	7911	7573	7923	7584	7935	7596	7947	7608	7959	7620	7970	7632	7982	7644
29	7849	7492	7861	7503	7873	7515	7885	7527	7896	7539	7908	7551	7920	7563	7932	7575	7944	7587	7956	7599
30	0.7823	0.7446	0.7835	0.7458	0.7847	0.7469	0.7858	0.7481	0.7870	0.7493	0.7882	0.7505	0.7894	0.7517	0.7906	0.7529	0.7918	0.7541	0.7930	0.7552
31	7797	7399	7809	7411	7821	7423	7833	7435	7844	7446	7856	7458	7868	7470	7880	7482	7892	7494	7903	7505
32	7772	7352	7783	7363	7795	7375	7807	7387	7819	7399	7830	7410	7842	7422	7854	7434	7866	7446	7877	7458
33	7746	7303	7758	7315	7770	7327	7781	7338	7793	7350	7805	7362	7817	7374	7828	7385	7840	7397	7852	7409
34	7721	7254	7733	7266	7744	7277	7756	7289	7768	7301	7779	7313	7791	7324	7803	7336	7814	7348	7826	7359
35	0.7696	0.7204	0.7707	0.7216	0.7719	0.7227	0.7731	0.7239	0.7742	0.7251	0.7754	0.7262	0.7766	0.7274	0.7777	0.7286	0.7789	0.7297	0.7801	0.7309
36	7671	7153	7682	7164	7694	7176	7706	7188	7717	7199	7729	7211	7740	7223	7752	7234	7764	7246	7775	7257
37	7646	7101	7658	7112	7669	7124	7681	7135	7692	7147	7704	7159	7715	7170	7727	7182	7739	7193	7750	7205
38	7621	7048	7633	7059	7644	7071	7656	7082	7668	7094	7679	7105	7691	7117	7702	7128	7714	7140	7725	7151
39	7597	6993	7608	7005	7620	7016	7631	7028	7643	7039	7654	7051	7666	7062	7677	7074	7689	7085	7700	7097
40	0.7573	0.6938	0.7584	0.6949	0.7596	0.6961	0.7607	0.6972	0.7618	0.6984	0.7630	0.6995	0.7641	0.7007	0.7653	0.7018	0.7664	0.7030	0.7676	0.7041
41	7548	6881	7560	6893	7571	6904	7583	6915	7594	6927	7606	6938	7617	6950	7628	6961	7640	6973	7651	6984
42	7524	6823	7536	6835	7547	6846	7559	6857	7570	6869	7581	6880	7593	6892	7604	6903	7616	6914	7627	6926

mm Hg	670		671		672		673		674		675		676		677		678		679	
°C	dry	sat.	dry	sat.	dry	sat.	dry	sat.	dry	sat.	dry	sat.	dry	sat.	dry	sat.	dry	sat.	dry	sat.
0	0.8816	0.8756	0.8829	0.8769	0.8842	0.8782	0.8855	0.8795	0.8868	0.8808	0.8882	0.8821	0.8895	0.8834	0.8908	0.8848	0.8921	0.8861	0.8934	0.8874
1	8784	8719	8797	8732	8810	8745	8823	8758	8836	8771	8849	8785	8862	8798	8875	8811	8888	8824	8902	8837
2	8752	8682	8765	8695	8778	8709	8791	8722	8804	8735	8817	8748	8830	8761	8843	8774	8856	8787	8869	8800
3	8720	8646	8733	8659	8746	8672	8759	8685	8772	8698	8785	8711	8798	8724	8811	8737	8824	8750	8837	8763
4	8688	8609	8701	8622	8714	8635	8727	8648	8740	8661	8753	8674	8766	8687	8779	8700	8792	8713	8805	8726
5	0.8657	0.8572	0.8670	0.8585	0.8683	0.8598	0.8696	0.8611	0.8709	0.8624	0.8722	0.8637	0.8734	0.8650	0.8747	0.8663	0.8760	0.8676	0.8773	0.8689
6	8626	8536	8639	8548	8652	8561	8664	8574	8677	8587	8690	8600	8703	8613	8716	8626	8729	8639	8742	8651
7	8595	8499	8608	8511	8621	8524	8633	8537	8646	8550	8659	8563	8672	8576	8685	8588	8698	8601	8710	8614
8	8564	8462	8577	8474	8590	8487	8603	8500	8615	8513	8628	8525	8641	8538	8654	8551	8667	8564	8679	8577
9	8534	8424	8547	8437	8559	8450	8572	8462	8585	8475	8598	8488	8610	8501	8623	8513	8636	8526	8649	8539
10	0.8504	0.8387	0.8516	0.8400	0.8529	0.8412	0.8542	0.8425	0.8554	0.8438	0.8567	0.8450	0.8580	0.8463	0.8593	0.8476	0.8605	0.8488	0.8618	0.8501
11	8474	8349	8486	8362	8499	8375	8512	8387	8524	8400	8537	8412	8550	8425	8562	8438	8575	8450	8588	8463
12	8444	8311	8457	8324	8469	8337	8482	8349	8494	8362	8507	8374	8520	8387	8532	8400	8545	8412	8557	8425
13	8414	8273	8427	8286	8439	8298	8452	8311	8465	8324	8477	8336	8490	8349	8502	8361	8515	8374	8527	8386
14	8385	8235	8397	8247	8410	8260	8423	8272	8435	8285	8448	8298	8460	8310	8473	8323	8485	8335	8498	8348
15	0.8356	0.8196	0.8368	0.8209	0.8381	0.8221	0.8393	0.8234	0.8406	0.8246	0.8418	0.8259	0.8431	0.8271	0.8443	0.8284	0.8456	0.8296	0.8468	0.8309
16	8327	8157	8339	8170	8352	8182	8364	8195	8377	8207	8389	8220	8401	8232	8414	8244	8426	8257	8439	8269
17	8298	8118	8310	8131	8323	8143	8335	8155	8348	8168	8360	8180	8372	8192	8385	8205	8397	8217	8410	8230
18	8270	8078	8282	8091	8294	8103	8307	8116	8319	8128	8331	8140	8344	8153	8356	8165	8368	8177	8381	8190
19	8241	8038	8253	8051	8266	8063	8278	8075	8290	8088	8303	8100	8315	8112	8327	8125	8340	8137	8352	8149
20	0.8213	0.7998	0.8225	0.8010	0.8237	0.8023	0.8250	0.8035	0.8262	0.8047	0.8274	0.8059	0.8287	0.8072	0.8299	0.8084	0.8311	0.8096	0.8323	0.8108
21	8185	7957	8197	7969	8209	7982	8222	7994	8234	8006	8246	8018	8258	8030	8270	8043	8283	8055	8295	8067
22	8157	7916	8169	7928	8182	7940	8194	7952	8206	7964	8218	7977	8230	7989	8242	8001	8255	8013	8267	8025
23	8130	7874	8142	7886	8154	7898	8166	7910	8178	7922	8190	7935	8202	7947	8215	7959	8227	7971	8239	7983
24	8102	7832	8114	7844	8126	7856	8138	7868	8151	7880	8163	7892	8175	7904	8187	7916	8199	7928	8211	7940
25	0.8075	0.7789	0.8087	0.7801	0.8099	0.7813	0.8111	0.7825	0.8123	0.7837	0.8135	0.7849	0.8147	0.7861	0.8159	0.7873	0.8171	0.7885	0.8183	0.7897
26	8048	7745	8060	7757	8072	7769	8084	7781	8096	7793	8108	7805	8120	7817	8132	7829	8144	7841	8156	7853
27	8021	7701	8033	7713	8045	7725	8057	7737	8069	7749	8081	7761	8093	7773	8105	7785	8117	7797	8129	7809
28	7994	7656	8006	7668	8018	7680	8030	7692	8042	7704	8054	7716	8066	7728	8078	7740	8090	7751	8102	7763
29	7968	7611	7980	7622	7992	7634	8003	7646	8015	7658	8027	7670	8039	7682	8051	7694	8063	7706	8075	7718
30	0.7941	0.7564	0.7953	0.7576	0.7965	0.7588	0.7977	0.7600	0.7989	0.7612	0.8001	0.7623	0.8013	0.7635	0.8024	0.7647	0.8036	0.7659	0.8048	0.7671
31	7915	7517	7927	7529	7939	7541	7951	7553	7963	7564	7974	7576	7986	7588	7998	7600	8010	7612	8022	7624
32	7889	7469	7901	7481	7913	7493	7925	7505	7936	7516	7948	7528	7960	7540	7972	7552	7983	7564	7995	7575
33	7863	7421	7875	7432	7887	7444	7899	7456	7910	7468	7922	7479	7934	7491	7946	7503	7957	7515	7969	7526
34	7838	7371	7849	7383	7861	7394	7873	7406	7885	7418	7896	7430	7908	7441	7920	7453	7931	7465	7943	7476
35	0.7812	0.7321	0.7824	0.7332	0.7836	0.7344	0.7847	0.7356	0.7859	0.7367	0.7871	0.7379	0.7882	0.7390	0.7894	0.7402	0.7906	0.7414	0.7917	0.7425
36	7787	7269	7799	7281	7810	7292	7822	7304	7833	7316	7845	7327	7857	7339	7868	7350	7880	7362	7892	7374
37	7762	7217	7773	7228	7785	7240	7797	7251	7808	7263	7820	7274	7831	7286	7843	7298	7854	7309	7866	7321
38	7737	7163	7748	7175	7760	7186	7771	7198	7783	7209	7795	7221	7806	7232	7818	7244	7829	7255	7841	7267
39	7712	7108	7723	7120	7735	7131	7747	7143	7758	7154	7770	7166	7781	7177	7793	7189	7805	7200	7816	7212
40	0.7687	0.7053	0.7699	0.7064	0.7710	0.7075	0.7722	0.7087	0.7733	0.7098	0.7745	0.7110	0.7756	0.7121	0.7768	0.7133	0.7779	0.7144	0.7791	0.7156
41	7663	6996	7674	7007	7686	7018	7697	7030	7709	7041	7720	7053	7731	7064	7743	7076	7754	7087	7766	7098
42	7638	6937	7650	6949	7661	6960	7673	6971	7684	6983	7695	6994	7707	7006	7718	7017	7730	7028	7741	7040

mm Hg	680		681		682		683		684		685		686		687		688		689	
°C	dry	sat.	dry	sat.	dry	sat.	dry	sat.	dry	sat.	dry	sat.	dry	sat.	dry	sat.	dry	sat.	dry	sat.
0	0.8947	0.8887	0.8961	0.8900	0.8974	0.8913	0.8987	0.8927	0.9000	0.8940	0.9013	0.8953	0.9026	0.8966	0.9039	0.8979	0.9053	0.8992	0.9066	0.9006
1	8915	8850	8928	8863	8941	8876	8954	8889	8967	8903	8980	8916	8993	8929	9006	8942	9020	8955	9033	8968
2	8882	8813	8895	8826	8908	8839	8921	8852	8934	8865	8947	8878	8961	8891	8974	8904	8987	8918	9000	8931
3	8850	8776	8863	8789	8876	8802	8889	8815	8902	8828	8915	8841	8928	8854	8941	8867	8954	8880	8967	8893
4	8818	8739	8831	8752	8844	8765	8857	8778	8870	8791	8883	8804	8896	8817	8909	8830	8922	8843	8935	8856
5	0.8786	0.8702	0.8799	0.8715	0.8812	0.8727	0.8825	0.8740	0.8838	0.8753	0.8851	0.8766	0.8864	0.8779	0.8877	0.8792	0.8890	0.8805	0.8902	0.8818
6	8755	8664	8767	8677	8780	8690	8793	8703	8806	8716	8819	8729	8832	8742	8845	8754	8858	8767	8870	8780
7	8723	8627	8736	8640	8749	8653	8762	8665	8775	8678	8787	8691	8800	8704	8813	8717	8826	8730	8839	8742
8	8692	8589	8705	8602	8718	8615	8731	8628	8743	8640	8756	8653	8769	8666	8782	8679	8794	8692	8807	8704
9	8661	8552	8674	8564	8687	8577	8699	8590	8712	8603	8725	8615	8738	8628	8750	8641	8763	8654	8776	8666
10	0.8631	0.8514	0.8643	0.8526	0.8656	0.8539	0.8669	0.8552	0.8681	0.8565	0.8694	0.8577	0.8707	0.8590	0.8719	0.8603	0.8732	0.8615	0.8745	0.8628
11	8600	8476	8613	8488	8625	8501	8638	8514	8651	8526	8663	8539	8676	8552	8689	8564	8701	8577	8714	8590
12	8570	8437	8583	8450	8595	8463	8608	8475	8620	8488	8633	8500	8646	8513	8658	8526	8671	8538	8683	8551
13	8540	8399	8552	8411	8565	8424	8578	8437	8590	8449	8603	8462	8615	8474	8628	8487	8640	8499	8653	8512
14	8510	8360	8523	8373	8535	8385	8548	8398	8560	8410	8573	8423	8585	8435	8598	8448	8610	8460	8623	8473
15	0.8481	0.8321	0.8493	0.8334	0.8505	0.8346	0.8518	0.8358	0.8530	0.8371	0.8543	0.8383	0.8555	0.8396	0.8568	0.8408	0.8580	0.8421	0.8593	0.8433
16	8451	8282	8464	8294	8476	8307	8488	8319	8501	8331	8513	8344	8526	8356	8538	8369	8551	8381	8563	8394
17	8422	8242	8434	8254	8447	8267	8459	8279	8471	8292	8484	8304	8496	8316	8509	8329	8521	8341	8533	8353
18	8393	8202	8405	8214	8418	8227	8430	8239	8442	8251	8455	8264	8467	8276	8479	8288	8492	8301	8504	8313
19	8364	8161	8376	8174	8389	8186	8401	8198	8413	8211	8426	8223	8438	8235	8450	8248	8463	8260	8475	8272
20	0.8336	0.8121	0.8348	0.8133	0.8360	0.8145	0.8372	0.8157	0.8385	0.8170	0.8397	0.8182	0.8409	0.8194	0.8421	0.8206	0.8434	0.8219	0.8446	0.8231
21	8307	8079	8319	8092	8332	8104	8344	8116	8356	8128	8368	8140	8380	8153	8393	8165	8405	8177	8417	8189
22	8279	8038	8291	8050	8303	8062	8315	8074	8328	8086	8340	8098	8352	8111	8364	8123	8376	8135	8389	8147
23	8251	7995	8263	8007	8275	8020	8287	8032	8299	8044	8312	8056	8324	8068	8336	8080	8348	8092	8360	8104
24	8223	7952	8235	7965	8247	7977	8259	7989	8271	8001	8284	8013	8296	8025	8308	8037	8320	8049	8332	8061
25	0.8195	0.7909	0.8207	0.7921	0.8220	0.7933	0.8232	0.7945	0.8244	0.7957	0.8256	0.7969	0.8268	0.7981	0.8280	0.7993	0.8292	0.8006	0.8304	0.8018
26	8168	7865	8180	7877	8192	7889	8204	7901	8216	7913	8228	7925	8240	7937	8252	7949	8264	7961	8276	7973
27	8141	7821	8153	7833	8165	7845	8177	7857	8189	7868	8201	7880	8213	7892	8225	7904	8236	7916	8248	7928
28	8114	7775	8126	7787	8137	7799	8149	7811	8161	7823	8173	7835	8185	7847	8197	7859	8209	7871	8221	7883
29	8087	7729	8099	7741	8110	7753	8122	7765	8134	7777	8146	7789	8158	7801	8170	7813	8182	7825	8194	7836
30	0.8060	0.7683	0.8072	0.7695	0.8084	0.7706	0.8096	0.7718	0.8107	0.7730	0.8119	0.7742	0.8131	0.7754	0.8143	0.7766	0.8155	0.7778	0.8167	0.7789
31	8033	7635	8045	7647	8057	7659	8069	7671	8081	7683	8092	7694	8104	7706	8116	7718	8128	7730	8140	7742
32	8007	7587	8019	7599	8031	7611	8042	7622	8054	7634	8066	7646	8078	7658	8089	7670	8101	7681	8113	7693
33	7981	7538	7993	7550	8004	7561	8016	7573	8028	7585	8039	7597	8051	7608	8063	7620	8075	7632	8086	7644
34	7955	7488	7966	7500	7978	7511	7990	7523	8002	7535	8013	7547	8025	7558	8037	7570	8048	7582	8060	7593
35	0.7929	0.7437	0.7941	0.7449	0.7952	0.7460	0.7964	0.7472	0.7976	0.7484	0.7987	0.7495	0.7999	0.7507	0.8011	0.7519	0.8022	0.7530	0.8034	0.7542
36	7903	7385	7915	7397	7926	7409	7938	7420	7950	7432	7961	7443	7973	7455	7985	7467	7996	7478	8008	7490
37	7878	7332	7889	7344	7901	7356	7912	7367	7924	7379	7936	7390	7947	7402	7959	7413	7970	7425	7982	7437
38	7852	7278	7864	7290	7875	7302	7887	7313	7898	7325	7910	7336	7922	7348	7933	7359	7945	7371	7956	7382
39	7827	7223	7839	7235	7850	7246	7862	7258	7873	7269	7885	7281	7896	7293	7908	7304	7919	7316	7931	7327
40	0.7802	0.7167	0.7814	0.7179	0.7825	0.7190	0.7836	0.7202	0.7848	0.7213	0.7859	0.7225	0.7871	0.7236	0.7882	0.7248	0.7894	0.7259	0.7905	0.7271
41	7777	7110	7789	7121	7800	7133	7811	7144	7823	7156	7834	7167	7846	7179	7857	7190	7869	7201	7880	7213
42	7752	7051	7764	7063	7775	7074	7787	7085	7798	7097	7809	7108	7821	7120	7832	7131	7844	7142	7855	7154

mm Hg	690		691		692		693		694		695		696		697		698		699	
°C	dry	sat.	dry	sat.	dry	sat.	dry	sat.	dry	sat.	dry	sat.	dry	sat.	dry	sat.	dry	sat.	dry	sat.
0	0.9079	0.9019	0.9092	0.9032	0.9105	0.9045	0.9118	0.9058	0.9132	0.9071	0.9145	0.9084	0.9158	0.9098	0.9171	0.9111	0.9184	0.9124	0.9197	0.9137
1	9046	8981	9059	8994	9072	9007	9085	9020	9098	9034	9111	9047	9124	9060	9138	9073	9151	9086	9164	9099
2	9013	8944	9026	8957	9039	8970	9052	8983	9065	8996	9078	9009	9091	9022	9104	9035	9117	9048	9130	9061
3	8980	8906	8993	8919	9006	8932	9019	8945	9032	8958	9045	8971	9058	8984	9071	8997	9084	9010	9097	9023
4	8948	8868	8961	8881	8974	8894	8986	8907	8999	8920	9012	8933	9025	8946	9038	8959	9051	8972	9064	8985
5	0.8915	0.8831	0.8928	0.8844	0.8941	0.8857	0.8954	0.8870	0.8967	0.8882	0.8980	0.8895	0.8993	0.8908	0.9006	0.8921	0.9019	0.8934	0.9032	0.8947
6	8883	8793	8896	8806	8909	8819	8922	8832	8935	8845	8948	8857	8961	8870	8973	8883	8986	8896	8999	8909
7	8852	8755	8864	8768	8877	8781	8890	8794	8903	8806	8916	8819	8929	8832	8941	8845	8954	8858	8967	8871
8	8820	8717	8833	8730	8846	8743	8858	8756	8871	8768	8884	8781	8897	8794	8909	8807	8922	8819	8935	8832
9	8789	8679	8801	8692	8814	8704	8827	8717	8840	8730	8852	8743	8865	8755	8878	8768	8891	8781	8903	8794
10	0.8758	0.8641	0.8770	0.8653	0.8783	0.8666	0.8796	0.8679	0.8808	0.8691	0.8821	0.8704	0.8834	0.8717	0.8846	0.8730	0.8859	0.8742	0.8872	0.8755
11	8727	8602	8739	8615	8752	8627	8765	8640	8777	8653	8790	8665	8803	8678	8815	8691	8828	8703	8840	8716
12	8696	8563	8709	8576	8721	8589	8734	8601	8746	8614	8759	8626	8772	8639	8784	8652	8797	8664	8809	8677
13	8666	8524	8678	8537	8691	8550	8703	8562	8716	8575	8728	8587	8741	8600	8753	8612	8766	8625	8779	8637
14	8635	8485	8648	8498	8660	8510	8673	8523	8685	8535	8698	8548	8710	8560	8723	8573	8735	8585	8748	8598
15	0.8605	0.8446	0.8618	0.8458	0.8630	0.8471	0.8643	0.8483	0.8655	0.8496	0.8668	0.8508	0.8680	0.8521	0.8693	0.8533	0.8705	0.8546	0.8717	0.8558
16	8575	8406	8588	8418	8600	8431	8613	8443	8625	8456	8638	8468	8650	8481	8662	8493	8675	8505	8687	8518
17	8546	8366	8558	8378	8571	8391	8583	8403	8595	8415	8608	8428	8620	8440	8632	8453	8645	8465	8657	8477
18	8516	8325	8529	8338	8541	8350	8553	8362	8566	8375	8578	8387	8590	8399	8603	8412	8615	8424	8627	8436
19	8487	8284	8499	8297	8512	8309	8524	8321	8536	8334	8549	8346	8561	8358	8573	8371	8586	8383	8598	8395
20	0.8458	0.8243	0.8470	0.8255	0.8483	0.8268	0.8495	0.8280	0.8507	0.8292	0.8519	0.8304	0.8532	0.8317	0.8544	0.8329	0.8556	0.8341	0.8568	0.8353
21	8429	8201	8442	8214	8454	8226	8466	8238	8478	8250	8490	8263	8503	8275	8515	8287	8527	8299	8539	8311
22	8401	8159	8413	8171	8425	8184	8437	8196	8449	8208	8462	8220	8474	8232	8486	8245	8498	8257	8510	8269
23	8372	8117	8384	8129	8397	8141	8409	8153	8421	8165	8433	8177	8445	8189	8457	8202	8469	8214	8481	8226
24	8344	8073	8356	8086	8368	8098	8380	8110	8392	8122	8404	8134	8417	8146	8429	8158	8441	8170	8453	8182
25	0.8316	0.8030	0.8328	0.8042	0.8340	0.8054	0.8352	0.8066	0.8364	0.8078	0.8376	0.8090	0.8388	0.8102	0.8400	0.8114	0.8412	0.8126	0.8424	0.8138
26	8288	7985	8300	7997	8312	8009	8324	8021	8336	8033	8348	8045	8360	8057	8372	8069	8384	8081	8396	8093
27	8260	7940	8272	7952	8284	7964	8296	7976	8308	7988	8320	8000	8332	8012	8344	8024	8356	8036	8368	8048
28	8233	7895	8245	7907	8257	7919	8269	7930	8281	7942	8293	7954	8305	7966	8316	7978	8328	7990	8340	8002
29	8206	7848	8218	7860	8229	7872	8241	7884	8253	7896	8265	7908	8277	7920	8289	7932	8301	7943	8313	7955
30	0.8178	0.7801	0.8190	0.7813	0.8202	0.7825	0.8214	0.7837	0.8226	0.7849	0.8238	0.7861	0.8250	0.7872	0.8261	0.7884	0.8273	0.7896	0.8285	0.7908
31	8152	7753	8163	7765	8175	7777	8187	7789	8199	7801	8211	7813	8222	7824	8234	7836	8246	7848	8258	7860
32	8125	7705	8137	7717	8148	7728	8160	7740	8172	7752	8184	7764	8195	7775	8207	7787	8219	7799	8231	7811
33	8098	7655	8110	7667	8122	7679	8133	7691	8145	7702	8157	7714	8169	7726	8180	7738	8192	7749	8204	7761
34	8072	7605	8083	7617	8095	7628	8107	7640	8119	7652	8130	7664	8142	7675	8154	7687	8165	7699	8177	7710
35	0.8046	0.7554	0.8057	0.7565	0.8069	0.7577	0.8080	0.7589	0.8092	0.7600	0.8104	0.7612	0.8115	0.7624	0.8127	0.7635	0.8139	0.7647	0.8150	0.7659
36	8019	7501	8031	7513	8043	7525	8054	7536	8066	7548	8078	7560	8089	7571	8101	7583	8112	7594	8124	7606
37	7994	7448	8005	7460	8017	7471	8028	7483	8040	7495	8051	7506	8063	7518	8075	7529	8086	7541	8098	7553
38	7968	7394	7979	7405	7991	7417	8002	7429	8014	7440	8026	7452	8037	7463	8049	7475	8060	7486	8072	7498
39	7942	7339	7954	7350	7965	7362	7977	7373	7988	7385	8000	7396	8011	7408	8023	7419	8034	7431	8046	7442
40	0.7917	0.7282	0.7928	0.7293	0.7940	0.7305	0.7951	0.7316	0.7963	0.7328	0.7974	0.7339	0.7986	0.7351	0.7997	0.7362	0.8009	0.7374	0.8020	0.7385
41	7892	7224	7903	7236	7914	7247	7926	7259	7937	7270	7949	7281	7960	7293	7972	7304	7983	7316	7994	7327
42	7866	7165	7878	7177	7889	7188	7901	7199	7912	7211	7923	7222	7935	7234	7946	7245	7958	7256	7969	7268

°C	700		701		702		703		704		705		706		707		708		709	
0	0.9211	0.9150	0.9224	0.9163	0.9237	0.9177	0.9250	0.9190	0.9263	0.9203	0.9276	0.9216	0.9289	0.9229	0.9303	0.9242	0.9316	0.9256	0.9329	0.9269
1	9177	9112	9190	9125	9203	9138	9216	9152	9229	9165	9242	9178	9256	9191	9269	9204	9282	9217	9295	9230
2	9143	9074	9156	9087	9170	9100	9183	9113	9196	9127	9209	9140	9222	9153	9235	9166	9248	9179	9261	9192
3	9110	9036	9123	9049	9136	9062	9149	9075	9162	9088	9175	9101	9188	9114	9201	9127	9214	9140	9227	9153
4	9077	8998	9090	9011	9103	9024	9116	9037	9129	9050	9142	9063	9155	9076	9168	9089	9181	9102	9194	9115
5	0.9045	0.8960	0.9057	0.8973	0.9070	0.8986	0.9083	0.8999	0.9096	0.9012	0.9109	0.9025	0.9122	0.9038	0.9135	0.9050	0.9148	0.9063	0.9161	0.9076
6	9012	8922	9025	8935	9038	8948	9051	8960	9064	8973	9076	8986	9089	8999	9102	9012	9115	9025	9128	9038
7	8980	8883	8993	8896	9005	8909	9018	8922	9031	8935	9044	8948	9057	8960	9070	8973	9082	8986	9095	8999
8	8948	8845	8961	8858	8973	8871	8986	8883	8999	8896	9012	8909	9025	8922	9037	8934	9050	8947	9063	8960
9	8916	8806	8929	8819	8942	8832	8954	8845	8967	8857	8980	8870	8992	8883	9005	8896	9018	8908	9031	8921
10	0.8884	0.8768	0.8897	0.8780	0.8910	0.8793	0.8923	0.8806	0.8935	0.8818	0.8948	0.8831	0.8961	0.8844	0.8973	0.8856	0.8986	0.8869	0.8999	0.8882
11	8853	8729	8866	8741	8878	8754	8891	8767	8904	8779	8916	8792	8929	8805	8942	8817	8954	8830	8967	8842
12	8822	8689	8835	8702	8847	8715	8860	8727	8872	8740	8885	8752	8898	8765	8910	8778	8923	8790	8935	8803
13	8791	8650	8801	8663	8816	8675	8829	8688	8841	8700	8854	8713	8866	8725	8879	8738	8892	8751	8904	8763
14	8760	8610	8773	8623	8785	8635	8798	8648	8810	8660	8823	8673	8836	8685	8848	8698	8861	8711	8873	8723
15	0.8730	0.8570	0.8742	0.8583	0.8755	0.8595	0.8767	0.8608	0.8780	0.8620	0.8792	0.8633	0.8805	0.8645	0.8817	0.8658	0.8830	0.8670	0.8842	0.8683
16	8700	8530	8712	8543	8725	8555	8737	8568	8749	8580	8762	8592	8774	8605	8787	8617	8799	8630	8812	8642
17	8670	8490	8682	8502	8694	8514	8707	8527	8719	8539	8732	8552	8744	8564	8756	8576	8769	8589	8781	8601
18	8640	8449	8652	8461	8664	8473	8677	8486	8689	8498	8701	8510	8714	8523	8726	8535	8739	8547	8751	8560
19	8610	8407	8622	8420	8635	8432	8647	8444	8659	8457	8672	8469	8684	8481	8696	8494	8709	8506	8721	8518
20	0.8581	0.8366	0.8593	0.8378	0.8605	0.8390	0.8617	0.8403	0.8630	0.8415	0.8642	0.8427	0.8654	0.8439	0.8667	0.8452	0.8679	0.8464	0.8691	0.8476
21	8551	8324	8564	8336	8576	8348	8588	8360	8600	8372	8613	8385	8625	8397	8637	8409	8649	8421	8661	8434
22	8522	8281	8535	8293	8547	8305	8559	8318	8571	8330	8583	8342	8595	8354	8608	8366	8620	8378	8632	8391
23	8494	8238	8506	8250	8518	8262	8530	8274	8542	8286	8554	8299	8566	8311	8579	8323	8591	8335	8603	8347
24	8465	8194	8477	8206	8489	8219	8501	8231	8513	8243	8525	8255	8537	8267	8550	8279	8562	8291	8574	8303
25	0.8436	0.8150	0.8449	0.8162	0.8461	0.8174	0.8473	0.8186	0.8485	0.8198	0.8497	0.8210	0.8509	0.8222	0.8521	0.8235	0.8533	0.8247	0.8545	0.8259
26	8408	8105	8420	8117	8432	8129	8444	8141	8456	8153	8468	8165	8480	8177	8492	8189	8504	8202	8516	8214
27	8380	8060	8392	8072	8404	8084	8416	8096	8428	8108	8440	8120	8452	8132	8464	8144	8476	8156	8488	8168
28	8352	8014	8364	8026	8376	8038	8388	8050	8400	8062	8412	8074	8424	8086	8436	8098	8448	8109	8460	8121
29	8325	7967	8336	7979	8348	7991	8360	8003	8372	8015	8384	8027	8396	8039	8408	8051	8420	8062	8432	8074
30	0.8297	0.7920	0.8309	0.7932	0.8321	0.7944	0.8333	0.7955	0.8344	0.7967	0.8356	0.7979	0.8368	0.7991	0.8380	0.8003	0.8392	0.8015	0.8404	0.8026
31	8270	7872	8281	7883	8293	7895	8305	7907	8317	7919	8329	7931	8341	7943	8352	7954	8364	7966	8376	7978
32	8243	7823	8254	7834	8266	7846	8278	7858	8290	7870	8301	7881	8313	7893	8325	7905	8337	7917	8348	7929
33	8216	7773	8227	7784	8239	7796	8251	7808	8262	7820	8274	7831	8286	7843	8298	7855	8309	7867	8321	7878
34	8189	7722	8200	7734	8212	7745	8224	7757	8236	7769	8247	7780	8259	7792	8271	7804	8282	7816	8294	7827
35	0.8162	0.7670	0.8174	0.7682	0.8185	0.7694	0.8197	0.7705	0.8209	0.7717	0.8220	0.7729	0.8232	0.7740	0.8244	0.7752	0.8255	0.7764	0.8267	0.7775
36	8136	7618	8147	7629	8159	7641	8171	7653	8182	7664	8194	7676	8205	7687	8217	7699	8229	7711	8240	7722
37	8109	7564	8121	7576	8133	7587	8144	7599	8156	7610	8167	7622	8179	7634	8190	7645	8202	7657	8214	7668
38	8083	7509	8095	7521	8106	7533	8118	7544	8129	7556	8141	7567	8153	7579	8164	7590	8176	7602	8187	7613
39	8057	7454	8069	7465	8080	7477	8092	7488	8103	7500	8115	7511	8126	7523	8138	7534	8149	7546	8161	7557
40	0.8032	0.7397	0.8043	0.7408	0.8054	0.7420	0.8066	0.7431	0.8077	0.7443	0.8089	0.7454	0.8100	0.7466	0.8112	0.7477	0.8123	0.7489	0.8135	0.7500
41	8006	7339	8017	7350	8029	7362	8040	7373	8052	7384	8063	7396	8075	7407	8086	7419	8097	7430	8109	7442
42	7980	7279	7992	7291	8003	7302	8015	7313	8026	7325	8037	7336	8049	7348	8060	7359	8072	7370	8083	7382

mm Hg	710		711		712		713		714		715		716		717		718		719	
°C	dry	*sat.*	dry	*sat.*	dry	*sat.*	dry	*sat.*	dry	*sat.*	dry	*sat.*	dry	*sat.*	dry	*sat.*	dry	*sat.*	dry	*sat.*
0	0.9342	*0.9282*	0.9355	*0.9295*	0.9368	*0.9308*	0.9382	*0.9321*	0.9395	*0.9334*	0.9408	*0.9348*	0.9421	*0.9361*	0.9434	*0.9374*	0.9447	*0.9387*	0.9461	*0.9400*
1	9308	*9243*	9321	*9256*	9334	*9270*	9347	*9283*	9360	*9296*	9373	*9309*	9387	*9322*	9400	*9335*	9413	*9348*	9426	*9361*
2	9274	*9205*	9287	*9218*	9300	*9231*	9313	*9244*	9326	*9257*	9339	*9270*	9352	*9283*	9365	*9296*	9379	*9309*	9392	*9322*
3	9240	*9166*	9253	*9179*	9266	*9192*	9279	*9205*	9292	*9218*	9305	*9231*	9318	*9244*	9331	*9257*	9344	*9270*	9358	*9284*
4	9207	*9128*	9220	*9141*	9233	*9154*	9246	*9167*	9259	*9180*	9272	*9193*	9285	*9206*	9298	*9219*	9311	*9232*	9324	*9245*
5	0.9174	*0.9089*	0.9187	*0.9102*	0.9200	*0.9115*	0.9213	*0.9128*	0.9225	*0.9141*	0.9238	*0.9154*	0.9251	*0.9167*	0.9264	*0.9180*	0.9277	*0.9193*	0.9290	*0.9206*
6	9141	*9051*	9154	*9063*	9167	*9076*	9179	*9089*	9192	*9102*	9205	*9115*	9218	*9128*	9231	*9141*	9244	*9154*	9257	*9166*
7	9108	*9012*	9121	*9025*	9134	*9037*	9147	*9050*	9159	*9063*	9172	*9076*	9185	*9089*	9198	*9102*	9211	*9114*	9224	*9127*
8	9076	*8973*	9088	*8986*	9101	*8998*	9114	*9011*	9127	*9024*	9140	*9037*	9152	*9050*	9165	*9062*	9178	*9075*	9191	*9088*
9	9043	*8934*	9056	*8946*	9069	*8959*	9082	*8972*	9094	*8985*	9107	*8997*	9120	*9010*	9133	*9023*	9145	*9036*	9158	*9048*
10	0.9011	*0.8895*	0.9024	*0.8907*	0.9037	*0.8920*	0.9049	*0.8933*	0.9062	*0.8945*	0.9075	*0.8958*	0.9088	*0.8971*	0.9100	*0.8983*	0.9113	*0.8996*	0.9126	*0.9009*
11	8980	*8855*	8992	*8868*	9005	*8880*	9018	*8893*	9030	*8906*	9043	*8918*	9055	*8931*	9068	*8944*	9081	*8956*	9093	*8969*
12	8948	*8815*	8961	*8828*	8973	*8841*	8986	*8853*	8998	*8866*	9011	*8878*	9024	*8891*	9036	*8904*	9049	*8916*	9061	*8929*
13	8917	*8776*	8929	*8788*	8942	*8801*	8954	*8813*	8967	*8826*	8979	*8838*	8992	*8851*	9005	*8864*	9017	*8876*	9030	*8889*
14	8886	*8736*	8898	*8748*	8911	*8761*	8923	*8773*	8936	*8786*	8948	*8798*	8961	*8811*	8973	*8823*	8986	*8836*	8998	*8848*
15	0.8855	*0.8695*	0.8867	*0.8708*	0.8880	*0.8720*	0.8892	*0.8733*	0.8905	*0.8745*	0.8917	*0.8758*	0.8929	*0.8770*	0.8942	*0.8782*	0.8954	*0.8795*	0.8967	*0.8807*
16	8824	*8655*	8836	*8667*	8849	*8679*	8861	*8692*	8874	*8704*	8886	*8717*	8899	*8729*	8911	*8742*	8923	*8754*	8936	*8766*
17	8793	*8614*	8806	*8626*	8818	*8638*	8831	*8651*	8843	*8663*	8855	*8675*	8868	*8688*	8880	*8700*	8893	*8713*	8905	*8725*
18	8763	*8572*	8776	*8585*	8788	*8597*	8800	*8609*	8813	*8622*	8825	*8634*	8837	*8646*	8850	*8659*	8862	*8671*	8874	*8683*
19	8733	*8530*	8745	*8543*	8758	*8555*	8770	*8567*	8782	*8580*	8795	*8592*	8807	*8604*	8819	*8617*	8832	*8629*	8844	*8641*
20	0.8703	*0.8488*	0.8716	*0.8501*	0.8728	*0.8513*	0.8740	*0.8525*	0.8752	*0.8537*	0.8765	*0.8550*	0.8777	*0.8562*	0.8789	*0.8574*	0.8801	*0.8586*	0.8814	*0.8599*
21	8674	*8446*	8686	*8458*	8698	*8470*	8710	*8482*	8722	*8495*	8735	*8507*	8747	*8519*	8759	*8531*	8771	*8544*	8784	*8556*
22	8644	*8403*	8656	*8415*	8669	*8427*	8681	*8439*	8693	*8451*	8705	*8464*	8717	*8476*	8729	*8488*	8742	*8500*	8754	*8512*
23	8615	*8359*	8627	*8371*	8639	*8384*	8651	*8396*	8663	*8408*	8676	*8420*	8688	*8432*	8700	*8444*	8712	*8456*	8724	*8468*
24	8586	*8315*	8598	*8327*	8610	*8339*	8622	*8352*	8634	*8364*	8646	*8376*	8658	*8388*	8671	*8400*	8683	*8412*	8695	*8424*
25	0.8557	*0.8271*	0.8569	*0.8283*	0.8581	*0.8295*	0.8593	*0.8307*	0.8605	*0.8319*	0.8617	*0.8331*	0.8629	*0.8343*	0.8641	*0.8355*	0.8653	*0.8367*	0.8665	*0.8379*
26	8528	*8226*	8540	*8238*	8552	*8250*	8564	*8262*	8576	*8274*	8588	*8286*	8600	*8298*	8612	*8310*	8624	*8322*	8636	*8334*
27	8500	*8180*	8512	*8192*	8524	*8204*	8536	*8216*	8548	*8228*	8560	*8240*	8572	*8252*	8584	*8264*	8596	*8276*	8608	*8287*
28	8472	*8133*	8483	*8145*	8495	*8157*	8507	*8169*	8519	*8181*	8531	*8193*	8543	*8205*	8555	*8217*	8567	*8229*	8579	*8241*
29	8443	*8086*	8455	*8098*	8467	*8110*	8479	*8122*	8491	*8134*	8503	*8146*	8515	*8158*	8527	*8169*	8539	*8181*	8550	*8193*
30	0.8416	*0.8038*	0.8427	*0.8050*	0.8439	*0.8062*	0.8451	*0.8074*	0.8463	*0.8086*	0.8475	*0.8098*	0.8487	*0.8109*	0.8499	*0.8121*	0.8510	*0.8133*	0.8522	*0.8145*
31	8388	*7990*	8400	*8002*	8411	*8013*	8423	*8025*	8435	*8037*	8447	*8049*	8459	*8061*	8471	*8072*	8482	*8084*	8494	*8096*
32	8360	*7940*	8372	*7952*	8384	*7964*	8396	*7976*	8407	*7987*	8419	*7999*	8431	*8011*	8443	*8023*	8454	*8035*	8466	*8046*
33	8333	*7890*	8345	*7902*	8356	*7914*	8368	*7925*	8380	*7937*	8392	*7949*	8403	*7961*	8415	*7972*	8427	*7984*	8439	*7996*
34	8306	*7839*	8317	*7851*	8329	*7862*	8341	*7874*	8353	*7886*	8364	*7897*	8376	*7909*	8388	*7921*	8399	*7933*	8411	*7944*
35	0.8279	*0.7787*	0.8290	*0.7799*	0.8302	*0.7810*	0.8314	*0.7822*	0.8325	*0.7834*	0.8337	*0.7845*	0.8349	*0.7857*	0.8360	*0.7869*	0.8372	*0.7880*	0.8384	*0.7892*
36	8252	*7734*	8263	*7746*	8275	*7757*	8287	*7769*	8298	*7780*	8310	*7792*	8322	*7804*	8333	*7815*	8345	*7827*	8356	*7839*
37	8225	*7680*	8237	*7692*	8248	*7703*	8260	*7715*	8272	*7726*	8283	*7738*	8295	*7749*	8306	*7761*	8318	*7773*	8329	*7784*
38	8199	*7625*	8210	*7636*	8222	*7648*	8233	*7660*	8245	*7671*	8256	*7683*	8268	*7694*	8280	*7706*	8291	*7717*	8303	*7729*
39	8172	*7569*	8184	*7580*	8195	*7592*	8207	*7603*	8218	*7615*	8230	*7626*	8241	*7638*	8253	*7649*	8264	*7661*	8276	*7672*
40	0.8146	*0.7511*	0.8158	*0.7523*	0.8169	*0.7534*	0.8181	*0.7546*	0.8192	*0.7557*	0.8204	*0.7569*	0.8215	*0.7580*	0.8227	*0.7592*	0.8238	*0.7603*	0.8249	*0.7615*
41	8120	*7453*	8132	*7464*	8143	*7476*	8155	*7487*	8166	*7499*	8177	*7510*	8189	*7522*	8200	*7533*	8212	*7545*	8223	*7556*
42	8094	*7393*	8106	*7405*	8117	*7416*	8129	*7427*	8140	*7439*	8151	*7450*	8163	*7462*	8174	*7473*	8186	*7484*	8197	*7496*

	720		721		722		723		724		725		726		727		728		729	
0	0.9474	*0.9413*	0.9487	*0.9427*	0.9500	*0.9440*	0.9513	*0.9453*	0.9526	*0.9466*	0.9539	*0.9479*	0.9553	*0.9492*	0.9566	*0.9506*	0.9579	*0.9519*	0.9592	*0.9532*
1	9439	*9374*	9452	*9388*	9465	*9401*	9478	*9414*	9491	*9427*	9505	*9440*	9518	*9453*	9531	*9466*	9544	*9479*	9557	*9492*
2	9405	*9336*	9418	*9349*	9431	*9362*	9444	*9375*	9457	*9388*	9470	*9401*	9483	*9414*	9496	*9427*	9509	*9440*	9522	*9453*
3	9371	*9297*	9384	*9310*	9397	*9323*	9410	*9336*	9423	*9349*	9436	*9362*	9449	*9375*	9462	*9388*	9475	*9401*	9488	*9414*
4	9337	*9258*	9350	*9270*	9363	*9283*	9376	*9296*	9388	*9309*	9401	*9322*	9414	*9335*	9427	*9348*	9440	*9361*	9453	*9374*
5	0.9303	*0.9218*	0.9316	*0.9231*	0.9329	*0.9244*	0.9342	*0.9257*	0.9355	*0.9270*	0.9368	*0.9283*	0.9380	*0.9296*	0.9393	*0.9309*	0.9406	*0.9322*	0.9419	*0.9335*
6	9270	*9179*	9282	*9192*	9295	*9205*	9308	*9218*	9321	*9231*	9334	*9244*	9347	*9257*	9360	*9269*	9373	*9282*	9385	*9295*
7	9236	*9140*	9249	*9153*	9262	*9166*	9275	*9179*	9288	*9191*	9301	*9204*	9313	*9217*	9326	*9230*	9339	*9243*	9352	*9255*
8	9203	*9101*	9216	*9113*	9229	*9126*	9242	*9139*	9255	*9152*	9267	*9165*	9280	*9177*	9293	*9190*	9306	*9203*	9319	*9216*
9	9171	*9061*	9184	*9074*	9196	*9087*	9209	*9099*	9222	*9112*	9234	*9125*	9247	*9138*	9260	*9150*	9273	*9163*	9285	*9176*
10	0.9138	*0.9021*	0.9151	*0.9034*	0.9164	*0.9047*	0.9176	*0.9060*	0.9189	*0.9072*	0.9202	*0.9085*	0.9214	*0.9098*	0.9227	*0.9110*	0.9240	*0.9123*	0.9253	*0.9136*
11	9106	*8982*	9119	*8994*	9131	*9007*	9144	*9020*	9157	*9032*	9169	*9045*	9182	*9057*	9195	*9070*	9207	*9083*	9220	*9095*
12	9074	*8942*	9087	*8954*	9099	*8967*	9112	*8979*	9124	*8992*	9137	*9005*	9150	*9017*	9162	*9030*	9175	*9042*	9187	*9055*
13	9042	*8901*	9055	*8914*	9067	*8926*	9080	*8939*	9093	*8951*	9105	*8964*	9118	*8977*	9130	*8989*	9143	*9002*	9155	*9014*
14	9011	*8861*	9023	*8873*	9036	*8886*	9048	*8898*	9061	*8911*	9073	*8923*	9086	*8936*	9098	*8948*	9111	*8961*	9123	*8973*
15	0.8979	*0.8820*	0.8992	*0.8832*	0.9004	*0.8845*	0.9017	*0.8857*	0.9029	*0.8870*	0.9042	*0.8882*	0.9054	*0.8895*	0.9067	*0.8907*	0.9079	*0.8920*	0.9092	*0.8932*
16	8948	*8779*	8961	*8791*	8973	*8804*	8986	*8816*	8998	*8829*	9010	*8841*	9023	*8853*	9035	*8866*	9048	*8878*	9060	*8891*
17	8917	*8737*	8930	*8750*	8942	*8762*	8954	*8775*	8967	*8787*	8979	*8799*	8992	*8812*	9004	*8824*	9016	*8836*	9029	*8849*
18	8887	*8696*	8899	*8708*	8911	*8720*	8924	*8733*	8936	*8745*	8948	*8757*	8961	*8770*	8973	*8782*	8985	*8794*	8998	*8807*
19	8856	*8653*	8868	*8666*	8881	*8678*	8893	*8690*	8905	*8703*	8918	*8715*	8930	*8727*	8942	*8740*	8955	*8752*	8967	*8764*
20	0.8826	*0.8611*	0.8838	*0.8623*	0.8850	*0.8635*	0.8863	*0.8648*	0.8875	*0.8660*	0.8887	*0.8672*	0.8899	*0.8684*	0.8912	*0.8697*	0.8924	*0.8709*	0.8936	*0.8721*
21	8796	*8568*	8808	*8580*	8820	*8592*	8832	*8605*	8845	*8617*	8857	*8629*	8869	*8641*	8881	*8653*	8894	*8666*	8906	*8678*
22	8766	*8525*	8778	*8537*	8790	*8549*	8802	*8561*	8815	*8573*	8827	*8585*	8839	*8598*	8851	*8610*	8863	*8622*	8875	*8634*
23	8736	*8481*	8748	*8493*	8761	*8505*	8773	*8517*	8785	*8529*	8797	*8541*	8809	*8553*	8821	*8566*	8833	*8578*	8845	*8590*
24	8707	*8436*	8719	*8448*	8731	*8460*	8743	*8472*	8755	*8485*	8767	*8497*	8779	*8509*	8791	*8521*	8804	*8533*	8816	*8545*
25	0.8678	*0.8391*	0.8690	*0.8403*	0.8702	*0.8415*	0.8714	*0.8427*	0.8726	*0.8439*	0.8738	*0.8451*	0.8750	*0.8464*	0.8762	*0.8476*	0.8774	*0.8488*	0.8786	*0.8500*
26	8648	*8346*	8660	*8358*	8672	*8370*	8684	*8382*	8696	*8394*	8709	*8406*	8721	*8418*	8733	*8430*	8745	*8442*	8757	*8454*
27	8620	*8299*	8632	*8311*	8644	*8323*	8655	*8335*	8667	*8347*	8679	*8359*	8691	*8371*	8703	*8383*	8715	*8395*	8727	*8407*
28	8591	*8253*	8603	*8265*	8615	*8276*	8627	*8288*	8639	*8300*	8651	*8312*	8662	*8324*	8674	*8336*	8686	*8348*	8698	*8360*
29	8562	*8205*	8574	*8217*	8586	*8229*	8598	*8241*	8610	*8253*	8622	*8265*	8634	*8276*	8646	*8288*	8658	*8300*	8669	*8312*
30	0.8534	*0.8157*	0.8546	*0.8169*	0.8558	*0.8181*	0.8570	*0.8192*	0.8581	*0.8204*	0.8593	*0.8216*	0.8605	*0.8228*	0.8617	*0.8240*	0.8629	*0.8252*	0.8641	*0.8264*
31	8506	*8108*	8518	*8120*	8530	*8132*	8541	*8143*	8553	*8155*	8565	*8167*	8577	*8179*	8589	*8191*	8600	*8202*	8612	*8214*
32	8478	*8058*	8490	*8070*	8502	*8082*	8513	*8093*	8525	*8105*	8537	*8117*	8549	*8129*	8560	*8141*	8572	*8152*	8584	*8164*
33	8450	*8007*	8462	*8019*	8474	*8031*	8485	*8043*	8497	*8054*	8509	*8066*	8521	*8078*	8532	*8090*	8544	*8101*	8556	*8113*
34	8423	*7956*	8434	*7968*	8446	*7979*	8458	*7991*	8469	*8003*	8481	*8014*	8493	*8026*	8505	*8038*	8516	*8050*	8528	*8061*
35	0.8395	*0.7904*	0.8407	*0.7915*	0.8419	*0.7927*	0.8430	*0.7939*	0.8442	*0.7950*	0.8454	*0.7962*	0.8465	*0.7974*	0.8477	*0.7985*	0.8489	*0.7997*	0.8500	*0.8008*
36	8368	*7850*	8380	*7862*	8391	*7873*	8403	*7885*	8415	*7897*	8426	*7908*	8438	*7920*	8449	*7932*	8461	*7943*	8473	*7955*
37	8341	*7796*	8353	*7807*	8364	*7819*	8376	*7831*	8387	*7842*	8399	*7854*	8411	*7865*	8422	*7877*	8434	*7888*	8445	*7900*
38	8314	*7740*	8326	*7752*	8337	*7763*	8349	*7775*	8360	*7787*	8372	*7798*	8383	*7810*	8395	*7821*	8407	*7833*	8418	*7844*
39	8287	*7684*	8299	*7695*	8311	*7707*	8322	*7718*	8334	*7730*	8345	*7741*	8357	*7753*	8368	*7764*	8380	*7776*	8391	*7787*
40	0.8261	*0.7626*	0.8272	*0.7638*	0.8284	*0.7649*	0.8295	*0.7661*	0.8307	*0.7672*	0.8318	*0.7684*	0.8330	*0.7695*	0.8341	*0.7707*	0.8353	*0.7718*	0.8364	*0.7729*
41	8235	*7567*	8246	*7579*	8257	*7590*	8269	*7602*	8280	*7613*	8292	*7625*	8303	*7636*	8315	*7647*	8326	*7659*	8338	*7670*
42	8208	*7507*	8220	*7519*	8231	*7530*	8243	*7542*	8254	*7553*	8265	*7564*	8277	*7576*	8288	*7587*	8300	*7599*	8311	*7610*

mm Hg	730		731		732		733		734		735		736		737		738		739	
°C	dry	sat.	dry	sat.	dry	sat.	dry	sat.	dry	sat.	dry	sat.	dry	sat.	dry	sat.	dry	sat.	dry	sat.
0	0.9605	0.9545	0.9618	0.9558	0.9632	0.9571	0.9645	0.9584	0.9658	0.9598	0.9671	0.9611	0.9684	0.9624	0.9697	0.9637	0.9711	0.9650	0.9724	0.9663
1	9570	9506	9583	9519	9596	9532	9609	9545	9623	9558	9636	9571	9649	9584	9662	9597	9675	9610	9688	9624
2	9535	9466	9548	9479	9561	9492	9574	9505	9588	9518	9601	9531	9614	9544	9627	9558	9640	9571	9653	9584
3	9501	9427	9514	9440	9527	9453	9540	9466	9553	9479	9566	9492	9579	9505	9592	9518	9605	9531	9618	9544
4	9466	9387	9479	9400	9492	9413	9505	9426	9518	9439	9531	9452	9544	9465	9557	9478	9570	9491	9583	9504
5	0.9432	0.9348	0.9445	0.9361	0.9458	0.9373	0.9471	0.9386	0.9484	0.9399	0.9497	0.9412	0.9510	0.9425	0.9523	0.9438	0.9536	0.9451	0.9548	0.9464
6	9398	9308	9411	9321	9424	9334	9437	9347	9450	9360	9463	9372	9476	9385	9488	9398	9501	9411	9514	9424
7	9365	9268	9378	9281	9390	9294	9403	9307	9416	9320	9429	9332	9442	9345	9454	9358	9467	9371	9480	9384
8	9331	9228	9344	9241	9357	9254	9370	9267	9382	9280	9395	9292	9408	9305	9421	9318	9434	9331	9446	9344
9	9298	9188	9311	9201	9324	9214	9336	9227	9349	9239	9362	9252	9375	9265	9387	9278	9400	9290	9413	9303
10	0.9265	0.9148	0.9278	0.9161	0.9291	0.9174	0.9303	0.9186	0.9316	0.9199	0.9329	0.9212	0.9341	0.9225	0.9354	0.9237	0.9367	0.9250	0.9379	0.9263
11	9233	9108	9245	9121	9258	9133	9270	9146	9283	9159	9296	9171	9308	9184	9321	9197	9334	9209	9346	9222
12	9200	9068	9213	9080	9225	9093	9238	9105	9251	9118	9263	9131	9276	9143	9288	9156	9301	9168	9314	9181
13	9168	9027	9180	9039	9193	9052	9206	9064	9218	9077	9231	9090	9243	9102	9256	9115	9268	9127	9281	9140
14	9136	8986	9148	8998	9161	9011	9173	9023	9186	9036	9198	9048	9211	9061	9223	9073	9236	9086	9248	9098
15	0.9104	0.8945	0.9117	0.8957	0.9129	0.8970	0.9141	0.8982	0.9154	0.8994	0.9166	0.9007	0.9179	0.9019	0.9191	0.9032	0.9204	0.9044	0.9216	0.9057
16	9073	8903	9085	8916	9097	8928	9110	8940	9122	8953	9135	8965	9147	8978	9160	8990	9172	9003	9184	9015
17	9041	8861	9054	8874	9066	8886	9078	8898	9091	8911	9103	8923	9115	8936	9128	8948	9140	8960	9153	8973
18	9010	8819	9022	8831	9035	8844	9047	8856	9059	8868	9072	8881	9084	8893	9096	8905	9109	8918	9121	8930
19	8979	8776	8991	8789	9004	8801	9016	8813	9028	8826	9041	8838	9053	8850	9065	8863	9078	8875	9090	8887
20	0.8948	0.8734	0.8961	0.8746	0.8973	0.8758	0.8985	0.8770	0.8997	0.8783	0.9010	0.8795	0.9022	0.8807	0.9034	0.8819	0.9047	0.8832	0.9059	0.8844
21	8918	8690	8930	8702	8942	8715	8955	8727	8967	8739	8979	8751	8991	8763	9003	8776	9016	8788	9028	8800
22	8888	8646	8900	8658	8912	8671	8924	8683	8936	8695	8949	8707	8961	8719	8973	8732	8985	8744	8997	8756
23	8858	8602	8870	8614	8882	8626	8894	8638	8906	8650	8918	8663	8930	8675	8943	8687	8955	8699	8967	8711
24	8828	8557	8840	8569	8852	8581	8864	8593	8876	8605	8888	8618	8900	8630	8912	8642	8924	8654	8937	8666
25	0.8798	0.8512	0.8810	0.8524	0.8822	0.8536	0.8834	0.8548	0.8846	0.8560	0.8858	0.8572	0.8870	0.8584	0.8882	0.8596	0.8894	0.8608	0.8907	0.8620
26	8769	8466	8781	8478	8793	8490	8805	8502	8817	8514	8829	8526	8841	8538	8853	8550	8865	8562	8877	8574
27	8739	8419	8751	8431	8763	8443	8775	8455	8787	8467	8799	8479	8811	8491	8823	8503	8835	8515	8847	8527
28	8710	8372	8722	8384	8734	8396	8746	8408	8758	8420	8770	8432	8782	8444	8794	8455	8806	8467	8818	8479
29	8681	8324	8693	8336	8705	8348	8717	8360	8729	8372	8741	8383	8753	8395	8765	8407	8776	8419	8788	8431
30	0.8653	0.8275	0.8664	0.8287	0.8676	0.8299	0.8688	0.8311	0.8700	0.8323	0.8712	0.8335	0.8724	0.8347	0.8736	0.8358	0.8747	0.8370	0.8759	0.8382
31	8624	8226	8636	8238	8648	8250	8660	8261	8671	8273	8683	8285	8695	8297	8707	8309	8719	8321	8730	8332
32	8596	8176	8608	8188	8619	8199	8631	8211	8643	8223	8655	8235	8666	8246	8678	8258	8690	8270	8702	8282
33	8568	8125	8579	8137	8591	8148	8603	8160	8615	8172	8626	8184	8638	8195	8650	8207	8662	8219	8673	8230
34	8540	8073	8551	8085	8563	8096	8575	8108	8586	8120	8598	8131	8610	8143	8622	8155	8633	8167	8645	8178
35	0.8512	0.8020	0.8524	0.8032	0.8535	0.8043	0.8547	0.8055	0.8559	0.8067	0.8570	0.8078	0.8582	0.8090	0.8594	0.8102	0.8605	0.8113	0.8617	0.8125
36	8484	7966	8496	7978	8508	7990	8519	8001	8531	8013	8542	8025	8554	8036	8566	8048	8577	8059	8589	8071
37	8457	7912	8468	7923	8480	7935	8492	7946	8503	7958	8515	7970	8526	7981	8538	7993	8550	8004	8561	8016
38	8430	7856	8441	7867	8453	7879	8464	7890	8476	7902	8487	7914	8499	7925	8510	7937	8522	7948	8534	7960
39	8403	7799	8414	7810	8426	7822	8437	7834	8449	7845	8460	7857	8472	7868	8483	7880	8495	7891	8506	7903
40	0.8376	0.7741	0.8387	0.7752	0.8399	0.7764	0.8410	0.7775	0.8422	0.7787	0.8433	0.7798	0.8445	0.7810	0.8456	0.7821	0.8467	0.7833	0.8479	0.7844
41	8349	7682	8360	7693	8372	7705	8383	7716	8395	7728	8406	7739	8418	7750	8429	7762	8440	7773	8452	7785
42	8322	7621	8334	7633	8345	7644	8357	7656	8368	7667	8379	7678	8391	7690	8402	7701	8414	7713	8425	7724

mm Hg	740		741		742		743		744		745		746		747		748		749	
°C	dry	sat.	dry	sat.	dry	sat.	dry	sat.	dry	sat.	dry	sat.	dry	sat.	dry	sat.	dry	sat.	dry	sat.
0	0.9737	0.9677	0.9750	0.9690	0.9763	0.9703	0.9776	0.9716	0.9789	0.9729	0.9803	0.9742	0.9816	0.9756	0.9829	0.9769	0.9842	0.9782	0.9855	0.9795
1	9701	9637	9714	9650	9727	9663	9741	9676	9754	9689	9767	9702	9780	9715	9793	9728	9806	9742	9819	9755
2	9666	9597	9679	9610	9692	9623	9705	9636	9718	9649	9731	9662	9744	9675	9757	9688	9770	9701	9783	9714
3	9631	9557	9644	9570	9657	9583	9670	9596	9683	9609	9696	9622	9709	9635	9722	9648	9735	9661	9748	9674
4	9596	9517	9609	9530	9622	9543	9635	9556	9648	9569	9661	9582	9674	9595	9687	9608	9700	9621	9713	9634
5	0.9561	0.9477	0.9574	0.9490	0.9587	0.9503	0.9600	0.9516	0.9613	0.9529	0.9626	0.9541	0.9639	0.9554	0.9652	0.9567	0.9665	0.9580	0.9678	0.9593
6	9527	9437	9540	9450	9553	9463	9566	9475	9579	9488	9591	9501	9604	9514	9617	9527	9630	9540	9643	9553
7	9493	9397	9506	9409	9519	9422	9531	9435	9544	9448	9557	9461	9570	9474	9583	9486	9596	9499	9608	9512
8	9459	9356	9472	9369	9485	9382	9497	9395	9510	9407	9523	9420	9536	9433	9549	9446	9561	9459	9574	9471
9	9426	9316	9438	9329	9451	9341	9464	9354	9476	9367	9489	9380	9502	9392	9515	9405	9527	9418	9540	9430
10	0.9392	0.9275	0.9405	0.9288	0.9418	0.9301	0.9430	0.9313	0.9443	0.9326	0.9456	0.9339	0.9468	0.9351	0.9481	0.9364	0.9494	0.9377	0.9506	0.9389
11	9359	9235	9372	9247	9384	9260	9397	9272	9410	9285	9422	9298	9435	9310	9448	9323	9460	9336	9473	9348
12	9326	9194	9339	9206	9351	9219	9364	9231	9377	9244	9389	9257	9402	9269	9414	9282	9427	9294	9440	9307
13	9293	9152	9306	9165	9319	9178	9331	9190	9344	9203	9356	9215	9369	9228	9381	9240	9394	9253	9406	9265
14	9261	9111	9274	9124	9286	9136	9299	9149	9311	9161	9324	9174	9336	9186	9349	9199	9361	9211	9374	9224
15	0.9229	0.9069	0.9241	0.9082	0.9254	0.9094	0.9266	0.9107	0.9279	0.9119	0.9291	0.9132	0.9304	0.9144	0.9316	0.9157	0.9329	0.9169	0.9341	0.9182
16	9197	9027	9209	9040	9222	9052	9234	9065	9247	9077	9259	9090	9271	9102	9284	9114	9296	9127	9309	9139
17	9165	8985	9177	8997	9190	9010	9202	9022	9215	9035	9227	9047	9239	9059	9252	9072	9264	9084	9277	9097
18	9133	8942	9146	8955	9158	8967	9171	8979	9183	8992	9195	9004	9208	9017	9220	9029	9232	9041	9245	9054
19	9102	8899	9114	8912	9127	8924	9139	8936	9151	8949	9164	8961	9176	8973	9188	8986	9201	8998	9213	9010
20	0.9071	0.8856	0.9083	0.8868	0.9096	0.8881	0.9108	0.8893	0.9120	0.8905	0.9132	0.8917	0.9145	0.8930	0.9157	0.8942	0.9169	0.8954	0.9181	0.8966
21	9040	8812	9052	8825	9065	8837	9077	8849	9089	8861	9101	8873	9113	8886	9126	8898	9138	8910	9150	8922
22	9009	8768	9022	8780	9034	8792	9046	8805	9058	8817	9070	8829	9082	8841	9095	8853	9107	8865	9119	8878
23	8979	8723	8991	8735	9003	8748	9015	8760	9027	8772	9040	8784	9052	8796	9064	8808	9076	8820	9088	8833
24	8949	8678	8961	8690	8973	8702	8985	8714	8997	8726	9009	8739	9021	8751	9033	8763	9045	8775	9057	8787
25	0.8919	0.8632	0.8931	0.8644	0.8943	0.8656	0.8955	0.8668	0.8967	0.8680	0.8979	0.8693	0.8991	0.8705	0.9003	0.8717	0.9015	0.8729	0.9027	0.8741
26	8889	8586	8901	8598	8913	8610	8925	8622	8937	8634	8949	8646	8961	8658	8973	8670	8985	8682	8997	8694
27	8859	8539	8871	8551	8883	8563	8895	8575	8907	8587	8919	8599	8931	8611	8943	8623	8955	8635	8967	8647
28	8830	8491	8841	8503	8853	8515	8865	8527	8877	8539	8889	8551	8901	8563	8913	8575	8925	8587	8937	8599
29	8800	8443	8812	8455	8824	8467	8836	8479	8848	8491	8860	8502	8872	8514	8883	8526	8895	8538	8907	8550
30	0.8771	0.8394	0.8783	0.8406	0.8795	0.8418	0.8807	0.8429	0.8819	0.8441	0.8830	0.8453	0.8842	0.8465	0.8854	0.8477	0.8866	0.8489	0.8878	0.8501
31	8742	8344	8754	8356	8766	8368	8778	8380	8789	8391	8801	8403	8813	8415	8825	8427	8837	8439	8849	8450
32	8714	8294	8725	8305	8737	8317	8749	8329	8761	8341	8772	8352	8784	8364	8796	8376	8808	8388	8820	8400
33	8685	8242	8697	8254	8708	8266	8720	8277	8732	8289	8744	8301	8755	8313	8767	8324	8779	8336	8791	8348
34	8657	8190	8668	8202	8680	8213	8692	8225	8703	8237	8715	8248	8727	8260	8739	8272	8750	8284	8762	8295
35	0.8629	0.8137	0.8640	0.8148	0.8652	0.8160	0.8663	0.8172	0.8675	0.8183	0.8687	0.8195	0.8698	0.8207	0.8710	0.8218	0.8722	0.8230	0.8733	0.8242
36	8601	8083	8612	8094	8624	8106	8635	8117	8647	8129	8659	8141	8670	8152	8682	8164	8694	8176	8705	8187
37	8573	8027	8584	8039	8596	8051	8608	8062	8619	8074	8631	8085	8642	8097	8654	8109	8665	8120	8677	8132
38	8545	7971	8557	7983	8568	7994	8580	8006	8591	8018	8603	8029	8614	8041	8626	8052	8638	8064	8649	8075
39	8518	7914	8529	7926	8541	7937	8552	7949	8564	7960	8575	7972	8587	7983	8598	7995	8610	8006	8621	8018
40	0.8490	0.7856	0.8502	0.7867	0.8513	0.7879	0.8525	0.7890	0.8536	0.7902	0.8548	0.7913	0.8559	0.7925	0.8571	0.7936	0.8582	0.7947	0.8594	0.7959
41	8463	7796	8475	7808	8486	7819	8498	7830	8509	7842	8521	7853	8532	7865	8543	7876	8555	7888	8566	7899
42	8436	7735	8448	7747	8459	7758	8471	7770	8482	7781	8493	7792	8505	7804	8516	7815	8528	7827	8539	7838

mm Hg	750		751		752		753		754		755		756		757		758		759	
°C	dry	*sat.*	dry	*sat.*	dry	*sat.*	dry	*sat.*	dry	*sat.*	dry	*sat.*	dry	*sat.*	dry	*sat.*	dry	*sat.*	dry	*sat.*
0	0.9868	*0.9808*	0.9882	*0.9821*	0.9895	*0.9834*	0.9908	*0.9848*	0.9921	*0.9861*	0.9934	*0.9874*	0.9947	*0.9887*	0.9961	*0.9900*	0.9974	*0.9913*	0.9987	*0.9927*
1	9832	*9768*	9845	*9781*	9859	*9794*	9872	*9807*	9885	*9820*	9898	*9833*	9911	*9846*	9924	*9860*	9937	*9873*	9950	*9886*
2	9797	*9727*	9810	*9740*	9823	*9753*	9836	*9767*	9849	*9780*	9862	*9793*	9875	*9806*	9888	*9819*	9901	*9832*	9914	*9845*
3	9761	*9687*	9774	*9700*	9787	*9713*	9800	*9726*	9813	*9739*	9826	*9752*	9839	*9765*	9852	*9778*	9865	*9791*	9878	*9804*
4	9726	*9647*	9739	*9660*	9752	*9672*	9765	*9685*	9778	*9698*	9790	*9711*	9803	*9724*	9816	*9737*	9829	*9750*	9842	*9763*
5	0.9691	*0.9606*	0.9704	*0.9619*	0.9716	*0.9632*	0.9729	*0.9645*	0.9742	*0.9658*	0.9755	*0.9671*	0.9768	*0.9684*	0.9781	*0.9697*	0.9794	*0.9709*	0.9807	*0.9722*
6	9656	*9566*	9669	*9578*	9682	*9591*	9694	*9604*	9707	*9617*	9720	*9630*	9733	*9643*	9746	*9656*	9759	*9669*	9772	*9681*
7	9621	*9525*	9634	*9538*	9647	*9551*	9660	*9563*	9673	*9576*	9685	*9589*	9698	*9602*	9711	*9615*	9724	*9627*	9737	*9640*
8	9587	*9484*	9600	*9497*	9613	*9510*	9625	*9522*	9638	*9535*	9651	*9548*	9664	*9561*	9676	*9574*	9689	*9586*	9702	*9599*
9	9553	*9443*	9566	*9456*	9578	*9469*	9591	*9481*	9604	*9494*	9617	*9507*	9629	*9520*	9642	*9532*	9655	*9545*	9668	*9558*
10	0.9519	*0.9402*	0.9532	*0.9415*	0.9544	*0.9428*	0.9557	*0.9440*	0.9570	*0.9453*	0.9583	*0.9466*	0.9595	*0.9478*	0.9608	*0.9491*	0.9621	*0.9504*	0.9633	*0.9516*
11	9485	*9361*	9498	*9374*	9511	*9386*	9523	*9399*	9536	*9412*	9549	*9424*	9561	*9437*	9574	*9450*	9587	*9462*	9599	*9475*
12	9452	*9320*	9465	*9332*	9477	*9345*	9490	*9357*	9503	*9370*	9515	*9383*	9528	*9395*	9540	*9408*	9553	*9420*	9566	*9433*
13	9419	*9278*	9432	*9291*	9444	*9303*	9457	*9316*	9469	*9328*	9482	*9341*	9494	*9353*	9507	*9366*	9520	*9378*	9532	*9391*
14	9386	*9236*	9399	*9249*	9411	*9261*	9424	*9274*	9436	*9286*	9449	*9299*	9461	*9311*	9474	*9324*	9486	*9336*	9499	*9349*
15	0.9354	*0.9194*	0.9366	*0.9206*	0.9378	*0.9219*	0.9391	*0.9231*	0.9403	*0.9244*	0.9416	*0.9256*	0.9428	*0.9269*	0.9441	*0.9281*	0.9453	*0.9294*	0.9466	*0.9306*
16	9321	*9152*	9334	*9164*	9346	*9176*	9358	*9189*	9371	*9201*	9383	*9214*	9396	*9226*	9408	*9239*	9421	*9251*	9433	*9263*
17	9289	*9109*	9301	*9121*	9314	*9134*	9326	*9146*	9338	*9158*	9351	*9171*	9363	*9183*	9376	*9196*	9388	*9208*	9400	*9220*
18	9257	*9066*	9269	*9078*	9282	*9091*	9294	*9103*	9306	*9115*	9319	*9128*	9331	*9140*	9343	*9152*	9356	*9165*	9368	*9177*
19	9225	*9022*	9237	*9035*	9250	*9047*	9262	*9059*	9274	*9072*	9287	*9084*	9299	*9096*	9311	*9109*	9324	*9121*	9336	*9133*
20	0.9194	*0.8979*	0.9206	*0.8991*	0.9218	*0.9003*	0.9230	*0.9015*	0.9243	*0.9028*	0.9255	*0.9040*	0.9267	*0.9052*	0.9279	*0.9064*	0.9292	*0.9077*	0.9304	*0.9089*
21	9162	*8934*	9175	*8947*	9187	*8959*	9199	*8971*	9211	*8983*	9223	*8996*	9236	*9008*	9248	*9020*	9260	*9032*	9272	*9044*
22	9131	*8890*	9143	*8902*	9156	*8914*	9168	*8926*	9180	*8938*	9192	*8951*	9204	*8963*	9216	*8975*	9229	*8987*	9241	*8999*
23	9100	*8845*	9112	*8857*	9125	*8869*	9137	*8881*	9149	*8893*	9161	*8905*	9173	*8917*	9185	*8930*	9197	*8942*	9209	*8954*
24	9070	*8799*	9082	*8811*	9094	*8823*	9106	*8835*	9118	*8847*	9130	*8859*	9142	*8872*	9154	*8884*	9166	*8896*	9178	*8908*
25	0.9039	*0.8753*	0.9051	*0.8765*	0.9063	*0.8777*	0.9075	*0.8789*	0.9087	*0.8801*	0.9099	*0.8813*	0.9111	*0.8825*	0.9123	*0.8837*	0.9136	*0.8849*	0.9148	*0.8861*
26	9009	*8706*	9021	*8718*	9033	*8730*	9045	*8742*	9057	*8754*	9069	*8766*	9081	*8778*	9093	*8790*	9105	*8802*	9117	*8814*
27	8979	*8659*	8991	*8671*	9003	*8683*	9015	*8695*	9027	*8706*	9039	*8718*	9051	*8730*	9063	*8742*	9074	*8754*	9086	*8766*
28	8949	*8611*	8961	*8623*	8973	*8634*	8985	*8646*	8997	*8658*	9008	*8670*	9020	*8682*	9032	*8694*	9044	*8706*	9056	*8718*
29	8919	*8562*	8931	*8574*	8943	*8586*	8955	*8598*	8967	*8609*	8979	*8621*	8991	*8633*	9002	*8645*	9014	*8657*	9026	*8669*
30	0.8890	*0.8512*	0.8902	*0.8524*	0.8913	*0.8536*	0.8925	*0.8548*	0.8937	*0.8560*	0.8949	*0.8572*	0.8961	*0.8584*	0.8973	*0.8595*	0.8984	*0.8607*	0.8996	*0.8619*
31	8860	*8462*	8872	*8474*	8884	*8486*	8896	*8498*	8908	*8510*	8919	*8521*	8931	*8533*	8943	*8545*	8955	*8557*	8967	*8569*
32	8831	*8411*	8843	*8423*	8855	*8435*	8867	*8447*	8878	*8458*	8890	*8470*	8902	*8482*	8914	*8494*	8925	*8506*	8937	*8517*
33	8802	*8360*	8814	*8371*	8826	*8383*	8838	*8395*	8849	*8407*	8861	*8418*	8873	*8430*	8885	*8442*	8896	*8453*	8908	*8465*
34	8774	*8307*	8785	*8319*	8797	*8330*	8809	*8342*	8820	*8354*	8832	*8365*	8844	*8377*	8856	*8389*	8867	*8400*	8879	*8412*
35	0.8745	*0.8253*	0.8757	*0.8265*	0.8768	*0.8277*	0.8780	*0.8288*	0.8792	*0.8300*	0.8803	*0.8312*	0.8815	*0.8323*	0.8827	*0.8335*	0.8838	*0.8347*	0.8850	*0.8358*
36	8717	*8199*	8728	*8210*	8740	*8222*	8752	*8234*	8763	*8245*	8775	*8257*	8786	*8269*	8798	*8280*	8810	*8292*	8821	*8303*
37	8689	*8143*	8700	*8155*	8712	*8167*	8723	*8178*	8735	*8190*	8747	*8201*	8758	*8213*	8770	*8224*	8781	*8236*	8793	*8248*
38	8661	*8087*	8672	*8098*	8684	*8110*	8695	*8121*	8707	*8133*	8718	*8145*	8730	*8156*	8741	*8168*	8753	*8179*	8765	*8191*
39	8633	*8029*	8644	*8041*	8656	*8052*	8667	*8064*	8679	*8075*	8690	*8087*	8702	*8098*	8713	*8110*	8725	*8121*	8736	*8133*
40	0.8605	*0.7970*	0.8617	*0.7982*	0.8628	*0.7993*	0.8640	*0.8005*	0.8651	*0.8016*	0.8663	*0.8028*	0.8674	*0.8039*	0.8685	*0.8051*	0.8697	*0.8062*	0.8708	*0.8074*
41	8578	*7910*	8589	*7922*	8601	*7933*	8612	*7945*	8623	*7956*	8635	*7968*	8646	*7979*	8658	*7991*	8669	*8002*	8681	*8013*
42	8550	*7849*	8562	*7861*	8573	*7872*	8585	*7884*	8596	*7895*	8607	*7906*	8619	*7918*	8630	*7929*	8642	*7941*	8653	*7952*

mm Hg	760		761		762		763		764		765		766		767		768		769	
°C	dry	*sat.*	dry	*sat.*	dry	*sat.*	dry	*sat.*	dry	*sat.*	dry	*sat.*	dry	*sat.*	dry	*sat.*	dry	*sat.*	dry	*sat.*
0	1.0000	*0.9940*	1.0013	*0.9953*	1.0026	*0.9966*	1.0039	*0.9979*	1.0053	*0.9992*	1.0066	*1.0006*	1.0079	*1.0019*	1.0092	*1.0032*	1.0105	*1.0045*	1.0118	*1.0058*
1	0.9963	*9899*	0.9977	*9912*	0.9990	*9925*	0003	*9938*	0016	*9951*	0029	*0.9964*	0042	*0.9978*	0055	*0.9991*	0068	*0004*	0081	*0017*
2	9927	*9858*	9940	*9871*	9953	*9884*	0.9966	*9897*	0.9979	*9910*	0.9992	*9923*	0006	*9936*	0019	*9949*	0032	*0.9962*	0045	*0.9976*
3	9891	*9817*	9904	*9830*	9917	*9843*	9930	*9856*	9943	*9869*	9956	*9882*	0.9969	*9895*	0.9982	*9908*	0.9995	*9921*	0008	*9934*
4	9855	*9776*	9868	*9789*	9881	*9802*	9894	*9815*	9907	*9828*	9920	*9841*	9933	*9854*	9946	*9867*	9959	*9880*	0.9972	*9893*
5	0.9820	*0.9735*	0.9833	*0.9748*	0.9846	*0.9761*	0.9859	*0.9774*	0.9871	*0.9787*	0.9884	*0.9800*	0.9897	*0.9813*	0.9910	*0.9826*	0.9923	*0.9839*	0.9936	*0.9852*
6	9785	*9694*	9797	*9707*	9810	*9720*	9823	*9733*	9836	*9746*	9849	*9759*	9862	*9772*	9875	*9784*	9888	*9797*	9900	*9810*
7	9750	*9653*	9762	*9666*	9775	*9679*	9788	*9692*	9801	*9704*	9814	*9717*	9827	*9730*	9839	*9743*	9852	*9756*	9865	*9769*
8	9715	*9612*	9728	*9625*	9740	*9638*	9753	*9650*	9766	*9663*	9779	*9676*	9791	*9689*	9804	*9701*	9817	*9714*	9830	*9727*
9	9680	*9571*	9693	*9583*	9706	*9596*	9718	*9609*	9731	*9622*	9744	*9634*	9757	*9647*	9769	*9660*	9782	*9673*	9795	*9685*
10	0.9646	*0.9529*	0.9659	*0.9542*	0.9671	*0.9554*	0.9684	*0.9567*	0.9697	*0.9580*	0.9709	*0.9593*	0.9722	*0.9605*	0.9735	*0.9618*	0.9748	*0.9631*	0.9760	*0.9643*
11	9612	*9487*	9625	*9500*	9637	*9513*	9650	*9525*	9663	*9538*	9675	*9551*	9688	*9563*	9700	*9576*	9713	*9589*	9726	*9601*
12	9578	*9446*	9591	*9458*	9603	*9471*	9616	*9483*	9629	*9496*	9641	*9509*	9654	*9521*	9666	*9534*	9679	*9546*	9692	*9559*
13	9545	*9404*	9557	*9416*	9570	*9429*	9582	*9441*	9595	*9454*	9607	*9466*	9620	*9479*	9633	*9491*	9645	*9504*	9658	*9517*
14	9511	*9361*	9524	*9374*	9536	*9386*	9549	*9399*	9561	*9411*	9574	*9424*	9586	*9436*	9599	*9449*	9611	*9461*	9624	*9474*
15	0.9478	*0.9319*	0.9491	*0.9331*	0.9503	*0.9344*	0.9516	*0.9356*	0.9528	*0.9369*	0.9541	*0.9381*	0.9553	*0.9394*	0.9566	*0.9406*	0.9578	*0.9419*	0.9590	*0.9431*
16	9445	*9276*	9458	*9288*	9470	*9301*	9483	*9313*	9495	*9326*	9508	*9338*	9520	*9350*	9532	*9363*	9545	*9375*	9557	*9388*
17	9413	*9233*	9425	*9245*	9438	*9258*	9450	*9270*	9462	*9282*	9475	*9295*	9487	*9307*	9499	*9319*	9512	*9332*	9524	*9344*
18	9380	*9189*	9393	*9202*	9405	*9214*	9417	*9226*	9430	*9239*	9442	*9251*	9454	*9263*	9467	*9276*	9479	*9288*	9491	*9300*
19	9348	*9145*	9360	*9158*	9373	*9170*	9385	*9182*	9397	*9195*	9410	*9207*	9422	*9219*	9434	*9232*	9447	*9244*	9459	*9256*
20	0.9316	*0.9101*	0.9328	*0.9114*	0.9341	*0.9126*	0.9353	*0.9138*	0.9365	*0.9150*	0.9377	*0.9163*	0.9390	*0.9175*	0.9402	*0.9187*	0.9414	*0.9199*	0.9427	*0.9212*
21	9284	*9057*	9297	*9069*	9309	*9081*	9321	*9093*	9333	*9105*	9346	*9118*	9358	*9130*	9370	*9142*	9382	*9154*	9394	*9167*
22	9253	*9012*	9265	*9024*	9277	*9036*	9289	*9048*	9302	*9060*	9314	*9072*	9326	*9085*	9338	*9097*	9350	*9109*	9362	*9121*
23	9222	*8966*	9234	*8978*	9246	*8990*	9258	*9002*	9270	*9015*	9282	*9027*	9294	*9039*	9307	*9051*	9319	*9063*	9331	*9075*
24	9191	*8920*	9203	*8932*	9215	*8944*	9227	*8956*	9239	*8968*	9251	*8980*	9263	*8992*	9275	*9005*	9287	*9017*	9299	*9029*
25	0.9160	*0.8873*	0.9172	*0.8885*	0.9184	*0.8897*	0.9196	*0.8909*	0.9208	*0.8922*	0.9220	*0.8934*	0.9232	*0.8946*	0.9244	*0.8958*	0.9256	*0.8970*	0.9268	*0.8982*
26	9129	*8826*	9141	*8838*	9153	*8850*	9165	*8862*	9177	*8874*	9189	*8886*	9201	*8898*	9213	*8910*	9225	*8922*	9237	*8934*
27	9098	*8778*	9110	*8790*	9122	*8802*	9134	*8814*	9146	*8826*	9158	*8838*	9170	*8850*	9182	*8862*	9194	*8874*	9206	*8886*
28	9068	*8730*	9080	*8742*	9092	*8754*	9104	*8766*	9116	*8778*	9128	*8790*	9140	*8801*	9152	*8813*	9164	*8825*	9176	*8837*
29	9038	*8681*	9050	*8693*	9062	*8705*	9074	*8716*	9086	*8728*	9098	*8740*	9109	*8752*	9121	*8764*	9133	*8776*	9145	*8788*
30	0.9008	*0.8631*	0.9020	*0.8643*	0.9032	*0.8655*	0.9044	*0.8667*	0.9056	*0.8678*	0.9067	*0.8690*	0.9079	*0.8702*	0.9091	*0.8714*	0.9103	*0.8726*	0.9115	*0.8738*
31	8979	*8580*	8990	*8592*	9002	*8604*	9014	*8616*	9026	*8628*	9038	*8640*	9049	*8651*	9061	*8663*	9073	*8675*	9085	*8687*
32	8949	*8529*	8961	*8541*	8973	*8553*	8984	*8564*	8996	*8576*	9008	*8588*	9020	*8600*	9031	*8612*	9043	*8623*	9055	*8635*
33	8920	*8477*	8931	*8489*	8943	*8500*	8955	*8512*	8967	*8524*	8978	*8536*	8990	*8547*	9002	*8559*	9014	*8571*	9025	*8583*
34	8891	*8424*	8902	*8436*	8914	*8447*	8926	*8459*	8937	*8471*	8949	*8482*	8961	*8494*	8973	*8506*	8984	*8517*	8996	*8529*
35	0.8862	*0.8370*	0.8873	*0.8382*	0.8885	*0.8393*	0.8897	*0.8405*	0.8908	*0.8417*	0.8920	*0.8428*	0.8932	*0.8440*	0.8943	*0.8452*	0.8955	*0.8463*	0.8967	*0.8475*
36	8833	*8315*	8845	*8327*	8856	*8338*	8868	*8350*	8879	*8362*	8891	*8373*	8903	*8385*	8914	*8396*	8926	*8408*	8938	*8420*
37	8804	*8259*	8816	*8271*	8828	*8282*	8839	*8294*	8851	*8306*	8862	*8317*	8874	*8329*	8886	*8340*	8897	*8352*	8909	*8363*
38	8776	*8202*	8788	*8214*	8799	*8225*	8811	*8237*	8822	*8248*	8834	*8260*	8845	*8272*	8857	*8283*	8868	*8295*	8880	*8306*
39	8748	*8144*	8759	*8156*	8771	*8167*	8782	*8179*	8794	*8190*	8805	*8202*	8817	*8213*	8828	*8225*	8840	*8236*	8852	*8248*
40	0.8720	*0.8085*	0.8731	*0.8097*	0.8743	*0.8108*	0.8754	*0.8120*	0.8766	*0.8131*	0.8777	*0.8143*	0.8789	*0.8154*	0.8800	*0.8165*	0.8812	*0.8177*	0.8823	*0.8188*
41	8692	*8025*	8704	*8036*	8715	*8048*	8726	*8059*	8738	*8071*	8749	*8082*	8761	*8093*	8772	*8105*	8784	*8116*	8795	*8128*
42	8664	*7963*	8676	*7975*	8687	*7986*	8699	*7998*	8710	*8009*	8721	*8020*	8733	*8032*	8744	*8043*	8756	*8055*	8767	*8066*

mm Hg	770		771		772		773		774		775		776		777		778		779	
°C	dry	*sat.*	dry	*sat.*	dry	*sat.*	dry	*sat.*	dry	*sat.*	dry	*sat.*	dry	*sat.*	dry	*sat.*	dry	*sat.*	dry	*sat.*
0	1.0132	*1.0071*	1.0145	*1.0084*	1.0158	*1.0098*	1.0171	*1.0111*	1.0184	*1.0124*	1.0197	*1.0137*	1.0211	*1.0150*	1.0224	*1.0163*	1.0237	*1.0177*	1.0250	*1.0190*
1	0095	*0030*	0108	*0043*	0121	*0056*	0134	*0069*	0147	*0082*	0160	*0096*	0173	*0109*	0186	*0122*	0199	*0135*	0213	*0148*
2	0058	*0.9989*	0071	*0002*	0084	*0015*	0097	*0028*	0110	*0041*	0123	*0054*	0136	*0067*	0149	*0080*	0162	*0093*	0175	*0106*
3	0021	*9947*	0034	*0.9960*	0047	*0.9973*	0060	*0.9986*	0073	*0.9999*	0086	*0012*	0099	*0025*	0112	*0038*	0125	*0051*	0138	*0064*
4	0.9985	*9906*	0.9998	*9919*	0011	*9932*	0024	*9945*	0037	*9958*	0050	*0.9971*	0063	*0.9984*	0076	*0.9997*	0089	*0010*	0102	*0023*
5	0.9949	*0.9864*	0.9962	*0.9877*	0.9975	*0.9890*	0.9988	*0.9903*	1.0001	*0.9916*	1.0014	*0.9929*	1.0027	*0.9942*	1.0039	*0.9955*	1.0052	*0.9968*	1.0065	*0.9981*
6	9913	*9823*	9926	*9836*	9939	*9849*	9952	*9862*	0.9965	*9874*	0.9978	*9887*	0.9991	*9900*	0003	*9913*	0016	*9926*	0029	*9939*
7	9878	*9781*	9891	*9794*	9903	*9807*	9916	*9820*	9929	*9833*	9942	*9846*	9955	*9858*	0.9968	*9871*	0.9980	*9884*	0.9993	*9897*
8	9843	*9740*	9855	*9753*	9868	*9765*	9881	*9778*	9894	*9791*	9907	*9804*	9919	*9816*	9932	*9829*	9945	*9842*	9958	*9855*
9	9808	*9698*	9820	*9711*	9833	*9723*	9846	*9736*	9859	*9749*	9871	*9762*	9884	*9774*	9897	*9787*	9910	*9800*	9922	*9813*
10	0.9773	*0.9656*	0.9786	*0.9669*	0.9798	*0.9681*	0.9811	*0.9694*	0.9824	*0.9707*	0.9836	*0.9719*	0.9849	*0.9732*	0.9862	*0.9745*	0.9874	*0.9758*	0.9887	*0.9770*
11	9738	*9614*	9751	*9627*	9764	*9639*	9776	*9652*	9789	*9665*	9802	*9677*	9814	*9690*	9827	*9702*	9840	*9715*	9852	*9728*
12	9704	*9572*	9717	*9584*	9729	*9597*	9742	*9609*	9755	*9622*	9767	*9635*	9780	*9647*	9792	*9660*	9805	*9672*	9818	*9685*
13	9670	*9529*	9683	*9542*	9695	*9554*	9708	*9567*	9720	*9579*	9733	*9592*	9746	*9605*	9758	*9617*	9771	*9630*	9783	*9642*
14	9636	*9486*	9649	*9499*	9661	*9511*	9674	*9524*	9687	*9537*	9699	*9549*	9712	*9562*	9724	*9574*	9737	*9587*	9749	*9599*
15	0.9603	*0.9443*	0.9615	*0.9456*	0.9628	*0.9468*	0.9640	*0.9481*	0.9653	*0.9493*	0.9665	*0.9506*	0.9678	*0.9518*	0.9690	*0.9531*	0.9703	*0.9543*	0.9715	*0.9556*
16	9570	*9400*	9582	*9413*	9595	*9425*	9607	*9437*	9619	*9450*	9632	*9462*	9644	*9475*	9657	*9487*	9669	*9500*	9682	*9512*
17	9537	*9357*	9549	*9369*	9561	*9381*	9574	*9394*	9586	*9406*	9599	*9419*	9611	*9431*	9623	*9443*	9636	*9456*	9648	*9468*
18	9504	*9313*	9516	*9325*	9528	*9337*	9541	*9350*	9553	*9362*	9565	*9374*	9578	*9387*	9590	*9399*	9603	*9411*	9615	*9424*
19	9471	*9268*	9483	*9281*	9496	*9293*	9508	*9305*	9520	*9318*	9533	*9330*	9545	*9342*	9557	*9355*	9570	*9367*	9582	*9379*
20	0.9439	*0.9224*	0.9451	*0.9236*	0.9463	*0.9248*	0.9476	*0.9261*	0.9488	*0.9273*	0.9500	*0.9285*	0.9512	*0.9297*	0.9525	*0.9310*	0.9537	*0.9322*	0.9549	*0.9334*
21	9407	*9179*	9419	*9191*	9431	*9203*	9443	*9215*	9455	*9228*	9468	*9240*	9480	*9252*	9492	*9264*	9504	*9277*	9517	*9289*
22	9375	*9133*	9387	*9145*	9399	*9158*	9411	*9170*	9423	*9182*	9436	*9194*	9448	*9206*	9460	*9219*	9472	*9231*	9484	*9243*
23	9343	*9087*	9355	*9099*	9367	*9112*	9379	*9124*	9391	*9136*	9404	*9148*	9416	*9160*	9428	*9172*	9440	*9184*	9452	*9197*
24	9311	*9041*	9324	*9053*	9336	*9065*	9348	*9077*	9360	*9089*	9372	*9101*	9384	*9113*	9396	*9125*	9408	*9138*	9420	*9150*
25	0.9280	*0.8994*	0.9292	*0.9006*	0.9304	*0.9018*	0.9316	*0.9030*	0.9328	*0.9042*	0.9340	*0.9054*	0.9352	*0.9066*	0.9364	*0.9078*	0.9377	*0.9090*	0.9389	*0.9102*
26	9249	*8946*	9261	*8958*	9273	*8970*	9285	*8982*	9297	*8994*	9309	*9006*	9321	*9018*	9333	*9030*	9345	*9042*	9357	*9054*
27	9218	*8898*	9230	*8910*	9242	*8922*	9254	*8934*	9266	*8946*	9278	*8958*	9290	*8970*	9302	*8982*	9314	*8994*	9326	*9006*
28	9187	*8849*	9199	*8861*	9211	*8873*	9223	*8885*	9235	*8897*	9247	*8909*	9259	*8921*	9271	*8933*	9283	*8945*	9295	*8957*
29	9157	*8800*	9169	*8812*	9181	*8824*	9193	*8835*	9205	*8847*	9216	*8859*	9228	*8871*	9240	*8883*	9252	*8895*	9264	*8907*
30	0.9127	*0.8750*	0.9139	*0.8761*	0.9150	*0.8773*	0.9162	*0.8785*	0.9174	*0.8797*	0.9186	*0.8809*	0.9198	*0.8821*	0.9210	*0.8832*	0.9222	*0.8844*	0.9233	*0.8856*
31	9097	*8699*	9108	*8710*	9120	*8722*	9132	*8734*	9144	*8746*	9156	*8758*	9168	*8769*	9179	*8781*	9191	*8793*	9203	*8805*
32	9067	*8647*	9079	*8659*	9090	*8670*	9102	*8682*	9114	*8694*	9126	*8706*	9137	*8717*	9149	*8729*	9161	*8741*	9173	*8753*
33	9037	*8594*	9049	*8606*	9061	*8618*	9072	*8629*	9084	*8641*	9096	*8653*	9108	*8665*	9119	*8676*	9131	*8688*	9143	*8700*
34	9008	*8541*	9019	*8553*	9031	*8564*	9043	*8576*	9054	*8588*	9066	*8599*	9078	*8611*	9089	*8623*	9101	*8634*	9113	*8646*
35	0.8978	*0.8487*	0.8990	*0.8498*	0.9002	*0.8510*	0.9013	*0.8522*	0.9025	*0.8533*	0.9037	*0.8545*	0.9048	*0.8557*	0.9060	*0.8568*	0.9072	*0.8580*	0.9083	*0.8591*
36	8949	*8431*	8961	*8443*	8972	*8455*	8984	*8466*	8996	*8478*	9007	*8489*	9019	*8501*	9031	*8513*	9042	*8524*	9054	*8536*
37	8920	*8375*	8932	*8387*	8943	*8398*	8955	*8410*	8967	*8421*	8978	*8433*	8990	*8445*	9001	*8456*	9013	*8468*	9025	*8479*
38	8892	*8318*	8903	*8329*	8915	*8341*	8926	*8352*	8938	*8364*	8949	*8375*	8961	*8387*	8972	*8399*	8984	*8410*	8995	*8422*
39	8863	*8259*	8875	*8271*	8886	*8282*	8898	*8294*	8909	*8305*	8921	*8317*	8932	*8328*	8944	*8340*	8955	*8351*	8967	*8363*
40	0.8835	*0.8200*	0.8846	*0.8211*	0.8858	*0.8223*	0.8869	*0.8234*	0.8881	*0.8246*	0.8892	*0.8257*	0.8903	*0.8269*	0.8915	*0.8280*	0.8926	*0.8292*	0.8938	*0.8303*
41	8806	*8139*	8818	*8151*	8829	*8162*	8841	*8174*	8852	*8185*	8864	*8196*	8875	*8208*	8887	*8219*	8898	*8231*	8909	*8242*
42	8778	*8077*	8790	*8089*	8801	*8100*	8813	*8112*	8824	*8123*	8835	*8134*	8847	*8146*	8858	*8157*	8870	*8169*	8881	*8180*

mm Hg	780		781		782		783		784		785		786		787		788		789	
°C	dry	*sat.*	dry	*sat.*	dry	*sat.*	dry	*sat.*	dry	*sat.*	dry	*sat.*	dry	*sat.*	dry	*sat.*	dry	*sat.*	dry	*sat.*
0	1.0263	*1.0203*	1.0276	*1.0216*	1.0289	*1.0229*	1.0303	*1.0242*	1.0316	*1.0256*	1.0329	*1.0269*	1.0342	*1.0282*	1.0355	*1.0295*	1.0368	*1.0308*	1.0382	*1.0321*
1	0226	*0161*	0239	*0174*	0252	*0187*	0265	*0200*	0278	*0213*	0291	*0227*	0304	*0240*	0317	*0253*	0331	*0266*	0344	*0279*
2	0188	*0119*	0201	*0132*	0214	*0145*	0228	*0158*	0241	*0171*	0254	*0185*	0267	*0198*	0280	*0211*	0293	*0224*	0306	*0237*
3	0151	*0077*	0164	*0090*	0177	*0103*	0190	*0116*	0203	*0129*	0216	*0142*	0229	*0155*	0242	*0169*	0256	*0182*	0269	*0195*
4	0115	*0036*	0128	*0049*	0141	*0061*	0154	*0074*	0167	*0087*	0180	*0100*	0192	*0113*	0205	*0126*	0218	*0139*	0231	*0152*
5	1.0078	*0.9994*	1.0091	*1.0007*	1.0104	*1.0020*	1.0117	*1.0032*	1.0130	*1.0045*	1.0143	*1.0058*	1.0156	*1.0071*	1.0169	*1.0084*	1.0182	*1.0097*	1.0195	*1.0110*
6	0042	*9952*	0055	*0.9965*	0068	*0.9977*	0081	*0.9990*	0094	*0003*	0106	*0016*	0119	*0029*	0132	*0042*	0145	*0055*	0158	*0068*
7	0006	*9910*	0019	*9923*	0032	*9935*	0045	*9948*	0057	*0.9961*	0070	*0.9974*	0083	*0.9987*	0096	*0000*	0109	*0012*	0122	*0025*
8	0.9970	*9868*	0.9983	*9880*	0.9996	*9893*	0009	*9906*	0022	*9919*	0034	*9932*	0047	*9944*	0060	*0.9957*	0073	*0.9970*	0085	*0.9983*
9	9935	*9825*	9948	*9838*	9960	*9851*	0.9973	*9864*	0.9986	*9876*	0.9999	*9889*	0011	*9902*	0024	*9915*	0037	*9927*	0050	*9940*
10	0.9900	*0.9783*	0.9913	*0.9796*	0.9925	*0.9808*	0.9938	*0.9821*	0.9951	*0.9834*	0.9963	*0.9846*	0.9976	*0.9859*	0.9989	*0.9872*	1.0001	*0.9884*	1.0014	*0.9897*
11	9865	*9740*	9878	*9753*	9890	*9766*	9903	*9778*	9916	*9791*	9928	*9804*	9941	*9816*	9953	*9829*	0.9966	*9842*	0.9979	*9854*
12	9830	*9698*	9843	*9710*	9855	*9723*	9868	*9735*	9881	*9748*	9893	*9761*	9906	*9773*	9918	*9786*	9931	*9799*	9944	*9811*
13	9796	*9655*	9808	*9667*	9821	*9680*	9833	*9692*	9846	*9705*	9859	*9718*	9871	*9730*	9884	*9743*	9896	*9755*	9909	*9768*
14	9762	*9612*	9774	*9624*	9787	*9637*	9799	*9649*	9812	*9662*	9824	*9674*	9837	*9687*	9849	*9699*	9862	*9712*	9874	*9724*
15	0.9728	*0.9568*	0.9740	*0.9581*	0.9753	*0.9593*	0.9765	*0.9606*	0.9778	*0.9618*	0.9790	*0.9631*	0.9802	*0.9643*	0.9815	*0.9655*	0.9827	*0.9668*	0.9840	*0.9680*
16	9694	*9524*	9706	*9537*	9719	*9549*	9731	*9562*	9744	*9574*	9756	*9587*	9768	*9599*	9781	*9611*	9793	*9624*	9806	*9636*
17	9660	*9480*	9673	*9493*	9685	*9505*	9698	*9518*	9710	*9530*	9722	*9542*	9735	*9555*	9747	*9567*	9760	*9580*	9772	*9592*
18	9627	*9436*	9640	*9449*	9652	*9461*	9664	*9473*	9677	*9486*	9689	*9498*	9701	*9510*	9714	*9523*	9726	*9535*	9738	*9547*
19	9594	*9391*	9606	*9404*	9619	*9416*	9631	*9428*	9643	*9441*	9656	*9453*	9668	*9465*	9680	*9478*	9693	*9490*	9705	*9502*
20	0.9561	*0.9346*	0.9574	*0.9359*	0.9586	*0.9371*	0.9598	*0.9383*	0.9610	*0.9395*	0.9623	*0.9408*	0.9635	*0.9420*	0.9647	*0.9432*	0.9659	*0.9444*	0.9672	*0.9457*
21	9529	*9301*	9541	*9313*	9553	*9325*	9565	*9338*	9578	*9350*	9590	*9362*	9602	*9374*	9614	*9386*	9627	*9399*	9639	*9411*
22	9496	*9255*	9509	*9267*	9521	*9279*	9533	*9292*	9545	*9304*	9557	*9316*	9569	*9328*	9582	*9340*	9594	*9352*	9606	*9365*
23	9464	*9209*	9476	*9221*	9489	*9233*	9501	*9245*	9513	*9257*	9525	*9269*	9537	*9281*	9549	*9294*	9561	*9306*	9573	*9318*
24	9432	*9162*	9444	*9174*	9457	*9186*	9469	*9198*	9481	*9210*	9493	*9222*	9505	*9234*	9517	*9246*	9529	*9258*	9541	*9271*
25	0.9401	*0.9114*	0.9413	*0.9126*	0.9425	*0.9138*	0.9437	*0.9150*	0.9449	*0.9163*	0.9461	*0.9175*	0.9473	*0.9187*	0.9485	*0.9199*	0.9497	*0.9211*	0.9509	*0.9223*
26	9369	*9066*	9381	*9078*	9393	*9090*	9405	*9102*	9417	*9114*	9429	*9126*	9441	*9138*	9453	*9150*	9465	*9162*	9477	*9174*
27	9338	*9018*	9350	*9030*	9362	*9042*	9374	*9054*	9386	*9066*	9398	*9078*	9410	*9090*	9422	*9102*	9434	*9114*	9446	*9126*
28	9307	*8969*	9319	*8980*	9331	*8992*	9343	*9004*	9355	*9016*	9366	*9028*	9378	*9040*	9390	*9052*	9402	*9064*	9414	*9076*
29	9276	*8919*	9288	*8931*	9300	*8942*	9312	*8954*	9323	*8966*	9335	*8978*	9347	*8990*	9359	*9002*	9371	*9014*	9383	*9026*
30	0.9245	*0.8868*	0.9257	*0.8880*	0.9269	*0.8892*	0.9281	*0.8904*	0.9293	*0.8915*	0.9305	*0.8927*	0.9316	*0.8939*	0.9328	*0.8951*	0.9340	*0.8963*	0.9352	*0.8975*
31	9215	*8817*	9227	*8829*	9238	*8840*	9250	*8852*	9262	*8864*	9274	*8876*	9286	*8888*	9297	*8899*	9309	*8911*	9321	*8923*
32	9185	*8765*	9196	*8776*	9208	*8788*	9220	*8800*	9232	*8812*	9243	*8823*	9255	*8835*	9267	*8847*	9279	*8859*	9291	*8871*
33	9154	*8712*	9166	*8723*	9178	*8735*	9190	*8747*	9201	*8759*	9213	*8770*	9225	*8782*	9237	*8794*	9248	*8806*	9260	*8817*
34	9125	*8658*	9136	*8670*	9148	*8681*	9160	*8693*	9171	*8705*	9183	*8716*	9195	*8728*	9206	*8740*	9218	*8751*	9230	*8763*
35	0.9095	*0.8603*	0.9107	*0.8615*	0.9118	*0.8626*	0.9130	*0.8638*	0.9142	*0.8650*	0.9153	*0.8661*	0.9165	*0.8673*	0.9177	*0.8685*	0.9188	*0.8696*	0.9200	*0.8708*
36	9065	*8548*	9077	*8559*	9089	*8571*	9100	*8582*	9112	*8594*	9124	*8606*	9135	*8617*	9147	*8629*	9158	*8640*	9170	*8652*
37	9036	*8491*	9048	*8502*	9059	*8514*	9071	*8526*	9082	*8537*	9094	*8549*	9106	*8560*	9117	*8572*	9129	*8584*	9140	*8595*
38	9007	*8433*	9019	*8445*	9030	*8456*	9042	*8468*	9053	*8479*	9065	*8491*	9076	*8503*	9088	*8514*	9099	*8526*	9111	*8537*
39	8978	*8374*	8990	*8386*	9001	*8398*	9013	*8409*	9024	*8421*	9036	*8432*	9047	*8444*	9059	*8455*	9070	*8467*	9082	*8478*
40	0.8949	*0.8315*	0.8961	*0.8326*	0.8972	*0.8338*	0.8984	*0.8349*	0.8995	*0.8361*	0.9007	*0.8372*	0.9018	*0.8383*	0.9030	*0.8395*	0.9041	*0.8406*	0.9053	*0.8418*
41	8921	*8254*	8932	*8265*	8944	*8276*	8955	*8288*	8967	*8299*	8978	*8311*	8989	*8322*	9001	*8334*	9012	*8345*	9024	*8357*
42	8892	*8191*	8904	*8203*	8915	*8214*	8927	*8226*	8938	*8237*	8949	*8248*	8961	*8260*	8972	*8271*	8984	*8283*	8995	*8294*

The vital functions of highly developed organisms are closely dependent on the internal aqueous medium and on the maintenance in it of extreme constancy of chemical and physical properties. For the physician a knowledge of some of the properties of aqueous solutions is therefore essential to an understanding of water and electrolyte balance and how it may be modified clinically.

In spite of the advances made in physical chemistry there remain considerable gaps in our knowledge of aqueous solutions. The properties of solutions with concentrations up to 0.01 mol/kg can now be calculated with great accuracy, but for solutions of higher concentration it is necessary to introduce empirical correction factors in order to reconcile measured with theoretical values. In biology and medicine, however, this is of little importance since the approximate formulae derived from theory are sufficiently accurate for most practical purposes.

This section should be read in conjunction with the tables on pages 272–276 and with the chapter 'Water and Electrolyte Balance' (pages 523–530).

Definitions of the concepts atom, molecule and ion

A molecule of a substance is that group of elementary particles existing as kinetic unit in the gaseous phase of the substance at low concentration. The number of molecules per unit volume and their kinetic energy determine the mechanical and thermal properties of ideal gases. Molecules can be made up of one kind of element only or of various elements in combination. The smallest part of an element identifiable in compounds of which the element forms a part is known as an atom.

The 'chemical bonds' binding atoms together to form molecules are usually more than one order of magnitude stronger than the attractive forces between molecules. For this reason the molecules of a substance are often recognizable as units even in the condensed state. This does not apply, however, to many groups of substances, in particular metals and salts; here the term molecule is used in the purely formal sense as the sum of the atoms given in the empirical formula.

Salts are not made up of atoms bound together by orientated forces but of electrically charged atoms – known as ions – situated at the centre of a spherically symmetrical electric field. Atoms are transformed into positive ions (cations) by loss of electrons and into negative ions (anions) by capture of electrons. Since the chemical properties of a particle are determined by the number of electrons it possesses, the properties of ions are completely different from those of the corresponding atoms.

Electrolytes

When an electric current is passed through a salt or its solution in water (or other polar solvent) chemical changes occur at the places where the current enters and leaves (the electrodes). This process is known as electrolysis, a substance undergoing it as an electrolyte. Current passing through an electrolyte is carried by material particles, the ions. Positively charged ions (cations), which migrate in the electric field to the cathode, are indicated by one or more plus signs, depending on their valency, placed after their symbol; in the same way negatively charged ions (anions), which migrate to the anode, are indicated by minus signs (for example, magnesium ion = Mg^{++}, nitrate ion = NO_3^-).

That the ions already exist in the solution and are not formed when the electric field is applied can be demonstrated by measuring properties dependent only on the number of particles present in the solution, such as osmotic pressure, freezing-point depression, etc. (see below). The dissolution of a salt is therefore understood as the statistical distribution of the positive and negative ions forming the solid crystal lattice. This separation of oppositely charged particles is made easier by (1) a higher dielectric constant of the solvent, and (2) a stronger ion–dipole interaction between the ions of the solute and the polar molecules of the solvent (known as solvation or, for water, hydration of the ions). In respect of both (1) and (2) water occupies an almost unique position among solvents.

A solution in which the solute consists of (solvated or hydrated) ions is known as a 'strong' electrolyte (the term electrolyte is also used to describe the solute itself). If ν is the number of ions into which such a solute dissociates, then n mole (see page 226) of the solute will form $n\nu$ mole of particles in solution (positive and negative ions together). Thus for NaCl $\nu = 2$, for $CaCl_2$ $\nu = 3$, while for $K_3Fe(CN)_6$ $\nu = 4$ since $[Fe(CN)_6]^{---}$ is a single complex ion.

Other substances dissociate in solution partly into ions and partly into molecules. These and their solutions are known as 'weak' electrolytes. They include particularly the weak acids and bases (almost all organic acids and bases, carbonic acid, hydrogen sulphide, etc.). The fraction of the total number of molecules dissociated into ions is known as the degree of dissociation α. Dissolution of n mole of a weak electrolyte results in the formation of n $(\nu\alpha + 1 - \alpha)$ mole of particles. The degree of dissociation α depends to a great extent on the concentration of the solution: the weaker the solution the more complete the dissociation and the closer the degree of dissociation approaches to unity.

Ideal dilute solutions

The thermodynamic treatment of dilute solutions makes use of the concept of the ideal dilute solution. This is a solution in which the molecules of the solute are completely surrounded by solvent molecules, so that any further addition of solvent results in no further interactions between solvent and solute. Under these conditions the properties of the solvent molecules in the solution depend only on the number of dissolved particles and not on their individual properties. Thus the lowering of the vapour pressure of the solvent due to the presence of the solute is proportional to the molar concentration of the solute, and the same applies to the osmotic pressure, freezing-point depression and boiling-point elevation.

The osmotic pressure and freezing-point depression of an ideal dilute aqueous solution are expressed as follows:

$$\text{\textit{Osmotic pressure} (ideal) in atm} = P_{id} = 0.082055 \times T \times \frac{M}{V_m} \times m_2 \times \nu \qquad (1)$$

$$\text{\textit{Freezing-point depression} (ideal) in °C} = \Delta T_{id} = 1.86 \times m_2 \times \nu \qquad (2)$$

where 0.082055 = the gas constant R in litre atmosphere; T = absolute temperature in kelvin (K) = 273.15 + °C; 1.86 = the cryoscopic constant (molal freezing-point depression of water); m_2 = molality of the solute (number of moles of undissociated solute per 1000 g water); ν = number of particles into which the solute dissociates at complete dissociation (to be replaced by the factor $\nu\alpha + 1 - \alpha$ when dissociation is not complete); M/V_m = ratio of molar mass to molar volume for water (= 1 at a good approximation). For osmotic pressure and freezing-point depression data for osmotic concentrations of 10–740 mmol/1000 g water see page 272.

From (1) and (2) it follows that

$$P_{(atm)} = 0.0441 \times T \times \Delta T \qquad (3)$$

$$\text{or } P_{(atm,\ at\ 0\,°C)} = 12.05 \times \Delta T \qquad (4)$$

In contrast to (1) and (2), equations (3) and (4) are valid for a wider range of concentrations than those to which the concept of the ideal dilute solution applies, and for this reason the symbols P and ΔT do not bear the index $_{id}$ (ideal).

Real solutions

The higher the solute concentration the wider the solution diverges from the concept of the ideal dilute solution. This divergence can be compensated for by means of a correction factor known as the osmotic coefficient g (= 1 for ideal dilute solutions). At any given concentration a real solution diverges the more widely from the ideal solution the stronger the interactions between the particles in it. For ionic solutions the coefficient g is therefore greater than for solutions of undissociated molecules, and for solutions containing multivalent ions it is particularly large.

For very dilute ionic solutions the coefficient g can be calculated by means of the Debye-Hückel limiting law. Experimentally, it can be obtained from the relationship

$$g = \frac{\Delta T}{\Delta T_{id}} = \frac{\Delta T}{1.86\, m_2 \nu} \qquad (5)$$

where ΔT is the measured freezing-point depression. Most reference books (*International Critical Tables*, *Handbook of Chemistry and Physics*, *Landolt-Börnstein*, etc.) give the latter as a function of the molality m_2, whence g can be obtained by dividing by 1.86 ν in accordance with (5).

In solutions of weak electrolytes the osmotic properties (freezing-point depression, osmotic pressure, etc.) depend mainly on the number of particles, which is a function of the concentration, in other words, they vary with the degree of dissociation α. In this case the divergence from the ideal dilute solution is of importance only in very precise physicochemical measurements, particularly as the ionic concentration remains low.

Measures of concentration

The concentration of a dilute solution is usually expressed as its molality (mole per 1000 g solvent) or molarity (mole per 1000 ml solution, analogous with the normality).

The use of 1000 ml solution as reference unit has great advantages in volumetric analysis but also the disadvantage of being temperature-dependent (see page 251). Giving concentrations in equivalents instead of moles (normality instead of molarity) is always necessary when valency or valency change is involved, particularly in acid–base reactions, oxidations and reductions, but it should be borne in mind that the normality of a solution can differ in different types of reaction (data on decinormal solutions for titrimetric analysis are given on page 277).

Freezing-point depression data are always given for concentrations expressed as molality.

In extremely dilute aqueous solutions the molality and molarity can be assumed to be equal; with rising concentration they deviate more and more to an extent depending on the specific volume of the solute(s). Thus the molarity of serum differs from its molality owing to the high specific volume of proteins. In order to calculate the molality of any particular serum component, its concentration, e.g., in mg/l serum, must be converted into its concentration in the serum water.

This conversion can be made by means of either the specific gravity or the protein content of serum. The former method is the more accurate and the appropriate factors are given on page 557. On the basis of protein content the conversion is made by means of the following formula[1]:

$$\text{Water content of serum in g/l serum} = 984.0 - \left(\begin{matrix}0.718 \times \text{protein content}\\ \text{in g/l serum}\end{matrix}\right) \qquad \textbf{(6)}$$

(The figure of 984 instead of 1000 represents a correction for the volume occupied by inorganic and other constituents.)

Example. The freezing-point depression of serum is 0.56 °C, corresponding to a molality of 300 mmol (300 mmol/1000 g water). The molarity of a normal serum is accordingly 300 × 0.940 = 282 mmol/l serum (table on page 557, factor in column 3 divided by 1000, specific gravity 1.026).

In the following only the molality will be used. It should be noted that molality and molarity are sometimes confused even by reputable authors, so that it is advisable always to examine carefully what is meant by the expression 'molarity' in any particular case.

In order to avoid this confusion the molarity and molality should always be related to the *undissociated* solute; otherwise they should be clearly specified, for instance 'the molality of all osmotically active particles'.

Osmolarity, osmolality

These terms indicate respectively the molarity and molality an ideal solution of a non-dissociating substance must possess in order to exert the same osmotic pressure as the solution under consideration. Osmolarity and osmolality are not used in the physicochemical field but find considerable application in the sphere of biology and medicine[2]. As is clear from the definition, the (real) osmolality is a quantity capable of experimental determination. It can also be calculated from the molality of the solution provided (1) the number of molecular fragments (for weak electrolytes the degree of dissociation α) and (2) the correction factor (osmotic coefficient g) from the ideal to the real state are known.

If weak electrolytes are excluded, the ideal osmolality can be obtained by multiplying the molality by the number of molecular fragments. Multiplication of this by the osmotic coefficient g gives the (real) osmolality as defined above:

$$\text{ideal osmolality} = m_2\,\nu \qquad \textbf{(7)}$$

$$\text{(real) osmolality} = \text{ideal osmolality} \times g = m_2\,\nu\,g = \Delta T/1.86 \qquad \textbf{(8)}$$

For mixed solutions $m_2\nu$ is replaced by the sum $\sum_{i=2}^{n} m_i\nu_i = m_2\nu_2 + m_3\nu_3 + \ldots$ for each of the component solutes. For the sake of simplicity it is assumed that there is no change in the osmotic coefficient when passing from a simple to a mixed solution.

In analogy with the mole, the unit of osmolarity and osmolality is the osmole (osm).

Applications

To obtain freezing-point depression and osmotic pressure from osmolality see the table on page 272.

Osmolality of blood serum from freezing-point depression (0.56 °C) (table on page 272)

Columns 5 and 6 of the table show that the (real) osmolality of serum is 302.1 mmol.

Sodium chloride and glucose solutions (table on page 273)

(*a*) *The weights* of NaCl and glucose (or fructose) *corresponding to given ideal osmolalities* are obtained from columns 1/2 and 1/6. Column 7 gives the corresponding calorific values for glucose and fructose.

(*b*) *The ideal osmolalities corresponding to given weights* of NaCl and glucose (or fructose) are obtained from columns 11/12 and 11/13. The corresponding calorific values for glucose and fructose are given in column 14.

(*c*) *The osmotic coefficient* g (or $1/g$) is obtained for NaCl from columns 1/4 (or 1/5) and for glucose from columns 1/9 (or 1/10), the values in column 1 in this case being read as real osmolalities.

Example 1. Required is the weight of NaCl necessary to yield a solution with a real osmolality of 500 mmol.

From equation **(7)** the ideal osmolality = real osmolality/g = 500/0.9180 = 500 × 1.0893 = 544.65 mmol. The corresponding weight of NaCl from (*a*) above lies between 15.780 and 16.072 at ca. 15.9 g. This is therefore the quantity of NaCl which must be dissolved in 1000 g water in order to yield an osmolality of 500 mmol.

The inconvenience of first calculating the ideal osmolality can be avoided by calculating the required weight direct from column 2 (for NaCl) or column 6 (for glucose). To do this, the weight given in column 2 obtained by entering the real osmolality in column 1 is multiplied by the corresponding value for $1/g$. The above example, with a real osmolality of 500 mmol, thus gives the result: 14.611 × 1.0893 = 15.916 g NaCl.

Example 2. It is required to increase to 500 mmol the osmolality of a solution of 400 mmol by addition of NaCl. Here the calculation is simplified by assuming that the factor g does not change when the solution becomes a mixed solution. $1/g$ for NaCl for 500 mmol/1000 g water is 1.0893. Since 100 mmol are to be added by means of NaCl, the required weight (see example 1) is 2.922 × 1.0893 = 3.183 g NaCl.

(*d*) *Isotonic solutions.* The concentrations required to yield these can be calculated as in examples 1 and 2 or simply read off from the table in columns 1/3 (NaCl) and 1/8 (glucose).

Example 1. In order to obtain an isotonic NaCl or glucose solution (osmolality 300 mmol), 9.463 g NaCl or 53.312 g glucose must be dissolved in 1000 g water.

Example 2. It is required to render a solution of osmolality 200 mmol isotonic with serum by addition of NaCl, i.e., to increase the osmolality to 300 mmol. Since the additional osmolality is 100 mmol (column 1) the necessary weight of NaCl is 3.154 g (column 3). The figure for glucose can be calculated in a similar manner.

References

1 Welt, L. G., in Duncan, G. G. (Ed.), *Diseases of Metabolism*, 5th ed., Saunders, Philadelphia, 1964, page 449.

2 Netter, H., *Theoretische Biochemie*, Springer, Berlin, 1959, page 108.

Aqueous Solutions – Calculation of Freezing-point Depression and Osmotic Pressure

(For explanation see pages 270–271)

Real osmolality (mmol/1000 g water)	Freezing-point depression (Δ T °C)	Osmotic pressure at 0 °C (atm)	Osmotic pressure at 38 °C* (atm)	Freezing-point depression (Δ T °C)	Real osmolality (mmol/1000 g water)	Osmotic pressure at 0 °C (atm)	Osmotic pressure at 38 °C* (atm)
1	2	3	4	5	6	7	8
10	0.019	0.22	0.26	0.01	5.4	0.12	0.14
20	0.037	0.45	0.51	02	10.7	0.24	0.28
30	0.056	0.67	0.77	03	16.1	0.36	0.41
40	0.074	0.90	1.01	04	21.5	0.48	0.55
50	0.093	1.12	1.27	0.05	26.9	0.60	0.69
60	0.112	1.35	1.52	06	32.3	0.72	0.82
70	0.130	1.57	1.78	07	37.6	0.84	0.95
80	0.149	1.79	2.03	08	43.0	0.97	1.09
90	0.167	2.02	2.28	09	48.4	1.09	1.23
100	0.186	2.24	2.54	**0.10**	53.8	1.21	1.37
10	0.205	2.47	2.79	11	59.2	1.33	1.50
20	0.223	2.69	3.05	12	64.6	1.45	1.64
30	0.242	2.91	3.30	13	70.0	1.57	1.78
40	0.260	3.14	3.55	14	75.3	1.69	1.92
50	0.279	3.36	3.80	0.15	80.7	1.81	2.05
60	0.297	3.59	4.06	16	86.1	1.93	2.18
70	0.316	3.81	4.31	17	91.5	2.05	2.32
80	0.334	4.03	4.57	18	96.9	2.17	2.46
90	0.353	4.26	4.83	19	102.3	2.29	2.59
200	0.371	4.48	5.07	**0.20**	107.7	2.41	2.73
10	0.390	4.71	5.33	21	113.0	2.53	2.87
20	0.408	4.93	5.58	22	118.4	2.65	3.01
30	0.427	5.16	5.84	23	123.8	2.77	3.14
40	0.445	5.38	6.09	24	129.2	2.89	3.28
50	0.464	5.60	6.34	0.25	134.6	3.02	3.42
60	0.482	5.83	6.59	26	140.0	3.14	3.56
70	0.501	6.05	6.85	27	145.4	3.26	3.68
80	0.519	6.28	7.10	28	150.8	3.38	3.82
90	0.537	6.50	7.36	29	156.2	3.50	3.96
300	0.556	6.72	7.62	**0.30**	161.6	3.62	4.10
10	0.574	6.95	7.87	31	167.0	3.74	4.23
20	0.593	7.17	8.12	32	172.4	3.86	4.37
30	0.611	7.40	8.37	33	177.8	3.98	4.51
40	0.630	7.62	8.63	34	183.2	4.10	4.65
50	0.648	7.84	8.88	0.35	188.6	4.23	4.78
60	0.667	8.07	9.14	36	194.0	4.35	4.92
70	0.685	8.29	9.39	37	199.4	4.47	5.06
80	0.704	8.52	9.64	38	204.8	4.59	5.20
90	0.722	8.74	9.90	39	210.2	4.71	5.33
400	0.741	8.97	10.15	**0.40**	215.5	4.84	5.47
10	0.759	9.19	10.40	41	220.9	4.96	5.61
20	0.778	9.41	10.66	42	226.3	5.08	5.75
30	0.796	9.64	10.92	43	231.8	5.20	5.88
40	0.815	9.86	11.16	44	237.2	5.32	6.02
50	0.833	10.09	11.42	0.45	242.6	5.44	6.16
60	0.851	10.31	11.67	46	248.0	5.56	6.30
70	0.870	10.53	11.93	47	253.4	5.68	6.43
80	0.887	10.76	12.17	48	258.8	5.80	6.57
90	0.906	10.98	12.43	49	264.2	5.92	6.71
500	0.925	11.21	12.69	**0.50**	269.6	6.04	6.85
10	0.943	11.43	12.94	51	275.0	6.16	6.98
20	0.962	11.66	13.20	52	280.4	6.28	7.11
30	0.980	11.88	13.45	53	285.8	6.40	7.25
40	0.998	12.10	13.70	54	291.2	6.52	7.39
50	1.017	12.33	13.95	0.55	296.7	6.64	7.53
60	1.035	12.55	14.21	56	302.1	6.77	7.66
70	1.054	12.78	14.47	57	307.5	6.89	7.80
80	1.072	13.00	14.72	58	312.9	7.02	7.94
90	1.090	13.22	14.97	59	318.3	7.14	8.07
600	1.109	13.45	15.22	**0.60**	323.7	7.26	8.21
10	1.127	13.67	15.48	61	329.2	7.38	8.35
20	1.146	13.90	15.73	62	334.6	7.49	8.49
30	1.164	14.12	15.99	63	340.0	7.62	8.62
40	1.182	14.34	16.24	64	345.4	7.74	8.76
50	1.201	14.57	16.49	0.65	350.8	7.86	8.90
60	1.219	14.79	16.75	66	356.2	7.98	9.04
70	1.238	15.02	17.00	67	361.6	8.10	9.17
80	1.256	15.24	17.26	68	367.0	8.22	9.31
90	1.274	15.47	17.51	69	372.5	8.34	9.45
700	1.292	15.69	17.77	**0.70**	377.9	8.47	9.59
10	1.311	15.91	18.01	71	383.3	8.59	9.72
20	1.329	16.14	18.27	72	388.7	8.71	9.86
30	1.347	16.36	18.52	73	394.2	8.84	10.00
40	1.365	16.59	18.78	74	399.6	8.96	10.14

* Normal blood temperature = ca. 38 °C = 311.15 K.

(For explanation see page 271)

Values in columns 3–5 and 8–10 have been calculated for the osmolalities in column 1 read as real osmotic concentrations (millimoles or grammes per 1000 g water). The osmotic coefficients *g* have been obtained by interpolation from the data of Scatchard and Prentiss, *J. Amer. chem. Soc.*, **55**, 4355 (1933), for NaCl and Roth, W. A., *Z. phys. Chem.*, **43**, 539 (1903), for glucose

	Common salt (NaCl, mol. wt. 58.443)				D-Glucose* ($C_6H_{12}O_6$, mol. wt. 180.16)						Common salt (NaCl)	D-Glucose* ($C_6H_{12}O_6$)	
Osmolality (ideal)	Corresponds to a weight of	Weight necessary when the mmol in column 1 are required to be added to bring the total osmolality to 300 mmol	Osmotic coefficient corresponding to the osmolality in column 1 read as real osmolality		Corresponds to a weight of	Corresponds to a calorific value of	Weight necessary when the mmol in column 1 are required to be added to bring the total osmolality to 300 mmol	Osmotic coefficient corresponding to the osmolality in column 1 read as real osmolality			Corresponds to an ideal osmolality of	Corresponds to an ideal osmolality of	Corresponds to a calorific value of
mmol	g	g	*g*	1/*g*	g	cal**	g	*g*	1/*g*	g	mmol	mmol	cal**
1	2	3	4	5	6	7	8	9	10	11	12	13	14
10	0.292	0.315	0.9778	1.0227	1.802	7.53	1.777	1.0005	0.9995	1	34.22	5.55	4.18
20	0.584	0.630	0.9703	1.0306	3.603	15.07	3.554	1.0009	0.9991	2	68.44	11.10	8.36
30	0.877	0.947	0.9653	1.0359	5.405	22.60	5.331	1.0014	0.9986	3	102.66	16.65	12.55
40	1.169	1.262	0.9612	1.0404	7.206	30.14	7.108	1.0018	0.9982	4	136.89	22.20	16.73
50	1.461	1.577	0.9579	1.0440	9.008	37.67	8.885	1.0023	0.9977	5	171.11	27.75	20.91
60	1.753	1.892	0.9550	1.0471	10.810	45.21	10.662	1.0028	0.9972	6	205.33	33.30	25.09
70	2.046	2.208	0.9525	1.0499	12.611	52.74	12.439	1.0032	0.9968	7	239.55	38.85	29.27
80	2.338	2.524	0.9503	1.0523	14.413	60.27	14.217	1.0037	0.9963	8	273.77	44.41	33.46
90	2.630	2.839	0.9482	1.0546	16.214	67.81	15.994	1.0041	0.9959	9	307.99	49.96	37.64
100	2.922	3.154	0.9463	1.0567	18.016	75.34	17.771	1.0046	0.9954	**10**	342.22	55.51	41.82
10	3.214	3.469	0.9448	1.0584	19.818	82.88	19.548	1.0051	0.9949	11	376.44	61.06	46.00
20	3.507	3.785	0.9432	1.0602	21.619	90.41	21.325	1.0055	0.9945	12	410.66	66.61	50.18
30	3.799	4.101	0.9418	1.0618	23.421	97.95	23.102	1.0060	0.9940	13	444.88	72.16	54.37
40	4.091	4.416	0.9405	1.0633	25.222	105.48	24.879	1.0064	0.9936	14	479.10	77.71	58.55
50	4.383	4.731	0.9392	1.0647	27.024	113.01	26.656	1.0069	0.9931	15	513.32	83.26	62.73
60	4.675	5.047	0.9380	1.0661	28.826	120.55	28.433	1.0074	0.9927	16	547.54	88.81	66.91
70	4.968	5.362	0.9368	1.0675	30.627	128.08	30.210	1.0078	0.9923	17	581.77	94.36	71.09
80	5.260	5.678	0.9357	1.0687	32.429	135.62	31.987	1.0083	0.9918	18	615.99	99.91	75.28
90	5.552	5.993	0.9347	1.0699	34.230	143.15	33.764	1.0087	0.9914	19	650.21	105.46	79.46
200	5.844	6.308	0.9337	1.0710	36.032	150.68	35.541	1.0092	0.9909	**20**	684.43	111.01	83.64
10	6.137	6.624	0.9328	1.0720	37.834	158.22	37.318	1.0097	0.9904	21	718.65	116.56	87.82
20	6.429	6.939	0.9319	1.0731	39.635	165.75	39.096	1.0101	0.9900	22	752.87	122.11	92.00
30	6.721	7.255	0.9311	1.0740	41.437	173.29	40.873	1.0106	0.9895	23	787.09	127.66	96.19
40	7.013	7.570	0.9304	1.0748	43.238	180.82	42.650	1.0110	0.9891	24	821.32	133.22	100.37
50	7.305	7.885	0.9297	1.0756	45.040	188.36	44.427	1.0115	0.9886	25	855.54	138.77	104.55
60	7.598	8.201	0.9290	1.0764	46.842	195.89	46.204	1.0120	0.9881	26	889.76	144.32	108.73
70	7.890	8.516	0.9283	1.0772	48.643	203.43	47.981	1.0124	0.9878	27	923.98	149.87	112.91
80	8.182	8.832	0.9276	1.0780	50.445	210.96	49.758	1.0129	0.9873	28	958.20	155.42	117.10
90	8.474	9.147	0.9270	1.0787	52.246	218.49	51.535	1.0133	0.9869	29	992.42	160.97	121.28
300	8.766	9.463	0.9264	1.0794	54.048	226.03	53.312	1.0138	0.9864	**30**	1026.65	166.52	125.46
10	9.059		0.9258	1.0801	55.850	233.56		1.0143	0.9859	31	1060.87	172.06	129.64
20	9.351		0.9252	1.0808	57.651	241.10		1.0147	0.9855	32	1095.09	177.62	133.82
30	9.643		0.9246	1.0815	59.453	248.63		1.0152	0.9850	33	1129.31	183.17	138.01
40	9.935		0.9241	1.0821	61.254	256.17		1.0156	0.9846	34	1163.53	188.72	142.19
50	10.228		0.9236	1.0827	63.056	263.70		1.0161	0.9842	35	1197.75	194.27	146.37
60	10.520		0.9232	1.0832	64.858	271.23		1.0166	0.9837	36	1231.97	199.82	150.55
70	10.812		0.9227	1.0838	66.659	278.77		1.0170	0.9833	37	1266.20	205.37	154.73
80	11.104		0.9223	1.0842	68.461	286.30		1.0175	0.9828	38	1300.42	210.92	158.92
90	11.396		0.9219	1.0847	70.262	293.84		1.0179	0.9824	39	1334.64	216.47	163.10
400	11.689		0.9215	1.0852	72.064	301.37		1.0183	0.9820	**40**	1368.86	222.03	167.28
10	11.981		0.9211	1.0857	73.866	308.91		1.0187	0.9816	41	1403.08	227.58	171.46
20	12.273		0.9207	1.0861	75.667	316.44		1.0192	0.9812	42	1437.30	233.13	175.64
30	12.565		0.9204	1.0864	77.469	323.98		1.0196	0.9808	43	1471.52	238.68	179.82
40	12.857		0.9200	1.0868	79.270	331.51		1.0201	0.9803	44	1505.75	244.23	184.00
50	13.150		0.9196	1.0874	81.072	339.04		1.0205	0.9799	45	1539.97	249.78	188.19
60	13.442		0.9192	1.0878	82.874	346.58		1.0209	0.9795	46	1574.19	255.33	192.37
70	13.734		0.9189	1.0882	84.675	354.11		1.0214	0.9790	47	1608.41	260.88	196.55
80	14.026		0.9185	1.0887	86.477	361.64		1.0218	0.9787	48	1642.63	266.43	200.74
90	14.319		0.9182	1.0891	88.278	369.18		1.0222	0.9783	49	1676.85	271.98	204.92
500	14.611		0.9180	1.0893	90.080	376.72		1.0226	0.9779	**50**	1711.08	277.53	209.10
10	14.903		0.9177	1.0897	91.882	384.25		1.0230	0.9775	51	1745.30	283.08	213.28
20	15.195		0.9174	1.0900	93.683	391.78		1.0234	0.9771	52	1779.52	288.63	217.46
30	15.487		0.9172	1.0903	95.485	399.32		1.0238	0.9767	53	1813.74	294.18	221.65
40	15.780		0.9170	1.0905	97.286	406.85		1.0242	0.9764	54	1847.96	299.73	225.82
50	16.072		0.9167	1.0908	99.088	414.39		1.0245	0.9761	55	1882.18	305.28	230.01
60	16.364		0.9165	1.0911	100.890	421.92		1.0249	0.9757	56	1916.40	310.84	234.19
70	16.656		0.9163	1.0913	102.691	429.45		1.0253	0.9753	57	1950.63	316.39	238.37
80	16.948		0.9161	1.0916	104.493	436.98		1.0256	0.9750	58	1984.85	321.94	242.56
90	17.241		0.9159	1.0918	106.294	444.52		1.0260	0.9747	59	2019.07	327.49	246.73
600	17.533		0.9157	1.0921	108.096	452.06		1.0263	0.9744	**60**	2053.29	333.04	250.92
10	17.825		0.9155	1.0923	109.898	459.59		1.0267	0.9740	61	2087.51	338.59	255.10
20	18.117		0.9153	1.0925	111.699	467.13		1.0270	0.9737	62	2121.73	344.14	259.28
30	18.410		0.9152	1.0927	113.501	474.66		1.0273	0.9734	63	2155.95	349.69	263.47
40	18.702		0.9150	1.0929	115.302	482.19		1.0276	0.9731	64	2190.18	355.24	267.65
50	18.994		0.9148	1.0931	117.104	489.73		1.0279	0.9729	65	2224.40	360.79	271.83
60	19.286		0.9146	1.0934	118.906	497.26		1.0282	0.9726	66	2258.62	366.34	276.01
70	19.578		0.9145	1.0935	120.707	504.80		1.0285	0.9723	67	2292.84	371.89	280.19
80	19.871		0.9144	1.0936	122.509	512.33		1.0288	0.9720	68	2327.06	377.44	284.38
90	20.163		0.9142	1.0938	124.310	519.87		1.0291	0.9717	69	2361.28	382.99	288.56
700	20.455		0.9140	1.0941	126.112	527.40		1.0293	0.9715	**70**	2395.51	388.55	292.74
10	20.747		0.9139	1.0942	127.914	534.93		1.0296	0.9713	71	2429.73	394.09	296.92
20	21.039		0.9137	1.0945	129.715	542.47		1.0298	0.9711	72	2463.95	399.65	301.10
30	21.332		0.9135	1.0947	131.517	550.00		1.0300	0.9709	73	2498.17	405.20	305.29
40	21.624		0.9134	1.0948	133.318	557.54		1.0302	0.9707	74	2532.39	410.75	309.47

Column 3 (below 300): These values are obtained by dividing the values in column 2 by 0.926 4 or multiplying them by 1.079 4 (*g* or 1/*g* for NaCl at an osmolality of 300 mmol or mosm).

Column 8 (below 300): These values are obtained by dividing the values in column 6 by 1.013 8 or multiplying them by 0.986 4 (*g* or 1/*g* for glucose at an osmolality of 300 mmol or mosm).

* Since the elementary composition of fructose is the same as that of glucose, columns 6, 7, 13 and 14 can also be used for fructose. Note that the osmotic coefficient *g* for fructose is not the same as that for glucose.

** Loewy's value for the calorific equivalent of carbohydrates (4.182 calories per gramme) has been used.

No.	Electrolyte (data for **1 g** unless otherwise stated)		Molecular weight	Undissociated solute	Solubility† (gramme per 1000 ml water)		Cation			Anion			Milliosmoles††
				mmol	cold	hot	mEq	mg		mEq	mg		
	Calcium (Ca)												
1	acetate	$Ca(C_2H_3O_2)_2 + H_2O$	176.19	5.68	436^{20}	331^{100}	11.35	227	Ca^{++}	11.35	670	$C_2H_3O_2^-$	17.03
2		$Ca(C_2H_3O_2)_2 + 2\,H_2O$	194.20	5.15	459^{0}	411^{80}	10.30	206	Ca^{++}	10.30	608	$C_2H_3O_2^-$	15.45
3	chloride	$CaCl_2 + 2\,H_2O$	147.02	6.80	1812^{60}	2106^{100}	13.60	273	Ca^{++}	13.60	482	Cl^-	20.40
4		$CaCl_2 + 6\,H_2O$	219.08	4.56	1175^{0}	2013^{30}	9.13	183	Ca^{++}	9.13	324	Cl^-	13.69
5	citrate	$Ca_3(C_6H_5O_7)_2 + 4\,H_2O$	570.51	1.75	8.5^{18}	9.6^{23}	10.52	211	Ca^{++}	10.52	663	$C_6H_5O_7^{---}$	8.76
6	D-gluconate	$Ca(C_6H_{11}O_7)_2 + H_2O$	448.40	2.23	33^{15}		4.46	89	Ca^{++}	4.46	870	$C_6H_{11}O_7^-$	6.69
7	lactate	$Ca(C_3H_5O_3)_2 + 5\,H_2O$	308.30	3.24	31^{0}	79^{30}	6.49	130	Ca^{++}	6.49	578	$C_3H_5O_3^-$	9.73
8	laevulinate	$Ca(C_5H_7O_3)_2 + 2\,H_2O$	306.33	3.26	400		6.53	131	Ca^{++}	6.53	752	$C_5H_7O_3^-$	9.79
9	oxide (lime)*	CaO	56.08	17.83	1.31^{10}d	0.7^{80}d	35.66	715	Ca^{++}				
10	phosphate, dibasic	$CaHPO_4 + 2\,H_2O$	172.09	5.81	0.2^{25}	0.75^{100}	11.62	233	Ca^{++}	11.62	558/180	HPO_4^{--} / P	11.62
11	thiosulphate	$CaS_2O_3 + 6\,H_2O$	260.30	3.84	1000^{3}	d	7.68	154	Ca^{++}	7.68	431/246	$S_2O_3^{--}$ / S	7.68
	Chlorine (Cl)												
12	Ammonium chloride	NH_4Cl	53.49	18.69	294^{0}	773^{100}	18.69	337	NH_4^+	18.69	663	Cl^-	37.39
13	Hydrochloric acid (10 % solution)												
	1 g	(0.1 g HCl)	36.46	2.74	∞	∞	2.74	2.8	H^+	2.74	97.2	Cl^-	5.48
	1 ml	(0.1047 g HCl)	36.46	2.87	∞	∞	2.87	2.9	H^+	2.87	101.8	Cl^-	5.74
	See also Calcium (**3, 4**), Magnesium (**14, 15**), Potassium (**22**) and Sodium (**35**)												
	Magnesium (Mg)												
14	chloride	$MgCl_2$	95.21	10.50	542.5^{20}	727^{100}	21.00	255	Mg^{++}	21.0	745	Cl^-	31.50
15		$MgCl_2 + 6\,H_2O$	203.30	4.92	1127^{0}	1559^{100}	9.84	120	Mg^{++}	9.84	349	Cl^-	14.76
16	hydroxide	$Mg(OH)_2$	58.32	17.14	0.009^{18}	0.04^{100}	34.29	417	Mg^{++}				
17	oxide (magnesia)*	MgO	40.30	24.80	0.0062	0.086^{30}	49.60	603	Mg^{++}				
18	sulphate (Epsom salts)	$MgSO_4 + 7\,H_2O$	246.47	4.06	483^{10}	641^{40}	8.11	98.6	Mg^{++}	8.11	390/130	SO_4^{--} / S	8.11
	Phosphorus (P)												
	See Calcium (**10**), Potassium (**26, 27**) and Sodium (**30, 31, 40–42**)												
	Potassium (K)												
19	acetate	$K(C_2H_3O_2)$	98.15	10.19	2530^{20}	4920^{62}	10.19	398	K^+	10.19	602	$C_2H_3O_2^-$	20.38
20	bicarbonate	$KHCO_3$	100.12	9.99	183^{0}	375^{60}	9.99	391	K^+	9.99	609	HCO_3^-	19.98
21	bromide	KBr	119.01	8.40	535^{0}	1040^{100}	8.40	329	K^+	8.40	671	Br^-	16.81
22	chloride	KCl	74.56	13.41	276^{0}	567^{100}	13.41	524	K^+	13.41	476	Cl^-	26.83
23	citrate	$K_3(C_6H_5O_7) + H_2O$	324.42	3.08	1670^{15}	1997^{31}	9.25	362	K^+	9.25	583	$C_6H_5O_7^{---}$	12.33
24	D-gluconate	$K(C_6H_{11}O_7)$	234.25	4.27			4.27	167	K^+	4.27	833	$C_6H_{11}O_7^-$	8.54
25	oxide*	K_2O	94.20	10.62	d	d	21.23	830					
26	phosphate, monobasic	KH_2PO_4	136.09	7.35	330^{25}	v.s.	7.35 7.35	287 7.4	K^+ H^+	14.70	705/228	HPO_4^{--} / P	22.04
27	phosphate, dibasic	K_2HPO_4	174.18	5.74	1670^{20}	v.s.	11.48	449	K^+	11.48	551/178	HPO_4^{--} / P	17.22
	Sodium (Na)												
28	acetate	$Na(C_2H_3O_2) + 3\,H_2O$	136.08	7.35	602^{0}	2306^{60}	7.35	169	Na^+	7.35	434	$C_2H_3O_2^-$	14.70
29	acid citrate	$Na_2H(C_6H_5O_7) + 1\frac{1}{2}\,H_2O$	263.11	3.80	v.s.	v.s.	7.60	175	Na^+	7.60	723	$H(C_6H_5O_7)^{--}$	11.40
							7.60 3.80	175 3.83	Na^+ H^+	11.4	719	$C_6H_5O_7^{---}$	15.20
30	acid phosphate	$NaH_2PO_4 + H_2O$	137.99	7.25	599^{0}	1824^{50}	7.25 7.25	167 7.3	Na^+ H^+	14.49	696/224	HPO_4^{--} / P	21.74
31		$NaH_2PO_4 + 2\,H_2O$	156.01	6.41	753^{0}	1797^{40}	6.41 6.41	147 6.5	Na^+ H^+	12.82	615/199	HPO_4^{--} / P	19.23
32	aminosalicylate	$Na(C_7H_6O_3N) + 2\,H_2O$	211.15	4.74			4.74	109	Na^+	4.74	720	$C_7H_6O_3N^-$	9.47
33	bicarbonate**	$NaHCO_3$	84.01	11.90	69^{0}	164^{60}	11.90	274	Na^+	11.90	726	HCO_3^-	23.81
34	bromide	$NaBr$	102.89	9.72	542^{80}	548^{100}	9.72	223	Na^+	9.72	777	Br^-	19.44
35	chloride (common salt)	$NaCl$	58.44	17.11	357^{0}	398^{100}	17.11	393	Na^+	17.11	607	Cl^-	34.22
36	citrate	$Na_3(C_6H_5O_7) + 2\,H_2O$	294.10	3.40	720^{25}	1670^{100}	10.19	235	Na^+	10.19	643	$C_6H_5O_7^{---}$	13.60
37		$Na_3(C_6H_5O_7) + 5\frac{1}{2}\,H_2O$	357.16	2.80	926^{25}	2500^{100}	8.40	193	Na^+	8.40	529	$C_6H_5O_7^{---}$	11.20
38	lactate**	$Na(C_3H_5O_3)$	112.06	8.92	v.s.		8.92	205	Na^+	8.92	795	$C_3H_5O_3^-$	17.84
39	oxide*	Na_2O	61.98	16.13	d	d	32.26	742	Na^+				
40	phosphate	Na_2HPO_4	141.96	7.04		1022^{100}	14.09	324	Na^+	14.09	676/218	HPO_4^{--} / P	21.13
41		$Na_2HPO_4 + 2\,H_2O$	177.99	5.62	1006^{50}	1290^{90}	11.24	258	Na^+	11.24	539/174	HPO_4^{--} / P	16.85
42		$Na_2HPO_4 + 12\,H_2O$	358.14	2.79	42.1^{0}	525^{30}	5.58	128	Na^+	5.58	268/86.5	HPO_4^{--} / P	8.38
43	salicylate	$Na(C_7H_5O_3)$	160.11	6.25	1110^{15}	1250^{25}	6.25	144	Na^+	6.25	856	$C_7H_5O_3^-$	12.49
44	sulphate (anhydrous)	Na_2SO_4	142.04	7.04	488^{40}	425^{100}	14.08	324	Na^+	14.08	676/226	SO_4^{--} / S	21.12
45	sulphate (Glauber's salt)	$Na_2SO_4 + 10\,H_2O$	322.19	3.10	113^{0}	925^{30}	6.21	143	Na^+	6.21	298/100	SO_4^{--} / S	9.31
46	thiosulphate	$Na_2S_2O_3$	158.11	6.32	525^{0}	2660^{100}	12.65	291	Na^+	12.65	709/406	$S_2O_3^{--}$ / S	18.97
	Sulphur (S)												
	See Calcium (**11**), Magnesium (**18**) and Sodium (**44–46**)												

† The index figures are the temperatures in °C; v.s. = very soluble; d = decomposes.
†† On the assumption of complete dissociation.
* The oxides have been included in view of the continuing use of the older nutritional tables.

** The sodium content of 1 g sodium bicarbonate corresponds to that of 1.33 g sodium lactate. The sodium content of 1 g sodium lactate corresponds to that of 0.75 g sodium bicarbonate.

	Electrolyte (data for **10 mosm of solute*** unless otherwise stated)		Undissociated solute		Cation			Anion		
			g	mmol	mEq	mg		mEq	mg	
	Calcium (Ca)									
1	acetate	$Ca(C_2H_3O_2)_2 + H_2O$	0.587	3⅓	6⅔	134	Ca^{++}	6⅔	394	$C_2H_3O_2^-$
2		$Ca(C_2H_3O_2)_2 + 2\,H_2O$	0.647	3⅓	6⅔	134	Ca^{++}	6⅔	394	$C_2H_3O_2^-$
3	chloride	$CaCl_2 + 2\,H_2O$	0.490	3⅓	6⅔	134	Ca^{++}	6⅔	236	Cl^-
4		$CaCl_2 + 6\,H_2O$	0.730	3⅓	6⅔	134	Ca^{++}	6⅔	236	Cl^-
5	citrate	$Ca_3(C_6H_5O_7)_2 + 4\,H_2O$	1.141	2	12	240	Ca^{++}	12	756	$C_6H_5O_7^{---}$
6	D-gluconate	$Ca(C_6H_{11}O_7)_2 + H_2O$	1.495	3⅓	6⅔	134	Ca^{++}	6⅔	1301	$C_6H_{11}O_7^-$
7	lactate	$Ca(C_3H_5O_3)_2 + 5\,H_2O$	1.028	3⅓	6⅔	134	Ca^{++}	6⅔	594	$C_3H_5O_3^-$
8	laevulinate	$Ca(C_5H_7O_3)_2 + 2\,H_2O$	1.021	3⅓	6⅔	134	Ca^{++}	6⅔	767	$C_5H_7O_3^-$
10	phosphate, dibasic	$CaHPO_4 + 2\,H_2O$	0.860	5	10	200	Ca^{++}	10	480	HPO_4^{--}
									155	P
11	thiosulphate	$CaS_2O_3 + 6\,H_2O$	1.302	5	10	200	Ca^{++}	10	561	$S_2O_3^{--}$
									321	S
	Chlorine (Cl)									
12	Ammonium chloride	NH_4Cl	0.267	5	5	90	NH_4^+	5	177	Cl^-
13	Hydrochloric acid (10 % solution)									
	1 g	(0.1 g HCl/g)	1.823	5	5	5	H^+	5	177	Cl^-
	1 ml	(0.1047 g HCl/ml)	1.741	5	5	5	H^+	5	177	Cl^-
	See also Calcium (**3, 4**), Magnesium (**14, 15**), Potassium (**22**) and Sodium (**35**)									
	Magnesium (Mg)									
14	chloride	$MgCl_2$	0.317	3⅓	6⅔	81	Mg^{++}	6⅔	236	Cl^-
15		$MgCl_2 + 6\,H_2O$	0.678	3⅓	6⅔	81	Mg^{++}	6⅔	236	Cl^-
18	sulphate	$MgSO_4 + 7\,H_2O$	1.232	5	10	122	Mg^{++}	10	480	SO_4^{--}
									160	S
	Phosphorus (P)									
	See Calcium (**10**), Potassium (**26, 27**) and Sodium (**30, 31, 40–42**)									
	Potassium (K)									
19	acetate	$K(C_2H_3O_2)$	0.491	5	5	196	K^+	5	295	$C_2H_3O_2^-$
20	bicarbonate	$KHCO_3$	0.501	5	5	196	K^+	5	305	HCO_3^-
21	bromide	KBr	0.595	5	5	196	K^+	5	400	Br^-
22	chloride	KCl	0.373	5	5	196	K^+	5	177	Cl^-
23	citrate	$K_3(C_6H_5O_7) + H_2O$	0.811	2½	7½	293	K^+	7½	473	$C_6H_5O_7^{---}$
24	D-gluconate	$K(C_6H_{11}O_7)$	1.171	5	5	196	K^+	5	976	$C_6H_{11}O_7^-$
26	phosphate, monobasic	KH_2PO_4	0.454	3⅓	3⅓	130	K^+	6⅔	320	HPO_4^{--}
									103	P
27	phosphate, dibasic	K_2HPO_4	0.581	3⅓	6⅔	261	K^+	6⅔	320	HPO_4^{--}
									103	P
	Sodium (Na)									
28	acetate	$Na(C_2H_3O_2) + 3\,H_2O$	0.680	5	5	115	Na^+	5	295	$C_2H_3O_2^-$
29	acid citrate	$Na_2H(C_6H_5O_7) + 1\tfrac{1}{2}\,H_2O$	0.658	2½	5	115	Na^+	7½	473	$C_6H_5O_7^{---}$
30	acid phosphate	$NaH_2PO_4 + H_2O$	0.460	3⅓	3⅓	77	Na^+	6⅔	320	HPO_4^{--}
31		$NaH_2PO_4 + 2\,H_2O$	0.520	3⅓	3⅓	77	Na^+	6⅔	320	HPO_4^{--}
									103	P
32	aminosalicylate	$Na(C_7H_6O_3N) + 2\,H_2O$	1.056	5	5	115	Na^+	5	761	$C_7H_6O_3N^-$
33	bicarbonate	$NaHCO_3$	0.420	5	5	115	Na^+	5	305	HCO_3^-
34	bromide	$NaBr$	0.514	5	5	115	Na^+	5	400	Br^-
35	chloride	$NaCl$	0.292	5	5	115	Na^+	5	177	Cl^-
36	citrate	$Na_3(C_6H_5O_7) + 2\,H_2O$	0.735	2½	7½	172	Na^+	7½	473	$C_6H_5O_7^{---}$
37		$Na_3(C_6H_5O_7) + 5\tfrac{1}{2}\,H_2O$	0.893	2½	7½	172	Na^+	7½	473	$C_6H_5O_7^{---}$
38	lactate	$Na(C_3H_5O_3)$	0.560	5	5	115	Na^+	5	445	$C_3H_5O_3^-$
40	phosphate	Na_2HPO_4	0.473	3⅓	6⅔	153	Na^+	6⅔	320	HPO_4^{--}
									103	P
41		$Na_2HPO_4 + 2\,H_2O$	0.593	3⅓	6⅔	153	Na^+	6⅔	320	HPO_4^{--}
									103	P
42		$Na_2HPO_4 + 12\,H_2O$	1.194	3⅓	6⅔	153	Na^+	6⅔	320	HPO_4^{--}
									103	P
43	salicylate	$Na(C_7H_5O_3)$	0.801	5	5	115	Na^+	5	686	$C_7H_5O_3^-$
44	sulphate (anhydrous)	Na_2SO_4	0.473	3⅓	6⅔	153	Na^+	6⅔	320	SO_4^{--}
									107	S
45	sulphate	$Na_2SO_4 + 10\,H_2O$	1.074	3⅓	6⅔	153	Na^+	6⅔	320	SO_4^{--}
									107	S
46	thiosulphate	$Na_2S_2O_3$	0.527	3⅓	6⅔	153	Na^+	6⅔	374	$S_2O_3^{--}$
									214	S
	Sulphur (S)									
	See Calcium (**11**), Magnesium (**18**) and Sodium (**44–46**)									

* On the assumption of complete dissociation.

Left-hand column: Given: weight of the inorganic ions. Required: corresponding weight of the salt.
Right-hand column: Given: milliequivalents of the ions. Required: corresponding weight of the salt.

Inorganic ions

No.	Left-hand column	Formula	Right-hand column	Formula
1	**1 g = 49.90 mEq Calcium (Ca^{++}) corresponds to**		**1 mEq = 20.04 mg Calcium (Ca^{++}) corresponds to**	
2	4.396 g Calcium acetate	$Ca(C_2H_3O_2)_2 + H_2O$	88.09 mg Calcium acetate	$Ca(C_2H_3O_2)_2 + H_2O$
3	4.845 g Calcium acetate dihydrate	$Ca(C_2H_3O_2)_2 + 2\,H_2O$	97.10 mg Calcium acetate dihydrate	$Ca(C_2H_3O_2)_2 + 2\,H_2O$
4	3.668 g Calcium chloride	$CaCl_2 + 2\,H_2O$	73.51 mg Calcium chloride	$CaCl_2 + 2\,H_2O$
5	5.466 g Calcium chloride hexahydrate	$CaCl_2 + 6\,H_2O$	109.54 mg Calcium chloride hexahydrate	$CaCl_2 + 6\,H_2O$
6	4.745 g Calcium citrate	$Ca_3(C_6H_5O_7)_2 + 4\,H_2O$	95.08 mg Calcium citrate	$Ca_3(C_6H_5O_7)_2 + 4\,H_2O$
7	11.188 g Calcium D-gluconate	$Ca(C_6H_{11}O_7)_2 + H_2O$	224.20 mg Calcium D-gluconate	$Ca(C_6H_{11}O_7)_2 + H_2O$
8	7.692 g Calcium lactate	$Ca(C_3H_5O_3)_2 + 5\,H_2O$	154.15 mg Calcium lactate	$Ca(C_3H_5O_3)_2 + 5\,H_2O$
9	7.643 g Calcium laevulinate	$Ca(C_5H_7O_3)_2 + 2H_2O$	153.17 mg Calcium laevulinate	$Ca(C_5H_7O_3)_2 + 2\,H_2O$
11	4.294 g Calcium phosphate, dibasic	$CaHPO_4 + 2\,H_2O$	86.05 mg Calcium phosphate, dibasic	$CaHPO_4 + 2\,H_2O$
12	6.495 g Calcium thiosulphate	$CaS_2O_3 + 6\,H_2O$	130.15 mg Calcium thiosulphate	$CaS_2O_3 + 6\,H_2O$
	1 g Carbon dioxide (CO_2) corresponds to 1.387 g = 22.72 mEq bicarbonate ions (HCO_3^-) **1 vol% Carbon dioxide (CO_2)** at 0 °C and 760 mm Hg corresponds to 27.41 mg/l = 0.449 mEq/l bicarbonate ions (HCO_3^-)*		**1 mEq = 61.02 mg Bicarbonate ions** (HCO_3^-) corresponds to 44.01 mg carbon dioxide (CO_2) **1 mEq/l = 61.02 mg/l Bicarbonate ions** (HCO_3^-) corresponds at 0 °C and 760 mm Hg to 2.23 vol% carbon dioxide (CO_2)*	
13	**1 g = 28.21 mEq Chloride (Cl^-) corresponds to**		**1 mEq = 35.453 mg Chloride (Cl^-) corresponds to**	
14	1.509 g Ammonium chloride	NH_4Cl	53.49 mg Ammonium chloride	NH_4Cl
4	2.073 g Calcium chloride	$CaCl_2 + 2\,H_2O$	73.51 mg Calcium chloride	$CaCl_2 + 2\,H_2O$
5	3.090 g Calcium chloride hexahydrate	$CaCl_2 + 6\,H_2O$	109.55 mg Calcium chloride hexahydrate	$CaCl_2 + 6\,H_2O$
15	10.28 g or 9.823 ml Hydrochloric acid 10 %		364.6 mg or 348.24 µl Hydrochloric acid 10%	
17	1.343 g Magnesium chloride	$MgCl_2$	47.61 mg Magnesium chloride	$MgCl_2$
18	2.867 g Magnesium chloride hexahydrate	$MgCl_2 + 6\,H_2O$	101.66 mg Magnesium chloride hexahydrate	$MgCl_2 + 6\,H_2O$
27	2.103 g Potassium chloride	KCl	74.56 mg Potassium chloride	KCl
41	1.648 g Sodium chloride	$NaCl$	58.44 mg Sodium chloride	$NaCl$
16	**1 g = 82.3 mEq Magnesium (Mg^{++}) corresponds to**		**1 mEq = 12.15 mg Magnesium (Mg^{++}) corresponds to**	
17	3.917 g Magnesium chloride	$MgCl_2$	47.61 mg Magnesium chloride	$MgCl_2$
18	8.364 g Magnesium chloride hexahydrate	$MgCl_2 + 6\,H_2O$	101.65 mg Magnesium chloride hexahydrate	$MgCl_2 + 6\,H_2O$
21	10.138 g Magnesium sulphate	$MgSO_4 + 7\,H_2O$	123.24 mg Magnesium sulphate	$MgSO_4 + 7\,H_2O$
22	**1 g Phosphorus (P) corresponds to**		At pH 4.3 **1 g Phosphorus (P)** corresponds to 32.28 mEq $H_2PO_4^-$ ions, and **1 mEq $H_2PO_4^-$ ions** corresponds to 30.97 mg phosphorus (with only a small error these figures can be used for urine). At pH 9.6 **1 g Phosphorus (P)** corresponds to 64.57 mEq HPO_4^{--} ions, and **1 mEq HPO_4^{--} ions** corresponds to 15.49 mg phosphorus. At pH 7.4 and 38 °C **1 g Phosphorus** corresponds to 58.1 mEq phosphate ions, and **1 mEq Phosphate ions** corresponds to 17.2 mg phosphorus (ca. 20% $H_2PO_4^-$ ions and ca. 80% HPO_4^{--} ions).	
11	5.556 g Calcium phosphate, dibasic	$CaHPO_4 + 2\,H_2O$		
31	4.394 g Potassium phosphate, monobasic	KH_2PO_4		
32	5.624 g Potassium phosphate, dibasic	K_2HPO_4		
36	4.455 g Sodium acid phosphate	$NaH_2PO_4 + H_2O$		
37	•5.037 g Sodium acid phosphate dihydrate	$NaH_2PO_4 + 2\,H_2O$		
46	4.583 g Sodium phosphate	Na_2HPO_4		
47	5.746 g Sodium phosphate dihydrate	$Na_2HPO_4 + 2\,H_2O$		
48	11.563 g Sodium phosphate dodecahydrate	$Na_2HPO_4 + 12\,H_2O$		
23	**1 g = 25.57 mEq Potassium (K^+) corresponds to**		**1 mEq = 39.10 mg Potassium (K^+) corresponds to**	
24	2.510 g Potassium acetate	$K(C_2H_3O_2)$	98.15 mg Potassium acetate	$K(C_2H_3O_2)$
25	2.560 g Potassium bicarbonate	$KHCO_3$	100.12 mg Potassium bicarbonate	$KHCO_3$
26	3.044 g Potassium bromide	KBr	119.01 mg Potassium bromide	KBr
27	1.907 g Potassium chloride	KCl	74.56 mg Potassium chloride	KCl
28	2.766 g Potassium citrate	$K_3(C_6H_5O_7) + H_2O$	108.14 mg Potassium citrate	$K_3(C_6H_5O_7) + H_2O$
29	5.991 g Potassium D-gluconate	$K(C_6H_{11}O_7)$	234.25 mg Potassium D-gluconate	$K(C_6H_{11}O_7)$
31	3.480 g Potassium phosphate, monobasic	KH_2PO_4	136.09 mg Potassium phosphate, monobasic	KH_2PO_4
32	2.227 g Potassium phosphate, dibasic	K_2HPO_4	87.09 mg Potassium phosphate, dibasic	K_2HPO_4
33	**1 g = 43.50 mEq Sodium (Na^+) corresponds to**		**1 mEq = 22.99 mg Sodium (Na^+) corresponds to**	
34	5.919 g Sodium acetate	$Na(C_2H_3O_2) + 3\,H_2O$	136.08 mg Sodium acetate	$Na(C_2H_3O_2) + 3\,H_2O$
35	5.722 g Sodium acid citrate	$Na_2H(C_6H_5O_7) + 1\frac{1}{2}\,H_2O$	131.56 mg Sodium acid citrate	$Na_2H(C_6H_5O_7) + 1\frac{1}{2}\,H_2O$
36	6.002 g Sodium acid phosphate	$NaH_2PO_4 + H_2O$	137.99 mg Sodium acid phosphate	$NaH_2PO_4 + H_2O$
37	6.786 g Sodium acid phosphate dihydrate	$NaH_2PO_4 + 2\,H_2O$	156.01 mg Sodium acid phosphate dihydrate	$NaH_2PO_4 + 2\,H_2O$
38	9.185 g Sodium aminosalicylate	$Na(C_7H_6O_3N) + 2\,H_2O$	211.15 mg Sodium aminosalicylate	$Na(C_7H_6O_3N) + 2\,H_2O$
39	3.654 g Sodium bicarbonate	$NaHCO_3$	84.01 mg Sodium bicarbonate	$NaHCO_3$
41	2.542 g Sodium chloride	$NaCl$	58.44 mg Sodium chloride	$NaCl$
42	4.264 g Sodium citrate	$Na_3(C_6H_5O_7) + 2\,H_2O$	98.03 mg Sodium citrate	$Na_3(C_6H_5O_7) + 2\,H_2O$
43	5.178 g Sodium citrate	$Na_3(C_6H_5O_7) + 5\frac{1}{2}\,H_2O$	119.05 mg Sodium citrate	$Na_3(C_6H_5O_7) + 5\frac{1}{2}\,H_2O$
44	4.874 g Sodium lactate	$Na(C_3H_5O_3)$	112.06 mg Sodium lactate	$Na(C_3H_5O_3)$
46	3.087 g Sodium phosphate	Na_2HPO_4	70.98 mg Sodium phosphate	Na_2HPO_4
47	3.781 g Sodium phosphate dihydrate	$Na_2HPO_4 + 2\,H_2O$	88.99 mg Sodium phosphate dihydrate	$Na_2HPO_4 + 2\,H_2O$
48	7.789 g Sodium phosphate dodecahydrate	$Na_2HPO_4 + 12\,H_2O$	179.07 mg Sodium phosphate dodecahydrate	$Na_2HPO_4 + 12\,H_2O$
49	6.964 g Sodium salicylate	$Na(C_7H_5O_3)$	160.11 mg Sodium salicylate	$Na(C_7H_5O_3)$
50	3.089 g Sodium sulphate (anhydrous)	Na_2SO_4	71.02 mg Sodium sulphate (anhydrous)	Na_2SO_4
51	7.007 g Sodium sulphate	$Na_2SO_4 + 10\,H_2O$	161.10 mg Sodium sulphate	$Na_2SO_4 + 10\,H_2O$
52	3.439 g Sodium thiosulphate	$Na_2S_2O_3$	79.05 mg Sodium thiosulphate	$Na_2S_2O_3$
53	**1 g Sulphur (S) corresponds to**		**1 g Sulphur (S)** corresponds to 62.37 mEq SO_4^{--} ions and **1 mEq SO_4^{--}** ions corresponds to 16.03 mg sulphur. At pH 7.4 and 38 °C and with an albumin/globulin ratio of 1.6, **1 g of serum proteins** corresponds to 0.241 basic mEq of ionized serum proteins, and **1 mEq** of ionized serum proteins corresponds to 4.15 g of serum proteins[1].	
12	4.059 g Calcium thiosulphate	$CaS_2O_3 + 6\,H_2O$		
21	7.687 g Magnesium sulphate	$MgSO_4 + 7\,H_2O$		
50	4.430 g Sodium sulphate (anhydrous)	Na_2SO_4		
51	10.048 g Sodium sulphate	$Na_2SO_4 + 10\,H_2O$		
52	2.465 g Sodium thiosulphate	$Na_2S_2O_3$		

* The conversion factors (0.449 and 2.23) given here for vol% CO_2 into mmol CO_2/l and mEq CO_2/l (bicarbonate-CO_2) are derived from the molar volume of this gas (22.257 l at 0 °C and 760 mm Hg). The conversion factor 2.24 often used in medical literature is mistakenly based on the molar volume of ideal gases (22.414 l). For practical purposes the difference between these two factors is negligible.

[1] From VAN SLYKE et al., *J. biol. Chem.*, **79**, 768 (1928).

Name	Molecular weight	Hydrogen equivalent	1 l of 0.1-N solution contains (gramme)	Mantissa of $\log_{10}$ of equivalent weight*
Acetic acid	60.05	$C_2H_4O_2$	6.005	7785
Ammonia	17.03	NH_3	1.703	2312
Ammonium chloride	53.49	NH_4Cl	5.349	7283
Ammonium hydroxide	35.05	NH_4OH	3.505	5447
Ammonium nitrate	80.04	NH_4NO_3	8.004	9033
Ammonium sulphate	132.14	$^1/_2\,(NH_4)_2SO_4$	6.607	8200
Ammonium thiocyanate	76.12	NH_4CNS	7.612	8815
Barium carbonate	197.35	$^1/_2\,BaCO_3$	9.868	9942
Barium chloride	244.28	$^1/_2\,[BaCl_2 + 2H_2O]$	12.214	0869
Barium hydroxide	315.48	$^1/_2\,[Ba(OH)_2 + 8H_2O]$	15.774	1979
Barium oxide	153.34	$^1/_2\,BaO$	7.667	8846
Borax. See Sodium tetraborate decahydrate				
Boric acid	61.83	$^1/_3\,H_3BO_3$	2.061	3141
Bromine	159.81	$^1/_2\,Br_2$	7.991	9026
Calcium carbonate	100.09	$^1/_2\,CaCO_3$	5.005	6994
Calcium chloride	110.99	$^1/_2\,CaCl_2$	5.550	7443
Calcium chloride hexahydrate	219.08	$^1/_2\,[CaCl_2 + 6H_2O]$	10.954	0396
Calcium hydroxide	74.09	$^1/_2\,Ca(OH)_2$	3.705	5688
Calcium oxide	56.08	$^1/_2\,CaO$	2.804	4478
Carbon dioxide	44.01	$^1/_2\,CO_2$	2.201	3426
Chlorine	70.91	$^1/_2\,Cl_2$	3.546	5497
Citric acid	210.14	$^1/_3\,[C_6H_8O_7 + H_2O]$	7.005	8454
Copper oxide	79.55	$^1/_2\,CuO$	3.978	5997
Copper sulphate	249.68	$^1/_2\,[CuSO_4 + 5H_2O]$	12.484	0964
Hydriodic acid	127.91	HI	12.791	1069
Hydrobromic acid	80.91	HBr	8.091	9080
Hydrochloric acid	36.46	HCl	3.646	5618
Hydrocyanic acid	27.03	HCN	2.703	4318
Iodine	253.81	$^1/_2\,I_2$	12.691	1035
Lactic acid	90.08	$C_3H_6O_3$	9.008	9546
Lead carbonate	267.20	$^1/_2\,PbCO_3$	13.360	1258
Lead oxide	223.19	$^1/_2\,PbO$	11.160	0477
Magnesium carbonate	84.31	$^1/_2\,MgCO_3$	4.216	6249
Magnesium chloride	95.21	$^1/_2\,MgCl_2$	4.761	6777
Magnesium chloride hexahydrate	203.30	$^1/_2\,[MgCl_2 + 6H_2O]$	10.165	0071_5
Magnesium oxide	40.31	$^1/_2\,MgO$	2.016	3045
Malic acid	134.09	$^1/_2\,C_4H_6O_5$	6.705	8264
Manganese sulphate	151.00	$^1/_2\,MnSO_4$	7.550	8779
Mercuric chloride (corrosive sublimate)	271.50	$^1/_2\,HgCl_2$	13.575	1327
Nitric acid	63.01	HNO_3	6.301	7994
Nitrous acid	47.01	HNO_2	4.701	6722
Oxalic acid	90.04	$^1/_2\,C_2H_2O_4$	4.502	6534
Oxalic acid dihydrate	126.07	$^1/_2\,[C_2H_2O_4 + 2H_2O]$	6.304	7996
Phosphoric acid	98.00	$^1/_3\,H_3PO_4$	3.267	5141
Potassium bicarbonate	100.12	$KHCO_3$	10.012	0005_2
Potassium bitartrate	188.18	$C_4H_5O_6K$	18.818	2746
Potassium carbonate	138.21	$^1/_2\,K_2CO_3$	6.911	8395
Potassium chloride	74.56	KCl	7.456	8725
Potassium cyanide	65.12	KCN	6.512	8137
Potassium dichromate	294.19	$^1/_6\,K_2Cr_2O_7$	4.903	6905
Potassium hydroxide	56.11	KOH	5.611	7490
Potassium oxide	94.20	$^1/_2\,K_2O$	4.710	6730
Potassium permanganate in acid medium	158.04	$^1/_5\,KMnO_4$	3.161	4998
Potassium permanganate for Mn determination	158.04	$^1/_3\,KMnO_4$	5.268	7216
Potassium tartrate	226.28	$^1/_2\,C_4H_4O_6K_2$	11.314	0536
Potassium tetroxalate	254.20	$^1/_3\,[KH_3(C_2O_4)_2 + 2H_2O]$	8.473	9280
Silver nitrate	169.87	$AgNO_3$	16.987	2301
Sodium bicarbonate	84.01	$NaHCO_3$	8.401	9243
Sodium carbonate	105.99	$^1/_2\,Na_2CO_3$	5.300	7243
Sodium chloride	58.44	$NaCl$	5.844	7667
Sodium hydroxide	40.00	$NaOH$	4.000	6021
Sodium oxide	61.98	$^1/_2\,Na_2O$	3.099	4912
Sodium phosphate (disodium phosphate)	177.99	$^1/_2\,[Na_2HPO_4 + 2H_2O]$	8.900	9494
Sodium phosphate (trisodium phosphate)	380.12	$^1/_3\,[Na_3PO_4 + 12H_2O]$	12.671	1028
Sodium sulphide	78.04	$^1/_2\,Na_2S$	3.902	5913
Sodium tetraborate	201.22	$^1/_2\,Na_2B_4O_7$	10.061	0026_4
Sodium tetraborate decahydrate (borax)	381.37	$^1/_2\,[Na_2B_4O_7 + 10H_2O]$	19.069	2803
Succinic acid	118.09	$^1/_2\,C_4H_6O_4$	5.905	7712
Sulphuric acid	98.08	$^1/_2\,H_2SO_4$	4.904	6906
Sulphur trioxide	80.06	$^1/_2\,SO_3$	4.003	6024
Tartaric acid	150.09	$^1/_2\,C_4H_6O_6$	7.505	8754
Zinc sulphate	287.54	$^1/_2\,[ZnSO_4 + 7H_2O]$	14.377	1577

* For logarithms see page 10.

Definitions of pH scales [1, 2]

A. Dissociation constant of water

The relationship between the concentrations of hydrogen ions* and hydroxyl ions in an aqueous medium is fixed by the dissociation equilibrium of water:

$$H_2O \rightleftharpoons H^+ + OH^- \quad (1)$$

If solutes are present in such small concentrations that the activity of water is practically unity**, the ion product constant*** of water is given by

$$K_W = a_H a_{OH} = m_H \gamma_H m_{OH} \gamma_{OH} \quad (2)$$

where a = ionic activity, γ = activity coefficient, m = molality.

The dissociation of pure water is extremely small***, and if no solutes are present

$$\gamma_H = \gamma_{OH} \approx 1 \quad (3)$$

Since the value of K_W at 25 °C is 1.008×10^{-14} it follows that for pure water

$$m_H = m_{OH} = \sqrt{K_W} \cong 1 \times 10^{-7} \quad (4)$$

In water the molarity c of the ions is practically identical with the molality m (see page 271), so that for pure water

$$c_H \cong m_H \cong 1 \times 10^{-7} \quad (5)$$

In aqueous solutions the solutes may give rise to additional H^+ ions (dissociation of acids, hydrolysis of salts, etc.), with the result that the equilibrium (1) is displaced and the concentration of OH^- ions reduced. In the same way additional OH^- ions cause a decrease in the concentration of H^+ ions, so that $c_H \ll 1 \times 10^{-7}$. In the former case the solution is said to be 'acid', in the latter 'alkaline'. Since the ion product constant K_W is markedly temperature-dependent the same applies to the neutral point of c_H, the value of which at 0 °C is $1 \times 10^{-7.5}$, at 60 °C $1 \times 10^{-6.6}$.

Temperature dependence of the ion product constant of water (K_W)[3]

°C	$K_W \times 10^{14}$	$-\log K_W$	°C	$K_W \times 10^{14}$	$-\log K_W$
0	0.1139	14.943	35	2.089	13.680
5	0.1846	14.734	40	2.919	13.535
10	0.2920	14.535	45	4.018	13.396
15	0.4505	14.346	50	5.474	13.262
20	0.6809	14.167	55	7.297	13.137
25	1.008	13.996	60	9.614	13.017
30	1.469	13.833			

B. The Sørensen *pH scale*

Sørensen was the first to realize the importance of hydrogen ion concentration in biochemical processes, and he devised colorimetric and potentiometric methods of measuring quantities which – in the light of the thermodynamic concepts of the time (1909) – were considered as strictly equal to the molarity of the hydrogen ion. At the same time he introduced the abbreviation now written as pH:

$$\mathrm{pH} = -\log_{10} c_H \quad (6)$$

As the actual means of measuring pH, Sørensen chose the cell

$$\text{Pt; } H_2\text{, Solution } X \;\Big|\; \text{KCl bridge solution}^{\dagger} \;\Big|\; \text{0.1-N Calomel electrode} \quad (7)$$

the e.m.f. of which (E) is compared with that (E') of a similar cell containing a solution†† of $c_H = 1$ in place of the solution X. For this purpose the hydrogen electrode could be replaced by any other electrode responsive to H^+ ions (a quinhydrone or glass electrode for instance). Other reference electrodes could likewise be used in place of the calomel electrode. It is necessary only that the comparison be made under the same conditions, such as constancy of temperature. According to Sørensen, the pH value of the solution X is given by

$$\mathrm{pH}_{\text{SØRENSEN}} = \frac{(E - E')F}{RT \ln 10} \quad (8)$$

where F is the Faraday constant, R the molar gas constant, T the absolute temperature, and $\ln 10 = 2.30259$. Values of $(RT \ln 10)/F$ at various temperatures are given on the opposite page.

C. The conventional pH scale

It is now known that the e.m.f. of the cell (7) is dependent not only on the concentration of H^+ ions but also on their activity, on the activity of the Cl^- ions, and on the transference numbers of the ions (variation of the diffusion potential with ionic concentration). For this reason comparison is no longer made with a reference solution whose c_H value is assumed to be unity but with a standard solution S whose pH value (pH_S) is fixed by convention. The pH value of the solution X is then defined conventionally as

$$\mathrm{pH}_X = \frac{(E_X - E_S)F}{RT \ln 10} + \mathrm{pH}_S \quad (9)$$

In the United Kingdom[4] and Japan[5] the primary standard solution is 1/20-molar potassium hydrogen phthalate, while in the USA[6] five standard solutions are in use (all these standards use the same conventions). The five US standard solutions have assigned pH_S values between 3.5 and 9.5. This allows of an alternative definition of pH through comparison of the solution X with two standards S and S', when pH_X is obtained from the following formula:

$$\frac{\mathrm{pH}_X - \mathrm{pH}_S}{\mathrm{pH}_{S'} - \mathrm{pH}_S} = \frac{E - E_S}{E_{S'} - E_S} \quad (10)$$

This procedure is especially recommended when the H^+ ion-responsive electrode is a glass electrode. Differences in measured values of pH obtained by the use of different standard solutions are too small to be of practical significance.

Values of pH on the Sørensen and conventional scales differ by a constant amount as follows[2]:

$$\mathrm{pH} = \mathrm{pH}_{\text{SØRENSEN}} + 0.04 \quad (11)$$

D. Thermodynamic interpretation of the conventional pH scale

It is clear from the above that there exists no definite relationship between the conventional pH scale and any true thermodynamic measurement of the acidity of a solution such as H^+ ion molality (m_H). This scale meets all practical needs, however, so that there is little value in introducing more complicated methods of measurement for the sake of thermodynamic principles. The difficulty lies in the fact that while only the product $\gamma_c \gamma_a$ of the activity coefficients of the cation and anion has any clear thermodynamic meaning, this is a quantity which cannot be measured by means of arrangements like the cell (7). The difficulty has been overcome by defining the activity of the *chloride* ion by

$$\log \gamma_{Cl} = -\frac{A\sqrt{I}}{1 + B'\sqrt{I}} \quad (12)$$

where A is the Debye-Hückel constant[7] $= 1.82 \times 10^6/(\varepsilon T)^{3/2}$ (ε = dielectric constant of the solution), B' a constant depending on the finite size of the ion, and I the ionic strength (not exceeding 0.1) defined as $\frac{1}{2}\sum_i m_i z_i^2$ for all the ionic species present. On the basis of this equation it can be assumed that for solutions with an ionic strength less than 0.1 and pH values between 2 and 12

$$\mathrm{pH} = -\log(m_H \gamma_H) = -\log a_H \quad (13)$$

* For the sake of simplicity the expressions hydrogen ion and hydroxyl ion are here used, although these ions never occur in the free state but only associated with water molecules (mainly in the form of $H_9O_4^+$ and $H_7O_4^-$).

** The activity of water in an aqueous solution is $p/p°$, where p and $p°$ are the pressures of water vapour in equilibrium respectively with the solution and with pure water at the temperature in question, provided that p and $p°$ are so small that water vapour can be considered an ideal gas[2].

*** The dissociation constant of water, rarely to be found in the literature, is given by K_W/m_{H_2O}, the value of m_{H_2O} being 55.51.

† The KCl solution is usually contained in a tube connecting the two halves of the cell and prevented from mixing with the other two solutions by means of agar plugs. Diffusion potentials arise at the two liquid junctions but these are of opposite sign and almost equal because of the similar transference numbers of the K^+ and Cl^- ions. Sørensen originally attempted to measure E for various concentrations of the KCl bridge and to extrapolate to a zero diffusion potential. Under the present convention, the KCl bridge must have a concentration of at least 3.5-N (saturated KCl is 4.2-N) maintained constant in comparative measurements.

†† Sørensen used HCl, with a correction based on conductivity measurements for its presumed incomplete dissociation.

Values of $(RT \ln 10)/F$ from 0° to 100 °C*[2]

°C	$RT \ln 10/F$	°C	$RT \ln 10/F$
0	0.054197	50	0.064118
5	0.055189	55	0.065110
10	0.056181	60	0.066102
15	0.057173	65	0.067094
20	0.058165	70	0.068086
25	0.059157	75	0.069078
30	0.060149	80	0.070070
35	0.061141	85	0.071062
38	0.061737	90	0.072054
40	0.062133	95	0.073046
45	0.063126	100	0.074038

* ln10 = 2.30259; $R = 8.3143$ J mol^{-1} deg^{-1}; $F = 96\,487.0$ C mol^{-1}; $T =$ °C + 273.15.

pH values of standard solutions at 25 °C on different pH scales[2]

Solution	Scale of: Hitchcock and Taylor	MacInnes et al.	National Bureau of Standards
Potassium bitartrate, 0.03-molar	3.567	–	3.569
Potassium biphthalate, 0.05-molar	4.010	4.000	4.008
Acetic acid 0.1-molar, Sodium acetate 0.1-molar.	4.645	4.640	4.652
KH_2PO_4 0.025-molar, NaH_2PO_4 0.025-molar	6.855	–	6.865
Sodium tetraborate decahydrate 0.05-molar (borax)	9.180	–	9.196

pH_S values of NBS primary standards from 0° to 95 °C[2]

Temperature (°C)	Potassium bitartrate (saturated at 25 °C)	Potassium biphthalate 0.05-molal	KH_2PO_4 0.025-molal Na_2HPO_4 0.025-molal	KH_2PO_4 0.008695-molal Na_2HPO_4 0.03043-molal	Sodium tetraborate decahydrate (borax) 0.01-molal
0	–	4.003	6.984	7.534	9.464
5	–	3.999	6.951	7.500	9.395
10	–	3.998	6.923	7.472	9.332
15	–	3.999	6.900	7.448	9.276
20	–	4.002	6.881	7.429	9.225
25	3.557	4.008	6.865	7.413	9.180
30	3.552	4.015	6.853	7.400	9.139
35	3.549	4.024	6.844	7.389	9.102
38	3.548	4.030	6.840	7.384	9.081
40	3.547	4.035	6.838	7.380	9.068
45	3.547	4.047	6.834	7.373	9.038
50	3.549	4.060	6.833	7.367	9.011
55	3.554	4.075	6.834	–	8.985
60	3.560	4.091	6.836	–	8.962
70	3.580	4.126	6.845	–	8.921
80	3.609	4.164	6.859	–	8.885
90	3.650	4.205	6.877	–	8.850
95	3.674	4.227	6.886	–	8.833

pH values of secondary British standards[2]

Solution	12 °C	25 °C	38 °C
Potassium tetroxalate 0.1-molar	–	1.48	1.50
HCl 0.01-molar, KCl 0.09-molar	–	2.07	2.08
Acetic acid 0.1-molar, Sodium acetate 0.1-molar	4.65	4.64	4.65
Acetic acid 0.01-molar, Sodium acetate 0.01-molar	4.71	4.70	4.72
KH_2PO_4 0.025-molar, Na_2HPO_4 0.025-molar	–	6.85	6.84
Sodium tetraborate decahydrate (borax) 0.05-molar	–	9.18	9.07
$NaHCO_3$ 0.025-molar, Na_2CO_3 0.025-molar	–	10.00	–

Approximate pH values of common reagent solutions at or near room temperature[2]

Solution	Molarity	pH
Ammonia water	0.1	11.3
Ammonium chloride	0.1	4.6
Ammonium dihydrogen phosphate	0.1	4.0
Ammonium oxalate	0.1	6.4
Ammonium sulphate	0.1	5.5
Barbital sodium	0.1	9.4
Benzoic acid	saturated	2.8
Boric acid	0.1	5.3
Calcium hydroxide	saturated	12.4
Citric acid	0.1	2.1
Diammonium hydrogen phosphate	0.1	7.9
Disodium hydrogen phosphate	0.1	9.2
Hydrochloric acid	0.1	1.1
Oxalic acid	0.1	1.3
Potassium acetate	0.1	9.7
Potassium aluminium sulphate	0.1	4.2
Potassium bicarbonate	0.1	8.2
Potassium carbonate	0.1	11.5
Potassium dihydrogen phosphate	0.1	4.5
Salicylic acid	saturated	2.4
Sodium acetate	0.1	8.9
Sodium benzoate	0.1	8.0
Sodium bicarbonate	0.1	8.3
Sodium bisulphate	0.1	1.4
Sodium carbonate	0.1	11.5
Sodium dihydrogen phosphate	0.1	4.5
Sodium hydroxide	0.1	12.9
Sodium tetraborate decahydrate	0.1	9.4
Succinic acid	0.1	2.7
Tartaric acid	0.1	2.0
Trichloracetic acid	0.1	1.2

References

1 Bates and Guggenheim, *Pure appl. Chem.*, **1**, 163 (1960).
2 Bates, R. G., *Determination of pH*, Wiley, New York, 1964.
3 Harned and Owen, *The Physical Chemistry of Electrolytic Solutions*, 3rd ed., Reinhold, New York, 1958.
4 *British Standard 1647: 1950*, British Standards Institution, London, 1950.
5 *Japanese Industrial Standard Z 8802-1958.*
6 *A.S.T.M. Method E70-52T*, American Society for Testing Materials, Philadelphia, 1952.
7 For values see Manov et al., *J. Amer. chem. Soc.*, **65**, 1765 (1943).

Buffer Solutions*

Buffer solutions (or buffers) are solutions whose pH value is to a large degree insensitive to the addition of other substances. It is important to realize, however, that the pH value of a buffer solution does not change only when acids or bases are added or on dilution but also when the temperature changes or neutral salts are added. In accurate work therefore, it is important to check the pH value electrometrically after all the ingredients have been added. The extent to which the pH values of buffer solutions vary when acids or bases are added or the temperature changes is shown in the tables which follow. In general, dilution to half the concentration changes the pH value by only some hundredths of a unit (Buffer No. 1 in the table is an exception in that the change amounts to ca. pH 0.15); addition of 0.1-molar neutral salt solution may change the pH value by ca. 0.1.

In the table opposite the solutions are classified into general buffers (mostly in use for the last 50 years), universal buffers with a low buffering capacity but a wide pH range, and buffers for biological media with a moderate pH range but containing stable ingredients (phosphate and borate, for example, often undergo side reactions with biological media). An important property is often the transparency to ultraviolet light. Occasionally it is desirable to have a volatile buffer which can be readily removed[1] (examples are buffers Nos. 20 and 21) but the use of very volatile systems makes a close control of the pH essential. Most of the pH data to be found in the literature relate to the SØRENSEN scale, and it should be noted that the values given in the following table of buffers are on the conventional pH scale (cf. 'pH Standards', page 278).

Both stock and buffer solutions should be made up with distilled water free of CO_2. Only standard reagents should be used. If there is any doubt as to the purity or water content of solutions their molarity must be checked by titration. The amounts x of stock solutions required to make up a buffer solution of the desired pH value are given in the table on page 282.

* This section (pages 280–282) has been compiled by F. KOHLER, Department of Physical Chemistry, University of Vienna.

Reference

[1] For a list of volatile buffers see MICHL, H., in HEFTMANN, E. (Ed.), *Chromatography*, part 1, Reinhold, New York, 1961, page 250.

No.	Name	pH range	Temperature	pH change per °C
	General buffers			
1	KCl/HCl (CLARK and LUBS)[1]	1.0– 2.2	Room	0
2	Glycine/HCl (SØRENSEN)[2]	1.2– 3.4	Room	0
3	Na citrate/HCl (SØRENSEN)[2]	1.2– 5.0	Room	0
4	K biphthalate/HCl (CLARK and LUBS)[1]	2.4– 4.0	20 °C	+0.001
5	K biphthalate/NaOH (Clark and LUBS)[1]	4.2– 6.2	20 °C	
6	Na citrate/NaOH (SØRENSEN)[2]	5.2– 6.6	20 °C	+0.004
7	Phosphate (SØRENSEN)[2]	5.0– 8.0	20 °C	−0.003
8	Barbital-Na/HCl (MICHAELIS)[3]	7.0– 9.0	18 °C	
9	Na borate/HCl (SØRENSEN)[2]	7.8– 9.2	20 °C	−0.005
10	Glycine/NaOH (SØRENSEN)[2]	8.6–12.8	20 °C	−0.025
11	Na borate/NaOH (SØRENSEN)[2]	9.4–10.6	20 °C	−0.01
	Universal buffers			
12	Citric acid/phosphate (McILVAINE)[4]	2.2– 7.8	21 °C	
13	Citrate-phosphate-borate/HCl (TEORELL and STENHAGEN)[5]	2.0–12.0	20 °C	
14	BRITTON-ROBINSON[6]	2.6–11.8	25 °C	at low pH 0 at high pH −0.02
	Buffers for biological media			
15	Acetate (WALPOLE)[7–9]	3.8– 5.6	25 °C	
16	Dimethylglutaric acid/NaOH[10]	3.2– 7.6	21 °C	
17	Piperazine/HCl[11,12]	4.6– 6.4 8.8–10.6	20 °C	
18	Tetraethylethylenediamine*[12]	5.0– 6.8 8.2–10.0	20 °C	
19	Trismaleate[7,13]	5.2– 8.6	23 °C	
20	Dimethylaminoethylamine*[12]	5.6– 7.4 8.6–10.4	20 °C	
21	Imidazole/HCl[14]	6.2– 7.8	25 °C	
22	Triethanolamine/HCl[15]	7.0– 8.8	25 °C	
23	*N*-Dimethylaminoleucylglycine/NaOH[16]	7.0– 8.8	23 °C	−0.015
24	Tris/HCl[7]	7.2– 9.0	23 °C	−0.02
25	2-Amino-2-methylpropane-1,3-diol/HCl[7,13]	7.8–10.0	23 °C	
26	Carbonate (DELORY and KING)[7,17]	9.2–10.8	20 °C	

* Can be combined with tris buffer to give a cationic universal buffer (cf. SEMENZA et al.[12]).

References

[1] CLARK and LUBS, *J. Bact.*, **2**, 1 (1917).
[2] SØRENSEN, S.P.L., *Biochem. Z.*, **21**, 131 (1909), and **22**, 352 (1909); *Ergebn. Physiol.*, **12**, 393 (1912); WALBUM, L.E., *Biochem. Z.*, **107**, 219 (1920).
[3] MICHAELIS, L., *J. biol. Chem.*, **87**, 33 (1930).
[4] McILVAINE, T.C., *J. biol. Chem.*, **49**, 183 (1921).
[5] TEORELL and STENHAGEN, *Biochem. Z.*, **299**, 416 (1938).
[6] BRITTON and WELFORD, *J. chem. Soc.*, **1937**, 1848.
[7] GOMORI, G., in COLOWICK and KAPLAN (Eds.), *Methods in Enzymology*, vol. 1, Academic Press, New York, 1955, page 138.
[8] WALPOLE, G.S., *J. chem. Soc.*, **105**, 2501 (1914).
[9] GREEN, A.A., *J. Amer. chem. Soc.*, **55**, 2331 (1933).
[10] STAFFORD et al., *Biochim. biophys. Acta*, **18**, 319 (1955); KREBS, H.A., unpublished, 1957.
[11] SMITH and SMITH, *Biol. Bull.*, **96**, 233 (1949).
[12] SEMENZA et al., *Helv. chim. Acta*, **45**, 2306 (1962).
[13] GOMORI, G., *Proc. Soc. exp. Biol. (N.Y.)*, **68**, 354 (1948).
[14] MERTZ and OWEN, *Proc. Soc. exp. Biol. (N.Y.)*, **43**, 204 (1940), quoted by RAUEN, H.M. (Ed.), *Biochemisches Taschenbuch*, 2nd ed., part 2, Springer, Berlin, 1964, page 90.
[15] BEISENHERZ et al., *Z. Naturforsch.*, **8b**, 555 (1953).
[16] LEONIS, J., *C. R. Lab. Carlsberg, Sér. Chim.*, **26**, 357 (1948).
[17] DELORY and KING, *Biochem. J.*, **39**, 245 (1945).

When not otherwise specified, both stock and buffer solutions should be made up with distilled water free of CO_2. Only standard reagents should be used. If there is any doubt as to the purity or water content of solutions their molarity must be checked by titration. The amounts x of stock solutions required to make up a buffer solution of the desired pH value are given in the table on page 282.

Buffer No.	Stock solutions A	Stock solutions B	Composition of the buffer
1	KCl 0.2-N (14.91 g/l)	HCl 0.2-N	25 ml A + x ml B made up to 100 ml
2	Glycine 0.1-molar in NaCl 0.1-N (7.507 g glycine + 5.844 g NaCl/l)	HCl 0.1-N	x ml A + (100 − x) ml B
3	Disodium citrate 0.1-molar (21.01 g $C_6H_8O_7 \cdot 1H_2O$ + 200 ml NaOH 1-N per litre)	HCl 0.1-N	x ml A + (100 − x) ml B
4	Potassium biphthalate 0.1-molar (20.42 g $KHC_8H_4O_4$/l)	HCl 0.1-N	50 ml A + x ml B made up to 100 ml
5	As No. 4	NaOH 0.1-N	50 ml A + x ml B made up to 100 ml
6	As No. 3	NaOH 0.1-N	x ml A + (100 − x) ml B
7	Monopotassium phosphate $^1/_{15}$-molar (9.073 g KH_2PO_4/l)	Disodium phosphate $^1/_{15}$-molar (11.87 g $Na_2HPO_4 \cdot 2H_2O$/l)	x ml A + (100 − x) ml B
8	Barbital sodium 0.1-molar (20.62 g/l)	HCl 0.1-N	x ml A + (100 − x) ml B
9	Boric acid, half-neutralized, 0.2-molar (corr. to 0.05-molar borax: 12.37 g boric acid + 100 ml NaOH 1-N per litre)	HCl 0.1-N	x ml A + (100 − x) ml B
10	As No. 2	NaOH 0.1-N	x ml A + (100 − x) ml B
11	As No. 9	NaOH 0.1-N	x ml A + (100 − x) ml B
12	Citric acid 0.1-molar (21.01 g $C_6H_8O_7 \cdot 1H_2O$/l)	Disodium phosphate 0.2-molar (35.60 g $Na_2HPO_4 \cdot 2H_2O$/l)	x ml A + (100 − x) ml B
13	To citric acid and phosphoric acid solutions (ca. 100 ml), each equivalent to 100 ml NaOH 1-N, add 3.54 g cryst. orthoboric acid and 343 ml NaOH 1-N, and make up the mixture to 1 l	HCl 0.1-N	20 ml A + x ml B made up to 100 ml
14	Citric acid, monopotassium phosphate, barbital, boric acid, all 0.028 57-molar (6.004 g $C_6H_8O_7 \cdot 1H_2O$, 3.888 g KH_2PO_4, 5.263 g barbital, 1.767 g H_3BO_3/l)	NaOH 0.2-N	100 ml A + x ml B
15	Sodium acetate 0.1-N (8.204 g $C_2H_3O_2Na$ or 13.61 g $C_2H_3O_2Na \cdot 3H_2O$/l)	Acetic acid 0.1-N (6.005 g/l)	x ml A + (100 − x) ml B
16	ββ-Dimethylglutaric acid 0.1-molar (16.02 g/l)	NaOH 0.2-N	(a) 100 ml A + x ml B made up to 1000 ml (b) 100 ml A + x ml B + 5.844 g NaCl made up to 1000 ml (NaCl ≙ 0.1-molar)
17	Piperazine 1-molar (86.14 g/l)	HCl 0.1-N	5 ml A + x ml B made up to 100 ml
18	Tetraethylethylenediamine 1-molar (172.32 g/l)	HCl 0.1-N	5 ml A + x ml B made up to 100 ml
19	Tris acid maleate 0.2-molar (24.23 g tris[hydroxymethyl]-aminomethane + 23.21 g maleic acid or 19.61 g maleic anhydride/l)	NaOH 0.2-N	25 ml A + x ml B made up to 100 ml
20	Dimethylaminoethylamine 1-molar (88 g/l)	HCl 0.1-N	5 ml A + x ml B made up to 100 ml
21	Imidazole 0.2-molar (13.62 g/l)	HCl 0.1-N	25 ml A + x ml B made up to 100 ml
22	Triethanolamine 0.5-molar (76.11 g/l) containing 20 g/l ethylenediaminetetra-acetic acid disodium salt ($C_{10}H_{14}O_8N_2Na_2 \cdot 2H_2O$)	HCl 0.05-N	10 ml A + x ml B made up to 100 ml
23	*N*-Dimethylaminoleucylglycine 0.1-molar (24.33 g $C_{10}H_{20}O_3N_2 \cdot {}^3/_2H_2O$/l) containing NaCl 0.2-N (11.69 g/l)	NaOH 1-N 100 ml made up to 1 l with A	x ml A + (100 − x) ml B
24	Tris 0.2-molar (24.23 g tris[hydroxymethyl]aminomethane/l)	HCl 0.1-N	25 ml A + x ml B made up to 100 ml
25	2-Amino-2-methylpropane-1,3-diol 0.1-molar (10.51 g/l)	HCl 0.1-N	50 ml A + x ml B made up to 100 ml
26	Sodium carbonate anhydrous 0.1-molar (10.60 g/l)	Sodium bicarbonate 0.1-molar (8.401 g/l)	x ml A + (100 − x) ml B

The table gives the amounts (x ml) of the stock solutions listed on page 281 required to make up a buffer solution of the desired pH value

pH	1	2	3	4	5	6	7	8	9	10	11	12	13	14	15	16a	16b	17	18	19	20	21	22	23	24	25	26	pH
1.0	54.2	...	...	...	...	...	...	...	...	...	...	...	...	...	...	...	...	...	...	...	...	...	...	...	...	...	...	1.0
1.2	36.0	11.1	9.0	...	...	...	...	...	...	...	...	...	...	...	...	...	...	...	...	...	...	...	...	...	...	...	...	1.2
1.4	23.2	26.4	17.9	...	...	...	...	...	...	...	...	...	...	...	...	...	...	...	...	...	...	...	...	...	...	...	...	1.4
1.6	14.7	36.2	23.6	...	...	...	...	...	...	...	...	...	...	...	...	...	...	...	...	...	...	...	...	...	...	...	...	1.6
1.8	9.3	43.9	27.6	...	...	...	...	...	...	...	...	...	...	...	...	...	...	...	...	...	...	...	...	...	...	...	...	1.8
2.0	5.9	50.7	30.2	...	...	...	...	...	...	...	...	...	74.4	...	...	...	...	...	...	...	...	...	...	...	...	...	...	2.0
2.2	3.8	56.5	32.2	...	...	...	...	...	...	...	...	98.8	68.8	...	...	...	...	...	...	...	...	...	...	...	...	...	...	2.2
2.4	...	62.3	34.1	41.0	...	...	...	...	...	...	...	94.5	64.6	...	...	...	...	...	...	...	...	...	...	...	...	...	...	2.4
2.6	...	68.4	36.0	34.3	...	...	...	...	...	...	...	90.0	61.3	1.6	...	...	...	...	...	...	...	...	...	...	...	...	...	2.6
2.8	...	74.7	37.9	27.8	...	...	...	...	...	...	...	85.1	58.9	3.6	...	...	...	...	...	...	...	...	...	...	...	...	...	2.8
3.0	...	81.0	39.9	21.6	...	...	...	...	...	...	...	80.3	56.9	5.7	...	...	...	...	...	...	...	...	...	...	...	...	...	3.0
3.2	...	86.2	42.1	15.9	...	...	...	...	...	...	...	76.0	55.2	7.8	...	7.0	14.4	...	...	...	...	...	...	...	...	...	...	3.2
3.4	...	90.3	44.8	10.9	...	...	...	...	...	...	...	72.0	53.9	9.9	...	13.3	20.9	...	...	...	...	...	...	...	...	...	...	3.4
3.6	...	...	47.8	6.7	...	...	...	...	...	...	...	68.4	52.9	11.7	...	20.7	26.8	...	...	...	...	...	...	...	...	...	...	3.6
3.8	...	...	51.2	3.3	...	...	...	...	...	...	...	65.1	51.8	13.5	10.9	26.3	32.4	...	...	...	...	...	...	...	...	...	...	3.8
4.0	...	...	55.1	0.0	...	...	...	...	...	...	...	62.0	50.7	15.3	16.6	32.4	36.6	...	...	...	...	...	...	...	...	...	...	4.0
4.2	...	...	60.0	...	3.0	...	...	...	...	...	...	59.1	49.7	17.5	23.9	36.2	40.3	...	...	...	...	...	...	...	...	...	...	4.2
4.4	...	...	66.4	...	6.7	...	...	...	...	...	...	56.4	48.6	19.7	33.5	39.3	43.1	...	...	...	...	...	...	...	...	...	...	4.4
4.6	...	...	74.9	...	11.1	...	...	...	...	...	...	53.7	47.5	21.9	44.9	41.3	45.7	94.3	...	...	...	...	...	...	...	...	...	4.6
4.8	...	...	85.6	...	16.5	...	...	...	...	...	...	51.2	46.4	24.1	56.6	43.5	48.3	91.5	...	...	...	...	...	...	...	...	...	4.8
5.0	...	...	100.0	...	22.6	...	99.2	...	...	...	...	49.0	45.4	26.3	67.8	45.7	51.5	87.8	94.3	...	...	...	...	...	...	...	...	5.0
5.2	...	...	...	...	28.8	87.1	98.4	...	...	...	...	46.9	44.3	28.6	76.8	48.4	53.6	83.6	91.5	3.2	...	...	...	...	...	...	...	5.2
5.4	...	...	...	...	34.4	78.0	97.3	...	...	...	...	44.7	43.2	31.0	84.0	51.3	58.2	77.6	87.8	5.0	...	...	...	...	...	...	...	5.4
5.6	...	...	...	...	39.1	70.3	95.5	...	...	...	...	42.4	42.0	33.4	89.3	55.0	63.6	71.8	83.1	7.3	94.3	...	...	...	...	...	...	5.6
5.8	...	...	...	...	42.4	64.5	92.8	...	...	...	...	40.0	40.8	35.8	...	58.8	68.7	66.5	77.6	9.7	91.7	...	...	...	...	...	...	5.8
6.0	...	...	...	...	45.0	60.3	88.9	...	...	...	...	37.4	39.7	38.3	...	63.9	73.6	61.8	71.7	12.4	88.0	...	...	...	...	...	...	6.0
6.2	...	...	...	...	46.7	57.2	83.0	...	...	...	...	34.5	38.4	40.8	...	69.5	78.5	58.2	66.4	15.2	83.3	43.4	...	...	...	...	...	6.2
6.4	...	...	...	...	...	54.8	75.4	...	...	...	...	31.4	37.0	43.3	...	74.1	83.3	55.5	61.7	17.9	77.9	40.4	...	...	...	...	...	6.4
6.6	...	...	...	...	...	53.2	65.3	...	...	...	...	27.9	35.6	45.8	...	83.5	87.4	...	58.0	20.8	72.0	36.5	...	...	...	...	...	6.6
6.8	...	...	...	...	...	...	53.4	...	...	...	...	23.5	34.2	48.3	...	87.4	91.0	...	55.3	22.2	66.6	31.4	...	...	...	...	...	6.8
7.0	...	...	...	...	...	...	41.3	53.3	...	...	...	19.0	32.9	50.9	...	90.0	93.2	...	...	23.7	61.9	25.4	86.2	86.4	...	...	...	7.0
7.2	...	...	...	...	...	...	29.6	55.0	...	...	...	13.8	31.7	53.4	...	91.8	94.9	...	...	25.2	58.1	19.6	79.6	80.6	44.7	...	...	7.2
7.4	...	...	...	...	...	...	19.7	57.6	...	...	...	9.8	30.6	55.8	...	93.0	95.8	...	...	26.7	55.3	14.6	71.3	72.8	42.0	...	...	7.4
7.6	...	...	...	...	...	...	12.8	60.8	...	...	...	6.8	29.6	58.2	...	93.8	96.8	...	...	28.6	...	10.2	62.0	63.2	39.3	...	...	7.6
7.8	...	...	...	...	...	...	7.4	65.2	53.0	...	...	4.6	28.8	60.5	...	...	...	...	...	31.2	...	6.6	52.0	52.1	33.7	43.9	...	7.8
8.0	...	...	...	...	...	...	3.7	70.6	55.4	...	...	...	28.1	62.8	...	...	...	...	...	33.9	...	...	42.0	41.1	27.9	41.6	...	8.0
8.2	...	...	...	...	...	...	...	75.9	58.0	...	...	...	27.6	65.0	...	...	...	...	46.4	36.9	...	...	31.9	31.4	22.9	38.4	...	8.2
8.4	...	...	...	...	...	...	...	81.2	62.1	...	...	...	27.0	67.2	...	...	...	...	43.9	39.9	...	...	22.5	23.0	17.3	34.8	...	8.4
8.6	...	...	...	...	...	...	...	86.2	66.9	94.7	...	...	26.3	69.3	...	...	...	...	40.9	42.7	45.4	...	16.0	15.9	13.0	30.7	...	8.6
8.8	...	...	...	...	...	...	...	90.1	73.6	92.0	...	...	25.2	71.3	...	...	...	45.5	36.8	...	42.8	...	11.7	10.3	8.8	23.3	...	8.8
9.0	...	...	...	...	...	...	...	93.2	83.5	88.4	...	...	24.0	73.2	...	...	...	43.2	31.8	...	39.2	...	...	...	5.3	17.7	...	9.0
9.2	...	...	...	...	...	...	...	...	95.6	84.0	...	...	22.6	75.1	...	...	...	40.0	26.2	...	34.7	...	...	...	...	13.3	10.0	9.2
9.4	...	...	...	...	...	...	...	...	...	78.9	87.0	...	21.4	77.0	...	...	...	35.8	20.4	...	29.3	...	...	...	...	9.2	18.4	9.4
9.6	...	...	...	...	...	...	...	...	...	73.2	75.5	...	20.2	78.8	...	...	...	30.8	15.2	...	23.6	...	...	...	...	5.2	29.3	9.6
9.8	...	...	...	...	...	...	...	...	...	67.2	65.1	...	19.0	80.4	...	...	...	25.0	10.8	...	19.0	...	...	...	...	4.1	42.0	9.8
10.0	...	...	...	...	...	...	...	...	...	62.5	59.6	...	18.1	81.8	...	...	...	19.4	7.4	...	13.1	...	...	...	...	2.3	53.4	10.0
10.2	...	...	...	...	...	...	...	...	...	58.8	56.4	...	17.1	83.1	...	...	...	14.3	...	...	9.2	...	...	...	...	...	63.7	10.2
10.4	...	...	...	...	...	...	...	...	...	55.7	54.1	...	16.5	84.3	...	...	...	10.0	...	...	6.2	...	...	...	...	...	73.1	10.4
10.6	...	...	...	...	...	...	...	...	...	53.6	52.3	...	16.0	85.4	...	...	...	6.9	...	...	...	...	...	...	...	...	81.2	10.6
10.8	...	...	...	...	...	...	...	...	...	52.2	...	...	15.5	86.5	...	...	...	...	...	...	...	...	...	...	...	...	87.9	10.8
11.0	...	...	...	...	...	...	...	...	...	51.2	...	...	14.7	87.8	...	...	...	...	...	...	...	...	...	...	...	...	...	11.0
11.2	...	...	...	...	...	...	...	...	...	50.4	...	...	13.5	89.3	...	...	...	...	...	...	...	...	...	...	...	...	...	11.2
11.4	...	...	...	...	...	...	...	...	...	49.5	...	...	11.7	91.3	...	...	...	...	...	...	...	...	...	...	...	...	...	11.4
11.6	...	...	...	...	...	...	...	...	...	48.7	...	...	9.1	94.5	...	...	...	...	...	...	...	...	...	...	...	...	...	11.6
11.8	...	...	...	...	...	...	...	...	...	47.6	...	...	5.5	99.0	...	...	...	...	...	...	...	...	...	...	...	...	...	11.8
12.0	...	...	...	...	...	...	...	...	...	46.0	...	...	1.3	...	...	...	...	...	...	...	...	...	...	...	...	...	...	12.0
12.2	...	...	...	...	...	...	...	...	...	43.2	...	...	...	...	...	...	...	...	...	...	...	...	...	...	...	...	...	12.2
12.4	...	...	...	...	...	...	...	...	...	39.1	...	...	...	...	...	...	...	...	...	...	...	...	...	...	...	...	...	12.4
12.6	...	...	...	...	...	...	...	...	...	31.8	...	...	...	...	...	...	...	...	...	...	...	...	...	...	...	...	...	12.6
12.8	...	...	...	...	...	...	...	...	...	21.4	...	...	...	...	...	...	...	...	...	...	...	...	...	...	...	...	...	12.8

Indicators are usually made up as 0.1% solutions in water with the addition of ethanol until solution is complete. For titrations to an end-point of definite pH it is advantageous to use mixed indicators as described in the literature[1].

References

[1] DATTA and GRZYBOWSKI, in LONG, C. (Ed.), *Biochemists' Handbook*, Spon, London, 1961, page 53; KOLTHOFF and MENZEL, *Die Maßanalyse*, part 2: *Die Praxis der Maßanalyse*, 2nd ed., Springer, Berlin, 1931, page 64.

Indicator	Acid side	pH range	Alkaline side
Cresol red, 1st range	red	0.2– 1.8	yellow
m-Cresol purple, 1st range	red	1.2– 2.8	yellow
Thymol blue, 1st range	red	1.2– 2.8	yellow
Metanil yellow	red	1.2– 2.3	yellow
Tropaeolin 00 (orange IV)	red	1.4– 3.2	yellow
2,6-Dinitrophenol	colourless	1.7– 4.4	yellow
Benzyl orange	red	1.9– 3.3	yellow
2,4-Dinitrophenol	colourless	2.0– 4.7	yellow
p-Dimethylaminoazobenzene	red	2.9– 4.0	yellow
Bromophenol blue	yellow	3.0– 4.6	violet
Congo red	blue	3.0– 5.0	red
Bromochlorophenol blue	yellow	3.0– 4.6	purple
Methyl orange	red	3.1– 4.4	yellow
Bromocresol green	yellow	3.8– 5.4	blue
2,5-Dinitrophenol	colourless	4.0– 5.8	yellow
Methyl red	red	4.2– 6.3	yellow
Azolitmin (litmus)	red	4.4– 6.6	blue
Propyl red	red	4.6– 6.6	yellow
p-Nitrophenol	colourless	4.7– 7.9	yellow
Bromocresol purple	yellow	4.8– 6.8	purple
Bromophenol red	yellow	4.8– 6.8	purple
Chlorophenol red	yellow	5.0– 6.9	purple
Bromothymol blue	yellow	6.0– 7.6	blue
m-Nitrophenol	colourless	6.6– 8.6	yellow
Neutral red	red	6.8– 8.0	yellow
Phenol red	yellow	6.8– 8.4	red
Rosolic acid	brown	6.9– 8.0	red
Cresol red, 2nd range	yellow	7.2– 8.8	purple
α-Naphtholphthalein	brown	7.3– 8.7	green
Orange I (Tropaeolin 000 No. 1)	yellow	7.6– 8.9	rose
m-Cresol purple, 2nd range	yellow	7.6– 9.2	purple
Thymol blue, 2nd range	yellow	8.0– 9.6	blue
o-Cresolphthalein	colourless	8.2– 9.8	red
Phenolphthalein	colourless	8.3–10.0	red
Thymolphthalein	colourless	9.3–10.5	blue
β-Naphthol violet	yellow	10.0–12.0	violet
Alizarin yellow R	yellow	10.0–12.1	brown
Alizarin yellow GG	yellow	10.0–12.0	orange
Nitramine	colourless	10.8–13.0	brown
POIRRIER blue	blue	11.0–13.0	red
Tropaeolin 0 (resorcin yellow)	yellow	11.1–12.7	orange

Many of the spectral emission lines listed in the tables below are readily detectable only in the hotter flames such as oxy-hydrogen or oxy-acetylene and in some cases only in the inner cone.

For further data on flame photometry see the literature[1].

References

[1] MAVRODINEANU and BOITEUX, *L'analyse spectrale quantitative par la flamme*, Masson, Paris, 1954; DEAN, J.A., *Flame Photometry*, McGraw-Hill, New York, 1960; MACINTYRE, I., *Advanc. clin. Chem.*, 4, 1 (1961).

[2] From MACINTYRE, I., in LONG, C. (Ed.), *Biochemists' Handbook*, Spon, London, 1961, page 10. Reproduced by kind permission of the author and publishers.

Flame lines and bands of analytical importance[2]

The emissions are arranged in order of wave length. Inclusion does not necessarily mean that the emission is suitable for quantitative measurement of the element concerned. Band emissions are given at the most sensitive wave length and are marked '*b*'.

Wave length (nm)	Element	Wave length (nm)	Element	Wave length (nm)	Element
228.8	Cd	375.8	Fe	495 *b*	B
253.7	Hg	377.6	Tl	497 *b*	Ti
285.2	Mg	378.6	Ru	500 *b*	Zn
303.4	Sn	383 *b*	Mg	510 *b*	Be
307.6	Zn	385.6	Fe	518 *b*	Ti
317.5	Sn	386.0	Fe	520.5	Cr
324.8	Cu	387.3	Co	520.6	Cr
326.1	Cd	387.4	Co	520.8	Cr
327.4	Cu	396.2	Al	521 *b*	B
328.1	Ag	403.3	Ga	535.0	Tl
330.2	Na	403.5	Mn	540 *b*	Mo
330.3	Na	404.4	K	548 *b*	B
338.3	Ag	404.7	K	550 *b*	U
340.5	Pd	405.8	Pb	552 *b*	Dy
341.2	Co	407.8	Sr	553.6	Ba
341.5	Ni	410.2	In	554 *b*	Ca
343.5	Rh	417.2	Ga	560 *b*	La
344.6	K	420.2	Rb	562 *b*	Pr
344.7	K	421.6	Sr	565 *b*	Tb
349 *b*	Sn	422.7	Ca	570 *b*	Gd
350.2	Co	425.4	Cr	570 *b*	Dy
350.3	Rh	427.5	Cr	571 *b*	Pr
351.5	Ni	429.0	Cr	576 *b*	V
352.4	Ni	430.4	Nd	589.0	Na
352.5	Ni	438 *b*	La	589.5	Na
353.0	Co	442 *b*	La	600 *b*	Mo
360.5	Cr	444 *b*	Y	600 *b*	Tb
361.0	Pd	450 *b*	Nb	622 *b*	Ca
363.5	Pd	450 *b*	Gd	653 *b*	Sm
364 *b*	Te	451.1	In	660 *b*	Nd
368.4	Pb	455.4	Ba	670.8	Li
369.2	Rh	455.5	Cs	681 *b*	Sr
371 *b*	Mg	460.7	Sr	715 *b*	Ti
372 *b*	Te	460.9	Sc	766.5	K
372.0	Fe	462 *b*	Gd	769.9	K
372.3	Fe	462 *b*	Nb	780.0	Rb
372.8	Ru	466.2	Eu	794.8	Rb
373.3	Fe	467 *b*	Al	818.3	Na
373.5	Fe	471 *b*	Be	819.5	Na
373.7	Fe	472.3	Bi	852.1	Cs
374.3	Fe	481 *b*	Ce	873 *b*	Ba
374.6	Fe	483 *b*	Y	894.3	Cs
374.8	Fe	484 *b*	Al		
374.9	Fe	493.4	Ba		

Detailed flame spectra of sodium, potassium, calcium and magnesium[2]

The ionization potential of the neutral atom and excitation potential of the singly ionized atom (expressed in eV) are given in brackets. '*r*' represents a transition to ground state. The most suitable wave lengths for analysis are given in *italics*. 'I' signifies the neutral atom, 'II' the singly ionized atom.

Element	Wave length (nm)	Emitter	Excitation potential (eV)
Na	285.3 *r*	I	4.06
(5.14; 33.3)	330.2 *r*	I	3.75
	330.3 *r*	I	3.75
	568.3	I	4.03
	568.8	I	4.03
	589.0 *r*	I	2.10
	589.5 *r*	I	2.10
	818.3	I	3.61
	819.5	I	3.61
K	344.6 *r*	I	3.59
(4.34; 20.6)	344.7 *r*	I	3.59
	404.4 *r*	I	3.06
	404.7 *r*	I	3.06
	693.9	I	3.40
	696.4	I	3.40
	766.5 *r*	I	1.61
	769.9 *r*	I	1.61
Ca	*422.7* *r*	I	2.93
(6.11; 3.12)	393.4 *r*	II	3.15
	396.8 *r*	II	3.12
	622	CaO	1.97
	554	CaO	
Mg	277.7	I	7.17
(7.64; 4.42)	277.8	I	7.17
	278.0	I	7.17
	278.1	I	7.17
	278.3	I	7.17
	285.2 *r*	I	4.34
	333.0	I	6.43
	333.2	I	6.43
	333.7	I	6.43
	382.9	I	5.85
	383.2	I	5.85
	383.8	I	5.85
	279.6 *r*	II	4.43
	280.3 *r*	II	4.42
	371	MgO	3.49
	383	MgO	3.38

(For references see page 291)

Principles[1] **

Chemical properties of radioactive nuclides

The artificial isotopes of a chemical element have the same properties as the natural ones and also a similar metabolic activity. Quantitative dissimilarities may occur, however, since differences in the mass number may result in differences in the diffusion and dissociation constants and thus in the rate of reaction both in vivo and in vitro. The more the relative atomic mass (atomic weight) of the isotope differs from that of the natural element, the greater is this 'isotope effect'. For the same reason, the greater the number of isotopic atoms a molecule contains, the more will its metabolic turnover differ from that of the ordinary molecule.

Metabolically, many nuclides behave qualitatively (but possibly not quantitatively) in the same way as the chemically distinct elements of the same or a neighbouring group in the Periodic System. These similarities have become important, particularly because artificial radionuclides, though given usually in very small and thus nontoxic doses, are easily identified by their radioactivity wherever they accumulate.

The replacement of a stable by a radioactive atom in the molecule of a chemical compound is known as 'tagging' or 'labelling', the resulting isotope as a 'tracer'. Biosynthesis by living organisms and enzymatic synthesis in vitro are the least harmful methods of tagging organic substances; unfortunately, with a few exceptions the compounds so produced have a much lower specific activity than that obtainable by purely chemical methods using carrier-free radionuclides in vitro.

Compounds of very high specific activity tagged with carrier-free, short-lived radionuclides should not contain more than *one* radioactive atom per molecule. For statistical reasons it is even better if only every fifth to tenth molecule is tagged with a radioactive atom. If there is multiple substitution the radiochemical isotope effect occurring when any unstable radionuclide disintegrates may take place. The disintegration of all radionuclides – except for isomeric transitions (see below) – results in the formation of new elements by emission of a β^- or β^+ particle together with reactive organic radicals. The remaining radioactive indicators then show a change in their molecular structure. Thus after the disintegration of one of the two radioactive iodine atoms in a di-iodotyrosine molecule tagged in this fashion, the disintegration of the remaining one indicates not di-iodotyrosine but monoiodotyrosine or a reaction product arising from the corresponding radical.

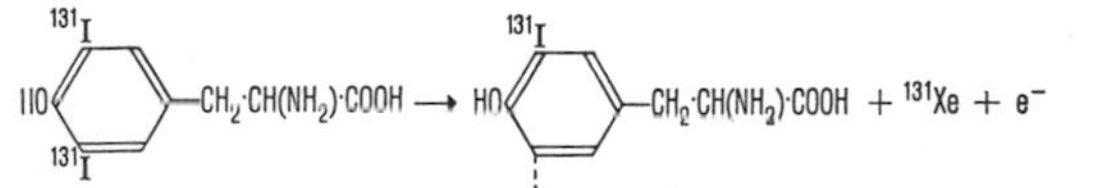

Another disadvantage of high specific activities is that organic compounds may be decomposed by their own radiation.

Radionuclides are designated 'carrier-free' when they are not contaminated by any other isotope of the same element. Most of the radionuclides commercially available are not absolutely carrier-free owing to the unavoidable adsorption phenomena occurring at the surfaces of pipettes and other glassware at the extremely low concentrations used in their preparation. Apart from this, apparatus and solvents often contain traces of the stable isotopes. For this reason, the specific activity of many 'carrier-free' radionuclides falls during storage.

Half-life

The time taken for half the atoms in a quantity of a radionuclide to disintegrate is known as the half-life (see also page 217 and the Isotope Decay Tables on pages 294–306). It follows that after a time equal to x times the half-life the proportion of the radionuclide remaining unchanged is $1:2^x$; after a time equal to 10 times the half-life only one-thousandth of the original radionuclide therefore remains.

The concept of the half-life is also applicable to the biological disappearance (from an organism, organ, organ preparation, enzyme system in vitro, etc.) of a substance tagged with the radionuclide – as it is to that of any substance in a biological system (biological half-life). This disappearance, at least initially, is often not a uniformly exponential process, in which case it may be possible to distinguish two or more component processes by graphical treatment.

The effective half-life, which is always shorter than both the biological (T_b) and physical ($T_{1/2}$) half-lives, can be calculated from the following formula:

$$\frac{T_{1/2} \times T_b}{T_{1/2} + T_b} = T_{eff}$$

This formula is valid only for uniform systems. Often it suffices to estimate T_{eff} by graphical means.

Radioactive disintegration

α-Emitters emit helium nuclei of mass number 4 and atomic number 2, so that their daughter nuclides, with a mass 4 units less, are elements two steps lower down in the Periodic System, for example $^{226}_{88}Ra \rightarrow {}^{222}_{86}Rn + {}^{4}_{2}He$ (= α). α-Disintegration is not always accompanied by measurable γ-emission. Since α-particles have a mass some 7400 times that of electrons their range is short; on the other hand, their ionization density is very much greater than that of β-particles or γ-quanta of the same energy. Unlike the β-emission, the α-emission of a nuclide is rigorously monochromatic and of very short range.

β-Emitters emit either electrons (e^-; β^-; negatrons) or positrons (e^+; β^+). In both cases the reduction in the mass number is negligible, though measurable. In β^--disintegration the nucleus gains a positive charge, so that the daughter nuclide is one step higher in the Periodic System, for example $^1_0n \rightarrow {}^1_1H + e^-$; in β^+-disintegration the nucleus loses a positive charge, and the daughter nuclide is one step lower in the Periodic System, for example $^{11}C \rightarrow {}^{11}B + e^+$. The positron emitted in β^+-disintegration is slowed down by other atoms and molecules and finally unites with an electron, either free or in an electron shell, with emission of the characteristic annihilation radiation, namely two γ-quanta each of 0.511 MeV.

Unlike α- and γ-radiation, β-emission is accompanied by loss of neutrinos and by radiation with a continuous, asymmetrically distributed energy spectrum (an exception are the electrons resulting from internal conversions). The mean β-energy $\bar{E}$ is generally 25–45% of the maximum β-energy (E_{max}). The spectral distribution of the X-ray bremsstrahlung depends on the β-energy and the nature of the material producing it. β-Disintegration is also often accompanied by emission of γ-rays.

In *K-capture*, as in positron emission, the nucleus loses a positive charge because the nucleus gains a shell electron, e^-. This process is initially accompanied not by the emission of radiation but by the loss of a neutrino; only *after* the electron capture does the *daughter* nuclide start to emit γ-rays and its specific K, L or M radiation (X rays), for instance $^{125}I \xrightarrow{K} {}^{125}Te$ (+ Te X rays of 0.027 MeV + γ-rays of 0.035 MeV). Often several kinds of disintegration take place simultaneously, for example:

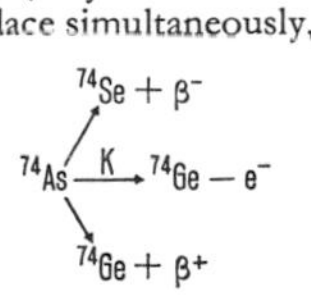

In *isomeric transition* a metastable nuclide is converted into another nuclide of the same element with emission of γ-rays, for example:

$$^{99}Tc^m \xrightarrow[6.0\ h]{\gamma} {}^{99}Tc \xrightarrow[2.2 \times 10^5\ y]{e^-} {}^{99}Ru$$

The process is often accompanied by internal conversion in which the excitation energy of the nucleus ionizes the K, L or M electron shell, with the emission of conversion electrons of uniform energy. In addition, the characteristic X rays are emitted when an electron is captured to fill the empty place in the shell.

In all radioactive processes a certain amount of energy is liberated in the form of heat and as a result of recoil effects and ionization, so that the *chemical* reactivity of the nuclide or daughter nuclide may be increased. In addition, the radiation causes ionization in the surrounding medium (air, solvent).

On units of radioactivity see page 217.

Detection of radioactivity

Ionization

The passage of high-energy radiation through matter results in the formation of ions as a result of collision of electrons with atoms. So much energy is transferred to the orbital electrons that one es-

* The sections 'Principles' and 'Diagnostic Uses' have been compiled in collaboration with E. Kallee, Isotope Laboratory, University Medical Clinic, Tübingen, the section 'Therapeutic uses' in collaboration with H. Lüthy, University Department of Radiology, Municipal Hospital, Basle.

** See also the section 'Radioactivity' and 'Radiation Dosimetry', page 217 sq.

(For references see page 291)

capes from the atom, giving rise to a slow, positively charged ion and a very fast secondary electron. If the ions and electrons are not immediately separated by means of an electric field they recombine and remain undetected. Electrons slowed by multiple collisions can be captured by reactive gas molecules and give rise to negative ions. Furthermore, an ion strongly accelerated in an electric field may collide with a neutral gas molecule and thereby give rise to a fresh positive ion and electron (see GEIGER counters, below). X and γ-rays must also first give rise to free electrons before they can be detected, and since the probability of ionization occurring decreases rapidly with increasing quantum energy, the harder such radiation is, the more difficult it is to detect.

Ionization chambers. While ionization chamber measurements form the absolute basis of dosimetry (see below), the method is too slow and insensitive for detecting short-lived radioactivity in the μCi range and lower.

Geiger counters. These are gas-filled counters operating at reduced pressure. They do not measure continuous currents like ionization chambers but register collision ionizations. The primary ions in the counter gas are multiplied by applying an electric field of 800–2000 V (ion 'avalanche'). In the range of roughly 200–600 V the number of ions present is strictly proportional to the number of primary ions (proportional region), and for this reason proportional counters can be used to distinguish β-rays from highly ionizing particles. At higher voltages (> 800 V) a 'plateau' region is reached in which the ion avalanche is largely independent of the intensity of primary ionization. The life-time of a gas-filled counter is limited by the capacity of the gas to a total of 10^9–10^{10} collision discharges; for halogen-filled tubes it is about 10^{12}. During a collision ionization, which lasts about 0.1 ms, the counter is refractory to additional ionizations (counter dead time). In the plateau region the resolving time – or minimum time between two counted discharges – is about 0.2 ms, in the proportional region about 1 μs.

Semiconductor detectors. When silicon or germanium crystals are irradiated, ionization occurs and secondary electrons are released. With the aid of electron donors (for example lithium) these can be conducted to electrodes and measured as current pulses. Such drift detectors are suitable for detecting corpuscular and low-energy X and γ-rays at room temperature. On account of their extremely small size they can even be implanted.

Scintillation

This is the name given to the light flashes emitted by luminescent substances when excited by high-energy radiation. The flashes can in turn liberate photoelectrons from photosensitive substances (for instance caesium/antimony phosphors); the photoelectrons are amplified 10^7–10^8 times by means of a phototube multiplier before being converted into current pulses. The pulse height depends on the energy of the original γ- or corpuscular radiation, and the pulses can thus be sorted by means of a discriminator (pulse height analyser). By using different discriminator channels the different nuclides in a mixture of isotopes can be determined either successively or simultaneously.

Solid scintillators. The commonest type in use in nuclear medicine consists of single crystals of thallium-activated sodium iodide. Since the decay time of the fluorescence is only 0.25 μs the scintillation crystals have a resolving power about a thousand times greater than gas-filled counters. Moreover, the pulse yield for X and γ-rays is 10–1000 times greater – depending on the crystal volume and surface – as a result of the higher density of the material. Since there is no dissipation of the crystals the life-time of these scintillation detectors is limited only by that of the replaceable multiplier and its semi-permanent photosensitive layer. The wave length of the luminescent radiation is about 410 nm. Organic scintillators and plastic scintillators have a decay time of 5–24 ns, their secondary luminescence a wave length of 410–440 nm.

Liquid scintillators. The radiation from preparations emitting β-rays, soft X rays or γ-rays can be measured with particularly high pulse yield if they are mixed directly with a scintillator solution.

Only a few highly purified alkylbenzenes (mainly toluene and xylene) and ethers (anisole, veratrole, dioxan) are suitable as *solvents*. They transmit the radiation energy to the scintillators by ionization via metastable (10^{-12}–10^{-9} s) excited states. This type of energy transmission is subject to interference by fluorescence quenching.

The *'first' scintillator* usually consists of a solution of 2,5-diphenyloxazole (PPO) in toluene (4 g/l). Its fluorescence, which is highly subject to quenching, has a maximum at 380 nm. Since the photocathodes of many multipliers develop optimum activity only at wave lengths above 400 nm the spectrum of the primary fluorescence must be displaced to higher wave lengths by using a second fluorescent substance. Other suitable first scintillators are 2-phenyl-5-(4-diphenyl)-1,3,4-oxadiazole (PBD or PBO) (in toluene, 12 g/l; 360 nm) and *p*-terphenyl (8 g/l; 350 nm). 2,5-Bis-(2-[5-*tert.*-butylbenzoxazolyl])thiophen (BBOT) emits light at 435 nm and therefore needs no second scintillator.

The *'second' scintillator* converts the ultraviolet radiation from the first by fluorescence into radiation with a wave length of about 420 nm. It usually consists of 1,4-di-(2-[5-phenyloxazolyl])benzene (POPOP) in toluene at a concentration of 0.1–2.0 g/l. A small part of the fluorescence of this substance is due to primary radioactivity and reduces quenching in the first scintillator.

If the radioactive preparation in question is insoluble in the solvent, other substances must be added to make it soluble. Like water, however, these substances considerably reduce the pulse yield by fluorescence quenching. Since the latter also causes spectral displacement, however, it can be detected and corrected by discriminatory measurements in two channels or by comparison with internal or external standard radiators.

Autoradiography

The oldest method of detecting radioactivity is the photographic one. Both electromagnetic and corpuscular radiation cause electrons to be expelled from the halogen atoms in the silver halide grains in a gelatin emulsion. Each electron reduces a silver ion (Ag^+) to metallic silver. The sites at which this occurs in the silver halide grains constitute 'development centres' where the developer begins the reduction of the whole grain to black metallic silver. The resulting degree of intensification is about 10^{12}.

Macroscopic autoradiography is used in nuclear medicine mainly for radiation exposure monitors (film badges); another use is the localization of radioactivity in chromatograms and in organ sections of large surface area. The film used is high-sensitivity X-ray film; for pure γ-ray sources an intensifying screen is usually necessary, though this reduces the sharpness of the image. Image intensity is dependent on a great many factors, so that the exposure time must be decided empirically in each case. As an example, an autoradiograph taken by a ^{131}I isotope with a radioactivity of 10 nCi/cm² requires an exposure time of 2–4 days.

Microscopic autoradiography of sections 5–10 μm thick requires an activity concentration in the tissue of about 10 μCi/ml (assuming uniform distribution) if satisfactory blackening of films is to be obtained in 2–16 days. In the case of weakly radioactive sources, self-exposure times longer than three times the half-life are pointless. The activity of weak β-emitters (^3H, ^{14}C, ^{35}S) can be determined semiquantitatively by counting the blackened grains.

Dosimetry of incorporated nuclides (see also pages 218–221)

If a β-emitter is uniformly distributed throughout an organ or the whole body, and if the range of its β-rays is small compared with the volume of matter concerned, then the absorbed dose D_∞ for complete disintegration is given by

$$D_\infty = K_\beta \times \alpha_0 \times \frac{T_{eff}}{T_{1/2}}\ [\text{rd}]$$

where α_0 is the initial activity concentration A_0/m (in μCi/g), T_{eff} the effective half-life (in days), $T_{1/2}$ the physical half-life (in days), K_β a characteristic constant for each β-emitter (see the table on pages 292 and 293). K_β is given by

$$K_\beta = 73.9 \times \bar{E}_\beta \times T_{1/2}\ [\text{rd g μCi}^{-1}]$$

where $T_{1/2}$ is in days and E_β is the mean energy in MeV of the β-emission ($\approx 0.3\ E_{max}$; see the table on pages 292 and 293).

The hourly absorbed dose rate after the lapse of a time t from incorporation is given by

$$\dot{D}_\beta = 0.0288 \times K_\beta \times \alpha_0 \times \frac{1}{T_{1/2}} \times e^{-0.693\frac{t}{T_{eff}}}\ [\text{rd h}^{-1}]$$

where $T_{1/2}$ is in days, t and T_{eff} in any time unit provided it is the same for both. For values of $t \ll T_{eff}$ the exponential factor can be assumed to be unity.

The absorbed dose D_∞ for complete disintegration of a uniformly distributed γ-emitter is given by

$$D_\infty = K_\gamma \times \alpha_0 \times \frac{T_{eff}}{T_{1/2}} \times \varrho_0 \times g\ [\text{rd}]$$

$$K_\gamma = 0.0338 \times \Gamma \times T_{1/2}\ [\text{rd cm}^2\ \text{μCi}^{-1}]$$

where ϱ_0 is the density of the medium in g ml^{-1}, Γ the specific γ-ray constant for the nuclide in R cm^2 h^{-1} mCi^{-1} (see the table on pages 292 and 293). For irradiations in vitro $T_{eff} \equiv T_{1/2}$.

The absorbed dose rate at any point within a sphere containing a uniformly distributed γ-emitter is obtained by the use of a geometrical factor g proportional to the radius r of the sphere. If g_0 is the value at the centre of the sphere, then it can be shown that the value at the surface of the sphere is $g_0/2$ and that the *average value* $\bar{g}$ *over the whole sphere* is $3\,g_0/4$, so that the corresponding dose rates are in these proportions. Values of g_0 for spheres of radius $r = 2$ cm and 4 cm are respectively 25 cm and 50 cm. For the human body containing a uniformly distributed γ-emitter, approximation of the trunk to a cylinder gives values of $\bar{g}$ between 110 and 140 cm, depending on the body weight.

The hourly absorbed dose rate is given by

$$\dot{D}_\gamma = 0.877 \times 10^{-3} \times \alpha_0 \times \Gamma \times \varrho_0 \times g \text{ [rd h}^{-1}\text{]}$$

The linear range R_L of β-rays in materials of low atomic number ($Z \approx 20$ or less) is dependent only on the density, so that for two media of density ϱ_1 and ϱ_2

$$R_{L1} = R_{L2} \times \frac{\varrho_2}{\varrho_1}$$

For β-rays it is usual to give the mass range R_D, or mass per unit area of a layer of thickness equal to the linear range. This is obtained by multiplying the linear range (cm) by the density (mg cm^{-3}) and is therefore expressed in mg cm^{-2}. Linear ranges of the β-radiation of various nuclides in water are given in the table on pages 292 and 293.

The intensity of both corpuscular and electromagnetic radiation from a point source *in vacuo* decreases with the square of the distance. Thus for γ-rays the dose rate at distance r can be calculated from the following formula (A_0 = initial activity) if the specific γ-ray constant Γ is known:

$$\dot{D}_\gamma = \frac{\Gamma \times A_0}{r^2} \text{ [R h}^{-1}\text{]}$$

For γ- and X rays this formula also holds approximately in air.

Diagnostic uses[1]

Thyroid[2]

Functional tests with radio-iodine

The dietary iodine intake of adults is about 50–200 μg/day, in some countries as much as 600–800 μg/day. Iodine can also be absorbed via the lungs and skin. The intestinal wall absorbs iodide very rapidly, the average rate at which it is taken up by the thyroid being 75 μg/day (0.2–10 μg/h). Above a critical serum iodide concentration of 200–350 μg/l the thyroid ceases to take up further iodide. Two days after administration of carrier-free radio-iodine the concentration of activity is about 10000 times higher in the thyroid than in the serum.

In clinical radio-iodine tests, adults are given 20–50 μCi (children 2–10 μCi) of ^{131}I in the form of 'carrier-free' iodide either orally on an empty stomach or by intravenous injection (owing to its short half-life, ^{132}I is given by the intravenous route only). The weight of the ^{131}I test dose varies from 1–100 ng, depending on the extent to which it has been freed from ^{127}I and ^{129}I, but in any case it is an amount negligibly small in comparison with that already present in the body fluids (10–40 μg/l).

The radio-iodide is completely absorbed by the alimentary-tract mucosa within 1–2 hours under normal conditions and passes into the blood in the same way as other iodide. During the next 24 hours about 20–40% of the test dose is then excreted by the healthy kidneys and about 40–70% stored by the healthy thyroid. The remainder is distributed throughout the extravascular space, whence it is also removed gradually by these two organs. In addition, some of the iodide enters a cycle involving the salivary and gastric glands. In hyperthyroidism the kidneys excrete less than 20% of the dose, in hypothyroidism – except in cases where there is a disturbance of hormone synthesis – over 40%.

About 2 hours after taking the test dose the activity in the blood rises for a short time to a level corresponding to about 3–5% (depending on the body weight and plasma volume) of the total activity administered per litre of the serum or plasma and then falls during the next 48 hours to a figure of 0.1–0.3%. At this time over two-thirds of this activity is contained in thyroid hormones. The proteins carrying this hormonal iodine can be precipitated by trichloracetic acid or other substances (protein-bound ^{131}I, PB^{131}I) and thus separated from the unbound ^{131}I$^-$. Another and more complicated procedure is extraction of the hormones with butanol (butanol-extractable ^{131}I, BE^{131}I). This method also permits separation of the iodinated peptides and proteins sometimes present in the blood in thyroiditis, carcinoma and autochthonous disturbances of thyroid hormone synthesis.

About 48 hours after the test dose the PB^{131}I – representing the newly-formed thyroid hormones – normally amounts to 0.05–0.2% of the total ^{131}I administered per litre of the serum. The proportion of the total activity accounted for by the PB^{131}I – the so-called conversion rate – is 65–90%. The conversion rate is lowered in most cases of hypothyroidism as well as after the ingestion of iodine.

The first 2–12 hours after giving radio-iodine are known as the 'iodide phase' since most of the serum iodine is still in the form of iodide. This is succeeded by the 'hormone phase' as soon as measurable amounts of PB^{131}I appear in the serum. Although there is of course no sharp division between these two phases, an empirical distinction is justified on clinical grounds since the iodide phase is shortened in hyperthyroidism and lengthened in uncomplicated hypothyroidism. For this reason the ^{131}I activity of the thyroid is measured in the routine radio-iodine test first of all at 2, 4 or 6 hours after the test dose and then again after 24 hours. If it is intended to give radio-iodine therapeutically, further measurements after 48 and 72 hours are necessary so that the correct dosage can be estimated from the rate at which the activity disappears.

Normal values for radio-iodine uptake by the thyroid are 10–50% after 6 hours and 25–65% after 24 hours (see the uptake curves on page 288). These wide ranges are partly due to differences in the characteristics of measuring instruments, and for this reason the International Atomic Energy Agency in 1964 published a guide to the optimal constitution of collimators[3]. Other causes of discrepancies are a high dietary intake of iodine (sea foods, sweet cherries, iodinated salt), the avidity of the thyroid in persons living in iodine-deficiency areas where table salt is not iodinated, and the presence in some foods (cabbages, milk) and even drinking water of thyrostatic substances (thiouracil and its derivatives, vinylthio-oxazolidone, pteridines).

Radio-iodine tests are also subject to interference by many drugs containing inorganic or organic iodine compounds as well as by ACTH, adrenaline, androgens, arsenic, *p*-aminobenzoic acid, *p*-aminosalicylic acid, bismuth, brominated compounds (iodine content > 0.02%), carbutamide, chloramphenicol, chloroquine, chlortetracycline, cobalt, corticosteroids, diphenylhydantoin, Evans blue, fluphenazine, glutethimide, manganese, meprobamate, mercury, methylphenobarbitone, morphine, phenobarbitone, phenylbutazone, resorcinol, salicylates, sulphobromophthalein, sulphonamides, thiocyanates, thionine, tolbutamide, tranquillizers and vitamin A.

Tri-iodothyronine test (T_3 test; Hamolsky test)[4]

The ^{131}I-T_3 test in vitro is based on equilibria in the distribution of the thyroid hormones on the carrier proteins. In the plasma the inter-α-globulin (thyroxine-binding globulin, TBG), prealbumin and albumin possess to some extent identical binding sites for thyroxine (T_4) and tri-iodothyronine (T_3). Since T_4 is more strongly bound to these proteins than T_3 it is able to displace T_3 from these sites. These two hormones are less strongly bound to the erythrocyte proteins than to the serum proteins. Moreover, the former have separate binding sites for T_3 and T_4, and their potential binding capacity for T_3 is rather high at 37 °C; in the absence of the plasma proteins they can take up 60–70% of a test dose of ^{131}I-T_3 if this is given at a concentration of about 1–10 ng/ml erythrocytes. In the presence of the plasma proteins an equilibrium is established between the T_3 bound to these proteins and that bound to the erythrocyte proteins; thus in heparinized whole blood under normal conditions only 5.5–6.5% of the test dose of ^{131}I-T_3 is erythrocyte-bound. Adjustment to a haematocrit of 100% gives a value for the relative T_3 uptake (T_H) of 12–16%, a range which covers the original normal values given by Hamolsky et al. Pathological changes in the haematocrit require additional adjustment by means of the binding coefficient K of Adams et al.[5]:

$$K = \frac{F\,(1-H)}{H\,(1-F)}$$

K values	
Normal	0.10–0.18
Hypothyroidism	0.06–0.10
Hyperthyroidism	0.18–0.35

(For references see page 291)

Typical radio-iodine test results

I Normal values
Ia Normal range in iodine-deficiency areas
Ib Normal range in iodine-surplus areas
II Rapid iodine turnover in the rebound effect, severe hyperthyroidism and hereditary myxoedema (curves occasionally seen are shown by broken lines)
III Hyperthyroidism (curves occasionally seen are shown by broken lines)
IV Ingestion of drugs containing iodine, thyroid block, hypothyroidism
V Iodine deficiency

Radio-iodine uptake by the thyroid

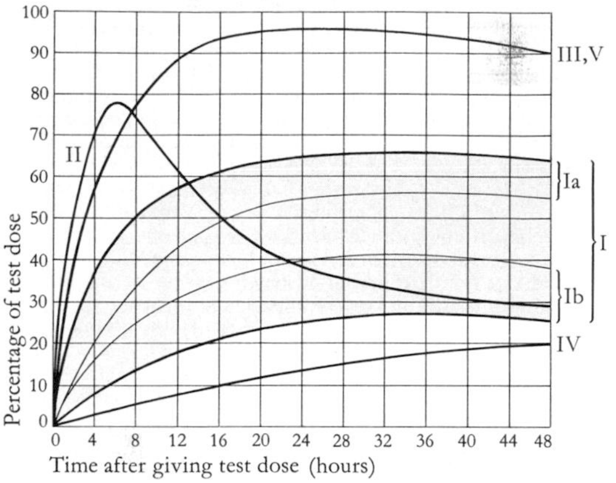

PB¹³¹I (trichloracetic acid precipitation)

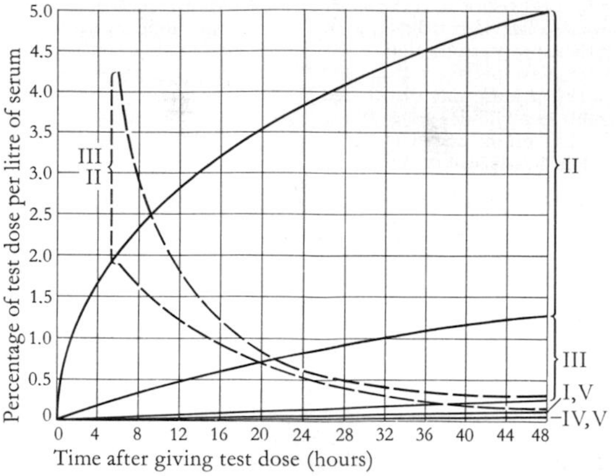

where F is the fraction of ^{131}I-T_3 taken up by the cells and H the haematocrit value.

In order to be able to compare T_H values with older values in the literature converted to a normal haematocrit value of 40% (T_{40}), Wechselberger et al.[6] have introduced another coefficient K': $T_{40} = T_H + K'$. K' is calculated from one of the following two formulae, depending on whether the pathological haematocrit is above or below 40%:

For H = 20–40%, $K' = +0.15\,(40 - H)$

For H = 40–80%, $K' = -6.5 \times 10^{-3}\,(H^2 - 50\,H + 400)$

K' values for various values of H are as follows:

H	K′	H	K′	H	K′
20%	+3.00	45%	−1.13	70%	−11.70
25%	+2.25	50%	−2.60	75%	−14.78
30%	+1.50	55%	−4.38	80%	−18.20
35%	+0.75	60%	−6.50		
40%	+0.00	65%	−8.93		

Variants of the T_3 test often use synthetic resins, dextran gels and other adsorbents in place of erythrocytes. Whatever form the test takes, however, the adsorption of free T_3 depends mainly on two variables: the concentration of T_4 or any other substance capable of displacing T_3, and the TBG, prealbumin and albumin concentrations. The concentration of T_3 in the plasma usually has practically no effect. When the various extrathyroidal factors affecting the results are allowed for, relative T_H values of over 16–17% point in all probability to hyperthyroidism, values below 10–12% to hypothyroidism. Normal values fluctuate slightly, depending on how often the erythrocytes are washed and other procedural differences.

During pregnancy the T_H value is greatly decreased, often also during menstruation. Pathological values are seen in some extrathyroidal diseases, particularly disturbances of the plasma proteins, some types of leukaemia, and uraemic, hepatic and diabetic coma. The following drugs also affect the T_H value: anabolic agents, androgens, anticoagulants, corticosteroids, diphenylhydantoin, Evans blue, furosemide, gestagens (ovulation inhibitors), oestrogens, phenothiazine, phenylbutazone and derivatives, salicylates, sulphobromophthalein, sulphonamides, thyroxine, tri-iodothyronine and thyrotropin, as well as many radionuclides given for diagnostic or therapeutic purposes.

'Free' thyroxine in blood[7]

The serum of euthyroidal persons contains about 50 ng of protein-bound iodine per millilitre, made up principally of thyroxine (T_4). After addition of ^{131}I-T_4, only about 0.05% of the serum activity is dialysable against aqueous buffer solution, the remaining 99.95% being fairly firmly bound to protein. It follows that normal serum contains about 0.025 ng of dialysable ('free') T_4 per millilitre. In hyperthyroidism this is increased to about 0.13 ng/ml, in hypothyroidism decreased to about 0.004 ng/ml. Unlike the T_H value, the serum T_4 level changes little in pregnancy. Its determination is subject to the errors common to all chemical methods of determining protein-bound iodine.

Thyroxine metabolism[8]

In healthy subjects the biological half-life of intravenously injected ^{131}I-T_4 after reaching diffusion equilibrium is about 7 (4–9) days. The extrathyroidal reserve of T_4 has been estimated at 800 µg, of which about 100 µg is broken down per day. In hyperthyroidism the *extra*thyroidal T_4 reserve is increased to about 1800 µg in spite of the augmented rate of breakdown (about 330 µg/day; half-life about 4 days). In hypothyroidism the reserve is reduced to about 360 µg, and the rate of breakdown to about 30 µg/day, with the half-life increased to about 8½ days. Determination of the initial rapid rate of disappearance of ^{131}I-T_4 is also of value in differential diagnosis. In vivo studies of T_4 are subject to interference by disturbances of liver function and by changes in the protein binding.

Thyroid scintigraphy

Two methods of obtaining scintigrams of the thyroid are in current use. In the older and more usual method a collimated scintillation crystal scans the thyroid in a horizontal plane. The impulses picked up are recorded simultaneously on paper, in some instruments in different colours showing the rate at which the impulses are received. The other method (scintillation camera) uses either a very large, fixed scintillation crystal about 25 cm in diameter and carrying some 20 photomultipliers, or a group of ten or more scintillation detectors which scan the object simultaneously. The impulses are usually stored for a period ranging from a few seconds to minutes before being converted into a photographic image.

The principal radioactive sources used in thyroid scintigraphy are $^{131}I^-$ and $^{99}Tc^mO_4^-$. ^{131}I scintigraphy is usually combined with the radio-iodine test, the scintigram being taken 12–48 hours after giving a test dose of 30 µCi Na^{131}I (2–10 µCi in children).

Although the use of ^{99}Tc^m requires a tenfold larger dose, the magnitude of the radiation load on the thyroid is about 100 times

(For references see page 291)

less than with ^{131}I since the former isotope disintegrates without β-radiation and has a shorter effective half-life. $^{99}Tc^{m}$ also gives sharper scintigrams on account of its monochromatic γ-radiation and the fact that this shows little scattering. It gives no quantitative indication, however, of the state of iodine metabolism.

The areas of radioactivity revealed by scintigraphy of the thyroid are roughly classified into 'cold' or 'hot' nodes according to their intensity. The only information they afford is the intensity of the activity in relation to that in the surrounding tissue. A 'cold' node could therefore just as well represent a cyst, fibroma, abscess, haematoma, epithelial connective tissue or 'burnt-out' adenoma as a malignant tumour. A 'hot' node usually represents an adenoma, but it could also be an epithelial residue capable of taking up iodine and surrounded by tissue of low functional activity. Since thyroid adenomas, particularly the 'toxic' variety, have a largely autonomous metabolism independent of anterior pituitary control, suppression for three days with daily doses of 50–100 μg of tri-iodothyronine may be helpful; an adenoma may then be more clearly seen in a second scintigram. Multiple adenomas may be difficult to distinguish by scintigraphy alone from nodular goitre, differentiated or undifferentiated carcinomas, thyroid tumours, or florid or irregularly healed inflammatory areas in a goitrous gland.

For whole-body scintigraphy aimed at locating an aberrant goitre the usual test dose of 30 μCi of ^{131}I suffices. Diffuse metastases of 'benign' thyroid tumours or (rare) thyroid carcinomas with functional activity require doses of 50–100 μCi. Most thyroid carcinomas do not take up iodine; stimulation with thyrotropin is indicated only when there is no danger of compression.

Kidneys [9]

Radiography of the kidneys at present makes use principally of *o*-iodohippuric acid (IHA). With ^{131}IHA the applied dose is about 0.2 μCi/kg body weight, with ^{125}IHA usually 0.4 μCi/kg body weight. The nephrogram reveals two main phases, both of which can be evaluated:

(a) A rising phase commencing about 10–15 seconds after the injection and reaching a maximum in 4–6 minutes. This phase represents the uptake, storage and secretion of the IHA and can often be divided into a very steep part (initial phase) and rather less steep part (functional phase) separated by a more or less sharp break.

(b) A falling phase following the maximum and with a roughly exponential course (half-life normally about 15 minutes).

IHA nephrography is the best tolerated and fastest method of diagnosing major renal disturbances. It also enables a comparison to be made of the functional capacity of the two kidneys. Anatomical details are shown up better with ^{203}Hg- or ^{197}Hg-chlormerodrin scintigraphy than with IHA.

Liver [10]

Intravenous injection of 10–30 μCi ^{131}I-Bengal red is followed by measurement of the rate of disappearance of serum activity and rate of uptake of the dye by the liver. The half-life in the serum is normally only a few minutes. In the scintigram the storage maximum is reached about 20–30 minutes after the injection; after 40–90 minutes the activity is concentrated in the gallbladder region. The rise and fall in the activity are determined by the blood flow and functional capacity of the liver. Scintigraphy of the liver can also be carried out with colloidal radiogold (^{198}Au, 40–100 μCi i.v.), which is phagocytosed by the cells of the reticuloendothelial system, but this isotope gives no picture of the gallbladder.

Brain [11]

Suitable isotopes for the diagnosis of tumours and abscesses of the brain are the positron-emitters ^{74}As (1.5 mCi of Na_3AsO_4) and ^{68}Ga (250 μCi of Ga-EDTA) and the γ-emitters ^{197}Hg (0.5–1.0 mCi of chlormerodrin) and $^{99}Tc^{m}$ (5–10 mCi of TcO_4^-). In searching for brain tumours with ^{197}Hg a conventional scintigram suffices, but with $^{99}Tc^{m}$ a scintigraph with a very high scanning speed or a scintillation camera is necessary. ^{74}As can be used only in conjunction with a positron scintigraph with two detectors for coincidence counting; ^{68}Ga requires an ANGER positron camera.

Gastroenterology

Enteral excretion of plasma proteins or polyvinylpyrrolidone (PVP) [12]

In 4 days, normal persons excrete 0.3–1.0% of a tracer dose of 5–10 μCi ^{131}I-PVP or 20–30 μCi ^{51}Cr-albumin in the faeces. After 6 days the upper limit of the total activity excreted is about 1.5% of the dose. In diseases accompanied by enteral loss of protein the corresponding figure may be over 10%. Although ^{51}Cr-human albumin is a nonphysiological polymer it is the indicator of choice on account of its low dose constant and medium half-life.

Schilling's vitamin B_{12} excretion test [13]

In the presence of calcium and the gastrogenic 'intrinsic factor', vitamin B_{12} (cyanocobalamin) is absorbed from the diet and from the intestinal bacteria in the ileum, whence it is transported to the liver and stored (see also page 484). Since the liver can store additional cyanocobalamin, SCHILLING's test uses an oral dose of 0.1–0.5 μg of ^{57}Co-cyanocobalamin (≈0.1–0.5 μCi) given to the fasting patient. Two hours later an intramuscular injection of 1000 μg cyanocobalamin is given in order to saturate the liver and serum proteins with the vitamin. Normally, the kidneys now excrete over 5% (range 6–30%) of the activity administered. If the renal excretion is less than 6% the test must be repeated a week later with the simultaneous administration of intrinsic factor. If the renal excretion is now within the normal range there is a deficiency of intrinsic factor, as in pernicious anaemia, atrophy of the gastric mucosa and carcinoma of the stomach. If it is still low the patient is suffering from impaired intestinal absorption.

Haematology

Iron metabolism [14]

In healthy women the iron reserve amounts to about 40 mg/kg body weight, in men to about 50 mg/kg body weight, so that the total reserves in an adult are 2–4 g of iron. The dose of 5–10 μCi (≈ 1 μg) of ^{59}Fe usually given in metabolic iron studies is therefore negligible. The daily dietary intake of iron is about 17 mg, of which 2–12% (0.5–2.0 mg) is absorbed. The daily iron turnover in the plasma, which contains a total of 7–15 g of transferrin and 2–5 mg of iron, is 25–40 mg, or many times more than the amount absorbed from the diet. The rate of iron turnover can be calculated from the serum iron concentration (SI) and the biological half-life (T_b) of ^{59}Fe in milligrammes per day per 100 ml of whole blood in accordance with the following formula:

$$\frac{\text{SI (in } \mu\text{g/100 ml)}}{T_b \text{ (in min)}} \times \frac{100 - \text{haematocrit}}{100}$$

In spite of the stability of the transferrin binding, ^{59}Fe passes into the tissues with a half-life of 60–120 minutes, and within 8–24 hours most of it has been taken up by the bone marrow. Within 6–14 days some 70–90% of the ^{59}Fe administered has reappeared in the blood in newly formed erythrocytes. Extramedullary blood-forming tissue or iron deposits can be revealed by radioactivity measurements on the sacrum, liver and spleen. Determination of the ferrokinetic parameters requires an observation time of 2–4 weeks.

Erythrocyte breakdown and erythrocyte volume [15,16]

Routine determination of the rate of disappearance of tagged erythrocytes uses $Na_2{}^{51}CrO_4$, 50–95% of the chromium of which becomes bound to the β helix of globin, the amount depending on the method. The determination takes 10–25 days and requires a dose of 30–60 μCi of ^{51}Cr. In normal adults the half-life of the erythrocytes is 29 days (range 24–35 days). At the same time the uptake of ^{51}Cr by the spleen, liver and sacrum is determined by surface activity measurements. The uptake by the spleen must be regarded as pathological if the spleen/liver activity ratio exceeds 1.2.

The *erythrocyte volume* can be measured at the same time as the half-life if desired, and requires merely 1–3 activity measurements and haematocrit determinations 10–20 minutes after intravenous injection of at least 15–30 μCi of ^{51}Cr-tagged erythrocytes. For normal values see page 555.

Plasma volume [16]

The plasma volume can be rapidly and simply determined by intravenous injection of 2.5–5.0 μCi of tagged (^{131}I, ^{125}I) human albumin or human γ-globulin, or of 10–30 μCi of ^{51}Cr-albumin. During the first 10–30 minutes after the injection the rate at which the activity disappears from the plasma is mainly dependent on the rate of mixing of the tagged protein with the normal protein in the vessels. At the same time there is a gradual movement of activity into the extravascular space. By extrapolating the activity curve plotted on logarithmic ordinates the activity concentration at the moment of the injection can be approximately calculated. For normal values see page 555.

Radioimmunological methods[17]

Insulin antibodies

Humoral antibodies in the γ-globulin range that reversibly adsorb insulin instead of precipitating it appear in the blood of only those persons who have previously been given this drug – usually during the 3–6 weeks after the first insulin injection. The binding capacity of these antibodies can be determined by electrophoretic, chromatographic or adsorption-equilibrium methods using insulin tagged with radio-iodine. Binding capacities of over 0.8–1.0 mg of ^{131}I-insulin per litre serum (≈ 20–25 IU/l serum) are often, but not always, associated with intractable diabetes, very high values with insulin resistance. These antibodies are active not only against the homologous (sensitizing) insulin but also against insulin from other species. Thus anti-beef insulin human γ-globulin – formed in man when beef insulin is injected – binds not only the latter but also human and hog insulins. All quantitative immunological methods of determining the concentration of the hormone depend both on this nonspecificity and on the reversibility of the antigen-antibody binding.

Determination of hormone levels

Nonprecipitating antibodies to insulin and other hormone antigens are usually obtained from guinea-pigs. These antibodies bind the corresponding tagged hormones reversibly, for addition of non-radioactive hormone antigen causes the tagged hormone to be displaced from its binding with the species-nonspecific antibody. The higher the concentration of hormone, the less therefore is the amount of antigen activity carried by the antibody γ-globulins. The γ-globulin–hormone complexes can be separated from the unbound ('free') hormone by electrophoresis, chromatography, the adsorption-equilibrium method, immunoprecipitation or other selective precipitation techniques. Hormones that are adequately homogeneous and particularly suitable for determination by radioimmunological methods are insulin, glucagon, ACTH and growth hormone. The lower limit of determination lies in the nanogramme to picogramme range and is dependent on the specific activity of the tagged hormone antigens (5–50 mCi of radio-iodine per milligramme of hormone) and on the hormone-binding capacity of the antibody γ-globulins.

Therapeutic uses[1]

In contrast to the natural radioactive isotopes, which on account of their gaseous decay products can only be used for therapeutic purposes when enclosed in a gastight container (needles, tubes or plaques of platinum, gold or monel metal), the artificial isotopes can mostly be used without enclosure and in either the solid or liquid form. The placing of the radioisotope in a circumscribed focus of disease with maximum possible protection of the surrounding healthy tissue can be achieved by various methods.

Teletherapy (γ-emitters)

Isotope ^{60}Co. Sources with a specific activity of 20–100 Ci/g are used, usually as cylinders 10×10 mm up to 25×25 mm. The source as purchased is fully shielded in a tungsten or lead container, the emergent radiation being controlled by an adjustable or exchangeable tungsten diaphragm. Exposure time is adjusted by a remote-controlled tungsten shutter. Irradiation distance: 20–100 cm according to the activity. Field size: somewhat smaller than in deep X-ray therapy. Crossfire technique, rotation therapy or arc therapy. Advantages over 200 kV X-ray therapy are: higher relative depth dose; sharper lateral limitation of the field; absorption in bone practically the same as in soft tissues (less injury to the bones); maximum dose 4–5 mm *beneath* the skin (dose on skin surface 25–30% of maximum, with correspondingly milder skin reaction). The biological effectiveness of the radiation from ^{60}Co is about 80% of that of 200 kV X rays, so that the dosages given are usually somewhat higher.

Isotope ^{137}Cs. Sources may be contaminated with the shorter-lived isotope ^{134}Cs (half-life 2.3 y compared with 30 y for ^{137}Cs), in which case there is a more rapid loss of activity. The advantage of this isotope lies in its longer half-life than ^{60}Co; its disadvantages are its much lower specific activity, necessitating larger sources and therefore larger penumbra, and its lower γ-energy, resulting in more injury to the skin and bones.

Contact therapy (β- and γ-emitters)

Pure β-*emitters* are used for the irradiation of surface foci of infection in dermatology and ophthalmology and are applied directly to the lesion in suitable forms.

Isotopes ^{32}P *and* ^{90}Sr/^{90}Y. Maximum depth of penetration 5–8 mm, effective range ca. 3 mm. Commercially available in the form of flexible plastic foils containing 20% red phosphorus which have been activated in a reactor.

The Sr/Y mixture is available in metal capsules with a silver foil filter over the exit surface. Activity is due to the β-radiation of the daughter isotope ^{90}Y. Ophthalmological applicators shaped to fit the corneal curvature are available.

A greater depth effect is obtained with γ-*emitters* applied to the surface to be treated. Commercially available is ^{60}Co granulate in a soft plastic mass (Plastobalt) or as plastic spheres enclosed in 6-mm gold foil. These provide optimal adaptation to surfaces of complex shape. The dose of γ-emitters decreases sharply with increasing depth since the intensity is inversely proportional to the square of the distance. ^{182}Ta is available in the form of wire in a plastic tube and is particularly suitable for ring sources for epibulbar irradiation.

Interstitial irradiation

Needles of solid γ-emitters. ^{60}Co is supplied as wire of the ductile alloy 'Cobanic' (55% nickel+45% cobalt) in steel needles or nylon tubes. These 'threads' are sewn into the lesion and have marked advantages over rigid carriers.

^{182}Ta wire (0.4 mm diameter with platinum envelope 0.1 mm thick) is formed into hairpin-shaped loops which are inserted into tumour tissue, particularly in the wall of the bladder.

^{192}Ir is also very suitable for interstitial application in this way. The threads are withdrawn from the tissues at the end of the irradiation period.

For tumours accessible for only a short time, 'seeds' of radiogold (^{198}Au) ca. 2.5 mm long and 0.8 mm in diameter are used, the β-radiation being filtered out by means of an inactive gold or platinum coating. Such seeds can be quickly and accurately placed in the tissue with the aid of a 'pistol' for which filled 'magazines' are available. The magazines must be sterilized before placing in the pistol. Another equipment allows pieces of any desired length to be cut under shielding from radiogold wire coated with inactive gold. The pieces are then inserted into the tissue through a special tube. Radiogold seeds have important advantages over radon seeds.

Needles of solid β-emitters. ^{90}Y (pure β-emitter) in the form of ceramic bodies (1 mm Y_2O_3 spheres) is particularly suitable for irradiation of the pituitary, either via the nose or by stereotaxis. Uniform distribution of the dose over the pituitary can be achieved by implanting about 40 spheres. The total dose required for radiohypophysectomy is about 10 mCi.

Infiltration methods (β-emitters). The radioactive substance is injected directly into the tumour tissue in the form of a stabilized colloidal solution. The irradiation can be assumed to be practically homogeneous when the individual depots are not more than 3 mm apart. Isotopes used: colloidal radiogold (^{198}Au), colloidal ^{32}P as $Cr^{32}PO_4$, colloidal ^{90}Y. There is some loss of activity via the lymph ducts with concentration in the neighbouring lymph glands.

For dosage calculation see pages 286 and 287.

Intracavitary irradiation

(*a*) Colloidal suspensions of radiogold (^{198}Au) are used for intraperitoneal and intrapleural infusion in superficial or disseminated carcinomatosis. Individual doses of 100–150 mCi are given, repeated if necessary after several months up to a total dose of 500 mCi. The main activity is due to the β-radiation, with a small depth effect up to ca. 3 mm. This technique has recently been used for irradiation of the inner wall of the bladder, using 300 mCi of radiogold for a 4-hour period. The dosage can be obtained from a nomogram[18].

(*b*) Solid applicators in the form of plastic masses containing ^{60}Co grains of diameter ca. 1 mm are used principally for irradiation of tumours of the mouth, nose and pharyngeal cavities. Beads of ^{60}Co of diameter 6 mm are strung together for insertion into the oesophagus, or can be packed into natural or surgically opened body cavities.

(*c*) Gynaecology: Sealed radium carriers (platinum filter capsules, total content 50–130 mg of ^{226}Ra) introduced into the vagina, cervix and/or uterus.

Enteral and intravenous applications

A therapeutic effect from intravenous or peroral administration of isotopes is only obtainable when the isotope can be concentrated sufficiently in the tissue to be treated. The only successful application so far is that of radio-iodine (^{131}I), 30–50% of the amount administered being stored in the healthy thyroid. In some cases of primary tumours or metastases (at the most 10% of all thyroid tumours) sufficient of the isotope has been concentrated in the lesion to provide an adequate radiation dose. The usual dose is 100–150 mCi given by mouth.

Hyperthyroidism is treated by administration of peroral doses of 4–10 mCi radio-iodine, repeated if necessary under regular clinical control. The dose achieved depends on the percentage uptake (determined by tracer test), the effective half-life of the isotope and the size of the thyroid. The concentration of the isotope may vary a hundredfold within the gland so that theoretical calculations are useless and dosage must be estimated on an empirical clinical basis.

In the treatment of blood diseases (polycythaemia vera, leucosis), ^{32}P is the isotope of choice. Assuming 20–40% excretion in urine after intravenous injection, the total radiation to which a 70-kg man is exposed per millicurie of the isotope corresponds to 10 R. The dosage is adjusted in accordance with the changes in the blood picture observed.

References

1 ATTIX and ROESCH (Eds.), *Radiation Dosimetry*, 2nd ed., Academic Press, New York, 1968; FIELDS and SEED (Eds.), *Clinical Use of Radioisotopes*, 2nd ed., Year Book Medical Publishers, Chicago, 1961; FRANCIS et al., *Isotopic Tracers – A Theoretical and Practical Manual for Biological Students and Research Workers*, 2nd ed., Athlone Press, London, 1959; GLOCKER and MACHERAUCH, *Röntgen- und Kernphysik für Mediziner und Biophysiker*, 2nd ed., Thieme, Stuttgart, 1965; HAYTER, C. J., *Abstr. Wld Med.*, **42**, 1 (1968); HUNTER and FOECKLER, *Progr. clin. Path.*, **1**, 154 (1966); KAZEM et al., *Brit. J. Radiol.*, **40**, 292 (1967); OWEN, C. A., *Diagnostic Radioisotopes*, Blackwell, Oxford, 1959; SILVER, S., *Radioactive Isotopes in Medicine and Biology*, 2nd ed., Kimpton, London, 1962; SILVER, S., *Nucleonics*, **23**, No. 8, 106 (1965); WHYTE, G. N., *Principles of Radiation Dosimetry*, Wiley, London, 1959; VEALL and VETTER, *Radioisotope Techniques in Clinical Research and Diagnosis*, Butterworth, London, 1958.

2 FOLDENAUER et al., *Dtsch. med. Wschr.*, **92**, 745 (1967); GOOLDEN et al., *Lancet*, **1**, 12 (1967); GRAYSON, R. R., *Amer. J. Med.*, **28**, 397 (1960); KALLEE, E., *Acta isotop. (Padova)*, **6**, suppl. 1 (1966); MEANS et al., *The Thyroid and Its Diseases*, 3rd ed., McGraw-Hill, New York, 1963; QUINN, J. L. (Ed.), *Scintillation Scanning in Clinical Medicine*, Saunders, Philadelphia, 1964; SCAZZIGA and LEMARCHAND-BÉRAUD, Physiopathology of the Thyroid, *Documenta Geigy, Acta clinica*, No. 5, Basle, 1967; WERNER, S. C., *The Thyroid*, 2nd ed., Hoeber-Harper, New York, 1962.

3 BELCHER et al., *Nucl.-Med. (Stuttg.)*, **4**, 78 (1964).

4 HAMOLSKY et al., *J. clin. Invest.*, **36**, 1486 (1957); HAMOLSKY et al., *J. clin. Endocr.*, **17**, 33 (1957); HAMOLSKY et al., *J. clin. Endocr.*, **19**, 103 (1959).

5 ADAMS et al., *J. clin. Endocr.*, **20**, 1366 (1960).

6 WECHSELBERGER et al., *Acta isotop. (Padova)*, **6**, 159 (1966).

7 STERLING and BRENNER, *J. clin. Invest.*, **45**, 153 (1966).

8 INADA et al., *J. clin. Endocr.*, **24**, 775 (1964); KLEIN, E., *Der endogene Jodhaushalt des Menschen und seine Störungen*, Thieme, Stuttgart, 1960; LENNON et al., *J. clin. Invest.*, **40**, 996 (1961); STERLING et al., *J. clin. Invest.*, **33**, 1031 (1954); STERLING and CHODOS, *J. clin. Invest.*, **35**, 806 (1956).

9 BURBANK et al., *Circulation*, **27**, 328 (1963); FEINE et al., *Ärztl. Forsch.*, **21**, 15 (1967); MCAFEE and WAGNER, *Radiology*, **75**, 820 (1960); NORDYKE and TONCHEN, *J. Amer. med. Ass.*, **183**, 440 (1963); REBA et al., *Medicine (Baltimore)*, **42**, 269 (1963); TAPLIN et al., *Nucl. Sci. Abstr.*, **10**, 492 (1956); WERDEN et al., *Amer. J. Med.*, **34**, 765 (1963).

10 CZERNIAK et al., *J. nucl. Med.*, **2**, 121 (1961); LOKEN et al., *J. nucl. Med.*, **5**, 375 (1964); von OLDERSHAUSEN, H. F., *Gastroenterologia (Basel)*, **95**, supplement, 361 (1961); STIRRETT et al., *Radiology*, **61**, 930 (1953).

11 BLAU and BENDER, *J. nucl. Med.*, **1**, 106 (1960), and **3**, 83 (1962); DI CHIRO, G., *J. Amer. med. Ass.*, **188**, 524 (1964); MAGALOTTI and HUMMON, *Amer. J. Roentgenol.*, **83**, 135 (1960); SHY et al., *External Collimation Detection of Intracranial Neoplasia with Unstable Nuclides*, Williams & Wilkins, Baltimore, 1958; SWEET and BROWNELL, *J. Amer. med. Ass.*, **157**, 1183 (1955); TAPLIN et al., *J. nucl. Med.*, **5**, 366 (1964); WITCOFSKI et al., *J. nucl. Med.*, **6**, 121 (1965).

12 GORDON, R. S., *Lancet*, **1**, 325 (1959); GLAUBITT, D., *Dtsch. med. Wschr.*, **92**, 1373 (1967); STEINFELD et al., *Amer. J. Med.*, **29**, 405 (1960); WALDMANN, T. A., *Lancet*, **2**, 121 (1961).

13 CASTRILLÓN-OBERNDORFER et al., in HOFFMANN, G. (Ed.), *Radioisotope in der Gastroenterologie*, Schattauer, Stuttgart, 1967, page 85; DOSCHERHOLMEN and HAGEN, *J. clin. Invest.*, **35**, 699 (1956); GLASS et al., *Arch. Biochem.*, **51**, 251 (1954); HEINLE et al., *Trans. Ass. Amer. Phycns*, **65**, 214 (1952); SCHILLING et al., *J. Lab. clin. Med.*, **45**, 926 (1955).

14 MOORE and BROWN, Le métabolisme du fer, *Documenta Geigy, Acta clinica*, No. 7, Basle, 1967.

15 BOVE and EBAUGH, *Clin. Res. Proc.*, **5**, 142 (1957); CLINE and BERLIN, *Blood*, **22**, 459 (1963); DORNHORST, A. C., *Blood*, **6**, 1284 (1951); EBAUGH et al., *J. clin. Invest.*, **32**, 1260 (1953); LAJTHA, L. G., *The Use of Isotopes in Haematology*, Blackwell, Oxford, 1961.

16 ALBERT, S. N., *Blood Volume*, Thomas, Springfield, 1963.

17 BERSON and YALOW, in PINCUS et al. (Eds.), *The Hormones*, vol. 4, Academic Press, New York, 1964, page 557; FELBER et al., *Schweiz. med. Wschr.*, **95**, 757 (1965); GREENWOOD, F. C., in GARDINER-HILL, H. (Ed.), *Modern Trends in Endocrinology*, vol. 3, Butterworth, London, 1967, page 288; POTTS et al., *Advanc. intern. Med.*, **13**, 183 (1967).

18 ELLIS and OLIVER, *Brit. med. J.*, **1**, 136 (1955).

Characteristics of radioactive nuclides with medical applications[1]

Nuclide	Half-life	Mode of decay	β-Radiation		E_β^{tot}	γ-Radiation[2] (energies in MeV)	Dose constants			β-range in water[3] (mm)	Reciprocal specific activity[4] $\left[\frac{pg}{\mu Ci}\right]$
			E_{max}	$\bar{E}_\beta$			K_β $\left[\frac{rd\,g}{\mu Ci}\right]$	Γ $\left[\frac{R\,cm^2}{h\,mCi}\right]$	K_γ[3] $\left[\frac{rd\,cm^2}{\mu Ci}\right]$		
1	2	3	4	5	6	7	8	9	10	11	12
^{3}H	12.36 y	β^-	0.018 (100)	0.005_5	0.005_5	–	1835	–	–	0.007	103
^{14}C	5568 y	β^-	0.156 (100)	0.049_6	0.049_6	–	7450×10^3	–	–	0.24	218×10^3
^{22}Na	2.58 y	β^+, EC, γ	+0.54 (89)	0.188	0.188	1.28 (100); 0.51 (178)	13100	11.7	3.72×10^2	2.1	160
^{24}Na	15 h	β^-, γ	1.39 (100)	0.550	0.550	2.75 (100); 1.37 (100)	25.6	18.1	0.39	6.4	0.113
^{32}P	14.4 d	β^-	1.71 (100)	0.695	0.695	–	739	–	–	8.0	3.52
^{35}S	87.5 d	β^-	0.167 (100)	0.049	0.049	–	316	–	–	0.3	23.4
^{36}Cl	2.85×10^5 y	β^-, EC	0.71 (98)	0.247	0.247	–	1900×10^6	–	–	2.7	30.5×10^6
^{42}K	12.47 h	β^-, γ	3.55 (82); 1.98 (18)	1.469	1.469	1.53 (18)	56.3	1.35	0.024	19	0.167
^{45}Ca	159 d	β^-	0.258 (100)	0.078	0.078	–	915	–	–	0.6	56.6
^{47}Ca	4.7 d	β^-, γ	2.00 (18); 0.69 (82)			1.30 (76); 0.81 (6); 0.50 (6)		5.1	0.81	9.6	1.69
^{51}Cr	27.8 d	EC, γ	–	–	0.0049	0.32 (9)	10	0.18	0.17	–	10.9
^{52}Mn	5.67 d	β^+, EC, γ	+0.58 (34)	0.084_5	0.088	1.46 (100); 0.94 (100); 0.73 (100); 0.51 (68)	36.9	18.5	3.6	2.2	2.27
^{54}Mn	297 d	EC, γ	–	–	0.0054	0.84 (100)	118.7	4.7	47	–	122.6
^{55}Fe	2.77 y	EC	–	–	0.0059	–	441	–	–	–	414
^{57}Co	267 d	EC, γ	–	–		0.136 (9); 0.122 (89); 0.0144 (6)		0.61	5.5	–	118
^{58}Co	71 d	β^+, EC, γ	+0.49 (15)			1.6 (5); 0.81 (99.5); 0.51		5.585	13.4	1.5	31.6
^{59}Fe	45 d	β^-, γ	1.56 (0.3); 0.462 (54); 0.271 (46)	0.128	0.128	1.29 (43); 1.10 (57); 0.19 (3)	432	6.2	9.4	1.5	20.6
^{60}Co	5.23 y	β^-, γ	1.48 (0.2); 0.312 (99.8)	0.095	0.095	1.33 (100); 1.17 (100)	1340	12.9	8.32×10^2	0.8	884
^{64}Cu	12.8 h	β^-, β^+, EC, γ	0.57 (39); +0.65 (19)	0.126	0.130	1.35 (0.5); 0.51 (38)	5.1	1.15	0.021	2.6	0.226
^{65}Zn	245 d	β^+, EC, γ	+0.324 (1.5)	0.002	0.010	1.12 (46); 0.51 (3)	181	2.8	23	1.2	122
^{74}As	18 d	β^-, β^+, EC, γ	1.36 (17.7); 0.72 (14.5); +1.5 (3.6); +0.91 (26.1)			0.635 (14.5); 0.596 (61); 0.51		4.4	2.6	7.0	9.93
^{75}Se	120 d	EC, γ	–	–		0.405 (15); 0.308 (1); 0.281 (28); 0.269 (54); 0.20 (2); 0.136 (40); 0.122 (12); 0.097 (2); 0.066 (7) and other weak lines		1.5	6.1	–	69
^{76}As	26.45 h	β^-, γ	2.97 (50); 2.41 (31); 1.76 (16); 0.36 (3)	1.078	1.078	2.06 (2); 1.41 (1); 1.21 (12); 0.65 (5); 0.56 (38)	87.8	2.4	0.089	15.7	0.642
^{82}Br	35.7 h	β^-, γ	0.45 (100)	0.134	0.134	1.48 (17); 1.32 (28); 1.04 (27); 0.83 (27); 0.78 (83); 0.70 (27); 0.62 (44); 0.55 (73)	14.7	14.5	0.73	1.6	0.942
^{85}Kr	10.6 y	β^-, γ	0.672 (<99.3); 0.15 (>0.7)			0.514 (~0.7)		0.02	2.6	2.5	2520
^{86}Rb	18.66 d	β^-, γ	1.78 (84); 0.71 (15); 0.23 (1)	0.627	0.627	1.08 (9)	864	0.51	0.32	8.7	12.3
^{89}Sr	51.5 d	β^-	1.46 (100)	0.555	0.555	–	2260	–	–	6.8	34.7
^{90}Sr	28.0 y	β^-	0.54 (100)	0.174	0.174 (0.20)	–	(1510×10^2)	–	–	2.2	7050
^{90}Y	64.5 h	β^-	2.26 (100)	0.917	0.917	–	182	–	–	11	1.86
^{99}Mo	67 h	β^-, γ	1.23 (85); 0.87 (~1); 0.45 (14)			0.780 (4); 0.741 (10); 0.181 (2); 0.041 (1)		0.73	0.17	5.4	2.16

$^{99}Tc^{m}$	6 h	γ	–	–		0.142 (1); 0.140 (88)		0.67	0.0057	–	0.19
^{111}Ag	7.5 d	β⁻, γ	1.04 (91); 0.80 (1); 0.70 (8)	0.356	0.356	0.34 (8); 0.24 (1)	197	0.17	0.043	4.0	6.35
^{113}Sn	119 d	EC, γ	–	–	0.120	0.39 (69)	1058	3.34	13	11.7	103
^{121}Te	17 d	EC, γ	–	–	0.009	0.57 (87) 0.51 (13); 0.07 (2)	6.3	4.4	2.5	–	15.7
^{124}Sb	60.5 d	β⁻, γ	0.97 (9); 0.61 (49); 0.24 (14)	0.371	0.371	2.09 (9); 1.69 (45); 1.33 (3); 0.97 (4); 0.72 (22); 0.65 (9); 0.60 (92)	1666	9.3	19	4.1	57
^{125}I	60 d	EC, γ	–	–		0.035 (7) [0.027 (93) Te X rays]		0.67	1.35	–	57
^{130}I	12.5 h	β⁻, γ	1.02 (46); 0.60 (54)	0.267	0.276	1.15 (31); 0.74 (69); 0.66 (100); 0.53 (100); 0.41 (23)	10.5	12.1	0.21	4.5	0.52
^{131}I	8.09 d	β⁻, γ	0.815 (0.7); 0.608 (87.2); 0.335 (9.3); 0.250 (2.8)	0.181	0.188	0.722 (3); 0.637 (9); 0.364 (80); 0.284 (5); 0.08 (2)	112.2	2.2	0.60	2.2	8.1
^{132}I	2.3 h	β⁻, γ	2.22; 2.14 (81); 1.61 (21); 1.49 (12); 1.22 (12); 1.04 (15); 0.80 (21)			1.40 (8); 1.14 (4); 0.95 (19); 0.78 (82); 0.72 (7); 0.67 (99); 0.65 (26); 0.62 (5); 0.52 (19) and other weak lines		11.12	0.036	10.7	0.095
^{132}Te	78 h	β⁻, γ	0.22 (100)			0.23 (92); 0.052 (~16)		12.74	1.4	0.5	3.28
^{137}Cs	30 y	β⁻, γ	1.17 (8); 0.51 (92)	0.179	0.235	0.662 (84)	1900×10²	3.30	1.2×10³	5.0	10900
^{170}Tm	120 d	β⁻, EC, γ	0.97 (77); 0.885 (23)	0.323	0.328	0.084 (9)	2860	0.08	0.3	4.0	156
^{182}Ta	113 d	β⁻, γ	0.514 (52.1); 0.44 (34.3); 0.36 (14.6)	0.142	–	1.23; 1.22; 1.19; 1.12; 0.22; 0.15; 0.10; 0.07 and other weak lines	1183*	6.0	23	1.8	159
^{192}Ir	74.5 d	β⁻, EC	0.67 (50); 0.54 (35); 0.26 (8); 0.097 (1)	0.169	–	0.61; 0.60; 0.48; 0.47; 0.32; 0.31; 0.30; and other weak lines	930*	5.0	13	2.5	109
^{197}Hg	65.5 h	EC, γ	–	–	0.012	1.92 (1); 0.077 (28)	2.4	0.66	0.06	–	4.08
^{198}Au	2.7 d	β⁻, γ	0.96 (98.6); 0.29 (1.4)	0.312	0.321	1.09 (0.3); 0.67 (1.2); 0.41 (97)	64.0	2.35	0.21	3.8	4.1
^{199}Au	3.15 d	β⁻, γ	0.46 (6.4); 0.302 (69.3); 0.25 (24.3)	0.085	0.110	0.208 (16); 0.158 (77); 0.05 (0.6)	26.4	0.86	0.09	1.5	4.8
^{203}Hg	46.5 d	β⁻, γ	0.208 (100)	0.057	0.086	0.279 (86)	296	1.37	2.15	0.45	73.3
^{204}Tl	4.1 y	β⁻, EC	0.764 (98)	0.238	0.238	–	263×10²	0.007	0.35	2.9	2330

* β-Rays only.

References

[1] Modified from GLOCKER and MACHERAUCH, *Röntgen- und Kernphysik für Mediziner und Biophysiker*, 2nd ed., Thieme, Stuttgart, 1965, pages 39, 40, 42 and 238.
[2] Values mainly from STROMINGER et al., *Rev. mod. Phys.*, **30**, 585 (1958), and (where no value is given in column 6) *International Directory of Isotopes*, 3rd ed., International Atomic Energy Agency, Vienna, 1964.
[3] WECHSELBERGER, E., Tübingen, personal communication, 1967.
[4] Theoretical values for the carrier-free nuclides from E. KALLEE, Tübingen, 1967.

Notes

Column 3: β⁺ = positron emission, EC = orbital electron capture.

Column 4: E_{max} = maximum β-energy in MeV. ⁺ = positron emission. Numbers in brackets are the frequencies of electron or positron emission as percentage of disintegrations.

Column 5: $\bar{E}_{\beta}$ = mean value of the energies of all the β-rays emitted per disintegration. Calculated from E_{max} on the basis of theoretical data of I. H. MARSHALL (*Nucleonics*, **13**, 34 [1955]).

Column 6: $\bar{E}_{\beta}^{tot}$ = sum of $\bar{E}_{\beta}$, the K energy (from internal conversions and electron capture), the energies of the conversion and AUGER electrons, and the L and M energies. For nuclides with atomic numbers greater than 35, the K energy is usually included in calculating the γ dose. For ^{90}Sr, HINE has calculated a correction factor of 1.17 to take account of forbidden transitions.

Column 7: The numbers in brackets are the frequencies of the transitions as percentage of disintegrations. Transitions with frequencies < 0.1% have been disregarded. Energies with a value of 0.51 MeV are annihilation radiations. The effect of internal conversions has been allowed for.

Column 8: Calculated from the equation given on page 286.

Column 9: Calculated from the equation $\Gamma = 194 \times E_{\gamma} \times (\mu_K/\varrho)_L$ [R cm² h⁻¹ mCi⁻¹], (where E_{γ} = γ-energy and $[\mu_K/\varrho]_L$ = mass energy transfer coefficient for air), and including the K energy (from internal conversions and electron capture) for nuclides of atomic number greater than 35 (except for those for which no value is given in column 6). See also page 221.

Column 10: Calculated from the equation given on page 286.

Column 12: Theoretical values for the carrier-free nuclides.

Explanation of the tables on pages 294–306 *

Column 1 — t = elapsed time $(t - t_0)$ in days (d), hours (h) and minutes (min).

Column 2 — N_t = amount of isotope not disintegrated at time t expressed as percentage of N_0 (the values apply equally to the activities A_t and A_0).

Columns 3 and 4 — Factors and their logarithms for calculating N_0 (or A_0) from N_t (or A_t):

$$N_0 = \frac{N_0}{N_t} N_t \quad \text{or} \quad A_0 = \frac{A_0}{A_t} A_t$$

The half-lives ($T_{1/2}$) of $^{99}Tc^m$, ^{132}Te and ^{197}Hg are taken from the *Handbook of Chemistry and Physics*[1], all others from the *Catalogue of Radioactive Products*[2].

* Reproduction of data on pages 294–306 only by permission of the publishers of these *Scientific Tables*.

Decay data for ^3H and ^{226}Ra have also been calculated and may be obtained on application to the publishers of these *Scientific Tables*.

The data in the tables have been calculated by computer using the following relationships (see also page 217):

Column 2 $$\ln \frac{N_t}{N_0} = \frac{-\ln 2}{T_{1/2}} t$$

Columns 3 and 4 $$\ln \frac{N_0}{N_t} = \frac{\ln 2}{T_{1/2}} t$$

$$\left(\text{Disintegration constant } \lambda_t = \frac{\ln 2}{T_{1/2}}\right)$$

References

[1] Heath, R.L., in Weast et al. (Eds.), *Handbook of Chemistry and Physics*, 49th ed., The Chemical Rubber Co., Cleveland, 1968, page B-4.

[2] Radiochemical Centre, *Catalogue of Radioactive Products*, RC.11, Amersham, Bucks., 1967/68.

Sodium-22
half-life 2.6 y

t (d)	N_t	N_0/N_t	$\log_{10} N_0/N_t$
0	100.00	1.000	0.00000
50	96.42	1.037	0.01585
100	92.96	1.076	0.03170
150	89.63	1.116	0.04755
200	86.42	1.157	0.06340
250	83.32	1.200	0.07925
300	80.33	1.245	0.09510
400	74.68	1.339	0.12680
500	69.42	1.440	0.15850
600	64.54	1.550	0.19020
700	59.99	1.667	0.22190
800	55.77	1.793	0.25360
900	51.84	1.929	0.28530
1000	48.19	2.075	0.31700
1100	44.80	2.232	0.34870
1200	41.65	2.401	0.38040
1300	38.72	2.583	0.41210
1400	35.99	2.778	0.44380
1500	33.46	2.989	0.47550
1600	31.10	3.215	0.50720
1800	26.88	3.720	0.57060
2000	23.23	4.305	0.63400
2250	19.35	5.167	0.71325
2500	16.13	6.201	0.79250
2750	13.44	7.443	0.87175
3000	11.19	8.933	0.95100
3250	9.33	10.721	1.03025
3500	7.77	12.868	1.10949
3750	6.48	15.443	1.18874
4000	5.40	18.535	1.26799
4250	4.50	22.246	1.34724
4500	3.75	26.699	1.42649
4750	3.12	32.044	1.50574
5000	2.60	38.459	1.58499
5250	2.17	46.158	1.66424
5500	1.81	55.398	1.74349
5750	1.50	66.488	1.82274
6000	1.25	79.798	1.90199
6250	1.04	95.773	1.98124
6500	0.87	114.945	2.06049
6750	0.72	137.956	2.13974
7000	0.60	165.573	2.21899
7250	0.50	198.719	2.29824

Sodium-24
half-life 15 h

d	h	min	N_t	N_0/N_t	$\log_{10} N_0/N_t$
		0	100.00	1.000	0.00000
		10	99.23	1.007	0.00335
		20	98.47	1.015	0.00669
		30	97.72	1.023	0.01003
		40	96.97	1.031	0.01338
		50	96.22	1.039	0.01672
	1	0	95.48	1.047	0.02007
		10	94.75	1.055	0.02341
		20	94.02	1.063	0.02676
		30	93.30	1.071	0.03010
		40	92.59	1.080	0.03345
		50	91.88	1.088	0.03679
	2	0	91.17	1.096	0.04014
		10	90.47	1.105	0.04348
		20	89.78	1.113	0.04683
		30	89.09	1.122	0.05017
		40	88.41	1.131	0.05352
		50	87.73	1.139	0.05686
	3	0	87.06	1.148	0.06021
		10	86.39	1.157	0.06355
		20	85.72	1.166	0.06690
		30	85.07	1.175	0.07024
		40	84.41	1.184	0.07359
		50	83.77	1.193	0.07693
	4	0	83.12	1.203	0.08028
		10	82.49	1.212	0.08362
		20	81.85	1.221	0.08696
		30	81.23	1.231	0.09031
		40	80.60	1.240	0.09365
		50	79.98	1.250	0.09700
	5	0	79.37	1.259	0.10034
		10	78.76	1.269	0.10369
		20	78.16	1.279	0.10703
		30	77.56	1.289	0.11038
		40	76.96	1.299	0.11372
		50	76.37	1.309	0.11707
	6	0	75.79	1.319	0.12041
		10	75.20	1.329	0.12376
		20	74.63	1.339	0.12710
		30	74.05	1.350	0.13045
		40	73.49	1.360	0.13379
		50	72.92	1.371	0.13714
	7	0	72.36	1.381	0.14048
		10	71.81	1.392	0.14383
		20	71.26	1.403	0.14717
		30	70.71	1.414	0.15052
		40	70.17	1.425	0.15386
		50	69.63	1.436	0.15720
	8	0	69.10	1.447	0.16055
		10	68.57	1.458	0.16389
		20	68.04	1.469	0.16724
		30	67.52	1.481	0.17058
		40	67.00	1.492	0.17393
		50	66.49	1.504	0.17727
	9	0	65.98	1.515	0.18062
		10	65.47	1.527	0.18396
		20	64.97	1.539	0.18731
		30	64.47	1.551	0.19065
		40	63.97	1.563	0.19400
		50	63.48	1.575	0.19734
	10	0	63.00	1.587	0.20069
		10	62.51	1.599	0.20403
		20	62.03	1.612	0.20738
		30	61.56	1.624	0.21072
		40	61.08	1.637	0.21407
		50	60.62	1.649	0.21741
	11	0	60.15	1.662	0.22076
		10	59.69	1.675	0.22410
		20	59.23	1.688	0.22745
		30	58.78	1.701	0.23079
		40	58.33	1.714	0.23413
		50	57.88	1.727	0.23748
	12	0	57.43	1.741	0.24082
		10	56.99	1.754	0.24417
		20	56.56	1.768	0.24751
		30	56.12	1.781	0.25086
		40	55.69	1.795	0.25420
		50	55.27	1.809	0.25755
	13	0	54.84	1.823	0.26089
		10	54.42	1.837	0.26424
		20	54.00	1.851	0.26758
		30	53.59	1.866	0.27093
		40	53.18	1.880	0.27427
		50	52.77	1.895	0.27762
	14	0	52.36	1.909	0.28096
		10	51.96	1.924	0.28431
		20	51.56	1.939	0.28765
		30	51.17	1.954	0.29100
		40	50.78	1.969	0.29434
		50	50.39	1.984	0.29769
	15	0	50.00	2.000	0.30103
		10	49.62	2.015	0.30438
		20	49.24	2.031	0.30772
		30	48.86	2.046	0.31106
		40	48.48	2.062	0.31441
		50	48.11	2.078	0.31775
	16	0	47.74	2.094	0.32110
		10	47.38	2.110	0.32444
		20	47.01	2.127	0.32779
		30	46.65	2.143	0.33113
		40	46.29	2.160	0.33448
		50	45.94	2.176	0.33782
	17	0	45.59	2.193	0.34117
		10	45.24	2.210	0.34451
		20	44.89	2.227	0.34786
		30	44.54	2.244	0.35120
		40	44.20	2.262	0.35455
		50	43.86	2.279	0.35789
	18	0	43.53	2.297	0.36124
		10	43.19	2.315	0.36458
		20	42.86	2.333	0.36793
		30	42.53	2.351	0.37127
		40	42.21	2.369	0.37462
		50	41.88	2.387	0.37796
	19	0	41.56	2.406	0.38131
		10	41.24	2.424	0.38465
		20	40.93	2.443	0.38799
		30	40.61	2.462	0.39134
		40	40.30	2.481	0.39468
		50	39.99	2.500	0.39803
	20	0	39.69	2.519	0.40137
		10	39.38	2.539	0.40472
		20	39.08	2.558	0.40806
		30	38.78	2.578	0.41141
		40	38.48	2.598	0.41475
		50	38.19	2.618	0.41810
	21	0	37.89	2.639	0.42144
		10	37.60	2.659	0.42479
		20	37.31	2.679	0.42813
		30	37.03	2.700	0.43148
		40	36.74	2.721	0.43482
		50	36.46	2.742	0.43817
	22	0	36.18	2.763	0.44151
		10	35.90	2.785	0.44486
		20	35.63	2.806	0.44820
		30	35.36	2.828	0.45155
		40	35.08	2.850	0.45489
		50	34.81	2.872	0.45823
	23	0	34.55	2.894	0.46158
		10	34.28	2.916	0.46492
		20	34.02	2.939	0.46827
		30	33.76	2.962	0.47161
		40	33.50	2.985	0.47496
		50	33.24	3.008	0.47830
1	0		32.99	3.031	0.48165
	1		31.50	3.174	0.50172
	2		30.08	3.324	0.52179
	3		28.72	3.482	0.54185
	4		27.42	3.646	0.56192
	5		26.18	3.819	0.58199
	6		25.00	3.999	0.60206
	7		23.87	4.189	0.62213
	8		22.79	4.387	0.64220
	9		21.76	4.594	0.66227
	10		20.78	4.812	0.68233
	11		19.84	5.039	0.70240
	12		18.95	5.278	0.72247
	13		18.09	5.527	0.74254
	14		17.27	5.789	0.76261
	15		16.49	6.062	0.78268
	16		15.75	6.349	0.80274
	17		15.04	6.649	0.82281
	18		14.36	6.964	0.84288
	19		13.71	7.293	0.86295
	20		13.09	7.638	0.88302
	21		12.50	7.999	0.90308
	22		11.94	8.378	0.92315
	23		11.40	8.774	0.94322
2	0		10.88	9.189	0.96329
	1		10.39	9.623	0.98335
	2		9.92	10.079	1.00343
	3		9.47	10.556	1.02350
	4		9.05	11.055	1.04357
	5		8.64	11.578	1.06364
	6		8.25	12.125	1.08371
	7		7.87	12.699	1.10378
	8		7.52	13.299	1.12385
	9		7.18	13.928	1.14391
	10		6.86	14.587	1.16398
	11		6.55	15.277	1.18405
	12		6.25	16.000	1.20412
	13		5.97	16.756	1.22419
	14		5.70	17.549	1.24426
	15		5.44	18.379	1.26433
	16		5.20	19.248	1.28439
	17		4.96	20.158	1.30446
	18		4.74	21.112	1.32453
	19		4.52	22.110	1.34460
	20		4.32	23.156	1.36467
	21		4.12	24 251	1.38474
	22		3.94	25.398	1.40481
	23		3.76	26.599	1.42488
3	0		3.59	27.857	1.44494
	1		3.43	29.175	1.46501
	2		3.27	30.554	1.48508
	3		3.13	32.000	1.50515
	4		2.98	33.513	1.52522
	5		2.85	35.098	1.54529
	6		2.72	36.758	1.56536
	7		2.60	38.496	1.58542
	8		2.48	40.317	1.60549
	9		2.37	42.224	1.62556
	10		2.26	44.221	1.64563
	11		2.16	46.312	1.66570
	12		2.06	48.502	1.68577
	13		1.97	50.796	1.70584
	14		1.88	53.199	1.72590
	15		1.79	55.714	1.74597
	16		1.71	58.349	1.76604
	17		1.64	61.109	1.78611
	18		1.56	63.999	1.80618
	19		1.49	67.026	1.82625
	20		1.42	70.196	1.84631
	21		1.36	73.515	1.86638
	22		1.30	76.992	1.88645
	23		1.24	80.634	1.90652
4	0		1.18	84.447	1.92659
	1		1.13	88.440	1.94665
	2		1.08	92.623	1.96672
	3		1.03	97.003	1.98679
	4		0.98	101.594	2.00687
	5		0.94	106.398	2.02694
	6		0.90	111.430	2.04700
	7		0.86	116.701	2.06708
	8		0.82	122.219	2.08714
	9		0.78	128.000	2.10721
	10		0.75	134.053	2.12728
	11		0.71	140.394	2.14735
	12		0.68	147.032	2.16741
	13		0.65	153.988	2.18749
	14		0.62	161.269	2.20755
	15		0.59	168.896	2.22762
	16		0.57	176.884	2.24769
	17		0.54	185.250	2.26776
	18		0.52	194.012	2.28783
	19		0.49	203.185	2.30789
	20		0.47	212.797	2.32797
	21		0.45	222.861	2.34803
	22		0.43	233.399	2.36810
	23		0.41	244.439	2.38817

Phosphorus-32

half-life 14.3 d

t: d	t: h	N_t	N_0/N_t	$\log_{10} N_0/N_t$
	0	100.00	1.000	0.00000
	3	99.40	1.006	0.00263
	6	98.80	1.012	0.00526
	9	98.20	1.018	0.00789
	12	97.61	1.025	0.01053
	15	97.02	1.031	0.01316
	18	96.43	1.037	0.01579
	21	95.85	1.043	0.01842
1	0	95.27	1.050	0.02105
	12	92.99	1.075	0.03158
2	0	90.76	1.102	0.04210
	12	88.59	1.129	0.05263
3	0	86.47	1.157	0.06315
	12	84.40	1.185	0.07368
4	0	82.38	1.214	0.08420
	12	80.40	1.244	0.09473
5	0	78.48	1.274	0.10526
	12	76.60	1.306	0.11578
6	0	74.76	1.338	0.12631
	12	72.97	1.370	0.13683
7	0	71.23	1.404	0.14736
	12	69.52	1.438	0.15788
8	0	67.86	1.474	0.16841
	12	66.23	1.510	0.17893
9	0	64.65	1.547	0.18946
	12	63.10	1.585	0.19999
10	0	61.59	1.624	0.21051
	12	60.11	1.664	0.22104
11	0	58.67	1.704	0.23156
	12	57.27	1.746	0.24209
12	0	55.90	1.789	0.25261
	12	54.56	1.833	0.26314
13	0	53.25	1.878	0.27366
	12	51.98	1.924	0.28419
14	0	50.73	1.971	0.29472
	12	49.52	2.019	0.30524
15	0	48.33	2.069	0.31577
	12	47.17	2.120	0.32629
16		46.04	2.172	0.33682
17		43.87	2.280	0.35787
18		41.79	2.393	0.37892
19		39.81	2.512	0.39997
20		37.93	2.636	0.42102
21		36.13	2.767	0.44207
22		34.43	2.905	0.46312
23		32.80	3.049	0.48418
24		31.24	3.201	0.50523
25		29.77	3.360	0.52628
26		28.36	3.526	0.54733
27		27.02	3.702	0.56838
28		25.74	3.885	0.58943
29		24.52	4.078	0.61048
30		23.36	4.281	0.63153
32		21.20	4.717	0.67364
34		19.24	5.197	0.71574
36		17.46	5.726	0.75784
38		15.85	6.309	0.79994
40		14.39	6.951	0.84205
42		13.06	7.659	0.88415
44		11.85	8.438	0.92625
46		10.76	9.297	0.96835
48		9.76	10.244	1.01045
50		8.86	11.286	1.05256
52		8.04	12.435	1.09466
54		7.30	13.701	1.13676
56		6.62	15.096	1.17886
58		6.01	16.633	1.22097
60		5.46	18.326	1.26307
65		4.28	23.352	1.36832
70		3.36	29.756	1.47358
75		2.64	37.917	1.57884
80		2.07	48.316	1.68409
85		1.62	61.567	1.78935
90		1.27	78.452	1.89460
100		0.79	127.384	2.10511
110		0.48	206.835	2.31562

Sulphur-35

half-life 87.2 d

t: d	N_t	N_0/N_t	$\log_{10} N_0/N_t$
0	100.00	1.000	0.00000
5	96.10	1.041	0.01726
10	92.36	1.083	0.03452
15	88.76	1.127	0.05178
20	85.30	1.172	0.06904
25	81.98	1.220	0.08630
30	78.78	1.269	0.10357
35	75.71	1.321	0.12083
40	72.76	1.374	0.13809
50	67.20	1.488	0.17261
60	62.07	1.611	0.20713
70	57.33	1.744	0.24165
80	52.94	1.889	0.27618
90	48.90	2.045	0.31070
100	45.16	2.214	0.34522
110	41.71	2.397	0.37974
120	38.52	2.596	0.41426
130	35.58	2.811	0.44879
140	32.86	3.043	0.48331
150	30.35	3.295	0.51783
160	28.03	3.567	0.55235
180	23.91	4.182	0.62139
200	20.40	4.903	0.69044
225	16.72	5.981	0.77674
250	13.71	7.295	0.86305
275	11.24	8.899	0.94935
300	9.21	10.856	1.03566
325	7.55	13.242	1.12196
350	6.19	16.154	1.20827
375	5.07	19.705	1.29457
400	4.16	24.037	1.38088
425	3.41	29.321	1.46718
450	2.80	35.767	1.55349
475	2.29	43.631	1.63979
500	1.88	53.223	1.72610
525	1.54	64.923	1.81240
550	1.26	79.197	1.89871
575	1.04	96.608	1.98501
600	0.85	117.846	2.07132
625	0.70	143.754	2.15762
650	0.57	175.358	2.24393

Potassium-42

half-life 12.4 h

t: d	t: h	t: min	N_t	N_0/N_t	$\log_{10} N_0/N_t$
		0	100.00	1.000	0.00000
		10	99.07	1.009	0.00405
		20	98.15	1.019	0.00809
		30	97.24	1.028	0.01214
		40	96.34	1.038	0.01618
		50	95.45	1.048	0.02023
	1	0	94.56	1.057	0.02428
		10	93.69	1.067	0.02832
		20	92.82	1.077	0.03237
		30	91.96	1.087	0.03642
		40	91.10	1.098	0.04046
		50	90.26	1.108	0.04451
	2	0	89.42	1.118	0.04855
		10	88.59	1.129	0.05260
		20	87.77	1.139	0.05665
		30	86.96	1.150	0.06069
		40	86.15	1.161	0.06474
		50	85.35	1.172	0.06878
	3	0	84.56	1.183	0.07283
		10	83.78	1.194	0.07688
		20	83.00	1.205	0.08092
		30	82.23	1.216	0.08497
		40	81.47	1.227	0.08901
		50	80.71	1.239	0.09306
	4	0	79.96	1.251	0.09711
		10	79.22	1.262	0.10115
		20	78.49	1.274	0.10520
		30	77.76	1.286	0.10925
		40	77.04	1.298	0.11329
		50	76.32	1.310	0.11734
	5	0	75.62	1.322	0.12138
		10	74.92	1.335	0.12543
		20	74.22	1.347	0.12948
		30	73.53	1.360	0.13352
		40	72.85	1.373	0.13757
		50	72.17	1.386	0.14161
	6	0	71.51	1.398	0.14566
		10	70.84	1.412	0.14971
		20	70.19	1.425	0.15375
		30	69.53	1.438	0.15780
		40	68.89	1.452	0.16184
		50	68.25	1.465	0.16589
	7	0	67.62	1.479	0.16994
		10	66.99	1.493	0.17398
		20	66.37	1.507	0.17803
		30	65.75	1.521	0.18208
		40	65.14	1.535	0.18612
		50	64.54	1.549	0.19017
	8	0	63.94	1.564	0.19421
		10	63.35	1.579	0.19826
		20	62.76	1.593	0.20231
		30	62.18	1.608	0.20635
		40	61.60	1.623	0.21040
		50	61.03	1.638	0.21444
	9	0	60.47	1.654	0.21849
		10	59.91	1.669	0.22254
		20	59.35	1.685	0.22658
		30	58.80	1.701	0.23063
		40	58.25	1.717	0.23467
		50	57.71	1.733	0.23872
	10	0	57.18	1.749	0.24277
		10	56.65	1.765	0.24681
		20	56.12	1.782	0.25086
		30	55.60	1.798	0.25491
		40	55.09	1.815	0.25895
		50	54.58	1.832	0.26300
	11	0	54.07	1.849	0.26704
		10	53.57	1.867	0.27109
		20	53.07	1.884	0.27514
		30	52.58	1.902	0.27918
		40	52.09	1.920	0.28323
		50	51.61	1.938	0.28727
	12	0	51.13	1.956	0.29132
		20	50.19	1.993	0.29941
		40	49.26	2.030	0.30750
	13	0	48.35	2.068	0.31560
		20	47.46	2.107	0.32369
		40	46.58	2.147	0.33178
	14	0	45.72	2.187	0.33987
		20	44.88	2.228	0.34797
		40	44.05	2.270	0.35606
	15	0	43.24	2.313	0.36415
		20	42.44	2.356	0.37224
		40	41.65	2.401	0.38034
	16	0	40.89	2.446	0.38843
		20	40.13	2.492	0.39652
		40	39.39	2.539	0.40461
	17	0	38.66	2.586	0.41270
		20	37.95	2.635	0.42080
		40	37.25	2.685	0.42889
	18	0	36.56	2.735	0.43698
		20	35.89	2.787	0.44507
		40	35.22	2.839	0.45317
	19	0	34.57	2.892	0.46126
		20	33.94	2.947	0.46935
		40	33.31	3.002	0.47744
	20	0	32.69	3.059	0.48553
		20	32.09	3.116	0.49363
		40	31.50	3.175	0.50172
	21	0	30.92	3.235	0.50981
		20	30.35	3.295	0.51790
		40	29.79	3.357	0.52600
	22	0	29.24	3.420	0.53409
		20	28.70	3.485	0.54218
		40	28.17	3.550	0.55027
	23	0	27.65	3.617	0.55836
		20	27.14	3.685	0.56646
		40	26.63	3.754	0.57455
1	0	0	26.14	3.825	0.58264
		20	25.66	3.897	0.59073
		40	25.19	3.970	0.59883
	1	0	24.72	4.045	0.60692
		20	24.27	4.121	0.61501
		40	23.82	4.199	0.62310
	2	0	23.38	4.278	0.63119
		20	22.95	4.358	0.63929
		40	22.52	4.440	0.64738
	3	0	22.11	4.523	0.65547
		20	21.70	4.609	0.66356
		40	21.30	4.695	0.67166
	4	0	20.91	4.784	0.67975
		20	20.52	4.873	0.68784
		40	20.14	4.965	0.69593
	5	0	19.77	5.059	0.70402
		20	19.40	5.154	0.71212
		40	19.05	5.251	0.72021
	6	0	18.69	5.349	0.72830
		20	18.35	5.450	0.73639
		40	18.01	5.552	0.74449
	7	0	17.68	5.657	0.75258
		20	17.35	5.763	0.76067
		40	17.03	5.872	0.76876
	8	0	16.72	5.982	0.77685
		20	16.41	6.095	0.78495
		40	16.11	6.209	0.79304
	9	0	15.81	6.326	0.80113
		20	15.52	6.445	0.80922
		40	15.23	6.566	0.81732
	10	0	14.95	6.690	0.82541
		20	14.67	6.816	0.83350
		40	14.40	6.944	0.84159
	11	0	14.14	7.074	0.84968
		20	13.87	7.207	0.85778
		40	13.62	7.343	0.86587
	12		13.37	7.481	0.87396
	13		12.64	7.911	0.89824
	14		11.95	8.366	0.92252
	15		11.30	8.847	0.94679
	16		10.69	9.356	0.97107
	17		10.11	9.893	0.99535
	18		9.56	10.462	1.01962
	19		9.04	11.064	1.04390
	20		8.55	11.700	1.06818
	21		8.08	12.372	1.09245
	22		7.64	13.084	1.11673
	23		7.23	13.836	1.14101
2	0		6.83	14.631	1.16528
	1		6.46	15.472	1.18956
	2		6.11	16.362	1.21384
	3		5.78	17.303	1.23811
	4		5.47	18.297	1.26239
	5		5.17	19.349	1.28667
	6		4.89	20.462	1.31094
	7		4.62	21.638	1.33522
	8		4.37	22.882	1.35950
	9		4.13	24.198	1.38377
	10		3.91	25.589	1.40805
	11		3.70	27.060	1.43233
	12		3.49	28.616	1.45660
	13		3.30	30.261	1.48088
	14		3.12	32.000	1.50516
	15		2.96	33.840	1.52943
	16		2.79	35.786	1.55371
	17		2.64	37.843	1.57799
	18		2.50	40.019	1.60226
	19		2.36	42.319	1.62654
	20		2.23	44.752	1.65082
	21		2.11	47.325	1.67509
	22		2.00	50.046	1.69937
	23		1.89	52.923	1.72365
3	0		1.79	55.966	1.74792
	1		1.69	59.183	1.77220
	2		1.60	62.586	1.79648
	3		1.51	66.184	1.82075
	4		1.43	69.989	1.84503
	5		1.35	74.013	1.86931
	6		1.28	78.268	1.89358
	7		1.21	82.768	1.91786
	8		1.14	87.526	1.94214
	9		1.08	92.558	1.96641
	10		1.02	97.879	1.99069
	11		0.97	103.506	2.01497
	12		0.91	109.457	2.03924
	13		0.86	115.750	2.06352
	14		0.82	122.404	2.08780
	15		0.77	129.442	2.11207
	16		0.73	136.883	2.13635
	17		0.69	144.753	2.16063
	18		0.65	153.075	2.18490
	19		0.62	161.875	2.20918
	20		0.58	171.182	2.23346
	21		0.55	181.023	2.25773
	22		0.52	191.430	2.28201
	23		0.49	202.436	2.30629

Calcium-45

half-life 165 d

t: d	N_t	N_0/N_t	$\log_{10} N_0/N_t$
0	100.00	1.000	0.00000
10	95.89	1.043	0.01824
20	91.94	1.088	0.03649
30	88.16	1.134	0.05473
40	84.53	1.183	0.07298
50	81.05	1.234	0.09122
60	77.72	1.287	0.10947
70	74.52	1.342	0.12771
80	71.46	1.399	0.14595
90	68.52	1.459	0.16420
100	65.70	1.522	0.18244
110	63.00	1.587	0.20069
120	60.40	1.656	0.21893
130	57.92	1.727	0.23718
140	55.54	1.801	0.25542
150	53.25	1.878	0.27366
160	51.06	1.958	0.29191
180	46.95	2.130	0.32840
200	43.16	2.317	0.36489
220	39.68	2.520	0.40137
240	36.49	2.741	0.43786
260	33.55	2.981	0.47435
280	30.84	3.242	0.51084
300	28.36	3.526	0.54733
320	26.07	3.835	0.58382
340	23.97	4.172	0.62031
360	22.04	4.537	0.65680
380	20.26	4.935	0.69328
400	18.63	5.368	0.72977
425	16.77	5.962	0.77538
450	15.10	6.622	0.82099
475	13.60	7.355	0.86660
500	12.24	8.170	0.91222
525	11.02	9.075	0.95783
550	9.92	10.079	1.00344
575	8.93	11.196	1.04905
600	8.04	12.435	1.09466
625	7.24	13.812	1.14027
650	6.52	15.342	1.18588
675	5.87	17.041	1.23149
700	5.28	18.928	1.27710

t (d)	N_t	N_0/N_t	$\log_{10} N_0/N_t$
725	4.76	21.024	1.32271
750	4.28	23.352	1.36832
775	3.86	25.938	1.41393
800	3.47	28.810	1.45955
850	2.81	35.544	1.55077
900	2.28	43.852	1.64199
950	1.85	54.102	1.73321
1000	1.50	66.747	1.82443
1050	1.21	82.348	1.91565
1100	0.98	101.596	2.00687
1150	0.80	125.342	2.09810
1200	0.65	154.639	2.18932
1250	0.52	190.783	2.28054

Calcium-47
half-life 4.7 d

d	h	min	N_t	N_0/N_t	$\log_{10} N_0/N_t$
	0		100.00	1.000	0.00000
	3		98.17	1.019	0.00801
	6		96.38	1.038	0.01601
	9		94.62	1.057	0.02402
	12		92.89	1.077	0.03202
	15		91.19	1.097	0.04003
	18		89.53	1.117	0.04804
	21		87.89	1.138	0.05604
1	0		86.29	1.159	0.06405
	3		84.71	1.180	0.07206
	6		83.16	1.202	0.08006
	9		81.65	1.225	0.08807
	12		80.15	1.248	0.09607
	15		78.69	1.271	0.10408
	18		77.25	1.294	0.11209
	21		75.84	1.319	0.12009
2	0		74.46	1.343	0.12810
	3		73.10	1.368	0.13610
	6		71.76	1.394	0.14411
	9		70.45	1.419	0.15212
	12		69.16	1.446	0.16012
	15		67.90	1.473	0.16813
	18		66.66	1.500	0.17614
	21		65.44	1.528	0.18414
3	0		64.25	1.556	0.19215
	3		63.07	1.585	0.20015
	6		61.92	1.615	0.20816
	9		60.79	1.645	0.21617
	12		59.68	1.676	0.22417
	15		58.59	1.707	0.23218
	18		57.52	1.739	0.24018
	21		56.47	1.771	0.24819
4	0		55.44	1.804	0.25620
	3		54.42	1.837	0.26420
	6		53.43	1.872	0.27221
	9		52.45	1.906	0.28022
	12		51.50	1.942	0.28822
	15		50.56	1.978	0.29623
	18		49.63	2.015	0.30423
	21		48.73	2.052	0.31224
5	0		47.84	2.090	0.32025
	3		46.96	2.129	0.32825
	6		46.10	2.169	0.33626
	9		45.26	2.209	0.34426
	12		44.44	2.250	0.35227
	15		43.62	2.292	0.36028
	18		42.83	2.335	0.36828
	21		42.04	2.378	0.37629
6	0		41.28	2.423	0.38430
	3		40.52	2.468	0.39230
	6		39.78	2.514	0.40031
	9		39.06	2.560	0.40831
	12		38.34	2.608	0.41632
	15		37.64	2.657	0.42433
	18		36.95	2.706	0.43233
	21		36.28	2.756	0.44034
7	0		35.62	2.808	0.44834
	3		34.97	2.860	0.45635
	6		34.33	2.913	0.46436
	9		33.70	2.967	0.47236
	12		33.08	3.023	0.48037
	15		32.48	3.079	0.48838
	18		31.89	3.136	0.49638
	21		31.30	3.194	0.50439
8	0		30.73	3.254	0.51239
	12		28.55	3.503	0.54442
9	0		26.52	3.771	0.57644
	12		24.63	4.059	0.60847
10	0		22.88	4.370	0.64049
	12		21.26	4.705	0.67252
11	0		19.75	5.065	0.70454
	12		18.34	5.452	0.73657
12	0		17.04	5.869	0.76859
	12		15.83	6.319	0.80061
13	0		14.70	6.802	0.83264
	12		13.66	7.323	0.86466
14			12.69	7.883	0.89669
15			10.95	9.136	0.96074
16			9.45	10.587	1.02479
17			8.15	12.270	1.08884
18			7.03	14.220	1.15289
19			6.07	16.479	1.21693
20			5.24	19.098	1.28098
22			3.90	25.650	1.40908
24			2.90	34.449	1.53718
26			2.16	46.268	1.66528
28			1.61	62.141	1.79338
30			1.20	83.460	1.92148
32			0.89	112.092	2.04957
34			0.66	150.547	2.17767
36			0.49	202.195	2.30577

Chromium-51
half-life 27.8 d

d	h	min	N_t	N_0/N_t	$\log_{10} N_0/N_t$
	0		100.00	1.000	0.00000
	6		99.38	1.006	0.00271
	12		98.76	1.013	0.00541
	18		98.15	1.019	0.00812
1	0		97.54	1.025	0.01083
	6		96.93	1.032	0.01354
	12		96.33	1.038	0.01624
	18		95.73	1.045	0.01895
2	0		95.14	1.051	0.02166
	12		93.96	1.064	0.02707
3	0		92.79	1.078	0.03249
	12		91.64	1.091	0.03790
4	0		90.51	1.105	0.04331
	12		89.39	1.119	0.04873
5	0		88.28	1.133	0.05414
	12		87.19	1.147	0.05956
6	0		86.11	1.161	0.06497
	12		85.04	1.176	0.07038
7	0		83.98	1.191	0.07580
	12		82.94	1.206	0.08121
8	0		81.92	1.221	0.08663
	12		80.90	1.236	0.09204
9	0		79.90	1.252	0.09746
	12		78.91	1.267	0.10287
10	0		77.93	1.283	0.10828
	12		76.97	1.299	0.11370
11	0		76.01	1.316	0.11911
	12		75.07	1.332	0.12453
12	0		74.14	1.349	0.12994
	12		73.22	1.366	0.13536
13	0		72.32	1.383	0.14077
	12		71.42	1.400	0.14618
14	0		70.53	1.418	0.15160
	12		69.66	1.436	0.15701
15	0		68.80	1.454	0.16243
	12		67.95	1.472	0.16784
16	0		67.10	1.490	0.17326
	12		66.27	1.509	0.17867
17	0		65.45	1.528	0.18408
	12		64.64	1.547	0.18950
18	0		63.84	1.566	0.19491
	12		63.05	1.586	0.20033
19	0		62.27	1.606	0.20574
	12		61.50	1.626	0.21115
20	0		60.73	1.647	0.21657
	12		59.98	1.667	0.22198
21	0		59.24	1.688	0.22740
	12		58.50	1.709	0.23281
22	0		57.78	1.731	0.23823
	12		57.06	1.752	0.24364
23	0		56.36	1.774	0.24905
	12		55.66	1.797	0.25447
24	0		54.97	1.819	0.25988
	12		54.29	1.842	0.26530
25	0		53.62	1.865	0.27071
	12		52.95	1.889	0.27613
26	0		52.29	1.912	0.28154
	12		51.65	1.936	0.28695
27	0		51.01	1.961	0.29237
	12		50.38	1.985	0.29778
28	0		49.75	2.010	0.30320
	12		49.13	2.035	0.30861
29	0		48.53	2.061	0.31403
	12		47.92	2.087	0.31944
30			47.33	2.113	0.32485
31			46.17	2.166	0.33568
32			45.03	2.221	0.34651
33			43.92	2.277	0.35734
34			42.84	2.334	0.36817
35			41.78	2.393	0.37900
36			40.75	2.454	0.38982
37			39.75	2.516	0.40065
38			38.77	2.579	0.41148
39			37.82	2.644	0.42231
40			36.89	2.711	0.43314
41			35.98	2.780	0.44397
42			35.09	2.850	0.45480
43			34.23	2.922	0.46562
44			33.38	2.995	0.47645
45			32.56	3.071	0.48728
46			31.76	3.149	0.49811
47			30.98	3.228	0.50894
48			30.22	3.310	0.51977
49			29.47	3.393	0.53059
50			28.75	3.479	0.54142
51			28.04	3.567	0.55225
52			27.35	3.657	0.56308
53			26.67	3.749	0.57391
54			26.02	3.844	0.58474
55			25.38	3.941	0.59557
56			24.75	4.040	0.60639
57			24.14	4.142	0.61722
58			23.55	4.247	0.62805
59			22.97	4.354	0.63888
60			22.40	4.464	0.64971
62			21.31	4.692	0.67136
64			20.28	4.932	0.69302
66			19.29	5.184	0.71468
68			18.35	5.449	0.73634
70			17.46	5.728	0.75799
72			16.61	6.021	0.77965
74			15.80	6.329	0.80131
76			15.03	6.652	0.82296
78			14.30	6.992	0.84462
80			13.61	7.350	0.86628
82			12.94	7.726	0.88793
84			12.31	8.121	0.90959
86			11.72	8.536	0.93125
88			11.15	8.972	0.95290
90			10.60	9.431	0.97456
92			10.09	9.913	0.99622
94			9.60	10.420	1.01788
96			9.13	10.953	1.03953
98			8.69	11.513	1.06119
100			8.26	12.102	1.08285
105			7.29	13.708	1.13699
110			6.44	15.529	1.19113
115			5.68	17.590	1.24527
120			5.02	19.926	1.29942
125			4.43	22.571	1.35356
130			3.91	25.568	1.40770
135			3.45	28.963	1.46184
140			3.05	32.808	1.51598
145			2.69	37.164	1.57013
150			2.38	42.099	1.62427
155			2.10	47.688	1.67841
160			1.85	54.020	1.73255
165			1.63	61.192	1.78670
170			1.44	69.317	1.84084
175			1.27	78.520	1.89498
180			1.12	88.945	1.94912
185			0.99	100.755	2.00327
190			0.88	114.132	2.05741
195			0.77	129.286	2.11155
200			0.68	146.451	2.16569
205			0.60	165.895	2.21983
210			0.53	187.922	2.27398
215			0.47	212.872	2.32812

Manganese-52
half-life 5.7 d

d	h	min	N_t	N_0/N_t	$\log_{10} N_0/N_t$
	0		100.00	1.000	0.00000
	6		97.01	1.030	0.01320
	12		94.10	1.062	0.02641
	18		91.28	1.095	0.03961
1	0		88.55	1.129	0.05281
	6		85.90	1.164	0.06602
	12		83.33	1.200	0.07922
	18		80.83	1.237	0.09242
2	0		78.41	1.275	0.10563
	6		76.06	1.314	0.11883
	12		73.79	1.355	0.13203
	18		71.58	1.397	0.14523
3	0		69.43	1.440	0.15844
	6		67.35	1.484	0.17164
	12		65.34	1.530	0.18484
	18		63.38	1.577	0.19805
4	0		61.48	1.626	0.21125
	6		59.64	1.676	0.22445
	12		57.86	1.728	0.23766
	18		56.12	1.781	0.25086
5			54.44	1.836	0.26406
6			48.21	2.074	0.31687
7			42.69	2.342	0.36969
8			37.80	2.645	0.42250
9			33.47	2.987	0.47531
10			29.64	3.373	0.52812
11			26.25	3.810	0.58094
12			23.24	4.302	0.63375
13			20.58	4.859	0.68656
14			18.22	5.487	0.73937
15			16.14	6.197	0.79218
16			14.29	6.998	0.84499
17			12.65	7.903	0.89780
18			11.20	8.925	0.95061
19			9.92	10.079	1.00343
20			8.79	11.382	1.05625
25			4.78	20.907	1.32031
30			2.60	38.403	1.58437
35			1.42	70.538	1.84843
40			0.77	129.565	2.11249
45			0.42	237.987	2.37655
50			0.23	437.139	2.64062

Manganese-54
half-life 314 d

d	N_t	N_0/N_t	$\log_{10} N_0/N_t$
0	100.00	1.000	0.00000
10	97.82	1.022	0.00959
20	95.68	1.045	0.01917
30	93.59	1.068	0.02876
40	91.55	1.092	0.03835
50	89.55	1.117	0.04793
60	87.59	1.142	0.05752
70	85.68	1.167	0.06711
80	83.81	1.193	0.07670
90	81.98	1.220	0.08628
100	80.19	1.247	0.09587
110	78.44	1.275	0.10546
120	76.73	1.303	0.11504
130	75.05	1.332	0.12463
140	73.41	1.362	0.13422
150	71.81	1.393	0.14380
160	70.24	1.424	0.15339
170	68.71	1.455	0.16298
180	67.21	1.488	0.17257
190	65.74	1.521	0.18215
200	64.31	1.555	0.19174
210	62.90	1.590	0.20133
220	61.53	1.625	0.21091
230	60.19	1.662	0.22050
240	58.87	1.699	0.23009
250	57.59	1.736	0.23967
260	56.33	1.775	0.24926
270	55.10	1.815	0.25885
280	53.90	1.855	0.26844
290	52.72	1.897	0.27802
300	51.57	1.939	0.28761
320	49.34	2.027	0.30678
340	47.21	2.118	0.32596
360	45.17	2.214	0.34513
380	43.22	2.314	0.36431
400	41.35	2.418	0.38348
420	39.57	2.527	0.40265
440	37.86	2.641	0.42183
460	36.22	2.761	0.44100
480	34.66	2.885	0.46018
500	33.16	3.015	0.47935
520	31.73	3.152	0.49852
540	30.36	3.294	0.51770
560	29.05	3.442	0.53687
580	27.79	3.598	0.55604
600	26.59	3.760	0.57522
640	24.35	4.107	0.61357
680	22.29	4.487	0.65191
720	20.41	4.901	0.69026
760	18.68	5.353	0.72861
800	17.10	5.847	0.76696
840	15.66	6.387	0.80531
880	14.33	6.977	0.84365
920	13.12	7.621	0.88200
960	12.01	8.324	0.92035
1000	11.00	9.093	0.95870
1100	8.82	11.339	1.05457
1200	7.07	14.140	1.15044
1300	5.67	17.632	1.24631
1400	4.55	21.988	1.34218
1500	3.65	27.419	1.43805
1700	2.35	42.637	1.62979
1900	1.51	66.302	1.82153
2000	1.21	82.679	1.91740
2500	0.40	249.313	2.39675

Iron-59
half-life 45 d

d	h	min	N_t	N_0/N_t	$\log_{10} N_0/N_t$
	0		100.00	1.000	0.00000
	12		99.23	1.007	0.00335
1	0		98.47	1.015	0.00669
	12		97.72	1.023	0.01003
2	0		96.97	1.031	0.01338
	12		96.22	1.039	0.01672

t (d)	t (h)	t (min)	N_t	N_0/N_t	$\log_{10} N_0/N_t$
3	0		95.48	1.047	0.02007
	12		94.75	1.055	0.02341
4	0		94.02	1.063	0.02676
	12		93.30	1.071	0.03010
5	0		92.59	1.080	0.03345
	12		91.88	1.088	0.03679
6	0		91.17	1.096	0.04014
	12		90.47	1.105	0.04348
7	0		89.78	1.113	0.04683
	12		89.09	1.122	0.05017
8	0		88.41	1.131	0.05352
	12		87.73	1.139	0.05686
9	0		87.06	1.148	0.06021
	12		86.39	1.157	0.06355
10	0		85.72	1.166	0.06690
	12		85.07	1.175	0.07024
11	0		84.41	1.184	0.07359
	12		83.77	1.193	0.07693
12	0		83.12	1.203	0.08028
	12		82.49	1.212	0.08362
13	0		81.85	1.221	0.08696
	12		81.23	1.231	0.09031
14	0		80.60	1.240	0.09365
	12		79.98	1.250	0.09700
15	0		79.37	1.259	0.10034
	12		78.76	1.269	0.10369
16	0		78.16	1.279	0.10703
	12		77.56	1.289	0.11038
17	0		76.96	1.299	0.11372
	12		76.37	1.309	0.11707
18	0		75.79	1.319	0.12041
	12		75.20	1.329	0.12376
19	0		74.63	1.339	0.12710
	12		74.05	1.350	0.13045
20			73.49	1.360	0.13379
22			71.26	1.403	0.14717
24			69.10	1.447	0.16055
26			67.00	1.492	0.17393
28			64.97	1.539	0.18731
30			63.00	1.587	0.20069
32			61.08	1.637	0.21407
34			59.23	1.688	0.22745
36			57.43	1.741	0.24082
38			55.69	1.795	0.25420
40			54.00	1.851	0.26758
42			52.36	1.909	0.28096
44			50.78	1.969	0.29434
46			49.24	2.031	0.30772
48			47.74	2.094	0.32110
50			46.29	2.160	0.33448
52			44.89	2.227	0.34786
54			43.53	2.297	0.36124
56			42.21	2.369	0.37462
58			40.93	2.443	0.38799
60			39.69	2.519	0.40137
62			38.48	2.598	0.41475
64			37.31	2.679	0.42813
66			36.18	2.763	0.44151
68			35.08	2.850	0.45489
70			34.02	2.939	0.46827
72			32.99	3.031	0.48165
74			31.99	3.126	0.49503
76			31.02	3.224	0.50841
78			30.08	3.324	0.52179
80			29.16	3.428	0.53516
82			28.28	3.536	0.54854
84			27.42	3.646	0.56192
86			26.59	3.760	0.57530
88			25.78	3.878	0.58868
90			25.00	3.999	0.60206
92			24.24	4.125	0.61544
94			23.51	4.254	0.62882
96			22.79	4.387	0.64220
98			22.10	4.524	0.65558
100			21.43	4.666	0.66896
102			20.78	4.812	0.68233
104			20.15	4.962	0.69571
106			19.54	5.117	0.70909
108			18.95	5.278	0.72247
110			18.37	5.443	0.73585
112			17.81	5.613	0.74923
114			17.27	5.789	0.76261
116			16.75	5.970	0.77599
118			16.24	6.156	0.78937
120			15.75	6.349	0.80274
122			15.27	6.548	0.81612
124			14.81	6.753	0.82950
126			14.36	6.964	0.84288
128			13.92	7.182	0.85626
130			13.50	7.406	0.86964
132			13.09	7.638	0.88302
134			12.69	7.877	0.89640
136			12.31	8.124	0.90977
138			11.94	8.378	0.92315
140			11.57	8.640	0.93653
144			10.88	9.189	0.96329
148			10.23	9.773	0.99004
152			9.62	10.394	1.01681
156			9.05	11.055	1.04357
160			8.50	11.757	1.07033
164			8.00	12.505	1.09709
168			7.52	13.299	1.12385
172			7.07	14.145	1.15060
176			6.65	15.043	1.17736
180			6.25	16.000	1.20412
184			5.88	17.016	1.23088
188			5.53	18.098	1.25764
192			5.20	19.248	1.28439
196			4.88	20.471	1.31115
200			4.59	21.772	1.33791
210			3.94	25.398	1.40481
220			3.38	29.627	1.47170
230			2.89	34.561	1.53860
240			2.48	40.317	1.60549
250			2.13	47.031	1.67239
260			1.82	54.863	1.73928
270			1.56	63.999	1.80618
280			1.34	74.656	1.87307
290			1.15	87.089	1.93996
300			0.98	101.594	2.00687
320			0.72	138.247	2.14066
340			0.53	188.125	2.27445
360			0.39	255.996	2.40823
380			0.29	348.359	2.54203
400			0.21	474.045	2.67582

Cobalt-57

half-life 270 d

t (d)	N_t	N_0/N_t	$\log_{10} N_0/N_t$
0	100.00	1.000	0.00000
10	97.47	1.026	0.01115
20	95.00	1.053	0.02230
30	92.59	1.080	0.03345
40	90.24	1.108	0.04460
50	87.95	1.137	0.05575
60	85.72	1.167	0.06690
70	83.55	1.197	0.07805
80	81.43	1.228	0.08919
90	79.37	1.260	0.10034
100	77.36	1.293	0.11149
110	75.40	1.326	0.12264
120	73.49	1.361	0.13379
130	71.62	1.396	0.14494
140	69.81	1.432	0.15609
150	68.04	1.470	0.16724
160	66.31	1.508	0.17839
170	64.63	1.547	0.18954
180	63.00	1.587	0.20069
190	61.40	1.629	0.21184
200	59.84	1.671	0.22299
210	58.33	1.714	0.23414
220	56.85	1.759	0.24528
230	55.41	1.805	0.25643
240	54.00	1.852	0.26758
250	52.63	1.900	0.27873
260	51.30	1.949	0.28988
270	50.00	2.000	0.30103
280	48.73	2.052	0.31218
290	47.50	2.105	0.32333
300	46.29	2.160	0.33448
320	43.98	2.274	0.35678
340	41.78	2.394	0.37908
360	39.68	2.520	0.40137
380	37.70	2.653	0.42367
400	35.81	2.792	0.44597
420	34.02	2.939	0.46827
440	32.32	3.094	0.49057
460	30.70	3.257	0.51287
480	29.16	3.429	0.53517
500	27.70	3.610	0.55747
540	25.00	4.000	0.60206
580	22.56	4.433	0.64666
620	20.36	4.912	0.69126
660	18.37	5.443	0.73585
700	16.58	6.032	0.78045
740	14.96	6.684	0.82505
780	13.50	7.407	0.86965
820	12.18	8.208	0.91424
860	10.99	9.096	0.95884
900	9.92	10.079	1.00344
950	8.73	11.460	1.05918
1000	7.67	13.030	1.11493
1050	6.75	14.814	1.17068
1100	5.94	16.843	1.22642
1150	5.22	19.150	1.28217
1200	4.59	21.773	1.33792
1250	4.04	24.755	1.39366
1300	3.55	28.146	1.44941
1350	3.12	32.000	1.50516
1400	2.75	36.383	1.56090
1450	2.42	41.367	1.61665
1500	2.13	47.032	1.67240
1600	1.64	60.798	1.78389
1700	1.27	78.593	1.89538
1800	0.98	101.596	2.00687
1900	0.76	131.331	2.11837
2000	0.59	169.770	2.22986

Cobalt-58

half-life 71 d

t (d)	N_t	N_0/N_t	$\log_{10} N_0/N_t$
0	100.00	1.000	0.00000
1	99.03	1.010	0.00424
2	98.07	1.020	0.00848
3	97.11	1.030	0.01272
4	96.17	1.040	0.01696
5	95.24	1.050	0.02120
6	94.31	1.060	0.02544
7	93.39	1.071	0.02968
8	92.49	1.081	0.03392
9	91.59	1.092	0.03816
10	90.70	1.103	0.04240
11	89.82	1.113	0.04664
12	88.94	1.124	0.05088
13	88.08	1.135	0.05512
14	87.23	1.146	0.05936
15	86.38	1.158	0.06360
16	85.54	1.169	0.06784
17	84.71	1.181	0.07208
18	83.88	1.192	0.07632
19	83.07	1.204	0.08056
20	82.26	1.216	0.08480
21	81.46	1.228	0.08904
22	80.67	1.240	0.09328
23	79.89	1.252	0.09752
24	79.11	1.264	0.10176
25	78.34	1.276	0.10600
26	77.58	1.289	0.11024
27	76.83	1.302	0.11448
28	76.08	1.314	0.11872
29	75.34	1.327	0.12296
30	74.61	1.340	0.12720
31	73.89	1.353	0.13144
32	73.17	1.367	0.13568
33	72.46	1.380	0.13992
34	71.75	1.394	0.14416
35	71.06	1.407	0.14840
36	70.37	1.421	0.15264
37	69.68	1.435	0.15688
38	69.01	1.449	0.16112
39	68.34	1.463	0.16536
40	67.67	1.478	0.16960
41	67.01	1.492	0.17383
42	66.36	1.507	0.17807
43	65.72	1.522	0.18231
44	65.08	1.537	0.18655
45	64.45	1.552	0.19079
46	63.82	1.567	0.19503
47	63.20	1.582	0.19927
48	62.59	1.598	0.20351
49	61.98	1.613	0.20775
50	61.38	1.629	0.21199
52	60.19	1.661	0.22047
54	59.03	1.694	0.22895
56	57.89	1.728	0.23743
58	56.77	1.762	0.24591
60	55.67	1.796	0.25439
62	54.59	1.832	0.26287
64	53.54	1.868	0.27135
66	52.50	1.905	0.27983
68	51.49	1.942	0.28831
70	50.49	1.981	0.29679
72	49.51	2.020	0.30527
74	48.56	2.059	0.31375
76	47.62	2.100	0.32223
78	46.70	2.141	0.33071
80	45.79	2.184	0.33919
82	44.91	2.227	0.34767
84	44.04	2.271	0.35615
86	43.19	2.315	0.36463
88	42.35	2.361	0.37311
90	41.53	2.408	0.38159
92	40.73	2.455	0.39007
94	39.94	2.504	0.39855
96	39.17	2.553	0.40703
98	38.41	2.603	0.41551
100	37.67	2.655	0.42399
102	36.94	2.707	0.43247
104	36.23	2.760	0.44095
106	35.53	2.815	0.44943
108	34.84	2.870	0.45791
110	34.17	2.927	0.46639
112	33.51	2.984	0.47487
114	32.86	3.043	0.48335
116	32.22	3.103	0.49183
118	31.60	3.165	0.50031
120	30.99	3.227	0.50879
122	30.39	3.291	0.51726
124	29.80	3.355	0.52574
126	29.23	3.422	0.53422
128	28.66	3.489	0.54270
130	28.11	3.558	0.55118
132	27.56	3.628	0.55966
134	27.03	3.700	0.56814
136	26.51	3.772	0.57662
138	26.00	3.847	0.58510
140	25.49	3.923	0.59358
142	25.00	4.000	0.60206
144	24.52	4.079	0.61054
146	24.04	4.159	0.61902
148	23.58	4.241	0.62750
150	23.12	4.325	0.63598
152	22.67	4.410	0.64446
154	22.24	4.497	0.65294
156	21.81	4.586	0.66142
158	21.38	4.676	0.66990
160	20.97	4.768	0.67838
165	19.97	5.007	0.69958
170	19.02	5.257	0.72078
175	18.11	5.520	0.74198
180	17.25	5.797	0.76318
185	16.43	6.087	0.78438
190	15.65	6.391	0.80558
195	14.90	6.711	0.82678
200	14.19	7.047	0.84798
205	13.52	7.399	0.86917
210	12.87	7.769	0.89037
215	12.26	8.158	0.91157
220	11.67	8.566	0.93277
225	11.12	8.994	0.95397
230	10.59	9.444	0.97517
235	10.08	9.917	0.99637
240	9.60	10.413	1.01757
245	9.15	10.934	1.03877
250	8.71	11.481	1.05997
255	8.30	12.055	1.08117
260	7.90	12.658	1.10237
265	7.52	13.291	1.12357
270	7.17	13.956	1.14477
275	6.82	14.654	1.16597
280	6.50	15.387	1.18717
285	6.19	16.157	1.20836
290	5.89	16.965	1.22956
295	5.61	17.814	1.25076
300	5.35	18.705	1.27196
305	5.09	19.641	1.29316
310	4.85	20.623	1.31436
315	4.62	21.655	1.33556
320	4.40	22.738	1.35676
325	4.19	23.876	1.37796
330	3.99	25.070	1.39916
335	3.80	26.324	1.42036
340	3.62	27.641	1.44156
345	3.45	29.024	1.46276
350	3.28	30.476	1.48396
355	3.12	32.000	1.50516
360	2.98	33.601	1.52636
365	2.83	35.282	1.54755
370	2.70	37.047	1.56875
375	2.57	38.900	1.58995
380	2.45	40.846	1.61115
385	2.33	42.890	1.63235
390	2.22	45.035	1.65355
395	2.11	47.288	1.67475
400	2.01	49.654	1.69595
405	1.92	52.137	1.71715
410	1.83	54.746	1.73835
415	1.74	57.484	1.75955
420	1.66	60.360	1.78075
425	1.58	63.379	1.80195
430	1.50	66.550	1.82315
435	1.43	69.879	1.84435
440	1.36	73.375	1.86555
445	1.30	77.045	1.88674
450	1.24	80.899	1.90794
455	1.18	84.946	1.92914
460	1.12	89.196	1.95034
465	1.07	93.657	1.97154
470	1.02	98.343	1.99274
475	0.97	103.262	2.01394
480	0.92	108.428	2.03514
485	0.88	113.852	2.05634
490	0.84	119.547	2.07754
495	0.80	125.527	2.09874
500	0.76	131.807	2.11994
505	0.72	138.400	2.14114
510	0.69	145.324	2.16234
515	0.66	152.594	2.18354
520	0.62	160.227	2.20474
525	0.59	168.242	2.22594
530	0.57	176.658	2.24713
535	0.54	185.496	2.26833
540	0.51	194.775	2.28953
545	0.49	204.518	2.31073

Cobalt-60

half-life 5.26 y

t (d)	N_t	N_0/N_t	$\log_{10} N_0/N_t$
0	100.00	1.000	0.00000
20	99.28	1.007	0.00313
40	98.57	1.015	0.00627
60	97.86	1.022	0.00940
80	97.15	1.029	0.01254
100	96.46	1.037	0.01567
120	95.76	1.044	0.01880
140	95.07	1.052	0.02194
160	94.39	1.059	0.02507
180	93.71	1.067	0.02820
200	93.04	1.075	0.03134
220	92.37	1.083	0.03447
240	91.71	1.090	0.03761
260	91.05	1.098	0.04074
280	90.39	1.106	0.04387
300	89.74	1.114	0.04701
320	89.10	1.122	0.05014
340	88.46	1.131	0.05328
360	87.82	1.139	0.05641
380	87.19	1.147	0.05954
400	86.56	1.155	0.06268
420	85.94	1.164	0.06581
440	85.32	1.172	0.06894
460	84.71	1.181	0.07208
480	84.10	1.189	0.07521
500	83.49	1.198	0.07835
520	82.89	1.206	0.08148
540	82.30	1.215	0.08461
560	81.71	1.224	0.08775
580	81.12	1.233	0.09088
600	80.54	1.242	0.09401
620	79.96	1.251	0.09715
640	79.38	1.260	0.10028
660	78.81	1.269	0.10342
680	78.24	1.278	0.10655
700	77.68	1.287	0.10968
720	77.12	1.297	0.11282
740	76.57	1.306	0.11595
760	76.02	1.315	0.11909
780	75.47	1.325	0.12222
800	74.93	1.335	0.12535
820	74.39	1.344	0.12849
840	73.85	1.354	0.13162
860	73.32	1.364	0.13475
880	72.80	1.374	0.13789
900	72.27	1.384	0.14102
920	71.75	1.394	0.14416
940	71.24	1.404	0.14729
960	70.73	1.414	0.15042
980	70.22	1.424	0.15356
1000	69.71	1.434	0.15669
1020	69.21	1.445	0.15983
1040	68.71	1.455	0.16296
1060	68.22	1.466	0.16609
1080	67.73	1.476	0.16923
1100	67.24	1.487	0.17236
1120	66.76	1.498	0.17549
1140	66.28	1.509	0.17863
1160	65.80	1.520	0.18176
1180	65.33	1.531	0.18490
1200	64.86	1.542	0.18803
1250	63.70	1.570	0.19586
1300	62.56	1.598	0.20370
1350	61.44	1.628	0.21153
1400	60.34	1.657	0.21937
1450	59.26	1.687	0.22720
1500	58.21	1.718	0.23504
1550	57.16	1.749	0.24287
1600	56.14	1.781	0.25071
1650	55.14	1.814	0.25854
1700	54.15	1.847	0.26638
1750	53.19	1.880	0.27421
1800	52.23	1.914	0.28204
1850	51.30	1.949	0.28988
1900	50.38	1.985	0.29771
1950	49.48	2.021	0.30555
2000	48.60	2.058	0.31338
2050	47.73	2.095	0.32122
2100	46.88	2.133	0.32905
2150	46.04	2.172	0.33689
2200	45.21	2.212	0.34472
2250	44.41	2.252	0.35256
2300	43.61	2.293	0.36039
2350	42.83	2.335	0.36822
2400	42.07	2.377	0.37606
2450	41.31	2.420	0.38389
2500	40.58	2.464	0.39173
2550	39.85	2.509	0.39956
2600	39.14	2.555	0.40740
2650	38.44	2.602	0.41523
2700	37.75	2.649	0.42307
2750	37.08	2.697	0.43090
2800	36.41	2.746	0.43874
2850	35.76	2.796	0.44657
2900	35.12	2.847	0.45440
2950	34.50	2.899	0.46224
3000	33.88	2.952	0.47007
3050	33.27	3.005	0.47791
3100	32.68	3.060	0.48574
3150	32.09	3.116	0.49358
3200	31.52	3.173	0.50141
3250	30.96	3.230	0.50925
3300	30.40	3.289	0.51708
3350	29.86	3.349	0.52492
3400	29.33	3.410	0.53275
3450	28.80	3.472	0.54058
3500	28.29	3.535	0.54842
3550	27.78	3.600	0.55625
3600	27.28	3.665	0.56409
3650	26.80	3.732	0.57192
3700	26.32	3.800	0.57976
3750	25.85	3.869	0.58759
3800	25.38	3.939	0.59543
3850	24.93	4.011	0.60326
3900	24.49	4.084	0.61110
3950	24.05	4.158	0.61893
4000	23.62	4.234	0.62677
4050	23.20	4.311	0.63460
4100	22.78	4.390	0.64243
4150	22.37	4.470	0.65027
4200	21.97	4.551	0.65810
4250	21.58	4.634	0.66594
4300	21.19	4.718	0.67377
4350	20.82	4.804	0.68161
4400	20.44	4.891	0.68944
4450	20.08	4.981	0.69728
4500	19.72	5.071	0.70511
4550	19.37	5.164	0.71295
4600	19.02	5.258	0.72078
4650	18.68	5.353	0.72861
4700	18.35	5.451	0.73645
4750	18.02	5.550	0.74428
4800	17.70	5.651	0.75212
4850	17.38	5.754	0.75995
4900	17.07	5.859	0.76779
4950	16.76	5.965	0.77562
5000	16.46	6.074	0.78346
5050	16.17	6.184	0.79129
5100	15.88	6.297	0.79913
5150	15.60	6.412	0.80696
5200	15.32	6.528	0.81479
5250	15.04	6.647	0.82263
5300	14.78	6.768	0.83046
5350	14.51	6.891	0.83830
5400	14.25	7.017	0.84613
5450	14.00	7.144	0.85397
5500	13.75	7.274	0.86180
5550	13.50	7.407	0.86964
5600	13.26	7.542	0.87747
5650	13.02	7.679	0.88531
5700	12.79	7.819	0.89314
5750	12.56	7.961	0.90097
5800	12.34	8.106	0.90881
5850	12.12	8.254	0.91664
5900	11.90	8.404	0.92448
5950	11.69	8.557	0.93231
6000	11.48	8.713	0.94015
6050	11.27	8.871	0.94798
6100	11.07	9.033	0.95582
6150	10.87	9.197	0.96365
6200	10.68	9.365	0.97149
6250	10.49	9.535	0.97932
6300	10.30	9.709	0.98716
6350	10.12	9.885	0.99499
6400	9.94	10.065	1.00282
6450	9.76	10.248	1.01066
6500	9.58	10.435	1.01849
6550	9.41	10.625	1.02633
6600	9.24	10.818	1.03416
6650	9.08	11.015	1.04200
6700	8.92	11.216	1.04983
6750	8.76	11.420	1.05767
6800	8.60	11.628	1.06550
6850	8.45	11.840	1.07334
6900	8.30	12.055	1.08117
6950	8.15	12.275	1.08900
7000	8.00	12.498	1.09684
7050	7.86	12.725	1.10467
7100	7.72	12.957	1.11251
7150	7.58	13.193	1.12034
7200	7.44	13.433	1.12818
7250	7.31	13.678	1.13601
7300	7.18	13.927	1.14385
7350	7.05	14.180	1.15168
7400	6.93	14.438	1.15952
7450	6.80	14.701	1.16735
7500	6.68	14.969	1.17518
7550	6.56	15.241	1.18302
7600	6.44	15.519	1.19085
7650	6.33	15.801	1.19869
7700	6.22	16.089	1.20652
7750	6.10	16.382	1.21436
7800	6.00	16.680	1.22219
7850	5.89	16.983	1.23003
7900	5.78	17.293	1.23786
7950	5.68	17.607	1.24570
8000	5.58	17.928	1.25353
8050	5.48	18.254	1.26136
8100	5.38	18.587	1.26920
8150	5.28	18.925	1.27703
8200	5.19	19.269	1.28487
8250	5.10	19.620	1.29270
8300	5.01	19.977	1.30054
8350	4.92	20.341	1.30837
8400	4.83	20.711	1.31621
8450	4.74	21.088	1.32404
8500	4.66	21.472	1.33188
8550	4.57	21.863	1.33971
8600	4.49	22.261	1.34755
8650	4.41	22.666	1.35538
8700	4.33	23.079	1.36321
8750	4.26	23.499	1.37105
8800	4.18	23.927	1.37888
8850	4.10	24.362	1.38672
8900	4.03	24.806	1.39455
8950	3.96	25.257	1.40239
9000	3.89	25.717	1.41022
9050	3.82	26.185	1.41806
9100	3.75	26.662	1.42589
9150	3.68	27.147	1.43373
9200	3.62	27.641	1.44156
9250	3.55	28.145	1.44939
9300	3.49	28.657	1.45723
9350	3.43	29.179	1.46506
9400	3.37	29.710	1.47290
9450	3.31	30.251	1.48073
9500	3.25	30.801	1.48857
9550	3.19	31.362	1.49640
9600	3.13	31.933	1.50424
9650	3.08	32.514	1.51207
9700	3.02	33.106	1.51991
9750	2.97	33.709	1.52774
9800	2.91	34.322	1.53557
9850	2.86	34.947	1.54341
9900	2.81	35.583	1.55124
9950	2.76	36.231	1.55908
10000	2.71	36.890	1.56691
10050	2.66	37.562	1.57475
10100	2.61	38.246	1.58258
10150	2.57	38.942	1.59042
10200	2.52	39.651	1.59825
10250	2.48	40.373	1.60609
10300	2.43	41.107	1.61392
10350	2.39	41.856	1.62175
10400	2.35	42.618	1.62959
10450	2.30	43.393	1.63742
10500	2.26	44.183	1.64526
10550	2.22	44.988	1.65309
10600	2.18	45.807	1.66093
10650	2.14	46.640	1.66876
10700	2.11	47.489	1.67660
10750	2.07	48.354	1.68443
10800	2.03	49.234	1.69227
10850	1.99	50.130	1.70010
10900	1.96	51.043	1.70794
10950	1.92	51.972	1.71577
11000	1.89	52.918	1.72360
11050	1.86	53.881	1.73144
11100	1.82	54.862	1.73927
11150	1.79	55.861	1.74711
11200	1.76	56.878	1.75494
11250	1.73	57.913	1.76278
11300	1.70	58.967	1.77061
11350	1.67	60.041	1.77845
11400	1.64	61.134	1.78628
11450	1.61	62.247	1.79412
11500	1.58	63.380	1.80195
11550	1.55	64.533	1.80978
11600	1.52	65.708	1.81762
11650	1.49	66.904	1.82545
11700	1.47	68.122	1.83329
11750	1.44	69.362	1.84112
11800	1.42	70.625	1.84896
11850	1.39	71.910	1.85679
11900	1.37	73.219	1.86463
11950	1.34	74.552	1.87246
12000	1.32	75.909	1.88030
12050	1.29	77.291	1.88813
12100	1.27	78.698	1.89596
12150	1.25	80.131	1.90380
12200	1.23	81.589	1.91163
12250	1.20	83.075	1.91947
12300	1.18	84.587	1.92730
12350	1.16	86.127	1.93514
12400	1.14	87.694	1.94297
12450	1.12	89.291	1.95081
12500	1.10	90.916	1.95864
12550	1.08	92.571	1.96648
12600	1.06	94.256	1.97431
12650	1.04	95.972	1.98214
12700	1.02	97.719	1.98998
12750	1.01	99.498	1.99781
12800	0.99	101.309	2.00565
12850	0.97	103.153	2.01348
12900	0.95	105.031	2.02132
12950	0.94	106.943	2.02915
13000	0.92	108.890	2.03699
13050	0.90	110.872	2.04482
13100	0.89	112.890	2.05266
13150	0.87	114.945	2.06049
13200	0.85	117.037	2.06832
13250	0.84	119.168	2.07616
13300	0.82	121.337	2.08399
13350	0.81	123.546	2.09183
13400	0.79	125.795	2.09966
13450	0.78	128.085	2.10750
13500	0.77	130.416	2.11533
13550	0.75	132.790	2.12317
13600	0.74	135.208	2.13100
13650	0.73	137.669	2.13884
13700	0.71	140.175	2.14667
13750	0.70	142.727	2.15451
13800	0.69	145.325	2.16234
13850	0.68	147.970	2.17017
13900	0.66	150.664	2.17801
13950	0.65	153.406	2.18584
14000	0.64	156.199	2.19368
14050	0.63	159.042	2.20151
14100	0.62	161.937	2.20935
14150	0.61	164.885	2.21718
14200	0.60	167.887	2.22502
14250	0.58	170.943	2.23285
14300	0.57	174.055	2.24069
14350	0.56	177.223	2.24852
14400	0.55	180.449	2.25635
14450	0.54	183.734	2.26419
14500	0.53	187.078	2.27202
14550	0.52	190.484	2.27986
14600	0.52	193.951	2.28769
14650	0.51	197.482	2.29553
14700	0.50	201.077	2.30336

Copper-64

half-life 12.84 h

d	h	min	N_t	N_0/N_t	$\log_{10} N_0/N_t$
		0	100.00	1.000	0.00000
		20	98.22	1.018	0.00781
		40	96.47	1.037	0.01563
	1	0	94.74	1.055	0.02344
		20	93.06	1.075	0.03126
		40	91.40	1.094	0.03907
	2	0	89.77	1.114	0.04689
		20	88.16	1.134	0.05470
		40	86.59	1.155	0.06252
	3	0	85.05	1.176	0.07033
		20	83.53	1.197	0.07815
		40	82.04	1.219	0.08596
	4	0	80.58	1.241	0.09378
		20	79.14	1.264	0.10159
		40	77.73	1.286	0.10941
	5	0	76.34	1.310	0.11722
		20	74.98	1.334	0.12504
		40	73.65	1.358	0.13285
	6	0	72.33	1.383	0.14067
		20	71.04	1.408	0.14848
		40	69.78	1.433	0.15630
	7	0	68.53	1.459	0.16411
		20	67.31	1.486	0.17193
		40	66.11	1.513	0.17974
	8	0	64.93	1.540	0.18756
		20	63.77	1.568	0.19537
		40	62.63	1.597	0.20319
	9	0	61.52	1.626	0.21100
		20	60.42	1.655	0.21882
		40	59.34	1.685	0.22663
	10	0	58.28	1.716	0.23445
		20	57.24	1.747	0.24226
		40	56.22	1.779	0.25008
	11	0	55.22	1.811	0.25789
		20	54.24	1.844	0.26571
		40	53.27	1.877	0.27352
	12		52.32	1.911	0.28134
	13		49.57	2.017	0.30478
	14		46.96	2.129	0.32823
	15		44.50	2.247	0.35167
	16		42.16	2.372	0.37512
	17		39.94	2.504	0.39856
	18		37.84	2.642	0.42201
	19		35.85	2.789	0.44545
	20		33.97	2.944	0.46890
	21		32.19	3.107	0.49234
	22		30.49	3.279	0.51579
	23		28.89	3.461	0.53923
1	0		27.37	3.653	0.56268
	1		25.93	3.856	0.58612

t d	t h	t min	N_t	N_0/N_t	$\log_{10} N_0/N_t$
	2		24.57	4.070	0.60956
	3		23.28	4.295	0.63301
	4		22.06	4.534	0.65645
	5		20.90	4.785	0.67990
	6		19.80	5.051	0.70334
	7		18.76	5.331	0.72679
	8		17.77	5.626	0.75023
	9		16.84	5.939	0.77368
	10		15.95	6.268	0.79712
	11		15.12	6.616	0.82057
	12		14.32	6.983	0.84401
	15		12.18	8.210	0.91435
	18		10.36	9.653	0.98468
	21		8.81	11.351	1.05502
2	0		7.49	13.346	1.12535
	3		6.37	15.692	1.19568
	6		5.42	18.451	1.26602
	9		4.61	21.695	1.33635
	12		3.92	25.509	1.40669
	15		3.33	29.993	1.47702
	18		2.84	35.266	1.54736
	21		2.41	41.466	1.61769
3	0		2.05	48.756	1.68803
	3		1.74	57.327	1.75836
	6		1.48	67.405	1.82869
	9		1.26	79.255	1.89903
	12		1.07	93.189	1.96936
	15		0.91	109.571	2.03970
	18		0.78	128.834	2.11003
	21		0.66	151.484	2.18037
4	0		0.56	178.115	2.25070

Zinc-65

half-life 245 d

t d	N_t	N_0/N_t	$\log_{10} N_0/N_t$
0	100.00	1.000	0.00000
10	97.21	1.028	0.01229
20	94.50	1.058	0.02457
30	91.86	1.088	0.03686
40	89.30	1.119	0.04915
50	86.81	1.151	0.06144
60	84.39	1.185	0.07372
70	82.03	1.219	0.08601
80	79.75	1.253	0.09830
90	77.52	1.289	0.11058
100	75.36	1.326	0.12287
110	73.26	1.365	0.13516
120	71.21	1.404	0.14744
130	69.23	1.444	0.15973
140	67.30	1.485	0.17202
150	65.42	1.528	0.18430
160	63.59	1.572	0.19659
170	61.82	1.617	0.20888
180	60.09	1.664	0.22117
190	58.42	1.711	0.23345
200	56.79	1.760	0.24574
210	55.20	1.811	0.25803
220	53.66	1.863	0.27031
230	52.17	1.916	0.28260
240	50.71	1.971	0.29489
250	49.30	2.028	0.30717
260	47.92	2.086	0.31946
270	46.59	2.146	0.33175
280	45.29	2.208	0.34403
290	44.02	2.271	0.35632
300	42.79	2.336	0.36861
310	41.60	2.403	0.38090
320	40.44	2.472	0.39318
330	39.31	2.543	0.40547
340	38.22	2.616	0.41776
350	37.15	2.691	0.43004
360	36.11	2.769	0.44233
370	35.11	2.848	0.45462
380	34.13	2.930	0.46690
390	33.17	3.014	0.47919
400	32.25	3.100	0.49148
410	31.35	3.189	0.50376
420	30.48	3.281	0.51605
430	29.63	3.375	0.52834
440	28.80	3.472	0.54063
450	28.00	3.572	0.55291
460	27.21	3.674	0.56520
470	26.46	3.779	0.57749
480	25.72	3.888	0.58977
490	25.00	3.999	0.60206
500	24.30	4.114	0.61435
510	23.62	4.232	0.62663
520	22.97	4.354	0.63892
530	22.33	4.479	0.65121
540	21.70	4.607	0.66349
550	21.10	4.740	0.67578
560	20.51	4.876	0.68807
570	19.94	5.015	0.70035
580	19.38	5.159	0.71264
590	18.84	5.307	0.72493
600	18.31	5.460	0.73722
610	17.80	5.616	0.74950
620	17.31	5.778	0.76179
630	16.82	5.943	0.77408
640	16.35	6.114	0.78636
650	15.90	6.289	0.79865
660	15.45	6.470	0.81094
670	15.02	6.656	0.82322
680	14.60	6.847	0.83551
690	14.20	7.043	0.84780
700	13.80	7.245	0.86008
720	13.04	7.667	0.88466
740	12.32	8.113	0.90923
760	11.65	8.586	0.93380
780	11.01	9.085	0.95837
800	10.40	9.614	0.98295
820	9.83	10.174	1.00753
840	9.29	10.767	1.03210
860	8.78	11.394	1.05668
880	8.29	12.057	1.08125
900	7.84	12.759	1.10583
920	7.41	13.502	1.13040
940	7.00	14.288	1.15497
960	6.61	15.119	1.17955
980	6.25	16.000	1.20412
1000	5.91	16.931	1.22869
1040	5.27	18.960	1.27784
1080	4.71	21.231	1.32699
1120	4.21	23.775	1.37614
1160	3.76	26.624	1.42529
1200	3.35	29.814	1.47443
1240	3.00	33.387	1.52358
1280	2.67	37.387	1.57273
1320	2.39	41.867	1.62188
1360	2.13	46.883	1.67102
1400	1.90	52.501	1.72017
1500	1.44	69.668	1.84304
1600	1.08	92.448	1.96590
1700	0.82	122.681	2.08878
1800	0.61	162.797	2.21165
1900	0.46	216.034	2.33452

Selenium-75

half-life 121 d

t d	N_t	N_0/N_t	$\log_{10} N_0/N_t$
0	100.00	1.000	0.00000
4	97.73	1.023	0.00995
8	95.52	1.047	0.01990
12	93.36	1.071	0.02985
16	91.24	1.096	0.03981
20	89.17	1.121	0.04976
24	87.15	1.147	0.05971
28	85.18	1.174	0.06966
32	83.25	1.201	0.07961
36	81.36	1.229	0.08956
40	79.52	1.258	0.09951
44	77.72	1.287	0.10947
48	75.96	1.316	0.11942
52	74.24	1.347	0.12937
56	72.56	1.378	0.13932
60	70.91	1.410	0.14927
64	69.31	1.443	0.15922
68	67.74	1.476	0.16917
72	66.20	1.511	0.17913
76	64.70	1.546	0.18908
80	63.24	1.581	0.19903
84	61.80	1.618	0.20898
88	60.40	1.656	0.21893
92	59.04	1.694	0.22888
96	57.70	1.733	0.23883
100	56.39	1.773	0.24879
104	55.11	1.814	0.25874
108	53.87	1.856	0.26869
112	52.65	1.900	0.27864
116	51.45	1.944	0.28859
120	50.29	1.989	0.29854
124	49.15	2.035	0.30849
128	48.03	2.082	0.31845
132	46.95	2.130	0.32840
136	45.88	2.179	0.33835
140	44.84	2.230	0.34830
144	43.83	2.282	0.35825
148	42.83	2.335	0.36820
152	41.86	2.389	0.37815
156	40.92	2.444	0.38811
160	39.99	2.501	0.39806
170	37.76	2.648	0.42294
180	35.66	2.804	0.44782
190	33.67	2.970	0.47269
200	31.80	3.145	0.49757
210	30.03	3.330	0.52245
220	28.36	3.526	0.54733
230	26.78	3.734	0.57221
240	25.29	3.954	0.59709
250	23.88	4.188	0.62197
260	22.55	4.434	0.64684
270	21.29	4.696	0.67172
280	20.11	4.973	0.69660
290	18.99	5.266	0.72148
300	17.93	5.576	0.74636
310	16.93	5.905	0.77124
320	15.99	6.253	0.79612
330	15.10	6.622	0.82099
340	14.26	7.012	0.84587
350	13.47	7.426	0.87075
360	12.72	7.864	0.89563
370	12.01	8.327	0.92051
380	11.34	8.818	0.94539
390	10.71	9.338	0.97027
400	10.11	9.889	0.99514
410	9.55	10.472	1.02002
420	9.02	11.089	1.04490
430	8.52	11.743	1.06978
440	8.04	12.435	1.09466
450	7.59	13.169	1.11954
460	7.17	13.945	1.14442
470	6.77	14.767	1.16929
480	6.39	15.638	1.19417
490	6.04	16.560	1.21905
500	5.70	17.536	1.24393
510	5.39	18.570	1.26881
520	5.09	19.665	1.29369
530	4.80	20.824	1.31857
540	4.53	22.052	1.34345
550	4.28	23.352	1.36832
560	4.04	24.729	1.39320
570	3.82	26.187	1.41808
580	3.61	27.731	1.44296
590	3.41	29.366	1.46784
600	3.22	31.097	1.49272
610	3.04	32.930	1.51760
620	2.87	34.872	1.54247
630	2.71	36.928	1.56735
640	2.56	39.105	1.59223
650	2.41	41.410	1.61711
660	2.28	43.852	1.64199
670	2.15	46.437	1.66687
680	2.03	49.175	1.69175
690	1.92	52.074	1.71662
700	1.81	55.145	1.74150
710	1.71	58.396	1.76638
720	1.62	61.839	1.79126
730	1.53	65.485	1.81614
740	1.44	69.345	1.84102
750	1.36	73.434	1.86590
760	1.29	77.763	1.89077
770	1.21	82.348	1.91565
780	1.15	87.203	1.94053
790	1.08	92.344	1.96541
800	1.02	97.789	1.99029
810	0.97	103.554	2.01517
820	0.91	109.659	2.04005
830	0.86	116.125	2.06492
840	0.81	122.971	2.08980
850	0.77	130.221	2.11468
860	0.73	137.899	2.13956
870	0.68	146.029	2.16444
880	0.65	154.639	2.18932
890	0.61	163.756	2.21420
900	0.58	173.410	2.23908
910	0.54	183.634	2.26395
920	0.51	194.461	2.28883

Bromine-82

half-life 35.4 h

t d	t h	t min	N_t	N_0/N_t	$\log_{10} N_0/N_t$
		0	100.00	1.000	0.00000
		20	99.35	1.007	0.00283
		40	98.70	1.013	0.00567
	1	0	98.06	1.020	0.00850
		20	97.42	1.026	0.01134
		40	96.79	1.033	0.01417
	2	0	96.16	1.040	0.01701
		20	95.53	1.047	0.01984
		40	94.91	1.054	0.02268
	3	0	94.30	1.061	0.02551
		20	93.68	1.067	0.02835
		40	93.07	1.074	0.03118
	4	0	92.47	1.081	0.03401
		20	91.87	1.089	0.03685
		40	91.27	1.096	0.03968
	5	0	90.67	1.103	0.04252
		20	90.08	1.110	0.04535
		40	89.50	1.117	0.04819
	6	0	88.92	1.125	0.05102
		20	88.34	1.132	0.05386
		40	87.76	1.139	0.05669
	7	0	87.19	1.147	0.05953
		20	86.62	1.154	0.06236
		40	86.06	1.162	0.06520
	8	0	85.50	1.170	0.06803
		20	84.94	1.177	0.07086
		40	84.39	1.185	0.07370
	9	0	83.84	1.193	0.07653
		20	83.30	1.201	0.07937
		40	82.76	1.208	0.08220
	10	0	82.22	1.216	0.08504
		20	81.68	1.224	0.08787
		40	81.15	1.232	0.09071
	11	0	80.62	1.240	0.09354
		20	80.10	1.248	0.09638
		40	79.58	1.257	0.09921
	12	0	79.06	1.265	0.10204
		20	78.55	1.273	0.10488
		40	78.03	1.281	0.10771
	13	0	77.53	1.290	0.11055
		20	77.02	1.298	0.11338
		40	76.52	1.307	0.11622
	14	0	76.02	1.315	0.11905
		20	75.53	1.324	0.12189
		40	75.04	1.333	0.12472
	15	0	74.55	1.341	0.12756
		20	74.06	1.350	0.13039
		40	73.58	1.359	0.13322
	16	0	73.10	1.368	0.13606
		20	72.63	1.377	0.13889
		40	72.16	1.386	0.14173
	17	0	71.69	1.395	0.14456
		20	71.22	1.404	0.14740
		40	70.76	1.413	0.15023
	18	0	70.30	1.423	0.15307
		20	69.84	1.432	0.15590
		40	69.38	1.441	0.15874
	19	0	68.93	1.451	0.16157
		20	68.48	1.460	0.16440
		40	68.04	1.470	0.16724
	20	0	67.60	1.479	0.17007
		20	67.16	1.489	0.17291
		40	66.72	1.499	0.17574
	21	0	66.29	1.509	0.17858
		20	65.85	1.518	0.18141
		40	65.43	1.528	0.18425
	22	0	65.00	1.538	0.18708
		20	64.58	1.549	0.18992
		40	64.16	1.559	0.19275
	23	0	63.74	1.569	0.19559
		20	63.33	1.579	0.19842
		40	62.91	1.589	0.20125
1	0	0	62.50	1.600	0.20409
		20	62.10	1.610	0.20692
		40	61.69	1.621	0.20976
	1	0	61.29	1.632	0.21259
		20	60.89	1.642	0.21543
		40	60.50	1.653	0.21826
	2	0	60.10	1.664	0.22110
		20	59.71	1.675	0.22393
		40	59.32	1.686	0.22677
	3	0	58.94	1.697	0.22960
		20	58.56	1.708	0.23243
		40	58.17	1.719	0.23527
	4	0	57.80	1.730	0.23810
		20	57.42	1.742	0.24094
		40	57.05	1.753	0.24377
	5	0	56.68	1.764	0.24661
		20	56.31	1.776	0.24944
		40	55.94	1.788	0.25228
	6	0	55.58	1.799	0.25511
		20	55.21	1.811	0.25795
		40	54.86	1.823	0.26078
	7	0	54.50	1.835	0.26361
		20	54.14	1.847	0.26645
		40	53.79	1.859	0.26928
	8	0	53.44	1.871	0.27212
		20	53.09	1.883	0.27495
		40	52.75	1.896	0.27779
	9	0	52.41	1.908	0.28062
		20	52.06	1.921	0.28346
		40	51.73	1.933	0.28629
	10	0	51.39	1.946	0.28913
		20	51.06	1.959	0.29196
		40	50.72	1.971	0.29480
	11	0	50.39	1.984	0.29763
		20	50.07	1.997	0.30046
		40	49.74	2.010	0.30330
	12		49.42	2.024	0.30613
	13		48.46	2.064	0.31464
	14		47.52	2.104	0.32314
	15		46.60	2.146	0.33164
	16		45.69	2.189	0.34015
	17		44.81	2.232	0.34865
	18		43.94	2.276	0.35716
	19		43.09	2.321	0.36566
	20		42.25	2.367	0.37416
	21		41.43	2.414	0.38267
	22		40.63	2.461	0.39117
	23		39.84	2.510	0.39967

t d	t h	t min	N_t	N_0/N_t	$\log_{10} N_0/N_t$
2	0		39.07	2.560	0.40818
	1		38.31	2.610	0.41668
	2		37.57	2.662	0.42519
	3		36.84	2.714	0.43369
	4		36.12	2.768	0.44219
	5		35.42	2.823	0.45070
	6		34.74	2.879	0.45920
	7		34.06	2.936	0.46770
	8		33.40	2.994	0.47621
	9		32.76	3.053	0.48471
	10		32.12	3.113	0.49321
	11		31.50	3.175	0.50172
	12		30.89	3.238	0.51022
	13		30.29	3.302	0.51873
	14		29.70	3.367	0.52723
	15		29.13	3.433	0.53573
	16		28.56	3.501	0.54424
	17		28.01	3.571	0.55274
	18		27.46	3.641	0.56124
	19		26.93	3.713	0.56975
	20		26.41	3.787	0.57825
	21		25.90	3.861	0.58676
	22		25.39	3.938	0.59526
	23		24.90	4.016	0.60376
3	0		24.42	4.095	0.61227
	1		23.95	4.176	0.62077
	2		23.48	4.259	0.62927
	3		23.03	4.343	0.63778
	4		22.58	4.429	0.64628
	5		22.14	4.516	0.65479
	6		21.71	4.606	0.66329
	7		21.29	4.697	0.67179
	8		20.88	4.790	0.68030
	9		20.47	4.884	0.68880
	10		20.08	4.981	0.69730
	11		19.69	5.079	0.70581
	12		19.31	5.180	0.71431
	13		18.93	5.282	0.72282
	14		18.56	5.387	0.73132
	15		18.20	5.493	0.73982
	16		17.85	5.602	0.74833
	17		17.51	5.713	0.75683
	18		17.17	5.826	0.76533
	19		16.83	5.941	0.77384
	20		16.51	6.058	0.78234
	21		16.19	6.178	0.79084
	22		15.87	6.300	0.79935
	23		15.56	6.425	0.80785
4	0		15.26	6.552	0.81636
	1		14.97	6.681	0.82486
	2		14.68	6.813	0.83336
	3		14.39	6.948	0.84187
	4		14.11	7.086	0.85037
	5		13.84	7.226	0.85887
	6		13.57	7.368	0.86738
	7		13.31	7.514	0.87588
	8		13.05	7.663	0.88439
	9		12.80	7.814	0.89289
	10		12.55	7.969	0.90139
	11		12.31	8.126	0.90990
	12		12.07	8.287	0.91840
	13		11.83	8.451	0.92690
	14		11.60	8.618	0.93541
	15		11.38	8.788	0.94391
	16		11.16	8.962	0.95242
	17		10.94	9.139	0.96092
	18		10.73	9.320	0.96942
	19		10.52	9.504	0.97793
	20		10.32	9.692	0.98643
	21		10.12	9.884	0.99493
	22		9.92	10.079	1.00344
	23		9.73	10.279	1.01194
5	0		9.54	10.482	1.02044
	6		8.48	11.789	1.07147
	12		7.54	13.258	1.12249
	18		6.71	14.911	1.17351
6	0		5.96	16.770	1.22453
	6		5.30	18.861	1.27556
	12		4.71	21.212	1.32658
	18		4.19	23.856	1.37760
7	0		3.73	26.830	1.42862
	6		3.31	30.175	1.47964
	12		2.95	33.937	1.53067
	18		2.62	38.167	1.58169
8	0		2.33	42.925	1.63271
	6		2.07	48.276	1.68373
	12		1.84	54.295	1.73476
	18		1.64	61.063	1.78578
9	0		1.46	68.675	1.83680
	6		1.29	77.237	1.88782
	12		1.15	86.865	1.93885
	18		1.02	97.694	1.98987
10	0		0.91	109.873	2.04089
	6		0.81	123.570	2.09191
	12		0.72	138.974	2.14293
	18		0.64	156.299	2.19396
11	0		0.57	175.784	2.24498
	6		0.51	197.697	2.29600
	12		0.45	222.343	2.34702

Krypton-85

half-life 10.6 y

t d	N_t	N_0/N_t	$\log_{10} N_0/N_t$
0	100.00	1.000	0.00000
100	98.23	1.018	0.00778
200	96.48	1.036	0.01555
300	94.77	1.055	0.02333
400	93.09	1.074	0.03110
500	91.44	1.094	0.03888
600	89.81	1.113	0.04665
700	88.22	1.134	0.05443
800	86.66	1.154	0.06220
900	85.12	1.175	0.06998
1000	83.61	1.196	0.07775
1100	82.12	1.218	0.08553
1200	80.67	1.240	0.09331
1300	79.24	1.262	0.10108
1400	77.83	1.285	0.10886
1500	76.45	1.308	0.11663
1600	75.09	1.332	0.12441
1700	73.76	1.356	0.13218
1800	72.45	1.380	0.13996
1900	71.17	1.405	0.14773
2000	69.90	1.431	0.15551
2100	68.66	1.456	0.16328
2200	67.44	1.483	0.17106
2300	66.25	1.510	0.17884
2400	65.07	1.537	0.18661
2600	62.78	1.593	0.20216
2800	60.57	1.651	0.21771
3000	58.44	1.711	0.23326
3200	56.39	1.773	0.24881
3400	54.40	1.838	0.26436
3600	52.49	1.905	0.27992
3800	50.64	1.975	0.29547
4000	48.86	2.047	0.31102
4200	47.14	2.121	0.32657
4400	45.49	2.198	0.34212
4600	43.89	2.279	0.35767
4800	42.34	2.362	0.37322
5000	40.85	2.448	0.38877
5200	39.42	2.537	0.40432
5400	38.03	2.630	0.41987
5600	36.69	2.725	0.43542
5800	35.40	2.825	0.45098
6000	34.16	2.928	0.46653
6400	31.80	3.145	0.49763
6800	29.60	3.379	0.52873
7200	27.55	3.629	0.55983
7600	25.65	3.899	0.59093
8000	23.88	4.188	0.62203
8400	22.23	4.499	0.65314
8800	20.69	4.833	0.68424
9200	19.26	5.192	0.71534
9600	17.93	5.578	0.74644
10000	16.69	5.992	0.77754
10400	15.54	6.436	0.80865
10800	14.46	6.914	0.83975
11200	13.46	7.428	0.87085
11600	12.53	7.979	0.90195
12000	11.67	8.571	0.93305
13000	9.75	10.252	1.01081
14000	8.16	12.262	1.08856
15000	6.82	14.666	1.16632
16000	5.70	17.542	1.24407
17000	4.77	20.981	1.32182
18000	3.98	25.094	1.39958
19000	3.33	30.015	1.47733
20000	2.79	35.899	1.55509
21000	2.33	42.938	1.63284
22000	1.95	51.357	1.71060
23000	1.63	61.426	1.78835
24000	1.36	73.469	1.86610
25000	1.14	87.874	1.94386
26000	0.95	105.103	2.02161
27000	0.80	125.709	2.09937
28000	0.67	150.356	2.17712
29000	0.56	179.836	2.25488
30000	0.46	215.095	2.33263

Strontium-89

half-life 51 d

t d	N_t	N_0/N_t	$\log_{10} N_0/N_t$
0	100.00	1.000	0.00000
1	98.65	1.014	0.00590
2	97.32	1.028	0.01181
3	96.00	1.042	0.01771
4	94.71	1.056	0.02361
5	93.43	1.070	0.02951
6	92.17	1.085	0.03542
7	90.92	1.100	0.04132
8	89.70	1.115	0.04722
9	88.49	1.130	0.05312
10	87.29	1.146	0.05903
12	84.95	1.177	0.07083
14	82.67	1.210	0.08264
16	80.46	1.243	0.09444
18	78.30	1.277	0.10625
20	76.20	1.312	0.11805
22	74.16	1.349	0.12986
24	72.17	1.386	0.14166
26	70.23	1.424	0.15347
28	68.35	1.463	0.16527
30	66.52	1.503	0.17708
32	64.73	1.545	0.18888
34	63.00	1.587	0.20069
36	61.31	1.631	0.21249
38	59.66	1.676	0.22430
40	58.06	1.722	0.23610
42	56.51	1.770	0.24791
44	54.99	1.818	0.25971
46	53.52	1.869	0.27152
48	52.08	1.920	0.28332
50	50.68	1.973	0.29513
52	49.32	2.027	0.30693
54	48.00	2.083	0.31874
56	46.71	2.141	0.33054
58	45.46	2.200	0.34235
60	44.24	2.260	0.35415
64	41.90	2.387	0.37776
68	39.68	2.520	0.40137
72	37.59	2.661	0.42499
76	35.60	2.809	0.44860
80	33.71	2.966	0.47221
84	31.93	3.132	0.49582
88	30.24	3.307	0.51943
92	28.64	3.492	0.54304
96	27.12	3.687	0.56665
100	25.69	3.893	0.59026
104	24.33	4.110	0.61387
108	23.04	4.340	0.63748
112	21.82	4.582	0.66109
116	20.67	4.838	0.68470
120	19.57	5.109	0.70831
124	18.54	5.394	0.73192
128	17.56	5.695	0.75553
132	16.63	6.014	0.77914
136	15.75	6.350	0.80275
140	14.92	6.704	0.82636
150	13.02	7.680	0.88539
160	11.37	8.799	0.94441
170	9.92	10.079	1.00344
180	8.66	11.547	1.06246
190	7.56	13.228	1.12149
200	6.60	15.154	1.18051
210	5.76	17.360	1.23954
220	5.03	19.887	1.29857
230	4.39	22.782	1.35759
240	3.83	26.099	1.41662
250	3.34	29.898	1.47564
260	2.92	34.251	1.53467
270	2.55	39.237	1.59369
280	2.22	44.949	1.65272
290	1.94	51.493	1.71175
300	1.70	58.989	1.77077
310	1.48	67.577	1.82980
320	1.29	77.415	1.88882
330	1.13	88.685	1.94785
340	0.98	101.596	2.00687
350	0.86	116.386	2.06590
360	0.75	133.329	2.12493
370	0.65	152.740	2.18395
380	0.57	174.976	2.24298
390	0.50	200.449	2.30200

Strontium-90

half-life 28 y

t d	N_t	N_0/N_t	$\log_{10} N_0/N_t$
0	100.00	1.000	0.00000
100	99.32	1.007	0.00294
200	98.65	1.014	0.00589
300	97.99	1.021	0.00883
400	97.33	1.027	0.01177
500	96.67	1.034	0.01472
600	96.01	1.042	0.01766
700	95.37	1.049	0.02060
800	94.72	1.056	0.02355
900	94.08	1.063	0.02649
1000	93.45	1.070	0.02944
1100	92.82	1.077	0.03238
1200	92.19	1.085	0.03532
1300	91.57	1.092	0.03827
1400	90.95	1.100	0.04121
1500	90.33	1.107	0.04415
1600	89.72	1.115	0.04710
1700	89.12	1.122	0.05004
1800	88.51	1.130	0.05298
1900	87.92	1.137	0.05593
2000	87.32	1.145	0.05887
2200	86.15	1.161	0.06476
2400	84.99	1.177	0.07065
2600	83.84	1.193	0.07653
2800	82.71	1.209	0.08242
3000	81.60	1.225	0.08831
3200	80.50	1.242	0.09419
3400	79.42	1.259	0.10008
3600	78.35	1.276	0.10597
3800	77.29	1.294	0.11186
4000	76.25	1.311	0.11774
4200	75.23	1.329	0.12363
4400	74.21	1.347	0.12952
4600	73.21	1.366	0.13540
4800	72.23	1.384	0.14129
5000	71.26	1.403	0.14718
5200	70.30	1.423	0.15307
5400	69.35	1.442	0.15895
5600	68.42	1.462	0.16484
5800	67.50	1.482	0.17073
6000	66.59	1.502	0.17661
6200	65.69	1.522	0.18250
6400	64.81	1.543	0.18839
6600	63.93	1.564	0.19427
6800	63.07	1.585	0.20016
7000	62.22	1.607	0.20605
7200	61.39	1.629	0.21194
7400	60.56	1.651	0.21782
7600	59.74	1.674	0.22371
7800	58.94	1.697	0.22960
8000	58.15	1.720	0.23548
8200	57.36	1.743	0.24137
8400	56.59	1.767	0.24726
8600	55.83	1.791	0.25315
8800	55.08	1.816	0.25903
9000	54.34	1.840	0.26492
9200	53.60	1.866	0.27081
9400	52.88	1.891	0.27669
9600	52.17	1.917	0.28258
9800	51.47	1.943	0.28847
10000	50.77	1.969	0.29436
10200	50.09	1.996	0.30024
10400	49.42	2.024	0.30613
10600	48.75	2.051	0.31202
10800	48.09	2.079	0.31790
11000	47.45	2.108	0.32379
11200	46.81	2.136	0.32968
11400	46.18	2.166	0.33557
11600	45.56	2.195	0.34145
11800	44.94	2.225	0.34734
12000	44.34	2.255	0.35323
12200	43.74	2.286	0.35911
12400	43.15	2.317	0.36500
12600	42.57	2.349	0.37089
12800	42.00	2.381	0.37678
13000	41.43	2.414	0.38266
13200	40.87	2.447	0.38855
13400	40.32	2.480	0.39444
13600	39.78	2.514	0.40032
13800	39.25	2.548	0.40621
14000	38.72	2.583	0.41210
14200	38.20	2.618	0.41799
14400	37.68	2.654	0.42387
14600	37.17	2.690	0.42976
14800	36.67	2.727	0.43565
15000	36.18	2.764	0.44153
15200	35.69	2.802	0.44742
15400	35.21	2.840	0.45331
15600	34.74	2.879	0.45919
15800	34.27	2.918	0.46508
16000	33.81	2.958	0.47097
16500	32.68	3.060	0.48569
17000	31.59	3.165	0.50040
17500	30.54	3.274	0.51512
18000	29.52	3.387	0.52984
18500	28.54	3.504	0.54456
19000	27.59	3.625	0.55928
19500	26.67	3.750	0.57399
20000	25.78	3.879	0.58871
20500	24.92	4.013	0.60343
21000	24.09	4.151	0.61815
21500	23.29	4.294	0.63286
22000	22.51	4.442	0.64758
22500	21.76	4.595	0.66230
23000	21.04	4.754	0.67702
23500	20.34	4.917	0.69174
24000	19.66	5.087	0.70645
24500	19.00	5.262	0.72117
25000	18.37	5.444	0.73589
25500	17.76	5.631	0.75061
26000	17.17	5.825	0.76532
26500	16.59	6.026	0.78004
27000	16.04	6.234	0.79476
27500	15.51	6.449	0.80948
28000	14.99	6.671	0.82420
28500	14.49	6.901	0.83891
29000	14.01	7.139	0.85363
29500	13.54	7.385	0.86835

t (d)	N_t	N_0/N_t	$\log_{10} N_0/N_t$
30000	13.09	7.640	0.88307
30500	12.65	7.903	0.89779
31000	12.23	8.175	0.91250
31500	11.82	8.457	0.92722
32000	11.43	8.749	0.94194
32500	11.05	9.050	0.95666
33000	10.68	9.362	0.97137
33500	10.33	9.685	0.98609
34000	9.98	10.019	1.00081
34500	9.65	10.364	1.01553
35000	9.33	10.721	1.03025
35500	9.02	11.091	1.04496
36000	8.72	11.473	1.05968
36500	8.43	11.869	1.07440
37000	8.14	12.278	1.08912
37500	7.87	12.701	1.10383
38000	7.61	13.139	1.11855
38500	7.36	13.592	1.13327
39000	7.11	14.060	1.14799
39500	6.88	14.545	1.16271
40000	6.65	15.046	1.17742
40500	6.42	15.565	1.19214
41000	6.21	16.101	1.20686
41500	6.00	16.656	1.22158
42000	5.80	17.230	1.23629
42500	5.61	17.824	1.25101
43000	5.42	18.439	1.26573
43500	5.24	19.074	1.28045
44000	5.07	19.732	1.29517
44500	4.90	20.412	1.30988
45000	4.74	21.115	1.32460
45500	4.58	21.843	1.33932
46000	4.43	22.596	1.35404
46500	4.28	23.375	1.36875
47000	4.14	24.181	1.38347
47500	4.00	25.014	1.39819
48000	3.86	25.877	1.41291
48500	3.74	26.769	1.42763
49000	3.61	27.691	1.44234
49500	3.49	28.646	1.45706
50000	3.37	29.633	1.47178
50500	3.26	30.655	1.48650
51000	3.15	31.711	1.50121
51500	3.05	32.804	1.51593
52000	2.95	33.935	1.53065
52500	2.85	35.105	1.54537
53000	2.75	36.315	1.56009
53500	2.66	37.567	1.57480
54000	2.57	38.862	1.58952
54500	2.49	40.201	1.60424
55000	2.40	41.587	1.61896
55500	2.32	43.020	1.63367
56000	2.25	44.503	1.64839
56500	2.17	46.037	1.66311
57000	2.10	47.624	1.67783
57500	2.03	49.266	1.69255
58000	1.96	50.964	1.70726
58500	1.90	52.721	1.72198
59000	1.83	54.538	1.73670
59500	1.77	56.418	1.75142
60000	1.71	58.363	1.76613
60500	1.66	60.374	1.78085
61000	1.60	62.455	1.79557
61500	1.55	64.608	1.81029
62000	1.50	66.835	1.82501
62500	1.45	69.139	1.83972
63000	1.40	71.522	1.85444
63500	1.35	73.988	1.86916
64000	1.31	76.538	1.88388
64500	1.26	79.176	1.89859
65000	1.22	81.905	1.91331
65500	1.18	84.729	1.92803
66000	1.14	87.649	1.94275
66500	1.10	90.670	1.95747
67000	1.07	93.796	1.97218
67500	1.03	97.029	1.98690
68000	1.00	100.374	2.00162
68500	0.96	103.833	2.01634
69000	0.93	107.413	2.03105
69500	0.90	111.115	2.04577
70000	0.87	114.945	2.06049
70500	0.84	118.907	2.07521
71000	0.81	123.006	2.08993
71500	0.79	127.246	2.10464
72000	0.76	131.632	2.11936
72500	0.73	136.169	2.13408
73000	0.71	140.863	2.14880
73500	0.69	145.719	2.16351
74000	0.66	150.741	2.17823
74500	0.64	155.938	2.19295
75000	0.62	161.313	2.20767
75500	0.60	166.873	2.22239
76000	0.58	172.625	2.23710
76500	0.56	178.575	2.25182
77000	0.54	184.731	2.26654
77500	0.52	191.098	2.28126
78000	0.51	197.686	2.29598
78500	0.49	204.500	2.31069

Yttrium-90

half-life 64.2 h

t (d)	t (h)	t (min)	N_t	N_0/N_t	$\log_{10} N_0/N_t$
	0		100.00	1.000	0.00000
	1		98.93	1.011	0.00469
	2		97.86	1.022	0.00938
	3		96.81	1.033	0.01407
	4		95.77	1.044	0.01876
	5		94.74	1.055	0.02344
	6		93.73	1.067	0.02813
	7		92.72	1.079	0.03282
	8		91.73	1.090	0.03751
	9		90.74	1.102	0.04220
	10		89.77	1.114	0.04689
	11		88.80	1.126	0.05158
	12		87.85	1.138	0.05627
	13		86.90	1.151	0.06096
	14		85.97	1.163	0.06565
	15		85.05	1.176	0.07033
	16		84.13	1.189	0.07502
	17		83.23	1.201	0.07971
	18		82.34	1.215	0.08440
	19		81.45	1.228	0.08909
	20		80.58	1.241	0.09378
	21		79.71	1.254	0.09847
	22		78.86	1.268	0.10316
	23		78.01	1.282	0.10785
1	0		77.17	1.296	0.11254
	1		76.34	1.310	0.11722
	2		75.52	1.324	0.12191
	3		74.71	1.338	0.12660
	4		73.91	1.353	0.13129
	5		73.12	1.368	0.13598
	6		72.33	1.383	0.14067
	7		71.56	1.398	0.14536
	8		70.79	1.413	0.15005
	9		70.03	1.428	0.15474
	10		69.27	1.444	0.15942
	11		68.53	1.459	0.16411
	12		67.79	1.475	0.16880
	13		67.07	1.491	0.17349
	14		66.35	1.507	0.17818
	15		65.63	1.524	0.18287
	16		64.93	1.540	0.18756
	17		64.23	1.557	0.19225
	18		63.54	1.574	0.19694
	19		62.86	1.591	0.20163
	20		62.19	1.608	0.20631
	21		61.52	1.626	0.21100
	22		60.86	1.643	0.21569
	23		60.20	1.661	0.22038
2	0		59.56	1.679	0.22507
	1		58.92	1.697	0.22976
	2		58.28	1.716	0.23445
	3		57.66	1.734	0.23914
	4		57.04	1.753	0.24383
	5		56.43	1.772	0.24851
	6		55.82	1.791	0.25320
	7		55.22	1.811	0.25789
	8		54.63	1.831	0.26258
	9		54.04	1.850	0.26727
	10		53.46	1.871	0.27196
	11		52.89	1.891	0.27665
	12		52.32	1.911	0.28134
	13		51.76	1.932	0.28603
	14		51.20	1.953	0.29072
	15		50.65	1.974	0.29540
	16		50.11	1.996	0.30009
	17		49.57	2.017	0.30478
	18		49.04	2.039	0.30947
	19		48.51	2.061	0.31416
	20		47.99	2.084	0.31885
	21		47.47	2.106	0.32354
	22		46.96	2.129	0.32823
	23		46.46	2.152	0.33292
3	0		45.96	2.176	0.33761
	1		45.47	2.199	0.34229
	2		44.98	2.223	0.34698
	3		44.50	2.247	0.35167
	4		44.02	2.272	0.35636
	5		43.55	2.296	0.36105
	6		43.08	2.321	0.36574
	7		42.62	2.347	0.37043
	8		42.16	2.372	0.37512
	9		41.71	2.398	0.37981
	10		41.26	2.424	0.38449
	11		40.81	2.450	0.38918
	12		40.38	2.477	0.39387
	13		39.94	2.504	0.39856
	14		39.51	2.531	0.40325
	15		39.09	2.558	0.40794
	16		38.67	2.586	0.41263
	17		38.25	2.614	0.41732
	18		37.84	2.642	0.42201
	19		37.44	2.671	0.42670
	20		37.04	2.700	0.43138
	21		36.64	2.729	0.43607
	22		36.24	2.759	0.44076
	23		35.85	2.789	0.44545

t (d)	t (h)	t (min)	N_t	N_0/N_t	$\log_{10} N_0/N_t$
4	0		35.47	2.819	0.45014
	1		35.09	2.850	0.45483
	2		34.71	2.881	0.45952
	3		34.34	2.912	0.46421
	4		33.97	2.944	0.46890
	5		33.61	2.976	0.47358
	6		33.24	3.008	0.47827
	7		32.89	3.041	0.48296
	8		32.53	3.074	0.48765
	9		32.19	3.107	0.49234
	10		31.84	3.141	0.49703
	11		31.50	3.175	0.50172
	12		31.16	3.209	0.50641
	13		30.83	3.244	0.51110
	14		30.49	3.279	0.51579
	15		30.17	3.315	0.52047
	16		29.84	3.351	0.52516
	17		29.52	3.387	0.52985
	18		29.21	3.424	0.53454
	19		28.89	3.461	0.53923
	20		28.58	3.499	0.54392
	21		28.27	3.537	0.54861
	22		27.97	3.575	0.55330
	23		27.67	3.614	0.55799
5	0		27.37	3.653	0.56268
	1		27.08	3.693	0.56736
	2		26.79	3.733	0.57205
	3		26.50	3.773	0.57674
	4		26.22	3.814	0.58143
	5		25.93	3.856	0.58612
	6		25.66	3.898	0.59081
	7		25.38	3.940	0.59550
	8		25.11	3.983	0.60019
	9		24.84	4.026	0.60488
	10		24.57	4.070	0.60956
	11		24.31	4.114	0.61425
	12		24.05	4.159	0.61894
	13		23.79	4.204	0.62363
	14		23.53	4.249	0.62832
	15		23.28	4.295	0.63301
	16		23.03	4.342	0.63770
	17		22.78	4.389	0.64239
	18		22.54	4.437	0.64708
	19		22.30	4.485	0.65177
	20		22.06	4.534	0.65645
	21		21.82	4.583	0.66114
	22		21.59	4.633	0.66583
	23		21.35	4.683	0.67052
6	0		21.12	4.734	0.67521
	1		20.90	4.785	0.67990
	2		20.67	4.837	0.68459
	3		20.45	4.890	0.68928
	4		20.23	4.943	0.69397
	5		20.01	4.996	0.69865
	6		19.80	5.051	0.70334
	7		19.59	5.105	0.70803
	8		19.38	5.161	0.71272
	9		19.17	5.217	0.71741
	10		18.96	5.274	0.72210
	11		18.76	5.331	0.72679
	12		18.56	5.389	0.73148
	13		18.36	5.447	0.73617
	14		18.16	5.506	0.74086
	15		17.97	5.566	0.74554
	16		17.77	5.626	0.75023
	17		17.58	5.688	0.75492
	18		17.39	5.749	0.75961
	19		17.21	5.812	0.76430
	20		17.02	5.875	0.76899
	21		16.84	5.939	0.77368
	22		16.66	6.003	0.77837
	23		16.48	6.068	0.78306
7	0		16.30	6.134	0.78775
	6		15.28	6.545	0.81588
	12		14.32	6.983	0.84401
	18		13.42	7.450	0.87215
8	0		12.58	7.948	0.90028
	6		11.79	8.480	0.92841
	12		11.05	9.048	0.95655
	18		10.36	9.653	0.98468
9	0		9.71	10.299	1.01282
	6		9.10	10.989	1.04095
	12		8.53	11.724	1.06908
	18		7.99	12.509	1.09722
10	0		7.49	13.346	1.12535
	12		6.58	15.192	1.18162
11	0		5.78	17.294	1.23789
	12		5.08	19.686	1.29415
12	0		4.46	22.409	1.35042
	12		3.92	25.509	1.40669
13	0		3.44	29.037	1.46296
	12		3.03	33.054	1.51922
14	0		2.66	37.626	1.57549
	12		2.33	42.831	1.63176
15	0		2.05	48.756	1.68803
	12		1.80	55.500	1.74429
16	0		1.58	63.177	1.80056
	12		1.39	71.916	1.85683
17	0		1.22	81.864	1.91310
	12		1.07	93.189	1.96936
18	0		0.94	106.079	2.02563
	12		0.83	120.753	2.08190
19	0		0.73	137.457	2.13817
	12		0.64	156.471	2.19443
20	0		0.56	178.115	2.25070
	12		0.49	202.753	2.30697

Molybdenum-99

half-life 67 h

t (d)	t (h)	t (min)	N_t	N_0/N_t	$\log_{10} N_0/N_t$
	0		100.00	1.000	0.00000
	1		98.97	1.010	0.00449
	2		97.95	1.021	0.00899
	3		96.94	1.032	0.01348
	4		95.95	1.042	0.01797
	5		94.96	1.053	0.02246
	6		93.98	1.064	0.02696
	7		93.01	1.075	0.03145
	8		92.06	1.086	0.03594
	9		91.11	1.098	0.04044
	10		90.17	1.109	0.04493
	11		89.24	1.121	0.04942
	12		88.33	1.132	0.05392
	13		87.42	1.144	0.05841
	14		86.52	1.156	0.06290
	15		85.63	1.168	0.06740
	16		84.74	1.180	0.07189
	17		83.87	1.192	0.07638
	18		83.01	1.205	0.08087
	19		82.15	1.217	0.08537
	20		81.31	1.230	0.08986
	21		80.47	1.243	0.09435
	22		79.64	1.256	0.09885
	23		78.82	1.269	0.10334
1	0		78.01	1.282	0.10783
	1		77.21	1.295	0.11233
	2		76.42	1.309	0.11682
	3		75.63	1.322	0.12131
	4		74.85	1.336	0.12580
	5		74.08	1.350	0.13030
	6		73.32	1.364	0.13479
	7		72.56	1.378	0.13928
	8		71.82	1.392	0.14378
	9		71.08	1.407	0.14827
	10		70.35	1.422	0.15276
	11		69.62	1.436	0.15726
	12		68.91	1.451	0.16175
	13		68.20	1.466	0.16624
	14		67.49	1.482	0.17073
	15		66.80	1.497	0.17523
	16		66.11	1.513	0.17972
	17		65.43	1.528	0.18421
	18		64.76	1.544	0.18871
	19		64.09	1.560	0.19320
	20		63.43	1.576	0.19769
	21		62.78	1.593	0.20219
	22		62.13	1.609	0.20668
	23		61.49	1.626	0.21117
2	0		60.86	1.643	0.21566
	1		60.23	1.660	0.22016
	2		59.61	1.677	0.22465
	3		59.00	1.695	0.22914
	4		58.39	1.713	0.23364
	5		57.79	1.730	0.23813
	6		57.20	1.748	0.24262
	7		56.61	1.767	0.24712
	8		56.03	1.785	0.25161
	9		55.45	1.803	0.25610
	10		54.88	1.822	0.26059
	11		54.31	1.841	0.26509
	12		53.76	1.860	0.26958
	13		53.20	1.880	0.27407
	14		52.65	1.899	0.27857
	15		52.11	1.919	0.28306
	16		51.58	1.939	0.28755
	17		51.05	1.959	0.29205
	18		50.52	1.979	0.29654
	19		50.00	2.000	0.30103
	20		49.49	2.021	0.30552
	21		48.98	2.042	0.31002
	22		48.47	2.063	0.31451
	23		47.97	2.085	0.31900
3	0		47.48	2.106	0.32350
	1		46.99	2.128	0.32799
	2		46.51	2.150	0.33248
	3		46.03	2.173	0.33698
	4		45.55	2.195	0.34147
	5		45.09	2.218	0.34596
	6		44.62	2.241	0.35045
	7		44.16	2.264	0.35495
	8		43.71	2.288	0.35944
	9		43.26	2.312	0.36393
	10		42.81	2.336	0.36843
	11		42.37	2.360	0.37292
	12		41.94	2.385	0.37741
	13		41.50	2.409	0.38191

t: d	t: h	t: min	N_t	N_0/N_t	$\log_{10} N_0/N_t$
	14		41.08	2.434	0.38640
	15		40.65	2.460	0.39089
	16		40.24	2.485	0.39538
	17		39.82	2.511	0.39988
	18		39.41	2.537	0.40437
	19		39.01	2.564	0.40886
	20		38.61	2.590	0.41336
	21		38.21	2.617	0.41785
	22		37.81	2.644	0.42234
	23		37.43	2.672	0.42684
4	0		37.04	2.700	0.43133
	1		36.66	2.728	0.43582
	2		36.28	2.756	0.44031
	3		35.91	2.785	0.44481
	4		35.54	2.814	0.44930
	5		35.17	2.843	0.45379
	6		34.81	2.873	0.45829
	7		34.45	2.903	0.46278
	8		34.10	2.933	0.46727
	9		33.75	2.963	0.47177
	10		33.40	2.994	0.47626
	11		33.06	3.025	0.48075
	12		32.72	3.057	0.48524
	13		32.38	3.088	0.48974
	14		32.05	3.121	0.49423
	15		31.72	3.153	0.49872
	16		31.39	3.186	0.50322
	17		31.07	3.219	0.50771
	18		30.75	3.252	0.51220
	19		30.43	3.286	0.51670
	20		30.12	3.320	0.52119
	21		29.81	3.355	0.52568
	22		29.50	3.390	0.53017
	23		29.20	3.425	0.53467
5	0		28.90	3.461	0.53916
	1		28.60	3.497	0.54365
	2		28.30	3.533	0.54815
	3		28.01	3.570	0.55264
	4		27.72	3.607	0.55713
	5		27.44	3.644	0.56163
	6		27.16	3.682	0.56612
	7		26.88	3.721	0.57061
	8		26.60	3.759	0.57510
	9		26.33	3.798	0.57960
	10		26.06	3.838	0.58409
	11		25.79	3.878	0.58858
	12		25.52	3.918	0.59308
	13		25.26	3.959	0.59757
	14		25.00	4.000	0.60206
	15		24.74	4.042	0.60656
	16		24.49	4.084	0.61105
	17		24.24	4.126	0.61554
	18		23.99	4.169	0.62003
	19		23.74	4.212	0.62453
	20		23.50	4.256	0.62902
	21		23.25	4.300	0.63351
	22		23.01	4.345	0.63801
	23		22.78	4.390	0.64250
6	0		22.54	4.436	0.64699
	1		22.31	4.482	0.65149
	2		22.08	4.529	0.65598
	3		21.85	4.576	0.66047
	4		21.63	4.623	0.66496
	5		21.41	4.672	0.66946
	6		21.19	4.720	0.67395
	7		20.97	4.769	0.67844
	8		20.75	4.819	0.68294
	9		20.54	4.869	0.68743
	10		20.33	4.920	0.69192
	11		20.12	4.971	0.69642
	12		19.91	5.022	0.70091
	13		19.71	5.075	0.70540
	14		19.50	5.127	0.70989
	15		19.30	5.181	0.71439
	16		19.10	5.235	0.71888
	17		18.91	5.289	0.72337
	18		18.71	5.344	0.72787
	19		18.52	5.400	0.73236
	20		18.33	5.456	0.73685
	21		18.14	5.512	0.74135
	22		17.95	5.570	0.74584
	23		17.77	5.628	0.75033
7	0		17.59	5.686	0.75482
	6		16.53	6.050	0.78178
	12		15.53	6.438	0.80874
	18		14.60	6.850	0.83570
8	0		13.72	7.289	0.86266
	6		12.89	7.756	0.88961
	12		12.12	8.252	0.91657
	18		11.39	8.781	0.94353
9	0		10.70	9.343	0.97049
	6		10.06	9.941	0.99745
	12		9.45	10.578	1.02440
	18		8.88	11.255	1.05136
10	0		8.35	11.976	1.07832
	12		7.38	13.559	1.13224
11	0		6.51	15.352	1.18615
	12		5.75	17.381	1.24007
12	0		5.08	19.678	1.29398
	12		4.49	22.279	1.34790
13	0		3.96	25.224	1.40182
	12		3.50	28.558	1.45573
14	0		3.09	32.333	1.50965
	12		2.73	36.607	1.56357
15	0		2.41	41.446	1.61748
	12		2.13	46.924	1.67140
16	0		1.88	53.127	1.72531
	12		1.66	60.149	1.77923
17	0		1.47	68.100	1.83315
	12		1.30	77.101	1.88706
18	0		1.15	87.293	1.94098
	12		1.01	98.831	1.99489
19	0		0.89	111.895	2.04881
	12		0.79	126.685	2.10273
20	0		0.70	143.431	2.15664
	12		0.62	162.389	2.21056
21	0		0.54	183.854	2.26447
	12		0.48	208.156	2.31839

Technetium-99m

half-life 6 h

t: d	t: h	t: min	N_t	N_0/N_t	$\log_{10} N_0/N_t$
		0	100.00	1.000	0.00000
		5	99.04	1.010	0.00418
		10	98.09	1.019	0.00836
		15	97.15	1.029	0.01254
		20	96.22	1.039	0.01672
		25	95.30	1.049	0.02090
		30	94.39	1.059	0.02509
		35	93.48	1.070	0.02927
		40	92.59	1.080	0.03345
		45	91.70	1.091	0.03763
		50	90.82	1.101	0.04181
		55	89.95	1.112	0.04599
	1	0	89.09	1.122	0.05017
		5	88.24	1.133	0.05435
		10	87.39	1.144	0.05853
		15	86.55	1.155	0.06271
		20	85.72	1.167	0.06690
		25	84.90	1.178	0.07108
		30	84.09	1.189	0.07526
		35	83.28	1.201	0.07944
		40	82.49	1.212	0.08362
		45	81.70	1.224	0.08780
		50	80.91	1.236	0.09198
		55	80.14	1.248	0.09616
	2	0	79.37	1.260	0.10034
		5	78.61	1.272	0.10452
		10	77.86	1.284	0.10871
		15	77.11	1.297	0.11289
		20	76.37	1.309	0.11707
		25	75.64	1.322	0.12125
		30	74.92	1.335	0.12543
		35	74.20	1.348	0.12961
		40	73.49	1.361	0.13379
		45	72.78	1.374	0.13797
		50	72.09	1.387	0.14215
		55	71.39	1.401	0.14633
	3	0	70.71	1.414	0.15052
		5	70.03	1.428	0.15470
		10	69.36	1.442	0.15888
		15	68.70	1.456	0.16306
		20	68.04	1.470	0.16724
		25	67.39	1.484	0.17142
		30	66.74	1.498	0.17560
		35	66.10	1.513	0.17978
		40	65.47	1.527	0.18396
		45	64.84	1.542	0.18814
		50	64.22	1.557	0.19233
		55	63.61	1.572	0.19651
	4	0	63.00	1.587	0.20069
		5	62.39	1.603	0.20487
		10	61.79	1.618	0.20905
		15	61.20	1.634	0.21323
		20	60.62	1.650	0.21741
		25	60.04	1.666	0.22159
		30	59.46	1.682	0.22577
		35	58.89	1.698	0.22995
		40	58.33	1.714	0.23414
		45	57.77	1.731	0.23832
		50	57.21	1.748	0.24250
		55	56.67	1.765	0.24668
	5	0	56.12	1.782	0.25086
		10	55.05	1.816	0.25922
		20	54.00	1.852	0.26758
		30	52.97	1.888	0.27595
		40	51.96	1.924	0.28431
		50	50.97	1.962	0.29267
	6	0	50.00	2.000	0.30103
		10	49.05	2.039	0.30939
		20	48.11	2.079	0.31776
		30	47.19	2.119	0.32612
		40	46.29	2.160	0.33448
		50	45.41	2.202	0.34284
	7	0	44.54	2.245	0.35120
		10	43.70	2.289	0.35957
		20	42.86	2.333	0.36793
		30	42.04	2.378	0.37629
		40	41.24	2.425	0.38465
		50	40.46	2.472	0.39301
	8	0	39.68	2.520	0.40137
		10	38.93	2.569	0.40974
		20	38.19	2.619	0.41810
		30	37.46	2.670	0.42646
		40	36.74	2.722	0.43482
		50	36.04	2.775	0.44318
	9	0	35.36	2.828	0.45155
		10	34.68	2.883	0.45991
		20	34.02	2.939	0.46827
		30	33.37	2.997	0.47663
		40	32.73	3.055	0.48499
		50	32.11	3.114	0.49336
	10	0	31.50	3.175	0.50172
		10	30.90	3.237	0.51008
		20	30.31	3.299	0.51844
		30	29.73	3.364	0.52680
		40	29.16	3.429	0.53517
		50	28.61	3.496	0.54353
	11	0	28.06	3.564	0.55189
		10	27.53	3.633	0.56025
		20	27.00	3.704	0.56861
		30	26.49	3.776	0.57698
		40	25.98	3.849	0.58534
		50	25.49	3.924	0.59370
	12	0	25.00	4.000	0.60206
		20	24.06	4.157	0.61879
		40	23.15	4.320	0.63551
	13	0	22.27	4.490	0.65223
		20	21.43	4.666	0.66896
		40	20.62	4.849	0.68568
	14	0	19.84	5.040	0.70241
		20	19.09	5.238	0.71913
		40	18.37	5.443	0.73585
	15	0	17.68	5.657	0.75258
		20	17.01	5.879	0.76930
		40	16.37	6.110	0.78603
	16	0	15.75	6.350	0.80275
		20	15.15	6.599	0.81947
		40	14.58	6.858	0.83620
	17	0	14.03	7.127	0.85292
		20	13.50	7.407	0.86965
		40	12.99	7.698	0.88637
	18	0	12.50	8.000	0.90309
		20	12.03	8.314	0.91982
		40	11.57	8.641	0.93654
	19	0	11.14	8.980	0.95327
		20	10.72	9.332	0.96999
		40	10.31	9.699	0.98671
	20	0	9.92	10.079	1.00344
		20	9.55	10.475	1.02016
		40	9.19	10.886	1.03689
	21	0	8.84	11.314	1.05361
		20	8.50	11.758	1.07033
		40	8.18	12.220	1.08706
	22	0	7.87	12.699	1.10378
		20	7.58	13.198	1.12051
		40	7.29	13.716	1.13723
	23	0	7.02	14.255	1.15395
		20	6.75	14.814	1.17068
		40	6.50	15.396	1.18740
1	0		6.25	16.000	1.20412
	1		5.57	17.960	1.25430
	2		4.96	20.159	1.30447
	3		4.42	22.628	1.35464
	4		3.94	25.399	1.40481
	5		3.51	28.509	1.45498
	6		3.12	32.000	1.50516
	7		2.78	35.919	1.55533
	8		2.48	40.318	1.60550
	9		2.21	45.256	1.65567
	10		1.97	50.798	1.70584
	11		1.75	57.018	1.75602
	12		1.56	64.001	1.80619
	13		1.39	71.839	1.85636
	14		1.24	80.636	1.90653
	15		1.10	90.511	1.95670
	16		0.98	101.596	2.00687
	17		0.88	114.037	2.05705
	18		0.78	128.003	2.10722
	19		0.70	143.678	2.15739
	20		0.62	161.273	2.20756
	21		0.55	181.023	2.25773
	22		0.49	203.192	2.30791

Tellurium-132

half-life 78 h

t: d	t: h	t: min	N_t	N_0/N_t	$\log_{10} N_0/N_t$
	0		100.00	1.000	0.00000
	1		99.12	1.009	0.00386
	2		98.24	1.018	0.00772
	3		97.37	1.027	0.01158
	4		96.51	1.036	0.01544
	5		95.65	1.045	0.01930
	6		94.81	1.055	0.02316
	7		93.97	1.064	0.02702
	8		93.14	1.074	0.03087
	9		92.31	1.083	0.03473
	10		91.50	1.093	0.03859
	11		90.69	1.103	0.04245
	12		89.89	1.113	0.04631
	13		89.09	1.122	0.05017
	14		88.30	1.132	0.05403
	15		87.52	1.143	0.05789
	16		86.75	1.153	0.06175
	17		85.98	1.163	0.06561
	18		85.22	1.173	0.06947
	19		84.46	1.184	0.07333
	20		83.72	1.195	0.07719
	21		82.98	1.205	0.08105
	22		82.24	1.216	0.08491
	23		81.51	1.227	0.08877
1	0		80.79	1.238	0.09262
	1		80.08	1.249	0.09648
	2		79.37	1.260	0.10034
	3		78.67	1.271	0.10420
	4		77.97	1.283	0.10806
	5		77.28	1.294	0.11192
	6		76.60	1.306	0.11578
	7		75.92	1.317	0.11964
	8		75.25	1.329	0.12350
	9		74.58	1.341	0.12736
	10		73.92	1.353	0.13122
	11		73.27	1.365	0.13508
	12		72.62	1.377	0.13894
	13		71.98	1.389	0.14280
	14		71.34	1.402	0.14666
	15		70.71	1.414	0.15052
	16		70.08	1.427	0.15437
	17		69.46	1.440	0.15823
	18		68.85	1.452	0.16209
	19		68.24	1.465	0.16595
	20		67.64	1.478	0.16981
	21		67.04	1.492	0.17367
	22		66.45	1.505	0.17753
	23		65.86	1.518	0.18139
2	0		65.28	1.532	0.18525
	1		64.70	1.546	0.18911
	2		64.13	1.559	0.19297
	3		63.56	1.573	0.19683
	4		63.00	1.587	0.20069
	5		62.44	1.602	0.20455
	6		61.89	1.616	0.20841
	7		61.34	1.630	0.21227
	8		60.80	1.645	0.21612
	9		60.26	1.660	0.21998
	10		59.73	1.674	0.22384
	11		59.20	1.689	0.22770
	12		58.67	1.704	0.23156
	13		58.15	1.720	0.23542
	14		57.64	1.735	0.23928
	15		57.13	1.750	0.24314
	16		56.62	1.766	0.24700
	17		56.12	1.782	0.25086
	18		55.63	1.798	0.25472
	19		55.13	1.814	0.25858
	20		54.65	1.830	0.26244
	21		54.16	1.846	0.26630
	22		53.68	1.863	0.27016
	23		53.21	1.879	0.27402
3	0		52.74	1.896	0.27787
	1		52.27	1.913	0.28173
	2		51.81	1.930	0.28559
	3		51.35	1.947	0.28945
	4		50.90	1.965	0.29331
	5		50.45	1.982	0.29717
	6		50.00	2.000	0.30103
	7		49.56	2.018	0.30489
	8		49.12	2.036	0.30875
	9		48.68	2.054	0.31261
	10		48.25	2.072	0.31647
	11		47.83	2.091	0.32033
	12		47.40	2.110	0.32419
	13		46.98	2.128	0.32805
	14		46.57	2.147	0.33191
	15		46.16	2.167	0.33577
	16		45.75	2.186	0.33962
	17		45.34	2.205	0.34348
	18		44.94	2.225	0.34734
	19		44.54	2.245	0.35120
	20		44.15	2.265	0.35506
	21		43.76	2.285	0.35892
	22		43.37	2.306	0.36278
	23		42.99	2.326	0.36664
4	0		42.61	2.347	0.37050
	1		42.23	2.368	0.37436
	2		41.86	2.389	0.37822
	3		41.49	2.410	0.38208
	4		41.12	2.432	0.38594
	5		40.76	2.454	0.38980
	6		40.40	2.475	0.39366

t d	t h	t min	N_t	N_0/N_t	$\log_{10} N_0/N_t$
	7		40.04	2.498	0.39752
	8		39.68	2.520	0.40137
	9		39.33	2.542	0.40523
	10		38.99	2.565	0.40909
	11		38.64	2.588	0.41295
	12		38.30	2.611	0.41681
	13		37.96	2.634	0.42067
	14		37.62	2.658	0.42453
	15		37.29	2.682	0.42839
	16		36.96	2.706	0.43225
	17		36.63	2.730	0.43611
	18		36.31	2.754	0.43997
	19		35.99	2.779	0.44383
	20		35.67	2.803	0.44769
	21		35.36	2.828	0.45155
	22		35.04	2.854	0.45541
	23		34.73	2.879	0.45927
5	0		34.43	2.905	0.46312
	1		34.12	2.931	0.46698
	2		33.82	2.957	0.47084
	3		33.52	2.983	0.47470
	4		33.22	3.010	0.47856
	5		32.93	3.037	0.48242
	6		32.64	3.064	0.48628
	7		32.35	3.091	0.49014
	8		32.06	3.119	0.49400
	9		31.78	3.147	0.49786
	10		31.50	3.175	0.50172
	11		31.22	3.203	0.50558
	12		30.94	3.232	0.50944
	13		30.67	3.261	0.51330
	14		30.40	3.290	0.51716
	15		30.13	3.319	0.52102
	16		29.86	3.349	0.52487
	17		29.60	3.379	0.52873
	18		29.34	3.409	0.53259
	19		29.08	3.439	0.53645
	20		28.82	3.470	0.54031
	21		28.56	3.501	0.54417
	22		28.31	3.532	0.54803
	23		28.06	3.564	0.55189
6	0		27.81	3.595	0.55575
	1		27.57	3.628	0.55961
	2		27.32	3.660	0.56347
	3		27.08	3.693	0.56733
	4		26.84	3.726	0.57119
	5		26.60	3.759	0.57505
	6		26.37	3.792	0.57891
	7		26.14	3.826	0.58277
	8		25.90	3.860	0.58662
	9		25.68	3.895	0.59048
	10		25.45	3.930	0.59434
	11		25.22	3.965	0.59820
	12		25.00	4.000	0.60206
	13		24.78	4.036	0.60592
	14		24.56	4.072	0.60978
	15		24.34	4.108	0.61364
	16		24.13	4.145	0.61750
	17		23.91	4.182	0.62136
	18		23.70	4.219	0.62522
	19		23.49	4.257	0.62908
	20		23.28	4.295	0.63294
	21		23.08	4.333	0.63680
	22		22.87	4.372	0.64066
	23		22.67	4.411	0.64452
7	0		22.47	4.450	0.64837
	6		21.30	4.694	0.67153
	12		20.20	4.951	0.69469
	18		19.15	5.222	0.71784
8	0		18.16	5.508	0.74100
	6		17.21	5.810	0.76416
	12		16.32	6.128	0.78731
	18		15.47	6.464	0.81047
9	0		14.67	6.817	0.83362
	6		13.91	7.191	0.85678
	12		13.18	7.585	0.87994
	18		12.50	8.000	0.90309
10	0		11.85	8.438	0.92625
	12		10.65	9.388	0.97256
11	0		9.57	10.444	1.01887
	12		8.61	11.619	1.06519
12	0		7.74	12.927	1.11150
	12		6.95	14.382	1.15781
13	0		6.25	16.000	1.20412
	12		5.62	17.801	1.25044
14	0		5.05	19.804	1.29675
	12		4.54	22.032	1.34306
15			4.08	24.512	1.38937
16			3.30	30.339	1.48200
17			2.66	37.551	1.57462
18			2.15	46.478	1.66725
19			1.74	57.527	1.75987
20			1.40	71.203	1.85250
25			0.48	206.835	2.31562

Iodine-125

half-life 60 d

t d	N_t	N_0/N_t	$\log_{10} N_0/N_t$
0	100.00	1.000	0.00000
1	98.85	1.012	0.00502
2	97.72	1.023	0.01003
3	96.59	1.035	0.01505
4	95.48	1.047	0.02007
5	94.39	1.059	0.02509
6	93.30	1.072	0.03010
7	92.23	1.084	0.03512
8	91.17	1.097	0.04014
9	90.13	1.110	0.04515
10	89.09	1.122	0.05017
11	88.07	1.136	0.05519
12	87.06	1.149	0.06021
13	86.06	1.162	0.06522
14	85.07	1.176	0.07024
15	84.09	1.189	0.07526
16	83.12	1.203	0.08027
17	82.17	1.217	0.08529
18	81.23	1.231	0.09031
19	80.29	1.245	0.09533
20	79.37	1.260	0.10034
21	78.46	1.275	0.10536
22	77.56	1.289	0.11038
23	76.67	1.304	0.11540
24	75.79	1.320	0.12041
25	74.92	1.335	0.12543
26	74.05	1.350	0.13045
27	73.20	1.366	0.13546
28	72.36	1.382	0.14048
29	71.53	1.398	0.14550
30	70.71	1.414	0.15052
31	69.90	1.431	0.15553
32	69.10	1.447	0.16055
33	68.30	1.464	0.16557
34	67.52	1.481	0.17058
35	66.74	1.498	0.17560
36	65.98	1.516	0.18062
37	65.22	1.533	0.18564
38	64.47	1.551	0.19065
39	63.73	1.569	0.19567
40	63.00	1.587	0.20069
41	62.27	1.606	0.20570
42	61.56	1.625	0.21072
43	60.85	1.643	0.21574
44	60.15	1.662	0.22076
45	59.46	1.682	0.22577
46	58.78	1.701	0.23079
47	58.10	1.721	0.23581
48	57.43	1.741	0.24082
49	56.78	1.761	0.24584
50	56.12	1.782	0.25086
51	55.48	1.803	0.25588
52	54.84	1.823	0.26089
53	54.21	1.845	0.26591
54	53.59	1.866	0.27093
55	52.97	1.888	0.27595
56	52.36	1.910	0.28096
57	51.76	1.932	0.28598
58	51.17	1.954	0.29100
59	50.58	1.977	0.29601
60	50.00	2.000	0.30103
62	48.86	2.047	0.31107
64	47.74	2.095	0.32110
66	46.65	2.144	0.33113
68	45.59	2.194	0.34117
70	44.54	2.245	0.35120
72	43.53	2.297	0.36124
74	42.53	2.351	0.37127
76	41.56	2.406	0.38131
78	40.61	2.462	0.39134
80	39.68	2.520	0.40137
82	38.78	2.579	0.41141
84	37.89	2.639	0.42144
86	37.03	2.701	0.43148
88	36.18	2.764	0.44151
90	35.36	2.828	0.45155
92	34.55	2.895	0.46158
94	33.76	2.962	0.47162
96	32.99	3.031	0.48165
98	32.23	3.102	0.49168
100	31.50	3.175	0.50172
102	30.78	3.249	0.51175
104	30.08	3.325	0.52179
106	29.39	3.403	0.53182
108	28.72	3.482	0.54186
110	28.06	3.564	0.55189
112	27.42	3.647	0.56192
114	26.79	3.732	0.57196
116	26.18	3.819	0.58199
118	25.58	3.909	0.59203
120	25.00	4.000	0.60206
122	24.43	4.094	0.61210
124	23.87	4.189	0.62213
126	23.33	4.287	0.63217
128	22.79	4.387	0.64220
130	22.27	4.490	0.65223
132	21.76	4.595	0.66227
134	21.27	4.702	0.67230
136	20.78	4.812	0.68234
138	20.31	4.925	0.69237
140	19.84	5.040	0.70241
145	18.73	5.339	0.72749
150	17.68	5.657	0.75258
155	16.69	5.993	0.77766
160	15.75	6.350	0.80275
165	14.86	6.727	0.82784
170	14.03	7.127	0.85292
175	13.24	7.551	0.87801
180	12.50	8.000	0.90309
185	11.80	8.476	0.92818
190	11.14	8.980	0.95327
195	10.51	9.514	0.97835
200	9.92	10.079	1.00344
205	9.36	10.679	1.02852
210	8.84	11.314	1.05361
215	8.34	11.987	1.07870
220	7.87	12.699	1.10378
225	7.43	13.454	1.12887
230	7.02	14.255	1.15395
235	6.62	15.102	1.17904
240	6.25	16.000	1.20412
245	5.90	16.952	1.22921
250	5.57	17.960	1.25430
255	5.26	19.028	1.27938
260	4.96	20.159	1.30447
265	4.68	21.358	1.32955
270	4.42	22.628	1.35464
275	4.17	23.973	1.37973
280	3.94	25.399	1.40481
285	3.72	26.909	1.42990
290	3.51	28.509	1.45498
295	3.31	30.204	1.48007
300	3.12	32.000	1.50516
310	2.78	35.919	1.55533
320	2.48	40.318	1.60550
330	2.21	45.256	1.65567
340	1.97	50.798	1.70584
350	1.75	57.018	1.75602
360	1.56	64.001	1.80619
370	1.39	71.839	1.85636
380	1.24	80.636	1.90653
390	1.10	90.511	1.95670
400	0.98	101.596	2.00687
410	0.88	114.037	2.05705
420	0.78	128.003	2.10722
430	0.70	143.678	2.15739
440	0.62	161.273	2.20756
450	0.55	181.023	2.25773
460	0.49	203.192	2.30791

Iodine-131

half-life 8.04 d

d	h	min	N_t	N_0/N_t	$\log_{10} N_0/N_t$
	0		100.00	1.000	0.00000
	3		98.93	1.011	0.00468
	6		97.87	1.022	0.00936
	9		96.82	1.033	0.01404
	12		95.78	1.044	0.01872
	15		94.75	1.055	0.02340
	18		93.74	1.067	0.02808
	21		92.73	1.078	0.03276
1	0		91.74	1.090	0.03744
	3		90.76	1.102	0.04212
	6		89.78	1.114	0.04680
	9		88.82	1.126	0.05148
	12		87.87	1.138	0.05616
	15		86.93	1.150	0.06084
	18		86.00	1.163	0.06552
	21		85.07	1.175	0.07020
2	0		84.16	1.188	0.07488
	3		83.26	1.201	0.07956
	6		82.37	1.214	0.08424
	9		81.48	1.227	0.08892
	12		80.61	1.241	0.09360
	15		79.75	1.254	0.09828
	18		78.89	1.268	0.10296
	21		78.05	1.281	0.10764
3	0		77.21	1.295	0.11233
	3		76.38	1.309	0.11701
	6		75.56	1.323	0.12169
	9		74.75	1.338	0.12637
	12		73.95	1.352	0.13105
	15		73.16	1.367	0.13573
	18		72.38	1.382	0.14041
	21		71.60	1.397	0.14509
4	0		70.83	1.412	0.14977
	3		70.07	1.427	0.15445
	6		69.32	1.443	0.15913
	9		68.58	1.458	0.16381
	12		67.84	1.474	0.16849
	15		67.12	1.490	0.17317
	18		66.40	1.506	0.17785
	21		65.69	1.522	0.18253
5	0		64.98	1.539	0.18721
	3		64.29	1.556	0.19189
	6		63.60	1.572	0.19657
	9		62.91	1.589	0.20125
	12		62.24	1.607	0.20593
	15		61.57	1.624	0.21061
	18		60.91	1.642	0.21529
	21		60.26	1.659	0.21997
6	0		59.61	1.677	0.22465
	3		58.98	1.696	0.22933
	6		58.34	1.714	0.23401
	9		57.72	1.733	0.23869
	12		57.10	1.751	0.24337
	15		56.49	1.770	0.24805
	18		55.88	1.789	0.25273
	21		55.28	1.809	0.25741
7	0		54.69	1.828	0.26209
	6		53.52	1.868	0.27145
	12		52.38	1.909	0.28081
	18		51.27	1.951	0.29017
8	0		50.17	1.993	0.29953
	6		49.10	2.037	0.30889
	12		48.06	2.081	0.31825
	18		47.03	2.126	0.32761
9	0		46.03	2.173	0.33698
	6		45.05	2.220	0.34634
	12		44.09	2.268	0.35570
	18		43.15	2.318	0.36506
10	0		42.23	2.368	0.37442
	6		41.33	2.420	0.38378
	12		40.44	2.473	0.39314
	18		39.58	2.526	0.40250
11	0		38.74	2.581	0.41186
	6		37.91	2.638	0.42122
	12		37.10	2.695	0.43058
	18		36.31	2.754	0.43994
12	0		35.54	2.814	0.44930
	6		34.78	2.875	0.45866
	12		34.04	2.938	0.46802
	18		33.31	3.002	0.47738
13	0		32.60	3.067	0.48674
	6		31.91	3.134	0.49610
	12		31.23	3.202	0.50546
	18		30.56	3.272	0.51482
14	0		29.91	3.343	0.52418
	6		29.27	3.416	0.53354
	12		28.65	3.491	0.54290
	18		28.04	3.567	0.55226
15	0		27.44	3.644	0.56163
	6		26.85	3.724	0.57099
	12		26.28	3.805	0.58035
	18		25.72	3.888	0.58971
16	0		25.17	3.973	0.59907
	12		24.11	4.148	0.61779
17	0		23.09	4.330	0.63651
	12		22.12	4.521	0.65523
18	0		21.19	4.720	0.67395
	12		20.29	4.928	0.69267
19	0		19.44	5.145	0.71139
	12		18.62	5.372	0.73011
20	0		17.83	5.608	0.74883
	12		17.08	5.855	0.76755
21	0		16.36	6.113	0.78628
	12		15.67	6.383	0.80500
22	0		15.01	6.664	0.82372
	12		14.37	6.957	0.84244
23	0		13.77	7.264	0.86116
	12		13.19	7.584	0.87988
24	0		12.63	7.918	0.89860
	12		12.10	8.266	0.91732
25			11.59	8.631	0.93604
26			10.63	9.408	0.97348
27			9.75	10.255	1.01093
28			8.95	11.178	1.04837
29			8.21	12.185	1.08581
30			7.53	13.282	1.12325
32			6.34	15.781	1.19813
34			5.33	18.751	1.27302
36			4.49	22.279	1.34790
38			3.78	26.472	1.42278
40			3.18	31.453	1.49767
45			2.07	48.403	1.68488
50			1.34	74.488	1.87208
55			0.87	114.629	2.05929
60			0.57	176.401	2.24650
65			0.37	271.463	2.43371

Iodine-132
half-life 2.3 h

t d	t h	t min	N_t	N_0/N_t	$\log_{10} N_0/N_t$
		0	100.00	1.000	0.00000
		2	99.00	1.010	0.00436
		4	98.01	1.020	0.00873
		6	97.03	1.031	0.01309
		8	96.06	1.041	0.01745
		10	95.10	1.052	0.02181
		12	94.15	1.062	0.02618
		14	93.21	1.073	0.03054
		16	92.28	1.084	0.03490
		18	91.36	1.095	0.03926
		20	90.44	1.106	0.04363
		22	89.54	1.117	0.04799
		24	88.64	1.128	0.05235
		26	87.76	1.140	0.05672
		28	86.88	1.151	0.06108
		30	86.01	1.163	0.06544
		32	85.15	1.174	0.06980
		34	84.30	1.186	0.07417
		36	83.46	1.198	0.07853
		38	82.62	1.210	0.08289
		40	81.80	1.223	0.08726
		42	80.98	1.235	0.09162
		44	80.17	1.247	0.09598
		46	79.37	1.260	0.10034
		48	78.58	1.273	0.10471
		50	77.79	1.285	0.10907
		52	77.01	1.298	0.11343
		54	76.24	1.312	0.11779
		56	75.48	1.325	0.12216
		58	74.73	1.338	0.12652
	1	0	73.98	1.352	0.13088
		2	73.24	1.365	0.13525
		4	72.51	1.379	0.13961
		6	71.78	1.393	0.14397
		8	71.07	1.407	0.14833
		10	70.36	1.421	0.15270
		12	69.65	1.436	0.15706
		14	68.96	1.450	0.16142
		16	68.27	1.465	0.16579
		18	67.59	1.480	0.17015
		20	66.91	1.495	0.17451
		22	66.24	1.510	0.17887
		24	65.58	1.525	0.18324
		26	64.92	1.540	0.18760
		28	64.27	1.556	0.19196
		30	63.63	1.572	0.19632
		32	63.00	1.587	0.20069
		34	62.37	1.603	0.20505
		36	61.74	1.620	0.20941
		38	61.13	1.636	0.21378
		40	60.51	1.652	0.21814
		42	59.91	1.669	0.22250
		44	59.31	1.686	0.22686
		46	58.72	1.703	0.23123
		48	58.13	1.720	0.23559
		50	57.55	1.738	0.23995
		52	56.98	1.755	0.24432
		54	56.41	1.773	0.24868
		56	55.84	1.791	0.25304
		58	55.28	1.809	0.25740
	2	0	54.73	1.827	0.26177
		2	54.18	1.846	0.26613
		4	53.64	1.864	0.27049
		6	53.11	1.883	0.27485
		8	52.58	1.902	0.27922
		10	52.05	1.921	0.28358
		12	51.53	1.941	0.28794
		14	51.01	1.960	0.29231
		16	50.50	1.980	0.29667
		18	50.00	2.000	0.30103
		20	49.50	2.020	0.30539
		22	49.01	2.041	0.30976
		24	48.52	2.061	0.31412
		26	48.03	2.082	0.31848
		28	47.55	2.103	0.32285
		30	47.08	2.124	0.32721
		32	46.60	2.146	0.33157
		34	46.14	2.167	0.33593
		36	45.68	2.189	0.34030
		38	45.22	2.211	0.34466
		40	44.77	2.234	0.34902
		45	43.66	2.290	0.35993
		50	42.58	2.349	0.37084
		55	41.52	2.408	0.38174
	3	0	40.49	2.470	0.39265
		5	39.49	2.533	0.40356
		10	38.51	2.597	0.41446
		15	37.55	2.663	0.42537
		20	36.62	2.731	0.43628
		25	35.71	2.800	0.44718
		30	34.83	2.871	0.45809
		35	33.96	2.944	0.46900
		40	33.12	3.019	0.47990
		45	32.30	3.096	0.49081
		50	31.50	3.175	0.50172
		55	30.72	3.256	0.51263
	4	0	29.95	3.338	0.52353
		5	29.21	3.423	0.53444
		10	28.49	3.510	0.54535
		15	27.78	3.600	0.55625
		20	27.09	3.691	0.56716
		25	26.42	3.785	0.57807
		30	25.76	3.881	0.58897
		35	25.13	3.980	0.59988
		40	24.50	4.081	0.61079
		45	23.89	4.185	0.62169
		50	23.30	4.291	0.63260
		55	22.72	4.401	0.64351
	5	0	22.16	4.512	0.65442
		5	21.61	4.627	0.66532
		10	21.08	4.745	0.67623
		15	20.55	4.866	0.68714
		20	20.04	4.989	0.69804
		25	19.55	5.116	0.70895
		30	19.06	5.246	0.71986
		35	18.59	5.380	0.73076
		40	18.13	5.517	0.74167
		45	17.68	5.657	0.75258
		50	17.24	5.801	0.76348
		55	16.81	5.948	0.77439
	6	0	16.39	6.100	0.78530
		5	15.99	6.255	0.79621
		10	15.59	6.414	0.80711
		15	15.20	6.577	0.81802
		20	14.83	6.744	0.82893
		25	14.46	6.916	0.83983
		30	14.10	7.092	0.85074
		35	13.75	7.272	0.86165
		40	13.41	7.457	0.87255
		45	13.08	7.646	0.88346
		50	12.75	7.841	0.89437
		55	12.44	8.040	0.90527
	7	0	12.13	8.245	0.91618
		5	11.83	8.455	0.92709
		10	11.53	8.670	0.93800
		15	11.25	8.890	0.94890
		20	10.97	9.116	0.95981
		25	10.70	9.348	0.97072
		30	10.43	9.586	0.98162
		35	10.17	9.829	0.99253
		40	9.92	10.079	1.00344
		45	9.68	10.336	1.01434
		50	9.44	10.599	1.02525
		55	9.20	10.868	1.03616
	8	0	8.97	11.145	1.04707
		5	8.75	11.428	1.05797
		10	8.53	11.719	1.06888
		15	8.32	12.017	1.07979
		20	8.12	12.322	1.09069
		25	7.91	12.636	1.10160
		30	7.72	12.957	1.11251
		35	7.53	13.287	1.12341
		40	7.34	13.624	1.13432
		45	7.16	13.971	1.14523
		50	6.98	14.326	1.15613
		55	6.81	14.691	1.16704
	9	0	6.64	15.064	1.17795
		5	6.47	15.447	1.18886
		10	6.31	15.840	1.19976
		15	6.16	16.243	1.21067
		20	6.00	16.656	1.22158
		25	5.85	17.080	1.23248
		30	5.71	17.514	1.24339
		35	5.57	17.960	1.25430
		40	5.43	18.416	1.26520
		45	5.30	18.885	1.27611
		50	5.16	19.365	1.28702
		55	5.04	19.857	1.29792
	10	0	4.91	20.363	1.30883
		10	4.67	21.411	1.33065
		20	4.44	22.514	1.35246
		30	4.22	23.674	1.37427
		40	4.02	24.894	1.39609
		50	3.82	26.176	1.41790
	11	0	3.63	27.524	1.43971
		10	3.46	28.942	1.46153
		20	3.29	30.433	1.48334
		30	3.12	32.000	1.50516
		40	2.97	33.649	1.52697
		50	2.83	35.382	1.54878
	12	0	2.69	37.205	1.57060
		10	2.56	39.121	1.59241
		20	2.43	41.136	1.61423
		30	2.31	43.255	1.63604
		40	2.20	45.483	1.65785
		50	2.09	47.826	1.67967
	13	0	1.99	50.290	1.70148
		10	1.89	52.880	1.72329
		20	1.80	55.604	1.74511
		30	1.71	58.469	1.76692
		40	1.63	61.480	1.78874
		50	1.55	64.647	1.81055
	14	0	1.47	67.977	1.83236
		10	1.40	71.479	1.85418
		20	1.33	75.161	1.87599
		30	1.27	79.032	1.89781
		40	1.20	83.103	1.91962
		50	1.14	87.384	1.94143
	15	0	1.09	91.886	1.96325
		10	1.03	96.619	1.98506
		20	0.98	101.596	2.00687
		30	0.94	106.829	2.02869
		40	0.89	112.332	2.05050
		50	0.85	118.118	2.07232
	16	0	0.81	124.202	2.09413
		10	0.77	130.600	2.11594
		20	0.73	137.328	2.13776
		30	0.69	144.402	2.15957
		40	0.66	151.840	2.18139
		50	0.63	159.661	2.20320
	17	0	0.60	167.886	2.22501
		10	0.57	176.534	2.24683
		20	0.54	185.627	2.26864
		30	0.51	195.189	2.29045

Caesium-137
half-life 30 y

t d	N_t	N_0/N_t	$\log_{10} N_0/N_t$
0	100.00	1.000	0.00000
100	99.37	1.006	0.00275
200	98.74	1.012	0.00550
300	98.12	1.019	0.00824
400	97.50	1.025	0.01099
500	96.89	1.032	0.01374
600	96.28	1.038	0.01648
700	95.67	1.045	0.01923
800	95.07	1.051	0.02198
900	94.47	1.058	0.02473
1000	93.87	1.065	0.02747
1100	93.28	1.072	0.03022
1200	92.69	1.078	0.03297
1300	92.11	1.085	0.03572
1400	91.52	1.092	0.03846
1500	90.95	1.099	0.04121
1600	90.37	1.106	0.04396
1700	89.80	1.113	0.04670
1800	89.24	1.120	0.04945
1900	88.67	1.127	0.05220
2000	88.12	1.134	0.05495
2200	87.01	1.149	0.06044
2400	85.91	1.163	0.06594
2600	84.83	1.178	0.07143
2800	83.77	1.193	0.07693
3000	82.71	1.208	0.08242
3200	81.67	1.224	0.08792
3400	80.65	1.239	0.09341
3600	79.63	1.255	0.09890
3800	78.63	1.271	0.10440
4000	77.64	1.287	0.10989
4200	76.67	1.304	0.11539
4400	75.70	1.320	0.12088
4600	74.75	1.337	0.12638
4800	73.81	1.354	0.13187
5000	72.88	1.372	0.13737
5200	71.97	1.389	0.14286
5400	71.06	1.407	0.14836
5600	70.17	1.425	0.15385
5800	69.29	1.443	0.15935
6000	68.42	1.461	0.16484
6200	67.56	1.480	0.17033
6400	66.71	1.499	0.17583
6600	65.87	1.518	0.18132
6800	65.04	1.537	0.18682
7000	64.22	1.557	0.19231
7200	63.42	1.576	0.19781
7400	62.62	1.596	0.20330
7600	61.83	1.617	0.20880
7800	61.05	1.637	0.21429
8000	60.29	1.658	0.21979
8200	59.53	1.679	0.22528
8400	58.78	1.701	0.23078
8600	58.04	1.722	0.23627
8800	57.31	1.744	0.24177
9000	56.59	1.767	0.24726
9200	55.88	1.789	0.25275
9400	55.18	1.812	0.25825
9600	54.48	1.835	0.26374
9800	53.80	1.858	0.26924
10000	53.12	1.882	0.27473
10200	52.45	1.906	0.28023
10400	51.79	1.930	0.28572
10600	51.14	1.955	0.29122
10800	50.50	1.980	0.29671
11000	49.86	2.005	0.30221
11200	49.24	2.030	0.30770
11400	48.62	2.056	0.31320
11600	48.01	2.083	0.31869
11800	47.40	2.109	0.32419
12000	46.81	2.136	0.32968
12200	46.22	2.163	0.33517
12400	45.64	2.191	0.34067
12600	45.06	2.219	0.34616
12800	44.50	2.247	0.35166
13000	43.94	2.275	0.35715
13200	43.39	2.304	0.36265
13400	42.84	2.334	0.36814
13600	42.30	2.363	0.37364
13800	41.77	2.394	0.37913
14000	41.25	2.424	0.38463
14200	40.73	2.455	0.39012
14400	40.21	2.486	0.39562
14600	39.71	2.518	0.40111
14800	39.21	2.550	0.40660
15000	38.72	2.582	0.41210
15200	38.23	2.615	0.41759
15400	37.75	2.649	0.42309
15600	37.27	2.682	0.42858
15800	36.81	2.716	0.43408
16000	36.34	2.751	0.43957
16500	35.21	2.839	0.45331
17000	34.12	2.931	0.46705
17500	33.05	3.025	0.48078
18000	32.02	3.122	0.49452
18500	31.03	3.222	0.50826
19000	30.06	3.326	0.52199
19500	29.13	3.433	0.53573
20000	28.22	3.543	0.54947
20500	27.34	3.657	0.56320
21000	26.49	3.775	0.57694
21500	25.66	3.896	0.59068
22000	24.87	4.021	0.60441
22500	24.09	4.150	0.61815
23000	23.34	4.284	0.63189
23500	22.61	4.422	0.64562
24000	21.91	4.564	0.65936
24500	21.23	4.710	0.67309
25000	20.57	4.862	0.68683
25500	19.93	5.018	0.70057
26000	19.31	5.179	0.71430
26500	18.71	5.346	0.72804
27000	18.12	5.517	0.74178
27500	17.56	5.695	0.75551
28000	17.01	5.878	0.76925
28500	16.48	6.067	0.78299
29000	15.97	6.262	0.79672
29500	15.47	6.463	0.81046
30000	14.99	6.671	0.82420
30500	14.52	6.885	0.83793
31000	14.07	7.106	0.85167
31500	13.63	7.335	0.86540
32000	13.21	7.570	0.87914
32500	12.80	7.814	0.89288
33000	12.40	8.065	0.90661
33500	12.01	8.324	0.92035
34000	11.64	8.591	0.93408
34500	11.28	8.867	0.94782
35000	10.93	9.152	0.96156
35500	10.59	9.446	0.97529
36000	10.26	9.750	0.98903
36500	9.94	10.064	1.00277
37000	9.63	10.387	1.01651
37500	9.33	10.721	1.03025
38000	9.04	11.065	1.04398
38500	8.76	11.421	1.05772
39000	8.48	11.788	1.07146
39500	8.22	12.167	1.08519
40000	7.96	12.558	1.09893
40500	7.71	12.961	1.11267
41000	7.47	13.378	1.12640
41500	7.24	13.808	1.14014
42000	7.02	14.252	1.15388
42500	6.80	14.710	1.16761
43000	6.59	15.182	1.18135
43500	6.38	15.670	1.19509
44000	6.18	16.174	1.20882
44500	5.99	16.693	1.22256
45000	5.80	17.230	1.23630
45500	5.62	17.784	1.25003
46000	5.45	18.355	1.26377
46500	5.28	18.945	1.27751
47000	5.11	19.554	1.29124
47500	4.95	20.182	1.30498
48000	4.80	20.831	1.31872
48500	4.65	21.500	1.33245
49000	4.51	22.191	1.34619
49500	4.37	22.904	1.35993
50000	4.23	23.640	1.37366
50500	4.10	24.400	1.38740
51000	3.97	25.184	1.40114
51500	3.85	25.994	1.41487
52000	3.73	26.829	1.42861
52500	3.61	27.691	1.44235
53000	3.50	28.581	1.45608
53500	3.39	29.499	1.46982
54000	3.28	30.447	1.48356
54500	3.18	31.426	1.49729
55000	3.08	32.436	1.51103
55500	2.99	33.478	1.52477

t (d)	N_t	N_0/N_t	$\log_{10} N_0/N_t$
56000	2.89	34.554	1.53850
56500	2.80	35.664	1.55224
57000	2.72	36.810	1.56598
57500	2.63	37.993	1.57971
58000	2.55	39.214	1.59345
58500	2.47	40.474	1.60719
59000	2.39	41.775	1.62092
59500	2.32	43.117	1.63466
60000	2.25	44.503	1.64840
60500	2.18	45.933	1.66213
61000	2.11	47.409	1.67587
61500	2.04	48.933	1.68960
62000	1.98	50.505	1.70334
62500	1.92	52.128	1.71708
63000	1.86	53.803	1.73081
63500	1.80	55.533	1.74455
64000	1.74	57.317	1.75829
64500	1.69	59.159	1.77202
65000	1.64	61.060	1.78576
65500	1.59	63.022	1.79950
66000	1.54	65.047	1.81323
66500	1.49	67.137	1.82697
67000	1.44	69.295	1.84071
67500	1.40	71.522	1.85444
68000	1.35	73.820	1.86818
68500	1.31	76.192	1.88191
69000	1.27	78.641	1.89565
69500	1.23	81.168	1.90939
70000	1.19	83.776	1.92312
70500	1.16	86.468	1.93686
71000	1.12	89.246	1.95059
71500	1.09	92.114	1.96433
72000	1.05	95.074	1.97806
72500	1.02	98.129	1.99180
73000	0.99	101.285	2.00555
73500	0.96	104.540	2.01928
74000	0.93	107.900	2.03302
74500	0.90	111.367	2.04676
75000	0.87	114.946	2.06050
76000	0.82	122.452	2.08797
77000	0.77	130.449	2.11544
78000	0.72	138.968	2.14292
79000	0.68	148.042	2.17039
80000	0.63	157.711	2.19786
81000	0.60	168.010	2.22534
82000	0.56	178.980	2.25281
83000	0.52	190.668	2.28028
84000	0.49	203.119	2.30775
85000	0.46	216.384	2.33523
86000	0.43	230.515	2.36270
87000	0.41	245.567	2.39017
88000	0.38	261.602	2.41764
89000	0.36	278.691	2.44512
90000	0.34	296.885	2.47259
91000	0.32	316.275	2.50007
92000	0.30	336.927	2.52754
93000	0.28	358.937	2.55502
94000	0.26	382.365	2.58248
95000	0.25	407.348	2.60997
96000	0.23	433.933	2.63742
97000	0.22	462.278	2.66490
98000	0.20	492.465	2.69238
99000	0.19	524.631	2.71985
100000	0.18	558.877	2.74732

Iridium-192

half-life 74 d

t (d)	N_t	N_0/N_t	$\log_{10} N_0/N_t$
0	100.00	1.000	0.00000
2	98.14	1.019	0.00814
4	96.32	1.038	0.01627
6	94.53	1.058	0.02441
8	92.78	1.078	0.03254
10	91.06	1.098	0.04068
12	89.37	1.119	0.04882
14	87.71	1.140	0.05695
16	86.08	1.162	0.06509
18	84.48	1.184	0.07322
20	82.92	1.206	0.08136
22	81.38	1.229	0.08950
24	79.87	1.252	0.09763
26	78.38	1.276	0.10577
28	76.93	1.300	0.11390
30	75.50	1.324	0.12204
32	74.10	1.350	0.13018
34	72.73	1.375	0.13831
36	71.38	1.401	0.14645
38	70.05	1.428	0.15458
40	68.75	1.455	0.16272
42	67.48	1.482	0.17086
44	66.22	1.510	0.17899
46	64.99	1.539	0.18713
48	63.79	1.568	0.19526
50	62.60	1.597	0.20340
52	61.44	1.628	0.21154
54	60.30	1.658	0.21967
56	59.18	1.690	0.22781
58	58.08	1.722	0.23594
60	57.01	1.754	0.24408
64	54.91	1.821	0.26035
68	52.89	1.891	0.27662
72	50.95	1.963	0.29290
76	49.07	2.038	0.30917
80	47.27	2.116	0.32544
84	45.53	2.196	0.34171
88	43.85	2.280	0.35798
92	42.24	2.367	0.37426
96	40.69	2.458	0.39053
100	39.19	2.552	0.40680
104	37.75	2.649	0.42307
108	36.36	2.750	0.43934
112	35.03	2.855	0.45561
116	33.74	2.964	0.47189
120	32.50	3.077	0.48816
124	31.30	3.195	0.50443
128	30.15	3.317	0.52070
132	29.04	3.443	0.53697
136	27.97	3.575	0.55325
140	26.95	3.711	0.56952
144	25.95	3.853	0.58579
148	25.00	4.000	0.60206
152	24.08	4.153	0.61833
156	23.19	4.311	0.63461
160	22.34	4.476	0.65088
170	20.34	4.915	0.69156
180	18.53	5.398	0.73224
190	16.87	5.928	0.77292
200	15.36	6.510	0.81360
210	13.99	7.150	0.85428
220	12.74	7.852	0.89496
230	11.60	8.623	0.93564
240	10.56	9.469	0.97632
250	9.62	10.399	1.01700
260	8.76	11.420	1.05768
270	7.97	12.542	1.09836
280	7.26	13.773	1.13904
290	6.61	15.126	1.17972
300	6.02	16.611	1.22040
310	5.48	18.242	1.26108
320	4.99	20.033	1.30176
330	4.55	22.001	1.34244
340	4.14	24.161	1.38312
350	3.77	26.534	1.42380
360	3.43	29.139	1.46448
370	3.12	32.000	1.50516
380	2.85	35.143	1.54584
390	2.59	38.594	1.58652
400	2.36	42.383	1.62720
410	2.15	46.545	1.66788
420	1.96	51.116	1.70856
430	1.78	56.135	1.74924
440	1.62	61.647	1.78992
450	1.48	67.701	1.83060
460	1.35	74.349	1.87128
470	1.22	81.650	1.91195
480	1.12	89.667	1.95263
490	1.02	98.472	1.99331
500	0.92	108.142	2.03399
510	0.84	118.761	2.07467
520	0.77	130.423	2.11535
530	0.70	143.230	2.15603
540	0.64	157.295	2.19671
550	0.58	172.741	2.23739
560	0.53	189.703	2.27807
570	0.48	208.331	2.31875

Gold-198

half-life 2.7 d

t: d	h	min	N_t	N_0/N_t	$\log_{10} N_0/N_t$
	0		100.00	1.000	0.00000
	1		98.94	1.010	0.00465
	2		97.88	1.021	0.00929
	3		96.84	1.032	0.01394
	4		95.81	1.043	0.01858
	5		94.79	1.054	0.02323
	6		93.78	1.066	0.02787
	7		92.79	1.077	0.03252
	8		91.80	1.089	0.03716
	9		90.82	1.101	0.04181
	10		89.86	1.112	0.04646
	11		88.90	1.124	0.05110
	12		87.95	1.136	0.05575
	13		87.02	1.149	0.06039
	14		86.09	1.161	0.06504
	15		85.18	1.174	0.06968
	16		84.27	1.186	0.07433
	17		83.37	1.199	0.07897
	18		82.49	1.212	0.08362
	19		81.61	1.225	0.08827
	20		80.74	1.238	0.09291
	21		79.88	1.251	0.09756
	22		79.03	1.265	0.10220
	23		78.19	1.278	0.10685
1	0		77.36	1.292	0.11149
	1		76.54	1.306	0.11614
	2		75.72	1.320	0.12078
	3		74.92	1.334	0.12543
	4		74.12	1.349	0.13008
	5		73.33	1.363	0.13472
	6		72.55	1.378	0.13937
	7		71.78	1.393	0.14401
	8		71.01	1.408	0.14866
	9		70.26	1.423	0.15330
	10		69.51	1.438	0.15795
	11		68.77	1.454	0.16259
	12		68.04	1.469	0.16724
	13		67.32	1.485	0.17188
	14		66.60	1.501	0.17653
	15		65.89	1.517	0.18118
	16		65.19	1.533	0.18582
	17		64.50	1.550	0.19047
	18		63.81	1.567	0.19511
	19		63.13	1.584	0.19976
	20		62.46	1.601	0.20440
	21		61.79	1.618	0.20905
	22		61.14	1.635	0.21369
	23		60.49	1.653	0.21834
2	0		59.84	1.671	0.22299
	1		59.21	1.689	0.22763
	2		58.58	1.707	0.23228
	3		57.95	1.725	0.23692
	4		57.34	1.744	0.24157
	5		56.73	1.762	0.24621
	6		56.12	1.781	0.25086
	7		55.53	1.800	0.25550
	8		54.94	1.820	0.26015
	9		54.35	1.839	0.26480
	10		53.77	1.859	0.26944
	11		53.20	1.879	0.27409
	12		52.63	1.899	0.27873
	13		52.07	1.920	0.28338
	14		51.52	1.940	0.28802
	15		50.97	1.961	0.29267
	16		50.43	1.982	0.29731
	17		49.89	2.004	0.30196
	18		49.36	2.025	0.30661
	19		48.84	2.047	0.31125
	20		48.32	2.069	0.31590
	21		47.80	2.091	0.32054
	22		47.29	2.114	0.32519
	23		46.79	2.137	0.32983
3	0		46.29	2.160	0.33448
	1		45.80	2.183	0.33912
	2		45.31	2.206	0.34377
	3		44.83	2.230	0.34841
	4		44.35	2.254	0.35306
	5		43.88	2.278	0.35771
	6		43.42	2.303	0.36235
	7		42.95	2.328	0.36700
	8		42.50	2.353	0.37164
	9		42.04	2.378	0.37629
	10		41.60	2.403	0.38093
	11		41.15	2.429	0.38558
	12		40.72	2.455	0.39022
	13		40.28	2.482	0.39487
	14		39.86	2.509	0.39952
	15		39.43	2.536	0.40416
	16		39.01	2.563	0.40881
	17		38.60	2.590	0.41345
	18		38.19	2.618	0.41810
	19		37.78	2.646	0.42274
	20		37.38	2.675	0.42739
	21		36.98	2.704	0.43203
	22		36.59	2.733	0.43668
	23		36.20	2.762	0.44133
4	0		35.81	2.792	0.44597
	1		35.43	2.822	0.45062
	2		35.05	2.852	0.45526
	3		34.68	2.883	0.45991
	4		34.31	2.914	0.46455
	5		33.95	2.945	0.46920
	6		33.59	2.977	0.47384
	7		33.23	3.009	0.47849
	8		32.87	3.041	0.48313
	9		32.53	3.074	0.48778
	10		32.18	3.107	0.49243
	11		31.84	3.141	0.49707
	12		31.50	3.174	0.50172
	13		31.16	3.208	0.50636
	14		30.83	3.243	0.51101
	15		30.50	3.278	0.51565
	16		30.18	3.313	0.52030
	17		29.86	3.349	0.52494
	18		29.54	3.385	0.52959
	19		29.23	3.421	0.53424
	20		28.91	3.458	0.53888
	21		28.61	3.495	0.54353
	22		28.30	3.533	0.54817
	23		28.00	3.571	0.55282
5	0		27.70	3.609	0.55746
	6		25.98	3.848	0.58534
	12		24.37	4.104	0.61321
	18		22.85	4.376	0.64108
6	0		21.43	4.666	0.66896
	6		20.10	4.975	0.69683
	12		18.85	5.305	0.72470
	18		17.68	5.656	0.75257
7	0		16.58	6.031	0.78045
	6		15.55	6.431	0.80832
	12		14.58	6.857	0.83619
	18		13.68	7.312	0.86406
8	0		12.83	7.797	0.89194
	6		12.03	8.313	0.91981
	12		11.28	8.865	0.94768
	18		10.58	9.452	0.97555
9	0		9.92	10.079	1.00343
	6		9.30	10.747	1.03131
	12		8.73	11.459	1.05918
	18		8.18	12.219	1.08705
10	0		7.67	13.029	1.11493
	6		7.20	13.893	1.14280
	12		6.75	14.814	1.17067
	18		6.33	15.795	1.19855
11	0		5.94	16.842	1.22642
	6		5.57	17.959	1.25429
	12		5.22	19.149	1.28217
	18		4.90	20.419	1.31004
12	0		4.59	21.772	1.33791
	6		4.31	23.215	1.36578
	12		4.04	24.754	1.39366
	18		3.79	26.395	1.42153
13	0		3.55	28.145	1.44940
	6		3.33	30.010	1.47728
	12		3.13	32.000	1.50515
	18		2.93	34.121	1.53302
14	0		2.75	36.382	1.56090
	6		2.58	38.794	1.58877
	12		2.42	41.365	1.61664
	18		2.27	44.107	1.64452
15	0		2.13	47.031	1.67239
	6		1.99	50.148	1.70026
	12		1.87	53.473	1.72814
	18		1.75	57.017	1.75601
16	0		1.64	60.796	1.78388
	6		1.54	64.826	1.81175
	12		1.45	69.123	1.83963
	18		1.36	73.705	1.86750
17	0		1.27	78.590	1.89537
	6		1.19	83.799	1.92324
	12		1.12	89.353	1.95111
	18		1.05	95.276	1.97899
18	0		0.98	101.594	2.00687
	6		0.92	108.328	2.03474
	12		0.87	115.508	2.06261
	18		0.81	123.164	2.09049
19	0		0.76	131.328	2.11836
	6		0.71	140.034	2.14624
	12		0.67	149.316	2.17411
	18		0.63	159.212	2.20198
20			0.59	169.767	2.22986
25			0.16	612.782	2.78731
30			0.05	2211.900	3.34477
35			0.01	7987.220	3.90240

Mercury-197

half-life 65 h

t: d	h	min	N_t	N_0/N_t	$\log_{10} N_0/N_t$
	0		100.00	1.000	0.00000
	1		98.94	1.011	0.00463
	2		97.89	1.022	0.00926
	3		96.85	1.033	0.01389
	4		95.82	1.044	0.01852
	5		94.81	1.055	0.02316
	6		93.80	1.066	0.02779
	7		92.81	1.078	0.03242
	8		91.82	1.089	0.03705
	9		90.85	1.101	0.04168
	10		89.89	1.113	0.04631
	11		88.93	1.124	0.05094
	12		87.99	1.137	0.05557
	13		87.06	1.149	0.06021
	14		86.13	1.161	0.06484
	15		85.22	1.173	0.06947
	16		84.31	1.186	0.07410
	17		83.42	1.199	0.07873
	18		82.53	1.212	0.08336
	19		81.66	1.225	0.08799
	20		80.79	1.238	0.09262
	21		79.94	1.251	0.09726
	22		79.09	1.264	0.10189
	23		78.25	1.278	0.10652
1	0		77.42	1.292	0.11115
	1		76.60	1.306	0.11578
	2		75.79	1.320	0.12041
	3		74.98	1.334	0.12504

t: d	t: h	t: min	N_t	N_0/N_t	$\log_{10} N_0/N_t$
	4		74.19	1.348	0.12967
	5		73.40	1.362	0.13431
	6		72.62	1.377	0.13894
	7		71.85	1.392	0.14357
	8		71.09	1.407	0.14820
	9		70.33	1.422	0.15283
	10		69.59	1.437	0.15746
	11		68.85	1.452	0.16209
	12		68.12	1.468	0.16672
	13		67.40	1.484	0.17136
	14		66.68	1.500	0.17599
	15		65.98	1.516	0.18062
	16		65.28	1.532	0.18525
	17		64.58	1.548	0.18988
	18		63.90	1.565	0.19451
	19		63.22	1.582	0.19914
	20		62.55	1.599	0.20377
	21		61.89	1.616	0.20841
	22		61.23	1.633	0.21304
	23		60.58	1.651	0.21767
2	0		59.94	1.668	0.22230
	1		59.30	1.686	0.22693
	2		58.67	1.704	0.23156
	3		58.05	1.723	0.23619
	4		57.43	1.741	0.24082
	5		56.83	1.760	0.24546
	6		56.22	1.779	0.25009
	7		55.63	1.798	0.25472
	8		55.04	1.817	0.25935
	9		54.45	1.836	0.26398
	10		53.88	1.856	0.26861
	11		53.30	1.876	0.27324
	12		52.74	1.896	0.27787
	13		52.18	1.916	0.28251
	14		51.63	1.937	0.28714
	15		51.08	1.958	0.29177
	16		50.54	1.979	0.29640
	17		50.00	2.000	0.30103
	18		49.47	2.021	0.30566
	19		48.94	2.043	0.31029
	20		48.43	2.065	0.31492
	21		47.91	2.087	0.31956
	22		47.40	2.110	0.32419
	23		46.90	2.132	0.32882
3	0		46.40	2.155	0.33345
	1		45.91	2.178	0.33808
	2		45.42	2.201	0.34271
	3		44.94	2.225	0.34734
	4		44.47	2.249	0.35197
	5		43.99	2.273	0.35661
	6		43.53	2.297	0.36124
	7		43.07	2.322	0.36587
	8		42.61	2.347	0.37050
	9		42.16	2.372	0.37513
	10		41.71	2.398	0.37976
	11		41.27	2.423	0.38439
	12		40.83	2.449	0.38902
	13		40.40	2.475	0.39366
	14		39.97	2.502	0.39829
	15		39.54	2.529	0.40292
	16		39.12	2.556	0.40755
	17		38.71	2.583	0.41218
	18		38.30	2.611	0.41681
	19		37.89	2.639	0.42144
	20		37.49	2.667	0.42607
	21		37.09	2.696	0.43071
	22		36.70	2.725	0.43534
	23		36.31	2.754	0.43997
4	0		35.93	2.784	0.44460
	1		35.54	2.813	0.44923
	2		35.17	2.844	0.45386
	3		34.79	2.874	0.45849
	4		34.43	2.905	0.46312
	5		34.06	2.936	0.46776
	6		33.70	2.967	0.47239
	7		33.34	2.999	0.47702
	8		32.99	3.031	0.48165
	9		32.64	3.064	0.48628
	10		32.29	3.097	0.49091
	11		31.95	3.130	0.49554
	12		31.61	3.164	0.50017
	13		31.27	3.197	0.50481
	14		30.94	3.232	0.50944
	15		30.61	3.266	0.51407
	16		30.29	3.301	0.51870
	17		29.97	3.337	0.52333
	18		29.65	3.373	0.52796
	19		29.34	3.409	0.53259
	20		29.03	3.445	0.53722
	21		28.72	3.482	0.54186
	22		28.41	3.520	0.54649
	23		28.11	3.557	0.55112
5	0		27.81	3.595	0.55575
	1		27.52	3.634	0.56038
	2		27.23	3.673	0.56501
	3		26.94	3.712	0.56964
	4		26.65	3.752	0.57427
	5		26.37	3.792	0.57891
	6		26.09	3.833	0.58354
	7		25.81	3.874	0.58817
	8		25.54	3.916	0.59280
	9		25.27	3.958	0.59743
	10		25.00	4.000	0.60206
	11		24.73	4.043	0.60669
	12		24.47	4.086	0.61132
	13		24.21	4.130	0.61596
	14		23.96	4.174	0.62059
	15		23.70	4.219	0.62522
	16		23.45	4.264	0.62985
	17		23.20	4.310	0.63448
	18		22.96	4.356	0.63911
	19		22.71	4.403	0.64374
	20		22.47	4.450	0.64837
	21		22.23	4.498	0.65301
	22		22.00	4.546	0.65764
	23		21.76	4.595	0.66227
6	0		21.53	4.644	0.66690
	1		21.30	4.694	0.67153
	2		21.08	4.744	0.67616
	3		20.85	4.795	0.68079
	4		20.63	4.846	0.68542
	5		20.41	4.898	0.69006
	6		20.20	4.951	0.69469
	7		19.98	5.004	0.69932
	8		19.77	5.058	0.70395
	9		19.56	5.112	0.70858
	10		19.35	5.167	0.71321
	11		19.15	5.222	0.71784
	12		18.95	5.278	0.72247
	13		18.75	5.335	0.72711
	14		18.55	5.392	0.73174
	15		18.35	5.450	0.73637
	16		18.16	5.508	0.74100
	17		17.96	5.567	0.74563
	18		17.77	5.627	0.75026
	19		17.58	5.687	0.75489
	20		17.40	5.748	0.75952
	21		17.21	5.810	0.76416
	22		17.03	5.872	0.76879
	23		16.85	5.935	0.77342
7	0		16.67	5.999	0.77805
	6		15.64	6.395	0.80584
	12		14.67	6.817	0.83362
	18		13.76	7.268	0.86141
8	0		12.91	7.748	0.88920
	6		12.11	8.260	0.91699
	12		11.36	8.806	0.94477
	18		10.65	9.388	0.97256
9	0		9.99	10.008	1.00035
	6		9.37	10.669	1.02814
	12		8.79	11.374	1.05592
	18		8.25	12.126	1.08371
10	0		7.74	12.927	1.11150
	12		6.81	14.692	1.16707
11	0		5.99	16.697	1.22265
	12		5.27	18.977	1.27822
12	0		4.64	21.568	1.33380
	12		4.08	24.512	1.38937
13	0		3.59	27.858	1.44495
	12		3.16	31.661	1.50052
14	0		2.78	35.983	1.55610
	12		2.45	40.895	1.61167
15	0		2.15	46.478	1.66725
	12		1.89	52.823	1.72282
16	0		1.67	60.034	1.77840
	12		1.47	68.230	1.83397
17	0		1.29	77.544	1.88955
	12		1.13	88.130	1.94512
18	0		1.00	100.161	2.00070
	12		0.88	113.835	2.05627
19	0		0.77	129.375	2.11185
	12		0.68	147.036	2.16742
20	0		0.60	167.109	2.22300
	12		0.53	189.922	2.27857
21	0		0.46	215.849	2.33415

Mercury-203

half-life 47 d

t: d	t: h	t: min	N_t	N_0/N_t	$\log_{10} N_0/N_t$
0	0		100.00	1.000	0.00000
	12		99.27	1.007	0.00320
1	0		98.54	1.015	0.00640
	12		97.81	1.022	0.00961
2	0		97.09	1.030	0.01281
	12		96.38	1.038	0.01601
3	0		95.67	1.045	0.01921
	12		94.97	1.053	0.02242
4	0		94.27	1.061	0.02562
	12		93.58	1.069	0.02882
5	0		92.89	1.077	0.03202
	12		92.21	1.084	0.03523
6	0		91.53	1.093	0.03843
	12		90.86	1.101	0.04163
7	0		90.19	1.109	0.04483
	12		89.53	1.117	0.04804
8	0		88.87	1.125	0.05124
	12		88.22	1.134	0.05444
9	0		87.57	1.142	0.05764
	12		86.93	1.150	0.06085
10	0		86.29	1.159	0.06405
	12		85.65	1.167	0.06725
11	0		85.02	1.176	0.07045
	12		84.40	1.185	0.07366
12	0		83.78	1.194	0.07686
	12		83.16	1.202	0.08006
13	0		82.55	1.211	0.08326
	12		81.95	1.220	0.08647
14	0		81.35	1.229	0.08967
	12		80.75	1.238	0.09287
15			80.15	1.248	0.09607
16			78.98	1.266	0.10248
17			77.82	1.285	0.10888
18			76.69	1.304	0.11529
19			75.56	1.323	0.12169
20			74.46	1.343	0.12810
21			73.37	1.363	0.13450
22			72.29	1.383	0.14091
23			71.23	1.404	0.14731
24			70.19	1.425	0.15372
25			69.16	1.446	0.16012
26			68.15	1.467	0.16653
27			67.15	1.489	0.17293
28			66.17	1.511	0.17934
29			65.20	1.534	0.18574
30			64.25	1.556	0.19215
31			63.31	1.580	0.19855
32			62.38	1.603	0.20496
33			61.47	1.627	0.21136
34			60.57	1.651	0.21777
35			59.68	1.676	0.22417
36			58.81	1.701	0.23058
37			57.95	1.726	0.23698
38			57.10	1.751	0.24339
39			56.26	1.777	0.24979
40			55.44	1.804	0.25620
41			54.63	1.831	0.26260
42			53.83	1.858	0.26901
43			53.04	1.885	0.27541
44			52.26	1.913	0.28182
45			51.50	1.942	0.28822
46			50.74	1.971	0.29463
47			50.00	2.000	0.30103
48			49.27	2.030	0.30744
49			48.55	2.060	0.31384
50			47.84	2.090	0.32025
51			47.14	2.122	0.32665
52			46.45	2.153	0.33306
53			45.77	2.185	0.33946
54			45.10	2.218	0.34587
55			44.44	2.250	0.35227
56			43.78	2.284	0.35868
57			43.14	2.318	0.36508
58			42.51	2.352	0.37149
59			41.89	2.387	0.37789
60			41.28	2.423	0.38430
62			40.08	2.495	0.39710
64			38.91	2.570	0.40991
66			37.78	2.647	0.42272
68			36.68	2.726	0.43553
70			35.62	2.808	0.44834
72			34.58	2.892	0.46115
74			33.58	2.978	0.47396
76			32.60	3.067	0.48677
78			31.65	3.159	0.49958
80			30.73	3.254	0.51239
82			29.84	3.351	0.52520
84			28.97	3.452	0.53801
86			28.13	3.555	0.55082
88			27.31	3.661	0.56363
90			26.52	3.771	0.57644
92			25.75	3.884	0.58925
94			25.00	4.000	0.60206
96			24.27	4.120	0.61487
98			23.57	4.243	0.62768
100			22.88	4.370	0.64049
102			22.22	4.501	0.65330
104			21.57	4.636	0.66611
106			20.94	4.774	0.67892
108			20.34	4.917	0.69173
110			19.75	5.065	0.70454
112			19.17	5.216	0.71735
114			18.61	5.372	0.73016
116			18.07	5.533	0.74297
118			17.55	5.699	0.75578
120			17.04	5.869	0.76859
122			16.54	6.045	0.78140
124			16.06	6.226	0.79421
126			15.59	6.412	0.80702
128			15.14	6.604	0.81983
130			14.70	6.802	0.83264
132			14.27	7.006	0.84545
134			13.86	7.215	0.85826
136			13.46	7.431	0.87107
138			13.07	7.654	0.88388
140			12.69	7.883	0.89669
145			11.78	8.486	0.92871
150			10.95	9.136	0.96074
155			10.17	9.835	0.99276
160			9.45	10.587	1.02479
165			8.77	11.398	1.05681
170			8.15	12.270	1.08884
175			7.57	13.209	1.12086
180			7.03	14.220	1.15289
185			6.53	15.308	1.18491
190			6.07	16.479	1.21693
195			5.64	17.740	1.24896
200			5.24	19.098	1.28098
205			4.86	20.559	1.31301
210			4.52	22.133	1.34503
215			4.20	23.826	1.37706
220			3.90	25.650	1.40908
225			3.62	27.613	1.44111
230			3.36	29.726	1.47313
235			3.12	32.000	1.50516
240			2.90	34.449	1.53718
245			2.70	37.086	1.56921
250			2.50	39.924	1.60123
255			2.33	42.979	1.63325
260			2.16	46.268	1.66528
265			2.01	49.809	1.69730
270			1.86	53.620	1.72933
275			1.73	57.724	1.76135
280			1.61	62.141	1.79338
285			1.49	66.896	1.82540
290			1.39	72.016	1.85743
295			1.29	77.527	1.88945
300			1.20	83.460	1.92148
305			1.11	89.846	1.95350
310			1.03	96.722	1.98552
315			0.96	104.124	2.01755
320			0.89	112.092	2.04957
325			0.83	120.670	2.08160
330			0.77	129.904	2.11362
335			0.72	139.845	2.14565
340			0.66	150.547	2.17767
345			0.62	162.068	2.20970
350			0.57	174.470	2.24172
355			0.53	187.822	2.27375
360			0.49	202.195	2.30577

Constituents of Living Matter

Carbohydrates 308
Monosaccharides 308
Stereochemistry of sugars 308
Amino sugars 311
Sugar phosphates 312
Polyhydric alcohols 312
Primary oxidation products of carbohydrates 312
Oligosaccharides 312
Polysaccharides 312

Amino acids 329
Polypeptides 329

Nucleosides and nucleotides 336

Nucleic acids 351
Synthesis of deoxyribonucleic acid (DNA) 351
Synthesis of ribonucleic acid (RNA) 352
Synthesis of proteins 353
Minor constituents of nucleic acids 354

Porphyrins 355
Iron porphyrins (haem derivatives) 359
Bile pigments 362
Chlorophylls 362
Cyanocobalamin (vitamin B_{12}) 363

Lipids 365
Fatty acids 373
Prostaglandins 373
Acylglycerols (fats) 374
Alkoxydiglycerides 374
Glycoglycerides 375
Phospholipids (phosphatides) 375
Sphingolipids 376
Waxes 377

Steroids 378

Enzymes 382
Nomenclature of enzymes 382
Specificity of enzymes 382
Structure of enzymes and mechanism of enzyme action 382
Enzyme kinetics 382
Classification and numbering of enzymes 385

Metabolism

General aspects 387
Energy metabolism 387
Cell metabolism 388

Energy-supplying reactions 389
Intermediary stages of carbohydrate degradation 389
Oxidative degradation of fat 391
Intermediary stages of the degradation of amino acids 391
Degradation of individual amino acids 394
Degradation of food constituents other than carbohydrate, fat and protein 399
Degradation of the principal foodstuffs 401
Mechanism of biological oxidations 402
The key position of adenosine triphosphate (ATP) in biological energy transformations 404

Digestive enzymes 405
Proteolytic enzymes (proteases, peptide hydrolases) 405
Glycoside hydrolases (glycosidases) 405
Lipases and other ester hydrolases (esterases) 405
Nucleases 406

Synthesis of cell constituents from glucose 420
The oxidative pentose phosphate cycle 420
Glucuronic acid and iduronic acid 423
Formation of glucosamine and related amino sugars 423
Biosynthesis of L-fucose in mammalian tissues 423
Formation and utilization of hexosamines and *N*-acetylneuraminic acid in mammals 424
Extension of carbon chains by carbon dioxide fixation 424
Fatty acid synthesis 424
Formation of lecithin and cephalin 425
Formation of triglyceride 426
Biosynthesis of cholesterol 426
Biosynthesis and metabolism of steroid hormones of the adrenal cortex and gonads 428
Biosynthesis and metabolism of oestrogens 430
Formation of serine and glycine 432
Formation of glutamic acid 432
Formation of proline and hydroxyproline 432
Formation of histidine 432

Synthesis of cell constituents from amino acids 433
Formation of purines 433
Transfer of groups containing one carbon atom 436
Formation of porphyrins 437
Formation of creatine 437
Formation of glutathione 438
Formation of bile acid conjugates 438
Formation of taurine 438
Formation of pyrimidines 438
Conversion of phenylalanine to tyrosine 439
Formation of noradrenaline and adrenaline 440
Formation of thyroid hormones 440
Formation of melanin 440
Formation and degradation of 5-hydroxytryptamine (serotonin) 441
Synthesis of carbohydrate from amino acids and other non-carbohydrate precursors (gluconeogenesis) 441

Detoxication mechanisms 442
Synthesis of urea 442
Acetylation of amines 444
Formation of glycine conjugates 444
Formation of esters of sulphuric acid 445
Formation of phenacetylglutamine 445
Formation of mercapturic acids 445

Inborn Errors of Metabolism

Introduction 446
Haemoglobinopathies 446
Inborn errors of amino-acid metabolism 448
Inborn errors of carbohydrate metabolism 450
Inborn defects of renal transport mechanisms 452
Inborn errors of purine and pyrimidine metabolism 453
Hyperbilirubinaemia and porphyria 454
Lipidoses 455
Inborn errors of corticosteroid metabolism 456

(For references see page 312)

Carbohydrates [1]

Carbohydrates are carbon compounds containing hydrogen and oxygen in the ratio 2:1, their general empirical formula being $C_x(H_2O)_y$**. The term is also extended, however, to oxidation and reduction products of carbohydrates proper, as well as to their simple derivatives such as amino and phosphorylated sugars.

Carbohydrates are frequently referred to as 'sugars' (saccharides) because many of them possess a sweet taste*** but actually the term 'sugar' is only loosely defined and may denote a wide variety of carbohydrate compounds. To the carbohydrate chemist, however, it means a mono- or oligosaccharide but *not* a polysaccharide (see below). Mono- and oligosaccharides are given names with the suffix '-ose', e.g., glucose, fructose, lactose.

Monosaccharides

Carbohydrates that cannot be split further by hydrolysis are called simple sugars or monosaccharides. Their general empirical formula is $[C(H_2O)]_n$ and they are classed as aldehydic alcohols (aldoses) or ketonic alcohols (ketoses). Those of importance to mammals are listed in Table 1 (pages 313–316).

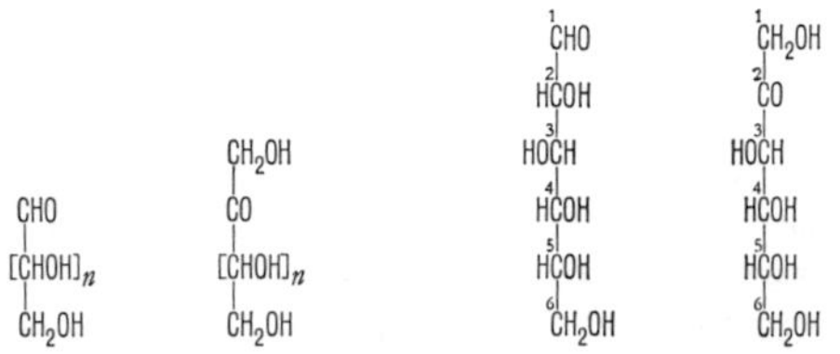

Aldose Ketose Glucose Fructose

Sugars with chain lengths of 3, 4, 5, 6, etc. carbon atoms are known as trioses, tetroses, pentoses, hexoses, etc.†. The numbering convention is shown above in the structures of glucose and fructose.

The open-chain form of sugars (aldehyde or ketone form) normally occurs only in aqueous solution, where it is a transitional form in equilibrium with the ring form. The latter is the rule with carbohydrates of longer chain length, and with few exceptions the ring is usually 5- or 6-membered. By analogy with the similar heterocyclic compounds†† furan and pyran, these ring forms are known as *furanoses* and *pyranoses* respectively:

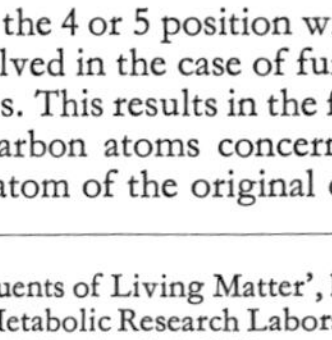

Furan Pyran

The ring forms are formed from chain forms by the reaction of the hydroxyl group in the 4 or 5 position with the carbonyl group. Carbon atom 4 is involved in the case of furanoses, carbon atom 5 in the case of pyranoses. This results in the formation of an oxygen bridge between the carbon atoms concerned and of a hydroxyl group on the carbon atom of the original carbonyl group:

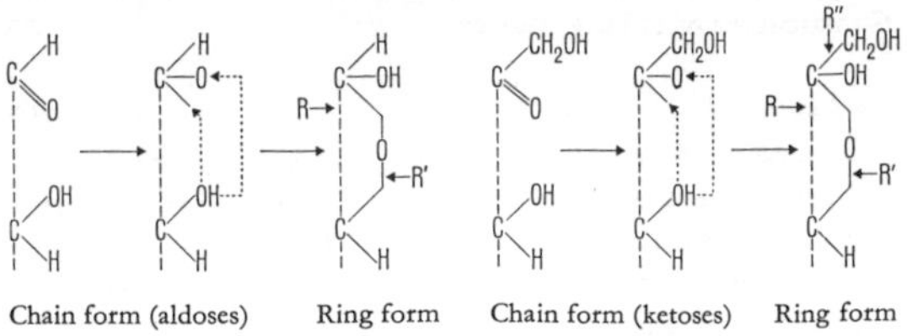

Chain form (aldoses) Ring form Chain form (ketoses) Ring form

The compound formed is an intramolecular hemiacetal (when derived from an aldose) or hemiketal (when derived from a ketose).

Acetal Hemiacetal Ketal Hemiketal

The hydroxyl group attached to the hemiacetal or hemiketal carbon atom (C-1 or C-2 respectively) is particularly reactive and is known as the glycosidic hydroxyl. It combines readily with the alcoholic or phenolic groups of other molecules, and when this reaction takes place with a compound that is not another sugar (an aglycon), the resulting compound is known as a *glycoside:*

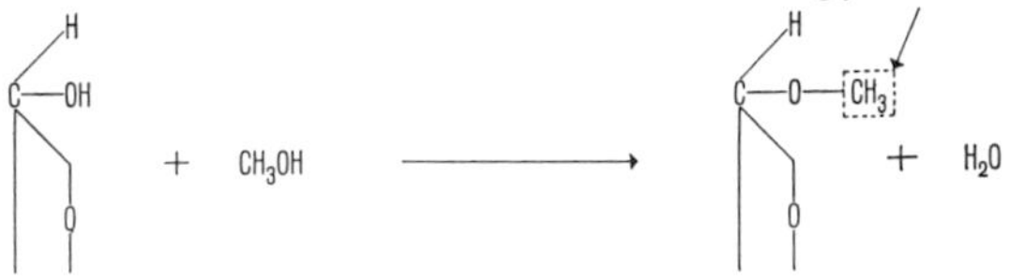

Sugar Aglycon (here methanol) Glycoside (methylglycoside)

When the reaction takes place with a molecule of another sugar the resulting compound is known not as a glycoside but as a disaccharide (cf. 'Oligo- and Polysaccharides', page 312).

Stereochemistry of sugars

The stereoisomerism of sugars and related substances is of particular importance in biochemistry*, and for this reason it will be dealt with in some detail here. For a more thorough treatment of the subject see HONEYMAN[2]. A carbon atom with four different substituents, for example C-2 of glyceraldehyde, is known as an *asymmetric* carbon atom. This grouping cannot be superimposed on its mirror image and the resulting lack of symmetry gives rise to a type of isomerism associated with optical activity. The two possible spatial configurations of the substituents can be readily seen if one imagines the asymmetric C atom to be in the middle of a regular tetrahedron with the valencies pointing to the corners. The two possible configurations of glyceraldehyde shown as an example in Figure 1 cannot in any way be superimposed one upon the other. They are related to one another as an object to its mirror image, and are known as enantiomorphs. No such asymmetry exists with a carbon atom possessing at least two identical substituents.

Enantiomorphic isomers are optically active, i.e., in solution one of the isomers rotates the plane of polarized light to the right, the other an equal amount to the left. The degree of rotation depends on the length of the polarimeter tube, on the wave length of the polarized light, on the concentration, and on the solvent and its temperature**. The direction of rotation was originally indicated by prefixing the name of the isomer by *dextro* (*d*-) and *laevo* (*l*-)

---

* This chapter, 'Constituents of Living Matter', has been written in consultation with H. A. KREBS (Metabolic Research Laboratory, Nuffield Department of Clinical Medicine, Oxford, England), I. O. WALKER (Department of Biochemistry, University of Oxford, England), L. I. WOOLF (Faculty of Medicine, University of British Columbia), J. R. QUAYLE (Department of Microbiology, University of Sheffield, England), J. M. LOWENSTEIN (Graduate Department of Biochemistry, Brandeis University, Waltham, Mass., USA) and P. R. RAGGATT (Department of Biochemistry, University of Oxford, England).

** There are compounds with this empirical formula that do not fall into the category of carbohydrates, such as acetic acid, lactic acid, phloroglucinol.

*** The sweetest of the sugars is fructose. Polysaccharides have no taste.

† According to BEILSTEIN (1938) these names are derived from the number of oxygen atoms. In the case of 'ordinary' monosaccharides $[C(H_2O)]_n$ both nomenclatures are identical. They are different in the case of substituted and deoxy sugars. In general the nomenclature based on the number of carbon atoms is the more commonly used and permits a better understanding of carbohydrate metabolism (anabolism of the carbon chain from small molecules and its subsequent catabolism).

†† Heterocycles are ring molecules in which apart from carbon atoms the ring contains at least one atom of another element.

* Stereoisomerism is of importance in nature not only for carbohydrates but for all compounds where stereoisomers are possible. This is because as a rule only specific stereoisomers are synthesized or degraded in naturally occurring reactions (this is a characteristic difference compared to laboratory synthesis). One reason is the stereospecificity of many enzymes, but the fundamental mechanism is unknown.

** The specific rotation $[\alpha]$ is defined as the rotation in degrees of 1g of substance in 1ml of solution in a tube with a length of 10 cm. The D-line of sodium is as a rule used as a source of light. The temperature, wave length of the incident light, nature of the solvent and the concentration must also be included where these diverge from the definition, e.g., $[\alpha]_D^{25°}$, 20% (H_2O) = + 12°.

(For references see page 312)

Fig. 1 Stereoisomerism of glyceraldehyde

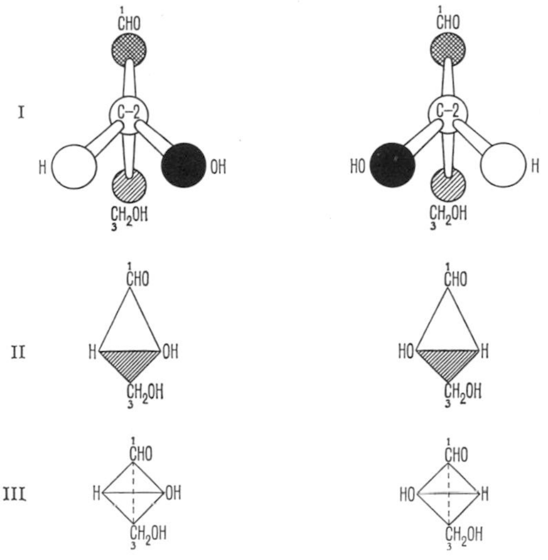

I Atomic models.

II Tetrahedral representation of I. The edge of the tetrahedron joining C-1 and C-3 (imagined to be in or below the plane of the paper) is invisible, as is also the asymmetric carbon atom C-2 lying inside the tetrahedron.

III Conventional representation of the tetrahedron. The edge between C-1 and C-3 in the plane of the paper is indicated by a broken line, the other edges (all above the plane of the paper) by full lines.

respectively. The alternative symbols (+) and (−) are now more commonly used*.

In a mixture containing equal amounts of an enantiomorphic pair of isomers the rotations due to the isomers cancel each other out. An optically *inactive* substance of this kind is known as a *racemate* and is indicated by the prefix *dl* or DL*.

A racemate must not be confused with an optically inactive *meso* form. A *meso* form may arise in the case of a molecule possessing more than one asymmetric centre where the configuration is such that there is a plane or centre of symmetry in the molecule as a whole. The various directions of rotation then cancel each other out within the molecule (internal compensation). These racemic and meso forms are illustrated by the cases of tartaric acid and hexahydrohexahydroxybenzene:

Isomers of tartaric acid

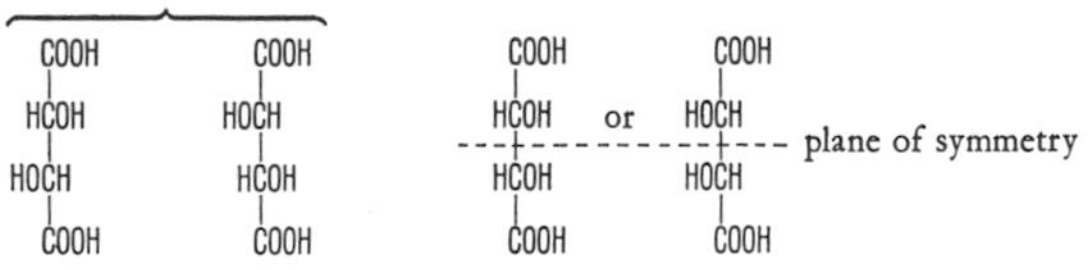

dextro *laevo* *meso*

(mirror-image forms) (identical forms, as can be seen by turning one through 180° in the plane of the paper)

Isomers of hexahydrohexahydroxybenzene (inositol)

meso forms**:

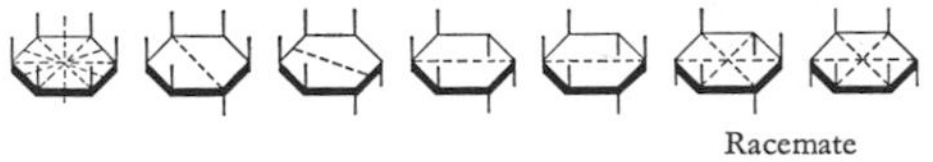

Racemate

Optically active enantiomorphs:

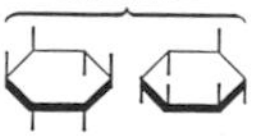

(The vertical lines indicate the positions of the OH groups, the broken lines the planes of symmetry.)

* The use of the letters *d* and *l* to denote optical rotation is now discouraged in favour of *dextro* and *laevo*, or better (+) and (−). DL is likewise preferred for racemates.

** Although all structures are *meso* forms and optically inactive, the name mesoinositol is confined to the fifth compound from the left.

Meso forms do not occur in the case of sugars since the carbonyl group on one side of the ring renders meso-symmetry impossible.

The classification of carbohydrate molecules is based on their relationship to the simplest optically active sugar, glyceraldehyde, to which ROSANOFF[3] arbitrarily assigned the following configurations:

Projection formulae (FISCHER)

Dextrorotatory glyceraldehyde Laevorotatory glyceraldehyde

(With the carbonyl group at the top, the hydroxyl group is written on the right of the asymmetric carbon atom in the case of the dextrorotatory compound, and on the left in the case of the laevorotatory compound.)

Sugars with longer carbon chains can be considered to be derived from dextro- or laevorotatory glyceraldehyde by the successive addition of secondary alcohol groups (–CHOH) to the carbonyl carbon. With each additional asymmetric centre the number of possible isomers is increased, while the optical rotation relative to the parent substance can increase or decrease or even be reversed in sign. To designate the direction of rotation of a sugar as *d* or *l* therefore in no way indicates whether it is derived from dextro- or laevorotatory glyceraldehyde. The designations D and L, introduced by ROSANOFF, make clear this genetic relationship. According to this usage, all sugars (and related substances such as tartaric acid) are assigned to the D-series, irrespective of their direction of rotation, if the secondary alcohol group (–CHOH) furthest from the principal function (i.e., the aldehydo, keto, carbonyl group, etc.) possesses the same spatial configuration as that of dextrorotatory glyceraldehyde. They are assigned to the L-series if this group has the configuration of laevorotatory glyceraldehyde. This arbitrary configuration has been found to correspond absolutely with the true configuration in the case of tartaric acid, the absolute structure of which has been determined by BIJVOET[4] by physical methods.

With a few exceptions, all naturally occurring sugars belong to the D-series. The D-series of aldoses and ketoses with a carbon chain length up to 6 are shown in Figures 2 and 3.

The D- or L-designation thus gives no indication of the direction of rotation of a substance, and if it is desired to show this the appropriate prefix is added, e.g., D-(+)-glyceraldehyde, D-(−)-erythrose. In the case of tartaric acid, the dextrorotatory form belongs to the L-series, the laevorotatory form to the D-series, so that they are designated L-(+)-tartaric acid and D-(−)-tartaric acid respectively. L-isomers are enantiomorphs of D-isomers, with opposite rotations, so that a DL-substance is a racemate.

On ring closure of a straight-chain carbohydrate molecule a secondary alcohol group is formed from the original carbonyl group, thus introducing an additional asymmetric centre. The two stereoisomers of a cyclic sugar molecule arising in this way are denoted by the symbols α and β (after HUDSON[5]), the designation α being given to the isomer in the D-series that is more strongly *dextro*rotatory and to the isomer in the L-series that is more strongly *laevo*rotatory. In the FISCHER projection formula the OH group is again arbitrarily written on the right of the asymmetric carbon atom in the case of the more strongly dextrorotatory isomers (α-D- or β-L-configuration) and on the left in the case of the more strongly laevorotatory isomers (β-D- or α-L-configuration):

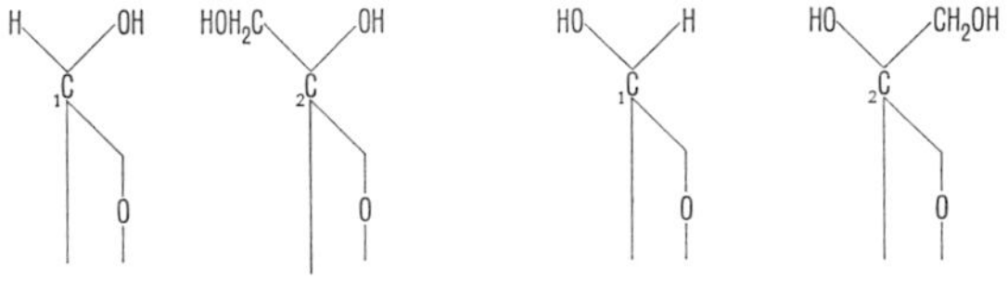

Aldose Ketose Aldose Ketose

α-D or β-L β-D or α-L

The α- and β-isomers yield corresponding α- and β-glycosides. This is of importance insofar as many glycoside hydrolases have been found to be α- or β-specific in their action.

The representation of cyclic sugars by the FISCHER projection convention is best illustrated by the example of D-glucose:

(For references see page 312)

Fig. 2 Configurational relationships of the D-aldo-sugars

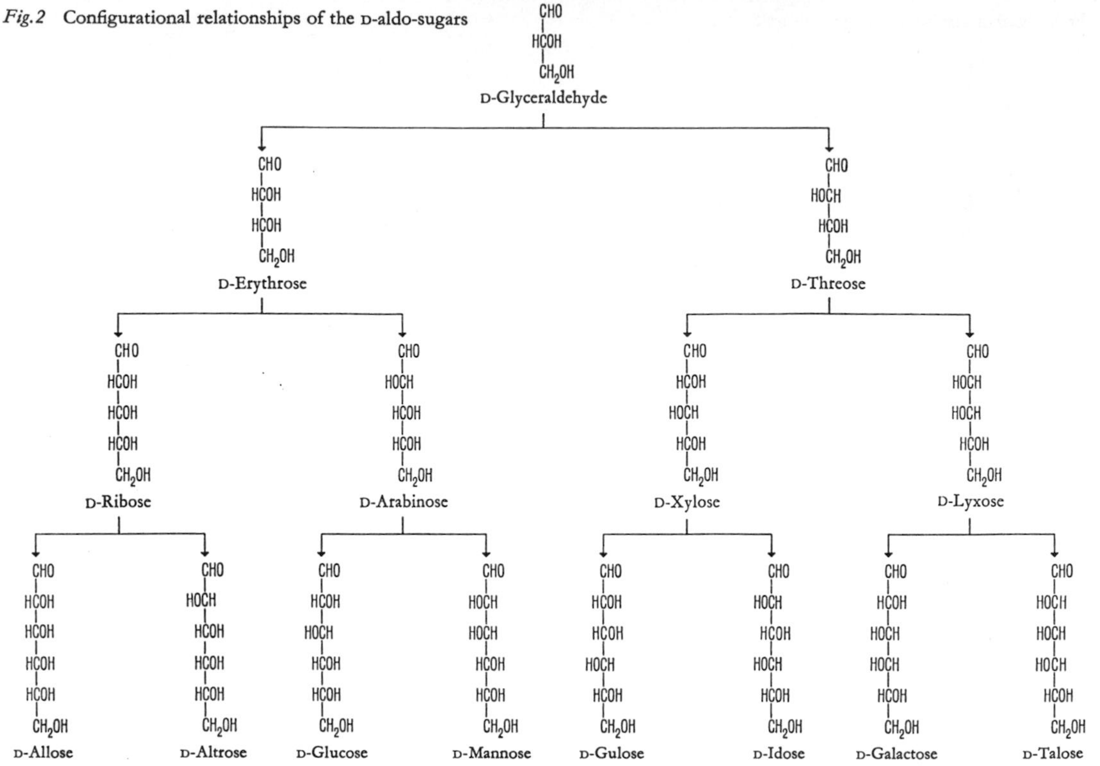

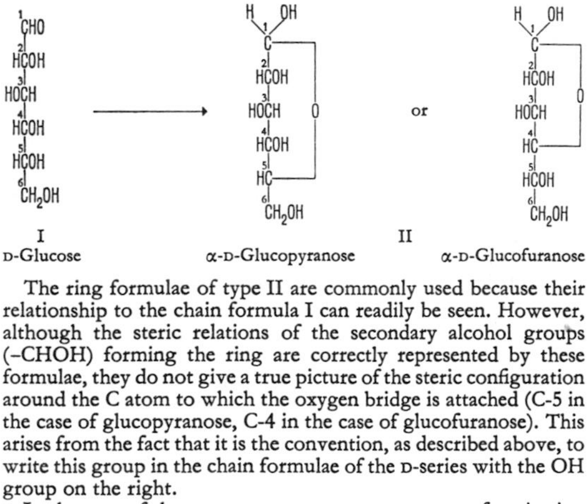

The ring formulae of type II are commonly used because their relationship to the chain formula I can readily be seen. However, although the steric relations of the secondary alcohol groups (–CHOH) forming the ring are correctly represented by these formulae, they do not give a true picture of the steric configuration around the C atom to which the oxygen bridge is attached (C-5 in the case of glucopyranose, C-4 in the case of glucofuranose). This arises from the fact that it is the convention, as described above, to write this group in the chain formulae of the D-series with the OH group on the right.

In the case of the pyranoses, a more correct type of projection formula is that illustrated by III and IV for glucose (derived by imagining the bond between C-4 and C-5 to be rotated through 180° before ring closure):

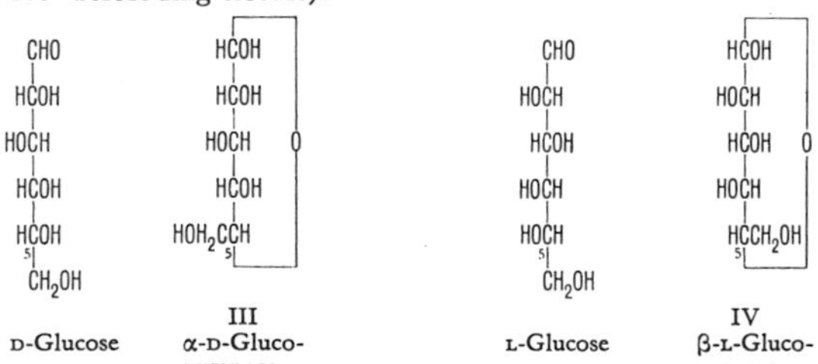

In formulae III and IV, however, the D- and L-configurations respectively of the OH group attached to C-5 are no longer readily recognizable. These defects of the FISCHER projection formulae led HAWORTH to introduce a type of ring formula in which the steric relations of the groups are shown unequivocally. The ring is imagined as being looked at obliquely from above, the three thickened edges being those nearest to the observer:

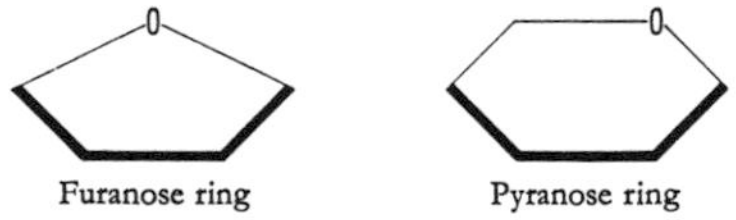

The positions of the substituents correspond to those in formulae of type III and IV:

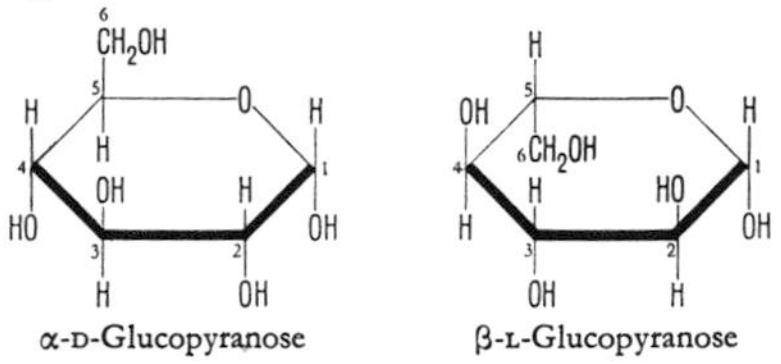

In the case of the furanose forms of hexoses, ring closure results in the formation of a side chain. When, as in the case of glucofuranose, this side chain contains an asymmetric carbon atom, its configuration in the HAWORTH formula must be shown by means of an appropriate convention. The derivation from the projection formula is best illustrated by the example of α-D-glucofuranose:

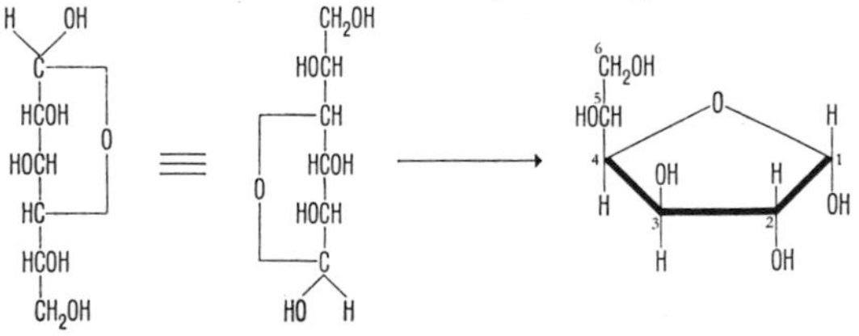

For convenience in writing the formulae of polysaccharides and other complex sugar compounds, the HAWORTH rings are some-

(For references see page 312)

Fig. 3 Configurational relationships of the D-keto-sugars

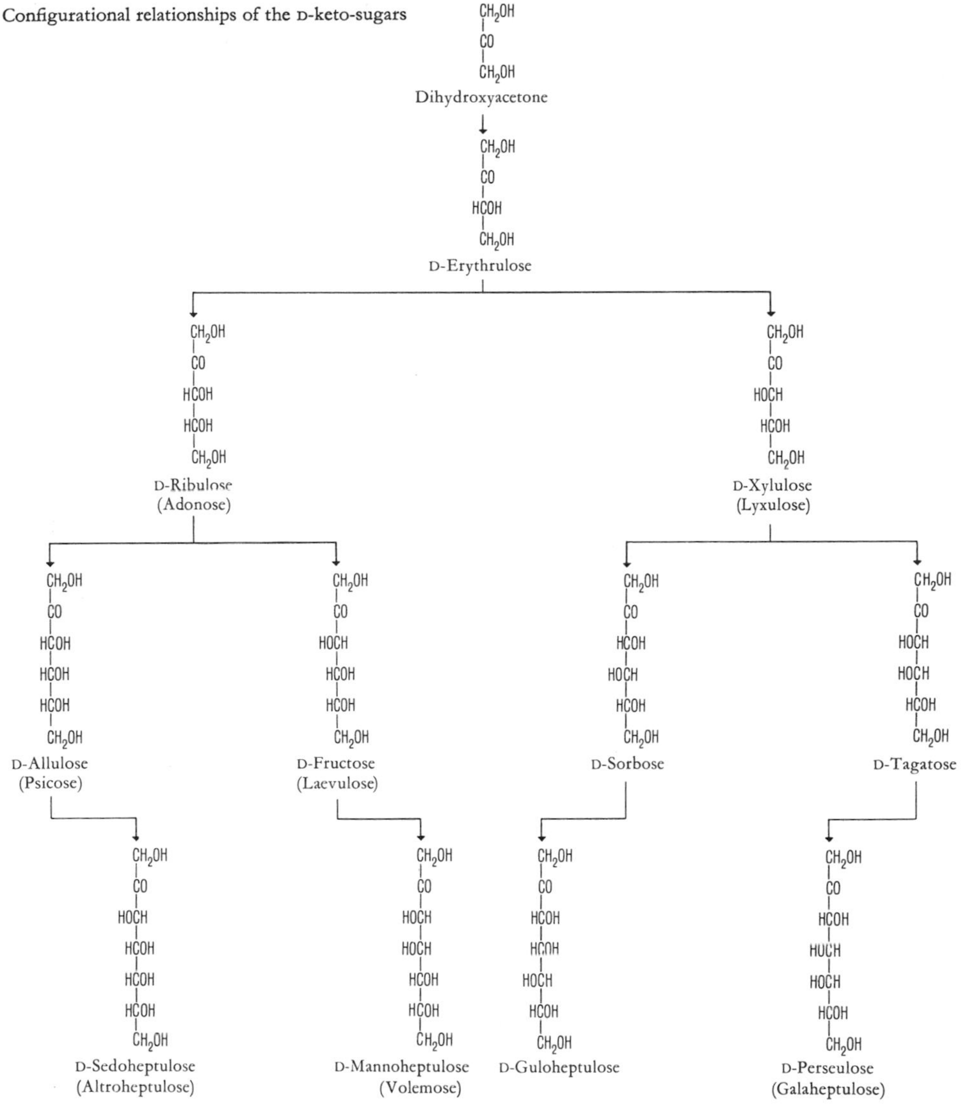

times written upside down or back to front with respect to the examples shown above, i.e., in the positions obtained by rotating the ring through 180° about two axes in the plane of the ring or about an axis passing vertically through the centre of it. The alternative positions for α-D-glucopyranose are as follows:

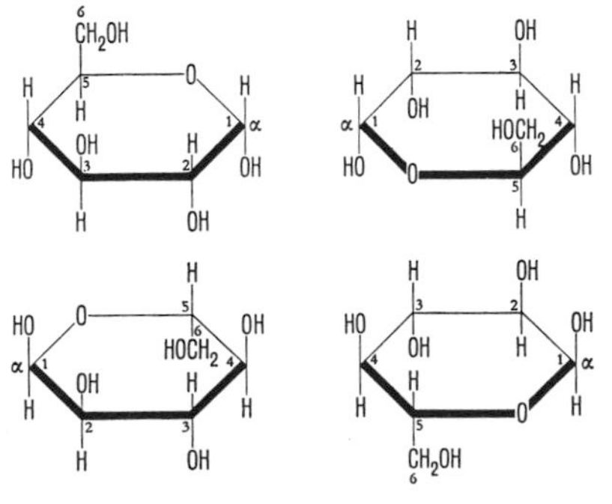

It is now known that the pyranose ring is not planar, and most of its properties can be explained on the assumption that it has the 'chair' form. The furanose ring is usually planar. For further details of the conformational analysis see the literature[6].

Amino sugars[7]

Amino sugars are components of polysaccharides (see below), for example structural polysaccharides[18], mucopolysaccharides, bacterial capsular polysaccharides, teichoic acids, glycolipids, glycoproteins. Until recently, glucosamine, galactosamine and the sialic acids were the only known naturally occurring amino sugars (see Table 1, pages 313–316), but in the last few years several others, for instance muramic acid, mannosamine, talosamine and fucosamine, have been found in the polysaccharides of bacterial cells. Further 'novel' amino sugars have been isolated as components of antibiotics[8].

The sialic acids, which are mucopolysaccharides containing N-acylated neuraminic acid, are found in glandular secretions, blood serum and as constituents of cell surfaces. They provide the groupings that attract and bind influenza virus particles to the surface of host cells as a preliminary to infection[9].

Sugar phosphates[10]

Phosphorylated sugars are intermediates in glycolysis; they are components of nucleic acids, nucleotides and polysaccharides[11] (see Table 2, pages 317–321).

The stability of phosphate groups toward acid or alkaline hydrolysis varies over a wide range[12] and, as yet, detailed correlation between the rates of hydrolysis and the position of the groups has not been made. Under conditions of acid or alkaline hydrolysis, migration of the phosphate group may occur, e.g., in the case of the phosphoglyceric acids[13].

Polyhydric alcohols[14]

These compounds, which may be considered as reduction products of the monosaccharides, are of wide occurrence in plants but of limited occurrence in mammalian tissue. They are mostly crystalline compounds, generally possessing a sweet taste and devoid of any reducing properties. Those of importance to mammals are listed in Table 3 (page 322).

Primary oxidation products of carbohydrates

The nomenclature of the products of the oxidation of the terminal groups of aldoses is derived as follows:

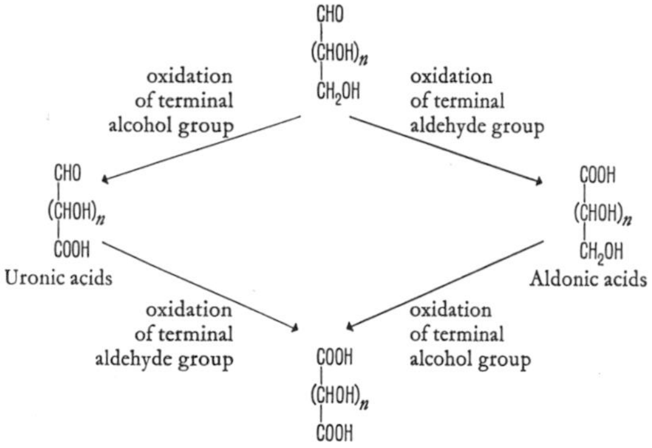

Saccharic acids (aric acids)

Oxidation products of carbohydrates of importance to mammals are listed in Table 4 (page 323).

Oligosaccharides

Oligosaccharides are composed of monosaccharide molecules or their derivatives linked together through glycosidic linkages. The linkages may be glycosidic on one side only or on both sides. In the nomenclature of oligosaccharides, the sugar units in compounds of the former type are given the suffixes '-osido' and '-ose', while those in the latter type are indicated by '-osido' and '-oside'. This is illustrated by the following scheme:

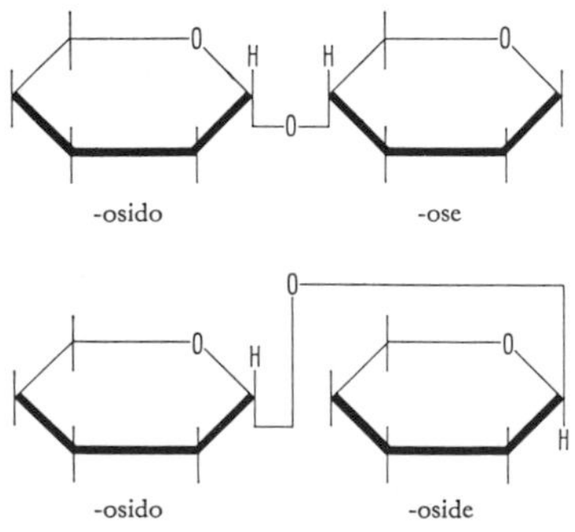

The term oligosaccharide is generally used to designate compounds containing between two and ten monosaccharide units per molecule. Oligosaccharides may be reducing or nonreducing, depending on the presence or absence of free hemiacetal hydroxyl groups. The constituent monosaccharides are set free from an oligosaccharide by acid or enzymic hydrolysis.

The principal oligosaccharides of importance to mammals are given in Table 5 (page 324). A great variety of oligosaccharides is encountered in the plant kingdom.

Polysaccharides[15]

Polysaccharides, like oligosaccharides, are built up from a variety of monosaccharide units and their derivatives. They differ from oligosaccharides in that their molecules contain from ten up to several thousand monosaccharide units. The most commonly occurring constituent is D-glucose. However, D-mannose, D- and L-galactose, D-xylose, L-arabinose, uronic acids (D-glucuronic, D-galacturonic and D-mannuronic acids), amino sugars (D-glucosamine, D-galactosamine, their N-acetyl derivatives and sulphate esters) are also found. In contrast with the oligosaccharides many of the polysaccharides are insoluble and nonreducing.

Their structure has been investigated by chemical methods[15], e.g., by methylation and subsequent hydrolysis, by periodate oxidation, and by enzymic methods[16]. The determination of the molecular size of polysaccharides involves physical measurements of properties such as osmotic pressure, behaviour on ultracentrifuging, viscosity and light scattering[17].

Polysaccharides may serve as:

(*a*) structural materials, e.g., cellulose (plants), chitin (insects and crustaceae), chondroitin sulphate (cartilage)[18],
(*b*) food storage, e.g., glycogen (animals), starch (plants),
(*c*) lubricants in synovial fluids, constituents of special tissues (vitreous body of the eye; connective tissue), components of mucus, heparin, blood-group substances[18].

The principal polysaccharides of importance to mammals are listed in Table 6 (pages 325–328).

References

1 For reviews see Gilman et al. (Eds.), *Organic Chemistry: An Advanced Treatise*, vol. 2, 2nd ed., Wiley, New York, 1943, page 1532; Percival, E.G.V., *Structural Carbohydrate Chemistry*, Prentice-Hall, New York, 1950; Pigman, W. (Ed.), *The Carbohydrates*, Academic Press, New York, 1957.
2 Honeyman, J., *An Introduction to the Chemistry of Carbohydrates*, Oxford University Press, Oxford, 1948.
3 Rosanoff, M.A., *J.Amer.chem.Soc.*, **28**, 114 (1906).
4 Bijvoet, J.M., *Endeavour*, **14**, 71 (1955).
5 Hudson, C.S., *Advanc.Carbohyd.Chem.*, **3**, 1 (1948).
6 Mills, J.A., *Advanc.Carbohyd.Chem.*, **10**, 1 (1955); Capon and Overend, *Advanc.Carbohyd.Chem.*, **15**, 11 (1960).
7 Salton, M.R.J., *Ann. Rev.Biochem.*, **34**, 143 (1965); Jeanloz and Balasz, *The Amino Sugars*, vol. 2A, Academic Press, New York, 1965.
8 Dutcher, J.D., *Advanc.Carbohyd.Chem.*, **18**, 259 (1963).
9 Gottschalk, A., *The Chemistry and Biology of Sialic Acids and Related Substances*, Cambridge University Press, Cambridge, 1960.
10 For reviews see Leloir, L.F., in Zechmeister, L. (Ed.), *Progress in the Chemistry of Organic Natural Products*, vol. 8, Springer, Vienna, 1951, page 47; Foster and Overend, *Quart.Rev.chem.Soc.Lond.*, **11**, 61 (1957).
11 For a general account see Avison and Hawkins, *Quart.Rev.chem.Soc.Lond.*, **5**, 171 (1951).
12 See Leloir, L.F., in Zechmeister, L. (Ed.), *Progress in the Chemistry of Organic Natural Products*, vol. 8, Springer, Vienna, 1951, page 47.
13 See Ballou and Fischer, *J.Amer.chem.Soc.*, **76**, 3188 (1954).
14 For a review see Lohmar, R.L., in Pigman, W. (Ed.), *The Carbohydrates*, Academic Press, New York, 1957, page 241; Touster and Shaw, *Physiol. Rev.*, **42**, 181 (1962).
15 For reviews see Stacey and Barker, *Polysaccharides of Micro-Organisms*, Oxford University Press, Oxford, 1960; Stacey and Barker, *Carbohydrates of Living Tissues*, Van Nostrand, London, 1962; Manners, D.J., *Advanc. Carbohyd.Chem.*, **12**, 261 (1957); Bouveng and Lindberg, *Advanc.Carbohyd. Chem.*, **15**, 53 (1960); Aspinall, G.O., *Ann.Rev.Biochem.*, **31**, 79 (1962).
16 Manners, D.J., *Quart.Rev.chem.Soc.Lond.*, **9**, 73 (1955); Manners, D.J., *Advanc.Carbohyd.Chem.*, **17**, 371 (1962).
17 Greenwood, C.T., *Advanc.Carbohyd.Chem.*, **7**, 289 (1952).
18 Cf. Kent and Whitehouse, *Biochemistry of the Aminosugars*, Butterworth, London, 1955; *Biochem.Soc.Symp.*, No. 20 (1961); Baschang, G., in Zechmeister, L. (Ed.), *Progress in the Chemistry of Organic Natural Products*, vol. 20, Springer, Vienna, 1962, page 200.

Table 1 Monosaccharides of importance to mammals

Some of the more important sugars that are constituents of substances of medical interest are also included in this table.

Name	Formula and mol. wt.	Structure	Specific rotation	Occurrence
		Trioses		
D-Glyceraldehyde (2,3-dihydroxy-propanal)	$C_3H_6O_3$ 90.08	CHO HCOH CH_2OH	$[\alpha]_D^{20}$ + 13.5°	As phosphate ester (see Table 2, page 317)
s-Dihydroxyacetone (1,3-dihydroxy-propan-2-one)	$C_3H_6O_3$ 90.08	CH_2OH CO CH_2OH or CH_2OH C(OH) CHOH	Inactive	As phosphate ester (see Table 2, page 317)
		Tetroses		
D-Erythrose	$C_4H_8O_4$ 120.11	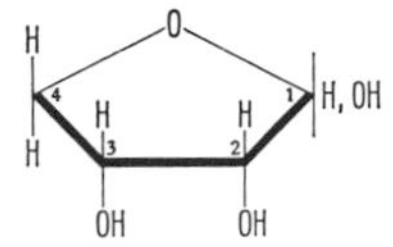	$[\alpha]_D^{20}$ – 14.8°	As phosphate ester (see Table 2, page 317)
L-Erythrulose	$C_4H_8O_4$ 120.11	CH_2OH CO HOCH CH_2OH	$[\alpha]_D^{20}$ + 12°	As metabolically active phosphate ester (see Table 2, page 317)
2-Deoxy-D-ribose (2-deoxy-D-*erythro*pentose, thyminose, deoxyarabinose)	$C_5H_{10}O_4$ 134.13	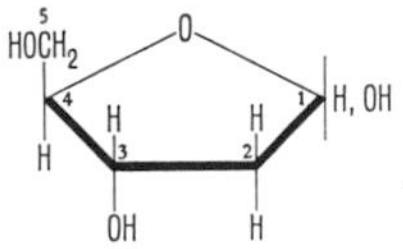	$[\alpha]_D^{25}$ – 50°	Universal occurrence as constituent of nucleosides, nucleotides and nucleic acids. For phosphates see Table 2, page 318
D-Digitoxose (2-deoxy-D-*altro*methylose)	$C_6H_{12}O_4$ 148.16	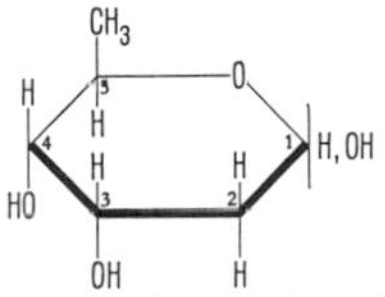	$[\alpha]_D^{20}$ + 46.5°	Component of digitalis glycosides
		Pentoses		
β-D-Arabinose	$C_5H_{10}O_5$ 150.13	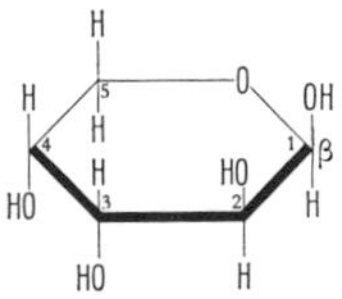	$[\alpha]_D^{20}$ – 105°	In glycosides of aloe and tubercle bacilli
L-Fucose (6-deoxy-L-galactose)	$C_6H_{12}O_5$ 164.16	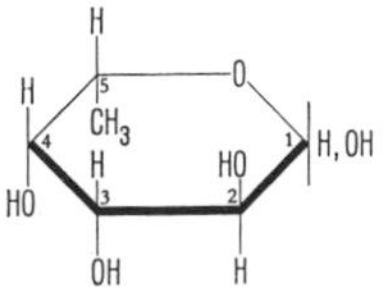	$[\alpha]_D^{20}$ – 153° → + 76°	Component of polysaccharides of human milk, blood-group substances, marine algae, gum tragacanth (see Table 5, page 324)
L-Rhamnose (6-deoxy-L-mannose, *iso*dulcitol)	$C_6H_{12}O_5$ 164.16	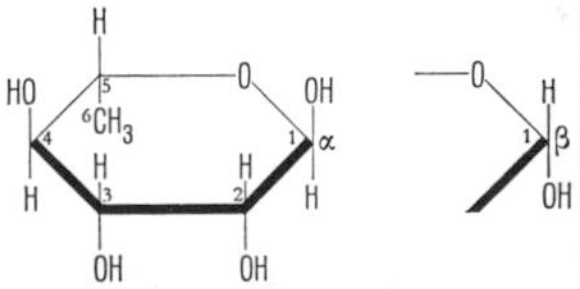	α-form, 1 H_2O: $[\alpha]_D^{20}$ – 9° β-form: $[\alpha]_D^{20}$ + 38°	As glycoside in plant pigments, gums and mucilages. Common component of cardiac glycosides

Table 1 (continued) Monosaccharides of importance to mammals

Name*	Formula and mol. wt.	Structure	Specific rotation	Occurrence
D-Ribose (Rib) (D-ribofuranose)	$C_5H_{10}O_5$ 150.13	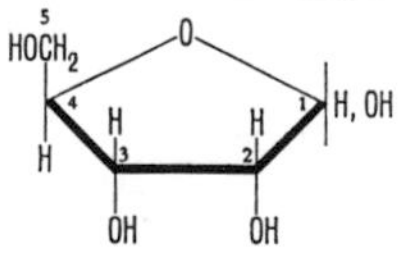	$[\alpha]_D^{20}$ − 23.7° (4% soln.)	Universal occurrence as constituent of nucleosides, nucleotides and nucleic acids. For phosphates see Table 2, pages 317–318
D-Ribulose (D-*erythro*pentulose, D-adonose, D-arabulose)	$C_5H_{10}O_5$ 150.13	CH_2OH CO HCOH HCOH CH_2OH	–	As phosphate esters (see Table 2, page 318). Intermediary metabolite in glucose oxidation
D-Xylulose (D-*threo*pentulose, D-xyloketose, D-lyxulose, D-lyxoketose)	$C_5H_{10}O_5$ 150.13	CH_2OH CO HOCH HCOH CH_2OH	$[\alpha]_D^{20}$ − 33°	As phosphate ester (see Table 2, page 318)
L-Xylulose (L-*threo*pentulose, L-xyloketose, L-lyxulose, L-lyxoketose)	$C_5H_{10}O_5$ 150.13	CH_2OH CO HCOH HOCH CH_2OH	$[\alpha]_D^{20}$ + 33°	In urine in pentosuria
		Hexoses		
D-Fructose (Fru) (2-keto-D-arabohexose, laevulose, fruit sugar)	$C_6H_{12}O_6$ 180.16	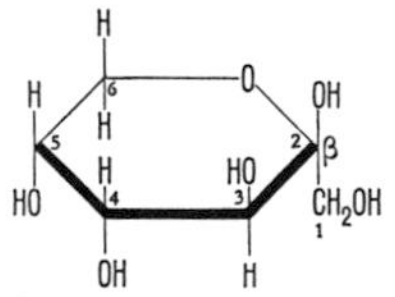 β-D-Fructopyranose 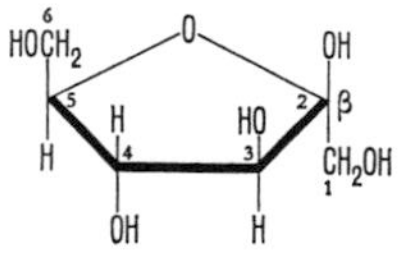 β-D-Fructofuranose	β-form: $[\alpha]_D^{20}$ − 133.5° → − 92°	As phosphate esters (see Table 2, pages 318–319). Component of many polysaccharides (combined with glucose in sucrose). Has pyranose form when crystalline but furanose form in all natural products. Sweetest of all known sugars
D-Galactose (Gal) (cerebrose, brain sugar)	$C_6H_{12}O_6$ 180.16	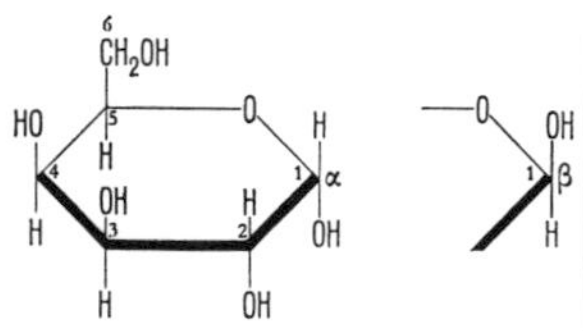	α-form: $[\alpha]_D^{20}$ + 144° → + 80.5° β-form: $[\alpha]_D^{20}$ + 54° → + 80.5°	Present in mammalian tissues as phosphate ester (see Table 2, page 319). Component of cerebrosides and gangliosides, and of polysaccharides both as sugar and derived amino sugar (e.g., lactose, raffinose, stachyose)
D-Galactosamine (GalN) (D-chondrosamine, 2-amino-2-deoxy-D-galactose)	$C_6H_{13}NO_5$ 179.17	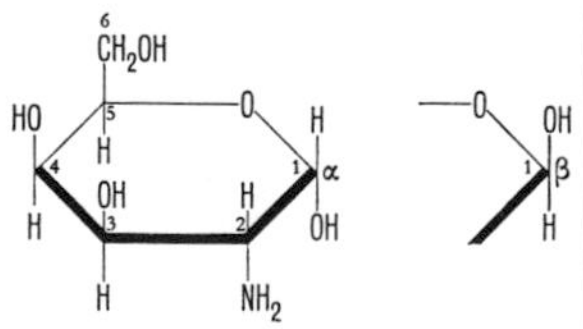	α-form, 1 HCl: $[\alpha]_D^{20}$ + 135° → + 93° β-form, 1 HCl: $[\alpha]_D^{20}$ + 39° → + 93°	Widely distributed in nature as component of hyaluronic acid, mucopolysaccharides, cartilage, tendons (chondroitin), β-heparin, lipoids, cerebral gangliosides, blood-group substances, glycoproteins (see Table 6, pages 326–328)

* The three-letter symbols are those recommended by the Combined Commission on Biochemical Nomenclature of the International Union of Pure and Applied Chemistry and the International Union of Biochemistry (*J. biol. Chem.*, **241**, 527 [1966]).

Table 1 (continued) Monosaccharides of importance to mammals

Name*	Formula and mol. wt.	Structure	Specific rotation	Occurrence
N-Acetyl-D-galactosamine	$C_8H_{15}NO_6$ 221.21	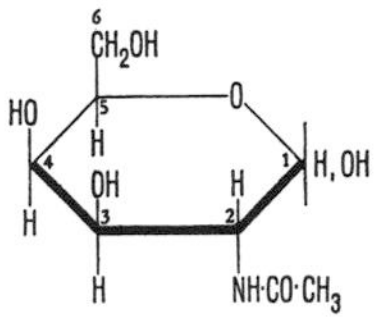	$[\alpha]_D^{20}$ + 115 ° → + 80 °	Form in which D-galactosamine (page 314) occurs as component of hyaluronic acid, etc.
D-Glucose (Glc, G) (dextrose, blood sugar, grape sugar, corn sugar)	$C_6H_{12}O_6$ 180.16	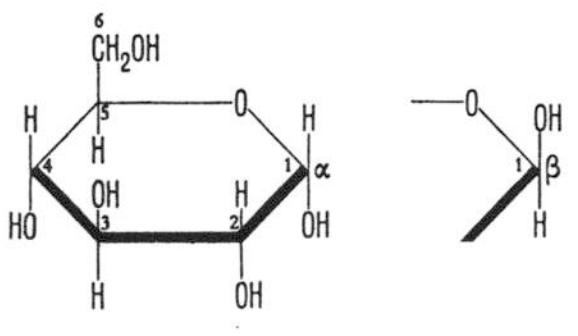	α-form: $[\alpha]_D^{20}$ + 113.4 ° → + 52.5 ° β-form: $[\alpha]_D^{20}$ + 19.3 ° → + 52.5 °	As phosphate esters (see Table 2, page 319). Most widely distributed of all sugars. Found free in many biological fluids, e.g., blood, lymph, cerebrospinal fluid. Component of polysaccharides both as sugar and amino sugar (see 'D-Glucosamine', below)
D-Glucosamine (GlcN) (chitosamine, 2-amino-2-deoxy-D-glucose)	$C_6H_{13}NO_5$ 179.17	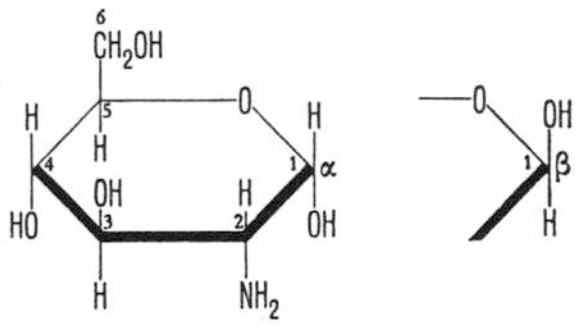	α-form: $[\alpha]_D^{20}$ + 100 ° → + 47.5 ° β-form $[\alpha]_D^{20}$ + 14 ° → + 47.5 °	Component of chitin, heparin, glycoproteins, blood-group polysaccharides, oligosaccharides of human milk, etc. (see Table 6, pages 325–328)
N-Acetyl-D-glucosamine	$C_8H_{15}NO_6$ 221.21	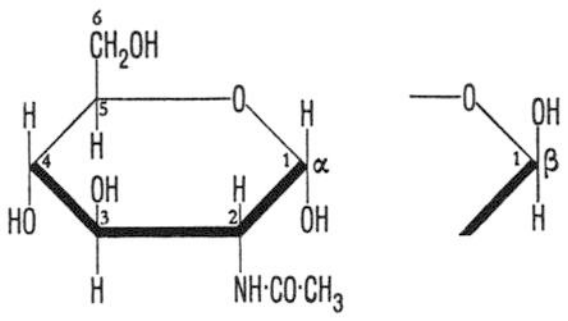	–	Form in which D-glucosamine occurs as component of chitin, etc.
3-*O*-Carbethoxyglucosamine (muramic acid)	$C_9H_{17}NO_7$ 251.24	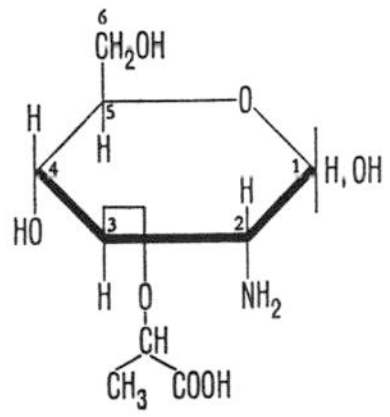	$[\alpha]_D^{20}$ + 109 ° (water)	Component of bacterial cell walls[1]
N-Methyl-L-glucosamine	$C_7H_{15}NO_5$ 193.20	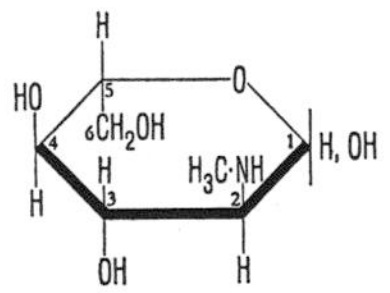	–	Component of streptomycin
D-Mannose (Man) (seminose)	$C_6H_{12}O_6$ 180.16	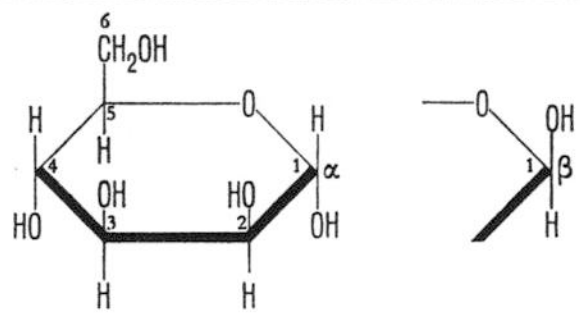	α-form: $[\alpha]_D^{20}$ + 29.9 ° → + 14.5 ° β-form: $[\alpha]_D^{20}$ − 16.3 ° → + 14.5 °	As phosphate ester (see Table 2, page 320). Widely distributed as component of mannans and hemicelluloses. Limited occurrence as component of glycoproteins

* See footnote, page 314.

[1] Rogers, H. J., *Biochem. Soc. Symp.*, No. 22, 55 (1963).

Table 1 (concluded) Monosaccharides of importance to mammals

Name	Formula and mol. wt.	Structure	Specific rotation	Occurrence
N-Acetyl-D-mannosamine	$C_8H_{15}NO_6$ 221.21	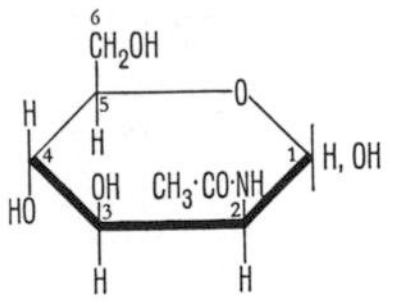	$[\alpha]_D^{20}$ − 9.4° → + 9.7°	Intermediate in biosynthesis of *N*-acetylneuraminic acid
		Heptose		
D-Sedoheptulose (D-*altro*ketoheptose, D-*altro*heptulose)	$C_7H_{14}O_7$ 210.19	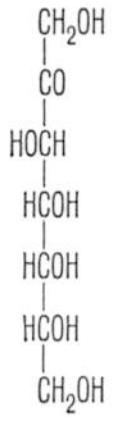	$[\alpha]_D^{20}$ + 2–3° Ba salt: $[\alpha]_{5461}^{20}$ + 8°	As phosphate esters (see Table 2, page 321)
		Nonoses		
N-Acetylneuraminic acid	$C_{11}H_{19}NO_9$ 309.28	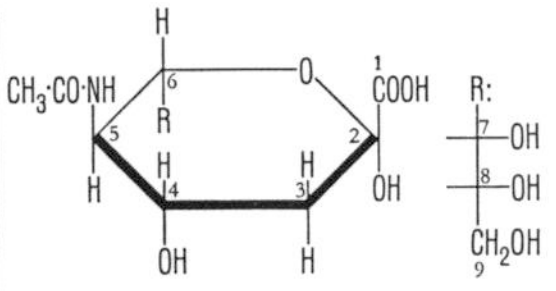	$[\alpha]_D^{22}$ − 32° No mutarotation	Component of mucins of epithelial secretions (e.g., digestive and urinary tracts), serum glycoproteins, milk oligosaccharides, brain gangliosides, erythrocyte stroma, bacterial cell walls
N-Glycolylneuraminic acid	$C_{11}H_{19}NO_{10}$ 325.27	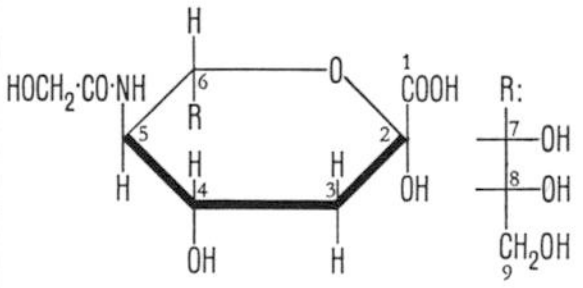	$[\alpha]_D^{22}$ − 32°	Component of mucins of epithelial secretions, serum glycoproteins, erythrocyte stroma. Often in the same molecule as *N*-acetylneuraminic acid
5-*N*,4-*O*-Diacetylneuraminic acid	$C_{13}H_{21}NO_{10}$ 351.31	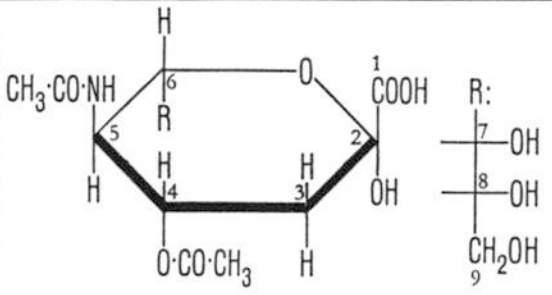	$[\alpha]_D^{22}$ − 61° No mutarotation	Equine submaxillary mucin
5-*N*,7-*O*-Diacetylneuraminic acid	$C_{13}H_{21}NO_{10}$ 351.31	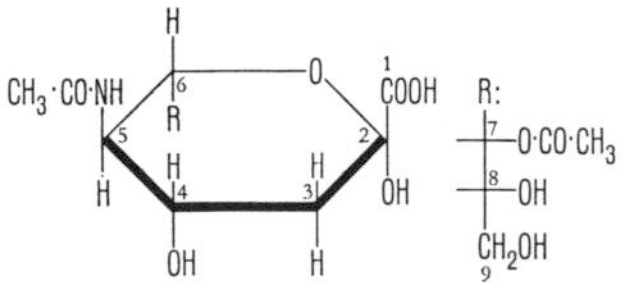	$[\alpha]_D^{22}$ + 8° After 400 h − 17°	Bovine submaxillary mucin
5-*N*-Acetyl,*O*-diacetylneuraminic acid	$C_{15}H_{23}NO_{11}$ 393.35	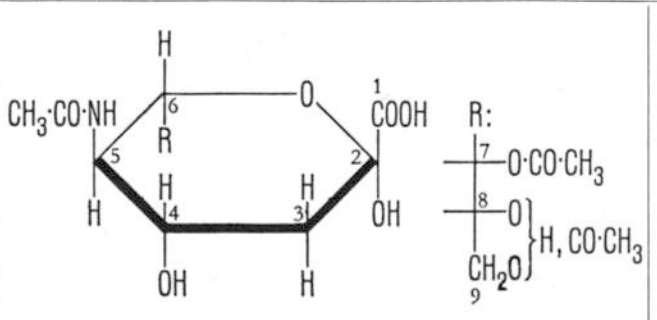	$[\alpha]_D^{22}$ + 9°	Bovine submaxillary mucin

Table 2 Sugar phosphates of importance to mammals
(Not including nucleotides, for which see Tables 10c, 11 and 12, pages 342–350)

Name	Formula and mol. wt.	Structure	Elementary composition C	H	P	Specific rotation	Biological function	Reference (see page 321)
Dihydroxyacetone phosphate	$C_3H_7O_6P$ 170.06	CH_2OH – CO – $CH_2OPO_3H_2$	21.19	4.15	18.21	–	Intermediate of glycolysis	1
D-Glyceraldehyde 3-phosphate ('FISCHER-BAER ester')	$C_3H_7O_6P$ 170.06	CHO – HCOH – $CH_2OPO_3H_2$	21.19	4.15	18.21	$[\alpha]_D^{20}$ + 14°	Intermediate of glycolysis	2
L-Glycerol 1-phosphate	$C_3H_9O_6P$ 172.08	$CH_2OPO_3H_2$ – HOCH – CH_2OH	20.94	5.27	18.00	$[\alpha]_D^{20}$ – 1.45° (Ba salt)	Intermediate of fat metabolism. Component of phospholipids	3
D-Glyceric acid 2-phosphate ('KIESSLING ester')	$C_3H_7O_7P$ 186.06	COOH – $HCOPO_3H_2$ – CH_2OH	19.37	3.79	16.65	$[\alpha]_D^{20}$ + 13° (1-N HCl) $[\alpha]_D^{22}$ + 3.6° (water)	Intermediate of glycolysis	4
D-Glyceric acid 3-phosphate	$C_3H_7O_7P$ 186.06	COOH – HCOH – $CH_2OPO_3H_2$	19.37	3.79	16.65	$[\alpha]_D^{20}$ – 14.5° (1-N HCl)	Intermediate of glycolysis	5
D-Glyceric acid 1,3-diphosphate	$C_3H_8O_{10}P_2$ 266.04	$COOPO_3H_2$ – HCOH – $CH_2OPO_3H_2$	13.54	3.03	23.29	$[\alpha]_D^{20}$ – 2.3°	Intermediate of glycolysis	6
D-Glyceric acid 2,3-diphosphate	$C_3H_8O_{10}P_2$ 266.04	COOH – $HCOPO_3H_2$ – $CH_2OPO_3H_2$	13.54	3.03	23.29	$[\alpha]_D^{20}$ – 2.3°	Intermediate of glycolysis	7
Pyruvic acid enol phosphate (phosphopyruvic acid)	$C_3H_5O_6P$ 168.04	COOH – $COPO_3H_2$ = CH_2	21.44	3.00	18.43	–	Intermediate of glycolysis	8
D-Erythrose 4-phosphate	$C_4H_9O_7P$ 200.09	CHO – HCOH – HCOH – $CH_2OPO_3H_2$	24.01	4.53	15.48	–	Intermediate of pentose phosphate cycle	9
L-Erythrulose 1-phosphate	$C_4H_9O_7P$ 200.09	$CH_2OPO_3H_2$ – CO – HOCH – CH_2OH	24.01	4.53	15.48	–	Function not known	10
α-D-Ribose 1-phosphate (furanose form)	$C_5H_{11}O_8P$ 230.11	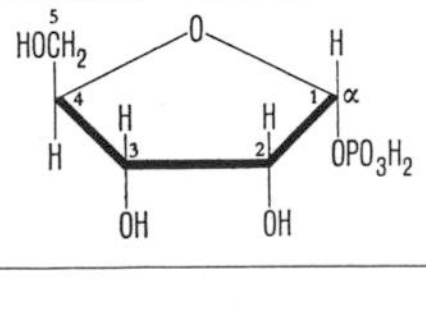	26.10	4.82	13.46	–	Intermediate of nucleotide metabolism	11

Table 2 (continued) Sugar phosphates of importance to mammals

Name	Formula and mol. wt.	Structure	Elementary composition C	Elementary composition H	Elementary composition P	Specific rotation	Biological function	Reference (see page 321)
D-Ribose 5-phosphate (furanose form)	$C_5H_{11}O_8P$ 230.11	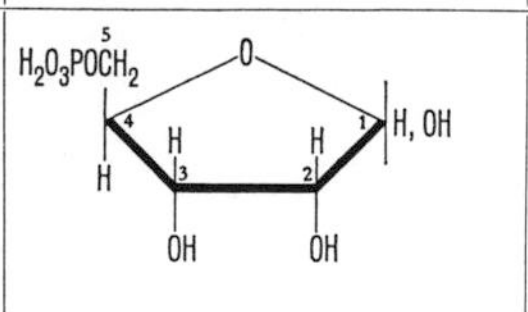	26.10	4.82	13.46	$[\alpha]_D^{20}$ + 16.5°	Intermediate of pentose phosphate cycle and nucleotide synthesis	12
D-Ribose 1,5-diphosphate (furanose form)	$C_5H_{12}O_{11}P_2$ 310.09	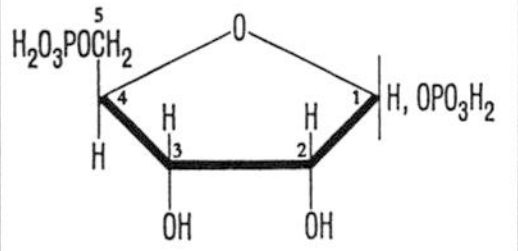	19.37	3.90	19.98	–	Intermediate of interconversion of ribose 1-phosphate and ribose 5-phosphate	13
D-Ribose 5-phosphate-1-pyrophosphate (5-phosphoribosyl-1-pyrophosphate)	$C_5H_{13}O_{14}P_3$ 390.07	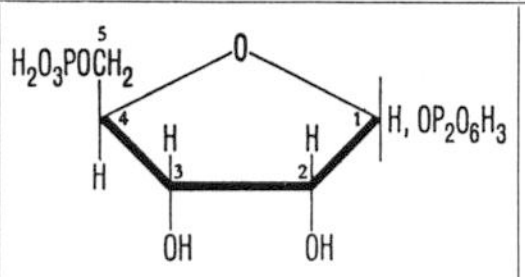	15.40	3.36	23.82	–	Intermediate of nucleotide synthesis	14
Deoxyribose 1-phosphate (furanose form)	$C_5H_{11}O_7P$ 214.11	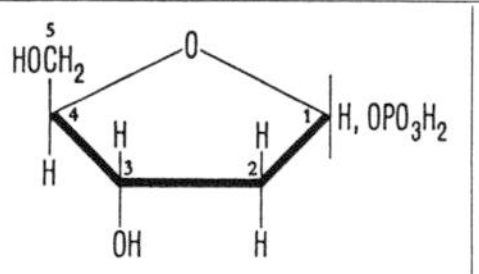	28.05	5.18	14.47	–	Product of nucleoside degradation	15
Deoxyribose 5-phosphate (furanose form)	$C_5H_{11}O_7P$ 214.11	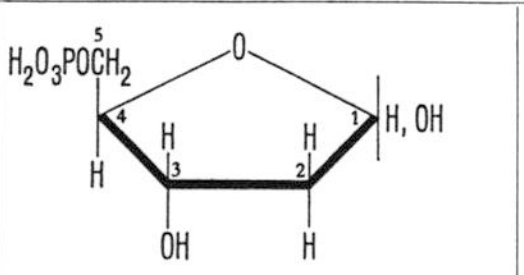	28.05	5.18	14.47	–	Component of deoxynucleic acids and deoxynucleotides	16
D-Ribulose 5-phosphate	$C_5H_{11}O_8P$ 230.11	CH_2OH CO HCOH HCOH $CH_2OPO_3H_2$	26.10	4.82	13.46	$[\alpha]_D^{20}$ – 40°	Intermediate of pentose phosphate cycle	17
D-Xylulose 5-phosphate	$C_5H_{11}O_8P$ 230.11	CH_2OH CO HOCH HCOH $CH_2OPO_3H_2$	26.10	4.82	13.46	–	Intermediate of pentose phosphate cycle	18
D-Fructose 1-phosphate (pyranose form) ('ROBISON-TANKO ester')	$C_6H_{13}O_9P$ 260.14	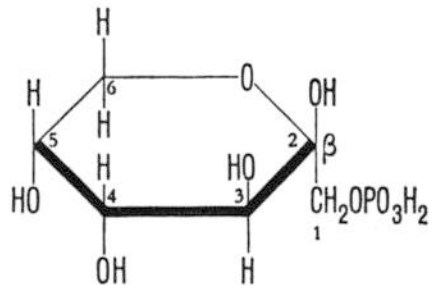	27.70	5.04	11.91	$[\alpha]_D^{26}$ – 30.4°	Intermediate of glycolysis	19

Table 2 (continued) Sugar phosphates of importance to mammals

Name	Formula and mol. wt.	Structure	Elementary composition			Specific rotation	Biological function	Reference (see page 321)
			C	H	P			
D-Fructose 6-phosphate (furanose form) ('NEUBERG ester')	$C_6H_{13}O_9P$ 260.14	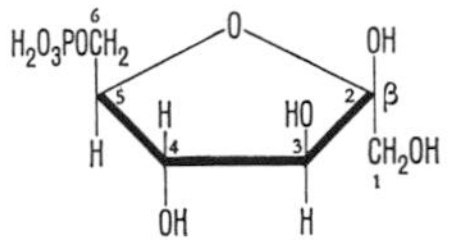	27.70	5.04	11.91	$[\alpha]_D^{19}$ + 3.58° (Ba salt)	Intermediate of glycolysis	20
D-Fructose 1,6-diphosphate (furanose form) ('HARDEN-YOUNG ester')	$C_6H_{14}O_{12}P_2$ 340.12	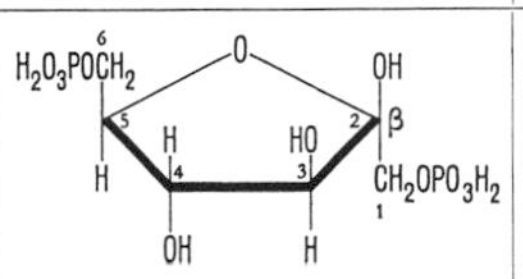	21.19	4.15	18.21	$[\alpha]_D^{17}$ + 4.1°	Intermediate of glycolysis	21
α-D-Galactose 1-phosphate (pyranose form)	$C_6H_{13}O_9P$ 260.14	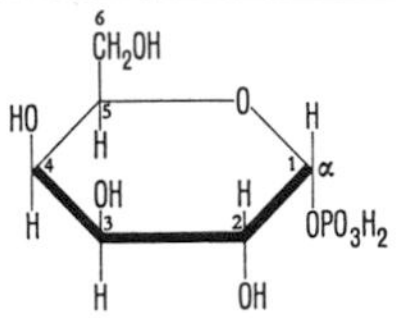	27.70	5.04	11.91	$[\alpha]_D^{18}$ + 148.5°	Intermediate of galactose metabolism	22
D-Galactosamine 1-phosphate	$C_6H_{14}NO_8P$ 259.15	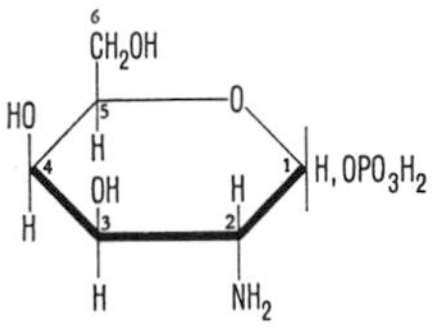	27.81	5.45	11.95	–	Formed from galactosamine in brain tissue extracts and *Saccharomyces fragilis*	23
α-D-Glucose 1-phosphate (pyranose form) ('CORI ester')	$C_6H_{13}O_9P$ 260.14	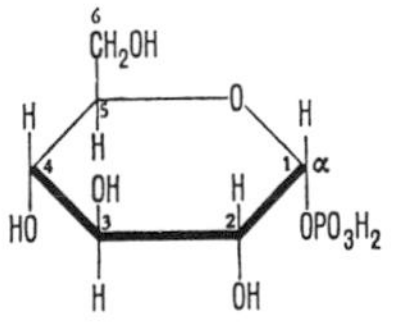	27.70	5.04	11.91	$[\alpha]_D^{25}$ + 120°	Intermediate of glucose–glycogen interconversion	24
D-Glucose 6-phosphate (pyranose form) ('ROBISON ester')	$C_6H_{13}O_9P$ 260.14	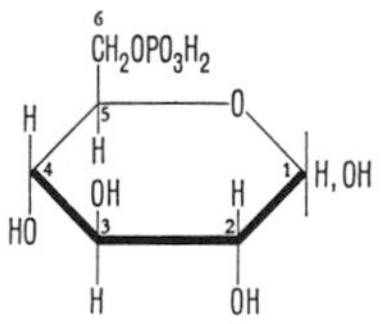	27.70	5.04	11.91	$[\alpha]_D^{25}$ + 34.2°	Intermediate of glycolysis	25
β-D-Glucose 1,6-diphosphate (pyranose form)	$C_6H_{14}O_{12}P_2$ 340.12	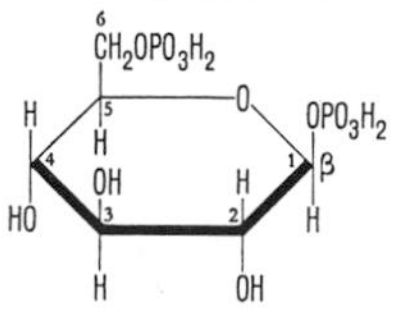	21.19	4.15	18.21	$[\alpha]_D^{20}$ – 19° (pH 8)	Intermediate of glucose–glycogen interconversion	26

Table 2 (continued) Sugar phosphates of importance to mammals

Name	Formula and mol. wt.	Structure	Elementary composition			Specific rotation	Biological function	Reference
			C	H	P			
D-Glucosamine 6-phosphate	$C_6H_{14}NO_8P$ 259.15	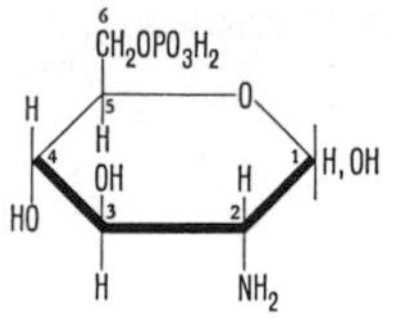	27.81	5.45	11.95	$[\alpha]_{D}^{25}$ + 56°	Formed from D-glucosamine by yeast enzyme preparations and by hexokinase	27
D-Gluconic acid 6-phosphate	$C_6H_{13}O_{10}P$ 276.14	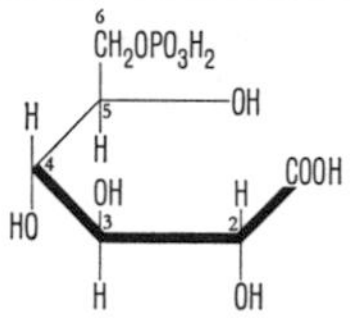	26.10	4.75	11.22	$[\alpha]_{5461}^{20}$ + 0.2°	Intermediate of pentose phosphate cycle	28
N-Acetylglucosamine 1-phosphate	$C_8H_{16}NO_9P$ 301.19	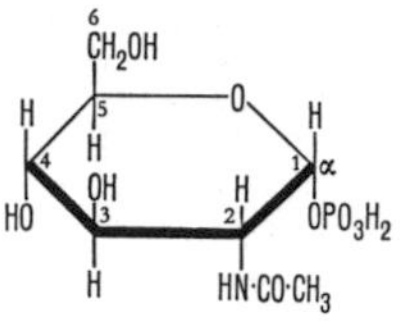	31.90	5.35	10.28	$[\alpha]_{D}^{25}$ + 79°	Intermediate in the formation of UDP *N*-acetylglucosamine and *N*-acetylneuraminic acid	29
N-Acetylglucosamine 6-phosphate	$C_8H_{16}NO_9P$ 301.19	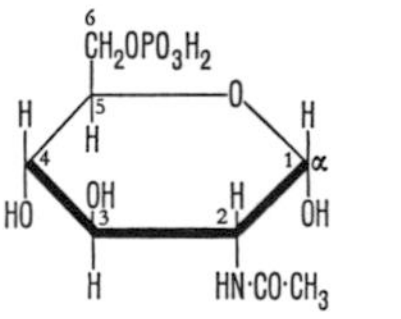	31.90	5.35	10.28	$[\alpha]_{D}^{25}$ + 29.5°	Intermediate in the formation of *N*-acetylglucosamine and *N*-acetylneuraminic acid	30
D-Mannose 6-phosphate (pyranose form)	$C_6H_{13}O_9P$ 260.14	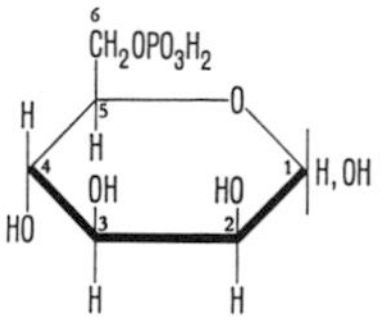	27.70	5.04	11.91	$[\alpha]_{5461}^{20}$ + 15.1°	Intermediate of mannose metabolism	31
N-Acetylmannosamine 6-phosphate	$C_8H_{16}NO_9P$ 301.19	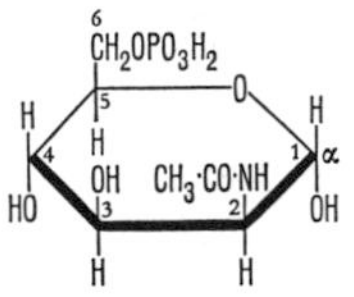	31.90	5.35	10.28	$[\alpha]_{D}^{23}$ + 11.2°	Intermediate in biosynthesis of *N*-acetylneuraminic acid	32
N-Acetylneuraminic acid 9-phosphate	$C_{11}H_{20}NO_{12}P$ 389.26	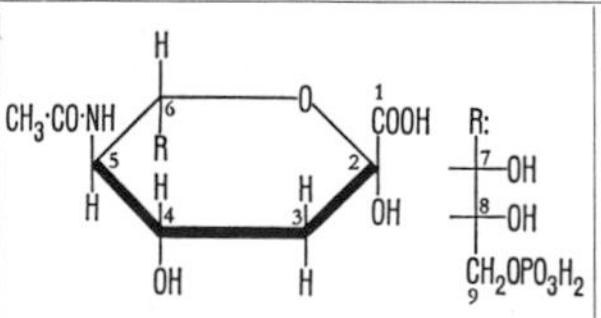	33.94	5.18	7.96	–	Intermediate in formation of *N*-acetylneuraminic acid from *N*-acetylmannosamine	33

Table 2 (concluded) Sugar phosphates of importance to mammals

Name	Formula and mol. wt.	Structure	Elementary composition			Specific rotation	Biological function	Reference
			C	H	P			
D-Sedoheptulose 7-phosphate	$C_7H_{15}O_{10}P$ 290.17	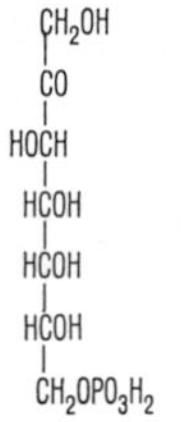	28.98	5.21	10.67	–	Intermediate of pentose phosphate cycle	34
D-Sedoheptulose 1,7-diphosphate	$C_7H_{16}O_{13}P_2$ 370.15	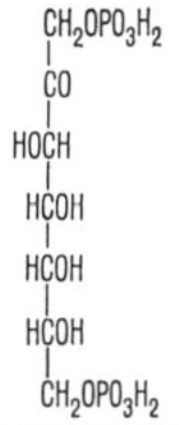	22.71	4.36	16.74	–	Intermediate of pentose phosphate cycle	35
Lactose 1-phosphate	$C_{12}H_{23}O_{14}P$ 422.28	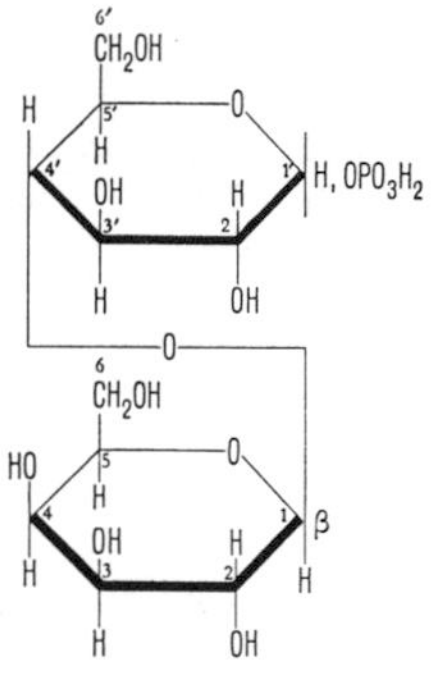 (probable structure)	34.13	5.49	7.33	$[\alpha]_D^{23}$ + 99.5°	Possible intermediate in lactose synthesis. Formed from UDP galactose and glucose 1-phosphate	36

References

1 BALLOU, C.E., in LARDY et al. (Eds.), *Biochemical Preparations*, vol. 7, Wiley, New York, 1960, page 45.
2 MEYERHOF, O., *Bull. Soc. Chim. biol. (Paris)*, **20**, 1033 and 1345 (1938); BALLOU and FISCHER, *J. Amer. chem. Soc.*, **77**, 3329 (1955).
3 BAER and FISCHER, *J. biol. Chem.*, **128**, 491 (1939); BAER and FISCHER, in BALL et al. (Eds.), *Biochemical Preparations*, vol. 2, Wiley, New York, 1952, page 31.
4 KIESSLING, W., *Ber. dtsch. chem. Ges.*, **68**, 243 (1935); BALLOU, C.E., in SHEMIN et al. (Eds.), *Biochemical Preparations*, vol. 5, Wiley, New York, 1957, page 66.
5 NEUBERG and LUSTIG, *Arch. Biochem.*, **1**, 311 (1942); BALLOU and FISCHER, *Abstr. chem. Soc. 126th Meeting*, 1954, page 7D.
6 NEGELEIN and BRÖMEL, *Biochem. Z.*, **301**, 135 (1939).
7 BAER, E., *J. biol. Chem.*, **185**, 763 (1950).
8 LOHMANN and MEYERHOF, *Biochem. Z.*, **273**, 60 (1934); BAER and FISCHER, *J. biol. Chem.*, **180**, 145 (1949); BAER and FISCHER, in BALL et al. (Eds.), *Biochemical Preparations*, vol. 2, Wiley, New York, 1952, page 25.
9 BALLOU et al., *J. Amer. chem. Soc.*, **77**, 2658 (1955).
10 GILLETT and BALLOU, *Biochemistry*, **2**, 547 (1963).
11 KALCKAR, H.M., *J. biol. Chem.*, **167**, 477 (1947); WRIGHT and KHORANA, *J. Amer. chem. Soc.*, **78**, 811 (1956).
12 LELOIR, L.F., in ZECHMEISTER, L. (Ed.), *Progress in the Chemistry of Organic Natural Products*, vol. 8, Springer, Vienna, 1951, page 70.
13 KLENOW, H., *Arch. Biochem.*, **46**, 186 (1953).
14 KORNBERG and KHORANA, in MEISTER et al. (Eds.), *Biochemical Preparations*, vol. 8, Wiley, New York, 1961, page 110.
15 FRIEDKIN, M., *J. biol. Chem.*, **184**, 449 (1950).
16 PRICER and HORECKER, in COON et al. (Eds.), *Biochemical Preparations*, vol. 9, Wiley, New York, 1962, page 35.
17 PONTREMOLI and MANGIAROTTI, *J. biol. Chem.*, **237**, 643 (1962).
18 DICKENS and WILLIAMSON, *Nature*, **176**, 400 (1955).
19 POGELL, B.M., in LARDY et al. (Eds.), *Biochemical Preparations*, vol. 7, Wiley, New York, 1960, page 58.
20 NEUBERG et al., *Arch. Biochem.*, **3**, 33 (1944); TANKO, B., *Abstracts of the Communications of the 1st International Congress of Biochemistry*, Cambridge, 1949, page 222.
21 SABLE, H.Z., in BALL et al. (Eds.), *Biochemical Preparations*, vol. 2, Wiley, New York, 1952, page 52.
22 KOSTERLITZ, H.W., *Biochem. J.*, **37**, 318 (1943); HANSEN et al., in WESTERFELD et al. (Eds.), *Biochemical Preparations*, vol. 4, Wiley, New York, 1955, page 1.
23 CARDINI and LELOIR, *Arch. Biochem.*, **45**, 55 (1953).
24 CORI et al., *J. biol. Chem.*, **121**, 465 (1937); WOLFROM and PLETCHER, *J. Amer. chem. Soc.*, **63**, 1050 (1941); KRAHL and CORI, in CARTER et al. (Eds.), *Biochemical Preparations*, vol. 1, Wiley, New York, 1949, page 33; MCCREADY and HASSID, in WESTERFELD et al. (Eds.), *Biochemical Preparations*, vol. 4, Wiley, New York, 1955, page 63.
25 LELOIR, L.F., in ZECHMEISTER, L. (Ed.), *Progress in the Chemistry of Organic Natural Products*, vol. 8, Springer, Vienna, 1951, page 76; LARDY and FISCHER, in BALL et al. (Eds.), *Biochemical Preparations*, vol. 2, Wiley, New York, 1952, page 39; WOOD and HORECKER, in SNELL et al. (Eds.), *Biochemical Preparations*, vol. 3, Wiley, New York, 1953, page 71.
26 CARDINI et al., *Arch. Biochem.*, **22**, 87 (1949); POSTERNAK, T., *J. biol. Chem.*, **180**, 1269 (1949).
27 JOURDIAN and ROSEMAN, in COON et al. (Eds.), *Biochemical Preparations*, vol. 9, Wiley, New York, 1962, page 44.
28 ROBISON and KING, *Biochem. J.*, **25**, 323 (1931).
29 O'BRIEN, P.J., *Biochim. biophys. Acta (Amst.)*, **86**, 628 (1964).
30 DISTLER et al., *J. biol. Chem.*, **230**, 497 (1958).
31 ROBISON, R., *Biochem. J.*, **26**, 2191 (1932); SLEIN, M.W., *J. biol. Chem.*, **186**, 753 (1950).
32 GHOSH and ROSEMAN, *Proc. nat. Acad. Sci. (Wash.)*, **47**, 955 (1961).
33 ROSEMAN et al., *Proc. nat. Acad. Sci. (Wash.)*, **47**, 958 (1961).
34 HORECKER and SMYRNIOTIS, *J. biol. Chem.*, **212**, 811 (1955).
35 HORECKER et al., *J. biol. Chem.*, **212**, 827 (1955).
36 MCGEOWN and MALPRESS, *Biochem. J.*, **52**, 606 (1952); GANDER et al., *Arch. Biochem.*, **60**, 259 (1956) and **69**, 85 (1957).

Table 3 Polyhydric alcohols of importance to mammals

Name	Formula and mol. wt.	Structure	Specific rotation	Occurrence
Glycerol	$C_3H_8O_3$ 92.10	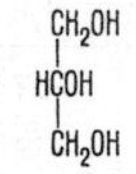	–	Wide occurrence in lipids of mammalian tissues. Sweet taste. Component of cell walls of many GRAM-positive bacteria[1]
Erythritol	$C_4H_{10}O_4$ 122.12	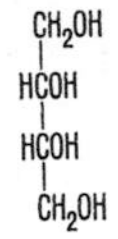	Inactive	Isolated from human urine[3]
Ribitol (adonitol)	$C_5H_{12}O_5$ 152.15	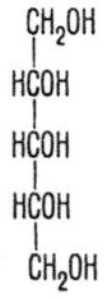	–	Component of riboflavin (vitamin B_2, see page 472). Also found in *Adonis vernalis*. Component of cell walls of many GRAM-positive bacteria[1]
L-Arabitol	$C_5H_{12}O_5$ 152.15	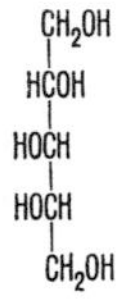	$[\alpha]_D$ – 7.2	Isolated from human urine in pentosuria[4]
Sorbitol (D-glucitol)	$C_6H_{14}O_6$ 182.17	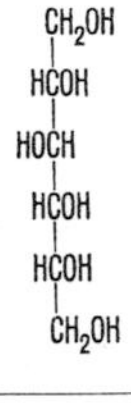	$[\alpha]_D$ – 1.8	Constituent of seminal plasma in many species including man
Myoinositol[2] ('mesoinositol')	$C_6H_{12}O_6$ 180.16	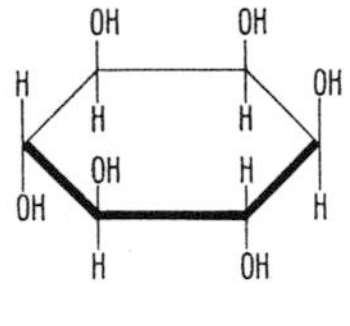	Inactive	Widely distributed in plant and animal kingdoms. Found both free and combined in muscle, heart, liver and other tissues. Component of brain cephalin. The hexaphosphate (phytin) is the organic phosphorus reserve material of green plants. (See also page 491)
Streptidine	$C_8H_{18}N_6O_4$ 262.27	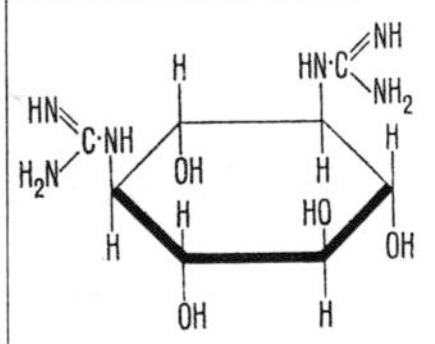	–	Component of streptomycin

References

[1] ROGERS, H.J., *Biochem. Soc. Symp.*, No. 22, 55 (1963).
[2] ANGYAL and ANDERSON, *Advanc. Carbohyd. Chem.*, **14**, 135 (1959).
[3] TOUSTER et al., *J. biol. Chem.*, **235**, 951 (1960).
[4] TOUSTER and HARWELL, *J. biol. Chem.*, **230**, 103 (1958).

Table 4 Oxidation products of carbohydrates

Name	Formula and mol. wt.	Structure	Specific rotation	Occurrence
		Aldonic acids		
D-Glyceric acid (D-α,β-dihydroxy-propionic acid)	$C_3H_6O_4$ 106.08	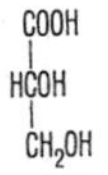	–	As phosphate esters (see Table 2, page 317) which are intermediates in glycolysis
L-Ascorbic acid (L-xyloascorbic acid, vitamin C)	$C_6H_8O_6$ 176.13	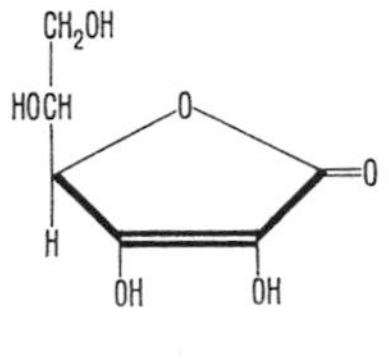	$[\alpha]^{20}_{D}$ + 49°	See under 'Vitamins', page 489
D-Gluconic acid (dextronic acid)	$C_6H_{12}O_7$ 196.16	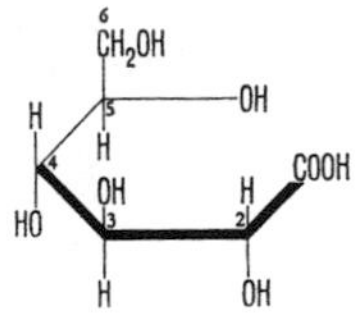	$[\alpha]^{20}_{D}$ − 6.7° → + 17.5°	As phosphate ester (see Table 2, page 320), intermediate in pentose phosphate cycle
		Uronic acids		
α-D-Galacturonic acid	$C_6H_{10}O_7$ 194.14	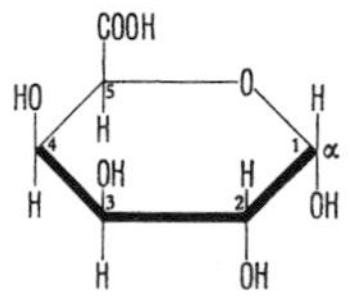	$[\alpha]^{21}_{D}$ + 100° → + 68°	Main component of pectins. Also occurs in some plant gums and mucilages and bacterial polysaccharides (see Table 6, pages 325 and 328)
β-D-Glucuronic acid	$C_6H_{10}O_7$ 194.14	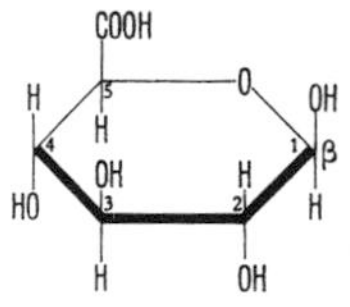	$[\alpha]^{20}_{D}$ + 12° → + 36°	Component of mucopolysaccharides (see Table 6, pages 325, 327 and 328). Many aliphatic and aromatic hydroxy compounds and acids are excreted as glucuronides[1] (see also page 442). Has pyranose form in natural products
L-Iduronic acid	$C_6H_{10}O_7$ 194.14	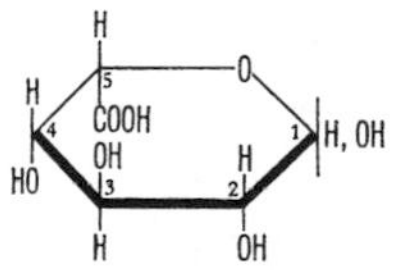	–	Component of chondroitin sulphate B (see Table 6, page 326)

References [1] TEAGUE, R. S., *Advanc. Carbohyd. Chem.*, **9**, 185 (1954); WILLIAMS, R. T., *Detoxication Mechanisms*, 2nd ed., Chapman & Hall, London, 1959.

Table 5 Oligosaccharides of importance to mammals[1]

Name	Formula and mol. wt.	Structure	Specific rotation	Remarks
		Disaccharides		
Cellobiose (4′-[β-D-gluco-pyranosido]-β-D-glucopyranose)	$C_{12}H_{22}O_{11}$ 342.30	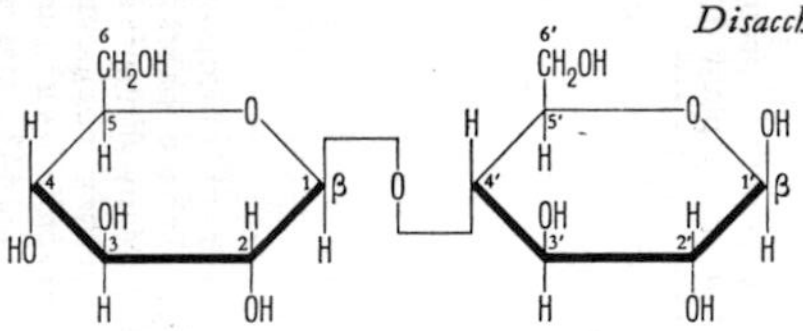	$[\alpha]_D^{20}$ + 14.2° → + 34.6°	Breakdown product of cellulose arising in herbivores in the course of digestion. Component also of lichenin
Lactose (4′-[β-D-galacto-pyranosido]-D-glucopyranose)	$C_{12}H_{22}O_{11}$ 342.30	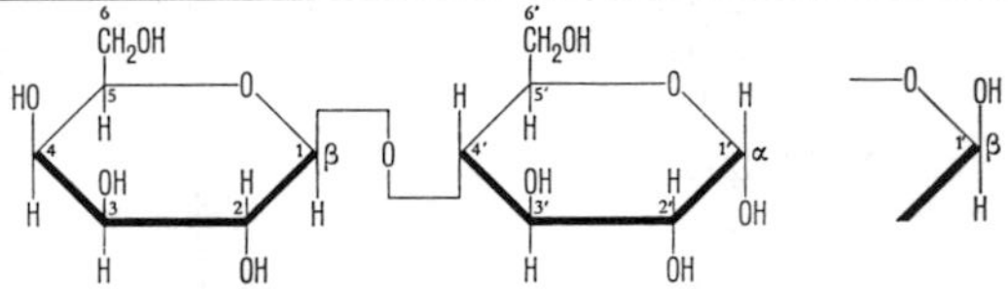	α-form, 1 H_2O: $[\alpha]_D^{20}$ + 85° → + 52.6° β-form: $[\alpha]_D^{20}$ + 34.9° → + 55.4°	Constituent of mammalian milk (4–8%). Only faintly sweet
Maltose (4′-[α-D-gluco-pyranosido]-β-D-glucopyranose)	$C_{12}H_{22}O_{11}$ 342.30	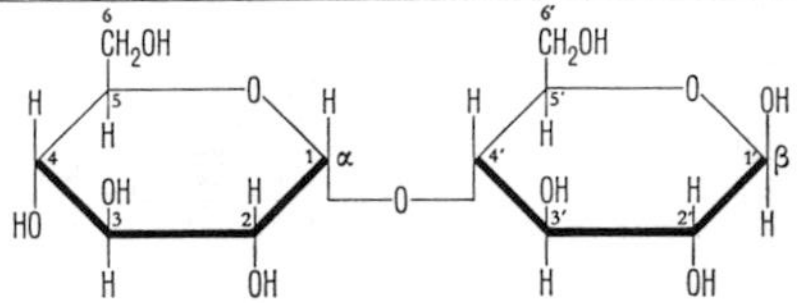	β-form, 1 H_2O: $[\alpha]_D^{20}$ + 111.7° → + 130.4°	Breakdown product of starch and glycogen arising in the course of digestion. Found free in some plants (barley) and in honey
Sucrose (saccharose, cane sugar, beet sugar, α-D-glucopyranosido-β-D-fructofuranoside)	$C_{12}H_{22}O_{11}$ 342.30	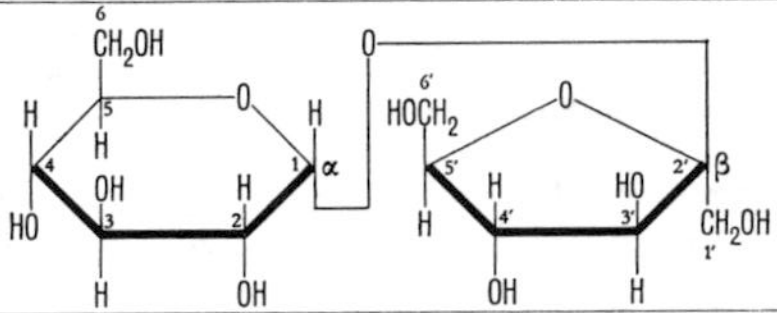	$[\alpha]_D^{20}$ + 66.53°	Almost universal occurrence in the vegetable kingdom
		Trisaccharide		
Fucosidolactose (2-[α-L-fuco-pyranosido]lactose)	$C_{18}H_{32}O_{15}$ 488.44	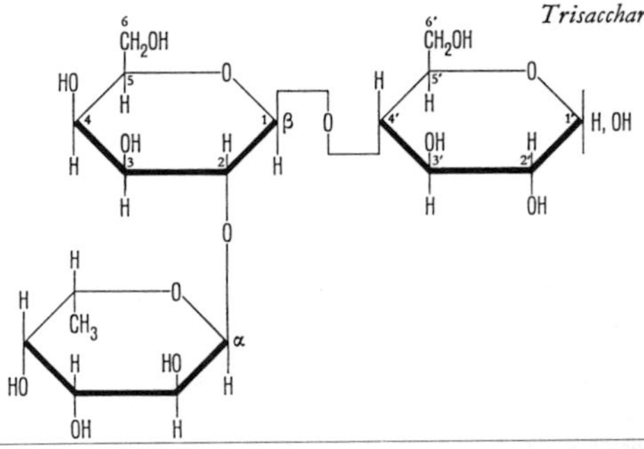	–	Occurs in traces in human milk along with other di-, tri-, penta- and hexasaccharides[2]

References [1] For a detailed and comprehensive review of the structure and occurrence of oligosaccharides see Bailey and Pridham, *Advanc. Carbohyd. Chem.*, **17**, 121 (1962). [2] Stacey and Barker, *Carbohydrates of Living Tissues*, Van Nostrand, London, 1962, page 122.

Table 6 Polysaccharides of importance to mammals (*for references see page 328*)

Name	Mol. wt.	Structure	Specific rotation	Remarks	References
Amylopectin (α-amylose, B-fraction of starch)	Up to 52×10^6 for potato amylopectin	Highly-branched molecule composed of several hundred unit-chains, each of which comprises 20–26 α-1:4-linked glucose residues; the unit-chains are interlinked by glycosidic bonds from the reducing group to C-6 of a glucose residue in an adjacent chain: 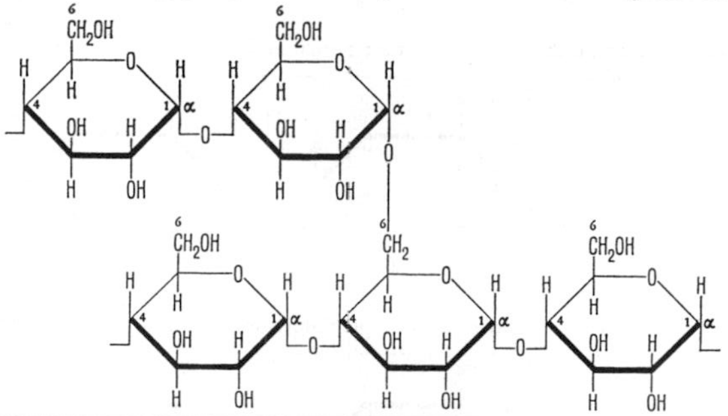	$[\alpha]_D^{20}$ + 150°	Main constituent of starch (usually ca. 80%)	1–3
Amylose (β-amylose, A-fraction of starch)	$(323)_n$, up to 1×10^6	Essentially a linear chain of α-1:4-linked glucose residues: 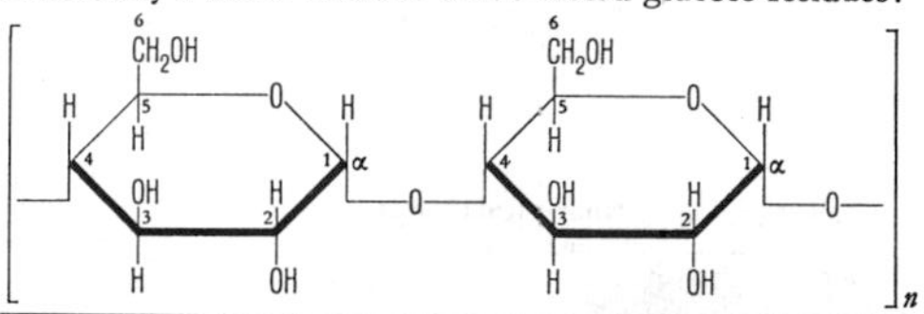	$[\alpha]_D^{20}$ + 220°	Constituent of starch (ca. 20%). Absent in some starches, e.g., that of 'waxy' maize (corn)	1–3
Bacterial capsule polysaccharides	–	Polymers with a composition depending on the type of organism. Thus the polysaccharide of pneumococcus type II is composed of glucose, glucuronic acid and rhamnose, that of pneumococcus type III of glucose and glucuronic acid, that of pneumococcus type XIV of glucose, galactose and *N*-acetylglucosamine, that of streptococci groups A and C of glucuronic acid and *N*-acetylglucosamine, that of *Haemophilus influenzae* of ribose phosphate. Probable structure of the polysaccharide of pneumococcus type III: 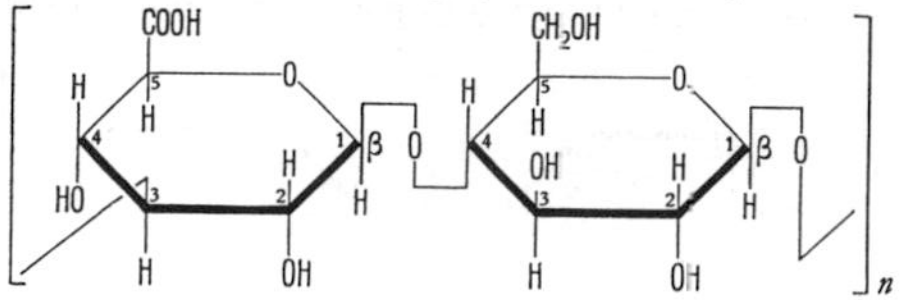	–	Specific oligosaccharide units of the capsular polysaccharides are responsible for the specific antigenic properties of each bacterial type	9, 10, 12
Bacterial cell-wall polysaccharides (mureins)	–	Very large macromolecules of complex structure. The amino sugars *N*-acetylglucosamine and *N*-acetylmuramic acid form strands of linear unbranched muropolysaccharides making up the backbone of the murein. These strands are attached by amide bonds to the carboxylic groups of the muramic acids and carry short oligopeptide side chains. Additional peptide bonds occur between different side chains of neighbouring muropolysaccharide strands, so that a close two- or three-dimensional mesh is formed	–	Found particularly in GRAM-positive bacteria, in smaller amount also in some GRAM-negative bacteria	10, 11

Table 6 (continued) Polysaccharides of importance to mammals *(for references see page 328)*

Name	Mol. wt.	Structure	Specific rotation	Remarks	References
Cellulose	$(323)_n$, up to 1.7×10^6	Linear chain of β-1:4-linked glucose residues: 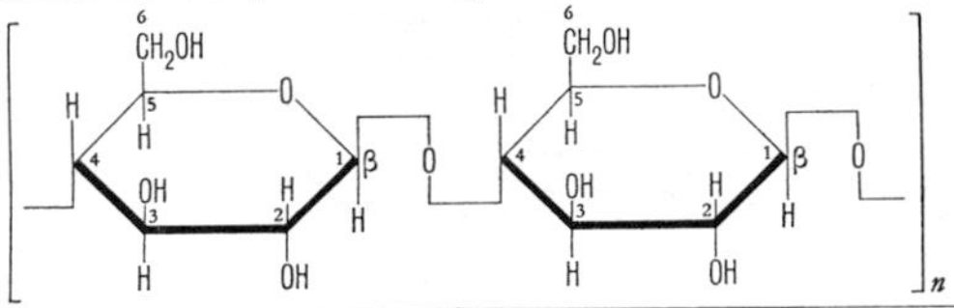	–	Chief structural polysaccharide of plants. Also found in algae, bacterial membranes, and as tunicin in some lower animals. Not digested by man	3
Chitin	$(203.19)_n$, ca. 4×10^5	Linear chain of β-1:4-linked *N*-acetyl-D-glucosamine residues: 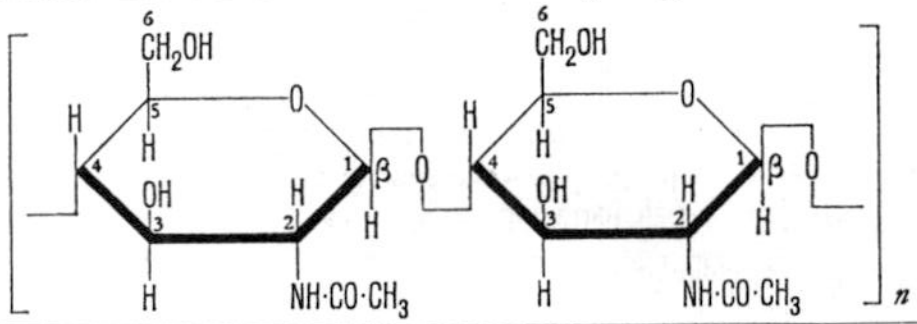	$[\alpha]_D^{20}$ − 14.7° (in HCl)	Skeletal substance of molluscs and insects. Also found in lower plants and fungi	4
Chondroitin sulphate A (chondroitin 4-sulphate)	Polydisperse	Polymer composed of D-glucuronic acid, *N*-acetyl-D-galactosamine and sulphate residues. Probable structure: 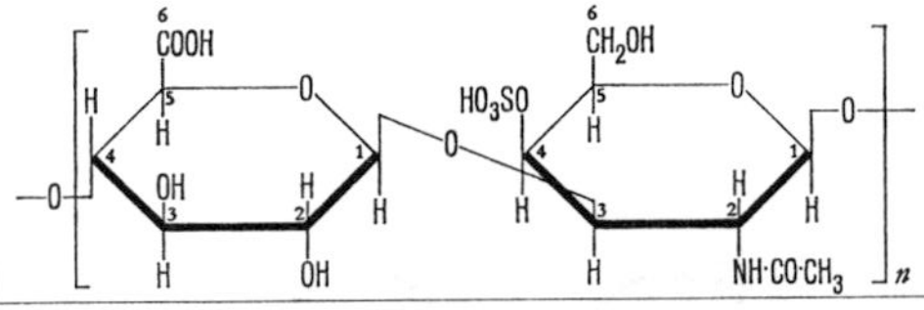	$[\alpha]_D$ − 28° to − 32°	Present in mammalian cartilaginous tissue	5, 6
Chondroitin sulphate B (β-heparin, dermatan sulphate)	Polydisperse	Polymer composed of L-iduronic acid, *N*-acetyl-D-galactosamine and sulphate residues. Probable structure: 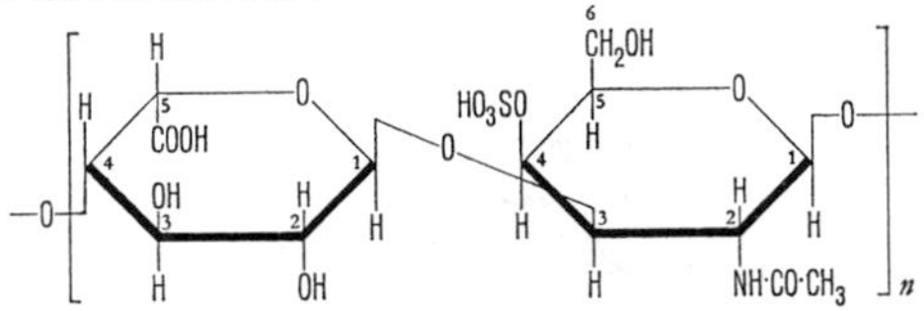	$[\alpha]_D$ − 60° to − 32°	Present in mammalian cartilaginous tissue	5, 6
Chondroitin sulphate C (chondroitin 6-sulphate)	Polydisperse	Polymer composed of D-glucuronic acid, *N*-acetyl-D-galactosamine and sulphate residues. Probable structure: 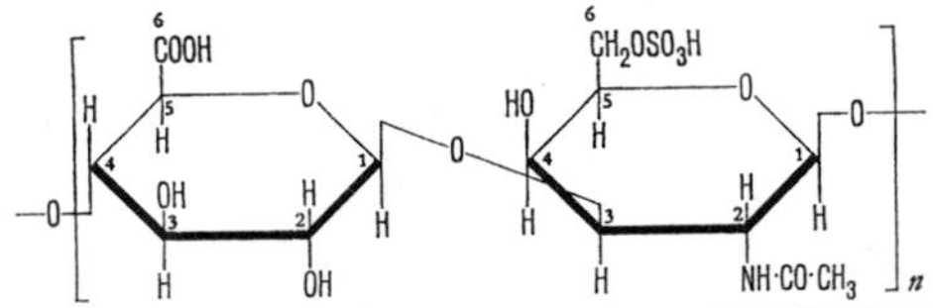	$[\alpha]_D$ − 16° to − 22°	Present in mammalian cartilaginous tissue	5, 6

Dextrans	$(323)_n$, ca. 4×10^6	Probably α-1:6-linked glucose residues in branched or straight chains, for instance: 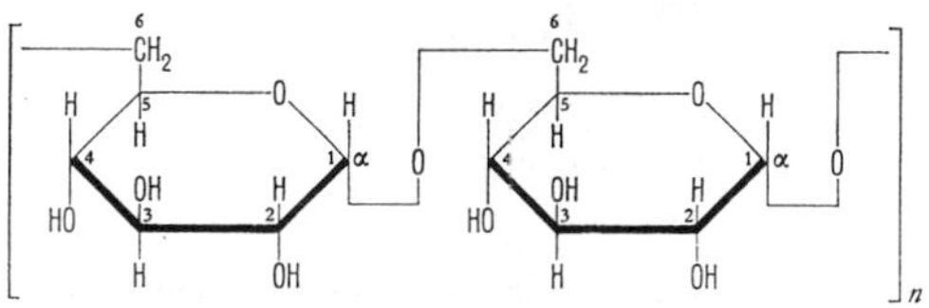	–	Produced extracellularly by bacteria, e.g., *Leuconostoc mesenteroides*. Partially degraded dextrans are used as blood-plasma substitutes	7
Glycogen (liver starch)	Polydisperse; for most glycogens at least 2×10^6	Highly-branched molecule resembling amylopectin and consisting of unit chains of α-1:4-linked glucose residues interlinked by α-1:6-glycosidic bonds: 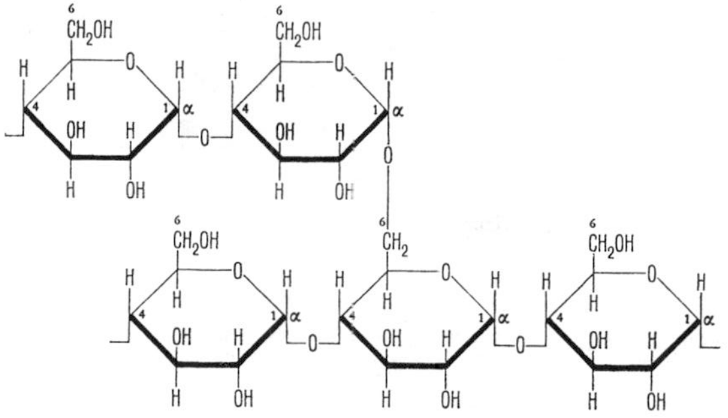	$[\alpha]_D^{20}$ ca. + 200° (water)	Reserve carbohydrate of animal tissues. Converted in muscle to lactic acid during glycolysis (see page 389). Also present in yeast. Has been synthesized by action of heart or liver phosphorylase on glucose 1-phosphate	2, 3, 5
Glycoproteins	–	Proteins containing covalently bound carbohydrate residues other than uronic acids. The carbohydrates are D-galactose, D-mannose, D-glucosamine, D-galactosamine, L-fucose and sialic acid; some plant glycoproteins contain also arabinose and xylose. The carbohydrate content ranges from 2–3% in γG-globulin up to 75% in the blood-group substances. In many glycoproteins aspartic acid serves as the linking residue between the protein and carbohydrate moieties. In orosomucoid, transferrin, fibrinogen and ovalbumin there seems to be a common structure consisting of (a) a core of D-mannose and D-glucosamine, the latter linked to aspartic acid, and (b) an outer envelope containing D-galactose, L-fucose and in some cases sialic acid	–	Widely distributed in nature. The majority of plasma proteins, many milk and egg proteins, mucins, connective tissue components, hormones and a number of enzymes (bovine pancreatic ribonuclease, horse serum cholinesterase, human serum alkaline phosphatases) have been characterized as glycoproteins	12
Heparin	ca. 17000	Polymer composed of D-glucosamine, D-glucuronic acid and sulphate residues. Probable structure: 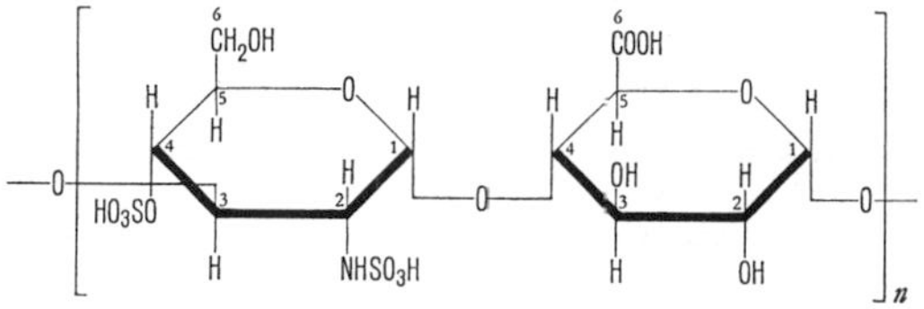	–	Occurs in animal tissues. Blood anticoagulant	5, 6

Table 6 (concluded) Polysaccharides of importance to mammals

Name	Mol. wt.	Structure	Specific rotation	Remarks	Reference
Hyaluronic acid	ca. 1×10^6	Polymer composed of *N*-acetyl-D-galactosamine and D-glucuronic acid residues. Probable structure: 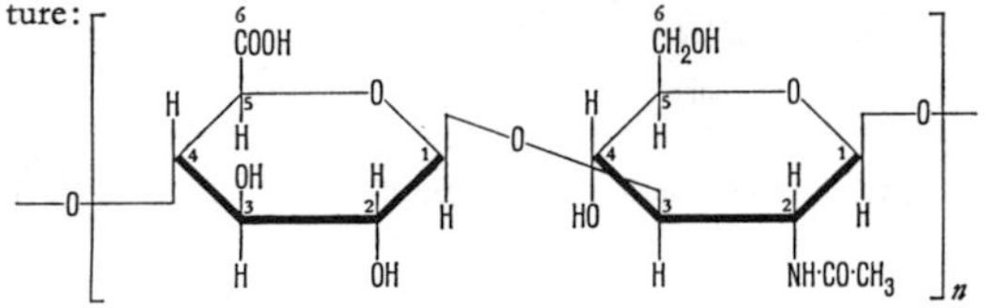	–	Widely distributed in tissues and intercellular fluids	5, 6
Inulin	$(162.14)_n$, ca. 5000	Linear chain of about 30 β-1:2-linked fructofuranose units: 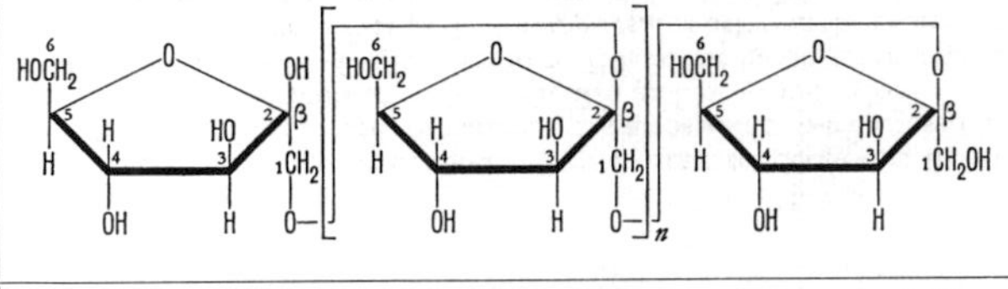	$[\alpha]_D^{20}$ − 40°	Reserve carbohydrate of many plants, alone or with starch	3
Keratan sulphate (keratosulphate)	Polydisperse	Polymer composed of D-galactose, *N*-acetyl-D-glucosamine and sulphate residues. It is probably (1 → 3)-*O*-β-D-galactopyranosyl-(1 → 4)-2-acetamido-2-deoxy-6-*O*-sulpho-β-D-glucopyranose	–	Originally isolated from the bovine cornea. Occurs in animal connective tissues, e.g., nucleus pulposus, costal cartilage	6
Pectic acid (pectins)	$(346)_n$, up to 5×10^4	Probably a linear chain of α-1:4-linked D-galacturonic acid residues: 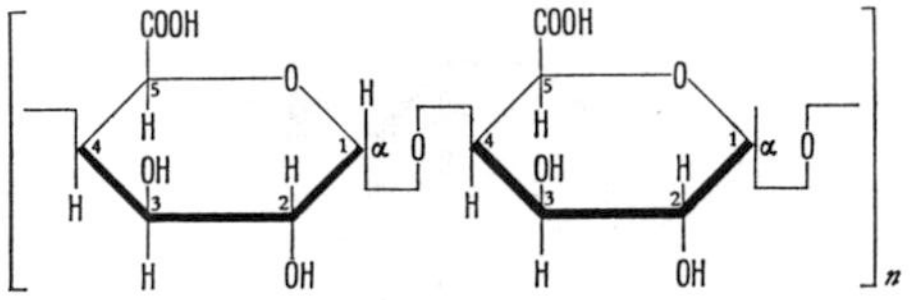	$[\alpha]_D^{20}$ ca. + 240°	Important cell-wall constituent of plants. Occurs as Ca salt or methyl ester	8
Teichoic acids	–	Linear polymers of either glycerol or ribitol phosphate subunits connected in 1,3- or 1,5-phosphodiester linkages respectively. The hydroxyl groups of the polyol monomers may be substituted with D-alanine in an ester bond and with different glycosidically linked mono- or oligosaccharides functioning as the determinant groups of the teichoic acid antigens	–	In cell walls of some bacteria (e.g., *Staphylococcus aureus*), where the teichoic acid is covalently bound to the muropolysaccharide strands of murein	11

References

[1] For review of starch chemistry see WHELAN, W. J., in RUHLAND, W. (Ed.), *Encyclopedia of Plant Physiology*, vol. 6, Springer, Berlin, 1958, page 154.
[2] MANNERS, D. J., *Advanc. Carbohyd. Chem.*, **17**, 371 (1962).
[3] HIRST, E. L., *Biochem. Soc. Symp.*, No. 21, 45 (1962).
[4] FOSTER and WEBBER, *Advanc. Carbohyd. Chem.*, **15**, 371 (1960).
[5] STACEY and BARKER, *Carbohyd. of Living Tissues*, Van Nostrand, London, 1962.
[6] BRIMACOMBE and STACEY, *Advanc. clin. Chem.*, **7**, 199 (1964); JEANLOZ, R. W., *Expos. ann. Biochim. méd.*, **24**, 1 (1963); REES, D. A., *Ann. Rep. Progr. Chem.*, **62**, 469 (1966).
[7] NEELY, W. B., *Advanc. Carbohyd. Chem.*, **15**, 341 (1960).
[8] HIRST and JONES, *Advanc. Carbohyd. Chem.*, **2**, 235 (1946); HINTON, C. L., *Ann. Rev. Biochem.*, **20**, 67 (1951); WOOD, R. K. S., *Ann. Rev. Plant Physiol.*, **11**, 299 (1960).
[9] HEIDELBERGER, M., *Ann. Rev. Biochem.*, **25**, 641 (1956).
[10] WEIBULL, C., in DUBOS and HIRSCH (Eds.), *Bacterial and Mycotic Infections of Man*, 4th ed., Pitman, London, 1965, page 37.
[11] MARTIN, H. H., *Ann. Rev. Biochem.*, **35**, 457 (1966).
[12] SHARON, N., *Ann. Rev. Biochem.*, **35**, 485 (1966).

Amino acids [1]

An amino acid is any compound containing one or more amino groups and one or more carboxylic acid groups. Those of biological importance generally contain an amino group in the α-position to a carboxyl group, i.e., they are of the general structure:

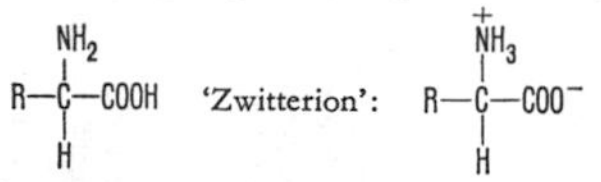

The asymmetry about the α-carbon atom renders the amino acids optically active, except when R = H, as in glycine. Their nomenclature is similar to that adopted for the carbohydrate series and involves the use of the small capital letters D and L to indicate their configuration about the α-carbon atom, sometimes followed by the sign of optical rotation in parentheses, e.g., L-(+)-alanine. In the case of amino acids possessing two asymmetric centres, four stereoisomers are possible, and the isomer which has been found in proteins is referred to simply as the L-isomer. This is not, of course, a complete configurational description of this particular acid. (For the stereochemical configurations of amino acids see NEUBERGER [2].) The value of the specific rotation for any particular amino acid varies with concentration, temperature and hydrogen-ion concentration. A precise control of the experimental conditions is thus necessary for indicating the identity and purity of an acid by means of specific rotation values [3].

The majority of amino acids are stable compounds and melt above 200 °C with decomposition; they are insoluble in the common neutral solvents except water, and can usually be recrystallized from aqueous ethanol. Their salt-like behaviour can be ascribed to their existence as internal salts, or 'zwitterions' (see above).

The amino acids behave as amphoteric compounds and possess characteristic isoelectric points; many of their physical properties exhibit maxima and minima at these points.

Amino acid analysis may be carried out by adsorption chromatography on starch, partition chromatography on silica gel and paper, ion-exchange chromatography, electrophoresis, thin-film chromatography, and vapour-phase chromatography [1,4]. A single ion-exchange column is now sufficient for the separation of all the common amino acids and an automatic analyser based on this procedure is now commercially available. Many methods exist for the quantitative estimation of amino acids: isotope dilution, enzymatic assay, microbial assay and chemical methods [1,4].

There are three methods of quantitative estimation applicable to the majority of amino acids:

(*a*) Amino acids containing a primary amino group react with nitrous acid to give nitrogen:

$$R{-}CH(NH_2){\cdot}COOH + HNO_2 \longrightarrow R{-}CH(OH){\cdot}COOH + N_2 + H_2O$$

This forms the basis of VAN SLYKE's method of estimation, the nitrogen being measured volumetrically [5] or manometrically [6].

(*b*) Amino acids containing free carboxylic and primary α-amino groups are oxidized on heating with ninhydrin:

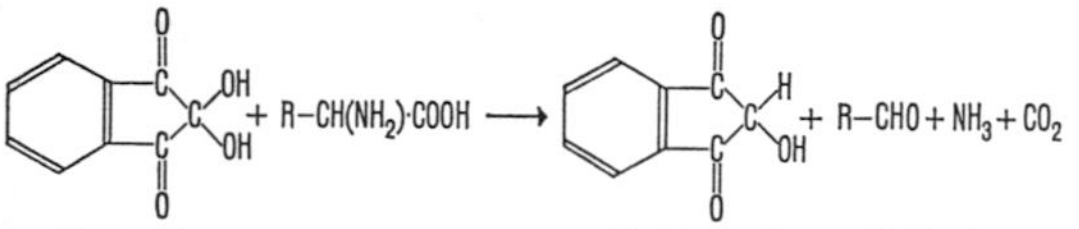

Ninhydrin (triketohydrindene hydrate) — Hydrindantin — Aldehyde

Either NH_3 or CO_2 can be quantitatively measured [7]. Alternatively, the blue colour forming above pH 2 when the reaction mixture is heated, due to the following reaction, can be used for quantitative estimations [8]:

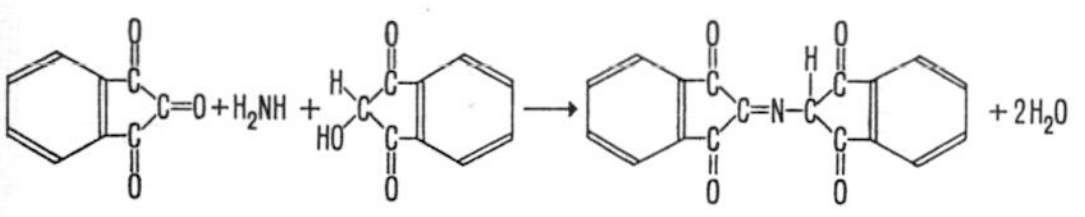

Triketohydrindene — Hydrindantin — Diketohydrindylidene-diketohydrindamine

(*c*) Formaldehyde reacts with the amino groups of an amino acid and thus reduces their basicity; this allows the acid to be directly titrated with alkali using phenolphthalein as indicator [9].

The amino acids are the structural units of protein molecules and just over twenty have been established in this role (Table 7, pages 330–333). These are all α-amino acids of the L-configuration and there is no conclusive evidence that any other type of amino acid is a protein constituent [2]. However, D-amino acids have been isolated from plants and microorganisms [10]. The latter frequently elaborate polypeptides (often possessing antibiotic properties) containing D-amino acids; and indeed, the capsules of certain bacilli, e.g., *Bacillus anthracis*, consist almost wholly of polypeptides of D-glutamic acid. The amino acids listed in Table 8, pages 334 and 335, are not found in proteins but occur as intermediary metabolites or constituents of physiologically active compounds.

Polypeptides

Polypeptides are compounds built up of the repeating unit

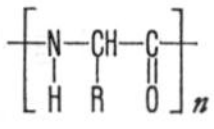

They are derived from amino acids by elimination of water, which gives rise to the peptide bond –HN · CO– between adjacent units. Within this broad classification fall the naturally occurring *proteins* including the enzymes. On protein synthesis see pages 353–354.

The *simple proteins* yield only α-amino acids on hydrolysis, whereas *conjugated proteins* yield other compounds in addition. The conjugated proteins include the *glycoproteins* and *mucoproteins* containing carbohydrate residues, *lipoproteins* containing fatty acids, cholesterol and phospholipids, *haem proteins* containing iron-porphyrin groups, and *nucleoproteins* in which proteins are associated with nucleic acids. According to their solubility in various solvents the proteins can be classified into *albumins*, which are readily soluble in pure water, *globulins*, which are insoluble in water but dissolve readily in aqueous salt solutions, *prolamines*, which are soluble in alcohol–water mixtures but not in pure alcohol or pure water, and various other classes.

The sequence of constituent amino acids in a protein is known as the *primary structure*, any regular or fairly regular folding of the polypeptide chain, which is usually constrained by hydrogen bonds between the N–H and C=O groups of the peptide backbone, as the *secondary structure*, the arrangement of the polypeptide chain in space, as determined by various types of non-covalent interactions between the amino-acid side chains, as the *tertiary structure*, and the aggregation of protein molecules (as subunits) into oligomers as the *quaternary structure*. Since the terms secondary structure and tertiary structure both refer to the spatial folding of the protein the use of the general term *protein conformation* for both levels of structure is preferable [11].

A compilation of the protein amino-acid sequences elucidated up to 1968 is available [12]. The conformations of several proteins in the crystalline state have been determined by X-ray diffraction [13]. The conformations of proteins in solution are usually studied by spectrophotometric methods [14].

References

1 For detailed and comprehensive information on all aspects of amino acid chemistry see GREENSTEIN and WINITZ, *Chemistry of the Amino Acids*, 3 vols., Academic Press, New York, 1961.

2 NEUBERGER, A., *Advanc. Protein Chem.*, **4**, 297 (1948).

3 For resolution of α-amino acids see GREENSTEIN, J.P., *Advanc. Protein Chem.*, **9**, 121 (1954).

4 BLOCK and BOLLING, *The Amino Acid Composition of Proteins and Foods*, 2nd ed., Thomas, Springfield, 1951; LEDERER and LEDERER, *Chromatography*, 2nd ed., Elsevier, Amsterdam, 1957; BLOCK et al., *A Manual of Paper Chromatography and Paper Electrophoresis*, 2nd ed., Academic Press, New York, 1958; ALEXANDER and BLOCK, *A Laboratory Manual of Analytical Methods of Protein Chemistry*, 3 vols., Pergamon, Oxford, 1960–61; BURCHFIELD and STORRS, *Biochemical Applications of Gas Chromatography*, Academic Press, New York, 1962; TRUTER, E.V., *Thin Film Chromatography*, Cleaver-Hume, London, 1963.

5 VAN SLYKE, D.D., *J. biol. Chem.*, **9**, 185 (1911); **12**, 275 (1912).

6 VAN SLYKE, D.D., *J. biol. Chem.*, **83**, 425 (1929).

7 VAN SLYKE et al., *J. biol. Chem.*, **141**, 627, 671 (1941); **150**, 251 (1943).

8 MOORE and STEIN, *J. biol. Chem.*, **176**, 367 (1948).

9 OLCOTT, H.S., in GREENBERG, D.M. (Ed.), *Amino Acids and Proteins*, Thomas, Springfield, 1951, page 80.

10 THORNE, C.B., *Ann. Rev. Microbiol.*, **10**, 331 (1956).

11 NÉMETHY, G., in WILLIAMS and LANSFORD (Eds.), *The Encyclopedia of Biochemistry*, Reinhold, New York, 1967, page 687.

12 DAYHOFF and ECK, *Atlas of Protein Sequence and Structure, 1967–68*, National Biomedical Research Foundation, Silver Spring, Md., 1968.

13 STRYER, L., *Ann. Rev. Biochem.*, **37**, 25 (1968).

14 TIMASHEFF and GORBUNOFF, *Ann. Rev. Biochem.*, **36**, 13 (1967).

Table 7 Physical and chemical properties of amino acids occurring as protein constituents (*for references see page 333*)

Name	Symbol*	Formula and mol. wt.	Structure	Elementary composition (%) C	H	N	Solubility (grammes per 100 g water at 25 °C)	Specific rotation: Temperature (°C)	Concentration**	Solvent	$[\alpha]_D$	Special properties / *Organism for microbiological assay*	Special occurrence and biological function
α-Alanine (α-amino-propionic acid)	Ala	$C_3H_7NO_2$ 89.09	$CH_3{\cdot}CH(NH_2){\cdot}COOH$	40.44	7.92	15.72	16.72	25 25 20	2.06 10.00 1.78	6-N HCl Water 3-N NaOH	+ 13.70 + 2.41 + 3.0	*Leuconostoc (Lactobacillus) citrovorum* 8081	–
Arginine (α-amino-δ-guanido-*n*-valeric acid)	Arg	$C_6H_{14}N_4O_2$ 174.20	$HN{=}C(H_2N){\cdot}NH{\cdot}[CH_2]_3{\cdot}CH(NH_2){\cdot}COOH$	41.37	8.10	32.16	15	23.3 20 20	1.65 3.48 0.87	6-N HCl Water 0.5-N NaOH	+ 27.58 + 12.5 + 11.8	Basic. Gives SAKAGUCHI colour reaction with α-naphthol and sodium hypohalite *Streptococcus faecalis* 9790; *Leuconostoc citrovorum*	Intermediate in ornithine cycle of urea synthesis (see pages 442–444) and in creatine synthesis (see pages 437–438)
Asparagine (aspartic acid β-monoamide; α-amino-β-carbamyl-propionic acid)	Asn or Asp(NH₂) Asp | NH₂	$C_4H_8N_2O_3$ 132.12	$NH_2{\cdot}CO{\cdot}CH_2{\cdot}CH(NH_2){\cdot}COOH$	36.36	6.10	21.20	2.46	20 20 20	2.24 1.41 11.23	3.4-N HCl Water 2.5-N NaOH	+ 34.26 – 5.30 – 6.35	Hydrolysed by hot acid or specific enzymes to give NH_3 + aspartic acid	Found in free state in many plant tissues, especially etiolated seedlings
Aspartic acid (aminosuccinic acid)	Asp	$C_4H_7NO_4$ 133.10	$HOOC{\cdot}CH_2{\cdot}CH(NH_2){\cdot}COOH$	36.10	5.30	10.52	0.50	24 18 18	2.02 1.33 1.33	6-N HCl Water 3-N NaOH	+ 24.6 + 4.7 – 1.7	Acidic. Yields 2 moles of CO_2 and 1 mole of NH_3 in ninhydrin reaction *Leuconostoc mesenteroides* P-60, 8042	Involved in transformation of citrulline to arginine (see pages 442–444), and in biosynthesis of purines and pyrimidines (see pages 433 and 438–439)
Cysteine (α-amino-β-thiolpropionic acid)	Cys	$C_3H_7NO_2S$ 121.16	$HS{\cdot}CH_2{\cdot}CH(NH_2){\cdot}COOH$	29.74	5.82	11.56	Very soluble	26	12.1	1-N HCl	+ 7.6	Readily autoxidized in neutral or basic solution to cystine	Interconvertible with cystine by oxido-reduction. Component of glutathione (see page 438). Some aromatic compounds are excreted in urine as derivatives of *N*-acetylcysteine (mercapturic acids) (see page 445)
				Sulphur 26.46									
Cystine (di-[α-amino-propionic]-β-disulphide)	Cys | Cys	$C_6H_{12}N_2O_4S_2$ 240.30	$S{\cdot}CH_2{\cdot}CH(NH_2){\cdot}COOH$ | $S{\cdot}CH_2{\cdot}CH(NH_2){\cdot}COOH$	29.99	5.03	11.66	0.011	24 18.5	1.0 0.4	1-N HCl 0.2-N NaOH	–214.4 – 70.0	Readily reduced to cysteine *Leuconostoc mesenteroides* P-60, 8042; *Lactobacillus arabinosus*	Occurs abundantly in hair, keratin and insulin. The disulphide bond links together different polypeptide chains or different parts of the same polypeptide chain within the protein molecule
				Sulphur 26.69									
3,5-Di-iodo-tyrosine***	–	$C_9H_9NO_3I_2$ 432.99	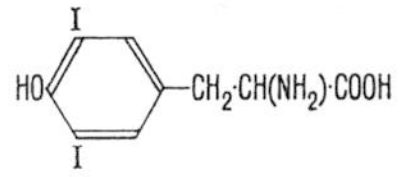	24.97	2.10	3.23	0.062	20 20	5.08 4.41	1.1-N HCl 3.4-N NH_4OH	+ 2.89 + 2.27	–	Occurrence confined to protein of thyroid gland (thyroid hormones; see page 440)
				Iodine 58.62									

Glutamic acid (α-aminoglutaric acid)	Glu	$C_5H_9NO_4$ 147.13	$HOOC\cdot(CH_2)_2\cdot CH(NH_2)\cdot COOH$	40.82	6.17	9.52	0.843	22.4 18 18	1.00 1.47 1.47	6-N HCl Water 1-N NaOH	+ 31.2 + 11.5 + 10.96	Acidic. On boiling in solution over a wide pH range (4–10) cyclizes to pyrrolidonecarboxylic acid *Leuconostoc mesenteroides* P-60, 8042; *Lactobacillus arabinosus*	Component of glutathione (see page 438) and of the folic acid vitamins (see page 479). Present in high concentration in tissues. More readily dehydrogenated in animal tissue than any other amino acid, and also more reactive in enzymic transamination reactions
Glutamine (glutamic acid β-monoamide; α-amino-γ-carbamyl-butyric acid)	Gln or Glu(NH₂) or Glu | NH₂	$C_5H_{10}N_2O_3$ 146.15	$NH_2\cdot CO\cdot(CH_2)_2\cdot CH(NH_2)\cdot COOH$	41.09	6.90	19.17	3.6 (at 18 °C)	22	3.6	Water	+ 5.0	On heating in solution to ca. 100 °C at near neutrality cyclizes to ammonium salt of pyrrolidonecarboxylic acid. Amide group reacts with nitrous acid in presence of acetic acid to release N_2. Hydrolysed by specific enzyme to ammonium glutamate	Occurs in the free state in animal tissues and many plants, e.g., sugar beet. Phenylacetic acid is excreted by man as phenacetylglutamine (see page 445). Intermediate carrier of amino groups. See also page 434
Glycine (aminoacetic acid)	Gly	$C_2H_5NO_2$ 75.07	$NH_2\cdot CH_2\cdot COOH$	32.00	6.71	18.66	24.99	–	–	–	–	Optically inactive. Gives green colour with *o*-phthalaldehyde *Leuconostoc mesenteroides* P-60, 8042	In many animals benzoic acid is excreted as benzoylglycine (hippuric acid) (see pages 444 and 445). Component of glutathione (see page 438). Metabolite in synthesis of creatine, porphyrins, purines (see page 434). Formed from serine in mammals (see page 432)
Histidine (α-amino-β-[4-imidazole]-propionic acid)	His	$C_6H_9N_3O_2$ 155.16	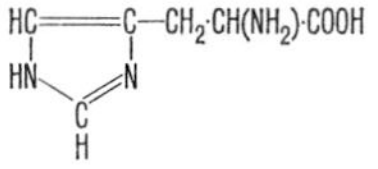	46.45	5.85	27.08	4.29	25 25 20	1.00–4.05 0.75–3.77 0.77	6.1-N HCl Water 0.5-N NaOH	+ 13.34 – 38.95 – 10.9	Basic. Gives biuret test; couples with diazotized sulphanilic acid to give intense red colour (Pauly reaction) *Leuconostoc mesenteroides* P-60, 8042	Decarboxylated to histamine. Constituent of the carnosine (β-alanylhistidine) found in muscle
δ-Hydroxylysine (α,ε-diamino-δ-hydroxy-*n*-caproic acid)	Hyl	$C_6H_{14}N_2O_3$ 162.19	$NH_2\cdot CH_2\cdot CH(OH)\cdot(CH_2)_2\cdot CH(NH_2)\cdot COOH$	44.43	8.70	17.27	–	25	2.0	6-N HCl	+ 14.5	Reacts with periodate to yield formaldehyde and ammonia	Has been found as protein constituent only in collagen and gelatin. Phosphate ester occurs naturally[3]
Hydroxyproline (γ-hydroxy-pyrrolidine-α-carboxylic acid)	Hyp	$C_5H_9NO_3$ 131.13	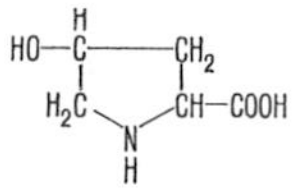	45.80	6.92	10.68	36.11	20 22.5 20	1.31 1.00 0.65	1-N HCl Water 0.5-N NaOH	– 47.3 – 75.2 – 70.6	Has no primary α-amino group and therefore differs in many respects from primary amino acids, e.g., with nitrous acid does not release nitrogen. Oxidized by hypochlorite to give hydroxypyrroline. Decarboxylated by ninhydrin to give reddish colour below pH 4.4, yellowish colour at higher pH. Forms bright blue condensation product with isatin	Component of gelatin, collagen and urinary di- and tri-peptides[2]. See also page 432

* Recommended by the Combined Commission on Biochemical Nomenclature of the International Union of Pure and Applied Chemistry and the International Union of Biochemistry (*J. biol. Chem.*, **241**, 527 [1966]) and used in the description of amino-acid sequences in polypeptide and protein molecules.

** As grammes per 100 ml solution unless otherwise stated.

*** For chromatographic separation from other iodinated amino acids and estimation see Block and Weiss[1].

Table 7 (continued) Physical and chemical properties of amino acids occurring as protein constituents

Name	Symbol*	Formula and mol. wt.	Structure	Elementary composition (%)			Solubility (grammes per 100 g water at 25 °C)	Specific rotation				Special properties *Organism for microbiological assay*	Special occurrence and biological function
				C	H	N		Tem-pera-ture (°C)	Concen-tration**	Solvent	[α]D		
Leucine (α-amino-*iso*caproic acid)	Leu	$C_6H_{13}NO_2$ 131.18	$(CH_3)_2CH{\cdot}CH_2{\cdot}CH(NH_2){\cdot}COOH$	54.94	9.99	10.68	2.19	25 25 20	2.00 2.00 1.31	6-N HCl Water 3-N NaOH	+ 15.20 − 10.57 + 7.6	*Lactobacillus arabinosus* 17–5, 8014; *Lactobacillus helveticus*; *Streptococcus faecalis*; *Leuconostoc mesenteroides* P-60, 8042	–
Isoleucine (α-amino-β-methyl-*n*-valeric acid)	Ile	$C_6H_{13}NO_2$ 131.18	$CH_3{\cdot}CH_2{\cdot}CH(CH_3){\cdot}CH(NH_2){\cdot}COOH$	54.94	9.99	10.68	2.93 (at 20 °C)	20 20 20	5.09 3.10 3.34	6.1-N HCl Water 0.33-N NaOH	+ 40.61 + 11.29 + 11.09	*Lactobacillus arabinosus* 17–5, 8014; *Lactobacillus helveticus*; *Streptococcus faecalis*; *Leuconostoc mesenteroides* P-60, 8042	–
Lysine (α,ε-diamino-*n*-caproic acid)	Lys	$C_6H_{14}N_2O_2$ 146.19	$NH_2{\cdot}(CH_2)_4{\cdot}CH(NH_2){\cdot}COOH$	49.30	9.65	19.16	Very soluble	23 20	2.00 6.50	6-N HCl Water	+ 25.9 + 14.6	Basic. Can be precipitated with phosphotungstic acid. Dry heating of proteins containing lysine causes an apparent loss of lysine *Streptococcus faecalis* 9790; *Leuconostoc mesenteroides* P-60, 8042	–
Methionine (α-amino-γ-methylthiol-*n*-butyric acid)	Met	$C_5H_{11}NO_2S$ 149.21	$CH_3{\cdot}S{\cdot}CH_2{\cdot}CH_2{\cdot}CH(NH_2){\cdot}COOH$	40.25 Sulphur 21.49	7.43	9.39	3.35 (for DL-acid)	20 25	5.00 0.80	3-N HCl Water	+ 23.40 − 8.11	*Leuconostoc mesenteroides* P-60, 8042; *Lactobacillus fermenti* 36 (for DL-acid)	Provides the sulphur atom for cysteine biosynthesis (see 'Cystathionine', Table 8, page 335). Carrier of 'active' methyl groups
3-Monoiodo-tyrosine	–	$C_9H_{10}NO_3I$ 307.09	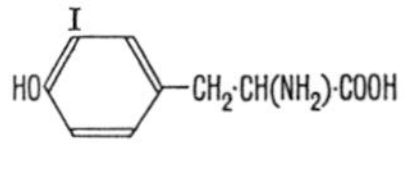	35.20 Iodine 41.32	3.28	4.56	–	20	5.00	1-N HCl	− 4.4	–	Occurrence confined to protein of thyroid gland (thyroid hormones; see page 440)
Norleucine (α-aminocaproic acid)	–	$C_6H_{13}NO_2$ 131.18	$CH_3{\cdot}(CH_2)_3{\cdot}CH(NH_2){\cdot}COOH$	54.94	9.99	10.68	1.15 (at 18 °C)	20	4.3	6-N HCl	+ 21.3	–	Has not been proved to be a protein constituent[4]
Phenylalanine (α-amino-β-phenyl-propionic acid)	Phe	$C_9H_{11}NO_2$ 165.19	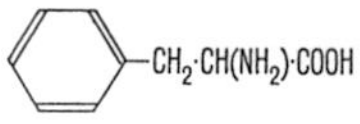	65.44	6.71	8.48	2.965	20	1.93	Water	− 35.14	*Leuconostoc mesenteroides* P-60, 8042	Can be converted to tyrosine in the human body (see page 398)
Proline (pyrrolidine-α-carboxylic acid)	Pro	$C_5H_9NO_2$ 115.13	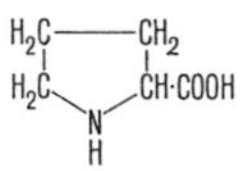	52.16	7.88	12.17	162.3	20 23.4 20	0.57 1.00 2.42	0.5-N HCl Water 0.6-N KOH	− 52.6 − 85.0 − 93.0	Neutral. Soluble in alcohol. Chemically very similar to hydroxyproline *Leuconostoc mesenteroides* P-60, 8042; *Lactobacillus brevis*	Protein constituent. See also page 432

Serine (α-amino-β-hydroxy-propionic acid)	Ser	$C_3H_7NO_3$ 105.09	$HO{\cdot}CH_2{\cdot}CH(NH_2){\cdot}COOH$	34.29	6.71	13.33	5.023 (for DL-acid)	25 20	9.34 10.41	1-N HCl Water	+ 14.95 – 6.83	Split by periodate or lead tetra-acetate to formaldehyde and glyoxylic acid. Gives biuret test. Acid hydrolysis of protein leads to partial destruction *Leuconostoc mesenteroides* P-60, 8042; *Lactobacillus delbrueckii* LD 5; *Lactobacillus helveticus*	Most of the serine in phosphoproteins (vitellin, casein) occurs in form of phosphoserine[5]. Phosphatidylserine is a component of some phospholipids
Threonine (β-methylserine; α-amino-β-hydroxy-butyric acid)	Thr	$C_4H_9NO_3$ 119.12	$CH_3{\cdot}CH(OH){\cdot}CH(NH_2){\cdot}COOH$	40.33	7.62	11.76	–	26	1.63 (g solute per 100 g solution)	Water	– 9.1	Some properties similar to those of serine. Oxidized by periodate to acetaldehyde and glyoxylic acid *Streptococcus faecalis* 9790; *Leuconostoc mesenteroides* P-60,8042	Phosphothreonine has been found in casein hydrolysates[6]
Thyroxine (3,5,3′,5′-tetraiodo thyronine)	–	$C_{15}H_{11}NO_4I_4$ 776.88	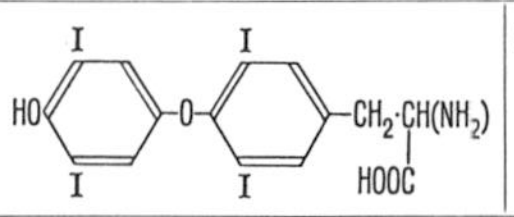	23.19 Iodine 65.34	1.43	1.80	0.001	–	3 (g solute per 100 g solution)	0.13-N NaOH in 70% ethanol	– 4.4	–	Occurrence confined to protein of thyroid gland (thyroid hormones; see page 440)
3,5,3′-Tri-iodo-thyronine	–	$C_{15}H_{12}NO_4I_3$ 650.98	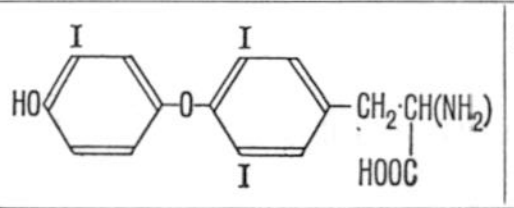	27.68 Iodine 58.48	1.86	2.15	–	29.5	4.75 (as hydro-chloride)	1-N HCl-ethanol (1:2)	+ 21.5	–	Occurrence confined to protein of thyroid gland (thyroid hormones; see page 440)
Tryptophan (α-amino-β-[3-indolyl]-propionic acid)	Trp	$C_{11}H_{12}N_2O_2$ 204.23	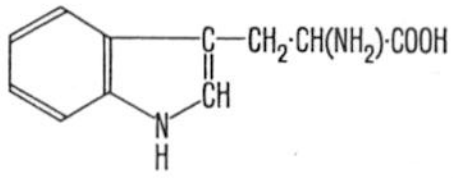	64.69	5.92	13.72	1.14	20 22.7 20	1.02 1.00 2.42	0.5-N HCl Water 0.5-N NaOH	+ 2.4 – 31.5 + 6.17	Destroyed on prolonged heating in hot acid. Gives MILLON reaction (see Tyrosine, below) and FOLIN test. Gives colour reaction with *p*-dimethyl-aminobenzaldehyde and nitrous acid (EHRLICH test) *Lactobacillus arabinosus* 17–5, 8014; *Streptococcus faecalis*	–
Tyrosine (α-amino-β-[*p*-hydroxyphenyl]-propionic acid)	Tyr	$C_9H_{11}NO_3$ 181.19	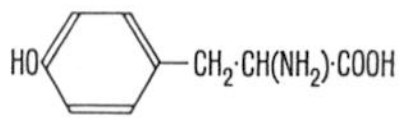	59.66	6.12	7.73	0.045	20 18	4.40 0.90	6.3-N HCl 3.0-N NaOH	– 8.64 – 13.2	Reacts with Hg salts and nitrous acid to give red colour (MILLON reaction). Other less specific colour tests are: reaction with α-nitroso-β-naphthol; reaction with FOLIN phenol reagent *Leuconostoc mesenteroides* P-60, 8042	Precursor of thyroxine, adrenaline and melanin (see page 440)
Valine (α-amino-*iso*valeric acid)	Val	$C_5H_{11}NO_2$ 117.15	$(CH_3)_2CH{\cdot}CH(NH_2){\cdot}COOH$	51.26	9.46	11.96	8.85	20 20	3.4 3.58	6-N HCl Water	+ 28.8 + 6.42	*Lactobacillus arabinosus* 17–5, 8014; *Lactobacillus helveticus*; *Streptococcus faecalis*	–

* Recommended by the Combined Commission on Biochemical Nomenclature of the International Union of Pure and Applied Chemistry and the International Union of Biochemistry (*J. biol. Chem.*, **241**, 527 [1966]) and used in the description of amino-acid sequences in polypeptide and protein molecules.
** As grammes per 100 ml solution unless otherwise stated.

References

1 ROCHE et al., in GLICK, D. (Ed.), *Methods of Biochemical Analysis*, vol.1, Wiley, New York, 1954, page 243; BLOCK and WEISS, *Amino Acid Handbook*, Thomas, Springfield, 1956, page 37.
2 MEILMAN et al., *J. clin. Invest.*, **42**, 40 (1963).
3 ASTRUP et al., *Acta physiol. scand.*, **24**, 202 (1952).
4 CONSDEN et al., *Biochem. J.*, **39**, 251 (1945).
5 ÅGREN et al., *Acta chem. scand.*, **5**, 324 (1951).
6 DE VERDIER, C.-H., *Nature*, **170**, 804 (1952).

Table 8 Physical and chemical properties of some amino acids not occurring in proteins but found in the free form

Name	Formula and mol. wt.	Structure	Elementary composition (%)			Solubility (grammes per 100 g water at 25 °C)	Specific rotation				Special properties	Occurrence and biological function
			C	H	N		Temperature (°C)	Concentration (g per 100 ml solution)	Solvent	$[\alpha]_D$		
β-Alanine (β-amino-propionic acid)	$C_3H_7NO_2$ 89.09	$NH_2 \cdot CH_2 \cdot CH_2 \cdot COOH$	40.44	7.92	15.72	Very soluble	–	–	–	–	–	Breakdown product of pyrimidines (see page 401). Occurs as constituent of pantothenic acid, coenzyme A, carnosine and anserine. See also page 434
α-Aminoadipic acid	$C_6H_{11}NO_4$ 161.16	$HOOC \cdot (CH_2)_3 \cdot CH(NH_2) \cdot COOH$	44.72	6.88	8.69	0.22 (at 20 °C)	–	–	–	–	Decomposes on heating to α-piperidone-α′-carboxylic acid	Intermediate in breakdown of lysine (see page 398)
α-Amino-*n*-butyric acid	$C_4H_9NO_2$ 103.12	$CH_3 \cdot CH_2 \cdot CH(NH_2) \cdot COOH$	46.59	8.80	13.58	28 (for DL-acid)	20	5.46	Water	+ 7.86	–	Found in brain preparations[1]. Occurs as constituent of tripeptide ophthalmic acid in lens tissue[2]
γ-Amino-*n*-butyric acid	$C_4H_9NO_2$ 103.12	$NH_2 \cdot (CH_2)_3 \cdot COOH$	46.59	8.80	13.58	–	–	–	–	–	–	Found in brain[3], lung and heart[1] preparations
β-Amino*iso*butyric acid	$C_4H_9NO_2$ 103.12	$NH_2 \cdot CH_2 \cdot CH(CH_3) \cdot COOH$	46.59	8.80	13.58	–	–	–	–	–	–	Breakdown product of thymine (see page 401)
δ-Aminolaevulinic acid (γ-keto-δ-amino-*n*-valeric acid)	$C_5H_9NO_3$ 131.13	$NH_2 \cdot CH_2 \cdot CO \cdot CH_2 \cdot CH_2 \cdot COOH$	45.80	6.92	10.68	–	–	–	–	–	Reduces BENEDICT's solution in the cold. Split by periodate to formaldehyde and succinic acid	Intermediate in porphyrin biosynthesis (see page 437)
Argininosuccinic acid	$C_{10}H_{18}N_4O_6$ 290.28	$HOOC \cdot CH(NH_2) \cdot (CH_2)_3 \cdot NH \cdot C(=NH) \cdot NH \cdot CH(COOH) \cdot CH_2 \cdot COOH$	41.38	6.25	19.30	–	24 24 24	2.9 2.9 2.9	Water 0.5-N NaOH 0.5-N HCl	+ 16.4 + 26.6 + 5.2	In aqueous solution cyclizes spontaneously with loss of water	Intermediary metabolite in ornithine cycle of urea synthesis[4] (see pages 442 and 444). Excreted in the urine of some mental defectives[5] (see page 449)
Carbamylaspartic acid (ureidosuccinic acid)	$C_5H_8N_2O_5$ 176.13	$HOOC \cdot CH_2 \cdot CH(COOH) \cdot NH \cdot CO \cdot NH_2$	34.10	4.58	15.90	0.4 (at 20 °C)	25	–	Water (Ba salt)	+ 24.1	–	Intermediate in biosynthesis of pyrimidines from aspartic acid in mammals and bacteria (see page 439)
Citrulline (α-amino-δ-ureido-*n*-valeric acid)	$C_6H_{13}N_3O_3$ 175.19	$NH_2 \cdot CO \cdot NH \cdot (CH_2)_3 \cdot CH(NH_2) \cdot COOH$	41.14	7.48	23.99	–	21 21	5.00 5.00	0.3-N HCl Water	+ 17.9 + 3.5	Converted to ornithine by alkaline hydrolysis	Intermediate in ornithine cycle of urea synthesis (see pages 442–443)
Creatine (methyl-glycocyamine)	$C_4H_9N_3O_2$ 131.14	$HN{=}C(NH_2) \cdot N(CH_3) \cdot CH_2 \cdot COOH$	36.64	6.92	32.04	1.35 (at 18 °C)	–	–	–	–	Weakly basic. Gives creatinine on heating with dilute acids	Cell constituent. Creatine phosphate acts as store of 'phosphate bond energy' in vertebrate muscle (see page 437)
Creatinine (1-methylglyco-cyamidine)	$C_4H_7N_3O$ 113.12	$HN{=}C \cdot N(CH_3) \cdot CH_2 \cdot CO$ (ring closed through NH)	42.47	6.24	37.15	8.7 (at 16 °C)	–	–	–	–	Strongly basic	Present in urine

Cystathionine	$C_7H_{14}N_2O_4S$ 222.26	HOOC·CH(NH$_2$)·CH$_2$·S·CH$_2$·CH$_2$·CH(NH$_2$)·COOH	37.83	6.35	12.60	–	22	1.0	1-N HCl	+ 23.7	–	Intermediate in transsulphuration of methionine with serine (see page 398)
			Sulphur 14.43									
Cysteic acid	$C_3H_7NO_5S$ 169.16	HO$_3$S·CH$_2$·CH(NH$_2$)·COOH	21.30	4.17	8.28	–	28	6.0	Water	+ 7.8	–	Intermediate in formation of taurine, a bile constituent (see below), from cysteine
			Sulphur 18.96									
Ergothioneine (betaine of thiolhistidine)	$C_9H_{15}N_3O_2S$ 229.30	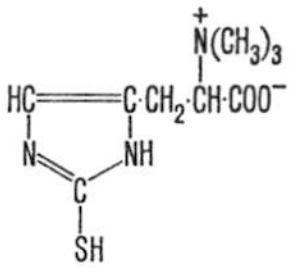	47.14	6.59	18.33	–	21	5.0	Water	+116.0	Basic. Stable to alkalis; thiol group is readily oxidized to sulphate under acid conditions. Gives reddish purple colour with diazotized sulphanilic acid and alkali	Occurs in erythrocytes, liver, kidney, other tissues, and in urine and semen[6]. Constituent of ergot
			Sulphur 13.98									
Glycocyamine (guanidinoacetic acid)	$C_3H_7N_3O_2$ 117.11	HN=C(NH$_2$)·NH·CH$_2$·COOH	30.77	6.03	35.88	Slightly soluble	–	–	–	–	–	In urine. Formed in kidney from arginine and glycine. Precursor of creatine and creatinine (see page 437)
Homoserine (α-amino-γ-hydroxy-*n*-butyric acid)	$C_4H_9NO_3$ 119.12	HO·CH$_2$·CH$_2$·CH(NH$_2$)·COOH	40.33	7.62	11.76	–	24 to 26	0.25	5-N HCl	+ 18.3	–	Intermediate in methionine and homocysteine metabolism (see pages 397–398)
1-Methylhistidine	$C_7H_{11}N_3O_2$ 169.18	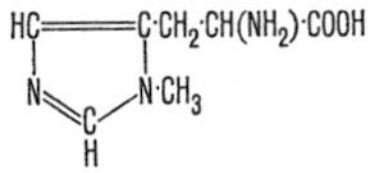	49.70	6.55	24.84	20	18	3.72	Water	− 26	–	Free acid isolated from normal urine[7]. In combination with β-alanine forms the dipeptide anserine found in animal muscle[8]
3-Methylhistidine	$C_7H_{11}N_3O_2$ 169.18	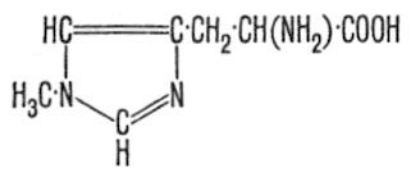	49.70	6.35	24.84	–	26	–	Water	− 25.4 to − 26.5	–	Isolated from normal urine[9]
Ornithine (2,5-diamino-*n*-valeric acid)	$C_5H_{12}N_2O_2$ 132.16	NH$_2$·(CH$_2$)$_3$·CH(NH$_2$)·COOH	45.44	9.15	21.20	Very soluble	20	0.84	0.45-N HCl	+ 14.1	Formed from arginine by alkaline hydrolysis	Intermediate in ornithine cycle of urea synthesis (see pages 442–443). Benzoic acid is excreted by the fowl as *N,N'*-dibenzoylornithine
Taurine (2-aminoethane-sulphonic acid)	$C_2H_7NO_3S$ 125.15	NH$_2$·CH$_2$·CH$_2$·SO$_3$H	19.20	5.64	11.19	8.78 (at 20 °C)	–	–	–	–	–	In muscle tissue of invertebrates. Formed in mammalian liver from cysteine (see page 438). Component of taurocholic acid (bile acid)
			Sulphur 25.62									

References

1 WALKER, D.M., *Biochem. J.*, **52**, 679 (1952).
2 WALEY, S.G., *Biochem. J.*, **64**, 715 (1956).
3 UDENFRIEND, S., *J. biol. Chem.*, **187**, 65 (1950).
4 RATNER et al., *J. biol. Chem.*, **204**, 95 (1953).
5 WESTALL, R.G., *Biochem. J.*, **77**, 135 (1960).
6 For review see BELL, D.J., *Ann. Rep. Progr. Chem.*, **52**, 285 (1955).
7 SEARLE and WESTALL, *Biochem. J.*, **48**, 1 (1951).
8 LONG, C. (Ed.), *Biochemists' Handbook*, Spon, London, 1961, page 668.
9 WESTALL, R.G., *Biochem. J.*, **52**, 638 (1952); TALLAN et al., *J. biol. Chem.*, **206**, 825 (1954).

Nucleosides and nucleotides

A *nucleoside* is a sugar linked to a heterocyclic base. A *nucleotide* is a nucleoside in which the sugar is esterified with phosphoric acid.

base — sugar

Nucleoside

base — sugar — phosphate

Nucleotide

The bases found in nucleosides and nucleotides are most commonly purines and pyrimidines. Others include pyridines and isoalloxazines. The parent compounds of these bases are:

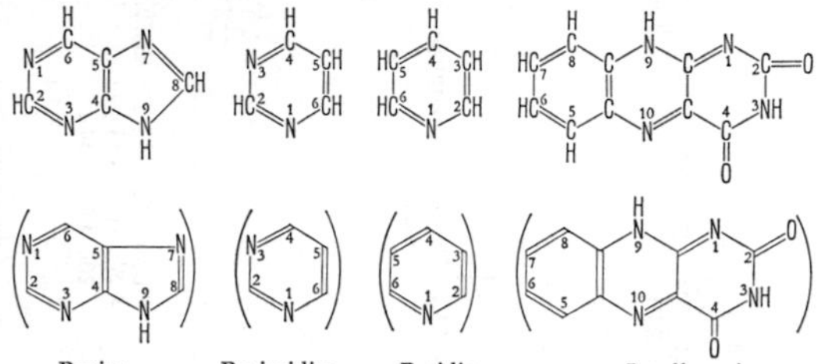

Purine | Pyrimidine (1,3-diazine) | Pyridine | Isoalloxazine

The sugars found in nucleosides and nucleotides are most commonly either ribose or 2-deoxyribose:

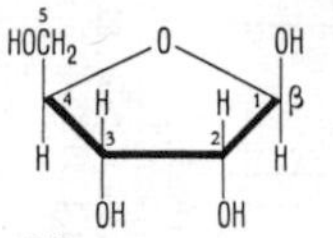

Ribose
(β-D-ribofuranose)

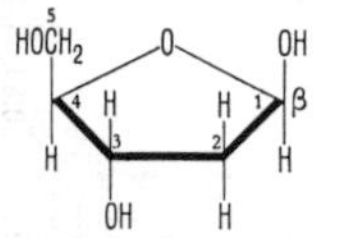

2-Deoxyribose
(β-D-2-deoxyribofuranose)

The base–glycoside linkage of nucleosides and nucleotides occupies the 9-position in the case of purines and the 3-position in the case of pyrimidines. Esterification of nucleosides is not confined to orthophosphoric acid. It occurs also with pyrophosphoric (diphosphoric) acid and triphosphoric acid.

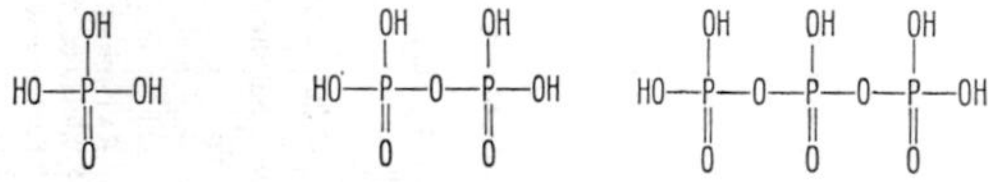

Orthophosphoric acid (monophosphoric acid) | Pyrophosphoric acid (diphosphoric acid) | Triphosphoric acid

The nomenclature of the nucleosides and nucleotides is demonstrated by the examples given in Table 9 opposite.

The naturally occurring nucleoside mono-, di- and triphosphates have the sugar–phosphate ester linkage in the 5′-position. Exceptions are the nucleoside 3′-monophosphates and the nucleoside 3′,5′-diphosphates formed during enzymatic digestion of ribonucleic acids. In the case of certain coenzymes, a nucleoside 2′,5′-diphosphate or nucleoside 3′,5′-diphosphate structure is also encountered (see Table 12, pages 344–350).

Nucleotides and polynucleotides (see Nucleic acids, pages 351 to 354) occur in all living cells. Certain naturally occurring bases, nucleosides and nucleotides have no known function apart from being intermediates in the synthesis or breakdown of other nucleotides (Tables 10a, b, c, pages 338–342).

Nucleoside di- or triphosphates are precursors of the nucleic acids. They act also as carriers of the free energy of pyrophosphate bonds. In this capacity, nucleotides may be regarded as coenzymes of the free-energy transfer that occurs in many synthetic and degradative reactions. Nucleoside diphosphates are formed from the corresponding monophosphates by nucleoside monophosphate kinase. This enzyme is analogous in action to adenylate kinase and catalyses the general reaction[1]:

nucleoside monophosphate + adenosine triphosphate
⇅
nucleoside diphosphate + adenosine diphosphate

Nucleoside triphosphates are formed in turn from the corresponding diphosphates by nucleoside diphosphate kinase[1]:

nucleoside diphosphate + adenosine triphosphate
⇅
nucleoside triphosphate + adenosine diphosphate

A list of nucleoside mono-, di- and triphosphates and their functions is given in Table 11, page 343.

The nucleotide coenzymes act as carriers of hydrogen (codehydrogenases) and as carriers of the active forms of sugars, amino acids, fatty acids, dicarboxylic acids, carbon dioxide, and sulphate. The roles and modes of formation of nucleotide coenzymes are listed in Table 12, pages 344–350.

References

[1] LIEBERMAN et al., *J. biol. Chem.*, **215**, 429 (1955); GIBSON et al., *Biochim. biophys. Acta (Amst.)*, **21**, 86 (1956).

Table 9 Nomenclature of nucleosides and nucleotides

The group names are the names which can be applied to any compound of the type shown. In general the terms nucleoside and nucleotide are reserved for derivatives of heterocyclic bases, whilst the terms ribonucleoside and ribonucleotide apply to any type of base (the terms 'riboside' and 'ribotide' should no longer be used). The term *nucleotide* is expanded to *mononucleotide* when it is necessary to distinguish between *mononucleotides* and *polynucleotides* (cf. 'Nucleic acids', page 351). When necessary the position of the phosphate ester linkage may be indicated. For example, the nucleotide shown is a 5′-nucleotide or, more fully, a 5′-ribonucleotide. The use of the bracketed group names is confined to occasions when it is necessary to distinguish between *monophosphates* and *polyphosphates*.

When the *nucleoside* or *nucleotide* under consideration contains deoxyribose in place of ribose, this is made clear by prefixing the syllable *deoxy* to the name of the compound, for example, *deoxyadenosine*, *deoxyadenylic acid.*

Structural formula	Group name	Alternative group name	Specific name	Specific alternatives
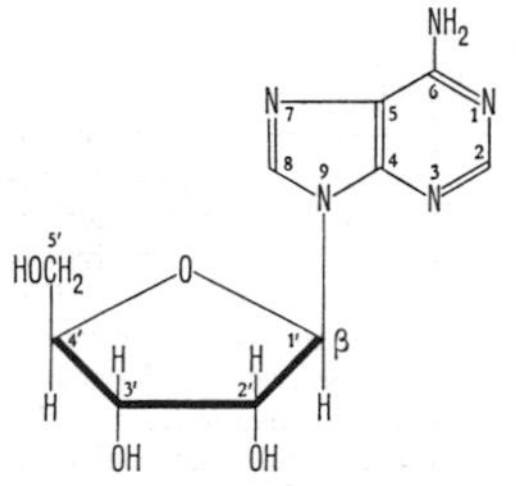	Nucleoside	Ribonucleoside (ribosylbase)	Adenosine	Ribosyladenine
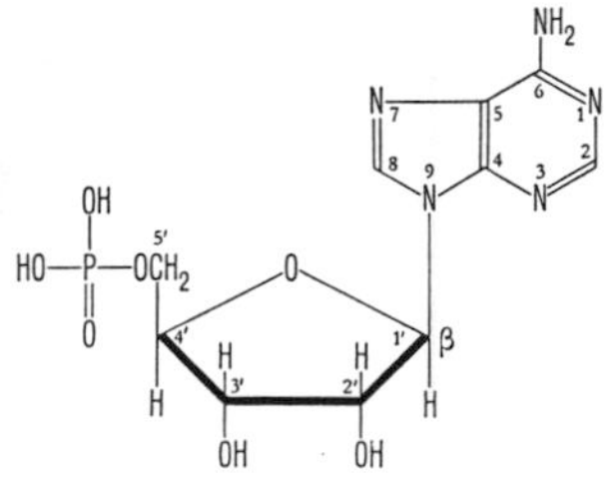	Nucleotide (nucleoside mono-phosphate)	Ribonucleotide (ribosylbase mono-phosphate)	5′-Adenylic acid (AMP)	Adenosine 5′-phosphate (adenosine monophos-phate) Adenine nucleotide Ribosyladenine 5′-phosphate
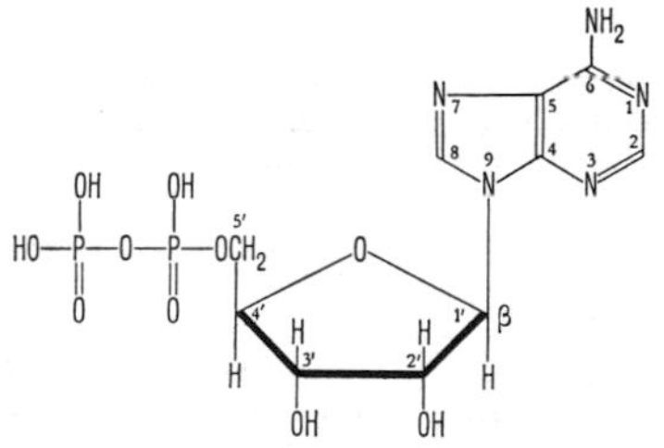	Nucleoside diphosphate	Ribosylbase diphosphate	Adenosine diphosphate (ADP)	Adenosine 5′-pyro-phosphate
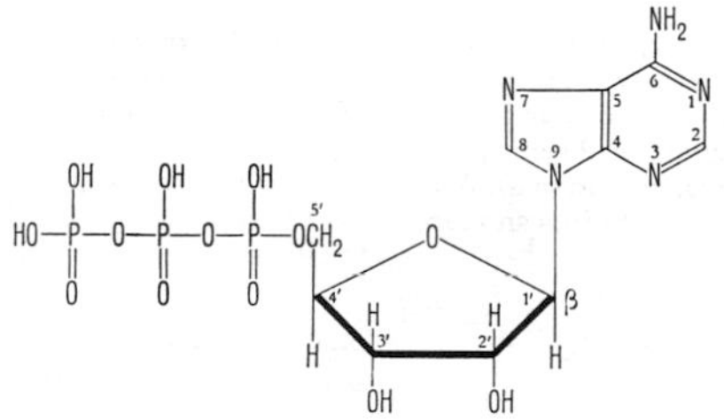	Nucleoside triphosphate	Ribosylbase triphosphate	Adenosine triphosphate (ATP)	

Table 10a Compounds involved in the biosynthesis and breakdown of purine and pyrimidine nucleotides: Purines and pyrimidines

Name	Formula and mol. wt.	Structure	Properties	Occurrence	Function
Adenine (6-amino-purine)	$C_5H_5N_5$ 135.13	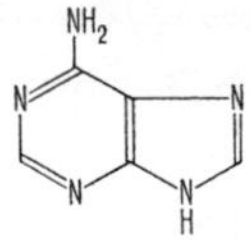	m.p. 365 °C (decomp.); picrate 298 °C	Occurs in tea, sugar beet, yeast, various animal organs	These bases are the products of the degradation of the corresponding nucleotides. They are further degraded by the pathways shown on pages 399–401. In mammals only adenine can be converted back to the corresponding nucleotide under normal conditions but the extent to which this occurs is uncertain
Guanine (2-amino-6-hydroxy-purine)	$C_5H_5N_5O$ 151.13	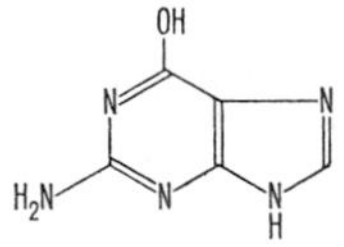	m.p. 365 °C (decomp.); picrate 258–260 °C	Occurs in scales and flesh of fish	
Uracil (2,6-dihydroxypyrimidine)	$C_4H_4N_2O_2$ 112.09	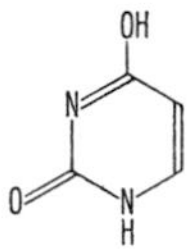	m.p. 338 °C (decomp.)	–	
Cytosine (6-amino-2-hydroxy-pyrimidine)	$C_4H_5N_3O$ 111.10	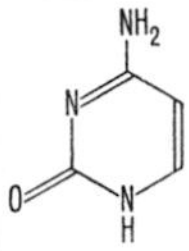	m.p. 320–325 °C (decomp.); picrate 333 °C	–	
Thymine (2,6-dihydroxy-5-methyl-pyrimidine)	$C_5H_6N_2O_2$ 126.12	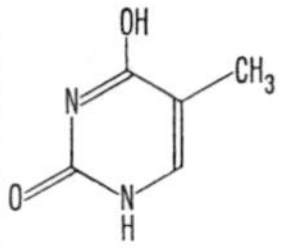	m.p. 321–325 °C	–	
5-Methyl-cytosine (5-methyl-6-amino-2-hydroxy-pyrimidine)	$C_5H_7N_3O$ 125.13	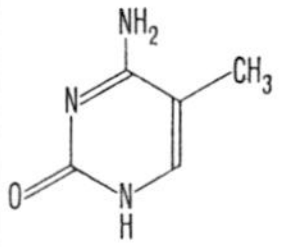	m.p. 270 °C (decomp.); picrate 290–291 °C	Occurs in calf thymus nucleic acid and wheat germ deoxyribonucleic acid	–
Hypoxanthine (6-hydroxy-purine)	$C_5H_4N_4O$ 136.11	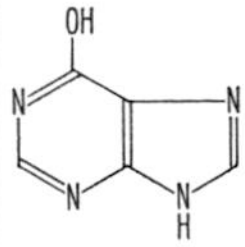	m.p. 150 °C (decomp.); picrate 246 °C	Occurs in muscle, meat extracts, blood, urine (the latter especially in leukaemia)	Product of deamination of adenine; precursor of xanthine
Xanthine (2,6-dihydroxypurine)	$C_5H_4N_4O_2$ 152.11	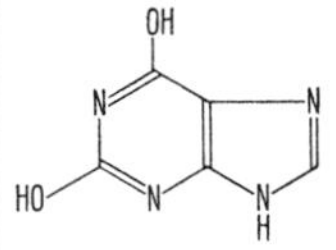	m.p. 262–264 °C (perchlorate)	Occurs in small quantities in plants, blood, liver, urine, yeast. Component of butterfly pigments and rare urinary calculi	Formed by oxidation of hypoxanthine, or by deamination of guanine; precursor of uric acid
Uric acid (2,6,8-tri-hydroxy-purine)	$C_5H_4N_4O_3$ 168.11	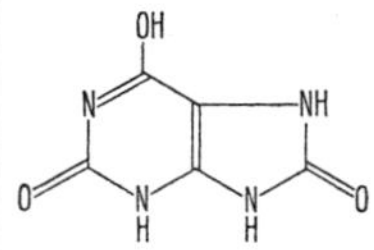	m.p. > 400 °C (decomp.) d^{25} 1.836	Occurs in urine and renal and urinary calculi (increased in urine and blood in gout, leukaemia, nephritis, pneumonia). Also in faeces of birds and reptiles	Formed by oxidation of xanthine. Chief product of nitrogen excretion in reptiles and birds. In mammals other than primates further degraded to allantoin (see page 400)
Orotic acid (2,6-dihydroxypyrimidine-4-carboxylic acid)	$C_5H_4N_2O_4$ 156.10	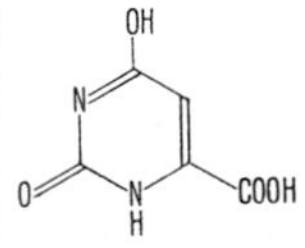	m.p. 345–347 °C (decomp.); ethyl ester 200 °C	Occurs in milk	Precursor of orotidylic acid (see pages 438–439)

Table 10b Compounds involved in the biosynthesis and breakdown of purine and pyrimidine nucleotides: Nucleosides

The purine nucleosides listed in this table all contain 9-*N*-β-riboside or -deoxyriboside linkages, the pyrimidine nucleosides 3-*N*-β-riboside or -deoxyriboside linkages. For explanation of the nomenclature see Table 9, page 337.

Name*	Formula and mol.wt.	Structure	Specific rotation	Function in mammalian tissue
Adenosine (Ado, A) (ribosyladenine)	$C_{10}H_{13}N_5O_4$ 267.25	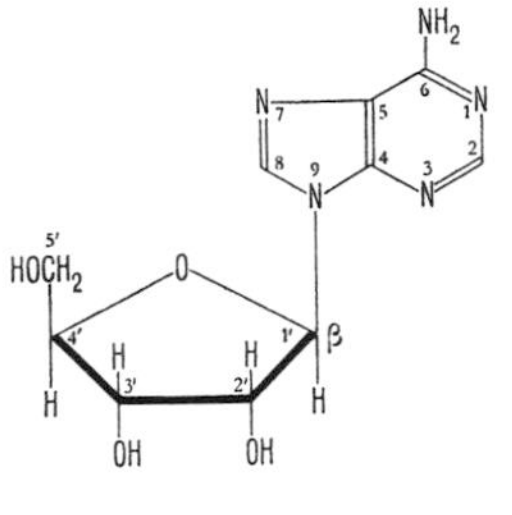	$[\alpha]_D^{20}$ − 67.3° (0.1-N NaOH)	
Deoxyadenosine (deoxyribosyl-adenine)	$C_{10}H_{13}N_5O_3$ 251.25	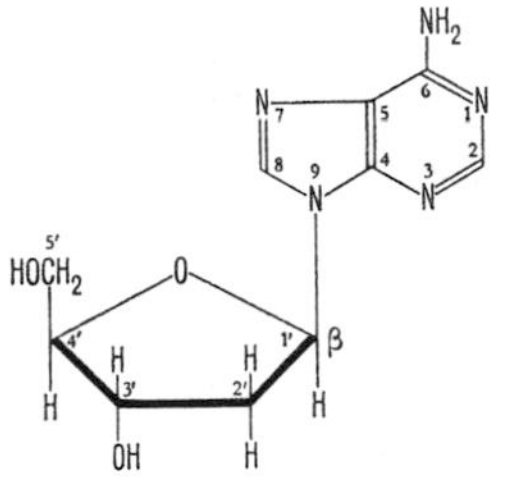	$[\alpha]_D^{21}$ − 26°	
Guanosine (Guo, G) (ribosylguanine)	$C_{10}H_{13}N_5O_5$ 283.25	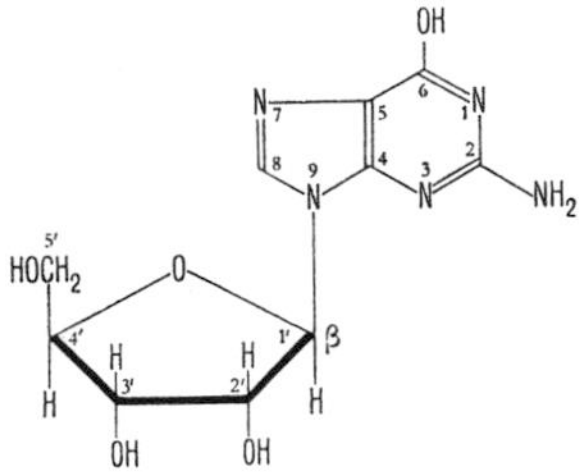	$[\alpha]_D^{20}$ − 60° (2% solution)	These nucleosides are products of the enzymic hydrolysis of the corresponding 3′- and 5′-nucleotides. The nucleosides in turn are broken down further by phosphorolysis to yield ribose 1-phosphate or deoxyribose 1-phosphate and the corresponding base. Nucleoside kinases that form 5′-nucleotides from nucleosides plus ATP are known to occur in yeast and in some animal tissues. Their importance in mammals has not at present been assessed
Deoxyguanosine (deoxyribosyl-guanine)	$C_{10}H_{13}N_5O_4$ 267.25	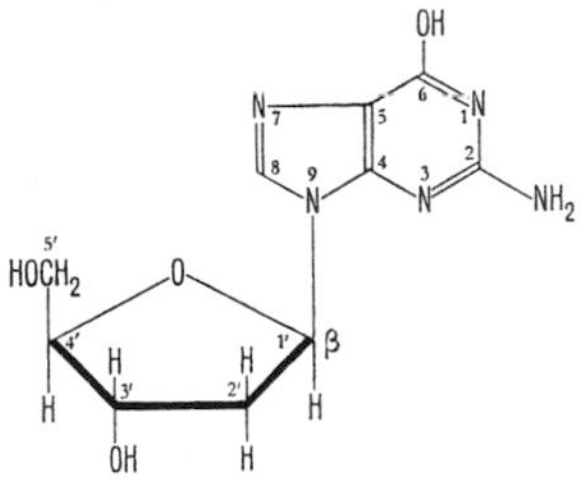	$[\alpha]_D^{19}$ − 47.7° (1-N NaOH)	
Cytidine (Cyd, C) (ribosylcytosine)	$C_9H_{13}N_3O_5$ 243.22	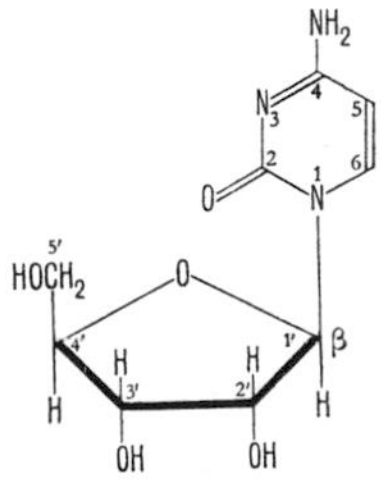	$[\alpha]_D^{20}$ + 29.6°	

* The three-letter symbols are those recommended by the Combined Commission on Biochemical Nomenclature of the International Union of Pure and Applied Chemistry and the International Union of Biochemistry (*J. biol. Chem.*, **241**, 527 [1966]). Other symbols are Thd or T for ribosylthymine and Ψrd or Ψ for 5-ribosyluridine (pseudouridine). Deoxy compounds can be indicated by the prefix d (for example dAdo or dA for deoxyadenosine).

Table 10b (continued) Compounds involved in the biosynthesis and breakdown of purine and pyrimidine nucleotides: Nucleosides

Name*	Formula and mol.wt.	Structure	Specific rotation	Function in mammalian tissue
Deoxycytidine (deoxyribosyl-cytosine)	$C_9H_{13}N_3O_4$ 227.22	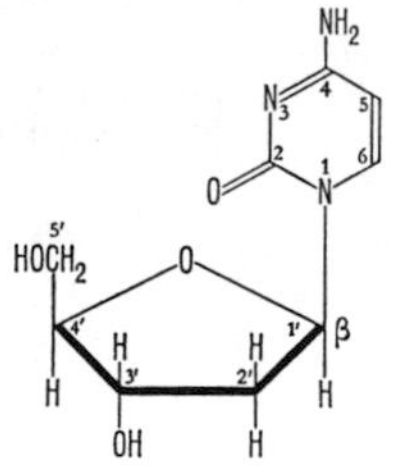	$[\alpha]_D^{25}$ + 40 °	
Uridine (Urd, U) (ribosyluracil)	$C_9H_{12}N_2O_6$ 244.21	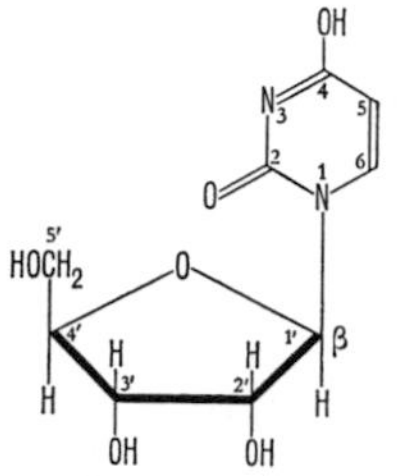	$[\alpha]_D^{16}$ + 9.6 °	These nucleosides are products of the enzymic hydrolysis of the corresponding 3′- and 5′-nucleotides. The nucleosides in turn are broken down further by phosphorolysis to yield ribose 1-phosphate or deoxyribose 1-phosphate and the corresponding base. Nucleoside kinases that form 5′-nucleotides from nucleosides plus ATP are known to occur in yeast and in some animal tissues. Their importance in mammals has not at present been assessed
Deoxythymidine (deoxyribosyl-thymine)	$C_{10}H_{14}N_2O_5$ 242.23	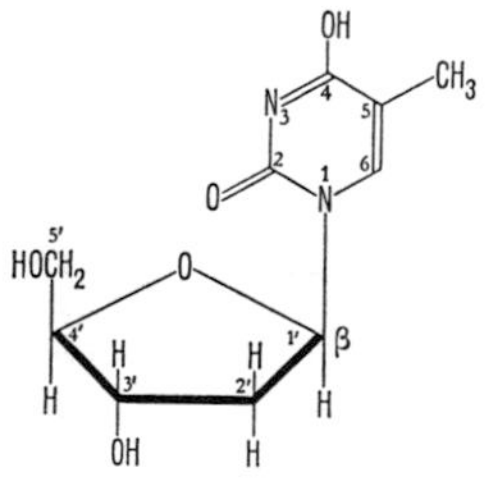	$[\alpha]_D^{16}$ + 32.50 ° (1-N NaOH)	
Inosine (Ino, I) (ribosyl-hypoxanthine)	$C_{10}H_{12}N_4O_5$ 268.23	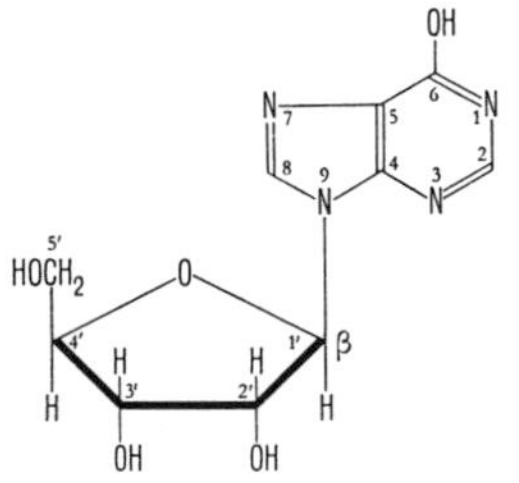	$[\alpha]_D^{18}$ − 72.45 ° (0.1-N NaOH)	This nucleoside has no known function other than its role as intermediate in the synthesis or breakdown of nucleotides (see page 400)

* See footnote page 339.

Table 10b (concluded) Compounds involved in the biosynthesis and breakdown of purine and pyrimidine nucleotides: Nucleosides

Name*	Formula and mol.wt.	Structure	Specific rotation	Function in mammalian tissue
Deoxyinosine (deoxyribosyl-hypoxanthine)	$C_{10}H_{12}N_4O_4$ 252.23	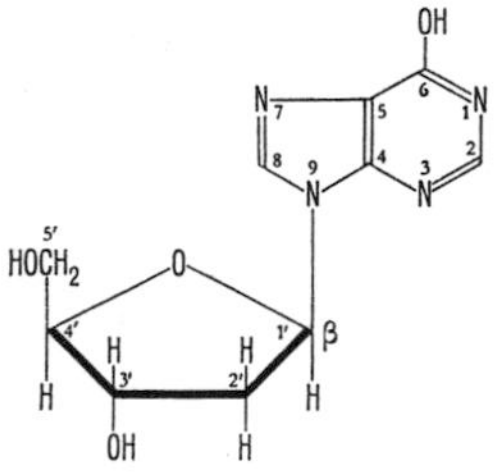	$[\alpha]_D^{19}$ − 22.9° (1-N NaOH)	
Xanthosine (Xao, X) (ribosylxanthine)	$C_{10}H_{12}N_4O_6$ 284.23	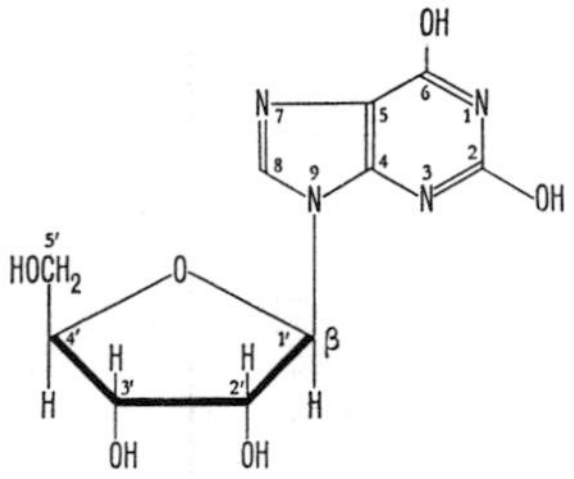	$[\alpha]_D^{30}$ − 51.21°	These nucleosides have no known function other than their role as intermediates in the synthesis or breakdown of nucleotides (see page 400)
Deoxyxanthosine (deoxyribosyl-xanthine)	$C_{10}H_{12}N_4O_5$ 268.23	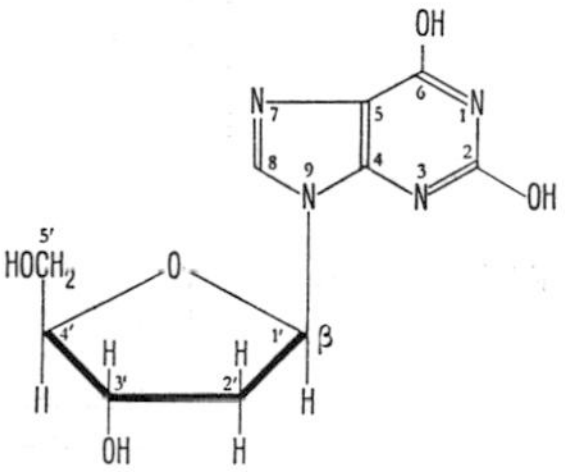	–	
Ribosyluric acid	$C_{10}H_{12}N_4O_7$ 300.23	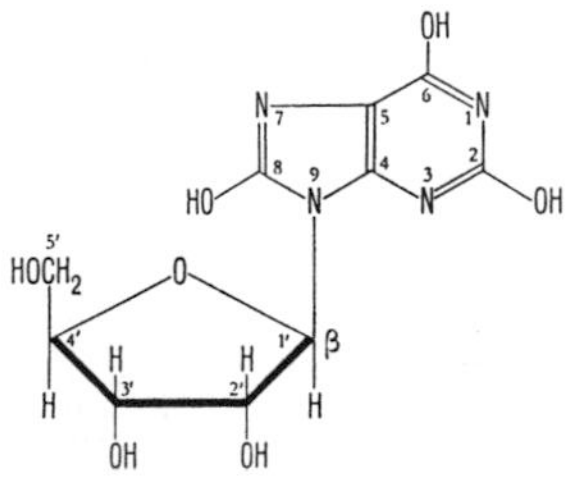	$[\alpha]_D^{20}$ − 40.8° (0.1-N NaOH)	

* See footnote page 339.

Table 10c Compounds involved in the biosynthesis and breakdown of purine and pyrimidine nucleotides: Nucleotides
With the exception of inosinic acid, the compounds listed here have no known coenzyme activity.

Name	Formula and mol.wt.	Structure*	Function
Orotidylic acid (OMP) (ribosylorotic acid 5′-phosphate)	$C_{10}H_{13}N_2O_{11}P$ 368.20	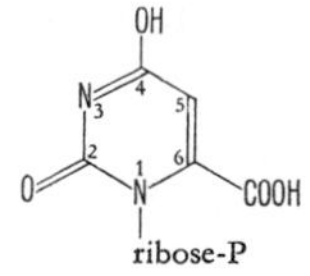	Intermediate in biosynthesis of pyrimidine nucleotides. Formed from orotic acid (see pages 438–439)
5-Phosphoribosylamine (D-ribosylamine 5′-phosphate)	$C_5H_{12}NO_7P$ 229.13	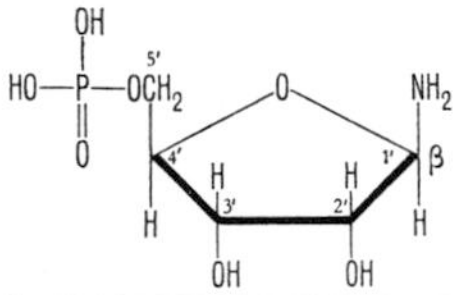	
Ribosylglycinamide 5′-phosphate	$C_7H_{15}N_2O_8P$ 286.18	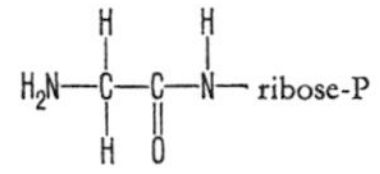	
Ribosylformylglycinamide 5′-phosphate	$C_8H_{15}N_2O_9P$ 314.19	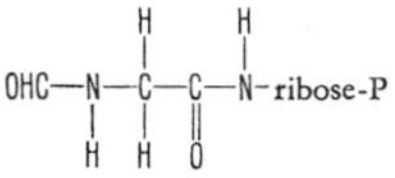	Intermediates in biosynthesis of inosinic acid (see pages 433 and 435)
Ribosylformylglycinamidine 5′-phosphate	$C_8H_{16}N_3O_8P$ 313.21	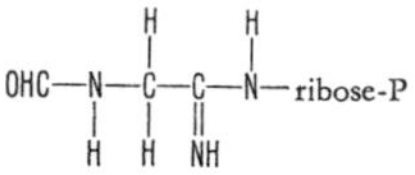	
1-Ribosyl-5-aminoimidazole 5′-phosphate	$C_8H_{14}N_3O_7P$ 295.19	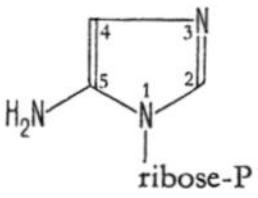	
1-Ribosyl-5-aminoimidazole-4-carboxamide 5′-phosphate	$C_9H_{15}N_4O_8P$ 338.22	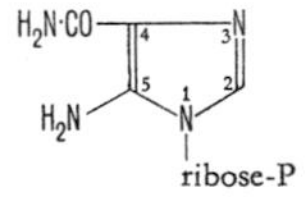	
Inosinic acid (IMP) (inosine 5′-phosphate)	$C_{10}H_{13}N_4O_8P$ 348.21	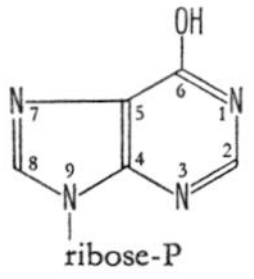	Precursor of adenosine 5′-phosphate (AMP) and guanosine 5′phosphate (GMP) (see Table 11, page 343). Can partially replace certain coenzyme functions of other nucleotides
Succinyladenylic acid (succinyladenosine 5′-phosphate)	$C_{14}H_{18}N_5O_{11}P$ 463.30	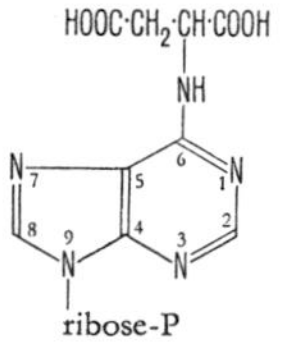	Intermediate in synthesis of adenosine 5′-phosphate (AMP) from inosinic acid (see pages 435–436)
Xanthylic acid (XMP) (xanthosine 5′-phosphate)	$C_{10}H_{13}N_4O_9P$ 364.21	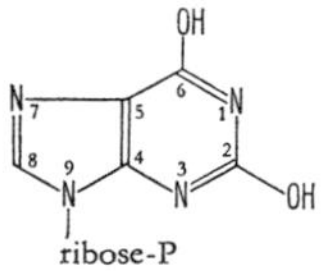	Intermediate in synthesis of guanosine 5′-phosphate (GMP) from inosinic acid (see page 436)

* For structure of the 'ribose-P' portion of the molecule see Table 9, page 337.

Table 11 Nucleoside 5′-mono-, di- and triphosphates (5′-nucleotides)

Name	Abbreviation	Formula	Mol.wt.	Function
Adenosine monophosphate (adenylic acid)	AMP	$C_{10}H_{14}N_5O_7P$	347.23	Precursor of ADP. Activates phosphorylase b
Adenosine diphosphate	ADP	$C_{10}H_{15}N_5O_{10}P_2$	427.21	Immediate precursor of polynucleotides. For other functions see page 404
Adenosine triphosphate	ATP	$C_{10}H_{16}N_5O_{13}P_3$	507.19	Precursor of adenosine coenzymes (see Table 12, pages 344–346). For other functions see page 404
Deoxyadenosine monophosphate	dAMP	$C_{10}H_{14}N_5O_6P$	331.23	Precursor of deoxyadenosine diphosphate
Deoxyadenosine diphosphate	dADP	$C_{10}H_{15}N_5O_9P_2$	411.21	Precursor of deoxyadenosine triphosphate
Deoxyadenosine triphosphate	dATP	$C_{10}H_{16}N_5O_{12}P_3$	491.19	Immediate precursor of deoxyribosepolynucleotides
Guanosine monophosphate (guanylic acid)	GMP	$C_{10}H_{14}N_5O_8P$	363.23	Precursor of guanosine diphosphate
Guanosine diphosphate	GDP	$C_{10}H_{15}N_5O_{11}P_2$	443.21	Immediate precursor of polynucleotides. Yields guanosine triphosphate during cleavage of succinyl-coenzyme A
Guanosine triphosphate	GTP	$C_{10}H_{16}N_5O_{14}P_3$	523.19	Precursor of guanosine coenzymes (see Table 12, page 347). Formed from orthophosphate and guanosine diphosphate during cleavage of succinyl-coenzyme A
Deoxyguanosine monophosphate (desoxyguanylic acid)	dGMP	$C_{10}H_{14}N_5O_7P$	347.23	Precursor of deoxyguanosine diphosphate
Deoxyguanosine diphosphate	dGDP	$C_{10}H_{15}N_5O_{10}P_2$	427.21	Precursor of deoxyguanosine triphosphate
Deoxyguanosine triphosphate	dGTP	$C_{10}H_{16}N_5O_{13}P_3$	507.19	Immediate precursor of deoxyribosepolynucleotides
Cytidine monophosphate (cytidylic acid)	CMP	$C_9H_{14}N_3O_8P$	323.20	Precursor of cytidine diphosphate
Cytidine diphosphate	CDP	$C_9H_{15}N_3O_{11}P_2$	403.18	Immediate precursor of polynucleotides. Precursor of cytidine triphosphate
Cytidine triphosphate	CTP	$C_9H_{16}N_3O_{14}P_3$	483.16	Precursor of cytidine coenzymes (see Table 12, pages 349–350)
Deoxycytidine monophosphate (deoxycytidylic acid)	dCMP	$C_9H_{14}N_3O_7P$	307.20	Precursor of deoxycytidine diphosphate
Deoxycytidine diphosphate	dCDP	$C_9H_{15}N_3O_{10}P_2$	387.18	Precursor of deoxycytidine triphosphate
Deoxycytidine triphosphate	dCTP	$C_9H_{16}N_3O_{13}P_3$	467.16	Immediate precursor of deoxyribosepolynucleotides
Uridine monophosphate (uridylic acid)	UMP	$C_9H_{13}N_2O_9P$	324.19	Precursor of uridine diphosphate
Uridine diphosphate	UDP	$C_9H_{14}N_2O_{12}P_2$	404.17	Immediate precursor of polynucleotides. Precursor of uridine triphosphate
Uridine triphosphate	UTP	$C_9H_{15}N_2O_{15}P_3$	484.15	Precursor of uridine coenzymes (see Table 12, pages 347–349)
Deoxythymidine monophosphate (thymidylic acid)	dTMP	$C_{10}H_{15}N_2O_8P$	322.21	Precursor of deoxythymidine diphosphate
Deoxythymidine diphosphate	dTDP	$C_{10}H_{16}N_2O_{11}P_2$	402.19	Precursor of deoxythymidine triphosphate
Deoxythymidine triphosphate	dTTP	$C_{10}H_{17}N_2O_{14}P_3$	482.17	Immediate precursor of deoxyribosepolynucleotides
Deoxy-5-hydroxymethylcytidine monophosphate	dHMCMP	$C_{10}H_{16}N_3O_8P$	337.23	Constituent nucleotide of the deoxyribonucleic acid of T_2, T_4 and T_6 bacteriophages of *Escherichia coli*, in which it replaces deoxycytidine monophosphate
Deoxy-5-methylcytidine monophosphate	dMCMP	$C_{10}H_{16}N_3O_7P$	321.23	Constituent of the deoxyribonucleic acid of wheat germ, in which it partially replaces deoxycytidine monophosphate

Table 12 Nucleotides with coenzyme functions

Name	Formula and mol.wt.	Structure	Functions	Reference (see page 350)
Nicotinamide mononucleotide (NMN)	$C_{11}H_{15}N_2O_8P$ 334.22	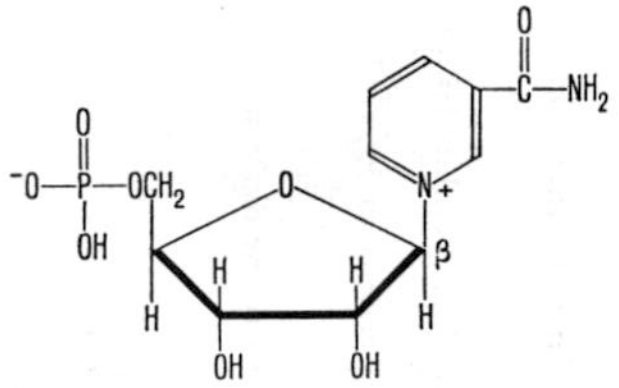	Constituent of nicotinamide-adenine dinucleotide (NAD) and nicotinamide-adenine dinucleotide phosphate (NADP) (see below)	1
Nicotinamide-adenine dinucleotide (NAD) (diphosphopyridine nucleotide, DPN; codehydrogenase I; coenzyme I, Co I; cozymase)	$C_{21}H_{27}N_7O_{14}P_2$ 663.44	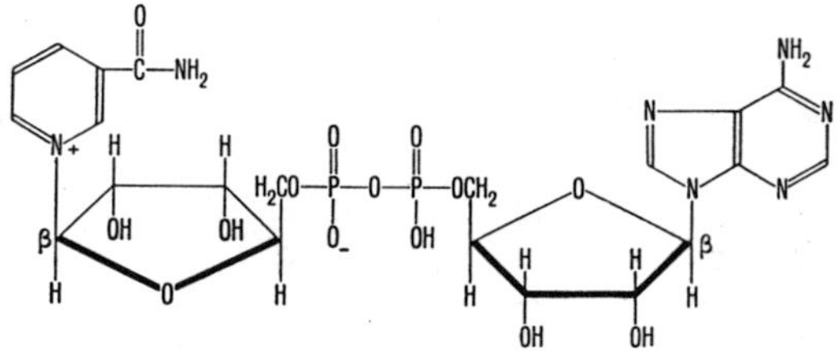	Formed by the reaction: nicotinamide mononucleotide + ATP→ NAD + pyrophosphate. Coenzyme of many dehydrogenases, in which function the pyridine ring of the molecule is reduced reversibly as follows: 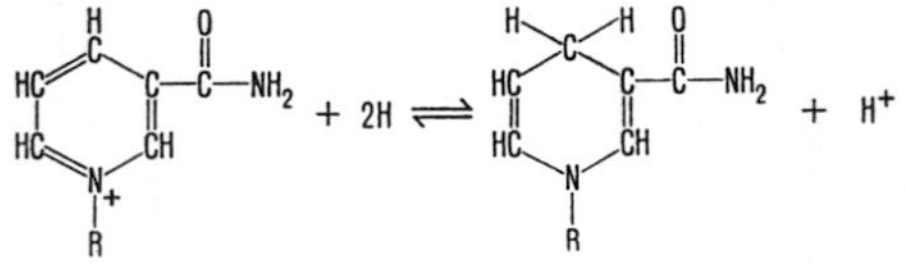	1
Nicotinamide-adenine dinucleotide phosphate (NADP) (triphosphopyridine nucleotide, TPN; codehydrogenase II; coenzyme II, Co II; phosphocozymase)	$C_{21}H_{28}N_7O_{17}P_3$ 743.42	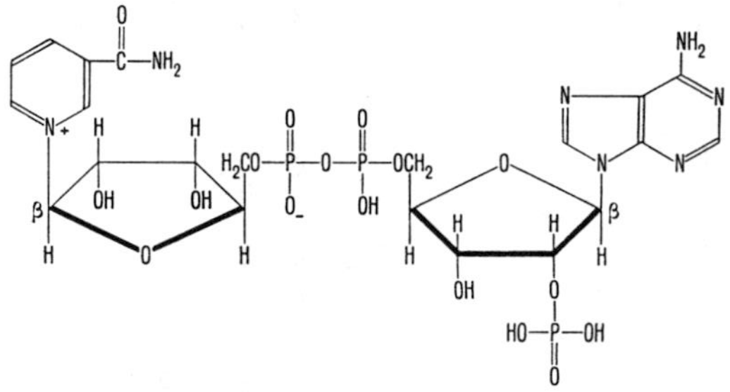	Formed by the reaction: NAD + ATP→ NADP + ADP. Coenzyme of many dehydrogenases, in which function the pyridine ring of the molecule is reduced reversibly as shown above	1

Flavin mononucleotide (FMN) (riboflavin 5′-phosphate, flavin ribityl phosphate)	$C_{17}H_{21}N_4O_9P$ 456.35	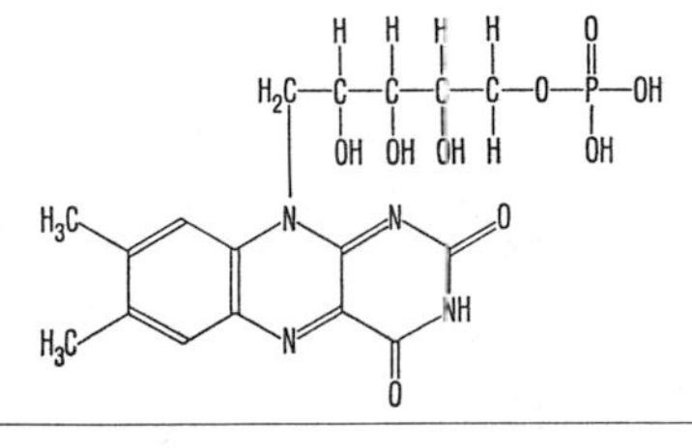	Constituent of flavin adenine dinucleotide (see below)	2
Flavin adenine dinucleotide (FAD) (adenosine diphosphoflavin ribitol)	$C_{27}H_{33}N_9O_{15}P_2$ 785.56	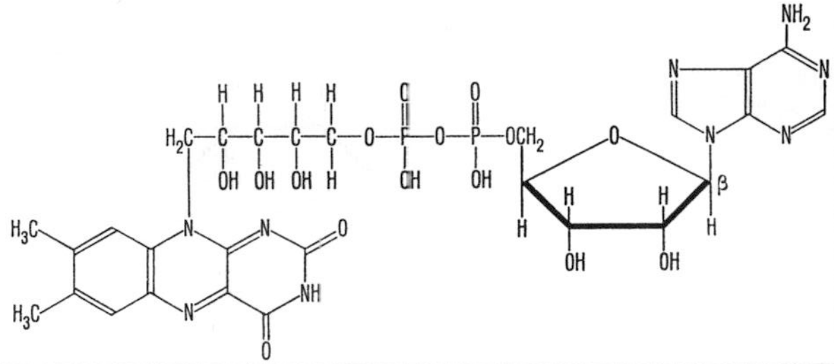	Formed by the reaction: flavin mononucleotide + ATP → flavin adenine dinucleotide + pyrophosphate. Prosthetic group of flavin enzymes (e.g., NAD- and NADP-cytochrome reductases, D-amino-acid oxidase, succinic dehydrogenase, xanthine oxidase)	2
Coenzyme A (CoA, CoASH)	$C_{21}H_{36}N_7O_{16}P_3S$ 767.54	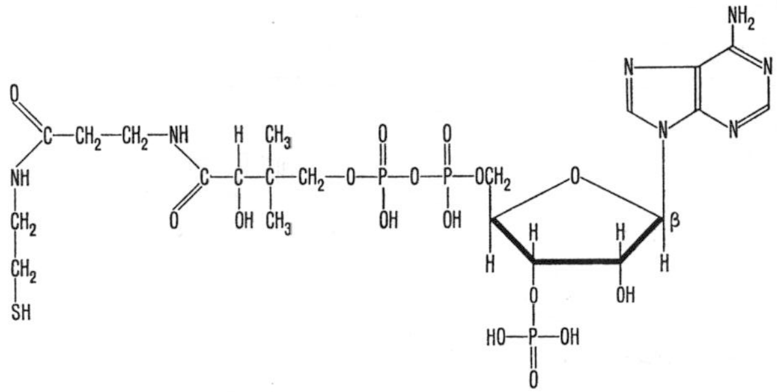	Coenzyme of acyl-group transfer. Formed from pantothenic acid, cysteine and ATP. Acyl groups combine with the sulphhydryl group of CoA to form thiol esters, e.g., $AMP - CO \cdot CH_3 + R \cdot SH \rightarrow AMP + R \cdot S \cdot CO \cdot CH_3$ CoA is involved in the following reactions: formation of citrate from oxaloacetate and acetate (pages 390 and 424), oxidation of pyruvate (page 391), and α-ketoglutarate (page 390), oxidation and synthesis of fatty acids (pages 391–392 and 424–425), synthesis of triglycerides (page 426), cholesterol (page 426) and phospholipids (page 425), and acetylation of amines (page 444), choline (page 434) and glucosamine	3
Cyclic adenosine monophosphate	$C_{10}H_{12}N_5O_6P$ 329.21	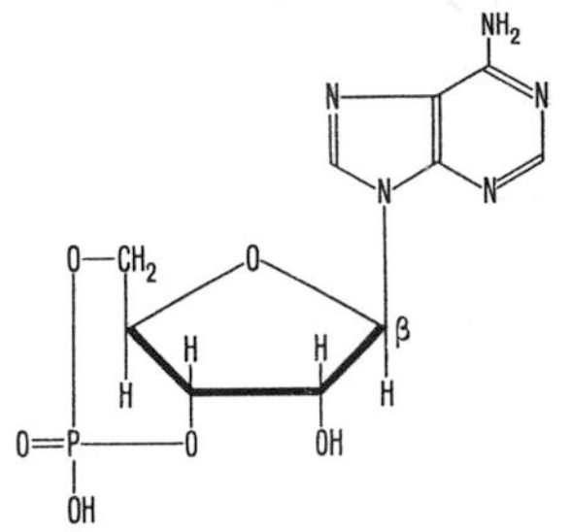	Formed enzymatically from ATP in a reaction that requires magnesium and is activated by several hormones including adrenaline and glucagon. The metabolic effects of these hormones are probably mediated by cyclic AMP, which increases the rate of formation of active phosphorylase from inactive phosphorylase	19

Table 12 (continued) Nucleotides with coenzyme functions

Name	Formula and mol.wt.	Structure	Functions	Reference (see page 350)
Acyl adenosine monophosphates (acyl-adenylates)	–	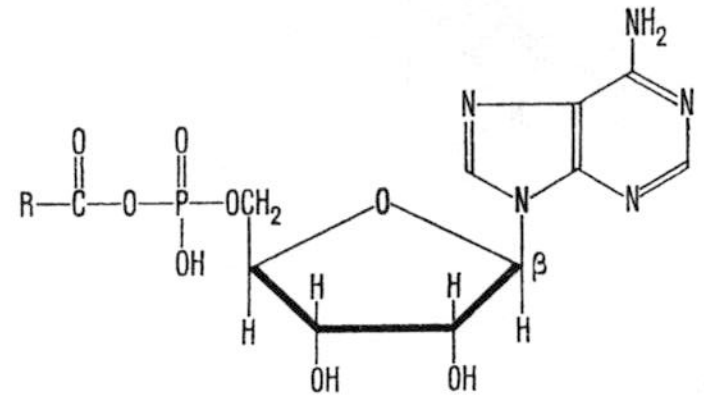 where R = $CH_3 \cdot (CH_2)_n$—	Formed by the reaction: fatty acid + ATP → acyl adenosine monophosphate + pyrophosphate. Intermediate in activation of acetic acid and other fatty acids (page 391)	4
Aminoacyl adenosine monophosphates	–	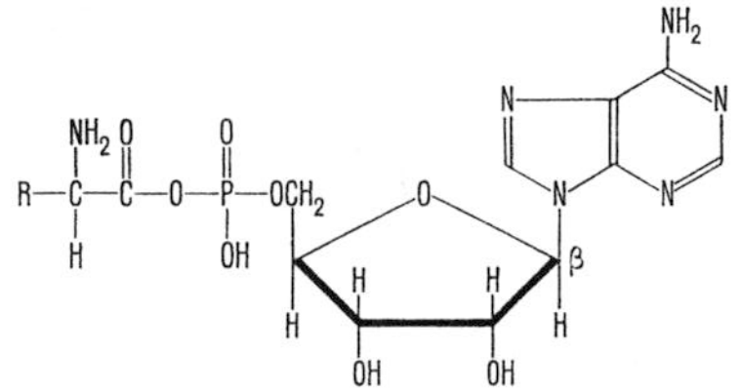 where R = amino-acid residue	Intermediate in activation of amino acids for protein synthesis	5
Adenosine 5′-phosphosulphate	$C_{10}H_{14}N_5O_{10}PS$ 427.29	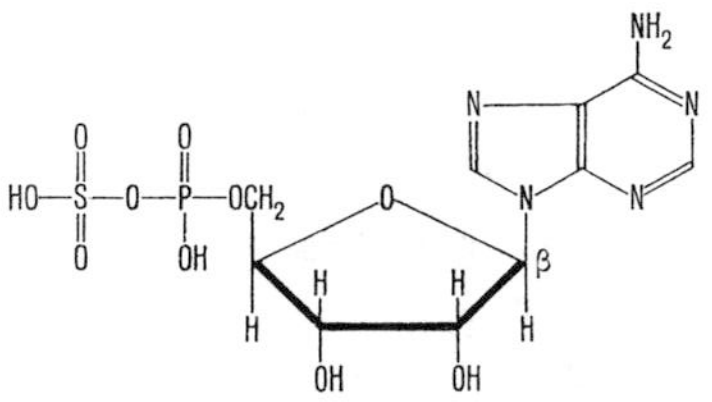	Formed from ATP and inorganic sulphate. Intermediate in sulphate ester synthesis (see page 445)	6
Adenosine 3′-phosphate 5′-phosphosulphate	$C_{10}H_{15}N_5O_{13}P_2S$ 507.27	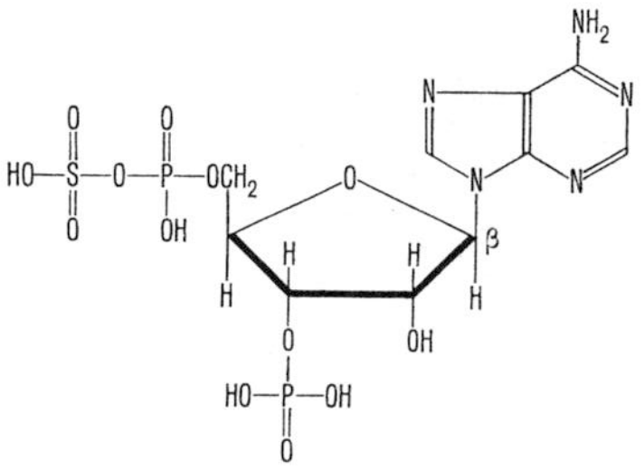	Formed from adenosine 5′-phosphosulphate and ATP. Donor of sulphate group in formation of esters of sulphuric acid (see page 445)	6

Guanosine diphosphate mannose	$C_{16}H_{25}N_5O_{16}P_2$ 605.35	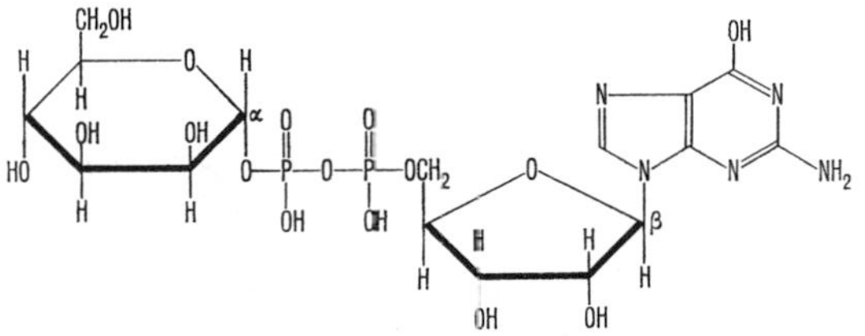	Probably intermediate in interconversions involving mannose. Formed from mannose 1-phosphate and guanosine triphosphate	7
Guanosine diphosphate L-fucose	$C_{16}H_{25}N_5O_{15}P_2$ 589.35	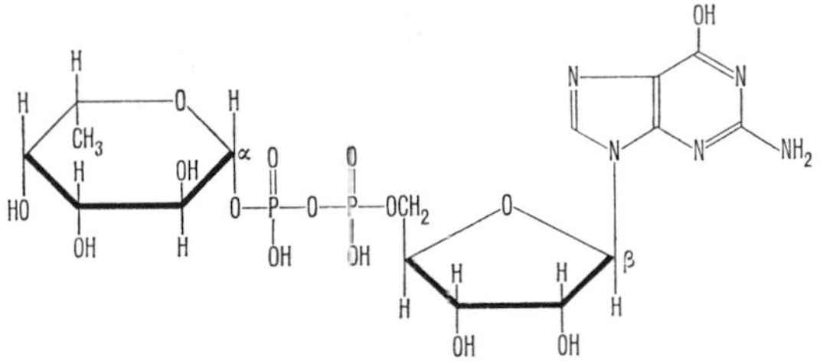	Naturally occurring precursor of L-fucose and form in which L-fucose is incorporated into milk oligosaccharides and probably other glycoproteins	8
Uridine diphosphate glucose (UDPG)	$C_{15}H_{24}N_2O_{17}P_2$ 566.31	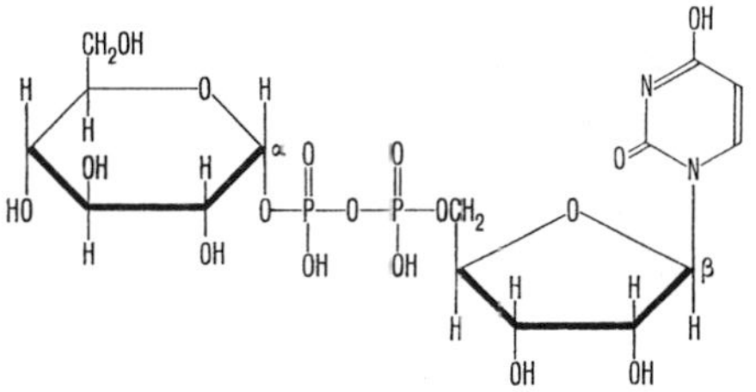	Formed by the reaction: glucose 1-phosphate + UTP → uridine diphosphate glucose + pyrophosphate. Precursor of uridine diphosphate glucuronic acid (see page 348). Intermediate in interconversion of glucose and galactose: uridine diphosphate glucose $\overset{NAD}{\rightleftharpoons}$ uridine diphosphate galactose. In this reaction NAD is required for the consecutive oxidation and reduction of the 4-position of the hexose ring: 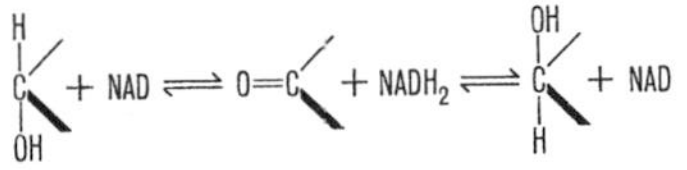	9
Uridine diphosphate galactose	$C_{15}H_{24}N_2O_{17}P_2$ 566.31	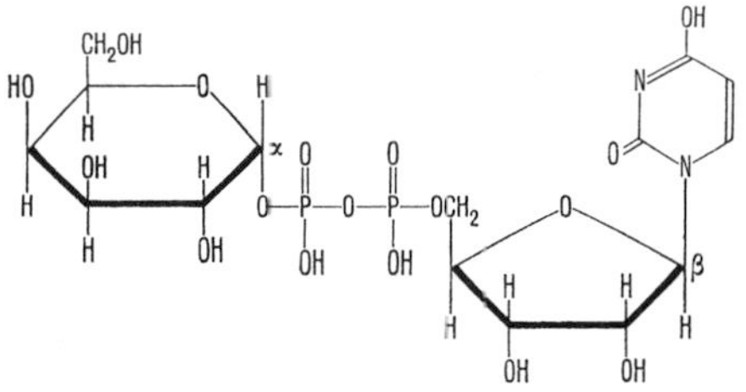	Intermediate in interconversion of galactose and glucose (see under 'Uridine diphosphate glucose' above). Probable intermediate in formation of lactose	9

Table 12 (continued) Nucleotides with coenzyme functions

Name	Formula and mol.wt.	Structure	Functions	Reference (see page 350)
Uridine diphosphate glucosamine	$C_{15}H_{25}N_3O_{16}P_2$ 565.32	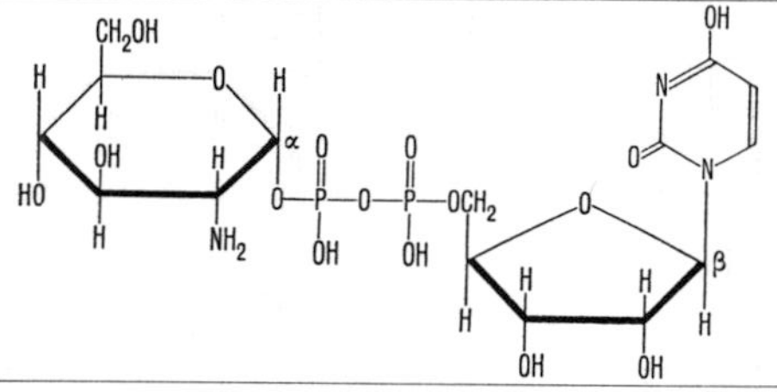	Intermediate in synthesis of mucopolysaccharides. Formed from uridine triphosphate and glucosamine 1-phosphate	10
Uridine diphosphate *N*-acetyl-glucosamine	$C_{17}H_{27}N_3O_{17}P_2$ 607.36	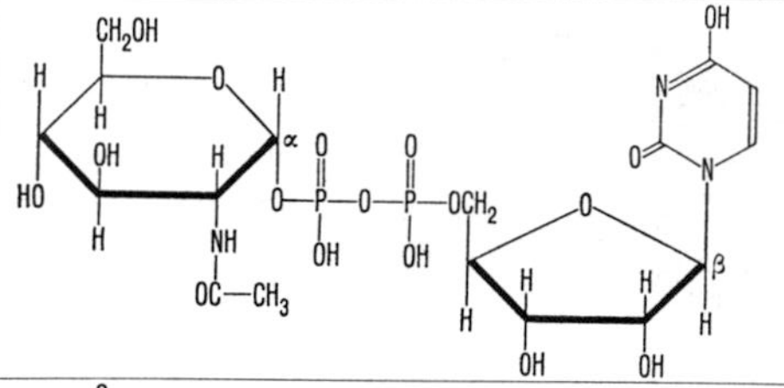	Intermediate in synthesis of mucopolysaccharides and glycoproteins	11
Uridine diphosphate acetylglucosamine phosphate	$C_{17}H_{28}N_3O_{20}P_3$ 687.34	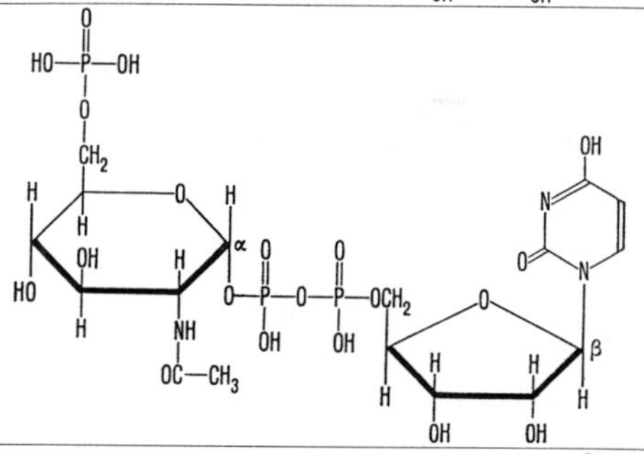	Intermediate in synthesis of mucopolysaccharides and glycoproteins	12
Uridine diphosphate glucuronic acid	$C_{15}H_{22}N_2O_{18}P_2$ 580.29	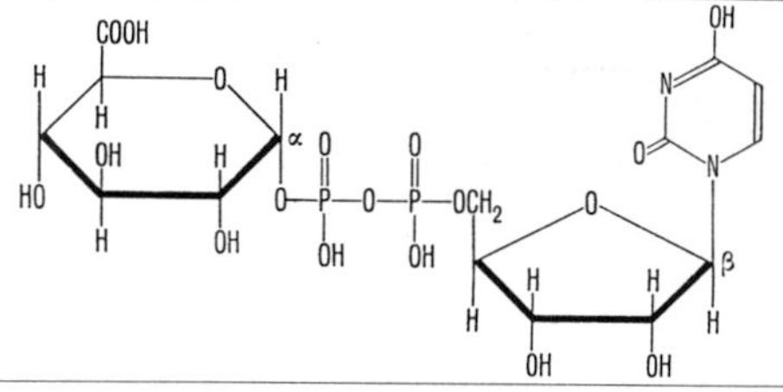	Formed from uridine diphosphate glucose by NAD-dependent oxidation. Donor of glucuronic acid in formation of glucuronide detoxication products, and probably also in formation of polysaccharides containing glucuronic acid (see page 423)	13

Uridine diphosphate *N*-acetyl-galactosamine	$C_{17}H_{27}N_3O_{17}P_2$ 607.36	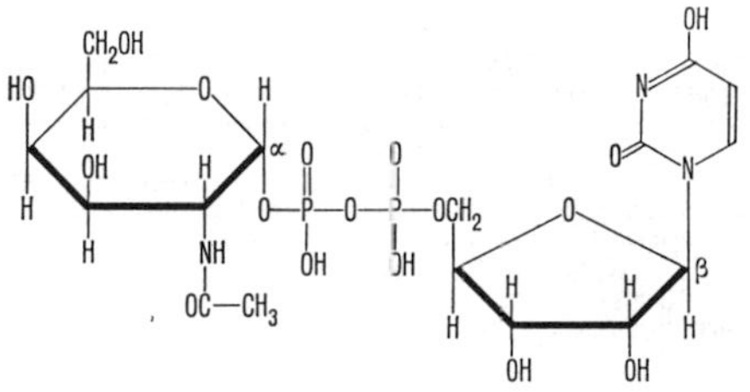	Probable intermediate in synthesis of mucopolysaccharides	14
Uridine diphosphate *N*-acetyl-galactosamine sulphate	$C_{17}H_{27}N_3O_{20}P_2S$ 687.42	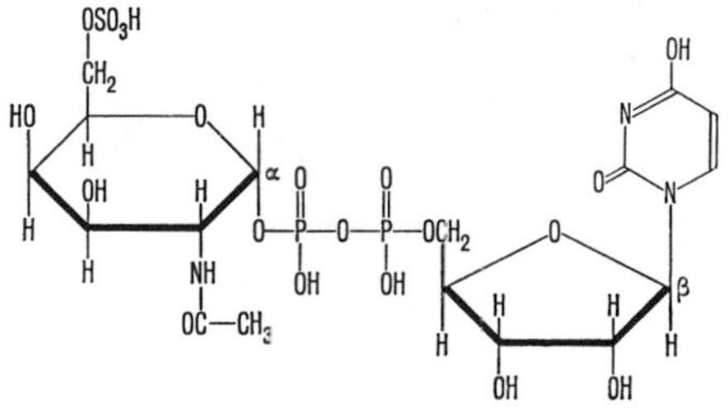	Intermediate in synthesis of mucopolysaccharides	15
Cytidine diphosphate glycerol	$C_{12}H_{21}N_3O_{13}P_2$ 477.26	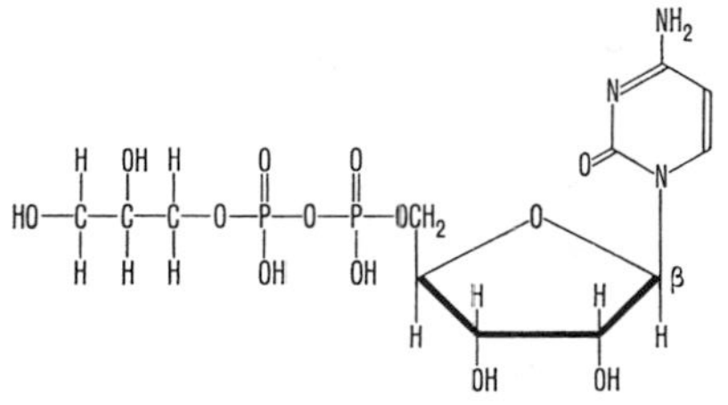	Probable intermediate in formation of glycerol teichoic acids, polymers found in the cell wall of many bacteria	16
Cytidine diphosphate ribitol	$C_{14}H_{25}N_3O_{15}P_2$ 537.31	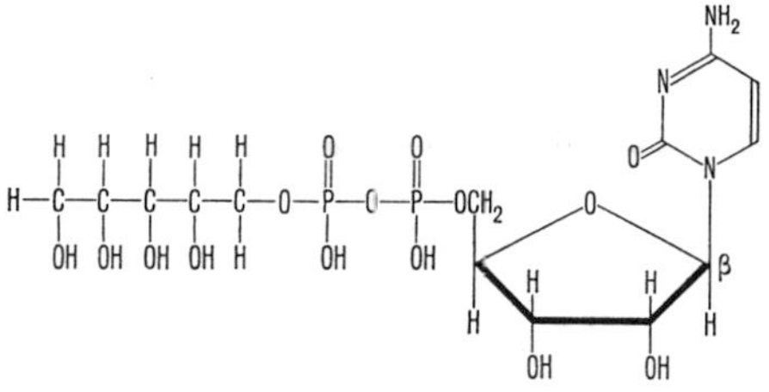	Probable intermediate in formation of ribitol teichoic acids, polymers found in the cell wall of many bacteria	16

Table 12 (concluded) Nucleotides with coenzyme functions

Name	Formula and mol.wt.	Structure	Functions	Reference
Cytidine diphosphate choline	$C_{14}H_{26}N_4O_{11}P_2$ 488.33	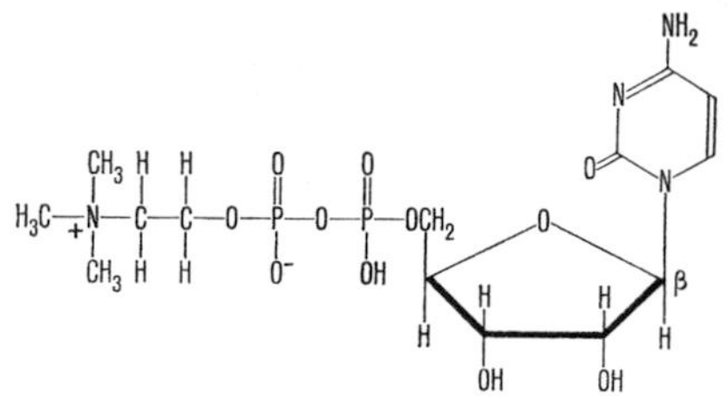	Formed from cytidine triphosphate and phosphorylcholine. Involved in formation of lecithin: cytidine diphosphate choline + α,β-diglyceride → lecithin + cytidine monophosphate (see page 425)	17
Cytidine diphosphate ethanolamine	$C_{11}H_{20}N_4O_{11}P_2$ 446.25	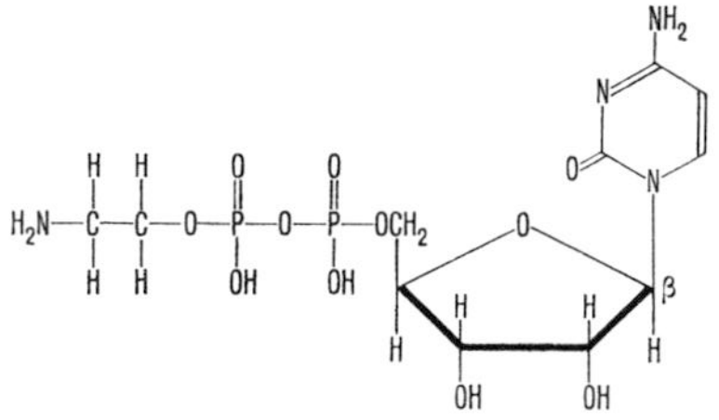	Formed from cytidine triphosphate and phosphorylethanolamine. Involved in formation of cephalin (phosphatidylethanolamine) (see page 425)	17
Cytidine monophosphate *N*-acetylneuraminic acid	$C_{20}H_{31}N_4O_{16}P$ 614.46	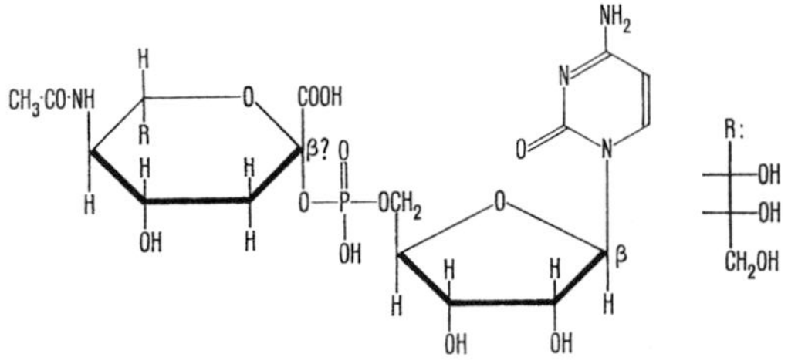	Intermediate in incorporation of *N*-acetylneuraminic acid into milk oligosaccharides and other glycoproteins	18

References

1 Racker, E., *Physiol. Rev.*, **35**, 1 (1955).
2 White et al., *Principles of Biochemistry*, London, McGraw-Hill, 1954.
3 Lipmann, F., *Bact. Rev.*, **17**, 1 (1953); Ward et al., *J. biol. Chem.*, **213**, 869, (1955); Hoagland and Novelli, *J. biol. Chem.*, **207**, 767 (1954).
4 Berg, P., *J. biol. Chem.*, **222**, 991, 1015 (1956).
5 Hoagland et al., *J. biol. Chem.*, **218**, 345 (1956); Keller and Zamecnik, *J. biol. Chem.*, **221**, 45 (1956); Berg, P., *J. biol. Chem.*, **222**, 1025 (1956).
6 Robbins and Lipmann, *J. Amer. chem. Soc.*, **78**, 2652, 6409 (1956); Bandurski et al., *J. Amer. chem. Soc.*, **78**, 6408 (1956).
7 Cabib and Leloir, *J. biol. Chem.*, **206**, 779 (1953); Strominger, J.L., *Fed. Proc.*, **13**, 307 (1954); Munch-Petersen, A., *Arch. Biochem. Biophys.*, **55**, 592 (1955).
8 Grollman et al., *J. biol. Chem.*, **240**, 975 (1965).
9 Caputto et al., *J. biol. Chem.*, **184**, 333 (1950); Maxwell, E.S., *J. Amer. chem. Soc.*, **78**, 1074 (1956); Park, J.T., *J. biol. Chem.*, **194**, 885 (1952); Gander et al., *Arch. Biochem. Biophys.*, **60**, 259 (1956).
10 Maley et al., *J. Amer. chem. Soc.*, **78**, 5303 (1956).
11 Cabib et al., *J. biol. Chem.*, **203**, 1055 (1953).
12 Strominger, J.L., *Biochim. biophys. Acta (Amst.)*, **17**, 283 (1955).
13 Storey and Dutton, *Biochem. J.*, **59**, 279 (1955); Smith and Mills, *Biochim. biophys. Acta (Amst.)*, **13**, 386 (1954); Strominger et al., *J. biol. Chem.*, **224**, 79 (1957).
14 Pontis, H.G., *J. biol. Chem.*, **216**, 195 (1955).
15 Strominger, J.L., *Biochim. biophys. Acta (Amst.)*, **17**, 283 (1955).
16 Baddiley et al., *J. chem. Soc. Lond.*, **1956**, 4186, 4583; *Biochem. J.*, **63**, 15P (1956); Touster and Shaw, *Physiol. Rev.*, **42**, 181 (1962).
17 Kennedy, E.P., *J. biol. Chem.*, **222**, 185 (1956); Kennedy and Weiss, *J. biol. Chem.*, **222**, 193 (1956).
18 Comb et al., *J. Amer. Chem. Soc.*, **81**, 5513 (1959).
19 Robison et al., *Ann. Rev. Biochem.*, **37**, 149 (1968).

Nucleic acids

Nucleic acid is the generic name given to a group of substances that, chemically speaking, are *polynucleotides*. Two types of nucleic acid are known: the *ribonucleic acids* (RNA), found in the cytoplasm and in small amounts in the nucleus of the cell, and the *deoxyribonucleic acids* (DNA), found in the nucleus of the cell. The polynucleotide structure of RNA and DNA is formed by the esterification of the phosphate group of 5′-nucleotides with the 3′-position of adjacent nucleotides. Four main types of nucleotide units are found in RNA: adenylic acid, guanylic acid, cytidylic acid and uridylic acid. Four main types of deoxyribonucleotide units are found in most kinds of DNA: deoxyadenylic acid, deoxyguanylic acid, deoxycytidylic acid and deoxythymidylic acid. The latter deoxyribonucleotide is still referred to simply as 'thymidylic acid' because no ribonucleotide containing the base thymine was believed to occur in nature. Since this compound has been detected in certain kinds of RNA this practice can no longer be justified. In certain types of DNA and RNA one of the common bases is replaced partially or wholly by a different one. Some of these exceptions are indicated in Table 11, page 343, and Table 13, page 354. Portions of RNA and DNA polynucleotides are shown in Figure 4.

Fig. 4 Portions of RNA and DNA polynucleotides

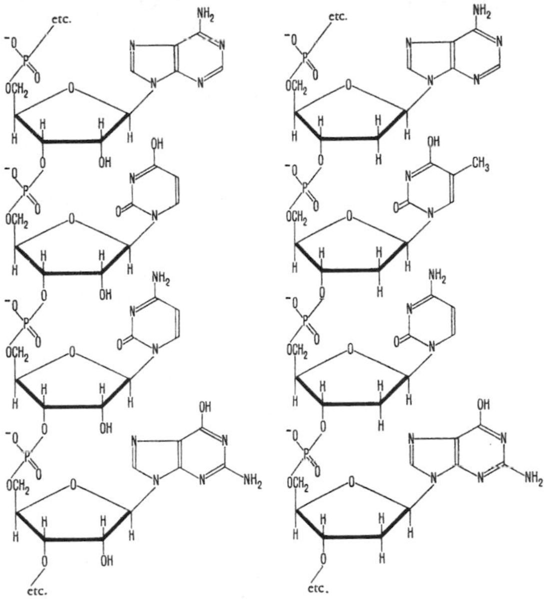

Portion of ribonucleic acid molecule — Portion of deoxyribonucleic acid molecule

Deoxyribonucleic acid (DNA)

DNA contains equal amounts of deoxyguanylic acid and deoxycytidylic acid and also of deoxyadenylic acid and deoxythymidylic acid, the second pair being present in somewhat larger amounts in animals than in other organisms.

The DNA molecule consists of a pair of polynucleotide chains aligned in the form of a double helix. The alignment is such that bases in one chain are linked to bases in the other chain by hydrogen bonds, adenine being linked to thymine and guanine to cytosine. DNA combined with protein (deoxyribonucleoprotein) makes up part or all of the constituent material of the chromosomes and genes[1]. According to current theory it forms both the storehouse of genetic information and the 'master templates' of cell reproduction[2]. It has been calculated that for a polynucleotide consisting of 300 mononucleotide units there can exist about 4×10^{87} different nucleic acids, assuming that there is complete freedom of choice in the arrangement of the four different mononucleotides[3]. The nucleic acids are thus capable of great specificity, and this specificity can be transferred to proteins during their synthesis. The chemical basis of heredity is believed to lie in the sequences of nucleotides in the polynucleotide chain, different sequences of nucleotides reflecting specific types of information; i.e., the sequence of amino acids in the proteins depends on the sequence of nucleotides.

Ribonucleic acid (RNA)

RNA is found in all the major parts of the cell. Several different kinds of RNA exist, each with a different function:

Ribosomal RNA. The cell contains small granules called ribosomes. They contain 40–65% RNA. The remainder of the ribosome is almost wholly protein. In animal cells the ribosomes are either free or attached to the endoplasmic reticulum. Ribosomal RNA accounts for 80–90% of the RNA of liver.

Ribosomes can be separated into two main types differing in size and therefore in their sedimentation constant (S): 80 S ribosomes in the cells of the higher plants, animals and some micro-organisms, 70 S ribosomes in most bacteria. Each of these types of ribosome dissociates readily into two subunits, the 80 S ribosomes into 40 S and 60 S subunits, the 70 S ribosomes into 30 S and 50 S subunits. The 40 S and 60 S subunits consist respectively of 18 S and 28 S RNA, the 30 S and 50 S subunits of 16 S and 23 S RNA. A low-molecular 5 S RNA consisting of about 120 bases has also been discovered[4].

When the base composition of ribosomal RNA is compared with the base composition of all of the DNA found in the same cell no correlation is observed[5]. However, hybridization experiments show that about 0.3% of the total DNA is complementary to the two types of ribosomal RNA[6].

Amino acid acceptor RNA. This type of RNA, which is also referred to as *soluble RNA* (s-RNA) or *transfer RNA* (t-RNA), accounts for 10–20% of the total RNA of the cell. It has a chain length of approximately 70–90 nucleotide units. There is no correlation between the base composition of s-RNA and the base composition of all the DNA found in the same cell. However, hybridization experiments show that about 0.025% of the total DNA is complementary to a particular type of s-RNA[7].

s-RNA acts as a carrier for amino acids during protein synthesis. There is at least one specific s-RNA for each of the 20 common amino acids, but some amino acids have several different, specific types of s-RNA. The amino acid is esterified either to the 2′- or the 3′-hydroxyl group of the terminal adenylic acid[8].

In addition to the four common bases, s-RNA contains small amounts of methylated derivatives of these bases together with pseudouridine (see page 354). The complete base sequence of alanyl-transfer RNA from yeast has been elucidated[9], and the primary structure of some other types of transfer RNA is also now known[10]. They all have in common the nucleotide sequence –CMP–CMP–AMP at the amino-acid accepting end of the molecule and the clover-leaf form of the base chain.

Messenger RNA. Another type of RNA can be distinguished by the rapid synthesis and breakdown (rapid turnover) it untergoes during protein synthesis. On a percentage basis this type of RNA (m-RNA) accounts for only 5% or less of the total RNA found in the cell. There is a close relation between the base composition of m-RNA and that of DNA of the same cell type[11]. The function of m-RNA is to transfer genetic information stored in DNA to the assembly site of protein synthesis, namely the ribosomes (see page 353). During protein synthesis much of the m-RNA of the cell is associated with the ribosomes[12].

References

1 For a review see Sinsheimer, R.L., *Science*, **125**, 1123 (1957).
2 Crick et al., *Nature*, **192**, 1227 (1961).
3 Dounce, A.L., *Enzymologia*, **15**, 251 (1952).
4 Brownlee et al., *Nature*, **215**, 735 (1967).
5 Grunberg-Manago, M., *Progr. Biophys. molec. Biol.*, **13**, 175 (1963).
6 Yankofsky and Spiegelman, *Proc. nat. Acad. Sci. (Wash.)*, **49**, 538 (1963).
7 Giacomoni and Spiegelman, *Science*, **138**, 1328 (1962).
8 Zachan et al., *Proc. nat. Acad. Sci. (Wash.)*, **44**, 885 (1958); Preiss et al., *Proc. nat. Acad. Sci. (Wash.)*, **45**, 319 (1959); Hecht et al., *Proc. nat. Acad. Sci. (Wash.)*, **45**, 505 (1959).
9 Holley et al., *Science*, **147**, 1462 (1965).
10 Madison, J.T., *Ann. Rev. Biochem.*, **37**, 131 (1968).
11 Brenner et al., *Nature*, **190**, 576 (1961); Gros et al., *Nature*, **190**, 581 (1961); Hayashi and Spiegelman, *Proc. nat. Acad. Sci. (Wash.)*, **47**, 1564 (1961); Volkin, E., *Fed. Proc.*, **21**, 112 (1962); Spiegelman, S., *Sci. Amer.*, **210**, No. 5, 48 (1964).
12 Risebrough et al., *Proc. nat. Acad. Sci. (Wash.)*, **48**, 430 (1962).

Synthesis of DNA

The synthesis of DNA has been studied mainly with bacterial enzymes, but the mechanism of DNA synthesis in animals resembles that of bacteria. The reaction catalysed by the enzyme DNA nucleotidyltransferase (DNA polymerase) can be formulated as follows (cf. Table 11, page 343):

$$x\text{dATP} + x\text{dTTP} + y\text{dGTP} + y\text{dCTP} \underset{\text{DNA primer}}{\overset{Mg^{++}}{\rightleftharpoons}} \text{DNA} + (2x+2y)\text{pyrophosphate}$$

The enzyme has an absolute requirement for magnesium ions as well as for a 'primer' consisting of DNA. It requires all four deoxyribonucleotides if a primer containing all four deoxyribonucleotides is used. The enzyme is specific for the four *deoxyribo*nucleoside *tri*phosphates. Mono- and diphosphates are inactive, as are all ribonucleotides[1,2].

The base composition of the enzymatically formed DNA is a complementary copy of the base composition of the DNA used as primer, regardless of the relative amounts of each deoxyribonucleoside triphosphate added to the reaction mixture[3]. This and other evidence[4] shows that the enzymatic synthesis occurs by 'base-pairing' with the primer DNA. In other words, the role of the primer DNA is that of a DNA template. Where the DNA template contains the base adenine, the nucleotide inserted into the new molecule is the base thymine, and vice versa. Where the template contains the base guanine, the nucleotide inserted into the new molecule is cytosine, and vice versa[2]. Such assembly can occur in two directions. In one direction the newly synthesized molecule of DNA has *opposite polarity* to the template molecule, i.e., the 3',5'-phosphodiester bridges in the template point in the opposite direction to the 3',5'-phosphodiester bridges of the newly synthesized molecule. In the other direction the newly synthesized molecule of DNA has *similar polarity*. Here the 3',5'-phosphodiester bridges of template DNA and newly formed DNA point in the same direction (Fig. 5). Experimental evidence shows that the newly synthesized DNA has the *opposite* polarity of the template. The product is double-stranded DNA. When the primer is double-stranded DNA it must presumably be 'unwound' into single-strand DNA before it can act as a template for DNA synthesis. The mechanism for such 'unwinding' is not understood, but one possibility is that the 'unwinding' occurs just ahead of the growth of the new DNA chain[5].

Using pure DNA polymerase, the total synthesis of infective viral DNA starting from the four deoxynucleoside triphosphates has been accomplished in vitro[6].

Fig. 5 Double-stranded DNA of opposite polarity (upper diagram) and of similar polarity (lower diagram). Experimental evidence shows that during the synthesis of DNA the new strand is of opposite polarity[4]

A Adenine; T Thymine; G Guanine; C Cytosine; P Phosphate

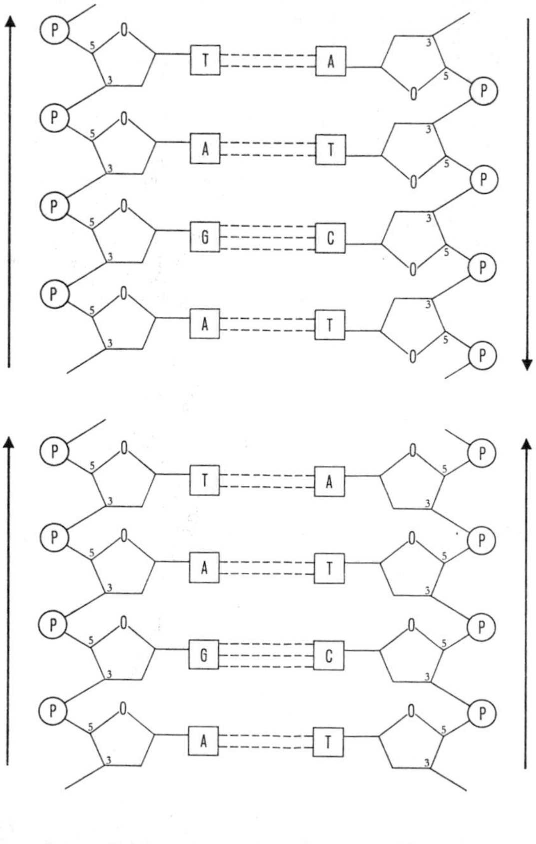

References

[1] Lehman et al., *J. biol. Chem.*, **233**, 163 (1958); Bessman et al., *J. biol. Chem.*, **233**, 171 (1958); Adler et al., *Proc. nat. Acad. Sci. (Wash.)*, **44**, 641 (1958); Bollum, F. J., *Fed. Proc.*, **17**, 193 (1958); Bollum and Potter, *J. biol. Chem.*, **233**, 478 (1958); Kornberg, A., *Harvey Lect. 1957–1958*, **53**, 83 (1959); Smellie et al., *Biochim. biophys. Acta (Amst.)*, **35**, 389 (1959); Smellie et al., *Biochim. biophys. Acta (Amst.)*, **37**, 243 (1960); Grunberg-Manago, M., *Progr. Biophys. molec. Biol.*, **13**, 175 (1963).
[2] Kornberg, A., *Science*, **131**, 1503 (1960).
[3] Lehman et al., *Proc. nat. Acad. Sci. (Wash.)*, **44**, 1191 (1958); Lehman, I. R., *Ann. N. Y. Acad. Sci.*, **81**, 745 (1959).
[4] Josse et al., *J. biol. Chem.*, **236**, 864 (1961).
[5] Spiegelman, S., *Sci. Amer.*, **210**, No. 5, 48 (1964).
[6] Kornberg, A., *Sci. Amer.*, **219**, No. 4, 64 (1968).

Synthesis of RNA

RNA nucleotidyltransferase (RNA polymerase). This enzyme catalyses the formation of RNA from nucleoside 5'-triphosphates[1]:

$$x(\text{ATP} + \text{GTP} + \text{UTP} + \text{CTP}) \underset{\text{DNA primer}}{\overset{Mn^{++}}{\rightleftharpoons}} \text{RNA} + 4x \text{ pyrophosphate}$$

The reaction requires all four ribonucleoside triphosphates and a DNA primer. The product is RNA with a base composition that is a complementary copy of the DNA primer[2]. The enzyme requires a bivalent metal ion, manganese being more effective than magnesium. The chief physiological function of this enzyme is probably to make messenger RNA for protein synthesis[3], in other words, to transcribe information contained in the DNA code into RNA ('transcription'). This enzyme is also responsible for the synthesis of ribosomal RNA and s-RNA[4]. The nature of the RNA actually synthesized is determined by specific factors that adapt the enzyme to specific template DNA[5].

Other types of RNA polymerases also exist. For example, viruses that contain RNA but not DNA can duplicate in host cells. In this case viral RNA acts as the template and DNA is not required for the *de novo* synthesis of RNA[6].

Polyribonucleotide nucleotidyltransferase (polynucleotide phosphorylase). This enzyme catalyses the synthesis of polyribonucleotides from nucleoside 5'-diphosphates. The reverse reaction is termed phosphorolysis:

$$x \text{ nucleoside diphosphate} \overset{Mg^{++}}{\rightleftharpoons} \text{RNA} + x \text{ orthophosphate}$$

The RNA formed according to this equation will contain x mononucleotide units. The enzyme is specific for *ribo*nucleoside *di*phosphates. Nucleoside mono- and triphosphates are inactive; also inactive are deoxyribonucleoside diphosphates[7]. The enzyme is relatively unspecific with respect to the base of the nucleoside diphosphate[8]. It can make polymers containing one or more bases. When the four ribonucleoside diphosphates containing adenine (A), guanine (G), cytidine (C), and uracil (U) are used, an RNA-like polymer results in which the base-sequence is random[9]. The synthesis of RNA shows a lag period that is abolished if an RNA primer is added[10,11]. When a primer is supplied the enzyme adds new nucleotides to the ends of the primer molecules[11].

The function of this enzyme reaction is not yet understood. Its chief role may be not to synthesize but to degrade RNA. s-RNA is very resistant to phosphorolysis by polynucleotide phosphorylase, but the rapid breakdown of m-RNA may be catalysed by this enzyme[8].

References

[1] Hurwitz et al., *Biochem. biophys. Res. Commun.*, **3**, 15 (1960); Stevens, A., *Biochem. biophys. Res. Commun.*, **3**, 92 (1960); Weiss, S. B., *Proc. nat. Acad. Sci. (Wash.)*, **46**, 1020 (1960); Weiss and Nakamoto, *J. biol. Chem.*, **236**, PC18 (1961); Weiss, S. B., *Fed. Proc.*, **21**, 120 (1962).
[2] Weiss and Nakamoto, *Proc. nat. Acad. Sci. (Wash.)*, **47**, 1400 (1961); Chamberlin and Berg, *Proc. nat. Acad. Sci. (Wash.)*, **48**, 81 (1962); Geiduschek et al., *Proc. nat. Acad. Sci. (Wash.)*, **48**, 1078 (1962); Furth et al., *Fed. Proc.*, **21**, 371 (1962).

[3] EISENSTADT et al., *Proc.nat.Acad.Sci.(Wash.)*, **48**, 652 (1962); KAMEYAMA and NOVELLI, *Proc.nat.Acad.Sci.(Wash.)*, **48**, 659 (1962); NISMAN et al., *Biochim. biophys. Acta (Amst.)*, **55**, 704 (1962); OISHI et al., *Biochem.biophys. Res. Commun.*, **8**, 342 (1962); RUECKERT et al., *J.molec.Biol.*, **5**, 10 (1962).
[4] YANKOFSKY and SPIEGELMAN, *Proc.nat.Acad.Sci.(Wash.)*, **48**, 1069 and 1466 (1962); **49**, 538 (1963).
[5] TOCHINI-VALENTINI et al., *Nature*, **220**, 275 (1968); BURGESS and TRAVERS, *Nature*, **221**, 43 (1969).
[6] NAKAMOTO and WEISS, *Proc.nat.Acad.Sci.(Wash.)*, **48**, 880 (1962).
[7] GRUNBERG-MANAGO and OCHOA, *J. Amer.chem.Soc.*, **77**, 3165 (1955); GRUNBERG-MANAGO et al., *Biochim.biophys.Acta (Amst.)*, **20**, 269 (1956); LITTAUER and KORNBERG, *J.biol.Chem.*, **226**, 1077 (1957); OCHOA, S., *Angew.Chem.*, **72**, 225 (1960); OCHOA et al., in COLOWICK and KAPLAN (Eds.), *Methods in Enzymology*, vol. 6, Academic Press, New York, 1963, page 3.
[8] GRUNBERG-MANAGO, M., *Progr.Biophys.molec.Biol.*, **13**, 175 (1963).
[9] COX, A.R., Acides ribonucléiques et polyphosphates; structure, synthèse et fonctions, *Colloques internationaux du CNRS*, Paris, 1961, page 92.
[10] MII and OCHOA, *Biochim.biophys.Acta (Amst.)*, **26**, 445 (1957); SINGER et al., *Biochim.biophys.Acta (Amst.)*, **26**, 447 (1957); SINGER et al., *J.biol.Chem.*, **235**, 738 and 751 (1960); SINGER and GUSS, *J.biol.Chem.*, **237**, 182 (1962).
[11] BEERS, R.F., *Nature*, **183**, 1335 (1959).

Fig. 6 Diagrammatic representation of protein synthesis

Polypeptide s-RNA is transferred to the new aminoacyl-s-RNA. The growing polypeptide s-RNA together with the m-RNA then moves along the ribosome from right to left by one division. A molecule of s-RNA is released.

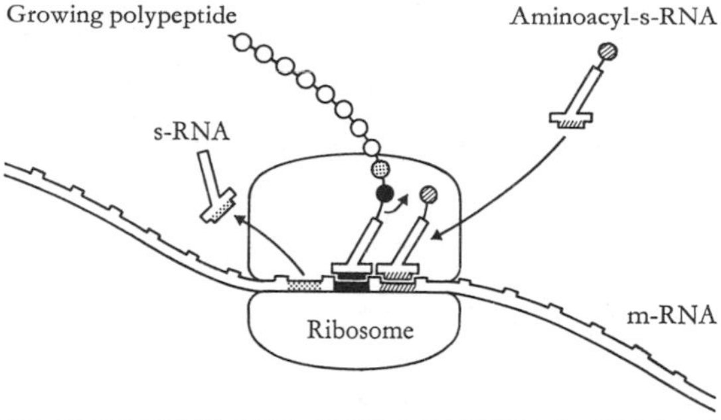

Synthesis of proteins [1–3]

Protein synthesis involves the linking together of 20 different amino acids in specific sequences containing hundreds of amino acids. The amino-acid sequence of a particular protein is reproduced exactly over and over again in each protein molecule synthesized. Errors in amino-acid sequence are exceedingly rare. The exact position of each amino acid in a protein molecule is determined genetically by the information stored in the form of DNA. In other words, DNA contains coded information for protein synthesis. The 'alphabet' of the DNA code consists of only four 'letters', corresponding to the four bases found in DNA, namely adenine (A), thymine (T), guanine (G) and cytosine (C) [4].

The code 'message' contained in DNA is not transmitted to the site of protein synthesis in the form of DNA. It is first transcribed into messenger RNA (m-RNA) by an enzyme, RNA polymerase, that requires DNA as a primer. This enzyme copies the base sequence of DNA into RNA. Each molecule of DNA is thus transcribed into many molecules of m-RNA ('transcription'). The base sequence of m-RNA is complementary to the DNA template. A in the DNA is copied as uracil (U) in the m-RNA, T is copied as A, G is copied as C, and C is copied as A. The strand of messenger RNA leaves the DNA template and becomes attached to the structural unit of protein synthesis, the ribosome.

Amino acids are activated by attachment to another kind of RNA, namely soluble RNA (s-RNA, transfer-RNA) [5] (see page 351):

$$\begin{matrix}\text{amino}\\ \text{acid}\end{matrix} + \text{ATP} + \text{s-RNA} \rightleftharpoons \begin{matrix}\text{aminoacyl}\\ \text{s-RNA}\end{matrix} + \text{AMP} + \begin{matrix}\text{pyro-}\\ \text{phosphate}\end{matrix}$$

The reaction proceeds through the intermediate formation of aminoacyl AMP. For each amino acid there are at least one specific activating enzyme and one specific type of s-RNA. Each amino acid activating enzyme thus recognizes one specific amino acid and one specific s-RNA [6,7]. For some amino acids there may be more than one activating enzyme and more than one type of s-RNA [7,8].

The activated amino acids are condensed into polypeptides as follows:

The scheme shows that proteins grow by the stepwise addition of amino acids, starting with the amino-terminal amino acid and ending with the carboxyl-terminal amino acid [9]. It shows further that the growing polypeptide always contains a molecule of s-RNA corresponding to the last amino acid to be inserted. The specific amino acid added to the growing polypeptide is determined by the base sequence of m-RNA ('translation'). Each specific s-RNA has in it a region which 'recognizes' part of the amino-acid code contained in the m-RNA molecule. Such recognition occurs by correct base-pairing of a sequence of three nucleotides of m-RNA (a 'codon') with a sequence of three nucleotides of aminoacyl-s-RNA (an 'anticodon' or 'nodoc') [4,10]. In bacteria, protein chains (codons AUG, GUG) have been shown to be initiated by formyl-methionyl-s-RNA.

The assembly of the polypeptide occurs on the ribosome. The function of the ribosome is that of a framework on which m-RNA and aminoacyl-s-RNA are brought together. This can be pictured as shown in Figure 6 above.

In Figure 6 the divisions along the m-RNA are intended to represent coding information equivalent to one amino acid. Only one new aminoacyl-s-RNA can fit into the ribosomal framework. The *specific* kind of aminoacyl-s-RNA is determined by the segment of amino acid code of m-RNA on the ribosome. The new aminoacyl-s-RNA is correctly aligned with the m-RNA on the ribosome. The polypeptide chain is then transferred from the polypeptide s-RNA to the new aminoacyl-s-RNA. One molecule of s-RNA is liberated and dissociates from the ribosome. This process requires transfer enzymes [11–13]. The m-RNA and polypeptide s-RNA must now move along the ribosomal framework by one segment, and the process is then repeated. When the synthetic mechanism reaches the end of the newly synthesized protein molecule the last s-RNA must be lost by hydrolysis, but the details of the release of the protein molecule from the ribosome are not clear at present. UAA, UAG and UGA are thought to be the triplets that terminate polypeptide synthesis [16].

$$\mathrm{H_2N \cdot AA_1 \cdot CO \cdot s\text{-}RNA_1}$$

$$\downarrow + \mathrm{H_2N \cdot AA_m \cdot CO \cdot s\text{-}RNA_m}$$

$$\mathrm{H_2N \cdot AA_1 \cdot CO \cdot NH \cdot AA_m \cdot CO \cdot s\text{-}RNA_m + s\text{-}RNA_1}$$

$$\downarrow + \mathrm{H_2N \cdot AA_n \cdot s\text{-}RNA_n}$$

$$\mathrm{H_2N \cdot AA_1 \cdot CO \cdot NH \cdot AA_m \cdot CO \cdot NH \cdot AA_n \cdot CO \cdot s\text{-}RNA_n + s\text{-}RNA_m}$$

$$\downarrow + \mathrm{H_2N \cdot AA_o \cdot s\text{-}RNA_o}$$

$$\mathrm{H_2N \cdot AA_1 \cdot CO \cdot NH \cdot AA_m \cdot CO \cdot NH \cdot AA_n \cdot CO \cdot NH \cdot AA_o \cdot s\text{-}RNA_o + s\text{-}RNA_n}$$

$$\downarrow + \mathrm{H_2N \cdot AA_p \cdot s\text{-}RNA_p}$$

etc.

The transfer of amino acid from aminoacyl-s-RNA to ribosomal polypeptide requires GTP[11,12]. The role of GTP in this reaction is not understood.

Electron microscopy reveals that ribosomes actively engaged in protein synthesis appear like beads strung on a thread[14]. It has also been shown that ribosomes active in protein synthesis have a much higher molecular weight than those not active[15]. This evidence has been interpreted to show that more than one ribosome can be attached to each molecule of m-RNA. The assembly of one molecule of protein starts before the assembly of another, further along the molecule of m-RNA, has been completed.

References

1 Watson, J.D., *Science*, **140**, 17 (1963).
2 Arnstein, H.R.V., *Brit. med. Bull.*, **21**, 217 (1965).
3 Hoagland, M.B., in Stanbury et al. (Eds.), *The Metabolic Basis of Inherited Disease*, McGraw-Hill, New York, 1966.
4 Crick et al., *Nature*, **192**, 1227 (1961).
5 Hoagland et al., *Biochim. biophys. Acta (Amst.)*, **24**, 215 (1957); Hoagland et al., *J. biol. Chem.*, **231**, 241 (1958).
6 Zamecnik et al., *Proc. nat. Acad. Sci. (Wash.)*, **44**, 73 (1958); Berg and Ofengand, *Proc. nat. Acad. Sci. (Wash.)*, **44**, 78 (1958); Allen et al., *J. biol. Chem.*, **235**, 1061 and 1068 (1960); Bergmann et al., *J. biol. Chem.*, **236**, 1735 (1961).
7 Berg et al., *J. biol. Chem.*, **236**, 1726 (1961).
8 Doctor et al., *J. biol. Chem.*, **236**, 1117 (1961).
9 Bishop et al., *Proc. nat. Acad. Sci. (Wash.)*, **46**, 1030 (1960); Dintzis, H. M., *Proc. nat. Acad. Sci. (Wash.)*, **47**, 247 (1961); Naughton and Dintzis, *Proc. nat. Acad. Sci. (Wash.)*, **48**, 1822 (1962); Canfield and Anfinsen, *Biochemistry*, **2**, 1073 (1963); Capechi, M.R., *Proc. nat. Acad. Sci. (Wash.)*, **55**, 1517 (1966); Clark and Marcker, *J. molec. Biol.*, **17**, 394 (1966); Gosh et al., *J. molec. Biol.*, **25**, 275 (1967).
10 Brenner et al., *Nature*, **190**, 576 (1961); Gros et al., *Nature*, **190**, 581 (1961); Hayashi and Spiegelman, *Proc. nat. Acad. Sci. (Wash.)*, **47**, 1564 (1961); Spiegelman, S., *Sci. Amer.*, **210**, No. 5, 48 (1964); Nirenberg and Leder, *Science*, **145**, 1399 (1964); Bernfield and Nirenberg, *Science*, **147**, 479 (1965).
11 Zamecnik, P.C., *Harvey Lect. 1958–59*, **54**, 256 (1960).
12 Nathans et al., *Fed. Proc.*, **21**, 127 (1962).
13 Hardesty et al., *Cold Spr. Harb. Symp. quant. Biol.*, **28**, 215 (1963); Nakamoto et al., *Cold Spr. Harb. Symp. quant. Biol.*, **28**, 227 (1963); Moldave, K., *Ann. Rev. Biochem.*, **34**, 419 (1965).
14 Warner et al., *Science*, **138**, 1399 (1962).
15 Barondes and Nirenberg, *Science*, **138**, 813 (1962); Spyrides and Lipmann, *Proc. nat. Acad. Sci. (Wash.)*, **48**, 1977 (1962); Risebrough et al., *Proc. nat. Acad. Sci. (Wash.)*, **48**, 430 (1962); Warner et al., *Proc. nat. Acad. Sci. (Wash.)*, **49**, 122 (1963).
16 Weigert et al., *Cold Spr. Harb. Symp. quant. Biol.*, **31**, 145 (1966); Brenner et al., *Nature*, **213**, 449 (1967).

Minor (infrequently occurring) constituents of nucleic acids

More than 20 minor purine and pyrimidine nucleosides have been found in hydrolysates of RNA isolated from various organisms. There are several classes of these minor components. In the largest class the bases are methylated. The majority of the theoretically possible methylated derivatives of the common bases have been found. Another class has the sugar linked to an unusual position of the base. Yet another class has a hydroxyl group of the sugar methylated. Of these minor constituents 18 have been isolated from a single source, namely s-RNA from yeast[1].

The minor constituents arise by direct methylation of the RNA molecule, and the enzymes responsible are referred to as RNA methylases. At least 8 separate RNA methylases have been demonstrated. These enzymes are widely distributed in living organisms[2]. The methylated bases are not distributed at random but are specifically located in the RNA molecule. The biological significance of the methylated bases is not known, but it has been suggested that they constitute part of the recognition mechanism in the transfer of genetic information[2].

Several minor components have also been found in addition to the four common bases of DNA. The DNA of animals and plants contains 5-methylcytosine[3] and that of certain bacteria contains 6-methyladenosine[4]. These constituents arise by direct methylation of DNA. At least two DNA methylases exist. One methylates adenine and the other cytosine of DNA[2].

A summary of these minor nucleosides of the nucleic acids is given in Table 13[5].

References

1 Hall, R.M., *Biochemistry*, **4**, 661 (1965).
2 Gold et al., *Proc. nat. Acad. Sci. (Wash.)*, **52**, 292 (1964).
3 Wyatt, R., *Biochem. J.*, **48**, 584 (1951).
4 Dunn and Smith, *Biochem. J.*, **68**, 627 (1958).
5 Littlefield and Dunn, *Biochem. J.*, **70**, 642 (1958); Dunn, D.B., *Biochem. J.*, **86**, 14P (1963); Srinivasan and Borek, *Science*, **145**, 548 (1964); Hemmens, W.F., *Biochim. biophys. Acta (Amst.)*, **91**, 332 (1964).

Table 13 Minor (infrequently occurring) nucleosides found in nucleic acids

The minor nucleosides are listed below the formula of the parent compound. Although shown as a parent compound, inosine is itself one of the minor nucleosides.

Adenosine	Guanosine	Inosine	Cytidine	Uridine
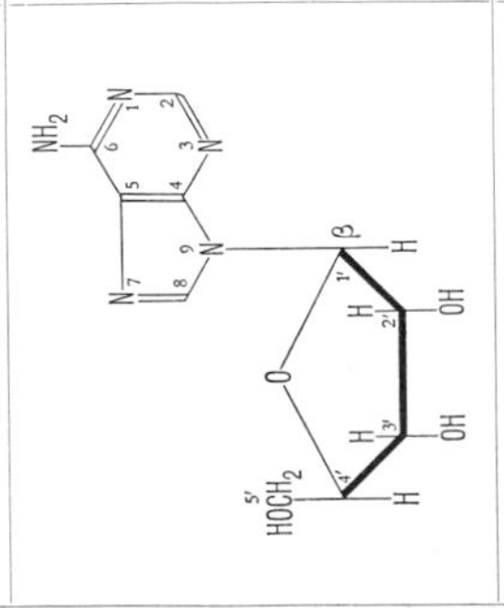	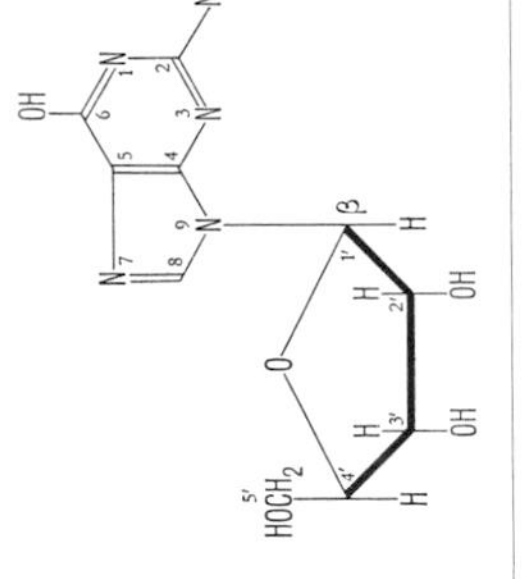	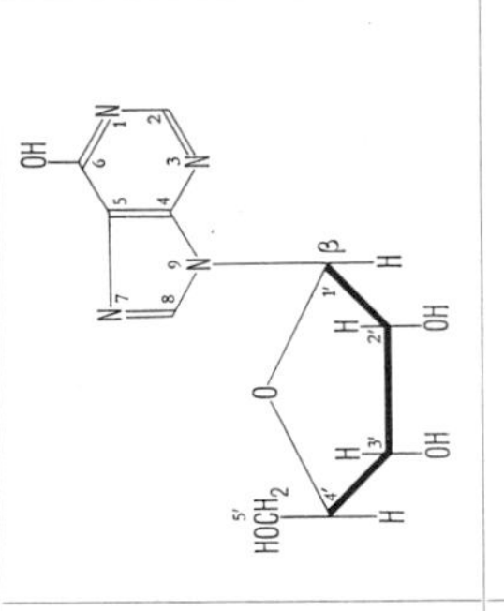	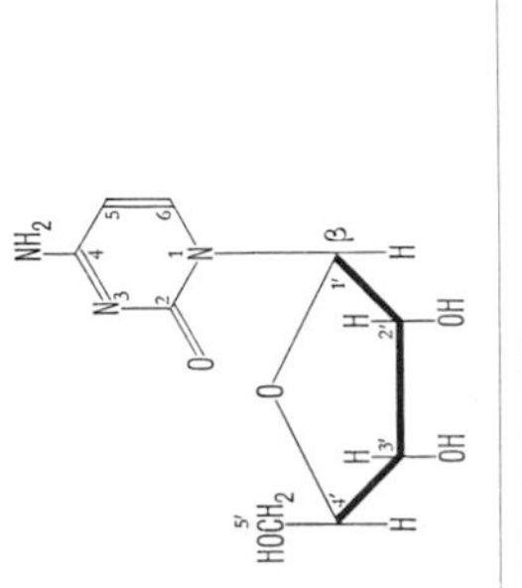	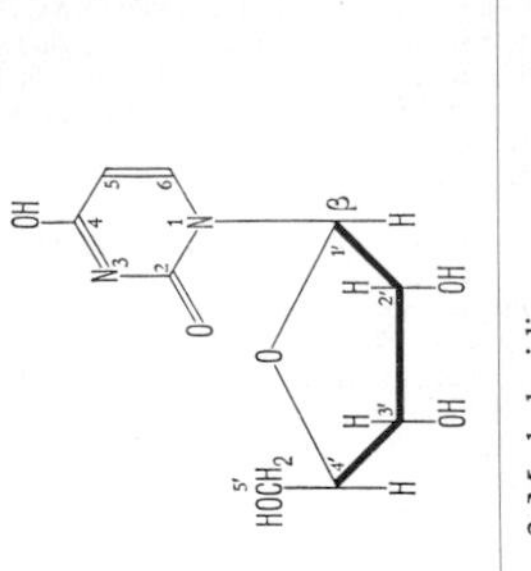
*N*⁶-Methyladenosine *N*⁶,*N*⁶-Dimethyladenosine 2-Methyladenosine 2′-*O*-Methyladenosine	1-Methylguanosine 7-Methylguanosine *N*²-Methylguanosine *N*²,*N*²-Dimethylguanosine 2′-*O*-Methylguanosine *N*²-Ribosylguanine	1-Methylinosine	3-Methylcytidine 5-Methylcytidine 2′-*O*-Methylcytidine	3-Methyluridine 5-Methyluridine* 2′-*O*-Methyluridine Pseudouridine** 2′-*O*-Methylpseudouridine**

* This compound is the ribose-containing analogue of thymidine. ** Pseudouridine is 5-ribosyluracil.

(For references see page 363)

Porphyrins [1,2]

Porphyrins are tetrapyrrolic pigments sometimes found free in nature but more commonly occurring as divalent metal-ion complexes, usually conjugated with proteins. Such proteins often function as enzymes.

The parent compound of the porphyrins is *porphin*, in the molecule of which one pyrrole ring and 3 pyrrole-like rings are linked together through their α-carbon atoms by means of methene (=CH–) bridges:

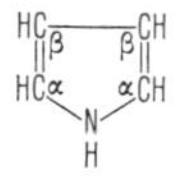

Pyrrole

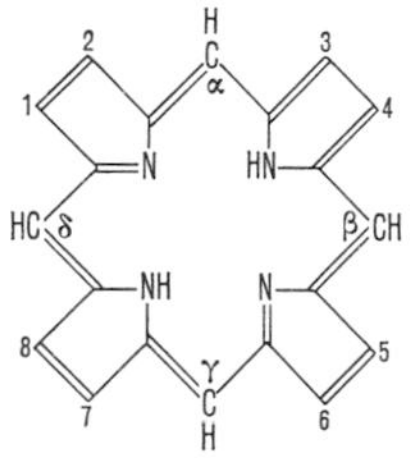

Porphin

The porphyrin molecule thus forms a closed ring of carbon and nitrogen atoms lying in one plane and containing a central 16-membered ring of 12 carbon and 4 nitrogen atoms.

The simplest of the porphyrins is aetioporphyrin, which has 4 methyl and 4 ethyl groups in positions 1 to 8 of the porphin ring. Depending on the arrangement of the attached groups, 4 isomeric forms of aetioporphyrin are possible[3]:

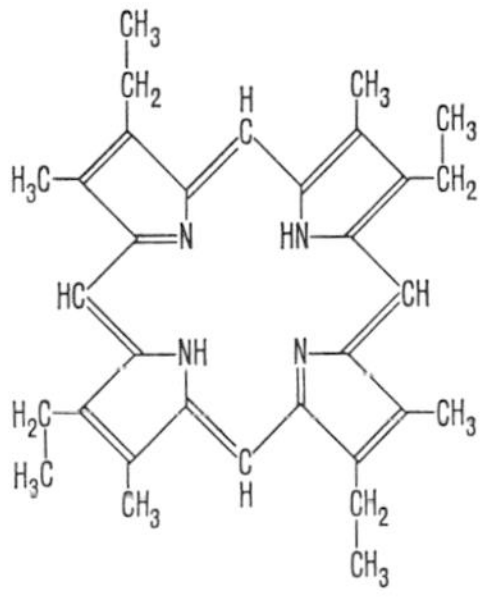

I

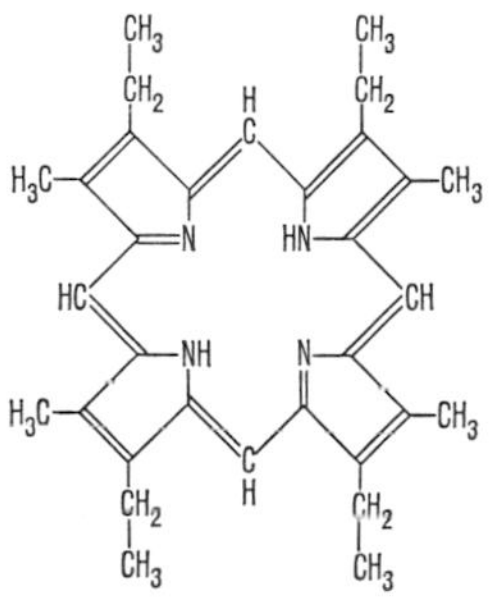

II

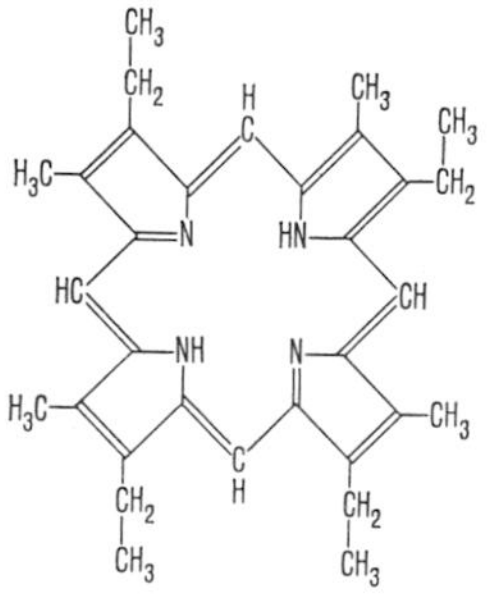

III

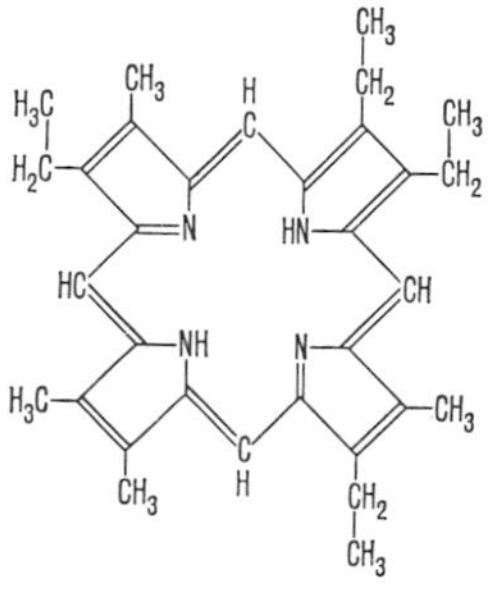

IV

These isomers, known as types I–IV porphyrins, provide the basis for the classification of the naturally occurring porphyrins.

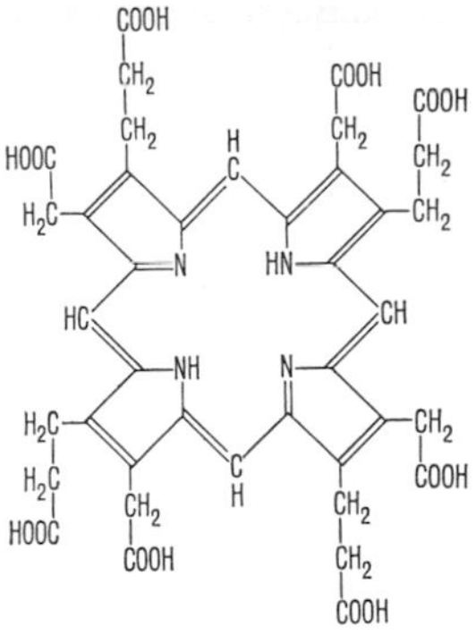

Uroporphyrin I

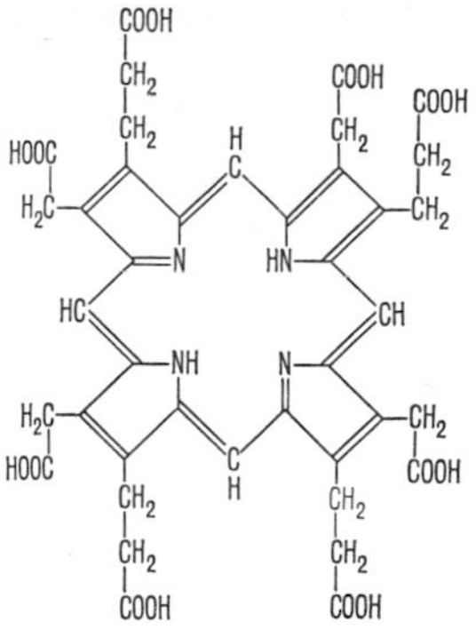

Uroporphyrin III

All porphyrins occurring in the animal body are derived from porphobilinogen (see Table 14, page 356) and are related structurally to *uroporphyrin I* or *uroporphyrin III*, compounds in which the 8 β-hydrogen atoms of porphin are replaced by 4 acetic acid and 4 propionic acid groups.

Decarboxylation of the 4 acetic acid groups gives rise to the *coproporphyrins*, which contain 4 methyl and 4 propionic acid groups:

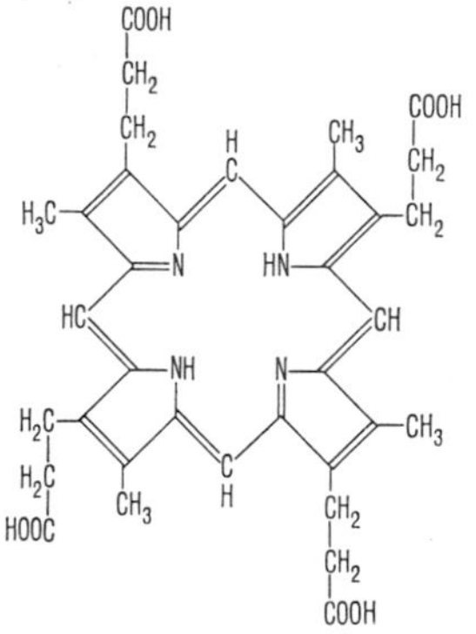

Coproporphyrin I

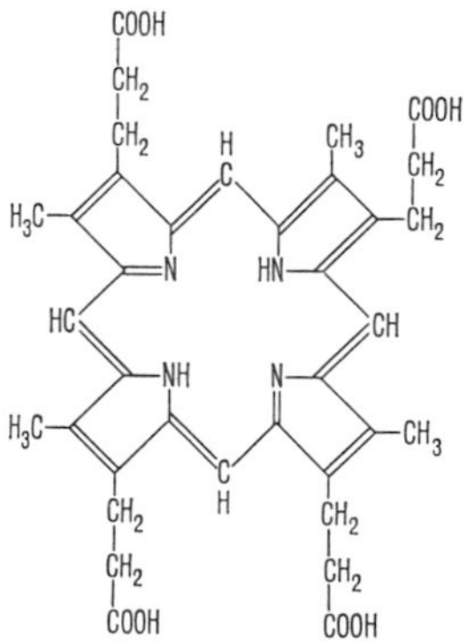

Coproporphyrin III

Decarboxylation and dehydrogenation of two of the propionic acid groups of coproporphyrin III yield *protoporphyrin IX*, which contains 4 methyl, 2 vinyl and 2 propionic acid groups:

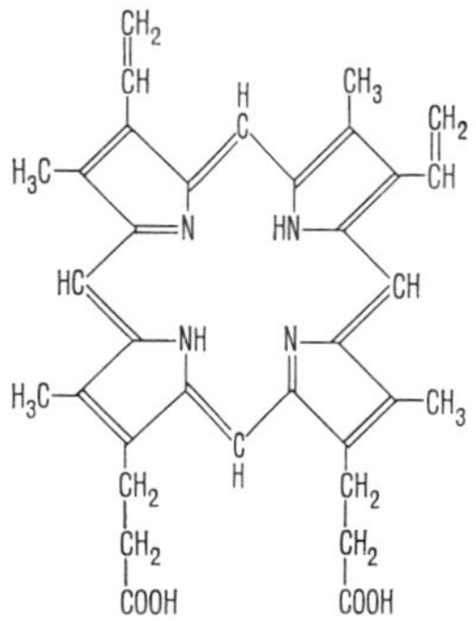

Protoporphyrin IX

Protoporphyrin IX, one of 15 possible isomers that differ only in the arrangement of the 8 groups attached to the porphin ring, is the only protoporphyrin so far found in nature. In the form of its iron complex (haem) it constitutes the prosthetic group of haemoglobin and other biologically important proteins (see Table 16, pages 360–361).

Data on the naturally occurring porphyrins are summarized in Table 14 on pages 356–359. On the biosynthesis of porphyrins see page 436; on the porphyrias see pages 454–455.

Table 14 Porphyrins of biological importance (and their precursors)

Porphyrin	Structure	Occurrence
Porphobilinogen $C_{10}H_{14}N_2O_4$	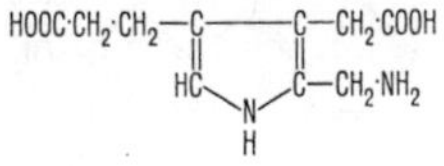	Obligatory precursor for the biosynthesis of porphyrins and haem. Present in urine in hepatic porphyria, and in poisoning by lead and monoureide sedatives
Uroporphyrinogen I $C_{40}H_{44}N_4O_{16}$	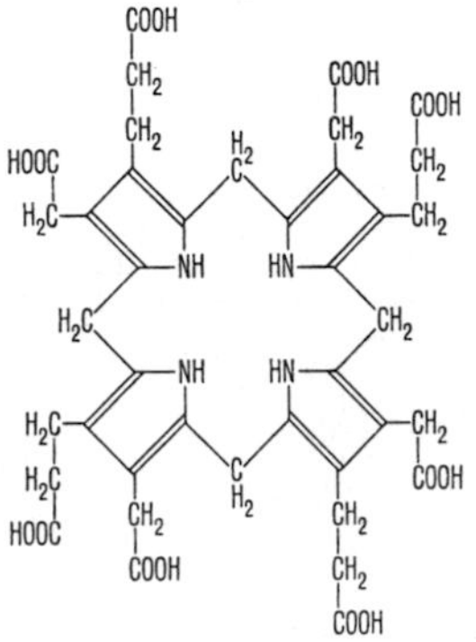	Metabolite of porphobilinogen
Uroporphyrinogen III $C_{40}H_{44}N_4O_{16}$	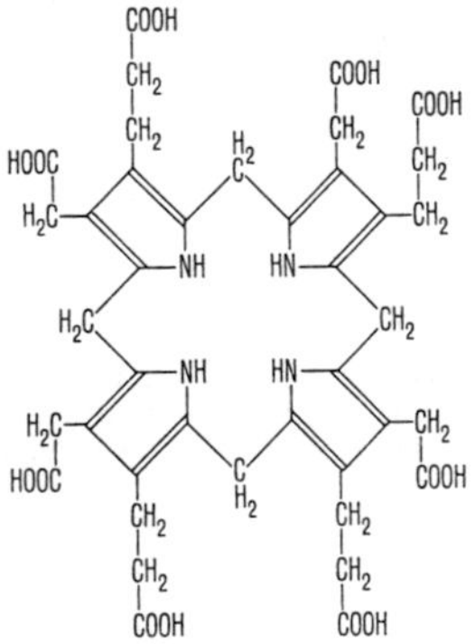	Metabolite of porphobilinogen
Coproporphyrinogen I $C_{36}H_{44}N_4O_8$	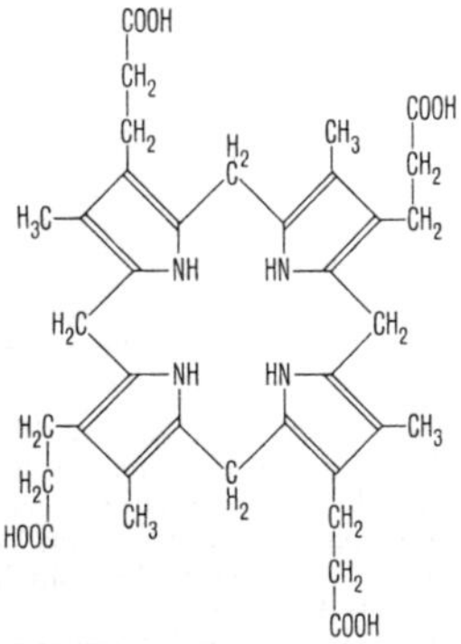	Metabolite of porphobilinogen

Table 14 (continued) Porphyrins of biological importance (and their precursors)

Porphyrin	Structure	Occurrence
Coproporphyrinogen III $C_{36}H_{44}N_4O_8$	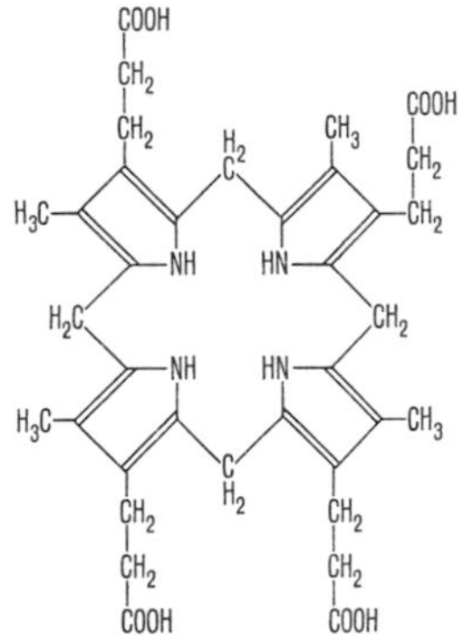	Metabolite of porphobilinogen
Uroporphyrin I $C_{40}H_{38}N_4O_{16}$	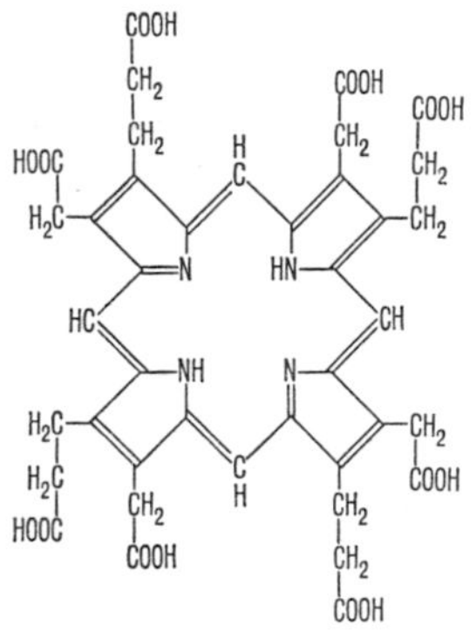	Found in large amounts in erythrocytes and other tissues, especially the teeth and bones of patients with erythropoietic porphyria. Also present in small amounts in urine
Uroporphyrin III $C_{40}H_{38}N_4O_{16}$	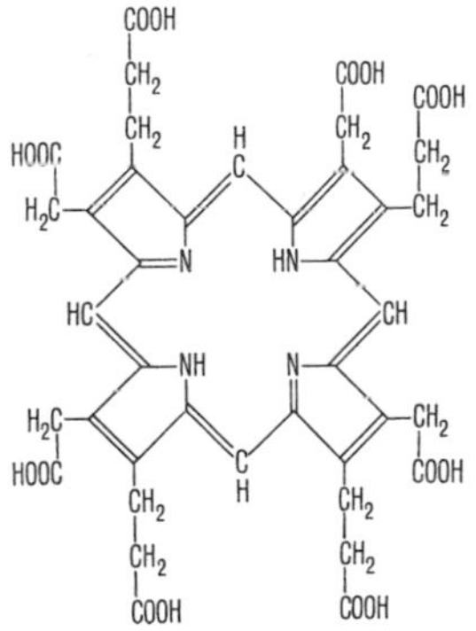	Found in very small amounts in human urine, in larger amounts in some forms of porphyria and lead poisoning
Coproporphyrin I $C_{36}H_{38}N_4O_8$	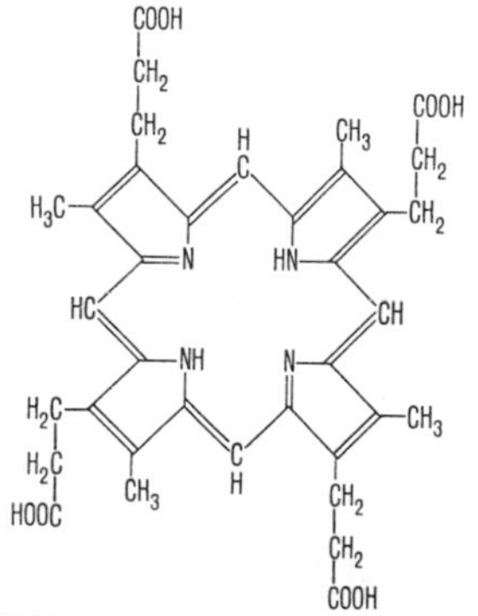	Found in large amounts in erythrocytes and other tissues, especially the teeth and bones of patients with erythropoietic porphyria. Also present in faeces, urine, bile, yeast and bacteria. Product of putrefaction of meat

Table 14 (continued) Porphyrins of biological importance

Porphyrin	Structure	Occurrence
Coproporphyrin III $C_{36}H_{38}N_4O_8$	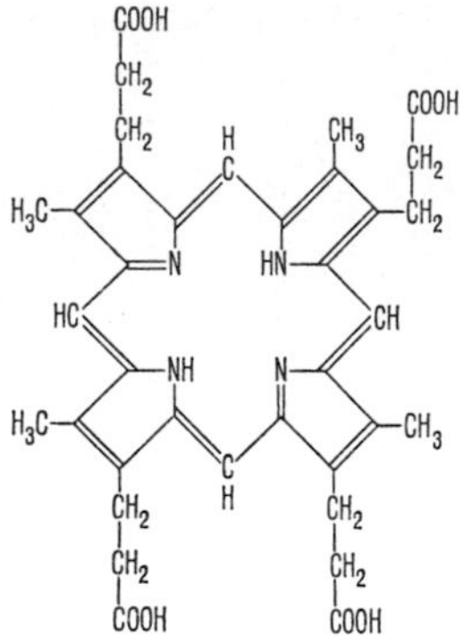	Found free in faeces, urine, erythrocytes, bile, yeast and bacteria. Increased pathologically in porphyrinuria and porphyria. Also formed in the putrefaction of meat
Protoporphyrin IX $C_{34}H_{34}N_4O_4$	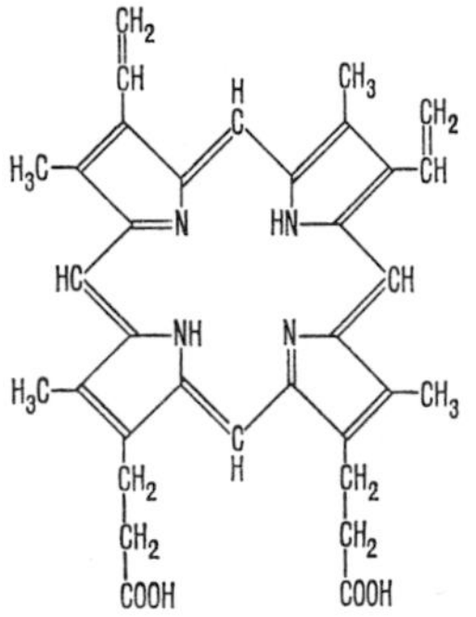	Found in bone marrow, erythrocytes, liver and faeces. The iron complexes form the prosthetic groups of haemoglobin, myoglobin, catalase, peroxidases and cytochrome b. Also formed in the putrefaction of meat
Mesoporphyrin IX $C_{34}H_{38}N_4O_4$	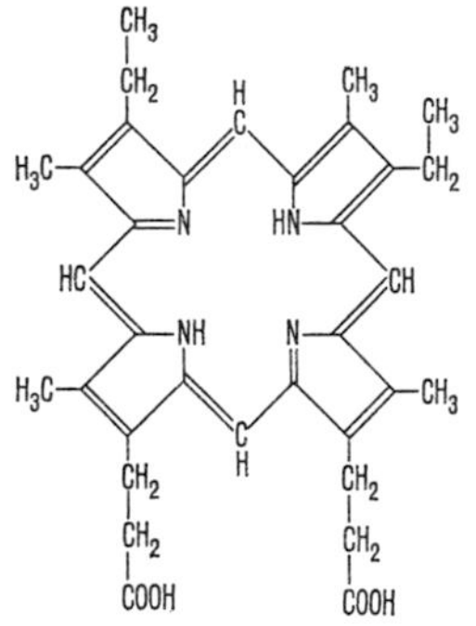	Occurs in normal human faeces, possibly also in human fistula bile
Deuteroporphyrin IX $C_{30}H_{30}N_4O_4$	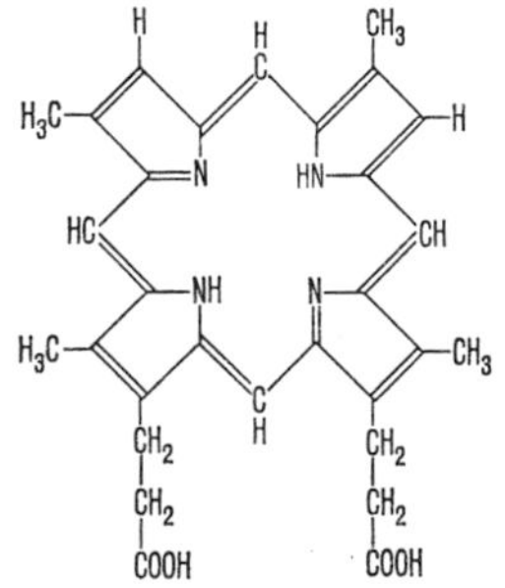	Occurs in human faeces after ingestion of blood or following haemorrhages of the gastro-intestinal tract. Formed together with protoporphyrin and coproporphyrin in the putrefaction of meat

(For references see page 363)

Table 14 (concluded) Porphyrins of biological importance

Porphyrin	Structure	Occurrence
Haematoporphyrin IX $C_{34}H_{38}N_4O_6$	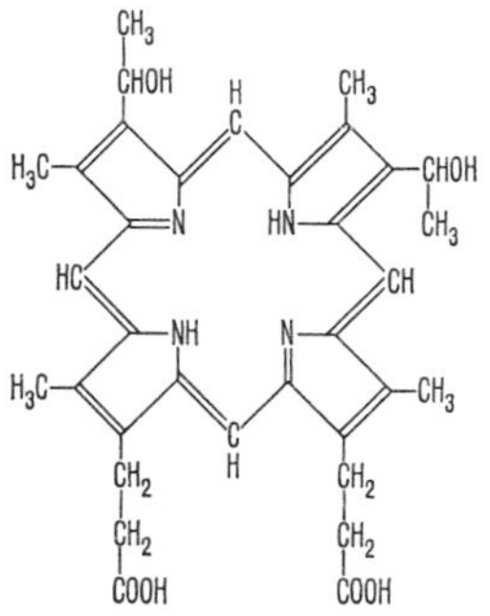	Probably not of biological importance. Natural occurrence not definitely established, but may be present in natural coproporphyrin and deuteroporphyrin fractions
Phylloerythrin $C_{33}H_{34}N_4O_3$	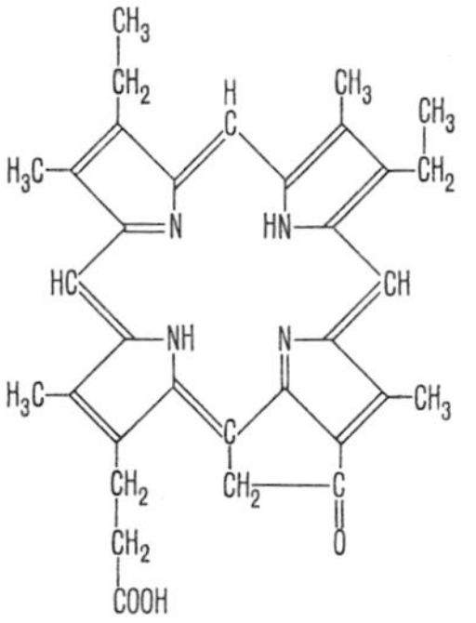	Occurs in large amounts in bile and faeces of ruminants. Causes photosensitization if bile flow is impeded

Table 15 Nomenclature of iron porphyrins

Valency of iron atom	Coordination position occupied by		Authors		
	(a)	(b)	Lemberg and Legge[7]	Pauling[4], Barron[5]	Anson[6], Keilin[7]
2	H_2O	H_2O	Heme*	Ferroheme	Haem
3	OH	H_2O	Hematin**	Ferriheme hydroxide	Haematin
3	Cl	–	Hemin	Ferriheme chloride	Haemin
2	*N*-Compound	*N*-Compound	Hemochrome	Ferro-hemochromogen	Haemochromogen
3	*N*-Compound	*N*-Compound	Hemichrome	Ferri-hemochromogen	Parahaematin
2	Globin	H_2O	Hemoglobin	Hemoglobin	Haemoglobin
2	Globin	O_2	Oxyhemoglobin	Oxyhemoglobin	Oxyhaemoglobin
3	Globin	H_2O	Hemiglobin	Ferrihemoglobin	Acid methaemoglobin
3	Globin	OH	Hemiglobin hydroxide	Ferrihemoglobin hydroxide	Alkaline methaemoglobin
2	Globin	CO	Carboxyhemoglobin	Carbon monoxide hemoglobin	–

* Also referred to by some authors as ferroprotoporphyrin. ** Also referred to by some authors as ferriprotoporphyrin hydroxide.

Iron porphyrins (haem derivatives)

The tendency of porphyrins to form complexes with divalent metal ions is one of their most characteristic properties. In the iron–porphyrin complexes, known collectively as *haem derivatives* (see Tables 15 and 16), the two central hydrogen atoms of the porphyrin ring are replaced by an atom of iron, bound to the ring by 4 coordination bonds. The remaining 2 coordination bonds of the iron atom can be occupied by various molecules or groups (a and b in Table 15). The term *haem* itself is used to designate the complex of protoporphyrin IX with ferrous iron (Fe^{++}), where the two coordination positions are occupied by water molecules (not shown in the formula). This compound is also known as protohaem in order to distinguish it from other haem-like compounds.

The complex of protoporphyrin with ferric iron (Fe^{+++}) is known as *ferrihaem*. It forms a hydroxide, *haematin*, and a chloride, *haemin:*

(continued on page 362)

(For references see page 363)

Table 16 Iron porphyrins and haem proteins of biological importance

Substance	General nature	Spectral characteristics		Remarks
		Solvent	Absorption maxima in nm	
Haem (protohaem) $C_{34}H_{32}N_4O_4Fe$	Ferrous iron complex of protoporphyrin IX. Extremely unstable. Easily oxidized to haematin. See also pages 359 and 362	Phosphate buffer pH 7.0	575 550 415	Prosthetic group of haemoglobin. Combines with many nitrogenous bases to form haemochromes
Haematin $C_{34}H_{32}N_4O_4Fe$ (OH)	Ferric iron complex of protoporphyrin IX. Moderately stable. See also pages 359 and 362	Acetic acid 10% NaOH Ether	630–635 540 510 400 580 650	Formed from haemoglobin in blood under many different conditions. The pigment of the malarial parasite *Plasmodium* has been shown to consist of haematin[8]
Haemoglobin (Hb) (deoxyhaemoglobin)	Compound of globin with 4 molecules of haem. Iron is in the ferrous state and readily oxidized. Globin portion consists of 4 polypeptide chains in the form of 2 pairs of identical chains. The great variety of abnormal haemoglobins is accounted for by differences in the amino-acid sequence and in the way the chains are combined[9] (see also pages 446–448). On the spatial arrangement of the haemoglobin molecule see the literature[18]	Water	560 430	Oxygen carrier in erythrocytes of all vertebrates. One erythrocyte contains ca. 280 million Hb molecules. Combines reversibly with oxygen to form oxyhaemoglobin, and with carbon monoxide to form carboxyhaemoglobin (affinity for carbon monoxide over 100 times that for oxygen)
Myoglobin (myohaemoglobin, deoxymyoglobin)	Unlike haemoglobin, consists of one haem molecule combined with a polypeptide of 153 amino-acid residues[9]. Iron is in the ferrous state. On the spatial arrangement of the myoglobin molecule see the literature[19]	Water	555 435	Found in muscles of higher vertebrates, nematodes and molluscs, where its main function is oxygen storage. Completely saturated with oxygen at low pressures. The affinity of myoglobin for oxygen is greater than that of haemoglobin
Oxyhaemoglobin	Compound of haemoglobin with 4 molecules of oxygen available physiologically. Iron is in the ferrous state	Water	577 540 412	Present in fresh blood of all vertebrates (see also under 'Haemoglobin' above)
Carboxyhaemoglobin	Compound of 4 molecules of carbon monoxide with the 4 iron atoms of haemoglobin	Water	568–572 538 418	Rapidly formed in the body during exposure to carbon monoxide, resulting in failure of oxygen transport by haemoglobin (see also under 'Haemoglobin' above)
Haemiglobin (methaemoglobin)	Similar to haemoglobin except that iron is in the ferric state	Acid solution Alkaline solution	630 500 405 577 540 411	Formed reversibly from haemoglobin by oxidation (ferricyanide, nitrites, chlorates, etc.). Occurs in erythrocytes in larger amounts in some pathological conditions[10]
Choleglobin (verdoglobin A, verdohaemoglobin)	Haemoglobin-like compound in which the α-methene bridge is oxidized; formed by coupled oxidation of haemoglobin	Water	670 630	Possibly a normal haemoglobin degradation product and intermediary in bile pigment formation

(For references see page 363)

Table 16 (continued) Iron porphyrins and haem proteins of biological importance

Substance	General nature	Spectral characteristics		Remarks
		Solvent	Absorption maxima in nm	
Sulphaemoglobin (verdoglobin S)	Chemical structure not known	Water	620	Formed irreversibly from haemoglobin by action of hydrogen sulphide. Present in erythrocytes after ingestion of sulphur, sulphonamides, aromatic amines, occasionally trinitrotoluene; also in septicaemia (especially *Clostridium perfringens* bacteraemia) and severe constipation
Cytochrome a group: a, a_3	Prosthetic group is a haem containing a formyl side chain	Water	(Ferro-ferri difference spectrum) Cytochrome a: 605 (α) 444 (γ) Cytochrome a_3: 605 (α) 445 (γ)	Cytochromes a and a_3 are components of the cytochrome c oxidase of the mitochondria of animals, plants and yeast [20]. Ferrocytochrome a_3 combines with cyanide and carbon monoxide, whereas ferrocytochrome a does not. The cyanide compound of ferrocytochrome a_3 is autoxidizable. Cytochromes a and a_3 may be part of the same protein ('cytochrome aa'')
Cytochrome c group: c, c_1	Possess covalent linkages between haem side chains and protein. Only thioether linkages are so far known, and the prosthetic groups can be called 'substituted mesohaems'	Water	Ferrocytochrome c: 550 (α) 520 (β) 415 (γ) Ferrocytochrome c_1: 553 (α)	Cytochromes c and c_1 are found in the mitochondria of animals, plants and yeast. At neutral pH the former is relatively heat-stable, the latter not. Cytochrome c has an isoelectric point above pH 7 and the oxidation of its ferro form by oxygen is catalysed by cytochrome oxidase; the oxidation–reduction potential over most of the physiological pH range is ca. + 0.25 V
Cytochrome b group: b, b_5	Prosthetic group is protohaem	Water	Ferrocytochrome b: 564 (α) Ferrocytochrome b_5: 556 (α)	Cytochrome b occurs in the mitochondria of animals, plants and yeast. Cytochrome b_5 is found in animal microsomes. It is reduced by NADH in the presence of cytochrome b_5 reductase
Cytochrome d group: d (a_2)	Prosthetic group is an iron-dihydroporphyrin (phytochlorin) complex	Water	Ferrocytochrome d: 645	Found in some bacteria (e.g., *E.coli*, *Acetobacter peroxidans*). The ferro form is autoxidizable and combines with carbon monoxide
Peroxidases	Prosthetic group is haematin or a related compound	Weak acids	645 583 548 498 (horse-radish peroxidase)	Occur in plants and animals. Biological functions not well known
Catalase	Prosthetic group is haematin	Water	629 544 506 409 280	Decomposes hydrogen peroxide. Present in respiring cells; highly active in liver, erythrocytes, etc. Catalytic activity inhibited by cyanide, hydrogen sulphide, hydroxylamine, azides, aminophenols and 2,4-dichlorophenol

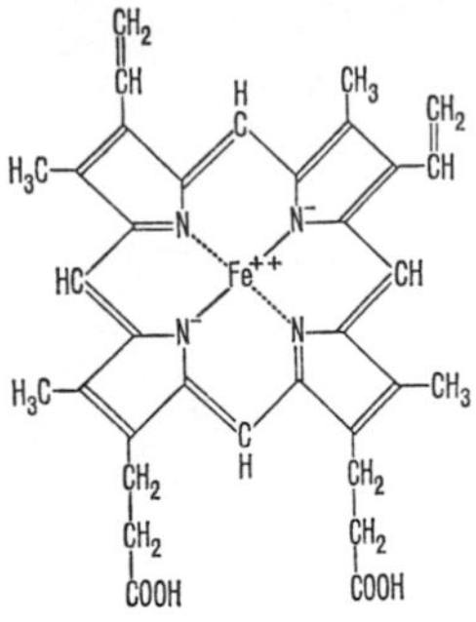

Haem (protohaem)

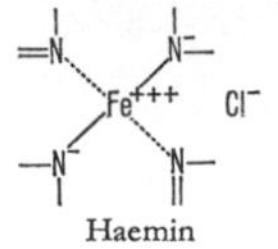

Haemin

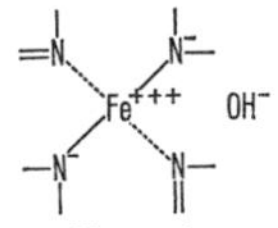

Haematin

Haem and other ferrous complexes of the porphyrins readily react with bases such as primary amines, pyridine, ammonia, imidazole compounds (e.g., histidine) and hydrazine, the resulting products being known as *haemochromes*.

Haemoproteins are conjugated proteins in which the prosthetic group is haem. They are of two types: 'haemochromes', in which the two free coordination bonds of the haem iron atom are occupied by nitrogen atoms of basic side chains of the protein, and 'open' type haemoproteins, in which at least one of these bonds is not so occupied. Haemoglobin and myoglobin are haemoproteins of the open type, as are catalases and peroxidases, though in the latter the nature of the iron-coordinating groups is not known for certain.

Three types of physiologically active haemoproteins, depending on the valency state of the iron, can be distinguished:

1. Fe remains divalent:	haemoglobin, myoglobin
2. Fe is reversibly oxidized and reduced:	cytochromes
3. Fe remains trivalent:	catalase and peroxidases

Haemoglobin is the principal representative of a class of haemoproteins whose function is to combine reversibly with oxygen; this reaction does not involve rapid oxidation of the haem iron atom. *Catalases* and *peroxidases* are enzymes responsible for catalysis of electron and/or hydrogen transport, the hydrogen acceptor being either hydrogen peroxide or one of its alkyl derivatives. *Cytochromes* are by definition haemoproteins whose characteristic function is also electron and/or hydrogen transport, but by means of a reversible valency change in their haem iron atom (ferrocytochrome ⇌ ferricytochrome). For further data on haemoproteins see Table 16, pages 360–361.

Bile pigments[1,11]

The metabolic breakdown of the haemoglobin released by the disintegration of erythrocytes results in the formation of bile pigments. The breakdown occurs by the oxidative cleavage of the porphyrin ring with the loss of a carbon atom to form open-chain tetrapyrroles. Bile pigments are generally represented as linear tetrapyrrolic chains with terminal hydroxyl groups:

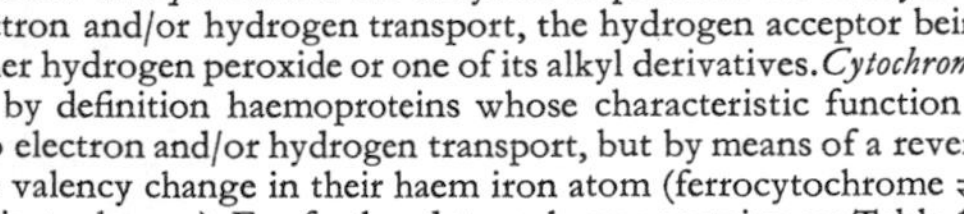

(*a*) Linear tetrapyrrolic structure of bile pigments

but their structure is more correctly represented by a tetrapyrrolic 'ring', closed by a hydrogen bond between oxygen atoms:

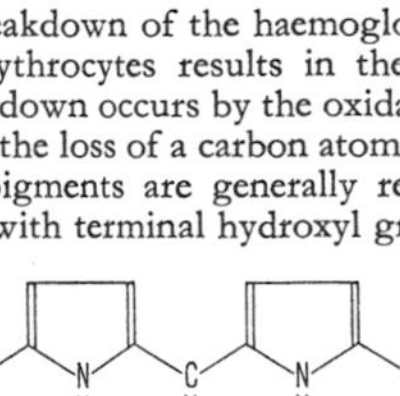

(*b*) 'Ring' structure of bile pigments

All naturally occurring bile pigments are derived from protoporphyrin IX by fission at the α-methene link. The possibility exists that the oxidative cleavage of the porphyrin ring occurs before the protoporphyrin is released from the globin, with choleglobin as intermediate[12]. The iron released by the catabolism of haemoglobin is largely retained in the body in the form of the protein ferritin, while the bile pigments are excreted. Current views about the formation in the organism of the various bile pigments (see also Table 17, pages 363–364) can be summarized as follows[13]:

Haemoglobin → Choleglobin; Haemoglobin → Biliverdin

Choleglobin → Bilirubin; Biliverdin → Bilirubin

Bilirubin → Mesobilirubin

Mesobilirubin → Urobilinogen IX-α (Mesobilirubinogen)

(+)-Urobilinogen ← Urobilinogen IX-α (Mesobilirubinogen) → Stercobilinogen

(+)-Urobilinogen → (+)-Urobilin; Urobilinogen IX-α → Urobilin IX-α; Stercobilinogen → Stercobilin

The principal sites of conversion of the haem portion of haemoglobin to bilirubin are believed to be the reticuloendothelial cells of the liver, spleen and bone marrow. In the blood, bilirubin becomes bound to serum albumin (see also pages 576–577) and is rapidly taken up by the liver, whence it reaches the intestine via the bile. The further degradation takes place mainly in the intestine.

van den Bergh and Müller[14] were the first to observe that there is a difference between serum bilirubin and the bilirubin-like pigments excreted in bile in respect of their coupling with diazotized sulphanilic acid, the latter pigments reacting directly whereas serum bilirubin requires the presence of ethanol (direct and indirect van den Bergh reactions respectively). Subsequently it was shown[15] that bilirubin undergoes conjugation in the liver cells with glucuronic acid (and possibly other substances) and is excreted into the bile mainly as the diglucuronide and to a smaller extent as the monoglucuronide. This conjugated bilirubin is water-soluble, whereas bilirubin itself is soluble in lipids but insoluble in water. This difference in solubility explains not only the difference in the van den Bergh reaction but also that in the physiological behaviour of the two types of pigment. Thus it accounts for the fact that bile pigments are excreted in the urine in obstructive jaundice and hepatitis but not in haemolytic jaundice (see below). Since lipids have an affinity for brain tissue, it also explains why a great excess of bilirubin in the blood of infants results in kernicterus.

Jaundice

Jaundice may broadly be classified into the haemolytic, obstructive and hepatogenous varieties. In haemolytic jaundice the excessive rate of breakdown of erythrocyte haemoglobin causes bilirubin to pass into the blood stream at a rate greater than that at which it can be conjugated and removed by the liver. Obstructive jaundice occurs when there is obstruction to the outflow of bile from the liver through the biliary ducts. In hepatogenous jaundice destruction of the normal architecture of the liver causes bile pigment to enter the blood stream. In both the latter cases the water-soluble bile pigment is excreted in the urine. See also pages 576–577.

Bilirubinoids

The various intermediates (bilirubinoids) in the conversion of bilirubin to stercobilin by the reductive enzymes of the intestinal bacteria may be partly reabsorbed in the intestinal tract and either returned to the liver or excreted in the urine. Data on the most important of these compounds are summarized in Table 17, pages 363 and 364.

Chlorophylls

Other metallo-phorphyrins occurring in nature include the magnesium porphyrin compounds that are components of the chlorophyll of green plants. The latter has been shown to consist mainly of a mixture of chlorophyll a and chlorophyll b, both of which contain a porphyrin esterified with the long-chain optically active fatty alcohol phytol and magnesium. The porphyrins are characterized by the presence of an additional isocyclic ring.

Phytol is also a component of vitamin K_1 (see page 468). Spectral data have indicated the existence of two further chlorophylls,

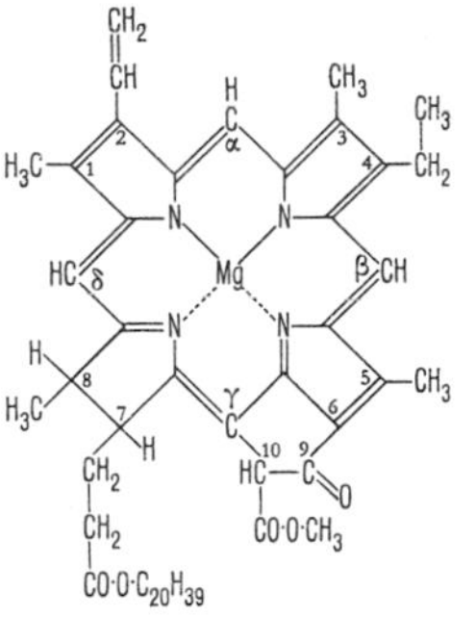

Chlorophyll a

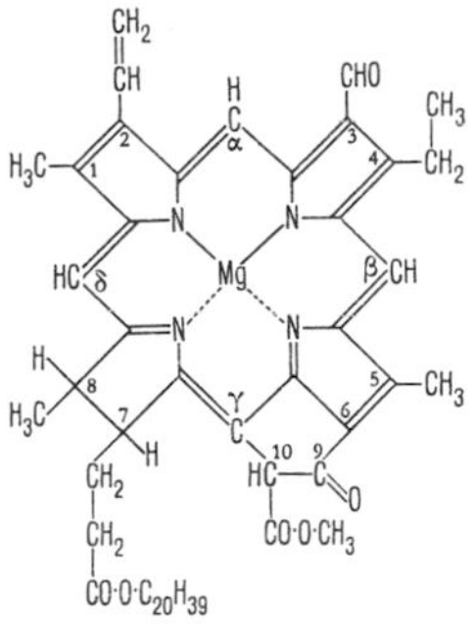

Chlorophyll b

c and d. In leaf tissue, chlorophylls exist in the form of a protein complex, chloroplastin, which has been isolated[16].

The photosynthetic purple sulphur bacteria contain the pigment bacteriochlorophyll. This has been shown to differ from chlorophyll a only in the presence of an acetyl group in place of the vinyl group in position 2 and in the hydrogenation of the 3,4 double bond.

Cyanocobalamin (vitamin B_{12})

Cyanocobalamin, the cobalt-containing principle of liver extracts used in the treatment of pernicious anaemia (see 'Vitamin B_{12} group', page 482) is a highly substituted and partially hydrogenated tetrapyrrole linked to the nucleotide 5,6-dimethyl-1-(α-ribofuranosyl)benzimidazole 3′-phosphate. The six coordinate valencies of the cobalt atom are satisfied by the four nitrogen atoms of the tetrapyrrole, a nitrogen atom of the nucleotide, and a cyanide ion[17].

References

1 For reviews see LEMBERG and LEGGE, *Hematin Compounds and Bile Pigments*, Interscience, New York, 1949.
2 THEORELL, H., *Advanc. Enzymol.*, 7, 265 (1947); GRANICK and GILDER, *Advanc. Enzymol.*, 7, 305 (1947); WYMAN, J., *Advanc. Protein Chem.*, **4**, 407 (1948); MARGOLIASH, E., *Ann. Rev. Biochem.*, **30**, 549 (1961); ROSSI FANELLI et al., *Advanc. Protein Chem.*, **19**, 73 (1964); SCHMID, R., in STANBURY et al. (Eds.), *The Metabolic Basis of Inherited Disease*, 2nd ed., MCGRAW-HILL, New York, 1966; GOLDBERG and RIMINGTON, *Diseases of Porphyrin Metabolism*, Thomas, Springfield, Ill., 1962; CAUGHEY, W.S., *Ann. Rev. Biochem.*, **36**, 611 (1967).
3 FISCHER and ORTH, *Die Chemie des Pyrrols*, vol. 2, part 1, Akademische Verlagsgesellschaft, Leipzig, 1937, page 176.
4 PAULING and CORYELL, *Proc. nat. Acad. Sci. (Wash.)*, **22**, 159 (1936).
5 BARRON, E.S.G., *J. biol. Chem.*, **121**, 285 (1937).
6 ANSON, M.L., *J. gen. Physiol.*, **23**, 239 (1939).
7 KEILIN, D., *Proc. roy. Soc. B*, **100**, 129 (1926).
8 RIMINGTON et al., *Biochem. J.*, **41**, 619 (1947).
9 LEHMANN and HUNTSMAN, *Man's Haemoglobins*, North-Holland Publishing Company, Amsterdam, 1966.
10 GIBSON and HARRISON, *Lancet*, **2**, 941 (1947); GIBSON, Q.H., *Biochem. J.*, **42**, 13 (1948).
11 GRAY, C.H., *The Bile Pigments*, Methuen, London, 1953; GRAY, C.H., *Bile Pigments in Health and Disease*, Thomas, Springfield, Ill., 1961; WITH, T.K., *Bile Pigments*, Academic Press, New York, 1968; SCHMID, R., in STANBURY et al. (Eds.), *The Metabolic Basis of Inherited Disease*, 2nd ed., MCGRAW-HILL, New York, 1966.
12 LEMBERG et al., *Biochem. J.*, **33**, 754 (1939).
13 CARTWRIGHT, G.E., in WINTROBE, M.M. (Ed.), *Clinical Hematology*, 6th ed., Lea & Febiger, Philadelphia, 1967, page 168.
14 VAN DEN BERGH and MÜLLER, *Biochem. Z.*, **77**, 90 (1916).
15 TALAFANT, E., *Nature*, **178**, 312 (1956); BILLING et al., *Biochem. J.*, **65**, 774 (1957); SCHMIDT, R., *Helv. med. Acta*, **24**, 273 (1957); SCHMIDT et al., *Arch. Biochem.*, **70**, 285 (1957).
16 STOLL and WIEDEMANN, in ZECHMEISTER, L. (Ed.), *Progress in the Chemistry of Organic Natural Products*, vol. 1, Springer, Vienna, 1938, page 159; STOLL and WIEDEMANN, *Schweiz. med. Wschr.*, **77**, 664 (1947).
17 ARMITAGE et al., *J. chem. Soc.*, **4**, 3849 (1953); HODGKIN et al., *Nature*, **176**, 325 (1955) and **178**, 64 (1956); BONNETT et al., *J. chem. Soc.*, **1**, 1158 and 1168 (1957).
18 MUIRHEAD and PERUTZ, *Nature*, **199**, 633 (1963).
19 KENDREW et al., *Nature*, **185**, 422 (1960); NOBBS et al., *Nature*, **209**, 339 (1966).
20 LEMBERG, M.R., *Physiol. Rev.*, **49**, 48 (1969).

Table 17 Bilirubinoids and related compounds

Substance	Structure	Remarks
Bilirubin $C_{33}H_{36}N_4O_6$	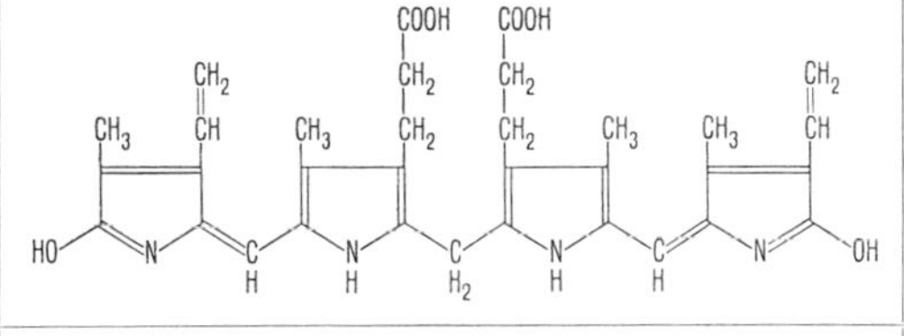	Breakdown product of haemoglobin and other haem compounds in reticuloendothelial system. Present in excess in serum and tissues in haemolytic jaundice. Also found in urine and faeces of infants. Conjugated in liver cells with glucuronic acid to form bile pigment
Biliverdin $C_{33}H_{34}N_4O_6$	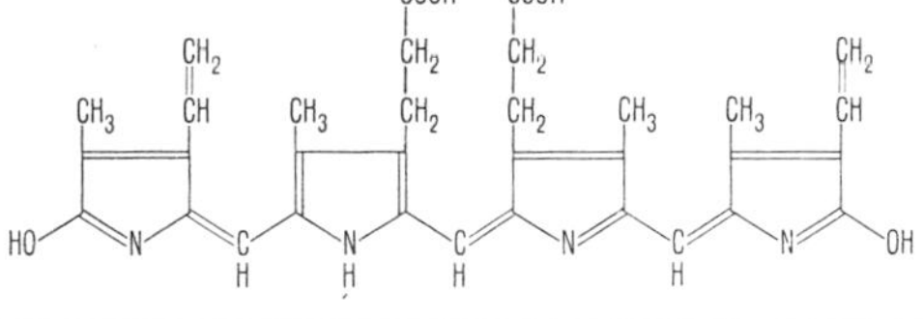	Breakdown product of haemoglobin, reduced enzymatically in liver to bilirubin. Not found in blood, but present in bile of some animals, in placenta of some mammals (uteroverdin) and in egg shells of many birds (oocyan). Also found in meconium of foetus and newborn and in bile after death. An iron complex may be the prosthetic group of inactive liver catalase
Mesobilirubin $C_{33}H_{40}N_4O_6$	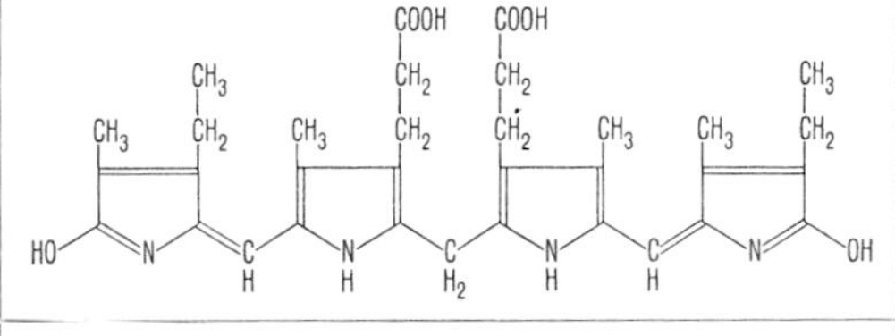	May be present in the small intestine as reduction product of bilirubin
Mesobilane (mesobilirubinogen, urobilinogen IX-α) $C_{33}H_{44}N_4O_6$	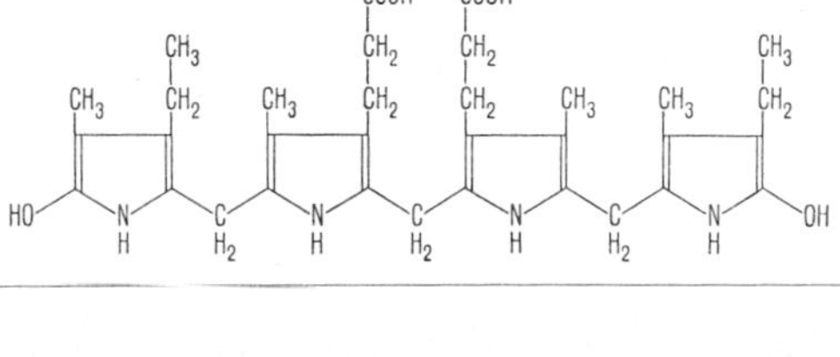	Degradation product of bilirubin in liver. Present in normal bile, urine and faeces; increased in pathological conditions

Table 17 (continued) Bilirubinoids and related compounds

Substance	Structure	Remarks
Mesobilene-(b) (urobilin IX-α) $C_{33}H_{42}N_4O_6$	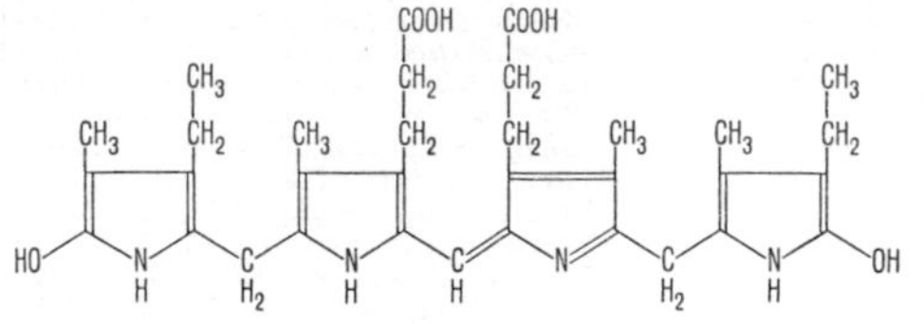	Oxidation product of mesobilane. Present in normal urine and faeces
(−)-Tetrahydro-mesobilane (stercobilinogen) $C_{33}H_{48}N_4O_6$	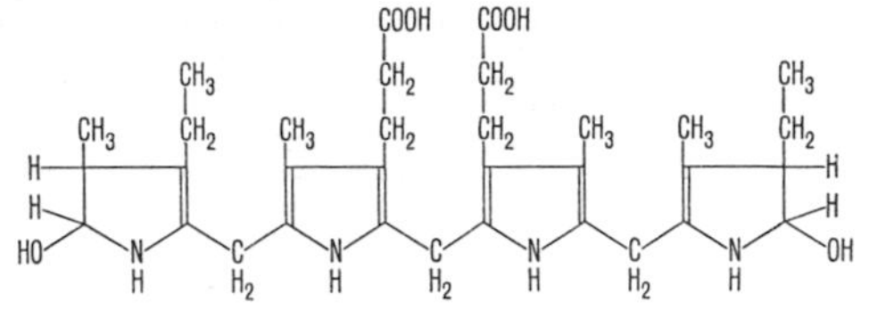	Reduction product of mesobilane. Main excretory product of haemoglobin in most vertebrates
(−)-Tetrahydro-mesobilene-(b) (stercobilin) $C_{33}H_{46}N_4O_6$	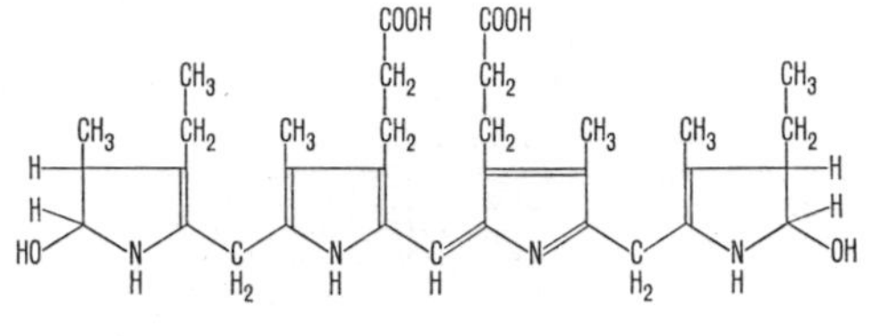	Oxidation product of tetrahydromesobilane (stercobilinogen). Constituent of normal faeces and urine
Mesobiliviolin $C_{33}H_{40}N_4O_6$	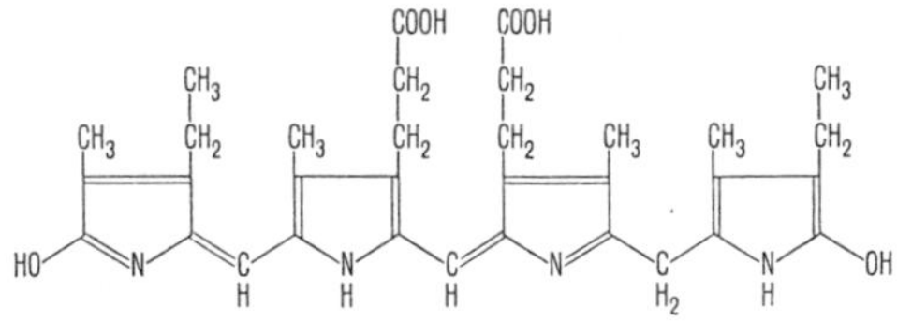	Found in human faeces, probably derived from mesobilane. Forms prosthetic group of the phycocyanins (chromoproteins of red and blue algae) that act as efficient photo-sensitizers in algal photosynthesis
Mesobilierythrin (mesobilirhodin) $C_{33}H_{40}N_4O_6$	Not established with certainty	Prosthetic group of phycoerythrin of red and some blue algae. A sensitizer in algae photosynthesis
Mesobilifuscins Bilifuscins Propentdyopents $C_{16}H_{18-20}N_2O_{4-5}$	Not definitely established, but known to be dipyrroles containing the skeleton: 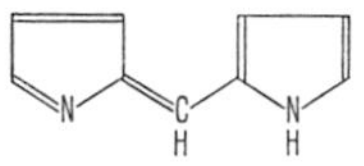	Secondary products of oxidation of bile pigments and haem compounds, excreted in urine and faeces in jaundice and liver disease; present in gallstones
(+)-Urobilin $C_{33}H_{40}N_4O_6$	Not established with certainty. Strongly dextrorotatory	Isolated from infected bile, where it presumably arises from bilirubin[1]
(+)-Urobilinogen $C_{33}H_{42}N_4O_6$	Not established with certainty. Strongly dextrorotatory	Isolated from infected bile, where it presumably arises from bilirubin[1]

[1] WATSON, C.J., *J. Lab. clin. Med.*, **54**, 1 (1959).

Lipids

Lipids is the general term for a group of natural products that are soluble in relatively nonpolar solvents, such as mixtures of chloroform and methanol, but insoluble in water. This classification is not a rigid definition: for example, gangliosides are extracted with water from solution in chloroform/methanol. Most lipids are esters or amides of long-chain fatty acids and yield soaps on alkaline hydrolysis. Any classification of the lipids is to some extent arbitrary, according to whether it is on the basis of physical properties, chemical structure and reactions, or biological occurrence and function. A classification of saponifiable lipids is given in Table 18 below.

In addition to the saponifiable lipids there are several groups of nonsaponifiable compounds which must also be classified as lipids:

(a) fatty acids (see pages 366–373), a group including also the prostaglandins (see page 373)
(b) higher straight-chain alcohols, e.g., cetyl (C_{16}), stearyl (C_{18}), ceryl (C_{26}) and myricyl (C_{30}) alcohols
(c) sterols (see page 377), i.e., alcohols containing the cyclopentanoperhydrophenanthrene nucleus, e.g., cholesterol (see page 374), sitosterol, stigmasterol and ergosterol
(d) hydrocarbons, e.g., squalene (see page 374) and the carotenes
(e) the fat-soluble vitamins A, D, E and K (see under 'Vitamins', pages 457–469).

Further reading

Deuel, H. J., *The Lipids*, vol. 1, Interscience, New York, 1951; Hilditch, T. P., *The Chemical Constitution of Natural Fats*, 4th ed., Chapman & Hall, London, 1964; Lovern, J. A., *The Chemistry of Lipids of Biochemical Significance*, 2nd ed., Methuen, London, 1957; Popják, G. (Ed.), *Biochemistry of Lipids*, Pergamon, Oxford, 1960; Hanahan, D. J., *Lipide Chemistry*, Wiley-Interscience, New York, 1960.

Table 18 Classification and structural components of saponifiable lipids

Classification of lipids*		Structural components (other than fatty acids)**		
		Ester or amide of	Nitrogenous base	Other
Acylglycerols (fats)	(i) Monoglycerides (ii) Diglycerides (iii) Triglycerides (neutral fats)	Glycerol	—	—
Alkoxydiglycerides		Glycerol	—	Higher aliphatic alcohol
Glycoglycerides		Glycerol	—	Galactose
Glycerophosphatides	(i) Phosphatidic acids	Glycerol	—	Phosphoric acid
	(ii) Phosphatidyl esters: Phosphatidylcholines	Glycerol	Choline	Phosphoric acid
	Phosphatidylethanolamines	Glycerol	Ethanolamine	Phosphoric acid
	Phosphatidylserines	Glycerol	Serine	Phosphoric acid
	(iii) Lysophosphatides	Glycerol	Choline Ethanolamine Serine	Phosphoric acid
	(iv) Inositol phosphatides: Mono-, Di-, Tri-	Glycerol	—	Phosphoric acid, inositol
	(v) Acetal phosphatides	Glycerol	(As for lysophosphatides)	Phosphoric acid, α,β-unsaturated higher aliphatic alcohol
	(vi) Alkyl lysophosphatide ethers	Glycerol	(As for lysophosphatides)	Phosphoric acid, saturated higher aliphatic alcohol
Sphingolipids	(i) Sphingomyelins	Sphingosine and dihydrosphingosine	Choline	Phosphoric acid
	(ii) Cerebrosides		—	Hexose or di- or trisaccharide
	(iii) Sulphatides		—	Galactose, sulphuric acid
	(iv) Aminoglycolipids		*N*-Acetylgalactosamine	Glucose, galactose
	(v) Gangliosides		*N*-Acetylgalactosamine	Glucose, galactose, neuraminic acid
Waxes	(i) True waxes	Long-chain aliphatic alcohols	—	—
	(ii) Steryl esters, vitamin A and D_3 esters	Complex cyclic alcohols	—	—

* In Bloor's classification (*Chem. Rev.*, **2**, 243 [1925/26]) the triglycerides (neutral fats) and waxes together constitute the 'simple lipids', while the remaining classes listed above are collectively designated 'compound lipids' (phospholipids, cerebrosides, gangliosides). The phospholipids or phosphatides comprise the glycerophosphatides and sphingomyelins, grouped together by virtue of their sole common component, the phosphate group. The classification of the sphingomyelins with the other sphingolipids (derivatives of sphingosine) is more rational.

** All compounds yield fatty acids on hydrolysis, with the possible exception of some acetal phosphatides.

Table 19 Fatty acids

Name	Formula and mol.wt.	Structure	Physical properties	Remarks
		Saturated straight-chain monocarboxylic acids		
Formic acid (methanoic acid)	CH_2O_2 46.03	H·COOH	m.p. 8.6°C b.p. 100.8°C d^{20} 1.220 n_D^{20} 1.371 4	Occurs in human urine and many plant materials
Acetic acid (ethanoic acid)	$C_2H_4O_2$ 60.05	CH_3·COOH	m.p. 16.5°C b.p. 118.1°C d^{20} 1.049 2 n_D^{25} 1.369 76	Present in most biological materials. Formed from ethanol by many species of aerobic bacteria and from pentoses by some anaerobic species
Propionic acid (propanoic acid)	$C_3H_6O_2$ 74.08	CH_3·CH_2·COOH	m.p. −22°C b.p. 140.9°C d^{20} 0.992 $n_D^{19.9}$ 1.387 36	Formed by bacterial decomposition of carbohydrates
n-Butyric acid (butanoic acid)	$C_4H_8O_2$ 88.11	CH_3·$(CH_2)_2$·COOH	m.p. −7.9°C b.p. 163°C d^{20} 0.958 7 n_D^{20} 1.399 06	Occurs in traces in many fats
n-Valeric acid (pentanoic acid)	$C_5H_{10}O_2$ 102.13	CH_3·$(CH_2)_3$·COOH	m.p. −34.5°C b.p. 186.4°C d^{20} 0.938 7 n_D^{20} 1.408 6	
Caproic acid (hexoic acid, hexanoic acid)	$C_6H_{12}O_2$ 116.16	CH_3·$(CH_2)_4$·COOH	m.p. −4°C b.p. 205°C d^{20} 0.929 n_D^{20} 1.416 35	Occurs in traces in many fats
Enanthic acid (heptanoic acid)	$C_7H_{14}O_2$ 130.19	CH_3·$(CH_2)_5$·COOH	m.p. −7.46°C b.p. 223°C d^{14} 0.921 6 $n_D^{19.8}$ 1.421 62	
Caprylic acid (octanoic acid)	$C_8H_{16}O_2$ 144.22	CH_3·$(CH_2)_6$·COOH	m.p. 16°C b.p. 239°C d^{20} 0.908 8 n_D^{20} 1.428 5	Component of many fats
Pelargonic acid (nonanoic acid)	$C_9H_{18}O_2$ 158.24	CH_3·$(CH_2)_7$·COOH	m.p. 12.3°C b.p. 254°C d^{20} 0.905 5 n_D^{20} 1.433 0	Occurs in oil of rue, Japan wax, fusel oils, leaves of *Pelargonium roseum*
Capric acid (decanoic acid)	$C_{10}H_{20}O_2$ 172.27	CH_3·$(CH_2)_8$·COOH	m.p. 31.3°C b.p. 269°C d^{40} 0.885 8 n_D^{40} 1.428 55	Component of many animal and vegetable fats
Undecylic acid (hendecanoic acid)	$C_{11}H_{22}O_2$ 186.30	CH_3·$(CH_2)_9$·COOH	m.p. 28.5°C b.p. 284°C d^{20} 0.890 5 $n_D^{45.2}$ 1.429 4	Found in *Pseudomonas*
Lauric acid (dodecanoic acid)	$C_{12}H_{24}O_2$ 200.32	CH_3·$(CH_2)_{10}$·COOH	m.p. 43.5°C b.p. 225°C/100 d^{20} 0.883 $n_D^{82.1}$ 1.418 3	Major component of vegetable fats (esp. laurel). In smaller quantities in depot fat of animals, milk fat, fishliver oils
Tridecylic acid (tridecanoic acid)	$C_{13}H_{26}O_2$ 214.35	CH_3·$(CH_2)_{11}$·COOH	m.p. 51°C b.p. 312.4°C n_D^{70} 1.424 9	Occurs in animal fats in very small traces
Myristic acid (tetradecanoic acid)	$C_{14}H_{28}O_2$ 228.38	CH_3·$(CH_2)_{12}$·COOH	m.p. 54.4°C b.p. 250.5°C/100 d^{54} 0.862 2 n_D^{60} 1.430 8	Component of almost all animal fats (1–5%) and vegetable fats, esp. milk fat, fish oils, palm oil, nutmegs

Table 19 (continued) Fatty acids

Name	Formula and mol.wt.	Structure	Physical properties	Remarks
Pentadecylic acid (pentadecanoic acid)	$C_{15}H_{30}O_2$ 242.41	$CH_3{\cdot}(CH_2)_{13}{\cdot}COOH$	m.p. 52.1°C b.p. 257°C/100 d^{80} 0.8423 n_D^{70} 1.4270	Occurs in traces in animal fats, esp. liver fats
Palmitic acid (hexadecanoic acid)	$C_{16}H_{32}O_2$ 256.43	$CH_3{\cdot}(CH_2)_{14}{\cdot}COOH$	m.p. 62.85°C b.p. 268.5°C/100 d^{70} 0.8487 $n_D^{79.8}$ 1.4273	Widely distributed in nature. Present in almost all fats
Margaric acid (heptadecanoic acid)	$C_{17}H_{34}O_2$ 270.46	$CH_3{\cdot}(CH_2)_{15}{\cdot}COOH$	m.p. 62°C b.p. 227°C/100 d^{60} 0.8579 n_D^{70} 1.4319	Occurs in traces in mutton fat
Stearic acid (octadecanoic acid)	$C_{18}H_{36}O_2$ 284.49	$CH_3{\cdot}(CH_2)_{16}{\cdot}COOH$	m.p. 69.6°C b.p. 298°C/100 d^{20} 0.9408 $n_D^{80.2}$ 1.4299	Found abundantly in important edible fats. Also occurs in vegetable fats
Nondecylic acid (nonadecanoic acid)	$C_{19}H_{38}O_2$ 298.51	$CH_3{\cdot}(CH_2)_{17}{\cdot}COOH$	m.p. 68–69°C b.p. 298°C/100	
Arachidic acid (eicosanoic acid)	$C_{20}H_{40}O_2$ 312.54	$CH_3{\cdot}(CH_2)_{18}{\cdot}COOH$	m.p. 75.4°C b.p. 328°C d^{100} 0.824 n_D^{100} 1.4250	Occurs in traces in many seed and animal fats
Heneicosanoic acid	$C_{21}H_{42}O_2$ 326.57	$CH_3{\cdot}(CH_2)_{19}{\cdot}COOH$	m.p. 75.1°C	
Behenic acid (docosanoic acid)	$C_{22}H_{44}O_2$ 340.59	$CH_3{\cdot}(CH_2)_{20}{\cdot}COOH$	m.p. 80°C b.p. 306°C/60 d^{100} 0.8221 n_D^{100} 1.4270	Present in traces in animal fats and seed fats. Constitutes 50% of the spleen cerebrosides in GAUCHER's disease (see page 455)
Tricosanoic acid	$C_{23}H_{46}O_2$ 354.62	$CH_3{\cdot}(CH_2)_{21}{\cdot}COOH$	m.p. 79.1°C	
Lignoceric acid (tetracosanoic acid)	$C_{24}H_{48}O_2$ 368.65	$CH_3{\cdot}(CH_2)_{22}{\cdot}COOH$	m.p. 84.2°C d^{20} 0.8207 n_D^{100} 1.4287	Component of sphingomyelins and of kerasin (spleen cerebroside in GAUCHER's disease; see page 455). Also found in some vegetable fats and bacterial and insect waxes
Pentacosanoic acid	$C_{25}H_{50}O_2$ 382.68	$CH_3{\cdot}(CH_2)_{23}{\cdot}COOH$	m.p. 83°C	
Cerotic acid (hexacosanoic acid)	$C_{26}H_{52}O_2$ 396.70	$CH_3{\cdot}(CH_2)_{24}{\cdot}COOH$	m.p. 87.7°C d^{100} 0.8198 n_D^{100} 1.4301	Occurs free and combined. In Chinese wax (cetyl ester), beeswax, wool fat
Heptacosanoic acid	$C_{27}H_{54}O_2$ 410.73	$CH_3{\cdot}(CH_2)_{25}{\cdot}COOH$	m.p. 87.6°C	
Montanic acid (octacosanoic acid)	$C_{28}H_{56}O_2$ 424.76	$CH_3{\cdot}(CH_2)_{26}{\cdot}COOH$	m.p. 90.9°C d^{100} 0.8191 n_D^{100} 1.4313	Component of montan wax, beeswax, Chinese wax
Nonacosanoic acid	$C_{29}H_{58}O_2$ 438.78	$CH_3{\cdot}(CH_2)_{27}{\cdot}COOH$	m.p. 90.3°C	
Melissic acid (triacontanoic acid)	$C_{30}H_{60}O_2$ 452.81	$CH_3{\cdot}(CH_2)_{28}{\cdot}COOH$	m.p. 93.6°C n_D^{100} 1.4323	Occurs in beeswax

Table 19 (continued) Fatty acids

Name	Formula and mol.wt.	Structure	Physical properties	Remarks
Lacceroic acid (dotriacontanoic acid)	$C_{32}H_{64}O_2$ 480.87	$CH_3{\cdot}(CH_2)_{30}{\cdot}COOH$	m.p. 96.2°C	Occurs in stick-lac wax (from *Tachardia lacca*) and other natural waxes
Unsaturated (mono-olefinic) straight-chain monocarboxylic acids				
Acrylic acid (propenoic acid)	$C_3H_4O_2$ 72.06	$CH_2{=}CH{\cdot}COOH$	m.p. 13°C b.p. 141°C d^{16} 1.062 n_D^{20} 1.4224	
trans-(α-)Crotonic acid (*trans*-butenoic acid)	$C_4H_6O_2$ 86.09	$CH_3{\cdot}CH{=}HC{\cdot}COOH$ (CH₃·CH over HC·COOH, double bond)	m.p. 72°C b.p. 189°C d^{72} 0.973 $n_D^{79.7}$ 1.4228	Constituent of croton oil (from *Croton tiglium* seeds)
Iso-(β-)crotonic acid (*cis*-butenoic acid)	$C_4H_6O_2$ 86.09	$HC{\cdot}CH_3{=}HC{\cdot}COOH$ (HC·CH₃ over HC·COOH, double bond)	m.p. 15.5°C b.p. 169°C d^{15} 1.0312 n_D^{20} 1.4457	Readily isomerizes to the *trans*-acid
Δ^2-Hexenoic acid	$C_6H_{10}O_2$ 114.15	$CH_3{\cdot}(CH_2)_2{\cdot}CH{=}CH{\cdot}COOH$	m.p. 32°C b.p. 217°C d^{40} 0.9627 n_D^{40} 1.4601	Occurs in Japanese peppermint oil
Δ^4-Decenoic acid (obtusilic acid)	$C_{10}H_{18}O_2$ 170.25	$CH_3{\cdot}(CH_2)_4{\cdot}CH{=}CH{\cdot}(CH_2)_2{\cdot}COOH$	b.p. 148–150°C/13 d^{20} 0.9197 n_D^{20} 1.4497	Occurs in seed fat of *Lindera obtusiloba*
Δ^9-Decenoic acid	$C_{10}H_{18}O_2$ 170.25	$CH_2{=}CH{\cdot}(CH_2)_7{\cdot}COOH$	b.p. 143–148°C/15 d^{15} 0.9238 n_D^{20} 1.4488	Occurs in butter and milk fats and in sperm head oil
Δ^4-Dodecenoic acid (linderic acid)	$C_{12}H_{22}O_2$ 198.31	$CH_3{\cdot}(CH_2)_6{\cdot}CH{=}CH{\cdot}(CH_2)_2{\cdot}COOH$	m.p. 1–1.3°C b.p. 170–172°C/13 d^{20} 0.9081 n_D^{20} 1.4529	Occurs in various seed oils, e.g., *Lindera obtusiloba*
Δ^5-Dodecenoic acid (lauroleic acid)	$C_{12}H_{22}O_2$ 198.31	$CH_3{\cdot}(CH_2)_5{\cdot}CH{=}CH{\cdot}(CH_2)_3{\cdot}COOH$	d^{15} 0.9130 n_D^{15} 1.4535	Occurs in sperm blubber and head oil
Δ^9-Dodecenoic acid	$C_{12}H_{22}O_2$ 198.31	$CH_3{\cdot}CH_2{\cdot}CH{=}CH{\cdot}(CH_2)_7{\cdot}COOH$	–	Occurs in fat of cow's milk
Δ^4-Tetradecenoic acid (tsuzuic acid)	$C_{14}H_{26}O_2$ 226.36	$CH_3{\cdot}(CH_2)_8{\cdot}CH{=}CH{\cdot}(CH_2)_2{\cdot}COOH$	m.p. 18–18.5°C b.p. 185–188°C/13 d^{20} 0.9024 n_D^{20} 1.4557	Occurs in various tropical plant oils, esp. tsuzu oil
Δ^5-Tetradecenoic acid (physeteric acid)	$C_{14}H_{26}O_2$ 226.36	$CH_3{\cdot}(CH_2)_7{\cdot}CH{=}CH{\cdot}(CH_2)_3{\cdot}COOH$	d^{20} 0.9046 n_D^{20} 1.4552	Occurs in whale blubber and sardine oil
Δ^9-Tetradecenoic acid (myristoleic acid)	$C_{14}H_{26}O_2$ 226.36	$CH_3{\cdot}(CH_2)_3{\cdot}CH{=}CH{\cdot}(CH_2)_7{\cdot}COOH$	d^{20} 0.9018 n_D^{20} 1.4549	Occurs in milk fat and depot and liver fat of many animals
Δ^9-Hexadecenoic acid (palmitoleic acid)	$C_{16}H_{30}O_2$ 254.42	$CH_3{\cdot}(CH_2)_5{\cdot}CH{=}CH{\cdot}(CH_2)_7{\cdot}COOH$	m.p. 1°C b.p. 218–220°C d^{15} 0.9003	Widely distributed. In marine oils (15–20% of total fatty acids), in depot and milk fat of animals, vegetable oils and fats

Table 19 (continued) Fatty acids

Name	Formula and mol.wt.	Structure	Physical properties	Remarks (for references see page 372)
cis-Δ^6-Octadecenoic acid (petroselinic acid)	$C_{18}H_{34}O_2$ 282.47	$CH_3{\cdot}(CH_2)_{10}{\cdot}CH{=}CH{\cdot}(CH_2)_4{\cdot}COOH$	m.p. 32–33°C b.p. 208–210°C/10 d^{35} 0.8824 n_D^{47} 1.4535	Occurs in seeds of aromatic plants (parsley, celery, etc.) and in some umbellate fats
Oleic acid (*cis*-Δ^9-octadecenoic acid)	$C_{18}H_{34}O_2$ 282.47	$CH{\cdot}(CH_2)_7{\cdot}COOH$ ‖ $CH{\cdot}(CH_2)_7{\cdot}CH_3$	m.p. 13°C b.p. 286°C/100 d^{20} 0.895 n_D^{20} 1.45823	Most abundant of the unsaturated fatty acids. Present in nearly all natural fats (one-third of fatty acids of cow's milk; phosphatides). Occurs in traces in human urine
Elaidic acid (*trans*-Δ^9-octadecenoic acid)	$C_{18}H_{34}O_2$ 282.47	$CH_3{\cdot}(CH_2)_7{\cdot}CH$ ‖ $CH{\cdot}(CH_2)_7{\cdot}COOH$	m.p. 44–45°C b.p. 288°C/100 d^{79} 0.851 n_D^{70} 1.4405	Formed by isomerization of oleic acid
trans-Vaccenic acid (*trans*-Δ^{11}-octadecenoic acid)	$C_{18}H_{34}O_2$ 282.47	$CH_3{\cdot}(CH_2)_5{\cdot}CH$ ‖ $CH{\cdot}(CH_2)_9{\cdot}COOH$	m.p. 42.5°C d^{70} 0.8560 n_D^{60} 1.4439	Occurs in many animal fats and vegetable oils
cis-Vaccenic acid (*cis*-Δ^{11}-octadecenoic acid)	$C_{18}H_{34}O_2$ 282.47	$CH{\cdot}(CH_2)_9{\cdot}COOH$ ‖ $CH{\cdot}(CH_2)_5{\cdot}CH_3$	m.p. 12.4–13°C	Has been shown to be the haemolytic acid occurring in plasma and various animal tissues [1]. Also present in *Lactobacillus* species [2]
Δ^{12}-Octadecenoic acid	$C_{18}H_{34}O_2$ 282.47	$CH_3{\cdot}(CH_2)_4{\cdot}CH{=}CH{\cdot}(CH_2)_{10}{\cdot}COOH$	–	Occurs in partially hydrogenated peanut oil
Gadoleic acid (Δ^9-eicosenoic acid)	$C_{20}H_{38}O_2$ 310.52	$CH_3{\cdot}(CH_2)_9{\cdot}CH{=}CH{\cdot}(CH_2)_7{\cdot}COOH$	m.p. 24.5°C	*Cis* and *trans* forms. In many fish and marine animal oils, in vegetable oils, in brain phosphatides
Δ^{11}-Eicosenoic acid	$C_{20}H_{38}O_2$ 310.52	$CH_3{\cdot}(CH_2)_7{\cdot}CH{=}CH{\cdot}(CH_2)_9{\cdot}COOH$	m.p. *cis* 22°C *trans* 52–53°C	Principal acid of jojoba nuts ('goat nuts'), also in seed oil of *Conringia orientalis*, rape- and mustard seed oils, fish oils
Cetoleic acid (Δ^{11}-docosenoic acid)	$C_{22}H_{42}O_2$ 338.58	$CH_3{\cdot}(CH_2)_9{\cdot}CH{=}CH{\cdot}(CH_2)_9{\cdot}COOH$	m.p. 32–33°C	Occurs in various marine oils
Erucic acid (*cis*-Δ^{13}-docosenoic acid)	$C_{22}H_{42}O_2$ 338.58	$CH{\cdot}(CH_2)_{11}{\cdot}COOH$ ‖ $CH{\cdot}(CH_2)_7{\cdot}CH_3$	m.p. 33.5°C b.p. 281°C/30 d^{55} 0.860 n_D^{64} 1.4480	Occurs in seed oils, esp. rapeseed oil
Brassidic acid (*trans*-Δ^{13}-docosenoic acid)	$C_{22}H_{42}O_2$ 338.58	$CH_3{\cdot}(CH_2)_7{\cdot}CH$ ‖ $CH{\cdot}(CH_2)_{11}{\cdot}COOH$	m.p. 61.5°C b.p. 282°C/30 d^{57} 0.8585 n_D^{100} 1.4347	Formed by isomerization of erucic acid
Selacholeic acid (nervonic acid, *cis*-Δ^{15}-tetracosenoic acid)	$C_{24}H_{46}O_2$ 366.63	$CH{\cdot}(CH_2)_{13}{\cdot}COOH$ ‖ $CH{\cdot}(CH_2)_7{\cdot}CH_3$	m.p. 40.5–41°C n_D^{46} 1.4535	Occurs in shark and ray liver oils, in brain cerebrosides (nervone) and sphingomyelins [3]
Ximenic acid (Δ^{17}-hexacosenoic acid)	$C_{26}H_{50}O_2$ 394.69	$CH_3{\cdot}(CH_2)_7{\cdot}CH{=}CH{\cdot}(CH_2)_{15}{\cdot}COOH$	m.p. 45°C	Occurs in *Ximenia americana* (tallow-wood). A hexacosenoic acid is found with nervonic acid in brain cerebrosides

Table 19 (continued) Fatty acids

Name	Formula and mol.wt.	Structure	Physical properties	Remarks
		Unsaturated (polyolefinic) straight-chain monocarboxylic acids		
Sorbic acid ($\Delta^{2,4}$-hexadienoic acid)	$C_6H_8O_2$ 112.13	$CH_3 \cdot CH{=}CH \cdot CH{=}CH \cdot COOH$	m.p. 134.5°C b.p. 228°C (decomp.)	Occurs as lactone in oil of unripe mountain ash berries
Linoleic acid (*cis-cis*-$\Delta^{9,12}$-octadecadienoic acid)	$C_{18}H_{32}O_2$ 280.45	$CH_3 \cdot (CH_2)_4 \cdot CH$ ‖ $CH \cdot CH_2 \cdot CH$ ‖ $CH \cdot (CH_2)_7 \cdot COOH$	m.p. −11 (−5)°C b.p. 230°C/16 d^{20} 0.9025 n_D^{20} 1.4699	Widely distributed in plants, esp. in linseed, hemp and cottonseed oils. Also in lipids of animals (component of phosphatides, etc.). Essential dietary component
Hiragonic acid ($\Delta^{6,10,14}$-hexadecatrienoic acid)	$C_{16}H_{26}O_2$ 250.38	$CH \cdot (CH_2)_2 \cdot CH{=}CH \cdot CH_3$ ‖ $CH \cdot (CH_2)_2 \cdot CH{=}CH \cdot (CH_2)_4 \cdot COOH$	d^{20} 0.9288 n_D^{20} 1.4855	Occurs in sardine oil
α-Eleostearic acid (*cis*-$\Delta^{9,11,13}$-octadecatrienoic acid)	$C_{18}H_{30}O_2$ 278.44	$CH_3 \cdot (CH_2)_3 \cdot (CH{=}CH)_3 \cdot (CH_2)_7 \cdot COOH$	m.p. 48°C b.p. 235°C/12 d^{56} 0.8980 n_D^{56} 1.5080	Occurs in vegetable oils, esp. tung oil
β-Eleostearic acid (*trans*-$\Delta^{9,11,13}$-octadecatrienoic acid)	$C_{18}H_{30}O_2$ 278.44		m.p. 71°C d^{80} 0.8839 n_D^{74} 1.5000	Formed from α-eleostearic acid by action of light, heat and chemical reagents
Linolenic acid ($\Delta^{9,12,15}$-octadecatrienoic acid)	$C_{18}H_{30}O_2$ 278.44	$CH \cdot CH_2 \cdot CH{=}CH \cdot CH_2 \cdot CH_3$ ‖ $CH \cdot CH_2 \cdot CH{=}CH \cdot (CH_2)_7 \cdot COOH$	m.p. −11.2 to −11°C b.p. 230–232°C/17 d^{20} 0.9046 n_D^{20} 1.4780	Occurs in many vegetable oils, esp. drying oils such as linseed oil. Also in traces in animal fats (phosphatides)
Stearidonic acid (moroctic acid, $\Delta^{4,8,12,15}$-octadecatetraenoic acid)	$C_{18}H_{28}O_2$ 276.42	$CH_3 \cdot CH_2 \cdot CH{=}CH \cdot CH_2 \cdot CH$ ‖ $CH \cdot (CH_2)_2 \cdot CH{=}CH \cdot (CH_2)_2 \cdot CH$ ‖ $CH \cdot (CH_2)_2 \cdot COOH$	d^{20} 0.9297 n_D^{20} 1.4911	Occurs in fish oils. The position of the double bonds is not confirmed
Timnodonic acid ($\Delta^{4,8,12,15,18}$-eicosapentaenoic acid)	$C_{20}H_{30}O_2$ 302.46	$CH_3 \cdot CH{=}CH \cdot CH_2 \cdot CH{=}CH$ | $CH \cdot (CH_2)_2 \cdot CH{=}CH \cdot CH_2$ ‖ $CH \cdot (CH_2)_2 \cdot CH{=}CH \cdot (CH_2)_2 \cdot COOH$	–	Occurs in sardine oil, cod-liver oil, pilot whale oil and oil from *Squalus sucklei* (spiny dog fish)
Arachidonic acid ($\Delta^{5,8,11,14}$-eicosatetraenoic acid)	$C_{20}H_{32}O_2$ 304.48	$CH_3 \cdot (CH_2)_4 \cdot CH{=}CH \cdot CH_2 \cdot CH$ ‖ $CH \cdot CH_2 \cdot CH{=}CH \cdot CH_2 \cdot CH$ ‖ $CH \cdot (CH_2)_3 \cdot COOH$	m.p. −49.5°C n_D^{20} 1.8482	Occurs in animal lipids (liver, phosphatides). 'Essential' acid. Synthesized in animals from dietary linoleic acid
Clupanodonic acid ($\Delta^{4,8,12,15,19}$-docosapentaenoic acid)	$C_{22}H_{34}O_2$ 330.52	$CH_3 \cdot CH_2 \cdot CH{=}CH \cdot (CH_2)_2 \cdot CH$ ‖ $CH \cdot (CH_2)_2 \cdot CH{=}CH \cdot CH_2 \cdot CH$ ‖ $CH \cdot (CH_2)_2 \cdot CH{=}CH \cdot (CH_2)_2 \cdot COOH$	m.p. < −78°C b.p. 236°C/5 d^{20} 0.9290 n_D^{20} 1.4868	Occurs in fish oils
Nisinic acid ($\Delta^{4,8,12,15,18,21}$-tetracosahexaenoic acid)	$C_{24}H_{36}O_2$ 356.55	$CH_3 \cdot CH_2 \cdot CH{=}CH \cdot CH_2 \cdot CH{=}CH \cdot CH_2$ | $CH \cdot (CH_2)_2 \cdot CH{=}CH \cdot CH_2 \cdot CH{=}CH$ ‖ $CH \cdot (CH_2)_2 \cdot CH{=}CH \cdot (CH_2)_2 \cdot COOH$	–	Occurs in tunny oil
Thynnic acid ($\Delta^?$-hexacosahexaenoic acid)	$C_{26}H_{40}O_2$ 384.61	–	d^{20} 0.9433 n_D^{20} 1.5022	Occurs in tunny oil

Table 19 (continued) Fatty acids

Name	Formula and mol.wt.	Structure	Physical properties	Remarks (for references see page 372)
		Unsaturated (acetylenic) straight-chain monocarboxylic acids		
Tariric acid (6-stearolic acid, 6-octadecynoic acid)	$C_{18}H_{32}O_2$ 280.45	$CH_3\cdot(CH_2)_{10}\cdot C{\equiv}C\cdot(CH_2)_4\cdot COOH$	m.p. 50.5°C	Occurs in fat of *Picramnia* spp. (tariri) (bitter-bush oil)
Stearolic acid (9-octadecynoic acid)	$C_{18}H_{32}O_2$ 280.45	$CH_3\cdot(CH_2)_7\cdot C{\equiv}C\cdot(CH_2)_7\cdot COOH$	m.p. 48.5°C b.p. 260°C	Formed by oxidation of oleic or elaidic acid
Behenolic acid (13-docosynoic acid)	$C_{22}H_{40}O_2$ 336.56	$CH_3\cdot(CH_2)_7\cdot C{\equiv}C\cdot(CH_2)_{11}\cdot COOH$	m.p. 57.5°C	Formed by oxidation of erucic or brassidic acid
		Branched-chain monocarboxylic acids		
Isobutyric acid (2-methyl-propanoic acid)	$C_4H_8O_2$ 88.11	CH_3 $\quad\rangle CH\cdot COOH$ CH_3	m.p. −47°C b.p. 154.4°C d^{20} 0.949 n_D^{20} 1.393	Occurs free in carob beans (*Ceratonia siliqua*), as ethyl ester in croton oil; also in faeces and as product of enzymic breakdown of proteins. Intermediate in metabolism of valine (see page 396)
Isovaleric acid (3-methylbutanoic acid)	$C_5H_{10}O_2$ 102.13	CH_3 $\quad\rangle CH\cdot CH_2\cdot COOH$ CH_3	m.p. −51°C b.p. 176.7°C d^{15} 0.937 $n_D^{22.4}$ 1.501 78	Occurs in root of valerian, tobacco leaves, volatile oils, depot fat of dolphins and porpoises, as glyceride in human faeces. Formed from leucine in bacterial degradation of proteins. Intermediate in metabolism of leucine (see page 395)
Tiglic acid (*cis*-2-methyl-Δ^2-butenoic acid)	$C_5H_8O_2$ 100.12	$CH_3\cdot CH{=}C\cdot COOH$ $\qquad\qquad |$ $\qquad\quad CH_3$	m.p. 64.5°C b.p. 198.5°C d^{76} 0.964 n_D^{81} 1.434 2	Occurs in croton oil (glyceride); in Roman cumin oil (esters), in geranium oils. Intermediate in metabolism of isoleucine (see page 396)
Isomyristic acid (13-methyltri-decanoic acid)	$C_{14}H_{28}O_2$ 228.38	$CH_3\cdot CH\cdot(CH_2)_{10}\cdot COOH$ $\qquad |$ $\quad CH_3$	m.p. 51°C	Occurs together with other even-numbered *iso* acids from $C_{10:br}$ to $C_{28:br}$ as esters in wool wax[4]
*ante*Isomargaric acid (14-methylhexa-decanoic acid)	$C_{17}H_{34}O_2$ 270.46	$CH_3\cdot CH_2\cdot CH\cdot(CH_2)_{12}\cdot COOH$ $\qquad\qquad |$ $\qquad\quad CH_3$	m.p. 36.8°C $[\alpha]_D$ +5.2°	Occurs together with other odd-numbered *ante-iso* acids from $C_{9:br}$ to $C_{31:br}$ as esters in wool wax[4]
Tuberculostearic acid (D-[−]-10-methyl-octadecanoic acid)	$C_{19}H_{38}O_2$ 298.51	$CH_3\cdot(CH_2)_7\cdot CH\cdot(CH_2)_8\cdot COOH$ $\qquad\qquad\quad |$ $\qquad\qquad CH_3$	m.p. 12.5–12.9 (23.5–25.8)°C b.p. 180°C/0.1 d^{24} 0.877 1 n_D^{25} 1.451 2 $[\alpha]_D^{19}$ −0.08°	Occurs free in lipids of tubercle bacilli and *Mycobacterium leprae*[5]
Phytanic acid (3,7,11,15-tetra-methylhexa-decanoic acid)	$C_{20}H_{40}O_2$ 312.54	$CH_3\cdot CH\cdot(CH_2)_3\cdot CH\cdot(CH_2)_3\cdot CH\cdot(CH_2)_3\cdot CH\cdot CH_2\cdot COOH$ $\quad |\qquad\qquad\quad |\qquad\qquad\quad |\qquad\qquad\quad |$ $CH_3\qquad\quad CH_3\qquad\quad CH_3\qquad\quad CH_3$	m.p. −6 to −7°C	Present in traces in animal fats, butter and in blood serum (increased in REFSUM's syndrome)[6]

Table 19 (concluded) Fatty acids

Name	Formula and mol.wt.	Structure	Physical properties	Remarks
Mycolipenic acid ([+]-2,4,6-tri-methyltetracos-2-enoic acid)	$C_{27}H_{52}O_2$ 408.71	$CH_3{\cdot}(CH_2)_{17}{\cdot}CH(CH_3){\cdot}CH_2{\cdot}CH(CH_3){\cdot}CH{=}C(CH_3){\cdot}COOH$	–	One of the 3 phthioic acids of tubercle bacilli[7]
Mycoceranic acid	$C_{32}H_{64}O_2$ 480.87	$CH_3{\cdot}(CH_2)_{22}{\cdot}CH(CH_3){\cdot}CH_2{\cdot}CH(CH_3){\cdot}CH_2{\cdot}CH(CH_3){\cdot}COOH$	–	In the lipids of tubercle bacilli[7]
Hydroxy acids				
α-Hydroxymyristic acid (2-hydroxytetra-decanoic acid)	$C_{14}H_{28}O_3$ 244.38	$CH_3{\cdot}(CH_2)_{11}{\cdot}CH(OH){\cdot}COOH$	m.p. 81–82°C	Occurs as esters in wool wax[4]
α-Hydroxypalmitic acid (2-hydroxyhexa-decanoic acid)	$C_{16}H_{32}O_3$ 272.43	$CH_3{\cdot}(CH_2)_{13}{\cdot}CH(OH){\cdot}COOH$	m.p. 86°C $[\alpha]_D$ −1.0°	Occurs as esters in wool wax[4]
α-Hydroxystearic acid (2-hydroxyocta-decanoic acid)	$C_{18}H_{36}O_3$ 300.49	$CH_3{\cdot}(CH_2)_{15}{\cdot}CH(OH){\cdot}COOH$	m.p. 93°C	Minor component of cerebrosides of normal human brain
Ricinoleic acid (*cis*-12-hydroxy-Δ^9-octadecenoic acid)	$C_{18}H_{34}O_3$ 298.47	$CH{\cdot}CH_2{\cdot}CH(OH){\cdot}(CH_2)_5{\cdot}CH_3$ ‖ $CH{\cdot}(CH_2)_7{\cdot}COOH$	m.p. 5, 7.7 and 16°C (3 forms) b.p. 250°C/15 n_D^{20} 1.4711 $[\alpha]_D^{20}$ +7.8°	As glyceride, chief constituent of castor oil
2-Hydroxytrico-sanoic acid	$C_{23}H_{46}O_3$ 370.62	$CH_3{\cdot}(CH_2)_{20}{\cdot}CH(OH){\cdot}COOH$	–	Component of normal brain cerebrosides to extent of about 7% of total fatty acids
Cerebronic acid (phrenosinic acid, 2-hydroxytetra-cosanoic acid)	$C_{24}H_{48}O_3$ 384.65	$CH_3{\cdot}(CH_2)_{21}{\cdot}CH(OH){\cdot}COOH$	m.p. 90–93 (102)°C $[\alpha]_D^{22}$ +3.33°	Component of cerebroside phrenosin (cerebron). About 15% of total fatty acids of brain cerebrosides[8]
2-Hydroxynervonic acid (2-hydroxy-Δ^{15}-tetracosenoic acid)	$C_{24}H_{46}O_3$ 382.63	$CH_3{\cdot}(CH_2)_7{\cdot}CH{=}CH{\cdot}(CH_2)_{12}{\cdot}CH(OH){\cdot}COOH$	m.p. 65°C $[\alpha]_D^{20}$ +2.87°	Component of cerebroside hydroxynervone (of which the isomeric Δ^{17}-acid is also a component). About 12% of total fatty acids of brain cerebrosides

References

1 Laser, H., *J. Physiol. (Lond.)*, **110**, 338 (1949); Morton and Todd, *Biochem. J.*, **47**, 327 (1950).
2 Bounds et al., *J. chem. Soc.*, **1954**, 448.
3 Hofmann and Sax, *J. biol. Chem.*, **205**, 55 (1953).
4 Truter, E.V., *Quart. Rev. chem. Soc. Lond.*, **5**, 390 (1951).
5 Schmidt and Shirley, *J. Amer. chem. Soc.*, **71**, 3804 (1949); Linstead et al., *J. chem. Soc.*, **1951**, 1130.
6 Klenk and Kahlke, *Hoppe-Seylers Z. physiol. Chem.*, **333**, 133 (1963); Avigan, J., *Biochim. biophys. Acta (Amst.)*, **116**, 391 (1966).
7 Polgár, N., *J. chem. Soc.*, **1954**, 1008, 1011; Asselineau et al., *Acta chem. scand.*, **11**, 196 (1957); Lederer, E., *Angew. Chem.*, **72**, 372 (1960); Asselineau, J., in Rauen, H.M. (Ed.), *Biochemisches Taschenbuch*, 2nd ed., part 1, Springer, Berlin, 1964, page 258.
8 Chibnall et al., *Biochem. J.*, **55**, 707 (1953); Mislow and Bleicher, *J. Amer. chem. Soc.*, **76**, 2825 (1954).

(For references see page 377)

Fatty acids[1]

Fatty acids are aliphatic monocarboxylic acids, R·COOH, where R is a saturated or unsaturated, straight-chain or branched radical. In a few cases they contain a hydroxyl group or, very rarely, keto, fluoro-, cyclic or acetylenic linkings. Straight-chain fatty acids are much more abundant than branched-chain ones, which occur in traces in many fats and in larger amounts in wool wax and the lipids of mycobacteria. Fatty acids containing an even number of carbon atoms are far more abundant than odd-numbered ones, a circumstance which is in accordance with the concept that the biosynthesis of fatty acids takes place by the condensation of 2-carbon units (acetate) with other 2-carbon units or with larger units that were themselves built up from 2-carbon units[2]. Data on the principal fatty acid components of lipids are given in Table 19 on pages 366–372.

A fatty acid is often represented by the symbol $C_{x:y}$, where x is the total number of carbon atoms and y the number of double bonds. Thus C_{16} is palmitic acid, $C_{18:1}$ oleic acid or one of its isomers, and so on. If the chain is branched, this is indicated for example by $C_{4:br}$ (isobutyric acid).

The naturally occurring unsaturated fatty acids are the *cis* geometrical isomers, although the *trans* forms of some have been detected in trace amounts, e.g., elaidic acid (*trans* isomer of oleic acid) and vaccenic acid (*trans*-11-octadecenoic acid). *Cis-trans* geometrical isomerism is illustrated by the case of oleic and elaidic acids:

CH·(CH$_2$)$_7$·COOH
‖
CH·(CH$_2$)$_7$·CH$_3$
Oleic acid (*cis*)

CH·(CH$_2$)$_7$·COOH
‖
CH$_3$·(CH$_2$)$_7$·CH
Elaidic acid (*trans*)

Unsaturated fatty acids with more than one double bond (polyolefinic or polyethenoid acids) play an important role in animal nutrition; some are apparently not synthesized in the organism at a rate sufficient to meet the requirements of growth and are therefore essential constituents of the diet. The most important of these are *cis-cis*-linoleic and arachidonic acids, the so-called 'essential fatty acids', the ingestion of any of which is effective in preventing or curing the fat-deficiency syndrome due to a completely fat-free diet (see page 492).

Prostaglandins[3]

Prostaglandins are a special class of unsaturated fatty acids with high physiological activity (lowering of blood pressure, stimulation of smooth muscle such as that of the uterus and intestine, inhibition of the release of fatty acid by adipose tissue stimulated by adrenaline or glucagon). They were first found by von Euler[4] in semen (at least 13 different ones have since been identified in human seminal plasma), but are now known to be widely distributed in the animal body. They are formed enzymatically from long-chain unsaturated fatty acids, arachidonic acid for instance, and all have a 5-membered ring, 1–3 hydroxyl groups and a *trans* double bond in position Δ-13. The structures of the 6 primary prostaglandins are shown in Table 20 below.

Table 20 Prostaglandins

Trivial name	Formula and mol. wt.	Chemical name	Structure
Prostaglandin E_1	$C_{20}H_{34}O_5$ 354.49	11α,15-Dihydroxy-9-ketoprost-13-enoic acid	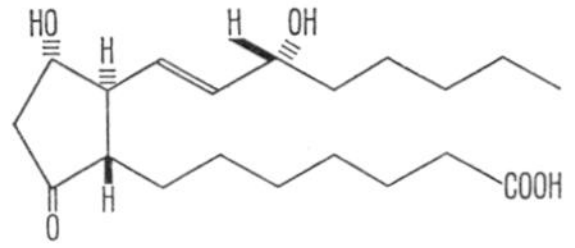
Prostaglandin E_2	$C_{20}H_{32}O_5$ 352.48	11α,15-Dihydroxy-9-ketoprosta-5,13-dienoic acid	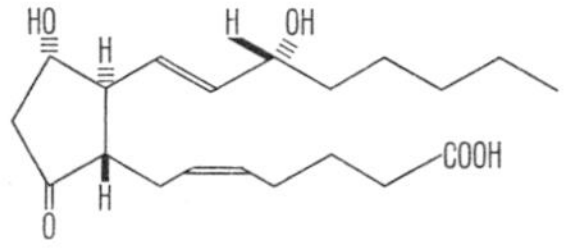
Prostaglandin E_3	$C_{20}H_{30}O_5$ 350.46	11α,15-Dihydroxy-9-ketoprosta-5,13,17-trienoic acid	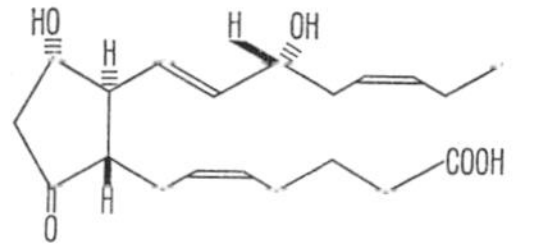
Prostaglandin $F_{1\alpha}$	$C_{20}H_{36}O_5$ 355.50	9α,11α,15-Trihydroxyprost-13-enoic acid	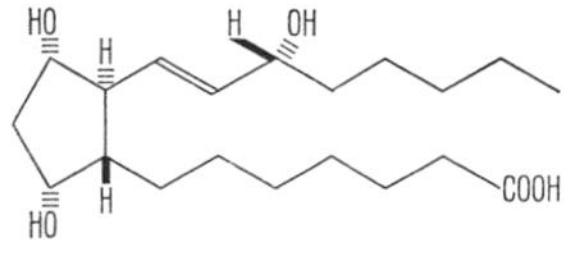
Prostaglandin $F_{2\alpha}$	$C_{20}H_{33}O_5$ 353.48	9α,11α,15-Trihydroxyprosta-5,13-dienoic acid	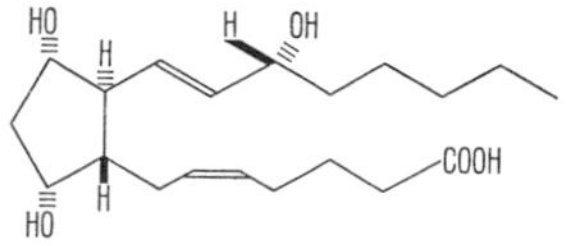
Prostaglandin $F_{3\alpha}$	$C_{20}H_{31}O_5$ 351.47	9α,11α,15-Trihydroxyprosta-5,13,17-trienoic acid	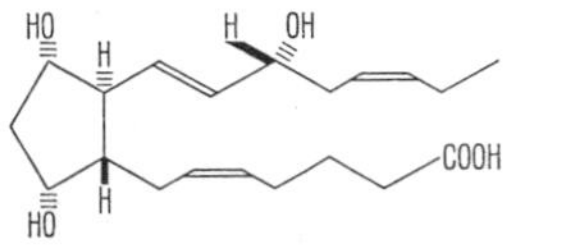

(For references see page 377)

Acylglycerols (fats)

The acylglycerols are formed by esterification of glycerol with one, two or three fatty-acid residues, yielding respectively a mono-, di- or triglyceride.

The natural fats are composed almost exclusively of triglycerides (neutral fats) together with traces of mono- and diglycerides. Lipids of the two latter types are formed during digestion and absorption of triglycerides and are found among the circulating lipids of the plasma.

At room temperature natural fats may be solid or liquid, and most contain at least 5 and up to 12 or more different fatty-acid residues. Chemically, they are complex mixtures of mixed triglycerides.

$CH_2{\cdot}O{\cdot}CO{\cdot}R$	$CH_2{\cdot}OH$	$CH_2{\cdot}O{\cdot}CO{\cdot}R$	$CH_2{\cdot}O{\cdot}CO{\cdot}R$	$CH_2{\cdot}O{\cdot}CO{\cdot}R$
$CH{\cdot}OH$	$CH{\cdot}O{\cdot}CO{\cdot}R$	$CH{\cdot}O{\cdot}CO{\cdot}R'$	$CH{\cdot}OH$	$CH{\cdot}O{\cdot}CO{\cdot}R'$
$CH_2{\cdot}OH$	$CH_2{\cdot}OH$	$CH_2{\cdot}OH$	$CH_2{\cdot}O{\cdot}CO{\cdot}R'$	$CH_2{\cdot}O{\cdot}CO{\cdot}R''$
α-Monoglyceride (1-acylglycerol)	β-Monoglyceride (2-acylglycerol)	α,β-Diglyceride (1,2-diacylglycerol)	α,α'-Diglyceride (1,3-diacylglycerol)	Triglyceride (1,2,3-triacylglycerol)

The tendency in all natural fats is towards maximum heterogeneity in the composition of the constituent triglycerides.

The fatty acids of most natural fats consist of mixtures of saturated and unsaturated acids. In general, the higher the proportion of saturated to unsaturated acids, the higher the melting point of the fat.

From the standpoint of their fatty-acid composition, the depot fats of land mammals are characterized by a preponderance of oleic acid, palmitic acid and in some important cases (e.g., ox, sheep) stearic acid. In the milk fat of land mammals this preponderance is diminished to an extent corresponding to the additional presence of the lower saturated fatty acids C_{12} down to C_4 (butyric acid). The depot fat of man contains the following percentages (by weight) of fatty acids: oleic 45, palmitic 25, linoleic 8, palmitoleic 7, stearic 6. The fats of aquatic animals contain mainly the higher unsaturated acids C_{16} to C_{22} together with usually 10–18% of palmitic acid.

Vegetable oils are often rich in the unsaturated C_{18} acids oleic ($C_{18:1}$), linoleic ($C_{18:2}$) and linolenic ($C_{18:3}$). The seed fats of the *Palmae* are rich in lower saturated fatty acids (e.g., 37–51% C_{12}, some C_{10} and C_8 in coconut oil), and the *Myristicaceae* yield much myristic acid (60–77% C_{14} in nutmeg oil).

In any particular tissue in the same species of animal the composition of the fat shows variations, and it is known that this is due at least in part to dietary differences. An example is the 'soft pork' produced from swine fed on soybean oil.

Absorption, transport and storage of fats [5]

The dietary triglycerides, which contain long-chain or medium-chain fatty acids, are hydrolysed in the intestine by pancreatic lipase in the presence of conjugated bile salts to yield β-monoglycerides and free fatty acids. The β-monoglycerides may in small part be isomerized to their α-isomers. The reaction products, in the form of bile-salt micelles, are mainly absorbed in the upper gut. Both α- and β-monoglycerides are readily absorbed by the intestinal mucosa. A small part is hydrolysed and some is converted into phospholipids. The major portion, however, is directly acylated to triglycerides by enzymes present in the brush border or in the microsomes. This resynthesis of triglycerides is not a random process and certain fatty acids are preferred in given positions of the glycerol molecule. Medium-chain fatty acids are not re-esterified by the intestinal mucosa but transported via the portal circulation to the liver, where they are largely oxidized. Most of the reformed triglycerides pass from the villi via the lacteals, the intestinal lymphatics, the thoracic duct and the subclavian vein into the systemic blood stream, but a small portion may reach the liver via the portal circulation.

Blood fats. Fats are transported in the body by the blood stream in the form of fine droplets of 1 μm or less in diameter known as *chylomicrons*. They are surrounded by a stabilizing film of protein (α- and β-globulins) and can be separated by centrifuging. The level of fats (and of other lipids) in the blood (see pages 590 sq.) rises after digestion of a meal containing fat. Hyperlipaemia also occurs after several days' fasting, when it is due to increased metabolism of depot fat following the exhaustion of glycogen reserves. Ingestion of alcohol, as well as the administration of various narcotics, also causes a marked increase in blood fats.

The chylomicrons are rapidly removed from the blood stream in the adipose tissue, heart muscle and liver. In the adipose tissue the triglycerides rapidly undergo considerable degradation, and their constituent fatty acids are used for resynthesis of new triglycerides and phospholipids and also for combustion to CO_2. Since the body's capacity to metabolize the fatty acids is limited, drastic changes in the fatty-acid composition of dietary fats may affect that of the depot fats.

Depot fats. The principal locations of depot fats in the body are subcutaneous, intramuscular, in the omentum, and in association with various organs such as the heart, kidney, mesentery, ovaries, etc. Their main function is that of an energy reserve, for which purpose they are more efficient than carbohydrates or proteins. In warm-blooded animals, subcutaneous fat often provides insulation against heat loss which is essential for survival. Adipose tissue also affords some protection against mechanical injury to important organs. In certain species, notably some marine animals, triglycerides are almost entirely replaced as energy reserves by other lipids, for example waxes. In any particular animal the amount of depot fat laid down is dependent on the state of nutrition and other factors and it is being continuously utilized and replaced.

In addition to dietary fat, triglycerides synthesized in the body itself are also stored, the fatty acids arising from carbohydrates and thus indirectly also from proteins, and the glycerol mainly from the splitting of blood glucose.

Unsaponifiable matter of fats

Natural fats contain a proportion of *unsaponifiable matter* varying from 0.1 to 5%. This consists chiefly of cholesterol and other sterols, carotenoids (hydrocarbons related to carotene), and the fat-soluble vitamins (see pages 457–469). The reasons for the occurrence of these substances in natural fats are presumably their solubility in triglycerides and insolubility in water. Many fats contain steryl esters of fatty acids (see under 'Waxes', page 377) in addition to free sterols.

Cholesterol is a normal constituent of all animal tissues and a major constituent of brain and nerve tissue in particular. Dietary cholesteryl esters are hydrolysed in the intestine and the free sterol is absorbed by the brush border. It is then transferred to the mucosal cells by a displacement mechanism, re-esterified and transported to the lymph [25]. Most of the body's cholesterol is synthesized endogenously, however, from acetyl-coenzyme A (see pages 426 to 427), principally in the liver. In the plasma, cholesterol circulates as a component of lipoproteins (see page 601).

The hydrocarbon *squalene* occurs in the liver oils of many elasmobranch fish, particularly sharks (up to 57% has been reported), also in olive oil, yeast fat and human skin. Its role as a precursor of cholesterol in the animal liver has been demonstrated (see page 426).

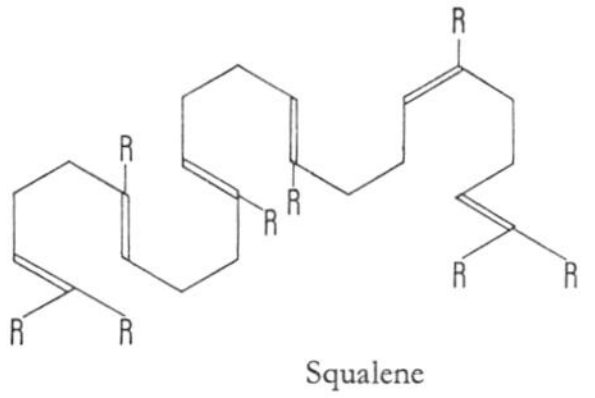

($R = CH_3$)

Squalene

Alkoxydiglycerides

The liver oils of Elasmobranch fish contain considerable proportions of compounds differing from the triglycerides in containing an ether linkage. They are diglycerides in which the remaining hydroxyl group has formed an ether with a higher aliphatic alcohol (R·OH) and may therefore be designated either as alkoxydiglycerides or as fatty acid esters of glyceryl ethers:

$$\begin{array}{l} CH_2{\cdot}O{\cdot}R \\ | \\ CH{\cdot}O{\cdot}CO{\cdot}R' \\ | \\ CH_2{\cdot}O{\cdot}CO{\cdot}R'' \end{array}$$

Alkoxydiglycerides

Ratfish liver oil consists almost exclusively of such compounds and contains practically no triglycerides. Diglyceride ethers of α,β-unsaturated higher aliphatic alcohols occur in the plasmalogen fraction (see page 376).

(For references see page 377)

Glycoglycerides

These compounds are widely distributed throughout the vegetable kingdom. They consist of two fatty-acid residues esterified with glycerol, the third (primary) alcohol group forming a glycoside, often a D-galactopyranoside. Mono- and digalactosyldiglycerides, and a sulphonic acid derivative of the former are major lipids of the chloroplasts of all green plants.

Phospholipids (phosphatides)

Broadly speaking, the phospholipids (phosphatides) are esters of fatty acids in which the alcohol component of the molecule contains a phosphate group as an integral part. They comprise principally the glycerophosphatides, containing glycerol, and the sphingomyelins containing sphingosine. They are constituents of all organs, especially brain and nerve tissue, but are notably absent from depot fats. They are involved in a great many metabolic processes and may be regarded as a form in which fats undergo metabolic change or are transported in the body. Thus they have been shown to be involved in intestinal fat absorption, fatty acid transport and oxidation, and the development of fatty livers. They have also been implicated as structural components of organs and in the process of blood coagulation. Phospholipids are readily synthesized in the organism, mainly in the liver and small intestine.

Glycerophosphatides

The glycerophosphatides are of universal occurrence. Chemically, they consist of α-glycerophosphoric acid esterified with fatty acids and/or other constituents.

Both the α and β forms of glycerophosphoric acid are known, but contrary to the statements made in most reference books it is now considered doubtful whether β-glycerophosphoric acid or β-glycerophosphatides or other derivatives occur in nature. Thus it has been shown[6] that in the hydrolysis of lecithins (see below) there is a reversible migration of the phosphate group resulting in the formation of mixtures of α- and β-glycerophosphoric acids. A similar change probably takes place during chemical isolation procedures. The migration of the phosphate group is thought to proceed as follows[7]:

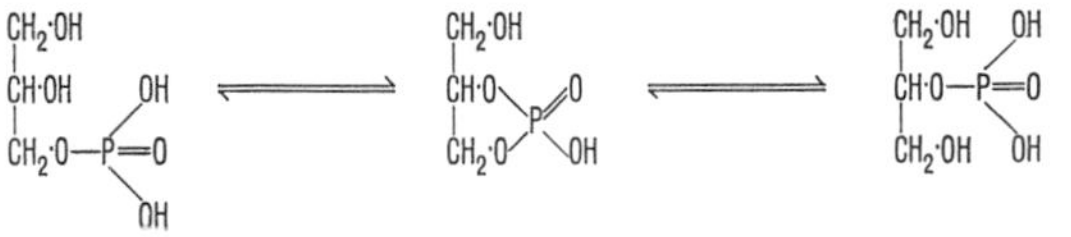

α-Glycerophosphoric acid — Glyceric-1,2-cyclic phosphoric acid — β-Glycerophosphoric acid

(*a*) *Phosphatidic acids*. Phosphatidic acids, the simplest of the glycerophosphatides and those most similar chemically to the triglycerides, are derived from α-glycerophosphoric acid by esterification of the two hydroxyl groups with fatty acids. Alternatively, they may be envisaged as triglycerides in which one of the fatty acid residues has been replaced by a phosphoric acid residue:

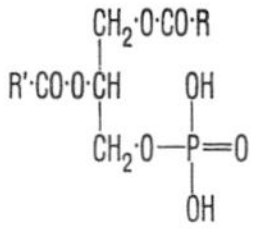

α-Phosphatidic acids
(where R·CO and R′·CO are fatty-acid residues)

Phosphatidic acids have been isolated from a wide range of plant tissues and have been shown to occur in animal tissues[8]. Their biosynthesis from fatty acids, glycerol and adenosine triphosphate (ATP) has been demonstrated[9].

α-Phosphatidylglycerols are compounds widely distributed in nature consisting of triglycerides in which one of the ester residues is a phosphatidic acid[10].

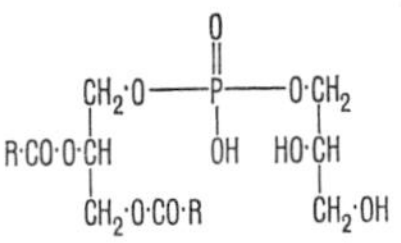

α-Phosphatidylglycerols

A phosphatidic acid derivative of importance is cardiolipin, which plays a role in the WASSERMANN reaction. First isolated from heart muscle, it consists of an α,α′-diglyceride in which the ester residues are both phosphatidic acids[11].

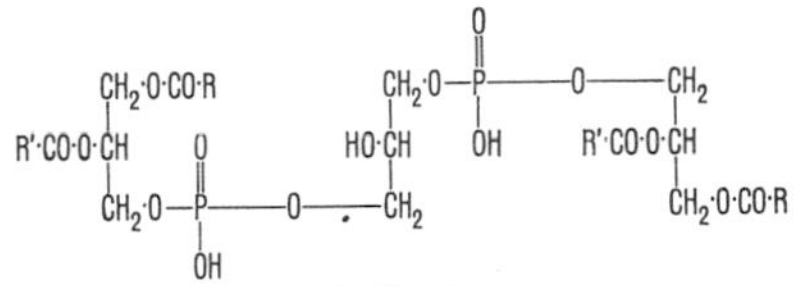

Cardiolipin

The fatty acids of cardiolipin consist almost entirely of oleic and linoleic acids in the ratio 1:5. *E. coli* is capable of forming cardiolipin from α-phosphatidylglycerols[12].

(*b*) *Phosphatidyl esters*. These substances are phosphatidic acids esterified with the hydroxyl groups of ethanolamine, choline or serine:

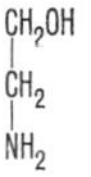

Ethanolamine

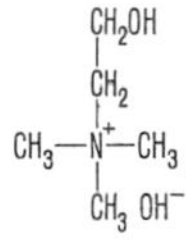

Choline

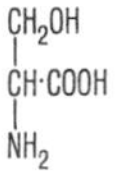

Serine

The resulting three types of phosphatidyl ester are:

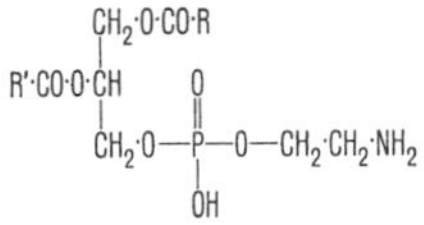

α-Phosphatidylethanolamines (cephalins)

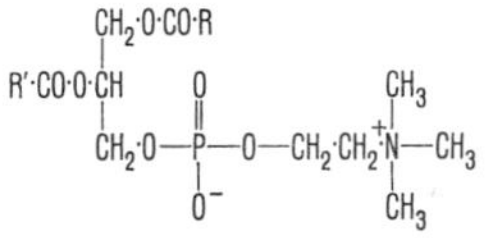

α-Phosphatidylcholines (lecithins)

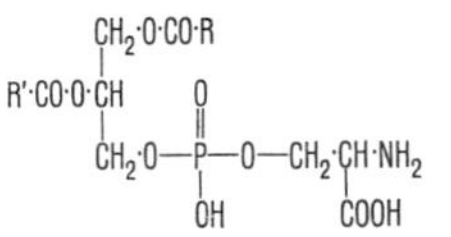

α-Phosphatidylserines

The term 'cephalin' was originally given to an ethanol-insoluble lipid fraction isolated from brain and containing both α-phosphatidylethanolamines and α-phosphatidyl-L-serines. The fatty-acid residues in the cephalins are predominantly those of oleic and stearic acids[13].

The lecithins obtained from many sources have all been shown to have the L-α-glycerophosphorylcholine skeleton given above[6], with the fatty acids as the only variant. The long-chain fatty acids (R·COOH and R′·COOH) are similar to those that predominate in triglycerides (oleic, palmitic, stearic and linoleic acids). The tetraethenoid fatty acid, arachidonic acid, is also found in some lecithins.

The lecithins of brain differ from those of other organs in their greater content of highly unsaturated fatty acids of chain length greater than C_{20}. Most lecithins contain both a saturated and an unsaturated fatty-acid residue, but some[14] contain either two saturated or two unsaturated fatty-acid residues.

The nature of the fatty-acid residues markedly affects the solubility of different lecithins in nonpolar solvents.

(*c*) *Lysophosphatides*. The lysophosphatides consist of partially hydrolysed glycerophosphatides (see page 417). Snake venoms contain an enzyme that splits one and only one of the two fatty acids from lecithins, yielding lysolecithins:

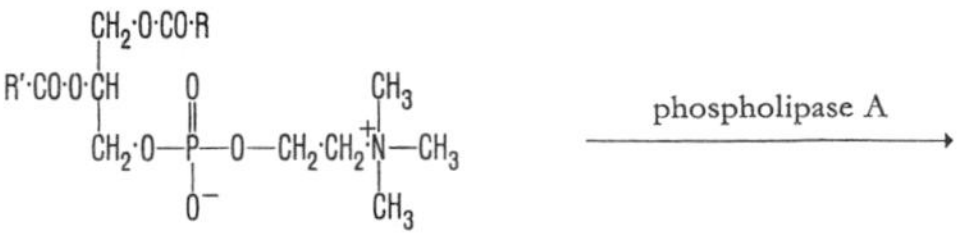

α-Phosphatidylcholines (lecithins)

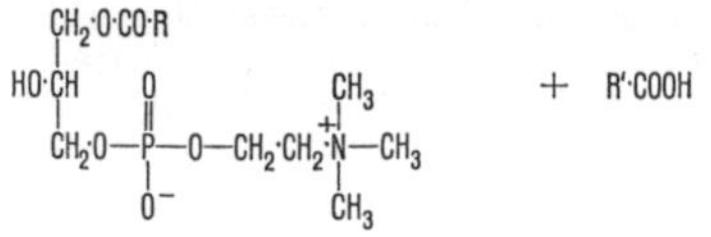

Lysolecithins Fatty acid

(*d*) *α-Glycerophosphoryl compounds* that lack both of the fatty acids present in phosphatidyl esters occur in mammalian tissues and fluids[15]. They are α-glycerophosphorylethanolamine and α-glycerophosphorylcholine:

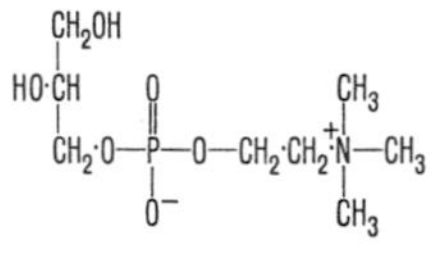

α-Glycerophosphorylcholine

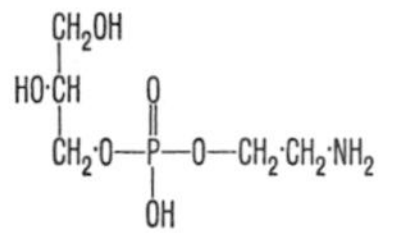

α-Glycerophosphorylethanolamine

(*e*) *Phosphatidylinositides*[16]. At least three distinct inositides have been described. These have been differentiated on the basis of the inositol derivatives obtained on hydrolysis. One type, the phosphatidylinositols (phosphoinositides)[17], are analogous to the glycerophosphatides. They occur in liver, heart, wheat germ and soybean, and have the following structure:

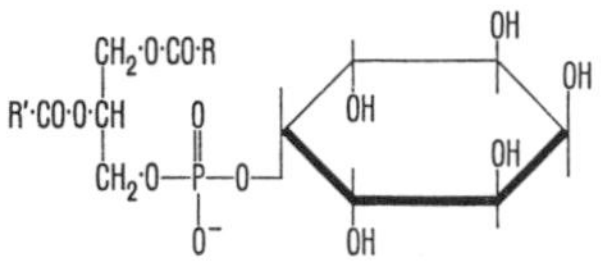

α-Phosphatidylinositols

Di- and triphosphoinositides have a similar structure with, in addition, either one or two phosphoric acid groups esterified with the inositol moiety[18].

Phosphoinositides are important metabolically active components of the myelin sheath, with a high turnover rate. They are bound to neurokeratin and to peptides (phosphatidopeptides) containing β-alanine[18].

(*f*) *Acetal phosphatides* (plasmalogens). These compounds are closely related to the phosphatidyl esters. Plasmalogens containing ethanolamine (phosphatidal ethanolamine) predominate in nature, but compounds in which ethanolamine is replaced by either serine (phosphatidal serine) or choline (phosphatidal choline) are also widely distributed in many tissues. Phosphatidal ethanolamine is the major ethanolamine-containing lipid of myelin.

Plasmalogens give a positive reaction for aldehydes, and the aldehydes corresponding to stearic and palmitic acids have been isolated from the crystalline acetal phosphatides of brain. About 20 different aldehydogenic chains occur in plasmalogens, 25–35% of them branched[18]. They have been shown[19] to contain two long-chain alkyl groups, one of which is present in ester linkage and the other in an unsaturated vinyl ether linkage:

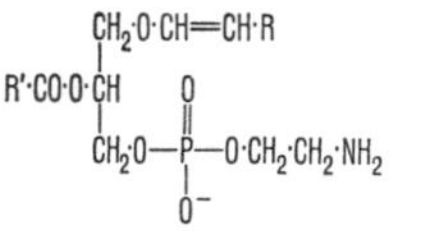

Acetal phosphatides (plasmalogens)

The existence of a phospholipid in malignant tumours has been reported. The compound, which possesses a marked affinity for protoporphyrin III, is composed of choline, spermine, phosphoric acid and fatty acid. The following structure has been proposed[20]:

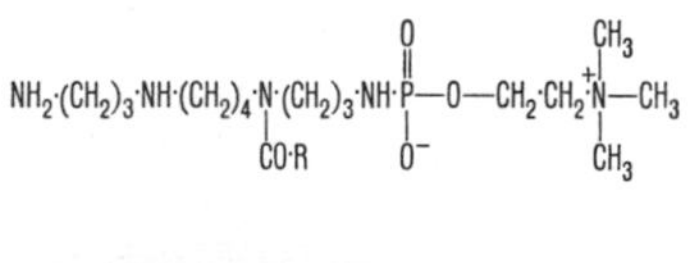

(*g*) *Alkyloxylysophosphatides*[21]. Analogues of acetal phosphatides, with a saturated α,β-bond in the ethereal alkyl group, occur in myelin and other tissues. They may be regarded as alkyl ethers of lysophosphatides, e.g., glycerol 1-hexadecyloxy-2-acyl-3-phosphorylethanolamine. They lack aldehydogenic properties, resist some hydrolytic procedures, and are important components of the cephalin B complex of glycerophosphatides, which is difficult to separate from sphingomyelin.

Sphingolipids

In the sphingolipid group, the base sphingosine (*erythro-trans*-1,3-dihydroxy-2-aminooctadec-4-ene) replaces glycerol. A single fatty acid radical is attached to the nitrogen by an amide linkage; the acylsphingosines are known as *ceramides*. Some sphingolipids are phosphatides, but others contain no phosphorus.

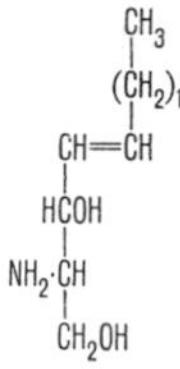

Sphingosine

In some members of the sphingolipid group, sphingosine is replaced by dihydrosphingosine (in which the double bond of sphingosine is saturated), or by the 4-hydroxy derivative of dihydrosphingosine (1,3,4-trihydroxy-2-amino-octadecane), phytosphingosine or its C_{20} homologue.

(*a*) *Sphingomyelin*. The only sphingolipids resembling the glycerophosphatides are the sphingomyelins:

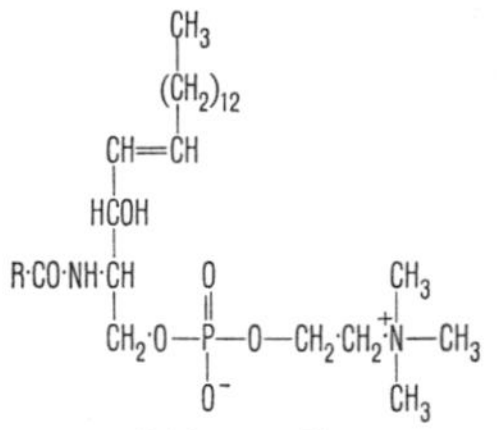

Sphingomyelins

Sphingomyelin is an important component of the myelin sheath. The sphingomyelin of grey matter contains mainly stearic acid[22], that of white matter mainly $C_{24:1}$ acid with lesser amounts of $C_{25:1}$, $C_{26:1}$, C_{24}, C_{25} and C_{16} acids.

(*b*) *Cerebrosides*[26]. Cerebrosides are widely distributed in nature. They consist of ceramide attached by a β-glycosidic linkage to a sugar, usually galactose or glucose but sometimes a di- or trisaccharide. Myelin contains large amounts of galactocerebrosides (ceramide galactoside), separable into four classes on the basis of the fatty acid linked to sphingosine. A proportion of each galactocerebroside contains dihydrosphingosine in place of sphingosine.

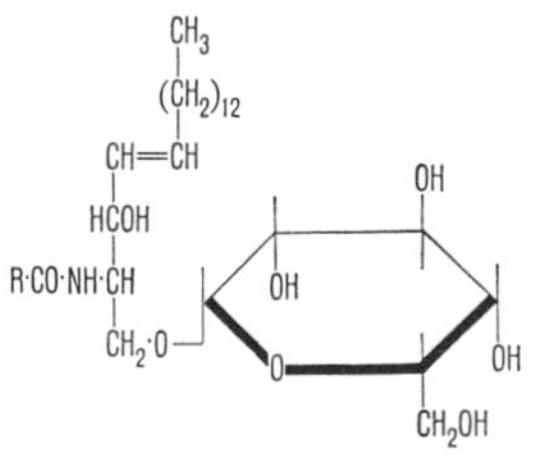

Cerebrosides

Other fatty acids, ranging from C_{14} to C_{26}, as well as the corresponding α-hydroxy acids, also occur[23, 25]. The α-hydroxy acids constitute 50–60% of the total fatty acids.

Cerebroside	Constituent fatty acid
Kerasin	Lignoceric acid $CH_3\cdot(CH_2)_{22}\cdot COOH$
Phrenosin	Cerebronic acid $CH_3\cdot(CH_2)_{21}\cdot CH(OH)\cdot COOH$
Nervone	Nervonic acid $CH_3\cdot(CH_2)_7\cdot CH{=}CH\cdot(CH_2)_{13}\cdot COOH$
Hydroxynervone	Hydroxynervonic acid $CH_3\cdot(CH_2)_7\cdot CH{=}CH\cdot(CH_2)_{12}\cdot CH(OH)\cdot COOH$

In GAUCHER's disease (see page 455) a glucocerebroside (ceramide glucoside) is deposited in various tissues. The sphingosine has the normal *erythro-trans* configuration and the fatty acids are usually mainly saturated and nonhydroxy, e.g., C_{22}. Moderately small amounts of ceramide lactoside accompany the glucocerebroside in some cases, and in a few the dihexoside is a major component.

Ceramide lactoside has been isolated from tumours and has antigenic properties [18, 25]. Small amounts of ceramide lactoside occur in normal ox and human spleen, blood serum, liver and erythrocyte stroma, accompanied in each case by traces of ceramide glucoside and ceramide trihexoside. The trihexoside contains one glucose and two galactose residues. The fatty acids of these glycolipids from normal spleen, etc. are mixtures of unsubstituted and α-hydroxy acids in the ratio of about 5:1. A ceramide trimannoside occurs in wheat flour.

(*c*) *Sulphatides*. Sulphatides are sulphuric acid esters of galactocerebrosides, with the sulphate group attached to the galactose ring [18, 25]. They occur in the grey and white matter of the brain and are strong acids. Sulphatides continue to be formed as long as myelination continues, but once formed they do not normally undergo further changes.

In metachromatic leucodystrophy the content of sulphatides is raised two- to five-fold, but other lipids are markedly reduced in amount. The sulphatides are of normal structure [22].

(*d*) *Aminoglycolipids* [23, 25]. These are neutral lipids composed of ceramide linked to one glucose, one *N*-acetylgalactosamine and two galactose residues. Stearic acid is the main fatty acid of normal brain aminoglycolipid, with smaller amounts of C_{20}, $C_{18:1}$ and C_{16} acids; α-hydroxy acids have not been found.

Aminoglycolipids occur in normal brain, spleen, liver, erythrocyte stroma and blood serum. In TAY-SACHS' disease (see page 455) the amount of aminoglycolipid in the brain is increased about 120-fold and its properties are not identical with normal brain aminoglycolipid [22].

Globoside, the most abundant glycolipid in the stroma of human erythrocytes, is an *N*-acetylgalactosamine containing sphingolipid.

(*e*) *Gangliosides (mucolipids)* [23, 25]. Gangliosides are acidic glycosphingolipids containing sialic acids (acylated neuraminic acids; see page 316). The non-ceramide portion of the ganglioside molecule resembles some mucoids, and for this reason the name 'mucolipids' has been used for the ganglioside group and aminoglycolipids. The fatty acids and general structure of gangliosides resemble those of brain aminoglycolipids except for the presence of additional *N*-acetylneuraminic acid residues. Though gangliosides are monomeric, with a molecular weight of about 1500, they form micelles in water.

Gangliosides of varying structure occur in the brain, spleen, liver, and erythrocyte stroma. The four major gangliosides isolated from human and beef brain have a common basic structure, viz., galactosyl-*N*-acetylgalactosaminylgalactosylglucosylceramide bound to 1–3 molecules of sialic acid. Enzymic hydrolysis with neuraminidase transforms the trisialoganglioside and the two disialogangliosides into the same monosialoganglioside. In the latter, the sialic acid residue occupies position 3 on the middle galactose molecule. An outstanding characteristic of the brain gangliosides is the large amount of stearic acid they contain (86–95% of the fatty acids); other fatty acids present are palmitic acid (1–3%) and arachidic acid (2–12%).

The erythrocyte stroma of the horse, cat and dog contains gangliosides composed of fatty acid, sphingosine, glucose, galactose and *N*-acetylneuraminic acid, but no hexosamine. The fatty acids are mostly $C_{24:1}$, C_{24} and C_{22}. Human, sheep and guinea-pig erythrocytes contain aminoglycolipids but no gangliosides.

In TAY-SACHS' disease (see page 455) the monosialoganglioside content of both the grey and white matter of the brain is increased about 20 times [23], in addition to the increase in aminoglycolipids. The gangliosides react abnormally with gangliosidase and have different solubilities and higher R_F values than normal brain gangliosides, but yield the same components on hydrolysis; the fatty-acid distribution is the same [22].

Waxes

The saponifiable waxes (as distinct from the hydrocarbon waxes) are conveniently divisible into the so-called *true waxes*, which are long-chain fatty-acid esters of long-chain aliphatic alcohols, and the *steryl esters*, long-chain fatty-acid esters of the complex cyclic alcohols, known as *sterols*. With the second group may be included the naturally occurring long-chain fatty-acid esters of vitamin A (see page 457) and vitamin D_3 (see page 462).

In general, the true waxes are products excreted by the epidermis of animals and plants for the purpose of providing a protective covering either to prevent water loss or wetting. Examples of the former are the surface waxes of plants in arid climates, of the latter the lanolin present on the skin and fur of almost all fur-bearing animals as well as the surface wax of fruits in moist climates (e.g., apples). In certain animals, notably the sperm whale, waxes almost entirely replace triglycerides as the energy reserve material.

True waxes. These are mixtures of fatty-acid esters of the higher aliphatic straight-chain monohydric alcohols, usually cetyl alcohol (hexadecanol, $CH_3\cdot[CH_2]_{14}\cdot CH_2OH$) and octadecyl alcohol (octadecanol, $CH_3\cdot[CH_2]_{16}\cdot CH_2OH$), but often including higher alcohols up to C_{36}. The fatty acids are usually of the saturated type, the commonest being cerotic acid (hexacosanoic acid, $CH_3\cdot[CH_2]_{24}\cdot COOH$), although acids containing a hydroxyl group are occasionally found. In many natural waxes the fatty acid and alcohol components have the same chain length.

Sterols. These substances, which also occur free as constituents of the unsaponifiable matter of fats, are alcohols belonging to the larger group known as *steroids*, compounds characterized by possession of the 17-carbon cyclopentanophenanthrene ring and dealt with in the section that follows.

References

1 ASSELINEAU and LEDERER, *Ann. Rev. Biochem.*, **30**, 71 (1961); MARKLEY, K.S. (Ed.), *Fatty Acids: Their Chemistry, Properties, Production and Uses*, 2nd ed., part 1, Wiley-Interscience, New York, 1960.

2 GREEN and GIBSON, in GREENBERG, D.M. (Ed.), *Metabolic Pathways*, vol. 1, Academic Press, New York, 1960, page 301.

3 For a review see BERGSTRÖM and SAMUELSSON, *Ann. Rev. Biochem.*, **34**, 101 (1965); HORTON, E.W., *Experientia (Basel)*, **21**, 113 (1965); BERGSTRÖM, S., *Science*, **157**, 382 (1967).

4 VON EULER, U.S., *Naunyn-Schmiedeberg's Arch. exp. Path. Pharmak.*, **175**, 78 (1934); VON EULER, U.S., *Klin. Wschr.*, **14**, 1182 (1935).

5 DOLE and HAMLIN, *Physiol. Rev.*, **42**, 674 (1962); ALSON, J.A., *Ann. Rev. Biochem.*, **35**, 559 (1966); SHAPIRO, B., *Ann. Rev. Biochem.*, **36**, 247 (1967).

6 BAER and KATES, *J. biol. Chem.*, **185**, 615 (1950); BAER et al., *J. Amer. chem. Soc.*, **78**, 232 (1956).

7 BAILLY, M.-C., *C. R. Acad. Sci. (Paris)*, **206**, 1902 (1938); **208**, 443, 1820 (1939); VERKADE et al., *Rec. Trav. chim. Pays-Bas*, **59**, 886 (1940); CHARGAFF, E., *J. biol. Chem.*, **144**, 455 (1942).

8 HOKIN and HOKIN, *J. biol. Chem.*, **233**, 800 (1958).

9 KORNBERG and PRICER, *J. biol. Chem.*, **204**, 345 (1953); BUBLITZ and KENNEDY, *J. biol. Chem.*, **211**, 951 (1954).

10 BENSON, A.A., *Ann. Rev. Plant Physiol.*, **15**, 1 (1964); CARTER et al., *Ann. Rev. Biochem.*, **34**, 109 (1965).

11 VAN DEENEN and DE HAAS, *Ann. Rev. Biochem.*, **35**, 157 (1966).

12 STANACEV et al., *J. biol. Chem.*, **242**, 3018 (1967).

13 FOLCH, J., *J. biol. Chem.*, **174**, 439 (1948).

14 HANAHAN and JAYKO, *J. Amer. chem. Soc.*, **74**, 5070 (1952); HANAHAN, D.J., *J. biol. Chem.*, **211**, 313 (1954).

15 DAWSON, R.M.C., *Biochem. J.*, **65**, 627 (1957).

16 FOLCH and LEBARON, *Canad. J. Biochem.*, **34**, 305 (1956).

17 HAWTHORNE, J.N., *Biochem. J.*, **59**, ii (1955).

18 RAPPORT and NORTON, *Ann. Rev. Biochem.*, **31**, 103 (1962).

19 GRAY, G.M., *Biochem. J.*, **70**, 425 (1958).

20 KOSAKI et al., *Science*, **127**, 1176 (1958).

21 ANSELL and SPANNER, *Biochem. J.*, **88**, 56 (1963).

22 FOLCH-PI and BAUER (Eds.), *Brain Lipids and Lipoproteins, and the Leucodystrophies*, Proceedings of the 7th International Congress of Neurology, Rome 1961, Elsevier, Amsterdam, 1963.

23 ARONSON and VOLK (Eds.), *Cerebral Sphingolipidoses*, Academic Press, New York, 1962.

24 DAVID et al., *Biochem. J.*, **98**, 662 (1966).

25 CARTER et al., *Ann. Rev. Biochem.*, **34**, 109 (1965).

Steroids [1]

Stereochemistry

The naturally occurring steroids include the sex hormones, the adrenocortical hormones and progesterone as well as cholesterol and the bile acids. All steroids possess the cyclopentanoperhydrophenanthrene ring system, a fairly flat structure conveniently represented as planar:

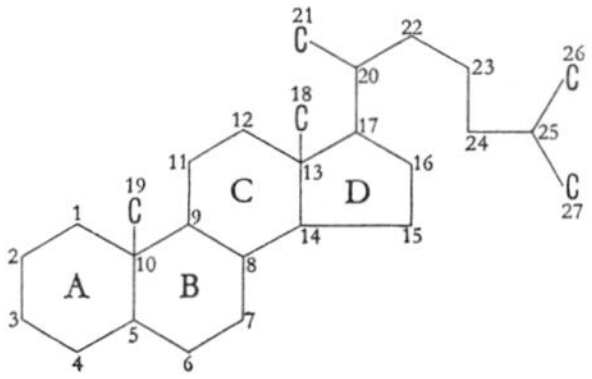

Cyclopentanoperhydrophenanthrene ring system

The skeleton (nucleus) of the steroid molecule consists of three six-membered rings A, B and C and a five-membered ring D. Each of the six-membered rings is in the 'chair' conformation:

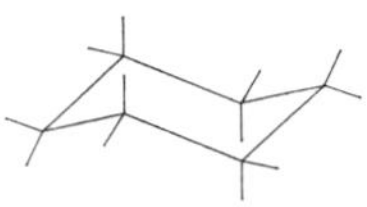

'Chair' conformation

There may be methyl or other groups at C-10 and C-13 and a side chain at C-17 of up to eight carbons. In the oestrogens ring A is aromatic. The system of numbering is shown in the figure above.

In these structures all the carbon atoms shared by two rings are asymmetric and, in addition, replacement of hydrogen atoms on other carbon atoms by other monovalent groups introduces further asymmetry. Since the biological activity of steroids is dependent on the stereochemical configuration it is essential to give precise designations. In the skeleton as shown in the figure the side nearer the observer is designated 'β' and the other side 'α'; thus in cholesterol the hydroxyl group projects towards the observer from the plane of the steroid skeleton when arranged as in the figure and so is 'above' it and thus 'β'. The systematic name for cholesterol is therefore cholest-5-en-3β-ol. In structural formulae, groups with β configuration are shown as attached to the steroid skeleton by a continuous line (——), those with α configuration by a dotted or broken line (- - -). Groups of unknown configuration are shown attached by a wavy line (~~~) and designated in names by the Greek letter. The prefix 'epi-' is used trivially to indicate inversion

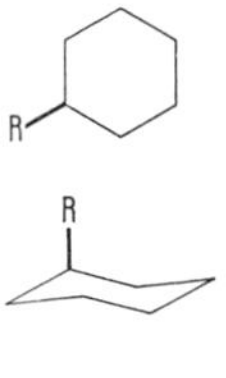

β configuration (R above the plane of the ring)

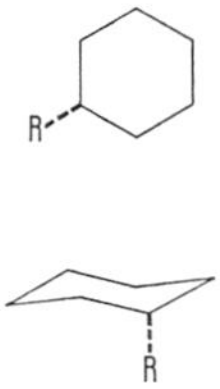

α configuration (R below the plane of the ring)

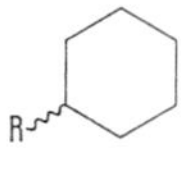

ξ configuration (configuration unknown)

of a substituent; thus the more common natural form of oestradiol is the 17β-hydroxy compound (17β-oestradiol) while the less common 17α-hydroxy form is often referred to as 17-epioestradiol or simply epioestradiol.

There are two distinct series of naturally occurring steroids saturated at C-5 which differ in their stereochemistry at the junction of the A and B rings. The series in which the A:B junction is *trans* is designated '5α' because the hydrogen attached to C-5 is on the α side and is *trans* with respect to the methyl group attached to C-10. The series in which the A:B junction is *cis* is designated '5β' because the hydrogen attached to C-5 is on the β side and is *cis* with respect to the methyl group attached to C-10. In steroids unsaturated at C-5, i.e., with a double bond between C-4 and C-5

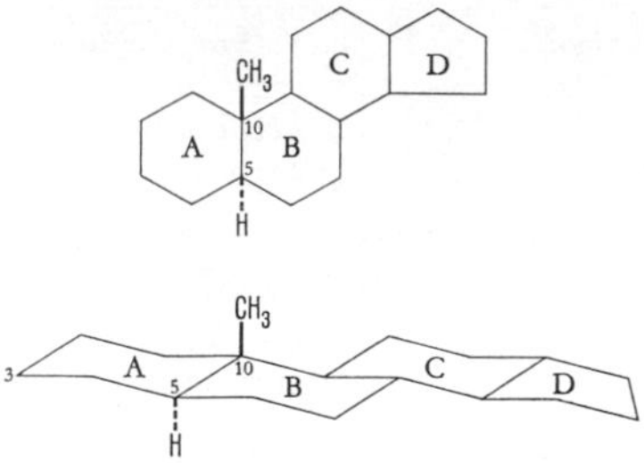

5α series of steroids saturated at C-5

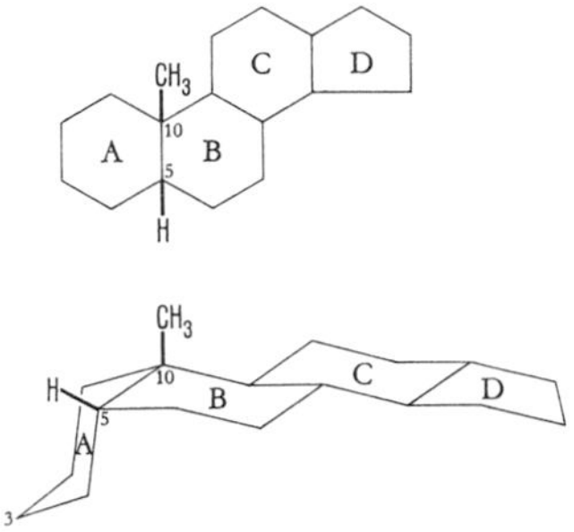

5β series of steroids saturated at C-5

or between C-5 and C-6, there is no hydrogen at C-5 and hence no stereoisomerism at the A:B ring junction. The prefix 'allo-' was formerly used to denote the 5α configuration. The C_{27} steroid skeleton with 5α configuration was formerly called coprostane while the 5β configuration was called cholestane; the names 5α-cholestane and 5β-cholestane are now used. The C_{19}-steroid skeleton with 5α configuration was formerly called androstane while the 5β configuration was called aetiocholane or aetiane; they are now known as 5α-androstane and 5β-androstane.

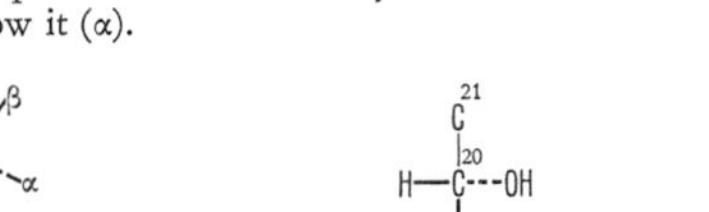

Δ^4-Steroids

The symbols α and β are also used to denote stereoisomerism at C-20. For this purpose the carbon atoms C-20 and C-21 are assumed to lie in a plane parallel to and above the skeleton; monovalent groups attached to C-20 may then be either above this plane (β) or below it (α).

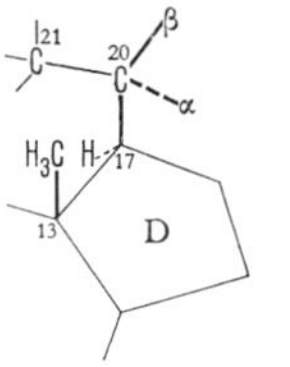

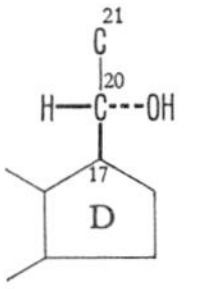

20α-Hydroxy-

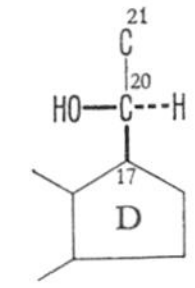

20β-Hydroxy-

Classification

Steroids are classified both by the total number of carbon atoms in the molecule and according to their function (see opposite).

C_{17}-Steroids – parent compound *gonane*; no groups at C-10, C-13 or C-17.

C_{18}-Steroids – parent compound *oestrane*; methyl group at C-13 and no side chain at C-17; include the naturally occurring oestrogens.

C_{19}-Steroids – parent compound *androstane*; methyl groups at C-10 and C-13 but no side chain at C-17; include the naturally occurring androgens.

C_{21}-Steroids — parent compound *pregnane*; methyl groups at C-10 and C-13 and a 2-carbon side chain at C-17; include the naturally occurring corticosteroids.

C_{24}-Steroids — parent compound *cholane*; methyl groups at C-10 and C-13 and a branched 5-carbon side chain at C-17; include many naturally occurring bile acids.

C_{27}-Steroids — parent compound *cholestane*; methyl groups at C-10 and C-13 and a branched 8-carbon side chain at C-17, e.g., cholesterol.

Names of parent compounds of other naturally occurring steroids are *ergostane* (24-methyl-5α-cholestane), *stigmastane* (24-ethyl-5α-cholestane), *lanostane* (4,4,14α-trimethyl-5α-cholestane).

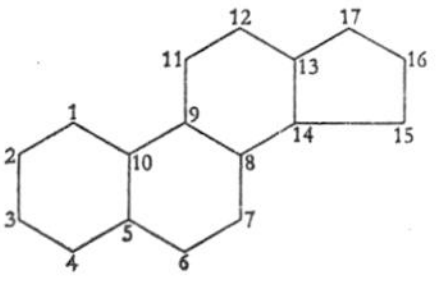

Gonane

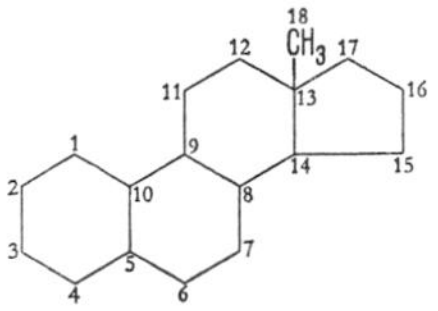

Oestrane

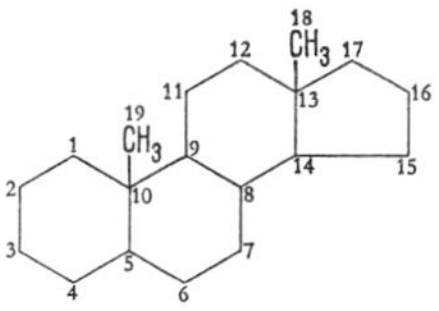

Androstane

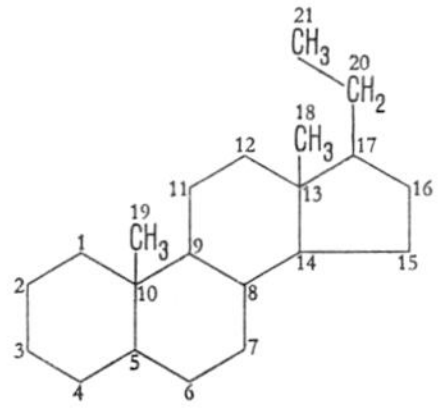

Pregnane

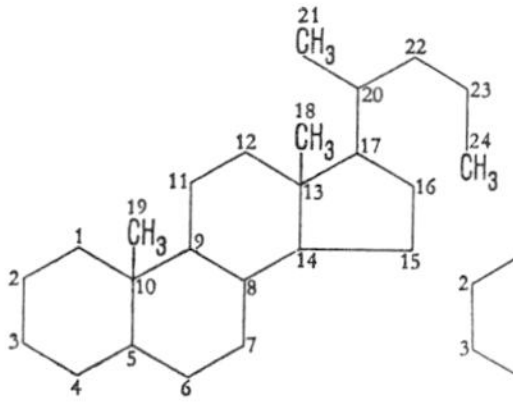

Cholane

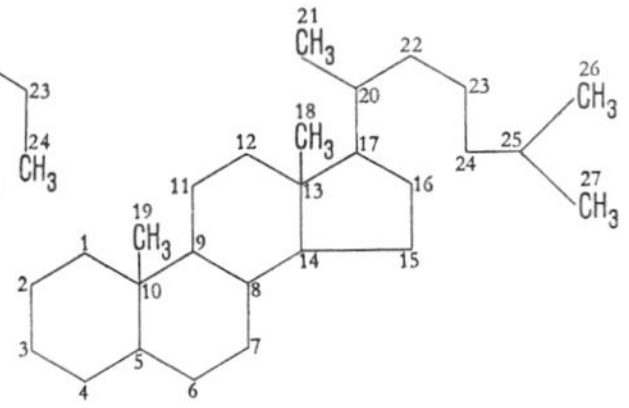

Cholestane

Table 21 Prefixes and suffixes in steroid nomenclature

Chemical group	Prefix	Suffix
double bond	Δ (in trivial names only)	changes -ane to *-ene*
triple bond	–	changes -ane to *-yne*
hydroxyl	hydroxy-	-ol
acetate ester	acetoxy-	-yl acetate
benzoate ester	benzoyloxy-	-yl benzoate
sulphate ester	–	-yl sulphate
glucuronoside (glucuronide)	–	-glucuronide
carbonyl	oxo- (formerly keto-)	-one
aldehyde	–	-al
carboxylic acid	carboxy-	-oic acid
amine	amino	-amine
halogen (e.g., chlorine)	halogeno- (e.g., chloro-)	halide (e.g., chloride, in trivial names only)
epoxide	epoxy-	–
ethyne (–C ≡ CH)	ethynyl-	–

Systematic nomenclature

Steroids are named systematically[2] by adding prefixes and suffixes to the names of the parent hydrocarbons. The Greek letter Δ was formerly used to denote an olefinic double bond and is still common in trivial usage; thus pregnenolone, formerly Δ^5-pregnen-3β-ol-20-one, is now pregn-5-en-3β-ol-20-one. For double bonds between atoms with successive numbers (e.g., 5 and 6) only the *lower* number is used (thus pregn-5-en-3β-ol-20-one or Δ^5-pregnenolone). When the carbon atoms have non-successive numbers (e.g., 5 and 10) the second (higher) number is added in brackets [thus cholest-5(10)-ene or $\Delta^{5(10)}$-cholestene]. Table 22 lists the trivial and systematic names of important steroids together with their hormonal activity.

Prefixes and suffixes used in steroid nomenclature are listed in Table 21.

Other *prefixes* in trivial or systematic use are

allo- (in trivial names): formerly used to denote the 5α-series of saturated steroids

anhydro- (in trivial names): loss of H and OH from adjacent carbon atoms with formation of a double bond

dehydro- (in trivial names): loss of 2H from adjacent carbon atoms with formation of a double bond

deoxy- or *desoxy-* (in trivial names): replacement of OH by H

de-: removal of a whole ring, e.g., de-D

dihydro- (in trivial names): addition of 2H to a double bond

epi- (in trivial names): inversion of a substituent from α to β or from β to α

homo-: ring enlargement, e.g., D-homo- means a six membered D ring

nor- (preceded by carbon number or ring letter): removal of one carbon atom

seco-: ring fission with addition of one H to each of the two terminal groups (preceded by the numbers of the atoms forming the bond cleaved)

Steroid hormones

Steroid hormones are found in all classes of vertebrates[3] and in insects[4]. In vertebrates the hormone-producing organs are the adrenal cortex, the ovaries, the testes and the placenta. Each gland produces a large number of steroids (over 40 have been isolated from the adrenal cortex), but not all of them are hormonally active. Since the steps in the metabolic pathway leading to the various classes of hormones are qualitatively the same in each organ, it is not surprising to find differing amounts of the same metabolites in different organs. Each organ has characteristic steroid hormones but also produces others that may or may not be physiologically significant. Thus cortisol and aldosterone are the characteristic hormones of the adrenal cortex, but this organ also produces dehydroepiandrosterone sulphate, an androgen. 17β-Oestradiol is the characteristic oestrogen of the ovaries, which also produce physiologically significant amounts of progesterone. Progesterone is the characteristic hormone of the placenta, which also produces oestrogens. The characteristic hormone of the testes is testosterone.

The steroid hormones are also classified according to function into *oestrogens* (female sex hormones; C_{18}-steroids with an aromatic A ring), *androgens* (male sex hormones; C_{19}-steroids) and *corticosteroids* (hormones of the adrenal cortex; C_{21}-steroids). Among the last-named a distinction is often made between *mineralocorticoids* (e.g., aldosterone) and *glucocorticoids* (e.g., cortisol), the basis for which is that physiological doses of these steroids in man have essentially one effect. However, the effects of the various hormones overlap considerably and differ from species to species; they differ also from individual to individual depending on the previous dietary and hormonal history.

References

[1] For reviews see Fieser and Fieser, *Steroids*, Reinhold, New York, 1959; Klyne, W., *The Chemistry of the Steroids*, Methuen, London, 1957 and 1965.

[2] International Union of Pure and Applied Chemistry, *Definitive Rules for Nomenclature of Steroids*, Butterworth, London, 1958, page 71; International Union of Pure and Applied Chemistry, Nomenclature of Organic Chemistry, *J. Amer. chem. Soc.*, **82**, 5575 (1960).

[3] Dorfman and Ungar, *Metabolism of Steroid Hormones*, Academic Press, New York, 1965.

[4] Karlson and Sekeris, *Recent Progr. Hormone Res.*, **22**, 473 (1966).

Table 22 Names, formulae and hormonal activity of important steroids

Trivial name	Systematic name	Formula (mol.wt.)	Hormonal activity*
Adrenosterone	Androst-4-ene-3,11,17-trione	$C_{19}H_{24}O_3$ (300.40)	♂
Aetianedione (aetiocholanedione)	5β-Androstane-3,17-dione	$C_{19}H_{28}O_2$ (288.43)	–
Aetiocholanolone	3α-Hydroxy-5β-androstan-17-one	$C_{19}H_{30}O_2$ (290.45)	–
3β-Aetiocholanolone	3β-Hydroxy-5β-androstan-17-one	$C_{19}H_{30}O_2$ (290.45)	–
Aldosterone	11β,21-Dihydroxypregn-4-en-18-al-3,20-dione	$C_{21}H_{28}O_5$ (360.45)	*G, M*
Allocortol	5α-Pregnane-3α,11β,17α,20α,21-pentol	$C_{21}H_{36}O_5$ (368.52)	–
β-Allocortol	5α-Pregnane-3α,11β,17α,20β,21-pentol	$C_{21}H_{36}O_5$ (368.52)	–
Allocortolone	3α,17α,20α,21-Tetrahydroxy-5α-pregnan-11-one	$C_{21}H_{34}O_5$ (366.50)	–
β-Allocortolone	3α,17α,20β,21-Tetrahydroxy-5α-pregnan-11-one	$C_{21}H_{34}O_5$ (366.50)	–
α-Allopregnanediol	3α,20α-Dihydroxy-5α-pregnane	$C_{21}H_{36}O_2$ (320.52)	–
β-Allopregnanediol	3β,20α-Dihydroxy-5α-pregnane	$C_{21}H_{36}O_2$ (320.52)	–
α-Allopregnanolone	3α-Hydroxy-5α-pregnan-20-one	$C_{21}H_{34}O_2$ (318.50)	–
Allotetrahydrocortisol	3α,11β,17α,21-Tetrahydroxy-5α-pregnan-20-one	$C_{21}H_{34}O_5$ (366.50)	–
Androstanedione	5α-Androstane-3,17-dione	$C_{19}H_{28}O_2$ (288.43)	♂
Androstenedione	Androst-4-ene-3,17-dione	$C_{19}H_{26}O_2$ (286.42)	♂
Androsterone	3α-Hydroxy-5α-androstan-17-one	$C_{19}H_{30}O_2$ (290.45)	♂
*Betamethasone***	9α-Fluoro-11β,17,21-trihydroxy-16β-methylpregna-1,4-diene-3,20-dione	–	*G, A*
Cholecalciferol	See Vitamin D_3		
Cholesterol	Cholest-5-en-3β-ol	$C_{27}H_{46}O$ (386.67)	–
Cortexolone	See 11-Deoxycortisol		
Cortexone	See Deoxycorticosterone		
Corticosterone (compound B)	11β,21-Dihydroxypregn-4-ene-3,20-dione	$C_{21}H_{30}O_4$ (346.47)	*G, M*
Cortisol (hydrocortisone, 17α-hydroxy-corticosterone, compound F)	11β,17α,21-Trihydroxypregn-4-ene-3,20-dione	$C_{21}H_{30}O_5$ (362.47)	*G, A, M*
Cortisone (compound E)	17α,21-Dihydroxypregn-4-ene-13,11,20-trione	$C_{21}H_{28}O_5$ (360.45)	*G, A, M*
α-Cortol	5β-Pregnane-3α,11β,17α,20α,21-pentol	$C_{21}H_{36}O_5$ (368.52)	–
β-Cortol	5β-Pregnane-3α,11β,17α,20β,21-pentol	$C_{21}H_{36}O_5$ (368.52)	–
α-Cortolone	3α,17α,20α,21-Tetrahydroxy-5β-pregnan-11-one	$C_{21}H_{34}O_5$ (366.50)	–
β-Cortolone	3α,17α,20β,21-Tetrahydroxy-5β-pregnan-11-one	$C_{21}H_{34}O_5$ (366.50)	–
11-Dehydrocorticosterone (compound A)	21-Hydroxypregn-4-ene-3,11,20-trione	$C_{21}H_{28}O_4$ (344.45)	*G*
Dehydroepiandrosterone (dehydro*iso*androsterone, androstenolone)	3β-Hydroxyandrost-5-en-17-one	$C_{19}H_{29}O_2$ (289.44)	♂
Deoxycorticosterone (11-deoxycorticosterone, DOC, cortexone, 21-hydroxypregnen-olone)	21-Hydroxypregn-4-ene-3,20-dione	$C_{21}H_{30}O_3$ (330.47)	*G*
11-Deoxycortisol (cortexolone, substance S)	17α,21-Dihydroxypregn-4-ene-3,20-dione	$C_{21}H_{30}O_4$ (346.47)	*G*
21-Deoxycortisol	11β,17α-Dihydroxypregn-4-ene-3,20-dione	$C_{21}H_{30}O_4$ (346.47)	–
*Dexamethasone***	9α-Fluoro-16α-methyl-11β,17α,21-trihydroxypregna-1,4-diene-3,20-dione	$C_{22}H_{29}FO_5$ (392.47)	*A, G*
Epiandrosterone (*iso*androsterone)	3β-Hydroxy-5α-androstan-17-one	$C_{19}H_{30}O_2$ (290.45)	♂

* *A* Anti-inflammatory activity; *G* Glucocorticoid activity; *M* Mineralocorticoid activity; *P* Progestational activity; ♂ Androgenic activity; ♀ Oestrogenic activity

** Synthetic steroid; no known natural occurrence.

Table 22 Names, formulae and hormonal activity of important steroids

Trivial name	Systematic name	Formula (mol.wt.)	Hormonal activity*
Epioestradiol (17-epioestradiol, oestradiol-17α)	Oestra-1,3,5(10)-triene-3,17α-diol	$C_{18}H_{24}O_2$ (272.39)	♀
Epitestosterone	17α-Hydroxyandrost-4-en-3-one	$C_{19}H_{28}O_2$ (288.43)	–
Equilenin	3-Hydroxyoestra-1,3,5(10),6,8-penten-17-one	$C_{18}H_{18}O_2$ (266.34)	♀
Equilin	3-Hydroxyoestra-1,3,5(10),7-tetraen-17-one	$C_{18}H_{20}O_2$ (268.36)	♀
Ergocalciferol	See Vitamin D_2		
Ergosterol	24-Methylcholesta-5,7,22-trien-3β-ol	$C_{28}H_{44}O$ (396.66)	–
*Ethynyloestradiol***	17α-Ethynyloestra-1,3,5(10)-triene-3,17β-diol	–	♀
*Fluorocortisol*** (9α-fluorocortisol, 9α-fluoro-hydrocortisone)	9α-Fluoro-11β,17α,21-trihydroxypregn-4-ene-3,20-dione	–	*A*, *M*
*Fluorometholone*** (oxylone)	9α-Fluoro-6α-methyl-11β,17α-dihydroxypregna-1,4-diene-3,20-dione	–	*A*
*Fluoxymestrone***	9α-Fluoro-11β,17β-dihydroxy-17α-methylandrost-4-en-3-one	–	♂
17-α-Hydroxyprogesterone	17α-Hydroxypregn-4-ene-3,20-dione	$C_{21}H_{30}O_3$ (330.47)	♂, *P*
20α-Hydroxyprogesterone	20α-Hydroxypregn-4-en-3-one	$C_{21}H_{32}O_2$ (316.49)	*P*
20β-Hydroxyprogesterone	20β-Hydroxypregn-4-en-3-one	$C_{21}H_{32}O_2$ (316.49)	*P*
Lanosterol	4,4,14α-Trimethylcholesta-8,24-dien-3β-ol	$C_{30}H_{50}O$ (426.73)	–
*Methylprednisolone***	6α-Methyl-11β,17α,21-trihydroxypregna-1,4-diene-3,20-dione	$C_{22}H_{30}O_5$ (374.48)	*A*, *M*
*Norethandrolone***	17α-Ethyl-17β-hydroxy-19-norandrost-4-en-3-one	–	♂***
*Norethindrone*** (norethisterone)	17α-Ethynyl-17β-hydroxy-19-norandrost-4-en-3-one	–	*P*
*Norethynodrel***	17α-Ethynyl-17β-hydroxyoestr-5(10)-en-3-one	–	*P*
Oestradiol (oestradiol-17β)	Oestra-1,3,5(10)-triene-3,17β-diol	$C_{18}H_{24}O_2$ (272.39)	♀
Oestriol	Oestra-1,3,5(10)-triene-3,16α,17β-triol	$C_{18}H_{24}O_3$ (288.39)	♀
Oestrone	3-Hydroxyoestra-1,3,5(10)-trien-17-one	$C_{18}H_{22}O_2$ (270.37)	♀
*Prednisolone***	11β,17α,21-Trihydroxypregna-14-diene-3,20-dione	$C_{21}H_{28}O_5$ (360.45)	*A*, *M*
*Prednisone***	17α,21-Dihydroxypregna-1,4-diene-3,11,20-trione	$C_{21}H_{26}O_5$ (358.44)	*A*, *M*
Pregnanediol	5β-Pregnanc-3α,20α-diol	$C_{21}H_{36}O_2$ (320.52)	–
Pregnanetriol	5β-Pregnane-3α,17α,20α-triol	$C_{21}H_{36}O_3$ (336.52)	–
Pregnanolone	3α-Hydroxy-5β-pregnan-20-one	$C_{21}H_{34}O_2$ (318.50)	–
Pregnenolone (Δ⁵-pregnenolone)	3β-Hydroxypregn-5-en-20-one	$C_{21}H_{32}O_2$ (316.49)	–
Progesterone	Pregn-4-ene-3,20-dione	$C_{21}H_{30}O_2$ (314.47)	*P*
Testosterone	17β-Hydroxyandrost-4-en-3-one	$C_{19}H_{28}O_2$ (288.43)	♂
Tetrahydro-A	3α,21-Dihydroxy-5β-pregnane-11,20-dione	$C_{21}H_{32}O_4$ (348.49)	–
Tetrahydro-B	3α,11β,21-Trihydroxy-5β-pregnan-20-one	$C_{21}H_{34}O_4$ (350.50)	–
Tetrahydro-E	See Urocortisone		
Tetrahydro-F	See Urocortisol		
Tetrahydro-S	3α,17α,21-Trihydroxy-5β-pregnan-20-one	$C_{21}H_{34}O_4$ (350.50)	–
*Triamcinolone***	9α-Fluoro-11β,16α,17α,21-tetrahydroxypregna-1,4-diene-3,20-dione	$C_{21}H_{27}FO_6$ (394.44)	*A*
Uroaldosterone	3α,11β,21-Trihydroxy-20-oxo-5β-pregnan-18-al	$C_{21}H_{32}O_5$ (364.49)	–
Urocortisol (tetrahydro-F)	3α,11β,17α,21-Tetrahydroxy-5β-pregnan-20-onc	$C_{21}H_{34}O_5$ (366.50)	–
Urocortisone (tetrahydro-E)	3α,17α,21-Trihydroxy-5β-pregnane-11,20-dione	$C_{21}H_{32}O_5$ (364.49)	–
Vitamin D_2 (ergocalciferol)	24-Methyl-9,10-secocholesta-5,7,10(19),22-tetraen-3β-ol	$C_{28}H_{44}O$ (396.66)	–
Vitamin D_3 (cholecalciferol)	9,10-Secocholesta-5,7,10(19)-trien-3β-ol	$C_{27}H_{44}O$ (384.65)	–

* *A* Anti-inflammatory activity; *G* Glucocorticoid activity; *M* Mineralocorticoid activity; *P* Progestational activity; ♂ Androgenic activity; ♀ Oestrogenic activity

** Synthetic steroid; no known natural occurrence.

*** High anabolic activity, low androgenic activity.

(For references see page 385)

Enzymes

Enzymes are protein catalysts ranging in molecular weight from about 13 000 (ribonuclease) up to as much as one million (pyruvate decarboxylase). They are purified and isolated by the use of techniques for fractionating proteins[1]. Their general properties will be described in the section which follows*.

Nomenclature of enzymes

Enzymes are usually given names indicating both the principal substrate and the reaction catalysed (e.g., malate dehydrogenase). Many enzymes have, however, been given trivial names and these are often a cause of confusion. With the aim of eliminating the existing ambiguity, the Commission on Enzymes of the International Union of Biochemistry has worked out a systematic nomenclature[2] based on the reaction catalysed (see Table 24, page 385) and has given each enzyme a characteristic number indicating the nature of this reaction together with a recommended trivial name (these names have been used in the chapter on 'Metabolism' on pages 387–445).

The word 'enzyme' usually denotes a catalytic protein plus any component that cannot be readily removed from the protein without denaturing it. The usage is not very rigid, however, for in some contexts 'enzyme' is intended to include dissociable cofactors and in others to indicate the catalytic protein *per se*. If there is danger of ambiguity, the catalytic protein is denoted by the term '*apo-enzyme*' and the protein plus cofactors by '*holo-enzyme*'.

Coenzymes or *prosthetic groups* are nonprotein organic compounds which, in combination with the apo-enzyme, play an intimate part in the catalysis by the enzyme. There is no generally accepted distinction between coenzymes and prosthetic groups, but the latter name is usually reserved for groups that are bound relatively firmly by the protein. '*Activators*' are usually distinguished from coenzymes in being small ions that are required by some enzymes for full catalytic activity. Some enzymes do not appear to possess a prosthetic group or coenzyme nor do they require an activator.

Specificity of enzymes[3]

Although nearly all the individual reactions of intermediary metabolism are catalysed by separate enzymes (see pages 405–419), few of these enzymes are absolutely specific to the structure of their substrates. Most enzymes can act on close structural analogues of their physiological substrates, although usually at much reduced rates, whilst a few enzymes can act on a relatively wide group of substrates. Like any other catalyst, an enzyme catalyses both the forward and reverse reactions, but does not affect the final position of the equilibrium.

There are no completely general rules of enzyme specificity, for in different enzyme systems different parts of the substrate molecule appear to be important. Thus, the lipases require an ester bond in their substrates but there can be very considerable variation in the structures of the groups adjoining this susceptible bond. On the other hand, chymotrypsin and trypsin require certain configurations in the neighbourhood of the susceptible bond, but the nature of the bond itself can vary. For example, these enzymes will hydrolyse peptide bonds in protein substrates but in certain artificial substrates (e.g., methyl cinnamate) ester bonds can be hydrolysed.

An added complication is that those hydrolytic enzymes which can act on several substrates are usually capable of catalysing a transferring reaction in which an alcohol or an amine replaces the water. Many of these transfer reactions are unlikely to be of physiological significance because of the prevalence of water molecules under physiological conditions.

Many enzymes show stereochemical specificity in being unable to attack geometrical or optical isomers of their substrates. Less specific enzymes such as the esterases can, however, attack stereochemical isomers although usually at reduced rates.

Structure of enzymes and mechanism of enzyme action

In 1963 the complete sequence of the 124 amino-acid residues, together with the position of the sulphur bridges in the chain, was established for bovine ribonuclease[4]. Since that time the amino-acid sequence of many other enzymes has been elucidated[22]. The three-dimensional structure (conformation) of a few enzymes (e.g., lysozymes, ribonuclease, α-chymotrypsin) in the crystalline state has been determined by X-ray diffraction[23]. In 1969 the first total synthesis of an enzyme, that of ribonuclease, was accomplished[24].

It is now clear that the full catalytic activity of an enzyme depends on the integrity of the three-dimensional structure of the folded polypeptide chain. Denaturation of the enzyme, with concomitant destruction of the organization in the chain will usually result in loss of enzyme activity. The surface formed by the folding of the chain in the native structure thus enables the substrate molecule to combine with the enzyme at three or more points. Those amino-acid residues which contribute towards the formation of the enzyme–substrate complex and which take part in the catalytic process together constitute the 'active site' of the enzyme[5]. The folding of the peptide chain thus brings amino-acid residues which are remote from each other in sequence into close juxtaposition at the active site. Although the complete structures are unknown, the amino-acid sequences near the active sites of many enzymes have been determined (e.g., cytochrome c, trypsin, pancreatopeptidase E, phosphoglucomutase). Studies of this type reveal variations in the amino-acid sequences in the same enzyme from different species (e.g., ribonuclease)[6]. Some enzymes, for example those involved in biosynthetic pathways, appear to have two distinct active sites, one for combining with substrate and another for combining with an inhibitor[7] which may regulate the biological action of the enzyme. It is suggested that the formation of a complex between the inhibitor and the enzyme induces a conformational change in the enzyme structure that modifies the catalytic activity of the other active site, rendering the enzyme inactive. This class of proteins have been called 'allosteric'[8].

Although there is no instance in which the mechanism of action of an enzyme is fully understood, a large number of mechanisms have been proposed[9]. The most attractive ideas involve the formation of a covalently-bound enzyme–substrate compound in which nucleophilic or electrophilic attack on the substrate moiety is facilitated by the enzyme.

Enzyme kinetics[10]

When an enzyme is added to a suitable reaction mixture there is first a very short lag before a steady rate of reaction is attained[11]. This lag is so short that it is not detectable when the rate is obtained from measurements made at intervals of one minute or longer. Once established, the rate remains constant for a period which may sometimes be as long as several hours, although in other cases it may be only a few minutes. The rate of reaction begins to fall after this period because of reduced substrate concentration and/or the accumulation of products. This decrease in reaction rate is not easily analysed mathematically, and it is therefore usual to study only the constant reaction rate. The following discussion is confined to this constant reaction rate.

If the enzyme is susceptible to inhibition by excess substrate (see below) the rate may at first increase as the inhibition is relieved by removal of the substrate.

Enzyme concentration. The reaction rate is usually proportional to the concentration of enzyme. Strict linearity may not always be achieved experimentally, for instance because the enzyme preparation may contain a dissociable activator or inhibitor or the enzyme may be unstable at low concentrations. Alternatively, the reaction may have proceeded so far that the rate has already commenced to fall off at the highest enzyme concentrations.

Hydrogen-ion concentration. Most enzymes possess well-defined pH optima with appreciable activity over a range of only 2–3 pH units. Some enzymes are inhibited by one or other of the buffers in common use. It is therefore often worthwhile to compare the results in one buffer with those obtained in another type of buffer solution of the same pH range.

The study of kinetic data obtained at different pH values with different substrates and different concentrations of a single substrate is of use in investigating the details of enzyme mechanisms[12]. For other purposes, the variations in the pH curve with different substrates and substrate concentrations are not usually important.

Temperature. The rate of an enzyme-catalysed reaction increases by a factor which is usually 1.5–3 for every rise of 10°C. There is, however, an optimum temperature above which further increase reduces the amount of substrate reacting because the enzyme becomes inactivated. The optimum temperature for short-term experiments (e.g., of one hour's duration) is often about 50°C. Most

* The enzymes occurring in blood and various body tissues are described on pages 584–600, those responsible for digestion on pages 405–419. On enzyme units see page 584.

Fig. 7 Inhibition data plotted according to Table 23

Each line represents data for a series of substrate concentrations. One line of each graph is without inhibition and the other two are for two different concentrations of inhibitor.

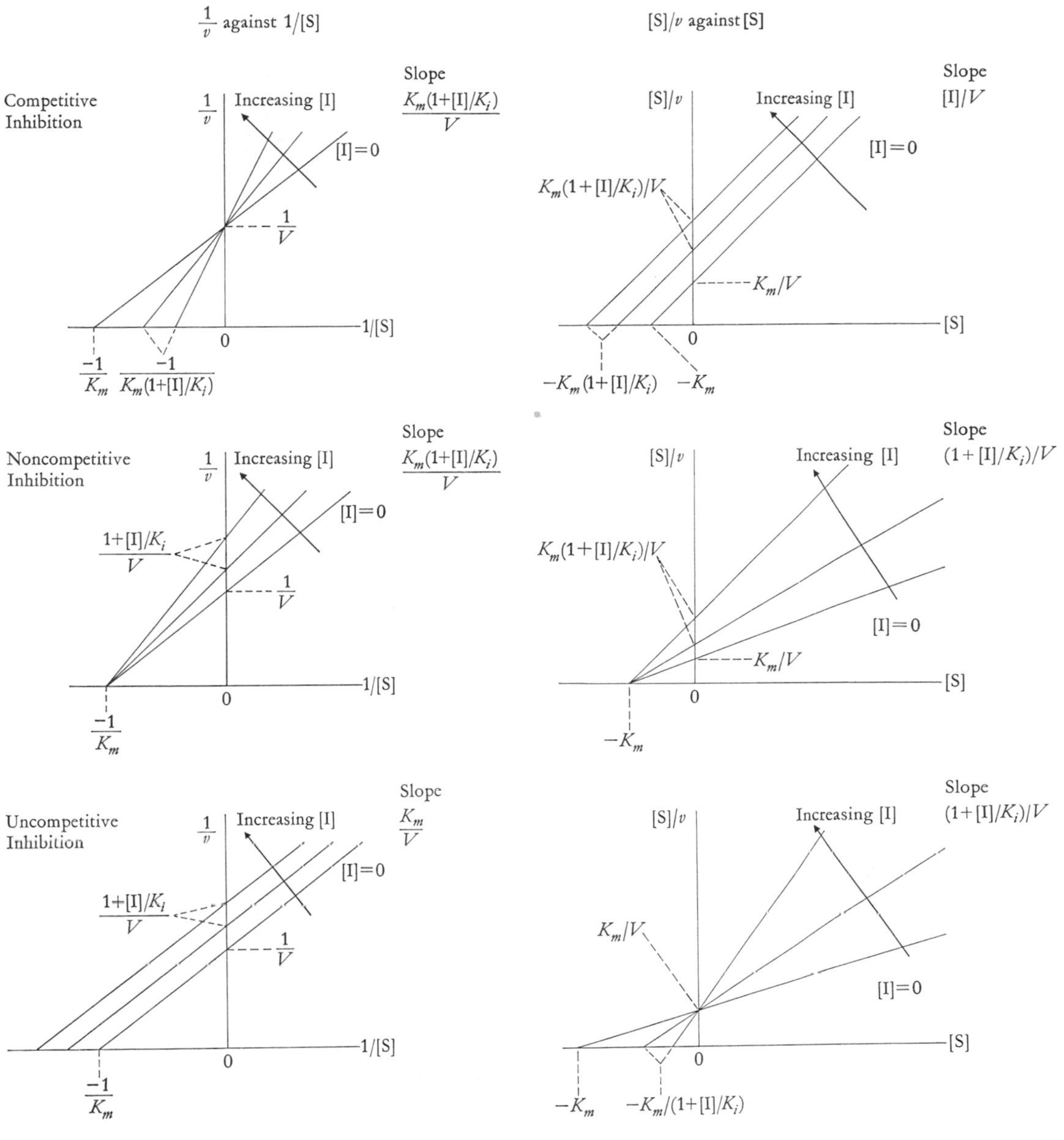

mammalian enzymes show little inactivation in the presence of their cofactors and substrates at 37 °C, so that this is usually a suitable temperature to study the reaction. It is not desirable to increase the temperature to the optimum because the rate of enzyme inactivation, and therefore the optimum temperature, is often greatly influenced by slight changes in the experimental conditions.

Substrate concentration. As the initial substrate concentration is increased, the rate of reaction is at first proportional to this concentration, but at higher values it usually becomes virtually independent of it. This relation can be justified theoretically by considering a mechanism such as

$$E + S \underset{k_{-1}}{\overset{k_1}{\rightleftharpoons}} ES \overset{k_2}{\rightarrow} E + P \qquad (1)$$

where E is the enzyme, S the substrate, ES the enzyme–substrate compound, P the products, and k_1, k_{-1} and k_2 the rate constants of the three reactions. The constant steady-state velocity v is given by

$$v = \frac{V[S]}{K_m + [S]} \qquad (2)$$

where V is the maximum velocity obtained at high substrate concentrations, [S] the concentration of substrate, and K_m a quantity termed the 'MICHAELIS constant' and equivalent to the substrate concentration at which the velocity is half the maximum velocity. [S] is strictly the concentration of substrate not combined with the enzyme, but the amount of enzyme is usually so low that there is virtually no difference between the concentrations of free and total substrate. Mathematically, V is given by k_2e where e is the total concentration of enzyme present. K_m is given by $(k_{-1} + k_2)/k_1$ and has the dimensions of concentration. Although K_m is independent of both [S] and e, it usually changes with pH, temperature, different substrates and the cofactor concentration. K_m may sometimes change with ionic strength or with different buffers and, like other characteristics of enzymes, it may differ for similar enzymes from different sources.

Equation (**2**) was first obtained theoretically by MICHAELIS and MENTEN[13], who assumed that the second reaction of mechanism (**1**) was the rate-limiting step. Under these conditions k_{-1} is much greater than k_2, and K_m becomes k_{-1}/k_1, which is the dissociation constant of the enzyme–substrate compound. This assumption is known to be valid for some enzymes but not for others[14].

Evaluation of Michaelis constant K_m and maximum velocity V. K_m may be evaluated by plotting the curve of v against [S]. The experimental data can, however, be used more efficiently by plotting certain functions of v and [S] as shown in Table 23[3,15]. These plots give straight lines if equation (**2**) is obeyed. The plot of $1/v$ against $1/[S]$ has the advantage that the variables are separate and the calculations for plotting are thus quicker. Unfortunately the points are not evenly spread and the errors at low values of v are accentuated. This method gives accurate values for V but less accurate estimates for K_m. A statistical evaluation[16] of the various graphical methods for determining K_m and V shows that the third method (Table 23) is the most satisfactory and gives the most accurate values of these quantities over the usual range of concentration and velocity available for experimentation.

Table 23 Linear plots for evaluating MICHAELIS constant K_m and maximum velocity V

Plot		Slope	Intercept	
Ordinate	Abscissa		Ordinate	Abscissa
$1/v$	$1/[S]$	K_m/V	$1/V$	$-1/K_m$
v	$v/[S]$	$-K_m$	V	V/K_m
$[S]/v$	$[S]$	$1/V$	K_m/V	$-K_m$

It is sometimes convenient, such as when comparing different substrates, to plot v against log [S]. This plot gives an S-shaped curve instead of a straight line; the inflection of this curve occurs at a value of log [S] equal to log K_m.

Inhibition by excess substrate. This phenomenon occurs with some enzymes and is usually explained by postulating that the enzyme–substrate compound (ES) combines with a second molecule of S to form an inactive complex which, unless it reverts to the original ES form, can yield products only slowly or not at all. When v is plotted against log [S], this mechanism predicts a symmetrical bell-shaped curve[17] if the rate can be reduced to zero by high substrate concentrations. This prediction agrees with experimental findings[18].

Another mechanism of substrate inhibition may occur if there is a dissociable cofactor such as Mg^{++} which can combine with the substrate. Increased substrate concentration may inhibit by removing the cofactor.

Inhibitors[15]. Two types of inhibition are commonly encountered, competitive and noncompetitive. In the competitive type, the inhibition is reduced by increasing the concentration of substrate. Many competitive inhibitors are structural analogues of the substrate, suggesting that the inhibitor and the substrate combine with the same site of the enzyme. Assuming that the inhibitor can react reversibly with the enzyme so as to prevent it combining with its substrate, it can be derived that on the basis of mechanism (**1**):

$$v = \frac{V[S]}{K_m(1 + [I]/K_i) + [S]} \qquad (3)$$

where [I] is the concentration of inhibitor and K_i is the dissociation constant of the enzyme–inhibitor compound. V and K_m are the values obtained in the absence of the inhibitor.

In a case of noncompetitive inhibition, the amount of inhibition is independent of the concentration of substrate and depends only on the concentration of inhibitor. An equation to fit this can be derived by assuming that the inhibitor combines reversibly and equally readily with both the enzyme and the enzyme–substrate compound:

$$v = \frac{V[S]}{(K_m + [S])\,(1 + [I]/K_i)} \qquad (4)$$

This mechanism suggests that a noncompetitive inhibitor does not combine with the active centre of the enzyme responsible for combination with the substrate.

It should be noted that, in competitive inhibition, the inhibitor increases the apparent MICHAELIS constant without affecting the maximum velocity, whereas in noncompetitive inhibition the inhibitor decreases the maximum velocity without changing the MICHAELIS constant.

A third and less common type of inhibition is that in which both the maximum velocity and the MICHAELIS constant are reduced to a similar extent, so that there is no change in the ratio K_m/V as evaluated from the plots of Table 23. This type of inhibition has been termed 'uncompetitive' and is illustrated by the action of azide on the oxidized form of cytochrome oxidase[19]. The appropriate equation is based on the assumption that the inhibitor combines only with the enzyme–substrate compound:

$$v = \frac{V[S]}{K_m + [S]\,(1 + [I]/K_i)} \qquad (5)$$

Plotting inhibition data. The different types of inhibition can be clearly differentiated by using any of the substrate plots of Table 23 and thus determining the effect of the inhibitor on the apparent K_m or V. Examples are shown in Figure 7 (page 383). K_i can be evaluated from the quantitative nature of this effect. To show that

Fig. 8 Inhibition data: plots of $1/v$ against [I][3,15]

Each line represents data for a series of inhibitor concentrations [I] but at different substrate concentrations [S].

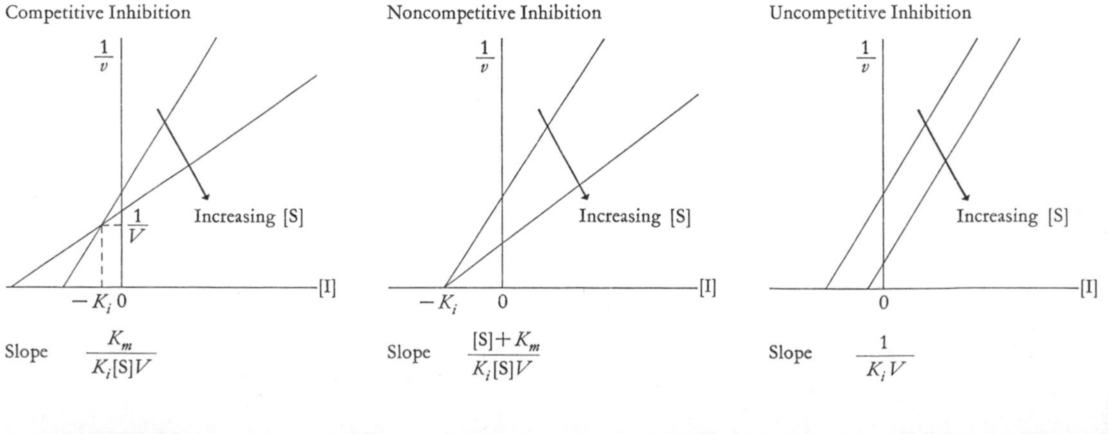

the appropriate equations are satisfactorily obeyed it is necessary either to obtain the same value of K_i for more than one concentration of inhibitor or to plot data for a series of inhibitor concentrations according to the plot shown in Figure 8 above. If a straight line is obtained and the value of K_i agrees with that expected from the Figure 7 plot, it is valid to conclude that the appropriate equation is satisfactorily obeyed. In cases of competitive inhibition it is desirable to check that, when the line is produced backwards, $[I] = -K_i$ at the point where $1/v = 1/V$.

The intersections between lines for different values of [S] can be used to evaluate K_i. If this method is used it is also necessary to check that equation (**2**) is obeyed by plotting according to one of the methods of Table 23. This need only be done with the data in the absence of inhibitor or at one inhibitor concentration.

Intermediate types of inhibition are to be expected theoretically and have, in fact, been described in careful work. These result from the inhibitor combining with both the free enzyme and the enzyme–substrate compound. Unlike strictly noncompetitive inhibition, the inhibitor has different affinities for the two forms of the enzyme. The two dissociation constants for the inhibitor (K_i from the EI compound, K_i' from the EIS compound) may be obtained from plots of $1/v$ against [I]. The straight lines obtained at different values of [S] intersect at the points $[I] = -K_i$ and $1/v = 1/V(1-K_i/K_i')$ when they are produced backwards. The inhibition tends to be competitive if, at the intersection, $1/v > 0$, or uncompetitive if $1/v < 0$. Converse relations are obtained from plots of $[S]/v$ against [I]; these intersect at the points $[I] = -K_i'$ and $[S]/v = K_m/V(1-K_i'/K_i)$.

Activators and coenzymes. When the concentration of a dissociable cofactor is varied the reaction rate usually changes according to equation (**2**), where [S] is then the concentration of the cofactor and not of the substrate. If, however, the cofactor is somewhat firmly bound to the enzyme, the activity–concentration relation may approach two straight lines[20]. Several instances have been reported of coenzyme analogues inhibiting by competing with the coenzyme[21].

When di- or trivalent metal ions are required as activators it is usually found that one or more of the substrates or cofactors spontaneously combine with the activator. This can introduce serious complications into the kinetic relations.

References

1 Colowick and Kaplan (Eds.), *Methods in Enzymology*, 7 vols., Academic Press, New York, 1955–1964.
2 International Union of Biochemistry, *Report of the Commission on Enzymes*, Pergamon Press, Oxford, 1961; International Union of Biochemistry, *Enzyme Nomenclature*, Recommendations 1964, Elsevier, Amsterdam, 1965.
3 Dixon and Webb, *Enzymes*, 2nd ed., Longmans, Green, London, 1964.
4 Smyth et al., *J. biol. Chem.*, **238**, 227 (1963).
5 Koshland, D.E., *Advanc. Enzymol.*, **22**, 45 (1960).
6 Anfinsen, C.B., *The Molecular Basis of Evolution*, Wiley, New York, 1959.
7 Changeux, J.-P., *Cold Spr. Harb. Symp. quant. Biol.*, **26**, 313 (1961).
8 Monod et al., *J. molec. Biol.*, **6**, 306 (1963).
9 Waley, S.G., *Mechanisms of Organic and Enzymic Reactions*, Oxford University Press, Oxford, 1961; Boyer et al. (Eds.), *The Enzymes*, 8 vols., 2nd ed., Academic Press, New York, 1959–1963; Massey and Veeger, *Ann. Rev. Biochem.*, **32**, 579 (1963); Jencks, W.P., *Ann. Rev. Biochem.*, **32**, 639 (1963); Rose, I.A., *Ann. Rev. Biochem.*, **35**, 23 (1966); Koshland and Neet, *Ann. Rev. Biochem.*, **37**, 359 (1968).
10 For more extensive treatments see Webb, J.L., *Enzyme and Metabolic Inhibitors*, vol. 1, Academic Press, New York, 1963; Dixon and Webb, *Enzymes*, 2nd ed., Longmans, London, 1964; Alberty, R.A., *Advanc. Enzymol.*, **17**, 1 (1956).
11 Gutfreund, H., *Disc. Faraday Soc.*, **20**, 167 (1955).
12 Laidler, K.J., *Trans. Faraday Soc.*, **51**, 528, 540, 550 (1955); Alberty, R.A., *Advanc. Enzymol.*, **17**, 1 (1956).
13 Michaelis and Menten, *Biochem. Z.*, **49**, 333 (1913).
14 Laidler, K.J., *Disc. Faraday Soc.*, **20**, 83 (1955).
15 For more extensive treatment see Webb, J.L., *Enzyme and Metabolic Inhibitors*, vol. 1, Academic Press, New York, 1963.
16 Wilkinson, G.N., *Biochem. J.*, **80**, 324 (1961).
17 Friedenwald and Maengwyn-Davies, in McElroy and Glass (Eds.), *The Mechanism of Enzyme Action*, Johns Hopkins, Baltimore, 1954, page 180.
18 For an example see Marcus and Talalay, *Proc. roy. Soc. B*, **144**, 116 (1955).
19 Winzler, R.J., *J. cell. comp. Physiol.*, **21**, 229 (1943).
20 Theorell, H., *Biochem. Z.*, **278**, 263 (1935).
21 For examples see Walaas and Walaas, *Acta chem. scand.*, **10**, 122 (1956).
22 Dayhoff and Eck, *Atlas of Protein Sequence and Structure, 1967–68*, National Biomedical Research Foundation, Silver Spring, Md., 1968.
23 Stryer, L., *Ann. Rev. Biochem.*, **37**, 25 (1968).
24 News and Views, *Nature*, **221**, 316 (1969).

Table 24 Classification and numbering of enzymes

The Enzyme Commission of the International Union of Biochemistry[1] has devised a system providing a classification of enzymes and at the same time a basis for numbering them. Each enzyme has been given a code number consisting of four figures separated by points. The first figure denotes the main enzyme division to which the enzyme belongs, the second the sub-class, the third the sub-sub-class, while the fourth figure is the serial number of the enzyme in its sub-sub-class.

1. Oxidoreductases

1.1 Acting on the HC–OH group of donors
- 1.1.1 With NAD or NADP as acceptor
- 1.1.2 With a cytochrome as an acceptor
- 1.1.3 With O_2 as acceptor
- 1.1.99 With other acceptors

1.2 Acting on the aldehyde or keto group of donors
- 1.2.1 With NAD or NADP as acceptor
- 1.2.2 With a cytochrome as an acceptor
- 1.2.3 With O_2 as acceptor
- 1.2.4 With lipoate as acceptor
- 1.2.99 With other acceptors

1.3 Acting on the HC–CH group of donors
- 1.3.1 With NAD or NADP as acceptor
- 1.3.2 With a cytochrome as an acceptor
- 1.3.3 With O_2 as acceptor
- 1.3.99 With other acceptors

1.4 Acting on the HC–NH_2 group of donors
- 1.4.1 With NAD or NADP as acceptor
- 1.4.3 With O_2 as acceptor

1.5 Acting on the C–NH group of donors
- 1.5.1 With NAD or NADP as acceptor
- 1.5.3 With O_2 as acceptor

1.6 Acting on reduced NAD or NADP as donor
- 1.6.1 With NAD or NADP as acceptor
- 1.6.2 With a cytochrome as an acceptor
- 1.6.4 With a disulphide compound as acceptor
- 1.6.5 With a quinone or related compound as acceptor
- 1.6.6 With a nitrogenous group as acceptor
- 1.6.99 With other acceptors

1.7 Acting on other nitrogenous compounds as donors
- 1.7.3 With O_2 as acceptor
- 1.7.99 With other acceptors

1.8 Acting on sulphur groups of donors
- 1.8.1 With NAD or NADP as acceptor
- 1.8.3 With O_2 as acceptor
- 1.8.4 With a disulphide compound as acceptor
- 1.8.5 With a quinone or related compound as acceptor
- 1.8.6 With a nitrogenous group as acceptor

1.9 Acting on haem groups of donors
- 1.9.3 With O_2 as acceptor
- 1.9.6 With a nitrogenous group as acceptor

1.10 Acting on diphenols and related substances as donors
- 1.10.3 With O_2 as acceptor

1.11 Acting on H_2O_2 as acceptor

1.12 Acting on hydrogen as donor

1.13 Acting on single donors with incorporation of oxygen (oxygenases)

1.14 Acting on paired donors with incorporation of oxygen into one donor (hydroxylases)
- 1.14.1 Using reduced NAD or NADP as one donor
- 1.14.2 Using ascorbate as one donor
- 1.14.3 Using reduced pteridine as one donor

2. Transferases

2.1 Transferring one-carbon groups
- 2.1.1 Methyltransferases
- 2.1.2 Hydroxymethyl-, formyl- and related transferases
- 2.1.3 Carboxyl- and carbamoyltransferases
- 2.1.4 Amidinotransferases

2.2 Transferring aldehydic or ketonic residues

2.3 Acyltransferases
- 2.3.1 Acyltransferases
- 2.3.2 Aminoacyltransferases

Table 24 (continued) Classification and numbering of enzymes

2. Transferases *(continued)*

2.4 Glycosyltransferases
- 2.4.1 Hexosyltransferases
- 2.4.2 Pentosyltransferases

2.5 Transferring alkyl or related groups

2.6 Transferring nitrogenous groups
- 2.6.1 Aminotransferases
- 2.6.3 Oximinotransferases

2.7 Transferring phosphorus-containing groups
- 2.7.1 Phosphotransferases with an alcohol group as acceptor
- 2.7.2 Phosphotransferases with a carboxyl group as acceptor
- 2.7.3 Phosphotransferases with a nitrogenous group as acceptor
- 2.7.4 Phosphotransferases with a phospho group as acceptor
- 2.7.5 Phosphotransferases, apparently intramolecular
- 2.7.6 Pyrophosphotransferases
- 2.7.7 Nucleotidyltransferases
- 2.7.8 Transferases for other substituted phospho groups

2.8 Transferring sulphur-containing groups
- 2.8.1 Sulphurtransferases
- 2.8.2 Sulphotransferases
- 2.8.3 CoA-transferases

3. Hydrolases

3.1 Acting on ester bonds
- 3.1.1 Carboxylic ester hydrolases
- 3.1.2 Thiolester hydrolases
- 3.1.3 Phosphoric monoester hydrolases
- 3.1.4 Phosphoric diester hydrolases
- 3.1.5 Triphosphoric monoester hydrolases
- 3.1.6 Sulphuric ester hydrolases

3.2 Acting on glycosyl compounds
- 3.2.1 Glycoside hydrolases
- 3.2.2 Hydrolysing *N*-glycosyl compounds
- 3.2.3 Hydrolysing *S*-glycosyl compounds

3.3 Acting on ether bonds
- 3.3.1 Thioether hydrolases

3.4 Acting on peptide bonds (peptide hydrolases)
- 3.4.1 α-Amino-acyl-peptide hydrolases
- 3.4.2 Peptidyl-amino-acid hydrolases
- 3.4.3 Dipeptide hydrolases
- 3.4.4 Peptidyl-peptide hydrolases

3.5 Acting on C–N bonds other than peptide bonds
- 3.5.1 In linear amides
- 3.5.2 In cyclic amides
- 3.5.3 In linear amidines
- 3.5.4 In cyclic amidines
- 3.5.5 In cyanides
- 3.5.99 In other compounds

3.6 Acting on acid–anhydride bonds
- 3.6.1 In phosphoryl-containing anhydrides

3.7 Acting on C–C bonds
- 3.7.1 In ketonic substances

3.8 Acting on halide bonds
- 3.8.1 In *C*-halide compounds
- 3.8.2 In *P*-halide compounds

3.9 Acting on P–N bonds

4. Lyases

4.1 Carbon–carbon lyases
- 4.1.1 Carboxy-lyases
- 4.1.2 Aldehyde-lyases
- 4.1.3 Ketoacid-lyases

4.2 Carbon–oxygen lyases
- 4.2.1 Hydro-lyases
- 4.2.99 Other carbon–oxygen lyases

4.3 Carbon–nitrogen lyases
- 4.3.1 Ammonia-lyases
- 4.3.2 Amidine-lyases

4.4 Carbon–sulphur lyases

4.5 Carbon–halide lyases

4.99 Other lyases

5. Isomerases

5.1 Racemases and epimerases
- 5.1.1 Acting on amino acids and derivatives
- 5.1.2 Acting on hydroxy acids and derivatives
- 5.1.3 Acting on carbohydrates and derivatives
- 5.1.99 Acting on other compounds

5.2 Cis-trans isomerases

5.3 Intramolecular oxidoreductases
- 5.3.1 Interconverting aldoses and ketoses
- 5.3.2 Interconverting keto and enol groups
- 5.3.3 Transposing C=C bonds

5.4 Intramolecular transferases
- 5.4.1 Transferring acyl groups
- 5.4.2 Transferring phosphoryl groups
- 5.4.99 Transferring other groups

5.5 Intramolecular lyases

5.99 Other isomerases

6. Ligases

6.1 Forming C–O bonds
- 6.1.1 Amino acid–RNA ligases

6.2 Forming C–S bonds
- 6.2.1 Acid–thiol ligases

6.3 Forming C–N bonds
- 6.3.1 Acid–ammonia ligases (amide synthetases)
- 6.3.2 Acid–amino-acid ligases (peptide synthetases)
- 6.3.3 Cyclo-ligases
- 6.3.4 Other C–N ligases
- 6.3.5 C–N ligases with glutamine as N donor

6.4 Forming C–C bonds

[1] International Union of Biochemistry, *Report of the Commission on Enzymes*, Pergamon Press, Oxford, 1961; International Union of Biochemistry, *Enzyme Nomenclature*, Recommendations 1964, Elsevier, Amsterdam, 1965.

General aspects of metabolism

Chemical changes taking place in living organisms are commonly referred to as *metabolism*. By far the greater part of metabolism arises directly or indirectly from the need of living cells for energy. A smaller proportion is due to the formation of new tissues in the growing organism; the synthesis of special substances such as hormones, antibodies, digestive enzymes, urea; the detoxication of drugs and other foreign substances; and the replacement of losses due to wear and tear of the body (for example of surface epithelia or of red and white blood cells).

Since all manifestations of life are accompanied by metabolic activities, the study of metabolism is a fundamental aspect of all branches of biology. It may be taken as axiomatic that all pathological events also involve metabolic changes, either qualitative or quantitative, and the study of the biochemistry of disease is therefore of the greatest importance to medicine. The concept that most diseases – those called organic – have an anatomical basis has long been established. Every anatomical change in turn has a material, that is chemical, basis and beyond the field covered by morbid anatomy there is therefore a 'molecular pathology' dealing with pathological changes in terms of chemical substances and chemical reactions. A pathological tissue is liable to possess an abnormal chemical composition as well as abnormal chemical activities, and the study of these chemical abnormalities provides a closer insight into the nature of the disorder. It may also supply information about 'functional' disorders where no morphological change is detectable, because not all chemical derangements are necessarily accompanied by morphological changes. In fact, at the molecular level the distinctions between organic and functional diseases are reduced to quantitative differences, organic diseases being those disorders where the molecular changes are large enough to come within the range of optical tools.

So far little more than a beginning has been made in the biochemical analysis of disease. The knowledge summarized in the following pages represents a foundation upon which molecular pathology will develop.

Energy metabolism

The need for energy springs from the fact that living matter is a thermodynamically unstable system that cannot be maintained unless energy is continuously added. Moreover, living matter is constantly engaged in performing various kinds of work, such as movement, chemical syntheses and transporting substances against concentration gradients. Activities of this kind cannot take place unless there is a supply of energy. Warm-blooded organisms need energy also to maintain the body temperature.

Energy is obtained by the degradation of foodstuffs. In higher organisms the overall effect of this degradation is essentially an oxidation of organic substances to carbon dioxide and water. This overall effect is the sum of many hundreds of separate chemical reactions many of which are now known in considerable detail.

Energy can also be obtained in the absence of air, i.e., anaerobically, by certain special degradation reactions of glucose and other hexoses. These are usually referred to as 'fermentations' or 'glycolysis'. The only form of fermentation occurring in animal tissues is the lactic acid fermentation, by which one molecule of glucose is split into two molecules of lactic acid:

$$C_6H_{12}O_6 \longrightarrow 2\ CH_3{\cdot}CH(OH){\cdot}COOH$$

Micro-organisms possess many forms of fermentation, among which the most important is the alcoholic fermentation:

$$C_6H_{12}O_6 \longrightarrow 2\ CH_3{\cdot}CH_2OH + 2\ CO_2$$

The energy made available by fermentations is only a small fraction of that liberated by the oxidation of sugar. The complete oxidation of one mole of glucose yields about 686 kcal of free energy, whilst the fermentation of the same amount of glucose to lactic acid yields about 45 kcal. Thus to obtain the same amount of energy by fermentation about 15 times more glucose has to be decomposed.

In most tissues of higher organisms, lactic acid fermentation is low in the presence of oxygen, but may be high in the absence of oxygen. The suppression of fermentation by oxygen, first observed by PASTEUR in yeast cells, is known as the PASTEUR effect.

Cell metabolism

The metabolism of the whole body is the result of the metabolic activities of the component tissues. Within the last 40 years methods have become available for the study of the metabolic activities of isolated tissues and organs. In particular, measurements have been made of the rate of respiration and lactic acid fermentation of many types of cells and tissues. A few representative figures for animal tissues are given in Tables 1 and 2.

Table 1 Rate of respiration (Q_{O_2}) of animal tissues*

Representative values, measured on isolated tissues, usually slices suspended in glucose–saline medium at 38–40 °C. Unless otherwise stated the data refer to rat tissues. For further data see the literature[1].

Tissue	Q_{O_2}	*Tissue*	Q_{O_2}
Kidney cortex	−25	ROUS sarcoma (chicken)	− 5
Kidney medulla (guinea-pig)	− 8	FLEXNER's carcinoma	− 8
Liver	−13	Erythrocytes	− 0.6
Brain cortex	−12	Leucocytes	− 9
Brain, white matter	− 6	Thrombocytes	− 7
Retina	−30	Bone marrow, red	−10
Spleen	−12	Adipose tissue**	− 0.5
Lung	− 8	Connective tissue (renal capsule, goat)	− 1
Submaxillary gland	−12	Cartilage (costal)	− 0.5
Pancreas	− 4	Skin (newborn rat)	− 1
Intestinal mucosa	−12	Striated muscle:	
Colonic mucosa	−10	– diaphragm	− 7
Adrenal gland	−10	– gastrocnemius	− 3
Pituitary gland	−12	– breast muscle (pigeon, minced)	−40
Thymus gland	− 5		
Thyroid (guinea-pig)	− 8	Smooth muscle (gizzard, pigeon)	− 4
Testis	−10		
JENSEN's sarcoma	−11	Cardiac muscle (sheep, minced)	−18

* The magnitude of respiration and fermentation is commonly expressed by the 'metabolic quotients', defined as follows:

$$Q_{O_2} = \frac{\text{microlitres of } O_2 \text{ used}}{\text{milligrammes dry weight} \times \text{hours}}$$

$$Q_{CO_2} = \frac{\text{microlitres of } CO_2 \text{ used or produced}}{\text{milligrammes dry weight} \times \text{hours}}$$

$$Q_{\text{lactic acid}} \text{ or } Q_L = \frac{\text{microlitres of lactic acid formed}}{\text{milligrammes dry weight} \times \text{hours}}$$

The disappearance of a substance is usually indicated by a negative sign, the formation by a positive sign. Anaerobic and aerobic conditions are denoted by the superscripts N_2 and O_2, e.g.: $Q_L^{N_2}$, $Q_L^{O_2}$.

A nongaseous substance like lactic acid is treated as if it were a gas on the assumption that 1 millimole is equivalent to 22 400 µl of gas. The reasoning in favour of this somewhat unusual connotation is that many of the measurements have been made by gasometric methods even when a substance like lactic acid is not a gas. Lactic acid production is usually measured in the presence of bicarbonate and the formation of acid is therefore followed by the production of an equivalent amount of CO_2. Some authors prefer to express the amounts metabolized in micromoles. To convert micromoles into microlitres, multiply micromoles by 22.4. The following calculation translates the Q values into quantities which can be readily understood and will illustrate the high intensity of the metabolism of some cells. Since 1 mg of lactic acid is equivalent to 250 µl of CO_2, a Q_L value of 25 means that the material produces 10% of its own dry weight of lactic acid per hour. Since 1 µl occupies roughly the space of 1 mg of tissue, and since the ratio of wet weight to dry weight is of the order of 5, a Q_{O_2} value of 5 means that the tissue uses about its own volume of oxygen per hour.

** Calculated for dry weight less ether-soluble matter.

[1] KREBS and JOHNSON, *Tab. biol. (Amst.)*, **19**, 100 (1948); ALBRITTON, E.C. (Ed.), *Standard Values in Nutrition and Metabolism*, Saunders, Philadelphia, 1954.

* The following review of metabolism has been written in consultation with H.A. KREBS and PATRICIA LUND (Metabolic Research Laboratory, Nuffield Department of Clinical Medicine, University of Oxford, England), E.A. NEWSHOLME (Department of Zoology, University of Oxford, England), H.L. KORNBERG, F.R.S., and R.A. COOPER (Department of Biochemistry, University of Leicester, England), J.M. LOWENSTEIN (Graduate Department of Biochemistry, Brandeis University, Waltham, Mass., U.S.A.) and R.B. CLAYTON (Department of Psychiatry, Stanford University, Palo Alto, Calif., U.S.A.).

Table 2 Rate of anaerobic lactic acid fermentation ($Q^{N_2}_{\text{lactic acid}}$) in animal tissues*

Representative values, measured on isolated tissues, usually slices suspended in glucose–saline medium at 38–40 °C. Unless otherwise stated the data refer to rat tissues. For further data see the literature [1].

Tissue	$Q^{N_2}_{L}$	*Tissue*	$Q^{N_2}_{L}$
Kidney cortex	3	Testis	8
Kidney medulla (guinea-pig)	28	JENSEN's sarcoma	32
Liver	3	ROUS sarcoma (chicken)	30
Brain cortex	18	FLEXNER's carcinoma	30
Retina	88	Erythrocytes	0.35
Retina (pigeon)	180	Leucocytes (polymorphonuclear, rabbit)	22
Spleen	8	Leucocytes (mononuclear, rabbit)	22
Lung (rat embryo)	10	Thrombocytes	26
Submaxillary gland	5	Bone marrow, red	21
Pancreas (rabbit)	3.5	Adipose tissue**	0.7
Intestinal mucosa	14	Cartilage (costal)	1.5
Adrenal gland	4	Skin (newborn rat)	7
Pituitary gland	13	Embryo	12
Thymus gland	8		

* See footnote * to Table 1, page 387.
** Calculated for dry weight less ether-soluble matter.

[1] KREBS and JOHNSON, *Tab. biol. (Amst.)*, **19**, 100 (1948); ALBRITTON, E.C. (Ed.), *Standard Values in Nutrition and Metabolism*, Saunders, Philadelphia, 1954.

There are wide variations in the metabolic activities of different materials. The highest rates of respiration and fermentation are found among micro-organisms. *Azotobacter*, for example, at 38 °C can give Q_{O_2} values of over 8000, and rates of 100–200 are common among bacteria. Anaerobic fermentation rates in micro-organisms reach figures up to 400. The maximum rate of lactic acid production in muscle can probably reach $Q^{N_2}_{L}$ values of well over 100 for short periods. Avian retina gives the highest continuous rate of lactic acid production among animal tissues ($Q^{N_2}_{L} = 180$ in pigeon retina).

Low metabolic rates are generally found in tissues of relatively low physiological activity. This is true for resting glands or muscle and in particular for tissues whose function, like that of connective tissue or bone, is largely structural or, like that of adipose tissue, is concerned with the storage of metabolically inert material.

The rates of respiration and fermentation increase with temperature, like the majority of other chemical reactions. At a critical temperature – in the case of warm-blooded animals at about 40 °C, in the case of cold-blooded animals somewhat below this temperature – a further rise in temperature reduces metabolism. In exceptional cases, those of the thermophilic bacteria, the critical temperature may be as high as 80 °C.

Among the factors which affect energy production in the intact warm-blooded animal, body size has long been recognized as being of major importance. The differences in the oxygen consumption of intact animals of different size are not exactly reflected in the rates of respiration of individual tissues. In general, the tissues of larger species have a somewhat lower metabolism than the tissues of smaller species, but the differences between the Q_{O_2} values of, for example, brain, kidney, liver, spleen and lung of different species are relatively small. The characteristic differences in the basal metabolic rate of animals of different size appear to be due mainly to differences in the resting metabolism of the musculature.

Energy-supplying reactions

The first stage in the utilization of foodstuffs either for the supply of energy or for other purposes consists of a hydrolytic breakdown of the large molecules of food to the small constituent units. Proteins are converted to amino acids, carbohydrates to hexoses, fats to glycerol and fatty acid, and nucleic acids to the constituent bases, pentoses and phosphate. This hydrolytic breakdown is commonly referred to as *digestion*. Biologically speaking, digestion results in the solubilization of the foodstuffs, a prerequisite to absorption from the intestine. Processes very similar to intestinal digestion also occur in most tissues when reserve materials are mobilized to serve as a source of energy, or when damaged tissues are 'autolysed'.

Digestion is brought about by the combined action of many specific enzymes each dealing with the hydrolysis of one compound or of a series of closely related compounds. The basic properties of these enzymes are described on pages 405–419.

Intermediary stages of carbohydrate degradation

Hexoses formed by digestion in the intestinal tract are absorbed and reach the various tissues through the blood circulation. The main reaction by which hexoses are degraded is the anaerobic fermentation to lactic acid, followed by the oxidation of the products of fermentation. An alternative pathway of oxidation exists in which glucose is oxidized without first undergoing fission to a 3-carbon compound, but this pathway, the 'pentose phosphate cycle' (see page 420), is not a major source of energy in higher animals; its main functions are probably the provision of a reducing agent in the form of reduced nicotinamide-adenine dinucleotide phosphate ($NADPH_2$) and of ribose phosphate required for the synthesis of nucleic acids (see page 351).

Table 3 Intermediary reactions of lactic acid fermentation (glycolysis) in animal tissues (for formulae of intermediates see Figure 1)
These reactions occur in all animal tissues and in many micro-organisms.

No.	Intermediary reactions			Enzyme catalysing the reaction*
1	glucose + adenosine triphosphate (ATP)	→	glucose 6-phosphate + adenosine diphosphate (ADP)	Hexokinase
2	glucose 6-phosphate	→	fructose 6-phosphate	Glucosephosphate isomerase
3	fructose 6-phosphate + ATP	→	fructose 1,6-diphosphate + ADP	Phosphofructokinase
4	fructose 1,6-diphosphate	→	dihydroxyacetone phosphate + 3-phosphoglyceraldehyde	Fructosediphosphate aldolase
5	dihydroxyacetone phosphate	→	3-phosphoglyceraldehyde	Triosephosphate isomerase
6	2 [3-phosphoglyceraldehyde + diphosphopyridine nucleotide (NAD) + phosphate	→	1,3-diphosphoglyceric acid + $NADH_2$]	Glyceraldehydephosphate dehydrogenase
7	2 [1,3-diphosphoglyceric acid + ADP	→	3-phosphoglyceric acid + ATP]	Phosphoglycerate kinase
8	2 [3-phosphoglyceric acid	→	2-phosphoglyceric acid]	Phosphoglycerate phosphomutase
9	2 [2-phosphoglyceric acid	→	phosphopyruvic acid + H_2O]	Phosphopyruvate hydratase
10	2 [phosphopyruvic acid + ADP	→	pyruvic acid + ATP]	Pyruvate kinase
11	2 [pyruvic acid + $NADH_2$	→	lactic acid + NAD]	Lactate dehydrogenase
	Balance: glucose + 2 ADP + 2 phosphate	→	2 lactic acid + 2 ATP + 2 H_2O	

* On enzyme nomenclature see page 382.

Fig. 1 The intermediates of glycolysis formed from glucose

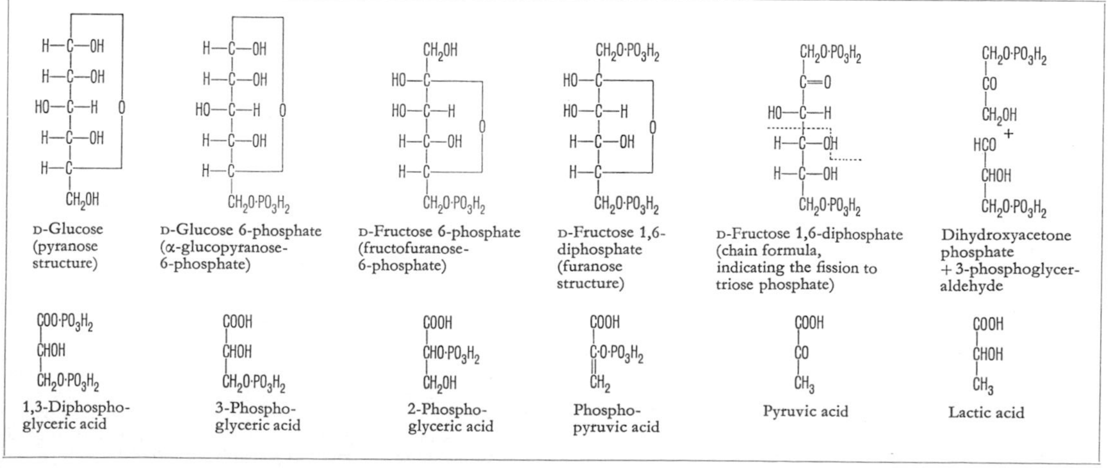

D-Glucose (pyranose structure); D-Glucose 6-phosphate (α-glucopyranose-6-phosphate); D-Fructose 6-phosphate (fructofuranose-6-phosphate); D-Fructose 1,6-diphosphate (furanose structure); D-Fructose 1,6-diphosphate (chain formula, indicating the fission to triose phosphate); Dihydroxyacetone phosphate + 3-phosphoglyceraldehyde

1,3-Diphosphoglyceric acid; 3-Phosphoglyceric acid; 2-Phosphoglyceric acid; Phosphopyruvic acid; Pyruvic acid; Lactic acid

Table 4 Ancillary reactions of lactic acid fermentation in animal tissues

No.	Intermediary reactions			Enzyme catalysing the reaction
1	glycogen$_n$ + phosphate	⇌	glucose 1-phosphate + glycogen$_{n-1}$	α-Glucan phosphorylase
2	glucose 1-phosphate	⇌	glucose 6-phosphate	Phosphoglucomutase
3	fructose + ATP	→	fructose 6-phosphate + ADP	Hexokinase*
4	galactose + ATP	→	galactose 1-phosphate + ADP	Galactokinase [2]
5	galactose 1-phosphate + uridine diphosphoglucose	⇌	glucose 1-phosphate + uridine diphosphogalactose	Hexose 1-phosphate uridylyl-transferase [3]
6	uridine diphosphogalactose	⇌	uridine diphosphoglucose	UDPglucose epimerase [4]
7	uridine diphosphoglucose + pyrophosphate	⇌	uridine triphosphate (UTP) + glucose 1-phosphate	UDPG pyrophosphorylase [5]
8	fructose + ATP	→	fructose 1-phosphate + ADP	Ketohexokinase [6]
9	fructose 1-phosphate	⇌	dihydroxyacetone phosphate + glyceraldehyde	Ketose 1-phosphate aldolase [7]
10	D-glyceraldehyde + ATP	→	glyceraldehyde 3-phosphate + ADP	Triokinase [8]

* Hexokinase reacts similarly with many other hexoses, e.g., mannose, 2-deoxyglucose [1].

References

[1] SOLS and CRANE, *J. biol. Chem.*, **210**, 581 (1954).
[2] TRUCCO et al., *Arch. Biochem.*, **18**, 137 (1948).
[3] KALCKAR et al., *Nature*, **172**, 1038 (1953); SMITH and MILLS, *Biochim. biophys. Acta (Amst.)*, **13**, 386 (1954).
[4] LELOIR, L.F., *Arch. Biochem.*, **33**, 186 (1951); KALCKAR, H.M., *Advanc. Enzymol.*, **20**, 111 (1958).
[5] MUNCH-PETERSEN et al., *Nature*, **172**, 1036 (1953); ISSELBACHER, K.J., *J. biol. Chem.*, **232**, 429 (1958).
[6] HERS and KUSAKA, *Biochim. biophys. Acta (Amst.)*, **11**, 427 (1953); PARKS et al., *J. biol. Chem.*, **227**, 231 (1957).
[7] PEANASKY and LARDY, *J. biol. Chem.*, **233**, 365 and 371 (1958).
[8] BERGMEYER et al., *Biochem. Z.*, **333**, 471 (1961).

Fig. 2 The individual stages of the tricarboxylic acid cycle
The names of the enzymes are given above the arrows, those of the coenzymes required below the arrows.

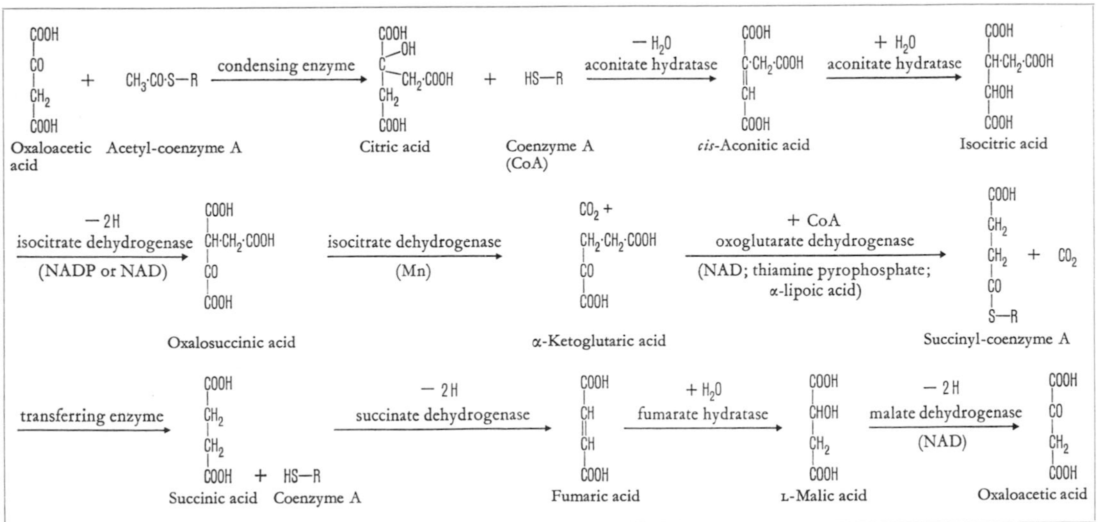

Anaerobic lactic acid fermentation (glycolysis). The intermediary reactions of the lactic acid fermentation are given in Table 3. The changes of the carbon skeleton are summarized in Figure 1. The alcoholic fermentation of yeasts, moulds, other micro-organisms and plants follows essentially the same pathway except that reaction 11 (Table 3) is replaced by the following two reactions:

pyruvic acid → acetaldehyde + CO_2
acetaldehyde + $NADH_2$ → ethanol + NAD

The balance reaction of the alcoholic fermentation (reactions 1–10 of Table 3, plus the above two reactions occurring twice each) is thus:

glucose + 2 ADP + 2 phosphate
→ 2 ethanol + 2 CO_2 + 2 ATP + 2 H_2O

Reactions related to the lactic acid fermentation are shown in Table 4. Some of these reactions are concerned with the fermentation of other starting materials such as glycogen, fructose or galactose. When glycogen (or starch) is the starting material the balance reaction is

glycogen (1 glucose equivalent) + 3 ADP + 3 phosphate
→ 2 lactic acid + 3 ATP + 3 H_2O

Oxidation of carbohydrate. As a rule, sugars are not oxidized as such but only after fermentation to lactic acid or triose phosphate. As already mentioned, the alternative pathway of glucose oxidation, the pentose phosphate cycle (see page 420), appears to be of limited significance as an energy-supplying mechanism.

Lactic acid is first converted into acetyl-coenzyme A via pyruvic acid. The intermediary stages are assumed to be as follows:

Lactic acid Pyruvic acid

The second step is assumed to be a reaction between pyruvate and thiamine pyrophosphate (TPP) in which an acetaldehyde-TPP complex ('active acetaldehyde'; see page 469) is formed and CO_2 liberated:

Pyruvic acid Thiamine pyrophosphate Acetaldehyde-TPP complex

In the succeeding reaction the aldehyde-TPP complex reacts with the disulphide form of α-lipoic acid in such a manner that the aldehyde group of the complex is oxidized to a carboxyl group and the disulphide reduced to the dimercaptan; further the nascent carboxyl and one of the nascent thiol groups condense to form *S*-acetyl-α-lipoic acid:

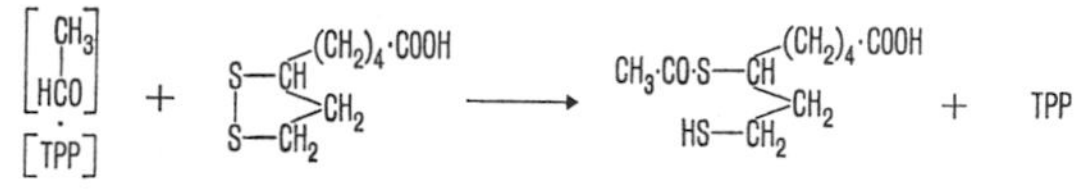

Acetaldehyde-TPP complex Disulphide form of α-lipoic acid *S*-Acetyl-α-lipoic acid

In the next stage the acetyl group is transferred from α-lipoic acid to coenzyme A, with the formation of reduced lipoic acid and acetyl-coenzyme A. The reduced lipoic acid is reoxidized by interaction with NAD, catalysed by lipoamide dehydrogenase:

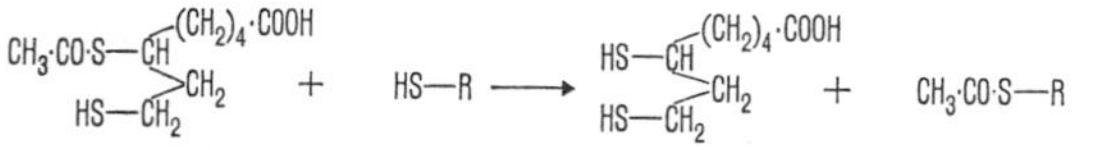

S-Acetyl-α-lipoic acid Coenzyme A Reduced α-lipoic acid Acetyl-coenzyme A

Reduced α-lipoic acid Oxidized α-lipoic acid

The sum of the last four reactions is:

pyruvic acid + NAD + coenzyme A
→ acetyl-coenzyme A + $NADH_2$ + CO_2

Analogous reactions probably occur whenever α-ketonic acids are oxidized. α-Ketonic acids arise in particular from α-amino acids; α-ketoglutarate is also formed during the tricarboxylic acid cycle.

Acetyl-coenzyme A is oxidized to completion by the tricarboxylic acid cycle (also referred to in the literature as the 'citric acid cycle' or 'Krebs cycle'). This cycle is initiated by a condensation of acetyl-coenzyme A and oxaloacetate leading to citrate. Citrate undergoes a series of reactions that, on balance, are oxidative and in which other tricarboxylic acids and dicarboxylic acids arise. They lead eventually to the regeneration of oxaloacetate, which thus becomes available for another turn of the cycle. This means that oxaloacetate reacts after the manner of a catalyst. The hydrogen atoms arising in the course of the cycle react ultimately with molecular oxygen to form water, and the overall effect of one turn of the cycle is therefore:

$$CH_3{\cdot}COOH + 2O_2 \longrightarrow 2CO_2 + 2H_2O$$

The component reactions of the cycle are given in Figure 2. The cycle itself is shown diagrammatically in Figure 3.

Fig. 3 The tricarboxylic acid cycle

Substances entering the cycle (coenzyme A, H_2O) after the initial condensation of 1 molecule of acetyl-coenzyme A and 1 molecule of oxaloacetate are written inside the cycle; substances arising in it are written outside. During one turn of the cycle, one acetic acid equivalent is completely oxidized. The four pairs of H atoms which arise react ultimately with O_2 to form water. For further details see Krebs and Lowenstein, in Greenberg, D. M. (Ed.), *Metabolic Pathways*, vol. 1, Academic Press, New York, 1960, page 129; and Krebs and Kornberg, *Ergebn. Physiol.*, **49**, 212 (1957).

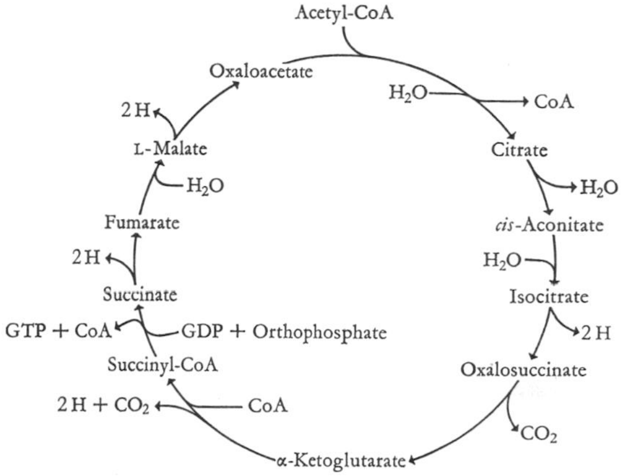

Oxidative degradation of fat[1] (for references see page 393)

Fats are not oxidized in the ester form in which they are deposited in tissues and present in foods. Prior to oxidation fat is hydrolysed to free fatty acids and glycerol, a reaction catalysed by lipases or other ester hydrolases.

The oxidation of the free fatty acids is initiated by a reaction resulting in the attachment of the fatty acid radical to the sulphur atom of coenzyme A. This reaction requires the participation of ATP and of specific enzyme systems (acyl-CoA-synthetase). Two stages of the reaction have been identified. The first leads to the formation of an adenyl fatty acid (acyl-adenosine monophosphate)[2]:

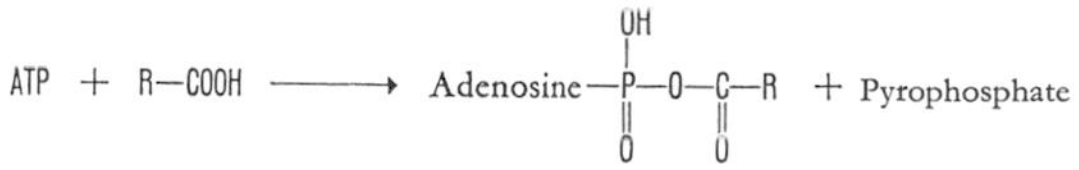

Fatty acid Acyl-adenylate

The second is a transfer of the acyl group from adenylic acid to coenzyme A:

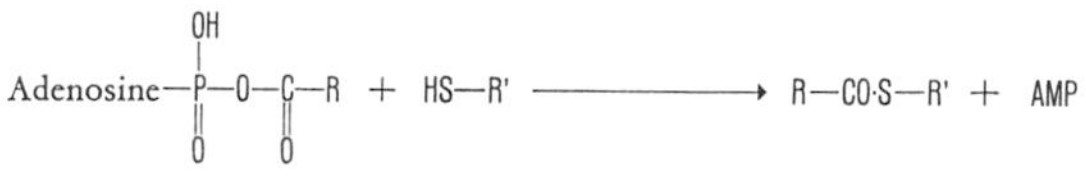

Acyl-adenylate Coenzyme A Acyl-coenzyme A

Several fatty acids, including acetic, propionic and higher fatty acids, have been shown to react in this way[3]. The acyl-coenzyme compounds thus formed represent the 'active' forms of fatty acids that in the presence of further specific enzymes undergo a characteristic sequence of reactions, summarily referred to as β-oxidation, because the oxidation occurs at the β-carbon atom of the chain. It leads to the stepwise removal of acetic acid equivalents from the carbon chain. The intermediary enzymic reactions of this process are given in Figure 4. As shown in this scheme, β-oxidation involves four separate steps. The first is the dehydrogenation in the α-β position, the second the addition of water to the double bond and the formation of a β-hydroxy acid. The third is the dehydrogenation of the β-hydroxyl group to form a β-keto acid, the last is a 'thiolysis', i.e., a fission of the carbon chain effected by the sulphydryl group of coenzyme A. It results in the formation of one molecule of acetyl-coenzyme A and an acyl-coenzyme A derivative shorter than the original chain by two carbon atoms. The shortened chain repeatedly undergoes the same sequence of reactions until the whole fatty-acid chain is reduced to a fragment of

Fig. 4 β-Oxidation of fatty acids

On enzyme nomenclature see page 382. Acyl-CoA-dehydrogenase is a flavoprotein, 3-hydroxyacyl-CoA-dehydrogenase requires NAD. All four reactions are reversible. The β-hydroxyacyl-coenzyme A compounds are optically active and belong to the L-series, in contrast to the free β-hydroxybutyrate in blood and urine which belongs to the D-series. The latter arises by reduction of free acetoacetate[4].

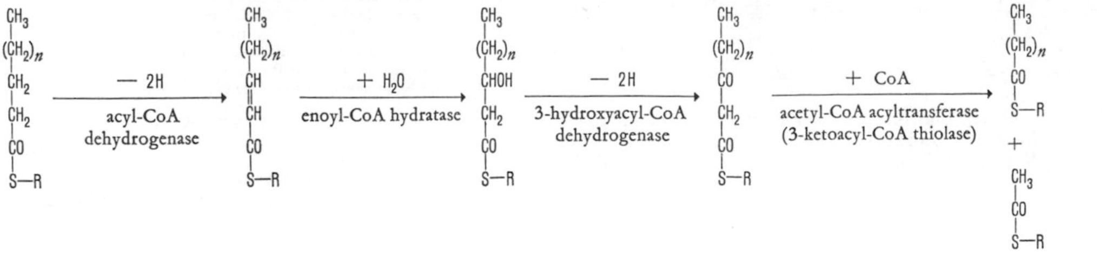

Fatty acyl-coenzyme A — α-β-Unsaturated fatty acyl-coenzyme A — β-Hydroxyacyl-coenzyme A — β-Ketoacyl-coenzyme A — Fatty acyl-coenzyme A + acetyl-coenzyme A

less than four carbon atoms. In the case of chains with even numbers of carbon atoms the last fragment is acetyl-coenzyme A, in the case of those with uneven numbers it is propionyl-coenzyme A.

The great majority of naturally occurring fatty acids contain an even number of carbon atoms and therefore yield acetyl-coenzyme A as the only product. The propionyl-coenzyme A formed from uneven chains is known to enter a CO_2-fixation reaction leading to succinic acid (see below).

The sequence of reactions by which fatty acids are oxidized has been referred to as the 'fatty-acid cycle'. It is not a cycle in the strict sense since the starting material is not regenerated by a full turn of the 'cycle'. What happens is a periodic repetition of the same *types* of reaction, but not of the same reactions. This is shown diagrammatically in Figure 5, from which it can be seen that the mechanism is a 'spiral' rather than a 'cycle'.

Carnitine (page 491) stimulates oxidation of fatty acids by promoting their transport from cytoplasm[13] to mitochondria through the formation of carnityl esters:

Acyl-CoA + carnitine ⇌ acylcarnitine + CoA

Unsaturated fatty acids are formed by desaturation of the coenzyme A esters of saturated fatty acids. This involves a coupled reaction in which both molecular oxygen and $NADPH_2$ are required[5]:

Fig. 5 Diagram of the 'spiral' of fatty-acid oxidation

C_{16}, C_{14}, etc.	= fatty acyl-coenzyme A
ΔC_{16}, ΔC_{14}, etc.	= unsaturated fatty acyl-coenzyme A
β-OH-C_{16}, β-OH-C_{14}, etc.	= β-hydroxyacyl-coenzyme A
β-O-C_{16}, β-O-C_{14}, etc.	= β-ketoacyl-coenzyme A
C_2	= acetyl-coenzyme A

The subscripts indicate the length of the carbon chain

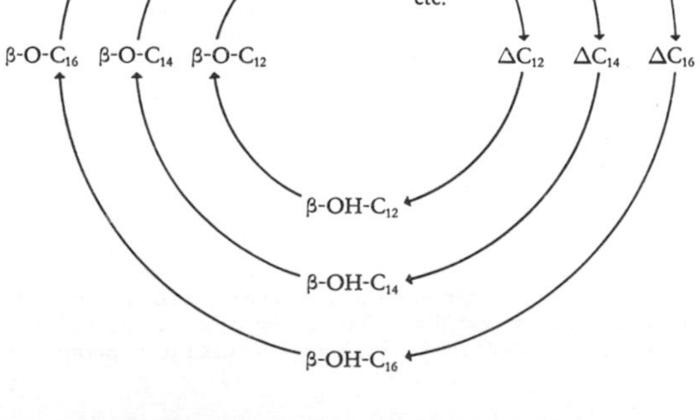

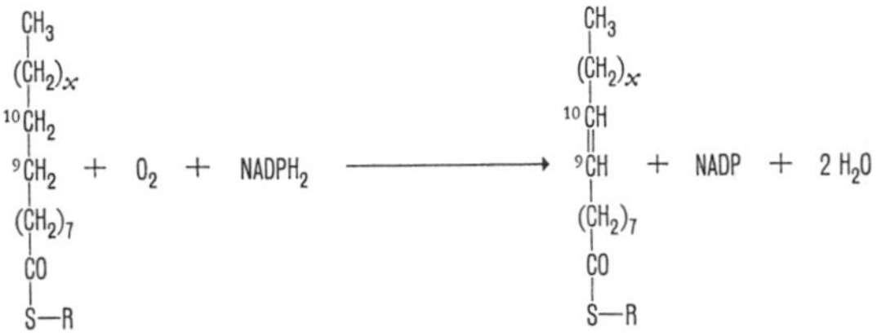

Unsaturated fatty acids are also degraded by β-oxidation[13]. The double bond necessitates two additional enzymes, an isomerase that transposes it and converts it from cis to trans configuration, and an epimerase that converts the β-hydroxyacyl-coenzyme A formed by addition of H_2O to the bond from the D- to the L-configuration. The latter is then degraded as shown in Figure 4.

Glycerol, the second constituent of neutral fats, is converted in liver primarily to α-glycerophosphate:

glycerol + ATP→ α-glycerophosphate + ADP

Alternatively, glycerol may be dehydrogenated to D-glyceraldehyde, which can yield glyceraldehyde 3-phosphate, or 2-phosphoglyceric acid via D-glycerate[6].

The triose phosphate formed from glycerol subsequently joins the reactions of triose phosphate arising from sugars.

Formation of succinic acid from propionyl-coenzyme A. As already mentioned, the propionyl-coenzyme A formed from fatty acids with uneven carbon chains yields succinic acid. This involves a CO_2-fixation reaction discovered by Ochoa et al.[7] followed by racemization and rearrangement of methylmalonyl-coenzyme A as follows[8]:

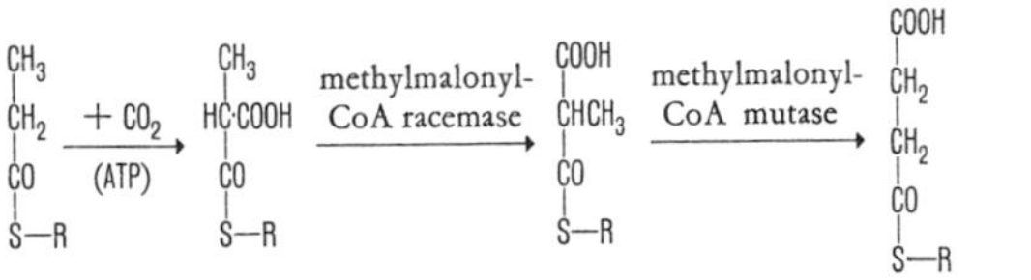

Propionyl-coenzyme A — Methylmalonyl-coenzyme A (a) — Methylmalonyl-coenzyme A (b) — Succinyl-coenzyme A

Hydrolysis of succinyl-coenzyme A then gives succinic acid.

Terminal oxidation of fat. The degradation reactions of fat so far considered bring about an incomplete oxidation of fatty acids and glycerol. The main product of this incomplete oxidation is acetic acid in the form of acetyl-coenzyme A. The only other product is succinic acid, which arises from the three terminal carbon atoms of the fatty-acid chain with odd numbers of carbon atoms. Since fatty acids with odd numbers of carbon atoms are uncommon in nature the total amount of succinate arising from fat is normally very small. Such fatty acids are uncommon because fatty-acid chains are usually synthesized from 2-carbon units.

Acetyl-coenzyme A and succinate are oxidized to completion by the reactions of the tricarboxylic acid cycle described on pages 390 and 391.

Ketosis. In ketosis due to starvation or diabetes or other causes, the 'ketone bodies', viz., acetoacetate ($CH_3 \cdot CO \cdot CH_2 \cdot COOH$), β-hydroxybutyrate ($CH_3 \cdot CHOH \cdot CH_2 \cdot COOH$) and acetone ($CH_3 \cdot CO \cdot CH_3$), accumulate in the tissues and body fluids. For reasons not fully understood more acetyl-coenzyme A is formed in ketosis, mainly from fatty acids, than can be oxidized through the tricarboxylic acid cycle. The surplus molecules of acetyl-coenzyme A condense in pairs to form acetoacetyl-coenzyme A which undergoes hydrolysis to free acetoacetate and coenzyme A (in liver free acetoacetate is not readily utilized):

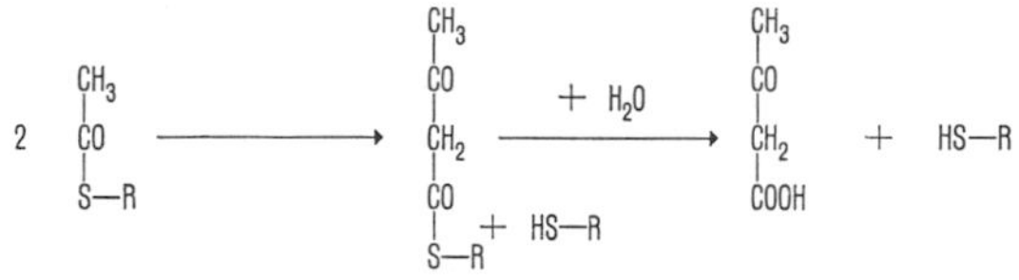

Acetyl-coenzyme A — Acetoacetyl-coenzyme A — Acetoacetic acid

Acetoacetate is the primary ketone body. β-Hydroxybutyrate is formed from it by reduction, acetone by decarboxylation. The latter reaction is mainly nonenzymic, and is due to the inherent instability of acetoacetate:

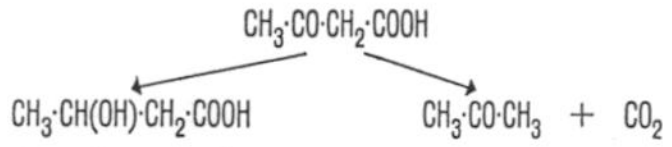

β-Hydroxybutyric acid — Acetone

The older view that acetoacetate arises directly from the four terminal carbon atoms of fatty acid chains is no longer tenable in view of isotope data demonstrating conclusively that *most* acetoacetate is formed by the condensation of two molecules of acetyl-coenzyme A.

It follows that all substances which can form acetyl-coenzyme A, including carbohydrate and many amino acids, can be parent substances of the ketone bodies. Why ketone bodies accumulate only when acetyl-coenzyme A is formed from fatty acids and the three ketogenic amino acids, and not when it is formed from carbohydrate and other amino acids, is not clear. Since the oxidation of acetyl-coenzyme A through the tricarboxylic acid cycle requires oxaloacetate it is likely that oxaloacetate is a key substance in the control of ketosis[9]. It has been assumed that a sufficient level of oxaloacetate for the optimal operation of the tricarboxylic acid cycle cannot be maintained unless carbohydrate is oxidized, but why this should be the case is still a matter of conjecture.

Ancillary reactions of fatty acid degradation. Some ancillary degradation reactions of fatty acids are the following:

(*a*) Acetoacetyl-CoA-hydrolase liberates free acetoacetate from the coenzyme A derivative:

acetoacetyl-coenzyme A + H_2O
→ acetoacetate + coenzyme A

This reaction is assumed to play a role in the appearance of the ketone bodies in blood and tissues in ketosis[10].

(*b*) 3-Hydroxybutyrate dehydrogenase catalyses the reversible interconversion of acetoacetate and β-hydroxybutyrate:

β-hydroxybutyrate + NAD ⇌ acetoacetate + $NADH_2$

and is responsible for the formation and removal of β-hydroxybutyrate.

(*c*) An enzyme transferring coenzyme A reversibly between acetoacetate and succinate (3-ketoacid-CoA-transferase) may initiate the breakdown of free acetoacetate:

acetoacetate + succinyl-coenzyme A
⇌ acetoacetyl-coenzyme A + succinate[11]

(*d*) Acetoacetate breakdown can also be initiated by the reaction

acetoacetate + coenzyme A + ATP
→ acetoacetyl-coenzyme A + AMP + pyrophosphate[12]

This is analogous to the reaction initiating the degradation of fatty acids (page 391) and may involve the same type of intermediary stages, i.e., the formation of acetoacetyl-adenylate.

References

1 LYNEN, F., *Harvey Lect. 1952/53*, **48**, 210 (1954); GREEN, D. E., *Biol. Rev.*, **29**, 330 (1954); POPJÁK and LE BRETON (Eds.), *Biochemical Problems of Lipids*, Proceedings of the Second International Conference, Gent 1955, Butterworth, London, 1956; BEINERT et al., *Biochem. J.*, **64**, 782 (1956).
2 BERG, P., *J. biol. Chem.*, **222**, 991, 1015, 1025 (1956).
3 PENG, C.H.L., *Biochim. biophys. Acta (Amst.)*, **22**, 42 (1956); JENCKS and LIPMANN, *J. biol. Chem.*, **225**, 207 (1957); WHITEHOUSE et al., *J. biol. Chem.*, **226**, 813 (1957).
4 LEHNINGER and GREVILLE, *Biochim. biophys. Acta (Amst.)*, **12**, 188 (1953).
5 STOFFEL, W., *Biochem. biophys. Res. Commun.*, **6**, 270 (1961); NUGTEREN, D.H., *Biochim. biophys. Acta (Amst.)*, **60**, 656 (1962).
6 HERS, H.G., in BOYER et al. (Eds.), *The Enzymes*, 2nd ed., vol. 6, Academic Press, New York, 1962, page 75.
7 FLAVIN et al., *Nature*, **176**, 823 (1955).
8 EGGERER et al., *J. Amer. chem. Soc.*, **82**, 2643 (1960); MAZUMDER et al., *J. biol. Chem.*, **237**, 3065 (1962).
9 KREBS, H.A., *Arch. intern. Med.*, **107**, 51 (1961); WIELAND and LÖFFLER, *Biochem. Z.*, **339**, 204 (1963).
10 GREEN, D.E., *Biol. Rev.*, **29**, 330 (1954).
11 STERN et al., *J. Amer. chem. Soc.*, **75**, 1517 (1953).
12 STERN and OCHOA, *J. biol. Chem.*, **191**, 161 (1951).
13 OLSON, J.A., *Ann. Rev. Biochem.*, **35**, 559 (1966).

Intermediary stages of the degradation of amino acids

As in the case of carbohydrate and fat, the degradation of amino acids consists of two major stages. In the first stage the amino acids are converted into an intermediate that can be oxidized through the tricarboxylic acid cycle. The second or terminal stage is the tricarboxylic acid cycle. The following account is concerned with the first stage.

General degradation reactions. Some degradation reactions are common to all or several amino acids. These are (*a*) oxidative deamination, (*b*) transamination, (*c*) nonoxidative decarboxylation.

Oxidative deamination. The general reaction scheme of oxidative deamination is as follows:

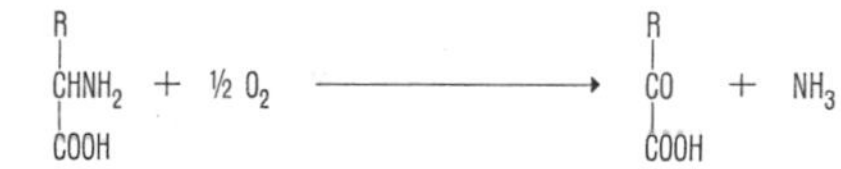

α-Amino acid — α-Ketonic acid

Liver and kidney contain enzymes that attack the majority of α-amino acids of both the D- and L-series in this way. In general the activity of the D-amino-acid oxidases is greater than that of the L-amino-acid oxidases, although D-amino acids occur very infrequently in natural products. One L-amino acid, however, reacts at a much greater rate than all other L-amino acids. This is glutamic acid, which is attacked by a specific glutamate dehydrogenase catalysing the following reaction:

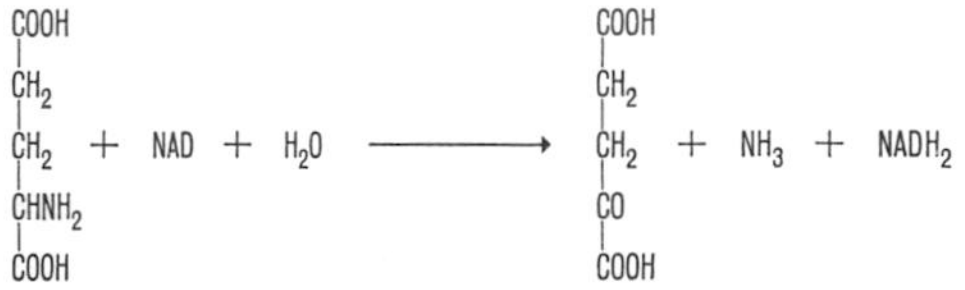

L-Glutamic acid — α-Ketoglutaric acid

This enzyme differs from all the other enzymes bringing about oxidative deamination in animal tissues in that it transfers hydrogen to NAD. In the case of oxidative deamination by the other enzymes, the primary acceptor is a flavoprotein. The L-amino-acid oxidases of animal tissues are comparatively weak and it is probable that deamination is generally effected by transamination of α-amino acids with α-ketoglutarate (see below) followed by the dehydrogenation of glutamate according to the above reaction.

Transamination. Transamination is a reversible reaction between amino and α-ketonic acids leading to the exchange of the amino and ketonic groups. An example is the following:

Table 5 Some transamination reactions in animal tissues[1]

Reactions			Remarks
α-ketoglutarate + L-α-amino acid	⇌	L-glutamate + α-ketonic acid	Most α-amino acids can react in this way in liver and many other tissues
α-ketoglutarate + L-ornithine	⇌	L-glutamate + L-glutamic γ-semialdehyde	Involves transfer of ω-amino groups; occurs in liver[2,3]
glyoxylate + L-ornithine	⇌	glycine + L-glutamic γ-semialdehyde	
pyruvate + L-ornithine	⇌	L-alanine + L-glutamic γ-semialdehyde	
L-glutamine + α-keto-γ-guanidinovaleric acid	⇌	α-ketoglutarate + L-arginine + NH_3	Occurs in liver[2]
L-alanine + hydroxypyruvate	⇌	pyruvate + L-serine	Occurs in liver and kidney[4]
α-ketoglutarate + γ-aminobutyrate	⇌	L-glutamate + succinic semialdehyde	Occurs in brain and liver[5]
α-ketoglutarate + β-alanine	⇌	L-glutamate + malonic semialdehyde	Occurs in brain and liver[6]

References

[1] For reviews see COHEN and SALLACH, in GREENBERG, D.M. (Ed.), *Metabolic Pathways*, vol. 2, Academic Press, New York, 1961, page 1; KREBS, H.A., in MUNRO and ALLISON (Eds.), *Mammalian Protein Metabolism*, vol. 1, Academic Press, New York, 1964, page 125; GUIRARD and SNELL, in FLORKIN and STOTZ (Eds.), *Comprehensive Biochemistry*, vol. 15, Elsevier, Amsterdam, 1964, page 138.

[2] MEISTER, A., *J. biol. Chem.*, **206**, 587 (1954).

[3] QUASTEL and WITTY, *Nature*, **167**, 556 (1951).

[4] SALLACH, H.J., *J. biol. Chem.*, **223**, 1101 (1956).

[5] ROBERTS et al., *J. biol. Chem.*, **203**, 195 (1953).

[6] ROBERTS and BREGOFF, *J. biol. Chem.*, **201**, 393 (1953).

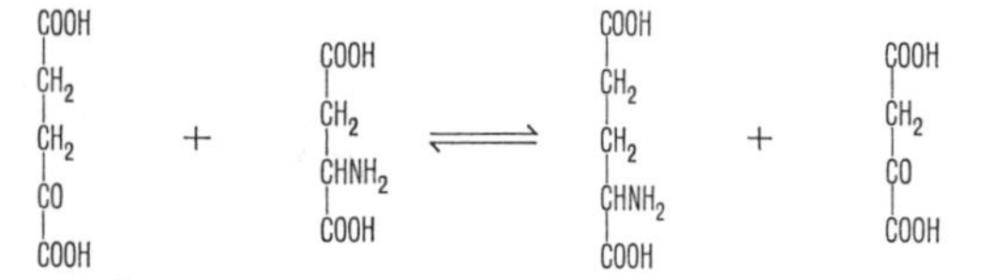

α-Ketoglutaric acid   L-Aspartic acid   L-Glutamic acid   Oxaloacetic acid

The majority of α-amino acids can replace aspartic acid in this type of reaction, according to the general scheme

α-ketoglutarate + α-amino acid
⇌ L-glutamate + α-ketonic acid

but the rate of reaction is by far the highest when aspartic acid is the amino group donor. Transaminases occur in most animal tissues as well as in micro-organisms and plants. Several tissues contain special types of transaminases. Some of these tissues are listed in Table 5.

Transaminases readily diffuse from tissues into the blood plasma when the tissue has suffered damage. This is the basis of a clinical test, the rise of the plasma level of transaminase in cardiac infarction. Pyridoxal phosphate is a prosthetic group of transaminases.

Decarboxylation. Decarboxylation of amino acids proceeds according to the following general scheme:

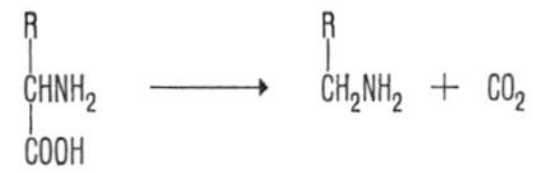

α-Amino acid   Primary amine

Decarboxylases occur in animal tissues and in many micro-organisms, but not every amino acid can undergo decarboxylation. Reactions that have been recorded are listed in Table 6. The significance of some of the decarboxylations occurring in animal tissues lies in the supply of essential metabolites, e.g., of taurine (required for the synthesis of bile acids), of histamine and serotonin (required for the functional activities of nervous tissue) or of ethanolamine (required for the synthesis of cephalins, choline and acetylcholine). Pyridoxal phosphate (see page 474) is a coenzyme also in most decarboxylation reactions. A notable exception is the decarboxylation of histidine.

Degradation of individual amino acids[1]

(for references see page 399)

L-*Glutamic acid,* L-*aspartic acid,* L-*alanine.* On oxidative deamination or transamination these three amino acids yield α-ketonic acids which also occur as intermediates in the metabolism of carbohydrate; they are α-ketoglutarate, oxaloacetate and pyruvate respectively.

Table 6 Decarboxylation of L-amino acids[1]

Most of the bacterial reactions listed below occur in the micro-organisms of the intestinal tract, e.g., *Escherichia coli, Streptococcus faecalis, Clostridium* species

Amino acid	Amine formed	Occurrence of enzyme
Histidine	Histamine	Animal tissues, bacteria
Cysteic acid	Taurine	Liver
Glutamic acid	γ-Aminobutyric acid	Brain, bacteria
5-Hydroxytryptophan	5-Hydroxytryptamine (serotonin)	Animal tissues
3,4-Dihydroxyphenylalanine	3,4-Dihydroxyphenylethylamine	Animal tissues
Serine	Ethanolamine	Animal tissues[2]
Lysine	Cadaverine	Bacteria
Ornithine	Putrescine	Bacteria
Tyrosine	Tyramine	Bacteria
Phenylalanine	Phenylethylamine	Bacteria
Aspartic acid	β-Alanine	Bacteria
α,ε-Diaminopimelic acid	Lysine	Bacteria[3]

References

[1] For reviews see GUIRARD and SNELL, in FLORKIN and STOTZ (Eds.), *Comprehensive Biochemistry*, vol. 15, Elsevier, Amsterdam, 1964, page 138; KREBS, H.A., in MUNRO and ALLISON (Eds.), *Mammalian Protein Metabolism*, vol. 1, Academic Press, New York, 1964, page 125.

[2] ARNSTEIN, H.R.V., *Biochem. J.*, **48**, 27 (1951).

[3] DEWEY and WORK, *Nature*, **169**, 533 (1952).

The degradation of the six amino acids L-*histidine,* L-*arginine,* L-*citrulline,* L-*ornithine,* L-*proline and* L-*hydroxyproline* leads in every case to glutamic acid and thence to α-ketoglutarate.

L-*Histidine* is converted to glutamic acid by an enzyme complex of liver tissue that includes tetrahydrofolic acid (THF) as a cofactor. The overall result of the action of this complex is an hydrolysis according to the following scheme:

(For references see page 399)

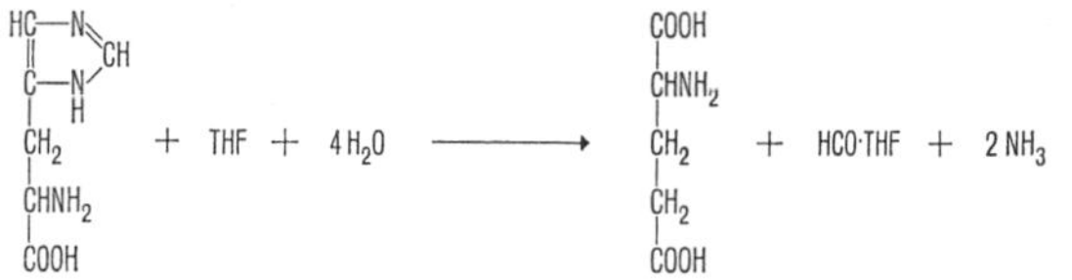

L-Histidine Tetrahydrofolic acid L-Glutamic acid 10-Formyltetrahydrofolic acid

Six intermediate stages have been identified[2], of which the first is the fission to ammonia and an unsaturated derivative of histidine.

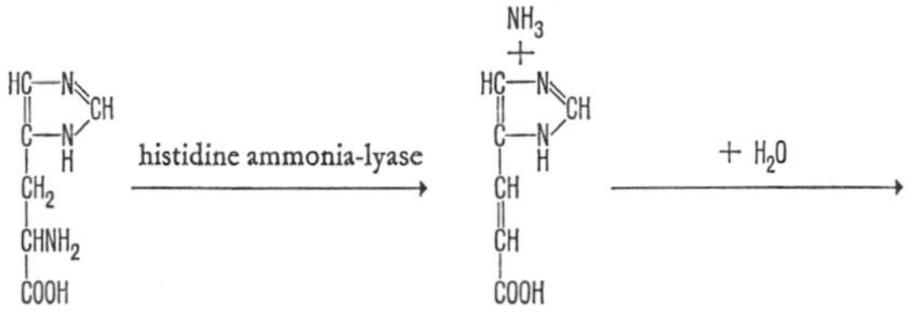

L-Histidine Urocanic acid

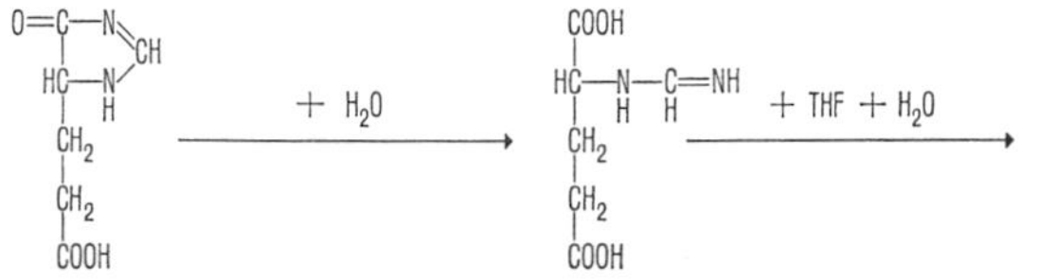

Imidazolonepropionic acid Formiminoglutamic acid

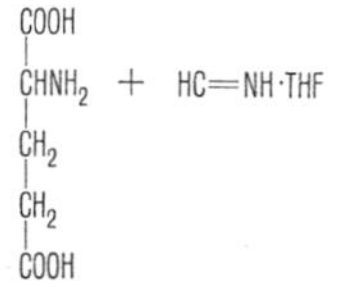

L-Glutamic acid Formiminotetrahydrofolic acid

Formimino-THF is converted into 5,10-methylidyne-THF and 10-formyl-THF. For these and further reactions see pages 436 and 437.

Oxidative deamination or transamination of histidine yields imidazolepyruvic acid[3], which may be further converted into imidazolelactic acid and imidazoleacetic acid.

A similar pathway of histidine degradation to glutamic acid has been shown in bacteria, although tetrahydrofolic acid does not appear to be involved.

L-*Citrulline* and L-*arginine* are converted in liver tissue into ornithine by the reactions of the ornithine cycle (see pages 442 and 443). L-*Ornithine* is known to yield glutamic γ-semialdehyde by transamination (see page 394) and the semialdehyde can form glutamic acid by dehydrogenation:

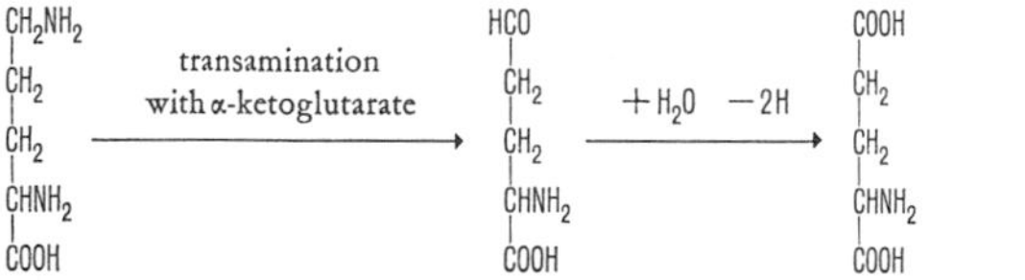

L-Ornithine L-Glutamic γ-semialdehyde L-Glutamic acid

D-*Ornithine*, under the influence of D-amino-acid oxidase, follows a different route, the primary step being the removal of the α-amino group:

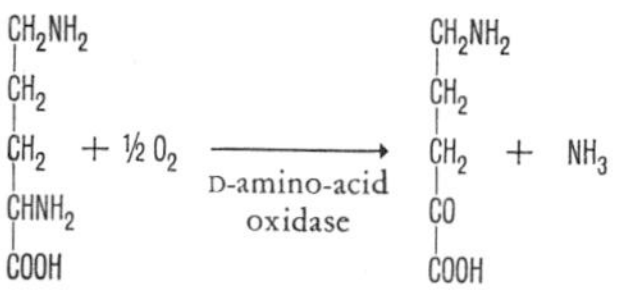

D-Ornithine α-Keto-δ-aminovaleric acid

L-*Proline* forms glutamic acid by the following three steps[4], which include two dehydrogenations:

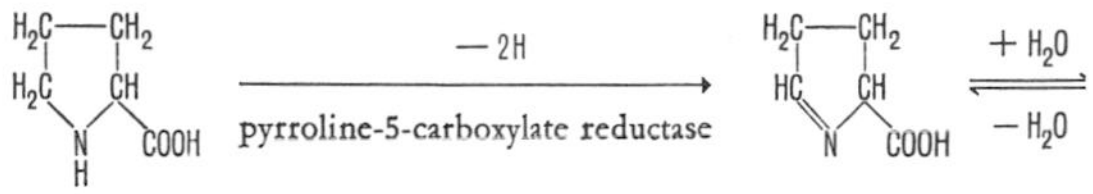

L-Proline L-Δ^1-Pyrroline-5-carboxylic acid

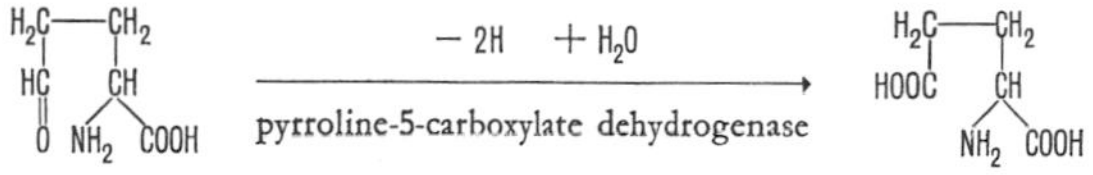

L-Glutamic γ-semialdehyde L-Glutamic acid

These reactions have been shown to occur in both liver and bacteria.

D-*Proline* reacts differently in mammalian liver or kidney and gives the same α-ketonic acid as D-ornithine. This is to be expected as the point of attack of D-amino-acid oxidase is always the α-carbon atom.

L-*Hydroxyproline*. γ-Hydroxyglutamic acid can be formed from hydroxyproline by a route analogous to that of glutamate formation from proline[5]. Transamination of γ-hydroxyglutamic acid with α-ketoglutaric acid yields γ-hydroxyglutaric acid, which may be split to form pyruvic and glyoxylic acids or decarboxylated to malate.

The degradation of the *leucines* and *valines* follows initially a common pattern. In every case transamination or oxidative deamination leads to the corresponding α-ketonic acid. This subsequently undergoes reactions analogous to those described for pyruvic acid (page 391), resulting in the formation of an acyl-coenzyme A derivative and CO_2. The acyl-coenzyme A derivative then reacts essentially in the same way as the acyl-coenzyme A derivative of long-chain fatty acids. Special reactions – CO_2-fixation and an aldol fission – follow in the case of leucine. The end-products are acetyl-coenzyme A and propionyl-coenzyme A. As already mentioned (page 392), propionyl-coenzyme A eventually yields succinate.

Leucine yields three molecules of acetyl-coenzyme A. The intermediate stages are as follows[6]:

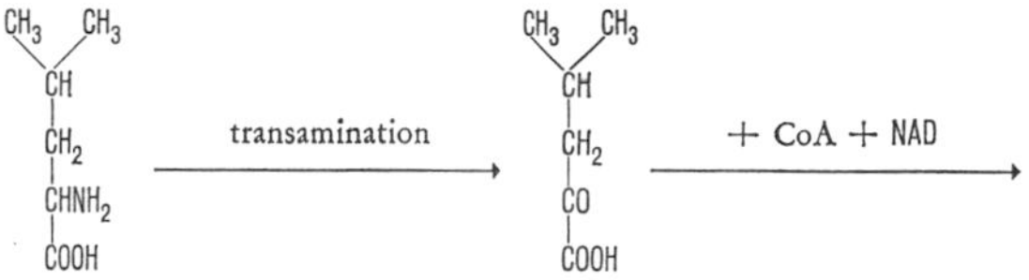

Leucine α-Ketoisocaproic acid

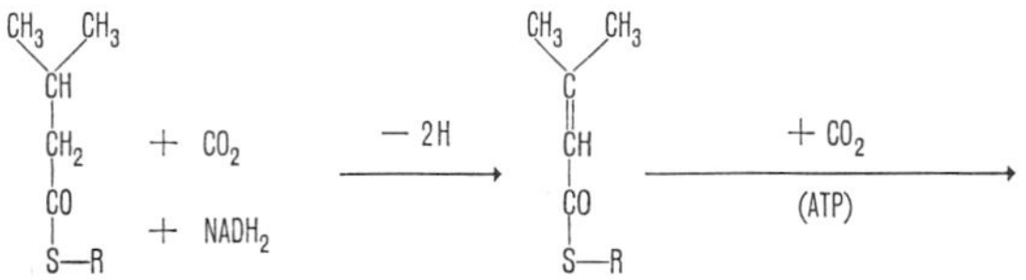

Isovaleryl-coenzyme A β-Methylcrotonyl-coenzyme A

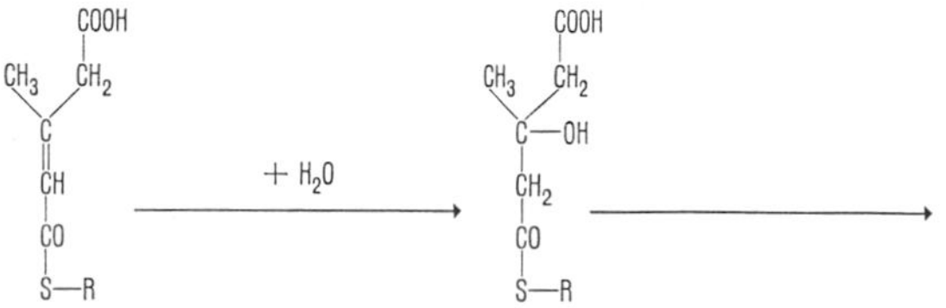

β-Methylglutaconyl-coenzyme A β-Hydroxy-β-methylglutaryl-coenzyme A

(For references see page 399)

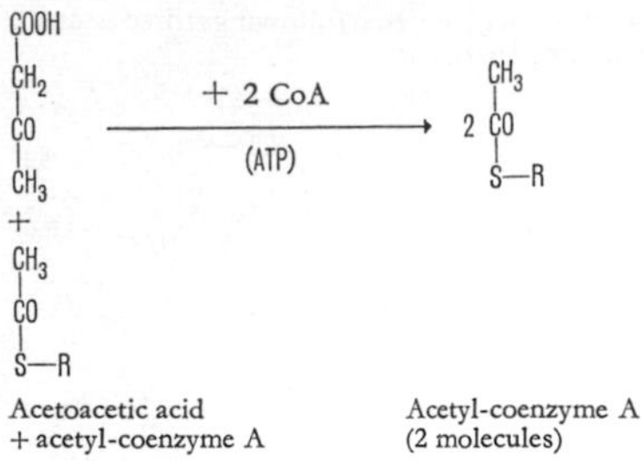

Isoleucine yields one molecule of acetyl-coenzyme A and one molecule of propionyl-coenzyme A[7]:

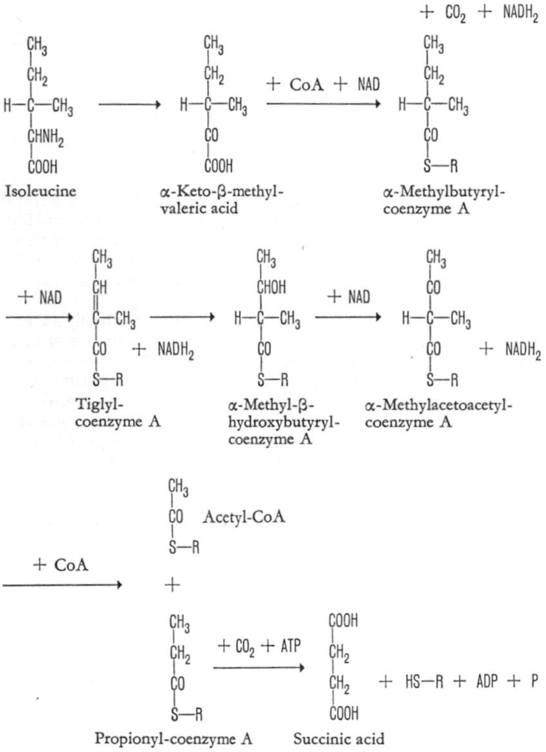

The mechanism of the last of these reactions is discussed on page 392.

Valine is degraded by analogous reactions to the stage of β-hydroxyisobutyryl-coenzyme A. This compound is hydrolysed by a thiol ester hydrolase to yield β-hydroxyisobutyric acid, which is further metabolized as shown below[8]:

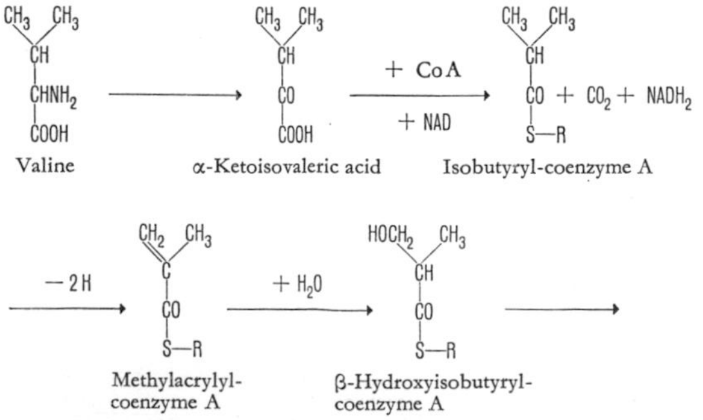

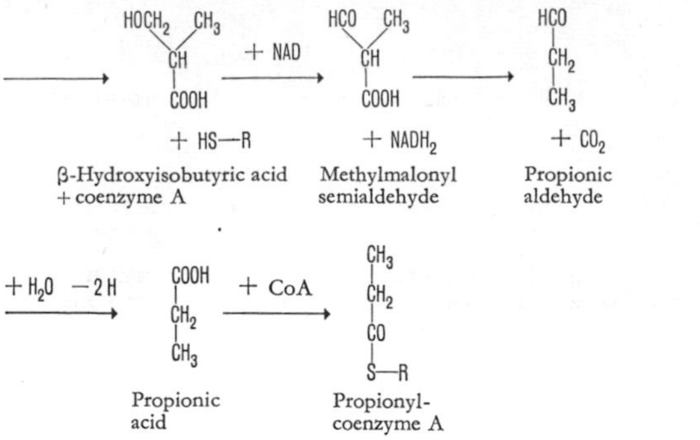

Norleucine (which is not a protein constituent) has not been studied in detail, but by analogy it is expected to undergo the following sequence of reactions leading to propionyl-coenzyme A and acetyl-coenzyme A:

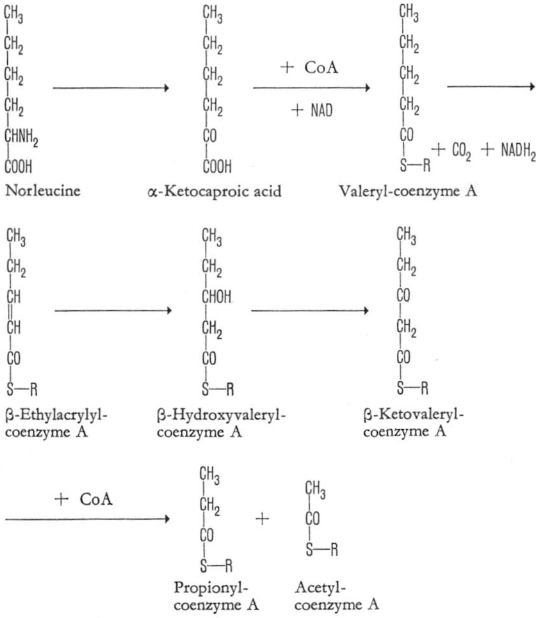

Norvaline, by the same types of reaction, forms two molecules of acetyl-coenzyme A:

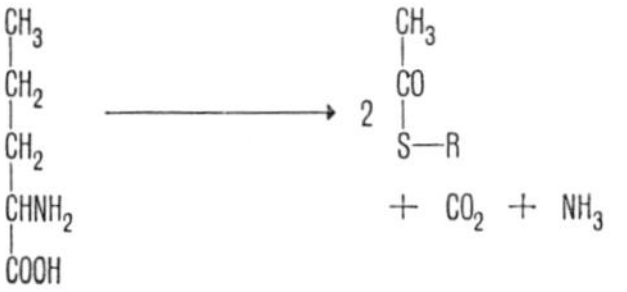

α-*Aminobutyric acid* by analogy forms propionyl-coenzyme A and thence succinate.

The *hydroxyamino acids* (serine, homoserine, threonine) and *glycine* react atypically in that the oxidative deamination is not the primary step.

Serine yields anaerobically ammonia and pyruvic acid in animal tissues as well as in micro-organisms. The intermediate steps are assumed to be as follows[9]:

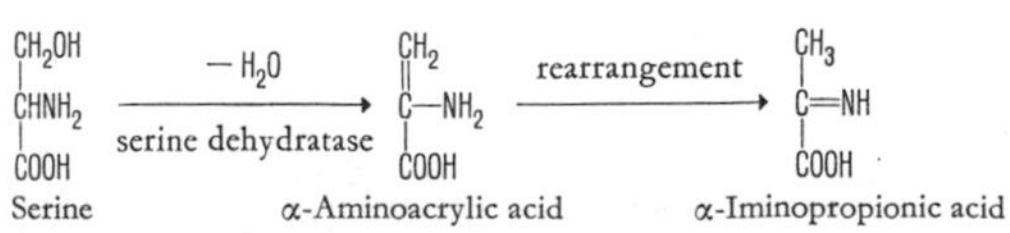

(For references see page 399)

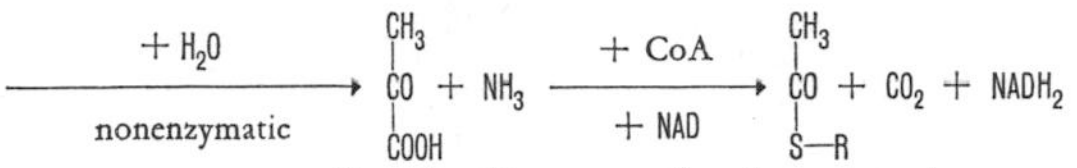

Pyruvic acid   Acetyl-coenzyme A

L-*Threonine* (an intermediate in the metabolism of methionine) is known to undergo an analogous nonoxidative deamination on incubation with liver extracts, yielding α-ketobutyric acid and ammonia[10]:

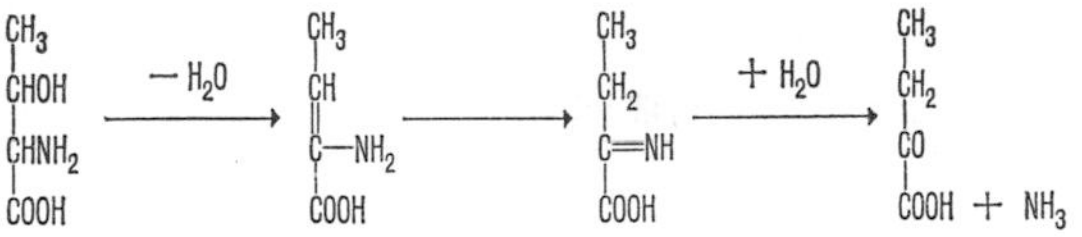

L-Threonine   α-Amino-crotonic acid   α-Imino-butyric acid   α-Keto-butyric acid

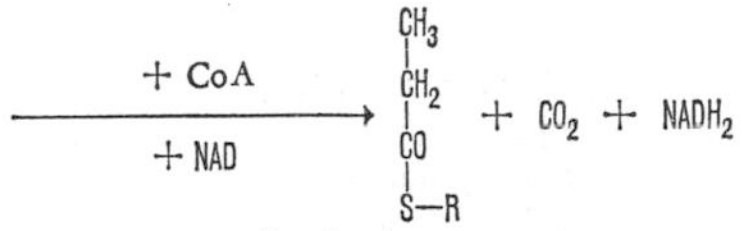

Propionyl-coenzyme A

It may also be split by an aldolase to give acetaldehyde and glycine[11].

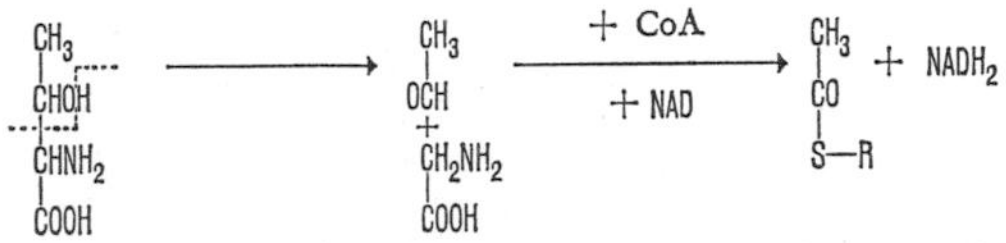

L-Threonine   Acetaldehyde + glycine   Acetyl-coenzyme A

The acetaldehyde formed can be converted into acetyl-coenzyme A, whilst the glycine reacts as described later.

Homoserine (an intermediate in the metabolism of methionine) yields α-ketobutyric acid and ammonia by a nonoxidative deamination analogous to that of serine[12]:

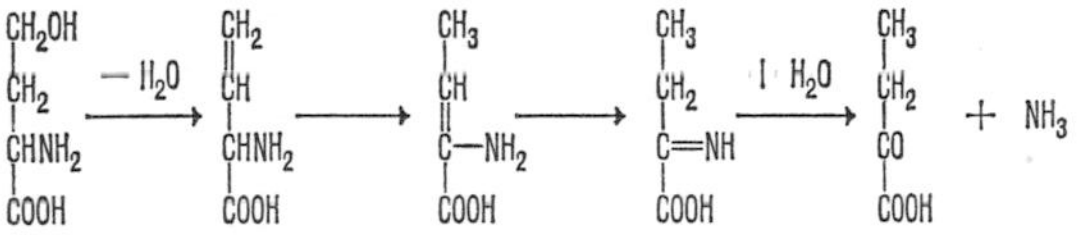

Homoserine   α-Amino-vinylacetic acid   α-Amino-crotonic acid   α-Imino-butyric acid   α-Ketobutyric acid

Glycine. The pathway of degradation of glycine is not yet fully clarified. One route is the conversion into serine by an aldol condensation with hydroxymethyltetrahydrofolic acid[13]:

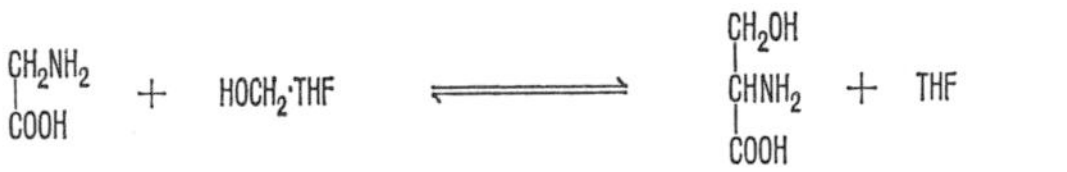

Glycine   Hydroxymethyltetra-hydrofolic acid   L-Serine   Tetrahydro-folic acid

The conversion of serine to glycine is important for the production of 'active' single carbon units in both animals and bacteria.

Transamination with α-ketoglutarate gives glyoxylic acid, which can yield oxalic acid by oxidation or formic acid by oxidative decarboxylation[14]. The latter reaction is probably that most commonly occurring in animal tissues:

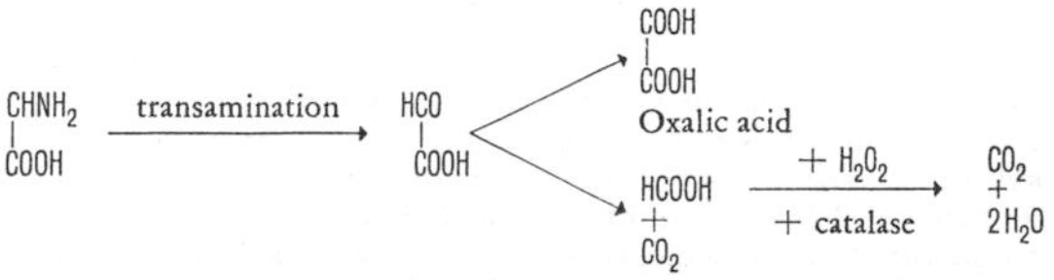

Glycine   Glyoxylic acid   Formic acid

Another possible pathway of glycine degradation is initiated by the condensation with succinyl-coenzyme A[15]:

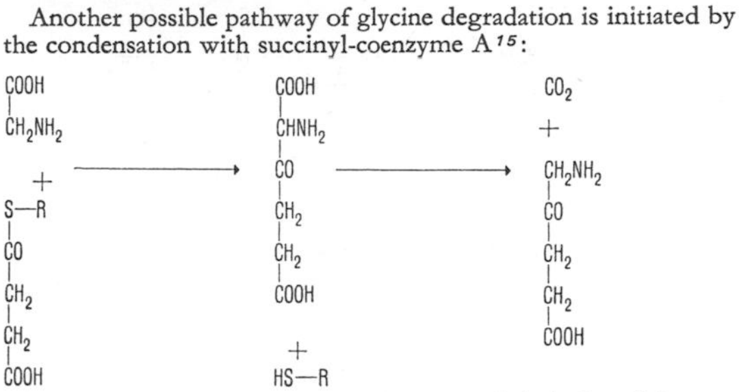

Glycine + succinyl-coenzyme A   α-Amino-β-ketoadipic acid + coenzyme A   δ-Aminolaevulinic acid

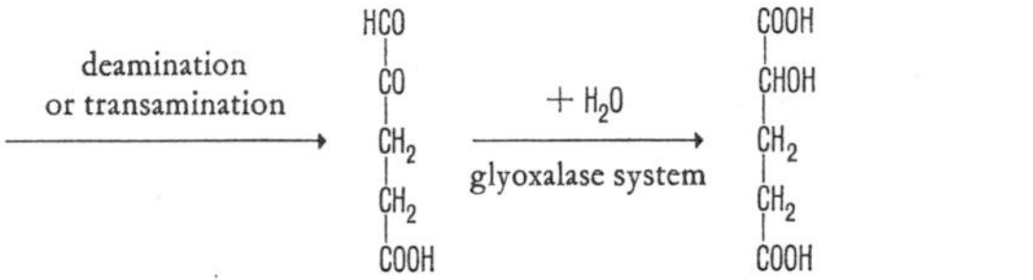

α-Ketoglutaric semialdehyde   α-Hydroxy-glutaric acid

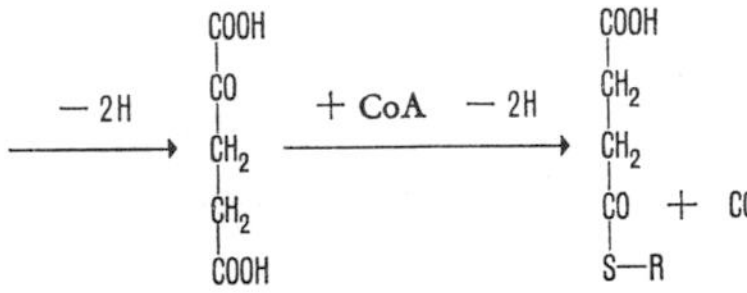

α-Keto-glutaric acid   Succinyl-coenzyme A

The reactions up to the stage of δ-aminolaevulinic acid have been firmly established but the pathway beyond δ-aminolaevulinic acid leading eventually to succinyl-coenzyme A is hypothetical and based on analogies.

L-*Cysteine* can be desulphurated, under the influence of the enzyme cysteine desulphhydrase, to yield pyruvate, NH_3 and H_2S[16]. The intermediate stages have been formulated as follows:

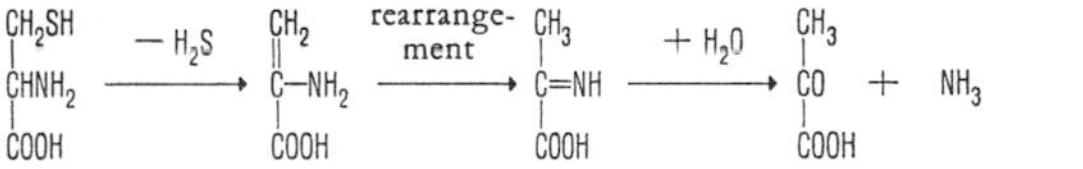

L-Cysteine   α-Aminoacrylic acid   α-Iminopropionic acid   Pyruvic acid

These reactions are closely analogous to those of serine.

A more important metabolic route involves oxidation at the sulphur atom:

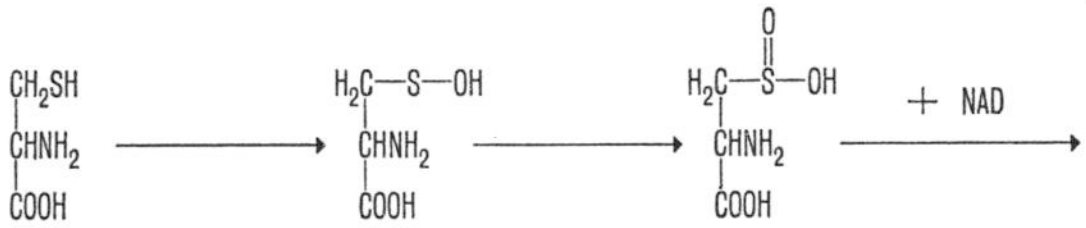

L-Cysteine   Cysteinesulphenic acid (hypothetical)   Cysteinesulphinic acid

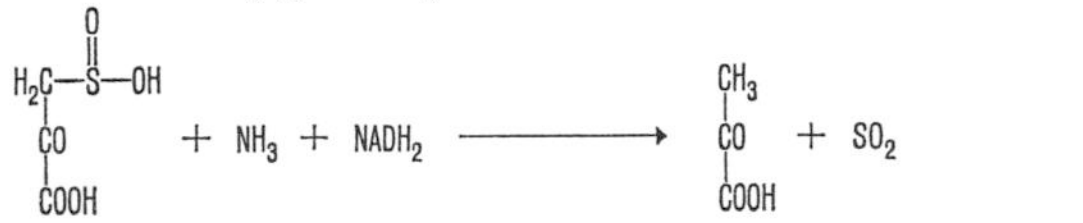

β-Sulphinyl-pyruvic acid   Pyruvic acid

Cystine is converted in liver tissue into the same products as cysteine; it is assumed that it undergoes reduction to cysteine before it is degraded.

L-*Homocysteine*, an intermediate in methionine oxidation, undergoes a transsulphuration reaction with cystathionine as intermediate[17]. In this way the methionine sulphur becomes that of cysteine, the pathway of degradation of which is shown above.

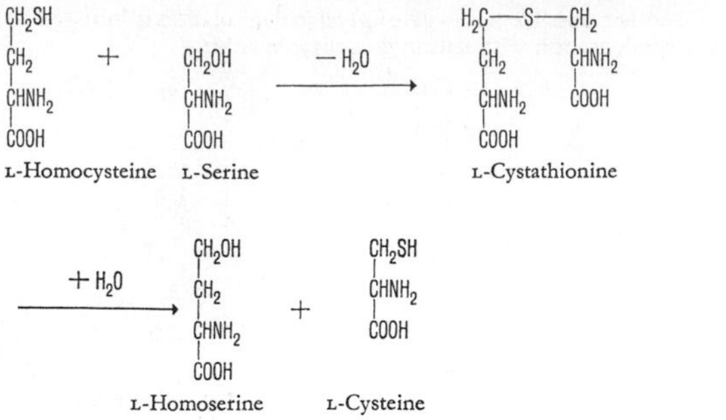

L-*Methionine* is first converted to an active form, a step requiring adenosine triphosphate (ATP)[18]. The product, *S*-adenosylmethionine, is a methyl group donor (in choline synthesis).

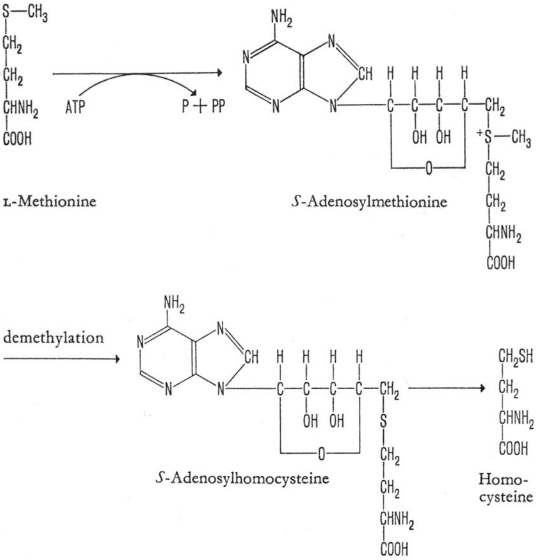

The fate of homocysteine has already been discussed.

L-*Lysine*. The following pathway of the degradation of lysine is essentially based on isotopic evidence and the isolation of most of the intermediates[19]:

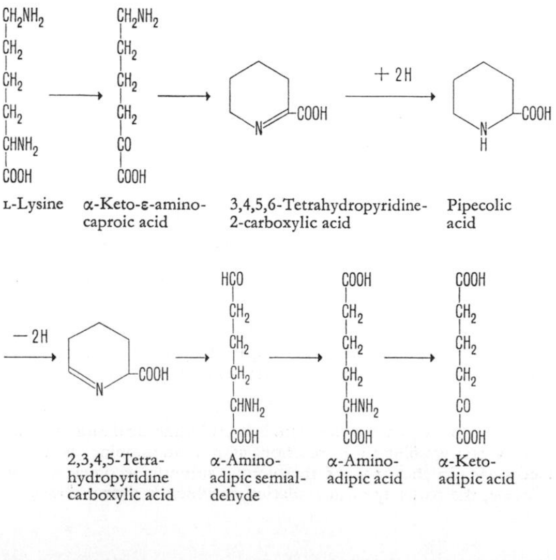

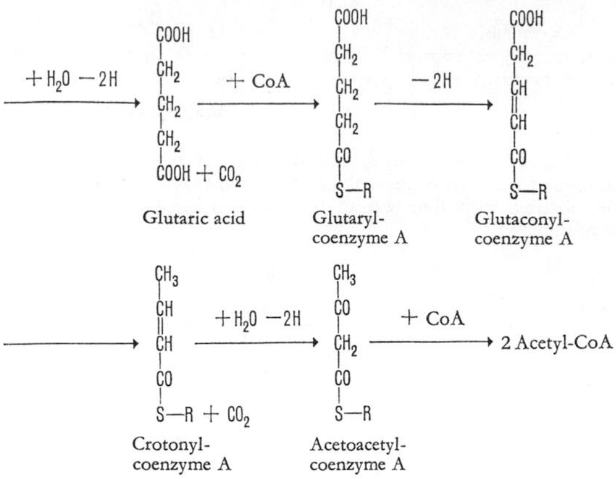

Phenylalanine and *tyrosine* are degraded in animal tissues by the reactions shown in the following scheme. Several unusual enzymes are involved. The end-products as formulated are oxaloacetic acid and acetyl-coenzyme A:

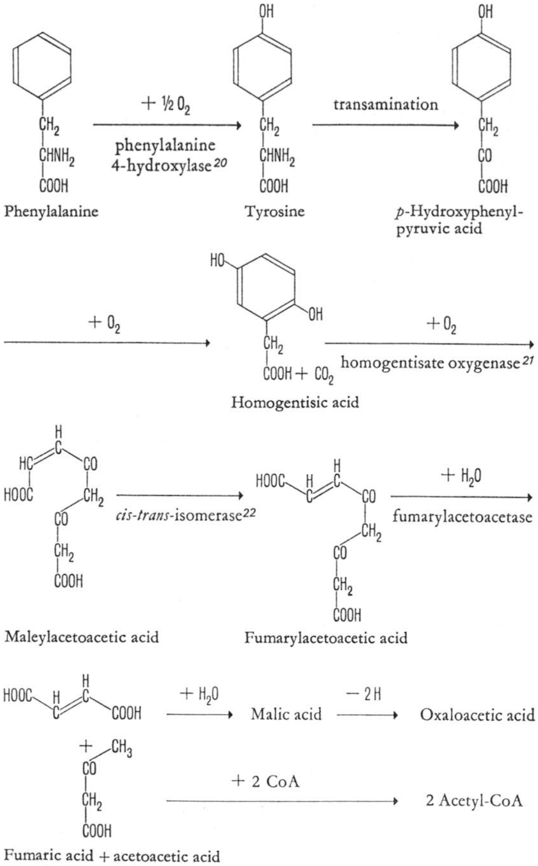

On inborn errors of phenylalanine and tyrosine metabolism see pages 448–449.

Tryptophan is incompletely burned in man and in most animals. Products of incomplete oxidation appearing in the urine are indole-3-acetic acid, anthranilic acid, kynurenine, hydroxykynurenine, kynurenic acid and 8-hydroxykynurenic ('xanthurenic') acid. Tryptophan and 3-hydroxyanthranilic acid (but not anthranilic acid) can be converted into nicotinic acid in some animals, though only in limited quantities. This involves a fission of the benzene ring of

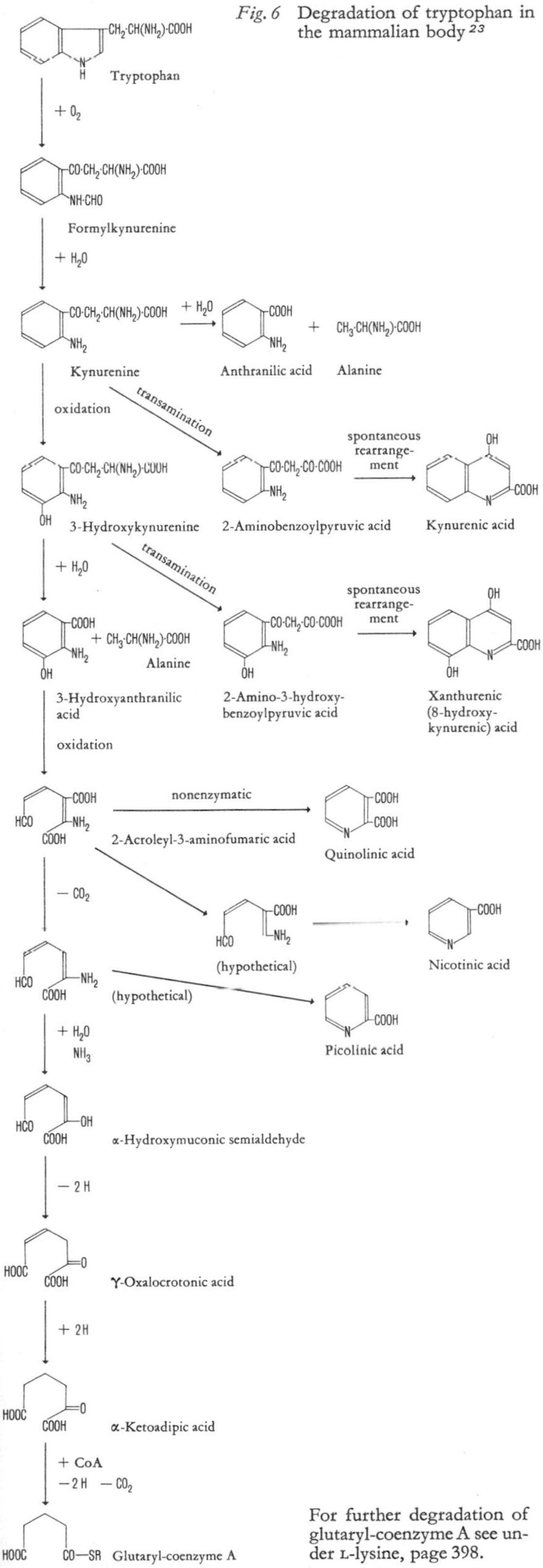

Fig. 6 Degradation of tryptophan in the mammalian body[23]

For further degradation of glutaryl-coenzyme A see under L-lysine, page 398.

3-hydroxyanthranilic acid and the formation of a pyridine ring, the nitrogen of which is derived from the amino group of anthranilic acid. The side chain of tryptophan can appear in the form of alanine. An outline of the probable pathways leading to the various products is given in Figure 6.

References

[1] For reviews see GREENBERG, D.M. (Ed.), *Metabolic Pathways*, vol. 2, Academic Press, New York, 1961; KREBS, H.A., in MUNRO and ALLISON (Eds.), *Mammalian Protein Metabolism*, vol. 1, Academic Press, New York, 1964, page 125.

[2] TABOR and WYNGARDEN, *J. biol. Chem.*, **234**, 1830 (1959).

[3] SPOLTER and BALDRIDGE, *J. biol. Chem.*, **238**, 2071 (1963).

[4] JOHNSON and STRECKER, *J. biol. Chem.*, **237**, 1876 (1962).

[5] ADAMS and GOLDSTONE, *J. biol. Chem.*, **235**, 3492 (1960); DEKKER, E.E., *Biochim. biophys. Acta (Amst.)*, **40**, 174 (1960); GOLDSTONE and ADAMS, *J. biol. Chem.*, **237**, 3476 (1962).

[6] BACHHAWAT et al., *J. biol. Chem.*, **216**, 727 (1955); **219**, 539 (1956); DEL CAMPILLO-CAMPBELL et al., *Biochim. biophys. Acta (Amst.)*, **31**, 290 (1959).

[7] COON et al., *J. biol. Chem.*, **199**, 75 (1954); ROBINSON et al., *J. biol. Chem.*, **218**, 391 (1956).

[8] KINNORY et al., *J. biol. Chem.*, **212**, 385 (1955); ROBINSON et al., *J. biol. Chem.*, **224**, 1 (1957); RENDINA and COON, *J. biol. Chem.*, **225**, 523 (1957).

[9] CHARGAFF and SPRINSON, *J. biol. Chem.*, **151**, 273 (1943); SELIM and GREENBERG, *J. biol. Chem.*, **234**, 1474 (1959).

[10] GOLDSTEIN et al., *J. biol. Chem.*, **237**, 2855 (1962).

[11] BRAUNSHTEIN and VILENKINA, *Dokl. Akad. Nauk SSSR, Otd. Biokh.*, **66**, 243 (1949); MELTZER and SPRINSON, *J. biol. Chem.*, **197**, 461 (1952).

[12] MATSUO et al., *J. biol. Chem.*, **221**, 679 (1956); MATSUO and GREENBERG, *J. biol. Chem.*, **230**, 545 (1958).

[13] GREENBERG, D.M., in GREENBERG, D.M. (Ed.), *Metabolic Pathways*, vol. 2, Academic Press, New York, 1961, page 173.

[14] NAKADA et al., *J. biol. Chem.*, **216**, 583 (1955); NAKADA and SUND, *J. biol. Chem.*, **233**, 8 (1958); CRAWHALL and WATTS, *Biochem. J.*, **85**, 163 (1962).

[15] SHEMIN and RUSSELL, *J. Amer. chem. Soc.*, **75**, 4873 (1953); SHEMIN, D., *Harvey Lect. 1954–55*, **50**, 258 (1956); RIMINGTON, C., *Brit. med. J.*, **2**, 189 (1956).

[16] KUN, E., in GREENBERG, D.M. (Ed.), *Metabolic Pathways*, vol. 2, Academic Press, New York, 1961, page 237.

[17] SELIM and GREENBERG, *J. biol. Chem.*, **234**, 1474 (1959).

[18] DE LA HABA and CANTONI, *J. biol. Chem.*, **234**, 603 (1959); KUN, E., in GREENBERG, D.M. (Ed.), *Metabolic Pathways*, vol. 2, Academic Press, New York, 1961, page 237.

[19] TUSTANOFF and STERN, *Fed. Proc.*, **20**, 272 (1961); BAGCHI et al., *J. biol. Chem.*, **236**, 370 (1961); ROTHSTEIN et al., *J. biol. Chem.*, **237**, 2828 (1962).

[20] MITOMA, C., *Arch. Biochem.*, **60**, 476 (1956).

[21] HAGER et al., *J. biol. Chem.*, **225**, 935 (1957).

[22] EDWARDS and KNOX, *J. biol. Chem.*, **220**, 79 (1956).

[23] GHOLSON et al., *J. biol. Chem.*, **237**, PC2043 (1962); KREBS, H.A., in MUNRO and ALLISON (Eds.), *Mammalian Protein Metabolism*, vol. 1, Academic Press, New York, 1964, page 125; JACOBY and LA DU, *Biochem. biophys. Res. Commun.*, **8**, 352 (1962).

Degradation of food constituents other than carbohydrate, fat and protein (for references see page 401)

Foods contain a number of substances built up from molecules other than hexoses, fatty acids or amino acids. Some of these are not broken down in the body, but others are. To the latter group belong the constituents of nucleic acids and nucleotides (pentoses, deoxypentoses, purine bases, pyrimidine bases) and part of the cholesterol molecule. Quantitatively these substances form a very small part of the food and their contribution to the supply of energy is almost negligible.

Pentoses, reacting in the form of ribose 5-phosphate, can be converted to glucose 6-phosphate and triose phosphate by reactions of the pentose phosphate cycle [reactions (**3**) to (**8**) of Table 19, page 422]. Three molecules of ribose 5-phosphate form two molecules of glucose 6-phosphate and one molecule of glyceraldehyde phosphate.

2-Deoxyribose 5-phosphate can be split by aldolase to acetaldehyde and glyceraldehyde phosphate[1]:

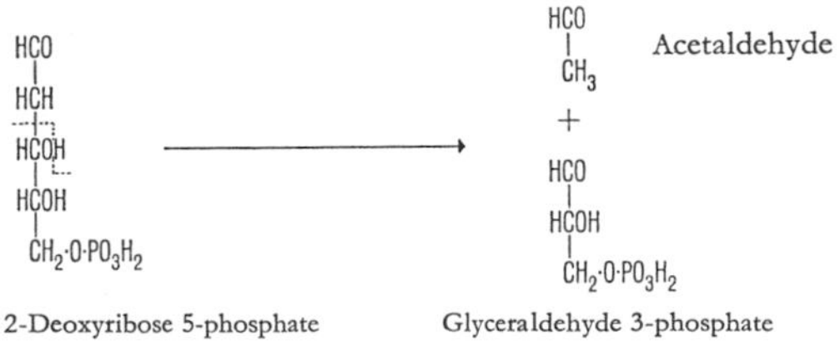

The acetaldehyde can be converted into acetyl-coenzyme A.

(continued on page 401)

Fig. 7 Degradation of purine bases in mammals

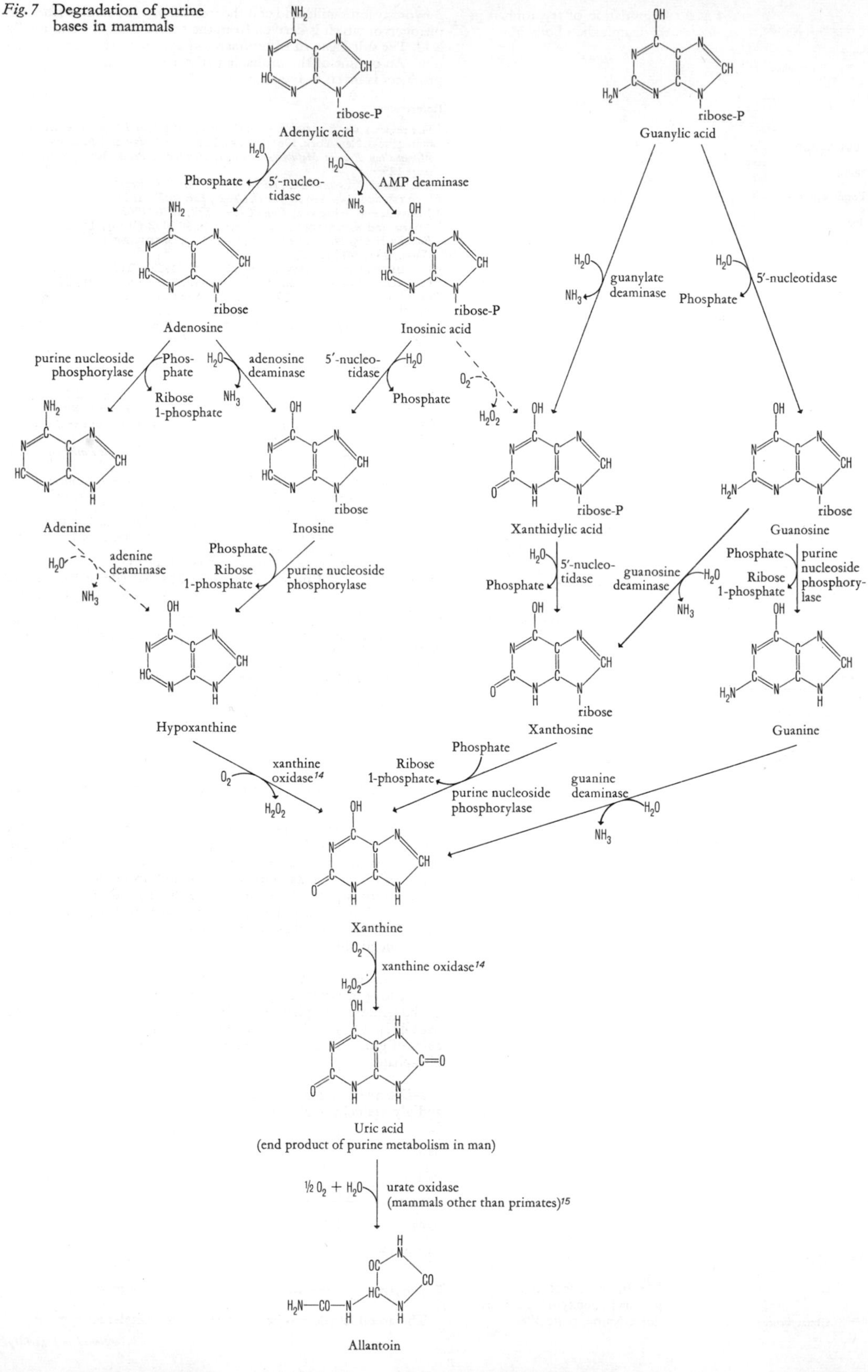

(continued from page 399)

Degradation of purine bases in man and mammals[12]. The degradation of the purine bases adenine and guanine involves hydrolytic deamination and oxidation. Both types of reactions can be entered by the respective nucleotides and nucleosides, and by the free purine bases. Deamination precedes oxidation but there are various pathways depending on whether deamination and oxidation precede or do not precede the fission of the nucleotide or nucleoside. The end-product of purine degradation is the same, irrespective of the route. It is uric acid in man and other primates, and allantoin in other mammals. Amphibians and fish degrade allantoin further to allantoic acid, urea and glyoxylic acid. Some lower species such as crustacea degrade urea to ammonia and carbon dioxide.

The various pathways are shown in Figure 7 opposite. The relative importance of the alternatives has not been accurately assessed. Reactions that occur readily and are widespread in mammals are indicated by full arrows, those that are of limited occurrence and relatively slow by broken arrows.

Purine deaminases. Three types of enzyme are known – adenine deaminase, adenosine deaminase and AMP deaminase – that hydrolyse adenine, adenosine and AMP respectively to yield ammonia and the corresponding derivative of hypoxanthine. Of these, the occurrence of adenine deaminase in mammals is uncertain. Adenosine deaminase occurs in most tissues of higher animals. AMP deaminase occurs abundantly in striated muscle but is relatively weak in other tissues, including heart muscle[13].

Three types of enzyme are known – guanine deaminase, guanosine deaminase, and guanylate deaminase – that hydrolyse guanine, guanosine and GMP respectively to yield ammonia and the corresponding derivative of xanthine. Each of these enzymes occurs in many tissues of higher animals. The relative contributions to purine catabolism of these different deamination reactions are not known.

Purine oxidases. The oxidation of purines can occur at the ribotide level or at the free base level. The oxidation of inosinic acid to xanthidylic acid is an intermediate stage in the synthesis of guanylic acid (see page 436), but the contribution of this reaction to the degradation of purines is probably very small, the chief oxidation reactions being those attacking the free purine bases.

Xanthine oxidase catalyses the oxidation of hypoxanthine to xanthine and of xanthine to uric acid. The enzyme occurs in milk and in many tissues[14].

Urate oxidase oxidizes uric acid to allantoin[15]. It occurs in liver and kidney of mammals other than man and primates.

Nucleotidases and purine nucleoside phosphorylases. The fission of nucleotides is hydrolytic, the products being nucleosides and inorganic phosphate. The fission of nucleosides in animals is phosphorolytic, the products being a purine base and ribose 1-phosphate. Micro-organisms also contain nucleoside hydrolases, but these have not so far been demonstrated in higher animals.

Degradation of pyrimidines. Cytosine and uracil are converted into β-alanine by the liver through the following reaction sequence[9]:

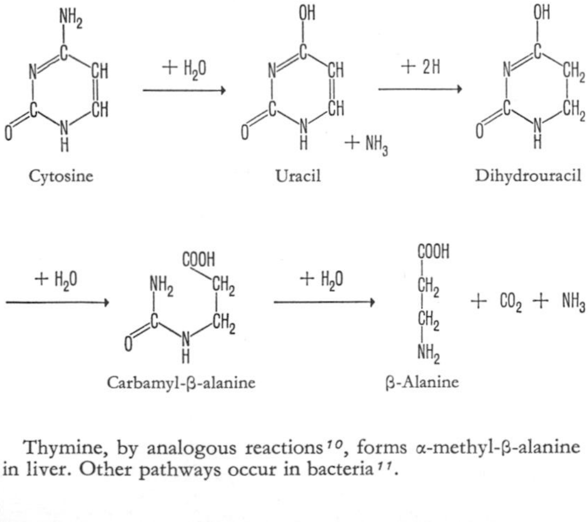

Thymine, by analogous reactions[10], forms α-methyl-β-alanine in liver. Other pathways occur in bacteria[11].

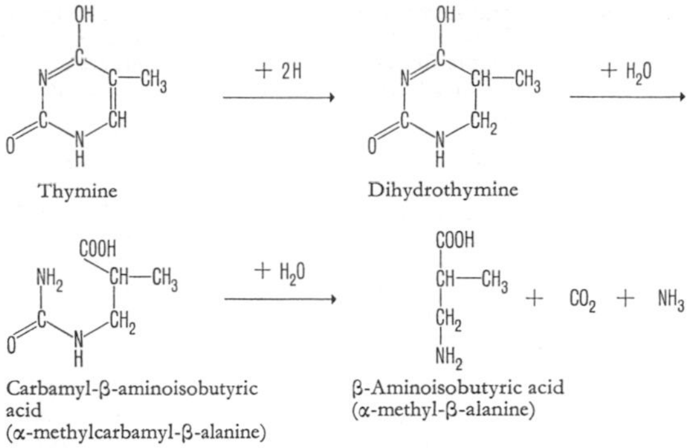

Both β-alanine and α-methyl-β-alanine can be further oxidized[2]. β-Alanine can enter a transamination reaction with α-ketoglutarate to form the semialdehyde of malonic acid, which is probably decarboxylated to acetaldehyde, a precursor of acetyl-coenzyme A[3]:

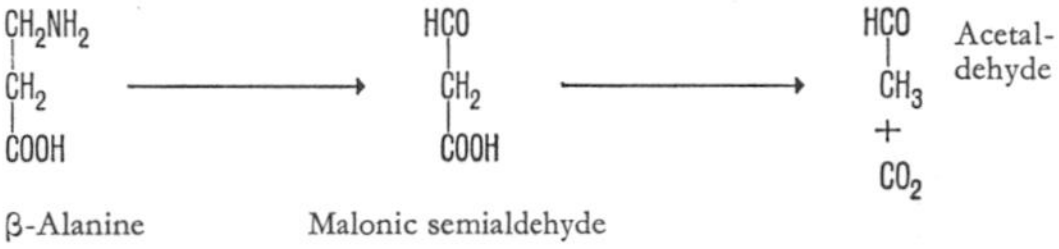

α-Methyl-β-alanine reacts in an analogous manner to give methylmalonic semialdehyde[4], which can form propionaldehyde and subsequently succinic acid via propionyl-coenzyme A.

About 5–10% of humans excrete α-methyl-β-alanine in the urine in quantities up to 300 mg daily[5]. This is assumed to be an inborn error of metabolism. It is probably due to an abnormality in the enzymes responsible for the degradation of α-methyl-β-alanine[6].

In *cholesterol*, only the side chain undergoes complete oxidation. A specific enzyme can cleave off the side chain, forming isocaproic acid and leaving the ring system in the form of pregnenolone[7]. Isocaproic acid in turn is broken down to propionic acid and acetyl-coenzyme A[8]. The ring system of cholesterol and the steroids is not oxidized to CO_2[7].

Other cell constituents that are essentially not oxidized in the body to CO_2 are the *iron porphyrins* (see pages 359 sq.) derived from haemoglobin and cytochromes (these are excreted in the form of bile pigments and their derivatives; see page 362), and the *uronic acids* (see page 323) contained in mucins, in hyaluronic acid and in the chondroitin sulphate of cartilage and tendons.

References

1 Racker, E., *J. biol. Chem.*, **196**, 347 (1952).
2 Roberts and Bregoff, *J. biol. Chem.*, **201**, 393 (1953).
3 Pihl and Fritzson, *J. biol. Chem.*, **215**, 345 (1955).
4 Kupiecki and Coon, *J. biol. Chem.*, **229**, 743 (1957).
5 Crumpler et al., *Nature*, **167**, 307 (1951).
6 Gartler, S.M., *Amer. J. hum. Genet.*, **11**, 257 (1959).
7 Siperstein and Chaikoff, *J. biol. Chem.*, **198**, 93 (1952); Staple et al., *J. biol. Chem.*, **219**, 845 (1956).
8 Atchley, W.A., *J. biol. Chem.*, **176**, 123 (1948).
9 Fink et al., *J. biol. Chem.*, **221**, 425 (1956); Canellakis, E.S., *J. biol. Chem.*, **221**, 315 (1956); Fritzson and Pihl, *J. biol. Chem.*, **226**, 229 (1957).
10 Fink et al., *Fed. Proc.*, **15**, 251 (1956).
11 Hayaishi and Kornberg, *J. biol. Chem.*, **197**, 717 (1952).
12 For a review see Schulman, M.P., in Greenberg, D.M. (Ed.), *Metabolic Pathways*, vol. 2, Academic Press, New York, 1961, page 389.
13 Conway and Cooke, *Biochem. J.*, **33**, 479 (1939).
14 For a review see Bray, R.C., in Boyer et al. (Eds.), *The Enzymes*, 2nd ed., vol. 7, Academic Press, New York, 1963, page 533.
15 For a review see Keilin, J., *Biol. Rev.*, **34**, 265 (1959); Mahler, H.R., in Boyer et al. (Eds.), *The Enzymes*, 2nd ed., vol. 8, Academic Press, New York, 1963, page 285.

Degradation of the principal foodstuffs

In surveying the reactions by which the basic constituents of foodstuffs are broken down it may be said that the degradation proceeds in two major stages. In the first stage the starting material – the small molecules produced by the process of digestion and consisting of several hexoses, glycerol, about twenty amino acids and a number of fatty acids – is incompletely burned. The products listed in Table 7, apart from carbon dioxide and water, are either acetic acid in the form of acetyl-coenzyme A or an intermediate of the tricarboxylic acid cycle, α-ketoglutarate, succinate, fumarate or oxaloacetate. Acetic acid constitutes the main product: two-thirds of the carbon of carbohydrate and glycerol, all the carbon of the common fatty acids and about half the carbon skeleton of amino acids yield acetyl-coenzyme A. α-Ketoglutarate arises from glutamic acid, histidine, arginine, citrulline, ornithine, proline and hydroxyproline; oxaloacetate from aspartate; fumarate from part of the benzene ring of tyrosine and phenylalanine; succinate from threonine, isoleucine, valine, methionine, α-aminobutyric acid, propionic acid and the three terminal carbon atoms of fatty acids with an odd number of carbon atoms.

The products of the first stage of the oxidative breakdown are completely oxidized in the second stage, the tricarboxylic acid cycle, which thus represents a common terminal pathway of oxidation shared by all foodstuffs. Almost two-thirds of the total energy released in the combustion of foodstuffs appears during the reactions of this cycle.

Any surplus oxaloacetate not required as a catalyst in the cycle can be decarboxylated to pyruvate, whence it is converted into acetyl-coenzyme A and undergoes complete oxidation.

Table 7 Survey of the products formed by the initial oxidative degradation reactions of the basic constituents of foodstuffs

These reactions all lead to acetyl-coenzyme A and/or the intermediates of the tricarboxylic acid cycle.

Starting material	Products of initial reactions (CO_2 omitted)
Glucose, other hexoses	2 acetyl-coenzyme A
Fatty acids (even-numbered chains of *n* C-atoms)	½ *n* acetyl-coenzyme A
Fatty acids (odd-numbered chains of *n* C-atoms)	½ (*n*−3) acetyl-coenzyme A 1 succinate (via propionyl-coenzyme A)
Glycerol, alanine, cysteine, cystine, serine	1 acetyl-coenzyme A
Glutamic acid, histidine, arginine, ornithine, citrulline, proline, hydroxyproline	1 α-ketoglutarate
Aspartic acid	1 oxaloacetate
Leucine	3 acetyl-coenzyme A
Isoleucine	1 acetyl-coenzyme A 1 succinate (via propionyl-coenzyme A)
Valine	1 succinate (via methyl-malonic semialdehyde
Norleucine	1 acetyl-coenzyme A
Norvaline	2 acetyl-coenzyme A 1 succinate (via propionyl-coenzyme A)
α-Aminobutyric acid, homoserine, homocysteine, methionine	1 succinate (via propionyl-coenzyme A)
Glycine*	1 acetyl-coenzyme A (via serine)
Threonine	1 succinate
Lysine	2 acetyl-coenzyme A
Phenylalanine, tyrosine	1 fumarate 2 acetyl-coenzyme A
Tryptophan	at most 3 acetyl-coenzyme A**

* Glycine may also be oxidized by a special cycle (see page 397).
** Other products are formed that are not oxidizable (see page 398).

In so far as substances other than carbohydrate, fat and amino acids can supply energy, their degradation follows pathways which, like those of carbohydrate, fat and amino acids, yield acetyl-coenzyme A and/or an intermediate of the tricarboxylic acid cycle.

Mechanism of biological oxidations

(for references see page 404)

General. The degradation reactions discussed so far take place when the foodstuff molecules are 'burned' by molecular oxygen. This 'combustion' is not, however, a direct reaction of molecular oxygen with the substrate but a transference of electrons, mediated by several complex enzyme systems, in which oxygen is the ultimate electron acceptor. In order to understand the action of these catalysts, it has to be borne in mind that biological oxidations include three types of reaction that at first sight appear to be different but are basically the same. The three types are illustrated by the following cases:

Case 1. Addition of oxygen atoms, for example:

$$CH_3\cdot CHO \xrightarrow{+O} CH_3\cdot COOH$$

Acetaldehyde → Acetic acid

Case 2. Removal of hydrogen atoms, for example:

$$CH_3\cdot CHOH\cdot COOH \xrightarrow{-2H} CH_3\cdot CO\cdot COOH$$

Lactic acid → Pyruvic acid

Case 3. Transformation of a metal from a lower to a higher valency state by removal of electrons, for example:

$$Fe^{++} \rightarrow Fe^{+++} + e^-$$

All three cases are seen to be basically similar – as removal of H atoms – if the participation of water is also considered:

Case 1 may then be formulated as

$$CH_3\cdot CHO + H_2O \rightarrow CH_3\cdot CH(OH)_2 \xrightarrow{-2H} CH_3\cdot COOH$$

Acetaldehyde; Hydrated form of acetaldehyde; Acetic acid

and case 3 as

$$2\,Fe^{++} + 2\,H_2O \xrightarrow{-2H} 2\,Fe^{+++} + 2\,OH^-$$

The common feature of all types of biological oxidations is a removal of electrons, although this is often either written as a removal of H (i.e., electron and proton) or as the addition of O atoms. There are instances in which neither H nor O atoms are directly involved, as in the oxidation of one heavy metal catalyst by another:

$$R\cdot Fe^{++} + R'\cdot Fe^{+++} \rightarrow R\cdot Fe^{+++} + R'\cdot Fe^{++}$$

Such reactions occur in living cells between iron porphyrins (cytochromes) in which the electrons travel more or less directly from one iron atom to another. Because there are cases where electron transfer is the only change, the formulation of oxidation as electron transport is looked upon as the most general and fundamental description of this process.

Biological oxidations may therefore be described in terms of the transfer of electrons, and the reactions whereby electrons are transferred from substrates to molecular oxygen are usually referred to as electron transport reactions.

The catalysts of biological oxidations[1,2]. Three major types of catalysts participate in biological oxidations. They are enzymes which have as prosthetic groups respectively pyridine nucleotides, flavin nucleotides and iron porphyrins. The prosthetic groups undergo reversible oxidation and reduction. The catalysts thus exist in (at least) two forms, oxidized and reduced. The mechanism of reduction is illustrated by reaction (**1**) for a pyridine nucleotide, and by reaction (**2**) for a flavin nucleotide:

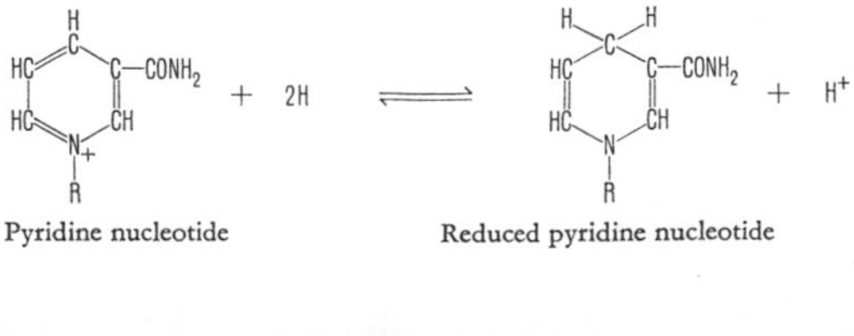

(**1**)

Pyridine nucleotide — Reduced pyridine nucleotide

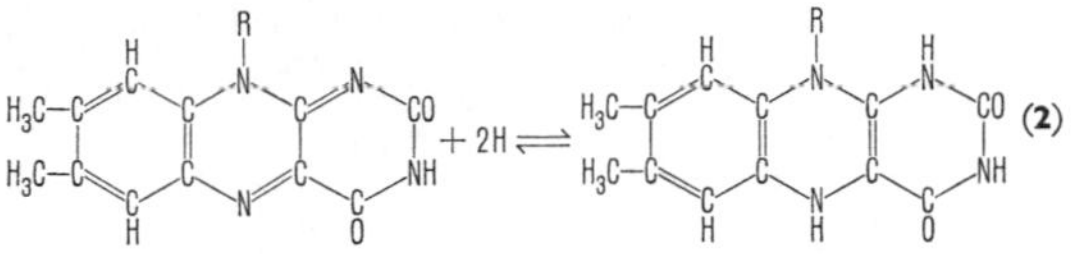

Flavin nucleotide Reduced flavin nucleotide

These reactions are written as similar to case 2 above. The iron atoms of iron porphyrin enzymes are reversibly oxidized and reduced as described in case 3 above.

When mediating the reactions between substrate and molecular oxygen, i.e., when transferring electrons (or H atoms) from substrate to oxygen, these catalysts react in a characteristic order governed by their thermodynamic properties. These properties are indicated by the oxidation–reduction potentials of the catalysts:

Catalyst	E'_0 (volts)
Oxygen electrode ($H_2O \rightleftharpoons \frac{1}{2}O_2 + 2H + 2e^-$)	+ 0.81
Cytochrome c	+ 0.25[3]
Flavin nucleotides (free)	− 0.20[3]
Pyridine nucleotides (free)	− 0.32[3]
Hydrogen electrode ($H_2 \rightleftharpoons 2H^+ + 2e^-$)	− 0.42

As seen from this table, the potentials of the electron carriers are such that the reduced form of pyridine nucleotides can act as reductant of the flavin nucleotides which, in turn, can act as reductant of the oxidized cytochromes. The order in which the catalysts transport electrons from the substrate to molecular oxygen may therefore be expressed in the following series of reactions:

Substrate + pyridine nucleotide → oxidized substrate + reduced pyridine nucleotide **(a)**

Reduced pyridine nucleotide + flavin nucleotide → pyridine nucleotide + reduced flavin nucleotide **(b)**

Reduced flavin nucleotide + 2 Fe^{+++}-porphyrin → flavin nucleotide + 2 Fe^{++}-porphyrin + 2 H^+ **(c)**

2 Fe^{++}-porphyrin + 2 H^+ + $\frac{1}{2}O_2$ → 2 Fe^{+++}-porphyrin + H_2O **(d)**

Sum: Substrate + $\frac{1}{2}O_2$ → oxidized substrate + H_2O

Reactions (**b**), (**c**) and (**d**) are referred to as the 'electron transport system' or the 'respiratory chain'.

There are many variants of this basic scheme; firstly, because there are two pyridine nucleotides, many flavoproteins (some containing nonhaem iron or molybdenum) and many iron porphyrins; secondly, because other types of reactions such as

flavoprotein 1 + reduced flavoprotein 2
→ reduced flavoprotein 1 + flavoprotein 2

or

ferrous iron porphyrin 1 + ferric iron porphyrin 2
→ ferric iron porphyrin 1 + ferrous iron porphyrin 2

can be interspersed in the above series; thirdly, because additional catalysts may take part. The most important among these are the recently discovered ubiquinones, also referred to as coenzyme Q[4]. A representative is 'Q_{10}':

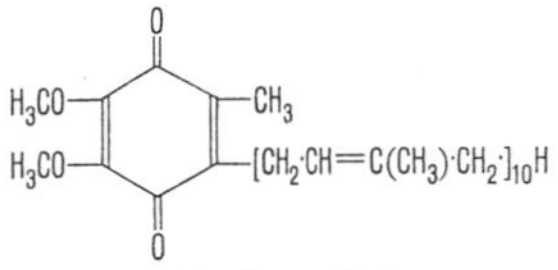

Ubiquinone (Q_{10})

Other ubiquinones differ from this structure by the number of isoprenoid units in the side chain and are accordingly called Q_4, Q_6, Q_8, etc. Hydrogen transfer by these coenzymes is effected by the reversible interconversion of the quinone and the hydroqui-

Fig. 8 Diagram of the pathway of electron transport showing the stages where ADP is converted to ATP and where specific inhibitors act

Electron carriers, the role of which cannot yet be clearly defined (ubiquinone, vitamin K, vitamin E) have been omitted. Where the sequence in which the catalysts are arranged is uncertain they are bracketed together.

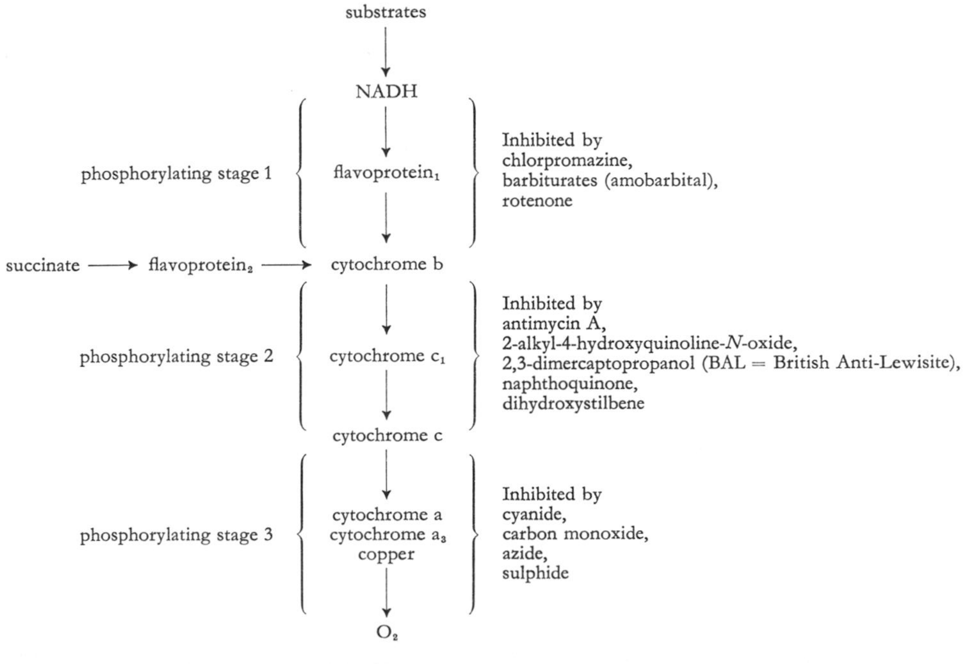

none. While the fact of reduction and reoxidation of ubiquinones is firmly established, the precise location of these catalysts in electron transport is not yet fully known. One of the places appears to be in the oxidation of succinate, another near cytochrome b[2]. There is evidence that vitamin E and vitamin K are also involved in the respiratory chain[5].

Figure 8 (page 403) illustrates schematically the pathway of electron transport and indicates the stages where ADP is converted to ATP and where specific inhibitors act.

References

[1] For reviews of earlier work see BALL, E.G., *Ann. N.Y.Acad. Sci.*, **45**, 363 (1944); HERBERT, D., *Ann. Rep. Progr. Chem.*, **47**, 335 (1951); SLATER, E.C., *Proceedings of the Third International Congress of Biochemistry, Brussels 1955*, New York, 1956, page 264; MAHLER and GREEN, *Science*, **120**, 7 (1954); MAHLER, H.R., *Proceedings of the Third International Congress of Biochemistry, Brussels 1955*, New York, 1956, page 252; LEHNINGER, A.L., *The Mitochondrion*, Benjamin, New York, 1964; ERNSTER and LEE, *Ann. Rev. Biochem.*, **33**, 729 (1964); RACKER, E., *Mechanisms in Bioenergetics*, Academic Press, New York, 1965.

[2] GRIFFITHS, D.E., in CAMPBELL and GREVILLE (Eds.), *Essays in Biochemistry*, vol. 1, Academic Press, London, 1965, page 91.

[3] Values from BURTON, K., in KREBS and KORNBERG, *Ergebn. Physiol.*, **49**, 212 (1957).

[4] WOLSTENHOLME and O'CONNOR (Eds.), *Ciba Foundation Symposium on Quinones in Electron Transport*, Churchill, London, 1961.

[5] DONALDSON et al., *J. biol. Chem.*, **233**, 572 (1958); CRANE, F. L., *Biochemistry*, **1**, 510 (1962).

The key position of adenosine triphosphate (ATP) in biological energy transformations[1]

One of the outstanding advances in the understanding of energy metabolism is the appreciation of the fact that the energy derived from the degradation of foodstuffs can be utilized for most purposes only if it is first transformed into a special type of chemical energy. This is the energy residing in the pyrophosphate bonds of adenosine triphosphate (ATP), which is released when these bonds are hydrolysed to form inorganic orthophosphate (P) or pyrophosphate (PP), adenosine diphosphate (ADP) and adenosine monophosphate (adenylic acid, AMP):

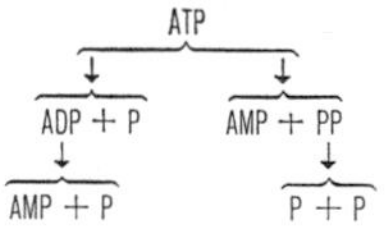

Pyrophosphate bonds release more free energy on hydrolysis (11–13 kcal according to conditions) than ester–phosphate bonds (2–4 kcal). They are therefore referred to as 'energy-rich'. It is the hydrolysis of the pyrophosphate bonds of ATP that provides the energy necessary for the various kinds of work performed by living cells, such as the contraction of muscle, the production of secretions, the activities of the nervous system and the synthesis of cell constituents.

The pyrophosphate bonds used up during the activities of the cells are resynthesized at the expense of the energy liberated by the degradation of foodstuffs. The synthesis of pyrophosphate bonds may in fact be looked upon as the first major object of the biological energy transformations. Special chemical mechanisms are required for the coupling between pyrophosphate bond synthesis and foodstuff degradation. It is evident that many hundreds of separate reactions occur when foodstuffs are degraded, but owing to the special arrangement of the metabolic processes coupling between degradation and pyrophosphate bond synthesis occurs only at a few stages. In all, six types of reaction are known in which energy becomes available for the synthesis of ATP. Two such stages occur in anaerobic glycolysis: when one molecule of glucose is converted into lactic acid two molecules of ATP are resynthesized from ADP and inorganic phosphate (Table 3, page 389). There are no more than four types of step in the course of all the oxidative reactions where ATP is synthesized. The oxidative degradation of the substrate itself, i.e., the removal of two hydrogen atoms and their transfer to pyridine nucleotide, as a rule does not supply energy. Energy is liberated when the hydrogen atoms or electrons are transferred from the pyridine nucleotides to molecular oxygen through the reactions (**b**), (**c**) and (**d**) discussed on page 403. Each of these three steps leads to the synthesis of one pyrophosphate bond ('oxidative phosphorylation'). The fourth step of the oxidative metabolism coupled with phosphorylation consists of reactions of type (**a**) (page 403) where the substrate is an α-ketonic acid. Reactions of this type where the substrate is not an α-ketonic acid do not yield appreciable amounts of energy and therefore cannot support the synthesis of pyrophosphate bonds.

In spite of intensive studies, the chemical mechanism by which the coupling between pyrophosphate synthesis and reactions (**b**), (**c**) and (**d**) is effected is still essentially unknown. For reviews of the present state of knowledge see the literature[3–5].

Some information is available about the coupling mechanism between ATP synthesis and reactions of type (**a**) with α-ketonic acids as substrates. In this case an acyl-coenzyme A derivative is formed from the α-ketonic acid by the reactions described for pyruvate on page 391. Thus α-ketoglutarate yields succinyl-coenzyme A. The latter reacts as follows:

succinyl-coenzyme A + guanosine diphosphate + P
→ succinate + coenzyme A + guanosine triphosphate

Phosphoryl succinate or phosphoryl-coenzyme A may be intermediates in this reaction though neither has as yet been identified[2]. Guanosine triphosphate can transfer phosphate to ADP:

guanosine triphosphate + ADP
→ guanosine diphosphate + ATP

ATP contains two 'energy-rich' pyrophosphate bonds. It is probable that only the terminal bond serves as an immediate source of energy, or can be directly resynthesized. The second pyrophosphate bond is used to re-phosphorylate ADP according to the reaction

$$2\,\text{ADP} \rightleftharpoons \text{AMP} + \text{ATP}$$

This reaction is catalysed by the enzyme adenylate kinase present in all tissues. The balance of this reaction plus the hydrolysis of ATP to ADP + P represents an hydrolysis of ADP to AMP + P. In reverse the reaction represents a mechanism for the re-phosphorylation of AMP.

References

[1] For bibliography see KREBS and KORNBERG, *Ergebn. Physiol.*, **49**, 212 (1957).

[2] SANADI et al., *Biochim. biophys. Acta (Amst.)*, **13**, 146 (1954); **14**, 434 (1954); KAUFMAN, S., *J. biol. Chem.*, **216**, 153 (1955); COHN, M., *Biochim. biophys. Acta (Amst.)*, **20**, 92 (1956).

[3] GRIFFITHS, D.E., in CAMPBELL and GREVILLE (Eds.), *Essays in Biochemistry*, vol. 1, Academic Press, London, 1965, page 91.

[4] RACKER, E., *Mechanisms in Bioenergetics*, Academic Press, New York, 1965.

[5] PULLMAN and SCHATZ, *Ann. Rev. Biochem.*, **36**, 539 (1967).

Digestive enzymes

This section describes the specific enzymes the combined action of which is responsible for the digestion of foodstuffs. Each enzyme catalyses the hydrolysis of one compound or of a series of closely related compounds. (For a general review of enzymes and enzyme action see pages 382–386.)

Proteolytic enzymes (proteases, peptide hydrolases [peptidases])

These are enzymes catalysing the hydrolytic cleavage of peptide bonds:

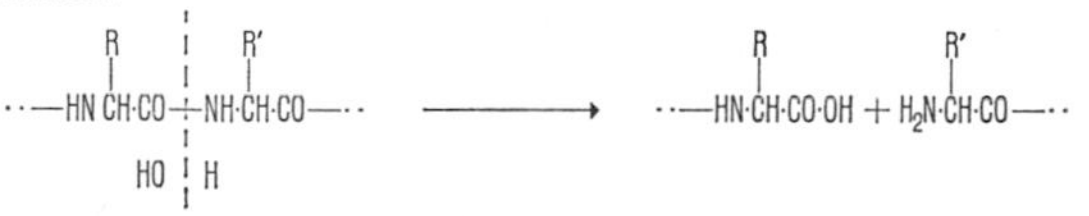

They may be divided into two main classes:

1. *Peptidyl-peptide hydrolases (endopeptidases)*, which act on proteins and peptides by hydrolysing 'internal' peptide linkages, i.e., those situated away from the ends of peptide chains.
2. *α-Amino-acyl-peptide hydrolases, peptidyl-amino-acid hydrolases (exopeptidases)*, which catalyse the hydrolysis of peptide bonds situated at the ends of peptide chains. These enzymes are specific for peptides possessing one or more free terminal α-amino or α-carboxyl groups.

Members of both classes of proteases are widely distributed in mammalian tissues. Those of the gastrointestinal tract are discussed in Tables 10 and 11, pages 406–409, those of other tissues in Table 12 (pages 410–411).

Glycoside hydrolases (glycosidases)

Carbohydrates are digested by these enzymes, which catalyse the hydrolysis of glycosidic bonds:

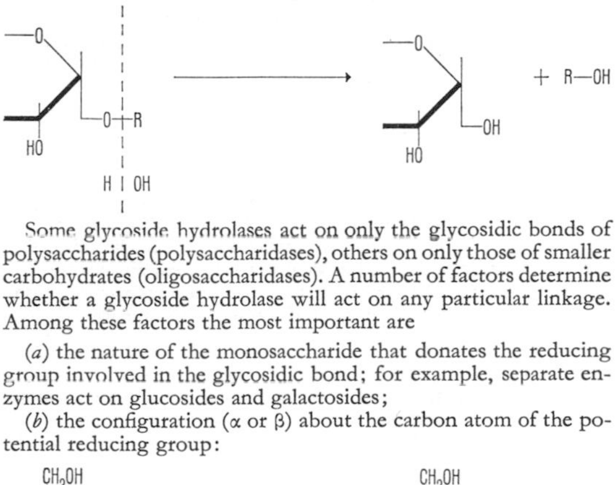

Some glycoside hydrolases act on only the glycosidic bonds of polysaccharides (polysaccharidases), others on only those of smaller carbohydrates (oligosaccharidases). A number of factors determine whether a glycoside hydrolase will act on any particular linkage. Among these factors the most important are

(*a*) the nature of the monosaccharide that donates the reducing group involved in the glycosidic bond; for example, separate enzymes act on glucosides and galactosides;

(*b*) the configuration (α or β) about the carbon atom of the potential reducing group:

α β

(*c*) the configuration (D or L) of the monosaccharide bearing the potential reducing group. In general, mammalian glycoside hydrolases act only at linkages of the D-configuration;

(*d*) the size of the heterocyclic sugar ring. Usually, glycosidases that act on aldohexosides are specific for linkages in which the aldohexose is in the pyranose form, whilst those acting on ketohexosides require the substrate to be in the furanose form:

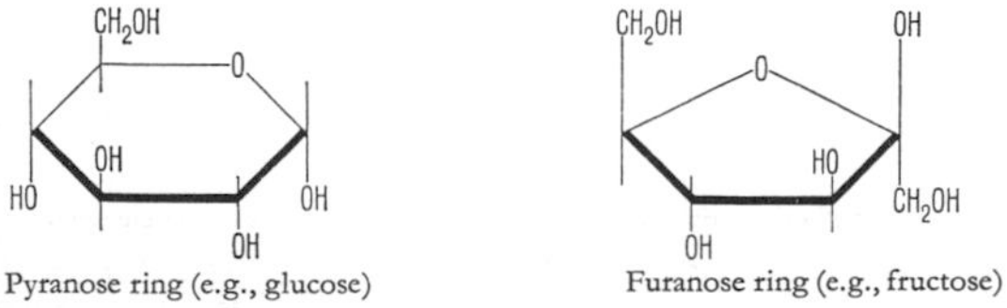

Pyranose ring (e.g., glucose) Furanose ring (e.g., fructose)

The general properties of mammalian glycoside hydrolases are described in Table 13 (pages 411–413). For their content in the mucosa of the human small intestine see page 413.

Lipases and other ester hydrolases (esterases)

Fats and other esters are hydrolysed by the action of enzymes that have been subdivided into

1. *Lipases*, thought to act predominantly on undissolved substrates (either fats or simple esters), and
2. *Fatty acid ester hydrolases (esterases proper)* acting on substrates in true solution (i.e., simple esters rather than fats)[7]. The general action of this group of enzymes is to hydrolyse ester linkages and may be formulated as follows:

Ester Fatty acid Alcohol

The fatty acid ester hydrolases of the gastrointestinal tract are discussed in Table 14 (page 414). Other lipases such as those of serum, leucocytes, erythrocytes, cerebrospinal fluid, milk, pleural effusions, lymph, liver, lung, brain, muscle, skin, testes, etc., behave similarly; like those of the gastrointestinal tract, they hydrolyse fats and short-chain fatty acid esters.

Phosphoric ester hydrolases (phosphatases)

Mammalian tissues contain a variety of unspecific esterases which have not yet been obtained in a pure form. Some of these enzymes catalyse the hydrolysis of the ester linkages between short-chain fatty acids and alcohol, others hydrolyse esters of the type R·OR′, where R is not a carboxylic acid. The largest group of these enzymes is formed by the *phosphatases*. These may be further classified as

1. *Phosphoric monoester hydrolases* (phosphomonoesterases), hydrolysing monoesters of phosphoric acid:

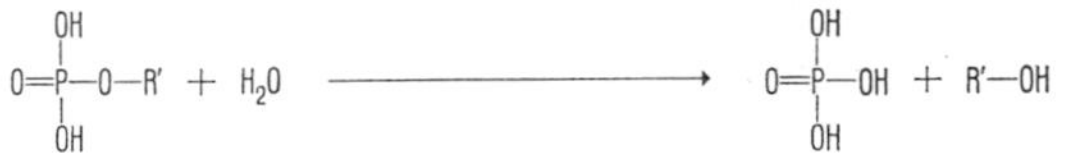

For example, glucose 6-phosphate is hydrolysed to glucose and phosphate.

2. *Phosphoric diester hydrolases* (phosphodiesterases), hydrolysing substrates such as nucleic acids, or the synthetic substrate diphenyl orthophosphate, at one of the ester linkages:

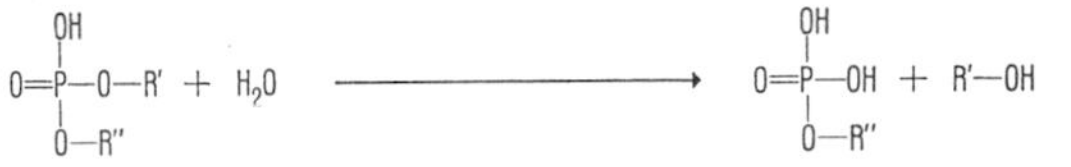

3. *Pyrophosphatases*, hydrolysing the pyrophosphate linkages of salts of pyrophosphoric acid and of pyrophosphate esters:

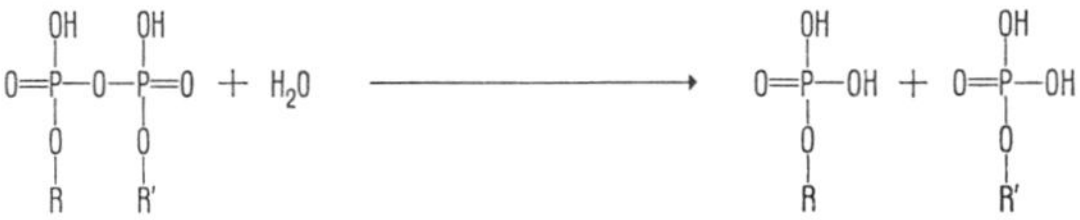

4. *Metaphosphatases*, hydrating metaphosphates to orthophosphates:

$$(HPO_3)_n + n\,H_2O \rightarrow n\,H_3PO_4$$

These have not been demonstrated to occur in the mammalian body.

The phosphoric ester hydrolases are described in Table 15 (pages 415–416), those acting on phospholipids and their metabolic products in Table 16 (page 417).

Sulphuric ester hydrolases (sulphatases)

These enzymes catalyse the hydrolysis of esters of sulphuric acid:

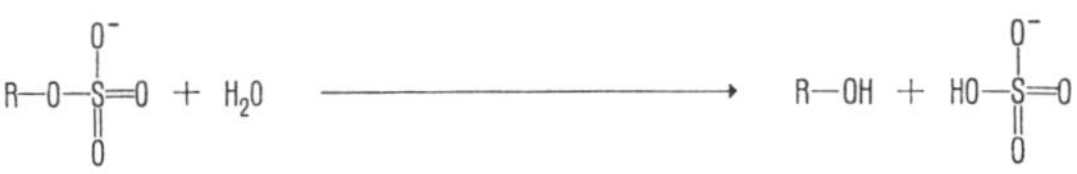

They may be distinguished according to the nature of the sulphuric acid esters they hydrolyse.

Nucleases

Ribonucleases (RNAases) and deoxyribonucleases (DNAases) catalyse the cleavage of ribonucleic acid (RNA) and deoxyribonucleic acid (DNA) respectively (Table 17, pages 418–419). They are present in most if not all tissues.

Of the RNAases only pancreatic RNAase has been studied extensively. The enzyme is a specific phosphodiesterase hydrolysing certain phosphoric ester linkages of RNA but not of DNA. The end-products of the prolonged action of pancreatic RNAase are 3′-uridylic acid, 3′-cytidylic acid, and a large number of dialysable polynucleotides of varying degrees of polymerization. The terminal nucleotides of these polynucleotides are all either 3′-uridylic acid or 3′-cytidylic acid.

The initial action of RNAase on RNA probably involves mainly the 'phosphotransferase' action of the enzyme. The first step consists of the cleavage of the phosphodiester bond between the 3′- and 5′-positions of the ribose moieties of the RNA molecule, with the formation of oligonucleotides terminated by cyclic 2′,3′-phosphates. These terminal groups are split off (when the preceding unit in the RNA chain contains pyrimidine) as free mononucleotide cyclic phosphates and are then hydrolysed with the formation of the corresponding nucleoside 3′-phosphate[2]. The mode of attack of the enzyme on a hypothetical part of an RNA molecule is shown in Figure 9. Several enzymes have been reported to attack RNA with the production of nucleoside 5′-phosphates.

Several types of DNAases are present in various tissues[3]; of these, pancreatic DNAase (DNAase I) has been studied most extensively. The enzyme is a specific phosphodiesterase that hydrolyses certain phosphoric ester linkages of DNA. Some preparations appear to act also on RNA. The end-products of the prolonged action of DNAase on DNA are mainly di- and tri-nucleotides as well as small amounts of mononucleotides and other polynucleotides. All the fragments produced are 5′-nucleotides. This indicates that pancreatic DNAase specifically hydrolyses nucleoside 5′-phosphodiesters with the resulting liberation of the corresponding nucleoside 5′-phosphates (Figure 10). The enzyme appears to have a preference for action on linkages between purine and pyrimidine nucleotides. A DNAase from spleen and thymus (DNAase II) differs from DNAase I in many of its properties. In particular, DNA digestion by DNAase II produces more mononucleotides, considerably fewer dinucleotides, and much larger amounts of the higher oligonucleotides. All these reaction products are terminated by 3′-phosphates.

The products of the action of RNAase and DNAase are broken down further by other phosphodiesterases and phosphatases (see Table 17, pages 418–419) to yield nucleotides and nucleosides. The latter are then degraded by phosphorolysis to yield purines and pyrimidines and pentose 1-phosphate, or by hydrolysis to yield purines and pyrimidines, pentose and inorganic phosphate.

Fig. 10 The specificity of pancreatic deoxyribonuclease

The ester linkage attacked by the enzyme is indicated by a broken arrow.

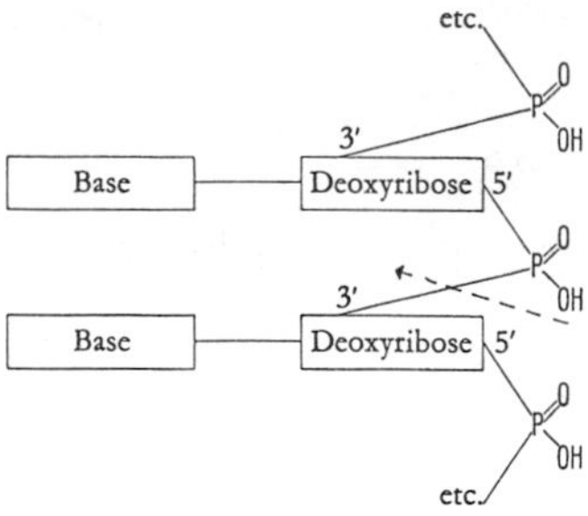

Fig. 9 Reactions catalysed by pancreatic ribonuclease

The 5′-ester linkages attacked are indicated by broken arrows, those not attacked by crossed arrows. The enzyme does not attack 3′-ester linkages.

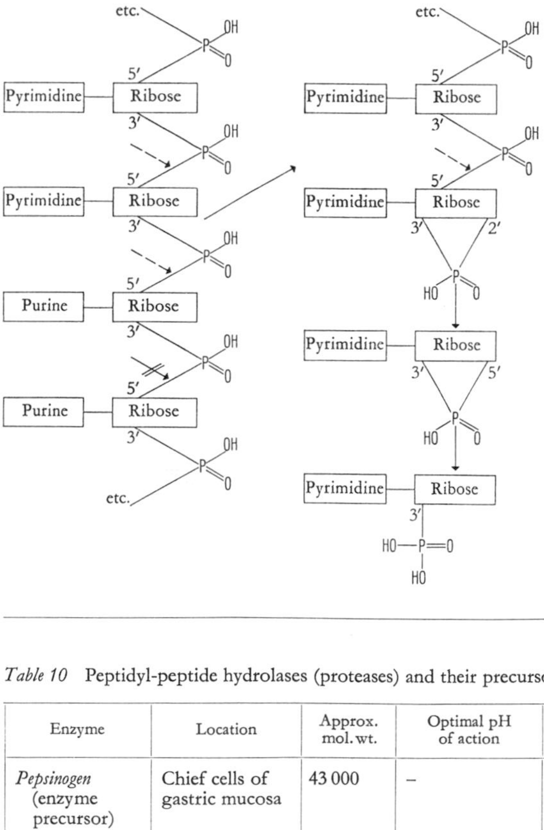

References

[1] Hofstee, B.H.J., in Boyer et al. (Eds.), *The Enzymes*, 2nd ed., vol. 4, Academic Press, New York, 1960, page 485.

[2] Anfinsen and White, in Boyer et al. (Eds.), *The Enzymes*, 2nd ed., vol. 5, Academic Press, New York, 1961, page 95.

[3] Laskowski, M., in Boyer et al. (Eds.), *The Enzymes*, 2nd ed., vol. 5, Academic Press, New York, 1961, page 123.

Table 10 Peptidyl-peptide hydrolases (proteases) and their precursors in the gastrointestinal tract *(for references see page 408)*

Enzyme	Location	Approx. mol. wt.	Optimal pH of action	Reaction catalysed*	Remarks
Pepsinogen (enzyme precursor)	Chief cells of gastric mucosa	43 000	–	–	Formation of pepsin from pepsinogen is autocatalytic at pH < 5 (maximally at pH 2)[1] with loss of (a) 'pepsin inhibitor', containing 29 amino acids, of mol.wt. 3242[2], and (b) 5 smaller peptides of aggregate mol.wt. ca. 4000[2,3]

* The specificity relationships listed are those elucidated by the action of the enzymes on synthetic peptides; they are not necessarily those of the enzymes acting on proteins *in vivo*.

Table 10 (continued) Peptidyl-peptide hydrolases (proteases) and their precursors in the gastrointestinal tract

Enzyme*	Location	Approx. mol.wt.	Optimal pH of action	Reaction catalysed**	Remarks
3.4.4.1 *Pepsin*	Gastric juice	36 000	1.8–4.4 Depends on the nature of the substrate[4]	—CO·NH·CH(R)·CO ⋮ NH·CH(R′)·CO— where R′ = *p*-hydroxybenzyl or benzyl (from L-tyrosine or L-phenylalanine; D-isomers not attacked)	Endopeptidase: attacks most proteins except some protamines and keratins. Denatured proteins are attacked more readily than native proteins, and the pH range of action is wider. It is assumed that the initial step of peptic hydrolysis is the unfolding of the peptide chain
3.4.4.2 *Pepsin B*[5]	Gastric juice	36 000	ca. 3	Similar to pepsin	Formerly known as parapepsin. Differs from pepsin in the N-terminal amino-acid residue, phosphorus content, and stability at pH 6.9[6]
3.4.4.22 *Gastricsin*[7]	Gastric juice	–	ca. 3	Similar to pepsin	More heat-stable than pepsin and has a lower electrophoretic mobility on starch gel; could be an autolysis product of pepsin[7]
3.4.4.3 *Rennin*	Stomach of young animals	40 000	Milk clotting ca. 5; proteolysis (haemoglobin) 3.7[8]	Similar to pepsin[9]. The crystalline enzyme (unlike commercial rennet) does not have phosphoamidase activity	Clots milk and liberates peptones from the α-casein contained therein
Trypsinogen (enzyme precursor)	Pancreas	24 500[10]	–	–	Nonenzymatic precursor of trypsin, into which it is converted by enteropeptidase and, autocatalytically, by trypsin, with elimination of a hexapeptide of structure Val–(Asp)$_4$–Lys from the N-terminal end by scission of a Lys–Ile bond
3.4.4.4 *Trypsin*	Intestinal secretion	23 800	7–8	—CO·NH·CH(R)·CO ⋮ X where R = δ-guanidino-*n*-propyl or ε-amino-*n*-butyl (from L-arginine or L-lysine)	An endopeptidase completely and reversibly inhibited by polypeptides, of mol.wt. ranging from 6000 to 30 000, occurring naturally in pancreas, colostrum, egg white (ovomucoid) and lima and soya beans[11]
Chymotrypsinogen A (enzyme precursor)	Acinar cells of pancreas	25 000[12]	–	–	Cationic at pH 8 (isoelectric point ca. 9.1). Converted to δ-chymotrypsin via a sequence involving (a) cleavage of the Arg–Ile bond of chymotrypsinogen A to form the highly active π-chymotrypsin; (b) autolytic cleavage of a (second) bond of the C-terminal sequence of π-chymotrypsin, with elimination of the dipeptide serylarginine, to form δ-chymotrypsin[13]. Subsequent attack, by autolysis and/or trypsin, may yield chymotrypsin(s) A[14]
Chymotrypsinogen B[15] (enzyme precursor)	Acinar cells of pancreas	21 600[16]	–	–	Anionic at pH 8 (isoelectric point ca. 5.2). Nonenzymic precursor of chymotrypsin B

* The numbers and trivial names are those recommended by the Enzyme Commission of the International Union of Biochemistry (see pages 385 and 386).

** The specificity relationships listed are those elucidated by the action of the enzymes on synthetic peptides; they are not necessarily those of the enzymes acting on proteins *in vivo*.

Table 10 (concluded) Peptidyl-peptide hydrolases (proteases) and their precursors in the gastrointestinal tract

Enzyme*	Location	Approx. mol. wt.	Optimal pH of action	Reaction catalysed**	Remarks
3.4.4.5 *Chymotrypsin A*	Pancreas	25 000	7.8	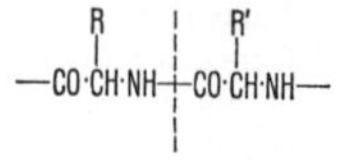 where for maximum activity R' is phenyl or substituted phenyl. However, other bonds (such as L-leucyl or L-asparaginyl)[14] are also split at high rates	Derived from chymotrypsinogen A; contains three open peptide chains held together by disulphide bridges. Unlike trypsin, clots milk but not blood. Irreversibly inhibited by *p*-nitrophenyl phosphate[17]
3.4.4.6 *Chymotrypsin B*	Pancreas	23 600[16]	ca. 8	Similar to chymotrypsin A	Unlike chymotrypsin A, splits acyl-tryptophan esters very slowly in presence of 30% methanol[18]
3.4.4.7 *Pancreatopeptidase E*[19]	Pancreas	–	ca. 8	Hydrolyses peptide linkages, preferentially those adjacent to neutral L-amino-acid residues	Formerly known as elastase
3.4.4.8 *Enteropeptidase*	Intestinal secretion	–	ca. 6	Converts trypsinogen to trypsin	Exact mode of action unknown, since maximal activation of trypsinogen occurs under conditions where autocatalytic activation is also maximal. Enteropeptidase is probably a glycoprotein[20]

* The numbers and trivial names are those recommended by the Enzyme Commission of the International Union of Biochemistry (see pages 385 and 386).
** The specificity relationships listed are those elucidated by the action of the enzymes on synthetic peptides; they are not necessarily those of the enzymes acting on proteins *in vivo*.

References

1 Herriott, R.M., *J. gen. Physiol.*, **22**, 65 (1938/39).
2 van Vunakis and Herriott, *Biochim. biophys. Acta (Amst.)*, **22**, 537 (1956).
3 van Vunakis and Herriott, *Biochim. biophys. Acta (Amst.)*, **23**, 600 (1957).
4 Northrop, J.H., *J. gen. Physiol.*, **5**, 263 (1922/23); Fruton and Bergmann, *J. biol. Chem.*, **127**, 627 (1939).
5 Sable and Guarino, *J. biol. Chem.*, **196**, 395 (1952).
6 Ryle and Porter, *Biochem. J.*, **73**, 75 (1959).
7 Tang et al., *J. biol. Chem.*, **234**, 1174 (1959).
8 Berridge, N.J., in Colowick and Kaplan (Eds.), *Methods in Enzymology*, vol. 2, Academic Press, New York, 1955, page 69.
9 Fish, J.C., *Nature*, **180**, 345 (1957).
10 Kay et al., *J. biol. Chem.*, **236**, 118 (1961).
11 For a review see Laskowski and Laskowski, *Advanc. Protein Chem.*, **9**, 203 (1954).
12 Bluhm and Kendrew, *Biochim. biophys. Acta (Amst.)*, **20**, 562 (1956).
13 Bettelheim and Neurath, *J. biol. Chem.*, **212**, 241 (1955).
14 Rovery et al., *Biochim. biophys. Acta (Amst.)*, **23**, 608 (1957).
15 Keith et al., *J. biol. Chem.*, **170**, 227 (1947).
16 Smith et al., *J. biol. Chem.*, **191**, 639 (1951).
17 Hartley and Kilby, *Biochem. J.*, **50**, 672 (1952).
18 Keller et al., *J. biol. Chem.*, **233**, 344 (1958).
19 Lewis et al., *J. biol. Chem.*, **222**, 705 (1956); **234**, 2304 (1959).
20 Yamashina, I., *Ark. Kemi*, **9**, 225 (1956); Yamashina, I., *Biochim. biophys. Acta (Amst.)*, **20**, 433 (1956).

Table 11 α-Aminoacyl-peptide hydrolases and peptidyl-amino-acid hydrolases in the gastrointestinal tract[1]

A large number of different exopeptidases have been recognized as occurring in the gastrointestinal tract. They are distinguished from each other mainly in their specificity of action on synthetic peptides. Relatively few have been purified extensively, and the list given here includes only those that have been well characterized.

Enzyme*	Location	Approx. mol. wt.	Optimal pH of action	Reaction catalysed**	Remarks
Dipeptidases: 3.4.3.1 *Glycyl-glycine dipeptidase* 3.4.3.6 *Iminodipeptidase* (prolinase) 3.4.3.7 *Imidodipeptidase* (prolidase)	Intestinal secretions	–	ca. 8	Hydrolyse dipeptides, with various degrees of specificity	The component members of this class of enzymes have not yet been sufficiently characterized to merit individual description. Glycyl-glycine dipeptidase[2] appears to be highly specific for this peptide linkage. Iminodipeptidase appears to act only on dipeptides which bear the free imino group of L-proline or hydroxy-L-proline[3], whereas imidodipeptidase splits peptide bonds involving the nitrogen of these compounds[2]

* The numbers and trivial names are those recommended by the Enzyme Commission of the International Union of Biochemistry (see pages 385 and 386).
** The specificity relationships listed are those elucidated by the action of the enzymes on synthetic peptides; they are not necessarily those of the enzymes acting on proteins *in vivo*.

Table 11 (continued) α-Aminoacyl-peptide hydrolases and peptidyl-amino-acid hydrolases in the gastrointestinal tract

Enzyme*	Location	Approx. mol. wt.	Optimal pH of action	Reaction catalysed**	Remarks
Procarboxypeptidase A (enzyme precursor)	Acinar cells of pancreas	96 000	–	–	Nonenzymatic precursor of carboxypeptidase A. Is more acidic and larger than the enzyme to which it is converted by trypsin. In this process, approx. 40 small peptides (average mol.wt. ca. 1500) are released, but the enzymatic activity is confined to carboxypeptidase A
3.4.2.1 *Carboxypeptidase A*	Pancreatic juice	34 000	7.5–8.5	R·CO ┆ NH·CH(R')·COOH Hydrolyses terminal peptide linkage adjacent to free carboxyl group. Though of wide specificity, maximally active when R′ = aromatic nucleus	Contains Zn (ca. 1.9 mg/g) as essential constituent
3.4.2.2 *Carboxypeptidase B*	Pancreatic juice	–	ca. 8	R·CO ┆ NH·CH(R')·COOH Acts uniquely on peptides containing R′ = arginine, lysine or ornithine. Again, carboxyl group must be free[4]	Formed from procarboxypeptidase B by tryptic activation[4]. Probably identical with 'protaminase'[5]
3.4.1.1 *Leucine aminopeptidase*	Small intestine	300 000[6]	ca. 8	H_2N·CH(R)·CO ┆ NH·CH(R')·COOH Wide specificity[7] but most active when R = L-leucine residue. Also attacks polypeptides, but more slowly	Also found in other tissues, plants and micro-organisms. Activated by Mg^{++} or Mn^{++}, inhibited by anions which will bind Mg^{++} or Mn^{++}, e.g., citrate, ethylenediamine tetra-acetate, pyrophosphate. Not affected by reagents reacting with sulphydryl groups
3.4.1.3 *Aminopeptidase*[2]	Small intestine	–	7.5–8.5	H_2N·CH(R)·CO ┆ NH·CH(R')·CO·NH·CH(R'')·COOH Hydrolyses a wide variety of tripeptides. Requires free amino group	Hydrolyses tripeptides at the bond adjacent to the essential free amino group to yield a free amino acid and a dipeptide. Has little or no action on tetra- or dipeptides. Inhibited by Cd^{++}

* The numbers and trivial names are those recommended by the Enzyme Commission of the International Union of Biochemistry (see pages 385 and 386).

** The specificity relationships listed are those elucidated by the action of the enzymes on synthetic peptides; they are not necessarily those of the enzymes acting on proteins *in vivo*.

References

1 For reviews see BOYER et al. (Eds.), *The Enzymes*, 2nd ed., vol. 4, Academic Press, New York, 1960.
2 For a review see SMITH, E.L., *Advanc. Enzymol.*, **12**, 191 (1951).
3 DAVIS and SMITH, *J. biol. Chem.*, **200**, 373 (1953); DAVIS and ADAMS, *Arch. Biochem.*, **57**, 301 (1955).
4 FOLK and GLADNER, *J. biol. Chem.*, **231**, 379 and 393 (1958).
5 WEIL and TELKA, *Arch. Biochem.*, **71**, 204 (1957).
6 SPACKMAN et al., *J. biol. Chem.*, **212**, 255 (1955).
7 SMITH and SPACKMAN, *J. biol. Chem.*, **212**, 271 (1955).

Table 12 Peptidyl-peptide hydrolases and exopeptidases in tissues other than the gastrointestinal tract

Enzyme*	Location	Optimal pH of action	Reaction catalysed**	Remarks
		Peptidyl-peptide hydrolases		
– *Cathepsins*** A and B*[1]	Ubiquitous component of animal tissues; particularly abundant in spleen, liver, kidney and lung	ca. 4 (A); 5–6 (B)	Similar in action to pepsin (A) and trypsin (B): can effect the activation of trypsinogen[2]	Whereas A requires no activator, B has an absolute requirement for –SH compounds
3.4.4.9 *Cathepsin C*	Ubiquitous but most abundant in spleen	ca. 5 (at higher pH, catalyses transamidation reactions[3])	Similar in action to chymotrypsin but more restricted in its specificity: attacks only peptide linkages at a specified distance from the free α-amino group[3]	Activated by –SH compounds and by cyanide
3.4.4.23 *Cathepsin D*[4]	Spleen	3.0 (acid-denatured haemoglobin); 4.2 (acid-denatured albumin)	Similar in action to pepsin, but more restricted in specificity	Does not hydrolyse the synthetic substrates[3] hydrolysed by cathepsins A, B and C. The enzyme is heat-labile and rapidly destroyed below pH 2.5
3.4.4.13 *Thrombin*	Blood serum	ca. 7	Hydrolyses peptides, amides and esters of L-arginine; converts fibrinogen to fibrin	Formed from the nonenzymic precursor prothrombin by a variety of factors[5]
3.4.4.14 *Plasmin*	Blood serum	ca. 7	Hydrolyses peptides and esters of L-arginine and L-lysine; converts fibrin into soluble products	Formed from plasminogen[6]
		Exopeptidases		
3.4.3.1 *Glycyl-glycine dipeptidase*	Many tissues; has been partially purified from rat muscle, human uterus and swine kidney[7]	7.6	Similar in action to the intestinal enzyme	Activity enhanced by addition of Co^{++} or, more weakly, of Mn^{++}. Preparations of this enzyme from rat muscle are exceedingly unstable, from human uterus less so[7]
3.4.3.2 *Glycyl-leucine dipeptidase*	Several tissues; has been partially purified from uterus[7]	ca. 8	Similar in action to the intestinal enzyme	Activity enhanced by Zn^{++} and phosphate
3.4.3.3 *Carnosinase*	Several tissues; has been partially purified from spleen, liver and swine kidney[7,8]	8.0–8.4 in presence of Mn^{++}; 7.8–7.9 in presence of Zn^{++}; 7.4–7.5 in absence of metal	A dipeptidase, hydrolysing L-alanyl-L-histidine > glycyl-L-histidine > β-alanyl-L-histidine > D-alanyl-L-histidine	Activity enhanced by Zn^{++} and Mn^{++}
3.4.3.6 *Iminodipeptidase* (prolinase)	Many tissues; has been partially purified from swine kidney[7]	ca. 8	Similar in action to the intestinal enzyme	Activity enhanced by Mn^{++} and Cd^{++}
3.4.3.7 *Imidodipeptidase* (prolidase)	Many tissues; has been found in skeletal and smooth muscle, erythrocytes, serum, pituitary, lung and kidney, and has been partially purified from equine erythrocytes and swine kidney[7]	7.8–8.0	Similar in action to the intestinal enzyme	Activity enhanced by Mn^{++}
3.4.2.1 *Carboxypeptidase A*	Most animal tissues	ca. 7	Homospecific with pancreatic carboxypeptidase A	Old name: cathepsin IV

* The numbers and trivial names are those recommended by the Enzyme Commission of the International Union of Biochemistry (see pages 385 and 386).

** The specificity relationships listed have been elucidated by the use of synthetic substrates; they are not necessarily those of the enzymes acting on proteins *in vivo*.

*** The term 'cathepsin' is applied to proteinases obtained from tissues other than the gastrointestinal tract. None of them has yet been crystallized and their physiological role is not established.

Table 12 (continued) Peptidyl-peptide hydrolases and exopeptidases in tissues other than the gastrointestinal tract

Enzyme*	Location	Optimal pH of action	Reaction catalysed**	Remarks
		Exopeptidases (continued)		
3.4.1.1 *Leucine aminopeptidase*	Many tissues; especially abundant in kidney	8–9	Similar in action to the intestinal enzyme	Old name: cathepsin III. The enzyme protein, isolated from swine kidney [9], is particularly rich in leucine (8.8%). Requires activation by Mg^{++} or Mn^{++}
3.4.1.3 *Aminopeptidase*	Most animal tissues	8.0	Similar in action to intestinal tripeptidase	Inhibited by cysteine, Cd^{++}, Hg^{++}. Rapidly inactivated in acid media

* The numbers and trivial names are those recommended by the Enzyme Commission of the International Union of Biochemistry (see pages 385 and 386).
** The specificity relationships listed have been elucidated by the use of synthetic substrates; they are not necessarily those of the enzymes acting on proteins *in vivo.*

References

1 For a review see Fruton, J.S., in Boyer et al. (Eds.), *The Enzymes*, 2nd ed., vol. 4, Academic Press, New York, 1960, page 233.
2 Greenbaum et al., *J. biol. Chem.*, **234**, 2885 (1959).
3 Fruton, J.S., *Harvey Lect. 1955–56*, **51**, 64 (1957).
4 Press et al., *Biochem. J.*, **74**, 501 (1960).
5 For a review see Waugh et al., in Boyer et al. (Eds.), *The Enzymes*, 2nd ed., vol. 4, Academic Press, New York, 1960, page 215.
6 For a review see Ablondi and Hagan, in Boyer et al. (Eds.), *The Enzymes*, 2nd ed., vol. 4, Academic Press, New York, 1960, page 175; Astrup, T., *Blood*, **11**, 781 (1956).
7 Smith, E.L., in Colowick and Kaplan (Eds.), *Methods in Enzymology*, vol. 2, Academic Press, New York, 1955, page 93.
8 Rosenberg, A., *Biochim. biophys. Acta (Amst.)*, **45**, 297 (1960).
9 Spackman et al., *J. biol. Chem.*, **212**, 255 (1955).

Table 13 Glycosyltransferases and glycoside hydrolases (glycosidases) *(for references see page 413)*

Enzyme*	Location	Optimal pH of action	Reaction catalysed	Remarks
2.4.1.1 *α-Glucan phosphorylase* [1] (glycogen phosphorylase)	Muscle, liver	6.9	Transfers D-glucose residues from non-reducing end of starch or glycogen chains to inorganic phosphate, D-glucose or oligosaccharides α-D-glucose 1-phosphate $+ [G]_n \rightleftharpoons [G]_{n+1} + H_3PO_4$	Acts on glycogen and amylopectin. Phosphorolysis of exterior chains giving 20–44% α-D-glucose 1-phosphate from various glycogens and 35–55% from various amylopectins and leaving a phosphorylase limit dextrin (Φ-dextrin). Most phosphorylases exist in more than one form, an *a* form active in the absence of adenosine 5′-phosphate and a *b* form dependent on adenosine 5′-phosphate for activity. Pyridoxal 5′-phosphate is a prosthetic group for *a* and *b* forms. Interconversion of *a* and *b* forms is an enzymic process involving the action of a specific phosphatase ($a \rightarrow b$) or a phosphokinase ($b \rightarrow a$). This change is accompanied by a gross change in molecular size
3.2.1.1 *α-Amylase* [1]	Saliva, pancreatic juice, blood	6.9	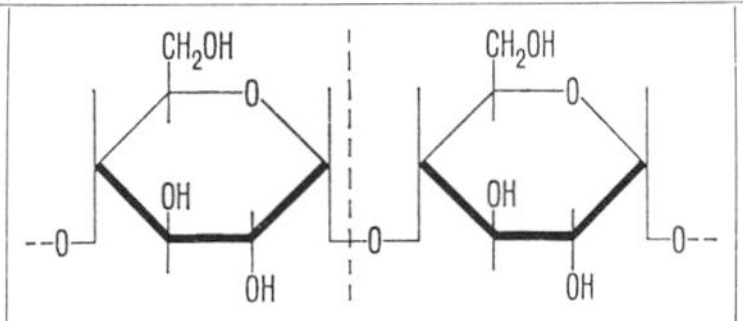	Hydrolyses in a random manner non-terminal α-1,4-glucosidic bonds in amylose, amylopectin, glycogen and dextrins. The initial stage of action of the enzyme is characterized by a rapid decrease in turbidity, viscosity and staining power with iodine. The final products of the enzyme reaction are maltose (70–90%), small amounts of D-glucose, and α-limit dextrins consisting of 4–8 glucose units and containing one or more α-1,6-glucosidic linkages [2]. The α-amylases are calcium metalloproteins whose activity is enhanced by $Cl^- > Br^- > I^- > NO_3^-$

* The numbers and trivial names are those recommended by the Enzyme Commission of the International Union of Biochemistry (see pages 385–386).

Table 13 (continued) Glycosyltransferases and glycoside hydrolases (glycosidases)

Enzyme*	Location	Optimal pH of action	Reaction catalysed	Remarks
3.2.1.10 *Oligo-1,6-glucosidase*[3]	Small intestine	6.3	Hydrolyses 1,6-glucoside linkages of isomaltose, panose, and α-amylase dextrins	Participates in the digestion of starch by hydrolysing the α-amylase limit-dextrins to smaller unbranched molecules that can be further degraded by α-amylase and α-glucosidase in the pancreatic juice. Has no action on glycogen, phosphorylase limit-dextrin or maltose
3.2.1.33 *Dextrin-1,6-glucosidase*[4] (a similar enzyme from plants is listed 3.2.1.9)	Muscle	ca. 7	Hydrolyses the outermost inter-chain linkages in a phosphorylase limit-dextrin to give glucose + polysaccharide	Originally known as amylo-1,6-glucosidase. Hydrolyses the α-1,6-glucosidic bonds of the limit-dextrin resulting from phosphorylase action. The enzyme liberates glucose plus a polysaccharide that can again be degraded by phosphorylase action. The concurrent action of dextrin-1,6-glucosidase and phosphorylase gives complete breakdown of the polysaccharide yielding > 90% α-D-glucose 1-phosphate and D-glucose (4–8%) from the α-1,6-linked residues. This enzyme differs from oligo-1,6-glucosidase in having no action on isomaltose, panose, or α-amylase limit-dextrin. In the relative absence of this enzyme, as in type 3 glycogen-storage disease (see pages 450 to 451), glycogen breakdown is incomplete and limited to the exterior chains
3.2.1.20 *α-Glucosidase*	Small intestine, pancreatic juice, blood, liver	6.6–7.0	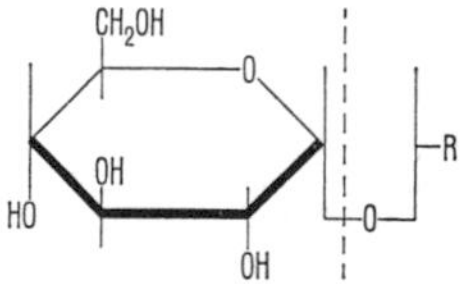 where R = glucose (in which case the compound is maltose), substituted hexoses, phenols, terpenes, etc.	Formerly called maltase: the maltose produced from the digestion of starch by α-amylase is hydrolysed to glucose by this enzyme. Inhibited by the glucose formed. Certain α-glucosidases hydrolyse sucrose and others do not. At least three intestinal 'maltases' have been separated from 'isomaltase'[3, 6]
3.2.1.21 *β-Glucosidase* 3.2.1.23 *β-Galactosidase*[5]	Kidney, liver, small intestine, blood	ca. 6	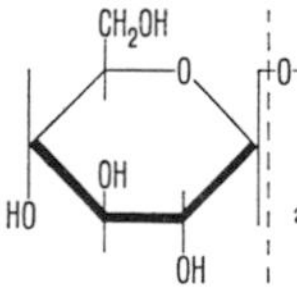 and 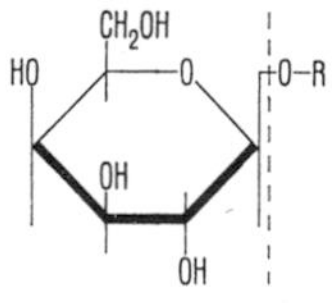	β-Glucosidase is widespread in plants and micro-organisms. In some preparations it appears to be identical with β-galactosidase[7]. β-Galactosidases can transfer galactose residues to a variety of acceptors (such as lactose, galactose and glucose) as well as to water
3.2.1.31 *β-Glucuronidase*[8]	All mammalian tissues and body fluids; especially high in liver, kidney, spleen, epididymis and cancer tissues	ca. 5	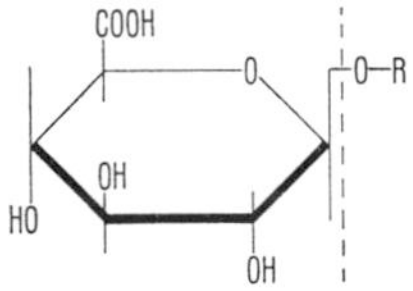 Hydrolyses steroid glucuronides and various β-glucuronides excreted in urine and bile	Possibly plays a role in mucopolysaccharide metabolism. Hydrolyses alkyl, aryl, alicyclic and acyl β-glucuronides and some β-galacturonides. Aldonolactones are powerful competitive inhibitors of the enzyme. Dilute solutions of the enzyme are activated non-specifically by a variety of high molecular weight compounds, the most reliable results being given by albumin. No action on α-glucuronides or β-glucosides. Shows some transferase reaction *in vitro* but unlikely to be of importance in glucuronide synthesis *in vivo*. After the action of testicular hyaluronidase on hyaluronic acid or chondroitin, the oligosaccharides formed are degraded stepwise from the non-reducing end by β-glucuronidase and β-acetylglucosaminase (below) acting alternately

* The numbers and trivial names are those recommended by the Enzyme Commission of the International Union of Biochemistry (see pages 385–386).

Table 13 (concluded) Glycosyltransferases and glycoside hydrolases (glycosidases)

Enzyme*	Location	Optimal pH of action	Reaction catalysed	Remarks
3.2.1.35 *Hyaluronate lyase* (hyaluronidase)[9]	Testes	ca. 7	Degrades hyaluronic acid by liberating the endoglucosaminyl group, i.e., is an endohexosaminidase. Also acts as a transglycosidase. The testicular enzyme acts on both hyaluronic acid and chondroitin sulphates	The end-products after exhaustive digestion of hyaluronic acid are 10–15% disaccharide and 80–85% of a tetrasaccharide. The oligosaccharides are composed of a β-1,3 linked glucuronic acid–*N*-acetylglucosamine unit. The end-products of action on chondroitin sulphates are tetrasaccharides, apparently still 4- and 6-sulphate esters. The hyaluronidase contained in the head of most mammalian spermatozoa probably plays a role in their penetration through the granulosa cell layer of the ovum
3.2.1.17 *Mucopeptide glucohydrolase*[10] (lysozyme)	Tears, nasal mucus, saliva, blood serum and plasma	6.2	Hydrolyses glycosidic linkages in bacterial mucopolysaccharides, especially those of GRAM-positive bacteria	Formerly called muramidase. Very stable at acid pH values and resists heating at 100°C for 3 min at pH 4.5. Very unstable at alkaline pH values. May play a role in defending mucus surfaces against bacterial invasion
3.2.1.19 *Heparinase*[11]	Liver and kidney	5.3–6.8	Hydrolyses α-1,4 links between D-glucosamine sulphate and D-glucuronic acid residues in heparin	A similar enzyme isolated from bacteria has been used to elucidate the structure of heparin[12]
3.2.1.30 β-*Acetylglucosaminase*[13]	Spleen, liver, kidney, lung, blood, heart, brain, testes	4.0–6.0	Hydrolyses β-phenylacetylaminodeoxyglucosides to phenol + acetylaminodeoxyglucose	Probably of importance in mucopolysaccharide breakdown. Acts on the blood group A and 0(H) substances of swine gastric mucin with the liberation of methylpentose constituents. The enzyme liberates acetylaminodeoxyglucose residues from A but not from 0(H)[14]. The same enzyme may act on β-acetylgalactosaminases

* The numbers and trivial names are those recommended by the Enzyme Commission of the International Union of Biochemistry (see pages 385 and 386).

References

1 MANNERS, D.J., *Advanc.Carbohyd.Chem.*, **17**, 371 (1962).
2 WALKER and WHELAN, *Biochem.J.*, **76**, 257 (1960).
3 LARNER and GILLESPIE, *J.biol.Chem.*, **223**, 709 (1956).
4 LARNER and SCHLISELFELD, *Biochim.biophys.Acta (Amst.)*, **20**, 53 (1956).
5 WALLENFELS and MALHOTRA, *Advanc.Carbohyd.Chem.*, **16**, 239 (1961).
6 DAHLQVIST, A., *Acta chem.scand.*, **14**, 1 and 72 (1960); DAHLQVIST, A., *J.clin.Invest.*, **41**, 463 (1962); SEMENZA and AURICCHIO, *Biochim.biophys. Acta (Amst.)*, **65**, 173 (1962); AURICCHIO et al., *Biochim.biophys.Acta (Amst.)*, **96**, 498 (1965).
7 DAHLQVIST, A., *Biochim.biophys.Acta (Amst.)*, **50**, 55 (1961).
8 LEVVY and MARSH, in BOYER et al. (Eds.), *The Enzymes*, 2nd ed., vol. 4, Academic Press, New York, 1960, page 397.
9 MEYER et al., in BOYER et al. (Eds.), *The Enzymes*, 2nd ed., vol. 4, Academic Press, New York, 1960, page 447.
10 JOLLES, A., in COLOWICK and KAPLAN (Eds.), *Methods in Enzymology*, vol. 5, Academic Press, New York, 1962, page 137.
11 CHO and JAQUES, *Canad.J.Biochem.*, **34**, 799 (1956).
12 KORN and PAYZA, *J.biol.Chem.*, **223**, 859 (1956).
13 WALKER et al., *Biochem.J.*, **79**, 288 (1961).
14 HOWE and KABAT, *J.Amer.chem.Soc.*, **75**, 5542 (1953).

Glycoside hydrolases of the mucosa of the human small intestine[1]

Age	Number	Protein (mg/g mucosa)	Enzyme activity (U/g protein)*					
			'Maltase'	'Saccharase'	'Isomaltase'	'Lactase'	'Cellobiase'	'Amylase'
Gestational age								
2–3 months . .	2	42.5	12.5 (2.1–23)	4 (0.6–7.5)	4 (0.6–7.4)	1	–	–
3–4 months . .	3	51 (47–55)	104 (80–124)	40 (34–48)	36 (36–37)	7 (5–9)	–	5
6 months	1	90	132	52	44	15	4.1	6.6
7–8 months . .	6	96 (58–150)	235 (100–481)	91 (31–201)	74 (35–145)	26 (15–37)	5.8 (4.4–8.5)	11.4 (8–18)
8–9 months . .	10	90 (77–129)	281 (138–422)	101 (51–150)	85 (37–113)	31 (16–77)	6.6 (3.2–16.2)	16.5 (8.8–32)
Adults	15	90 (84–121)	246 (70–456)	76 (24–152)	74 (27–136)	30 (5.9–54.5)	6.8 (1–11.6)	295 (78–1179)

* 1U = 1 μmol disaccharide hydrolysed per minute at 37°C and pH 5.8.

1 AURICCHIO et al., *Pediatrics*, **35**, 944 (1965).

Table 14 Fatty acid ester hydrolases (fatty acid esterases)

Enzyme*	Location	Optimal pH of action	Reaction catalysed	Remarks
3.1.1.1 *Carboxylesterase* [1]	Most tissues, high activity in liver	ca. 8	Hydrolyses carboxylic esters to give a carboxylic acid and an alcohol	Formerly called aliesterase. Hydrolyses dissolved triglycerides. Much more active on simple esters (e.g., methyl butyrate) than on acetylcholine. All esterases can catalyse the transfer of the acyl moiety of the substrate. In the presence of hydroxylamine the liver enzyme catalyses the formation of hydroxamic acids from fatty acids [2]
3.1.1.3 *Lipase* [3]	Pancreas, gastric juice, saliva	7–9	CH_2—O—CO—R CH—O—CO—R′ CH_2—O—CO—R″ where R, R′ and R″ are long-chain fatty acids. Attacks tri- > di- > monoglycerides	Splits preferentially the outer chains of the triglyceride so that hydrolysis proceeds via triglyceride → 1,2-diglyceride → 2-monoglyceride → glycerol. Pancreatic lipase acts only at an ester–water interface. Suspensions of methyl butyrate and triacetin are readily hydrolysed but the enzyme does not attack true solutions of methyl butyrate. Bile salts activate the enzyme, in part by emulsifying the water-insoluble substrate. The optimum reaction for hydrolysis of lower triglycerides is about pH 7. For higher triglycerides it is pH 8.8
3.1.1.6 *Acetylesterase* [1]	Widely distributed	ca. 7	Hydrolyses acetic esters to give an alcohol and acetic acid	Also attacks aromatic acetates. Less sensitive to eserine inhibition than cholinesterase
3.1.1.7 *Acetylcholinesterase* [4]	Most tissues, especially conductive tissues (e.g., brain, nerves), erythrocytes	ca. 7	Hydrolyses acetylcholine to give acetic acid and choline. Hydrolyses propionylcholine at the same rate but butyrylcholine only slowly	Has a well-defined optimum substrate concentration for acetylcholine of 4–7 µmol/ml and is inhibited at higher concentrations. Acetyl-β-methylcholine is rapidly hydrolysed, but the rate is considerably lower than with acetylcholine. Acts on a variety of acetic esters and catalyses transacetylations
3.1.1.8 *Cholinesterase* [5]	Most tissues, especially blood serum, pancreas, liver, ovary, placenta, intestinal mucosa, brain	ca. 7	Hydrolyses acylcholine to give choline and an acid	Hydrolyses butyryl- or propionylcholine more rapidly than acetylcholine. Also hydrolyses simple butyryl or propionyl esters. Does not act on acetyl-β-methylcholine. Does not have a well-defined substrate optimum, i.e., is not inhibited by excess substrate. The cholinesterases can be distinguished from the simple esterases by the effect of eserine (physostigmine). All types of cholinesterase are completely inhibited by 10^{-5}-molar eserine
3.1.1.13 *Cholesterol esterase* [6]	Pancreas, blood serum	ca. 8	Hydrolyses cholesterol esters to give cholesterol and an acid	The enzyme from pancreas has an absolute requirement for free cholic acid. The enzyme is much less stable than lipase. Purified enzyme has synthetic as well as hydrolytic activity. Cholesterol, dehydroandrosterone, dihydrocholesterol and cholestanol are readily esterified and all the sterol butyrates are rapidly hydrolysed. Cholesterol esterase may be identical with one of the carboxylesterases of the pancreas

* The numbers and trivial names are those recommended by the Enzyme Commission of the International Union of Biochemistry (see pages 385 and 386).

References

[1] Hofstee, B.H.J., in Boyer et al. (Eds.), *The Enzymes*, 2nd ed., vol. 4, Academic Press, New York, 1960, page 485.

[2] Lipmann and Tuttle, *Biochim. biophys. Acta (Amst.)*, 4, 301 (1950).

[3] Desnuelle, P., *Advanc. Enzymol.*, **23**, 129 (1961).

[4] Wilson, I.B., in Boyer et al. (Eds.), *The Enzymes*, 2nd ed., vol. 4, Academic Press, New York, 1960, page 501.

[5] Augustinsson, K.-B., in Boyer et al. (Eds.), *The Enzymes*, 2nd ed., vol. 4, Academic Press, New York, 1960, page 521.

[6] Hernandez and Chaikoff, *J. biol. Chem.*, **228**, 447 (1957).

Table 15 Phosphatases

Enzyme*	Location	Optimal pH of action	Reaction catalysed	Remarks
			3.1.3 Phosphoric acid monoester hydrolases (phosphomonoesterases)	
3.1.3.1 *Alkaline phosphatase* [1]	Most cells, particularly zones of growth of bones, intestinal mucosa, kidney, lactating mammary gland, milk	9–10, depending on substrate and concentration	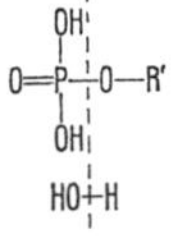	Has wide specificity. Activity is enhanced by divalent cations, e.g., Mg^{++}. In contrast to certain other groups of hydrolases, phosphomonoesterhydrolases and phosphodiesterases are not inhibited by di-isopropyl fluorophosphate. The enzyme shows transferase activity. In hypophosphatasia abnormally low amounts of the enzyme are present in all tissues and in blood serum. In bone destruction the amount in blood serum is considerably increased. Might serve to provide inorganic phosphate for metabolic, excretory and some secretory purposes
3.1.3.2 *Acid phosphatase* [2]	Lactating mammary gland, kidney, prostate, liver, spleen, erythrocytes	5.3–5.6	As for alkaline phosphatase	Has wide specificity. Many but not all acid phosphatases catalyse transfer of the phosphoryl group to organic hydroxyl compounds. Of the animal acid phosphatases only the enzyme from prostate glands is inhibited by (+)-tartrate
3.1.3.9 *Glucose-6-phosphatase* [3]	Liver, kidney, small intestine	6.5	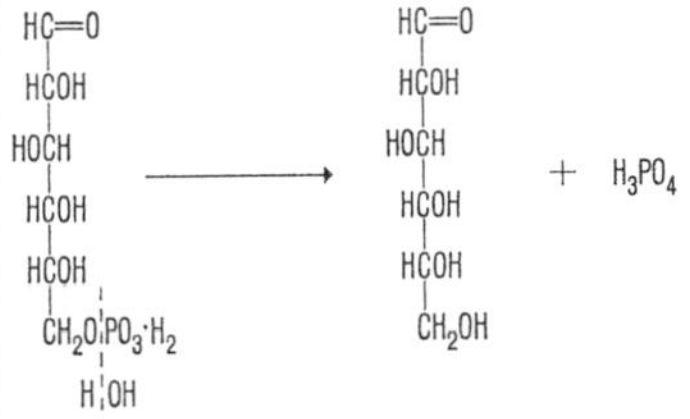 Glucose 6-phosphate → Glucose	Readily catalyses the transfer of a phosphoryl group from glucose 6-phosphate to glucose or fructose. Hydrolytic activity is inhibited by glucose. Appears to be solely associated with the microsomal fraction. Plays a role in the formation of glucose from glycogen and noncarbohydrate compounds (see Fig.17, page 441). Absent from, or weak in, the liver during glycogen storage disease [4]
3.1.3.11 *Hexosediphosphatase*	Kidney, liver	9.3–9.5	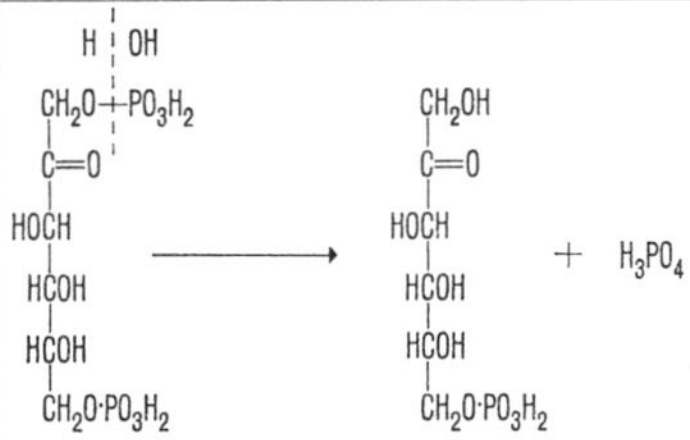 Fructose 1,6 diphosphate → Fructose 6-phosphate	Markedly specific for fructose 1,6-diphosphate [5]. Does not hydrolyse glucose 1-phosphate, glucose 6-phosphate, fructose 6-phosphate, L-sorbose 1-phosphate or phosphoglycerate. Fructose 1-phosphate and L-sorbose 1,6-diphosphate are hydrolysed at rates of 0.009 and 0.03 times the rate for fructose 1,6-diphosphate respectively. The enzyme is activated by Mg^{++} or Mn^{++} and inhibited by fructose 6-phosphate, fructose 1,6-diphosphate and adenosine monophosphate. Plays a role in the synthesis of glycogen from noncarbohydrate compounds (see Fig.17, page 441)

* The numbers and trivial names are those recommended by the Enzyme Commission of the International Union of Biochemistry (see pages 385–386).

Table 15 (continued) Phosphatases

Enzyme*	Location	Optimal pH of action	Reaction catalysed	Remarks
			3.1.4 Phosphoric acid diester hydrolases (phosphodiesterases)	
3.1.4 *Phosphodiesterases*	Widespread	–	Hydrolyses phosphoric diesters to a phosphoric monoester and an alcohol	The enzymes classified as phosphodiesterases are listed elsewhere, e.g., glycerophosphorylcholine diesterase, phospholipase C and phospholipase D in Table 16 opposite, and ribonuclease, deoxyribonuclease and phosphodiesterase in Table 17, page 441
			3.6.1 Hydrolases acting on anhydrides containing phosphoryl	
3.6.1.1 *Inorganic pyrophosphatase*[6]	Liver, brain, erythrocytes and other tissues	7.6–7.8	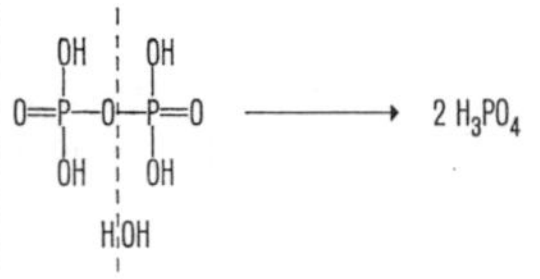	Has an absolute requirement for Mg^{++}. Some tissues contain a pyrophosphatase with an acid pH optimum, and this enzyme is not stimulated by Mg^{++}
3.6.1.7 *Acylphosphatase*[7]	Skeletal muscle, brain, kidney, liver, leucocytes	5.3	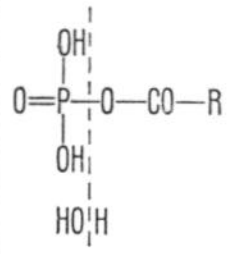 where R·CO = acetyl, butyryl, palmityl	Also catalyses the hydrolysis of 1,3-diphosphoglyceric acid and carbamyl phosphate. No reaction with glycerol phosphate, 3-phosphoglycerate or phosphoenolpyruvate. Stable to heat at acid pH values (no loss of activity after 15 min at 80 °C). Has a molecular weight of ca. 13000 and is similar to ribonuclease both in size and in its remarkable stability to various denaturing agents
3.6.1.9 *Nucleotide pyrophosphatase*[8]	Kidney, liver	ca. 8	Hydrolyses dinucleotides to give 2 mononucleotides	Acts rapidly on $NADH_2$, $NADPH_2$, FAD, adenosine diphosphate ribose and several analogues of $NADH_2$. The animal enzyme generally splits $NADH_2$ faster than NAD. The enzyme from potato also splits ADP, ATP and thiamine pyrophosphate

* The numbers and trivial names are those recommended by the Enzyme Commission of the International Union of Biochemistry (see pages 385 and 386).

References

1 Stadtman, T.C., in Boyer et al. (Eds.), *The Enzymes*, 2nd ed., vol. 5, Academic Press, New York, 1961, page 55.
2 Schmidt, G., in Boyer et al. (Eds.), *The Enzymes*, 2nd ed., vol. 5, Academic Press, New York, 1961, page 37.
3 Ashmore and Weber, *Vitam. and Horm.*, **17**, 91 (1959).
4 Cori and Cori, *J. biol. Chem.*, **199**, 661 (1952).
5 Mokrasch and McGilvery, *J. biol. Chem.*, **221**, 909 (1956).
6 Seal and Binkley, *J. biol. Chem.*, **228**, 193 (1957).
7 Raijman et al., *J. biol. Chem.*, **235**, 2340 (1960).
8 Jacobson and Kaplan, *J. biophys. biochem. Cytol.*, **3**, 31 (1957).

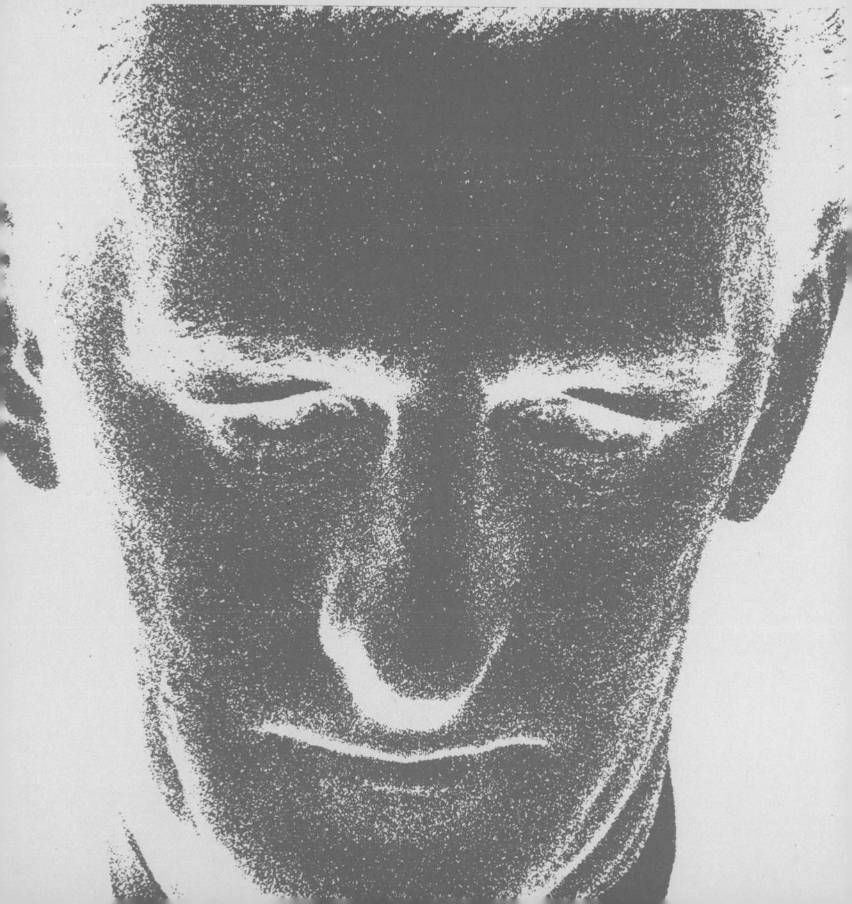

Table 16 Phospholipases

Typical phospholipids, such as lecithin or cephalin, may be represented by the general formula

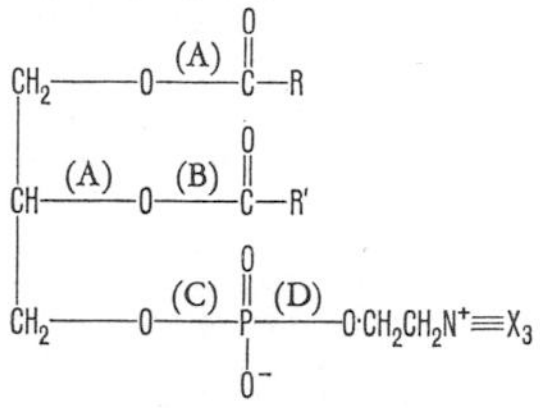

where $R-\overset{\overset{O}{\|}}{C}-O$ is a saturated, $R'-\overset{\overset{O}{\|}}{C}-O-$ an unsaturated, long-chain fatty acid; $X = CH_3$ for lecithin, H for cephalin. The corresponding enzymes capable of cleaving the four designated bonds in the formula are called phospholipases A, B, C and D. Since the term 'lipase' usually refers to the cleavage of a carboxyl ester, phospholipases C and D are in a strict sense phosphodiesterases.

Enzyme*	Location	Optimal pH of action	Reaction catalysed	Remarks
3.1.1.4 *Phospholipase A*[1]	Muscle, heart, liver, kidney, adrenals, pancreas	ca. 7	Cleavage of the phospholipid at the positions marked (A) in the formula	Removes only one fatty acid from phospholipids to give lysolipids, which can cause rapid haemolysis. One of the most widespread components of animal poisons, present in the poisonous secretions of snakes, echinoderms, scorpions, bees and wasps. For a long time thought only to split off the unsaturated fatty acids from the α-position. Now known to split off saturated acids from either the α- or β-position. Activated by Ca^{++} and albumin. Very heat-stable, can be boiled for 5 min at pH 5.9 without loss of activity. Cleaves the phospholipid–cytochrome complex within mitochondria, causing powerful inhibition of certain respiratory enzymes
3.1.1.5 *Phospholipase B*[1] (lysophospholipase)	Liver, pancreas	4.0–6.0	Cleavage of the phospholipid at the position marked (B) in the formula	Completely inactive towards lecithins and cephalins. Attacks only the lyso compounds. Forms glycerol phosphocholine, which has no haemolytic activity, from lysolecithin. Less heat stable than phospholipase A; rapidly destroyed above 41°C
3.1.4.3 *Phospholipase C*	*Clostridium* toxins, brain[2]	6.0–7.6	Cleavage of the phospholipid at the position marked (C) in the formula	Absolute specificity for hydrolysis of the linkage between glycerol and phosphate in phospholipids. Catalyses hydrolysis of phospholipid derivatives that still retain diesterified phosphate. Acts on lecithins, producing a diglyceride and choline phosphate. Catalyses hydrolysis of sphingomyelin to acylsphingosine and choline phosphate. Activated by Ca^{++}. Relatively heat stable: retains 50% of its activity after heating at 100°C for 10 min
3.1.4.4 *Phospholipase D*	Not present in mammalian tissues. Found in plants[3]	5.1–5.9	Cleavage of the phospholipid at the position marked (D) in the formula	Catalyses hydrolysis of the linkage between the base and phosphoric acid to form a phosphatidic acid and, in the case of lecithin, choline. Acts on both lecithin and cephalin. Heat stable: retains 30–40% of its activity after heating at 100 °C for 15 min
3.1.4.2 *Glycerophosphorylcholine diesterase*	Nervous tissue[4], liver and other tissues[5]	7.5–9.0	–	Catalyses hydrolysis of glycerol phosphorylcholine, produced by the joint action of phospholipase A and B, to glycerol phosphate and choline. Resembles phospholipase D in specificity. Also acts on glycerophosphoethanolamine. Requires Mg^{++}. The enzyme has been purified from bacterial extracts

* The numbers and trivial names are those recommended by the Enzyme Commission of the International Union of Biochemistry (see pages 385 and 386).

References

1 Slotta, K.H., in Boyer et al. (Eds.), *The Enzymes*, 2nd ed., vol. 4, Academic Press, New York, 1960, page 551.
2 Druzhinina and Kritsman, *Biokhimiya*, **17**, 77 (1952).
3 Hanahan and Chaikoff, *J. biol. Chem.*, **172**, 191 (1948).
4 Webster et al., *Biochem. J.*, **65**, 374 (1957).
5 Dawson, R.M., *Biochem. J.*, **62**, 689 (1956).

Table 17 Nucleases and other enzymes acting on nucleotides and nucleosides

Enzyme*	Location	Optimal pH of action	Reaction catalysed	Remarks
2.7.7.16 *Ribonuclease*[1] (RNAase)	Most tissues, highest activity in the pancreas *RNAase content of vertebrate pancreas* (μg/g)[11] Cow 1200 Sheep 1080 Goat 1000 Mouse 395 Lizard 380 Rat 260 Guinea-pig 240 Pig 80 Horse 25 Chicken 20 Whale 18 Monkey 2 Man 1 Cat 0.5 Dog 0.5 Rabbit 0.5	7.0–8.0	Catalyses the depolymerization of ribonucleic acid, producing nucleoside 3′-phosphates. The animal enzymes cannot attack purine nucleoside phosphate linkages and consequently produce a resistant 'core' rich in purine bases	First action of RNAase on internucleotide bonds is transesterification to form a pyrimidine nucleoside cyclic 2′,3′-phosphate ester. These terminal groups are split off as free mononucleotide cyclic phosphates, which are then hydrolysed with the formation of the corresponding nucleoside 3′-phosphates. Some enzymes produce nucleoside 5′-phosphates from RNA. Bovine pancreatic RNAase has been extensively studied
3.1.4.5 *Deoxyribonuclease*[2] (DNAase) 3.1.4.6 *Deoxyribonuclease II*[2] (DNAase II)	Many tissues, pancreas being the best source	ca. 7 4.5–5.5	Catalyse the depolymerization of deoxyribonucleic acids. Products include mononucleotides through to oligonucleotides. All four mononucleotides have been isolated from the enzyme digests. The nucleotides are terminated in 5′-phosphates in the case of DNAase and 3′-phosphates in the case of DNAase II	DNAase requires added Mg^{++} for activity, is inhibited by EDTA and has a pH optimum at ca. 7. DNAase II is inhibited by added Mg^{++}, often activated by EDTA and has a pH optimum at pH 4.5–5.5. Both DNAases can occur in the same tissue
3.1.4.1 *Phosphodiesterase*[3]	Intestine, spleen and other tissues	ca. 7	Hydrolyses phosphoric diesters to give a phosphoric monoester and an alcohol	Attacks both ribo- and deoxyribo-internucleotide bonds. Has wide specificity. The spleen enzyme forms 3′-nucleotides
3.1.3.5 *5′-Nucleotidase*[4]	Retina, nervous tissue, prostate, testes, sperm. In human tissues the highest activity is in the posterior pituitary gland	ca. 8	Hydrolyses all ribonucleoside and deoxyribonucleoside 5′-phosphates as well as nicotinamide mononucleotide to the corresponding nucleosides and orthophosphate	Preparations of the enzyme, especially from snake venom and bull seminal plasma, have been used to help establish the identity of nucleoside 5′-phosphates
2.4.2.1 *Purine nucleoside phosphorylase*[5]	Liver, brain, thymus, erythrocytes and other tissues	ca. 7	Pentose 1-phosphate + purine $\rightleftharpoons$ nucleoside + orthophosphate	Since the reaction is readily reversible the enzyme is often assayed as orthophosphate released on nucleoside formation. At least two classes of enzymes, purine and pyrimidine nucleoside phosphorylases, have been recognized. The specificity of the various enzymes has not been completely determined. It seems likely that these enzymes play a role in nucleic acid breakdown rather then in nucleoside synthesis

* The numbers and trivial names are those recommended by the Enzyme Commission of the International Union of Biochemistry (see pages 385–386).

Table 17 (continued) Nucleases and other enzymes acting on nucleotides and nucleosides

Enzyme*	Location	Optimal pH of action	Reaction catalysed	Remarks
3.5.4.6 *AMP deaminase*[6]	Muscle and other tissues	6.1–6.4	Deaminates adenylic acid to inosinic acid and ammonia	Acts only on 5′-adenylic acid and 5′-deoxyadenylic acid. The rate with the latter is about 1% of that with the former
3.5.4.4 *Adenosine deaminase*[7]	Muscle, liver, intestinal mucosa	ca. 7.5	Deaminates adenosine to inosine and ammonia	Deoxyadenosine is also deaminated
3.5.4.3 *Guanine deaminase*[7,8]	Liver, muscle	6–10	Deaminates guanine to xanthine and ammonia	Formerly called guanase. Acts on guanine and 8-azaguanine but not on guanosine or guanylic acid. Guanine deaminase in conjunction with xanthine oxidase can be used to determine micro-amounts of guanine
1.2.3.2 *Xanthine oxidase*[9]	Milk, liver, spleen, kidney, lung	7.4	The purified enzyme oxidizes hypoxanthine to xanthine, xanthine to uric acid, and aldehydes to acids	Contains flavin adenine dinucleotide, iron and molybdenum
1.7.3.3 *Urate oxidase*[10]	Liver and kidney of mammals. Absent in man and other primates	9.2	Oxidizes uric acid to allantoin according to the overall reaction: uric acid + O_2 + $2H_2O$ → allantoin + H_2O_2 + CO_2	Contains copper. The production of allantoin is dependent on the interaction of the reaction intermediates with the buffer ions. In phosphate and tris buffers the product is allantoin alone but in borate buffer only 30% of the product is allantoin

* The numbers and trivial names are those recommended by the Enzyme Commission of the International Union of Biochemistry (see pages 385 and 386).

References

1 Anfinsen and White, in Boyer et al. (Eds.), *The Enzymes*, 2nd ed., vol. 5, Academic Press, New York, 1961, page 95.
2 Laskowski, M., in Boyer et al. (Eds.), *The Enzymes*, 2nd ed., vol. 5, Academic Press, New York, 1961, page 123.
3 Razzell, W.E., in Colowick and Kaplan (Eds.), *Methods in Enzymology*, vol. 6, Academic Press, New York, 1963, page 236.
4 Heppel, L.A., in Boyer et al. (Eds.), *The Enzymes*, 2nd ed., vol. 5, Academic Press, New York, 1961, page 49.
5 Friedkin and Kalckar, in Boyer et al. (Eds.), *The Enzymes*, 2nd ed., vol. 5, Academic Press, New York, 1961, page 237.
6 Lee, Y.-P., *J. biol. Chem.*, **227**, 999 (1957).
7 Kalckar, H.M., *J. biol. Chem.*, **167**, 429, 445, 461, 477 (1947).
8 Schmidt, G., *Hoppe-Seylers Z. physiol. Chem.*, **208**, 185 (1932).
9 de Renzo, E.C., *Advanc. Enzymol.*, **17**, 293 (1956).
10 Hübscher et al., *Biochim. biophys. Acta (Amst.)*, **23**, 43 (1957).
11 Barnard, E.A., *Nature*, **221**, 340 (1969).

Synthesis of cell constituents

Apart from supplying energy, the products of digestion serve as precursors of many cell constituents. The mammalian body can form all cell constituents from:

1. The essential amino acids (see page 434)
2. Vitamins
3. The essential (highly unsaturated) fatty acids
4. Mineral salts
5. A bulk source of carbon (usually carbohydrate)
6. A source of nitrogen in the form of ammonia derived mainly from surplus amino acids, with small amounts supplied by purine bases, pyrimidines and amino sugars.

Carbohydrate as a bulk source of carbon can be largely replaced by protein and fat, especially in carnivores.

Much progress has been made in recent years in the elucidation of the pathways by which the basic constituents of food are converted into cell constituents, but many details still remain to be clarified. A synopsis of the available information is contained in the section which follows.

Synthesis of cell constituents from glucose

The principal products, their pathways of formation and their physiological functions are summarized in Table 18 below.

The oxidative pentose phosphate cycle

Glucose 6-phosphate (formed from glucose by the hexokinase reaction) can be oxidized in liver and some other animal tissues at the carbon atom 1 to yield 6-phosphogluconate. This initiates a sequence of reactions in which various pentose phosphates and other sugar phosphates are formed. In the course of these reactions

Table 18 Formation of basic cell constituents and metabolites from glucose

Product formed	Pathway of formation	Physiological function
Glycogen	From glucose 1-phosphate via UDP-glucose, catalysed by UDPG pyrophosphorylase and UDPG glycogenglucosyltransferase [1]	Storage of carbohydrate
Galactose	Reversal of reactions 4 and 5, Table 4, page 390	Constituent of lactose, cerebrosides
Lactose	Probably from UDP-galactose and glucose 1-phosphate, via lactose 1-phosphate	Milk constituent
Ribose 5-phosphate	Reactions of the pentose phosphate cycle (see opposite page)	Constituent of nucleic acid and nucleotides
Deoxyribose 5-phosphate	Probably by aldol condensation between glyceraldehyde phosphate and acetaldehyde (reversal of the reaction shown on page 399)	Constituent of nucleic acids
Glucuronic acid and iduronic acid	Formed via UDP-glucose (see page 423)	Constituent of mucins (hyaluronic acid and chondroitin sulphate) and of heparin; detoxicating agent
Glucosamine	From fructose 6-phosphate by transfer of the amido group of glutamine (see page 423)	Constituent of lipids, polysaccharides and glycoproteins
L-Fucose	From fructose 6-phosphate via GDP-mannose (see page 423)	Constituent of milk oligosaccharides and glycoproteins
Fructose	Reactions of glycolysis and hydrolysis of fructose 6-phosphate by phosphatase	Constituent of semen
Citric acid	CO_2-fixation by pyruvate (see page 424) and reactions of the tricarboxylic acid cycle (see page 390)	Constituent of bone, milk, semen
Fatty acids	From acetyl-coenzyme A (formed via pyruvate) by a route involving malonyl-coenzyme A	Constituents of fats and phospholipids
Glycerophosphates	Reduction of dihydroxyacetone phosphate, catalysed by glycerophosphate dehydrogenase	Constituents of phospholipids
Phospholipids	See page 425	Cell constituents
Glyceride fats	See page 426	Cell constituents
Sterols and steroids	See pages 426–432	Cell constituents; hormones
Nonessential amino acids:		
Glutamic acid	Glutamate dehydrogenase reaction (see page 432)	Constituent of proteins and special peptides (glutathione, folic acid)
Aspartic acid	CO_2-fixation by pyruvate (see page 424) and transamination between glutamate and oxaloacetate	Constituent of proteins
Alanine	Transamination between pyruvate and glutamate	Constituent of proteins
Glycine	From 3-phosphoglycerate by the reactions shown on page 432	Constituent of proteins
Serine	From 3-phosphoglycerate by the reactions shown on page 432	Constituent of proteins
Cysteine	From serine by transsulphuration from homocysteine derived from methionine (see pages 397–398)	Constituent of proteins
Proline	From glutamic acid or ornithine (see page 432)	Constituent of proteins
Hydroxyproline	Probably by oxidation of proline (see page 432)	Constituent of proteins

[1] Leloir and Cardini, *J. Amer. chem. Soc.*, **79**, 6340 (1957).

some glucose 6-phosphate is regenerated, implying a cyclic nature of the reaction sequence. The reactions of this cycle represent a partial oxidation of glucose 6-phosphate.

The main components of the cycle are eight different reactions. In the first reaction (**1**) glucose 6-phosphate is oxidized to 6-phosphogluconolactone, which is subsequently hydrolysed by a 'gluconolactonase' to 6-phosphogluconate[7]. NADP is reduced in this reaction.

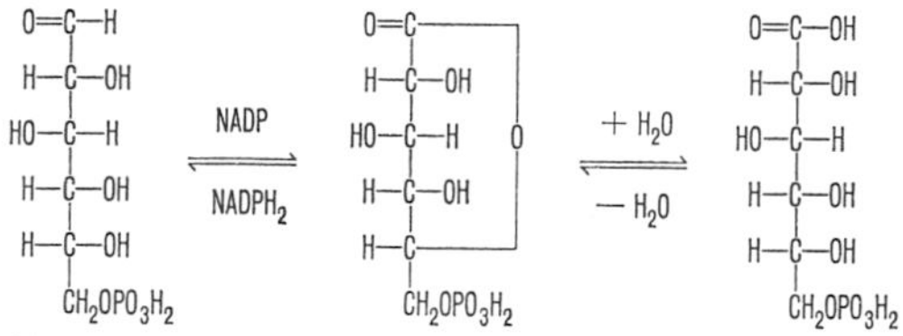

(**1**)

Glucose 6-phosphate — 6-Phosphoglucono-lactone — 6-Phosphogluconic acid

The 6-phosphogluconate formed is oxidatively decarboxylated (**2**) to yield ribulose 5-phosphate, while another molecule of NADP is reduced[2]:

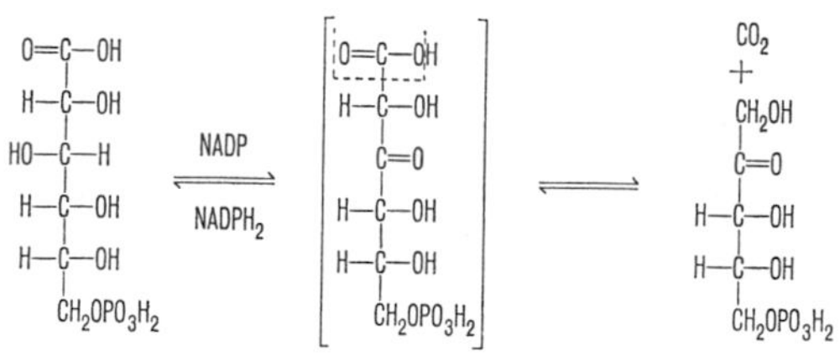

(**2**)

6-Phospho-gluconic acid — Hypothetical intermediate (3-keto-6-phosphogluconic acid) — Ribulose 5-phosphate

Ribulose 5-phosphate undergoes two different isomerizations, one to ribose 5-phosphate (**3**) catalysed by pentose phosphate isomerase[3]:

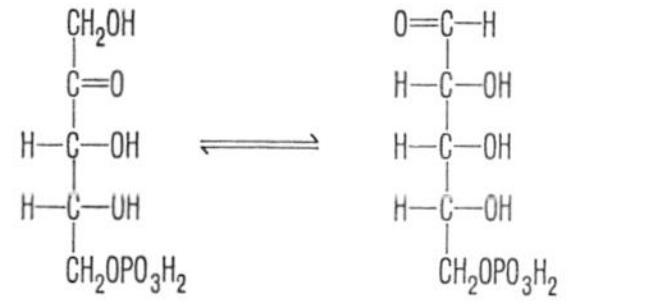

(**3**)

Ribulose 5-phosphate — Ribose 5-phosphate

and one (**4**) to xylulose 5-phosphate[4,5]:

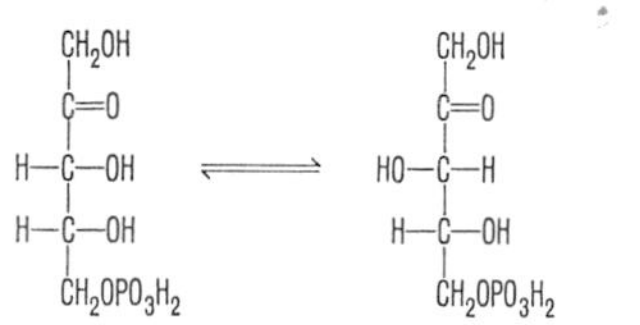

(**4**)

Ribulose 5-phosphate — Xylulose 5-phosphate

One molecule of xylulose 5-phosphate and one of ribose 5-phosphate, produced by reactions (**3**) and (**4**), interact to form sedoheptulose 7-phosphate and glyceraldehyde 3-phosphate (**5**)[4,6]. This reaction is catalysed by transketolase[7], an enzyme requiring thiamine pyrophosphate (TPP) as co-factor. It is thought that an 'active glycolaldehyde' may be an intermediate in this reaction[8]. This may therefore be written as:

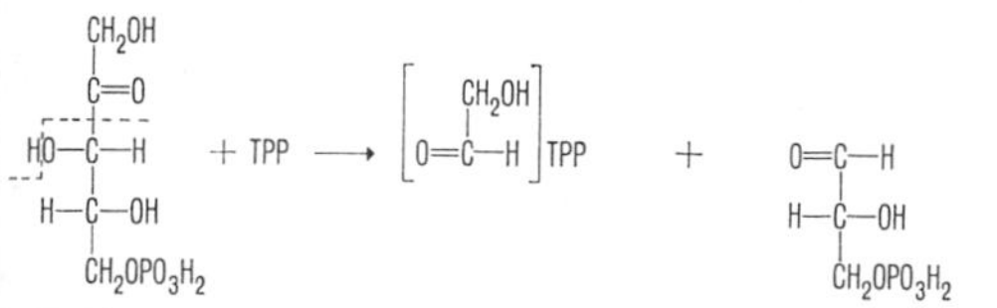

(**5**)

Xylulose 5-phosphate — 'Active glycolaldehyde' — Glyceraldehyde 3-phosphate

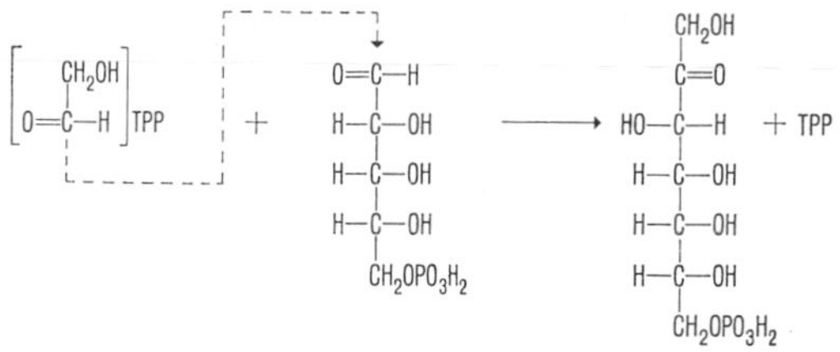

'Active glycol-aldehyde' — Ribose 5-phosphate — Sedoheptulose 7-phosphate

The glyceraldehyde 3-phosphate and sedoheptulose 7-phosphate interact further in a transfer reaction under the influence of transaldolase. The action of this enzyme is analogous to that of transketolase, except that the moiety transferred is not an 'active glycolaldehyde' but an 'active dihydroxyacetone'. In this reaction (**6**) fructose 6-phosphate and erythrose 4-phosphate are formed[9]:

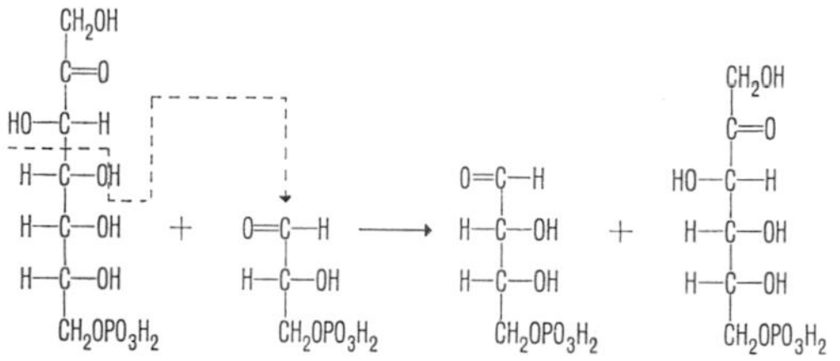

(**6**)

Sedoheptulose 7-phosphate — Glyceraldehyde 3-phosphate — Erythrose 4-phosphate — Fructose 6-phosphate

The erythrose 4-phosphate formed in (**6**) undergoes a transketolase reaction (**7**) with a molecule of xylulose 5-phosphate. This is analogous to reaction (**5**) and leads to fructose 6-phosphate and glyceraldehyde 3-phosphate[10]:

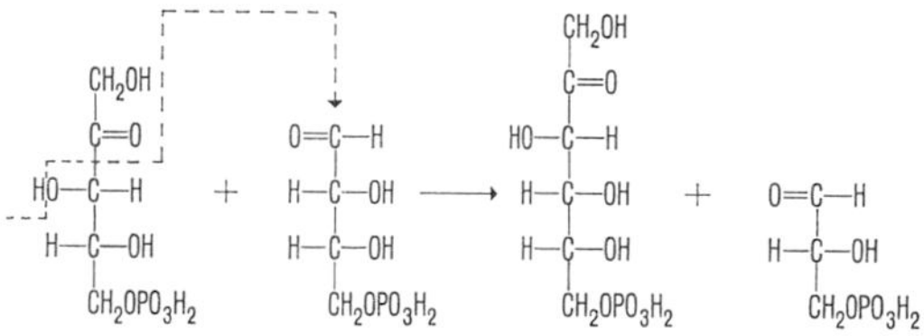

(**7**)

Xylulose 5-phosphate — Erythrose 4-phosphate — Fructose 6 phosphate — Glyceraldehyde 3 phosphate

The fructose 6-phosphate formed in reactions (**6**) and (**7**) is converted to glucose 6-phosphate by reaction (**8**), catalysed by glucose-phosphate isomerase:

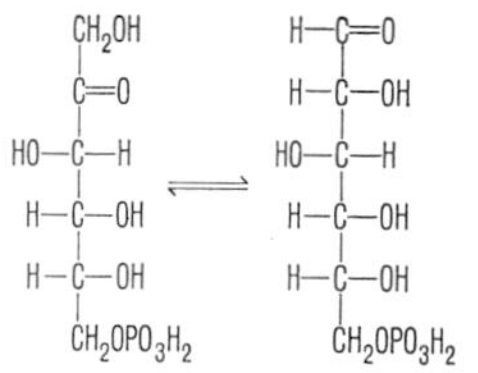

(**8**)

Fructose 6-phosphate — Glucose 6-phosphate

This reaction completes the cycle in that it leads to the (partial) regeneration of the starting material, glucose 6-phosphate. The interplay of the components of the cycle is somewhat complex. It is shown diagrammatically in Figure 11 and Table 19 (page 422).

In this scheme, the reactions catalysed by transketolase and transaldolase, (**5**), (**6**) and (**7**), are indicated by crossing arrows; of the three glucose 6-phosphate molecules required for each turn of the cycle, two are regenerated. While three molecules participate in reactions (**1**) and (**2**), two are involved in reactions (**4**) and (**8**) and only one each participates in the remaining reactions.

The net effect of one revolution of the cycle, as shown in Table 19, is therefore:

glucose 6-phosphate → glyceraldehyde 3-phosphate + 3 CO_2

Table 19 The component reactions of the pentose phosphate cycle and their quantitative relations

(**1**)	3 glucose 6-phosphate + 3 NADP	(glucose 6-phosphate dehydrogenase) →	3 6-phosphogluconate + 3 $NADPH_2$
(**2**)	3 6-phosphogluconate + 3 NADP	(phosphogluconate dehydrogenase) →	3 ribulose 5-phosphate + 3 CO_2 + 3 $NADPH_2$
(**3**)	ribulose 5-phosphate	(ribosephosphate isomerase) →	ribose 5-phosphate
(**4**)	2 ribulose 5-phosphate	(ribulosephosphate 3-epimerase) →	2 xylulose 5-phosphate
(**5**)	ribose 5-phosphate + xylulose 5-phosphate	(transketolase) →	sedoheptulose 7-phosphate + glyceraldehyde 3-phosphate
(**6**)	sedoheptulose 7-phosphate + glyceraldehyde 3-phosphate	(transaldolase) →	fructose 6-phosphate + erythrose 4-phosphate
(**7**)	xylulose 5-phosphate + erythrose 4-phosphate	(transketolase) →	fructose 6-phosphate + glyceraldehyde 3-phosphate
(**8**)	2 fructose 6-phosphate	(glucosephosphate isomerase) →	2 glucose 6-phosphate
Sum	glucose 6-phosphate + 6 NADP	→	3 CO_2 + glyceraldehyde 3-phosphate + 6 $NADPH_2$

Fig. 11 Diagram of the pentose phosphate cycle

Starting materials and end-products are shown enclosed. P = phosphate. The crossing arrows indicate transfer reactions. For further details see Table 19 and the text.

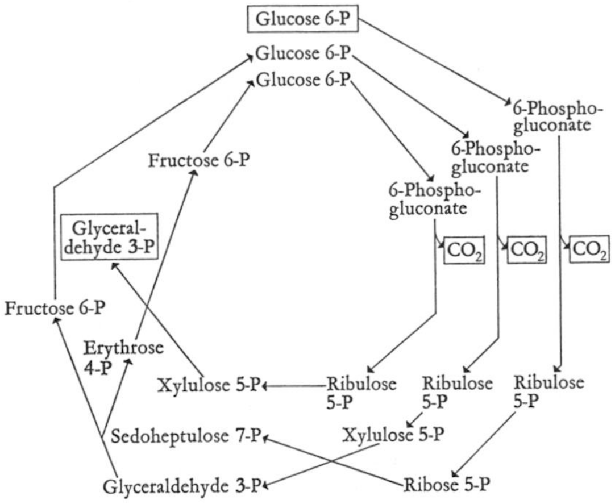

Fig. 12 Complete oxidation of glucose 6-phosphate via the pentose phosphate cycle and additional reactions catalysed by triosephosphate isomerase, fructosediphosphate aldolase, hexosediphosphatase and glucosephosphate isomerase

The first step shown in the diagram (conversion of glucose 6-phosphate into glyceraldehyde phosphate + 3 CO_2) represents the sum of the reactions shown in Table 19 and Figure 11. P = phosphate.

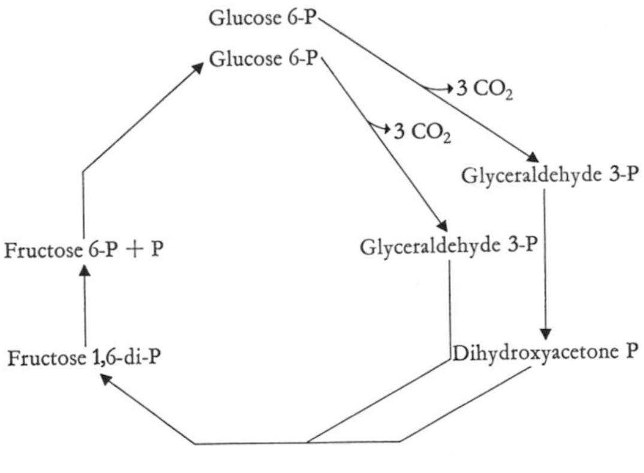

The glyceraldehyde 3-phosphate thus formed does not, however, accumulate in the organism. It can be converted into pyruvate and acetyl-coenzyme A and undergo complete oxidation. Alternatively, if triosephosphate isomerase, fructosediphosphate aldolase, hexosediphosphatase and glucosephosphate isomerase are present, the following sequence of reactions can occur:

glyceraldehyde 3-phosphate	→ dihydroxyacetone phosphate	(**9**)
glyceraldehyde 3-phosphate + dihydroxyacetone phosphate	→ fructose 1,6-diphosphate	(**10**)
fructose 1,6-diphosphate + H_2O	→ fructose 6-phosphate + H_3PO_4	(**11**)
fructose 6-phosphate	→ glucose 6-phosphate	(**8**)

Glucose 6-phosphate would thus be formed from two molecules of glyceraldehyde 3-phosphate, and could re-enter (and be oxidized by) the pentose phosphate cycle. Reactions (**1**)–(**11**) repeated several times would therefore result in a complete combustion of glucose 6-phosphate. This concept, which rests on the demonstration of all the required enzymes in liver[11], is illustrated in Figure 12.

Physiological significance of the oxidative pentose phosphate cycle. The oxidative pentose phosphate cycle is not a major source of energy. Its function is probably twofold: to supply (1) pentose phosphates required for the synthesis of nucleic acids, and (2) reduced NADP required as a source of hydrogen in many reductive syntheses. Quantitatively, the most important reductive synthesis in animal tissues is the formation of fatty acids from carbohydrates, and this is in accordance with the fact that the activity of the enzymes of the pentose phosphate cycle is particularly high at the sites of lipogenesis, for instance in the lactating mammary gland and in adipose tissue[12].

References

1 Warburg and Christian, *Biochem. Z.*, **287**, 440 (1936); Cori and Lipmann, *J. biol. Chem.*, **194**, 417 (1952).
2 Warburg and Christian, *Biochem. Z.*, **292**, 287 (1937); Horecker et al., *J. biol. Chem.*, **193**, 383 (1951).
3 Axelrod et al., *J. biol. Chem.*, **202**, 619 (1953).
4 Srere et al., *Arch. Biochem.*, **59**, 535 (1955).
5 Dickens and Williamson, *Nature*, **176**, 400 (1955).
6 Horecker et al., *J. Amer. chem. Soc.*, **78**, 692 (1956).
7 Racker et al., *J. Amer. chem. Soc.*, **75**, 1010 (1953); de la Haba et al., *J. biol. Chem.*, **214**, 409 (1955).

[8] HOLZER, H., *Angew. Chem.*, **73**, 721 (1961); HOLZER et al., *Ann. N.Y. Acad. Sci.*, **98**, 453 (1962).
[9] HORECKER and SMYRNIOTIS, *J. Amer. chem. Soc.*, **75**, 2021 (1953); HORECKER et al., *J. biol. Chem.*, **212**, 827 (1955); SRERE et al., *Fed. Proc.*, **14**, 285 (1955).
[10] KORNBERG and RACKER, *Biochem. J.*, **61**, III (1955).
[11] HORECKER et al., *J. biol. Chem.*, **207**, 393 (1954); GIBBS and HORECKER, *J. biol. Chem.*, **208**, 813 (1954).
[12] GIBSON et al., *Biochim. biophys. Acta (Amst.)*, **30**, 376 (1958); CAHILL et al., *J. biol. Chem.*, **230**, 125 (1958); CAHILL et al., *Ann. N.Y. Acad. Sci.*, **82**, 403 (1959); ABRAHAM and CHAIKOFF, *J. biol. Chem.*, **234**, 2246 (1959); MCLEAN, P., *Biochim. biophys. Acta (Amst.)*, **57**, 620 (1962).

Glucuronic acid and iduronic acid

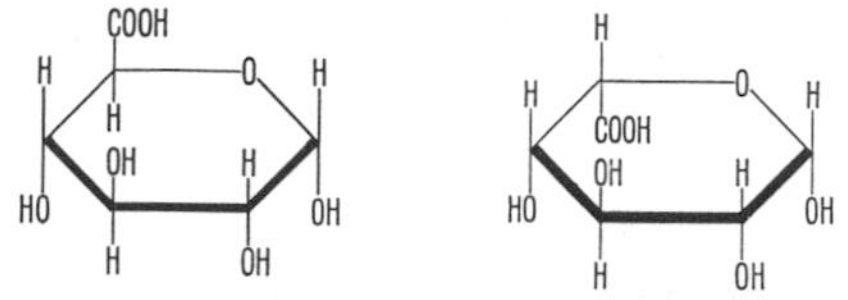

D-Glucuronic acid L-Iduronic acid

D-Glucuronic acid and L-iduronic acid are components of mucopolysaccharides, such as the chondroitin sulphates. Glucuronic acid is also a coupling agent in detoxication reactions. It couples with many substances possessing hydroxyl groups, such as alcohols and substances that are converted in the body into alcohols (salicylic acid, camphor, menthol, chloral hydrate, pregnanediol) or phenols (phenol, indoxyl). It also couples with carboxyl groups attached to an aromatic nucleus (benzoic acid, phenylacetic acid)[1], and with bile pigments[2].

The reactive form of glucuronic acid in the conjugation reactions, in the synthesis of mucopolysaccharides and in the interconversion of glucuronic and iduronic acids is UDP-glucuronic acid:

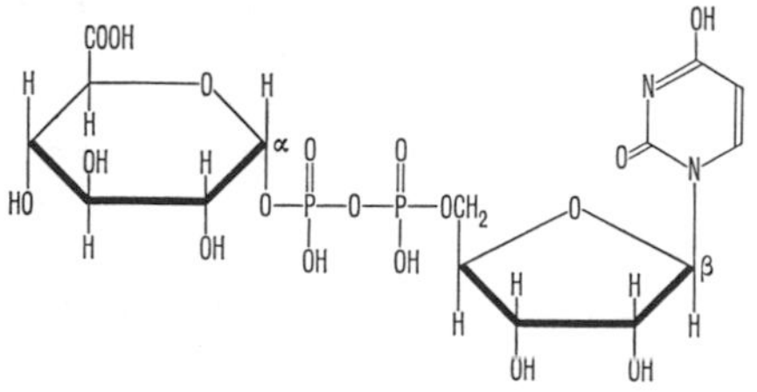

This arises from glucose by the following reactions[3,4]:

glucose + ATP	→ glucose 6-phosphate + ADP
glucose 6-phosphate	→ glucose 1-phosphate
glucose 1-phosphate + UTP	→ UDP-glucose + pyrophosphate
UDP-glucose + 2 NAD	→ UDP-glucuronic acid + 2 $NADH_2$

The synthesis of conjugated glucuronide may be represented as follows[5]:

UDP-glucuronate + ROH —WALDEN inversion→ glucuronosyl-OR + UDP

where ROH is an alcoholic or phenolic compound, or an aromatic carboxylic acid.

UDP-glucuronic acid is converted to uridine diphosphoiduronic acid by an epimerase that attacks the 5-position of the sugar ring. NAD acts catalytically[4].

References

[1] WILLIAMS, R.T., *Detoxication Mechanisms*, 2nd ed., Chapman & Hall, London, 1959.
[2] BILLING et al., *Biochem. J.*, **65**, 774 (1957).
[3] STROMINGER et al., *J. Amer. chem. Soc.*, **76**, 6411 (1954).
[4] JACOBSON and DAVIDSON, *J. biol. Chem.*, **237**, 635 (1962).
[5] SMITH and MILLS, *Biochim. biophys. Acta (Amst.)*, **13**, 386 (1954); STOREY and DUTTON, *Biochem. J.*, **59**, 279 (1955).

Formation of glucosamine and related amino sugars

Glucosamine, mannosamine, and their N-acetyl derivatives, as well as sialic acid, occur in lipids, polysaccharides and glycoproteins. Glucosamine is formed from fructose 6-phosphate by transfer of the amido group of glutamine. The amino sugar is then acetylated by an enzymatic reaction involving acetyl-coenzyme A:

fructose 6-phosphate + glutamine	→	glucosamine 6-phosphate + glutamic acid
glucosamine 6-phosphate + acetyl-coenzyme A	→	*N*-acetylglucosamine 6-phosphate + coenzyme A

The sugar *N*-acetylglucosamine is converted to *N*-acetylmannosamine, which is then phosphorylated with ATP to yield the 6-phosphate derivative. This reacts with phosphoenolpyruvate to yield a sialic acid:

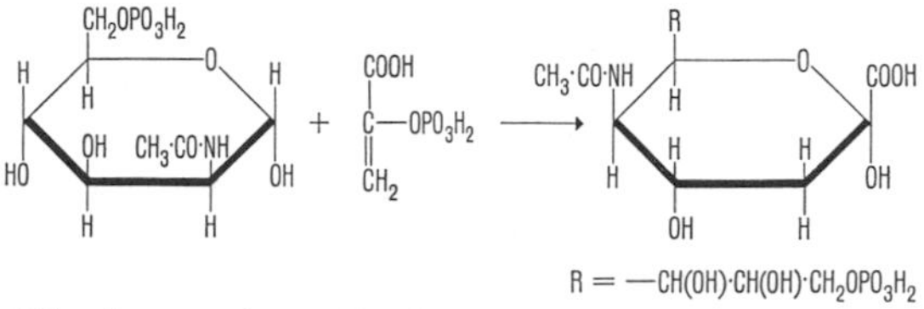

N-Acetylmannosamine 6-phosphate Phosphoenol-pyruvate *N*-Acetylneuraminic acid 9-phosphate (a sialic acid)

Biosynthesis of L-fucose in mammalian tissues[1]

L-Fucose is formed from fructose 6-phosphate by the following series of reactions (R = GDP residue):

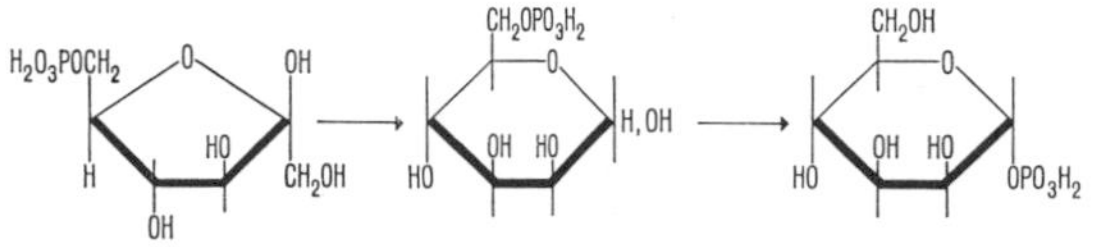

D-Fructose 6-phosphate D-Mannose 6-phosphate D-Mannose 1-phosphate

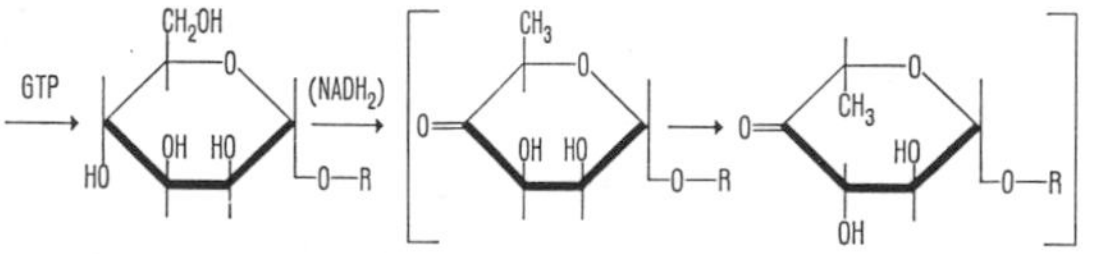

GDP-D-mannose GDP-4-keto-6-deoxy-D-mannose GDP-4-keto-6-deoxy-L-galactose

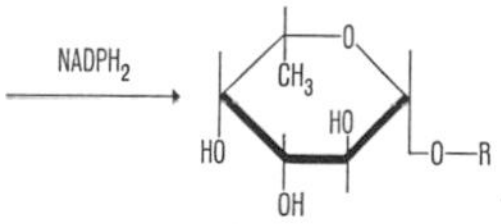

GDP-L-fucose

Incorporation of L-fucose into milk oligosaccharides and probably glycoproteins is via GDP-L-fucose:

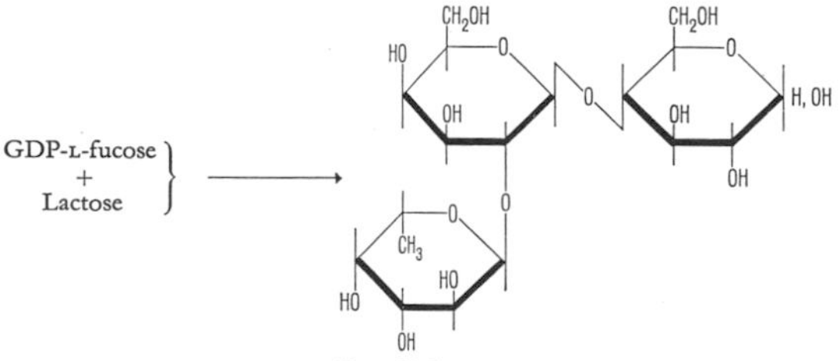

Fucosidolactose (2-[α-L-fucopyranosido]lactose)

References

[1] MUNCH-PETERSEN, A., *Acta chem. scand.*, **10**, 928 (1956); GLASER et al., *Biochim. biophys. Acta (Amst.)*, **33**, 522 (1959); GINSBURG, V., *J. biol. Chem.*, **236**, 2389 (1961); FOSTER and GINSBURG, *Biochim. biophys. Acta (Amst.)*, **54**, 376 (1961); GROLLMAN et al., *J. biol. Chem.*, **240**, 975 (1965).

Formation and utilization of hexosamines and *N*-acetylneuraminic acid in mammals

The following scheme illustrates the manner in which these amino sugars[1] are formed and utilized in the mammalian organism:

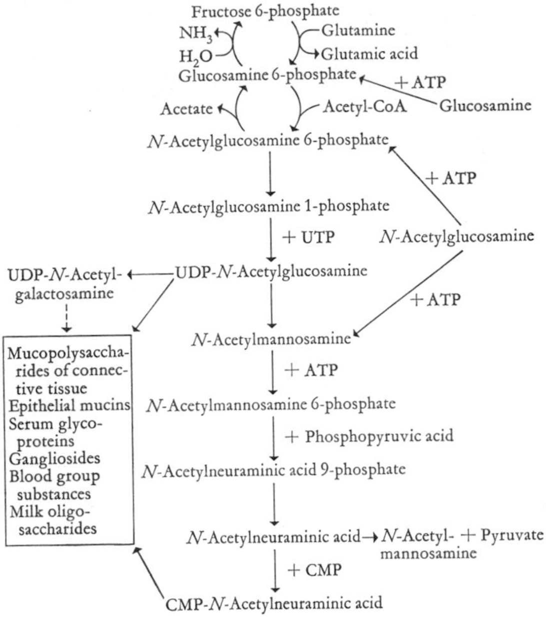

References

[1] On amino sugar metabolism in general see WOLSTENHOLME and O'CONNOR (Eds.), *Ciba Foundation Symposium on the Chemistry and Biology of Mucopolysaccharides*, Churchill, London, 1958; ROSEMAN, S., *Ann.Rev.Biochem.*, **28**, 545 (1959); GOTTSCHALK, A., *The Chemistry and Biology of Sialic Acids and Related Substances*, Cambridge University Press, London, 1960; WHITEHOUSE and ZILLIKEN, *Meth.biochem.Anal.*, **8**, 199 (1960); CLARK and GRANT (Eds.), *The Biochemistry of Mucopolysaccharides of Connective Tissue*, Biochem. Soc. Symp., No. 20 (1961); STACY and BARKER, *Carbohydrates of Living Tissues*, Van Nostrand, London, 1962; MCGARRAHAN and MALEY, *J.biol. Chem.*, **237**, 2458 (1962); SPIRO, R.G., *New Engl.J.Med.*, **269**, 566 (1963); Symposium on Mucous Secretions, *Ann.N.Y.Acad.Sci.*, **106**, 157 (1963); BRIMACOMBE and WEBBER, *Mucopolysaccharides*, Elsevier, Amsterdam, 1964; DORFMAN, A., *Biophys.J.*, **4**, suppl., 155 (1964); GINSBURG, V., *Advanc. Enzymol.*, **26**, 35 (1964); GRANT and SIMKIN, *Ann.Rep.chem.Soc.*, **61**, 491 (1964); KORNFELD et al., *Proc.nat.Acad.Sci.(Wash.)*, **52**, 371 (1964); SARCIONE, E.J., *J.biol.Chem.*, **239**, 1686 (1964); CARTER et al., *Ann.Rev.Biochem.*, **34**, 109 (1965); MOLNAR et al., *J.biol.Chem.*, **240**, 1882 (1965); JEANLOZ and BALAZS (Eds.), *The Amino Sugars*, 2 vols., Academic Press, New York, 1965/66; GOTTSCHALK, A., *Glycoproteins*, Elsevier, Amsterdam, 1966.

Extension of carbon chains by carbon dioxide fixation

An important link in the building-up of the carbon skeletons of cell constituents is the addition of CO_2 to pyruvate. There are at least two CO_2-fixation reactions in animal tissues by which 4-carbon chains arise from pyruvate. The first[1] is catalysed by the 'malic' enzyme; it requires reduced NADP and leads to L-malic acid:

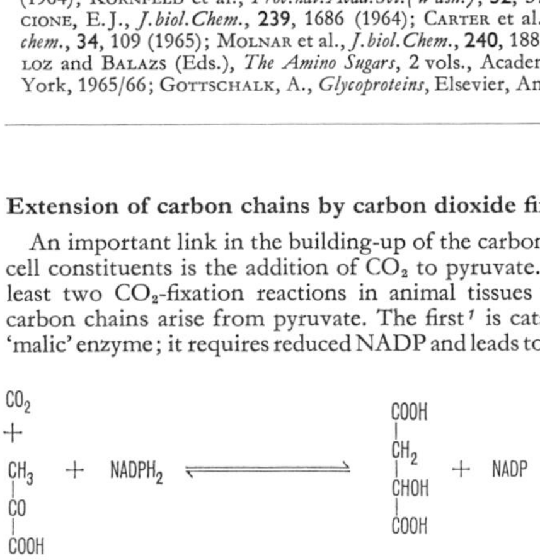

Pyruvic acid   L-Malic acid

The second reaction requires ATP and consists of the carboxylation of pyruvate to oxaloacetate, catalysed by the enzyme pyruvate carboxylase[2]:

Pyruvate   Oxaloacetate

Both reactions readily occur in liver tissue and also elsewhere. They are reversible. The malic and oxaloacetic acids formed can enter the tricarboxylic acid cycle and form citrate and α-ketoglutarate.

References

[1] OCHOA et al., *J.biol.Chem.*, **174**, 979 (1948); VEIGA SALLES and OCHOA, *J.biol.Chem.*, **187**, 849 (1950); HARARY et al., *J.biol.Chem.*, **203**, 595 (1953).
[2] UTTER and KEECH, *J.biol.Chem.*, **238**, 2603 (1963).

Fatty acid synthesis

Acetyl-coenzyme A formed from carbohydrate or amino acids, if not required for energy supply or special biosyntheses, can be converted to fatty acids. Most of the acetyl-coenzyme A is formed within the mitochondria, but the synthesis of fatty acids is an extramitochondrial process[1]. Acetyl groups must therefore be diverted from the mitochondria to the extramitochondrial space. This requires a special mechanism since acetyl-coenzyme A as such cannot diffuse into or out of the mitochondria[2]. The acetyl group is probably transferred as follows[3]:

Formation of citrate (intramitochondrial)

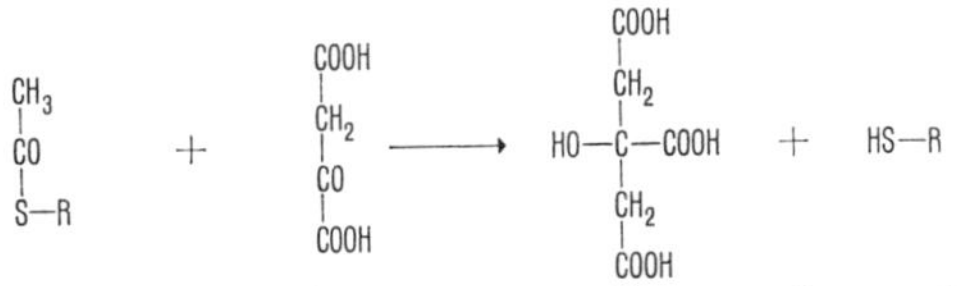 **(1)**

Acetyl-coenzyme A   Oxaloacetate   Citrate   Coenzyme A

Diffusion

Intramitochondrial citrate → extramitochondrial citrate **(2)**

Cleavage of citrate (extramitochondrial)

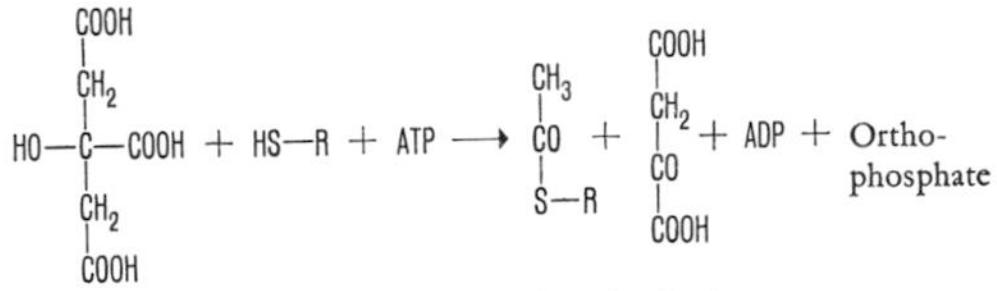 **(3)**

Citrate   Coenzyme A   Acetyl-coenzyme A   Oxalo-acetate

It is to be noted that reactions (**1**) and (**3**) are catalysed by different enzymes[4]. Reaction (**3**) is followed by the carboxylation of acetyl-coenzyme A to yield malonyl-coenzyme A[5]:

Acetyl-coenzyme A carboxylase reaction

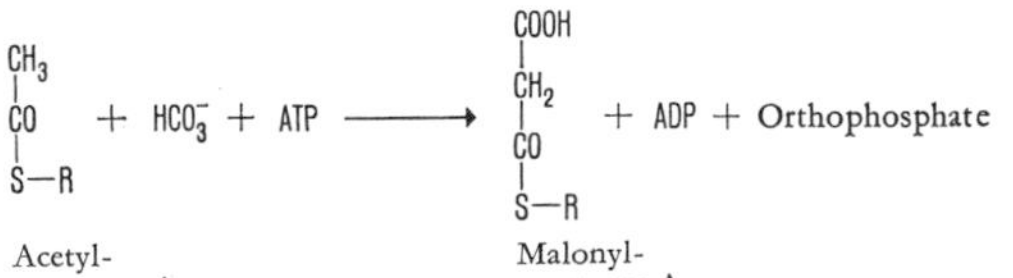 **(4)**

Acetyl-coenzyme A   Malonyl-coenzyme A

The enzyme catalysing this reaction contains biotin and requires citrate as an activator. Acetyl-coenzyme A and malonyl-coenzyme A then condense and are reduced according to the following stoichiometric equation[6]:

$$\text{acetyl-CoA} + 7\ \text{malonyl-CoA} + 14\ NADPH_2 \rightarrow \text{palmitate} + 7\ CO_2 + 14\ NADP + 8\ CoA \qquad (5)$$

This reaction is catalysed by a cytoplasmic enzyme complex[7] consisting of at least 6 or 7 different kinds of protein; these are tightly bound together in yeast and pigeon liver but readily dissociable in *E.coli* and several plant systems. An 'acyl carrier protein' (ACP) has been isolated from *E.coli* which binds acyl intermediates during the formation of long-chain fatty acids. ACP contains one free sulphydryl group per molecule, derived from 2-mercaptoethylamine, which binds the acyl derivative to form a thioester[8]. The individual steps of the fatty acid synthesis in *E.coli* are as follows:

acetyl·S·CoA + HS·ACP	→	acetyl·S·ACP + HS·CoA	(**5**a)
malonyl·S·CoA + HS·ACP	→	malonyl·S·ACP + HS·CoA	(**5**b)
acetyl·S·ACP + malonyl·S·ACP	→	acetoacetyl·S·ACP + HS·ACP + CO_2	(**5**c)
acetoacetyl·S·ACP + $NADPH_2$	→	D-β-hydroxybutyryl·S·ACP + NADP	(**5**d)
D-β-hydroxybutyryl·S·ACP	→	crotonyl·S·ACP + H_2O	(**5**e)
crotonyl·S·ACP + $NADPH_2$	→	butyryl·S·ACP + NADP	(**5**f)

Butyryl·S·ACP then undergoes condensation with another molecule of malonyl·S·ACP to yield β-ketohexanoyl·S·CoA. The reduction, dehydration and reduction steps are then repeated to yield hexanoyl·S·CoA. Another round of chain elongation then begins. The chain length at which chain elongation is terminated is determined enzymatically, presumably by the enzyme that catalyses reaction (**5**c). In higher animals the most common fatty acid made is palmitate. The final step is probably

palmityl·S·ACP + HS·CoA → palmityl·S·CoA + ACP (**5**g)

The palmityl group of palmityl-CoA may then be hydrolysed to palmitate or transferred to α-glycerophosphate and related compounds.

Steps (**3**), (**4**) and (**5**) of this process are summarized in Figure 13.

Fig. 13 Fatty acid synthesis from citrate

(*a*) Citrate cleavage enzyme. (*b*) Acetyl-coenzyme A carboxylase (activated by citrate). (*c*) Enzyme complex.

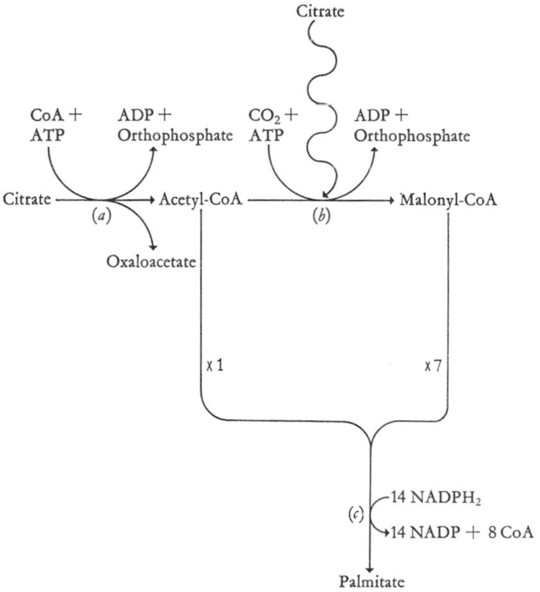

References

[1] Wakil, S.J., *Ann. Rev. Biochem.*, **31**, 369 (1962); Spencer et al., *Biochem. J.*, **93**, 378 (1964).
[2] Lowenstein, J.M., in Grant, J.K. (Ed.), *The Control of Lipid Metabolism*, Academic Press, New York, 1963, page 57; Fritz and Yue, *Amer. J. Physiol.*, **206**, 531 (1964).
[3] Spencer and Lowenstein, *J. biol. Chem.*, **237**, 3640 (1962); Bhaduri and Srere, *Biochim. biophys. Acta (Amst.)*, **70**, 221 (1963).
[4] Ochoa, S., in Colowick and Kaplan (Eds.), *Methods in Enzymology*, vol. 1, Academic Press, New York, 1955, page 685; Srere, P. A., *J. biol. Chem.*, **236**, 50 (1961).
[5] Waite and Wakil, *J. biol. Chem.*, **238**, 77 (1963); Vagelos et al., *J. biol. Chem.*, **238**, 533 (1963).
[6] Brady, R.O., *J. biol. Chem.*, **235**, 3099 (1960); Martin et al., *J. biol. Chem.*, **236**, 663 (1961); Bressler and Wakil, *J. biol. Chem.*, **236**, 1643 (1961).
[7] Majerus et al., *Proc. nat. Acad. Sci. (Wash.)*, **51**, 1231 (1964); Alberts et al., *Biochemistry*, **3**, 1563 (1964); Norris et al., *J. biol. Chem.*, **239**, 3653 (1964); Goldman, P., *J. biol. Chem.*, **239**, 3663 (1964); Olson, J.A., *Ann. Rev. Biochem.*, **35**, 559 (1966); Lynen, F., *Expos. ann. Biochim. méd.*, **28**, 1 (1967).
[8] Sauer et al., *Proc. nat. Acad. Sci. (Wash.)*, **52**, 1360 (1964).

Formation of lecithin and cephalin

The synthesis of lecithin in animal tissues from fatty acids, glycerophosphate and choline requires the participation as cofactors of ATP, coenzyme A and cytidine triphosphate:

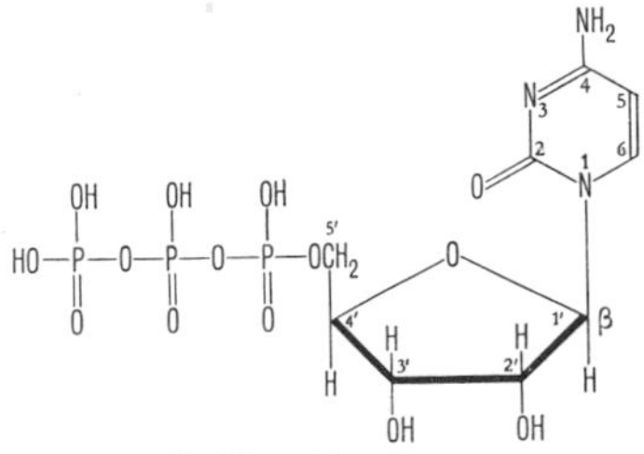

Cytidine triphosphate

The intermediary stages of the synthesis are as follows:

(*a*) 'Activation' of fatty acids[1]:

R·COOH + HS·R' + ATP → R·CO·S·R' + AMP + pyrophosphate

Fatty acid; Coenzyme A; Acyl-coenzyme A

(*b*) 'Activation' of choline by choline kinase[2]:

$CH_2N(CH_3)_3$–CH_2OH (Choline) + ATP → $CH_2N(CH_3)_3$–$CH_2O{\cdot}PO_3H_2$ (Phosphocholine) + ADP

(*c*) 'Activation' of phosphocholine[3]:

cytidine triphosphate + phosphocholine ⇌ cytidine diphosphocholine + pyrophosphate

(*d*) Synthesis of phosphatidic acid[3]:

CH_2OH–CHOH–$CH_2O{\cdot}PO_3H_2$ (α-Glycerophosphate) + R'·CO·SR, R''·CO·SR (2 Acyl-coenzyme A) → $CH_2{\cdot}O{\cdot}CO{\cdot}R'$–CH·O·CO·R''–$CH_2O{\cdot}PO_3H_2$ (Phosphatidic acid) + 2 HS·R (2 Coenzyme A)

(*e*) Dephosphorylation of phosphatidic acid[3]:

phosphatidic acid → D-α,β-diglyceride + phosphate

(*f*) Synthesis of lecithin[3]:

cytidine diphosphocholine + D-α,β-diglyceride → lecithin + cytidine monophosphate

(*g*) Rephosphorylation of cytidine monophosphate[4]:

cytidine monophosphate + 2 ATP → cytidine triphosphate + 2 ADP

Cephalin is synthesized by analogous reactions, choline being replaced by ethanolamine ($HO{\cdot}CH_2{\cdot}CH_2{\cdot}NH_2$).

References

[1] Kornberg and Pricer, *J. biol. Chem.*, **204**, 329 (1953).
[2] Wittenberg and Kornberg, *J. biol. Chem.*, **202**, 431 (1953).
[3] Kennedy and Weiss, *J. Amer. chem. Soc.*, **77**, 250 (1955); Kennedy and Weiss, *J. biol. Chem.*, **222**, 193 (1956); Kennedy, E.P., *J. biol. Chem.*, **222**, 185 (1956); Weiss et al., *Nature*, **178**, 594 (1956).
[4] Berg and Joklik, *J. biol. Chem.*, **210**, 657 (1954); Krebs and Hems, *Biochim. biophys. Acta (Amst.)*, **12**, 172 (1953); Krebs and Hems, *Biochem. J.*, **61**, 435 (1955); Lieberman et al., *J. biol. Chem.*, **215**, 429 (1955); Brumm et al., *J. biol. Chem.*, **220**, 713 (1956).

Formation of triglyceride[1]

The synthesis of triglyceride requires α-glycerophosphate. Two molecules of fatty acyl-coenzyme A condense with α-glycerophosphate to form phosphatidic acid, and then diglyceride, as described in the previous section. The final step is the reaction of diglyceride with another molecule of fatty acyl-coenzyme A to form triglyceride:

$CH_2·O·CO·R'$				$CH_2·O·CO·R'$		
$CH·O·CO·R''$	+	$R·CO·S·R$	⟶	$CH·O·CO·R''$	+	$HS·R$
CH_2OH				$CH_2·O·CO·R$		
Diglyceride		Fatty acyl-coenzyme A		Triglyceride		Coenzyme A

References

[1] STEIN and SHAPIRO, *Biochim. biophys. Acta (Amst.)*, **24**, 197 (1957); STEINBERG et al., *J. biol. Chem.*, **236**, 1631 (1961).

Biosynthesis of cholesterol[1]

Cholesterol[2] is by far the commonest sterol of the animal kingdom, though related sterols, notably Δ^7-sterols, are found to predominate in some primitive molluscs and starfish. Cholesterol is synthesized in almost all vertebrate tissues but most actively in the liver, intestine, adrenals and gonads. Synthesis does not take place in erythrocytes, and is reduced to extremely low levels in nerve and brain after myelination is completed. An important function of cholesterol is as a component of cell membranes and subcellular membrane structures, in which it is associated with phospholipids, glycolipids and proteins. The most likely type of interrelationship of these different components in membranes has been deduced from studies of the structure and composition of the myelin sheath and the erythrocyte membrane.

The rate of endogenous cholesterol synthesis is variable and in man has been estimated to range between 0.5 and 2 g per day[21]. The principal catabolic pathway for cholesterol is conversion to bile acids by the liver[22]. Some intact cholesterol leaves the body by excretion into the bile and some by direct loss through the intestinal wall and faeces. In the intestine some cholesterol is metabolized to coprosterol and coprostanone. A small proportion of the total cholesterol synthesized functions as a precursor of the steroid hormones of the adrenal cortex and of the steroid sex hormones.

The pathway of synthesis of cholesterol[3,4] has been studied primarily in the rat. Certain important reaction steps[5] have been studied *in vitro* with enzymes isolated from yeast, which synthesizes the related sterol, ergosterol. All the evidence assembled so far points to a unified mechanism of synthesis for the basic structure of all sterols. The sterols of plants (e.g., β-sitosterol) and fungi (e.g., ergosterol) differ from cholesterol in having extra carbon atoms in the side chain. These carbon atoms are added at a late stage in the synthesis by a mechanism so far not completely elucidated[6].

The individual steps in the biosynthesis of cholesterol as understood at present are as follows (Fig. 14 opposite):

The molecule is built up from acetate units which condense in the form of their coenzyme A derivatives; the first condensation yields acetoacetyl-coenzyme A (I), the second involves the further condensation of this compound with a third acetyl-coenzyme A molecule to give hydroxymethylglutaryl-coenzyme A (II). For several years it was recognized that by some mechanism this product must yield a five-carbon 'isoprenoid' fragment which forms the basis of the sterol structure, but it was only with the discovery of mevalonic acid (III) and the subsequent study of its conversion to sterol[7] that the details of this mechanism could be clarified. Hydroxymethylglutaryl-coenzyme A (II) is now known to be reduced by an NADP-dependent enzyme system to mevalonic acid (III). The occurrence of an aldehydic intermediate in this reduction is not certain. Mevalonic acid next undergoes at least two sequential phosphorylations yielding in turn mevalonic phosphate (IV) and mevalonic pyrophosphate (V), the phosphate group at each step being derived from a molecule of ATP. A third molecule of ATP is consumed in the next reaction, in which mevalonic pyrophosphate (V) undergoes both dehydration and decarboxylation to isopentenyl pyrophosphate (VII)[8]. This transformation probably involves the intermediate formation of the triphosphate (VI), but this compound has not been identified.

An isomerase converts the isopentenyl pyrophosphate (VII) to its dimethylallyl isomer[9] (VIII), and a condensation reaction between dimethylallyl pyrophosphate and isopentenyl pyrophosphate now takes place to give geranyl pyrophosphate (IX). This compound in turn condenses with a further dimethylallyl pyrophosphate molecule to give farnesyl pyrophosphate[10] (X). Each of these condensations takes place with elimination of the pyrophosphate group as the inorganic ion and the formation of a new double bond lying in the main chain allylic to the remaining pyrophosphate group. The steps probably involved in the first of these reactions are shown (VII + VIII). The second condensation (IX + VIII) follows by an analogous mechanism.

In some manner as yet undetermined, two molecules of farnesyl pyrophosphate condense to form the C_{30} triterpenoid hydrocarbon squalene (XI). This condensation is known to involve stereospecific addition of hydrogen from reduced NADP[11]. Squalene now undergoes a series of ill-defined cyclization and rearrangement reactions ending in lanosterol[12] (XII), with 2,3-oxidosqualene as intermediate[23].

Comparison of the structures of lanosterol (XII) and cholesterol (XIX) shows that the remaining biosynthetic steps must involve the removal of three methyl substituents from the 4α-, 4β- and 14α-positions of lanosterol. Other necessary changes are the saturation of the double bond in the side chain and the conversion of the Δ^8- to the Δ^5-nuclear structure. The three 'extra' methyl groups appear to be removed prior to the other changes in the molecule. In the pathway operating in the rat, the 14α-methyl group is removed first[13] and the two methyl substituents in position 4 are then removed in turn. The carbon atoms detached from the nucleus in these reactions are converted to CO_2[14] and the oxidation of each methyl to a carboxylic acid group seems likely to occur in each case. The final decarboxylation step is thought to be facilitated in the case of the 14α-methyl group by the proximity of the Δ^8-bond and in the case of the C_4-methyl groups by the transitory oxidation of the 3β-OH group to a ketone. Evidence for the latter step is the fact that the loss of the 4α-methyl group takes place with exchange of the 3α-hydrogen atom (demonstrated with 3α-tritium labelled substrates)[15].

The demethylation steps, if they occurred with no other changes in the molecule, would lead to the formation of $\Delta^{8,24}$-cholestadienol-(3β) (zymosterol) (XV). This compound is known as a minor sterol of yeast and evidence for its participation in the biosynthesis of cholesterol in the rat has been given[16]. The steps involved in the conversion of the Δ^8-structure of zymosterol to the Δ^5-structure of cholesterol are still unclear at many points. It seems likely that the Δ^8-bond is shifted to Δ^7 by some 'direct' mechanism involving hydrogen transfer. The conversion of Δ^7-cholestenol-(3β) to cholesterol probably takes place via the $\Delta^{5,7}$-derivative and is known to require oxygen, but the participation of a 6-hydroxylated derivative has not been demonstrated.

It has been suggested that in rat liver the conversion of zymosterol to cholesterol takes place via the $\Delta^{7,24}$-, $\Delta^{5,7,24}$- and $\Delta^{5,24}$-intermediates (XVI–XVIII) respectively, with the final step in the biosynthesis of cholesterol involving reduction of the Δ^{24}-bond[4]. The $\Delta^{5,24}$-sterol desmosterol (XVIII), known to occur naturally in trace amounts in adult mammalian tissues[17] and in larger amounts in embryonic chick tissues[18], accumulates in the liver of rats treated with the anticholesterogenic drug triparanol[19]. However, the question of whether the Δ^{24}-bond is retained until the last step in cholesterol synthesis must be regarded as unsettled at the present time. Evidence presented by several laboratories indicates that all the conversions from lanosterol onwards can be accomplished by enzymes of rat liver with substrates in which the Δ^{24}-bond is either present or absent. Moreover, normal rat skin contains a complex mixture of sterols with a saturated side chain but with nuclear structures representing nearly all the possible stages in the conversion of lanosterol to cholesterol. Triparanol treatment leads to the accumulation of the Δ^{24}-analogues of all these compounds in the skin[20]. It is possible that there are differences between tissues that determine whether cholesterol biosynthesis takes place predominantly via the Δ^{24}-series of compounds, including desmosterol (XVIII), or via the series of analogues in which the side chain is saturated, but whether it is necessary to envisage the process as occurring by one or the other of two mutually exclusive pathways is not clear.

References

[1] For reviews see CLAYTON, R.B., *Quart. Rev. chem. Soc.*, **19**, 168 (1965); BLOCH, K., *Science*, **150**, 19 (1965); FRANTZ and SCHROEPFER, *Ann. Rev. Biochem.*, **36**, 691 (1967).

[2] COOK, R.P. (Ed.), *Cholesterol; Chemistry, Biochemistry, and Pathology*, Academic Press, New York, 1958; BERGMANN, W., in FLORKIN and MASON (Eds.), *Comparative Biochemistry, a Comprehensive Treatise*, vol. 3, Academic Press, New York, 1962, page 103.

(continued on page 428)

Fig. 14 Biosynthesis of cholesterol

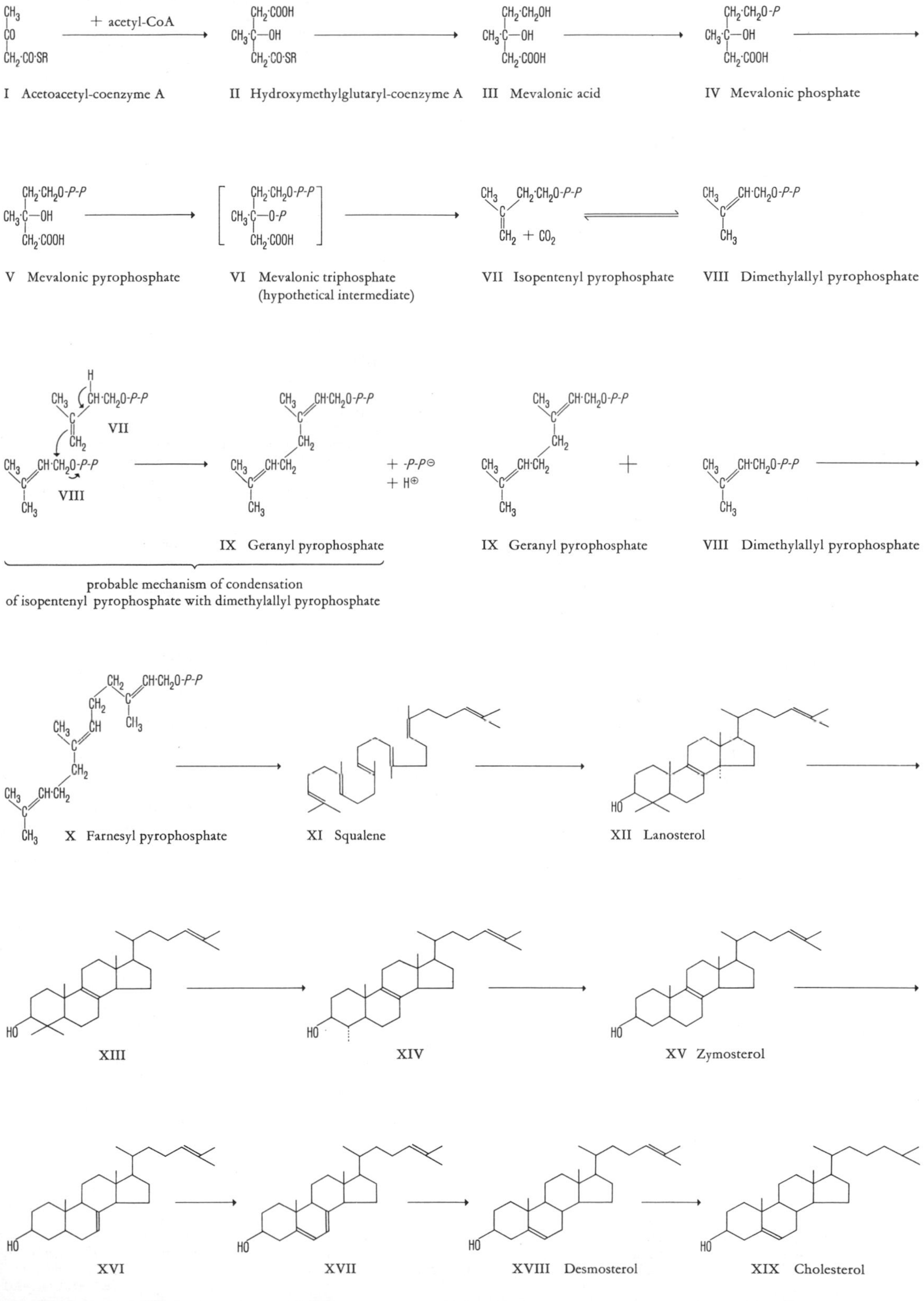

[3] Popják and Cornforth, *Advanc. Enzymol.*, **22**, 281 (1960).
[4] Bloch, K., *Vitam. and Horm.*, **15**, 119 (1957).
[5] Lynen, F., in Wolstenholme and O'Connor (Eds.), *Ciba Foundation Symposium on the Biosynthesis of Terpenes and Sterols*, Churchill, London, 1959, page 95; de Waard et al., *J. Amer. chem. Soc.*, **81**, 2913 (1959).
[6] Bader et al., *Proc. chem. Soc.*, **1964**, 16.
[7] Tavormina et al., *J. Amer. chem. Soc.*, **78**, 4498 (1956).
[8] Lynen et al., *Angew. Chem.*, **70**, 738 (1958).
[9] Lynen et al., *Angew. Chem.*, **71**, 657 (1959).
[10] Goodman and Popják, *Biochem. J.*, **74**, 35P (1960).
[11] Samuelsson and Goodman, *J. biol. Chem.*, **239**, 98 (1964).
[12] Tchen and Bloch, *J. biol. Chem.*, **226**, 921 (1957).
[13] Gautschi and Bloch, *J. biol. Chem.*, **233**, 1343 (1958).
[14] Olson et al., *J. biol. Chem.*, **226**, 941 (1957).
[15] Bloch, K., in Wolstenholme and O'Connor (Eds.), *Ciba Foundation Symposium on the Biosynthesis of Terpenes and Sterols*, Churchill, London, 1959, page 4.
[16] Johnston and Bloch, *J. Amer. chem. Soc.*, **79**, 1145 (1957).
[17] Stokes and Fish, *J. biol. Chem.*, **235**, 2604 (1960).
[18] Stokes et al., *J. biol. Chem.*, **220**, 415 (1956).
[19] Avigan et al., *J. biol. Chem.*, **235**, 3123 (1960).
[20] Clayton et al., *J. Lipid Res.*, **4**, 166 (1963).
[21] Food and Nutrition Board, *Dietary fat and human health*, National Academy of Sciences – National Research Council, Publication 1147, Washington, 1966.
[22] Danielsson, H., *Advanc. Lipid. Res.*, **1**, 335 (1963).
[23] Sih and Whitlock, *Ann. Rev. Biochem.*, **37**, 661 (1968).

Biosynthesis and metabolism of steroid hormones of the adrenal cortex and gonads (for references see page 430)

The normal adrenal cortex produces a wider variety of steroid hormones than either the ovary or the testis[1]. Besides producing eight C_{21}-steroids of known structure and proven 'corticoid' activity, it also produces many C_{21}-steroids of unknown physiological activity as well as progesterone, the oestrogens and the androgens of the $C_{19}O_2$- and $C_{19}O_3$-series[2–4]. Adrenal androgen formation[5] is at present more fully documented than the formation of adrenal oestrogens, and the pathway of testicular androgen formation appears to be clearly represented in the adrenal cortex. It is therefore convenient to outline the pathways of androgen synthesis together with the pathways of synthesis of C_{21}-steroids in a single scheme (Fig. 15), since these two aspects of steroid metabolism are closely interlinked. The oestrogenic steroids are further transformation products of the androgens and are more conveniently discussed separately (see page 430). The adrenal cortex, the testis, the ovary and the placenta are all capable of synthesizing their characteristic steroid hormones from acetate via cholesterol and pregnenolone, and it seems likely that most of the biosynthetic reactions involved in the synthesis of all classes of steroid hormones are possible in all the above-mentioned organs. However, it is not certain to what extent the hormones secreted normally in vivo are formed from acetate, from blood cholesterol or from steroid precursors synthesized in the adrenal cortex.

The C_{21}-corticoids have profound effects on carbohydrate and protein metabolism ('glucocorticoid' activity) and on sodium and potassium metabolism ('mineralocorticoid' activity). Most of these compounds exert effects of both types with one or the other predominating, according to their chemical structure. The more powerful glucocorticoids are those having oxygen functions at both C-11 and C-17. The glucocorticoid action of the human adrenal is considered to be accounted for almost wholly by the cortisol (hydrocortisone) it produces, since this is both the most potent naturally occurring steroid in this respect and also the most abundant product of the adrenal cortex in man. Corticosterone, the most abundant corticoid of the rat, has a less powerful glucocorticoid action. It is now clear that a portion of the cortisol or corticosterone output of the adrenal is in a protein-bound form in the blood[6]. It seems probable that the unbound portion is to be regarded as the physiologically active form, and various factors (for instance oestrogen levels) affecting the degree of protein-binding of the glucocorticoids may therefore exert important effects on their physiological function. The most potent hormone in the regulation of salt metabolism is aldosterone, a quantitatively minor product. Deoxycorticosterone has a much smaller but still detectable effect on salt metabolism. For further discussion of the adrenocortical steroids see pages 742 sq.

Figure 15 shows the most probable routes of biosynthesis of the physiologically active C_{21}-steroids of the adrenal and depicts the main pathways leading to the androgens testosterone, Δ^4-androstenedione, dehydroepiandrosterone, 11β-hydroxy-Δ^4-androstenedione and Δ^4-androstene-3,11,17-trione (adrenosterone). All these C_{19}-steroids may arise in the adrenal but the last two, having 11-oxygen functions, are probably specifically products of the adrenals. Testosterone is certainly the principal androgen of the testis but probably is formed in only trace amounts in the adrenal. Both the testis and adrenal give rise to some Δ^4-androstenedione and dehydroepiandrosterone (see page 751).

The pathways outlined in Figure 15 are largely based on evidence from *in vitro* work with adrenal and testis tissues, but the evidence of in vivo studies in man is consistent with the operation of these pathways. There is an extensive literature on steroid biosynthesis and metabolism in the adrenals and gonads in pathological states, especially in various types of tumours of these tissues and in abnormalities having a genetic basis. The major genetic abnormalities are briefly considered below, but metabolic studies with tumour tissues will not be discussed, though it should be noted that they frequently show abnormal biosynthetic patterns suggested by the symptoms to which the tumours give rise (for instance masculinizing adrenal tumours produce androgens; feminizing tumours produce oestrogens). Since such findings most probably represent an exaggeration of the normal biosynthetic potentialities rather than the addition of totally new features they provide valuable clues to the normal pathways of synthesis.

The C_{21}-steroids of the adrenals can all be derived from cholesterol via 20α-hydroxycholesterol and 20α,22ξ-dihydroxycholesterol. In the adrenals, the first identifiable C_{21}-steroid, pregnenolone, is mostly converted via progesterone into the more highly oxygenated C_{21}-corticoids. A minor pathway for pregnenolone in both the adrenals and testes involves its conversion to 17α-hydroxypregnenolone, which serves as a precursor of the weak androgen dehydroepiandrosterone. The conversion of progesterone into the C_{21}-corticoids takes place mainly by one of two divergent pathways depending upon whether hydroxylation takes place first at the 17α-position (giving 17α-hydroxyprogesterone) or the 21-position (giving deoxycorticosterone). Most of the data indicate that hydroxylation at C-17 proceeds more readily in the absence of the 21-hydroxyl group[7]. Both deoxycorticosterone and 17α-hydroxydeoxycorticosterone may undergo hydroxylation at the 11β-position giving respectively corticosterone and cortisol, which on further oxidation at C-11 yield minor amounts of two further physiologically active substances, 11-dehydrocorticosterone and cortisone. The pathway to aldosterone is still not clear, but its formation from deoxycorticosterone by hydroxylation at C-18 to 18-hydroxycorticosterone and subsequent oxidation has been demonstrated. Other synthetic pathways are also possible[8]. The mechanisms by which aldosterone and cortisol output are controlled (see page 430) are markedly different and in this connection it is probably significant that aldosterone secretion seems to be almost exclusively confined to the outer zone (zona glomerulosa) of the cortex, cortisol secretion to the inner zones.

Further metabolism of C_{21}-steroids and the formation of androgens. The physiologically active corticoids shown in Figure 15 undergo a multiplicity of further transformations, both in the adrenal itself and in other tissues, notably the liver and sex glands. It is not known at present whether these transformations are related to the hormonal function of these compounds. The catabolic reactions may be classified into four principal groups: oxidative degradation, hydroxylation, reduction and conjugation.

Oxidative degradation. The cleavage of the side chain in the C_{21}-steroids having the 17α-hydroxy-20-keto grouping is the main route by which the androgens arise in the testis, ovary and adrenal, as it is in the liver in the course of inactivation of the blood corticoids. It is because this cleavage reaction occurs in the liver that 17-ketosteroid excretion may be taken as a rough index of adrenocortical activity (see page 747). Dehydroepiandrosterone may be formed in the adrenal by cleavage of the side chain of 17-hydroxypregnenolone[9] and possibly of 17α,20α-dihydroxycholesterol[5]. Both these reactions probably occur in the testis also, but the major precursor of testosterone in the testis is progesterone, which is degraded via its 17α-hydroxy derivative. A second possible route from progesterone to testosterone involves its direct oxidation to testosterone acetate. This reaction has been observed microbiologically[10] and there is some evidence for its occurrence in humans.

Hydroxylation[3,4]. Besides the hydroxylations at C-11, C-17, C-18 and C-21 leading to the formation of the active C_{21}-corticoids, the adrenal cortex is also able to hydroxylate steroids of both the C_{19}- and C_{21}-series at the 6α-, 6β- and 19-positions. Hydroxylations at C-6 are also known to occur in rat liver, and the guinea-pig adrenal converts cortisol to 2α-hydroxycortisol. Urinary steroids (both

(continued on page 430)

Fig. 15 Biosynthesis of adrenal steroids and androgens

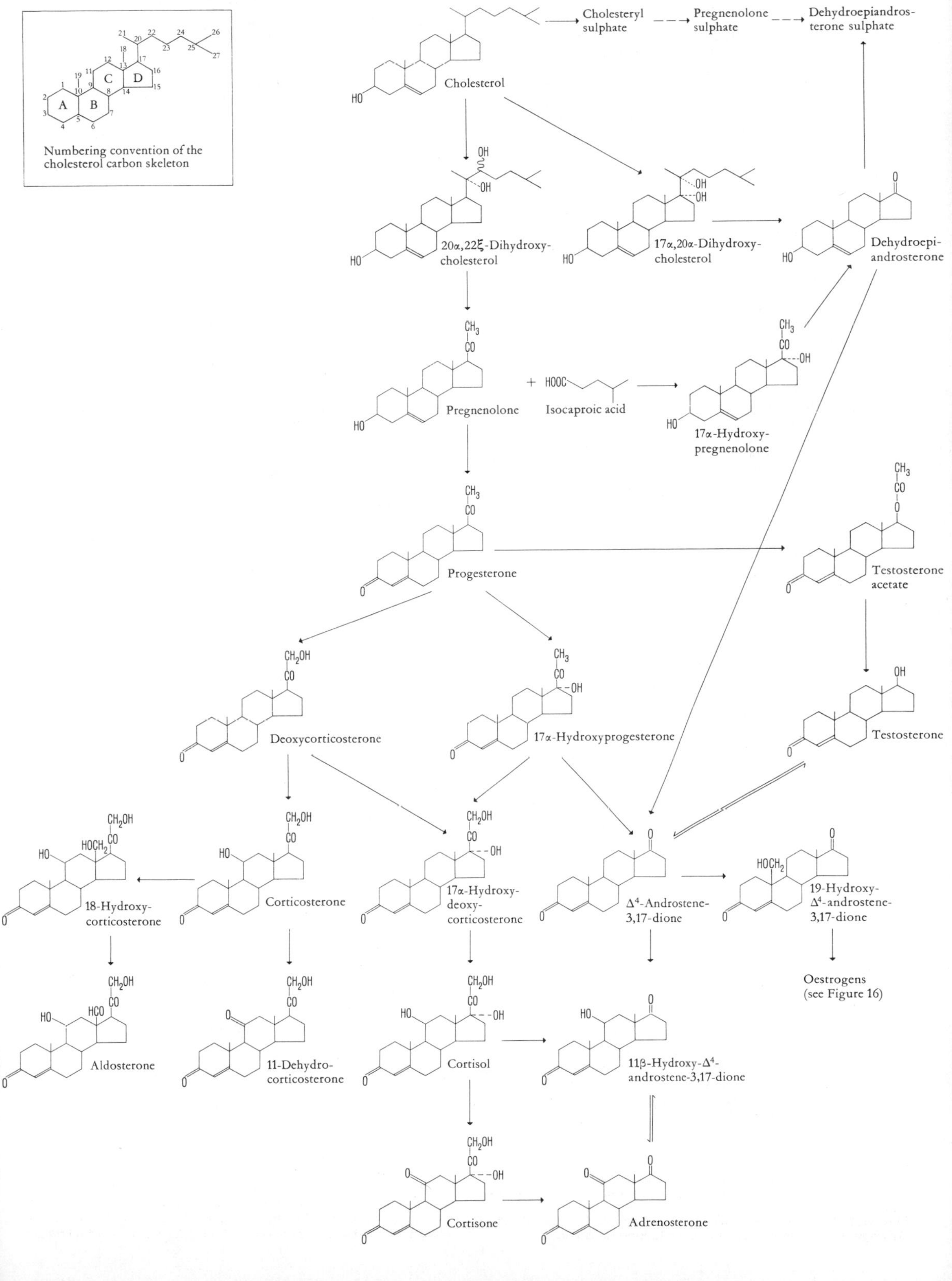

C_{19}- and C_{21}-) with 16α-hydroxy groups have also been isolated, and hog adrenal tissue is able to carry out hydroxylations at this position.

Reduction. In general, the body tends to eliminate steroid hormones in the form of metabolites in which the Δ^4-3-keto system of ring A is totally reduced (Fig. 15). Theoretically, this reduction may lead to products having either 3α- or 3β-hydroxy groups and the hydrogen atom at C-5 in either the 5α- or 5β-configuration. Actually, almost all reduced metabolites excreted by man are of the 3α-hydroxy-5β- (C_{21}: pregnane; C_{19}: aetiocholane) series. Minor quantities of steroids of the 3α-hydroxy-5α-(C_{21}: allopregnane; C_{19}: androstane) series are also excreted. Metabolism of steroid hormones by tissues of other species, in particular rat liver (*in vitro*) yields predominantly (but not exclusively) reduction products of the 5α-series having both 3α- and 3β-hydroxy groups. Reduction of the Δ^4-3-keto moiety apparently proceeds in stepwise fashion, the Δ^4-bond being reduced first[11]. Interesting sex differences have been observed in the intracellular distribution and overall concentration of Δ^5-steroid reductases in the rat[12].

Conversion of the 20-keto group to a 20-hydroxy group is a further important catabolic reduction of the C_{21}-steroids and also follows a course in most *in vitro* tissue preparations sterically different from that found in man. The product *in vitro* is generally a 20β-hydroxy derivative; that excreted by man is almost exclusively a 20α-hydroxy derivative.

Conjugation and excretion. The steroid excretion products of the urine are present largely in the form of conjugates with glucuronic acid or with sulphate. Dehydroepiandrosterone and androsterone are present in the urine to a major extent as sulphate conjugates. There is evidence for the secretion of some dehydroepiandrosterone as the sulphate[13]. Some of this material may arise via a series of intermediates derived directly from cholesteryl sulphate[14], but the quantitative importance of this pathway remains to be established. Cortisone and cortisol are apparently excreted in the urine largely in the free form, but the majority of the C_{21}-metabolites are excreted as β-glucuronides; the latter appear to arise primarily in the liver by a mechanism involving glucuronosyl transfer from uridine diphosphate glucuronic acid[15]. It has been demonstrated that about 50% of the blood cortisol is in the glucuronide form[16].

Pituitary control. The adrenal cortex is maintained in a normal functional state by the action of pituitary ACTH. Apart from this generalized influence on the metabolism of adrenal cortical tissue, ACTH also exerts a specific and immediate stimulating effect on the process of corticosteroid biogenesis. The precise point (or points) at which this influence is exerted is still in doubt. One important point of action is considered to be at a very early stage, probably in the conversion of cholesterol to pregnenolone[17]. It has also been observed that ACTH stimulation can alter the ratio of the amounts of cortisol and corticosterone secreted, but such an effect does not necessarily imply intervention of ACTH in the later stages of biosynthesis[18]. The mechanism of action of ACTH remains largely unknown at the present time despite intensive study[19]. For further discussion of this subject see page 717.

Aldosterone. Aldosterone, the steroid hormone mainly responsible for controlling electrolyte balance, is unique in that it has an aldehydic group at C-18 and is synthesized in the zona glomerulosa of the cortex. Aldosterone production has been demonstrated from a number of precursors but the major route is probably progesterone → deoxycorticosterone → corticosterone → aldosterone (Fig. 15). The major metabolic product seems to be tetrahydroaldosterone glucuronide[20]. The 18-hydroxytetrahydrocorticosterone found in human urine is a metabolite of 18-hydroxycorticosterone and not of aldosterone[21].

Since aldosterone output falls by only 30% after hypophysectomy ACTH would appear to have little effect on aldosterone secretion[22]. More important and more direct is probably the regulation by the sodium and potassium concentrations and the extracellular fluid volume of the body. Angiotensin also plays an important part[23] (see page 741).

References

1 WITSCHI, E., *Development of Vertebrates*, Saunders, Philadelphia, 1956.
2 PINCUS and THIMANN (Eds.), *The Hormones*, vol. 3, Academic Press, New York, 1955.
3 DEANE, H.W., *The Adrenocortical Hormones*, in EICHLER et al. (Eds.), *Handbook of Experimental Pharmacology*, vol. 14, part 1, Springer, Berlin, 1962.
4 SOFFER et al., *The Human Adrenal Gland*, Lea & Febiger, Philadelphia, 1961.
5 DORFMAN et al., *Recent Progr. Hormone Res.*, **19**, 251 (1963).
6 DAUGHADAY, W.H., *Physiol. Rev.*, **39**, 885 (1959).
7 LOMBARDO and HUDSON, *Endocrinology*, **65**, 417 (1959).
8 JAYLE et al., *Expos. ann. Biochim. méd.*, **28**, 163 (1967).
9 SOLOMON et al., *J. biol. Chem.*, **235**, 351 (1960).
10 FONKEN et al., *J. Amer. chem. Soc.*, **82**, 5507 (1960).
11 TOMKINS, G.M., *J. biol. Chem.*, **225**, 13 (1957).
12 FORCHIELLI et al., *Proc. Soc. exp. Biol. (N.Y.)*, **99**, 594 (1958).
13 WIELAND et al., *Biochim. biophys. Acta (Amst.)*, **78**, 566 (1963).
14 CALVIN et al., *Biochemistry*, **2**, 648 (1963); ROBERTS et al., *J. Amer. chem. Soc.*, **86**, 958 (1964).
15 ISSELBACHER, K.J., *Recent Progr. Hormone Res.*, **12**, 134 (1956).
16 BONGIOVANNI et al., *Proc. Soc. exp. Biol. (N.Y.)*, **87**, 282 (1954).
17 HAYANO et al., *Recent Progr. Hormone Res.*, **12**, 79 (1956).
18 KASS et al., *Proc. Soc. exp. Biol. (N.Y.)*, **85**, 583 (1954); GRANT et al., *J. clin. Endocr.*, **17**, 933 (1957).
19 PASTAN, I., *Ann. Rev. Biochem.*, **35**, 369 (1966).
20 SANDOR and LANTHIER, *Acta endocr. (Kbh.)*, **39**, 87 (1962).
21 ULICK and KUSCH, *J. Amer. chem. Soc.*, **82**, 6421 (1960).
22 BLAIR-WEST et al., *Recent Progr. Hormone Res.*, **19**, 311 (1963); GANONG et al., *Recent Progr. Hormone Res.*, **22**, 381 (1966).
23 DAVIS, J.O., *Recent Progr. Hormone Res.*, **17**, 293 (1961); DAVIS, J.O., *Circulation*, **25**, 1002 (1962); PEART, W.S., *Recent Progr. Hormone Res.*, **21**, 73 (1965); GROSS et al., *Recent Progr. Hormone Res.*, **21**, 119 (1965).

Biosynthesis and metabolism of oestrogens

(For references see page 432)

It is now evident that all the tissues active in the synthesis of steroid hormones are capable of some degree of oestrogen synthesis. Under more usual physiological conditions the ovaries are certainly the most active site of such synthesis, but their output is surpassed several hundred-fold by the placenta close to term.

The oestrogens are C_{18}-steroids in which ring A is aromatic, and there is now ample evidence for the biosynthesis[1,2] of these compounds from acetate via cholesterol, pregnenolone, progesterone and the C_{19}-steroids, according to the scheme outlined in Figure 16. The aromatization of ring A evidently takes place via a C_{19}-steroid intermediate in which the C-19 methyl group has been oxidized, though whether this intermediate has a hydroxylic or aldehydic oxygen function at C-19 has not been unequivocally established. The C-19 atom is released as formaldehyde[3], a finding interpreted as indicating that oxidation at C-19 proceeds to the aldehyde stage prior to rupture of the C-10 to C-19 bond, as shown. Several other mechanisms could, however, yield the same end products. There is evidence that the aromatizing enzyme system has rather low specificity with respect to the structure of the molecule as a whole. Thus, both 6α- and 6β-hydroxy-Δ^4-androstene-3,17-dione are converted to the corresponding 6-hydroxyoestrogens[4].

Intermediary metabolism of oestrogens

When radioactive oestrone or oestradiol-17β is administered to intact animals or incubated with animal tissues the oestrogenic activity is rapidly destroyed; considerably less than half of the administered radioactivity can be recovered in the ether-soluble fraction even after hydrolysis of the excreta or the incubation mixture with acid or with enzymes which release the oestrogens from their known conjugated forms[1,5]. The nature of the oestrogen derivatives that resist extraction with ether in such experiments is entirely unknown, and this fact should not be overlooked when considering the significance of the work relating to oestrogen metabolism summarized in the following sections.

When either oestradiol or oestrone is injected into a human subject, conjugates of the three steroids oestriol, oestrone and oestradiol-17β appear in the urine in the approximate proportions 45:45:10. The relative constancy of these proportions indicates a rapid equilibration of oestrone and oestradiol in the body tissues. The enzyme responsible for the interconversion in the human placenta has been studied extensively. It can utilize either NAD or NADP as cofactor, a finding that has prompted speculation as to the mode of physiological action of the oestrogenic hormones[6].

During the past few years, several other phenolic steroids besides the 'classical' oestrogens – oestradiol, oestrone and oestriol – have been isolated from various sources and have been characterized chemically. Thus it is now clear that hydroxylation of oestrone may occur at the 2-, 6-, 11-, 16- or 18-position. The interrelationships of these various compounds are shown in Figure 16. Hydroxylation at the 2-position is followed by methylation. Both reactions occur in the liver, and both 2-hydroxy- and 2-methoxyoestrone may be eliminated in the urine. The methylation reaction is catalyzed by an *O*-methyl transferase which, like other *O*-methyl trans-

Fig. 16 Biosynthesis and metabolism of oestrogens

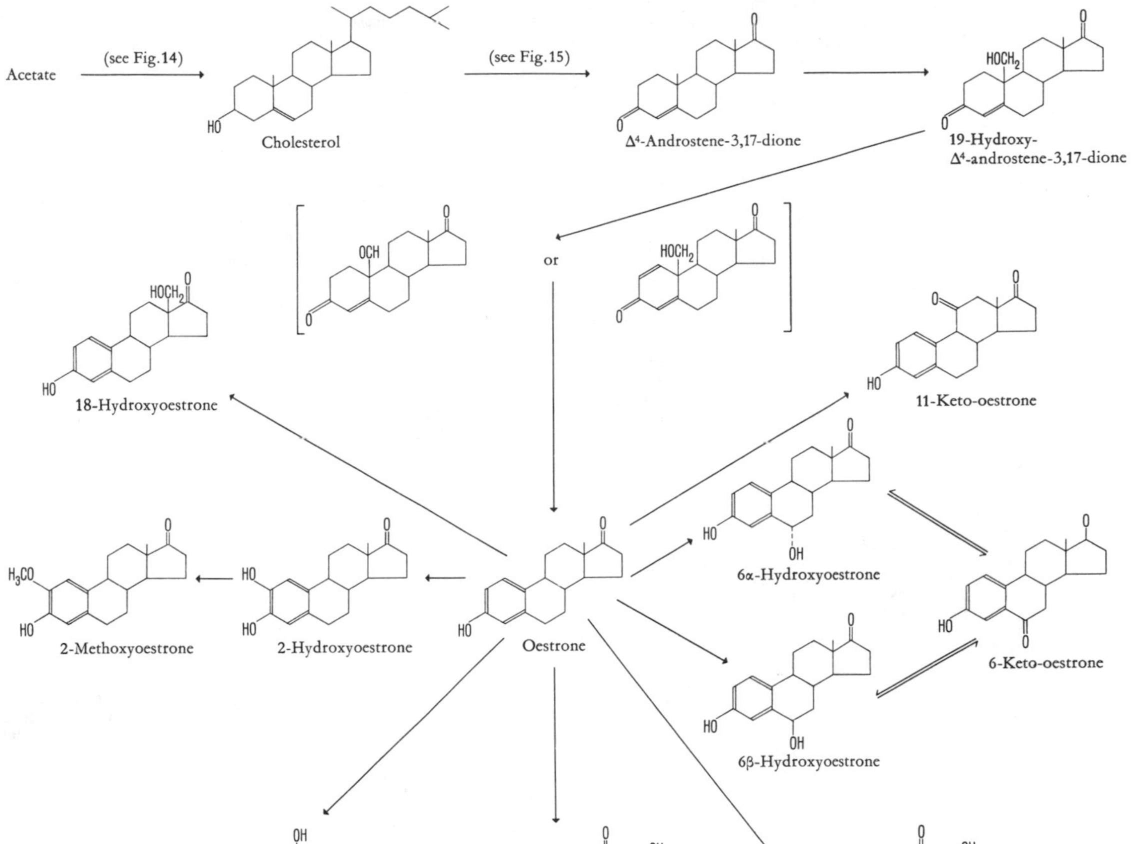

ferases (e.g., in the metabolism of catecholamines), utilizes *S*-methyladenosylmethionine as the methyl group donor[7].

Both 6α- and 6β-hydroxyoestrone have been obtained *in vitro* by the action of hydroxylating enzymes present in the livers of rats and humans. These two compounds are equilibrated via the 6-keto steroid through the activity of NADP-dependent dehydrogenases. Oestrogens oxygenated at C-6 are probably minor urinary excretory metabolites.

The formation of 11β-hydroxyoestrone by the action of ox adrenal homogenates on oestrone *in vitro* has been described, but the extent and physiological significance of this reaction in man are unknown[8].

The various 16-oxygenated steroids isolated and characterized in recent years may now be related to each other and to oestrone in a metabolic scheme as shown in Figure 16. Oestriol, long known as a major urinary oestrogen, is formed mainly from oestrone via

16α-hydroxyoestrone[9]. Very small amounts of 17-epioestriol are also formed. 16β-Hydroxyoestrone is a further product, but on enzymic reduction gives 16-epioestriol with 16,17-epioestriol as a minor product. 18-Hydroxyoestrone occurs in pregnancy urine[10] and there is evidence that this compound is of adrenal origin[11].

Equilin and equilenin are well known as urinary oestrogens of the pregnant mare, and equilenin has been identified as a metabolite of a feminizing adrenal tumour in man[12]. Evidence against the derivation of these compounds from oestrone has been put forward, but since it is based on *in vivo* work with horses it must be accepted with reservation.

Conjugates of oestrogen metabolites. The urinary oestrogens are excreted predominantly in the form of conjugates with glucuronic acid or sulphate. Oestriol is converted to both the 16- and 17-glucuronosides, but the involvement of the phenolic oxygen function in glucuronoside formation has definitely been established in the case of oestrone. This steroid accepts the glucuronic acid residue from UDP-glucuronic acid in a typical reaction catalysed by a glucuronyl transferase[1]. The formation of the sulphates involves the phenolic hydroxyl function in the case of oestriol and oestrone. The mechanism of this reaction has not been described, but the mechanism of formation of other sulphate esters has been extensively studied[13].

References

1 Breuer, H., *Vitam. and Horm.*, **20**, 285 (1962).
2 O'Donnell and Preedy, in Gray and Bacharach (Eds.), *Hormones in Blood*, Academic Press, New York, 1961, page 303.
3 Breuer and Grill, *Hoppe-Seylers Z. physiol. Chem.*, **324**, 254 (1961).
4 Breuer et al., *Biochim. biophys. Acta (Amst.)*, **40**, 560 (1960).
5 Beer and Gallagher, *J. biol. Chem.*, **214**, 335 (1955); Jellinck, P.H., *Biochem. J.*, **71**, 665 (1959).
6 Tallalay and Williams-Ashman, *Proc. nat. Acad. Sci. (Wash.)*, **44**, 15 (1958); Tomkins and Maxwell, *Ann. Rev. Biochem.*, **32**, 677 (1963).
7 Knuppen et al., *Hoppe-Seylers Z. physiol. Chem.*, **324**, 108 (1961).
8 Knuppen and Breuer, *Biochim. biophys. Acta (Amst.)*, **58**, 147 (1962).
9 Fishman et al., *J. biol. Chem.*, **235**, 3104 (1960); Fishman et al., *Acta endocr. (Kbh.)*, **37**, 57 (1961).
10 Loke et al., *Biochim. biophys. Acta (Amst.)*, **28**, 214 (1958).
11 Loke et al., *Biochim. biophys. Acta (Amst.)*, **26**, 230 (1957).
12 Salhanick and Berliner, *J. biol. Chem.*, **227**, 583 (1957).
13 Robbins and Lipmann, *J. biol. Chem.*, **229**, 837 (1957).

Formation of serine and glycine

Serine can be formed from glucose via phosphoglyceric acid. It is not certain at what stage the phosphate is removed from the ester link and the evidence is in accordance with several possibilities[1] as follows:

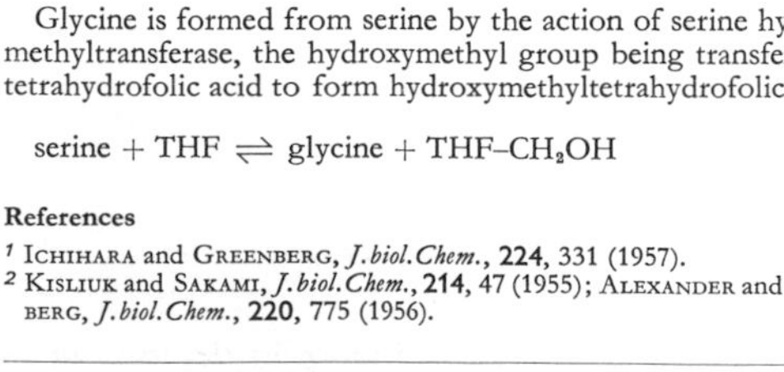

Glycine is formed from serine by the action of serine hydroxymethyltransferase, the hydroxymethyl group being transferred to tetrahydrofolic acid to form hydroxymethyltetrahydrofolic acid[2]:

$$\text{serine} + \text{THF} \rightleftharpoons \text{glycine} + \text{THF–CH}_2\text{OH}$$

References

1 Ichihara and Greenberg, *J. biol. Chem.*, **224**, 331 (1957).
2 Kisliuk and Sakami, *J. biol. Chem.*, **214**, 47 (1955); Alexander and Greenberg, *J. biol. Chem.*, **220**, 775 (1956).

Formation of glutamic acid

Glutamic acid is readily synthesized in liver and other animal tissues when α-ketoglutarate, ammonia and reduced NAD or NADP are available. The reaction is catalysed by glutamate dehydrogenase:

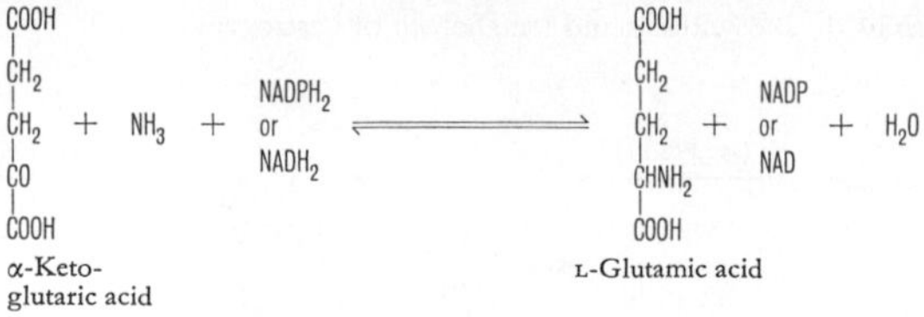

Glutamic acid is the only amino acid in animal tissues that can be directly synthesized from ammonia and the corresponding carbon skeleton (supplied in the form of the α-ketonic acid). All other nonessential amino acids are formed from the corresponding α-ketonic acids by transamination with glutamate. The reductive amination of α-ketoglutarate is thus the most important ammonia-binding reaction in the animal body.

Formation of proline and hydroxyproline

These amino acids are assumed to be formed from ornithine or glutamic acid via glutamic semialdehyde according to the following sequence of reactions:

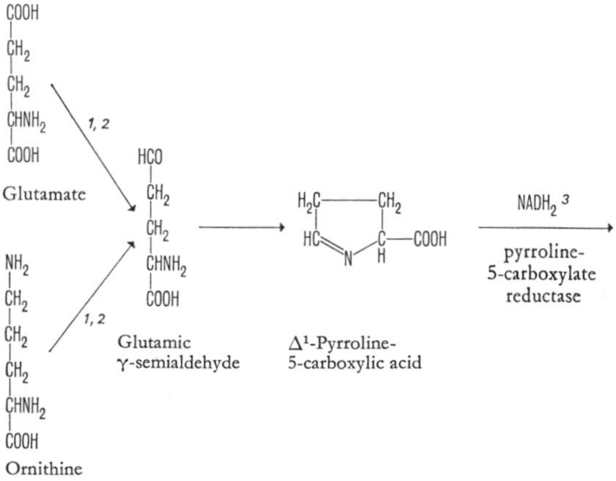

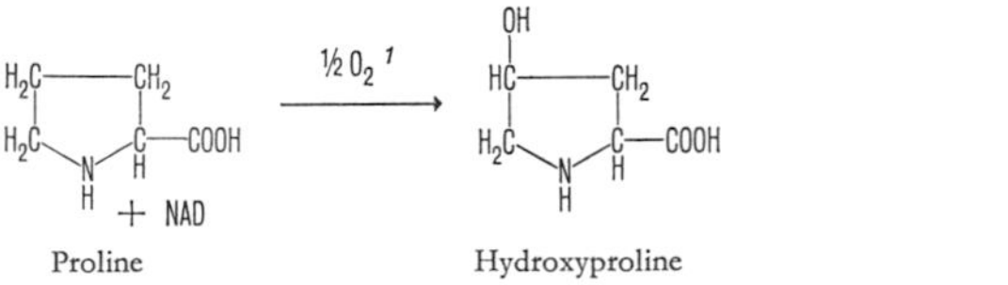

Collagen hydroxyproline is derived from proline by hydroxylation of prolyl residues in a precursor polypeptide, the so-called protocollagen[4]. In an analogous reaction hydroxylysine is derived from peptide-linked lysine[5].

References

1 Stetten, M.R., in McElroy and Glass (Eds.), *A Symposium on Amino Acid Metabolism*, Johns Hopkins Press, Baltimore, 1955, page 277; Vogel, H.J., *ibid.*, page 335.
2 Strecker and Mela, *Biochim. biophys. Acta (Amst.)*, **17**, 580 (1955).
3 Yura and Vogel, *Biochim. biophys. Acta (Amst.)*, **17**, 582 (1955); Smith and Greenberg, *J. biol. Chem.*, **226**, 317 (1957).
4 Udenfried, S., *Science*, **152**, 1335 (1966).
5 Popenoe et al., *J. biol. Chem.*, **240**, 3089 (1965).

Formation of histidine

The capacity of man to synthesize histidine has not been established. In micro-organisms this amino acid is synthesized from ATP, ribose 5-phosphate 1-pyrophosphate and glutamine in a ten-stage reaction[1].

Reference

1 Broquist and Trupin, *Ann. Rev. Biochem.*, **35**, 231 (1966).

(For references see page 436)

Synthesis of cell constituents from amino acids

The principal products, their pathways of formation and their physiological functions are summarized in Table 20 on page 434.

Formation of purines

Knowledge of the pathways shown below and on pages 435 and 436 is derived mainly from work done on pigeon liver. There is, however, no reason to doubt that the same pathway occurs in mammals. The purine skeleton is built up on the nitrogen atom of ribosylamine 5-phosphate. The substrates utilized in this process include glutamine, glycine, aspartic acid, carbon dioxide, and a one-carbon fragment equivalent to formaldehyde that is supplied in the form of a formyl derivative of tetrahydrofolic acid[1]. The first purine derivative to be formed is inosinic acid (reactions **1–11**). This is then converted into adenylic acid (reactions **12** and **13**) or into xanthylic acid (reaction **14**) and guanylic acid (reaction **15**). Only adenine is utilized directly when the naturally occurring purines are ingested as the free bases. It is probably converted into AMP by a reaction similar to the conversion of orotic acid to orotidylic acid (see page 439)[2]. Other purine bases such as guanine, hypoxanthine and xanthine are utilized to a very small extent or not at all[3].

Formation of inosinic acid (inosine monophosphate, IMP)

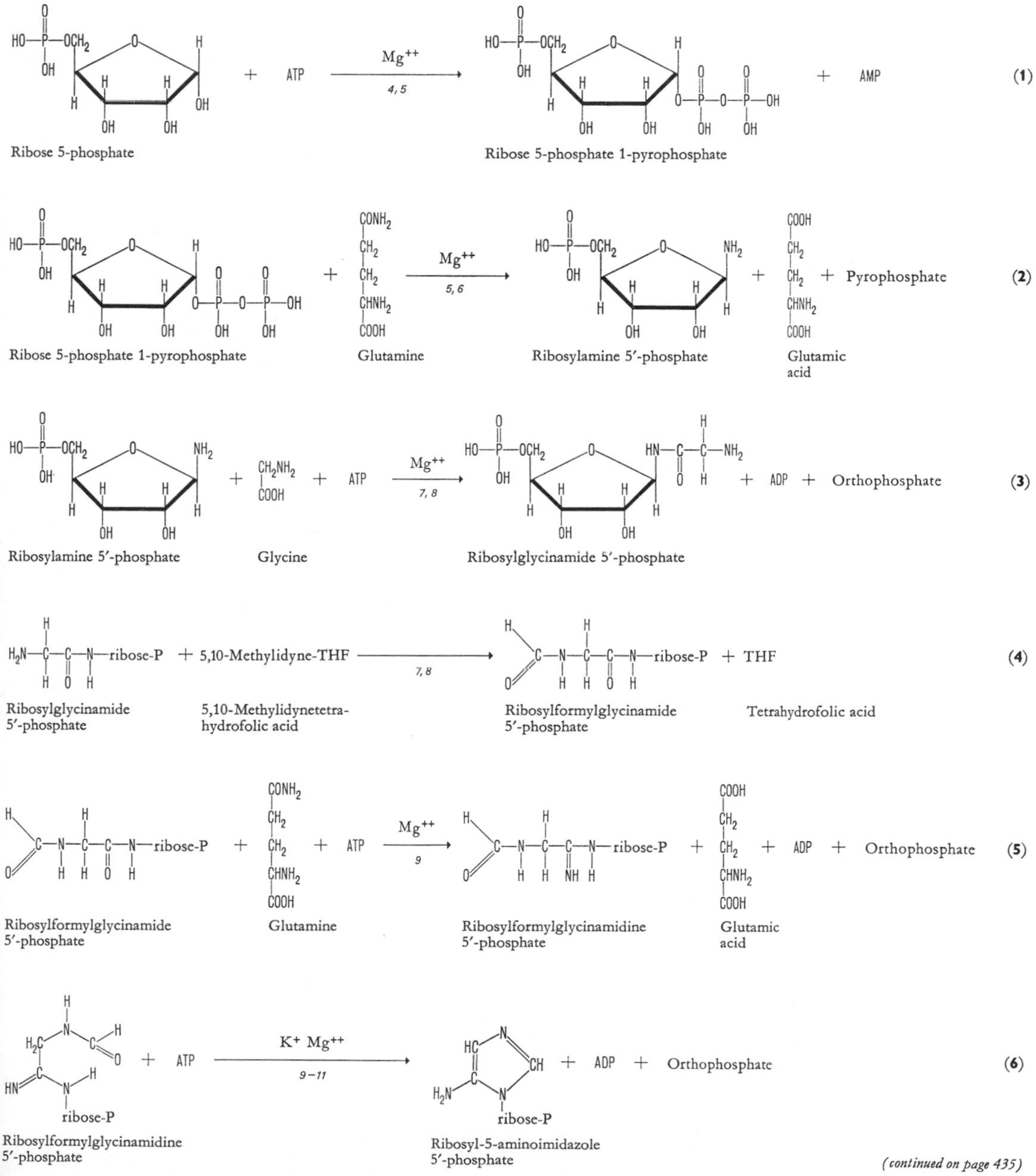

(continued on page 435)

Table 20 Formation of basic cell constituents and metabolites from amino acids
This list is not comprehensive; for carbohydrate synthesis from amino acids see page 441.

Amino acid serving as starting material	Product formed	Pathway of formation	Physiological function
Glycine	Purine bases	See page 433	Constituent of nucleic acids and nucleotides
	Porphyrins	See page 437	Constituent of haemoglobin and cytochromes
	Creatine	See page 437	Precursor of creatine phosphate, an energy store in muscle and other tissues
	Glutathione	See page 438	Coenzyme function in the glyoxalase system and for cis-trans isomerases and probably other enzymes
	Hippuric acid and related compounds	See page 445	Detoxication product of benzoic acid
	Bile acids	See page 438	Required for digestion of fats
Serine	Ethanolamine	Decarboxylation (see Table 6, page 394)	Constituent of phospholipids
	Choline	Methylation of ethanolamine, methionine acting as a methyl group donor	Constituent of phospholipids
	Acetylcholine	Acetylation of choline by acetyl-coenzyme A[1]	Transmitter substance at nerve endings
Cysteine	Taurine	See page 438	Constituent of bile acids
	Glutathione	See page 438	See above under 'Glycine'
Glutamic acid	Glutamine	From glutamic acid and ammonia in the presence of ATP[2]	Cell constituent. Intermediate carrier of amino groups in aminations and amidations
	γ-Aminobutyric acid	Decarboxylation (see Table 6, page 394)	Cell constituent, especially of brain
	Glutathione	See page 438	See above under 'Glycine'
	Proline	See page 432	Protein constituent
	Hydroxyproline	See page 432	Protein constituent
Arginine	Creatine	See page 437	See above under 'Glycine'
Methionine	Creatine	See page 437	See above under 'Glycine'
	Choline	Decarboxylation (see Table 6, page 394)	See above under 'Serine'
Histidine	Histamine	Decarboxylation (see Table 6, page 394)	Vasodilator. Stimulates gastric secretion
Aspartic acid	Pyrimidine bases	See page 439	Constituent of nucleic acids and nucleotides
	β-Alanine	Probably by α-decarboxylation	Constituent of special peptides (anserine, carnosine, coenzyme A, pantothenic acid)
Tyrosine	Adrenaline	See page 440	Hormone
	Noradrenaline	See page 440	Hormone and transmitter substance at nerve endings
	Thyroxine	See page 440	Hormone
	Melanins	See page 440	General pigments of hair and skin
Tryptophan	5-Hydroxytrypt-amine (serotonin)	See page 441	Transmitter substance at nerve endings in the CNS
	Nicotinic acid	See page 399 and 476	Constituent of nicotinamide-adenine dinucleotides
Glucogenic amino acids	Carbohydrates	See page 441	

References [1] Korkes et al., *J. biol. Chem.*, **198**, 215 (1952). [2] Elliott, W.H., *J. biol. Chem.*, **201**, 661 (1953).

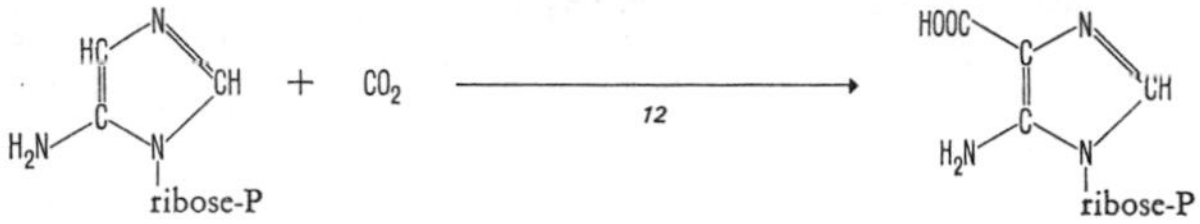

Ribosyl-5-aminoimidazole 5′-phosphate — Ribosyl-5-amino-4-carboxyimidazole 5′-phosphate

(7)

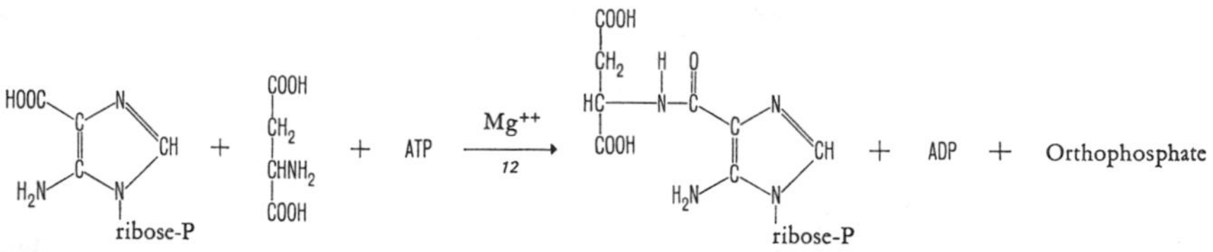

Ribosyl-5-amino-4-carboxyimidazole 5′-phosphate — Aspartic acid — Ribosyl-5-amino-4-succinocarboxamidoimidazole 5′-phosphate

(8)

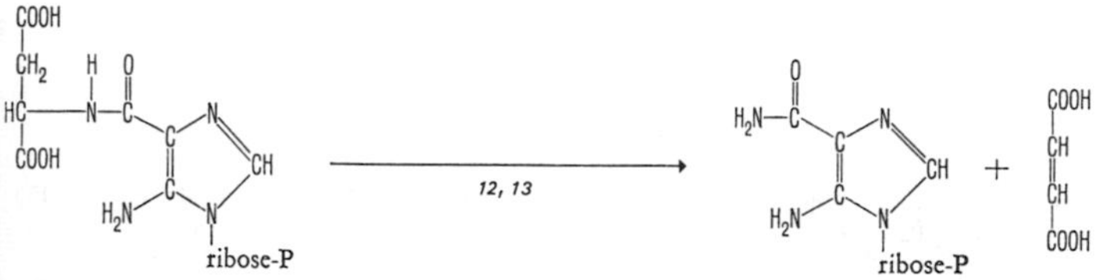

Ribosyl-5-amino-4-succinocarboxamidoimidazole 5′-phosphate — Ribosyl-5-amino-4-carboxamidoimidazole 5′-phosphate — Fumaric acid

(9)

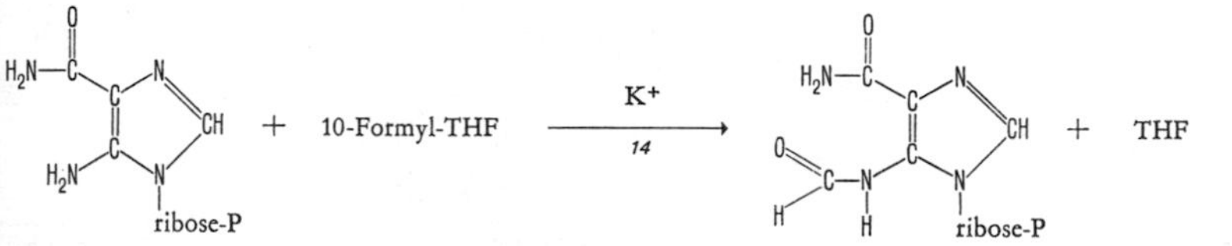

Ribosyl-5-amino-4-carboxamidoimidazole 5′-phosphate — Formyltetra hydrofolic acid — Ribosyl-5-formamido-4-carboxamidoimidazole 5′-phosphate — Tetrahydrofolic acid

(10)

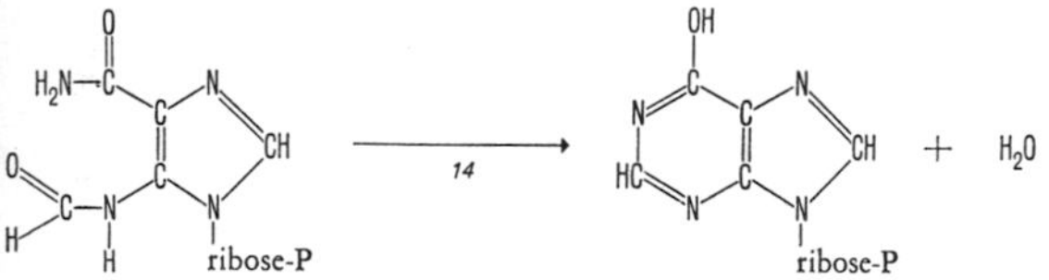

Ribosyl-5-formamido-4-carboxamidoimidazole 5′-phosphate — Inosinic acid

(11)

Formation of adenylic acid (adenosine monophosphate, AMP)

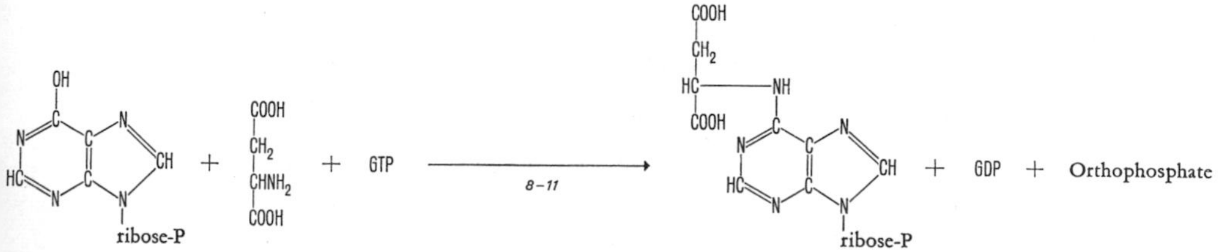

Inosinic acid — Aspartic acid — Adenylosuccinic acid (*N*-succinyladenylic acid)

(12)

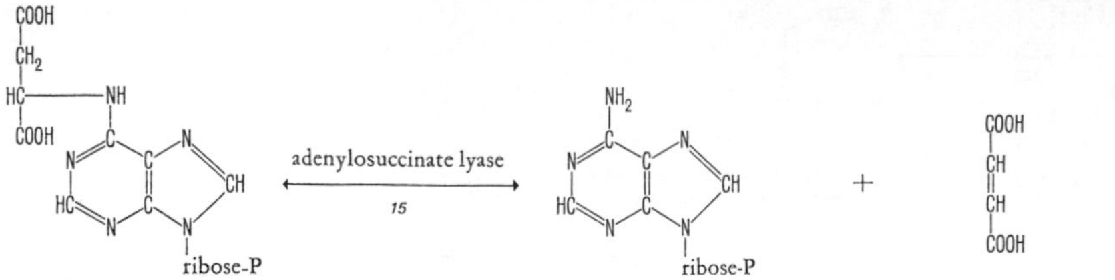

Adenylosuccinic acid (*N*-succinyladenylic acid) — Adenylic acid — Fumaric acid (13)

Formation of xanthylic acid (xanthosine monophosphate, XMP)

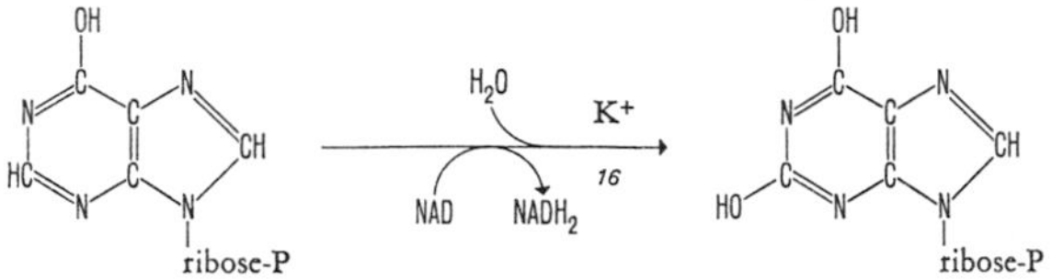

Inosinic acid — Xanthylic acid (14)

Formation of guanylic acid (guanosine monophosphate, GMP)

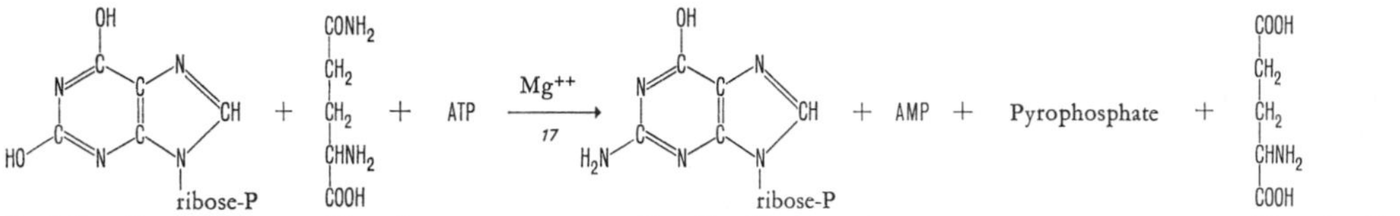

Xanthylic acid — Glutamine — Guanylic acid — Glutamic acid (15)

References

[1] Carter, C.E., *Ann. Rev. Biochem.*, **25**, 123 (1956); Buchanan and Hartman, *Advanc. Enzymol.*, **21**, 199 (1959); Hartman and Buchanan, *Ann. Rev. Biochem.*, **28**, 365 (1959).
[2] Kornberg et al., *J. biol. Chem.*, **215**, 417 (1955).
[3] Christman, A.A., *Physiol. Rev.*, **32**, 303 (1952).
[4] Kornberg et al., *J. biol. Chem.*, **215**, 389 (1955).
[5] Goldthwait et al., *Biochim. biophys. Acta (Amst.)*, **18**, 148 (1955).
[6] Goldthwait, D.A., *J. biol. Chem.*, **222**, 1051 (1956).
[7] Goldthwait et al., *J. biol. Chem.*, **221**, 569 (1956); Warren and Buchanan, *J. biol. Chem.*, **229**, 613 (1957).
[8] Hartman et al., *J. biol. Chem.*, **221**, 1057 (1956).
[9] Levenberg and Buchanan, *J. biol. Chem.*, **224**, 1005 and 1019 (1957).
[10] Melnick and Buchanan, *J. biol. Chem.*, **225**, 157 (1957).
[11] Goldthwait et al., in McElroy and Glass (Eds.), *A Symposium on Amino Acid Metabolism*, Johns Hopkins Press, Baltimore, 1955, page 765; Buchanan et al., in McElroy and Glass (Eds.), *A Symposium on Amino Acid Metabolism*, Johns Hopkins Press, Baltimore, 1955, page 743.
[12] Miller and Buchanan, *J. biol. Chem.*, **237**, 485 (1962).
[13] Miller et al., *J. Amer. chem. Soc.*, **79**, 1513 (1957).
[14] Flaks et al., *J. biol. Chem.*, **229**, 603 (1957).
[15] Lieberman, I., *J. biol. Chem.*, **223**, 327 (1956).
[16] Carter and Cohen, *J. biol. Chem.*, **222**, 17 (1956).
[17] Abrams and Bentley, *Arch. Biochem.*, **58**, 109 (1955); Lagerkvist, U., *Acta chem. scand.*, **9**, 1028 (1955); Gehring and Magasanik, *J. Amer. chem. Soc.*, **77**, 4685 (1955).

Transfer of groups containing one carbon atom [1]

Tetrahydrofolic acid (THF) is the coenzyme of many reactions involving the transfer of a group containing one carbon atom. In most cases the one-carbon fragment is attached to nitrogen atoms 5 or 10 of THF, or to both.

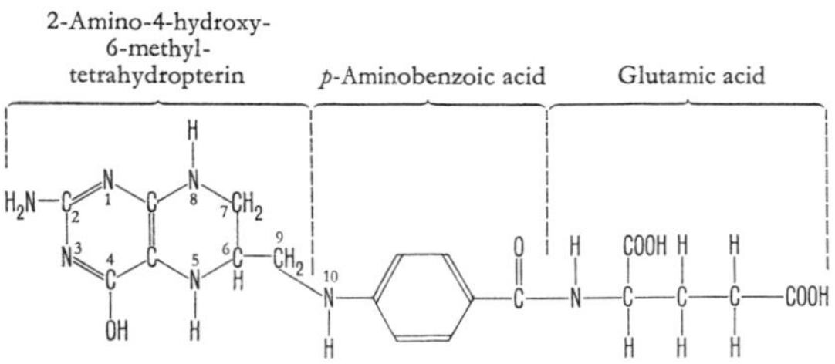

Tetrahydrofolic acid

For the sake of brevity it is common to draw only the portion of the THF molecule that includes these atoms:

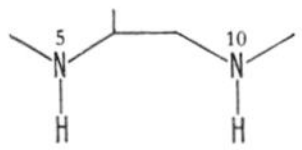

The groups most commonly transferred and their mode of attachment to THF are as follows:

Group attached to one N atom	Group attached to two N atoms	Oxidation state equivalent to
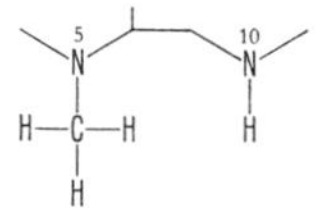 5-Methyl-THF		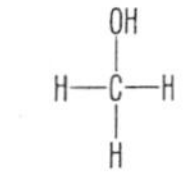 Methanol
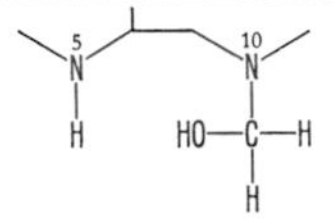 10-Hydroxymethyl-THF	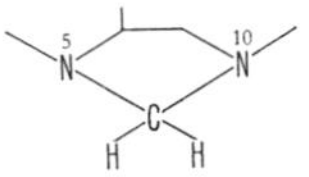 5,10-Methylene-THF	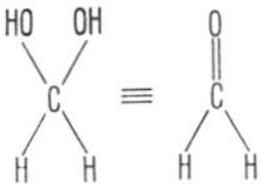 Formaldehyde
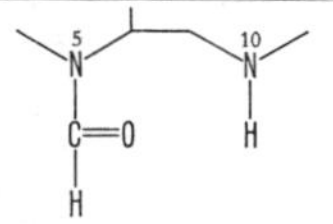 5-Formyl-THF (10-formyl-THF also occurs)	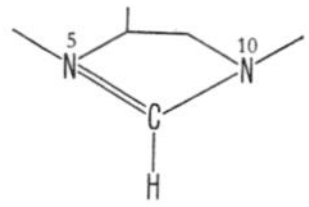 5,10-Methylidyne-THF	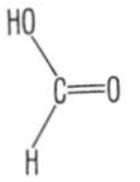 Formic acid
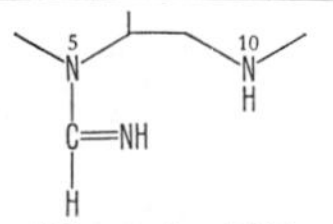 5-Formimino-THF	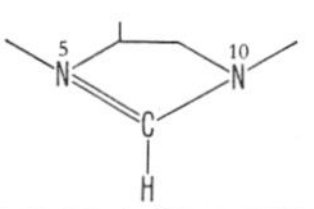 5,10-Methylidyne-THF	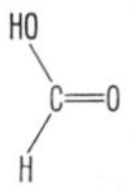 Formic acid

Formyl-THF, hydroxymethyl-THF and methyl-THF are enzymatically interconvertible. The reactions are catalysed by specific oxidoreductases:

$$\text{5,10-methylidyne-THF} + \text{NADPH} \rightleftharpoons \text{5,10-methylene-THF} + \text{NADP} \quad (1)$$

$$\text{5,10-methylene-THF} + \frac{\text{NADPH}}{(\text{NADH})} \rightleftharpoons \text{5-methyl-THF} + \frac{\text{NADP}}{(\text{NAD})} \quad (2)$$

5-Formyl-THF is converted to 5,10-methylidyne-THF by reaction (**3**), while 10-formyl-THF is converted to 5,10-methylidyne-THF by reaction (**4**). In addition, 10-formyl-THF can be formed by reaction (**5**). In mammals, this reaction is probably of minor importance.

$$\text{5-formyl-THF} + \text{ATP} \rightarrow \text{5,10-methylidyne-THF} + \text{ADP} + \text{orthophosphate} \quad (3)$$

$$\text{10-formyl-THF} \rightarrow \text{5,10-methylidyne-THF} + H_2O \quad (4)$$

$$\text{formate} + \text{ATP} + \text{THF} \rightarrow \text{10-formyl-THF} + \text{ADP} + \text{orthophosphate} \quad (5)$$

Among the most important one-carbon transfer reactions are the interconversion of serine and glycine (page 397), and the methylation of deoxyuridylic acid to thymidylic acid (page 439): In the latter reaction a pair of hydrogen atoms is transferred from THF, and one of the products is dihydrofolic acid (DHF). DHF is reduced to THF by tetrahydrofolate dehydrogenase (**6**):

$$\text{DHF} + \text{NADPH}_2 \rightarrow \text{THF} + \text{NADP} \quad (6)$$

Another important methylation reaction is the formation of methionine from homocysteine (**7**). Vitamin B_{12} is involved in this reaction:

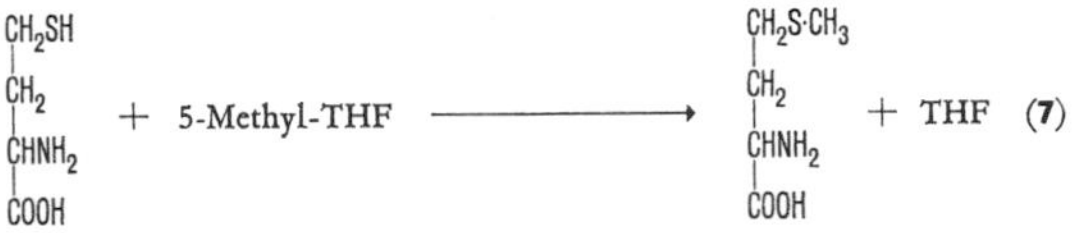

Homocysteine — Methionine

References

[1] Greenberg, D.M., *Advanc. Enzymol.*, **25**, 395 (1963); Huennekens, F.M., *Biochemistry*, **2**, 151 (1963).

Formation of porphyrins

Eight of the carbon atoms of the porphyrin molecule are derived from the α-carbon atom of glycine; the remaining twenty-six carbon atoms are derived from succinic acid. The four nitrogen atoms of the molecule are derived from the amino group of glycine[1]. The formation of this complex molecule has been demonstrated to proceed via δ-aminolaevulinic acid and porphobilinogen[2] by the following reactions:

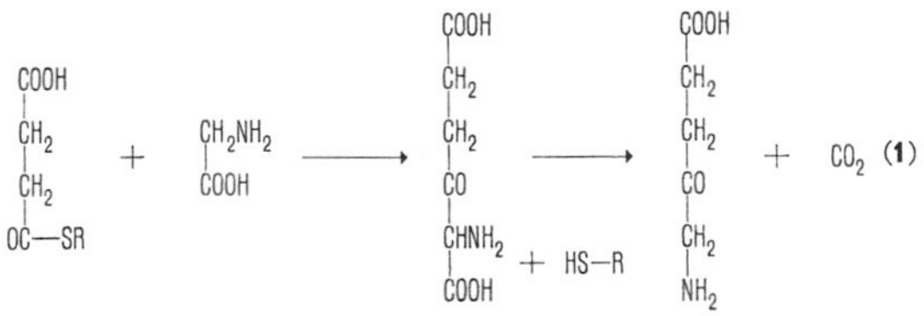

Succinyl-coenzyme A (see page 390) — Glycine — α-Amino-β-ketoadipic acid (hypothetical intermediate) — δ-Amino laevulinic acid

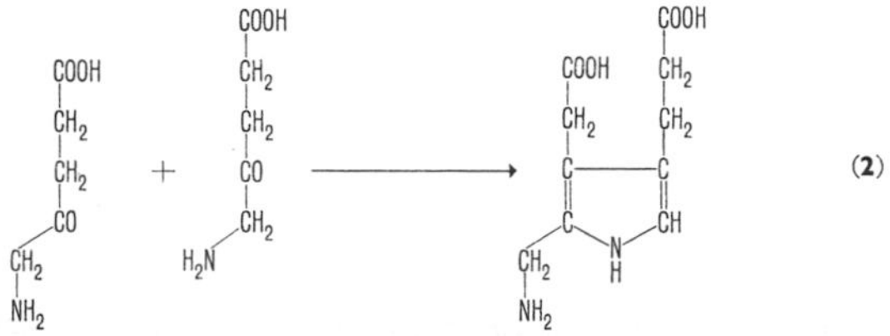

δ-Aminolaevulinic acid (2 molecules) — Porphobilinogen

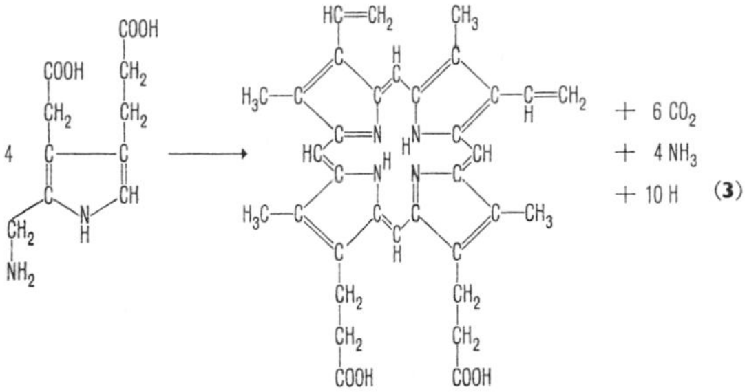

Porphobilinogen — Protoporphyrin IX

References

[1] Shemin, D., in McElroy and Glass (Eds.), *A Symposium on Amino Acid Metabolism*, Johns Hopkins Press, Baltimore, 1955, page 727; Shemin, D., *Ergebn. Physiol.*, **49**, 299 (1957).

[2] Berlin et al., *Biochem. J.*, **64**, 80 (1956); Wriston et al., *J. biol. Chem.*, **215**, 603 (1955); Falk et al., *Nature*, **172**, 292 (1953); Nemeth et al., *J. biol. Chem.*, **229**, 415 (1957); Gibson et al., *Biochem. J.*, **70**, 71 (1958).

Formation of creatine from glycine, arginine and methionine[1]

Creatine (which in the form of creatine phosphate serves as a store of 'phosphate bond energy') is formed by two transfer reactions. The basic skeleton of creatine is provided by glycine. In the first transfer reaction the group $HN=\underset{|}{C}-NH_2$ is transferred from arginine to glycine:

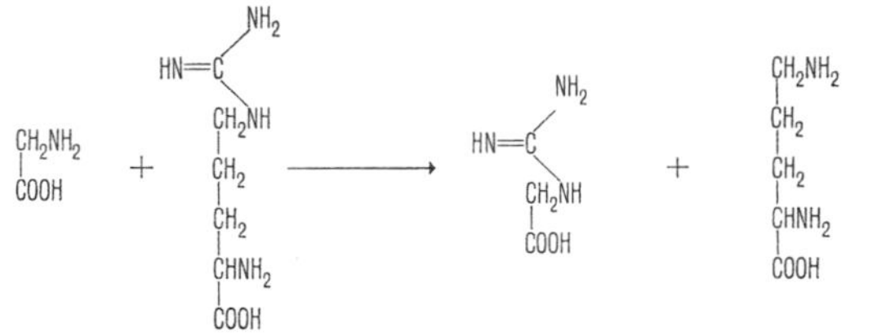

Glycine — Arginine — Guanidinoacetic acid (glycocyamine) — Ornithine

In the second reaction the methyl group of methionine is transferred to the guanidinoacetic acid formed in the first reaction:

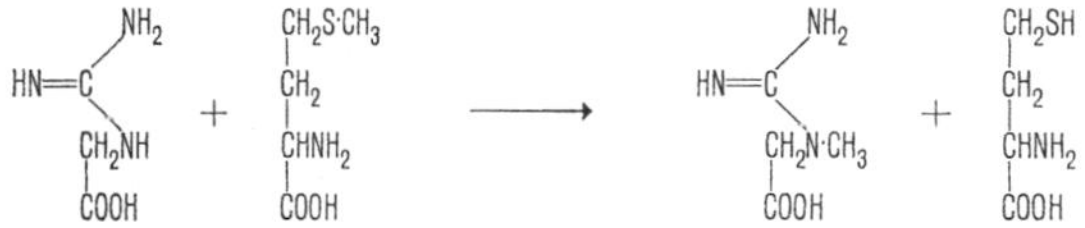

Guanidino-acetic acid — Methionine — Creatine — Homo-cysteine

Methionine does not react as the free amino acid but as the *S*-adenosyl derivative, formed from ATP and methionine[2]:

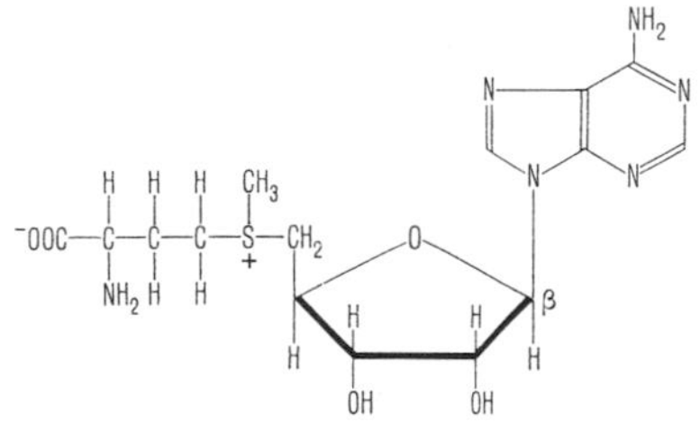

S-Adenosylmethionine

Homocysteine appears likewise as the adenosyl derivative in the transmethylation reaction formulated above[3].

Creatine interacts reversibly with ATP, especially in muscle, to form creatine phosphate:

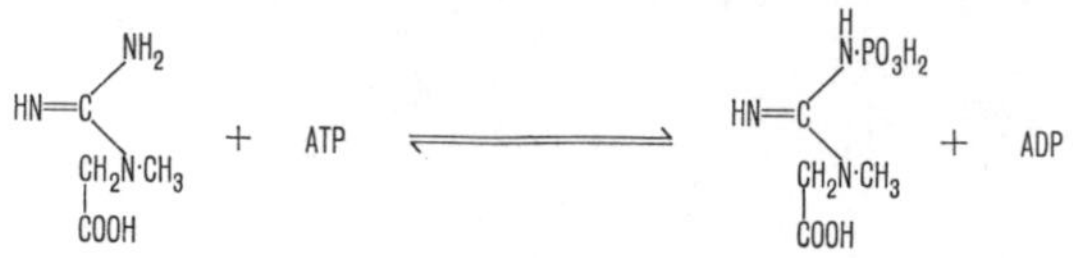

Creatine — Creatine phosphate

The reaction proceeds from left to right in resting muscle, and from right to left during prolonged contractions, regenerating ATP spent as an energy source in the process of contraction.

References

[1] For a review see ARNSTEIN, H.R.V., *Advanc. Protein Chem.*, **9**, 1 (1954).
[2] CANTONI, G.L., *J. biol. Chem.*, **204**, 403 (1953); CANTONI and SCARANO, *J. Amer. chem. Soc.*, **76**, 4744 (1954); CANTONI and VIGNOS, *J. biol. Chem.*, **209**, 647 (1954); MUDD and CANTONI, *J. biol. Chem.*, **231**, 481 (1958).
[3] CANTONI and SCARANO, *J. Amer. chem. Soc.*, **76**, 4744 (1954).

Formation of glutathione

Glutathione is formed in two main steps that have been demonstrated to occur in the liver. The first of these involves the formation of the dipeptide γ-L-glutamyl-L-cysteine from glutamic acid, cysteine and ATP[1]. This is followed by the formation of glutathione itself from γ-L-glutamyl-L-cysteine, glycine and ATP[2]:

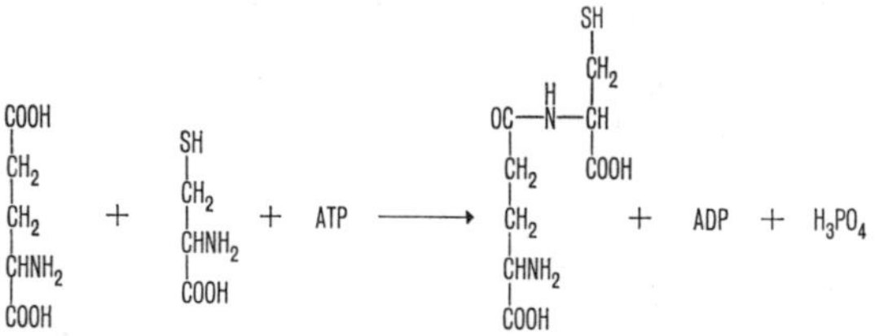

L-Glutamic acid — L-Cysteine — γ-L-Glutamyl-L-cysteine

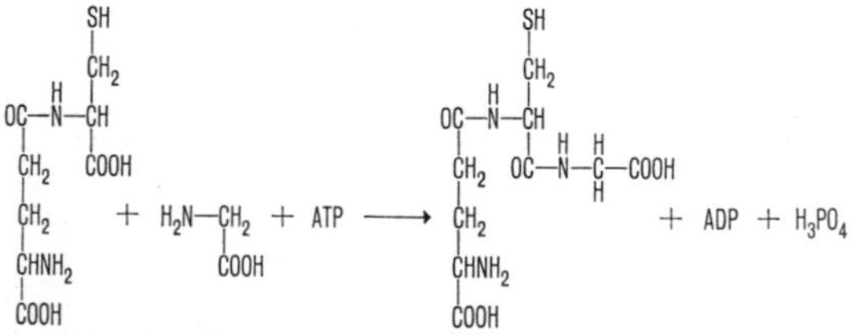

γ-L-Glutamyl-L-cysteine — Glycine — Glutathione

References

[1] MANDELES and BLOCH, *J. biol. Chem.*, **214**, 639 (1955).
[2] SNOKE, J.E., *J. biol. Chem.*, **213**, 813 (1955).

Formation of bile acid conjugates[1]

Bile acids such as cholic and deoxycholic acids are excreted into the intestine in the form of glycine or taurine conjugates. The major factor controlling the ratios of glycine and taurine conjugates appears to be the availability of taurine. The specificity and activity of the enzyme systems are such as to favour the formation of taurine conjugates[2]. The reactions require the presence of coenzyme A and ATP, and presumably proceed by a mechanism similar to that involved in the activation of acetate (page 391) and aromatic acids (page 444)[3]:

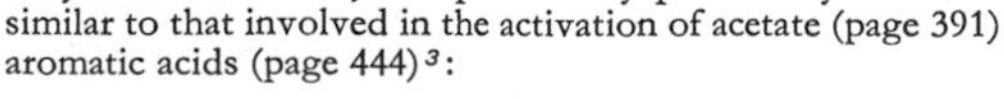 (1)

Bile acid — Coenzyme A — Bile acyl-coenzyme A — Pyrophosphoric acid

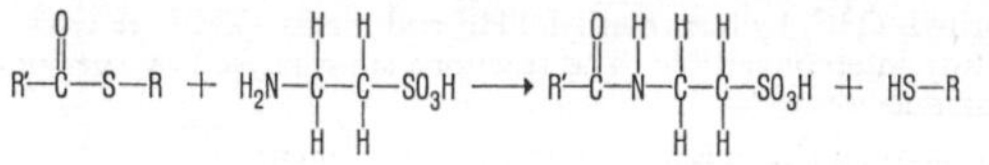 (2a)

Bile acyl-coenzyme A — Taurine — Bile acid–taurine conjugate (e.g., taurocholic acid) — Coenzyme A

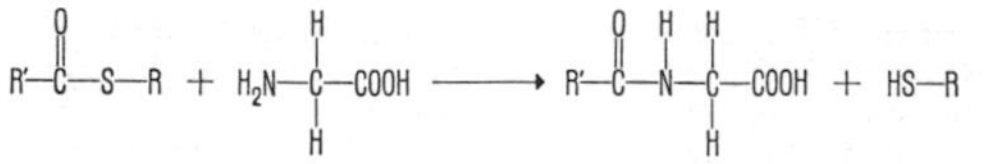 (2b)

Bile acyl-coenzyme A — Glycine — Bile acid–glycine conjugate (e.g., glycocholic acid) — Coenzyme A

References

[1] BERGSTRÖM and BORGSTRÖM, *Ann. Rev. Biochem.*, **25**, 187 (1956).
[2] BREMER, J., *Acta chem. scand.*, **9**, 268 (1955).
[3] BREMER, J., *Acta chem. scand.*, **9**, 1036 (1955); PIHL et al., *J. biol. Chem.*, **227**, 339 (1957); ELLIOTT, W.H., *Biochem. J.*, **62**, 427, 433 (1955); **65**, 315 (1957).

Formation of taurine

Taurine is formed from cysteine in the liver and possibly in other organs. The pathway in mammalian tissues is via cysteinesulphinic acid and hypotaurine[1]:

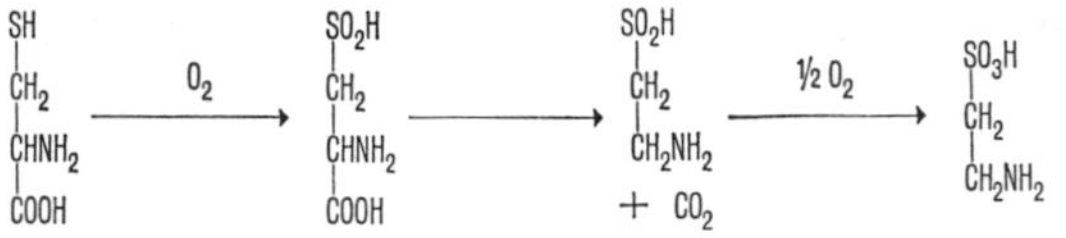

Cysteine — Cysteinesulphinic acid — Hypotaurine — Taurine

Cysteinesulphinic acid may also be formed from pyruvic acid, sulphur dioxide and glutamic acid by the following reactions[2]:

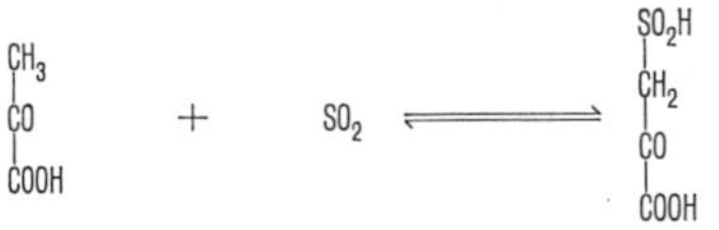

Pyruvic acid — β-Sulphinylpyruvic acid

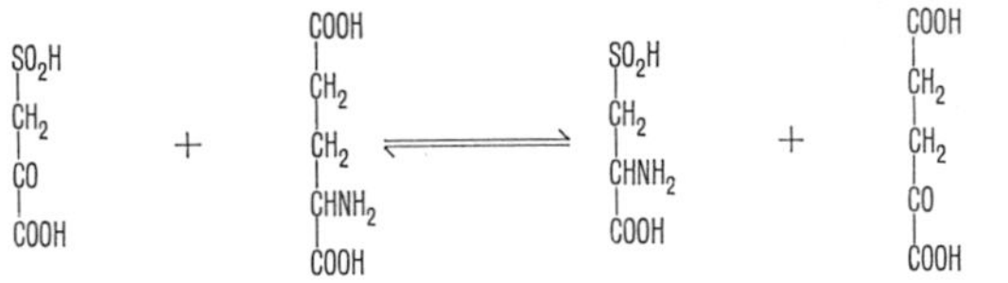

β-Sulphinylpyruvic acid — Glutamic acid — Cysteinesulphinic acid — α-Ketoglutaric acid

References

[1] AWAPARA and WINGO, *J. biol. Chem.*, **203**, 189 (1953); CAVALLINI et al., *J. biol. Chem.*, **216**, 577 (1955); HOPE, B.D., *Biochem. J.*, **59**, 497 (1955); BERGERET et al., *Biochim. biophys. Acta (Amst.)*, **17**, 128 (1955); CHAPEVILLE and FROMAGEOT, *Biochim. biophys. Acta (Amst.)*, **17**, 275 (1955).
[2] CHAPEVILLE and FROMAGEOT, *Biochim. biophys. Acta (Amst.)*, **14**, 415 (1954).

Formation of pyrimidines

The starting materials of pyrimidine synthesis are aspartic acid and carbamyl phosphate. The pathway shown below occurs in mammals[1] and bacteria[2]. Orotic acid is the first complete pyrimidine to be formed. This is converted to orotidylic acid (OMP)[3] and then to uridylic acid (UMP), cytidylic acid[4] and thymidylic acid* (TMP)[5].

* Strictly speaking, this compound should be termed deoxythymidylic acid (dTMP) since it contains deoxyribose.

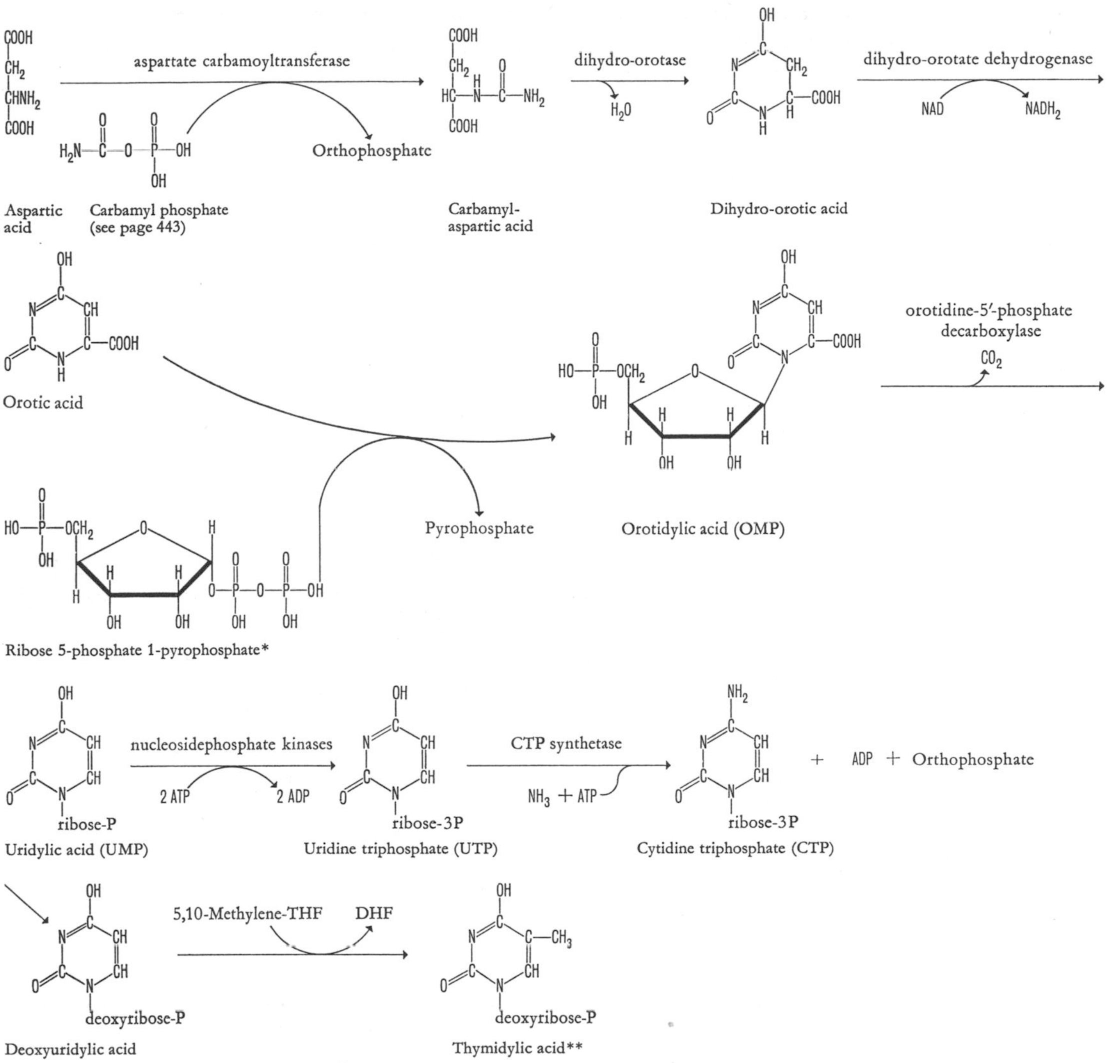

* This compound is formed by reaction (**1**), page 433.

** Strictly speaking, this compound should be termed deoxythymidylic acid (dTMP) since it contains deoxyribose.

References

[1] Carter, C.E., *Ann. Rev. Biochem.*, **25**, 123 (1956); Lowenstein and Cohen, *J. biol. Chem.*, **220**, 57 (1956); Cooper et al., *J. biol. Chem.*, **216**, 37 (1955).

[2] Lieberman and Kornberg, *J. biol. Chem.*, **207**, 911 (1954).

[3] Lieberman et al., *J. biol. Chem.*, **215**, 403 (1955).

[4] Lieberman, I., *J. biol. Chem.*, **222**, 765 (1956).

[5] Friedkin et al., *J. biol. Chem.*, **220**, 627 (1956); Humphreys and Greenberg, *Arch. Biochem.*, **78**, 275 (1958); Reichard, P., *Advanc. Enzymol.*, **21**, 263 (1959); Greenberg, D.M., *Advanc. Enzymol.*, **25**, 395 (1963).

Conversion of phenylalanine to tyrosine

The enzymic conversion of phenylalanine to tyrosine involves a pteridine cofactor. The reaction can be considered to proceed in two parts. The first consists of a hydroxylation involving molecular oxygen and a reduced cofactor, 4-hydroxytetrahydropteridine[1]. The products are tyrosine, the oxidized cofactor 4-hydroxydihydropteridine, and water. The second step consists of the regeneration of reduced cofactor, a reaction catalysed by tetrahydrofolate dehydrogenase:

	4-hydroxytetrahydropteridine + phenylalanine + O_2	$\rightarrow$ 4-hydroxydihydropteridine + tyrosine + H_2O	(**1**)
	4-hydroxydihydropteridine + $NADPH_2$	$\rightarrow$ 4-hydroxytetrahydropteridine + NADP	(**2**)
Sum	phenylalanine + O_2 + $NADPH_2$	$\rightarrow$ tyrosine + H_2O + NADP	(**3**)

A possible form of 4-hydroxydihydropteridine is shown below. A number of isomeric forms of 4-hydroxytetrahydropteridine are possible. The physiologically active isomer has not yet been identified.

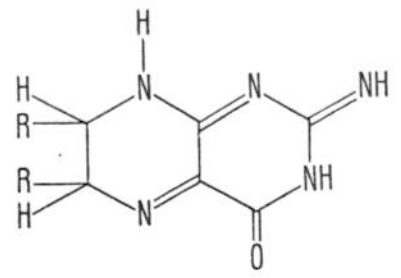

4-Hydroxydihydropteridine ('para-quinonoid' form)

Reference

[1] Kaufman, S., *J. biol. Chem.*, **239**, 332 (1964).

Formation of noradrenaline and adrenaline from tyrosine

Noradrenaline and adrenaline are formed from tyrosine (and thus from phenylalanine), the main pathway being as follows[1]:

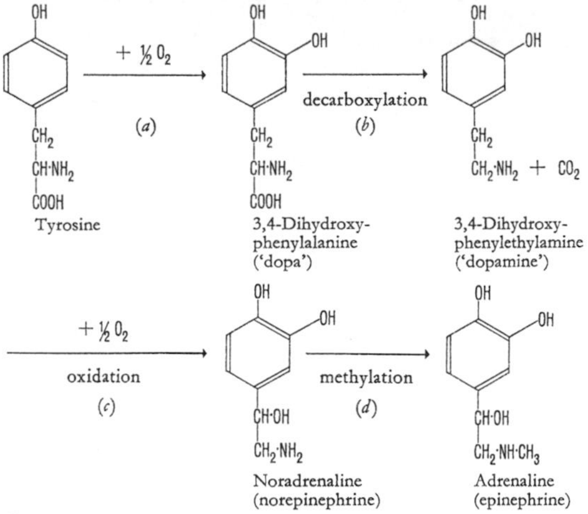

Enzymes

(*a*) tyrosine hydroxylase
(*b*) dopa decarboxylase
(*c*) dopamine hydroxylase
(*d*) phenylethanolamine *N*-methyltransferase

The reaction catalysed by tyrosine hydroxylase is probably the rate-limiting step[2]. The enzyme phenylethanolamine *N*-methyltransferase is found almost exclusively in the adrenal gland[3].

Alternative pathways have been proposed[4].

References

[1] For a review see Blaschko, H., *Pharmacol. Rev.*, **11**, 307 (1959).
[2] Levitt et al., *Pharmacol. exp. Ther.*, **198**, 1 (1965).
[3] Axelrod, J., *J. biol. Chem.*, **237**, 1657 (1962).
[4] Axelrod, J., *Science*, **190**, 499 (1963); Kopin, I.J., *Z. klin. Chem.*, **2**, 115 (1964); Iversen, L.L., *Nature*, **219**, 8 (1967).

Formation of thyroid hormones[1]

Iodide is absorbed in the gastrointestinal tract and rapidly distributed in the extracellular fluid. Except during the postprandial period the iodide concentration of plasma is less than 5 μg/l. This inorganic iodide of the plasma is removed almost entirely by the kidneys and thyroid gland. The concentration of readily exchangeable iodine in the normal thyroid in terms of whole tissue or of tissue water may be 20-40 or more times greater than that in the plasma. Prior to the iodination of the tyrosine molecule the iodide

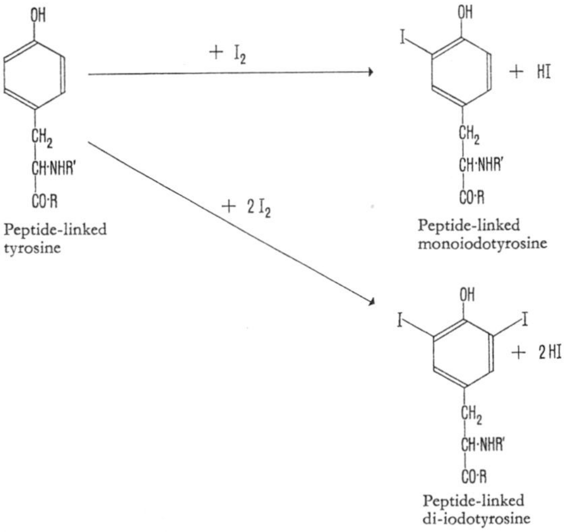

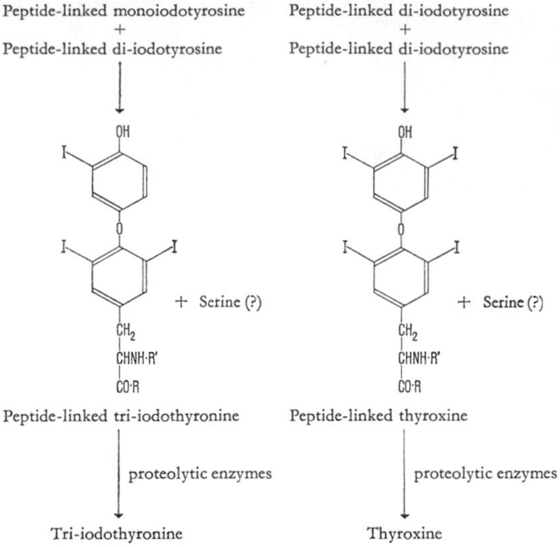

must be oxidized to free iodine or the iodinium ion, a reaction probably involving a peroxidase. The iodination of tyrosine to monoiodotyrosine and di-iodotyrosine probably takes place in peptide-linked tyrosyl residues. The thyroid hormones tri-iodothyronine and thyroxine are formed by condensation of iodotyrosyl residues, the side chain of one tyrosyl residue giving rise to serine in this coupling reaction.

Tri-iodothyronine and thyroxine are retained in the thyroid within the colloid as peptide-linked residues in the specific protein thyroglobulin. The thyroid hormones are released from the thyroglobulin pool by enzymatic hydrolysis as required. The further metabolism of these hormones is described on pages 726–727.

References

[1] For a review see Roche and Michel, *Physiol Rev.*, **35**, 583 (1955); Roche et al., in Florkin and Mason (Eds.), *Comparative Biochemistry*, vol 5, Academic Press, New York, 1963, page 514; Stanbury, J.B., in Stanbury et al. (Eds.), *The Metabolic Basis of Inherited Disease*, 2nd ed., McGraw-Hill, New York, 1966, page 215.

Formation of melanin from tyrosine[1]

Melanin is the pigment of vertebrate skin, hair, feathers and eyes (see page 722). It is a complex and nonhomogeneous substance. The chief basic unit is 5,6-dihydroxyindole, which undergoes polymerization and in the polymerized form combines with protein[2]. It is formed from tyrosine, probably by the following route (this route is blocked in albinism; cf. page 448):

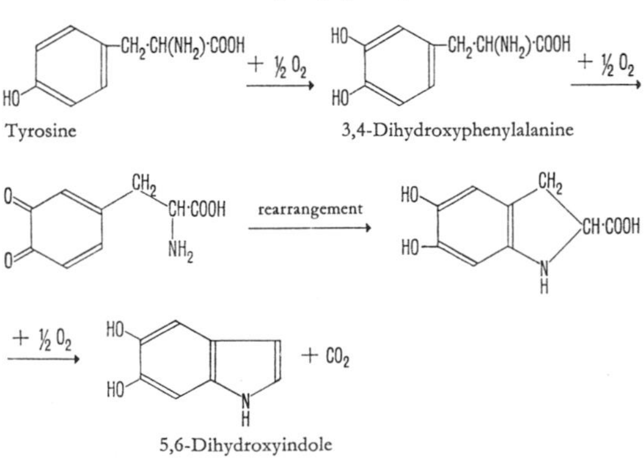

References

[1] For a review see Mason, H.S., *Advanc. Enzymol.*, **16**, 163 (1955); Dalgliesh, C.E., *Advanc. Protein Chem.*, **10**, 65 (1955).
[2] Cromartie and Harley-Mason, *Biochem. J.*, **66**, 713 (1957).

Formation and degradation of 5-hydroxytryptamine (serotonin)

5-Hydroxytryptamine (serotonin) is assumed to be a neurotransmittor substance in the CNS; it may play a role in haemostasis, in the control of renal activity, and has probably other functions[1]. It is found in relatively high concentrations in thrombocytes and in the argentaffine cells of the intestinal wall. Its degradation product, 5-hydroxyindoleacetic acid, appears in the urine in abnormal quantities in cases of tumours of the argentaffine cells (argentaffinoma, malignant carcinoid)[2]. 5-Hydroxytryptamine is assumed to be formed from tryptophan by the following reactions[3]:

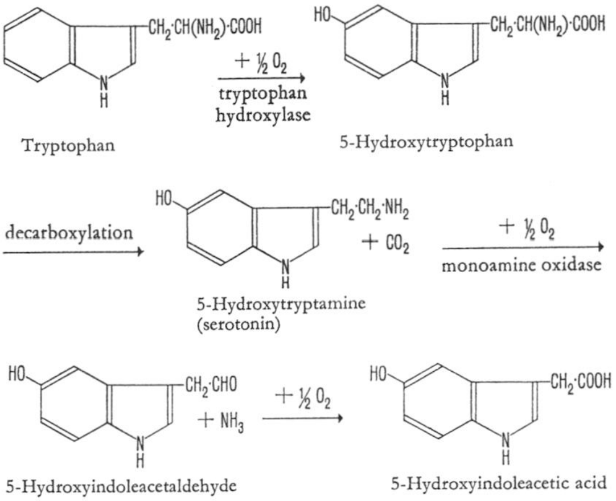

The reaction catalysed by the enzyme tryptophan hydroxylase is probably the rate-limiting step in the synthesis of serotonin[4].

Serotonin is the precursor of melatonin in the pineal gland (see page 730).

References

1 ERSPAMER, V., *Pharmacol. Rev.*, **6**, 425 (1954); SPECTOR and WILLOUGHBY, *Nature*, **179**, 318 (1957); PAGE, I.H., *Physiol. Rev.*, **38**, 277 (1958).
2 PAGE et al., *Lancet*, **1**, 198 (1955); PERNOW and WALDENSTRÖM, *Lancet*, **2**, 951 (1954).
3 UDENFRIEND et al., *J. Amer. chem. Soc.*, **75**, 501 (1953); DALGLIESH, C.E., *Advanc. Protein Chem.*, **10**, 103 (1955); *Biochem. J.*, **64**, 481 (1956); DALGLIESH and DUTTON, *Biochem. J.*, **65**, 21 P (1957); HENDERSON et al., in FLORKIN and MASON (Eds.), *Comparative Biochemistry*, vol. 4, Academic Press, New York, 1962, page 324.
4 JEQUIER et al., *Molec. Pharmacol.*, **3**, 274 (1967).

Synthesis of carbohydrate from amino acids and other non-carbohydrate precursors (gluconeogenesis)

Glucose can be formed from lactate, pyruvate, glycerol and a number of amino acids: glutamic acid, aspartic acid, alanine, arginine, proline, hydroxyproline, histidine, serine, glycine and valine. The common metabolic property of all glucose-formers is the ability to yield pyruvate (or phosphopyruvate). The pathway from pyruvate to glucose includes most steps of the anaerobic glycolysis (Table 3, page 389) in reverse, but at three stages special reactions occur[1] circumventing the energy barriers which would prevent a simple reversal of glycolysis:

(*a*) The formation of phosphopyruvate from pyruvate. The special reactions by which phosphopyruvate is formed are[2]:

pyruvate + ATP + CO_2 —(pyruvate carboxylase)→ oxaloacetate + ADP + phosphate

oxaloacetate + ATP or ITP —(phosphopyruvate carboxylase)→ phosphopyruvate + ADP or IDP

(*b*) Fructose 1,6-diphosphate is converted into fructose 6-phosphate by a specific phosphatase[3] (and not by transfer of phosphate to ADP):

Fig. 17 Pathways of carbohydrate breakdown and synthesis[1]

The pathways differ at four points. Breakdown reactions are indicated by the left-hand arrows, synthesis reactions by the right-hand arrows.

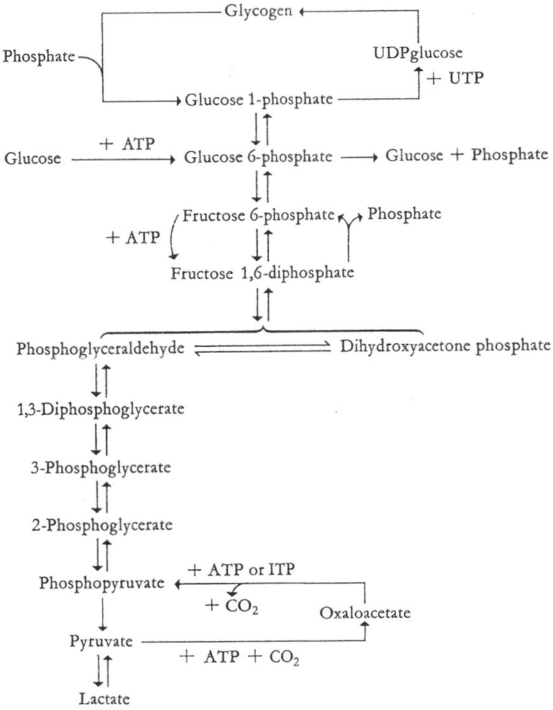

fructose 1,6-diphosphate —(hexosediphosphatase)→ fructose 6-phosphate + phosphate

(*c*) Glucose 6-phosphate is likewise dephosphorylated by a specific phosphatase[4] (and not by transfer to ADP):

glucose 6-phosphate —(glucose-6-phosphatase)→ glucose + phosphate

(*d*) Glucose 1-phosphate is converted into glycogen via UDP-glucose[5] and not by reversal of the phosphorylase reaction:

glucose 1-phosphate + UTP —(glucose-1-phosphate uridylyltransferase)→ UDP-glucose + pyrophosphate

UDP-glucose + $glycogen_n$ —(UDPglucose-glycogen glucosyltransferase)→ $glycogen_{n+1}$ + UDP

The stages of carbohydrate synthesis from pyruvate are summarized in Figure 17 above.

References

1 KREBS and KORNBERG, *Ergebn. Physiol.*, **49**, 212 (1957); for a review of gluconeogenesis see KREBS, H.A., *Proc. roy. Soc. B*, **159**, 545 (1964); LARDY, H.A., *Harvey Lect.*, *1964–1965*, **60**, 261 (1966).
2 UTTER and KURAHASHI, *J. biol. Chem.*, **207**, 821 (1954); UTTER and KEECH, *J. biol. Chem.*, **238**, 2603 (1963).
3 GOMORI, G., *J. biol. Chem.*, **148**, 139 (1943).
4 SWANSON, M.A., *J. biol. Chem.*, **184**, 647 (1950); CORI and CORI, *J. biol. Chem.*, **199**, 661 (1952).
5 LELOIR and CARDINI, *J. Amer. chem. Soc.*, **79**, 6340 (1957); VILLAR-PALASI and LARNER, *Biochim. biophys. Acta (Amst.)*, **30**, 449 (1958).

Detoxication mechanisms

A number of metabolic processes do not fall under the headings of either energy supply or synthesis of cell constituents. Their common feature is the disposal of potentially harmful substances. In other words they contribute towards the maintenance of the physiological environment. These metabolic processes are commonly referred to as 'detoxication mechanisms'.

Quantitatively the most important detoxication mechanism is the conversion of surplus nitrogen, in particular surplus ammonium ions, into urea (see below). Other detoxication reactions concern the disposal of certain ingested materials (e.g., benzoic acid) and of drugs. A recent review of drug metabolism can be found in GOLDSTEIN et al.[1]

Reference

[1] GOLDSTEIN et al., *Principles of Drug Action*, Harper & Row, New York, 1968.

Synthesis of urea[1] (for references see page 444)

Most of the surplus nitrogen arising in the mammalian body is excreted in the form of urea. The synthesis of urea from ammonia and carbon dioxide proceeds by a cyclical mechanism. The concept of the urea (or ornithine) cycle was originally based on the observation that ornithine, citrulline and arginine stimulate urea production in the presence of ammonia without being themselves consumed in the process[2]. Since it was proposed, this concept has received support from many other experiments[1]. The reactions of the cycle involve the stepwise building-up of the urea structure on the δ-amino group of ornithine. The building-up process is completed with the formation of arginine, which is then hydrolysed by arginase to yield urea and ornithine.

Before one molecule each of ammonia and carbon dioxide enter the cycle, they react to form carbamyl phosphate. The synthesis of this compound requires ATP and has been formulated as follows[3,4]:

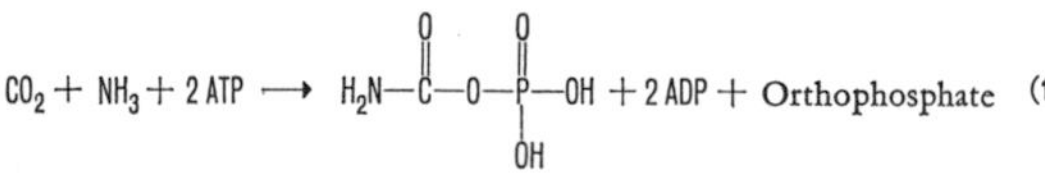

(1)

Carbamyl phosphate

Reaction (**1**) is stimulated by acetylglutamate and by other acylglutamates[5]. It is probable that acetylglutamate is the compound normally involved since it occurs in mammalian liver[6]. In bacteria the stimulation by acetylglutamate does not occur, and only one molecule of ATP is utilized per molecule of carbamyl phosphate formed. The nature of the action of acetylglutamate is obscure. Carbamyl phosphate reacts with ornithine to yield citrulline[3,7]:

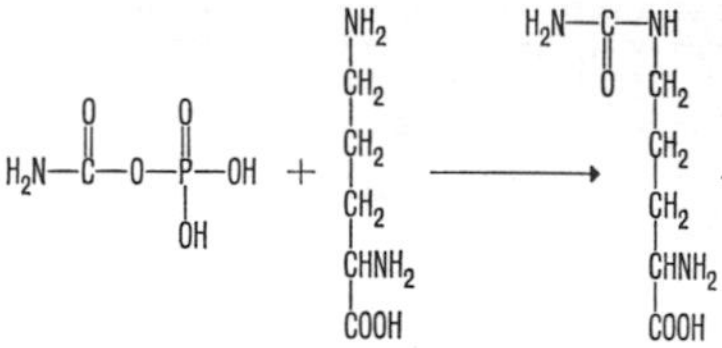

(2)

Carbamyl phosphate · Ornithine · Citrulline

Citrulline next condenses with aspartic acid to form argininosuccinic acid[8], a process that requires ATP:

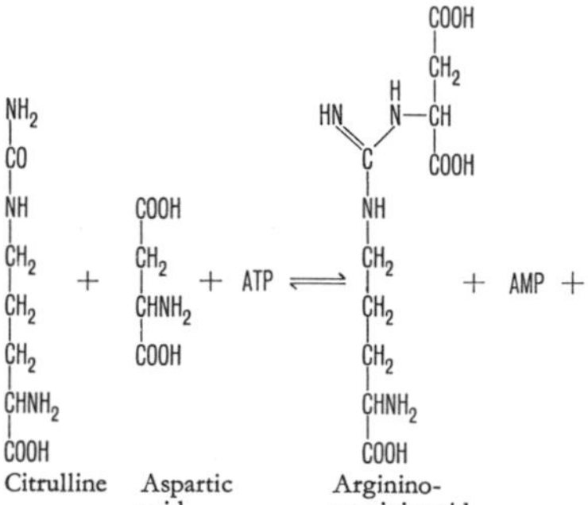

(3)

Citrulline · Aspartic acid · Argininosuccinic acid

Reaction (**3**) is freely reversible, but under physiological conditions it proceeds only from left to right because of the presence of a highly active pyrophosphatase[9]:

Table 21 Detoxication mechanisms

Reaction	Examples of compounds detoxicated	Product formed	Mechanism
Acetylation	Sulphanilamide	Acetylsulphanilamide	See page 444
Methylation	Nicotinamide	*N*-Methylnicotinamide	The methyl group is derived from methionine probably via *S*-adenosylmethionine (see page 437)
Glycine conjugation	Benzoic acid	Hippuric acid	See page 444
Alkyl- and arylglucuronide formation	Alcohols and phenols (menthol and phenol)	Menthyl- and phenyl-glucuronide	R·OH + UDPglucuronic acid → 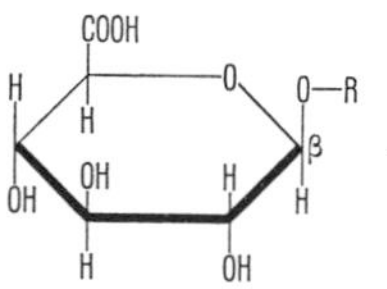 β-Glucuronide
Acylglucuronide formation	Aromatic acids (benzoic acid) and branched-chain aliphatic acids	Benzoylglucuronide	Not known
Sulphate ester formation	Phenols	Phenyl sulphate	See page 445
Glutamine conjugation	Phenylacetic acid	Phenacetylglutamine	See page 445
Mercapturic acid formation	Naphthalene, alkyl halides	Naphthylmercapturic acid	See page 445

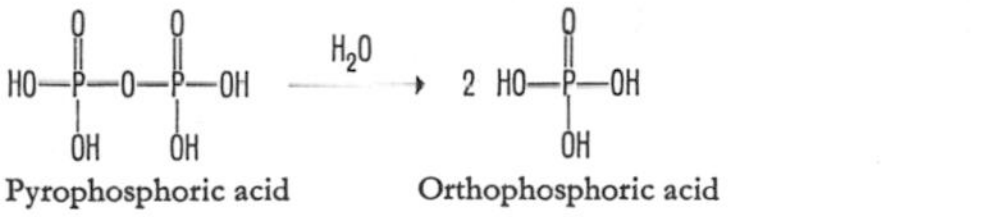

(4)

Argininosuccinate reacts further to give arginine and fumarate[10] by reaction (5):

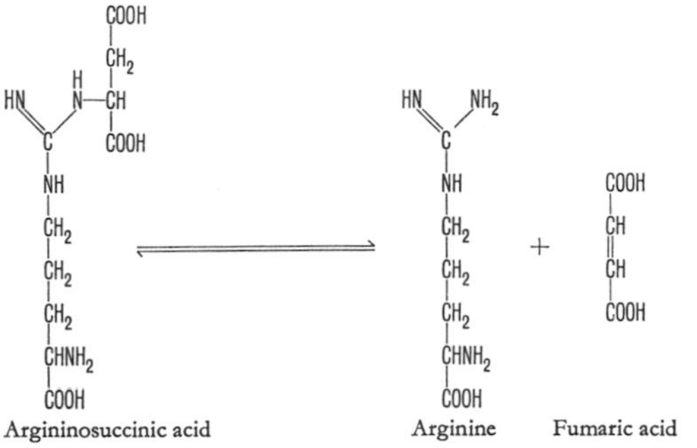

(5)

This is followed by the hydrolysis of arginine to ornithine and urea. Ornithine can then undergo the same sequence of reactions, starting with reaction (2):

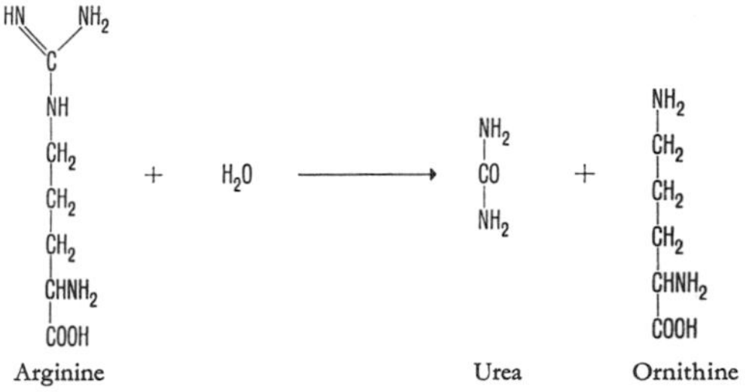

(6)

The cyclic sequence of the reactions is shown in Figure 18 below. As formulated here, one molecule each of carbon dioxide and ammonia are utilized for every molecule of urea produced. The second nitrogen atom of the urea molecule is supplied by aspartic acid. The latter is regenerated by transamination between glutamate and oxaloacetate. Glutamate in turn can be regenerated in two ways, either by transamination between various amino acids

Fig. 18 The urea cycle (ornithine cycle)
A list of the enzymes involved in the cycle is given below the diagram.

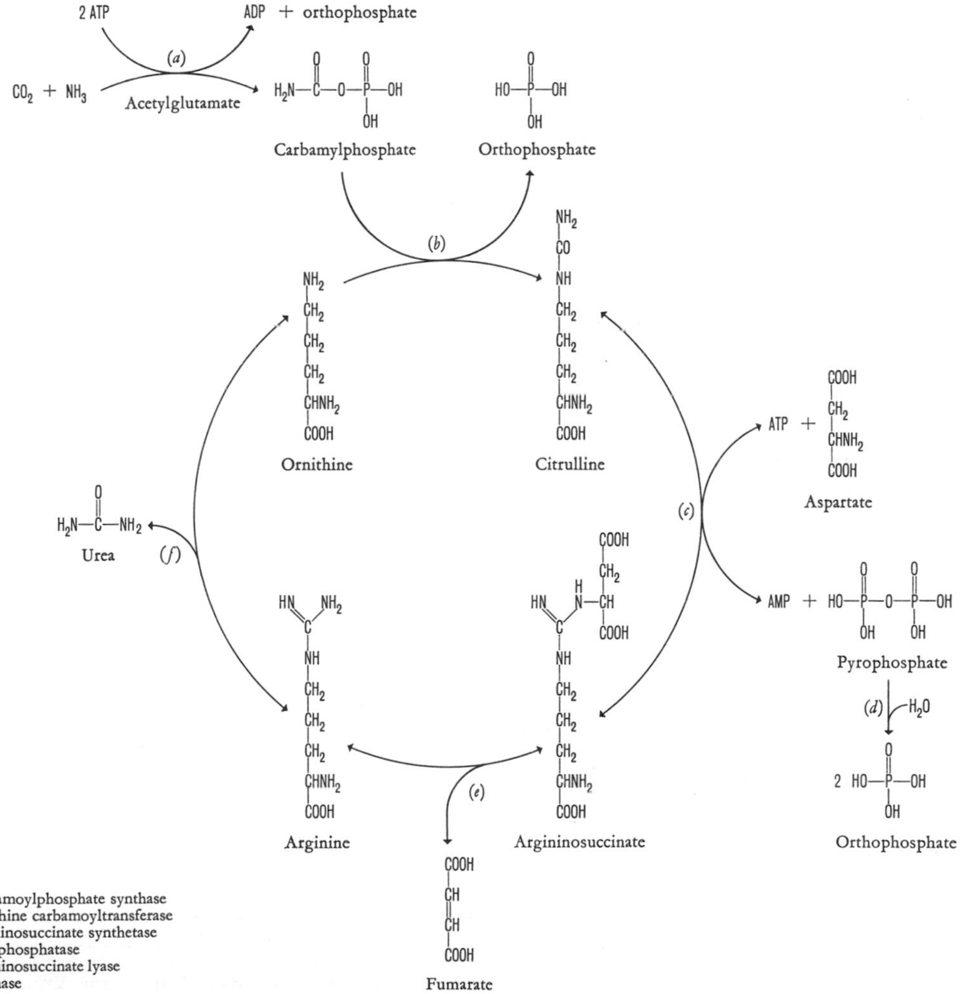

Enzymes
(*a*) carbamoylphosphate synthase
(*b*) ornithine carbamoyltransferase
(*c*) argininosuccinate synthetase
(*d*) pyrophosphatase
(*e*) argininosuccinate lyase
(*f*) arginase

Fig. 19 Utilization and regeneration of aspartate in the synthesis of urea

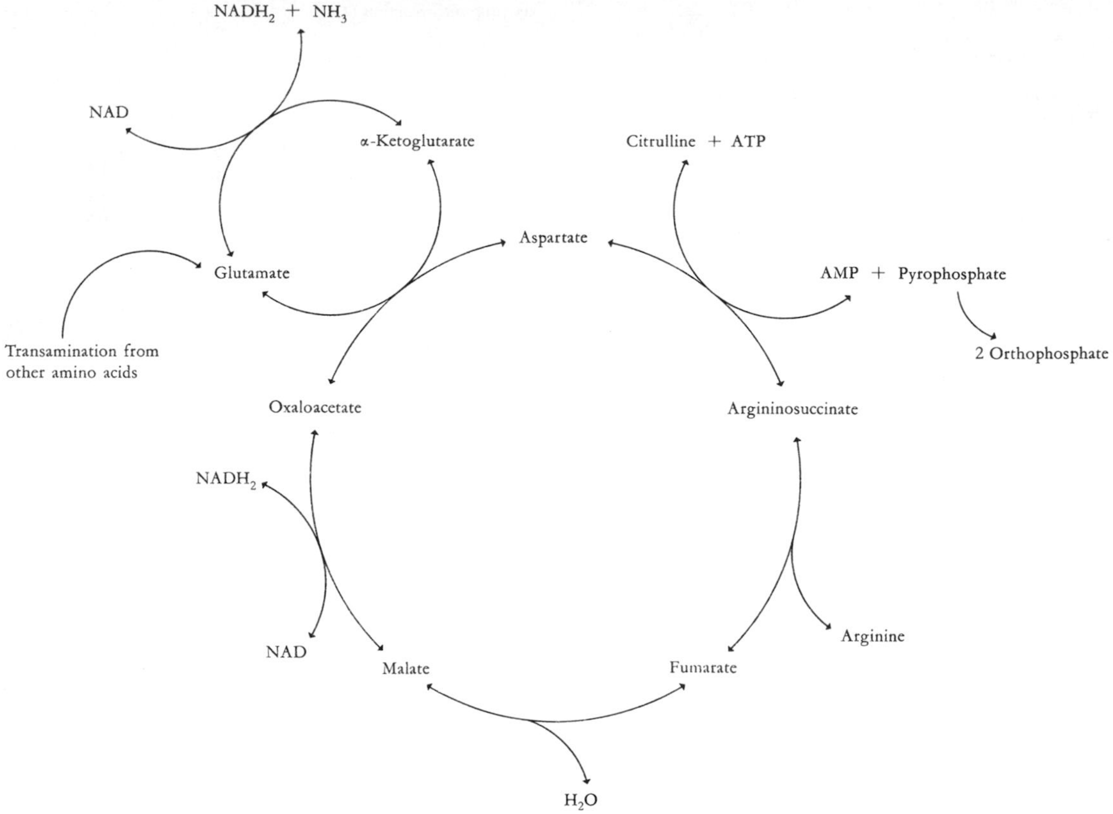

and α-ketoglutarate (see page 393) or by reductive amination from ammonia and α-ketoglutarate[11]:

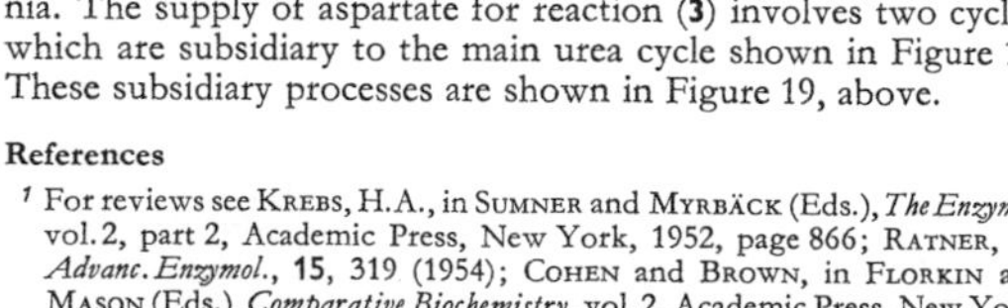

(7)

Ammonia α-Ketoglutaric acid Glutamic acid

The second nitrogen atom of urea must thus pass through glutamate and aspartate but not necessarily through the stage of ammonia. The supply of aspartate for reaction (**3**) involves two cycles, which are subsidiary to the main urea cycle shown in Figure 18. These subsidiary processes are shown in Figure 19, above.

References

[1] For reviews see KREBS, H.A., in SUMNER and MYRBÄCK (Eds.), *The Enzymes*, vol. 2, part 2, Academic Press, New York, 1952, page 866; RATNER, S., *Advanc. Enzymol.*, **15**, 319 (1954); COHEN and BROWN, in FLORKIN and MASON (Eds.), *Comparative Biochemistry*, vol. 2, Academic Press, New York, 1960, page 161; COHEN and SALLACH, in GREENBERG, D.M. (Ed.), *Metabolic Pathways*, Academic Press, New York, 1961, page 1.
[2] KREBS and HENSELEIT, *Hoppe-Seyl. Z. physiol. Chem.*, **210**, 33 (1932).
[3] JONES et al., *J. Amer. chem. Soc.*, **77**, 819 (1955).
[4] METZENBERG et al., *J. biol. Chem.*, **229**, 1019 (1957).
[5] GRISOLIA and COHEN, *J. biol. Chem.*, **204**, 753 (1953).
[6] HALL et al., *Nature*, **178**, 1468 (1956); HALL et al., *J. biol. Chem.*, **230**, 1013 (1958).
[7] BURNETT and COHEN, *J. biol. Chem.*, **229**, 337 (1957).
[8] RATNER et al., *J. biol. Chem.*, **204**, 95 (1953).
[9] RATNER and PETRACK, *Arch. Biochem.*, **65**, 582 (1956).
[10] RATNER et al., *J. biol. Chem.*, **204**, 115 (1953).
[11] OLSON and ANFINSEN, *J. biol. Chem.*, **202**, 841 (1953).

Acetylation of amines[1]

Many aromatic and aliphatic amines are acetylated in the body. These include sulphanilamide, *p*-aminobenzoic acid, *p*-nitraniline and others[2]. In general, the acetylated amines are less toxic than the unacetylated compounds. However, in some cases the low solubility of acetylated amines can render them harmful owing to their crystallization in the urinary tract.

The acetylation reaction proceeds via acetyl-coenzyme A (see page 391), for example:

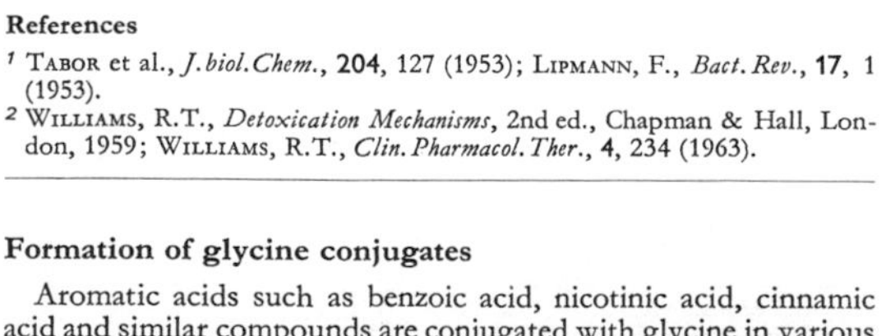

References

[1] TABOR et al., *J. biol. Chem.*, **204**, 127 (1953); LIPMANN, F., *Bact. Rev.*, **17**, 1 (1953).
[2] WILLIAMS, R.T., *Detoxication Mechanisms*, 2nd ed., Chapman & Hall, London, 1959; WILLIAMS, R.T., *Clin. Pharmacol. Ther.*, **4**, 234 (1963).

Formation of glycine conjugates

Aromatic acids such as benzoic acid, nicotinic acid, cinnamic acid and similar compounds are conjugated with glycine in various organs[1]. The reaction requires coenzyme A and ATP, and proceeds by a mechanism similar to that involved in the activation of acetate (see page 391), for example:

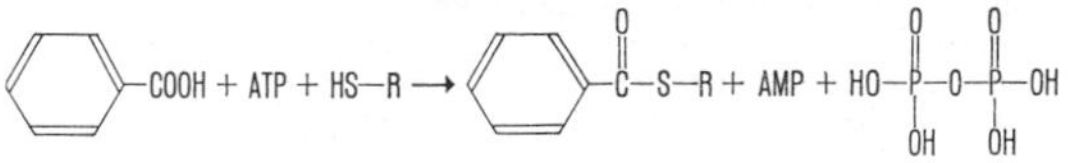

Benzoic acid | Coenzyme A | Benzoyl-coenzyme A | Pyrophosphoric acid

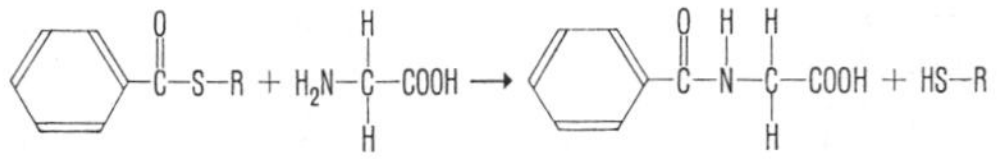

Benzoyl-coenzyme A | Glycine | Hippuric acid | Coenzyme A

References

[1] CHANTRENNE, H., *J. biol. Chem.*, **189**, 227 (1951); SCHACHTER and TAGGART, *J. biol. Chem.*, **208**, 263 (1954); MOLDAVE and MEISTER, *J. biol. Chem.*, **229**, 463 (1957).

Formation of esters of sulphuric acid

Naturally occurring sulphate esters include the polysaccharides chondroitin sulphate and heparin, steroid sulphates and phenyl sulphates (aryl sulphates). In addition to these substances, foreign phenols when ingested are esterified with sulphate to a greater or lesser extent, and the elimination of phenols in the form of phenyl sulphates constitutes one of several detoxication mechanisms of phenols[1]. Sulphate ester formation requires inorganic sulphate and ATP and involves the formation of two 'active sulphate' intermediates[2]:

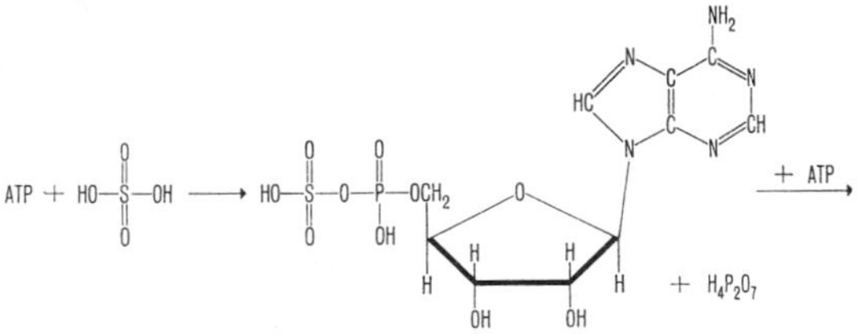

Adenosine 5'-phosphosulphate | Pyrophosphoric acid

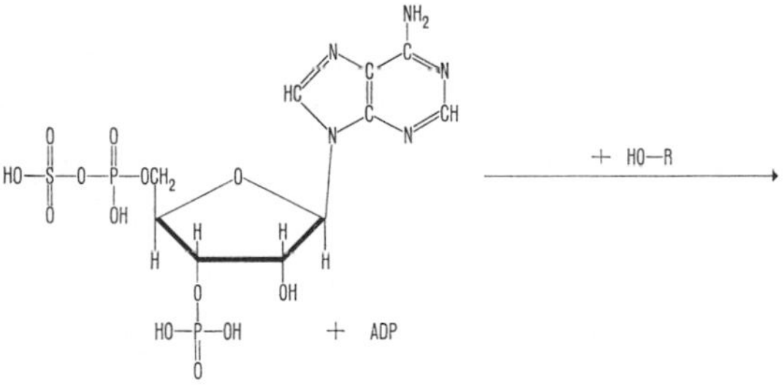

Adenosine 3'-phosphate 5'-phosphosulphate

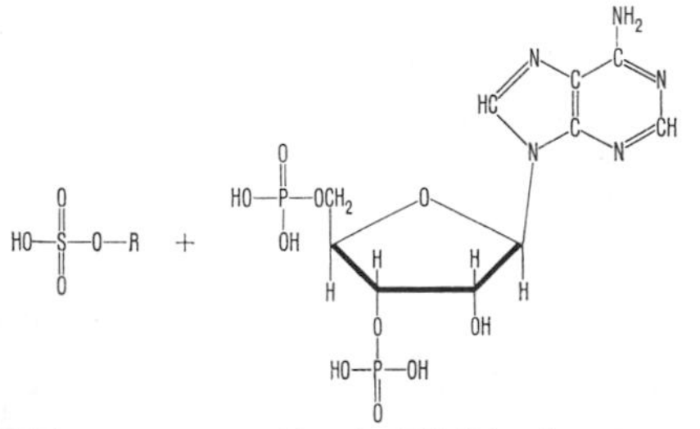

Sulphate ester | Adenosine 3',5'-diphosphate

References

[1] WILLIAMS, R.T., *Detoxication Mechanisms*, 2nd ed., Chapman & Hall, London, 1959.

[2] BANDURSKI et al., *J. Amer. chem. Soc.*, **78**, 6408 (1956); ROBBINS and LIPMANN, *J. Amer. chem. Soc.*, **78**, 2652, 6409 (1956); ROBBINS and LIPMANN, *J. biol. Chem.*, **229**, 837 (1957); GREGORY and LIPMANN, *J. biol. Chem.*, **229**, 1081 (1957).

Formation of phenacetylglutamine

This detoxication mechanism is peculiar to the detoxication of phenylacetic acid in anthropoid apes and man. The reaction requires coenzyme A and ATP, and proceeds by a mechanism similar to that involved in the activation of acetate (see page 391):

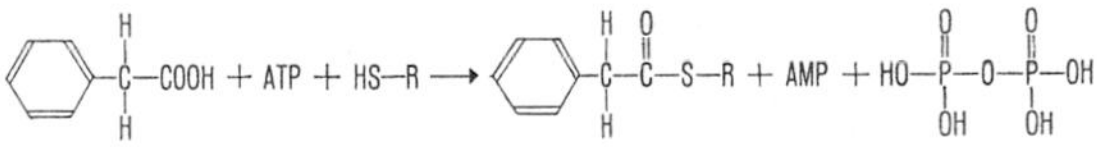

Phenylacetic acid | Coenzyme A | Phenylacetyl-coenzyme A | Pyrophosphoric acid

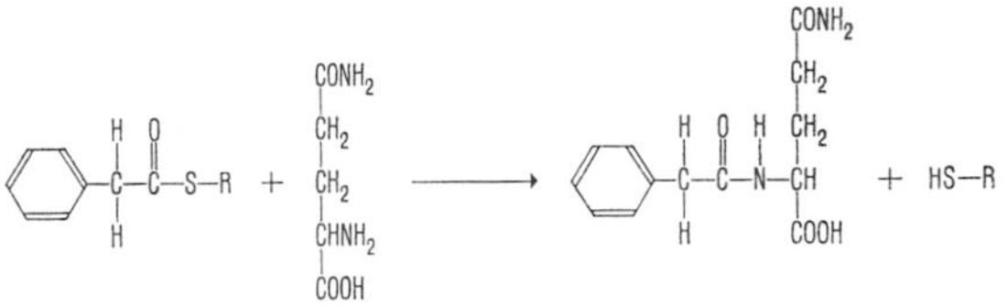

Phenylacetyl-coenzyme A | Glutamine | Phenylacetyl-glutamine | Coenzyme A

The first of these reactions occurs in beef as well as human tissues; the second, however, appears to be confined to human kidney and liver, and it has been found not to occur in rat and beef liver. As in the case of acetate activation, phenylacetic acid and ATP can be replaced by phenylacetyl-AMP, but an accumulation of the latter on incubating phenylacetic acid on ATP has not been demonstrated.

Formation of mercapturic acids

A number of aromatic compounds (e.g., halogenobenzenes, naphthalene) give rise on ingestion to mercapturic acids (*N*-acetyl-*S*-arylcysteines)[1]. The mechanism of formation of these compounds is as follows[2]:

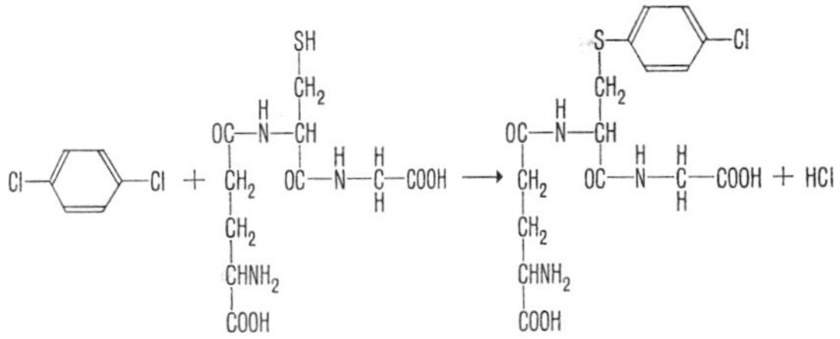

p-Dichlorobenzene | Glutathione | *S*-(*p*-Chlorobenzyl)-glutathione

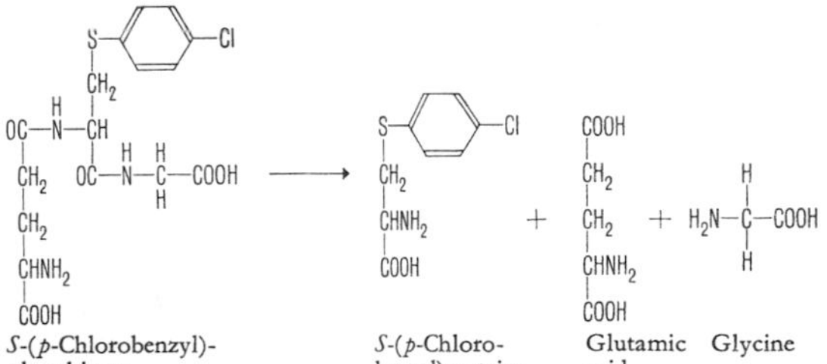

S-(*p*-Chlorobenzyl)-glutathione | *S*-(*p*-Chlorobenzyl)cysteine | Glutamic acid | Glycine

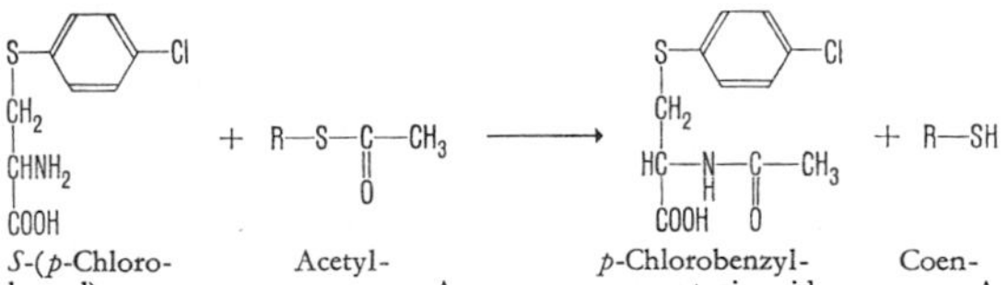

S-(*p*-Chlorobenzyl)-cysteine | Acetyl-coenzyme A | *p*-Chlorobenzyl-mercapturic acid (*N*-acetyl-*S*-*p*-chlorobenzylcysteine) | Coenzyme A

References

[1] WILLIAMS, R.T., *Detoxication Mechanisms*, 2nd ed., Chapman & Hall, London, 1959.

[2] BRAY et al., *Biochem. J.*, **71**, 690 (1959); BOOTH et al., *Biochem. J.*, **79**, 516 (1961).

Introduction

A number of diseases are now known to be caused by a failure of the body to synthesize sufficient quantities of one specific protein, often an enzyme, or by the synthesis of an abnormal protein in place of the normal one. Failure to synthesize an enzyme can cause a complete or partial block of a metabolic pathway and usually leads to the accumulation of the intermediary metabolite that is normally the substrate of the missing enzyme. In some cases the accumulation of this metabolite leads to abnormal side reactions. In phenylketonuria, for example, absence of phenylalanine 4-hydroxylase leads to accumulation of phenylalanine, some of which is converted to phenylpyruvic acid, and this undergoes further changes to *o*-hydroxyphenylacetic acid, phenyl-lactic acid and phenylacetylglutamine.

In some cases the defective protein is not an enzyme in the narrower sense, i.e., a catalyst bringing about a chemical change, but a substance concerned with the active transport of a metabolite from one compartment of the body to another. Examples are intestinal absorption and renal tubular reabsorption. In such cases the resulting disease or abnormality is not caused by a metabolic block but by a disturbance of transportation and the secondary effects of this disturbance. In Hartnup disease, for example, tryptophan is poorly absorbed from the intestine and is in consequence acted on by bacteria in the colon to produce abnormal indolic compounds that are absorbed. In this disease there is also a renal tubular defect leading to amino-aciduria.

These defects in the synthesis of an enzyme or transport mechanism are genetically determined and are referred to as inborn errors of metabolism. Some defects of this kind consisting of single enzyme failures can be acquired, like the action of a heavy metal poison on proximal renal tubular transport of amino acids and of hexachlorobenzene on porphyrin metabolism or the production of alkaptonuria in experimental animals by administration of α,α-dipyridyl. Such acquired defects are often temporary.

Some gene mutations lead to the formation of an abnormal structural protein rather than the absence of an enzyme. The clearest examples are the haemoglobinopathies, where the structure of some of the abnormal proteins has been completely elucidated. In the thalassaemias there is a relative failure to synthesize haemoglobin rather than production of an abnormal haemoglobin. Thalassaemia is thought to be caused by mutation of a 'controller' or 'tap' gene, abnormal haemoglobins by mutations of 'structural' genes. Inborn errors of metabolism may resemble either type of haemoglobinopathy: mutation of the relevant structural gene would produce in place of the normal enzyme a protein lacking catalytic properties, while a 'silent gene' mutation would produce neither the enzyme nor an abnormal protein.

Haemoglobinopathies[1]

Four major types of haemoglobin occur in normal erythrocytes: Hb-A_1 (or A), Hb-A_2, Hb-F and Hb-A_3. In the adult, Hb-A_1 constitutes over 85% of the normal haemoglobin and Hb-A_2 about 2½%. Hb-F is the major constituent in utero but is rarely detectable after the first year of extrauterine life. Hb-A_3 is a compound of Hb-A_1 and glutathione found in older erythrocytes and will not be further considered.

Each molecule of haemoglobin consists of four polypeptide chains of two different types and four haem groups. Hb-A_1 has two α^A and two β^A polypeptide chains; Hb-A_1 can be formulated as $\alpha_2^A\beta_2^A$, Hb-A_2 as $\alpha_2^A\delta_2^{A_2}$ and Hb-F as $\alpha_2^A\gamma_2^F$. The synthesis of each type of polypeptide chain, α, β, γ or δ, is controlled by a different pair of genes. Each polypeptide consists of between 140 and 150 amino-acid residues. The identity of the amino-acid residue at any point on the chain is determined by the structure of the triplet of deoxyribonucleotides at the corresponding point on the DNA chain constituting the gene. A change in this triplet (i.e., a mutation) may alter the identity of the amino acid incorporated at this point in the chain and thus produce a different polypeptide. Combination of this abnormal polypeptide with other polypeptide chains and haem groups produces an abnormal haemoglobin.

Over 100 different abnormal haemoglobins are known, each produced by a mutation affecting one type of polypeptide chain. In sickle-cell anaemia, for example, the β gene has undergone mutation to produce an abnormal β polypeptide (β^S) with valine in place of glutamic acid at position 6, but the α gene is normal. The major haemoglobin produced by the homozygote is therefore $\alpha_2^A\beta_2^S$, accompanied by normal $\alpha_2^A\gamma_2^F$ and $\alpha_2^A\delta_2^{A_2}$; the heterozygote has $\alpha_2^A\beta_2^A$ as well.

Hydrolysis of haemoglobin or its separated polypeptides with trypsin breaks up the chains wherever a lysine or arginine residue occurs, producing a series of oligopeptides. These can be separated by paper electrophoresis and chromatography to produce a two-dimensional pattern of peptides characteristic of the starting protein, a so-called 'fingerprint'. In an abnormal haemoglobin one tryptic peptide in general will differ from its normal counterpart in one of the constituent amino acids and hence in its position (and possibly reactions) on the 'fingerprint'. The relevant peptide spot can be cut out and further analysed.

An abnormal haemoglobin is first denoted by a letter or geographical location or by both, for example Hb-S, Hb-Norfolk, Hb-D_{Punjab}. When it is known which polypeptide chain is abnormal the nomenclature is modified, for example Hb-S $= \alpha_2^A\beta_2^S$, Hb-Norfolk $= \alpha_2^{Norfolk}\beta_2^A$. The tryptic peptides of the α chain are numbered αTpI to αTpXIV, those of the β chain βTpI to βTpXV; if known, the tryptic peptide containing the changed amino-acid residue is indicated, for example Hb-S $= \alpha_2^A\beta_2^S = \alpha_2^A\beta_2^{Tp\,I}$; Hb-Norfolk $= \alpha_2^{Norfolk}\beta_2^A = \alpha_2^{Tp\,VII}\beta_2^A$. The alteration in amino-acid composition, when known, is indicated by, for example, Hb-S $= \alpha_2^A\beta_2^{Tp\,I(Glu\rightarrow Val)}$, Hb-Norfolk $= \alpha_2^{Tp\,VII(Gly\rightarrow Asp)}\beta_2^A$. Finally, when the structure is completely elucidated, the notation used gives the amino acid substituted for the normal one in Hb-A and the position in the polypeptide at which the substitution occurs, for example, Hb-S $= \alpha_2^A\beta_2^{6Val}$, Hb-Norfolk $= \alpha_2^{57Asp}\beta_2^A$. A similar notation applies to the γ and δ chains, though as yet few abnormalities of these have been described.

The thalassaemias are a group of genetically determined anaemias in which the production of α chains, β chains or $\beta+\delta$ chains is greatly decreased or absent. Each type of thalassaemia is carried by a single autosomal gene with heterozygote expression and more marked homozygote expression.

Where α, β or δ chains are produced they are normal in structure; the various thalassaemias are probably caused by mutations of 'tap' genes controlling the activity of the α, β or $\beta+\delta$ structural genes respectively. If α chains are not made, Hb-A_1, Hb-A_2 and Hb-F cannot be formed. Homozygotes for α-thalassaemia probably all die in utero, while heterozygotes have more or less severe anaemia. Since surplus β, γ and δ chains are produced, α-thalassaemics sometimes possess abnormal haemoglobins with four β chains (Hb-H), four γ chains (Hb-Bart's) and, probably, four δ chains. In β-thalassaemia no abnormal haemoglobins are present but Hb-A_1 is decreased in amount or completely absent. In a pure β-thalassaemia, Hb-A_2 is increased in amount, as is Hb-F, but in thalassaemias where the activity of both β and δ genes is reduced, Hb-A_2 as well as Hb-A_1 is decreased in amount. Except in the High Hb-F condition, all homozygotes for β-thalassaemia and 95% of heterozygotes for α- or β-thalassaemia exhibit morphological abnormalities of the erythrocytes in the form of hypochromia, poikilocytosis, frequent target cells and microcythaemia. The erythrocytes show decreased osmotic fragility. The anaemia is caused both by reduced formation of the globin moiety of haemoglobin and by haemolysis.

Thalassaemias are classified on clinical grounds. Probably all homozygotes for β-thalassaemia have thalassaemia 'major', and the majority of heterozygotes thalassaemia 'minor', 'minima' or 'trait'. There is some overlapping, however, as with heterozygotes for α-thalassaemia, who may show any degree of anaemia from very mild to very severe.

The High Hb-F gene is classified with the thalassaemias since it suppresses formation of β and δ chains. However, it is clinically harmless even when combined with sickle-cell trait in double heterozygotes. The High Hb-F condition has been called 'nonmicrocythaemic thalassaemia'[2].

Hb-Lepore and related diseases in homozygous form closely resemble the β-thalassaemias clinically as well as in the morphology of the erythrocytes and in the high proportion of Hb-F in the blood. In the Hb-Lepore group, however, an abnormal haemoglobin is present in place of Hb-A_1 and Hb-A_2. This abnormal haemoglobin has normal α chains but in place of β or δ chains a hybrid of these two. These abnormal β/δ polypeptides are formed

---

* This chapter on 'Inborn Errors of Metabolism' has been written in collaboration with L.I. Woolf (Department of the Regius Professor of Medicine, Radcliffe Infirmary, Oxford).

probably by nonhomologous crossings over of the β and δ genes, which are adjacent[3].

Although most abnormal haemoglobins are found only very rarely, the genes for thalassaemia (Hb-S, Hb-C and Hb-E) occur with high frequency in some parts of the world. Some of these, however, are lethal recessive genes, so that homozygotes for thalassaemia or Hb-S only rarely survive into adult life and there is a steady loss of these genes. Almost all the other haemoglobinopathies cause some loss of survival fitness. The Hb-S gene occurs only in regions where malignant tertian malaria is rife and in descendants of emigrants from these regions. As a child the heterozygote is more resistant to malaria than a homozygous normal individual, so that the better survival fitness of the heterozygote balances the loss of homozygotes for sickling, giving a stable polymorphic population with a frequency of the sickle-cell gene of up to 20%[4]. The same is very probably true of thalassaemia. Similar explanations involving conditions other than malaria will probably be found for the markedly uneven geographical distribution of the genes for Hb-C and Hb-E.

Some representative haemoglobinopathies are listed in Table 1.

References

[1] INGRAM, V.M., *Hemoglobin and Its Abnormalities*, Thomas, Springfield, 1961; INGRAM, V.M., *The Hemoglobins in Genetics and Evolution*, Columbia University Press, New York, 1963; MARTI, H.R., *Normale und anomale menschliche Hämoglobine*, Springer, Berlin, 1963; HUISMAN, T.H.J., *Advanc. clin. Chem.*, **6**, 231 (1963); GERALD and SCOTT, in STANBURY et al. (Eds.), *The Metabolic Basis of Inherited Disease*, 2nd ed., McGraw-Hill, New York, 1966, page 1090; LEHMANN et al., in STANBURY et al. (Eds.), *The Metabolic Basis of Inherited Disease*, 2nd ed., McGraw-Hill, New York, 1966, page 1100; LEHMANN and CARRELL, *Brit. med. Bull.*, **25**, 14 (1969); WEATHERALL, D., *Brit. med. Bull.*, **25**, 24 (1969).

[2] MOTULSKY, A.G., *Nature*, **194**, 607 (1962).

[3] BAGLIONI, C., *Proc. nat. Acad. Sci. (Wash.)*, **48**, 1880 (1962).

[4] LAMBOTTE-LEGRAND and LAMBOTTE-LEGRAND, *Sang*, **23**, 560 (1952); ALLISON, A.C., *Brit. med. J.*, **1**, 290 (1954); ALLISON, A.C., *Ann. N.Y. Acad. Sci.*, **91**, 710 (1961).

Table 1 Haemoglobinopathies and thalassaemias

Condition or abnormal haemoglobin	Haemoglobins present		Clinical features	Original geographical distribution
Sickle-cell anaemia	$\alpha_2^A\beta_2^{6\,Val}$ (Hb-S) $\alpha_2^A\delta_2^{A_2}$ (Hb-A_2) $\alpha_2^A\gamma_2^F$ (Hb-F)	77–87% 2.5% 10–20%	Infarcts and haemolytic anaemia	Central and West Africa, India, South Arabia, Mediterranean lands
Sickle-cell trait (heterozygotes for above)	$\alpha_2^A\beta_2^A$ (Hb-A_1) $\alpha_2^A\beta_2^{6\,Val}$ (Hb-S)	56–76% 20–40%	Usually symptomless; sickling crises if anoxic	As above
Hb-C disease	$\alpha_2^A\beta_2^{6\,Lys}$ $\alpha_2^A\delta_2^{A_2}$ $\alpha_2^A\gamma_2^F$	88% 9% 2%	Fairly mild haemolytic anaemia; splenomegaly	Northern Ghana
Hb-SC disease (heterozygote for Hb-S and Hb-C)	$\alpha_2^A\beta_2^{6\,Val}$ $\alpha_2^A\beta_2^{6\,Lys}$ $\alpha_2^A\gamma_2^F$	52.5% 43.5% 3.5%	Severe haemolytic anaemia	Parts of Ghana and neighbouring countries
Hb-E	$\alpha_2^A\beta_2^{26\,Lys}$		Relatively mild anaemia	Thailand, South-east Asia
Hb-$G_{San\ José}$	$\alpha_2^A\beta_2^{7\,Gly}$		Symptomless	–
Hb-M group (at least 5 different types)	Hb-M_{Boston} $= \alpha_2^{Tp\ VII\ (His \rightarrow Tyr)}\beta_2^A$		Methaemoglobinaemia; fairly severe anaemia	Europe (?)
Hb-Zurich	$\alpha_2^A\beta_2^{63\,Arg}$		Sulphonamides produce haemolytic crises	Europe (?)
Hb-Lepore (at least 3 forms: Hb-$Lepore_{Boston}$ Hb-$Lepore_{Hollandia}$ Hb-Pylos)	Hb-Lepore $\alpha_2^A\gamma_2^F$	25% 75%	As in β-thalassaemia	–
δ-Thalassaemia	$\alpha_2^A\delta_2^{A_2}$	reduced (none in homozygotes)	None, unless combined with β- or (δβ)-thalassaemia	Greece
(δβ)-Thalassaemia (F-thalassaemia)	$\alpha_2^A\beta_2^A$ $\alpha_2^A\delta_2^{A_2}$ $\alpha_2^A\gamma_2^F$	none or reduced none or reduced up to 100% in homozygotes 5–15% in heterozygotes	As for β-thalassaemia	Greece, Central Africa

Table 1 (continued) Haemoglobinopathies and thalassaemias

Condition or abnormal haemoglobin	Haemoglobins present		Clinical features	Original geographical distribution
β-Chain thalassaemia (COOLEY's anaemia, Mediterranean anaemia, thalassaemia major, A_2-thalassaemia, etc.)	$\alpha_2^A\beta_2^A$ $\alpha_2^A\gamma_2^F$ $\alpha_2^A\delta_2^{A_2}$	none or low 5–95% 2–14%	Severe microcytic anaemia	Mediterranean lands, Asia south of latitude 40°N, Central Africa
High Hb-F (persistent foetal haemoglobin, F-gene, 'non-microcythaemic thalassaemia')	$\alpha_2^A\gamma_2^F$	100% in homozygotes 30% in heterozygotes	Symptomless; total Hb concentration normal even in homozygotes	Central Africa (?)
Heterozygotes for β-chain thalassaemia (COOLEY's trait, thalassaemia minor)	$\alpha_2^A\beta_2^A$ $\alpha_2^A\delta_2^{A_2}$ $\alpha_2^A\gamma_2^F$	reduced raised in 96% raised in 50%	Microcytic anaemia, varying from very mild to severe	Mediterranean lands, etc.
Heterozygotes for β-chain thalassaemia and Hb-S, Hb-C or Hb-E (sickle-cell thalassaemia, etc.)	$\alpha_2^A\beta_2^{6\,Val}$ or $\alpha_2^A\beta_2^{6\,Lys}$ or $\alpha_2^A\beta_2^{26\,Lys}$		Combine the features of both heterozygous diseases; often more severe than either alone	As for Hb-S, Hb-C or Hb-E
α-Chain thalassaemias, Hb-H, Hb-Bart's (COOLEY's anaemia, etc.)	$\alpha_2^A\beta_2^A$ β_4^A = Hb-H γ_4^F = Hb-Bart's $\delta_4^{A_2}$	in reduced amount	As in β-thalassaemia; probably only heterozygotes survive	Thailand, China, Greece

Inborn errors of amino-acid metabolism

In alkaptonuria the absence of homogentisate oxygenase prevents the catabolism of homogentisic acid to maleylacetoacetic acid with the result that homogentisic acid accumulates and is excreted in the urine. The renal clearance of homogentisic acid is very high.

Phenylketonuria, histidinaemia and maple syrup urine disease (leucinosis) resemble alkaptonuria in that each is caused by the genetically determined absence of an enzyme and the consequent accumulation of the relevant substrate. In each case, however, the substrate undergoes 'abnormal' reactions because of its high concentration, for example in phenylketonuria the transamination of phenylalanine to phenylpyruvic acid or β-imidazolylpyruvic acid and reduction to the α-hydroxy acids. Substrates of the missing enzymes in abnormally high concentrations, as well as the abnormal metabolites, are often toxic; they may cause brain damage in phenylketonuria and maple syrup urine disease, ochronosis and arthritis in alkaptonuria.

In albinism, though tyrosine is not converted to 3,4-dihydroxyphenylalanine (DOPA) and the latter is not converted to melanin, it is adequately metabolized by other pathways. The nature of the enzymatic defects in cystinosis, homocystinuria, hyperglycinaemia and oxalosis is still obscure.

Diseases arising from inborn errors of amino-acid metabolism are listed in Table 2. All involve some loss of survival fitness and many are virtually lethal. All are inherited as mendelian recessive characters, as would be expected in view of the fact that a mutant gene would tend not to survive if it produced a dominant character causing serious disability. Even recessively inherited lethal genes tend to vanish unless there is some compensating advantage to the heterozygote in some environments.

Table 2 Inborn errors of intermediary metabolism of amino acids

Condition	Defective enzyme	Biochemical features	Clinical features	Treatment	Reference
Alkaptonuria*	Homogentisate oxygenase	Urinary excretion of homogentisic acid	Urine darkens; ochronosis; arthritis in later life	None known	1, 2
Phenylketonuria**	Phenylalanine 4-hydroxylase	Phenylalanine accumulates in blood, CSF, etc.; urinary excretion of phenylpyruvic acid and related compounds	Severe mental deficiency, epilepsy, abnormal EEG, eczema, behavioural disorders	Diet low in phenylalanine beginning at early age	2, 3
Albinism***	*o*-Diphenol oxidase (tyrosinase)	Lack of melanin in skin, hair and eyes	Photophobia, nystagmus, carcinomata of the skin	None known	2, 4

* Incidence 1 in 100 000. ** Incidence varies from 1 in 3200 to 1 in 10^7 according to locality. *** Incidence 1 in 13 000.

Table 2 (continued) Inborn errors of intermediary metabolism of amino acids

Condition	Defective enzyme	Biochemical features	Clinical features	Treatment	Reference
Goitrous cretinism (several types)	(1) Tyrosine iodinase (2) Coupling enzyme (3) Deiodinase	Lack of thyroid hormone	Cretinism, goitre	Thyroid, thyroxine or tri-iodothyronine	5
Maple syrup urine disease (leucinosis)	Enzyme responsible for oxidative decarboxylation of α-ketoisocaproic, α-keto-β-methyl-n-valeric and α-keto-isovaleric acids	Leucine, isoleucine and valine accumulate in blood, CSF, etc.; urinary excretion of the 3 keto acids and related compounds	Cerebral degeneration; usually early death. Milder form with partial enzyme deficiency, symptomless except during infections, etc.	Diet low in leucine, isoleucine and valine	6
Cystinosis	Cystine reductase (?)	Cystine is deposited in reticulo-endothelial system; amino-aciduria, glucosuria, proteinuria, phosphaturia, dilute urine	Dwarfism, photophobia, renal acidosis, hypokalaemia, vitamin-resistant rickets; death before puberty. A benign (non-renal?) variant occurs in adults	Palliative: potassium salts, alkalis, vitamin D. Diet low in cystine and methionine (efficacy doubtful)	7
Homocystinuria	L-Serine dehydratase	Urinary excretion of homocystine	Mental retardation, retinal defects, dislocated lenses, malar flush, thromboses	Diet low in methionine, high in cystine. Pyridoxine	8
Hyperglycinaemia (several types)	(Uncertain, depends on type)	Glycine accumulates in blood, etc.; urinary excretion of glycine and, in one type, methylmalonic acid	Neonatal lethargy and ketosis, neutropenia, hypo-γ-globulinaemia; mental retardation	Diet low in protein	9
Oxalosis	Excessive conversion of glycine to oxalic acid	Calcium oxalate accumulates in kidneys, heart, bone marrow and cartilages	Nephrocalcinosis leading to progressive renal failure	None known	10
Histidinaemia	Histidine ammonia-lyase	Urinary excretion of β-imidazolylpyruvic acid and related compounds	Speech defects; mental retardation in some	Diet low in histidine	11
Familial tyrosinaemia	(Uncertain)	Tyrosine level in blood and urine raised; urinary excretion of phenolic acids related to tyrosine; generalized amino-aciduria; glucosuria; fructosuria	Rapidly enlarging liver; jaundice; hypoprothrombinaemia; death common in infancy; survivors may have vitamin D-resistant rickets and acidosis	Diet low in tyrosine and phenylalanine (efficacy doubtful)	12
Hyperprolinaemia Type I	Pyrroline-5-carboxylate reductase	Hyperprolinaemia; urinary excretion of proline, glycine and hydroxyproline	Mental retardation, convulsions, renal disease, deafness	None known	13
Type II	Pyrroline-5-carboxylate dehydrogenase				
Hydroxyprolinaemia	3-Hydroxypyrroline-5-carboxylate reductase (?)	High levels of hydroxyproline in blood and urine	Mental retardation (?)	None known	13
Citrullinaemia	Argininosuccinate synthetase	High blood and urinary levels of citrulline; blood ammonia increased; urea excretion normal	Mental retardation, epilepsy, vomiting, ammonia intoxication	Diet low in protein	14, 15
Argininosuccinic aciduria	Argininosuccinate lyase	Urinary excretion of argininosuccinic acid; high blood and CSF ammonia levels; urea excretion normal	Mental retardation, convulsions, hair abnormalities, ammonia intoxication	Diet low in protein	15, 16

Table 2 (concluded) Inborn errors of intermediary metabolism of amino acids

Condition	Defective enzyme	Biochemical features	Clinical features	Treatment	Reference
Hyperammonaemia Type I	Ornithine carbamoyltransferase	Blood ammonia about 10 mg/l; urea excretion normal	Mental retardation, ammonia intoxication	Diet low in protein (?)	17
Type II	Carbamoyl-phosphate synthase				18

References

1 O'Brien et al., *Amer.J.Med.*, **34**, 813 (1963); LaDu, B.N., in Stanbury et al. (Eds.), *The Metabolic Basis of Inherited Disease*, 2nd ed., McGraw-Hill, New York, 1966, page 303.
2 Woolf, L.I., *Advanc.clin.Chem.*, **6**, 97 (1963).
3 Lyman, F.L. (Ed.), *Phenylketonuria*, Thomas, Springfield, 1963; Knox, W.E., in Stanbury et al. (Eds.), *The Metabolic Basis of Inherited Disease*, 2nd ed., McGraw-Hill, New York, 1966, page 258.
4 Fitzpatrick and Quevedo, in Stanbury et al. (Eds.), *The Metabolic Basis of Inherited Disease*, 2nd ed., McGraw-Hill, New York, 1966, page 324.
5 Stanbury, J.B., in Stanbury et al. (Eds.), *The Metabolic Basis of Inherited Disease*, 2nd ed., McGraw-Hill, New York, 1966, page 215.
6 Woolf, L.I., in Linneweh, F. (Ed.), *Erbliche Stoffwechselkrankheiten*, Urban & Schwarzenberg, Munich, 1962, page 159; Dancis and Levitz, in Stanbury et al. (Eds.), *The Metabolic Basis of Inherited Disease*, 2nd ed., McGraw-Hill, New York, 1966, page 353; Morris et al., *Pediatrics*, **28**, 918 (1961); Kiil and Rokkones, *Acta paediat. (Uppsala)*, **53**, 356 (1964).
7 Linneweh, F., in Linneweh, F. (Ed.), *Erbliche Stoffwechselkrankheiten*, Urban & Schwarzenberg, Munich, 1962, page 141; Bauer and Antener, *Helv. paediat.Acta*, **21**, 19 (1966); Lietman et al., *Amer.J. Med.*, **40**, 511 (1966).
8 Gerritsen and Waisman, in Stanbury et al. (Eds.), *The Metabolic Basis of Inherited Disease*, 2nd ed., McGraw-Hill, New York, 1966, page 420; Cusworth and Dent, *Brit. med. Bull.*, **25**, 42 (1969).
9 Nyhan, W.L., in Linneweh, F. (Ed.), *Erbliche Stoffwechselkrankheiten*, Urban & Schwarzenberg, Munich, 1962, page 170; Schreier and Müller, *Dtsch. med. Wschr.*, **89**, 1739 (1964) and *Germ.med.Mth.*, **9**, 437 (1964).
10 Wyngaarden and Elder, in Stanbury et al. (Eds.), *The Metabolic Basis of Inherited Disease*, 2nd ed., McGraw-Hill, New York, 1966, page 189.
11 Ghadimi et al., *Pediatrics*, **29**, 714 (1962); La Du, B.N., in Stanbury et al. (Eds.), *The Metabolic Basis of Inherited Disease*, 2nd ed., McGraw-Hill, New York, 1966, page 366.
12 Gentz et al., *J. Pediat.*, **66**, 670 (1965); LaDu, B.N., in Stanbury et al. (Eds.), *The Metabolic Basis of Inherited Disease*, 2nd ed., McGraw-Hill, New York, 1966, page 295; Gjessing, L.R. (Ed.), *Symposium on Tyrosinosis*, Oslo University Press, Oslo, 1966.
13 Efron, M.L., in Stanbury et al. (Eds.), *The Metabolic Basis of Inherited Disease*, 2nd ed., McGraw-Hill, New York, 1966, page 376.
14 McMurray et al., *Pediatrics*, **32**, 347 (1963).
15 Efron, M.L., in Stanbury et al. (Eds.), *The Metabolic Basis of Inherited Disease*, 2nd ed., McGraw-Hill, New York, 1966, page 393.
16 Tomlinson and Westall, *Clin.Sci.*, **26**, 261 (1964); Schreier and Leuchte, *Dtsch.med. Wschr.*, **90**, 864 (1965).
17 Russell et al., *Lancet*, **2**, 699 (1962).
18 Freeman et al., *J. Pediat.*, **65**, 1039 (1964).

Inborn errors of carbohydrate metabolism

Genetically determined absence of the appropriate intestinal enzyme causes inability to split lactose, sucrose or limit dextrin. Consumption of these substances may lead to diarrhoea and sometimes injury of the intestinal mucosa.

In galactosaemia, galactose is not converted to glycogen because of the absence of galactose-1-phosphate uridylyltransferase. Galactose 1-phosphate therefore accumulates and has a toxic effect due to its inhibition of phosphoglucomutase and other enzymes. Similarly, in fructose intolerance the absence of fructose-1-phosphate aldolase results in accumulation of fructose-1-phosphate, which causes severe hypoglycaemia, probably by inhibition of glucose-6-phosphatase. Defects in the metabolism of carbohydrates other than glycogen are listed in Table 3. With the exception of hereditary leucine-sensitive hypoglycaemia, all are probably or certainly inherited as mendelian recessive characters.

There are at least seven diseases due to an abnormality of glycogen metabolism (Table 4). There may be failure to form this substance, or a glycogen of abnormal structure may be laid down, or the glycogen deposited in various tissues may not be broken down normally. In six of the seven diseases a specific enzymatic defect has been demonstrated, but not all of these resemble typical inborn errors of metabolism in which a mutant gene fails to produce a normal enzyme. In idiopathic generalized glycogenosis there is a deficiency of α-glucosidase. In some, more severe, cases of Gierke's disease, glucose-6-phosphatase is absent from the liver, but more often it is present in diminished amount. A second enzyme, glucose-6-phosphate dehydrogenase, is also absent in some but not all persons with Gierke's disease. Glucose-6-phosphatase deficiency and dextrin-1,6-glucosidase deficiency occur in the same families; in these families at least, the mutant gene is unlikely to be directly responsible for the enzymatic defects. The status of amylopectinosis and of hepatic glycogen phosphorylase deficiency is also somewhat uncertain.

Table 3 Inborn errors of metabolism of carbohydrates other than glycogen

Condition	Defective enzyme	Biochemical features	Clinical features	Treatment	Reference
Galactose diabetes	Galactokinase	Urinary excretion of galactose	Cataracts	Diet low in galactose from early infancy	1
Galactosaemia*	Galactose-1-phosphate uridylyltransferase	Galactose and galactose 1-phosphate accumulate in tissues and body fluids	Liver damage, cataracts, mental deficiency, renal tubular dysfunction; often early death	Diet free from galactose	2
Fructose intolerance	Fructose-1-phosphate aldolase	Fructose and fructose 1-phosphate accumulate	Severe hypoglycaemia after ingesting fructose, sucrose, etc.	Avoidance of fructose and fructose precursors such as sucrose	3, 4
Fructosuria	Fructokinase	Urinary excretion of ingested fructose	Benign	Unnecessary	3

* Incidence 1 in 70 000.

Table 3 (continued) Inborn errors of metabolism of carbohydrates other than glycogen

Condition	Defective enzyme	Biochemical features	Clinical features	Treatment	Reference
Pentosuria*	L-Xylulose reductase	Urinary excretion of L- xylulose	Benign	Unnecessary	5
Alactasia	β-Galactosidase (lactase) in intestinal mucosa (lifelong)	Lactose not hydrolysed in small intestine	Diarrhoea; failure to gain weight	Avoidance of lactose	6, 7
Lactose intolerance	Probably intestinal β-galactosidase (temporarily)	Lactose not utilized; lactosuria; amino-aciduria	Diarrhoea; possible death in infancy	Avoidance of lactose and sucrose	6, 7
Sucrose intolerance	β-Fructofuranosidase (saccharase) and oligo-1,6-glucosidase (isomaltase) in mucosa of small intestine	Sucrose and 1,6-α-oligo-saccharides not hydrolysed in intestines	Diarrhoea after ingesting sucrose; less severe diarrhoea after ingesting starch	Avoidance of sucrose; diet low in starch	7
Hereditary leucine-sensitive hypoglycaemia**	–	Hypoglycaemia accentuated by giving leucine or protein, through release of insulin	Hypoglycaemic convulsions; varying degrees of mental retardation; sometimes symptomless	Carbohydrates with every protein meal	8

* Incidence 1 in 50 000.
** Inherited as a dominant character causing 40–60% of cases of idiopathic infantile hypoglycaemia.

References

1 GITZELMANN, R., *Lancet*, **2**, 670 (1965).
2 WOOLF, L.I., *Advanc. clin. Chem.*, **5**, 1 (1962); ISSELBACHER, K.J., in STANBURY et al. (Eds.), *The Metabolic Basis of Inherited Disease*, 2nd ed., McGraw-Hill, New York, 1966, page 178.
3 FROESCH, E.R., in LINNEWEH, F. (Ed.), *Erbliche Stoffwechselkrankheiten*, Urban & Schwarzenberg, Munich, 1962, page 242; FROESCH, E.R., in STANBURY et al. (Eds.), *The Metabolic Basis of Inherited Disease*, 2nd ed., McGraw-Hill, New York, 1966, page 124.
4 HERS, H.G., in LINNEWEH, F. (Ed.), *Erbliche Stoffwechselkrankheiten*, Urban & Schwarzenberg, Munich, 1962, page 252.
5 HOLLMANN, S., in LINNEWEH, F. (Ed.), *Erbliche Stoffwechselkrankheiten*, Urban & Schwarzenberg, Munich, 1962, page 254; HIATT, H.H., in STANBURY et al. (Eds.), *The Metabolic Basis of Inherited Disease*, 2nd ed., McGraw-Hill, New York, 1966, page 109.
6 HOLZEL, A., in LINNEWEH, F. (Ed.), *Erbliche Stoffwechselkrankheiten*, Urban & Schwarzenberg, Munich, 1962, page 219.
7 AURICCHIO et al., *J. Pediat.*, **62**, 165 (1963); PRADER and AURICCHIO, *Ann. Rev. Med.*, **16**, 345 (1965); TOWNLEY, R.R.W., *Pediatrics*, **38**, 127 (1966).
8 PAYNE and WOOLF, *Mod. Probl. Pädiat.*, **4**, 369 (1959).

Table 4 Inborn errors of glycogen deposition or utilization [1]

Condition	CORI type	Biochemical features	Clinical features
Glucose-6-phosphatase deficiency (GIERKE's disease)	1	Normal glycogen accumulates in liver and kidney	Hepatomegaly, hypoglycaemia; stunted growth with retarded bone age, etc.
Idiopathic generalized glycogenosis (POMPE's disease)	2	Normal glycogen accumulates in all organs	Cardiac failure, muscle hypotonia, neurological disorders, death in infancy
Dextrin-1,6-glucosidase (debrancher) deficiency (limit dextrinosis; FORBES' disease)	3	Abnormal glycogen with short branches deposited in liver and, sometimes, skeletal and cardiac muscle	Hepatomegaly, hypoglycaemia; less severe than GIERKE's disease
α-Glucan-branching glycosyltransferase (brancher) deficiency (amylopectinosis; ANDERSEN's disease)	4	Abnormal carbohydrate with long inner and outer branches deposited in liver, spleen and lymph nodes	Hepatic cirrhosis; death within two years of birth
Glycogen phosphorylase (glycogen phosphorylase of the muscle) deficiency (MCARDLE's syndrome)	5	Moderate accumulation of normal glycogen in skeletal muscles; lactate and pyruvate levels in blood fall during exercise	Generalized muscular fatiguability and pain
Glycogen phosphorylase (hepatic glycogen phosphorylase) deficiency (HERS' disease)	6	Normal glycogen accumulates in liver; phosphorylase content of liver and leucocytes reduced	Hepatomegaly; relatively benign
Deficiency of UDPglucose–glycogen glucosyltransferase (glycogen synthetase)	–	Liver glycogen almost completely absent	Severe fasting hypoglycaemia

Reference

1 FIELD, R.A., in STANBURY et al. (Eds.), *The Metabolic Basis of Inherited Disease*, 2nd ed., McGraw-Hill, New York, 1966, page 141; HERS, H.G., *Advanc. metab. Disord.*, **1**, 1 (1964); *Control of Glycogen Metabolism*, Ciba Foundation Symposium, Churchill, London, 1964.

Inborn defects of renal transport mechanisms[1]

Many of the substances in the glomerular filtrate are normally reabsorbed with high efficiency in the proximal renal tubule. This active process requires specific receptor sites on the cells lining this region. One type of site absorbs cystine, lysine, arginine and ornithine. In cystinuria[2] these sites are absent or largely inactive, so that cystine, lysine, arginine and ornithine are very inefficiently reabsorbed from the glomerular filtrate and appear in the urine. Cystinuria is determined by a single pair of genes. Abnormal homozygotes excrete all four amino acids and tend to form cystine stones. Some heterozygotes excrete moderately increased amounts of cystine and lysine, others are completely normal.

In the Hartnup syndrome[3] the renal tubular reabsorption of a different, and larger, group of amino acids is defective. Moreover, since absorption of tryptophan from the gut is also defective, bacterial metabolites of tryptophan are excreted in abnormal amounts.

There are several conditions characterized by one or more of the following: renal glucosuria[4], phosphaturia[5], renal acidosis[6], generalized amino-aciduria[7]. Each is caused by loss of some specific function of the proximal renal tubule, often inherited in dominant fashion. With the exception of renal glucosuria, the tubular defect is associated with disease in some individuals. Phosphogluco-amino-aciduria[8] (DEBRÉ - DE TONI - FANCONI syndrome), 'benign amino-aciduria'[9] and osteomalacia with amino-aciduria[10] (adult FANCONI syndrome) were formerly considered to be separate entities, but the demonstration of renal loss of phosphate and bicarbonate in two cases of 'benign amino-aciduria'[9] closed the gaps between it and the other two conditions. It seems probable that all three are manifestations of the same primary renal tubular defect[11], the clinical effects varying markedly from individual to individual, both in age at onset and severity. Cystinosis must be distinguished from these conditions since the progressive loss of renal tubular function in cystinosis is secondary to some more fundamental metabolic defect, as in galactosaemia and WILSON's disease; these three diseases are recessively inherited.

Glycine is reabsorbed from the glomerular filtrate by a mechanism probably specific for glycine. In glycinuria[12] this mechanism is defective; the condition is dominantly inherited.

In nephrogenic diabetes insipidus[13] the distal tubule and collecting duct do not respond to vasopressin by becoming permeable to water.

In renal glucosuria and glucose-galactose malabsorption[14] there is a disturbance of the reabsorption of glucose from the renal tubules.

References

1 WOOLF, L.I., *Renal Tubular Dysfunction*, Thomas, Springfield, 1966.
2 KNOX, W.E., in STANBURY et al. (Eds.), *The Metabolic Basis of Inherited Disease*, 2nd ed., McGraw-Hill, New York, 1966, page 1262.
3 JEPSON, J.B., in STANBURY et al. (Eds.), *The Metabolic Basis of Inherited Disease*, 2nd ed., McGraw-Hill, New York, 1966, page 1283.
4 REUBI, F., in LINNEWEH, F. (Ed.), *Erbliche Stoffwechselkrankheiten*, Urban & Schwarzenberg, Munich, 1962, page 234; KRANE, S.M., in STANBURY et al. (Eds.), *The Metabolic Basis of Inherited Disease*, 2nd ed., McGraw-Hill, New York, 1966, page 1221.
5 LINNEROTH et al., *Acta paediat. (Uppsala)*, **47**, 568 (1958); WILLIAMS et al., in STANBURY et al. (Eds.), *The Metabolic Basis of Inherited Disease*, 2nd ed., McGraw-Hill, New York, 1966, page 1179.
6 SELDIN and WILSON, in STANBURY et al. (Eds.), *The Metabolic Basis of Inherited Disease*, 2nd ed., McGraw-Hill, New York, 1966, page 1230.
7 PAYNE, W.W., *Pediatrics*, **17**, 84 (1956); JAGENBURG, O.R., *Scand. J. clin. Lab. Invest.*, **11**, suppl. 43 (1959); WOOLF, L.I., *Brit. med. Bull.*, **17**, 224 (1961); TATUM, E.L., in *Papers and Discussions of the 1st Inter-American Conference on Congenital Defects*, 1962, Lippincott, Philadelphia, 1963, page 53.
8 DE TONI, G., *Ann. paediat. (Basel)*, **187**, 42 (1956).
9 LUDER and SHELDON, *Arch. Dis. Childh.*, **30**, 160 (1955); SHELDON et al., *Arch. Dis. Childh.*, **36**, 90 (1961).
10 DENT and HARRIS, *J. Bone Jt Surg.*, **38B**, 204 (1956).
11 LEAF, A., in STANBURY et al. (Eds.), *The Metabolic Basis of Inherited Disease*, 2nd ed., McGraw-Hill, New York, 1966, page 1205.
12 DE VRIES et al., *Amer. J. Med.*, **23**, 408 (1957); WYNGAARDEN and SEGAL, in STANBURY et al. (Eds.), *The Metabolic Basis of Inherited Disease*, 2nd ed., McGraw-Hill, New York, 1966, page 341.
13 ORLOFF and BURG, in STANBURY et al. (Eds.), *The Metabolic Basis of Inherited Disease*, 2nd ed., McGraw-Hill, New York, 1966, page 1247.
14 MARKS et al., *J. Pediat.*, **69**, 225 (1966).

Table 5 Some inborn defects of transport mechanisms

Condition	Site of defect	Biochemical signs	Clinical features	Treatment	Genetics
Cystinuria	Renal tubules and gut wall	Excessive urinary excretion of cystine, lysine, arginine and ornithine	Calculi of cystine in urinary tract. Often symptomless	High water intake, alkalinization; penicillamine	Two forms, both recessive
Hartnup disease	Renal tubules and gut wall	Delayed intestinal absorption of tryptophan, etc.; excessive urinary excretion of indoles and many amino acids	Cerebellar ataxia, photosensitive dermatitis	Nicotinamide	Recessive
Glucose-galactose malabsorption	Wall of intestine, renal tubules	Glucose, galactose and products of microbial fermentation in faeces; glucosuria	Diarrhoea; dehydration, sometimes fatal	Diet with fructose as sole carbohydrate	Autosomal recessive (?)
Glycinuria	Renal tubules	Glycine excretion increased	Probably benign	None known	Dominant
Renal glucosuria	Renal tubules	Glucosuria; reduced *Tm* (glucose) in type A; increased splay of glucose reabsorption curve in type B	Benign	None known	Dominant
Hypophosphataemia (phosphaturia)	Renal tubules	Urinary loss of phosphate	Rickets resistant to vitamin D; sometimes symptomless	Phosphate infusions; large doses of vitamin D or dihydrotachysterol	Sex-linked with expression in most hemizygotes, some heterozygotes

Table 5 (continued) Some inborn defects of transport mechanisms

Condition	Site of defect	Biochemical signs	Clinical features	Treatment	Genetics
Renal acidosis	Renal tubules	Impaired hydrogen-ion exchange in glomerular filtrate; hypercalcinuria	Hyperchloraemia, acidosis, nephrocalcinosis, nephrolithiasis, rickets or osteomalacia. Sometimes symptomless	Alkalis	Sometimes dominant
Phosphoglucoamino-aciduria (DEBRÉ-DE TONI-FANCONI syndrome) 'Benign familial amino-aciduria' Osteomalacia with amino-aciduria (adult FANCONI syndrome)	Renal tubules	Urinary loss of glucose, phosphate, amino acids, protein and bicarbonate	Sometimes benign; phosphate loss, if severe, causes vitamin D-resistant rickets and dwarfism in children, osteomalacia in adults; acidosis in many cases	Alkalis, vitamin D or dihydrotachysterol, phosphate infusions	Dominant
Nephrogenic diabetes insipidus	Distal renal tubules and collecting ducts	Urine dilute and copious	Dehydration, mental retardation	Water, diet low in salt and nitrogen, chlorothiazide	Sex-linked recessive

Inborn errors of purine and pyrimidine metabolism

Hyperuricaemia (gout) is one of the commonest of all inborn errors of metabolism. Experiments with isotopically-labelled precursors indicate that the rate of synthesis of uric acid is increased in hyperuricaemia, presumably because one of the mechanisms regulating the synthesis of purines is faulty. The defect may be at the stage of the synthesis of ribosylamine 5-phosphate (see page 433) a reaction inhibited and probably controlled by ATP, ADP and related compounds.

In the very rare condition of xanthinuria, xanthine and not uric acid is excreted as the end-product of purine metabolism owing to lack of the enzyme xanthine oxidase.

Orotic-aciduria is due to a failure to synthesize uridylic acid from orotic acid (see page 438). A consequence is megaloblastic anaemia and retarded growth.

β-Aminoisobutyric acid is a breakdown product of thymine (see page 401) and is excreted in excess whenever tissue breakdown and DNA turnover proceed at a high rate, for example in leukaemia. β-Aminoisobutyric-aciduria occurs in some healthy individuals, possibly owing to the lack of an enzyme necessary for degradation of β-aminoisobutyric acid.

Table 6 Inborn errors of purine and pyrimidine metabolism

Condition	Defective enzyme or system	Biochemical features	Clinical features	Incidence and genetics	Reference
Gout (hyperuricaemia)	Excessive synthesis of uric acid from precursors	Concentration of uric acid increased in serum and often in urine	Acute arthritic attacks, chronic arthritis with urate deposition in tissues; urinary urate calculi causing kidney damage; asymptomatic in 80% of cases	Hyperuricaemia in 1–2%, clinical gout in 2–4 per 1000; probably autosomal dominant with variable and sex-modified expression	1
Xanthinuria	Deficiency of xanthine oxidase and defective renal tubular reabsorption of xanthine	Xanthine excreted in large amounts	Xanthine calculi in urinary tract	Rare	2
Orotic-aciduria	Absence of orotidine-5′-phosphate pyrophosphorylase and/or decarboxylase	Orotic acid accumulates and is excreted in urine	Severe megaloblastic anaemia, orotic-acid crystalluria	Very rare; recessive	3
β-Aminoisobutyric-aciduria	Deficiency of a catabolic enzyme	High urinary excretion of β-aminoisobutyric acid	Harmless	0–46% depending on ethnic group; recessive	4

References

1 WYNGAARDEN, J.B., in STANBURY et al. (Eds.), *The Metabolic Basis of Inherited Disease*, 2nd ed., McGraw-Hill, New York, 1966, page 667.

2 WYNGAARDEN, J.B., in STANBURY et al. (Eds.), *The Metabolic Basis of Inherited Disease*, 2nd ed., McGraw-Hill, New York, 1966, page 729.

3 SMITH et al., in STANBURY et al. (Eds.), *The Metabolic Basis of Inherited Disease*, 2nd ed., McGraw-Hill, New York, 1966, page 739.

4 SUTTON, H.E., in STANBURY et al. (Eds.), *The Metabolic Basis of Inherited Disease*, 1st ed., McGraw-Hill, New York, 1960, page 792.

Hyperbilirubinaemia[1] and porphyria[2]

Several inborn errors of the metabolism of pyrrole derivatives are known. The main stages of the synthesis of haem from glycine and succinyl-coenzyme A are as follows (for fuller details see page 355):

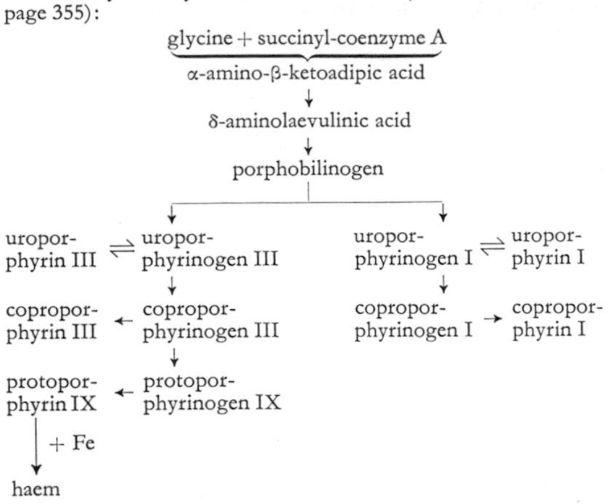

Complete failure of any of the enzymes leading to the formation of haem is incompatible with life since haem is an essential part not only of haemoglobin and myoglobin but also of a number of enzymes, especially the cytochromes. Deficiencies of the enzymes synthesizing haem can be due to inborn errors or the action of toxic substances. Thus among other effects, lead poisoning diminishes the activity of the enzymes metabolizing δ-aminolaevulinic acid, so that the latter is excreted in the urine.

In the commonest forms (intermittent acute porphyria and porphyria cutanea tarda hereditaria) the primary biochemical lesion is in the liver. These have been called respectively the Swedish and South African forms of hepatic porphyria, though both occur in all countries. Mixed porphyria and porphyria variegata are other terms applied, in particular, to the form of porphyria cutanea tarda hereditaria common in South Africa.

Hepatic porphyria (or cutaneous hepatic porphyria) is caused by oxidation of porphyrinogens to porphyrins in the liver. The porphyrins so produced cannot be used for haem synthesis and are excreted via the bile. The condition can be acquired by alcoholism, by ingestion of hexachlorobenzene, or as a result of liver disease.

Haem is normally broken down to bilirubin, which is conjugated with glucuronic acid in the liver and excreted as the conjugate in the bile. Free bilirubin in high concentration, in contrast to the conjugate, is toxic. Of the four known inherited conditions leading to hyperbilirubinaemia only one, the CRIGLER-NAJJAR syndrome, can be definitely attributed to the absence of an enzyme. The other three conditions may be the results of defects of a transport system.

References

[1] VEST, M., in LINNEWEH, F. (Ed.), *Erbliche Stoffwechselkrankheiten*, Urban & Schwarzenberg, Munich, 1962, page 333; SCHMID, R., in STANBURY et al. (Eds.), *The Metabolic Basis of Inherited Disease*, 2nd ed., McGraw-Hill, New York, 1966, page 871.

[2] GOLDBERG and RIMINGTON, *Diseases of Porphyrin Metabolism*, Thomas, Springfield, 1962; HAEGER-ARONSEN, B., *Amer. J. Med.*, **35**, 450 (1963); PERLROTH et al., *Amer. J. Med.*, **41**, 149 (1966); SCHMID, R., in STANBURY et al. (Eds.), *The Metabolic Basis of Inherited Disease*, 2nd ed., McGraw-Hill, New York, 1966, page 813; DEAN, G., *Brit. med. Bull.*, **25**, 48 (1969).

Table 7 Inborn defects of metabolism of pyrrole derivatives (hyperbilirubinaemia and porphyria)

Condition	Defective enzyme or system	Biochemical effects	Clinical features	Treatment	Incidence and genetics
Congenital non-haemolytic jaundice (CRIGLER-NAJJAR syndrome)	Bilirubin-glucuronic acid conjugating system	Serum bilirubin 150–400 mg/l (all free)	Severe kernicterus; often early death; sometimes symptomless	None known	Recessive
Constitutional hepatic dysfunction (GILBERT's disease)	Bilirubin-glucuronic acid conjugating system (?)	Serum bilirubin 10–30 mg/l (all free)	Probably harmless	None necessary	Probably dominant
Chronic idiopathic jaundice (DUBIN-JOHNSON syndrome)	Probably faulty hepatic excretion of pigment, etc. into the bile	Slight hyperbilirubinaemia (bilirubin all conjugated); unidentified brown pigment in liver parenchyma cells	Benign; sometimes liver enlargement and tenderness	None	Probably dominant
ROTOR syndrome	Possibly faulty hepatic excretion	Serum bilirubin 40–76 mg/l, half-free and half conjugated; no pigment in liver	Some liver tests abnormal	None	Probably dominant
Congenital erythropoietic porphyria (GÜNTHER's disease)	Probably uroporphyrinogen isomerase	Uroporphyrin I and coproporphyrin I in tissues, plasma, urine and faeces	Often early death; photosensitization leading to severe scarring, erythrodontia; haemolytic anaemia	Splenectomy, protection from sunlight	50 known cases; recessive
Intermittent acute porphyria	Large amounts of δ-aminolaevulinic acid synthetase in liver	Porphobilinogen and δ-aminolaevulinic acid excreted in urine	Often intermittent; abdominal pain, neurosis and psychosis, peripheral neuritis, paralysis, generalized demyelination; mortality high	Avoidance of barbiturates	Incidence 0.015–0.1%; dominant

Table 7 (continued) Inborn defects of metabolism of pyrrole derivatives (hyperbilirubinaemia and porphyria)

Condition	Defective enzyme or system	Biochemical effects	Clinical features	Treatment	Incidence and genetics
Porphyria cutanea tarda hereditaria	Excessive hepatic porphyrin production	Faecal porphyrins high in remission; urinary porphyrins (and possibly also porphobilinogen and δ-aminolaevulinic acid) high in relapse; liver porphyrins high	Symptomless unless accompanying hepatic dysfunction, when there is photosensitization leading to severe scarring, pigmentation of skin, hirsutism, oedema; jaundice, hepatic cirrhosis, sometimes mental symptoms	Protection from sunlight and skin trauma; avoidance of alcohol and barbiturates	Up to 1% in some regions; dominant
Idiopathic coproporphyria	Uncertain	Large amounts of coproporphyrin III in urine and faeces; amino-aciduria	Harmless	None	Rare; recessive
Erythropoietic protoporphyria	Uncertain	Large amounts of protoporphyrin in erythrocytes, normoblasts and (sometimes) faeces	Relatively mild photosensitive dermatitis, erythema, itching, mild oedema	Avoidance of bright sunlight	Rare; dominant

Lipidoses[1]

A group of pathological conditions, generally grouped together as 'lipidoses', are either caused by or result in a disturbance of lipid metabolism. Lipidoses are characterized by the accumulation of large quantities of some particular lipid. The accumulation occurs in one or more of the tissues, often selectively in the spleen.

Each of the lipidoses is a separate entity, though differential diagnosis often presents difficulties during life and, occasionally, on chemical analysis of the tissues after death.

The lipidoses are all genetically determined and thus belong to the group of inborn errors of metabolism, though little is known of the enzymatic defects underlying them. The three forms of GAUCHER's disease are distinct from one another genetically and in other ways. This is also true of the two forms of amaurotic familial idiocy. However, it is not certain that the different forms of NIEMANN-PICK disease are genetically distinct; they may differ only in site and rate of lipid deposition, and this may also be true of metachromatic leucodystrophy.

References

[1] VAN BOGAERT et al. (Eds.), *Cerebral Lipidoses*, Blackwell, Oxford, 1957; THANNHAUSER, S. J., *Lipidoses; Diseases of the Cellular Lipid Metabolism*, 3rd ed., Grune & Stratton, New York, 1958; ARONSON and VOLK (Eds.), *Cerebral Sphingolipidoses*, Academic Press, New York, 1962; ZÖLLNER and CUMINGS, in LINNEWEH, F. (Ed.), *Erbliche Stoffwechselkrankheiten*, Urban & Schwarzenberg, Munich, 1962, page 261; FOLCH-PI and BAUER (Eds.), *Brain Lipids and Lipoproteins, and the Leucodystrophies*, Proceedings of the 7th International Congress of Neurology, Rome 1961, Elsevier, Amsterdam, 1963; STANBURY et al. (Eds.), *The Metabolic Basis of Inherited Disease*, 2nd ed., McGraw-Hill, New York, 1966.

Table 8 Lipidoses

Condition	Lipid accumulating	Site	Clinical features	Age at which symptoms appear	Genetics	Reference
GAUCHER's disease (a) 'Adult' (b) Acute infantile (c) Juvenile and adult neurological	Glucocerebroside	Spleen, liver, bone marrow, leucocytes. Brain in (b) and (c); lung in (b)	Splenomegaly, often gross; hepatomegaly; anaemia; bone disorder; purpura; cerebral degeneration in (b) and (c)	(a) 1–60 years (b) 1st or 2nd half-year of life (c) 6–20 years	(a), (b) and (c) in different families; all recessive	1
TAY-SACHS' disease (infantile amaurotic familial idiocy)	Ganglioside G_{M2} (G_0), aminoglycolipid	White and grey matter of the brain	Cherry-red spot; progressive cerebral degeneration; death at age 1–5 years	Usually 4–6 months, sometimes earlier	Recessive	2
Juvenile and adult amaurotic familial idiocy	Ganglioside G_{M1} (G_1)	Brain (moderate increase)	Progressive loss of vision and cerebral degeneration	From 5 years onwards	Probably recessive	2

Table 8 (continued) Lipidoses

Condition	Lipid accumulating	Site	Clinical features	Age at which symptoms appear	Genetics	Reference
NIEMANN-PICK disease (a) Acute infantile (b) Cerebral juvenile (c) Noncerebral	Mainly sphingomyelin	Spleen, bone marrow, liver; usually also brain and retina	Often cherry-red spot; hepatosplenomegaly; hepatic cirrhosis; usually cerebral degeneration and death in first 2½ years. Some adult cases are without neurological involvement	(a) From birth (b) Childhood (c) Up to 30 years or later	(a) Recessive (b) Recessive (c) Uncertain	3
Metachromatic leucodystrophy (a) Infantile (b) Adult	Sulphatides	Brain, kidney, urine, gall-bladder	(a) Cerebral and cerebellar degeneration; spasticity; dementia; death after 1–6 years (b) Psychotic changes; blindness; aphasia; tetraplegia. Death after 3–12 years	(a) 1–2 years (b) Late childhood or adulthood	(a) Recessive (b) Uncertain	4
Essential familial hyperlipaemia	Triglycerides, lipoproteins	Blood plasma (chylomicrons)	Hepatosplenomegaly; sometimes xanthomata. Relatively benign	Usually early childhood	Complex	5
Hypercholesterolaemia	Cholesterol (free and esterified), phosphatides, sometimes triglycerides	Blood plasma (lipoproteins), tendons, skin, blood vessels	Cutaneous and tendinous xanthomata; atheroma of endocardium, coronary arteries or great vessels	From childhood onwards	Usually dominant	5, 6

References

1 FREDRICKSON, D.S., in STANBURY et al. (Eds.), *The Metabolic Basis of Inherited Disease*, 2nd ed., McGraw-Hill, New York, 1966, page 565.

2 FREDRICKSON and TRAMS, in STANBURY et al. (Eds.), *The Metabolic Basis of Inherited Disease*, 2nd ed., McGraw-Hill, New York, 1966, page 523.

3 FREDRICKSON, D.S., in STANBURY et al. (Eds.), *The Metabolic Basis of Inherited Disease*, 2nd ed., McGraw-Hill, New York, 1966, page 586.

4 MOSER and LEES, in STANBURY et al. (Eds.), *The Metabolic Basis of Inherited Disease*, 2nd ed., McGraw-Hill, New York, 1966, page 539.

5 FREDRICKSON and LEES, in STANBURY et al. (Eds.), *The Metabolic Basis of Inherited Disease*, 2nd. ed., McGraw-Hill, New York, 1966, page 429.

6 HARLAN et al., *Medicine (Baltimore)*, **45**, 77 (1966).

Inborn errors of corticosteroid metabolism[1]

Certain forms of adrenal hyperplasia have their origin in an inborn defect in the biosynthesis of steroids. The commonest is a defect in the hydroxylation of the steroid skeleton at C-21 due to a deficiency of steroid 21-hydroxylase, the result being a diminished synthesis of 21-hydroxysteroids. Since these steroids have no effect on the pituitary, the latter produces increased amounts of ACTH, resulting in further stimulation of the synthesis of 21-deoxysteroids. Some of these 21-deoxysteroids are precursors of androgens, the augmentation of which is the reason for the progressive virilization seen in these patients. When the deficiency of steroid 21-hydroxylase is very marked, practically no 21-hydroxysteroids are formed. This results in limitation also of aldosterone synthesis and the accumulation of progestogens, which act as aldosterone antagonists. The excretion of sodium by the kidneys is therefore increased, and in infants with this defect there is extreme loss of salt in the urine and possibly crises like those seen in ADDISON's disease.

A rarer form of inborn adrenal hyperplasia is due to deficiency of steroid 11β-hydroxylase, resulting in increased formation of 11-deoxycorticosterone and excessive excretion of metabolites of this substance in the urine. Unlike patients with the defect of 21-hydroxylation, such persons excrete only small amounts of 17-ketosteroids in the urine and they show hardly any increase in pregnanetriol. 11-Deoxycorticosterone causes sodium retention, and this is probably the cause of the arterial hypertension seen in these patients.

Deficiency of 3β-hydroxysteroid dehydrogenase is rare; this blocks the formation of progesterone from pregnenolone. As with the defect in 21-hydroxylation, the result is loss of salt in the urine, but clinically the condition differs from inborn adrenal hyperplasia in the manner in which it affects differentiation of the external genitalia in the foetus.

A case of deficiency of steroid 17α-hydroxylase has been reported[2]; here the adrenal cortex produced excessive amounts of corticosterone and deoxycorticosterone, with consequent arterial hypertension.

The various forms of inborn adrenal hyperplasia are probably each inherited through an autosomal recessive gene.

References

1 SOFFER et al., *The Human Adrenal Gland*, Lea & Febiger, Philadelphia, 1961; STEMPFEL and TOMKINS, in STANBURY et al. (Eds.), *The Metabolic Basis of Inherited Disease*, 2nd ed., McGraw-Hill, New York, 1966, page 635.

2 BIGLIERI et al., *J.clin.Invest.*, **45**, 1946 (1966).

(For references see pages 460–461)

Vitamin A[1,2]

Chemistry[3]

Vitamin A and the carotenes are soluble in fats, insoluble in water, and readily oxidized. In the absence of oxygen they are stable to acids, alkalis and heat. On the *cis-trans* isomerism of the carotenes and vitamin A see ZECHMEISTER[4]. For structure and properties of vitamin A and related compounds see the table on pages 458–459.

Assay

Biological[5]. Mainly by the standardized growth test on vitamin A-deficient rats.

Chemical[6]. Spectrophotometrically in pure solution (vitamin A at 328 nm, carotenes at ca. 450 nm) or colorimetrically, for instance with antimony trichloride (CARR-PRICE reaction); in biological material chromatographically after suitable extraction.

Units

Vitamin A. 1 International Unit (IU) = 0.344 μg *all-trans* vitamin A_1 acetate = 0.300 μg *all-trans* vitamin A_1. 1 US Pharmacopeia (USP) Unit = 1 International Unit.

Carotenes. 1 International Unit (IU) = 0.6 μg β-carotene, equivalent in activity to 1 IU vitamin A.

Biogenesis[7,8]

The carotenes are synthesized by the higher plants, algae and photosynthetic bacteria and are found in concentrated form in the chloroplasts. Acetate is converted by condensation and decarboxylation into isopentenyl pyrophosphate, from which a C_{20} terpenol pyrophosphate arises by condensation. This substance gives rise by further condensation to a carotenoid precursor with 40 C-atoms, probably phytoene. The various carotenes arise by dehydrogenation, cyclization, isomerization, hydration and hydroxylation. Carotenes with a β-ionone ring are broken down in the animal organism to vitamin A, more probably by fission in the middle of the chain than by successive β-oxidation from the end of the isoprenoid chain[9]. In the liver oils, vitamin A is present in the esterified form.

Intake and excretion

In the USA the daily diet contains ca. 7500–10000 IU (2.3–3 mg) of vitamin A[10,11]. About a half of the apparent vitamin intake is in the form of the provitamin.

The vitamin A esters are hydrolysed in the lumen of the duodenum, probably by esterases of the pancreatic juice. Bile is necessary for absorption of the carotenes but not of vitamin A; the absorption of the carotenes is promoted by fats. In the wall of the duodenum and upper jejunum the carotenes are broken down to vitamin A, with vitamin A aldehyde as an intermediate product[9,12]. In the intestinal wall vitamin A is probably mainly esterified with palmitic acid, the ester being transported by the lymph[13,14]. The carotenes are less easily absorbed than vitamin A and part of those ingested appears in the faeces. Under favourable conditions the biological activity of β-carotene amounts to about half that of vitamin A.

The vitamin A level in blood is at its highest about 4 hours after giving the vitamin[2]. The mean normal levels in serum are 850 μg carotene/l and 324 μg vitamin A/l (see page 609). In the serum, vitamin A is normally present to the extent of about 90% as the alcohol, the remainder as the ester; shortly after intake of vitamin A, however, the proportion of ester is increased[15]. Freshly absorbed vitamin A esters are transported by the lipoproteins S_f 10–400. Vitamin A alcohol is probably bound to albumin in the serum[14]. In breast milk vitamin A is about 90% esterified.

Vitamin A is stored in the liver, the carotenes mainly in the fatty tissues. About 90% of the whole vitamin A of the body is stored in the liver; the liver reserves (up to 300 μg vitamin A per gramme liver or more[16]) are sufficient to meet the body's requirements of the vitamin for one year or more[2]. These reserves, however, are rapidly used up in infections, hyperthermia and poisoning[2]. 90–95% of the vitamin A in the liver is present as palmitate, the remainder as aldehyde and alcohol[14,15]. When any organ requires vitamin A, the esters in the liver are hydrolysed and the free alcohol transported by the blood to where it is required. In the tissues, particularly in the liver, vitamin A alcohol and aldehyde are rapidly oxidized to vitamin A acid; this substance is not stored, however, but rapidly broken down[8,17]. An active metabolite of vitamin A acid has recently been identified but its composition is unknown[16]. After administration of tagged vitamin A to rats, radioactivity can be detected in the bile, urine and faeces[8]; the presence of vitamin A and/or its metabolites in bile points to enterohepatic circulation of the vitamin[18].

Metabolism of vitamin A

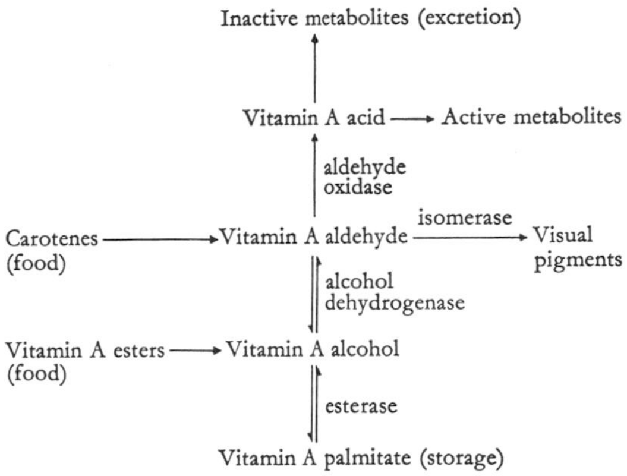

Function

Vitamin A is of great importance for maintenance of health and life, normal growth, the visual process and reproductivity. It appears to be necessary for the stability of the lipoprotein membrane of the cell and of the subcellular particles[19].

Vitamin A alcohol can be converted in the body to the aldehyde and acid and has a specific effect on the ability to reproduce. Vitamin A aldehyde is the prosthetic group of the visual pigments. Vitamin A acid, while very active in maintaining growth, is not capable of maintaining reproductivity.

Metabolic functions of vitamin A[20]

Active form	Biochemical reaction	Clinical effect
Vitamin A alcohol or other active form	Unknown	Reproduction in both sexes
Vitamin A aldehyde	Reaction with opsin	Visual process
Vitamin A acid or other active form	Liberation of proteolytic enzymes	Breakdown of cartilage
	Synthesis of mucopolysaccharides	Stimulation of mucous secretion in the epithelium
	Synthesis of corticosterone	Lesions in the adrenal cortex, interference with gluconeogenesis in deficiency states

The vitamin A aldehydes retinal and dehydroretinal form together with the protein opsin the light-sensitive pigments in the rods (night vision) and cones (day and colour vision) of the retina. The four main types of pigment[21,22] are rhodopsin (retinal + rod opsin) in terrestrial and aquatic animals, iodopsin (retinal + cone opsin) in terrestrial animals, porphyropsin (dehydroretinal + rod opsin) in fresh-water animals, and cyanopsin (dehydroretinal + cone opsin). Absorption of light by the visual pigments causes transformation of the 11-cis isomers of retinal or dehydroretinal into the *all-trans* form. The potential difference induced by this isomerization is responsible for the registration in the brain of the visual impressions from the rods and cones. 11-*cis*-Retinal is not only the prosthetic group of the visual pigment in the rods but also of the red- and green-sensitive pigments in the cones of the human eye[23]. The *cis-trans* isomerization of retinal proceeds as follows[21]:

(continued on page 460)

Structure and properties of vitamin A and related compounds

Names*	Formula and mol. wt.	Structure	Physical properties	Occurrence	Relative activity
α-Carotene	$C_{40}H_{56}$ 536.89	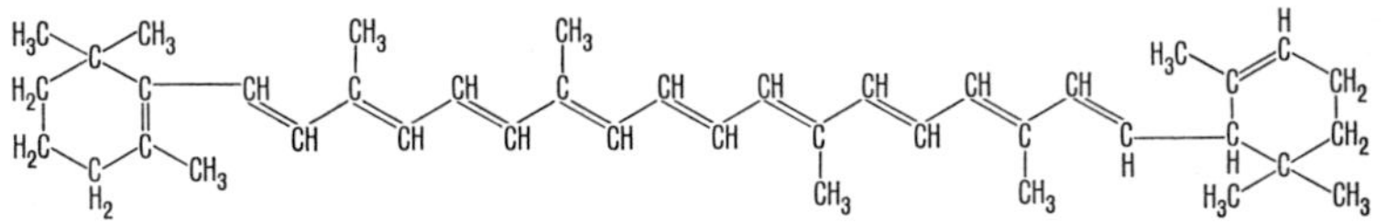	Violet to red crystals M. p. 187 °C (benzene/methanol)	Palm oil, mountain ash berries	50
β-Carotene	$C_{40}H_{56}$ 536.89	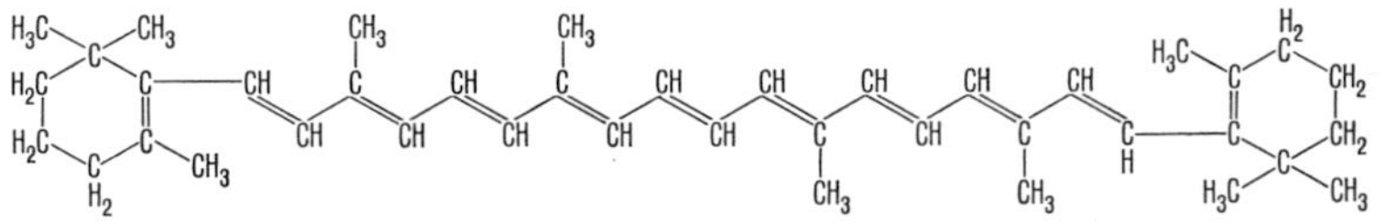	Violet to red crystals M. p. 180 °C	Plants, fruits	100
Cryptoxanthene (3-hydroxy-β-carotene)	$C_{40}H_{56}O$ 552.89	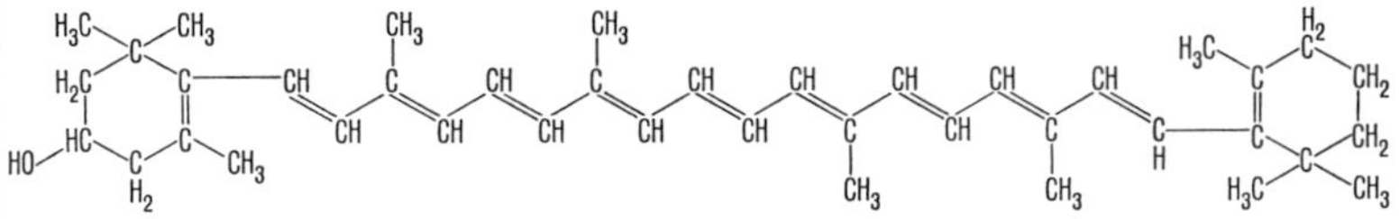	Red platelets M. p. 158 °C	Maize	50
Vitamin A_1 (*all-trans*) (retinol*, axerophthol)	$C_{20}H_{30}O$ 286.46	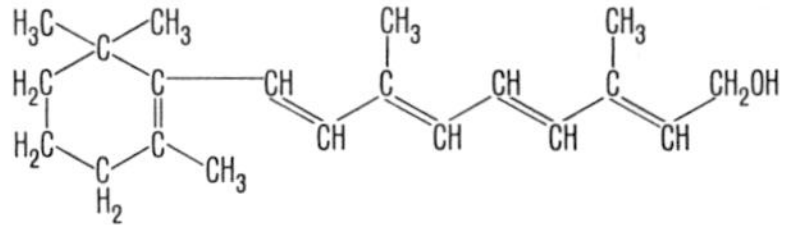	Yellow prisms M. p. 62–64 °C	Liver of marine fish	100
9-*cis*-Vitamin A_1 (*iso-a*)	$C_{20}H_{30}O$ 286.46	As *all-trans* vitamin A_1 but with double bond at C-9 in *cis* configuration	Yellow prisms M. p. 82 °C	–	21
11-*cis*-Vitamin A_1 (*neo-b*) (11-*cis*-retinol)	$C_{20}H_{30}O$ 286.46	As *all-trans* vitamin A_1 but with double bond at C-11 in *cis* configuration	Orange-yellow oil	Retina	23

13-*cis*-Vitamin A_1 (*neo-a*)	$C_{20}H_{30}O$ 286.46	As *all-trans* vitamin A_1 but with double bond at C-13 in *cis* configuration	Yellow prisms M. p. 58 °C	Fish liver	75
Vitamin-A_1 aldehyde (*all-trans*) (retinal*, retin-aldehyde*, β-retinene, retinene$_1$)	$C_{20}H_{28}O$ 284.45	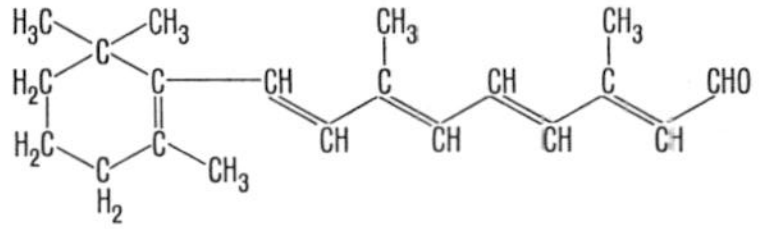	Orange prisms M. p. 58 °C	Citrus fruits, green vegetables, liver	91
11-*cis*-Vitamin-A_1 aldehyde (*neo-b*) (11-*cis*-retinal)	$C_{20}H_{28}O$ 284.45	As *all-trans* vitamin-A_1 aldehyde but with double bond at C-11 in *cis* configuration	Orange prisms M. p. 64 °C	Eyes of crustacea	48
Vitamin-A_1 carboxylic acid (*all-trans*) (retinic acid*)	$C_{20}H_{28}O_2$ 300.44	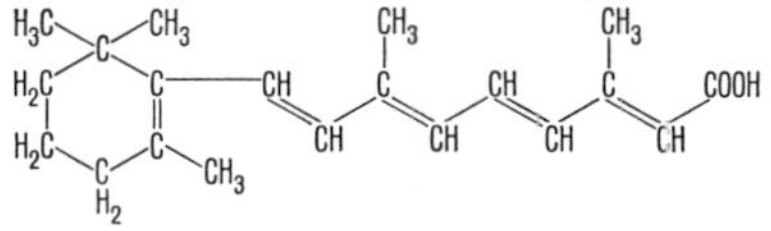	Yellow needles M. p. 179 °C	Tissues?	~65
Vitamin A_2 (3-dehydroretinol*)	$C_{20}H_{28}O$ 284.45	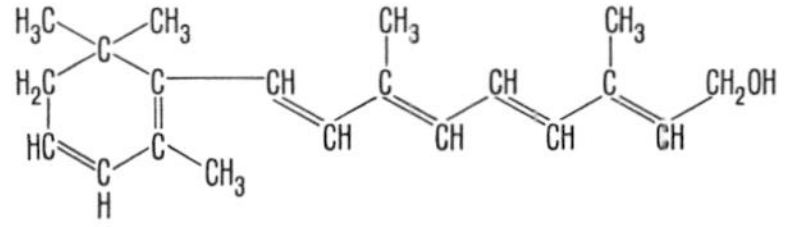	Yellow needles M. p. 63–65 °C	Liver of freshwater fish	40
Vitamin A_2 aldehyde (3-dehydroretinal*, 3-dehydroretinaldehyde*, α-retinene, retinene$_2$)	$C_{20}H_{26}O$ 282.43	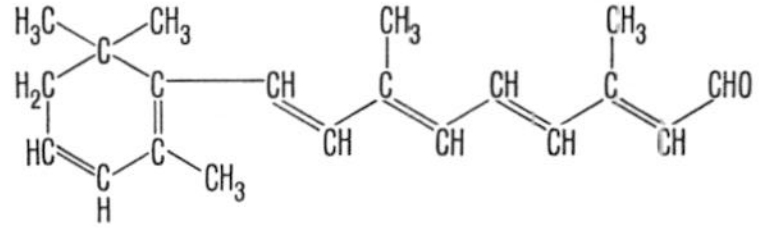	Orange-red prisms M. p. 78 °C	Retina in fish	

* Trivial names recommended by the Commission on Biochemical Nomenclature of the International Union of Pure and Applied Chemistry and the International Union of Biochemistry [*Biochim. biophys. Acta (Amst.)*, **107**, 1 (1965)].

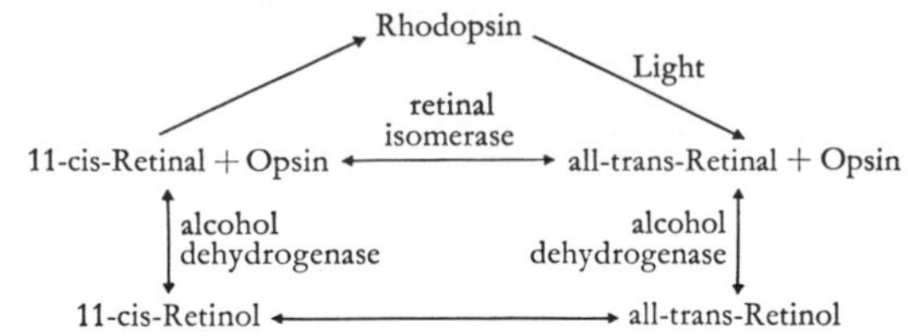

Vitamin A and carotene in their protein-bound form are thought to participate in an analogous manner in the sense of smell[24].

Requirements and deficiency symptoms

The requirement of vitamin A is proportional to the body weight. Daily requirements in health allowing for some reserve are 2500 IU vitamin A, 4000 IU carotene in fats, 7500 IU in green vegetables or 12000 IU in boiled carrots[26]. In 10- to 15-year-old boys 1700 IU vitamin A are sufficient to maintain a plasma level of 300 µg/l[27]. For infants from birth to 5 months it is assumed that exclusive breast-feeding can provide sufficient vitamin A[25]. For recommendations of official bodies see the tables on pages 493–494.

Good sources of vitamin A are the fish oils (cod 1000, herring 5000, halibut and tunny 50000–100000 IU/g), liver, milk fat and egg yolk; green vegetables and carrots are rich in carotenes. See also pages 499–515.

Causes of vitamin A deficiency[2] are inadequate dietary intake, impaired absorption (fat deficiency) or storage, disturbances in the conversion of carotene into vitamin A, or rapid depletion of the body's reserves. Impairment of absorption or storage is seen in coeliac disease, cystic fibrosis of the pancreas, ulcerative colitis, pancreatectomy, obstruction of the biliary ducts and cirrhosis of the liver. Conversion of carotenes may also be impaired in diabetes and hyperthyroidism. Some infections result in disappearance of vitamin A from the blood. The typical lesions of vitamin A deficiency[28] are night blindness, xerosis or keratinization of various membranes (particularly xerophthalmia) and the formation of defective bony tissue and dentine during growth. The most sensitive test for vitamin A deficiency is measurement of dark adaptation of the eye[26]; determination of vitamin A concentration in the serum is less reliable since the serum level does not fall until the body's reserves are fully depleted[2]. In many countries of South America, Asia and Africa xerophthalmia is still one of the commonest causes of blindness in children[29, 30]. Other manifestations of vitamin A deficiency are BITÔT's spots on the conjunctiva and roughness of the skin due to hyperkeratosis of the hair follicles. In animals vitamin A deficiency has serious effects in pregnancy and is a cause of infertility and congenital deformities[31].

Vitamin A deficiency symptoms in pregnancy and at various ages (modified from McLAREN and HALASA[30])

	Cause of deficiency	Symptoms
Pregnancy	Dietary carotene deficiency, increased requirement, depletion following repeated pregnancies	Low plasma level of vitamin A, low liver reserves, xerophthalmia (rare), BITÔT's spots (occasionally)
Foetus		Low liver reserves, xerophthalmia (rare), abortion (?), congenital deformities (?)
Up to 12 months	Inadequacy of breast milk, low vitamin A content of breast milk, bottle feeding, infections	Low plasma level of vitamin A, depletion of liver reserves, xerophthalmia (fairly common), BITÔT's spots (rare)
Up to 5 years	Breast feeding continued too long, dietary deficiency, infections	Commonest cause of conjunctival xerosis, xerophthalmia, BITÔT's spots (occasionally)
School age	Dietary deficiency of carotene, vitamin A, fats and proteins	Conjunctival xerosis and BITÔT's spots (main symptoms), night blindness, follicular hyperkeratosis (occasionally)
Adults	Dietary deficiency, infections, cirrhosis of the liver, pancreatic disease	Night blindness (main symptom), BITÔT's spots (occasionally), xerophthalmia (rare), follicular hyperkeratosis (occasionally)

Treatment and toxicity

Deficiency symptoms should be treated by giving vitamin A in doses of up to 25000 IU (corresponding to ca. 30 ml liver oil). Xerophthalmia calls for initially higher doses (5000 IU/kg body weight daily for 5 days)[29, 30]. When liver oils are given in large doses, vitamin D may be ingested in toxic amounts, even though it has been shown that vitamin A in large doses diminishes the toxic effect of vitamin D[32].

Protracted treatment with high doses of vitamin A (for instance 100000 IU or more per day in children) may result in toxic symptoms such as anorexia, alopecia, affections of the skin and mucosa, swelling of the bones and diaphyses of the limbs, anaemia, enlargement of the liver and spleen and headache. All these symptoms are reversible and disappear rapidly on cessation of the treatment[2]. In children overdosage of vitamin A may interfere with bone development and lead to premature fusion of the epiphyses[33].

In some countries vitamin A is given prophylactically to newborn children and infants in daily doses of 7500–10000 IU. Because of the danger of possible intoxication, however, it is better to restrict prophylactic doses to 2500 IU per day[34].

Acute vitamin A intoxication has been observed following the consumption of polar bear liver, which contains 20000 IU per gramme[35, 36]; whale liver contains 4400 IU vitamin A per gramme, swine's liver only 100–150 IU per gramme[36].

References

1 SEBRELL and HARRIS (Eds.), *The Vitamins*, vol. 1, Academic Press, New York, 1954, page 1; MOORE, T., *Vitamin A*, Elsevier, Amsterdam, 1957; Symposium on Vitamin A and Metabolism, *Vitam. and Horm.*, **18**, 289 (1960); DAM and SØNDERGAARD, in BEATON and MCHENRY (Eds.), *Nutrition*, vol. 2, Academic Press, New York, 1964, page 1.
2 KAGAN and GOODHART, in WOHL and GOODHART (Eds.), *Modern Nutrition in Health and Disease*, 3rd ed., Lea & Febiger, Philadelphia, 1964, page 341.
3 KARRER and JUCKER, *Carotenoids*, Elsevier, Amsterdam, 1950; FREYSCHLAG, H., in RAUEN, H. M. (Ed.), *Biochemisches Taschenbuch*, 2nd ed., part 1, Springer, Berlin, 1964, page 358.
4 ZECHMEISTER, L., *Cis-trans Isomeric Carotenoids, Vitamins A and Arylpolyenes*, Springer, Vienna, 1962.
5 HARRIS, P. L., *Vitam. and Horm.*, **18**, 341 (1960).
6 ISLER et al., *Vitam. and Horm.*, **18**, 295 (1960); GSTIRNER, F., *Chemisch-physikalische Vitaminbestimmungsmethoden*, 5th ed., Enke, Stuttgart, 1965, page 5.
7 GOODWIN, T. W., *The Biosynthesis of Vitamins and Related Compounds*, Academic Press, New York, 1963, page 270.
8 OLSON, J. A., *J. Lipid Res.*, **5**, 281 (1964).
9 GOODMAN and HUANG, *Science*, **149**, 879 (1965); GOODMAN et al., *J. biol. Chem.*, **241**, 1929 (1966).
10 STITT, K. R., *Nutr. Rev.*, **21**, 257 (1963).
11 Food and Nutrition Board, *Recommended Dietary Allowances*, 7th ed., National Academy of Sciences – National Research Council, Publication 1694, Washington, 1968, page 21.
12 GLOVER, J., *Vitam. and Horm.*, **18**, 371 (1960).
13 MAHADEVAN et al., *Biochem. J.*, **88**, 534 (1963).
14 MAHADEVAN et al., *Wld Rev. Nutr. Diet.*, **5**, 209 (1965).
15 GANGULY, J., *Vitam. and Horm.*, **18**, 387 (1960).
16 YAGISHITA et al., *Nature*, **203**, 411 (1964).
17 DESHMUKH et al., *Biochim. biophys. Acta (Amst.)*, **107**, 120 (1965).
18 ZACHMAN and OLSON, *Nature*, **201**, 1222 (1964).
19 LUCY and DINGLE, *Nature*, **204**, 156 (1964).
20 WOLF, G., *Nutr. Rev.*, **20**, 161 (1962); Colloquium on aspects of vitamin A function, *Biochem. J.*, **90**, 35 P (1964).
21 WALD, G., *Vitam. and Horm.*, **18**, 417 (1960).
22 DARTNALL and TANSLEY, *Ann. Rev. Physiol.*, **25**, 433 (1963).
23 BROWN and WALD, *Nature*, **200**, 37 (1963).
24 BRIGGS and DUNCAN, *Nature*, **191**, 1310 (1961); DUNCAN and BRIGGS, *Arch. Otolaryng.*, **75**, 116 (1962).
25 Joint FAO/WHO Expert Group, *Wld Hlth Org. techn. Rep. Ser.*, No. 362 (1967).
26 HUME and KREBS, *Spec. Rep. Ser. med. Res. Coun. (Lond.)*, No. 264 (1949).
27 ANISOVA, A. A., *Vop. Pitan.*, **23**, No. 3, 29 (1964), quoted in *Nutr. Rev.*, **22**, 349 (1964).

(For references see page 464)

28 Moore, T., *Vitam. and Horm.*, **18**, 499 (1960).
29 McLaren, D. S., *Nutr. Rev.*, **22**, 289 (1964).
30 McLaren and Halasa, *Postgrad. med. J.*, **40**, 711 (1964).
31 Watt and Barlow, *Vet. Rec.*, **68**, 780 (1956).
32 Clark and Basset, *J. exp. Med.*, **115**, 147 (1962).
33 Pease, C. N., *J. Amer. med. Ass.*, **182**, 980 (1962).
34 Tunell et al., *Acta paediat. scand.*, **54**, 61 (1965).
35 Rodahl and Moore, *Biochem. J.*, **37**, 166 (1943).
36 Notes, *Nutr. Rev.*, **19**, 318 (1961).

Vitamin D[1,2]

Chemistry[1,3]

The D vitamins are odourless crystals, soluble in fats and fat solvents, insoluble in water, and only slightly photosensitive. All show a wide absorption band at 260–290 nm. For structure and properties of vitamin D and related compounds see the table on pages 462–463.

Assay

Biological[1]. By its preventive or curative effect on young rats with experimental rickets.

Chemical[4]. Spectrophotometrically in pure solution at 265 nm; the individual D vitamins cannot be distinguished. Colorimetrically with antimony trichloride, in the presence of vitamin A after chromatographic separation. The individual D vitamins can be separated by column, paper or thin-layer chromatography.

Units

1 International Unit (IU) = 0.025 µg crystalline vitamin D_3. 1 US Pharmacopeia Unit = 1 International Unit (see also International Standard for Vitamin D_3, page 763). The earlier international unit equivalent to 1 mg of standardized irradiated ergosterol dissolved in a vegetable oil is now obsolete.

Biogenesis

Vitamin D_3 occurs solely in the higher animals and is formed photochemically from 7-dehydrocholesterol (provitamin D_3, animal provitamin). 7-Dehydrocholesterol is formed from cholesterol by a reaction that also takes place in the intestinal tissues[5]. Other D vitamins of known constitution and formed by ultraviolet irradiation at wave lengths of 275–300 nm are the following: D_2 from ergosterol, D_4 from 22-dihydroergosterol, D_5 from 7-dehydrositosterol, D_6 from 2-dehydrostigmasterol and D_7 from 7-dehydrocampesterol.

The conversion of provitamin D into vitamin D by irradiation occurs as follows[6]:

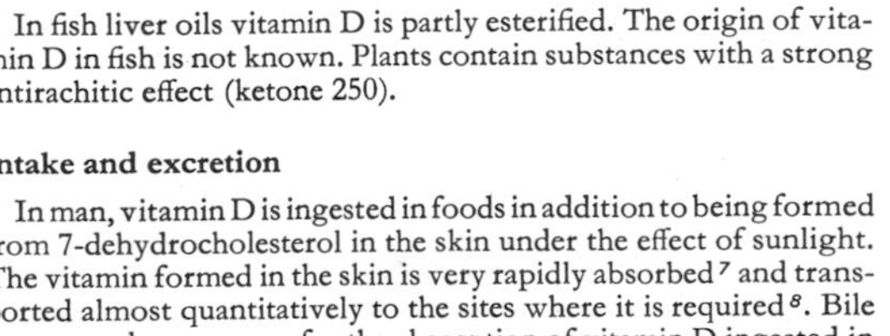

In fish liver oils vitamin D is partly esterified. The origin of vitamin D in fish is not known. Plants contain substances with a strong antirachitic effect (ketone 250).

Intake and excretion

In man, vitamin D is ingested in foods in addition to being formed from 7-dehydrocholesterol in the skin under the effect of sunlight. The vitamin formed in the skin is very rapidly absorbed[7] and transported almost quantitatively to the sites where it is required[8]. Bile appears to be necessary for the absorption of vitamin D ingested in foods. In rats, the vitamin is partly esterified during absorption and is transported by the lymph[9]. A similar process has also been observed in man[10]. In children the blood level is 860–2100 IU/l[11], in adults 700–3100 IU/l[36]. With a daily oral intake of 50 000–500 000 IU, the blood level in adults rises to 90 000–130 000 IU/l[12]. In the blood, the vitamin is transported bound to the α_2-globulins and albumin[13]. It is taken up by and metabolized in the liver, and is also present in other tissues such as the kidneys, intestine, adrenals and bones[13,14]. 24 hours after giving ^{14}C-tagged vitamin D, 10% of the activity was found in the tissues and 20% in the faeces, the remaining 70% being present as breakdown products[13]. In rats, some vitamin D is excreted in the bile bound to taurine and glycine and then partly reabsorbed. In man, the urine contains no vitamin D as such but up to 2–4% of the radioactivity of ingested tagged vitamin D has been found there[31].

The vitamin D content of the skin exposed to sunlight amounts to ca. 1 IU/cm². In the skin of the human back activation may reach the level of 15 IU/cm². 50–75% of the activity is found in the deeper layers of the epidermis and 25–50% in the parts of the coreum adjacent to the epidermis[8].

It has been suggested that the metabolic effect of vitamin D is due not to the vitamin itself but to a metabolite[14]. Such an active metabolite has been found in the nuclear fraction of the intestinal mucosa[32]. Recently a biologically active metabolite of vitamin D_3 has been identified as 25-hydroxycholecalciferol[33].

Function

The activity of vitamin D is closely related to that of parathyroid hormone and of calcitonin, all three factors being necessary for maintenance of calcium balance and a normal serum calcium level[14,16]. Vitamin D may be responsible for formation of the calcium transport system in bone cells; the control of serum calcium concentration by parathyroid hormone depends on the presence of vitamin D, whereas that by calcitonin does not[14]. It has been shown that the physiological expression of the action of vitamin D on intestinal calcium transport and bone mineral mobilization probably involves DNA transcription into messenger RNA and protein synthesis[14]. At the subcellular level, vitamin D causes release of the bound calcium in the mitochondria, probably as a result of its action on oxidative phosphorylation[15].

In rats, vitamin D has been shown to increase calcium absorption mainly in the intestine[17]. A vitamin D-dependent calcium-binding protein has been isolated from the intestinal mucosa of chicks[34]. There is evidence that vitamin D also favours the intestinal absorption of magnesium[18].

Vitamin D is also necessary for the development of normal bone and for the calcification of rachitic bone. The manner in which it acts is obscure but probably the defective calcification of newly formed bone in rickets and osteomalacia is due to a reduction of the calcium phosphate product in the tissue fluid surrounding the osteoid[19]. The increase in the serum citrate level caused by vitamin D is probably due to its effect on calcium metabolism[16].

It is not certain whether vitamin D has any effect on the renal transport of calcium; in any case this effect is small in comparison with that of parathyroid hormone[16]. Vitamin D is thought to favour the tubular reabsorption of phosphate[20].

Requirements and deficiency symptoms

In adults the body's needs of vitamin D are usually met by its own synthesis, provided this is not impaired by lack of daylight, as in night workers, miners, and people living in subpolar regions. During the period of active skeletal growth, in pregnancy and in lactation, there is an increase in both the calcium and vitamin D requirements, so that intake of exogenous vitamin D is advisable. In such cases, oral administration of 400 IU vitamin D per day is adequate[21] (see also pages 493–494).

The liver oils are rich in vitamin D: tunny fish 7000–50 000 IU per gramme, cod 60–300 IU per gramme; the mammalian liver contains only small quantities of vitamin D, egg yolk 1.5–5 IU per gramme (values from Dam and Søndergaard[1]).

Deficiency of vitamin D causes rickets, of which osteomalacia is the adult form[19,22]. Both diseases are marked by failure of mineralization in newly formed bone, leading to progressive demineralization and weakening of the skeleton. In children, bone growth is particularly rapid in the epiphyses and it is here that vitamin D deficiency is first manifested. In adults, on the other hand, there is slow breakdown of bone throughout the skeleton, so that the disease develops in a slower and more widespread fashion. Rickets and osteomalacia can be classified as follows[19]:

1. Rickets due to vitamin D deficiency
   (a) vitamin D deficiency in food and lack of sunlight
   (b) vitamin D deficiency in food with pigmentation of the skin
   (c) impaired absorption (idiopathic steatorrhoea, coeliac disease)
2. Vitamin D-resistant rickets
   (a) renotubular acidosis

(continued on page 464)

Structure and properties of vitamin D and related compounds

Names*	Formula and mol. wt.	Structure	Physical properties	Occurrence	Antirachitic activity
Ergosterol	$C_{28}H_{44}O$ 396.66	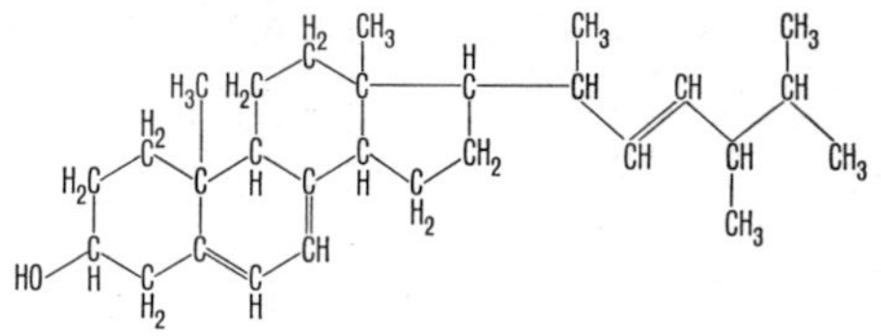	M. p. 168 °C (with 1½ H_2O)	Yeast, ergot, hens' eggs	None (provitamin D_2)
7-Dehydrocholesterol	$C_{27}H_{44}O$ 384.65	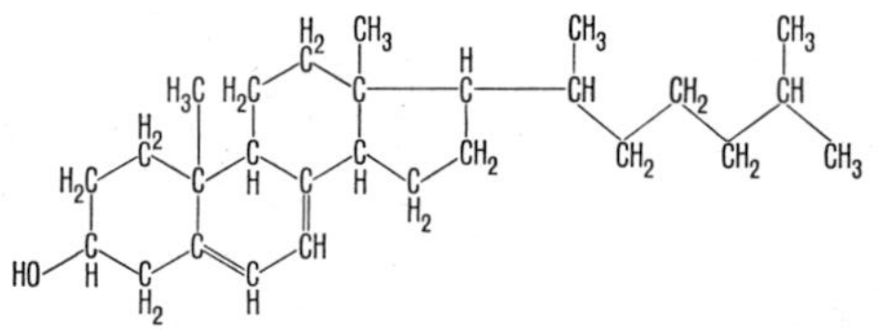	M. p. 150 °C (anhydrous)	Higher animals, man	None (provitamin D_3)
22-Dihydroergosterol	$C_{28}H_{46}O$ 398.68	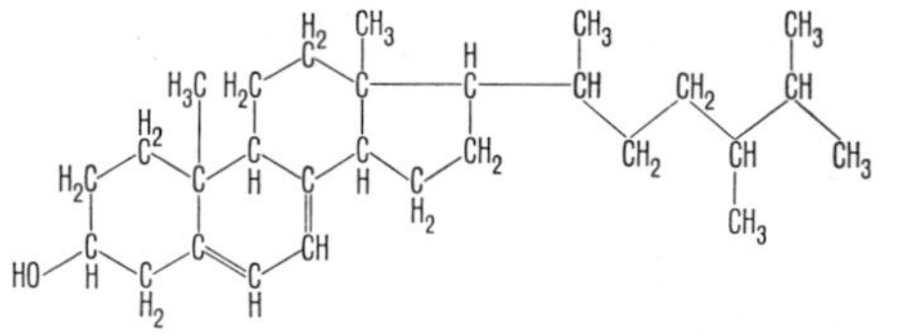	M. p. 152 °C	Synthetic	None (provitamin D_4)
Vitamin D_2 (ergocalciferol*)	$C_{28}H_{44}O$ 396.66	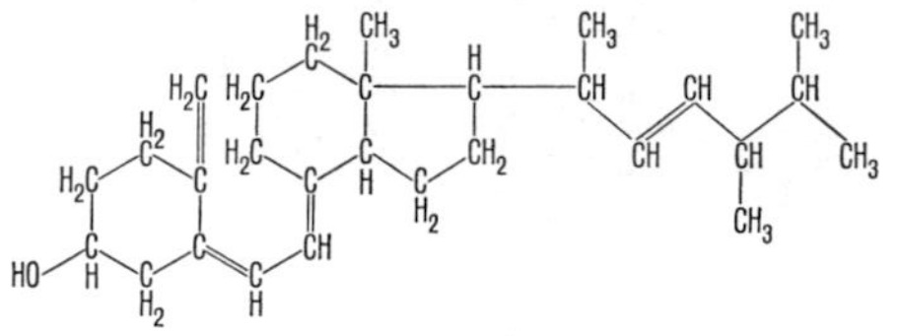	M. p. 115–118 °C	Formed by irradiation of ergosterol	In rats similar to, in chicks and apes less than that of vitamin D_3
Vitamin D_3 (cholecalciferol*)	$C_{27}H_{44}O$ 384.65	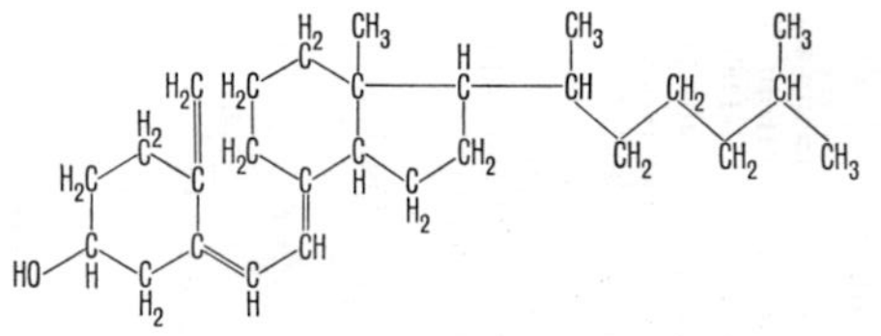	M. p. 84–85 °C	Formed by irradiation of 7-dehydrocholesterol. In fish-liver oils, egg yolk, milk	Antirachitic

Vitamin D_4	$C_{28}H_{46}O$ 398.68	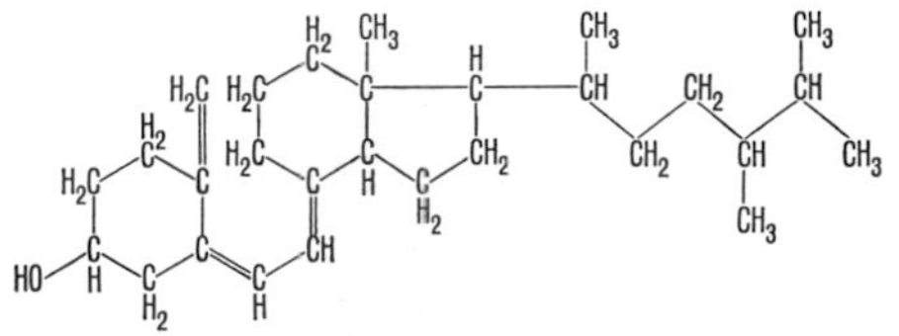	M. p. 96–98 °C	Formed by irradiation of 22-dihydroergosterol	Rather less than that of vitamin D_3
Ketone 250	$C_{27}H_{46}O_3$ 418.67	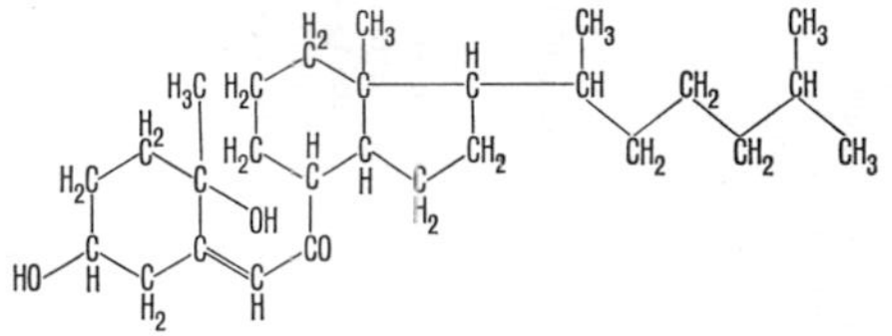	M. p. 73 °C	Plants, fish-liver oils	One-tenth that of vitamin D_3
Lumisterol	$C_{28}H_{44}O$ 396.66	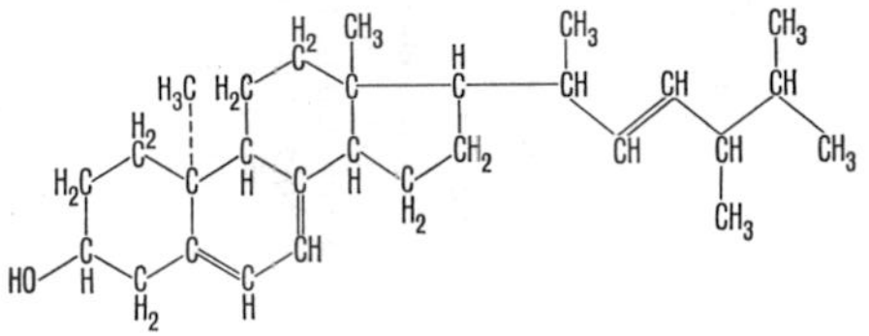	M. p. 118 °C	Formed by irradiation of ergosterol	None
Tachysterol	$C_{28}H_{44}O$ 396.66	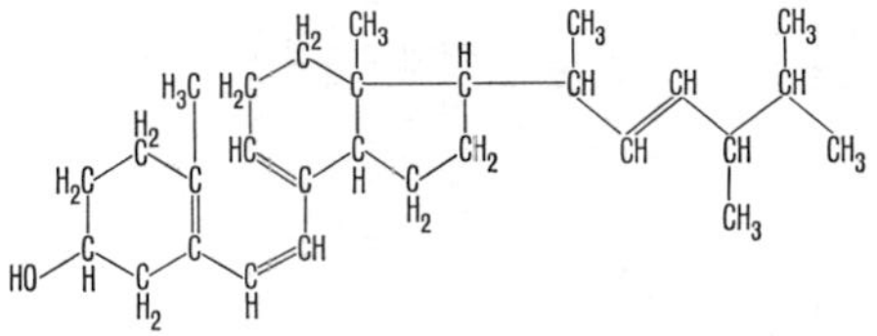	Oil, readily oxidizing in air	Formed by irradiation of ergosterol	None (hypercalcaemic effect)
Dihydrotachysterol	$C_{28}H_{46}O$ 398.68	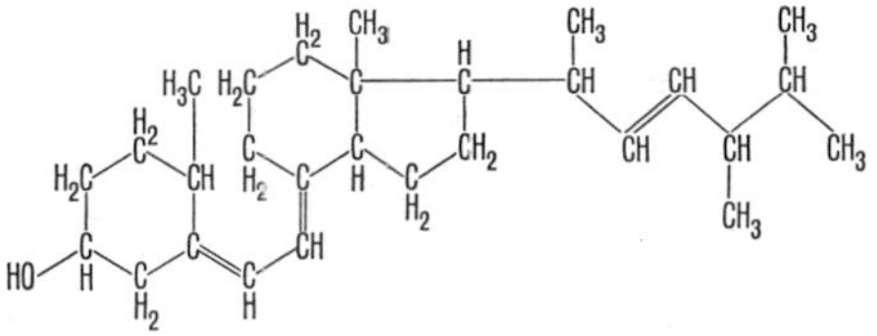	M. p. 125–127 °C	Synthetic	400 times less active than vitamin D_3 (same hyper-calcaemic effect)

* Trivial names recommended by the Commission on Biochemical Nomenclature of the International Union of Pure and Applied Chemistry and the International Union of Biochemistry [*Biochim. biophys. Acta (Amst.)*, **107**, 1 (1965)].

(b) Fanconi's syndrome
(c) primary vitamin D resistance
(d) renal insufficiency

The clinical symptoms of rickets are pain in the limbs, particularly the legs, genu valgum, bending of the long bones, thickening of the synchondroses of the ribs and of the joint epiphyses, and protuberance of the forehead. Tetany is also an occasional symptom. The radiological changes consist in widening of the epiphyses combined with disorganization of the epiphyseal disk, and appearance of a cup-shaped structure in place of the normal, distinct, straight boundary between metaphysis and epiphysis. The biochemical changes observed are slight lowering of the plasma calcium level, marked lowering of the plasma phosphate level, reduced urinary calcium excretion, increased phosphate clearance, increased phosphate excretion index and a rise in the plasma concentration of alkaline phosphatase; the calcium phosphate product in the plasma is lower than normal. One of the first signs of vitamin D deficiency is an increase in the amino-acid content of the urine[23].

Primary vitamin D-resistant rickets is congenital and usually hereditary. It is characterized by lower plasma phosphate levels and an increase in the phosphate excretion index. The vitamin D activity of the serum must be 10–20 times the normal value if the calcium metabolism is to be restored to normal[24]. This form of rickets may be due to a defect of vitamin D metabolism[25, 35] and excretion.

Treatment

Prophylaxis of rickets: Sun-baths or quartz lamp treatment, 400 IU vitamin D per day in the pure form or as cod-liver oil.

Treatment of rickets: Rickets and osteomalacia due to a simple deficiency of vitamin D respond to daily oral doses of 3000 IU vitamin D[19]; in premature infants and children with impaired absorption these should be given intramuscularly. Treatment with massive doses has the disadvantage that there is uncertainty as to the extent to which single high doses are absorbed. High vitamin D doses are called for in primary vitamin D-resistant rickets, and treatment should begin with 50 000 IU per day[26]. Complete disappearance of the radiological and biochemical symptoms has been reported with a total of 5–400 million IU, depending on the individual[24]. The maintenance dose, again depending on the individual, ranges from 1000 to 500 000 IU per day[24]. If growth of the long bones is to proceed normally, treatment must be started immediately after birth[27].

Treatment of lupus vulgaris with vitamin D in very massive dosage is now usual only if other tuberculostatic drugs cannot be given.

Toxicology

All the D vitamins are toxic in large quantities. High doses of vitamin D mobilize the bound calcium of the skeleton and bring about a considerable increase in the plasma calcium level as well as in the urinary excretion of phosphate and calcium. The calcium mobilized from the bones is taken up in the soft tissues, particularly the kidneys and media of the vessels. The clinical symptoms are loss of appetite, gastro-intestinal disturbances, pain in the head and joints and muscular weakness; in children other signs are a dry, loose skin, tremor of the limbs, loss of muscle tone with fibrillary spasms and arterial hypertension. When death occurs, this is usually due to renal failure. The symptoms of vitamin D poisoning are reversible when ingestion of the vitamin is stopped.

The toxic effect of vitamin D appears when daily doses exceed 1000–3000 IU per kg body weight and when these doses are given over several months; in infants, hypercalcaemia may appear even with total daily doses of 3000–4000 IU[21]. The clinical appearance of this idiopathic hypercalcaemia of infancy is very similar to that of vitamin D poisoning[28]. For this reason, infants and pregnant women (since idiopathic hypercalcaemia may already occur in utero) should not be given more than 400 IU vitamin D per day[21, 29]. Since enrichment of milk, margarine and baby foods with vitamin D is now quite common in many countries, the intake of this substance by infants and children is often excessive, for instance in the USA and Canada up to 2000 IU per day[21], in England up to 1200 IU per day[30].

Vitamin D_2 is less suitable for treating rickets since its hypercalcaemic effect at high dosage is greater than that of vitamin D_3. Although dihydrotachysterol has only a very slight antirachitic activity it is, like vitamin D, capable of increasing the serum calcium level. The danger of poisoning is the same, however, with both substances. In the treatment of hypercalcaemia it is essential that the serum calcium level should be watched.

References

1 Dam and Søndergaard, in Beaton and McHenry (Eds.), *Nutrition*, vol. 2, Academic Press, New York, 1964, page 1.
2 Sebrell and Harris (Eds.), *The Vitamins*, vol. 2, Academic Press, New York, 1954, page 131; Kagan and Goodhart, in Wohl and Goodhart (Eds.), *Modern Nutrition in Health and Disease*, 3rd ed., Lea & Febiger, Philadelphia, 1964, page 360.
3 Reuber, R., in Rauen, H. M. (Ed.), *Biochemisches Taschenbuch*, 2nd ed., part 1, Springer, Berlin, 1964, page 473.
4 Gstirner, F., *Chemisch-physikalische Vitaminbestimmungsmethoden*, 5th ed., Enke, Stuttgart, 1965, page 338.
5 Glover et al., *Biochem. J.*, **51**, 1 (1952).
6 Velluz et al., *C. R. Acad. Sci. (Paris)*, **240**, 2076 and 2156 (1955); Butenandt, A., *Angew. Chem.*, **72**, 645 (1960).
7 Cruickshank et al., *Proc. Nutr. Soc.*, **14**, VIII (1955).
8 Bekemeier, H., *Vitamin D der Haut*, Huber, Berne, 1966 (supplement 10 to *Int. Z. Vitaminforsch.*).
9 Bell and Bryan, *J. Lab. clin. Med.*, **66**, 852 (1965).
10 Thompson et al., *J. clin. Invest.*, **45**, 94 (1966).
11 Job et al., *Ann. Péd.*, **43**, 2412/P. 648 (1967).
12 Warkany et al., *J. Lab. clin. Med.*, **27**, 557 (1942).
13 Kodicek, E., in Wasserman, R. H. (Ed.), *Proceedings of a Conference on the Transfer of Calcium and Strontium Across Biological Membranes*, Ithaca, New York, 1962, Academic Press, New York, 1963.
14 DeLuca, H. F., *Vitam. and Horm.*, **25**, 315 (1967).
15 Rasmussen et al., *J. clin. Invest.*, **42**, 1940 (1963).
16 Harrison, M. T., *Postgrad. med. J.*, **40**, 497 (1964).
17 Schachter et al., *Amer. J. Physiol.*, **200**, 1263 (1961).
18 George et al., *Lancet*, **1**, 1300 (1962).
19 Nordin, B. E. C., Osteomalacia and Osteoporosis, in Calcium and Phosphate Metabolism, *Documenta Geigy, Acta clinica*, No. 2, Basle, 1965, page 45.
20 Harrison, H. E., *Helv. paediat. Acta*, **14**, 434 (1959).
21 American Academy of Pediatrics, Committee on Nutrition, *Pediatrics*, **31**, 512 (1963).
22 Engfeldt and Hjertquist, *Wld Rev. Nutr. Diet.*, **2**, 185 (1960).
23 Chisolm and Harrison, *J. Pediat.*, **60**, 206 (1962).
24 Gentil et al., *Sem. Hôp. Paris, Ann. Pédiat.*, **39**, 214 (1963).
25 Avioli et al., *J. clin. Invest.*, **45**, 982 (1966).
26 Pierce et al., *J. Bone Jt Surg.*, **46A**, 978 (1964).
27 Schoen, E. J., *J. Amer. med. Ass.*, **195**, 524 (1966).
28 Black, J. A., *Germ. med. Mth.*, **9**, 290 (1964).
29 American Academy of Pediatrics, Committee on Nutrition, *Pediatrics*, **35**, 1022 (1965).
30 Bransby et al., *Brit. med. J.*, **1**, 1661 (1964).
31 Avioli et al., *J. clin. Invest.*, **46**, 983 (1967).
32 Haussler et al., *J. biol. Chem.*, **243**, 4055 (1968).
33 Blunt et al., *Chem. Commun.*, **1968**, 801.
34 Wasserman et al., *J. biol. Chem.*, **243**, 3978 (1968).
35 Avioli et al., *J. clin. Invest.*, **47**, 2239 (1968).
36 Thomas et al., *J. clin. Invest.*, **38**, 1078 (1959).

Vitamin E[1-3] (for references see page 467)

Chemistry[4]

The tocopherols are viscous, yellowish oils readily soluble in organic solvents and insoluble in water. They are stable to acids, alkalis and heat, unstable to oxidizing agents, particularly when exposed to light. The ubiquinones and ubichromenols form yellow crystals. For structure and properties of vitamin E and related compounds see the table on pages 465–466.

Assay

Biological. Antisterility test on female rats[7]; dialuric acid haemolysis test on rats[8].

Chemical[9]. Using the reducing properties of the tocopherols, for instance reduction of ferric chloride (Emmerie-Engel reaction). When biological materials require to be assayed, prior separation of other reducing substances is necessary, for instance by molecular distillation or column chromatography. The individual tocopherols can be separated by column, thin-layer, paper or gas chromatography.

Unit

By weight. Formerly 1 International Unit (IU) = 1 mg *dl*-α-tocopherol acetate = 1 International Rat Unit = the amount required to be given orally to tocopherol-deficient rats to prevent absorption of the foetus in 50%[10].

1 IU = 1.00 mg *dl*-α-tocopherol acetate = 1.10 mg *dl*-α-tocopherol = 0.73 mg *d*-α-tocopherol acetate = 0.81 mg *d*-α-tocopherol.

Biogenesis

In young plants most of the vitamin E synthesized consists of α-tocopherol, whereas in seeds the other tocopherols predominate[11]. The individual steps of biogenesis are unknown but it is possible

(continued on page 466)

Structure and properties of vitamin E and related compounds

Names*	Formula and mol. wt.	Structure	Main source	Activity**
		Tocols		
		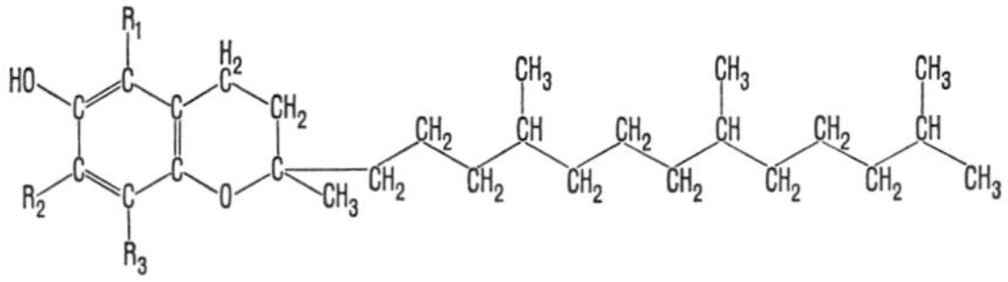		
Tocol	$C_{26}H_{44}O_2$ 388.64	$R_1 = H$, $R_2 = H$, $R_3 = H$	Synthetic	Inactive
8-Methyltocol (δ-tocopherol)	$C_{27}H_{46}O_2$ 402.67	$R_1 = H$, $R_2 = H$, $R_3 = CH_3$	Soybean oil	1
5,8-Dimethyltocol (β-tocopherol)	$C_{28}H_{48}O_2$ 416.69	$R_1 = CH_3$, $R_2 = H$, $R_3 = CH_3$	Wheat-germ oil	33
7,8-Dimethyltocol (γ-tocopherol)	$C_{28}H_{48}O_2$ 416.69	$R_1 = H$, $R_2 = CH_3$, $R_3 = CH_3$	Maize-germ oil	10
5,7,8-Trimethyl-tocol (α-tocopherol)	$C_{29}H_{50}O_2$ 430.72	$R_1 = CH_3$, $R_2 = CH_3$, $R_3 = CH_3$	Maize-germ oil, wheat-germ oil, etc., animal tissues	100
		Tocotrienols		
		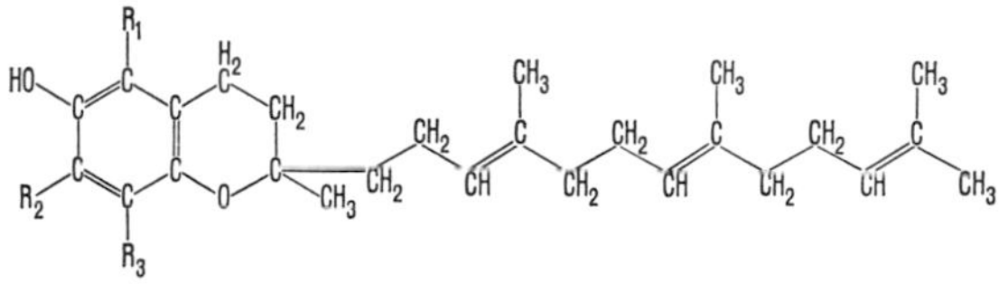		
8-Methyltoco-trienol (δ-tocotrienol)	$C_{27}H_{40}O_2$ 396.62	$R_1 = H$, $R_2 = H$, $R_3 = CH_3$	Palm oil	
5,8-Dimethyltoco-trienol (ε-tocopherol, β-tocotrienol)	$C_{28}H_{42}O_2$ 410.65	$R_1 = CH_3$, $R_2 = H$, $R_3 = CH_3$	Wheat	5
7,8-Dimethyltoco-trienol (γ-tocotrienol)	$C_{28}H_{42}O_2$ 410.65	$R_1 = H$, $R_2 = CH_3$, $R_3 = CH_3$	Rice	
5,7,8-Trimethyl-tocotrienol (ζ1-tocopherol, α-tocotrienol, tocochromanol-3)	$C_{29}H_{44}O_2$ 424.67	$R_1 = CH_3$, $R_2 = CH_3$, $R_3 = CH_3$	Wheat	30

* Trivial names recommended by the Commission on Biochemical Nomenclature of the International Union of Pure and Applied Chemistry and the International Union of Biochemistry [*Biochim. biophys. Acta (Amst.)*, **107**, 1 and 5 (1965)].
** Relative activity in antisterility test on rats.

Structure and properties of vitamin E and related compounds (continued)

Names*	Formula and mol. wt.	Structure	Main source	Activity**
		Tocopherol-like compounds		
α-Tocopheryl-quinone (α-tocopherol-quinone)	$C_{29}H_{50}O_3$ 446.72	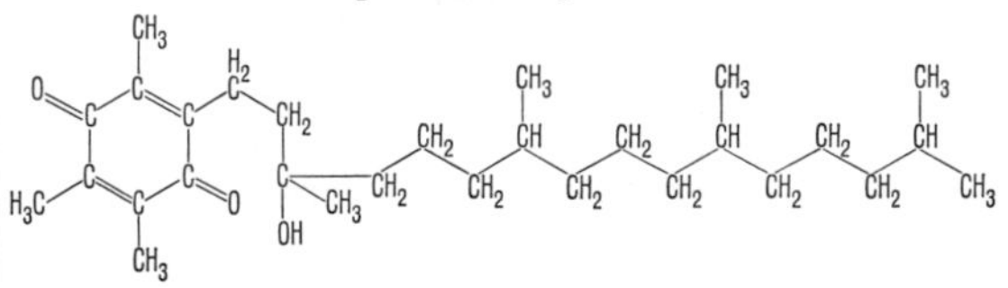	Oxidation product of α-tocopherol, green plants	Active[5]
Ubiquinones (coenzymes Q)		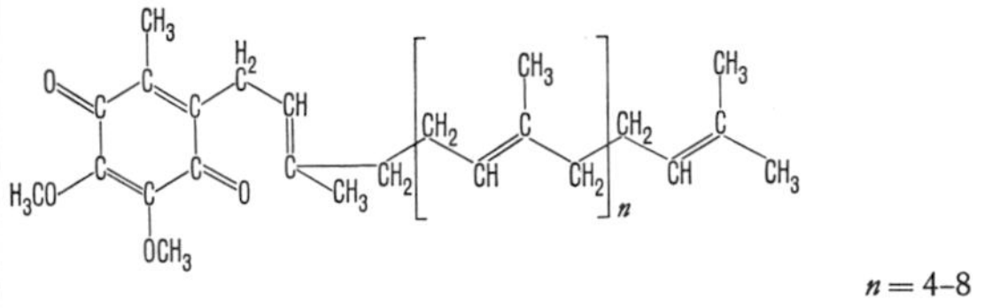 $n = 4–8$	Ubiquinone-9 (ubiquinone-45, coenzyme Q_9)*: leaves; ubiquinone-10 (ubiquinone-50, coenzyme Q_{10})*: liver, yeast	
Ubichromenols		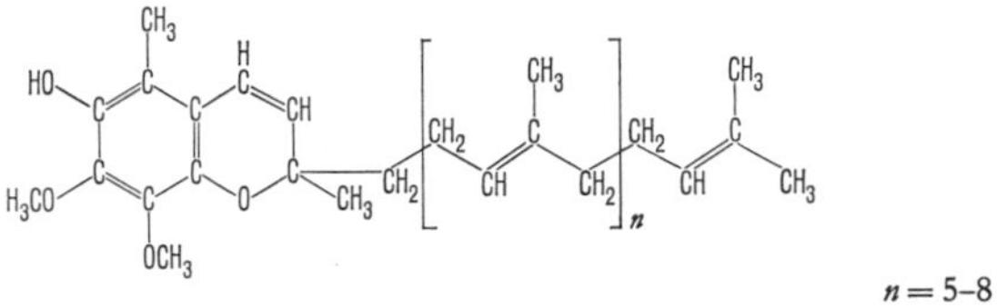 $n = 5–8$	As corresponding ubiquinones	Active[6]

*Trivial names recommended by the Commission on Biochemical Nomenclature of the International Union of Pure and Applied Chemistry and the International Union of Biochemistry [*Biochim. biophys. Acta (Amst.)*, **107**, 1 and 5 (1965)].
** Relative activity in antisterility test on rats.

that the process resembles the synthesis of the ubiquinones (formation of the terpenoid chain of mevalonic acid and of the aromatic ring from phenylalanine)[12].

Intake and excretion

The daily intake of adults in the USA has been estimated at 24 mg total tocopherols and 14 mg α-tocopherol[13], by another authority at 7.4 mg α-tocopherol[14]. The tocopherol esters are hydrolysed in the small intestine, and bile is necessary for their absorption. Probably only about 35% of the tocopherols in food is absorbed, the remainder being excreted in the faeces[15]. The normal concentration in adult serum is ca. 10 mg/l, in newborn infants ca. 5 mg/l (see page 609). The maximum blood level is reached 4–9 hours after giving tocopherols[16,17].

α-Tocopherol is stored in the liver and fatty tissues. High concentrations occur in the pituitary, adrenals, uterus and testes[18]. In the liver, tocopherol has been found in the mitochondria and microsomes[16]. The amount of tocopherols stored by the body is several grammes[2]. In the fatty tissues this is believed to include also α-tocopherylquinone, an oxidation product of α-tocopherol[19].

The metabolites tocopheronic acid and tocopheronolactone have been isolated in the form of glucuronides (Simon metabolite)[20] from the urine of persons given large amounts of tocopherol.

Function

The tocopherols act as antioxidants in the following processes both in vitro and in vivo[21, 22]:

(a) they prevent the oxidation of unsaturated fatty acids (linoleic acid) to peroxides; lipoperoxides are associated with the formation of the yellowish brown pigment in smooth muscle (ceroid pigment)
(b) they prevent the oxidation of vitamin A and the carotenes
(c) they prevent the oxidation of thiol groups, particularly in enzymes, presumably in conjunction with selenium[23].

The relationship between vitamin E and cholesterol metabolism is obscure[22]. The tocopherols may play a role in nucleic acid metabolism[24] and in erythropoiesis[25]. There may be a functional connection between the tocopherols and the ubiquinones, which are involved in electron transport[26], and the formation of adenosine triphosphate (see page 403)[27]. Vitamin E seems to have an effect on the transport and metabolism of vitamin B_{12}[28].

Requirements and deficiency symptoms

Healthy adults require 10–30 mg α-tocopherol per day[29] (see also page 494), depending on the intake of polyene fatty acids[30], 0.6 mg α-tocopherol at least being required per gramme polyene fatty acid[31]. The minimal requirement of infants is probably 0.5 mg per kg body weight[32], an amount normally absorbed with the breast milk.

Vegetable oils are rich in tocopherols, especially wheat-germ oil with 200–300 mg/100 g. Other good sources of tocopherols are cereals and eggs. Animal tissues contain little tocopherol, mainly as α-tocopherol.

Vitamin E deficiency results in various changes depending on the species, age and nutritional state. They include impaired reproductivity and absorption of the foetus (rats, mice, guinea-pigs), muscular dystrophy accompanied sometimes by marked creatinuria (monkeys, mice, etc.), formation of ceroid pigments (monkeys, mice, swine), increased haemolysis in vitro (rats, chickens), encephalomalacia (chickens), exudative diathesis (chickens), necrosis of the liver ('respiratory decline' in rats), renal autolysis (rats).

In human beings the signs of vitamin E deficiency are not very marked.

A measure of the vitamin E status is provided by the peroxide haemolysis test[33]. In many persons a lowered serum tocopherol level is associated with an increase of in vitro haemolysis[30]. A low serum level is common in newborn infants and particularly premature infants, and vitamin E deficiency is a possible cause of macrocytic anaemia[34] and haemolytic anaemia[35] in infants. Vitamin E deficiency may also be caused by impaired absorption of fats[3, 36]. Thus low tocopherol serum levels, often combined with creatinuria and the deposition of ceroid pigments in the smooth muscle (gastro-intestinal tract), have been observed in sprue, coeliac disease, biliary cirrhosis, pancreatitis and particularly cystic fibrosis of the pancreas. A definite relationship between muscular dystrophy and vitamin E deficiency has not been proved[37]. A very low vitamin E content in the fatty tissues of premature infants with oedema of the subcutaneous connective tissue has been reported[38].

Treatment[39]

Administration of tocopherols is indicated in intermittent claudication, in disturbances of fat absorption (particularly cystic fibrosis of the pancreas), in premature infants nurtured on cow's milk and in persons whose diet includes large amounts of unsaturated fatty acids. In cystic fibrosis of the pancreas at least 100 mg α-tocopherol should be given daily[17]. Inclusion of vitamin E in the diet of women before childbirth is considered to have a favourable effect on the capillary resistance of the infant[40]. The tocopherols do not appear to be toxic even in large doses.

References

1 SEBRELL and HARRIS (Eds.), *The Vitamins*, vol. 3, Academic Press, New York, 1954, page 481; VASINGTON et al., *Vitam. and Horm.*, **18**, 43 (1960); Symposium on Vitamin E and Metabolism, *Vitam. and Horm.*, **20**, 373 (1962).
2 DAM and SØNDERGAARD, in BEATON and MCHENRY (Eds.), *Nutrition*, vol. 2, Academic Press, New York, 1964, page 1.
3 GORDON and NITOWSKY, in WOHL and GOODHART (Eds.), *Modern Nutrition in Health and Disease*, 3rd ed., Lea & Febiger, Philadelphia, 1964, page 372.
4 ISLER et al., *Vitam. and Horm.*, **20**, 389 (1962); PENNOCK et al., *Biochem. biophys. Res. Commun.*, **17**, 542 (1964); MARTIUS and BOSSHARDT, in RAUEN, H. M. (Ed.), *Biochemisches Taschenbuch*, 2nd ed., part 1, Springer, Berlin, 1964, page 540.
5 GREEN et al., *Biochim. biophys. Acta (Amst.)*, **49**, 417 (1961).
6 JOHNSON et al., *Biochem. biophys. Res. Commun.*, **5**, 309 (1961).
7 EVANS et al., *J. biol. Chem.*, **108**, 515 (1934).
8 ROSE und GYÖRGY, *Fed. Proc.*, **8**, 244 (1949); FRIEDMAN et al., *J. Nutr.*, **65**, 143 (1958).
9 KOFLER et al., *Vitam. and Horm.*, **20**, 407 (1962); GSTIRNER, F., *Chemisch-physikalische Vitaminbestimmungsmethoden*, 5th ed., Enke, Stuttgart, 1965, page 367.
10 SIEBERT et al., in RAUEN, H. M. (Ed.), *Biochemisches Taschenbuch*, 2nd ed., part 2, Springer, Berlin, 1964, page 664.
11 GREEN, J., *J. Sci. Food. Agric.*, **9**, 801 (1958).
12 OLSON et al., *J. biol. Chem.*, **238**, 3146 (1963).
13 HARRIS et al., *J. Nutr.*, **40**, 367 (1950).
14 BUNNELL et al., *Amer. J. clin. Nutr.*, **17**, 1 (1965).
15 KLATSKIN and MOLANDER, *J. Lab. clin. Med.*, **39**, 802 (1952).
16 WISS et al., *Vitam. and Horm.*, **20**, 441 (1962).
17 GOLDBLOOM, R. B., *Pediatrics*, **32**, 36 (1963).
18 QUAIFE and DJU, *J. biol. Chem.*, **180**, 263 (1949); DJU et al., *Amer. J. clin. Nutr.*, **6**, 50 (1958).
19 WEBER and WISS, *Helv. physiol. Acta pharmacol.*, **21**, 131 (1963).
20 SIMON et al., *J. biol. Chem.*, **221**, 807 (1956).
21 TAPPEL, A. L., *Vitam. and Horm.*, **20**, 493 (1962).
22 ALFIN-SLATER and MORRIS, *Advanc. Lipid Res.*, **1**, 183 (1963).
23 SCHWARZ, K., *Vitam. and Horm.*, **20**, 463 (1962).
24 DINNING, J. S., *Vitam. and Horm.*, **20**, 511 (1962).
25 DINNING, J. S., *Nutr. Rev.*, **21**, 289 (1963).
26 MORTON, R. A., *Vitam. and Horm.*, **19**, 1 (1961); WOLSTENHOLME and O'CONNOR (Eds.), *Ciba Foundation Symposium on Quinones in Electron Transport*, Churchill, London, 1961.
27 MOORE and FOLKERS, *J. Amer. chem. Soc.*, **86**, 3393 (1964).
28 OSKI et al., *Amer. J. clin. Nutr.*, **18**, 307 (1966).
29 Food and Nutrition Board, *Recommended Dietary Allowances*, 7th ed., National Academy of Sciences – National Research Council, Publication 1694, Washington, 1969, page 27.
30 HORWITT, M. K., *Vitam. and Horm.*, **20**, 541 (1962).
31 HARRIS and EMBREE, *Amer. J. clin. Nutr.*, **13**, 385 (1963).
32 NITOWSKY et al., *Vitam. and Horm.*, **20**, 559 (1962).
33 GYÖRGY et al., *Proc. Soc. exp. Biol. (N. Y.)*, **81**, 536 (1952).
34 MAJAJ et al., *Amer. J. clin. Nutr.*, **12**, 374 (1963); MAJAJ, A. S., *Amer. J. clin. Nutr.*, **18**, 362 (1966).
35 OSKI and BARNESS, *J. Pediat.*, **70**, 211 (1967); RITCHIE et al., *New Engl. J. Med.*, **279**, 1185 (1968).
36 KOCH, E., in LANG, K. (Ed.), *Tocopherole*, 12th Symposium of the Deutsche Gesellschaft für Ernährung, Mainz 1965, Steinkopff, Darmstadt, 1967, page 108.
37 HORWITT, M. K., *Fed. Proc.*, **24**, 68 (1965).
38 GERLÓCZY et al., in *VII. Internationaler Ernährungskongreß*, Hamburg 1966, Summary of Papers, Pergamos-Druck, Hamburg, 1966, page 232.
39 MARKS, J., *Vitam. and Horm.*, **20**, 573 (1962).
40 BECKMANN et al., *Klin. Wschr.*, **41**, 1043 (1963).

Vitamin K[1,2]

Chemistry

The K vitamins are soluble in fats, fairly stable to heat but unstable to light. Solubility in water is confined to menadione sodium bisulphite and the tetrasodium salt of hydrovitamin K_1 diphosphate.

For structure and properties of vitamin K and related compounds see the table on page 468.

Assay

Biological. By curative effect on vitamin K-deficient chicks[2].

Chemical[3]. In pure solution spectrophotometrically, fluorimetrically, colorimetrically, polarographically, also oxidimetrically after reduction to the hydroquinone.

Assay of the vitamin in animal or vegetable material must be done chromatographically or after a suitable extraction process.

Unit

No international unit; by weight. The following units are occasionally used: 20 DAM units = 1 ANSBACHER unit = 0.000 8 mg menadione = the minimum amount required to normalize the prothrombin time within 6 hours in vitamin K-deficient chicks weighing 70–100 g.

Biogenesis

Vitamin K_1 is synthesized in green plants under the effect of light and accumulates mainly in the chloroplasts. The K_2 vitamins are synthesized by certain intestinal bacteria. It is not known how the naphthoquinone ring is formed.

Intake and excretion

Bile or bile acids are necessary for optimal absorption of vitamin K, both from foods and from the vitamin synthesized by the intestinal flora; menadione and the synthetic water-soluble preparations are absorbed without the intervention of bile. Vitamin K is transported by the lymph. According to MARTIUS[4], vitamin K of vegetable or bacterial origin undergoes a conversion in the animal organism in which the various side chains are replaced uniformly by an isoprenoid chain of 20 C-atoms. The original side chains are split off by the action of intestinal bacteria with the formation of methylnaphthoquinone. The latter is absorbed and converted in animal tissues into the specific vitamin $K_{2(20)}$ of the animal organism by introduction of the geranylgeranyl chain.

Vitamin K is not stored in the tissues when ingested in quantities comparable with those in the diet. When large doses are given, the vitamin accumulates in the liver and spleen[5]. After administration of radioactive vitamin K to rats, part of the activity has been found in the urine and bile[6]. Metabolites of the vitamin have been isolated from the bile of dogs[7].

Function

Vitamin K is involved in the blood coagulation mechanism and is responsible for the maintenance of a normal prothrombin time. It also affects the formation of prothrombin (factor II), factor VII, factor IX, factor X and perhaps also factor V[8]. Here the vitamin possibly acts by promoting the formation of the quaternary protein structure (S-S bridges)[9]; it may also be involved directly in prothrombin synthesis[10]. Whether the vitamin plays a role in oxidative phosphorylation is not yet clear[11], although such a role has been demonstrated in bacteria[12]. In the light of the quinone-hydroquinone structure of vitamin K and its ready conversion into a chromanol, the function of the vitamin is most likely that of an electron carrier[9].

Dicumarol and related components are vitamin K antagonists in blood coagulation, whence their use as anticoagulants; their anticoagulant effect can be inhibited by vitamin K.

Requirements and deficiency symptoms

The human requirement of vitamin K is unknown, but ample amounts appear to be available, except in newborn infants, from a normal diet combined with synthesis by the intestinal bacteria, though the latter does not seem to play any great role in man[13]. Tests have shown that in newborn infants 5 μg disodium 2-methyl-1,4-naphthohydroquinone disuccinate per day are adequate to ensure maximum prothrombin activity[14].

Vitamin K is found mainly in green vegetables such as spinach and cabbage; the amounts in tomatoes and liver are less, and very little is present in fruits, milk and meat. Cow's milk contains more of the vitamin than breast milk.

Vitamin K deficiency causes a hypoprothrombinaemia marked by an excessive prothrombin time and a tendency to bleeding. A reduced prothrombin activity due to vitamin K deficiency occurs

Structure and properties of vitamin K and related compounds

Names*	Formula and mol. wt.	Structure	Physical properties	Occurrence	Activity **
Vitamin $K_{1(20)}$ (phyllo-quinone*)	$C_{31}H_{46}O_2$ 450.71	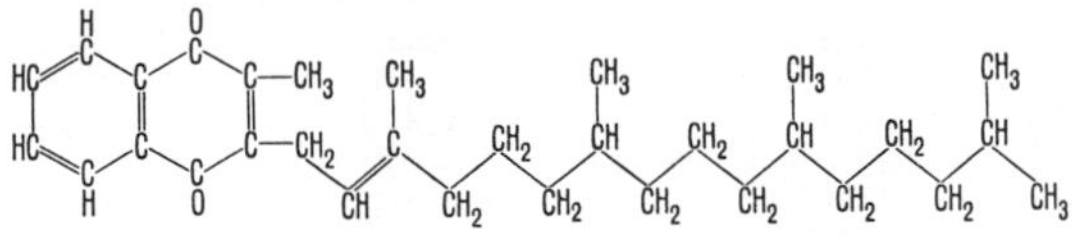	Yellow oil M.p. −20 °C	Green plants, tomatoes, some bacteria. Isolated from alfalfa	100
Vitamin $K_{2(30)}$ (mena-quinone-6*)	$C_{41}H_{56}O_2$ 580.90	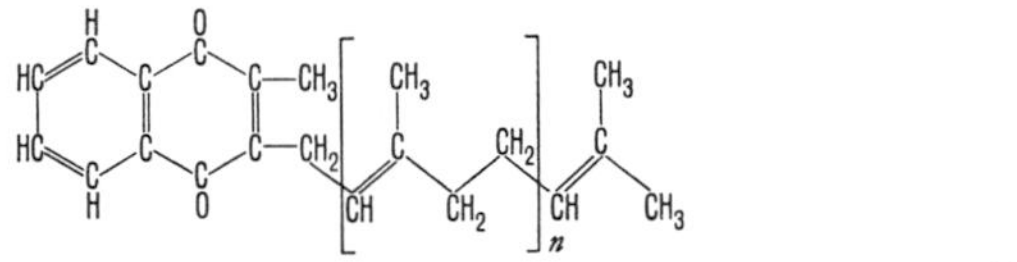 $n = 5$	Yellow crystals M.p. 50 °C	Isolated from putrid fishmeal	100
Vitamin $K_{2(35)}$ (mena-quinone-7*)	$C_{46}H_{64}O_2$ 649.02	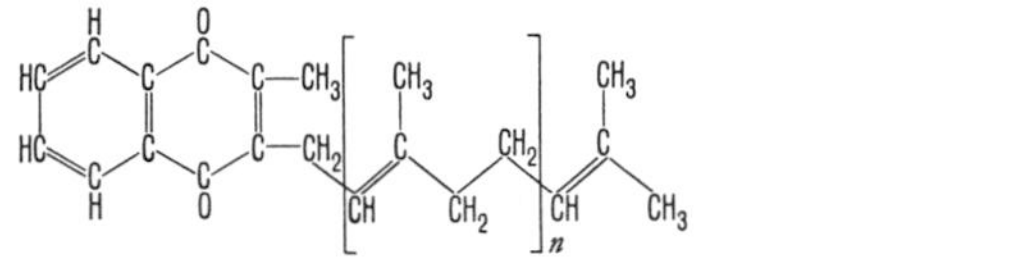 $n = 6$	Yellow crystals M.p. 54 °C	Some bacteria. Isolated from putrid fishmeal	70
Menadione (vitamin K_3, methyl-naphtho-quinone)	$C_{11}H_8O_2$ 172.19	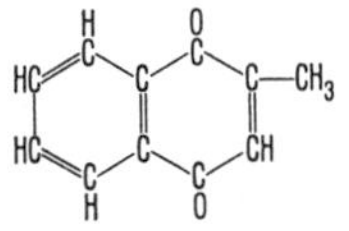	Yellow needles M.p. 106 °C	Synthetic. Possibly a metabolite	ca. 100

* Trivial names recommended by the Commission on Biochemical Nomenclature of the International Union of Pure and Applied Chemistry and the International Union of Biochemistry [*Biochim. biophys. Acta (Amst.)*, **107**, 5 (1965)].
** Relative activity in vitamin K-deficient chicks.

in some intestinal complaints like severe diarrhoea[15] and steatorrhoea[16], as well as in impaired absorption of the vitamin due to lack of bile (biliary fistula, obstruction of the bile ducts). The hypoprothrombinaemia associated with severe injury to the liver parenchyma is not due, however, to vitamin K deficiency and is also not reversed by administration of the vitamin; this forms the basis of a test of liver function. Vitamin K deficiency can also occur during long-term treatment with antibiotics or sulphonamides as a result of destruction of the intestinal flora.

During the first days of life the prothrombin activity of the plasma is 10–50% of that in adults[17], possibly because the intestinal flora is not sufficiently developed and intake of the vitamin with milk is small. Among newborn infants not given vitamin K, 0.1–1% suffer from bleeding, a proportion that has been shown to be reducible by vitamin K treatment[18,19].

Treatment

Vitamin K is given prophylactically to newborn infants, particularly premature infants and those with anoxia, the dosage of the vitamin (or of a water-soluble preparation) being 0.5–1 mg subcutaneously or intramuscularly or 1–2 mg orally at birth[18]. Double these doses may be necessary in children whose mothers have been treated with anticoagulants. Administration of the vitamin to mothers ante partum is not recommended[20]. The prophylactic use of the water-soluble menadione derivatives in pregnant women and newborn children is inadvisable on account of the danger of hyperbilirubinaemia and an increased tendency to kernicterus; these effects may be due not to the menadione derivatives themselves but to their intermediary metabolites.

The vitamin is given to correct low prothrombin activity due to a deficiency (see under 'Requirements and deficiency symptoms', above) as well as to overdosage of anticoagulants.

If possible, vitamin K should be given by the oral, intramuscular or subcutaneous route and not intravenously[21].

References

1 SEBRELL and HARRIS (Eds.), *The Vitamins*, vol. 2, Academic Press, New York, 1954, page 387; ISLER and WISS, *Vitam. and Horm.*, **17**, 53 (1959); KAGAN and GOODHART, in WOHL and GOODHART (Eds.), *Modern Nutrition in Health and Disease*, 3rd ed., Lea & Febiger, Philadelphia, 1964, page 367.
2 DAM and SØNDERGAARD, in BEATON and MCHENRY (Eds.), *Nutrition*, vol. 2, Academic Press, New York, 1964, page 1.
3 GSTIRNER, F., *Chemisch-physikalische Vitaminbestimmungsmethoden*, 5th ed., Enke, Stuttgart, 1965, page 400.
4 MARTIUS, C., *Schweiz. med. Wschr.*, **93**, 1264 (1963).
5 DAM et al., *Acta pharmacol. (Kbh.)*, **10**, 58 (1954) and **11**, 90 (1955).
6 JAQUES et al., *Schweiz. med. Wschr.*, **84**, 792 (1954); TAYLOR et al., *Canad. J. Biochem.*, **34**, 1143 (1956).
7 LOSITO et al., *Biochim. biophys. Acta (Amst.)*, **107**, 123 (1965).
8 ABALLI et al., *Amer. J. Dis. Child.*, **97**, 524 (1959).
9 JOHNSON, B. C., *Nutr. Rev.*, **22**, 225 (1964).
10 OLSON, R. E., *Science*, **145**, 926 (1964); HILL et al., *J. biol. Chem.*, **243**, 3930 (1968).
11 MARTIUS, C., *Dtsch. med. Wschr.*, **83**, 1701 (1958).
12 BRODIE, A. F., *Fed. Proc.*, **20**, 995 (1961).
13 UDALL, J. A., *J. Amer. med. Ass.*, **194**, 127 (1965).
14 LARSEN, E. H., *Svingningerne i prothrombinaktiviteten hos nyfødte med en analyse af prothrombinbestemmelsers teknik og vurdering*, Thesis, Munksgaard, Copenhagen, 1952.
15 MATOTH, Y., *Amer. J. Dis. Child.*, **80**, 944 (1950).
16 SHAW, S., *Brit. med. J.*, **2**, 647 (1960).
17 DAM and PLUM, *Postgrad. Med.*, **15**, 279 (1954); MCELFRESH, A. E., *Amer. J. med. Sci.*, **242**, 771 (1961).
18 American Academy of Pediatrics, Committee on Nutrition, *Pediatrics*, **28**, 501 (1961).
19 VIETTI et al., *J. Pediat.*, **56**, 343 (1955); WEFRING, K. W., *J. Pediat.*, **61**, 686 (1962).
20 *Med. Letter*, **5**, 47 (1963).
21 *Med. Letter*, **5**, 97 (1963).

(For references see page 471)

Thiamine[1-3]

Structure and properties of thiamine and related compounds

Compound	Formula and mol. wt.	Structure	Physical properties	Occurrence and activity
Thiamine (vitamin B_1, aneurin)	$C_{12}H_{17}N_4OS$ (cation) 265.36 $C_{12}H_{18}N_4OSCl_2$ (hydrochloride) 337.27	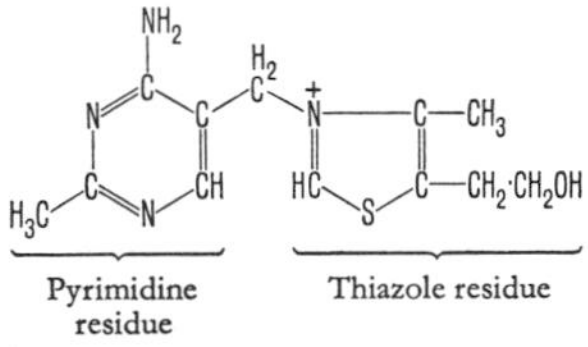	Colourless needles, readily soluble in water, odourless when pure, thermolabile in neutral and alkaline solution, stable to atmospheric oxygen, unstable to oxidizing agents and ultraviolet light M. p. 245–248 °C (hydrochloride)	Plants. In animal tissues as thiamine pyrophosphate
Thiamine diphosphate (TDP) Thiamine pyrophosphate (TPP) (cocarboxylase)	$C_{12}H_{18}N_4O_7P_2S$ 424.31	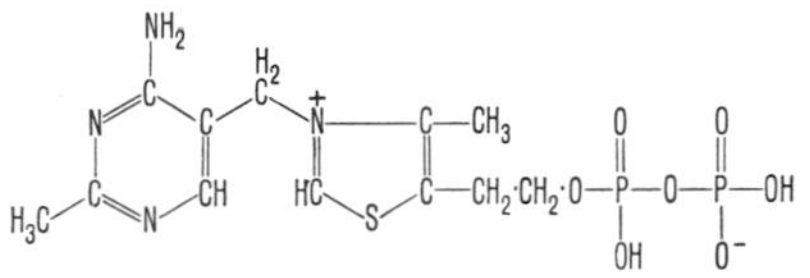	Pale yellow needles, readily soluble in water M. p. 242–244 °C	Animal tissues. Cofactor of decarboxylases and other enzymes
α-Hydroxyethyl-2-thiamine diphosphate α-Hydroxyethyl-2-thiamine pyrophosphate	$C_{14}H_{22}N_4O_8P_2S$ 468.37	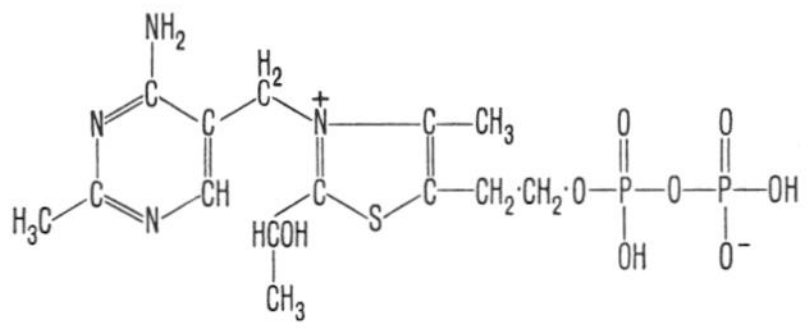		Micro-organisms; represents 60% of the total thiamine in *E. coli*[4]. Also known as 'active acetaldehyde' (see page 391)
Thiochrome	$C_{12}H_{14}N_4OS$ 262.34	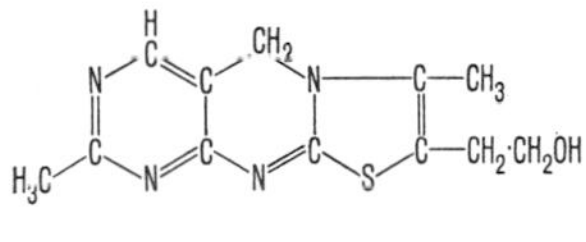	Yellow prisms showing blue fluorescence in solution M. p. 277–278 °C	Oxidation product of thiamine
Oxythiamine	$C_{12}H_{16}N_3O_2S$ 266.34	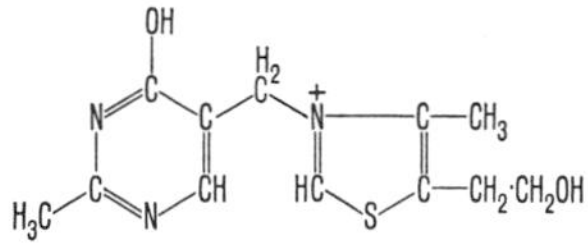	M. p. 195–200 °C	Antagonist of thiamine

Assay

Biological. Rat protection test, rat growth test; now little used.

Microbiological. Thiamine with *Ochromonas malhamensis*[5] or *Ochromonas danica*[6]; pyrimidine and thiazole residues with *Saccharomyces cerevisiae*[7].

Enzymatic. With apodecarboxylase from yeast[8].

Chemical[9]. Quantitatively in pure solution by titration of the chloride, gravimetrically as reineckate, colorimetrically via the azo derivatives from thiamine and diazonium salts, fluorimetrically with cyanogen bromide; in biological material by oxidation of thiamine to thiochrome, which shows strong blue fluorescence in ultraviolet light; with suitable modifications the thiochrome method can be used to determine the mono-, di- and triphosphates of thiamine as well as the protein-bound thiamine.

Units

No international unit; by weight. The former International Unit (= 0.003 mg thiamine hydrochloride = the U. S. Pharmacopeia Unit) is now obsolete.

Biogenesis[10]

Thiamine is synthesized by plants, many bacteria and algae, and by some fungi. Some micro-organisms can synthesize only the pyrimidine and/or thiazole residues, which are formed independently of one another in a manner largely unknown and then combine to form thiamine. The first product is thiamine monophosphate, which is then hydrolysed to thiamine.

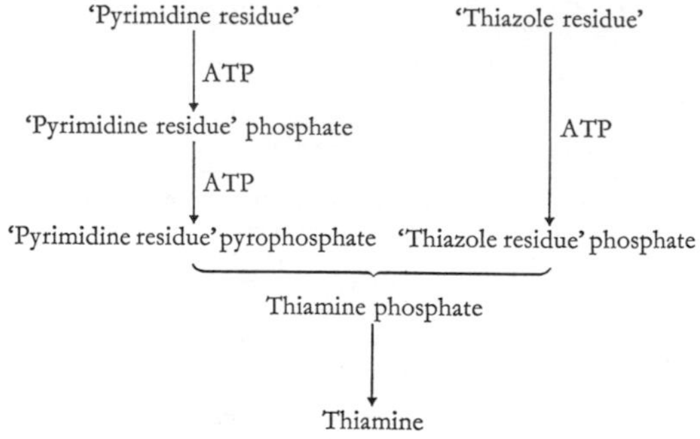

Thiamine, but not thiamine phosphate, is converted by ATP into thiamine pyrophosphate (for instance in yeast and intestinal tissue). ATP can also convert thiamine pyrophosphate into thiamine triphosphate (yeast). On the activation of aldehydes by thiamine pyrophosphate see under 'Function', below.

Intake and excretion

In the USA, the daily diet contains about 2.15 mg thiamine[11], in Germany about 1.8 mg[12]. Thiamine is readily absorbed in the small intestine and converted enzymatically in the intestinal mucosa into thiamine pyrophosphate. In rats, thiamine is synthesized by the intestinal flora[13], but in man it is unlikely that bacterial synthesis plays an important role.

In whole blood the thiamine content is 20–75 µg/l, in serum 18–62 µg/l, in spinal fluid 3–12 µg/l[6]. Erythrocytes contain 80 µg/l, leucocytes 675 µg/l[14]. The thiamine content of the serum in newborn children is very high (see page 609). Small amounts of free thiamine are present in the serum, whereas in the erythrocytes and tissues the main component is thiamine pyrophosphate. The presence of thiamine monophosphate and triphosphate and thiochrome in the tissues has often been reported[15]. The heart muscle is fairly rich in thiamine (2–3 µg/g), as are the brain, liver and kidneys (1 µg/g); smaller quantities are present in the skeletal muscles (0.5 µg/g)[16]. The human liver contains about 4 mg of thiamine[17].

When the daily dietary intake of thiamine rises above 0.5–0.6 mg the urinary excretion of the vitamin increases in proportion to the intake; on an ample diet it amounts to at least 100 µg/day[2,18] (see also page 676). The urine also contains breakdown products (pyrimidine and thiazole residues) the amounts of which are not proportional to the thiamine content of the diet, so that they are regarded as a measure of the rate at which body stores of thiamine are being depleted[19]. The thiamine content of breast milk (see page 689) depends on the thiamine intake and shows large individual variations.

Function

Thiamine pyrophosphate possesses coenzyme functions in the breakdown of carbohydrates (oxidative decarboxylation of pyruvate, see page 391), in the citric acid cycle (oxidative decarboxylation of α-ketoglutarate, see page 390), in the pentose phosphate cycle (transketolase reaction, see page 421) and other biochemical reactions[20]; at least 24 enzymes are known that contain thiamine pyrophosphate as coenzyme[2]. The active aldehyde group in these reactions is formed or transported by thiamine pyrophosphate enzymes and is bound to the C-2 atom of the thiazole ring (see table).

Reaction	Active aldehyde
Oxidative decarboxylation of pyruvate	Active pyruvate (α-lactyl-2-thiamine pyrophosphate)[21] Active acetaldehyde (α-hydroxyethyl-2-thiamine pyrophosphate)[21]
Oxidative decarboxylation of α-ketoglutarate	Active α-ketoglutarate (?) Active succinate semialdehyde (?)
Transketolase reaction	Active xylulose 5-phosphate (?) Active glycolaldehyde[21] Active sedoheptulose 7-phosphate (?)
Glyoxylate carboligase reaction	Active glyoxylate[22] Active formaldehyde[22] Active tartronic semialdehyde[22]

Thiamine pyrophosphate plays an important part in the production of stimuli in the peripheral nerves and in the recovery process after stimulation[23]; during stimulation of the peripheral nerves thiamine is liberated from thiamine pyrophosphate[24].

The thiamine-sparing effect of dietary fats probably derives from the fact that in thiamine deficiency the activity of pyruvate dehydrogenase is more rapidly inhibited than that of oxoglutarate dehydrogenase (α-ketoglutarate dehydrogenase)[2]; in thiamine deficiency, however, toxic products may also be formed from carbohydrates[20].

Various synthetic compounds resembling thiamine in structure, such as oxythiamine, pyrithiamine and neopyrithiamine, act as thiamine antagonists[25]; antithiamine factors of unknown structure occur in bacteria, plants and animals (particularly in cold-blooded animals, where the antimetabolite concerned is also known as 'thiaminase')[26].

Requirements and deficiency symptoms

The requirement of thiamine depends primarily on the intake of carbohydrates, although in practice it is usually related to the calorie intake. In adults the minimum requirement is about 0.27–0.33 mg per 1000 kcal[28]. In bottle-fed infants the maintenance dose has been given as 0.14–0.20 mg per day[29]. The Joint FAO/WHO Expert Group[27] recommends a daily thiamine intake of 0.4 mg per 1000 kcal for infants, children, adults and pregnant and lactating women (see page 493). The allowances of the Food and Nutrition Board (USA)[39] (see page 494) are based on a daily intake of 0.5 mg thiamine per 1000 kcal. The requirement of thiamine increases with the metabolic rate. The possible presence of antithiamine factors in the diet must also be allowed for.

Good sources of thiamine are yeast, pork, liver, kidneys and wholemeal cereals (see pages 507–508). The vitamin is partly destroyed during cooking, particularly in alkaline media, but is unaffected by deep freezing[1].

The classical symptoms of vitamin B_1 deficiency are incipient anorexia, nausea and vomiting. Other symptoms are fatigue, weakness, hypotonia of the gastrointestinal tract and disturbances of the peripheral nerves (weakness in the limbs, hyperaesthesia and paraesthesia, disturbances of coordination). Emotional disturbances are also observed, such as depression, irritability and impairment of memory and power of concentration.

Beriberi takes various forms according to the predominating symptoms:

(a) An exudative form, in which oedema is the first symptom. This may be followed by enlargement of the heart and right-sided heart failure with sudden death.

(b) A 'dry' form in which the main symptoms are polyneuritis of peripheral degenerative type and atrophy of the muscles of the limbs. In European latitudes thiamine deficiency is marked mainly by polyneuritis; it is seen for example in chronic alcoholism, although this condition is probably accompanied in general by deficiency of several of the B vitamins[30].

(c) A rare cerebral form with the symptoms of WERNICKE's disease, namely nystagmus, ocular paralysis and emotional disturbances (irritability, sleeplessness, loss of memory, disorientation, confabulation, hallucinations), followed by loss of consciousness and death. This disease is seen for instance in Europe among chronic alcoholics and occasionally in patients with cancer.

(d) An infantile form seen in the first year of life and a principal cause of the high infant mortality in southern and southeastern Asia; thus between 1954 and 1958 in the Philippines 15 000 children died each year from beriberi[31]. The chronic form is manifested by a slow growth rate, constipation, vomiting and oedema, the acute form by heart failure and death. Occasionally the symptoms resemble those of meningitis or encephalitis. The cause of this vitamin deficiency disease is still to some extent obscure. In most cases the mother suffers from thiamine deficiency so that the maternal milk is deficient in this vitamin; toxic substances in the milk may also play a role[32].

Biochemically, thiamine deficiency is characterized by a low urinary concentration of the vitamin (in beriberi 0–14 µg per 24 h), by disturbances of carbohydrate metabolism (increased blood pyruvate and α-ketoglutarate levels[33]) and by a low tissue concentration of thiamine pyrophosphate (erythrocytes[34], brain[35]). The thiamine pyrophosphate content of the erythrocytes can be measured by means of the transketolase activity, which in thiamine deficiency can be normalized by administering thiamine pyrophosphate[34]. The biochemical changes precede the pathological symptoms; it is not known, however, how the lesions in the vascular system of the heart and in the nervous system arise. Possibly the energy supply to the tissues is too low, or there may be an accumulation of toxic metabolites.

Order in which thiamine deficiency symptoms appear (0.2 mg thiamine per day)[34]

Days	Biochemical symptoms	Clinical symptoms
5	Urinary thiamine 50 µg/24 h	–
10	Urinary thiamine 25 µg/24 h, transketolase activity of erythrocytes somewhat low	–
21–28	Urinary thiamine 0–25 µg/24 h, transketolase activity of erythrocytes 15–25% lower	Loss of weight, sleeplessness, irritability
30–200	Urinary thiamine negligible, transketolase activity of erythrocytes 35% lower	Increasing weakness, loss of weight, polyneuritis, bradycardia, peripheral oedema, enlargement of heart, ophthalmoplegia
over 200	Urinary thiamine negligible, transketolase activity of erythrocytes over 45% lower	Histopathological changes as a result of the biochemical defects

Treatment

In adults beriberi is usually treated by administering thiamine at a dosage of 20–30 mg thiamine per day[36]. Oral administration is usually successful, but when the heart is severely affected the vitamin should be given initially by the parenteral route. In rare cases parenteral administration results in anaphylactic shock. The biochemical changes usually regress rapidly; the cardiovascular disturbances are normally reversible but recovery from polyneuritis is slow and there is occasional irreversible injury to the nerves. Thiamine has been used in the treatment of many diseases[37], but a condition of its successful application is the existence of a thiamine deficiency.

Since thiamine hydrochloride is only partly absorbed and is readily decomposed in alkaline media, biologically active derivatives with fewer disadvantages[38], for instance thiamine propyl disulphide, have been synthesized.

References

1 Horwitt, M.K., in Wohl and Goodhart (Eds.), *Modern Nutrition in Health and Disease*, 3rd ed., Lea & Febiger, Philadelphia, 1964, page 380.
2 Goldsmith, G.A., in Beaton and McHenry (Eds.), *Nutrition*, vol. 2, Academic Press, New York, 1964, page 109.
3 Sebrell and Harris (Eds.), *The Vitamins*, vol. 3, Academic Press, New York, 1954, page 403.
4 Carlson and Brown, *J. biol. Chem.*, **236**, 2099 (1961).
5 Baker and Sobotka, *Advanc. clin. Chem.*, **5**, 173 (1962).
6 Baker et al., *Amer. J. clin. Nutr.*, **14**, 197 (1964).
7 Ziporin et al., *Analyt. Biochem.*, **3**, 1 (1962).
8 Ochoa and Peters, *Biochem. J.*, **32**, 1501 (1938).
9 Gstirner, F., *Chemisch-physikalische Vitaminbestimmungsmethoden*, 5th ed., Enke, Stuttgart, 1965, page 68.
10 Brown and Reynolds, *Ann. Rev. Biochem.*, **32**, 419 (1963); Goodwin, T.W., *The Biosynthesis of Vitamins and Related Compounds*, Academic Press, New York, 1963, page 1.
11 Stitt, K.R., *Nutr. Rev.*, **21**, 257 (1963).
12 Wirths, W., *Ber. Landwirtsch.*, **40**, 845 (1962).
13 Wostmann et al., *Ann. N.Y. Acad. Sci.*, **98**, 516 (1962).
14 Burch et al., *J. biol. Chem.*, **198**, 477 (1952).
15 Wiss and Brubacher, *Ann. N.Y. Acad. Sci.*, **98**, 508 (1962).
16 Ferrebee et al., quoted by Goldsmith, G.A.[2].
17 Baker et al., *Amer. J. clin. Nutr.*, **14**, 1 (1964).
18 Pearson, W.N., *Amer. J. clin. Nutr.*, **20**, 514 (1967).
19 Ziporin et al., *J. Nutr.*, **85**, 287 and 297 (1965).
20 Handler, P., *Fed. Proc.*, **17**, suppl. 2, 31 (1958).
21 Holzer et al., *Ann. N.Y. Acad. Sci.*, **98**, 453 (1962); Krampitz et al., *Ann. N.Y. Acad. Sci.*, **98**, 466 (1962); Ullrich et al., *Int. Z. Vitaminforsch.*, **38**, 273 (1968).
22 Kohlhaw et al., *J. biol. Chem.*, **240**, 2135 (1965).
23 von Muralt, A., *Bibl. 'Nutr. et Dieta' (Basel)*, No. 1, 75 (1960).
24 von Muralt, A., *Ann. N.Y. Acad. Sci.*, **98**, 499 (1962).
25 Rogers, E.F., *Ann. N.Y. Acad. Sci.*, **98**, 412 (1962).
26 Somogyi, J.C., *Bibl. 'Nutr. et Dieta' (Basel)*, No. 1, 77 (1960).
27 Food and Nutrition Board, *Recommended Dietary Allowances*, 7th ed., National Academy of Sciences – National Research Council, Publication 1694, Washington, 1968, page 42.
28 Ziporin et al., *J. Nutr.*, **85**, 297 (1965).
29 Holt et al., *J. Nutr.*, **37**, 53 (1949).
30 Fennelly et al., *Brit. med. J.*, **2**, 1290 (1964).
31 Salcedo, J., *Ann. N.Y. Acad. Sci.*, **98**, 568 (1962).
32 Sebrell, W.H., *Ann. N.Y. Acad. Sci.*, **98**, 563 (1962); Bhuvaneswaran and Sreenivasan, *Ann. N.Y. Acad. Sci.*, **98**, 576 (1962).
33 Buckle, R.M., *Metabolism*, **14**, 141 (1965).
34 Brin, M., *J. Amer. med. Ass.*, **187**, 762 (1964).
35 Dreyfus and Victor, *Schweiz. med. Wschr.*, **93**, 1655 (1963).
36 To-day's Drugs, *Brit. med. J.*, **1**, 227 (1964).
37 Zbinden, G., *Ann. N.Y. Acad. Sci.*, **98**, 550 (1962).
38 Kawasaki, C., *Advanc. clin. Chem.*, **21**, 69 (1963).
39 Joint FAO/WHO Expert Group, *Wld Hlth Org. techn. Rep. Ser.*, No. 362 (1967).

Riboflavin[1–3] (for references see page 473)

Chemistry

For structure and properties of riboflavin and related compounds see the table on page 472.

Assay

Biological[5]. Growth test on rats or chicks.

Microbiological[6]. With *Lactobacillus helveticus* (*L. casei*), *Leuconostoc mesenteroides* or *Tetrahymena pyriformis*[7].

Chemical[4]. By mass analysis after oxidation with periodate; polarographically, spectrophotometrically in the UV range; by photometric measurement of the colour; by fluorometric measurement of the colour of the original vitamin or after conversion to lumiflavin by irradiation in alkaline solution. In biological materials assay is best carried out by the latter method after suitable pre-treatment. The individual flavins can be separated by paper chromatography, electrophoresis or ion exchange.

Unit

No international unit; by weight. 1 rat unit = 4 µg riboflavin.

Biogenesis[8]

Riboflavin is synthesized by bacteria (such as *Clostridium* spp., *Azotobacter* spp.), by fungi (such as ascomycetes and yeasts) and by plants. Purines, pyrimidines, riboflavin and pteridines are formed in a similar way from glycine, formic acid and carbon dioxide. Probable intermediate products of the biosynthesis are 4,5-diaminouracil and 6,7-dimethyl-8-ribityl-lumazine, so that the pyrimidine ring is the first product. The benzene ring is probably completed by the incorporation of acetate. Riboflavin is possibly synthesized at the FAD stage, with 4,5 diaminouracil adenine dinucleotide as intermediate. The conversion of riboflavin into flavin mononucleotide and flavin adenine dinucleotide is mediated by ATP and also occurs in animal tissues (intestine, liver).

Intake and excretion

In USA the daily diet contains on the average 2.65 mg riboflavin[9]. Riboflavin is absorbed in the small intestine in amounts proportional to the amounts of the vitamin ingested[10]. Riboflavin is also synthesized by the intestinal flora, particularly when the diet contains large amounts of carbohydrates that are not easily digested. A part of the riboflavin so formed may also be absorbed in man[11]. In rats, FAD is absorbed less easily than free riboflavin and FMN[12]. Free riboflavin is converted in the intestinal mucosa into FMN, which is then transformed into FAD in the liver[13].

The riboflavin content of whole blood[14] is 49–104 µg/l, of serum[15] 26–37 µg/l, of erythrocytes[15] 180–262 µg/l, of leucocytes[15] 2.27–2.93 mg/l, of liver[16] 25 µg/g, of heart muscle[16] 13 µg/g, of skeletal muscle[16] 2.7 µg/g, of the lens of the eye[16] 3.1 µg/g. In blood (see page 609) and in animal organs 70–90% of the riboflavin is present as FAD, 5–30% as FMN and 0.5–2% as free riboflavin[4]. In the presence of a positive nitrogen balance[17] flavoproteins are produced in the tissues (with decreasing urinary riboflavin concentration); in the presence of a negative nitrogen balance[17] or during fasting[18] flavoproteins are broken down in the tissues (with increasing urinary riboflavin concentration). The urinary excretion varies with the intake; when the latter is less than 1 mg riboflavin

Structure and properties of riboflavin and related compounds

Names	Formula and mol. wt.	Structure	Physical properties	Occurrence and activity
Riboflavin (vitamin B_2, lactoflavin, 7,8-dimethyl-10-[D-ribityl]-isoalloxazine)	$C_{17}H_{20}N_4O_6$ 376.37	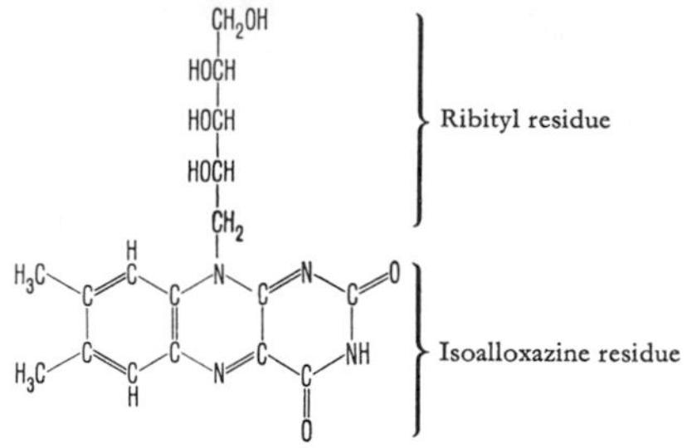	Orange-yellow needles, bitter taste, slightly soluble in water and ethanol, readily soluble in acids, stable to heat when dry and to acid media, very unstable to alkalis and light. Yellowish green fluorescence in solution M.p. 275–282 °C (decomp.)	Constituent of flavin mononucleotide and flavin adenine dinucleotide. Occurs in free form in some micro-organisms. Makes up 0.5–2% of total riboflavin of animal organs[4]. Present in urine
Flavinmononucleotide (FMN) (riboflavin-5′-phosphate)	See page 345	See page 345	Yellow powder, soluble in water	In micro-organisms as active group of flavoproteins, and in plants and animals. Makes up 5–30% of total riboflavin of animal organs[4]
Flavinadenine dinucleotide (FAD)	See page 345	See page 345	Yellow powder, readily soluble in water, insoluble in ethanol	In micro-organisms as active group of flavoproteins, and in plants and animals. Makes up 70–90% of riboflavin of animal organs[4]
Lumiflavin (7,8,10-trimethyl-isoalloxazine)	$C_{13}H_{12}N_4O_2$ 256.27	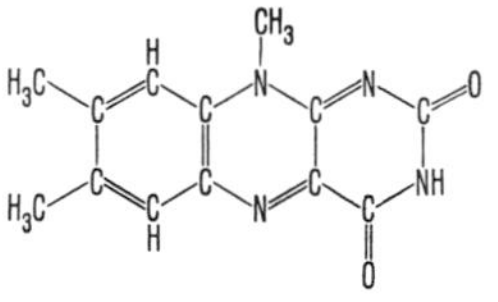	Yellow crystals, only slightly soluble in water. Blue fluorescence in solution M.p. 333 °C (decomp.)	Formed from riboflavin by irradiation in alkaline solution. Antagonist of riboflavin
Galactoflavin (7,8-dimethyl-10-[D-dulcityl]-isoalloxazine)	$C_{18}H_{22}N_4O_7$ 406.40	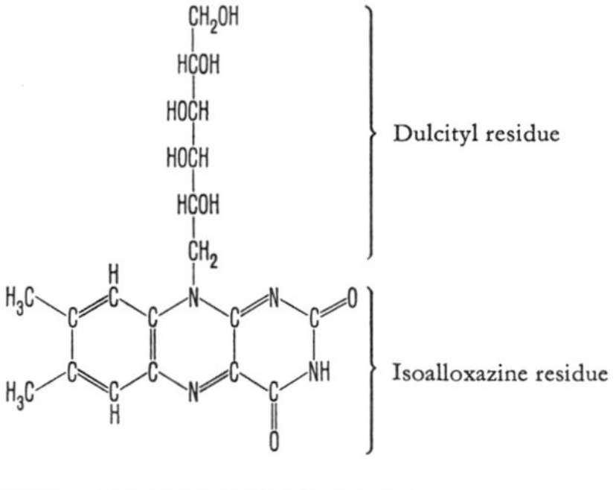	Yellow crystals, slightly soluble in water	Antagonist of riboflavin

per day, 10% of the intake is excreted; with an intake of 1.5 mg, about 20% is excreted, with an intake of 5–11 mg, about 60%[17,19] (see also page 676). The concentration of riboflavin in breast milk depends on the intake of the vitamin[20].

Function

In the form of flavin mononucleotide (FMN) and flavin adenine dinucleotide (FAD) riboflavin forms the active group of the flavoproteins, enzymes with an important function in biological oxidations (see pages 402–403). Here the isoalloxazine system acts as a reversible redox system. In the oxidized form (fluorescent) the flavoproteins take up two hydrogen atoms and pass into the leuco-form (non-fluorescent); in some reactions they take up only one hydrogen atom and become semiquinones. At least 40 flavoproteins are known[21], among them (active group in brackets) important oxidases such as aldehyde oxidase (FAD), xanthine oxidase (FAD), L-amino acid oxidase (FMN), D-amino acid oxidase (FAD), dehydrogenases like acyl-CoA-dehydrogenase (FAD) and succinate dehydrogenase (FAD), NAD(P)H_2 dehydrogenases (FAD), and glutathione reductase (FAD).

Riboflavin, in combination with protein, is necessary to prevent recurrent skin lesions such as those occurring in the corners of the mouth[1]. In erythropoiesis, it is possibly necessary for the formation or effective functioning of erythropoietin[22].

Requirements and deficiency symptoms

The requirement of riboflavin is usually based on the energy requirement[23] but can also be related to the protein requirement[24].

Depletion-repletion studies indicate that the body's needs of riboflavin are met by a daily intake of 0.44 mg/1000 kcal, and it is on this figure that the daily intake of 0.55 mg/1000 kcal recommended by a Joint FAO/WHO Expert Group[25] is based (see page 493). The Food and Nutrition Board (USA)[26] base their recommendations (page 494) on studies of riboflavin requirements that point to dependence of these on 'metabolic body size', represented as the 0.75th power of the body weight: infants 0.1 mg, children 10–12 years 0.09 mg, children 12–14 years 0.08 mg, adults 0.07 mg riboflavin/$kg^{0.75}$. For the requirements of pregnant and lactating women see the table on page 494.

Good sources of riboflavin are milk, liver, kidneys, heart, protein and green vegetables (see pages 499–515). The vitamin is fairly stable to cooking, but up to 85% of that in milk is destroyed on exposure to sunlight[2].

Experimental riboflavin deficiency in man has resulted in lesions of the intestinal mucosa (glossitis, inflammation of the bucco-pharyngeal mucosa, cheilitis, rhagades of the corners of the mouth), of the skin (severe pruritis, desquamation, rhagades, inflammation of the skin creases over joints, seborrhoeic dermatitis) and particularly of the anogenital region (inflammation, desquamation and severe pruritis of anus, vulva and scrotum); recent studies[27,28] have also indicated injury to the bone marrow (absence of mature erythrocytes) with normochromic and normocytic anaemia and deficiency of reticulocytes. Whether the vascularization of the cornea and capillary dilatation of the skin seen in endemic riboflavin deficiency (ariboflavinosis) are due to actual deficiency of the vitamin is uncertain[1,27], and these symptoms may be the result of a multiple nutritional defect. Biochemically, riboflavin deficiency can be recognized by the low riboflavin content in the erythrocytes (202–276 µg/l at a daily intake of 2.55–3.55 mg, 100–131 µg/l at a daily intake of 0.55 mg[29]) and by the reduced urinary excretion of the vitamin (below 40 µg/24 h[30]).

Treatment

The deficiency symptoms usually disappear after several days of giving riboflavin in doses of 5 mg 2–3 times a day[2]. The results of this treatment will confirm the diagnosis.

References

1 Horwitt, M.K., in Wohl and Goodhart (Eds.), *Modern Nutrition in Health and Disease*, 3rd ed., Lea & Febiger, Philadelphia, 1964, page 380.
2 Goldsmith, G.A., in Beaton and McHenry (Eds.), *Nutrition*, vol. 2, Academic Press, New York, 1964, page 109.
3 Sebrell and Harris (Eds.), *The Vitamins*, vol. 3, Academic Press, New York, 1954, page 299.
4 Gstirner, F., *Chemisch-physikalische Vitaminbestimmungsmethoden*, 5th ed., Enke, Stuttgart, 1965, page 112.
5 Bliss and György, in György, P. (Ed.), *Vitamin Methods*, vol. 2, Academic Press, New York, 1951, page 201.
6 Snell, E.E., in György, P. (Ed.), *Vitamin Methods*, vol. 1, Academic Press, New York, 1950, page 327.
7 Baker et al., *Amer. J. clin. Nutr.*, **19**, 17 (1966).
8 Brown and Reynolds, *Ann. Rev. Biochem.*, **32**, 419 (1963); Goodwin, T.W., *The Biosynthesis of Vitamins and Related Compounds*, Academic Press, New York, 1963, page 24.
9 Stitt, K.R., *Nutr. Rev.*, **21**, 257 (1963).
10 Campbell and Morrison, quoted by Stokstad, E.L.R., *Ann. Rev. Biochem.*, **31**, 451 (1962).
11 Najjar et al., *J. Amer. med. Ass.*, **126**, 357 (1944).
12 Chen and Yamauchi, *J. Vitaminol.*, **6**, 247 (1960).
13 Chen and Yamauchi, *J. Vitaminol.*, **7**, 163 (1961).
14 Kerppola, W., *Acta med. scand.*, **153**, 33 (1955).
15 Burch et al., *J. biol. Chem.*, **175**, 457 (1948).
16 Kirk, J.E., *Vitam. and Horm.*, **20**, 67 (1962).
17 Kraut et al., *Int. Z. Vitaminforsch.*, **32**, 25 (1961).
18 Windmueller et al., *Amer. J. clin. Nutr.*, **15**, 73 (1964).
19 Horwitt et al., *J. Nutr.*, **41**, 247 (1950); Morley et al., *J. Nutr.*, **69**, 191 (1959).
20 Belavady, B., *Indian J. med. Res.*, **50**, 104 (1962).
21 Dixon and Webb, *Enzymes*, 2nd ed., Longmans, London, 1964.
22 Review, *Nutr. Rev.*, **23**, 197 (1965).
23 Bro-Rasmussen, F., *Nutr. Abstr. Rev.*, **28**, 1 and 369 (1958).
24 Horwitt, M.K., *Amer. J. clin. Nutr.*, **18**, 458 (1966).
25 Joint FAO/WHO Expert Group, *Wld Hlth Org. techn. Rep. Ser.*, No. 362 (1967).
26 Food and Nutrition Board, *Recommended Dietary Allowances*, 7th ed., National Academy of Sciences – National Research Council, Publication 1694, Washington, 1968, page 40.
27 Lane et al., *J. clin. Invest.*, **43**, 357 (1964).
28 Lane and Alfrey, *Blood*, **25**, 432 (1965).
29 Bessey et al., *J. Nutr.*, **58**, 367 (1956).
30 Interdepartmental Committee on Nutrition, *Publ. Hlth Rep. (Wash.)*, **75**, 687 (1960).

Vitamin B_6[1,2] (for references see page 476)

Chemistry

For structure and properties of vitamin B_6 and related compounds see the table on page 474.

Assay[3,4]

Biological. Growth test on chicks and rats, curatively on rats with deficiency dermatitis.

Microbiological. With *Saccharomyces carlsbergensis* (same activity for pyridoxine, pyridoxamine and pyridoxal), *S. cerevisiae* (pyridoxal 46%, pyridoxamine 40% of activity of pyridoxine), *Lactobacillus casei* (pyridoxal activity only), *Streptococcus faecalis* (pyridoxamine and pyridoxal activity only), *Tetrahymena pyriformis*[5] (pyridoxamine and pyridoxal activity only).

Enzymatic. Pyridoxal phosphate by means of tyrosine decarboxylase.

Chemical[6]. Spectrophotometrically or colorimetrically in pure solution on the basis of the reactivity of the phenolic hydroxyl group; pyridoxal and pyridoxal phosphate fluorimetrically as cyanohydrin (pyridoxine is converted into pyridoxal by oxidation, pyridoxamine to the same compound by transamination); pyridoxic acid fluorimetrically as lactone (pyridoxamine can be converted into pyridoxine; pyridoxine and pyridoxal can be oxidized to pyridoxic acid); all the above forms of the vitamin can be separated by column, paper or thin-layer chromatography.

Unit

No international unit; by weight.

Biogenesis[7]

Practically nothing is known of the biosynthesis of the pyridine ring. Pyridoxine, pyridoxal, pyridoxamine and the phosphates are interconvertible in animal tissues and by micro-organisms in accordance with the scheme shown[8].

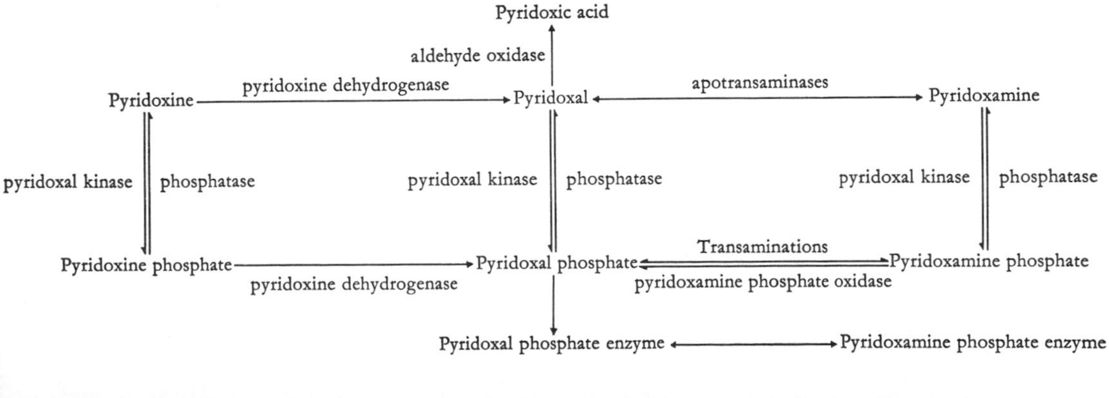

Structure and properties of vitamin B_6 and related compounds

Names*	Formula and mol. wt.	Structure	Physical properties	Occurrence and activity
Pyridoxine*, pyridoxol* (adermine)	$C_8H_{11}NO_3$ 169.18	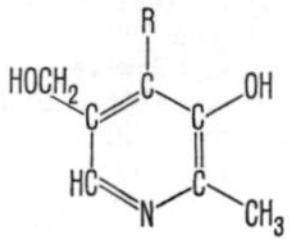 R = —CH_2OH	Colourless crystals, water-soluble, stable to heat, unstable to light M.p. 160 °C	Particularly in plants. Vitamin B_6 activity for higher plants and yeasts; only slight activity for bacteria
Pyridoxamine*	$C_8H_{12}N_2O_2$ 168.20	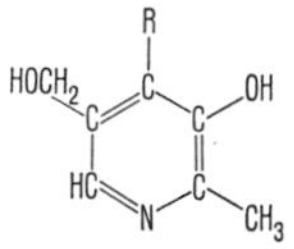 R = —CH_2NH_2	Colourless crystals, water-soluble, unstable to heat and light M.p. 193 °C	Particularly in animal tissues. Vitamin B_6 activity for micro-organisms and higher animals
Pyridoxal*	$C_8H_9NO_3$ 167.17	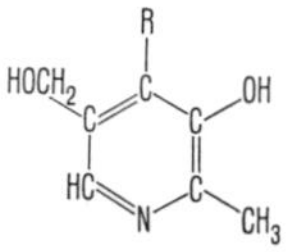 R = —CHO	Colourless crystals, water-soluble, unstable to heat and light	Particularly in animal tissues. Vitamin B_6 activity for micro-organisms and higher animals
Pyridoxamine phosphate	$C_8H_{13}N_2O_5P$ 248.18	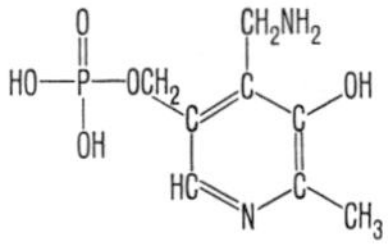	–	Coenzyme in transaminations
Pyridoxal phosphate (codecarboxylase)	$C_8H_{10}NO_6P$ 247.15	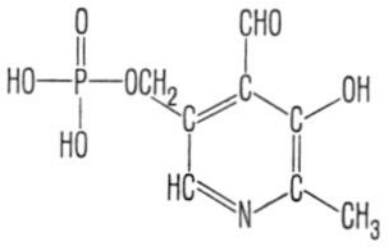	Yellow crystals, water-soluble M.p. > 270 °C	Particularly in muscle. Coenzyme in decarboxylations, transaminations and phosphorylations
Pyridoxic acid (4-pyridoxic acid)	$C_8H_9NO_4$ 183.17	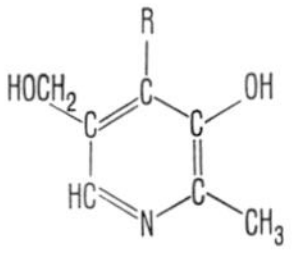 R = —COOH	White crystals, moderately soluble in water M.p. 247 °C	Particularly in urine (breakdown product). No vitamin B_6 activity
Deoxypyridoxine	$C_8H_{11}NO_2$ 153.18	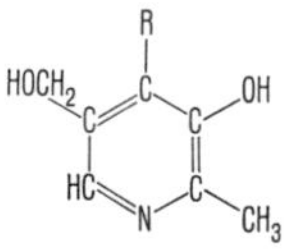 R = —CH_3	–	Vitamin B_6 antagonist in micro-organisms and animals

* Trivial names recommended by the Commission on Biochemical Nomenclature of the International Union of Pure and Applied Chemistry and the International Union of Biochemistry [*Biochim. biophys. Acta (Amst.)*, **107**, 1 (1965)].

Intake and excretion

An average daily diet contains about 2 mg vitamin B_6[2]. Vitamin B_6 phosphates from foods are probably hydrolysed in the intestine by phosphatases[9], and the non-phosphorylated compounds undergo absorption in the upper intestinal tract. Vitamin B_6 is formed also by the intestinal flora, though it is hardly likely that the body makes use of this source of the vitamin[10]. Excretion of vitamin B_6 in the faeces is largely independent of the intake and amounts in adults to 0.7–0.9 mg per day and in children to 0.15–0.30 mg per day[2]. For urinary excretion of the vitamin see page 676.

The non-phosphorylated compounds are converted into the phosphates in the tissues (mainly the brain, liver and kidneys), but probably not in the blood, by the action of the enzyme pyridoxal kinase and ATP[11]. The vitamin B_6 activity of whole blood amounts to 20–45 μg/l, of the serum 30–80 μg/l[12]. Pyridoxal phosphate occurs in the serum (ca. 10 μg/l) and leucocytes (see also pages 609–610). Pyridoxine does not seem to be present in the blood[4]. Pyridoxine administration results within 3 days in an increase in the pyridoxal phosphate content of whole blood and within 10 days in a similar increase in the leucocytes[2]. The human body can apparently convert a maximum of 7 mg pyridoxine per day into pyridoxal phosphate; higher intakes of pyridoxine do not cause any further increase in the pyridoxal phosphate content of the blood[13].

Vitamin B_6 is stored in the liver (5–20 μg/g), muscles (2–6 μg/g) and brain (12–25 μg/g)[12], and it may be present in the spinal fluid (see page 639). The vitamin B_6 content of the whole body has been estimated variously at 40–150 mg[14] and 16–32 mg[15]; about a half of the pyridoxal phosphate in the body appears to be bound to α-glucan phosphorylase in the muscles[16]. The daily turnover of vitamin B_6 is 2.2–4.4%, with a 2–3% depletion of the body's reserves[14].

Pyridoxal is converted in the liver by aldehyde oxidase to pyridoxic acid, which is excreted in the urine along with small amounts of pyridoxine, pyridoxal and pyridoxamine (see page 676). On a normal diet about a half or less of the vitamin B_6 turnover appears as pyridoxic acid in the urine[14,17].

Function[8,18]

Vitamin B_6 is involved as coenzyme in over 40 enzymatic reactions[19]. Pyridoxamine phosphate and pyridoxal phosphate act as coenzymes in transamination reactions important for the breakdown of γ-aminobutyric acid in the brain and for oxalic acid metabolism. Pyridoxal phosphate is the coenzyme in the decarboxylation of amino acids and for other reactions of amino acids (see the table below). Pyridoxal phosphate is also involved in various reactions of tryptophan metabolism (see figure), and this fact is made use of in the tryptophan loading test for diagnosis of vitamin B_6 deficiency[20]. Pyridoxal phosphate is also the coenzyme in the transport of one-carbon units from serine to tetrahydrofolic acid[21], and plays a role in the formation of circulating antibodies[22]. It is also involved with other cofactors in the synthesis of δ-aminolaevulinic acid, a precursor of the porphyrins (haemopoiesis)[23]. Pyridoxal phosphate is a component of α-glucan phosphorylase[16]. It is uncertain whether vitamin B_6 is directly involved in fat metabolism[24].

Deoxypyridoxine and other synthetic pyridoxines, hydrazides (such as isonicotinic acid hydrazide) and cycloserine act as vitamin B_6 antagonists[25], with various degrees of inactivation of the enzymes linked to pyridoxal phosphate.

Dependence of tryptophan metabolism on the B vitamins[20,26]

Bold arrows indicate the main breakdown route. In vitamin B_6 deficiency, kynureninase is inactivated more strongly than the transaminases, which are involved in the formation of xanthurenic acid[27].

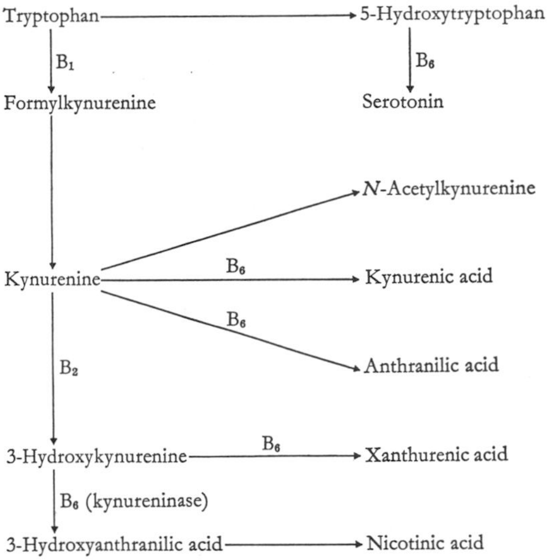

Requirements and deficiency symptoms

In adults the minimum requirement of pyridoxine hydrochloride is apparently about 1.25 mg per day with a daily protein intake of 30 g and 1.5 mg per day with a daily protein intake of 100 g, the optimal requirement being 1.75–2.0 mg per day with a daily protein intake of 100 g[28,29]. The requirement of the vitamin increases with the protein intake. In infants it is between 0.1 and 0.5 mg per day and is dependent on the protein intake (20 μg/g protein); the minimum requirement of children is 0.5–1.5 mg per day, that of adolescents 1.5–2 mg per day[34]. The Food and Nutrition Board (USA) recommend a vitamin B_6 intake of 2.0 mg per day when the daily protein intake is 100 g or more[30]. The human vitamin B_6 requirement has been the object of much discussion[31,32]; it is possible that even higher intakes than those given above are desirable. During pregnancy the requirement is probably increased[33], and a daily intake of 2.5 mg has been recommended for pregnant and lactating women[30]. See also page 494.

Vitamin B_6 occurs in practically all vegetable and animal foodstuffs (see pages 499–515). Good sources of vitamin B_6 are yeast, liver and cereals (wholemeal, since milling results in loss of 80–90% of the vitamin)[2].

The symptoms of vitamin B_6 deficiency vary greatly with the species and age of the individual. The great variety of deficiency symptoms observed is in part due to the fact that in progressive B_6 deficiency not all the enzyme systems are blocked simultaneously to

*Enzymatic reactions with pyridoxamine phosphate and pyridoxal phosphate as cofactors**

Enzyme	Reaction	Enzyme	Reaction
Diaminoxidase, histaminase	Oxidation of diamines and histamine	Decarboxylases	For example, decarboxylation of histidine to histamine, tyrosine to tyramine, dopa to dopamine, hydroxytryptophan to serotonin
Serine hydroxymethyl transferase	Formation of 5,10-methylene tetrahydrofolic acid	Threonine aldolase	Breakdown of threonine to glycine and acetaldehyde
α-Glucan phosphorylase	Phosphorolysis of glycogen	Dehydratases	Deamination of serine, homoserine, threonine, etc.
Transaminases	amino $acid_1$ + ketoic $acid_2$ ⇌ ketoic $acid_1$ + amino $acid_2$ (with all naturally occurring amino acids)	Desulphydrases	Deaminating desulphydration of cysteine and homocysteine
Synthases	Formation of tryptophan from serine and indole, of cysteine from serine, of methylcysteine from serine and methanethiol	Racemases	L-amino acid ⇌ D-amino acid (alanine, methionine, glutamic acid)

* Pyridoxamine phosphate acts as cofactor only in transaminations.

the same extent[27]. The following symptoms have been observed in experimental B₆ deficiency[31]: in rats, severe dermatitis (rat pellagra), occasionally haemolytic anaemia and overall loss of body fat; in rabbits, desquamating dermatitis of the ears, mild anaemia, convulsions, creatinuria, paralytic collapse and death[35]; in rhesus monkeys, arteriosclerosis, dental caries, fatty degeneration or cirrhosis of the liver, pancreatic sclerosis, disturbances of the central nervous system[36]; in man, (a) skin and mucosa: seborrhoeic and desquamative dermatitis of the mouth and eyes which may spread to the face, scalp, neck and loins; intertrigo of the breasts and inguinal region in women; stomatitis and glossitis; (b) nervous system: irritability, depression, somnolence, nausea, impairment of sensitivity to vibration and positional change; very rarely peripheral neuritis[37].

Spontaneous vitamin B₆ deficiency is rare in man. Among 300 infants who received only about 60 µg vitamin B₆ per litre of formula milk (as a result of a new sterilization process) hyperacusis, nervousness and epileptiform convulsions were observed[38]. Of possible genetic origin are the pyridoxine-dependent convulsions seen in infants (generalized convulsions with no clinical or electroencephalographic peculiarities appearing in the first days of life and occasionally developing into status epilepticus during the following weeks)[38–40]; these are probably due to an unsatisfied vitamin B₆ requirement or to a disturbance of vitamin B₆ utilization. Similar causes are probably at the root of the pyridoxine-deficiency anaemia and the pyridoxine-sensitive anaemia seen in man[38, 41, 42], but in contrast to the central nervous disturbances these are observed almost solely among adults. In pyridoxine-deficiency anaemia (a hypochromic microcytic anaemia with increased serum iron and organ haemosiderosis) there is a disturbance of δ-aminolaevulinic acid synthesis, with consequent reduction in the amount of protoporphyrin formed; this disease is also probably of genetic origin. In pyridoxine-sensitive anaemia (symptoms as in the deficiency anaemia but often including enlargement of the liver and spleen) there is a complex disturbance of porphyrin metabolism resembling that in sideroachrestic anaemia.

It is uncertain whether vitamin B₆ deficiency in man causes dental caries[43] or the formation of oxalate stones in the urinary tract[44].

Cystathionuria is probably due to a defect in the linkage of the coenzyme pyridoxal phosphate to the apoenzyme of homoserine dehydratase (cystathionase)[45].

Biochemically, vitamin B₆ deficiency is recognizable (a) by the increased excretion of xanthurenic acid and other tryptophan metabolites in urine, especially following oral doses of tryptophan (tryptophan loading test)[20]; this disturbance of tryptophan metabolism appears after only one week on a vitamin B₆-deficient diet[46]; (b) by a lowered pyridoxal phosphate level in the blood and a greatly reduced vitamin B₆ and pyridoxic acid excretion in the urine[47]; (c) by a reduced transaminase content of the serum[47] and erythrocytes[48]; (d) by an increased urinary oxalic acid excretion[44, 49] and a lowered urinary taurine excretion[49].

Treatment

When the vitamin B₆ deficiency is purely alimentary, daily doses of the vitamin at the level of the normal requirement suffice. In pyridoxine-dependent convulsions in infants pyridoxine should be given parenterally at the rate of 2–15 mg per day[40]; in pyridoxine-deficiency anaemia the dose should be at least 10 mg per day[41] and in pyridoxine-sensitive anaemia at least 500 mg per day[41]. Daily pyridoxine supplements of 10–15 mg may be helpful in overcoming disturbances of pregnancy such as severe vomiting and toxaemia, particularly when the diet is poor[50]. Pyridoxine doses of 100 mg have been recommended for the treatment of radiation sickness[51]. The success of treatment with pyridoxine is conditional on there being no disturbance of the conversion into pyridoxal (by the action of pyridoxine dehydrogenase) in the body[8].

References

1 Sebrell and Harris (Eds.), *The Vitamins*, vol. 3, Academic Press, New York, 1954, page 219; Chow, B. F., in Beaton and McHenry (Eds.), *Nutrition*, vol. 2, Academic Press, New York, 1964, page 207; International Symposium on Vitamin B₆, *Vitam. and Horm.*, **22**, 359 (1964).
2 Vilter, R. W., in Wohl and Goodhart (Eds.), *Modern Nutrition in Health and Disease*, 3rd ed., Lea & Febiger, Philadelphia, 1964, page 400.
3 Toepfer and Polansky, *Vitam. and Horm.*, **22**, 825 (1964).
4 Storvick and Peters, *Vitam. and Horm.*, **22**, 833 (1964).
5 Baker and Sobotka, *Advanc. clin. Chem.*, **5**, 173 (1962).
6 Gstirner, F., *Chemisch-physikalische Vitaminbestimmungsmethoden*, 5th ed., Enke, Stuttgart, 1965, page 145.
7 Brown and Reynolds, *Ann. Rev. Biochem.*, **32**, 419 (1963); Goodwin, T. W., *The Biosynthesis of Vitamins and Related Compounds*, Academic Press, New York, 1963, page 145.
8 Snell, E. E., *Vitam. and Horm.*, **22**, 485 (1964).
9 Turner, J. M., *Biochem. J.*, **80**, 663 (1961).
10 Wayne et al., *Arch. intern. Med.*, **101**, 143 (1958).
11 Roberts et al., *Vitam. and Horm.*, **22**, 503 (1964).
12 Baker et al., *Amer. J. clin. Nutr.*, **18**, 123 (1966).
13 Boxer et al., *J. Nutr.*, **63**, 623 (1957).
14 Johansson et al., *Amer. J. clin. Nutr.*, **18**, 185 (1966).
15 Sauberlich et al., in *VII. Internationaler Ernährungskongreß*, Hamburg 1966, Summaries of Papers, Pergamos-Druck, Hamburg, 1966, page 253.
16 Krebs and Fischer, *Vitam. and Horm.*, **22**, 399 (1964).
17 Reddy et al., *J. biol. Chem.*, **233**, 691 (1958); Udalov and Čelnokova, *Lab. Delo*, No. 3, 33 (1962), quoted in *Nutr. Abstr. Rev.*, **32**, 910 (1962).
18 Snell, E. E., *Vitam. and Horm.*, **16**, 77 (1958).
19 Dixon and Webb, *Enzymes*, 2nd ed., Longmans, London, 1964.
20 Musajo and Benassi, *Advanc. clin. Chem.*, **7**, 63 (1964).
21 Blakley, R. L., *Biochem. J.*, **77**, 459 (1960).
22 Axelrod and Trakatellis, *Vitam. and Horm.*, **22**, 591 (1964).
23 Schulman and Richert, *J. biol. Chem.*, **226**, 181 (1957).
24 Mueller, J. F., *Vitam. and Horm.*, **22**, 787 (1964).
25 Rosen et al., *Vitam. and Horm.*, **22**, 609 (1964).
26 Goodwin, T. W., *The Biosynthesis of Vitamins and Related Compounds*, Academic Press, New York, 1963, page 69.
27 Wiss and Weber, *Vitam. and Horm.*, **22**, 495 (1964); Wiss, J., *Biochem. J.*, **95**, 1P (1965).
28 Baker et al., *Amer. J. clin. Nutr.*, **15**, 59 (1964).
29 Sauberlich, H. E., *Vitam. and Horm.*, **22**, 807 (1964).
30 Food and Nutrition Board, *Recommended Dietary Allowances*, 7th ed., National Academy of Sciences – National Research Council, Publication 1694, Washington, 1968, page 43.
31 Leitch and Hepburn, *Nutr. Abstr. Rev.*, **31**, 389 (1961).
32 Borsook, H., *Vitam. and Horm.*, **22**, 855 (1964); Sebrell, W. H., *Vitam. and Horm.*, **22**, 875 (1964).
33 Wachstein, M., *Vitam. and Horm.*, **22**, 705 (1964).
34 American Academy of Pediatrics – Committee on Nutrition, *Pediatrics*, **38**, 1068 (1966).
35 Hove and Herndon, *J. Nutr.*, **61**, 127 (1957).
36 Greenberg, L. D., *Vitam. and Horm.*, **22**, 677 (1964).
37 Vilter et al., *J. Lab. clin. Med.*, **42**, 335 (1953); Vilter, R. W., *J. Amer. med. Ass.*, **159**, 1210 (1955).
38 Coursin, D. B., *Vitam. and Horm.*, **22**, 755 (1964).
39 Scriver, C. R., *Pediatrics*, **26**, 62 (1960).
40 Cramer, H., *Dtsch. med. Wschr.*, **87**, 1577 (1962).
41 Horrigan and Harris, *Advanc. intern. Med.*, **12**, 103 (1964); Harris and Horrigan, *Vitam. and Horm.*, **22**, 721 (1964).
42 Gehrmann, G., *Germ. med. Mth.*, **9**, 162 (1964); *Dtsch. med. Wschr.*, **88**, 2261 (1963).
43 Hillman, R. W., *Vitam. and Horm.*, **22**, 695 (1964).
44 Gershoff, S. N., *Vitam. and Horm.*, **22**, 581 (1964).
45 Review, *Nutr. Rev.*, **24**, 37 (1966).
46 Brown et al., *Fed. Proc.*, **23**, 137 (1964).
47 Baysal et al., *Fed. Proc.*, **23**, 137 (1964).
48 Raica and Sauberlich, *Amer. J. clin. Nutr.*, **15**, 67 (1964).
49 Johnston and Donald, *Fed. Proc.*, **23**, 137 (1964).
50 Diding and Melander, *Acta obstet. gynec. scand.*, **40**, 252 (1961).
51 Jones, P. O., *Practitioner*, **182**, 45 (1959).

Nicotinic acid[1–3] (for references see page 478)

Chemistry

For structure and properties of nicotinic acid and related compounds see the table opposite.

Assay

Biological[4]. Black tongue curative test in dogs, growth test in chicks.

Microbiological[5]. With *Lactobacillus plantarum* (earlier *L. arabinosus*) or *Tetrahymena pyriformis* for nicotinic acid and nicotinamide.

Chemical[6]. In pure solution spectrophotometrically, polarographically, by mass analysis, colorimetrically by the bromcyanogen (König) reaction or fluorometrically (the latter method particularly suitable for organs). Nicotinic acid and its metabolites can be separated by chromatographic methods. NAD and NADP must be hydrolysed before being determined as nicotinic acid; they can be estimated directly by the spectrophotometric or fluorimetric method through their blue fluorescence in alkaline solution.

Unit

No international unit; by weight.

Biogenesis[7, 8]

In plants nicotinic acid arises by condensation of 3- and 4-carbon units. In animals, fungi and a few bacteria (for instance, *Xanthomonas pruni*) nicotinic acid is formed from tryptophan by the action of thiamine, riboflavin and vitamin B₆ (see diagram on page 475). It is less likely that nicotinamide is formed directly from nicotinic acid than by the hydrolysis of nicotinamide dinucleotides. The latter compounds are formed in erythrocytes, liver, yeast, etc. in accordance with the following scheme:

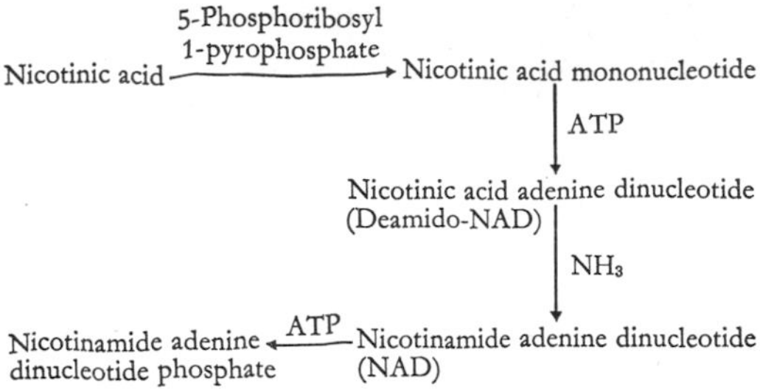

Intake and excretion

In the USA the daily average diet contains about 500–1000 mg tryptophan and 8–17 mg nicotinic acid[9]. Nicotinic acid and tryptophan are readily absorbed in the intestinal tract. Nicotinic acid is probably synthesized from tryptophan by the intestinal bacteria, though it is unlikely that the human body makes use of this source. In the body about 1 mg nicotinic acid is formed from every 60 mg tryptophan[1, 2]; the enzymes required for this transformation occur in the liver and erythrocytes. This conversion of tryptophan into nicotinic acid is increased in pregnancy[10].

The nicotinic acid content of whole blood is about 4–10 mg per litre and consists almost wholly of dinucleotides in the blood cells. The serum contains about 0.02–0.05 mg of free nicotinic acid[5] (see also page 610). The nicotinic acid level in the blood increases rapidly when nicotinic acid is given parenterally; oral doses of nicotinic acid or tryptophan raise the dinucleotide content of the erythrocytes. In the form of dinucleotides, nicotinic acid occurs in all tissues, particularly the liver. The human liver contains on the average 65 mg nicotinic acid[11].

In the liver, nicotinamide but not nicotinic acid is methylated to 1-methylnicotinamide with *S*-adenosylmethionine as methyl-group donor and is further oxidized to 1-methyl-2-pyridonecarboxylamide[8]. These compounds are excreted in the urine (per day normally 5–8 mg 1-methylnicotinamide and 7–10 mg 1-methyl-2-pyridonecarboxylamide as well as about 1 mg nicotinic acid[2]; see also page 676). After oral doses of 10–150 mg nicotinamide per day, on the average 57% has been found in the urine, consisting of 10–30% 1-methylnicotinamide and 70–90% 1-methyl-2-pyridonecarboxylamide[12]. Following high doses of nicotinic acid but not nicotinamide, nicotinic acid is also excreted in the urine bound to glycine (as nicotinuric acid).

Function

The active forms of nicotinic acid are the nicotinamide dinucleotides NAD and NADP. These are coenzymes (cosubstrates) of numerous dehydrogenases, particularly in fermentation, glycolysis and other reactions. They are responsible also for hydrogen transport within the cell, $NADPH_2$ providing the hydrogen necessary for biosynthesis while $NADH_2$ transports this hydrogen to the enzymes of the respiratory chain. The synthesis of ATP utilizes the reaction with oxygen to form water (oxidative phosphorylation); for details see pages 403–404.

Nicotinic acid but not nicotinamide has an inhibiting effect at high dosage on the synthesis of lipids, particularly cholesterol, but

Structure and properties of nicotinic acid and related compounds

Compound	Formula and mol. wt.	Structure	Physical properties	Occurrence and activity
Nicotinic acid* (niacin, pyridine-3-carboxylic acid, vitamin PP)	$C_6H_5NO_2$ 123.11	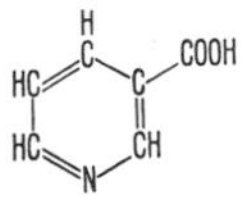	White crystals, acid taste, moderately soluble in water and ethanol, stable to heat and oxidation M.p. 234–237 °C	In plant and animal tissues; component of NAD and NADP
Nicotinamide* (nicotinic acid amide, niacinamide, pyridine-3-carboxylamide, vitamin PP)	$C_6H_6N_2O$ 122.13	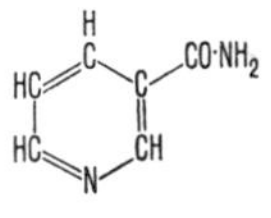	White crystals, salty taste, soluble in water and ethanol, stable to heat and oxidation M.p. 128–131 °C	In plant and animal tissues; component of NAD and NADP
1-Methylnicotinamide (N_1-methylnicotinamide)	$C_7H_9N_2O$ 137.16	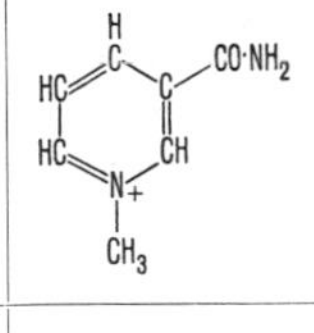		In urine; metabolite of nicotinic acid
1-Methyl-6-pyridone-3-carboxylamide (N_1-methyl-2-pyridone-5-carboxylamide)	$C_7H_8N_2O_2$ 152.15	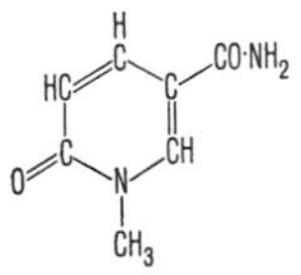	White crystals, soluble in water and ethanol M.p. 212–214 °C	In urine; metabolite of nicotinic acid
Nicotinamide adenine dinucleotide (NAD; reduced form $NADH_2$)	See page 344	See page 344	Colourless powder, soluble in water, insoluble in ethanol	In all animal and plant cells; coenzyme of many dehydrogenases
Nicotinamide adenine dinucleotide phosphate (NADP; reduced form $NADPH_2$)	See page 344	See page 344	Colourless powder, soluble in water, insoluble in ethanol	In all animal and plant cells; coenzyme of many dehydrogenases

* Trivial names recommended by the Commission on Biochemical Nomenclature of the International Union of Pure and Applied Chemistry and the International Union of Biochemistry [*Biochim. biophys. Acta (Amst.)*, **107**, 1 (1965)].

the mechanism of this effect is obscure[13]; the primary action of nicotinic acid is possibly the liberation of free fatty acids blocked in the tissues[14].

Requirements and deficiency symptoms

The nicotinic acid requirement can also be met by tryptophan, 60 mg of which corresponds to 1 mg nicotinic acid. The requirement of nicotinic acid depends on the calorie intake. The minimum requirement for preventing pellagra is 4.4 mg per 1000 kcal, or 9 mg for adults whose daily calorie intake is below 2000 kcal[9]. For children and adults the Food and Nutrition Board (USA)[9] recommend a daily intake of 6.6 mg per 1000 kcal; during pregnancy this should be increased by 2 mg per day, during lactation by 7 mg per day (see page 494). The same daily intake of 6.6 mg/1000 kcal for children and adults is recommended by the Joint FAO/WHO Expert Group[22] (see page 493); for infants the latter accept that breast feeding by well-nourished mothers will supply adequate niacin equivalents.

Good sources of nicotinic acid are yeast, liver, lean meat, groundnuts and leguminous plants (see pages 499–515). Plant proteins contain 0.8–1.4% tryptophan, animal proteins about 1.3% (see page 516). Maize is low in both nicotinic acid and tryptophan; nicotinic acid is also present in the combined form so that it is not available to the organism[15]. During the roasting of coffee considerable amounts of nicotinic acid are formed from trigonelline[16].

Nicotinic acid deficiency causes pellagra, the development of which is favoured by sunlight and heavy physical work. Alimentary nicotinic acid deficiency is common in areas where maize constitutes the principal foodstuff. Pellagra occasionally occurs in chronic alcoholism, cirrhosis of the liver, chronic diarrhoea, diabetes and neoplasias. In the presence of carcinoid tumours up to 60% (normally 1%) of the body's tryptophan is converted into serotonin, so that it is no longer available as a source of nicotinic acid[17]. Treatment with isoniazid can cause inhibition of the activity of pyridoxal phosphate and thus interfere with the synthesis of nicotinic acid from tryptophan. This synthesis is possibly also impaired by diets containing large amounts of leucine[18].

The following are the symptoms of pellagra: (a) A dark red erythema appearing symmetrically on the extremities, face, neck and all other regions exposed to air and light; the skin finally becomes dry, fissured, atrophic and brown-coloured. The lesions are marked by atrophy of the superficial layers of the corium with dilatation of the blood vessels, keratinization of the epidermis and a tendency for the latter to separate from the corium. Wounds of any kind exacerbate these symptoms. (b) Chronic inflammation of the mucosa and intestinal tract (stomatitis, glossitis, gastritis with low acid secretion); profuse and often bloody diarrhoea. (c) Emotional disturbances (delirium, hallucinations, confused mental states). Neurological disturbances, if present, are probably due to simultaneous deficiency of other vitamins since these symptoms have not been observed in experimental nicotinic acid deficiency[2].

The biochemical signs of nicotinic acid deficiency are the following: in pellagra a urinary excretion of 1-methylnicotinamide plus 1-methyl-2-pyridonecarboxylamide of usually less than 2 mg per day. Within 30–60 days the excretion of these metabolites falls to a minimum value and then remains constant; shortly after this minimum value is reached, the first clinical signs of deficiency appear[2]. On a standard diet (10 mg nicotinic acid plus 1000 mg tryptophan) the excretion of nicotinic acid metabolites is less than 3.0 mg in pellagra patients and 7–37 mg in healthy persons[19]. In nicotinic acid deficiency the concentration of nicotinamide dinucleotides in the muscles and liver falls, but not that in the erythrocytes[2, 20].

Treatment

In severe nicotinic acid deficiency, 300–500 mg nicotinamide should be given in daily oral doses of 50–100 mg; if there is difficulty in swallowing, 100 mg nicotinamide should be given three times per day intramuscularly[2]. Nicotinic acid should not be given intravenously in doses exceeding 25 mg owing to the danger of anaphylactic shock. In high doses nicotinic acid but not nicotinamide causes marked dilatation of the vessels and particularly of the capillaries and vessels of the upper half of the body; this is of therapeutic use in disturbances of the peripheral circulation. Nicotinic acid can be used to lower the serum cholesterol level and for this purpose is usually given at the rate of 1 g three times per day[21].

References

1 Horwitt, M.K., in Wohl and Goodhart (Eds.), *Modern Nutrition in Health and Disease*, 3rd ed., Lea & Febiger, Philadelphia, 1964, page 380.
2 Goldsmith, G.A., in Beaton and McHenry (Eds.), *Nutrition*, vol. 2, Academic Press, New York, 1964, page 109.
3 Sebrell and Harris (Eds.), *The Vitamins*, vol. 2, Academic Press, New York, 1954, page 449.
4 Bliss and György, in György, P. (Ed.), *Vitamin Methods*, vol. 2, Academic Press, New York, 1951, page 210.
5 Baker and Sobotka, *Advanc. clin. Chem.*, **5**, 173 (1962).
6 Gstirner, F., *Chemisch-physikalische Vitaminbestimmungsmethoden*, 5th ed., Enke, Stuttgart, 1965, page 196.
7 Brown and Reynolds, *Ann. Rev. Biochem.*, **32**, 419 (1963).
8 Goodwin, T.W., *The Biosynthesis of Vitamins and Related Compounds*, Academic Press, New York, 1963, page 69.
9 Food and Nutrition Board, *Recommended Dietary Allowances*, 7th ed., National Academy of Sciences – National Research Council, Publication 1694, Washington, 1968, page 37.
10 Wertz et al., *J. Nutr.*, **64**, 339 (1958).
11 Baker et al., *Amer. J. clin. Nutr.*, **14**, 1 (1964).
12 Goldsmith et al., *J. Nutr.*, **73**, 172 (1961).
13 Chiu, G.C., *Arch. intern. Med.*, **108**, 717 (1961); Goldsmith, G.A., *J. Amer. med. Ass.*, **194**, 167 (1965).
14 Eaton et al., *J. clin. Invest.*, **44**, 247 (1965).
15 Review, *Nutr. Rev.*, **19**, 240 (1961).
16 Bressani and Navarrete, *Food Res.*, **24**, 344 (1959).
17 Bridges et al., *Brit. J. Surg.*, **45**, 117 (1957).
18 Review, *Nutr. Rev.*, **21**, 334 (1963).
19 Goldsmith et al., *Amer. J. clin. Nutr.*, **4**, 151 (1956).
20 Axelrod et al., *J. biol. Chem.*, **138**, 667 (1941).
21 To-day's Drugs, *Brit. med. J.*, **2**, 1181 (1964).
22 Joint FAO/WHO Expert Group, *Wld Hlth Org. techn. Rep. Ser.*, No. 362 (1967).

Folic acid group[1–3]

Chemistry[4]

For structure and properties of folic acid and related compounds see the table on pages 480–481.

Assay

Biological. Curative test on chickens[5].

Microbiological[1, 6]. With *Lactobacillus casei* (total folic acid activity: pteroylglutamic acid, pteroyltriglutamic acid and higher conjugates, reduced folic acid including 5-methyltetrahydropteroylglutamic acid); with *Streptococcus faecalis* (pteroylglutamic acid, reduced folic acid, but not 5-methyltetrahydropteroylglutamic acid); with *Pediococcus cerevisiae* (reduced folic acid). In biological material, particularly foodstuffs, the conjugates can also be broken down enzymatically.

Chemical[7]. Photometrically after fission with zinc or potassium permanganate and subsequent diazotization; in pure solution also spectrophotometrically or polarographically.

Units

No international unit; by weight.

Biogenesis[8]

Folic acid is synthesized by higher plants, by micro-organisms (intestinal flora) and in animal tissues[9], probably in accordance with the following scheme:

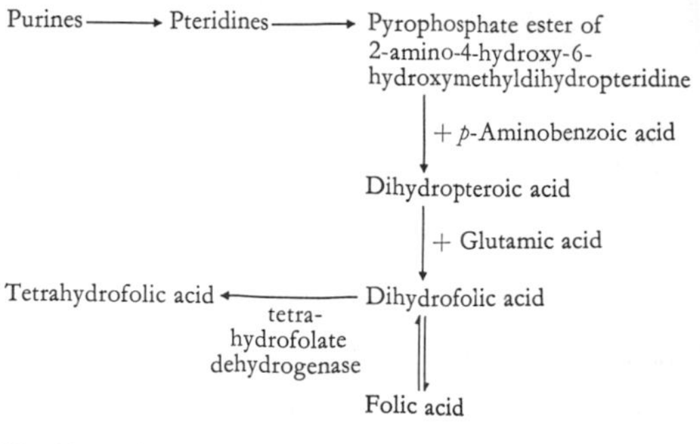

The biosynthesis of dihydrofolic acid is inhibited by sulphonamides[10]. Folic acid antagonists like aminopterin and substances with a structure resembling pyramidine (e.g., primidone and pyrimethamine) inhibit tetrahydrofolate dehydrogenase and thereby the formation of tetrahydrofolic acid.

Intake and excretion

In USA the daily diet contains about 150–200 µg folic acid activity[11,12]; this includes only about 20 µg pteroylglutamic acid[12].

The folic acid conjugates are hydrolysed in the upper intestinal tract. Both the folic acid derived from the diet and that formed by the intestinal flora are actively absorbed in all parts of the small intestine; large amounts also diffuse passively through the intestinal wall[13].

On the folic acid content of blood, erythrocytes and leucocytes see page 610. The maximum folic acid concentration in the serum is attained 2–4 hours after an oral dose of the vitamin[14]. The half-life of intravenous doses in the serum is about 6–10 minutes[15]. Oral administration of folic acid has no effect on the serum folinic acid level; the exogenous folic acid is reduced in the tissues and stored in small amounts. The total folic acid content of the human body has been estimated at 12–15 mg[16]; of this amount about 7 mg is contained in the liver[17]. In serum[18,19], erythrocytes[20] and liver[21], folic acid is predominantly present in the form of 5-methyltetrahydropteroylglutamic acid. The body's stores are probably sufficient to prevent the appearance of clinical deficiency symptoms for 4–5 months[19]. After an intravenous dose of tagged folic acid, radioactive folic acid and 10-formyltetrahydropteroylglutamic acid have been found in the urine as well as untagged 5-methyltetrahydropteroylglutamic acid originating from the tissues[22].

Function[23]

Tetrahydrofolic acid ($H_4PteGlu$) is an important carrier of one-carbon units. These units arise mainly from histidine and serine and are required for the synthesis of purines and methionine (see the scheme below and pages 433 and 436).

On account of the importance of folic acid for purine and nucleic acid synthesis it is understandable that the vitamin should play an essential part in all processes of cell division, particularly in haemopoiesis (stimulation of the reticulocytes). In folic acid deficiency the primary defect is probably a disturbance of the doubling of DNA in the nucleus during cell division. The role of the vitamin in maintaining normal pregnancy is still obscure, but it is possible that it alters the action of the ovarial hormones on the uterus.

Requirements

The folic acid requirement is not known for certain[24]. The daily minimum requirement of adults is probably about 50 µg, an amount sufficient to maintain the serum level[25]. Infants have a minimum requirement of about 5–20 µg[26] or more[27]. The requirement is increased in pregnancy (possibly 200–400 µg per day in the 3rd trimester when there is a deficiency of folate[28]). The Food and Nutrition Board (USA)[24] recommend a daily intake of 0.4 mg for adults, 0.8 mg for pregnant women, and 0.5 mg for lactating women; these are amounts determined in foods by *Lactobacillus casei* assay (see page 494).

Good sources of folic acid are liver, kidneys, dark-green leaf vegetables, yeast (see pages 499–515). The folic acid content of fresh breast and cow's milk is sufficient to meet the requirement in infancy[29]. Folic acid is very sensitive to heat and 50–95% of the activity is destroyed by cooking.

Deficiency[30, 31]

The following are causes of folic acid deficiency:

(a) Inadequate dietary intake (infants, alcoholics, cirrhotic patients)
(b) Disturbances of intestinal absorption (malabsorption syndrome, resection of the jejunum, haemochromatosis)
(c) An increased requirement (pregnancy, chronic haemolytic anaemia, malignant disease)
(d) Disturbances of folic acid metabolism (folic acid antagonists: see under 'Biogenesis' above).

A daily intake of 5 µg folic acid or less results in deficiency of the vitamin[32]. The clinical symptoms are megaloblastosis of the bone marrow, macrocytic anaemia, leucopenia, excessive segmentation of the leucocytes, thrombocytopenia, glossitis and gastrointestinal disturbances. Biochemical symptoms of use in diagnosis are lowered folic acid contents of the serum and erythrocytes (see page 610) and the increased urinary excretion of formiminoglutamic acid after histidine loading (see page 670). Folic acid deficiency can also be diagnosed by a therapeutic test (0.05–0.2 mg folic acid per day for 10 days orally or, in malabsorption, intramuscularly)[2]. Other methods are measurement of the folic acid absorption using tritium-tagged folic acid and of the plasma folic acid clearance.

Deficiency symptoms appear in the following order[33]:

Lowered serum folic acid level (< 7–16 µg/l)	2 weeks
Excessive segmentation of the leucocytes	6–10 weeks
Increased excretion of formiminoglutamic acid	12–18 weeks
Lowered erythrocyte folic acid content	17 weeks
Macroelliptocytosis	18 weeks
Megaloblastosis of the bone marrow	19 weeks
Macrocytic anaemia	20 weeks

Folic acid deficiency is a common cause of megaloblastic anaemia in pregnancy. It is also often seen in children in the tropics, the main symptoms being loss of appetite and slow growth rather than megaloblastic anaemia[31].

Secondary folic acid deficiency in vitamin B_{12} deficiency is probably due to blocking of tetrahydrofolic acid regeneration from 5-methyltetrahydrofolic acid, a step requiring vitamin B_{12}[13].

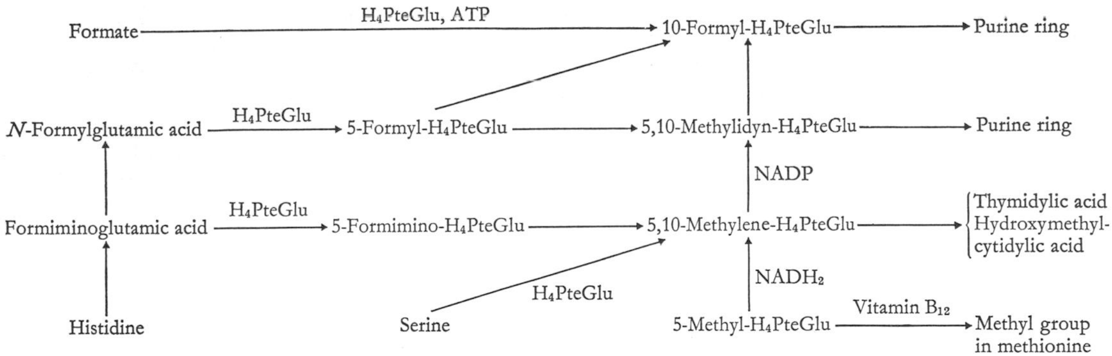

Treatment

Treatment of folic acid deficiency with doses of the vitamin should be adjusted as closely as possible to the severity of the deficiency[34]. In megaloblastic anaemia due to dietary deficiency of the vitamin, 0.25 mg folic acid per day is sufficient to normalize the blood picture[35]. Doses of folic acid exceeding 0.1 mg per day are required to prevent the appearance of anaemia in patients with vitamin B_{12} deficiency but are inadequate to protect the nervous system from subacute degenerative changes[24, 36]. In treatment employing folic acid antagonists (cancer) folic acid should be given in reduced form (for example as folinic acid)[37]. During pregnancy, prophylactic doses of 0.1–0.5 mg folic acid are recommended[16].

References

1 GIRDWOOD, R.H., *Advanc. clin. Chem.*, **3**, 235 (1960).
2 LUHBY and COOPERMAN, *Advanc. metab. Disord.*, **1**, 263 (1964).
3 SEBRELL and HARRIS (Eds.), *The Vitamins*, vol. 3, Academic Press, New York, 1954, page 87; CHOW, B.F., in BEATON and MCHENRY (Eds.), *Nutrition*, vol. 2, Academic Press, New York, 1964, page 207; VILTER, R.W., in WOHL and GOODHART (Eds.), *Modern Nutrition in Health and Disease*, 3rd ed., Lea & Febiger, Philadelphia, 1964, page 409.
4 PFLEIDERER, W., in RAUEN, H.M. (Ed.), *Biochemisches Taschenbuch*, 2nd ed., part 1, Springer, Berlin, 1964, page 647.
5 O'DELL and HOGAN, *J. biol. Chem.*, **149**, 323 (1943).
6 BAKER and SOBOTKA, *Advanc. clin. Chem.*, **5**, 173 (1962).
7 GSTIRNER, F., *Chemisch-physikalische Vitaminbestimmungsmethoden*, 5th ed., Enke, Stuttgart, 1965, page 188.

(continued on page 482)

Structure and properties of folic acid and related compounds

Names*	Formula and mol. wt.	Structure	Physical properties	Occurrence and biological properties
Rhizopterin (SLR factor)	$C_{15}H_{12}N_6O_4$ 340.30	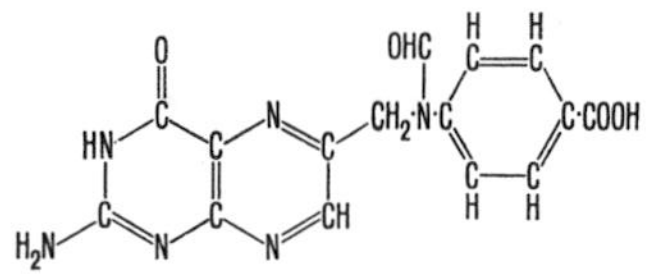	Light-yellow platelets	In fermentation juice of *Rhizopus nigrans*. Weak folic acid activity
Pteroylglutamic acid (folic acid, folacin, vitamin B_c, *p*-[2-amino-4-oxo-dihydropteridyl-(6)]-methylaminobenzoyl-L-glutamic acid)	$C_{19}H_{19}N_7O_6$ 441.41	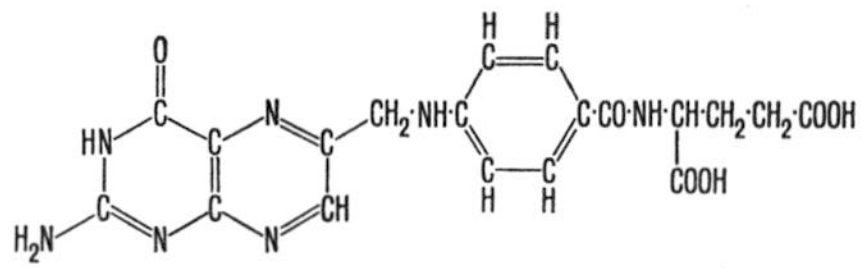	Orange-yellow needles or platelets, odourless and tasteless [α] + 20° in 0.1-N NaOH	In liver, yeast, green leaves. Growth factor for *Lactobacillus casei*, *Streptococcus faecalis R* and other micro-organisms. Anti-anaemic properties
Pteroyltriglutamic acid, $PteGlu_3$ (teropterin)	$C_{29}H_{33}N_9O_{12}$ 699.64	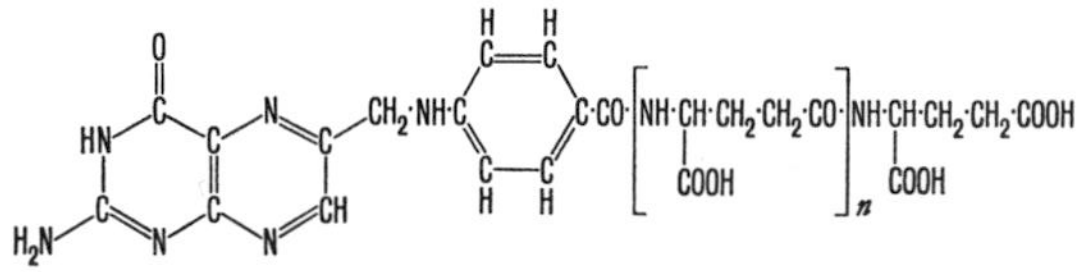 $n = 2$	Light-yellow amorphous powder	In micro-organisms; formed in fermentations induced by coryne-bacteria. Weak folic acid activity
Pteroylheptaglutamic acid, $PteGlu_7$ (vitamin B_c conjugate)	$C_{49}H_{61}N_{13}O_{24}$ 1216.11	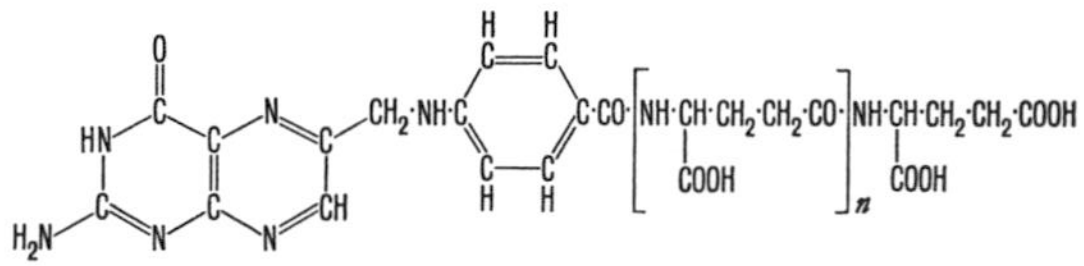 $n = 6$	Orange crystals	In yeast. Microbiologically inactive; presumably the form in which pteroylglutamic acid is stored
Dihydropteroylglutamic acid, $H_2PteGlu$ (dihydrofolic acid, DHF)	$C_{19}H_{21}N_7O_6$ 443.42	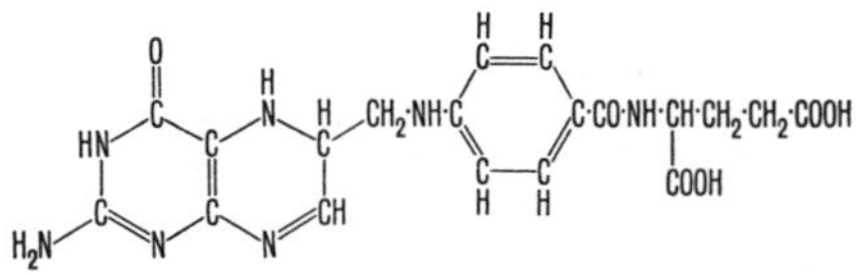	Light-yellow amorphous powder	Intermediary metabolite

Tetrahydropteroylglutamic acid, H_4PteGlu (tetrahydrofolic acid, THF)	$C_{19}H_{23}N_7O_6$ 445.44	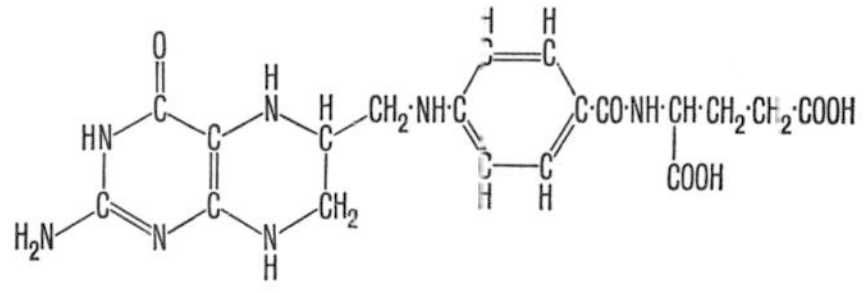	Pale cream-coloured powder, oxidizing in air, unstable to light, particularly in solution (−)-L-Form: $[\alpha]_D^{27}-16.9°$	Active form of folic acid
5-Formyltetrahydropteroylglutamic acid (citrovorum factor, folinic acid, leucovorin)	$C_{20}H_{23}N_7O_7$ 473.45	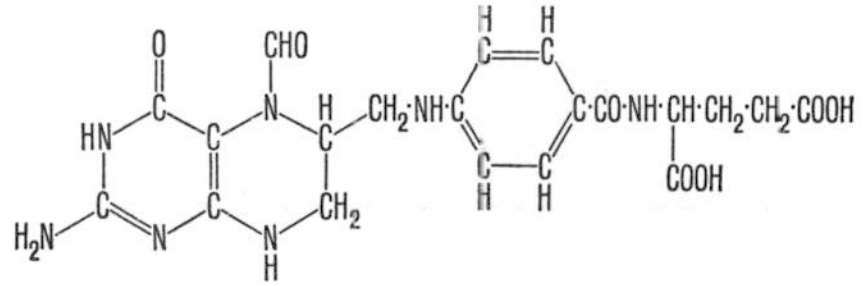	Colourless crystals $[\alpha]_D-15.1°$ (natural factor) $[\alpha]_D^{25}+16.76°$ (racemate, synthetic factor)	In micro-organisms. Growth factor for *Leuconostoc citrovorum*, *Lactobacillus casei*, *Streptococcus faecalis*, *Lactobacillus arabinosus*; carrier of one-carbon units
5,10-Methylenetetrahydropteroylglutamic acid ('active formaldehyde')	$C_{20}H_{23}N_7O_6$ 457.45	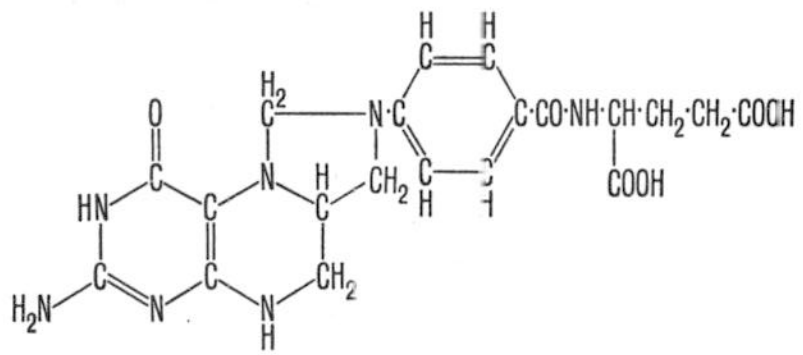	Unstable in acid and neutral media	Carrier of one-carbon units
5-Methyltetrahydropteroylglutamic acid	$C_{20}H_{25}N_7O_6$ 459.47	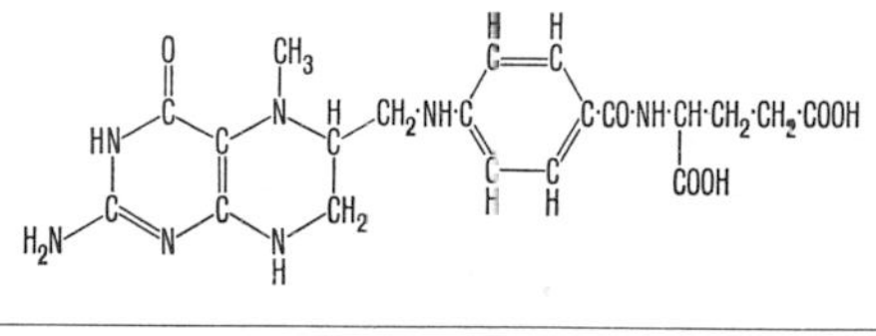		In serum and liver. Carrier of one-carbon units
4-Aminopteroylglutamic acid (aminopterin)	$C_{19}H_{20}N_8O_5$ 440.42	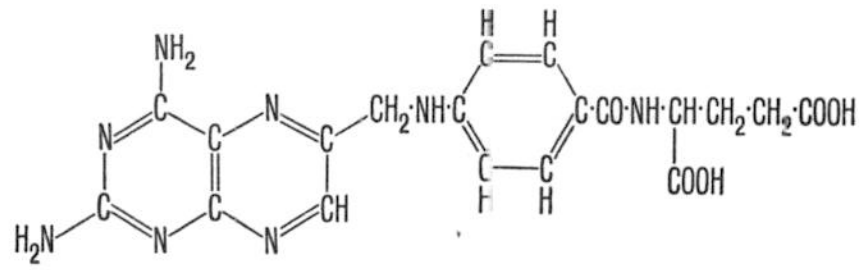	Yellow needles	Antagonist of folic acid; inhibits cell division

* In accordance with the recommendations of the Commission on Biochemical Nomenclature of the IUPAC (IUPAC-IUB Commission on Biochemical Nomenclature [*Biochim. biophys. Acta (Amst.)*, **107**, 11 (1965)] the names 'folic acid' and 'folates' should be used only as general designations for compounds of the group or mixtures of such compounds and not for any compound named on the basis of its structural formula.

8 Goodwin, T. W., *The Biosynthesis of Vitamins and Related Compounds*, Academic Press, New York, 1963, page 100; Brown and Reynolds, *Ann. Rev. Biochem.*, **32**, 419 (1963); Stokstad and Koch, *Physiol. Rev.*, **47**, 83 (1967).
9 Luckey et al., *J. Nutr.*, **55**, 105 (1955), and **57**, 169 (1955).
10 Hitchings and Burchall, *Advanc. Enzymol.*, **27**, 417 (1965).
11 Mangay Chung et al., *Amer. J. clin. Nutr.*, **9**, 573 (1961).
12 Butterworth et al., *J. clin. Invest.*, **42**, 1929 (1963).
13 Herbert, V., *Ann. Rev. Med.*, **16**, 359 (1965).
14 Baker et al., *J. Amer. med. Ass.*, **187**, 119 (1964).
15 Sheehy et al., *J. Lab. clin. Med.*, **61**, 650 (1963).
16 To-day's Drugs, *Brit. med. J.*, **2**, 1248, (1964).
17 Baker et al., *Amer. J. clin. Nutr.*, **14**, 1 (1964).
18 Herbert et al., *J. clin. Invest.*, **41**, 1134 (1962).
19 Herbert, V., *Proc. roy. Soc. Med.*, **57**, 377 (1964).
20 Noronha and Aboobaker, *Arch. Biochem.*, **101**, 445 (1963).
21 Chanarin et al., *Brit. med. J.*, **1**, 396 (1966).
22 McLean and Chanarin, *Blood*, **27**, 386 (1966).
23 Slavík, K., *Wld Rev. Nutr. Diet.*, **3**, 83 (1962); Friedkin, M., *Ann. Rev. Biochem.*, **32**, 185 (1963); Jaenicke, L., *Ann. Rev. Biochem.*, **33**, 287 (1964); Arnstein, H. R. V., *Scand. J. Haemat.*, suppl. *Ser. haemat.*, No. 3, 38 (1965); Stokstad and Koch, *Physiol. Rev.*, **47**, 83 (1967).
24 Food and Nutrition Board, *Recommended Dietary Allowances*, 7th ed., National Academy of Sciences – National Research Council, Publication 1694, Washington, 1968, page 35.
25 Herbert, V., *Arch. intern. Med.*, **110**, 649 (1962).
26 Velez et al., *Amer. J. clin. Nutr.*, **12**, 54 (1963).
27 Sullivan et al., *Amer. J. clin. Nutr.*, **18**, 311 (1966).
28 Alperin et al., *Arch. intern. Med.*, **117**, 681 (1966); Willoughby and Jewell, *Brit. med. J.*, **2**, 1568 (1966).
29 Matoth et al., *Amer. J. clin. Nutr.*, **16**, 356 (1965).
30 Mollin, D. L., *Ann. Rev. Med.*, **11**, 333 (1960); Heller and Venger, *Med. Clin. N. Amer.*, **46**, 121 (1962); Compston and Pitcher, in Baron et al. (Eds.), *Recent Advances in Medicine*, 14th ed., Churchill, London, 1964, page 171; Castle, W. B., *Med. Clin. N. Amer.*, **50**, 1245 (1966).
31 Rachmilewitz, M., *Scand. J. Haemat.*, suppl. *Ser. haemat.*, No. 3, 19 (1965).
32 Herbert, V., *Amer. J. clin. Nutr.*, **12**, 17 (1963).
33 Krehl and Hodges, *Amer. J. clin. Nutr.*, **17**, 191 (1965).
34 Herbert, V., *Med. Clin. N. Amer.*, **46**, 1365 (1962).
35 Davidson and Jandl, *Amer. J. clin. Nutr.*, **7**, 711 (1959).
36 Vilter et al., *Blood*, **5**, 695 (1950).
37 Delmonte and Jukes, *Pharmacol. Rev.*, **14**, 92 (1962).

Vitamin B₁₂ group (corrinoids)[1,2] (for references see page 485)

Chemistry[3]

All the complete B₁₂ vitamins contain an α-glycosidic nucleotide. The imidazole nitrogen atom of this nucleotide can become co-ordinated under suitable conditions with the cobalt atom. In the case of the incomplete types either the alkanolamine and nucleotide portion, or simply the latter, is lacking; in some cases the nucleotide portion is β-glycosidic, when the imidazole nitrogen atom cannot become co-ordinated with the cobalt atom. The B₁₂ coenzymes correspond to the complete B₁₂ types but in place of the inorganic group they possess an organic group linked directly via a carbon atom to the cobalt atom. The complete and incomplete B₁₂ types fairly stable to light and oxygen are presumably artefacts of the B₁₂ coenzymes.

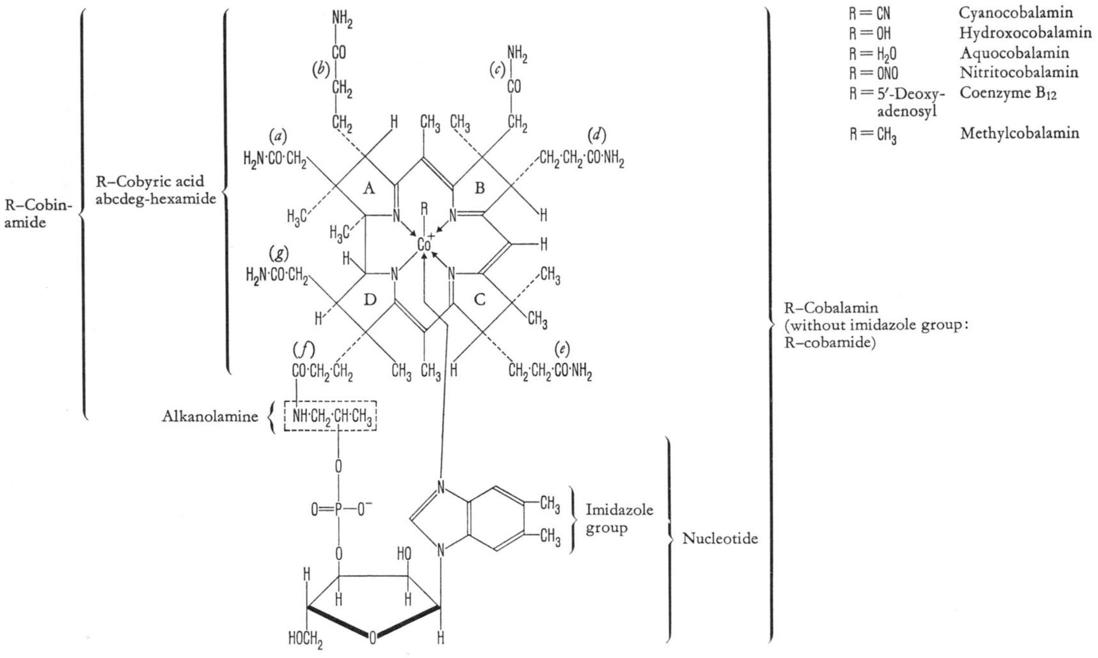

Names*	Formula and mol. wt.	Physical properties	Occurrence and biological properties
		Complete B₁₂ types	
Vitamin B₁₂ (cyanocobalamin, 5,6-dimethylbenzimidazolylcyanocobamide)	$C_{63}H_{88}N_{14}O_{14}PCo$ 1355.40	Red needles, stable on heating several hours at 100 °C. Spectral absorption in water: maxima at 278, 361, 550 nm	Occurs in nature as coenzyme. Can be isolated from animal tissues, many species of bacteria, sewage sludge, activated sludge. Stimulates maturation of erythrocytes in bone marrow; acts as *animal protein factor* in animals; promotes growth of many micro-organisms

* Trivial names recommended by the Commission on Biochemical Nomenclature of the International Union of Pure and Applied Chemistry and the International Union of Biochemistry [*Biochim. biophys. Acta (Amst.)*, **117**, 285 (1966)].

(For references see page 485)

Names*	Formula and mol. wt.	Physical properties	Occurrence and biological properties
Aquocobalamin (vitamin B_{12b}, 5,6-dimethylbenzimidazolylaquocobamide) Hydroxocobalamin (vitamin B_{12a}, 5,6-dimethylbenzimidazolylhydroxocobamide)	$C_{62}H_{90}N_{13}O_{15}PCo$ 1347.39	Red needles, aquo form in neutral solution, hydroxo form in alkaline solution Spectral absorption in water: maxima at 274, 350, 522 nm	Activity as for cyanocobalamin; depot form in the human body
5-Methylbenzimidazolylcyanocobamide		Red needles	In sewage sludge and activated sludge. Represents two-thirds of the cyanocobalamin activity in pernicious anaemia
Benzimidazolylcyanocobamide		Red needles	In sewage sludge and activated sludge. Represents two-thirds of the cyanocobalamin activity in pernicious anaemia
5-Hydroxybenzimidazolylcyanocobamide (Factor III)		Red needles	Inactivated sludge; weakly active in pernicious anaemia
Pseudovitamin B_{12} (adeninecyanocobamide)		Red needles	Inactivated sludge, faeces, stomach contents of ruminants; inactive in pernicious anaemia
2-Methyladeninecyanocobamide (Factor A)		Red needles	Inactivated sludge, faeces, stomach contents of ruminants; very weakly active in pernicious anaemia
		Incomplete B_{12} types	
Aetiocobalamin (Factor B, cyanocobinamide)		Amorphous	Inactivated sludge, faeces, stomach contents of ruminants; antagonist of cayanocobalamin in the chick test
		B_{12} coenzymes	
5′-Deoxyadenosylcobalamin (coenzyme B_{12})		Orange-yellow platelets, photosensitive	In many species of bacteria, in animal tissues (mainly liver). Biochemically active form of vitamin B_{12}. Growth promoting-activity for micro-organisms and chicks; activity in pernicious anaemia as for cyanocobalamin; depot action in the human body
Methylcobalamin		Orange-yellow platelets, photosensitive	In animal tissues (liver), blood serum. Coenzyme function

* Trivial names recommended by the Commission on Biochemical Nomenclature of the International Union of Pure and Applied Chemistry and the International Union of Biochemistry [*Biochim. biophys. Acta (Amst.)*, **117**, 285 (1966)].

Assay

Microbiological[1, 4]. With bacteria: *Escherichia coli* (cobalamins, cobamide pseudo-vitamin B_{12}), *Lactobacillus leichmannii* (cobalamins, pseudo-vitamin B_{12}). With protozoa: *Euglena gracilis* (cobalamins, pseudo-vitamin B_{12}), *Ochromonas malhamensis* (cobalamins only).

Chemical[5]. Spectrophotometrically or polarographically in pure solution; separation of the individual compounds by countercurrent diffusion, column chromatography or ion exchange.

Isotopic dilution method. Tagging of vitamin B_{12} with ^{57}Co, ^{58}Co or ^{60}Co.

Unit

No international unit; by weight. 1 μg vitamin B_{12} = 11000 LLD (*Lactobacillus lactis* DORNER) Units = 1 USP Unit (liver extract). 1 USP Unit is the daily dose that produces a clinically and haematologically satisfactory response in true pernicious anaemia. From the standpoint of activity, 1000 LLD Units corresponds roughly to 1 ml of a good liver extract.

For International Reference Preparation see page 763.

Biogenesis[6, 7]

Vitamin B_{12} is synthesized by many species of bacteria, in particular the propionibacteria and *Aerobacter aerogenes*. It is possibly also formed in animal tissues[8].

The biosynthesis is in accordance roughly with the following scheme:

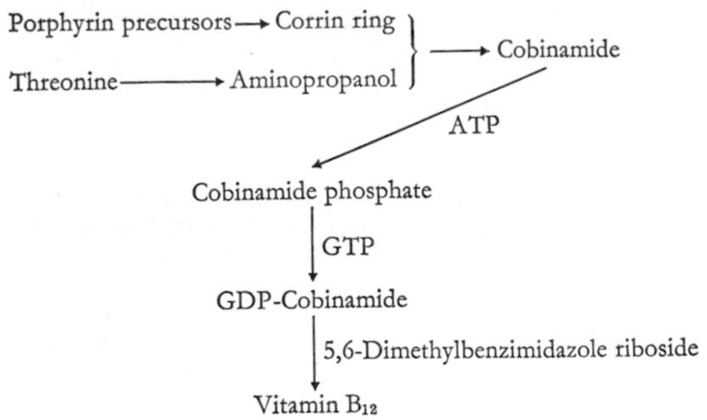

This process results in formation of the coenzyme forms of the vitamin; cyanocobalamin and hydroxocobalamin are probably only artefacts[9]; they can, however, be converted in animal tissues into the coenzymes:

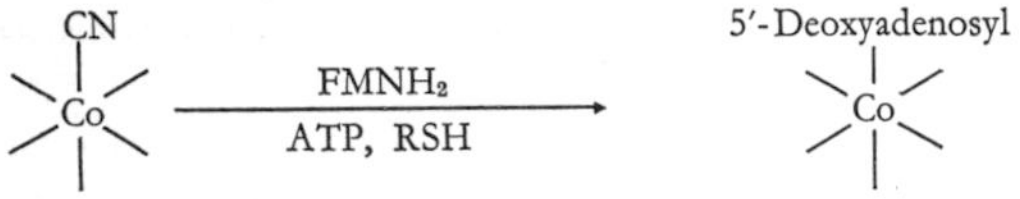

Intake and excretion

In the USA the average daily diet contains 15–30 µg vitamin B_{12}[10], of which perhaps 5 µg is absorbed. According to HEINRICH and WOLFSTELLER[12], of any dose of vitamin B_{12}, 1.5 µg is absorbed in the ileum with the aid of the so-called *intrinsic factor*, a mucoprotein of the gastric juice[11]; transport through the intestinal wall probably takes place together with the intrinsic factor[13]. In addition, there is passive diffusion through the intestinal wall[14] to an extent that increases logarithmically with increasing size of the dose up to a limiting value of 0.9% of the dose[12]. On a normal diet and three meals a day this means that 2–5 µg or more of vitamin B_{12} is absorbed daily[15] (see the figure below). Cyanocobalamin is rather more easily absorbed than coenzyme B_{12}[16]. Some 10–15 µg vitamin B_{12} is synthesized daily by bacteria in the human large intestine, and about the same quantity is excreted daily in the faeces; whether any of the quantity formed by bacterial synthesis is absorbed is doubtful[17].

The vitamin B_{12} content of the serum lies in the range 100–900 ng/l (see page 610); here the vitamin is mainly present as methylcobalamin, about 80% being bound to α-globulins (transcobalamin I). Exogenous vitamin B_{12} becomes bound for a short time to β-globulin (transcobalamin II)[18]. The half-life of intravenously administered cyanocobalamin in the serum is about 6 days[19]. Small doses of a few microgrammes of vitamin B_{12} are retained in the body but doses of a few milligrammes are rapidly excreted in the urine. Hydroxocobalamin given parenterally is retained in the body longer than cyanocobalamin or coenzyme B_{12}[16]. In the tissues the vitamin is probably stored as the coenzyme. The total body stores of the vitamin have been estimated at 2–5 mg (range 1–11 mg)[1,12,15]. The liver contains about 0.8 mg vitamin B_{12}[20] (the biological half-life of the vitamin in the liver is about 12 months[19]). 0.1% of the body's stores of vitamin B_{12} is excreted daily[15]. These stores probably suffice to prevent the appearance of clinical deficiency symptoms for 3–8 years[1,15]. Excretion of the vitamin is almost solely in the bile (see page 655), only very small amounts being found in the urine (0–0.27 µg per day)[1]. On SCHILLING's excretion test see pages 289 and 485.

Distribution of the total intestinal vitamin B_{12} absorption in healthy persons between absorption dependent on the intrinsic factor and absorption dependent on diffusion[12]

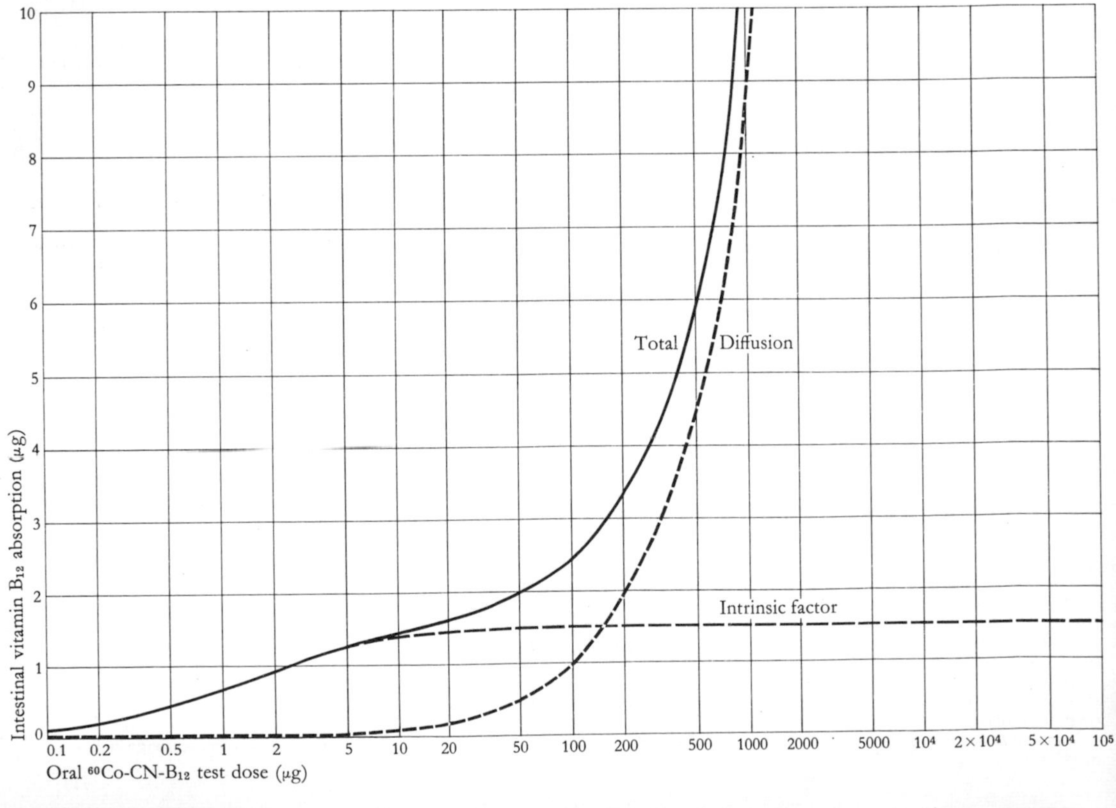

Function[7, 21]

Vitamin B$_{12}$ acts as coenzyme in various biological reactions:

Enzyme (reaction catalysed in brackets)	Coenzyme	Occurrence
Methylaspartate mutase (glutamic acid ⇌ β-methylaspartic acid)	5′-Deoxyadenosyl-cobalamin	Bacteria
Methylmalonyl-CoA-mutase (methylmalonyl-CoA ⇌ succinyl-CoA)	5′-Deoxyadenosyl-cobalamin	Bacteria, animal tissues
Glycol dehydrogenase (ethyleneglycol ⇌ acetaldehyde, 1,2-propane-diol ⇌ propionaldehyde)	5′-Deoxyadenosyl-cobalamin	Bacteria
5-Methyltetrahydrofolate homocysteine trans-methylase (Methionine formation)	Methylcobalamin (protein complex) as intermediate product	Bacteria, animal tissues
Ribonucleotide reductase (DNA formation)	5′-Deoxyadenosyl-cobalamin	Bacteria, animal tissues
(Thiol oxidation)	Unknown	Bacteria, animal tissues

Inside the cell, vitamin B$_{12}$ is located in the mitochondria[22] and is involved in a manner still largely unknown in protein and probably also lipid and carbohydrate metabolism. The role played by the vitamin in the formation of methionine is probably important in the regeneration of tetrahydrofolic acid (see page 437). Vitamin B$_{12}$ plays a very important part in haemopoiesis (stimulation of the reticulocytes) in that together with folic acid it is involved directly or indirectly in the formation of deoxyribonucleotides from ribonucleotides. The significance of the vitamin in normal reproduction is obscure (more is known of this role in animals than in man[23]), as is the part it plays in the maturation of the spermatozoa[24] and in growth[25].

Requirements

The daily requirement in adults appears to be amply covered by the absorption of 0.6–1.5 µg[15], but a desirable daily absorption level is 5 µg[26] (see page 494). In pregnant women the requirement may be higher since the mother's reserves are largely exhausted by the needs of the foetus; the Food and Nutrition Board (USA)[26] accordingly recommend a daily intake of 8 µg (see page 494).

The best sources of vitamin B$_{12}$ (in decreasing order of importance) are liver, kidneys, meat and milk; only small quantities are present in plants (see pages 499–515). Cooking destroys not more than 30% of the vitamin[15].

Deficiency[27]

Vitamin B$_{12}$ deficiency may arise from the following causes:

(a) Inadequate dietary intake (strict vegetarians)

(b) Absence or inadequacy of intrinsic factor secretion (pernicious anaemia, gastrectomy, gastroenterostomy; presence in the gastric juice of antibodies to the intrinsic factor[28])

(c) Inadequate ileal absorption (malabsorption syndrome, ileitis, tuberculosis, ileal resection)

(d) Interference with absorption by bacteria (intestinal congestion in blind loops, diverticulosis of the small intestine) or by the fish tapeworm.

The following are the deficiency symptoms: macrocytic anaemia, megaloblastosis of the bone marrow, leucopenia, thrombocytopenia, glossitis, morphological changes in the gastrointestinal tract and (in contrast to folic acid deficiency) progressive degeneration of the axis cylinders of the spinal-cord neurones. In adults, the cause of the pernicious anaemia is possibly immunological processes (the serum of many patients contains antibodies to the intrinsic factor) leading to atrophy of the gastric mucosa. Whereas in adults with pernicious anaemia there is absence of acid secretion in the stomach, in children secretion of the intrinsic factor itself may be absent – probably as a genetic defect – but acid secretion normal[29].

Biochemical deficiency symptoms of use in diagnosis are the lowered vitamin B$_{12}$ content of the serum (see page 610) and liver and the very much increased excretion of methylmalonic acid in the urine[30]. The amount of vitamin B$_{12}$ absorbed from the diet can be estimated by measurement of the total faecal excretion over a period of 5 or more days, of the excretion in a single faecal sample using a double isotope technique with a nonabsorbable marker, of the hepatic uptake of radioactivity, of the urinary excretion after a flushing dose of untagged vitamin B$_{12}$, or of the whole-body retention of radioactivity. In malabsorption the test is repeated with intrinsic factor to see if this improves absorption; alternatively vitamin B$_{12}$ and vitamin B$_{12}$ intrinsic factor tagged with two different cobalt isotopes can be given simultaneously[31]. SCHILLING's test (0.5 µg tagged vitamin B$_{12}$ orally followed one hour later by 1000 µg untagged vitamin B$_{12}$ intramuscularly) gives the following values[32]: normal 8–34%, in pernicious anaemia 0–3.5% of the radioactivity in the 24-hour urine.

Treatment

The blood picture in pernicious anaemia shows an improvement with parenteral doses of as little as 0.1 µg vitamin B$_{12}$ per day[33]; doses of 0.5–2.0 µg per day result in complete remission of the symptoms[34]. The body's reserves can be restored within 10 days by giving 5 doses each of 1000 µg subcutaneously. The usual maintenance dose is 100–400 µg parenterally once a month or 1000 µg orally twice a week[35]. Oral treatment with vitamin B$_{12}$ plus intrinsic factor is not recommended since the body eventually develops resistance. Oral treatment with a vitamin B$_{12}$-peptide complex has been suggested[36].

References

1 GRÄSBECK, R., *Advanc. clin. Chem.*, **3**, 299 (1960).
2 SEBRELL and HARRIS (Eds.), *The Vitamins*, vol. 1, Academic Press, New York, 1954, page 395; CHOW, B. F., in BEATON and MCHENRY (Eds.), *Nutrition*, vol. 2, Academic Press, New York, 1964, page 207; VILTER, R. W., in WOHL and GOODHART (Eds.), *Modern Nutrition in Health and Disease*, 3rd ed., Lea & Febiger, Philadelphia, 1964, page 421; SMITH, E. L., *Vitamin B$_{12}$*, 3rd ed., Methuen, London, 1965.
3 FRIEDRICH, W., in RAUEN, H. M. (Ed.), *Biochemisches Taschenbuch*, 2nd ed., part 1, Springer, Berlin, 1964, page 708.
4 BAKER and SOBOTKA, *Advanc. clin. Chem.*, **5**, 173 (1962).
5 GSTIRNER, F., *Chemisch-physikalische Vitaminbestimmungsmethoden*, 5th ed., Enke, Stuttgart, 1965, page 162.
6 GOODWIN, T. W., *The Biosynthesis of Vitamins and Related Compounds*, Academic Press, New York, 1963, page 167; BROWN and REYNOLDS, *Ann. Rev. Biochem.*, **32**, 419 (1963); BERNHAUER et al., *Advanc. Enzymol.*, **26**, 233 (1964).
7 JAENICKE, L., *Ann. Rev. Biochem.*, **33**, 287 (1964); WAGNER, F., *Ann. Rev. Biochem.*, **35**, 405 (1966).
8 BRADY and NEWTON, *Experientia (Basel)*, **19**, 398 (1963).
9 ROSENBLUM, C., *Scand. J. Haemat.*, suppl. *Ser. haemat.*, No. 3, 48 (1965).
10 MANGAY CHUNG et al., *Amer. J. clin. Nutr.*, **9**, 573 (1961).
11 GLASS, G. B. J., *Physiol. Rev.*, **43**, 529 (1963); ELLENBOGEN and HIGHLEY, *Vitam. and Horm.*, **21**, 1 (1963); HERBERT and CASTLE, *New Engl. J. Med.*, **270**, 1181 (1964); GLASS, G. B. J., *Scand. J. Haemat.*, suppl. *Ser. haemat.*, No. 3, 61 (1965).
12 HEINRICH and WOLFSTELLER, *Med. Klin.*, **61**, 756 (1966).
13 WILSON, T. H., *Nutr. Rev.*, **23**, 33 (1965).
14 HERBERT et al., *Medicine (Baltimore)*, **43**, 679 (1964).
15 HEYSSEL et al., *Amer. J. clin. Nutr.*, **18**, 176 (1966).
16 HERBERT and SULLIVAN, *Ann. N. Y. Acad. Sci.*, **112**, 855 (1964); HEINRICH and GABBE, *Ann. N. Y. Acad. Sci.*, **112**, 871 (1964).
17 MERZBACH and GROSSOWICZ, *J. Nutr.*, **87**, 41 (1965).
18 HALL and FINKLER, *J. Lab. clin. Med.*, **65**, 459 (1965).
19 ADAMS, J. F., *Nature*, **198**, 200 (1963).
20 BAKER et al., *Amer. J. clin. Nutr.*, **14**, 1 (1964).
21 WEISSBACH and DICKERMAN, *Physiol. Rev.*, **45**, 80 (1965); ARNSTEIN, H. R. V., *Scand. J. Haemat.*, suppl. *Ser. haemat.*, No. 3, 38 (1965).
22 SWEENSEID et al., *J. biol. Chem.*, **190**, 791 (1951).
23 FOX and CHOW, *Wld Rev. Nutr. Diet.*, **1**, 125 (1959).
24 WATSON, A. A., *Lancet*, **2**, 644 (1962); SHARP and WITTS, *Lancet*, **2**, 779 (1962).
25 Editorial, *Brit. med. J.*, **1**, 853 (1962).
26 Food and Nutrition Board, *Recommended Dietary Allowances*, 7th ed., National Academy of Sciences – National Research Council, Publication 1694, Washington, 1968, page 47.
27 ESTREN et al., *Advanc. intern. Med.*, **9**, 11 (1958); MOLLIN, D. L., *Ann. Rev. Med.*, **11**, 333 (1960); HELLER and VENGER, *Med. Clin. N. Amer.*, **46**, 121 (1962); COMPSTON and PITCHER, in BARON et al. (Eds.), *Recent Advances in Medicine*, 14th ed., Churchill, London, 1964, page 171; CASTLE, W. B., *Med. Clin. N. Amer.*, **50**, 1245 (1966); BAKER, S. J., *Wld Rev. Nutr. Diet.*, **8**, 62 (1967).
28 SCHADE et al., *New Engl. J. Med.*, **275**, 528 (1966).
29 MCINTYRE et al., *New Engl. J. Med.*, **272**, 981 (1965).
30 WHITE and COX, *Ann. N. Y. Acad. Sci.*, **112**, 915 (1964).
31 KATZ et al., *J. Lab. clin. Med.*, **61**, 266 (1963).
32 FRICK and BRUNNER, *Helv. med. Acta*, **31**, 345 (1964).
33 SULLIVAN and HERBERT, *New Engl. J. Med.*, **272**, 340 (1965).
34 DARBY et al., *Amer. J. Med.*, **25**, 726 (1958).
35 MCKENNA and ERSLEV, *Med. Clin. N. Amer.*, **49**, 1371 (1965).
36 Editorial, *Brit. med. J.*, **1**, 1559 (1963).

Biotin[1]

Chemistry

For structure and properties of biotin and related compounds see the table below.

Assay

Biological[3]. With *Saccharomyces cerevisiae*, *Lactobacillus casei*, *Lactobacillus arabinosus*, *Neurospora crassa*, etc.; in biological fluids preferably with *Ochromonas danica*.

Chemical. No methods in common use.

Unit

No international unit; by weight. 1 avidine unit = the smallest quantity that completely suppresses the growth-promoting effect in yeast of 1 μg biotin[4].

Biogenesis[2, 5]

Biotin is synthesized in plants (particularly in sprouting seeds) and various micro-organisms. Thus *Achromobacter* forms biotin from pimelyl-coenzyme A, cysteine and carbamyl phosphate; pimelyl-coenzyme A is formed from 3 molecules of malonyl-coenzyme A[6]. The carboxyl group of biotin is covalent and bound to the lysine residue of a protein. Biocytin is formed by the action of a proteinase on protein-bound biotin.

Intake and excretion

Biotin is formed by the intestinal flora in such large quantities that it is excreted in the faeces in an amount 2–5 times greater than the dietary intake[7]. The body appears to be capable of utilizing biotin formed in the intestine but to an unknown extent. The avidine present in raw egg-albumin combines with biotin, thus rendering it useless for the organism.

Biotin has been detected in whole blood and serum (see page 611) and in urine (see page 676). Small quantities are stored in the liver (about 0.2 mg) and in the brain[3, 8] (blood vessels 3–5 ng/g[9]). In the liver, biotin is mostly bound to protein (in rats 90%[5]). Little is known of the metabolism of biotin. In rats given injections of biotin 16% was found 4 hours later in the liver and 30% was excreted[5].

Function[5]

Biotin is essential for warm-blooded animals and some micro-organisms. It acts as coenzyme in CO_2-fixation and transcarboxylation reactions.

Structure and properties of biotin and related compounds

Names	Formula and mol. wt.	Structure	Physical properties	Occurrence	Activity
Biotin, *d*-biotin	$C_{10}H_{16}N_2O_3S$ 244.31	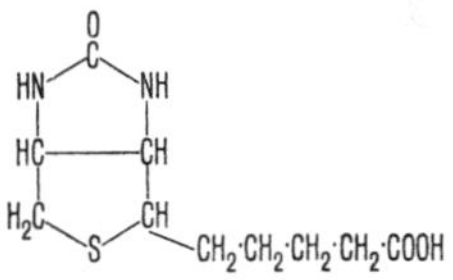	White needles, stable to heat, unstable to acids and alkalis M.p. 230–232 °C $[\alpha]_D^{26}+91°$ in 0.1-N NaOH	Various micro-organisms, for example yeasts, animal tissues, particularly liver, egg-yolk, plants	Growth factor for many bacteria, protozoa and probably all higher animals
Biocytin, *d*-biocytin (ε-*N*-biotinyl-L-lysine)	$C_{16}H_{28}N_4O_4S$ 372.49	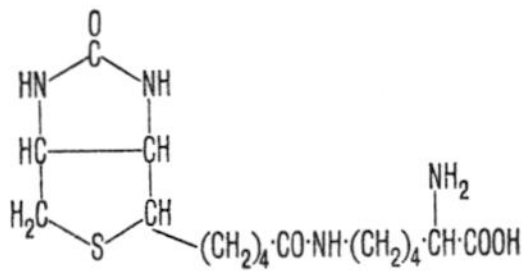	M.p. 245–252 °C	Yeasts	Growth factor for various micro-organisms
Biotin sulphoxide, *d*-biotin 1-sulphoxide (AN factor)	$C_{10}H_{16}N_2O_4S$ 260.31	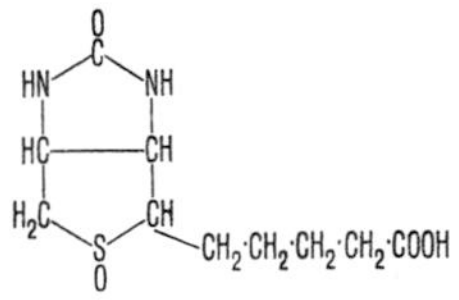		Cultures of *Aspergillus niger* and *Phycomyces blakesleeanus*	Growth factor for *Neurospora crassa*
Oxybiotin (oxobiotin)	$C_{10}H_{16}N_2O_4$ 228.25	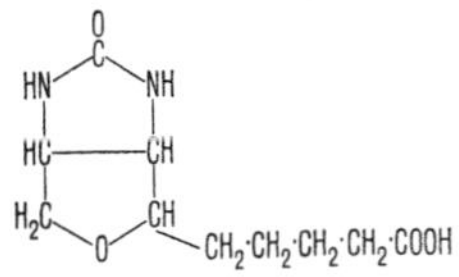	M.p. 205–207 °C		5–30% of activity of biotin[2]
1'-*N*-Carboxy-biotin (CO_2-biotin)	$C_{11}H_{16}N_2O_5S$ 288.33	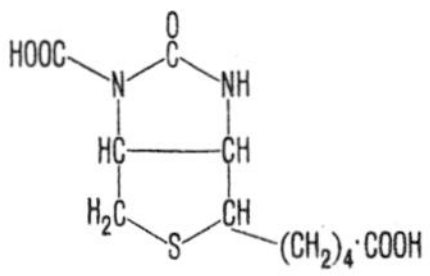		Unstable intermediate	Active form of CO_2 in carboxylations

Biotin enzymes

Enzyme	Reaction catalysed	Occurrence
Acetyl-CoA-carboxylase	acetyl-CoA + HCO_3^- + ATP ⇌ malonyl-CoA + ADP + P	Micro-organisms, chicken liver
β-Methylcrotonyl-CoA-carboxylase	β-methylcrotonyl-CoA + HCO_3^- + ATP ⇌ β-methylglutaconyl-CoA + ADP + P	Micro-organisms, rat liver mitochondria
Propionyl-CoA-carboxylase	propionyl-CoA + HCO_3^- + ATP ⇌ methylmalonyl-CoA + ADP + P	Swine heart, ox liver mitochondria
Methylmalonyl-CoA-carboxyl-transferase	methylmalonyl-CoA + pyruvate ⇌ propionyl-CoA + oxalacetate	Propionibacteria, skeletal muscle of dogs
Pyruvate carboxylase	pyruvate + HCO_3^- + ATP ⇌ oxalacetate + ADP + P	Micro-organisms, liver mitochondria, rabbit kidneys

The carboxylation reactions catalysed by the biotin enzymes have the general form

$$\text{Biotin enzyme} + CO_2 + \text{ATP} \xrightleftharpoons{Mg^{++}} CO_2\text{-biotin enzyme} + \text{ADP} + \text{P}$$

$$CO_2\text{-biotin enzyme} + X \rightleftharpoons \text{Biotin enzyme} + CO_2\text{-}X$$

(where X is for example β-methylcrotonyl-CoA) via a CO_2-biotin enzyme compound in which the CO_2 is linked to biotin (see 1′-*N*-carboxybiotin in the table opposite)[10]. In the carboxylation of acetyl-coenzyme A, on the other hand, the carbamide carbon atom of the biotin itself represents the active CO_2[11]; a compound known as 'diaminobiotin' is here assumed to arise as intermediate product.

The carboxylation of acetylcoenzyme A is an important starting point in the biosynthesis of fatty acids (see page 424). Biotin plays an important role in many other reactions in which, however, it acts only in an indirect manner. Examples of such reactions are the deamination of aspartate, serine and threonine in bacteria, deamination of serine in animals, reductive carboxylation of pyruvate, carboxylation of phosphoenol pyruvate, carbamylation reactions, tryptophan metabolism, purine synthesis, protein synthesis and carbohydrate metabolism.

Certain biotin homologues (homo-oxybiotin; biotinsulphone, in which the sulphur atom is replaced by a sulphone group) act as antivitamins[12].

Requirements and deficiency symptoms

The biotin requirement of man is unknown. In experimental biotin deficiency, doses of 150–300 μg per day sufficed to suppress the deficiency symptoms[13,14]; this amount is provided by a normal diet[15].

Substances rich in biotin are liver, kidneys, yeast and egg-yolk; the vitamin is also present in vegetables, nuts and cereals (see pages 498–515).

Biotin deficiency is manifested[16] in nervous disturbances (rats, pigs, chickens, man), hyperkeratosis (rats), seborrhoeic dermatitis (man), loss of hair (rats, mice), loss of hair pigment (rats, mice). Experimental biotin deficiency in man results in lethargy, loss of appetite, nausea, muscular pain and localized paraesthesia[14]. Spontaneous biotin deficiency has been reported following a diet rich in raw eggs[17,18] and also appears to be associated with liver cirrhosis[18].

Treatment

Biotin has been used to treat seborrhoeic dermatitis in young children (LEINER's disease)[19], which is possibly due to a deficiency of biotin in the breast milk together with loss of the vitamin due to persistent diarrhoea.

References

1 SEBRELL and HARRIS (Eds.), *The Vitamins*, vol. 1, Academic Press, New York, 1954, page 525; CHOW, B.F., in BEATON and MCHENRY (Eds.), *Nutrition*, vol. 2, Academic Press, New York, 1964, page 207; GOODHART, R.S., in WOHL and GOODHART (Eds.), *Modern Nutrition in Health and Disease*, 3rd ed., Lea & Febiger, Philadelphia, 1964, page 458.

2 GOODWIN, T.W., *The Biosynthesis of Vitamins and Related Compounds*, Academic Press, New York, 1963, page 145.

3 BAKER and SOBOTKA, *Advanc. clin. Chem.*, **5**, 173 (1962).

4 DHYSE, F.G., *Proc. Soc. exp. Biol. (N.Y.)*, **85**, 515 (1954).

5 MISTRY and DAKSHINAMURTI, *Vitam. and Horm.*, **22**, 1 (1964).

6 LEZIUS et al., *Biochem. Z.*, **336**, 510 (1963).

7 OPPEL, T.W., *Amer. J. med. Sci.*, **204**, 856 (1942).

8 BAKER et al., *Amer. J. clin. Nutr.*, **14**, 1 (1964).

9 KIRK and SANWALD, *J. Lab. clin. Med.*, **66**, 885 (1965).

10 LYNEN et al., in DE REUCK and O'CONNOR (Eds.), *The Mechanism of Action of Water-soluble Vitamins*, Ciba Foundation Study Group, No. 11, Churchill, London, 1961, page 80; KNAPPE et al., *Angew. Chem.*, **74**, 432 (1962).

11 WAITE and WAKIL, *J. biol. Chem.*, **238**, 81 (1963).

12 DORNOW and PETSCH, *Arzneimittel-Forsch.*, **5**, 536 (1955).

13 SYDENSTRICKER et al., *Science*, **95**, 176 (1942).

14 SYDENSTRICKER et al., *J. Amer. med. Ass.*, **118**, 1199 (1942).

15 Food and Nutrition Board, *Recommended Dietary Allowances*, 7th ed., National Academy of Sciences – National Research Council, Publication 1694, Washington, 1968, page 33.

16 TERROINE, T., *Vitam. and Horm.*, **18**, 1 (1960).

17 WILLIAMS, R.H., *New Engl. J. Med.*, **228**, 247 (1943).

18 BUTTERWORTH et al., *Amer. J. clin. Nutr.*, **20**, 364 (1967).

19 GAUTIER et al., *Int. Z. Vitaminforsch.*, **28**, 61 (1957); NISENSON, A., *J. Pediat.*, **51**, 537 (1957).

Pantothenic acid[1] (for references see page 489)

Chemistry

For structure and properties of pantothenic acid and related compounds see the table on page 488.

Assay

Biological. Growth test on chicks; microbiologically[3] with *Lactobacillus casei* or *L. plantarum* (*L. arabinosus*).

Chemical[4]. After hydrolysis by colorimetric determination of the β-alanine.

Unit

No international unit; by weight. 1 LIPMANN unit of coenzyme A = 2.4 μg of the pure compound (corresponding to 0.7 μg pantothenic acid)[5].

Biogenesis[6]

Pantothenic acid is formed by bacteria (e.g., *Escherichia coli*, *Bacterium linens*) from α-ketoisovaleric acid by addition of a one-carbon unit. The formation of pantothenic acid from pantoic acid and β-alanine is mediated by ATP (for instance in *Escherichia coli* and *Brucella abortus*) as follows:

$$\alpha\text{-Ketoisovaleric acid} \xrightarrow{HCHO} \alpha\text{-Ketopantoic acid} \xrightarrow{+2\,H} \text{Pantoic acid}$$

$$\text{Pantoic acid} + \beta\text{-Alanine} + \text{ATP} \rightarrow \text{Pantothenic acid} + \text{Pyrophosphate}$$

In animal tissues no pantothenic acid is formed; the vitamin is, however, incorporated in coenzyme A in both micro-organisms and animal tissues (for instance liver):

$$\text{Pantothenic acid} \xrightarrow{ATP} \text{4'-Phosphopantothenic acid}$$

$$\downarrow \text{ATP, Cysteine}$$

$$\text{4'-Phosphopantothenylcysteine}$$

$$\downarrow -CO_2$$

$$\text{Pantethein} \longleftrightarrow \text{4'-Phosphopantethein}$$

$$\downarrow \text{ATP}$$

$$\text{Dephospho-CoA}$$

$$\downarrow \text{ATP}$$

$$\text{CoA}$$

Intake and excretion

A 2500 kcal diet contains about 4–12 mg of free and 9–20 mg total pantothenic acid[7]. The vitamin is also synthesized in the human

Structure and properties of pantothenic acid and related compounds

Compound	Formula and mol. wt.	Structure	Physical properties	Occurrence and activity
Pantothenic acid (D-[+]-*N*-[α,γ-dihydroxy-ββ-dimethylbutyryl]-β-alanine, chick antidermatitis factor)	$C_9H_{17}NO_5$ 219.24	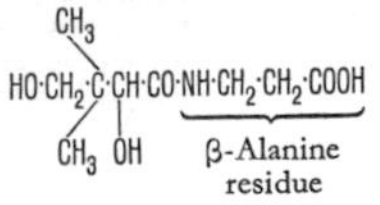	Yellow oil, unstable to heat, acids and alkalis $[\alpha]_D^{25}$ +37.5° Calcium salt: white crystals, stable to heat	Widely distributed in plants and animals. Growth factor for yeasts, many other micro-organisms and all higher animals; component of coenzyme A
Pantothenyl alcohol (panthenol, *N*-pantoyl-3-propanolamine)	$C_9H_{19}NO_4$ 205.26	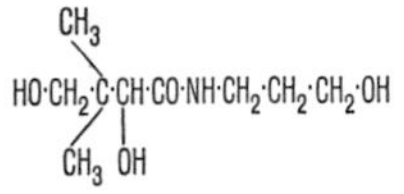	Viscous liquid $[\alpha]_D^{20}$ +29.5°	Synthetic. Shows 86% of activity of pantothenic acid in the chick test[2]
Pantethein (*N*-pantothenyl-β-aminoethanethiol)	$C_{11}H_{22}N_2O_4S$ 278.37	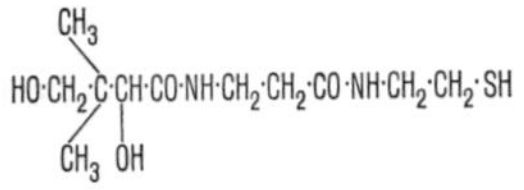	Amorphous powder soluble in water	Growth factor for *Lactobacillus bulgaricus*
Coenzyme A (CoA)	$C_{21}H_{36}N_7O_{16}P_3S$ 767.54	See page 345	Colourless powder soluble in water	Widely distributed in micro-organisms, plants and animals. See also text and page 345

intestine, though it is not known whether the body makes use of this source. The pantothenic acid content of whole blood is ca. 0.2–2 mg/l (see page 611), that of the spinal fluid about the same (see page 639). Urinary excretion of the vitamin amounts to 0.76–4.1 mg/l[3] (see also page 676). Four hours after giving a test dose of the vitamin there is a sharp rise in the blood and urine levels[8]. In blood and spinal fluid pantothenic acid is in the conjugated form, whereas in the urine it is in the free form[3]. The excretion in the faeces is very variable and depends on the nature of the diet.

Coenzyme A is not present in the circulating blood and appears to pass the cell membrane only with difficulty. It is probably formed within the cell when required. Coenzyme A occurs mainly in the following organs (in order of decreasing concentration): liver, adrenals, kidneys, brain, heart, testes. The pantothenic acid content of the human liver amounts to 28 mg, mainly as coenzyme A[9].

Function

The importance of pantothenic acid in metabolism is explained by its presence in coenzyme A. In the form of acetyl-coenzyme A ('active acetic acid') it is responsible for transport of two-carbon and other acyl groups (see page 345). Coenzyme A is involved in the following reactions: formation of citrate from oxalacetate and acetate (pages 390 and 424), oxidation of pyruvate (page 391), oxidation of α-ketoglutarate (page 390), oxidation and synthesis of fatty acids (pages 391 and 424), synthesis of triglycerides (page 426), phospholipids (page 425) and cholesterol (page 426), acetylation of amines (page 444), choline (page 434) and glucosamine (see page 424). Pantothenic acid plays an important part in the activity of the adrenal cortex[10] since the corticosteroids are formed from the cholesterol synthesized with the participation of coenzyme A (page 429).

Requirements and deficiency symptoms

The human pantothenic acid requirement is unknown, but in children and adults it is probably met by an intake of 5–10 mg per day[11], an amount normally present in the diet. The requirements of children are lower in accordance with their smaller intake of calories[12].

Pantothenic acid is present in almost all vegetables, cereals and animal foods. Good sources of the vitamin are yeast, liver, kidneys, heart (see pages 499–515) and particularly the jelly queen bees are fed on (royal jelly), containing 110–320 μg/g[13].

Pantothenic acid is so widely distributed in foods that deficiency is practically unknown in man. Deficiency symptoms in animals are degeneration of the neuromuscular structures and adrenal insufficiency, and death may ensue. An experimental deficiency has been produced in man by means of a diet low in the vitamin together with doses of the antagonist Ω-methylpantothenic acid[14], with the following symptoms: mild fatigue, headache, sleeplessness, nausea, epigastric pain, paraesthesia of the limbs, muscle spasms and coordination disturbances; other signs were absence of the eosinophile reaction of the blood to ACTH and an increased sensitivity to insulin. The pantothenic acid deficiency was evidenced by the reduced acetylating capacity of the blood after administration of sulphanilamide or para-aminobenzoic acid.

Treatment

The so-called 'burning feet' syndrome has been treated with pantothenic acid[15], though it is not certain that this syndrome is solely due to pantothenic acid deficiency. Pantothenic acid has been reported to be effective against the neurotoxicity of streptomycin[16]; its value in the treatment of emotional disturbances[17], diabetic neuropathy[17], skin diseases[17] and paralytic ileus[18] remains uncertain.

References ('Pantothenic acid', pages 487–488)

1 Sebrell and Harris (Eds.), *The Vitamins*, vol. 2, Academic Press, New York, 1954, page 589; Chow, B.F., in Beaton and McHenry (Eds.), *Nutrition*, vol. 2, Academic Press, New York, 1964, page 207; Vilter, R.W., in Wohl and Goodhart (Eds.), *Modern Nutrition in Health and Disease*, 3rd ed., Lea & Febiger, Philadelphia, 1964, page 395.
2 Hegsted, D.M., *Proc. Soc. exp. Biol. (N.Y.)*, **69**, 571 (1948).
3 Baker and Sobotka, *Advanc. clin. Chem.*, **5**, 173 (1962).
4 Gstirner, F., *Chemisch-physikalische Vitaminbestimmungsmethoden*, 5th ed., Enke, Stuttgart, 1965, page 231.
5 Kaplan and Lipmann, *J. biol. Chem.*, **174**, 37 (1948).
6 Goodwin, T.W., *The Biosynthesis of Vitamins and Related Compounds*, Academic Press, New York, 1963, page 131; Brown and Reynolds, *Ann. Rev. Biochem.*, **32**, 419 (1963).
7 Mangay Chung et al., *Amer. J. clin. Nutr.*, **9**, 573 (1961).
8 Gounelle and Richet, *C. R. Soc. Biol. (Paris)*, **150**, 2167 (1956), and **151**, 24 (1957).
9 Baker et al., *Amer. J. clin. Nutr.*, **14**, 1 (1964).
10 Langwell et al., *Endocrinology*, **62**, 565 (1958).
11 Food and Nutrition Board, *Recommended Dietary Allowances*, 7th ed., National Academy of Sciences – National Research Council, Publication 1694, Washington, 1968, page 38.
12 Szórády, I., *Mschr. Kinderheilk.*, **111**, 10 (1963).
13 Rembold, H., *Vitam. and Horm.*, **23**, 359 (1965).
14 Vilter and Will, *Ann. Rev. Med.*, **9**, 191 (1958); Hodges et al., *J. clin. Invest.*, **38**, 1421 (1959).
15 Gopalon, C., *Indian med. Gaz.*, **81**, 22 (1946).
16 Murray, I., *Practitioner*, **182**, 50 (1959).
17 Brock, J.F., in Brock, J.F. (Ed.), *Recent Advances in Human Nutrition*, Churchill, London, 1961, page 74.
18 Editorial, *Brit. med. J.*, **2**, 634 (1963).

Ascorbic acid[1–3] (for references see page 491)

Chemistry

Compound	Formula and mol. wt.	Structure	Physical properties	Occurrence and activity
L-Ascorbic acid (vitamin C)	$C_6H_8O_6$ 176.13	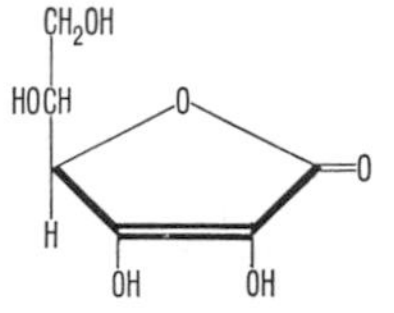	White crystals with an acid taste, soluble in water, rather insoluble in ethanol, sensitive to light, atmospheric oxygen and some heavy metals; strong reducing action M.p. 192 °C, $[\alpha]_D + 23°$	Probably present in all higher plants, particularly cabbage, citrus fruits, hawthorn berries; in small amounts in animal tissues. Antiscorbutic activity
Dehydroascorbic acid	$C_6H_6O_6$ 174.11	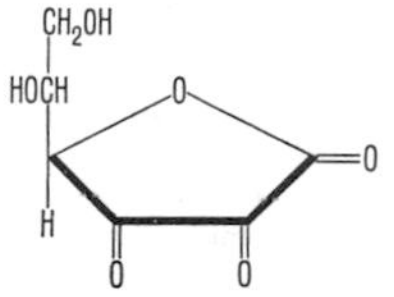	White crystals, soluble in water; readily hydrolysed to 2,3-diketo-L-gulonic acid M.p. 225 °C	Present with ascorbic acid in plants. Antiscorbutic activity
2-Keto-L-gulonic acid	$C_6H_{10}O_7$ 194.14	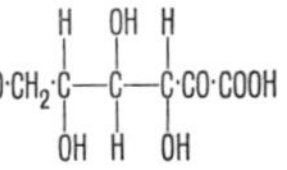	White crystals M.p. 171 °C	Precursor of ascorbic acid. No antiscorbutic activity

Assay

Biological[4]. In guinea-pigs either by histological study of tooth structure or by means of the preventive or curative growth test.

Chemical[5]. Polarographically; by mass analysis based on the ability of ascorbic acid to reduce 2,6-dichlorphenolindophenol or *N*-bromosuccinimide (dehydroascorbic acid must be reduced beforehand with, for instance, H_2S or homocysteine); photometrically using the 2,4-dinitrophenylhydrazones of dehydroascorbic acid and 2,3-diketo-L-gulonic acid, which give a red solution in concentrated sulphuric acid (ascorbic acid must be oxidized beforehand with, for instance, bromine or active charcoal). The vitamin is best extracted from biological materials with metaphosphoric acid solution. Ascorbic acid and dehydroascorbic acid can be separated from one another and from other substances by paper chromatography.

Unit

No international unit; by weight. The former International Unit (= 50 μg L-ascorbic acid) is now obsolete.

Biogenesis[6]

Ascorbic acid is synthesized by higher plants and all animals except the primates, guinea-pigs, the red-vented bubul (*Pycnonotus cafer*) and the Indian fruit bat (*Pteropus medius*). The vitamin is apparently not formed by micro-organisms, and is presumably not necessary for their growth. Biogenesis takes place in the following steps (there is some doubt as to whether these are valid for plants):

D-Glucose ⟶ D-Glucuronic acid ⟶ D-Glucuronolactone ⟶

L-Gulonolactone $\xrightarrow{\text{L-gulonolactone oxidase}}$ 2-Keto-L-gulonic acid ⟶ L-Ascorbic acid

In most animals ascorbic acid is synthesized in the liver, but in birds, reptiles and amphibia in the kidneys. Animals that do not form ascorbic acid do not possess the enzyme L-gulonolactone oxidase.

Intake and excretion

In the USA the daily intake of ascorbic acid is about 120 mg, half of which arises from citrus fruits and tomatoes[7]. In the gastro-intestinal tract ascorbic acid is absorbed in the same way as glucose and other carbohydrates[3]. Even with high intakes of ascorbic acid less than 10 mg of the vitamin is excreted per day in the faeces[8]. Equilibrium between ascorbic acid absorbed from the diet and that present in the tissues is reached in less than 4 hours. Ascorbic acid probably passes the cell membranes in the more lipid-soluble dehydroascorbic acid form, which is then again reduced to ascorbic acid in the cell[9,10]. When the tissues are saturated with ascorbic acid the overall body concentration of the vitamin is 50 mg per kg[11]. The ascorbic acid contents (mg/kg) of various tissues in human adults are as follows[12]: brain 150, pituitary 150, lens of the eye 250, adrenals 400, pancreas 150, liver 150, kidneys 50, heart muscle 50. Tissue levels of ascorbic acid are highest at birth and greatly reduced in old age[12]. The saturation level in leucocytes is 270–300 mg ascorbic acid per kg[11]; high doses of ascorbic acid have been reported to increase this concentration up to 600 mg per kg[13]. The whole blood and plasma levels (see page 611) depend on the degree of tissue saturation and on the dietary intake. High doses of ascorbic acid cause the plasma level to rise rapidly, possibly to 40 mg per litre; the normal plasma level is below 14 mg per litre, since at this concentration the threshold value for the kidneys is reached with a consequent steep rise in the ascorbic acid clearance[3,11]. In the plasma about 20% of the total ascorbic acid is in the form of dehydroascorbic acid[14] (page 611). Ascorbic acid also occurs in the aqueous humour of the eye (50–295 mg/l[15]), in gastric juice (see page 650) and in the synovial fluid (see page 642).

Dependence of ascorbic acid levels in serum and leucocytes on intake[2,3,11]

Daily intake (mg)	Serum (mg/l)	Leucocytes (mg/kg)	Tissue saturation (%)	Percentage of a test dose in the urine*
<10	<2	<120	0–40	<5
10–20	~2	~120	~40	<15
30–100	4–10	150–200	>50	20–60
>100	10–14	270–300	→100	60–80

* The usual loading tests consist either of giving 10 mg ascorbic acid orally per kg body weight followed by determination of ascorbic acid in the 24-hour urine, or of giving 100 mg ascorbic acid intravenously followed by determination of ascorbic acid in the 3-hour urine.

With an ascorbic acid concentration of 20 mg per kg body weight the daily turnover is about 1 mg per kg, corresponding to a half-life of 16 days[16]. In urine ascorbic acid appears mainly unchanged (see page 676), but part is hydrolysed to diketogulonic acid and appears finally as oxalic acid[3]. Other metabolites are L-xylonic and L-lyxonic acids, which arise by decarboxylation of ascorbic acid[17]. Radioactive CO_2 has been detected in expired air after giving doses of tagged ascorbic acid[18]. The ascorbic acid content of breast milk (page 689) depends largely on the dietary intake.

Function

Ascorbic acid and dehydroascorbic acid form a redox system with 'semidehydroascorbic acid' as highly reactive intermediate. The latter arises by the loss of a single electron by ascorbic acid or by the acceptance of a single electron by dehydroascorbic acid[10]. Almost all metabolic processes the disturbance of which gives rise to scurvy involve reactions in which ascorbic acid is oxidized. Of particular importance are the hydroxylation reactions dependent on ascorbic acid which require molecular oxygen.

The disturbances in the formation of connective tissue that appear in ascorbic acid deficiency are a result of failure of the ascorbic acid-dependent hydroxylation of proline to hydroxyproline, a component of collagen. The formation and maintenance of collagen is dependent on a normal ascorbic acid level[19]. Synthesis of collagen in human skin-tissue cultures is promoted by ascorbic acid[20]. In guinea-pigs with ascorbic acid deficiency the formation of hydroxyproline in granulation tissue commences only after ascorbic acid has been administered[21].

Another hydroxylation reaction dependent on ascorbic acid is the hydroxylation of the side chain of dopamine to noradrenaline; the enzyme catalysing this reaction has been found in the microsomes of beef adrenal cortex[22]. Ascorbic acid is probably involved also in the hydroxylations occurring in steroid synthesis in the adrenals, but little is known of this role[22,23].

Ascorbic acid is also concerned in tyrosine metabolism as reducing agent, although here it does not participate in a hydroxylation reaction. Its probable effect is that of protecting the enzyme para-hydroxyphenylpyruvic acid hydroxylase from inhibition by its substrate[24]. Ascorbic acid also plays a role as electron donor in the conversion of folic acid into tetrahydrofolic acid. This connection between ascorbic acid and tetrahydrofolic acid may be responsible for the appearance of macrocytic anaemia in scurvy[10]. The hypochromic anaemia of scurvy, on the other hand, is more likely to be due to an effect of ascorbic acid on iron metabolism, since the vitamin is necessary for the incorporation of iron into ferritin[25].

In contrast to the reactions dependent on ascorbic acid, the hydroxylation of tryptophan to 5-hydroxytryptophan, the precursor of serotonin, is mediated by dehydroascorbic acid, which is thereby reduced to ascorbic acid. The enzyme catalysing this reaction is dependent on copper ions for its activity and occurs mainly in the tissues of the small intestine[26]. The regeneration of ascorbic acid from dehydroascorbic acid in the tissues plays an important metabolic role. It takes place with the formation of semidehydroascorbic acid from ascorbic acid and dehydroascorbic acid, whereby an enzyme system present in the animal cell transfers electrons from $NADH_2$ to semidehydroascorbic acid and so regenerates ascorbic acid[10].

In the animal organism ascorbic acid seems to have a protective action against deficiencies of other vitamins (thiamine, riboflavin, pantothenic acid, biotin, folic acid, vitamin E, vitamin A); the relationships between these vitamins and ascorbic acid are, however, obscure[27].

Requirements and deficiency symptoms

The minimum intake of ascorbic acid required to prevent scurvy in infants is about 10 mg per day, in adults a little under 10 mg per day[28]. A daily intake of 30–40 mg results in moderate saturation of the tissues, one of 60–100 mg in almost complete saturation[28]. The recommended daily intakes of ascorbic acid in various countries are as follows: England[32]: infants 15 mg, children 20–30 mg, adults 30 mg; USA[29]: infants 35 mg, children 40–80 mg, adults 60 mg; Western Germany[30]: infants 30–35 mg, children 40–50 mg, adults 75 mg; Canada[31]: children 20–30 mg, adults 30 mg; Holland[33]: children 35–75 mg, adults 50 mg; Japan[34]: children 30–90 mg, adults 60–65 mg. For the recommendations of the Food and Nutrition Board (USA)[29] for pregnant and lactating women see the table on page 494. Workers in very cold climates should have an intake of 150–250 mg per day[35].

Good sources of ascorbic acid are cabbage, spinach, paprikas, citrus fruits, tomatoes, strawberries, red currants and liver (see pages 499–515). In vegetables the ascorbic acid falls rapidly during withering. Potatoes are an important source of ascorbic acid but the concentration decreases by up to 80% in winter storage. Fresh cow's milk contains up to 25 mg per litre; this is markedly reduced by pasteurization or boiling.

The most important symptoms of ascorbic acid deficiency are a marked tendency to bleeding with the appearance of extensive patches of haemorrhage under the skin and in the gums, muscles, fatty tissues and internal organs. Other symptoms are impairment of connective tissue formation with changes in bone structure and growth, defective tooth formation and fissuring and roughening of the skin; there are also often disturbances of iron absorption and anaemia. In infants ascorbic acid deficiency (Moeller-Barlow disease) is manifested mainly in the bones, which show a zone of destroyed bone extending over the margin of the metaphysis into the soft tissues, as well as by subperiostal bleeding, particularly in the metaphyseal zones of the long bones.

On a diet free of ascorbic acid the ascorbic acid content of the plasma falls after 40 days to less than 1 mg per litre, while after 120 days that of the leucocytes is almost zero[2]. At this time there is also enlargement and keratosis of the hair follicles, which in the succeeding 40 days gradually develop haemorrhages and the characteristic signs of scurvy; changes in the gingiva appear after 180 days[36].

An inadequate intake of ascorbic acid is best recognized by the lowered plasma level, whereas a severe deficiency of the vitamin is characterized by the low ascorbic acid concentration of the leucocytes (<120 mg/kg; see the table above). Various tests are available for measuring the extent to which ascorbic acid is provided by the diet; they depend on the degree of tissue saturation effected by a test dose of the vitamin as indicated by the plasma level and urinary excretion.

Treatment

In infants, doses of 20 mg ascorbic acid per day, for instance in the form of orange juice, are ample to prevent the appearance of scurvy; in infants with scurvy 25 mg should be given 4 times a day, in adults with the disease 100 mg 5 or 6 times a day[28]. In patients who have undergone extensive surgery 150–300 mg ascorbic acid per day is sufficient to produce adequate saturation of the tissues[37]. The reducing properties of ascorbic acid can be utilized in the treatment of methaemoglobinaemia and to promote the absorption of orally administered iron[38]. Russian workers have reported success in the treatment of coronary diseases with ascorbic acid[39].

References ('Ascorbic acid', pages 489–490)

1 Sebrell and Harris (Eds.), *The Vitamins*, vol. 1, Academic Press, New York, 1954, page 177; Knox and Goswami, *Advanc. clin. Chem.*, 4, 121 (1961).
2 Vilter, R. W., in Wohl and Goodhart (Eds.), *Modern Nutrition in Health and Disease*, 3rd ed., Lea & Febiger, Philadelphia, 1964, page 433.
3 Woodruff, C. W., in Beaton and McHenry (Eds.), *Nutrition*, vol. 2, Academic Press, New York, 1964, page 265.
4 Bliss and György, in György, P. (Ed.), *Vitamin Methods*, vol. 2, Academic Press, New York, 1951, page 244.
5 Roe, J. H., *Ann. N. Y. Acad. Sci.*, **92**, 277 (1961); Gstirner, F., *Chemisch-physikalische Vitaminbestimmungsmethoden*, 5th ed., Enke, Stuttgart, 1965, page 254.
6 Isherwood and Mapson, *Ann. Rev. Plant Physiol.*, **13**, 329 (1962); Goodwin, T. W., *The Biosynthesis of Vitamins and Related Compounds*, Academic Press, New York, 1963, page 210.
7 Stitt, K. R., *Nutr. Rev.*, **21**, 257 (1963).
8 Abt and Farmer, quoted in Vilter [2].
9 Martin, G. R., *Ann. N. Y. Acad. Sci.*, **92**, 141 (1961).
10 Schneider and Staudinger, *Klin. Wschr.*, **42**, 879 (1964).
11 Burch, H. B., *Ann. N. Y. Acad. Sci.*, **92**, 268 (1961).
12 Kirk, J. E., *Vitam. and Horm.*, **20**, 67 (1962).
13 Mašek and Hrubá, *Int. Z. Vitaminforsch.*, **34**, 39 (1964).
14 Linkswiler, H., *J. Nutr.*, **64**, 43 (1958).
15 Huber, A., in *Documenta Geigy, Scientific Tables*, 5th ed., Basle, 1956, page 363.
16 Hellman and Burns, *J. biol. Chem.*, **230**, 923 (1958).
17 Ashwell et al., *Ann. N. Y. Acad. Sci.*, **92**, 105 (1961).
18 Schuchling and Abt, *Proc. Soc. exp. Biol. (N. Y.)*, **118**, 30 (1965).
19 Robertson, W. van B., *Ann. N. Y. Acad. Sci.*, **92**, 159 (1961).
20 Green and Goldberg, *Proc. Soc. exp. Biol. (N. Y.)*, **117**, 258 (1964).
21 Gould, B. S., *Vitam. and Horm.*, **18**, 89 (1960).
22 Levin et al., *J. biol. Chem.*, **235**, 2080 (1960).
23 Chalopin et al., *Wld Rev. Nutr. Diet.*, **6**, 165 (1966).
24 La Du and Zannoni, *Ann. N. Y. Acad. Sci.*, **92**, 175 (1961).
25 Mazur, A., *Ann. N. Y. Acad. Sci.*, **92**, 223 (1961).
26 Cooper, J. R., *Ann. N. Y. Acad. Sci.*, **92**, 208 (1961).
27 Terroine, T., *Wld Rev. Nutr. Diet.*, **2**, 101 (1960).
28 Goldsmith, G. A., *Ann. N. Y. Acad. Sci.*, **92**, 230 (1961).
29 Food and Nutrition Board, *Recommended Dietary Allowances*, 7th ed., National Academy of Sciences – National Research Council, Publication 1694, Washington, 1968, page 31.
30 Deutsche Gesellschaft für Ernährung, *Die wünschenswerte Höhe der Nahrungszufuhr*, 2nd ed., Umschau Verlag, Frankfurt, 1962.
31 Canadian Council on Nutrition, May 1963, quoted by Young, E. G., in Beaton and McHenry (Eds.), *Nutrition*, vol. 2, Academic Press, New York, 1964, page 299.
32 Davidson and Passmore, *Human Nutrition and Dietetics*, 4th ed., Livingstone, Edinburgh, 1969, page 243.
33 Commissie van de Voedings-Organisatie T.N.O., *Voeding*, **19**, 66 (1958), and **22**, 210 (1961).
34 Ministry of Health and Welfare, *Nutrition in Japan*, Tokyo, 1961.
35 van der Merwe, A. le R., *S. Afr. med. J.*, **36**, 751 (1962).
36 Bartley et al., *Spec. Rep. Ser. med. Res. Coun. (Lond.)*, No. 280 (1953).
37 Crandon et al., *Ann. N. Y. Acad. Sci.*, **92**, 246 (1961); Coon, W. W., *Surg. Gynec. Obstet.*, **114**, 522 (1962).
38 Schroeder, H., *Ther. d. Gegenw.*, **100**, 224 (1961).
39 Simonson and Keys, *Circulation*, **24**, 1239 (1961).

Substances with vitamin-like action (vitaminoids)*

Compound	Formula, mol. wt. and physical properties	Occurrence	Function	Requirements and deficiency symptoms
Bioflavonoids [2] (vitamin P group, citrin)	Structure of the flavones: 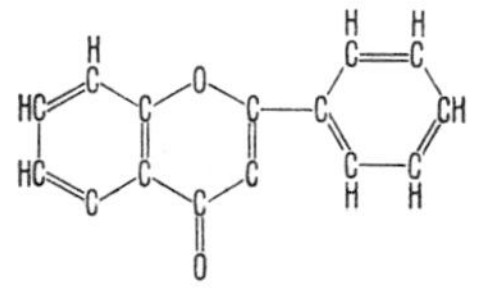 Substances like hesperidine and eriodictiol also belong to this group	Widely distributed in plants, particularly in fruits (e.g., lemons and black currants)	Biological function obscure. Views on pharmacological activity vary. Substances increasing capillary resistance probably possess antihistamine and antihyaluronidase activity [3]	
Mesoinositol [4] (myoinositol)	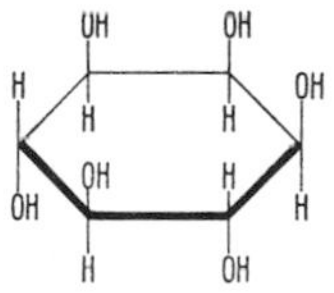 $C_6H_{12}O_6$ Mol. wt. 180.16 M. p. 225–227 °C	Probable component of all living cells. Component of phospholipids in leaves, seeds and animal tissues (particularly heart, brain and skeletal muscle); present as hexaphosphate (phytic acid) in plants	In the phospholipid form involved in cation transport through the cell membranes, in stimulation of nerves and in metabolism of the mitochondria [5]	Growth factor for yeasts and many kinds of animal cells in tissue culture. Synthesized in the animal organism. Significance in human nutrition obscure. Intake about 1 g per day
Carnitine [6] (β-hydroxy-γ-butyrobetaine, vitamin B_T)	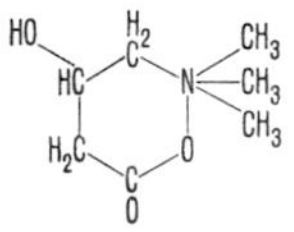 $C_7H_{15}NO_3$ Mol. wt. 161.20 $[\alpha]_D$ −20.9°	In all animal tissues (skeletal muscle 1, heart 0.6, kidneys 0.4, liver 0.3 mg/gramme dry substance); small amounts in blood, milk, plants and micro-organisms	Involved in intracellular fat metabolism in the form of acylcarnitines by (a) transporting acetyl-coenzyme A and acetoacetyl-coenzyme A from the mitochondria to the site of synthesis of long-chain fatty acids outside the mitochondria [7]; (b) transporting activated long-chain acyl groups from the cytoplasm to the mitochondria, where long-chain fatty acids are oxidized [8]	Growth factor for some insects, for instance mealworm, *Tenebrio molitor* and some bacterial species. Vertebrates can synthesize carnitine

* According to Bersin[1] these are substances that must be regarded as essential dietary components for many living organisms but that do not function in the form of enzymes.

Compound	Formula, mol. wt. and physical properties	Occurrence	Function	Requirements and deficiency symptoms
Choline[9] (β-hydroxy-ethyltrimethyl-ammonium hydroxide)	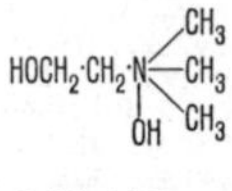 $C_5H_{15}NO_2$ Mol. wt. 121.18 M.p. 180 °C (decomp.)	Component of lecithin, plasmalogens, sphingomyelin and acylcholines. Widely distributed in plants and animals (egg-yolk 17, meat 6, cereals 1mg per gramme). See also pages 394 and 434	Methyl-group donor, replaceable by other sources of labile methyl groups or when synthesized from the latter in the body. Involved in transport of fatty acids from the liver to peripheral fat stores	Growth factor for various micro-organisms, also for rats, chickens and turkeys. Choline deficiency in animals results in injury to the liver and kidneys. Significance in human nutrition obscure. Intake about 0.5–0.9 g per day, an adequate amount in the light of the known requirement of 0.1–0.15 g per 100 g of food[10]
α-Lipoic acid[11] (thioctic acid)	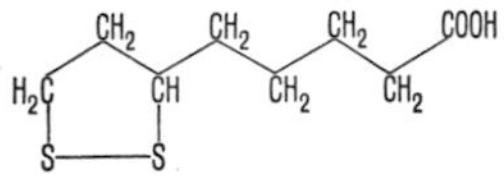 $C_8H_{14}O_2S_2$ Mol. wt. 206.33 M.p. 48 °C	In small amounts in vegetable and animal tissues, particularly yeasts and liver	Involved in the oxidative decarboxylation of pyruvic and α-ketoglutaric acids (see pages 390 and 391)	Growth factor for certain bacterial and protozoal species. Probably of no importance in nutrition of higher animals
Essential fatty acids[12] (vitamin F)	Linoleic and arachidonic acids (see page 370) Unsaturated fatty acids and related compounds such as the corresponding alcohols not synthesized by the body in adequate quantity but necessary for metabolism and growth	In the diet, particularly linoleic acid (plant oils, animal fats) and arachidonic acid (animal fats). Also active are linoleic acid precursors such as linoleyl alcohol and cis-2-octenic acid[13]; linolenic acid is almost inactive. Arachidonic acid is synthesized in the animal body from linoleic acid	Involved in formation of the cell membranes and possibly transport of fatty acids. Structurally essential components of phospholipids and precursors of prostaglandins. Play a role in metabolism of the mitochondria. Many polyene fatty acids such as linoleic and arachidonic acids but also others with no effect on growth are capable of lowering the serum cholesterol level	Deficiency symptoms: in young rats cessation of growth and eczema; in infants eczema[14]. The increased water intake in rats with deficiency can be utilized to measure activity[15]. In deficiency the triene acid content of the serum is increased (formation of 5,8,11- and 7,10,13-eicosatrienic acids), the tetraene acid content (arachidonic acid) lowered[16,17]. The minimum essential fatty acid requirement in man is about 1–2% of the calorie intake[16,18], or 1.2–2.4 g linoleic acid per 1000 kcal dietary intake. Optimal requirement in infancy: 4% of the calorie intake in the form of linoleic acid[19]. The tocopherol requirement rises with increasing intake of essential fatty acids (see page 466)

* See footnote, page 491.

References

1 Bersin, T., *Biochemie der Vitamine*, Akademische Verlagsgesellschaft, Frankfurt, 1966.
2 Vilter, R.W., in Wohl and Goodhart (Eds.), *Modern Nutrition in Health and Disease*, 3rd ed., Lea & Febiger, Philadelphia, 1964, page 452.
3 Ravina, A., *Presse méd.*, **72**, 2855 (1964).
4 Goodhart, R.S., in Wohl and Goodhart (Eds.), *Modern Nutrition in Health and Disease*, 3rd ed., Lea & Febiger, Philadelphia, 1964, page 455.
5 Hawthorne, J.N., *Vitam. and Horm.*, **22**, 57 (1964).
6 Fraenkel and Friedman, *Vitam. and Horm.*, **15**, 74 (1957); Goodhart, R.S., in Wohl and Goodhart (Eds.), *Modern Nutrition in Health and Disease*, 3rd ed., Lea & Febiger, Philadelphia, 1964, page 460.
7 Bressler and Katz, *J. clin. Invest.*, **44**, 840 (1965).
8 Fritz, I.B., *Advanc. Lipid Res.*, **1**, 285 (1964); Wittels and Bressler, *J. clin. Invest.*, **44**, 1639 (1965).
9 Goodhart, R.S., in Wohl and Goodhart (Eds.), *Modern Nutrition in Health and Disease*, 3rd ed., Lea & Febiger, Philadelphia, 1964, page 453.
10 Joint FAO/WHO Expert Group, *Wld Hlth Org. techn. Rep. Ser.*, No. 362 (1967).
11 Reed, L.J., *Vitam. and Horm.*, **20**, 1 (1962).
12 Aaes-Jørgensen, E., *Physiol. Rev.*, **41**, 1 (1961).
13 Sinclair, H., *Brit. med. J.*, **2**, 337 (1962).
14 Hansen et al., *J. Nutr.*, **66**, 565 (1958).
15 Thomasson, H.J., *Int. Z. Vitaminforsch.*, **25**, 62 (1953).
16 Holman, R.T., *J. Amer. med. Ass.*, **178**, 930 (1961).
17 Aaes-Jørgensen, E., *Nutr. Rev.*, **24**, 1 (1966).
18 Holman et al., *Amer. J. clin. Nutr.*, **14**, 70 (1964).
19 Adam et al., *J. Nutr.*, **66**, 555 (1958).

Nutritional Standards

(For references see page 497)

A *nutritional standard* is a statement of the amounts of certain nutrients (usually the average daily amounts) regarded as necessary for a person representative of the category of the population to which the standard applies[7]. Terms such as nutritional requirement and nutritional allowance are also used but must not always be regarded as synonymous. The resulting diets are referred to as minimum, average or desirable. Since it is at present impossible to define an individual's optimum requirement of any dietary constituent, other methods of evaluating nutritional standards have become necessary. In USA, the recommended dietary *allowances*[2] are designed to provide an adequate diet to cover individual variations among most normal persons of the population. Comparisons between the various standards laid down by national and international bodies are possible only when the purpose of the standards compared is known. In the tables below and on pages 494–495 the standards of the FAO[3] and the Joint FAO/WHO Expert Groups[4–6] and of the Food and Nutrition Board (USA) are given in detail. For other national standards (British, Canadian, Indian, South African, Australian, Dutch, Norwegian, Central American, Russian) see YOUNG[7]. A new UK standard has recently been published[38].

Recommended daily allowances of calories (FAO[3]) *and of vitamin A (retinol), thiamine, riboflavin and niacin** (Joint FAO/WHO Expert Group[6])

Age	Calories per day	Retinol† (mg)	Thiamine (mg)	Riboflavin (mg)	Niacin equivalents††
0–3 months **	120 per kg	–	–	–	–
4–6 months **	110 per kg	–	–	–	–
7–12 months	1000	300	0.4	0.6	6.6
1 year	1150	250	0.5	0.6	7.6
2 years	1300	250	0.5	0.7	8.6
3 years	1450	250	0.6	0.8	9.6
4–6 years	1700	300	0.7	0.9	11.2
7–9 years	2100	400	0.8	1.2	13.9
10–12 years	2500	575	1.0	1.4	16.5
13–15 (boys)	3100	725	1.2	1.7	20.4
(girls)	2600	725	1.0	1.4	17.2
16–19 (boys)	3600	750	1.4	2.0	23.8
(girls)	2400	750	1.0	1.3	15.8
Adults (men)	3200	750	1.3	1.8	21.1
(women)	2300	750	0.9	1.3	15.2

* The amounts given do not cover abnormal needs such as those due to infections, malabsorption, metabolic disturbances, extreme environmental conditions, etc. They are also applicable only when the requirements for calories and all other nutrients are fully met.

** For infants from 0 to 6 months, it is accepted that breast feeding by a well-nourished mother is the best way to satisfy the nutritional requirements for these vitamins.

† For diets containing both carotene and retinol, adjustment must be made as follows: recommended intake of mixed vitamin A-active compounds =

$$\frac{\text{recommended intake of retinol}}{0.167\,k + (1 - k)}, \text{ where } k = \frac{\beta\text{-carotene } (\mu g)}{\beta\text{-carotene } (\mu g) + \text{retinol } (\mu g)}$$

†† A niacin equivalent is 1 mg niacin or 60 mg L-tryptophan.

Daily protein requirements (FAO/WHO Expert Group[4])

Age	Grammes Reference Protein* per kilogramme body weight: Average	Range**
Infants†		
0–3 months	2.3	–
3–6 months	1.8	–
6–9 months	1.5	–
9–12 months	1.2	–
Juveniles		
1–3 years	0.88	0.70–1.06
4–6 years	0.81	0.65–0.97
7–9 years	0.77	0.62–0.92
10–12 years	0.72	0.58–0.86
13–15 years	0.70	0.56–0.84
16–19 years	0.64	0.51–0.77
Adults††	0.59	0.47–0.71

* The composition of the Reference Protein is given on page 516. The proteins of eggs, milk and meat all have the same biological value. The intake of proteins of lower biological value must be correspondingly increased.
** This range is based on the expected range of individual variation; the upper level is likely to cover the requirements of 95% of the population and can thus be regarded as a *practical allowance*.
† In terms of either breast milk or cow's milk protein.
†† During the second and third trimesters of pregnancy 6 g per day should be added, during lactation 15 g per day.

Desirable daily calcium allowances (FAO/WHO Expert Group[5])

Age	mg/day
0–12 months*	500– 600
1–9 years	400– 500
10–15 years	600– 700
16–19 years	500– 600
Adults	400– 500
Pregnancy, 3rd trimester	1000–1200
Lactation	1000–1200

* For infants not being breast-fed; the calcium requirement of an infant being breast-fed by a normally lactating mother is met by the breast milk.

Calories†

The body requires food energy for resting metabolism, synthesis of body tissues, physical activities, excretory processes and maintenance of thermal balance. The energy requirements at different levels of activity are given in the tables on page 495.

The calorie allowances of the Food and Nutrition Board (USA), like those of the FAO, are based on the concept of a 'reference' subject. In the case of the former this is a man aged 22 weighing 70 kg or a woman aged 22 weighing 58 kg with a 'light' level of physical activity in a mean environmental temperature of 20 °C. It is assumed that weight gains after this age are likely to be fat. Since it is difficult to estimate the degree of reduction in physical activity associated with advancing age the calorie allowances (see table on page 494) were obtained by making a reduction of 5% between the ages of 22 and 35, of 3% per decade between 35 and 55, and of 5% per decade between 55 and 75. A further reduction of 7% is recommended for persons aged 75 and over. The upper left-hand table on page 495 gives the adjustment for persons of other than the ideal weight.

Increased physical activity also requires an increase in the calorie intake, though more than an additional 1500 kcal over the allowances recommended in the table is rarely necessary. A lower level of physical activity (e.g., in persons with a sedentary occupation) calls for a lower calorie intake.

An environmental temperature lower than 20 °C necessitates little if any increase in calorie intake provided that adequate but not

† 1 $kcal_{15}$ = 4.185 5 kJ (see page 213).

(For references see page 497)

*Recommended daily dietary allowances** (Food and Nutrition Board, USA[2])

	Age** (years)	Weight (kg)	Weight *(lb)*	Height cm	Height *(in)*	Calories (kcal)	Protein (g)	Minerals: Calcium (g)	Minerals: Phosphorus (g)	Minerals: Iodine (μg)	Minerals: Iron (mg)	Minerals: Magnesium (mg)
Infants	0–1/6	4	*9*	55	*22*	kg × 120	kg × 2.2***	0.4	0.2	25	6	40
	1/6–1/2	7	*15*	63	*25*	kg × 110	kg × 2.0***	0.5	0.4	40	10	60
	1/2–1	9	*20*	72	*28*	kg × 100	kg × 1.8***	0.6	0.5	45	15	70
Children	1–2	12	*26*	81	*32*	1100	25	0.7	0.7	55	15	100
	2–3	14	*31*	91	*36*	1250	25	0.8	0.8	60	15	150
	3–4	16	*35*	100	*39*	1400	30	0.8	0.8	70	10	200
	4–6	19	*42*	110	*43*	1600	30	0.8	0.8	80	10	200
	6–8	23	*51*	121	*48*	2000	35	0.9	0.9	100	10	250
	8–10	28	*62*	131	*52*	2200	40	1.0	1.0	110	10	250
Males	10–12	35	*77*	140	*55*	2500	45	1.2	1.2	125	10	300
	12–14	43	*95*	151	*59*	2700	50	1.4	1.4	135	18	350
	14–18	59	*130*	170	*67*	3000	60	1.4	1.4	150	18	400
	18–22	67	*147*	175	*69*	2800	60	0.8	0.8	140	10	400
	22–35	70	*154*	175	*69*	2800	65	0.8	0.8	140	10	350
	35–55	70	*154*	173	*68*	2600	65	0.8	0.8	125	10	350
	55–75+	70	*154*	171	*67*	2400	65	0.8	0.8	110	10	350
Females	10–12	35	*77*	142	*56*	2250	50	1.2	1.2	110	18	300
	12–14	44	*97*	154	*61*	2300	50	1.3	1.3	115	18	350
	14–16	52	*114*	157	*62*	2400	55	1.3	1.3	120	18	350
	16–18	54	*119*	160	*63*	2300	55	1.3	1.3	115	18	350
	18–22	58	*128*	163	*64*	2000	55	0.8	0.8	100	18	350
	22–35	58	*128*	163	*64*	2000	55	0.8	0.8	100	18	300
	35–55	58	*128*	160	*63*	1850	55	0.8	0.8	90	18	300
	35–75+	58	*128*	157	*62*	1700	55	0.8	0.8	80	10	300
Pregnancy						+ 200	65	+0.4	+0.4	125	18	450
Lactation						+ 1000	75	+0.5	+0.5	150	18	450

		Fat-soluble vitamins: Vitamin A activity (IU)	Fat-soluble vitamins: Vitamin D (IU)	Fat-soluble vitamins: Vitamin E activity (IU)	Water-soluble vitamins: Ascorbic acid (mg)	Folacin† (mg)	Niacin†† (mEq)	Riboflavin (mg)	Thiamine (mg)	Vitamin B_6 (mg)	Vitamin B_{12} (μg)
Infants	0–1/6	1500	400	5	35	0.05	5	0.4	0.2	0.2	1.0
	1/6–1/2	1500	400	5	35	0.05	7	0.5	0.4	0.3	1.5
	1/2–1	1500	400	5	35	0.1	8	0.6	0.5	0.4	2.0
Children	1–2	2000	400	10	40	0.1	8	0.6	0.6	0.5	2.0
	2–3	2000	400	10	40	0.2	8	0.7	0.6	0.6	2.5
	3–4	2500	400	10	40	0.2	9	0.8	0.7	0.7	3
	4–6	2500	400	10	40	0.2	11	0.9	0.8	0.9	4
	6–8	3500	400	15	40	0.2	13	1.1	1.0	1.0	4
	8–10	3500	400	15	40	0.3	15	1.2	1.1	1.2	5
Males	10–12	4500	400	20	40	0.4	17	1.3	1.3	1.4	5
	12–14	5000	400	20	45	0.4	18	1.4	1.4	1.6	5
	14–18	5000	400	25	55	0.4	20	1.5	1.5	1.8	5
	18–22	5000	400	30	60	0.4	18	1.6	1.4	2.0	5
	22–35	5000	–	30	60	0.4	18	1.7	1.4	2.0	5
	35–55	5000	–	30	60	0.4	17	1.7	1.3	2.0	5
	55–75+	5000	–	30	60	0.4	14	1.7	1.2	2.0	6
Females	10–12	4500	400	20	40	0.4	15	1.3	1.1	1.4	5
	12–14	5000	400	20	45	0.4	15	1.4	1.2	1.6	5
	14–16	5000	400	25	50	0.4	16	1.4	1.2	1.8	5
	16–18	5000	400	25	50	0.4	15	1.5	1.2	2.0	5
	18–22	5000	400	25	55	0.4	13	1.5	1.0	2.0	5
	22–35	5000	–	25	55	0.4	13	1.5	1.0	2.0	5
	35–55	5000	–	25	55	0.4	13	1.5	1.0	2.0	5
	55–75+	5000	–	25	55	0.4	13	1.5	1.0	2.0	6
Pregnancy		6000	400	30	60	0.8	15	1.8	+0.1	2.5	8
Lactation		8000	400	30	60	0.5	20	2.0	+0.5	2.5	6

* The allowance levels are intended to cover individual variations among most normal persons as they live in the USA under usual environmental stresses. The recommended allowances can be attained with a variety of common foods providing other nutrients for which human requirements have been less well defined.

** Entries on lines for age range 22–35 years represent the 'reference' man and woman at age 22 (see under 'Calories', page 493). All other entries represent allowances for the midpoint of the specified age range.

*** Assumes protein equivalent to human milk. For proteins not 100% utilized, factors should be increased proportionately.

† The folacin allowances refer to dietary sources as determined by *Lactobacillus casei* assay. Pure forms of folacin may be effective in doses less than a quarter of the recommended allowance.

†† Niacin equivalents include dietary sources of the vitamin itself plus 1 mEq for each 60 mg of dietary tryptophan.

(For references see page 497)

Recommended daily calorie allowances (Food and Nutrition Board, USA[2]) (Light physical activity, mean environmental temperature 20 °C)

	Body weight (kg)	Body weight (*lb*)	RMR* at age 22	Age 22	Age 45	Age 65
Men	50	*110*	1540	2200	2000	1850
	55	*121*	1620	2350	2150	1950
	60	*132*	1720	2500	2300	2100
	65	*143*	1820	2650	2400	2200
	70	*154*	1880	2800	2600	2400
	75	*165*	1970	2950	2700	2500
	80	*176*	2020	3050	2800	2600
	85	*187*	2110	3200	2950	2700
	90	*198*	2210	3350	3100	2800
	95	*209*	2290	3500	3200	2900
	100	*220*	2380	3700	3400	3100
Women	40	*88*	1280	1550	1450	1300
	45	*99*	1380	1700	1550	1450
	50	*110*	1460	1800	1650	1500
	55	*121*	1560	1950	1800	1650
	58	*128*	1620	2000	1850	1700
	60	*132*	1640	2050	1900	1700
	65	*143*	1740	2200	2000	1850
	70	*154*	1830	2300	2100	1950

* RMR = resting metabolic rate, approximately 10% above the metabolic rate measured under basal conditions.

Energy requirements during various activities[7]

Light work (2.5–4.9 kcal/min)	Moderately heavy work (5.0–7.4 kcal/min)	Heavy work (7.5–9.9 kcal/min)	Very heavy work (over 10 kcal/min)
Light industrial and domestic work	Farm work	Mine-working	Felling trees
Gymnastics	Marching with pack	Playing football	Steelmaking
Tile-laying	Ballroom dancing		Swimming (crawl)
Painting	Playing tennis		Climbing
Tending agricultural machines	Cycling		
Driving goods vehicles			
Playing golf, bowling			

Normal energy requirements of recumbent adults[7]

Fat (%)	Body type: Men	Body type: Women	45 kg / *99 lb*	50 kg / *110 lb*	55 kg / *121 lb*	60 kg / *132 lb*	65 kg / *143 lb*	70 kg / *154 lb*	75 kg / *165 lb*	80 kg / *176 lb*
			Energy requirement (kcal/min)							
5– 9	Lean	–	–	0.99	1.06	1.12	1.19	1.26	1.32	1.39
10–14	Average	–	–	0.94	1.01	1.08	1.14	1.21	1.28	1.34
15–19	Heavily built	Lean	0.82	0.89	0.96	1.03	1.09	1.16	1.23	1.30
20–24	Corpulent	Average	0.78	0.84	0.91	0.98	1.05	1.11	1.18	1.25
25–29	–	Heavily built	–	0.80	0.86	0.93	1.00	1.07	1.13	1.20
>30	–	Corpulent	–	–	0.81	0.88	0.95	1.02	1.08	1.15

Normal energy requirements of adults sitting and at rest[7]

Age in years	Number of subjects	Energy requirement (kcal/min): Mean	Range	*s*
Men (65 kg = 143 lb)				
20–39	30	1.39	0.97–1.79	0.25
40–64	30	1.37	0.87–1.94	0.29
65 and over	23	1.29	0.91–1.94	0.25
Women (55 kg = 121 lb)				
20–39	30	1.15	0.75–1.68	0.28
40–59	30	1.07	0.78–1.56	0.19
60 and over	23	1.09	0.77–1.62	0.31

Normal energy requirements of adults during walking[7]

Rate of walking km/h	Rate of walking mi/h	45 kg / *99 lb*	55 kg / *121 lb*	65 kg / *143 lb*	75 kg / *165 lb*	85 kg / *187 lb*	95 kg / *209 lb*
		Energy requirement (kcal/min)					
3	*1.9*	2.1	2.5	2.8	3.2	3.5	3.8
4	*2.5*	2.7	3.2	3.6	4.0	4.3	4.6
5	*3.1*	3.2	3.7	4.2	4.7	5.1	5.5
6	*3.7*	3.8	4.4	4.9	5.4	5.9	6.4
7	*4.3*	4.4	5.0	5.5	6.1	6.6	7.1

unreasonably heavy clothing is worn. The calorie requirement increases with increasing environmental temperature; at temperatures between 30 °C and 40 °C the calorie intake should be raised by 0.5% per 1°C, but only when physical activity is undiminished.

The Food and Nutrition Board (USA) calorie allowances for infants and children are average and approximate. Even more than in the case of adult allowances, they may need to be adjusted in accordance with observations of appetite, activity and nature of growth as judged by amount of subcutaneous fat.

The calorie allowances recommended by the FAO (page 493) are higher than those of the Food and Nutrition Board (USA) as a result of an assumed greater physical activity. Energy requirements during various activities can be calculated by means of the tables on this page.

Protein

Dietary protein is the source of the nitrogen and essential amino acids, i.e., those necessary for the synthesis of the body proteins and other nitrogenous substances (see the table opposite). The dietary protein allowance for adults recommended by the Food and Nutrition Board (USA)[2] (page 494), based on a utilization value of 70% for food protein, is 0.9 g protein per kilogramme body weight per day, a value about nine times the minimum requirement of Reference Protein[4]. In the case of infants it is assumed that when lactation is normal sufficient protein is obtained from the breast milk, even though this provides little more than the minimum requirement. For the protein allowances recommended by the FAO/WHO Expert Group see page 493. For premature infants the recommended allowance[8] is between 2.5 g and a maximum of 6 g per kilogramme body weight per day.

Carbohydrate and fat[2]

The desirable intake of carbohydrate and fat, like the optimal fatty-acid composition of foods, is difficult to assess. Apart from the body's specific needs for carbohydrate (e.g., brain energy), this and fat appear to be interchangeable as dietary energy sources, and in the body they are interconvertible, except that fatty acids with an even number of C-atoms from neutral fat, etc. cannot be used to form carbohydrate. Adaptation to diets very low in carbohydrate is possible, but for persons accustomed to a normal diet at least 100 g carbohydrate per day appears to be necessary if metabolic disturbances like ketosis, excessive protein breakdown, etc. are to be avoided. Normally, less than 1800 kcal of carbohydrate is stored as glycogen, so that if there is not enough in the diet it must be derived largely from dietary or body protein.

Dietary fat is also a carrier of other nutrients, including vitamins A, D, E and K. Calories, whether derived from dietary carbohydrate or fat, are stored mainly as fat in adipose cells. Except for the central nervous system, almost all body tissues utilize fatty acids directly as a source of energy.

The polyunsaturated fatty acids like linoleic and arachidonic acids have been shown to be essential for animals, and are very probably also essential for man. The minimum human requirements of the essential fatty acids should probably represent about 2% of the total calorie intake[9], or about 2.4 g linoleic acid per 1000 kcal of nutrient intake. In infants, a subclinical deficiency of linoleic acid can be prevented by ensuring that the amount of this substance in the formula supplies 3% of the calories[10].

Essential amino acids

Of the 18 amino acids contained in food proteins 8 are essential in that the body is not capable of synthesizing them (tryptophan, phenylalanine, lysine, threonine, methionine, leucine, isoleucine, valine), 2 are semi-essential in that they are not synthesized in adequate amounts during growth (histidine, arginine), and 6 are non-essential in that the body can synthesize them from a nitrogen source such as any amino acid, ammonium salts or urea (aspartic acid, glutamic acid, proline, glycine, serine, alanine).

*Requirements of the essential amino acids**

Amino acid	Infants: Minimum requirement[11] (mg/kg/day)	Adults**: Minimum requirement, Young men[12] (g/day)	Adults**: Minimum requirement, Young women[13] (g/day)	Adults**: Recommended intake[12] (g/day)
L-Histidine	34	0	0	0
L-Tryptophan	22	0.25	0.16	0.50
L-Phenylalanine				
Tyrosine available†	90	0.30	0.22	–
Tyrosine not available	–	1.10	–	2.20
L-Lysine	103	0.80	0.50	1.60
L-Threonine	87	0.50	0.31	1.00
L-Methionine				
Cystine available††	45	0.20	0.35	–
Cystine not available	–	1.10	–	2.20
L-Leucine	150	1.10	0.62	2.20
L-Isoleucine	126	0.70	0.45	1.40
L-Valine	105	0.80	0.65	1.60

* Assuming that the nitrogen intake is adequate for the formation of the non-essential amino acids.
** The requirements are higher during pregnancy and lactation. The minimum requirement of men over 50 is higher than that of young men in respect of at least two amino acids (methionine 2.4–3.0 g/day, lysine 1.4–2.8 g/day)[14].
† 70–75% of the phenylalanine requirement can be met by tyrosine[12].
†† 80–90% of the methionine requirement can be met by cystine[12].

Water

The water requirement of the body is determined by the amount of heat it produces and by the load of solutes in the body fluids. It is closely linked to the intake of salt. The intake must replace water losses in the urine, faeces, sweat and insensible perspiration (skin and lungs). Under the most favourable conditions (low-solute diet, resting, no sweating) the total water supplied by the diet and metabolic processes should be at least 1.5 l/day[15]. A reasonable water allowance is 1 ml per calorie of food[2]. In hot, dry climates the water requirement can be considerably increased as a result of sweating. Under ordinary conditions, infants require proportionately more water than adults and should be given 1.5 ml per calorie of food[2].

See also 'Water and Electrolyte Balance', pages 523–530.

Sodium and chloride

The requirement of sodium and chloride is closely linked to the water balance of the body. Both the total body content and body-fluid concentration of sodium are homoeostatically controlled, moderate intakes being rapidly excreted in the urine while a reduction in intake causes excretion to drop quickly to a very low level[16]. Sodium deficiency is rare in healthy persons provided there is no abnormal loss. The normal recommended NaCl intake is 1 g per kilogramme of water[2]. Hard physical work in the tropics would require a daily intake of up to 19 g NaCl[17]. Normal diets in western Europe and USA contain 6–18 g NaCl.

Potassium

The minimum daily potassium requirement probably amounts to 0.8–1.3 g[2]. Normal diets in western countries provide 0.8–1.5 g potassium per 1000 kcal. An adequate potassium intake is important during prolonged intravenous feeding, recovery from severe diarrhoea, and diabetic acidosis; this should be met by an intake of 40–120 mg (1–3 mEq) per kg body weight per day.

Magnesium

The probable daily magnesium requirement[18] is 150 mg for children under 10 years and 200–300 mg for older children; with a daily protein intake of 70–80 g, men require 300–400, women 300 mg per day. The requirement seems to increase with increasing protein intake. For the recommendations of the Food and Nutrition Board (USA) see the table on page 494. An average diet provides 250–500 mg magnesium per day.

Calcium and phosphorus

Knowledge of the minimum requirements of calcium is inadequate, but it is well established that no injurious effects occur when the daily calcium intake lies between 300 mg and 2000 mg[19].

The desirable calcium intakes (*suggested practical allowances*) recommended by the FAO/WHO Expert Group (see table on page 493) are lower than those of the Food and Nutrition Board (USA)[2] (see table on page 494).

Although the calcium–phosphorus ratio in bone is 2:1 it is much lower in the soft tissues. This, and the fact that on a normal diet the intake of phosphorus always equals or exceeds that of calcium, have led to the recommendation[2] that the calcium and phosphorus allowances should be equal except in the case of young infants (see the table on page 494).

Iron

In order to remain in iron balance, the daily iron intake of men, as well as of women after the menopause, must be 0.5–1.0 mg; menstruating women require some 0.3–1.0 mg per day more[20]. The iron requirement is increased during pregnancy, particularly as a result of the increase in the total erythrocyte volume, and this need is met partly by mobilization of iron reserves. The latter are restored post partum when the total erythrocyte volume falls again.

During the first months of life the iron requirement of infants is met principally from endogenous sources. Special attention should be paid to the iron needs of growing girls, who have to meet not only the requirements of growth but also cover menstruation losses. Assuming that 10% of the dietary iron is absorbed, the following amounts must be available in the diet:

Dietary iron requirements (Committee on Iron Deficiency Anemia, American Medical Association[21])

	Iron requirement of body mg/day	Dietary iron content* mg/day
Men	0.5–1.0	5–10
Menstruating women	0.7–2.0	7–20
Pregnant women	2.0–4.8	20–48
Adolescents	1.0–2.0	10–20
Children	0.4–1.0	4–10
Infants	0.5–1.5	1.5 mg/kg**

* Assuming 10% absorption of dietary iron.
** Up to a maximum of 15 mg.

With the exception of those during pregnancy, these requirements are almost identical with the recommendation of the Food and Nutrition Board (USA) (page 494).

Estimates of dietary iron intake in the UK, USA, Australia and Canada have given values of 10–20 mg per person per day; various studies in the USA have shown that children aged 3–6 years have a daily iron intake of 3–11 mg[22].

In infants the iron requirement is not met by the normal intake of breast or cow's milk alone. Premature infants, as well as infants with iron deficiency, require additional iron from the 2nd to 3rd month of life on; this should be given in the form of enriched cereal products or possibly iron salts[23]. The iron requirement in pregnancy is likewise met only with difficulty from dietary sources.

Copper

Copper is an important component of various enzymes involved in oxygen transport. In USA and Europe the diet of adults contains an average of 1–5 mg copper per day[22]. The daily requirement of adults has been estimated at 1.5–2 mg[2, 22], that of infants and children at 0.04–0.14 mg per kilogramme body weight[24].

Manganese

Manganese is very probably an essential nutrient. The element appears to be involved in the synthesis of lipids and in oxidative phosphorylation[25]. The daily diet contains 2–5 mg manganese[26], an amount apparently sufficient to meet human requirements. In order to maintain a positive manganese balance, daily dietary intakes of 0.2–0.3 mg manganese per kilogramme body weight have been recommended for children[27].

Zinc

Zinc is an important component of enzymes, particularly dehydrogenases. The daily dietary intake necessary for maintaining a positive zinc balance is 10–15 mg[28]. The zinc content of breast milk falls during the course of lactation (see page 688) and may be inadequate to meet the infant's zinc requirement[29].

Cobalt

Cobalt is a component of vitamin B_{12} and as far as is known is not used by the human body in any other way. The treatment of anaemia by cobalt salts is of doubtful value[30].

Molybdenum

Molybdenum is an essential component of various enzymes, particularly xanthine oxidase[31]. The normal diet appears to contain sufficient molybdenum to meet the need for this element.

Vanadium

Vanadium is possibly an essential nutrient in that it may be involved in lipid metabolism. The daily dietary intake amounts to 2 mg[32].

Chromium

Chromium in its trivalent form is probably an essential nutrient since there appears to be a relationship between this element and insulin function[33]. The daily diet contains 30–100 µg of chromium, of which about 1% is absorbed, enough to meet any possible requirement[34].

Selenium

Selenium has not been shown to be a significant nutrient for man, though a role in the metabolism of tocopherol and amino acids containing sulphur has been reported[35].

Iodine

Iodine is a component of thyroid hormones (see pages 725 sq.). The minimum requirement of adults has been estimated at 50–75 µg per day; children and pregnant women have a higher requirement[2, 36]. On the basis of the iodine turnover of the whole body the optimum requirement of adults has been estimated at 114–357 µg per day[37]. For the recommendations of the Food and Nutrition Board (USA) see the table on page 494. The iodine content of foods varies with that of the soil from which the food has originated. The addition of iodine to table salt in the proportion of 1:10000 to 1:100000 (as potassium iodide) is probably sufficient to guarantee an adequate iodine intake[36]. On the average, iodinated table salt contains the following amounts of iodine (in µg/g NaCl): German Federal Republic and Poland $\leq$ 3.8; Switzerland, Netherlands, Italy, Jugoslavia 7.6; England and Wales 19; Argentina 25; New Zealand 38; USA and Canada, international shipping and aircraft 76.

Fluorine

Fluorine is a component of dental enamel and plays a role in its protection against dental caries[39]. When the drinking water contains 1 mg fluoride per litre the incidence of dental caries, especially in children aged 6–15 years, is less than when the drinking water is relatively poor in fluoride. With a drinking-water fluoride content of 1 mg/l the daily fluoride intake has been estimated at 1.4–1.8 mg for adults and 0.4–0.8 mg for children aged 1–3 years. The Canadian Council on Nutrition has recommended a daily fluoride intake of 0.25 mg for infants and 0.5–1.0 mg for children aged 1–14 years[40]. In areas where the fluoride content of the natural water is low, fluoridation of the drinking water, in the proportion 1:1000000, is recommended by the Food and Nutrition Board (USA)[2], though the desirability of this measure is still internationally debated.

Vitamins

Vitamin requirements are dealt with under the individual vitamins in the chapter 'Vitamins', pages 457–492. The recommendations of the FAO/WHO Expert Group regarding vitamin A, thiamine, riboflavin and niacin and of the Food and Nutrition Board (USA) regarding these and other important vitamins are shown in the tables on page 493 and 494 respectively.

References

1 Young, E.G., in Beaton and McHenry (Eds.), *Nutrition: A Comprehensive Treatise*, vol. 2, Academic Press, New York, 1964, page 299.
2 Food and Nutrition Board, *Recommended Dietary Allowances*, 7th ed., National Academy of Sciences – National Research Council, Publication 1694, Washington, 1968.
3 *Calorie Requirements*, Report of the Second Committee on Calorie Requirements, *FAO Nutritional Studies*, No. 15, Food and Agriculture Organization of the United Nations, Rome, 1957.
4 *Protein Requirements*, Report of a Joint FAO/WHO Expert Group, *Wld Hlth Org. techn. Rep. Ser.*, No. 301 (1965).
5 *Calcium Requirements*, Report of a Joint FAO/WHO Expert Group, *Wld Hlth Org. techn. Rep. Ser.*, No. 230 (1962).
6 *Requirements of Vitamin A, Thiamine, Riboflavine and Niacin*, Report of a Joint FAO/WHO Expert Group, Rome 1965, *Wld Hlth Org. techn. Rep. Ser.*, No. 362 (1967).
7 Passmore, R., *Nutr. et Dieta (Basel)*, **8**, 161 (1966).
8 Barness and György, *Wld Rev. Nutr. Diet.*, **3**, 1 (1962).
9 Holman, R.T., *J. Amer. med. Ass.*, **178**, 930 (1961).
10 Hansen et al., *Acta Paediat.*, **51**, suppl. 137, 1 (1962).
11 Holt et al., *Protein and Amino Acid Requirements in Early Life*, New York University Press, New York, 1960.
12 Rose, W.C., *Fed. Proc.*, **8**, 546 (1949), and *Nutr. Abstr. Rev.*, **27**, 631 (1957).
13 Williams, H.H., *J. Amer. diet. Ass.*, **35**, 929 (1959).
14 Tuttle et al., *Metabolism*, **6**, 564 (1957), and *Amer. J. clin. Nutr.*, **16**, 229 (1965); Bigwood, E.J., *Nutr. et Dieta (Basel)*, **8**, 226 (1966).
15 Cotlove and Hogben, in Comar and Bronner (Eds.), *Mineral Metabolism*, vol. 2, part B, Academic Press, New York, 1962, page 109.
16 Weisberg, H.F., *Water Electrolytes and Acid Base Balance, Normal and Pathological*, Williams & Wilkins, Baltimore, Md., 1962.
17 Malhotra, M.S., *Indian J. med. Res.*, **48**, 212 (1960).
18 *Magnesium in Human Nutrition*, Home Economics Research Report, No. 19, Agricultural Research Service, United States Department of Agriculture, Washington.
19 Council on Foods and Nutrition, *J. Amer. med. Ass.*, **185**, 588 (1963).
20 Moore and Brown, Le métabolisme du fer, *Documenta Geigy, Acta clinica*, No. 7, Basle, 1967.
21 Committee on Iron Deficiency Anemia, *J. Amer. med. Ass.*, **203**, 407 (1968).
22 Hawkins, W.W., in Beaton and McHenry (Eds.), *Nutrition*, Academic Press, New York, 1964, page 309.
23 Schulman, I., *J. Amer. med. Ass.*, **175**, 118 (1961).
24 Gubler, C.J., *J. Amer. med. Ass.*, **161**, 530 (1956); Cordano et al., *Pediatrics*, **34**, 324 (1964).
25 Cotzias, G.C., in Comar and Bronner (Eds.), *Mineral Metabolism*, vol. 2, part B, Academic Press, New York, 1962, page 403.
26 Schroeder et al., *J. chron. Dis.*, **19**, 545 (1966).
27 Review, *Nutr. Rev.*, **23**, 236 (1965).
28 Vallee, B.L., in Comar and Bronner (Eds.), *Mineral Metabolism*, vol. 2, part B, Academic Press, New York, 1962, page 443.
29 Strain et al., in *VII. Internationaler Ernährungskongreß*, Hamburg 1966, Summaries of Papers, Pergamos-Druck, Hamburg, 1966, page 269.
30 Smith, E.L., in Comar and Bronner (Eds.), *Mineral Metabolism*, vol. 2, part B, Academic Press, New York, 1962, page 349.
31 De Renzo, E.C., in Comar and Bronner (Eds.), *Mineral Metabolism*, vol. 2, part B, Academic Press, New York, 1962, page 483.
32 Schroeder et al., *J. chron. Dis.*, **16**, 1047 (1963).
33 Glinsmann et al., *Science*, **152**, 1243 (1966).
34 Schroeder et al., *J. chron. Dis.*, **15**, 941 (1962).
35 Scott, M.L., in Comar and Bronner (Eds.), *Mineral Metabolism*, vol. 2, part B, Academic Press, New York, 1962, page 543.
36 Stanbury and Ramalingaswami, in Beaton and McHenry (Eds.), *Nutrition*, vol. 1, Academic Press, New York, 1964, page 373.
37 Heinrich and Gabbe, *Klin. Wschr.*, **42**, 1248 (1964).
38 Davidson and Passmore, *Human Nutrition and Dietetics*, 4th ed., Livingstone, Edinburgh, 1969, page 243.
39 Nikiforuk and Grainger, in Beaton and McHenry (Eds.), *Nutrition*, vol. 1, Academic Press, New York, 1964, page 417; Duckworth, R., *Brit. med. J.*, **2**, 283 (1966).
40 Canadian Council on Nutrition, May 1963, quoted by Young, E.G., in Beaton and McHenry (Eds.), *Nutrition*, vol. 2, Academic Press, New York, 1964, page 299.

Amounts of principal nutrients, vitamins and minerals in various foods (tables on pages 499–515)

The extensive literature available on the chemical composition of foods has necessitated a critical selection of the most reliable and representative values for the various nutrients. The principal tables that have been made use of are those of the FAO[1], the US Department of Agriculture[2], the British Medical Research Council[3] and the West German Bundesministerium für Ernährung, Landwirtschaft und Forsten[4]. Data from various journals[5] have also been made use of. Detailed summaries of the nutrient contents of foods are also to be found in the works compiled by Church and Church[6], the Swiss Lebensmittelbuchkommission[7], Randoin et al.[8], Schall[9] and Schtenberg et al.[10], as well as in the monographs of Albritton[11], Mattice[12], Proudfit and Robinson[13], Turner[14], and others.

It is important to note that the actual concentration of a particular substance in a foodstuff can deviate from the value given in the tables since all foods are subject to large variations in composition. This is particularly the case with prepared foods such as preserves, chocolate, sausages, etc. With meat, the degree of fattening of the animal plays an important part (fat content), with vegetable foods the climate, nature of the soil and degree of ripening. The storage conditions of foods affect the extent to which their water and vitamin contents are conserved. Water loss results in a higher concentration of all nutrients.

Preparing and cooking foods can lead to loss of nutrients. Some vitamins are decomposed by heat and oxidation. Both vitamins and mineral constituents pass into water in which foods are cooked and are lost if this is discarded.

The values given in the food composition tables are the contents in 100 g of the edible portion, uncooked unless otherwise stated.

With the exception of the calorific value, the data indicate the total amounts of the components in the food as ingested and not in that part of it absorbed. Little is known of the extent to which minerals and vitamins are absorbed. Thus only 2–12% – depending on the type of foodstuff – of the iron contained in foods is absorbed; the element is more readily absorbed from lean meat, haemoglobin and soya beans than from eggs, cereals and vegetables[15]. A high oxalic acid content can seriously interfere with the absorption of calcium.

The *water content* is usually determined by measuring the loss of weight at high temperature, so that the values may include other readily volatile substances.

The *protein content* is obtained from the nitrogen content by multiplying by 6.25 for meat and eggs, by 6.38 for milk, and by various factors ranging from 5.18 to 6.25 for vegetables, cereals and nuts (for details see the US Department of Agriculture Handbook No. 8[2]).

The *fat content* is that part of the food extractable by fat solvents (for instance ether). The data for polyene fatty acids are either the sum of the linoleic and arachidonic acid contents or the difference between the oleic acid and total unsaturated fatty acid contents. The cholesterol content is roughly equivalent to the unsaponifiable part of the total fat. Cholesterol occurs only in animal products, however, so that 'cholesterol' values for nuts, cereals and other vegetable foods reflect their content of other sterols.

The *carbohydrate content* is usually determined by difference, namely as the total weight less water, protein, fat and ash. Data for fibre content vary greatly with the method of determination. Collected data on the amounts of the various carbohydrates in foods are available[16].

The *calorific value* is calculated from the fat, carbohydrate and protein (and any alcoholic) content by using a specific factor that takes account of the varying extent to which different foods are absorbed (for details see the report by the Food and Agriculture Organization[17]); the data therefore represent utilizable calories.

Vitamins. Amounts of vitamin A (including β-carotene) and vitamin D are given in international units (IU), those of all other vitamins in milligrammes. 1 IU vitamin A = 0.0003 mg vitamin A_1 or 0.0006 mg β-carotene; 1 IU vitamin D = 0.000025 mg vitamin D_3. The data under vitamin E are α-tocopherol values (when known) since this compound is responsible for most of the vitamin activity (see page 465).

Percentage vitamin losses during cooking[18]

	B_1	B_2	Nicotinic acid	C
Meats	35	20	25	–
Meats plus drippings	25	5	10	–
Eggs	25	10	0	–
Cereals	10	0	10	–
Legumes	20	0	0	–
Vegetables (leafy, green and yellow)	40	25	25	60
Vegetables, other	25	15	25	60
Tomatoes	5	5	5	15
Potatoes	40	25	25	60

Zero and unknown values. Zero values are indicated by 0 throughout. A dash (–) denotes that the value is unknown.

References

1 Chatfield, C., *Food Composition Tables for International Use*, FAO Nutritional Studies No. 3, Food and Agriculture Organization of the United Nations, Washington, 1949; Chatfield, C., *Food Composition Tables – Minerals and Vitamins – for International Use*, FAO Nutritional Studies No. 11, Food and Agriculture Organization of the United Nations, Rome, 1954.
2 Watt and Merrill, *Composition of Foods – Raw, Processed, Prepared*, United States Department of Agriculture, Agriculture Handbook No. 8, Washington, 1963.
3 McCance and Widdowson, *The Composition of Foods*, Med. Res. Coun. Spec. Rep. Ser., No. 297, HMSO, London, 1960.
4 Souci et al., *Die Zusammensetzung der Lebensmittel*, 2 vols., Wissenschaftliche Verlagsgesellschaft, Stuttgart, 1962 and 1964.
5 *Agricultural and Food Chemistry; Bulletin de la Société scientifique d'hygiène alimentaire et d'alimentation rationnelle; Food Research; Journal of the American Dietetic Association; Journal of Nutrition; Journal of the Science of Food and Agriculture; Mitteilungen aus dem Gebiete der Lebensmitteluntersuchung und Hygiene; Zeitschrift für Lebensmittel-Untersuchung und -Forschung.*
6 Church and Church, *Bowes and Church's Food Values of Portions Commonly Used*, 9th ed., Lippincott, Philadelphia, 1963.
7 Schweizerische Lebensmittelbuchkommission, *Schweizerisches Lebensmittelbuch*, 5th ed., vol. 1, Eidg. Drucksachen- u. Materialzentrale, Berne, 1964, page 736.
8 Randoin et al., *Tables de composition des aliments*, 3rd ed., Lanore, Paris, 1961.
9 Schall, H., *Nahrungsmitteltabelle*, 18th ed., Barth, Leipzig, 1962.
10 Schtenberg et al., *Chemische Zusammensetzung und Nährwert der Lebensmittel*, Akademie-Verlag, Berlin, 1959.
11 Albritton, E.C. (Ed.), *Standard Values in Nutrition and Metabolism*, Saunders, Philadelphia, 1954.
12 Mattice, M. R., *Bridges' Food and Beverage Analyses*, 3rd ed., Lea & Febiger, Philadelphia, 1950.
13 Robinson, C. H., *Proudfit-Robinson's Normal and Therapeutic Nutrition*, 13th ed., Macmillan, New York, 1967.
14 Turner, D. F., *Handbook of Diet Therapy*, 3rd ed., University of Chicago Press, Chicago, 1959.
15 Moore and Brown, Le métabolisme du fer, *Documenta Geigy, Acta clinica*, No. 7, Basle, 1967.
16 Hardinge et al., *J. Amer. diet. Ass.*, **46**, 197 (1965).
17 *Energy Yielding Components of Food and Computation of Caloric Values*, Food and Agriculture Organization, Nutrition Division, Washington, 1947.
18 Interdepartmental Committee on Nutrition, *Publ. Hlth Rep. (Wash.)*, **75**, 687 (1960).

Content per 100 grammes edible portion (unless otherwise stated)	Water g	Proteins g	Fats: Total g	Fats: Poly-unsaturated g	Carbohydrates: Total g	Carbohydrates: Fibre g	Calories* kcal	Vitamins: A** IU	Vitamins: B1 mg	Vitamins: B2 mg	Vitamins: B6 mg	Vitamins: Nicotinic acid mg	Vitamins: Pantothenic acid mg	Vitamins: C mg	Vitamins: Other vitamins*** mg	Other organic constituents: Malic acid mg	Other organic constituents: Citric acid mg	Other organic constituents: Oxalic acid mg	Excess acid A / Excess base B	Elements: Sodium Na mg	Elements: Potassium K mg	Elements: Calcium Ca mg	Elements: Magnesium Mg mg	Elements: Manganese Mn mg	Elements: Iron Fe mg	Elements: Copper Cu mg	Elements: Phosphorus P mg	Elements: Sulphur S mg	Elements: Chlorine Cl mg
Fruits, Fruit juices																													
Apples (sweet) (*Pirus malus*)	84.0	0.3	0.6	–	15.0	0.9	58	90	0.04	0.02	0.03	0.1	0.1	5[1]	E 0.3; biotin 0.001; FA 0.002	270–1020	0–30	1.5	B	1	116	7	5	0.07	0.3	0.08	10	5	4
per lb as purchased (refuse 18%)	*312*	*1.1*	*2.2*	–	*56*	*3.3*	*216*	*335*	*0.15*	*0.07*	*0.11*	*0.4*	*0.4*	*19*	*E 1.1; biotin 0.004; FA 0.007*	*1000–3790*	*0–112*	*5.6*	*B*	*4*	*431*	*26*	*19*	*0.26*	*1.1*	*0.29*	*37*	*19*	*15*
dried	20.4	3	0.7	–	73.6	4.0	281	–	0.05	0.08	0.16	0.5	–	10[1]	–	–	–	–	B	5	557	31	29	–	1.6	–	52	19	19
Apple juice, fresh	86.9	0.1	trace	–	13	–	47	–	0.01	0.02	0.03	0.5	0.02	1	FA 0.001; biotin 0.0005	700	230	0	B	2	100	6	–	–	0.6	0.35	9	–	–
Apple sauce, sweetened	75.7	0.2	0.1	–	23.8	0.5	91	60	0.01	0.01	–	trace	–	1	–	–	–	–	B	0.3	55	4	5	–	0.5	–	5	–	–
Apricots (*Prunus armeniaca*)	85.3	0.9	0.2	–	12.8	0.6	51	2700	0.03	0.05	0.07	0.7	0.3	7	FA 0.003	–	–	–	B	0.6	440	17	9	0.2	0.5	0.12	23	6	2
per lb as purchased (refuse 6%)	*364*	*3.8*	*0.9*	–	*55*	*2.6*	*217*	*11500*	*0.13*	*0.21*	*0.29*	*3.0*	*1.3*	*30*	*FA 0.013*	–	–	–	*B*	*3*	*1880*	*72*	*38*	*0.9*	*2.1*	*0.51*	*98*	*25*	*9*
canned, sweetened	76.9	0.6	0.1	–	22.0	0.4	86	1740	0.02	0.02	0.05	0.3	0.1	4	–	330	1060	–	B	2	256	11	7	0.08	0.3	0.05	15	1.0	2
dried	25.0	5.0	0.5	–	66.5	3.0	260	10900	0.01	0.16	0.25	3.3	0.7	12	FA 0.005	810	350	–	B	26	1700	67	65	0.28	5.5	0.4	119	164	35
Avocados (*Persea gratissima*)	73.6	2.2	17.0	2	6.0	1.5	171	290	0.11	0.20	0.61	1.6	0.9	14	FA 0.03	–	–	–	B	3	340	10	30	0.3–4.2	0.6	0.4	42	25	10
Bananas (*Musa sapientium*)	75.7	1.1	0.2	–	22.2	0.6	85	190	0.05	0.06	0.32	0.6	0.2	10	E 0.2; biotin 0.004; FA 0.01	500	150	6.4	B	1	420	8	31	0.64	0.7	0.2	28	12	125
per lb as purchased (refuse 32%)	*233*	*3.4*	*0.6*	–	*68*	*1.9*	*262*	*586*	*0.15*	*0.19*	*1.0*	*1.9*	*6.1*	*31*	*E 0.6; biotin 0.012; FA 0.03*	*1540*	*463*	*19.7*	*B*	*3*	*1300*	*25*	*96*	*1.97*	*2.2*	*0.6*	*86*	*37*	*386*
Blackberries (*Rubus fruticosus*)	84.5	1.2	0.9	–	12.9	4.1	58	200	0.03	0.04	0.05	0.4	0.25	21	biotin 0.0004; FA 0.012	160	trace	18	B	4	181	32	24	0.59	1.0	0.12	19	17	15
frozen, sweetened	74.3	0.8	0.3	–	24.4	1.8	96	140	0.02	0.10	–	0.6	–	8	–	–	–	–	B	1	105	17	12	–	0.6	–	17	–	–
Cantaloups (*Cucumis melo*)	91.2	0.7	0.1	–	7.5	0.3	30	3400[2]	0.04	0.03	0.036	0.6	0.26	33	biotin 0.003; FA 0.007	0	–	0	B	12	230	14	17	0.04	0.4	0.04	16	11.7	41
per lb as purchased (refuse 50%)	*207*	*1.6*	*0.2*	–	*1.7*	*0.7*	*68*	*7710*	*0.09*	*0.07*	*0.08*	*1.4*	*0.6*	*75*	*biotin 0.007; FA 0.016*	*0*	–	*0*	*B*	*27*	*522*	*32*	*39*	*0.09*	*0.9*	*0.09*	*36*	*27*	*93*
Cherries (*Prunus avium*)	83.4	1.2	0.4	–	14.6	0.5	60	1000	0.05	0.06	0.05	0.3	0.08	10	biotin 0.0004; FA 0.006	1250	10	trace	B	2	260	19	14	0.03	0.5	0.07	19	8	3
per lb as purchased (refuse 10%)	*340*	*4.9*	*1.6*	–	*59.6*	*2.0*	*245*	*4080*	*0.20*	*0.24*	*0.20*	*1.2*	*0.32*	*41*	*biotin 0.0016; FA 0.024*	*5100*	*41*	*trace*	*B*	*8*	*1060*	*78*	*57*	*0.12*	*2.0*	*0.29*	*78*	*33*	*12*
Cranberries (*Vaccinium macrocarpon*)	87.9	0.4	0.7	–	10.8	1.4	46	40	0.03	0.02	0.06	0.1	–	12	–	260	1120	–	B	1	65	14	8	0.3	0.5	0.09	11	7	5
Cranberry sauce	62.1	0.1	0.2	–	37.5	0.2	146	20	0.01	0.01	–	trace	–	2	–	–	–	–	B	1	17	6	2	–	0.2	–	4	–	–

* To convert to kJ (kilojoule) multiply the values given by 4.1855.
** Vitamin A activity due to vitamin A + carotenes; 1 IU vitamin A = 0.0006 mg β-carotene.
*** FA = folic acid; E = α-tocopherol unless otherwise stated.
[1] Wide variations between different varieties.
[2] Highly coloured variety.

Content per 100 grammes edible portion (unless otherwise stated)	Water	Proteins	Fats: Total	Fats: Poly-unsaturated	Carbo-hydrates: Total	Carbo-hydrates: Fibre	Calories*	Vitamins: A**	Vitamins: B₁	Vitamins: B₂	Vitamins: B₆	Vitamins: Nicotinic acid	Vitamins: Pantothenic acid	Vitamins: C	Vitamins: Other vitamins***	Other organic constituents: Malic acid	Other organic constituents: Citric acid	Other organic constituents: Oxalic acid	Excess acid A Excess base B	Elements: Sodium Na	Elements: Potassium K	Elements: Calcium Ca	Elements: Magnesium Mg	Elements: Manganese Mn	Elements: Iron Fe	Elements: Copper Cu	Elements: Phosphorus P	Elements: Sulphur S	Elements: Chlorine Cl
	g	g	g	g	g	g	kcal	IU	mg	mg	mg	mg	mg	mg	mg	mg	mg	mg		mg	mg	mg	mg	mg	mg	mg	mg	mg	mg
Currants																													
red and white (*Ribes rubrum*) . . .	85.7	1.4	0.2	–	12.1	3.4	50	120	0.04	0.02	0.05	0.3	0.06	41	biotin 0.0026	50	2300	19	B	2	275	36	15	0.6	1.0	0.12	23	29	13
black (*Ribes nigrum*)	82	1.0	0.1	–	16.1	5.7	62	220	0.05	0.03	0.08	0.3	–	136	–	400	3030	4	B	3	336	17	10	–	0.9	0.12	28	–	–
Dates (*Phoenix dactylifera*)																													
dried	22.5	2.2	0.5	–	72.9	2.3	274	50	0.09	0.10	0.1	2.2	0.8	0	FA 0.025	–	–	–	B	1	790	59	65	0.15	3.0	0.21	63	65	290
Elderberries, black (*Sambucus nigra*)	80.9	2.5	0.5	–	15.9	6.8	42	600	0.07	0.08	0.25	1.5	0.18	18	biotin 0.002; FA 0.017	–	–	–	B	0.5	305	35	–	–	1.6	–	57	–	–
Figs (*Ficus carica*)	81.7	1.2	0.4	–	16.1	1.4	65	75	0.09	0.08	0.13	0.63	0.4	2	FA 0.01	trace	340	–	B	2	190	35	21	–	0.8	0.06	22	12	14
dried	23.0	4.3	1.3	–	69.1	5.6	274	80	0.10	0.10	0.32	1.7	0.5	0	FA 0.03	–	–	–	B	34	780	126	82	0.35	4.0	0.35	116	69	105
Fruit cocktail																													
canned	79.6	0.4	0.1	–	19.7	0.4	76	140	0.02	0.01	–	0.4	–	2	–	–	–	–	B	5	160	9	8	–	0.4	0.03	12	2	3
Gooseberries (*Ribes grossularia*) . .	88.9	0.8	0.2	–	9.7	1.9	39	290	0.15	0.03	0.02	0.3	0.15	25	biotin 0.0005	500–2080	–	–	B	1	210	35	9	0.04	0.5	0.08	31	15	9
Grapes (*Vitis vinifera*)	81.4	0.6	0.3	–	17.3	0.5	67	100	0.05	0.02	0.1	0.3	0.08	4	biotin 0.002; FA 0.006	650	–	–	B	2	250	12	7	0.083	0.4	0.1	20	9	2
Grape juice	82.9	0.2	trace	–	16.6	trace	66	–	0.04	0.02	0.021	0.2	0.04	2	biotin 0.0003; FA 0.003	310	20	–	B	1	120	11	4	–	0.3	0.02	12	–	–
Grapefruit (*Citrus decumana*)	88.4	0.6	0.1	–	9.8	0.5	39	80	0.04	0.02	0.02	0.2	0.25	40	E 0.25; FA 0.003; biotin 0.003	80	1460	0	B	2	198	17	10	0.01	0.3	0.02	16	5	3
per lb as purchased (refuse 51%) . .	*197*	*1.3*	*0.2*	–	*22*	*1.1*	*87*	*178*	*0.09*	*0.04*	*0.04*	*0.4*	*0.56*	*89*	*E 0.56; FA 0.007; biotin 0.007*	*178*	*3250*	*0*	*B*	*5*	*441*	*38*	*22*	*0.02*	*0.7*	*0.04*	*36*	*11*	*7*
canned, sweetened	81.1	0.6	0.1	–	17.8	0.2	70	10	0.03	0.02	–	0.2	–	30	–	–	–	–	B	2	135	13	11	–	0.3	–	14	–	–
Grapefruit juice, fresh	89.2	0.4	0.1	–	9.8	0.1	41	10	0.03	0.02	0.014	0.2	0.16	45	biotin 0.0007; FA 0.001	–	–	–	B	2	150	8	12	–	0.4	–	14	5	2
Lemons (*Citrus medica*)	90.1	1.1	0.3	–	8.2	0.4	27	20	0.04	0.02	0.06	0.1	0.2	45	FA 0.007	trace	3840	–	B	6	148	26	9	0.04	0.6	0.26	16	8	4
Lemon juice	91.0	0.5	0.2	–	8.0	–	25	20	0.03	0.01	0.039	0.1	0.1	50	FA 0.001	290	6080	–	B	1	130	14	7	–	0.2	0.13	11	2	4
Lime juice (*Citrus aurantifolia*) . . .	90.3	0.3	–	–	9.0	–	26	10	0.02	0.01	0.05	0.1	–	32	–	–	–	–	B	1	100	9	–	–	0.2	–	11	–	39
Loganberries (*Rubus ursinus* var. *loganobaccus*)	83	1.0	0.6	–	14.9	3.0	62	200	0.03	0.04	–	0.4	–	24	–	–	–	–	B	1	170	35	25	–	1.2	0.14	17	18	16
Melons, water (*Citrullus vulgaris* var. *colocynthoides*)	92.6	0.5	0.2	–	6.4	0.3	26	590	0.03	0.03	0.033	0.2	0.3	7	biotin 0.004; FA 0.0006	200	–	0	B	0.3	100	7	8	0.02	0.5	0.07	10	9	8
Nectarines (*Prunus persica* var. *nectarina*)	81.8	0.6	trace	–	17.1	0.4	64	1650	–	–	–	–	–	13	–	–	–	–	B	6	294	4	13	–	0.5	0.06	24	10	5

* To convert to kJ (kilojoule) multiply the values given by 4.1855. ** Vitamin A activity due to vitamin A + carotenes; 1 IU vitamin A = 0.0006 mg β-carotene. *** FA = folic acid; E = α-tocopherol unless otherwise stated.

Content per 100 grammes edible portion (unless otherwise stated)	Water g	Proteins g	Fats: Total g	Fats: Poly-unsaturated g	Carbo-hydrates: Total g	Carbo-hydrates: Fibre g	Calories* kcal	Vitamins: A** IU	Vitamins: B_1 mg	Vitamins: B_2 mg	Vitamins: B_6 mg	Vitamins: Nicotinic acid mg	Vitamins: Pantothenic acid mg	Vitamins: C mg	Vitamins: Other vitamins*** mg	Other organic constituents: Malic acid mg	Other organic constituents: Citric acid mg	Other organic constituents: Oxalic acid mg	Excess acid A Excess base B	Elements: Sodium Na mg	Elements: Potassium K mg	Elements: Calcium Ca mg	Elements: Magnesium Mg mg	Elements: Manganese Mn mg	Elements: Iron Fe mg	Elements: Copper Cu mg	Elements: Phosphorus P mg	Elements: Sulphur S mg	Elements: Chlorine Cl mg
Olives (*Olea europaea*) green	78.2	1.4	12.7	1.0	1.3	1.3	116	300	0.03	0.08	0.02	0.5	0.02	0	FA 0.001	–	–	–	B	2400	55	61	22	0.05–1.0	1.6	0.46	17	32	3750
Oranges (*Citrus sinensis*)	87.1	1.0	0.2	–	12.2	0.5	49	200	0.10	0.03	0.03	0.2	0.2	50	E 0.23; biotin 0.001; FA 0.005	trace	980	24	B	0.3	170	41	10	0.025	0.4	0.07	23	8	4
per lb as purchased (refuse 27%)	*288*	*3.3*	*0.7*	–	*40*	*1.7*	*162*	*662*	*0.33*	*0.10*	*0.10*	*0.7*	*0.7*	*166*	*E 0.76; biotin 0.003; FA 0.017*	*trace*	*3250*	*79*	*B*	*1*	*563*	*136*	*33*	*0.083*	*1.3*	*0.23*	*76*	*26*	*13*
Orange juice, fresh	86	0.6	0.1	–	12.9	0.1	49	100	0.07	0.02	0.026	0.2	0.14	50[1]	biotin 0.0003; FA 0.002	–	–	–	B	0.5	190	11	11	–	0.3	0.08	17	8	4
Peaches (*Prunus persica*)	86.6	0.6	0.1	–	11.8	0.6	46	880	0.02	0.05	0.02	1.0	0.12	7	biotin 0.002; FA 0.004	370	370	trace	B	0.5	160	9	10	0.11	0.5	0.01	19	7	5
per lb as purchased (refuse 13%)	*342*	*2.4*	*0.4*	–	*47*	*2.4*	*182*	*3470*	*0.08*	*0.20*	*0.08*	*3.9*	*0.5*	*28*	*biotin 0.008; FA 0.016*	*1460*	*1460*	*trace*	*B*	*2*	*631*	*36*	*39*	*0.43*	*2.0*	*0.04*	*74*	*28*	*20*
canned, sweetened	79.1	0.4	0.1	–	20.1	0.4	78	430	0.01	0.02	0.02	0.6	0.05	4	biotin 0.0002; FA 0.0005	–	–	1.2	B	5	107	4	6.3	0.04	0.3	0.06	12	1	4
dried	25.0	3.0	0.7	–	68.3	3.1	262	3900	0.01	0.2	0.15	5.3	–	18	–	–	–	–	B	12	1100	48	54	0.67	6.0	0.3	117	240	11
Pears (*Pirus communis*)	83.2	0.5	0.4	–	15.5	1.5	61	20	0.02	0.04	0.02	0.1	0.05	4	biotin 0.0001; FA 0.002	120	240	3	B	2	129	8	9	0.06	0.3	0.13	11	7	4
per lb as purchased (refuse 9%)	*343*	*2.1*	*1.7*	–	*64*	*6.2*	*252*	*83*	*0.08*	*0.17*	*0.08*	*0.4*	*0.21*	*17*	*biotin 0.0004; FA 0.008*	*495*	*991*	*12*	*B*	*8*	*532*	*33*	*37*	*0.25*	*1.2*	*0.54*	*46*	*29*	*17*
canned, sweetened	79.8	0.2	0.2	–	19.6	0.6	76	trace	0.01	0.02	–	0.1	0.02	1	–	160	420	1.7	B	2	52	5	6	–	0.2	0.04	7	1.3	3
Persimmons, Japanese (kaki) (*Diospyros kaki*)	78.8	0.7	0.4	–	19.7	1.6	77	2710	0.03	0.02	–	0.1	–	11	–	–	–	–	B	6	174	6	8	–	0.3	–	26	–	–
Pineapples (*Ananas sativus*)	86.7	0.4	0.2	–	12.2	0.5	47	70	0.08	0.03	0.08	0.2	0.17	17	FA 0.004	120	770	–	B	0.3	210	17	17	1.07	0.5	0.07	8	2.5	46
canned, sweetened	79.9	0.3	0.1	–	19.4	0.3	74	50	0.08	0.02	0.07	0.2	–	7	FA 0.001	–	–	6.3	B	1	120	11	8	–	0.3	0.05	5	2.7	4.2
Pineapple juice, canned	85.6	0.4	0.1	–	13.5	0.1	55	50	0.05	0.02	0.1	0.2	0.1	7	FA 0.001	–	–	–	B	1	140	15	15	–	0.5	–	9	–	–
Plums (*Prunus domestica*)	85.7	0.7	0.1	–	12.3	0.7	50	250	0.07	0.04	0.05	0.5	0.13	6	biotin trace; FA 0.002	360–2390	30	10	B	2	167	13	13	0.1	0.4	0.3	23	5	2
per lb as purchased (refuse 6%)	*365*	*3.0*	*0.4*	–	*52*	*3.0*	*213*	*1070*	*0.30*	*0.17*	*0.21*	*2.1*	*0.55*	*26*	*biotin trace; FA 0.008*	*1540–10200*	*128*	*43*	*B*	*8*	*712*	*55*	*55*	*0.4*	*1.7*	*1.3*	*98*	*21*	*8*
canned, sweetened	77.4	0.4	0.1	–	21.6	0.3	83	230	0.02	0.02	0.027	0.4	0.08	2	FA 0.001	–	–	–	B	1	142	9	5	0.07	0.9	0.16	10	–	–
Prunes dried, uncooked	28.0	2.1	0.6	–	67.4	1.6	255	1600	0.1	0.17	0.5	1.6	0.35	3	FA 0.005	–	–	–	B	6	700	51	32	0.18	3.9	0.16	79	28	9
Quinces (*Cydonia oblonga, Cydonia vulgaris*)	84	0.3	0.3	–	14.9	2.4	57	30	0.03	0.02	–	0.2	–	15	–	680–1590	–	–	B	3	203	14	6	0.04	0.3	0.13	19	5	2

* To convert to kJ (kilojoule) multiply the values given by 4.1855.
** Vitamin A activity due to vitamin A + carotenes; 1 IU vitamin A = 0.0006 mg β-carotene.
*** FA = folic acid; E = α-tocopherol unless otherwise stated.
[1] In canned juice 12.

Content per 100 grammes edible portion (unless otherwise stated)	Water	Proteins	Fats		Carbohydrates		Calories*	Vitamins								Other organic constituents			Excess acid A / Excess base B	Elements									
			Total	Poly-unsaturated	Total	Fibre		A**	B_1	B_2	B_6	Nicotinic acid	Pantothenic acid	C	Other vitamins***	Malic acid	Citric acid	Oxalic acid		Sodium Na	Potassium K	Calcium Ca	Magnesium Mg	Manganese Mn	Iron Fe	Copper Cu	Phosphorus P	Sulphur S	Chlorine Cl
	g	g	g	g	g	g	kcal	IU	mg	mg	mg	mg	mg	mg	mg	mg	mg	mg		mg	mg	mg	mg	mg	mg	mg	mg	mg	mg
Raisins (*Vitis vinifera*) dried	18.0	2.5	0.2	–	77.4	0.9	289	20	0.11	0.08	0.3	0.5	0.09	1	biotin 0.005; FA 0.01	–	–	–	B	31	725	62	42	0.32	3.5	0.2	101	42	9
Raspberries (*Rubus idaeus*)	84.2	1.2	0.5	–	13.6	3.0	57	150	0.03	0.09	0.09	0.9	0.2	25	biotin 0.0019; FA 0.005	40	1300	15	B	3	190	49	23	0.51	1.0	0.13	22	18	22
frozen, sweetened	74.3	0.7	0.2	–	24.6	2.2	98	70	0.02	0.02	–	0.6	–	21	–	–	–	–	B	1	100	13	11	–	0.6	–	17	–	–
Raspberry juice, fresh	88	0.2	0	–	11	trace	40	120	0.02	–	–	–	–	20	–	–	–	–	B	7	141	29	18	–	1.0	–	14	7	10
Strawberries (*Fragaria* sp.)	89.9	0.7	0.5	–	8.4	1.3	37	60	0.03	0.07	0.04	0.6	0.26	60	biotin 0.0011; FA 0.005	160	1080	19	B	1	145	21	12	0.06	1.0	0.13	21	12	11
frozen, sweetened	75.7	0.4	0.2	–	23.5	0.6	92	30	0.02	0.06	–	0.5	–	53	–	–	–	–	B	1	104	13	–	–	0.6	–	16	–	–
Tangerines (*Citrus nobilis*)	87	0.8	0.2	–	11.6	0.5	46	420	0.07	0.02	0.07	0.2	–	31	–	–	–	–	B	2	110	40	11	0.04	0.4	0.1	18	10	2
per lb as purchased (refuse 26%)	*292*	*2.7*	*0.7*	–	*39*	*1.7*	*154*	*1410*	*0.23*	*0.07*	*0.23*	*0.7*	–	*104*	–	–	–	–	*B*	*7*	*369*	*134*	*37*	*0.13*	*1.3*	*0.3*	*60*	*34*	*7*
Whortleberries (*Vaccinium myrtillus*)	83.2	0.7	0.5	–	15.3	1.5	62	100	0.03	0.06	0.091	0.5	0.12	14	FA 0.008	100	1560	15	B	1	89	15	10	2.3	1.0	0.11	13	11	8
frozen, sweetened	72.3	0.6	0.3	–	26.5	0.9	105	30	0.04	0.05	–	0.4	–	8	–	–	–	–	B	1	66	6	4	–	0.4	–	11	–	–
Vegetables																													
Artichokes (*Cynara scolymus*)	85.5	2.7	0.2	–	10.6	2.4	49	160	0.08	0.05	–	1.0	0.4	9	–	170	100	–	B	43	430	51	–	0.36	1.3	0.2	94	20	22
Asparagus (*Asparagus officinalis*)	92.9	2.1	0.2	–	4.1	0.8	21	900	0.18	0.20	0.14	1.5	0.62	33	E 2.5; FA 0.11	100	110	5.2	B	2	240	22	20	0.19	1.0	0.14	62	46	53
per lb as purchased (refuse 44%)	*236*	*5.3*	*0.5*	–	*10.4*	*2.0*	*53*	*2290*	*0.46*	*0.51*	*0.36*	*3.8*	*1.57*	*84*	*E 6.4; FA 0.28*	*254*	*279*	*13.2*	*B*	*5*	*610*	*56*	*51*	*0.48*	*2.5*	*0.36*	*157*	*117*	*135*
canned, drained solids	92.5	2.4	0.4	–	3.4	0.8	21	800	0.06	0.10	0.03	0.8	0.15	15	biotin 0.002; FA 0.03	–	–	–	B	236[1]	166	19	–	–	1.9	–	53	–	–
Beans kidney (*Phaseolus vulgaris*)	11.6	21.3	1.6	–	61.6	4.0	338	0	0.6	0.22	0.28	2.1	0.98	2	E 4	–	–	–	B	2	1310	106	132	2.0	6.1	–	429	–	25
lima (*Phaseolus lunatus*)	67.5	8.4	0.5	–	22.1	1.8	123	290	0.24	0.12	0.55	1.4	1.3	29	biotin 0.01; FA 0.13	170	650	4.3	B	1	680	52	66	–	2.8	0.86	142	60	9
canned, drained solids	74.7	5.4	0.3	–	18.3	1.8	96	190	0.03	0.05	0.08	0.5	0.11	6	FA 0.013	–	–	–	B	236[2]	210	28	–	–	2.4	–	70	–	–
string (*Phaseolus vulgaris*)	90.1	1.9	0.2	–	7.1	1.0	32	600	0.07	0.11	0.14	0.5	0.2	19	E<0.1; K 0.29; FA 0.028	130	30	30	B	1.7	256	56	26	0.45	0.8	0.07	44	30	33
per lb as purchased (refuse 12%)	*360*	*7.6*	*0.8*	–	*28.3*	*4.0*	*128*	*2400*	*0.28*	*0.44*	*0.56*	*2.0*	*0.8*	*76*	*E< 0.4; K 1.2; FA 0.12*	*519*	*120*	*120*	*B*	*7*	*1020*	*223*	*104*	*1.8*	*3.2*	*0.28*	*176*	*120*	*132*
canned, drained solids	91.9	1.4	0.1	–	5.2	1.0	24	470	0.03	0.05	0.043	0.3	0.07	4	biotin 0.001; FA 0.012	–	–	–	B	236[3]	95	45	13	–	1.5	–	25	–	–

* To convert to kJ (kilojoule) multiply the values given by 4.1855.
** Vitamin A activity due to vitamin A + carotenes; 1 IU vitamin A = 0.0006 mg β-carotene.
*** FA = folic acid; E = α-tocopherol unless otherwise stated.
[1] Unsalted 3.
[2] Unsalted 4.
[3] Unsalted 2.

Content per 100 grammes edible portion (unless otherwise stated)	Water g	Proteins g	Fats: Total g	Fats: Poly-unsaturated g	Carbo-hydrates: Total g	Carbo-hydrates: Fibre g	Calories* kcal	Vitamins: A** IU	Vitamins: B_1 mg	Vitamins: B_2 mg	Vitamins: B_6 mg	Vitamins: Nicotinic acid mg	Vitamins: Pantothenic acid mg	Vitamins: C mg	Vitamins: Other vitamins*** mg	Other organic constituents: Malic acid mg	Other organic constituents: Citric acid mg	Other organic constituents: Oxalic acid mg	Excess acid A Excess base B	Elements: Sodium Na mg	Elements: Potassium K mg	Elements: Calcium Ca mg	Elements: Magnesium Mg mg	Elements: Manganese Mn mg	Elements: Iron Fe mg	Elements: Copper Cu mg	Elements: Phosphorus P mg	Elements: Sulphur S mg	Elements: Chlorine Cl mg
Beets (beetroots) *(Beta vulgaris)* peeled	87.3	1.6	0.1	–	9.9	0.8	43	20	0.03	0.04	0.05	0.4	0.12	10	FA 0.02	0	110	338	B	84	303	25	23	0.94	0.7	0.19	33	15	61
tops	90.9	2.2	0.3	–	4.6	1.3	24	6100	0.05	0.17	–	0.3	0.26	30	biotin 0.003; FA 0.06	–	–	916	B	130	570	119	71	1.3	3.3	0.09	40	35	40
Broadbeans, mature, dry *(Vicia faba)*	12.6	24.0	2.2	–	58.2	5.9	339	30	0.53	0.30	–	2.5	–	6	–	–	–	–	B	–	–	77	–	–	6.3	–	374	–	–
Broccoli *(Brassica oleracea var. botrytis)*	89.1	3.6	0.3	–	5.9	1.5	32	2500	0.1	0.23	0.17	0.9	1.3	113	FA 0.05	120	210	–	B	15	400	103	24	0.15	1.1	1.4	78	137	76
frozen	90.7	3.3	0.2	–	5.1	1.1	28	1900	0.07	0.13	–	0.6	–	78	–	–	–	–	B	13	244	43	21	–	0.7	–	60	–	–
Brussels sprouts *(Brassica oleracea var. gemmifera)*	84.8	4.7	0.4	–	8.7	1.2	47	550	0.1	0.16	0.16	0.9	0.72	100	E 1; K 0.8–3; biotin 0.0004; FA 0.05	200	240	–	B	12	450	29	20	0.27	1.5	0.1	80	78	40
per lb as purchased (refuse 8%)	*354*	*19.6*	*1.7*	–	*36.3*	*5.0*	*196*	*2300*	*0.4*	*0.67*	*0.67*	*3.8*	*3.0*	*417*	*E 4; K 3.3–13; biotin 0.0016; FA 0.21*	*835*	*1000*	–	*B*	*50*	*1880*	*121*	*83*	*1.13*	*6.3*	*0.4*	*334*	*326*	*167*
Cabbage red *(Brassica oleracea var. capitata rubra)*	91.8	1.5	0.2	–	5.9	1.1	26	50	0.07	0.05	0.15	0.4	0.32	50	E 0.2; biotin 0.002	–	–	–	B	4	266	35	18	0.1	0.5	0.06	30	–	100
white (var. *capitata alba*)	92.1	1.4	0.2	–	5.7	1.5	25	70	0.05	0.04	0.11	0.32	0.26	46	E 0.7; FA 0.08	–	–	–	B	13	227	46	23	0.1	0.5	0.06	27.5	–	37
Carrots *(Daucus carota)*	88.6	1.1	0.2	–	9.1	1.0	40	11000[1]	0.06	0.06	0.12	0.6	0.27	2–10	E 0.45; biotin 0.003; FA 0.008	24	90	33	B	50	311	37	21	0.06–0.25	0.7	0.08	36	21	40
per lb as purchased (refuse 18%)	*330*	*4.1*	*0.7*	–	*33.8*	*3.7*	*149*	*41000*	*0.22*	*0.22*	*0.45*	*2.2*	*1.0*	*7–37*	*E 1.67; biotin 0.011; FA 0.03*	*89*	*335*	*123*	*B*	*186*	*1160*	*138*	*78*	*0.22–0.93*	*2.6*	*0.30*	*134*	*78*	*149*
canned, drained solids	91.2	0.8	0.3	–	6.7	0.8	30	15000	0.03	0.02	0.04	0.3	0.11	3	biotin 0.002; FA 0.003	–	–	–	B	236[2]	110	26	5	–	0.7	0.04	22	–	445
Cauliflower *(Brassica oleracea var. botrytis)*	91.0	2.7	0.2	–	5.2	1.0	27	60	0.11	0.10	0.2	0.6	1.0	78	E 0.15; K 3.6; biotin 0.017; FA 0.022	390	210	0	B	16	400	25	7	0.17	1.1	0.14	56	29	30
Celery *(Apium graveolens)* leaves and stalks	94.1	0.9	0.1	–	3.9	0.6	17	240	0.05	0.03	–	0.4	–	9	E 0.7	170	10	50	B	96	291	39	25	0.16	0.5	0.01	40	22	137
root	88.4	1.8	0.3	–	8.5	1.3	40	16	0.03	0.03	–	0.7	–	8	E 0.2	–	–	34	B	100	300	60	12	0.16	0.9	0.15	60	–	50
Chard, Swiss *(Beta vulgaris var. cicla)*	90.8	1.6	0.4	–	5.6	1.0	27	6500	0.03	0.09	–	0.4	0.17	34	E 1.5; FA 0.03	–	–	690	B	147	550	110	65	0.3	2.7	0.11	29	–	–
Chicory *(Cichorium intybus)*	96.2	0.8	0.1	–	3.7	0.6	16	–	0.07	0.12	–	0.40	–	10	–	–	–	–	B	10	182	18	13	0.30	0.69	0.14	21	18	25

* To convert to kJ (kilojoule) multiply the values given by 4.1855.
** Vitamin A activity due to vitamin A + carotenes; 1 IU vitamin A = 0.0006 mg β-carotene.
*** FA = folic acid; E = α-tocopherol unless otherwise stated.
[1] Vitamin A content in dark varieties; in light varieties 2000.
[2] Unsalted 39.

Content per 100 grammes edible portion (unless otherwise stated)	Water	Proteins	Fats		Carbo-hydrates		Calories*	Vitamins								Other organic constituents			Excess acid A / Excess base B	Elements									
	g	g	Total g	Poly-unsaturated g	Total g	Fibre g	kcal	A** IU	B_1 mg	B_2 mg	B_6 mg	Nicotinic acid mg	Pantothenic acid mg	C mg	Other vitamins*** mg	Malic acid mg	Citric acid mg	Oxalic acid mg		Sodium Na mg	Potassium K mg	Calcium Ca mg	Magnesium Mg mg	Manganese Mn mg	Iron Fe mg	Copper Cu mg	Phosphorus P mg	Sulphur S mg	Chlorine Cl mg
Chives (*Allium schoenoprasum*)	91.3	1.8	0.3	–	5.8	1.1	28	5800	0.04	0.11	–	0.3	–	22	–	–	–	1.1	B	3	250	76	32	–	0.9	0.11	26	–	–
Corn (sweet). See Maize																													
Cress, garden (*Lepidium sativum* ssp. *sativum*)	89.4	2.6	0.7	–	5.5	1.1	32	9300	0.08	0.26	–	1.0	–	69	–	–	–	–	B	14	606	81	–	–	1.3	–	76	–	–
Cucumbers (*Cucumis sativus*)	95.6	0.8	0.1	–	3.0	0.6	13	300	0.04	0.05	0.04	0.2	0.3	8	biotin 0.001; FA 0.001	240	10	25	B	5	140	25	9	0.15	1.1	0.06	27	12	30
per lb as purchased (refuse 5%)	*412*	*3.4*	*0.4*	–	*13*	*2.6*	*56*	*1290*	*0.17*	*0.22*	*0.17*	*0.9*	*1.3*	*34*	*biotin 0.004; FA 0.004*	*1030*	*43*	*108*	*B*	*22*	*603*	*108*	*39*	*0.65*	*4.7*	*0.26*	*116*	*52*	*129*
Dandelion greens (*Taraxacum officinale*)	85.6	2.7	0.7	–	9.2	1.6	45	14000	0.19	0.26	–	–	–	36	–	–	–	25	B	76	430	187	–	0.3	3.1	0.15	66	17	99
Eggplants (*Solanum melongena*)	92.4	1.2	0.2	–	5.6	0.9	25	10	0.05	0.05	–	0.6	0.23	5	–	170	0	6.9	B	0.9	190	17	10	0.11	0.4	0.08	26	9	24
Endives (*Cichorium endivia*)	93.1	1.7	0.1	–	4.1	0.9	20	3300	0.10	0.20	–	0.72	–	10	–	–	–	27.3	B	18	400	104	13	0.22	1.7	0.09	38	26	71
Fennel (*Foeniculum vulgare*)	90	1.5	0.1	–	6.4	0.5	27	3500	0.23	0.11	0.10	0.2	0.25	31	FA 0.1; biotin 0.003	–	–	–	B	331	784	100	–	–	2.7	–	51	–	–
Garlic (*Allium sativum*) bulbs	63.8	5.3	0.2	–	29.3	1.1	129	trace	0.21	0.08	–	0.6	–	9	–	–	–	–	B	32	515	38	36	–	1.4	–	134	–	–
Horse-radishes (*Armoracia lapathifolia*)	76.6	2.8	0.3	–	18.1	2.8	80	30	0.06	0.11	0.18	0.6	–	120	–	–	–	–	B	9	554	105	33	–	2.0	0.14	70	212	18
Kale (*Brassica oleracea* var. *acephala*)	87.5	4.2	0.8	–	6.0	1.3	38	8900	0.16	0.26	0.19	2.0	0.1–1.4	115	E 8; biotin 0.0005; FA 0.05	50	350	13	B	75	410	179	37	0.5	2.2	0.09	73	115	122
Kohlrabi (*Brassica oleracea* var. *gongylodes*), tubers	90.3	2.0	0.1	–	6.6	1.0	29	20	0.06	0.04	0.12	0.3	0.1	53	FA 0.01	–	–	–	B	10	392	41	48	0.11	0.5	0.14	51	–	57
Leeks, leaves (*Allium porrum*)	87.8	2.0	0.3	–	9.4	1.2	44	50	0.06	0.04	–	0.5	–	18	E 1.0	–	–	–	B	5	300	60	18	0.07	1.0	0.3	50	72	40
Lentils, dried (*Lens esculenta*)	11.1	24.7	1.1	–	60.1	3.9	340	60	0.50	0.25	0.49	2.0	1.5	–	biotin 0.013; FA 0.1	–	–	–	B	36	810	79	77	–	8.6	0.7	377	122	64
Lettuce (*Lactuca sativa*), headed	95.1	1.3	0.2	–	2.5	0.5	14	970	0.06	0.07	0.07	0.3	0.1	8	E 0.6; biotin 0.003; FA 0.02	170	20	7.1	B	12	140	35	10	0.80	2.0	0.07	26	12	39–74
Maize (*Zea mays*)	72.7	3.5	1.0	–	22.1	0.7	96	400[1]	0.15	0.12	0.22	1.7	0.89	12	biotin 0.006; FA 0.03	0	0	5.2	B	0.4	300	3	38	0.15	0.7	0.06	111	32	14
canned, drained solids	75.9	2.6	0.8	–	19.8	0.8	84	350[1]	0.03	0.05	0.27	0.9	0.28	4	biotin 0.003; FA 0.008	–	–	–	B	236[2]	97	5	19	–	0.5	–	49	–	–
Mushrooms (champignons) (*Psalliota campestris*)	90.8	2.8[3]	0.24	–	3.7	0.9	22	0	0.1	0.44	0.05	6.2	2.1	5	E 0.83[4]; biotin 0.016; FA 0.03; D 150 IU	–	–	–	B	5	520	9	13	0.08	0.8	1.8	116	34	25

* To convert to kJ (kilojoule) multiply the values given by 4.1855.
** Vitamin A activity due to vitamin A + carotenes; 1 IU vitamin A = 0.0006 mg β-carotene.
*** FA = folic acid; E = α-tocopherol unless otherwise stated.
[1] Based on yellow maize; white contains only a trace.
[2] Unsalted 2.
[3] ⅔ N × 6.25.
[4] Total tocopherol.

Content per 100 grammes edible portion (unless otherwise stated)	Water g	Proteins g	Fats: Total g	Fats: Poly-unsaturated g	Carbo-hydrates: Total g	Carbo-hydrates: Fibre g	Calories* kcal	Vitamins: A** IU	Vitamins: B_1 mg	Vitamins: B_2 mg	Vitamins: B_6 mg	Vitamins: Nicotinic acid mg	Vitamins: Pantothenic acid mg	Vitamins: C mg	Vitamins: Other vitamins*** mg	Other organic constituents: Malic acid mg	Other organic constituents: Citric acid mg	Other organic constituents: Oxalic acid mg	Excess acid A Excess base B	Elements: Sodium Na mg	Elements: Potassium K mg	Elements: Calcium Ca mg	Elements: Magnesium Mg mg	Elements: Manganese Mn mg	Elements: Iron Fe mg	Elements: Copper Cu mg	Elements: Phosphorus P mg	Elements: Sulphur S mg	Elements: Chlorine Cl mg
Onions (*Allium cepa*) ripe	89.1	1.5	0.1	–	8.7	0.6	38	40	0.03	0.04	0.1	0.2	0.17	10	E 0.26; biotin 0.004; FA 0.01	170	20	23	A	10	130	27	8	0.36	0.5	0.13	36	51	24
dried	4	8.7	1.3	–	82.1	4.4	350	200	0.25	0.18	–	1.4	–	35	–	–	–	–	A	88	1383	158	–	–	3.1	–	256	–	–
Parsley (*Petroselinum crispum*)	85.1	3.6	0.6	–	8.5	1.5	44	8500	0.12	0.26	0.2	1.2	0.03	172	biotin 0.0004; FA 0.04	–	–	190	B	28	880	203	52	0.94	6.2	0.21	63	190	156
Parsnips (*Pastinaca sativa*)	79.1	1.7	0.5	–	17.5	2.0	76	30	0.08	0.09	0.1	0.2	0.5	16	biotin 0.0001; FA 0.02	350	130	10	B	17	342	50	22	0.03–0.34	0.7	0.10	77	26	30
Peas (*Pisum sativum*) green, unripe	75.0	6.3	0.4	–	17.0	2.0	84	640	0.32	0.15	0.18	2.5	0.82	27	E 0.6; K 0.3; biotin 0.009; FA 0.025	80	110	1.3	B	2	370	26	30	0.41	2.0	0.23	116	50	33
green, frozen	80.7	5.4	0.3	–	12.8	1.9	73	680	0.32	0.10	–	2.0	–	19	–	–	–	–	B	129	150	20	24	–	2.0	–	90	–	–
canned	82.3	3.4	0.4	–	12.7	1.3	67	450	0.11	0.06	0.05	0.9	0.17	9	E 0.02; biotin 0.002; FA 0.01	–	–	0.8	B	260[1]	201	25	25	–	1.8	0.21	67	44	318
dried, split	9.3	24.2	1.0	–	62.7	1.2	348	120	0.87	0.29	0.05	3.0	2.1	–	biotin 0.02; FA 0.03	–	–	–	B	42	880	73	116	2.0	6.0	0.8	303	129	60
edible, podded	86.2	2.6	0.1	–	10.5	1.5	53	55	0.06	0.10	–	0.8	–	30	–	–	–	–	B	–	–	44	–	–	1.4	–	54	–	–
Peppers (*Capsicum* spp.) green chillies	92.8	1.2	0.2	–	5.3	1.4	24	420	0.08	0.08	–	0.4	–	128	–	–	–	16	B	4.2	186	9	12	0.13	0.4	0.11	25	19	13
Potato chips	1.8	5.3	39.8	–	50.0	1.6	568	trace	0.21	0.07	–	4.8	–	16	–	–	–	–	B	340	880	40	48	–	1.8	0.36	139	–	–
Potatoes (*Solanum tuberosum*) raw	79.8	2.1	0.1	–	17.7	0.5	76	trace	0.11	0.04	0.2	1.2	0.3	20	E 0.06; K 0.08; biotin 0.0001; FA 0.006	0	510	5.7	B	3	410	14	27	0.17	0.8	0.16	53	29	35
per lb as purchased (refuse 19%)	*293*	*7.7*	*0.4*	–	*65*	*1.8*	*279*	*trace*	*0.40*	*0.15*	*0.7*	*4.4*	*1.1*	*73*	*E 0.22; K 0.29; biotin 0.0004; FA 0.022*	*0*	*1874*	*21*	*B*	*11*	*1510*	*51*	*99*	*0.62*	*2.9*	*0.59*	*195*	*107*	*129*
dried	7.1	8.3	0.6	–	80.4	1.4	352	trace	0.25	0.10	–	4.8	–	26	–	–	–	–	B	84	1600	44	–	–	2.4	–	203	–	–
Pumpkins (*Cucurbita* spp.)	95.0	0.8	0.1	–	3.5	0.6	15	1600	0.05	0.11	–	0.6	–	9	–	150	0	–	B	1	457	21	12	0.04	0.8	0.08	44	10	37
Purslane (*Portulaca oleracea* var. *sativa*)	92.5	1.7	0.4	–	3.8	0.9	21	2500	0.03	0.10	–	0.5	–	25	–	–	–	–	B	2	754	103	151	–	3.5	–	39	–	–
Radishes (*Raphanus sativus*)	93.7	1.1	0.1	–	3.6	0.7	18	10	0.04	0.04	0.1	0.3	0.18	26	FA 0.01	–	–	–	B	15	260	30	15	0.05	1.0	0.13	31	37	37
Rhubarb (*Rheum undulatum*)	94.9	0.5	0.1	–	3.8	0.7	16	100	0.01	0.03	0.03	0.1	0.08	9	E 0.2; FA 0.003	1770	410	230–500	B	3.5	286	96	14	0.15	0.8	0.05	18	8	53

* To convert to kJ (kilojoule) multiply the values given by 4.1855.
** Vitamin A activity due to vitamin A + carotenes; 1 IU vitamin A = 0.0006 mg β-carotene.
*** FA = folic acid; E = α-tocopherol unless otherwise stated.
[1] Unsalted 3.

Content per 100 grammes edible portion (unless otherwise stated)	Water	Proteins	Fats: Total	Fats: Poly-unsaturated	Carbo-hydrates: Total	Carbo-hydrates: Fibre	Calories*	Vitamins: A**	Vitamins: B_1	Vitamins: B_2	Vitamins: B_6	Vitamins: Nicotinic acid	Vitamins: Pantothenic acid	Vitamins: C	Vitamins: Other vitamins***	Other organic constituents: Malic acid	Other organic constituents: Citric acid	Other organic constituents: Oxalic acid	Excess acid A / Excess base B	Elements: Sodium Na	Elements: Potassium K	Elements: Calcium Ca	Elements: Magnesium Mg	Elements: Manganese Mn	Elements: Iron Fe	Elements: Copper Cu	Elements: Phosphorus P	Elements: Sulphur S	Elements: Chlorine Cl
	g	g	g	g	g	g	kcal	IU	mg	mg	mg	mg	mg	mg	mg	mg	mg	mg		mg	mg	mg	mg	mg	mg	mg	mg	mg	mg
Rutabagas (*Brassica napus* var. *napobrassica*)	87.0	1.1	0.1	–	11.0	1.1	46	580	0.07	0.07	–	1.1	–	43	–	–	–	–	B	5	239	66	15	0.04	0.4	0.08	39	–	–
Salsify (*Scorzonera hispanica*)	79	3.2	0.6	–	16.4	1.8	77	10	0.04	0.04	–	0.2	–	12	–	–	–	–	B	5	320	40	–	–	1.5	–	76	–	–
Sauerkraut	92.8	1.0	0.2	–	4.0	0.7	18	50	0.03	0.04	–	0.2	0.08	14	–	–[1]	–[1]	–[1]	B	650	140	36	–	–	0.5	0.1	18	–	–
Soybeans (*Glycine hispida*), dried	10.0	34.1	17.7	10.7	33.5	4.9	403	80	1.14	0.31	0.64	2.1	1.68	trace	E 6–11; biotin 0.06; FA 0.22	–	–	–	B	4	1900	226	235	–	8.4	0.11	554	–	–
Spinach (*Spinacia oleracea*)	90.7	3.2	0.3	–	4.3	0.6	26	8100	0.10	0.20	0.20	0.6	0.3	51	E 2.5; K 0.04–3; biotin 0.007; FA 0.075	90	80	460	B	62	662	106	62	0.82	3.1	0.20	51	27	65
per lb as purchased (refuse 8%)	*379*	*13.4*	*1.3*	–	*17.9*	*2.5*	*109*	*33800*	*0.42*	*0.83*	*0.83*	*2.5*	*1.3*	*213*	*E 10.4; K 0.17–12.5; biotin 0.029; FA 0.031*	*376*	*334*	*1920*	*B*	*259*	*2760*	*442*	*259*	*3.42*	*12.9*	*0.83*	*213*	*113*	*271*
canned	93.0	2.0	0.4	–	3.0	0.7	19	5500	0.02	0.06	0.095	0.3	0.06	14	biotin 0.002; FA 0.05	–	–	364	B	320[2]	260	85	–	–	2.1	–	26	–	–
frozen	91.3	3.0	0.3	–	4.2	0.8	25	8100	0.1	0.16	–	0.5	–	35	–	–	–	–	B	53	385	105	–	–	2.5	–	45	–	–
Squash, summer (zucchini) (*Cucurbita pepo* var. *medullosa*)	94.6	1.2	0.1	–	3.6	0.6	17	320[3]	0.05	0.09	–	1.0	–	19	–	–	–	–	B	1	202	28	–	0.14	0.4	–	29	–	–
Sweet potatoes (*Ipomoea batatas*)	70.6	1.7	0.4	–	26.3	0.7	114	8800	0.10	0.06	0.32	0.6	0.93	21	E 4.0; biotin 0.004; FA 0.012	0	70	56	B	5	530	32	31	0.15–0.52	0.7	0.15	47	15	85
canned	70.7	1.0	0.2	–	27.5	0.6	114	5000	0.03	0.03	–	0.6	–	8	–	–	–	–	B	48	120	13	–	–	0.7	–	29	–	–
Tomatoes (*Lycopersicon esculentum*)	93.5	1.1	0.2	–	4.7	0.5	22	900	0.06	0.04	0.1	0.6	0.31	23	E 0.27; biotin 0.004; FA 0.008	150	390	7.5	B	3	268	13	11	0.19	0.6	0.10	27	11	51
canned	93.7	1.0	0.2	–	4.3	0.4	21	900	0.06	0.03	0.07	0.7	0.2	17	biotin 0.0018; FA 0.003	–	–	–	B	130[4]	217	6	–	0.04	0.5	0.09	19	–	–
Tomato juice, canned	93.6	0.9	0.1	–	4.3	0.2	19	800	0.05	0.03	0.19	0.7	0.30	16	FA 0.007	23	336	–	B	230[4]	230	7	7	–	0.9	–	18	–	–
Tomato ketchup	68.6	2.0	0.4	–	25.4	0.5	106	1400	0.09	0.07	–	1.6	–	15	–	–	–	–	B	1042	363	22	21	–	0.8	–	50	–	–
Tomato puree	86.0	2.3	0.5	–	9.5	0.5	44	1200	0.09	0.06	0.18	1.5	–	9	–	–	–	–	B	590	1160	60	–	–	1.0	–	34	–	–
Turnips (*Brassica rapa*)	91.5	1.0	0.2	–	6.6	0.9	30	trace	0.04	0.07	0.11	0.6	0.02	36	E 0.02; biotin 0.0001; FA 0.004	230	0	0	B	37	230	39	7	0.04	0.5	0.07	30	22	41
greens	90.3	3.0	0.3	–	5.0	0.8	28	7600	0.21	0.39	0.98	0.8	0.38	139	E 2.3; FA 0.04	–	–	15	B	10	440	260	19	1.4	1.8	0.09	58	54	168
Watercress (*Nasturtium officinale*)	93.3	2.2	0.3	–	3.0	0.7	19	4000	0.1	0.27	–	0.9	0.1	75	–	–	–	–	B	60	301	151	17	0.54	2.0	0.04	46	147	109

* To convert to kJ (kilojoule) multiply the values given by 4.1855.
** Vitamin A activity due to vitamin A + carotenes; 1 IU vitamin A = 0.0006 mg β-carotene.
*** FA = folic acid; E = α-tocopherol unless otherwise stated.
[1] Lactic acid 1.6 g.
[2] Unsalted 34.
[3] Including skin.
[4] Unsalted 3.

Content per 100 grammes edible portion (unless otherwise stated)	Water	Proteins	Fats: Total	Fats: Poly-unsaturated	Carbo-hydrates: Total	Carbo-hydrates: Fibre	Calories*	Vitamins: A**	B1	B2	B6	Nicotinic acid	Pantothenic acid	C	Other vitamins***	Other organic constituents: Malic acid	Citric acid	Oxalic acid	Excess acid A Excess base B	Elements: Sodium Na	Potassium K	Calcium Ca	Magnesium Mg	Manganese Mn	Iron Fe	Copper Cu	Phosphorus P	Sulphur S	Chlorine Cl
	g	g	g	g	g	g	kcal	IU	mg	mg	mg	mg	mg	mg	mg	mg	mg	mg		mg	mg	mg	mg	mg	mg	mg	mg	mg	mg
Yeast (*Saccharomyces cerevisiae*)																													
baker's, compressed	71.0	12.1	0.4	–	11.0	–	86	trace	0.71	1.65	1.2	11.2	5.3	trace	biotin 0.4; FA 0.5	–	–	–	A	16	610	13	59	–	4.9	–	394	–	–
brewer's, dried	5.0	38.8	1.0	–	38.4	1.7	283	trace	15.5	4.28	4.2	37.9	9.5	trace	biotin 0.08; FA 2.4	–	–	–	A	121	1700	210	231	0.53	17.3	3.32	1753	–	–
Yeast, torula (*Torulopsis utilis*)	6.0	38.6	1.0	–	37.0	3.3	277	trace	15.0	5.0	3.5	50.0	10.0	–	biotin 0.1; FA 3.0	–	–	–	A	15	2046	424	165	–	20	–	1713	–	–
Nuts																													
Almonds (*Amygdalus communis*) dried	4.7	18.6	54.2	10.8	19.5	2.6	598	75	0.25	0.92	0.10	3.5	0.58	trace	E 15; biotin 0.02; FA 0.045	–	–	–	B	3	690	234	252	1.9	4.7	0.14	504	150	2
Brazil nuts (*Bertholletia excelsa*)	4.6	14.3	66.9	18.4	10.9	3.1	654	10	1.0	0.07	0.11	7.7	0.23	2	E 6.5; FA 0.005	–	–	–	A	2	670	127	225	2.8	2.8	1.1	600	198	61
Cashew nuts (*Anacardium occidentale*)	5.2	17.2	45.7	3	29.3	1.4	561	100	0.43	0.25	–	1.8	–	–	–	–	–	–	–	15	464	38	267	–	3.8	–	373	–	–
Chestnuts (*Castanea sativa*)	48	3.4	1.9	–	45.6	1.3	213	0	0.23	0.22	0.29	0.5	0.3	6	E 0.5; biotin 0.0013	–	–	–	B	2	410	46	42	3.7	1.4	0.06	74	29	11
dried	9.0	6.7	4.1	–	78.8	2.5	378	0	0.34	0.39	–	0.8	–	0	–	–	–	–	B	4	875	57	–	–	3.3	–	170	–	–
Coconuts (*Cocos nucifera*)	48	4.2	34	0.6	12.8	3.3	351	0	0.06	0.03	0.06	0.6	0.33	2	E 1; FA 0.028	–	–	–	B	17	363	13	39	1.31	1.7	0.32	95	44	114
dried	3.5	7.2	64.9	0.6	23.0	3.9	662	0	0.06	0.04	–	0.6	–	0	–	–	–	–	B	29	588	26	90	–	3.3	0.55	187	76	196
Coconut water	94.2	0.3	0.2	–	4.7	trace	22	0	trace	trace	–	0.1	–	2	–	–	–	–	–	25	147	20	28	–	0.3	–	13	–	–
Hazelnuts (*Corylus avellana*)	6.0	12.7	60.9	23	18	3.5	627	100	0.47	0.55	0.54	1.6	1.15	7.5	E 21; FA 0.067	–	–	–	B	3	618	250	150	4.2	4.5	1.35	320	198	10
Peanuts (*Arachis hypogaea*) roasted	1.8	26.2	48.7	14.0	20.6	2.7	582	360	0.32	0.13	0.3	17.1	2.14	0	biotin 0.034; FA 0.057; E 6.5	–	–	–	A	3	740	74	181	1.51	2.2	0.27	407	377	7
Pecans (*Carya illinoinensis*)	3.4	9.2	71.2	14	14.6	2.3	687	130	0.86	0.13	0.19	0.9	–	2	E 1.5	–	–	–	–	trace	603	73	142	3.5	2.4	–	289	–	–
Pine nuts (*Pinus pinea*)	3.1	13.0	60.5	–	20.5	1.1	635	30	1.28	0.23	–	4.5	–	–	–	–	–	–	–	–	–	12	–	–	5.2	–	604	–	–
Pistachio nuts (*Pistacia vera*)	5.3	19.3	53.7	10	19.0	1.9	594	230	0.67	–	–	1.4	–	–	–	–	–	–	–	–	972	131	158	–	7.3	–	500	–	–
Walnuts (*Juglans regia*)	3.5	14.8	64.0	47.5	15.8	2.1	651	30	0.3	0.13	1.0	1.0	0.7	2	biotin 0.037; FA 0.077; E 1.5	–	–	–	A	4	450	99	134	1.8	3.1	0.31	380	146	23
Cereals, Cereal products																													
Barley (*Hordeum* spp.), pearled	12.0	9.0	1.4	0.8	76.5	0.8	346	0	0.12	0.05	–	3.1	0.5	0	–	–	70	–	A	3	160	16	37	1.68	2.0	0.4	189	116	105
Bread																													
white, enriched, 4% nonfat milk solids	35.6	8.7	3.2	–	50.8	0.2	270	trace	0.25	0.21	–	2.4	–	trace	–	–	–	–	A	507	105	84	22	0.31	2.5	0.2	97	–	–
toasted	25.1	10.1	3.7	–	58.8	0.2	314	trace	0.23	0.24	–	2.8	–	trace	–	–	–	–	A	590	122	98	28	–	2.9	–	113	–	1040
wholemeal	36.4	9.1	2.6	–	49.3	1.5	241	trace	0.30	0.10	–	2.8	–	trace	–	–	–	–	A	530	256	84	78	–	2.3	–	254	–	–
French, unenriched	30.6	9.1	3.0	–	55.4	0.2	290	trace	0.08	0.08	–	0.8	–	trace	–	–	–	–	A	580	90	43	22	–	0.7	–	85	–	–

* To convert to kJ (kilojoule) multiply the values given by 4.1855. ** Vitamin A activity due to vitamin A + carotenes; 1 IU vitamin A = 0.0006 mg β-carotene. *** FA = folic acid; E = α-tocopherol unless otherwise stated.

Content per 100 grammes edible portion (unless otherwise stated)	Water	Proteins	Fats		Carbo-hydrates		Calories*	Vitamins								Other organic constituents			Excess acid A / Excess base B	Elements									
			Total	Poly-unsaturated	Total	Fibre		A**	B1	B2	B6	Nicotinic acid	Pantothenic acid	C	Other vitamins***	Malic acid	Citric acid	Oxalic acid		Sodium Na	Potas-sium K	Calcium Ca	Magne-sium Mg	Manga-nese Mn	Iron Fe	Copper Cu	Phos-phorus P	Sulphur S	Chlorine Cl
	g	g	g	g	g	g	kcal	IU	mg	mg	mg	mg	mg	mg	mg	mg	mg	mg		mg	mg	mg	mg	mg	mg	mg	mg	mg	mg
Bread (continued)																													
pumpernickel	34.0	9.1	1.2	–	53.1	1.1	246	–	0.23	0.14	–	1.2	–	–	–	–	–	–	A	569	454	84	71	–	2.4	–	229	–	–
rye, American	35.5	9.1	1.1	–	52.1	0.4	243	0	0.18	0.07	–	1.4	–	0	–	–	–	–	A	557	145	75	42	1.3	1.6	0.28	147	–	1025
zwieback	5.0	10.7	8.8	–	74.3	0.3	423	40	0.05	0.07	–	1.3	–	–	–	–	–	–	A	250	150	13	–	–	0.6	–	69	–	–
Cornflakes	3.8	7.9	0.4	–	85.3	0.7	385	0	0.43[1]	0.1	–	2.1	0.19	0	FA 0.006	–	–	5.6	A	660	160	10	17	0.05	1.4	0.17	45	93	–
Cornstarch	12.0	0.3	trace	–	87.9	0.1	362	0	trace	0.08	0.005	0.03	–	–	–	–	–	–	A	4	4	trace	2	–	0.5	–	30	–	6
Flour																													
buckwheat	14.1	11.7	2.7	–	70	2.6	327	0	0.58	0.15	–	2.9	1.5	–	–	–	–	–	A	1	680	33	–	2.09	2.2	0.7	263	–	–
farina, unenriched	10.3	11.4	0.9	–	77.0	0.4	371	0	0.06	0.10	–	0.7	–	–	–	–	–	–	A	2	83	25	25	–	1.5	–	107	–	–
maize (corn)	12.0	7.8	2.6	–	76.8	0.7	368	340[2]	0.20	0.06	0.06	1.4	0.55	0	biotin 0.006; FA 0.01; E 0.3	–	–	–	A	1	120	6	–	–	1.8	–	164	–	–
rye, light	11	9.4	1.0	–	77.9	0.4	357	0	0.15	0.07	–	0.6	–	–	–	–	–	–	A	1	156	22	73	–	1.1	–	185	–	–
rye, medium	11	11.4	1.7	–	74.8	1.0	325	0	0.30	0.12	–	2.9	–	–	–	–	–	–	A	1	203	27	83	–	2.6	–	262	–	–
soybean, full fat	8.0	36.7	20.3	–	30.2	2.4	347	110	0.85	0.31	0.66	2.1	1.68	0	biotin 0.07; FA 0.43	–	–	–	B	–	1660	199	235	–	8.4	–	558	–	–
medium fat	8.0	43.4	6.7	–	36.6	2.5	264	80	0.83	0.36	–	2.6	–	0	–	–	–	–	B	–	2025	244	286	–	9.1	–	634	–	–
wheat, whole	12	13.3	2.0	–	71.0	2.3	333	0	0.55	0.12	–	4.3	–	0	–	–	–	–	A	3	370	41	113	–	3.3	0.2	372	–	–
white, unenriched	12	10.5	1.0	–	76.1	0.3	363	0	0.06	0.05	–	0.9	–	0	–	–	–	–	A	2	95	16	25	–	0.8	–	87	–	–
white, enriched	12	10.5	1.0	–	76.1	0.3	364	0	0.44	0.26	–	3.5	–	0	–	–	–	–	A	2	95	16	25	–	2.9	–	87	–	–
white, self-raising, enriched	11.5	9.3	1.0	–	74.2	0.4	352	0	0.44	0.26	–	3.5	–	0	–	–	–	–	A	1079	90	265	–	–	2.9	–	466	–	–
Muffins (enriched flour)	38.0	7.8	10.1	–	42.3	0.1	294	100	0.17	0.23	–	1.4	–	trace	–	–	–	–	A	441	125	104	–	–	1.6	–	151	–	–
Noodles, unenriched, dry	10.1	13.0	2.9	–	73	0.4	376	100	0.2	0.08	–	2.1	–	–	–	–	–	–	A	7	157	20	–	–	2.1	–	196	–	–
Oatflakes	10.3	13.8	6.6	2.7	67.6	1.4	387	–	0.55	0.14	0.75	1.1	0.92	0	E 0.25	–	–	–	A	2	340	53	145	4.9	3.6	0.74	407	199	49
Pancakes (enriched flour)	50.1	7.1	7.0	–	34.1	0.1	231	120	0.17	0.22	–	1.3	–	trace	–	–	–	–	A	425	123	101	–	–	1.3	–	139	–	–
Piecrust, plain, unenriched, unbaked	20.9	5.7	31.0	–	40.7	0.1	464	0	0.03	0.03	–	0.5	–	0	–	–	–	–	–	568	46	13	–	–	0.4	–	47	–	–
Popcorn, popped	4.0	12.7	5.0	2.0	76.7	2.2	386	–	0.39	0.12	–	2.2	–	0	–	–	–	–	A	3	240	11	–	–	2.7	0.31	281	–	–
Pretzels	4.5	9.8	4.5	–	75.9	0.3	390	0	0.02	0.03	–	0.7	–	0	–	–	–	–	A	1680	130	22	–	–	1.5	–	131	–	–
Rice																													
whole	12.0	7.5	1.9	–	77.4	0.9	360	0	0.29	0.05	–	4.7	–	0	E 1.2	–	–	–	A	9	150	32	119	1.7	1.6	0.36	221	121	–
polished	12.0	6.7	0.4	–	80.4	0.3	362	0	0.07	0.03	0.15	1.6	0.63	–	E 0.35	–	–	–	A	6	113	24	28	1.08	0.8	0.06–0.19	94	79	27
polished, cooked	72.6	2.0	0.1	–	24.2	0.1	109	0	0.02	0.01	–	0.4	–	0	–	–	–	–	A	2[3]	38	10	8	–	0.2	–	28	27	9[3]
Semolina																													
maize	11.0	8.8	1.1	–	78.0	–	365	440[2]	0.15	0.05	0.05	0.5	–	–	–	–	–	–	A	1	80	4	20	–	1.0	–	73	–	–
wheat	13.1	10.3	0.8	–	76	–	362	0	0.12	0.04	0.085	1.3	–	–	E 1.8[4]	–	–	–	A	1	112	17	–	–	1	–	87	–	–
Spaghetti, unenriched, dry	10.4	12.5	1.2	–	75.2	0.3	369	0	0.09	0.06	–	2.0	–	–	–	–	–	–	A	5	–	22	–	–	1.5	–	165	–	–
Tapioca, dry	12.6	0.6	0.2	–	86.4	0.1	360	0	0	0.1	–	0	–	0	–	–	–	–	0	4	20	12	2	0.69	1.0	0.07	12	4	16
Wheat germ	11.5	26.6	10.9	2.9	46.7	2.5	363	650	2.0	0.68	0.92	4.2	2.2	0	FA 0.31; E 15[4]	–	340	–	A	2	780	72	336	–	9.4	1.3	1118	–	70

* To convert to kJ (kilojoule) multiply the values given by 4.1855.
** Vitamin A activity due to vitamin A + carotenes; 1 IU vitamin A = 0.0006 mg β-carotene.
*** FA = folic acid; E = α-tocopherol unless otherwise stated.
[1] Enriched.
[2] Based on yellow maize.
[3] Unsalted.
[4] Total tocopherol.

Content per 100 grammes edible portion (unless otherwise stated)	Water	Proteins	Fats		Carbo-hydrates		Calories*	Vitamins								Other organic constituents			Excess acid A Excess base B	Elements									
			Total	Poly-unsaturated	Total	Fibre		A**	B1	B2	B6	Nicotinic acid	Pantothenic acid	C	Other vitamins***	Malic acid	Citric acid	Oxalic acid		Sodium Na	Potassium K	Calcium Ca	Magnesium Mg	Manganese Mn	Iron Fe	Copper Cu	Phosphorus P	Sulphur S	Chlorine Cl
	g	g	g	g	g	g	kcal	IU	mg	mg	mg	mg	mg	mg	mg	mg	mg	mg		mg	mg	mg	mg	mg	mg	mg	mg	mg	mg
Confectionery, Sugar																													
Caramel[1]	7.6	4.0	10.2	–	76.6	0.2	399	10	0.03	0.17	–	0.2	–	trace	–	–	–	–	B	226	192	148	–	–	1.4	–	122	–	–
Chocolate																													
milk, sweetened	0.9	7.7	32.3	–	56.9	0.4	520	270	0.06	0.34	–	0.3	–	0	E 1.1	–	–	–	A	86	420	228	58	–	1.1	1.1	251	67	151
plain, sweetened	0.9	4.4	35.1	1.2	57.9	0.5	528	10	0.02	0.14	–	0.3	–	trace	–	–	–	–	A	19	397	63	107	–	1.4	1.1	142	32	–
Cocoa, dry powder	5.6	19.8	24.5	0.4	43.6	5.7	299	10	0.09	0.11	–	1.9	–	0	E 3.1[2]	–	–	450	A–B	60	900–3200	114	420	3.53	12.5	3.4	709	203	51
Dextrose, anhydrous	trace	0	0	–	99.5	0	385	0	0	0	–	0	–	0	–	–	–	–	0	1	0.4	–	–	–	–	–	–	–	–
Honey	17.2	0.3	0	–	82.3	–	304	0	trace	0.04	0.01	0.3	0.06	1	FA 0.003	–	–	–	0	7	51	5	3	0.03	0.5	0.2	6	–	29
Jams	29	0.6	0.1	–	70.0	1.0	272	10	0.01	0.03	–	0.2	–	2	–	–	–	–	B	16	112	12	10	–	1.0	0.23	9	6.5	9
Maple syrup	33	–	–	–	65	–	252	–	–	–	–	–	–	0	–	–	–	–	B	10	176	104	–	–	1.2	–	8	–	–
Molasses	24.0	–	–	–	60.0	–	232	–	0–0.08	0–0.16	0.27	2.8	0.5	0	biotin 0.009; FA 0.01	–	–	–	B	40	1500	273	–	0.04	6.7	1.9	69	–	317
Sugar																													
brown	2.1	0	0	–	96.4	–	373	0	0.01	0.03	–	0.2	–	0	–	–	–	–	B	24	230	85	–	–	3.4	–	19	–	–
cane or beet, white	trace	0	0	–	99.5	0	385	0	0	0	–	0	–	0	–	–	–	–	0	0.3	0.5	0	–	–	0.04	–	0	–	–
Beverages, nonalcoholic																													
Carbonated soft drinks[3]	88	–	–	–	12	0	46	–	–	–	–	–	–	–	–	–	–	–	0	1–15	1	–	–	–	–	–	–	–	–
Cola drinks	90	–	–	–	10	–	39	–	–	–	–	–	–	–	–	–	–	–	B	–	–	–	–	–	–	–	–	–	–
Coffee[4] (unsweetened)	98.5	0.3	0.1	–	0.8	–	5	0	0.01	0.01	–	0.9	–	0	–	18	29	1	B	1–6	80	5	9	0.09	0.2	–	5	–	0.6
Tea[5] (unsweetened)	99	0.1	0	–	0.4	–	2	0	0	0.04	–	0.1	–	1	–	–	–	10	0	0–2	16	0.3–5	1–13	0.69	0.2	–	1–4	–	0.4
Beverages, alcoholic			Alcohol[6]																										
Beer	90.6	0.5	3.6		4.8[7]	0	47	0	0.004	0.03	0.05	0.88	0.08	–	biotin 0.0005	–	–	–	B	5	38	4	–	–	–	–	–	–	–
Brandy	–	–	35–40		–	–	245–280	–	–	–	–	–	–	–	–	–	–	–	0	3	4	–	–	–	–	–	–	–	–
Fruit wine	–	–	5.2		1.0	–	40	–	–	–	–	–	–	–	–	–	–	–	B	7	72	–	–	–	–	–	–	–	–
Port wine	–	0.2	15.0		14.0	–	161	–	–	–	–	–	–	–	–	–	–	–	B	4	75	5	10	–	0.3	0.09	11	–	8
Rum	–	–	35.1		–	–	246	–	–	–	–	–	–	–	–	–	–	–	0	2	3	–	–	–	–	–	–	–	–
Whisky	–	–	35		–	–	245	–	–	–	–	–	–	–	–	–	–	–	0	0.3	1	–	–	–	–	–	–	–	–
Wine[8]	–	0	8.8–12.5		0.2–8.0	–	60–120	–	0.001 to 0.005	0.01	0.09	0.05	0.04	–	FA 0.001	0–280	6–58	–	B	4–7	20–120	7	7–16	0.3	0.3–5	0.05–0.25	10	15	2

* To convert to kJ (kilojoule) multiply the values given by 4.1855. ** Vitamin A activity due to vitamin A + carotenes; 1 IU vitamin A = 0.0006 mg β-carotene. *** FA = folic acid; E = α-tocopherol unless otherwise stated. [1] Full-cream products. [2] Total tocopherol. [3] Not true mineral waters. [4] Caffeine 75–100 mg, trigonelline 100 mg, acetic acid 20 mg, formic acid 12 mg, chlorogenic acid and other phenolic acids 200 mg. [5] Caffeine 40–60 mg. [6] Alcohol has a calorific value of 7 kcal/g. [7] Extract. [8] Tartaric acid 163–234 mg, lactic acid 71–248 mg, succinic acid 90–130 mg, aromatic acids 56–136 mg, glycerol 0.8–2.6 g.

Content per 100 grammes edible portion (unless otherwise stated)	Water	Proteins	Fats			Carbohydrates	Calories*	Vitamins								Purine nitrogen	Excess acid A / Excess base B	Elements									
			Total	Poly-unsaturated	Cholesterol			A**	B_1	B_2	B_6	Nicotinic acid	Pantothenic acid	C	Other vitamins***			Sodium Na	Potassium K	Calcium Ca	Magnesium Mg	Manganese Mn	Iron Fe	Copper Cu	Phosphorus P	Sulphur S	Chlorine Cl
	g	g	g	g	g	g	kcal	IU	mg	mg	mg	mg	mg	mg	mg	mg		mg	mg	mg	mg	mg	mg	mg	mg	mg	mg
Fats, Oils																											
Butter	17.4	0.6	81.0	4	0.28	0.7	716	3300	trace	0.01	trace	0.1	trace	trace	E 2.4; D 40 IU	–	A	10[1]	23	16	1	0.04	0.2	0.03	16	9	–
Cod-liver oil	0	0	99.9	–	0.85	0	901	85000	–	0	–	0	–	–	E 26[2]; D 8500 IU	–	0	0.1	–	–	–	–	–	–	–	–	–
Corn oil	trace	0	99.9	56	0	0	883	–	–	–	–	–	–	–	E ∼ 19	–	0	–	–	–	–	–	–	–	–	–	–
Cottonseed oil	trace	0	99.9	50	0	0	883	–	–	–	–	–	–	–	E ∼ 30	–	0	–	–	–	–	–	–	–	–	–	–
Lard	1.0	trace	99.0	10	0.1	0	901	0	0	0	–	0	–	0	E 2	–	A	0.3	0.2	1	–	–	0.1	0.02	3	25	4
Margarine, salted	15.5	0.6	81.0	14	–	0.4	720	3300	–	–	–	–	–	0	–	–	–	987	23	20	–	–	0	–	16	–	–
Mayonnaise	15.1	1.1	78.9	32[3]	–	3.0	718	280	0.02	0.04	–	trace	–	0	–	–	A	702	53	18	2	–	0.5	–	28	–	–
Mustard, brown	78.1	5.9	6.3	–	–	5.3	91	–	–	–	–	–	–	–	–	–	A	1307	130	124	48	–	1.8	–	134	–	–
Olive oil	trace	0	99.9	8	0	0	883	0	0	0	–	0	–	0	E ∼ 3	–	0	0.1	trace	0.5	–	–	0.08	0.07	–	–	–
Palm oil	trace	0	99.9	9	0	0	883	–	–	–	–	–	–	–	E 30	–	0	–	–	–	–	–	–	–	–	–	–
Peanut butter	1.8	27.8	49.4	11.9	0	17.2	581	–	0.13	0.13	0.30	15.7	2.5	0	biotin 0.04; FA 0.06	–	A	607[4]	670	63	178	–	2.0	–	407	225	–
Peanut oil	trace	0	99.9	29	0	0	883	–	–	–	–	–	–	–	E 13	–	0	–	–	–	–	–	–	–	–	–	–
Safflower oil	trace	0	99.9	72	0	0	883	–	–	–	–	–	–	–	E 31	–	0	–	–	–	–	–	–	–	–	–	–
Soybean oil	trace	0	99.9	60	0	0	883	–	–	–	–	–	–	–	E 18	–	0	–	–	–	–	–	–	–	–	–	–
Sunflower oil	trace	0	99.9	63	0	0	883	–	–	–	–	–	–	–	E 22	–	0	–	–	–	–	–	–	–	–	–	–
Vegetable fat	0	0	100	7	–	0	884	–	0	0	0	0	0	0	–	0	0	0	0	0	0	0	0	0	0	0	0
Dairy products, Eggs																											
Butter. See under 'Fats', above																											
Cheese																											
Camembert	51.3	18.7	22.8	–	–	1.8	287	1010	0.05	0.45	0.25	1.45	0.1–0.9	0	biotin 0.005	–	A	1150[4]	109	382	18	–	0.5	0.08	184	–	–
Cheddar	37	25.0	32.2	1	0.10	2.1	398	1310	0.03	0.46	0.07	0.1	0.40	10.0	biotin 0.004; FA 0.016	–	A	700	82	750	43	–	1.0	–	478	–	–
cottage, creamed	78.3	13.6	4.2	trace	0.015	2.9	106	170	0.03	0.25	–	0.1	–	0	–	–	A	229	85	94	–	–	0.3	–	152	–	–
cottage, uncreamed	79.0	17.0	0.3	–	–	2.7	86	10	0.03	0.82	0.01	0.1	–	1	biotin 0.002; FA 0.03	–	A	290	72	90	–	–	0.4	–	175	–	–
cream	51	8.0	37.7	1	0.12	2.1	374	1540	0.02	0.24	–	0.1	–	0	–	–	A	250	74	62	–	–	0.2	–	95	–	–
Parmesan	30.0	36.0	26.0	–	–	2.9	393	1060	0.02	0.73	–	0.2	–	0	–	–	A	755[4]	153	1140	50	–	0.4	0.36	781	251	1110[4]
Roquefort	40.0	21.0	32.0	–	–	1.8	378	800	0.06	0.3–0.7	–	0.4–0.9	0.5–0.7	0	biotin 0.003	–	A	–	–	700	–	–	1	–	–	–	–
Swiss (Emmentaler)	34.9	27.4	30.5	–	–	3.4	398	1140	0.05	0.33	0.09	0.1	–	0.5	E 0.35[2]; D 100 IU	–	A	620[4]	100	1180	55	–	0.9	0.13	860	–	1210[4]
Cream																											
heavy 30%	64.1	2.2	30.4	0.8	–	2.9	288	1100[5]	0.025	0.17	0.035	0.07	–	1	D 40 IU	–	B	38	78	75	–	–	0–0.1	–	63	–	–
Eggs																											
whole, raw	74.0	12.8	11.5	2.3	0.46	0.7	162	1180	0.12	0.34	0.25	0.1	1.6	0	D 200 IU; B_{12} 0.002; E 1; K 0.002; biotin 0.02; FA 0.005	–	A	135	138	54	13	0.05	2.3	0.03	205	197	159

* To convert to kJ (kilojoule) multiply the values given by 4.1855.
** Vitamin A activity due to vitamin A + carotenes; 1 IU vitamin A = 0.0006 mg β-carotene.
*** FA = folic acid; E = α-tocopherol unless otherwise stated.
[1] Unsalted.
[2] Total tocopherol.
[3] Prepared with corn oil.
[4] Variable, depends on salt content.
[5] In summer; in winter 500.

Content per 100 grammes edible portion (unless otherwise stated)	Water g	Proteins g	Fats: Total g	Fats: Poly-unsaturated g	Fats: Cholesterol g	Carbohydrates g	Calories* kcal	Vitamins: A** IU	B_1 mg	B_2 mg	B_6 mg	Nicotinic acid mg	Pantothenic acid mg	C mg	Other vitamins*** mg	Purine nitrogen mg	Excess acid A / Excess base B	Elements: Sodium Na mg	Potassium K mg	Calcium Ca mg	Magnesium Mg mg	Manganese Mn mg	Iron Fe mg	Copper Cu mg	Phosphorus P mg	Sulphur S mg	Chlorine Cl mg
Egg white, raw	87.6	10.9	0.2	–	0	0.8	51	0	0.02	0.23	0.22	0.1	0.14	0	biotin 0.007; FA 0.001	–	A	192	148	9	11	0.04	0.2	0.03	17	208	161
Egg yolk, raw	50.0	16.1	31.9	6.7	1.6	0.6	360	3400	0.32	0.52	0.30	0.02	4.2	0	B_{12} 0.002; E 3; D 350 IU; biotin 0.05; FA 0.013	–	A	50	123	141	16	0.09	7.2	0.02	569	194	142
1 egg, medium (48 grammes)	*35.5*	*6.1*	*5.5*	*1.1*	*0.22*	*0.4*	*77*	*580*	*0.06*	*0.16*	*0.12*	*0.04*	*0.8*	*0*	–[3]	–	*A*	*66*	*67*	*26*	*6*	*0.02*	*1.3*	*0.02*	*98*	*95*	*69*
1 egg white, medium (31 grammes)	*27.0*	*3.3*	*0.1*	–	*0*	*0.3*	*16*	*0*	*0.01*	*0.07*	*0.07*	*0.03*	*0.04*	*0*	–[3]	–	*A*	*57*	*46*	*3*	*3*	*0.01*	*0.06*	*0.01*	*5*	*64*	*48*
1 egg yolk, medium (17 grammes)	*8.5*	*2.8*	*5.4*	*1.1*	*0.22*	*0.1*	*61*	*580*	*0.05*	*0.09*	*0.05*	*trace*	*0.7*	*0*	–[3]	–	*A*	*9*	*21*	*23*	*3*	*0.01*	*1.2*	*0.01*	*93*	*32*	*21*
Egg powder	4.1	47.0	41.2	–	2.14	4.1	592	4460	0.35	1.23	0.08	0.2	7.4	0	D 240 IU	–	A	519	483	190	41	–	8.7	0.18	800	630	592
Milk (cow's)[1, 2] pasteurized, whole	88.5	3.2	3.7	0.1	0.01	4.6	64	140	0.04	0.15	0.05	0.07	0.33	1	E 0.06[4]; B_{12} 0.0006; biotin 0.002; D 0.5–4 IU; FA 0.0001	–	B	75	139	133	13	0.002	0.04	0.01	88	29	105
buttermilk, cultured	91.2	3.5	0.5	–	–	4.0	35	35	0.04	0.18	0.04	0.1	0.36	1	B_{12} 0.0003; E 0.05[4]; biotin 0.002; FA 0.0003	–	B	57	147	109	16	–	0.1	0.02	95	30	100
condensed (sweetened)	27.1	8.1	8.7	0.2	–	54.3	321	350	0.1	0.38	0.06	0.2	0.85	1	biotin 0.003; D 3.5 IU	–	B	140	340	262	25	–	0.1	–	206	–	–
canned, evaporated (unsweetened)	73.8	7.0	7.9	0.2	–	9.7	138	350	0.06	0.36	0.03	0.2	0.85	1	biotin 0.003; FA 0.0007; D 3.5 IU	–	B	100	270	252	25	–	0.2	–	205	–	–
dried, whole	2.0	26.4	27.5	0.7	–	38.2	502	1200	0.28	1.2	0.3	0.7	2.7	10	B_{12} 0.002; biotin 0.013	–	B	410	1330	909	112	–	0.6	0.16	708	234	784
nonfat	3.0	35.9	1.0	–	–	52.0	362	30	0.35	1.80	0.4	0.9	3.5	10	B_{12} 0.002; biotin 0.016; FA 0.0024	–	B	525	1335	1300	111	–	0.6	–	1016	300	1130
skimmed	90.9	3.5	0.07	–	0.003	4.8	34	7	0.038	0.17	0.05	0.1	0.28	2	E 0.03[4]; biotin 0.002	–	B	53	150	123	14	–	0.1	0.003	97	–	100
Breast milk[1, 2]	87.7	1.03	4.4	0.3	0.01–0.02	6.9	70	330	0.01	0.04	0.02	0.18	0.24	5	E 0.23[4]; B_{12} trace; biotin 0.001; FA 0.0001; D 0.4–9.7 IU	–	B	17	50	33	3	trace	0.05	0.05	14	14	36
Camel's milk[1]	87.1	3.7	4.2	–	–	4.1	69	120	–	–	–	–	–	6	–	–	B	–	–	–	–	–	–	–	–	–	–
Goat's milk[1]	86.6	3.6	4.2	–	–	4.8	71	120	0.05	0.12	0.027	0.2	0.35	2	B_{12} 0.0001; biotin 0.002; FA 0.0002; D 2 IU	–	B	34	180	129	13	0.008	0.1	0.04	103	16	150
Mare's milk[1]	91.1	2.1	1.25	–	–	6.3	44	45	0.03	0.02	0.03	0.05	0.30	10	B_{12} 0.0003; FA 0.0001	–	B	–	70	100	10	–	–	–	60	–	20
Sheep's milk[1]	81.6	5.6	7.5	–	–	4.4	107	200	0.07	0.50	–	0.50	0.35	3	B_{12} 0.0003; biotin 0.009; FA 0.0002	–	B	30	190	190	–	–	0.1	–	150	–	140
Whey	93.3	0.9	0.3	–	–	4.7	25	8–16	0.04	0.08	0.02	0.07	0.35	1.5	biotin 0.002; E 0.024[4]	–	B	45	129	50	1	–	–	–	53	–	–
Yoghurt[5]	86.1	4.8	3.8	–	–	4.5	71	145	0.045	0.024	0.05	0.18	–	2	–	–	B	62	190	150	–	–	0.2	–	135	–	–
Meat, Poultry (raw unless otherwise stated)																											
Bacon medium fat	20.0	9.1	65.0	6.5	0.22	trace	625	0	0.36	0.11	0.35	1.8	–	0	E 0.4	28	A	1770	225	13	15	–	1.2	–	108	–	–

[1] **Values per 100 g**	pH	Spec. grav.	Casein	Albumin	Total protein	Nonprotein-N	Ash
Breast milk	6.97	1.031	0.40 g	0.30 g	1.0–6.0 g	32.4 mg	0.21 g
Camel's milk	–	1.031	2.90 g	0.90 g	3.4–3.7 g	–	0.68 g
Cow's milk	6.60	1.031	2.80 g	0.40 g	2.0–6.0 g	13–14 mg	0.72 g
Goat's milk	–	1.031	2.87 g	0.89 g	3.6–3.8 g	40 mg	0.85 g
Mare's milk	7.20	1.034	1.40 g	–	2.13 g	–	0.36 g
Sheep's milk	6.54	1.036	4.17 g	0.98 g	4.5–5 g	42.5 mg	0.93 g

* To convert to kJ (kilojoule) multiply the values given by 4.1855.
** Vitamin A activity due to vitamin A + carotenes; 1 IU vitamin A = 0.0006 mg β-carotene.
*** FA = folic acid; E = α-tocopherol unless otherwise stated.

[2] See also pages 687–689.
[3] Can be calculated from the 100 g values.
[4] Total tocopherol.
[5] Citric acid 232 mg, lactic acid 487 mg, acetic acid 44 mg.

Content per 100 grammes edible portion (unless otherwise stated)	Water	Proteins	Fats			Carbohydrates	Calories*	Vitamins								Purine nitrogen	Excess acid A Excess base B	Elements									
			Total	Poly-unsaturated	Cholesterol			A**	B_1	B_2	B_6	Nicotinic acid	Pantothenic acid	C	Other vitamins***			Sodium Na	Potassium K	Calcium Ca	Magnesium Mg	Manganese Mn	Iron Fe	Copper Cu	Phosphorus P	Sulphur S	Chlorine Cl
	g	g	g	g	g	g	kcal	IU	mg	mg	mg	mg	mg	mg	mg	mg		mg	mg	mg	mg	mg	mg	mg	mg	mg	mg
Beef																											
loin, lean	69.7	21.1	8.2	–	–	0	164	20	0.09	0.19	–	5.1	–	–	–	–	A	65	355	12	24	–	3.2	–	196	–	–
rib, lean	66.8	20.7	11.6	–	–	0	193	20	0.09	0.18	–	5.0	–	–	–	–	A	65	355	12	24	–	3.1	–	208	–	–
round, total edible	69.0	19.5	12.5	0.3	0.12	–	196	–	0.08	0.17	0.50	4.7	0.52	–	biotin 0.003; FA 0.01; B_{12} 0.002	50	A	68	400	11	22	–	2.9	0.08	180	–	–
rump, total edible	56.5	17.4	25.3	–	–	0	303	50	0.08	0.16	–	4.2	–	–	–	–	A	–	–	10	21	–	2.6	–	160	–	–
sirloin, lean	71.8	21.5	5.7	–	–	0	143	10	0.09	0.19	–	5.2	–	–	–	–	A	65	355	12	24	–	3.2	–	200	–	–
canned, corned	59.3	25.3	12.0	–	–	0	216	0	0.02	0.2	–	3.4	–	0	–	36	A	1300	60	20	–	–	4.3	–	106	–	–
dried, salted	47.7	34.3	6.3	–	0.23	0	203	0	0.11	0.32	–	3.7	–	0	–	–	A	4300	200	20	–	–	5.1	–	404	–	–
hamburger, cooked	54.2	24.2	20.3	–	–	0	364	40	0.09	0.21	–	5.4	–	–	–	–	A	47	450	11	21	–	3.2	–	194	–	–
brain	79.4	10.4	8.0	–	2.36	0.8	120	580	0.15	0.23	0.16	4.0	1.8	14	biotin 0.007; B_{12} 0.005; FA 0.012	–	A	104	191	11	12	–	1.6	0.2	265	–	–
heart	75.5	16.8	6.0	0.2	0.15	0.6	128	20	0.53	0.88	0.29	6.8	2.0	6	biotin 0.007; B_{12} 0.01; FA 0.003	94	A	85	286	5	17	–	4.0	0.3	195	–	–
kidneys	75.9	15.4	6.7	–	0.41	0.9	130	1000	0.25	2.1	0.39	6.4	4	11	B_{12} 0.04; FA 0.06; biotin 0.009	94	A	245	231	11	11	0.08	5.5	0.35	219	161	256
liver	69.9	19.7	3.8	0.7	0.32	5.9	136	20000	0.30	2.9	0.7	13.6	7.3	31	E 1; B_{12} 0.065; biotin 0.10; FA 0.29	110	A	116	292	7	15	0.27	6.5	2.1	352	–	–
lungs	80.1	16.9	2.0	–	0.35	trace	90	–	0.09	0.32	–	4.0	1.4	0	B_{12} 0.003; biotin 0.006	–	A	–	–	12	–	–	6.6	–	196	–	–
pancreas	70.6	14.6	12.3	–	–	trace	173	17	0.10	0.40	–	4.2	3.5	58	B_{12} 0.014; FA 0.02; biotin 0.014	–	A	62	249	9	15	–	1.0	0.06	335	–	–
spleen	77	18.1	3.4	–	–	trace	108	–	0.13	0.28	0.12	4.2	1.2	6	B_{12} 0.005; biotin 0.006	–	A	99	379	7	–	–	8.9	–	236	–	–
tongue	68.0	16.4	15.0	–	–	0.4	207	0	0.14	0.27	0.13	5.0	2.0	0	biotin 0.003; B_{12} 0.003	55	A	80	260	8	10	–	3.0	0.07	182	–	13
tripe	78	19.0	2.0	–	0.15	0	99	0	0.01	0.09	–	3.0	–	0	–	22	A	46	19	69	–	–	0.9	–	132	–	–
Calf (see also 'Veal')																											
brain	79.4	10.2	8.3	–	–	0.8	122	–	0.20	0.20	0.16	3.7	2.5	18	biotin 0.06; B_{12} 0.002	–	A	172	265	9	14	–	2.6	0.14	353	–	–
heart	78.3	12.2	7.6	0.5	–	0.8	124	30	0.6	1.05	–	6.3	2.8	5	biotin 0.015; B_{12} 0.01; FA 0.01	–	A	120	230	16	18	–	2.2	0.34	350	–	–
kidneys	75.0	16.7	6.4	0.18	–	0.8	132	70	0.37	2.5	0.5	6.5	4.0	13	B_{12} 0.025; FA 0.04	–	A	200	290	10	–	–	3.4	0.51	171	–	–
liver	70.7	19.2	4.7	–	0.36	4.1	140	22500	0.28	2.72	1.2	17	9.7	32	E 0.9–1.6[1]; K 0.15; FA 0.05; B_{12} 0.06; biotin 0.075; D 50 IU	120	A	84	295	8	15	0.34	5.4	4.4	311	–	–
sweetbreads	75	19.6	3.0	–	0.28	0	111	–	0.08	0.17	–	2.6	–	–	–	400	A	73	519	–	–	–	0.9	0.08	–	–	–
tongue	74.3	18.5	5.3	–	–	0.9	130	–	–	–	–	–	–	–	–	–	A	84	200	9	–	–	3.0	–	190	–	–
Chicken, flesh and skin																											
fryers	72.7	20.6	5.6	1.2	0.09	–	138	170	0.1	0.2	0.50	6.8	0.80	2.5	E 0.21; biotin 0.011; FA 0.003	60	A	83	359	12	37	0.02	1.8	0.3	200	–	85
roasters	66.9	19.5	12.6	–	–	0	197	410	0.08	0.12	–	7.4	–	–	–	–	A	–	–	11	–	–	1.5	–	191	–	–
hens and cocks	61.3	19.0	18.8	–	–	0	251	610	0.06	0.13	–	9.2	–	–	–	–	A	–	–	11	–	–	1.3	–	182	–	–
liver	72.2	19.7	3.7	1.0	0.20	2.9	141	12100	0.4	2.5	0.80	10.8	4.1	35	FA 0.38; B_{12} 0.004; D 50 IU	–	A	85	179	12	13	0.18	7.9	0.32	236	–	–
Duck, medium fat	54.0	16	28.6	6.9	0.07	0	326	–	0.10	0.24	–	5.6	–	8	–	60	A	85	285	15	–	0.03	1.8	0.4	188	–	85

* To convert to kJ (kilojoule) multiply the values given by 4.1855.
** Vitamin A activity due to vitamin A + carotenes; 1 IU vitamin A = 0.0006 mg β-carotene.
*** FA = folic acid; E = α-tocopherol unless otherwise stated.
[1] Total tocopherol.

Tofranil® Geigy

Successful in the Treatment of Enuresis

Content per 100 grammes edible portion (unless otherwise stated)	Water	Proteins	Fats			Carbohydrates	Calories*	Vitamins								Purine nitrogen	Excess acid A Excess base B	Elements									
			Total	Poly-unsaturated	Cholesterol			A**	B_1	B_2	B_6	Nicotinic acid	Pantothenic acid	C	Other vitamins***			Sodium Na	Potassium K	Calcium Ca	Magnesium Mg	Manganese Mn	Iron Fe	Copper Cu	Phosphorus P	Sulphur S	Chlorine Cl
	g	g	g	g	g	g	kcal	IU	mg	mg	mg	mg	mg	mg	mg	mg		mg	mg	mg	mg	mg	mg	mg	mg	mg	mg
Gelatin, dry	13.0	85.6	0.1	–	–	0	335	0	0	0	–	0	–	0	–	0	0	–	–	–	–	–	–	–	–	–	–
Goat	70	18.7	9.4	0.4	–	0	165	0	0.17	0.32	–	5.6	–	0	–	–	A	–	–	11	–	–	2.2	–	–	–	–
Goose, medium fat	51.0	16.4	31.5	2.5	–	0	354	–	0.13	0.24	0.6	5.6	–	–	–	100	A	85	420	15	–	0.05	1.8	0.3	188	–	–
liver	66	17	10	–	0.49	5.5	184	–	0.02	–	0.9	4	–	–	–	–	A	140	230	10	–	–	–	–	180	–	–
Ham																											
raw	53.0	15.2	31.0	–	0.07–0.1	0	345	0	0.74	0.18	0.44	4.0	0.64	0	FA 0.01; B_{12} 0.001; biotin 0.005	49	A	76	339	9	18	0.06	2.3	0.31	168	–	–
boiled	57.0	19.5	20.6	2.0	0.07	0	269	0	0.54	0.26	–	4.2	0.53	0	–	45	A	876	348	10	–	–	2.5	–	150	–	–
smoked, raw	42.0	16.9	35.0	–	0.11	0.3	389	0	0.7	0.19	0.40	4.0	–	0	–	–	A	2530	248	10	20	–	2.5	–	207	–	2060
canned, spiced	65.0	18.3	12.3	–	0.07	1.5	193	0	0.53	0.19	–	3.8	–	0	–	–	A	1150	293	11	20	–	2.7	0.09	156	–	–
Hare	73	22.3	0.9′	–	0.08	0.2	103	0	0.09	0.19	–	5.0	–	–	–	–	A	50	400	12	–	–	3.2	–	157	–	–
Horse flesh, lean	74.3	21.7	2.6	–	–	0.9	120	–	0.07	0.12	–	4.3	0.50	1	E 0.5′; B_{12} 0.003	–	A	44	332	10	–	–	2.7	–	150	–	–
Lamb (medium fat)																											
chop	52.0	14.9	32.0	0.7	0.07	0	352	–	0.13	0.18	0.33	4.3	0.59	–	E 0.6	65	A	90	345	9	14	–	2.2	–	138	–	–
leg	64.0	18.0	18.0	0.5	0.07	0	239	–	0.16	0.22	0.32	5.2	0.62	–	biotin 0.006; B_{12} 0.003; FA 0.003	81	A	78	380	10	16	–	2.7	–	213	–	–
Pork (see also 'Bacon' and 'Ham')																											
cutlets	53.9	15.2	30.6	2.8	0.07	0	341	0	0.8	0.19	0.48	4.3	0.40	0	E 0.6; B_{12} 0.001; biotin 0.005; FA 0.002	–	A	62	326	10	19	0.06	2.6	–	193	–	–
loin, lean	71.2	18.6	9.9	–	–	–	168	–	1.1	0.31	–	6.5	–	–	–	–	A	74	348	12	22	–	3.0	–	234	–	–
loin or chops, cooked	50	23.0	26.0	–	–	0	333	0	0.33	0.24	–	5.0	–	0	–	–	A	–	–	11	–	–	3.0	–	235	–	–
ribs	52.6	14.6	32.0	1.6	0.10	0	351	–	0.92	0.18	–	3.9	0.65	2	B_{12} 0.001	–	A	76	252	5	0.06	–	2.2	–	157	–	–
spare ribs, total edible	53.9	15.2	30.6	2.8	0.07	0	341	0	0.3	0.19	0.48	4.3	0.40	0	E 0.6; B_{12} 0.001; biotin 0.005; FA 0.002	–	A	62	326	9	19	0.06	2.3	–	170	–	–
canned, strained	75.7	17.1	6.0	–	–	0	127	0	0.35	0.28	–	4.7	–	0	–	–	A	–	–	14	–	–	1.7	–	180	–	–
brain	78.0	10.6	9.0	–	–	trace	126	–	0.16	0.28	–	4.3	2.8	18	B_{12} 0.003	–	A	153	312	10	11	–	3.6	0.3	300	–	–
heart	76.8	16.9	4.8	0.27	–	0.4	117	30	0.43	1.24	0.43	6.6	2.5	3	E 1.4′; B_{12} 0.003; biotin 0.02	–	A	80	257	6	15	–	3.3	0.3	132	198	113
kidneys	77.8	16.3	5.2	0.29	–	0.8	120	130	0.34	1.8	0.55	9.8	3.1	12	B_{12} 0.015; biotin 0.13	–	A	173	242	11	16	0.10	6.7	0.38	218	–	190
liver	71.6	20.6	4.8	–	–	2.6	131	10900	0.43	2.7	0.85	16.4	7.0	27	E 1.0′; B_{12} 0.010; FA 0.22; biotin 0.10	–	A	77	350	10	18	0.3	19	0.85	316	228	102
tongue	66.1	16.8	15.6	–	–	0.5	215	–	0.17	0.29	0.35	5.0	–	–	–	–	A	93	234	9	–	–	1.4	–	186	–	–
Rabbit	70.4	20.4	8.0	1.5	0.12	0	159	30	0.04	0.18	0.6	12.8	0.8	0	E 1.0′	38	A	40	385	18	–	–	2.4	–	210	199	51
Sausages																											
beef	49.2	13.8	18.4	–	–	15.7	286	–	–	–	–	–	–	–	–	–	A	1130	255	21.2	16.6	–	4.1	0.17	168	163	1770
bologna	56.2	12.1	27.5	–	–	1.1	304	–	0.16	0.22	–	2.6	–	–	–	–	A	1300	230	7	–	–	1.8	–	128	–	–
frankfurter, cervelat	55.6	12.5	27.6	–	–	1.8	256	0	0.16	0.20	–	2.7	–	0	–	–	A	1100	230	7	–	–	1.9	–	133	–	–
canned	65.7	13.0	19.6	–	–	–	232	–	0.03	0.08	–	3.1	–	–	–	–	A	711	–	10	–	–	2.7	–	185	–	1100

* To convert to kJ (kilojoule) multiply the values given by 4.1855.
** Vitamin A activity due to vitamin A + carotenes; 1 IU vitamin A = 0.0006 mg β-carotene.
*** FA = folic acid; E = α-tocopherol unless otherwise stated.
′ Total tocopherol.

Content per 100 grammes edible portion (unless otherwise stated)	Water	Proteins	Fats: Total	Fats: Poly-unsaturated	Fats: Cholesterol	Carbohydrates	Calories*	Vitamins: A**	B₁	B₂	B₆	Nicotinic acid	Pantothenic acid	C	Other vitamins***	Purine nitrogen	Excess acid A Excess base B	Elements: Sodium Na	Potassium K	Calcium Ca	Magnesium Mg	Manganese Mn	Iron Fe	Copper Cu	Phosphorus P	Sulphur S	Chlorine Cl
	g	g	g	g	g	g	kcal	IU	mg	mg	mg	mg	mg	mg	mg	mg		mg	mg	mg	mg	mg	mg	mg	mg	mg	mg
Sausages (continued)																											
mortadella	52.3	12.4	32.8	–	–	–	349	–	0.10	0.15	–	3.1	–	0	–	–	A	668	207	12	–	–	3.1	–	238	–	920
pork																											
English	50.7	8.8	28.8	–	–	9.8	335	–	–	–	–	–	–	–	–	–	A	770	158	15	11.5	–	2.5	0.12	108	73	1070
American	38.1	9.4	50.8	–	–	trace	498	0	0.43	0.17	–	2.3	–	–	–	–	A	740	140	5	–	–	1.4	–	92	–	–
salami	27.7	17.8	49.7	–	–	–	524	–	0.18	0.20	–	2.6	–	–	E 0.11	–	A	1260	302	35	–	–	–	–	–	–	2390
Sheep (see also 'Lamb' and 'Mutton')																											
kidneys	77.7	16.8	3.3	–	–	0.9	105	690	0.51	2.42	–	7.4	4.3	15	B_{12} 0.063	103	A	151	205	13	13	0.09	7.5	0.3	218	–	–
liver	70.8	21.0	3.9	–	0.12	2.9	136	50500	0.4	3.28	0.37	16.9	7.1	33	biotin 0.13; FA 0.28	–	A	51	170	13	14	0.23	10.9	6.3	349	–	–
Turkey	64.2	20.1	14.7[1]	3.0	0.015	0.4	218	trace	0.13	0.14	–	7.9	0.75	0	FA 0.01	79	A	66	315	8	–	0.03	1.5	0.2	212	–	123
Veal																											
rib	70.0	19.5	9.0	0.6	–	0	164	–	0.14	0.26	0.43	6.5	0.50	0	biotin 0.002; FA 0.005; B_{12} 0.0007	50	A	90	301	11	16	0.03	2.9	0.25	200	–	–
round with rump	73.0	19.9	6	–	–	0	139	–	0.15	0.26	–	6.7	–	–	–	–	A	90	320	12	–	–	3.0	–	206	–	–
Venison	73.0	21.4	3.6	0.3	–	0	124	0	0.37	0.28	–	7.4	–	0	–	–	A	70	336	19	29	–	5.0	–	183	211	41
Whale meat	71	20.6	4.0	–	–	1	125	1860	0.03	0.1	–	4.4	–	8	–	–	A	78	–	12	–	–	2.4	–	144	–	–
Fish, Sea foods (raw unless otherwise stated)																											
Carp (*Cyprinus carpio*)	72.4	18.9	7.1	–	–	0	145	300	0.08	0.04	–	1.5	–	1	–	54	A	51	285	34	15	–	1	–	220	–	62
Caviar, pressed	46.0	26.9	15.0	–	0.3	3.3	262	–	0	–	–	–	–	–	–	40	A	2200	180	276	–	–	11.8	–	355	–	1800
Clams, long and round (*Mya arenaria, Ensis americana*)	83.1	10.5	1.3	–	0.12	3.1	70	–	0.1	0.19	0.08	1.5	0.6	–	biotin 0.002; FA 0.003	–	A	121	235	12	63	–	0.6	–	208	–	–
Cod (*Gadus callarias*)	81.2	17.6	0.3	–	0.05	0	78	0	0.06	0.07	0.20	2.2	0.12	2	biotin 0.0002; FA 0.001; B_{12} 0.0005	62	A	86	339	11	28	0.01	0.5	0.5	190	–	97
Crab (*Cancer pagurus*), canned or cooked, meat only	77.2	17.4	2.5	–	0.15	1.1	101	–	0.08	0.08	0.35	2.5	0.5	trace	biotin 0.005; B_{12} 0.0005; FA 0.0003	61	A	1000	110	45	48	–	0.8	1.3	182	–	–
Eel (*Anguilla anguilla*)	60.7	12.7	25.6	–	0.05	0	285	2000	0.15	0.31	0.28	2.2	–	1.8	D 5000 IU	–	A	78	247	18	18	0.03	0.7	0.03	166	130	35
smoked	50.3	18.6	27.8	–	–	0.8	333	2500	0.14	0.35	0.15	3.8	–	–	B_{12} 0.006; D 6400 IU	–	A	798	239	95	50	0.03	0.7	–	211	–	–
Flounder (*Platichthys flesus, Pleuronectes flesus*)	81.3	16.7	0.8	–	0.06	0	79	30	0.22	0.21	0.25	3.8	–	–	–	86	A	68	332	12	31	0.02	0.8	0.18	195	–	151
Frog legs (*Rana* spp.)	81.9	16.4	0.3	–	0.04	0	73	–	0.14	0.25	–	1.2	–	5	–	–	A	55	308	18	–	–	1.5	–	147	163	40
Haddock (*Melanogrammus aeglefinus*)	80.5	18.3	0.1	–	0.06	0	79	60	0.06	0.17	0.2	3.0	0.14	0	E 0.6; biotin 0.0003; B_{12} 0.001; FA 0.001	67	A	99	301	18	24	0.02	0.7	0.23	197	238	241
smoked	72.6	23.2	0.4	–	–	0	103	–	0.06	0.05	–	2.1	–	–	–	–	–	–	–	–	–	–	–	–	–	–	–
Halibut (*Hippoglossus hippoglossus*)	75.2	18.6	5.2	–	0.06	0	126	440	0.09	0.18	0.42	6	0.30	0	biotin 0.002; B_{12} 0.001; FA 0.002	68	A	56	340	13	–	0.01	0.7	0.23	211	–	–

* To convert to kJ (kilojoule) multiply the values given by 4.1855.
** Vitamin A activity due to vitamin A + carotenes; 1 IU vitamin A = 0.0006 mg β-carotene.
*** FA = folic acid; E = α-tocopherol unless otherwise stated.
[1] Lean meat 6.6.

Content per 100 grammes edible portion (unless otherwise stated)	Water g	Proteins g	Fats: Total g	Fats: Poly-unsaturated g	Fats: Cholesterol g	Carbohydrates g	Calories* kcal	Vitamins: A** IU	Vitamins: B_1 mg	Vitamins: B_2 mg	Vitamins: B_6 mg	Vitamins: Nicotinic acid mg	Vitamins: Pantothenic acid mg	Vitamins: C mg	Vitamins: Other vitamins*** mg	Purine nitrogen mg	Excess acid A / Excess base B	Elements: Sodium Na mg	Elements: Potassium K mg	Elements: Calcium Ca mg	Elements: Magnesium Mg mg	Elements: Manganese Mn mg	Elements: Iron Fe mg	Elements: Copper Cu mg	Elements: Phosphorus P mg	Elements: Sulphur S mg	Elements: Chlorine Cl mg
Herring (*Clupea harengus*)	62.8	17.3	18.8	–	–	0	243	130	0.06	0.24	0.45	4.3	1.0	0.5	E 2[1,2]; B_{12} 0.01; D 900 IU[1]	119	A	118	317	57	26	0.02	1.1	0.3	240	202	122
pickled	60.2	18.3	14	–	–	–	204	150	–	0.08	0.15	3.3	–	–	–	–	A	1000	–	30	9	–	–	–	150	–	1600
smoked	61.0	22.2	12.9	–	–	0	211	40	0.04	0.28	0.35	3.3	–	–	B_{12} 0.01	–	A	720	285	66	–	–	1.4	–	254	–	230
Lobster (*Homarus vulgaris*)	78.5	16.9	1.9	–	0.20	0.5	91	–	0.15	0.13	–	1.5	1.3	5	biotin 0.005; FA 0.0005	73	A	300	260	29	22	0.04	0.6	2.2	200	170	500
canned	77.2	18.4	1.3	–	–	0.4	92	–	0.16	0.14	–	2.2	–	4	–	–	A	–	–	65	–	–	0.8	–	192	–	–
Mackerel (*Scomber scombrus*)	67.2	19.0	12.2	–	0.08	0	191	450	0.15	0.35	0.70	7.7	0.46	0	E 1.6[2]; B_{12} 0.01; biotin 0.002; FA 0.001; D 50 IU	–	A	144	358	5	33	0.02	1.0	0.16	239	197	170
smoked	59.4	23.8	13.0	–	–	0	219	–	–	–	–	–	–	–	–	–	A	–	–	–	–	–	–	–	–	–	–
Mussels (*Mytilus edulis*)	84.1	11.7	1.9	–	0.15	2.2	76	180	0.16	0.22	–	1.6	–	–	–	199	A	290	315	88	23	0.25	5.8	3.2	250	367	460
Ocean perch, Atlantic (*Sebastes marinus*)	77.9	18.9	3.0	–	–	0	108	30	0.09	0.08	–	2.5	–	3	–	–	A	94	345	46	–	–	1.0	–	212	–	–
Octopus (*Octopus bimaculatus*)	82.2	15.3	0.8	–	0.17	0	73	–	0.02	0.06	–	1.8	–	–	–	–	A	–	–	29	–	–	0.19	0.44	173	–	–
Oysters (*Ostrea* spp.)	83.0	9.0	1.2	–	0.11–0.33	4.8	68	310	0.18	0.23	0.11	2.5	0.5	trace	biotin 0.001; FA 0.004; B_{12} 0.015; D 5 IU	29	A	73	110	94	42	0.2	5.5	1.2–3.7	143	–	–
Perch (*Perca fluviatilis*)	79.5	18.4	0.8	–	0.07	0	86	30	0.075	0.12	–	1.7	–	–	–	–	A	67	238	20	–	–	1	–	198	–	–
Pike (*Esox lucius*)	80.2	18.2	1.2	–	–	0	89	–	0.15	0.07	–	1.7	–	–	E 0.2	45	A	70	300	20	30	0.02	0.7	0.25	210	200	100
Salmon																											
Atlantic (*Salmo salar*)	65.5	19.9	13.6	5.3	0.06	0	208	220	0.17	0.17	0.98	7.5	0.8	1	biotin 0.001; D 650 IU; FA 0.002; B_{12} 0.003	47	A	48	391	29	29	0.01	0.8	0.2	266	190	64
canned, solids and liquid	64.2	21.7	12.2	–	–	0	203	60	0.03	0.18	0.45	6.5	0.5	trace	biotin 0.015; FA 0.0005; D 500 IU	101	A	540	330	67	30	–	1.3	0.05	285	–	865
chinook	64.2	19.1	15.6	–	–	0	222	310	0.10	0.23	–	–	–	–	–	–	A	45	399	–	–	–	–	–	301	–	–
canned, solids and liquid	64.4	19.6	14.0	–	–	0	210	230	0.03	0.14	–	7.3	–	–	–	–	A	–	366	154	27	–	0.9	–	289	–	–
sockeye																											
canned, solids and liquid	67.2	20.3	9.3	–	–	0	171	230	0.04	0.16	–	7.3	–	–	–	–	A	522	344	259	29	–	1.2	–	344	–	–
smoked	58.9	21.6	9.3	–	–	0	176	–	–	–	–	–	–	–	–	–	A	–	–	14	–	–	–	–	245	–	–
Sardines, canned in oil																											
solids and liquid	50.6	20.6	24.4	–	–	0.6	311	180	0.02	0.16	0.16	4.4	0.5	0	biotin 0.005; D 300 IU; B_{12} 0.01; FA 0.002	–	A	510	560	354	–	–	3.5	0.04	434	–	–
drained solids	61.8	24.0	11.1	3	0.07	1.2	214	290	0.03	0.20	0.28	5.4	0.6	0	biotin 0.02; D 250 IU	234	A	823	590	437	–	–	2.9	0.04	499	–	–
Scallops (*Pecten* spp.)	79.8	15.3	0.2	–	–	3.3	79	0	0.04	0.06	–	1.3	0.14	–	biotin 0.0003; FA 0.0005	117	A	150	420	26	–	–	1.8	–	208	342	–
Shrimps (*Crangon* spp.)	78.2	18.7	2.2	–	0.14	–	97	10	0.07	0.05	0.13	1.25	–	2	B_{12} 0.001	–	A	140	258	63	42	–	2.0	0.43	300	–	–
canned, drained solids	70.4	24.2	1.1	–	0.15	0.7	116	60	0.01	0.03	0.11	1.5	0.21	0	FA 0.002; D 105 IU	–	A	–	122	115	–	–	3.1	–	263	–	–
Snails (*Helix*)	82	15	0.8	–	–	2	75	–	–	–	–	–	–	–	–	–	A	–	–	170	250	1.6	3.5	0.4	–	140	–
Trout (*Salmo trutta*)	77.6	19.2	2.1	–	–	0	101	150	0.09	0.25	–	3.5	–	–	–	92	A	39	470	19	–	0.03	1.0	0.33	220	–	–
Tunny (*Thunnus thynnus*), canned, solids and liquid	52.5	23.8	20.9	–	–	0	290	90	0.05	0.06	0.25	10.8	0.2	0	biotin 0.0005; B_{12} 0.001; FA 0.003	–	A	361	343	7	–	–	1.2	–	294	–	–

* To convert to kJ (kilojoule) multiply the values given by 4.1855.
** Vitamin A activity due to vitamin A + carotenes; 1 IU vitamin A = 0.0006 mg β-carotene.
*** FA = folic acid; E = α-tocopherol unless otherwise stated.
[1] Without gonads.
[2] Total tocopherol.

Amino acids of foods

The amino-acid contents of foods listed in the table below have been taken from a publication[1] of the British Medical Research Council. Other collected data on the subject are available in the publications of BLOCK and BOLLING[2], BLOCK and WEISS[3], ORR and WATT[4], and HARVEY[5]. The amounts of the essential amino acids in foods are given in the tables of SOUCI et al.[6] and of CHURCH and CHURCH[7]. The amino-acid content of the FAO/WHO Reference Protein[8] is based on the minimum requirements of the individual essential amino acids.

Many of the proteins of meat and fish have a largely similar composition, like those of cereal and milk products, and it has therefore been unnecessary to list all these foods in detail. On the other hand, the amino-acid composition of the vegetable proteins shows wide variations, but since these proteins are quantitatively unimportant in the human diet the variations are without appreciable effect in nutrition. Too little is known of the amino-acid composition of fruits to justify their inclusion in the table. The phenylalanine content of fruits lies between 1.5 and 4 g/16 g N[9].

The values in the table are for the raw foods. Cooking has very little effect on the proteins of foods poor in carbohydrate. In bakery products the proteins in the crust have a lower utilizability. It is known that vegetables lose nitrogenous substances during cooking, but this loss has no practical significance.

References

1 MCCANCE and WIDDOWSON, *The Composition of Foods*, Med. Res. Coun. Spec. Rep. Ser., No. 297, HMSO, London, 1960.
2 BLOCK and BOLLING, *The Amino Acid Composition of Proteins and Foods*, 2nd ed., Thomas, Springfield, 1951.
3 BLOCK and WEISS, *Amino Acid Handbook*, Thomas, Springfield, 1956.
4 ORR and WATT, *Amino Acid Content of Foods*, United States Department of Agriculture, Home Economics Research Report, No. 4, Washington, 1957.
5 HARVEY, D., *Tables of the Amino Acids in Foods and Feedingstuffs*, Commonwealth Agricultural Bureaux, Techn. Communication No. 19, Farnham Royal, 1958.
6 SOUCI et al., *Die Zusammensetzung der Lebensmittel*, vol. 1, Wissenschaftliche Verlagsgesellschaft, Stuttgart, 1962.
7 CHURCH and CHURCH, *Bowes and Church's Food Values of Portions Commonly Used*, 9th ed., Lippincott, Philadelphia, 1963.
8 *Protein Requirements*, Report of a Joint FAO/WHO Expert Group, *Wld Hlth Org. techn. Rep. Ser.*, No. 301 (1965).
9 MILLER et al., *J. Amer. diet. Ass.*, **46**, 43 (1965).

Amino-acid contents of foods (g per 16 g nitrogen*)

	Arginine	Cystine	Histidine	Isoleucine	Leucine	Lysine	Methionine	Phenylalanine	Threonine	Tryptophan	Tyrosine	Valine	Alanine	Aspartic acid	Glutamic acid	Glycine	Proline	Serine
Vegetables																		
Beans, snap	5.9	1.1	2.9	5.4	7.7	5.4	0.5	3.4	2.6	1.0	3.0	5.1	2.6	6.6	1.4	3.7	4.5	5.8
haricot	5.8	1.0	3.2	6.1	8.2	7.0	1.3	6.2	4.6	1.3	–	6.6	–	–	–	–	–	–
Beets	1.8	–	1.4	3.2	3.4	3.4	0.5	1.4	2.4	1.0	–	3.0	–	–	–	–	–	–
Beets, tops	6.1	1.4	1.9	3.2	6.2	3.5	2.4	5.0	4.2	1.4	4.5	5.1	–	–	–	–	–	–
Broccoli	5.8	–	1.8	3.8	5.3	5.4	1.8	3.0	3.4	1.3	–	4.2	–	–	–	–	–	–
Brussels sprouts	6.2	–	2.2	4.2	4.3	4.3	1.0	3.4	3.4	1.0	–	4.3	–	–	–	–	–	–
Cabbage	7.5	1.6	1.8	2.9	4.2	3.7	1.0	2.6	2.7	0.8	2.1	3.4	–	–	–	–	–	–
Carrots	3.5	–	1.4	4.3	5.8	4.5	1.1	3.7	3.8	0.8	–	5.4	–	–	–	–	–	–
Cauliflower	4.2	–	0.2	4.3	6.2	5.4	2.1	3.4	4.2	1.3	–	5.8	–	–	–	–	–	–
Lentils	8.3	0.6	2.2	5.3	7.0	6.2	0.6	4.2	3.7	0.8	–	5.6	–	–	–	–	–	–
Peas	8.6	1.0	1.8	5.0	6.9	5.3	1.0	4.0	4.0	1.0	4.2	4.6	(3.8)	(8.6)	(3.2)	(6.1)	–	–
Potatoes	5.3	1.3	1.4	4.5	4.6	5.0	1.6	4.2	3.7	1.3	2.9	5.1	4.2	17.1	23.8	1.9	2.6	2.7
Spinach	4.5	–	1.4	4.0	6.4	5.1	1.8	4.5	4.0	1.8	–	5.1	–	–	–	–	–	–
Soybeans, soyflour	7.4	1.9	2.6	5.3	7.7	6.4	1.3	5.0	4.0	1.4	3.7	5.3	5.0	1.3	19.0	4.5	5.3	5.8
Nuts																		
Almonds	10.1	1.8	2.2	3.8	6.6	2.6	1.3	5.1	2.7	0.8	–	5.0	–	–	–	–	–	–
Brazil nuts	13.3	3.0	2.1	3.7	6.9	2.6	5.1	3.4	2.6	1.1	–	4.8	–	–	–	–	–	–
Coconuts	12.5	1.8	2.1	4.5	7.2	3.5	1.8	4.2	3.0	2.1	–	5.6	–	–	–	–	–	–
Hazelnuts	14.6	2.6	1.9	5.8	6.2	2.9	1.0	3.7	2.9	1.4	3.7	6.2	–	7.0	20.5	9.4	5.6	9.6
Peanuts	10.6	1.6	2.4	4.2	6.2	3.5	1.0	5.0	2.9	1.1	3.0	5.0	2.9	14.1	2.0	5.4	5.1	6.6
Walnuts	13.0	1.8	2.2	4.3	6.9	2.6	1.8	4.3	3.4	1.0	–	5.4	–	–	–	–	–	–
Cereals																		
Barley, whole grain	5.0	2.1	1.9	3.8	6.9	3.4[1]	1.4	5.0	3.7	1.4	3.5	5.0	4.5	5.9	20.5	43.2	9.3	3.7
Bread, wheat, white	3.4	2.2	2.1	3.7	7.4	1.9	1.9	5.0	2.9	–	3.2	4.2	3.0	4.2	33.0	3.4	11.5	4.5
Flour, wheat, whole	4.3	2.1	2.1	3.8	6.4	2.7	1.6	4.6	2.9	1.3	3.2	4.3	3.4	5.0	27.7	3.8	10.1	4.8
white	3.4	2.2	2.1	3.7	7.0	1.9	1.6	5.4	2.9	1.3	3.4	4.2	3.2	4.2	33.4	3.4	11.7	4.6
Maize, whole grain	5.0	2.1	2.4	4.0	12.0	3.0	2.1	5.0	4.2	0.8	3.8	5.6	9.9	12.3	15.4	3.0	8.3	4.2
Oats, whole grain	6.6	1.8	1.9	4.6	7.0	3.7	1.4	5.0	3.4	1.3	3.8	5.4	5.1	4.2	18.4	4.2	5.8	3.4
Rice, whole	8.5	1.8	2.2	4.8	8.2	4.2	2.1	4.6	3.5	1.4	5.8	6.2	–	–	–	–	–	–
polished	8.0	1.6	2.2	4.6	8.5	3.0	2.1	4.8	3.8	1.4	5.0	6.6	5.6	4.5	10.7	6.6	4.5	5.1
Rye, whole grain	5.0	1.8	2.1	3.8	6.1	3.7	1.6	4.6	3.4	1.3	4.2	5.0	–	–	19.7	–	–	3.8
Wheat germ	6.9	1.4	2.7	3.5	5.9	6.1	1.4	3.7	4.5	1.0	–	4.6	–	–	–	–	–	–
Eggs, Milk																		
Eggs, whole	6.4	2.1	2.6	5.8	9.0	6.7	3.0	5.3	5.3	1.8	4.3	7.2	–	10.7	12.3	3.8	4.3	7.7
Egg white	6.2	2.2	2.4	5.8	9.0	6.6	4.0	5.9	5.0	1.9	4.2	7.8	–	11.0	12.6	4.2	4.2	6.9
Egg yolk	7.0	1.8	2.6	5.8	8.5	6.7	2.2	4.6	5.8	1.8	4.6	6.9	–	–	12.0	3.4	4.3	8.8
Milk, cow's, and dairy products	3.7	0.8[2]	2.7	6.2	9.9	7.8	2.4	5.1	4.6	1.4	5.6	7.0	3.7	8.2	22.2	1.9	9.8	5.8
Breast milk	3.4	1.9	2.2	5.6	9.4	6.2	2.1	4.0	4.5	1.6	4.8	6.2	3.8	9.3	19.8	2.2	8.6	4.8
Meat, Fish																		
Fish	5.8[3]	11.2	2.1[4]	5.1	7.5	9.0	2.9	3.7	4.5	1.0	3.0	5.3	6.1	9.4	14.1	6.1	5.9	5.3
Gelatin	7.8	trace	6.9	1.4	2.9	4.0	0.8	2.1	1.9	–	0.3	2.2	9.8	5.9	10.1	24.2	26.7[5]	3.7
Meat and meat products	6.6	1.3	3.2	5.1	7.8	8.2	2.4	4.2	4.5	1.3	3.4	5.3	6.2	9.1	15.4	4.5	4.2	4.2
brain, liver, kidney	6.1	1.3	3.2	5.1	9.0	8.2	2.4	5.1	4.5	1.3	3.4	6.1	6.2	9.1	15.4	4.5	4.2	4.2
FAO/WHO Reference Protein	–	–	–	4.3	4.9	4.3	2.3	2.9	2.8	1.4	2.9	4.3	–	–	–	–	–	–

* Average nitrogen content per 100 g protein. [1] Barley, pearled 2.2. [2] Cheese 0.5. [3] Shrimps 9.4. [4] Mackerel 3.7; tunny 5.8. [5] Including hydroxyproline.

The body is a complex structure, made up of many organs and tissues. These contribute different proportions to the body weight at different ages – the muscle, for example, accounts for about 25% of the weight of the newborn baby and 43% of the weight of the adult, whereas the brain constitutes 13% of the weight of the baby but only 2% of that of the adult. The composition of each of the component parts of the body changes with age, and the parts do not all mature chemically at the same rate. The composition of the whole body at any age is the resultant of the composition of its tissues and of their contribution to the weight of the body at that age.

Methods of determining the composition of the whole body

The composition of the whole body may be determined by direct chemical analysis or by dilution techniques. Chemical analysis can be used only after the person is dead, whereas dilution methods are applicable only during life. Our knowledge of the changes in the composition of the body during prenatal life has been derived from chemical analysis of foetuses and stillborn babies. During postnatal life, however, it is extremely difficult to acquire bodies to deal with in this way, and it is still more difficult to obtain bodies of healthy individuals. In fact, up to the present time, only 8 adult bodies have been analysed chemically. During postnatal development we have much more information about the fluid components of the body than about the total amounts of fat or nitrogen or inorganic matter.

Dilution methods depend upon introducing into the body a known amount of a foreign substance, or of a tagged, naturally occurring one, and then determining it in the serum at one or more time intervals. Then, allowing for any loss that may have occurred in the urine or been due to metabolism of the substance or any other cause, the volume of fluid in which the substance has become distributed can be calculated. By the use of appropriate substances it is possible to estimate the amounts of total water, of extracellular water and of certain minerals in the body. A number of substances, for instance deuterium oxide, tritium oxide, antipyrine and urea, yield similar values for the amount of total body water in the same individual, and have also been shown in experimental animals to yield values close to the actual water content of the body as determined by desiccation. The determination of the volume of extracellular fluid is more difficult, and probably the ideal substance for measuring it has not yet been found. The values obtained differ according to the substance used, and the use of each involves certain assumptions (for discussion of these see the literature[1]).

* This chapter on the 'Composition of the Body' (pages 517–522) has been compiled by E. M. Widdowson and J. W. T. Dickerson, Department of Experimental Medicine, University of Cambridge, England.

The values given in the table for the volume of extracellular fluid include the plasma volume. This can be determined separately if desired (see page 554).

It should be emphasized that dilution methods yield not the total amount of any mineral in the body but only that fraction of it which is 'exchangeable'.

Determination of the composition of the tissues

The composition of the body tissues is determined by chemical analysis, using material obtained after death, small samples of material taken by biopsy during life, or occasionally organs removed at operation. More is known about the composition of the separate organs and tissues than about that of the body as a whole.

Changes in composition during development

The proportion of fat in the human body increases rapidly during the last 2 months of gestation and the full-term baby has about 16%. Adult men of normal weight have approximately the same proportion, but in those of abnormal weight the value may vary from about 8% to 50%. The bodies of women tend to contain higher proportions of fat than those of men. In view of this wide variation in the proportion of fat it is usual to consider the amounts of the other constituents per 100 g or per kilogramme of fat-free body tissue.

One of the characteristic changes that take place with development is a decrease in the proportion of water in the fat-free body tissue and an increase in that of solid matter. The fall in the proportion of total water is due to the large reduction in the amount of extracellular fluid that accompanies growth; this exceeds the small rise in the amount of water inside the cells due to the increase in the proportion of the body occupied by the cells.

In parallel with these changes there is a decrease in the extracellular constituents sodium and chloride, and an increase in the substances primarily inside the cells – potassium, phosphorus and nitrogen. This applies to all the soft tissues as well as to the body as a whole.

The proportion of the body weight contributed by the skeleton does not change appreciably between birth and adult life, but the composition of bone alters more after birth than the composition of almost any other tissue. Most of the calcium in the body is in the skeleton and the proportion of calcium in the body more than doubles during postnatal life.

References

1 Elkinton and Danowski, *The Body Fluids*, Williams & Wilkins, Baltimore, 1955; McCance, R. A., *Ned. T. Geneesk.*, **99**, 146 (1955); Moore et al., *Metabolism*, **5**, 447 (1956); Edelman and Leibman, *Amer. J. Med.*, **27**, 256 (1959); Moore et al., *The Body Cell Mass and its Supporting Environment*, Saunders, Philadelphia, 1963; Friis-Hansen, B., in Brožek, J. (Ed.), *Human Body Composition*, Pergamon, Oxford, 1965, page 191.

Composition of the whole body as determined by chemical analysis (values per kilogramme fat-free tissue unless otherwise stated)

	Body weight kg	Water* g	Fat* g	Water g	N g	Na mEq	K mEq	Cl mEq	Mg g	Ca g	P g	Fe mg	Cu mg	Zn mg	B mg	Co mg
Foetus	0.02	898	2	900	10.5	110	48	80	0.10	2.1	2.1	–	–	–	–	–
Foetus	0.20	876	5	880	13.0	102	42	76	0.14	3.5	2.5	54	3.3	20	–	–
Foetus	1.0	851	10	860	18.4	94	42	68	0.20	6.3	3.9	65	3.4	20	–	–
Foetus	2.0	790	60	840	21.0	88	45	62	0.24	7.8	4.8	84	4.0	20	–	–
Newborn, full-term	3.5	689	160	820	22.6	82	53	55	0.26	9.6	5.6	94	4.7	20	–	–
Adults	70	605	160	720	34.0	80	69	50	0.47	22.4	12.0	74	1.7	28	0.37	0.02

* Per kilogramme whole body weight.

References

Widdowson et al., *Clin. Sci.*, **10**, 113 (1951); Widdowson and Spray, *Arch. Dis. Childh.*, **26**, 205 (1951); Forbes et al., *J. biol. Chem.*, **203**, 359, (1953); Forbes et al., *J. biol. Chem.*, **209**, 857 (1954); Forbes and Lewis, *J. clin. Invest.*, **35**, 596 (1956); Forbes et al., *J. biol. Chem.*, **223**, 969 (1956); Widdowson and Dickerson, in Comar and Bronner (Eds.), *Mineral Metabolism*, vol. 2, part A, Academic Press, New York, 1964, page 1.

Composition of the whole body as determined by dilution methods

	Total water as percentage of body weight	Extracellular fluid as percentage of body weight	Exchangeable Na mEq/kg body weight	Exchangeable K mEq/kg body weight	Exchangeable Cl mEq/kg body weight
Newborn, 1–27 hours[1]	–	–	–	35.5	–
Newborn, 1 day[2]	79.0 (deuterium oxide)	43.9 (thiosulphate)	–	–	–
Infants, 2–4 weeks[3]	–	–	–	–	48.1
Infants, 2 weeks–2 months[4]	–	–	76.4	–	–
Men[5]	59.1 (deuterium oxide)	15.6 (inulin)	41.7	48.1	31.9
	59.6 (tritium oxide)	16.3 (thiosulphate)	–	–	–
	53.4 (antipyrine)	22.9 (thiocyanate)	–	–	–
	60.2 (urea)	–	–	–	–
Women[5]	51.0 (deuterium oxide)	16.0 (thiosulphate)	40.5	38.2	28.6
	43.4 (antipyrine)	20.9 (thiocyanate)	–	–	–
	57.0 (urea)	–	–	–	–

References
1 Christian and Talso, *Pediatrics*, **23**, 63 (1959).
2 Friis-Hansen, B., *Acta paediat. (Uppsala)*, **46**, suppl. 110 (1957).
3 Cheek, D.B., *Pediatrics*, **14**, 5 (1954).
4 Forbes and Perley, *J.clin.Invest.*, **30**, 566 (1951).
5 For details see Widdowson and Dickerson, in Comar and Bronner (Eds.), *Mineral Metabolism*, vol. 2, part A, Academic Press, New York, 1964, page 1.

Composition of muscular tissues (values per kilogramme fat-free tissue)

		Weight as percentage of body weight	Water g	N g	Na mEq	K mEq	Cl mEq	Mg mEq	Ca mEq	P mmol
Skeletal muscle[1]	Foetus, 14 weeks	–	907	11.5	101	56.3	76.4	11.7	5.6	36.5
	Foetus, 20–22 weeks	25	887	15.4	90.6	57.6	65.6	10.5	7.1	40.0
	Newborn	25	804	20.9	60.1	57.7	42.6	14.8	4.3	47.0
	Infants, 4–7 months	–	785	29.6	50.1	89.5	35.5	20.0	3.1	64.9
	Adults	43	792	31.4	36.3	92.2	22.1	16.7	2.8	58.8
Heart[2] Whole	Foetus, 20 weeks	0.6	860	14.0	46.1	81.1	41.0	–	–	49.7
	Newborn	0.5	841	19.6	64.2	54.3	45.2	10.9	7.4	47.0
	Infants, 4–7 months	–	830	21.0	59.8	49.3	49.3	11.0	8.2	49.5
	Adults	0.4	827	22.9	57.8	66.5	45.6	13.2	2.6	49.0
Left ventricle	Adults	–	789	–	44.7	78.5	38.0	17.0	3.9	63.5
Right ventricle	Adults	–	802	–	47.8	56.2	39.5	16.5	3.8	50.0
Auricles	Adults	–	812	–	52.2	35.7	42.2	–	–	30.6
Septum	Adults	–	792	–	40.5	79.0	33.8	–	–	51.8
Myometrium[3]	Non-pregnant	–	794	–	87.8	62.6	73.8	12.8	16.6	–
	Early pregnant	–	825	–	93.6	59.0	71.0	8.5	7.1	–
	At term	–	823	–	88.8	62.4	63.2	13.5	17.5	–

References
1 Dickerson and Widdowson, *Biochem.J.*, **74**, 247 (1960).
2 Wilkins and Cullen, *J.clin.Invest.*, **12**, 1063 (1933); Mangun et al., *Arch.intern.Med.*, **67**, 320 (1941); Alexander et al., *J.Lab.clin.Med.*, **36**, 796 (1950); Clarke and Mosher, *Circulation*, **5**, 907 (1952); Widdowson and Dickerson, *Biochem.J.*, **77**, 30 (1960).
3 Hawkins and Nixon, *J.Obstet.Gynaec.Brit.Emp.*, **65**, 895 (1958).

Composition of glandular organs (values per kilogramme fresh weight)

		Weight as percentage of body weight	Water g	N g	Na mEq	K mEq	Cl mEq	Mg mEq	Ca mEq	P mmol	Fe (inorganic) mg	Cu mg	Zn mg	Mn mg
Liver[1-3]	Foetus, 14 weeks ..	–	849	20.2	–	81.8	62.2	–	–	82.5	–	–	–	–
	Foetus, 20 weeks ..	4	812	22.1	54.8	92.9	57.1	14.7	2.3	88.0	–	–	–	–
	Newborn.........	5	786	22.6	59.8	58.7	55.8	10.4	3.0	56.5	300	41.5	68.6	0.9
	Infants, 4–7 months	4	764	24.4	51.0	66.2	42.8	11.8	4.4	82.5	170	8.6	–	–
	Adults	2	711	28.2	42.5	75.0	38.3	15.2	2.8	86.0	28–162	5.2	–	1.3
Kidneys[1,2,4]	Foetus, 20 weeks ..	0.7	884	14.2	68.0	66.5	59.6	8.6	17.4	65.5	–	–	–	–
	Newborn.........	1.0	841	19.2	75.5	56.0	56.4	8.7	7.7	61.0	32	3.7	–	–
	Adults	0.5	810	24.5	82.0	57.0	67.8	8.6	7.0	57.5	3.3–10.1	2.8	–	–
Spleen[1,3,5]	Adults	0.2	790	30.1	–	81.0	–	13.0	4.2	71.0	85–169	1.8	33.0	0.18

References

[1] Tompsett, S.L., *Biochem.J.*, **29**, 480 (1935).
[2] Brückmann and Zondek, *Biochem.J.*, **33**, 1845 (1939).
[3] Widdowson et al., *Clin.Sci.*, **10**, 113 (1951).
[4] Widdowson and Dickerson, *Biochem.J.*, **77**, 30 (1960).
[5] Richards, M.B., *Biochem.J.*, **24**, 1572 (1930); Forbes et al., *J.biol.Chem.*, **203**, 359 (1953).

Composition of the lungs (values per kilogramme fresh tissue)

	Weight as percentage of body weight	Water g	N g	Na mEq	K mEq	Cl mEq	Mg mEq	Ca mEq	P mmol	Fe (total) mg	Cu mg	Mn mg	B mg	Co mg	Be μg
Foetus, 20 weeks ...	–	888	10.3	89.0	71.0	67.5	–	–	56.5	70	–	–	–	–	–
Newborn	1.7	858	17.0	75.6	48.6	62.5	–	–	44.0	150	–	–	–	–	–
Adults	1.6	787	27.2	75.3	54.7	69.0	4.8	12.5	51.8	200	3.7	0.40	0.16	0.03	0.23

References

Richards, M.B., *Biochem.J.*, **24**, 1572 (1930); Chou and Adolph, *Biochem.J.*, **29**, 476 (1935); Forbes et al., *J.biol.Chem.*, **223**, 969 (1956); Widdowson and Dickerson, in Comar and Bronner (Eds.), *Mineral Metabolism*, vol.2, part A, Academic Press, New York, 1964, page 1.

Composition of the brain and nerves (values per kilogramme fresh weight unless otherwise stated)

		Weight as percentage of body weight	Water g	N g	Na mEq	K mEq	Cl mEq	Mg mEq	Ca mEq	P mmol	Cu[3] mg	Fe[3] mg	Mn[3] mg	Pb[3] mg
Brain Whole[1]	Foetus, 14 weeks	15.0	914	9.6	97.5	49.6	72.1	–	–	57.0	–	–	–	–
	Foetus, 20–22 weeks .	13.4	922	8.4	91.7	52.0	72.6	8.4	4.9	52.2	–	–	–	–
	Newborn	13.4	897	9.3	80.9	58.2	66.1	7.9	4.8	54.0	–	–	–	–
	Adults	2.3	774	17.1	55.2	84.6	40.5	11.4	4.0	109	3.6–50	–	–	0.4–17.3
Grey matter[2]	Adults	–	843	17.2	83.9	58.4	48.6	16.3	5.2	71.3	15.9–99.0* 19.4, 33.0**	328–461* 222**	1.12* 1.24**	– –
White matter[2]	Adults	–	706	17.5	68.6	59.4	41.2	21.6	7.1	127	9.2–82.0* 23.3**	269–507*	0.99*	–
Spinal cord[2]	Adults	0.04	644	16.0	87.4	92.2	42.8	31.6	9.0	177	–	177	–	–
Peripheral nerve[2]	Adults	–	557	–	–	49.6	–	–	9.9	119	12.3	15.6	–	–

* Cerebrum.
** Cerebellum.

References

[1] (Except values from Cu onwards) Widdowson and Dickerson, *Biochem.J.*, **77**, 30 (1960).
[2] (Except values from Cu onwards) Widdowson and Dickerson, in Comar and Bronner (Eds.), *Mineral Metabolism*, vol.2, part A, Academic Press, New York, 1964, page 1.
[3] Values per kilogramme dry weight from Tingey, A.H., *J.ment.Sci.*, **83**, 452 (1937); Cumings, J.N., *Brain*, **71**, 410 (1948); Cumings, J.N., *Heavy Metals and the Brain*, Blackwell, Oxford, 1959.

Organic composition of the adult brain and spinal cord (values per kilogramme fresh tissue unless otherwise stated)[1]

	Whole brain g	Grey matter g	White matter g	Spinal cord g
Total phospholipid P	250*	30.8	78.2	51–105†
Lecithin P	–	7.9–13.2	9–15	22† ††
Cephalin P	148–260*	18–22	27–35	61† ††
Diphosphoinositide P	–	1.96	4.14	–
Sphingomyelin P	–	2.7	10.8	–
Cerebrosides	–	6.3 ± 2.9	49.0**	12.9–19.6
		3.1 ± 0.2**		67††
Total lipids	104	57.9	179	–
Cholesterol	26–44	7.2	40.7	59††
Gangliosides (*N*-acetylsialic acid × 4.0)	–	3.3	1.25	–
Total protein	100–110	73–82	77–92	90
Soluble in 4.5% KCl (isoelectric point pH 5.6)	–	16.7–18.9	18.5–22.1	–
Soluble in water (isoelectric point pH 4.6)	–	21.9–24.6	14.6–17.5	–
Proteolipid protein[2]	–	16	42	–
Neurokeratin	–	3.1	11.2	–

* Values per kilogramme dry weight.
** 'True' cerebrosides.
† Not expressed as P.
†† White matter.

References
1 (Except proteolipid protein) ANSELL, G.B., in LONG, C. (Ed.), *Biochemists' Handbook*, Spon, London, 1961, page 640.
2 Approximate values calculated from FOLCH and LEES, *J. biol. Chem.*, **191**, 807 (1951).

Composition of skin, hair and nails (values per kilogramme fresh weight unless otherwise stated)

		Weight as percentage of body weight	Water g	N g	Na mEq	K mEq	Cl mEq	Mg mEq	Ca mEq	P mmol	Cu mg	Fe mg	Mn** mg	Pb mg	Si mg
Skin[1]	Foetus, 14 weeks	–	917	11.6	–	23.8	90.6	–	4.4	41.8	–	–	–	–	–
	Foetus, 20 weeks	13	901	11.9	120	36.0	96.0	3.8	6.1	28.2	–	–	–	–	–
	Newborn	15	828	26.5	87.1	45.0	66.9	4.7	10.0	31.7	–	–	–	–	–
	Infants, 3–5 months	–	675	54.5	65.4	43.7	72.3	7.4	11.4	34.9	–	–	–	–	–
	Adults	7	694	53.0	79.3	23.7	71.4	3.1	9.5	14.0	–	–	–	–	–
Epidermis[2]	Adults	–	645	–	49.6	81.4	–	15.0	7.5	–	–	–	–	–	–
Hair*[3]	Adults	–	–	–	–	–	–	0.8–8.4	94–245	–	4–128	0.8–170	0.000 01–46	17–508	150–3600
Nails*[4]	Adults	–	–	–	–	–	–	1.9–9.2	–	–	9–81	18–65	<1	97–240	1700–5400

* Hair and nails also contain Zn (9–562 and 116–3080 mg/kg respectively). The presence in hair of Al, Ni, Co and Cr together with traces of Ti, Sr and Ag has also been reported.
** Values per kilogramme dry weight.

References
1 WIDDOWSON and DICKERSON, *Biochem. J.*, **77**, 30 (1960).
2 SUNTZEFF and CARRUTHERS, *J. biol. Chem.*, **160**, 567 (1945); ZHEUTLIN and FOX, *Arch. Derm.*, **61**, 397 (1950).
3 FLESCH, P., in ROTHMAN, S. (Ed.), *Physiology and Biochemistry of the Skin*, University of Chicago Press, Chicago, 1954, page 601.
4 GOLDBLUM et al., *J. invest. Derm.*, **20**, 13 (1953), quoted by LORINCZ, A.L., in ROTHMAN, S. (Ed.), *Physiology and Biochemistry of the Skin*, University of Chicago Press, Chicago, 1954, page 662.

Composition of teeth and bones (values per 100 gramme dry fat-free tissue unless otherwise stated)

		Water* g	N g	Ca g	P g	Mg g	CO_3^{--} g	Cl g	F g	Na g	K g	Fe g	Cu g	Pb g
Teeth[1]														
Enamel	Adults	3	0.03	36	17	0.4	2.5	0.25	0.010–0.034	0.71–0.90	0.05–0.30	0.000 8–0.4	0.000 17–0.000 9	–
Dentine	Adults	10	3.4	27	13	0.9	3.3	0.00–0.03	0.024–0.076	0.30	0.07–0.10	0.007	–	0.005
Bone tissue[2]														
Cortex of femur	Foetus, 14 weeks	–	5.95	18.9	9.1	–	–	–	–	–	–	–	–	–
	Foetus, 20–24 weeks .	31.1	5.25	23.4	10.5	–	–	–	–	–	–	–	–	–
	Newborn	23.8	5.06	24.6	10.8	–	–	–	–	–	–	–	–	–
	Infants, 2–4½ months	23.0	5.28	23.7	10.8	–	–	–	0.049**	–	–	–	–	–
	Infants, 5–9 months ..	19.5	5.31	24.9	11.0	–	–	–	–	–	–	–	–	–
	Infants, 12–24 months	20.3	5.24	24.6	11.1	–	–	–	0.071**	–	–	–	–	–
	Children, 12 years	15.5	4.92	25.3	11.5	–	–	–	–	–	–	–	–	–
	Adults, 18–35 years ..	12.2	4.74	26.4	11.3	0.39	4.0	0.18	0.094–0.270**	0.18–0.6	0.05–0.3	0.011–0.017	0.000 2–0.004 8	0.001–0.01
Whole femur (excluding epiphyses)	Foetus, 14 weeks	56.0	5.69	15.8	7.1	–	–	–	–	–	–	–	–	–
	Foetus, 20–24 weeks .	54.6	5.95	19.1	8.2	–	–	–	–	–	–	–	–	–
	Newborn	48.8	5.94	23.6	9.9	–	–	–	–	–	–	–	–	–
	Infants, 2–4½ months	49.2	6.78	19.9	9.7	–	–	–	–	–	–	–	–	–
	Infants, 5–9 months ..	43.7	6.89	19.0	8.6	–	–	–	–	–	–	–	–	–
	Infants, 12–24 months	39.7	5.67	18.3	8.5	–	–	–	–	–	–	–	–	–
	Children, 12 years	30.7	5.21	27.2	12.4	–	–	–	–	–	–	–	–	–
	Adults, 18–35 years ..	22.7	5.20	25.1	10.7	–	–	–	–	–	–	–	–	–

* Per 100 gramme fat-free bone.
** Increases with age and with the amount in the drinking water. Values given are for ribs (JACKSON and WEIDMANN, *J. Path. Bact.*, **76**, 451 [1958]).

References
[1] EASTOE, J.E., in LONG, C. (Ed.), *Biochemists' Handbook*, Spon, London, 1961, page 720.
[2] EASTOE, J.E., in LONG, C. (Ed.), *Biochemists' Handbook*, Spon, London, 1961, page 715; DICKERSON, J.W.T., *Biochem. J.*, **82**, 56 (1962).

Strontium and barium contents of ashed bone (µg/g)

Age	Sr	Ba
0–3 months	79.1	7.0
1–13 years	73.8	7.6
19–33 years	107	5.1
33–74 years	114	8.5

Reference
SOWDEN and STITCH, *Biochem. J.*, **67**, 104 (1957).

Strontium-90: calcium ratio in bone (pCi ^{90}Sr : g Ca)

Age	Mean	Maximum
0–5 years	2	3.2
5–20 years	1	2.0
Over 20 years	0.3	0.6

Reference
SCHEUERMANN, W., *Z. Ernährungsw.*, **2**, 123 (1962). Values from Western Germany, 1960.

Organic components of soft and hard tissues (values per kilogramme fresh tissue unless otherwise stated)

		Non-protein N g	Sarcoplasmic protein N g	Fibrillar protein N g	Collagen N g	Glycogen g	Mucopoly-saccharides g	Cholesterol g
Skeletal muscle[1]	Foetus, 14 weeks	1.2	3.6	5.7	0.6 (Total extracellular protein N)	–	–	–
	Foetus, 20–22 weeks	1.7	3.7	8.7	1.8 (Total extracellular protein N)	–	–	–
	Newborn	2.4	3.9	10.9	3.8 (Total extracellular protein N)	–	–	–
	Infants, 4–7 months	3.2	5.0	17.0	4.6 (Total extracellular protein N)	–	–	–
	Adults	3.0	6.7	19.9	1.4 (Total extracellular protein N)	–	–	2.7**
Uterus[2]								
Muscle	Non-pregnant	–	–	5, 11, 4*	–	–	–	10**
	Pregnant, at term	–	–	13, 9, 15*	–	–	–	–
Mucous membrane	Proliferative phase	–	–	–	–	3.2	–	–
	Early differentiation phase	–	–	–	–	11.2	–	–
	Secretory phase	–	–	–	–	6.4	–	–
Skin[3]	Foetus, 20–22 weeks	–	–	–	2.4	–	–	–
	Newborn	–	–	–	16.8	–	2.9†	–
	Infants, 4–7 months	–	–	–	39.2	–	–	–
	Adults	–	–	–	45.7	–	2.0†	–
Bone[4]	Foetus, 14 weeks	–	–	–	29.2†	–	–	–
	Foetus, 20–24 weeks	–	–	–	40.6†	–	–	–
	Newborn	–	–	–	42.0†	–	–	–
	Infants, 2–4½ months	–	–	–	44.0†	–	–	–
	Infants, 5–9 months	–	–	–	42.7†	–	–	–
	Infants, 12–24 months	–	–	–	43.7†	–	2.3††	–
	Adults, 18–35 years	–	–	–	41.5†	–	1.6††	–
Teeth[5]								
Enamel	Adults	–	–	–	0.16**	–	1.0 (Soluble enamel protein)	–
Dentine	Adults	–	–	–	30.6–32.4**	–	2.0–6.0	4.0

* Values for actomyosin, myosin and actotropomyosin respectively.
** Per kilogramme dry tissue.
† Per kilogramme dry fat-free tissue.
†† Per kilogramme dry weight as glucosamine hydrochloride.

References
[1] DICKERSON and WIDDOWSON, *Biochem. J.*, **74**, 247 (1960).
[2] CSAPO, A., *Amer. J. Physiol.*, **160**, 46 (1950); NAESLUND and SNELLMAN, *Acta Soc. Med. upsalien.*, **59**, 349 (1954); ARRONET and LATOUR, *J. clin. Endocr.*, **17**, 261 (1957).
[3] WIDDOWSON and DICKERSON, *Biochem. J.*, **77**, 30 (1960); LOEWI, G., *Biochim. biophys. Acta*, **52**, 435 (1961).
[4] ROGERS, H. J., *Nature*, **164**, 625 (1949); DICKERSON, J. W. T., *Biochem. J.*, **82**, 56 (1962).
[5] EASTOE, J. E., in LONG, C., (Ed.), *Biochemists' Handbook*, Spon, London, 1961, page 720.

Composition of placenta and amniotic fluid (values per kilogramme fresh placenta and per litre amniotic fluid)

	Stage of gestation	Water g	N g	Na mEq	K mEq	Cl mEq	Mg mEq	Ca mEq	P mmol	Cu mg	Zn mg
Placenta[1]	20–40 weeks	866	18.5	98	40	–	6.6	12.4	30	1.5	10.0
Amniotic fluid[2]	First half	–	–	135	4.0	109	1.4	3.6	1.2	–	–
	Term	–	–	–	–	–	–	–	0.7	–	–

References
[1] WIDDOWSON and SPRAY, *Arch. Dis. Childh.*, **26**, 205 (1951); for further values see BERGER and VON HORNSTEIN, *Fortschr. Geburtsh. Gynäk.*, **14**, 1 (1961).
[2] MAKEPEACE et al., *Surg. Gynec. Obstet.*, **53**, 635 (1931); ECONOMOU-MAVROU and MCCANCE, *Biochem. J.*, **68**, 573 (1958); WESTIN et al., *Acta paediat. (Uppsala)*, **49**, 154 (1960).

(For references see page 530)

This chapter on 'Water and Electrolyte Balance' has been compiled by U. F. GRUBER and M. ALLGÖWER of the University Surgical Clinic, Basle. It should be read in conjunction with the chapter on 'Aqueous Solutions', pages 270–271.

The treatment of water and electrolyte disturbances is a matter of restoring a balance. In healthy adults the total intake of each element is equal to its total excretion. Treatment thus calls for a knowledge of the daily water, electrolyte and calorie requirements of the adult and of the ways and amounts in which they are excreted. In patients it is necessary to take into account not only the daily intakes but also the amounts of water and electrolytes which have been and are being excreted. The success of treatment is therefore dependent on precise determination of the total intake (food, drink, infusions, enemas) and excretion (urine, faeces, vomit, secretions, fistula and puncture fluids, etc.) as well as a knowledge of their exact composition. Of considerable help in detecting changes in water balance and metabolism is the daily weighing of the patient under standardized conditions. It is essential to rectify the whole electrolyte and water balance of the patient; the mere correction of particular abnormal plasma concentrations does not suffice.

Composition of the body

This is shown in detail in the chapter 'Composition of the Body' on pages 517–522.

Table 1 Approximate composition of the whole body and distribution of the body water expressed as percentage of the body weight

	Adults		Infants
	Men	Women	
Solids	40	50	25
Organic substances	35	45	–
Minerals	5	5	–
Total body water	60	50	75
Intracellular	40	30	40
Extracellular	20	20	35
(a) intravascular	4	4	5
(b) interstitial	16	16	30

Electrolyte composition of the body fluids

For a more detailed discussion of the serum electrolyte composition see under 'Blood', page 561 sq.

Table 2 Concentrations of the principal electrolytes in serum, serum water and the interstitial and intracellular fluids[1]

	Serum		Serum water	Interstitial fluid*	Intracellular fluid**
	mEq/l	mg/l	mEq/l	mEq/l	mEq/kg water
Cations					
Sodium	142	3265	152.7	145	10
Potassium	4	156	4.3	4	160
Calcium	5	100	5.4	5	2
Magnesium	2	24	2.2	2	26
Cations, total	153	3545	164.6	156	198
Anions					
Chloride	101	3581	108.5	114	3
Bicarbonate	27	1648	29.3	31	10
Phosphate ($HPO_4^{=}$)	2	96	2.2	2	100
Sulphate	1	48	1	1	20
Organic acids	6	210	6.4	7	–
Proteins	16	66300	17.2	1	65
Anions, total	153	71900	164.6	156	198

* The average GIBBS-DONNAN value of 0.95 applies only to univalent ions, so that the values given for the bivalent ions are not exact. In addition, no correction has been made for the nonionized fraction of Ca^{++} which does not gain access to the interstitial fluid.
** Values based on the intracellular water of skeletal muscle.

Table 3 Conversion factors for serum electrolytes (see also page 276)

	Serum concentrations				Conversion factors			
	mEq/l	mmol/l	mosm/l	mg/l	mg/l to mEq/l	mg/100 ml to mEq/l	mEq/l to mg/l	mEq/l to mg/100 ml
Cations								
Sodium	142	142	142	3265	0.0435	0.435	23.0	2.30
Potassium	4	4	4	156	0.0256	0.256	39.1	3.91
Calcium	5	2.5	2.5	100	0.0499	0.499	20.0	2.00
Magnesium	2	1	1	24	0.0823	0.823	12.2	1.22
Cations, total	153	149.5	149.5	3545	–	–	–	–
Anions								
Chloride	101	101	101	3581	0.0282	0.282	35.5	3.55
Bicarbonate	27	27	27	1648	0.0164*	0.164*	61.0*	6.10*
Phosphate ($HPO_4^{=}$)	2	1	1	96	0.0208	0.208	48.0	4.80
Sulphate	1	0.5	0.5	48	0.0208	0.208	48.0	4.80
Organic acids	6	6	6	210	0.0286	0.286	35	3.5
Proteins	16	2	2	66300	0.000241**	0.00241**	4145**	414.5**
Anions, total	153	137.5	137.5	71900	–	–	–	–
Total cations + total anions	306	287	287	75400	–	–	–	–

* For the conversion of vol% CO_2 into mmol CO_2 and vice versa see page 276.
** The VAN SLYKE factor of 2.41 for the conversion of serum protein (g/100 ml) into ionized serum protein (mEq/l) is valid for 38 °C, pH 7.4 and an albumin/globulin ratio of 1.6. When the distribution of the plasma protein fractions is abnormal, VAN SLYKE recommends calculation of the equivalent value for the albumins and globulins by means of the following factors[2]: 1 g albumin nitrogen = 1.745 mEq, 1 g globulin nitrogen = 1.205 mEq. According to BROCH[3] these factors give values that are too high.

(For references see page 530)

Water balance

Table 4 Average daily water turnover of an adult weighing 70 kg[4]

	Water intake (g)			Water output (g)	
	Obligatory	Facultative		Obligatory	Facultative
Drink	650	1000	Urine	700	1000
Food	750		Skin	500	
Oxidative	350		Lungs	400	
			Faeces	150	
Subtotal	1750	1000	Subtotal	1750	1000
Total	2750		Total	2750	

Table 5 Daily water requirements in millilitres per kilogramme body weight at various ages under normal conditions[5, 6]

Age	Body weight kg	Estimated water requirement ml/kg
3 days	3.0	80–100*
10 days	3.2	125–150*
3 months	5.4	140–160
6 months	7.3	130–155
9 months	8.6	125–145
1 year	9.5	120–135
2 years	11.8	115–125
4 years	16.2	100–110
6 years	20.0	90–100
10 years	28.7	70–85
14 years	45.0	50–60
18 years	54.0	40–50
Adults[7]	70.0	21–43

* Average value for breast-fed infants.

In adults, the daily water, electrolyte and calorie requirements can be calculated with sufficient accuracy from the body weight. In spite of the greater accuracy of values derived from body surface area this method offers no advantage since the actual requirements are also subject to other factors like age, sex, the functional state of the heart, kidneys and lungs, fever, disease, nutritional status and calorie consumption. In newborn as well as older children, however, the requirements should be calculated from the body surface area (see the nomogram on page 538) or the daily calorie turnover.

Table 6 Daily water requirements per square metre body surface area[6]

Minimum requirement	870 ml/m²
Average requirement	1500 ml/m²
Maximum tolerance	2730 ml/m²

Table 7 Average daily water turnover per 100 kcal[1]

Water intake	80–110 ml/100 kcal
Water of oxidation	10– 20 ml/100 kcal
Urine	50– 70 ml/100 kcal
Insensible water loss (see also Table 8)	40– 60 ml/100 kcal

Table 8 Average daily insensible water loss at different ages[1]

Age	ml/m²	ml/100 kcal
0–3 years	1150	59
3–8 years	950	49
8–16 years	700	45
Adults	550	40

At body temperatures above normal the insensible water loss increases by about 13% for each degree Centigrade[8] (7% for each degree Fahrenheit). For the water loss by sweating see page 679. In resting infants under 12 months the pulmonary water loss amounts to about 1 g/kg body weight per hour[5].

With normal bodily activity 25% of the total heat loss of the body is accounted for by evaporation of water (insensible water loss)[9]. The heat of evaporation of water is 0.58 kcal/ml (or 1 kcal/1.7 ml) at 37 °C, whence the water loss by evaporation can be calculated from the total calorie expenditure.

Table 9 Water of oxidation[1]

Metabolic breakdown of	gives rise to
100 g fat	107 ml water of oxidation
100 g protein	41 ml water of oxidation
100 g carbohydrate	55 ml water of oxidation
100 g nonfatty tissue	15 ml water of oxidation

That the proteins of nonfatty tissue are not fully oxidized is shown by the presence of a nonoxidized C-atom in the urea excreted in the urine. The breakdown of nonfatty tissue not only gives rise to water of oxidation but also releases the intracellular water (73 ml/100 g). Fatty tissue contains practically no water[10].

Table 10 Water arising from metabolic breakdown of body tissue

Metabolic breakdown of	gives rise to	
500 g fatty tissue	535 ml water of oxidation	–
500 g nonfatty tissue	75 ml water of oxidation	365 ml intracellular water
1000 g fatty and nonfatty tissue together	610 ml water of oxidation	365 ml intracellular water
	Total: 975 ml water	

The breakdown of 1 kg of the body's own tissue, assuming it is made up of equal parts of fatty and nonfatty tissue, thus gives rise to about 1 l of endogenous, practically sodium-free water. It is important that this should be allowed for in patients with a limited calorie consumption whose water excretion is low (e.g., after operations), since otherwise they may easily become waterlogged. A patient given only electrolytes and 5% glucose solution after an uncomplicated abdominal operation should therefore lose 200–400 g weight per day[10].

(For references see page 530)

Electrolyte balance

Table 11 Daily requirements, usual intake and average excretion of various electrolytes[1,7,10,11]

	Minimum requirement*	Usual intake	Average excretion**			
			With an intake of	Urine	Faeces	Sweat
	mEq/day	mEq/day	mEq/day	mEq/day	mEq/day	mEq/day
Sodium						
Adults	20	50–250	100	97	3	0–(10)
Per square metre body surface	12	29–145				
Per kilogramme body weight	0.3	0.7–3.6				
Potassium						
Adults	20–33	50–150	100	90	10	0–(5)
Per square metre body surface	12–19	29–87				
Per kilogramme body weight	0.3–0.5	0.7–2.1				
Calcium						
Adults	15	25–75	50	5	45	–
Per square metre body surface	9	14–43				
Per kilogramme body weight	0.2	0.4–1.1				
Magnesium						
Adults	16–25	20–50	30	10	20	–
Per square metre body surface	9–14	12–29				
Per kilogramme body weight	0.2–0.4	0.3–0.7				
Chloride						
Adults	20	50–250	100	97	3	0–(10)
Per square metre body surface	12	29–145				
Per kilogramme body weight	0.3	0.7–3.6				

* The values apply only to adults. The minimum requirement of sodium and chloride is not known; the amounts given are those contained in a very low-sodium diet. An extremely low-sodium diet (9 mEq sodium per day) calls for constant medical supervision.

** For details see under 'Urine', pages 662–664, 'Faeces', page 658, and 'Sweat', pages 679–680.

Table 12 Amounts and electrolyte contents of important body fluids*

	Amount	Sodium mEq/l	Potassium mEq/l	Chloride mEq/l	Bicarbonate mEq/l	pH
Saliva	500–1500 ml/24 h	10–25	15–40	10–40	2–13	–
Gastric juice	2000–3000 ml/24 h	–	–	–	–	–
with parietal-cell secretion	–	20–70	5–15	80–160	0	acid
without parietal-cell secretion	–	70–150	5–15	80–120	25–40	neutral to weakly alkaline
Pancreatic juice	300–1500 ml/24 h	140	6–9	110–130	25–45	alkaline
Bile	250–1100 ml/24 h	130–165	3–12	90–120	30	weakly alkaline
Intestinal secretions	3000 ml/24 h	–	–	–	–	weakly alkaline
Small intestine, MILLER-ABBOTT-tube	–	82–148	2–8	43–137	–	–
Ileostomy, recent	–	105–144	6–29	90–136	–	–
Ileostomy, adapted	–	46	3	21	–	–
Coecostomy	–	53	8	–	–	–
Intraluminal fluid	500 ml	70	35	–	–	–
Sweat	500–1000 ml/24 h	5–80	5–15	5–70	–	–
Cerebrospinal fluid	100–160 ml	130–150	2.5–4.5	122–128	25	weakly alkaline
Transudates**	–	130–145	2.5–5	90–110	–	–
Faecal water***	–	–	–	–	–	–

* These data are discussed more fully in the later chapters dealing with the individual body fluids. The values for the intestinal secretions and transudates are from LOCKWOOD and RANDALL[12], those for the intraluminal fluid from BLACK[13].

** The ratios of the electrolyte concentrations in transudate water to those in serum water amount on the average to 0.96 for sodium, 0.92 for potassium and 1.03 for chloride[14]. The values given have been calculated from the mean serum values with the aid of these ratios and on the assumption of a mean transudate protein content of 20 g/l.

*** In diarrhoea the electrolyte concentrations in the faeces approximate to those of an ileal secretion. The potassium concentration is fairly high, and values of 40–70 mEq/l have been reported[10].

(For references see page 530)

Table 13 Sodium and potassium exchange in a man weighing 70 kg[10,15]

	Sodium	Potassium
Total exchangeable*	2800 mEq	3400 mEq
In plasma.........	450 mEq	14 mEq
In interstitial fluid ..	1900 mEq	60 mEq
In intracellular fluid .	220 mEq	3300 mEq
Average intake	100 mEq/24 h**	100 mEq/24 h***
Average excretion ..	100 mEq/24 h	100 mEq/24 h
1 mEq corresponds to	23 mg	39 mg

* Including sodium in the bones, which is not otherwise included in the table. For further details see 'Composition of the Body', page 518.
** 1 l of physiological (isotonic) salt solution (0.85%) contains 145 mEq each of sodium and chloride, which is more than the daily requirement of salt.
*** 60 mEq/day is adequate if given parenterally and kidney function is unimpaired[10]. Patients with healthy kidneys can safely be given infusions of 20–25 mEq potassium per hour; in severe potassium deficiency it may be necessary to give 50–60 mEq per hour[16].

Osmotic relationships

The distribution of water and its solutes in the water spaces of the body is a result of the osmotic relationships. The membranes separating the various fluid phases of the body (the vascular endothelium and the cell membranes) are in general freely permeable to water, so that there is a uniform osmotic pressure throughout the body fluids. For a discussion of freezing-point depression, osmotic pressure, osmolarity and osmolality see pages 270–271. For conversion tables see pages 272–273.

Freezing-point depression of plasma at 38 °C: 0.540 °C
Osmotic pressure of plasma at 38 °C: 7.39 atm (5616 mm Hg)
Osmolality of plasma at 38 °C: 291.2 mosm/kg water

The theoretical osmolality of blood plasma calculated from its known components and assuming their complete electrolytic dissociation is 325 mosm/kg serum water. The difference between this value and the actual osmolality of 291.2 mosm/kg serum water (the numerical value is about twice that of the sodium concentration in serum in mEq/l) is due to the fact that the electrolytes are not completely dissociated in serum.

Tonicity. From the clinical standpoint, tonicity and osmolality are the same thing. A solution is described as *isotonic* when it is isosmotic with serum, i.e., has the same osmotic pressure as serum. In practice, both hypotonic and hypertonic solutions with osmolalities ranging from 140 to 1710 mosm/kg water can be administered intravenously without causing haemolysis[1]. $^1/_6$ molar, or $^1/_6$ normal, solutions of all salts having binary dissociation can be regarded for practical purposes as isotonic (333 mosm/l).

The maintenance of the plasma volume and the distribution of fluid between the plasma and the interstitial space is mainly dependent on the 'effective' osmotic pressure of the plasma proteins. The capillary endothelium is freely permeable to almost all the substances in solution in the extracellular fluid, the total osmotic pressure of which is determined mainly by the sodium and chloride ions. However, since these ions pass freely through the capillaries and become uniformly distributed by diffusion and filtration throughout the extracellular space they cannot contribute to the osmotic pressure gradients between the intravasal and extravasal spaces. On the other hand, the intravasal space contains almost all the large protein molecules. As a result of their effective osmotic pressure, these molecules prevent the passage of water out of the plasma in spite of the fact that they are responsible for only a small part of the total osmolality. This specific effect of the plasma proteins is known as the *colloid-osmotic* or *oncotic pressure.*

Oncotic pressure of plasma at 38 °C:	ca. 0.04 atm
	ca. 30 mm Hg
	ca. 400 mm H_2O

The albumins contribute about 85% of the colloid-osmotic pressure. Since fibrinogen has practically no osmotic effect because of its high molecular weight the colloid-osmotic pressure of serum can be assumed to be the same as that of plasma.

When the composition of the plasma proteins is abnormal the colloid-osmotic pressure can be calculated by means of the formula of Keys[17]:

$$\text{Colloid-osmotic pressure (in mm } H_2O) = f_c\,(4.52\,A + 1.886\,G) \times T/273.15$$

where A = albumin concentration in g/l, G = globulin concentration in g/l, T = absolute temperature in kelvin (K) = 273.15 + °C, f_c = a factor whose value depends on the total protein content of the serum as follows:

Total protein content of serum (g/l)	10	20	30	40	50	60	70	80
f_c	0.88	0.92	0.98	1.03	1.09	1.17	1.28	1.45

The colloid-osmotic pressure is counteracted by the hydrostatic pressure in the capillaries.

Capillary pressure at 38 °C (see also page 553):

Arterial limb	32 mm Hg
	435 mm H_2O
Venous limb.........................	12 mm Hg
	163 mm H_2O

For osmotic activity of serum electrolytes see Table 3, page 523.

Table 14 Osmotic activity of serum crystalloids[10]

1000 mg glucose/l serum	5.5 mosm/l
1000 mg urea/l serum	17.2 mosm/l

Table 15 Osmotic activity of serum colloids[10]

	g/l	mEq/l	mosm/l
Albumin	45	14	1.7
Globulin	15	2	0.3
Total proteins................	60	16	2.0

Infusions of plasma and blood are distributed throughout the intravascular space, those of isotonic electrolytes throughout the extracellular space, those of isotonic crystalloid solutions (e.g., glucose solutions) throughout the total body water.

Calorie requirements

The definition of the calorie and conversion tables will be found on pages 212–213, the daily calorie requirements on page 493, the calorific values of foods on pages 498–515, and the calorific values of fats, proteins and carbohydrates on page 539.

The calorie requirements in parenteral infusion therapy can be met by solutions of carbohydrates and amino acids and by emulsions of fats. Commercial preparations of known calorific value are available.

The human body cannot normally utilize more than ca. 0.5 g D-glucose per kilogramme body weight per hour[18].

Ethyl alcohol 95 vol% furnishes 5.6 kcal/g, lactate 0.31 kcal/mole.

250 ml of plasma contain 15 g protein, equivalent to ca. 60 kcal.

The total calorie consumption and expenditure of a hospital patient who is not bedridden but whose activity is limited amounts to approx. 2000 kcal per day.

Table 16 Daily calorie balance of a man weighing 70 kg[19]

Average intake		Average excretion	
500 g fat + carbohydrate + protein 550 l oxygen		12 g urea nitrogen 450 l carbon dioxide 300 ml water of oxidation	
	Energy in kcal		Energy in kcal
Fat	900	Bodily activity (light) ..	800
Carbohydrate..	1400	Specific dynamic effect .	200
Protein	300	Basal metabolism......	1600
Total.........	2600	Total	2600

Acid–base balance and pH

The concentration of hydrogen ions in the various water compartments of the body is determined by the amounts and proportions of acids and bases present*. It is maintained within definite limits by chemical and physiological regulatory mechanisms. Since hydrogen-ion concentration is not measurable with precision it is given in the form of a pH value (for definition see page 278). Chemical regulation of hydrogen-ion concentration is effected by means of buffer systems. The substances constituting these systems in plasma and interstitial fluid are mainly bicarbonate, phosphate and ionized protein, in the cells haemoglobin and other ionized proteins as well as organic phosphates (adenosine triphosphate, creatine phosphate, etc.); a chemical buffer action is also exerted by the apatite crystals of bone. Physiological regulation is by the lungs (expiration of CO_2) and kidneys (excretion of hydrogen ions or bicarbonate). Since the dissociation of acids and bases is dependent on other ions present, changes in the electrolyte content of the body fluids often cause changes in pH and vice versa.

Table 17 Buffer capacity (ΔmEq/ΔpH) of the body tissues[20]

Tissue	Buffer capacity per kilogramme tissue	Kilogramme tissue per kilogramme body weight	Buffer capacity per kilogramme body weight
Blood.............	18	0.10	1.8
Muscle............	5	0.65	3.25

Table 18 Relative buffer capacity of blood[21]

Whole blood 100%	Cells ... 79%		
	Plasma.. 21%	Ionized protein	13.6%
		Bicarbonate...	6.1%
		Phosphate	1.5%

On a normal mixed diet the body has a positive hydrogen-ion balance. The hydrogen ions arising from the breakdown of foods are excreted by the kidneys in the form of NH_4^+, $H_2PO_4^-$ and organic acids (together ca. 30–80 mEq per day, cf. page 536). Hydrogen ions are formed endogenously also by the oxidation of sulphur-containing amino acids to sulphuric acid, by the liberation of certain phosphate groups to form phosphoric acid, and by the breakdown of carbohydrates and fats into keto acids, lactic acid and other organic acids. Endogenously, hydrogen ions are used up in the combustion of organic anions such as citrate, malate and oxalate from fruit and vegetables. The CO_2 arising in the course of metabolism normally contributes nothing to the hydrogen-ion balance since it is excreted through the lungs, but it does affect the acid-base balance of the blood which transports it.

* According to the Brønsted-Lowry definition, acids are proton donors (hydrogen donors), bases proton acceptors.

For clinical purposes the acid–base balance of the body can be investigated by measurements of the CO_2-bicarbonate system. The intracellular buffer systems are probably at least as important as the extracellular systems[22] but their measurement involves considerable technical difficulties.

If two of the three values pH, total CO_2 content (in mmol/l) and CO_2 partial pressure (P_{CO_2} in mm Hg) determined at body temperature in plasma or serum from arterial blood drawn under anaerobic conditions, the third can be calculated[25] from the Henderson-Hasselbalch formula[23, 24]:

$$pH = 6.10 + \log \frac{[\text{total } CO_2]_P - 0.0301\,P_{CO_2}}{0.0301\,P_{CO_2}}$$

where $[\text{total } CO_2]_P$ = sum of the concentrations of dissolved CO_2 and HCO_3^- in the plasma (P = plasma) in mmol/l. Conversion into vol% is made as follows (see page 276):

$$\text{mmol/l} = \frac{\text{vol\%}}{2.226}$$

The sum of the concentrations of dissolved CO_2 and H_2CO_3 in the plasma (in mmol/l) can be calculated from the formula:

$$[CO_2]_P = 0.0301\,P_{CO_2}$$

The concentration of HCO_3^- in the plasma (in mmol/l) is obtained as the difference between the total CO_2 concentration and the concentrations of dissolved CO_2 and H_2CO_3:

$$[HCO_3^-]_P = [\text{total } CO_2]_P - [CO_2]_P$$

These relationships are shown diagrammatically in Figure 1 (page 528).

Table 19 Normal values for the CO_2-bicarbonate system in the arterial and venous blood of adults*[25, 27]

	Unit	Blood sample**	Mean	Range
pH	–	*v*	7.37	7.32–7.42
		a	7.40	7.35–7.45
$[HCO_3^-]_P$***	mmol/l	*v*	26	24–28
		a	24	22–26
P_{CO_2}	mm Hg	*v*	46	42–55
		a	40	34–46
$[\text{total } CO_2]_P$	mmol/l	*v*	27	25–29
		a	25	23–27
$[CO_2]_P$	mmol/l	*v*	1.38	1.26–1.65
		a	1.20	1.02–1.38

* For persons living at sea level. At higher altitudes P_{CO_2} is lower as a result of chronic hyperventilation, whereas the pH remains normal because of complete renal compensation, i.e., by lowering of the plasma bicarbonate concentration[25]. A detailed summary of the normal values will be found under 'Blood Gases', pages 570–571; for pH values see page 560.
** *a* = arterial blood, *v* = venous blood. Venous blood should be drawn without applying a tourniquet. Venous blood is not suitable for measurements in patients with circulatory or respiratory disturbances[25].
*** In women the plasma bicarbonate concentration is ca. 1 mmol/l lower than in men[25].

The respiratory components of the acid–base balance are adequately expressed by the P_{CO_2} value; whether the metabolic components are best expressed by the plasma bicarbonate content[28], by the buffer base content of the whole blood[29] (see page 571), or by the base excess of the whole blood[30] (see page 571) is a matter of discussion[31].

The following changes in acid–base balance are distinguished on the basis of the origin of the disturbance:

1. Respiratory alkalosis: Decrease in P_{CO_2} as a result of hyperventilation.
2. Respiratory acidosis: Increase in P_{CO_2} as a result of reduced CO_2 excretion by the lungs.

(For references see page 530)

3. Metabolic alkalosis: Increase in the base content or decrease in the acid content of the blood.
4. Metabolic acidosis: Increase in the acid content or decrease in the base content of the blood.

Two of these disturbances may appear at the same time (cf. Fig. 2).

Fig. 1 Nomogram for the evaluation of the HENDERSON-HASSELBALCH formula[26]

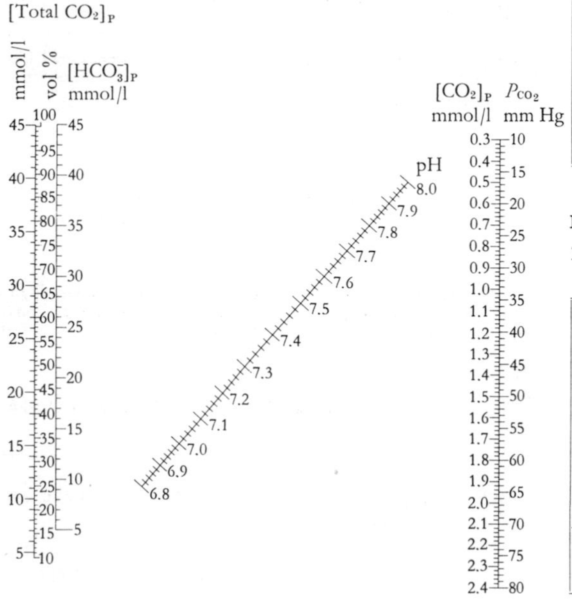

Fig. 2 The pH-bicarbonate diagram of DAVENPORT[25] as modified by PERRET[32]

The heavy line running from upper left to lower right is the normal plasma buffer curve, that running from lower left to upper right the P_{CO_2} isobar for normal plasma (40 mm Hg); other P_{CO_2} isobars are shown by thinner lines. The point of intersection of the plasma buffer curve and the 40 mm Hg isobar represents blood with the normal values pH = 7.40, bicarbonate concentration = 24 mmol/l, P_{CO_2} = 40 mm Hg.

The numbers in the diagram denote areas in which there is disturbance of acid–base balance: *1* Compensated respiratory acidosis. *2* Compensated metabolic alkalosis. *3* Compensated metabolic acidosis. *4* Compensated respiratory alkalosis. *5* Respiratory and metabolic acidosis. *6* Metabolic and respiratory alkalosis. *7* Fully compensated respiratory acidosis or metabolic alkalosis. *8* Fully compensated metabolic acidosis or respiratory alkalosis.

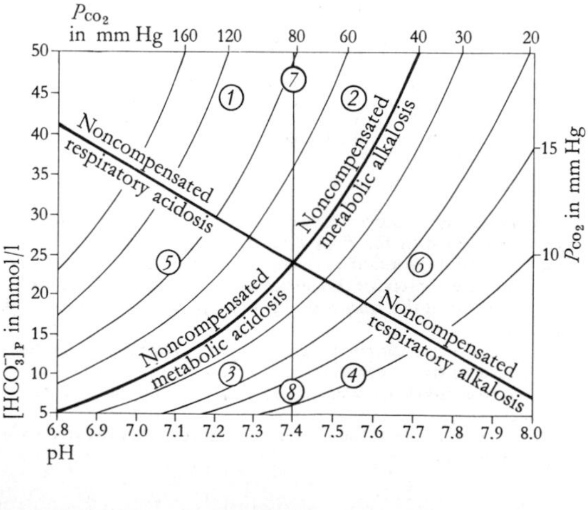

Blood volume

Table 20 Blood volume in health*[10]

Body build	Blood volume as percentage of body weight	
	Men	Women
Normal	7.0	6.5
Obese	6.0	5.5
Thin	6.5	6.0
Muscular	7.5	7.0

* Based on measurements of absolute blood volume made by separate and simultaneous determination of plasma volume and red cell volume using two different tracer substances and addition of the results. For a detailed discussion of blood volume see pages 554–555.

Body surface area

Table 21 Surface area of various parts of the body as percentage of total body surface[33]

Age in years	Head	Trunk*	Arms**	Legs
0	19	34	19	28
1	17	34	19	30
5	13	34	19	34
10	11	34	19	36
15	9	34	19	38
Adults	7	34	19	40

* Including the neck, genitals and buttocks.
** At all ages the palm of the hand is about 1% of the total body surface.

Table 22 Rule of nines for adults*[34]: Surface area of various parts of the body as percentage of total body surface

Head	9
Arms, each	9
Trunk, front	18
Trunk, back	18
Legs, each	18
Genitals	1
Total	100

* The buttocks are included in the lower limbs. The proportions are sufficiently accurate for clinical purposes.

Parenteral therapy

Patients should be fed by mouth as soon as this is feasible. When intravenous water and electrolyte infusions are necessary at least part of the patient's nourishment should be by mouth if possible.

Infusions should not be given subcutaneously; absorption is slow and irregular (diffusion of ions and water), the procedure is painful, the amount of fluid that can be given limited, and the risk of infection greater than when the intravenous route is used. If more than one infusion must be given, early installation of an intravenous tube is advisable. In the event that the tube must be left in situ for several days it is best to use the cephalic, basilic or jugular vein and introduce it as far as the superior vena cava. This method appears to involve less risk of thrombosis than the use of the saphenous vein and the inferior vena cava. The smaller veins of the arms or legs can be used, however, if the infusion is of short duration and the solutions are more or less isotonic.

Fig. 3 Nomogram for number of drops per minute[35]

The number of drops per minute required to administer a particular quantity of infusion solution in a certain time can be read off directly from this nomogram. The nomogram allows for the increase in drop size as the dropping rate increases and is based on the normal drop defined by the relationship: 20 drops distilled water at 15 °C = 1 g (± 0.05 g) when falling at the rate of 60/min. The dependence of drop size on dropping rate is allowed for by the increasing width of the scale units of the three abscissae as the dropping rate increases.

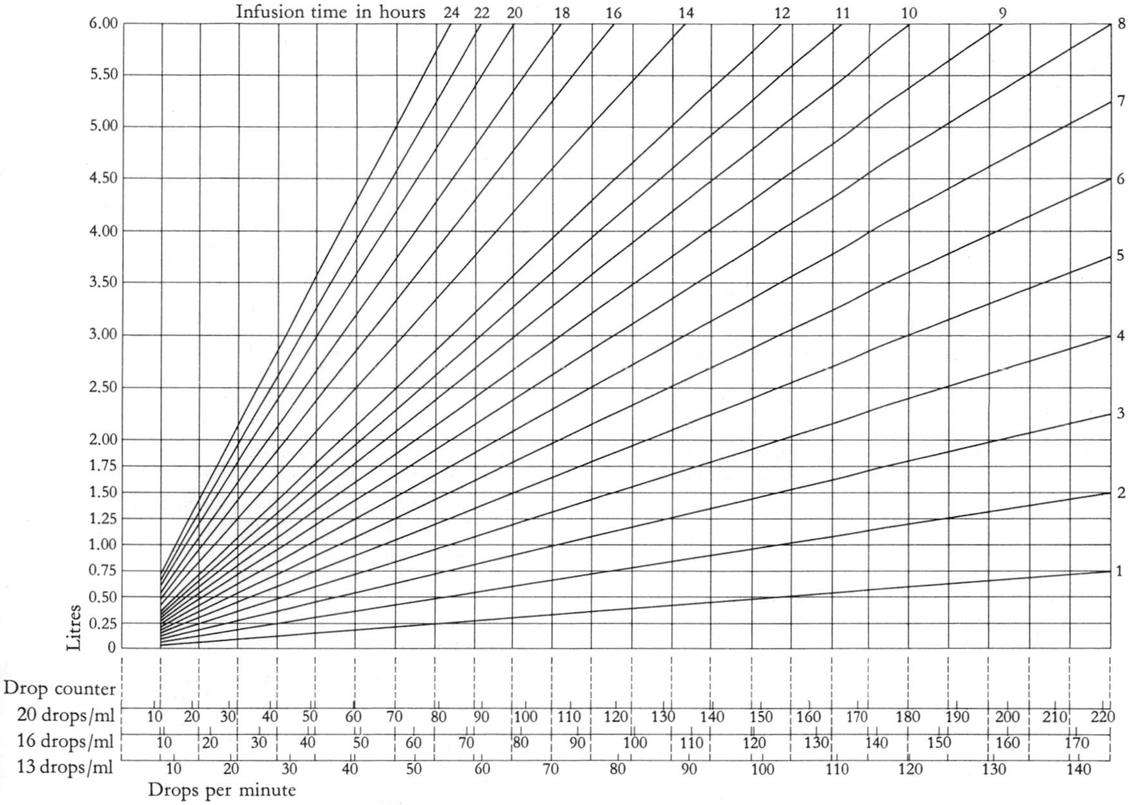

Table 23 Composition of some important parenteral infusion solutions

Solution	Solutes	g/l	Na^+ mEq/l	K^+ mEq/l	Ca^{++} mEq/l	Mg^{++} mEq/l	Cl^- mEq/l	HCO_3^- mEq/l	Lactate mEq/l	Total ions mEq/l	mosm/l	kcal/l
Glucose 5%	$C_6H_{12}O_6$	50	–	–	–	–	–	–	–	–	278	200
Salt 0.85%	NaCl	8.5	145	–	–	–	145	–	–	290	290	–
Ringer (USP)	NaCl	8.6	147	–	–	–	147	–	–	–	–	–
	KCl	0.3	–	4	–	–	4	–	–	–	–	–
	$CaCl_2 + 2H_2O$ ..	0.33	–	–	5	–	5	–	–	–	–	–
	Total	–	147	4	5	–	156	–	–	312	309	–
Ringer lactate (Hartmann)	NaCl	6.0	103	–	–	–	103	–	–	–	–	–
	KCl	0.4	–	5.4	–	–	5.4	–	–	–	–	–
	$CaCl_2 + 6H_2O$ ..	0.2	–	–	1.8	–	1.8	–	–	–	–	–
	Na lactate	3.05	27	–	–	–	–	–	27	–	–	9
	$MgCl_2$	0.2	–	–	–	2	2	–	–	–	–	–
	Total	–	130	5.4	1.8	2	112.2	–	27	278.4	276	9
Sodium bicarbonate 1/6 normal	$NaHCO_3$	14	167	–	–	–	–	167	–	334	334	–
Ammonium chloride 1/6 normal	NH_4Cl	9	–	–	–	–	169	–	–	338	338	–

Table 24 Order of priority in the parenteral therapy of acute disturbances of water and electrolyte balance[10]

1. Maintenance of blood volume	5. Administration of potassium (see Table 13)
2. Maintenance of colloid-osmotic pressure	6. Total body water and electrolytes: maintenance of requirements and elimination of deficits
3. Restoration of acid–base balance	
4. Restoration of total osmotic pressure	7. Provision of calories

A great variety of crystalloid and electrolyte solutions of known constitution are commercially available. The tendency is now to restrict parenteral infusion therapy to a minimum number of basic solutions meeting the daily water and electrolyte requirements. Ampoules containing other electrolytes are available for mixing with these solutions if the need arises. Potassium chloride and lactate, sodium chloride, bicarbonate and lactate, calcium chloride, magnesium sulphate and others are supplied in this form.

Metabolic disturbances of acid–base balance mostly require treatment with sodium bicarbonate, sodium lactate, ammonium chloride or arginine hydrochloride. An effective intracellular buffer is also now available in the form of tris-hydroxymethylaminomethane (THAM). Its 0.3-molar solution (36.3 g/l) is isotonic and is usually given at a dosage of 0.3–0.5 g/kg body weight over 3–4 hours[36].

The following colloidal solutions are in common use in parenteral infusion therapy:

1. Whole blood: available as stored citrated blood, fresh citrated blood, fresh blood drawn over cation exchangers, fresh heparinated blood, or blood given by direct transfusion.
2. Red-cell concentrates: in their own plasma or in isotonic electrolyte solutions.
3. Plasma and plasma fractions: available as dried human plasma (not free of hepatitis virus), pasteurized plasma protein solutions, fresh plasma, or solutions of albumin, fibrinogen, antihaemophilic globulin and gamma globulin.
4. Plasma expanders in the form of dextran solutions (average molecular weight of either 70 000 or 40 000).

References

1 Maxwell and Kleeman (Eds.), *Clinical Disorders of Fluid and Electrolyte Metabolism*, McGraw-Hill, New York, 1962.
2 van Slyke et al., *J. biol. Chem.*, **79**, 769 (1928).
3 Broch, O. J., *Scand. J. clin. Lab. Invest.*, **5**, 9 (1953).
4 Wolf, A. V., *Thirst*, Thomas, Springfield, 1958.
5 Bland, J. H., *Clinical Recognition and Management of Disturbances of Body Fluids*, Saunders, Philadelphia, 1956.
6 Talbot et al., *New Engl. J. Med.*, **248**, 1100 (1953), and **252**, 856 (1955).
7 Elkinton and Danowski, *The Body Fluids*, Williams & Wilkins, Baltimore, 1955.
8 Hayes et al., *Surgery*, **41**, 353 (1957).
9 Newburgh et al., *J. clin. Invest.*, **10**, 703 (1931).
10 Moore, F. D., *The Metabolic Care of the Surgical Patient*, Saunders, Philadelphia, 1959.
11 *Recommended Dietary Allowances*, A Report of the Food and Nutrition Board, National Academy of Sciences – National Research Council, 6th ed., Publication 1146, Washington, 1964; Wohl and Goodhart (Eds.), *Modern Nutrition in Health and Disease*, 3rd ed., Lea & Febiger, Philadelphia, 1964.
12 Lockwood and Randall, *Bull. N. Y. Acad. Med.*, **25**, 228 (1949).
13 Black, D. A. K., *Sci. Basis Med. Ann. Rev.*, **1964**, 291.
14 Peters, J. P., *Body Water: the Exchange of Fluids in Man*, Thomas, Springfield, 1935; Folk et al., *Amer. J. Physiol.*, **153**, 381 (1948).
15 Moore, F. D., in Brožek and Henschel (Eds.), *Techniques for Measuring Body Composition*, National Academy of Sciences – National Research Council, Washington, 1961; Moore et al., *The Body Cell Mass and Its Supporting Environment*, Saunders, Philadelphia, 1963.
16 Clementsen, H. J., *Lancet*, **2**, 175 (1962).
17 Keys, A., *J. phys. Chem.*, **42**, 11 (1938).
18 Felber et al., *Mod. Probl. Pädiat.*, **4**, 467 (1959).
19 Kinney, J. M., *Bull. N. Y. Acad. Med.*, **36**, 617 (1960).
20 Fenn, W. O., *Ann. N. Y. Acad. Sci.*, **92**, 547 (1961).
21 Ellison et al., *Clin. Chem.*, **4**, 452 (1958).
22 Robin, E. D., *New Engl. J. Med.*, **265**, 780 (1961); Bittar, E. E., *Cell pH*, Butterworth, London, 1964.
23 Henderson, L. J., *Blood*, Yale University Press, New Haven, 1928.
24 Hasselbalch, K. A., *Biochem. Z.*, **78**, 112 (1916).
25 Davenport, H. W., *The ABC of Acid-Base Chemistry*, The University of Chicago Press, Chicago, 1958.
26 McLean, F. C., *Physiol. Rev.*, **18**, 495 (1938).
27 Weisberg, H. F., *Water, Electrolyte and Acid-Base Balance*, 2nd ed., Williams & Wilkins, Baltimore, 1962.
28 Schwartz and Relman, *New Engl. J. Med.*, **268**, 1382 (1963).
29 Singer and Hastings, *Medicine (Baltimore)*, **27**, 223 (1948).
30 Astrup and Siggaard-Andersen, *Advanc. clin. Chem.*, **6**, 1 (1963).
31 Committee on Acid-Base Terminology, *Lancet*, **2**, 1010 (1965); *Ann. intern. Med.*, **63**, 885 (1965); *Ann. N. Y. Acad. Sci.*, **133**, 251 (1966).
32 Perret, C., *L'insuffisance respiratoire, Documenta Geigy, Acta clinica*, No. 6, Basle, 1966.
33 Lund and Browder, *Surg. Gynec. Obstet.*, **79**, 352 (1944).
34 Wallace, A. B., *Lancet*, **1**, 501 (1951).
35 Jeanneret et al., *Schweiz. med. Wschr.*, **86**, 1390 (1956); Jeanneret et al., *Pharm. Acta Helv.*, **32**, 118 (1957).
36 Nahas, G. G., *Ann. N. Y. Acad. Sci.*, **92**, 337 (1961).

Renal Function Values*

(For references see page 536)

The individual functions of the kidneys can be assessed by means of quantitative as well as so-called semiquantitative tests. The quantitative tests are mostly based on the clearance principle and their use is not in all cases practicable or necessary; some are very time-consuming and may involve referring the patient to a specialized clinic. The semiquantitative tests include determinations of nonprotein nitrogen (NPN) and 'true' endogenous creatinine in the plasma, the phenolsulphonphthalein (PSP) test, and the fluid deprivation test for determining the ability of the kidneys to concentrate urine. The sensitivity of semiquantitative tests can be established by comparing their results with those of precise quantitative methods of determining the renal functions concerned.

Renal haemodynamics

Quantitative methods

In these tests the plasma clearance (C)[1,2] of certain substances is calculated by means of the formula:

$$C = \frac{U \times V}{P} \tag{1}$$

where U and P are the concentrations of the clearance substance in the urine and plasma respectively in mg/l and V is the rate of urinary secretion in ml/min. A venous plasma concentration value is valid in the usual clearance formula only if measured under conditions of constancy of the concentrations of the clearance substance in the plasma and other body fluids. The standard plasma clearance of a substance is related to the 'normal' body surface area (1.73 m²)[3,4].

Provided that a clearance substance is neither synthesized nor destroyed in the body and is physiologically inert, its plasma clearance is a measure of the *glomerular filtration rate*. The most suitable substance in this respect so far found is *inulin*[5,6], though it has recently been shown[7] that a poly(fructose)saccharide resembling inulin gives equally good results. (The urea clearance is of no use in determining renal haemodynamic values since in addition to being filtered by the glomeruli, urea also undergoes tubular reabsorption to an extent depending on the urinary flow[8].)

On account of its physicochemical and physiological properties, *p-aminohippuric acid* (PAH) is superior to all other substances for the determination of the *effective renal plasma flow* (C_{PAH})[2,9]:

$$C_{PAH} = \frac{U_{PAH} \times V}{P_{PAH}} \tag{2}$$

The total renal plasma flow[2] is

$$RPF = \frac{C_{PAH}}{E_{PAH}} \tag{3}$$

E_{PAH} is the renal extraction: $E_{PAH} = \dfrac{Ka - Kv}{Ka}$

where Ka is the concentration of PAH in the arterial plasma, Kv that in the renal venous blood.

For plasma PAH concentrations up to 30 mg/l the normal value of E_{PAH} is 0.925 (range 0.875–1.000)[10].

$$\text{The effective renal blood flow}^{2} = \frac{C_{PAH}}{1 - Ht} \tag{4}$$

(Ht = peripheral haematocrit value)

The total renal blood flow[2] is

$$RBF = \frac{C_{PAH}}{E_{PAH}\,(1 - Ht)} \tag{5}$$

The 'normal' values of the renal inulin and PAH clearances (Table 1) are dependent on the water and salt balance[11,13] as well as on protein intake[14]. In the steady state, severe restriction of sodium intake causes C_{In} to fall markedly but has no effect on C_{PAH}. The diagnostically important filtration fraction (FF) is thus reduced:

$$FF = \frac{C_{In}}{C_{PAH}} \tag{6}$$

The clearances are increased on a protein-rich diet[14], as they are – without any characteristic change in the filtration fraction – when the daily urinary volume is high (hydration)[11,13]. Apart from this, the standard clearance values are dependent on age[15]. Between the 20th and 90th years of life C_{In} and C_{PAH} diminish roughly in proportion, so that the filtration fraction remains practically unchanged. The standard values at any age are given by the following equations:

$$C_{In} = 157.0 - (1.16 \times \text{age in years})$$
$$C_{PAH} = 820.2 - (6.75 \times \text{age in years})$$

The renal fraction of the minute output of the heart amounts normally to about 20%[2].

Semiquantitative methods

There exists no simple linear relationship between the glomerular filtration rate and the plasma creatinine or nonprotein nitrogen (NPN) levels[5,16–20] (Figs. 1 and 2), so that these determinations could fail to give an indication of even a considerable reduction in the glomerular function. A better indicator in this respect is the plasma concentration of *'true' endogenous creatinine* (P_{Cr}), which is largely independent of the nitrogen metabolism.

In general, P_{Cr} is sensitive to a reduction of two-thirds or more in the normal glomerular filtration rate[5,18,20] (Fig. 1). The plasma NPN on the other hand is dependent on both the nitrogen turnover and urinary output; it may even be increased in persons with healthy kidneys[6] and may fail to react to a reduction in the glomerular filtration rate until this has fallen to a quarter of the normal value[19] (Fig. 2). In individual cases even a minor disturbance of renal function may result in an increased plasma creatinine level[18,20], while in persons with healthy kidneys the value may vary according to the method of measurement (for the normal range see under 'Blood', page 572). The different values for the two sexes given by most authorities are due to differences in the muscle mass of the body, since it is in this tissue that most of the creatinine is formed[22]. In determining plasma creatinine care should always be taken that the reaction mixture is freed of non-creatinine chromogens (including acetone, acetoacetic acid, bromsulphophthalein, glucose, barbiturates, pyruvic acid), which are treated differently by the kidney. When the plasma creatinine level is normal these chromogens, the proportion of which in the plasma creatinine shows marked individual variations but is of the order of 15%[17,23], are a disturbing factor in the test, whereas in renal insufficiency their importance becomes less in inverse proportion to the true plasma creatinine level.

Table 1 Normal values in renal haemodynamics (based on a body surface area of 1.73 m²)

1. Normal conditions (mixed diet, urinary volume 1–3 ml/min)		
Women[2]	C_{In}	108.8 ± 13.5 ml/min
	C_{PAH}	592 ± 153 ml/min
	FF	0.194 ± 0.039
	RBF[1]	982 ± 184 ml/min
Men[2]	C_{In}	124.1 ± 25.8 ml/min
	C_{PAH}	654 ± 163 ml/min
	FF	0.192 ± 0.035
	RBF[1]	1209 ± 256 ml/min
Men and women[11]	C_{In}	124.5 ± 9.7 ml/min
	C_{PAH}	638.6 ± 84.5 ml/min
	FF	0.197 ± 0.018
	RBF[12]	1165 ml/min
2. Hydration (urinary volume 6–12 ml/min)		
Men and women[11]	C_{In}	152.6 ± 14.7 ml/min
	C_{PAH}	711.7 ± 136.5 ml/min
	FF	0.220 ± 0.037
3. Steady state in dietetic restriction of sodium to 30 mEq/day; protein intake 0.5–1.0 g/kg body weight/day; urinary volume 1–3 ml/min		
Men and women[11]	C_{In}	107.6 ± 11.4 ml/min
	C_{PAH}	631.2 ± 87.8 ml/min
	FF	0.172 ± 0.018

* This chapter on 'Renal Function Values' has been compiled by D.P. Mertz and H. Sarre, Medical Policlinic, University of Freiburg i.B. (Director: Prof. H. Sarre).

(For references see page 536)

The upper limit of the normal range of *plasma NPN concentration* is considered to be 40 mg/100 ml[24]. Increases in this level are known to be dependent on an increase in the *urea fraction.* The proportion of the NPN due to the urea fraction can be calculated roughly from the urea nitrogen by means of the formula of PETERS and VAN SLYKE[25]:

NPN (in mg/100 ml) $= 10 + (1.07 \times$ urea-N in mg/100 ml).

Here it should be borne in mind that in chronic renal insufficiency the rise in the NPN is not due to urea nitrogen to the extent indicated by the above formula. Whereas in acute renal failure up to 90% of the NPN is represented by urea, in chronic renal insufficiency there is a relatively larger increase in other NPN components.

The 15-minute *phenolsulphonphthalein test* (after a single i.v. injection of 6 mg of the dye) is not sufficiently sensitive to reveal small changes in the excretory function of the renal tubules[26]. The marked variance of the sample values around the regression line (Fig. 3) is due in the main to the combination of PSP with plasma proteins (dependent on various factors), the absence of a flow

Fig. 1 Nonlinear relationship between the concentration of 'true' endogenous creatinine in plasma (P_{Cr}, as measured by the method of LØKEN[21]) and the renal inulin clearance (C_{In}). $Ty = 95\%$ tolerance range for Y/x[18]

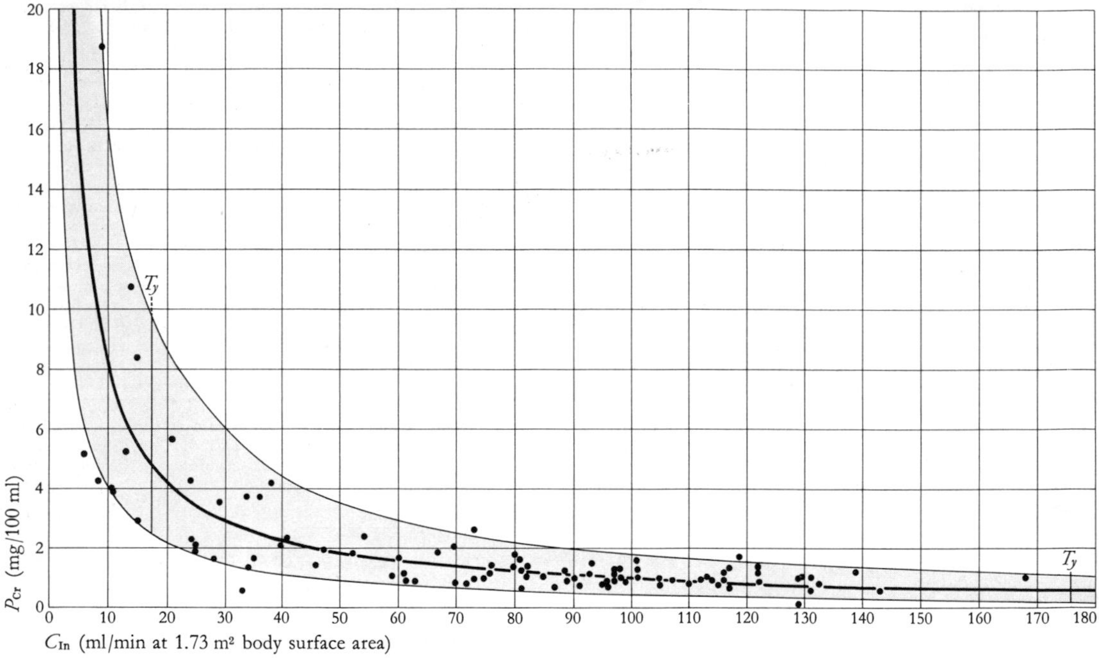

Fig. 2 Nonlinear relationship between the concentration of nonprotein nitrogen (NPN) in plasma and the renal inulin clearance (C_{In})[19]

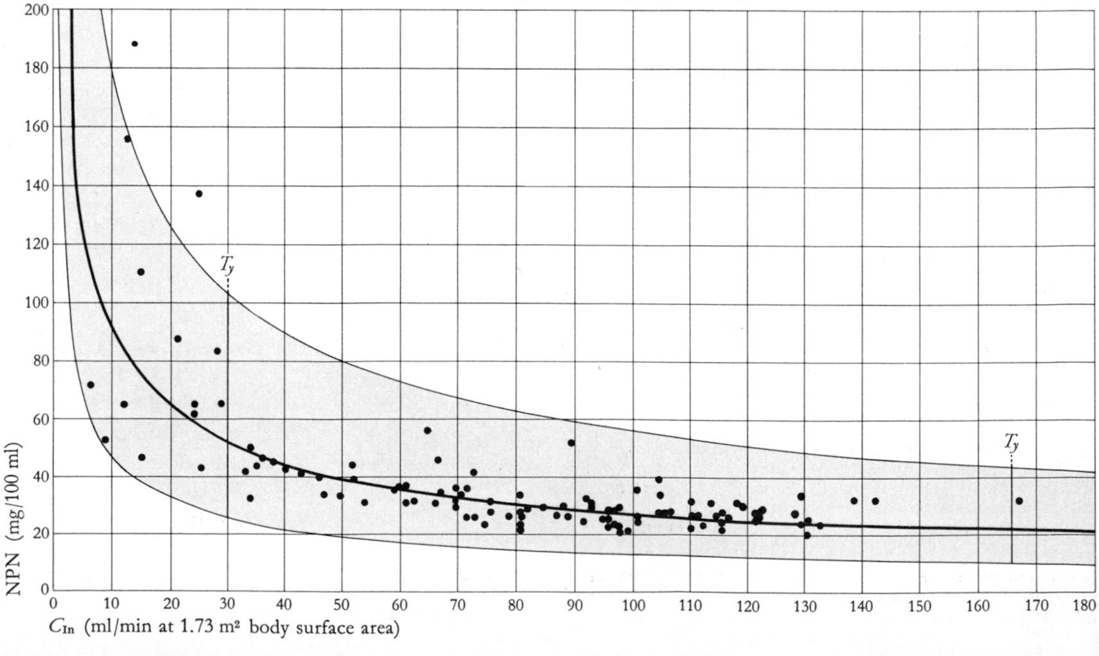

(For references see page 536)

Fig. 3 Linear relationship between the percentage excretion of phenolsulphonphthalein (PSP; 15-minute value after a single i.v. injection of 6 mg) and the renal PAH clearance (C_{PAH}). $Ty = 95\%$ tolerance range for Y/x[26]

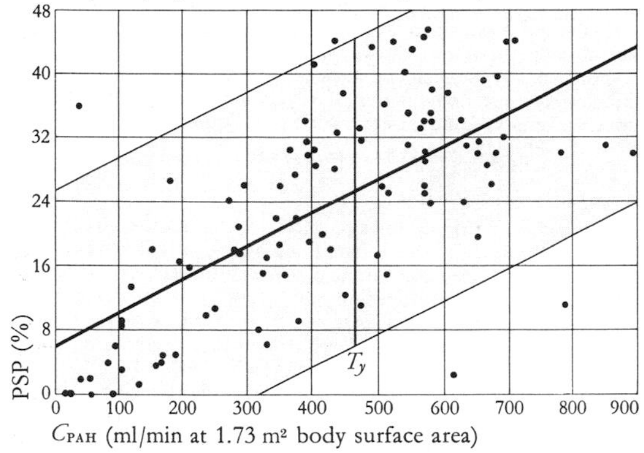

equilibrium of PSP in the body fluid compartments after a single injection, failure to take account of body weight in evaluating the results, and the use of spontaneous urine samples[26].

Dilution and concentration of urine

Tests of the diluting capacity of the kidneys are usually now dispensed with. If the organ can concentrate urine it must also be able to dilute it, and in any case concentration tests are less dependent on extrarenal factors and therefore more sensitive. Moreover, a dilution test could have a disturbing effect on a subsequent concentration test[20, 24, 27].

Quantitative methods

When ADH (antidiuretic hormone) activity is at a maximum, the urinary concentrating capacity is limited by two factors[28]: (a) during hydropenia and oliguria by the maximum value of the ratio between the osmotic concentrations of the urine and plasma (U_{osm}/P_{osm}), i.e., by the maximum osmotic concentration effect; (b) during osmotic diuresis, which does not normally occur under physiological conditions, by the maximum reabsorption of osmotically free water ($Tm^c_{H_2O}$) into the hypertonic interstices of the renal medulla. A number of conditions are known in which the latter is the more sensitive factor, and it may have a pathological value even when the concentration test (determination of maximum urinary osmolality) is still completely normal.

Normal values

Maximum urinary osmolarity...	900–1400 mosm/l[29–31]
	1027 ± 110 mosm/l[29]
	1067 (918–1230) mosm/l[32]
Maximum value of U_{osm}/P_{osm} ..	2.77 ± 0.36[33]
	3.63–4.65[34]
$Tm^c_{H_2O}$ (with i.v. infusion of hypertonic mannitol solution) ..	5.7 ± 2.0 ml/min[35]
$Tm^c_{H_2O} \times 100/C_{In}$ (with i.v. infusion of hypertonic mannitol solution)	5.1 ± 1.5[36]

With increasing osmolar clearance (C_{osm}) from 1 to 15 ml/min (for a body surface area of 1.73 m²), $T^c_{H_2O}$ increases steadily up to its maximum value $Tm^c_{H_2O}$. When C_{osm} exceeds about 25 ml/min it tends to diminish slightly[37].

It has recently been shown that with increasing osmotic saline diuresis the value of $T^c_{H_2O}$ rises continuously and not to the expected individual maximum. This applies not only to normotensive subjects with healthy kidneys[38, 39] but also to patients with essential hypertension[39] provided their renal function is not noticeably impaired. This progressive increase in $T^c_{H_2O}$ also occurs in the diuretic range where its value for mannitol diuresis already shows

Fig. 4 Plots of $T^c_{H_2O}$ during saline diuresis (——) and mannitol diuresis (- - -) in (*a*) a healthy man and (*b*) a man with essential hypertension[39]

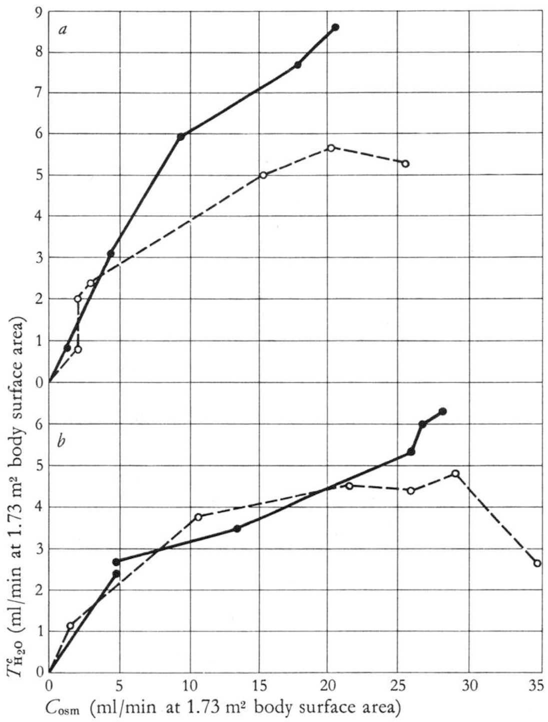

a tendency to decrease (Fig. 4). In contrast to the views of some authorities it therefore seems that in man the behaviour of $T^c_{H_2O}$ is not constant during osmotic diuresis with different substances such as sodium chloride, mannitol, urea or glucose under conditions of comparable total excretion of osmotically active material. The upper limit for the net withdrawal of osmotically free water during osmotic diuresis with mannitol, urea or glucose is a 'pseudo-maximum'. Sodium transport in the interstitium of the renal medulla is no more subject to a maximum value in man than it is in the experimental animal. In the view of the present author[39], the ratio U_{osm}/P_{osm} during hydropenia and oliguria affords the best measure of the concentrating capacity of the kidney. In many cases, determination of '$Tm^c_{H_2O}$' during hypertonic mannitol diuresis offers at best certain advantages over the usual methods in respect of localization of the site of disturbances in the urinary concentration mechanism.

At maximum diuresis the excess of osmotically free water compared to a hypothetical isosmotic urinary portion can be determined as the maximum free-water clearance ($Tm^d_{H_2O}$).

Normal values (1.73 m² body surface area)

$Tm^d_{H_2O}$ = maximum C_{H_2O}	17 ml/min[40]
	23 ml/min[41]

Method of WESSON and ANSLOW[42]:

$$\text{Hypothetical isosmotic urinary portion} = \text{Osmolar clearance } (C_{osm}) = \frac{U_{osm} \times V}{P_{osm}} \quad \textbf{(7)}$$

$$T^c_{H_2O} = C_{osm} - V \quad \textbf{(8)}$$

$$T^d_{H_2O} = C_{H_2O} = V - C_{osm} \quad \textbf{(9)}$$

$$U_{osm}/P_{osm} = 1 + \frac{T^c_{H_2O}}{V} \text{ (see Fig. 5)}^{36} \quad \textbf{(10)}$$

(For references see page 536)

Fig. 5 Diagram for reading off values of $Tm^c_{H_2O}$ from those of U_{osm}/P_{osm} and the simultaneous urinary minute volume in osmotic diuresis[43]

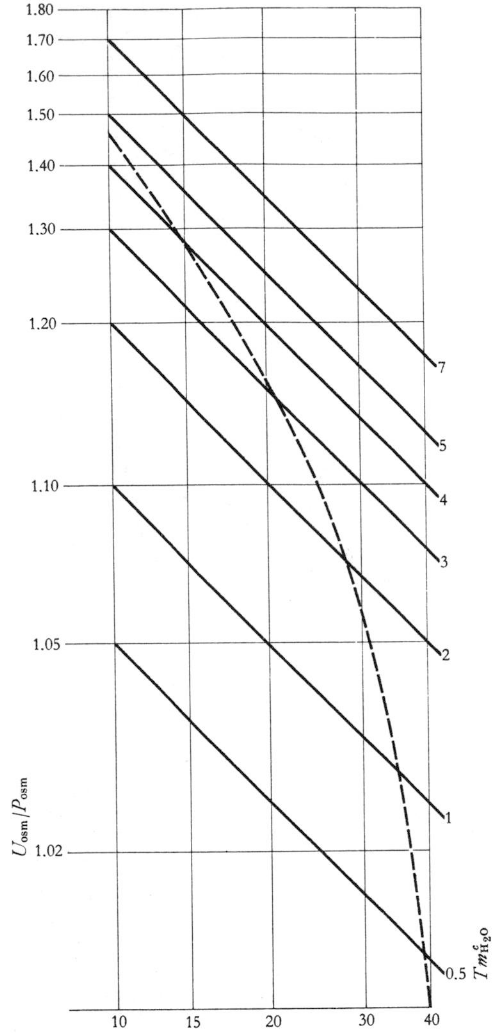

Fig. 6 Contributions of various urinary components to the specific gravity and osmolarity of the urine[49]

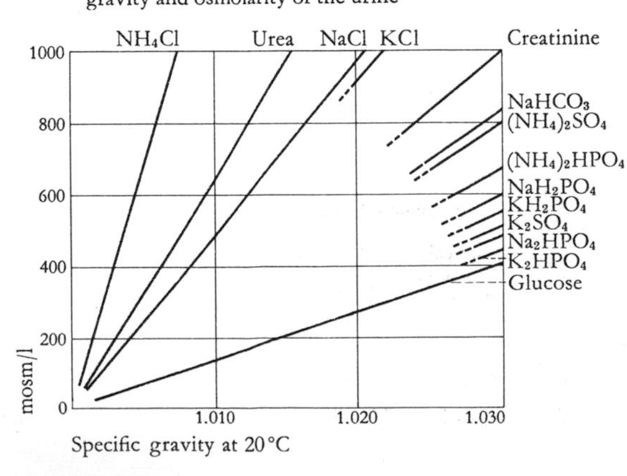

There are considerable discrepancies in the 'normal' values given in the literature for some of the parameters of renal concentrating capacity, a result of differences in the experimental methods. The concentrating capacity of the kidneys can be increased by means of a protein-rich diet[44]; it is decreased under conditions of inadequate dehydration[45] and in man (fluid deprivation test) is independent of the sodium chloride intake[46].

For persons between the ages of 24 and 72 years with healthy kidneys the age dependence of maximum urinary osmolality as found by a 24-hour fluid deprivation test is given by the formula[47]:

$$U_{osm} \text{ (in mosm/l)} = 1134 - (4.1 \times \text{age in years})$$

Semiquantitative methods

While the underlying physiological process in the concentration of urine consists of the removal of osmotically-free water, the various electrolytes and nonelectrolytes present contribute in different degrees to the specific gravity and osmotic pressure. The determination of the *maximum specific gravity of urine* in the fluid deprivation test[48] must therefore be regarded as a semiquantitative test of renal function.

Glucose, phosphate and sulphate cause a high specific gravity of urine at fairly low osmotic concentrations[49], whereas chloride and urea exert a relatively high osmotic pressure for a given urinary specific gravity (Fig. 6). In persons with healthy kidneys the maximum urinary osmolarity reached in the fluid deprivation test is only loosely related to the maximum specific gravity[29]. The variance in the relationship between these two parameters increases in renal disease (Fig. 7)[30].

Normal specific gravity of urine (24-hour fluid deprivation test)	1.035 ± 4[27]
Lower limit of the normal (healthy kidney)......	1.026[24, 27, 30]

The maximum urinary specific gravity falls from an average of 1.032 at 20 years to an average of 1.024 between 80 and 90 years[50].

Dependence of the 24-hour urinary volume on the amounts of solutes removed in the urine and the concentrating capacity of the kidneys

The amounts of solutes removed in the urine depend both on the dietary intake, particularly of proteins and salts, and on the calorie turnover of the body[51]. A mixed diet yields about 1200 mosm of urinary solutes per day[52], an amount reduced by fasting to about 800 mosm. In fasting subjects given 100 g glucose per day the urinary solutes fall to 400 mosm per day, while a diet low in protein and salt but rich in carbohydrates (with maintenance of the basal metabolic rate) results in a further reduction to 200 mosm per day. On the basis of a maximum urinary osmolarity of 1400 mosm/l the amounts of water required for the excretion of these amounts are 857, 571, 286 and 143 ml respectively. In isosthenuria (urinary osmolarity of 300 mosm/l) the renal elimination of 1200, 800, 400 and 200 mosm of urinary solutes requires respectively 4000, 2667, 1333 and 667 ml of water. The relationship between the renal water requirement and the urinary osmolarity for different daily amounts of solutes removed in the urine is shown in Figure 8[51].

Tubular transport functions

Clearance techniques enable an assessment to be made of the state of functioning of the active local transport mechanisms in the proximal tubular convolution. Both the tubular secretion of *p*-aminohippuric acid (PAH) and the reabsorption of glucose (G) from the tubular urine are limited by transport maxima (*Tm*)[1].

$$Tm_{PAH} = (U_{PAH} \times V) - (P_{PAH} \times C_{In} \times k)^{9} \quad \textbf{(11)}$$

where U_{PAH} and P_{PAH} are the concentrations of PAH in urine and plasma respectively and k is a correction factor for the plasma PAH fraction that is protein-bound and not filtrable by the glomeruli. The normal value of k is 0.83.

$$Tm_G = (P_G \times C_{In}) - (U_G \times V) \quad \textbf{(12)}$$

Normal values (for 1.73 m² body surface area)

Tm_{PAH}	Men....................	79.8 ± 16.7 mg/min[2]
	Women	77.2 ± 10.8 mg/min[2]
Tm_G	Men....................	375 ± 79.7 mg/min[1, 2]
	Women	303 ± 55.3 mg/min[1, 2]

Fig. 7 Relationship between the maximum urinary specific gravity (SU) achieved in the 18-hour fluid deprivation test and the corresponding osmolarity (U_{osm}) of the urine: $(SU - 1.000) \times 1000/U_{osm} = 0.0318 \pm 0.0053$[30]

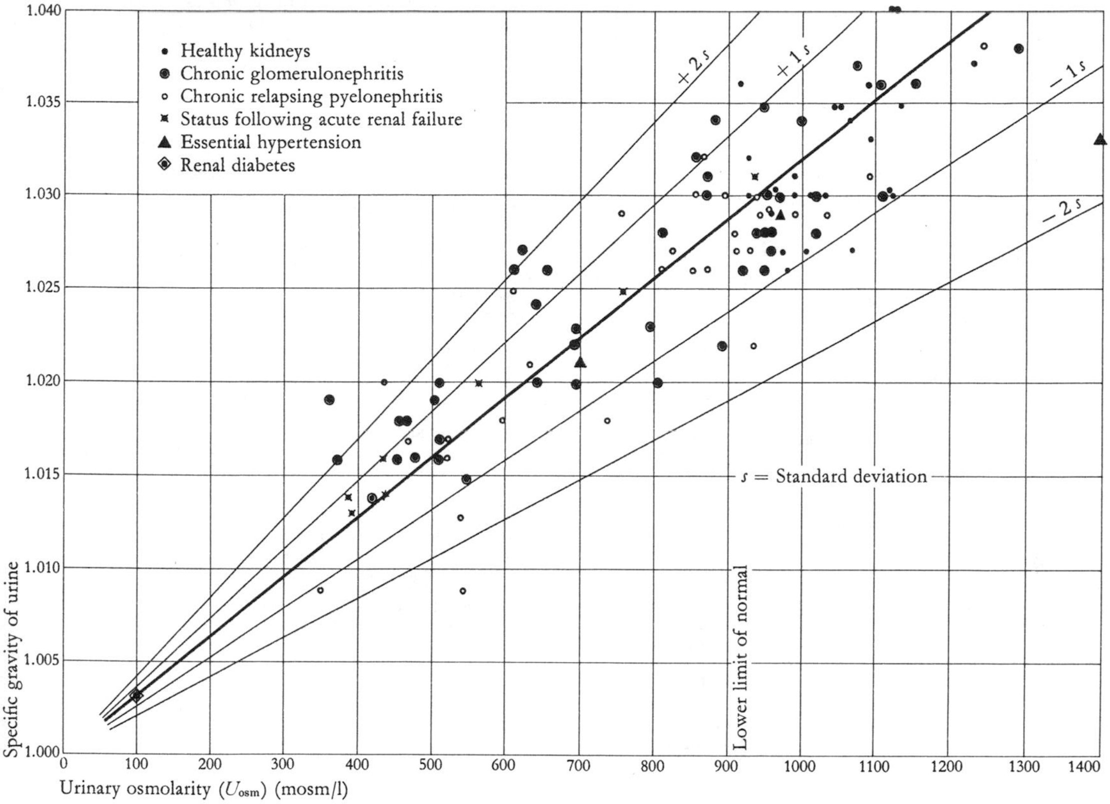

These renal functions can be differentiated more precisely by relating Tm_{PAH} (as a measure of the functioning secretory renal tissue) and Tm_G (as a measure of the reabsorptive renal tissue) to C_{In} and C_{PAH} respectively. The ratios C_{In}/Tm_{PAH}, C_{PAH}/Tm_{PAH} and Tm_G/C_{In} are measures of glomerular activity, i.e., of the effective renal plasma flow per unit of the secretory or reabsorptive tissue.

Normal values

C_{In}/Tm_{PAH}	1.54 ± 0.4 ml/mg[2]
C_{PAH}/Tm_{PAH}	8.28 ± 2.2 ml/mg[2]
Tm_G/C_{In}	2.41 ± 0.35 mg/ml[1]

All these functions show age regression between the 20th and 90th years of life:

$Tm_{PAH} = 120.6 - (0.865 \times \text{age in years})$[15]

$Tm_G = 432.8 - (2.604 \times \text{age in years})$[50]

$C_{In}/Tm_{PAH} = 1.382 - (0.00158 \times \text{age in years})$[50]

$C_{PAH}/Tm_{PAH} = 7.710 - (0.0278 \times \text{age in years})$[50]

Excretion of acids and electrolytes

The *total acid excretion* (A_{H^+}) is made up of potentially ionizable hydrogen ions (titratable acidity, TA) and bound (nonionizable) hydrogen ions in the form of ammonium ions (NH_4^+):

$$A_{H^+} = A_{TA} + A_{NH_4^+} \quad \textbf{(13)}$$

Fig. 8 Relationship between urinary volume and osmolarity at various solute concentrations[51, 52]

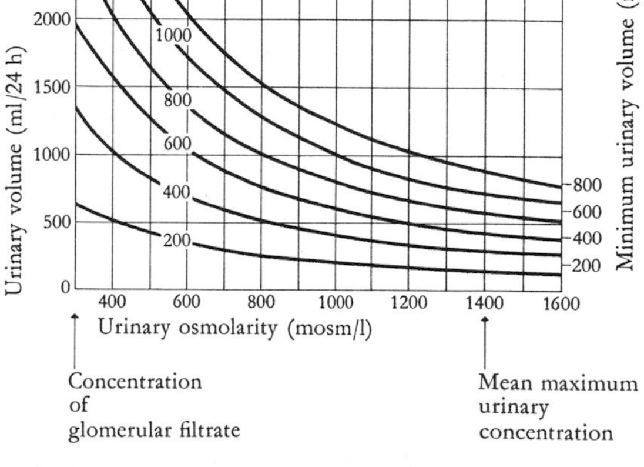

Normal values (on a mixed diet)

Total acid excretion (A_{H^+})	30–80 mEq/24 h[53]
Titratable acidity (A_{TA})	10–30 mEq/24 h[53]
NH_4^+ excretion ($A_{NH_4^+}$)	20–50 mEq/24 h[53]
$A_{NH_4^+}/A_{TA}$	1.0–2.5[53]
	1.28 ± 0.14[54]

The difference between the sum of the TA and NH_4^+ excretions and the bicarbonate excretion (HCO_3^-) is known as the *effective acid excretion* ($A_{H^+_{eff}}$).

$$A_{H^+_{eff}} = A_{H^+} - A_{HCO_3^-} = A_{TA} + A_{NH_4^+} - A_{HCO_3^-} \qquad \textbf{(14)}$$

In alkaline urine the effective acid excretion has a negative value since mainly bicarbonate ions are excreted.

The pH value of urine may vary between 4.6 and 8.2[2,55].

An accurate assessment of the tubular treatment of an *electrolyte* from the excreted proportion of the amount filtered by the glomeruli is possible only when the substance concerned is freely filtrable and is exclusively reabsorbed in the tubules and not secreted. The only important electrolytes at present considered to fulfil this condition in man are sodium, chloride and bicarbonate.

Table 2 gives the mean values for the glomerular filtration and total excretion of some electrolytes in the 24-hour urine[24].

The *glomerular filtration rate* (GFR) of a completely filtrable electrolyte (E) is calculated as follows:

$$GFR_E \text{ (in mEq/min)} = k \times P_E \times C_{In} \qquad \textbf{(15)}$$

where P_E is the plasma concentration of the electrolyte (in mEq/l) and k a correction factor for the small differences between the concentrations in plasma and glomerular filtrate resulting from the GIBBS-DONNAN equilibrium and the lowering of the water content of the plasma by the proteins.

The value of k is normally 1.02 for Cl^- and HCO_3^- [56], 0.96[57] for Na^+ and 0.92[57] for K^+.

For calculation of the amounts of partly plasma-protein-bound electrolytes filtered by the glomeruli it is important to know the filtrable part. This is dependent on the concentration and composition of the plasma proteins and on the pH value and other physicochemical conditions. 54% of the plasma calcium and 68% of the plasma magnesium are normally ultrafiltrable[58].

So-called 'normal' values for the clearance of electrolytes have little significance since they are very largely dependent on exogenous factors.

Table 2 Amounts of solutes excreted and reabsorbed assuming a glomerular filtrate of 130 ml/min

	Amount filtered	Amount excreted in urine
Urea	46 g	20–35 g
Uric acid	7.2 g	0.1–2 g
Amino acids	50 g	0.5–1 g
Creatinine	1.2 g	1.2–1.5 g
Glucose	180 g	–
Albumin	36 g	–
Sodium	600 g	4–6 g
Chloride	640 g	6–9 g
Potassium	7.2 g	2.5–3.5 g
Bicarbonate	4900 mEq	1–2 mEq
Calcium	uncertain	0.01–0.3 g
Inorganic phosphate (as P)	5.6 g	1–5 g
Inorganic sulphate (as S)	2.9 g	1.4–3.3 g
Water	180 l	1.5 l

References

1 SMITH, H.W., *Lectures on the Kidney*, University of Kansas, Lawrence, Kans., 1943.
2 SMITH, H.W., *The Kidney; Structure and Function in Health and Disease*, Oxford University Press, New York, 1951.
3 McINTOSH et al., *J.clin.Invest.*, **6**, 467 (1928).
4 MÖLLER et al., *J.clin.Invest.*, **6**, 427 (1928).
5 REUBI, F., *Schweiz.med.Wschr.*, **88**, 1084 (1958).
6 SARRE and SCHADKHU, *Klin.Wschr.*, **40**, 179 (1962).
7 HARTH, O., *Klin.Wschr.*, **41**, 769 (1963); MERTZ and SARRE, *Klin. Wschr.*, **41**, 868 (1963).
8 AUSTIN et al., *J.biol.Chem.*, **46**, 91 (1921).
9 SMITH et al., *J.clin.Invest.*, **24**, 388 (1945).
10 BRADLEY et al., *Fed.Proc.*, **6**, 79 (1947).
11 MERTZ, D.P., *Z.klin.Med.*, **157**, 1 (1961).
12 AAS and BLEGEN, *Scand.J.clin.Lab.Invest.*, **1**, 22 (1949).
13 MERTZ, D.P., *Die extrazelluläre Flüssigkeit*, Thieme, Stuttgart, 1962.
14 PULLMAN et al., *J.Lab.clin.Med.*, **44**, 320 (1954).
15 WATKIN and SHOCK, *J.clin.Invest.*, **34**, 969 (1955).
16 STEINITZ and TÜRKAND, *J.clin.Invest.*, **19**, 285 (1940); SARRE et al., *Dtsch. med.Wschr.*, **82**, 1093 (1957); EFFERSØE, P., *Acta med.scand.*, **156**, 429 (1957); EDWARDS and WHYTE, *Aust. Ann.Med.*, **8**, 218 (1959).
17 DOOLAN et al., *Amer.J.Med.*, **32**, 65 (1962).
18 MERTZ et al., *Klin.Wschr.*, **40**, 687 (1962).
19 MERTZ et al., *Klin.Wschr.*, **40**, 889 (1962).
20 REUBI, F., *Nierenkrankheiten*, Huber, Berne, 1960.
21 LØKEN, F., *Scand.J.clin.Lab.Invest.*, **6**, 325 (1954).
22 BORSOOK and DUBNOFF, *J.biol.Chem.*, **168**, 493 (1947).
23 MILLER and DUBOS, *J.biol.Chem.*, **121**, 457 (1937).
24 SARRE, H., *Nierenkrankheiten*, 2nd ed., Thieme, Stuttgart, 1959.
25 PETERS and VAN SLYKE, *Quantitative Clinical Chemistry*, 2nd ed., vol.1, Williams & Wilkins, Baltimore, 1946.
26 MERTZ and SARRE, *Klin.Wschr.*, **40**, 692 (1962).
27 BOCK and KRECKE, *Dtsch.Arch.klin.Med.*, **204**, 499 (1957).
28 SMITH, H.W., *Principles of Renal Physiology*, Oxford University Press, New York, 1956.
29 ISAACSON, L.C., *Lancet*, **1**, 467 (1960).
30 MERTZ, D.P., *Z.klin.Med.*, **157**, 517 and 529 (1963).
31 GAMBLE, J.L., *Proc.Amer.philos.Soc.*, **88**, 151 (1944); MCCANCE, R.A., *J.Physiol.(Lond.)*, **104**, 196 (1945).
32 HULET and SMITH, *Amer.J.Med.*, **30**, 8 (1961).
33 BOYARSKY and SMITH, *J.Urol.(Baltimore)*, **78**, 511 (1957).
34 RAISZ and SCHEER, *J.clin.Invest.*, **38**, 1 (1959).
35 ZAK et al., *J.clin.Invest.*, **33**, 1064 (1954).
36 BALDWIN et al., *J.clin.Invest.*, **34**, 800 (1955).
37 RAISZ et al., *J.clin.Invest.*, **38**, 1725 (1959); EISNER et al., *J.Mt Sinai Hosp.*, **29**, 38 (1962).
38 GOLDBERG et al., *J.clin.Invest.*, **44**, 182 (1965).
39 MERTZ, D.P., *Pflügers Arch.ges.Physiol.*, **290**, 1 (1966).
40 KLEEMAN et al., *J.clin.Invest.*, **35**, 749 (1956); BUCHBORN et al., *Klin.Wschr.*, **37**, 347 (1959).
41 KLEEMAN et al., *J.clin.Invest.*, **39**, 1472 (1960).
42 WESSON and ANSLOW, *Amer.J.Physiol.*, **170**, 255 (1952).
43 BUCHBORN and ANASTASAKIS, *Internist (Berl.)*, **2**, 611 (1961).
44 EPSTEIN et al., *J.clin.Invest.*, **36**, 635 (1957).
45 KLEEMAN and MAXWELL, *Clin.Res.Proc.*, **5**, 43 (1957); EPSTEIN et al., *J.clin. Invest.*, **36**, 629 (1957).
46 LEVITT et al., *J.clin.Invest.*, **38**, 463 (1959).
47 LINDEMAN et al., *New Engl.J.Med.*, **262**, 1306 (1960).
48 VOLHARD, F., *Verh.dtsch.Ges.inn.Med.*, **27**, 735 (1910).
49 ISAACSON, L.C., *Lancet*, **1**, 72 (1959).
50 SHOCK, N.W., in WOLSTENHOLME and O'CONNOR (Eds.), *Ciba Foundation Colloquia on Ageing*, vol.4, Churchill, London, 1958, page 229.
51 GAMBLE, J.L., *Chemical Anatomy, Physiology and Pathology of Extracellular Fluid*, 6th ed., Harvard University Press, Cambridge, 1954.
52 GAMBLE and BUTLER, *Trans.Ass.Amer.Phycns*, **58**, 157 (1944).
53 KRÜCK, F., *Klin.Wschr.*, **36**, 946 (1958).
54 SCHWAB, M., *Verh.dtsch.Ges.inn.Med.*, **67**, 595 (1961).
55 PITTS et al., *J.clin.Invest.*, **27**, 48 (1948).
56 HASTINGS et al., *J.gen.Physiol.*, **8**, 701 (1927).
57 FOLK et al., *Amer.J.Physiol.*, **153**, 381 (1948).
58 WALSER, M., *J.clin.Invest.*, **40**, 723 (1961).

Nomogram for determination of body surface area from height and weight

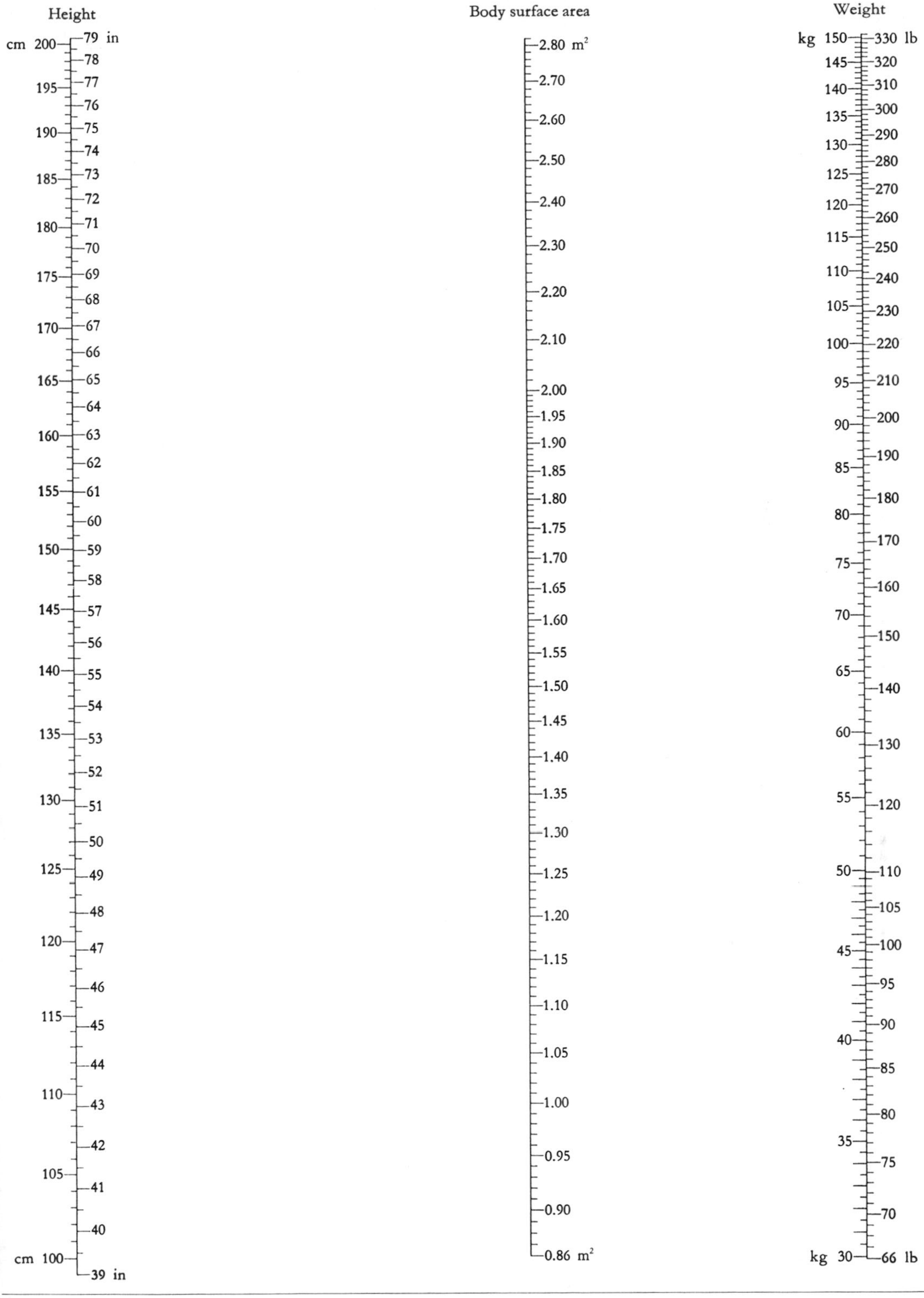

From the formula of Du Bois and Du Bois, *Arch. intern. Med.*, **17**, 863 (1916): $S = W^{0.425} \times H^{0.725} \times 71.84$, or
$\log S = \log W \times 0.425 + \log H \times 0.725 + 1.8564$ (S = body surface in cm², W = weight in kg, H = height in cm)

Nomogram for determination of body surface area from height and weight

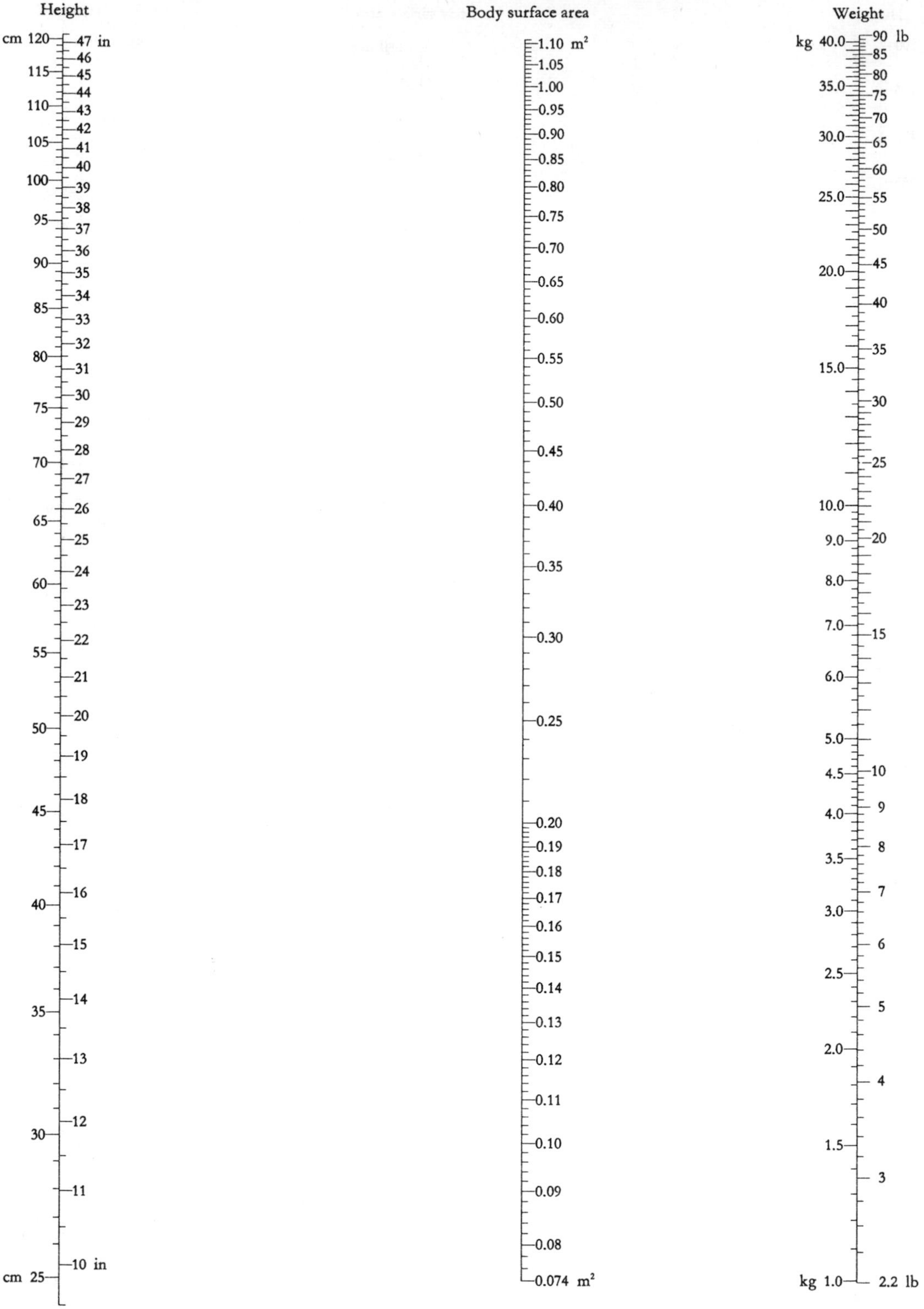

From the formula of Du Bois and Du Bois, *Arch. intern. Med.*, **17**, 863 (1916): $S = W^{0.425} \times H^{0.725} \times 71.84$, or
$\log S = \log W \times 0.425 + \log H \times 0.725 + 1.856\,4$ (S = body surface in cm², W = weight in kg, H = height in cm)

The basal metabolism (or basal metabolic rate, BMR) is the calorie requirement of the fasting body, physically and mentally at rest, at room temperature (ca. 20 °C). It corresponds to the unavoidable heat loss due to the cell metabolism plus the energy expended (even at rest) in maintaining the minimal functions of the body (circulation, respiration, digestion, involuntary muscle tone). A major part of the BMR is accounted for by the metabolism of the liver, as shown in the following table.

Contributions of various organs to the basal metabolism[1]

Organ	Weight (kg)	Proportion of body weight (%)	Oxygen consumption per kg (ml/min)	Oxygen consumption whole organ (ml/min)	Proportion of basal metabolism (%)
(a) Liver........	1.5	2.1	44	66	26.4
(b) Brain........	1.4	2.0	33	46	18.3
(c) Heart	0.3	0.43	94	23	9.2
(d) Kidneys	0.3	0.43	61	18	7.2
(a)–(d) together..	...	...	...	153	61.1
(e) Skeletal muscle	27.8	39.7	2.3	64	25.6
Total (a)–(e)	...	...	...	217	86.7

The BMR is dependent on many factors[2,3], particularly sex, height and weight, bodily constitution, age and hormonal balance. Daily and seasonal rhythms as well as climatic effects have also been observed. In women, slight variations occur during the course of the menstrual cycle[3,4], and there is an increase of about 20% towards the end of pregnancy[5]. Many standard values for the BMR have been published; in common use are those of HARRIS and BENEDICT[6], BOOTHBY, BERKSON and DUNN[7], ROBERTSON and REID[8], and FLEISCH[9]. Standard values for children have been published by SHOCK[10] and by LEWIS et al.[11]. The BMR of infants[12] and children[13] has been extensively investigated and that in the 50–90 year-old group has been the subject of a special study[14].

Standard values of the BMR are usually related to body surface area (for the determination of body surface area see pages 537 and 538), but more recently suggestions have been made to use the fat-free body mass (muscle mass or 'active tissue mass')[15], an accepted measure of which is the urinary creatinine excretion[16]. In infants the BMR is best related to body weight[17].

Pathological changes in the BMR occur chiefly as a result of disturbances of pituitary, thyroid or adrenocortical function. Hyperactivity of these glands causes an increase in the BMR, diminished activity a decrease. A specific form of increased BMR has been ascribed to a disturbance of mitochondrial respiration[18].

Measurement of BMR

Since the calorimetric determination of the BMR requires complicated apparatus, in practice it is usually calculated from the O_2 consumption, the CO_2 production and occasionally (when greater accuracy is required) the urinary nitrogen excretion. Gas volumes must be converted to STPD (see page 269).

The ratio of the CO_2 production ($\dot{V}_{CO_2}$) to the oxygen consumption ($\dot{V}_{O_2}$) is known as the *respiratory quotient* (RQ):

$$RQ = \frac{\dot{V}_{CO_2}}{\dot{V}_{O_2}}$$

Variation of RQ with age[19]

Newborn, first hours of life	0.90
first days of life	0.73
end of 1st week	0.82
Adults, postabsorptive (basal RQ)	0.82

The following formulae can be used for calculating the BMR ($\dot{E}$ = energy consumption in kilocalories per unit time; $\dot{V}_{O_2}$ = O_2 consumption in litres per unit time; $\dot{V}_{CO_2}$ = CO_2 production in litres per unit time; $\dot{H}_N$ = urinary nitrogen excretion in grammes per unit time):

$$\dot{E} = 4.825\ \dot{V}_{O_2} \quad (\mathbf{1})$$

(when only O_2 consumption is measured)

$$\dot{E} = 3.941\ \dot{V}_{O_2} + 1.106\ \dot{V}_{CO_2} \quad (\mathbf{2}a)$$

$$\dot{E} = 3.78\ \dot{V}_{O_2} + 1.16\ \dot{V}_{CO_2} \quad (\mathbf{2}b)$$

(when O_2 consumption and CO_2 production are measured)

$$\dot{E} = 3.941\ \dot{V}_{O_2} + 1.106\ \dot{V}_{CO_2} - 2.17\ \dot{H}_N \quad (\mathbf{3}a)$$

$$\dot{E} = 3.78\ \dot{V}_{O_2} + 1.16\ \dot{V}_{CO_2} - 2.98\ \dot{H}_N \quad (\mathbf{3}b)$$

(when protein breakdown is also determined)

Formula (**1**)[20] assumes a RQ of 0.82; the calorie values of LOEWY were used for formulae (**2**a) and (**3**a)[21], those of RUBNER for formulae (**2**b) and (**3**b)[22].

Calorific value, oxygen consumption and carbon dioxide production per gramme of protein, fat and carbohydrate burnt in the body and per gramme of nitrogen excreted in the urine[23]

	Oxygen consumed (ml/g)	Carbon dioxide produced (ml/g)	RQ	kcal/g from RUBNER	kcal/g from LOEWY	kcal/l Oxygen	kcal/l Carbon dioxide
Protein	966.3	773.9	0.801	4.10	4.316	4.485	5.579
Urinary N	5939.0	4757.0	0.801	25.63	26.54	4.485	5.579
Fat	2019.3	1427.3	0.707	9.3	9.461	4.686	6.629
Carbohydrate...	828.8	828.8	1.000	4.1	4.182	5.047	5.047

References

1 BROŽEK and GRANDE, quoted by KINNEY et al., *Ann. N. Y. Acad. Sci.*, **110**, 711 (1963).
2 KRAUT and ZIMMERMANN, in FLASCHENTRÄGER and LEHNARTZ (Eds.), *Physiologische Chemie*, vol. 2, part 2c, Springer, Berlin, 1959, page 220; TATA, J. R., *Advanc. metab. Disord.*, **1**, 153 (1964); SWIFT and FISHER, in BEATON and MCHENRY (Eds.), *Nutrition*, vol. 1, Academic Press, New York, 1964, page 181.
3 SUZUKI, S., *Wld Rev. Nutr. Diet.*, **1**, 103 (1959).
4 WAKEHAM, G., *J. biol. Chem.*, **56**, 555 (1923).
5 HYTTEN and LEITCH, *The Physiology of Human Pregnancy*, Blackwell, Oxford, 1964, page 96.
6 HARRIS and BENEDICT, *A Biometric Study of Basal Metabolism in Man*, Publication No. 279 of the Carnegie Institution, Washington, 1919.
7 BOOTHBY et al., *Amer. J. Physiol.*, **116**, 468 (1936).
8 ROBERTSON and REID, *Lancet*, **1**, 940 (1952).
9 FLEISCH, A., *Helv. med. Acta*, **18**, 23 (1951).
10 SHOCK, N. W., *Amer. J. Dis. Child.*, **64**, 19 (1942).
11 LEWIS et al., *J. Pediat.*, **23**, 1 (1943).
12 KARLBERG, P., *Acta paediat. (Uppsala)*, **41**, suppl. 89 (1952).
13 SARGENT, D. W., *An Evaluation of Basal Metabolic Data for Children and Youth in the United States*, Home Economics Research Report No. 14, United States Department of Agriculture, Washington, 1961.
14 BINET et al., *Bull. Acad. nat. Méd. (Paris)*, **144**, 355 (1960); BINET et al., *J. Physiol. (Paris)*, **54**, 687 (1962).
15 MILLER and BLYTH, *J. appl. Physiol.*, **5**, 311 (1953); MILLER, A. T., *Meth. med. Res.*, **6**, 74 (1954); KINNEY et al., *Ann. N. Y. Acad. Sci.*, **110**, 711 (1963).
16 TALBOT, N. B., *Amer. J. Dis. Child.*, **52**, 16 (1936); TALBOT et al., *Amer. J. Dis. Child.*, **58**, 506 (1939).

[17] HILL, J. R., in JONXIS et al. (Eds.), *Nutricia Symposium on the Adaptation of the Newborn Infant to Extra-Uterine Life*, Kroese, Leiden, 1964, page 223.
[18] ERNSTER and LUFT, *Advanc. metab. Disord.*, **1**, 95 (1964).
[19] SMITH, C. A., *The Physiology of the Newborn Infant*, 3rd ed., Blackwell, Oxford, 1959, page 203; BEHRENDT, H., *Diagnostic Tests in Infants and Children*, 2nd ed., Lea & Febiger, Philadelphia, 1962, page 33.
[20] LUSK, G., *J. biol. Chem.*, **59**, 41 (1924).
[21] WEIR, J. B. DE V., *J. Physiol. (Lond.)*, **109**, 1 (1949).
[22] CONSOLAZIO et al., *Physiological Measurements of Metabolic Functions in Man*, McGraw-Hill, New York, 1963, page 315.
[23] From PETERS and VAN SLYKE, *Quantitative Clinical Chemistry*, 2nd ed., vol. 1, Williams & Wilkins, Baltimore, 1946, page 3.

Standard BMR values

Age in years	kcal/m²/h: Men, Standard of *Handbook of Biological Data*[1]: Mean	Men, Standard of *Handbook of Biological Data*[1]: 95% range	Men, Standard of FLEISCH[2]: Mean	Women, Standard of *Handbook of Biological Data*[1]: Mean	Women, Standard of *Handbook of Biological Data*[1]: 95% range	Women, Standard of FLEISCH[2]: Mean
1	–	–	53.0	–	–	53.0
2	–	–	52.4	–	–	52.4
3	60.1	51.8–68.3	51.3	54.5	47.0–62.0	51.2
4	57.9	49.9–65.9	50.3	53.9	46.5–61.3	49.8
5	56.3	48.5–64.1	49.3	53.0	45.7–60.3	48.4
6	54.0	46.5–61.5	48.3	51.2	44.1–58.3	47.0
7	52.3	45.1–59.5	47.3	49.7	42.8–56.6	45.4
8	50.8	43.8–57.8	46.3	48.0	41.4–54.6	43.8
9	49.5	42.7–56.3	45.2	46.2	39.8–52.6	42.8
10	47.7	41.1–54.3	44.0	44.9	38.7–51.1	42.5
11	46.5	40.1–52.9	43.0	44.1	38.0–50.2	42.0
12	45.3	39.0–51.6	42.5	42.0	36.2–47.8	41.3
13	44.5	38.4–50.6	42.3	40.5	34.9–46.1	40.3
14	43.8	37.8–49.8	42.1	39.2	33.8–44.6	39.2
15	43.7	37.7–49.7	41.8	38.3	33.0–43.6	37.9
16	42.9	37.0–48.8	41.4	37.7	32.5–42.9	36.9
17	41.9	36.1–47.7	40.8	36.2	31.2–41.2	36.3
18	40.5	34.9–46.1	40.0	35.7	30.8–40.6	35.9
19	40.1	34.6–45.6	39.2	35.4	30.5–40.3	35.5
20	39.8	34.3–45.3	38.6	35.3	30.4–40.2	35.3
21	39.4	34.0–44.8	–	35.2	30.3–40.1	–
22	39.2	33.8–44.6	–	35.2	30.3–40.1	–
23	39.0	33.6–44.4	–	35.2	30.3–40.1	–
24	38.7	33.4–44.0	–	35.1	30.3–39.9	–
25	38.4	33.1–43.7	37.5	35.1	30.3–39.9	35.2
26	38.2	32.9–43.5	–	35.0	30.2–39.8	–
27	38.0	32.8–43.2	–	35.0	30.2–39.8	–
28	37.8	32.6–43.0	–	35.0	30.2–39.8	–
29	37.7	32.5–42.9	–	35.0	30.2–39.8	–
30	37.6	32.4–42.8	36.8	35.0	30.2–39.8	35.1
31	37.4	32.2–42.6	–	35.0	30.2–39.8	–
32	37.2	32.1–42.3	–	34.9	30.1–39.7	–
33	37.1	32.0–42.2	–	34.9	30.1–39.7	–
34	37.0	31.9–42.1	–	34.9	30.1–39.7	–
35	36.9	31.8–42.0	36.5	34.8	30.0–39.6	35.0
36	36.8	31.7–41.9	–	34.7	29.9–39.5	–
37	36.7	31.6–41.8	–	34.6	29.8–39.4	–
38	36.7	31.6–41.8	–	34.5	29.7–39.3	–
39	36.6	31.5–41.7	–	34.4	29.7–39.1	–
40	36.5	31.5–41.5	36.3	34.3	29.6–39.0	34.9
45	36.3	31.3–41.3	36.2	33.9	29.2–38.6	34.5
50	36.0	31.0–40.0	35.8	33.4	28.8–38.0	33.9
55	35.4	30.5–40.3	35.4	32.9	28.4–37.4	33.3
60	34.8	30.0–39.6	34.9	32.4	27.9–36.9	32.7
65	34.0	29.3–38.7	34.4	31.8	27.4–36.2	32.2
70	33.1	28.5–37.7	33.8	31.3	27.0–35.6	31.7
75 and over	31.8	27.4–36.2	33.2	31.1	26.8–35.4	31.3

Age in years	kJ/m²/h*: Men, Standard of *Handbook of Biological Data*[1]: Mean	Men, Standard of *Handbook of Biological Data*[1]: 95% range	Men, Standard of FLEISCH[2]: Mean	Women, Standard of *Handbook of Biological Data*[1]: Mean	Women, Standard of *Handbook of Biological Data*[1]: 95% range	Women, Standard of FLEISCH[2]: Mean
1	–	–	222	–	–	222
2	–	–	219	–	–	219
3	252	217–286	215	228	197–260	214
4	242	209–276	211	226	195–257	208
5	236	203–268	206	222	191–252	203
6	226	195–257	202	214	185–244	197
7	219	189–249	198	208	179–237	190
8	213	183–242	194	201	173–229	183
9	207	179–236	189	193	167–220	179
10	200	172–227	184	188	162–214	178
11	195	168–221	180	185	159–210	176
12	190	163–216	178	176	152–200	173
13	186	161–212	177	170	146–193	169
14	183	158–208	176	164	141–187	164
15	182	158–208	175	160	138–182	159
16	180	155–204	173	158	136–180	154
17	175	151–200	171	152	131–172	152
18	170	146–193	167	149	129–170	150
19	168	145–191	164	148	128–169	149
20	167	144–190	162	148	127–168	148
21	165	142–188	–	147	127–168	–
22	164	141–187	–	147	127–168	–
23	163	141–186	–	147	127–168	–
24	162	140–184	–	147	127–167	–
25	161	139–183	157	147	127–167	147
26	160	138–182	–	146	126–167	–
27	159	137–181	–	146	126–167	–
28	158	136–180	–	146	126–167	–
29	158	136–180	–	146	126–167	–
30	157	136–179	154	146	126–167	147
31	157	135–178	–	146	126–167	–
32	156	134–177	–	146	126–166	–
33	155	134–177	–	146	126–166	–
34	155	134–176	–	146	126–166	–
35	154	133–176	153	146	126–166	146
36	154	133–175	–	145	125–165	–
37	154	132–175	–	145	125–165	–
38	154	132–175	–	144	124–164	–
39	153	132–175	–	144	124–164	–
40	153	132–174	152	144	124–163	146
45	152	131–173	152	142	122–162	144
50	151	130–167	150	140	121–159	142
55	148	128–169	148	138	119–157	139
60	146	126–166	146	136	117–154	137
65	142	123–162	144	133	115–152	135
70	139	119–158	141	131	113–149	133
75 and over	133	115–152	139	130	112–148	131

* The values in kJ have been calculated by using the relationship 1 $kcal_{15}$ = 4.185 5 kJ (see page 213).

[1] BOOTHBY and DUBOIS, in ALBRITTON, E. C. (Ed.), *Standard Values in Nutrition and Metabolism*, Saunders, Philadelphia, 1954, page 241. The values are based on 4016 measurements. The normal range has been calculated using a mean coefficient of variation of 6.9. The following data were used: Mayo Foundation Standards of BOOTHBY, BERKSON and DUNN; standard of ROBERTSON and REID; Carnegie Nutrition Laboratory Standards of HARRISON and BENEDICT.
[2] FLEISCH, A., *Helv. med. Acta*, **18**, 23 (1951). Values based on 24 reports in the literature.

(For references see page 546)

Symbols used in respiratory physiology[1]

1. Gas phase

(a) Primary symbols (italic capitals)
(A point over a symbol indicates a time derivative, a bar a mean value)

V	Gas volume
$\dot{V}$	Gas volume per unit time
P	Gas pressure (partial pressure)
$\bar{P}$	Mean gas pressure
F	Fractional concentration in dry gas phase
f	Respiratory frequency (breaths per unit time)
D	Diffusing capacity

(b) Secondary symbols (small italic capitals) and abbreviations (small upright capitals)

I	Inspired gas
E	Expired gas
A	Alveolar gas
D	Dead-space gas
T	Tidal gas
B	Barometric pressure
STPD	Standard temperature and pressure, dry (gas at 0 °C, 760 mm Hg, dry)
BTPS	Body temperature and pressure, saturated with water vapour (gas at 37 °C, measured barometric pressure, saturated)
ATPS	Ambient temperature and pressure, saturated (gas at ambient temperature and pressure, saturated with water vapour)

2. Blood phase

(a) Primary symbols (italic capitals)

Q	Blood volume
$\dot{Q}$	Blood volume per unit time
S	O_2 or CO_2 saturation of haemoglobin (as percentage of O_2 or CO_2 capacity)

(b) Secondary symbols (italic small letters)

a	Arterial blood
v	Venous blood
c	Capillary blood

Respiratory variable	Definition	Unit	Remarks, normal values
Lung volumes and capacities	*Subdivisions of the lung volume*[1]		

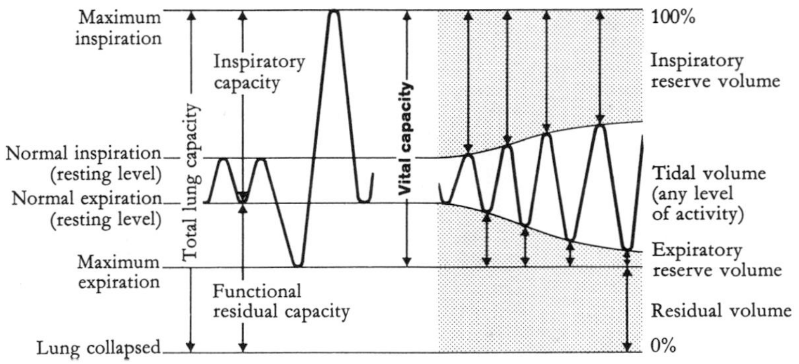

	The subdivisions on the right apply to all levels of respiratory effort and do not overlap. The capacities on the left include two or more of the primary subdivisions		All volumes to be corrected to BTPS (see also page 269). Measurements are usually made on the recumbent patient; rather higher values are obtained if the patient is sitting or standing[2]
Tidal volume (V_T)	The volume of air inspired and expired at each breath	1	For normal values see Table 1, page 550
Inspiratory reserve volume (IRV)	The maximum volume of air that can be additionally inspired after a normal inspiration	1	
Expiratory reserve volume (ERV)	The maximum volume of air that can be additional expired after a normal expiration	1	For normal values see Table 2, page 550

(For references see page 546)

Respiratory variable	Definition	Unit	Remarks, normal values
Residual volume (RV)	The volume of air remaining in the lungs after a maximum expiration	l	For normal values see Tables 2, 3 and 5, pages 550–551
Total lung capacity (TLC)	The volume of air contained in the lungs after a maximum inspiration	l	For normal values see Table 2, page 550, and Table 5, page 551. For determination in children see Figure 1, page 547. The total lung capacity can be calculated from the normal vital capacity as follows[3]: 15–34 years 0.8 35–49 years 0.75 } × vital capacity > 50 years 0.65
Vital capacity (VC)	The maximum volume of air that can be forcibly inspired after a maximum expiration (inspiratory vital capacity) or that can be forcibly expired after a maximum inspiration (expiratory vital capacity)	l	It is better to measure the inspiratory VC since this is reproducible even in diseased persons, whereas the expiratory VC may fluctuate as a result of the check-valve mechanism. For normal values see Table 2, page 550, and Tables 3–5, page 551. For measurement in ambulant or bedded patients with healthy lungs see Figures 3 and 4, page 547. The 'crying' VC of the newborn is about 0.14 l[4]
Inspiratory capacity (IC)	The maximum volume of air that can be inspired from the resting expiratory level	l	For normal values see Table 2, page 550
Functional residual capacity (FRC)	The volume of air in the lungs at the resting expiratory level	l	For normal values see Table 2, page 550. For determination in children see Figure 2, page 547. The FRC of the newborn is about 70 ml[4]
Ventilation			
Minute ventilation ($\dot{V}_T$)	The volume of air inspired or expired in one minute	$l\ min^{-1}$	Since the respiratory quotient in normal breathing at rest is less than 1, the inspiratory minute ventilation differs from the expiratory minute ventilation. The amount of the minute volume is a function mainly of the energy consumption of the body, the dead-space ventilation and the respiratory frequency, and is thus subject to large individual variations. For calculation of the normal value see ROSSIER et al.[5]. For normal measured values see Table 1, page 550
Alveolar ventilation ($\dot{V}_A$)	The volume of air entering the alveoli per minute, or the amount of alveolar air expired per minute	$l\ min^{-1}$	In a young man weighing 70 kg with an O_2 intake of 250 ml/min the alveolar ventilation must be at least 4.3 l/min if arterialization is to be complete[3]. The alveolar ventilation is calculated by means of BOHR's alveolar equation. The normal value is affected by postural changes and under resting conditions is 70–80%, under heavy loading about 85%, of the total ventilation; the remainder is the dead-space ventilation, or functional dead space[5, 6]

(For references see page 546)

Respiratory variable	Definition	Unit	Remarks, normal values
Respiratory time quotient	Ratio of the time of expiration to the time of inspiration		For normal values see Table 1, page 550
Mixing time	The time required for stabilization of the gas concentration in the lung–spirometer system		The mixing time is a measure of the degree of homogeneity of the intrapulmonary gas mixture and is obtained during determination of the residual volume by the closed-circuit method. Mixing is normally complete after 2–3 min. For helium methods see BRISCOE[7]
Tests of ventilatory function			
Maximum voluntary ventilation (MVV), *maximum breathing capacity* (MBC)	The maximum minute ventilation attainable by voluntary hyperventilation	$l\ min^{-1}$	Calculated from the value measured over 10–20 s. For determination from age and respiratory frequency see Figure 5, page 548. Normal value at a respiratory frequency of 50/min[8,9]: one-second forced expiratory volume × 37, or normal vital capacity × 30. For normal values in adults see Figure 6, page 548. For values used in the evaluation of permanent impairment see the literature[10]
Forced expiratory volume (FEV_t)	The volume of air expired per unit time during forced expiration following full inspiration	l	Usually measured during the first second (one-second volume, $FEV_{1.0}$). The following are also measured: $FEV_{0.5}$, $FEV_{3.0}$ and $FEV_{0.25-0.75}$. For normal values of $FEV_{1.0}$ in adults see Figure 7, page 548, and Table 5, page 551, in children Figure 10, page 549. For normal values in the UK and USA see the literature[10,11]
Percentage forced expiratory volume	The forced expiratory volume expressed as percentage of the vital capacity: $100\ FEV_t/VC$	%	For normal values see Table 5, page 551, and Figure 8, page 549
Maximum expiratory flow rate (MEFR), *peak flow rate*	The flow rate at a particular point during forced expiration	$l\ s^{-1}$	Measured directly by pneumotachograph or pneumatometer, or read off from spirograms. For normal values in adults and children see Table 6, page 551, and Figure 13, page 550
Maximum inspiratory flow rate (MIFR)	The flow rate at a particular point during forced inspiration	$l\ s^{-1}$	
Maximum mid-expiratory flow (MMF)	The flow rate during the middle half of a forced expiration	$l\ s^{-1}$	For normal values in adults see Figure 9, page 549
Pulmonary circulation			
Intravascular pressure	The ratio of the blood pressure in any part of the blood vessel to the atmospheric pressure	mm Hg	For normal values see page 553

(For references see page 546)

Respiratory variable	Definition	Unit	Remarks, normal values
Transmural pressure	The difference between the blood pressure in the vessel and the external pressure on the vessel	mm Hg	The pressure acting externally on the pulmonary arteries and veins is equal to the intrathoracic pressure
Driving pressure	The pressure difference between the two ends of any section of a blood vessel	mm Hg	
Vascular resistance	Ratio of the driving pressure in the pulmonary circulation to the minute volume	dyn s cm^{-5}	
Minute volume	The volume of blood passing through the lungs in one minute	l min^{-1}	Obtained by using FICK's principle, according to which the minute volume is equal to the ratio $\frac{O_2 \text{ intake (ml/min)}}{\text{arteriovenous } O_2 \text{ difference (ml/l)}}$ In resting adults the blood flow through the lungs is about 5 l/min
Intrapulmonary blood volume	The volume of blood contained between the origin of the pulmonary artery and the junction of the pulmonary veins with the left atrium	l	Normal value in adults about 900 ml. The volume of blood contained in the pulmonary capillaries in resting adults is 75–100 ml[3]. For normal values in children see BUCCI[12]
Ventilation/perfusion ratio ($\dot{V}_A/\dot{Q}$)	Ratio of the alveolar ventilation to the blood flow in the capillaries (perfusion)		In resting adults the alveolar ventilation is about 4 l/min and the blood flow about 5 l/min, so that the ventilation/perfusion ratio is about 0.8
Intrapulmonary shunt volume	Proportion of venous blood in the blood flowing through the aorta	vol%	Physiologically, the venous blood present derives from the bronchial venous blood flowing into the pulmonary veins, from intrapulmonary arteriovenous shunts, and to a lesser extent from coronary venous blood entering via the veins of THEBESIUS and via communications between the portal and pulmonary veins and the mediastinal and pulmonary veins. Normal value in young adults at rest 2 (0–4)%[13]
Blood gases and diffusion	The pressures given are partial pressures (the partial pressure of a component of a gas mixture is the pressure it would exert if it alone occupied the whole volume of the mixture). The pressure of an (ideal) gas mixture is equal to the sum of the partial pressures of its components		Most types of gas analysis apparatus give so-called dry percentages of the gases, also expressed as fractions F of the dry gas mixture. The pressure P of a component gas (in mm Hg) in the original mixture is given by $P_{gas} = F_{gas} (B - P_{H_2O})$, where B = barometric pressure (mm Hg), P_{H_2O} = 47 mm Hg at 37 °C
Alveolar O_2 pressure ($P_{A_{O_2}}$)		mm Hg	Adults[9]: 100 (95–105) mm Hg
Alveolar CO_2 pressure ($P_{A_{CO_2}}$)		mm Hg	Adults[9]: 40 (38–42) mm Hg
Arterial O_2 saturation (Sa_{O_2})		%	Adults[9]: 97 (95–99)%. See also page 570
Arterial O_2 pressure (Pa_{O_2})		mm Hg	Adults[9]: 80–100 mm Hg. See also page 570

Respiratory variable	Definition	Unit	Remarks, normal values
Arterial CO_2 pressure (Pa_{CO_2})		mm Hg	Adults[9]: 40 (38–42) mm Hg. See also page 570
Arterial pH value			Adults[9]: 7.4 (7.36–7.44). See also page 560
Diffusing capacity (D)	The rate at which a gas passes from the alveoli into the blood at a partial-pressure difference of 1 mm Hg	ml min^{-1} mm Hg^{-1}	Measured by using CO or O_2. The diffusing capacity is affected by constitution, age, lung volume, metabolic state and posture. For normal values in the lung itself (D_L) see Table 7, page 552. The value for CO in the lung is the sum of two components: (1) diffusion through the alveolar membrane (D_M), and (2) diffusion through the erythrocyte membrane into the lung capillaries and binding to haemoglobin ($\vartheta\, Vc$): $\frac{1}{D_L} = \frac{1}{D_M} + \frac{1}{\vartheta\, Vc}$ where ϑ is a velocity constant (dependent on Pc_{O_2}), Vc the volume of blood in the capillaries
Difference between alveolar and arterial partial pressure of O_2	$P_{AO_2} - Pa_{O_2}$	mm Hg	The normal value when breathing air is 10–15 mm Hg. The difference is due to (1) the admixture of venous blood with the arterialized blood from the alveoli (this mixture constitutes the arterial blood), (2) the non-uniformity of the ventilation-perfusion process in the different parts of the lung (even in healthy persons ventilation is in excess of perfusion or vice versa in some alveoli), and (3) the fall in partial pressure due to perfusion (of little consequence in healthy persons under normal conditions). The difficulty of calculating the last factor precisely is the reason for the wide fluctuations in published data on the diffusing capacity of the lungs for O_2
Respiratory mechanics			
Compliance (C)	The expansibility of the lungs and/or thorax expressed as the volume change per unit pressure change	l cm H_2O^{-1}	Normal values in *young men*[3]: Compliance of the lungs (C_L) about 0.2 l cm H_2O^{-1}; Compliance of the thorax (C_T) about 0.2 l cm H_2O^{-1}; Compliance of the lungs + thorax (C_{L+T}) about 0.1 l cm H_2O^{-1} where $\frac{1}{C_{L+T}} = \frac{1}{C_L} + \frac{1}{C_T}$. Compliance of the lungs in the *newborn*[4]: 5 ml cm H_2O^{-1}. Compliance of the lungs in *children*: see Figure 11, page 549. Compliance of the lungs in *adults*: see Table 9, page 552
Specific compliance	The ratio of compliance to functional residual capacity		Per litre of functional residual capacity[3]: Adults 0.05–0.06 l cm H_2O^{-1}; Newborn 0.065 l cm H_2O^{-1}
Elastance	Reciprocal of the compliance	cm H_2O l^{-1}	A measure of the elastic resistance of the lungs and thorax

Respiratory variable	Definition	Unit	Remarks, normal values
Nonelastic (viscous) resistances	Expressed as the pressure difference corresponding to unit ventilation	cm H_2O s l^{-1}	
Airway resistance	Resistance to flow in the airways		Can be measured by means of the body plethysmograph, usually with rapid superficial breathing (frequency 200/min). For normal values see Table 8, page 552. For values at normal respiratory frequency see JAEGER and OTIS[14]
Pulmonary tissue resistance	Frictional and deformational resistance of the pulmonary tissue		Obtained as the difference between the pulmonary total and airway resistances. For normal values see Table 8, page 552
Total pulmonary resistance	Airway resistance plus tissue resistance		Determined by measuring the intrathoracic or oesophageal pressure. In healthy younger subjects about 20% is tissue resistance and about 80% airway resistance. For normal values in children see Figure 12, page 549, in adults Table 8, page 552
Thoracic tissue resistance	Deformational resistance of the thoracic tissue		Obtained approximately as the difference between the total respiratory and total pulmonary resistances
Total (nonelastic) respiratory resistance	Total pulmonary resistance plus thoracic tissue resistance		Can be measured approximately by means of a pneumotachograph. Exact values can be obtained only by using a respirator ('iron lung') with complete relaxation of the muscles involved in respiration
Conductance	Reciprocal of the nonelastic resistance	l s^{-1} cm H_2O^{-1}	
Work of breathing (A)	The work required to overcome the elastic and nonelastic resistances of the lungs and thorax and the airway resistance: A = force × distance = pressure × volume	m kg or l atm	The total work of breathing can be precisely determined only by having the subject breathe passively in a respirator and measuring the pressures required for various minute ventilations. For a tidal volume of 500 ml and respiratory frequency of 15/min this method gives a total work of breathing of 0.315 kg m min^{-1} [15]. By ignoring the work required to overcome the thoracic tissue resistance, the work of breathing can be obtained from the respiratory loop (see the adjacent diagram). It is the sum of the products of the forces (measurable as pressures in the oesophagus) and corresponding tidal volumes. The respiratory loop can be calculated from the pneumotachogram and pressure curve or registered by means of a cathode-ray oscillograph or other directly recording instrument. For normal values of the components of the work of breathing for a single breath see Table 10, page 552

Volume–pressure diagram for a single breath (respiratory loop)[16]

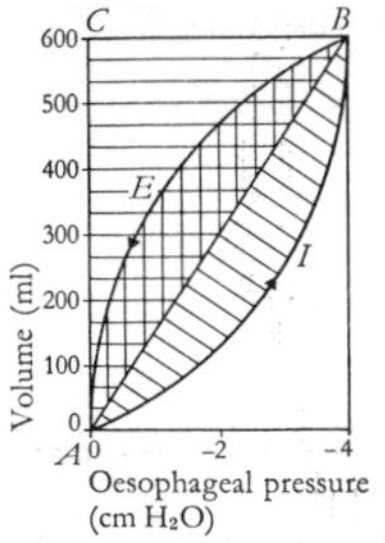

Area *AIBC* Total work done against the elastic and nonelastic resistances of the pulmonary tissue and the airway resistance

Area *AIB* Work done against the nonelastic resistance of the pulmonary tissue and the airway resistance during inspiration

Area *ABC* Work done against the elastic resistance of the pulmonary tissue during inspiration

Area *BEA* Work done against the nonelastic resistance of the pulmonary tissue and the airway resistance during expiration. Expiration does not require active work but takes place passively through the elastic contraction of the lung expanded during inspiration

References

1 PAPPENHEIMER et al., *Fed. Proc.*, **9**, 602 (1950).
2 WHITFIELD et al., *Brit. J. soc. Med.*, **4**, 86 (1950); HAMM and KLEINSORG, *Dtsch. Arch. klin. Med.*, **203**, 234 (1956); MORENO and LYONS, *J. appl. Physiol.*, **16**, 27 (1961); GEUBELLE and GOFFIN, *Acta paediat. (Uppsala)*, **51**, 255 (1962).
3 COMROE et al., *The Lung*, 2nd ed., Year Book Medical Publishers, Chicago, 1962.
4 COOK et al., *Advanc. Pediat.*, **11**, 11 (1960).
5 ROSSIER et al., *Physiologie und Pathophysiologie der Atmung*, 2nd ed., Springer, Berlin, 1958.
6 FRUHMANN and STURM, *Z. ges. exp. Med.*, **139**, 357 (1965).
7 BRISCOE, W. A., *Clin. Sci.*, **11**, 45 (1952).
8 BÜHLMANN et al., *Schweiz. med. Wschr.*, **91**, 105 (1961).
9 HERTZ, C.W., *Internist (Berl.)*, **1**, 80 (1960).
10 Committee on Rating of Mental and Physical Impairment, *J. Amer. med. Ass.*, **194**, 919 (1965).
11 COTES et al., *Brit. med. J.*, **1**, 1016 (1966).
12 BUCCI et al., *J. Pediat.*, **58**, 820 (1961).
13 FRUHMANN, G., *Z. ges. exp. Med.*, **139**, 391 (1965).
14 JAEGER and OTIS, *J. appl. Physiol.*, **19**, 813 (1964).
15 OTIS et al., *J. appl. Physiol.*, **2**, 592 (1950); OTIS, A.B., *Physiol. Rev.*, **34**, 449 (1954).
16 HAMM et al., *Z. klin. Med.*, **157**, 133 (1962).

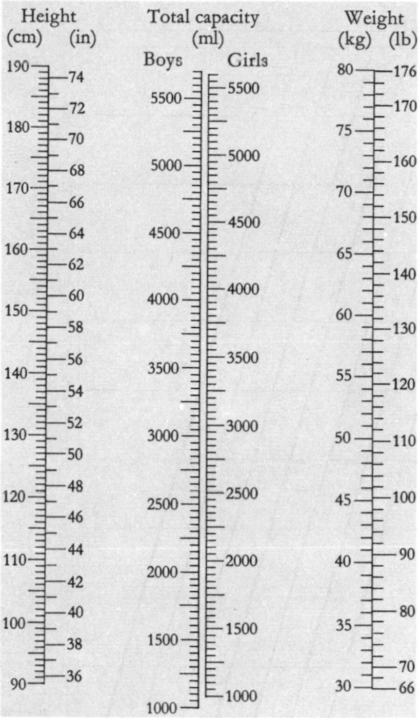

Fig. 1. Determination of total lung capacity in children (from LYONS and TANNER, *J. appl. Physiol.*, **17**, 601 [1962])

Fig. 2. Determination of functional residual capacity in children (from LYONS and TANNER, *J. appl. Physiol.*, **17**, 601 [1962]) ▼

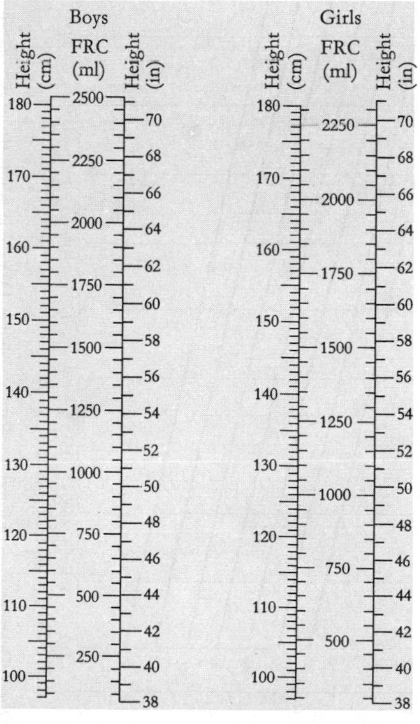

Fig. 3. Determination of vital capacity in healthy adults (from MILLER et al., *J. appl. Physiol.*, **14**, 157 [1959]) ▶

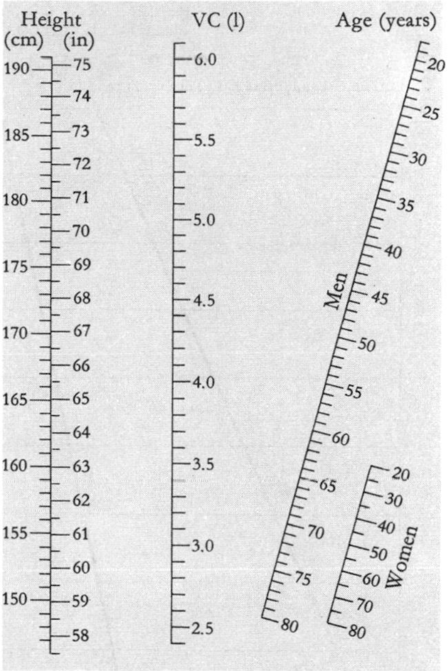

Fig. 4. Determination of vital capacity in recumbent healthy adults (from BALDWIN et al., *Medicine [Baltimore]*, **27**, 243 [1948]) ▼

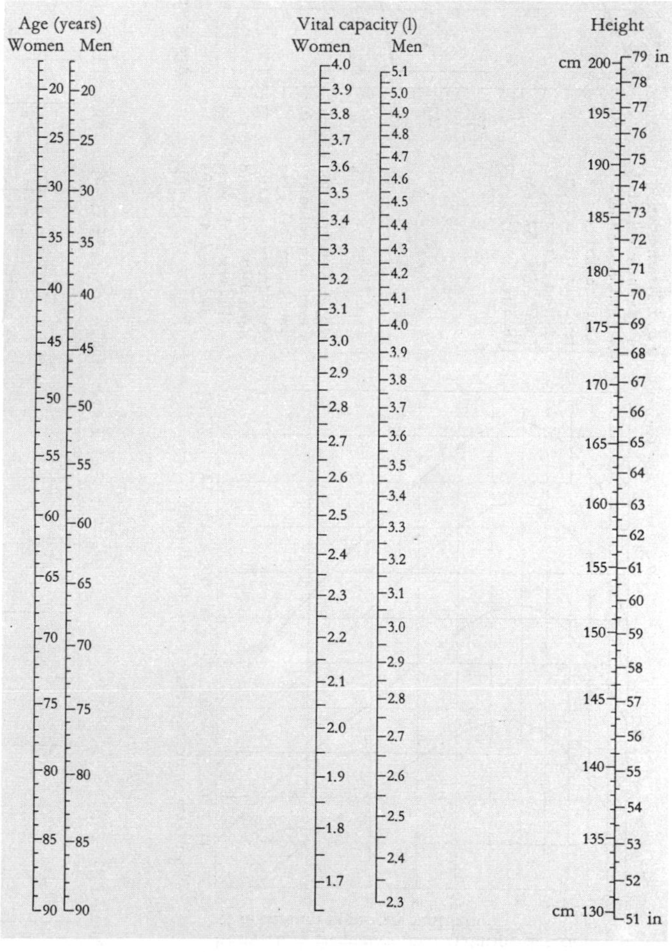

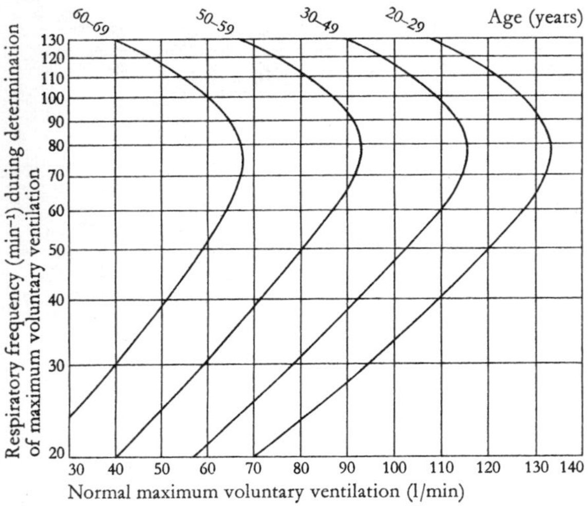

Fig. 5. Determination of maximum voluntary ventilation as a function of respiratory frequency (from FRUHMANN and ZIEGLER, *Z. klin. Med.*, **157**, 586 [1963])

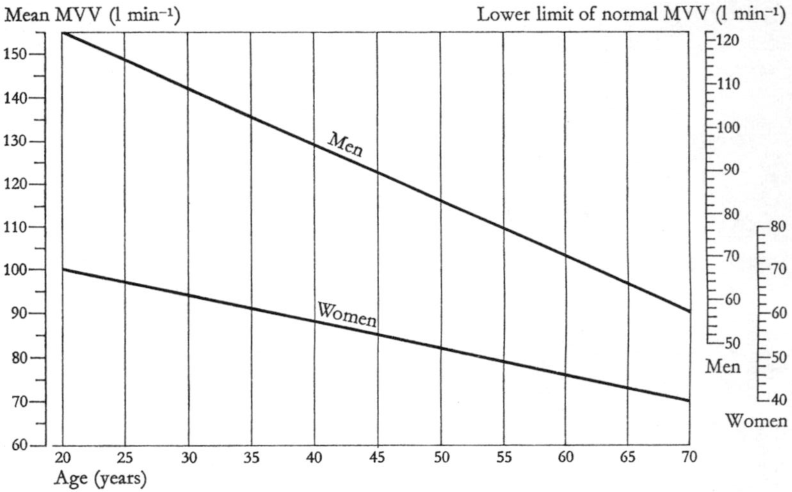

Fig. 6. Determination of maximum voluntary ventilation (MVV) in adults (respiratory frequency 40/min) (from BIRATH et al., *Acta med. scand.*, **173**, 193 [1963])

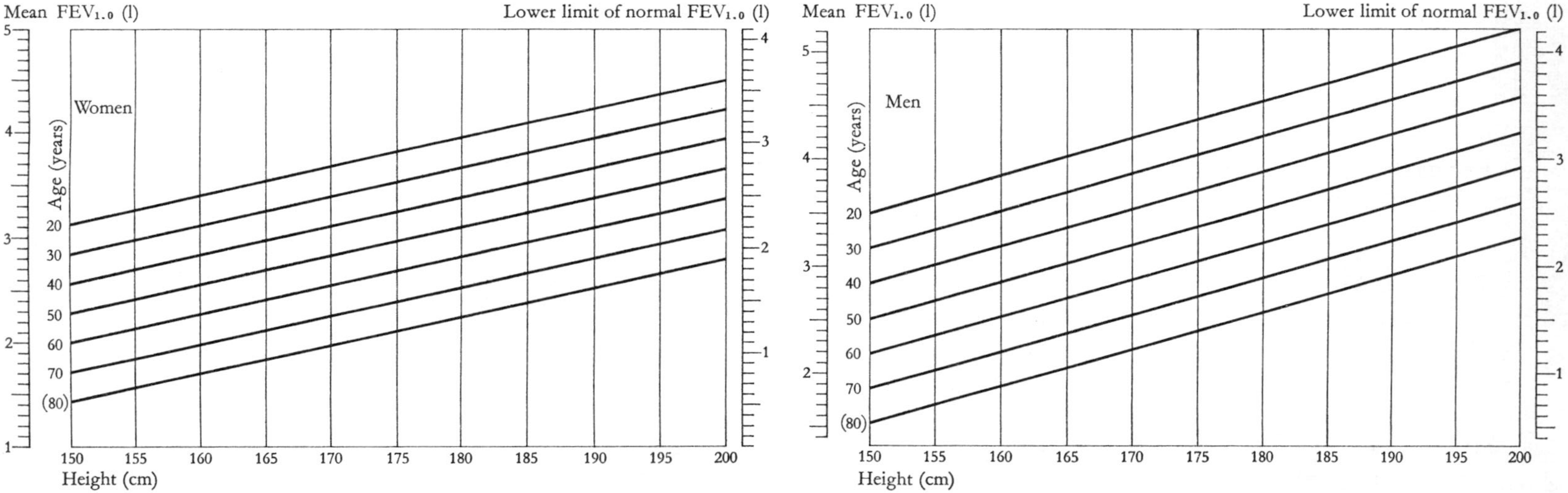

Fig. 7. Determination of forced expiratory volume ($FEV_{1.0}$) in adults (from BERGLUND et al., *Acta med. scand.*, **173**, 185 [1963])

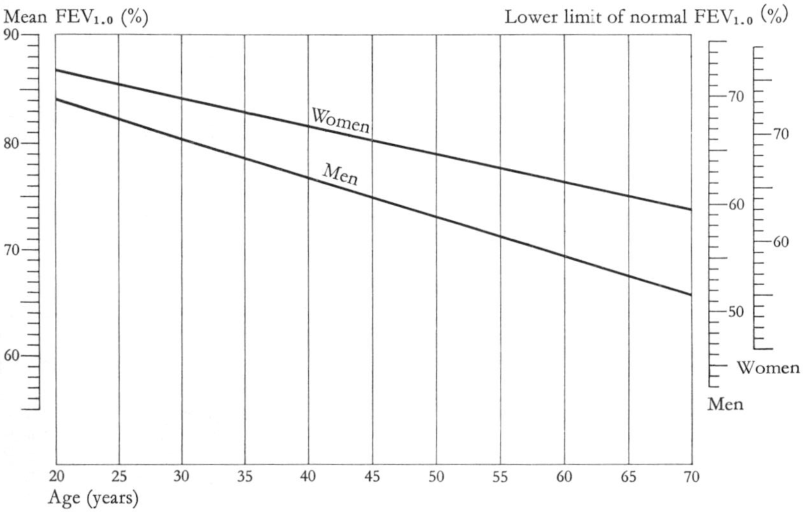

Fig. 8. Determination of percentage forced expiratory volume ($FEV_{1.0}$) in adults (from BERGLUND et al., *Acta med. scand.*, **173**, 185 [1963])

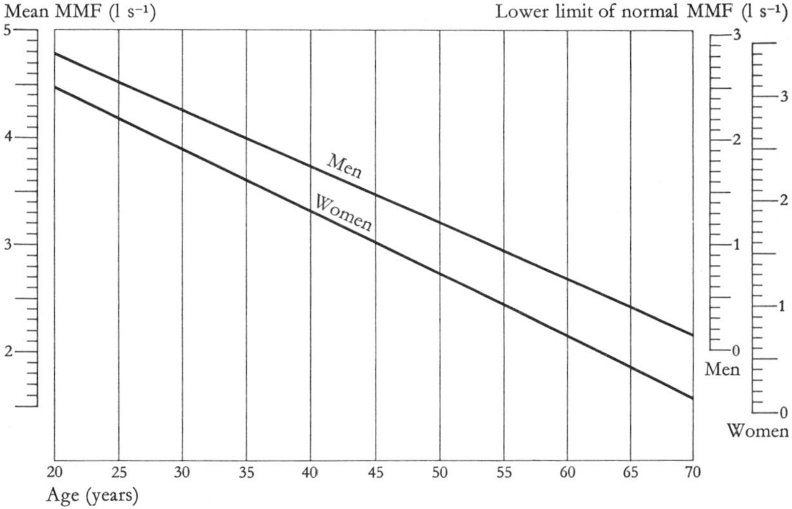

Fig. 9. Determination of maximum mid-expiratory flow (MMF) in adults (from BIRATH et al., *Acta med. scand.*, **173**, 193 [1963])

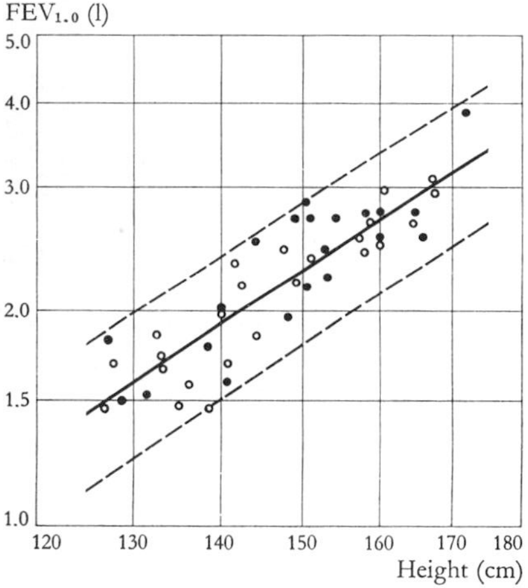

Fig. 10

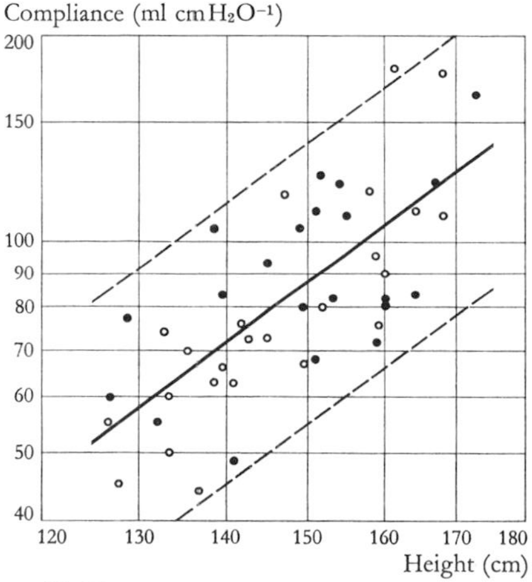

Fig. 11

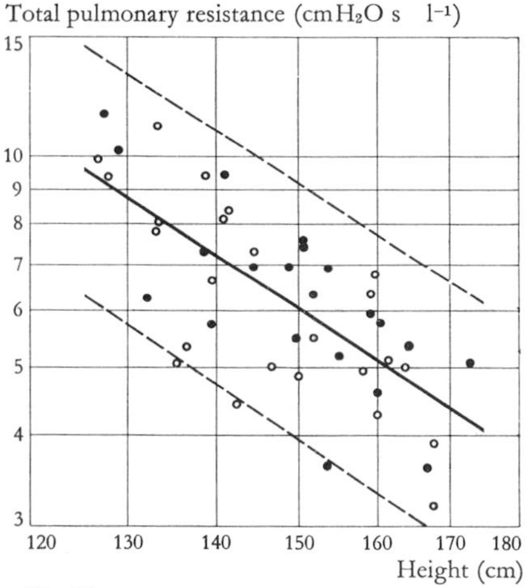

Fig. 12

Figs. 10–12. Determination of forced expiratory volume ($FEV_{1.0}$), compliance and total pulmonary resistance in children (from ENGSTRÖM et al., *Acta paediat. [Uppsala]*, **51**, 68 [1962])

● Boys
○ Girls
—— Regression line
----- 95% confidence limits

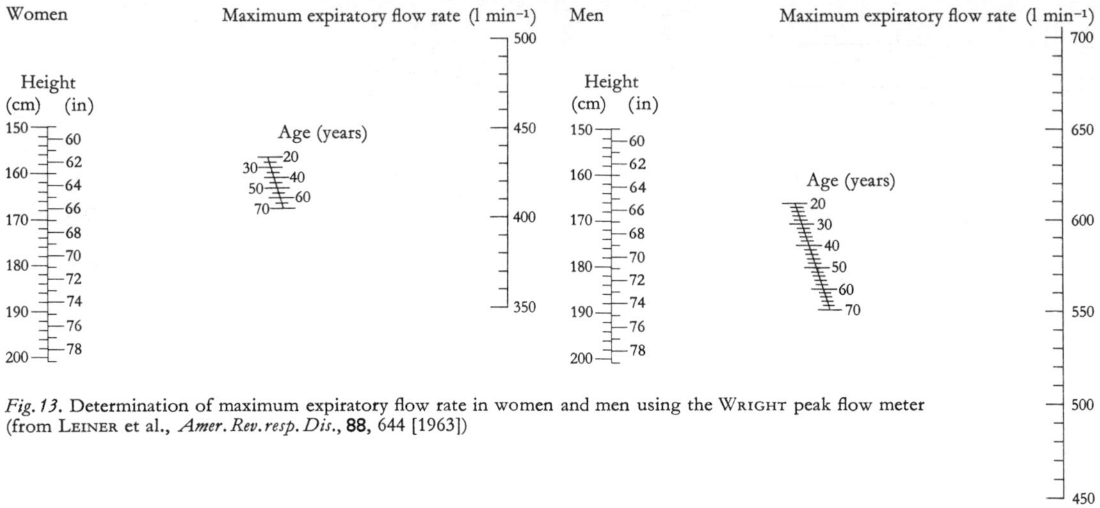

Fig. 13. Determination of maximum expiratory flow rate in women and men using the WRIGHT peak flow meter (from LEINER et al., *Amer. Rev. resp. Dis.*, **88**, 644 [1963])

Table 1 Respiratory frequency, tidal volume, minute ventilation and respiratory time quotient in children and adults*

	Respiratory frequency (min^{-1})		Tidal volume (ml)		Minute ventilation ($l\ min^{-1}$)		Respiratory time quotient		Reference
	Mean	95% range (extreme range in brackets)	Mean	95% range (extreme range in brackets)	Mean	95% range (extreme range in brackets)	Mean	95% range (extreme range in brackets)	
Newborn, 4–6 days	49.7	(28.0–69.0)	17.3	(9.5–25.9)	0.83	(0.50–1.48)	1.29	(0.97–2.09)	1
Infants, 11 weeks	62.8	(40.0–87.0)	17.5	(11.0–28.1)	1.03	(0.75–1.37)	1.27	(1.09–1.58)	1
Children, 2–3 years	23.7	(18.9–30.3)	122	(77–149)	2.8	(2.3–4.0)	1.46	(0.92–1.79)	1
Children, 4–5 years	23.2	(11.3–30.2)	138	(147–275)	4.0	(3.1–4.7)	1.43	(1.27–1.55)	1
Children, 6–7 years	21.1	(17.4–24.0)	203	(180–223)	4.3	(3.7–4.9)	1.60	(1.15–2.52)	1
Boys, 12 years	16.3	7.9–24.7	305	185–425	4.8	3.7–5.8	–	–	2
Girls, 12 years	16.1	9.8–22.4	289	189–389	4.5	3.1–6.0	–	–	2
Boys, 14 years	17.0	12.8–21.2	316	196–436	5.3	3.8–6.8	–	–	2
Girls, 14 years	15.6	11.4–19.8	315	235–395	4.9	3.6–6.1	–	–	2
Boys, 16 years	15.6	9.3–21.9	344	184–504	5.1	3.4–6.8	–	–	2
Girls, 16 years	15.2	8.9–21.5	282	162–402	4.2	2.5–5.9	–	–	2
Adults, 20–39 years	17.2	–	–	–	8.5	2.5–14.5	1.35	0.79–1.91	3
Adults, 40–59 years	16.9	–	–	–	9.5	–	1.33	0.85–1.81	3
Adults, 60 years and over	16.3	–	–	–	10.5	–	1.54	0.98–2.10	3
Men, resting	11.7	(10.1–13.1)	630	–	7.4	(5.8–10.3)	–	–	4
Men, light work (500 m kg min^{-1})	17.1	(15.7–18.2)	1670	–	28.6	(27.3–30.9)	–	–	4
Men, heavy work (800 m kg min^{-1})	21.2	(18.6–23.3)	2030	–	43	(39–45)	–	–	4
Women, resting	11.7	–	390	–	4.6	–	–	–	4
Women, light work (300 m kg min^{-1})	19.0	–	860	–	16.4	–	–	–	4

1 BLÖMER and HAHN, *Z. Kinderheilk.*, **87**, 466 (1963).
2 SHOCK, N.W., in DITTMER and GREBE (Eds.), *Handbook of Respiration*, Saunders, Philadelphia, 1958, page 44.
3 FRUHMANN, G., *Z. exp. Med.*, **138**, 1 (1964).
4 TAYLOR, C., *Amer. J. Physiol.*, **135**, 27 (1941).
* At rest unless otherwise stated.

Table 2 Lung volumes and capacities in resting adults

	50 young men[1] (recumbent)		50 young women[1] (recumbent)		11 men over 50 years[2] (semi-recumbent)	
	Mean	*s*	Mean	*s*	Mean	*s*
Age (years)	22.9	3.3	23.1	3.4	61.5	6.8
Height (in and *cm*)	69.3	2.0	64.3	1.7	66.3	1.9
	176.2	*5.1*	*163.4*	*4.2*	*169.0*	*4.8*
Weight (lb and *kg*)	159.5	24.7	126.2	20.4	145.2	27.4
	72.5	*11.2*	*57.2*	*9.4*	*65.9*	*12.4*
Inspiratory capacity (l)	3.79	0.52	2.42	0.36	2.61	0.61
Expiratory reserve volume (l)	0.98	0.26	0.73	0.19	1.01	0.38
Vital capacity (l)	4.78	0.59	3.14	0.41	3.48	0.48

	50 young men[1] (recumbent)		50 young women[1] (recumbent)		11 men over 50 years[2] (semi-recumbent)	
	Mean	*s*	Mean	*s*	Mean	*s*
Residual volume (l)	1.19	0.35	1.10	0.30	2.43	0.50
Functional residual capacity (l)	2.18	0.50	1.82	0.39	3.44	0.74
Total capacity (l)	5.97	0.81	4.24	0.57	5.92	0.57
Relative residual capacity (% of total capacity)	19.8	4.4	25.9	5.0	40.9	7.1

1 From KALTREIDER et al., *Amer. Rev. Tuberc.*, **37**, 662 (1938).
2 From GREIFENSTEIN et al., *J. appl. Physiol.*, **4**, 641 (1952).

Table 3 Residual volume and vital capacity as functions of age[1]

Age (years)	Number	Vital capacity (ml)		Residual volume (ml)		Residual volume as percentage of total lung capacity (%)	
		Mean	*s*	Mean	*s*	Mean	*s*
Men							
9–13	16	2690	520	540	180	17.3	4.3
14–19	9–10	4030	540	830	340	17.2	4.3
20–29	20–26	5440	720	1410	310	20.6	4.0
30–39	15–19	5030	700	1510	360	22.2	4.0
40–49	14–17	4530	500	1690	410	26.8	5.2
50–59	18	4650	970	1740	380	27.8	4.4
60–75	7–11	3860	810	1760	330	33.9	5.2
Women							
14–19	2–3	3330	(300)	820	(220)	19.5	(5.0)
20–29	9–11	3600	390	1290	340	25.7	6.2
30–39	3	3460	(380)	1310	(280)	28.0	(5.0)
40–49	3–4	3680	(710)	1390	(490)	30.0	(8.7)
50–59	4	3250	(370)	1300	(360)	28.8	(4.6)
60–64	2–3	3140	(400)	1200	(280)	29.5	(4.6)

[1] From Zehnder, H., *Helv. med. Acta*, **27**, 245 (1960).

Table 4 Vital capacity in children as a function of age and sex[1]

Age (years)	Number	Height (in)	Height (*cm*)	Vital capacity (ml)* Mean	*s*	Extreme range
Boys						
4.........	6	40.7	*103.4*	855	–	540– 970
5.........	20	42.0	*106.8*	1001	–	650–1240
6.........	62	44.2	*112.2*	1246	197	860–1730
7.........	112	46.0	*116.9*	1393	210	970–2380
8.........	98	47.9	*121.8*	1585	238	1130–2270
9.........	110	51.1	*129.9*	1852	266	1300–2480
10.........	87	52.5	*133.4*	2022	283	1510–2860
11.........	113	54.2	*137.8*	2150	292	1400–3020
12.........	114	56.1	*142.4*	2357	367	1400–3560
13.........	132	58.4	*148.7*	2655	464	1840–4300
14.........	177	60.9	*154.8*	2929	523	1510–4640
15.........	155	62.9	*159.9*	3397	595	2000–4750
16.........	67	65.8	*167.2*	3699	619	2270–4640
17.........	23	67.4	*171.4*	4078	–	2590–4860
Girls						
4.........	9	37.5	*95.4*	717	–	380– 920
5.........	26	41.9	*106.4*	959	–	650–1300
6.........	62	43.8	*111.5*	1172	176	760–1730
7.........	81	45.0	*114.4*	1326	196	970–1940
8.........	76	47.6	*121.0*	1513	215	860–2100
9.........	73	50.0	*127.0*	1634	247	1080–2430
10.........	117	52.0	*132.1*	1806	295	970–2590
11.........	119	53.4	*135.9*	1943	260	1350–2750
12.........	135	56.7	*144.0*	2217	370	1510–3130
13.........	162	59.6	*151.4*	2537	442	1670–3890
14.........	192	61.6	*156.6*	2816	390	2050–4100
15.........	131	62.1	*157.8*	2918	446	2050–4000
16.........	29	63.0	*160.1*	3000	–	2210–3780
17.........	7	64.0	*162.6*	3178	–	2430–3670

[1] From Stewart and Sheets, *Amer. J. Dis. Child.*, **24**, 83, 451 (1922).
* Original values increased by 8% as an approximate conversion to BTPS (cf. Bernstein et al., *J. Allergy*, **30**, 514 [1959]).

Table 5 Ratios of vital capacity (VC), residual volume (RV), total lung capacity (TLC) and forced expiratory volume ($FEV_{1.0}$) to the cube of the height, and other ratios (volumes in litres, heights in metres)[1]

Age (years)	$\frac{VC}{H^3}$	$\frac{RV}{H^3}$	$\frac{TLC}{H^3}$	$\frac{100\,RV}{TLC}$	$\frac{FEV_{1.0}}{H^3}$	$\frac{FEV_{1.0}}{VC}$
18–19	0.990	0.240	1.230	19.5	0.812	82.0
20–29	1.025	0.275	1.300	21.0	0.818	80.0
30–34	1.020	0.300	1.300	22.5	0.795	78.0
35–39	1.010	0.310	1.320	23.5	0.778	77.0
40–44	1.000	0.320	1.320	24.3	0.757	75.5
45–49	0.990	0.330	1.320	25.0	0.737	74.5
50–54	0.970	0.350	1.320	26.5	0.713	73.5
55–59	0.950	0.370	1.320	28.0	0.684	72.0
60–64	0.930	0.390	1.320	29.5	0.651	70.0
$2V \times 100$* .	17%	31%	22%	11%	19%	13%
Number	3153	1098	1098	1098	2536	2536

* V = Coefficient of variance (see page 159).

[1] From Cara and Martin, in Denolin et al. (Eds.), *L'exploration fonctionnelle pulmonaire*, Flammarion, Paris, 1964, page 112.

Table 6 Maximum expiratory flow rate (MEFR) in children and adults

Age (years)		Number	Method	MEFR ($l\ s^{-1}$) Mean	*s*	Reference
Children 3–5		30	Pneumotachograph	1.8	0.4	1
Men	9–13	16	Hadorn pneumatometer	5.0	0.8	2
	14–19	10		7.1	1.3	2
	20–29	20		8.0	0.9	2
	32–39	16		7.9	1.1	2
	40–49	16		7.6	1.0	2
	50–59	17		7.3	1.2	2
	60–75	11		6.8	1.2	2
Women	14–19	3		5.5	(0.9)	2
	20–29	11		5.8	0.7	2
	30–39	3		6.0	(0.8)	2
	40–49	4		5.1	(0.6)	2
	50–59	4		4.6	(0.5)	2
	60–64	3		5.0	(0.2)	2
Adults	40	37	'Minimus' pneumatometer	6.85	1.89	3

[1] Rivera and Snider, *Pediatrics*, **30**, 117 (1962).
[2] Zehnder, H., *Helv. med. Acta*, **87**, 245 (1960).
[3] Fabel and Hamm, *Dtsch. med. Wschr.*, **87**, 2361 (1962).

Table 7 Diffusing capacity of the lungs (D_L) in resting subjects

Method		Number	Age (years)	D_L (ml min^{-1} mm Hg^{-1}) Mean	95% range (extreme range in brackets)	Reference	Remarks
CO methods	'Steady state' method	5	23–45	17	(10.5–28.0)	1	Calculation of mean alveolar CO pressure
	'Steady state' method	18	18–41	17.6	(10.5–28.7)	2	Measurement of CO pressure in expired alveolar air
		7	26–36	20.6	9.6–31.6	3	
	Single-breath method	28	8–72	24.9	(11.0–37.5)	4	Breath-holding for 10 s
		20	4–13	17.4*	4.8–30.0	5	
		3	24–46	35.6	(28.4–41.6)	6	
	Continuous breathing method	15	24–60	25	(19–31)	7	Using ^{14}CO
O_2 methods	'Steady state' method	6	28–36	21	(12–36)	8	
		9	22–28	47	–	9	
	Single-breath method	5	24–46	33	(23–45)	6	Using $^{17}O_2$

* Dependent on body surface area:

Surface area (m^2)	D_L	Surface area (m^2)	D_L
0.8	12.8	1.4	25.4
1.0	17.0	1.6	29.6
1.2	21.2	1.8	33.8

[1] Filley et al., *J. clin. Invest.*, **33**, 530 (1954).
[2] Bates et al., *J. Physiol.*, **129**, 237 (1955).
[3] Macklem and Becklake, *Amer. Rev. resp. Dis.*, **87**, 47 (1963).
[4] Ogilvie et al., *J. clin. Invest.*, **36**, 1 (1957).
[5] Giammona and Daly, *Amer. J. Dis. Child.*, **110**, 144 (1965).
[6] Hyde et al., *J. clin. Invest.*, **45**, 1178 (1966).
[7] Kruhøffer, P., *Acta physiol. scand.*, **32**, 106 (1954).
[8] Lilienthal et al., *Amer. J. Physiol.*, **147**, 199 (1946).
[9] Haab et al., *Helv. physiol. pharmacol. Acta*, **23**, C23 (1965).

Table 8 Respiratory resistances in children and adults

	Number	Age (years)	Resistance (cm H_2O s l^{-1}) Mean	s	Reference
Airway resistance	5	4–6	1.93	0.5	1
	5	10–13	1.49	0.2	1
	5	10	2.26	0.73	2
	21	22–57	1.50	0.49	3
	12 men	24–46	0.96	0.27	2, 4
	7 women	18–30	1.46	0.47	2, 4
Pulmonary tissue resistance	5	10	1.31	0.37	2
	12 men	24–46	0.29	0.12	2, 4
	7 women	18–30	0.50	0.15	2, 4
Total pulmonary resistance	5	10	3.57	0.98	2
	12 men	24–46	1.25	0.28	2, 4
	7 women	18–30	1.96	0.45	2, 4
	11	18–47	1.9	0.6	5
	21	50–89	2.8	0.8	5
	7	26–36	1.7	1.1	6
	36	–	2.59	0.68	7
Thoracic tissue resistance	36	–	1.37	0.63	7
Total respiratory resistance	36	–	3.96	0.65	7

[1] Giammona and Daly, *Amer. J. Dis. Child.*, **110**, 144 (1965).
[2] Bachofen and Scherrer, *J. clin. Invest.*, **46**, 133 (1967).
[3] DuBois et al., *J. clin. Invest.*, **35**, 327 (1956).
[4] Bachofen, H., *Helv. med. Acta*, **33**, 108 (1966).
[5] Frank et al., *J. clin. Invest.*, **36**, 1680 (1957).
[6] Macklem and Becklake, *Amer. Rev. resp. Dis.*, **87**, 47 (1963).
[7] Jaeger, M., *Schweiz. med. Wschr.*, **92**, 67 (1962).

Table 9 Compliance of the lungs (C_L) in resting adults and children

Number	Age (years)	C_L (ml cm H_2O^{-1}) Mean	s	Reference	Remarks
11	18–47	150	27	1	
21	50–89	131	38	1	
12	39	213	60	2	Respiratory frequency 20/min
7	26–36	189	34	3	
12 men	24–46	260	60	4	
7 women	18–30	160	50	4, 5	
5	10	83	10.2	5	

[1] Frank et al., *J. clin. Invest.*, **36**, 1680 (1957).
[2] Hamm et al., *Z. klin. Med.*, **157**, 133 (1962).
[3] Macklem and Becklake, *Amer. Rev. resp. Dis.*, **87**, 47 (1963).
[4] Bachofen, H., *Helv. med. Acta*, **33**, 108 (1966).
[5] Bachofen and Scherrer, *J. clin. Invest.*, **46**, 133 (1967).

Table 10 Work of breathing per breath per millilitre tidal volume in adults[1]

	g cm ml^{-1} Mean	s
Total inspiratory work	2.40	0.50
Elastic inspiratory work	1.80	0.35
Nonelastic inspiratory plus nonelastic expiratory work	1.40	0.30

[1] Hamm and Schölmerich, *Klin. Wschr.*, **42**, 1108 (1964).

Blood pressure in various vessels (mm Hg)[1]

	Systolic pressure		Diastolic pressure		Mean pressure		Method
	Mean	Range	Mean	Range	Mean	Range	
Right atrium	–	–	–	–	3.5	2.5–6.0	Right heart catheterization
Left atrium	–	–	–	–	6.6	6–9	Left heart catheterization
Right ventricle	25	17.0–31.5	0	−0.5 to +7.0	–	–	Right heart catheterization
Left ventricle	120	105–150	0	−0.5 to +7.0	–	–	Left heart catheterization
Pulmonary artery ...	20	11–29	9	4–13	–	8–19	Right heart catheterization
Pulmonary arterioles	15	–	5	–	–	5–13	Right heart catheterization
Pulmonary veins....	4	–	8	–	5	3–8	Left or right heart catheterization
Vena cava	–	–	–	–	−1	−5 to +4	Right heart catheterization

Arterial blood pressure

Various methods of measuring blood pressure have been proposed[2–6], and special techniques have been developed for children[7]. When not otherwise defined, arterial blood pressure means that measured indirectly in the brachial artery of the upper arm. The method is usually Korotkoff's auscultatory method, but palpatory and oscillometric techniques can also be used. Standardization of the auscultatory method has been proposed by the American Heart Association and the Cardiological Society of Great Britain and Ireland[2] as well as by the World Health Organization[5]. Comparison with intra-arterial measurements has shown that in persons of normal weight the auscultatory method gives readings variously estimated at 10 mm Hg[4] and 25 mm Hg[8] too low for the systolic pressure and at a few mm Hg too high[4] and too low[8] for the diastolic pressure. The relationship between the circumference of the arm and the size of the cuff is important[4–7]. Exact blood pressure data are best obtained by continuous intra-arterial measurement. In infants the palpatory and oscillometric methods are better than the auscultatory[9].

Measured values of the arterial blood pressure depend on the level of the arm in relation to that of the heart[10], and determinations should therefore be made with the arm held at the level of the aortic valve. Occasionally there are differences in pressure between the two arms[11], so that at a first examination measurements should be made in both. There are also differences in pressure depending on whether the subject is lying down, sitting or standing. A precise determination of the resting blood pressure is not normally made, but its measurement under so-called 'basal' conditions has been suggested[2,5].

The arterial blood pressure varies during the course of the day[12] and is highest in the early evening, lowest during sleep between 1 a.m. and 4 a.m. In the newborn, the arterial blood pressure depends on the time of tying the umbilical cord and falls during the first hours of life[13,14]. Berger et al.[14] record mean values of 87 mm Hg for the systolic pressure and 59 mm Hg for the diastolic pressure a few minutes after birth; during the following 2 hours these pressures fell by 15–20 mm Hg after which they rose slowly again. In premature infants the arterial blood pressure tends to be lower than in full-term infants[15]. In children the arterial blood pressure increases gradually with age. Between 12 and 14 years, however, the diastolic pressure tends to fall[16,17], i.e., in the period when sex differences become well marked. In young persons the arterial blood pressure appears to depend mainly on the degree of maturity[17,18], and abnormally high values in the absence of organic disease point to vasomotor instability. The extent to which the arterial blood pressure in adults depends on age has also been studied[3,19–21]. Other factors probably affecting arterial blood pressure in adults are weight[19,21], bodily constitution[3,21], heredity[22] and environment[23]. Light or moderate physical activity seems to have little effect on the arterial blood pressure, but during very heavy work the systolic pressure often rises to over 180 mm Hg[24], whereas the diastolic pressure increases only slightly. The arterial blood pressure often rises during emotional stress[25]. In early pregnancy it tends to be low but rises towards term[26].

Hypertension. The limiting value for hypertension is usually taken as a systolic pressure of 140–150 mm Hg and a diastolic pressure of 90 mm Hg, regardless of age[6,27], whereby particular attention must be paid to the diastolic pressure (diastolic hypertension). According to Master et al.[3], the 'clinical' normal range of the systolic or diastolic blood pressure in adults is given by the mean value $+ 1.282\,s$, the lower limit of hypertension by the mean $+ 2\,s$. The blood pressure associated with the lowest mortality in men aged 30–59 and women aged 20–49 (according to the Society of Actuaries[28]) is $<$ 130 mm Hg systolic, $<$ 70 mm Hg diastolic.

Arterial blood pressure (mm Hg) at various ages

Age	Systolic				Diastolic				Reference
	Men		Women		Men		Women		
	Mean	s	Mean	s	Mean	s	Mean	s	
1 day..........	70	5							33
3 days.........	72	6							33
9 days.........	73	6							33
3 weeks	77	5							33
3 months	86	5							33
6–12 months ...	89	14.5	93	9.1	60	10.0	62	9.3	34
1 year	96	15.2	95	11.9	66	12.3	65	15.0	34
2 years	99	12.4	92	12.2	64	12.3	60	11.7	34
3 years	100	12.4	100	11.2	67	11.7	64	8.3	34
4 years	99	10.1	99	10.6	65	5.1	66	9.8	34
5 years	92	6.0	92	6.5	62	7.5	62	6.5	35
6 years	94	6.5	94	7.0	64	7.5	64	7.0	35
7 years	97	6.5	97	7.0	65	7.5	66	7.5	35
8 years	100	6.5	100	7.0	67	7.0	68	7.0	35
9 years	101	6.5	101	7.0	68	6.5	69	7.0	35
10 years	103	6.5	103	7.0	69	6.0	70	6.5	35
11 years	104	6.5	104	7.0	70	5.5	71	6.5	35
12 years	106	6.5	106	7.0	71	5.0	72	7.0	35
13 years	108	6.5	108	6.5	72	5.0	73	7.5	35
14 years	110	6.5	110	6.5	73	5.0	74	8.5	35
15 years	112	7.0	112	7.0	75	5.5	76	9.5	35

Age	Systolic				Diastolic				Reference
	Men		Women		Men		Women		
	Mean	s	Mean	s	Mean	s	Mean	s	
16 years	118	12.2	116	12.1	73	10.3	72	9.6	2
17 years	121	12.9	116	11.5	74	9.4	72	9.2	2
18 years	120	12.0	116	11.4	74	10.0	72	8.6	2
19 years	122	15.0	115	11.9	75	10.3	71	8.9	2
20–24 years	123	13.8	116	11.8	76	9.9	72	9.7	2
25–29 years	125	12.6	117	11.4	78	9.0	74	9.1	2
30–34 years	126	13.6	120	14.0	79	9.7	75	10.8	2
35–39 years	127	14.2	124	13.9	80	10.4	78	10.0	2
40–44 years	129	15.1	127	17.1	81	9.5	80	10.6	2
45–49 years	130	16.9	131	19.5	82	10.8	82	11.6	2
50–54 years	135	19.2	137	21.3	83	11.3	84	12.4	2
55–59 years	138	18.8	139	21.4	84	11.4	84	11.7	2
60–64 years	142	21.1	144	22.3	85	12.4	85	13.0	2
65–69 years	143	26.0	154	29.0	83	9.9	85	13.8	36
70–74 years	145	26.3	159	25.8	82	15.3	85	15.3	36
75–79 years	146	21.6	158	26.3	81	12.9	84	13.1	36
80–84 years	145	25.6	157	28.0	82	9.9	83	13.1	36
85–89 years	145	24.2	154	27.9	79	14.9	82	17.3	36
90–94 years	145	23.4	150	23.6	78	12.1	79	12.1	36
95–106 years ...	145	27.5	149	23.5	78	12.7	81	12.5	36

Venous blood pressure

The venous blood pressure rises with increasing distance from the heart, so that the highest pressure is in the peripheral vessels. It varies according to the position of the vein in relation to the right atrium, a result of the varying effect of gravity. The venous pressure is usually measured in the median basilic vein of the right arm at the level of the tricuspid valve. In the newborn the venous pressure depends on the time of tying of the umbilical cord[29].

Venous blood pressure (mm Hg)[30] (median basilic vein at elbow)

	Mean	Range
Children, 3–5 years	3.4	2.2– 4.6
5–10 years	4.3	2.4– 5.4
Adults, men	7.4	3.7–10.3
women	6.9	4.4– 9.4
Dorsal metacarpal veins	9.6	5.2–12.5
Femoral vein	8.2	7.2– 9.4
Abdominal veins	8.5	5.2–11.8
Long saphenous vein	11.0	8.1–14.0
Dorsal digital veins of foot	12.9	9.1–15.4

Capillary blood pressure (mm Hg) (at base of finger nail, hand at level of heart)

	Mean	Range
Direct measurement[31]		
arterial limb	32	21–48
venous limb	12	6–18
Indirect (bloodless) measurement[32]		
arterioles	47	–
capillaries	27	–

References

1 LUISADA, A. A., in DITTMER and GREBE (Eds.), *Handbook of Circulation*, Saunders, Philadelphia, 1959, page 112.
2 BORDLEY et al., *Circulation*, **4**, 503 (1951).
3 MASTER et al., *Normal Blood Pressure and Hypertension*, Lea & Febiger, Philadelphia, 1952.
4 PICKERING, G. W., *High Blood Pressure*, Churchill, London, 1955.
5 Expert Committee on Arterial Hypertension and Ischaemic Heart Disease, *Wld Hlth Org. techn. Rep. Ser.*, No. 231 (1962).
6 WOLLHEIM and MOELLER, in VON BERGMANN et al. (Eds.), *Handbuch der inneren Medizin*, vol. 9, part 5, Springer, Berlin, 1960; MOELLER, J., *Med. Klin.*, **58**, 1449 (1963).
7 MOSS and ADAMS, *Problems of Blood Pressure in Childhood*, Thomas, Springfield, 1962.
8 HOLLAND and HUMERFELT, *Brit. med. J.*, **2**, 1241 (1964).
9 KEUTH, U., *Z. Kinderheilk.*, **86**, 169 (1961); YOUNG, M., *Brit. med. Bull.*, **17**, 154 (1961).
10 MERENDINO and FINNERTY, *J. Amer. med. Ass.*, **175**, 51 (1961); KRAUSE and KLEPZIG, *Z. Kreisl.-Forsch.*, **52**, 927 (1963).
11 RUEGER, M. J., *Ann. intern. Med.*, **35**, 1023 (1951); REINLE, E., *Schweiz. med. Wschr.*, **93**, 1616 (1963).
12 PIERACH, A., *Münch. med. Wschr.*, **105**, 873 (1963); RICHARDSON et al., *Clin. Sci.*, **26**, 445 (1964).
13 ASHWORTH and NELIGAN, *Lancet*, **1**, 804 (1959).
14 BERGER et al., *Z. Kinderheilk.*, **86**, 247 (1962).
15 MOSS et al., *Pediatrics*, **32**, 175 (1963).
16 SHOCK, N. W., *Amer. J. Dis. Child.*, **68**, 16 (1944).
17 HEALD et al., *New Engl. J. Med.*, **268**, 299 (1963).
18 KATCHER, A. L., *Med. Clin. N. Amer.*, **48**, 1467 (1964).
19 SOLTH, K., *Med. Klin.*, **56**, 1281 (1961).
20 HAMILTON et al., *Clin. Sci.*, **13**, 11, 37 and 273 (1954); PICKERING, G., in WOLSTENHOLME et al. (Eds.), *Ciba Foundation Symposium on Significant Trends in Medical Research*, Churchill, London, 1959, page 273; LOWE and McKEOWN, *Lancet*, **1**, 1086 (1962); U.S. Department of Health, Education, and Welfare, *Blood Pressure of Adults by Age and Sex, United States 1960–1962*, National Center for Health Statistics, Series 11, No. 4, Washington, 1964; JOHNSON et al., *J. chron. Dis.*, **18**, 147 (1965).
21 HARLAN et al., *Circulation*, **26**, 530 (1962).
22 PICKERING, G. W., in BOCK and COTTIER (Eds.), *Essentielle Hypertonie*, Symposium, Springer, Berlin, 1960, page 34; PLATT, R., in BOCK and COTTIER (Eds.), *Essentielle Hypertonie*, Symposium, Springer, Berlin, 1960, page 45; McKUSICK, V. A., *Circulation*, **22**, 857 (1960); U.S. Department of Health, Education, and Welfare, *Blood Pressure of Adults by Age and Sex, United States 1960–1962*, National Center for Health Statistics, Series **11**, No. 5, Washington, 1964.
23 CRUZ-COKE, R., *Lancet*, **2**, 885 (1960); Annotation, *Lancet*, **1**, 383 (1961); SCHNECKLOTH et al., *Amer. Heart J.*, **63**, 607 (1962).
24 MAIDORN and MELLEROWICZ, *Z. Kreisl.-Forsch.*, **52**, 53 (1963); GUILD, W. R., *Med. Clin. N. Amer.*, **49**, 495 (1965).
25 VON UEXKÜLL and WICK, *Arch. Kreisl.-Forsch.*, **39**, 236 (1962).
26 HYTTEN and LEITCH, *The Physiology of Human Pregnancy*, Blackwell, Oxford, 1964, page 61.
27 Editorial, *Brit. med. J.*, **2**, 763 (1963).
28 Society of Actuaries, *Build and Blood Pressure Study*, vol. 1, Chicago, 1959, page 121.
29 TAYLOR et al., *Amer. J. Dis. Child.*, **96**, 545 (1958); JEGIER et al., *Acta paediat. (Uppsala)*, **52**, 485 (1963).
30 BURCH, G. E., *A Primer of Venous Pressure*, Lea & Febiger, Philadelphia, 1950, quoted by DITTMER and GREBE (Eds.), *Handbook of Circulation*, Saunders, Philadelphia, 1959, page 111.
31 LANDIS, E. M., *Heart*, **15**, 209 (1930).
32 KÜCHMEISTER, H., *Ergebn. inn. Med. Kinderheilk.*, **4**, 464 (1953).
33 HOLLAND and YOUNG, *Brit. med. J.*, **2**, 1331 (1956).
34 ALLEN-WILLIAMS, G. M., *Arch. Dis. Childh.*, **20**, 125 (1945).
35 FABER and JAMES, *Amer. J. Dis. Child.*, **22**, 7 (1921).
36 MASTER et al., *Ann. intern. Med.*, **48**, 284 (1958).

Blood volume

In men the normal blood volume amounts to 6–8%, in women 5.5–7%, of the body weight (see page 528), depending on the bodily constitution. Of the total quantity, 65–75% is in the venous system, 15–20% in the arteries and 5–7.5% in the capillary bed[1]. Blood volumes given by different authorities should not be compared without careful prior scrutiny of the methods of measurement used. The table on page 555 contains selected blood volume values for children and adults. The literature[1–3] should be consulted for more comprehensive reviews.

The most accurate method of determining the blood volume (BV) is by separate measurement of the plasma volume (PV) and erythrocyte volume (EV):

$$BV = PV + EV \qquad (1)$$

A less accurate method is by calculation from the plasma volume and body haematocrit (Ht):

$$BV = 100 \times \frac{PV}{100 - Ht} \qquad (2)$$

or from the erythrocyte volume and body haematocrit:

$$BV = 100 \times \frac{EV}{Ht} \qquad (3)$$

The body haematocrit is defined as

$$Ht = 100 \times \frac{EV}{PV + EV} \qquad (4)$$

and is calculated from the venous haematocrit (Ht_V):

$$Ht = Ht_V \times 0.97 \times 0.91 = Ht_V \times 0.88 \qquad (5)$$

The factor of 0.97 allows for the trapped plasma remaining in the erythrocyte column after centrifuging (micro-haematocrit technique[4]), the factor of 0.91 for the lower erythrocyte content in the blood as a whole than in venous blood.

Various methods are available for determining plasma and erythrocyte volume[3, 5]. The following indicators are used for plasma volume: Evans blue (T-1824), Coomassie blue[6], dextran, $^{51}CrCl_3$, ^{59}Fe citrate, ^{131}I-human serum albumin, ^{125}I-human serum albumin[7], alkaline phosphatase[8]; indicators for erythrocyte volume are carbon monoxide and erythrocytes tagged with ^{32}P, ^{42}K or ^{51}Cr.

Physiological variations

During the first years of life there are considerable differences between the blood volumes of individual children[9]. Divergences in published values for the blood volume of newborn infants[9–11] and children[12–14] are probably due to differences in the method of measurement. In the newborn the time of tying of the umbilical cord has an effect on the blood volume[11]. Regression equations for the blood volume in children in relation to height, weight and body surface area have been derived[13]. Up to puberty the blood volume increases in proportion to growth in both sexes; from puberty onwards it increases faster than the rate of growth and in boys to a greater extent than in girls[12]. Other workers, however, have reported that the relationship to body weight in adults is very similar to that in children[15].

In adults the blood volume is very closely related to the body mass, particularly the fat-free body mass[16]. It is a function of the metabolic tissue requirement and the metabolic rate[7]. In adults the relationship of the blood volume to the body mass is independent of age[17–19]. Regression equations for the dependence of the blood volume on height and weight have been derived for men[17, 20, 21] and women[18, 20, 21]. There appear to be racial differences in blood volume, since compared to whites negroes[22] have lower, eskimos[23] higher, blood and plasma volumes.

The blood volume is fairly constant, and intake of fluid by either the oral or intravenous route is followed by its very rapid normalization[24]. Bed-rest causes a diminution in the blood volume, mainly as a result of loss of plasma[25]. Active sports increase both the volume of the blood and its haemoglobin content[26]. With rising ambient temperature, vasodilatation and a resulting increase in the plasma and blood volume occurs, while a falling ambient temperature causes vasoconstriction and a decrease in the plasma and blood volume[23, 27]. Acclimatization at extreme altitudes causes an increase in the erythrocyte volume as a result of an increase in the number of cells (see under 'Erythrocytes', page 614).

During pregnancy the blood volume increases, the plasma volume rising by 25–80%[28, 29], the erythrocyte volume by 10–20%[28, 30]. The volume has returned to normal at 3–4 months post partum[28, 31].

References

1 Albert, S.N., *Blood Volume*, Thomas, Springfield, 1963.
2 Sjöstrand, T., *Physiol. Rev.*, **33**, 202 (1953); Wintrobe, M.M., *Clinical Hematology*, 6th ed., Lea & Febiger, Philadelphia, 1967, page 345.
3 Gregersen and Rawson, *Physiol. Rev.*, **39**, 307 (1959); Moens et al., *Schweiz. med. Wschr.*, **92**, 1660 and 1697 (1962).
4 Rustad, H., *Scand. J. clin. Lab. Invest.*, **16**, 677 (1964).
5 Root, W.S., *Meth. med. Res.*, **8**, 59 (1960); Wennesland et al., *Scand. J. clin. Lab. Invest.*, **14**, 355 (1962).
6 Martin, W.B., *Amer. J. med. Sci.*, **242**, 342 (1961); Martin and Fuller, *Amer. J. med. Sci.*, **245**, 556 (1963).
7 Button et al., *Transfusion (Philad.)*, **5**, 143 (1965); New Appliances, *Brit. med. J.*, **1**, 1374 (1965).
8 Posen et al., *J. Lab. clin. Med.*, **65**, 530 (1965).
9 Sisson et al., *J. Pediat.*, **55**, 163 (1959).
10 Mollison et al., *Arch. Dis. Childh.*, **25**, 242 (1950); Steele, M.W., *Amer. J. Dis. Child.*, **103**, 10 (1962); Low et al., *Amer. J. Obstet. Gynec.*, **86**, 886 (1963).
11 Usher et al., *Acta paediat. (Uppsala)*, **52**, 497 (1963).
12 Brines et al., *J. Pediat.*, **18**, 447 (1941).
13 Morse et al., *Amer. J. Physiol.*, **151**, 448 (1947).
14 Russell, S.J.M., *Arch. Dis. Childh.*, **24**, 88 (1949); Linden et al., *Ann. Paediat. Fenn.*, **6**, 119 (1960).
15 Graham, G.R., *Ann. roy. Coll. Surg. Engl.*, **33**, 149 (1963).
16 Börner et al., *Klin. Wschr.*, **38**, 21 (1960).
17 Wennesland et al., *J. clin. Invest.*, **38**, 1065 (1959).
18 Brown et al., *J. clin. Invest.*, **41**, 2182 (1962).
19 Yiengst and Shock, *J. appl. Physiol.*, **17**, 195 (1962).
20 Moore et al., *The Body Cell Mass and Its Supporting Environment*, Saunders, Philadelphia, 1963, page 58.
21 Nadler et al., *Surgery*, **51**, 224 (1962).
22 Bass et al., *J. appl. Physiol.*, **14**, 801 (1959).
23 Bass and Henschel, *Physiol. Rev.*, **36**, 128 (1956).
24 Kaltreider and Meneely, *J. clin. Invest.*, **19**, 627 (1940).
25 Taylor et al., *Amer. J. Physiol.*, **144**, 227 (1945).
26 Kjellberg et al., *Acta physiol. scand.*, **19**, 146 (1949); Musshoff et al., *Acta radiol. (Stockh.)*, **57**, 377 (1962).
27 Paloheimo, J.A., *Scand. J. clin. Lab. Invest.*, **15**, 563 (1963).
28 Hytten and Duncan, *Nutr. Abstr. Rev.*, **26**, 855 (1956).
29 Hytten and Paintin, *J. Obstet. Gynaec. Brit. Cwlth*, **70**, 402 (1963).
30 Gahres et al., *Amer. J. Obstet. Gynec.*, **84**, 770 (1962).
31 Pritchard et al., *Amer. J. Obstet. Gynec.*, **84**, 1271 (1962).

Blood, erythrocyte and plasma volumes (per kilogramme body weight or square metre body surface area)

	Number	Whole blood				Erythrocytes				Plasma				Ratio body haematocrit: venous haematocrit		Method*	Reference
		ml/kg		ml/m²		ml/kg		ml/m²		ml/kg		ml/m²					
		Mean	*s*	Mean	*s*	Mean	*s*	Mean	*s*	Mean	*s*	Mean	*s*	Mean	*s*		
Newborn, 15–30 minutes ..	50	76.5	7.81	–	–	35.0	5.60	–	–	41.5	3.98	–	–	–	–	T-1824, Ht	1
Newborn, 24 hours	61	83.3	8.2	–	–	37.7	6.4	–	–	45.6	4.3	–	–	–	–	T-1824, Ht	1
Children, 3 months	–	87	–	–	–	33	–	–	–	54	–	–	–	–	–	T-1824, Ht	2
Children, 6 months	–	86	–	–	–	31	–	–	–	55	–	–	–	–	–	T-1824, Ht	2
Children, 1 year ...	–	80	–	–	–	28	–	–	–	52	–	–	–	–	–	T-1824, Ht	2
Children, 6 years ..	–	80	–	–	–	29	–	–	–	51	–	–	–	–	–	T-1824, Ht	2
Children, 10 years .	–	75	–	–	–	30	–	–	–	45	–	–	–	–	–	T-1824, Ht	2
Children, 15 years .	–	71	–	–	–	30	–	–	–	41	–	–	–	–	–	T-1824, Ht	2
Men	–	71	–	–	–	33	–	–	–	38	–	–	–	–	–	T-1824, Ht	2
Women	–	70	–	–	–	29	–	–	–	41	–	–	–	–	–	T-1824, Ht	2
Men	30	69.1	–	2566	235	28.0	–	1039	123	41.1	–	1527	156	0.950	0.33	T-1824, ^{32}P	3
Women	30	62.1	–	2245	191	21.6	–	782	80	40.5	–	1463	162	0.930	0.51	T-1824, ^{32}P	3
Men	8	77.6	–	2857	–	31.7	–	1167	–	45.9	–	1690	–	0.913	0.036	^{131}I-HSA, ^{51}Cr	4
Women	4	78.7	–	2700	–	29.1	–	998	–	49.6	–	1702	–	0.913	0.036	^{131}I-HSA, ^{51}Cr	4
Men	22	77.8	6.6	2873	210	29.9	3.5	1109	111	48.0	4.9	1765	171	–	–	^{131}I-HSA, Ht	4
Women	12	72.7	13.4	2437	358	24.7	5.1	835	151	47.5	8.7	1586	214	–	–	^{131}I-HSA, Ht	4
Men, 23–54 years	10	69	–	–	–	27	–	–	–	42	–	–	–	–	–	T-1824, ^{51}Cr	5
Men, 71–84 years	7	70	–	–	–	25	–	–	–	45	–	–	–	–	–	T-1824, ^{51}Cr	5
Women, 23–51 years	10	64	–	–	–	22	–	–	–	42	–	–	–	–	–	T-1824, ^{51}Cr	5
Women, 60–74 years	7	57	–	–	–	20	–	–	–	37	–	–	–	–	–	T-1824, ^{51}Cr	5

* T-1824 = Evans blue; ^{131}I-HSA = ^{131}I-human serum albumin; Ht = haematocrit.

1 Low et al., *Amer. J. Obstet. Gynec.*, **86**, 886 (1963).
2 Osgood, E.E., *Pediatrics*, **15**, 733 (1955).
3 Samet et al., *Medicine (Baltimore)*, **36**, 211 (1957).
4 Moens et al., *Schweiz. med. Wschr.*, **92**, 1660 and 1697 (1962).
5 Moore et al., *The Body Cell Mass and Its Supporting Environment*, Saunders, Philadelphia, 1963.

Nomogram for obtaining blood, plasma and erythrocyte volumes from the age and body weight of adults [Dagher et al., *Advanc. Surg.*, 1, 69 (1965)]

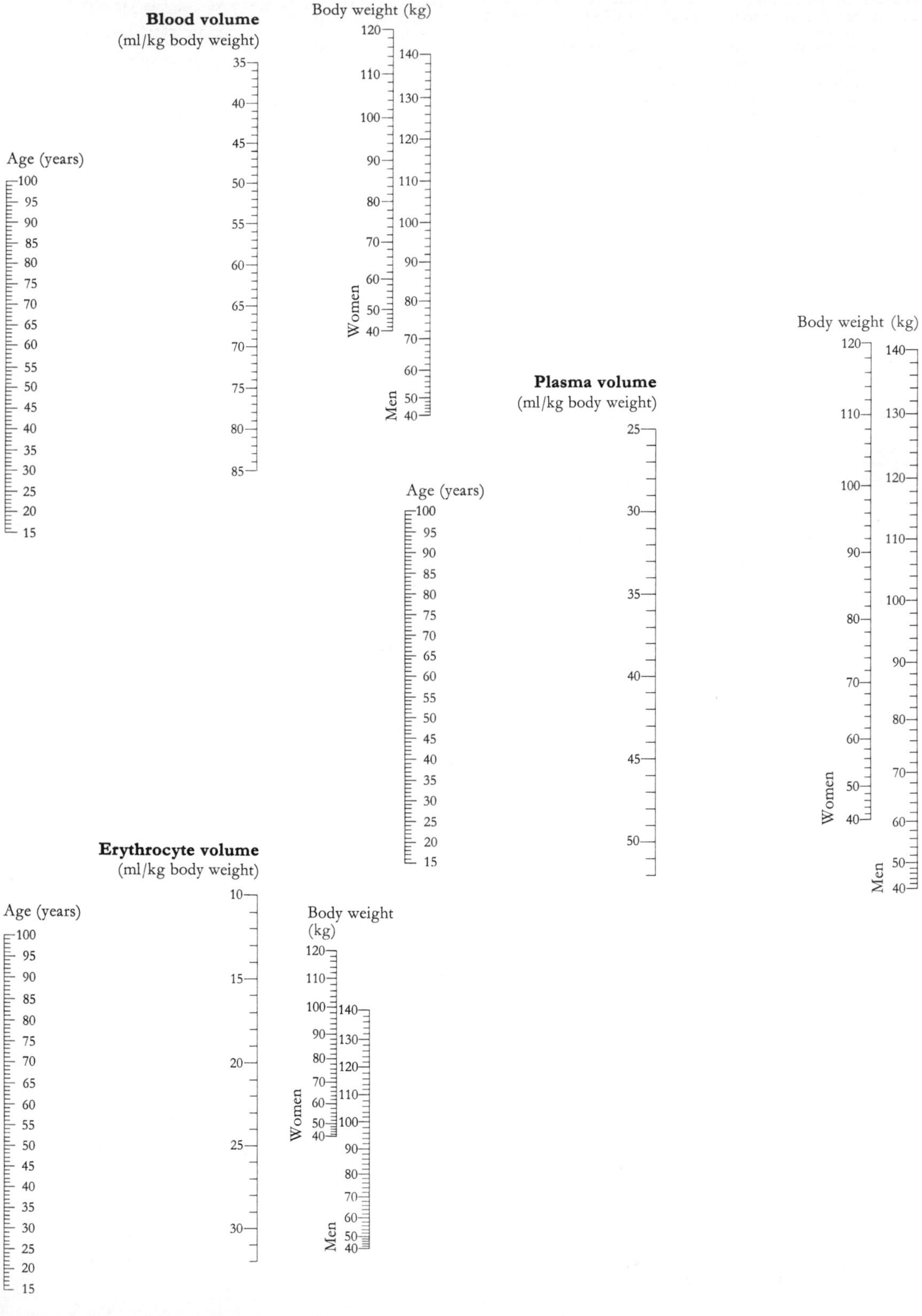

(For references see page 561)

	Mean	95% range (extreme range in brackets)	s	Reference	Remarks
Specific gravity (25 °C/4 °C)					
(a) Whole blood, men	1.0595	1.0553–1.0637	0.0021	1	Measured on (a, c, d) 20 subjects, (b) 17 subjects; values (a, b, c, d) by the copper sulphate method of PHILLIPS et al.[5] (cf. also POLLER[6]). The specific gravity of whole blood depends on the erythrocyte content, that of plasma and serum mainly on the protein content. The specific gravity of whole blood is rather lower in the afternoon and after meals, rather higher at night and after physical effort. The plasma specific gravity is pathologically *increased* in cholera, dysentery, severe burns and plasmacytoma, *decreased* in hydropic renal disease; the specific gravity of whole blood is pathologically *decreased* in anaemia.
(b) Whole blood, women		(1.0523–1.0604)		1	
(c) Plasma, men	1.0269	1.0251–1.0287	0.0009	1	
Serum	–	(1.024–1.028)	–	2	
(d) Erythrocytes, men	1.0964	1.0928–1.1000	0.0018	1	
Leucocytes	–	(1.07–1.08)	–	3	
Thrombocytes	1.03	–	–	4	
Freezing-point depression (°C)					
(a) Serum	0.540	0.512–0.568	0.014	7	Measured on (a) 75, (b) 50 subjects. Values in whole blood and serum are almost identical. The erythrocytes are in osmotic equilibrium with the serum[9].
(b) Serum	0.537	–	–	8	
Osmolality (mosm/kg H_2O)					
Serum	289	281–297	4	8	Measured on 50 subjects. The simplest method is by calculation from the freezing-point depression[10]. The electrolytes contribute about 96% of the osmolality, glucose and nonprotein nitrogenous substances about 4%. The osmolality is higher in the first two days of life[11]. Pathological changes are mainly accounted for by changes in the sodium content of the blood.
Osmotic pressure (at 0 °C)					
Serum (atm)	6.51	–	–	–	Calculated from the values (a) for the freezing-point depression (using the table on page 272). The osmotic pressure is mainly accounted for by the crystalloid components; the colloids contribute only about 0.5% of the total osmotic pressure.
Serum (mm Hg)	4950	–	–	–	

Specific gravity/Serum water/Solutes[22]

The table can be used to convert

(a) the concentration of a substance per litre serum into its concentration per kilogramme serum water: Multiply by the factor in column 4

(b) the concentration of a substance per kilogramme serum water into its concentration per litre serum: Multiply by the figure in column 3 and divide by 1000

Specific gravity	Water per kilogramme serum (g)	Water per litre serum (g)	Factor
1	2	3	4
1.015	952	966	1.035
1.016	948	964	1.038
1.017	945	961	1.040
1.018	942	959	1.043
1.019	939	957	1.045
1.020	936	954	1.048
1.021	932	952	1.051
1.022	929	949	1.053
1.023	926	947	1.056
1.024	923	945	1.059
1.025	919	942	1.061
1.026	916	940	1.064
1.027	913	938	1.067
1.028	910	935	1.069
1.029	906	933	1.072
1.030	903	930	1.075
1.031	900	928	1.078
1.032	897	925	1.081
1.033	894	923	1.083
1.034	890	921	1.086

Relationship between haematocrit and blood viscosity[17]

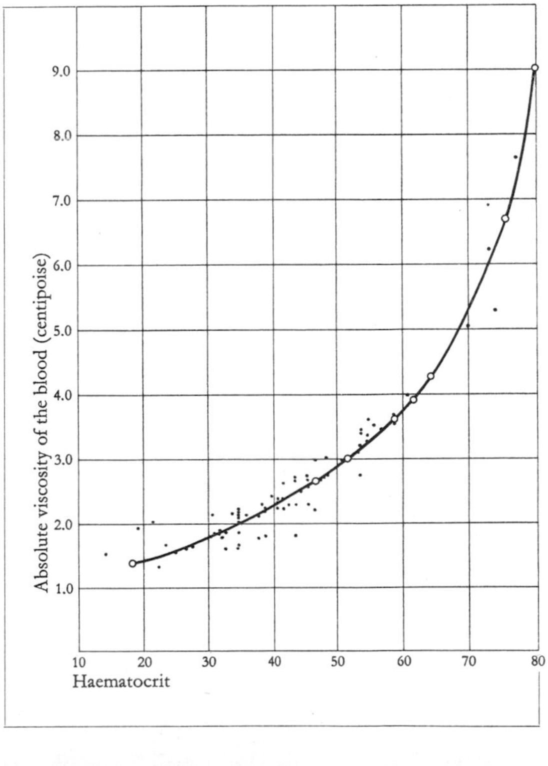

(For references see page 561)

	Mean	95% range (extreme range in brackets)	*s*	Reference	Remarks
Colloid-osmotic (oncotic) pressure (at 0 °C)					
Serum (mm Hg)	24.3	(20.6–35.3)	–	12	The colloid-osmotic pressure (COP) can be calculated approximately from the albumin and globulin contents by using the formula of Keys[13] (see page 526). Exact calculation requires measurement of the COP of the individual serum protein fractions[14]. The major part of the COP is accounted for by albumin; fibrinogen has no measurable effect on the COP of the plasma[15], so that the COP of the plasma can be equated with that of the serum.
Viscosity					
Relative viscosity (in vitro at 18 °C)					
(a) Whole blood	4.75	(3.80–5.70)	–	16	Measured on (a, b) 21, (c) 25 fasting subjects with the Hess viscosimeter; (d) in vivo by means of capillaries on subjects with a haematocrit of 40–45%; (e) with the Zeitfuchs capillary viscosimeter. Since blood is a non-Newtonian fluid, viscosity values measured by different methods are not comparable. The dependence of the dynamic viscosity on the shear rate between 10 and 200 s^{-1} has been studied by means of a cone-plate viscosimeter[19]; for any given haematocrit value the viscosity falls with increasing shear rate. The in vivo viscosity values (d) correspond to a shear rate of ca. 1700 s^{-1}. The rheological properties of blood have also been studied in vivo[20]. For determination of viscosity by the falling-ball viscosimeter see Krosch and Heidelmann[21]. The viscosity of whole blood depends mainly on the cell content, i.e., in healthy subjects on the erythrocyte content (see the diagram on page 557), that of plasma on the protein content. The relative viscosity of whole blood is about 0.5 higher in men than in women[23, 39], while in children it is rather lower than in adults[39]. The relative viscosity of venous blood is higher than that of arterial blood[39]. The viscosity of whole blood is pathologically *increased* in polycythaemia vera[24], sickle-cell anaemia[25] and leukaemia[26], that of the serum is *increased* in hyperglobulinaemia[18, 27], in the presence of a high titre of the rheumatoid factor[18], and particularly in macroglobulinaemia[18, 27].
(b) Plasma	2.01	1.67–2.35	0.17	16	
(c) Serum	1.88	1.58–2.18	0.15	16	
Dynamic viscosity (centipoise) (in vivo)					
(d) Whole blood	–	(2.30–2.75)	–	17	
Kinematic viscosity (centistoke) (in vitro at 37.5 °C)					
(e) Serum	1.15	(1.08–1.22)	–	18	
Erythrocyte sedimentation rate (sedimentation rate, ESR)	...	...	...	...	Values depend on the method of measurement (see the table below and text opposite).
Leucocyte sedimentation index (LSI) (mm/h)	13.58	3.72–23.4	4.93	28	Calculated from the formula ½($a+b/2$), where a = mm sedimentation in 1 hour, b = mm sedimentation in 2 hours; values from 300 adults. In the method used, a sample of leucocyte-rich plasma is layered on top of cell-free plasma. The LSI is dependent on the properties of the leucocytes but not on those of the plasma; immature leucocyte forms appear to settle out faster. The LSI is increased in acute forms of leukaemia, acute Hodgkin's disease, tuberculosis and other bacterial infections, and in carcinoma with liver metastases.

Erythrocyte sedimentation rate

		Westergren methods: Original[70]			Westergren methods: 'Wide tube' modification[71]		Westergren methods: Wintrobe's modification[39]		Linzenmeier's method[72]	
Methods	*Sedimentation tube*									
	Blood column	200 mm			100 mm		100 mm		50 mm	
	Diameter	2.5 mm			5 mm		2.5 mm		5 mm	
	Anticoagulant	Sodium citrate 3.8% solution			Sodium citrate 3.8% solution		2 parts potassium oxalate + 3 parts ammonium oxalate dry		Sodium citrate 5% solution	
	Quantity (mg/100 ml mixture)	760			760		200		1000	
	Resulting dilution of blood	20%			20%		0		20%	
Normal values (mornings, fasting)		Sedimentation after 1 hour (mm)	2 hours (mm)	24 hours (mm)	1 hour (mm)	2 hours (mm)	1 hour (mm)		Time for a sedimentation of 18 mm (h)	
		Range	Range	Range	Range	Range	Mean	Range	Mean[75]	Range[75]
	Newborn, 1st day	Up to 2[73]	–	–	–	–	–	Up to 2[73]	106	30–185
	Newborn, 4th day	–	–	–	–	–	–	–	45	6–120
	Newborn, 12th–21st day	–	–	–	–	–	–	–	11	2–40
	Males, 12–20 years	–	–	–	–	–	4.7[74]	Up to 20[74]	–	–
	Men	3–5	Up to 15	90	2–5	5–14	3.7	Up to 6.5	10	–
	Women	3–8	Up to 20	100–110	3–8	6–18	9.6	Up to 15	–	3½–5

(For references see page 561)

Erythrocyte sedimentation rate (ESR)

The mechanism of erythrocyte sedimentation[29, 30] is only partly understood. Three phases can be distinguished: In the first phase (agglomeration phase) a few cells sink under gravity but the majority form agglomerates (rouleaux) of various sizes. In the second phase the agglomerates sink rapidly, the rate of fall depending on their size; lack of uniformity in the size of the agglomerates may result in blurring of the level of the settled erythrocytes. In the third phase the rate of settling is slow owing to 'clogging' of the agglomerates.

The rate of sedimentation depends on the extent to which the cells agglomerate. The cause of the adherence of the cells is reversible adsorption of certain plasma proteins by so-called sedimentation receptors on the cell surface. These receptors probably consist of a cerebroside[31], while the plasma proteins involved can be divided into so-called agglomerins[32] and a supplement[33]. Except when they are present at very high concentrations, the agglomerins can bring about marked agglomeration only in the presence of the supplement. They include fibrinogen, caeruloplasmin, haptoglobin, certain paraproteins, cold agglutinins and autoagglutinins; it is not known whether other agglomerins not normally found in the plasma are present when the sedimentation rate is increased.

The α_1-lipoproteins of pathological blood sera as well as sera in which the sedimentation rate is normal contain a so-called pro-inhibitor[34] from which a lysophosphatide[35] (probably a lysolecithin) is split off on incubation with a specific serum enzyme at 37 °C. This lysophosphatide attaches itself to the serum albumin to form an albumin-lipid complex that inhibits sedimentation of the erythrocytes.

The biological significance of an increase in the sedimentation rate is still obscure. Since a number of substances that inhibit inflammation also inhibit an increase in the sedimentation rate in vitro it has been suggested that the agglomerins are inflammation activators, a view supported by the fact that inhibitors of inflammation exercise their inhibitory effect on sedimentation via inhibition of the plasma proteins involved in the sedimentation process[36].

Other factors affecting the sedimentation rate are

(a) size, shape (sickle-cell erythrocytes have a lower sedimentation rate than normal erythrocytes), haemoglobin content and number of the erythrocytes;
(b) length of the column of blood (a short column shows a slower rate of sedimentation since 'clogging' occurs relatively early);
(c) nature and amount of the anticoagulant used[37] (the rate is increased by too little citrate, decreased by too much);
(d) temperature (the rate increases with increasing temperature[38]);
(e) position of the tube (inclination of the tube greatly increases the rate).

Physiological variations. The sedimentation rate is more constant in men than in women; this is not due to the menstrual cycle, changes during which are small and of no clinical significance[29]. In pregnancy, the rate begins to increase at the 3rd to 4th month and does not return to normal until the 3rd or 4th week post partum[39, 40]. In the newborn the sedimentation rate is greatly reduced (see the table on page 558), in older adults rather high[41].

Pathological variations. The sedimentation rate is reduced in polycythaemia, congestive heart failure, diseases of the liver parenchyma, hyperbilirubinaemia, acute anaphylactic reactions and vagotonia. As a rule it is increased in all inflammatory conditions, in acute and chronic infections, in diseases accompanied by necrosis or tissue breakdown, in the presence of tumours, after exposure to ultraviolet light or X rays, and following stimulation therapy.

Guiding principles in practice[29]

1. In principle, this blood *plasma* test cannot be expected to yield more information than would be expected from such a simple, nonspecific, routine method. A thorough examination of the patient must be carried out even if the sedimentation rate is normal. In contrast to the rapid response shown by the blood picture, 20–30 hours usually elapse before a change in the sedimentation rate is observed.
2. Daily fluctuations in the sedimentation rate are insignificant; usually it is sufficient to measure the 1- and 2-hour values. In any particular blood sample the measured values vary from method to method. Values show marked differences in any one individual, so that a knowledge of his minimal values when in good health is important.
3. A marked increase in the sedimentation rate is an objective indication of a pathological process but cannot be interpreted as direct evidence of the presence of disease (it may, for instance, persist during convalescence). When there is a marked increase that cannot be explained, further examination of the patient is essential.
4. An exceptionally large and rapid increase in the sedimentation rate reaching a maximum in 15–20 minutes points strongly to a plasmacytoma or macroglobulinaemia.
5. A marked and persistent increase in the sedimentation rate that cannot be otherwise accounted for should raise suspicion of a carcinoma. In these circumstances the patient should continue to be examined at intervals until the cause of the increase is revealed.
6. A normal sedimentation rate never excludes the possibility of disease, even a severe progressive one such as tuberculosis or cancer; in particular, an increase in the rate is often very late in appearing in heart failure. In these circumstances electrophoresis will reveal marked abnormalities of the plasma proteins. Exceptionally low values of 1–3 mm in 1 or 2 hours are often observed in vagotonia.
7. In rare cases a marked increase in the sedimentation rate is accompanied by a completely normal plasma protein pattern, for instance in decompensated pernicious anaemia. There is no correlation, however, between the sedimentation rate and the fibrinogen, globulin or total protein content of the blood.
8. The full significance of a sedimentation rate measured at the climax of an illness is apparent only when it is compared with later measurements, so that in an acute illness there should be no unnecessary delay in making the test.
9. The sedimentation rate is often less affected by the disease itself than by the secondary complications, such as pneumonia, thrombophlebitis, infarction of the lung, intercurrent infections, etc. Anticoagulant therapy often delays normalization of the sedimentation rate for a considerable time. While drugs in general have no direct effect on the sedimentation rate they may have a secondary effect due to damage to the liver parenchyma.
10. Measurement of the sedimentation rate provides an opportunity of examining the plasma for colour and clarity (golden-yellow in haemolysis, unusually clear in iron deficiency, straw-coloured in pernicious anaemia, cloudy as a result of an increased fat content and protein changes in nephrosis and diabetes and after ingestion of fats). Pathological increases in the leucocyte count (over 50 000 per mm³ in leukaemia) may also be visible to the naked eye.

	Mean	95% range (extreme range in brackets)	s	Reference	Remarks
Surface tension (20 °C, dyn cm^{-1})					
Serum	56.2	–	–	42	Values measured by torsion balance in 82 fasting subjects between 20 and 30 years of age.
Refractive index (20 °C)	–	(1.348 46–1.351 32)	–	43	Measured by the PULFRICH refractometer. The refractive index of the serum depends mainly on the protein content and can therefore be used to determine the latter (as for instance by DRICKMAN and MCKEON[44]), though the method is unreliable when the blood urea, sugar, lipid and bilirubin levels are high.

	Mean	95% range (extreme range in brackets)	s	Reference	Remarks
Specific heat (cal deg⁻¹ g⁻¹)					
Whole blood	0.87	–	–	45	
Plasma	0.94	–	–	45	
Erythrocytes	0.77	–	–	45	
Specific conductivity (25 °C, S cm⁻¹)					
Serum	0.01190	(0.01173–0.01229)	–	46	The specific conductivity and total protein content of the serum can be used to calculate the total cations (see page 562).
Electrophoretic mobility (anodic) (μm s⁻¹ V⁻¹ cm)					
(a) Erythrocytes	1.080	1.064–1.096	0.008	47	Values from (a) 10 subjects (pH 7.2 in phosphate-buffered saline), (b) 28 subjects (citrated blood). The electrophoretic mobility of blood cells is determined mainly by the carboxyl groups of the sialic acid present on the cell surface[49–51]. Each type of cell has a characteristic mobility; that of the erythrocytes is independent of race, sex, age and blood grouping[52]. The leucocytes have an increased mobility[48, 51] in chronic and acute myelosis, lymphadenosis, HODGKIN's disease and in the presence of tumours with bone metastases. Erythrocytes have a lower mobility in the serum of cancer patients[53].
(b) Erythrocytes	1.270	1.236–1.304	0.017	48	
(b) Granulocytes	0.840	0.790–0.890	0.025	48	
(b) Lymphocytes	1.060	1.006–1.114	0.027	48	
(b) Thrombocytes	0.120	0.020–0.220	0.050	48	
Surface density of electric charge (esu cm⁻²)					
Erythrocytes	3500	–	–	50	Calculated from the electrophoretic mobility. Assuming the erythrocyte surface to be 163 μm², the electric charge per erythrocyte is 11.9 × 10⁶ esu.
Redox potential (mV)					
Whole venous blood					
(a) To calomel electrode	–	–260 to –300	–	54	The range given embraces 83% of 550 measurements made in vitro by the method of ZIEGLER[55] using a weakly polarized platinum electrode. The redox potential of blood is determined by the ratio of dehydroascorbic acid to ascorbic acid.
(b) To hydrogen electrode	–	–12 to –52	–	54	
pH value (38 °C)					
(a) Umbilical artery, whole blood	7.21	(7.05–7.38)	–	56	Values from (a) 19, (b) 12, (c) 13, (d) 15, (e) 29, (f, g, h, k) each 20, (i) 55 and (j) 9 subjects measured by pH electrode; values (d, f, g, h, k) are on the NBS pH scale, values (e, j) on the HITCHCOCK-TAYLOR pH scale. On the theoretical basis of pH measurement see page 278. The clinical measurement of pH has been much discussed[60, 65–67]. pH values are comparable only when the nature of the standard buffer used is known; use of the National Bureau of Standards buffer scale is recommended (for the NBS pH scale see page 279). Measurements should be made at 37 °C and not 38 °C[64]. Heparin is a suitable anticoagulant, but not oxalate, citrate or EDTA[66]. In completely resting subjects there is no difference between the values in plasma and whole blood[65], but during bodily activity the arterial plasma is slightly more alkaline than the arterial whole blood (maximum difference 0.10 pH units at an oxygen saturation of 98%). The pH value of the capillary blood is almost the same as that of the arterial blood[59, 60], the former being on the average 0.008 pH units more alkaline than the latter. In the limbs the venous plasma is up to 0.03 pH units less alkaline than the arterial plasma[59]. In the newborn the blood pH is low[56, 68], in pregnant women rather high[69]. In acute disturbances of acid–base balance the blood pH may briefly fall to 6.8 or rise to 7.8[60]; in chronic diseases it usually lies between 7.2 and 7.5. The pH value of the blood is extremely low in diabetic coma and severe renal insufficiency, very high in acute hyperventilation accompanied by anaesthesia and following protracted loss of hydrogen ions, for instance in vomiting.
(a) Umbilical vein, whole blood	7.32	(7.23–7.42)	–	56	
Arterial whole blood					
(b) Infants, 1–4 weeks	7.377	7.315–7.439	0.031	57	
(c) Infants, 4–16 months	7.432	7.366–7.498	0.033	57	
(d) Adults	7.424	7.386–7.462	0.019	58	
(e) Adults	7.392	–	–	59	
Capillary whole blood					
(f) Men	7.390	7.360–7.420	0.015	60	
(g) Women	7.398	7.366–7.430	0.016	60	
Arterial plasma					
(h) Adults	7.39	7.35–7.43	0.018	61	
Venous plasma					
(i) Adults	7.398	7.378–7.418	0.010	62	
Erythrocytes					
(j) Adults	7.209	7.175–7.243	0.017	63	
(k) Adults	7.19	7.15–7.23	0.022	61	
Capillary whole blood (37 °C)					
(f) Men	7.405	7.375–7.435	–	64	
(g) Women	7.412	7.391–7.435	–	64	

References

1 van Slyke et al., *J.biol.Chem.*, **183**, 349 (1950).
2 Leake et al., *Amer.J. Physiol.*, **81**, 493 (1927).
3 Graham et al., *Blood*, **10**, 467 (1955).
4 Tullis, J.L., *Blood*, **7**, 891 (1952).
5 Phillips et al., *J.biol.Chem.*, **183**, 305 (1950).
6 Poller, L., *Acta haemat. (Basel)*, **21**, 242 (1959).
7 Olmstead and Roth, *Amer.J.med.Sci.*, **233**, 392 (1957).
8 Hendry, E.B., *Clin.Chem.*, **7**, 156 (1961), and **8**, 246 (1962).
9 Williams et al., *J.clin.Invest.*, **38**, 1587 (1959).
10 Johnson et al., *Stand.Meth.clin. Chem.*, **5**, 159 (1965); Warhol et al., *Arch. intern. Med.*, **116**, 743 (1965).
11 Gautier, E., in Jonxis et al. (Eds.), *Nutricia Symposium on the Adaptation of the Newborn Infant to Extra-Uterine Life*, Kroese, Leiden, 1964, page 83.
12 Keys and Hill, *J.exp.Biol.*, **11**, 28 (1934).
13 Keys, A., *J.phys.Chem.*, **42**, 11 (1938).
14 Ott, H., *Klin. Wschr.*, **34**, 1079 (1956).
15 Wuhrmann and Märki, *Dysproteinämien und Paraproteinämien*, Schwabe, Basle, 1963, page 156.
16 Watson, W.C., *Lancet*, **2**, 366 (1957).
17 Pirofsky, B., *J.clin.Invest.*, **32**, 292 (1953).
18 Shearn et al., *Arch.intern.Med.*, **112**, 684 (1963); *J.Lab.clin.Med.*, **61**, 677 (1963).
19 Wells et al., *J.Lab.clin.Med.*, **57**, 646 (1961); Wells and Merrill, *J.clin. Invest.*, **41**, 1591 (1962).
20 Dreizen, P., *J.clin.Invest.*, **41**, 2036 (1962).
21 Krosch and Heidelmann, *Klin. Wschr.*, **33**, 947 (1955).
22 Sunderman, F.W., *J. biol. Chem.*, **113**, 111 (1936).
23 Swank, R.L., *Amer.J.clin.Nutr.*, **10**, 418 (1962).
24 Nygaard et al., *Amer.J.Physiol.*, **114**, 128 (1935).
25 McCord et al., *Proc.Soc.exp.Biol. (N.Y.)*, **69**, 19 (1948).
26 Stephens, D.J., *Proc.Soc.exp.Biol. (N.Y.)*, **35**, 251 (1936).
27 Steel, A.E., *Clin.chim.Acta*, **8**, 86 (1963).
28 Annotation, *Brit.med.J.*, **2**, 520 (1960); Storti, *Acta med.scand.*, **167**, 1 (1960).
29 Wuhrmann and Märki, *Dysproteinämien und Paraproteinämien*, Schwabe, Basle, 1963, page 699.
30 Saner, R., *Helv.med.Acta*, **28**, 775 (1961); Brittinger, G., *Med.Klin.*, **58**, 1057 (1963); Ruhenstroth-Bauer, G., *Klin. Wschr.*, **44**, 533 (1966).
31 Granzer, E., *Naturwissenschaften*, **51**, 244 (1964).
32 Ruhenstroth-Bauer et al., *Klin. Wschr.*, **40**, 1200 (1962).
33 Ruhenstroth-Bauer, G., *Klin. Wschr.*, **43**, 460 (1965).
34 Kayser et al., *Hoppe-Seylers Z.physiol.Chem.*, **331**, 95 (1963).
35 Bergenhem, B., *Acta path.microbiol.scand.*, suppl. 39, 220 (1938); Schiebel et al., *Hoppe-Seylers Z.physiol.Chem.*, **338**, 198 (1964).
36 Ruhenstroth-Bauer, G., Munich, personal communication, 1964.
37 Dawson, J.B., *Brit.med.J.*, **1**, 1697 (1960); Editorial, *Brit.med.J.*, **1**, 1717 (1960).
38 Manley, R.W., *J.clin.Path.*, **10**, 354 (1957).
39 Wintrobe, M.M., *Clinical Hematology*, 6th ed., Lea & Febiger, Philadelphia, 1967, page 354.
40 Katz and Leffkowitz, *Ergebn.inn.Med.Kinderheilk.*, **33**, 266 (1928); Viscolo, H.-C., *Méd.et Hyg. (Genève)*, **22**, 487 (1964).
41 Olbrich, O., *Edinb.med.J.*, **55**, 100 (1948); Undritz and Bragatsch, *Schweiz.med. Wschr.*, **92**, 388 (1962); Böttiger and Svedberg, *Brit.med.J.*, **2**, 85 (1967).
42 Künzel, O., *Ergebn.inn.Med.Kinderheilk.*, **60**, 565 (1941).
43 Frank, H., in Henning, N. (Ed.), *Klinische Laboratoriumsdiagnostik*, 2nd ed., Urban & Schwarzenberg, Munich, 1960, page 1.
44 Drickman and McKeon, *Amer.J.clin.Path.*, **38**, 392 (1962).
45 Mendlowitz, M., *Science*, **107**, 97 (1948).
46 Sunderman, F.W., *Amer.J.clin.Path.*, **15**, 219 (1945).
47 Sachtleben and Ruhenstroth-Bauer, *Nature*, **192**, 982 (1961).
48 Ruhenstroth-Bauer et al., *Münch.med.Wschr.*, **103**, 794 (1961).
49 Cook et al., *Nature*, **191**, 44 (1961).
50 Eylar et al., *J.biol.Chem.*, **237**, 1992 (1962).
51 Ruëff, F., *Die Zellelektrophorese in der klinischen Diagnostik*, Lehmann, Munich, 1964.
52 Bangham et al., *Nature*, **182**, 642 (1958).
53 Rottino and Angers, *Proc.N.Y.State Ass.publ.Hlth Laborat.*, **41**, 9 (1961); Rottino and Angers, *Clin.Chem.*, **8**, 579 (1962); Grace et al., *Amer. Rev. resp.Dis.*, **88**, 652 (1963).
54 Münker, G., *Redoxpotential-, Eisen-, Kupfer- und Vitamin-C-Veränderungen im Blut unter einer Behandlung, die Einfluß auf das redoxaktive Geschehen nimmt*, Thesis, Freiburg i.Br., 1962.
55 Ziegler, E., *The Redox Potential of the Blood In Vitro and In Vivo*, Thomas, Springfield, 1965.
56 Rooth, G., *Acta paediat. (Uppsala)*, **52**, 22 (1963).
57 Riegel, K., *Klin. Wschr.*, **41**, 249 (1963).
58 Schwab and Wisser, *Klin. Wschr.*, **40**, 713 (1962).
59 Gambino, S.R., *Amer.J.clin.Path.*, **32**, 298 (1959).
60 Siggaard-Andersen, O., *Scand.J.clin.Lab.Invest.*, **15**, suppl. 70 (1963); Astrup and Siggaard-Andersen, *Advanc.clin.Chem.*, **6**, 1 (1963).
61 Purcell et al., *Clin.Chem.*, **7**, 536 (1961).
62 Gambino, S.R., *Amer.J.clin.Path.*, **32**, 294 (1959).
63 Sommerkamp and Bomke, *Klin. Wschr.*, **42**, 392 (1964).
64 Gambino et al., *Ann.N.Y.Acad.Sci.*, **133**, 259 (1966).
65 Gambino, S.R., *Amer.J.clin.Path.*, **32**, 285 (1959).
66 Gambino et al., *Stand.Meth.clin.Chem.*, **5**, 169 (1965).
67 Woolmer, R.F. (Ed.), *A Symposium on pH and Blood Gas Measurement*, Churchill, London, 1959; Consolazio et al., *Physiological Measurements of Metabolic Functions in Man*, McGraw-Hill, New York, 1963, page 132; Bartels et al., *Lungenfunktionsprüfungen*, Springer, Berlin, 1959.
68 Reardon et al., *Pediatrics*, **6**, 753 (1950); Räihä, N.C.R., *Pediatrics*, **32**, 1025 (1963).
69 Sjöstedt, S., *Amer.J.Obstet.Gynec.*, **84**, 775 (1962).
70 Westergren, A., *Ergebn.inn.Med.Kinderheilk.*, **26**, 577 (1924).
71 Wuhrmann and Märki, *Dysproteinämien und Paraproteinämien*, Schwabe, Basle, 1963, page 221.
72 Linzenmeier, G., *Arch. Gynäk.*, **113**, 608 (1920).
73 Smith, C.H., *Amer.J.med.Sci.*, **192**, 73 (1936).
74 Gallagher, J.R., *Amer.J.med.Sci.*, **188**, 450 (1934).
75 Berg et al., in Henning, N. (Ed.), *Klinische Laboratoriumsdiagnostik*, 2nd ed., Urban & Schwarzenberg, Munich, 1960, page 10; Hurwitz et al., *J.Pediat.*, **12**, 785 (1938).

Inorganic substances (for references see pages 567–568)

	Whole blood				Plasma or serum				Remarks
	Mean	95% range (extreme range in brackets)	*s*	Reference	Mean	95% range (extreme range in brackets)	*s*	Reference	
Water									
(g/l)	850	(830–865)	–	1	945	(930–955)	–	1	Values (a) from 128 subjects. The water content of the erythrocytes increases as the haemoglobin content falls[4]. The water content of the plasma is highest in resting recumbent subjects and increases during physical effort. The water content of the leucocytes varies with the type and degree of maturity[5].
(g/l)	713	Erythrocytes: 693–733	10	2					
(g/kg)	681.3	654–709	13.6	3					
(a) (g/kg)	666	648–684	9.0	127					
Dry substance									
(a) (g/l)	210	–	–	–	80	–	–	–	Values (a) calculated from the water content and specific gravity, (b) measured in 128 subjects. About 90% of the dry substance of whole blood consists of organic substances.
(b) (g/kg)	334	Erythrocytes: 316–352	9.0	127					
Total cations									
(a) Arterial blood (mEq/l)	...	...	...	...	152.9	149–157	2.2	6	Values (a) from 44 men by electrodialysis, (b) calculated by addition of the potassium, sodium, magnesium and calcium ions. The total serum cations are increased in premature infants during the first weeks of life (mean 159 mEq/l)[7]. See the nomogram on page 562.
(a) Venous blood (mEq/l)	...	...	...	...	154.1	149–159	2.6	6	
(b) (mEq/kg H_2O)	156	Erythrocytes: –	–	3	163	–	–	3	

(For references see pages 567–568)

	Whole blood				Plasma or serum				Remarks
	Mean	95% range (extreme range in brackets)	*s*	Reference	Mean	95% range (extreme range in brackets)	*s*	Reference	
Bicarbonate (mEq/l)	11.2	Erythrocytes: 10.9–11.5	0.15	8	24.9	21.3–28.5	1.79	9	Erythrocyte values from 9, plasma values from 15 subjects. See also under 'Blood Gases', page 571.
Chloride (mEq/l)									
(a) Umbilical vein blood	...	...	...	...	103.3	94.1–113	4.6	10	Values from (a) 14, (b) 20, (c) 100, (d) 157, (f) 37 subjects measured (a) iodometrically, (b, c) mercurimetrically, (d, f) argentometrically. An automatic amperometric method of chloride determination has been described[16]. As soon as whole blood comes into contact with air, CO_2 passes out of the erythrocytes and is replaced by chloride from the plasma (chloride shift); in determining serum chloride the erythrocytes should therefore be separated as far as possible with the exclusion of air.
(a) Newborn, 2 days	...	...	...	...	102.8	88.6–117	7.1	10	
(b) Infants, 3 months	...	...	...	...	113.6	83.2–144	15.2	11	
(c) Adults	–	(77–88)	–	12	102.7	(99–110)	–	12	
(d) Adults	...	...	...	...	106	101–111	2.5	13	
(e) Adults	–	Erythrocytes: (52–65)	–	14					
(f) Adults	67.9	58.9–76.9	4.5	15					

The chloride content of cord blood is roughly the same as that of the maternal blood[17]; that of the serum rather higher in infants than in adults[11].

The serum chloride level is pathologically *increased* after protracted dehydration, in renal hyperchloraemic acidosis (Lightwood and Albright types), in respiratory alkalosis, after head injuries and during treatment with corticosteroids; it is *decreased* by severe sweating without adequate chloride intake, by loss of digestive juices (especially gastric juice), by burns, by expansion of the extracellular fluid (pneumonia, water intoxication), in injury to the renal tubules, in adrenocortical insufficiency (Addison's disease), during medication with certain diuretic agents, in respiratory acidosis and occasionally in diabetic ketosis accompanied by diuresis.

Nomogram for obtaining the serum cation concentration from the specific conductivity and protein content of the serum (from Lufkin and Sunderman, *Techn. Bull. Registry med. Technologists*, **7**, 118 [1946], supplement to *Amer. J. clin. Path.*, **16** [1946])

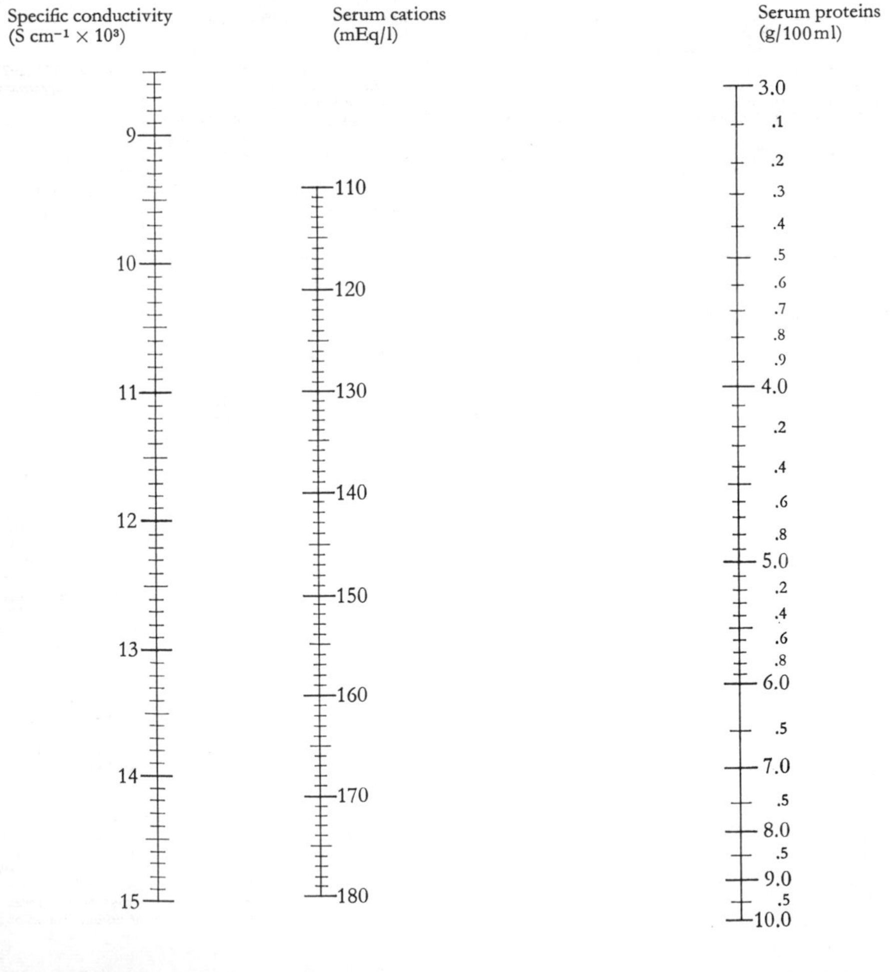

(For references see pages 567–568)

	Whole blood				Plasma or serum				Remarks
	Mean	95% range (extreme range in brackets)	*s*	Reference	Mean	95% range (extreme range in brackets)	*s*	Reference	
Phosphorus (mg/l)									
(a) Total phosphorus	370	(314–443)	–	18	112	(89–149)	–	18	Values from (a) 42, (b) 464, (c) 121, (d, whole blood) 42, (d, serum) 22, (e) 30, (f) 42, (g, erythrocytes) 20, (g, serum) 42 subjects; values (f) exclude lipid phosphorus. The phosphorus of the erythrocytes consists mainly of phosphoric acid esters (nucleotides, sugar phosphates and glycerol diphosphate), with only small amounts of inorganic phosphate. In the serum, lipid phosphorus predominates (see under 'Phosphatides', page 601). *Serum inorganic phosphate.* Determinations should be made in fasting serum. For methods see the literature[24]. The serum phosphate consists of about 80% primary phosphate and about 20% secondary phosphate, depending on the pH; small amounts are protein-bound[25]. The serum phosphate level is high during the first days of life[17,19,26]; in children it is markedly higher than in adults but falls to the adult level when ossification of the skeleton is complete[27,28]. The level begins to increase at about the age of 50[28]. In men and women the levels are about the same[28] except during pregnancy, when there is a marked reduction[29]. On phosphate metabolism see the literature[30]. The serum phosphate level is pathologically *increased* in hypoparathyroidism, pseudohypoparathyroidism, renal insufficiency, vitamin D intoxication, and occasionally in idiopathic hypercalcaemia; it is *decreased* in hyperparathyroidism, impaired calcium and phosphate absorption, vitamin D-deficient rickets, renal tubular acidosis (ALBRIGHT type), the FANCONI syndrome and phosphate diabetes.
	719	Erythrocytes: (609–867)	–	18					
Inorganic phosphorus		Whole blood:							
(b) Newborn, 1 week	...	...	...	...	60.3	(37–85)	–	19	
(c) Juveniles, 1–19 years	...	...	...	...	48	(36–59)	–	20	
(d) Adults	29	(21–38)	–	18	33.6	25.6–41.6	4.0	21	
(a)	24	Erythrocytes: (9.1–33)	–	18					
(e)	2.7	0.5–4.9	1.1	22					
(f) Phosphoric ester phosphorus	231	Whole blood: (186–286)	–	18	34	(25–45)	–	18	
	497	Erythrocytes: (385–587)	–	18					
(g) Lipid phosphorus	137	Erythrocytes: 124–150	6.5	23	83	(69–97)	–	18	
Sulphur (mg/l)									
(a) Total sulphur	1221	–	–	31	780	–	–	–	Plasma values (a) calculated from the whole blood and erythrocyte values; values (b) from 16, (c) from 88 young adults. About 95% of the sulphur in blood is contained in the proteins. The sulphuric ester fraction contains 3-indoxylsulphuric acid (see page 575) and other conjugated sulphuric acids; the neutral sulphur fraction includes amino acids, glutathione, ergothioneine and other compounds. The serum inorganic sulphate level is increased in renal failure[33].
	1900	Erythrocytes: –	–	31					
(a) Protein sulphur	1180	Whole blood: –	–	31	740	–	–	–	
	1859	Erythrocytes: –	–	31					
(b) Nonprotein sulphur	...	...	...	...	33.8	(29.5–37.5)	–	32	
Inorganic sulphate sulphur	...	...	...	...	15.7	(10.0–18.5)	–	32	
Sulphuric ester sulphur	...	...	...	...	3.9	(2.5–6.5)	–	32	
Neutral sulphur	...	...	...	...	14.2	(9.0–19.5)	–	32	
(c) Inorganic sulphate (mEq/l)	...	...	...	...	0.65	0.31–0.99	0.17	33	
Bromide (mg/l)	3.72	(2.27–5.27)	–	34	2.8	(0.7–13.3)	--	35	Values (a) from 5 subjects determined by neutron activation. The bromide content of the blood appears to fluctuate widely from one individual to another. It is increased by medication with bromine compounds; levels over 2.5 g/l serum are definitely toxic[37].
(a) (mg/kg)	3.9	0–7.9	2.0	36					
Fluoride (mg/l)									
(a)	0.18	(0.04–0.36)	–	38	–	(0.14–0.19)	–	39	Values (a) for whole blood from 37 women; lower values have been recorded in the newborn and their mothers. Serum values from subjects whose drinking water contained 0.15–2.5 mg fluoride per litre; the serum level is largely independent of the intake[40]. Values (b) from 14 subjects.
(b)	...	...	...	...	0.014	–	0.008	128	

(For references see pages 567–568)

	Whole blood				Plasma or serum				Remarks
	Mean	95% range (extreme range in brackets)	s	Reference	Mean	95% range (extreme range in brackets)	s	Reference	
Iodine (μg/l)									
(a) Total iodine	...	...	...	...	52.1	(38–60)	–	41	Values from (a) 12, (b) 11, (c) 8, (d) 125, (e) 12, (f) 38, (g) 91, (h) 29 and (i) 52 subjects; values determined by (a, c) alkaline digestion, (b) ^{132}I tracer, (d) chloric acid digestion, (e–i) permanganate digestion. For methods see the literature[47, 48].
(b) Inorganic iodine	...	...	...	...	2.8	(1.0–5.2)	–	42	
Protein-bound iodine									
(c) Cord blood	...	...	...	...	79	(67–92)	–	43	
(a) Adults	...	...	...	...	48.1	(35–56)	–	41	
(d) Adults	...	...	...	...	52	32–72	10	44	
Butanol-extractable iodine									
(e) Newborn, 2–6 days	...	...	...	...	–	(70–117)	–	45	
(f) Children, 1 month–10 years	...	...	...	...	55	39–71	8	46	
(g) Juveniles, 11–18 years	...	...	...	...	42	30–54	6	46	
(h) Men	...	...	...	...	50.0	33.0–67.0	8.5	46	
(i) Women	...	...	...	...	44.6	31.8–57.4	6.4	46	

The inorganic serum iodine level depends on the iodine intake; with a normal intake the serum iodine is almost exclusively organic. The protein-bound iodine consists of the tetra-, tri- and di-iodothyronines and part of the mono-iodothyronine, while the butanol-extractable iodine comprises only tetra- and tri-iodothyronine. The serum protein-bound iodine is higher in old age[49] and during pregnancy[43, 50], and also higher in newborn than in older children[43, 45]; it is *increased* in hyperthyroidism (80–300 μg/l) and *decreased* in hypothyroidism (0–40 μg/l)[47]. On iodine metabolism see the literature[51].

	Mean	95% range (extreme range in brackets)	s	Reference	Mean	95% range (extreme range in brackets)	s	Reference	Remarks
Thiocyanate (mg/l)	...	...	...	...	0.80	(0.44–1.14)	–	52	Values from 52 nonsmokers. Higher values are found in smokers and in patients with hyperplasia of the thyroid.
Borate (as boron, mg/l)	0.25	(0.00–1.25)	–	53	...	...	...	...	Values from 34 children; larger amounts, due for instance to excessive absorption through the skin from using boric acid preparations, are toxic.
Nitrite (μg/l)	8	(0–16)	–	54					
Silicate (as SiO_2, mg/l)	8.3	3.5–13.1	2.4	55	...	...	...	...	Values from 264 subjects; no differences due to age, sex or disease (including silicosis) were found.
Potassium (mEq/l)		Erythrocytes:							
(a) Umbilical vein blood	99.6	97–102	–	10	7.79	3.79–11.8	2.0	10	Values from (a, erythrocytes) 3, (a, serum) 14, (b) 12, (c) 13, (d, erythrocytes) 20, (d, serum) 157, (e) 37, (f, plasma) 106, (g, serum) 22, (h) 128, (i) 40 subjects, all by flame photometry; for details of method[59] and the effect of thrombocytes on potassium determination in serum see the literature[57, 60].
(a) Newborn, 1 day	105	100–108	–	10	6.19	4.73–7.65	0.73	10	
(a) Newborn, 2 days	107	100–114	–	10	5.92	4.32–7.52	0.8	10	
(b) Children, 3 months	...	...	...	...	5.24	4.30–6.18	0.47	11	
(c) Children, 18 months	...	...	...	...	4.72	3.54–5.90	0.59	11	
(d) Adults	81.7	68.3–95.1	6.7	56	4.30	3.40–5.20	0.45	13	
(e) Adults	88	76–100	6	15	4.05	3.37–4.73	0.34	15	
(f) Adults	...	...	...	...	3.7	3.1–4.3	0.31	127	
(g) Adults	...	...	...	...	4.4	3.6–5.2	0.39	127	
(h) (mEq/kg)	89.6	82–97	3.6	127					
		Thrombocytes:							
(i) (mEq/kg)	89.7	73.9–106	7.9	57					
(k) (mEq/kg)	69.1	65–71	–	58					

The potassium content of the cord serum is significantly higher than that of the maternal serum[17]; in infants it is significantly higher than in adults[11]. There is no noticeable change in the potassium level in the blood between the ages of 25 and 97[61].

The serum potassium level is pathologically *increased* by rapid infusion of potassium salts and in massive haemolysis, acute tissue breakdown, adrenocortical insufficiency (Addison's disease, hypoaldosteronism), renal failure accompanied by oliguria or anuria and untreated diabetic ketosis; it is pathologically *decreased* by inadequate potassium intake or absorption, by loss of digestive juices (diarrhoea, vomiting), and in adrenocortical hyperfunctioning (hyperaldosteronism, Cushing's syndrome, corticosteroid therapy), kidney disease accompanied by polyuria, medication with diuretic agents, renal tubular acidosis, Fanconi's syndrome, and diabetic ketosis during insulin treatment.

(For references see pages 567–568)

	Whole blood				Plasma or serum				Remarks
	Mean	95% range (extreme range in brackets)	*s*	Reference	Mean	95% range (extreme range in brackets)	*s*	Reference	
Sodium (mEq/l)									
(a) Umbilical vein blood	...	...	...	...	146.8	131–163	8.1	10	Values from (a) 14, (b) 20, (c) 37, (d) 157, (e) 20, (f) 106, (g) 128 subjects by (a–d, f, g) flame photometry, (e) neutron activation. On the flame photometric method[59] and the effect of serum proteins on assay see the literature[62, 63].
(a) Newborn, 1 day	...	...	...	...	146.4	133–159	6.5	10	
(a) Newborn, 2 days	...	...	...	...	148.7	140–157	4.3	10	
(b) Adults	16.4	Erythrocytes: 10–22	3.0	56	144.5	138–151	3.3	56	
(c) Adults	8.7	5.1–13.1	–	15	143.1	136–151	3.8	15	
(d) Adults	...	...	...	...	138	132–144	3	13	
(e) Adults	...	...	...	...	142.6	138–148	2.45	62	
(f) Adults	...	...	...	...	138.4	132–145	3.07	127	
(g) (mEq/kg)	10.9	8.3–13.5	1.3	127					
(h) (mEq/kg)	27.0	Thrombocytes: 25–28	–	58					

The sodium content of the erythrocytes is rather low during pregnancy[17]. The serum sodium level is much the same in the newborn infant and its mother, whereas the sodium content of the erythrocytes is higher in the infant than in the mother[17]. The serum sodium level is practically the same in infants as in adults[11]. There is an extensive literature on the physiological and clinical significance of the serum sodium[64].

The serum sodium level is pathologically *increased* in dehydration, sodium intoxication (for infants particularly a danger), adrenocortical hyperfunctioning, corticosteroid therapy, brain injury, brain haemorrhage and encephalitis; it is *decreased* by severe sweating without adequate sodium intake and by loss of digestive juices (diarrhoea, vomiting), and in burns, expansion of the extracellular fluid (water intoxication, pneumonia), severe renal tubular injury, adrenocortical insufficiency (ADDISON's disease), medication with diuretic agents, and diabetic ketosis.

	Whole blood				Plasma or serum				Remarks
	Mean	95% range (extreme range in brackets)	*s*	Reference	Mean	95% range (extreme range in brackets)	*s*	Reference	
Calcium (mEq/l)									
(a) Cord blood	...	...	...	...	5.5	–	–	65	Values from (a) 3, (b) 48, (d) 70, (e) 21, (f) 35, (g) 50 subjects by (a, d, e, f) EDTA titration, (b) oxalate precipitation, (c, g) flame photometry. The oxalate-precipitation and flame photometric methods give rather higher values than EDTA titration[67, 69]. On the flame photometric method see MACINTYRE[70, 71].
(b) Adults	...	...	...	...	5.09	4.7–5.5	0.22	66	
(c) Adults	...	...	...	...	5.2	4.8–5.6	0.2	67	
(d) 16–59 years	...	...	...	...	4.74	4.56–4.92	0.09	129	
(e) 60–70 years	...	...	...	...	4.60	4.36–4.84	0.12	129	
(f) Adults	...	...	...	...	4.9	4.6–5.2	0.13	68	
Protein-bound	...	...	...	...	1.8	1.4–2.2	0.18	68	
Ionized	...	...	...	...	2.9	2.7–3.1	0.10	68	
Complex	...	...	...	...	0.1	0–0.3	0.10	68	
(g) (mEq/kg)	0.12	Erythrocytes: 0.05–0.19	0.034	3					

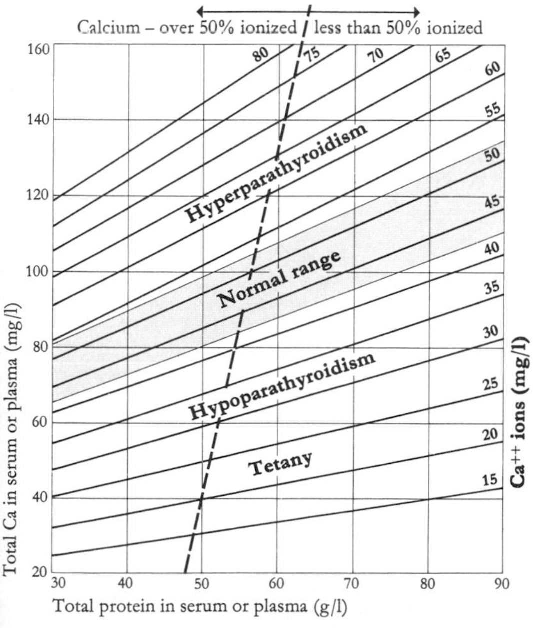

The serum calcium is 35–50% protein-bound, 50–60% ionized and 5–10% in the form of complexes with organic acids[72]. The ionized calcium can be determined directly by colorimetry[73] or read off from nomograms[74], though the usefulness of the latter is limited when the pH and protein content of the serum deviate widely from the normal. The serum calcium level is low during pregnancy[29], in the newborn markedly higher than in the mother[65] and in infants rather higher than in adults[11]. There is an extensive literature on calcium metabolism[30, 72].

The serum calcium is pathologically *increased* in hyperparathyroidism, vitamin D intoxication, bone tumours and metastases, idiopathic hypercalcaemia[75], sarcoidosis and acute bony atrophy as well as by a high intake of calcium (milk-alkali diet); it is pathologically *decreased* in hypoparathyroidism, pseudohypoparathyroidism and disturbances of calcium absorption, and occasionally in renal insufficiency with phosphate retention. Tetany occurs at serum calcium levels lower than 3–3.5 mEq/l. The proportion of ionized calcium is dependent on the protein and especially the albumin content of the serum; when the serum albumin level is low, lower calcium concentrations can be tolerated before tetany occurs.

Determination of Ca++ ions from the total protein and calcium contents of the serum or plasma (from MCLEAN and HASTINGS[74])

	Whole blood				Plasma or serum				Remarks
	Mean	95% range (extreme range in brackets)	s	Reference	Mean	95% range (extreme range in brackets)	s	Reference	
Magnesium (mEq/l)		Erythrocytes:							
(a) Cord blood	4.4	–	–	65	1.64	–	–	65	Values from (a) 3, (b) 77, (c, erythrocytes) 54, (c, serum) 46, (d) 40, (e) 76, (f) 100, (g) 58, (h) 97 subjects by (a, b) EDTA titration, (c, h) titanium yellow method, (d) ammonium phosphate precipitation, (e) emission flame photometry, (f, i, k) absorption flame photometry, (g) fluorometrically with 8-hydroxyquinoline. On the emission flame photometric method see MACINTYRE[70].
(b) Adults	5.3	4.24–6.36	0.53	65	2.00	1.70–2.30	0.15	65	
(c) Adults	4.78	3.30–6.26	0.74	76	1.70	1.30–2.10	0.20	76	
(d) Adults	4.93	3.87–5.99	0.53	76	1.73	1.45–2.01	0.14	76	
(e) Adults	...	...	...	...	1.66	1.50–1.82	0.08	77	
(f) Adults	...	...	...	...	1.74	1.52–1.96	0.11	78	
(g) Adults	...	...	...	...	1.89	1.6–2.2	–	79	
(h) Adults	...	...	...	...	1.80	1.28–2.32	0.26	80	
(i) Before puberty	3.76	(2.86–4.30)	–	83	1.69	(1.50–1.99)	–	83	
(k) After puberty	4.26	(3.68–5.26)	–	83	1.65	(1.36–2.07)	–	83	

For discussion of the discrepancies in the serum magnesium values see the literature[81]. The serum magnesium is about 30% protein-bound, 55–60% ionized and 10–15% in the form of complexes[25, 82]. The serum magnesium level is lower in the newborn and their mothers than in adults[65]. No age or sex differences have been observed in adults[78]. There is an extensive literature on magnesium metabolism[76, 77, 84, 85].
The serum magnesium is pathologically *increased* in kidney disease (the erythrocyte magnesium is also increased) and hypothyroidism; it is pathologically *decreased* in disturbances of magnesium absorption, severe vomiting and diarrhoea, hyperparathyroidism, thyrotoxicosis, chronic alcoholism, primary aldosteronism and renal tubular acidosis, and occasionally in liver cirrhosis. Serum magnesium levels below 1.3 mEq/l are marked by acute convulsions[84] but the peripheral muscle cramps seen in hypocalcaemia do not occur.

	WB Mean	WB 95% range	WB s	WB Ref.	P/S Mean	P/S 95% range	P/S s	P/S Ref.	Remarks
Cobalt (μg/l)	0.35	–	–	86	0.29	–	–	87	
Iron (mg/l)									
(a) Cord blood	...	...	...	...	1.93	–	–	88	Serum values from (a) 21, (b) 17, (c) 160, (d) 161, (e) 33 subjects by (a, b, e) colorimetry with *o*-phenanthroline[93], (c, d) dipyridyl method[92]. Serum iron can also be determined with bathophenanthroline[94].
(b) Children, 3–10 years	...	...	...	...	0.86	0.20–1.52	0.33	88	
(c) Boys, 12–19 years	...	...	...	...	0.946	0.19–1.70	0.376	89	
(d) Girls, 12–19 years	...	...	...	...	0.917	0.25–1.59	0.335	89	
(e) Men	–	(440–560)	–	90	1.34	0.58–2.10	0.38	88	
(f) Women	–	(420–480)	–	90					
(g) Adults	...	...	...	...	–	0.75–1.75	–	91	
Total iron-binding capacity (= latent or unsaturated iron-binding capacity + serum iron) (mg/l)									
(b) Children, 3–10 years	...	...	...	...	4.0	(1.9–4.5)	–	88	
(g) Adults	...	...	...	...	–	2.5–4.0	–	92	

Most of the iron in the blood is contained in the haemoglobin of the erythrocytes; haemoglobin contains 0.347% iron. The serum iron is in the ferric form and is almost completely contained in the protein transferrin.
Serum iron. There are wide diurnal fluctuations[95], with values 10–30% higher in the morning than in the evening. In women the values are 10–15% lower than in men[92] and vary during the menstrual cycle[96]. In pregnant women approaching term the serum iron is 35% lower than in nonpregnant women[97]. In the newborn the level is at first high but falls rapidly during the first 12 hours[88]; it rises again during the first month, falls during the 2nd to 6th months, and often remains low up to the age of 2 years before rising to the adult level at school age[98]. On iron metabolism see the literature[92, 99].
The serum iron is pathologically *increased* in haemolytic anaemia, untreated pernicious anaemia, acute hepatitis and idiopathic haemochromatosis, pathologically *decreased* in iron-deficiency anaemia, infections, the nephrotic syndrome and chronic bleeding.

	WB Mean	WB 95% range	WB s	WB Ref.	P/S Mean	P/S 95% range	P/S s	P/S Ref.	Remarks
Copper (mg/l)		Erythrocytes:							
(a) Cord blood	1.03	–	–	100	0.51	–	–	88	Erythrocyte values from (a) 3, (d, e) 10 subjects; serum values from (a) 22, (b) 17, (c) 31, (d) 120, (e) 85 subjects. All values determined colorimetrically with dithizone. Copper can also be determined with bathocuproine[94] or oxalyl dihydrazide[102].
(b) Children, 3–10 years	...	...	...	...	1.31	0.77–1.85 (0.99–1.58)	0.27	88	
(c) Men	...	...	...	...	0.92	0.50–1.34	0.21	88	
(d) Men	0.89	0.72–1.06	0.085	100	1.10	0.79–1.41	0.157	101	
(e) Women	0.89	0.64–1.14	0.127	100	1.20	0.84–1.56	0.178	101	

Some 60% of the erythrocyte copper is contained in the erythrocuprein, 94% of the serum copper in the caeruloplasmin; both these proteins contain 0.32–0.36% copper. The copper content of the erythrocytes is much more constant than that of the serum, and there is no correlation between the two.
Serum copper. There may be wide fluctuations up to 0.3 mg/l from day to day[103]. During pregnancy the level rises by about 100% and then falls within two weeks post partum to the nonpregnancy level[100]. In the newborn it is much lower than in the mother because of the inability of caeruloplasmin to pass the placental barrier. The level rises steeply during the first year and is significantly higher in children than in adults[104]. There is an extensive literature on copper metabolism[105].
The serum copper is pathologically *increased* in infections, lupus erythematodes, glomerulonephritis, myocardial infarction, haemochromatosis, cirrhosis of various organs, HODGKIN's disease, acute leukaemia, aplastic anaemia and thyrotoxicosis, as well as during oestrogen therapy; it is pathologically *decreased* in disturbances of copper absorption, kwashiorkor, hepatolenticular degeneration, idiopathic hypoproteinaemia and loss of caeruloplasmin in the kidneys (in the nephrotic syndrome). In hepatolenticular degeneration the copper not bound to caeruloplasmin is increased.

	Whole blood				Plasma or serum				Remarks
	Mean	95% range (extreme range in brackets)	*s*	Reference	Mean	95% range (extreme range in brackets)	*s*	Reference	
Manganese (µg/l)									
(a)	–	(8.6–16.5)	–	106	–	(1.8–3.1)	–	106	Values (a) by neutron activation, (b) by colorimetry.
		Erythrocytes:							
(b)	~200	–	–	107	~100	–	–	107	
Molybdenum (µg/kg)	3.3	0–8.3	2.5	36	...	...	...	...	Values from 5 subjects by neutron activation.
Zinc (mg/l)		Erythrocytes:							
(a) Cord blood	3.76	1.56–5.96	1.10	108	1.25	0.59–1.91	0.33	108	Values for whole blood and cells from (a) 32, (b) 16, (c) 12, (d) 84, (e) 27, (f, g) 29 subjects, for serum from (a) 39, (b) 15, (c) 11, (d) 126, (e) 40 subjects; values (e, whole blood) determined by neutron activation, all others colorimetrically. About 35% of the serum zinc is bound to proteins. During pregnancy the serum zinc level falls by about 20%[108,111] but that of the erythrocytes and leucocytes remains fairly constant[112]. There is a considerable literature on zinc metabolism[113]. The serum zinc is pathologically *decreased* in atrophic cirrhosis of the liver, infections, myocardial infarction and untreated pernicious anaemia. The zinc content of the leucocytes is pathologically *decreased* in leukaemia[109,112] and cirrhosis of the liver[112,114].
(b) Children, 4–11 months	7.77	4.37–11.17	1.70	108	1.27	0.69–1.85	0.29	108	
(c) Children, 1–5 years	10.55	7.51–13.59	1.52	108	1.30	0.66–1.94	0.32	108	
(d) Adults	12.44	8.84–16.04	1.80	108	1.09	0.69–1.49	0.20	108	
		Whole blood:							
(e)	5.9	3.7–8.1	1.1	109	1.21	0.83–1.59	0.19	110	
		Erythrocytes:							
(f) (mg/10^{12} cells)	0.97	0.65–1.29	0.16	109					
		Leucocytes:							
(g) (mg/10^{12} cells)	14.0	0–34.8 (3.7–43.5)	10.4	109					
Aluminium (µg/l)	140	0–380	120	115	172	156–188	8	116	Serum values from 536 subjects. No dependence on age or sex has been observed.
Arsenic (µg/l)	–	(60–200)	–	117	...	...	...	...	Values (a) from 8 subjects by neutron activation.
(a) (µg/kg)	4	0–10	3.1	36					
Lead (µg/l)									
(a)	270	170–370	50	115	29	–	–	115	Values (b) from 100 adults (90% of the values under 100 µg/l); values (a) determined spectrographically, (b, c) colorimetrically. Most of the blood lead is in the erythrocytes[115]. Whole-blood values exceeding 400 µg/l indicate an abnormally high lead absorption[118].
(b)	–	(0–200)	–	118					
(c)	–	(<300–400)	–	119					
Lithium (µg/l)	...	...	...	...	–	(3–44)	–	120	
Selenium (µg/kg)	120	20–220	50	36	...	...	...	...	Values from 6 subjects by neutron activation.
Other elements	...	...	...	...	...	...	...	...	For a detailed list of the elements so far determined in blood see Bowen[121]. Recent assays have been made of barium[122,123], cadmium[124], chromium[123–125], gold[36], mercury[126], rubidium[123] and tin[115].

References

1 Davis et al., *Science*, **118**, 276 (1953).
2 Kessler et al., *J. Lab. clin. Med.*, **57**, 32 (1961).
3 Valberg et al., *J. clin. Invest.*, **44**, 379 (1965).
4 von Bubnoff and Riecker, *Klin. Wschr.*, **39**, 724 (1961).
5 Rigas, D. A., *J. Lab. clin. Med.*, **58**, 234 (1961).
6 Gibbs et al., *J. biol. Chem.*, **144**, 325 (1942).
7 Reardon et al., *Pediatrics*, **6**, 753 (1950).
8 Sommerkamp and Bomke, *Klin. Wschr.*, **42**, 392 (1964).
9 Schwab, M., *Klin. Wschr.*, **40**, 765 (1962).
10 Acharya and Payne, *Arch. Dis. Childh.*, **40**, 430 (1965).
11 Gyllenswärd and Josephson, *Scand. J. clin. Lab. Invest.*, **9**, 21 (1957).
12 Schales et al., *Stand. Meth. clin. Chem.*, **1**, 37 (1953).
13 Flear and Hughes, *Brit. Heart J.*, **25**, 166 (1963).
14 von Bubnoff and Riecker, *Biochem. Z.*, **331**, 577 (1959).
15 Marongiu et al., *Klin. Wschr.*, **44**, 1405 (1966).
16 Cotlove et al., *Stand. Meth. clin. Chem.*, **3**, 81 (1961).
17 Österlund, K., *Ann. Paediat. Fenn.*, **1**, suppl. 4 (1955).
18 Helve, O., *Acta med. scand.*, **125**, 505 (1946).
19 Todd et al., *Amer. J. Dis. Child.*, **57**, 1278 (1939).
20 Bullock, J. K., *Amer. J. Dis. Child.*, **40**, 725 (1930).
21 Wertheim et al., *J. clin. Invest.*, **33**, 565 (1954).
22 Skaug and Natvig, *Scand. J. clin. Lab. Invest.*, **9**, 39 (1957).
23 Reed et al., *J. Lab. clin. Med.*, **56**, 281 (1960).
24 Power and Young, *Stand. Meth. clin. Chem.*, **1**, 84 (1953); Dryer et al., *Stand. Meth. clin. Chem.*, **4**, 191 (1963).
25 Walser, M., *J. clin. Invest.*, **40**, 723 (1961).
26 Connelly et al., *Pediatrics*, **30**, 425 (1962).
27 Stearns and Warweg, *J. biol. Chem.*, **102**, 749 (1933).
28 Greenberg et al., *J. clin. Endocr.*, **20**, 364 (1960).
29 Kerr et al., *Amer. J. Obstet. Gynec.*, **83**, 2 (1962).
30 Nordin, B. E. C., *Advanc. clin. Chem.*, **4**, 275 (1961); Borle et al., Calcium and Phosphate Metabolism, *Documenta Geigy, Acta clinica*, No. 2, Basle, 1965.

31 LARIZZA, P., *Fisiol. e Med.*, **6**, 203 (1935), quoted by FLASCHENTRÄGER and LEHNARTZ (Eds.), *Physiologische Chemie*, vol. 2, part 1a, Springer, Berlin, 1954, page 415.
32 STURM and POTHMANN, *Z. klin. Med.*, **137**, 467 (1940).
33 MILLER et al., *J. Lab. clin. Med.*, **58**, 656 (1961).
34 CONWAY and FLOOD, *Biochem. J.*, **30**, 716 (1936).
35 CRETIUS and BEYERMANN, *Klin. Wschr.*, **40**, 89 (1962).
36 BRUNE et al., *Clin. chim. Acta*, **13**, 285 (1966).
37 ARIEFF, A. J., *J. Amer. med. Ass.*, **180**, 1075 (1962).
38 GEDALIA et al., *Proc. Soc. exp. Biol. (N.Y.)*, **106**, 147 (1961).
39 SINGER and ARMSTRONG, *J. appl. Physiol.*, **15**, 508 (1960).
40 SOGNNAES, R. F., *Science*, **150**, 989 (1965).
41 SANZ et al., *Clin. chim. Acta*, **1**, 570 (1956).
42 HARDEN and ALEXANDER, *Clin. Sci.*, **25**, 79 (1963).
43 DOWLING et al., *J. clin. Invest.*, **35**, 1263 (1956).
44 FARRELL and RICHMOND, *Clin. chim. Acta*, **6**, 620 (1961).
45 MAN et al., *Pediatrics*, **9**, 32 (1952).
46 MAN, E. B., *J. Lab. clin. Med.*, **59**, 528 (1962).
47 CHANEY, A. L., *Advanc. clin. Chem.*, **1**, 81 (1958).
48 KINGSLEY et al., *Stand. Meth. clin. Chem.*, **2**, 147 (1958); FOSS et al., *Stand. Meth. clin. Chem.*, **4**, 125 (1963).
49 SCAZZIGA et al., *Schweiz. med. Wschr.*, **94**, 1778 (1964).
50 ABOUL-KHAIR et al., *Clin. Sci.*, **27**, 195 (1964).
51 WAYNE et al., *Clinical Aspects of Iodine Metabolism*, Blackwell, Oxford, 1964; GROSS, J., in COMAR and BRONNER (Eds.), *Mineral Metabolism*, vol. 2, part B, Academic Press, New York, 1962, page 221.
52 REINWEIN and LIEBERMEISTER, *Klin. Wschr.*, **39**, 130 (1961).
53 FISHER and FREIMUTH, *J. invest. Derm.*, **30**, 85 (1958).
54 HINSBERG, K., in FLASCHENTRÄGER and LEHNARTZ (Eds.), *Physiologische Chemie*, vol. 2, part 1a, Springer, Berlin, 1954, page 415.
55 WORTH, G., *Klin. Wschr.*, **30**, 82 (1952).
56 GESSLER, U., *Klin. Wschr.*, **39**, 232 (1961).
57 PFLEIDERER, T., *Klin. Wschr.*, **42**, 640 (1964).
58 HARTMANN et al., *J. clin. Invest.*, **37**, 699 (1958).
59 HALD and MASON, *Stand. Meth. clin. Chem.*, **2**, 165 (1958); HALD, P. M., *Meth. med. Res.*, **4**, 79 (1951).
60 STAIB et al., *Chirurg*, **32**, 453 (1961).
61 VIDEBAEK and ACKERMANN, *J. Geront.*, **8**, 63 (1953).
62 BERGSTRÖM and HULTMAN, *Lancet*, **1**, 1132 (1962).
63 BERGMAN et al., *Lancet*, **1**, 892 (1963).
64 LEAF, A., *New Engl. J. Med.*, **267**, 24 and 77 (1962).
65 WALLACH et al., *J. Lab. clin. Med.*, **59**, 195 (1962).
66 STUTZMAN and AMATUZIO, *Arch. Biochem.*, **39**, 271 (1952).
67 STEWART and DUNLOP, *Clinical Chemistry in Practical Medicine*, 6th ed., Livingstone, Edinburgh, 1962, page 236.
68 FOWLER et al., *Lancet*, **2**, 284 (1961).
69 WILKINSON, R. H., *J. clin. Path.*, **10**, 126 (1957).
70 MACINTYRE, I., *Advanc. clin. Chem.*, **4**, 1 (1961).
71 MACINTYRE, I., *Biochem. J.*, **67**, 164 (1957).
72 MYERS, W. P. L., *Advanc. intern. Med.*, **11**, 163 (1962).
73 LUMB, G. A., *Clin. chim. Acta*, **8**, 33 (1963).
74 MCLEAN and HASTINGS, *Amer. J. med. Sci.*, **189**, 601 (1935); FANCONI and ROSE, *Quart. J. Med.*, NS**27**, 463 (1958); HANNA et al., *Clin. Chem.*, **10**, 235 (1964).
75 FORFAR and TOMPSETT, *Advanc. clin. Chem.*, **2**, 167 (1959).
76 HÄNZE, S., *Der Magnesiumstoffwechsel*, Thieme, Stuttgart, 1962.
77 MACINTYRE, I., *Sci. Basis Med. Ann. Rev.*, **1963**, 216.
78 STEWART et al., *J. Lab. clin. Med.*, **61**, 858 (1963).
79 THIERS et al., *Stand. Meth. clin. Chem.*, **5**, 131 (1965).
80 BASINSKI et al., *Stand. Meth. clin. Chem.*, **5**, 137 (1965).
81 ALCOCK et al., *Nature*, **206**, 89 (1965); PURDEN et al., *Clin. chem.*, **12**, 613 (1966).
82 PRASAD et al., *J. Lab. clin. Med.*, **58**, 531 (1961).
83 BOELLNER et al., *Amer. J. Dis. Child.*, **110**, 172 (1965).
84 WACKER and VALLEE, *Med. Clin. N. Amer.*, **44**, 1357 (1960).
85 WACKER and VALLEE, in COMAR and BRONNER (Eds.), *Mineral Metabolism*, vol. 2, part A, Academic Press, New York, 1964, page 483.
86 HAERDI et al., *Helv. chim. Acta*, **43**, 869 (1960).
87 PARR and TAYLOR, *Biochem. J.*, **91**, 424 (1964).
88 STURGEON, P., *Pediatrics*, **13**, 107 (1954).
89 SELTZER et al., *Amer. J. clin. Nutr.*, **13**, 343 (1963).
90 SACHS et al., *Arch. intern. Med.*, **52**, 366 (1933); **55**, 227 (1935); **71**, 489 (1943).
91 BEUTLER, E., *New Engl. J. Med.*, **256**, 692 (1957).
92 RAMSAY, W. N. M., *Advanc. clin. Chem.*, **1**, 1 (1958).
93 SCHALES et al., *Stand. Meth. clin. Chem.*, **2**, 69 (1958).
94 ZAK, B., *Clin. chim. Acta*, **3**, 328 (1958); SCHADE, A. L., *Meth. med. Res.*, **8**, 53 (1960); GIOVANNIELLO et al., *Stand. Meth. clin. Chem.*, **4**, 139 (1963); LAUBER, K., *Z. klin. Chem.*, **3**, 96 (1965).
95 BOWIE et al., *Amer. J. clin. Path.*, **40**, 491 (1963).
96 ZILVA and PATSTON, *Lancet*, **1**, 459 (1966).
97 HYTTEN and LEITCH, *The Physiology of Human Pregnancy*, Blackwell, Oxford, 1964, page 34.
98 GLADTKE and RIND, *Klin. Wschr.*, **44**, 88 (1966).
99 MOORE and DUBACH, in COMAR and BRONNER (Eds.), *Mineral Metabolism*, vol. 2, part B, Academic Press, New York, 1962, page 287; BOTHWELL and FINCH, *Iron Metabolism*, Little, Brown, Boston, 1962; BEUTLER et al., *Clinical Disorders of Iron Metabolism*, Grune & Stratton, New York, 1963: MOORE, F. D., Le métabolisme du fer, *Documenta Geigy, Acta clinica*, No. 7, Basle, 1967.
100 SHIELDS et al., *J. clin. Invest.*, **40**, 2007 (1961).
101 CARTWRIGHT et al., *Amer. J. Med.*, **28**, 555 (1960).
102 RICE et al., *Stand. Meth. clin. Chem.*, **4**, 57 (1963).
103 RICE, E. W., *Amer. J. med. Sci.*, **243**, 593 (1962).
104 BAKWIN et al., *Pediatrics*, **27**, 642 (1961).
105 MCELROY and GLASS (Eds.), *Copper Metabolism; a Symposium on Animal, Plant and Soil Relationships*, Johns Hopkins Press, Baltimore, 1950; ADELSTEIN and VALLEE, *New Engl. J. Med.*, **265**, 892 and 941 (1961); ADELSTEIN and VALLEE, in COMAR and BRONNER (Eds.), *Mineral Metabolism*, vol. 2, part B, Academic Press, New York, 1962, page 371; WALSHE and CUMINGS (Eds.), *Wilson's Disease*, Blackwell, Oxford, 1961.
106 COTZIAS and PAPAVASILIOU, *Nature*, **195**, 823 (1962).
107 MILLER and YOE, *Analyt. chim. Acta*, **26**, 224 (1962).
108 BERFENSTAM, R., *Acta paediat. (Uppsala)*, **41**, suppl. 87 (1952).
109 DENNES et al., *Biochem. J.*, **78**, 578 (1961).
110 VALLEE et al., *Ann. intern. Med.*, **50**, 1077 (1959).
111 JOHNSON, N. C., *Proc. Soc. exp. Biol. (N.Y.)*, **108**, 518 (1961).
112 FREDRICKS et al., *J. clin. Invest.*, **43**, 304 (1964).
113 VALLEE, B. L., *Physiol. Rev.*, **39**, 443 (1959); VALLEE, B. L., in COMAR and BRONNER (Eds.), *Mineral Metabolism*, vol. 2, part B, Academic Press, New York, 1962, page 443.
114 FREDRICKS et al., *J. clin. Invest.*, **39**, 1651 (1960).
115 KEHOE et al., *J. Nutr.*, **19**, 579 (1940); **20**, 85 (1940).
116 SEIBOLD, M., *Klin. Wschr.*, **38**, 117 (1960).
117 LEIFHEIT and FLETCHER, *Stand. Meth. clin. Chem.*, **3**, 23 (1961).
118 BERMAN, E., *Amer. J. clin. Path.*, **36**, 549 (1961).
119 RICE et al., *Stand. Meth. clin. Chem.*, **5**, 121 (1965).
120 LANG and HERRMANN, *Z. ges. exp. Med.*, **139**, 200 (1965).
121 BOWEN, H. J. M., *The Elementary Composition of Mammalian Blood*, United Kingdom Atomic Energy Authority Research Group, R 4196, Harwell, 1963.
122 THOMAS and CHITTENDEN, *Lancet*, **2**, 209 (1960).
123 NIEDERMEIER et al., *Arthr. and Rheum.*, **5**, 439 (1962).
124 IMBUS et al., *Arch. environm. Hlth*, **6**, 286 (1963).
125 PAIXAO and YOE, *Clin. chim. Acta*, **4**, 507 (1959); HERRING et al., *Amer. J. clin. Nutr.*, **8**, 846 and 855 (1960).
126 GOLDWATER et al., *Arch. environm. Hlth*, **5**, 537 (1962); KELLERSHOHN et al., *J. Lab. clin. Med.*, **66**, 168 (1965).
127 FUNDER and WIETH, *Scand. J. clin. Lab. Invest.*, **18**, 167 (1966).
128 TAVES, D. R., *Nature*, **211**, 192 (1966).
129 BAUDITZ, W., *Z. ges. exp. Med.*, **142**, 9 (1967).

Blood gases (for blood pH values see page 560; for references see page 571)

The normal values given in the table on pages 570 and 571 are for sea level and can be used at altitudes up to 200 m without adjustment. In persons resident at high altitudes the value of P_{CO_2} is reduced as a result of chronic hyperventilation while the pH remains normal owing to complete renal compensation, so that the plasma bicarbonate concentration is also reduced (cf. 'Water and Electrolyte Balance', page 527).

Blood samples for gas analysis must be drawn under anaerobic conditions. Even when they are stored under anaerobic conditions, however, it must be borne in mind that changes due to clotting, glycolysis, autoxidation and sedimentation will occur. Blood from the peripheral subcutaneous veins is not usually suitable for gas analysis. Venous mixed blood is drawn from the pulmonary arteries. Arterial blood should be drawn from the femoral, brachial or radial arteries. For the micro methods, capillary blood obtained by deep puncture of the warmed finger tip or of the lobe of the ear is suitable since its gas content is almost identical with that of arterial blood[1]. It has recently been recommended[2] that blood gas values should be measured at 37 °C instead of 38 °C, or converted to the former temperature.

Methods[3–5]. Carbon dioxide, oxygen, nitrogen and carbon monoxide are usually determined manometrically by VAN SLYKE's method or the KOPP-NATELSON micro modification of this method. Carbon dioxide and oxygen can also be measured by mass spectrography or gas chromatography, oxygen capacity and oxygen saturation by spectrophotometry, bicarbonate by titration, oxygen pressure polarographically, carbon dioxide pressure potentiometrically. Components of the CO_2-bicarbonate system not measured directly can be obtained by calculation using the dissociation equilibrium of carbonic acid (page 527) or by means of nomograms (pages 528 and 569).

Nomogram for the acid–base balance of human blood at 37 °C (from SINGER and HASTINGS, *Medicine [Baltimore]*, **27**, 223 [1948])

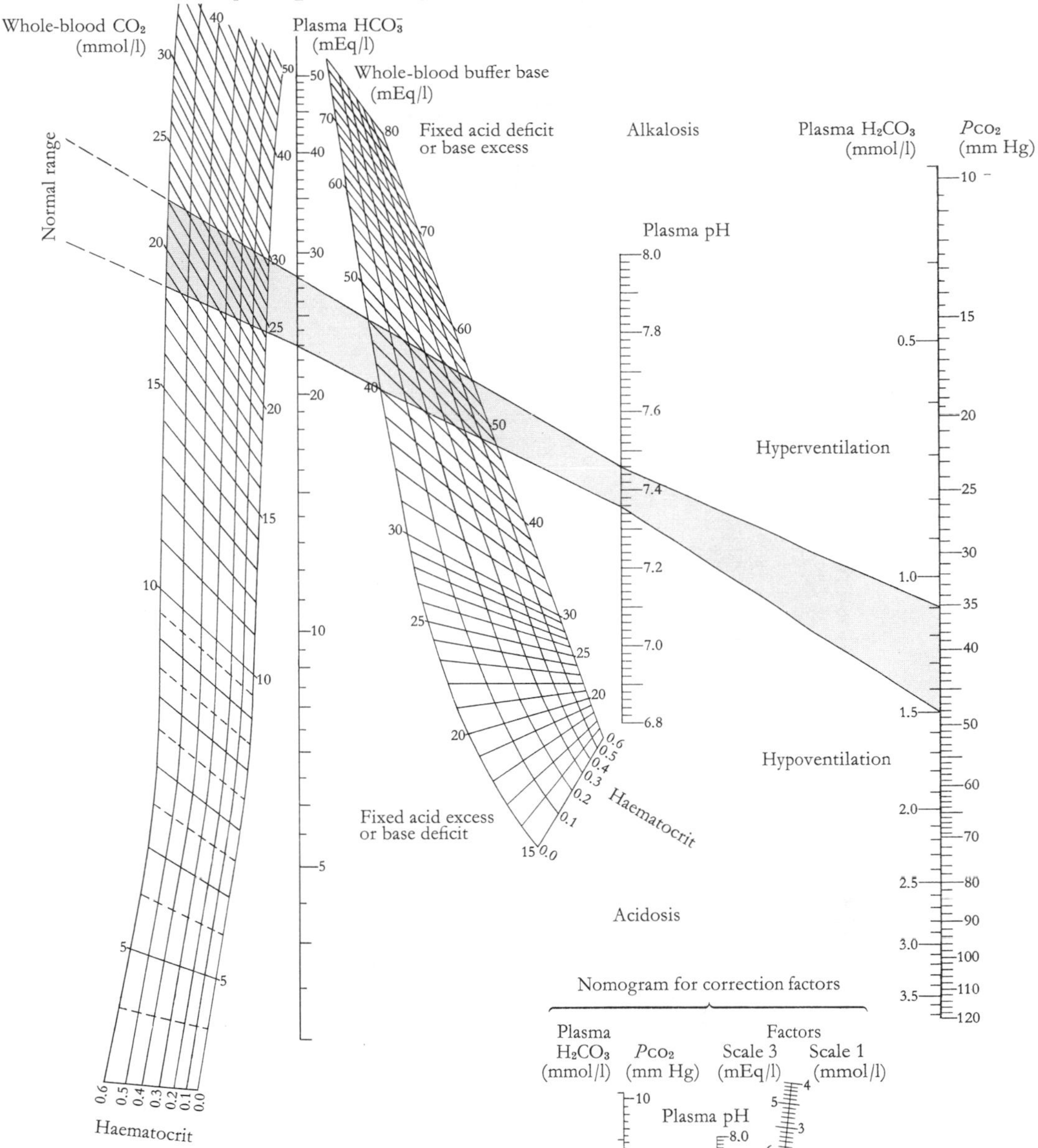

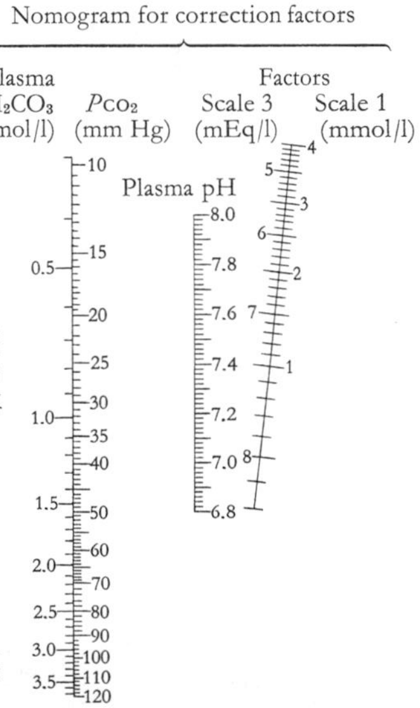

A straight line through points given on two of the scales intersects the remaining scales at simultaneously occurring values of the other variables of the acid–base balance. The normal range is for arterial, not venous, blood. If measurements are made on venous blood or blood not completely saturated with oxygen the appropriate corrected values for whole-blood CO_2 and whole-blood buffer base* are obtained by means of the correction factors f from the lower nomogram, as follows:

$$(\text{whole-blood } CO_2)_{\text{corrected}} = \text{whole-blood } CO_2 + (f_{\text{scale 1}} \times U \times \text{Ht})$$

$$(\text{whole-blood buffer base})_{\text{corrected}} = \text{whole-blood buffer base} - (f_{\text{scale 3}} \times U \times \text{Ht})$$

$$\text{Ht} = \text{haematocrit} = \frac{\text{vol\% of erythrocytes in whole blood}}{100}$$

$$U = 1 - \frac{O_2 \text{ saturation in \%}}{100}$$

* By whole-blood buffer base is understood the base equivalent of the sum of the buffering anions (bicarbonate, haemoglobin, plasma proteinate).

	Source of sample (blood unless otherwise stated)	Method	Number	Mean	95% range (extreme range in brackets)	s	Reference	Remarks
Oxygen								
Oxygen pressure (mm Hg)	Umbilical artery	Polarographic	25	9.2	0–19.2	5.0	6	Partial pressure of oxygen in a gaseous phase in equilibrium with blood (symbol P_{O_2} or p_{O_2}).
	Umbilical vein	Polarographic	25	22.4	12.8–32.0	4.8	6	
	Children, 1–4 weeks, arterial	Polarographic	12	85.6	70.7–101	7.45	7	
	Children, 4–16 months, arterial	Polarographic	13	78.0	55.0–101	11.51	7	
	Men, < 30 years, arterial	Polarographic	28	91.0	74.4–108	8.3	8	
	Men, > 60 years, arterial	Polarographic	10	79.7	62.7–96.7	8.5	8	
Oxygen content (vol%)	Umbilical artery	Manometric (van Slyke)	25	2.9	0–6.9	2.0	6	Oxygen content of blood drawn and tested under exclusion of air. About 99% is bound to haemoglobin, the remainder in physical solution (for details see Albritton[13]).
	Umbilical artery	Gas chromatographic	29	4.1	(0.4–7.7)	–	9	
	Umbilical vein	Manometric (van Slyke)	25	10.6	4.2–17.0	3.2	6	
	Umbilical vein	Gas chromatographic	32	12.3	(6.2–16.6)	–	9	
	Children, 3–11 years, arterial	Manometric (van Slyke)	9	15.6	13.7–17.5	0.93	10	
	Men, arterial	Manometric (van Slyke)	50	19.6	17.2–22.0	1.2	11	
	Men, venous	Manometric (van Slyke)	50	12.9	10.3–15.5	1.3	11	
Oxygen capacity (vol%)	Umbilical artery	Manometric (van Slyke)	25	22.15	17.9–26.4	2.11	6	Oxygen content of blood saturated with oxygen (maximum content possible). The O_2 in physical solution is often ignored and the oxygen capacity equated with the amount capable of being bound by the haemoglobin, from the content of which it is then calculated.
	Children, 1–4 weeks, arterial	Manometric (van Slyke)	12	20.38	14.5–26.2	2.93	7	
	Children, 4–16 months, arterial	Manometric (van Slyke)	13	13.89	10.3–17.5	1.78	7	
	Men, arterial	Manometric (van Slyke)	50	20.9	18.3–23.5	1.3	11	
	Men, venous	Manometric (van Slyke)	50	20.8	18.2–23.4	1.3	11	
Oxygen saturation (%)	Umbilical artery	Manometric (van Slyke)	25	13.7	0–32.1	9.2	6	Percentage saturation of the haemoglobin with oxygen (100 × O_2 content/O_2 capacity).
	Umbilical vein	Manometric (van Slyke)	25	47.7	19.5–75.9	14.1	6	
	Children, 1–4 weeks, arterial	Manometric (van Slyke)	12	95.2	89.0–101	3.11	7	
	Children, 4–16 months, arterial	Manometric (van Slyke)	13	92.5	86.0–99.0	3.23	7	
	Men, arterial	Manometric (van Slyke)	50	93.9	91.9–95.9	1.0	11	
	Men, venous	Manometric (van Slyke)	50	61.8	54.4–69.2	3.7	11	
	Adults, capillary	Spectrophotometric	40	96.6	94.2–99.0	1.2	4	
Carbon dioxide								
Carbon dioxide pressure (mm Hg)	Umbilical artery	Calculated	25	60.4	43.2–77.6	8.6	6	Partial pressure of carbon dioxide in a gaseous phase in equilibrium with blood (symbol P_{CO_2} or p_{CO_2}).
	Umbilical vein	Calculated	25	44.9	28.9–60.9	8.0	6	
	Children, 1–4 weeks, arterial	Calculated	12	36.7	28.5–44.9	4.08	7	
	Children, 4–16 months, arterial	Calculated	13	32.1	24.6–39.6	3.77	7	
	Children, 2–12 months, capillary	Calculated	10	32.8	28.7–36.9	2.05	12	
	Adults, arterial	Calculated	15	37.5	33.0–42.0	2.23	14	
	Men, < 30 years, arterial	Potentiometric	24	39.3	31.9–46.7	3.7	8	
	Men, > 60 years, arterial	Potentiometric	11	38.8	32.5–45.1	3.16	8	
	Men, arterial	Calculated	50	39.9	36.3–43.5	1.8	11	
	Men, venous	Calculated	50	49.9	46.1–53.7	1.9	11	
	Men, capillary (38 °C)	Calculated	20	41.2	35.8–46.6	2.7	4	
	Women, capillary (38 °C)	Calculated	20	38.1	32.5–43.7	2.8	4	
	Men, capillary (37 °C)	Calculated	–	39.3	–	–	2	
	Women, capillary (37 °C)	Calculated	–	36.4	31.0–41.7	–	2	

Carbon dioxide content (mmol/l)	Umbilical artery	Manometric (van Slyke)	25	21.4	17.0–25.8	2.2	6	Amount of CO_2 extractable by strong acid from blood drawn and tested under exclusion of air. In plasma about 5% is in physical solution, 94% as bicarbonate and 1% as carbamino compounds; in the erythrocytes the corresponding figures are 7%, 82% and 11% (for details see Albritton[13]). The proportion of carbonic acid (H_2CO_3) and carbonate (CO_3^{-}) is very small. To convert the values given into vol% multiply by 2.226.
	Umbilical artery	Gas chromatographic	29	19.8	(13.3–25.6)	–	9	
	Umbilical vein	Manometric (van Slyke)	25	18.3	13.9–22.7	2.2	6	
	Umbilical vein	Gas chromatographic	32	17.0	(11.1–21.2)	–	9	
	Children, 3–11 years, arterial	Manometric (van Slyke)	9	20.4	18.2–22.6	1.1	10	
	Men, arterial	Manometric (van Slyke)	50	21.6	20.4–22.8	0.6	11	
	Men, venous	Manometric (van Slyke)	50	24.6	23.2–26.0	0.7	11	
	Adults, arterial (plasma)	Manometric (van Slyke)	15	26.1	22.4–29.8	1.83	14	
	Men, arterial (plasma)	Manometric (van Slyke)	50	26.6	24.6–28.6	0.99	5	
	Women, arterial (plasma)	Manometric (van Slyke)	50	25.6	22.7–28.5	1.43	5	
	Men, venous (plasma)	Manometric (Kopp-Natelson)	7	30.3	27.7–32.9	1.31	15	
	Women, venous (plasma)	Manometric (Kopp-Natelson)	8	27.8	24.9–30.7	1.45	15	
Bicarbonate content (mEq/l)	Adults (plasma)	Titrimetric	–	–	21–30	–	16	The bicarbonate content of the plasma is usually calculated from the carbon dioxide content by subtracting the physically dissolved CO_2, but not the carbamino CO_2, from the total carbon dioxide. The values so obtained agree fairly well with those measured by titration.
	Adults, arterial (plasma)	Calculated	15	24.9	21.3–28.5	1.79	14	
	Adults (erythrocytes)	Calculated	9	11.2	10.9–11.5	0.15	17	
Standard bicarbonate (mEq/l)	Umbilical vein	Calculated	–	16.6	11.8–21.4	–	18	Bicarbonate content of the plasma of whole blood containing oxygen-saturated haemoglobin and equilibrated at a P_{CO_2} of 40 mm Hg at 37 °C. The standard bicarbonate can also be obtained from nomograms[4, 5]. The alkali reserve (carbon dioxide combining power) is the CO_2 content of the anaerobically separated plasma equilibrated at a P_{CO_2} of 40 mm Hg at room temperature; the values obtained are not absolutely reproducible.
	Children, 1–4 weeks, arterial (plasma)	Calculated	12	21.1	17.8–24.4	1.67	7	
	Children, 4–16 months, arterial (plasma)	Calculated	13	21.0	19.0–23.0	0.99	7	
	Adults, arterial (plasma)	Manometric (van Slyke)	15	25.2	22.4–28.0	1.40	14	
	Men, capillary (plasma)	Calculated	20	–	22.1–25.8	–	5	
	Women, capillary (plasma)	Calculated	20	–	21.3–25.0	–	5	
Base excess (mEq/l)	Umbilical artery	Calculated	16	−9.9	–	–	9	Base concentration as measured by titration with strong acid up to pH 7.40 at a P_{CO_2} of 40 mm Hg (at 37 °C). Negative values are those measured by titration with a strong base (also called base deficit). For a Hb content of 150 g/l blood the following approximate relationship holds between the deviation of the standard bicarbonate from normal and the base excess: Δ standard bicarbonate × 1.2 = base excess.
	Umbilical vein	Calculated	16	−6.4	–	–	9	
	Umbilical vein	Calculated	–	−9.5	−16.6 to −2.5	–	18	
	Men, capillary	Calculated	20	−0.1	−2.4 to 2.3	–	4	
	Women, capillary	Calculated	20	−1.0	−3.3 to 1.2	–	4	
Buffer base (mEq/l)	Umbilical vein	Calculated	–	37.2	30.8–43.7	–	18	Sum of the basic buffer anions in whole blood, namely bicarbonate, haemoglobin and plasma proteinate. Obtained by use of the nomogram on page 569.
	Men, arterial	Calculated	153	48.4	46–52	–	19	
	Men, capillary	Calculated	180	50.1	47–53	–	19	
	Women, capillary	Calculated	24	48.0	45–51	–	19	

1 Singer et al., *Clin. Chem.*, **1**, 287 (1955); Gambino, S. R., *Amer. J. clin. Path.*, **35**, 175 (1961); Maas and van Heijst, *Clin. chim. Acta*, **6**, 31 (1961).
2 Gambino et al., *Ann. N. Y. Acad. Sci.*, **133**, 259 (1966).
3 Bartels et al., *Lungenfunktionsprüfungen*, Springer, Berlin, 1959; Woolmer, R. F. (Ed.), *A Symposium on pH and Blood Gas Measurement*, Churchill, London, 1959; Gaensler, E. A., *Ann. Rev. Med.*, **12**, 385 (1961); Severinghaus, J. W., *Ann. Rev. Physiol.*, **24**, 421 (1962); Consolazio et al., *Physiological Measurements of Metabolic Functions in Man*, McGraw-Hill, New York, 1963, page 99 and 132.
4 Siggaard-Andersen, O., *Scand. J. clin. Lab. Invest.*, **15**, suppl. 70 (1963).
5 Astrup and Siggaard-Andersen, *Advanc. clin. Chem.*, **6**, 1 (1963).
6 Beer et al., *Pflügers Arch. ges. Physiol.*, **260**, 306 (1955).
7 Riegel, K., *Klin. Wschr.*, **41**, 249 (1963).
8 Ulmer and Reichel, *Klin. Wschr.*, **41**, 1 (1963).
9 Rooth, G., *Acta paediat. (Uppsala)*, **52**, 22 (1963).
10 Kennedy and Sokoloff, *J. clin. Invest.*, **36**, 1130 (1957).
11 Gibbs et al., *J. biol. Chem.*, **144**, 325 (1942).
12 Proença and Wenner, *Klin. Wschr.*, **40**, 898 (1962).
13 Albritton, E. C. (Ed.), *Standard Values in Blood*, Saunders, Philadelphia, 1952, page 120; Dittmer and Grebe (Eds.), *Handbook of Respiration*, Saunders, Philadelphia, 1958, page 56.
14 Schwab, M., *Klin. Wschr.*, **40**, 765 (1962).
15 Gambino, S. R., *Amer. J. clin. Path.*, **32**, 294 (1959).
16 Hodes et al., *Stand. Meth. clin. Chem.*, **1**, 19 (1953).
17 Sommerkamp and Bomke, *Klin. Wschr.*, **42**, 392 (1964).
18 Saling, E., *Das Kind im Bereich der Geburtshilfe*, Thieme, Stuttgart, 1966.
19 Singer and Hastings, in Dittmer, D. S. (Ed.), *Blood and Other Body Fluids*, Biological Handbooks, Federation of American Societies for Experimental Biology, Washington, 1961, page 183.

(For references see page 578)

	Whole blood				Plasma or serum				Remarks
	Mean	95% range (extreme range in brackets)	*s*	Reference	Mean	95% range (extreme range in brackets)	*s*	Reference	
Total nitrogen (g/l)	34.3	(30.0–41.0)	–	1	13.1	(12.0–14.3)	–	1	Comprises the chemically bound nitrogen. Because of the fibrinogen the total nitrogen of the plasma is slightly higher than the serum value given here. For the KJELDAHL method of N determination see ARCHIBALD et al.[6]. The proportion of protein N in the total N is over 99% in the erythrocytes, over 96% in the serum, about 80% in the leucocytes and about 90% in the thrombocytes; in the erythrocytes 94% of the total N is contained in the haemoglobin.
		Erythrocytes:							
(g/l)	–	(57–62)	–	2					
(g/kg)	55.3	51.7–58.9	1.8	3					
(mg/10^9 cells)	4.61	3.77–5.45	0.42	4					
		Leucocytes:							
	10.0	0–23.8	6.9	4					
		Thrombocytes:							
	–	(0.31–0.39)	–	5					
Nonprotein nitrogen (NPN) (mg/l)									
(a) Cord blood	311	244–378	33.4	7	...	...	...	...	Values from (a) 25, (b) 21, (c) 25, (d) 30, (e) 58, (f) 46 subjects by (a–d) method of FOLIN[9], (e, f) method of RAPPAPORT[10]. On a high-protein diet the NPN content is increased and the proportion of urea N is up to 90%; on a low-protein diet the NPN content is reduced and the proportion of urea N is 50% or less[11]. Towards the end of pregnancy the NPN content of the blood decreases and the proportion of urea N is small[11]. The NPN is pathologically *increased* in various kidney diseases, obstruction of the urinary tract, burns and shock, *decreased* in severe liver damage. See also under 'Urea', below, and page 531.
(b) Newborn, 5–6 days	266	201–331	32.3	7					
(c) Children, 1–6 years	324	253–395	35.7	7					
(d) Adults	331	219–443	56.0	7					
(e) Men	276	202–350	36.9	8	249	177–321	35.9	8	
(f) Women	261	183–339	39.1	8	223	139–307	42.0	8	
		Erythrocytes:							
(e) Men	309	211–407	48.9	8					
(f) Women	318	189–447	64.7	8					
Urea (mg/l)									
(a) Cord blood	294	148–440	73	12	216	158–274	29	7	Values from (a, whole blood) 13, (a, serum) 25, (b) 21, (c) 25, (d) 30, (e) 42, (f) 31, (g) 10 subjects by cleavage with urease and determination of NH_3 by NESSLER's reagent[14] or better BERTHELOT's reagent[15,16]. In an automatic series of assays using diacetylmonoxime[17] 90% of the values were below 200 mg/l serum. For calculation of the urea content from the NPN see page 532. The urea content of the blood depends mainly on the protein intake, the amount of urine excreted and the functional state of the kidneys. The concentration in the cord blood is determined by that in the maternal blood[12]; in pregnant women it appears to be rather low[7]. The urea content is *increased* when protein breakdown in organs is increased (for instance in fever and after operations), in disturbances of renal excretion and in obstruction of the urinary tract; it is *decreased* frequently in dehydrated patients given N-free solutions[18].
(a) Newborn, 3 hours	257	71–443	93	12					
(a) Newborn, 24 hours	318	60–576	129	12					
(b) Newborn, 5–6 days	...	...	...	...	201	139–263	31	7	
(c) Children, 1–6 years	...	...	...	...	313	241–385	36	7	
(d) Adults	...	...	...	...	328	230–426	49	7	
(e) Men	272	156–388	58	8	305	177–433	64	8	
(f) Women	241	131–351	55	8	238	122–354	58	8	
		Erythrocytes:							
(e) Men	232	114–350	59	8					
(f) Women	178	58–298	60	8					
(g) In relation to protein intake									
0.5 g protein/kg body weight/day	...	...	...	...	193	135–251	29	13	
1.5 g protein/kg body weight/day	...	...	...	...	386	244–528	71	13	
2.5 g protein/kg body weight/day	...	...	...	...	455	311–599	72	13	
Creatine (mg/l)									
Children, 1–14 weeks	...	...	...	...	–	(2.2–12.5)	–	19	Serum values by (a) JAFFÉ reaction, (b) fluorometry with ninhydrin. On the JAFFÉ reaction see below under 'Creatinine'. The serum creatine level is somewhat increased on a diet rich in meat.
Adults									
(a)	27	–	–	20	–	(1.6–4.0)	–	21	
(b)	...	...	...	...	–	(1.9–7.9)	–	22	
		Erythrocytes:							
	56.2	–	–	23					
Creatinine (mg/l)									
(a) Cord blood	...	...	...	...	11.8	6.4–17.2	2.7	7	Serum values from (a) 25, (b) 18, (c) 25, (d) 30, (e) 39, (f) 28 subjects; values (e, f) by an automatic method. The JAFFÉ reaction often used to determine creatine and creatinine is not specific and is subject to interference by glucose, acetoacetic acid, acetone, ascorbic acid, pyruvate, etc. Values also depend on how the sample is prepared; those measured by the enzymatic[25] and ion-exchange[26] methods (true creatinine) are about 10–20% less than the JAFFÉ reaction values. For further discussion of methods see the literature[21, 27].
(b) Children, 4–21 weeks	...	...	...	...	9.5	7.9–11.1	0.8	7	
(c) Children, 1–6 years	...	...	...	...	11.9	7.5–16.3	2.2	7	
(d) Adults	6	–	–	20	12.4	6.6–18.2	2.9	7	
(e) Men	...	...	...	...	8.55	5.3–11.9	1.69	24	
(f) Women	...	...	...	...	7.12	5.6–8.6	0.77	24	
		Erythrocytes:							
	4.5	–	–	23					

The serum creatinine level is *increased* by ingestion of creatinine (for instance in roast meat); it is largely proportional to the muscle mass and therefore higher in men than in women (see also page 531). The level is pathologically *increased* when endogenous synthesis is increased (as in acromegaly) and when excretion is impaired.

(For references see page 578)

	Whole blood				Plasma or serum				Remarks
	Mean	95% range (extreme range in brackets)	*s*	Reference	Mean	95% range (extreme range in brackets)	*s*	Reference	
Guanidine (mg/l)	–	(< 0.4)	–	*20*					
Guanidinoacetic acid (mg/l)	–	(< 3)	–	*20*	–	(2.4–4.4)	–	*28*	Absent from the erythrocytes[23].
Methylguanidine (mg/l)	–	(< 0.2)	–	*20*					
Ammonia (mg/l)									
(a) Newborn, 0–14 days	–	(0.9–1.5)	–	*29*	...	...	...	...	Values from (b, whole blood) 25, (b, serum) 30, (c) 20, (d) 50, (e) 25 subjects by (a, d, e) diffusion method, (b, c) ion-exchange chromatography. In the newborn the blood ammonia level is higher than in the mother[34]; it is high in premature infants and newborn with icterus[29], very often also in patients with incipient hepatic coma[35].
(a) Children	–	(0.07–0.63)	–	*29*					
(b) Adults	0.48	0.22–0.74	0.13	*30*	0.20	(0.04–0.33)	–	*31*	
(c) Adults	...	...	...	...	0.19	0.08–0.30	0.055	*32*	
(d) Adults, venous blood	1.02	0.56–1.48	0.23	*33*					
(e) Adults, arterial blood	1.06	0.76–1.36	0.15	*33*					
Free amino acids (as α-amino-N) (mg/l)									
(a) Cord blood	...	...	...	...	76.8	36.8–116.8	20	*36*	Values from (a) 25, (b) 32, (c, d) 53 subjects by colorimetric method with ninhydrin. A measure of the amino-acid content is the α-amino-N content, best determined by the gasometric ninhydrin method[37], though this also measures the α-amino groups of peptides and other substances. In serum the α-amino-N value depends on the manner in which the proteins are precipitated[38]; it is rather higher than in the plasma owing to release of amino acids from the thrombocytes during coagulation. (For individual amino acids in blood see page 574.)
(b) Children, 6–11 years	...	...	...	...	50.1	24.1–76.1	13	*36*	
(c) Men	61	48.4–73.6	6.3	*8*	42	33.4–50.6	4.3	*8*	
(d) Women	59	48.2–69.8	5.4	*8*	39	28.0–50.0	5.5	*8*	
		Erythrocytes:							
(c) Men	87	71.8–102.2	7.6	*8*					
(d) Women	90	75.0–105.0	7.5	*8*					
Carnitine (mg/l)	...	...	...	...	–	(8.6–13.3)	–	*49*	
Ergothioneine (mg/l)		Erythrocytes:							
(a) Adults	96	34–158	31	*50*	...	...	...	...	Values from (a) 94 measurements and (b) 4, (c) 10, (d) 15, (e) 13 subjects. The blood level depends on the ergothioneine content of the diet. Pathological variations have been reported[50, 51].
(μmol/kg water)									
(b) Cord blood	162	26–298	68	*45*					
(c) Children, 4 days–1 year	125	17–233	54	*45*					
(d) Children, 1–12 years	200	0–410	105	*45*					
(e) Adults	458	90–826	184	*41*	–	(< 10)	–	*41*	
		Leucocytes:							
	–	(< 300)	–	*41*					
Glutathione (mg/l)									
(a) Adults	354	(269–414)	–	*52*	...	...	...	...	Values from (a) 10, (b) 102, (c) 10 subjects. Glutathione occurs only in the erythrocytes. In its reduced form it accounts for some 30% of the nonsugar reducing substances of whole blood. There appears to be a close relationship between glutathione stability and the sensitivity of the cells to haemolysis[56].
		Erythrocytes:							
(b) Newborn, < 48 hours	782	748–816	16.9	*53*					
(b) Newborn, > 48 hours	697	662–732	17.6	*53*					
(c) Adults	–	(586–689)	–	*54*					
(μmol/10^{12} cells)									
Reduced (GSH)	210	144–276	33	*55*					
Oxidized (GSSG)	22	10–34	6	*55*					
Aliphatic amines (as N) (mg/l)	0.30	0.08–0.52	0.11	*57*	...	...	...	...	Values from 35 subjects. Ethanolamine and dimethylamine predominate.
Ethanolamine (μmol/kg water)	–	Erythrocytes: (< 10)	–	*41*	–	(< 10)	–	*41*	For plasma values see also the table on page 574.
	–	Leucocytes: (< 250)	–	*41*					
Phosphoethanolamine (mg/l)									
Cord blood	...	...	...	...	2.7	0–5.5	1.4	*47*	
Maternal blood	...	...	...	...	0.5	0–1.1	0.3	*47*	
		Leucocytes:							
(μmol/kg water)	2651	451–4851	1100	*41*					

(For references see page 578)

Amino acids

Individual amino acids can be determined by microbiological methods[39] or after separation by paper chromatography[40, 41] or column chromatography[42, 43]; for a few there are also specific chemical methods. STEIN and MOORE's column-chromatographic separation usually yields 26 amino acids in serum, with a further 6 ninhydrin-positive substances occurring in traces. Normal values are shown in the table below. For further data see the literature (reviews[43, 44], values in children[45, 46], cord-blood values[47]).

Physiological variations. The amino-acid content of the blood is increased for several hours after a protein-rich meal. It is higher in newborn and particularly premature infants than in older children; in children in general it is rather lower than in adults, though there are wide individual variations. Values for glutamic acid are higher in children than in adults. In women the amino-acid content of the blood shows some dependence on the menstrual cycle: at the start of the luteal phase the alanine, serine, lysine, threonine and proline contents are low, while during pregnancy most amino acids are present in rather lower amount than in the luteal phase.

Pathological variations. The serum amino-acid content is *increased* in liver disease, particularly acute yellow atrophy of the liver, severe burns and shock, in diabetes with ketosis and in kwashiorkor (especially β-aminobutyric acid), *decreased* somewhat in nephrosis. The contents of some amino acids are increased in hereditary disturbances of amino-acid metabolism (see pages 448–450). For further discussion of the pathological variations see the literature[48].

Free amino acids in the plasma and blood cells of newborn, children and adults (by ion-exchange column chromatography)

	Newborn* 1st day		Adults*		Children** 9 months–2 years		Adults†	Men††			
	Plasma		Plasma		Plasma		Plasma	Plasma[42]	Erythrocytes	Leucocytes	Thrombocytes
	Mean	Range	Mean	Range	Mean	Range	Range	Mean			
	mg/l	mg/l	mg/l	mg/l	µmol/l	µmol/l	µmol/l	µmol/kg	µmol/kg	µmol/kg	µmol/kg
Alanine	29.4	21.0–36.5	30.7	22.2–44.7	219	99–313	213–472	420	350	6610	2700
β-Alanine	1.3	–	0.8	–	0	0	–	–	–	–	–
α-Aminobutyric acid	1.5	0.6–3.0	1.7	1.0–2.4	5	0–17	10–35	–	–	–	–
β-Aminoisobutyric acid	–	–	–	–	5	0–22	trace	–	–	–	–
Arginine	9.4	3.8–15.3	14.3	8.6–26.3	31	11–65	40–140	100	0	330	530
Asparagine	6.0	–	5.7	–	–	–	–	–	–	–	–
Aspartic acid	1.1	trace–2.2	2.2	trace–7.2	2	0–9	1–11	2	370	3500	2700
Citrulline	2.8	1.5–5.0	5.3	2.1–9.7	–	–	10–17	–	–	–	–
Cystine §	14.7	8.5–20.2	17.7	11.5–33.7	4	0–40	70–108	110	0	370	0
Ethanolamine	3.2	1.6–5.6	0.1	trace–0.7	–	–	–	–	–	–	–
Glutamic acid	7.6	3.0–15.7	8.6	2.5–17.3	–	–	(20–90)	(50)	(320)	(7360)	(3160)
Glutamine	112	79–140	83	61–102	135	46–290	(140–570)	–	–	–	–
Glycine	25.8	16.8–38.6	17.4	10.8–36.6	170	56–308	179–587	220	370	5080	3650
Histidine	11.9	7.6–17.7	12.4	9.7–14.5	64	24–112	32–97	80	140	630	310
Hydroxyproline	4.2	–	0.92 §§	0.69–1.20 §§	–	–	–	–	–	–	–
Isoleucine	5.2	3.5–6.9	7.1	4.6–11.5	44	26–94	40–99	70	40	2900	1200
Leucine	9.5	6.1–14.3	13.2	9.3–17.8	75	45–155	78–176	140	400	6300	1880
Lysine	29.3	16.7–39.3	25.4	21.1–30.9	87	45–144	105–207	200	130	2360	1220
Methionine	4.4	1.3–6.1	3.2	2.3–3.9	21	3–29	11–30	30	trace	1750	380
1-Methylhistidine	–	–	–	–	0	0	0–10	–	–	–	–
3-Methylhistidine	–	–	–	–	0	0	0–8	–	–	–	–
Ornithine	12.1	6.5–20.0	9.2	4.3–16.7	40	10–107	30–64	–	–	–	–
Phenylalanine	13.0	6.9–18.2	9.5	6.3–19.2	40	23–69	38–73	50	40	2480	850
Proline	21.3	12.3–31.9	27.1	12.8–51.4	115	51–185	103–290	220	170	2100	1020
Serine	17.2	9.9–25.5	11.8	6.8–20.3	92	24–172	76–164	120	150	5100	3650
Taurine	17.6	9.3–27.0	8.3	5.7–17.3	49	19–91	32–138	50	36	26000	21000
Threonine	25.9	13.6–39.9	19.4	12.2–29.3	60	33–128	76–194	130	160	3400	1550
Tryptophan	6.5	trace–13.7	9.8	5.1–14.9	–	–	–	–	–	–	–
Tyrosine	12.6	7.6–18.0	9.1	6.5–11.3	45	11–122	22–83	60	50	1970	780
Valine	16.0	9.4–28.8	19.9	13.6–26.6	127	57–262	168–317	270	330	3750	1500

* Values from 25 infants before the first feed and 8 adults[129].
** Fasting values from 20 children (VIS, H., quoted by SOUPART, P.[43]).
† Fasting values from 30 adults assembled from the literature[43].
†† Blood-cell values from one man[43].

§ Values in µmol are for cystine ½ + cysteine. The plasma of adults contains about 10 mg cystine and about 4 mg cysteine per litre[130].
§§ Fasting values from 10 men[131].

Blood – Nitrogenous Substances

(For references see page 578)

	Whole blood				Plasma or serum				Remarks
	Mean	95% range (extreme range in brackets)	s	Reference	Mean	95% range (extreme range in brackets)	s	Reference	
Cystamine (mg/l)	2.9	–	–	58					
Spermine (mg/l)	1.34	1.14–1.54	0.10	59	...	...	...	...	Values from 30 subjects. Both amines are found only in the cells.
Spermidine (mg/l)	0.96	0.86–1.06	0.05	59	...	...	...	...	
Acetylcholine (µg/l)	...	...	...	...	12.8	0–36.8 (3.2–48.0)	12.0	60	Values from 14 subjects. Higher in asthmatic patients.
Choline (mg/l)									
Total choline	...	...	...	...	–	(244–542)	–	61	The serum choline is almost all in the form of phospholipids.
Free choline	...	...	...	...	4.4	(2.5–9.9)	–	62	
Catecholamines	...	...	...	...	...	...	...	...	See pages 731 and 733.
Histamine (µg/l)	–	(16–89)	–	63	2.6	(0–15)	–	63	Histamine occurs mainly in the leucocytes[64] (values in µg per 10^9 cells): neutrophils 3.3, basophils 1080, eosinophils 160, lymphocytes 0.6, monocytes 1.2, thrombocytes 0.009. The blood histamine is increased in the carcinoid syndrome[65] and particularly in chronic myeloid leukaemia owing to the increased number of basophils[64].
Bufotenine (µg/l)	–	(0–27)	–	66					
Tryptamine	...	...	...	...	...	...	...	...	Tryptamine has been found in the blood of a patient with a carcinoid tumour[67].
***N, N*-Dimethyltryptamine** (µg/l)	39	27–51	6	68	...	...	...	...	Values from 50 subjects.
Serotonin (µg/l)	–	(90–180)	–	69	13	1–25	6	70	Most of the blood serotonin is adsorbed on the thrombocytes. It is increased in the carcinoid syndrome[72], with thrombocyte values up to 18.5 µg/10^9 cells[71].
(µg/10^9 cells)	0.336	Thrombocytes: 0.148–0.524	0.094	70					
	0.45	0.13–0.77	0.16	71					
3-Indoxylsulphuric acid (indican) (mg/l)									
(a) Men	...	...	...	...	3	1.2–4.8	0.9	73	Values from (a) 56, (b) 44 subjects. The serum indican is increased in the nephrotic syndrome[74].
(b) Women	...	...	...	...	3	0.6–5.4	1.2	73	
6-Sulphatoxyskatole (mg/l)	...	...	...	...	–	(0–1)	–	75	
Indolyl-3-acetic acid (mg/l)	...	...	...	...	–	(1–2)	–	75	
Indolyl-3-lactic acid (mg/l)	...	...	...	...	–	(0.1–1)	–	75	
Porphyrins									
δ-Aminolaevulinic acid (mg/l)	–	Erythrocytes: (0.25–0.45)	–	76	0.19	0.11–0.27	0.04	77	Serum values from 50 men. Aminoacetone is also formed in the erythrocytes during the biosynthesis of δ-aminolaevulinic acid[78].
Porphobilinogen (mg/l)	–	Erythrocytes: (0.15–0.40)	–	76					
Coproporphyrin (µg/l)									
(a) Cord blood	28	Erythrocytes: 0–60 (11–72)	16	79	15	1–29 (7–32)	7	79	Erythrocyte values from (a) 20, (b) 10, (c, d) 20 subjects; serum values from (a) 16, (c, d) 11 subjects. The coproporphyrin content of the erythrocytes shows good correlation with the reticulocyte count[80]. It is often markedly increased in congenital erythropoietic porphyria, coproporphyria[81], and sideroachrestic anaemia[82], increased in haemolytic anaemia, slightly increased in iron-deficiency anaemia, while zero values are found in untreated pernicious anaemia[80]. The serum coproporphyrin is increased in porphyria[83].
(b) Newborn, 9–15 days	8	–	–	79					
(c) Men	13	5–21 (7–23)	4	79					
(d) Women	12	0–26 (3–23)	7	79	8	2–14 (4–15)	3	79	

(For references see page 578)

	Whole blood				Plasma or serum				Remarks
	Mean	95% range (extreme range in brackets)	*s*	Reference	Mean	95% range (extreme range in brackets)	*s*	Reference	
Protoporphyrin (μg/l)		Erythrocytes:							
(a) Cord blood	540	40–1040 (320–1350)	250	79	...	...	...	...	Values from (a) 20, (b) 10, (c) 8, (d, e) 20 subjects. Protoporphyrin is almost absent from the serum[83]. The protoporphyrin content of the erythrocytes is not so closely correlated with the reticulocyte count as the coproporphyrin content[80]. It is markedly increased in erythropoietic protoporphyria[81] and iron-deficiency anaemia, slightly increased in haemolytic anaemia, shows very high values in lead poisoning, and remains within the normal limits in pernicious anaemia[80].
(b) Newborn, 9–15 days	510	–	–	79					
(c) Children, 1–2 years	320	–	–	79					
(d) Men	300	150–450 (160–520)	75	79					
(e) Women	370	170–570 (180–510)	100	79					
Uroporphyrin (μg/l)	–	Erythrocytes: (0–20)	–	76					
Haemoglobin									
Cord blood (mg/l)	...	...	...	...	80	–	–	84	Values (a) from blood drawn by careful puncture of the heel, (b) from 25 subjects by the benzidine reaction. The serum haemoglobin is increased during bodily activity and may reach 30 times the normal value in highly-trained athletes. The serum haemoglobin is bound to haptoglobin; the maximum binding capacity is 1.4 g/l serum[87]. Values (c) from 200 subjects. See also pages 611 and 613.
(a) Newborn (mg/l)	...	...	...	...	–	(1000–1310)	–	84	
(b) Adults (mg/l)	...	...	...	...	3.1	(1.6–5.8)	–	85	
(c) Adults (g/l)	158.5	134–173	–	86					
(c) Adults (g/l)	328	Erythrocytes: 299–357	–	86					
Haemiglobin (methaemoglobin) (as % of the haemoglobin)	0.4	(0.0–1.1)	–	88	...	...	...	...	For spectrophotometric determination see HAINLINE et al.[90]. Clinical symptoms (cyanosis) appear at 20% and higher concentrations of haemiglobin[91], and there is danger to life at 70%[92]. On toxic and congenital haemiglobinaemia (methaemoglobinaemia) see JAFFÉ and HELLER[92].
	0.65	0.25–1.05	0.20	89					
Carboxyhaemoglobin (as % of the haemoglobin)									
(a) Newborn	0.42	0–1.54 (0.1–1.8)	0.56	93	...	...	...	...	Values (a) from 20 infants up to 4 days old (infants with Rh and AB0 incompatibilities had values from 1.9 to 11.9%[93]), (b) measured in a CO-free atmosphere, (c) measured in a normal atmosphere. Values of 12% and more have been measured in car drivers. Clinical symptoms appear at 15–25%, danger to life at 65%[91].
(b) Adults	0.55	–	–	94					
(c) Adults	3.4	0–8.2	2.4	95					
Verdoglobin (mg/l)	4	–	–	96					
Bilirubin (mg/l)									
Direct-reacting									
(a) Adults	...	...	...	...	1.0	(0.5–2.4)	–	97	Values from (a, b) 110, (c) 49, (d) 150, (e) 11, (f) 10, (g) 11, (h) 6, (i) 61, (j) 53 subjects. Determination by VAN DEN BERGH reaction; for modification of MALLOY and EVELYN (denaturing with methanol) see MACDONALD et al.[101], for that of JENDRASSIK and GROF (acceleration with acetate, benzoate and caffeine) see GAMBINO et al.[102]. In the newborn a direct spectrophotometric method has been used[15,103]. On methods in general see the literature[15,104]; purity of the bilirubin standard is all-important[15,105]. The direct-reacting bilirubin of the diazo reaction represents roughly the conjugated bilirubin (bilirubin diglucuronide, smaller amounts of bilirubin monoglucuronide and sulphate), the difference between the total bilirubin and direct-reacting bilirubin (indirect bilirubin) the free bilirubin. It is uncertain whether direct-reacting bilirubin is present in the serum of healthy persons.
Total									
(b) Adults	...	...	...	...	6.0	(2.6–14)	–	97	
(c) Premature infants, cord blood	...	...	...	...	18.5	2.9–34.1	7.8	98	
(d) Newborn, cord blood	...	...	...	...	15.1	1.7–28.5	6.7	98	
(e) Newborn, 1 day	...	...	...	...	26.8	0–60.0	16.6	99	
(f) Newborn, 3 days	...	...	...	...	58.5	2.5–114.5	28.0	99	
(g) Newborn, 5 days	...	...	...	...	60.6	1.0–120.2	29.8	99	
(h) Newborn, 7 days	...	...	...	...	50.0	1.4–98.6	24.3	99	
Free									
(i) Men	...	...	...	...	4.0	1.5–10.5	–	100	
(j) Women	...	...	...	...	2.8	1.1–7.0	–	100	

The free (unconjugated) bilirubin is normally bound to albumin, the binding capacity of which can be determined[106]. The bilirubin of pathological sera can be separated chromatographically into 4 fractions[107], namely free, mono-conjugated, diconjugated and albumin-bound. On the physiology and pathology of bilirubin metabolism see the literature[108,109], also pages 363–364 and the table on the opposite page.

Simple jaundice of infants. Owing to deficiency of UDP glucuronyl transferase the liver is incapable of conjugating all the bilirubin present, so that the serum

level of free bilirubin increases. About 40% of newborn infants have a serum bilirubin level of over 40 mg/l during the first week[110]. The bilirubin level is higher in the umbilical arterial serum than in the umbilical venous serum[111].
Haemolytic jaundice of the newborn. With increasing haemoglobin breakdown the serum bilirubin level rises; as soon as the binding capacity of the albumin is exceeded, kernicterus may develop. Exchange transfusions are recommended when the serum bilirubin exceeds 190–250 mg/l, depending on the age and health of the child. For further discussion of haemolytic jaundice and kernicterus see the literature[98,109,112].

Disturbances of bilirubin metabolism

Type of jaundice	Nature of metabolic disturbance	Site	Free bilirubin in serum (↑ increased)	Conjugated bilirubin in serum (↑ increased)
Acholuric familial jaundice (familial haemolytic jaundice)	Increased haemoglobin breakdown	Reticular system	↑	(↑)
Acquired haemolytic anaemia			↑	(↑)
Haemolytic jaundice of newborn			↑↑	–
Congenital haemolytic jaundice (GILBERT's syndrome)	Impaired transport of free bilirubin	Liver (lysosomes)	↑	–
Posthepatic hyperbilirubinaemia			↑	–
Simple jaundice of infants (neonatal jaundice)	Incomplete conjugation of free bilirubin	Liver (microsomes)	↑	–
CRIGLER-NAJJAR syndrome			↑↑	–
Cholestatic jaundice	Impaired excretion of bilirubin glucuronides	Bile capillaries	(↑)	↑
DUBIN-JOHNSON syndrome			(↑)	↑
ROTOR syndrome			↑	↑
Obstructive jaundice	Impaired transport of bilirubin glucuronides into the duodenum	Bile ducts	(↑)	↑↑
Hepatitis, cirrhosis	At several stages of bilirubin metabolism		↑	↑↑

	Whole blood: Mean	95% range (extreme range in brackets)	s	Reference	Plasma or serum: Mean	95% range (extreme range in brackets)	s	Reference	Remarks
Purines, nucleotides									
Allantoin (mg/l)	...	...	...	...	–	(3–6)	–	113	
Uric acid (mg/l)									
(a) Newborn, up to 4 days	...	...	...	...	55	–	–	114	Serum values from (a) 70, (b) 224, (c) 874, (d) 899 subjects by uricase method; whole-blood values from (c) 13, (d) 8 subjects by chromatography; age range of subjects (c, d) 4–88 years. For discussion of methods of uric acid determination see the literature[118].
(b) Children, 4–9 years	...	...	...	...	37.3	–	–	115	
(c) Males	23.6	16.0–31.2	3.8	116	48.6	20.8–76.4	13.9	115	
(d) Females	22.7	13.7–31.7	4.5	116	41.8	18.2–65.4	11.8	115	
		Erythrocytes:							
	25	–	–	117					

The serum uric acid level is high in the newborn, in children rather lower than in adults. In men it remains fairly constant throughout life; in women it is lower before the menopause than in men, higher after it. The upper limit of the normal (uricase method) is 75 mg/l serum in men, 60 mg/l serum in women aged 20–40[119]. There is an extensive literature on uric acid metabolism[120].
The serum uric acid level is pathologically *increased* in gout, in renal injury, and when nucleic acid metabolism is increased (as for instance in myeloic leukaemia and polycythaemia), *decreased* in WILSON's disease and the FANCONI syndrome and by the administration of uricosuric drugs.

	Whole blood: Mean	95% range	s	Reference	Plasma or serum: Mean	95% range	s	Reference	Remarks
Xanthine and hypoxanthine (mg/l)	...	...	...	...	–	(∼1–2)	–	121	
Nucleotides (μmol/l)									
Adenosine monophosphate	–	(2–14)	–	116	...	...	...	...	Values from 13 men and 8 women after chromatographic separation. Nucleotides are found only in the cells, and the plasma contains traces at most. Various nucleotides have been determined in whole blood and erythrocytes[124], leucocytes[125] and thrombocytes[126]. A hereditary type of increased erythrocyte ATP content has been reported[127].
Adenosine diphosphate	–	(32–73)	–	116					
Adenosine triphosphate	–	(287–586)	–	116					
Guanosine triphosphate	–	(13–36)	–	116					
Inosine triphosphate	3	–	–	123					
Uridine diphosphate	4.5	–	–	123					
Nicotinamide-adenine dinucleotide	–	(22–40)	–	116					
As NAD	33.0	–	–	122					
As $NADH_2$	4.6	–	–	122					
Nicotinamide-adenine dinucleotide phosphate	–	(2–15)	–	116					
As NADP	11.6	–	–	122					
As $NADPH_2$	16.0	–	–	122					

	Whole blood				Plasma or serum				Remarks
	Mean	95% range	s	Reference	Mean	95% range	s	Reference	
Nucleic acids (mg/10^9 cells)		Leucocytes:							
Ribonucleic acid	8.19	0.91–15.47	3.64	128					
Deoxyribonucleic acid	6.86	4.52–9.20	1.17	128					

References

1 GRAM, H.C., *Amer.J.med.Sci.*, **168**, 511 (1924).
2 HINSBERG and BERENDT, in FLASCHENTRÄGER and LEHNARTZ (Eds.), *Physiologische Chemie*, vol. 2, part 1a, Springer, Berlin, 1954, page 416.
3 VALBERG et al., *J.clin.Invest.*, **44**, 379 (1965).
4 DENNES et al., *Biochem.J.*, **78**, 578 (1961).
5 NOUR-ELDIN, F., *Nature*, **196**, 1219 (1962).
6 ARCHIBALD et al., *Stand.Meth.clin.Chem.*, **2**, 91 (1958).
7 JOSEPHSON et al., *Acta paediat. (Uppsala)*, **51**, suppl. 135, 111 (1962).
8 BJÖRNESJÖ, K.B., *Scand.J.clin.Lab.Invest.*, **15**, suppl. 69, 25 (1963).
9 BEACH et al., *Stand.Meth.clin.Chem.*, **2**, 100 (1958).
10 RAPPAPORT and EICHHORN, *J.Lab.clin.Med.*, **32**, 1034 (1947).
11 EASTHAM, R.D., *Biochemical Values in Clinical Medicine*, 2nd ed., Wright, Bristol, 1963, page 77.
12 ACHARYA and PAYNE, *Arch.Dis.Childh.*, **40**, 430 (1965).
13 ADDIS et al., *J.clin.Invest.*, **26**, 869 (1947).
14 SCHALES et al., *Stand.Meth.clin.Chem.*, **1**, 118 (1953); SÜDHOF et al., *Klin. Wschr.*, **40**, 208 (1962).
15 RICHTERICH, R., *Klinische Chemie*, Karger, Basle, 1965.
16 KAPLAN et al., *Stand.Meth.clin.Chem.*, **5**, 245 (1965).
17 SEARCY et al., *Lancet*, **2**, 1114 (1962).
18 GALLAGHER and SELIGSON, *New Engl.J.Med.*, **266**, 492 (1962).
19 COHEN et al., *Amer.J.Dis.Child.*, **86**, 752 (1953).
20 VAN PILSUM et al., *J.biol.Chem.*, **222**, 225 (1956).
21 TAUSSKY and BRAHEN, *Stand.Meth.clin.Chem.*, **3**, 99 (1961).
22 CONN, R.B., *Clin.Chem.*, **6**, 537 (1960).
23 SANDBERG et al., *Metabolism*, **2**, 22 (1953).
24 ZENDER and FALBRIARD, *Clin.chim.Acta*, **12**, 183 (1965).
25 MILLER and DUBOS, *J.biol.Chem.*, **121**, 457 (1937).
26 TEGER-NILSSON, A.-C., *Scand.J.clin.Lab.Invest.*, **13**, 326 (1961).
27 SCHIRMEISTER et al., *Klin.Wschr.*, **41**, 878 (1963).
28 HOBERMAN, H.D., *J.biol.Chem.*, **167**, 721 (1947); LEVEDAHL and SAMUELS, *J.biol.Chem.*, **176**, 327 (1948).
29 O'BRIEN and IBBOTT (Eds.), *Laboratory Manual of Pediatric Micro- and Ultramicro-Biochemical Techniques*, 3rd ed., Hoeber, Harper & Row, New York, 1962, page 31.
30 HUTCHINSON and LABBY, *J.Lab.clin.Med.*, **60**, 170 (1962).
31 FENTON, J.C.B., *Clin.chim.Acta*, **7**, 163 (1962).
32 SECCHI et al., *Clin.chim.Acta*, **12**, 235 (1965).
33 CONN et al., *Stand.Meth.clin.Chem.*, **5**, 43 (1965).
34 MCGOVERN et al., *Pediatrics*, **23**, 1160 (1959).
35 BESSMAN, S.P., *Advanc.clin.Chem.*, **2**, 135 (1959); GABUZDA, G.J., *Advanc. intern.Med.*, **11**, 11 (1962); STAHL, J., *Ann.intern.Med.*, **58**, 1 (1963).
36 ANDREWS et al., *J.Pediat.*, **60**, 201 (1962).
37 FRAME et al., *Stand.Meth.clin.Chem.*, **4**, 1 (1963).
38 OEPEN and OEPEN, *Klin.Wschr.*, **41**, 921 (1963).
39 JOHNSON and BERGEIM, *J.biol.Chem.*, **188**, 833 (1951).
40 MCMENAMY et al., *J.clin.Invest.*, **36**, 1672 (1957).
41 MCMENAMY et al., *J.clin.Invest.*, **39**, 1675 (1960).
42 STEIN and MOORE, *J.biol.Chem.*, **211**, 915 (1954).
43 SOUPART, P., in HOLDEN, J.T. (Ed.), *Amino Acid Pools*, Elsevier, Amsterdam, 1962, page 220.
44 ZILVERSMIT, D.B., *Expos.ann.Biochim.méd.*, **23**, 1 (1961).
45 NICOLAIDOU et al., *Arch.Biochem.*, **96**, 613 (1962).
46 SCHREIER, K., in HOLDEN, J.T. (Ed.), *Amino Acid Pools*, Elsevier, Amsterdam, 1962, page 263.
47 GHADIMI and PECORA, *Pediatrics*, **33**, 500 (1964).
48 BICKEL, H., *Schweiz.med.Wschr.*, **91**, 1597 (1961).
49 GOODHART, R.S., in WOHL and GOODHART (Eds.), *Modern Nutrition in Health and Disease*, 3rd ed., Lea & Febiger, Philadelphia, 1964, page 460.
50 FRASER, R.S., *J.Lab.clin.Med.*, **35**, 960 (1950); **37**, 199 (1951).
51 MELVILLE, D.B., *Vitam.and Horm.*, **17**, 155 (1959).
52 CAREN and CARNE, *Amer.J.med.Sci.*, **221**, 307 (1951).
53 SILVERBERG et al., *Ann.N.Y.Acad.Sci.*, **111**, 472 (1963).
54 BEUTLER et al., *J.Lab.clin.Med.*, **61**, 882 (1963).
55 WALLER, H.D., *Scand.J.Haemat.*, suppl. *Ser.haemat.*, No. 2, 34 (1965).
56 BEUTLER, E., *J.Lab.clin.Med.*, **49**, 84 (1957).
57 SIMENHOFF et al., *Clin.Sci.*, **25**, 65 (1963).
58 MONDOVÌ et al., *Ital.J.Biochem.*, **10**, 42 (1961).
59 RAINA, A., *Scand.J.clin.Lab.Invest.*, **14**, 318 (1962).
60 SCUDAMORE et al., *J.Lab.clin.Med.*, **37**, 860 (1951).
61 COHEN, L., *J.Lab.clin.Med.*, **53**, 629 (1959).
62 APPLETON et al., *J.biol.Chem.*, **205**, 803 (1953).
63 VAN ARSDEL and BEALL, *Arch.intern.Med.*, **106**, 714 (1960).
64 GRAHAM et al., *Blood*, **10**, 467 (1955).
65 HAVERBACK et al., *J.clin.Invest.*, **41**, 1364 (1962).
66 GROSS and FRANZEN, *Biochem.Z.*, **340**, 403 (1964).
67 ECCLESTON et al., *Nature*, **197**, 502 (1963).
68 GROSS and FRANZEN, *Z.klin.Chem.*, **3**, 99 (1965).
69 WAALKES, T.P., *J.Lab.clin.Med.*, **53**, 824 (1959).
70 CRAWFORD, N., *Clin.chim.Acta*, **12**, 274 (1965).
71 GIRARD, J.-P., *Schweiz.med.Wschr.*, **93**, 1456 (1963).
72 DALGLIESH, C.E., *Advanc.clin.Chem.*, **1**, 193 (1958); RESNICK and GRAY, *Med.Clin.N.Amer.*, **44**, 1323 (1960).
73 MÜTING et al., *Z.klin.Med.*, **157**, 538 (1963).
74 MÜTING et al., *Z.klin.Med.*, **157**, 544 (1963).
75 RODNIGHT, R., *Int.Rev.Neurobiol.*, **3**, 251 (1961).
76 HEILMEYER, L., *Schweiz.med.Wschr.*, **92**, 1285 (1962).
77 HAEGER, B., *Scand.J.clin.Lab.Invest.*, **12**, suppl. 47 (1960).
78 DRUYAN and HAEGER-ARONSEN, *Scand.J.clin.Lab.Invest.*, **16**, 498 (1964).
79 WRANNE, L., *Acta paediat. (Uppsala)*, **49**, suppl. 124 (1960).
80 WATSON, C.J., *Arch.intern.Med.*, **86**, 797 (1950).
81 GRANICK and LEVERE, *Progr.Hemat.*, **4**, 1 (1964); STICH, W., *Verh.dtsch. Ges.inn.Med.*, **70**, 522 (1964).
82 VERLOOP et al., *Scand.J.Haemat.*, suppl. *Ser.haemat.*, No. 5, 76 (1965).
83 SCHLENKER et al., *Amer.J.clin.Path.*, **36**, 31 (1961).
84 MICHAËLSSON and SJÖLIN, *Acta paediat.scand.*, **54**, 325 (1965).
85 CHAPLIN et al., *J.Lab.clin.Med.*, **57**, 612 (1961).
86 DITTRICH, H., *Med.Klin.*, **58**, 1882 (1963).
87 JAYLE and MORETTI, *Progr.Hemat.*, **3**, 342 (1962).
88 VAN SLYKE et al., *J.biol.Chem.*, **166**, 121 (1946).
89 WALLER et al., *Klin.Wschr.*, **37**, 898 (1959).
90 HAINLINE et al., *Stand.Meth.clin.Chem.*, **5**, 143 (1965).
91 SCHWERD, W., *Der rote Blutfarbstoff und seine wichtigsten Derivate*, Schmidt-Römhild, Lübeck, 1962, page 73.
92 JAFFÉ and HELLER, *Progr.Hemat.*, **4**, 48 (1964).
93 OSKI and ALTMAN, *J.Pediat.*, **61**, 709 (1962).
94 SJÖSTRAND, T., *Acta physiol.scand.*, **26**, 338 (1952).
95 PACE et al., *Amer.J.Physiol.*, **147**, 352 (1946).
96 KIESE, M., *Klin.Wschr.*, **21**, 565 (1942).
97 NOSSLIN, B., *Scand.J.clin.Lab.Invest.*, **12**, suppl. 49 (1960).
98 VEST, M., *Bibl.paediat. (Basel)*, No. 69 (1959).
99 OBRINSKY et al., *Amer.J.Dis.Child.*, **87**, 305 (1954).
100 BRODERSEN et al., *Scand.J.clin.Lab.Invest.*, **15**, 523 (1963).
101 MACDONALD et al., *Stand.Meth.clin.Chem.*, **5**, 65 (1965).
102 GAMBINO et al., *Stand.Meth.clin.Chem.*, **5**, 55 (1965).
103 EBERLEIN, W.R., *Pediatrics*, **25**, 878 (1960).
104 MATHER, A., *Pediatrics*, **26**, 350 (1960); WATSON and ROGERS, *J.clin.Path.*, **14**, 271 (1961); MCKAY, R.J., *Pediatrics*, **30**, 1 (1962); LUCEY et al., *Pediatrics*, **30**, 3 (1962); WESTPHAL et al., *Pediatrics*, **30**, 12 (1962); SCHELLONG, G., *Dtsch.med.Wschr.*, **88**, 1145 (1963), and *Germ.med.Mth.*, **8**, 274 (1963); HENRY, R.J., *Clinical Chemistry*, Hoeber, Harper & Row, New York, 1964; MICHAËLSSON et al., *Pediatrics*, **35**, 925 (1965).
105 Committee on Fetus and Newborn, *Pediatrics*, **31**, 878 (1963); Recommendation on a Uniform Bilirubin Standard, *Stand.Meth.clin.Chem.*, **5**, 75 (1965).
106 WATERS and PORTER, *Pediatrics*, **33**, 749 (1964).
107 KUENZLE et al., *J.Lab.clin.Med.*, **67**, 282 and 294 (1966).
108 BILLING, B.H., *Advanc.clin.Chem.*, **2**, 267 (1959); WITH, T.K., *Bile Pigments*, Academic Press, New York, 1968, page 259; ARIAS, I.M., *Med.Clin. N.Amer.*, **44**, 607 (1960); KLATSKIN, G., *Ann.Rev.Med.*, **12**, 211 (1961); BILLING, B.H., *Sci.Basis Med.Ann.Rev.*, **1963**, 197; STICH, W., *Med.Klin.*, **58**, 648 (1963).
109 ARIAS, I.M., *Advanc.clin.Chem.*, **3**, 35 (1960).
110 CLAIREAUX, A.E., *Brit.med.J.*, **1**, 1528 (1960).
111 DÖRING, G.K., *Dtsch.med.Wschr.*, **89**, 293 (1964).
112 LUCEY, J.F., *Pediatrics*, **25**, 690 (1960); Leading article, *Lancet*, **1**, 1281 (1962); Survey, *Lancet*, **1**, 1291 (1962); Annotation, *Lancet*, **2**, 1283 (1964).
113 ARCHIBALD, R.M., *J.biol.Chem.*, **156**, 121 (1944).
114 CHRISTIANSSON and JOSEPHSON, *Acta paediat. (Uppsala)*, **49**, 633 (1960).
115 MIKKELSEN et al., *J.Lab.clin.Med.*, **60**, 999 (1962).
116 BISHOP et al., *J.biol.Chem.*, **234**, 1233 (1959).
117 JØRGENSEN and NIELSEN, *Scand.J.clin.Lab.Invest.*, **8**, 108 (1956).
118 CARAWAY and HALD, *Stand.Meth.clin.Chem.*, **4**, 239 (1963); ZÖLLNER, N., *Z.klin.Chem.*, **1**, 178 (1963).
119 OTT, H., *Schweiz.med.Wschr.*, **94**, 1597 (1964).
120 SEEGMILLER et al., *New Engl.J.Med.*, **268**, 712, 764 and 821 (1963).
121 GOLDFINGER et al., *J.clin.Invest.*, **44**, 623 (1965).
122 LÖHR and WALLER, *Dtsch.med.Wschr.*, **86**, 27 and 87 (1961), and *Germ. med.Mth.*, **6**, 37 (1961).
123 VANDERHEIDEN, B.S., *Biochem.biophys.Res.Commun.*, **21**, 265 (1965).
124 VOGEL, G., *Klin.Wschr.*, **36**, 975 (1958); SCHEIBE, O., *Klin.Wschr.*, **40**, 303 (1962); PAPENBERG et al., *Klin.Wschr.*, **40**, 936 (1962); BOCK et al., *Schweiz.med.Wschr.*, **92**, 1213 (1962).
125 SILBER et al., *J.clin.Invest.*, **41**, 230 (1962).
126 SCHMITZ et al., *Klin.Wschr.*, **40**, 13 (1962).
127 BREWER, G.J., *J.clin.Invest.*, **43**, 1287 (1964); BREWER and POWELL, *J.Lab. clin.Med.*, **64**, 844 (1964).
128 FREI et al., *Blood*, **18**, 317 (1961).
129 DICKINSON et al., *Pediatrics*, **36**, 2 (1965).
130 BRIGHAM et al., *J.clin.Invest.*, **39**, 1633 (1960).
131 ØYE, I., *Scand.J.clin.Lab.Invest.*, **14**, 259 (1962).

	Whole blood				Plasma or serum				Remarks
	Mean	95% range (extreme range in brackets)	s	Reference	Mean	95% range (extreme range in brackets)	s	Reference	
Total proteins									
(g/l)	–	180–210	–	1	–	Serum: 65–80	–	1	In whole blood the haemoglobin of the erythrocytes predominates. It makes up about 94% of the erythrocyte protein, the remainder consisting of stroma albumin, free globin and various enzymes. For data on the haemoglobin content see page 617. The proteins of the erythrocytes[4] and leucocytes[5] can be separated by electrophoresis. On the plasma proteins see below and pages 580–583.
	–	Erythrocytes: 330–390	–	1					
(mg/10⁹ cells)	100	Leucocytes: –	–	2					
	–	Thrombocytes: (1.6–1.8)	–	3					
Fibrinogen (g/l)	...	...	...	...	2.95	Plasma: 2.6–3.3 (2.0–4.0)	0.17	6	Values from 20 subjects. Occurs also in the thrombocytes[7].

Plasma proteins[8, 9]

Methods. For the determination of total proteins by the KJELDAHL method see ARCHIBALD et al.[10], by the biuret reaction see REINHOLD et al.[11], by refractometry see page 559. The proteins can be separated into fractions by salting out (for instance by HOWE's method), precipitation with water-miscible organic solvents (COHN's ethanol method), ultracentrifuging, chromatography on ion-exchangers, gel filtration or various methods of electrophoresis (method of TISELIUS or using filter paper, starch gel, agar gel, cellulose acetate foil, etc., as carrier). Individual proteins can be identified by immunochemical methods such as antibody consumption, antigen fixation, complement fixation and immune precipitate formation. Particularly effective is the combination of carrier electrophoresis with immune precipitate formation (immunoelectrophoresis[12]), whereby up to 30 different serum protein fractions can be separated. Enzymes can be determined by means of their biochemical activity (see page 584). For the simple separation of the albumins from the globulins by salting out see REINHOLD et al.[11]. With the exception of erythrocyte sedimentation (see pages 558–559), serum lability reactions are no longer used.

Physiological variations. Procedural differences make it desirable for every laboratory to establish its own normal range. The plasma protein concentration is subject to changes in the water content of the plasma; it is lowest when the subject is recumbent, about 8% higher when standing, and rises by a further 10% after a brief spell of exercise[9]. In infants the results of plasma protein determinations are particularly subject to changes in the plasma water content. When taking blood samples, prolonged venous stasis should be avoided since the blood concentration and therefore the protein level rise. In infants up to 2 years the blood should be sampled by percutaneous puncture of the heel[9]. Intake of food affects mainly the lipoprotein content. Marked changes in the protein content and composition occur particularly during the first year of life[9, 13] (see page 583) and in pregnancy[14] (see page 691). The adult plasma protein level is reached at the age of about 3 years[13]. In old age the albumin content falls while the β-globulin content rises[15] (see page 582). Differences in the plasma protein level between whites and negroes have often been observed[16].

Several of the serum proteins exhibit allotypy (see under 'Serum Groups', page 634).

References

1 Usual values in the literature.
2 HINSBERG and BERENDT, in FLASCHENTRÄGER and LEHNARTZ (Eds.), *Physiologische Chemie*, vol. 2, part 1a, Springer, Berlin, 1954, page 416.
3 MARCUS and ZUCKER, *The Physiology of Blood Platelets*, Grune & Stratton, New York, 1965.
4 BOTTINI and HUEHNS, *Clin. chim. Acta*, **8**, 127 (1963); TODOROW and DIKOW, in PEETERS, H. (Ed.), *Protides of the Biological Fluids*, 11th Colloquium, Elsevier, Amsterdam, 1964, page 502.
5 ANDERSEN, V., in PEETERS, H. (Ed.), *Protides of the Biological Fluids*, 10th Colloquium, Elsevier, Amsterdam, 1963, page 54.
6 REINER et al., *Stand. Meth. clin. Chem.*, 3, 114 (1961).
7 NACHMAN, R. L., *Blood*, **25**, 703 (1965).
8 PUTNAM, F. W. (Ed.), *The Plasma Proteins*, 2 vols., Academic Press, New York, 1960; RIVA, G., *Das Serumeiweißbild*, 2nd ed., Huber, Berne, 1960; Schweizerische Akademie der Medizinischen Wissenschaften, *Biochemie und Klinik der menschlichen Bluteiweiße*, Symposium, Schwabe, Basle, 1961; FURNESS et al., *Ann. N. Y. Acad. Sci.*, **94**, Art. 1 (1961); SCHEIFFARTH et al., *Papierelektrophorese in Klinik und Praxis*, Urban & Schwarzenberg, Munich, 1962; KAZAL, L. A., *Progr. Hemat.*, 3, 294 (1962); WUHRMANN and MÄRKI, *Dysproteinämien und Paraproteinämien*, Schwabe, Basle, 1963.
9 HITZIG, W. H., *Die Plasmaproteine in der klinischen Medizin*, Springer, Berlin, 1963.
10 ARCHIBALD et al., *Stand. Meth. clin. Chem.*, 2, 91 (1958).
11 REINHOLD et al., *Stand. Meth. clin. Chem.*, 1, 88 (1953).
12 WUNDERLY, C., *Advanc. clin. Chem.*, 4, 207 (1961).
13 OBERMAN et al., *New Engl. J. Med.*, **255**, 743 (1956).
14 MACK, H. C., *The Plasma Proteins in Pregnancy*, Thomas, Springfield, 1955; HYTTEN and LEITCH, *The Physiology of Human Pregnancy*, Blackwell, Oxford, 1964.
15 RAFSKY et al., *Amer. J. med. Sci.*, **224**, 522 (1952); BIRREN et al. (Eds.), *Human Aging*, Public Health Service Publication No. 986, U. S. Department of Health, Education, and Welfare, Bethesda, 1963, page 37.
16 POLLAK et al., *J. Lab. clin. Med.*, **58**, 353 (1961); ASSHAVER, E., *Med. Klin.*, **61**, 130 (1966).

Metabolism of the plasma proteins[1]

	Amount (g/kg body weight)	Synthesized in	Half-life (days)	Breakdown (% per day)	Breakdown (site)
Albumin	1.1–1.7	Liver	~15	5–8	Gastrointestinal tract
γ-Globulins	0.54	Plasma cells	γG 23	3	Liver, gastrointestinal tract
			γA 6	12	
			γM 5	14	
α- and β-Globulins	–	Liver	~ 5	–	Liver? Gut?
Fibrinogen	0.7–0.8	Liver	~ 5	–	–

1 For detailed discussion see WUHRMANN and MÄRKI, *Dysproteinämien und Paraproteinämien*, Schwabe, Basle, 1963; ANKER, H. S., in PUTNAM, F. W. (Ed.), *The Plasma Proteins*, vol. 2, Academic Press, New York, 1960, page 267. Data on the immunoglobulins from FAHEY, J. L., *J. Amer. med. Ass.*, **194**, 255 (1965).

Physicochemical and biological characteristics of defined plasma proteins[1]

(For lipoproteins see page 602, for glycoproteins see page 606)

	Grammes per 100 g plasma proteins (%)	Iso-electric point (pH)	Electro-phoretic mobility* (10^{-5} cm² V^{-1} s^{-1})	Sedimentation constant $S_{20}w$ (10^{-13} cm² s^{-1} dyn^{-1})	Diffusion constant $D_{20}w$ (10^{-7} cm² s^{-1})	Approximate molecular weight	Function
Prealbumin (tryptophan-rich)	0.1–0.5	–	9.0	4.2	–	61 000	Thyroxine-binding (?)
Albumin..................	50–65	4.9	5.9	4.6	5.9	69 000	Colloid-osmotic pressure; carrier and reserve protein
Acid α_1-glycoprotein (α_1-seromucoid, orosomucoid)	0.5–1.5	2.7	5.1	3.1	5.3	44 100	Tissue-breakdown product (?)
α_1-Antitrypsin.............	1.9–4.0	–	–	3.4	–	45 000	Inhibition of trypsin
α_2-Macroglobulin..........	1.5–4.5	5.4	4.2	19.4	2.4	900 000	Inhibition of proteinase
α_2-Haptoglobin............	0.3–1.9	4.1	3.3	4.1	4.7	85 000	Haemoglobin-binding
α_2-Caeruloplasmin	0.3–0.5	4.4	4.6	7.2	4.7	150 000	Oxidase activity (?); copper content 0.34%
β_1-Siderophilin (transferrin) .	3.0–6.5	5.8	3.1	6.1	6.2	88 000	Iron transport; defence against infection (?)
α_1-Lipoprotein							
density 1.093	4.5–8	–	–	5.5	–	435 000	Lipid transport
density 1.149				5.0	–	195 000	
α_2-Lipoprotein	0.5–1.5	–	–	S_f>12	–	3 400 000	Lipid transport
β_1-Lipoprotein	4–14	5.4	3.1	S_f=0–12	–	2 500 000	Lipid transport
γA, IgA (β_{2A}-globulin, γ_{1A}-globulin)............	0.8–2.8	–	−2.2	7 (10, 13, 15, 17)	–	180 000–500 000	Immunoglobulins: carriers of specific humoral antibodies***
γM, IgM (β_{2M}-globulin, γ_{1M}-globulin, γ_1-macroglobulin, 19 S γ)..	0.6–1.7	–	−2	18–20	–	950 000	
γG, IgG (γ-globulin, γ_2-globulin, γ_{ss}-globulin, 7 S γ)...................	13–22	7.3	−0.8	6.5–7	4.0	150 000	
γD, IgD..................	<0.5	–	–	6–7	–	150 000 (?)	
γE, IgE**	<0.002	–	–	8	–	200 000	
Fibrinogen................	2.5–5.0	5.4	2.1	8.5	2.0	340 000	Coagulation

* pH 8.6; ionic strength 0.1.
** Identical with IgND.

[1] From summaries in HITZIG, W.H., *Die Plasmaproteine in der klinischen Medizin*, Springer, Berlin, 1963, page 45; PHELPS and PUTNAM, in PUTNAM, F.W. (Ed.), *The Plasma Proteins*, vol. 1, Academic Press, New York, 1960, page 143; WUHRMANN and MÄRKI, *Dysproteinämien und Paraproteinämien*, Schwabe, Basle, 1963, page 55; SCHWICK and STÖRIKO, *Laboratoriumsblätter für die medizinische Diagnostik*, Behringwerke AG., Marburg-Lahn, June 1965; EDELMAN and GALL, *Ann. Rev. Biochem.*, **38**, 415 (1969).

*** Some of the antibodies in this group are:
γA Various insulin antibodies, tetanus antitoxin, polio I/III antibodies, certain isoagglutinins
γM Isoantibodies anti-A and anti-B, agglutinating Rh antibodies, specific and nonspecific cold-agglutinins, heterophilic agglutinins, WASSERMANN antibodies, antinuclear antibodies, rheumatoid factor, conglutinins (properdin)
γG Incomplete Rh antibodies, incomplete antibodies anti-A and anti-B, LE-factor (?), blocking antibodies
γD Nature unknown
γE Reagins

Structure of the immunoglobulins[1]

Chains* H	γ		α		δ		ε		μ		–	–
Chains* L	κ	λ	κ	λ	κ	λ	κ	λ	κ	λ	κ	λ
Molecular type	K	L	K	L	K	L	K	L	K	L	K	L
Chain combination	$\kappa_2\gamma_2$	$\lambda_2\gamma_2$	$[\kappa_2\alpha_2]_n$	$[\lambda_2\alpha_2]_n$	$\kappa_2\delta_2$	$\lambda_2\delta_2$	$\kappa_2\varepsilon_2$	$\lambda_2\varepsilon_2$	$[\kappa_2\mu_2]_n$	$[\lambda_2\mu_2]_n$	κ_2	λ_2
			$n = 1, 2, 3$						$n = 5$			
Normal immunoglobulin	γG-Globulin		γA-Globulin		γD-Globulin		γE-Globulin		γM-Globulin		γU-Globulin	
Paraprotein**	Myeloma globulins								Macroglobulin		BENCE-JONES globulin	

* Both the H chain (heavy chain; mol. wt. ca. 50000) and L chain (light chain; mol. wt. ca. 20000) consist of a variable sequence determining the antibody specificity and an almost invariable sequence characteristic of the species and determining the class of immunoglobulin as well as polymorphism within the class. The type K molecule, containing the κ light chain, is also known as type I, 1 or B, the type L molecule, containing the γ light chain, as type II, 2 or A. The heavy chain possesses the Gm activity, the κ light chain the InV activity.

** Paraproteins are proteins of abnormal structure in the immunoglobulin group appearing in neoplastic diseases of the reticuloendothelial system.

[1] HEIDE, K., in *Die gelben Hefte*, Immunbiologische Informationen der Behringwerke AG., No. 9, Marburg-Lahn, 1965, page 321; PUTNAM, F. W., *Scand. J. Haemat.*, suppl. *Ser. haemat.*, No. 4, 1 (1965); FAHEY, J. L., *J. Amer. med. Ass.*, **194**, 71 (1965); LENNOX and COHN, *Ann. Rev. Biochem.*, **36**, 365 (1967); EDELMAN and GALL, *Ann. Rev. Biochem.*, **38**, 415 (1969).

Amino-acid and carbohydrate composition of human serum proteins (g/100 g protein)[1]

	Pre-albumin	Albumin	Acid α_1-glycoprotein	α_1-Antitrypsin	Haptoglobin	Caeruloplasmin	α_2-Macroglobulin	Transferrin	γG-Globulin	γM-Globulin	γA-Globulin
Lysine	6.96	10.95	4.48	7.15	8.17	5.84	5.34	9.65	6.96	4.88	4.57
Histidine	3.62	3.17	1.12	2.92	3.12	3.93	2.70	3.33	2.28	1.83	1.93
Ammonia	1.00	0.94	1.49	1.04	1.40	1.40	1.37	1.23	1.46	1.23	2.02
Arginine	4.27	5.38	3.44	1.85	2.23	4.38	3.82	5.15	4.02	5.05	4.55
Aspartic acid	6.44	9.05	5.72	8.02	9.53	9.45	7.16	11.40	7.69	7.12	6.15
Threonine	9.17	4.31	4.02	4.97	4.42	5.35	5.35	3.71	7.18	7.23	7.65
Serine	7.36	3.15	1.44	2.98	3.50	3.64	5.50	4.38	9.69	6.95	7.93
Glutamic acid	10.91	15.85	10.50	10.90	9.70	10.88	12.30	10.22	11.26	10.62	10.52
Proline	5.31	3.65	1.81	2.69	4.19	3.21	4.07	3.82	6.05	5.27	6.26
Glycine	3.94	1.05	1.03	2.03	2.90	2.98	2.75	3.44	3.35	3.06	3.22
Alanine	6.25	6.67	1.52	2.89	3.53	2.44	3.44	5.00	3.18	3.51	3.87
Cystine ½	0	5.09	0.68	0	2.05	0.72	1.14	5.07	2.20	1.58	2.10
Valine	8.44	6.17	2.14	3.86	6.25	4.10	6.80	5.40	8.10	6.49	6.00
Methionine	0.86	1.08	0.37	1.66	1.04	1.98	1.53	1.31	0.85	1.16	0.80
Isoleucine	3.68	1.31	2.46	3.32	3.38	4.13	3.09	2.10	2.14	2.70	1.74
Leucine	5.50	10.30	3.92	8.25	6.03	5.51	7.76	8.21	7.21	6.33	7.76
Tyrosine	5.51	4.03	4.08	1.87	5.55	7.55	4.84	4.61	5.97	4.21	4.38
Phenylalanine	5.11	6.74	3.31	6.37	2.36	5.07	5.37	5.07	4.29	3.96	3.66
Tryptophan	2.40	0.13	1.40	0.55	2.60	2.30	1.30	2.10	3.83	2.80	3.30
Sum	96.73	99.02	54.93	73.32	81.95	84.86	85.63	95.20	97.71	85.98	88.41
Hexoses	0.4	0.05	14.70	4.70	7.80	3.00	3.6	2.40	1.10	5.40	3.20
Acetylhexosamine	0.1	0.03	13.90	3.90	5.30	2.40	2.9	2.00	1.30	4.40	2.90
Acetylneuraminic acid	0	0	12.10	3.60	5.30	2.40	1.8	1.40	0.30	1.30	1.80
Fucose	0	0	0.70	0.20	0.20	0.18	0.1	0.07	0.20	0.70	0.22
Sum	97.23	99.10	96.33	85.72	100.55	92.84	94.03	101.07	100.61	97.78	96.53

[1] HEIMBURGER et al., *Clin. chim. Acta*, **10**, 293 (1964).

Serum and plasma protein fractions of adults

Free electrophoresis of serum and plasma proteins[1]

	Serum (30 subjects)						Plasma (7 subjects)			
	Absolute values (g/l serum)			Relative values (g/100 g total protein)			Absolute values (g/l plasma)	Relative values (g/100 g total protein)		
	Mean	Extreme range	s	Mean	Extreme range	s	Extreme range	Mean	Extreme range	s
Total protein	73	68–82	3.7	100	–	–	~69–85	100	–	–
Albumin	46.2	42.2–53.9	2.9	63.5	59.7–68.6	2.32	–	61.2	57.0–65.8	3.2
Globulins	26.8	22.5–31.0	2.2	36.5	31.4–40.3	2.32	–	38.8	32.2–43.0	3.2
α-Globulin	6.8	5.1–9.8	1.1	9.2	7.0–12.2	1.43	–	9.2	8.1–10.5	0.83
α_1-Globulin	–	–	–	2.0	1.1–3.0	0.52	–	–	–	–
α_2-Globulin	–	–	–	7.3	5.5–9.8	1.15	–	–	–	–
β-Globulin	8.2	5.5–10.1	1.1	11.3	7.7–14.0	1.40	–	11.5	10.5–12.9	1.3
γ-Globulin	11.6	8.8–15.0	1.4	15.9	12.3–18.9	1.6	–	14.1	12.7–17.0	1.5
Fibrinogen	–	–	–	–	–	–	~2–4	4.0	2.2–5.8	1.1
Albumin: globulin ratio	–	–	–	1.74	1.49–2.19	0.17	–	1.59	1.32–1.92	0.21

[1] RIVA, G., *Das Serumeiweißbild*, 2nd ed., Huber, Berne, 1960, page 257.

Electrophoresis of serum proteins on paper[1] *or cellulose acetate*[2]

	Paper electrophoresis (12 subjects)			Electrophoresis on cellulose acetate (40 subjects)			
	Relative values (g/100 g total protein)			Absolute values (g/l serum)		Relative values (g/100 g total protein)	
	Mean	Extreme range	s	Mean	95% range	Mean	95% range
Total protein	100	–	–	75.0	66–84	100	–
Albumin	65.2	58.0–71.9	4.35	44.7	37–52	59.6	52.2–67.0
Globulins	34.8	28.1–42.0	4.35	–	–	–	–
α-Globulin	10.9	8.4–14.2	2.0	–	–	–	–
α_1-Globulin	4.1	3.1–6.6	1.14	2.5	1–4	3.5	2.4–4.6
α_2-Globulin	6.7	5.2–9.1	1.28	7.5	5–10	10.1	6.6–13.6
β-Globulin	9.8	6.1–12.0	1.64	9.0	6–12	11.9	9.1–14.7
γ-Globulin	14.1	10.3–18.4	2.92	11.1	6–16	14.8	9.0–20.6
Fibrinogen	–	–	–	–	–	–	–
Albumin: globulin ratio	1.92	1.42–2.59	0.38	–	–	1.48	–

[1] RIVA, G., *Das Serumeiweißbild*, 2nd ed., Huber, Berne, 1960, page 257.
[2] KAPLAN and SAVORY, *Clin. Chem.*, **11**, 937 (1965).

Serum proteins of men at various ages (g/l)[1]

	Number	Total protein		Albumin		α_1-Globulin		α_2-Globulin		β-Globulin		γ-Globulin	
		Mean	95% range	Mean	95% range	Mean	95% range	Mean	95% range	Mean	95% range	Mean	95% range
18–36 years	22	71.9	62.1–81.7	38.1	29.9–46.3	3.7	2.3–5.4	7.6	3.8–11.3	9.9	6.7–17	12.5	7.3–17
65–92 years	43	69.3	58.4–89.2	32.7	26.9–38.5	3.8	2.4–5.2	8.8	5.8–11.8	11.3	8.7–13.9	13.0	6.6–19.4

[1] Paper electrophoresis values from National Institute of Mental Health, Bethesda, Maryland, in BIRREN et al. (Eds.), *Human Aging*, Public Health Service Publication No. 986, U.S. Department of Health, Education and Welfare, Bethesda, 1963, page 37.

Serum proteins at various ages (g/l)

	Reference	Total protein	Albumin*	α_1-Globulins*	α_1-Lipoprotein**	α_2-Globulins*	α_2-Macroglobulin**	α_2-Haptoglobin***	α_2-Caeruloplasmin†	β-Globulins*	β_1-Lipoprotein**	β_1-Siderophilin††	γA-Globulin**	γM-Globulin**	γG-Globulin††
		Mean (*s* in brackets)													
Maternal blood .	1	59.31	27.46	3.97	2.36	7.30	4.33	1.44	0.89	10.85	4.89	4.80	1.05	0.96	10.9
		(3.54)	(3.00)	(0.71)	(2.24)	(1.45)	(1.45)	(0.69)	(0.27)	(1.26)	(1.93)	(0.64)	–	(0.46)	(0.8)
Cord blood.	1	54.81	32.16	2.31	0.28	4.51	4.54	0.26	0.11	4.66	1.16	3.33	<0.02	<0.09	12.5
		(3.24)	(3.38)	(0.31)	(0.22)	(0.58)	(1.44)	(0.38)	(0.06)	(0.86)	(0.47)	(0.24)	–	–	(2.0)
Children															
0–14 days	1	51.30	30.06	2.33	0.65	4.89	5.17	0.15	0.17	4.32	2.50	2.70	<0.02	0.22	9.9
		(5.10)	(3.64)	(0.39)	(0.27)	(0.62)	(1.12)	(0.07)	(0.05)	(0.79)	(0.74)	(0.09)	–	(0.06)	(0.8)
2–4 weeks . . .	1	50.78	29.71	2.59	0.40	4.86	4.55	0.41	0.20	5.01	1.38	2.74	0.09	0.27	9.5
		(3.74)	(3.54)	(0.66)	(0.17)	(1.16)	(2.70)	(0.37)	(0.08)	(0.75)	(0.43)	(0.26)	(0.12)	(0.09)	(0.6)
5–9 weeks . . .	1	53.37	35.10	2.60	0.33	5.13	3.60	0.25	0.24	5.25	1.42	3.03	0.45	0.26	6.3
		(3.04)	(2.64)	(0.48)	(0.15)	(0.82)	(1.70)	(0.24)	(0.06)	(0.61)	(0.46)	(0.23)	(0.25)	(0.11)	(1.8)
2–6 months . .	1	56.50	35.02	2.01	0.61	6.78	5.44	0.73	0.25	6.75	2.36	3.59	0.50	0.35	5.8
		(3.98)	(2.78)	(0.72)	(0.31)	(1.15)	(1.81)	(0.41)	(0.11)	(1.27)	(1.03)	(0.35)	(0.20)	(0.13)	(1.2)
6–13 months .	1	60.56	36.09	2.19	0.89	7.55	5.60	1.17	0.39	7.81	3.26	3.94	0.69	0.55	7.5
		(3.31)	(2.63)	(0.61)	(0.39)	(1.37)	(2.01)	(0.57)	(0.17)	(0.82)	(1.03)	(0.38)	(0.27)	(0.23)	(1.3)
1¼–3 years . .	2	64.40	36.20	3.26	–	8.15	5.00	0.95	0.51	8.92	4.60	3.53	–	0.67	8.66
		(4.31)	(3.39)	(0.72)	–	(1.27)	(1.41)	(0.46)	(0.09)	(1.38)	(1.71)	(0.41)	–	(0.36)	(2.42)
3–7 years	2	66.90	36.58	3.40	–	7.59	4.72	0.68	0.51	8.89	4.22	3.53	–	0.64	13.00
		(4.56)	(2.59)	(0.65)	–	(1.08)	(1.27)	(0.32)	(0.12)	(0.23)	(1.73)	(0.44)	–	(0.18)	(2.81)
7–11 years . . .	2	68.86	37.96	3.15	–	7.15	4.50	0.61	0.44	8.78	4.12	3.57	–	0.61	14.20
		(2.64)	(2.60)	(0.53)	–	(1.18)	(1.50)	(0.41)	(0.14)	(1.50)	(1.66)	(0.56)	–	(0.25)	(2.71)
11–16 years . .	2	69.17	37.50	3.32	–	6.81	3.46	0.47	0.41	8.94	3.78	3.41	–	0.55	13.85
		(2.79)	(2.11)	(0.56)	–	(0.96)	(0.87)	(0.30)	(0.11)	(1.56)	(1.48)	(0.37)	–	(0.25)	(1.83)
Adults	2	69.86	36.58	3.11	–	6.76	2.92	0.81	0.38	8.74	3.56	3.00	–	0.68	13.14
		(1.43)	(2.81)	(0.41)	–	(1.27)	(0.98)	(0.46)	(0.08)	(1.07)	(1.90)	(0.38)	–	(0.29)	(2.02)
Adults	1	69.25	35.75	3.58	0.80	7.08	3.56	1.10	0.32	8.66	2.18	3.66	0.80	0.66	11.7
		(1.86)	(2.11)	(0.54)	(0.16)	(0.50)	(0.29)	(0.82)	(0.06)	(0.54)	(0.44)	(0.13)	–	(0.19)	(0.4)

* Paper electrophoresis.
** Ouchterlony's two-dimensional immunodiffusion.
*** Chemically by Jayle's method.
† Values with reference[1] by Ouchterlony's method, reference[2] by Ravin's enzymatic method.
†† Oudin's one-dimensional immunodiffusion.

[1] Hitzig, W.H., *Die Plasmaproteine in der klinischen Medizin*, Springer, Berlin, 1963, page 110.
[2] Weiss, W.A., *Klin. Wschr.*, 43, 273 (1965).

(For references see pages 588–589)

Enzymes are proteins with particular catalytic functions. They are identifiable and measurable by their activity, i.e., their ability to transform a particular substrate. The greater the rate at which the substrate is transformed, the higher the activity of the enzyme. For further discussion of enzyme kinetics see the section on pages 382–386, in which this and other aspects of enzymes (notably nomenclature, specificity and structure) are dealt with.

Enzyme units. At the present time a large number of enzyme units are in use, a situation that makes it difficult to compare the values from different laboratories even when the same method is used. For this reason the International Union of Biochemistry (IUB)[1] has recommended the use of a standard unit (U)** defined as follows:

1 U of any enzyme is that amount which will catalyse the transformation of 1 μmol of the substrate per minute under standard conditions.

The usual multiples kU, mU, μU, etc. are used. The recommended standard conditions are 30 °C (formerly 25 °C) and, if possible, optimal pH and substrate concentration. The IUB has also defined a number of other quantities in terms of the unit of enzyme:

Enzyme concentration:	U/ml solution (U/l solution, U/kg tissue and U/g tissue are also in use)
Specific activity:	U/mg enzyme preparation
Molecular activity:	U/μmol enzyme

Table 1 gives factors for converting some of the units at present in use into U/l (≡mU/ml) (temperature differences have not been allowed for), while Table 2 lists temperature correction factors for some important enzymes.

About 90% of the total cell protein consists of enzymes. The various organs and tissues are equipped with a specific set of enzymes depending on their particular function. The differences between these sets of enzymes are mainly of a quantitative nature[2], and the function of an organ or tissue derives from its possession of an enzyme pattern in which important elements are not single enzymes but 'constant-proportion' groups of enzymes[3]. The enzymes involved in the principal energy-supplying metabolic reactions constitute a basic pattern that is complemented by other, variable enzymes. Depending on the metabolic type of the tissue concerned, the relationship of the latter – for instance lactate dehydrogenase, α-glycerophosphate dehydrogenase or the enzymes of the hexose monophosphate cycle – to the basic metabolic pattern is very variable. Their activity may differ by several orders of magnitude from one organ to another.

The variable enzymes of organs, especially the parenchymatous organs, naturally include all those that are carriers of specific organ properties. With some of these the differences in activity from organ to organ are so large that the description of 'organ-specific' or 'tissue-specific' enzyme is justified, examples being the 'liver enzymes' iditol dehydrogenase and ketose-1-phosphate aldolase and the 'muscle enzyme' creatine kinase. With the aid of these enzymes and the differing relationships between the ubiquitous metabolic enzymes it is possible to recognize the enzyme pattern peculiar to an organ from a very small part of it; this may be as little as 3–4 enzymes if these are suitably chosen[4].

'Isozyme'[5] (or 'isoenzyme') is the term given to enzymes having the same catalytic function but different structures and therefore different properties[6]. The fact that the proportions of the total activity of an enzyme attributable to its various isoenzymes differ markedly from one organ to another presents a further means of distinguishing between the enzymatic equipment of different organs. The best-known example is provided by the enzyme lactate dehydrogenase[7], whose isozyme distribution in the heart differs considerably from that in the liver. A large number of enzymes are known to possess isozymes, among them malate dehydrogenase[8,9], aspartate aminotransferase[9,10], isocitrate dehydrogenase[9,11], glucose-6-phosphate dehydrogenase[11], glycerophosphate dehydrogenase[11], phosphopyruvate hydratase[12], leucinaminopeptidase[13], alkaline phosphatase[14,15], acid phosphatase[14,16], cholinesterase[17], ribonuclease[18], glutamate dehydrogenase[19], phosphogluconate dehydrogenase[20], creatine kinase[21], pyruvate kinase[22], phosphoglucomutase[23] and amylase[24].

Within the cell the enzymes are located in various compartments, namely the cytoplasm, mitochondria, lysosomes, microsomes and nucleus, and are classified into types I and II. Type I enzymes are easily extractable and probably only loosely bound to the hyalo-

Table 1 Conversion factors for some enzyme units

To convert from the unit given to the standard unit (U/l) multiply by the factor. The normal ranges given in the literature for enzymes differ according to the method of measurement used (independently of the unit chosen).

Unit given	Conversion factor
*1. NAD/NADP-dependent reactions**	
Method of BÜCHER[131] 25 °C, $E^{366}_{0.100}$/100 s × 1 ml	18.3
Method of KARMEN and WRÓBLEWSKI[132] 23 °C, $E^{340}_{0.001}$/1 min × 3 ml	0.48
Method of AMELUNG and HORN[101] 25 °C, 1 μmol/1 h × 1 ml	16.7
Method of HOLZER and GERLACH[133] 24 °C, $E^{366}_{0.001}$/1 min × 3 ml	0.91
2. Fructosediphosphate aldolase	
Method of BRUNS[134] 37 °C, 1 μl fructose-1,6-diphosphate solution/1 h × 1 ml	0.61
Method of SIBLEY and LEHNINGER[135] 38 °C, 1 μl fructose solution/30 min × 0.04 ml	0.74
Method of SCHAPIRA[136] 37 °C, 1 mg triosephosphate-P/1 min × 1000 ml	16.00
3. Alkaline phosphatase	
KING-ARMSTRONG method[137,138] 37.5 °C, 1 mg phenol/15 min × 100 ml	7.1
Method of SHINOWARA[139] 37 °C, 1 mg P/1 h × 100 ml	5.4
BESSEY-LOWRY method (also for acid phosphatase)[140] 38 °C, 1 mmol *p*-nitrophenol/1 h × 1000 ml	16.7
Method of BODANSKY (also for acid phosphatase)[141] 37.5 °C, 1 mg P/1 h × 100 ml	5.4
4. Acid phosphatase	
KING-ARMSTRONG method[137] 37.5 °C, 1 mg phenol/1 h × 100 ml	1.8
5. Amylase (diastase)	
Method of SOMOGYI[142] 37 °C, 5 mg starch/15 min × 100 ml	20.6
Method of WOHLGEMUTH[143] 38 °C, 1 mg starch/30 min × 1 ml	206.0

* The units of activity are expressed as the decrease (subscript) in optical density (or extinction, E) at the given wave length (superscript) over the given time and light path.

* The data on pages 584–600 have been compiled in conjunction with E. SCHMIDT and F. W. SCHMIDT, Gastroenterological Department, Medical Clinic, Medizinische Hochschule, Hannover. The enzymes are referred to throughout by the trivial names recommended by the Enzyme Commission (EC) of the International Union of Biochemistry (see page 385). In particular, the trivial names aspartate aminotransferase for the former glutamate-oxalacetate transaminase and alanine aminotransferase for the former glutamate-pyruvate transaminase should be noted.

** Also known as the International Unit (IU). The International Union of Pure and Applied Chemistry and the International Federation for Clinical Chemistry have jointly recommended the enzyme unit catal (catalytic amount; symbol cat) defined as follows[1a]:

1 cat = the catalytic amount of a system which catalyses as many cycles per second of a stated reaction scheme as there are atoms in 0.012 kg of the pure nuclide ^{12}C. It follows that 1 U = 16.67 ncat (n = nano).

(For references see pages 588–589)

Table 2 Correction factors for conversion of activity values to 25 °C

Temperature of measurement	Lactate dehydrogenase[144]	Alanine aminotransferase[144]	Aspartate aminotransferase[144]	Malate dehydrogenase[33]	Glucose-6-phosphate dehydrogenase and phosphogluconate dehydrogenase[33]	Cholinesterase[33]
20 °C	1.470	1.400	1.390	1.520	1.300	1.360
21 °C	1.350	1.310	1.300	1.390	1.240	1.280
22 °C	1.250	1.220	1.220	1.280	1.180	1.200
23 °C	1.160	1.140	1.150	1.180	1.120	1.120
24 °C	1.080	1.060	1.070	1.090	1.060	1.055
25 °C	1.000	1.000	1.000	1.000	1.000	1.000
26 °C	0.928	0.930	0.936	0.920	0.950	0.950
27 °C	0.862	0.874	0.878	0.860	0.900	0.900
28 °C	0.802	0.817	0.821	0.800	0.850	0.855
29 °C	0.742	0.767	0.770	0.740	0.800	0.815
30 °C	0.694	0.716	0.719	0.680	0.760	0.775
31 °C	0.640	0.672	0.675	0.630	0.720	0.740
32 °C	0.598	0.628	0.636	0.580	0.680	0.700
33 °C	0.556	0.591	0.599	0.540	0.650	0.670
34 °C	0.520	0.553	0.560	0.500	0.620	0.635
35 °C	0.485	0.516	0.528	0.460	0.590	0.605
36 °C	0.449	0.484	0.497	0.430	0.560	0.575
37 °C	0.419	0.459	0.465	0.400	0.530	0.545

plasm, like lactate dehydrogenase and alanine aminotransferase, whereas type II enzymes are released only when the cell is severely disrupted, like the mitochondrial enzyme glutamate dehydrogenase. Aspartate aminotransferase, malate dehydrogenase and isocitrate dehydrogenase probably belong to a further class (type III) since their cytoplasmic isozymes are very soluble and their mitochondrial isozymes rather insoluble[25]. Other enzymes, like those of the respiratory chain, are so strongly bound to the cell that they cannot be separated without losing their activity.

In view of the great difference in enzyme concentration inside and outside the cell – maintained only by continuous expenditure of energy by the cell – it is understandable that even under physiological conditions small activities of the readily soluble cytoplasmic enzymes should be present in the serum. Any considerable increase in these activities, or the appearance in the serum of mitochondrial enzymes, is always a sign of severe damage to the cells.

The manner in which the physiological serum enzyme level is maintained remains for the most part obscure, but probably many organs contribute to it. The part played by normal breakdown of the erythrocytes has been overestimated[26], and it is likely that the increased release of enzymes during muscular work is more important[27].

Physiological variations in enzyme activity (see also the main table on pages 590–600)

The concentrations of the various enzymes in the body fluids have lognormal rather than normal distributions; for this reason the data in the main table do not include the usual 95% range calculated from the mean and standard deviation.

Sex differences. Most of the enzymes present in the plasma show no sex-dependent differences. Women have rather lower serum acid phosphatase[28], cholinesterase[29] and β-glucuronidase[30] activities than men, and they have also been reported to have slightly lower normal values for aspartate aminotransferase[31], alanine aminotransferase[31] and creatine kinase[32]. For almost all the diagnostically useful enzymes, however, men and women can be assumed to have the same normal limits[33, 34].

Age differences. Many enzymes have higher serum values in the immediate postnatal period and early infancy. In the 2nd to 3rd years of life, however, the only difference of practical interest is the markedly higher alkaline phosphatase level. During the growth period the serum level of this enzyme shows a close correlation with the state of bone growth[35].

Higher concentrations of malate dehydrogenase, aspartate aminotransferase and alanine aminotransferase have been reported in old age[36], though these are probably a result of the increased incidence of subclinical ailments.

Daily variations. Data on diurnal changes in serum enzyme levels are conflicting. Fluctuations of up to 40% (though with very wide

Table 3 Enzyme activities (in U/g tissue[4, 145] or U/10¹¹ cells[146])

Tissue	Hexokinase	Iditol dehydrogenase	Ketose-1-phosphate aldolase	Fructosediphosphate aldolase	Glycerophosphate dehydrogenase	Alcohol dehydrogenase	Glyceraldehydephosphate dehydrogenase	Phosphopyruvate hydratase	Pyruvate kinase	Lactate dehydrogenase	Malate dehydrogenase	Isocitrate dehydrogenase	Glutamate dehydrogenase	Aspartate aminotransferase	Alanine aminotransferase	Glucose-6-phosphate dehydrogenase	Phosphogluconate dehydrogenase	Phosphoglycerate kinase	Phosphoglycerate phosphomutase
Liver	25.2	71.9	3.4	5.7	14.8	30.5	75.2	22.2	15.5	156	202	36.2	60.2	96.0	58.7	0.93	1.39	217	134
Skeletal muscle	3.5	0.01	0.9	98.1	2.3	0.01	175	21.4	67.6	148	93.8	6.8	0.5	36.7	3.4	0.01	0.01	33.8	35.0
Cardiac muscle	2.0	0.01	0.3	5.0	0.6	0.01	62.6	1.7	29.0	125	482	5.2	1.1	52.5	3.0	0.2	0.1	0	0
Uterus	2.2	0.01	0.01	0.9	0.01	0.01	37.5	2.7	11.1	25.6	33.8	1.1	1.1	4.1	0.9	0.9	0.01	15.0	23.1
Stomach muscles	2.3	0.3	0.1	2.6	0.05	0.01	57.4	5.2	17.6	54.1	49.8	2.8	0.7	4.3	0.05	0.5	0.1	0	0
Gastric mucosa	1.1	1.2	0.05	1.1	0.1	0.9	69.8	6.4	22.2	65.7	113	11.0	3.0	28.9	1.1	0.7	0.3	0	0
Pancreas	0.4	0.2	0.09	0.04	0.04	0.1	37.7	3.5	9.8	50.8	47.7	1.8	0.5	3.0	0.7	0.4	0.2	0	0
Renal cortex	2.1	3.6	0.5	1.8	2.4	0.01	108	9.1	15.6	114	105	6.1	6.7	10.6	2.0	0.7	0.5	0	0
Renal medulla	1.1	0.6	0.1	0.7	0.2	0.05	57.8	3.3	23.5	101	49.2	4.4	2.2	8.2	0.7	0.3	0.3	0	0
Cerebral cortex	3.2	0.2	0.1	5.3	0.09	0.01	69.3	10.5	28.5	54.6	117	0.8	4.1	20.3	0.1	0.3	0.3	0	0
Cerebrum	1.0	0.2	0.04	2.5	0.2	0.01	69.1	7.7	27.9	40.1	61.8	0.9	2.3	9.3	0.01	0.2	0.1	0	0
Cerebellar hemispheres	1.8	0.1	0.07	4.7	0.01	0.01	69.7	12.4	34.9	64.7	78.4	0.2	1.5	21.6	0.07	0.3	0.3	0	0
Lungs	1.6	1.6	0.04	0.5	0.1	0.3	27.3	2.6	8.6	27.4	27.3	1.1	2.5	1.1	0.3	0.6	0.5	0	0
Fatty tissues	0.7	0.01	0.1	1.6	4.3	0.2	19.4	1.6	3.8	52.8	72.7	1.7	1.3	5.2	1.9	1.5	1.2	0	0
Lymph glands	3.7	0.2	0.09	3.4	0.1	0.2	75.3	10.8	30.4	84.0	69.7	4.1	2.7	7.4	0.07	0.9	0.5	0	0
Erythrocytes	2.0	0	0	10.3	0	0	198	18.9	32.8	171	125	1.2	0	6.8	1.4	13.2	7.1	289	64.2
foetal	1.5	0	0	14.9	1.9	0	284	30.3	23.3	357	304	2.7	0	14.3	1.3	28.5	8.2	600	75.4
Thrombocytes	4.5	0	0	8.2	1.2	0	39.0	23.6	120	97.7	37.2	3.3	0.7	1.6	0.8	6.9	0.9	82.7	39.4
Granulocytes	174	0	0	406	159	0	5.29×10^3	3.38×10^3	368	9.92×10^3	2.43×10^3	166	23.8	271	82.3	926	342	11.7×10^3	4.16×10^3

(For references see pages 588–589)

Table 4 Enzyme concentration gradients[4]

	Skeletal muscle/ serum	Liver/ serum
Fructosediphosphate aldolase	21800:1	2700:1
Pyruvate kinase	6200:1	1400:1
Lactate dehydrogenase	1400:1	1400:1
Malate dehydrogenase	2000:1	2600:1
Aspartate aminotransferase	5700:1	9000:1
Alanine aminotransferase	750:1	7600:1

variance in the values) between maximum nocturnal and minimum noon levels have been reported[37] as well as marked constancy throughout the day[38].

Muscular work. Heavy muscular work causes a marked rise in serum enzyme activities. In untrained test subjects, long-continued work resulted in considerable increases in the levels of aspartate aminotransferase, alanine aminotransferase, lactate dehydrogenase, fructosediphosphate aldolase, malate dehydrogenase, pyruvate kinase and creatine kinase[27, 39–41], the last-named enzyme being markedly sensitive even to quite mild physical exertion[39, 42]. Alkaline and acid phosphatases, as well as amylase, show no change[33].

Pregnancy. During uneventful pregnancy the serum activities of many enzymes – for instance aspartate aminotransferase, alanine aminotransferase, fructosediphosphate aldolase, isocitrate dehydrogenase, malate dehydrogenase and α-hydroxybutyrate dehydrogenase–remain within the normal range[43–50]. There have been reports of irregular increases in aspartate aminotransferase[47], creatine kinase[49] and especially lactate dehydrogenase[47, 48, 51] during the last weeks of gestation, but these have not been confirmed by other workers[44–46, 52].

A number of hydrolytically active enzymes (alkaline phosphatase[45, 47, 53], leucine aminopeptidase[50, 54], oxytocinase[55], β-glucuronidase[50, 56]) as well as histaminase[57] show increases up to many times the normal serum value during pregnancy, with a subsequent return to normal in a few days post partum.

Serum enzyme activities

Most of the diagnostically useful enzymes except those concerned in blood coagulation are best determined in the serum since in the plasma their activity may be inhibited by the presence of added citrate, oxalate, heparin, fluoride, etc.[33]. Even slight haemolysis interferes with the determination of the enzymes present at high activities in the erythrocytes, such as lactate dehydrogenase, glucose-6-phosphate dehydrogenase, phosphogluconate dehydrogenase, fructosediphosphate aldolase, arginase, etc., but it can be tolerated in the case of enzymes whose serum and erythrocyte concentrations differ by much less, such as aspartate aminotransferase, alanine aminotransferase, glutamate dehydrogenase, ketose-1-phosphate aldolase, etc.

In general, determinations should be carried out immediately after collection of the serum sample since enzymes may be unstable in the serum. Most of the diagnostically useful enzymes, however, show little change in activity during the first 24 hours if the serum is kept at +4 °C or even room temperature[33, 34]. Exceptions are glucose-6-phosphatase, glucose-6-phosphate dehydrogenase, phosphogluconate dehydrogenase and creatine kinase[33]. For methods of enzyme determination see the literature[33, 58].

Elimination of enzymes from the serum

The serum levels of enzymes normally remain fairly constant. Injection of enzymes into the blood is followed by a rapid return to normal values[59–62]. The reduction takes place in two phases[61], a faster phase of distribution over the whole intercellular space and a slower one of actual elimination. The half-lives in human serum, so far known only approximately, of various enzymes are[63–66]: aspartate aminotransferase 46–58 hours, alanine aminotransferase 63–88 hours, lactate dehydrogenase ca. 52 hours.

The mechanism of elimination remains obscure. Alkaline phosphatase and leucine aminopeptidase are excreted in the bile, amylase, pepsinogen and other enzymes of low molecular weight in the urine. Nevertheless, the rates of excretion of yet other enzymes like aspartate aminotransferase, alanine aminotransferase and lactate dehydrogenase remain unchanged by bilateral nephrectomy, by hepatectomy or by splenectomy[59, 61, 63, 67]. The reticuloendothelial system may play an important part in enzyme elimination from the blood[68].

Diagnostic use of enzymes

Maintenance of the normal difference between the enzyme concentrations in the cells and serum is a process closely linked to the energy metabolism of the cell. Impairment of energy production – as in injury to the cell – results in movement of enzymes out of the cell[59, 60, 69], the rate depending on the concentration gradient, molecular weight and location of the particular enzyme. The relative importance of these factors varies with the severity of the injury to the cell. When it is acute and severe – as in cardiac infarction – the enzyme pattern of the organ appears in the serum, whereas in less acute and less severe injury the increase in serum enzyme activity is mainly accounted for by the readily extractable cytoplasmic enzymes; in the latter case the characteristic enzyme pattern is soon effaced as a result of the different rates at which the enzymes are eliminated[41, 70–72].

The extent to which the serum enzyme activity increases reflects the severity and scope of the cell injury[64, 66, 73]. The seat of the disease can be established by identifying the typical enzyme pattern of the organ in the serum, or by determining 'organ-specific' enzymes or tissue-specific isozyme distributions[74].

Of the many enzymes present in the serum only a few have proved to be of lasting diagnostic value. In order of practical importance these are: aspartate aminotransferase, alanine aminotransferase, alkaline phosphatase, acid phosphatase, amylase, creatine kinase, glutamate dehydrogenase, lactate dehydrogenase (and its isozymes), iditol dehydrogenase and fructosediphosphate aldolase. Enzyme determinations now play an indispensable part in the diagnosis of liver, heart, muscle and pancreatic diseases.

1. Liver disease. In *acute hepatitis* there is an increase in most of the serum enzymes so far studied[75]. Aspartate aminotransferase activity rises 10–150 times, that of alanine aminotransferase 20–200 times. The increase in alkaline phosphatase activity is comparatively small and reflects the accompanying biliary obstruction[76]. There is a decrease in the plasma cholinesterase activity originating in the liver[77]. The increase in enzyme activity precedes the rise in the bilirubin concentration and thus allows diagnosis of hepatitis in anicteric patients[78]. The course of the disease can readily be followed with the aid of enzyme determinations, an aggravation or relapse always being manifested by a renewed rise in the serum enzyme levels[76]. Failure of the aminotransferase activities to return to normal in spite of apparent clinical healing is an indication that hepatitis persists in a subchronic form[76].

A smaller rise in serum aminotransferase activities (2–8 times the normal) occurs in active *chronic hepatitis* and *cirrhosis of the liver*[76, 79–81]. In cases of long standing the aspartate aminotransferase level is usually higher than the alanine aminotransferase level, with a fairly marked rise in glutamate dehydrogenase activity[76]. These enzyme changes are quite distinct from those seen in acute hepatitis and are characteristic of the necrotic type of cell injury[72].

Any aggravation of the disease, whether marked by jaundice or not, results in an immediate rise in serum enzyme activities[76, 79, 81, 82]. In protracted *hepatic coma* a fall in aminotransferase activity must be regarded as an unfavourable sign[81, 83–85]; other enzymes – lactate dehydrogenase, malate dehydrogenase, ketose-1-phosphate aldolase, etc. – show large increases in activity[76, 85].

In the terminal stages of *cirrhosis of the liver with ascites* the overall enzyme activity shows little pathological change; the aspartate aminotransferase activity is always higher than the alanine aminotransferase activity, however, while glutamate dehydrogenase can often be detected. These very small increases in aminotransferase activity enable the terminal stages to be distinguished from the so-called 'early' ascites accompanying acute aggravations of the disease, in which aminotransferase activity is very markedly increased owing to the severe injury to the cells[76].

In *adipohepatic liver* there are merely slight changes in serum enzyme activities. Marked increases are seen only in very severe fatty degeneration or in the presence of secondary inflammation[76, 86]. Extremely high increases – up to 10 000 U/l for aspartate and alanine aminotransferases and lactate dehydrogenase – occur in *acute poisoning*, especially with organic solvents[64, 87]. A rise in serum enzyme activities following acute *alcohol intoxication* is seen only in alcoholics and cannot be produced experimentally in healthy persons[88].

Primary *carcinoma of the liver* in the presence of cirrhosis of the liver is not marked by any further change in the serum enzyme pattern[81, 89]. In *carcinomatous metastases of the liver* there is a moderate overall increase in enzyme activity, with higher aspartate aminotransferase than alanine aminotransferase activity[75, 76], and a distinct increase in glutamate dehydrogenase activity[76], while lactate dehydrogenase levels often exceed 500 U/l[75, 76]. High alkaline phosphatase values are often also found in the absence of jaundice[90, 91].

In *obstructive jaundice*, diagnostic criteria are the markedly lower increase in aminotransferase activities compared to acute hepatitis[81, 91, 92] and the rise in alkaline phosphatase[93] and leucine aminopeptidase[94, 95] activities. Quite often, however, particularly following biliary colic, there are rises in aminotransferase activity like those seen in the milder forms of acute hepatitis[41, 81, 96]. Another feature often seen is absence of any corresponding increase in alkaline phosphatase activity. The diagnosis can be strengthened by measuring the ratio (aspartate aminotransferase + alanine aminotransferase)/glutamate dehydrogenase[97]; in inflammatory icteric liver disease this is over 30, in obstructive jaundice less than 15.

2. Heart disease. A rise in serum enzyme activity is a constant (95–100% of patients) and reliable sign of *cardiac infarction*[98, 99]. When injury to the cells is acute and short-lived the timely measurement of enzyme activities is particularly important[75].

The relatively small mass of muscle damaged in cardiac infarction means that the increase in enzyme activity is markedly less than in acute liver disease. In general, the creatine kinase and aspartate aminotransferase activities reach values 10 times the normal, the lactate dehydrogenase and fructosediphosphate aldolase activities values 3–6 times the normal[74, 75]. The clear correlation between the size of the infarct and the level of serum enzyme activity observed in experimental animals[100] is seen also in man, though in some patients circulatory collapse and increasing heart failure cause release of enzymes from other organs as well. Care must therefore be taken in drawing prognostic conclusions from the extent of the rise in enzyme activity[75]. The enzyme pattern in the serum resembles that in the myocardium, namely higher aspartate aminotransferase than alanine aminotransferase activity and a relatively high creatine kinase level. A fresh infarct can be distinguished from incipient decompensation if this characteristic enzyme pattern is recognized when enzyme activities again increase. In decompensation, apart from usually lower creatine kinase values, the alanine aminotransferase activity rises until it equals and possibly exceeds the aspartate aminotransferase activity[75].

In *angina pectoris*, serum enzyme activities remain unchanged[101]. If the symptoms are severe and an increase in enzyme activity is observed, there is a high probability that infarction has occurred even though the typical ECG changes are not recorded[102].

Changes in serum enzyme activity are also associated with various types of *tachycardia* of frequency exceeding 160/min[99, 103] and are due to congestion of the liver.

Pulmonary embolism can be distinguished from cardiac infarction by means of the following criteria: In about 60% of cases there is no increase in aminotransferases. When this does occur the difference in the levels characteristic of infarction is absent, and the alanine aminotransferase activity equals or exceeds the aspartate aminotransferase activity. Furthermore, there is no increase in creatine kinase, and the isozymes of lactate dehydrogenase show an increase not in the 'cardiac' fraction but in the 'hepatic' fraction[75].

Cardiac infarction must also be distinguished from acute upper abdominal disease, characterized by a typical serum 'liver enzyme pattern' consisting of higher alanine than aspartate aminotransferase activity and a slight increase in lactate dehydrogenase accounted for by the 'hepatic' isozyme fraction and liver-specific enzymes, such as ketose-1-phosphate aldolase and iditol dehydrogenase. Other diagnostic aids are the determination of amylase (pancreatic disease) and of alkaline phosphatase and glutamate dehydrogenase (bile duct disease).

In *pericarditis* due to a variety of causes there is usually no increase in serum enzyme activities[104], and any slight rise is indicative of involvement of the heart muscle in the inflammation[66, 105]. Small increases in aspartate aminotransferase and lactate dehydrogenase activities are seen in myocarditis[106], and surprisingly high values may be met with in the myocarditis of diphtheria[107].

Most patients with *myogenic heart failure* have more or less normal serum aminotransferase activities. Any increase points to hypoxic injury to the liver cells due to congestion. However, other organs (for instance the skeletal muscles) certainly contribute to the enzyme changes observed. In predominantly right heart failure the serum enzyme pattern bears more resemblance to the liver pattern than in left ventricular heart failure[108].

Table 5 Serum enzyme activities following cardiac infarction[74,75]

	Starts to rise at (hours)	Maximum activity at (hours)	Returns to normal after (days)
Creatine kinase	2–4	24–36	3–6
Aspartate aminotransferase	4–6	24–48	4–7
Lactate dehydrogenase	8–10	48–72	8–9
Lactate dehydrogenase isozymes 1 and 2	8–10	24–92	10–12
Fructosediphosphate aldolase	4–6	24–48	2–9

3. Muscular disease. After severe *muscular injury* there is a slight rise particularly in those enzymes with a high activity in muscle, namely creatine kinase, aspartate aminotransferase and fructosediphosphate aldolase. Very marked increases in activity are observed in *muscular dystrophy*, especially of the DUCHENNE type[109–112]; in other types the rise is distinctly smaller and more irregular[109–112]. The extent of the increase in enzyme activity depends on the severity of the disease process and on the stage reached. Highest values are seen at the start of the disease[112]. The greater the extent to which fatty and connective tissue are involved in place of muscle as the disease progresses, the lower the enzyme activities; in bedridden patients the values may fall in the normal range. Enzyme determinations have proved useful in hereditary studies; thus female relatives of boys with progressive muscular dystrophy (DUCHENNE type) on the average have higher fructosediphosphate aldolase, creatine kinase and lactate dehydrogenase activities than unrelated women and girls[111–113].

An increase in serum enzyme activities is also seen in *chronic polymyositis*[110,114,115], in *dystrophia myotonica*[110,114,116] and in *dermatomyositis*; in the latter disease, lactate dehydrogenase and glucosephosphate isomerase are especially prominent, and the aminotransferase activity may reach 400–600 U/l[117].

4. Pancreatic disease. The enzyme determinations of choice are still those of amylase and lipase. Increases in other enzymes – aspartate aminotransferase, alanine aminotransferase, lactate dehydrogenase, alkaline phosphatase, leucine aminopeptidase – are not characteristic and are indicative merely of primary or secondary involvement of the liver[95,118].

In *acute pancreatitis* the serum amylase and lipase activities start to rise within 3–6 hours and attain a maximum after 20–30 hours. Increased activities are still observed after 48–72 hours, after which the values return to normal – in milder forms of the disease as a result of restoration of the integrity of the cells, in severe forms as a result of failure to form new enzymes[119]. The enzymes released into the serum are excreted in the urine, where enzyme changes similar to those seen in the serum are observed 6–10 hours later.

The unreliability of enzyme determinations in the diagnosis of *chronic pancreatitis* and *pancreatic carcinoma*, in which serum enzyme changes occur only occasionally during painful episodes, has led to the use of provocation tests[120]. In these, an increased release of enzymes by the injured organ into the plasma is attained by means of a powerful secretory stimulus; their efficacy is dependent on the pancreas being able to form enzymes in adequate amount.

5. Blood disease. Characteristic of *pernicious anaemia* is the increase, often extremely high, in the serum lactate dehydrogenase activity[83,121,122]. In untreated patients values over 700 U/l are almost always found[123]. Values over 1200 U/l are diagnostically conclusive provided extensive metastatic carcinomas, severe poisoning and shock can be excluded[123]. After treatment with vitamin B_{12} the lactate dehydrogenase activity falls before the reticulocyte count begins to rise and returns to normal within 2–3 weeks, before normalization of the blood picture[83,123].

In *congenital haemolytic anaemia*, *haemorrhagic anaemia* and *aplastic anaemia* there is little or no change in serum enzyme activities[83,124]. *Erythrocytosis* and *polycythaemia*[122,125] are likewise as a rule not marked by serum enzyme changes, though treatment with X rays or ^{32}P causes a short-lived increase in activity[125].

In *acute leucosis* an increase in enzyme activity is a common but not constant symptom[126,127]. *Chronic myeloid leukaemia* is accompanied by only a slight increase. In *chronic lymphadenosis*, lactate dehydrogenase activity is often normal, while other enzyme activities are usually so[126].

6. Tumours. Earlier hopes that a carcinoma could be detected with certainty by determination of enzymes[128], particularly lactate dehydrogenase, have not been fulfilled. The frequency with which an increased lactate dehydrogenase activity occurs in patients with tumours varies between 40% and 90%[129]. The values for this enzyme, among 26 whose activities in the serum of patients with tumours of very different kinds were studied, proved to be the most regular in their behaviour[130]. They constitute no reliable index, however, since an increase in the lactate dehydrogenase activity is not a constant observation even when tumours are widely disseminated; it is also a feature of a great many other diseases.

The characteristic enzyme pattern seen in carcinomatous metastases of the liver has already been mentioned.

Apart from the diseases mentioned in this chapter, there are many others in which serum enzyme determinations can play a valuable role in the diagnosis and in following the course of the disease. This is particularly so when measurements are made not on a *single* enzyme but on a selected group of two, three or more enzymes whose relationship to the other symptoms of the disease has been established[76].

References

1 International Union of Biochemistry, *Report of the Commission on Enzymes*, Pergamon Press, Oxford, 1961; International Union of Biochemistry, *Enzyme Nomenclature*, Recommendations 1964, Elsevier, Amsterdam, 1965.
1a Dybkaer and Jørgensen, *Quantities and Units in Clinical Chemistry*, Munksgaard, Copenhagen, 1967, page 28.
2 Greenstein, J.P., *Biochemistry of Cancer*, 2nd ed., Academic Press, New York, 1954, chapter 8.
3 Pette et al., *Biochem.biophys.Res.Commun.*, **7**, 419 (1962); Pette et al., *Biochem.biophys.Res.Commun.*, **7**, 425 (1962); Klingenberg and Pette, *Biochem.biophys.Res.Commun.*, **7**, 430 (1962); Pette and Luh, *Biochem. biophys.Res.Commun.*, **8**, 283 (1962).
4 Schmidt and Schmidt, *Klin.Wschr.*, **38**, 957 (1960).
5 Markert and Møller, *Proc.nat.Acad.Sci.(Wash.)*, **45**, 753 (1959).
6 Neilands, J.B., *Science*, **115**, 143 (1952); Neilands, J.B., *J.biol.Chem.*, **199**, 373 (1952); Krebs, E.G., *J.biol.Chem.*, **200**, 471 (1953); Vesell and Bearn, *Proc.Soc.exp.Biol.(N.Y.)*, **94**, 96 (1957).
7 Pfleiderer and Jeckel, *Biochem.Z.*, **329**, 370 (1957); Wieland and Pfleiderer, *Biochem.Z.*, **329**, 112 (1957); Wieland et al., *Biochem.Z.*, **332**, 1 (1959); Wieme, R.J., *Clin.chim.Acta*, **4**, 317 (1959); Plagemann et al., *J.biol.Chem.*, **235**, 2282 (1960); Hess and Walter, *Klin.Wschr.*, **38**, 1080 (1960); Richterich et al., *Clin.chim.Acta*, **8**, 178 (1963).
8 Delbrück et al., *Biochem.Z.*, **331**, 297 (1959); Thorne, C.J.R., *Biochim. biophys.Acta (Amst.)*, **42**, 175 (1960).
9 Schmidt et al., *Klin.Wschr.*, **40**, 1133 (1962).
10 Eichel and Bukovsky, *Nature*, **191**, 243 (1961).
11 Tsao, M.U., *Arch.Biochem.*, **90**, 234 (1960).
12 Malmström, B.G., *Arch.Biochem.*, **70**, 58 (1957).
13 Kowlessar et al., *J.clin.Invest.*, **39**, 671 (1960); Schobel and Wewalka, *Klin.Wschr.*, **40**, 1048 (1962).
14 Latner, A.L., in Ruyssen and Vandendriessche (Eds.), *Enzymes in Clinical Chemistry*, West-European Symposia on Clinical Chemistry, Ghent 1964, vol.4, Elsevier, Amsterdam, 1965.
15 Keiding, N.R., *Scand.J.clin.Lab.Invest.*, **11**, 106 (1959).
16 Reith et al., *Klin.Wschr.*, **42**, 915 (1964).
17 Dubbs et al., *Science*, **131**, 1529 (1960).
18 Hakim, A.A., *Arch.Biochem.*, **83**, 390 (1959).
19 van der Helm, *Nature*, **194**, 773 (1962).
20 Fildes and Parr, *Nature*, **200**, 890 (1963).
21 Deul and van Breemen, *Clin.chim.Acta*, **10**, 276 (1964).
22 von Fellenberg et al., *Enzymol.biol.clin.(Basel)*, **3**, 240 (1963).
23 Spencer et al., *Nature*, **204**, 742 (1964).
24 McGeachin and Lewis, *J.biol.Chem.*, **234**, 795 (1959).
25 Delbrück et al., *Biochem.Z.*, **331**, 273 (1959).
26 Hof and Woller, *Klin.Wschr.*, **34**, 98 (1956).
27 Otto et al., *Klin.Wschr.*, **42**, 75 (1964).
28 Richterich et al., *Schweiz.med.Wschr.*, **92**, 1496 (1962).
29 Reinhold et al., *Amer.J.clin.Path.*, **23**, 645 (1953); Breuer and Schönfelder, *Clin.chim.Acta*, **6**, 515 (1961).
30 Cohen and Huseby, *Cancer Res.*, **11**, 52 (1951); Goldbarg et al., *Gastroenterology*, **36**, 193 (1959); Plaice, C.H., *J.clin.Path.*, **14**, 661 (1961).
31 Siekert and Fleisher, *Proc.Mayo Clin.*, **31**, 459 (1956).
32 Hughes, B.P., *Clin.chim.Acta*, **7**, 597 (1962).
33 King, J., *Practical Clinical Enzymology*, Van Nostrand, London, 1965.
34 Feissli et al., *Klin.Wschr.*, **44**, 390 (1966).
35 Clark and Beck, *J.Pediat.*, **36**, 335 (1950).
36 Merten and Solbach, *Mitteilungsdienst der Gesellschaft zur Bekämpfung der Krebskrankheiten in Nordrhein-Westfalen*, No.5/6, 388 (1961).
37 Vetter et al., *Z.ges.inn.Med.*, **16**, 359 (1961).
38 Schmidt and Schmidt, unpublished studies; Massarrat, S., personal communication.
39 Baumann et al., *Schweiz.Z.Sportmed.*, **10**, 33 (1962).
40 Cantone and Cerretelli, *Int.Z.angew.Physiol.*, **18**, 107 (1960); Altland and Highman, *Amer.J.Physiol.*, **201**, 393 (1961); Richterich et al., *Schweiz.med.Wschr.*, **91**, 601 (1961); Fowler et al., *J.appl.Physiol.*, **17**, 943 (1962); Schneider and Heise, *Dtsch.med.Wschr.*, **88**, 520 (1963), and *Germ. med.Mth.*, **8**, 397 (1963).
41 Schmidt and Schmidt, in Wildhirt, E. (Ed.), *Fortschritte der Gastroenterologie*, Urban & Schwarzenberg, Munich, 1960.
42 Colombo et al., *Klin.Wschr.*, **40**, 37 (1962).
43 Bompiani, A., *Ann.Ostet.Ginec.*, **78**, 705 (1956); Johansson et al., *Nord. Med.*, **59**, 442 (1958); Dubach and Stamm, *Arch.Gynäk.*, **190**, 394 (1958); Borglin, N.E., *J.clin.Endocr.*, **18**, 872 (1958); Borglin, N.E., *J.clin. Endocr.*, **19**, 425 (1959); Ferrario and Fumagalli, *Minerva ginec.*, **11**, 260 (1959); Klimek et al., *Ginek.pol.*, **30**, 345 (1959); Kucker and Richter, *Gynaecologia (Basel)*, **148**, 142 (1959); Normann et al., *Nord.Med.*, **63**, 259 (1960); Kubli, F., *Arch.Gynäk.*, **194**, 406 and 413 (1961); von Muralt and Richter, *Gynaecologia (Basel)*, **151**, 124 (1961); Dawkins and Wigglesworth, *J.Obstet.Gynaec.Brit.Cwlth*, **68**, 264 (1961); Little and Kirpalani, *Amer.J.Obstet.Gynec.*, **83**, 1346 (1962); Tobin, S.M., *Amer.J.Obstet.Gynec.*, **87**, 213 (1963).
44 West and Zimmerman, *Amer.J.med.Sci.*, **235**, 443 (1958).
45 Knutson et al., *J.Lab.clin.Med.*, **51**, 773 (1958).
46 Crisp et al., *Obstet.and Gynec.*, **13**, 487 (1959); Neumann and Kyank, *Zbl. Gynäk.*, **83**, 1909 (1961).
47 Friedman et al., *Amer.J.Obstet.Gynec.*, **82**, 132 (1961).
48 Theisen et al., *Obstet.and Gynec.*, **17**, 183 (1961).
49 Konttinen and Pyörälä, *Scand.J.clin.Lab.Invest.*, **15**, 429 (1963).
50 Carol and Bonow, *Zbl.Gynäk.*, **87**, 426 (1965).
51 Hagerman and Wellington, *Amer.J.Obstet.Gynec.*, **77**, 348 (1959); Stone et al., *Amer.J.Obstet.Gynec.*, **80**, 104 (1960); Romalis and Claman, *Amer. J.Obstet.Gynec.*, **84**, 1104 (1962).
52 Little, W.A., *Obstet.and Gynec.*, **13**, 152 (1959); Smith et al., *Obstet.and Gynec.*, **13**, 163 (1959); Emery and Pascasio, *Amer.J.Obstet.Gynec.*, **91**, 18 (1965).
53 Meranze et al., *Amer.J.Obstet.Gynec.*, **33**, 444 (1937); Waronski and Kudla, *Ginek.pol.*, **32**, 521 (1961).
54 Goldbarg and Rutenburg, *Cancer*, **11**, 283 (1958); Sabatini and Marimpietri-Pienabarca, *Monit.ostet.-ginec.*, NS **33**, 471 (1962); Kokot and Cekański, *Zbl.Gynäk.*, **85**, 1638 (1963).
55 Werle and Effkemann, *Arch.Gynäk.*, **171**, 286 (1941); Semm, K., *Naunyn-Schmiedeberg's Arch.exp.Path.Pharmak.*, **220**, 447 (1953); Tuppy and Wintersberger, *Mh.Chem.*, **91**, 1001 (1961); Tuppy et al., *Hoppe-Seylers Z.physiol.Chem.*, **329**, 278 (1962); Bernhard and Semm, *Zbl.Gynäk.*, **86**, 1691 (1964).
56 McDonald and Odell, *J.clin.Endocr.*, **7**, 535 (1947); Yamada and Hayakawa, *Nagoya J.med.Sci.*, **16**, 203 (1953); Kasdon et al., *Obstet.Gynec.*, **15**, 367 (1960).
57 Werle and Effkemann, *Arch.Gynäk.*, **170**, 82 (1940); Ahlmark, A., *Acta physiol.scand.*, **9**, suppl.28 (1944); Vignes and Cariou, *Gynéc. et Obstét.*, **57**, 399 (1958); Swanberg, H., *Acta physiol.scand.*, **23**, suppl.79 (1958); Borglin and Willert, *Cancer*, **15**, 271 (1962).
58 Colowick and Kaplan (Eds.), *Methods in Enzymology*, 7 vols., Academic Press, New York, 1955–1964; Henry et al., *Amer.J.clin.Path.*, **34**, 381 (1960); Bergmeyer, H.-U. (Ed.), *Methods of Enzymatic Analysis*, Academic Press, New York, 1963; Schmidt and Schmidt, *Enzymol.biol.clin.*, **2**, 201 (1962); Richterich, R., *Clinical Chemistry, Theory and Practice*, Karger, Basle, and Academic Press, New York, 1969.
59 Sibley, J.A., *Ann.N.Y.Acad.Sci.*, **75**, 339 (1958).
60 Bruns and Neuhaus, *Arch.Biochem.*, **55**, 588 (1955).
61 Dunn et al., *J.Lab.clin.Med.*, **51**, 259 (1958).
62 Sibley and Fleisher, *Proc.Mayo Clin.*, **29**, 591 (1954); Wróblewski and LaDue, *Proc.Soc.exp.Biol.(N.Y.)*, **90**, 210 (1955); Amelung et al., *Klin. Wschr.*, **36**, 963 (1958); Sampson, J.J., *Progr.cardiovasc.Dis.*, **1**, 187 (1958); Wolfson et al., *Ann.N.Y.Acad.Sci.*, **75**, 260 (1958/59).
63 Amelung, D., *Hoppe-Seylers Z.physiol.Chem.*, **318**, 219 (1960).
64 Molander et al., *J.Lab.clin.Med.*, **46**, 831 (1955).
65 Neuhaus et al., *Klin.Wschr.*, **41**, 619 (1963).
66 Nydick et al., *Circulation*, **15**, 324 (1957).
67 Strandjord et al., *J.clin.Invest.*, **38**, 2111 (1959); Reichard, H., *J.Lab. clin.Med.*, **53**, 417 (1959); Cleeve, H., *J.clin.Path.*, **15**, 93 (1962).
68 Fleisher and Wakim, *J.Lab.clin.Med.*, **61**, 76, 86, 98, 107 (1963).
69 Warburg and Christian, *Biochem.Z.*, **314**, 399 (1943); Warburg and Hiepler, *Z.Naturforsch.*, **7b**, 193 (1952); Schade, A.L., *Biochim.biophys. Acta (Amst.)*, **12**, 163 (1953); Warburg et al., *Z.Naturforsch.*, **9b**, 109 (1954); Zierler, K.L., *Amer.J.Physiol.*, **185**, 12 (1956); Zierler, K.L., *Amer.J.Physiol.*, **190**, 201 (1957); Bruns, F.H., *Clin.chim.Acta*, **2**, 257 (1957); Zierler, K.L., *Amer.J.Physiol.*, **192**, 283 (1958); Zierler, K.L., *Bull.Johns Hopk.Hosp.*, **102**, 17 (1958); Zierler, K.L., *Ann.N.Y.Acad. Sci.*, **75**, 227 (1958); Wu and Racker, *Fed.Proc.*, **17**, 399 (1958); Wu, R., *Cancer Res.*, **19**, 1217 (1959); Bruns et al., *Klin.Wschr.*, **39**, 342 (1961).
70 Bücher et al., in *Transactions of the 9th Middle East Medical Assembly*, Beirut, 1959.
71 Schmidt and Schmidt, in *Verhandlungen des 1. Europäischen Symposiums über medizinische Enzymologie*, Milan 1960, Karger, Basle, 1961, page 100; Schmidt and Schmidt, *Bibl.gastroent.(Basel)*, **4**, 15 (1961); Schmidt and Schmidt, in *Transactions du 7e Congrès international de gastroentérologie*, Brussels, 1964, page 116; Schmidt, F.W., *Verh.dtsch.Ges.inn.Med.*, **70**, 612 (1964).
72 Schmidt and Schmidt, *Regensburg.Jb.ärztl.Fortbild.*, **12**, 4, 207 (1964).
73 Wróblewski and LaDue, *Cancer*, **8**, 1155 (1955); Friend et al., *J.exp. Med.*, **102**, 699 (1955); Nydick et al., *Circulation*, **12**, 161 (1955); Bruns and Neuhaus, *Biochem.Z.*, **326**, 242 (1955); Rudolph et al., *J.Lab.clin. Med.*, **49**, 31 (1957); Asada, M., *Med.J.Osaka Univ.*, **9**, 45 (1958); De Ritis et al., *G.Mal.infett.*, **11**, 469 (1959).
74 Schmidt et al., in Bergmeyer, H.-U. (Ed.), *Methoden der enzymatischen Analyse*, Verlag Chemie, Weinheim/Bergstr., 1962, page 651.
75 Amelung, D., *Fermentdiagnostik interner Erkrankungen*, Thieme, Stuttgart, 1964.
76 Schmidt and Schmidt, *Enzymol.biol.clin.(Basel)*, **3**, 1 (1963).
77 Antopol et al., *Proc.Soc.exp.Biol.(N.Y.)*, **38**, 363 (1938); Molander et al., *Ann.intern.Med.*, **41**, 1139 (1954); Kommerell and Franken, *Dtsch. med.Wschr.*, **81**, 1959 (1956); Pietschmann, H., *Wien.Z.inn.Med.*, **41**, 409 (1960).

[78] Bang et al., *Nord. Med.*, **58**, 1013 (1957); Tolentino and Rossi, *G. Mal. infett.*, **9**, 552 (1957); Delkeskamp et al., *Dtsch. med. Wschr.*, **84**, 188 (1959), and *Germ. med. Mth.*, **4**, 44 (1959); De Ritis et al., *Bull. Wld Hlth Org.*, **20**, 589 (1959); Manning et al., *Amer. J. med. Sci.*, **241**, 454 (1961).
[79] Schmidt et al., *Klin. Wschr.*, **36**, 280 (1958).
[80] De Ritis et al., *Recenti Progr. Med.*, **20**, 533 (1956).
[81] Wróblewski, F., *Amer. J. Med.*, **27**, 911 (1959).
[82] Molander et al., *J. Amer. med. Ass.*, **163**, 1461 (1957); Donato, R. A., *Amer. J. clin. Path.*, **28**, 377 (1957); Baier et al., *Klin. Wschr.*, **39**, 117 (1961).
[83] Beyreder and Rettenbacher-Däubner, *Wien. klin. Wschr.*, **71**, 686 (1959).
[84] Franken, F. H., *Klin. Wschr.*, **35**, 1203 (1957).
[85] Schmidt and Schmidt, *Gastroenterologia (Basel)*, **90**, suppl. 69 (1958).
[86] Bradus et al., *Amer. J. med. Sci.*, **246**, 35 (1963).
[87] Lindner, H., *Klin. Wschr.*, **36**, 877 (1958); Baier, H., *Medizinische*, **1959**, 2222; Petersen, V. P., *Acta med. scand.*, **164**, 131 (1959); Krentz, K., *Internist (Berl.)*, **2**, 261 (1961); Dawborn et al., *Brit. med. J.*, **2**, 493 (1961).
[88] Bang et al., *J. Amer. med. Ass.*, **168**, 156 (1958); Linde, S., *Scand. J. Lab. clin. Invest.*, **10**, 303 (1958); Madsen et al., *Brit. med. J.*, **1**, 543 (1958); Hed, R., *Acta med. scand.*, **165**, 161 (1959); von Oldershausen and Regoeczi, *Bibl. gastroent. (Basel)*, **4**, 79 (1961).
[89] Klein, H. G., *Wien. med. Wschr.*, **109**, 179 (1959).
[90] Mendelsohn and Bodansky, *Cancer*, **5**, 1 (1952); Gibbons, T. B., *J. Amer. med. Ass.*, **164**, 22 (1957); Molander et al., *Acta Un. int. Cancr.*, **16**, 1478 (1960).
[91] Gutman, A. B., *Amer. J. Med.*, **27**, 875 (1959).
[92] Wróblewski and LaDue, *Ann. intern. Med.*, **43**, 345 (1955); Eismann, J., *Dtsch. med. J.*, **7**, 204 (1956); De Ritis et al., *Minerva med.*, **47**, 167 (1956); Horn and Amelung, *Dtsch. med. Wschr.*, **82**, 619 (1957).
[93] Latner and Smith, *Lancet*, **2**, 915 (1958); Martini and Strohmeyer, *Med. Klin.*, **54**, 1489 (1959); Leipold et al., *Dtsch. med. Wschr.*, **86**, 1341 (1961).
[94] Banks et al., *New Engl. J. Med.*, **263**, 1277 (1960); Bressler et al., *J. Lab. clin. Med.*, **56**, 417 (1960).
[95] Göggel et al., *Dtsch. med. Wschr.*, **85**, 1756 and 1808 (1960), and *Germ. med. Mth.*, **6**, 399 (1961).
[96] Lindner, H., *Dtsch. med. J.*, **12**, 15 and 33 (1961); Demeulenaere, L., in *Verhandlungen des 1. Europäischen Symposiums über medizinische Enzymologie*, Milan 1960, Karger, Basle, 1961, page 260; Mossberg and Ross, *Gastroenterology*, **45**, 345 (1963).
[97] Schmidt and Schmidt, *Klin. Wschr.*, **40**, 962 (1962); Filippa, G., *Enzymol. biol. clin. (Basel)*, **3**, 97 (1963).
[98] Kattus et al., *Circulation*, **15**, 502 (1957); Lass et al., *Medizinische*, **1958**, 1767; Forster, G., *Praxis*, **47**, 1013 (1958); LaDue, J. S., *Amer. J. Cardiol.*, **1**, 308 (1958); Rudolph et al., *N. Y. St. J. Med.*, **58**, 2520 (1958); Wood et al., *Northw. Med. (Seattle)*, **57**, 1447 (1958); Snodgrass et al., *New Engl. J. Med.*, **261**, 1259 (1959).
[99] Chinsky and Sherry, *Arch. intern. Med.*, **99**, 556 (1957).
[100] Glassner et al., *Amer. J. Physiol.*, **179**, 639 (1954); Lemley-Stone et al., *Amer. J. Physiol.*, **183**, 555 (1955); Siegel and Bing, *Proc. Soc. exp. Biol. (N. Y.)*, **91**, 604 (1956); Wróblewski, F., *Amer. Heart J.*, **54**, 219 (1957); Coltorti et al., *Minerva cardioangiol.*, **5**, 1 (1957); Ruegsegger et al., *Circulat. Res.*, **7**, 4 (1959).
[101] Amelung and Horn, *Dtsch. med. Wschr.*, **81**, 1701 (1956).
[102] LaDue et al., *Mod. Conc. cardiov. Dis.*, **25**, 333 (1956).
[103] Carcassi and Pitzus, *Minerva med.*, **48**, 2449 (1957); Bruyet et al., *Arch. Mal. Cœur*, **51**, 758 (1958); Dewar et al., *Brit. med. J.*, **2**, 1121 (1958).
[104] Chinsky et al., *J. Lab. clin. Med.*, **47**, 108 (1956); Fremont et al., *Amer. J. Cardiol.*, **1**, 480 (1958); Weissmann, C., *Schweiz. med. Wschr.*, **89**, 777 and 811 (1959).
[105] Agress et al., *Proc. Soc. exp. Biol. (N. Y.)*, **92**, 826 (1956).
[106] Nydick et al., *Circulation*, **12**, 795 (1955); Baron et al., *Quart. J. Med.*, **27**, 533 (1958); Cattaneo et al., *Reumatismo*, **10**, 366 (1958).
[107] Choremis and Leonidas, *Acta paediat. (Uppsala)*, **51**, 293 (1962).
[108] West et al., *Amer. J. med. Sci.*, **241**, 350 (1961).
[109] Schapira and Dreyfus, in Bourne and Golarz (Eds.), *Muscular Dystrophy in Man and Animals*, Karger, Basle, 1963, page 48.
[110] Dreyfus and Schapira, in Gigon and Ludwig (Eds.), *Enzymatische Regulationen in der Klinik*, Schwabe, Basle, 1961, page 145.
[111] Chung et al., *Amer. J. hum. Genet.*, **12**, 52 (1960).
[112] Aebi et al., *Helv. paediat. Acta*, **16**, 543 (1961).
[113] Aebi et al., *Enzymol. biol. clin. (Basel)*, **1**, 61 (1961/62); Schapira et al., *Enzymol. biol. clin. (Basel)*, **2**, 45 (1962/63).
[114] Heyck and Laudahn, *Klin. Wschr.*, **41**, 905 (1963).
[115] Matzelt and Mertens, *Verh. dtsch. Ges. inn. Med.*, **68**, 285 (1962).
[116] Kuhn et al., *Klin. Wschr.*, **40**, 744 (1962).
[117] Wüst et al., *Derm. Wschr.*, **137**, 288 (1958).
[118] Foulk and Fleisher, *Gastroenterology*, **35**, 375 (1958); Harkness et al., *Brit. med. J.*, **1**, 1787 (1960); Pojer et al., *Gastroenterologia (Basel)*, **95**, 73 (1961); Klaus, D., *Med. Welt*, **12**, 644 (1962).
[119] Gülzow, M., *Internist (Berl.)*, **5**, 88 (1964).
[120] Popper et al., *Surg. Gynec. Obstet.*, **77**, 471 (1943); Knight et al., *Gastroenterology*, **12**, 34 (1949); Sanchez-Ubeda and Rousselot, *Surg. Gynec. Obstet.*, **93**, 283 (1951); Steinmann and Widmer, *Schweiz. med. Wschr.*, **85**, 411 (1955).
[121] Hess and Gehm, *Klin. Wschr.*, **33**, 91 (1959); Heller et al., *J. Lab. clin. Med.*, **55**, 425 (1960).
[122] Levitan et al., *Clin. Res.*, **7**, 217 (1959).
[123] Amelung, D., *Dtsch. med. Wschr.*, **85**, 1629 (1960), and *Germ. med. Mth.*, **5**, 334 (1960).
[124] Hennemann and Klaus, *Klin. Wschr.*, **36**, 516 (1958); Horn, H. D., *Verh. dtsch. Ges. inn. Med.*, **64**, 315 (1958); Schlief et al., *Medizinische*, **1959**, 669.
[125] Vetter and Griesche, *Z. ges. inn. Med.*, **15**, 367 (1960).
[126] Englhardt-Gölkel et al., *Klin. Wschr.*, **36**, 462 (1958).
[127] Englhardt-Gölkel et al., *Klin. Wschr.*, **36**, 576 (1958).
[128] Hill and Levi, *Cancer Res.*, **14**, 513 (1954).
[129] Hsieh et al., *Proc. Soc. exp. Biol. (N. Y.)*, **89**, 627 (1955), correction: **90**, 554 (1955); White, L. P., *J. nat. Cancer Inst.*, **21**, 671 and 685 (1958); Horn and Langrehr, *Z. Geburtsh. Gynäk.*, **150**, 311 (1958); Gullino et al., *Minerva chir.*, **16**, 274 (1961); Rose et al., *Cancer*, **14**, 726 (1961).
[130] Merten and Solbach, *Klin. Wschr.*, **39**, 222 (1961).
[131] Beisenherz et al., *Z. Naturforsch.*, **8b**, 555 (1953).
[132] Karmen et al., *J. clin. Invest.*, **34**, 126 (1955).
[133] Holzer et al., *Biochem. Z.*, **326**, 451 (1955); Gerlach, U., *Klin. Wschr.*, **37**, 93 (1959).
[134] Bruns, F., *Biochem. Z.*, **325**, 156 (1954).
[135] Sibley and Lehninger, *J. biol. Chem.*, **177**, 859 (1949).
[136] Schapira et al., *Amer. J. phys. Med.*, **34**, 313 (1955).
[137] King and Armstrong, *Canad. med. Ass. J.*, **31**, 376 (1934).
[138] King and Wootton, *Microanalysis in Medical Biochemistry*, 3rd ed., Churchill, London, 1959.
[139] Shinowara et al., *J. biol. Chem.*, **142**, 921 (1942).
[140] Bessey et al., *J. biol. Chem.*, **164**, 321 (1946).
[141] Bodansky, A., *J. biol. Chem.*, **101**, 93 (1933).
[142] Somogyi, M., *J. biol. Chem.*, **125**, 399 (1938).
[143] Wohlgemuth, J., *Biochem. Z.*, **9**, 1 (1908).
[144] Henry et al., *Amer. J. clin. Path.*, **34**, 381 (1960).
[145] Schmidt and Schmidt, *Enzymol. biol. clin. (Basel)*, **2**, 201 (1962).
[146] Löhr, G. W., *Folia haemat. (Frankfurt)*, NF **6**, 49 (1961); Löhr and Waller, *Z. Geburtsh.*, **159**, supplement (1962).

Normal values in **U/l plasma or serum** of adults unless otherwise stated (for definition of the unit U see page 584)

EC number Systematic name **Recommended trivial name** In brackets: abbreviation and non-recommended trivial name	Method	Number	Mean	95% range (extreme range in brackets)	*s*	Reference	Remarks (see also text on pages 584–588)
1.1.1.1							
Alcohol: NAD oxidoreductase **Alcohol dehydrogenase** (ADH)	Optical[1], modified, 25 °C ...	7	1.8			2	Slight haemolysis does not interfere. Clinical importance small up to now. Markedly increased in serum in acute hepatitis and other acute liver disease of a severe nature[2,3].
1.1.1.8							
L-Glycerol-3-phosphate: NAD oxidoreductase **Glycerophosphate dehydrogenase** (GDH)	Optical[4], modified, 25 °C ...	19	2.7	(1.6–6.6)		2, 5	Slight haemolysis does not interfere. Increased in serum in acute hepatitis and severe liver disease[2].
1.1.1.14							
L-Iditol: NAD oxidoreductase **L-Iditol dehydrogenase** (Sorbitol dehydrogenase [SDH])	Optical[6], modified, 24 °C ...	16	0.9			7	Owing to the low activity of the enzyme in the erythrocytes slight haemolysis does not interfere. Activity high in liver only. A rise in the serum activity is fairly specific for liver damage[5,7,9].
	Optical[7], modified, 25 °C ...	12	1.1			5	
	Optical[7], modified, 25 °C ...	91	0.06	(0–0.4)	0.1	8	
	Optical[7], modified, 37 °C ...	32	0.08	(0–0.6)		9	
	Optical[7], modified, 25 °C						
	Adults			0–3.0		10	
	Cord blood			0–4.5		10	
	Children			0–6.0		10	
1.1.1.27							
L-Lactate: NAD oxidoreductase **Lactate dehydrogenase** (LDH)	Optical[11], modified, 24–27 °C	161	225	(120–419)		12	Owing to the high activity of this enzyme in the erythrocytes even slight haemolysis results in 'false' high serum values. Present in all organs at high activity, so that an increase in the serum activity follows severe organic injury of any kind. 5 isozymes have been identified in organs and serum. Determination of total lactate dehydrogenase activity is clinically useful in diagnosis of cardiac infarction, in differential diagnosis of anaemia (highest values in pernicious anaemia) and to some extent in liver disease; for further discussion see the literature[20]. For normal values of the isozyme distribution see JORDAN and WHITE[20a].
	Optical[13], modified, 25 °C...	130		(125–379)		14	
	Optical[11], modified, 25 °C...	180	88	(36–130)		5	
	Optical[11], modified, room temperature	107	71		6.2	15	
	Optical[11], modified, 25 °C...			(30–120)		16	
	Colorimetric (2,4-diphenylhydrazine), 37 °C			(70–240)		16	
	Optical[11], modified, 25 °C...	209	100		22	8	
	Optical[11], modified, 25 °C...	175	144		28.8	17	
	Optical[11], modified, 25 °C						
	Adults	100	140		45	10	
	Cord blood	29	306		118	10	
	1 month	6	306		89	10	
	2–3 months	13	221		44	10	
	4–6 months	12	217		41	10	
	6–12 months	14	197		44	10	
	2 years	12	230		57	10	
	2–16 years	24	145		45	10	
	Optical[11], modified, 25 °C						
	Cord blood	202		(87–580)		18	
	Optical[11], modified, 25 °C						
	Premature infants	25	126			19	
	Newborn	19	114		61	19	
	Infants	36	49		27	19	
	Children	38	42		12	19	

[1] NEGELEIN and WULFF, *Biochem. Z.*, **293**, 351 (1937).
[2] SCHMIDT et al., *Klin. Wschr.*, **36**, 280 (1958).
[3] WOLFSON et al., *Ann. N. Y. Acad. Sci.*, **75**, 260 (1958/59).
[4] BÜCHER, T., in COLOWICK and KAPLAN (Eds.), *Methods in Enzymology*, vol. 1, Academic Press, New York, 1955, page 415.
[5] SCHMIDT et al., in BERGMEYER, H.-U. (Ed.), *Methoden der enzymatischen Analyse*, Verlag Chemie, Weinheim/Bergstr., 1962, page 703.
[6] HOLZER et al., *Biochem. Z.*, **326**, 451 (1955).
[7] GERLACH, U., *Klin. Wschr.*, **37**, 93 (1959).
[8] FEISSLI et al., *Klin. Wschr.*, **44**, 390 (1966).
[9] WÜST and SCHÖN, *Klin. Wschr.*, **39**, 280 (1961).
[10] GAUTIER et al., *Helv. paediat. Acta*, **17**, 415 (1962).
[11] KUBOWITZ and OTT, *Biochem. Z.*, **314**, 94 (1943).
[12] WRÓBLEWSKI and LADUE, *Proc. Soc. exp. Biol. (N. Y.)*, **90**, 210 (1955).
[13] STROMINGER and LOWRY, *J. biol. Chem.*, **213**, 635 (1955).
[14] HSIEH and BLUMENTHAL, *Proc. Soc. exp. Biol. (N. Y.)*, **91**, 626 (1956).
[15] ENGLHARDT-GÖLKEL et al., *Klin. Wschr.*, **36**, 462 (1958).
[16] KING, J., *Practical Clinical Enzymology*, Van Nostrand, London, 1965.
[17] SCHNEIDER et al., *Med. Klin.*, **60**, 6 (1965).
[18] HAUG and KLUGE, *Klin. Wschr.*, **43**, 680 (1965).
[19] STAVE, U., *Z. Kinderheilk.*, **81**, 472 (1958).
[20] WILKINSON, J. H., *An Introduction to Diagnostic Enzymology*, Arnold, London, 1962; HESS, B., *Enzyme im Blutplasma*, Thieme, Stuttgart, 1962; AMELUNG, D., *Fermentdiagnostik interner Erkrankungen*, Thieme, Stuttgart, 1964.
[20a] JORDAN and WHITE, *Clin. chim. Acta*, **15**, 457 (1967).

Normal values in **U/l plasma or serum** of adults unless otherwise stated (for definition of the unit U see page 584)

EC number Systematic name **Recommended trivial name** In brackets: abbreviation and non-recommended trivial name	Method	Number	Mean	95% range (extreme range in brackets)	*s*	Reference	Remarks (see also text on pages 584–588)
[α-Hydroxybutyrate dehydrogenase] (HBDH)	Optical[21,22], 25 °C	42	90		38	23	Not in itself an enzyme but derives from the simple method of determining the electrophoretically fast-migrating isozymes of lactate dehydrogenase[21]. These are present at high activity in heart muscle and brain and oxidize hydroxybutyrate to a much greater extent than the isozymes mainly present in skeletal muscle and liver. For practical purposes the ratio LDH/HBDH equals the ratio total LDH isozymes/heart-muscle specific LDH isozymes; normal value in 42 adults[23] 1.40, in 155 adults[17] 1.34.
	Optical[21,22], 25 °C	175	108		23.5	17	
	Optical[21,22], 25 °C	100	77		36	24	
	Optical[21,22], 25 °C						
	Adults	152	76		30	25	
	Cord blood	15	211		164	25	
1.1.1.37 L-Malate: NAD oxidoreductase **Malate dehydrogenase** (MDH)	Optical[26], modified, 25 °C ..	28	37.9	(17.0–57.3)		5	Owing to the high activity of this enzyme in the erythrocytes even slight haemolysis results in 'false' high serum values. In the neonatal period the upper limit of the normal may be up to 100 U/l[28]. Diagnostic importance so far slight. Present in all organs at high activity, so that an increase in the serum activity follows severe organic injury of any kind, for instance cardiac infarction, liver damage, blood disease. For reviews see the literature[20].
	Optical[27], modified, 25 °C ..	107	23.5		3.4	15	
	Optical[26], modified, 25 °C ..	88	71		17	8	
	Optical[26], modified, 25 °C						
	Adults			(12.5–50)		16	
	Cord blood	202		(93.4–265)		18	
1.1.1.38 (40) L-Malate: NAD(P) oxidoreductase (decarboxylating) **Malate dehydrogenase (decarboxylating)** ('Malic' enzyme)	Optical[29], 25 °C	30		(0–0.5)		30	
1.1.1.42 *threo*-D$_s$-Isocitrate: NADP oxidoreductase (decarboxylating) **Isocitrate dehydrogenase** (ICDH)	Optical[31], 25 °C	44	2.0	(0.86–4.8)		31	Slight haemolysis does not interfere. In cord blood the activity is much higher than in the blood of adults but falls within 10 days[16]; other studies[33] showed little difference. The serum activity increases in liver damage[2]. In cardiac infarction it is either unchanged[34] or shows only a slight and transient rise[35].
	Optical[32], room temperature	38	1.3	(0.96–1.9)		32	
	Optical[27], modified, 25 °C						
	Adults	13	3.5	(1.0–7.3)		5	
	Cord blood	30	3.7		2.6	33	
1.1.1.44 6-Phospho-D-gluconate: NADP oxidoreductase (decarboxylating) **Phosphogluconate dehydrogenase (decarboxylating)** (PGDH)	Optical[31], 25 °C	26	2.5	(0.7–4.0)		31	Owing to the high activity of this enzyme in the erythrocytes even slight haemolysis results in 'false' high serum values. The serum activity is normal during pregnancy, in cord blood rather higher than in the blood of adults. Diagnostic importance so far small. The activity increases in acute hepatitis[2,3] and blood disease[37]. Its determination in vaginal fluid has been suggested as a test for gynaecological cancer[38].
	Optical[36], modified, 25 °C ..	17	1.0			5	

21 Rosalki and Wilkinson, *Nature*, **188**, 1110 (1960).
22 Elliott and Wilkinson, *Lancet*, **1**, 698 (1961).
23 Elliott et al., *Clin. Sci.*, **23**, 305 (1962).
24 Richterich, R., *Klinische Chemie; Theorie und Praxis*, Karger, Basle, 1965.
25 Konttinen and Pyörälä, *Scand. J. clin. Lab. Invest.*, **15**, 429 (1963).
26 Mehler et al., *J. biol. Chem.*, **174**, 961 (1948).
27 Ochoa, S., *J. biol. Chem.*, **174**, 133 (1948).
28 King and Morris, *Arch. Dis. Childh.*, **36**, 604 (1961).
29 Ochoa et al., *J. biol. Chem.*, **174**, 979 (1948).
30 Merten and Solbach, *Klin. Wschr.*, **39**, 222 (1961).
31 Wolfson and Williams-Ashman, *Proc. Soc. exp. Biol. (N.Y.)*, **96**, 231 (1957).
32 Kerppola et al., *Acta med. scand.*, **164**, 357 (1959).
33 Pehrson, S. L., *Acta obstet. gynec. scand.*, **43**, 69 (1964).
34 Bowers and MacDuffee, *Clin. Chem.*, **5**, 369 (1959).
35 Strandjord et al., *J. clin. Invest.*, **38**, 2111 (1959).
36 Horecker and Smyrniotis, in Colowick and Kaplan (Eds.), *Methods in Enzymology*, vol. 1, Academic Press, New York, 1955, page 323.
37 Heller et al., *J. Lab. clin. Med.*, **55**, 425 (1960).
38 Bonham and Gibbs, *Brit. med. J.*, **2**, 823 (1962).

Normal values in U/l **plasma or serum** of adults unless otherwise stated (for definition of the unit U see page 584)

EC number Systematic name **Recommended trivial name** In brackets: abbreviation and non-recommended trivial name	Method	Number	Mean	95% range (extreme range in brackets)	s	Reference	Remarks (see also text on pages 584–588)
1.1.1.49							
D-Glucose-6-phosphate: NADP oxidoreductase	Optical[39], room temperature	67	1.4	(0.5–2.4)		32	Even slight haemolysis results in 'false' high serum values. Serum activity increased in acute hepatitis[2], cardiac infarction[40] and other severe tissue damage. Clinically useful when deficiency of this enzyme in the erythrocytes[40, 41] is suspected (primaquine sensitivity), as in favism and kernicterus.
Glucose-6-phosphate dehydrogenase	Optical[39], modified, 25 °C ..	18	1.0			5	
(G-6-PDH)	Optical[39], modified, 25 °C ..	38	0.24		0.29	8	
('Zwischenferment' [ZF])							
1.2.1.12							
D-Glyceraldehyde-3-phosphate: NAD oxidoreductase (phosphorylating) **Glyceraldehyde-phosphate dehydrogenase** **Triosephosphate dehydrogenase** (GAPDH)	Optical[42], modified, 25 °C ..	20	7.1	(1.0–11.2)		5	Even slight haemolysis interferes considerably. Clinical importance so far small. Serum activity is increased in acute hepatitis[2], infectious mononucleosis[43] and various kinds of tumour[30].
1.2.3.2							
Xanthine: oxygen oxidoreductase **Xanthine oxidase** (Hypoxanthine oxidase)	Substrate: 8-^{14}C-xanthine[44], 25 °C	20		(0–0.000 5)		44	Clinical importance so far small. Serum activity increased in liver damage[44].
1.3.99.1							
Succinate: (acceptor) oxidoreductase **Succinate dehydrogenase**	Optical[45]			Not detectable		15	Structurally bound enzyme. So far not detected in serum even in severe organic injury.
1.4.1.3							
L-Glutamate: NAD(P) oxidoreductase (deaminating)	Optical[6], modified, 25 °C ...		1.0			46	Slight haemolysis does not interfere. Largely specific to the liver. Serum activity increased in inflammatory liver disease and obstructive jaundice[46, 47], which can be differentiated by means of the ratio (aspartate aminotransferase + alanine aminotransferase)/glutamate dehydrogenase[47–49].
Glutamate dehydrogenase	Optical[6], modified, 25 °C ...	127	1.0			47	
(GLDH)	Optical (Boehringer), 25 °C .	243	0.39	< 0.8	0.28	8	
1.6.4.2							
Reduced-NAD(P): oxidized-glutathione oxidoreductase	Optical[50]			(5–35)		16	Serum activity markedly increased in acute hepatitis and leukaemia[32], less so in cirrhosis. Also increased in 35–80% of patients with disseminated carcinomas[32, 52]. In primaquine-sensitive patients, whose erythrocytes are poor in glucose-6-phosphate dehydrogenase, the glutathione reductase activity of the cells is doubled[53].
Glutathione reductase	Optical[51], 25 °C						
(GR)	NAD	10	7.0	(3.3–10.2)		51	
	NADP	10	12.6	(4.3–17.4)		51	
	Optical[50], NADP..........	98	19.2		7.2	52	

39 KORNBERG and HORECKER, in COLOWICK and KAPLAN (Eds.), *Methods in Enzymology*, vol. 1, Academic Press, New York, 1955, page 323.
40 CARSON et al., *Science*, **124**, 484 (1956).
41 SMITH and VELLA, *Lancet*, **1**, 1133 (1960).
42 BEISENHERZ et al., *Z. Naturforsch.*, **8b**, 555 (1953).
43 KALK et al., *Klin. Wschr.*, **38**, 421 (1960).
44 SHAMMA'A et al., *Gastroenterology*, **48**, 226 (1965).
45 SLATER and BORNER, *Biochem. J.*, **52**, 185 (1952).
46 GERLACH, U., *Klin. Wschr.*, **35**, 1144 (1957).
47 SCHMIDT and SCHMIDT, *Klin. Wschr.*, **40**, 962 (1962).
48 FILIPPA, G., *Enzymol. biol. clin. (Basel)*, **3**, 97 (1963).
49 SCHMIDT and SCHMIDT, *Enzymol. biol. clin. (Basel)*, **3**, 1 (1963).
50 RACKER, E., in COLOWICK and KAPLAN (Eds.), *Methods in Enzymology*, vol. 2, Academic Press, New York, 1955, page 722.
51 HORN and BRUNS, *Biochem. Z.*, **331**, 58 (1958).
52 MANSO and WRÓBLEWSKI, *J. clin. Invest.*, **37**, 214 (1958).
53 SCHRIER et al., *J. Lab. clin. Med.*, **52**, 109 (1958).

Normal values in **U/l plasma or serum** of adults unless otherwise stated (for definition of the unit U see page 584)

EC number Systematic name **Recommended trivial name** In brackets: abbreviation and non-recommended trivial name	Method	Number	Mean	95% range (extreme range in brackets)	s	Reference	Remarks (see also text on pages 584–588)
–							
(Caeruloplasmin)	Colorimetric (*p*-phenylene-diamine)[54], 37 °C						Caeruloplasmin has the properties of *p*-diphenol oxidase. In pregnancy the caeruloplasmin activity is 2–3 times higher than normal[55]. A deficiency of the enzyme is characteristic of hepatolenticular degeneration[56], but is also found in the nephrotic syndrome, kwashiorkor[57] and sprue[58]. The serum activity is increased in cardiac infarction, infectious diseases, leukaemia, etc.[16].
	Adults			19–45		10	
	Cord blood			3.3–16.7		10	
	1-3 months			12.1–39		10	
	Children			19.2–60		10	
2.1.3.3 Carbamoylphosphate: L-ornithine carbamoyltransferase **Ornithine carbamoyltransferase** (OCT)	Microdiffusion[59], modified[60], 37 °C			(0–0.25)		16	Increased in 25% of normal pregnancies. In cord blood the activity is the same as in normal adults. The observation of an increase in serum activity from the age of 24 years on[63] has not been confirmed[64]. The high activity of the enzyme in the liver renders the serum activity a specific index of severe liver damage.
	Colorimetric[61], 37 °C			(8–20)		61	
	Isotopic[62], 37 °C			(0–0.07)		62	
2.2.1.1 Sedoheptulose-7-phosphate: D-glyceraldehyde-3-phosphate glycolaldehydetransferase **Transketolase** **Glycolaldehydetransferase**	Colorimetric (assay of sedoheptulose 7-phosphate)[65], 37 °C	15	0.82	(0.38–1.42)		65	Serum activity increased in uraemia and often in acute hepatitis, normal in cardiac infarction, cirrhosis of the liver and obstructive jaundice[65].
		21	0.29	(0.17–0.60)		66	
2.6.1.1 L-Aspartate: 2-oxoglutarate aminotransferase **Aspartate aminotransferase** (Glutamate-oxalacetate transaminase [GOT])	Optical[67], 20–22 °C	500	10.6	(2.4–19.2)	3.2	68	Slight haemolysis interferes hardly at all. The clinical importance of this enzyme lies in the marked improvement it has brought about in the diagnosis of cardiac infarction and liver disease. For reviews see the literature[20, 49, 72].
	Optical[67], 38 °C	160	16.6		0.4	69	
	Optical[67], modified, 25 °C	105	8.0	(3.6–17.0)		5	
	Optical (Boehringer), 25 °C, blood donors	950	12.0	(6.2–22.0)		70	
	Optical[67], 25 °C, blood donors	100	13.6		3.2	10	
	Optical[67], 25 °C			(4–15)		16	
	Colorimetric[71], modified, 25 °C			(5–18)		16	
	Optical (Boehringer), 25 °C	577	7.67		1.8	8	
	Optical[67], 25 °C						
	Cord blood	44	21.3		9.5	10	
	Up to 1 month	12	20.4		9.7	10	
	2–3 months	13	22.6		6.3	10	
	4–6 months	12	24.3		5.5	10	
	7–12 months	16	19.3		5.4	10	
	2 years	6	15.7		4.8	10	
	2–16 years	58	14.1		3.9	10	
	16 years	49	14.4		4.0	10	
	Cord blood	15	12.6		9.0	25	
	Cord blood	202		(0–29)		18	
	Optical[67], 25 °C						
	Premature infants	25	9.2		9.4	19	
	Newborn	20	8.8		4.5	19	
	Infants	41	4.8		2.6	19	
	Children	43	3.7		2.6	19	

54 Ravin, H. A., *Lancet*, **1**, 726 (1956).
55 Holmberg and Laurell, *Scand. J. clin. Lab. Invest.*, **3**, 103 (1951).
56 Scheinberg and Gitlin, *Science*, **116**, 484 (1952).
57 Reiff and Schnieden, *Blood*, **14**, 967 (1959).
58 Gubler, C. J., *J. Amer. med. Ass.*, **161**, 530 (1956).
59 Reichard and Reichard, *J. Lab. clin. Med.*, **52**, 709 (1958).
60 Ballan et al., *Presse méd.*, **67**, 2353 (1959).
61 Brown and Grisolia, *J. Lab. clin. Med.*, **54**, 617 (1959).
62 Reichard, H., *J. Lab. clin. Med.*, **57**, 78 (1961).
63 Reichard, H., *Enzymol. biol. clin. (Basel)*, **1**, 47 (1961).
64 Demange et al., *Presse méd.*, **70**, 1032 (1962).
65 Bruns et al., *Biochem. Z.*, **330**, 497 (1958).
66 Englhardt-Gölkel and Withöft, *Klin. Wschr.*, **40**, 642 (1962).
67 Karmen, A., *J. clin. Invest.*, **34**, 131 (1955).
68 Wróblewski and LaDue, *Ann. intern. Med.*, **43**, 345 (1955).
69 Fleisher et al., *Proc. Mayo Clin.*, **32**, 188 (1957).
70 Lindner, H., *Dtsch. med. J.*, **12**, 15 and 33 (1961).
71 Reitman and Frankel, *Amer. J. clin. Path.*, **28**, 56 (1957).
72 Wróblewski, F., *Amer. J. Med.*, **27**, 911 (1959).

Normal values in **U/l plasma or serum** of adults unless otherwise stated (for definition of the unit U see page 584)

EC number Systematic name **Recommended trivial name** In brackets: abbreviation and non-recommended trivial name	Method	Number	Mean	95% range (extreme range in brackets)	s	Reference	Remarks (see also text on pages 584–588)
2.6.1.2 L-Alanine:2-oxoglutarate aminotransferase	Optical[73], modified, room temperature	54	3.7		2.1	74	Slight haemolysis does not interfere. High activity in liver, practically none in erythrocytes. Serum activity increased markedly in liver disease, in the diagnosis of which it is the most important enzyme. For reviews see the literature[20, 49, 72].
Alanine aminotransferase	Optical[73], 20–22 °C	260	7.7	(2.4–16.8)		73	
(Glutamate–pyruvate-transaminase [GPT])	Optical[73], modified, 25 °C	122	6.9	(2.9–16.1)		5	
	Optical (Boehringer), 25 °C, blood donors	2400		(6.4–16.0)		70	
	Optical[73], 25 °C, blood donors	2400		(6.4–16.0)		75	
	Optical (Boehringer), 25 °C	722	5.54		1.7	8	
	Cord blood	44	5.0		2.3	10	
	1 month	11	4.0		3.0	10	
	2–3 months	11	7.5		1.6	10	
	4–12 months	14	6.2		2.7	10	
	From 1 year	31	6.8		3.3	10	
	Cord blood	202		0.5–9.6		18	
2.7.1.1 ATP:D-hexose 6-phosphotransferase **Hexokinase** (HK)	Optical, with glucose 6-phosphate dehydrogenase, 25 °C	30		Not detectable		15	Haemolysis interferes. No clinical usefulness so far. Serum activity increased in acute hepatitis[2].
	Optical, 25 °C	7	0.1			5	
2.7.1.3 ATP:D-fructose 1-phosphotransferase **Ketohexokinase** (Fructokinase [FK])	Optical[76], modified, 25 °C	30		Not detectable		30	No clinical usefulness so far. Serum activity increased in acute hepatitis[30].
2.7.1.40 ATP:pyruvate phosphotransferase **Pyruvate kinase** (PK)	Optical[42], modified, 25 °C	19	16.4	(3.8–34.8)		5	No clinical significance. In acute hepatitis the serum activity shows a non-significant reduction (due to bed-rest?)[2], in patients with tumours an increase[30]. In non-spherocytic haemolytic anaemia the erythrocytes have been shown to be deficient in this enzyme[78].
	Optical[42]	20	29.9	(15.7–49.6)		77	
	Optical[42], modified, 25 °C	30	15.8		6.0	30	
2.7.2.3 ATP:3-phospho-D-glycerate 1-phosphotransferase **Phosphoglycerate kinase** (PGK)	Optical[4], modified, room temperature	107	11.2		3.1	15	Serum activity increased in leukaemia[15]. In cardiac infarction and acute hepatitis normal[15] as well as higher values[49] have been found.
2.7.3.2 ATP:creatine phosphotransferase	Colorimetric[79], 37 °C			(3.3–23.7)		79	Slight haemolysis does not interfere. Higher serum activities are found following physical effort[83, 85]. In men the normal value is slightly higher than in women[8, 80]. Creatine kinase is a sensitive pointer in the diagnosis of cardiac and muscular diseases. For reviews see the literature[20].
Creatine kinase	Colorimetric[80], 37 °C			(5.5–75)		81	
(Creatine phosphokinase [CPK])	Optical[82], 37 °C	254	0.40		1.3	83	
	Optical (Boehringer), 25 °C	257	0.30	<1.0	0.30	8	
	Optical (Boehringer), 25 °C	30		(0–0.48)		84	
	Optical[82], 37 °C						
	Adults		1.0		0.8	25	
	Cord blood		2.1		1.8	25	
	Pregnancy, 3rd trimester		2.9		5.6	25	

73 Wróblewski and LaDue, *Proc. Soc. exp. Biol. (N.Y.)*, **91**, 569 (1956).
74 Henley and Pollard, *J. Lab. clin. Med.*, **46**, 785 (1955).
75 Richterich et al., *Schweiz. med. Wschr.*, **91**, 601 (1961).
76 Waller et al., *Thrombos. Diathes. haemorrh. (Stuttg.)*, **3**, 520 (1959).
77 van Rymenant and Robert, *Cancer*, **12**, 1087 (1959).
78 Tanaka et al., *Blood*, **19**, 267 (1962).
79 Dreyfus et al., *Rev. franç. Etud. clin. biol.*, **5**, 384 (1960).
80 Goldbarg et al., *Gastroenterology*, **36**, 193 (1959).
81 Hughes, B. P., *Clin. chim. Acta*, **7**, 597 (1962).
82 Kuby et al., *J. biol. Chem.*, **209**, 191 (1954); Tanzer and Gilvarg, *J. biol. Chem.*, **234**, 3201 (1959).
83 Richterich et al., *Amer. J. hum. Genet.*, **15**, 133 (1963).
84 Forster and Escher, *Helv. med. Acta*, **28**, 513 (1961).
85 Griffiths, P. D., *Clin. chim. Acta*, **13**, 413 (1966).

Normal values in **U/l plasma or serum** of adults unless otherwise stated (for definition of the unit U see page 584)

EC number Systematic name **Recommended trivial name** In brackets: abbreviation and non-recommended trivial name	Method	Number	Mean	95% range (extreme range in brackets)	*s*	Reference	Remarks (see also text on pages 584–588)
2.7.4.3 ATP:AMP phosphotransferase **Adenylate kinase** (Myokinase [MK])	Optical[86], 25 °C	25	8.7		3.1	87	In striped muscle the absolute activity of adenylate kinase is higher than that of creatine kinase[88]. Occurs at relatively high activities in leucocytes and thrombocytes. The usefulness of serum determinations in the diagnosis of cardiac and muscular diseases is limited by the necessity of using serum completely free of haemolysis[87].
2.7.5.1 α-D-Glucose-1,6-diphosphate: α-D-glucose-1-phosphate phosphotransferase **Phosphoglucomutase** **Glucose phosphomutase** (PGluM)	Fructose 6-phosphate assay[89], 37 °C	10	8.3	(1.7–23.4)		89	Slight haemolysis does not interfere. In cord blood, values only half as high as in adults have been found. Little clinical importance. Increased in liver damage[91].
	Fructose 6-phosphate assay[89], 37 °C	30	9.8		5.2	30	
	Glucose 1-phosphate assay[90], 37 °C		9.2	(4–17)	3.4	90	
3.1.1.3 Glycerol-ester hydrolase **Lipase**	Titrimetric (substrate olive oil), 37 °C	68	78		29	92	Haemolysis interferes because of inhibition of the reaction by the haemoglobin. No sex-specific differences have been observed[93]. The marked increase in the serum activity in acute pancreatitis has so far found little diagnostic application[94]. In chronic pancreatitis the changes are not reliable; better results are obtained with provocation tests[95]. Slight increases in serum lipase activity are seen in inflammatory liver diseases[96].
	Titrimetric (substrate olive oil), 37 °C			(18–285)		16	
	Titrimetric (substrate phenyl laurate), 37 °C			(9–20)		16	
3.1.1.8 Acylcholine acyl-hydrolase **Cholinesterase** (CHE)	Colorimetric (acetylcholine bromide), 37 °C			(2000–5200)		97	Slight haemolysis does not interfere. In cord blood the serum activity is rather low but becomes normal after the 10th day; after 2 months the value is about 25% higher than in adults. Serum activity is lower in hepatitis and cirrhosis, in accordance with the reduced serum albumin level[102]. Determination of serum cholinesterase activity has its most important application in detecting poisoning by organic phosphorus compounds (insecticides[103]) and assessing tolerance to muscle relaxants[104]. Hereditary deficiency of the enzyme, in which atypical enzyme variants may occur, can be detected by determining the dibucaine number:
	Optical (benzoylcholine), 25 °C			(620–1370)		98	
	Colorimetric (phenyl benzoate), 37 °C			(3200–7000)		99	
	Optical (benzoylcholine), 25 °C	60	1026		233	24	
	Colorimetric (acetylcholine), 37 °C	250	1530		333	100	
	Colorimetric (benzoylcholine), 37 °C	250	1560		333	100	
	Colorimetric (α-naphthyl propionate), 37 °C	250	3050		466	100	
	Colorimetric (β-naphthyl propionate), 37 °C	250	1750		383	100	
	Colorimetric (phenyl acetate), 37 °C	250	16600		3830	100	
	Colorimetric (monosuccinylcholine), 37 °C	250		<20		100	
	Colorimetric (disuccinylcholine), 37 °C	250		<20		100	
	Titrimetric (acetylcholine chloride), 37 °C						
	Men (blood donors)	25	4440		620	101	
	Women (blood donors)	25	3640		680	101	

	King[16]	Richterich[24]
Normal	80±3	62–90
Heterozygotes	62±8	30–60
Atypical homozygotes	22±6	30

86 Schmidt, F. H., *Klin. Wschr.*, **42**, 476 (1964).
87 Schreiber, F. K., *Klin. Wschr.*, **42**, 478 (1964).
88 Oliver, I. T., *Biochem. J.*, **61**, 116 (1955).
89 Noltmann and Bruns, *Hoppe-Seylers Z. physiol. Chem.*, **313**, 194 (1958).
90 Bodansky, O., *Cancer*, **10**, 859 (1957).
91 De Ritis et al., *Boll. Soc. ital. Biol. sper.*, **32**, 386 (1956); De Ritis et al., *G. Mal. infett.*, **9**, 240 (1957).
92 Weber, H., *Dtsch. med. Wschr.*, **90**, 1170 (1965), and *Germ. med. Mth.*, **11**, 8 (1966).
93 Comfort and Osterberg, *Proc. Mayo Clin.*, **15**, 427 (1940).
94 Tietz et al., *Amer. J. clin. Path.*, **31**, 148 (1959).
95 Burton et al., *Gut*, **1**, 125 (1960).
96 Cummins and Bockus, *Gastroenterology*, **18**, 518 (1951).
97 de la Huerga et al., *Amer. J. clin. Path.*, **22**, 1126 (1952).
98 Kalow and Genest, *Canad. J. Biochem.*, **35**, 339 (1957).
99 Smith et al., *Clin. chim. Acta*, **4**, 384 (1959).
100 Pilz, W., *Z. klin. Chem.*, **3**, 89 (1965).
101 Regulations of the firm Radiometer A/S, Copenhagen.
102 Kunkel and Ward, *J. exp. Med.*, **86**, 325 (1947); Burnett, W., *Gut*, **1**, 294 (1960).
103 Aldridge and Davies, *Brit. med. J.*, **1**, 945 (1952).
104 Evans et al., *Lancet*, **1**, 1229 (1952).

Normal values in **U/l plasma or serum** of adults unless otherwise stated (for definition of the unit U see page 584)

EC number Systematic name **Recommended trivial name** In brackets: abbreviation and non-recommended trivial name	Method	Number	Mean	95% range (extreme range in brackets)	*s*	Reference	Remarks (see also text on pages 584–588)
3.1.3.1 Orthophosphoric monoester phosphohydrolase **Alkaline phosphatase**	Substrate phenyl phosphate, 37 °C			(25–92)		105	Serum activity increased in childhood[16,110] and towards term in pregnancy (see page 586). The most important application of serum alkaline phosphatase determination is in the diagnosis of liver and bone diseases, in the former as indicator of the degree of intra- or extrahepatic biliary obstruction, in the latter as confirmation (when increased) of rickets and to a lesser extent of osteomalacia. High activities are also seen in bone tumours and their metastases marked by an increase in osteoblasts. For reviews see the literature[113].
	Substrate *p*-nitrophenyl phosphate, 37 °C			(13.4–38)		106	
	Substrate phenolphthalein phosphate, 37 °C			(0.6–4.2)		107	
	Substrate β-glycerophosphate, 37 °C			(15.1–46.4)		108	
	Substrate β-glycerophosphate, 37 °C			(8.2–21.8)		109	
	Substrate *p*-nitrophenyl phosphate, 37 °C						
	Adults	100	29		8	110	
	Cord blood	15	60		19	110	
	1 month	3	59			110	
	2–3 months	17	98		29	110	
	4–6 months	14	98		32	110	
	7–12 months	15	92		29	110	
	2–15 years	142	88		26	110	
	Substrate phenyl phosphate, 37 °C						
	Newborn			(35–105)		16	
	1 month			(70–250)		16	
	1–3 years			(70–210)		16	
	3–10 years			(70–180)		16	
	10–16 years			(100–275)		16	
	Substrate *p*-nitrophenyl phosphate, optimum conditions[111], 25 °C	73	102	61–171		112	
3.1.3.2 Orthophosphoric monoester phosphohydrolase **Acid phosphatase**	Substrate *p*-nitrophenyl phosphate, 37 °C						
	Total						
	Serum, men		9.15		4.40	114	The acid phosphatase of serum originates from various sources (erythrocytes, thrombocytes, leucocytes, prostate, bone) which can be identified by the difference in behaviour towards formol and L-tartrate. Serum acid phosphatase determination is important in the diagnosis of prostate carcinoma, though in most cases an increase occurs only in the presence of bony metastases. The diagnosis can be established with greater certainty by determining the formol-stable and tartrate-labile fractions, especially the latter. For reviews see the literature[116].
	Serum, women		8.00		2.94	114	
	Plasma, men		5.08		3.54	114	
	Plasma, women		4.41		1.60	114	
	Prostatic						
	Serum, men		1.84		1.80	114	
	Serum, women		1.85		1.58	114	
	Plasma, men		0.32		0.64	114	
	Plasma, women		0.33		0.60	114	
	Substrate phenyl phosphate, 37 °C						
	Formol-stable		4.25			115	
	Tartrate-labile		1.25			115	
	Total		5.5			115	
	Newborn			(3–6)		16	
	1 month			(6.5–11)		16	
	1–3 years			(6.5–11)		16	
	3–10 years			(3.5–9)		16	
	10–16 years			(3–10)		16	

[105] King and Wootton, *Microanalysis in Medical Biochemistry*, 3rd ed., Churchill, London, 1959.
[106] Bessey et al., *J. biol. Chem.*, **164**, 321 (1946).
[107] Klein et al., *Clin. Chem.*, **6**, 269 (1960).
[108] Shinowara et al., *J. biol. Chem.*, **142**, 921 (1942).
[109] Bodansky, A., *J. biol. Chem.*, **101**, 93 (1933).
[110] Richterich and Gautier, *Schweiz. med. Wschr.*, **92**, 781 (1962).
[111] Rick and Hausamen, *Z. analyt. Chem.*, **212**, 267 (1965).
[112] Hausamen et al., *Clin. chim. Acta*, **15**, 241 (1967).
[113] King, E. J., *Brit. med. Bull.*, **9**, 160 (1953); Gutman, A. B., *Amer. J. Med.*, **27**, 875 (1959).
[114] Richterich et al., *Schweiz. med. Wschr.*, **92**, 1496 (1962).
[115] Joplin and Jegatheesan, *Brit. med. J.*, **1**, 827 (1962).
[116] Woodard, H. Q., *Amer. J. Med.*, **27**, 902 (1959).

Normal values in **U/l plasma or serum** of adults unless otherwise stated (for definition of the unit U see page 584)

EC number Systematic name **Recommended trivial name** In brackets: abbreviation and non-recommended trivial name	Method	Number	Mean	95% range (extreme range in brackets)	*s*	Reference	Remarks (see also text on pages 584–588)
3.1.3.5 5′-Ribonucleotide phosphohydrolase **5′-Nucleotidase**	Colorimetric[117], 37 °C			(2–15)		117	Values in children the same as in adults. Like alkaline phosphatase, this enzyme shows a large rise in serum activity in obstructive jaundice[118] and a smaller one in hepatogenic jaundice[119]. Unlike alkaline phosphatase it shows no increase in bone disease[118].
3.1.3.9 D-Glucose-6-phosphate phosphohydrolase **Glucose-6-phosphatase**	Colorimetric[120], 37 °C		8			120	Haemolysis interferes because of the rise in nonspecific phosphatases. Serum activity increased in acute hepatitis and chronic liver disease[120].
3.1.4.5 Deoxyribonucleate oligonucleotidohydrolase **Deoxyribonuclease** (DNAase, DNase)	Colorimetric, 37 °C		0.65	(0–1.8)		121	
3.1.4.6 Deoxyribonucleate 3′-nucleotidohydrolase **Deoxyribonuclease II** (DNAase II)	Colorimetric, 37 °C		0.56	(0–1.2)		121	
3.2.1.1 α-1,4-Glucan 4-glucanohydrolase **α-Amylase**	Amyloclastic[122], modified, 37 °C	100	1500		615	24	Haemolysis interferes because of inhibition of the reaction by haemoglobin. Serum activity is low in the newborn but rises to the adult level during the first year[24]. It is pathologically increased in acute pancreatitis and pancreatic carcinoma, occasionally also in other abdominal conditions, severe renal failure, and mumps. It is rather lower in chronic pancreatic insufficiency. The most important enzyme in the diagnosis of pancreatic disease. For reviews see the literature[123].
3.2.1.31 β-D-Glucuronide glucuronohydrolase **β-Glucuronidase**	Colorimetric (phenolphthalein mono-β-D-glucuronate), 37 °C						Slight haemolysis does not interfere. Serum activity increases in the 3rd trimester of pregnancy but returns to normal post partum (see page 586). High levels are seen in pre-eclampsia[125] and carcinoma of the pancreatic head; in other forms of carcinoma the rise is smaller[80]. Serum activity also increased in pancreatitis and liver damage[80], less so in advanced cirrhosis and disseminated liver metastases[126]. Determination of the enzyme in the vaginal secretion has been suggested as an aid to the diagnosis of carcinoma[127].
	Men			(0.2–0.55)		16	
	Women			(0.09–0.4)		16	
	Men		0.62		0.15	124	
	Women		0.46		0.12	124	
	Colorimetric (*p*-nitrophenyl β-D-glucuronate), 25 °C						
	Men	52		0.35–1.32		124a	
	Women	53		0.22–0.99		124a	

117 Campbell, D.M., *Biochem.J.*, **82**, 34P (1962).
118 Dixon and Purdom, *Nature*, **170**, 500 (1952); Dixon and Purdom, *J.clin. Path.*, **7**, 341 (1954).
119 Wachstein and Sigismondi, *Amer.J.clin.Path.*, **30**, 523 (1958); Young, I.I., *Ann.N.Y.Acad.Sci.*, **75**, 357 (1958/59).
120 Koide and Oda, *Clin.chim.Acta*, **4**, 554 (1959).
121 Gavosto et al., *Clin.chim.Acta*, **4**, 192 (1959).
122 Smith and Roe, *J.biol.Chem.*, **227**, 357 (1957).
123 Janowitz and Dreiling, *Amer.J.Med.*, **27**, 924 (1959); Webster and Zieve, *New Engl.J.Med.*, **267**, 604 and 654 (1962).
124 Schön and Leipold, *Klin.Wschr.*, **40**, 292 (1962).
124a Szász, G., *Clin.chim.Acta*, **15**, 275 (1967).
125 Odell and McDonald, *Amer.J.Obstet.Gynec.*, **56**, 74 (1948).
126 Pineda et al., *Gastroenterology*, **36**, 202 (1959).
127 Odell et al., *Science*, **109**, 564 (1949).

Normal values in **U/l plasma or serum** of adults unless otherwise stated (for definition of the unit U see page 584)

EC number Systematic name **Recommended trivial name** In brackets: abbreviation and non-recommended trivial name	Method	Number	Mean	95% range (extreme range in brackets)	*s*	Reference	Remarks (see also text on pages 584–588)
3.4.1.1 L-Leucyl-peptide hydrolase **Leucine aminopeptidase** (LAP)	Colorimetric (substrate L-leucyl-β-naphthylamide), 37 °C			(15–50)		16	Slight haemolysis does not interfere. Values are somewhat lower in women, though some workers[129] regard the difference as clinically insignificant and others[130] have found no difference. Serum activity greatly increased in pregnancy (see page 586) and in biliary obstruction of extra- or intrahepatic origin. No increase in carcinoma of the pancreatic head in the absence of biliary obstruction and liver metastases[131]. Slight increase in inflammatory liver disease and acute pancreatitis.
	Colorimetric (substrate L-leucylglycine), 37 °C	82	16.4		0.67	128	
– [Oxytocin-cleaving aminoacylpeptidase] (Oxytocinase)	Colorimetric (substrate L-cystine-bis-β-naphthylamide[132] or L-cystine-bis-*p*-nitroanilide[133])						Serum activity increased many times in pregnancy (see page 586). The cystine aminopeptidase activity of normal serum probably depends on the leucine aminopeptidase activity[134].
3.4.1.3 Amino-acyl-dipeptide hydrolase **Aminopeptidase** (Aminotripeptidase)	Colorimetric (substrate glycylglycylglycine), 37 °C	39	64.7		4.2	128	
3.4.4.1 **Pepsin**	Colorimetric (substrate beef haemoglobin), 37 °C	45	1.72		0.91	135	Formed from pepsinogen. Serum activity rather higher in men than in women[137]. It is low or absent in gastric atrophy, increased in the presence of duodenal ulcers[137,138].
	Colorimetric (substrate beef haemoglobin), 37 °C						
	1 week		2.76	(0.60–8.26)		136	
	3 weeks–6 years		2.41	(1.05–3.08)		136	
3.4.4.4 **Trypsin**							The serum contains no active trypsin[139]. The trypsin-inhibiting capacity of 1 ml of serum is sufficient to inhibit on the average 1 mg of trypsin.
3.4.4.15 **Renin**							Formed in the juxtaglomerular apparatus of the kidneys and released into the plasma, where it is involved in the formation of angiotensin from angiotensinogen (see pages 740–741).
3.5.3.1 L-Arginine amidinohydrolase **Arginase**	Colorimetric[140], 37 °C			(0–12)		16	Haemolysis interferes because of the high activity of this enzyme in the erythrocytes. Serum activity increased in acute and chronic injury to the liver parenchyma; no increase in obstructive jaundice[140,141].
3.5.4.3 Guanine aminohydrolase **Guanine deaminase** (Guanase)	Optical[142], 37 °C			0–3		143	Haemolysis does not interfere. Serum activity increased in liver damage.

[128] FLEISHER et al., *Ann.N.Y.Acad.Sci.*, **75**, 363 (1958/59).
[129] MILLER and WORSLEY, *Brit.med.J.*, **2**, 1419 (1960).
[130] BRESSLER et al., *J.Lab.clin.Med.*, **56**, 417 (1960).
[131] FLEISHER et al., *Proc.Mayo Clin.*, **32**, 410 (1957); HARKNESS et al., *Brit.med.J.*, **1**, 1787 (1960).
[132] TUPPY and NESVADBA, *Mh.Chem.*, **88**, 977 (1957).
[133] TUPPY et al., *Hoppe-Seylers Z.physiol.Chem.*, **329**, 278 (1962).
[134] GOEBELSMAN and BELLER, *Z.klin.Chem.*, **3**, 49 (1965).
[135] HIRSCHOWITZ, B.I., *J.Lab.clin.Med.*, **46**, 568 (1955).
[136] GRAYZEL et al., *Amer.J.Dis.Childh.*, **103**, 759 (1962).
[137] VAN GOIDSENHOVEN et al., *Gastroenterology*, **34**, 421 (1958).
[138] EDWARDS et al., *Brit.med.J.*, **1**, 30 (1960); VICKERS and KENNEDY, *Brit.med.J.*, **1**, 1453 (1962).
[139] ROMAN and FAVILLA, *Enzymologia*, **26**, 249 (1963).
[140] MANNING and GRISOLIA, *Proc.Soc.exp.Biol.(N.Y.)*, **95**, 225 (1957).
[141] UGARTE et al., *J.Lab.clin.Med.*, **57**, 359 (1961); PELIKÁN et al., *Clin.chim.Acta*, **9**, 141 (1964).
[142] HUE and FREE, *Clin.Chem.*, **10**, 631 (1964).
[143] KNIGHTS et al., *J.Lab.clin.Med.*, **65**, 355 (1965).

Normal values in U/l **plasma or serum** of adults unless otherwise stated (for definition of the unit U see page 584)

EC number Systematic name **Recommended trivial name** In brackets: abbreviation and non-recommended trivial name	Method	Number	Mean	95% range (extreme range in brackets)	s	Reference	Remarks (see also text on pages 581–588)
3.5.4.4 Adenosine aminohydrolase **Adenosine deaminase**	Colorimetric[144], 25 °C	70	2.6	(1.4–4.7)	0.54	145	Haemolysis interferes because of the activity of this enzyme in the erythrocytes. Serum activity increased in liver disease, as also in haemoblastosis, reticulosis and acute renal disease.
4.1.2.7 Ketose-1-phosphate aldehyde-lyase **Ketose-1-phosphate aldolase** (Phosphofructaldolase [PFA], aldolase)	Optical[146], modified, 25 °C	18	1.0			5	Activity of this enzyme in the liver far exceeds that in other organs, so that an increase in the serum activity is specific for liver disease. Serum activity is high in acute hepatitis, less so in chronic liver disease and obstructive jaundice[147].
4.1.2.13 Fructose-1,6-diphosphate D-glyceraldehyde-3-phosphate-lyase **Fructosediphosphate aldolase** (Aldolase [ALD], zymohexase)	Colorimetric[148], 38 °C	115	4.4	(2.2–7.4)		148	Haemolysis interferes because of the activity of this enzyme in the erythrocytes. The serum activity rises to a maximum on the 3rd day of life and then falls again to the cord blood value within 3 weeks[16]. It is higher in children than in adults[10, 16, 151] (but see also STAVE[19]). Physical effort results in a moderate increase in serum activity[152]. Determination of the serum activity is diagnostically useful in diseases of the skeletal musculature, heart muscle and liver. Increased particularly in muscular dystrophy of DUCHENNE type, often also in the patient's mother, brothers and sisters[153]. For reviews see the literature[20].
	Colorimetric[148], modified, 37 °C	21	3.3	(1.8–4.9)		149	
	Optical[42], modified, 25 °C	23	2.7	(1–9.7)		5	
	Optical[42], 25 °C	48	1.8		0.65	8	
	Optical[42], 25 °C blood donors	100	6.4		2.4	10	
	Optical[42], 25 °C	30	5.0		2.5	30	
	Colorimetric[150], 37 °C						
	Adults		3.2		0.4	151	
	Children		6.4		0.5	151	
	Colorimetric, 37 °C						
	Cord blood		9.0	(4.0–17.5)		16	
	1 year		17.5			16	
	2 years		15.2			16	
	6 years		12.0			16	
	12 years		8.7			16	
	18 years		6.6			16	
	Optical[42], 25 °C						
	Infants	50	5.3		1.3	10	
	Children	43	3.6		1.5	10	
	Optical[42], modified, 25 °C						
	Premature infants	25	7.1			19	
	Newborn	18	6.4		2.9	19	
	Infants	54	3.5		1.5	19	
	Children	45	2.4		0.7	19	
4.2.1.2 L-Malate hydro-lyase **Fumarate hydratase** (Fumarase)	Optical[154], 37 °C			Not detectable		155	Serum activity slightly increased in hepatitis[156]. No definite increase in carcinoma, even in the late stage[30].
	Optical[154], 37 °C	30		(0–0.7)		30	
4.2.1.3 Citrate (isocitrate) hydro-lyase **Aconitate hydratase** (Aconitase)	Optical[157], 37 °C	30		Not detectable		30	No increase in plasma activity in cardiac infarction, hepatitis or cirrhosis[158].

[144] MARTINEK, R. G., *Clin. Chem.*, **9**, 620 (1963).
[145] MÜLLER-BEISSENHIRTZ and KELLER, *Dtsch. med. Wschr.*, **91**, 159 (1966).
[146] LEUTHARDT et al., *Helv. chim. Acta*, **36**, 227 (1953).
[147] WOLF et al., *Gastroenterologia (Basel)*, **87**, 172 (1957); RICK and OESTERLE, *Verh. dtsch. Ges. inn. Med.*, **65**, 692 (1959); FORSTER and JENNY, *Helv. med. Acta*, **26**, 673 (1959); SCHNEIDERBAUR and RETTENBACHER, *Wien. med. Wschr.*, **111**, 322 (1961).
[148] SIBLEY and LEHNINGER, *J. biol. Chem.*, **177**, 859 (1949).
[149] BRUNS and PULS, *Klin. Wschr.*, **32**, 656 (1954).
[150] MEYERHOF and LOHMANN, *Biochem. Z.*, **271**, 89 (1934).
[151] SCHAPIRA et al., *Amer. J. phys. Med.*, **34**, 313 (1955).
[152] CANTONE and CERRETELLI, *Int. Z. angew. Physiol.*, **18**, 107 (1960); BAUMANN et al., *Schweiz. Z. Sportmed.*, **10**, 33 (1962); FOWLER et al., *J. appl. Physiol.*, **17**, 943 (1962); OTTO et al., *Klin. Wschr.*, **42**, 75 (1964).
[153] SCHAPIRA and SCHAPIRA, *Ann. Biol. clin.*, **18**, 1 (1960); CHUNG et al., *Amer. J. hum. Genet.*, **12**, 52 (1960); LEYBURN et al., *Ann. hum. Genet.*, **25**, 41 (1961).
[154] RACKER, E., *Biochim. biophys. Acta*, **4**, 20 (1950).
[155] DE RITIS et al., *Clin. chim. Acta (Amst.)*, **4**, 213 (1959).
[156] DE RITIS et al., *Boll. Soc. ital. Biol. sper.*, **32**, 642 (1956).
[157] RACKER, E., *Biochim. biophys. Acta (Amst.)*, **4**, 211 (1950).
[158] BEUTLER and YEH, *J. Lab. clin. Med.*, **54**, 456 (1959).

Enzymes: Normal values in **U/l plasma or serum** of adults unless otherwise stated (for definition of the unit U see page 584)

EC number Systematic name **Recommended trivial name** In brackets: abbreviation and non-recommended trivial name	Method	Number	Mean	95% range (extreme range in brackets)	s	Reference	Remarks (see also text on pages 584–588)
4.2.1.11 2-Phospho-D-glycerate hydro-lyase **Phosphopyruvate hydratase** (Enolase [ENO])	Optical[42], modified, 25 °C	15	3.1	(1–6.0)		5	Serum activity increased in liver disease, cardiac infarction and metastatic carcinoma[2, 30].
	Optical[42], 25 °C	30	10.5		3.3	30	
5.3.1.1 D-Glyceraldehyde-3-phosphate ketol-isomerase **Triosephosphate isomerase** (TIM)	Optical[42], 34 °C	21	142		58	159	Serum activity increased in viral hepatitis and progressive muscular dystrophy[159, 161], also in generalized neoplastic disease and especially liver metastases[160].
	Optical[42], 25 °C	30	42.8		15	30	
	Optical[42], modified, 25 °C	26	234	(100–400)	58	160	
5.3.1.6 D-Ribose-5-phosphate ketol-isomerase **Ribosephosphate isomerase** (Phosphoriboisomerase)	Colorimetric[162], 37 °C	11	58.4	(33.4–90.2)		162	Serum activity increased in liver disease, nephritis and lymphosarcoma[162].
5.3.1.9 D-Glucose-6-phosphate ketolisomerase **Glucosephosphate isomerase** (Phosphohexose isomerase [PHI], hexosephosphate isomerase)	Colorimetric[163], 37 °C		50.8		24.2	30	Serum activity higher in early childhood than in adults. Increased in cardiac infarction[165, 166], and acute hepatitis[166, 167], slightly so in chronic liver disease and obstructive jaundice[166, 167]. Also increased in leukaemia[168], megaloblastic anaemia[78], muscular dystrophy[151], severe thyrotoxicosis[169] and carcinoma[167, 169, 170].
	Colorimetric[164], 37 °C						
	Adults		46.5	(13.5–86.0)		16	
	Cord blood			(45–170)		16	
5.4.2.1 D-Phosphoglycerate 2,3-phosphomutase **Phosphoglycerate phosphomutase** (PGM)	Optical[171], modified, 25 °C	30		Not detectable		30	No definite changes in serum activity in heart or liver disease or in the presence of tumours[30].

[159] GIUSTI and PICCININO, *Acta hepato-splenol. (Stuttg.)*, **10**, 166 (1963).
[160] ROBERT et al., *Cancer*, **14**, 1166 (1961).
[161] GIUSTI, G., *Boll. Soc. ital. Biol. sper.*, **38**, 10 (1962).
[162] BRUNS, F. H., *Biochem. Z.*, **327**, 523 (1956).
[163] BRUNS and HINSBERG, *Biochem. Z.*, **325**, 532 (1954).
[164] HORROCKS et al., *J. clin. Path.*, **16**, 248 (1963).
[165] SIEGEL and BING, *Proc. Soc. exp. Biol. (N.Y.)*, **91**, 604 (1956).
[166] BING et al., *J. Amer. med. Ass.*, **164**, 647 (1957).
[167] BRUNS and JACOB, *Klin. Wschr.*, **32**, 1041 (1954).
[168] BLANCHAER et al., *Blood*, **13**, 245 (1958).
[169] WHITE, L. P., *J. nat. Cancer Inst.*, **21**, 671 (1958).
[170] SCHWARTZ et al., *Cancer*, **15**, 347 (1962).
[171] SUTHERLAND et al., *J. biol. Chem.*, **181**, 153 (1949).

Lipids (for references see page 602)

	Erythrocytes				Plasma or serum				Remarks
	Mean	95% range	s	Reference	Mean	95% range	s	Reference	
Total lipids (g/l)	5.10	4.08–6.12	0.51	1	–	3.5–8.5	–	2	See text opposite.
Fatty acids (g/l)*									
Total	2.0	–	–	1	–	1.0–5.0	–	2	See text opposite.
Non-esterified ('free')	0.08	–	–	3	–	0.10–0.35	–	2	
Cholesterol (g/l)									
Total	1.20	1.02–1.38	0.09	1	–	1.0–3.0	–	2	See text opposite.
Free	–	–	–	–	–	0.3–1.0	–	2	

* 1 mmol (mEq)/l ≈ 0.28 g/l, or 1 g/l ≈ 3.57 mmol (mEq)/l.

(For references see page 602)

	Erythrocytes				Plasma or serum				Remarks
	Mean	95% range	s	Reference	Mean	95% range (extreme range in brackets)	s	Reference	
Phosphatides (g/l)	2.98	2.58–3.38	0.20	1	–	1.5–3.5	–	2	See text below.
Triglycerides (g/l)	~0.2	–	–	4	–	0.5–2.2	–	2	See text below.
Bile acids (mg/l)									
Trihydroxycholanic acid (cholic acid)	...	...	...	...	1.4	(0–3.4)	–	5	The serum bile acid content is normally less than 10 mg/l[6] and is *increased* in diseases resulting in disturbance of bile secretion[7], with values up to 400 mg/l.
Dihydroxycholanic acids (chenodeoxycholic acid and deoxycholic acid)	...	...	...	...	0.8	(0–1.9)	–	5	

Total lipids

The blood lipids consist of free fatty acids, mono-, di- and triglycerides, phosphatides, sterols (cholesterol, bile acids, steroid hormones), carotenoids and fat-soluble vitamins.

Various methods have been proposed for determining the individual lipid fractions[8]. The total lipids are best determined gravimetrically after suitable extraction[9].

Of the erythrocyte lipids, 90% are contained in the cell membrane. In the leucocytes they account for 5–10% of the dry substance[10], in the thrombocytes about 15%[11]. The thrombocyte lipids have a similar composition to the erythrocyte lipids[12]. The serum lipids are mostly bound to proteins (α- and β-lipoproteins; see the tables on page 602). For further discussion of the serum lipids see the literature[13].

The lipid content of the serum depends on various factors, particularly age, sex, race, diet, hormonal balance, stress, climate, physical exercise and occupation. The serum lipid content is lower at birth and in childhood than in adult life, and rises steadily up to the age of about 60 years; it is increased in pregnancy[14]. Its relationship to body weight, constitution and blood pressure has been studied[15]. There is a positive correlation between the incidence of atherosclerosis and the lipid (or low-density lipoprotein, cholesterol and glyceride) content of the serum[16,17], though no causal connection has been conclusively demonstrated. The diet should therefore be so adjusted as to avoid an excessive rise in the serum lipid content.

Fatty acids

From about 3% up to about 10% of the serum fatty acids are nonesterified[18]; they consist in the main of components of glycerides, phosphatides and cholesteryl esters. Small amounts of free fatty acids are also present in the erythrocytes. Unlike the protein-bound lipids of the other fractions, the free fatty acids of serum are mostly bound loosely as anions to albumin.

The free-fatty acid content of the serum rises within a few hours of birth to a level three times as high as that in the cord blood[38]. It is rather higher in children before puberty than in adults[19]; in pregnancy it rises towards term and falls to normal by the second day post partum[20].

For the fatty acid content of the lipid fractions see the literature[21].

Cholesterol

In the serum about one-third of the cholesterol is in the free state, about two-thirds esterified; some 0.7% consists of dihydrocholesterol[22]. The cholesteryl sulphate content of the serum is less than 5 mg/l[23]. The ratio of the esterified to the total cholesterol (ester quotient) in the serum is extremely constant; in the thrombocytes and leucocytes it varies widely[24]. Various colorimetric methods have been developed for the assay of cholesterol, but none is very specific[25]; most used are those of Schoenheimer and Sperry[26], Abell[27] and Zak[28].

Like the total lipid content, the cholesterol content of the serum depends on various factors, with the diet and bodily activity playing a particularly important role. The serum cholesterol level is affected less by the cholesterol content of the diet – most of the serum cholesterol is of endogenous origin – than by the fat content and fatty acid composition of the diet. Foods whose fat contains a larger proportion of polyene fatty acids tend to lower the serum cholesterol level. To reduce the chances of developing atherosclerosis it is desirable to keep the serum cholesterol level below 2.0 g/l[17].

At birth the serum cholesterol content is low but starts to rise within hours or days[29]. There is an extensive literature on the relationship between serum cholesterol and age and sex[13,17,30–32]. Studies of persons in New York of European descent showed that in men the level rises from about 2.0 g/l at 20 years to 2.5 g/l at 50 years and falls again in old age; in women it rises from about 2.0 g/l at 20 years to 2.8 g/l at 55 years and likewise falls again in old age (median values)[30]. During pregnancy the serum level of both free and esterified cholesterol is high[14].

Phosphatides (phospholipids)

The phosphatides account for about 60% of the total lipids of the erythrocytes[7], about 50% of those of the leucocytes[10] and about 75% of those of the thrombocytes[11]. They are usually determined from the lipid phosphorus by the method of Zilversmit[33] or that of Fiske and Subbarow[34].

The serum phosphatide level is low at birth, high during pregnancy[14]. Its age- and sex-dependence has been studied in a large group of subjects aged 2–77 years[32]. In both men and women the concentration increases with advancing age.

Glycerides

The erythrocytes contain only small amounts of glycerides. Of those in the serum, 5–10% consist of mono- and diglycerides[35], the remainder of triglycerides.

The lack of precise methods of determination has led to wide discrepancies in the serum glyceride values to be found in the literature. The glyceride content, also known as 'neutral fat' or 'residual fat', is usually obtained as a difference[36]:

Neutral fat (mg/l) = mg total lipids per litre – (mg free cholesterol per litre + 1.68 mg cholesteryl esters per litre + [25 × mg lipid phosphorus per litre])

A more exact method is determination via the ester-bound fatty acids[36]:

Neutral fat (mg/l) = mg fatty acid esters per litre – ([0.764 × mg cholesteryl esters per litre] + [14.2 × mg lipid phosphorus per litre])

or via the bound glycerol[36]:

Neutral fat (mg/l) = 885 × (mmol total glycerol per litre – mmol free glycerol per litre)

The serum glyceride content rises during the first few months of life and then remains constant during childhood[37]. Studies of persons in New York of European descent showed that the serum glyceride level is higher in men than in women at all ages and that in men there is a marked rise in the 5th decade followed by a fall in the 6th decade[30].

References ('Lipids', pages 600–601)

1 FARQUHAR, J.W., *Biochim. biophys. Acta (Amst.)*, **60**, 80 (1962).
2 Usual values found in the literature.
3 WAYS and HANAHAN, *J. Lipid Res.*, **5**, 318 (1964).
4 WAYS and REED, *Scand. J. Haemat.*, suppl. *Ser. haemat.*, No. 10, 34 (1965).
5 CAREY, J.B., *J. clin. Invest.*, **37**, 1494 (1958).
6 MACINTYRE and WOOTTON, *Ann. Rev. Biochem.*, **29**, 635 (1960); OSBORN et al., *Lancet*, **2**, 1049 (1959).
7 VAN ITALLIE and HASHIM, *Med. Clin. N. Amer.*, **47**, 629 (1963).
8 SUNDERMAN and SUNDERMAN (Eds.), *Lipids and the Steroid Hormones in Clinical Medicine*, Lippincott, Philadelphia, 1960; ZÖLLNER and EBERHAGEN (Eds.), *Untersuchung und Bestimmung der Lipoide im Blut*, Springer, Berlin, 1965.
9 SPERRY et al., *Stand. Meth. clin. Chem.*, **4**, 173 (1963).
10 HINSBERG and BERENDT, in FLASCHENTRÄGER and LEHNARTZ (Eds.), *Physiologische Chemie*, vol. 2, part 1a, Springer, Berlin, 1954, page 461.
11 BARKHAN and SILVER, *Progr. Hemat.*, **3**, 170 (1962).
12 TROUP et al., in JOHNSON et al. (Eds.), *Blood Platelets*, Little, Brown, Boston, 1961, page 265.
13 LINDGREN and NICHOLS, in PUTNAM, F.W. (Ed.), *The Plasma Proteins*, vol. 2, Academic Press, New York, 1960, page 1; PEZOLD, F.A., *Lipide und Lipoproteide im Blutplasma*, Springer, Berlin, 1961.
14 BOYD, E.M., *J. clin. Invest.*, **13**, 347 (1934); OLIVER and BOYD, *Clin. Sci.*, **14**, 15 (1955).
15 HARTMANN et al., *Z. Kreisl.-Forsch.*, **52**, 425 (1963).
16 KUO, P.T., *Med. Clin. N. Amer.*, **44**, 1635 (1960).
17 STAMLER et al., *Med. Clin. N. Amer.*, **47**, 3 (1963).
18 EGGSTEIN, M., *Z. klin. Chem.*, **4**, 12 (1966).
19 LOEB et al., *Rev. franç. Etud. clin. biol.*, **5**, 916 (1960).
20 BURT, R.L., *Obstet. and Gynec.*, **15**, 460 (1960).
21 SCHRADE, W., *Med. u. Ernähr.*, **1**, 267 (1960); SCHRADE et al., *Klin. Wschr.*, **38**, 739 (1960); LINDGREN and NICHOLS, *Ann. N. Y. Acad. Sci.*, **94**, 55 (1961).
22 CHATTOPADHYAY and MOSBACH, *Analyt. Biochem.*, **10**, 435 (1965).
23 DRAYER and LIEBERMAN, *Biochem. biophys. Res. Commun.*, **18**, 126 (1965); MOSER et al., *Biochim. biophys. Acta (Amst.)*, **116**, 146 (1966).
24 HAWTHORNE et al., *J. Nutr.*, **81**, 241 (1963).
25 KRITCHEVSKY et al., *J. Lab. clin. Med.*, **63**, 511 (1964).
26 KASER et al., *Stand. Meth. clin. Chem.*, **1**, 43 (1953).
27 ABELL et al., *Stand. Meth. clin. Chem.*, **2**, 26 (1958).
28 LEFFLER et al., in SUNDERMAN and SUNDERMAN (Eds.), *Lipids and the Steroid Hormones in Clinical Medicine*, Lippincott, Philadelphia, 1960, page 18; ZAK et al., *Stand. Meth. clin. Chem.*, **5**, 79 (1965).
29 THALME, B., *Acta paediat. (Uppsala)*, **51**, 649 (1962).
30 SCHAEFER, L.E., *Amer. J. Med.*, **36**, 262 (1964).
31 KEYS et al., *J. clin. Invest.*, **29**, 1347 (1950); KEYS et al., *Clin. Chem.*, **1**, 34 (1955); LEWIS et al., *Circulation*, **16**, 227 (1957).
32 ADLERSBERG et al., *J. Amer. med. Ass.*, **162**, 619 (1956).
33 ZILVERSMIT et al., *Stand. Meth. clin. Chem.*, **2**, 132 (1958).
34 SUNDERMAN et al., in SUNDERMAN and SUNDERMAN (Eds.), *Lipids and the Steroid Hormones in Clinical Medicine*, Lippincott, Philadelphia, 1960, page 28.
35 CARLSON and WADSTRÖM, *Clin. chim. Acta*, **4**, 197 (1959).
36 EGGSTEIN, M., in ZÖLLNER and EBERHAGEN (Eds.), *Untersuchung und Bestimmung der Lipoide im Blut*, Springer, Berlin, 1965, page 289.
37 BROWN et al., in WOLLHEIM and SCHLEGEL (Eds.), *VIIth International Congress of Internal Medicine*, Munich 1962, vol. 1, Thieme, Stuttgart, 1963, page 176.
38 KEELE et al., *Pediatrics*, **37**, 597 (1966).

Serum lipoproteins and their composition[1]

Fraction		Content* (g/l serum)	Density	S_f**	$-S$**	Free electrophoresis (fraction)	COHN fraction (method 10)	Lipoprotein composition: Protein (%)	Lipids (%)	Lipid fraction as percentage of total lipids: Glycerides	Phosphatides	Cholesteryl esters	Free cholesterol	Nonesterified fatty acids
Chylomicrons		0–0.5	<0.96	10^4–10^5	–	–	I+II	1	99	88	8	3	1	–
β-*Lipoproteins, low-density*	LDF$_1$	1.5	0.96 –1.006	20–400	>70	α_2	I+II	7	93	56	20	15	8	1
	LDF$_2$	0.5	1.006–1.019	12–20	40–70	α_2	I+III	11	89	29	26	34	9	1
	LDF$_3$	3.5	1.019–1.063	0–12***	20–40	β	III	21	79	13	28	48	10	1
α-*Lipoproteins, high-density*	HDL$_2$	0.5	1.063–1.125	–	4–20	α_1	IV+V	33	67	16	43	31	10	–
	HDL$_3$	3.0	1.125–1.210	–	0–4	α_1	IV+V	57	43	13	46	29	6	6
Nonesterified fatty acids-albumin		40.0	–	–	–	–	V	99	1	0	0	0	0	100

1 OLSON and VESTER, *Physiol. Rev.*, **40**, 677 (1960).
* Average post-absorptive values for a healthy, well-nourished man aged 40 years.
** S_f = SVEDBERG flotation units ($-S \times 10^{-13}$ s) at a density of 1.063 and t = 26 °C; $-S$ = SVEDBERG flotation units at a density of 1.21 and t = 26 °C.
*** Fractions 0–2 are high-density lipoproteins (HDL$_1$).

Serum lipoprotein concentrations at various ages (g/l)[1]

Age	Number	S_f 100–400 Mean	s	S_f 20–100 Mean	s	S_f 12–20 Mean	s	S_f 0–12 Mean	s	HDL$_1$ Mean	s	HDL$_2$ Mean	s	HDL$_3$ Mean	s
							Men								
17–29	585	0.37	0.43	0.75	0.41	0.40	0.21	3.22	0.86	0.23	0.07	0.37	0.28	2.17	0.40
30–39	834	0.51	0.64	0.91	0.54	0.51	0.23	3.55	0.84	0.24	0.15	0.36	0.28	2.19	0.42
40–49	399	0.66	0.91	1.07	0.66	0.57	0.23	3.80	0.84	0.25	0.15	0.37	0.28	2.26	0.50
50–65	143	0.58	0.70	1.03	0.58	0.56	0.24	3.83	0.75	0.27	0.22	0.42	0.32	2.24	0.51
							Women								
17–29	190	0.09	0.14	0.44	0.29	0.30	0.16	2.83	0.68	0.21	0.07	0.80	0.41	2.28	0.38
30–39	99	0.13	0.17	0.51	0.36	0.41	0.22	3.24	0.86	0.22	0.09	0.81	0.45	2.35	0.38
40–49	37	0.18	0.24	0.65	0.51	0.42	0.21	3.46	0.67	0.23	0.05	0.89	0.53	2.41	0.43
50–65	10	0.32	0.37	0.77	0.48	0.93	0.36	4.37	0.40	0.25	0.07	1.17	0.66	2.70	0.54

1 LINDGREN and NICHOLS, in PUTNAM, F.W. (Ed.), *The Plasma Proteins*, vol. 2, Academic Press, New York, 1960, page 1 (values determined in healthy employees of the University of California Radiation Laboratory, Livermore, Calif.).

Serum lipid concentrations at various ages

	Number	Total lipids (g/l)			Total cholesterol (g/l)			Free cholesterol (g/l)			Phosphatides (g/l)			Glycerides (g/l)			Nonesterified fatty acids (mmol/l)		Reference
		Mean	Extreme range	s	Mean	95% range (extreme range in brackets)	s	Mean	Extreme range	s	Mean	Extreme range	s	Mean	95% range	s	Mean	s	
Mothers	36	9.03	–	–	2.60	–	–	0.66	–	–	2.76	–	–	2.28	–	–	–	–	1
Cord blood	21	2.91	–	–	0.75	–	–	0.15	–	–	0.99	–	–	0.69	–	–	–	–	1
Children, 6–8 weeks																			
Milk and meat diet	10	5.74	–	–	1.36	–	–	0.30	–	–	1.77	–	–	1.83	–	–	–	–	1
Vegetable diet	10	3.83	–	–	0.89	–	–	0.17	–	–	1.32	–	–	1.10	–	–	–	–	1
Cord blood	15	3.13	(1.70–4.40)	–	0.74	(0.48–0.98)	–	0.26	(0.19–0.38)	–	1.24	(0.76–1.70)	–	–	–	–	–	–	2
Children, 3–10 days (breast-fed)	15	6.08	(4.30–7.60)	–	1.34	(1.10–1.67)	–	0.49	(0.37–0.59)	–	2.07	(1.60–2.60)	–	–	–	–	–	–	2
Children, 1–12 months	37	6.06	(2.40–8.00)	–	1.30	(0.69–1.73)	–	0.40	(0.27–0.66)	–	1.88	(1.22–2.76)	–	–	–	–	–	–	2
Children, 2–14 years	25	8.38	(4.90–10.90)	–	1.88	(1.38–2.42)	–	0.54	(0.39–0.69)	–	2.35	(1.88–2.92)	–	–	–	–	–	–	2
Children, 10–13 years	635	–	–	–	1.54	1.07–2.06	–	–	–	–	–	–	–	0.75	0.33–1.74	–	–	–	3
Men, 16–35 years	62	6.10	–	1.20	1.92	–	0.57	0.64	–	0.19	2.08	–	0.35	0.84	–	0.34	0.750	0.233	4
Women, 16–35 years	29	6.48	–	1.14	1.85	–	0.38	0.58	–	0.18	2.32	–	0.44	0.88	–	–	0.781	0.174	4
Adults, 20–35 years	62	–	–	–	1.78	–	0.26	0.46	–	–	1.78	–	0.23	1.23	–	0.49	0.405	0.081	5
Adults, 45–70 years	30	–	–	–	2.09	–	0.29	0.61	–	–	2.50	–	0.28	–	–	–	–	–	5

	Total lipids* (g/l)						Total cholesterol* (g/l)						Phosphatides* (g/l)						Glycerides* (g/l)						Reference
	Number	2.5%	5%	50%	95%	97.5%	Number	2.5%	5%	50%	95%	97.5%	Number	2.5%	5%	50%	95%	97.5%	Number	2.5%	5%	50%	95%	97.5%	
Men, 15–24 years	150	3.95	4.15	5.82	8.29	8.63	148	1.21	1.42	1.87	2.59	2.78	150	1.45	1.51	1.93	2.57	2.74	142	0.07	0.10	0.98	2.49	2.83	6
Men, 25–34 years	383	4.58	4.81	6.50	9.35	9.95	379	1.47	1.62	2.11	2.94	3.12	383	1.58	1.66	2.15	2.76	2.98	371	0.11	0.22	1.17	2.98	3.77	6
Men, 35–44 years	497	4.93	5.18	7.12	10.91	11.89	494	1.60	1.76	2.37	3.31	3.54	495	1.70	1.82	2.32	3.00	3.18	488	0.20	0.28	1.27	3.43	4.78	6
Men, 45–54 years	499	5.16	5.33	7.44	10.26	11.24	497	1.61	1.77	2.45	3.34	3.49	499	1.77	1.86	2.39	3.09	3.21	491	0.16	0.24	1.32	3.08	3.54	6
Men, 55–64 years	301	5.33	5.55	7.69	10.50	11.73	301	1.75	1.83	2.54	3.28	3.55	303	1.80	1.94	2.43	3.06	3.30	292	0.23	0.31	1.36	3.59	4.07	6

* Sample percentiles.

1 Sweeney et al., *Pediatrics*, **27**, 765 (1961) (inmates of a Tennessee orphans' home).

2 Rafstedt and Swahn, *Acta paediat. (Uppsala)*, **43**, 221 (1954); Rafstedt, S., *Acta paediat. (Uppsala)*, **44**, suppl. 102 (1955) (healthy children in Lund, Sweden).

3 Baker et al., *Amer. J. clin. Nutr.*, **20**, 850 (1967) (schoolchildren in New York City).

4 Svanborg et al., *Acta med. scand.*, **169**, 43 (1961) (healthy adults in Göteborg, Sweden).

5 Eggstein, M., *Klin. Wschr.*, **43**, 1031 (1965); **44**, 267 (1966); nonesterified fatty acids from Eggstein et al., *Klin. Wschr.*, **45**, 943 (1967).

6 Hartmann, G., personal communication, 1967 (able-bodied men in Basle, Switzerland).

Fatty acid composition of the serum lipid fractions of adults[1]

	Non-esterified fatty acids	Cholesteryl esters	Phosphatides	Triglycerides
Lipid fraction (g/l serum)	0.29	2.24	2.09	1.73
Fatty acids of lipid fraction (g/l serum)	0.29	0.72	1.11	1.44
Fatty acids (% of total)				
Myristic acid	2.0	1.1	0.9	1.6
Palmitic acid	27.9	12.1	30.7	28.1
Palmitoleic acid	7.2	6.8	3.3	7.6
Stearic acid	14.9	2.6	11.9	3.7
Oleic acid	25.5	18.9	15.1	36.8
Linoleic acid	13.1	47.1	21.5	12.2
Triene acids (C_{18} and C_{20})	0.9	0.9	0.8	0.9
Arachidonic acid	2.4	5.0	8.8	3.1
Pentaene acids (C_{20} and C_{22})	1.2	1.4	2.0	1.2
Hexaene acids (C_{22}) ...	1.8	1.9	3.1	1.9
Other	3.1	2.2	2.1	2.9

[1] Schrade, W., *Med. u. Ernähr.*, **1**, 267 (1960); Schrade et al., *Klin. Wschr.*, **38**, 739 (1960) (mean values from 16 healthy subjects aged 18–41 years).
For the fatty acid composition of the lipid fractions in the newborn see Zöllner et al., *Klin. Wschr.*, **44**, 380 (1966), in the newborn and infants in relation to diet see Pikaar and Fernandes, *Amer. J. clin. Nutr.*, **19**, 194 (1966).

Phosphatides in the plasma and erythrocytes[1]

	Plasma (15 adults*)		Erythrocytes (13 adults)	
	Mean	*s*	Mean	*s*
Lipid phosphorus (mg/l)	99.8	15.2	139.5	11.2
Phosphatides (% of lipid phosphorus)				
Cephalin**	5.0	0.6	42.4	1.0
Lecithin	68.2	1.7	32.7	2.0
Sphingomyelin	19.0	1.9	23.1	1.9
Lysolecithin	7.7	1.5	1.8	0.2

* Fasting values. In the cord plasma the proportion of lecithin is lower, that of the other fractions higher[2].
** In the serum[3] about one-third of the cephalin fraction consists of plasmalogens, in the erythrocytes[4] about one-half.
[1] Phillips, G. B., *J. Lab. clin. Med.*, **59**, 357 (1962).
[2] Zöllner et al., *Klin. Wschr.*, **44**, 380 (1966).
[3] Phillips, G. B., *Biochim. biophys. Acta (Amst.)*, **29**, 594 (1958).
[4] Farquhar, J. W., *Biochim. biophys. Acta*, **60**, 80 (1962).

Suggested nomenclature of changes in the serum lipid content[1]

	Designation for an increase in the serum concentration
Cholesterol	Hypercholesterolaemia
Lipid phosphorus	Hyperphosphatidaemia
Neutral fat	Hyperlipaemia
Free fatty acids	Hyperlipacidaemia
Total lipids	Hyperlipidaemia
Clouding by neutral fat	Lipaemia

[1] Klenk et al., *Clin. chim. Acta*, **7**, 446 (1962).

Carbohydrates (for references see page 606)

Glucose, fasting values (mg/l)

	Determined in	Method	Number	Mean	95% range	*s*	Reference
Pregnancy	Capillary blood	Hagedorn-Jensen	19	931	878–984	26.7	1
		Glucose oxidase	19	867	788–946	39.5	1
Newborn	Cord blood	Hagedorn-Jensen	20	856	790–922	33.2	1
		Glucose oxidase	20	671	588–754	41.5	1
1st hour	Capillary blood	Hagedorn-Jensen	20	558	489–627	34.4	1
		Glucose oxidase	20	263	190–336	36.5	1
6th day	Capillary blood	Hagedorn-Jensen	16	708	653–763	27.5	1
		Glucose oxidase	16	447	381–513	32.8	1
Newborn	Cord blood	Somogyi-Nelson	14	730	392–1068	169	2
1 hour	Capillary blood	Somogyi-Nelson	14	626	224–1028	201	2
2 hours	Capillary blood	Somogyi-Nelson	14	589	209–969	190	2
9 hours	Capillary blood	Somogyi-Nelson	14	590	310–870	140	2
24 hours	Capillary blood	Somogyi-Nelson	14	579	301–857	139	2
48 hours	Capillary blood	Somogyi-Nelson	14	591	321–861	135	2
Newborn 1–78 hours ...	Blood	Hagedorn-Jensen	63	841	–	–	3
		Somogyi-Nelson	63	598	–	–	3
Children 1–17 months .	Blood	Hagedorn-Jensen	10	948	–	–	3
		Somogyi-Nelson	10	796	–	–	3

Remarks:

Methods. Reduction methods of determining 'blood sugar' – for instance Hagedorn-Jensen, Hoffman, Folin-Wu, Somogyi-Nelson – determine other hexoses (fructose, mannose, galactose), pentoses, glucuronic acid, glutathione, uric acid, creatine and creatinine, ascorbic acid and various drugs in addition to glucose. Aldohexoses can be determined colorimetrically with *o*-toluidine[7,10] or triphenyltetrazolium chloride[11]. Most specific are the enzymatic methods using either glucose oxidase with peroxidase[8,12,13] or hexokinase with glucose-6-phosphate dehydrogenase[13].
Physiological and pathological variations. After 12 hours fasting the glucose level in the capillary blood approximates to that in the venous blood; after glucose intake it is higher in the capillary and arterial than in the venous blood. In leucocytosis there may be a false appearance of hypoglycaemia owing to glycolysis in the leucocytes[14]. The concentration of glucose is the same in the serum water and erythrocyte

Glucose, fasting values (mg/l) *(continued)*

	Determined in	Method	Number	Mean	95% range	*s*	Reference	Remarks (continued)
Children 2–14 years ...	Blood	HAGEDORN-JENSEN	15	933	–	–	3	water. The blood glucose level falls during the first hours of life and then rises slowly over the next few days[1,2,15]; this hypoglycaemia of the newborn is particularly marked in premature infants[16,17], in poorly nourished children[18] and in children of diabetic mothers[16]. The blood glucose level is pathologically *increased* in diabetes and adrenocortical (CUSHING's syndrome) or pituitary disorders (acromegaly), after administration of ACTH, by an increase in the amount of circulating adrenaline, and in WERNICKE's encephalopathy; it is *decreased* in insulin excess, the dumping syndrome, impairment of adrenocortical (ADDISON's disease) or pituitary function, lesions of the hypothalamus and some liver diseases.
		SOMOGYI-NELSON	15	843	–	–	3	
Adults	Blood	HAGEDORN-JENSEN	21	1072	–	–	3	
		SOMOGYI-NELSON	21	1000	–	–	3	
Children 8–14 years ...	Venous blood	Glucose oxidase	12	800	600–1000	–	4	
Adults	Venous plasma	SOMOGYI-NELSON	33	995	819–1171	88	5	
		Glucose oxidase	33	909	751–1067	79	5	
Adults	Venous blood	Glucose oxidase	38	800	668–932	66	6	
Adults	Blood	*o*-Toluidine	21	–	630–870	–	7	
Adults	Blood	Glucose oxidase	94	810	630–990	90	8	
Birth–29 years ..	Capillary blood	HOFFMAN	41	859	683–1035	88	9	
30–49 years	Capillary blood	HOFFMAN	103	878	650–1106	114	9	
50–69 years	Capillary blood	HOFFMAN	155	897	623–1171	137	9	
70 years and over	Capillary blood	HOFFMAN	46	991	665–1317	163	9	
17–45 years	Capillary blood	Hexokinase	199	828	700–950	65.6	13	

	Whole blood				Plasma or serum				Remarks
	Mean	95% range (extreme range in brackets)	*s*	Reference	Mean	95% range	*s*	Reference	
Pentoses (mg/l)	...	...	...	...	6.6	0.2–13.0	3.2	19	Values from 28 subjects, determined with orcinol.
L-Xylulose	...	...	...	...	1.4	0–5.0	1.8	20	Values from 36 subjects. Increased in diabetes.
Galactose (mg/l)..........	15.9	3.4–28.4	6.25	48					Values from 100 subjects, determined enzymatically.
Mesoinositol (mg/l)	...	...	...	...	10.9	6.7–15.1	2.1	21	Values from 18 subjects, determined enzymatically.
Sugar phosphates (µmol/l)		Erythrocytes:							
Diphosphoglyceric acid	4420	600–8240	1910	22					
Phosphoenolpyruvic acid ..	8.8	3.6–14.0	2.6	22					
2-Phosphoglyceric acid	4.3	0.7–7.9	1.8	22					
3-Phosphoglyceric acid	61.2	36.4–86.0	12.4	22					
Glyceraldehyde 3-phosphate	2.6	1.2–4.0	0.7	22					
Dihydroxyacetone phosphate	4.9	0–11.9	3.5	22					
Glucose 6-phosphate	24.8	5.2–44.4	9.8	22					
Fructose 6-phosphate......	5.4	3.4–7.4	1.0	22					
Fructose 1,6-diphosphate ..	4.6	2.6–6.6	1.0	22					
Pentose 5-phosphate	18	0–36	9	23					
Nucleotide pentose........	3800	2630–4980	590	23					
Sedoheptulose 1,7-diphosphate	9	–	–	24					
Octulose 1,8-diphosphate ..	3	–	–	24					
Galactose 1-phosphate (mg/l)	...	...	...	...	...	...	...	...	Increased in galactosaemia.
Cord blood	17	1–33	8	25					
Children, adults	0	0–6	3	25					
Glucuronic acid, total (mg/l)									
(a) Children.............	...	...	...	...	65	–	–	26	Values from (b) 56, (c) 44 subjects determined with (a) carbazole, (b, c, d) naphthoresorcinol. Component of glycoproteins (see page 606); in serum occurs mainly bound to glycosides, but part is free[29]. The serum glucuronic acid level is decreased in the nephrotic syndrome[30].
(b) Men	...	...	...	...	32	19.6–44.4	6.2	27	
(c) Women	...	...	...	...	32	23–41	4.5	27	
(d).....................	–	Erythrocytes: (0–20)	–	28					

	Whole blood				Plasma or serum				Remarks
	Mean	95% range (extreme range in brackets)	s	Reference	Mean	95% range (extreme range in brackets)	s	Reference	
Glycogen (mg/l)	55	(12–162)	–	31	0	–	–	31	In glycogen storage disease the glycogen content of the erythrocytes may be increased[32, 34].
(μg/g haemoglobin)		Erythrocytes:							
Newborn, 1st day	155	(48–361)	–	32					
Children, 1–12 months	86	(32–151)	–	32					
Adults	56	(26–105)	–	32					
		Granulocytes:							
(mg/10^9 cells)	7.5	(4.7–11.9)	–	33					
Heparin (mg/l)	...	...	...	...	–	(1.0–2.4)	–	35	
Protein-bound carbohydrates (glycoproteins) (mg/l)									
Total	...	...	...	...	2739	–	–	36	Various proteins in the serum, erythrocytes, leucocytes and thrombocytes contain carbohydrates[38, 39]. For the carbohydrate content of the serum glycoproteins see page 581. The hexoses of the serum glycoproteins are galactose and mannose, the hexosamines galactosamine and glucosamine (in the ratio 1:6[40]).
Hexoses	...	...	...	...	1210	1170–1250	21	36	
Hexosamines	...	...	...	...	830	750–910	40	36	
Sialic acid	...	...	...	...	600	526–674	37	36	
Fucose	...	...	...	...	89	77–101	6	36	
Uronic acids	...	...	...	...	2.3	0.8–3.8	0.75	37	

The serum level of protein-bound carbohydrates is the same in men and women[41] (there is an increase towards term in pregnancy[42]); that of sialic acid[41, 43] and hexoses[42, 44] increases with age. The serum sialic acid level in the newborn is lower than in the mother[45, 46] and attains the adult level within 4 months[46]. The serum glycoprotein level is *increased* in diseases accompanied by tissue breakdown, in the collagen diseases, and in inflammatory and degenerative disorders. For further discussion of the pathological changes in the glycoproteins see the literature[38, 42, 47].

References

1 Wolf, H., *Klin. Wschr.*, **38**, 87 (1960).
2 Acharya and Payne, *Arch. Dis. Childh.*, **40**, 430 (1965).
3 Hallman, N., *Mod. Probl. Pädiat.*, **4**, 535 (1959).
4 Öckerman, P. A., *Clin. chim. Acta*, **12**, 370 (1965).
5 Saifer and Gerstenfeld, *J. Lab. clin Med.*, **51**, 448 (1958).
6 Sunderman and Sunderman, *Amer. J. clin. Path.*, **36**, 75 (1961).
7 Hyvärinen and Nikkilä, *Clin. chim. Acta*, **7**, 140 (1962).
8 Fales and Seligson, *Stand. Meth. clin. Chem.*, **4**, 101 (1963).
9 Diabetes Survey Working Party, *Brit. med. J.*, **2**, 655 (1963).
10 Zender, R., *Clin. chim. Acta*, **8**, 351 (1963).
11 Lorentz, K., *Clin. chim. Acta*, **13**, 660 (1966).
12 Richterich and Colombo, *Klin. Wschr.*, **40**, 1208 (1962); Free, A. H., *Advanc. clin. Chem.*, **6**, 67 (1963); Meites et al., *Stand. Meth. clin. Chem.*, **5**, 113 (1965).
13 Schmidt, F. H., *Internist (Berl.)*, **4**, 554 (1963); personal communication, 1967.
14 Hanrahan et al., *Amer. J. clin. Path.*, **40**, 43 (1963).
15 Creery and Parkinson, *Arch. Dis. Childh.*, **28**, 134 (1953); Farquhar, J. W., *Arch. Dis. Childh.*, **29**, 519 (1954).
16 Zetterström, R., in Wolstenholme and O'Connor (Eds.), *Ciba Foundation Symposium on Somatic Stability in the Newly Born*, Churchill, London, 1961, page 59.
17 Baens et al., *Pediatrics*, **31**, 580 (1963).
18 Neligan et al., *Lancet*, **1**, 1282 (1963).
19 McKay, E., *Clin. chim. Acta*, **10**, 320 (1964).
20 Winegrad et al., *Diabetes*, **14**, 311 (1965).
21 Garcia-Buñuel and Garcia-Buñuel, *J. Lab. clin. Med.*, **64**, 461 (1964).
22 Oski et al., *Pediatrics*, **44**, 84 (1969).
23 Fornaini et al., *J. clin. Invest.*, **41**, 1446 (1962).
24 Vanderheiden, B. S., *Biochem. biophys. Res. Commun.*, **21**, 265 (1965).
25 Woolf, L. I., *Advanc. clin. Chem.*, **5**, 1 (1962).
26 Vest, M., *Bibl. paediat. (Basel)*, No. 69 (1959).
27 Müting et al., *Z. klin. Med.*, **157**, 538 (1963).
28 Deichmann and Dierker, *J. biol. Chem.*, **163**, 753 (1946).
29 Green et al., *Biochim. biophys. Acta (Amst.)*, **62**, 574 (1962).
30 Müting et al., *Z. klin. Med.*, **157**, 544 (1963).
31 Wagner, R., *Arch. Biochem.*, **11**, 249 (1946).
32 Sidbury et al., *Helv. paediat. Acta*, **16**, 506 (1961).
33 Valentine et al., *J. clin. Invest.*, **32**, 251 (1953).
34 Hers, H. G., *Advanc. metab. Disord.*, **1**, 1 (1964).
35 Engelberg, H., *Circulation*, **23**, 578 (1961).
36 Winzler, R. J., in Putnam, F. W. (Ed.), *The Plasma Proteins*, vol. 1, Academic Press, New York, 1960, page 309.
37 Kerby, G. P., *J. clin. Invest.*, **37**, 962 (1958).
38 Stary, Z., *Ergebn. Physiol.*, **50**, 174 (1959).
39 Magalini and Mascioli, *J. Lab. clin. Med.*, **62**, 961 (1963).
40 Hirayama et al., *Lancet*, **1**, 532 (1961).
41 Böttiger and Holmström, *J. Lab. clin. Med.*, **63**, 772 (1964).
42 Shetlar, M. R., *Ann. N. Y. Acad. Sci.*, **94**, 44 (1961).
43 Böttiger and Carlson, *Clin. chim. Acta*, **5**, 664 (1960).
44 Pearce et al., *Clin. Chem.*, **10**, 1066 (1964).
45 Löhr and Pullig, *Klin. Wschr.*, **37**, 633 (1959).
46 Cabezas et al., *Clin. chim. Acta*, **7**, 406 and 448 (1962).
47 Heiskell et al., *Ann. N. Y. Acad. Sci.*, **94**, 183 (1961).
48 Rommel et al., *Klin. Wschr.*, **46**, 1042 (1968).

Non-nitrogenous metabolites (for references see page 608)

	Whole blood				Plasma or serum				Remarks
	Mean	95% range (extreme range in brackets)	s	Reference	Mean	95% range	s	Reference	
Ethyl alcohol (mg/l)	–	(< 1.5)	–	34	...	...	...	...	For colorimetric determination see Sunshine et al.[35].
Acetaldehyde (mg/l)	2.3	(0.5–4.0)	–	36	...	...	...	...	*Increased* in alcoholic poisoning. Can be detected in the breath when the blood concentration exceeds 5 mg/l.
Acetoin (mg/l)	0.10	–	–	37					

	Whole blood				Plasma or serum				Remarks
	Mean	95% range (extreme range in brackets)	*s*	Reference	Mean	95% range (extreme range in brackets)	*s*	Reference	
2,3-Butylene glycol (mg/l)	1.17	–	–	37					
Glycerol (mg/l)									
(a) Children, 8–14 years	...	...	...	...	5.5	0.9–10	–	38	Values from (a) 12, (b) 15, (c) 57 subjects for the free glycerol. Glycerol is mainly present as a component of the glycerides (see under 'Lipids', page 601).
(b) Adults	...	...	...	...	7.5	2.9–12.1	2.3	39	
(c) Adults	...	...	...	...	11	0–23	6	40	
Volatile acids (mg/l)	17	–	–	1	...	...	...	...	About 25% consists of formic acid, 75% of acetic acid and 0–5% of propionic acid.
Fatty acids	...	...	...	...	...	...	...	...	See under 'Lipids', page 601.
Malic acid (mg/l)	4.6	(2.4–7.5)	–	2	0.43	0.19–0.67	0.12	3	Serum values from 14 subjects determined enzymatically. Increased in renal insufficiency.
Succinic acid (mg/l)	...	...	...	...	5	–	–	4	
Citric acid (mg/l)									
Umbilical vein	16.9	4.3–29.5	6.3	5	...	...	...	...	Values (a) from 29 fasting subjects. Increases by 4–9 mg/l after a meal.
Umbilical artery	13.0	8.2–17.8	2.4	5					
Adults	–	(13.0–16.7)	–	6	–	(19.2–26.0)	–	6	
(a) Adults	...	...	...	...	26	(17–31)	–	7	

In adults the citrate level of whole blood falls with increasing age and is independent of sex[7, 8]. In the serum the citrate is present mainly as a complex with calcium and magnesium, and only about 20% is free[9]. An increase in the serum citrate level results in a decrease in ionized calcium (citrate poisoning). The blood citrate is *increased* after physical effort, often in primary hyperparathyroidism, and occasionally in cardiac infarction and liver damage; it is *decreased* occasionally in diabetes, in the presence of visceral neoplasms and in acute renal insufficiency. For a review see Nordmann and Nordmann[10].

	Mean	95% range	*s*	Ref.	Mean	95% range	*s*	Ref.	Remarks
Lactic acid (mg/l)									
(a) Umbilical vein	196	60–332	68	11	...	...	...	...	Values from (a) 14, (b) 69 subjects. Values (b) in arterial blood of fasting subjects completely at rest, (c) in venous blood under the usual conditions. For colorimetric assay see Barker et al.[14], for enzymatic methods see Olson[15] and Bergmeyer[16].
(a) Newborn, 1 hour	160	40–280	60	11					
(a) Newborn, 1 day	144	28–260	58	11					
(a) Newborn, 2 days	135	41–229	47	11					
(b) Adults	56	42.2–69.8	6.9	12					
(c) Adults	90	68.4–112	10.8	12					
		Erythrocytes:							
	76	32–120	22	13					

The blood lactate level is *increased* by muscular activity and emotional excitement, in the newborn (especially in the arterial cord blood)[5, 11, 17], and towards term in pregnancy[18], often *decreased* in renal insufficiency[3]. A syndrome associated with a high blood lactate level (lactacidosis) has been described[19].

	Mean	95% range	*s*	Ref.	Mean	95% range	*s*	Ref.	Remarks
Oxalic acid (mg/l)	–	(2.0–3.2)	–	20	–	(1.4–2.8)	–	20	Values from 15 adults on a normal diet.
Glyoxylic acid	...	...	...	...	0	–	–	20	
Pyruvic acid (mg/l)									
Umbilical vein	7.1	1.1–13.1	3.0	5	...	...	...	...	Values from (a) 120, (b) 21 subjects; values (b) determined enzymatically in venous blood of fasting subjects at complete rest. Pyruvic and other keto acids are unstable and should therefore be determined in whole blood rather than in serum.
(a) Children, 2–13 years	6.73	4.93–8.53	0.90	21					
(b) Adults	5.6	1.2–10.0	2.2	22	6.4	2.6–10.2	1.9	22	
		Erythrocytes:							
	8.2	2.6–13.8	2.8	13					

The blood pyruvate level is high in the newborn and falls during the first days of life[17, 23]. It is increased by glucose intake, muscular effort and emotional excitement. Pathological increases are seen in vitamin B_1 deficiency, respiratory alkalosis, severe cardiovascular disturbances, arsenic and mercury poisoning and liver disease. For a review see Nordmann and Nordmann[10].

	Mean	95% range	*s*	Ref.	Mean	95% range	*s*	Ref.	Remarks
α-Ketoglutaric acid (mg/l)									
Cord blood	2	–	–	5	...	...	...	...	Values from (a) 120, (b) 40 subjects. The physiological and pathological changes in the blood α-ketoglutarate level are much the same as those in the pyruvate level.
(a) Children, 2–13 years	1.36	0.70–2.02	0.33	21					
(b) Children, adults	1.3	0.5–2.1	0.4	24					
α-Ketoisovaleric acid (mg/l)	1.3	0.9–1.7	0.2	24	...	...	...	...	Values from 40 children and adults.

	Whole blood				Plasma or serum				Remarks
	Mean	95% range (extreme range in brackets)	*s*	Reference	Mean	95% range (extreme range in brackets)	*s*	Reference	
α-Ketoisocaproic acid and **α-keto-β-methylvaleric acid** (mg/l)	3.8	1.8–5.8	1.0	24	...	...	...	...	Values from 40 children and adults.
Oxaloacetic acid (mg/l)	1.2	–	–	25					
Ketone bodies (μmol/l)									
(a) Newborn, < 4 hours	90	(40–180)	–	26	...	...	...	...	Values (a) in capillary blood, fasting, (b) from 94, (c) from 19 subjects; calculation from values (b) gives 8.3 mg acetone or 14.9 mg β-hydroxybutyric acid per litre. Few methods of determining ketone bodies are satisfactory[28]. Acetoacetic and β-hydroxybutyric acids can be determined by specific enzymatic methods (see values below).
(a) Newborn, 2–6 days	670	(90–1900)	–	26					
(a) Children, 1 week–1 year	250	(30–890)	–	26					
(a) Children, 1–2 years	540	(40–2300)	–	26					
(a) Children, 2–6 years	290	(30–1100)	–	26					
(a) Children, 6–15 years	130	(10–540)	–	26					
(b) Adults, fasting	143	5–281	69	27					
(c) Adults, non-fasting	107	0–247	70	27					

25–35% of the blood ketone bodies consist of acetoacetic acid and acetone, 65–75% of β-hydroxybutyric acid[29, 30]. The level is increased by long fasting. For the biochemical basis of ketone-body formation see the literature[31].

The ketone bodies of blood are pathologically *increased* in untreated diabetes, glycogen storage disease, alkalosis, CUSHING's syndrome and under the action of growth hormone.

Acetone (mg/l)									
(a) Children, 1–3 years	...	...	...	...	12	(0–37)	–	28	Values from (a) 50, (b) 47, (c) 11 subjects.
(b) Children, 10–15 years	...	...	...	...	9	(0–34)	–	28	
(c) Adults	...	...	...	...	2.9	2.3–3.5	0.3	32	
Acetoacetic acid (mg/l)*									
(a) Children, 1–3 years	...	...	...	...	6	(0–32)	–	28	Values from (a) 45, (b) 43, (c) 5, (d) 16, (e) 7 subjects; values (d, e) determined enzymatically.
(b) Children, 10–15 years	...	...	...	...	3	(0–28)	–	28	
(c) Adults	–	(0.55–2.6)	–	33	–	(0.80–2.8)	–	33	
(d) Adults, non-fasting	1.7	(0.5–4.6)	–	30					
(e) Adults, fasting	3.2	(1.8–7.8)	–	30					
β-Hydroxybutyric acid (mg/l)**									
(a) Children, 1–3 years	...	...	...	...	13	(0–35)	–	28	Values from (a) 11, (b) 17, (c) 16, (d) 7 subjects; values (c, d) determined enzymatically.
(b) Children, 10–15 years	...	...	...	...	9	(0–25)	–	28	
(c) Adults, non-fasting	3.7	(1.4–9.9)	–	30					
(d) Adults, fasting	9.4	(5.8–17.1)	–	30					
Lipoic acid (μg/l)	...	...	...	...	15.8	8.8–22.8	3.5	41	Values from 10 subjects.

* 1 mg/l = 9.8 μmol/l. ** 1 mg/l = 9.6 μmol/l.

References

1 ANNISON, E. F., *Biochem. J.*, **58**, 670 (1954).
2 HUMMEL, J. P., *J. biol. Chem.*, **180**, 1225 (1949).
3 NORDMANN et al., *Clin. chim. Acta*, **12**, 304 (1965).
4 KREBS, H. A., *Ann. Rev. Biochem.*, **19**, 417 (1950).
5 RÄIHÄ, N. C. R., *Pediatrics*, **32**, 1025 (1963).
6 NATELSON et al., *J. biol. Chem.*, **170**, 597 (1947).
7 HODGKINSON, A., *Clin. Sci.*, **24**, 167 (1963).
8 RECHENBERGER and BENNDORF, *Z. klin. Med.*, **154**, 648 (1957).
9 WALSER, M., *J. clin. Invest.*, **40**, 723 (1961).
10 NORDMANN and NORDMANN, *Advanc. clin. Chem.*, **4**, 53 (1961).
11 ACHARYA and PAYNE, *Arch. Dis. Childh.*, **40**, 430 (1965).
12 HUCKABEE, W. E., *J. clin. Invest.*, **37**, 244 (1958); *Amer. J. Med.*, **30**, 833 (1961).
13 FORNAINI et al., *J. clin. Invest.*, **41**, 1446 (1962).
14 BARKER et al., *Stand. Meth. clin. Chem.*, **3**, 167 (1961).
15 OLSON, G. F., *Clin. Chem.*, **8**, 1 (1962).
16 BERGMEYER, H.-U. (Ed.), *Methods of Enzymatic Analysis*, Academic Press, New York, 1963.
17 STAVE and FRIOLET, *Klin. Wschr.*, **38**, 1198 (1960).
18 BURT et al., *Obstet. and Gynec.*, **17**, 80 (1961).
19 HUCKABEE, W. E., *Amer. J. Med.*, **30**, 840 (1961); DÉROT et al., *Presse méd.*, **73**, 1269 (1965).
20 ZAREMBSKI and HODGKINSON, *Biochem. J.*, **96**, 717 (1965).
21 VERSÉ, H., *Z. Kinderheilk.*, **86**, 347 (1962).
22 TSIRIMBAS and STICH, *Klin. Wschr.*, **38**, 1196 (1960).
23 BONCOMPAGNI et al., *Minerva pediat.*, **13**, 176 (1961).
24 KÄSER, H., *Clin. chim. Acta*, **6**, 337 (1961).
25 GRÜNDIG, E., *Clin. chim. Acta*, **6**, 331 (1961).
26 ÅKERBLOM et al., *Ann. Paediat. Fenn.*, **11**, 108 (1965).
27 WERK and KNOWLES, *Diabetes*, **10**, 22 (1961).
28 PEDEN, V. H., *J. Lab. clin. Med.*, **63**, 332 (1964).
29 WILLIAMSON et al., *Biochem. J.*, **82**, 90 (1962); WAKIL and BRESSLER, *Metabolism*, **11**, 742 (1962).
30 BERGMEYER and BERNT, *Enzymol. biol. clin. (Basel)*, **5**, 65 (1965).
31 PASSMORE, R., *Lancet*, **1**, 839 (1961); SIDBURY and DONG, *J. Pediat.*, **60**, 294 (1962).
32 LEVEY et al., *J. Lab. clin. Med.*, **63**, 574 (1964).
33 ROSENTHAL, S. M., *J. biol. Chem.*, **179**, 1235 (1949).
34 Review, *Nutr. Rev.*, **21**, 324 (1963).
35 SUNSHINE et al., *Stand. Meth. clin. Chem.*, **3**, 1 (1961).
36 KLEIN and KORZIS, *Medizinische*, **1958**, 345.
37 THÖLEN et al., *Experientia (Basel)*, **18**, 454 (1962).
38 ÖCKERMAN, P. A., *Clin. chim. Acta*, **12**, 445 (1965).
39 MUELLER and EVANS, *J. Lab. clin. Med.*, **61**, 953 (1963).
40 EGGSTEIN, M., *Klin. Wschr.*, **44**, 267 (1966).
41 SHIGETA et al., *J. Vitaminol.*, **7**, 48 (1961).

(For references see page 611)

	Whole blood				Plasma or serum				Remarks
	Mean	95% range (extreme range in brackets)	s	Reference	Mean	95% range (extreme range in brackets)	s	Reference	
Carotenes (μg/l)	...	...	...	...	850	(200–1990)	–	1	Values from 133 adults on a diet with a normal carotene content.

The serum carotene level is rather high towards term in pregnancy[2]; in cord blood it is about 25% of that in the maternal blood[3]. In infants it is often *increased*, probably as a result of the high intake of milk and vegetables. Values for children are within the above normal range[4].

	WB Mean	WB 95% range	WB s	WB Ref.	PS Mean	PS 95% range	PS s	PS Ref.	Remarks
Vitamin A (μg/l)	...	...	...	...	324	(207–471)	–	1	Values from 133 adults on a diet with a normal carotene and vitamin A content.

The serum vitamin A level is about 25% lower towards term in pregnancy[2, 3]; in cord blood it is about 50% of that in the maternal blood[3]. In children aged 3–12 years values are within the above normal range[4]. In adults differences from decade to decade have been observed, in particular a reduction in men over 70[5]. In winter, values are rather lower than in the autumn[5]. In the serum about 90% of the vitamin A is present as alcohol, the remainder as ester; almost all is bound to the plasma proteins (see page 457). So long as the body's reserves of the vitamin are not exhausted, the serum level remains constant. It is pathologically decreased in infections; in lobular pneumonia vitamin A may disappear completely from the serum[6].

	WB Mean	WB 95% range	WB s	WB Ref.	PS Mean	PS 95% range	PS s	PS Ref.	Remarks
Vitamin D (IU/l)									
Children	...	...	...	...	–	(860–2100)	–	10	Values by biological method (rat test). In the serum, vitamin D is bound to α_2-globulins and albumin (see page 461).
Adults	...	...	...	...	2000	(700–3100)	–	7	
Tocopherol (mg/l)									
(a) Cord blood	...	...	...	...	5.7	(1.0–11.2)	–	8	Values from (a) 46, (b) 71, (c) 61 subjects by (a) method of NAIR and MAGAR[10] and (b, c) method of FARBER et al.[11].
(b) Men	...	...	...	...	10.6	5.6–15.6	2.5	9	
(c) Women	...	...	...	...	10.4	5.0–15.8	2.7	9	

The serum tocopherol is 88% α-, the remainder β- and γ-tocopherol[12]. The serum level is increased in pregnancy[13]; it is decreased in the newborn and various tocopherol-deficiency states, particularly cystic pancreatic fibrosis (see page 466)[14]. Breast-fed infants have higher serum levels than those on cow's milk[14].

	WB Mean	WB 95% range	WB s	WB Ref.	PS Mean	PS 95% range	PS s	PS Ref.	Remarks
Ubiquinone (mg/l)	...	...	...	...	0.73	(0.40–1.15)	–	15	The serum contains ubiquinone-50[16].
Thiamine (μg/l)									
(a) Total	28	(20–75)	–	17	21	(18–62)	–	17	Values (a) from 138 (whole blood) and 128 (serum) subjects determined by *Ochromonas danica*; values (b) from 28 subjects determined by *Ochromonas malhamensis*; values (c) from 11 subjects by thiochrome method. Total thiamine is determined after hydrolysis of the thiamine pyrophosphate.
(b) Total	–	(20–41)	–	18	–	(3–15)	–	18	
(c) Total	–	(40–70)	–	19					
(c) Free	–	(6.5–11.4)	–	19					

The thiamine of the erythrocytes and leucocytes is mainly pyrophosphate (see page 470). The serum thiamine level is lower towards term in pregnancy (mean 11.5 μg/l), higher in the newborn (mean 55 μg/l)[20]. The fall in the erythrocyte thiamine pyrophosphate level in thiamine deficiency is made use of diagnostically in the transketolase test (see page 470). The blood thiamine level is low in insulin-dependent diabetics[21].

	WB Mean	WB 95% range	WB s	WB Ref.	PS Mean	PS 95% range	PS s	PS Ref.	Remarks
Riboflavin (μg/l)									
(a) Total	66.8	(49–104)	–	22	...	...	...	...	Values (a) from 18 men and 42 women by the lumiflavin method; values (b) from 13, (c, d) from 12 subjects, all by photometric analysis; values (e) from 8 subjects by using *Lactobacillus casei*. In cord blood serum the level of free riboflavin is 4 times, that of FMN 3 times, that of FAD half, as high as in the maternal serum[25]. A lowered erythrocyte riboflavin level indicates riboflavin deficiency[26] (see page 473).
(a) As FMN and FAD	55.1	(43–71)	–	22					
(b) Total	...	...	...	...	32	(26–37)		23	
(b) As FAD	...	...	...	...	24	(18–30)		23	
(b) Free and as FMN	...	...	...	...	8	(3–13)	–	23	
(c)	224	Erythrocytes: (180–262)	–	23					
(d)	2520	Leucocytes: (2270–2930)	–	23					
(e) (μg/10^9 cells)	0.62	0.18–1.06	0.22	24					
Vitamin B_6									
Total activity (μg/l)									
(a)	37	(20–45)	–	27	44	(30–80)	–	27	Values determined by means of (a) *Tetrahymena pyriformis*, (b, c) *Saccharomyces carlsbergensis*; values from (b) 30, (c) 15 subjects. For methods of determining vitamin B_6 see the literature[29, 30] and page 473.
(b) Men	19.2	(6.8–77)	–	28					
(c) Women	17.7	(4.4–76)	–	28					
(a)	20	Erythrocytes: (13–31)	–	27					

The vitamin B_6 activity of the blood is probably mainly due to pyridoxal phosphate; pyridoxol appears to be absent[31]. The blood level is rather low during pregnancy[28, 32]; in the cord blood the concentration is about 4 times that in the maternal blood[28].

	Whole blood				Plasma or serum				Remarks
	Mean	95% range (extreme range in brackets)	*s*	Reference	Mean	95% range (extreme range in brackets)	*s*	Reference	
Pyridoxal phosphate (μg/l)									
(a) Birth–1 year	...	...	...	...	16.3	(6.5–57.1)	16.7	33	Values from (a) 14, (b) 13, (c) 11, (d) 21, (e) 40 subjects by the tyrosine decarboxylase method.
(b) 20–29 years	...	...	...	...	11.3	(3.8–21.6)	5.7	33	
(c) 30–59 years	...	...	...	...	7.1	(2.4–12.4)	3.0	33	
(d) 60 years and over	...	...	...	...	3.4	(0–13.5)	3.0	33	
(e) (μg/10^9 cells)	–	Leucocytes: (0.14–0.36)	–	34					
Pyridoxic acid (μg/l)	–	(100–130)	–	31	...	...	...	...	Values from 3 subjects determined fluorometrically.
Nicotinic acid (mg/l)									
(a)	–	(3.9–9.6)	–	29	–	(0.016–0.05)	–	29	Values from (a) 28, (b) 39, (c) 46 subjects by means of (a) *Tetrahymena pyriformis*, (b, c) *Lactobacillus arabinosus*. In whole blood the nicotinic acid occurs almost exclusively as nicotinamide dinucleotides (NAD and NADP) in the cells (in the erythrocytes 60–90 mg/l, in the leucocytes 88 mg/l, expressed as NAD[36]).
(b) Men	6.55	5.32–7.78	0.615	35					
(c) Women	6.05	4.59–7.51	0.730	35					
1-Methylnicotinamide (mg/l)	...	...	...	...	0.017	–	–	36	After ingestion of nicotinamide the metabolites 1-methyl-2-pyridone-5-carboxylamide and 1 methyl-4-pyridone-5-carboxylamide are found in the plasma[37].
Vitamin B_{12} (ng/l)									
(a)	...	...	...	...	611	277–945	167	38	Values from (a) 39, (b) 223, (c) 28, (d) 3, (e) 50 subjects determined by using (a) isotope dilution, (b) *Euglena gracilis*, (c, d) *Ochromonas malhamensis*, (e) *Lactobacillus leichmannii*. For discussion of methods see the literature[29, 43].
(b)	...	...	...	...	356	(100–900)	–	39	
(c)	–	(120–450)	–	18	–	(140–640)	–	18	
(d)	74	Erythrocytes: (59–88)	–	40					
(e)	213	(110–500)	–	41					
(ng/kg)	–	Leucocytes: (500–4300)	–	42					
(ng/10^9 cells)	–	(2.45–6.65)	–	42					

About 80% of the vitamin B_{12} of the serum is not utilizable by micro-organisms unless it is first liberated by heating. This part is bound to α_1- and α_2-globulins[44]. Most of the vitamin B_{12} activity of the serum appears to be due to methylcobalamin[45]. The serum values show a lognormal distribution[46].
The serum level is rather low during pregnancy[47, 48]; in the cord blood it is higher than in the maternal blood[49].

The serum level is pathologically *decreased* in pernicious anaemia, cancer of the stomach, gastric resection, lesions of the small intestine (malabsorption syndrome), fish-tapeworm carriers and alimentary vitamin B_{12} deficiency (for example in vegetarians); it is *increased* in liver and renal diseases, diabetes and leukaemia[39, 43, 46]. Serum values below 100 ng/l are indicative of severe deficiency of the vitamin (megaloblastic anaemia).

	Mean	95% range	*s*	Reference	Mean	95% range	*s*	Reference	Remarks
Folic acid (μg/l)									
(a)	12.0	(3.0–20.0)	–	50	...	...	...	...	Values from (a–c) 43, (d) 27, (e) 24 subjects determined by means of (a) *Streptococcus faecalis*, (b) *Pediococcus cerevisiae*, (c–e) *Lactobacillus casei*. Only with the latter can 5-methyltetrahydropteroylglutamic acid, the most important member of the folic acid group in blood, be determined (see page 478). For methods of determination see the literature[29, 53].
(b)	6.35	(1.5–25.0)	–	50					
(c)	89	(47–149)	–	50	8.2	(3.5–15.0)	–	50	
(d)	327	Erythrocytes: (184–655)	–	51	9.4	(5.2–23.8)	–	51	
(ng/10^9 cells)									
(e)	2.6	–	1.8	52					
(e)	64	Leucocytes: –	42.5	52					

Of the serum folic acid 64% is protein-bound[54].
During pregnancy the serum level is often low[47, 50]; in the cord blood it is higher than in the maternal blood[55], but falls during the first weeks of life[56]. It is pathologically *decreased* in diseases of the small intestine, chronic polyarthritis, myelofibrosis, carcinomatosis and dietary deficiency of the vitamin; values below 3 μg/l indicate severe folic acid deficiency (megaloblastic anaemia)[50, 51]. The folic acid content of the leucocytes is increased in myeloid leukaemia[57]. The concentration in the erythrocytes and whole blood is an indication of the amount of the vitamin stored by the body[58].

	Mean	95% range	*s*	Reference	Mean	95% range	*s*	Reference	Remarks
Unconjugated pterins (μg/l)	–	(27–70)	–	18	–	(11–43)	–	18	Determined by means of *Crithidia fasciculata*.
(ng/10^9 cells)	6.0	Erythrocytes: (4.3–11.8)	–	52					
	117	Leucocytes: (77–167)	–	52					

	Whole blood				Plasma or serum				Remarks
	Mean	95% range (extreme range in brackets)	s	Reference	Mean	95% range (extreme range in brackets)	s	Reference	
Biotin (ng/l)									
(a) Infants	324	(147–555)	114	71	...	...	...	...	Values from (a) 30, (b) 25, (c) 12 subjects by means of (a, b) *Lactobacillus plantarum*, (c) *Ochromonas danica*.
(b) Adults	258	(120–422)	74	71					
(c)	–	170–279	–	29	–	213–404	–	29	
Pantothenic acid (µg/l)									
(a) Total	–	(230–2075)	–	18	–	(200–1650)	–	18	Values from (a) 28, (b) 30 subjects by means of *Lactobacillus plantarum*.
(b) Total	464	382–546	41	59					
(b) Free	28.7	0–58.7	15	59					

During pregnancy the blood level lies within the above normal range[20,60]; in the newborn the level is about 5 times higher than in the maternal blood[20]. The blood level is *increased* – with reduction of the liver content – in fatty or acute cirrhotic liver[61], *decreased* in rheumatoid arthritis[62].

	Whole blood				Plasma or serum				Remarks
Ascorbic acid (mg/l)									
(a) Men, 20–30 years	5.07	(2.24–8.80)	–	63	4.76	(1.96–8.76)	–	63	Values from (a) 11, (b) 7, (c) 558, (d) 25, (e) 50 subjects; values (a–c) determined with 2,4-dinitrophenylhydrazine. For methods see Roe et al.[65].
(b) Women, 20–30 years	8.84	(5.17–12.8)	–	63	8.97	(6.24–14.1)	–	63	
(c) Children, 10–13 years	...	...	...	...	6	0–15	–	72	
(µg/10^9 cells)		Leucocytes:							
(d) 18–45 years	350	210–530	–	64					
(e) 60–91 years	134	20–360	–	64					

The ascorbic acid content of the blood and plasma depends on the extent of tissue saturation and on the dietary intake (see page 490). The serum and leucocyte levels in the newborn are higher than in the maternal blood[66]. The serum ascorbic acid includes 21% (range 7–41%) of dehydroascorbic acid[67]; in women this proportion fluctuates during the menstrual cycle[68]. Administration of corticosteroids causes dehydroascorbic acid to disappear from the serum[69].

References

1 Campbell and Tonks, *Brit.J.Ophthal.*, **46**, 151 (1962).
2 Pulliam et al., *Proc.Soc.exp.Biol.(N.Y.)*, **109**, 913 (1962).
3 Lübke and Finkbeiner, *Int.Z.Vitaminforsch.*, **29**, 45 (1958).
4 Chikhalikar et al., *Indian J.Child Hlth*, **10**, 161 (1961).
5 Leitner et al., *Brit.J.Nutr.*, **14**, 157 (1960).
6 Kagan and Goodhart, in Wohl and Goodhart (Eds.), *Modern Nutrition in Health and Disease*, 3rd ed., Lea & Febiger, Philadelphia, 1964, page 341.
7 Thomas et al., *J.clin.Invest.*, **38**, 1078 (1959).
8 Toyama, R., *Acta pediat.esp.*, **22**, 283 (1964).
9 Bieri et al., *Proc.Soc.exp.Biol.(N.Y.)*, **117**, 131 (1964).
10 Nair and Magar, *Indian J.med.Res.*, **42**, 577 (1954).
11 Farber et al., *Proc.Soc.exp.Biol.(N.Y.)*, **79**, 225 (1952).
12 Bieri and Prival, *Proc.Soc.exp.Biol.(N.Y.)*, **120**, 554 (1965).
13 Ferguson et al., *J.Nutr.*, **55**, 305 (1955).
14 Goldbloom, R.B., *Canad.med.Ass.J.*, **82**, 1114 (1960).
15 Bieri, J.G., *Nutr.Rev.*, **21**, 129 (1963).
16 Dinning et al., *Amer.J.clin.Nutr.*, **13**, 169 (1963).
17 Baker et al., *Amer.J.clin.Nutr.*, **14**, 197 (1964).
18 Baker et al., *Nature*, **191**, 78 (1961).
19 Haugen, H.N., *Scand.J.clin.Lab.Invest.*, **13**, 50 (1961).
20 Baker et al., *Proc.Soc.exp.Biol.(N.Y.)*, **103**, 321 (1960).
21 Haugen, H.N., *Scand.J.clin.Lab.Invest.*, **16**, 260 (1964).
22 Kerppola, W., *Acta med.scand.*, **153**, 33 (1955).
23 Burch et al., *J.biol.Chem.*, **175**, 457 (1948).
24 Prager et al., *J.Lab.clin.Med.*, **53**, 926 (1959).
25 Lust et al., *J.clin.Invest.*, **33**, 38 (1954).
26 Bessey et al., *J.Nutr.*, **58**, 367 (1956).
27 Baker et al., *Amer.J.clin.Nutr.*, **18**, 123 (1966).
28 Karlin, R., *C.R.Soc.Biol.(Paris)*, **156**, 858 (1962).
29 Baker and Sobotka, *Advanc.clin.Chem.*, **5**, 173 (1962).
30 Storvick and Peters, *Vitam.and Horm.*, **22**, 833 (1964).
31 Fujita and Fujino, quoted by Storvick and Peters [30].
32 Wachstein, M., *Vitam.and Horm.*, **22**, 705 (1964).
33 Hamfelt, A., *Clin.chim.Acta*, **10**, 48 (1964).
34 Wachstein et al., *Proc.Soc.exp.Biol.(N.Y.)*, **105**, 563 (1960).
35 Karlin, R., *C.R.Soc.Biol.(Paris)*, **153**, 1044 (1959).
36 Goldsmith, G.A., in Beaton and McHenry (Eds.), *Nutrition*, vol. 2, Academic Press, New York, 1964, page 109.
37 Abelson et al., *J.biol.Chem.*, **238**, 717 (1963); *Clin.chim.Acta*, **8**, 603 (1963).
38 Barakat and Ekins, *Blood*, **21**, 70 (1963).
39 Mollin and Ross, in Heinrich, H.C. (Ed.), *Vitamin B_{12} und Intrinsic Factor*, 1. Europäisches Symposium über Vitamin B_{12} und Intrinsic Factor, Hamburg 1956, Enke, Stuttgart, 1957, page 413.
40 Baker et al., *Nature*, **180**, 1043 (1957).
41 Biggs et al., *Brit.J.Haemat.*, **10**, 36 (1964).
42 Mollin and Ross, *Brit.J.Haemat.*, **1**, 155 (1955).
43 Gräsbeck, R., *Advanc.clin.Chem.*, 3, 299 (1960); Baker et al., *Clin.Chem.*, **6**, 578 (1960).
44 Meyer, L.M., *Scand.J.Haemat.*, suppl. *Ser.haemat.*, No. 3, 91 (1965).
45 Ståhlberg, K.G., *Scand.J.Haemat.*, **1**, 220 (1964).
46 Panders et al., *Ned.T.Geneesk.*, **109**, 1291 (1965).
47 Ball and Giles, *J.clin.Path.*, **17**, 165 (1964).
48 Boger et al., *Proc.Soc.exp.Biol.(N.Y.)*, **92**, 140 (1956).
49 Boger et al., *New Engl.J.Med.*, **256**, 1085 (1957); Baker et al., *Proc.Soc.exp.Biol.(N.Y.)*, **103**, 321 (1960); Chow and Okuda, *J.Amer.med.Ass.*, **172**, 422 (1960).
50 Rachmilewitz, M., *Scand.J.Haemat.*, suppl. *Ser.haemat.*, No. 3, 19 (1965).
51 Mollin and Hoffbrand, *Scand.J.Haemat.*, suppl. *Ser. haemat.*, No. 3, 1 (1965).
52 James and Hart, *Amer.J.clin.Nutr.*, **18**, 309 (1966).
53 Girdwood, R.H., *Advanc.clin.Chem.*, 3, 235 (1960).
54 Johns et al., *J.clin.Invest.*, **40**, 1684 (1961).
55 Matoth et al., *Pediatrics*, **33**, 507 (1964).
56 Strelling et al., *Lancet*, **1**, 898 (1966).
57 Swendseid et al., *Cancer Res.*, **11**, 864 (1951).
58 Herbert, V., *Ann.Rev.Med.*, **16**, 359 (1965).
59 Hatano, M., *J. Vitaminol.*, **8**, 134 (1962).
60 Ishiguro, K., *Tohoku J.exp.Med.*, **78**, 7 (1962), quoted in *Nutr.Abstr.Rev.*, **33**, 815 (1963).
61 Leevy et al., *J.clin.Invest.*, **39**, 1005 (1960).
62 Barton-Wright and Elliott, *Lancet*, **2**, 862 (1963).
63 Spathis and Hallpike, *Guy's Hosp.Rep.*, **110**, 148 (1961).
64 Denson and Bowers, *Clin.Sci.*, **21**, 157 (1961).
65 Roe et al., *Stand.Meth.clin.Chem.*, 3, 35 (1961).
66 Dłużniewska et al., *Rocz. Państwowego Zakt.Hig.*, **14**, 443 (1963), quoted in *Nutr.Abstr.Rev.*, **34**, 1103 (1964).
67 Linkswiler, H., *J.Nutr.*, **64**, 43 (1958).
68 Kofoed et al., *Amer.J.Obstet.Gynec.*, **91**, 95 (1965).
69 Stewart et al., *Biochem.J.*, **53**, 254 (1953).
70 Job et al., *Ann.Péd.*, **43**, 2412/P.648 (1967).
71 Bhagavan and Coursin, *Amer.J.clin.Nutr.*, **20**, 903 (1967).
72 Baker et al., *Amer.J.clin. Nutr.*, **20**, 850 (1967).

Erythroblasts

Erythroblasts are all nucleated precursors of the erythrocytes; the term includes the pro-erythroblasts, the erythroblasts proper and the normoblasts. Under physiological conditions the peripheral blood contains only the last-named – and only during the first two days of life. The normoblasts closely resemble the erythrocytes in respect of plasma-staining, haemoglobin content and size. The erythroblasts proper are polychromatic in plasma-staining, the pro-erythroblasts basophile.

By *erythroblastosis* is understood the entry of erythroblasts into the peripheral blood; it is always a sign of increased erythropoiesis and is therefore usually accompanied by reticulocytosis. In the newborn (including premature babies and young infants) they are an indication of persistence or recurrence of extramedullary blood formation and at the same time of an abnormal relationship between the intensive erythrocyte formation on the one hand and the absolute and relatively small bone-marrow volume at this age on the other. Severe erythroblastosis of 50–100–500 or more erythroblasts per 100 leucocytes in the early days of life is almost always a sign of severe haemolysis due to blood-group incompatibility between mother and child. In later infancy and childhood the main causes of peripheral erythroblastosis are haemolytic anaemia, haemorrhagic anaemia, and occasionally leucosis or cyanotic heart defects.

	Mean	Extreme range	s	Reference	Remarks
Number (per 100 leucocytes)					
Cord blood	3.2	(0–30)	–	1	Method: Counting in GIEMSA-stained blood smears.
Newborn, 1–10 hours	1.6	(0–16)	–	1	
Newborn, 2 days	–	(0–1)	–	1	
Adults	0	–	–	1	

Reference [1] v. BOROVICZÉNY and BALLÓ, *Wien. Z. inn. Med.*, **38**, 196 (1957).

Reticulocytes

Synonyms: Vital-granulated erythrocytes, vital-staining erythrocytes, pro-erythrocytes (UNDRITZ[7]), polychromatic erythrocytes.

The reticulocytes are erythrocytes of more than average size and more resistant to haemolysis. There is a sex difference in the reticulocyte count of 3–5 per thousand (see table below). The number of reticulocytes increases with any increase in erythrocyte formation, i.e., continuously in chronic haemolytic or haemorrhagic anaemia, suddenly and persistently for days or weeks in the reparative phase of pernicious anaemia and erythroblastopenia, to a lesser extent also in iron-deficiency anaemia. The number of reticulocytes decreases in aplastic and hypoplastic anaemia, after transfusions and after long-continued administration of oxygen. The extent to which reticulocytes are released from the bone marrow is in general a measure of the extent of erythrocyte formation.

The wide fluctuations in the data given in the table below for normal reticulocyte counts are due to differences in the methods of measurement. The better the method of staining, the higher the reticulocyte count obtained (as in counts in smears stained with brilliant cresol blue).

	Mean	95% range (extreme range in brackets)	s	Reference	Remarks
Number					
(per µl)	–	10 000–50 000	–	2	Values for adults by direct measurement. For newborn values see below.
(per 10^3 erythrocytes)	7.5	1.3–13.7	3.1	3	Values for adults. For newborn values see below, for values in children and other adult values see the opposite page. (Values for children in agreement with WASHBURN[4].)
Diameter (µm)	–	(8.0–9.0)	–	5	1.0–1.5 µm greater than that of erythrocytes (≡ 1.1–1.2 times erythrocyte diameter).
Thickness (µm)	–	(4.5–5.5)	–	6	Erythrocytes 1.8–2.2 µm.
Volume (fl ≡ μm^3)					
Infants	–	(200–230)	–	6	Erythrocytes 5 μm^3.
Adults	–	(250–310)	–	6	Erythrocytes 85 μm^3.

Reticulocyte count during 1st day of life[7]

Hours	Per 10^3 erythrocytes	Per µl
At birth	25.4	126 000
2	35.9	168 000
4	40.0	190 000
6	26.6	148 000
8	25.1	119 000
10	15.7	86 000

Reticulocyte count in newborn (values per 10^3 erythrocytes)

Days	FAXÉN[8]	SEIP[13]	GAIRDNER et al.[10]
1	22	52	37
2	20.4	50	–
3	16.6	52	–
4	10.7	45	27.5
5	5.3	33	–
6	4.8	18	–
7	3.8	13	–
9	–	–	7.9

Reticulocyte count in childhood (per 10^3 erythrocytes[11])

Age	Mean	95% range	s
1–24 hours	39.2	–	–
1–7 days	22.3	–	–
7–10 days	10.6	–	–
10–30 days	7.9	0.3–15.5	3.8
1–2 months	12.9	0–27.7	7.4
2–6 months	10.6	0–24.8	7.1
6–12 months	7.5	0–17.3	4.9
1 year	7.5	0–16.3	4.4
2 years	7.1	0–15.1	4.0
3 years	7.2	0–15.4	4.1
4 years	8.1	0–18.1	5.0
5 years	8.2	0–17.2	4.5
6 years	7.5	0–15.5	4.0
7 years	7.6	0.6–14.6	3.5
8 years	6.8	0.4–13.2	3.2
9 years	7.5	0.9–14.1	3.3
10 years	7.6	1.2–14.0	3.2
11–15 years	7.4	0–15.4	4.0

Reticulocyte count in adults (values per 10^3 erythrocytes)

	SEIP[9]		WATSON[3]	
	Mean	Extreme range	Mean	95% range
Men and women	15.7	9.6–23.8	7.5	1.3–13.7
Men	13.5	9.6–18.4	6	1.6–10.4
Women	17.3	10.4–23.8	9	2.6–15.4

Maturity of reticulocytes (per 10^3 erythrocytes)

Degree	SEIP[9]		NIZET[12]	
	Mean	Extreme range	Mean	Extreme range
I	0.02	0–0.2	0	–
II	1.1	0–2.6	1.6	0–5.6
III	5.0	1.8–10.8	3.6	0.2–12.3
IV	9.5	5.8–12.0	12.5	–

References

1 UNDRITZ, E., *Dtsch.med. Wschr.*, **63**, 1686 (1937).
2 BJÖRKMAN, S. E., *Xe Congrès de la Société européenne d'hématologie*, Strasbourg, 1965, page 225.
3 WATSON, C. J., *Arch.intern.Med.*, **86**, 797 (1950).
4 WASHBURN, A. H., *Amer.J.Dis.Child.*, **62**, 530 (1941).
5 PERSONS, E. L., *J.clin.Invest.*, **7**, 615 (1929).
6 WEICKER and FICHSEL, *Klin. Wschr.*, **33**, 1074 (1955).
7 WEGELIUS, R., *Acta paediat. (Uppsala)*, **35**, suppl. 4, 1 (1948).
8 FAXÉN, N., *Acta paediat. (Uppsala)*, **19**, suppl. 1, 1 (1937).
9 SEIP, M., *Acta med. scand.*, **146**, suppl. 282, 1 (1953).
10 GAIRDNER et al., *Arch. Dis. Childh.*, **27**, 214 (1952).
11 DE CHASTONAY, E., *Helv. paediat. Acta*, **6**, 257 (1951).
12 NIZET, A., *Acta med. scand.*, **127**, 424 and 565 (1947).
13 SEIP, M., *Acta paediat. (Uppsala)*, **44**, 355 (1955).

Erythrocytes

(For other physical and chemical data see under 'Blood', pages 557–611; for references see page 616)

	Mean	95% range	s	Reference	Remarks
Erythrocyte count (red blood count, RBC)	...	...	...	...	See text below and table, page 617.
Haematocrit value (Ht) (packed cell volume, PCV)	...	...	...	...	See text, page 614, and table, page 617.
Diameter (μm)					
(a)	8.56	8.14–8.98	0.21	1	Microscopic measurements on erythrocytes of 10 persons: (a) individual cells, wet preparations; (b) dry preparations; (c) rouleaux. See text, page 614, and table, page 617.
(b)	7.11	6.31–7.91	0.40	1	
(c)	8.70	8.12–9.28	0.29	1	
Thickness (μm)					
(a)	1.9	1.75–2.1	–	2	(a) and (b) calculated from the single-cell volume and the cell diameter; (a) wet preparations, (b) dry preparations; (c) microscopic measurements on 10 persons. See also text, page 614.
(b)	2.1	1.9–2.3	–	2	
(c)	1.64	1.50–1.78	0.07	1	
Surface area (μm^2)	145.0	128–162	8.3	1	Calculated from the cell diameter and cell thickness. The total surface area of the erythrocytes of an average man is ca. 3820 m^2 or some 2000 times the body surface area.
	163	–	–	3	
Volume ($fl \equiv \mu m^3$)	86.1	73.5–98.7	6.3	1	Calculated from the cell diameter and cell thickness. See text, pages 614–615, and table, page 617.
Weight (pg)	96.8	–	7.02	4	Values have lognormal distribution.
Haemoglobin (Hb) content	...	...	...	...	See text, page 615, and table, page 617.

Erythrocyte count

Methods

The visual counting methods still used in most laboratories are subject to considerable error, the coefficient of variation in the results given by different methods being 10–15%[5]. Automatic counting apparatus is more precise, though this applies properly speaking only to the action of counting. The errors associated with preparation of the sample (squeezing-out of capillary blood, inaccurate filling of pipettes and failure to dab off the surplus blood) are much more important. Thus a coefficient of variation between repeated measurements on the same blood sample of 2–2.5% bears no relationship to the reliability of the sampling technique.

Counts made with the aid of ^{32}P-tagged erythrocytes have given considerably lower figures for the total numbers of circulating erythrocytes than calculations from the concentration in the peripheral venous blood. The erythrocyte concentration of the peripheral blood therefore represents an absolute value of practical diagnostic use only when the total blood volume is measured at the same time. This is shown clearly for example in the first hours of life, when the erythrocyte count often rises to over one million per microlitre while the total blood volume is reduced.

For details of the various methods of counting see the literature[6].

Physiological characteristics

In the newborn the erythrocyte count fluctuates to a greater extent than at any other time of life, even under constant sampling conditions. It is also dependent on the site from which blood is drawn. During the first days of life the capillary blood has up to half-a-million more erythrocytes than the cord or venous blood[7]. The time at which the cord is clamped has an effect on the count. Immediate clamping prevents the passage of a quarter to one-third of the total blood volume available to the newborn child in the placenta. For this reason the erythrocyte count after a few hours in such children may lie about 1–1½ million per microlitre below the normal level. In the newborn the erythrocyte count rises to a maximum after a few hours since the initially high blood volume is reduced by the passage of blood plasma into the tissues[8]. The erythrocyte count falls steadily from the middle of the first week of life up to the middle of the third month owing to the gradual slowing-down of erythropoiesis. The physiological polyglobulinaemia of the newborn is followed by physiological oligoglobulinaemia in the 3-month child.

During pregnancy the erythrocyte count falls[9]. In general the erythrocyte count is dependent on the partial oxygen pressure of the atmosphere and therefore on the altitude. Thus the Indians of the uplands of Peru show marked polyglobulinaemia, beginning in childhood. A very considerable increase in altitude is thus equivalent to an anoxic stimulus to erythropoiesis, descent from a high altitude (like administration of oxygen) to an inhibition. Emotional effects like anxiety and excitement can result in 'stress erythrocytosis', probably as a result of the movement of plasma into the tissues.

During puberty a sex difference in the erythrocyte count of about half-a-million develops.

Haematocrit value

The haematocrit value is the proportion of the volume of the peripheral venous or capillary whole blood occupied by the erythrocytes. On the body haematocrit see page 554. The haematocrit value is dependent on three factors, namely the erythrocyte count, the mean corpuscular volume (see below) and the plasma volume. Since the ratio between the mean corpuscular haemoglobin (see the opposite page) and the mean corpuscular volume varies between only narrow limits, the haematocrit value has almost the same significance as the haemoglobin content of the whole blood.

Measurement

The haematocrit can be measured by a variety of macro- and micro-methods. The best methods are those using high-speed haematocrit centrifuges and microhaematocrit capillaries[10]. The haematocrit value depends on the speed of the centrifuge, the time of centrifuging and the viscosity of the blood. The amount of plasma trapped between the packed erythrocytes is 1–9%, depending on the method[11]; the proportion after centrifuging at 14 000 g_n for 40 minutes is only 0.45%[12].

See also the literature on haematocrit measurement[13].

Physiological characteristics

By its nature the haematocrit varies in a manner similar to the erythrocyte count in newborn children; thus it is dependent on the time the cord is clamped[14], rises during the first hours of life and falls up to the third month. From this time onwards, however, it behaves differently to the erythrocyte count. Whereas the latter remains more or less constant or rises slightly, the haematocrit falls somewhat because the newly-formed erythrocytes are low in haemoglobin and therefore smaller in volume. The haematocrit also resembles the erythrocyte count in respect of sex difference, behaviour during pregnancy and dependence on partial oxygen pressure of the atmosphere.

Erythrocyte diameter

Measurement

Two basically different methods are used to measure the mean erythrocyte diameter, micrometry and halometry[15]. The latter method is simple, time-saving and adequate for routine use. Measurement on blood smears or on optical projections of smears have the advantage that the distribution as well as the mean value is obtained; as in blood-volume measurements the former may be of diagnostic importance. Distribution values, however, should be based on measurements on at least 1500–2000 cells[16].

On methods of measurement see also the literature[17].

Physiological characteristics

In the newborn the erythrocyte diameter is likewise high, though unlike the erythrocyte count it continues to fall not only up to the third month of life but, as a result of the formation of new erythrocytes low in haemoglobin, up to the end of the first year. The value may fall to a mean value of less than 7 μm.

Pathological characteristics

In pernicious and similar anaemias the erythrocyte diameter is high and shows a particularly wide variance. It is fairly high in aplastic anaemia, low in iron-deficiency and sideroachrestic anaemias and spherocytosis; in the latter condition a particularly important characteristic is the normal erythrocyte volume.

Numerical eccentricity

Deviation of the shape of the erythrocytes from the truly spherical is expressed as either the axis coefficient K or the numerical eccentricity ε as follows:

$$K = 1 - \frac{b}{a}; \quad \varepsilon = \sqrt{1 - \left(\frac{b}{a}\right)^2}$$

where a = the larger, b = the smaller diameter. For the determination of these values by nomogram see v. Boroviczény[18]. Normally 74.4% of the erythrocytes are spherical, 14.9% non-spherical, 8.2% elliptical and 2.5% grossly elliptical.

Predominance of regularly oval forms is known as elliptocytosis, and is a dominant inheritable anomaly of no clinical significance in which all erythrocytes are similar in appearance. Symptomatic elliptocytosis of varying morphological and numerical degrees of severity occurs, usually associated with poikilocytosis, in pernicious and similar anaemias, occasionally in leukaemia and rarely in severe infections.

Morphological variations

Poikilocytes are erythrocytes of irregular shape and have an extremely wide range of size. Usually they indicate a disturbance of erythropoiesis and are probably formed by the extrusion of a mass of erythroblastic or normoblastic plasma.

Round cells (spherocytes), basket cells, target cells and sickle cells are mostly phenotypic manifestations of haemolytic anaemia due to metabolic disturbances.

Erythrocyte thickness

The thickness of an erythrocyte is an arbitrary dimension since the erythrocyte is not a true rotation ellipsoid but a disk with bilateral indentations. It is of significance only when showing extreme deviations, namely in spherocytosis of hereditary origin and in phenocopy. During haemolysis the thickness increases to 4–5 μm while the volume remains constant; this results in a lowering of the osmotic resistance of the cell. In iron-deficiency and sideroachrestic anaemias the thickness of the erythrocytes is less than 1.5 μm, so that there is an increase in the osmotic resistance.

Measurement

By direct microscopic measurement or calculation from the erythrocyte volume (mean corpuscular volume) by dividing by the square of the radius × π.

Mean corpuscular volume (MCV)

In contrast to the erythrocyte count and haematocrit, which are dependent on various factors, the mean corpuscular volume is an absolute quantity, i.e., it has an individual though almost constant value. Measured values are of course mean values and like other biological data exhibit variance. With the aid of modern automatic erythrocyte counting instruments it is possible to obtain distribution curves of the mean corpuscular volume. In the diagnosis of anaemia such curves are capable of giving even more information than the itself very useful mean corpuscular volume. Thus in aplastic, hypoplastic and especially pernicious and similar anaemias the mean corpuscular volume is high, whereas in iron-deficiency and sideroachrestic anaemias it is low. A high mean corpuscular volume can be simulated by a high reticulocyte count since the mean reticulocyte volume is three times greater than the mean corpuscular volume. Macrocytic haemolytic anaemia usually consists of normocytic anaemia accompanied by reticulocytosis. The high mean corpuscular volume of the newborn is also partly a result of the relatively high reticulocyte count.

Measurement

The mean corpuscular volume is calculated by dividing the haematocrit value (in litres per litre) by the number of erythrocytes in 1 litre of whole blood. The normal range so calculated is 80–90 fl ($\equiv \mu m^3$).

Mean corpuscular haemoglobin concentration (MCHC)

The mean corpuscular haemoglobin concentration is a 'natural constant'[19] not only in man but widely elsewhere in the animal kingdom. The value varies only when there is a high percentage of reticulocytes, since the latter have a low haemoglobin content. Even under pathological conditions there is little variation, so that true diminutions of concentration by 30%, such as are found in extreme iron deficiency, are of considerable diagnostic significance.

Measurement

The mean corpuscular haemoglobin concentration (in grammes per litre erythrocytes) is calculated by dividing the haemoglobin concentration of the whole blood (in grammes per litre) by the haematocrit value (in litres per litre).

The sole *physiological characteristic* is the fairly high value at birth; this falls to normal by the end of the first month of life.

Mean corpuscular haemoglobin (MCH, Hb_E)

Like the mean corpuscular volume, the mean corpuscular haemoglobin (mean haemoglobin content of a single erythrocyte) is a real quantity. It gives some direct indication of the state of erythropoiesis and is independent of the volumes of the whole blood and plasma. Values of over 35 pg are referred to as hyperchromia and are characteristic of pernicious and similar anaemias as well as of aplastic and hypoplastic anaemias. Any considerable diminution below 30 pg is known as hypochromia and is characteristic of iron-deficiency and sideroachrestic anaemias.

Measurement

The mean corpuscular haemoglobin is calculated by dividing the haemoglobin concentration of the whole blood (in grammes per litre) by the number of erythrocytes in 1 litre. The normal value is 30–32 pg (pg $\equiv 10^{-12}$ g).

Physiological characteristics

The mean corpuscular haemoglobin is likewise high in the newborn and undergoes no change during the first day of life. It then falls to normal by the third month and to moderately hypochromic values by the end of the first year. Subsequently it rises to the normal value again by puberty. In premature infants hypochromic values are reached in as little as 4–8 weeks and are lower than in full-term infants since they receive less iron from the mother.

An increase or decrease in the supply of respiratory oxygen (oxygen administration or a large increase in altitude) has no effect on the mean corpuscular haemoglobin since the haemoglobin content of the whole blood and the erythrocyte count undergo parallel changes.

The so-called colour index (haemoglobin content of the blood expressed as percentage of the normal divided by the erythrocyte count similarly expressed), which in principle is a measure of the mean corpuscular haemoglobin, should no longer be used, and the same applies to the use of values expressed as 'Sahli percentages'. The colour index must be corrected by several factors if it is to give the same information as the mean corpuscular haemoglobin.

Haemoglobin content of the whole blood

The haemoglobin content of the whole blood is the mean corpuscular haemoglobin multiplied by the number of erythrocytes in the volume unit used. For this reason it rises and falls both with the erythrocyte count and with the mean corpuscular haemoglobin. The various values for the haemoglobin content of whole blood given in the literature have been obtained by different methods of measurement and are not necessarily comparable.

Measurement

The recommended standard method is that of photometric determination as haemiglobin cyanide[20]. Measurements are made at 540 nm or 546 nm using a mercury lamp; the millimolar extinction coefficient of haemiglobin cyanide at 540 nm is 44.0, the molecular weight of haemoglobin 64458. Standard solutions of haemiglobin cyanide are available from the various standardization committees. The photometric method measures all the haemoglobin derivatives present in the blood with the exception of verdoglobins.

When other methods of measurement are used, for instance assay as oxyhaemoglobin or from the iron content, care must be taken that the results obtained are comparable with those given by the haemiglobin cyanide method. The determination of haemoglobin as acid haematin is not advisable because of the inaccuracy of the method. The haemoglobin content of whole blood can be expressed in grammes or in millimoles per unit volume; on no account should values in 'Sahli percentages' be used.

For details of methods see the literature[5, 21].

Physiological characteristics

The haemoglobin content is subject to much the same variations as the erythrocyte count (pages 613–614) and haematocrit value (page 614), particularly the latter. Thus cord blood contains about 160 g/l, venous blood on the first day of life about 182 g/l and capillary blood about 200 g/l[22]. When the cord is clamped immediately after birth the haemoglobin content during the first day of life is about 20 g/l lower than when the cord is clamped only after it has been stripped[23]. Like the erythrocyte count, the haemoglobin content rises during the first hours of life, remains high for some days and begins to fall in the middle of the first week. The physiological minimum is reached at 9–11 weeks[8] and maintained up to the end of the 2nd year. From the 2nd to the 12th year it rises continuously, remains stationary in girls but reaches the normal value in boys at puberty[5, 24].

During pregnancy the haemoglobin content falls to a minimum of 120 g/l in the 30th–35th weeks. Lowered and increased partial oxygen pressures cause respectively an increase and decrease of the haemoglobin content, which in this respect behaves like the erythrocyte count[9, 25].

Since the haemoglobin content of the whole blood in general runs parallel with the erythrocyte count, any deviation from this behaviour is of diagnostic significance. Thus in pernicious and similar anaemias and to a lesser extent in aplastic and hypoplastic anaemias the erythrocyte count falls more sharply than the haemoglobin content. A marked fall in the haemoglobin content accompanied by absence of or only a slight decrease in the erythrocyte count is typical of iron-deficiency and sideroachrestic anaemias.

Foetal haemoglobin

The blood of the very early foetus contains practically only foetal haemoglobin (Hb-F), whereas the embryonic blood contains a different transitional form, the so-called embryonic haemoglobin. In the 4th month of development the normal adult form of haemoglobin (Hb-A) appears; at the 5th month it constitutes about 10% of the total haemoglobin and remains roughly at this figure up to the 33rd week. Subsequently the proportion of Hb-A increases, until at birth only some 60–80% of Hb-F is present. After birth the proportion of Hb-F continues to fall until at 5 months it is only about 10%, at 2 years 1.8%, in adults 0.5% (maximum 2%)[26]. This relationship between the proportions of Hb-F and Hb-A remains practically unaltered whether birth is premature or at term.

The proportion of Hb-F can be determined on the basis of the alkali resistance. Hb-A can be separated in fixed blood smears by means of acid buffers, which have no effect on the Hb-F in the cells.

(For other physical and chemical data see under 'Blood', pages 557–611)

	Mean	95% range (extreme range in brackets)	*s*	Reference	Remarks
Lifetime (days)					
(a) Premature infants	–	(70–90)	–	27	Measurement: (a) and (b) by ASHBY's differential agglutination method, (c) and (d) with ^{15}N-glycine. The best method is that using ^{32}P-di-isopropyl fluorophosphate; for details of methods see the literature[29, 30]. A lifetime of 120 days corresponds to an erythrocyte turnover of 0.83% per day. Pathological changes in the lifetime are exclusively reductions[29].
(b) Adults	117	(110–135)	–	5	
(c) Men	120	–	–	28	
(d) Women	109	–	–	28	
Half-life (days)					
Premature infants	16	–	–	27	Measured by means of ^{51}Cr-tagged erythrocytes. In adults the half-life amounts to about a quarter of the mean lifetime.
Newborn	24	–	–	27	
Infants, 3 months	28	–	–	27	
Adults	29	(25–40)	–	29	
Osmotic resistance (concentration [%] of the NaCl solution used)					
(a) Cord blood					Measured on (a) 16, (b) 14 and (c) 18 subjects. For details of methods see the literature[5, 32]; the results are affected by the temperature, nature of the anticoagulant used, pH value of the haemolysing solution and bilirubin content of the blood. Complete haemolysis of the erythrocytes occurs in 0.33–0.30% NaCl solution (see diagram below). The more nearly spherical the erythrocytes, the lower the osmotic resistance[5, 32, 33]. Spherocytes are therefore more readily haemolysed, whereas the thinner erythrocytes are more resistant. Young mature erythrocytes are more resistant in hypotonic media than old erythrocytes[34]. Erythrocytes from venous blood have a lower resistance than those from arterial blood[35]. *Pathological changes*[5, 32]. Markedly reduced in congenital haemolytic jaundice and occasionally in haemolytic jaundice due to the presence of abnormal antibodies[36], increased in polycythaemia vera, thalassaemia major (resistance increased up to a NaCl concentration of 0.03%) and in sickle-cell and hypochromic anaemias.
5% haemolysis	0.502	0.46–0.55	0.022	31	
50% haemolysis	0.422	0.38–0.46	0.021	31	
(b) Newborn, 2–5 days					
5% haemolysis	0.474	0.34–0.51	0.019	31	
50% haemolysis	0.395	0.36–0.43	0.016	31	
(c) Adults					
5% haemolysis	0.475	0.45–0.50	0.012	31	
50% haemolysis	0.424	0.40–0.44	0.010	31	
Metabolism (μmol per 10^{11} erythrocytes)					
O_2 uptake per hour	2.7	0–5.5	1.4	37	
CO_2 formation per hour	2.5	0.3–4.7	1.1	37	
Pyruvate formation per hour	1.9	1.1–2.7	0.4	37	
Lactate formation per hour	38.4	26.6–50.2	5.9	37	

Osmotic resistance of erythrocytes[35]

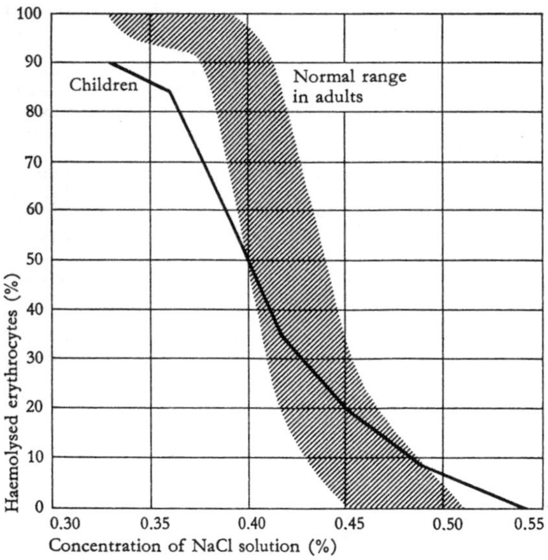

References

1 WESTERMAN et al., *J. Lab. clin. Med.*, **57**, 819 (1961).
2 v. BOROVICZÉNY, K.G., *Pädiat. Prax.*, **3**, 537 (1964); *Tägl. Prax.*, **6**, 477 (1965).
3 EYLAR et al., *J. biol. Chem.*, **237**, 1992 (1962).
4 CH'IN, C.-T., *J. Lab. clin. Med.*, **32**, 66 (1947).
5 WINTROBE, M.M., *Clinical Hematology*, 5th ed., Lea & Febiger, Philadelphia, 1961.
6 Symposium on Erythrocytometric Methods and Their Standardization, *Bibl. haemat. (Basel)*, No. 18, 15 (1964); Colloquium on Standardization of Blood Cell Counts and of Packed Cell Volume Determination, *Bibl. haemat. (Basel)*, No. 24, 2 (1966).
7 DEMARSH et al., *J. Amer. med. Ass.*, **116**, 2568 (1941).
8 BETKE, K., *Arch. Kinderheilk.*, **159**, 51 (1959).
9 HYTTEN and DUNCAN, *Nutr. Abstr. Rev.*, **26**, 855 (1956).
10 DITTRICH, H., *Langenbecks Arch. klin. Chir.*, **302**, 118 (1963); STRUMIA et al., *Amer. J. clin. Path.*, **24**, 1016 (1954).
11 KLEINE, N., *Bibl. haemat. (Basel)*, No. 18, 29 (1964).
12 KLEINE, N., *Bibl. haemat. (Basel)*, No. 24, 118 (1966).
13 Colloquium on Standardization of Blood Cell Counts and of Packed Cell Volume Determination, *Bibl. haemat. (Basel)*, No. 24, 83 (1966).
14 USHER et al., *Acta paediat. (Uppsala)*, **52**, 497 (1963); OH and LIND, *Acta paediat. (Uppsala)*, **55**, 38 (1966).
15 v. BOROVICZÉNY and SAFFAR, *Schweiz. med. Wschr.*, **92**, 1327 (1962).
16 BEHNKEN and v. BOROVICZÉNY, *Schweiz. med. Wschr.*, **93**, 1509 (1963).
17 Symposium on Erythrocytometric Methods and Their Standardization, *Bibl. haemat. (Basel)*, No. 18, 40 (1964).
18 v. BOROVICZÉNY, K.G., *Schweiz. med. Wschr.*, **93**, 1499 (1963).
19 STENGLE et al., *Bibl. haemat. (Basel)*, No. 21, 4 (1965).
20 Deutsche Gesellschaft für innere Medizin, *Acta haemat. (Basel)*, **27**, 369 (1962); Division of Medical Science of the National Academy of Sciences – National Research Council, *Blood*, **26**, 104 (1965); Symposium on Standardization, Documentation and Normal Values in Haematology, *Bibl. haemat. (Basel)*, No. 21, 213 (1965).
21 HAINLINE et al., *Stand. Meth. clin. Chem.*, **2**, 49 (1958); LEGOWSKI and v. BOROVICZÉNY, *Dtsch. med. Wschr.*, **87**, 1953 (1962); SCHWERD, W., *Der rote Blutfarbstoff und seine wichtigsten Derivate*, Schmidt-Römhild, Lübeck, 1962; Symposium on Standardization, Documentation and Normal Values in Haematology, *Bibl. haemat. (Basel)*, No. 18, 59 (1964); Symposium on Erythrocytometric Methods and Their Standardization, *Bibl. haemat. (Basel)*, No. 18, 86 (1964); Symposium on Standardization, Documentation and Normal Values in Haematology, *Bibl. haemat. (Basel)*, No. 21, 2, 25, 62 (1965).
22 JOSEPHS, H.W., *Acta paediat. (Uppsala)*, **48**, 403 (1959).
23 LANZKOWSKY, P., *Brit. med. J.*, **2**, 1777 (1960).
24 DE WIJN and RUSBACH, *Ned. T. Geneesk.*, **105**, 1028 (1961).
25 PAABY, P., *Acta obstet. gynec. scand.*, **37**, 69 (1958); MORGAN, E.H., *Lancet*, **1**, 9 (1961).
26 GOLDBERG and BOVE, *Stand. Meth. clin. Chem.*, **3**, 131 (1961); ZIPURSKY et al., *Pediatrics*, **30**, 262 (1962); BETKE, K., in WIESENER, H. (Ed.), *Einführung in die Entwicklungsphysiologie des Kindes*, Springer, Berlin, 1964, page 92.
27 VEST, M., *Bibl. paediat. (Basel)*, No. 69 (1959).
28 RICKENBERG, D., *J. biol. Chem.*, **179**, 463 (1949).
29 BERLIN et al., *Physiol. Rev.*, **39**, 577 (1959); BERLIN, N.I., *J. Amer. med. Ass.*, **188**, 375 (1964).
30 ROOT, W.S., *Meth. med. Res.*, **8**, 92 (1960).
31 CRAWFORD et al., *Blood*, **8**, 620 (1953).
32 HADEN, R.L., *Amer. J. med. Sci.*, **188**, 441 (1934).
33 DAMESHEK, W., *Blood*, Special Issue, No. 2, 43 (1948).
34 MARKS and JOHNSON, *J. clin. Invest.*, **37**, 1542 (1958).
35 WHITBY and HYNES, *J. Path. Bact.*, **40**, 219 (1935).
36 SPIESS and WOLF, *Klin. Wschr.*, **41**, 30 (1963).
37 WALLER, H.D., *Scand. J. Haemat.*, suppl. *Ser. haemat.*, No. **2**, 34 (1965).

Erythrocyte count, erythrocyte size and haemoglobin content at various ages*

Age	Reference	Erythrocyte count (millions/μl)		Haematocrit value (l/l)		Erythrocyte ∅ (μm)	Mean corpuscular volume (fl)		Haemoglobin content: g/l whole blood		Haemoglobin content: g/l erythrocytes		Haemoglobin content: pg per single erythrocyte	
		Mean	95% range (extreme range in brackets)	Mean	95% range (extreme range in brackets)	Mean	Mean	95% range (extreme range in brackets)	Mean	95% range (extreme range in brackets)	Mean	95% range (extreme range in brackets)	Mean	95% range (extreme range in brackets)
1 day	1	5.6	(4.7–7.0)	0.561	–	8.6	106	–	212	(177–265)	378	–	38	–
1 week	1	5.3	(4.5–6.4)	0.527	–	–	101	–	196	(162–255)	372	–	37	–
2 weeks	1	5.1	(4.3–6.0)	0.496	–		96	–	180	(145–242)	363	–	35	–
3 weeks	1	4.9	(4.1–6.0)	0.466	–	8.1	93	–	166	(132–230)	356	–	34	–
4 weeks	1	4.7	(3.9–5.9)	0.446	–		91	–	156	(120–218)	350	–	33	–
2 months	1	4.5	(3.8–5.8)	0.389	–		85	–	133	(108–180)	342	–	30	–
4 months	1	4.5	(3.8–5.3)	0.365	–	7.7	79	–	124	(102–150)	340	–	27	–
6 months	1	4.6	(3.9–5.3)	0.362	–		78	–	123	(100–150)	340	–	27	–
8 months	1	4.6	(4.0–5.4)	0.358	–		77	–	121	(98–150)	338	–	26	–
10 months	1	4.6	(4.0–5.5)	0.355	–	7.4	77	–	119	(84–149)	335	–	26	–
12 months	1	4.6	(4.0–5.5)	0.352	–		77	–	116	(90–146)	330	–	25	–
2 years	1	4.7	(3.8–5.4)	0.355	–	7.3	78	–	117	(92–155)	330	–	25	–
4 years	1	4.7	(3.8–5.4)	0.371	–		80	–	126	(96–155)	340	–	27	–
6 years	1	4.7	(3.8–5.4)	0.379	–		80	–	127	(100–155)	335	–	27	–
8 years	1	4.7	(3.8–5.4)	0.389	–	7.4	80	–	129	(103–155)	332	–	27	–
10 years	1	4.8	(3.8–5.4)	0.390	–		80	–	130	(107–155)	333	–	27	–
12 years	1	4.8	(3.8–5.4)	0.396	–		81	–	134	(110–165)	338	–	28	–
Males, 14 years and over	1	5.4	4.6–6.2	0.47	0.40–0.54	7.5	87	–	158	140–180	335	–	29	–
Females, 14 years and over	1	4.8	4.2–5.4	0.42	0.37–0.47	7.5	87	–	139	115–160	335	–	29	–
2 years	2	–	–	0.368	0.332–0.404	–	79	72–86	123	122–124	–	–	26.3	23.5–29.1
3 years	2	–	–	0.376	0.340–0.412	–	80	73–87	125	124–126	–	–	27.2	24.4–30.0
4–5 years	2	–	–	0.377	0.341–0.413	–	81	74–88	128	127–129	–	–	27.5	24.7–30.3
6–8 years	2	–	–	0.389	0.353–0.425	–	83	76–90	134	133–135	–	–	28.8	26.0–31.6
9–11 years	2	–	–	0.401	0.365–0.437	–	84	77–91	140	139–141	–	–	29.4	26.6–32.2
Men	3	5.2	4.4–6.0	0.46	0.41–0.51	–	88	80–96	150	130–170	330	310–350	29	26–32
Men and women	4	–	–	0.481	0.336–0.576	–	–	–	159	134–173	328	299–357	–	–
Males, 10–20 years	5	4.8	(3.9–5.9)	0.460	(0.37–0.54)	–	97	(82–107)	146	(121–172)	319	(233–368)	30.7	(28–35)
Men, 20–40 years	5	5.1	(4.1–6.0)	0.479	(0.41–0.55)	–	96	(83–110)	158	(133–182)	331	(291–361)	31.4	(27–38)
Men, over 40 years	5	5.0	(4.2–5.6)	0.463	(0.41–0.52)	–	93	(87–103)	156	(141–170)	336	(308–358)	31.2	(29–36)
Females, 10–20 years	5	4.5	(3.9–5.0)	0.436	(0.38–0.50)	–	98	(77–116)	139	(120–164)	320	(283–368)	31.1	(26–36)
Women, 20–40 years	5	4.5	(3.9–5.5)	0.429	(0.35–0.49)	–	95	(88–109)	141	(118–175)	329	(296–356)	31.2	(28–34)
Women, over 40 years	5	4.4	(4.0–5.0)	0.443	(0.40–0.52)	–	100	(92–117)	139	(127–163)	319	(270–360)	31.9	(30–35)
Men at sea level	6	5.1	(4.3–5.9)	0.468	–	7.5	91	–	160	(140–183)	341	–	31	–
Men at 4540 m	6	6.2	(5.0–7.6)	0.599	–	7.7	97.5	–	208	(181–254)	347	–	34	–

* When not otherwise stated, the values are for persons at an altitude between sea level and 200 m. The values from DITTMER[1] and WINTROBE[1] have been summarized from earlier publications in the USA; the values of BETKE et al.[2] and DITTRICH[4] derive from studies made in Germany, those of GREENDYKE et al.[3] from studies in the USA, those of PLUM[5] from studies in Denmark (in references[2–5] haemoglobin was determined by the haemiglobin cyanide method); the values of HURTADO et al.[6] are from studies in the Andes (at sea level [Lima] and at 4540 m [Morococha]). In recent years other normal values have been published in Switzerland[7] (for age groups between 19 and 93 years), in USA[8] (for age groups between 12 and 17 years), in Japan[9] (for adults) and in Turkey[10] (for adults). For erythrocyte data during pregnancy see HOLLY[11] and page 691.

References

1 DITTMER, D. S. (Ed.), *Blood and Other Body Fluids*, Federation of American Societies for Experimental Biology, Washington, 1961, page 109; WINTROBE, M. M., *Clinical Hematology*, 6th ed., Lea & Febiger, Philadelphia, 1967, page 85.
2 BETKE et al., *Dtsch.med.Wschr.*, **89**, 1197 (1964); *Germ.med.Mth.*, **9**, 313 (1964).
3 GREENDYKE et al., *Amer.J.clin.Path.*, **37**, 429 (1962).
4 DITTRICH, H., *Med.Klin.*, **58**, 1882 (1963).
5 PLUM, C. M., *Bibl.haemat.(Basel)*, No. 21, 165 (1965).
6 HURTADO et al., *Arch.intern.Med.*, **75**, 284 (1945).
7 UNDRITZ and BRAGATSCH, *Schweiz.med.Wschr.*, **92**, 388 (1962).
8 KASPER and WALLERSTEIN, *Amer.J.clin.Nutr.*, **18**, 286 (1966).
9 HOSHINO, T., *Bibl.haemat.(Basel)*, No. 21, 135 (1965); TAKIKAWA et al., *Bibl.haemat.(Basel)*, No. 21, 142 (1965); KAWAKITA, Y., *Bibl.haemat.(Basel)*, No. 21, 151 (1965).
10 REIMANN, F., *Bibl.haemat.(Basel)*, No. 21, 132 (1965).
11 HOLLY, R. G., *Obstet.and Gynec.*, **2**, 119 (1953).

Leucocytes

(For other physical and chemical data see under 'Blood', pages 557–611; for references see page 620)

	Mean	95% range	s	Reference	Remarks
Leucocyte count (white blood count, WBC)	...	...	...	...	See text below and table opposite.
Leucocytocrit (ml/l) (leucocyte packing volume)	~2.5	...	...	...	Proportion of volume of the whole blood occupied by the leucocytes; calculated from the leucocyte count and mean leucocyte volume.
Diameter	...	...	...	...	See table below
Volume	...	...	...	...	
Half-life (hours)					
Granulocytes	6.6	3.8–9.4	1.4	3	Measured on 45 men by the ^{32}P-di-isopropyl fluorophosphate (DFP) method.
Osmotic resistance	...	...	...	...	After 6 minutes' exposure to 0.2% NaCl solution 55–75% of the leucocytes remain unchanged[4]; mononuclear cells are less resistant than granulocytes. The resistance increases with age. It is increased in inflammatory leucocytosis as a result of the increased number of young cells and in most forms of myelosis, decreased in leucopenia and pancytopenia.
Metabolism (mmol/10^{11} leucocytes)					
O_2 uptake per hour	4.0	–	–	5	Values depend on the composition of the incubation medium.
Glucose consumption per hour	14.0	–	–	5	
Lactate formation per hour	30.1	–	–	5	

	Diameter[1] (μm)	Volume[2] (μm³ [≡ fl])
Neutrophils	10–15	450
Eosinophils	10–15	450
Basophils	10–15	450
Lymphocytes	7–18	230
Monocytes	12–20	470
Neutrophil myelocytes	12–18	–

Leucocyte count (see also the table opposite)

Measurement

Visual counting in a counting chamber or automatically using a blood-cell counting apparatus. In respect of the range of error and counting differences the remarks on pages 613–614 on erythrocyte counting also apply. For discussion of methods and bibliography see the literature[7].

Physiological characteristics

Like the erythrocyte count the leucocyte count in the newborn rises by one-fifth to one-quarter during the first hours of life (see diagram). As with the erythrocytes, there is a difference between the leucocyte count in the capillary and venous blood in the period following birth, the count in the venous blood being 1000–1500 lower. During the first days of life there is marked neutrophilia and to a lesser extent monocytosis; the period from the 2nd week up to the 4th year is accompanied by lymphocytosis.

Slight neutrophilia occurs towards the end of pregnancy, during physical work, emotional excitement and convulsions, and after taking adrenaline.

There is no sex difference in the leucocyte count[8]. Daily rhythms as well as seasonal and climatic fluctuations have been reported.

Pathological characteristics

Leucocytosis usually consists of an increase in the number of neutrophils. It occurs in many infectious diseases, in all suppurative conditions due to cocci, in poisoning by various metals and drugs, in diabetic ketosis, in many cases of malignant tumours, in gastric and duodenal ulcers, in gout and in coronary thrombosis. Excessive leucocytosis with a very marked shift to the left in the granulocytes occurs in tuberculous disease with typhoid-like symptoms. Myeloid leukaemia may be variously marked by the presence of myeloblasts, promyelocytes or monocytes, or by a mixture of these cells. Leucocytosis consisting of an increase in the lymphocytes in children is seen mainly in whooping cough and acute infectious lymphocytosis. Leucocytosis due to the presence of lymphoid monocytes is characteristic of infectious mononucleosis.

Leucopenia due to agranulocytosis or granulocytopenia occurs in salmonellosis, in typhoid (more so than in paratyphoid), very occasionally in septicaemia and miliary tuberculosis, in anaphylactic shock and in severe bone-marrow disturbances due for instance to radiation. Leucopenia consisting of lymphocytopenia or even alymphocytosis is characteristic of many antibody-deficiency syndromes[9].

Leucocyte count per microlitre from birth until 15 years[6]

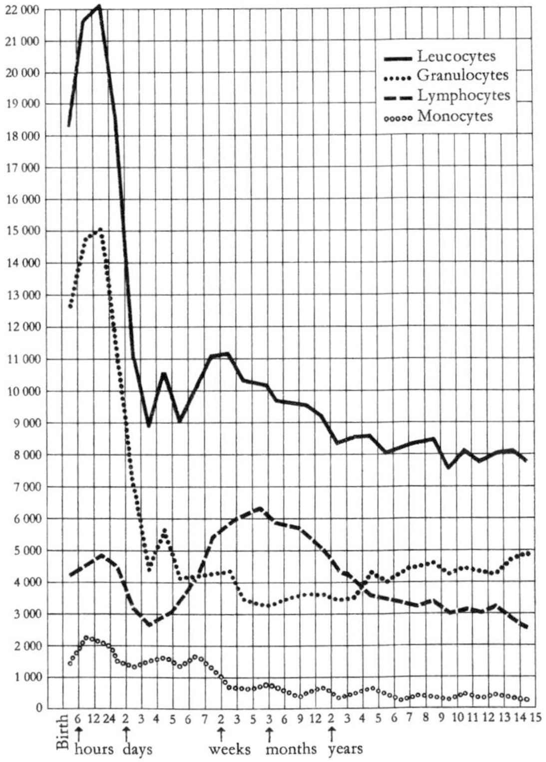

(For other physical and chemical data see under 'Blood', pages 557–611)

Total leucocyte count and distribution at various ages

Age		Reference	Total leucocytes		Neutrophil granulocytes: Total		Neutrophil granulocytes: Stab cells	Neutrophil granulocytes: Segmented cells	Eosinophil granulocytes		Basophil granulocytes		Lymphocytes		Monocytes		Neutrophil myelocytes*	
			Mean	95% range (extreme range in brackets)	Mean	95% range (extreme range in brackets)	Mean	Mean	Mean	95% range (extreme range in brackets)	Mean	95% range (extreme range in brackets)	Mean	95% range (extreme range in brackets)	Mean	95% range (extreme range in brackets)	Mean	95% range (extreme range in brackets)
Birth	number/μl	1,2	18100	(9000–30000)	11000	(6000–26000)	1650	9400	400	(20–850)	100	(0–640)	5500	(2000–11000)	1050	(400–3100)	–	
	per cent . .				61		9.1	52	2.2		0.6		31		5.8			
12 hours	number/μl	1,2	22800	(13000–38000)	15500	(6000–28000)	2330	13200	450	(20–950)	100	(0–500)	5500	(2000–11000)	1200	(400–3600)	–	0–1908
	per cent . .				68		10.2	58	2.0		0.4		24		5.3			0–10
24 hours	number/μl	1,2	18900	(9400–34000)	11500	(5000–21000)	1750	9800	450	(50–1000)	100	(0–300)	5800	(2000–11500)	1100	(200–3100)	–	
	per cent . .				61		9.2	52	2.4		0.5		31		5.8			
1 week	number/μl	1,2	12200	(5000–21000)	5500	(1500–10000)	830	4700	500	(70–1100)	50	(0–250)	5000	(2000–17000)	1100	(300–2700)	–	0–437
	per cent . .				45		6.8	39	4.1		0.4		41		9.1			0–3
2 weeks	number/μl	1,2	11400	(5000–20000)	4500	(1000–9500)	630	3900	350	(70–1000)	50	(0–230)	5500	(2000–17000)	1000	(200–2400)	–	0–102
	per cent . .				40		5.5	34	3.1		0.4		48		8.8			0–1
4 weeks	number/μl	1	10800	(5000–19500)	3800	(1000–9000)	490	3300	300	(70–900)	50	(0–200)	6000	(2500–16500)	700	(150–2000)	–	–
	per cent . .				35		4.5	30	2.8		0.5		56		6.5			
2 months	number/μl	1	11000	(5500–18000)	3800	(1000–9000)	490	3300	300	(70–850)	50	(0–200)	6300	(3000–16000)	650	(130–1800)	–	–
	per cent . .				34		4.4	30	2.7		0.5		57		5.9			
4 months	number/μl	1	11500	(6000–17500)	3800	(1000–9000)	450	3300	300	(70–800)	50	(0–200)	6800	(3500–14500)	600	(100–1500)	–	–
	per cent . .				33		3.9	29	2.6		0.4		59		5.2			
6 months	number/μl	1	11900	(6000–17500)	3800	(1000–8500)	450	3300	300	(70–750)	50	(0–200)	7300	(4000–13500)	580	(100–1300)	–	–
	per cent . .				32		3.8	28	2.5		0.4		61		4.8			
8 months	number/μl	1	12200	(6000–17500)	3700	(1000–8500)	410	3300	300	(70–700)	50	(0–200)	7600	(4500–12500)	580	(80–1200)	–	–
	per cent . .				30		3.3	27	2.5		0.4		62		4.7			
10 months	number/μl	1	12000	(6000–17500)	3600	(1000–8500)	400	3200	300	(60–700)	50	(0–200)	7500	(4500–11500)	550	(50–1200)	–	–
	per cent . .				30		3.3	27	2.5		0.4		63		4.6			
12 months	number/μl	1	11400	(6000–17500)	3500	(1500–8500)	350	3200	300	(50–700)	50	(0–200)	7000	(4000–10500)	550	(50–1100)	–	–
	per cent . .				31		3.1	28	2.6		0.4		61		4.8			
2 years	number/μl	1	10600	(6000–17000)	3500	(1500–8500)	320	3200	280	(40–650)	50	(0–200)	6300	(3000–9500)	530	(50–1000)	–	–
	per cent . .				33		3.0	30	2.6		0.5		59		5.0			
4 years	number/μl	1	9100	(5500–15500)	3800	(1500–8500)	270	3500	250	(20–650)	50	(0–200)	4500	(2000–8000)	450	(0–800)	–	–
	per cent . .				42		3.0	39	2.8		0.6		50		5.0			
6 years	number/μl	1	8500	(5000–14500)	4300	(1500–8000)	250	4000	230	(0–650)	50	(0–200)	3500	(1500–7000)	400	(0–800)	–	–
	per cent . .				51		3.0	48	2.7		0.6		42		4.7			
8 years	number/μl	1	8300	(4500–13500)	4400	(1500–8000)	250	4100	200	(0–600)	50	(0–200)	3300	(1500–6800)	350	(0–800)	–	–
	per cent . .				53		3.0	50	2.4		0.6		39		4.2			
10 years	number/μl	1	8100	(4500–13500)	4400	(1800–8000)	240	4200	200	(0–600)	40	(0–200)	3100	(1500–6500)	350	(0–800)	–	–
	per cent . .				54		3.0	51	2.4		0.5		38		4.3			
12 years	number/μl	1	8000	(4500–13500)	4400	(1800–8000)	240	4200	200	(0–550)	40	(0–200)	3000	(1200–6000)	350	(0–800)	–	–
	per cent . .				55		3.0	52	2.5		0.5		38		4.4			
14 years	number/μl	1	7900	(4500–13000)	4400	(1800–8000)	240	4200	200	(0–500)	40	(0–200)	2900	(1200–5800)	380	(0–800)	–	–
	per cent . .				56		3.0	53	2.5		0.5		37		4.7			
16 years	number/μl	1	7800	(4500–13000)	4400	(1800–8000)	230	4200	200	(0–500)	40	(0–200)	2800	(1200–5200)	400	(0–800)	–	–
	per cent . .				57		3.0	54	2.6		0.5		35		5.1			
18 years	number/μl	1	7700	(4500–12500)	4400	(1800–7700)	230	4200	200	(0–450)	40	(0–200)	2700	(1000–5000)	400	(0–800)	–	–
	per cent . .				57		3.0	54	2.6		0.5		35		5.2			
20 years	number/μl	1	7500	(4500–11500)	4400	(1800–7700)	230	4200	200	(0–450)	40	(0–200)	2500	(1000–4800)	380	(0–800)	–	–
	per cent . .				59		3.0	56	2.7		0.5		33		5.0			
21 years	number/μl	1	7400	(4500–11000)	4400	(1800–7700)	220	4200	200	(0–450)	40	(0–200)	2500	(1000–4800)	300	(0–800)	–	–
	per cent . .				59		3.0	56	2.7		0.5		34		4.0			
Adults	number/μl	3	7000	2800–11200	4150	712–7588	–	–	165	0–397	44	0–112	2185	1029–3341	456	66–846	0	0
	per cent . .				59				2.4		0.6		31		6.5			

* These cells are also included in the stab neutrophils.

[1] Dittmer, D. S. (Ed.), *Blood and Other Body Fluids*, Federation of American Societies for Experimental Biology, Washington, 1961, page 125.

[2] Forkner, C. E., *Bull. Johns Hopk. Hosp.*, **45**, 75 (1929).

[3] Graham et al., *Blood*, **10**, 467 (1955).

(For other physical and chemical data see under 'Blood', pages 557–611)

Basophil count[10]

Physiological and pathological characteristics

1. Increased greatly in chronic myeloid leukaemia and polycythaemia, significantly in diabetes and myxoedema.
2. Decreased greatly in hyperthyroidism, after administration of glucocorticoids and during pregnancy.

Eosinophil count[11]

Physiological characteristics

1. Subject to fluctuations at intervals of a few minutes with a range exceeding the error inherent in the method of measurement.
2. Subject to marked daily periodicity with low values in the late afternoon and early morning (down to about 20% of the mean 24-hour value) and a maximum at midnight (up to about 30% of the same mean value). This periodicity is mainly seen in *fasting* subjects.
3. Subject to seasonal fluctuations (increase in the early part of the year and autumn).
4. Subject to change during the course of the menstrual cycle (menstrual peak, low point following ovulation).

Pathological characteristics

1. Eosinophilia occurs in parasitic infestations, in allergic reactions, in functional disturbances of the spleen, and in diseases of the blood-forming organs and central nervous system.
2. Eosinopenia arises from increased migration into the tissues with inadequate replacement, in suppression or aplasia of myelopoiesis due to increased corticosteroid secretion or corticosteroid administration.
3. Aneosinophilia occurs during the peak period of typhoid fever.

Schilling's haemogram

Normal relationship of immature neutrophils (myelocytes + young neutrophils + stab neutrophils) to mature (segmented) neutrophils = $^1/_{13}$ or less	Basophils	Eosinophils	Myelocytes	Neutrophils			Lymphocytes	Monocytes
				Young cells	Stab cells	Segmented cells		
Normal range (%)	0.5–1.5	2–4	0	0–1	3–5	51–67	20–30	5–10

In order to simplify the recording of results of differential counts SCHILLING's haemogram can be written: '–,–/–,–,–,–/–,–', where the dashes represent the percentage values in the order given in the above table of the haemogram. This enables the differential blood picture to be rapidly evaluated.

References

[1] WINTROBE, M.M., *Clinical Hematology*, 6th ed., Lea & Febiger, Philadelphia, 1967, page 224.
[2] TIVEY et al., *Blood*, **6**, 1013 (1951).
[3] MAUER et al., *J. clin. Invest.*, **39**, 1481 (1960).
[4] BRÜSCHKE and HERRMANN, *Dtsch. Gesundh.-Wes.*, **15**, 1719 (1960); BRÜSCHKE, G., *Schweiz. med. Wschr.*, **91**, 1150 (1961).
[5] VALENTINE, W.N., *Progr. Hemat.*, **1**, 293 (1956).
[6] KATO, K., *J. Pediat.*, **7**, 7 (1935).
[7] Colloquium on Standardization of Blood Cell Counts and of Packed Cell Volume Determination, *Bibl. haemat. (Basel)*, No. 24, 2 (1966).
[8] UNDRITZ and BRAGATSCH, *Schweiz. med. Wschr.*, **92**, 388 (1962).
[9] GASSER, C., *Pädiatr. Fortbildungskurse (Basel)*, No. 11–12, 16 (1964).
[10] BRAUNSTEINER, H., in BRAUNSTEINER, H. (Ed.), *The Physiology and Pathology of Leucocytes*, Grune & Stratton, New York, 1962.
[11] GROSS, R., in BRAUNSTEINER, H. (Ed.), *The Physiology and Pathology of Leucocytes*, Grune & Stratton, New York, 1962.

Thrombocytes (Platelets)

(For other physical and chemical data see under 'Blood', pages 557–579)

	Mean	95% range (extreme range in brackets)	s	Reference	Remarks
Thrombocyte count (in thousands per μl)					
Cord blood	227	149–305	39	1	Determined by the direct method. There are no marked differences as far as sex or age are concerned[3]. The thrombocyte count is rather low prior to and at the start of menstruation and rises after cessation of menstruation[4]. Differences in the count due to constitution, physical exercise, altitude and ambient temperature have been reported. The thrombocyte count is *increased* after injury and in chronic myeloid leukaemia, *decreased* in thrombopenic purpura.
Children					
1 week (cutaneous blood)	233	143–323	45	1	
1 month (cutaneous blood)	277	175–379	51	1	
3 months (cutaneous blood)	348	220–476	64	1	
12 months (cutaneous blood)	339	219–459	60	1	
Adults					
cutaneous blood	250	133–367	58.5	2	
venous blood	310	286–334	11.9	2	
arterial blood	350	322–378	13.9	2	
Thrombocytocrit value (thrombocyte packing volume) (ml/l)	4.8	(3.3–8.3)	–	5	Proportion of the peripheral venous blood volume occupied by the thrombocytes.
Diameter (μm)	–	(2–4)	–	2, 6	Normally the thrombocytes are spherical or egg-shaped. They undergo change of shape even after brief contact with a wettable surface[5,7].
Volume (fl ≡ μm³)	–	(10–12)	–	2	Dependent on temperature and on concentration of anticoagulants[8]. *Increased* in thrombopenic purpura and a few other diseases[5].
	16.2	(10.3–19.7)	–	5	
	5.8	–	–	8	
Lifetime (days)	–	(8–14)	–	9	Measured by the ^{32}P-di-isopropyl fluorophosphate (DFP) method. Reduced in polycythaemia vera accompanied by thrombopenia[10].
Half-life (days)	–	(5–6)	–	11	Measured by means of ^{14}C-serotonin.
Osmotic resistance	...	...	...	...	Morphological changes in the thrombocytes occur with NaCl concentrations of 0.44% and below; at a concentration of 0.1% almost all the thrombocytes are in the form of ghosts[12]. The osmotic resistance is lowered in idiopathic thrombocytopenia[12], increased in thrombopathic conditions[12] and altered also in some infectious diseases[13].

Thrombocytes (Platelets)

(For other physical and chemical data see under 'Blood', pages 557–579)

	Mean	95% range	s	Reference	Remarks
Metabolism (μmol per 10^{11} thrombocytes)					
O_2 uptake per hour.........	86.3	73.5–99.1	6.4	14	Values depend on the composition of the incubation medium.
CO_2 formation per hour	95.7	74.9–117	10.4	14	
Pyruvate formation per hour	3.9	3.1–4.7	0.4	14	
Lactate formation per hour ..	76.4	52.6–100	11.9	14	

Thrombocyte count during menstruation[15]

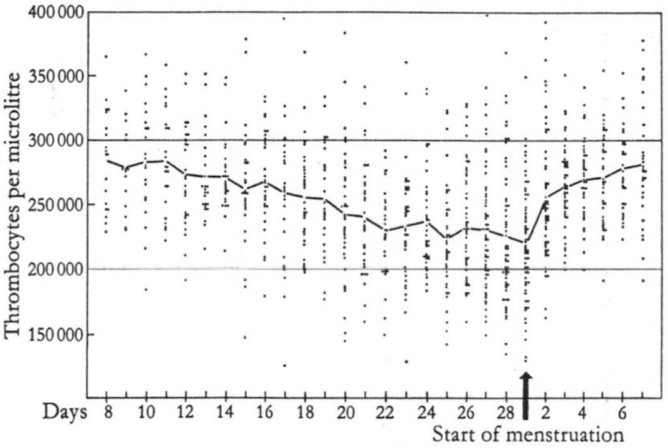

References

1 MERRITT and DAVIDSON, *Amer. J. Dis. Child.*, **46**, 990 (1933).
2 TOCANTINS, L. M., *Medicine (Baltimore)*, **17**, 155 (1938).
3 UNDRITZ and BRAGATSCH, *Schweiz. med. Wschr.*, **92**, 388 (1962).
4 POHLE, F. J., *Amer. J. med. Sci.*, **197**, 40 (1939).
5 REBUCK et al., in JOHNSON et al. (Eds.), *Blood Platelets*, Henry Ford Hospital International Symposium, Little, Brown, Boston, 1961, page 533.
6 OLEF, I., *J. Lab. clin. Med.*, **23**, 166 (1937).
7 BRAUNSTEINER, H., in JOHNSON et al. (Eds.), *Blood Platelets*, Henry Ford Hospital International Symposium, Little, Brown, Boston, 1961, page 617.
8 BULL and ZUCKER, *Proc. Soc. exp. Biol. (N.Y.)*, **120**, 296 (1965).
9 ZUCKER et al., *J. Lab. clin. Med.*, **58**, 405 (1961).
10 ODELL and KNISELEY, *Progr. Hemat.*, **3**, 203 (1962).
11 HEYSSEL, R. M., *J. clin. Invest.*, **40**, 2134 (1961).
12 NELKEN et al., *J. Lab. clin. Med.*, **56**, 120 (1960).
13 ROGNER, G., *Klin. Wschr.*, **41**, 290 (1963).
14 WALLER et al., *Thrombos. Diathes. haemorrh. (Stuttg.)*, **3**, 520 (1959).
15 POHLE, F. J., *Amer. J. med. Sci.*, **197**, 40 (1939).

Bone marrow

Nowhere in haematology are such conflicting data to be found as among the percentages of the various types of cell present in human bone marrow. This is a result of differences in counting techniques. The greater the amount of marrow aspirated, the greater the volume of blood entering the syringe. The proportions of erythroblasts and granuloblasts fall while those of the stab and segmented cells and lymphocytes rise. The last three types of cell are really constituents of the marrow blood and their numbers can therefore be enriched at any time from the peripheral blood. On values in adults see particularly the monograph by ROHR[1].

Myelogram at various ages[2]

Type of cell	24 hours		End of newborn period		Infancy		Early childhood		School age		Adults	
	Range (%)	Mean (%)	Range (%)	Mean (%)	Range (%)	Mean (%)	Range (%)	Mean (%)	Range (%)	Mean (%)	Range (%)	Mean (%)
Erythroblasts												
basophil.........	0.5–10.0	5.0	0.0– 3.0	1.0	0.5– 5.0	2.5	1.0– 6.0	2.5	1.0– 8.0	3.0	0.5– 7.5	3.5
polychromatic....	7.5–30.0	15.0	0.0–10.0	3.0	5.0–20.0	10.0	3.0–10.0	5.0	3.0–10.0	6.0	2.0–15.0	7.0
oxyphil.........	7.5–30.0	15.0	2.0–20.0	6.0	5.0–12.5	7.5	5.0–20.0	10.0	5.0–20.0	11.0	5.0–25.0	12.0
Total	...	35.0	...	10.0	...	20.0	...	17.5	...	20.0	...	22.5
Granulopoiesis												
Myeloblasts......	0.2– 5.0	2.5	0.2– 5.0	2.0	0.2– 5.0	1.5	0.2– 5.0	1.0	0.2– 5.0	1.0	0.5– 5.0	1.0
Promyelocytes ...	0.2– 5.0	3.0	0.5– 7.5	3.5	0.5–10.0	2.5	0.5– 7.5	2.5	0.5–10.0	3.0	0 – 7.5	3.0
Myelocytes	2.0–20.0	6.0	5.0–20.0	10.0	5.0–15.0	10.0	5.0–20.0	12.5	5.0–25.0	15.0	5.0–25.0	15.0
Metamyelocytes ..	5.0–25.0	12.5	5.0–25.0	12.5	5.0–15.0	10.0	5.0–20.0	12.5	5.0–25.0	15.0	5.0–20.0	15.0
Stab cells	5.0–25.0	12.5	10.0–25.0	15.0	5.0–15.0	8.0	5.0–15.0	10.0	5.0–20.0	12.5	5.0–25.0	15.0
Segmented cells ..	10.0–30.0	15.0	10.0–25.0	15.0	1.0–15.0	7.0	1.0–15.0	8.5	1.0–15.0	8.0	0.5–15.0	7.0
Eosinophils......	0.0– 5.0	1.0	0.5– 7.5	2.5	1.0– 7.5	4.0	1.5– 7.5	5.0	1.0– 7.0	4.0	1.5– 7.5	4.0
Basophils........	0.0– 0.5	0.05	0.0– 1.0	0.05	0 – 1.0	<0.05	0 – 0.5	<0.1	0 – 1.0	<0.2	0 – 1.0	<0.5
Total	...	52.5	...	60.0	...	43.0	...	52.0	...	58.5	...	60.5
Monocytes*	3.0–15.0	7.5	2.0–10.0	5.0	0.5– 5.0	2.0	1.0– 5.0	3.0	0.5– 4.0	1.5	0.5– 3.0	2.0
Lymphocytes**	...	...	...	...	...	...	...	...	...	...	2.5–15.0	7.5
Reticular cells**	0.0–10.0	5.0	10.0–40.0	25.0	15.0–50.0	35.0	15.0–40.0	27.5	10.0–35.0	20.0	1.5–20.0	6.5
Plasmacytes........	0.0– 1.0	0.1	0.0– 1.5	0.1	0 – 2.0	<0.5	0 – 2.5	<0.5	0.2– 2.5	0.5	0.5– 3.0	1.0
Megakaryocytes	...	0.1	...	0.1	...	<0.5	...	<0.5	...	<0.5	...	<0.5

* The high value for monocytes in the marrow of the newborn is probably synchronous with the peripheral monocytosis of the first weeks of life.

** Here no distinction is made between lymphoid reticulum and lymphocytes since the data in the literature show large discrepancies.

References

1 ROHR, K., *Das menschliche Knochenmark*, 3rd ed., Thieme, Stuttgart, 1960.
2 OPITZ and WEICKER, in BROCK, J. (Ed.), *Biologische Daten für den Kinderarzt*, 2nd ed., vol. 1, Springer, Berlin, 1954, page 160.

Blood Coagulation*

(For references see page 625)

Physiology

The processes involved in the coagulation of blood are still to some extent obscure, so that the diagrammatic representation shown here (Fig. 1) should not be regarded as conclusive.

Normally, the blood begins to coagulate when it escapes as a result of injury to a vessel and comes into contact with a foreign, wettable surface, for instance damaged tissue. In the presence of calcium ions, contact of the blood with such a surface results in the activation of Factor XII, which in turn initiates the viscous metamorphosis of the thrombocytes in a manner as yet unknown. The thrombocytes become labile, and as a consequence agglutinate to the foreign surface, to one another and to other cells. The result is the formation of a platelet thrombus and the release of a number of active substances, including a lipoid factor. At the same time, and also in the presence of calcium ions, the activated Factor XII causes the activation in succession of Factors XI, IX, VIII and X in a chain reaction. The activated Factor X, together with the lipoid factor of the thrombocytes, forms active plasma thromboplastin (the so-called intrinsic system).

Factor X is likewise activated in the presence of calcium ions by the tissue fluid in conjunction with Factor VII. The Factor X activated by this system (the so-called extrinsic system) brings about the formation of active tissue thromboplastin. The formation of both these active thromboplastins is accelerated by Factor V.

In the first phase of coagulation the two active thromboplastins – plasma thromboplastin and tissue thromboplastin – act on the prothrombin and convert it into thrombin.

Heparin inhibits the activity of both the thromboplastins and thrombin. At this stage other antithrombins likewise function as antagonists in the coagulation process.

In the second stage of coagulation thrombin acts on the fibrinogen, which is thereby converted into monomeric, soluble fibrin. The latter now polymerizes and is converted under the action of Factor XIII and calcium ions into stable fibrin.

In the third phase the fibrin clot undergoes retraction under the action of the agglutinated thrombocytes.

The retracted clot may eventually be broken down by plasmin to yield soluble products. Plasmin is a rather nonspecific proteolytic enzyme; under pathological conditions it is also capable of breaking down fibrinogen and other protein components of the coagulation system. Plasmin is formed from plasminogen as a result of a complicated series of activation processes, commencing with the formation of an activator by the action of lysokinases – present in both blood and tissues – on a proactivator of the blood. This activator converts plasminogen into plasmin. The latter can also arise from plasminogen directly via a tissue activator. Lysokinases are inhibited by antilysokinases, plasmin activity by antiplasmin.

Physiological variations

The coagulation process does not function fully in all newborn children. On the average, the concentrations of fibrinogen and Factors II, VII, IX and X are low, especially during the first few days of life; there are considerable individual variations, however, and values above normal may even be encountered[7].

The number and functional state of the thrombocytes are both within the normal range in newborn infants, both full-term and premature (see also page 620).

Ageing as such does not appear to involve any alteration in the coagulation process. Pathological changes are probably in most cases due to changes in either the coagulation process or the vessels. Impairment of the coagulation system due to certain foodstuffs appears to be commoner in old age; an example is the increased tendency to coagulation after a meal rich in fats[2].

During pregnancy the concentrations of Factors VII and X in the blood are often increased. The occasional rise in the blood levels of Factor IX and fibrinogen, combined with an enhanced tendency of the thrombocytes to agglutinate in the presence of an increased blood phospholipid concentration, may lead to thrombo-embolic complications during pregnancy[3].

Pathology

The pathology of blood coagulation comprises three main types of disease: thrombosis with the concomitant danger of embolism, the haemorrhagic diatheses, and cardiac infarction.

* This chapter (pages 622–625) has been compiled by C. MONTIGEL, Research Laboratories of J. R. Geigy S.A., Basle (Switzerland).

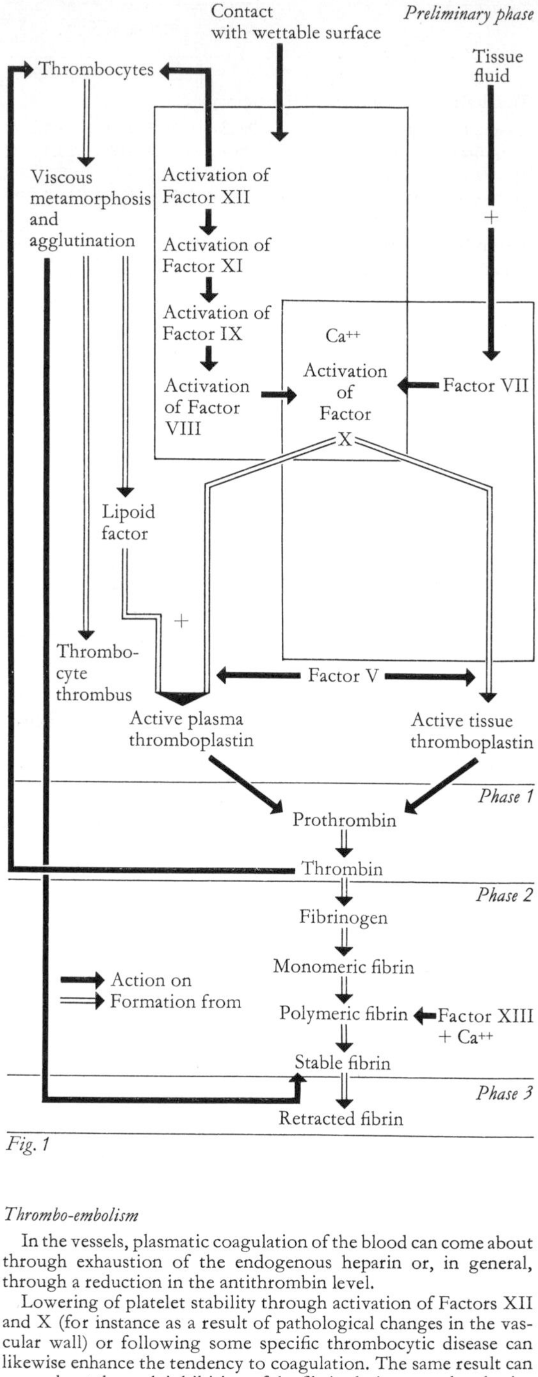

Fig. 1

Thrombo-embolism

In the vessels, plasmatic coagulation of the blood can come about through exhaustion of the endogenous heparin or, in general, through a reduction in the antithrombin level.

Lowering of platelet stability through activation of Factors XII and X (for instance as a result of pathological changes in the vascular wall) or following some specific thrombocytic disease can likewise enhance the tendency to coagulation. The same result can come about through inhibition of the fibrinolytic system by physiological inhibitors, drugs or disease. Stasis due to a diminished rate of blood flow also favours thrombosis.

The sites where thromboses are most likely to occur are shown in order of frequency in Figure 2.

Theoretically feasible methods of treatment are first a reduction in the plasmatic coagulation potential by means of oral anticoagulants, secondly inhibition of the activity of the thromboplastins and thrombin by means of heparin, thirdly stabilization of the thrombocytes, i.e., inhibition of the contact activation process (inhibition of the activity of Factor XII), and lastly an increase in fibrinolytic activity.

(For references see page 625)

Haemorrhagic diatheses

An increased tendency to bleeding may be due to an abnormal increase in fibrinolytic activity (caused by physiological activators, disease or drugs), to enhanced stability of the thrombocytes, to thrombocytopenia or hereditary thrombo-asthenia, and finally to inhibition of the plasmatic coagulation process as a result of an increase in endogenous heparin, a rise in the antithrombin titre, a deficiency of certain factors, or drug action.

1 Deep and superficial vessels of the lower limbs
2 Coronary vessels
3 Pelvic vessels
4 Mesenteric vessels
5 Endocardium and heart valves
6 Cerebral veins and arteries, large cervical vessels
7 Deep vessels of the arm
8 Superficial vessels of the arm
9 Subclavian and pulmonary vessels

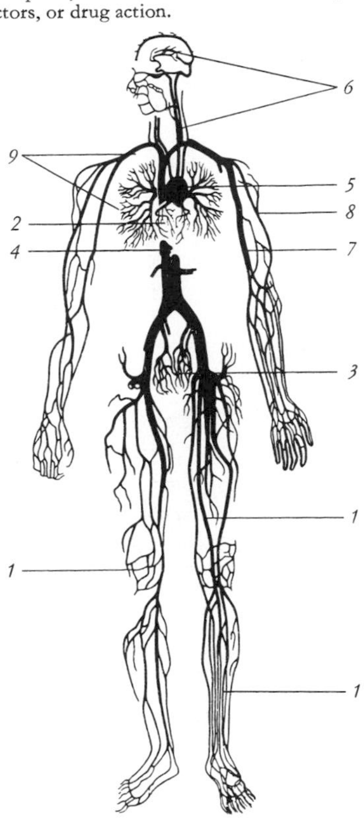

Fig. 2

Increased fibrinolytic activity can be controlled by administering fibrinolysis inhibitors such as ε-aminocaproic acid. Pathologically high thrombocyte stability, like thrombocytopenia and thrombo-asthenia, is not susceptible to medication. Inhibition of the plasmatic coagulation system by an excess of endogenous heparin or heparin-like inhibitors can be overcome by administering protamine sulphate. Administration of a single coagulation factor or of the whole plasmatic coagulation system when one or more of the plasmatic factors is missing from the blood is effective only for a limited time. If the coagulability of the blood has been too strongly impaired by the use of oral anticoagulants the condition can be corrected by administering vitamin K_1 (see also page 468).

Figure 3 shows what disturbances in the plasmatic, thrombocytic and fibrinolytic coagulation systems increase the likelihood of either bleeding or intravascular clotting. The diagram also makes it clear that the normal interplay of the various coagulation factors results in a dynamic equilibrium between the thrombophilic and haemorrhagic tendencies. It is now known that the stability of the vascular wall and of the blood cells, particularly the thrombocytes, plays a very important part in the maintenance of this equilibrium.

Endogenous amines like serotonin, histamine and adrenaline, as well as endogenous and exogenous thromboplastic lipids and ACTH, increase the lability of the vascular wall and the thrombocytes. Carriers of negative charges, like heparin, on the other hand, have a stabilizing effect on the vascular endothelium and thrombocytes when supported by stabilizers such as cortisone or cortisol. The present concept of the mechanisms involved in the regulation and maintenance of the normal equilibrium is shown in Figure 4. The formation and release of heparin in the mast cells is subject to neurovegetative control via the sympathetic nervous system. The ACTH-cortisone equilibrium, which is disturbed by exogenous stimuli like climatic and weather changes and stress, is regulated by the diencephalon via the pituitary and adrenal cortex (see also page 717).

Cardiac infarction

In spite of certain common external causes and initiating mechanisms, the pathogenesis of cardiac infarction differs considerably from that of thrombosis[4]. Only in rare cases are primary coagulation thrombi found in cardiac infarction. Many aspects of the disease are still unexplained.

The primary cause of an infarct is usually stress, shock or, indirectly, drug action. The following series of effects then occur in a very short space of time: An increase in sympathetic nervous tone mediated by the brain stem leads to an increased release of catecholamines from the adrenal medulla. The ensuing hypoxaemia

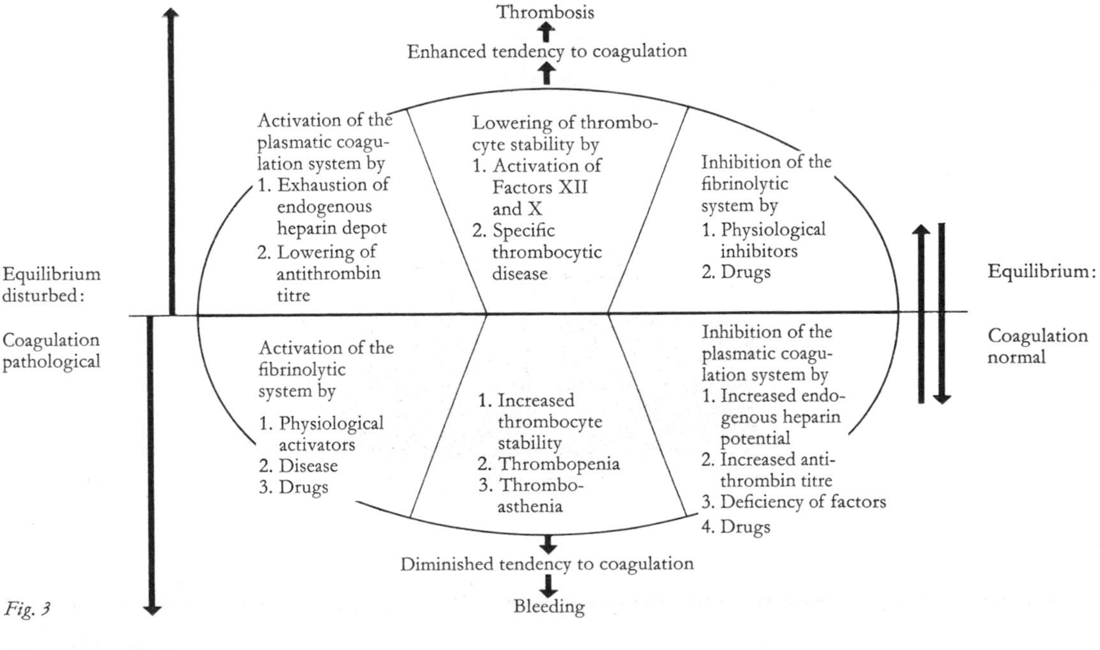

Fig. 3

Fig. 4

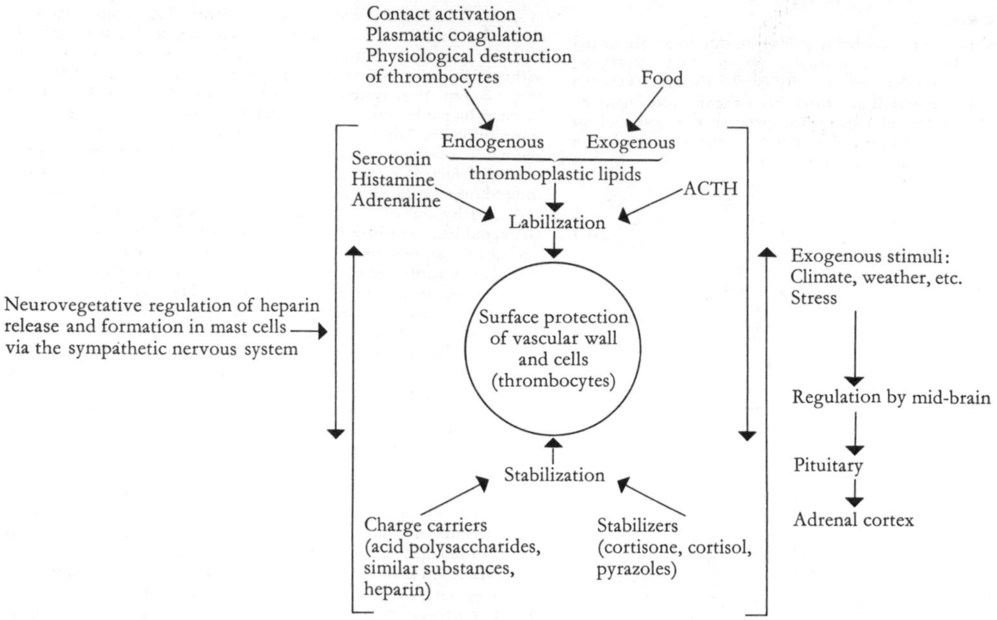

results in the formation of necrotic areas in the vascular walls and in the heart, particularly beneath the endocardium, in the wall of the left ventricle, in the septum and in the apex, in fact in any part where a high concentration of monoamine oxidase can be demonstrated histologically[5]. This necrosis causes a manifest infarct either directly or via the development of oedema in the coronary vessels. The action of catecholamines in causing necrosis, oedema and thus infarction is also favoured by the hypertension, spasms, stasis and ischaemia that commonly result from a disturbance of haemodynamics and cardiac activity.

The process of infarction initiated in this way is intensified by mechanisms under central nervous control and mediated by the pituitary and vasomotor centre[6]. The pituitary releases larger amounts of vasoconstrictor substances, with the result that the haemodynamic equilibrium is disturbed. At the same time the regulation of cardiac activity and of haemodynamics by the vasomotor centre is impaired. The increased release of ACTH by the pituitary blocks the release of corticosteroids by the adrenal cortex, so that the stability of the vascular wall is endangered (Fig. 5).

Methods

The coagulation process can be studied by various *routine methods* suitable for any laboratory:

Bleeding time. Measured by making a small wound in a capillary, small vein or arteriole. The results depend on the condition of the plasmatic, thrombocytic and fibrinolytic coagulation systems. Differentiation is not possible.

Fig. 5

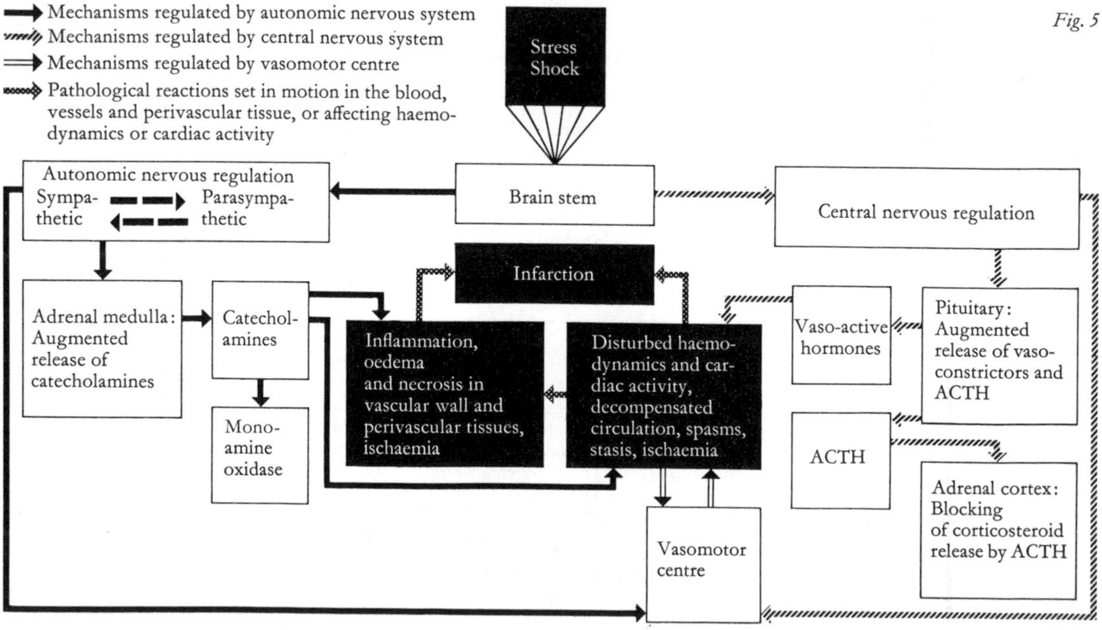

Recalcification time. This method is particularly useful for measuring the effect of heparin and heparinoids on the plasmatic coagulation system.

Prothrombin time. This method reveals changes in the plasmatic coagulation Factors II, V, VII and X and is used exclusively for checking on the action of oral anticoagulants.

Retraction. The measurement of clot retraction is of clinical interest since it is modified in certain thrombocytic diseases as well as during treatment with heparin.

Heparin tolerance test. By measuring the coagulability of the blood this test makes it possible to assess the patient's tendency to thrombosis.

A number of *special methods*, suitable only for appropriately equipped laboratories, are available for determining individual factors and functions involved in the physiological coagulation process. They require the use of either expensive apparatus like the thrombo-elastograph and thrombocyte aggregometer or special reagents which must be prepared in the laboratory itself. Those special methods whose reliability is now established are listed in the table below. For a detailed description of the techniques involved see MONTIGEL[7].

References

[1] MCELFRESH, A.E., *Amer.J.med.Sci.*, **242**, 771 (1961); ŠILKO, N.A., quoted in *Abstr. Wld Med.*, **33**, 74 (1963); LANDBECK, G., in WIESENER, H. (Ed.), *Einführung in die Entwicklungsphysiologie des Kindes*, Springer, Berlin, 1964, page 118.
[2] OLLENDORFF et al., *Acta med.scand.*, **175**, 621 (1964).
[3] PECHET and ALEXANDER, *New Engl.J.Med.*, **265**, 1093 (1961).
[4] Report, *Dtsch.med.J.*, **17**, 736 (1966).
[5] MÜLLER, E., *Naunyn-Schmiedeberg's Arch.exp.Path.Pharmak.*, **254**, 439 (1966).
[6] SELYE, H., *Practitioner*, **172**, 5 (1954).
[7] MONTIGEL, C., *Die Analytik der Blutgerinnung* (in preparation).

Special methods of studying blood coagulation

Phase of coagulation	Factor or phase tested	Method	Reagent	Remarks
Preliminary phase, intrinsic system, thrombocytic process	Thrombocyte function	Thrombo-elastograph Thrombocyte aggregometer (BREDDIN's method)		
Preliminary phase, intrinsic system, plasmatic process	Contact activation Factor XII	Thrombo-elastograph Thrombocyte aggregometer		
Preliminary phase, intrinsic system, plasmatic process	Factor X	Measurement of coagulation	Factor X-free plasma + viper toxin + phospholipids	
extrinsic system, plasmatic process			Factor X-free plasma + tissue thromboplastin	Only when Factor VII is present in adequate amount
Preliminary phase, extrinsic system	Factor VII	Measurement of coagulation	Factor VII-free plasma + tissue thromboplastin	
Preliminary phase, plasmatic process	Factor V	Measurement of coagulation	Factor V-free plasma + tissue thromboplastin	
Preliminary phase, plasmatic process, inhibitors	Antithrombin II	Measurement of coagulation after addition of fibrinogen	Fibrinogen solution	
Phase 1	Factor II Prothrombin	Measurement of coagulation	Factor II-free plasma + tissue thromboplastin	
Phase 2	Factor I			No satisfactory routine method
Phase 3	Retraction potential of thrombocytes	Measurement of clot retraction		
Phase 4	Fibrinolytic potential	Plasmolysis time		
		Euglobulolysis time		Inhibitors removed

Blood Groups*

(For references see pages 633–634)

The blood groups[1] consist of inherited characters of the blood corpuscles, particularly the erythrocytes, identifiable as antigens by means of their reaction with specific antibodies. The genes responsible for the presence of these antigens are inherited in accordance with Mendelian principles. Most of the blood-group characters are already identifiable in the young embryo and remain unchanged throughout life. They are unaffected by external factors like climate or, in general, disease[2].

The blood-group characters can be arranged into systems, those so far recognized being the AB0, MNSs, P, Rh, Lutheran, Kell, Lewis, Duffy, Kidd, Diego, Ii, Auberger, Xg, Yt and Dombrock systems. With one exception, each of these systems is inherited independently of the others as an autosomal character; the exception is the Xg group, which is located on the X chromosome. Also known are blood-group antigens of very rare occurrence ('private antigens'), like the Levay, Jobbins, Becker, Ven, Rm, Chr^a, Wr^a, Be^a, By, Sw^a, Good, Bi and Tr^a antigens, as well as others only rarely absent from human erythrocytes, like Vel, Ge, Lan and Sm ('public antigens').

An individual's blood-group characters are identifiable by means of test sera containing antibodies. These may be of human origin (iso-antibodies) and contain either agglutinins or incomplete antibodies. The antibodies are either naturally occurring, i.e., they have not arisen from any known immunizing stimulus, or they are immune antibodies due to an immunizing stimulus such as pregnancy or blood transfusion or injection. Test sera containing hetero-antibodies may also be produced by immunizing suitable animals. Finally, certain reagents of vegetable origin (phytagglutinins) can be used to identify particular blood-group characters (A_1, A_2, H, M, N, etc.).

An antigen-antibody reaction takes place between the test serum and the antigen-carrying erythrocytes leading either to agglutination or, occasionally, in the presence of complement, to haemolysis.

At the right temperature, the agglutinins react with erythrocytes suspended in physiological salt solution. Reaction with incomplete antibodies may be demonstrated

(a) in viscous reaction media, 22–30% beef albumin being a particularly suitable one; other substances used for this purpose include human serum or plasma free of antibodies, gelatin, dextran, polyvinylpyrrolidone, gum arabic, etc.
(b) in the fermentation test; in the main the following proteolytic enzymes are used: trypsin, papain, bromelain and ficin.
(c) in the indirect antiglobulin test (COOMBS' test).

Combinations of tests (for instance a trypsin test combined with an indirect antiglobulin test) are particularly sensitive.

The AB0 blood-group system (LANDSTEINER, 1900[3])

The iso-antibodies anti-A and anti-B are normal and regular constituents of appropriate human blood sera. Two antigens (agglutinogens) A and B, reacting respectively with anti-A and anti-B, enable an individual's blood to be assigned to one of the four groups A, B, AB or 0.

Table 1

Reaction with anti-A ...	+	–	+	–
Reaction with anti-B	–	+	+	–
Blood group	A	B	AB	0

The antigen is located on the surface of the erythrocytes, while the serum contains the iso-antibody, either anti-A or anti-B, corresponding to the antigen not carried by the erythrocytes; if both antigens are carried, or both lacking, the serum contains respectively neither iso-antibody, or both:

Table 2

Blood group	Antigen carried by erythrocytes	Antibodies in serum
0	–	anti-A + anti-B
A.............	A	anti-B
B.............	B	anti-A
AB	A and B	neither

From the genetic aspect, an allelic gene (*A*, *B* or *0*) is situated at a chromosomal locus, the blood group being determined by the combined effect of the two genes situated at the equivalent loci. Phenotypically, the character 0 is found only in the homozygotic form.

The four blood groups (phenotypes) arise from the six possible genotypes, as shown in Table 3. It is impossible to distinguish serologically between *AA* and *A0* or between *BB* and *B0*.

Table 3

Blood group (phenotype)	Genotype
0	*00*
A	*AA* or *A0*
B	*BB* or *B0*
AB	*AB*

The frequencies with which the various blood groups occur within a population differ widely. From these phenotype frequencies the corresponding gene frequencies can be calculated (for formulae see RACE and SANGER[1]). Such data are of great importance in anthropological studies.

Subgroups of the AB0 system

The blood group A can be subdivided into A_1 and A_2 (VON DUNGERN and HIRSZFELD[4]), the blood group AB into A_1B and A_2B. Anti-A sera (from B individuals) consist of two components, anti-A and anti-A_1. Anti-A_1 reacts only with erythrocytes of groups A_1 and A_1B, anti-A on the other hand with groups A_1, A_2, A_1B and A_2B. This subdivision of A increases the number of possible AB0 blood groups from four to six, namely 0, A_1, A_2, B, A_1B and A_2B. There are 10 genotypes corresponding to these phenotypes (Table 4).

Table 4

Blood group (phenotype)	Genotype
0	*00*
A_1	A_1A_1, A_1A_2, A_10
A_2	A_2A_2, A_20
B	*BB*, *B0*
A_1B	A_1B
A_2B	A_2B

Anti-A_1 is present as an irregular antibody in the serum of 1–2% of A_2 individuals and about 26% of A_2B individuals.

Table 5 summarizes the serological data of the A_1A_2B0 groups.

Table 5

Blood group	Reaction with test serum			Antibodies regularly present in serum	Antibodies occasionally present in serum
	anti-A	anti-A_1	anti-B		
0	–	–	–	anti-A (+ anti-A_1) anti-B	–
A_1.....	+	+	–	anti-B	–
A_2.....	+	–	–	anti-B	anti-A_1 in about 1–2%
B......	–	–	+	anti-A (+ anti-A_1)	–
A_1B ...	+	+	+	none	–
A_2B ...	+	–	+	none	anti-A_1 in about 26%

The A subgroups can also be determined by means of phytagglutinins. *Dolichos biflorus* extract reacts specifically with A_1, and an extract of *Lotus tetragonolobus* seeds can be used as anti-A_2 reagent.

* The chapters on 'Blood Groups' and 'Serum Groups' (pages 626–634) have been compiled by L. P. HOLLÄNDER, Blood Donor Centre of the Swiss Red Cross, Basle.

In very rare cases a blood cannot be assigned to one of the A subgroups, when it is assumed to belong to an intermediary subgroup (A_{int}).

The A_3 group is found only rarely, about once in 1000 A individuals (GAMMELGAARD[5]). Erythrocytes of blood group A_3 are agglutinated by anti-A (from B or 0 individuals) in a characteristic manner, with numerous nonagglutinated cells interspersed among small clumps. The differentiation from chimera blood[6] or group change in leukaemia[2] may present difficulties. Still weaker subgroups of A are A_x (also known as A_4, A_5, A_z or A_0) and A_m. Serological data of the A subgroups are summarized in Table 6.

Table 6

Test serum	A_1	A_2	A_3	A_x	A_m
Reaction with test sera anti-A (blood group B)	+	+	+*	−(+)	−(+)
anti-A+B (blood group 0)......	+	+	+*	+	−(+)
anti-A_1	+	—	—	—	—
Reaction of serum with erythrocytes A_1	—	(+)	—	+	—
A_2	—	—	—	—	—
B	+	+	+	+	+
'A' substance present in saliva of secretors	Yes	Yes	Yes	No	Yes

* Mixed agglutination.

Variants of blood group B are also known that react weakly or negatively with anti-B test sera. In such individuals the serum contains an anti-B (not reacting with the individual's own B) as well as B substance. B bloods with no anti-B in the serum have also been reported; these have been designated B_w (LEVINE et al.[7]) or B_x (YOKOYAMA et al.[8]). Such individuals secrete B substance in the saliva. A weak B property (B_3) of the erythrocytes, with secretion of H substance but not of B substance, has been described (MOULLEC et al.[9]).

In the very rare *'Bombay'* or *Oh phenotypes* the ABH properties of the erythrocytes and secretions are suppressed, supposedly as a result of the presence of the gene *x* in homozygotic form (*xx*). The serum of these individuals contains anti-A, anti-B and anti-H. The *Xx* genes are now often designated *H* and *h*.

The A and B antigens have also been identified on thrombocytes and leucocytes. The chemical constitution of the A, B and H group substances has been largely elucidated.

The MNSs blood-group system (LANDSTEINER and LEVINE, 1927[10])

The M and N antigens of human erythrocytes can be identified by means of heterospecific immune sera from rabbits. Phenotypes and genotypes of the M and N properties are shown in Table 7.

Table 7

Reaction with anti-M..........	+	+	—
Reaction with anti-N..........	—	+	+
Phenotype (blood group)	M	MN	N
Genotype	*MM*	*MN*	*NN*

SANGER and RACE were able to show that a serum described by WALSH and MONTGOMERY[11] defines an antigen closely related to M and N. This antigen they designated S.

LEVINE et al.[12] discovered an antibody that reacted with the antigen s whose existence had already been assumed. Anti-M and anti-N also occur in human sera as irregular specific cold agglutinins. Anti-S and anti-s cannot be produced experimentally in animals. The use of the four antisera anti-M, anti-N, anti-S and anti-s enables nine genotypes to be distinguished (Table 8). The genotypes *MS/Ns* and *Ms/NS* cannot be distinguished serologically.

Table 8

	MS/MS	*MS/Ms*	*Ms/Ms*	*MS/NS*	*Ms/Ns*	*MS/Ns* or *Ms/NS*	*NS/NS*	*NS/Ns*	*Ns/Ns*
anti-M	+	+	+	+	+	+	—	—	—
anti-N	—	—	—	+	+	+	+	+	+
anti-S.....	+	+	—	+	—	+	+	+	—
anti-s	—	+	+	—	+	+	—	+	+

Weak forms of M or N (M_2, N_2) are occasionally met with. They are characterized by reacting only weakly with anti-M or anti-N sera. M^c (DUNSFORD et al.[13]) reacts with most anti-M and some anti-N sera and is considered to be intermediate between M and N. The M_1 antigen (JACK et al.[14]) is qualitatively different from M and is commoner among negroes than among the white races. A true allele of M and N is the rare M^g, which reacts neither with anti-M nor with anti-N (ALLEN et al.[15]). The corresponding antibody anti-M^g is fairly common in normal sera. WIENER et al.[16] found antibodies in the serum of a negress which reacted with all blood samples except those that were negative to anti-S and anti-s. This so-called anti-U behaves like an inseparable mixture of anti-S and anti-s. Individuals who form anti-U possess neither S nor s. The antigen Hu (Hunter[17]) was found mainly among members of the negro race, the antigen He (Henshaw)[18] exclusively so. Both belong to the MNSs system, though the exact location of the corresponding genes is still unknown. Anti-Mi^a (LEVINE et al.[19]), anti-Vw (VAN DER HART et al.[20]) and anti-Mu (CLEGHORN[21]) react with antigens likewise belonging to the MNSs system but their genetic interrelationships have not yet been fully elucidated. M^k is a silent allele at the MN locus (METAXAS and METAXAS-BÜHLER[22]), whereas the antigen reacting with anti-Vr (VAN DER HART et al.[23]) is not an allele of M or N, S or s, though also forming part of the MNSs complex. Further antigens belonging to this system are Ri^a and St^a (CLEGHORN[24]), Mt^a[25], Cl^a[26] and Ny^a[27].

The P blood-group system (LANDSTEINER and LEVINE, 1927[28])

Human bloods react either positively or negatively with anti-P sera. In the serum of P-negative individuals there are cold-active but often only weak anti-P antibodies. A natural anti-P also occurs in animal sera (horse, rabbit, swine, ox), and most anti-P test sera are obtained by immunizing such animals. The phenotypes and genotypes are shown in Table 9.

Table 9

		Phenotype	Genotype
anti-P	+	P+	*PP* or *Pp*
	—	P—	*pp*

In 1951, LEVINE et al.[29] described a haemolysing antibody, anti-Tj^a, that reacted with 99.99% of the erythrocyte samples against which it was tested. In 1955, SANGER[30] was able to show that the antigen Tj^a belonged to the P system. Individuals who form anti-Tj^a are P-negative. Adsorption of anti-Tj^a on P-negative erythrocytes leaves a part of the antibody with anti-P specificity. The P blood-group system is now regarded as genetically analogous to the A_1A_20 groups. The three alleles are P_1 (alias P), P_2 (alias p) and p (alias Tj[a−]). The anti-Tj^a formed by the rare pp individuals corresponds to anti-P + P_1. Table 10 shows the system in summary form.

In 1959, MATSON et al.[31] described the extremely rare antigen P^k; this belongs to the P system but its precise genetic interpretation has not yet been possible. Most anti-P + P_1 and anti-P_1 sera contain an anti-P^k component.

Table 10

Reaction with anti-P_1 (anti-P)	+	–	–
Reaction with anti-P + P_1 (anti-Tj^a)	+	+	–
Genotype	$P_1P_1(PP)$ $P_1P_2(Pp)$ $P_1p(PTj^b)$	$P_2P_2(pp)$ $P_2p(pTj^b)$	$pp(Tj^bTj^b)$
Phenotype	P_1	P_2	p

The designation in brackets is that usual prior to 1955.

The Rhesus blood-group system (LANDSTEINER and WIENER, 1940[32])

The discovery of the Rh blood-group system proved to be of great practical importance in view of the fact that Rh-negative persons form Rh antibodies fairly frequently after contact with the Rh antigen (transfusion or injection of blood, pregnancy). A second transfusion with Rh-positive blood may result in a haemolytic transfusion reaction. In women the result may be haemolytic disease in her newborn children (LEVINE et al., 1941[119]). For clinical purposes the distinction between Rh-positive and Rh-negative is usually sufficient, but in fact the Rh blood-group system is extremely complex. This complexity is one of the reasons why various genetic explanations of the Rh groups have been put forward and at least three different nomenclatures are in use. WIENER's concept[33] assumes the existence of a single gene locus on the chromosome with multiple alleles. Each allele results in the formation of an agglutinogen possessing several factors. These factors act as antigens and can be detected by means of the corresponding antibodies. On the other hand, according to FISHER and to RACE[34] the Rh group to which a blood belongs is determined by three closely linked gene pairs. Each individual inherits three Rh genes from his parents, namely *C* or *c*, *D* or *d* and *E* or *e*, in the form of an indivisible gene complex. For instance, an individual inherits *CDe* from one parent and *cde* from the other. Table 11 (from RACE and SANGER[7]) illustrates the two concepts using CDe as an example.

Table 11

	Gene	Agglutinogen	Factors	Antibodies
WIENER			Rh_0	anti-Rh_0
	R^1	Rh_1	rh′	anti-rh′
			hr″	anti-hr″
FISHER and RACE	*C*	C		anti-C
	D	D		anti-D
	e	e		anti-e

The correspondence between WIENER's factors and the antigens of FISHER and RACE, together with that between the respective antibodies, is shown in Table 12.

Table 12

Rh_0 = D	anti-Rh_0 = anti-D
rh′ = C	anti-rh′ = anti-C
rh″ = E	anti-rh″ = anti-E
hr′ = c	anti-hr′ = anti-c
hr″ = e	anti-hr″ = anti-e

Antigens have since been discovered which correspond partially to further alleles on the same single gene locus.

Alleles and variants of D

STRATTON[35] has described the antigen D^u, which reacts positively with some anti-D sera, negatively with others. D^u occurs in various strengths (high-grade and low-grade) and appears to be identical with WIENER's intermediate form ($\mathfrak{R}h_0$). In D^u individuals the antigen D can cause the formation of anti-D. The fact that D-positive individuals can also form anti-D (ARGALL et al.[36]) led WIENER and UNGER[37] to assume the existence of partial antigens of D. Individuals not possessing one of these partial factors can form antibodies against it. $\mathfrak{R}h^a$ indicates a blood in which the partial factor Rh^A is missing and which reacts with anti-Rh_0 and also with anti-Rh^B, anti-Rh^C and anti-Rh^D. These variants and their reactions are shown in Table 13.

Table 13

Variant	Reaction with anti-Rh_0	anti-Rh^A	anti-Rh^B	anti-Rh^C	anti-Rh^D
$\mathfrak{R}h^a$	+	–	+	+	+
$\mathfrak{R}h^b$	+	+	–	+	+
$\mathfrak{R}h^c$	+	+	+	–	+
$\mathfrak{R}h^d$	+	+	+	+	–
$\mathfrak{R}h^{ab}$	+	–	–	+	+
$\mathfrak{R}h^{abc}$......	+	–	–	–	+
$\mathfrak{R}h^{ac}$	+	–	+	–	+

The antigen described by CHOWN et al.[38] as reacting with the antibody anti-Wiel appears to be a further partial antigen of D^u.

Alleles and variants of C and c

C^W (CALLENDER and RACE[39]) is a third allele and reacts with a specific anti-C^W serum. Most anti-C sera also possess an anti-C^W component. A rare and weakly reacting antigen is C^u (RACE et al.[40]), a parallel to D^u. Anti-C^x is a not very rare antibody reacting with the very rare antigen C^x (STRATTON and RENTON[41]).

Alleles and variants of E and e

The antigen E^u (CEPPELLINI et al.[42]) is analogous to D^u and C^u. E^W (GREENWALT and SANGER[43]) has so far been found only in a very few families, e^s (SANGER et al.[44]) only in members of the negro race. SHAPIRO[45] found the antibody anti-hr^s in the serum of a Bantu woman; the factor hr^s occurs not only among the Bantu but also in white races. The antigen e^1 was found among the Columbian Indians (LAYRISSE et al.[46]).

Table 14 shows WIENER's analysis of the Rh phenotypes occurring in the white population of New York City[47], Table 15 their distribution among the English people as determined by RACE et al.[48].

During the last few years compound antigens of the Rh system have been discovered, for instance ce, which reacts with the antiserum originally designated anti-f (ROSENFIELD et al.[49]). Other compound antigens are rh_i or Ce (ROSENFIELD and HABER[50]), CE (TIPPETT et al.[51]) and ce^s, which reacts with the serum originally designated anti-V (DENATALE et al.[52]). The antigen G described by ALLEN and TIPPETT[53] is not a compound antigen in the same sense; it is closely related to C and D, since most C- or D-positive individuals are also G-positive. Anti-G is found in the serum of cde and cdE individuals, most of whom also form the antibody anti-D + C.

The first case of a 'deficient' Rh chromosome was described by RACE et al.[54] and designated by them –D– ($\overline{R}h_0$ in WIENER's nomenclature). Others have since come to light, namely C^wD– (GUNSON and DONOHUE[55]), cD– (TATE et al.[56]), – – – (VOS et al.[57]). It is not known whether these are cases of gene suppression or gene depression.

The antigen contents of the individual gene complexes are summarized in Table 16 (page 631) (from RACE and SANGER[7]).

An Rh complex with gene depression has been given the designation r^G (ALLEN and TIPPETT[53]). Similar behaviour is shown by the antigens of the complexes r^M (TIPPETT et al.[51]) and r^L (METAXAS and METAXAS-BÜHLER[58]).

In 1962, ROSENFIELD et al.[59] proposed a new terminology for the Rh groups in which the Rh antibodies were given numbers in the chronological order of their identification. The original publication listed 21 antibodies, since when the number has risen to 27 (KEITH et al.[60]). This nomenclature is without prejudice to any

Table 14 Rh—Hr phenomena and genotypes (from WIENER and WEXLER[47]; 'international' nomenclature according to WIENER)

2 Rh phenotypes			12 Rh phenotypes					28 Rh–Hr phenotypes					55 genotypes
Designation	Approximate frequency among New York City whites %	Reaction with anti-**Rh$_0$** or anti-rhesus	Type	Approximate frequency among New York City whites %	Reaction with anti-**rh'**	anti-**rh''**	anti-**rh^w**	Designation	Approximate frequency among New York City whites %	Reaction with anti-**hr'**	anti-**hr''**	anti-**hr**	
Rh-negative	15	—	rh	14.4	—	—	—	rh	14.4	+	+	+	rr
			rh'	0.46	+	—	—	rh'rh	0.46	+	+	+	$r'r$
								rh'rh'	0.003 6	—	+	—	$r'r'$
			rh'^{w}	0.004	+	—	+	rh'^{w}rh	0.004	+	+	+	$r'^w r$
								rh'^{w}rh'	0.000 06	—	+	—	$r'^w r'$ or $r'^w r'^w$
			rh''	0.38	—	+	—	rh''rh	0.38	+	+	+	$r''r$
								rh''rh''	0.002 5	+	—	—	$r''r''$
			rh$_y$	0.01	+	+	—	rh'rh''	0.006	+	+	—	$r'r''$
								rh$_y$rh	0.008	+	+	+	$r^y r$
								rh$_y$rh'	0.000 1	—	+	—	$r^y r'$
								rh$_y$rh''	0.000 1	+	—	—	$r^y r''$
								rh$_y$rh$_y$	0.000 001	—	—	—	$r^y r^y$
			rh$_y^w$	0.000 05	+	+	+	rh'^{w}rh''	0.000 05	+	+	—	$r'^w r''$
								rh$_y^w$rh'	0.000 001	—	+	—	$r'^w r^y$
Rh-positive	85	+	Rh$_0$	2.1	—	—	—	Rh$_0$	2.1	+	+	+	R^0R^0 or R^0r
			Rh$_1$	50.7	+	—	—	Rh$_1$rh	33.4	+	+	+	R^1r, R^1R^0 or R^0r'
								Rh$_1$Rh$_1$	17.3	—	+	—	R^1R^1 or R^1r'
			Rh$_1^w$	3.3	+	—	+	Rh$_1^w$rh	1.6	+	+	+	$R^{1w}r$, $R^{1w}R^0$ or $R^0r'^w$
								Rh$_1^w$Rh$_1$	1.7	—	+	—	$R^{1w}R^1$, $R^1r'^w$, $R^{1w}r'$, $R^{1w}R^{1w}$ or $R^{1w}r'^w$
			Rh$_2$	14.6	—	+	—	Rh$_2$rh	12.2	+	+	+	R^2r, R^2R^0 or R^0r''
								Rh$_2$Rh$_2$	2.4	+	—	—	R^2R^2 or R^2r''
			Rh$_z$	13.4	+	+	—	Rh$_1$Rh$_2$	12.9	+	+	—	R^1R^2, R^1r'' or R^2r'
								Rh$_z$rh	0.2	+	+	+	R^zr, R^zR^0 or R^0r^y
								Rh$_z$Rh$_1$	0.2	—	+	—	R^zR^1, R^zr' or R^1r^y
								Rh$_z$Rh$_2$	0.07	+	—	—	R^zR^2, R^zr'' or R^2r^y
								Rh$_z$Rh$_z$	0.000 4	—	—	—	R^zR^z or R^zr^y
			Rh$_z^w$	0.6	+	+	+	Rh$_1^w$Rh$_2$	0.6	+	+	—	$R^{1w}R^2$, $R^{1w}r''$ or $R^2r'^w$
								Rh$_z^w$Rh$_1$	0.008	—	+	—	$R^{1w}R^z$, $R^{1w}r^y$ or $R^zr'^w$

(For references see pages 633–634)

Table 15 The Rh genotypes of English people (from RACE et al.[48])

Calculated group frequency (if only first 4 sera used) %	Reaction with the 4 antisera fairly widely available: CC^w	c	D	E	Reaction with rarer antisera: pure C	pure C^w	e	f	d	Genetic and antigenic constitution	Short symbols: much used	WIENER and WEXLER[47]	Calculated genotype frequency %
15.1020	—	+	—	—	—	—	+	+	+	cde/cde	rr	rr	15.1020
2.0609	—	+	+	—	—	—	+	+	+	cDe/cde	R_0r	R^0r	1.9950
					—	—	+	+	—	cDe/cDe	R_0R_0	R^0R^0	0.0659
0.9376	—	+	—	+	—	—	+	+	+	cdE/cde	$R''r$	$r''r$	0.9235
					—	—	—	—	+	cdE/cdE	$R''R''$	$r''r''$	0.0141
14.0769	—	+	+	+	—	—	—	—	—	cDE/cDE	R_2R_2	R^2R^2	1.9906
					—	—	—	—	+	cDE/cdE	R_2R''	R^2r''	0.3353
					—	—	+	+	—	cDE/cDe	R_2R_0	R^2R^0	0.7243
					—	—	+	+	+	{ cDE/cde	R_2r	R^2r	10.9657
										{ cDe/cdE	R_0R''	R^0r''	0.0610
0.7644	+	+	—	—	+	—	+	+	+	Cde/cde	$R'r$	$r'r$	0.7644
					—	+	+	+	+	C^wde/cde	R'^wr	r'^w	0.0000
34.8899	+	+	+	—	+	—	+	+	—	CDe/cDe	R_1R_0	R^1R^0	2.0922
					+	—	+	+	+	{ CDe/cde	R_1r	R^1r	31.6759
										{ cDe/Cde	R_0R'	R^0r'	0.0505
					—	+	+	+	—	C^wDe/cDe	$R_1^wR_0$	$R^{1w}R^0$	0.0664
					—	+	+	+	+	{ C^wDe/cde	R_1^wr	$R^{1w}r$	1.0049
										{ C^wde/cDe	R'^wR_0	r'^wR^0	0.0000
0.0234	+	+	—	+	+	—	+	—	+	cdE/Cde	$R''R'$	$r''r'$	0.0234
					+	—	+	+	+	CdE/cde	R_yr	r^yr	0.0000
					+	—	—	—	+	CdE/cdE	R_yR''	r^yr''	0.0000
					—	+	+	—	+	C^wde/cdE	R'^wR''	r'^wr''	0.0000
13.4178	+	+	+	+	+	—	+	—	—	CDe/cDE	R_1R_2	R^1R^2	11.5000
					+	—	+	+	—	cDe/CDE	R_0R_z	R^0R^z	0.0125
					+	—	+	—	+	{ CDe/cdE	R_1R''	R^1r''	0.9685
										{ cDE/Cde	R_2R'	R^2r'	0.2775
					+	—	+	+	+	{ CDE/cde	R_zr	R_zr	0.1893
										{ CdE/cDe	R_yR_0	r^yR^0	0.0000
					+	—	—	—	—	cDE/CDE	R_2R_z	R^2R^z	0.0687
					+	—	—	—	+	{ cdE/CDE	$R''R_z$	$r''R^z$	0.0058
										{ CdE/cDE	R_yR_2	r_yR^2	0.0000
					—	+	+	—	—	C^wDe/cDE	$R_1^wR_2$	$R^{1w}R^2$	0.3648
					—	+	+	—	+	{ C^wDe/cdE	R_1^wR''	$R^{1w}r''$	0.0307
										{ C^wde/cDE	R'^wR_2	r'^wR^2	0.0000
0.0097	+	—	—	—	+	—	+	—	+	Cde/Cde	$R'R'$	$r'r'$	0.0097
					+	+	+	—	+	C^wde/Cde	R'^wR'	r'^wr'	0.0000
					—	+	+	—	+	C^wde/C^wde	$R'^wR'^w$	$r'^wr'^w$	0.0000
18.5073	+	—	+	—	+	—	+	—	—	CDe/CDe	R_1R_1	R^1R^1	16.6097
					+	—	+	—	+	CDe/Cde	R_1R'	R^1r'	0.8016
					+	+	+	—	—	CDe/C^wDe	$R_1R_1^w$	R^1R^{1w}	1.0539
					+	+	+	—	+	{ C^wDe/Cde	R_1^wR'	$R^{1w}r'$	0.0254
										{ C^wde/CDe	R'^wR_1	r'^wR^1	0.0000
					—	+	+	—	—	C^wDe/C^wDe	$R_1^wR_1^w$	$R^{1w}R^{1w}$	0.0167
					—	+	+	—	+	C^wde/C^wDe	$R'^wR_1^w$	r'^wR^{1w}	0.0000
0.2101	+	—	+	+	+	—	+	—	—	CDe/CDE	R_1R_z	R^1R^z	0.1985
					+	—	+	—	+	{ Cde/CDE	$R'R_z$	$r'R^z$	0.0048
										{ CdE/CDe	R_yR_1	r^yR^1	0.0000
					+	—	—	—	—	CDE/CDE	R_zR_z	R^zR^z	0.0006
					+	+	+	—	—	C^wDe/CDE	$R_1^wR_z$	$R^{1w}R^z$	0.0062
					+	—	—	—	+	CdE/CDE	R_yR_z	r^yR^z	0.0000
					+	+	+	—	+	{ CdE/C^wDe	$R_yR_1^w$	r^yR^{1w}	0.0000
										{ C^wde/CDE	R'^wR_z	r'^wR^z	0.0000
0.0000	+	—	—	+	+	—	+	—	+	CdE/Cde	R_yR'	r^yr'	0.0000
					+	—	—	—	+	CdE/CdE	R_yR_y	r^yr^y	0.0000
					+	+	+	—	+	CdE/C^wde	$R_yR'^w$	$r^yr'^w$	0.0000

Table 16

Gene complexes		Antigens				
R_0	*cDe*	D	G	c	ce	e
R_1	*CDe*	D	G	C	Ce	e
R_2	*cDE*	D	G	c	?	E
R_z	*CDE*	D	G	C	CE	E
r	*cde*	—	—	c	ce	e
R′	*Cde*	—	G	C	Ce	e
R″	*cdE*	—	—	c	?	E
R_y	*CdE*	—	G	C	CE	E
R_1^w	C^wDe	D	G	C^w	?	e
R_0^u	cD^ue	(D)	(G)	c	ce	e
r^v	cde^s	—	—	c	ce^s	e^s
R_0^v	cDe^s	D	G	c	ce^s	e^s
R'^s	Cde^s	—	G	C	ce	e^s
	—D—	D	G	—	—	—
	C^wD—	D	G	(C^w)	—	—
	cD—	D	G	(c)	(ce)	—
	— — —	—	—	—	—	—
r^G	*(C)d(e)*	—	G	(C)	—	(e)

eventual solution of the genetic problems and simply indicates the phenotype. Thus Rh: 1, 2, −3, 4, 5 denotes a blood giving the following reactions: anti-D+, anti-C+, anti-E−, anti-c+, anti-e+ (in the nomenclature of Fisher and Race CDe/cde, in that of Wiener Rh_1rh). The designations of the most important antigens of the Rh blood groups under the three systems of nomenclature are given in Table 17 (mainly from Rosenfield et al.[59]).

Table 17

Rosenfield et al.	Fisher and Race (CDE)	Wiener (Rh–Hr)	Rosenfield et al.	Fisher and Race (CDE)	Wiener (Rh–Hr)	Rosenfield et al.	Fisher and Race (CDE)	Wiener (Rh–Hr)
Rh1	D	Rh_0	Rh10	V, ce^s	hr^v	Rh19		hr^s
Rh2	C	rh′	Rh11	E^w	rh^{2w}	Rh20	VS, e^s	
Rh3	E	rh″	Rh12	G	rh^G	Rh21	C^G	
Rh4	c	hr′	Rh13	*	Rh^A	Rh22	CE	
Rh5	e	hr″	Rh14	*	Rh^B	Rh23	Wiel, D^w	
Rh6	f, ce	hr	Rh15	*	Rh^C	Rh24	E^T	
Rh7	Ce	rh_i	Rh16	*	Rh^D	Rh25	LW	
Rh8	C^w	rh^{1w}	Rh17	**	Hr_0	Rh26		
Rh9	C^x	rh^x	Rh18		Hr	Rh27	cE	

* Corresponds to some of the apparent anti-D formed by anti-D individuals.
** Corresponds to an antibody formed by —D—/—D— and other individuals.

The Lutheran blood-group system (Callender and Race, 1946[39])

This system is determined by the two allelic genes Lu^a and Lu^b. The corresponding antigens Lu^a and Lu^b react with the antibodies anti-Lu^a (Callender and Race[39]) and anti-Lu^b (Cutbush and Chanarin[61]) respectively. The following phenotypes are possible: Lu(a+b−), Lu(a+b+) and Lu(a−b+), corresponding to the genotypes Lu^aLu^a, Lu^aLu^b and Lu^bLu^b. Crawford et al.[62] described the rare phenotype Lu(a−b−) in a family in whom the Kidd group reactions were also unusual. An autosomal linkage between the Lutheran and Lewis genes has been suggested by Mohr[63]. According to Sanger and Race[64], such a linkage exists between the genes of the Lutheran groups and those determining the secretion of the ABH blood-group substances.

The Kell blood-group system (Coombs et al., 1946[65])

The discovery of the antibody anti-K by Coombs et al.[65] was followed by the description (Levine et al.[66]) of the antithetic antibody anti-k. The simple Kell system, with the phenotypes K+k−, K+k+ and K−k+, became more complicated with the finding of the antibodies anti-Kp^a and anti-Kp^b (Allen and Lewis[67]). In addition a phenotype was found giving negative reactions with all four Kell antibodies: K−k−Kp(a−b−) (Chown et al.[68]), designated by the symbol K^0. The antibody anti-Ku (Corcoran et al.[69]) reacts with all bloods except the very rare K^0 blood. A further and similarly rare phenotype (McLeod) was described by Allen et al.[70] in which the antigens k and Kp^b were only weakly active; the erythrocytes did not react with anti-Ku.

The observation that K^0 blood does not react with the antibodies anti-Js^a and anti-Js^b of the Sutter blood-group system (Giblett[71]) showed that the Js groups (so far found only among negroes) are part of the Kell blood-group system (Stroup et al.[72]).

Allen and Rosenfield[73] have proposed a nomenclature for the Kell system analogous to their Rh nomenclature, namely K = K1, k = K2, Kp(a+) = K3, Kp(b+) = K4. For instance, their designation K: −1, 2, −3, 4 is equivalent to K−k+Kp(a−b+).

The antigens of the Kell blood-group system, as enlarged by the Sutter properties, are listed in Table 18.

Table 18

K	K1 (Kell)
k	K2 (Cellano)
Kp^a	K3 (Penney)
Kp^b	K4 (Rautenberg)
Ku	K5 (Peltz)
Js^a	K6 (Sutter)
Js^b	K7 (Js^b = Matthews)

Present knowledge of the Kell blood-group system is summarized in Table 19 (with slight modification from Allen and Rosenfield[73]). This does not take account of the relationship with the Js system.

Table 19

Designation	Designation according to Allen and Rosenfield[73]	Antigenic structure of the phenotypes forming the antisera				
		anti-K K1	anti-k K2	anti-Kp^a K3	anti-Kp^b K4	anti-Ku K5
K+	K: 1, 2, −3, 4, 5	+	+	—	+	+
K−	K: 1, 2, −3, 4, 5	—	+	—	+	+
k−	K: 1, 2, −3, 4, 5	+	—	—	+	+
Kp(a+) ...	K: −1, 2, 3, 4, 5	—	+	+	+	+
K+Kp(a+)	K: 1, w 2, 3, 4, 5	+	w	+	+	+
Kp(b−) ...	K: −1, w 2, 3, 4, 5	—	w	+	—	+
K^0	K: −1, −2, −3, −4, −5	—	—	—	—	—
McLeod ...	K: 1, w 2, −3, w 4, −5	—	w	—	w	—

w = weak reaction

The secretor character for ABH substances

Secretors and nonsecretors

The A, B and H substances of the AB0 blood groups are present in water-soluble form in the body fluids and organs of so-called secretors. This property is determined by the gene *Se*. An alcohol-soluble form of these antigenic substances occurs on the erythrocytes and in all tissues except the brain, but not in the body fluids; its presence is unaffected by the *Se* gene (Friedenreich and Hartmann[74]).

The secretor and nonsecretor properties (genes *Se* and *se*) were shown to be related to the Lewis blood groups by Grubb[75].

The Lewis blood-group system (Mourant, 1946[76])

The discovery of the two antibodies anti-Le^a (Mourant[76]) and anti-Le^b (Andresen[77]) made it possible to distinguish four phenotypes of the erythrocytes (Table 20). The antibody anti-X (Andresen and Jordal[78]) possesses anti-Le^a + Le^b specificity.

Table 20

Reaction with anti-Le^a	Reaction with anti-Le^b	Phenotypes
+	—	Le(a+b−)
—	+	Le(a−b+)
—	—	Le(a−b−)
+	+	Le(a+b+)*

* In individuals of groups 0 and A_2.

The Lewis antigens are primarily substances present in the saliva and serum (GRUBB[79]), and the erythrocytes obtain them by absorption from the latter (SNEATH and SNEATH[80]). Since the Lewis phenotype depends on the secretor genotype, a nonsecretor (*se se*) inheriting the Lewis gene *Le* has blood of the Lewis phenotype Le(a+b−), while under the same circumstances the blood of a secretor (*Se se* or *Se Se*) will be Le(a−b+). The prominence of the Lewis phenotype is also affected by the AB0 group of the blood. Thus the A_1 gene interferes with both the Le^b (ANDRESEN[77]) and Le^a (CUTBUSH et al.[81]) antigens (cf. Table 20). The genetic relationships between the Lewis groups of the erythrocytes and the secretion of Lewis and ABH substances in the saliva have been studied by GRUBB[79] and by CEPPELLINI[82]; their views are summarized in Table 21.

Table 21

Genotype	Antigens in saliva: ABH	Le^a	Le^{bL}	Le^{bH}	on erythrocytes
Se Se Le Le, *Se Se Le le*, *Se se Le Le*, *Se se Le le*	+	+	+	+	Le(a−b+)
se se Le Le, *se se Le le*	—	+	—	—	Le(a+b−)
Se Se le le, *Se se le le*	+	—	—	+	Le(a−b−)
se se le le	—	—	—	—	Le(a−b−)

The Duffy blood-group system (CUTBUSH et al., 1950[83])

The antibodies anti-Fy^a (CUTBUSH et al.[83]) and anti-Fy^b (IKIN et al.[84]) react respectively with the human erythrocyte antigens Fy^a and Fy^b. The latter are determined by a pair of allelic genes Fy^a and Fy^b. SANGER et al.[85] described the phenotype Fy(a−b−), of common occurrence among negroes as well as the Jewish population of the Yemen. The Duffy blood groups are summarized in Table 22.

Table 22

Reaction with anti-Fy^a	Reaction with anti-Fy^b	Phenotype	Genotype
+	—	Fy(a+b−)	Fy^aFy^a
+	+	Fy(a+b+)	Fy^aFy^b
—	+	Fy(a−b+)	Fy^bFy^b
—	—	Fy(a−b−)	*FyFy*

The Kidd blood-group system (ALLEN et al., 1951[86])

The antibodies anti-Jk^a (ALLEN et al.[86]) and anti-Jk^b (PLAUT et al.[87]) react respectively with the human erythrocyte antigens Jk^a and Jk^b, determined by the allelic genes Jk^a and Jk^b. In the Kidd groups individuals have likewise been found whose blood reacts neither with anti-Jk^a nor with anti-Jk^b, i.e., of phenotype Jk (a−b−). The serum of such persons may contain the antibody anti-Jk^aJk^b (PINKERTON et al.[88]). The Kidd blood groups are summarized in Table 23.

Table 23

Reaction with anti-Jk^a	Reaction with anti-Jk^b	Phenotype	Genotype
+	—	Jk(a+b−)	Jk^aJk^a
+	+	Jk(a+b+)	Jk^aJk^b
—	+	Jk(a−b+)	Jk^bJk^b
—	—	Jk(a−b−)	*JkJk*

The Diego blood-group system (LAYRISSE et al., 1955[89])

Anti-Di^a, first found in Venezuela by LAYRISSE et al.[89], defines an antigen Di^a so far detected on the erythrocytes of mongoloid peoples, particularly the South American Indians. Anti-Di^b has also been described (THOMPSON et al.[90]).

The Auberger blood-group system (SALMON et al., 1961[91])

The antibody anti-Au^a has been found only once (SALMON et al.[91]). The antigen Au^a is equally common among whites and negroes.

The Dombrock blood-group system (SWANSON et al., 1964[92])

SWANSON et al.[92] described the antibody anti-Do^a, reacting with a hitherto unknown erythrocyte antigen Do^a present in about two-thirds of the bloods tested.

The Ii blood-group system (WIENER et al., 1956[93])

Anti-I is formed by those individuals whose erythrocytes carry the very small quantities of the antigen I (WIENER et al.[93]). Anti-I consists either of autoantibodies or of rare, naturally occurring iso-antibodies of cold type. Cord-blood erythrocytes react only weakly with anti-I; the normal antigenic reaction develops gradually and reaches the adult level at 18 months. Anti-i was discovered by MARSH and JENKINS[94]. There are various degrees of prominence among I carriers. A distinction is also made between i_1 (rare among whites) and i_2 (rare among negroes). A connection between the I and i characters and the AB0 blood groups is likely (TIPPETT et al.[95]).

The Xg blood-group system (MANN et al., 1962[96])

The Xg blood group is of particular genetic interest as the only one so far known that is inherited through the X chromosome. The antibody Xg^a is very rare. The antigen Xg^a, located on the short arm of the X chromosome, has contributed greatly to new knowledge of the topography of this chromosome.

The Yt blood-group system (EATON et al., 1956[97])

An antibody reacting with 99.6% of English bloods was discovered by EATON et al.[97] and named by them anti-Yt^a. Anti-Yt^b, which reacts with about 8% of bloods, was described by GILES and METAXAS[98].

Antigens of infrequent occurrence (private antigens)

Antibodies have repeatedly been found which react with antigens often confined to a single family. The genetic classification of the genes corresponding to these family antigens presents difficulty, and usually it is only possible to demonstrate their serological independence of the blood-group characters described above in this chapter and of other individual, private or family antigens. The hereditary character of most of these antigens has been established, namely Levay[39], Jobbins[99], Becker[100], Ven[101], Wr^a[102], Be^a[103], Rm[20], By[104], Chr^a[105], Sw^a[106], Good[107], Bi[108], Tr^a[109]. In others, inheritance has not been proved, namely Stobo[110], Ot[111], Ho[112], Price[113] and the antigens of the Bennett, Goodspeed, Sturgeon and Donna groups[114].

Widely distributed antigens (public antigens)

These are antigens whose absence from human erythrocytes is an extremely rare occurrence. Examples are Vel[115], Ge[116], Lan[112] and Sm[117].

Clinical significance of the blood groups

Blood-group specific antibodies may bring about haemolytic reactions during blood transfusions or be the cause of haemolytic disease of the newborn. The most important and most widely distributed of the blood-group specific antibodies and their role in the causation of the haemolytic transfusion reaction (HTR) and haemolytic disease of the newborn (HDN) are summarized in Table 24.

Table 24 Clinical importance of the blood-group specific antibodies (adapted from METAXAS[118])

Blood-group system	Antibody	HTR	HDN
AB0.........	anti-A	Yes	Yes
	anti-B	Yes	Rare
	anti-A$_1$	Very rare	No
	anti-H	No	No
MNSs	anti-M	Very rare	Very rare
	anti-N	No	No
	anti-S	Very rare	Rare
	anti-s	Very rare	Rare
	anti-U (S+s)	Very rare	Very rare
P	anti-P$_1$	Very rare	No
Rh..........	anti-D	Yes	Yes
	anti-C	Yes	Rare
	anti-c	Yes	Yes
	anti-C^w	Yes	Rare
	anti-E	Yes	Yes
	anti-e	Rare	Very rare
Lutheran.....	anti-Lu^a	No	No
	anti-Lu^b	Yes	Very rare

Blood-group system	Antibody	HTR	HDN
Kell.........	anti-K	Yes	Yes
	anti-k	Very rare	Very rare
	anti-Kp^a	No	No
	anti-Kp^b	No	Very rare
	anti-Js^a	Rare	No
Lewis	anti-Le^a	Yes	No
	anti-Le^b	Rare	No
	anti-X (Le^a+Le^b)	Yes	No
Duffy........	anti-Fy^a	Yes	Very rare
	anti-Fy^b	?	No
Kidd	anti-Jk^a	Yes	Rare
	anti-Jk^b	Rare	Very rare
	anti-Jk^{a}Jk^b	Rare	?
Diego	anti-Di^a	Yes	?
Auberger	anti-Au^a	?	?

References

1 Recent publications on blood groups and related fields: BOORMAN and DODD, *An Introduction to Blood Group Serology*, 3rd ed., Churchill, London, 1966; DUNSFORD and BOWLEY, *Techniques in Blood Grouping*, 2nd ed., Thomas, Springfield, 1965; MOLLISON, P.L., *Blood Transfusion in Clinical Medicine*, 4th ed., Blackwell, Oxford, 1967; MOURANT, A.E., *The Distribution of the Human Blood Groups*, Blackwell, Oxford, 1954; PROKOP and UHLENBRUCK, *Lehrbuch der menschlichen Blut- und Serumgruppen*, 2nd ed., Fischer, Jena, 1966; RACE and SANGER, *Blood Groups in Man*, 5th ed., Blackwell, Oxford, 1968; STRATTON and RENTON, *Practical Blood Grouping*, 2nd ed., Blackwell, Oxford (in preparation); WIENER, A.S., *Blood Groups and Transfusion*, 3rd ed., Thomas, Springfield, 1943; WIENER and WEXLER, *Heredity of the Blood Groups*, Grune & Stratton, New York, 1958.
2 For a review of blood-group changes in leukaemia see GOLD and HOLLÄNDER, *Blut*, **9**, 188 (1963).
3 LANDSTEINER, K., *Zbl. Bakt., I. Abt. Orig.*, **27**, 357 (1900).
4 VON DUNGERN and HIRSZFELD, *Z. Immun.-Forsch.*, **8**, 526 (1911).
5 GAMMELGAARD, A., *Hos Mennesket*, Nyt Nordisk Forlag, Copenhagen, 1942.
6 DUNSFORD et al., *Brit. med. J.*, **2**, 81 (1953).
7 LEVINE et al., in HOLLÄNDER, L.P. (Ed.), *Proceedings of the 6th Congress of the International Society of Blood Transfusion*, Boston 1956, Karger, Basle, 1958, page 132 (*Bibl. haemat. [Basel]*, No. 7).
8 YOKOYAMA et al., *Vox Sang. (Basel)*, NF **2**, 348 (1957).
9 MOULLEC et al., *Rev. Hémat.*, **10**, 574 (1955).
10 LANDSTEINER and LEVINE, *Proc. Soc. exp. Biol. (N.Y.)*, **24**, 600 (1927).
11 WALSH and MONTGOMERY, *Nature*, **160**, 504 (1947).
12 LEVINE et al., *Proc. Soc. exp. Biol. (N.Y.)*, **78**, 218 (1951).
13 DUNSFORD et al., *Nature*, **172**, 688 (1953).
14 JACK et al., *Nature*, **186**, 642 (1960).
15 ALLEN et al., *Vox Sang. (Basel)*, NF **3**, 81 (1958).
16 WIENER et al., *J. Amer. med. Ass.*, **153**, 1444 (1953).
17 LANDSTEINER et al., *J. Immunol.*, **27**, 469 (1934).
18 IKIN and MOURANT, *Brit. med. J.*, **1**, 456 (1951).
19 LEVINE et al., *Proc. Soc. exp. Biol. (N.Y.)*, **77**, 402 (1951).
20 VAN DER HART et al., *Vox Sang. (Basel)*, **4**, 108 (1954).
21 CLEGHORN, T.E., *The Occurrence of Certain Rare Blood Group Factors in Britain*, Thesis, Sheffield, 1961.
22 METAXAS and METAXAS-BÜHLER, *Nature*, **202**, 1123 (1964).
23 VAN DER HART et al., *Vox Sang. (Basel)*, NF **3**, 261 (1958).
24 CLEGHORN, T.E., *Nature*, **195**, 297 (1962).
25 SWANSON and MATSON, *Vox Sang. (Basel)*, NF **7**, 585 (1962).
26 WALLACE and IZATT, *Nature*, **200**, 689 (1963).
27 ÖRJASAETER et al., *Nature*, **201**, 832 (1964).
28 LANDSTEINER and LEVINE, *Proc. Soc. exp. Biol. (N.Y.)*, **24**, 941 (1927).
29 LEVINE et al., *Proc. Soc. exp. Biol. (N.Y.)*, **77**, 403 (1951).
30 SANGER, R., *Nature*, **176**, 1163 (1955).
31 MATSON et al., *Amer. J. hum. Genet.*, **11**, 26 (1959).
32 LANDSTEINER and WIENER, *Proc. Soc. exp. Biol. (N.Y.)*, **43**, 223 (1940).
33 WIENER, A.S., *Proc. Soc. exp. Biol. (N.Y.)*, **54**, 316 (1943).
34 RACE, R.R., *Nature*, **153**, 771 (1944).
35 STRATTON, F., *Nature*, **158**, 25 (1946).
36 ARGALL et al., *J. Lab. clin. Med.*, **41**, 895 (1953).
37 WIENER and UNGER, *J. Amer. med. Ass.*, **169**, 696 (1959).
38 CHOWN et al., *Transfusion (Philad.)*, **2**, 150 (1962).
39 CALLENDER and RACE, *Ann. Eugen. (Lond.)*, **13**, 102 (1946).
40 RACE et al., *Nature*, **161**, 316 (1948).
41 STRATTON and RENTON, *Brit. med. J.*, **1**, 962 (1954).
42 CEPPELLINI et al., *Boll. Ist. sieroter. milan.*, **29**, 123 (1950).
43 GREENWALT and SANGER, *Brit. J. Haemat.*, **1**, 52 (1955).
44 SANGER et al., *Nature*, **186**, 171 (1960).
45 SHAPIRO, M., *J. forens. Med.*, **7**, 96 (1960).
46 LAYRISSE et al., *Nature*, **191**, 503 (1961).
47 WIENER and WEXLER, *L. Geddas Novant' Anni delle Leggi Mendeliane*, Istituto Gregorio Mendel, Rome, 1956, page 147.
48 RACE et al., *Blood*, **3**, 689 (1948).
49 ROSENFIELD et al., *Brit. med. J.*, **1**, 975 (1953).
50 ROSENFIELD and HABER, *Amer. J. hum. Genet.*, **10**, 474 (1958).
51 TIPPETT et al., *Vox Sang. (Basel)*, NF **6**, 21 (1961).
52 DENATALE et al., *J. Amer. med. Ass.*, **159**, 247 (1955).
53 ALLEN and TIPPETT, *Vox Sang. (Basel)*, NF **3**, 321 (1958).
54 RACE et al., *Nature*, **166**, 520 (1950).
55 GUNSON and DONOHUE, *Vox Sang. (Basel)*, NF **2**, 320 (1957).
56 TATE et al., *Vox Sang. (Basel)*, NF **5**, 398 (1960).
57 VOS et al., *Lancet*, **1**, 14 (1961).
58 METAXAS and METAXAS-BÜHLER, *Vox Sang. (Basel)*, NF **6**, 136 (1961).
59 ROSENFIELD et al., *Transfusion (Philad.)*, **2**, 287 (1962).
60 KEITH et al., *Vox Sang. (Basel)*, NF **10**, 528 (1965).
61 CUTBUSH and CHANARIN, *Nature*, **178**, 855 (1956).
62 CRAWFORD et al., *Transfusion (Philad.)*, **1**, 228 (1961).
63 MOHR, J., *Acta path. microbiol. scand.*, **29**, 339 (1951).
64 SANGER and RACE, *Heredity*, **12**, 513 (1958).
65 COOMBS et al., *Lancet*, **1**, 264 (1946).
66 LEVINE et al., *Science*, **109**, 464 (1949).
67 ALLEN and LEWIS, *Vox Sang. (Basel)*, NF **2**, 81 (1957).
68 CHOWN et al., *Nature*, **180**, 711 (1957).
69 CORCORAN et al., *Transfusion (Philad.)*, **1**, 181 (1961).
70 ALLEN et al., *Vox Sang. (Basel)*, NF **6**, 555 (1961).
71 GIBLETT, E.R., *Nature*, **181**, 1221 (1958).
72 STROUP et al., *Transfusion (Philad.)*, **5**, 309 (1965).
73 ALLEN and ROSENFIELD, *Transfusion (Philad.)*, **1**, 305 (1961).
74 FRIEDENREICH and HARTMANN, *Z. Immun.-Forsch.*, **92**, 141 (1938).
75 GRUBB, R., *Nature*, **162**, 933 (1948).
76 MOURANT, A.E., *Nature*, **158**, 237 (1946).
77 ANDRESEN, P.H., *Acta path. microbiol. scand.*, **25**, 728 (1948).
78 ANDRESEN and JORDAL, *Acta path. microbiol. scand.*, **26**, 636 (1949).
79 GRUBB, R., *Acta path. microbiol. scand.*, **28**, 61 (1951).
80 SNEATH and SNEATH, *Nature*, **176**, 172 (1955).
81 CUTBUSH et al., *Brit. J. Haemat.*, **2**, 210 (1956).
82 CEPPELLINI, R., *Proceedings of the 5th Congress of the International Society of Blood Transfusion*, Paris, 1955, page 207.
83 CUTBUSH et al., *Nature*, **165**, 188 (1950).
84 IKIN et al., *Nature*, **168**, 1077 (1951).
85 SANGER et al., *Brit. J. Haemat.*, **1**, 370 (1955).
86 ALLEN et al., *Nature*, **167**, 482 (1951).
87 PLAUT et al., *Nature*, **171**, 431 (1953).
88 PINKERTON et al., *Vox Sang. (Basel)*, NF **4**, 155 (1959).
89 LAYRISSE et al., *Acta med. venez.*, **3**, 132 (1955).
90 THOMPSON et al., *Vox Sang. (Basel)*, NF **13**, 314 (1967).
91 SALMON et al., *Nouv. Rev. franç. Hémat.*, **1**, 649 (1961).
92 SWANSON et al., *Nature*, **206**, 313 (1965).
93 WIENER et al., *Ann. intern. Med.*, **44**, 221 (1956).
94 MARSH and JENKINS, *Nature*, **188**, 753 (1960).
95 TIPPETT et al., *Vox Sang. (Basel)*, NF **5**, 107 (1960).
96 MANN et al., *Lancet*, **1**, 8 (1962).
97 EATON et al., *Brit. J. Haemat.*, **2**, 333 (1956).
98 GILES and METAXAS, *Nature*, **202**, 1122 (1964).

(continued at foot of page 634)

Serum groups[1]

Some serum proteins exhibit a genetically determined allotypy that allows serum groups to be distinguished. Such proteins include the γ-globulins (Gm groups), the α_2-globulins (haptoglobins and Gc groups), the lipoproteins (Ag, Lp and Ld groups), the transferrins and serum cholinesterase. Polymorphism occurs not only among the serum enzymes but also among those of the erythrocytes, such as acid phosphatase[26], phosphoglucomutase[27], esterases[28] and lactate dehydrogenase[29].

Gm serum groups (GRUBB and LAURELL[2]) (genetic factors of the immune globulins)

The Gm serum groups are determined by the Gm factors located on the H chain and the Inv factors located on the L chain of the immune globulins (see also page 581). The Gm and Inv factors can be detected by means of the agglutination-inhibition reaction with Rh-positive erythrocytes carrying incomplete anti-D antibodies. A further character of the immune globulins, located on the H chain of the γ_{2b} type and independent of the Gm and Inv factors, is detected by a serum known as anti-ISf. So far, 22 Gm and 3 Inv characters have been described. The most important Gm factors are Gm^a (GRUBB and LAURELL[2]), Gm^b (HARBOE[3]), Gm^x (HARBOE and LUNDEVALL[4]) and Gm^t (GOLD et al.[5]). In 1965 a new nomenclature was proposed under which these Gm factors would become Gm(1), Gm(5), Gm(2) and Gm(4) respectively, while the original Inv(l) factor would be redesignated Inv(1).

Haptoglobin groups (SMITHIES[6])

When the α_2-globulins are separated electrophoretically in starch gel the haptoglobin bands show group-specific differences. These allow three Hp phenotypes to be distinguished, corresponding to three genotypes (Table 1).

Table 1

Phenotype	Genotype
Hp 1–1	Hp^1/Hp^1
Hp 2–1	Hp^1/Hp^2
Hp 2–2	Hp^2/Hp^2

Haptoglobins are normally absent from the blood of the newborn. Ahaptoglobinaemia may also result from intravascular haemolysis. True ahaptoglobinaemia, a defect in the blood proteins, is extremely rare.

A few rare variants of the haptoglobin groups have been reported, such as Hp-Ca (GALATIUS-JENSEN[7]) and the Johnson type (GIBLETT[8]); the latter occurs in two different modifications (1 and 2).

Group-specific components (Gc groups) (HIRSCHFELD[9])

By immunoelectrophoretic separation of the α_2-globulins HIRSCHFELD[9] was able to show that these proteins exhibited an allotypy he designated Gc grouping. A rapidly migrating Gc-1-1 type is distinguished from an intermediate Gc-2-1 type and a slowly migrating Gc-2-2 type.

Corresponding to these phenotypes are three genotypes owing their existence to the autosomal genes Gc^1 and Gc^2: Gc^1Gc^1, Gc^1Gc^2 and Gc^2Gc^2. Very rare variants are Gc^x (HIRSCHFELD[10]), Gc^y (HIRSCHFELD[11]) and Gc^z (HENNIG and HOPPE[12]).

Lipoprotein groups (Ag groups [ALLISON and BLUMBERG[13]]; Lp groups [BERG[14]])

In the complex class of lipoproteins a distinction is made between high-density lipoproteins and low-density lipoproteins (LDL). The latter also show a genetically determined allotypy that can be demonstrated by means of precipitating immune sera. The first precipitating anti-LSL antibody was found by ALLISON and BLUMBERG[13] in the serum of a patient who had received a large number of blood transfusions and named by them anti-Ag. Iso-precipitins with anti-Ag specificity were also found in the blood of women who had had at least four pregnancies (DÜRWALD et al.[15]). Various Ag specificities have since been described in addition to the original Ag(a)[13], namely Ag(b)[16], Ag(x)[17], Ag(a_1)[18] and Ag(z)[18]. More recently, BERG[19] has proposed the designation Ld(a) for yet another Ag specificity.

It has not proved possible to produce a heterospecific anti-Ag serum from animals, though by immunizing rabbits BERG[14] obtained heterospecific anti-LDL sera reacting with a further LDL antigen, Lp. The genetic independence of the Ag and Lp characters appears to have been confirmed[19]. Isoimmunization against an Lp factor has not yet been reported. An anti-Lp serum has also been produced from horses[20]. Whereas the original anti-Lp serum[14] defined the factor Lp(a), the heterospecific anti-Lp horse serum[20] reacts with the factor Lp(x).

Transferrin groups (SMITHIES[21])

The transferrin groups (Tf groups) are due to polymorphism of the iron-binding β_1-globulin transferrin (siderophilin). Up to eight types of transferrin distinguished by their different electrophoretic mobilities are known (SMITHIES and HILLER[22], GIBLETT et al.[23]). Each transferrin corresponds to an autosomal gene, of which each individual possesses a pair. Most members of the white races are homozygotic for the gene Tf^c.

Cholinesterase groups (LEHMANN and RYAN[24], KALOW and GENEST[25])

Group-specific differences in the activity of the serum enzyme cholinesterase give rise to the cholinesterase groups. Their genetic interpretation is still obscure.

References

1 For a review see PROKOP and UHLENBRUCK, *Lehrbuch der menschlichen Blut- und Serumgruppen*, Fischer, Jena, 1963.
2 GRUBB and LAURELL, *Acta path. microbiol. scand.*, **39**, 390 (1956).
3 HARBOE, M., *Acta path. microbiol. scand.*, **47**, 191 (1959).
4 HARBOE and LUNDEVALL, *Acta path. microbiol. scand.*, **45**, 357 (1959).
5 GOLD et al., *Vox Sang. (Basel)*, **10**, 299 (1965).
6 SMITHIES, O., *Biochem. J.*, **61**, 629 (1955).
7 GALATIUS-JENSEN, F., *The Haptoglobins; a Genetical Study*, Dansk Videnskabs Forlag, Copenhagen, 1960.
8 GIBLETT, E. R., *Nature*, **183**, 192 (1959).
9 HIRSCHFELD, J., *Acta path. microbiol. scand.*, **47**, 160 (1959).
10 HIRSCHFELD, J., *Progr. Allergy*, **6**, 155 (1962).
11 HIRSCHFELD, J., *Sci. Tools*, **8**, 17 (1962).
12 HENNIG and HOPPE, *Vox Sang. (Basel)*, NF **10**, 214 (1965).
13 ALLISON and BLUMBERG, *Lancet*, **1**, 634 (1961).
14 BERG, K., *Acta path. microbiol. scand.*, **59**, 369 (1963).
15 DÜRWALD et al., *Vox Sang. (Basel)*, NF **10**, 94 (1965).
16 BLUMBERG and RIDDELL, *J. clin. Invest.*, **42**, 867 (1963).
17 HIRSCHFELD and BLOMBÄCK, *Nature*, **201**, 1337 (1964).
18 HIRSCHFELD et al., *Nature*, **202**, 706 (1964).
19 BERG, K., *Vox Sang. (Basel)*, NF **11**, 419 (1966).
20 BUNDSCHUH, G., *Ärztl. Lab.*, **10**, 309 (1964).
21 SMITHIES, O., *Nature*, **180**, 1482 (1957).
22 SMITHIES and HILLER, *Biochem. J.*, **72**, 121 (1959).
23 GIBLETT et al., *Nature*, **183**, 1589 (1959).
24 LEHMANN and RYAN, *Lancet*, **2**, 124 (1956).
25 KALOW and GENEST, *Canad. J. Biochem.*, **35**, 339 (1957).
26 HOPKINSON et al., *Nature*, **199**, 969 (1963).
27 SPENCER et al., *Nature*, **204**, 742 (1964).
28 SHAW et al., *Science*, **138**, 31 (1962); TASHIAN and SHAW, *Amer. J. hum. Genet.*, **14**, 295 (1962).
29 VESELL, E. S., *Progr. med. Genet.*, **4**, 128 (1965).

99 GILBEY, B. E., *Nature*, **160**, 362 (1947).
100 ELBEL and PROKOP, *Z. Hyg. Infekt.-Kr.*, **132**, 120 (1951).
101 VAN LOGHEM and VAN DER HART, *Bulletin van het Centraal Laboratorium van de Bloedtransfusiedienst van het Nederlandse Rode Kruis*, **2**, 225 (1952).
102 HOLMAN, C. A., *Lancet*, **2**, 119 (1953).
103 DAVIDSOHN et al., *Blood*, **8**, 747 (1953).
104 SIMMONS and WERE, *Med. J. Aust.*, **2**, 55 (1955).
105 KISSMEYER-NIELSEN, F., *Vox Sang. (Basel)*, **5**, 102 (1955).
106 CLEGHORN, T. E., *Brit. J. Haemat.*, **6**, 433 (1960).
107 FRUMIN et al., *Blood*, **15**, 681 (1960).
108 WADLINGTON et al., *Amer. J. Dis. Child.*, **101**, 623 (1961).
109 CLEGHORN, T. E., quoted by RACE and SANGER, *Blood Groups in Man*, 5th ed., Blackwell, Oxford, 1968.
110 WALLACE and MILNE, in HOLLÄNDER, L. P. (Ed.), *Proceedings of the 7th Congress of the International Society of Blood Transfusion*, Rome 1958, Karger, Basle, 1959, page 587 (*Bibl. haemat. [Basel]*, No. 10).
111 DORFMEIJER et al., in HOLLÄNDER, L. P. [110], page 608.
112 VAN DER HART et al., quoted by RACE and SANGER [109], page 298.
113 DUNSFORD, I., quoted by RACE and SANGER [109], page 298.
114 BUCHANAN and AFAGANIS, *Vox Sang. (Basel)*, NF **8**, 213 (1963).
115 SUSSMAN and MILLER, *Rev. Hémat.*, **7**, 368 (1952).
116 ROSENFIELD et al., *Brit. J. Haemat.*, **6**, 344 (1960).
117 SCHMIDT et al., quoted by RACE and SANGER [109], page 396.
118 METAXAS, M. N., *Méd. et Hyg. (Genève)*, **20**, 999 (1962).
119 LEVINE et al., *J. Amer. med. Ass.*, **116**, 825 (1941); LEVINE et al., *Science*, **94**, 371 (1941).

Cerebrospinal Fluid

(For references see pages 639–640)

Unless otherwise stated, the following data apply to the lumbar fluid of adults drawn from the spinal subarachnoid space between the 3rd and 4th lumbar vertebrae. As a result of variations in the secretory, transudatory and resorptive processes there are some differences in the composition of the fluid in the various spaces, i.e., between that of lumbar fluid, cisternal fluid and ventricular fluid. For further details the reader is referred to the specialized literature[1–6].

	Mean	95% range (extreme range in brackets)	*s*	Reference	Remarks
Physicochemical data					
Pressure (mm Hg)					
Children	–	(3.0–7.5)	–	5	Determined with the subject lying on his side. Measured values are affected by the position of the subject, by breathing and by the heart beat. The pressure is increased by inhalation of CO_2 and by alkalosis, decreased by inhalation of O_2 and hyperventilation[7]. *Queckenstedt test:* the pressure is increased on compression of both jugular veins and returns to normal as soon as the compression is released. If the pressure of the spinal fluid increases on compression of a single jugular vein, this indicates thrombosis of the lateral venous sinus on the opposite side.
Adults	–	(4.5–13.5)	–	5	
Volume (ml)					
Infants	–	(40–60)	–	5	In adults the volume is made up of about 35 ml in the ventricles, 25 ml in the subarachnoid space and the cisternae, and 75 ml in the spinal canal.
Young children	–	(60–100)	–	5	
Older children	–	(80–120)	–	5	
Adults	135	(100–160)	–	5	
Appearance	...	...	...	...	The fluid is normally water-white and clear. Colour or cloudiness indicates disease except when due to bleeding during puncture. Cloudiness of the fluid commences with 200 leucocytes per microlitre. It is coloured red (erythrochromia) when containing blood acquired from the puncture or from some other cause a maximum of 5–6 hours previously (provided there are more than 30 erythrocytes per microlitre). A yellow coloration (xanthochromia) occurs when the fluid is admixed with blood more than 6 hours before puncture; it may also be due to increased permeability of the meninges to substances like bilirubin and the carotins (for instance in meningitis or circulatory block of the spinal fluid). A brown coloration may be due to a melanosarcoma of the central nervous system or meninges.
Leucocyte count (per µl)					
Newborn (0–14 days)					
Lumbar fluid	7.5	(0–15)	–	8	Values from (a) 60, (b) 20 subjects, in agreement with those of SAYK[10]. The leucocyte count is often markedly increased in newborn[8] and particularly premature infants[11] during the first weeks of life; from the third month onwards it is the same as in adults. In children 58% of the cells are polynuclear; in adults the proportion of lymphocytes is 70–90% (a), 85–95% (b), 95–100% (c), that of monocytes 10–20% (a), 5–15% (b), 0–5% (c).
Adults					
(a) Lumbar fluid	1.1	0–5.3	–	9	
(b) Cisternal fluid	0.9	0–3.6	–	9	
(c) Ventricular fluid	–	(0–1)	–	10	
Erythrocyte count (per µl)					
Newborn (0–14 days)	120	(0–675)	–	8	Except in the newborn period, the presence of erythrocytes in the fluid always indicates disease, provided that those almost always entering during puncture can be positively excluded.
Specific gravity	1.0070	(1.0062–1.0082)	–	12	Values from 150 subjects.
Freezing-point depression (°C)	0.569	(0.540–0.603)	–	13	Values from 47 subjects. The freezing-point depression and osmolality of the spinal fluid are both somewhat greater than in the serum.
Osmolality (mosm/kg H_2O)	306	–	–	13	
Refractive index	–	(1.33494–1.33510)	–	14	
Surface tension (20 °C, dyn cm^{-1})	61.5	60.0–63.0	0.75	15	Measured by torsion balance.
Relative viscosity (38 °C)	–	(1.020–1.027)	–	16	
Specific conductivity (18 °C, S cm^{-1})	0.01190	–	–	17	
Dry substance (g/kg)	10.8	(8.5–17.0)	–	13	Values from 28 subjects. The dry substance consists mainly of sodium chloride.
pH value					
Cisternal fluid	7.349	7.327–7.371	0.011	18	Values from 15 subjects on the NBS scale. Arterial blood has a mean pH value of 7.424. The cisternal and lumbar fluids have the same pH value[19]. The pH value of the spinal fluid remains fairly constant during disturbances of acid-base balance[20] as a result of a change in the bicarbonate concentration.

Cerebrospinal Fluid

(For references see pages 639–640)

	Mean	95% range (extreme range in brackets)	s	Reference	Remarks
Inorganic substances					
Bicarbonate (mEq/l)					
Cisternal fluid	23.6	21.3–25.9	1.17	18	Values from 15 subjects; the serum had a mean bicarbonate concentration of 24.9 mEq/l. The cisternal and lumbar fluids have identical bicarbonate concentrations[19].
CO_2 (mmol/l)					
Cisternal fluid	25.1	22.6–27.6	1.25	18	Determined by manometer in 15 subjects; the serum had a mean CO_2 content of 26.1 mmol/l.
CO_2 pressure (mm Hg)					
Cisternal fluid	45.2	39.5–50.9	2.84	18	Calculated values from 15 subjects; the arterial blood had a mean CO_2 pressure of 37.5 mm Hg. The cisternal and lumbar fluids have identical CO_2 pressures[19].
Chloride (mEq/l)					
(a)	124	(122–128)	–	21	Determined (a) argentometrically in 15 samples, (b) mercurimetrically in 23 subjects. The chloride concentration of the spinal fluid is about 20% higher than that of the serum.
(b)	119.4	110–129	4.81	22	
Phosphorus (mg/l)					
Total	–	(13.7–21.5)	–	23	Values for inorganic phosphorus determined on 70 subjects. The inorganic phosphorus is increased in inflammatory diseases of the central nervous system and in cerebral arteriosclerosis.
Inorganic	16.1	11.5–20.7	2.3	24	
Lipid phosphorus	0.16	–	–	25	
Sulphur, inorganic (mg/l)	6	–	–	26	Values from patients with neurological disease.
Bromide (mg/l)	2.3	(1.4–3.8)	–	27	The bromide concentration of the ventricular fluid is less than that of the lumbar fluid[28].
Iodine (μg/l)	2	–	–	29	Some of the iodine is present as iodide but most consists of thyroxine[30]. The iodine concentration of the spinal fluid is about 2% of that of the serum.
Thiocyanate (mg/l)	–	(0.3–2.9)	–	1	
Potassium (mEq/l)					
(a)	3.0	2.64–3.36	0.18	22	Values from (a) 23, (b) 20 subjects; in (b) the mean potassium content of the serum was 4.46 mEq/l. The potassium concentration of the spinal fluid is largely independent of that of the serum. In infants it is generally lower than in adults[32].
(b)	2.96	2.06–3.86 (2.33–4.59)	0.45	31	
Sodium (mEq/l)					
(a)	146	135–157	5.69	22	Values from (a) 23, (b) 20 subjects; in (b) the mean sodium content of the serum was 140.6 mEq/l. The sodium concentration of the spinal fluid is proportional to that of the serum except in severe diseases of the central nervous system[31].
(b)	141.2	129–153 (128–152)	6.0	31	
Calcium (mEq/l)	2.28	1.96–2.60	0.16	33	Values from 38 subjects. The concentration of calcium in the spinal fluid is roughly equal to that of ionized calcium in the serum. The various spinal fluid fractions have largely the same calcium content.
Magnesium (mEq/l)	2.23	0.45–4.01	0.89	33	Values from 38 subjects; the mean magnesium content of the serum was 1.61 mEq/l. The various spinal fluid fractions have largely the same magnesium concentration.
Iron (mg/l)	–	(0.23–0.52)	–	5	
Copper (μg/l)					
(a)	62	14–110	24	34	Values from 15 subjects in each case by (a) colorimetric, (b) neutron activation method.
(b)	16	8–24	4	87	
Manganese (μg/l)	–	(0.83–1.50)	–	35	Determined by neutron activation method.
Nitrogenous substances					
Total nitrogen (mg/l)	185	(157–220)	–	1	The spinal fluid contains only small amounts of protein. The nonprotein nitrogen consists mainly of urea and amino acids.
Nonprotein nitrogen (mg/l)	–	(110–200)	–	1	
Ammonia (mg/l)	0.264	0.062–0.466	0.101	36	Values from 15 subjects. The ammonia concentration of the spinal fluid is increased in cirrhosis of the liver.
Amino acids					
As α-amino-N (mg/l)	12.4	9.6–15.2 (10.0–14.7)	1.4	37	Determined colorimetrically with ninhydrin in 20 subjects. Data on the amounts of the individual free amino acids in the spinal fluid[38, 39] show only moderate agreement. Column chromatography by the method of STEIN and MOORE yields 35 ninhydrin-positive compounds[39], including 25 amino acids and 7 substances of unknown constitution. The glutamine concentration of the spinal fluid is similar to that of the serum; most other amino acids are present in concentrations 5–15% of their serum concentrations[39].

(For references see pages 639–640)

	Mean	95% range (extreme range in brackets)	s	Reference	Remarks
Ethanolamine (mg/l)	–	(0.5–1.5)	–	40	The spinal fluid contains more ethanolamine than the serum.
Creatine (mg/l)	–	(4.6–18.7)	–	41	
Creatinine (mg/l)	–	(6–14)	–	41	
Urea (mg/l)	250	(138–364)	–	42	Values from 106 subjects by the urease method. The urea concentration of the spinal fluid is about three-quarters of that of the serum[42, 43]. It is increased in diseases accompanied by nitrogen retention.
Uric acid (mg/l)	–	(5–26)	–	5	
Acetylcholine (μg/l)	–	(<20)	–	44	
Histamine (μg/l)	9.7	(2–30)	–	45	
Serotonin (μg/l)	1.04	0.66–1.42	0.19	46	Values from 48 subjects by a biological method.
Indoxylsulphuric acid (mg/l)	1.0	0.6–1.4	0.2	47	Values from 50 subjects. Increased in renal insufficiency.
Bilirubin (mg/l)					
Newborn	2.4	0.4–4.4	1.0	48	Values from 34 newborn infants with a bilirubin serum level of 67 mg/l. The bilirubin concentration of the spinal fluid rises with that of the serum (correlation coefficient 0.58[48]). Most of the bilirubin in the spinal fluid is in the unconjugated form[48, 50].
Adults	–	(<0.1)	–	49	
Proteins (mg/l)					
Children					
(a) 1–5 days	700	(250–900)	–	51	Values from (a) 35, (b) 7, (c) 98, (d) 21, (e) 25, (f) 13 and (g) 7 subjects by (a) biuret reaction, (b) precipitation with trichloracetic acid, (c, e) biuret reaction-FOLIN method, (d, f, g) precipitation with sulphosalicylic acid. Values vary somewhat with the method used[52, 54, 55]. The spinal fluid contains little protein in comparison with the serum. Immunoelectrophoretic analysis yields over 30 fractions[3, 4, 56], agar-gel electrophoresis about 20 fractions[57]. In nervous diseases the spinal fluid contains additionally proteins not present in the serum[56, 57]. The prealbumin concentration is much higher than that of the serum, whereas fibrinogen and most lipoproteins and proteins with a higher molecular weight than γG-globulin are normally absent. The protein concentration of the spinal fluid is increased in newborn and particularly premature infants[8, 11, 48, 51] but from about the 6th month it is the same as that in adults. In subjects over 65 years of age the lumbar fluid may contain over 600 mg protein per litre[55]. Data on sex differences are conflicting. In disease the protein concentration of the spinal fluid is always increased; the prealbumin fraction is sometimes diminished, while in inflammation and multiple sclerosis the γ-globulin fraction is increased[6, 57–59]. Leucoencephalitis, multiple sclerosis and neurosyphilis can be distinguished by agar-gel electrophoresis of the γ-globulins of the spinal fluid[57].
(b) 5–8 months	204	156–252	24	8	
Adults					
(c) Lumbar fluid	244	156–333	44	52	
(d) Lumbar fluid	313	123–503	95	53	
(e) Cisternal fluid	218	127–310	46	52	
(f) Cisternal fluid	183	97–269	43	53	
(g) Ventricular fluid	171	0–369	99	53	
Mucoproteins (mg/l)	51	15–87	18	60	Protein fraction soluble in perchloric acid.
Sialic acid (mg/l)	5.1	3.3–6.9	0.9	61	Determined in 15 samples by the thiobarbituric acid method. The spinal fluid contains no free sialic acid.
β-Lipoproteins (mg/l)	0.39	(0.10–0.62)	0.18	62	Values from 12 subjects.

Paper-electrophoretic protein fractions of spinal fluid (as percentages of the total protein)

	Number	Prealbumin		Albumin		α_1-Globulins		α_2-Globulins		β-Globulins		γ-Globulin		Reference
		Mean	s	Mean	s	Mean	s	Mean	s	Mean	s	Mean	s	
Children (1–5 days)	35	2.5		47.4		6.8		8.8		14.5		20.0		51
Adults														
Lumbar fluid	22	3.4	1.98	54.8	6.95	8.8	0.24	7.9	1.77	{9.8 / 5.8}*	{1.71 / 1.53}*	9.8	2.88	58
	21	4.6	1.3	49.5	6.5	6.7	2.0	8.3	2.1	18.5	4.8	11.2	2.7	53
Cisternal fluid	13	4.6	1.6	44.6	7.3	6.7	1.0	9.5	3.7	21.3	4.5	13.4	4.0	53
Ventricular fluid	7	6.3	1.8	46.4	6.5	8.1	1.7	7.9	2.8	19.1	2.0	10.3	2.7	53

* Total β-fraction; first value β-fraction, second value β_L-fraction.

	Mean	95% range (extreme range in brackets)	s	Reference	Remarks
Enzymes*	...	...	...	...	About 30 enzymes have so far been identified in the spinal fluid[4,6]. In addition to those listed, the spinal fluid contains various esterases (e.g., cholinesterase), lipases, ribonuclease, isocitrate dehydrogenase and succinate dehydrogenase. There is no direct relationship between the enzyme activity of the serum and that of the spinal fluid. Disturbances of the permeability of the blood-brain and blood-spinal fluid barriers may result in transudation of enzymes from the serum and cerebral parenchyma into the spinal fluid.
1.1.1.14 **L-Iditol dehydrogenase** (U/l, 25 °C)	1.0	0.54–1.46	0.23	63	Values from children aged 2–15 years.
1.1.1.27 **Lactate dehydrogenase** (U/l, 25 °C)	18.4	6.8–30.0	5.8	64	The proportions of the individual isoenzymes in the spinal fluid are much the same as in the serum[65]. No significant age differences have been observed in children[63].
1.1.1.37 **Malate dehydrogenase** (U/l, 25 °C)	20.8	12.8–28.8	4.0	64	
2.1.3.3 **Ornithine carbamoyltransferase** (U/l, 37 °C)	0.31	0.05–0.57	0.13	66	Values from 77 children.
2.6.1.1 **Aspartate aminotransferase** (U/l, 25 °C)	–	(0–10)	–	67	Determined spectrophotometrically. Significant age differences have not been observed in children[63].
2.6.1.2 **Alanine aminotransferase** (U/l, 25 °C)	–	(0–9)	–	67	
3.4.1.1 **Leucine aminopeptidase** (U/l, 37 °C)	0.17	(0.05–0.28)	–	68	
4.1.2.13 **Fructose diphosphate aldolase** (U/l, 37 °C)	0.29	0–0.73	0.22	64	
5.3.1.6 **Ribose phosphate isomerase** (U/l, 37 °C)	1.2	(0.5–1.3)	–	69	
5.3.1.9 **Glucose phosphate isomerase** (U/l, 37 °C)	15	(2.5–38)	–	69	
Lipids					
Total lipids (mg/l)	12.52	7.66–17.4	2.43	59	The spinal fluid contains triglycerides, phospholipids, cholesterol and cholesteryl esters. The fatty acid composition of the spinal fluid lipids is qualitatively similar to that of the plasma lipids; the proportion of linoleic acid in the spinal fluid fatty acids (4%) is lower than that in the plasma fatty acids (24%)[70].
Neutral fats (mg/l)	4.17	0–9.01	2.42	59	Calculated by difference. Probably consist mainly of triglycerides.
Cholesterol (mg/l)					
(a)	3.95	2.19–5.71	0.88	59	The proportion of free cholesterol was (a) 33%, (b) 44%.
(b)	4.63	1.55–7.71	1.54	71	
Phospholipids					
(mg/l)	5.49	2.09–8.89	1.70	71	The phospholipids of the spinal fluid consist of lecithins, cephalins, plasmalogens, sphingomyelins and small amounts of lysolecithins[59,72]. In nervous diseases the phospholipid concentration of the spinal fluid is often increased; in diseases accompanied by breakdown of myelin in the nervous tissue the cephalin concentration of the spinal fluid is increased[73].
(μmol/l)	5.21	3.41–7.01	0.90	59	
Total fatty acids (μmol/l)	70	42–98	14	74	

* Given are the numbers and trivial names recommended by the Enzyme Commission of the International Union of Biochemistry (see pages 385–386). For definition of the unit U see page 584.

	Mean	95% range (extreme range in brackets)	s	Reference	Remarks
Carbohydrates and non-nitrogenous metabolites					
Glucose (mg/l)					
(a) Lumbar fluid	615	487–743	64	75	Determined by (a) glucose oxidase method, (b) FOLIN-WU method, (c) HAGEDORN-JENSEN method. Glucose can also be determined by the *o*-toluidine method[76] since galactose and mannose are lacking in the spinal fluid of adults. About 90% of the reducing substances in the spinal fluid consist of glucose. The glucose concentration of the spinal fluid is about two-thirds of that of the serum; in the newborn it is often low, in diabetes and in encephalitis lethargica it is increased, in bacterial meningitis decreased.
(b) Lumbar fluid	670	480–860	95	75	
(c) Lumbar fluid	–	(500–800)	–	10	
(c) Cisternal fluid	–	(500–900)	–	10	
(c) Ventricular fluid	–	(500–900)	–	10	
Fructose (mg/l)	34	(24–42)	–	77	
Glucosamine (mg/l)	90	(50–180)	–	78	
Inositol (mg/l)	25.5	13.7–37.3	5.9	79	Values from 14 subjects.
Pyruvic acid (mg/l)	–	(4–7)	–	80	Diagnostic use of this assay has been suggested[81].
α-Ketoglutaric acid (mg/l)	–	(0.3–2.9)	–	80	
Oxaloacetic acid (mg/l)	–	(0.8–1.1)	–	80	
Succinic acid (mg/l)	–	(2.8–3.9)	–	82	
Citric acid (mg/l)					
Lumbar fluid	54	–	–	83	Values from 30-year old subjects. The citric acid concentration of the spinal fluid increases with age.
Cisternal fluid	37	–	–	83	
Lactic acid (mEq/l)	1.6	0.84–2.36	0.38	22	Values by an enzyme method from 23 subjects whose serum lactic acid level was 1.4 mEq/l.
Acetoacetic acid (mg/l)	2.67	(1.61–5.46)	1.26	88	Values by an enzyme method from 11 subjects.
β-Hydroxybutyric acid (mg/l)	4.83	(2.47–9.80)	2.49	88	Values by an enzyme method from 11 subjects.
Vitamins					
Thiamine (μg/l)					
(a)	–	(13–17)		84	Values from (a) 45 subjects with *Ochromonas malhamensis*, (b) 36 subjects with *Ochromonas danica*. In the spinal fluid thiamine occurs in both the free and phosphorylated form[7].
(b)	4	(3–12)	–	85	
Vitamin B_6 (μg/l)	–	(0–0.75)	–	84	Determined with *Tetrahymena pyriformis*.
Nicotinic acid (mg/l)	–	(0.1–0.5)	–	1	
Folic acid (μg/l)					
(a)	–	(10–30)	–	86	Determined with (a) *Lactobacillus casei*, (b) *Pediococcus cerevisiae*. For methods see page 478.
(b)	–	(1–5)	–	86	
Vitamin B_{12} (ng/l)	–	(0–30)	–	86	Determined with *Ochromonas malhamensis*.
Pantothenic acid (mg/l)	0.52	(0.10–1.7)	–	84	Values from 103 subjects determined with *Lactobacillus plantarum*. Present mainly in the combined form.
Ascorbic acid (mg/l)	–	(3–21)	–	1	Present in the reduced form.

References

1 HINSBERG and GEINITZ, in LANG et al. (Eds.), *Hoppe-Seyler/Thierfelder Handbuch der physiologisch- und pathologisch-chemischen Analyse*, 10th ed., vol.5, Springer, Berlin, 1953, page 300.

2 HINSBERG, K., in FLASCHENTRÄGER and LEHNARTZ (Eds.), *Physiologische Chemie*, vol.2, part 1a, Springer, Berlin, 1954, page 564; WOLSTENHOLME and O'CONNOR (Eds.), *The Cerebrospinal Fluid*, Ciba Foundation Symposium, Churchill, London, 1958; BOWSHER, D., *Cerebrospinal Fluid Dynamics in Health and Disease*, American Lecture Series, No. 413, Thomas, Springfield, 1960; HENLY, A. A., in LONG et al. (Eds.), *Biochemists' Handbook*, Spon, London, 1961, page 892; DAVSON, H., *Physiology of the Cerebrospinal Fluid*, Churchill, London, 1967; DAVSON, H., *Ergebn. Physiol.*, **52**, 20 (1963).

3 BAUER, H., *Internist (Berl.)*, **4**, 535 (1963).

4 BAUER and HABECK, *Internist (Berl.)*, **4**, 535 (1963).

5 LUPS and HAAN, *The Cerebrospinal Fluid*, Elsevier, Amsterdam, 1954.

6 MCALPINE et al., *Multiple Sclerosis*, Livingstone, Edinburgh, 1965.

7 RICH et al., *Circulat. Res.*, **1**, 389 (1953).

8 WIDELL, S., *Acta paediat. (Uppsala)*, **47**, suppl. 115 (1958).

9 RIEDER, H. P., University Neurological Clinic, Basle. Unpublished.

10 SAYK, J., *Cytologie der Cerebrospinalflüssigkeit*, Fischer, Jena, 1960, page 24.

11 GYLLENSWÄRD and MALMSTRÖM, *Acta paediat. (Uppsala)*, suppl. 135, 54 (1962).

12 WOLMAN et al., *Techn. Bull. Reg. med. Technol.*, **7**, 33 (1946).

13 FREMONT-SMITH et al., *Arch. Neurol. Psychiat. (Chic.)*, **25**, 1271 (1931).

14 HALLMANN, L., *Klinische Chemie und Mikroskopie*, 9th ed., Thieme, Stuttgart, 1960.

15 KÜNZEL, O., *Ergebn. inn. Med. Kinderheilk.*, **60**, 565 (1941).

16 LEVINSON, A., *Cerebrospinal Fluid in Health and in Disease*, 2nd ed., Mosby, St. Louis, 1923.

17 TESCHLER, L., *Dtsch. Z. Nervenheilk.*, **103**, 87 (1928).

18 SCHWAB, M., *Klin. Wschr.*, **40**, 765 (1962).

19 FISHER and CHRISTIANSON, *J. appl. Physiol.*, **18**, 712 (1963).

20 MITCHELL et al., *J. appl. Physiol.*, **20**, 443 (1965).

21 COTLOVE et al., *Stand. Meth. clin. Chem.*, **3**, 81 (1961).

[22] MONTANI and PERRET, *Schweiz. med. Wschr.*, **94**, 1552 (1964).
[23] TROPP et al., *Biochem. Z.*, **290**, 320 (1937).
[24] FRIEDMAN and LEVINSON, *Arch. Neurol. Psychiat. (Chic.)*, **74**, 424 (1955).
[25] TOURTELLOTTE, W. W., *Neurology (Minneap.)*, **9**, 375 (1959).
[26] WATCHORN and MCCANCE, *Biochem. J.*, **29**, 2291 (1935).
[27] DITTMER, D. S. (Ed.), *Blood and Other Body Fluids*, Biological Handbooks, Federation of American Societies for Experimental Biology, Washington, 1961, page 315.
[28] SMITH et al., *J. Neurol. Neurosurg. Psychiat.*, **18**, 237 (1955).
[29] GILDEA and MAN, *Arch. Neurol. Psychiat. (Chic.)*, **49**, 93 (1943).
[30] ALPERS and RALL, *J. clin. Endocr.*, **15**, 1482 (1955).
[31] COOPER et al., *Amer. J. Med.*, **18**, 613 (1955).
[32] GIUSTI, M., *Riv. Clin. pediat.*, **56**, 49 (1955).
[33] HUNTER and SMITH, *Nature*, **186**, 161 (1960).
[34] GUBLER et al., *J. clin. Invest.*, **36**, 1208 (1957).
[35] COTZIAS and PAPAVASILIOU, *Nature*, **195**, 823 (1962).
[36] SCHWAB and DAMMASCHKE, *Klin. Wschr.*, **40**, 184 (1962).
[37] WILLIAMS et al., *Clin. chim. Acta*, **12**, 468 (1965).
[38] GRÜNDIG, E., *Clin. chim. Acta*, **7**, 498 (1962); SCHREIER, K., in HOLDEN, J.T. (Ed.), *Amino Acid Pools*, Elsevier, Amsterdam, 1962, page 263.
[39] PERRY and JONES, *J. clin. Invest.*, **40**, 1363 (1961).
[40] KNAUFF and ZICKGRAF, *Hoppe-Seylers Z. physiol. Chem.*, **312**, 264 (1958).
[41] STRAUBE, G., *Dtsch. Z. Nervenheilk.*, **134**, 288 (1934).
[42] STRAUBE and HOFMANN, *Klin. Wschr.*, **13**, 1377 (1934).
[43] BRADBURY et al., *Clin. Sci.*, **25**, 97 (1963).
[44] TURNER and MAUSS, *Arch. gen. Psychiat.*, **1**, 646 (1959).
[45] JACKSON and ROSE, *J. Lab. clin. Med.*, **34**, 250 (1949).
[46] SINGH et al., *Nature*, **206**, 206 (1965).
[47] MÜTING, D., *Clin. chim. Acta*, **12**, 551 (1965).
[48] NASRALLA et al., *J. clin. Invest.*, **37**, 1403 (1958).
[49] BERMAN et al., *J. Lab. clin. Med.*, **44**, 273 (1954).
[50] STEMPFEL and ZETTERSTRÖM, *Pediatrics*, **16**, 184 (1955).
[51] PILIERO and LENDING, *Amer. J. Dis. Child.*, **97**, 785 (1959).
[52] RIEDER, H. P., *Klin. Wschr.*, **44**, 1036 (1966).
[53] GOLDSTEIN et al., *Med. Clin. N. Amer.*, **44**, 1053 (1960).
[54] FRIEDMAN et al., *Stand. Meth. clin. Chem.*, **5**, 223 (1965).
[55] RICE et al., *Stand. Meth. clin. Chem.*, **5**, 231 (1965).
[56] DENCKER and SWAHN, *Nature*, **194**, 288 (1962).
[57] LOWENTHAL, A., *Agar Gel Electrophoresis in Neurology*, Elsevier, Amsterdam, 1964.
[58] SCHEIFFARTH et al., *Papierelektrophorese in Klinik und Praxis*, Urban & Schwarzenberg, Munich, 1962, page 78.
[59] TOURTELLOTTE, W. W., *Med. Clin. N. Amer.*, **47**, 1619 (1963).
[60] ZLOTNICK et al., *J. Lab. clin. Med.*, **54**, 207 (1959).
[61] SAIFER and GERSTENFELD, *Clin. chim. Acta*, **7**, 467 (1962).
[62] CLAUSEN, J., in PEETERS, H. (Ed.), *Protides of the Biological Fluids*, Proceedings of the 13th Colloquium, Brussels 1965, Elsevier, Amsterdam, 1966, page 85.
[63] VERREY, F., *Enzymol. biol. clin. (Basel)*, **2**, 233 (1962/63).
[64] CONCONI et al., *Acta vitamin. (Milano)*, **15**, 197 (1961).
[65] VAN DER HELM et al., *Clin. chim. Acta*, **8**, 193 (1963).
[66] WEBER, H., *Klin. Wschr.*, **41**, 37 (1963).
[67] WRÓBLEWSKI, F., *Advanc. clin. Chem.*, **1**, 313 (1958).
[68] GREEN and PERRY, *Neurology (Minneap.)*, **13**, 924 (1963).
[69] BRUNS et al., *Clin. chim. Acta*, **1**, 63 (1956).
[70] TUNA et al., *Neurology (Minneap.)*, **13**, 331 and 381 (1963).
[71] SHIN, Y. S., *Analyt. Biochem.*, **5**, 369 (1963).
[72] HACK and HELMY, *Proc. Soc. exp. Biol. (N.Y.)*, **111**, 421 (1962); PHILLIPS and ROBINSON, *Clin. chim. Acta*, **8**, 832 (1963).
[73] Annotation, *Lancet*, **1**, 1363 (1963).
[74] FARSTAD, M., *Scand. J. clin. Lab. Invest.*, **16**, 554 (1964).
[75] MARKS, V., *Clin. chim. Acta*, **4**, 395 (1959).
[76] HYVÄRINEN and NIKKILÄ, *Clin. chim. Acta*, **7**, 140 (1962).
[77] PAPADOPOULOS and HESS, *Arch. Biochem.*, **88**, 167 (1960).
[78] EASTHAM and KEAY, *J. clin. Path.*, **5**, 319 (1952).
[79] GARCIA-BUÑUEL and GARCIA-BUÑUEL, *J. Lab. clin. Med.*, **64**, 461 (1964).
[80] GRÜNDIG, E., *Clin. chim. Acta*, **7**, 498 (1962).
[81] LASCH, F., *Klin. Wschr.*, **31**, 941 (1953).
[82] THUNBERG, T., *Acta med. scand.*, suppl. 90, 122 (1938).
[83] MÅRTENSSON and THUNBERG, *Acta med. scand.*, **140**, 454 (1951).
[84] BAKER and SOBOTKA, *Advanc. clin. Chem.*, **5**, 173 (1962).
[85] BAKER et al., *Amer. J. clin. Nutr.*, **14**, 197 (1964).
[86] SOBOTKA et al., *Proc. Soc. exp. Biol. (N.Y.)*, **103**, 801 (1960).
[87] KJELLIN, K., *J. Neurochem.*, **10**, 89 (1963).
[88] SCHMIDT and SCHWARZ, personal communication.

Synovial Fluid

(For references see page 642)

The synovial fluid consists of a serum ultrafiltrate together with a secretion formed by the cells of the synovial membrane; the latter component contains mucopolysaccharides. Normal values for the synovial fluid have been assembled by ROPES and BAUER[1] and by DITTMER[2]. For changes in the composition of the synovial fluid in joint disease see the literature[1,3,4].

Unless otherwise stated, the data given below refer to synovial fluid from the *knee joint.*

	Mean	95% range (extreme range in brackets)	*s*	Reference	Remarks
Physical data					
Volume (ml)	1.1	(0.13–4.00)	–	2	Often increased to 10–30 ml in joint disease.
Specific gravity (20 °C/20 °C)	–	(1.008 1–1.015)	–	5	Postmortem values in 25 subjects.
Viscosity					
Relative viscosity (37 °C)	–	(>300)	–	6	The viscosity is dependent on the hyaluronic acid content. It is often diminished in joint disease[6,7].
Intrinsic viscosity (37 °C)	46.3	26.9–65.7	9.7	6	
Cells (per μl)	63	(13–180)	–	8	Consist of 63% mononuclear phagocytes, 25% lymphocytes, 6.5% polymorphonuclear leucocytes and 4% synovial cells; any erythrocytes normally arise from injury during aspiration. The various kinds of cell present in the fluid in rheumatic diseases have been studied[9].
pH value	7.434	(7.31–7.64)	–	10	Measured in vivo. The pH is lower in inflammatory joint disease.
Water (g/kg)	–	(960–988)	–	5	Postmortem values in 25 subjects.
Dry substance (g/kg)	34	(12–48)	–	2	
Inorganic substances					
Carbon dioxide (mmol/l)	–	(19.3–30.6)	–	11	In accordance with the DONNAN equilibrium the bicarbonate concentration of the synovial fluid is higher than that of the serum[7].
Chloride (mEq/l)	107.4	(87–138)	–	7	In accordance with the DONNAN equilibrium the chloride concentration of the synovial fluid is higher than that of the serum[7].

(For references see pages 650–651)

Owing to the difficulty of collecting pure gastric juice the exact composition of this body fluid is not known for certain. The use of a gastric tube or even a gastric fistula yields not pure gastric juice but simply the gastric contents, almost always containing saliva, food remnants and occasionally also bile, pancreatic juice and intestinal contents. Unless otherwise stated, the following values apply to unstimulated gastric juice obtained from fasting subjects by means of permanent intubation.

The gastric juice consists of a mixture of the various secretions of the cells of the gastric mucosa. The parietal cells of the fundus glands secrete mainly hydrochloric acid, the chief cells of the glands mainly pepsinogen, while the mucosal cells of the covering epithelium and the other cells of the glands secrete an alkaline mucous juice. The gastric juice can be roughly divided into two components, that of the parietal cells (parietal secretion) and that of the other cells (nonparietal secretion)[1,2]. Both these components are roughly isotonic with the serum. The volumes of the two components are related as follows:

$$V_P = V_{total}\,(0.219 + 4.88\,A)$$
$$V_{NP} = V_{total} - V_P$$

(V_{total} = total secretion [ml]; V_P = parietal secretion [ml]; V_{NP} = nonparietal secretion [ml]; A = acidity [mEq/ml].)

The composition of the gastric juice thus depends on the proportions of the individual cellular secretions, the amounts and compositions of which are in turn dependent on the nature of the stimulus. There is a considerable literature on the composition of the gastric juice[2–6]; on the diagnostic aspects of gastric juice analysis see the literature[7,8].

	Mean	95% range (extreme range in brackets)	s	Reference	Remarks
Physicochemical data					
Fasting volume (ml)					
(a) Newborn	2.65	(0.4–12.3)	2.05	9	Values from (a) 154 newborn children, (b) 98 samples from 3 infants, (c) 695 samples from 59 children (mean age 9 years).
(b) Infants	2.4	(1.0–3.5)	0.7	10	
(c) Children	8.8	(0.4–[80])	8.2	10	
(d) Adults	50	(0–180)	–	5	
Appearance	...	...	...	...	Pure fistular juice is a clear to slightly turbid, almost colourless liquid with a slightly acid taste and odour. The fasting juice is slightly turbid, mucous and occasionally coloured green due to reflux of bile. Free hydrochloric acid is normally absent from the fasting juice of the unstimulated stomach. Traces of fresh blood may be due to injury during intubation. Pathological blood in the fasting juice is usually dark brown and resembles coffee grounds.
Secretion rate (ml/h)					
(a) Infants	18.6	(6–54)	18	10	Values from (a) 98 samples from 3 infants, (b) 10 children (mean age 21 months), (c) 695 samples from 59 children (mean age 9 years). The basal secretion is less in women than in men, falls in adults with advancing age, and varies according to the time of day and degree of stimulation (see also the table on page 648). The amount of gastric juice formed during 24 hours is about 2–3 l, or about 35 ml per kilogramme body weight[5]. Secretion is often *decreased* in diabetics[11] and patients with cancer of the stomach[12] or cirrhosis[13], *increased* in patients with duodenal ulcer[12,14,15] (particularly during the night[15]) or the ZOLLINGER-ELLISON syndrome[16].
(b) Young children					
Fasting (basal)	31	(10–64)	–	27	
After histamine (maximal)	52	(28–105)	–	27	
(c) Children	50.4	(6–180)	25.2	10	
(d) Adults					
Fasting (basal)	74	(0–176)	–	5	
At night	46	(12–99)	–	5	
After meals	101	(13–217)	–	5	
After histamine	117	(2–256)	–	5	
After insulin	124	(70–204)	–	5	
Specific gravity	–	(1.004–1.010)	–	5	
Freezing-point depression (°C)	0.47	(0.30–0.82)	–	5	The osmolality of the individual secretions is much the same as that of the serum. The mixing of the acid secretion of the parietal cells with the secretion containing bicarbonate causes liberation of CO_2, so that gastric juice of low acidity is often hypotonic[17].
Water (g/l)	–	(994–995)	–	3	
Dry substance (g/l)	5.6	–	–	3	Consists of roughly ¼ inorganic and ¾ organic substances.
pH value					
(a) Newborn	2.52	(1.2–7.4)	1.53	9	Values from (a) 154 newborn children, (b) 695 samples from 59 children (mean age 9 years), (c) 25 adults, (d) 12 adults. At birth the gastric juice is almost neutral and the values given for newborn children are reached 4–6 hours later[18,19]. The pH value of the parietal secretion is about 0.8, corresponding to an acidity of 160 mEq/l[2,17], that of the nonparietal secretion 7.7, corresponding to a bicarbonate concentration of 45 mEq/l[2,17]. The pH value is increased by saliva and intestinal contents. A method of measuring the intragastric pH value by means of a radio-transmitting capsule has been described[20].
(b) Children	3.27	(0.9–7.7)	2.01	10	
(c) Men	1.92	–	1.28	11	
(d) Women	2.59	–	2.08	11	

Gastric Juice

(For references see pages 650–651)

	Mean	Extreme range	s	Reference	Remarks
Acidity					
Total acid (mEq/l)					
(b) Children	38.2	(4–126)	21.6	10	Values from (a) 154 newborn children, (b) 695 samples from 59 children (mean age 9 years), (c) 15 men and 4 women (aged 20–25), (d) 10 children (mean age 21 months). The acid secreted by the parietal cells consists exclusively of hydrochloric acid, which is partly neutralized, buffered and diluted by the secretion of the other cells. The total acid corresponds to a titration end-point of pH 7–8, the free acid to one of pH 2.5–3.5. The difference between the total and free acid is known as bound acid and corresponds roughly to the buffered part of the hydrochloric acid; whether this distinction is a valid one, however, is doubtful. The present preferred method is to titrate the acid to the neutral point using phenol red or the electrometric technique up to pH 7.4[24, 25]. The earlier 'clinical unit' was mEq acid per litre, corresponding to millilitre of 0.1-NaOH per 100 ml.
(c) Adults	–	(5–118)	–	14	
Free acid (mEq/l)					
(a) Newborn	21.4	–	11.7	9	
(b) Children	28.1	(0–100)	17.9	10	
(c) Adults	–	(0–115)	–	14	
Free acid (mEq/h)					
(d) Young children					
Fasting (basal)	0.48	(0.00–1.32)	–	27	
After histamine (maximal)	2.59	(0.80–3.73)	–	27	
(e) Men					
Fasting (basal)	2.4	–	–	8	
At night	1.7	–	–	8	
After betazol (submaximal)	11.6	–	–	8	
After histamine (submaximal)	11.8	–	–	8	
After histamine (maximal)	22.4	–	–	8	
After insulin	16.5	–	–	8	

Gastric juice secretion under maximal histamine stimulation (augmented histamine test). The acid secretion is determined both under basal conditions and following a subcutaneous dose of 0.04 mg histamine monophosphate per kilogramme body weight[22, 23, 69]. The following are measured (all in mEq acid per unit of time):

- one-hour morning basal acid output (MBAO or BAO) = acid secretion during one hour in the morning without stimulation
- maximum acid output (MAO) or maximal secretory response (MSR) = acid secretion during one hour after maximum stimulation with histamine
- maximal histamine response (MHR) = acid secretion during the second and third quarter-hours after maximum stimulation with histamine
- peak acid output (PAO) = 2 × MHR

The acid secretion can also be stimulated[29] by betazol given subcutaneously (values for submaximal stimulation are given in the table below), by histamine given by the continuous intravenous route, by insulin or 2-deoxy-D-glucose (under vagus stimulation), or by gastrin or another synthetic pentapeptide of this type.

The acidity of both unstimulated and stimulated gastric juice varies with age and sex (see the tables below). The basal acid secretion varies with the time of day and is least at about 2 a.m.[17]. The highest acidity values found in man are around 150 mEq/l[21]. At birth the acid content of the gastric juice is very low but rises to the value given in the table during the first hours of life[19]. In children there is good correlation between the acid secretion under histamine stimulation and body weight (about 2 mEq/h per 10 kg body weight)[27, 28]. The maximum acid output is largely constant in any one individual and provides a measure of the total parietal cell mass[30]; about 40 million parietal cells are necessary to produce 1 mEq of hydrochloric acid per hour under maximum stimulation.

There has been much discussion of the usefulness of the acid secretion level for the diagnosis of gastric and intestinal ulcers[25, 31]. If the basal acid output exceeds 60% of the maximum acid output the patient is almost certainly suffering from the ZOLLINGER-ELLISON syndrome[22]. Anacidity (pH > 6) under maximum stimulation with histamine is rare[32] and seen only in severe atrophy of the gastric mucosa, as for instance in pernicious anaemia.

Acid secretion in adults before and after maximum histamine stimulation (subcutaneous dose of 0.04 mg histamine monophosphate per kilogramme body weight)

	Number of subjects	Volume (ml/h)		Total acid (mEq/h)		Free acid (mEq/h)	
		mean	s	mean	s	mean	s
From DOTEVALL[11]							
Basal secretion							
Men	30	64.0	21.4	3.70*	2.12	2.59	1.97
Women	12	54.2	24.2	2.24*	1.76	1.48	1.33
After histamine							
Men	24	201.6	53.4	23.3**	6.9	20.5	6.8
Women	12	153.7	33.3	17.7**	5.4	15.7	5.1
From BARON[69]							
Basal secretion							
Men	20	38.7	23.01	1.3*	1.59	–	–
Women	20	40.6	38.8	1.1*	1.75	–	–
After histamine							
Men	20	177	73.3	17.1**	11.94	–	–
Women	20	107	57.7	9.4**	7.20	–	–

* Basal acid output (BAO). ** Maximal acid output (MAO).

Acid secretion in adults before and after betazol stimulation[70] (subcutaneous dose of 0.5 mg betazol hydrochloride per kilogramme body weight)

Age	Men				Women			
	Number	Free acid (mEq/h)			Number	Free acid (mEq/h)		
		Extreme range	Mean	s		Extreme range	Mean	s
Basal secretion								
20–29	74	0–17.1	2.50	2.81	65	0– 8.6	1.74	2.06
30–39	157	0–14.9	2.63	2.70	145	0–15.0	1.58	2.32
40–49	156	0–12.3	2.83	3.01	184	0–13.5	1.43	2.24
50–59	158	0–17.0	2.25	3.04	162	0– 6.7	0.98	1.53
> 60	70	0– 9.9	1.48	2.18	78	0– 7.6	0.95	1.43
All ages	615	0–17.1	2.44	2.85	634	0–15.0	1.33	2.00
After betazol								
20–29	74	0–29.6	11.46	6.69	65	0.3–20.8	7.79	4.57
30–39	157	0–31.3	12.83	6.69	145	0–22.1	7.83	4.51
40–49	156	0–48.4	13.29	8.66	184	0–24.7	8.12	5.42
50–59	158	0–31.5	10.67	7.11	162	0–22.8	6.90	5.59
> 60	70	0–24.8	7.67	7.56	78	0–20.0	6.67	5.40
All ages	615	0–48.4	11.64	7.62	634	0–24.7	7.53	5.20

	Mean	95% range (extreme range in brackets)	s	Reference	Remarks
Inorganic substances					
Bicarbonate	...	...	...	...	The secretion of the covering cells is reported to contain 45 mEq bicarbonate per litre[17].
Chloride (mEq/l)	–	(77.6–159)	–	14	The chloride content of the parietal secretion is about 170 mEq/l, that of the nonparietal secretion about 125 mEq/l[2,17]. Values below 130 mEq/l point to contamination of the gastric juice by saliva and intestinal contents[2].
Phosphorus (mg/l)	70	([6]–[180])	–	33	From measurements on several hundred subjects; the lowest value was in a patient with hypersecretion, the highest value in a patient with stomach cancer. At least 95% of the total phosphorus consists of inorganic phosphate[33]; the nonparietal secretion contains this ion at a concentration of about 6.4 mEq/l but there is none in the parietal secretion[2,17].
Bromide (mg/l)	–	(0.6–9.0)	–	34	
Fluoride (mg/l)	–	(0.4–0.7)	–	35	
Thiocyanate	...	...	...	...	The presence of thiocyanate in the gastric juice indicates probable contamination with saliva[36].
Potassium (mEq/l)	11.6	(6.4–16.6)	–	37	Values from 50 men. Potassium is secreted in about the same concentration by the parietal cells as by the other cells. Changes in the potassium content under histamine stimulation are variable[38]. High values indicate contamination with saliva.
Sodium (mEq/l)	49	(18.7–69.5)	–	37	Values from 50 men. Sodium is secreted at a concentration of about 160 mEq/l by the cells of the covering epithelium but is absent from the parietal secretion[2,17]; the sodium content of the gastric juice therefore falls under histamine stimulation.
Calcium (mEq/l)	3.6	(2.0–4.8)	–	37	Values from 50 men. The calcium is found in the parietal secretion. Low calcium values indicate contamination by saliva.
Magnesium (mEq/l)	1.5	(0.3–3.0)	–	39	Values from 43 subjects.
Copper (mg/l)	–	(0.1–0.4)	–	40	Values from 7 subjects.
Organic substances					
Total nitrogen (mg/l)					
(a)	752	–	–	41	Values from (a) 21 patients with healthy stomachs, (b) 6 young men.
(b)	–	(910–2180)	–	14	
Nonprotein nitrogen (mg/l)					
(a)	415	–	–	41	Values from (a) 21 patients with healthy stomachs, (b) 10 subjects. The nonprotein nitrogen represents about 20–80% of the total nitrogen (in both subjects with healthy stomachs and patients with gastric complaints)[41].
(b)	–	(150–320)	–	42	
Peptide nitrogen (mg/l)	–	(38–70)	–	42	Values from 10 subjects.
Amino-acid nitrogen (mg/l)	–	(16–75)	–	42	Values from 10 subjects.
Free amino acids (mg/l)	316	–	–	43	Values from 15 subjects; 18 amino acids were determined. Hyperacidic gastric juice has an increased content of free amino acids. For a review see the literature[44].
Ammonia (mg/l)	97	67–127	15	45	Values from 24 subjects. The ammonia content is increased in uraemia[45] and liver cirrhosis[46].
Urea (mg/l)	84	–	15	45	Values from 24 subjects. The urea content is increased in uraemia[45].
Creatinine (mg/l)	–	(12–33)	–	5	
Uric acid (mg/l)	–	(8–69)	–	42	

	Mean	95% range (extreme range in brackets)	*s*	Reference	Remarks
Histamine (µg/l)	–	(7–48)	–	47	
Proteins (g/l)	2.8	2.2–3.4	0.3	48	Determined by the biuret reaction; values in agreement with those obtained by other methods[36,49,50].
Albumin (g/24 h)	–	(0.02–0.69)	–	51	The proteins of gastric juice are a very heterogeneous mixture[52,53] and include mucins rich in carbohydrate, enzymes and plasma proteins (albumin, γG-globulin, γA-globulin and others[54]). At low pH values they are readily broken down by enzymes into peptides and amino acids. Increased albumin values occur often in cancer of the stomach, in atrophic gastritis and always in MÉNÉTRIER's disease[52,55]. On the rate of flow of plasma into the stomach see WETTERFORS[55].
γ-Globulin (g/24 h)	–	(0.03–0.38)	–	51	
Mucins (g/l)	–	(0.6–15.0)	–	5	The mucins are contained in the covering-cell secretion (visible mucus) but are also secreted by the other cells of the glands except the parietal cells (glandular mucoproteins, mucoproteoses). The mucous substances are chemically very heterogeneous[52,53,56,57] and consist mainly of mucoproteins rich in sialic acid and mucopolysaccharides rich in fucose (including the blood-group specific substances). The intrinsic factor (see page 484) and various vitamin B_{12}-binding substances are also mucoproteins. Determination of the intrinsic factor secretion is a diagnostic aid in pernicious anaemia[58].
Undissolved substances	1.4	–	–	56	
Trichloracetic acid precipitate	1.0	–	–	56	
Mucoproteins	0.5	–	–	56	
Mucoproteoses	1.2	–	–	56	
Carbohydrates, bound (mg/l)					
(a) Hexoses	321	–	–	50	Values from (a) 16, (b) 10, (c) 15, (d) 13 and (e) 12 subjects. The carbohydrates are components of the mucoproteins and mucopolysaccharides. Their distribution has been studied by electrophoretic separation of the protein fractions[59]. An increase in the carbohydrate content of the gastric juice has been observed in cancer of the stomach and pernicious anaemia[50].
(b) Hexosamines	327	–	–	50	
(c) Fucose	138	–	–	50	
(d) Sialic acid	73	–	–	50	
(e) Glucuronic acid	20	–	–	50	
Lactic acid	...	...	...	...	Lactic acid arises from the carbohydrates by bacterial action, but only in anacidic and hypoacidic gastric juice.
Lipids	...	...	...	...	The gastric juice appears to contain small amounts of lipids[60] but these have not been further investigated.
Enzymes	...	...	...	...	The gastric juice contains mainly protein-splitting enzymes[52]. Other enzymes present are lipase[61], lysozyme[62], lactate dehydrogenase[63,64], isocitrate dehydrogenase[64], aminotransferases[64], fructosediphosphate aldolase[64], alkaline phosphatase[64], leucine aminopeptidase[64], oxoglutarate dehydrogenase[64], glucosephosphate isomerase[64], β-glucuronidase[64] and ribonuclease[64]; the urease[46] is probably of bacterial origin. The lactate dehydrogenase and β-glucuronidase contents are increased in cancer of the stomach.
Pepsin (kU/24 h, 37 °C)					
Men	28.8	–	13.5	65	Values from 10 men and 10 women (for definition of the unit U see page 584). The gastric juice in man contains at least 3 protein-splitting enzymes[52,53], namely 2 pepsins and a protease with a maximum activity at pH 7. According to TAYLOR[66] one pepsin is secreted by the chief cells of the fundus glands, the other by the pylorus glands. According to TANG and WOLF[67] the proteolytic activity at pH 2 is due to the pepsins, that at pH 3.5 to gastricsin. The pepsin content of the gastric juice is greatly reduced after histamine stimulation and greatly increased after vagus stimulation; it is decreased in cancer of the stomach and atrophy of the gastric mucosa[12,66].
Women	18.9	–	7.5	65	
Vitamins					
Vitamin B_{12} (µg/l)	–	(0.06–3.0)	–	68	
Ascorbic acid (mg/l)	–	(1.5–15.0)	–	5	

References

1 HOLLANDER, F., *Fed. Proc.*, **11**, 706 (1952).
2 HUNT, J. N., *Physiol. Rev.*, **39**, 491 (1959).
3 KRZYWANEK and FLASCHENTRÄGER, in FLASCHENTRÄGER and LEHNARTZ (Eds.), *Physiologische Chemie*, vol. 2, part 1a, Springer, Berlin, 1954, page 2.
4 HINSBERG and BRUNS, in LANG et al. (Eds.), *Hoppe-Seyler/Thierfelder Handbuch der physiologisch- und pathologisch-chemischen Analyse*, 10th ed., vol. 5, Springer, Berlin, 1953, page 372.
5 LEACH, A. A., in LONG et al. (Eds.), *Biochemists' Handbook*, Spon, London, 1961, page 911.
6 DITTMER, D. S. (Ed.), *Blood and Other Body Fluids*, Biological Handbooks, Federation of American Societies for Experimental Biology, Washington, 1961, page 404.
7 ROVELSTAD, R. A., *Gastroenterology*, **45**, 90 (1963).
8 SPARBERG and KIRSNER, *Arch. intern. Med.*, **114**, 508 (1964).
9 THOMSON, J., *Arch. Dis. Childh.*, **26**, 558 (1951).
10 WOLMAN, I. J., *Amer. J. Dis. Child.*, **71**, 394 (1946).
11 DOTEVALL, G., *Acta med. scand.*, **170**, 59 (1961).
12 HIRSCHOWITZ, B. I., *Amer. J. dig. Dis.*, **6**, 199 (1961).
13 SCOBIE and SUMMERSKILL, *Gut*, **5**, 422 (1964).
14 IHRE, B., *Acta med. scand.*, suppl. 95 (1938).
15 DRAGSTEDT, L. R., *Ann. N. Y. Acad. Sci.*, **99**, 190 (1962).
16 ZOLLINGER and ELLISON, *Proceedings of the Third World Congress of Gastroenterology*, vol. 1, Williams & Wilkins, Baltimore, 1959, page 419.
17 DAVENPORT, H. W., *Physiology of the Digestive Tract*, 2nd ed., Year Book Medical Publishers, Chicago, 1966, page 93.
18 EBERS et al., *Pediatrics*, **18**, 800 (1956); AVERY et al., *Pediatrics*, **37**, 1005 (1966).

[19] Montes-Gallo and Saari, *Ann. paediat. Fenn.*, **6**, 185 (1960).
[20] Noeller, H.G., *Germ. med. Mth.*, **6**, 3 (1961), and *Dtsch. med. Wschr.*, **85**, 1707 (1960); Ottenjann, R., *Med. Klin.*, **58**, 1999 (1963); Hochberg et al., *Münch. med. Wschr.*, **106**, 789 (1964).
[21] Nordgren, B., *Acta physiol. scand.*, **58**, suppl. 202 (1963).
[22] Marks, I.N., *Gastroenterology*, **41**, 599 (1961).
[23] Kay, A.W., *Brit. med. J.*, **2**, 77 (1953).
[24] Baron, J.H., *Gastroenterology*, **45**, 118 (1963).
[25] Perrier et al., *Schweiz. med. Wschr.*, **95**, 876 (1965).
[26] Lawrie et al., *Lancet*, **2**, 270 (1964); Lawrie and Forrest, *Postgrad. med. J.*, **41**, 408 (1965).
[27] Rødbro et al., *Lancet*, **2**, 730 (1966).
[28] Ghai et al., *Arch. Dis. Childh.*, **40**, 77 (1965).
[29] Makhlouf et al., *Gut*, **5**, 379 (1964); Zaterka and Neves, *Gastroenterology*, **47**, 251 (1964); Scobie, B.A., *Brit. med. J.*, **1**, 1287 (1965); Duke et al., *Lancet*, **2**, 871 (1965); Makhlouf et al., *Gut*, **6**, 525 (1965); Makhlouf et al., *Gastroenterology*, **51**, 149 (1966); Abernethy et al., *Lancet*, **1**, 291 (1967).
[30] Card and Marks, *Clin. Sci.*, **19**, 147 (1960).
[31] Baron, J.H., *Clin. Sci.*, **24**, 357 (1963); Baron, J.H., *Gut*, **4**, 243 (1963); Johnson et al., *Gut*, **5**, 402 (1964).
[32] Leading article, *Lancet*, **2**, 27 (1960).
[33] Hoesch, K., *Dtsch. Arch. klin. Med.*, **165**, 201 (1929).
[34] Cornbleet, T., *J. invest. Derm.*, **1**, 399 (1938).
[35] Goldemberg and Schraiber, *Rev. Soc. argent. Biol.*, **11**, 111 (1935).
[36] Teichmann, W., *Dtsch. Z. Verdau.- u. Stoffwechselkr.*, **13**, 203 (1953).
[37] Bernstein, R.E., *J. Lab. clin. Med.*, **40**, 707 (1952).
[38] Hollander, F., *Gastroenterology*, **40**, 477 (1961).
[39] Mahler, P., *Wien. Arch. inn. Med.*, **19**, 413 (1930).
[40] van Ravesteyn, A.H., *Acta med. scand.*, **118**, 163 (1944).
[41] Norpoth, L., *Klin. Wschr.*, **26**, 406 (1948).
[42] Nagl, F., *Z. klin. Med.*, **151**, 429 (1954).
[43] Müting, D., *Naturwissenschaften*, **41**, 580 (1954).
[44] Heathcote and Washington, *Nature*, **207**, 941 (1965).
[45] Lieber and Lefèvre, *J. clin. Invest.*, **38**, 1271 (1959).
[46] Rappoport and Kern, *J. Lab. clin. Med.*, **61**, 550 (1963).
[47] Farendin et al., *Gastroenterologia (Basel)*, **79**, 185 (1953).
[48] Berg, G., *Bibl. gastroent. (Basel)*, **5**, 195 (1962).
[49] Teichmann, W., *Z. ges. inn. Med.*, **7**, 908 (1952).
[50] Richmond et al., *Gastroenterology*, **29**, 1017 (1955).
[51] Horowitz and Hollander, *Ann. N.Y. Acad. Sci.*, **99**, 67 (1962).
[52] Glass, G.B.J., *Advanc. clin. Chem.*, **7**, 236 (1964).
[53] Glass, G.B.J., *Advanc. clin. Chem.*, **7**, 373 (1964).
[54] Barandun et al., *Schweiz. med. Wschr.*, **92**, 316 and 353 (1962); Hirsch-Marie and Burtin, in Peeters, H. (Ed.), *Protides of the Biological Fluids*, Proceedings of the 11th Colloquium, Brussels 1963, Elsevier, Amsterdam, 1964, page 256; Peeters et al., in Peeters, H. (Ed.), *Protides of the Biological Fluids*, Proceedings of the 11th Colloquium, Brussels 1963, Elsevier, Amsterdam, 1964, page 261.
[55] Wetterfors, J., *Acta med. scand.*, suppl. 430 (1965).
[56] Kent, P.W., *Gastroenterology*, **43**, 292 (1962).
[57] Hollander, F., *Gastroenterology*, **43**, 304 (1962).
[58] Irvine et al., *Lancet*, **2**, 397 (1965).
[59] Glass et al., *Clin. chim. Acta*, **9**, 509 (1964).
[60] Horowitz, M.I., *Ann. N.Y. Acad. Sci.*, **106**, 278 (1963).
[61] Schønheyder and Volqvartz, *Acta physiol. scand.*, **11**, 349 (1946); Bank et al., *Gut*, **5**, 480 (1964).
[62] Lobstein and Fogelson, *Amer. J. dig. Dis.*, **18**, 282 (1951).
[63] Smyrniotis et al., *Amer. J. dig. Dis.*, **7**, 712 (1962).
[64] Piper et al., *Gastroenterology*, **45**, 614 (1963); *Amer. J. dig. Dis.*, **8**, 701 (1963).
[65] van Goidsenhoven et al., *Gastroenterology*, **34**, 421 (1958).
[66] Taylor, W.H., *Physiol. Rev.*, **42**, 519 (1962).
[67] Tang and Wolf, *Gastroenterology*, **44**, 908 (1963).
[68] Pendl and Franz, *Acta haemat. (Basel)*, **13**, 207 (1955).
[69] Baron, J.H., *Gut*, **4**, 136 (1963).

Pancreatic Juice

(For references see page 653)

The pancreatic juice probably arises from two different types of cells: the one type, presumably the epithelial cells of the ducts, secrete a very watery juice rich in bicarbonate, whereas the other type, the epithelial cells of the acini, produce a viscous secretion rich in enzymes. Various stimuli, for instance acids, bring about the liberation of secretin and pancreozymin from the duodenal mucosa. Secretin stimulates mainly the secretion of fluid and bicarbonate, while pancreozymin, acetylcholine and vagus stimulation cause an increase in the liberation of enzymes. Unless otherwise stated, the data given in the table below apply to unstimulated pancreatic juice obtained either by means of intubation (here designated duodenal contents) or an external pancreatic fistula. For further data on the pancreatic juice see the literature[1–3].

	Mean	95% range (extreme range in brackets)	s	Reference	Remarks
Physicochemical data					
Appearance	...	...	...	...	Watery, colourless, thin fluid, clear or slightly opalescent. Because of its similarity to saliva, the pancreatic juice is also known as abdominal saliva.
Secretion rate (ml/h)					
Young children	–	(4–13)	–	4	
Adults	36	(>0–99)	–	2	The secretion of pancreatic juice never ceases completely; under strictly basal conditions it is probably less than 6 ml/h in adults[5]. A copious flow of pancreatic juice usually starts several minutes after commencing a meal and continues for about 3 hours. The daily volume of pancreatic juice produced when the rhythm of eating and sleeping is normal has been assessed at 700–2500 ml[5] or 17–20 ml/kg body weight[2]. Daily quantities of up to 3300 ml of fistular juice have been measured[5]. The secretion of pancreatic juice increases after intravenous injection of secretin.
Secretin test[6–9]					
(ml/h)	176	38–314	69	9	Values from 47 adults with a healthy pancreas, obtained by analysing the pancreatic juice during the hour following intravenous injection of 2 units of secretin per kilogramme body weight. The results of the test in adults are almost independent of sex and age[10]. Lower values are often found in patients with carcinoma of the head of the pancreas.
(ml/h/kg body weight)	2.68	1.04–4.32	0.82	9	
Specific gravity	–	(1.008–1.011)	–	11–13	
Freezing-point depression (°C)	–	(0.55–0.63)	–	12, 13	The pancreatic juice is roughly isotonic with the serum.
Water (g/l)	987	–	–	11	
Dry substance (g/l)	13.0	(7.5–15.7)	–	14	Values from fistular juice in 2 subjects. About 50–60% of the dry substance is inorganic.
pH value	–	(7.5–8.8)	–	15, 16	

	Mean	95% range (extreme range in brackets)	s	Reference	Remarks
Inorganic substances					
Bicarbonate (mEq/l).......	–	(25–[150])	–	17	The bicarbonate content of pancreatic juice rises in the form of a hyperbolic curve from 25 mEq/l at a secretory rate of 40 ml/h up to 130–150 mEq/l at a secretory rate of 300 ml/h. The sum of the bicarbonate and chloride concentrations is constant and amounts to about 154 mEq/kg water[17].
Secretin test[6–9]					
(mEq/h)..................	13.5	0–27.1	6.8	9	Values from 47 adults with a healthy pancreas, obtained by analysing the pancreatic juice during the hour following intravenous injection of 2 units of secretin per kilogramme body weight. The results of the test in adults are almost independent of sex and age[10]. The bicarbonate concentration is decreased in chronic pancreatitis.
(mEq/h/kg body weight) ...	0.199	0.047–0.351	0.076	9	
(mEq/l)	76	62–90	7	9	
Chloride (mEq/l)..........	–	([4]–129)	–	17	The chloride content of pancreatic juice is determined by the bicarbonate content (see under 'Bicarbonate' above). With increasing secretory rate the chloride content falls in the form of a hyperbolic curve.
Phosphate (mmol/kg water)	0.8	0–1.6	0.4	17	From analysis of the duodenal contents. The values accord with those for fistular juice[16].
Potassium (mEq/l)					
(a)........................	–	(6–9)	–	17	In (a) duodenal contents, (b) fistular juice.
(b)........................	–	(4.1–5.5)	–	16	
Sodium (mEq/l)	–	(139–143)	–	17	From analysis of the duodenal contents; in agreement with values from the fistular juice of 3 subjects[15]. The sodium content of the pancreatic juice largely parallels that of the serum.
Calcium (mEq/kg water)...	3.4	2.2–4.6	0.6	17	From analysis of the duodenal contents; in agreement with values from the fistular juice of 3 subjects[15].
Magnesium (mEq/kg water)	1.0	–	–	17	From analysis of the duodenal contents.
Other minerals	...	...	...	...	The following have also been found in the fistular juice[1]: sulphur (but no sulphate[15]), silicic acid, zinc (a component of carboxypeptidase A) and traces of copper.
Organic substances					
Total nitrogen (g/l)	–	(0.76–0.98)	–	1	Results of analyses of fistular juice made during the period 1902–1912.
Nonprotein nitrogen (g/l) .	0.14	–	–	15	From the fistular juice in 3 subjects.
Proteins (g/l)					
(a)........................	–	(4.8–5.3)	–	18	Values from (a) duodenal contents of 3 subjects, (b) fistular juice of 3 subjects. The greater part of the proteins in pancreatic juice are enzymes and their precursors, the remainder plasma- and mucoproteins. Electrophoretic separation has yielded up to 7 fractions[14].
(b)........................	–	(1.9–3.4)	–	15	
(b) Albumin	0.6	–	–	15	
(b) Globulin	0.4	–	–	15	
Urea (mg/l)...............	107	–	–	15	From the fistular juice in 3 subjects.
Creatinine	trace	–	–	16	
Uric acid (mg/l)...........	2	–	–	15	
Reducing substances (as glucose) (mg/l)	–	(85–180)	–	16	From the fistular juice in 1 subject.
Lipids (mg/l)	5.2	–	–	2	Cholesterol has not been found in the fistular juice[15].
Enzymes	...	...	...	...	Pancreatic juice is rich in enzymes and their precursors. The principal enzymes are the zymogens of proteases and peptidases such as trypsinogen, chymotrypsinogen and procarboxypeptidases; small amounts of amylase, lipase, phospholipase, ribonuclease, deoxyribonuclease, clostridiopeptidase A and pancreatopeptidase E are also present[19]. The fistular juice contains proteolytic enzymes[20] as well as amylase and lipase[14,21]. The presence of a trypsin inhibitor in the pancreatic juice has also been reported[22]. The pancreatic juice is often free of enzymes, and their absence is not a specific feature of cystic fibrosis[4,23]. The enzyme content is increased after injection of acetylcholine or pancreozymin and after vagus stimulation.
By pancreozymin test[7,8,24,25]:					
Amylase (mg/min)	0.62	0.29–1.30	–	25	See remarks under 'Chymotrypsin', 'Trypsin' and 'Lipase' opposite.
Carboxypeptidase A (mg/min)...............	0.72	0.36–1.45	–	25	

	Mean	95% range	s	Reference	Remarks
By pancreozymin test[7,8,24,25]:					
Chymotrypsin (mg/min) ...	3.0	1.22–7.6	–	25	Values from 36 adults with a healthy pancreas (for definition of the unit U see page 584). The mean volume secreted after stimulation with pancreozymin is 3.1 ml/min, the normal range 1.6–5.8 ml/min. Like those in the serum, the enzyme values are lognormally distributed. The data for amylase refer to crystalline amylase from the human pancreas, those for carboxypeptidase A, chymotrypsin and trypsin to the crystalline enzyme proteins from ox pancreas. The secretion of enzymes is often lowered in chronic pancreatitis.
Trypsin (mg/min)	0.73	0.38–1.42	–	25	
Lipase (kU/min, 25 °C)	1.65	0.78–3.50	–	25	

References

1 Krzywanek and Flaschenträger, in Flaschenträger and Lehnartz (Eds.), *Physiologische Chemie*, vol.2, part 1a, Springer, Berlin, 1954, page 155.
2 Leach, A. A., in Long et al. (Eds.), *Biochemists' Handbook*, Spon, London, 1961, page 914.
3 Hinsberg and Bruns, in Lang et al. (Eds.), *Hoppe-Seyler/Thierfelder Handbuch der physiologisch- und pathologisch-chemischen Analyse*, 10th ed., vol. 5, Springer, Berlin, 1953, page 389; Dittmer, D. S. (Ed.), *Blood and Other Body Fluids*, Biological Handbooks, Federation of American Societies for Experimental Biology, Washington, 1961, page 414.
4 Vink, C. L. J., in de Reuck and Cameron (Eds.), *Ciba Foundation Symposium on the Exocrine Pancreas*, Churchill, London, 1962, page 310.
5 Elmslie et al., *Ann. Surg.*, **160**, 937 (1964).
6 Ågren and Lagerlöf, *Acta med. scand.*, **90**, 1 (1936); Sarles et al., *Gastroenterologia (Basel)*, **99**, 279 (1963); Perrier et al., *Helv. med. Acta*, **31**, 573 (1964).
7 Dreiling and Janowitz, in de Reuck and Cameron (Eds.), *Ciba Foundation Symposium on the Exocrine Pancreas*, Churchill, London, 1962, page 225.
8 Dreiling et al., *Pancreatic Inflammatory Disease*, Evanston, New York, 1964.
9 Hartley et al., *Gastroenterology*, **48**, 312 (1965); *Amer. J. dig. Dis.*, **11**, 27 (1966).
10 Rosenberg et al., *Gastroenterology*, **50**, 191 (1966).
11 Glaessner, K., *Hoppe-Seylers Z. physiol. Chem.*, **40**, 465 (1903/04).
12 Luckhardt et al., *Amer. J. Physiol.*, **63**, 397 (1923).
13 Mangeot et al., *Ann. Méd.*, **54**, 604 (1953).
14 Verschure, J. C. M., *Clin. chim. Acta*, **4**, 38 (1959).
15 Miller and Wiper, *Ann. Surg.*, **120**, 852 (1944).
16 Kogut et al., *J. clin. Invest.*, **15**, 393 (1936).
17 Janowitz and Dreiling, in de Reuck and Cameron (Eds.), *Ciba Foundation Symposium on the Exocrine Pancreas*, Churchill, London, 1962, page 115.
18 Bartelheimer et al., *Klin. Wschr.*, **33**, 160 (1955).
19 Kowlessar, O. D., *Med. Clin. N. Amer.*, **44**, 817 (1960); Messer and Anderson, *Clin. chim. Acta*, **6**, 276 (1961); Zieve and Vogel, *J. Lab. clin. Med.*, **57**, 586 (1961); Neurath, H., in de Reuck and Cameron (Eds.), *Ciba Foundation Symposium on the Exocrine Pancreas*, Churchill, London, 1962, page 67; Lundh and Borgström, in de Reuck and Cameron (Eds.), *Ciba Foundation Symposium on the Exocrine Pancreas*, Churchill, London, 1962, page 259.
20 Troll and Doubilet, *Gastroenterology*, **19**, 326 (1951).
21 Tindel et al., *Nature*, **195**, 288 (1962).
22 Haverback et al., *Amer. J. Med.*, **29**, 421 (1960); Forell and Stahlheber, *Klin. Wschr.*, **42**, 321 (1964).
23 di Sant'Agnese and Lepore, *Gastroenterology*, **40**, 64 (1961).
24 Sarles et al., *Gastroenterologia (Basel)*, **99**, 279 (1963); Rick, W., in Henning et al. (Eds.), *Pathogenese, Diagnostik, Klinik und Therapie der Erkrankungen des exokrinen Pankreas*, Europäisches Pankreas-Symposion, Erlangen 1963, Schattauer, Stuttgart, 1964; Creutzfeldt, W., *Verh. dtsch. Ges. inn. Med.*, **70**, 781 (1964).
25 Rick, W., *Zur Physiologie und Pathologie der Enzymsekretion des Pankreas*, Thesis, Giessen, 1963; Rick, W., *Dtsch. med. Wschr.*, **89**, 190 (1964).

Bile

(For references see page 656)

Very pure hepatic bile can be obtained by means of a bile fistula, very pure gallbladder bile by puncture. Duodenal intubation in fasting subjects yields a yellow to light-brown fluid (A fraction) consisting of hepatic bile, pancreatic juice and duodenal secretion. When concentrated magnesium sulphate solution is injected into the tube a dark-brown viscous fluid (B fraction) consisting of gallbladder bile mixed with duodenal contents can be aspirated. Gallbladder bile is more concentrated than hepatic bile since water is absorbed in the gallbladder and the gallbladder epithelium liberates mucopolysaccharides. For further information on the composition of bile see the literature[1,2].

	Hepatic bile				Gallbladder bile				Remarks
	Mean	Extreme range	s	Reference	Mean	Extreme range	s	Reference	
Physicochemical data									
Appearance	...	...	...	...	...	...	...	...	Hepatic bile: golden-yellow to orange-yellow; gallbladder bile: brownish-black to brownish-green.
Secretion rate (ml/24 h) ...	–	(250–1100)	–	3	...	...	...	...	Bile formation by the liver is subject to rhythmic fluctuations during the course of the day[1]; less is produced during the night and morning than during the rest of the day, and more is produced after meals. The gallbladder contains about 50–65 ml in adults and about 8.5 ml in children aged 1–3 years[4].
Specific gravity	–	(0.995–1.008)	–	5	–	(1.008–1.034)	–	5	Measured at 37 °C.
Surface tension (dyn cm^{-1})	42.6	(39.6–44.0)	–	5	42.0	(40.8–44.2)	–	5	Measured at 37 °C.
Relative viscosity	1.27	(1.07–1.75)	0.24	6	2.85	(1.31–5.42)	1.63	6	
Freezing-point depression (°C)	–	(0.56–0.61)	–	1	...	...	...	...	The freezing-point depression changes little during concentration of the bile in the gallbladder. The bile is roughly isotonic with the serum.

Bile

(For references see page 656)

	Hepatic bile				Gallbladder bile				Remarks
	Mean	95% range (extreme range in brackets)	s	Reference	Mean	95% range (extreme range in brackets)	s	Reference	
Dry substance (g/l)	20 – 33.9	(8–34) (23–33) 28.9–38.9	9 – 2.5	6 7 8	136 180 166	(70–248) – (144–219)	60 – –	6 7 9	About 85–95% of the dry substance is organic. Water and salts are absorbed in the gallbladder, so that the increase of concentration of the gallbladder bile involves mainly the organic constituents; concentration is also aided by the release of mucopolysaccharides from the gallbladder epithelium.
pH value	7.15 7.5	– (6.2–8.5)	– –	10 11	6.89 6.0	– (5.6–8.0)	– –	10 11	Gallbladder bile is rather more acid than hepatic bile, possibly as a result of the enzymatic formation of lactic acid in the gallbladder.
Inorganic substances									
Bicarbonate (mEq/l)	30	–	–	10	19	–	–	10	Like the bicarbonate content of the pancreatic juice, that of the bile increases as the rate of secretion increases[3].
Chloride (mEq/l)	100.6	(89–118)	–	12	31	(7–110)	–	13	
Total phosphorus (g/l)	0.148	0.060–0.236	0.044	7	1.40	–	–	7	Most of the phosphorus is contained in phospholipids.
Potassium (mEq/l)	4.98	(2.6–12.0)	–	12	13.5	(8.4–17.5)	–	13	
Sodium (mEq/l)	148.9	(131–164)	–	12	220	(146–360)	–	13	
Calcium (mEq/l)	–	(3.3–4.1)	–	14	15.4	(3.9–33.2)	–	13	
Magnesium	...	...	...	...	...	...	...	...	The magnesium content of the bile is roughly the same as that of the serum[15].
Iron (mg/l)	–	(0.4–3.1)	–	1	–	(0.6–3.8)	–	1	
Copper (mg/l)	–	(0.35–2.05)	–	16					
Other minerals	...	...	...	...	...	...	...	...	The bile contains small amounts of zinc and manganese.
Organic substances									
Total nitrogen (g/l)	0.72 0.77	(0.24–1.45) (0.68–0.92)	0.31 –	6 7	3.49 4.9 2.8	(1.88–6.00) – (1.6–3.3)	1.45 – –	6 7 17	The total nitrogen of gallbladder bile fluctuates widely because of the variable bilirubin and protein content. About 40% of the nitrogen of gallbladder bile is dialysable[18].
Nonprotein nitrogen (g/l)	0.46	–	–	19	– 2.7	(0.68–0.94) –	– –	19 17	Most of the nonprotein nitrogen is due to bilirubin, choline (component of the phospholipids), urea and amino acids (mainly glycine and taurine as components of the bile-acid conjugates).
Peptide nitrogen (mg/l)	140	–	–	19	–	(39–270)	–	19	
Amino-acid nitrogen (mg/l)	54	–	–	19	–	(60–216)	–	19	
Urea (mg/l)	236	–	–	19	–	(200–450)	–	19	
Choline (g/l)	0.57	0.22–0.92 (0.35–0.89)	0.175	7	5.5	–	–	7	Choline is contained in the phospholipids.
Bilirubin (g/l)	0.65 –	(0.12–1.35) (0.26–0.41)	0.13 –	6 7	2.94	(0.36–6.30)	1.94	6	Free bilirubin does not occur in the bile; 70–80% of the bilirubin of gallbladder bile and over 90% of that of hepatic bile occur as bilirubin diglucuronide, the remainder as bilirubin monoglucuronide[20]. Apart from bilirubin, bile contains also small amounts of other bile pigments[1,21]. The bilirubin content of gallbladder bile is decreased in cirrhosis of the liver[22].
Porphyrins (μg/l)	...	...	...	...	101	–	–	23	The porphyrins consist of coproporphyrin I and III[1].

	Hepatic bile				Gallbladder bile				Remarks
	Mean	95% range (extreme range in brackets)	s	Reference	Mean	95% range (extreme range in brackets)	s	Reference	
Proteins (g/l)	1.8	(1.4–2.7)	–	7	4.5	–	–	7	The bile proteins consist of plasma proteins, mucopolysaccharides and enzymes. The presence of various plasma proteins has been demonstrated immunologically [17,24], namely albumin, orosomucoid, α_2-haptoglobin, transferrin and γG-globulin, as well as others specific to bile[25]. The albumin fraction of hepatic bile is diminished in acute icterogenic hepatitis, while the other protein fractions are increased[26].
Enzymes	...	...	...	...	...	...	...	...	The bile contains many enzymes[10,27,28], including esterases, phospholipase A, lipase, amylase, lactate dehydrogenase, malate dehydrogenase, transaminases, alkaline phosphatase, acid phosphatase, leucine aminopeptidase, L-iditol dehydrogenase, glucose 6-phosphate dehydrogenase, creatine kinase, and fructosediphosphate aldolase. The concentration of many of these enzymes in gallbladder bile is about 10 times their concentration in the serum[27].
Total carbohydrates (g/l)	–	(0.35–0.91)	–	7	2.4	–	–	7	The carbohydrates in hepatic bile mainly consist of glycoproteins[8] (see also under 'Proteins', above), those in gallbladder bile of mucopolysaccharides[18,28]. These mucopolysaccharides form a complex with the lipids and bilirubin[18,29]. Also found in gallbladder bile are galactose, glucose, small amounts of arabinose, fucose and ribose, glucosamine, galactosamine and uronic acids[18]. The carbohydrate content of gallbladder bile is markedly lower in the presence of stone[18].
Hexosamine, bound (mg/l)	57	(5–160)	49	6	83	(30–180)	53	6	
Reducing substances (as glucose) (g/l)	–	(0.17–0.52)	–	7	0.8	–	–	7	The reducing substances probably consist mainly of glucose[18].
Lactic acid (mg/l)	...	...	...	...	–	(130–480)	–	30	
Lipids	...	...	...	...	...	...	...	...	In addition to bile acids the main lipids of bile are lecithin and cholesterol; also present are triglycerides, diglycerides and nonesterified fatty acids[31,32].
Total fatty acids (g/l)	2.7	(1.6–4.1)	–	7	24	–	–	7	About 80% of the fatty acids consist of palmitic, oleic and linoleic acids[33]. Nonesterified fatty acids make up only about 0.3% of the total lipids[32].
Phospholipids (g/l)	–	(1.0–4.3)	–	7	34	(15–53)	–	34	Lecithin accounts for about 98% of the phospholipids, the remainder consisting of cephalins and lysolecithins[31]. In acute icterogenic hepatitis the phospholipid content of the bile is reduced[26].
Cholesterol (g/l)									
Children	–	(0.20–0.22)	–	35	–	(0.78–0.81)	–	35	In gallbladder bile about 4% of the total cholesterol is esterified, the remainder free[32]. In acute icterogenic hepatitis the cholesterol content of the bile is reduced[26].
Adults	–	(0.8–1.8)	–	7	6.3	(3.1–16.2)	–	34	
Bile acids (g/l)	–	(6.5–14)	–	7	115	–	–	7	For other values see page 656. The bile acids in bile are mostly conjugated with glycine and taurine, only a small proportion being in the free form[37]. In bile the bile acids are present as the anions. They include small quantities of trihydroxycoprostanic acid[38], which arises in the liver from cholesterol, the primary bile acids (cholic and chenodeoxycholic acids), which are likewise formed in the liver, and the secondary bile acids (deoxycholic, lithocholic and ursodeoxycholic acids), which are formed in the intestine by bacterial action from the primary bile acids, are there absorbed and again excreted in the bile[39]. Since bacteria are absent from the newborn intestine the bile of newborn infants contains no secondary bile acids. In cirrhosis of the liver the bile acid content of gallbladder bile is reduced[22].
					32.1	0–65.9	16.9	36	
Folic acid (µg/l)	33	(8–65)	–	40	...	...	...	...	Determined by means of *Lactobacillus casei* in the duodenal juice of 8 subjects.
Vitamin B_{12} (µg/l)	–	(3–10)	–	41					

Bile acid content of the bile in children and adults

Age	Number of subjects	Bile acids (mEq/l)*		Ratio glycine : taurine		Ratio cholic acid : chenodeoxycholic acid : deoxycholic acid
		Mean	Range	Mean	Range	
Hepatic bile (A fraction)[42]						
1–4 days	13	10.7	4.6–26.7	0.47	0.21–0.86	2.5:1:-
5–7 days	17	11.3	2.0–29.2	0.95	0.34–2.30	2.5:1:-
7–12 months	8	8.8	2.2–19.7	2.4	1.4 –3.1	1.1:1:-
4–10 years	3	3.4	2.4– 5.2	1.7	1.3 –2.4	2.0:1:0.9
20 years	19	8.1	2.8–20.0	3.1	1.9 –5.0	1.2:1:0.6
Gallbladder bile[37]						
Over 20 years	4	121	31.5–222	3.0	1.0 –6.6	1.0:1:0.5

* 1 mEq corresponds to ca. 0.4 g free bile acids.

References

1 STARY, Z., in FLASCHENTRÄGER and LEHNARTZ (Eds.), *Physiologische Chemie*, vol. 2, part 2a, Springer, Berlin, 1956, page 527.
2 HINSBERG and BRUNS, in LANG et al. (Eds.), *Hoppe-Seyler / Thierfelder Handbuch der physiologisch- und pathologisch-chemischen Analyse*, 10th ed., vol. 5, Springer, Berlin, 1953, page 390; POPPER and SCHAFFNER, *Liver: Structure and Function*, McGRAW-Hill, New York, 1957, page 80; KÜHN, H. A., in BÜCHNER et al. (Eds.), *Handbuch der allgemeinen Pathologie*, vol. 5, part 2, Springer, Berlin, 1959, page 390; DITTMER, D. S. (Ed.), *Blood and Other Body Fluids*, Biological Handbooks, Federation of American Societies for Experimental Biology, Washington, 1961, page 409; LATHE, G. H., in LONG et al. (Eds.), *Biochemists' Handbook*, Spon, London, 1961, page 917.
3 DAVENPORT, H. W., *Physiology of the Digestive Tract*, 2nd ed., Year Book Medical Publishers, Chicago, 1966, page 141.
4 ADAM, A., in BROCK, J. (Ed.), *Biologische Daten für den Kinderarzt*, 2nd ed., vol. 1, Springer, Berlin, 1954, page 559.
5 DE PALMA et al., *J. Amer. med. Ass.*, **195**, 943 (1966).
6 BOUCHIER et al., *Gastroenterology*, **49**, 343 (1965).
7 POLONOVSKI and BOURRILLON, *Bull. Soc. Chim. biol. (Paris)*, **34**, 703 (1952).
8 MIHAESCU and MIHAESCU, *Nature*, **186**, 394 (1960).
9 CRAWFORD and BROOKE, *Lancet*, **1**, 1096 (1955).
10 DIETRICH and ANDERS, *Hoppe-Seylers Z. physiol. Chem.*, **309**, 60 (1957).
11 SOBOTKA, H., *Physiological Chemistry of the Bile*, Baillière, London, 1937.
12 LOCKWOOD and RANDALL, *Bull. N. Y. Acad. Med.*, **25**, 228 (1949).
13 LARGE et al., *Amer. J. med. Sci.*, **239**, 713 (1960).
14 LICHTWITZ and BOCK, *Dtsch. med. Wschr.*, **41**, 1215 (1915).
15 WHEELER, H. O., *Med. Clin. N. Amer.*, **47**, 607 (1963).
16 VAN RAVESTEYN, A. H., *Acta med. scand.*, **118**, 163 (1944).
17 RUSSELL et al., *Clin. chim. Acta*, **10**, 210 (1964).
18 GILES et al., *J. Lab. clin. Med.*, **55**, 38 (1960).
19 NAGL, F., *Z. klin. Med.*, **151**, 429 (1954).
20 BILLING, B. H., *Advanc. clin. Chem.*, **2**, 267 (1959); HOFFMAN et al., *J. clin. Invest.*, **39**, 132 (1960); SCHACHTER, D., *Med. Clin. N. Amer.*, **47**, 621 (1963); KUENZLE et al., *J. Lab. clin. Med.*, **67**, 294 (1966).
21 WITH, T. K., *Bile Pigments*, Academic Press, New York, 1968.
22 WANNAGAT, L., in KALK and BOECKER (Eds.), *Gallenblase und Gallenwege*, Thieme, Stuttgart, 1963, page 63.
23 BRUGSCH, J., *Z. ges. inn. Med.*, **7**, 321 (1952).
24 CLAUSEN, J., in PEETERS, H. (Ed.), *Protides of the Biological Fluids*, Proceedings of the 10th Colloquium, Brussels 1962, Elsevier, Amsterdam, 1963, page 211; RUSSELL and BURNETT, *Gastroenterology*, **45**, 730 (1963); HARDWICKE et al., in PEETERS, H. (Ed.), *Protides of the Biological Fluids*, Proceedings of the 11th Colloquium, Brussels 1963, Elsevier, Amsterdam, 1964, page 264; HARDWICKE et al., *Clin. Sci.*, **26**, 509 (1964).
25 DUCK-SUN YOON et al., *J. Lab. clin. Med.*, **67**, 640 (1966).
26 SOTGIU et al., *Rev. int. Hépat.*, **12**, 575 (1962).
27 ZIEVE and VOGEL, *J. Lab. clin. Med.*, **57**, 586 (1961); CHIANDUSSI et al., *Clin. Sci.*, **22**, 425 (1962); LORENTZ, K., *Klin. Wschr.*, **41**, 18 (1963).
28 CLAUSEN and GÜTTLER, in PEETERS, H. (Ed.), *Protides of the Biological Fluids*, Proceedings of the 11th Colloquium, Brussels 1963, Elsevier, Amsterdam, 1964, page 323.
29 VERSCHURE and MIJNLIEFF, *Clin. chim. Acta*, **1**, 154 (1956).
30 HINSBERG and BRUNS, in LANG et al. (Eds.), *Hoppe-Seyler / Thierfelder Handbuch der physiologisch- und pathologisch-chemischen Analyse*, 10th ed., vol. 5, Springer, Berlin, 1953, page 390.
31 PHILLIPS, G. B., *Biochim. biophys. Acta*, **41**, 361 (1960).
32 NAKAYAMA and JOHNSTON, *J. Lab. clin. Med.*, **59**, 364 (1962).
33 BLOMSTRAND and EKDAHL, *Proc. Soc. exp. Biol. (N. Y.)*, **104**, 205 (1960).
34 ISAKSSON, B., *Acta Soc. Med. upsalien.*, **59**, 277 (1954).
35 KOSTIN, O. S., quoted in *Gastroenterology*, **40**, 836 (1961).
36 SINGER and FISCHER, *Analyt. Biochem.*, **2**, 292 (1961).
37 SJÖVALL, J., *Clin. chim. Acta*, **5**, 33 (1960).
38 CAREY and HASLEWOOD, *J. biol. Chem.*, **238**, PC 855 (1963).
39 HELLSTRÖM and SJÖVALL, *Acta physiol. scand.*, **51**, 218 (1961); VAN ITALLIE and HASHIM, *Med. Clin. N. Amer.*, **47**, 629 (1963); CAREY and WILLIAMS, *J. clin. Invest.*, **42**, 450 (1963).
40 BAKER et al., *Lancet*, **1**, 685 (1965).
41 GRÄSBECK, R., *Advanc. clin. Chem.*, **3**, 299 (1960).
42 ENCRANTZ and SJÖVALL, *Clin. chim. Acta*, **4**, 793 (1959).

Intestinal Juice

The composition of the secretions of the various parts of the healthy human gut is unknown since it is impossible to obtain pure samples. The composition of the intestinal contents, however, has been determined[1]. The main constituents of the intestinal juice, apart from electrolytes, are proteins[2] (albumin, γ-globulins, mucoproteins, enzymes) and lipids[2]. The rate of flow of plasma into the jejunum is about 0.20 ml/10 cm/h, or 0.036 ml/cm²/24 h[3].

Electrolyte content of the intestinal secretion in dogs[4]

	Duodenum	Jejunum	Ileum	Colon		Duodenum	Jejunum	Ileum	Colon
Volume (ml/h)	6–38	4–88	11–42	1–10	Chloride (mEq/l)	103–139	141–155	68–88	60–88
pH	6.5–7.6	6.3–7.3	7.6	7.9–8.0	Potassium (mEq/l)	5–9	4–10	5	6–9
Carbon dioxide (mmol/l)	–	5–27	70–97	86–93	Sodium (mEq/l)	138–156	126–152	146–156	136–151
					Calcium (mEq/l)	–	2–3	5	4–5

References

1 SUNDERMAN and BOERNER, *Normal Values in Clinical Medicine*, Saunders, Philadelphia, 1950, page 243; HINSBERG and BRUNS, in LANG et al. (Eds.), *Hoppe-Seyler / Thierfelder Handbuch der physiologisch- und pathologisch-chemischen Analyse*, 10th ed., vol. 5, Springer, Berlin, 1953, page 383; DITTMER, D. S. (Ed.), *Blood and Other Body Fluids*, Biological Handbooks, Federation of American Societies for Experimental Biology, Washington, 1961, pages 416 and 418.
2 RIVA et al., in PEETERS, H. (Ed.), *Protides of the Biological Fluids*, Proceedings of the 11th Colloquium, Brussels 1963, Elsevier, Amsterdam, 1964, page 168.
3 WETTERFORS, J., *Acta med. scand.*, suppl. 430 (1965).
4 DAVENPORT, H. W., *Physiology of the Digestive Tract*, 2nd ed., Year Book Medical Publishers, Chicago, 1966, page 149.

(For references see page 660)

Faeces consist of a complex mixture of food residues, digestive-tract secretions, and cells shed from the intestinal wall; representatives of the intestinal flora are also present. Unlike the faeces following food intake, the fasting faeces – on which only a few older studies exist[1] – contain no food residues; the meconium discharged from the bowel of the newborn infant is also free of bacteria. Unless otherwise stated the data here given for faeces apply to adults on a mixed diet. Detailed studies of the faeces have been published by KRZYWANEK and FLASCHENTRÄGER[1] and by HINSBERG et al.[2], and there is a tabular summary due to ALBRITTON[3].

	Mean	95% range (extreme range in brackets)	s	Reference	Remarks
Physicochemical data					
Appearance	...	...	...	...	Meconium: Soft, sticky, homogeneous mass, odourless and *greenish brown* to *black* in colour. Infants' stools: *Golden yellow* (bilirubin) on breast milk, turning *green* (biliverdin) on long standing; *brown* (stercobilin) on cow's milk. Adult stools: *Brown* (stercobilin, bilifuscin, mesobilifuscin), darkening on exposure to air; darker on low-residue meat diets, lighter on high-residue vegetable diets. *Black* from plant juices (whortleberries), charcoal, iron (ferric sulphide). *Pitchblack* when haematin content is high (black pudding, in haemorrhage of stomach or upper intestinal tract). *Light grey* when fat content is high (colour not due to fat but to breakdown products of bile pigments[4]).
Odour	...	...	...	...	Typical odour is due to volatile degradation products of protein.
Amount					
Meconium (g)	–	(70–90)	–	5	Values from (a) 44 children, (b) 24 male adults. The amount excreted daily depends on the amount and nature of the diet: infants on breast milk excrete less faeces (ca. 15–25 g/24 h[5]) than those on cow's milk (ca. 30–40 g/24 h[5]); for adults the daily amount after long fasting falls to 9.5–22 g, on a purely meat diet it is 54–64 g, on a purely vegetable diet ca. 370 g; in disease daily amounts of 500–1200 g or more occur[8].
(a) Children's stools, 2 months–6 years (g/24 h)	–	(6.6–54.1)	–	6	
(b) Adult stools (g/24 h)	115.3	33.1–197.5	41.1	7	
Number of stools per day					
Children					
1 day	–	(3–4)	–	9	69% of 500 healthy newborn infants had their first stools within 12 hours, 94% within 24 hours[10].
1 week	–	(4–5)	–	9	
2 weeks	–	(3–4)	–	9	
3–6 weeks	–	(2–3)	–	9	
7–13 weeks	–	(1–2)	–	9	
Water					
(a) Meconium (g/kg)	774	712–836	31	11	Values from (a) 12, (b) 44, (c) 7 subjects.
(b) Children's stools, 2 months–6 years (g/kg)	–	(623–857)	–	6	
(c) Adult stools					
(g/kg)	750	–	–	12	
(g/24 h)	111	–	–	12	
Dry substance					
Meconium (g/kg)	276	–	–	13	Values from (a) 44, (b) 24, (c) 7 subjects. In adult stools[1,8,12,14] 14–30% or more of the dry substance consists of dead bacteria, 25–40% of food residues (cellulose, muscle fibres, etc.); about $^1/_3$ of the dry substance is inorganic material, $^1/_3$ nitrogenous substances, $^1/_6$ lipids, $^1/_6$ cellulose and similar substances.
(a) Children's stools, 2 months–6 years (g/24 h)	–	(2.0–12.9)	–	6	
(b) Adult stools (g/24 h)	34.0	1.6–66.4	16.2	7	
(c) Adult stools (g/24 h)	21	11–31	5	12	
Ash (% of dry substance)					
Meconium	4.0	–	–	13	
Adults	20	–	–	1	
Calorific value					
(kcal/g dry substance)	5.15	(4.21–5.99)	–	15	Values of over 6 kcal/g dry substance are pathological and indicate inadequate utilization of food.
(kcal/24 h)	139	< 213 (upper limit of normal)	–	15	
pH value					
Meconium	6.1	(5.7–6.4)	–	16	The pH depends on the type of food and its rate of passage through the intestinal tract as well as on the intestinal flora, etc. Infants on breast milk have acid stools, those on cow's milk neutral or alkaline stools[18]. Adult stools with the pH given are soft and formed, whereas acid stools are rather unformed, alkaline stools rather hard[19].
Infants' stools, 6 days (on breast milk)	4.9	(4.6–5.2)	–	16	
Adult stools	7.15	5.85–8.45	0.65	17	

(For references see page 660)

	Mean	95% range (extreme range in brackets)	s	Reference	Remarks
Ions					
(mEq/kg) (anions or cations in solution)	–	(180–220)	–	20	Among the cations in solution are the sodium, potassium and ammonium and part of the calcium and magnesium, among the anions organic acids, free fatty acids, bicarbonate, chloride and part of the phosphate[21–23].
Inorganic substances					
Bicarbonate (mEq/kg)	< 30	–	–	22	
Chloride (mEq/24 h)	–	(0.5–3.0)	–	24	With an average chloride intake of 50–150 mEq/24 h.
Phosphorus					
(a) Meconium (mmol/kg)	5.28	2.38–8.18	1.45	11	Values from (a) 12 infants, (b) persons with an average phosphorus intake of 25–50 mmol/24 h. Most of the phosphorus is present as calcium phosphate, a small part as phosphate ion in solution[22, 23].
(b) Adult stools (mmol/24 h)	–	(10–25)	–	24	
Sulphate	0	–	–	22	
Fluoride (mg/24 h)	–	(0.5–2.2)	–	25	With an average fluorine intake of 1.5–4.7 mg/24 h.
Iodine (µg/24 h)	–	(10–57)	–	26	Values from 7 persons.
Potassium					
(a) Meconium (mEq/kg)	31.4	11.8–51.0	9.8	11	Values from (a) 12 infants, (b) persons with an average potassium intake of 50–75 mEq/24 h, (c) 7 adults.
(b) Adult stools (mEq/24 h)	–	(5–15)	–	24	
(c) Adult stools (mEq/24 h)	11.3	3.3–19.3	4	12	
Sodium					
(a) Meconium (mEq/kg)	136	90–182	23	11	Values from (a) 12 infants, (b) persons with an average sodium intake of 50–150 mEq/24 h, (c) 7 adults.
(b) Adult stools (mEq/24 h)	–	(0.5–5.0)	–	24	
(c) Adult stools (mEq/24 h)	6.5	0.5–12.5	3	12	
Calcium					
(a) Meconium (mEq/kg)	23.2	6.5–39.9	8.35	11	Values from (a) 12 infants, (b) persons with an average calcium intake of 25–75 mEq/24 h. In adult stools about 10 mEq/24 h is of endogenous origin (intestinal secretions)[27].
(b) Adult stools (mEq/24 h)	–	(15–65)	–	24	
Magnesium					
(a) Meconium (mEq/kg)	39.2	18.2–60.2	10.5	11	Values from (a) 12 infants, (b) persons with an average magnesium intake of 20–40 mEq/24 h.
(b) Adult stools (mEq/24 h)	–	(10–30)	–	24	
Iron					
(a) Meconium (mg/kg)	16.8	(12.0–27.1)	–	28	Values from (a) 6 infants, (b) persons with an average iron intake of 7 mg/24 h.
(b) Adult stools (mg/24 h)	–	(5.7–6.7)	–	29	
Copper					
Meconium (mg/kg)	17.0	(9.5–24.7)	–	28	Values from 6 infants.
Adult stools (mg/24 h)	1.96	0–4.62	1.33	30	
Zinc					
Meconium (mg/kg)	65.0	(38.8–117)	–	28	
Adult stools (mg/24 h)	–	(5.1–10.3)	–	31	
Cobalt (µg/24 h)	–	(0.19–1.21)	–	32	
Manganese (mg/24 h)	3.69	0–8.29	2.30	30	
Other elements	...	...	...	...	The amounts of aluminium, lead and tin are of the same order as those in the food[30]. On strontium excretion see SCHMID and ZIPF[33], on strontium in meconium see WIDDOWSON[11].
Nitrogenous substances					
Nitrogen					
Meconium (g/kg)	19	–	–	13	Values from (a) 24, (b) 7 persons. The nitrogenous components are from mucus and epithelial cells of the intestinal wall and from digestive juices, bacteria and food. 17% of the nitrogen is in the bacterial fraction; about 47% of it is water-soluble[12]. During fasting about 0.25 g nitrogen per day is excreted in the stools[1]. The nitrogen content is *increased* in some types of diarrhoea, as well as in pancreatic disease and steatorrhoea.
Infants' stools (g/24 h)					
On breast milk	0.16	–	–	1	
On cow's milk	0.4	–	–	1	
Adult stools (g/24 h)					
(a)	1.8	–	0.2	7	
(b)	1.1	–	–	12	

	Mean	95% range (extreme range in brackets)	s	Reference	Remarks
Proteins	...	...	...	...	The proteins consist mainly of undigested nutrient proteins and bacterial proteins, with only a very small proportion of plasma proteins, most of which enter the intestine with the digestive secretions and are broken down by bacteria and absorbed. The following have been demonstrated immunologically in meconium and to some extent in children's faeces[34]: prealbumin, albumin, γG-globulin, α_2-macroglobulin and siderophilin. Faeces, and especially meconium[35], also contain mucopolysaccharides, including blood-group specific substances.
Amino acids	...	...	...	...	In children's stools free amino acids represent only a small part of the total nitrogen[36].
Ammonia (mg/kg)	–	(251–884)	–	37	Ammonia arises in the terminal intestine from bacterial action.
Porphyrins					
Coproporphyrin (mg/24 h)	0.422	0.012–0.832	0.205	38	Deutero- and mesoporphyrin are also present[38]. The porphyrin content is often *increased* in idiopathic steatorrhoea[38] and some porphyrias[39].
Protoporphyrin (mg/24 h)	0.955	0–2.09	0.567	38	
Bilirubin					
Meconium (mg/kg)	585	(252–1020)	–	40	The bilirubin content of the meconium falls as that of the plasma rises (the values given are for a plasma bilirubin level of less than 50 mg/l). Towards the end of the first year of life, when the intestinal flora has developed, the bilirubin content of the stools reaches the adult level[42]. Disturbances of the intestinal flora by broad-spectrum antibiotics cause an increase in the bilirubin content of adult stools.
Adult stools (mg/24 h)	–	(5–20)	–	41	
Urobilinogen (mg/24 h)					
Men	101	(57–200)	–	43	As determined, 'urobilinogen' includes various colourless and coloured bacterial breakdown products of bilirubin (particularly stercobilinogen and stercobilin). Urobilinogen is rarely found in the stools in the first week of life and is present only in small and fluctuating quantity during the first year[41]. On bilirubin breakdown see page 362.
Women	40	(80–150)	–	43	
Purine bases					
As nitrogen (mg/24 h)	–	(63–73)	–	44	Uric acid is also present in small amount in the stools and meconium[7].
Enzymes	...	...	...	...	The enzymes arise from digestive secretions, cells of the intestinal wall and bacteria.
Trypsin (mg/g)	0.065	–	–	45	Meconium contains no trypsin[46]. In chronic pancreatitis the trypsin and chymotrypsin content of the stools is often lowered[45].
Chymotrypsin (mg/g)	0.421	–	–	45	
Non-nitrogenous substances					
Carbohydrates (g/kg)					
Children, up to 1 year	–	(< 8)	–	47	In the faeces of healthy adults these consist solely of indigestible polysaccharides from food, such as cellulose and hemicellulose. Mono- and disaccharides are found occasionally in infants' stools, glucuronic acid in the stools of newborn.
Adults	0	–	–	47	
Organic acids (mEq/kg)	150	(100–400)	–	22	Organic acids make up rather more than 50% of the anions of faeces and arise from bacterial decomposition of carbohydrates. See also below under 'Volatile fatty acids' and 'Lactic acid'.
Lactic acid (mg/24 h)					
(a) Children	160	(4.5–370)	–	36	Values from (a) 11, (b) 28 subjects. Often increased when absorption of carbohydrate is disturbed.
(b) Adults	32.4	0–76.4	22	48	
Phenols (mg/24 h)	–	(20–80)	–	49	Breakdown products of aromatic amino acids.
Lipids	...	...	...	...	The lipid fraction consists of free (41.9%) and saponified fatty acids, mono-, di- and triglycerides (15.9%), phospholipids (6.3%), free sterols (28.7%), sterol esters (7.2%)[63], bile acids, carotenoids, higher alcohols and hydrocarbons. The fatty acids of faeces are to a large extent endogenous[50]; their composition depends on the fatty acid composition of the diet[63].

	Mean	95% range (extreme range in brackets)	s	Reference	Remarks
Total fats (g/24 h)					
(a) Children, 2 months–6 years	–	(0.29–1.79)	–	6	Values from (a) 44 children by the SPERRY method, (b) 14 and (c) 24 adults by the method of VAN DE KAMER et al.[52]. On a fat-free diet the daily fat excretion is about 2 g[53]. In adult stools about 15% of the lipids are in the bacterial fraction[12]. The fat content is *increased* in various forms of malabsorption, in too rapid passage of food through the intestine, in biliary and pancreatic disease and in obstruction of the flow of lymph from the intestine. Steatorrhoea is better diagnosed by determining the fat content of the 24-hour stools than from the dry substance[4]; the microscopic examination of undigested food residues is diagnostically useless[4,54].
(b) Adults	5.54	0.14–10.94	2.7	51	
(c) Adults	4.0	0.8–7.2	1.6	7	
As percentage of dry substance					
(a) Children, 2–6 months	–	(5.2–43.1)	–	6	
(a) Children, 6 months–6 years	–	(6.1–25.8)	–	6	
(c) Adults	13.3	–	8.07	7	
Free fatty acids (g/24 h)					
(a) Children, 2 months–6 years	–	(0.14–1.38)	–	6	
(b) Adults	3.96	–	2.28	50	
Volatile fatty acids (mEq/24 h)	–	(9.8–31.2)	–	55	Acetic, propionic, butyric, valeric and other volatile fatty acids arise from bacterial decomposition of carbohydrates in the intestine; they are *increased* in sprue.
Neutral sterols					
Meconium (g/kg)	7.9	–	–	56	The ratio of sterol esters to free sterols is about 0.15. In adults the sterols consist of about 60% coprosterol, 15% cholesterol + cholestanol, 4% 7-dehydrocholesterol + Δ^7-cholestenol, 17% plant sterols[63].
Children's stools (g/24 h)					
1st week	0.24	–	–	56	
7 weeks–10 months	0.10	–	–	56	
Adult stools (g/24 h)	–	(0.39–0.76)	–	57	
Bile acids (g/24 h)	–	(0.27–0.48)	–	57	Estimated range. The following bile acids have been identified in faeces[58]: chenodeoxycholic acid, cholic acid, deoxycholic acid and lithocholic acid. The bile acid content varies with the nature of the nutrient fat[59].
Vitamins					
Vitamin B$_6$ (mg/24 h)					
Infants	–	(0.15–0.30)	–	60	
Adults	–	(0.7–0.9)	–	60	
Vitamin B$_{12}$ (µg/24 h)	~10	–	–	61	
Ascorbic acid (mg/24 h)	–	(< 10)	–	62	

References

1 KRZYWANEK and FLASCHENTRÄGER, in FLASCHENTRÄGER and LEHNARTZ (Eds.), *Physiologische Chemie*, vol. 2, part 2b, Springer, Berlin, 1957, page 202.
2 HINSBERG et al., in LANG et al. (Eds.), *Hoppe-Seyler/Thierfelder Handbuch der physiologisch- und pathologisch-chemischen Analyse*, 10th ed., vol. 5, Springer, Berlin, 1953, page 401.
3 ALBRITTON, E. C. (Ed.), *Standard Values in Nutrition and Metabolism*, Saunders, Philadelphia, 1954.
4 HAEMMERLI and AMMANN, *Schweiz. med. Wschr.*, **93**, 1517 (1963).
5 ADAM, A., in BROCK, J. (Ed.), *Biologische Daten für den Kinderarzt*, 2nd ed., vol. 1, Springer, Berlin, 1954, page 598.
6 ANDERSEN, D. H., *Amer. J. Dis. Child.*, **69**, 141 (1945).
7 PIMPARKAR et al., *Amer. J. Med.*, **30**, 910 and 927 (1961).
8 HARRISON, G. A., *Chemical Methods in Clinical Medicine*, 4th ed., Churchill, London, 1957, page 507.
9 GONCE and LEWIS, *Amer. J. Dis. Child.*, **80**, 274 (1950).
10 SHERRY and KRAMER, *J. Pediat.*, **46**, 158 (1955).
11 WIDDOWSON et al., *Lancet*, **2**, 373 (1962).
12 TRÉMOLIÈRES et al., *Nutr. et Dieta (Basel)*, **3**, 281 (1961).
13 BUCHANAN and RAPOPORT, *Pediatrics*, **9**, 304 (1952).
14 RÜEDI, W. F., *Schweiz. med. Wschr.*, **93**, 1065 (1963).
15 WOLF, F., *Bibl. gastroent. (Basel)*, **5**, 293 (1962).
16 NORTON and SHOHL, *Amer. J. Dis. Child.*, **32**, 183 (1926).
17 KERN et al., *J. Lab. clin. Med.*, **64**, 874 (1964).
18 BARNESS and GYÖRGY, *Wld Rev. Nutr. Diet.*, **3**, 1 (1962).
19 SHOSHKES, M., *Gastroenterology*, **9**, 765 (1947).
20 GOIFFON et al., *Gastroenterologia (Basel)*, **96**, 217 (1961).
21 GOIFFON et al., *Gastroenterologia (Basel)*, **96**, 223 (1961).
22 GOIFFON et al., *Gastroenterologia (Basel)*, **96**, 312 (1961).
23 GOIFFON et al., *Gastroenterologia (Basel)*, **96**, 326 (1961).
24 BERGER, E. Y., in COMAR and BRONNER (Eds.), *Mineral Metabolism*, vol. 1, part A, Academic Press, New York, 1960, page 249.
25 MCCLURE et al., *J. industr. Hyg.*, **27**, 159 (1945).
26 VAN MIDDLESWORTH, L., in ASTWOOD, E. B. (Ed.), *Clinical Endocrinology*, vol. 1, Grune & Stratton, New York, 1960, page 103.
27 SKILLMAN and HEANEY, *J. Lab. clin. Med.*, **60**, 1018 (1962).
28 CAVELL and WIDDOWSON, *Arch. Dis. Childh.*, **39**, 496 (1964).
29 JOHNSTON et al., *J. Nutr.*, **38**, 479 (1949).
30 KEHOE et al., *J. Nutr.*, **19**, 579 (1940).
31 VALLEE, B. L., *Physiol. Rev.*, **39**, 443 (1959).
32 HARP and SCOULAR, *J. Nutr.*, **47**, 67 (1952).
33 SCHMID and ZIPF, *Med. u. Ernähr.*, **3**, 173 (1962).
34 BARANDUN et al., *Schweiz. med. Wschr.*, **92**, 316 and 353 (1962); DE MURALT and ROULET, in PEETERS, H. (Ed.), *Protides of the Biological Fluids*, Proceedings of the 11th Colloquium, Brussels 1963, Elsevier, Amsterdam, 1964, page 216.
35 BUCHANAN and RAPOPORT, *J. biol. Chem.*, **192**, 251 (1951).
36 HOOFT et al., *Ann. paediat.*, **205**, 73 (1965).
37 ROBINSON, C. S., *J. biol. Chem.*, **52**, 445 (1922).
38 ENGLAND et al., *Clin. Sci.*, **22**, 447 (1962).
39 HAEGER-ARONSEN, B., *Scand. J. clin. Lab. Invest.*, **14**, 397 (1962).
40 FASHENA, G. J., *Amer. J. Dis. Child.*, **76**, 196 (1948).
41 WITH, T. K., *Bile Pigments*, Academic Press, New York, 1968, page 585.
42 SCHACHTER, D., *Med. Clin. N. Amer.*, **47**, 621 (1963).
43 BALIKOV, B., *Clin. Chem.*, **3**, 145 (1957); *Stand. Meth. clin. Chem.*, **2**, 192 (1958).
44 MENDEL and LYMAN, *J. biol. Chem.*, **8**, 115 (1910/11).
45 HAVERBACK et al., *Amer. J. dig. Dis.*, **7**, 972 (1962).
46 DE FILIPPI et al., *Pediatrics*, **14**, 114 (1954).
47 GRYBOSKI et al., *Gastroenterology*, **47**, 26 (1964).
48 KERN et al., *J. Lab. clin. Med.*, **64**, 874 (1964).
49 FOLIN and DENIS, *J. biol. Chem.*, **26**, 507 (1916).
50 JAMES et al., *Biochem. J.*, **78**, 333 (1961).
51 BERNDT et al., *Dtsch. med. J.*, **88**, 225 (1963).
52 VAN DE KAMER et al., *J. biol. Chem.*, **177**, 347 (1949).
53 LEWIS, G. T., *J. Lab. clin. Med.*, **44**, 91 (1954).
54 CREUTZFELDT, W., *Verh. dtsch. Ges. inn. Med.*, **70**, 781 (1964).
55 ASENJO et al., *Amer. J. dig. Dis.*, **7**, 974 (1962).
56 FOX and GARDNER, *Proc. roy. Soc. B*, **98**, 76 (1925/26).
57 AYLWARD et al., *Brit. J. Nutr.*, **16**, 339 and 345 (1962).
58 MOSETTIG et al., *Science*, **128**, 1433 (1958).
59 MOORE et al., *J. Lab. clin. Med.*, **60**, 1000 (1962).
60 VILTER, R. W., in WOHL and GOODHART (Eds.), *Modern Nutrition in Health and Disease*, 3rd ed., Lea & Febiger, Philadelphia, 1964, page 400.
61 CALLENDER and SPRAY, *Lancet*, **1**, 1391 (1951).
62 VILTER, R. W., in WOHL and GOODHART (Eds.), *Modern Nutrition in Health and Disease*, 3rd ed., Lea & Febiger, Philadelphia, 1964, page 433.
63 BÖHLE and STARCK, *Med. u. Ernähr.*, **8**, 81 (1967).

The physical properties and chemical composition of urine are very variable and change considerably with the amount and nature of the diet, while the amounts of endogenous metabolites present depend also on the body weight. The composition of individual urine samples does not tally precisely with that of the 24-hour urine since the excretion of many constituents is subject to a day-and-night rhythm[1–3]. Unless otherwise stated, the data given in this chapter are for adults on a mixed diet. There is an extensive literature on the properties and composition of urine[4–6].

Appearance

At the moment of voiding, the urine is usually clear and transparent, though a highly alkalinizing meal may sometimes cause it to be more or less cloudy. When clear urine has stood for a while a flocculent turbidity (nubecula) appears; this is due to the presence of mucus from the urinary tract and, in alkaline urine, of various crystals (metallic phosphates). Turbidity of the urine may also be due to lipids.

The cell content of urine is discussed on page 677, urinary sediments on pages 677–678.

Colour

Urine normally has a more or less intense yellow colour, but the nature of the substances (urochromes) responsible for this is unknown. Abnormal colorations occur in certain diseases or as a result of the ingestion of colouring matters. The following abnormalities of colour have been observed[7]:

Almost colourless: In diabetes insipidus, occasionally also in diabetes mellitus and arteriosclerotic kidney; in the polyuric phase following renal insufficiency; from diuretic agents.
Deep yellow to yellowish red: Very common in feverish illness or after severe sweating.
Yellowish red to brick red: In the presence of urobilinogens or porphyrins; deepens as the porphyrin content rises.
Yellowish green to greenish brown: In the presence of bilirubin.
Brownish red: In the presence of erythrocytes (deposit separable by sedimentation) or dissolved haemoglobin (methaemoglobin) or myoglobin; following ingestion of senna, phenolphthalein, santonin, amidopyrine or related drugs, azo-dyes.
Dark brown: In the presence of homogentisic acid or melanin, often darkening on addition of alkali or on exposure to air.
Brownish green: In poisoning with phenolic substances.
Greenish blue: Following ingestion of methylene blue, for instance in the form of capsules given to test gastric function (SAHLI).
Reddish purple: In the presence of phenolphthalein or phenolsulphonphthalein.
Blue: In the presence of indigo carmine.

Odour

Urine normally has a slight, usually aromatic odour due to unidentified constituents. Ingestion of certain substances, for instance coffee, garlic or asparagus, changes the odour completely. In the presence of acetone the urine has a fruity smell; decomposition causes a fetid odour or one of ammonia or hydrogen sulphide.

	Mean	95% range (extreme range in brackets)	*s*	Reference	Remarks
Amount (ml/24 h)					
Newborn, infants					
1 day	17	(0–68)	–	8	Values from (a) 60, (b) 40 and (c) 27 subjects (the last group over 90 years of age). At birth the bladder contains up to 44 ml (mean 5.7 ml) of urine[12]. Premature infants secrete less urine than full-term infants of the same age[13]. The secretion of urine is *increased* on a high water and salt intake and on protein-rich diets, *decreased* when water intake is low, on carbohydrate-rich diets, and during severe sweating. In adults the amount of urine voided shows a day-and-night rhythm, the greatest amounts being voided towards 6 p.m., the smallest between 3 a.m. and 6 a.m.[14]; this rhythm is reversed in adrenocortical and anterior pituitary insufficiency[15]. The urinary excretion is pathologically *increased* (polyuria) in central and nephrogenic diabetes insipidus, diabetes mellitus, adrenocortical insufficiency and advanced chronic nephritis; it is *decreased* (oliguria) in dehydration, hypotension, cardiac decompensation, acute renal injury and obstruction of the urinary tract. Any condition in which the urinary excretion is less than 50 ml per day is known as anuria. The amount of urine excreted is also discussed on pages 531–536.
2 days	34	(0–84)	–	8	
3–10 days	–	100–300	–	9	
10 days–2 months	–	250–450	–	9	
2–12 months	–	400–500	–	9	
Children					
1–3 years	–	500–600	–	9	
3–5 years	–	600–700	–	9	
5–8 years	–	650–1000	–	9	
8–14 years	–	800–1400	–	9	
(a) Men	1015	(510–2000)	–	10	
(b) Women	989	(500–1875)	–	10	
(c) Aged persons	853	(273–2400)	–	11	
(ml/kg body weight/24 h)					
(a) Newborn, 1st day	8.5	1.5–15.5	3.5	16	Values from (a) 9 infants, (b) 16 infants (breast-fed) and (c) 11 men.
(b) Newborn, 7th day	76	42–110	17	16	
(c) Young men	20	13.6–26.4	3.2	16	
Specific gravity					
Newborn, first days	1.012	–	–	9	The specific gravity of individual samples of urine can vary between 1.001 and 1.050[4]. For calculation of the amounts of solutes from the specific gravity see under 'Dry substance' on page 662. The maximum specific gravity in the fluid deprivation test is discussed under 'Renal Function Values' on page 530. The specific gravity of urine is greatly *reduced* in diabetes insipidus but *increased* in diabetes mellitus, fever and the nephrotic syndrome (as a result of proteinuria).
Infants	–	(1.002–1.006)	–	9	
Adults	–	(1.010–1.025)	–	17	
Relative viscosity	–	(1.0–1.14)	–	18	See table below. The viscosity is increased when the urine contains increased amounts of albumin, blood or erythrocytes.
Surface tension (dyn/cm⁻¹)	–	(64–69)	–	4	

Specific gravity	Relative viscosity	
1.005	1.0	(Viscosity of distilled water = 1.00)
1.016	1.02	
1.022	1.09	
1.024	1.14	

The viscosity is increased when the urine contains increased amounts of albumin, blood or erythrocytes.

	Mean	95% range (extreme range in brackets)	s	Reference	Remarks
Freezing-point depression (°C)					
(a)	–	(0.1–2.5)	–	19	Values (a) are for the limiting dilution and concentration capacities of the kidneys, values (b) for adults with maximum urinary concentration. For methods of determination see JOHNSON et al.[21]. The osmolarity and osmolality of urine are almost equal. Newborn infants, and particularly premature infants, can concentrate the urine only up to 700–1100 mosm/l depending on the urea concentration[22].
(b)	–	(1.6–2.5)	–	20	
Osmolarity (mosm/l)					
(a)	–	(50–1400)	–	19	
(b)	–	(855–1335)	–	20	
pH value					
Newborn	6.2	–	–	23	Normal urine usually has an acid reaction due to the phosphoric and sulphuric acids arising from breakdown of proteins. On a vegetable diet it may become alkaline as a result of breakdown of organic acids from fruit and vegetables to bicarbonate. The pH value (and the titratable acidity) is subject to a day-and-night rhythm[1,26]. The urine is least acid (sometimes alkaline) on waking in the morning and most acid towards midnight. It may also become alkaline owing to bacterial decomposition of urea.
Infants	6.0	(5.1–6.8)	–	23, 24	
Children	–	(5.3–7.2)	–	24	
Men	5.7	(4.8–7.5)	–	19, 25	
Women	5.8				
Titratable acidity (mEq/kg body weight/24 h)					
(a) Newborn	0.30	–	–	23	Titration up to pH 7.4; values from (a) 20, (b) 220 and (c) 11 subjects. The titratable acidity depends on the amounts of acids (uric, lactic and keto acids) and primary phosphates present. In the newborn the urine has only a small titratable content[16,28]. In adults the total acidity (titratable acidity + NH_4^+) on a mixed diet averages 50–60 mEq/24 h[29] (see also pages 535–536). In severe nonrenal acidosis up to 1000 mEq hydrogen ions may be excreted daily, while in alkalosis bicarbonate excretion may result in a daily saving of up to 250 mEq hydrogen ions. In stationary renal acidosis an average of 19 mEq hydrogen ions is retained daily[30].
(b) Infants	0.96	–	–	23	
(c) Young men	0.64	0.39–0.89	0.125	16	
Men (mEq/24 h)	38	(20–40)	–	25, 27	
Women (mEq/24 h)	28				
Dry substance (g/24 h)	–	(50–72)	–	2	The amount of solutes in the urine can be calculated roughly from the specific gravity by multiplying the second and third decimal places by 2.6 (1.6 for small children). Example: specific gravity 1.020; dry weight ≃ 20 × 2.6 = 52 g/24 h (adults)[6].

References
1 MILLS, J.N., in CREESE, R. (Ed.), *Recent Advances in Physiology*, 8th ed., Churchill, London, 1963, page 295.
2 DE VRIES et al., in STEWART and STRENGERS (Eds.), *Symposium on Water and Electrolyte Metabolism*, Elsevier, Amsterdam, 1961, page 77.
3 DE VRIES et al., *Clin.chim.Acta*, **5**, 915 (1960); Review, *Nutr. Rev.*, **20**, 13 (1962); HEATON and HODGKINSON, *Clin.chim.Acta*, **8**, 246 (1963); MERTZ, D.P., *Dtsch.med. Wschr.*, **89**, 2327 (1964).
4 WEHRLE and SCHIEVELBEIN, in FLASCHENTRÄGER and LEHNARTZ (Eds.), *Physiologische Chemie*, vol.2, part 2b, Springer, Berlin, 1957, page 1.
5 DITTMER, D.S. (Ed.), *Blood and Other Body Fluids*, Biological Handbooks, Federation of American Societies for Experimental Biology, Washington, 1961, page 363; COCKBURN, B.J., in LONG et al. (Eds.), *Biochemists' Handbook*, Spon, London, 1961, page 918.
6 HINSBERG, K., in LANG et al. (Eds.), *Hoppe-Seyler/Thierfelder Handbuch der physiologisch- und pathologisch-chemischen Analyse*, 10th ed., vol.5, Springer, Berlin, 1953, page 181.
7 FISCHLER and SCHLEMMER, *Anleitung zur Harnuntersuchung*, 4th ed., Bergmann, Munich, 1960, page 5.
8 AAS, K., *Acta paediat. (Uppsala)*, **50**, 361 (1961).
9 RUBIN, M.I., in NELSON, W.E. (Ed.), *Textbook of Pediatrics*, 7th ed., Saunders, Philadelphia, 1959, page 1010.
10 MÜTING et al., *Z.klin. Med.*, **157**, 391 (1962).
11 HOWELL, T.H., *J. Geront.*, **11**, 61 (1956).
12 ALEXANDER and NIXON, *Brit.med.Bull.*, **17**, 112 (1961).
13 CRANNY and CRANNY, *Amer.J. Dis.Child.*, **99**, 507 (1960).
14 METZ and MOURS-LAROCHE, *C.R.Soc.Biol. (Paris)*, **149**, 1026 (1955).
15 SIGLER and RUBINI, *J. Lab.clin.Med.*, **59**, 833 (1962).
16 MCCANCE and WIDDOWSON, *Acta paediat. (Uppsala)*, **49**, 409 (1960).
17 STEWART and DUNLOP, *Clinical Chemistry in Practical Medicine*, 6th ed., Livingstone, Edinburgh, 1962, page 299.
18 POSNER, C., *Berl.klin. Wschr.*, **52**, 1106 (1915).
19 CONSOLAZIO et al., *Physiological Measurements of Metabolic Functions in Man*, McGraw-Hill, New York, 1963, page 437.
20 JACOBSON et al., *Arch.intern.Med.*, **110**, 83 (1962).
21 JOHNSON et al., *Stand.Meth.clin.Chem.*, **5**, 159 (1965).
22 VESTERDAL, J., in WOLSTENHOLME and O'CONNOR (Eds.), *Ciba Foundation Symposium on Somatic Stability in the Newly Born*, Churchill, London, 1961, page 16.
23 WEBER, H., *Helv.paediat.Acta*, **15**, 186 (1960).
24 PEONIDES et al., *Arch.Dis.Childh.*, **40**, 33 (1965).
25 SCHWAB and KÜHNS, *Die Störungen des Wasser- und Elektrolytstoffwechsels*, Springer, Berlin, 1959, page 171.
26 VIOLLE, P.-L., *Rev.Prat. (Paris)*, **7**, 644 (1957).
27 SPEIER, F., *Laboratoriumsdiagnostik*, Bernecker, Melsungen, undated.
28 MCCANCE and HATEMI, *Lancet*, **1**, 293 (1961).
29 LANGENDORF, H., in AUERSWALD, W. (Ed.), *Aktuelle Probleme des Mineralstoffwechsels*, suppl. 1 to *Z. Ernährungsw.*, Steinkopff, Darmstadt, 1961, page 1; Editorial, *Lancet*, **1**, 92 (1961).
30 GOODMAN et al., *J.clin.Invest.*, **44**, 495 (1965).

Inorganic substances (for references see pages 664–665)

	Mean	95% range (extreme range in brackets)	s	Reference	Remarks
Chloride (mEq/kg body weight/24 h)					
(a) Newborn, 1st day	0.43	0.07–0.79	0.18	1	Values from (a) 9 infants, (b) 16 infants (breast-fed) and (c) 11 men. About 80–95% of the ingested chloride is excreted in the urine. The chloride excretion is *increased* on a high-salt diet, by the action of diuretic agents, in renal tubular injury (salt-losing nephritis) and in ADDISON's disease; it is *decreased* on low-salt diets, in chloride loss due to vomiting, sweating or diarrhoea, in CUSHING's syndrome and corticosteroid treatment, and in all forms of salt retention such as oedema.
(b) Newborn, 7th day	2.08	0.08–4.08	1.00	1	
(c) Young men	2.80	1.56–4.04	0.62	1	
Men (mEq/24 h)	184	(120–240)	–	2, 3	
Women (mEq/24 h)	132				

	Mean	95% range (extreme range in brackets)	s	Reference	Remarks
Phosphorus (mg/kg body weight/24 h)					
(a) Newborn, 1st day	0.12	0.06–0.18	0.03	1	Values from (a) 9 infants, (b) 16 infants (breast-fed; about 10 times higher on cow's milk) and (c) 11 men. The urine secreted in utero contains only little phosphorus[1]. About 95–100% of the urinary phosphorus is in the inorganic form[5], mainly as primary phosphate (increasingly as secondary phosphate as the pH value rises) and to a smaller extent as pyrophosphate[6]. The urinary phosphate excretion is subject to a day-and-night rhythm[7,8] with a minimum during the morning and higher values during the night. The urinary phosphorus arises mainly from food and to a lesser extent from the metabolism of organic phosphates. About 50–80% of the dietary phosphate appears in the urine[5]. Phosphate excretion is under parathyroid hormonal control (see page 728) and is also dependent on renal function. The phosphate excretion can be determined by measuring the phosphate clearance, the percentage of phosphate reabsorption, or the phosphate excretion index[9]; for values measured in children see Janse et al.[10]. For further data on phosphorus excretion see Nordin[11] and Borle[11].
(b) Newborn, 7th day	0.32	0–0.7	0.19	1	
(c) Young men	16.5	10.1–22.9	3.2	1	
Adults (g/24 h)	–	(0.8–2.0)	–	4	
Sulphur (g/24 h)					
Total S	1.32	(1.24–1.49)	–	12	Values from (a) 9 infants, (b) 16 infants (breast-fed; 3 times higher on cow's milk) and (c) 11 men. The urinary sulphur consists mainly of free sulphate, with small amounts as organic esters (indoxylsulphuric acid)[12,13]. The neutral sulphur consists of thiocyanate, mercaptans, diethyl sulphide and sulphur amino acids[5]. Sulphate excretion is increased on albumin-rich diets and decreased in the nephrotic syndrome[14].
Inorganic sulphate-S	1.17	(1.07–1.30)	–	12	
Sulphuric ester-S	0.09	(0.08–0.10)	–	12	
Neutral S	0.07	(0.05–0.08)	–	12	
Inorganic sulphate-S (mg/kg body weight/24 h)					
(a) Newborn, 1st day	3.4	0–6.8	1.7	1	
(b) Newborn, 7th day	6.0	1.8–10.2	2.1	1	
(c) Young men	19.2	10.8–27.6	4.2	1	
SO_4^{--} (mEq/24 h)					
Men	45	(30–70)	–	2, 3	
Women	36				
Bromide (mg/l)	6.56	(2.97–8.55)	–	15	Values from 8 subjects.
Fluoride (mg/l)					
(a) Children, 1–3 years	0.14	(0.05–0.30)	–	16	Values from (a) 31 infants, (b) 28 infants, (c) 34 adults with a drinking-water fluoride content of 0.5–0.6 mg/l, (d) 5 adults with a fluoride intake of 1.5–4.7 mg/24 h. Fluoride excretion falls at the 4th month of pregnancy (to 0.22 mg/l at the 8th month) and rises after parturition to normal in 16 weeks[18].
(b) Children, 4–6 years	0.27	(0.05–0.70)	–	16	
(c) Adults	0.52	(0.30–0.85)	–	16	
(d) Adults (mg/24 h)	–	(0.9–2.9)	–	17	
Iodide (mg/24 h)	0.191	(0.018–0.483)	0.138	19	
Thiocyanate (mg/l)	4	(0–6)	–	20	In nonsmokers; higher in smokers.
Cyanide (µg/24 h)	–	(2–6)	–	21	
Carbon dioxide (mmol/24 h)	–	(0.3–3.0)	–	3	In physical solution in urine at pH 5.5–6.0; with rising pH carbon dioxide is increasingly present as bicarbonate. See also under 'pH value' and 'Titratable acidity' above.
Potassium (mEq/kg body weight/24 h)					
(a) Newborn, 1st day	0.36	0.08–0.64	0.14	1	Values from (a) 9 infants, (b) 16 infants (breast-fed; about twice as high on cow's milk) and (c) 11 men. About 80% of the ingested potassium is excreted in the urine. On a potassium-free diet the potassium excretion falls to 10 mEq/24 h after 48 hours. The potassium excretion is subject to a day-and-night rhythm with a maximum in the late morning and a minimum after midnight[8,22]. It is pathologically *decreased* in renal diseases such as glomerulonephritis, pyelonephritis and 'salt-losing' nephritis, in extrarenal uraemia, in Addison's disease and chronic extrarenal potassium loss (for instance in diarrhoea); it is *increased* by the action of steroid hormones (Cushing's syndrome, primary hyperaldosteronism), in renal diseases such as Fanconi's syndrome, tubular acidosis, by the action of diuretic agents, in metabolic acidosis (for instance in diabetes) and metabolic alkalosis (for instance in vomiting) as well as in hunger as a result of increased cell breakdown.
(b) Newborn, 7th day	0.95	0–2.25	0.65	1	
(c) Young men	1.05	0.79–1.31	0.13	1	
Men (mEq/24 h)	57	(35–80)	–	2, 3	
Women (mEq/24 h)	47				
Sodium (mEq/kg body weight/24 h)					
(a) Newborn, 1st day	0.25	0.11–0.39	0.07	1	Values from (a) 9 infants, (b) 16 infants (breast-fed; about 1½ times higher on cow's milk) and (c) 11 men. About 90–95% of the ingested sodium appears in the urine[23]. The sodium excretion is *increased* on the ingestion of much salt, *decreased* when the salt intake is low and during sweating; it is subject to a day-and-night rhythm with a maximum in the evening and a minimum between 3.0 and 6 a.m.[8]. It is pathologically *increased* in adrenocortical insufficiency, in 'salt-losing' nephritis, in tubular acidosis, by the action of diuretic agents, in alkalosis and in cerebral injury in the hypothalamic region; it is *decreased* in extrarenal sodium loss and by the action of steroid hormones (stress, Cushing's syndrome).
(b) Newborn, 7th day	1.78	0–4.36	1.29	1	
(c) Young men	2.66	1.58–3.74	0.54	1	
Men (mEq/24 h)	177	(120–220)	–	2, 3	
Women (mEq/24 h)	128				

	Mean	95% range (extreme range in brackets)	s	Reference	Remarks
Calcium (mEq/kg body weight/24 h)					
(a) Newborn, 1st day	0.02	0.01–0.03	0.005	24	Values from (a) 12 infants, (b) 9 infants (breast-fed; about one-half as much on cow's milk), (c) 104 children, (d) 121 adults and (e) 13 adults. 0–33%, mean 22%, of the urinary calcium is ionized, the remainder bound to organic acids[29]. Calcium excretion is subject to a day-and-night rhythm with a maximum during the morning and a minimum during the night[7,8], probably an effect of meals[30]. It is more dependent on the degree of absorption from food than on the calcium content of the diet; with an intake of 700 mg calcium per day about 30% is excreted in the urine. In adults the calcium excretion is *decreased* when the calcium content of the diet is low and also in persons of advanced age[31]. Unlike the serum calcium level, calcium excretion does not change significantly during pregnancy[32]. It is pathologically *increased* in hyperparathyroidism, various forms of osteoporosis, bone metastases, tubular acidosis, idiopathic hypercalcaemia and vitamin-D poisoning, *decreased* when the calcium serum level is low (as in hypoparathyroidism and osteomalacia with steatorrhoea) and in renal insufficiency (for instance in the nephrotic syndrome). On calcium excretion see the literature[11,33].
(b) Newborn, 7th day	0.26	0.18–0.34	0.04	25	
(c) Children, 1 year	0.10	(0.01–0.40)	–	26	
(d) Adults	–	(0.05–0.31)	–	27	
(e) Adults (mEq/24 h)	11.5	6.5–16.5	2.5	28	
Magnesium (mEq/kg body weight/24 h)					
(a) Newborn, 1st day	0.004	0.0004–0.0076	0.0018	24	Values from (a) 12 infants, (b) 13 infants (breast-fed; about one-half as much on cow's milk), (c) 91 men, (d) 61 women. The magnesium excretion is subject to a day-and-night rhythm with a maximum during the morning and a minimum during the night[8,37], probably an effect of meals[30]. Of the magnesium in the diet about one-third is absorbed and excreted in the urine. An increase in magnesium excretion has been recorded during medication with diuretic agents[38].
(b) Newborn, 7th day	0.050	0–0.118	0.034	34	
(c) Men (mEq/24 h)	10.7	4.7–16.7	3.0	35	
(d) Women (mEq/24 h)	8.8	3.4–14.2	2.7	35	
(e) Adults (mEq/24 h)	–	(4.9–16.5)	–	36	
Iron (µg/24 h)					
(a)	55	–	–	39	Values (b) from 10 subjects determined with bathophenanthroline. The iron arises mainly from erythrocytes and from epithelial cells of the renal tubules and vesical mucosa. Iron excretion is increased in diseases involving intravascular haemolysis[41].
(b)	100	(40–150)	–	40	
Copper (µg/24 h)					
(a) Children	12	(6–17)	–	42	Values from (a) 12 children, (b) 20 adults, (c) 12 adults and (d) 16 subjects; values (a) and (b) determined with oxalyl dihydrazide, (c) with dithizone, (d) by neutron activation analysis. Copper excretion is at a maximum in the afternoon. It is pathologically *increased* in WILSON's disease, portal vein cirrhosis and proteinuria (for instance in the nephrotic syndrome), with 60–80% of the copper present as caeruloplasmin.
(b) Adults	14	(8–22)	–	42	
(c) Adults	18	3.6–32.4	7.2	43	
(d)	50.4	28.2–72.6	11.1	44	
Manganese (µg/24 h)	0.8	0.2–1.4	0.3	44	Values from 16 subjects determined by neutron activation analysis. See also KEHOE et al.[45] and SCHROEDER[46].
Molybdenum (µg/l)	16.3	0–42.7	13.2	47	Values from 16 subjects determined by emission spectrography. See also SCHROEDER[46] and MELTZER et al.[48].
Zinc (µg/24 h)					
(a)	457	217–697	120	49	Values from (a) 14, (b) 16 subjects. Zinc excretion is increased in liver cirrhosis due to alcohol[49], in diabetes[48] and in cancer[47].
(b)	430	138–722	146	47	
Other elements	...	...	...	...	Urine also contains silicate[5], nitrite and nitrate[5], and borate[50]. The arsenic content is normally less than 0.1 mg/l[51], the lead content 30–80 µg/l[46,52]; the mercury content should not exceed 30 µg/l[53]. The following elements have also been determined in urine: aluminium[45], cadmium[46,48,50], chromium[46,50], cobalt[48], nickel[45,46,50,54], silver[46], strontium[24,25,55], titanium[46], vanadium[46], bismuth[48] and tin[45,46,48].

References

1 McCANCE and WIDDOWSON, *Acta paediat. (Uppsala)*, **49**, 409 (1960).
2 SCHWAB and KÜHNS, *Die Störungen des Wasser- und Elektrolytstoffwechsels*, Springer, Berlin, 1959.
3 SPEIER, F., *Laboratoriumsdiagnostik*, Bernecker, Melsungen, undated.
4 CONSOLAZIO et al., *Physiological Measurements of Metabolic Functions in Man*, McGraw-Hill, New York, 1963, page 437.
5 WEHRLE and SCHIEVELBEIN, in FLASCHENTRÄGER and LEHNARTZ (Eds.), *Physiologische Chemie*, vol.2, part 2b, Springer, Berlin, 1957, page 1.
6 FLEISCH and BISAZ, *Nature*, **195**, 911 (1962); *Helv.physiol.pharmacol.Acta*, **21**, 88 (1963).
7 SCHÄFER et al., *Z.klin.Med.*, **157**, 372 (1962).
8 HEATON and HODGKINSON, *Clin.chim.Acta*, **8**, 246 (1963).
9 KYLE et al., *Ann.intern.Med.*, **57**, 957 (1962); HAAS, H.G., *Helv.med.Acta*, **33**, 91 (1966).
10 JANSE et al., *Arch.Dis.Childh.*, **41**, 541 (1966).
11 NORDIN, B.E.C., *Advanc.clin.Chem.*, **4**, 275 (1961); BORLE et al., Calcium and Phosphorus Metabolism, *Documenta Geigy*, *Acta clinica*, No.2, Basle, 1965.
12 FOLIN, O., *Amer.J.Physiol.*, **13**, 45 (1905).
13 MÜTING et al., *Z.klin.Med.*, **157**, 391 (1962).
14 MÜTING et al., *Z.klin.Med.*, **157**, 544 (1963).
15 CONWAY and FLOOD, *Biochem.J.*, **30**, 716 (1936).
16 GEDALIA, I., *J.dent.Res.*, **37**, 601 (1957).
17 McCLURE et al., *J.industr.Hyg.*, **27**, 159 (1945).
18 GEDALIA et al., *J.dent.Res.*, **38**, 548 (1959).
19 BRUGER et al., *J.Lab.clin.Med.*, **26**, 1942 (1941).
20 RHEINWALD, U., *Dtsch.zahnärztl.Z.*, **10**, 477 (1955).
21 BOXER and RICKARDS, *Arch.Biochem.*, **30**, 392 (1951).
22 MILLS, J.N., in CREESE, R. (Ed.), *Recent Advances in Physiology*, 8th ed., Churchill, London, 1963, page 295.
23 FORBES, G.B., in COMAR and BRONNER (Eds.), *Mineral Metabolism*, vol.2, part B, Academic Press, New York, 1962, page 1.
24 WIDDOWSON et al., *Lancet*, **2**, 373 (1962).
25 WIDDOWSON et al., *Lancet*, **2**, 941 (1960).
26 LELONG et al., *Sem.Hôp.Paris, Ann.Pédiat.*, **38**, 1125 (1962).
27 NORDIN, B.E.C., *Lancet*, **2**, 368 (1959).
28 BHANDARKAR and NORDIN, *Brit.med.J.*, **1**, 145 (1962).
29 NORDIN and TRIBEDI, *Lancet*, **1**, 409 (1962).
30 HODGKINSON and HEATON, *Clin.chim.Acta*, **11**, 354 (1965).
31 PANSU et al., in HIOCO, D. J. (Ed.), *L'ostéoporose*, Symposium, Masson, Paris, 1964, page 176.

32 Kerr et al., *Amer. J. Obstet. Gynec.*, **83**, 2 (1962).
33 Nordin and Hodgkinson, *Advanc. intern. Med.*, **13**, 155 (1967).
34 Slater, J. E., *Brit. J. Nutr.*, **15**, 83 (1961).
35 Evans and Watson, *Lancet*, **1**, 522 (1966).
36 Wacker and Vallee, *Med. Clin. N. Amer.*, **44**, 1357 (1960).
37 Metz and Mours-Laroche, *C. R. Soc. Biol. (Paris)*, **149**, 1026 (1955).
38 Wacker, W. E. C., *J. clin. Invest.*, **40**, 1086 (1961); Hänze, S., *Der Magnesiumstoffwechsel*, Thieme, Stuttgart, 1962.
39 Plötner and Petzel, *Klin. Wschr.*, **32**, 821 (1954).
40 Hwang and Brown, *Arch. intern. Med.*, **114**, 741 (1964).
41 Moore and Brown, Le métabolisme du fer, *Documenta Geigy, Acta clinica*, No. 7, Basle, 1967.
42 Wilson and Klassen, *Clin. chim. Acta*, **13**, 766 (1966).
43 Butler and Newman, *J. clin. Path.*, **9**, 157 (1956).
44 Kanabrocki et al., *J. nucl. Med.*, **6**, 780 (1965).
45 Kehoe et al., *J. Nutr.*, **19**, 579 (1940).
46 Schroeder, H. A., *Advanc. intern. Med.*, **8**, 259 (1956).
47 Pfeilsticker, K., *Z. klin. Chem.*, **3**, 145 (1965).
48 Meltzer et al., *Amer. J. med. Sci.*, **244**, 282 (1962).
49 Vallee et al., *Ann. intern. Med.*, **50**, 1077 (1959).
50 Imbus et al., *Arch. environm. Hlth*, **6**, 286 (1963).
51 Leifheit and Fletcher, *Stand. Meth. clin. Chem.*, **3**, 23 (1961).
52 Rice et al., *Stand. Meth. clin. Chem.*, **5**, 121 (1965).
53 Nobel and Leifheit, *Stand. Meth. clin. Chem.*, **3**, 176 (1961).
54 Sunderman, F. W., *Amer. J. clin. Path.*, **44**, 182 (1965).
55 Schmid and Zipf, *Med. u. Ernähr.*, **3**, 173 (1962).

Nitrogenous substances (for references see pages 671–672)

	Mean	95% range (extreme range in brackets)	*s*	Reference	Remarks
Total nitrogen (g/l)					
(a) Newborn, at birth	0.74	0.02–1.46	0.36	1	Values from (a) 7 infants, (b) 9 infants, (c) 12 adults, (d) 16 infants (breast-fed; twice as much on cow's milk), (e) 11 men, (f) 12 children, (g) 54 adults. On a protein-rich diet 90% of the urinary nitrogen consists of urea, 4% of creatinine and 3% of ammonium ions, on a low-protein diet 60% of urea, 11% of ammonium ions and 17% of creatinine. About 1–2% is in the form of uric acid and 2% as free amino acids; urine contains only small amounts of protein. On a nitrogen-free diet adults excrete about 3.5 g nitrogen per day[5].
(b) Newborn, 2nd day	6.40	3.44–9.36	1.48	1	
(c) Adults	9.19	–	–	2	
(mg/kg body weight/24 h)					
(b) Newborn, 1st day	38.9	2.1–75.7	18.4	1	
(b) Newborn, 2nd day	75.4	23.6–127	25.9	1	
(d) Newborn, 7th day	108	65.8–150	21.1	1	
(e) Young men	207	159–255	24.2	1	
(g/24 h)					
(f) Children, 3–11 years	–	(5.3–20.9)	–	3	
(g) Adults	11.5	6.9–16.1	2.3	4	
Urea (mg/kg body weight/24 h)					
(a) Newborn, 0–2 days	39	–	–	2	Values from (a) 8 infants, (b) 8 infants (breast-fed), (c) 4 adults and (d) 53 adults. The urea excretion is proportional to the protein content of the diet. It is *increased* when there is increased breakdown of body proteins, *decreased* when there is increased formation of body proteins (for instance during growth or pregnancy) as well as in renal insufficiency and liver disease.
(b) Newborn, 4–6 days	73	–	–	2	
(c) Adults	358	–	–	2	
(d) Adults (g/24 h)	20.6	12.6–28.6	4.0	4	
Creatine (mg/kg body weight/24 h)					
(a) Premature infants, 2–12 weeks	2.3	(0.3–4.3)	–	6	Values from (a) 10, (b) 6, (c) 5, (d) 13, and (e) 19 subjects; values (f) determined fluorometrically with ninhydrin, (g) enzymatically, all others by the Jaffé reaction[9,13] (see also page 572). Creatine excretion is greater in growing children than in adults, in girls and women somewhat greater than in boys and men. In women it fluctuates during the menstrual cycle and is increased during pregnancy and at the beginning of the puerperium. Following 11–17 days immobilization by bed-rest, values up to 800 mg/24 h have been recorded[14]. Creatine excretion is pathologically *increased* in muscle diseases, in endocrine disturbances marked by an excess of thyroxine, ACTH or cortisone, as well as in disturbances of renal reabsorption (such as diabetes, acromegaly and Cushing's syndrome), *decreased* in hypothyroidism and treatment with testosterone.
(b) Newborn, 2–12 weeks	28.0	(15.2–35.8)	–	7	
(c) Infants, 6–12 months	10.6	(3.6–15.3)	–	7	
(d) Children, 6–11 years	4.0	(2.2–7.4)	–	8	
(mg/24 h)					
(e)	–	(0–50)	–	9	
(f)	–	(18.6–58.5)	–	10	
(g) Men	52.1	(11–189)	–	11	
(g) Women	92.1	(19–270)	–	11	
(h) Persons over 90 years	90	(25–230)	–	12	
Creatinine (mg/kg body weight/24 h)					
(a) Premature infants, 2–12 weeks	14.3	(8.3–19.9)	–	6	Values from (a) 10, (b) 6, (c) 5, (d) 13, (e) 8 and (f) 10 subjects. On a creatinine-free diet the excretion is fairly constant and proportional to the muscle mass. It is pathologically *increased* in hypothyroidism, acromegaly and diabetes, *decreased* in muscle diseases, hyperthyroidism and advanced renal injury.
(b) Newborn, 2–12 weeks	11.9	(11.0–14.6)	–	7	
(c) Infants, 6–12 months	9.8	(5.2–20.4)	–	7	
(d) Children, 6–11 years	16.3	(6.4–21.9)	–	8	
(g/24 h)					
(e) Men, 20–45 years	1.80	1.1–2.5	0.35	15	
(f) Women, 20–45 years	1.17	1.01–1.33	0.08	15	
(g) Persons over 90 years	0.47	(0.04–1.0)	–	12	

Urine – Nitrogenous Substances

(For references see pages 671–672)

	Mean	95% range (extreme range in brackets)	s	Reference	Remarks
Guanidine (mg/24 h)	–	(<2)	–	16	
Guanidinoacetic acid					
(a) Newborn, 2–12 weeks (mg/kg body weight/24 h)	2.6	(1.7–3.6)	–	17	Values (a) by chromatographic separation in 11 infants, (b) colorimetrically in 5 adults.
(b) Adults (mg/24 h)	27	(11–56)	–	18	
Methylguanidine (mg/24 h)	–	(<1)	–	16	
Ammonia (mg/24 h)					
Men	680	(340–1200)	–	19	Values from (a) 9 infants, (b) 16 infants (breast-fed) and (c) 11 men. Abnormally low values are found in alkaline urine as a result of loss of ammonia, abnormally high values in old urine samples as a result of bacterial formation of ammonia. The ammonia excretion is proportional to the anionic content of the diet (for instance phosphates and sulphur in meat); it is therefore higher in acid than in alkaline urine. It is pathologically *increased* in metabolic and respiratory acidosis, *decreased* in metabolic and respiratory alkalosis and in injury to the distal renal tubules.
Women	510				
(mEq/24 h)					
Men	40	(20–70)	–	19	
Women	30				
(mEq/kg body weight/24 h)					
(a) Newborn, 1st day	0.26	0.02–0.50	0.12	1	
(b) Newborn, 7th day	0.56	0.26–0.86	0.15	1	
(c) Young men	0.80	0.52–1.08	0.14	1	
Amino acids, total					
(mg/24 h)	2255	(1337–3150)	–	20	Calculated from the amounts of the individual amino acids in hydrolysed urine.
(mg α-amino-N/24 h)	261	–	–	20	
Amino acids, free (mg/24 h)					
(a)	800	(350–1180)	–	21	Values (a) calculated from the amounts of the individual free amino acids (see the table on page 667); values (b), (d), (e) determined colorimetrically with ninhydrin; values (c) determined as the copper complex; values (d) from 8, (e) from 18 subjects. For details see page 667.
(mg α-amino-N/24 h)					
(b) Children, 2–4 years	33	(16–54)	–	22	
(a) Adults	90	(41–133)	–	21	
(mg α-amino-N/kg body weight/24 h)					
(c) Premature infants, 2–12 weeks	20.7	(10.0–26.8)	–	6	
(c) Newborn, 2–12 weeks	12.9	(6.8–20.7)	–	7	
(c) Infants, 6–12 months	6.3	(3.4–8.5)	–	7	
(c) Children	1.8	(0.9–2.9)	–	23	
(a) Adults	1.4	(0.6–2.1)	–	21	
(mg α-amino-N/mg creatinine-N)					
(d) Children	0.46	0.14–0.78	0.16	24	
(e) Adults	0.17	0.08–0.26	0.045	24	
Amino acids, bound (excluding peptides)					
o-Aminohippuric acid (mg/24 h)	1.14	(0.4–1.7)	–	28	Values from 20 subjects. See also under '*o*-Aminobenzoic acid', page 669.
Hippuric acid (g/24 h)	–	(1.0–2.5)	–	29	Represents about 70% of the bound glycine. The benzoic acid from which the hippuric acid arises mostly originates from aromatic components of vegetable foods. Hippuric acid excretion is *increased* after ingestion of large amounts of fruit and vegetables, pathologically *decreased* in renal insufficiency.
m-Hydroxyhippuric acid (mg/24 h)	6	(2–150)	–	30	
Phenylacetylglutamine (g/24 h)	–	(0.25–0.50)	–	29	Represents about 50% of the bound glutamic acid. The phenylacetic acid formed by bacterial decomposition of protein is excreted as phenylacetylglutamine.
Peptides (mg/24 h)					
Anserine	–	(5–7)	–	31	For a summary of data see SKARŻYŃSKI and SARNECKA-KELLER[33].
Carnosine	–	(2–3)	–	31	
Homocarnosine	1.1	(0.5–2.4)	–	32	
Peptides containing hydroxyproline (as hydroxyproline)	25.1	(14.0–38.7)	–	34	Values from 12 adults. The excretion is increased in growing children[35]. Only traces of free hydroxyproline are present in urine. The hydroxyproline excretion is a measure of the collagen metabolism.

(For references see pages 671–672)

Free amino acids in urine

About one-third of each of the urinary amino acids is present in the free form, about one-third in the non-peptide-bound form (e.g., hippuric acid, phenylacetylglutamine) and about one-third in the peptide bound form (peptides and proteins). The amino-acid content can be determined by measuring the α-amino nitrogen, though this method also embraces the free amino groups of the peptides and other substances; for this purpose, gasometric (with ninhydrin or nitric acid), titrimetric (formol titration) and colorimetric (with ninhydrin or sodium β-naphthoquinone-4-sulphonate or as copper complex) procedures have been devised, but these do not yield concordant results[21, 23, 25]. The individual amino acids can be determined microbiologically or by electrophoretic, paper-chromatographic or column-chromatographic separation; for a few amino acids there are also specific chemical methods. The automatic column-chromatographic separation method of STEIN and MOORE reveals up to 80 substances reacting with ninhydrin, of which 29 are well-known amino acids[26].

There are individual differences in the amino-acid content of the urine, but this is little affected by the diet or the urinary volume. On a protein-rich diet the amount of methylhistidine increases, in hunger and malnutrition that of β-aminoisobutyric acid. When measured as the nitrogen content of the urine, the amino-acid excretion of newborn and infants (particularly that of premature infants) is greater than that of adults. In women the amino-acid content of the urine varies during the menstrual cycle, the histidine excretion showing a maximum at the 15th–20th day, coinciding with the maximum oestrogen excretion. During pregnancy the amino-acid excretion, particularly that of histidine, is *increased*. It is pathologically *increased* when the amino-acid level of the blood is increased provided renal function is normal (for instance in liver diseases, increased protein catabolism, phenylketonuria) as well as in various renal disturbances (poisoning, rickets, various hereditary metabolic anomalies). There is a considerable literature on the amino-acid content of urine[21, 23, 27].

Genetic anomalies of the urinary amino acids are discussed on pages 448–450.

Amino acid	mg/24 h						µmol/kg body weight/24 h ***				
	Children* (9–24 months)		Men**		Women**		Premature infants, bottle-fed	Full-term babies and infants		Children	Adults
	Mean	Extreme range	Mean	Extreme range	Mean	Extreme range		Bottle-fed	Breast-fed		
Alanine	10	5–15	22	5–32	24	9–44	18.6–125	14.2–30.2	9.6–15.3	3.2–18.2	3.6–9.8
β-Alanine	ca. 0.3	–	6	3–10	3	2–9	–	–	–	–	–
α-Aminoadipic acid	ca. 0.5	–	8	5–13	4	0–13	–	–	–	–	–
α-Aminobutyric acid	ca. 0.3	–	–	–	–	–	–	–	–	–	–
γ-Aminobutyric acid	ca. 0.3	–	–	trace	–	trace	–	–	–	–	–
β-Aminoisobutyric acid	5	0–9	22	6–37	29	10–52	–	<2.7	3.2–12.2	1.4–9.4	–
Arginine	ca. 0.5	–	6	0–14	4	0–11	<3.1	<1.3–7.1	<1.0	–	<0.7–2.0
Asparagine	–	–	–	–	–	–	–	–	–	–	3.9–7.8
Aspartic acid	–	<4	8	3–29	4	2–11	–	–	–	–	<1.2
Citrulline	–	–	–	–	–	–	–	3.9–6.2	4.4	–	–
Cystine	–	–	–	–	–	–	<3.1–8.1	1.1–7.7	<2.9	0.6–4.1	<0.5–1.2
Cystine+cysteine†	–	<4	14	3–33	6	0–13	–	–	–	–	–
Glutamic acid	–	–	–	–	–	–	2.3–31	2.3–13.1	5.2	1.5–1.6	<0.7–2.8
Glutamine	–	–	–	–	–	–	–	–	–	4.0–33.4	–
Glutamine+asparagine	25	2–60	73	42–103	62	43–88	–	–	–	–	–
Glutamine+asparagine +serine	–	–	–	–	–	–	21.0–264	8.9–60.0	13.8–14.5	–	–
Glycine	28	11–42	104	53–189	142	67–312	42.6–484	46.0–117	27.6–33.8	4.3–53.1	13.8–36.6
Histidine	47	15–83	138	20–213	128	79–208	13.7–34.5	9.3–56.0	18.9–22.8	8.0–46.0	11.9–22.5
Homocitrulline††	10	1–65	–	trace	–	trace	–	–	–	–	–
Hydroxyproline†††	–	0.8–1.4	–	<0.5	–	<0.5	–	–	–	–	–
Isoleucine	–	<4	15	8–24	10	5–20	2.5–16.8	1.3–2.3	<1.5	0.5–2.3	1.1–2.7
Leucine	–	<4	11	6–20	9	2–16	3.2–21	2.5–6.6	<3.7	0.7–3.1	1.0–2.3
Lysine	10	1.5–20	7	0–14	8	0–16	–	–	–	1.8–23.5	0.7–4.5
Lysine+1-methylhistidine	–	–	–	–	–	–	10.6–35	7.0–27.0	9.7–10.1	–	–
Methionine	–	<5	7	5–11	5	3–12	<2.6	0.5–1.3	<1.0	0.6–3.9	<0.6–1.2
1-Methylhistidine	9	0–43	73	22–114	65	26–155	–	–	–	0.8–9.8	–
3-Methylhistidine	–	<5	65	35–87	48	30–69	5.1–5.2	2.2–4.7	2.1–5.2	1.5–8.9	–
Ornithine	–	<4	1	0–4	2	0–11	–	–	–	–	–
Phenylalanine	–	<5	13	8–15	13	6–41	2.4–28	1.3–4.5	2.0–3.1	0.8–4.4	0.8–2.6
Proline	ca. 0.3	–	–	–	–	–	0–108	0–37.6	0	0	<1.4
Serine	10	7–13	42	27–65	37	22–61	–	–	–	4.1–22.4	3.9–7.8
Taurine	7	2–14	123	44–231	87	27–161	<31	<16.5	3.5–7.3	2.2–45.3	9.1–38.6
Threonine	6	3–9	17	2–35	23	5–33	11.3–140	4.0–20.0	3.8–5.6	2.4–10.3	1.9–5.0
Tryptophan§	–	–	21	10–32	16	5–27	–	–	–	–	–
Tyrosine	–	<5	19	7–27	15	9–26	12.6–61	2.0–14.0	1.1–2.9	1.3–7.0	1.3–4.3
Valine	ca. 0.3	–	10	4–17	6	0–30	1.9–23	<3.7	<1.9	0.5–2.0	<1.4

* Values from 8 boys and 7 girls, determined by ion exchange (SOUPART, P., in HOLDEN, J. T. [Ed.], *Amino Acid Pools*, Elsevier, Amsterdam, 1962, page 220).
** Values from 6 men and 9 women, determined by ion exchange (SOUPART, P., *Clin. chim. Acta*, 4, 265 [1959]).
*** Summary of various values, determined in 5 premature infants, 8 bottle-fed full-term babies and infants (2 of them fed breast-milk), 14 children and 8 adults (O'BRIEN and IBBOTT [Eds.], *Laboratory Manual of Pediatric Micro- and Ultramicro-Biochemical Techniques*, 3rd ed., Hoeber, Harper & Row, New York, 1962, page 30).

† Cystine 10–15 mg/l; cysteine 2–4 mg/l; determined by ion exchange (BRIGHAM et al., *J. clin. Invest.*, **39**, 1633 [1960]).
†† Determined by ion exchange (GERRITSEN et al., *Arch. Biochem.*, **97**, 34 [1962]). Homocitrulline is formed from lysine in cow's milk infant foods during the canning process (GERRITSEN et al., *Arch. Biochem.*, **100**, 298 [1963]).
††† Determined colorimetrically (RAVENNI et al., *Boll. Soc. ital. Biol. sper.*, **38**, 263 [1962]).
§ Determined microbiologically (ULRICH, J. A., *Proc. Mayo Clin.*, **29**, 210 [1954]).

Urine – Nitrogenous Substances

(For references see pages 671–672)

	Mean	95% range (extreme range in brackets)	s	Reference	Remarks
Proteins (mg/24 h)					
Total non-dialysable material					
(a) Newborn	87.9	34.3–142	26.8	36	Values from (a) 7, (b) 3, (c) 11, (d) 7 subjects; values (a, b, c) by fractionation into protein and uromucoid by millipore filter; values (d) calculated from the N-content of the non-dialysable material; values (e) by the biuret reaction[40]; values (f) include about 80% chondroitin sulphate A. The discrepancy in the values for high-molecular substances (between 30 and 750 mg/24 h[41]) are due in large part to the difficulty of concentrating the urine. These substances include 30–40% of carbohydrates[37, 42], i.e., glycoproteins, glycopeptides and mucopolysaccharides. In electrophoretic separation of the proteins about 25% appear in the albumin fraction, 17% in the α_1-globulin fraction, 24% in the α_2-globulin fraction, 16% in the β-globulin fraction and 12% in the γ-globulin fraction[43]. Up to 25 serum proteins have been identified in urine[44], including transferrin, γA-globulin and γG-globulin and also low-molecular γ-globulin chains; the other proteins present arise from the kidneys[45]. The urinary protein content is physiologically *increased* in the newborn[46] (particularly in premature infants), after standing erect with hyperlordosis and following physical effort; it is pathologically *increased* in fever, severe shock and renal diseases (particularly the nephrotic syndrome[47]). In multiple myeloma a low-molecular protein (BENCE-JONES protein; for identification see SNAPPER and ORES[48] and NAUMANN[48]) often appears in readily identifiable amounts (precipitation with sulphosalicylic acid, disappearance of the precipitate at 90–100 °C). For a detailed discussion of the proteins and mucopolysaccharides of urine see the literature[41, 49].
(b) Infants	125	–	–	36	
(c) Adults	474	420–528	27	36	
(d)	433	203–663	115	37	
Proteins					
(a) Newborn	10.5	8.82–12.2	0.84	36	
(b) Infants	13.0	–	–	36	
(c) Adults	61.6	47.0–76.2	7.3	36	
(d)	204	–	–	37	
(e)	–	(30–60)	–	38	
Uromucoids					
(a) Newborn	4.75	3.27–6.23	0.74	36	
(b) Infants	14.8	–	–	36	
(c) Adults	70.5	47.7–93.3	11.4	36	
Mucopolysaccharides					
(f)	–	(3–15)	–	39	
Amines, betaines					
Ethanolamine (mg/24 h)					
(a) Children, 3–11 years	13.1	(3.6–18.7)	–	3	Determined (a) by column chromatography on 12 children, (b) by paper chromatography on 14 adults. Phosphoethanolamine occurs in the urine when the blood phosphatase level is low[50].
(b) Adults	20.6	(11.5–35.2)	–	18	
Methylamine (mg/24 h)	5.0	(4.6–6.0)	–	51	
Dimethylamine (mg/24 h)	17.0	(15.2–19.3)	–	51	
Cystamine (mg/24 h)	1.4	–	–	52	
Piperidine (mg/24 h)	5.7	(4.7–7.1)	–	51	Probably in the main of bacterial origin (large intestine)[53].
Choline (mg/24 h)	–	(5.6–9.0)	–	54	Present exclusively in the free form.
Carnitine (mg/24 h)	–	(80–130)	–	55	
Acetonitrile (μg/l)	2.9	–	–	56	Values from nonsmokers; in smokers 118 μg/l.
Tyramine (mg/24 h)	1.3	(0.8–2.6)	–	57	Probably in the main of bacterial origin (large intestine)[53].
Para-aminobenzoic acid (mg/24 h)	0.76	(0.31–1.32)	–	58	
Catecholamines (μg/24 h)					
Adrenaline free	1	–	–	59	Calculated from measurements on 41 samples of nocturnal urine. The catecholamines in urine are partly free, partly bound to sulphuric or glucuronic acid. See also page 733.
Noradrenaline free	57	–	–	59	
Dopamine free	197	–	–	59	
Metanephrine free	30	–	–	59	
total	88	–	–	59	
Normetanephrine free	205	–	–	59	
total	420	–	–	59	
Tryptophan metabolites	...	...	...	...	In vitamin B_6 deficiency (see also pages 475–476) there is increased excretion of xanthurenic acid and other tryptophan metabolites, particularly after oral administration of tryptophan (tryptophan loading test)[60, 61].
3-Hydroxyanthranilic acid (mg/24 h)	0.36	(0.1–1.1)	–	61	

(For references see pages 671–672)

	Mean	95% range (extreme range in brackets)	s	Reference	Remarks
3-Hydroxykynurenine (mg/24 h)	0.49	(0–2.3)	–	61	In women the excretion of this substance falls after menstruation[62].
Acetylkynurenine (mg/24 h)	2.2	–	–	62	Values from 7 women.
Kynurenine (mg/24 h)					
(a) Infants	2.32	(0.19–27.7)	–	63	Values from (a) 17, (b) 19, (c) 20 subjects.
(b) Children	1.8	(0.50–3.8)	–	64	
(c) Adults	1.14	(0.3–2.6)	–	61	
Kynurenic acid (mg/24 h)					
(a) Infants	1.81	(0–4.75)	–	63	Values from (a) 17, (b) 19, (c) 20 subjects.
(b) Children	5.0	(0.00–8.8)	–	64	
(c) Adults	2.83	(1.0–4.2)	–	61	
Xanthurenic acid (mg/24 h)					
(a) Children	6.4	(3.2–13.0)	–	64	Values from (a) 19, (b) 20 subjects. Found in only one of a group of 9 infants (1.5 mg/24 h)[63].
(b) Adults	0.66	(0.3–1.8)	–	61	
***o*-Aminobenzoic acid** (anthranilic acid) (mg/24 h)	0.89	(0.32–2.24)	–	58	Mainly present as *o*-aminohippuric acid (see page 666).
Nicotinic acid	...	...	...	...	See under 'Vitamins', page 477.
Indoles					
Tryptamine (μg/24 h)					
(a) Children	–	(66–370)	–	65	Values from (a) 20, (b) 13, (c) 6 subjects. Probably in the main of bacterial origin (large intestine)[53].
(b) Men	64	(20–120)	–	66	
(c) Women	56	(40–72)	–	66	
***N,N*-Dimethyltryptamine** (μg/24 h)	43.0	25.8–60.2	8.6	67	Values from 50 subjects.
Serotonin (5-hydroxytryptamine) (μg/24 h)					
Free					
(a) Children	83	(43–123)	–	64	Values from (a) 6, (b) 20, (c) 6, (d) 21 subjects. The excretion of conjugated serotonin in particular is increased in carcinoid tumours.
(b) Men	72	(45–110)	–	66	
(c) Women	55	(10–85)	–	66	
(d)	131	(31–296)	–	68	
As glucuronide	93	(21–355)	–	68	
As sulphate	59	(0–127)	–	68	
5-Hydroxyindoleacetic acid (mg/24 h)					
(a) Children	8.6	(1.4–13.2)	–	64	Values from (a) 19, (b) 30, (c) 15 subjects. The excretion of this serotonin metabolite is *increased* after the ingestion of serotonin in the diet (in bananas, tomatoes, plums, walnuts) and following medication by various drugs (for instance caffeine, nicotine)[69,71]; it is pathologically *increased* in carcinoid tumours (from 30 up to 1500 mg/24 h)[72].
(b) Adults	–	(1.0–14.7)	–	69	
(c) Adults	4.5	2.3–6.7	1.1	70	
5-Methoxytryptamine	0	–	–	64	50 μg/24 h has been found in the urine of a rheumatic fever patient.
Bufotenine (μg/24 h)	63	49–77	7	73	Values from 50 subjects.
Indoxylsulphuric acid (mg/24 h)					
(a) Children	420	(148–620)	–	64	Values from (a) 19, (b) 8, (c) 56, (d) 44 subjects. The excretion is *increased* when bacterial decomposition of the intestinal contents is increased (for instance in intestinal obstruction)[75] and in the nephrotic syndrome[76], *decreased* in rheumatic fever[64].
(b) Adults	200	(140–250)	–	64	
(c) Men	64	28–100	18	74	
(d) Women	57	13–101	22	74	
6-Sulphatoxyskatole (mg/24 h)	24	(5–130)	–	66	

	Mean	95% range (extreme range in brackets)	*s*	Reference	Remarks
Indole-3-acetic acid (mg/24 h)					
(a) Total	–	(5.2–13.8)	–	77	Values from (a, b) 11 subjects; (a) after hydrolysis of the urine.
(b) Free	–	(3.1–8.1)	–	77	
Indole-3-lactic acid (mg/24 h)	–	(0.3–3)	–	78	
Indoleacetylglutamine (mg/24 h)	–	(1–8)	–	78	
Indoleformylglucuronide (mg/24 h)	–	(0–60)	–	79	
Imidazoles, histidine metabolites					
***N*-Acetylhistamine** (µg/24 h)					
(a) Children	–	(17–1840)	–	65	Values from (a) 20, (b) 17 subjects. Probably in the main of bacterial origin (large intestine)[53].
(b) Adults	22.0	(2.3–56)	–	80	
Histamine (µg/24 h)	11.9	(6.1–19)	–	80	The excretion of histamine and its metabolite 1,4-methylimidazoleacetic acid is considerably increased in mastocytosis[81, 82].
	–	(5–30)	–	81	
Imidazolelactic acid (mg/g creatinine)	19.8	9.6–30.0	5.1	83	Values from 12 subjects.
Urocanic acid (mg/24 h)	0.62	(0–1.7)	–	84	
Formiminoglutamic acid (formamidinoglutaric acid) (mg/24 h)	1.25	(0–2.1)	–	84	The excretion of this histidine metabolite is *increased* in folic acid deficiency (see page 479), sometimes also in vitamin B_{12} deficiency, diseases of the liver and sarcoidosis.
Porphyrins and related compounds					
Aminoacetone (mg/l)	2.2	(1.5–3.1)	–	85	
δ-Aminolaevulinic acid					
(a) Children (mg/l)	2.57	0.27–4.87	1.15	86	Values from (a) 50 children under 15 years, (b) 100 adults, (c) 13 adults. On the excretion in children of various ages see Käser et al.[89]. It is *increased* in some porphyrias[90] (see also pages 454–455) and in lead poisoning. Determination of this component in urine enables an increased absorption of lead to be recognized in time; concentrations of 13–20 mg/l urine correspond to 150–200 µg of lead per litre of urine and indicate that lead poisoning is imminent.
(b) Adults (mg/l)	2.9	0.1–5.7	1.4	87	
(c) Adults (mg/24 h)	2.63	0–5.33 (1.43–6.97)	1.35	88	
Porphobilinogen					
(a) Children (mg/l)	1.05	0.13–1.97	0.46	86	Values from (a) 50 children under 15 years, (b) 100 adults, (c) 13 adults. On the excretion in children of various ages see Käser et al.[89]. It is *increased* in some porphyrias[90] (see also pages 454–455) and there is a slight increase in liver disease; it is not increased in lead poisoning.
(b) Adults (mg/l)	1.0	0–2.0	0.5	87	
(c) Adults (mg/24 h)	1.40	0.38–2.42	0.51	88	
Coproporphyrin					
(a) (µg/l)	70	0–150	40	87	Values from (a) 100, (b) 9, (c) 72 subjects. Spectrophotometric methods give lower values than fluorometric methods (b)[93]. The excretion of coproporphyrin is proportional to the body weight[91]. 50–90% of the urinary coproporphyrin consists of coproporphyrin III, 10–40% of coproporphyrin I[94]. The excretion is *increased* in some porphyrias[90] (see also pages 454–455), liver disease and lead poisoning.
(b) (µg/24 h)	130	(80–220)	–	91	
(c) (µg/24 h)	36	6–66	15	92	
Uroporphyrin					
(a) (µg/l)	–	(0–15)	–	86	Values from (a) 25, (b) 9, (c) 72 subjects. Spectrophotometric methods give lower values than fluorometric methods (b)[93]. The excretion of uroporphyrin is *increased* in some porphyrias[90] (see also pages 454–455).
(b) (µg/24 h)	39	(28–63)	–	91	
(c) (µg/24 h)	12	4–20	4	92	
Bilirubin (mg/l)					
Children	0.9	–	–	95	
Adults	–	(0.02–1.9)	–	96	
Urobilinogen (mg/24 h)	0.36	0.05–2.5	–	97	Values from 46 subjects; the distribution is lognormal. Urobilinogen excretion is *decreased* in obstruction of the bile passages, *increased* in liver injury and intravascular haemolysis[97, 98].

	Mean	95% range (extreme range in brackets)	s	Reference	Remarks
Haemoglobin	0	–	–	–	Free haemoglobin (mainly present as methaemoglobin) not bound to the erythrocytes is present in urine only when the haemoglobin-binding capacity of the serum haptoglobin is exceeded, i.e., at concentrations of about 0.5–1.4 g haemoglobin per litre serum and above[99]. Haemoglobin may appear in the urine in blackwater fever, in transfusions as a result of blood incompatibility, and in athletes after intensive track work[100]; a paroxysmal nocturnal form of haemoglobinuria is also known. In blackwater fever a reddish-brown colouring matter with no peroxidase activity may also be excreted[101].
Myoglobin	0	–	–	–	Myoglobin appears in the urine when the serum level exceeds 0.15–0.2 g/l, for instance after very severe physical effort or serious injuries involving the muscles; an idiopathic paroxysmal form of myoglobinuria is also known[102].
Purines and related compounds					
Aminoimidazole carboxamide (mg/24 h)	0.4	(0.1–1.0)	–	103	Aminoimidazole carboxamide is an intermediate in the biosynthesis of purine; the excretion of this substance is *increased* in vitamin B_{12} deficiency.
	0.90	(0.36–1.58)	–	104	
Xanthine (mg/24 h)	4.9	(2.1–12.0)	–	105	Values determined in the urine of 7 subjects by chromatographic separation. For the enzymatic determination of xanthine and hypoxanthine see PETERSEN et al.[106] (applies to Xanthine through Adenine)
Hypoxanthine (mg/24 h)	6.8	(2.6–12.5)	–	105	
1-Methylhypoxanthine (mg/24 h)	–	(trace)	–	105	
Guanine (mg/24 h)	0.5	(0–0.7)	–	105	
1-Methylguanine (mg/24 h)	1.2	(0–2.1)	–	105	
7-Methylguanine (mg/24 h)	3.6	(1.0–7.7)	–	105	
Adenine (mg/24 h)	1.5	(0.7–3.6)	–	105	
Uric acid (mg/kg body weight/24 h)					
(a) Newborn, 0–2 days	4.8	–	–	2	Values from (a) 8, (b) 4, (c) 20 subjects on a normal diet. The uric acid excretion is dependent on the purine content of the diet; a purine-rich diet may result in the excretion of 2 g or more of uric acid per day[108]. Uric acid excretion is pathologically *increased* in gout chronic granulocytic leukaemia and various forms of acute leukaemia (but not in chronic lymphocytic leukaemia[105]), in polycythaemia vera, in WILSON's disease and occasionally in psoriasis[109].
(b) Adults	8.7	–	–	2	
(c) Adults (mg/24 h)	528	80–976	224	107	
Allantoin (mg/24 h)	–	(25–30)	–	110	
Pyrimidines and related compounds					
5-Ribosyluracil (pseudouridine) (mg/24 h)	46	(24–75)	–	111	Values from 26 healthy subjects on a purine-free diet. The excretion of pseudouridine is *increased* in gout and also in many patients with leukaemia and psoriasis.
Orotic acid (mg/24 h)	1.4	–	–	112	Present in the urine of infants up to 1.5 g/24 h as familial metabolic defect[113].

References

1 McCANCE and WIDDOWSON, *Acta paediat. (Uppsala)*, **49**, 409 (1960).
2 BARLOW and McCANCE, *Arch. Dis. Childh.*, **23**, 225 (1948).
3 CARVER and PASKA, *Clin. chim. Acta*, **6**, 721 (1961).
4 JELLINEK and LOONEY, *J. biol. Chem.*, **128**, 621 (1939).
5 WEHRLE and SCHIEVELBEIN, in FLASCHENTRÄGER and LEHNARTZ (Eds.), *Physiologische Chemie*, vol. 2, part 2b, Springer, Berlin, 1957, page 1.
6 BERGSTEDT et al., *J. Pediat.*, **56**, 635 (1960).
7 DE LEO and DI FRANCESCO, *Pediatria (Napoli)*, **67**, 239 (1959).
8 KENNEDY, W. P., *Arch. Dis. Childh.*, **36**, 325 (1961).
9 TAUSSKY and BRAHEN, *Stand. Meth. clin. Chem.*, **3**, 99 (1961).
10 CONN, R. B., *Clin. Chem.*, **6**, 537 (1960).
11 KIBRICK, A. C., *Clin. chim. Acta*, **11**, 408 (1965).
12 HOWELL, T. H., *J. Geront.*, **11**, 61 (1956).
13 TAUSSKY, H. H., *Clin. chim. Acta*, **1**, 210 (1956).
14 HEILSKOV and SCHØNHEYDER, *Acta med. scand.*, **151**, 51 (1955).
15 VESTERGAARD and LEVERETT, *J. Lab. clin. Med.*, **51**, 211 (1958).
16 VAN PILSUM et al., *J. biol. Chem.*, **222**, 225 (1956).
17 COHEN et al., *Amer. J. Dis. Child.*, **86**, 752 (1953).
18 McMENAMY et al., *J. clin. Invest.*, **39**, 1675 (1960).
19 SCHWAB and KÜHNS, *Die Störungen des Wasser- und Elektrolytstoffwechsels*, Springer, Berlin, 1959, page 171; EASTHAM, R. D., *Biochemical Values in Clinical Medicine*, 2nd ed., Wright, Bristol, 1963, page 13.
20 MÜTING, D., *Hoppe-Seylers Z. physiol. Chem.*, **297**, 61 (1954).
21 BIGWOOD et al., *Advanc. clin. Chem.*, **2**, 201 (1959).
22 GHADIMI and SHWACHMAN, *Amer. J. Dis. Child.*, **99**, 457 (1960).
23 O'BRIEN and IBBOTT, *Laboratory Manual of Pediatric Micro- and Ultramicro-Biochemical Techniques*, 3rd ed., Hoeber, Harper & Row, New York, 1962.
24 KHACHADURIAN et al., *J. Lab. clin. Med.*, **56**, 321 (1960).
25 VAN SLYKE et al., *J. biol. Chem.*, **150**, 251 (1943); OPIEŃSKA-BLAUTH, J., *Clin. chim. Acta*, **4**, 841 (1959); FRAME et al., *Stand. Meth. clin. Chem.*, **4**, 1 (1963).

26 KING, J. S., *Clin. chim. Acta*, **9**, 441 (1964).
27 SNYDERMAN and HOLT, *Advanc. Pediat.*, **11**, 209 (1960); ZILVERSMIT, D. B., *Expos. ann. Biochim. méd.*, **23**, 1 (1961); SCHREIER, K., in HOLDEN, J. T. (Ed.), *Amino Acid Pools*, Elsevier, Amsterdam, 1962, page 263; SOUPART, P., in HOLDEN, J. T. (Ed.), *Amino Acid Pools*, Elsevier, Amsterdam, 1962, page 220; SCRIVER, C. R., *Progr. med. Genet.*, **2**, 83 (1962).
28 MUSAJO and BENASSI, *Advanc. clin. Chem.*, **7**, 63 (1964).
29 STEIN et al., *J. Amer. chem. Soc.*, **76**, 2848 (1954).
30 ARMSTRONG et al., *J. biol. Chem.*, **218**, 921 (1956).
31 WESTALL, R. G., *Biochem. J.*, **60**, 247 (1955).
32 ABRAHAM et al., *Arch. Biochem.*, **99**, 210 (1962).
33 SKARŻYŃSKI and SARNECKA-KELLER, *Advanc. clin. Chem.*, **5**, 107 (1962).
34 MITOMA et al., *J. Lab. clin. Med.*, **53**, 970 (1959).
35 JASIN et al., *J. clin. Invest.*, **41**, 1928 (1962); GOIDANICH et al., *Clin. chim. Acta*, **11**, 35 (1965); ALLISON et al., *Clin. chim. Acta*, **14**, 729 (1966).
36 KEUTEL and KING, *Clin. chim. Acta*, **11**, 341 (1965).
37 KING et al., *J. clin. Invest.*, **37**, 315 and 1658 (1958).
38 SPEIER, F., *Laboratoriumsdiagnostik*, Bernecker, Melsungen, undated, p. 123.
39 MCKUSICK et al., *Medicine (Baltimore)*, **44**, 445 (1965).
40 FOSTER et al., *J. Lab. clin. Med.*, **39**, 618 (1952).
41 MAXFIELD, M., *Ann. Rev. Med.*, **14**, 99 (1963).
42 BOURRILLON and KAPLAN, *Clin. chim. Acta*, **5**, 732 (1960).
43 WEBB et al., *Canad. J. Biochem.*, **36**, 1159 (1958).
44 BERGGÅRD et al., *Clin. chim. Acta*, **10**, 1 (1964).
45 HERMANN and DE VAUX ST. CYR, in PEETERS, H. (Ed.), *Protides of the Biological Fluids*, Proceedings of the 11th Colloquium, Brussels 1963, Elsevier, Amsterdam, 1964, page 494.
46 RHODES et al., *J. Pediat.*, **60**, 18 (1962).
47 TIDSTRØM, B., in PEETERS, H. (Ed.), *Protides of the Biological Fluids*, Proceedings of the 12th Colloquium, Brussels 1964, Elsevier, Amsterdam, 1965, page 311.
48 SNAPPER and ORES, *J. Amer. med. Ass.*, **173**, 1137 (1960); NAUMANN, H. N., *Amer. J. clin. Path.*, **44**, 413 (1965).
49 HITZIG, W. H., *Die Plasmaproteine in der klinischen Medizin*, Springer, Berlin, 1963, page 209; KING and BOYCE, *High Molecular Weight Substances in Human Urine*, Thomas, Springfield, 1963.
50 MCCANCE et al., *Lancet*, **1**, 131 (1955); BLOCKEY, N. J., *Lancet*, **1**, 286 (1955).
51 BLAU, K., *Biochem. J.*, **80**, 193 (1961).
52 MONDOVÌ et al., *Ital. J. Biochem.*, **10**, 42 (1961).
53 PERRY et al., *Clin. chim. Acta*, **14**, 116 (1966).
54 LUECKE and PEARSON, *J. biol. Chem.*, **153**, 259 (1944).
55 GOODHART, R. S., in WOHL and GOODHART (Eds.), *Modern Nutrition in Health and Disease*, 3rd ed., Lea & Febiger, Philadelphia, 1964, page 460.
56 Medical News, *J. Amer. med. Ass.*, **181**, No. 5, 26 (1962).
57 TOMPSETT, S. L., *Clin. chim. Acta*, **7**, 50 (1962).
58 TOMPSETT, S. L., *Clin. chim. Acta*, **5**, 415 (1960).
59 MATTOK et al., *Clin. chim. Acta*, **14**, 99 (1966).
60 PRICE et al., *Advanc. metab. Disord.*, **2**, 159 (1965).
61 MUSAJO and BENASSI, *Advanc. clin. Chem.*, **7**, 63 (1964).
62 BROWN et al., *J. clin. Invest.*, **40**, 617 (1961).
63 CAREDDU et al., *Acta vitamin. (Milano)*, **18**, 241 (1964).
64 HADDOX and SASLAW, *J. clin. Invest.*, **42**, 435 (1963).
65 PERRY et al., *Pediatrics*, **30**, 576 (1962).
66 RODNIGHT, R., *Int. Rev. Neurobiol.*, **3**, 251 (1961).
67 GROSS and FRANZEN, *Z. klin. Chem.*, **3**, 99 (1965).
68 DAVIS et al., *J. Lab. clin. Med.*, **66**, 390 (1965).
69 STURM, A., *Clin. chim. Acta*, **7**, 714 (1962).
70 MUSTALA et al., *Scand. J. clin. Lab. Invest.*, **16**, 655 (1964).
71 SCHIEVELBEIN et al., *Klin. Wschr.*, **40**, 52 (1962).
72 DALGLIESH, C. E., *Advanc. clin. Chem.*, **1**, 193 (1958); RESNICK and GRAY, *Med. Clin. N. Amer.*, **44**, 1323 (1960); WEISSBACH et al., *Stand. Meth. clin. Chem.*, **4**, 121 (1963).
73 GROSS and FRANZEN, *Biochem. Z.*, **340**, 403 (1964).
74 MÜTING et al., *Z. klin. Med.*, **157**, 538 (1963).
75 CURZON and WALSH, *Clin. chim. Acta*, **7**, 657 (1962).
76 MÜTING et al., *Z. klin. Med.*, **157**, 544 (1963).
77 WEISSBACH et al., *J. biol. Chem.*, **234**, 81 (1959).
78 ARMSTRONG et al., *J. biol. Chem.*, **232**, 17 (1958).
79 BALAKRISHNAN and RODNIGHT, *Biochem. J.*, **76**, 61 P (1960).
80 DUNER and PERNOW, *Scand. J. clin. Lab. Invest.*, **8**, 296 (1956).
81 DEMIS et al., *Arch. intern. Med.*, **111**, 309 (1963).
82 DEMIS, D. J., in *XXII International Congress of Physiological Sciences*, Leiden 1962, vol. 2, Excerpta Medica Foundation, Amsterdam, 1962, Abstract No. 695.
83 DUBOVSKÝ and DUBOVSKÁ, *Clin. chim. Acta*, **12**, 360 (1965).
84 MERRITT et al., *J. clin. Invest.*, **41**, 1472 (1962).
85 WALDRON, H. A., *J. clin. Path.*, **18**, 230 (1965).
86 HAEGER, B., *Lancet*, **2**, 606 (1958).
87 HAEGER, B., *Scand. J. clin. Lab. Invest.*, **12**, suppl. 47 (1960).
88 MALOOLY and HIGHTOWER, *J. Lab. clin. Med.*, **59**, 568 (1962).
89 KÄSER et al., *Schweiz. med. Wschr.*, **93**, 1052 (1963).
90 WALDENSTRÖM and HAEGER-ARONSEN, *Münch. med. Wschr.*, **106**, 1333 (1964).
91 TALMAN and SCHWARTZ, *Stand. Meth. clin. Chem.*, **2**, 137 (1958).
92 REINKINGH and VAN KAMPEN, *Clin. chim. Acta*, **9**, 592 (1964).
93 FERNANDEZ et al., *Clin. Chem.*, **12**, 463 (1966)
94 AZIZ et al., *J. Lab. clin. Med.*, **63**, 585 (1964).
95 MICHAËLSSON, M., *Scand. J. clin. Lab. Invest.*, **13**, suppl. 56 (1961).
96 GUNDERMANN and KÜBLER, *Dtsch. med. Wschr.*, **87**, 306 (1962).
97 BALIKOV et al., *Stand. Meth. clin. Chem.*, **2**, 192 (1958).
98 ROOT, W. S., *Meth. med. Res.*, **8**, 122 (1960).
99 LAURELL and NYMAN, *Blood*, **12**, 493 (1957).
100 SCHLATTER and FORSTER, *Schweiz. med. Wschr.*, **95**, 979 (1965).
101 RICK, W., Düsseldorf, personal communication.
102 Editorial, *Lancet*, **1**, 704 (1961); BOROIAN et al., *J. Pediat.*, **67**, 69 (1965).
103 LUHBY and COOPERMAN, *Lancet*, **2**, 1381 (1962).
104 COWARD and SMITH, *Clin. chim. Acta*, **12**, 206 (1965).
105 KRAKOFF et al., *Med. Clin. N. Amer.*, **45**, 521 (1961).
106 PETERSEN et al., *Scand. J. clin. Lab. Invest.*, **17**, 454 and 460 (1965).
107 KUHL et al., *Metabolism*, **4**, 143 (1955).
108 NATELSON et al., *Stand. Meth. clin. Chem.*, **1**, 123 (1953).
109 EISEN and SEEGMILLER, *J. clin. Invest.*, **40**, 1486 (1961).
110 LARSON, H. W., *J. biol. Chem.*, **94**, 727 (1931).
111 WEISSMAN et al., *J. Lab. clin. Med.*, **59**, 852 (1962).
112 LOTZ et al., *Nature*, **197**, 194 (1963).
113 HUGULEY et al., *Blood*, **14**, 615 (1959); BECROFT and PHILLIPS, *Brit. med. J.*, **1**, 547 (1965).

Enzymes (for definition of the unit U see page 584)

The healthy kidney excretes low-molecular enzymes and their precursors, such as amylase and uropepsinogen; if high-molecular enzymes are excreted at all they include lactate dehydrogenase[1–3], aspartate aminotransferase[2,4], ribonuclease[5], alkaline phosphatase[3,6,7], acid phosphatase[6], arylsulphatases[8], β-glucuronidase[9] and aminopeptidase[10]. In renal injury the amounts of these enzymes in the urine are often increased. When determining enzymes in urine the urinary volume and diuretic state must be taken into account; thus the activity of some enzymes measured per unit volume of urine is higher in antidiuresis than in diuresis[11].

	Mean	95% range (extreme range in brackets)	s	Reference	Remarks
Amylase (kU/24 h, 37 °C)...	6.03	(2.06–11.8)	–	12	Frequently *increased* in acute pancreatitis.
Uropepsinogen (U/24 h, 37 °C)					
(a) Men	40	2–78	19	13	Values from (a) 21, (b) 18 subjects; substrate haemoglobin. A small part of the pepsinogen secreted in the gastric mucosa enters the blood and is excreted by the kidneys; there is, however, little correlation between the uropepsinogen excretion and the pepsinogen content of the gastric juice. Absence of uropepsinogen in the urine indicates atrophy of the gastric mucosa.
(b) Women	23	0–51	14	13	

References

1 WACKER and DORFMAN, *J. Amer. med. Ass.*, **181**, 972 (1962); BRENNER and GILBERT, *Amer. J. med. Sci.*, **245**, 31 (1963); GÜTTLER and CLAUSEN, *Enzymol. biol. clin. (Basel)*, **5**, 55 (1965).
2 ROSALKI and WILKINSON, *Lancet*, **2**, 327 (1959).
3 AMADOR et al., *Ann. intern. Med.*, **62**, 30 (1965).
4 SEPAHA et al., *Indian J. med. Res.*, **49**, 68 (1961).
5 LEVY and ROTTINO, *Clin. Chem.*, **6**, 43 (1960).
6 BURGEN, A. S. V., *Lancet*, **1**, 329 (1947).
7 AMADOR, E., *J. Amer. med. Ass.*, **185**, 769 (1963); BUTTERWORTH et al., *Clin. chim. Acta*, **11**, 212 (1965); DIETZ and HODGES, *Clin. chim. Acta*, **15**, 393 (1967).
8 BAUM et al., *Clin. chim. Acta*, **4**, 453 (1959); DZIAŁOSZYŃSKI and GNIOT-SZULŻYCKA, *Clin. chim. Acta*, **15**, 381 (1967).
9 LEWIS and PLAICE, *Nature*, **184**, 1249 (1959); PULKKINEN et al., *Ann. Paediat. Fenn.*, **8**, 50 (1962).
10 ROTH, M., *Clin. chim. Acta*, **9**, 448 (1964); BERGMANN and SCHELER, *Klin. Wschr.*, **42**, 275 (1964).
11 BÖSCH and DUBACH, *Clin. chim. Acta*, **15**, 325 (1967).
12 TIERNEY et al., *Ann. intern. Med.*, **58**, 229 (1963).
13 VAN GOIDSENHOVEN et al., *Gastroenterology*, **34**, 421 (1958).

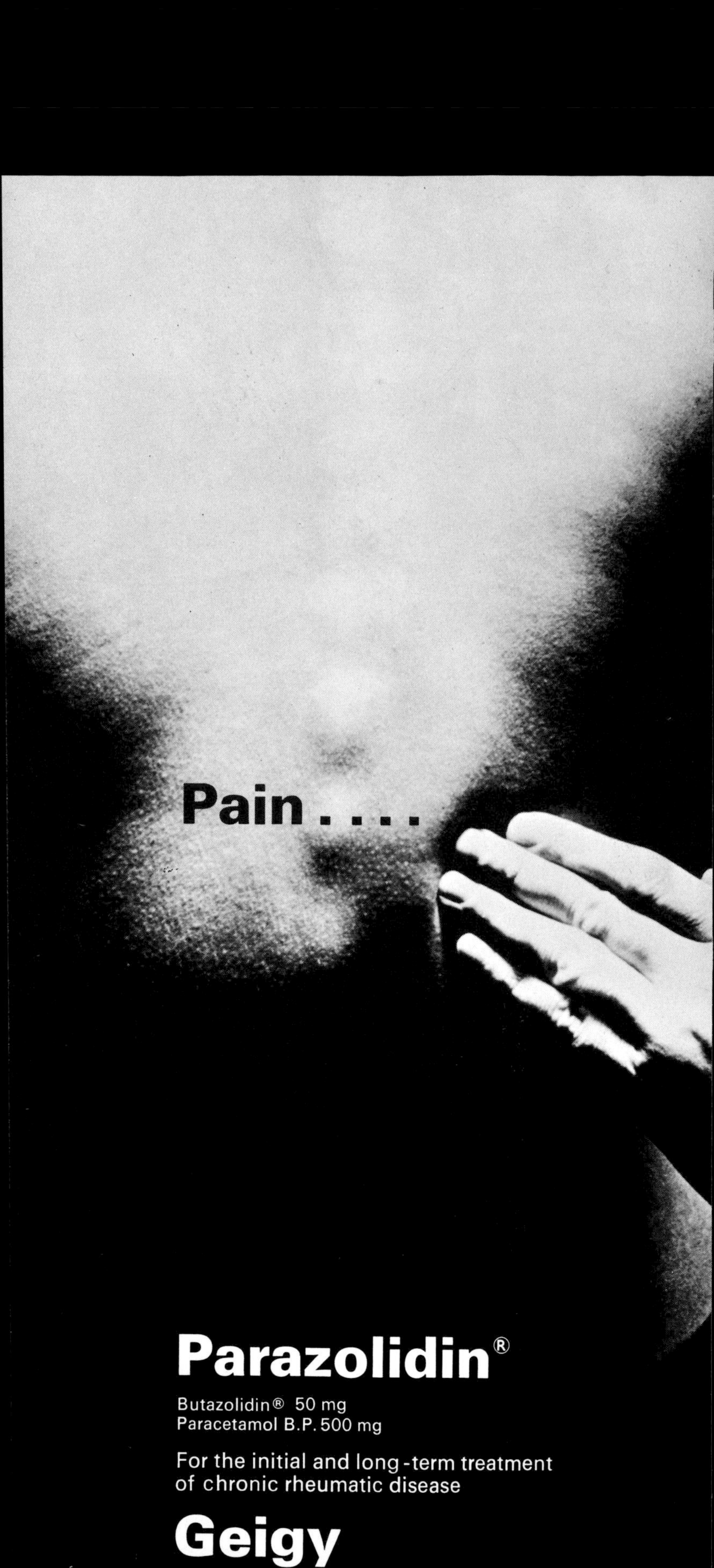

Pain....
Parazolidin®
Butazolidin® 50 mg
Paracetamol B.P. 500 mg
For the initial and long-term treatment
of chronic rheumatic disease
Geigy

The urinary carbohydrates are present partly in the free form, partly as components of glycoproteins, mucopolysaccharides and glycopeptides, partly as glucuronic acid bound to phenols and acids. On free sugars in urine see SIDBURY[1].

	Mean	95% range (extreme range in brackets)	s	Reference	Remarks
Reducing substances ('sugar') (mg/24 h)	515	(242–845)	–	2	Values from 30 subjects by the NELSON-SOMOGYI method. The classical methods of determining 'sugar' are based on the reducing power of certain carbohydrates. They are not specific for glucose, but give positive results also with other urinary components like uric acid, creatinine, glucuronic acid, homogentisic acid, ascorbic acid, fructose, lactose and pentoses. They can also be positive in patients treated with certain antibiotics[3] (penicillin, streptomycin, tetracyclines but not dihydrostreptomycin or chloramphenicol). Methods largely specific for glucose are the glucose oxidase–peroxidase reaction[4], the hexokinase–pyruvate kinase reaction[4] and the hexokinase–glucose-6-phosphate dehydrogenase reaction[5].
Glucose (mg/l)					
(a) Newborn, 1st week	–	(<250)	–	6	Values (a) by paper chromatography, (b) from 30 subjects by the glucose oxidase method. Glucose excretion is *increased* when the glucose intake is high, as also in some kinds of renal injury, various endocrine diseases (diabetes, CUSHING's syndrome, adrenocortical hyperplasia), head injury and intracranial tumours.
(a) Newborn, 2nd week	–	(<200)	–	6	
(b) Adults (mg/24 h)	72	(16–132)	–	2	
Galactose (mg/l)					
(a) Newborn, 1st week	–	(<250)	–	6	Values (a) by paper chromatography, (b) from 10 adults on an average diet. Infants on a milk diet may excrete up to 400 mg galactose per litre urine, those with galactosaemia up to 10 g per litre[8].
(a) Newborn, 2nd week	–	(<200)	–	6	
(b) Adults	14	(3–25)	–	7	
Fructose (mg/l)					
Newborn, 1st week	–	(<700)	–	6	Values by paper chromatography. Fructose excretion is *increased* with a high fructose intake; idiopathic fructosuria is also known.
Newborn, 2nd week	–	(<50)	–	6	
Lactose (mg/l)					
(a) Newborn, 1st week	–	(<1200)	–	6	Values (a) by paper chromatography, (b) from subjects on a mixed diet. No lactose is excreted when the diet is lactose-free. Endogenous lactose appears in the urine in late pregnancy and during lactation (up to 500 mg/l)[10].
(a) Newborn, 2nd week	–	(<100)	–	6	
(b) Adults (mg/24 h)	28	(0–91)	–	9	
Sucrose	...	...	...	...	Sucrose may appear in the urine after oral intake[11].
Xylose (mg/24 h)	49	(14–111)	–	7	Values from 10 adults on an average diet. The excretion of xylose and arabinose is *increased* after consuming fruit[6].
Arabinose (mg/24 h)	38	(12–56)	–	7	
Ketopentoses (mg/24 h)	4.3	0.5–8.1	1.9	12	Values from 15 men. The ketopentoses consist mainly of L-xylulose with traces of ribulose and sedoheptulose. In essential pentosuria 1–5 g L-xylulose per day is excreted independently of the diet[13].
Inositol (mg/l)	–	(35–85)	–	14	Chromatographic studies showed mesoinositol in all samples and scyllitol in 67%.
Glucuronic acid, total (mg/24 h)					
(a) Men	431	271–591	80	15	Values in hydrolysed urine from (a) 56, (b) 44, (c) 14 and (d) 10 subjects. Most of the glucuronic acid is bound to phenolic substances (including steroid hormones) and acids. The liver is capable of secreting large amounts of glucuronic acid for the detoxication and excretion of such substances. In women glucuronic acid excretion fluctuates during the menstrual cycle[17]. It is *increased* in severe burns and malignant neoplastic diseases[18], *decreased* in rheumatic diseases[17], liver diseases[19] and the nephrotic syndrome[20].
(b) Women	371	193–549	89	15	
(mg/kg body weight/24 h)					
(c) Newborn, 0–2 weeks	16.4	12.2–20.6	2.12	16	
(d) Newborn, 2–7 weeks	8.5	5.54–11.5	1.48	16	
Non-dialysable carbohydrates (mg/24 h)					
Hexoses	72.6	34.4–111	19.1	21	These carbohydrates consist of glycoproteins, mucopolysaccharides and glycopeptides (see also under 'Proteins', page 668). The following hexoses have been identified: galactose, mannose, glucose and fucose, together with the hexosamines glucosamine and galactosamine.
Hexosamines	26.5	14.3–38.7	6.1	21	
Sialic acid	40.7	25.7–55.7	7.5	21	
Glucuronic acid, children	–	(4.1–14.7)	–	22	
Glucuronic acid, adults	–	(2.7–7.3)	–	22	

References

1 SIDBURY, J. B., *Advanc. clin. Chem.*, **4**, 29 (1961).
2 FROESCH et al., *Diabetes*, **5**, 1 (1956).
3 FISHER et al., *Ann. paediat. (Basel)*, **185**, 254 (1955).
4 SCHMIDT, F. H., *Internist (Berl.)*, **4**, 554 (1963).
5 RENSCHLER et al., *Germ. med. Mth.*, **11**, 237 (1966); *Dtsch. med. Wschr.*, **90**, 2349 (1965).
6 BICKEL, H., *Mod. Probl. Pädiat.*, **4**, 136 (1959).
7 DATE, J. W., *Scand. J. clin. Lab. Invest.*, **10**, 155 (1958).
8 WOOLF, L. I., *Advanc. clin. Chem.*, **5**, 1 (1962).
9 STUHLFAUTH et al., *Klin. Wschr.*, **40**, 1151 (1962).
10 RIFFART et al., *Arch. Gynäk.*, **181**, 607 (1952).
11 HAWORTH, J. C., *Lancet*, **2**, 725 (1962).
12 BAKER et al., *Metabolism*, **9**, 478 (1960).
13 Annotation, *Brit. med. J.*, **1**, 1628 (1963).
14 MALANGEAU, P., *Bull. Soc. Chim. biol. (Paris)*, **38**, 729 (1956).
15 MÜTING et al., *Z. klin. Med.*, **157**, 538 (1963).
16 PULKKINEN et al., *Ann. Paediat. Fenn.*, **8**, 50 (1962).
17 HOLOPAINEN, T., *Ann. Med. exp. biol. Fenniae*, **36**, suppl. 8 (1958).
18 CORNILLOT, P., *Clin. chim. Acta*, **7**, 42 (1962).
19 MÜTING, D., *Germ. med. Mth.*, **8**, 198 (1963); *Dtsch. med. Wschr.*, **88**, 130 (1963).
20 MÜTING et al., *Z. klin. Med.*, **157**, 544 (1963).
21 KING et al., *J. clin. Invest.*, **37**, 315 (1958).
22 DIFERRANTE and RICH, *J. Lab. clin. Med.*, **48**, 491 (1956).

	Mean	95% range (extreme range in brackets)	s	Reference	Remarks
Organic acids (mEq/24 h)					
Men	55	–	–	1	Urine contains a large number of aliphatic and aromatic acids; in infants the former dominate, in adults – depending on the intake of fruit and vegetables – the latter. The aromatic acids are mainly bound to amino acids (page 666). For details see the literature[2, 3].
Women	64	–	–	1	
Volatile acids (mg/24 h)	–	(8–50)	–	4	In the main formic acid, a little acetic acid and traces of butyric acid[3].
Formic acid (mg/l)	13	–	–	5	
Adipic acid (mg/24 h)	–	(1.3–2.5)	–	6	
Malic acid (mg/24 h)	5.4	–	–	7	
Succinic acid (mg/24 h)	–	(2–12)	–	8	
Pyruvic acid (mg/24 h)					
(a) Children	5.6	1.9–9.3	1.83	9	Values from (a) 21 children aged 5–10 years, (b) 3 men, (c) 3 women and (d) children aged 3 months to 4 years. *Increased* in non-compensated diabetes.
(b) Men	9.6	–	–	10	
(c) Women	11.4	–	–	10	
(mg/kg body weight/24 h)					
(d) Children	–	(0.16–0.52)	–	11	
Citric acid					
(a) Adults (mg/24 h)	462	90–834	186	12	Values from (a) 12 adults, (b) children aged 3 months to 4 years. Higher on a carbohydrate diet than on one rich in proteins, *increased* in treatment with oestrogens (whence its fluctuation during the menstrual cycle) and vitamin D, *decreased* in severe muscular activity, acidosis, diabetes, hypoparathyroidism and chronic renal insufficiency[7].
(b) Children (mg/kg body weight/24 h)	–	(4–12)	–	11	
Furane-2,5-dicarboxylic acid (mg/24 h)	–	(3–4)	–	13	
Glutaric acid (mg/24 h)	2.5	–	–	15	
α-Ketoglutaric acid (mg/24 h)					
(a) Children	9.3	0.5–18.1	4.4	9	Values from (a) 21 children aged 5–10 years, (b) 3 men, (c) 3 women and (d) children aged 3 months to 4 years. *Decreased* in chronic renal insufficiency[7].
(b) Men	12.0	–	–	10	
(c) Women	18.7	–	–	10	
(d) Children (mg/kg body weight/24 h)	–	(0.5–2.0)	–	11	
Methylmalonic acid (mg/24 h)	5.8	(0–11.2)	–	14	*Increased* in vitamin B_{12} deficiency.
Lactic acid (mg/24 h)	–	100–600	–	4	Often absent from the urine. *Increased* during severe muscular activity, also following epileptic attacks and in fever.
Glycolic acid (mg/24 h)	42	–	–	16	Values from 15 children, adjusted to a body surface area of 1.73 m^2.
Glyoxylic acid (mg/24 h)	–	(1.4–4.7)	–	17	
Oxalic acid (mg/24 h)					
(a) Children	–	(10–45)	–	18	Values from (a) 25, (b) 18, (c) 60 subjects. In primary hyperoxaluria 100–400 mg per day is excreted[21].
(b)	31	13–49	9	19	
(c)	–	(9.0–28.5)	–	20	
Ketone bodies (as acetone) (mg/24 h)					
(a)	–	(10–100)	–	22	Values (a) usual in adults; values (b) in young men. The ketone bodies consist of acetoacetic acid, β-hydroxybutyric acid (which must be oxidized before determination as ketone) and acetone; the proportion of β-hydroxybutyric acid increases as the total ketone-body excretion rises. *Increased* during fasting, especially when physical work is done at the same time and when the ambiant temperature is low; *decreased* in dehydration. It is *pathologically increased* in diabetes (up to 50 g/l in poorly adjusted patients), thyreotoxicosis and fever. Children are more inclined to hyperketonuria than adults.
(b)	209	(< 400)	–	23	
Acetone (mg/l)	0.8	(0.2–2.5)	–	24	

	Mean	95% range (extreme range in brackets)	s	Reference	Remarks
Phenols, aromatic acids	...	...	...	...	The aromatic acids are partly bound to amino acids (page 666), the phenols to glucuronic acid (page 673).
Phenol (mg/24 h)..........	10	(8–13)	–	25	
***p*-Cresol** (mg/24 h).........	87	(64–117)	–	25	
Pyrocatechol (mg/24 h)	5.7	–	–	26	
3-Methoxy-4-hydroxyphenylglycol (mg/24 h).......	3.0	(1.4–4.6)	0.8	27	Values from 18 subjects.
3-Methoxy-4-hydroxyphenylacetic acid (homovanillic acid) (mg/24 h)	5.35	3.2–7.6	1.1	28	Values from 15 young adults.
Vanillic acid (mg/24 h)	–	(<5)	–	29	
3-Methoxy-4-hydroxymandelic acid (mg/24 h) .	3.6	–	–	30	For further data see page 733.
Dihydroxyphenylacetic acid (mg/24 h)	0.7	–	–	31	
Dihydroxymandelic acid (mg/24 h)...............	0.4	–	–	30	
Homogentisic acid	...	...	...	...	Excreted in urine in measurable amount only in alkaptonuria (3–5 g/24 h)[32].
***m*-Hydroxybenzoic acid** (mg/24 h)...............	–	(10–16)	–	33	
***p*-Hydroxyphenylacetic acid** (mg/24 h)	–	(15–31)	–	33	
Lipids					
Non-dialysable lipids (mg/24 h)...............	15.6	0–31.8	8.1	34	Lipid content of the non-dialysable material in urine (see page 668), consisting of cholesterol, phospholipids and fatty acids; triglycerides are not normally present. Lipid excretion is increased in some kidney diseases, particularly the nephrotic syndrome.
Cholesterol (mg/24 h)	2.7	(1.2–3.8)	–	35	Values from 5 subjects.
Phospholipids (mg/24 h)...	9.5	(7.0–13.3)	–	35	Values from 5 subjects.

References

1 Schwab and Kühns, *Die Störungen des Wasser- und Elektrolytstoffwechsels*, Springer, Berlin, 1959, page 171.
2 Nordmann and Nordmann, *Advanc.clin.Chem.*, **4**, 53 (1961).
3 Wehrle and Schievelbein, in Flaschenträger and Lehnartz (Eds.), *Physiologische Chemie*, vol.2, part 2b, Springer, Berlin, 1957, page 1.
4 Hinsberg, K., in Lang et al. (Eds.), *Hoppe-Seyler / Thierfelder Handbuch der physiologisch- und pathologisch-chemischen Analyse*, 10th ed., vol.5, Springer, Berlin, 1953, page 181.
5 Rietbrock and Hinrichs, *Klin. Wschr.*, **42**, 981 (1964).
6 Thomas et al., *Hoppe-Seylers Z.physiol.Chem.*, **317**, 276 (1959).
7 Nordmann et al., *Clin.chim.Acta*, **12**, 304 (1965).
8 Weitzel, G., *Hoppe-Seylers Z.physiol.Chem.*, **282**, 174 (1947).
9 Zelnicek, E., *Clin.chim.Acta*, **7**, 592 (1962).
10 Zelnicek, E., *Nature*, **185**, 928 (1960).
11 Schaerer and Antener, *Ann.paediat.(Basel)*, **203**, suppl.1 (1964).
12 Canary et al., *J.Lab.clin.Med.*, **57**, 230 (1961).
13 Flaschenträger and Bernhard, *Hoppe-Seylers Z.physiol.Chem.*, **246**, 124 (1937).
14 Cox and White, *Lancet*, **2**, 853 (1962); Giorgio and Plaut, *J. Lab.clin.Med.*, **66**, 667 (1965).
15 Thomas and Stalder, *Hoppe-Seylers Z.physiol.Chem.*, **317**, 269 (1959).
16 Hockaday et al., *J.Lab.clin.Med.*, **65**, 677 (1965).
17 Zarembski and Hodgkinson, *Biochem.J.*, **96**, 218 (1965).
18 Pik and Kerckhoffs, *Clin.chim.Acta*, **8**, 300 (1963).
19 Dempsey et al., *Metabolism*, **9**, 52 (1960).
20 Zarembski and Hodgkinson, *Biochem.J.*, **96**, 717 (1965).
21 Editorial, *Brit.med.J.*, **1**, 259 (1960).
22 Consolazio et al., *Physiological Measurements of Metabolic Functions in Man*, McGraw-Hill, New York, 1963, page 437.
23 Passmore, R., *Lancet*, **1**, 839 (1961).
24 Levey et al., *J.Lab.clin.Med.*, **63**, 574 (1964).
25 Schmidt, E.G., *J.biol.Chem.*, **179**, 211 (1949).
26 Smith, A.A., *Nature*, **190**, 167 (1961).
27 Ruthven and Sandler, *Clin.chim.Acta*, **12**, 318 (1965).
28 Ruthven and Sandler, *Clin.chim.Acta*, **14**, 511 (1966).
29 Sturm, A., *Germ.med.Mth.*, **8**, 234 (1963); *Dtsch.med.Wschr.*, **88**, 1000 (1963).
30 DeQuattro et al., *J.Lab.clin.Med.*, **63**, 864 (1964).
31 von Euler et al., *Upsala Läk.-Fören.Förh.*, **64**, 217 (1959).
32 Neuberger et al., *Biochem.J.*, **41**, 438 (1947).
33 Tompsett, S.L., *Clin.chim.Acta*, **3**, 149 (1958).
34 King et al., *J.clin.Invest.*, **37**, 315 (1958).
35 Klahr et al., *J.clin.Invest.*, **46**, 1475 (1967).

	Mean	95% range (extreme range in brackets)	s	Reference	Remarks
Coenzyme Q_{10} (μg/24 h) ...	15.4	(0–58)	–	1	
Thiamine (μg/l)					
(a) ...	900	(800–2400)	–	2	Values (a) from 31 subjects, using *Ochromonas danica*[2]; values (b) from 27 subjects, using *Ochromonas malhamensis*[3]; values (c) on 24 infants during the first three days. Except in dietary thiamine deficiency, the urinary thiamine excretion increases linearly with the intake. In thiamine deficiency it falls rapidly, whereas the excretion of thiamine metabolites remains largely constant (see page 470). In beri-beri 0–14 μg thiamine are excreted daily[5]. Thiamine excretion is increased in diuretic treatment with mercury salts but not with thiazides[6].
(b) ...	–	(110–370)	–	3	
(c) Newborn ...	96	52–140	22	4	
Riboflavin					
(a) Newborn (μg/l) ...	219	157–281	31	4	Values from (a) 24 infants during the first three days, (b) 31 children, in most of whom values were below 300 μg. Riboflavin excretion varies with the dietary intake (see pages 471–472).
(b) Children, 3–7 years (μg/24 h) ...	–	(50–650)	–	7	
(c) Adults (μg/24 h) ...	–	(150–2000)	–	5	
Vitamin B_6 (μg/24 h) ...	40	(20–120)	–	8	Determined by means of *Tetrahymena pyriformis*.
(nmol/kg/h)					
Total ...	–	(0.55–1.24)	–	9	Values from 3 children and 3 adults. The free vitamin was determined before hydrolysis, the total vitamin after hydrolysis, in both cases using *Saccharomyces carlsbergensis*.
Free ...	–	(0.08–0.29)	–	9	
Pyridoxic acid ...	–	(1.7–8.0)	–	9	
Nicotinic acid					
(a) Children (mg/24 h) ...	2.3	(1.8–2.9)	–	10	Values determined (a) chemically, (b) microbiologically with *Tetrahymena pyriformis*.
(b) Adults (mg/l) ...	–	(1.16–1.54)	–	3	
1-Methylnicotinamide (mg/24 h)					
(a) Newborn, 4–50 days ...	1.71	(0.55–4.87)	–	11	Values from (a) 14, (b) 29, (c) 25 subjects. The excretion of this nicotinic acid metabolite is decreased in pellagra (see page 477).
(b) Children, 6–11 years...	2.70	(0.77–5.45)	–	12	
(c) Men, under 35 years...	7.38	(2.85–12.3)	–	13	
(c) Women, under 35 years..	6.05	(2.34–12.7)	–	13	
(c) Men, over 50 years...	3.60	(1.76–10.5)	–	13	
(c) Women, over 50 years ...	3.45	(1.50–9.20)	–	13	
1-Methyl-2-pyridone 5-carboxylamide (mg/24 h)					
(a) Newborn, 4–50 days ...	1.64	(0.30–6.67)	–	11	Values from (a) 14, (b) 29, (c) 25 subjects. The isomeric compound 1-methyl-4-pyridone 5-carboxylamide is also present in urine[14]. The excretion of 1-methyl-2-pyridone 5-carboxylamide is increased during pregnancy[15] and fluctuates during the menstrual cycle[15,16]; it is pathologically decreased in diabetes[17] and pellagra (see page 477).
(b) Children, 6–11 years...	4.47	(1.55–11.8)	–	12	
(c) Men, under 35 years...	13.29	(4.44–29.2)	–	13	
(c) Women, under 35 years..	11.14	(4.30–32.2)	–	13	
(c) Men, over 50 years...	6.20	(0.80–21.1)	–	13	
(c) Women, over 50 years ...	12.28	(1.75–29.2)	–	13	
Vitamin B_{12} (ng/24 h) ...	–	(0–27)	–	19	On a normal diet.
Folic acid (μg/24 h) ...	4	(2–7)	–	18	On a normal diet.
Biotin (μg/l) ...	–	(6.26–32.7)	–	3	Values determined with *Ochromonas danica*. Present in the urine in the free form.
Pantothenic acid (mg/l)...	2.90	(0.76–4.1)	–	3	Values determined with *Lactobacillus plantarum*. Present in the urine in the free form.
Ascorbic acid					
(a) Newborn (mg/l) ...	45.4	31.8–59.0	6.8	4	Values (a) from 24 infants during the first three days. The values (b) for adults are dependent on the degree of tissue saturation and on the dietary intake (see pages 489–490).
(b) Adults (mg/24 h) ...	–	(10–100)	–	–	

References

1 NAPIER et al., *Nature*, **202**, 806 (1964).
2 BAKER et al., *Amer. J. clin. Nutr.*, **14**, 197 (1964).
3 BAKER and SOBOTKA, *Advanc. clin. Chem.*, **5**, 173 (1962).
4 DAHL et al., *Acta paediat. (Uppsala)*, **50**, 127 (1961).
5 GOLDSMITH, G.A., in BEATON and MCHENRY (Eds.), *Nutrition*, vol. 2, Academic Press, New York, 1964, page 109.
6 DUBEL and SOLOFF, *Amer. J. med. Sci.*, **245**, 58 (1963).
7 MASLENIKOVA and KOSENKO, *Vop. Pitan.*, **21**, No. 5, 31 (1962), quoted in *Nutr. Abstr. Rev.*, **33**, 521 (1963).
8 BAKER et al., *Amer. J. clin. Nutr.*, **18**, 123 (1966).
9 SCRIVER and CULLEN, *Pediatrics*, **36**, 14 (1965).
10 HADDOX and SASLAW, *J. clin. Invest.*, **42**, 435 (1963).
11 APOLLONIO et al., *Acta vitamin. (Milano)*, **17**, 65 (1963).
12 MAINARDI et al., *Acta vitamin. (Milano)*, **17**, 153 (1963).
13 MAINARDI et al., *Acta vitamin. (Milano)*, **16**, 255 (1962).
14 CHANG and JOHNSON, *J. biol. Chem.*, **236**, 2096 (1961).
15 BROWN et al., *J. clin. Invest.*, **40**, 617 (1961).
16 MAINARDI et al., *Acta vitamin. (Milano)*, **19**, 15 (1965).
17 PASQUARIELLO, G., *Acta vitamin. (Milano)*, **18**, 225 (1964).
18 REGISTER and SARETT, *Proc. Soc. exp. Biol. (N.Y.)*, **77**, 837 (1951).
19 GRÄSBECK, R., *Advanc. clin. Chem.*, **3**, 299 (1960).

	Mean	95% range (extreme range in brackets)	s	Reference	Remarks
Erythrocytes (per ml)......	–	0–2500	–	1	On the erythrocyte content of the urine of newborn infants see AAS[3], on that of pregnancy urine see SCHOLZ[4]. The erythrocyte content may be increased in spastic contraction of the renal veins (as for instance in haematuria due to lordotic congestion) as also in various diseases of the kidneys and urinary tract, including kidney stone and bladder stone.
Per 24 h	130000	–	–	2	
Leucocytes (per ml)	–	0–3000	–	1	On the leucocyte content of the urine of newborn infants see AAS[3], on that of pregnancy urine see SCHOLZ[4]. The leucocyte content is increased in all inflammatory renal diseases.
Men (per h)	46000	(0–220000)	–	5	
Women (per h)	74000	(0–574000)	–	5	
Per 24 h	650000	–	–	2	
Hyaline casts (per 24 h)....	2000	–	–	2	73% of all sediments contain no hyaline casts.
Bacteria..................	...	...	...	...	Urine obtained by bladder puncture is normally sterile; in samples obtained by 'clean' micturition the limiting value between normal bacterial contamination and true infection of the urinary tract is regarded as 100000 cells per millilitre[6].

References

1 BROSIG et al., *Urologe*, **4**, 241 (1965).

2 LIPPMAN, R.W., *Urine and the Urinary Sediment*, 2nd ed., Thomas, Springfield, 1957.

3 AAS, K., *Acta paediat. (Uppsala)*, **50**, 361 (1961).

4 SCHOLZ, B., *Geburtsh. u. Frauenheilk.*, **25**, 743 (1965).

5 LITTLE, P. J., *Lancet*, **1**, 1149 (1962).

6 MCGEACHIE and KENNEDY, *J. clin. Path.*, **16**, 32 (1963); REUTTER et al., *Helv. med. Acta*, **31**, 478 (1964); STAMEY et al., *Medicine (Baltimore)*, **44**, 1 (1965); THIEL, G., *Schweiz. med. Wschr.*, **95**, 922 (1965).

Amorphous and crystalline chemical sediments

Sediment	Characteristics	Occurrence	Solubility (○ = readily soluble, ● = sparingly soluble)						
			Heating	Alkalis	Mineral acids	Acetic acid	Alcohol	Acetone	Ether
Uric acid.......	Crystals mostly, but not always, coloured yellow by absorption of urinary pigments	Acid urine	○ (60 °C)	○	●	●	●	●	●
Urates.........	Calcium, magnesium and potassium urates, mostly amorphous, in concentrated acid urine. Colour and chemical behaviour as for uric acid	Ammonium urate in alkaline urines. All other urates in acid urines	○ (60 °C)	○	●	●	●	●	●
Phosphates									
Calcium phosphate........	Rare...............................	Alkaline urine	●	●	○	○	●	●	●
Ammonium magnesium phosphate ...	Commoner	Alkaline urine	●	●	○	○	●	●	●
Calcium oxalate.	Size about that of erythrocytes	Usually in acid urine, also in neutral and weakly alkaline	●	●	○	●	●	●	●
Cystine	Colourless crystals (distinction from uric acid crystals, when of similar form). Must be looked for in fresh urine since cystine is rapidly destroyed by bacteria	Acid urine	●	○ esp. ammonia	○	●	●	●	●
Tyrosine.......	Often yellow-coloured since they are associated with jaundice. Mostly accompanied by leucine. Occur in acute yellow atrophy of the liver, also in cirrhosis, acute phosphorus poisoning, leukaemia	Acid urine	● (relative)	○ precipitated on neutralization	○	○	●	●	●
Leucine........	See tyrosine. Crystals in urine are impure. Pure leucine crystallizes in hexagonal platelets	Acid urine	○ (relative)	○	○	○	●	●	●
Bilirubin....... (haematoidin)	Colours any uric acid crystals present and changes their shape	Acid urine	●	○ readily soluble in chloroform	○	○	●	○	●
Indigotin	Rare. Also colours other crystals and thus appears to crystallize in various forms. Pure indigo in urine is amorphous or as *b* in the figure on page 678. Crystallizes from chloroform as *c* in this figure	Alkaline or acid urine.......	very soluble in chloroform				●	–	○
Cholesterol.....	Very rare..........................	Acid urine	very soluble in chloroform				●	–	○
Hippuric acid...	Very rare..........................	....	○	○	●	●	●	–	●
Sulphonamides .	Easily distinguished from uric acid crystals by solubility in acetone	....	–	–	–	–	–	○	–

Amorphous and crystalline chemical sediments[1]

Various crystalline forms of uric acid

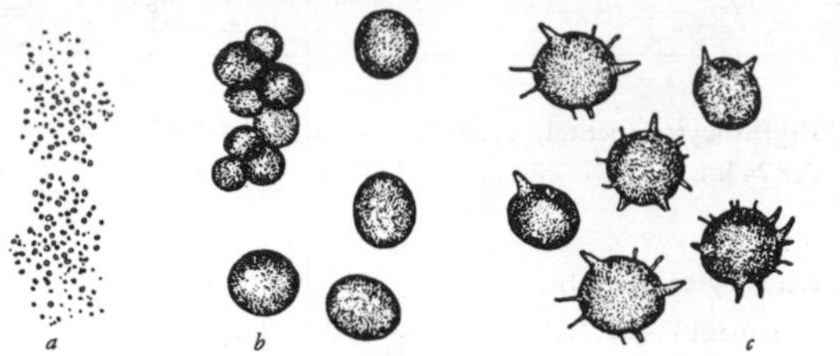

Urates

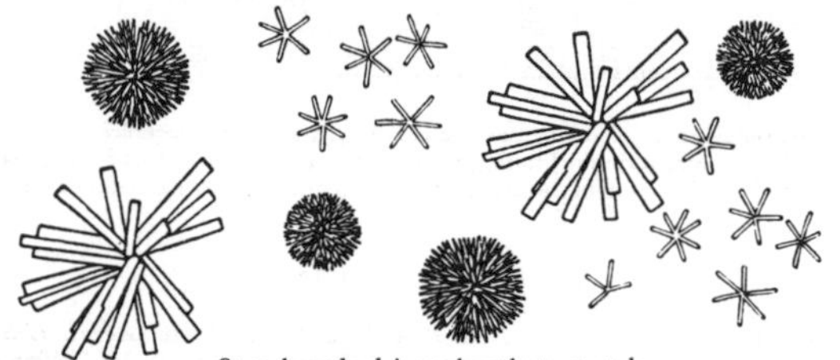

Star-shaped calcium phosphate crystals

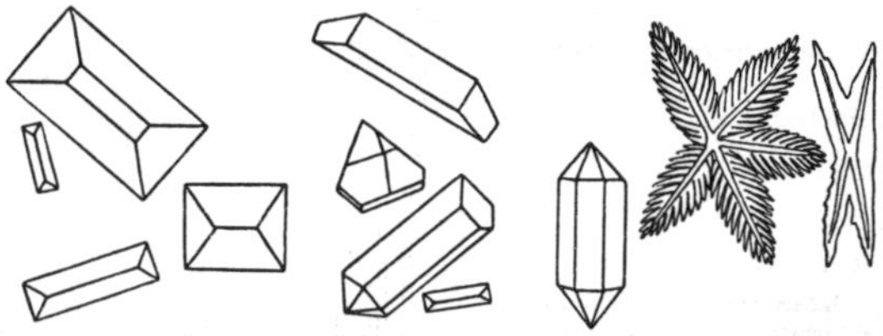

Ammonium magnesium phosphate crystals

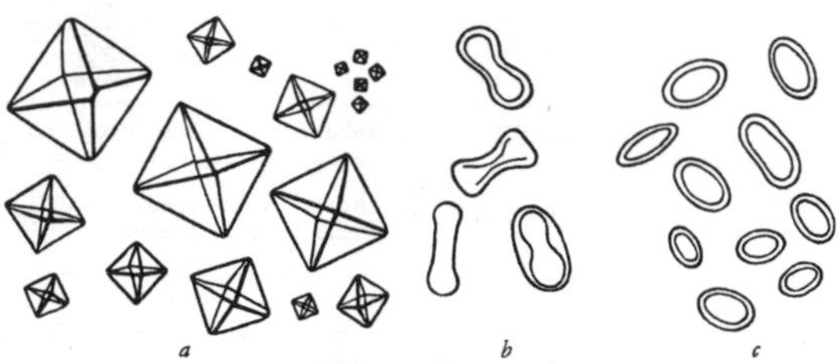

Calcium oxalate crystals

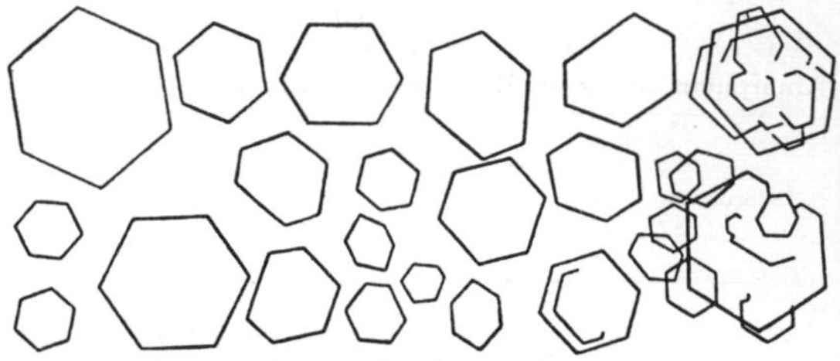

Hexagonal cystine crystals

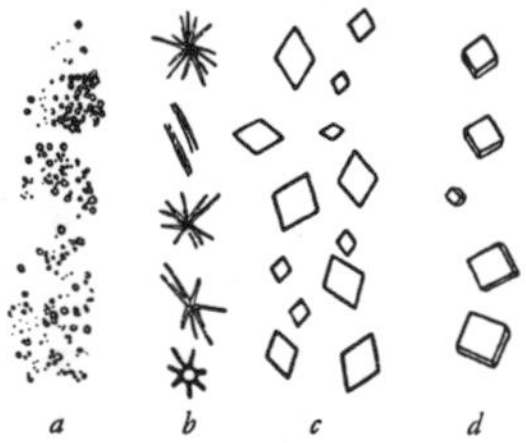

Bilirubin

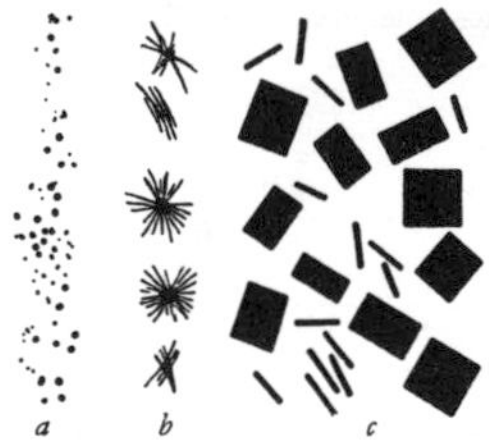

Indigotin

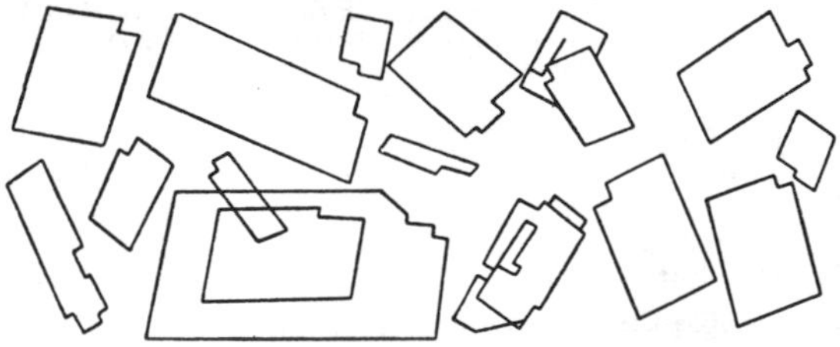

Jagged cholesterol platelets

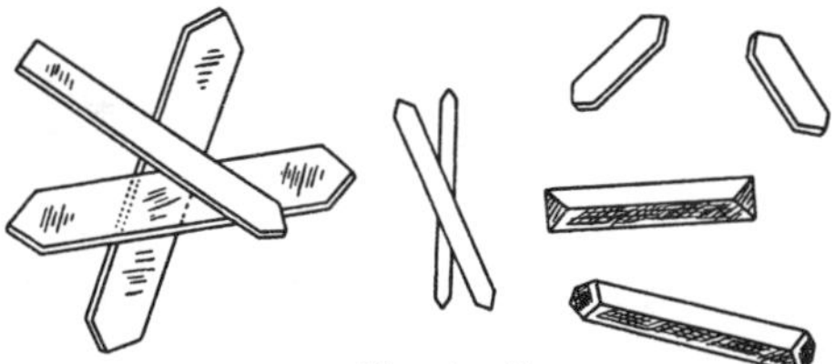

Hippuric acid

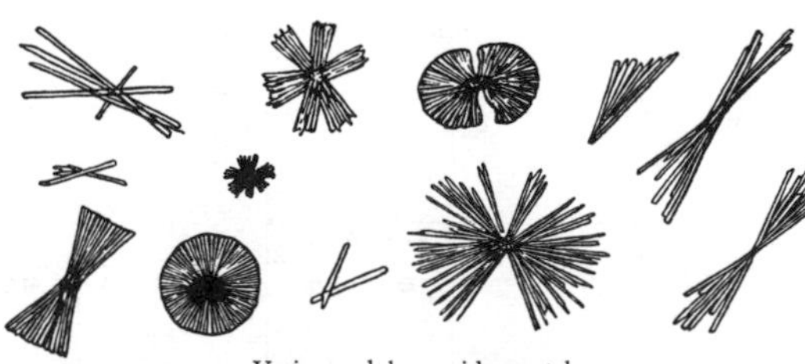

Various sulphonamide crystals

Urates	*a* calcium, magnesium and potassium urates, mostly amorphous
	b ammonium urate (spherical forms)
	c sodium urate (thorn-apple forms)
Calcium oxalate	*a* octahedra, often flattened (commonest form)
	b dumb-bell forms
	c ring forms
Bilirubin *reddish brown*	*a* amorphous
	b masses of needles
	c rhombic forms
	d cubic forms
Indigotin *blue*	*a* amorphous } urine
	b masses of needles } urine
	c rectangular platelets from chloroform

[1] From Harrison, G. A., *Chemical Methods in Clinical Medicine*, 4th ed., Churchill, London, 1957, pages 100 et seq.

(For references see page 681)

Sweat is secreted by two kinds of gland, the small, eccrine sweat glands and the larger, apocrine sweat glands. The former are much more numerous than the latter and are mainly found in the hairless parts of the skin, whereas the apocrine glands are confined mainly to the hairy areas, especially the axillae. The secretions of the two types of gland differ in composition. Little is known of that of apocrine sweat[7], so that unless otherwise stated the data in the following tables refer to eccrine sweat. Samples of sweat can be obtained by thermal excitation (heat sweat), strenuous bodily activity (work sweat) or by pharmacological means (for example, pilocarpine sweat). The composition varies with the method of collection, the rate of secretion and the location. There is an extensive literature on the composition of eccrine sweat[2–8].

Approximate numbers of sweat glands[9]

Total	2 million
Flexure of elbow	751/cm²
Palm of hand	373/cm²
Chest	155–250/cm²
Buttocks	57/cm²

Eccrine sweat unless otherwise stated	Mean	95% range (extreme range in brackets)	s	Reference	Remarks
Physicochemical data					
Appearance	...	...	...	...	Eccrine sweat: clear, watery, odourless. Apocrine sweat: cloudy, viscous, often slightly yellow and fluorescent, sometimes bluish or blackish (chromhidrosis = excessive coloration); sterile apocrine sweat is odourless but rapidly acquires its characteristic smell from bacterial action (bromhidrosis or osmidrosis = development of excessive odour).
Amount (l/24 h)					
(a)	0.3–0.5	–	–	7	(a) Insensible perspiration = macroscopically invisible sweat and transepidermal water loss under normal conditions; (b) measured on a 65 kg man doing light work in an environmental temperature of 29 °C. In children the amount per unit body surface area is about twice that in adults[6]. Transepidermal water loss from nonsweating skin is small[10] (0.2 mg/cm²/h, or 80–100 ml/24 h). Over short periods the maximum rate of sweating is 2–4 l/h or 8–15 l/24 h[6, 7]. Increasing tolerance to heat is accompanied by an appropriate reduction in sweating.
(b)	(2–3)	–	–	7	
Specific gravity	–	(1.001–1.008)	–	7	
Freezing-point depression (°C)	–	(0.32–0.37)	–	2	NaCl contributes about 80%, lactic acid about 11% of the osmolarity of sweat[4]. In healthy subjects the sweat is hypotonic, in patients with cystic pancreatic fibrosis isotonic with the extracellular fluid[11]. The osmolarity of sweat rises with increasing rate of secretion as a result of the increasing NaCl content.
Surface tension (dyn cm⁻¹)	–	(69–70)	–	12	Measured at 37–38 °C.
Water (g/l)	–	(990–995)	–	2	
Dry substance (g/l)	–	(3–10)	–	7	Consists of 50% organic and 50% inorganic matter.
pH value	–	(4–6.8)	–	5	Apocrine sweat is about 0.5 pH less acid than eccrine sweat[7], possibly because of its higher ammonia content[13].
Inorganic substances					
Chloride (mEq/l)					
(a) Newborn, 1st day	39	14–64	12.5	14	Measured in pilocarpine sweat from (a) 100, (b) 43, (c) 107, (d) 17, (e) 63 and (f) 31 subjects. On the method of determination see Ibbott et al.[17]. On physiological and pathological changes in the chloride content of sweat see under 'Sodium', page 680.
(b) Children, 1–12 months	12.3	2.5–22.1	4.9	15	
(c) Children, 1–10 years	15.3	0–31.5	8.1	15	
(d) Children, 10–16 years	19.9	1.5–38.3	9.2	15	
(e) Adults, 17–50 years	29.7	0–65.1	17.7	15	
(f) Adults, over 50 years	38.9	34.3–43.5	2.3	16	
Phosphate (mg/l)	14	(10–17)	–	18	Measured on 4 children. Data on the phosphate content of sweat vary widely[6, 7].
Sulphate (mg/l)	–	(7–190)	–	7	Less than 50% is inorganic sulphate.
Bromide (mg/l)	–	(0.182–0.502)	–	19	
Fluoride (mg/l)	–	(0.2–1.8)	–	20	
Iodine (µg/l)	9.5	(5.4–12.2)	–	21	*Increased* in cystic pancreatic fibrosis[22].

Eccrine sweat unless otherwise stated	Mean	95% range (extreme range in brackets)	s	Reference	Remarks
Potassium (mEq/l)					
(a) Newborn, 1st day	8	2–14	3	14	Measured in pilocarpine sweat from (a) 100, (b) 43, (c) 107, (d) 17, (e) 14 and (f) 6 subjects. The potassium content decreases slightly with increasing rate of secretion[24]. It is moderately *increased* in cystic pancreatic fibrosis[18, 23, 25], but the change is not as characteristic as that in the sodium or chloride content.
(b) Children, 1–12 months	11.2	4.4–18.0	3.4	15	
(c) Children, 1–10 years	9.6	4.0–15.2	2.8	15	
(d) Children, 10–16 years	8.5	3.7–13.3	2.4	15	
(e) Men, 20–60 years	7.5	4.3–10.7	1.6	23	
(f) Women, 20–60 years	10.0	5.8–14.2	2.1	23	
Sodium (mEq/l)					
(a) Newborn, 1st day	36	10–62	13	14	Measured in pilocarpine sweat from (a) 100, (b) 43, (c) 107, (d) 17, (e) 33, (f) 26 and (g) 21 subjects. The amounts of sodium and chloride in sweat are dependent on many factors[27], such as hereditary disposition, age, season, site of collection and diet; they increase as the rate of secretion increases and are higher in heat sweat than in pilocarpine sweat[18]. The sodium/chloride ratio is 1.0–1.3[7]. In children and young adults the upper limit of the normal range of sodium concentration in heat sweat is reported to be 70–80 mEq/l, the corresponding figure for chloride being 60–70 mEq/l[11, 25, 27, 28]; during the first days of life this limit is somewhat higher[14]. In cystic pancreatic fibrosis the sodium and chloride contents of sweat almost always exceed these limiting values; a less characteristic increase in the sodium content is seen in hypofunctioning of the adrenal cortex[8] (this can be corrected by giving aldosterone). The sodium and chloride contents are lowered in primary hyperaldosteronism[29].
(b) Children, 1–12 months	14.5	5.1–23.9	4.7	15	
(c) Children, 1–10 years	19.5	3.3–35.7	8.1	15	
(d) Children, 10–16 years	29.2	6.0–52.4	11.6	15	
(e) Men, 20–60 years	51.9	9.7–94.1	21.1	23	
(f) Women, 20–60 years	36.5	0–73.9	18.7	23	
(g) Adults, over 65 years	55.5	7.5–104	24.0	26	
Calcium (mEq/l)	–	(0.2–6)	–	7	The calcium content increases with increasing rate of sweat secretion. Prolonged severe sweating may result in serious loss of calcium[30].
Magnesium (mEq/l)	–	(0.03–4)	–	7	
Iron (mg/l)					
Men	1.15	(0.63–1.88)	–	31	About ¼ of the ingested iron is excreted in the sweat when this is free of cells, the iron content of heat sweat from the arms being 190 μg/l, from the feet 250 μg/l[33].
Women	1.61	(1.21–2.30)	–	32	
Copper (mg/l)	0.058	–	–	34	
Manganese (mg/l)	0.060	–	–	34	
Zinc (mg/l)	1.15	0.55–1.75	0.30	35	Heat sweat from 10 subjects.
Nitrogenous substances					
Total nitrogen (mg/l)	–	(230–400)	–	5	The nitrogen content of sweat varies widely, published values lying between 170 and 1960 mg/l, including 50–1500 mg/l urea-N, 10–350 mg/l ammonia-N and 10–100 mg/l amino-acid-N[7].
Urea (mg/l)	–	(260–1220)	–	5	The urea content of sweat varies widely, published values lying between 30 and 2000 mg/l[8]; in general it is about twice that of the serum[7].
Creatinine (mg/l)	4.6	(2.1–8.4)	–	18	Values from heat sweat of 4 children. Published values range from 0 to 67 mg/l, with a mean of about 4 mg/l[5, 7].
Ammonia (mg/l)	–	(60–110)	–	5	The ammonia content of sweat varies widely, published values lying between 12 and 425 mg/l[7]; this is partly due to differences in the extent to which urea is broken down by bacteria. It is 25–200 times greater than the ammonia content of the serum[7].
Amino acids (g/l)					
(a) Children	1.40	1.23–1.58	0.087	18	(a) Calculated as leucine in the pilocarpine sweat of 18 children (in heat sweat the mean value is 2.65 g/l). (b) Heat sweat of 4 men. (c) Pilocarpine sweat of 151 men and women; the following were quantitatively determined (in order of decreasing concentration): citrulline, serine, glutamic acid, aspartic acid, arginine, threonine, alanine, leucine, glycine, histidine, ornithine, lysine, valine; also detected in some samples were phenylalanine, tyrosine, proline, tryptophan, taurine.
(b) Adults	1.38	(0.54–2.59)	–	36	
(c) Adults	0.476	0.27–0.68	0.102	37	
Uric acid (mg/l)	–	(0–15)	–	5	Other studies[38] found no uric acid in sweat.
Urocanic acid (mg/l)	57	1–113	28	18	Pilocarpine sweat of 18 children (mean value in heat sweat 148 mg/l).

Eccrine sweat unless otherwise stated	Mean	95% range (extreme range in brackets)	s	Reference	Remarks
Acetylcholine (μg/l)	6.5	(2–20)	–	39	Heat sweat of 13 children; increased tenfold in cystic pancreatic fibrosis.
Mucoproteins (mg/l)	–	(200–400)	–	40	
Enzymes	...	...	...	...	Alkaline phosphatase has been found in eccrine sweat[41].
Non-nitrogenous substances					
Reducing substances (as glucose) (mg/l)	30	(0–110)	–	7	Not more than 25% of the reducing substances of sweat consists of glucose. The heat sweat of children has a glucose content of 2 mg/l[18], while that of adults contains less than 10 mg/l[42].
Pyruvic acid (mg/l)	–	(9–70)	–	7	This value represents about 10 times the serum pyruvic acid content.
Lactic acid (g/l)					
(a) Children...............	1.47	0.43–1.51	0.52	18	(a) Pilocarpine sweat of 18 children (mean value in heat sweat 2.30 g/l); (b) range of published mean values, representing about 4–40 times the serum lactic acid content. The lactic acid content is higher in men than in women[13] and falls as the rate of secretion increases. The lactic acid arises from anaerobic breakdown of glucose and glycogen in the sweat glands.
(b) Adults	–	(0.36–3.60)	–	7	
Lipids	...	...	...	...	Lipids are present in the apocrine sweat[1,6] but not in the eccrine sweat.

References (pages 679–681)

1 Hurley and Shelley, *The Human Apocrine Sweat Gland in Health and Disease*, Thomas, Springfield, 1960.
2 Schaaf, F., in Flaschenträger and Lehnartz (Eds.), *Physiologische Chemie*, vol.2, part 2b, Springer, Berlin, 1957, page 302.
3 Cremer and Führ, in Lang et al. (Eds.), *Hoppe-Seyler/Thierfelder Handbuch der physiologisch- und pathologisch-chemischen Analyse*, 10th ed., vol. 5, Springer, Berlin, 1953, page 603; Albritton, E.C. (Ed.), *Standard Values in Nutrition and Metabolism*, Saunders, Philadelphia, 1954; Montagna, W., *The Structure and Function of Skin*, Academic Press, New York, 1956.
4 Rothman, S., *Physiology and Biochemistry of the Skin*, University of Chicago Press, Chicago, 1954.
5 Robinson and Robinson, *Physiol. Rev.*, **34**, 202 (1954).
6 Kuno, Y., *Human Perspiration*, Thomas, Springfield, 1956.
7 Schwartz, I. L., in Comar and Bronner (Eds.), *Mineral Metabolism*, vol. 1, part A, Academic Press, New York, 1960, page 346.
8 Lobitz and Dobson, *Ann. Rev. Med.*, **12**, 289 (1961).
9 Stüttgen, G., *Die normale und pathologische Physiologie der Haut*, Fischer, Stuttgart, 1965, page 268.
10 Blank et al., in Montagna et al. (Eds.), *Advances in Biology of Skin*, vol. 3: *Eccrine Sweat Glands and Eccrine Sweating*, Pergamon, Oxford, 1962, page 97.
11 Vink, C. L. J., in de Reuck and Cameron (Eds.), *Ciba Foundation Symposium on the Exocrine Pancreas*, Churchill, London, 1962, page 310.
12 Randall and Calman, *J. invest. Derm.*, **23**, 113 (1954).
13 Thurmon and Ottenstein, *J. invest. Derm.*, **18**, 333 (1952).
14 Stur, O., *Öst. Z. Kinderheilk.*, **6**, 347 (1961).
15 Shwachman et al., *Pediatrics*, **32**, 85 (1963).
16 de Haller et al., *Schweiz. med. Wschr.*, **92**, 1493 (1962).
17 Ibbott et al., *Stand. Meth. clin. Chem.*, **5**, 101 (1965).
18 Clarke et al., *Amer. J. Dis. Child.*, **101**, 490 (1961).
19 Cornbleet, T., *J. invest. Derm.*, **1**, 399 (1938).
20 McClure et al., *J. industr. Hyg.*, **27**, 159 (1945).
21 Spector et al., *J. biol. Chem.*, **161**, 137 (1945).
22 Brodkey and Gibbs, *J. appl. Physiol.*, **15**, 501 (1960).
23 Lobeck and Huebner, *Pediatrics*, **30**, 172 (1962).
24 Collins, K. J., *Clin. Sci.*, **30**, 207 (1966).
25 di Sant'Agnese and Gibson, in Montagna et al. (Eds.), *Advances in Biology of Skin*, vol. 3: *Eccrine Sweat Glands and Eccrine Sweating*, Pergamon, Oxford, 1962, page 229.
26 McKendrick, T., *Lancet*, **1**, 183 (1962).
27 Shwachman, H., *Pediatrics*, **30**, 167 (1962).
28 Koch et al., *Internist (Berl.)*, **1**, 35 (1960); Siegenthaler et al., *Lancet*, **1**, 538 (1962); Siegenthaler and de Haller, *Helv. med. Acta*, **32**, 1 (1965).
29 Crane et al., *J. Lab. clin. Med.*, **61**, 51 (1963).
30 Consolazio et al., *J. Nutr.*, **78**, 78 (1962).
31 Hussain et al., *Indian J. med. Res.*, **48**, 235 (1960).
32 Hussain and Patwardhan, *Lancet*, **1**, 1073 (1959).
33 Apte and Venkatachalam, *Indian J. med. Res.*, **50**, 817 (1962).
34 Mitchell and Hamilton, *J. biol. Chem.*, **178**, 345 (1949).
35 Prasad et al., *J. Lab. clin. Med.*, **62**, 84 (1963).
36 Bosse and Paschen, *Klin. Wschr.*, **42**, 1196 (1964).
37 Coltman et al., *Amer. J. clin. Nutr.*, **18**, 373 (1966).
38 Seegmiller et al., *New Engl. J. Med.*, **268**, 712 (1963).
39 Eyerman et al., *Nature*, **192**, 77 (1961).
40 Jirka and Kotas, *Clin. chim. Acta*, **2**, 292 (1957).
41 Loewenthal and Politzer, *Nature*, **195**, 902 (1962).
42 Schulze and Kunz, *Arch. Derm. Syph. (Chic.)*, **181**, 486 (1940).

Semen

(For references see page 685)

The ejaculate (total semen) is a suspension of spermatozoa in a liquid medium, the seminal plasma. The latter consists of the various secretions of the accessory reproductive organs, namely the testes, epididymides, vasa deferentia, seminal vesicles, prostate and urethral and bulbo-urethral glands. The composition of the total semen depends on the amounts of these individual secretions contained in it. Those of the three principal fractions can be calculated from the content of acid phosphatase, characteristic of the prostate secretion, from the number of spermatozoa, characteristic of the testicular and epididymal secretions, and from the content of fructose, characteristic of the secretion of the seminal vesicles[1]. The method of collection also has some effect on the composition.

In ejaculation a few drops of the urethral and bulbo-urethral gland secretions are first discharged. This is followed by the prostate secretion, usually free of spermatozoa, then by the middle portion of the seminal vesical secretion containing the spermatozoa, and finally by the highly viscous part of the latter secretion[2]. Immediately after ejaculation the semen coagulates as a result of the action of an enzyme from the prostate on a fibrinogen-like protein from the seminal vesicles. Within 15 minutes of ejaculation the semen liquefies as a result of fibrinolysis of the coagulum, a process involving a plasmin-like enzyme from the prostate; this is followed by hydrolysis of the proteins to amino acids and ammonia.

Unless otherwise stated, the data in the following table refer to the liquefied ejaculate. There is an extensive literature on the composition and properties of semen[3–5].

Total semen unless otherwise stated	Mean	95% range (extreme range in brackets)	s	Reference	Remarks
Physicochemical data	...	...	...	...	For further data on spermatozoa see page 686.
Appearance	...	...	...	...	The fresh ejaculate is milky, slightly opalescent, and contains glassy, sticky threads as well as sago- and tapioca-like particles. The seminal vesical secretion occasionally contains yellow pigments (flavins).
Volume of the ejaculate (ml)	3.4	0.2–6.6	1.6	6	Values from 1000 measurements after continence of at least 3 days. Very variable in the same subject. Repeated coitus causes a reduction in the volume, long continence an increase (up to 13 ml). 13–33% of the ejaculate volume is from the prostate, 46–80% from the seminal vesicles, about 10% from the epididymides[1,3].
Specific gravity	1.028	(1.020–1.040)	–	5, 7	The specific gravity of the whole ejaculate depends on the spermatozoal content.
	1.035	(1.031–1.039)	–	8	
Prostate secretion	1.022	(1.018–1.027)	–	8	
Seminal vesical secretion	1.037	–	–	8	
Freezing-point depression (°C)					
(a)	–	(0.56–0.58)	–	9	(a) 1 hour, (b) 16 hours after ejaculation.
(b)	–	(0.74–0.78)	–	9	
Osmolality (mosm/kg H_2O)					
Seminal plasma	296	–	–	10	
Spermatozoa	296	–	–	10	
Relative viscosity at 20 °C	6.45	–	–	9	The viscosity of the whole ejaculate is largely dependent on the spermatozoal content; that of the prostate secretion is low, that of the seminal vesical secretion high. The ability to form threads is characteristic of the secretions of the urethral and bulbo-urethral glands[2].
Surface tension (dyn cm^{-1})					
At 20 °C	66	–	–	9	
At 15 °C	–	(52–59.5)	–	11	
Specific conductivity (S cm^{-1}) at 20 °C	–	(0.0088–0.0108)	–	9	
Water (g/l)	918	(891–944)	–	8	
Prostate secretion	932	(927–936)	–	8	
Seminal vesical secretion	890	–	–	8	
Spermatozoa (g/kg)	830	–	–	10	
Dry substance (g/l)	–	(80–130)	–	8	Consists of about 10% inorganic and 90% organic matter[12].
pH value	7.19	(6.9–7.36)	–	8	Loss of CO_2 on long standing causes semen to become alkaline (pH 7.6–8.0).
Prostate secretion	6.45	(6.3–6.6)	–	8	
Seminal vesical secretion	7.29	–	–	8	
Inorganic substances					
Carbon dioxide (mmol/l)	24	(19.2–33.2)	–	8	
Prostate secretion (mmol/l)	4.2	(3.1–5.4)	–	8	
Spermatozoa (mmol/kg)	10.5	–	–	10	
Chloride (mEq/l)	42.8	(28.3–57.3)	–	8	
Prostate secretion (mEq/l)	38.1	(34.8–46.1)	–	8	
Spermatozoa (mEq/kg)	33	–	–	10	

(For references see page 685)

Total semen unless otherwise stated	Mean	95% range (extreme range in brackets)	s	Reference	Remarks
Phosphorus (g/l)	1.12	–	–	5	
Acid-soluble phosphorus	0.57	(0.28–0.94)	–	5	The acid-soluble phosphorus of the seminal plasma consists mainly of phosphorylcholine and glycerylphosphorylcholine.
Prostate secretion	0.03	(0.02–0.06)	–	13	
Seminal vesical secretion	0.46	(0.30–0.62)	–	13	
Spermatozoa (g/kg)	1.6	–	–	10	
Inorganic phosphorus	0.11	–	–	5	
Lipid phosphorus	0.06	–	–	5	
Potassium (mEq/l)	31.3	–	–	14	
	22.9	(17–27.4)	–	8	
Prostate secretion	48.3	(28.7–61.4)	–	8	
Seminal vesical secretion	17.8	–	–	8	
Spermatozoa (mEq/kg)	35	–	–	10	
Sodium (mEq/l)	117	(100–133)	–	8	
Prostate secretion	153	(149–158)	–	8	
Seminal vesical secretion	103	–	–	8	
Spermatozoa (mEq/kg)	110	–	–	10	
Calcium (mEq/l)	12.4	(10.6–14.3)	–	8	
Prostate secretion	60.4	(57.4–65.4)	–	8	
Seminal vesical secretion	7	–	–	1	
Magnesium (mEq/l)	11.5	–	–	5	
Copper (mg/l)	–	(0.06–0.24)	–	15	
Zinc (mg/g dry substance)					
Seminal plasma	3.1	–	–	16	
Prostate secretion	7.2	–	–	17	
Spermatozoa	2.0	–	–	18	
Nitrogenous substances					
Total nitrogen (g/l)	9.13	(5.60–12.25)	–	8	
Prostate secretion	4.16	(2.95–5.11)	–	8	
Seminal vesical secretion	12.84	(12.33–13.43)	–	8	
Nonprotein nitrogen (g/l)	0.96	(0.73–1.30)	–	8	
Prostate secretion	0.54	(0.30–0.90)	–	8	
Seminal vesical secretion	0.99	–	–	8	
Ammonia (mg/l)	20	–	–	1	Increases on prolonged incubation at 37 °C as a result of progressive decomposition of proteins.
Urea (mg/l)					
Seminal plasma	720	–	–	19	
Creatine (mg/l)					
Seminal plasma	170	–	–	20	
Arginine (mg/l)					
Seminal plasma	900	–	–	20	
Amino acids (g/l)					
Seminal plasma	12.6	–	–	21	Total of 19 free and peptide-bound amino acids determined by column chromatography. All amino acids are present in considerably higher concentrations than in the blood plasma. 24 amino acids have been identified in semen by thin-layer chromatography[22].
Choline (free) (g/l)	0.70	–	–	23	2 minutes after ejaculation; increases to more than 20 g/l 6 hours later as a result of liberation of choline from phosphorylcholine under the action of acid phosphatase.
Phosphorylcholine (g/l)	3.06	(2.86–3.80)	–	24	
Glycerylphosphorylcholine (g/l)	0.66	(0.54–0.90)	–	24	

Total semen unless otherwise stated	Mean	95% range (extreme range in brackets)	s	Reference	Remarks
Spermine (g/l)	–	(0.5–3.5)	–	5	Includes about 10% of the diamines spermidine, 1,3-propanediamine and putrescine[25].
Ergothioneine (mg/l)					
Seminal plasma	15	–	–	26	
Seminal vesical secretion	–	(<10)	–	5	
Glutathione (mg/l)					
Seminal plasma	300	–	–	27	
Uric acid (mg/l)	60	–	–	5	
Proteins (g/l) (a)	45.0	(32.9–68.5)	–	8	(a) (Total nitrogen – nonprotein nitrogen) × 6.25; (b) determined gravimetrically; (c) determined by biuret reaction. As immunoelectrophoretic studies [28–30] have shown, the seminal plasma contains various serum proteins (albumin, α_1-globulin, α_2-globulin, transferrin and γG-globulin) as well as organ-specific proteins arising partly from the prostate[29,31], partly from the seminal vesicles[29]. After ejaculation the seminal proteins are rapidly broken down by the action of proteolytic enzymes. The proteins of the spermatozoa consist mainly of nucleoproteins and enzymes.
(b)	58.0	(43.0–77.4)	–	8	
Seminal plasma (c)	–	(18–47)	–	28	
Prostate secretion (a)	21.7	(16.6–29.3)	–	8	
(b)	25.5	(24.6–26.4)	–	8	
Seminal vesical secretion (a)	77.8	–	–	8	
(b)	90.4	–	–	8	
Mucoproteins (g/l)					
Seminal plasma	9	–	–	32	The semen probably also contains other mucoproteins in addition to this fraction adsorbable on benzoic acid.
Sialic acid (g/l)	–	(0.60–1.05)	–	33	Only about 4% of this is dialysable[34], indicating that the sialic acid is a component of the mucoproteins.
Prostate secretion	–	(0.75–1.05)	–	33	
Seminal vesical secretion	–	(<1.3)	–	33	
Deoxyribonucleic acid (pg per spermatozoal nucleus)	2.5	–	–	35	The amount of DNA, an integral component of the chromosomes, in the spermatozoa of men of normal fertility is constant and fairly uniform, whereas in those of men with doubtful fertility it is inconstant and varies widely from one individual to another[35,36]
Enzymes	...	...	...	...	The *spermatozoa* are rich in various enzymes[5] such as cytochromes, succinate dehydrogenase, lactate dehydrogenase, malate dehydrogenase and adenosine triphosphatase. The spermatozoal head contains hyaluronate lyase lightly bound to the cell surface and readily released into the seminal fluid. The *seminal plasma* contains many enzymes; quantitatively determined have been lactate dehydrogenase[37], malate dehydrogenase[37], isocitrate dehydrogenase[37], glutathione reductase[37], aspartate aminotransferase[38], alanine aminotransferase[38], creatine kinase[39], phosphatases[40], α-glucosidase[41], β-galactosidase[42], α-mannosidase[42], β-mannosidase[42], chitobiase[42], β-glucuronidase[42]. The seminal plasma has a high fibrinolytic and proteolytic activity[5] but the enzymes responsible have not been clearly identified.
Alkaline phosphatase (U/l, 37 °C)					
Seminal plasma	–	(18–177)	–	40	For definition of the unit U see page 584.
Acid phosphatase (kU/l, 37 °C)					
Seminal plasma	–	(96–750)	–	40	For definition of the unit U see page 584. The acid phosphatase of semen arises mainly from the prostate. The phosphatase content is fairly constant in different ejaculates of the same individual but may vary widely in different individuals.
Prostate secretion					
Boys, 11 years	9	–	–	43	
Boys, 16 years	1540	–	–	43	
Men, 20–40 years	2560	–	–	44	
Men, 40–100 years	660	–	–	44	
Non-nitrogenous substances					
Fructose (g/l)	2.24	(0.91–5.20)	–	5	The fructose content of semen arises mainly from the seminal vesicles and varies widely. None is detectable before puberty or after castration. Values below 1.2 g/l indicate impaired functioning of the interstitial cells of LEYDIG.
Seminal vesical secretion	3.15	(1.7–8.2)	–	1, 5	
Glycogen (g/l)					
Seminal plasma	–	(0.14–5.5)	–	41	
Inositol (g/l)					
Seminal plasma	0.6	–	–	45	

Total semen unless otherwise stated	Mean	95% range (extreme range in brackets)	s	Reference	Remarks
Sorbitol (g/l)					
Seminal plasma	0.1	–	–	46	
Pyruvic acid (g/l)					
Seminal plasma	0.29	(0.11–0.56)	–	37	
Citric acid (g/l)	3.76	(0.96–14.3)	–	5	The citric acid content of the semen is a measure of androgenic activity; that of the prostate secretion gradually diminishes after castration.
Prostate secretion	–	(4.80–26.9)	–	8	
Seminal vesical secretion	–	(0.15–0.22)	–	5	
Lactic acid (g/l)	0.37	(0.28–0.52)	–	1	
Prostate secretion	0.50	–	–	1	
Lipids					
Total lipids (g/l)					
Seminal plasma	1.88	(1.67–2.06)	–	47	The spermatozoa are rich in various lipids[5] (lipoproteins, triglycerides, free fatty acids, sterols, phospholipids – particularly acetalphosphatides – heptacosan). The lipids of the seminal plasma arise mainly from the prostate and are partly contained in the formed elements of the secretion.
Prostate secretion	2.86	(2.60–3.10)	–	47	
Phospholipids (g/l)					
Seminal plasma	0.84	(0.48–1.33)	–	47	
Prostate secretion	1.80	(1.44–2.25)	–	47	
Cholesterol (g/l)					
Seminal plasma	1.03	(0.70–1.20)	–	47	
Prostate secretion	0.80	(0.62–1.05)	–	47	
Prostaglandins (mg/l)					
Seminal plasma	...	...	...	...	Primary prostaglandins: PGE compounds 53.5 mg/l, PGF compounds 8 mg/l; also metabolites of PGE compounds 250 mg/l[48].
Vitamins					
Tocopherol (mg/kg)	9.8	–	–	49	
Vitamin B$_{12}$ (µg/l)					
Seminal plasma	–	(0.30–0.60)	–	50	Determined with *Euglena gracilis*. Values are from semen with morphologically normal spermatozoa.
Ascorbic acid (mg/l)	43	(18–72)	–	51	The ascorbic acid probably arises from the seminal vesicles rather than from the prostate[52].

References (pages 682–685)

1 Lundquist, F., *Acta physiol. scand.*, **19**, suppl. 66 (1949).
2 Oettle, A. G., *Fertil. and Steril.*, **5**, 227 (1954).
3 Junkmann, K., in Flaschenträger and Lehnartz (Eds.), *Physiologische Chemie*, vol. 2, part 2b, Springer, Berlin, 1954, page 563.
4 Doepfmer, R., in Jadassohn, J. (Ed.), *Handbuch der Haut- und Geschlechtskrankheiten*, supplement, vol. 6, part 3, Springer, Berlin, 1960, page 281; Dittmer, D. S. (Ed.), *Blood and Other Body Fluids*, Biological Handbooks, Federation of American Societies for Experimental Biology, Washington, 1961, page 425; Silló-Seidl, G., *Fortschr. Geburtsh. Gynäk.*, **15**, 1 (1963).
5 Mann, T., *The Biochemistry of Semen and of the Male Reproductive Tract*, Methuen, London, 1964.
6 MacLeod, J., *Fertil. and Steril.*, **2**, 115 (1951).
7 Belonoschkin, B., *Zeugung beim Menschen*, Sjöberg, Stockholm, 1949, page 117.
8 Huggins et al., *Amer. J. Physiol.*, **136**, 467 (1942).
9 Zagami, V., *Arch. Sci. biol. (Bologna)*, **25**, 208 (1939).
10 Keitel and Jones, *J. Lab. clin. Med.*, **47**, 917 (1956).
11 Shedlovsky et al., *Proceedings of the 2nd Conference on Biology of the Spermatozoa*, National Committee on Maternal Health, New York, 1940.
12 Weisman, A. I., *Spermatozoa and Sterility*, Hoeber, New York, 1941.
13 Huggins and Johnson, *Amer. J. Physiol.*, **103**, 574 (1933).
14 Sheth and Rao, *Experientia (Basel)*, **18**, 324 (1962).
15 Munch-Petersen, S., *Scand. J. clin. Lab. Invest.*, **2**, 335 (1950).
16 Mawson and Fischer, *Nature*, **177**, 190 (1956).
17 Mackenzie et al., *Nature*, **193**, 72 (1962).
18 Mawson and Fischer, *Biochem. J.*, **55**, 696 (1953).
19 Goldblatt, M. W., *Biochem. J.*, **29**, 1346 (1935).
20 White and Griffiths, *Aust. J. exp. Biol. med. Sci.*, **36**, 97 (1958).
21 Krampitz and Doepfmer, *Nature*, **194**, 684 (1962).
22 Keller and Pataki, *Helv. chim. Acta*, **46**, 1688 (1963).
23 Kahane and Lévy, *Bull. Soc. Chim. biol. (Paris)*, **19**, 959 (1937).
24 Dawson et al., *Biochem. J.*, **65**, 627 (1957).
25 Weaver and Herbst, *J. biol. Chem.*, **231**, 637 (1958).
26 Haag and MacLeod, *J. appl. Physiol.*, **14**, 27 (1959).
27 Infantellina, F., *Boll. Soc. ital. Biol. sper.*, **20**, 322 (1945).
28 Searcy et al., *Fertil. and Steril.*, **15**, 1 (1964).
29 Grant and Everall, in Peeters, H. (Ed.), *Protides of the Biological Fluids*, Proceedings of the 10th Colloquium, Brussels 1962, Elsevier, Amsterdam, 1963, page 237.
30 Klopstock et al., *Fertil. and Steril.*, **14**, 530 (1963); Licht and Keutel, *Z. Urol.*, **56**, 401 (1963).
31 Barnes et al., *J. Lab. clin. Med.*, **61**, 578 (1963).
32 Anderson and Maclagan, *Biochem. J.*, **59**, 638 (1955).
33 Eliasson, R., *Nature*, **203**, 980 (1964).
34 Warren, L., *J. clin. Invest.*, **38**, 755 (1959).
35 Leuchtenberger et al., *Lab. Invest.*, **5**, 422 (1956).
36 Weir and Leuchtenberger, *Fertil. and Steril.*, **8**, 373 (1957).
37 Rhodes and Williams-Ashman, *Med. exp. (Basel)*, **3**, 123 (1960).
38 Searcy et al., *Lancet*, **1**, 1413 (1962).
39 Lehmann and Griffiths, *Lancet*, **2**, 498 (1963).
40 Gutman and Gutman, *Endocrinology*, **28**, 115 (1941).
41 Sheth and Rao, *Experientia (Basel)*, **18**, 370 (1962).
42 Conchie and Mann, *Nature*, **179**, 1190 (1957).
43 Kirk et al., *J. clin. Endocr.*, **12**, 338 (1952).
44 Kirk, E., *J. Geront.*, **3**, 98 (1948).
45 Hartree, E. F., *Biochem. J.*, **66**, 131 (1957).
46 King and Mann, *Proc. roy. Soc. B*, **151**, 226 (1959).
47 Scott, W. W., *J. Urol. (Baltimore)*, **53**, 712 (1945).
48 Bergström, S., *Recent Progr. Hormone Res.*, **22**, 153 (1966).
49 Silló-Seidl, G., *Int. Z. Vitaminforsch.*, **32**, 381 (1962).
50 Watson, A. A., *Lancet*, **2**, 644 (1962).
51 Koets and Michelson, *Fertil. and Steril.*, **7**, 15 (1956).
52 Berg et al., *Amer. J. Physiol.*, **133**, 82 (1941).

Spermatozoa

(For other data see pages 682–685)

	Mean	95% range (extreme range in brackets)	s	Reference	Remarks
Number (millions/ml)					
(a)	106.6	0–256	74.5	1	(a) 1000 measurements. The spermatozoal concentration may vary widely in the same individual and is depressed particularly by emotional excitement and physical effort. In some cases long continence also lowers the concentration (but increases the proportion of abnormal forms), as does too high a testicular temperature (cause of testicular degeneration in cryptorchism). Seasonal variations have also been observed (diminished spermatozoal concentration during the warm months) but are not statistically significant. There is no absolute correlation between spermatozoal concentration and fertility or infertility, but in general the spermatozoal content of the ejaculate is lower in infertile men. To this may be added an absolute reduction in the number of spermatozoa due to a smaller volume of the ejaculate, or a dilution of the spermatozoa when the volume of the ejaculate is excessive. The minimum spermatozoal concentration for a fertile semen is regarded as 20–25 million/ml[3].
(b)	–	(28–225)	–	2	
Spermatocrit (ml spermatozoa/l semen)	~10	–	–	4	
Electrophoretic mobility (10^{-5} cm^2 s^{-1} V^{-1})	-	(6.1–8.7)	–	5	At pH 7.8 and 20 °C. The spermatozoa migrate to the anode.
Motility					
In vitro (s mm^{-1})	–	(40–50)	–	6	Normokinetic spermatozoa maintain their motility even 12 hours after ejaculation[6]. In the female genital tract motility is probably maintained for 48 hours. Spermatozoa can be classified according to their motility as follows[11]: 1. Nonmotile (dead), 15%; 2. only slightly motile, 15%; 3. moderately and 4. very motile, together at least 75%. A fertile semen should contain at least 40–60% of normally motile spermatozoa[3].
In vitro (mm min^{-1})	–	(0.3–0.6)	–	7	
In vivo (mm min^{-1})	–	(1.3–2.6)	–	7	
Spermatozoal forms (%)					
Oval	89.8	(66–99)	–	8	A fertile semen should contain at least 60% of morphologically normal spermatozoa and not more than 10% of spermiocytogenic cells[3].
Tapering	3.6	(0–24)	–	8	
Round	1.6	(0–9)	–	8	
Duplicate	1.8	(0–11)	–	8	
Giant and pinhead	0.6	(0–8)	–	8	
Amorphous	2.1	(0–12)	–	8	
Spermatozoal dimensions					
Weight (pg)	37	–	–	9	
Head					
Length (µm)	4.4	(3.3–6.2)	–	9	
Width (µm)	3.2	–	–	9	
Thickness (µm)	2.0	–	–	9	
Volume (µm^3)	6.4	–	–	9	
Middle piece					
Length (µm)	4.0	–	–	9	
Diameter (µm)	1.0	–	–	9	
Volume (µm^3)	3.1	–	–	9	
Tail					
Length (µm)	–	(40–60)	–	9	
Diameter (µm)	–	(0.4–0.7)	–	9	
Volume (µm^3)	–	(4.5–6.8)	–	9	
End piece					
Length (µm)	–	(6–10)	–	9	
Diameter (µm)	0.2	–	–	9	
Volume (µm^3)	0.16	–	–	9	

Diagram of the human spermatozoon[10]

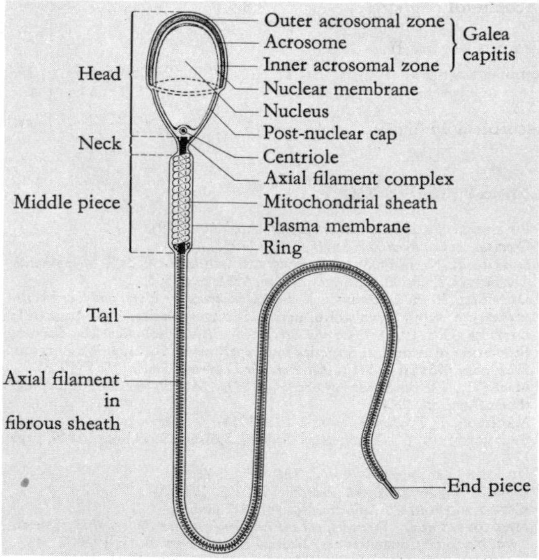

References

1 MacLeod, J., *Fertil. and Steril.*, **2**, 115 (1951).
2 Kaufman, S. A., *Hum. Fertil.*, **11**, 3 (1946).
3 MacLeod and Gold, *Int. J. Fertil.*, **3**, 382 (1958); Joël, C. A., *Fertil. and Steril.*, **11**, 384 (1960).
4 Lundquist, F., in Long, C. (Ed.), *Biochemists' Handbook*, Spon, London, 1961, page 904.
5 Joël et al., *Experientia (Basel)*, **7**, 274 (1951).
6 Silló-Seidl, G., *Fortschr. Geburtsh. Gynäk.*, **15**, 1 (1963).
7 Casares Ponce and Botella Llusiá, *Arch. Med. exp. (Madr.)*, **16**, 459 (1953).
8 Hotchkiss, R. S., *Fertility in Men*, Lippincott, Philadelphia, 1944, page 117.
9 van Duijn, C., *J. roy. micr. Soc.*, **77**, 12 (1957).
10 Modified from Mann, T., *The Biochemistry of Semen and of the Male Reproductive Tract*, Methuen, London, 1964, page 20.
11 Weisman, A. I., *Spermatozoa and Sterility*, Hoeber, New York, 1941.

Yield

In clinical practice it is usual to estimate the volume of milk produced during a given feed by weighing the baby before and after it is put to the breast ('test-weighing'). Provided the weighing is careful and there are no losses of urine, faeces or vomit, this gives a reasonable assessment, and if the breasts are empty after the feed the difference in weight corresponds to milk production. Milk left in the breasts may be expressed and measured.

Yield has also been measured by milking the breasts but there is reason to doubt whether either hand or mechanical methods will remove all the milk without disturbing the course of lactation. The sucking of the baby has, for the mother, emotional overtones beyond the mere stimulation of the nipple and areola; and the mechanical replacement of this local stimulus, however ingenious, cannot possibly be an entirely effective substitute. This has been confirmed experimentally[1]. Published estimates of yield must therefore be examined carefully in the light of their method of measurement.

In general the yield corresponds to the needs of the infant, amounting to about 850 ml per day for a body weight of 5–6 kg.

Composition (see pages 688 and 689)

It is easy to obtain some milk for chemical analysis, and many published data relate to 'spot' samples taken before, during or after a feed, but it is now recognized that such data have little or no relevance to the overall composition of a day's milk supply. The composition of the milk changes both during a feed[2] and in the course of the day[3]. For example, the fat content of milk rises steadily from beginning to end of a feed[2], and a change from less than 10 g/l to 60 g/l or more is common. Other major constituents show less dramatic changes, but the lactose content and soluble protein tend to fall as the fat content rises; casein tends to rise.

The daily variation in composition mainly concerns the fat content[3, 4]. In one study[3] this was usually lowest at 6 a.m., highest at 10 a.m. and somewhat variable during the rest of the day. The extreme differences may commonly be of the order of 25 g/l at 6 a.m. and 40 g/l at 10 a.m. for milk averaging 35 g/l for the whole day.

The differences in composition at different stages of lactation are well known but changes may be rapid in the first two weeks and times must be carefully standardized if valid comparisons are to be made between subjects[4, 5].

The collection of a 24-hour milk sample means removing the child from the breast during that time and emptying the breasts, preferably by pump. The administrative difficulties involved have led some workers to leave the child on one breast while sampling the contents of the other. But even this may mislead; the composition of milk from the two breasts is not necessarily the same[6].

There is no escape from the necessity of obtaining complete 24-hour samples from both breasts if misleading measurements are to be avoided. But since this is seldom done, comparisons between milk analyses reported in the literature must be made with the utmost caution.

The composition of breast milk is described in detail by Macy[7], Macy and Kelly[8] and Lintzel[9]. Data have also been published by the Committee on Nutrition of the American Academy of Pediatrics[10].

References

1 Hytten, F.E., *Brit. med. J.*, **1**, 175 (1954).
2 Hytten, F.E., *Brit. med. J.*, **1**, 176 (1954).
3 Hytten, F.E., *Brit. med. J.*, **1**, 179 (1954).
4 Roland and Freiesleben, *Med. u. Ernähr.*, **4**, 11 (1963).
5 Hytten, F.E., *Brit. med. J.*, **1**, 249 (1954).
6 Hytten, F.E., *Proc. Nutr. Soc.*, **15**, vi (1956).
7 Macy et al., *The Composition of Milks*, National Research Council, Publication 254, Washington, 1953.
8 Macy and Kelly, in Kon and Cowie (Eds.), *Milk: the Mammary Gland and Its Secretion*, vol. 2, Academic Press, New York, 1961, page 265.
9 Lintzel, W., in Flaschenträger and Lehnartz (Eds.), *Physiologische Chemie*, vol. 2, part 2b, Springer, Berlin, 1957, page 326.
10 Committee on Nutrition, *Pediatrics*, **26**, 1039 (1960).

Fatty acids (as percentage by weight of total fatty acids)*

	Mature milk			Colostrum 3rd day			Colostrum 2nd day			Colostrum 1st day			Cow's milk		
	Mean	s	Reference	Mean	s	Reference	Mean	s	Reference	Mean	s	Reference	Mean	s	Reference
Butyric acid	0.4	–	1	0.3	–	1	0.2	–	1	0.2	–	1	2.7	0.5	2
Caproic acid	0.1	0.1	2	0.1	–	1	0.1	–	1	0.1	–	1	2.0	0.2	2
Caprylic acid	0.1	0.2	2	0.1	–	1	0.8	–	1	0.8	–	1	1.2	0.2	2
Capric acid	0.8	0.4	2	0.9	–	1	3.5	–	1	3.5	–	1	3.2	0.7	2
Lauric acid	4.7	2.2	2	2.5	1.1	4	1.8	1.2	4	1.1	0.5	4	3.6	1.1	2
Myristic acid	7.9	1.5	2	5.7	1.7	4	3.6	1.3	4	3.7	1.3	4	11.8	1.5	2
Palmitic acid	26.7	2.7	2	26.1	3.0	4	26.1	2.7	4	26.9	2.8	4	36.6	4.7	2
Stearic acid	8.3	1.7	2	5.8	0.9	4	6.5	1.4	4	7.0	1.0	4	8.1	3.2	2
Arachidic acid	1.3	–	3	–	–	–	–	–	–	–	–	–	1.7	–	5
Decenoic acid	0.1	–	1	0.1	–	1	0.2	–	1	0.2	–	1	0.3	–	5
Dodecenoic acid	0.1	–	1	0.1	–	1	0.1	–	1	0.1	–	1	0.2	–	5
Myristoleic acid	0.24	–	3	0.2	–	1	0.1	–	1	0.1	–	1	1.5	–	5
Palmitoleic acid	3.4	1.0	2	5.4	0.8	4	4.4	1.5	4	4.3	1.6	4	3.2	0.7	2
Oleic acid	37.4	3.7	2	43.1	4.5	4	44.2	3.4	4	44.0	4.4	4	17.7	4.6	2
Eicosenoic acid	0.89	–	3	–	–	–	–	–	–	–	–	–	1.0	–	5
Linoleic acid	10.6	2.9	2	9.0	1.8	4	11.4	1.7	4	11.9	3.0	4	2.1	0.7	2
Linolenic acid	0.85	–	3	0.3	–	1	0.3	–	1	0.3	–	1	1.7	0.7	2
Arachidonic acid	0.57	–	3	1.6	–	1	1.8	–	1	1.8	–	1	0.4	–	5

References

1 Baldwin and Longenecker, *J. biol. Chem.*, **154**, 255 (1944).
2 Committee on Nutrition, *Pediatrics*, **26**, 1039 (1960).
3 Insull and Ahrens, *Biochem. J.*, **72**, 27 (1959).
4 Read and Sarrif, *Amer. J. clin. Nutr.*, **17**, 177 (1965).
5 Jack, E.L., *J. Agric. Food Chem.*, **8**, 377 (1960).
6 Pieraccini and Morgantini, *Riv. Clin. pediat.*, **68**, 241 (1961).
7 Pieraccini and Morgantini, *Riv. Clin. pediat.*, **68**, 386 (1961).
8 Read et al., *Amer. J. clin. Nutr.*, **17**, 180 and 184 (1965).

* For other fatty acids present in breast milk in traces see Insull and Ahrens[3] and Pieraccini and Morgantini[6]; similar data for cow's milk are given by Jack[5] and Pieraccini and Morgantini[7]. After a meal rich in carbohydrates the lauric and myristic acid contents of breast milk are increased. Most of the palmitic acid of breast milk probably originates from the blood rather than from synthesis in the mammary gland[8].

	Mature milk (15 days to 15 months post partum)				Transitional milk (6–10 days post partum)				Colostrum (first 5 days post partum)				Cow's milk			
	Mean	Experimental range	*s*	Reference	Mean	Experimental range	*s*	Reference	Mean	Experimental range	*s*	Reference	Mean	Experimental range	*s*	Reference
Calories																
(kcal/l)	747	446–1192	93	1	735	678–830	36	1	671	588–730	–	1	701	587–876	–	2
(MJ/l)	3.127	1.867–4.989	0.389	Ed	3.076	2.838–3.474	0.151	Ed	2.808	2.461–3.055	–	Ed	2.934	2.457–3.666	–	Ed
Specific gravity	1.031	1.026–1.037	0.002	1	1.035	1.034–1.036	–	1	1.034	–	–	38	1.031	1.028–1.033	–	3
pH	7.01	6.4–7.6	–	4	–	–	–	–	–	–	–	–	6.6	–	–	5
Solids, total (g/l)	129	103–175	11	1	133	105–156	8	1	128	100–167	13	1	124	119–142	–	3
Ash, total (g/l)	2.02	1.6–2.66	0.18	1	2.67	2.31–3.38	0.32	1	3.08	2.47–3.50	–	1	7.15	6.81–7.71	–	6
Minerals																
(a) Electropositive elements (mEq/l)	41	–	–	1	55	–	–	1	68	–	–	1	149	–	–	Ed
Sodium (g/l)	0.172	0.064–0.436	0.045	1	0.294	0.192–0.539	0.076	1	0.501	0.265–1.37	0.28	1	0.768	0.392–1.39	–	7
	0.189	0.080–0.350	0.066	39	0.536	0.170–1.21	0.271	39	0.956	0.330–2.24	0.377	39	–	–	–	–
Potassium (g/l)	0.512	0.373–0.635	0.085	1	0.636	0.528–0.769	0.068	1	0.745	0.658–0.870	–	1	1.43	0.38–2.87	–	8
	0.553	0.425–0.735	0.070	39	0.692	0.450–0.910	0.099	39	0.581	0.220–0.790	0.120	39	–	–	–	–
Calcium (g/l)	0.344	0.173–0.609	0.067	1	0.464	0.23–0.628	0.095	1	0.481	0.242–0.656	0.121	1	1.37	0.56–3.81	–	8
	0.271	0.207–0.372	0.030	39	0.320	0.166–0.420	0.045	39	0.261	0.180–0.364	0.026	39	–	–	–	–
Magnesium (g/l)	0.035	0.018–0.057	0.007	1	0.035	0.026–0.054	0.006	1	0.042	0.031–0.082	0.013	1	0.13	0.07–0.22	–	8
(b) Electronegative elements (mEq/l)	28	–	–	1	37	–	–	1	40	–	–	1	108	–	–	Ed
Phosphorus (g/l)	0.141	0.068–0.268	0.025	1	0.198	0.097–0.317	0.047	1	0.157	0.085–0.251	0.047	1	0.91	0.56–1.12	–	8
Sulphur (g/l)	0.14	0.05–0.30	0.03	1	0.20	0.15–0.23	0.02	1	0.23	0.20–0.26	–	1	0.30	0.24–0.36	–	8
Chlorine (g/l)	0.375	0.088–0.734	0.09	1	0.457	0.305–0.721	0.109	1	0.586	0.435–1.01	–	1	1.08	0.93–1.41	–	8
(c) Excess electropositive elements (mEq/l)	13	–	–	1	18	–	–	1	28	–	–	1	41	–	–	Ed
(d) Trace elements																
Cobalt (µg/l)	trace	–	–	–	–	–	–	–	–	–	–	–	0.6	–	–	9
Iron (mg/l)	0.50	0.20–0.80	–	10	0.59	0.29–1.45	–	40	1.0	–	–	11	0.45	0.25–0.75	–	10
Copper (mg/l)	0.51	–	0.046	11	1.04	–	0.073	11	1.34	–	0.112	11	0.102	–	–	11
Manganese (mg/l)	trace	–	–	12	trace	–	–	13	trace	–	–	13	0.02	0.005–0.067	–	14
Zinc (mg/l)	1.18	0.17–3.02	–	8	3.82	0.39–5.88	–	8	5.59	0.72–9.81	–	8	3.9	1.7–6.6	–	8
Fluorine (mg/l)	0.107	0.0–0.24	–	15	–	–	–	–	0.131	0.0–0.35	–	15	–	0.10–0.28	–	16
Iodine (mg/l)	0.061	0.044–0.093	–	17	–	–	–	–	–	0.045–0.450	–	18	0.116	0.036–1.05	–	17
Selenium (mg/l)	0.021	–	–	41	–	–	–	–	–	–	–	–	0.04	0.005–0.067	–	41
Protein																
Total (g/l)	10.6	7.3–20	4.6	1	15.9	12.7–18.9	9.8	1	22.9	14.6–68.0	12.6	1	32.46	28.16–36.76	–	19
	–	–	–	–	–	–	–	–	55	14–215	–	20	–	–	–	–
Casein (g/l)	3.7	1.4–6.8	0.8	1	5.1	4.2–5.9	–	1	21	7.3–52	–	20	24.9	21.9–28.0	–	19
Whey protein* (g/l)	7	4–10	–	21	–	–	–	–	–	–	–	–	7	6–10	–	21
'Lactalbumin' (g/l)	3.6	1.4–6.0	1.0	1	7.8	6.9–8.6	–	1	–	–	–	–	2.4	1.4–3.3	–	19
'Lactoglobulin' (g/l)	–	–	–	–	5.0	2.1–13.6	–	20	35	4.2–133	–	20	1.7	0.7–3.7	–	19
Blood-serum albumin (g/l)	0.32	0.20–0.47	–	22	0.37	0.26–0.65	–	22	2.5	–	–	42	0.4	–	–	43
Blood-serum immunoglobulin (g/l)	0.09	0.02–0.27	–	22	0.36	0.01–0.96	–	22	1.0	–	–	42	0.8	–	–	43
Amino acids																
Total (g/l)	12.8	9.0–16.0	–	23	9.4	6.0–10.0	–	23	12.0	7.0–40.0	–	23	33.0	27.0–41.0	–	23
Alanine (g/l)	–	0.36–0.42	–	24	–	–	–	–	–	–	–	–	0.75	–	–	44
Arginine (g/l)	0.43	0.28–0.64	0.088	1	0.63	0.48–0.73	0.069	1	0.74	0.62–0.96	–	1	1.4	1.2–1.6	–	25
Aspartic acid (g/l)	–	0.89–0.98	–	24	–	–	–	–	–	–	–	–	1.7	–	–	44
Cystine (g/l)	–	0.23–0.25	–	24	–	–	–	–	–	–	–	–	–	–	–	–
Glutamic acid (g/l)	–	1.89–2.00	–	24	–	–	–	–	–	–	–	–	6.8	–	–	44
Glycine (g/l)	–	0.23–0.24	–	24	–	–	–	–	–	–	–	–	0.11	–	–	44
Histidine (g/l)	0.24	0.12–0.30	0.041	1	0.38	0.29–0.45	0.046	1	0.41	0.35–0.46	–	1	1.2	1.1–1.3	–	25
Isoleucine (g/l)	0.61	0.41–0.92	0.121	1	0.97	0.73–1.21	0.110	1	1.01	0.88–1.15	–	1	2.5	2.1–2.9	–	25
Leucine (g/l)	0.97	0.65–1.47	0.174	1	1.51	1.13–1.97	0.219	1	1.66	1.33–2.14	–	1	3.6	3.2–3.9	–	25
Lysine (g/l)	0.70	0.36–0.93	0.127	1	1.13	0.88–1.48	0.157	1	1.18	0.95–1.41	–	1	2.6	2.3–3.1	–	25
Methionine (g/l)	0.12	0.07–0.16	0.023	1	0.24	0.16–0.34	0.040	1	0.25	0.19–0.36	–	1	0.8	0.6–0.9	–	25
Phenylalanine (g/l)	0.40	0.24–0.58	0.069	1	0.62	0.48–0.71	0.062	1	0.70	0.60–0.84	–	1	1.8	1.5–2.2	–	25
Proline (g/l)	–	0.84–0.94	–	24	–	–	–	–	–	–	–	–	2.5	–	–	44
Serine (g/l)	–	0.47–0.51	–	24	–	–	–	–	–	–	–	–	1.6	–	–	44
Threonine (g/l)	0.52	0.30–0.66	0.085	1	0.78	0.61–0.91	0.079	1	0.85	0.75–1.04	–	1	1.7	1.3–2.2	–	25
Tryptophan (g/l)	0.19	0.14–0.26	0.030	1	0.28	0.23–0.32	0.024	1	0.32	0.25–0.42	–	1	0.6	0.4–0.8	–	25
Tyrosine (g/l)	–	0.46–0.52	–	24	–	–	–	–	–	–	–	–	–	–	–	–
Valine (g/l)	0.73	0.45–1.14	0.155	1	1.05	0.77–1.36	0.122	1	1.17	0.98–1.49	–	1	2.6	2.4–2.8	–	25
Nonprotein nitrogen																
Total (mg/l)	324	173–604	57	1	479	425–533	–	1	910	510–1270	–	20	252	181–323	–	19
Urea-N (mg/l)	180	127–235	24	1	111	–	–	1	–	–	–	–	132.7	61.3–204	–	19
Uric acid-N (mg/l)	22	13–41	5	1	–	–	–	–	–	–	–	–	24.1	11.3–36.9	–	19
Creatinine-N (mg/l)	11	8–19	2	1	–	–	–	–	–	–	–	–	7.05	1.9–12.2	–	19
Creatine-N (mg/l)	11	2–41	7	1	–	–	–	–	–	–	–	–	40.35	24.5–56.2	–	19
Amino acid-N** (mg/l)	50	28–113	14	1	44	–	–	1	–	40–120	–	45,46	6.8	1.7–11.9	–	19
Choline-N*** (mg/l)	10.3	6.2–16.8	2.7	1	–	–	–	–	–	–	–	–	12	5–19	–	8
Enzymes†																
Lysozyme (mg/l)	390	30–3000	–	47	–	–	–	–	460	90–1020	–	47	0.13	0.00–2.6	–	47

	Mature milk (15 days to 15 months post partum)				Transitional milk (6–10 days post partum)				Colostrum (first 5 days post partum)				Cow's milk			
	Mean	Experimental range	s	Reference	Mean	Experimental range	s	Reference	Mean	Experimental range	s	Reference	Mean	Experimental range	s	Reference
Carbohydrates																
Lactose																
Directly estimated (g/l)	71	49–95	4	1	64	61–67	–	1	57	11–79	–	26	47	45–50	–	6
As difference (g/l)	68	50–92	6	1	64	60–68	–	1	–	–	–	–	–	–	–	–
Fucose†† (g/l)	1.3	–	–	27	–	–	–	–	–	–	–	–	–	–	–	–
Glucosamine (g/l)	–	0.7–0.8	–	24	–	–	–	–	–	1.4–4.3	–	24	0	–	–	24
Galactosamine (g/l)	–	0.0–0.4	–	24	–	–	–	–	–	0.04–0.7	–	24	0	–	–	24
Inositol (g/l)	0.45	0.39–0.56	–	1	–	–	–	–	–	–	–	–	0.08	0.06–0.12	–	8
Citric acid (g/l)	–	0.35–1.25	–	28	–	–	–	–	–	–	–	–	2.54	2.15–2.90	–	31
Fats, total (g/l)	45.4	13.4–82.9	10.0	1	35.2	27.3–51.8	7.3	1	29.5	24.7–31.8	–	1	38.0	34.0–61.0	–	3
Cholesterol (mg/l)	139	88–202	25	46	241	126–320	62	46	280	180–345	70	46	110	70–170	–	29
Free cholesterol (as per cent of total)	76.1	–	–	46	76.5	–	–	46	79.5	–	–	46	–	90–95	–	48
Lipid phosphorus (mg/l)	10.5	7–14	0.6	46	15.5	11–20	0.9	46	12	6–17	1	46	–	53–70	–	30
Vitamins																
Vitamin A (mg/l)	0.61	0.15–2.26	0.23	1	0.88	0.58–1.83	0.31	1	1.61	0.75–3.05	0.63	1	0.27	0.17–0.38	–	3
Carotenes (mg/l)	0.25	0.02–0.77	0.11	1	0.38	0.23–0.63	0.10	1	1.37	0.41–3.85	0.84	1	0.37	0.12–0.79	–	3
Vitamin D (IU/l)	–	4–100	–	33	–	–	–	–	–	–	–	–	–	5–40	–	33
Tocopherol (mg/l)	2.4	1.0–4.8	–	34	8.9	4.0–18.5	–	35	14.8	2.8–30.0	–	36	0.6	0.2–1.0	–	35
Thiamine (mg/l)	0.142	0.081–0.227	0.024	1	0.059	0.023–0.105	0.022	1	0.019	0.009–0.034	0.006	1	0.43	0.28–0.90	–	3
Riboflavin (mg/l)	0.373	0.198–0.790	0.087	1	0.369	0.275–0.490	0.053	1	0.302	0.120–0.453	0.087	1	1.56	1.16–2.02	–	3
Vitamin B_6 (mg/l)	0.18	0.10–0.22	–	1	–	–	–	–	–	–	–	–	0.51	0.40–0.63	–	8
Nicotinic acid (mg/l)	1.83	0.66–3.30	0.48	1	1.75	0.60–3.60	0.77	1	0.75	0.50–1.45	0.22	1	0.74	0.50–0.86	–	37
Vitamin B_{12}††† (μg/l)	–	trace	–	32	0.36	0.03–0.70	–	32	0.45	0.10–1.5	–	32	6.6	3.2–12.4	–	32
Folic acid§ (μg/l)																
(a)	1.4	0.9–1.8	–	32	0.2	0.15–0.25	–	32	0.5	0.10–1.5	–	32	1.3	0.2–4.0	–	32
(b)	24.0	7.4–61.0	–	49	–	–	–	–	–	–	–	–	37.7	16.8–63.2	–	49
(c)	7.3	2.4–17.6	–	49	–	–	–	–	–	–	–	–	12.6	2.8–43.6	–	49
Biotin (μg/l)	2	1–3	–	50	–	–	–	–	–	–	–	–	22	14–29	–	37
Pantothenic acid (mg/l)	2.46	0.86–5.84	0.63	1	2.88	1.35–4.12	0.57	1	1.83	0.29–3.02	0.86	1	3.4	2.2–5.5	–	37
Ascorbic acid§§ (mg/l)	52	0–112	19	1	71	45–90	12	1	72	47–104	18	1	11	3–23	–	3

* Little is known of the composition of the proteins of breast-milk serum. They include milk-specific proteins, like α-lactalbumin and lactotransferrin, as well as blood-serum proteins such as albumin and immunoglobulins (particularly IgA-globulin)[22, 42, 51].

** Data for individual free amino acids in breast and cow's milk are given by Ghadimi and Pecora[45], Tarjan et al.[46] and Armstrong and Yates[52].

*** Corresponding to 54–145 mg choline per litre breast milk and 40–160 mg choline per litre cow's milk.

† Various enzymes have been determined in breast milk: lactate dehydrogenase[53, 54], malate dehydrogenase[53, 54], glucose-6-phosphate dehydrogenase[55], xanthine oxidase[54], catalase[56], peroxidase[56], aspartate aminotransferase[57], alanine aminotransferase[57], arylesterase[56], lipase[57, 58], acetylesterase[56], cholinesterase[56], alkaline phosphatase[53, 57], acid phosphatase[57], amylase[57], peptide hydrolases[59], inorganic pyrophosphatase[56], ATPase[56], fructosediphosphate aldolase[57], glucosephosphate isomerase[57].

†† In the form of oligosaccharides (6 g per litre breast milk).

††† Determined with *Lactobacillus leichmannii.*

§ Determined with (a) *Streptococcus faecalis*, (b) *Lactobacillus casei*, (c) *Pediococcus cerevisiae.*

§§ Subject to wide fluctuations in breast milk as a result of variations in the ascorbic acid intake.

References

Ed Calculated by the editors.

1 Macy, I. G., *Amer. J. Dis. Child.*, **78**, 589 (1949).
2 Kahlenberg, O. J., *J. Agric. Res.*, **43**, 749 (1931).
3 Dahlberg et al., *Sanitary Milk Control in Relation to Sanitary, Nutritive, and Other Qualities of Milk*, National Research Council, Publication 250, Washington, 1952.
4 Modde et al., *Arch. Gynäk.*, **196**, 343 (1961).
5 Ling et al., in Kon and Cowie (Eds.), *Milk: the Mammary Gland and Its Secretion*, vol. 2, Academic Press, New York, 1961, page 195.
6 Meigs and Marsh, *J. biol. Chem.*, **16**, 147 (1913/14).
7 Jones and Davies, *Biochem. J.*, **29**, 978 (1935).
8 Macy, I. G., quoted by Macy et al., *The Composition of Milks*, National Research Council, Publication 254, Washington, 1953.
9 Archibald, J. G., *J. Dairy Sci.*, **30**, 293 (1947).
10 Feuillen and Plumier, *Acta paediat. (Uppsala)*, **41**, 138 (1952).
11 Kleinbaum, H., *Z. Kinderheilk.*, **86**, 655 (1962).
12 Dingle and Sheldon, *Biochem. J.*, **32**, 1078 (1938).
13 Castellanos and Lizarralde, *Rev. Asoc. argent. Diet.*, **1**, 199 (1943).
14 Kiermeier and Johannsmann, *Z. Lebensmitt.-Untersuch.*, **118**, 304 (1962).
15 Bercovici et al., *Obstet. and Gynec.*, **16**, 319 (1960).
16 Evans and Phillips, *J. Dairy Sci.*, **22**, 621 (1939).
17 Souci et al. (Eds.), *Die Zusammensetzung der Lebensmittel*, Wissenschaftliche Verlagsgesellschaft, Stuttgart, 1962.
18 Elmer and Rychlik, *C. R. Soc. Biol. (Paris)*, **117**, 530 (1934).
19 Shahani and Sommer, *J. Dairy Sci.*, **34**, 1010 (1951).
20 Waller et al., *Biochem. J.*, **35**, 272 (1941).
21 Plimmer and Lowndes, *Biochem. J.*, **31**, 1751 (1937).
22 Schwick et al., *Behringwerk-Mitteilungen*, No. 37, 11 (1959).
23 Albritton, E. C. (Ed.), *Standard Values in Nutrition and Metabolism*, Saunders, Philadelphia, 1954, page 111.
24 Bigwood, E. J., *Wld Rev. Nutr. Diet.*, **4**, 93 (1963).
25 Sarkar et al., *J. Dairy Sci.*, **32**, 671 (1949).
26 Widdows et al., *Biochem. J.*, **29**, 1145 (1935).
27 Malpress and Hytten, *Biochem. J.*, **68**, 708 (1958).
28 Jerlov, E., *Svenska Läk.-Tidn.*, **1**, 17 (1929), quoted by Macy et al., *The Composition of Milks*, National Research Council, Publication 254, Washington, 1953.
29 Nataf et al., *J. Nutr.*, **36**, 495 (1948).
30 Hess and Helman, *J. biol. Chem.*, **64**, 781 (1925).
31 Fabris, A., *Il Mondo del latte*, **1951**, 598.
32 Collins et al., *J. Nutr.*, **43**, 313 (1951).
33 Lawrence et al., *Amer. J. Dis. Child.*, **70**, 193 (1945).
34 Harris et al., *J. Nutr.*, **46**, 459 (1952).
35 Abderhalden, R., *Biochem. Z.*, **318**, 47 (1948).
36 Neuweiler, W., *Int. Z. Vitaminforsch.*, **20**, 108 (1948).
37 Lawrence et al., *J. Nutr.*, **32**, 73 (1946).
38 Castellanos and Lizarralde, *Rev. Asoc. argent. Diet.*, **1**, 199 (1943), quoted by Macy et al., *The Composition of Milks*, National Research Council, Publication 254, Washington, 1953.
39 Terheggen, H.-G., *Z. Kinderheilk.*, **92**, 193 (1965).
40 Cavell and Widdowson, *Arch. Dis. Childh.*, **39**, 496 (1964).
41 Hadjimarkos, D. M., *Méd. et Hyg. (Genève)*, **24**, 721 (1966).
42 Gugler and von Muralt, *Schweiz. med. Wschr.*, **89**, 925 (1959).
43 Brunner et al., *J. Dairy Sci.*, **43**, 901 (1960).
44 Williamson, M. B., *J. biol. Chem.*, **156**, 47 (1944).
45 Ghadimi and Pecora, *Amer. J. clin. Nutr.*, **13**, 75 (1963).
46 Tarjan et al., *Nutr. et Dieta (Basel)*, **7**, 136 (1965).
47 Chandan et al., *Nature*, **204**, 76 (1964).
48 de Man, J. M., *Z. Ernährungsw.*, **5**, 1 (1964).
49 Matoth et al., *Amer. J. clin. Nutr.*, **16**, 356 (1965).
50 Neuweiler and Ritter, *Int. Z. Vitaminforsch.*, **21**, 239 (1949).
51 Tomasi and Zigelbaum, *J. clin. Invest.*, **42**, 1552 (1963); Bell and McKenzie, *Nature*, **204**, 1275 (1964); Got, R., *Clin. chim. Acta*, **11**, 432 (1965).
52 Armstrong and Yates, *Proc. Soc. exp. Biol. (N. Y.)*, **113**, 680 (1963).
53 Deodhar et al., *Ann. Biochem.*, **23**, 479 (1964).
54 Deodhar et al., *Acta paediat. (Uppsala)*, **53**, 101 (1964).
55 Sklavunu-Zurukzoglu et al., *Helv. paediat. Acta*, **20**, 193 (1965).
56 Heyndrickx, G. V., *Pediatrics*, **31**, 1019 (1963).
57 Heyndrickx, G. V., *Ann. paediat. (Basel)*, **198**, 356 (1962).
58 Behrendt, H., *Biochem. Z.*, **128**, 450 (1922); Karmarkar et al., *Acta paediat. (Uppsala)*, **52**, 554 (1963); Tarassuk et al., *Nature*, **201**, 298 (1964).
59 Gründig and Rumler, *Klin. Wschr.*, **43**, 1010 (1965).

Weight gain in pregnancy (per 4-week period)[1]

4-week period of pregnancy	USA 1940[2] lb	USA 1940[2] *kg*	England 1957[3] lb	England 1957[3] *kg*	India 1959[4] lb	India 1959[4] *kg*	Desirable gain[5] lb	Desirable gain[5] *kg*
12–16	3.5	*1.6*	3.1	*1.4*	2.0	*0.9*	2.4	*1.1*
17–20	5.1	*2.3*	4.2	*1.9*	2.4	*1.1*	2.9	*1.3*
21–24	5.1	*2.3*	4.6	*2.1*	3.3	*1.5*	3.3	*1.5*
25–28	4.6	*2.1*	4.2	*1.9*	2.0	*0.9*	4.2	*1.9*
29–32	4.0	*1.8*	3.3	*1.5*	2.0	*0.9*	4.4	*2.0*
33–36	4.0	*1.8*	3.5	*1.6*	1.8	*0.8*	4.4	*2.0*
37–40	3.3	*1.5*	3.3	*1.5*	0.7	*0.3*	2.6	*1.2*

[1] For other values see Hytten and Leitch, *The Physiology of Human Pregnancy*, Blackwell, Oxford, 1964, page 214.
[2] Stander and Pastore, *Amer. J. Obstet. Gynec.*, **39**, 928 (1940) (2324 subjects).
[3] Thomson and Billewicz, *Brit. med. J.*, **1**, 243 (1957) (2868 subjects).
[4] Venkatachalam et al., *Indian J. med. Res.*, **48**, 511 (1960) (130 subjects).
[5] Hüter et al., *Geburtsh. u. Frauenheilk.*, **25**, 385 (1965). According to these workers, the gain in weight in healthy women (overall mean 10.2 kg) is independent of age, body size and parity.

Weight gain in pregnancy (per week) from a study on primigravidae made in the Aberdeen Maternity Hospital between 1950 and 1955[1] (P = percentile)

Weeks of pregnancy	Number	P_{10} lb	P_{10} *kg*	P_{25} lb	P_{25} *kg*	P_{50} lb	P_{50} *kg*	P_{75} lb	P_{75} *kg*	P_{90} lb	P_{90} *kg*
		80 %									
				50 %							
13–20	2868	0.42	*0.19*	0.64	*0.29*	0.93	*0.42*	1.19	*0.54*	1.45	*0.66*
20–30	2868	0.60	*0.27*	0.90	*0.41*	1.06	*0.48*	1.32	*0.60*	1.59	*0.72*
30–36	2868	0.35	*0.16*	0.62	*0.28*	0.93	*0.42*	1.28	*0.58*	1.59	*0.72*
36–40	2868	0.04	*0.02*	0.42	*0.19*	0.82	*0.37*	1.24	*0.56*	1.43	*0.65*
20-term (39, 40 or 41 weeks)*..................	486	0.31	*0.14*	0.75	*0.34*	0.97	*0.44*	1.24	*0.56*	1.50	*0.68*

* Group aged 20–29 years, healthy, no major clinical abnormality.

[1] Hytten and Leitch, *The Physiology of Human Pregnancy*, Blackwell, Oxford, 1964, page 214; Hytten, F. E., personal communication.

Analysis of weight gain in pregnancy (some values are estimates)[1]

Weeks of pregnancy	Whole body	Foetus	Placenta	Amniotic fluid	Uterus	Breasts	Plasma	Erythrocytes	Extracellular, extravascular water
Total weight gain (g)							Plasma + Erythrocytes		
10	650	5	20	30	135	34	100		0
20	4000	300	170	250	585	180	600		0
30	8500	1500	430	600	810	360	1300		0
40	12500	3300	650	800	900	405	1250		1200
Protein storage (g)							Plasma + Erythrocytes		
10	35	0.3	2	0	23	9	0		–
20	210	27	16	0.5	100	36	30		–
30	535	160	60	2	139	72	102		–
40	910	435	100	3	154	81	137		–
Fat storage (g)									
10	367	Insignificant	Insignificant	–	0.5	1.4	0.4	–	–
20	1930	2	1	–	2.3	5.4	3.9	–	–
30	3613	80	3	–	3.2	10.8	17.4	–	–
40	4464	430	4	–	3.6	12.2	19.6	–	–
Gain in water (ml)									
40	7000	2343	540	792	743	304	920	163	1195
Gain in extracellular water (ml)									
40	5165	1360	260	792	490	148	920	0	1195
Gain in intracellular water (ml)									
40	1835	983	280	0	253	156	0	163	0
Sodium storage (mEq)									
40	850	280	57	100	78	35	140	5	155
Potassium storage (mEq)									
40	316	154	42	3	49	35	4	24	5
Calcium storage (g)									
40	29.6	28.0	0.65	Insignificant	0.22	0.06	0.12	0.38	0.15

[1] Hytten and Leitch, *The Physiology of Human Pregnancy*, Blackwell, Oxford, 1964.

Protein and lipid contents of the plasma before, during and after pregnancy (g/l) [1]

	Number	Albumin		α_2-Globulin		β-Globulin		γ-Globulin		Fibrinogen		Total lipids	
		Mean	s	Mean	s	Mean	s	Mean	s	Mean	s	Mean	s
Nonpregnant women	17	38.3	2.7	5.9	0.98	8.8	1.3	14.1	2.4	3.6	0.85	6.2	0.74
Pregnant women (weeks)													
9–10	15	32.6	2.8	6.8	1.3	9.4	1.0	16.1	2.7	3.9	0.7	5.9	1.0
11–12	28	30.1	3.2	7.0	1.3	10.0	1.8	15.5	2.3	4.5	0.7	5.7	1.2
13–15	22	28.7	3.8	7.6	1.2	9.6	1.8	15.2	2.8	4.3	0.8	6.1	1.2
17–22	16	25.3	2.8	7.8	1.5	10.8	1.7	13.7	2.0	4.8	1.0	7.8	1.7
23–24	22	25.9	3.0	7.4	1.2	11.0	1.5	14.7	2.7	5.1	1.2	8.1	1.4
25–26	22	23.3	2.6	7.1	1.1	10.6	1.4	14.4	2.4	4.5	0.9	8.7	1.3
27–30	18	24.8	2.7	6.5	1.0	11.0	1.6	13.3	3.6	4.6	1.0	8.8	1.3
31–33	15	22.9	2.8	7.3	1.0	10.6	1.5	13.7	1.8	5.0	1.1	9.4	1.8
34	20	23.5	3.0	7.5	1.0	11.7	1.5	14.1	2.4	5.5	1.1	9.5	1.2
35–36	24	23.0	2.2	7.7	1.1	11.9	1.5	14.1	2.3	5.2	1.5	10.0	1.4
37–38	21	23.7	2.8	7.3	1.1	11.0	1.4	14.0	2.0	5.5	1.4	10.0	1.9
39–41	18	24.0	3.3	7.4	1.0	12.0	1.6	13.6	2.8	5.8	1.3	9.9	1.4
Post partum													
6–11 hours	15	21.6	2.5	7.1	1.0	10.1	1.7	14.1	2.0	5.0	1.0	8.6	1.1
12–16 hours	36	20.3	3.2	7.3	1.0	10.4	1.6	13.3	3.0	5.5	1.9	9.2	2.0
17–23 hours	26	21.0	2.9	7.4	1.2	10.5	1.5	13.9	2.2	5.9	1.4	8.9	1.3
24–33 hours	16	22.1	2.5	7.7	1.1	10.8	1.4	12.3	3.5	5.7	1.6	9.1	1.0
43 hours to 6½ days ...	40	22.9	3.3	8.5	1.7	11.6	1.5	15.3	3.4	6.1	1.9	9.4	2.0
7–8 days	52	25.2	2.8	9.1	1.3	12.1	1.6	16.6	2.9	6.0	1.6	9.1	1.7
8½–18 days	10	26.2	1.7	9.0	2.1	11.6	1.2	17.1	3.6	6.0	2.1	8.3	1.1
30–60 days	13	33.3	3.0	6.8	1.2	9.1	1.6	17.8	3.7	3.8	0.8	6.6	1.1

[1] Reboud et al., *Amer.J.Obstet.Gynec.*, **86**, 820 (1963).

Blood values in pregnancy [1]

	Plasma volume (ml)	Erythrocyte volume (ml)	Total blood volume (ml)	Body haematocrit (ml/l)	Venous haematocrit (ml/l)	Haemoglobin (calculated) (g/l blood)
Nonpregnant women ...	2600	1400	4000	350	398	131
Pregnant women (weeks)						
20	3150	1450	4600	315	358	118
30	3750	1550	5200	298	340	112
34	3830	1600	5430	295	335	111
40	3600	1650	5250	315	358	118

[1] Hytten and Leitch, *The Physiology of Human Pregnancy*, Blackwell, Oxford, 1964, page 24.

Size and weight of the embryo and foetus [1]

Embryonic age	Crown to rump length (mm)	Crown to heel length (mm)	External diameter of chorionic sac (mm)	Weight (g)	Foetal age	Crown to rump length (mm)	Crown to heel length (mm)	External diameter of chorionic sac (mm)	Weight (g)
1 week	0.1*	–	0.2	–	12 weeks	56.0	73.0	–	14
2 weeks	0.2*	–	3	–	16 weeks	112.0	157.0	–	105
3 weeks	2.0	–	10	–	20 weeks	160.0	239.0	–	310
4 weeks	5.0	–	20	0.02	24 weeks	203.0	296.0	–	640
5 weeks	8.0	–	25	–	28 weeks	242.0	355.0	–	1080
6 weeks	12.0	–	30	–	32 weeks	277.0	409.0	–	1670
7 weeks	17.0	19.0	40	–	36 weeks	313.0	458.0	–	2400
8 weeks	23.0	30.0	50	1	Full term (38 weeks).	350.0	500.0	–	3300

* Total length of the embryonic disk. [1] Arey, L.B., *Developmental Anatomy*, 7th ed., Saunders, Philadelphia, 1965, page 104.

Intrauterine growth*

Number	P_{10}	P_{25}	P_{50}	P_{75}	P_{90}	Weeks of pregnancy	Number	P_{10}	P_{25}	P_{50}	P_{75}	P_{90}
	80% (50%: P_{25}–P_{75})							80% (50%: P_{25}–P_{75})				
Males: Weight (kg)[1]							Females: Weight (kg)[1]					
13	0.610	0.730	0.830	1.020	1.230	24	11	0.490	0.645	0.760	0.980	1.250
12	0.685	0.790	0.880	1.040	1.260	25	15	0.600	0.740	0.845	1.050	1.295
43	0.760	0.875	0.965	1.110	1.330	26	25	0.700	0.830	0.935	1.125	1.350
38	0.835	0.970	1.080	1.215	1.435	27	34	0.790	0.925	1.035	1.210	1.420
64	0.915	1.075	1.205	1.350	1.570	28	54	0.870	1.020	1.140	1.320	1.530
80	0.995	1.180	1.330	1.495	1.720	29	63	0.945	1.115	1.255	1.455	1.690
61	1.085	1.290	1.465	1.650	1.875	30	48	1.025	1.215	1.380	1.600	1.880
88	1.195	1.415	1.600	1.830	2.050	31	59	1.125	1.330	1.515	1.760	2.100
66	1.320	1.550	1.760	2.045	2.280	32	58	1.250	1.465	1.675	1.970	2.330
62	1.470	1.710	1.970	2.310	2.575	33	56	1.400	1.630	1.875	2.275	2.620
74	1.645	1.920	2.220	2.620	2.920	34	71	1.550	1.825	2.155	2.555	2.920
104	1.875	2.180	2.520	2.885	3.190	35	84	1.730	2.060	2.410	2.795	3.160
118	2.105	2.410	2.745	3.090	3.385	36	84	1.960	2.320	2.630	2.980	3.335
188	2.330	2.625	2.930	3.245	3.540	37	184	2.220	2.520	2.800	3.120	3.450
354	2.505	2.795	3.080	3.380	3.665	38	282	2.405	2.680	2.940	3.235	3.545
504	2.630	2.915	3.200	3.505	3.780	39	506	2.540	2.810	3.060	3.340	3.640
576	2.700	2.995	3.290	3.610	3.880	40	588	2.630	2.905	3.160	3.440	3.720
312	2.735	3.035	3.330	3.670	3.940	41	320	2.660	2.950	3.210	3.520	3.795
164	2.730	3.005	3.310	3.660	3.995	42	172	2.630	2.940	3.210	3.550	3.840
Males and females: Length (cm)[2]							Males and females: Head circumference (cm)[2]					
30	30.8	32.9	35.5	37.5	39.9	26	24	22.4	23.6	25.2	26.6	28.5
21	31.8	34.1	36.6	38.6	41.0	27	20	23.2	24.4	25.8	27.2	28.9
46	33.0	35.5	37.8	39.8	42.2	28	40	24.3	25.4	26.7	28.0	29.4
53	34.4	36.8	39.0	40.9	43.1	29	49	25.3	26.4	27.6	28.8	30.2
47	36.1	38.3	40.3	42.2	44.5	30	49	26.2	27.4	28.6	29.7	31.1
54	37.5	39.7	41.6	43.5	45.9	31	53	26.9	28.2	29.6	30.5	31.9
62	38.8	41.1	43.2	45.0	47.2	32	58	27.6	29.0	30.4	31.4	32.7
69	39.9	42.3	44.7	46.2	48.4	33	65	28.4	29.8	31.2	32.1	33.4
111	41.0	43.4	45.8	47.3	49.4	34	103	29.2	30.6	31.9	32.9	34.0
149	42.0	44.6	46.7	48.1	50.2	35	149	30.0	31.3	32.5	33.4	34.5
189	43.1	45.6	47.4	48.8	50.9	36	186	30.6	31.8	32.9	33.8	34.9
345	44.1	46.5	48.0	49.3	51.3	37	353	31.1	32.3	33.2	34.1	35.2
595	44.9	47.1	48.4	49.8	51.7	38	611	31.4	32.5	33.4	34.3	35.4
957	45.5	47.6	48.8	50.1	52.0	39	961	31.6	32.8	33.7	34.6	35.7
1084	45.8	47.9	49.2	50.5	52.3	40	1097	31.8	33.0	34.0	34.8	35.9
589	46.0	48.1	49.5	50.8	52.6	41	587	32.0	33.2	34.2	35.0	36.0
315	46.2	48.2	49.7	51.0	52.8	42	315	32.1	33.4	34.3	35.1	36.2

* Live births in the Colorado General Hospital, Denver, between 1948 and 1961 (P = percentile).

[1] LUBCHENCO et al., *Pediatrics*, **32**, 793 (1963).
[2] LUBCHENCO et al., *Pediatrics*, **37**, 403 (1966).

Weight loss during the first days of life[1]

	Average weight at birth (g)	Weight loss as per cent of birth weight: 3rd day, Mean	3rd day, s	5th day, Mean	5th day, s	7th day, Mean	7th day, s
Normal birth	3465	7.22	2.52	7.29	3.14	5.72	3.29
Caesarean section with labour pains..	3580	7.19	2.09	7.65	2.83	6.06	3.31
Caesarean section without labour pains	3550	7.27	2.33	7.97	2.17	7.66	3.34

[1] Births in the Helsinki Women's Hospital between 1947 and 1952; from FURUHJELM, U., *Etud. néo-natal.*, **3**, 93 (1954).

Mean weekly weight gains (in ounces and *grammes*) of infants with low birth weight[1]

Age in months	Boys, Birth weight 2–<3 lb *0.91–<1.36 kg*	Boys, 3–<4 lb *1.36–<1.81 kg*	Boys, 4–<5 lb *1.81–<2.27 kg*	Boys, 5–<6 lb *2.27–<2.72 kg*	Boys, Full term	Girls, Birth weight 2–<3 lb *0.91–<1.36 kg*	Girls, 3–<4 lb *1.36–<1.81 kg*	Girls, 4–<5 lb *1.81–<2.27 kg*	Girls, 5–<6 lb *2.27–<2.72 kg*	Girls, Full term
0–1......	4.0 *113*	4.9 *139*	5.6 *159*	5.8 *164*	– –	4.0 *113*	4.9 *139*	5.6 *159*	5.1 *145*	– –
1–3......	7.2 *204*	7.8 *221*	8.3 *235*	8.5 *241*	8.3 *235*	6.6 *187*	6.9 *196*	6.8 *193*	7.0 *198*	7.1 *201*
3–6......	8.1 *230*	7.5 *213*	6.7 *190*	6.1 *173*	5.3 *150*	7.1 *201*	6.6 *187*	6.3 *179*	6.1 *173*	5.1 *145*
6–9......	5.1 *145*	4.7 *133*	4.4 *125*	4.0 *113*	3.7 *105*	5.5 *156*	5.1 *145*	5.0 *142*	4.6 *130*	3.6 *102*
9–12.....	3.5 *99*	3.2 *91*	3.0 *85*	2.9 *82*	2.5 *71*	3.7 *105*	3.2 *91*	2.8 *79*	2.4 *68*	2.4 *68*

[1] LEVIN et al., *Weight Gains, Serum Protein Levels and Health of Breast Fed and Artificially Fed Infants*, Medical Research Council, Special Report Series, No. 296, HMSO, London, 1959, pages 102 and 104.

Normal Measurements During Growth – Birth to 6 Months[1]

Weight in pounds and *kilogrammes*; other measurements in inches and *centimetres* (P = percentile)

Boys: Number	P_{05}	P_{10}	P_{25}	P_{50}	P_{75}	P_{90}	P_{95}		Girls: Number	P_{05}	P_{10}	P_{25}	P_{50}	P_{75}	P_{90}	P_{95}
								At birth								
123	5.7	6.2	6.8	7.5	8.2	8.6	8.8	Weight	121	5.8	6.0	6.5	7.1	7.8	8.7	9.0
	2.60	*2.80*	*3.10*	*3.40*	*3.70*	*3.90*	*4.01*			*2.64*	*2.70*	*2.95*	*3.20*	*3.53*	*3.96*	*4.06*
121	18.5	19.3	19.3	19.9	20.5	20.7	20.9	Length	118	18.5	18.5	19.2	19.5	20.1	20.5	20.9
	47.0	*49.0*	*49.0*	*50.5*	*52.0*	*52.5*	*53.0*			*47.0*	*47.0*	*48.7*	*49.5*	*51.0*	*52.0*	*53.0*
								1 month								
54	7.5	7.9	8.2	8.9	9.5	10.1	10.4	Weight	48	7.4	7.6	8.0	8.5	9.0	9.7	9.9
	3.42	*3.57*	*3.72*	*4.04*	*4.29*	*4.58*	*4.73*			*3.36*	*3.44*	*3.63*	*3.86*	*4.08*	*4.42*	*4.50*
54	20.5	20.7	20.9	21.5	22.0	22.4	22.4	Length	49	20.0	20.2	20.7	20.9	21.5	21.9	22.3
	52.0	*52.5*	*53.2*	*54.5*	*55.8*	*56.8*	*57.0*			*50.7*	*51.4*	*52.5*	*53.2*	*54.5*	*55.5*	*56.7*
51	13.3	13.4	13.8	14.2	14.4	14.6	14.8	Sitting height	42	13.0	13.2	13.5	13.8	14.2	14.5	14.9
	33.7	*34.0*	*35.0*	*36.0*	*36.5*	*37.0*	*37.7*			*33.0*	*33.5*	*34.2*	*35.0*	*36.0*	*36.9*	*37.9*
54	13.9	14.2	14.4	14.8	15.0	15.4	15.4	Head circ.	44	13.5	13.9	14.2	14.4	14.6	15.0	15.1
	35.3	*36.0*	*36.5*	*37.5*	*38.0*	*39.0*	*39.0*			*34.2*	*35.3*	*36.0*	*36.5*	*37.0*	*38.1*	*38.4*
								2 months								
65	9.4	9.8	10.4	11.0	11.8	12.4	12.5	Weight	57	9.0	9.2	9.9	10.5	11.1	11.7	12.1
	4.27	*4.43*	*4.73*	*4.98*	*5.34*	*5.64*	*5.69*			*4.07*	*4.19*	*4.48*	*4.75*	*5.02*	*5.31*	*5.50*
64	21.9	22.0	22.4	22.8	23.2	23.4	23.8	Length	56	21.2	21.5	22.0	22.2	22.6	23.0	23.4
	55.5	*56.0*	*57.0*	*58.0*	*59.0*	*59.5*	*60.4*			*53.9*	*54.5*	*56.0*	*56.5*	*57.5*	*58.5*	*59.5*
60	14.0	14.4	14.6	15.0	15.4	15.6	15.7	Sitting height	50	13.9	14.0	14.4	14.8	15.0	15.2	15.4
	35.5	*36.5*	*37.0*	*38.0*	*39.0*	*39.5*	*40.0*			*35.2*	*35.5*	*36.5*	*37.5*	*38.0*	*38.5*	*39.0*
63	14.8	15.0	15.2	15.4	15.7	15.9	16.0	Head circ.	53	14.3	14.6	14.8	15.2	15.4	15.6	15.7
	37.5	*38.0*	*38.5*	*39.0*	*40.0*	*40.5*	*40.7*			*36.3*	*37.0*	*37.5*	*38.5*	*39.0*	*39.5*	*40.0*
								3 months								
75	11.4	11.9	12.6	13.2	13.9	14.7	15.2	Weight	60	10.6	10.8	11.5	12.2	13.1	13.7	14.2
	5.18	*5.40*	*5.73*	*6.00*	*6.32*	*6.66*	*6.90*			*4.80*	*4.89*	*5.20*	*5.53*	*5.95*	*6.23*	*6.46*
75	23.0	23.2	23.8	24.0	24.6	24.9	25.0	Length	58	22.6	22.8	23.0	23.4	23.8	24.3	24.8
	58.3	*59.0*	*60.5*	*61.0*	*62.5*	*63.2*	*63.6*			*57.4*	*58.0*	*58.5*	*59.5*	*60.5*	*61.6*	*63.0*
74	15.0	15.2	15.6	15.9	16.1	16.3	16.5	Sitting height	55	14.8	14.8	15.2	15.4	15.7	15.9	16.2
	38.0	*38.5*	*39.5*	*40.5*	*41.0*	*41.5*	*42.0*			*37.5*	*37.5*	*38.5*	*39.0*	*40.0*	*40.5*	*41.1*
74	15.4	15.6	15.7	15.9	16.3	16.5	16.7	Head circ.	55	15.0	15.0	15.4	15.7	15.9	16.1	16.2
	39.0	*39.5*	*40.0*	*40.5*	*41.5*	*42.0*	*42.5*			*38.0*	*38.2*	*39.0*	*40.0*	*40.5*	*41.0*	*41.2*
26	15.0	15.2	15.6	16.1	16.2	16.5	16.5	Chest circ.	16	14.7	15.0	15.2	15.7	15.9	16.1	16.2
	38.0	*38.6*	*39.7*	*41.0*	*41.2*	*42.0*	*42.0*			*37.4*	*38.0*	*38.5*	*40.0*	*40.5*	*41.0*	*41.2*
								4 months								
63	12.8	13.0	14.0	15.1	15.9	16.5	17.1	Weight	58	11.5	11.9	12.7	13.8	15.1	15.7	16.4
	5.82	*5.91*	*6.35*	*6.84*	*7.23*	*7.49*	*7.77*			*5.22*	*5.42*	*5.77*	*6.24*	*6.85*	*7.13*	*7.43*
63	23.7	24.1	25.0	25.4	25.8	26.1	26.4	Length	58	23.4	23.6	23.8	24.4	25.0	25.4	25.4
	60.1	*61.3*	*63.5*	*64.5*	*65.5*	*66.3*	*67.0*			*59.5*	*60.0*	*60.5*	*62.0*	*63.5*	*64.5*	*64.6*
60	15.6	15.7	16.1	16.5	16.9	17.1	17.3	Sitting height	56	15.0	15.4	15.7	15.9	16.3	16.5	16.6
	39.5	*40.0*	*41.0*	*42.0*	*43.0*	*43.5*	*44.0*			*38.0*	*39.0*	*40.0*	*40.5*	*41.5*	*42.0*	*42.1*
60	15.7	15.9	16.1	16.3	16.7	16.9	17.1	Head circ.	55	15.4	15.4	15.7	16.1	16.4	16.7	16.9
	40.0	*40.5*	*41.0*	*41.5*	*42.5*	*43.0*	*43.5*			*39.0*	*39.2*	*40.0*	*41.0*	*41.6*	*42.5*	*43.0*
								5 months								
61	13.6	14.4	15.2	16.2	17.4	17.7	18.3	Weight	62	13.2	13.3	14.3	15.4	16.3	17.0	17.3
	6.19	*6.52*	*6.91*	*7.37*	*7.90*	*8.04*	*8.29*			*6.00*	*6.05*	*6.50*	*7.00*	*7.40*	*7.71*	*7.86*
61	24.6	25.0	25.8	26.2	26.6	27.1	27.2	Length	61	24.4	24.6	25.0	25.2	25.8	26.2	26.4
	62.5	*63.5*	*65.5*	*66.5*	*67.5*	*68.9*	*69.0*			*62.0*	*62.5*	*63.5*	*64.0*	*65.5*	*66.5*	*67.0*
58	16.1	16.3	16.6	17.1	17.3	17.6	17.7	Sitting height	59	15.9	15.9	16.1	16.5	16.7	17.1	17.3
	40.9	*41.5*	*42.2*	*43.5*	*44.0*	*44.6*	*45.0*			*40.5*	*40.5*	*41.0*	*42.0*	*42.5*	*43.5*	*44.0*
57	16.1	16.1	16.5	16.9	17.1	17.3	17.5	Head circ.	59	15.7	15.9	16.1	16.5	16.7	16.9	17.3
	41.0	*41.0*	*42.0*	*43.0*	*43.5*	*44.0*	*44.5*			*40.0*	*40.5*	*41.0*	*42.0*	*42.5*	*43.0*	*44.0*
								6 months								
73	14.9	15.4	16.5	17.9	18.7	19.3	19.8	Weight	74	14.0	14.4	15.3	16.5	17.5	18.2	19.0
	6.74	*7.00*	*7.48*	*8.12*	*8.49*	*8.77*	*8.98*			*6.34*	*6.53*	*6.92*	*7.48*	*7.93*	*8.27*	*8.62*
73	25.2	25.6	26.4	27.0	27.4	28.1	28.2	Length	74	25.0	25.2	25.6	26.2	26.6	27.3	27.4
	64.1	*65.1*	*67.1*	*68.5*	*69.5*	*71.3*	*71.6*			*63.5*	*64.0*	*65.0*	*66.5*	*67.5*	*69.3*	*69.6*
73	16.5	16.7	17.1	17.5	17.7	18.1	18.3	Sitting height	73	16.1	16.3	16.7	16.9	17.3	17.6	17.7
	41.8	*42.5*	*43.5*	*44.5*	*45.0*	*46.0*	*46.5*			*41.0*	*41.5*	*42.5*	*43.0*	*44.0*	*44.7*	*45.0*
73	16.5	16.7	16.9	17.1	17.5	17.7	17.9	Head circ.	73	16.1	16.3	16.5	16.9	17.1	17.3	17.5
	41.8	*42.5*	*43.0*	*43.5*	*44.5*	*45.0*	*45.5*			*40.8*	*41.5*	*42.0*	*43.0*	*43.5*	*44.0*	*44.5*
28	16.5	16.7	16.9	17.3	17.7	18.1	18.1	Chest circ.	23	15.5	16.1	16.5	16.9	17.3	17.6	17.7
	42.0	*42.4*	*43.0*	*44.0*	*45.0*	*46.0*	*46.0*			*39.3*	*41.0*	*41.8*	*43.0*	*44.0*	*44.7*	*45.0*

(Percentile ranges: 90% = P_{05}–P_{95}; 80% = P_{10}–P_{90}; 50% = P_{25}–P_{75}.)

[1] HEIMENDINGER, J., *Helv. paediat. Acta*, **19**, 406 (1964). From measurements made in the period 1957–1962 in northwest Switzerland on 341 boys and 326 girls mostly of German-Swiss descent.

Normal Measurements During Growth – 7 Months to 12 Months[1]

Weight in pounds and *kilogrammes*; other measurements in inches and *centimetres* (*P* = percentile)

Boys									Girls							
Number	P_{05}	P_{10} (90%)	P_{25} (80%)	P_{50} (50%)	P_{75} (50%)	P_{90} (80%)	P_{95} (90%)		Number	P_{05}	P_{10} (90%)	P_{25} (80%)	P_{50} (50%)	P_{75} (50%)	P_{90} (80%)	P_{95} (90%)
								7 months								
50	15.9	16.3	17.3	18.4	19.5	19.9	20.2	Weight	47	14.8	15.1	16.0	17.4	18.3	19.5	20.1
	7.19	*7.41*	*7.86*	*8.36*	*8.85*	*9.02*	*9.15*			*6.72*	*6.87*	*7.28*	*7.87*	*8.31*	*8.86*	*9.13*
49	25.7	26.2	27.0	27.6	28.0	28.3	28.8	Length	47	25.6	25.8	26.2	26.8	27.4	27.8	28.0
	65.2	*66.5*	*68.7*	*70.0*	*71.0*	*72.0*	*73.2*			*65.1*	*65.5*	*66.5*	*68.0*	*69.5*	*70.5*	*71.0*
48	16.9	17.1	17.5	17.7	18.1	18.5	18.6	Sitting height	46	16.6	16.9	17.1	17.3	17.7	18.0	18.4
	43.0	*43.5*	*44.5*	*45.0*	*46.0*	*47.0*	*47.3*			*42.1*	*42.8*	*43.5*	*44.0*	*45.0*	*45.7*	*46.8*
48	16.7	16.9	17.1	17.3	17.7	18.0	18.1	Head circ.	46	16.3	16.5	16.9	17.1	17.5	17.7	17.8
	42.5	*42.9*	*43.5*	*44.0*	*45.0*	*45.6*	*46.0*			*41.5*	*42.0*	*43.0*	*43.5*	*44.5*	*45.0*	*45.3*
20	16.5	16.7	16.9	17.3	17.7	18.1	18.1	Chest circ.	16	15.7	16.1	16.7	17.3	17.7	17.7	17.8
	42.0	*42.5*	*43.0*	*44.0*	*45.0*	*46.0*	*46.0*			*39.8*	*41.0*	*42.5*	*44.0*	*45.0*	*45.0*	*45.2*
								8 months								
59	16.8	17.8	18.4	19.8	20.7	21.3	21.8	Weight	56	15.7	15.8	16.7	18.2	19.4	20.5	21.5
	7.63	*8.06*	*8.35*	*8.97*	*9.37*	*9.66*	*9.88*			*7.10*	*7.16*	*7.56*	*8.24*	*8.78*	*9.30*	*9.74*
59	26.3	26.8	27.8	28.1	28.6	29.1	29.3	Length	55	26.2	26.4	26.8	27.4	28.0	28.4	28.7
	66.9	*68.0*	*70.5*	*71.5*	*72.6*	*74.0*	*74.5*			*66.5*	*67.0*	*68.0*	*69.5*	*71.0*	*72.2*	*73.0*
57	17.1	17.3	17.7	18.1	18.5	18.7	18.9	Sitting height	55	16.9	17.1	17.5	17.7	18.1	18.4	18.5
	43.4	*44.0*	*45.0*	*46.0*	*47.0*	*47.5*	*48.0*			*42.8*	*43.5*	*44.5*	*45.0*	*46.0*	*46.7*	*47.0*
56	16.9	16.9	17.5	17.7	18.1	18.3	18.3	Head circ.	55	16.5	16.8	17.1	17.5	17.7	18.1	18.1
	43.0	*43.0*	*44.5*	*45.0*	*46.0*	*46.5*	*46.5*			*42.0*	*42.7*	*43.5*	*44.5*	*45.0*	*46.0*	*46.0*
19	16.9	16.9	17.3	17.7	18.1	18.3	18.5	Chest circ.	20	16.7	16.7	16.9	17.7	18.1	18.5	18.7
	42.8	*43.0*	*44.0*	*45.0*	*46.0*	*46.5*	*46.9*			*42.5*	*42.5*	*43.0*	*45.0*	*46.0*	*47.0*	*47.5*
								9 months								
66	17.6	18.3	19.2	20.7	21.6	22.8	22.9	Weight	72	16.1	16.8	17.4	18.9	20.3	21.4	21.8
	8.00	*8.30*	*8.71*	*9.37*	*9.82*	*10.36*	*10.40*			*7.30*	*7.62*	*7.90*	*8.58*	*9.23*	*9.71*	*9.88*
66	27.1	28.0	28.3	28.7	29.1	29.5	29.8	Length	72	26.7	27.0	27.4	28.0	28.3	28.9	29.1
	68.8	*71.0*	*72.0*	*73.0*	*74.0*	*75.0*	*75.8*			*67.9*	*68.6*	*69.5*	*71.0*	*72.0*	*73.5*	*74.0*
63	17.5	17.7	18.1	18.3	18.7	19.0	19.3	Sitting height	72	17.0	17.3	17.7	17.9	18.3	18.5	18.8
	44.5	*45.0*	*46.0*	*46.5*	*47.5*	*48.3*	*49.0*			*43.3*	*44.0*	*45.0*	*45.5*	*46.5*	*47.0*	*47.7*
65	17.3	17.3	17.7	18.1	18.3	18.5	18.7	Head circ.	72	16.9	16.9	17.3	17.7	17.9	18.1	18.3
	44.0	*44.0*	*45.0*	*46.0*	*46.5*	*47.0*	*47.5*			*42.8*	*43.0*	*44.0*	*45.0*	*45.5*	*46.0*	*46.5*
24	17.2	17.3	17.3	17.9	18.5	18.5	18.8	Chest circ.	26	16.7	16.9	17.3	17.7	18.2	18.6	18.8
	43.6	*44.0*	*44.0*	*45.5*	*47.0*	*47.0*	*47.8*			*42.5*	*43.0*	*44.0*	*45.0*	*46.2*	*47.2*	*47.8*
								10 months								
36	17.6	18.3	19.5	20.7	21.6	22.9	23.5	Weight	36	16.8	17.3	18.3	19.3	20.4	21.8	22.2
	8.00	*8.30*	*8.85*	*9.40*	*9.82*	*10.41*	*10.66*			*7.60*	*7.84*	*8.30*	*8.74*	*9.25*	*9.90*	*10.07*
36	27.5	28.0	28.5	28.9	29.3	30.1	30.4	Length	36	27.0	27.2	27.8	28.3	28.7	29.1	29.4
	69.9	*71.0*	*72.5*	*73.5*	*74.5*	*76.4*	*77.1*			*68.5*	*69.1*	*70.5*	*72.0*	*73.0*	*74.0*	*74.7*
34	17.7	17.7	18.1	18.3	18.7	19.1	19.3	Sitting height	36	17.2	17.4	17.7	18.1	18.5	18.6	18.9
	45.0	*45.0*	*46.0*	*46.5*	*47.5*	*48.5*	*49.0*			*43.8*	*44.3*	*45.0*	*46.0*	*47.0*	*47.2*	*48.0*
36	17.3	17.3	17.7	18.1	18.5	18.5	18.8	Head circ.	34	16.9	16.9	17.3	17.7	18.0	18.1	18.3
	44.0	*44.0*	*45.0*	*46.0*	*47.0*	*47.0*	*47.8*			*43.0*	*43.0*	*44.0*	*45.0*	*45.7*	*46.0*	*46.5*
								11 months								
28	18.7	19.5	20.7	22.0	23.1	23.5	23.9	Weight	34	17.1	17.6	18.6	20.2	22.0	23.3	24.0
	8.50	*8.86*	*9.37*	*10.00*	*10.46*	*10.64*	*10.86*			*7.77*	*8.00*	*8.43*	*9.14*	*9.99*	*10.59*	*10.90*
28	28.1	28.9	29.1	29.7	29.9	30.4	30.6	Length	34	27.8	27.9	28.1	28.9	29.4	29.7	30.2
	71.3	*73.3*	*74.0*	*75.5*	*76.0*	*77.1*	*77.8*			*70.5*	*70.8*	*71.5*	*73.5*	*74.7*	*75.5*	*76.6*
28	17.9	18.1	18.3	18.7	18.9	19.3	19.5	Sitting height	33	17.4	17.6	18.0	18.4	18.7	19.0	19.2
	45.4	*46.0*	*46.5*	*47.5*	*48.0*	*49.0*	*49.6*			*44.3*	*44.6*	*45.6*	*46.7*	*47.5*	*48.3*	*48.8*
27	17.5	17.7	17.9	18.5	18.7	18.9	18.9	Head circ.	33	17.2	17.3	17.5	17.9	18.1	18.5	18.5
	44.5	*45.0*	*45.5*	*47.0*	*47.5*	*48.0*	*48.0*			*43.8*	*44.0*	*44.5*	*45.5*	*46.0*	*46.9*	*47.1*
								12 months								
58	18.7	20.2	21.1	22.2	23.8	24.5	25.0	Weight	73	18.1	18.5	19.5	21.0	22.1	24.4	25.0
	8.50	*9.17*	*9.57*	*10.09*	*10.78*	*11.13*	*11.36*			*8.22*	*8.40*	*8.86*	*9.51*	*10.04*	*11.05*	*11.33*
58	28.1	28.9	29.5	30.1	30.5	31.1	31.3	Length	72	28.0	28.3	28.7	29.4	29.9	30.3	30.5
	71.4	*73.4*	*75.0*	*76.5*	*77.5*	*79.0*	*79.5*			*71.0*	*72.0*	*73.0*	*74.7*	*76.0*	*77.0*	*77.5*
56	18.0	18.3	18.7	18.9	19.3	20.0	20.1	Sitting height	71	17.5	17.7	18.2	18.7	18.9	19.3	19.5
	45.8	*46.5*	*47.5*	*48.0*	*49.0*	*50.7*	*51.1*			*44.5*	*45.0*	*46.3*	*47.5*	*48.0*	*48.9*	*49.5*
58	17.5	17.7	18.1	18.5	18.9	19.1	19.1	Head circ.	72	17.2	17.5	17.7	18.1	18.3	18.5	18.7
	44.5	*45.0*	*46.0*	*47.0*	*48.0*	*48.5*	*48.5*			*43.8*	*44.5*	*45.0*	*46.0*	*46.5*	*47.0*	*47.5*
26	17.5	17.6	18.1	18.5	18.9	19.3	19.6	Chest circ.	31	16.7	17.3	17.8	18.1	18.5	18.7	19.0
	44.5	*44.8*	*46.0*	*47.0*	*48.0*	*49.0*	*49.7*			*42.5*	*44.0*	*45.3*	*46.0*	*47.1*	*47.5*	*48.2*

[1] Heimendinger, J., *Helv. paediat. Acta*, **19**, 406 (1964). From measurements made in the period 1957–1962 in northwest Switzerland on 341 boys and 326 girls mostly of German-Swiss descent.

Normal Measurements During Growth – 15 Months to 2 Years

Weight in pounds and *kilogrammes*; other measurements in inches and *centimetres* (*P* = percentile)

Boys: Number	P_{05}	P_{10}	P_{25}	P_{50}	P_{75}	P_{90}	P_{95}		Girls: Number	P_{05}	P_{10}	P_{25}	P_{50}	P_{75}	P_{90}	P_{95}
	90% (P_{05}–P_{95})									90% (P_{05}–P_{95})						
		80% (P_{10}–P_{90})									80% (P_{10}–P_{90})					
			50% (P_{25}–P_{75})									50% (P_{25}–P_{75})				
								15 months [1]								
50	20.8	21.6	22.5	24.0	25.3	26.9	28.5	Weight	46	19.7	20.0	21.4	22.4	24.1	24.9	25.6
	9.45	*9.80*	*10.20*	*10.90*	*11.48*	*12.20*	*12.93*			*8.92*	*9.06*	*9.69*	*10.15*	*10.92*	*11.29*	*11.61*
50	29.6	30.4	30.9	31.5	31.9	32.3	32.5	Length	46	29.5	29.7	30.1	30.7	31.3	31.7	31.9
	75.2	*77.2*	*78.4*	*80.0*	*81.0*	*82.0*	*82.5*			*75.0*	*75.5*	*76.5*	*78.0*	*79.5*	*80.5*	*81.0*
49	18.8	19.3	19.5	19.7	20.1	20.5	20.6	Sitting height	46	18.3	18.3	18.9	19.1	19.5	20.0	20.2
	47.8	*48.9*	*49.5*	*50.0*	*51.0*	*52.0*	*52.2*			*46.5*	*46.5*	*48.0*	*48.5*	*49.5*	*50.7*	*51.3*
50	17.9	18.3	18.5	18.9	19.1	19.5	19.5	Head circ.	45	17.5	17.7	18.1	18.5	18.7	18.9	19.1
	45.5	*46.4*	*47.0*	*48.0*	*48.5*	*49.5*	*49.5*			*44.5*	*45.0*	*46.0*	*47.0*	*47.5*	*48.0*	*48.5*
24	17.9	18.0	18.5	19.1	19.3	19.7	19.8	Chest circ.	28	17.1	17.6	18.1	18.5	18.7	18.9	19.4
	45.5	*45.7*	*47.0*	*48.5*	*49.0*	*50.0*	*50.4*			*43.4*	*44.8*	*46.0*	*47.0*	*47.5*	*48.1*	*49.4*
								18 months [1]								
39	22.3	22.8	24.1	24.9	26.5	28.5	29.3	Weight	40	21.1	22.4	23.1	24.1	26.2	27.4	28.7
	10.12	*10.36*	*10.91*	*11.31*	*12.02*	*12.91*	*13.29*			*9.56*	*10.15*	*10.47*	*10.95*	*11.90*	*12.42*	*13.00*
39	30.9	31.5	32.1	32.7	33.1	33.9	34.1	Length	40	30.7	30.9	31.5	32.1	32.7	33.5	33.9
	78.4	*79.9*	*81.5*	*83.0*	*84.1*	*86.0*	*86.5*			*78.0*	*78.5*	*80.0*	*81.5*	*83.0*	*85.0*	*86.0*
39	19.3	19.5	19.9	20.3	20.7	21.1	21.3	Sitting height	40	18.5	19.3	19.5	19.9	20.5	20.9	21.1
	49.0	*49.5*	*50.5*	*51.5*	*52.5*	*53.5*	*54.0*			*47.0*	*49.0*	*49.5*	*50.5*	*52.0*	*53.0*	*53.5*
39	17.9	18.3	18.7	19.3	19.3	19.7	19.7	Head circ.	40	17.7	18.3	18.5	18.7	19.1	19.3	19.3
	45.5	*46.5*	*47.5*	*49.0*	*49.0*	*50.0*	*50.0*			*45.0*	*46.5*	*47.0*	*47.5*	*48.5*	*49.0*	*49.0*
20	18.1	18.5	18.9	19.3	19.7	20.1	20.5	Chest circ.	22	17.6	17.8	18.4	18.9	19.4	20.1	20.2
	46.0	*47.0*	*48.0*	*49.0*	*50.0*	*51.0*	*52.0*			*44.8*	*45.1*	*46.7*	*48.0*	*49.2*	*51.0*	*51.4*
								2 years [1]								
23	24.1	25.0	26.1	27.6	29.5	30.7	31.8	Weight	24	22.1	23.3	24.7	26.7	28.6	30.2	31.0
	10.91	*11.33*	*11.82*	*12.53*	*13.39*	*13.93*	*14.43*			*10.03*	*10.59*	*11.22*	*12.10*	*12.96*	*13.70*	*14.05*
24	33.1	33.1	33.9	34.4	35.4	36.6	37.1	Height	24	32.7	33.0	33.5	34.6	35.2	35.7	36.0
	84.0	*84.0*	*86.0*	*87.5*	*90.0*	*92.9*	*94.3*			*83.0*	*83.9*	*85.0*	*88.0*	*89.5*	*90.8*	*91.4*
24	20.1	20.3	20.7	21.3	21.7	22.0	22.2	Sitting height	24	19.7	20.0	20.5	21.1	21.3	21.8	22.0
	51.1	*51.5*	*52.5*	*54.0*	*55.0*	*56.0*	*56.4*			*50.1*	*50.9*	*52.0*	*53.5*	*54.0*	*55.3*	*55.9*
24	18.5	18.8	18.9	19.5	19.7	20.2	20.3	Head circ.	24	18.1	18.5	18.7	19.1	19.3	19.5	19.6
	47.1	*47.7*	*48.0*	*49.5*	*50.0*	*51.3*	*51.5*			*46.1*	*46.9*	*47.5*	*48.5*	*49.0*	*49.5*	*49.9*
20	18.7	18.9	19.3	19.7	19.9	20.1	20.5	Chest circ.	10	–	18.5	18.9	19.5	19.9	20.1	–
	47.5	*48.0*	*49.0*	*50.0*	*50.5*	*51.0*	*52.0*			–	*47.0*	*48.0*	*49.5*	*50.5*	*51.0*	–

$P_{2.5}$	P_{10}	P_{25}	P_{50}	P_{75}	P_{90}	$P_{97.5}$	s		$P_{2.5}$	P_{10}	P_{25}	P_{50}	P_{75}	P_{90}	$P_{97.5}$	s
95% ($P_{2.5}$–$P_{97.5}$)									95% ($P_{2.5}$–$P_{97.5}$)							
	80% (P_{10}–P_{90})									80% (P_{10}–P_{90})						
		50% (P_{25}–P_{75})									50% (P_{25}–P_{75})					
								2 years [2]								
18.3	21.4	24.3	27.3	30.4	33.3	36.4	4.5	Weight	20.1	22.3	24.0	26.2	28.4	30.2	32.4	3.1
8.3	*9.7*	*11.0*	*12.4*	*13.8*	*15.1*	*16.5*	*2.05*		*9.1*	*10.1*	*10.9*	*11.9*	*12.9*	*13.7*	*14.7*	*1.4*
31.1	32.2	33.1	34.3	35.4	36.3	37.4	1.6	Height	31.0	32.0	33.0	34.1	35.1	36.1	37.1	1.5
78.9	*81.7*	*84.2*	*87.0*	*89.8*	*92.3*	*95.1*	*4.1*		*78.8*	*81.4*	*83.8*	*86.5*	*89.2*	*91.6*	*94.2*	*3.9*
18.9	19.6	20.2	20.8	21.5	22.0	22.7	0.9	Sitting height	18.3	19.1	19.9	20.7	21.6	22.4	23.2	1.3
48.1	*49.8*	*51.3*	*52.9*	*54.5*	*56.0*	*57.7*	*2.4*		*46.4*	*48.6*	*50.5*	*52.7*	*54.9*	*56.8*	*59.0*	*3.2*
4.9	5.8	6.7	7.6	8.5	9.4	10.3	1.4	Shoulder width	5.9	6.6	7.2	7.9	8.5	9.1	9.8	1.0
12.4	*14.8*	*16.9*	*19.3*	*21.7*	*23.8*	*26.2*	*3.5*		*15.0*	*16.8*	*18.3*	*20.0*	*21.7*	*23.2*	*25.0*	*2.5*
4.6	5.4	6.1	6.9	7.7	8.5	9.3	1.2	Pelvic width	4.9	5.5	6.0	6.6	7.2	7.7	8.4	0.9
11.7	*13.7*	*15.6*	*17.6*	*19.6*	*21.5*	*23.5*	*3.0*		*12.4*	*14.0*	*15.3*	*16.8*	*18.3*	*19.6*	*21.2*	*2.2*
18.3	18.7	19.0	19.4	19.8	20.1	20.5	0.6	Head circ.	17.6	18.0	18.3	18.7	19.1	19.4	19.8	0.6
46.4	*47.4*	*48.2*	*49.2*	*50.2*	*51.0*	*52.0*	*1.4*		*44.6*	*45.6*	*46.4*	*47.4*	*48.4*	*49.2*	*50.2*	*1.4*
17.8	18.4	18.9	19.5	20.1	20.6	21.3	0.9	Chest circ.	17.1	17.8	18.4	19.0	19.6	20.2	20.9	0.9
45.2	*46.8*	*48.1*	*49.6*	*51.1*	*52.4*	*54.0*	*2.2*		*43.5*	*45.2*	*46.7*	*48.3*	*49.9*	*51.4*	*53.1*	*2.4*
5.3	5.6	5.8	6.1	6.4	6.6	6.9	0.4	Upper arm circ.	4.1	4.7	5.2	5.8	6.3	6.9	7.4	0.8
13.5	*14.2*	*14.8*	*15.5*	*16.2*	*16.8*	*17.5*	*1.0*		*10.5*	*12.0*	*13.3*	*14.7*	*16.1*	*17.4*	*18.9*	*2.1*
1.6	2.4	3.1	3.9	4.7	5.5	6.3	1.2	Wrist circ.	1.6	2.4	3.0	3.8	4.5	5.2	5.9	1.1
4.1	*6.1*	*8.0*	*10.0*	*12.0*	*13.9*	*15.9*	*3.0*		*4.1*	*6.0*	*7.7*	*9.6*	*11.5*	*13.2*	*15.1*	*2.8*
6.7	7.0	7.2	7.5	7.8	8.0	8.3	0.4	Calf circ.	5.6	6.2	6.7	7.3	7.9	8.4	9.0	0.9
17.0	*17.7*	*18.3*	*19.0*	*19.7*	*20.3*	*21.0*	*1.0*		*14.1*	*15.7*	*17.0*	*18.5*	*20.0*	*21.3*	*22.9*	*2.2*

[1] HEIMENDINGER, J., *Helv. paediat. Acta*, **19**, 406 (1964). From measurements made in the period 1957–1962 in northwest Switzerland on 341 boys and 326 girls mostly of German-Swiss descent.

[2] HEIMENDINGER, J., *Helv. paediat. Acta*, **19**, suppl. 13 (1964). From measurements made in the period 1956–1957 on 2150 boys and 2150 girls in Basle, Switzerland.

Normal Measurements During Growth – 2½ Years to 3½ Years[1]

Weight in pounds and *kilogrammes*; other measurements in inches and *centimetres* (P = percentile)

Boys									Girls							
	95%									95%						
		80%									80%					
			50%									50%				
$P_{2.5}$	P_{10}	P_{25}	P_{50}	P_{75}	P_{90}	$P_{97.5}$	s		$P_{2.5}$	P_{10}	P_{25}	P_{50}	P_{75}	P_{90}	$P_{97.5}$	s
								2½ years								
20.5	23.8	26.7	29.8	32.8	35.7	39.0	4.7	Weight	21.4	24.0	26.2	28.9	31.5	33.7	36.4	3.7
9.3	*10.8*	*12.1*	*13.5*	*14.9*	*16.2*	*17.7*	*2.11*		*9.7*	*10.9*	*11.9*	*13.1*	*14.3*	*15.3*	*16.5*	*1.7*
33.1	34.3	35.2	36.4	37.5	38.5	39.6	1.7	Height	32.6	33.7	34.7	35.8	36.9	37.9	39.0	1.6
84.1	*87.0*	*89.5*	*92.4*	*95.3*	*97.8*	*100.7*	*4.2*		*82.9*	*85.7*	*88.2*	*91.0*	*93.8*	*96.3*	*99.1*	*4.1*
19.6	20.3	20.9	21.6	22.3	23.0	23.6	1.0	Sitting height	18.8	19.6	20.4	21.2	22.0	22.8	23.6	1.2
49.8	*51.5*	*53.1*	*54.9*	*56.7*	*58.3*	*60.0*	*2.6*		*47.7*	*49.8*	*51.7*	*53.8*	*55.9*	*57.8*	*59.9*	*3.1*
5.2	6.1	7.0	8.0	8.9	9.8	10.7	1.4	Shoulder width	6.2	6.9	7.5	8.1	8.8	9.4	10.1	1.0
13.1	*15.5*	*17.7*	*20.2*	*22.7*	*24.9*	*27.3*	*3.6*		*15.7*	*17.5*	*19.0*	*20.7*	*22.4*	*23.9*	*25.7*	*2.5*
4.5	5.4	6.1	7.0	7.9	8.6	9.5	1.3	Pelvic width	5.0	5.6	6.2	6.8	7.4	8.0	8.6	0.9
11.5	*13.7*	*15.6*	*17.8*	*20.0*	*21.9*	*24.1*	*3.2*		*12.7*	*14.3*	*15.7*	*17.3*	*18.9*	*20.3*	*21.9*	*2.3*
18.4	18.8	19.1	19.5	19.9	20.2	20.6	0.6	Head circ.	17.8	18.2	18.5	18.9	19.3	19.6	20.0	0.6
46.8	*47.8*	*48.6*	*49.6*	*50.6*	*51.4*	*52.4*	*1.4*		*45.3*	*46.3*	*47.1*	*48.1*	*49.1*	*49.9*	*50.9*	*1.4*
17.9	18.5	19.1	19.8	20.4	21.0	21.7	0.9	Chest circ.	17.5	18.2	18.8	19.4	20.0	20.6	21.3	0.9
45.4	*47.1*	*48.6*	*50.2*	*51.8*	*53.3*	*55.0*	*2.4*		*44.5*	*46.2*	*47.7*	*49.3*	*50.9*	*52.4*	*54.1*	*2.4*
5.2	5.5	5.8	6.1	6.5	6.8	7.1	0.5	Upper arm circ.	4.3	4.9	5.4	5.9	6.5	6.9	7.5	0.8
13.2	*14.0*	*14.8*	*15.6*	*16.4*	*17.2*	*18.0*	*1.2*		*11.0*	*12.4*	*13.6*	*15.0*	*16.4*	*17.6*	*19.0*	*2.0*
1.7	2.5	3.2	4.0	4.8	5.6	6.3	1.2	Wrist circ.	1.5	2.3	3.0	3.8	4.6	5.3	6.0	1.1
4.3	*6.3*	*8.2*	*10.2*	*12.2*	*14.1*	*16.1*	*3.0*		*3.9*	*5.8*	*7.6*	*9.6*	*11.6*	*13.4*	*15.3*	*2.9*
6.1	6.7	7.1	7.7	8.2	8.7	9.3	0.8	Calf circ.	5.8	6.4	6.9	7.5	8.1	8.6	9.3	0.9
15.5	*16.9*	*18.1*	*19.5*	*20.9*	*22.1*	*23.5*	*2.0*		*14.7*	*16.3*	*17.6*	*19.1*	*20.6*	*21.9*	*23.5*	*2.2*
								3 years								
23.1	26.2	29.1	32.2	35.3	38.1	41.2	4.5	Weight	22.7	25.8	28.4	31.5	34.6	37.3	40.3	4.4
10.5	*11.9*	*13.2*	*14.6*	*16.0*	*17.3*	*18.7*	*2.06*		*10.3*	*11.7*	*12.9*	*14.3*	*15.7*	*16.9*	*18.3*	*2.0*
34.7	35.8	36.8	37.9	39.0	40.0	41.1	1.6	Height	34.1	35.3	36.3	37.5	38.6	39.7	40.8	1.7
88.2	*91.0*	*93.5*	*96.3*	*99.1*	*101.6*	*104.4*	*4.1*		*86.7*	*89.6*	*92.3*	*95.2*	*98.1*	*100.8*	*103.7*	*4.3*
19.7	20.5	21.3	22.1	22.9	23.7	24.5	1.2	Sitting height	19.4	20.1	20.8	21.6	22.4	23.1	23.9	1.1
50.0	*52.1*	*54.0*	*56.1*	*58.2*	*60.1*	*62.2*	*3.1*		*49.2*	*51.1*	*52.9*	*54.9*	*56.9*	*58.7*	*60.6*	*2.9*
5.4	6.4	7.3	8.3	9.3	10.2	11.2	1.5	Shoulder width	6.4	7.0	7.7	8.4	9.1	9.7	10.4	1.0
13.8	*16.3*	*18.6*	*21.1*	*23.6*	*25.9*	*28.4*	*3.7*		*16.2*	*17.9*	*19.5*	*21.3*	*23.1*	*24.7*	*26.4*	*2.6*
4.4	5.4	6.2	7.1	8.1	8.9	9.8	1.4	Pelvic width	5.2	5.8	6.3	7.0	7.6	8.1	8.8	0.9
11.2	*13.6*	*15.7*	*18.1*	*20.5*	*22.6*	*25.0*	*3.5*		*13.1*	*14.7*	*16.1*	*17.7*	*19.3*	*20.7*	*22.3*	*2.3*
18.5	18.9	19.3	19.6	20.0	20.4	20.7	0.6	Head circ.	18.0	18.4	18.7	19.1	19.5	19.9	20.3	0.6
47.1	*48.1*	*48.9*	*49.9*	*50.9*	*51.7*	*52.7*	*1.4*		*45.6*	*46.7*	*47.6*	*48.6*	*49.6*	*50.5*	*51.6*	*1.5*
17.3	18.2	19.1	20.0	20.9	21.8	22.7	1.4	Chest circ.	17.9	18.6	19.2	19.8	20.5	21.1	21.8	1.0
43.9	*46.3*	*48.4*	*50.8*	*53.2*	*55.3*	*57.7*	*3.5*		*45.4*	*47.2*	*48.7*	*50.4*	*52.1*	*53.6*	*55.4*	*2.5*
5.1	5.5	5.8	6.2	6.6	6.9	7.3	0.6	Upper arm circ.	4.5	5.0	5.5	6.0	6.5	7.0	7.5	0.7
12.9	*13.9*	*14.7*	*15.7*	*16.7*	*17.5*	*18.5*	*1.4*		*11.5*	*12.8*	*14.0*	*15.3*	*16.6*	*17.8*	*19.1*	*1.9*
1.7	2.5	3.3	4.1	4.9	5.7	6.5	1.2	Wrist circ.	1.5	2.3	3.1	3.9	4.6	5.4	6.2	1.2
4.3	*6.4*	*8.3*	*10.4*	*12.5*	*14.4*	*16.5*	*3.1*		*3.9*	*5.9*	*7.8*	*9.8*	*11.8*	*13.7*	*15.7*	*3.0*
6.2	6.8	7.3	7.8	8.4	8.9	9.5	0.8	Calf circ.	6.2	6.7	7.2	7.7	8.2	8.7	9.2	0.7
15.7	*17.2*	*18.5*	*19.9*	*21.3*	*22.6*	*24.1*	*2.1*		*15.8*	*17.1*	*18.3*	*19.6*	*20.9*	*22.1*	*23.4*	*1.9*
								3½ years								
25.8	28.9	31.5	34.6	37.7	40.3	43.4	4.5	Weight	24.0	27.6	30.4	33.7	37.0	39.9	43.4	4.9
11.7	*13.1*	*14.3*	*15.7*	*17.1*	*18.3*	*19.7*	*2.03*		*10.9*	*12.5*	*13.8*	*15.3*	*16.8*	*18.1*	*19.7*	*2.2*
36.1	37.2	38.2	39.4	40.5	41.5	42.6	1.7	Height	35.5	36.7	37.7	38.9	40.1	41.1	42.3	1.7
91.7	*94.6*	*97.1*	*100.0*	*102.9*	*105.4*	*108.3*	*4.2*		*90.1*	*93.1*	*95.8*	*98.8*	*101.8*	*104.5*	*107.5*	*4.4*
19.5	20.5	21.5	22.5	23.6	24.5	25.6	1.5	Sitting height	19.9	20.6	21.3	22.0	22.8	23.5	24.2	1.1
49.5	*52.1*	*54.5*	*57.2*	*59.9*	*62.3*	*64.9*	*3.9*		*50.5*	*52.4*	*54.1*	*56.0*	*57.9*	*59.6*	*61.5*	*2.8*
5.8	6.8	7.6	8.6	9.6	10.5	11.4	1.4	Shoulder width	6.7	7.3	8.0	8.7	9.4	10.0	10.7	1.0
14.8	*17.2*	*19.4*	*21.9*	*24.4*	*26.6*	*29.0*	*3.6*		*16.9*	*18.6*	*20.2*	*22.0*	*23.8*	*25.4*	*27.1*	*2.6*
4.2	5.2	6.2	7.2	8.3	9.3	10.3	1.5	Pelvic width	5.4	6.0	6.5	7.1	7.7	8.2	8.9	0.9
10.7	*13.3*	*15.7*	*18.4*	*21.1*	*23.5*	*26.1*	*3.9*		*13.7*	*15.3*	*16.6*	*18.1*	*19.6*	*20.9*	*22.5*	*2.2*
18.7	19.1	19.4	19.8	20.2	20.5	20.9	0.6	Head circ.	18.3	18.7	19.0	19.3	19.7	20.0	20.4	0.5
47.5	*48.5*	*49.3*	*50.3*	*51.3*	*52.1*	*53.1*	*1.4*		*46.5*	*47.4*	*48.2*	*49.1*	*50.0*	*50.8*	*51.7*	*1.3*
15.2	17.0	18.5	20.2	22.0	23.5	25.2	2.5	Chest circ.	18.2	18.9	19.5	20.2	20.9	21.5	22.2	1.0
38.7	*43.1*	*47.0*	*51.4*	*55.8*	*59.7*	*64.1*	*6.4*		*46.3*	*48.1*	*49.6*	*51.3*	*53.0*	*54.5*	*56.3*	*2.5*
4.8	5.3	5.7	6.2	6.7	7.1	7.6	0.7	Upper arm circ.	4.8	5.3	5.7	6.1	6.6	7.0	7.5	0.7
12.2	*13.5*	*14.6*	*15.8*	*17.0*	*18.1*	*19.4*	*1.8*		*12.2*	*13.4*	*14.4*	*15.6*	*16.8*	*17.8*	*19.0*	*1.7*
1.8	2.6	3.3	4.2	5.0	5.7	6.6	1.2	Wrist circ.	1.6	2.4	3.1	3.9	4.7	5.5	6.3	1.2
4.5	*6.6*	*8.5*	*10.6*	*12.7*	*14.6*	*16.7*	*3.1*		*4.1*	*6.1*	*8.0*	*10.0*	*12.0*	*13.9*	*15.9*	*3.0*
6.3	6.9	7.4	8.0	8.6	9.1	9.8	0.9	Calf circ.	6.7	7.2	7.5	7.9	8.3	8.7	9.1	0.6
16.0	*17.6*	*18.9*	*20.4*	*21.9*	*23.2*	*24.8*	*2.2*		*17.1*	*18.2*	*19.1*	*20.1*	*21.1*	*22.0*	*23.1*	*1.5*

[1] Heimendinger, J., *Helv. paediat. Acta*, **19**, suppl. 13 (1964). From measurements made in the period 1956–1957 on 2150 boys and 2150 girls in Basle, Switzerland.

Normal Measurements During Growth – 4 Years to 5 Years[1]

Weight in pounds and *kilogrammes*; other measurements in inches and *centimetres* (*P* = percentile)

Boys									Girls							
95%									95%							
	80%									80%						
		50%									50%					
$P_{2.5}$	P_{10}	P_{25}	P_{50}	P_{75}	P_{90}	$P_{97.5}$	s		$P_{2.5}$	P_{10}	P_{25}	P_{50}	P_{75}	P_{90}	$P_{97.5}$	s
								4 years								
27.8	30.9	33.7	36.8	39.9	42.8	45.9	4.5	Weight	25.8	29.3	32.4	35.9	39.5	42.5	46.1	5.1
12.6	*14.0*	*15.3*	*16.7*	*18.1*	*19.4*	*20.8*	*2.05*		*11.7*	*13.3*	*14.7*	*16.3*	*17.9*	*19.3*	*20.9*	*2.3*
37.4	38.5	39.6	40.7	41.9	43.0	44.1	1.7	Height	36.8	38.0	39.1	40.3	41.5	42.6	43.8	1.8
95.0	*97.9*	*100.6*	*103.5*	*106.4*	*109.1*	*112.0*	*4.3*		*93.4*	*96.5*	*99.2*	*102.3*	*105.4*	*108.1*	*111.2*	*4.5*
19.8	20.9	21.9	22.9	24.0	25.0	26.0	1.6	Sitting height	20.4	21.1	21.8	22.5	23.2	23.9	24.6	1.1
50.3	*53.0*	*55.5*	*58.2*	*60.9*	*63.4*	*66.1*	*4.0*		*51.8*	*53.6*	*55.3*	*57.1*	*58.9*	*60.6*	*62.4*	*2.7*
6.5	7.5	8.2	8.9	9.7	10.4	10.8	1.1	Shoulder width	6.9	7.6	8.2	8.9	9.6	10.3	10.9	1.0
16.4	*19.1*	*20.8*	*22.7*	*24.6*	*26.3*	*27.4*	*2.8*		*17.6*	*19.3*	*20.9*	*22.7*	*24.5*	*26.1*	*27.8*	*2.6*
4.8	5.7	6.5	7.4	8.3	9.1	10.0	1.3	Pelvic width	5.6	6.2	6.7	7.3	7.8	8.3	8.7	0.8
12.3	*14.5*	*16.6*	*18.8*	*21.0*	*23.1*	*25.3*	*3.3*		*14.3*	*15.8*	*17.1*	*18.5*	*19.9*	*21.2*	*22.2*	*2.1*
18.8	19.2	19.5	19.9	20.3	20.6	21.0	0.6	Head circ.	18.5	18.9	19.2	19.5	19.9	20.2	20.6	0.5
47.8	*48.8*	*49.6*	*50.6*	*51.6*	*52.4*	*53.4*	*1.4*		*47.0*	*47.9*	*48.7*	*49.6*	*50.5*	*51.3*	*52.2*	*1.3*
15.2	17.0	18.7	20.5	22.3	24.0	25.8	2.7	Chest circ.	18.4	19.1	19.7	20.4	21.0	21.6	22.3	1.0
38.6	*43.3*	*47.5*	*52.1*	*56.7*	*60.9*	*65.6*	*6.8*		*46.7*	*48.5*	*50.0*	*51.7*	*53.4*	*54.9*	*56.7*	*2.5*
4.5	5.2	5.7	6.3	6.9	7.4	8.0	0.9	Upper arm circ.	5.2	5.6	5.9	6.3	6.7	7.0	7.4	0.6
11.5	*13.1*	*14.4*	*15.9*	*17.4*	*18.7*	*20.3*	*2.2*		*13.1*	*14.1*	*14.9*	*15.9*	*16.9*	*17.7*	*18.7*	*1.4*
1.9	2.7	3.5	4.3	5.0	5.8	6.6	1.2	Wrist circ.	1.8	2.6	3.3	4.1	4.8	5.6	6.3	1.1
4.9	*6.9*	*8.8*	*10.8*	*12.8*	*14.7*	*16.7*	*3.0*		*4.6*	*6.5*	*8.3*	*10.3*	*12.3*	*14.1*	*16.0*	*2.9*
6.4	7.0	7.6	8.2	8.9	9.4	10.0	0.9	Calf circ.	7.0	7.4	7.8	8.1	8.5	8.9	9.3	0.6
16.3	*17.9*	*19.3*	*20.9*	*22.5*	*23.9*	*25.5*	*2.3*		*17.9*	*18.9*	*19.7*	*20.7*	*21.7*	*22.5*	*23.5*	*1.4*
								4½ years								
30.0	33.3	36.2	39.2	42.3	45.2	48.5	4.7	Weight	27.6	31.3	34.6	38.1	41.7	45.0	48.7	5.3
13.6	*15.1*	*16.4*	*17.8*	*19.2*	*20.5*	*22.0*	*2.12*		*12.5*	*14.2*	*15.7*	*17.3*	*18.9*	*20.4*	*22.1*	*2.4*
38.6	39.8	40.9	42.1	43.3	44.4	45.6	1.8	Height	38.1	39.4	40.4	41.7	42.9	43.9	45.2	1.8
98.0	*101.1*	*103.8*	*106.9*	*110.0*	*112.7*	*115.8*	*4.5*		*96.9*	*100.0*	*102.7*	*105.8*	*108.9*	*111.6*	*114.7*	*4.5*
20.7	21.6	22.4	23.3	24.2	25.0	25.9	1.3	Sitting height	20.7	21.4	22.1	22.9	23.7	24.4	25.2	1.1
52.7	*54.9*	*57.0*	*59.2*	*61.4*	*63.5*	*65.7*	*3.3*		*52.5*	*54.4*	*56.2*	*58.2*	*60.2*	*62.0*	*63.9*	*2.9*
7.0	8.0	8.6	9.3	9.9	10.5	10.9	1.0	Shoulder width	7.3	8.0	8.5	9.2	9.8	10.4	11.1	0.9
17.7	*20.3*	*21.8*	*23.5*	*25.2*	*26.7*	*27.7*	*2.5*		*18.5*	*20.2*	*21.7*	*23.3*	*24.9*	*26.4*	*28.1*	*2.4*
5.6	6.3	6.9	7.5	8.2	8.8	9.5	1.0	Pelvic width	6.0	6.5	7.0	7.4	7.9	8.3	8.9	0.7
14.1	*15.9*	*17.4*	*19.1*	*20.8*	*22.3*	*24.1*	*2.5*		*15.3*	*16.6*	*17.7*	*18.9*	*20.1*	*21.2*	*22.5*	*1.8*
18.9	19.3	19.6	20.0	20.4	20.7	21.1	0.6	Head circ.	18.6	19.0	19.3	19.7	20.1	20.4	20.8	0.6
48.0	*49.0*	*49.8*	*50.8*	*51.8*	*52.6*	*53.6*	*1.4*		*47.2*	*48.2*	*49.0*	*50.0*	*51.0*	*51.8*	*52.8*	*1.4*
15.4	17.3	18.9	20.7	22.6	24.2	26.1	2.7	Chest circ.	18.5	19.2	19.8	20.5	21.2	21.9	22.5	1.0
39.2	*43.9*	*48.1*	*52.7*	*57.3*	*61.5*	*66.2*	*6.8*		*47.0*	*48.7*	*50.3*	*52.1*	*53.9*	*55.5*	*57.2*	*2.6*
4.6	5.2	5.7	6.3	6.9	7.4	8.1	0.9	Upper arm circ.	5.4	5.7	6.1	6.4	6.7	7.0	7.3	0.5
11.7	*13.3*	*14.6*	*16.1*	*17.6*	*18.9*	*20.5*	*2.2*		*13.8*	*14.6*	*15.4*	*16.2*	*17.0*	*17.8*	*18.6*	*1.2*
2.0	2.8	3.6	4.4	5.2	5.9	6.7	1.2	Wrist circ.	2.2	2.9	3.5	4.3	5.0	5.6	6.3	1.1
5.2	*7.2*	*9.1*	*11.1*	*13.1*	*15.0*	*17.0*	*3.0*		*5.5*	*7.3*	*9.0*	*10.8*	*12.6*	*14.3*	*16.1*	*2.7*
6.5	7.2	7.8	8.4	9.1	9.6	10.2	0.9	Calf circ.	7.2	7.6	8.0	8.3	8.7	9.1	9.4	0.6
16.6	*18.3*	*19.8*	*21.4*	*23.0*	*24.5*	*26.0*	*2.4*		*18.4*	*19.4*	*20.2*	*21.2*	*22.2*	*23.0*	*24.0*	*1.4*
								5 years								
32.2	35.5	38.4	41.7	45.0	47.8	51.1	4.8	Weight	29.8	33.5	36.8	40.3	43.9	47.2	50.9	5.3
14.6	*16.1*	*17.4*	*18.9*	*20.4*	*21.7*	*23.2*	*2.19*		*13.5*	*15.2*	*16.7*	*18.3*	*19.9*	*21.4*	*23.1*	*2.4*
39.8	41.0	42.2	43.4	44.6	45.7	47.0	1.8	Height	39.6	40.7	41.8	43.0	44.2	45.2	46.4	1.7
101.1	*104.2*	*107.1*	*110.2*	*113.3*	*116.2*	*119.3*	*4.6*		*100.5*	*103.5*	*106.2*	*109.2*	*112.2*	*114.9*	*117.9*	*4.4*
21.5	22.2	22.9	23.7	24.5	25.2	25.9	1.1	Sitting height	20.9	21.8	22.5	23.3	24.2	24.9	25.7	1.2
54.5	*56.4*	*58.2*	*60.2*	*62.2*	*64.0*	*65.9*	*2.9*		*53.2*	*55.3*	*57.2*	*59.3*	*61.4*	*63.3*	*65.4*	*3.1*
7.4	8.3	8.9	9.5	10.2	10.7	11.1	0.9	Shoulder width	7.8	8.4	8.9	9.4	10.0	10.5	11.1	0.8
18.9	*21.2*	*22.6*	*24.2*	*25.8*	*27.2*	*28.1*	*2.3*		*19.8*	*21.3*	*22.6*	*24.0*	*25.4*	*26.7*	*28.2*	*2.1*
5.9	6.6	7.1	7.7	8.3	8.8	9.4	0.9	Pelvic width	6.4	6.8	7.2	7.6	8.1	8.5	8.9	0.6
15.1	*16.7*	*18.0*	*19.5*	*21.0*	*22.3*	*23.9*	*2.2*		*16.2*	*17.3*	*18.3*	*19.4*	*20.5*	*21.5*	*22.6*	*1.6*
18.9	19.3	19.7	20.1	20.5	20.8	21.3	0.6	Head circ.	18.7	19.1	19.4	19.8	20.2	20.5	20.9	0.6
48.0	*49.1*	*50.0*	*51.0*	*52.0*	*52.9*	*54.0*	*1.5*		*47.5*	*48.5*	*49.3*	*50.3*	*51.3*	*52.1*	*53.1*	*1.4*
15.9	17.7	19.3	21.0	22.8	24.3	26.1	2.6	Chest circ.	18.7	19.3	20.0	20.7	21.4	22.0	22.7	1.0
40.5	*45.0*	*49.0*	*53.4*	*57.8*	*61.8*	*66.3*	*6.5*		*47.4*	*49.1*	*50.7*	*52.5*	*54.3*	*55.9*	*57.6*	*2.6*
5.0	5.5	5.9	6.4	6.9	7.3	7.8	0.7	Upper arm circ.	5.7	6.0	6.3	6.5	6.8	7.1	7.4	0.4
12.7	*14.0*	*15.1*	*16.3*	*17.5*	*18.6*	*19.9*	*1.8*		*14.4*	*15.2*	*15.9*	*16.6*	*17.3*	*18.0*	*18.8*	*1.1*
2.2	3.0	3.7	4.4	5.2	5.9	6.7	1.1	Wrist circ.	2.6	3.3	3.8	4.4	5.0	5.5	6.1	0.9
5.6	*7.5*	*9.3*	*11.3*	*13.3*	*15.1*	*17.0*	*2.9*		*6.7*	*8.3*	*9.6*	*11.1*	*12.6*	*13.9*	*15.5*	*2.2*
6.7	7.4	8.0	8.6	9.2	9.8	10.5	0.9	Calf circ.	7.5	7.9	8.2	8.6	9.0	9.3	9.7	0.6
17.0	*18.7*	*20.2*	*21.8*	*23.4*	*24.9*	*26.6*	*2.4*		*19.0*	*20.0*	*20.8*	*21.8*	*22.8*	*23.6*	*24.6*	*1.4*

[1] Heimendinger, J., *Helv. paediat. Acta*, **19**, suppl. 13 (1964). From measurements made in the period 1956–1957 on 2150 boys and 2150 girls in Basle, Switzerland.

Normal Measurements During Growth – 5½ Years to 6½ Years[1]

Weight in pounds and *kilogrammes*; other measurements in inches and *centimetres* (P = percentile)

Boys									Girls							
95%									95%							
	80%									80%						
		50%									50%					
$P_{2.5}$	P_{10}	P_{25}	P_{50}	P_{75}	P_{90}	$P_{97.5}$	s		$P_{2.5}$	P_{10}	P_{25}	P_{50}	P_{75}	P_{90}	$P_{97.5}$	s
								5½ years								
34.2	37.7	40.8	44.1	47.4	50.5	54.0	5.0	Weight	31.7	35.7	39.0	42.8	46.5	49.8	53.8	5.5
15.5	17.1	18.5	20.0	21.5	22.9	24.5	2.25		14.4	16.2	17.7	19.4	21.1	22.6	24.4	2.5
40.9	42.2	43.3	44.6	45.9	47.1	48.4	1.9	Height	40.8	42.0	43.1	44.3	45.6	46.6	47.8	1.8
103.9	107.2	110.1	113.4	116.7	119.6	122.9	4.8		103.7	106.8	109.5	112.6	115.7	118.4	121.5	4.5
21.8	22.6	23.3	24.1	24.9	25.6	26.4	1.2	Sitting height	21.3	22.2	22.9	23.8	24.6	25.4	26.3	1.3
55.3	57.3	59.2	61.2	63.2	65.1	67.1	3.0		54.1	56.3	58.2	60.4	62.6	64.5	66.7	3.2
7.8	8.7	9.2	9.8	10.4	10.9	11.3	0.9	Shoulder width	8.1	8.7	9.2	9.7	10.3	10.7	11.3	0.8
19.8	22.1	23.4	24.9	26.4	27.7	28.6	2.2		20.7	22.1	23.3	24.7	26.1	27.3	28.7	2.0
6.1	6.7	7.2	7.8	8.3	8.9	9.4	0.8	Pelvic width	6.5	6.9	7.3	7.8	8.3	8.7	9.1	0.7
15.6	17.1	18.4	19.8	21.2	22.5	24.0	2.1		16.4	17.6	18.6	19.8	21.0	22.0	23.2	1.7
18.9	19.3	19.7	20.2	20.6	21.0	21.4	0.6	Head circ.	18.7	19.1	19.5	19.9	20.4	20.7	21.2	0.6
48.0	49.1	50.1	51.2	52.3	53.3	54.4	1.6		47.4	48.5	49.5	50.6	51.7	52.7	53.8	1.6
18.0	19.1	20.2	21.3	22.5	23.5	24.7	1.7	Chest circ.	18.7	19.4	20.1	20.8	21.5	22.2	22.9	1.1
45.7	48.6	51.3	54.2	57.1	59.8	62.7	4.3		47.6	49.4	51.1	52.9	54.7	56.4	58.2	2.7
5.6	5.9	6.2	6.5	6.9	7.2	7.5	0.5	Upper arm circ.	5.8	6.1	6.4	6.7	6.9	7.2	7.5	0.4
14.2	15.0	15.8	16.6	17.4	18.2	19.0	1.2		14.7	15.5	16.2	16.9	17.6	18.3	19.1	1.1
2.6	3.3	3.9	4.5	5.2	5.8	6.5	1.0	Wrist circ.	3.2	3.6	4.0	4.4	4.9	5.3	5.7	0.6
6.5	8.3	9.8	11.5	13.2	14.7	16.5	2.5		8.1	9.2	10.2	11.3	12.4	13.4	14.5	1.6
6.9	7.6	8.1	8.8	9.4	10.0	10.7	0.9	Calf circ.	7.6	8.0	8.4	8.8	9.2	9.5	10.0	0.6
17.5	19.2	20.7	22.3	23.9	25.4	27.1	2.4		19.3	20.4	21.3	22.3	23.3	24.2	25.3	1.5
								6 years								
36.2	39.7	42.8	46.3	49.8	52.9	56.4	5.1	Weight	32.8	37.0	41.0	45.4	49.8	53.8	58.0	6.4
16.4	18.0	19.4	21.0	22.6	24.0	25.6	2.32		14.9	16.8	18.6	20.6	22.6	24.4	26.3	2.9
42.0	43.4	44.6	45.9	47.2	48.3	49.7	1.9	Height	41.7	43.1	44.3	45.6	47.0	48.2	49.5	2.0
106.8	110.2	113.2	116.5	119.8	122.8	126.2	4.9		106.0	109.4	112.5	115.9	119.3	122.4	125.8	5.0
22.0	22.9	23.6	24.5	25.4	26.1	27.0	1.3	Sitting height	21.8	22.6	23.4	24.2	25.0	25.8	26.6	1.2
55.9	58.1	60.0	62.2	64.4	66.3	68.5	3.2		55.4	57.5	59.4	61.5	63.6	65.5	67.6	3.1
8.2	9.0	9.5	10.0	10.6	11.1	11.4	0.8	Shoulder width	8.4	8.9	9.4	10.0	10.5	11.0	11.5	0.8
20.9	22.9	24.1	25.5	26.9	28.1	28.9	2.0		21.3	22.7	23.9	25.3	26.7	27.9	29.3	2.0
6.4	6.9	7.4	8.0	8.5	9.0	9.5	0.8	Pelvic width	6.5	7.0	7.5	8.0	8.4	8.9	9.4	0.7
16.2	17.6	18.8	20.2	21.6	22.8	24.2	2.0		16.6	17.9	19.0	20.2	21.4	22.5	23.8	1.8
18.4	19.1	19.6	20.2	20.9	21.4	22.0	0.9	Head circ.	18.6	19.1	19.5	20.0	20.5	20.9	21.4	0.7
46.8	48.4	49.8	51.4	53.0	54.4	56.0	2.3		47.2	48.5	49.6	50.8	52.0	53.1	54.4	1.8
19.5	20.2	20.9	21.6	22.3	23.0	23.7	1.1	Chest circ.	18.8	19.5	20.2	21.0	21.8	22.5	23.3	1.1
49.6	51.4	53.1	54.9	56.7	58.4	60.2	2.7		47.7	49.6	51.4	53.4	55.4	57.2	59.1	2.9
5.7	6.1	6.3	6.6	6.9	7.2	7.5	0.4	Upper arm circ.	5.8	6.1	6.5	6.8	7.1	7.4	7.7	0.5
14.6	15.4	16.1	16.8	17.5	18.2	19.0	1.1		14.8	15.6	16.4	17.2	18.0	18.8	19.6	1.2
3.0	3.5	4.1	4.6	5.2	5.7	6.3	0.8	Wrist circ.	3.5	3.8	4.1	4.5	4.8	5.2	5.5	0.5
7.5	9.0	10.3	11.7	13.1	14.4	15.9	2.1		8.8	9.7	10.5	11.4	12.3	13.1	14.0	1.3
7.2	7.8	8.3	9.0	9.6	10.2	10.8	0.9	Calf circ.	7.8	8.2	8.6	9.0	9.4	9.8	10.3	0.6
18.2	19.8	21.2	22.8	24.4	25.8	27.4	2.3		19.7	20.8	21.8	22.9	24.0	25.0	26.1	1.6
								6½ years								
37.7	41.4	45.0	48.7	52.5	56.0	59.7	5.6	Weight	32.8	38.1	42.8	48.1	53.4	58.0	63.3	7.7
17.1	18.8	20.4	22.1	23.8	25.4	27.1	2.53		14.9	17.3	19.4	21.8	24.2	26.3	28.7	3.5
43.1	44.5	45.7	47.0	48.4	49.6	50.9	2.0	Height	42.6	44.1	45.5	46.9	48.4	49.7	51.2	2.2
109.6	113.0	116.1	119.5	122.9	126.0	129.4	5.0		108.3	112.1	115.5	119.2	122.9	126.3	130.1	5.5
22.4	23.3	24.0	24.9	25.7	26.5	27.4	1.3	Sitting height	22.2	23.1	23.8	24.6	25.5	26.2	27.0	1.2
56.9	59.1	61.0	63.2	65.4	67.3	69.5	3.2		56.5	58.6	60.5	62.6	64.7	66.6	68.7	3.1
8.5	9.3	9.8	10.3	10.8	11.3	11.5	0.7	Shoulder width	8.5	9.1	9.6	10.2	10.8	11.3	12.0	0.9
21.7	23.7	24.9	26.2	27.5	28.7	29.3	1.9		21.6	23.2	24.5	26.0	27.5	28.8	30.4	2.2
6.5	7.0	7.5	8.1	8.6	9.1	9.6	0.8	Pelvic width	6.7	7.2	7.6	8.1	8.6	9.0	9.5	0.7
16.5	17.9	19.1	20.5	21.9	23.1	24.5	2.0		17.0	18.3	19.4	20.6	21.8	22.9	24.2	1.8
18.3	18.9	19.6	20.3	21.0	21.6	22.3	1.0	Head circ.	18.4	19.0	19.5	20.1	20.6	21.1	21.7	0.8
46.4	48.1	49.7	51.5	53.3	54.9	56.6	2.6		46.8	48.3	49.6	51.0	52.4	53.7	55.2	2.1
19.9	20.6	21.2	21.9	22.6	23.3	23.9	1.0	Chest circ.	18.8	19.6	20.5	21.3	22.2	23.0	23.9	1.3
50.6	52.3	53.9	55.7	57.5	59.1	60.8	2.6		47.7	49.9	52.0	54.2	56.4	58.5	60.7	3.3
5.8	6.1	6.4	6.7	7.0	7.2	7.6	0.4	Upper arm circ.	5.8	6.2	6.5	6.9	7.3	7.6	8.0	0.6
14.8	15.6	16.3	17.0	17.7	18.4	19.2	1.1		14.7	15.7	16.5	17.5	18.5	19.3	20.3	1.4
3.3	3.8	4.2	4.7	5.2	5.6	6.1	0.7	Wrist circ.	3.8	4.1	4.3	4.6	4.8	5.1	5.4	0.4
8.3	9.6	10.7	11.9	13.1	14.2	15.5	1.8		9.6	10.3	10.9	11.6	12.3	12.9	13.6	1.0
7.4	8.0	8.5	9.2	9.8	10.4	11.0	0.9	Calf circ.	8.0	8.4	8.8	9.2	9.6	10.0	10.5	0.6
18.7	20.3	21.7	23.3	24.9	26.3	27.9	2.3		20.2	21.3	22.3	23.4	24.5	25.5	26.6	1.6

[1] HEIMENDINGER, J., *Helv. paediat. Acta*, **19**, suppl. 13 (1964). From measurements made in the period 1956–1957 on 2150 boys and 2150 girls in Basle, Switzerland.

Normal Measurements During Growth – 7 Years to 8 Years[1]

Weight in pounds and *kilogrammes*; other measurements in inches and *centimetres* (P = percentile)

Boys									Girls							
	95%									95%						
		80%									80%					
			50%									50%				
$P_{2.5}$	P_{10}	P_{25}	P_{50}	P_{75}	P_{90}	$P_{97.5}$	s		$P_{2.5}$	P_{10}	P_{25}	P_{50}	P_{75}	P_{90}	$P_{97.5}$	s
								7 years								
39.7	43.7	47.2	51.1	55.1	58.6	62.6	5.8	Weight	34.8	40.6	45.9	51.8	57.8	63.1	68.8	8.6
18.0	*19.8*	*21.4*	*23.2*	*25.0*	*26.6*	*28.4*	*2.61*		*15.8*	*18.4*	*20.8*	*23.5*	*26.2*	*28.6*	*31.2*	*3.9*
44.2	45.6	46.8	48.2	49.6	50.8	52.2	2.0	Height	43.9	45.4	46.7	48.2	49.6	51.0	52.5	2.2
112.3	*115.8*	*118.9*	*122.4*	*125.9*	*129.0*	*132.5*	*5.1*		*111.5*	*115.3*	*118.7*	*122.4*	*126.1*	*129.5*	*133.3*	*5.5*
23.0	23.7	24.5	25.3	26.1	26.8	27.6	1.2	Sitting height	22.7	23.5	24.3	25.1	25.9	26.7	27.5	1.2
58.3	*60.3*	*62.2*	*64.2*	*66.2*	*68.1*	*70.1*	*3.0*		*57.6*	*59.7*	*61.6*	*63.7*	*65.8*	*67.7*	*69.8*	*3.1*
8.9	9.6	10.1	10.6	11.0	11.5	11.7	0.7	Shoulder width	8.8	9.4	9.9	10.5	11.1	11.6	12.2	0.9
22.6	*24.5*	*25.6*	*26.8*	*28.0*	*29.1*	*29.8*	*1.8*		*22.3*	*23.9*	*25.2*	*26.7*	*28.2*	*29.5*	*31.1*	*2.2*
6.7	7.2	7.7	8.2	8.7	9.2	9.7	0.7	Pelvic width	6.9	7.4	7.8	8.3	8.7	9.2	9.7	0.7
17.1	*18.4*	*19.6*	*20.9*	*22.2*	*23.4*	*24.7*	*1.9*		*17.4*	*18.7*	*19.8*	*21.0*	*22.2*	*23.3*	*24.6*	*1.8*
18.2	18.9	19.6	20.3	21.0	21.7	22.4	1.1	Head circ.	18.5	19.1	19.6	20.2	20.7	21.2	21.8	0.8
46.3	*48.1*	*49.8*	*51.6*	*53.4*	*55.1*	*56.9*	*2.7*		*47.0*	*48.5*	*49.8*	*51.2*	*52.6*	*53.9*	*55.4*	*2.1*
20.2	20.9	21.5	22.2	23.0	23.6	24.3	1.1	Chest circ.	19.0	20.0	20.8	21.7	22.7	23.5	24.4	1.4
51.2	*53.0*	*54.7*	*56.5*	*58.3*	*60.0*	*61.8*	*2.7*		*48.3*	*50.7*	*52.8*	*55.2*	*57.6*	*59.7*	*62.1*	*3.5*
5.8	6.1	6.5	6.8	7.1	7.4	7.7	0.5	Upper arm circ.	5.7	6.2	6.6	7.0	7.4	7.8	8.3	0.6
14.8	*15.6*	*16.4*	*17.2*	*18.0*	*18.8*	*19.6*	*1.2*		*14.6*	*15.7*	*16.7*	*17.8*	*18.9*	*19.9*	*21.0*	*1.6*
3.5	3.9	4.3	4.8	5.2	5.6	6.0	0.6	Wrist circ.	3.7	4.0	4.3	4.7	5.0	5.4	5.7	0.5
8.9	*10.0*	*11.0*	*12.1*	*13.2*	*14.2*	*15.3*	*1.6*		*9.3*	*10.2*	*11.0*	*11.9*	*12.8*	*13.6*	*14.5*	*1.3*
7.5	8.1	8.7	9.3	10.0	10.5	11.1	0.9	Calf circ.	8.1	8.6	9.0	9.5	10.0	10.4	10.9	0.7
19.1	*20.7*	*22.1*	*23.7*	*25.3*	*26.7*	*28.3*	*2.3*		*20.5*	*21.8*	*22.9*	*24.1*	*25.3*	*26.4*	*27.7*	*1.8*
								7½ years								
40.3	45.0	48.9	53.6	58.2	62.2	66.8	6.7	Weight	36.8	43.2	49.2	55.6	61.9	67.9	74.3	9.5
18.3	*20.4*	*22.2*	*24.3*	*26.4*	*28.2*	*30.3*	*3.05*		*16.7*	*19.6*	*22.3*	*25.2*	*28.1*	*30.8*	*33.7*	*4.3*
45.3	46.7	47.9	49.3	50.7	51.9	53.3	2.0	Height	45.2	46.7	48.0	49.4	50.8	52.1	53.5	2.1
115.1	*118.6*	*121.7*	*125.2*	*128.7*	*131.8*	*135.3*	*5.1*		*114.9*	*118.5*	*121.8*	*125.4*	*129.0*	*132.3*	*135.9*	*5.3*
23.3	24.1	24.9	25.7	26.5	27.2	28.0	1.2	Sitting height	23.3	24.0	24.7	25.5	26.3	27.0	27.8	1.1
59.3	*61.3*	*63.2*	*65.2*	*67.2*	*69.1*	*71.1*	*3.0*		*59.1*	*61.0*	*62.8*	*64.8*	*66.8*	*68.6*	*70.5*	*2.9*
9.1	9.9	10.4	10.8	11.3	11.7	12.0	0.7	Shoulder width	9.3	9.8	10.2	10.7	11.3	11.7	12.2	0.7
23.2	*25.2*	*26.3*	*27.5*	*28.7*	*29.8*	*30.4*	*1.8*		*23.5*	*24.8*	*26.0*	*27.3*	*28.6*	*29.8*	*31.1*	*1.9*
6.9	7.4	7.9	8.3	8.8	9.3	9.8	0.7	Pelvic width	7.1	7.6	8.0	8.5	8.9	9.3	9.8	0.7
17.6	*18.9*	*20.0*	*21.2*	*22.4*	*23.5*	*24.8*	*1.8*		*18.1*	*19.3*	*20.3*	*21.5*	*22.7*	*23.7*	*24.9*	*1.7*
18.3	19.0	19.6	20.4	21.1	21.7	22.4	1.1	Head circ.	18.6	19.2	19.7	20.2	20.8	21.3	21.9	0.8
46.4	*48.2*	*49.9*	*51.7*	*53.5*	*55.2*	*57.0*	*2.7*		*47.2*	*48.7*	*50.0*	*51.4*	*52.8*	*54.1*	*55.6*	*2.1*
20.3	21.1	21.8	22.6	23.3	24.1	24.8	1.1	Chest circ.	19.3	20.2	21.1	22.1	23.1	24.0	25.0	1.5
51.6	*53.5*	*55.3*	*57.3*	*59.3*	*61.1*	*63.0*	*2.9*		*48.9*	*51.4*	*53.7*	*56.2*	*58.7*	*61.0*	*63.5*	*3.7*
5.8	6.2	6.5	6.9	7.3	7.6	8.0	0.6	Upper arm circ.	5.7	6.3	6.7	7.2	7.6	8.1	8.6	0.7
14.7	*15.7*	*16.5*	*17.5*	*18.5*	*19.3*	*20.3*	*1.4*		*14.6*	*15.9*	*17.0*	*18.2*	*19.4*	*20.5*	*21.8*	*1.8*
3.7	4.1	4.4	4.8	5.2	5.6	5.9	0.6	Wrist circ.	3.3	3.8	4.3	4.8	5.4	5.9	6.4	0.8
9.5	*10.5*	*11.3*	*12.3*	*13.3*	*14.1*	*15.1*	*1.4*		*8.3*	*9.7*	*10.9*	*12.3*	*13.7*	*14.9*	*16.3*	*2.0*
7.7	8.3	8.9	9.5	10.2	10.7	11.3	0.9	Calf circ.	8.3	8.8	9.3	9.8	10.4	10.9	11.4	0.8
19.6	*21.2*	*22.6*	*24.2*	*25.8*	*27.2*	*28.8*	*2.3*		*21.0*	*22.4*	*23.6*	*25.0*	*26.4*	*27.6*	*29.0*	*2.0*
								8 years								
40.6	45.9	50.5	55.8	61.1	65.7	71.0	7.7	Weight	38.8	45.6	52.0	58.9	65.7	72.1	78.9	10.1
18.4	*20.8*	*22.9*	*25.3*	*27.7*	*29.8*	*32.2*	*3.49*		*17.6*	*20.7*	*23.6*	*26.7*	*29.8*	*32.7*	*35.8*	*4.6*
46.3	47.8	49.0	50.4	51.8	53.0	54.4	2.0	Height	46.6	47.9	49.1	50.5	51.8	53.0	54.4	2.0
117.7	*121.3*	*124.5*	*128.0*	*131.5*	*134.7*	*138.3*	*5.2*		*118.3*	*121.7*	*124.8*	*128.2*	*131.6*	*134.7*	*138.1*	*5.0*
23.6	24.4	25.2	26.1	26.9	27.7	28.5	1.3	Sitting height	23.8	24.5	25.2	25.9	26.7	27.4	28.1	1.1
59.9	*62.1*	*64.0*	*66.2*	*68.4*	*70.3*	*72.5*	*3.2*		*60.4*	*62.3*	*64.0*	*65.9*	*67.8*	*69.5*	*71.4*	*2.8*
9.5	10.2	10.6	11.1	11.5	11.9	12.2	0.7	Shoulder width	9.7	10.2	10.6	11.0	11.5	11.9	12.4	0.7
24.1	*25.9*	*26.9*	*28.1*	*29.3*	*30.3*	*30.9*	*1.7*		*24.6*	*25.8*	*26.8*	*28.0*	*29.2*	*30.2*	*31.4*	*1.7*
7.3	7.8	8.1	8.5	8.9	9.3	9.7	0.6	Pelvic width	7.4	7.8	8.2	8.6	9.1	9.4	9.8	0.6
18.6	*19.7*	*20.6*	*21.6*	*22.6*	*23.5*	*24.6*	*1.5*		*18.8*	*19.8*	*20.8*	*21.9*	*23.0*	*24.0*	*25.0*	*1.6*
18.3	19.0	19.7	20.4	21.1	21.8	22.5	1.1	Head circ.	18.5	19.1	19.6	20.3	20.9	21.5	22.1	0.9
46.5	*48.3*	*50.0*	*51.8*	*53.6*	*55.3*	*57.1*	*2.7*		*46.9*	*48.5*	*49.9*	*51.5*	*53.1*	*54.5*	*56.1*	*2.3*
20.5	21.3	22.0	22.9	23.7	24.4	25.3	1.2	Chest circ.	19.4	20.5	21.4	22.5	23.5	24.5	25.5	1.5
52.0	*54.1*	*56.0*	*58.1*	*60.2*	*62.1*	*64.2*	*3.1*		*49.4*	*52.0*	*54.4*	*57.1*	*59.8*	*62.2*	*64.8*	*3.9*
5.8	6.3	6.6	7.0	7.4	7.8	8.2	0.6	Upper arm circ.	5.7	6.3	6.7	7.3	7.8	8.3	8.9	0.8
14.8	*15.9*	*16.8*	*17.8*	*18.8*	*19.7*	*20.8*	*1.5*		*14.5*	*15.9*	*17.1*	*18.5*	*19.9*	*21.1*	*22.5*	*2.0*
3.9	4.3	4.6	4.9	5.3	5.6	5.9	0.5	Wrist circ.	3.4	3.9	4.4	5.0	5.5	6.0	6.5	0.8
9.9	*10.8*	*11.6*	*12.5*	*13.4*	*14.2*	*15.1*	*1.3*		*8.6*	*10.0*	*11.2*	*12.6*	*14.0*	*15.2*	*16.6*	*2.0*
7.9	8.5	9.1	9.7	10.4	10.9	11.5	0.9	Calf circ.	8.3	9.0	9.5	10.1	10.7	11.2	11.8	0.9
20.1	*21.7*	*23.1*	*24.7*	*26.3*	*27.7*	*29.3*	*2.3*		*21.2*	*22.8*	*24.1*	*25.6*	*27.1*	*28.4*	*30.0*	*2.2*

[1] HEIMENDINGER, J., *Helv. paediat. Acta*, **19**, suppl. 13 (1964). From measurements made in the period 1956–1957 on 2150 boys and 2150 girls in Basle, Switzerland.

Normal Measurements During Growth – 8½ Years to 9½ Years[1]

Weight in pounds and *kilogrammes*; other measurements in inches and *centimetres* (*P* = percentile)

Boys									Girls							
	95%									95%						
		80%									80%					
			50%									50%				
$P_{2.5}$	P_{10}	P_{25}	P_{50}	P_{75}	P_{90}	$P_{97.5}$	s		$P_{2.5}$	P_{10}	P_{25}	P_{50}	P_{75}	P_{90}	$P_{97.5}$	s
								8½ years								
39.0	45.6	51.6	58.2	64.8	70.8	77.4	9.6	Weight	40.3	47.6	54.0	61.3	68.6	75.0	82.2	10.6
17.7	*20.7*	*23.4*	*26.4*	*29.4*	*32.1*	*35.1*	*4.37*		*18.3*	*21.6*	*24.5*	*27.8*	*31.1*	*34.0*	*37.3*	*4.8*
47.5	48.9	50.1	51.5	52.8	54.1	55.4	2.0	Height	47.5	48.9	50.1	51.5	52.9	54.1	55.5	2.0
120.6	*124.1*	*127.2*	*130.7*	*134.2*	*137.3*	*140.8*	*5.1*		*120.7*	*124.2*	*127.3*	*130.8*	*134.3*	*137.4*	*140.9*	*5.1*
23.8	24.7	25.6	26.5	27.4	28.2	29.1	1.3	Sitting height	24.3	25.0	25.7	26.4	27.1	27.8	28.5	1.1
60.5	*62.8*	*64.9*	*67.2*	*69.5*	*71.6*	*73.9*	*3.4*		*61.7*	*63.5*	*65.2*	*67.0*	*68.8*	*70.5*	*72.3*	*2.7*
9.8	10.5	10.9	11.3	11.7	12.1	12.3	0.6	Shoulder width	9.9	10.4	10.8	11.3	11.7	12.1	12.6	0.7
24.9	*26.6*	*27.6*	*28.7*	*29.8*	*30.8*	*31.3*	*1.6*		*25.2*	*26.4*	*27.4*	*28.6*	*29.8*	*30.8*	*32.0*	*1.7*
7.6	8.0	8.3	8.7	9.0	9.3	9.7	0.5	Pelvic width	7.6	8.0	8.3	8.8	9.2	9.6	10.0	0.6
19.4	*20.3*	*21.1*	*22.0*	*22.9*	*23.7*	*24.6*	*1.3*		*19.2*	*20.2*	*21.2*	*22.3*	*23.4*	*24.4*	*25.4*	*1.6*
18.3	19.0	19.7	20.4	21.2	21.9	22.6	1.1	Head circ.	18.1	18.9	19.6	20.3	21.1	21.7	22.5	1.1
46.4	*48.3*	*50.0*	*51.9*	*53.8*	*55.5*	*57.4*	*2.8*		*46.1*	*48.0*	*49.7*	*51.6*	*53.5*	*55.2*	*57.1*	*2.8*
20.7	21.6	22.4	23.2	24.1	24.8	25.7	1.3	Chest circ.	19.5	20.7	21.7	22.8	23.9	24.9	26.1	1.7
52.7	*54.9*	*56.8*	*59.0*	*61.2*	*63.1*	*65.3*	*3.2*		*49.6*	*52.5*	*55.0*	*57.9*	*60.8*	*63.3*	*66.2*	*4.2*
5.9	6.4	6.7	7.1	7.5	7.9	8.3	0.6	Upper arm circ.	5.7	6.3	6.9	7.4	8.0	8.5	9.1	0.8
15.1	*16.2*	*17.1*	*18.1*	*19.1*	*20.0*	*21.1*	*1.5*		*14.6*	*16.1*	*17.4*	*18.8*	*20.2*	*21.5*	*23.0*	*2.1*
4.0	4.3	4.6	5.0	5.4	5.7	6.0	0.5	Wrist circ.	3.7	4.1	4.5	5.0	5.5	5.9	6.3	0.7
10.1	*11.0*	*11.8*	*12.7*	*13.6*	*14.4*	*15.3*	*1.3*		*9.3*	*10.5*	*11.5*	*12.7*	*13.9*	*14.9*	*16.1*	*1.7*
8.1	8.7	9.3	9.9	10.6	11.1	11.7	0.9	Calf circ.	8.4	9.0	9.6	10.2	10.8	11.4	12.0	0.9
20.6	*22.2*	*23.6*	*25.2*	*26.8*	*28.2*	*29.8*	*2.3*		*21.3*	*22.9*	*24.3*	*25.9*	*27.5*	*28.9*	*30.5*	*2.3*
								9 years								
41.2	47.8	54.0	60.6	67.2	73.4	80.0	9.8	Weight	42.5	49.8	56.2	63.5	70.8	77.2	84.4	10.6
18.7	*21.7*	*24.5*	*27.5*	*30.5*	*33.3*	*36.3*	*4.46*		*19.3*	*22.6*	*25.5*	*28.8*	*32.1*	*35.0*	*38.3*	*4.8*
48.5	49.9	51.1	52.5	53.9	55.1	56.5	2.0	Height	48.4	49.8	51.1	52.4	53.8	55.1	56.5	2.0
123.2	*126.7*	*129.8*	*133.3*	*136.8*	*139.9*	*143.4*	*5.1*		*122.9*	*126.5*	*129.7*	*133.2*	*136.7*	*139.9*	*143.5*	*5.2*
23.9	24.9	25.8	26.8	27.8	28.7	29.7	1.5	Sitting height	24.4	25.2	25.9	26.8	27.6	28.3	29.2	1.2
60.8	*63.3*	*65.6*	*68.1*	*70.6*	*72.9*	*75.4*	*3.7*		*61.9*	*64.0*	*65.9*	*68.0*	*70.1*	*72.0*	*74.1*	*3.1*
10.0	10.7	11.1	11.5	12.0	12.4	12.6	0.6	Shoulder width	10.0	10.6	11.0	11.5	11.9	12.4	12.9	0.7
25.5	*27.2*	*28.2*	*29.3*	*30.4*	*31.4*	*31.9*	*1.6*		*25.5*	*26.8*	*27.9*	*29.1*	*30.3*	*31.4*	*32.7*	*1.8*
7.9	8.2	8.5	8.8	9.1	9.4	9.8	0.5	Pelvic width	7.7	8.1	8.5	8.9	9.4	9.8	10.2	0.6
20.0	*20.8*	*21.6*	*22.4*	*23.2*	*24.0*	*24.8*	*1.2*		*19.6*	*20.6*	*21.6*	*22.7*	*23.8*	*24.8*	*25.8*	*1.6*
18.3	19.1	19.7	20.5	21.2	21.9	22.6	1.1	Head circ.	17.8	18.7	19.5	20.4	21.3	22.1	23.0	1.3
46.5	*48.4*	*50.1*	*52.0*	*53.9*	*55.6*	*57.5*	*2.8*		*45.1*	*47.4*	*49.5*	*51.8*	*54.1*	*56.2*	*58.5*	*3.4*
21.2	22.1	22.8	23.7	24.6	25.3	26.2	1.3	Chest circ.	19.3	20.6	21.8	23.1	24.4	25.6	26.9	1.9
53.9	*56.1*	*58.0*	*60.2*	*62.4*	*64.3*	*66.5*	*3.2*		*48.9*	*52.3*	*55.3*	*58.6*	*61.9*	*64.9*	*68.3*	*4.9*
6.1	6.5	6.9	7.2	7.6	8.0	8.3	0.6	Upper arm circ.	5.8	6.4	6.9	7.5	8.1	8.6	9.3	0.9
15.6	*16.6*	*17.4*	*18.4*	*19.4*	*20.2*	*21.2*	*1.4*		*14.7*	*16.3*	*17.6*	*19.1*	*20.6*	*21.9*	*23.5*	*2.2*
4.1	4.4	4.8	5.1	5.4	5.7	6.0	0.5	Wrist circ.	3.9	4.3	4.6	5.0	5.4	5.7	6.1	0.6
10.5	*11.3*	*12.1*	*12.9*	*13.7*	*14.5*	*15.3*	*1.2*		*9.9*	*10.9*	*11.7*	*12.7*	*13.7*	*14.5*	*15.5*	*1.4*
8.3	8.9	9.4	10.1	10.7	11.3	11.9	0.9	Calf circ.	8.4	9.1	9.7	10.3	10.9	11.5	12.2	0.9
21.0	*22.6*	*24.0*	*25.6*	*27.2*	*28.6*	*30.2*	*2.3*		*21.4*	*23.1*	*24.6*	*26.2*	*27.8*	*29.3*	*31.0*	*2.4*
								9½ years								
41.9	49.2	55.8	63.1	70.3	76.9	84.2	10.7	Weight	45.2	52.5	58.9	66.1	73.4	79.8	87.1	10.6
19.0	*22.3*	*25.3*	*28.6*	*31.9*	*34.9*	*38.2*	*4.86*		*20.5*	*23.8*	*26.7*	*30.0*	*33.3*	*36.2*	*39.5*	*4.8*
49.3	50.7	52.0	53.5	54.9	56.2	57.6	2.1	Height	49.1	50.6	51.9	53.3	54.8	56.1	57.5	2.1
125.3	*128.9*	*132.2*	*135.8*	*139.4*	*142.7*	*146.3*	*5.3*		*124.7*	*128.4*	*131.7*	*135.4*	*139.1*	*142.4*	*146.1*	*5.4*
24.0	25.1	26.1	27.2	28.3	29.3	30.4	1.6	Sitting height	24.0	25.1	26.1	27.2	28.3	29.3	30.4	1.6
61.0	*63.8*	*66.3*	*69.1*	*71.9*	*74.4*	*77.2*	*4.1*		*61.0*	*63.8*	*66.3*	*69.1*	*71.9*	*74.4*	*77.2*	*4.1*
10.5	10.9	11.3	11.8	12.2	12.6	13.0	0.6	Shoulder width	10.1	10.6	11.1	11.6	12.1	12.6	13.1	0.7
26.7	*27.8*	*28.8*	*29.9*	*31.0*	*32.0*	*33.1*	*1.6*		*25.7*	*27.0*	*28.2*	*29.5*	*30.8*	*32.0*	*33.3*	*1.9*
8.0	8.3	8.6	9.0	9.3	9.6	10.0	0.5	Pelvic width	7.9	8.3	8.7	9.1	9.5	9.9	10.3	0.6
20.2	*21.1*	*21.9*	*22.8*	*23.7*	*24.5*	*25.4*	*1.3*		*20.0*	*21.0*	*22.0*	*23.1*	*24.2*	*25.2*	*26.2*	*1.6*
18.3	19.1	19.8	20.5	21.3	21.9	22.7	1.1	Head circ.	17.5	18.5	19.4	20.4	21.5	22.4	23.4	1.5
46.6	*48.5*	*50.2*	*52.1*	*54.0*	*55.7*	*57.6*	*2.8*		*44.4*	*47.0*	*49.3*	*51.9*	*54.5*	*56.8*	*59.4*	*3.8*
21.7	22.5	23.3	24.1	25.0	25.7	26.6	1.3	Chest circ.	19.1	20.6	21.9	23.4	24.8	26.2	27.7	2.2
55.0	*57.2*	*59.1*	*61.3*	*63.5*	*65.4*	*67.6*	*3.2*		*48.5*	*52.3*	*55.7*	*59.4*	*63.1*	*66.5*	*70.3*	*5.5*
6.3	6.7	7.0	7.4	7.8	8.1	8.5	0.6	Upper arm circ.	5.8	6.5	7.0	7.6	8.3	8.8	9.4	0.9
15.9	*16.9*	*17.7*	*18.7*	*19.7*	*20.5*	*21.5*	*1.4*		*14.8*	*16.4*	*17.8*	*19.4*	*21.0*	*22.4*	*24.0*	*2.3*
4.2	4.5	4.8	5.2	5.5	5.8	6.1	0.5	Wrist circ.	3.9	4.3	4.7	5.1	5.5	5.8	6.3	0.6
10.7	*11.5*	*12.3*	*13.1*	*13.9*	*14.7*	*15.5*	*1.2*		*9.9*	*11.0*	*11.9*	*12.9*	*13.9*	*14.8*	*15.9*	*1.5*
8.5	9.1	9.6	10.3	10.9	11.5	12.1	0.9	Calf circ.	8.6	9.3	9.8	10.5	11.1	11.7	12.4	0.9
21.5	*23.1*	*24.5*	*26.1*	*27.7*	*29.1*	*30.7*	*2.3*		*21.8*	*23.5*	*25.0*	*26.6*	*28.2*	*29.7*	*31.4*	*2.4*

[1] HEIMENDINGER, J., *Helv. paediat. Acta*, **19**, suppl. 13 (1964). From measurements made in the period 1956–1957 on 2150 boys and 2150 girls in Basle, Switzerland.

Weight in pounds and *kilogrammes*; other measurements in inches and *centimetres* (P = percentile)

Boys									Girls							
			95%									95%				
			80%									80%				
			50%									50%				
$P_{2.5}$	P_{10}	P_{25}	P_{50}	P_{75}	P_{90}	$P_{97.5}$	s		$P_{2.5}$	P_{10}	P_{25}	P_{50}	P_{75}	P_{90}	$P_{97.5}$	s
								10 years								
43.9	51.8	59.1	67.2	75.4	82.7	90.6	11.8	Weight	46.7	54.7	61.7	69.4	77.2	84.2	92.2	11.5
19.9	*23.5*	*26.8*	*30.5*	*34.2*	*37.5*	*41.1*	*5.37*		*21.2*	*24.8*	*28.0*	*31.5*	*35.0*	*38.2*	*41.8*	*5.2*
50.2	51.7	53.0	54.4	55.9	57.2	58.7	2.2	Height	49.8	51.3	52.6	54.1	55.6	57.0	58.5	2.2
127.4	*131.2*	*134.6*	*138.3*	*142.0*	*145.4*	*149.2*	*5.5*		*126.4*	*130.2*	*133.7*	*137.5*	*141.3*	*144.8*	*148.6*	*5.6*
23.9	25.2	26.3	27.6	28.9	30.0	31.3	1.9	Sitting height	23.9	25.2	26.3	27.6	28.9	30.1	31.4	1.9
60.8	*64.0*	*66.9*	*70.1*	*73.3*	*76.2*	*79.4*	*4.7*		*60.7*	*64.0*	*66.9*	*70.2*	*73.5*	*76.4*	*79.7*	*4.8*
10.7	11.2	11.6	12.0	12.4	12.8	13.3	0.6	Shoulder width	10.2	10.8	11.3	11.8	12.4	12.8	13.4	0.8
27.3	*28.4*	*29.4*	*30.5*	*31.6*	*32.6*	*33.7*	*1.6*		*26.0*	*27.4*	*28.6*	*30.0*	*31.4*	*32.6*	*34.0*	*2.0*
8.1	8.5	8.7	9.2	9.2	9.9	10.3	0.6	Pelvic width	8.0	8.4	8.8	9.3	9.8	10.2	10.6	0.7
20.5	*21.5*	*22.2*	*23.3*	*23.4*	*25.1*	*26.1*	*1.4*		*20.2*	*21.4*	*22.4*	*23.6*	*24.8*	*25.8*	*27.0*	*1.7*
18.4	19.2	19.8	20.6	21.3	22.0	22.8	1.1	Head circ.	17.3	18.4	19.4	20.5	21.6	22.6	23.7	1.6
46.8	*48.7*	*50.4*	*52.3*	*54.2*	*55.9*	*57.8*	*2.8*		*43.9*	*46.7*	*49.2*	*52.0*	*54.8*	*57.3*	*60.1*	*4.1*
21.9	22.8	23.6	24.5	25.4	26.2	27.1	1.3	Chest circ.	19.1	20.7	22.1	23.7	25.2	26.6	28.2	2.3
55.5	*57.8*	*59.9*	*62.2*	*64.5*	*66.6*	*68.9*	*3.4*		*48.6*	*52.6*	*56.1*	*60.1*	*64.1*	*67.6*	*71.6*	*5.8*
6.3	6.8	7.1	7.5	7.9	8.3	8.7	0.6	Upper arm circ.	5.8	6.5	7.1	7.8	8.5	9.1	9.8	1.0
16.1	*17.2*	*18.1*	*19.1*	*20.1*	*21.0*	*22.1*	*1.5*		*14.8*	*16.6*	*18.1*	*19.8*	*21.5*	*23.0*	*24.8*	*2.5*
4.2	4.6	4.9	5.2	5.6	5.9	6.3	0.5	Wrist circ.	3.3	3.9	4.5	5.2	5.8	6.4	7.0	0.9
10.7	*11.6*	*12.4*	*13.3*	*14.2*	*15.0*	*15.9*	*1.3*		*8.3*	*10.0*	*11.5*	*13.1*	*14.7*	*16.2*	*17.9*	*2.4*
8.7	9.3	9.8	10.5	11.1	11.7	12.3	0.9	Calf circ.	8.7	9.4	10.0	10.7	11.3	11.9	12.6	1.0
22.0	*23.6*	*25.0*	*26.6*	*28.2*	*29.6*	*31.2*	*2.3*		*22.1*	*23.9*	*25.4*	*27.1*	*28.8*	*30.3*	*32.1*	*2.5*
								10½ years								
45.4	54.7	62.8	72.1	81.3	89.5	98.8	13.4	Weight	47.0	56.0	63.9	72.8	81.6	89.5	98.5	13.0
20.6	*24.8*	*28.5*	*32.7*	*36.9*	*40.6*	*44.8*	*6.10*		*21.3*	*25.4*	*29.0*	*33.0*	*37.0*	*40.6*	*44.7*	*5.9*
50.8	52.4	53.8	55.4	56.9	58.3	59.9	2.3	Height	50.2	51.8	53.3	54.9	56.6	58.0	59.7	2.4
129.1	*133.1*	*136.6*	*140.6*	*144.6*	*148.1*	*152.1*	*5.8*		*127.4*	*131.6*	*135.3*	*139.5*	*143.7*	*147.4*	*151.6*	*6.1*
24.1	25.4	26.7	28.0	29.3	30.6	31.9	2.0	Sitting height	24.0	25.4	26.7	28.1	29.4	30.7	32.1	2.0
61.2	*64.6*	*67.7*	*71.1*	*74.5*	*77.6*	*81.0*	*5.0*		*61.0*	*64.6*	*67.8*	*71.3*	*74.8*	*78.0*	*81.6*	*5.2*
10.9	11.4	11.8	12.2	12.7	13.1	13.6	0.7	Shoulder width	10.3	10.9	11.4	12.0	12.6	13.1	13.7	0.8
27.7	*28.9*	*29.9*	*31.1*	*32.3*	*33.3*	*34.5*	*1.7*		*26.2*	*27.7*	*29.0*	*30.5*	*32.0*	*33.3*	*34.8*	*2.1*
8.1	8.5	8.9	9.3	9.8	10.2	10.6	0.6	Pelvic width	8.0	8.5	9.0	9.4	9.9	10.4	10.9	0.7
20.5	*21.6*	*22.6*	*23.7*	*24.8*	*25.8*	*26.9*	*1.6*		*20.4*	*21.7*	*22.8*	*24.0*	*25.2*	*26.3*	*27.6*	*1.8*
18.6	19.3	19.9	20.6	21.3	22.0	22.6	1.0	Head circ.	17.4	18.5	19.4	20.6	21.7	22.6	23.7	1.6
47.3	*49.0*	*50.6*	*52.4*	*54.2*	*55.8*	*57.5*	*2.6*		*44.1*	*46.9*	*49.4*	*52.2*	*55.0*	*57.5*	*60.3*	*4.1*
21.8	22.8	23.7	24.7	25.7	26.7	27.7	1.5	Chest circ.	19.3	20.9	22.4	24.0	25.6	27.0	28.7	2.4
55.3	*57.9*	*60.2*	*62.8*	*65.4*	*67.7*	*70.3*	*3.8*		*49.0*	*53.1*	*56.8*	*60.9*	*65.0*	*68.7*	*72.8*	*6.0*
6.3	6.8	7.2	7.7	8.1	8.5	9.0	0.7	Upper arm circ.	5.9	6.6	7.2	7.9	8.6	9.3	9.9	1.0
16.1	*17.3*	*18.3*	*19.5*	*20.7*	*21.7*	*22.9*	*1.7*		*15.0*	*16.7*	*18.3*	*20.1*	*21.9*	*23.5*	*25.2*	*2.6*
4.2	4.6	4.9	5.3	5.7	6.0	6.4	0.6	Wrist circ.	3.2	3.9	4.6	5.3	6.0	6.7	7.4	1.1
10.7	*11.7*	*12.5*	*13.5*	*14.5*	*15.3*	*16.3*	*1.4*		*8.1*	*9.9*	*11.6*	*13.4*	*15.2*	*16.9*	*18.7*	*2.7*
8.9	9.5	10.0	10.7	11.3	11.9	12.5	0.9	Calf circ.	8.8	9.5	10.2	10.9	11.7	12.4	13.1	1.1
22.5	*24.1*	*25.5*	*27.1*	*28.7*	*30.1*	*31.7*	*2.3*		*22.3*	*24.2*	*25.9*	*27.8*	*29.7*	*31.4*	*33.3*	*2.8*
								11 years								
50.5	59.7	67.9	77.2	86.4	94.6	103.8	13.5	Weight	48.3	58.2	67.0	76.7	86.4	95.2	105.2	14.3
22.9	*27.1*	*30.8*	*35.0*	*39.2*	*42.9*	*47.1*	*6.12*		*21.9*	*26.4*	*30.4*	*34.8*	*39.2*	*43.2*	*47.7*	*6.5*
51.5	53.1	54.6	56.2	57.8	59.3	60.9	2.4	Height	50.7	52.5	54.1	55.8	57.6	59.1	60.9	2.6
130.8	*134.9*	*138.6*	*142.7*	*146.8*	*150.5*	*154.6*	*6.0*		*128.9*	*133.4*	*137.4*	*141.8*	*146.2*	*150.2*	*154.7*	*6.5*
24.3	25.7	27.0	28.4	29.8	31.0	32.4	2.0	Sitting height	24.3	25.7	27.0	28.5	30.0	31.3	32.7	2.1
61.8	*65.4*	*68.6*	*72.1*	*75.6*	*78.8*	*82.4*	*5.2*		*61.7*	*65.4*	*68.7*	*72.4*	*76.1*	*79.4*	*83.1*	*5.4*
10.9	11.5	11.9	12.4	13.0	13.4	13.9	0.7	Shoulder width	10.4	11.0	11.6	12.2	12.8	13.4	14.0	0.9
27.8	*29.1*	*30.3*	*31.6*	*32.9*	*34.1*	*35.4*	*1.9*		*26.4*	*28.0*	*29.4*	*31.0*	*32.6*	*34.0*	*35.6*	*2.3*
8.0	8.5	9.0	9.5	10.0	10.5	11.0	0.7	Pelvic width	8.1	8.7	9.1	9.6	10.2	10.6	11.1	0.7
20.3	*21.6*	*22.8*	*24.1*	*25.4*	*26.6*	*27.9*	*1.9*		*20.7*	*22.2*	*23.2*	*24.5*	*25.8*	*26.8*	*28.3*	*1.9*
18.9	19.6	20.1	20.7	21.3	21.8	22.4	0.9	Head circ.	17.6	18.7	19.6	20.6	21.6	22.5	23.5	1.5
48.1	*49.7*	*51.0*	*52.5*	*54.0*	*55.3*	*56.9*	*2.2*		*44.8*	*47.4*	*49.7*	*52.3*	*54.9*	*57.2*	*59.8*	*3.8*
21.8	22.9	23.9	25.0	26.1	27.0	28.1	1.6	Chest circ.	19.4	21.1	22.6	24.3	25.9	27.4	29.1	2.4
55.3	*58.1*	*60.6*	*63.4*	*66.2*	*68.7*	*71.5*	*4.1*		*49.3*	*53.6*	*57.4*	*61.6*	*65.8*	*69.6*	*73.9*	*6.2*
6.3	6.9	7.3	7.8	8.3	8.8	9.3	0.7	Upper arm circ.	5.9	6.7	7.3	8.0	8.8	9.4	10.1	1.1
16.1	*17.4*	*18.6*	*19.9*	*21.2*	*22.4*	*23.7*	*1.9*		*15.1*	*16.9*	*18.5*	*20.4*	*22.3*	*23.9*	*25.7*	*2.7*
4.2	4.6	5.0	5.4	5.7	6.1	6.5	0.6	Wrist circ.	3.9	4.4	4.8	5.3	5.8	6.2	6.7	0.7
10.6	*11.7*	*12.6*	*13.6*	*14.6*	*15.5*	*16.6*	*1.5*		*9.9*	*11.2*	*12.3*	*13.5*	*14.7*	*15.8*	*17.1*	*1.8*
9.0	9.6	10.2	10.8	11.5	12.0	12.6	0.9	Calf circ.	8.9	9.6	10.3	11.1	11.8	12.5	13.2	1.1
22.9	*24.5*	*25.9*	*27.5*	*29.1*	*30.5*	*32.1*	*2.3*		*22.6*	*24.5*	*26.2*	*28.1*	*30.0*	*31.7*	*33.6*	*2.8*

[1] HEIMENDINGER, J., *Helv. paediat. Acta*, **19**, suppl. 13 (1964). From measurements made in the period 1956–1957 on 2150 boys and 2150 girls in Basle, Switzerland.

Normal Measurements During Growth – 11½ Years to 12½ Years[1]

Weight in pounds and *kilogrammes*; other measurements in inches and *centimetres* (*P* = percentile)

Boys									Girls							
	95% (P10–P90 span: 80%; P25–P75 span: 50%)									95% (P10–P90 span: 80%; P25–P75 span: 50%)						
$P_{2.5}$	P_{10}	P_{25}	P_{50}	P_{75}	P_{90}	$P_{97.5}$	*s*		$P_{2.5}$	P_{10}	P_{25}	P_{50}	P_{75}	P_{90}	$P_{97.5}$	*s*
								11½ years								
53.6	63.5	72.3	82.2	92.2	101.0	110.9	14.5	Weight	50.5	61.1	70.5	81.1	91.7	101.2	111.8	15.4
24.3	*28.8*	*32.8*	*37.3*	*41.8*	*45.8*	*50.3*	*6.59*		*22.9*	*27.7*	*32.0*	*36.8*	*41.6*	*45.9*	*50.7*	*7.0*
52.0	53.7	55.2	57.0	58.7	60.2	62.0	2.5	Height	51.5	53.4	55.1	57.0	58.9	60.6	62.6	2.8
132.0	*136.4*	*140.3*	*144.7*	*149.1*	*153.0*	*157.4*	*6.4*		*130.7*	*135.6*	*140.0*	*144.8*	*149.6*	*154.0*	*158.9*	*7.1*
24.8	26.2	27.4	28.8	30.2	31.4	32.8	2.0	Sitting height	25.0	26.3	27.6	28.9	30.3	31.5	32.9	2.0
63.0	*66.5*	*69.6*	*73.1*	*76.6*	*79.7*	*83.2*	*5.1*		*63.4*	*66.9*	*70.0*	*73.5*	*77.0*	*80.1*	*83.6*	*5.1*
10.8	11.5	12.0	12.6	13.3	13.8	14.4	0.9	Shoulder width	10.6	11.2	11.8	12.4	13.1	13.7	14.3	0.9
27.5	*29.1*	*30.5*	*32.1*	*33.7*	*35.1*	*36.7*	*2.3*		*26.8*	*28.5*	*30.0*	*31.6*	*33.2*	*34.7*	*36.4*	*2.4*
7.8	8.5	9.1	9.7	10.3	10.9	11.6	0.9	Pelvic width	8.3	8.9	9.3	9.9	10.4	10.8	11.5	0.8
19.8	*21.5*	*23.0*	*24.6*	*26.2*	*27.7*	*29.4*	*2.4*		*21.1*	*22.7*	*23.7*	*25.1*	*26.5*	*27.5*	*29.1*	*2.0*
19.3	19.8	20.2	20.7	21.2	21.6	22.1	0.7	Head circ.	18.2	19.1	19.8	20.6	21.5	22.2	23.0	1.2
49.0	*50.3*	*51.4*	*52.6*	*53.8*	*54.9*	*56.2*	*1.8*		*46.3*	*48.4*	*50.3*	*52.4*	*54.5*	*56.4*	*58.5*	*3.1*
21.9	23.0	24.1	25.3	26.5	27.5	28.7	1.7	Chest circ.	19.7	21.4	22.9	24.6	26.2	27.7	29.4	2.4
55.5	*58.5*	*61.2*	*64.2*	*67.2*	*69.9*	*72.9*	*4.4*		*50.1*	*54.4*	*58.2*	*62.4*	*66.6*	*70.4*	*74.7*	*6.2*
6.2	6.8	7.4	8.0	8.6	9.2	9.8	0.9	Upper arm circ.	6.1	6.8	7.4	8.1	8.9	9.5	10.2	1.0
15.7	*17.3*	*18.7*	*20.3*	*21.9*	*23.3*	*24.9*	*2.3*		*15.5*	*17.3*	*18.9*	*20.7*	*22.5*	*24.1*	*25.9*	*2.6*
3.9	4.4	4.9	5.4	5.9	6.4	6.9	0.7	Wrist circ.	4.6	4.8	5.1	5.4	5.6	5.9	6.1	0.4
9.9	*11.2*	*12.4*	*13.7*	*15.0*	*16.2*	*17.5*	*1.9*		*11.6*	*12.3*	*12.9*	*13.6*	*14.3*	*14.9*	*15.6*	*1.0*
9.1	9.8	10.4	11.0	11.7	12.2	12.9	0.9	Calf circ.	8.9	9.7	10.4	11.2	12.0	12.7	13.4	1.1
23.2	*24.9*	*26.4*	*28.0*	*29.6*	*31.1*	*32.8*	*2.4*		*22.7*	*24.6*	*26.4*	*28.4*	*30.4*	*32.2*	*34.1*	*2.9*
								12 years								
56.9	67.5	76.7	87.1	97.4	106.7	117.3	15.2	Weight	53.6	64.8	75.0	86.0	97.0	107.1	118.4	16.3
25.8	*30.6*	*34.8*	*39.5*	*44.2*	*48.4*	*53.2*	*6.91*		*24.3*	*29.4*	*34.0*	*39.0*	*44.0*	*48.6*	*53.7*	*7.4*
52.6	54.4	56.1	57.9	59.7	61.3	63.2	2.7	Height	52.6	54.6	56.4	58.5	60.5	62.3	64.4	3.0
133.5	*138.2*	*142.4*	*147.0*	*151.6*	*155.8*	*160.5*	*6.8*		*133.5*	*138.7*	*143.3*	*148.5*	*153.7*	*158.3*	*163.5*	*7.6*
25.4	26.7	27.9	29.2	30.5	31.6	32.9	1.9	Sitting height	25.6	26.9	28.1	29.4	30.7	31.8	33.1	1.9
64.6	*67.9*	*70.8*	*74.1*	*77.4*	*80.3*	*83.6*	*4.8*		*65.1*	*68.4*	*71.3*	*74.6*	*77.9*	*80.8*	*84.1*	*4.8*
10.5	11.3	12.0	12.8	13.6	14.3	15.1	1.2	Shoulder width	10.7	11.5	12.0	12.7	13.4	14.0	14.7	1.0
26.6	*28.6*	*30.5*	*32.5*	*34.5*	*36.4*	*38.4*	*3.0*		*27.3*	*29.1*	*30.6*	*32.3*	*34.0*	*35.5*	*37.3*	*2.5*
7.6	8.4	9.1	9.9	10.7	11.4	12.1	1.1	Pelvic width	8.5	9.2	9.6	10.2	10.7	11.2	11.9	0.8
19.4	*21.3*	*23.1*	*25.1*	*27.1*	*28.9*	*30.8*	*2.9*		*21.7*	*23.4*	*24.5*	*25.9*	*27.3*	*28.4*	*30.1*	*2.1*
19.4	19.9	20.3	20.7	21.2	21.6	22.1	0.7	Head circ.	19.0	19.6	20.1	20.7	21.2	21.7	22.3	0.8
49.3	*50.5*	*51.5*	*52.7*	*53.9*	*54.9*	*56.1*	*1.7*		*48.3*	*49.8*	*51.1*	*52.5*	*53.9*	*55.2*	*56.7*	*2.1*
22.1	23.3	24.4	25.6	26.8	27.9	29.1	1.8	Chest circ.	19.9	21.6	23.1	24.8	26.5	28.1	29.8	2.5
56.1	*59.2*	*61.9*	*65.0*	*68.1*	*70.8*	*73.9*	*4.5*		*50.6*	*54.9*	*58.8*	*63.1*	*67.4*	*71.3*	*75.6*	*6.3*
6.0	6.7	7.4	8.1	8.9	9.6	10.3	1.1	Upper arm circ.	6.2	6.9	7.6	8.3	9.0	9.6	10.3	1.0
15.2	*17.1*	*18.8*	*20.7*	*22.6*	*24.3*	*26.2*	*2.8*		*15.8*	*17.6*	*19.2*	*21.0*	*22.8*	*24.4*	*26.2*	*2.6*
3.6	4.2	4.8	5.4	6.0	6.6	7.2	0.9	Wrist circ.	4.6	4.9	5.2	5.4	5.7	5.9	6.2	0.4
9.1	*10.7*	*12.1*	*13.7*	*15.3*	*16.7*	*18.3*	*2.3*		*11.8*	*12.5*	*13.1*	*13.8*	*14.5*	*15.1*	*15.8*	*1.0*
9.3	10.0	10.6	11.2	11.9	12.4	13.1	0.9	Calf circ.	9.1	9.8	10.5	11.3	12.1	12.8	13.5	1.1
23.7	*25.4*	*26.9*	*28.5*	*30.1*	*31.6*	*33.3*	*2.4*		*23.0*	*24.9*	*26.7*	*28.7*	*30.7*	*32.5*	*34.4*	*2.9*
								12½ years								
59.3	70.8	80.9	92.2	103.4	113.5	125.0	16.5	Weight	56.9	68.8	79.4	91.3	103.2	113.8	125.7	17.4
26.9	*32.1*	*36.7*	*41.8*	*46.9*	*51.5*	*56.7*	*7.50*		*25.8*	*31.2*	*36.0*	*41.4*	*46.8*	*51.6*	*57.0*	*7.9*
53.3	55.3	57.1	59.1	61.0	62.8	64.8	2.9	Height	53.7	55.7	57.6	59.6	61.7	63.6	65.6	3.0
135.3	*140.4*	*145.0*	*150.0*	*155.0*	*159.6*	*164.7*	*7.4*		*136.3*	*141.5*	*146.3*	*151.5*	*156.7*	*161.5*	*166.7*	*7.7*
26.1	27.3	28.4	29.6	30.7	31.8	33.0	1.7	Sitting height	26.5	27.6	28.7	29.8	30.9	32.0	33.1	1.7
66.4	*69.4*	*72.1*	*75.1*	*78.1*	*80.8*	*83.8*	*4.4*		*67.2*	*70.1*	*72.8*	*75.7*	*78.6*	*81.3*	*84.2*	*4.3*
9.5	10.7	11.7	12.9	14.0	15.1	16.2	1.7	Shoulder width	11.0	11.7	12.3	13.0	13.6	14.2	14.9	1.0
24.2	*27.1*	*29.8*	*32.7*	*35.6*	*38.3*	*41.2*	*4.3*		*27.9*	*29.7*	*31.2*	*32.9*	*34.6*	*36.1*	*37.9*	*2.5*
7.6	8.4	9.3	10.1	11.0	11.8	12.7	1.3	Pelvic width	8.8	9.5	10.0	10.6	11.1	11.6	12.3	0.9
19.2	*21.4*	*23.5*	*25.7*	*27.9*	*30.0*	*32.2*	*3.3*		*22.4*	*24.2*	*25.3*	*26.8*	*28.3*	*29.4*	*31.2*	*2.2*
19.5	20.0	20.4	20.8	21.2	21.6	22.0	0.6	Head circ.	19.4	19.9	20.3	20.7	21.2	21.6	22.1	0.7
49.6	*50.7*	*51.7*	*52.8*	*53.9*	*54.9*	*56.0*	*1.6*		*49.3*	*50.5*	*51.5*	*52.7*	*53.9*	*54.9*	*56.1*	*1.7*
22.3	23.6	24.8	26.1	27.4	28.5	29.8	1.9	Chest circ.	20.2	21.9	23.5	25.2	26.9	28.5	30.2	2.5
56.7	*60.0*	*62.9*	*66.2*	*69.5*	*72.4*	*75.7*	*4.8*		*51.3*	*55.7*	*59.6*	*64.0*	*68.4*	*72.3*	*76.6*	*6.4*
5.7	6.6	7.4	8.3	9.1	10.0	10.8	1.3	Upper arm circ.	6.3	7.0	7.7	8.4	9.1	9.7	10.4	1.0
14.5	*16.7*	*18.8*	*21.0*	*23.2*	*25.3*	*27.5*	*3.3*		*16.1*	*17.9*	*19.5*	*21.3*	*23.1*	*24.7*	*26.5*	*2.6*
3.5	4.2	4.8	5.4	6.1	6.7	7.4	1.0	Wrist circ.	4.8	5.0	5.3	5.6	5.8	6.1	6.3	0.4
8.8	*10.6*	*12.1*	*13.8*	*15.5*	*17.0*	*18.8*	*2.5*		*12.1*	*12.8*	*13.4*	*14.1*	*14.8*	*15.4*	*16.1*	*1.0*
9.3	10.0	10.7	11.4	12.1	12.8	13.5	1.1	Calf circ.	9.3	10.0	10.7	11.5	12.3	13.0	13.7	1.1
23.7	*25.5*	*27.2*	*29.0*	*30.8*	*32.5*	*34.3*	*2.7*		*23.5*	*25.4*	*27.2*	*29.2*	*31.2*	*33.0*	*34.9*	*2.9*

[1] HEIMENDINGER, J., *Helv. paediat. Acta*, **19**, suppl. 13 (1964). From measurements made in the period 1956–1957 on 2150 boys and 2150 girls in Basle, Switzerland.

Normal Measurements During Growth – 13 Years to 14 Years[1]

Weight in pounds and *kilogrammes*; other measurements in inches and *centimetres* (*P* = percentile)

Boys									Girls							
95% (P2.5–P97.5)									95% (P2.5–P97.5)							
	80% (P10–P90)									80% (P10–P90)						
		50% (P25–P75)									50% (P25–P75)					
$P_{2.5}$	P_{10}	P_{25}	P_{50}	P_{75}	P_{90}	$P_{97.5}$	s		$P_{2.5}$	P_{10}	P_{25}	P_{50}	P_{75}	P_{90}	$P_{97.5}$	s
								13 years								
63.7	75.4	85.8	97.2	108.7	119.1	130.7	16.9	Weight	61.5	74.1	85.1	97.7	110.2	121.3	133.8	18.3
28.9	*34.2*	*38.9*	*44.1*	*49.3*	*54.0*	*59.3*	*7.67*		*27.9*	*33.6*	*38.6*	*44.3*	*50.0*	*55.0*	*60.7*	*8.3*
54.3	56.4	58.3	60.4	62.5	64.4	66.5	3.1	Height	55.0	57.0	58.7	60.7	62.6	64.3	66.3	2.8
138.0	*143.3*	*148.1*	*153.4*	*158.7*	*163.5*	*168.8*	*7.8*		*139.8*	*144.8*	*149.2*	*154.1*	*159.0*	*163.4*	*168.4*	*7.2*
26.7	27.8	28.9	30.0	31.2	32.2	33.4	1.7	Sitting height	27.2	28.2	29.2	30.2	31.3	32.2	33.3	1.5
67.8	*70.7*	*73.4*	*76.3*	*79.2*	*81.9*	*84.8*	*4.3*		*69.1*	*71.7*	*74.1*	*76.8*	*79.5*	*81.9*	*84.5*	*3.9*
8.9	10.4	11.7	13.0	14.4	15.6	16.9	2.0	Shoulder width	11.2	11.9	12.5	13.2	13.9	14.5	15.2	1.0
22.6	*26.5*	*29.6*	*33.1*	*36.6*	*39.7*	*42.8*	*5.1*		*28.5*	*30.3*	*31.8*	*33.6*	*35.4*	*36.9*	*38.7*	*2.6*
7.4	8.4	9.3	10.4	11.4	12.3	13.1	1.5	Pelvic width	9.1	9.8	10.3	10.9	11.5	11.9	12.6	0.9
18.8	*21.4*	*23.7*	*26.3*	*28.9*	*31.2*	*33.3*	*3.8*		*23.2*	*25.0*	*26.1*	*27.6*	*29.1*	*30.2*	*32.0*	*2.2*
19.6	20.1	20.4	20.8	21.2	21.6	22.0	0.6	Head circ.	19.5	20.0	20.4	20.8	21.2	21.6	22.0	0.6
49.9	*51.0*	*51.9*	*52.9*	*53.9*	*54.8*	*55.9*	*1.5*		*49.6*	*50.7*	*51.7*	*52.8*	*53.9*	*54.9*	*56.0*	*1.6*
21.8	23.4	24.9	26.5	28.2	29.6	31.3	2.4	Chest circ.	20.6	22.4	23.9	25.7	27.4	29.0	30.7	2.6
55.3	*59.5*	*63.2*	*67.4*	*71.6*	*75.3*	*79.5*	*6.1*		*52.3*	*56.8*	*60.8*	*65.2*	*69.6*	*73.6*	*78.1*	*6.5*
5.8	6.7	7.5	8.3	9.2	10.0	10.9	1.3	Upper arm circ.	6.6	7.3	7.9	8.5	9.2	9.8	10.5	1.0
14.7	*16.9*	*19.0*	*21.2*	*23.4*	*25.5*	*27.7*	*3.3*		*16.7*	*18.5*	*20.0*	*21.7*	*23.4*	*24.9*	*26.7*	*2.5*
3.6	4.3	4.9	5.6	6.2	6.8	7.5	1.0	Wrist circ.	–	–	–	5.6	–	–	–	0.4
9.1	*10.9*	*12.4*	*14.1*	*15.8*	*17.3*	*19.1*	*2.5*		–	–	–	*14.2*	–	–	–	*0.9*
8.9	9.8	10.6	11.6	12.5	13.3	14.3	1.4	Calf circ.	9.5	10.3	11.0	11.8	12.6	13.3	14.1	1.2
22.5	*24.9*	*27.0*	*29.4*	*31.8*	*33.9*	*36.3*	*3.5*		*24.1*	*26.1*	*28.0*	*30.0*	*32.0*	*33.9*	*35.9*	*3.0*
								13½ years								
67.9	79.8	90.4	102.1	113.8	124.3	136.2	17.2	Weight	66.8	79.8	91.3	104.3	117.3	128.7	141.8	19.0
30.8	*36.2*	*41.0*	*46.3*	*51.6*	*56.4*	*61.8*	*7.81*		*30.3*	*36.2*	*41.4*	*47.3*	*53.2*	*58.4*	*64.3*	*8.6*
55.6	57.7	59.7	61.8	63.9	65.9	68.0	3.1	Height	56.5	58.3	59.8	61.5	63.3	64.7	66.5	2.5
141.2	*146.6*	*151.6*	*157.0*	*162.4*	*167.4*	*172.8*	*8.0*		*143.6*	*148.0*	*151.9*	*156.3*	*160.7*	*164.4*	*169.0*	*6.4*
27.3	28.4	29.5	30.6	31.8	32.8	34.0	1.7	Sitting height	27.9	28.8	29.7	30.7	31.7	32.5	33.5	1.4
69.3	*72.2*	*74.9*	*77.8*	*80.7*	*83.4*	*86.3*	*4.3*		*70.8*	*73.2*	*75.4*	*77.9*	*80.4*	*82.6*	*85.0*	*3.6*
9.8	11.3	12.3	13.4	14.6	15.6	16.3	1.7	Shoulder width	11.5	12.2	12.8	13.5	14.1	14.7	15.4	1.0
24.8	*28.7*	*31.2*	*34.1*	*37.0*	*39.5*	*41.4*	*4.2*		*29.2*	*31.0*	*32.5*	*34.2*	*35.9*	*37.4*	*39.2*	*2.5*
7.9	8.9	9.7	10.6	11.6	12.4	13.3	1.4	Pelvic width	9.6	10.2	10.7	11.2	11.8	12.2	12.9	0.8
20.1	*22.5*	*24.6*	*27.0*	*29.4*	*31.5*	*33.9*	*3.5*		*24.3*	*26.0*	*27.1*	*28.5*	*29.9*	*31.0*	*32.7*	*2.1*
19.7	20.1	20.5	20.9	21.3	21.6	22.0	0.6	Head circ.	19.7	20.1	20.5	20.9	21.3	21.6	22.0	0.6
50.0	*51.1*	*52.0*	*53.0*	*54.0*	*54.9*	*56.0*	*1.5*		*50.0*	*51.1*	*52.0*	*53.0*	*54.0*	*54.9*	*56.0*	*1.5*
21.3	23.4	25.2	27.2	29.3	31.1	33.1	3.0	Chest circ.	21.0	22.8	24.3	26.1	27.8	29.4	31.1	2.6
54.2	*59.4*	*64.0*	*69.2*	*74.4*	*79.0*	*84.2*	*7.6*		*53.3*	*57.8*	*61.8*	*66.2*	*70.6*	*74.6*	*79.1*	*6.5*
6.3	7.0	7.7	8.5	9.2	9.9	10.6	1.1	Upper arm circ.	6.8	7.4	8.0	8.7	9.3	9.9	10.6	0.9
16.0	*17.9*	*19.6*	*21.5*	*23.4*	*25.1*	*27.0*	*2.8*		*17.2*	*18.9*	*20.4*	*22.0*	*23.6*	*25.1*	*26.8*	*2.4*
3.9	4.5	5.1	5.7	6.3	6.9	7.5	0.9	Wrist circ.	–	–	–	5.6	–	–	–	0.4
9.9	*11.5*	*12.9*	*14.5*	*16.1*	*17.5*	*19.1*	*2.3*		–	–	–	*14.3*	–	–	–	*0.9*
8.9	9.9	10.8	11.8	12.8	13.7	14.7	1.5	Calf circ.	9.8	10.6	11.3	12.2	13.0	13.7	14.6	1.2
22.7	*25.2*	*27.5*	*30.0*	*32.5*	*34.8*	*37.3*	*3.7*		*24.8*	*26.9*	*28.8*	*30.9*	*33.0*	*34.9*	*37.0*	*3.1*
								14 years								
72.5	84.4	95.2	107.1	119.0	129.9	141.8	17.5	Weight	74.3	86.9	97.9	110.5	123.0	134.0	146.6	18.3
32.9	*38.3*	*43.2*	*48.6*	*54.0*	*58.9*	*64.3*	*7.92*		*33.7*	*39.4*	*44.4*	*50.1*	*55.8*	*60.8*	*66.5*	*8.3*
57.0	59.1	61.1	63.2	65.4	67.3	69.4	3.1	Height	57.8	59.4	60.7	62.3	63.8	65.2	66.7	2.2
144.8	*150.2*	*155.2*	*160.6*	*166.0*	*171.0*	*176.4*	*8.0*		*146.9*	*150.8*	*154.3*	*158.2*	*162.1*	*165.6*	*169.5*	*5.7*
27.8	29.0	30.0	31.2	32.4	33.5	34.6	1.7	Sitting height	28.5	29.4	30.2	31.1	32.0	32.8	33.7	1.3
70.6	*73.6*	*76.3*	*79.3*	*82.3*	*85.0*	*88.0*	*4.4*		*72.3*	*74.6*	*76.7*	*79.0*	*81.3*	*83.4*	*85.7*	*3.4*
11.3	12.6	13.2	13.9	14.6	15.3	15.5	1.1	Shoulder width	11.9	12.5	13.1	13.7	14.4	15.0	15.6	0.9
28.8	*31.9*	*33.6*	*35.4*	*37.2*	*38.9*	*39.4*	*2.7*		*30.1*	*31.8*	*33.3*	*34.9*	*36.5*	*38.0*	*39.7*	*2.4*
9.1	9.8	10.4	11.0	11.7	12.3	13.0	1.0	Pelvic width	10.0	10.5	11.0	11.5	12.1	12.6	13.1	0.8
23.0	*24.8*	*26.3*	*28.0*	*29.7*	*31.2*	*33.0*	*2.5*		*25.3*	*26.7*	*27.9*	*29.3*	*30.7*	*31.9*	*33.3*	*2.0*
19.7	20.2	20.5	20.9	21.3	21.7	22.1	0.6	Head circ.	19.8	20.2	20.6	20.9	21.3	21.7	22.1	0.6
50.1	*51.2*	*52.1*	*53.1*	*54.1*	*55.0*	*56.1*	*1.5*		*50.2*	*51.3*	*52.2*	*53.2*	*54.2*	*55.1*	*56.2*	*1.5*
22.8	24.6	26.1	27.9	29.7	31.3	33.1	2.6	Chest circ.	21.4	23.1	24.6	26.4	28.1	29.6	31.4	2.5
57.8	*62.4*	*66.4*	*70.9*	*75.4*	*79.4*	*84.0*	*6.6*		*54.3*	*58.7*	*62.6*	*67.0*	*71.4*	*75.3*	*79.7*	*6.4*
7.2	7.7	8.1	8.7	9.2	9.6	10.2	0.7	Upper arm circ.	7.0	7.6	8.1	8.8	9.4	10.0	10.6	0.9
18.2	*19.5*	*20.7*	*22.0*	*23.3*	*24.5*	*25.8*	*1.9*		*17.7*	*19.3*	*20.7*	*22.3*	*23.9*	*25.3*	*26.9*	*2.3*
4.3	4.9	5.4	5.9	6.5	6.9	7.5	0.8	Wrist circ.	–	–	–	5.7	–	–	–	0.4
11.0	*12.4*	*13.6*	*15.0*	*16.4*	*17.6*	*19.0*	*2.0*		–	–	–	*14.4*	–	–	–	*0.9*
10.0	10.7	11.4	12.1	12.8	13.5	14.2	1.1	Calf circ.	10.2	10.9	11.7	12.5	13.3	14.0	14.8	1.2
25.5	*27.3*	*29.0*	*30.8*	*32.6*	*34.3*	*36.1*	*2.7*		*25.8*	*27.8*	*29.7*	*31.7*	*33.7*	*35.6*	*37.6*	*3.0*

[1] Heimendinger, J., *Helv. paediat. Acta*, **19**, suppl. 13 (1964). From measurements made in the period 1956–1957 on 2150 boys and 2150 girls in Basle, Switzerland.

Normal Measurements During Growth – 14½ Years to 15½ Years[1]

Weight in pounds and *kilogrammes*; other measurements in inches and *centimetres* (P = percentile)

Boys									Girls							
	95%									95%						
		80%									80%					
			50%									50%				
$P_{2.5}$	P_{10}	P_{25}	P_{50}	P_{75}	P_{90}	$P_{97.5}$	s		$P_{2.5}$	P_{10}	P_{25}	P_{50}	P_{75}	P_{90}	$P_{97.5}$	s
								14½ years								
75.6	88.4	99.6	112.2	124.8	136.0	148.8	18.5	Weight	81.3	92.8	103.0	114.2	125.4	135.6	147.0	16.5
34.3	*40.1*	*45.2*	*50.9*	*56.6*	*61.7*	*67.5*	*8.37*		*36.9*	*42.1*	*46.7*	*51.8*	*56.9*	*61.5*	*66.7*	*7.5*
58.3	60.5	62.4	64.5	66.6	68.5	70.6	3.1	Height	58.9	60.0	61.4	62.9	64.4	65.8	66.9	2.2
148.2	*153.6*	*158.4*	*163.8*	*169.2*	*174.0*	*179.4*	*7.9*		*149.7*	*152.5*	*156.0*	*159.8*	*163.6*	*167.1*	*169.9*	*5.6*
28.4	29.6	30.6	31.8	33.0	34.1	35.2	1.7	Sitting height	29.0	29.8	30.7	31.5	32.4	33.2	34.1	1.3
72.1	*75.1*	*77.8*	*80.8*	*83.8*	*86.5*	*89.5*	*4.4*		*73.6*	*75.8*	*77.9*	*80.1*	*82.3*	*84.4*	*86.6*	*3.3*
12.5	13.1	13.7	14.4	15.0	15.6	16.3	0.9	Shoulder width	12.2	12.8	13.4	14.0	14.6	15.2	15.8	0.9
31.7	*33.4*	*34.9*	*36.5*	*38.1*	*39.6*	*41.3*	*2.4*		*31.0*	*32.6*	*34.0*	*35.6*	*37.2*	*38.6*	*40.2*	*2.3*
9.8	10.4	10.9	11.4	12.0	12.5	13.1	0.8	Pelvic width	10.3	10.8	11.3	11.8	12.3	12.8	13.3	0.7
24.8	*26.3*	*27.6*	*29.0*	*30.4*	*31.7*	*33.2*	*2.1*		*26.1*	*27.4*	*28.6*	*29.9*	*31.2*	*32.4*	*33.7*	*1.9*
19.8	20.2	20.6	21.0	21.4	21.7	22.2	0.6	Head circ.	19.8	20.2	20.6	21.0	21.5	21.9	22.3	0.6
50.3	*51.4*	*52.3*	*53.3*	*54.3*	*55.2*	*56.3*	*1.5*		*50.2*	*51.3*	*52.3*	*53.4*	*54.5*	*55.5*	*56.6*	*1.5*
24.2	25.7	27.0	28.5	30.0	31.3	32.8	2.2	Chest circ.	21.7	23.4	25.0	26.7	28.3	29.9	31.6	2.5
61.5	*65.3*	*68.7*	*72.4*	*76.1*	*79.5*	*83.3*	*5.5*		*55.2*	*59.5*	*63.4*	*67.7*	*72.0*	*75.9*	*80.2*	*6.3*
7.4	8.0	8.4	8.9	9.4	9.9	10.4	0.7	Upper arm circ.	7.2	7.8	8.3	8.9	9.4	10.0	10.6	0.8
18.9	*20.2*	*21.4*	*22.7*	*24.0*	*25.2*	*26.5*	*1.9*		*18.4*	*19.9*	*21.2*	*22.6*	*24.0*	*25.3*	*26.8*	*2.1*
4.8	5.2	5.6	6.0	6.5	6.9	7.3	0.6	Wrist circ.	–	–	–	5.7	–	–	–	0.4
12.1	*13.2*	*14.2*	*15.3*	*16.4*	*17.4*	*18.5*	*1.6*		–	–	–	*14.5*	–	–	–	*0.9*
10.6	11.3	11.9	12.6	13.3	13.9	14.6	1.0	Calf circ.	10.4	11.1	11.9	12.6	13.4	14.1	14.9	1.1
27.0	*28.8*	*30.3*	*32.0*	*33.7*	*35.2*	*37.0*	*2.5*		*26.4*	*28.3*	*30.1*	*32.1*	*34.1*	*35.9*	*37.8*	*2.9*
								15 years								
81.1	93.7	104.7	117.1	129.4	140.4	153.0	18.1	Weight	87.1	97.7	106.9	117.3	127.6	136.9	147.5	15.2
36.8	*42.5*	*47.5*	*53.1*	*58.7*	*63.7*	*69.4*	*8.22*		*39.5*	*44.3*	*48.5*	*53.2*	*57.9*	*62.1*	*66.9*	*6.9*
59.8	61.9	63.7	65.7	67.7	69.5	71.5	3.0	Height	59.4	60.6	61.9	63.4	64.9	66.3	67.4	2.2
151.9	*157.1*	*161.7*	*166.8*	*171.9*	*176.5*	*181.7*	*7.5*		*151.0*	*153.8*	*157.3*	*161.1*	*164.9*	*168.4*	*171.2*	*5.6*
28.9	30.1	31.1	32.4	33.6	34.6	35.9	1.8	Sitting height	29.5	30.4	31.1	32.0	32.8	33.6	34.4	1.3
73.3	*76.4*	*79.1*	*82.2*	*85.3*	*88.0*	*91.1*	*4.5*		*74.9*	*77.1*	*79.0*	*81.2*	*83.4*	*85.3*	*87.5*	*3.2*
13.0	13.6	14.1	14.7	15.3	15.8	16.5	0.9	Shoulder width	12.4	13.1	13.6	14.2	14.8	15.3	15.9	0.9
33.0	*34.6*	*35.9*	*37.4*	*38.9*	*40.2*	*41.8*	*2.2*		*31.6*	*33.2*	*34.5*	*36.0*	*37.5*	*38.8*	*40.4*	*2.2*
10.0	10.6	11.1	11.7	12.2	12.8	13.3	0.8	Pelvic width	10.5	10.9	11.4	11.9	12.4	12.9	13.3	0.7
25.5	*27.0*	*28.3*	*29.7*	*31.1*	*32.4*	*33.9*	*2.1*		*26.6*	*27.7*	*28.9*	*30.2*	*31.5*	*32.7*	*33.8*	*1.9*
19.8	20.3	20.6	21.0	21.4	21.8	22.2	0.6	Head circ.	19.9	20.3	20.7	21.1	21.5	21.8	22.2	0.6
50.4	*51.5*	*52.4*	*53.4*	*54.4*	*55.3*	*56.4*	*1.5*		*50.5*	*51.6*	*52.5*	*53.5*	*54.5*	*55.4*	*56.5*	*1.5*
25.2	26.5	27.8	29.1	30.4	31.7	33.0	2.0	Chest circ.	22.1	23.8	25.2	26.9	28.5	30.0	31.7	2.4
64.0	*67.4*	*70.5*	*73.9*	*77.3*	*80.4*	*83.8*	*5.0*		*56.2*	*60.4*	*64.1*	*68.3*	*72.5*	*76.2*	*80.4*	*6.1*
7.6	8.1	8.6	9.2	9.7	10.2	10.7	0.8	Upper arm circ.	7.4	8.0	8.5	9.0	9.6	10.0	10.6	0.8
19.3	*20.7*	*21.9*	*23.3*	*24.7*	*25.9*	*27.3*	*2.0*		*18.9*	*20.3*	*21.5*	*22.9*	*24.3*	*25.5*	*26.9*	*2.0*
5.1	5.4	5.7	6.1	6.5	6.8	7.1	0.5	Wrist circ.	–	–	–	5.7	–	–	–	0.4
12.9	*13.8*	*14.6*	*15.5*	*16.4*	*17.2*	*18.1*	*1.3*		–	–	–	*14.5*	–	–	–	*0.9*
11.0	11.7	12.2	12.9	13.5	14.1	14.8	0.9	Calf circ.	10.7	11.4	12.0	12.7	13.4	14.1	14.7	1.0
27.9	*29.6*	*31.1*	*32.7*	*34.3*	*35.8*	*37.5*	*2.4*		*27.2*	*28.9*	*30.5*	*32.3*	*34.1*	*35.7*	*37.4*	*2.6*
								15½ years								
86.9	99.0	110.0	122.1	134.3	145.3	157.4	17.8	Weight	90.4	100.5	109.6	119.7	129.9	138.9	149.0	14.8
39.4	*44.9*	*49.9*	*55.4*	*60.9*	*65.9*	*71.4*	*8.09*		*41.0*	*45.6*	*49.7*	*54.3*	*58.9*	*63.0*	*67.6*	*6.7*
61.3	63.2	64.9	66.7	68.6	70.2	72.1	2.7	Height	59.3	60.9	62.2	63.8	65.4	66.8	68.3	2.3
155.8	*160.6*	*164.8*	*169.5*	*174.2*	*178.4*	*183.2*	*6.9*		*150.6*	*154.6*	*158.1*	*162.1*	*166.1*	*169.6*	*173.6*	*5.8*
29.5	30.7	31.8	33.0	34.1	35.2	36.4	1.7	Sitting height	29.9	30.8	31.5	32.4	33.3	34.0	34.9	1.3
75.0	*78.0*	*80.7*	*83.7*	*86.7*	*89.4*	*92.4*	*4.4*		*76.0*	*78.2*	*80.1*	*82.3*	*84.5*	*86.4*	*88.6*	*3.2*
13.1	14.0	14.5	15.0	15.6	16.1	16.4	0.8	Shoulder width	12.6	13.2	13.7	14.3	14.8	15.3	15.9	0.8
33.2	*35.5*	*36.8*	*38.2*	*39.6*	*40.9*	*41.6*	*2.1*		*32.0*	*33.5*	*34.8*	*36.2*	*37.6*	*38.9*	*40.4*	*2.1*
10.3	10.9	11.4	11.9	12.5	13.0	13.6	0.8	Pelvic width	10.6	11.1	11.5	12.0	12.5	12.9	13.4	0.7
26.1	*27.6*	*28.9*	*30.3*	*31.7*	*33.0*	*34.5*	*2.1*		*26.9*	*28.2*	*29.3*	*30.5*	*31.7*	*32.8*	*34.1*	*1.8*
20.0	20.4	20.7	21.1	21.5	21.8	22.2	0.6	Head circ.	20.0	20.4	20.7	21.1	21.5	21.9	22.2	0.6
50.7	*51.7*	*52.5*	*53.5*	*54.5*	*55.3*	*56.3*	*1.4*		*50.9*	*51.9*	*52.7*	*53.7*	*54.7*	*55.5*	*56.5*	*1.4*
25.9	27.2	28.3	29.6	30.9	32.0	33.3	1.9	Chest circ.	22.6	24.1	25.5	27.1	28.7	30.0	31.6	2.3
65.9	*69.1*	*72.0*	*75.2*	*78.4*	*81.3*	*84.5*	*4.7*		*57.3*	*61.3*	*64.8*	*68.8*	*72.8*	*76.3*	*80.3*	*5.8*
7.6	8.2	8.7	9.3	9.9	10.4	11.0	0.9	Upper arm circ.	7.8	8.3	8.7	9.2	9.6	10.1	10.6	0.7
19.2	*20.8*	*22.1*	*23.6*	*25.1*	*26.4*	*28.0*	*2.2*		*19.7*	*21.0*	*22.1*	*23.3*	*24.5*	*25.6*	*26.9*	*1.8*
5.3	5.6	5.9	6.1	6.4	6.7	7.0	0.4	Wrist circ.	–	–	–	5.7	–	–	–	0.4
13.4	*14.2*	*14.9*	*15.6*	*16.3*	*17.0*	*17.8*	*1.1*		–	–	–	*14.5*	–	–	–	*0.9*
11.2	11.9	12.4	13.0	13.7	14.2	14.8	0.9	Calf circ.	10.9	11.6	12.2	12.8	13.4	14.0	14.7	0.9
28.5	*30.1*	*31.5*	*33.1*	*34.7*	*36.1*	*37.7*	*2.3*		*27.7*	*29.4*	*30.9*	*32.5*	*34.1*	*35.6*	*37.3*	*2.4*

[1] HEIMENDINGER, J., *Helv. paediat. Acta*, **19**, suppl. 13 (1964). From measurements made in the period 1956–1957 on 2150 boys and 2150 girls in Basle, Switzerland.

Normal Measurements During Growth – 16 Years to 17 Years[1]

Weight in pounds and *kilogrammes*; other measurements in inches and *centimetres* (P = percentile)

Boys									Girls							
	95%									95%						
		80%									80%					
			50%									50%				
$P_{2.5}$	P_{10}	P_{25}	P_{50}	P_{75}	P_{90}	$P_{97.5}$	s		$P_{2.5}$	P_{10}	P_{25}	P_{50}	P_{75}	P_{90}	$P_{97.5}$	s
								16 years								
92.4	104.5	115.3	127.2	139.1	149.9	162.0	17.6	Weight	92.2	102.3	111.3	121.5	131.6	140.7	150.8	14.8
41.9	47.4	52.3	57.7	63.1	68.0	73.5	7.98		41.8	46.4	50.5	55.1	59.7	63.8	68.4	6.7
62.5	64.3	65.9	67.6	69.3	70.9	72.7	2.6	Height	59.5	61.1	62.6	64.1	65.7	67.1	68.7	2.3
158.8	163.3	167.3	171.7	176.1	180.1	184.6	6.5		151.2	155.3	158.9	162.9	166.9	170.5	174.6	5.9
30.4	31.5	32.4	33.5	34.6	35.6	36.7	1.6	Sitting height	30.2	31.1	31.8	32.7	33.5	34.3	35.2	1.3
77.1	79.9	82.4	85.2	88.0	90.5	93.3	4.1		76.7	78.9	80.8	83.0	85.2	87.1	89.3	3.2
13.5	14.3	14.8	15.3	15.9	16.3	16.6	0.8	Shoulder width	12.8	13.3	13.8	14.3	14.9	15.4	15.9	0.8
34.2	36.3	37.5	38.9	40.3	41.5	42.2	2.0		32.4	33.8	35.0	36.4	37.8	39.0	40.4	2.0
10.7	11.2	11.7	12.2	12.7	13.1	13.7	0.7	Pelvic width	10.7	11.3	11.7	12.2	12.6	13.1	13.6	0.7
27.1	28.4	29.6	30.9	32.2	33.4	34.7	1.9		27.3	28.6	29.7	30.9	32.1	33.2	34.5	1.8
20.0	20.4	20.7	21.1	21.5	21.8	22.2	0.6	Head circ.	20.1	20.5	20.8	21.1	21.5	21.8	22.2	0.6
50.8	51.8	52.6	53.6	54.6	55.4	56.4	1.4		51.1	52.0	52.8	53.7	54.6	55.4	56.3	1.4
26.7	27.8	28.9	30.1	31.3	32.3	33.5	1.7	Chest circ.	23.0	24.4	25.8	27.2	28.7	30.0	31.5	2.2
67.7	70.7	73.4	76.4	79.4	82.1	85.1	4.4		58.3	62.1	65.5	69.2	72.9	76.3	80.1	5.5
7.6	8.2	8.8	9.4	10.0	10.6	11.2	0.9	Upper arm circ.	7.9	8.4	8.8	9.3	9.8	10.2	10.7	0.7
19.3	20.9	22.3	23.9	25.5	26.9	28.5	2.3		20.0	21.3	22.4	23.6	24.8	25.9	27.2	1.8
5.4	5.7	5.9	6.2	6.5	6.7	7.0	0.4	Wrist circ.	–	–	–	5.7	–	–	–	0.3
13.7	14.4	15.0	15.7	16.4	17.0	17.7	1.0		–	–	–	14.5	–	–	–	0.7
11.4	12.0	12.5	13.1	13.7	14.2	14.8	0.9	Calf circ.	11.0	11.7	12.2	12.8	13.5	14.0	14.6	0.9
28.9	30.5	31.8	33.3	34.8	36.1	37.7	2.2		28.0	29.6	31.0	32.6	34.2	35.6	37.2	2.3
								16½ years								
99.9	110.9	121.0	132.1	143.1	153.2	164.2	16.3	Weight	93.5	103.8	113.1	123.2	133.4	142.6	153.0	15.0
45.3	50.3	54.9	59.9	64.9	69.5	74.5	7.38		42.4	47.1	51.3	55.9	60.5	64.7	69.4	6.8
63.5	65.2	66.6	68.3	69.9	71.4	73.0	2.4	Height	59.7	61.3	62.8	64.4	66.0	67.4	69.1	2.4
161.3	165.5	169.2	173.4	177.6	181.3	185.5	6.1		151.6	155.7	159.4	163.5	167.6	171.3	175.4	6.0
31.4	32.2	33.0	34.0	34.9	35.7	36.8	1.4	Sitting height	30.3	31.2	31.9	32.8	33.7	34.4	35.3	1.3
79.7	81.8	83.9	86.3	88.7	90.8	93.5	3.5		77.0	79.2	81.1	83.3	85.5	87.4	89.6	3.2
14.0	14.5	15.0	15.6	16.1	16.6	17.1	0.8	Shoulder width	12.8	13.3	13.8	14.3	14.8	15.3	15.8	0.7
35.5	36.9	38.1	39.5	40.9	42.1	43.5	2.0		32.6	33.9	35.1	36.4	37.7	38.9	40.2	1.9
11.0	11.5	11.9	12.3	12.8	13.2	13.7	0.7	Pelvic width	10.9	11.4	11.8	12.3	12.8	13.2	13.7	0.7
27.9	29.1	30.1	31.3	32.5	33.5	34.7	1.7		27.6	28.9	30.0	31.2	32.4	33.5	34.8	1.8
20.0	20.4	20.7	21.1	21.5	21.9	22.2	0.6	Head circ.	20.1	20.5	20.8	21.1	21.5	21.8	22.2	0.6
50.9	51.9	52.7	53.7	54.7	55.5	56.5	1.4		51.1	52.0	52.8	53.7	54.6	55.4	56.3	1.4
27.2	28.3	29.3	30.5	31.6	32.6	33.7	1.7	Chest circ.	23.3	24.7	25.9	27.3	28.7	30.0	31.4	2.0
69.1	72.0	74.5	77.4	80.3	82.8	85.7	4.2		59.1	62.7	65.9	69.4	72.9	76.1	79.7	5.2
7.8	8.4	8.9	9.5	10.1	10.6	11.2	0.9	Upper arm circ.	8.0	8.5	8.9	9.4	9.9	10.3	10.8	0.7
19.7	21.3	22.6	24.1	25.6	26.9	28.5	2.2		20.3	21.6	22.7	23.9	25.1	26.2	27.5	1.8
5.4	5.7	5.9	6.2	6.5	6.7	7.0	0.4	Wrist circ.	–	–	–	5.7	–	–	–	0.3
13.8	14.5	15.1	15.8	16.5	17.1	17.8	1.0		–	–	–	14.5	–	–	–	0.7
11.4	12.0	12.6	13.1	13.7	14.3	14.9	0.9	Calf circ.	11.1	11.7	12.2	12.9	13.5	14.1	14.7	0.9
29.0	30.6	31.9	33.4	34.9	36.2	37.8	2.2		28.1	29.7	31.1	32.7	34.3	35.7	37.3	2.3
								17 years								
104.9	114.9	123.9	134.0	144.2	153.2	163.1	14.7	Weight	94.8	105.2	114.4	124.6	134.7	144.0	154.3	15.0
47.6	52.1	56.2	60.8	65.4	69.5	74.0	6.69		43.0	47.7	51.9	56.5	61.1	65.3	70.0	6.8
64.0	65.6	67.0	68.6	70.2	71.6	73.2	2.3	Height	59.7	61.3	62.8	64.5	66.1	67.6	69.3	2.4
162.6	166.7	170.3	174.3	178.3	181.9	186.0	5.9		151.7	155.8	159.6	163.8	168.0	171.8	175.9	6.1
31.5	32.4	33.2	34.1	35.0	35.8	36.7	1.3	Sitting height	30.4	31.3	32.0	32.9	33.7	34.5	35.4	1.3
79.9	82.2	84.3	86.6	88.9	91.0	93.3	3.4		77.2	79.4	81.3	83.5	85.7	87.6	89.8	3.2
14.3	14.8	15.2	15.7	16.3	16.7	17.2	0.7	Shoulder width	12.9	13.4	13.9	14.4	14.9	15.4	15.9	0.7
36.2	37.5	38.7	40.0	41.3	42.5	43.8	1.9		32.7	34.0	35.2	36.5	37.8	39.0	40.3	1.9
11.3	11.7	12.0	12.4	12.8	13.2	13.6	0.6	Pelvic width	11.0	11.5	11.9	12.4	12.9	13.3	13.8	0.7
28.6	29.7	30.6	31.6	32.6	33.5	34.6	1.5		27.9	29.2	30.3	31.5	32.7	33.8	35.1	1.8
20.0	20.4	20.8	21.2	21.6	21.9	22.4	0.6	Head circ.	20.1	20.5	20.8	21.1	21.5	21.8	22.2	0.6
50.8	51.9	52.8	53.8	54.8	55.7	56.8	1.5		51.1	52.0	52.8	53.7	54.6	55.4	56.3	1.4
27.6	28.7	29.7	30.9	32.0	33.0	34.1	1.7	Chest circ.	23.5	24.9	26.1	27.4	28.7	29.8	31.2	1.9
70.1	73.0	75.5	78.4	81.3	83.8	86.7	4.2		59.8	63.2	66.2	69.5	72.8	75.8	79.2	4.9
7.9	8.5	9.0	9.5	10.1	10.6	11.2	0.8	Upper arm circ.	8.1	8.6	9.1	9.5	10.0	10.4	10.9	0.7
20.0	21.5	22.8	24.2	25.6	26.9	28.4	2.1		20.6	21.9	23.0	24.2	25.4	26.5	27.8	1.8
5.5	5.7	6.0	6.2	6.5	6.7	6.9	0.4	Wrist circ.	–	–	–	5.7	–	–	–	0.3
14.0	14.6	15.2	15.8	16.4	17.0	17.6	0.9		–	–	–	14.5	–	–	–	0.7
11.5	12.1	12.6	13.2	13.7	14.3	14.8	0.8	Calf circ.	11.1	11.7	12.3	12.9	13.5	14.1	14.7	0.9
29.3	30.8	32.1	33.5	34.9	36.2	37.7	2.1		28.2	29.8	31.2	32.8	34.4	35.8	37.4	2.3

[1] HEIMENDINGER, J., *Helv. paediat. Acta*, **19**, suppl. 13 (1964). From measurements made in the period 1956–1957 on 2150 boys and 2150 girls in Basle, Switzerland.

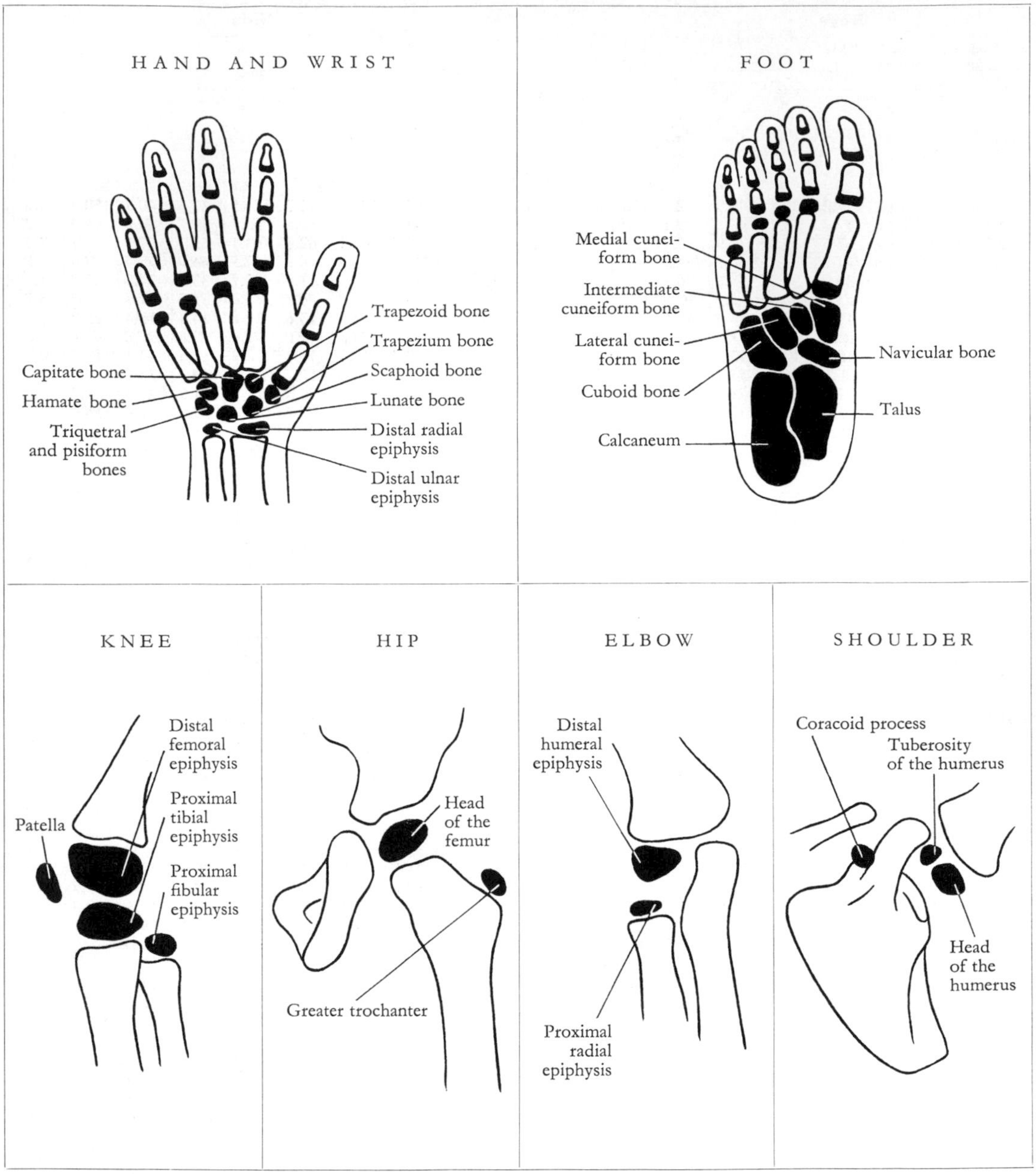

In many clinical situations the assessment of skeletal development is a matter of considerable importance. Various regional ossification processes occurring between birth and maturity can be utilized for this purpose.

For routine clinical purposes the following indications constitute a reliable guide to skeletal development.

Newborn

In the full-term infant, knee X-rays (anteroposterior or lateral) should reveal a distinct and well-formed distal femoral epiphysis.

Bone age in childhood[1–6]

The extent to which regional epiphyses are early or late in appearing can be determined by means of the table on page 707. In doing so it must be borne in mind that the range of physiological variation is rather wide, and that a discordance in the time of appearance of various ossification centres is commonly met with. For this reason, diagnostic X-rays should include several regions of the body (wrist, knee and foot, possibly others).

Bone age in the hand can be readily assessed by means of the table on page 708. For other bones and for a more detailed evaluation of bone age see the special atlases[1–4].

In assessing bone development at and during puberty it must be remembered that girls have a bone age about two years in advance of that of boys of the same age.

Bone development and the onset of puberty

The onset of puberty can be predicted far more reliably from the state of bone development than from height, while chronological age is an even more unreliable guide. When bone development is

* The data on pages 706–708 have been compiled in collaboration with H. J. Kaufmann, Children's Hospital, Basle.

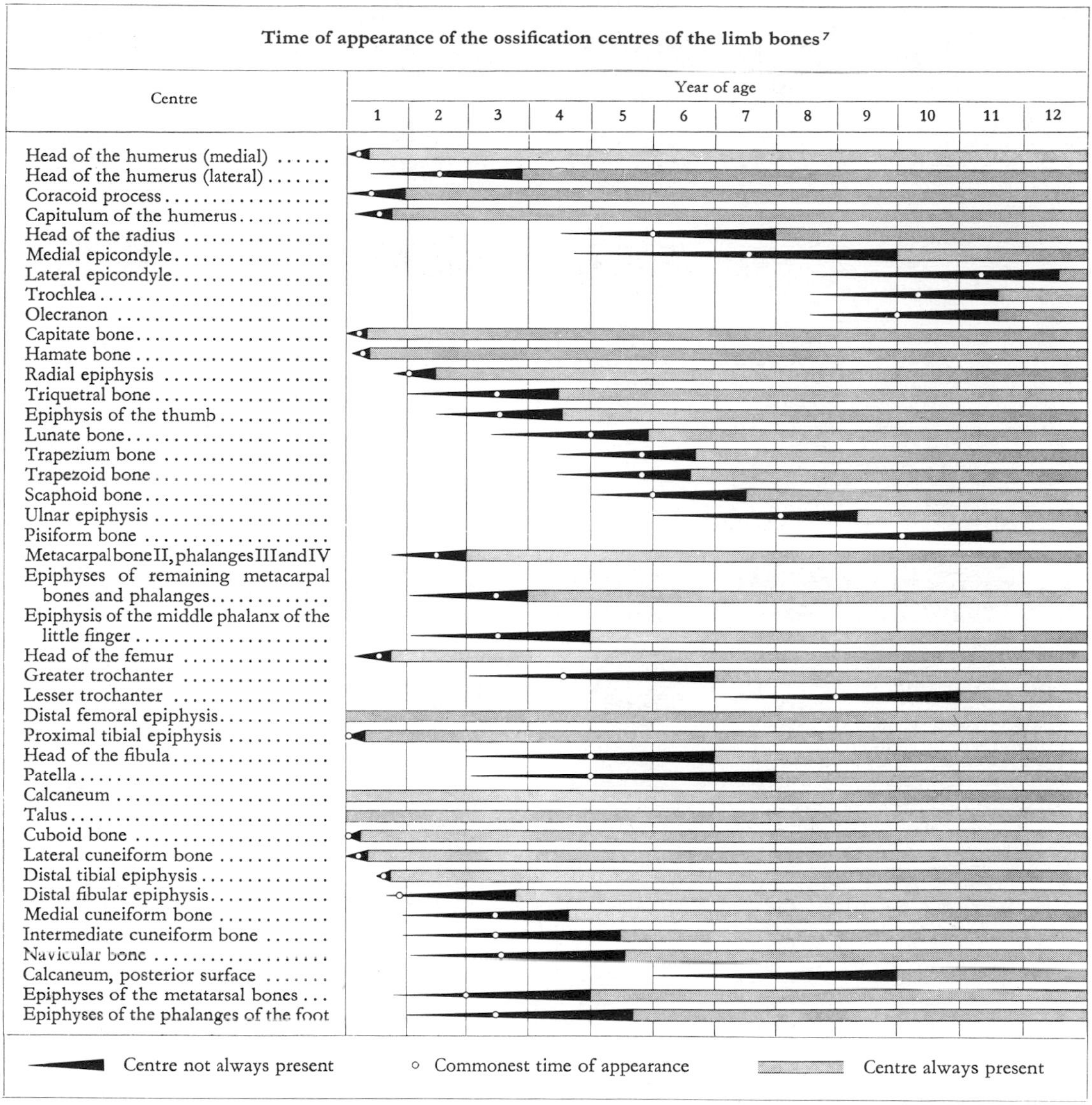

rapid and uninterrupted the onset of puberty will be early, and vice versa. In a similar way the time of appearance and state of development of the various ossification centres are directly related to the individual's eventual height. Thus from the age of 6 years onwards the adult height can be calculated with a fair degree of accuracy from the data given in the atlas of GREULICH and PYLE [1]. A useful clinical guide is the close relationship between the appearance of the sesamoid bones in the thumb and the onset of puberty. In girls the onset of the menarche can be expected within six months of the commencement of ossification of the apophysis of the iliac crest.

Conditions in which it is important to determine bone age

Hypothyroidism. This is marked by a distinct delay in the appearance of the ossification centres. Serial determinations of bone age should accompany treatment. Excessively rapid skeletal development involves the danger of dwarfism.

Pituitary dwarfism. Bone age and longitudinal growth are delayed to the same extent.

Primordial dwarfism. Longitudinal growth is delayed but ossification remains practically normal for the child's age.

Pituitary gigantism. Again due to discordance, longitudinal growth being very advanced while ossification is normal for the child's age.

Adrenogenital syndrome (with precocious puberty). The bone age is far in advance of longitudinal growth; the consequent premature union of the epiphyses results in the height being below normal.

Pseudo-precocious puberty. Here both bone development and longitudinal growth are abnormally rapid, the former more so than the latter.

References

1 GREULICH and PYLE, *Radiographic Atlas of Skeletal Development of the Hand and Wrist*, Stanford University Press, Stanford, 1950.
2 SCHMID and MOLL, *Atlas der normalen und pathologischen Handskeletentwicklung*, Springer, Berlin, 1960.
3 HOERR et al., *Radiographic Atlas of Skeletal Development of the Foot and Ankle*, Thomas, Springfield, 1962.
4 PYLE and HOERR, *Radiographic Atlas of Skeletal Development of the Knee*, Thomas, Springfield, 1955.
5 SCHMID and WEBER, *Röntgendiagnostik im Kindesalter*, Bergmann, Munich, 1955.
6 CAFFEY, J., *Pediatric X-Ray Diagnosis*, 4th ed., Year Book Medical Publishers, Chicago, 1961.
7 SCHMID and HALDEN, *Fortschr. Röntgenstr.*, **71**, 975 (1949).

Appearance of the Secondary Ossification Centres in the Hand[1]

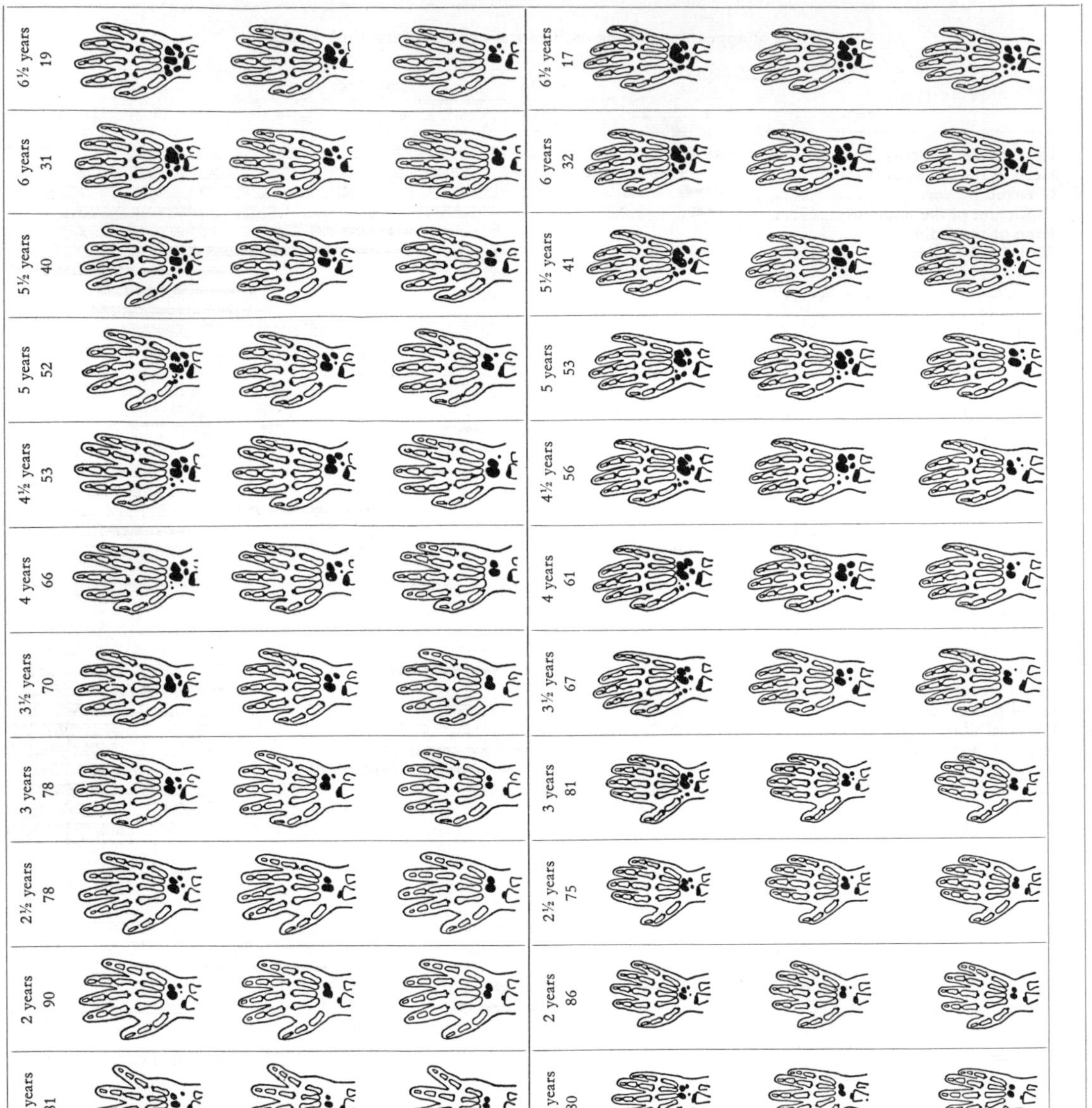

[1] Vogt and Vickers, *Radiology*, **31**, 441 (1938). P = percentile.

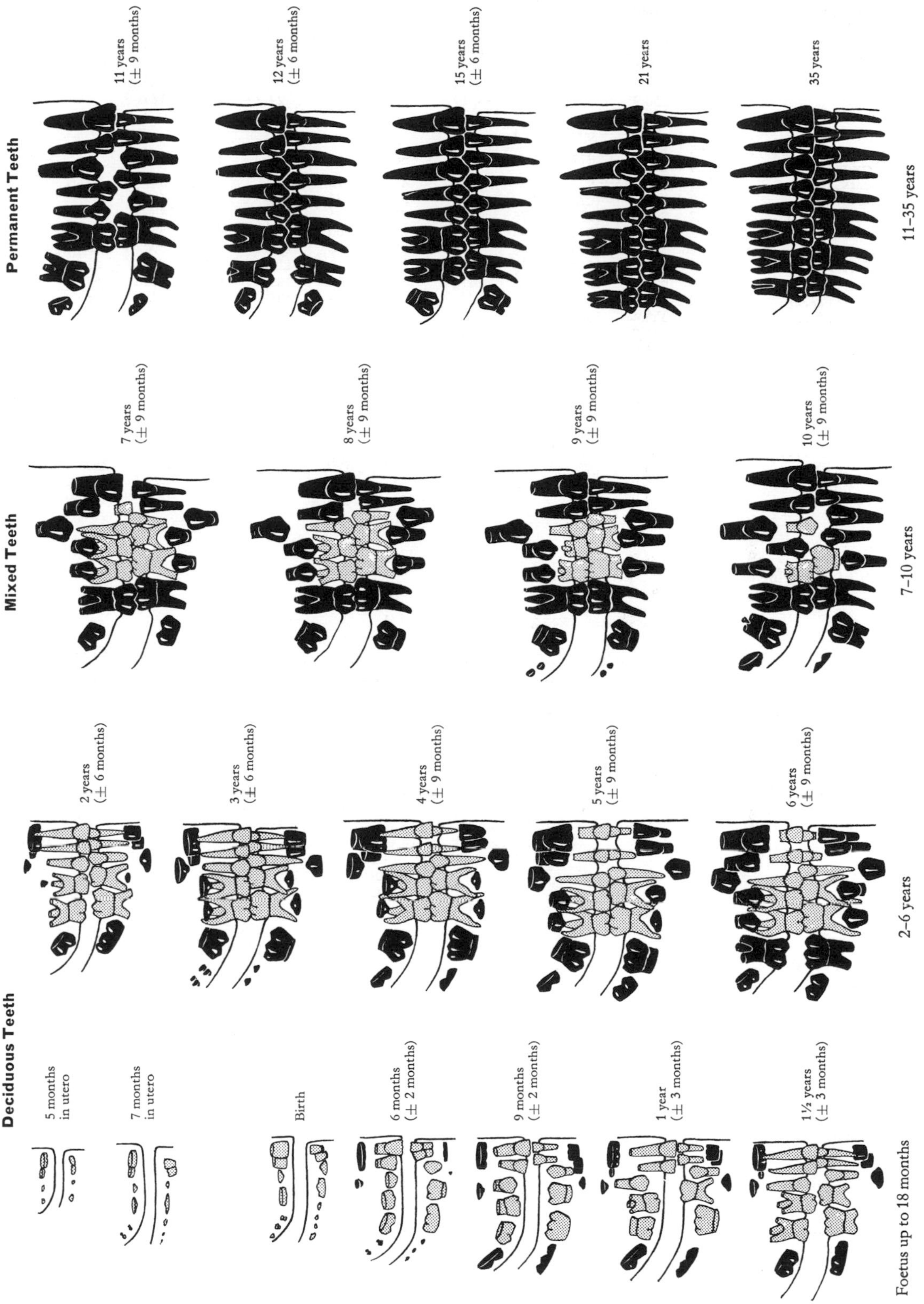

[1] From SCHOUR and MASSLER, *J. Amer. dent. Ass.*, **28**, 1153 (1941).

Organ weights at various ages (in grammes)[1]

	Lungs		Brain		Heart		Kidneys		Liver		Spleen	
	Men	Women	Men	Women	Men	Women	Men	Women	Men	Women	Men	Women
Newborn	51.7	50.9	353	347	19	20	24	24	124	125	8	6
0–3 months	68.8	63.6	435	411	–	–	–	–	–	–	–	–
3–6 months	94.1	93.3	600	534	–	–	–	–	–	–	–	–
6–9 months 9–12 months	128.5 142.4	114.7 142.1	877	726	41	36	60	52	300	240	26	25
1–2 years	170.3	175.3	971	894	54	48	72	65	400	390	35	34
2–3 years	245.9	244.3	1076	1012	63	62	85	75	460	450	42	41
3–4 years	304.7	265.5	1179	1076	73	71	93	84	510	500	48	47
4–5 years	314.2	311.7	1290	1156	83	80	100	93	555	550	53	52
5–6 years	260.6	319.9	1275	1206	95	90	106	102	595	590	58	57
6–7 years	399.5	357.5	1313	1225	103	100	112	112	630	635	62	62
7–8 years	365.4	404.4	1338	1265	110	113	120	123	665	685	64	67
8–9 years	405.0	382.1	1294	1208	122	126	128	135	715	745	68	71
9–10 years	376.4	358.4	1360	1226	132	140	138	148	770	810	73	77
10–11 years	474.5	571.2	1378	1247	144	154	150	163	850	880	82	85
11–12 years	465.6	535.0	1348	1259	157	168	164	180	950	960	91	93
12–13 years	458.8	681.7	1383	1256	180	188	178	195	1050	1080	101	103
13–14 years	504.5	602.3	1382	1243	202	207	196	210	1150	1180	111	112
14–15 years	692.8	517.0	1356	1318	238	226	212	222	1240	1270	121	120
15–16 years	691.7	708.8	1407	1271	258	238	229	230	1315	1330	135	127
16–17 years	747.3	626.5	1419	1300	282	243	244	236	1380	1360	145	134
17–18 years	776.9	694.5	1409	1254	300	247	260	240	1450	1380	152	140
18–19 years	874.7	654.9	1426	1312	310	250	270	244	1510	1395	157	146
19–20 years	1035.6	785.2	1430	1294	318	251	282	247	1580	1405	160	151
20–21 years	953.0	792.8	–	–	322	252	290	248	1630	1415	162	155

Weights of endocrine organs (in grammes) (values are for both sexes)[1]

	Adrenals	Pituitary	Thymus	Pancreas	Thyroid
Newborn	9.04	–	10.9	2.77	2.09
2–14 days	5.19	–	–	–	–
0–1 month	–	–	–	2.42	–
1–2 months	–	–	–	2.63	–
0–3 months	–	–	–	–	1.71
2–3 months	–	–	–	4.46	–
0–6 months	–	0.113	–	–	–
3–6 months	3.91	–	–	5.38	2.11
1 day to 12 months	–	–	19.5	–	–
6–12 months	4.73	0.127	–	9.24	2.04
1–2 years	3.56	0.148	–	13.54	2.53
1–3 years	–	–	23.0	–	–
2–3 years	–	–	–	–	3.40

	Adrenals	Pituitary	Thymus	Pancreas	Thyroid
2–4 years	–	–	–	19.44	–
2–5 years	4.71	0.194	–	–	–
3–5 years	–	–	28.0	–	–
4–6 years	–	–	–	22.44	5.24
6–8 years	–	–	–	28.46	7.05
5–10 years	5.19	0.257	28.5	–	–
8–10 years	–	–	–	26.53	9.30
10–12 years	–	–	–	29.25	8.69
12–14 years	–	–	–	–	14.82
10–15 years	7.00	0.380	29.5	–	–
14–16 years	–	–	–	–	14.48
16–18 years	–	–	–	–	16.62
15–20 years	10.00	0.556	21.0	68.33	–
18–20 years	–	–	–	–	18.33
20–25 years	–	–	18.6	–	–

Weights of reproductive organs (in grammes)[1]

	Testes	Testes and epididymides	Seminal vesicles	Prostate	Ovaries	Uterine tubes	Uterus
Newborn	0.85	0.91	0.050	0.82	0.33	0.29	3.90
0–1 year	1.03	1.33	0.052	0.9	0.62	0.26	1.42
1–2 years	–	–	–	–	0.84	0.29	1.50
1–3 years	1.48	1.82	–	1.2	–	–	–
2–4 years	–	–	–	–	1.12	–	2.30
3–5 years	1.64	1.76	–	1.1	–	–	–
4–7 years	–	–	–	–	1.90	–	2.80
5–10 years	1.67	2.24	0.099	1.3	–	–	–
10–12 years	2.00	4.00	0.120	1.9	–	–	–
7–14 years	–	–	–	–	3.30	0.49	4.30
12–14 years	6.96	8.15	–	3.3	–	–	–
14–16 years	15.56	19.3	0.900	4.3	–	–	–
16–18 years	–	32.0	–	8.8	–	–	–
14–20 years	–	–	–	–	6.03	1.05	32.50
20–30 years	34.66	–	–	16.6	10.71	2.13	49.50

[1] Boyd, E., in Altman and Dittmer (Eds.), *Growth, Including Reproduction and Morphological Development*, Biological Handbooks, Federation of American Societies for Experimental Biology, Washington, 1962, pages 346–348.

Average Weights of Adults[1]

Height (in shoes)		Average weights in pounds and *kilogrammes* (in indoor clothing)															
		15–16 years		17–19 years		20–24 years		25–29 years		30–39 years		40–49 years		50–59 years		60–69 years	
ft in	*cm*	lb	*kg*	lb	*kg*	lb	*kg*	lb	*kg*	lb	*kg*	lb	*kg*	lb	*kg*	lb	*kg*
Men																	
5 0	152.4	98	44.5	113	51.3	122	55.3	128	58.1	131	59.4	134	60.8	136	61.7	133	60.3
5 0½	153.7	100	45.4	114.5	51.9	123.5	56	129.5	58.7	132.5	60.1	135.5	61.5	137.5	62.4	134.5	61
5 1	154.9	102	46.3	116	52.6	125	56.7	131	59.4	134	60.8	137	62.1	139	63	136	61.7
5 1½	156.2	104.5	47.4	117.5	53.3	126.5	57.4	132.5	60.1	135.5	61.5	138.5	62.8	140.5	63.7	137.5	62.4
5 2	157.5	107	48.5	119	54	128	58.1	134	60.8	137	62.1	140	63.5	142	64.4	139	63
5 2½	158.8	109.5	49.7	121	54.9	130	59	136	61.7	139	63	142	64.4	143.5	65.1	140.5	63.7
5 3	160	112	50.8	123	55.8	132	59.9	138	62.6	141	64	144	65.3	145	65.8	142	64.4
5 3½	161.3	114.5	51.9	125	56.7	134	60.8	139.5	63.3	143	64.9	146	66.2	147	66.7	144	65.3
5 4	162.6	117	53.1	127	57.6	136	61.7	141	64	145	65.8	148	67.1	149	67.6	146	66.2
5 4½	163.8	119.5	54.2	129	58.5	137.5	62.4	142.5	64.6	147	66.7	150	68	151	68.5	148	67.1
5 5	165.1	122	55.3	131	59.4	139	63	144	65.3	149	67.6	152	68.9	153	69.4	150	68
5 5½	166.4	124.5	56.5	133	60.3	140.5	63.7	146	66.2	151	68.5	154	69.9	155	70.3	152	68.9
5 6	167.6	127	57.6	135	61.2	142	64.4	148	67.1	153	69.4	156	70.8	157	71.2	154	69.9
5 6½	168.9	129.5	58.7	137	62.1	143.5	65.1	149.5	67.8	155	70.3	158.5	71.9	159.5	72.3	156.5	71
5 7	170.2	132	59.9	139	63	145	65.8	151	68.5	157	71.2	161	73	162	73.5	159	72.1
5 7½	171.5	134.5	61	141	64	147	66.7	153	69.4	159	72.1	163	73.9	164	74.4	161	73
5 8	172.7	137	62.1	143	64.9	149	67.6	155	70.3	161	73	165	74.8	166	75.3	163	73.9
5 8½	174	139.5	63.3	145	65.8	151	68.5	157	71.2	163	73.9	167	75.8	168	76.2	165.5	75.1
5 9	175.3	142	64.4	147	66.7	153	69.4	159	72.1	165	74.8	169	76.7	170	77.1	168	76.2
5 9½	176.5	144	65.3	149	67.6	155	70.3	161	73	167.5	76	171.5	77.8	172.5	78.2	170.5	77.3
5 10	177.8	146	66.2	151	68.5	157	71.2	163	73.9	170	77.1	174	78.9	175	79.4	173	78.5
5 10½	179.1	148	67.1	153	69.4	159	72.1	165	74.8	172	78	176	79.8	177.5	80.5	175.5	79.6
5 11	180.3	150	68	155	70.3	161	73	167	75.8	174	78.9	178	80.8	180	81.6	178	80.8
5 11½	181.6	152	68.9	157.5	71.4	163.5	74.2	169.5	76.9	176.5	80.1	180.5	81.9	182.5	82.8	180.5	81.9
6 0	182.9	154	69.9	160	72.6	166	75.3	172	78	179	81.2	183	83	185	83.9	183	83
6 0½	184.2	156.5	71	162	73.5	168	76.2	174.5	79.2	181	82.1	185	83.9	187	84.8	185.5	84.1
6 1	185.4	159	72.1	164	74.4	170	77.1	177	80.3	183	83	187	84.8	189	85.7	188	85.3
6 1½	186.7	161.5	73.3	166	75.3	172	78	179.5	81.4	185.5	84.1	189.5	86	191.5	86.9	190.5	86.4
6 2	188	164	74.4	168	76.2	174	78.9	182	82.6	188	85.3	192	87.1	194	88	193	87.5
6 2½	189.2	166.5	75.5	170	77.1	176	79.8	184	83.5	190.5	86.4	194.5	88.2	196.5	89.1	195.5	88.7
6 3	190.5	169	76.7	172	78	178	80.8	186	84.4	193	87.5	197	89.4	199	90.3	198	89.8
6 3½	191.8	–	–	174	78.9	179.5	81.4	188	85.3	196	88.9	200	90.7	202	91.6	201	91.2
6 4	193	–	–	176	79.8	181	82.1	190	86.2	199	90.3	203	92.1	205	93	204	92.5
Women																	
4 10	147.3	97	44	99	44.9	102	46.3	107	48.5	115	52.2	122	55.3	125	56.7	127	57.6
4 10½	148.6	98.5	44.7	100.5	45.6	103.5	46.9	108.5	49.2	116	52.6	123	55.8	126	57.2	128	58.1
4 11	149.9	100	45.4	102	46.3	105	47.6	110	49.9	117	53.1	124	56.2	127	57.6	129	58.5
4 11½	151.1	101.5	46	103.5	46.9	106.5	48.3	111.5	50.6	118.5	53.8	125.5	56.9	128.5	58.3	130	59
5 0	152.4	103	46.7	105	47.6	108	49	113	51.3	120	54.4	127	57.6	130	59	131	59.4
5 0½	153.7	105	47.6	107	48.5	110	49.9	114.5	51.9	121.5	55.1	128.5	58.3	131.5	59.6	132.5	60.1
5 1	154.9	107	48.5	109	49.4	112	50.8	116	52.6	123	55.8	130	59	133	60.3	134	60.8
5 1½	156.2	109	49.4	111	50.3	113.5	51.5	117.5	53.3	124.5	56.5	131.5	59.6	134.5	61	135.5	61.5
5 2	157.5	111	50.3	113	51.3	115	52.2	119	54	126	57.2	133	60.3	136	61.7	137	62.1
5 2½	158.8	112.5	51	114.5	51.9	116.5	52.8	120.5	54.7	127.5	57.8	134.5	61	138	62.6	139	63
5 3	160	114	51.7	116	52.6	118	53.5	122	55.3	129	58.5	136	61.7	140	63.5	141	64
5 3½	161.3	115.5	52.4	118	53.5	119.5	54.2	123.5	56	130.5	59.2	138	62.6	142	64.4	143	64.9
5 4	162.6	117	53.1	120	54.4	121	54.9	125	56.7	132	59.9	140	63.5	144	65.3	145	65.8
5 4½	163.8	119	54	122	55.3	123	55.8	127	57.6	133.5	60.6	141.5	64.2	146	66.2	147	66.7
5 5	165.1	121	54.9	124	56.2	125	56.7	129	58.5	135	61.2	143	64.9	148	67.1	149	67.6
5 5½	166.4	123	55.8	125.5	56.9	127	57.6	131	59.4	137	62.1	145	65.8	150	68	151	68.5
5 6	167.6	125	56.7	127	57.6	129	58.5	133	60.3	139	63	147	66.7	152	68.9	153	69.4
5 6½	168.9	126.5	57.4	128.5	58.3	130.5	59.2	134.5	61	140.5	63.7	149	67.6	154	69.9	155	70.3
5 7	170.2	128	58.1	130	59	132	59.9	136	61.7	142	64.4	151	68.5	156	70.8	157	71.2
5 7½	171.5	130	59	132	59.9	134	60.8	138	62.6	144	65.3	153	69.4	158	71.7	159	72.1
5 8	172.7	132	59.9	134	60.8	136	61.7	140	63.5	146	66.2	155	70.3	160	72.6	161	73
5 8½	174	134	60.8	136	61.7	138	62.6	142	64.4	148	67.1	157	71.2	162	73.5	163	73.9
5 9	175.3	136	61.7	138	62.6	140	63.5	144	65.3	150	68	159	72.1	164	74.4	165	74.8
5 9½	176.5	–	–	140	63.5	142	64.4	146	66.2	152	68.9	161.5	73.3	166.5	75.5	–	–
5 10	177.8	–	–	142	64.4	144	65.3	148	67.1	154	69.9	164	74.4	169	76.7	–	–
5 10½	179.1	–	–	144.5	65.5	146.5	66.5	150.5	68.3	156.5	71	166.5	75.5	171.5	77.8	–	–
5 11	180.3	–	–	147	66.7	149	67.6	153	69.4	159	72.1	169	76.7	174	78.9	–	–
5 11½	181.6	–	–	149.5	67.8	151.5	68.7	155.5	70.5	161.5	73.3	171.5	77.8	177	80.3	–	–
6 0	182.9	–	–	152	68.9	154	69.9	158	71.7	164	74.4	174	78.9	180	81.6	–	–

[1] Insured persons in the United States (Society of Actuaries, *Build and Blood Pressure Study*, vol. 1, Chicago, 1959, page 16, with interpolations by the editors of these *Scientific Tables*). Compare the *desirable* weights in a similar population given in the table on page 712.

Desirable Weights of Adults[1]

Height (in shoes)		Desirable weight in pounds and *kilogrammes* (in indoor clothing), ages 25 and over					
		Small frame		Medium frame		Large frame	
ft in	*cm*	lb	*kg*	lb	*kg*	lb	*kg*
				Men			
5 2	*157.5*	112–120	*50.8–54.4*	118–129	*53.5–58.5*	126–141	*57.2–64*
5 3	*160*	115–123	*52.2–55.8*	121–133	*54.9–60.3*	129–144	*58.5–65.3*
5 4	*162.6*	118–126	*53.5–57.2*	124–136	*56.2–61.7*	132–148	*59.9–67.1*
5 5	*165.1*	121–129	*54.9–58.5*	127–139	*57.6–63*	135–152	*61.2–68.9*
5 6	*167.6*	124–133	*56.2–60.3*	130–143	*59 –64.9*	138–156	*62.6–70.8*
5 7	*170.2*	128–137	*58.1–62.1*	134–147	*60.8–66.7*	142–161	*64.4–73*
5 8	*172.7*	132–141	*59.9–64*	138–152	*62.6–68.9*	147–166	*66.7–75.3*
5 9	*175.3*	136–145	*61.7–65.8*	142–156	*64.4–70.8*	151–170	*68.5–77.1*
5 10	*177.8*	140–150	*63.5–68*	146–160	*66.2–72.6*	155–174	*70.3–78.9*
5 11	*180.3*	144–154	*65.3–69.9*	150–165	*68 –74.8*	159–179	*72.1–81.2*
6 0	*182.9*	148–158	*67.1–71.7*	154–170	*69.9–77.1*	164–184	*74.4–83.5*
6 1	*185.4*	152–162	*68.9–73.5*	158–175	*71.7–79.4*	168–189	*76.2–85.7*
6 2	*188*	156–167	*70.8–75.7*	162–180	*73.5–81.6*	173–194	*78.5–88*
6 3	*190.5*	160–171	*72.6–77.6*	167–185	*75.7–83.5*	178–199	*80.7–90.3*
6 4	*193*	164–175	*74.4–79.4*	172–190	*78.1–86.2*	182–204	*82.7–92.5*
				Women			
4 10	*147.3*	92– 98	*41.7–44.5*	96–107	*43.5–48.5*	104–119	*47.2–54*
4 11	*149.9*	94–101	*42.6–45.8*	98–110	*44.5–49.9*	106–122	*48.1–55.3*
5 0	*152.4*	96–104	*43.5–47.2*	101–113	*45.8–51.3*	109–125	*49.4–56.7*
5 1	*154.9*	99–107	*44.9–48.5*	104–116	*47.2–52.6*	112–128	*50.8–58.1*
5 2	*157.5*	102–110	*46.3–49.9*	107–119	*48.5–54*	115–131	*52.2–59.4*
5 3	*160*	105–113	*47.6–51.3*	110–122	*49.9–55.3*	118–134	*53.5–60.8*
5 4	*162.6*	108–116	*49 –52.6*	113–126	*51.3–57.2*	121–138	*54.9–62.6*
5 5	*165.1*	111–119	*50.3–54*	116–130	*49 –59*	125–142	*49.4–64.4*
5 6	*167.6*	114–123	*51.7–55.8*	120–135	*54.4–61.2*	129–146	*58.5–66.2*
5 7	*170.2*	118–127	*53.5–57.6*	124–139	*56.2–63*	133–150	*60.3–68*
5 8	*172.7*	122–131	*55.3–59.4*	128–143	*58.1–64.9*	137–154	*62.1–69.9*
5 9	*175.3*	126–135	*57.2–61.2*	132–147	*59.9–66.7*	141–158	*64 –71.7*
5 10	*177.8*	130–140	*59 –63.5*	136–151	*61.7–68.5*	145–163	*65.8–73.9*
5 11	*180.3*	134–144	*60.8–65.3*	140–155	*63.5–70.3*	149–168	*67.6–76.2*
6 0	*182.9*	138–148	*62.6–67.1*	144–159	*65.3–72.1*	153–173	*69.4–78.5*

[1] Weights of insured persons in the United States associated with lowest mortality (*Statist. Bull. Metrop. Life Insur. Co.*, **40**, Nov.–Dec. 1959).

Hormones

Hormones are substances with specific biological activity synthesized in glands or tissues specially adapted to this purpose and released into the blood. Chemically, they are glycoproteins, polypeptides, amino-acid derivatives or steroids. The observable physiological effects of hormones are the results of a primary biochemical process, such as an alteration of the permeability of the cell membrane or the stimulation of certain gene loci resulting in the synthesis of particular enzymes[1].

Reference

1 KARLSON, P. (Ed.), *Mechanisms of Hormone Action*, NATO Advanced Study Institute, Academic Press, New York, 1965.

Gonadotropins of the anterior pituitary[1,2]

Follicle-stimulating hormone

(FSH, follicle-ripening hormone)

Luteinizing hormone

(LH, interstitial cell-stimulating hormone = ICSH, corpus luteum-ripening hormone)

Chemistry

The gonadotropins are glycoproteins with a molecular weight (monomers) of 16000–17000[3,4]; higher figures are probably molecular weights of dimers or tetramers. The carbohydrate content of human LH is about 17%, that of human FSH about 24%[5]; present are mannose, galactose, fucose, *N*-acetylhexosamines and *N*-acetylneuraminic acid. LH has a much higher proline content than FSH[5]. The gonadotropins in the pituitary and urine can be isolated by appropriate extraction, fractional precipitation, gel filtration and gel electrophoresis. More highly purified preparations can be obtained from pituitary tissue than from urine.

Activity of various human gonadotropin preparations[5]

Origin	FSH preparations		
	Activity (IU/mg)	LH content (IU/mg)	Prepared by
Pituitary	1000	<10	BUTT
Menopausal urine	597	11	DONINI
	789	< 0.03	STEVENS
Male urine	59.5	24.2	DONINI
Origin	**LH preparations**		
	Activity (IU/mg)	FSH content (IU/mg)	Prepared by
Pituitary	7500	< 1	HARTREE
Menopausal urine	447	18.9	DONINI
Male urine	53.6	6.7	DONINI

Units, methods of assay

The following reference preparations are available[6]:

1st International Reference Preparation of Human Menopausal Gonadotropin (IRP-HMG), known previously as HMG-24.

2nd International Reference Preparation of Human Menopausal Gonadotropin (IRP-HMG), earlier known as Pergonal-23. 1 International Unit (IU) of human urinary FSH or human urinary LH is contained in 0.2295 mg of the reference preparation (see page 763).

Human Pituitary Gonadotropin (NIH-HPG-UE) of the National Institutes of Health, Endocrinology Study Section, Bethesda, USA. Obtained from the urine of eunuchs.

National Institutes of Health FSH from sheep pituitary: 3 preparations so far distributed (NIH-FSH-S1, -S2 and -S3).

National Institutes of Health LH from sheep pituitary (NIH-LH-S1).

Human Pituitary Gonadotropin: An International Reference Preparation is in course of development.

Conversion factors for reference preparations (as mg or IU equivalent to 1 mg of 2nd IRP-HMG)[44]

Reference preparation	FSH*	LH**
2nd IRP-HMG	1	1
1st IRP-HMG	56	16
NIH-FSH-S1	0.31	–
NIH-LH-S1	–	0.0053
International Unit	8	8

* Assayed by the ovarian augmentation method in rodents.
** Assayed by the rat ovarian ascorbic acid depletion method.

There is a considerable literature on the assay and extraction of gonadotropins in body fluids[6,7]. The following methods are in common use:

Total gonadotropic activity. Increase in the weight of the uterus in intact immature mice[8] or of the ovaries in intact immature rats[9].

FSH activity. Increase in ovarian weight in intact immature rats treated with HCG[10]. HCG and LH have similar biological properties; after an overdose the ovaries become refractory to LH and react only to FSH.

LH activity. Increase in ventral prostatic weight in immature hypophysectomized rats[11]; depletion of ovarian ascorbic acid[12] or cholesterol[13] in pseudo-pregnant immature rats after intravenous or subcutaneous injection of the hormone.

Immunological methods. LH[14] and FSH[15] can be determined by inhibition of haemagglutination, LH also by inhibition of latex-particle agglutination[16]. Radioimmunological methods have recently been developed for LH[17,20] and FSH[18,23]. Reliability criteria of immunological methods for both hormones remain to be established.

Biosynthesis, secretion, metabolism

In the anterior pituitary the gonadotropins are formed in the Δ-cells forming part of the basophile β-cells[19]. Small amounts are present in the circulating blood, where radioimmunological methods now provide a possible technique for their determination. In one such study LH serum levels of 4.8–26 mIU 2nd IRP-HMG/ml were found in men and in women not in the middle of the menstrual cycle[20]. At midcycle, shortly before the rise in the basal temperature, an increase of the plasma LH level to 30–150 mU/ml for a period of up to 24–28 hours has been observed[21]. Before puberty plasma LH levels are either low or undetectable in both boys and girls[22], while in postmenopausal women the plasma LH level is considerably increased[20,22]. Determinations by radioimmunoassay[45] have shown serum FSH levels of 5–25 2nd IRP-HMG mIU/ml, together with slight fluctuations during the menstrual cycle; in children the level was lower, while in postmenopausal women it rose to 40–250 mIU/ml. FSH has also been found to be present in the serum of pregnant women[46]. Results of FSH determinations by radioimmunoassay must at present be accepted with some reservation.

Little is known of the metabolism of the gonadotropins. They are excreted through the kidneys in spite of their being high-molecular glycoproteins. It has been reported that the mean renal clearance of FSH is 0.68 ml/min, of LH 0.14 ml/min[24]. Only a small proportion of the LH produced by the pituitary appears in the urine[25].

Normal values for gonadotropin excretion are given in the table below. Small amounts of 'total gonadotropins' as well as of LH

* This chapter on 'Hormones' (pages 713–758) has been compiled in collaboration with Sir HANS KREBS, F.R.S., and P.R. RAGGATT (Department of Biochemistry, University of Oxford, England); J.M. LOWENSTEIN (Graduate Department of Biochemistry, Brandeis University, Waltham, Mass., USA); M. ALIAPOULIOS (Peter Bent Brigham Hospital, Boston, Mass., USA); H.M. GOODMAN, W. ROTH and W.J. REDDY (Harvard Medical School, Boston, Mass., USA); M.J. HERRERA and J. STEINKE (Joslin Research Laboratory, Boston, Mass., USA); J. SOLOMON (Chestnut Hill, Mass., USA); J.R. WILLIAMSON (Department of Biophysics and Physical Biochemistry, The Johnson Foundation, Philadelphia, Pa., USA); L. BRAVERMAN (St. Elizabeth's Hospital, Boston, Mass., USA); J.A. LORAINE (Medical Research Council Clinical Endocrinology Research Unit, University of Edinburgh); H. STUDER (University Medical Clinic, Berne); R. VEYRAT (Department of Clinical Pathology, University of Geneva).

have been detected in the urine of prepuberal children[26]. In women, gonadotropin excretion shows characteristic fluctuations during the menstrual cycle with a maximum during the ovulatory phase shortly before the rise in basal temperature[27]. LH is present in the urine in all phases of the cycle and like total gonadotropin excretion rises to a maximum at midcycle[28–30]. FSH is also found in the urine in all phases of the cycle but the excretion is not subject to any marked rhythmic change[28, 29]. After the menopause gonadotropin excretion is increased, with wide daily variations, as a result of the almost complete cessation of ovarian oestrogen secretion[31]. In male urine FSH and LH are present in about the same proportion as in menopausal urine[29].

Total gonadotropin excretion in urine

	Mean	Range	s	Reference
	mg 1st IRP-HMG/24 h			
Men, 18–40 years	7.7	3.8–18.1	–	47
Women, 18–35 years	4.9	2.7–7.1	–	47
Girls, 14–15 years	0.8	–	–	47
Girls, 10 years	0.3	–	–	47
Boy, 8 ½ years	0.5	–	–	47
	U 1st IRP-HMG/24 h			
Women, menstruating	9.0	3.0–15.7	–	48
Women, proliferation phase	9.2	2.8–30.4	–	48
Women, ovulation phase	10.5	2.8–31.6	–	48
Women, luteal phase	7.4	2.9–14.9	–	48
Women, postmenopausal	76	35–158*	–	49
Men, 20–60 years	11	5–23*	–	50

* 95% range.

Gonadotropin assay in urine enables primary gonadal insufficiency (increased excretion) to be distinguished from secondary gonadal insufficiency due to disturbance of pituitary function (decreased excretion).

The urine of both children and adults contains a gonadotropin-inhibiting factor, but the precise physiological significance of this substance is not known[32, 43].

Regulation of gonadotropin secretion. Gonadotropin secretion is regulated by neurohumoral factors from the hypothalamus, the so-called 'gonadotropin-releasing factors' (GRF)[33]. These reach the cells of the anterior lobe of the pituitary via the portal circulation of the gland[34]. At present the best-known factor is LH-RF, a polypeptide of molecular weight between 1200 and 2500[35]. When given to rats this factor causes a rise in the plasma LH level[36]. Formation of LH-RF is inhibited by oestrogens and, at high dosage, by progesterone and testosterone[35]. Direct inhibition of LH release through the action of oestrogens on the pituitary may also occur[37]. Inhibition of FSH-RF formation appears to require larger amounts of oestrogens than that of LH-RF formation[38] and is also caused by testosterone[39]. The regulation of gonadotropin secretion is subject to the influence of nervous impulses of central and peripheral origin[40, 41]. The interaction of the gonadal steroids with the hypothalamus and pituitary not only takes the form of a negative feedback mechanism but in some circumstances may result in stimulation of these glands (positive feedback)[2, 40].

Biological activity

The gonadotropins act directly on the gonads of both sexes and indirectly on the male and female reproductive organs by stimulating the secretion of gonadal steroids. In both sexes FSH is responsible for maintaining gametogenesis, LH for stimulating the interstitial ovarian tissue, ovulation, corpus luteum formation and the production of androgens in the cells of Leydig. The interplay of the various regulatory mechanisms in the course of the menstrual cycle is still not fully understood. Together with LH, FSH induces growth of the follicle and secretion of oestrogens. Sudden release of LH results in ovulation and suppresses oestrogen secretion, but such a release can be inhibited by high blood levels of oestrogens and progestational substances; this is one reason for their use in ovulation-inhibiting preparations. Administration of FSH preparations from the human pituitary tissue followed by HCG has repeatedly been shown to induce ovulation[42].

References

1 Cole, H.H. (Ed.), *Gonadotropins, Their Chemical and Biological Properties and Secretory Control*, Freeman, London, 1964; Apostolakis and Voigt, *Gonadotropine*, Thieme, Stuttgart, 1965; Harris and Donovan (Eds.), *The Pituitary Gland*, vols. 1 and 2, Butterworth, London, 1966.
2 Mauvais-Jarvis, P., *Presse méd.*, **75**, 225 and 283 (1967).
3 Li and Starman, *Nature*, **202**, 291 (1964).
4 Jutisz, M., Discussion in Wolstenholme and Knight (Eds.), *Gonadotropins: Physicochemical and Immunological Properties*, Ciba Foundation Study Group, No. 22, Churchill, London, 1965, page 113.
5 Butt, W.R., in Bell and Loraine (Eds.), *Recent Research on Gonadotrophic Hormones*, Proceedings of 5th Gonadotrophin Club Meeting, Edinburgh 1966, Livingstone, Edinburgh, 1967, page 129.
6 Loraine and Bell, *Hormone Assays and Their Clinical Application*, 2nd ed., Livingstone, Edinburgh, 1966.
7 Lauritzen, C., *Med. Klin.*, **58**, 822 and 863 (1963); Bell, E.T., *Vitam. and Horm.*, **24**, 63 (1966).
8 Klinefelter et al., *J. clin. Endocr.*, **3**, 529 (1943).
9 Albert, A., *Fertil. and Steril.*, **10**, 60 (1959).
10 Steelman and Pohley, *Endocrinology*, **53**, 604 (1953).
11 Greep et al., *Endocrinology*, **30**, 635 (1942).
12 Parlow, A.F., in Albert, A. (Ed.), *Human Pituitary Gonadotropins*, Thomas, Springfield, 1961, page 300.
13 Bell et al., *J. Endocr.*, **28**, 321 (1964).
14 Wide et al., *Acta endocr. (Kbh.)*, **37**, 445 (1961); Wide and Gemzell, *Ciba Found. Coll. Endocr.*, **14**, 296 (1962).
15 Wolf, A., *Nature*, **211**, 942 (1966).
16 Rizkallah et al., *J. clin. Endocr.*, **25**, 943 (1965).
17 Odell et al., *Metabolism*, **15**, 287 (1966); Bagshawe et al., *Lancet*, **1**, 1118 (1966); Midgley, A.R., *Endocrinology*, **79**, 10 (1966).
18 Odell and Parlow, *Clin. Res.*, **15**, 125 (1967); Midgley, A.R., *J. clin. Endocr.*, **27**, 295 (1967).
19 Ezrin, C., in Netter, P.H. (Ed.), *Endocrine System and Selected Metabolic Diseases*, Ciba Collection of Medical Illustrations, vol. 4, Ciba, New York, 1965, page 10.
20 Odell et al., *J. clin. Invest.*, **46**, 248 (1967).
21 Midgley and Jaffe, *J. clin. Endocr.*, **26**, 1375 (1966); Ross et al., *Science*, **155**, 1679 (1967).
22 Schalch et al., *J. clin. Invest.*, **47**, 665 (1968).
23 Faiman and Ryan, *J. clin. Endocr.*, **27**, 444 (1967); Faiman and Ryan, *Nature*, **215**, 857 (1967).
24 Keller, P.J., *Schweiz. med. Wschr.*, **97**, 221 (1967).
25 Kohler et al., *J. clin. Invest.*, **46**, 1079 (1967).
26 Carletti and Kehyayan, *Minerva pediat.*, **14**, 21 (1962); Fitschen and Clayton, *Arch. Dis. Childh.*, **40**, 16 (1965); Bell and Mukerji, quoted by Loraine and Bell [6].
27 Kaiser et al., *Arch. Gynäk.*, **199**, 414 (1964).
28 Fukushima et al., *J. clin. Endocr.*, **24**, 205 (1964); Rosemberg and Keller, *J. clin. Endocr.*, **25**, 1262 (1965); Rosemberg et al., *J. clin. Endocr.*, **28**, 1419 (1968).
29 Becker and Albert, *J. clin. Endocr.*, **25**, 962 (1965).
30 Stevens et al., *Metabolism*, **14**, 327 (1965); Loraine and Bell, *Fertility and Contraception in the Human Female*, Livingstone, Edinburgh, 1968.
31 Brown, P.S., *J. Endocr.*, **25**, 427 (1963); Albert and Mendoza, *J. clin. Endocr.*, **26**, 371 (1966).
32 Landau et al., *Metabolism*, **9**, 85 (1960); Soffer and Fogel, *J. clin. Endocr.*, **23**, 870 (1963); Saito, A., *Canad. J. Biochem.*, **43**, 1711 (1965); Davis et al., *J. clin. Endocr.*, **26**, 1123 (1966).
33 Guillemin, R., *Recent Progr. Hormone Res.*, **20**, 89 (1964); Guillemin, R., *Ann. Rev. Physiol.*, **29**, 313 (1967).
34 Harris, G.W., in *Proceedings of the 23rd International Congress on Physiological Sciences*, Tokyo 1965, Excerpta Medica Foundation, International Congress Series, No. 87, Amsterdam, 1965.
35 McCann et al., in *Second International Congress on Hormonal Steroids*, Milan 1966, Excerpta Medica Foundation, Amsterdam, 1966, page 79.
36 Antunes-Rodrigues et al., *Proc. Soc. exp. Biol. (N.Y.)*, **122**, 1001 (1966).
37 Flerkó, B., in Szentágothai et al. (Eds.), *Hypothalamic Control of the Anterior Pituitary*, Hungarian Academy of Sciences, Budapest, 1963; Bogdanove, E.M., *Endocrinology*, **73**, 696 (1963).
38 Parlow, A.F., *Endocrinology*, **75**, 1 (1964).
39 Mittler and Meites, *Endocrinology*, **78**, 500 (1966).
40 Bogdanove, E.M., *Vitam. and Horm.*, **22**, 205 (1964).
41 Everett, J.W., *Physiol. Rev.*, **44**, 373 (1964).
42 Gemzell, C., *Recent Progr. Hormone Res.*, **21**, 179 (1965); Crooke, A.C., in Gardiner-Hill, H. (Ed.), *Modern Trends in Endocrinology*, vol. 3, Butterworth, London, 1967, page 111; Lunenfeld et al., *Advanc. metab. Dis.*, **3**, 153 (1968).
43 Krishnamurti and Bell, *J. Reprod. Fert.*, **13**, 149 (1967).
44 Butt et al., in Wolstenholme and Knight (Eds.), *Gonadotropins: Physicochemical and Immunological Properties*, Ciba Foundation Study Group, No. 22, Churchill, London, 1965, page 85.
45 Odell et al., *J. clin. Invest.*, **47**, 2551 (1968).
46 Faiman et al., *J. clin. Endocr.*, **28**, 1323 (1968).
47 Fitschen and Clayton, *Arch. Dis. Childh.*, **40**, 16 (1965).
48 Loraine and Bell, *Lancet*, **1**, 1340 (1963).
49 Apostolakis and Loraine, *J. clin. Endocr.*, **20**, 1437 (1960).
50 Loraine, J.A., quoted by Loraine and Bell [6].

Human chorionic gonadotropin[1,2]
(HCG)

Chemistry

An HCG preparation from pregnancy urine had a reported molecular weight of about 30000 and activity of 12000 IU/mg[3]; the glycoprotein contained 11% hexoses, 9% hexosamines, 1% fucose and 8.5% *N*-acetylneuraminic acid[3]. Another highly-purified HCG preparation from pregnancy urine had a reported activity of 18800 IU/mg[4]. The urine of patients with trophoblastic tumours yielded a preparation with an activity of 19000 IU/mg[5].

Units, methods of assay

1 International Unit (IU) is equal to 0.001279 mg of the 2nd International Standard (see page 763).

Many biological methods of assay have been described[6]. Immature rats or mice are usually used for the quantitative assay of HCG in blood or urine, as for instance in the hyperaemia test on rats[7] and the prostatic weight test on rats[8]. Diagnostic tests for pregnancy use mice (ASCHHEIM-ZONDEK test), rats (KUPPERMAN test), rabbits (FRIEDMAN test) or amphibians (GALLI-MAININI test). More recently these tests have been supplemented by immunological methods[9] based on inhibition of haemagglutination[10], inhibition of latex-particle agglutination[11] or the complement-fixation reaction[12]. Radioimmunological methods have also been described[13], including one that claims to distinguish HCG from luteotropic hormone[14].

Comparisons between immunological methods and those using experimental animals have repeatedly shown that the former often give higher values for HCG activity[15], possibly because they also measure the biologically inactive part of the hormone. It is therefore not justifiable to equate 'immunologically active HCG' with the biologically active hormone.

Biosynthesis, secretion, metabolism

HCG is almost certainly formed in the layer of LANGHANS cells (cytotrophoblast) of the chorionic villi of the placenta, commencing as early as 8 days after conception. In the second and third months of pregnancy the HCG content of the placenta rises to a peak of about 600 IU/g, thereafter falling to a fairly constant level of 20 IU/g during the second and third trimesters. In the peak period, HCG is released at the rate of about 500000–1000000 IU/24 h, during the second trimester at about 100000 IU/24 h[1]. In the serum, the HCG concentration starts to rise steeply about 30–40 days after the last menstruation and reaches a peak about 40 days later; thereafter the serum level falls rapidly until a few weeks before term, when it rises slightly again[7,16,17] (see the figure on this page). With the expulsion of the placenta, HCG disappears from the maternal blood within a few days. HCG is present in the blood of newborn during the first few days but rapidly becomes inactivated[19].

About 10% of the circulating HCG is probably excreted in the urine[1], and a clearance value for HCG of 0.18–1.2 ml/min has been reported[6]. The rise in the HCG excretion during pregnancy very largely parallels the rise in the plasma level, the maximum being reached on the 40th–90th day with values ranging from 20000–500000 IU/24 h[1,7,16,20]; during the second and third trimesters the rate of excretion is 5000–10000 IU/24 h. After parturition, HCG disappears from the urine within about 3 days[7]; its persistence in the urine may be due to the presence of a hydatidiform mole or chorionepithelioma. A testicular chorionepithelioma may also result in high urinary HCG levels. During pregnancy, HCG is present not only in the blood and urine but also in almost all the maternal body fluids and tissues, for instance spinal fluid, saliva, colostrum and vaginal secretion[1].

The manner in which HCG formation in the placenta is regulated is not known with certainty.

Concentration of HCG in the serum during the first 6 months of pregnancy[18] (mean and 95% confidence limits)

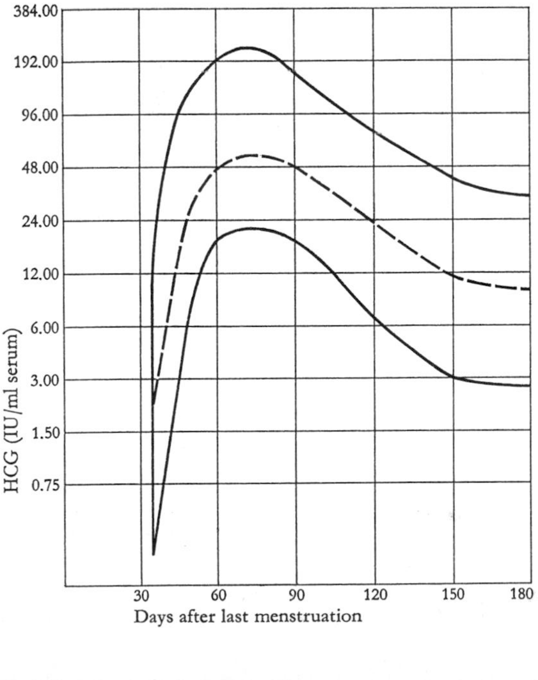

Biological activity

HCG administration in the proliferative phase of the menstrual cycle is without effect but the hormone can bring about rupture of the follicle and formation of the corpus luteum in the secretory phase. HCG lengthens the life of a fresh corpus luteum and therefore extends the menstrual cycle. At the start of pregnancy, HCG is thought to promote formation of progesterone by the corpus luteum, but its function during the second and third trimesters remains obscure. It has been suggested that in the foetus HCG has an adrenocorticotropic action resulting in the formation of dehydroepiandrosterone, a substance utilized by the placenta to produce oestrogens[19].

In male subjects exogenous HCG stimulates androgen synthesis in the interstitial cells of the testes.

Following medication with FSH, doses of HCG have been used to produce ovulation[21].

References

1 DICZFALUSY and TROEN, *Vitam. and Horm.*, **19**, 229 (1961).
2 COLE, H.H. (Ed.), *Gonadotropins, Their Chemical and Biological Properties and Secretory Control*, Freeman, London, 1963; APOSTOLAKIS and VOIGT, *Gonadotropine*, Thieme, Stuttgart, 1965.
3 GOT, R., *Gonadotropine choriale humaine; isolement et caractérisation*, Thesis, Paris, 1959; GOT and BOURRILLON, *Biochim. biophys. Acta*, **39**, 241 (1960).
4 VAN HELL et al., *Nature*, **212**, 261 (1966).
5 WILDE and BAGSHAWE, in WOLSTENHOLME and KNIGHT (Eds.), *Gonadotropins: Physicochemical and Immunological Properties*, Ciba Foundation Study Group, No. 22, Churchill, London, 1965, page 46.
6 LORAINE and BELL, *Hormone Assays and Their Clinical Application*, 2nd ed., Livingstone, Edinburgh, 1966.
7 ALBERT and BERKSON, *J. clin. Endocr.*, **11**, 805 (1951).
8 LORAINE, J.A., *J. Endocr.*, **6**, 319 (1950).
9 BERSON and YALOW, in PINCUS et al. (Eds.), *The Hormones*, vol. 4, Academic Press, New York, 1964, page 557; KELLER and PLETSCHER, *Schweiz. med. Wschr.*, **95**, 929 (1965); LOEWIT, K., *Dtsch. med. Wschr.*, **91**, 1609 (1966).
10 WIDE and GEMZELL, *Acta endocr. (Kbh.)*, **35**, 261 (1960); WIDE and GEMZELL, *Ciba Found. Coll. Endocr.*, **14**, 296 (1962).
11 TYLER et al., *Fertil. and Steril.*, **15**, 119 (1964); GOSS and TAYMOR, *Fertil. and Steril.*, **16**, 151 (1965).
12 BRODY and CARLSTRÖM, *Lancet*, **2**, 99 (1960); BRODY and CARLSTRÖM, *Ciba Found. Coll. Endocr.*, **14**, 296 (1962).
13 WILDE et al., *Nature*, **205**, 191 (1965); BAGSHAWE et al., *Lancet*, **1**, 1118 (1966).
14 MIDGLEY et al., *Nature*, **213**, 733 (1967).
15 BORTH et al., *Acta endocr. (Kbh.)*, **50**, 335 (1965).
16 LORAINE, J.A., *Ciba Found. Coll. Endocr.*, **11**, 19 (1957); FAIMAN et al., *J. clin. Endocr.*, **28**, 1323 (1968).
17 BRODY and CARLSTRÖM, *J. clin. Endocr.*, **25**, 792 (1965).
18 BRODY and CARLSTRÖM, in WOLSTENHOLME and KNIGHT (Eds.), *Gonadotropins: Physicochemical and Immunological Properties*, Ciba Foundation Study Group, No. 22, Churchill, London, 1965, page 70.
19 LAURITZEN, C., in *Second International Congress on Hormonal Steroids*, Milan 1966, Excerpta Medica Foundation, Amsterdam, 1966, page 294.
20 MISHELL and DAVAJAN, *Amer. J. Obstet. Gynec.*, **96**, 231 (1966); TAYMOR et al., *Fertil. and Steril.*, **17**, 613 (1966).
21 GEMZELL, C., *Recent Progr. Hormone Res.*, **21**, 179 (1965); CROOKE, A.C., in GARDINER-HILL, H. (Ed.), *Modern Trends in Endocrinology*, vol. 3, Butterworth, London, 1967, page 111.

Corticotropin[1,2]

(corticotropic hormone, adrenocorticotropin, adrenocorticotropic hormone = ACTH)

Chemistry[1,3]

The corticotropins isolated from the pituitary gland of various animal species are all single-chain peptides made up of 39 amino-acid residues. Structurally very similar, they differ only in part of the amino-acid sequence of the molecule (see the table below). The structure of the β-corticotropin from pigs was elucidated in 1956[4], and in 1963 its complete synthesis was reported[5]; it has a molecular weight of 4567. In the pituitary, ACTH probably occurs not only in the free state but also in a protein-bound form[6]. In 1967 the amino-acid chain characteristic of human α-ACTH was synthesized[44].

Possession of the complete amino-acid chain of the natural hormones is not an essential condition for corticotropic biological activity; very active peptides have been synthesized containing only the first 20–24 amino-acid residues of ACTH. Part of the amino-acid sequence of the corticotropins is identical with part of the sequence in the melanotropins (see page 721), and in fact the corticotropins have some melanocyte-stimulating activity. Whereas the biological activity of ACTH rests in the first 20–24 amino acids, it is the remaining part of the chain that is responsible for the immunological properties[7]. An ectopic ACTH is formed by some nonpituitary tumours and has been shown to be very similar to pituitary ACTH both chemically and immunologically[8].

Lipotropin

During the isolation of ACTH from the pituitary two further biologically active peptides have recently come to light. These were found to consist of 59 and 90 amino-acid residues respectively and on account of their lipolytic activity have been named γ- and β-lipotropins (lipotropic hormone, LPH)[9]. LPH possesses only slight corticotropic activity but resembles ACTH in melanocyte-stimulating activity.

Units, methods of assay[10,11]

1 International Unit (IU) of corticotropin is equal to 1 mg of the 3rd International Standard (see page 762). Of the many methods of determining the hormone, those most suitable for clinical purposes are the ascorbic acid depletion test of Sayers et al.[12] (diminution in the ascorbic acid content of the adrenals of hypophysectomized rats after administration of ACTH) and the test of Lipscomb and Nelson[13] (increase in the corticosteroid content of the adrenal cortex of hypophysectomized rats after administration of ACTH). The activity of ACTH preparations can also be determined by the in vitro method of Saffran and Schally[14] (corticosteroid formation in adrenal preparations from rats). Radioimmunological methods of determining ACTH in body fluids have recently been described[15].

Biosynthesis, secretion, metabolism

The site of ACTH formation in the pituitary is not known with certainty, but it is probably the chromophobic β^3 cells of the anterior lobe[16], though the hormone is also found in the basophile β^1 cells of the anterior and posterior lobes of the gland[17]. ACTH has been shown to be already present in the pituitary of the 16 weeks foetus[18]. The adult pituitary contains 7–38 IU of ACTH[6]. Data on the ACTH content of blood vary with the methods of determination and extraction; recent work[19,20] indicates that the blood level in man at rest lies between 1 mIU and 10 mIU per litre plasma. Radioimmunoassay has shown plasma levels of 10–80 ng/l (in terms of porcine ACTH; 1 mIU ≈ 10 ng)[15]. The level is higher in stress[21], in untreated adrenocortical insufficiency, in the advanced stage of Cushing's disease and particularly following bilateral adrenalectomy[10,11,22]. In man, the blood level at rest is subject to a day-and-night rhythm, with higher values in the morning and lower values in the evening[20,23]. Little is known of the fate of the ACTH circulating in the blood; exogenous ACTH is reported to have a half-life of 5 min or less[24], and in rats 75% of the endogenous circulating hormone was found to have disappeared within 3 min[25]. Peptidases, which may be responsible for the breakdown of ACTH,

Variation of the cortisol and ACTH contents of the plasma with age[43]

	Cortisol (μg/l)		ACTH (mIU/l)	
	Mean	*s*	Mean	*s*
1–5 years	244	64	1.9	0.8
6–10 years	193	58	1.6	0.4
11–15½ years ..	165	66	2.5	1.2
16–41 years	164	44	2.2	1.1

Structure and biological activity of corticotropins

	Amino-acid sequence*	ACTH activity (IU/mg)	
		in vitro†	in vivo††
α-ACTH (cattle)	NH$_2$ (on Glu 33) Ser·[A]·Asp·Gly·Glu·Ala·Glu·Asp·Ser·Ala·Glu·[B]·Phe 1 25 26 27 28 29 30 31 32 33 39	140	–
α-ACTH (sheep)	NH$_2$ (on Glu 33) Ser·[A]·Ala·Gly·Glu·Asp·Asp·Glu·Ala·Ser·Glu·[B]·Phe 1 25 26 27 28 29 30 31 32 33 39	177	100–150
α-ACTH (pig) .... (corticotropin A**, β-corticotropin)	NH$_2$ (on Glu 30) Ser·[A]·Asp·Gly·Ala·Glu·Asp·Glu·Leu·Ala·Glu·[B]·Phe 1 25 26 27 28 29 30 31 32 33 39	90–150	80–150
α-ACTH (man)	NH$_2$ (on Glu 28) Ser·[A]·Asp·Ala·Gly·Glu·Asp·Glu·Ser·Ala·Glu·[B]·Phe 1 25 26 27 28 29 30 31 32 33 39	52	26
β^{1-39}-Corticotropin (synthetic)	As α-ACTH (pig)	–	115
β^{1-24}-Corticotropin (synthetic) .... (tetracosactrin)	Ser·[A]	–	106

* [A] = Tyr·Ser·Met·Glu·His·Phe·Arg·Trp·Gly·Lys·Pro·Val·Gly·Lys·Lys·Arg·Arg·Pro·Val·Lys·Val·Tyr·Pro
2 3 4 5 6 7 8 9 10 11 12 13 14 15 16 17 18 19 20 21 22 23 24

[B] = Ala·Phe·Pro·Leu·Glu
34 35 36 37 38

** Unlike β-corticotropin, corticotropin A has no amide group at Glu^{30}.

† Determined by steroid genesis.
†† Determined by ascorbic acid test.

have been found in the fatty tissue and in pituitaries[26]. Small amounts of ACTH (ca. 0.07 mIU/24 h) are probably excreted in the urine[27].

Regulation of ACTH secretion[21,26,28,29]. Pituitary ACTH secretion is regulated by at least three factors: the time of day, noxious stimuli (stress), and the negative feedback mechanism (via the corticosteroid and possibly ACTH content of the blood).

The negative feedback mechanism arises from the fact that the corticosteroids secreted by the adrenal cortex under the influence of ACTH themselves inhibit the secretion of this substance by the pituitary. Corticosteroids secreted by an autonomous adrenocortical tumour have the same effect, with the result that the other adrenal atrophies. The various corticosteroids possess different inhibitory activities. Synthetic steroids are also active in this respect, and weight for weight, dexamethasone has 30 times the activity of cortisol[28]. Little is known of the so-called autofeedback mechanism, by which a high ACTH blood level is thought to inhibit pituitary ACTH secretion[26,30].

The increased ACTH secretion under stress is largely independent of the corticosteroid concentration in the blood; thus in animals under stress, ACTH secretion occurs in the presence of circulating corticosteroids at a concentration at which it would normally be suppressed.

ACTH secretion is to some extent regulated by the hypothalamus, in the postsynaptic neurones of which the so-called corticotropin-releasing factors (CRF) are formed (see page 725). These enter the portal vein system of the pituitary and stimulate the release of ACTH from this gland. In rats under stress, CRF activity has also been observed in the peripheral plasma[31].

Functional tests

The secretory capacity of the pituitary for ACTH can be measured indirectly by means of the metyrapone test[32,33]. Metyrapone (2-methyl-1,2-bis-[3-pyridyl]-1-propanone) inhibits the enzyme steroid-11β-hydroxylase and thus the hydroxylation of 11-deoxycortisol to cortisol in the adrenal cortex. Since pituitary ACTH secretion is inhibited only by cortisol, and therefore not by 11-deoxycortisol, administration of metyrapone to persons with a normally functioning pituitary causes an increase in ACTH secretion, which in turn results in a further increase in the release of 11-deoxycortisol. The increased amounts of 11-deoxycortisol and its metabolite tetrahydro-S can readily be determined in the urine as 17-hydroxysteroids. Other indirect tests for measuring pituitary ACTH secretion are based on the increase in the plasma cortisol level under the action of bacterial pyrogens (a noxious stimulus)[33] or of lysine-vasopressin[34].

Biological activity

Action on the adrenals. ACTH stimulates the growth of the adrenal cortex, particularly the zona fasciculata and zona reticularis. When the pituitary is removed the adrenal cortex becomes atrophied, though it still retains sufficient residual functional capacity to maintain life. The morphological changes resulting from hypophysectomy can be reversed by administration of ACTH. In healthy animals injections of ACTH cause hypertrophy of the adrenal cortex. Under the action of ACTH the cholesterol and ascorbic acid contents of the adrenal cortex diminish, and the synthesis and secretion of the glucocorticoids is stimulated. There appears to be a close connection, as yet unexplained, between the two effects of ACTH in promoting the formation of both steroids and proteins in the adrenal cortex[35,36].

The principal site of stimulation of adrenal corticosteroid synthesis by ACTH is cleavage of the side chain of the cholesterol molecule (see page 428)[38]. Further sites are the hydroxylation of progesterone to 17α-hydroxyprogesterone and the hydroxylation of 17α-hydroxydeoxycorticosterone to cortisol[1]. Aldosterone synthesis is only slightly affected by ACTH, infusions of which into the adrenal arteries bring about aldosterone formation only after cortisol and corticosterone have reached a high level[39]. ACTH causes an increase in the concentration of cyclic adenosine monophosphate in the adrenals, and this latter substance has been found to have an effect on corticosteroid synthesis similar to that of ACTH[40]. It is not yet known, however, whether the promotion of steroid synthesis is effected via the series of reactions comprising activation of phosphorylase (see also under 'Catecholamines', page 733), increase in glycogenolysis and formation of NADH[36,41].

In man the short-term effects of ACTH on the adrenal cortex differ from the long-term ones[1,37]. Short-term administration (less than 90 min) causes release of cortisol and corticosterone in the ratio 2:1 together with an increase in the blood supply to the cortex; long-term administration (4 days) markedly promotes steroid synthesis, with a cortisol/corticosterone ratio of up to 10:1, while at the same time the adrenals increase in weight.

Extra-adrenal effects[42]. ACTH exerts an effect on lipid metabolism (adipokinetic effect, consisting of increased liberation of free fatty acids from the fatty tissues, rise in the plasma free fatty acid level, increase in the fat content of the liver, ketosis) and on carbohydrate metabolism (hypoglycaemia with improved glucose tolerance, increase in glycogen content of the fatty tissues). Other extra-adrenal effects of ACTH are the melanocyte-stimulating activity (see the opposite page) and the inhibition of its own secretion by the pituitary (see above).

The *indirect effects* of ACTH stem from the increased corticosteroid secretion (see above). The anti-inflammatory action of ACTH has found therapeutic application.

References

1 Schwyzer, R., *Ann. Rev. Biochem.*, **33**, 259 (1964).
2 Venning, E.H., *Ann. Rev. Physiol.*, **27**, 107 (1965); Rosselin et al., *Presse méd.*, **74**, 813 and 873 (1966); Harris and Donovan (Eds.), *The Pituitary Gland*, vols. 1 and 2, Butterworth, London, 1966.
3 Li, C.H., *Recent Progr. Hormone Res.*, **18**, 1 (1962); Hofmann and Yajima, *Recent Progr. Hormone Res.*, **18**, 41 (1962); Schroeder and Luebke, *The Peptides*, vol. 2, Academic Press, New York, 1966, page 194.
4 Shepherd et al., *J. Amer. chem. Soc.*, **78**, 5067 (1956).
5 Schwyzer and Sieber, *Nature*, **199**, 172 (1963).
6 Currie et al., *Acta endocr. (Kbh.)*, **43**, 255 (1963).
7 Imura et al., *J. clin. Endocr.*, **25**, 1361 (1965).
8 Liddle et al., *Cancer Res.*, **25**, 1057 (1965); Fleischer et al., *Endocrinology*, **78**, 1067 (1966).
9 Li, C.H., *Nature*, **201**, 924 (1964); Anselmino and Hoffmann, *Dtsch. med. Wschr.*, **90**, 1697 (1965), and *Germ. med. Mth.*, **11**, 177 (1966); Li et al., *Nature*, **208**, 1093 (1965).
10 Munson, P.L., in Antoniades, H.N. (Ed.), *Hormones in Human Plasma*, Little, Brown, Boston, 1960, page 149; Sayers, G., in Gray and Bacharach (Eds.), *Hormones in Blood*, 2nd ed., vol. 1, Academic Press, London, 1967, page 169; Ruf, K., *Schweiz. med. Wschr.*, **96**, 684 (1966).
11 Loraine and Bell, *Hormone Assays and Their Clinical Application*, 2nd ed., Livingstone, Edinburgh, 1966.
12 Sayers et al., *Endocrinology*, **42**, 379 (1948); Munson et al., *J. clin. Endocr.*, **8**, 586 (1948); Schuler et al., *Schweiz. med. Wschr.*, **93**, 1027 (1963).
13 Lipscomb and Nelson, *Endocrinology*, **71**, 13 (1962).
14 Saffran and Schally, *Endocrinology*, **56**, 523 (1955).
15 Felber, J.P., *Experientia (Basel)*, **19**, 227 (1963); Yalow et al., *J. clin. Endocr.*, **24**, 1219 (1964); Landon, J., in James, V.H.T. (Ed.), *Recent Advances in Endocrinology*, 8th ed., Churchill, London, 1968, page 240.
16 Siperstein, E.R., *J. cell. Biol.*, **17**, 521 (1963).
17 Leznoff et al., *J. clin. Invest.*, **41**, 1720 (1962); Pearse and van Noorden, *Canad. med. Ass. J.*, **88**, 462 (1963).
18 Taylor et al., *J. Endocr.*, **9**, 334 (1953).
19 Vance et al., *J. clin. Invest.*, **41**, 20 (1962); Davies, B.M.A., *Acta endocr. (Kbh.)*, **45**, 55 (1964); Binoux et al., *Ann. Pédiat. Sem. Hôp. Paris*, **41**, 1603 (1965).
20 Retiene et al., *Klin. Wschr.*, **43**, 205 (1965); Berson and Yalow, *J. clin. Invest.*, **47**, 2725 (1968).
21 Estep, H.L., in Bajusz, E. (Ed.), *An Introduction to Clinical Neuroendocrinology*, Karger, Basle, 1967, page 106.
22 Nelson et al., *J. clin. Endocr.*, **26**, 722 (1966).
23 Ney et al., *J. clin. Invest.*, **42**, 1669 (1963); Binoux et al., *Ann. Pédiat. Sem. Hôp. Paris*, **41**, 1614 (1965).
24 Greenspan et al., *Endocrinology*, **46**, 261 (1950); Gemzell, C.A., *Ciba Found. Coll. Endocr.*, **14**, 287 (1962).
25 Sydnor and Sayers, *Proc. Soc. exp. Biol. (N.Y.)*, **83**, 729 (1953).
26 Vernikos-Danellis, J., *Vitam. and Horm.*, **23**, 97 (1965).
27 Ibayashi et al., in Bajusz, E. (Ed.), *An Introduction to Clinical Neuroendocrinology*, Karger, Basle, 1967, page 216.
28 Liddle et al., *Recent Progr. Hormone Res.*, **18**, 125 (1962).
29 Retiene et al., *Klin. Wschr.*, **44**, 716 (1966).
30 Plager, J.E., in Bajusz, E. (Ed.), *An Introduction to Clinical Neuroendocrinology*, Karger, Basle, 1967, page 232.
31 Anderson, E., *Science*, **152**, 379 (1966).
32 Liddle et al., *J. clin. Endocr.*, **19**, 875 (1959); Tamm, J., in Küchmeister et al. (Eds.), *Klinische Funktionsdiagnostik*, 3rd ed., Thieme, Stuttgart, 1967, page 44; Metcalf and Beaven, *Amer. J. Med.*, **45**, 176 (1968).
33 Brinck-Johnsen, T., in Bajusz, E. (Ed.), *An Introduction to Clinical Neuroendocrinology*, Karger, Basle, 1967, page 186.
34 Gwinup, G., *Metabolism*, **14**, 1282 (1965); Landon et al., *Lancet*, **2**, 1156 (1965).
35 Farese, R.V., *Endocrinology*, **74**, 579 (1964).
36 Scriba, P.C., *Klin. Wschr.*, **42**, 463 (1964).
37 Symington, T., *Brit. med. Bull.*, **18**, 117 (1962).
38 Hayano et al., *Recent Progr. Hormone Res.*, **12**, 79 (1956); Bransome, E.D., *Ann. Rev. Physiol.*, **30**, 171 (1968).
39 Blair-West et al., *Recent Progr. Hormone Res.*, **19**, 311 (1963).
40 Haynes and Berthet, *J. biol. Chem.*, **225**, 115 (1957); Haynes et al., *Recent Progr. Hormone Res.*, **16**, 121 (1960).
41 Pastan, I., *Ann. Rev. Biochem.*, **35**, 369 (1966).
42 Engel, F.L., *Vitam. and Horm.*, **19**, 189 (1961); Engel and Lebovitz, *Amer. J. Med.*, **35**, 721 (1963).
43 Binoux et al., *Ann. Pédiat. Sem. Hôp. Paris*, **41**, 1603 (1965).
44 Bajusz et al., *Acta Chim. Acad. Sci. Hung.*, **52**, 335 (1967).

Thyrotropin[1,2]

(thyrotropic hormone, thyroid-stimulating hormone = TSH)

Chemistry[3]

Bovine and human thyrotropins are glycoproteins of molecular weight ca. 28000; in addition to amino acids the molecule contains glucosamine, galactosamine and mannose. A highly purified but unstable preparation from the human pituitary had an activity of 20 IU/mg[3]. Bovine TSH is biologically active in all vertebrates but the activity varies with the species. A substance similar to TSH has been isolated from mammalian pituitaries and given the name heterothyrotropic factor (HTF)[4]; it has little TSH activity in mammals but is highly active in fish.

Units[5]

1 International Unit (IU) is equal to 13.5 mg of the 1st International Standard (see page 762). 1 IU = 1 USP Unit = ca. 10 JUNKMANN-SCHÖLLER Units (JSU).

Methods of assay[2,3,5]

TSH activity can be determined in vivo or in vitro by means of the histological or physiological effects on the thyroid. In vitro methods in common use are those of BAKKE et al.[6] (weight change of thyroid slices) and of KIRKHAM[7] and BOTTARI et al.[8] (release of ^{131}I from thyroid slices). In body fluids, TSH concentration can now also be measured by radioimmunoassay[9,10].

Biosynthesis, secretion, metabolism

TSH is formed in the basophile β^2-cells of the anterior pituitary[11]. The rate of secretion is regulated by the concentration of thyroid hormone in the circulating blood through a negative feedback mechanism (see page 727), a rise in the blood level of free thyroxine depressing TSH secretion, a fall accelerating it. Regulation of TSH secretion involves a neurohumoral mechanism depending on the formation of a thyrotropin-releasing factor (TRF)[12]. This neurohormone, probably a weakly basic polypeptide[13], is secreted by the nuclei of the anterior hypothalamus and discharged into the portal arteries of the anterior pituitary, where it stimulates the release and possibly also the synthesis of TSH[14]. In adults the rate of secretion of TSH has been estimated at 50–225 µg/24 h[15], corresponding to a half-life for TSH of 39–68 min.

Serum TSH levels. There is disagreement over the absolute levels[2,3]. Serum concentrations of less than 3 µg/l have been measured by radioimmunoassay in 50 euthyroid subjects, 10 hypophysectomized subjects and 12 pregnant women[9]; in the same study the levels in patients with hypothyroidism were 3–100 times higher, in those with hyperthyroidism within the normal range. The serum level in children is the same as in adults[16,26] but higher in the newborn[26] and old people[16]. The high plasma levels in hypothyroid patients are due to prolonged survival of TSH in the circulation and increased pituitary secretion of the hormone[15].

Whether TSH is excreted in measurable amount in the urine is still uncertain.

Long-acting thyroid stimulator (= LATS; thyroid-stimulating globulin = TSG). This factor is probably involved in the pathogenesis of GRAVES' disease[17,18]. In the bioassay of TSH its presence is revealed by the long duration of its stimulating action compared to TSH. LATS appears to be a γG-globulin[19]; it is formed in the lymphatic system and has a half-life in the rat of 7½ h[17].

Exophthalmos is certainly not due to TSH and probably not to LATS; a possible cause is a substance secreted by the pituitary[20] (EPS = exophthalmos-producing substance).

Biological activity

TSH brings about both histological and metabolic changes in the thyroid. The former comprise a diminution in the colloid content and enlargement of the epithelial cells, while under long-continued TSH stimulation the vessels become more numerous and larger and the gland becomes hypertrophic. The metabolic changes appear within 5–30 min of administering TSH[21] and include increased oxygen consumption, glucose oxidation, phospholipid turnover, RNA synthesis and sodium uptake as well as stimulation of the various steps in the formation and release of thyroid hormone, particularly the organic binding of iodine[22], the formation of iodothyronines from iodotyrosines[23], the liberation of thyroid hormone from thyroglobulin[24], and the release of iodine from iodotyrosines[22]. The effects of LATS on the thyroid are similar to those of TSH but are delayed[17,25].

References

1 SONENBERG, M., *Vitam. and Horm.*, **16**, 205 (1958); WERNER, S.C. (Ed.), *Thyrotropin*, Thomas, Springfield, 1963; HARRIS and DONOVAN (Eds.), *The Pituitary Gland*, vols. 1 and 2, Butterworth, London, 1966.
2 KIRKHAM, K.E., *Vitam. and Horm.*, **24**, 173 (1966).
3 CONDLIFFE and ROBBINS, in GRAY and BACHARACH (Eds.), *Hormones in Blood*, 2nd ed., vol. 1, Academic Press, London, 1967, page 333.
4 FONTAINE and LOPEZ, *Ann. Endocr. (Paris)*, **26**, 719 (1965).
5 CRIGLER, J.F., in ANTONIADES, H.N. (Ed.), *Hormones in Human Plasma*, Little, Brown, Boston, 1960, page 201; LORAINE and BELL, *Hormone Assays and Their Clinical Application*, 2nd ed., Livingstone, Edinburgh, 1966.
6 BAKKE et al., *Endocrinology*, **61**, 352 (1957).
7 KIRKHAM, K.E., *J. Endocr.*, **25**, 259 (1962).
8 BOTTARI et al., *J. Physiol.*, **169**, 278 (1963).
9 ODELL et al., *J. clin. Endocr.*, **25**, 1179 (1965).
10 UTIGER, R.D., *J. clin. Invest.*, **44**, 1277 (1965); LEMARCHAND-BÉRAUD et al., *Schweiz. med. Wschr.*, **95**, 772 (1965).
11 MURRAY and EZRIN, *J. clin. Endocr.*, **26**, 287 (1966).
12 D'ANGELO, S.A., in NALBANDOV, A.V. (Ed.), *Advances in Neuroendocrinology*, University of Illinois Press, Urbana, 1963, page 158; REICHLIN, S., in CAMERON and O'CONNOR (Eds.), *Brain-Thyroid Relationships*, Ciba Foundation Study Group, No. 18, Churchill, London, 1964, page 17; GUILLEMIN, R., *Recent Progr. Hormone Res.*, **20**, 89 (1964).
13 SCHALLY et al., *Endocrinology*, **78**, 726 (1966).
14 SINHA and MEITES, *Endocrinology*, **78**, 1002 (1966).
15 ODELL et al., *Recent Progr. Hormone Res.*, **23**, 47 (1967).
16 LEMARCHAND-BÉRAUD et al., *Schweiz. med. Wschr.*, **96**, 718 (1966).
17 ADAMS, D.D., *Brit. med. J.*, **1**, 1015 (1965).
18 MCKENZIE, J.M., *J. clin. Endocr.*, **25**, 424 (1965).
19 MIYAI and WERNER, *J. clin. Endocr.*, **26**, 504 (1966); KRISS, J.P., *Advanc. metab. Dis.*, **3**, 209 (1968).
20 SCHWARZ et al., *Acta endocr. (Kbh.)*, **51**, 359 (1966); HORSTER et al., *Dtsch. med. Wschr.*, **92**, 661 and 673 (1967), and *Germ. med. Mth.*, **12**, 384 (1967).
21 PASTAN, I., *Ann. Rev. Biochem.*, **35**, 369 (1966).
22 ROSENBERG et al., *Recent Progr. Hormone Res.*, **21**, 33 (1965).
23 SHIMODA et al., *Endocrinology*, **79**, 921 (1966).
24 DEISS et al., *Endocrinology*, **79**, 19 (1966).
25 PINCHERA et al., *J. clin. Endocr.*, **25**, 189 (1965).
26 UTIGER et al., *J. clin. Invest.*, **47**, 97a (1968).

Prolactin[1,2]

(lactogenic hormone, luteotropin, mammotropin, prolactin hormone = PH, luteotropic hormone = LTH, luteomammotropic hormone = LMTH)

Chemistry

Prolactin as isolated from the anterior pituitary of sheep, cattle and pigs is a polypeptide of molecular weight ca. 25000[3,4]. The prolactin molecule from sheep and cattle contains 211 amino-acid residues arranged as a single chain[3]; that from pigs has a considerably higher cysteine content[4].

Whether a primate prolactin exists is still uncertain[5]. Growth hormone from man and monkeys has been shown to have prolactin-like activity, and this activity is intrinsic to the growth hormone molecule. Other studies indicate that human growth hormone and prolactin are potentially separable[6]. A high prolactin activity but low growth hormone activity has been demonstrated in a human pituitary tumour[21], thus providing further evidence that the two hormones are not identical.

Luteotropin, formerly thought to be a distinct hormone, is now regarded as identical with prolactin.

Units, methods of assay

1 International Unit (IU) is equal to 0.04545 mg of the 2nd International Standard (see page 762), obtained from the anterior pituitary of sheep.

Biological assay[5,7,8]. Proliferation test on the pigeon crop[9]. Determination of mammotropic activity in rabbits[10] or mice[11]. Determination of luteotropic activity in rats[12] or mice[13]. Immunological methods have been devised[14] but have not yet found clinical application.

Biosynthesis, secretion, metabolism[2]

Prolactin is formed in the acidophile cells (staining with azocarmine or erythrosin) of the anterior pituitary. In mammals these cells exhibit increasing secretory activity during pregnancy and particularly lactation. Data on prolactin activity in the blood and urine of both men and women are to be found in the literature but in view of the difficulties of hormone extraction and determination they are of questionable reliability[8].

Regulation of prolactin secretion[2]. In contrast to its effect on the secretion of the other anterior pituitary hormones, the hypothalamus has an inhibitory action on prolactin secretion. This is shown by the increased amounts of prolactin formed in the rat or mouse pituitary when shielded from the hypothalamus[15]. A 'prolactin-inhibiting factor' has been demonstrated in hypothalamic extracts from various mammals[16]. In rats, the amount of this factor in the hypothalamus is reduced by oestrogens[17], which also have a direct effect on the anterior pituitary in that they increase the secretion of prolactin[18]. The latter is likewise stimulated by thyroid hormones[19]. The similar effect produced by large doses of progesterone, androgens and corticosteroids is probably an indirect one.

Biological activity[2]

In rats and mice, prolactin has a luteotropic effect similar to that of the gonadotropins, while its mammotropic and lactogenic effects are seen in various mammals. In pigeons and doves, prolactin stimulates crop growth and production of crop 'milk'. In some amphibious species injections of prolactin cause the animal to move from land to water (water-drive phenomenon).

In mammals, prolactin plays an important part in the growth of the mammary glands. In ovarectomized rats, administration of prolactin together with growth hormone results in complete lobulo-alveolar development of the mammary glands. In rats, the steroids of the ovaries are probably of only secondary significance for mammary growth since they probably act mainly by stimulating the secretion of prolactin and growth hormone. At about the time of parturition increased amounts of prolactin, ACTH and corticosteroids are released and together cause the onset of lactation. Secretion of these hormones in increased amounts then continues as a result of the suckling stimulus, so that lactation is maintained.

In male guinea-pigs and rats, prolactin has been reported to promote the growth of the prostate and seminal vesicles, but the physiological role played by the hormone in the male animal remains obscure.

In man, prolactin from sheep has effects similar to those of growth hormone of human origin[20].

References

1 Dixon and Li, *Metabolism*, **13**, suppl., 1093 (1964); Harris and Donovan (Eds.), *The Pituitary Gland*, vols. 1 and 2, Butterworth, London, 1966.
2 Meites and Nicoll, *Ann. Rev. Physiol.*, **28**, 57 (1966).
3 Li, C.H., *Advanc. Protein Chem.*, **12**, 269 (1957); Sluyser and Li, *Arch. Biochem.*, **104**, 50 (1964).
4 Eppstein, S., *Nature*, **202**, 899 (1964).
5 Forsyth, I.A., in Gray and Bacharach (Eds.), *Hormones in Blood*, 2nd ed., vol. 1, Academic Press, London, 1967, page 233.
6 Pasteels, J.L., *Arch. Biol. (Liège)*, **74**, 439 (1963); Apostolakis, M., *Acta endocr. (Kbh.)*, **49**, 1 (1965).
7 Bates, R.W., *Extrait de l'Acta Union internationale contre le cancer*, **18**, 280 (1962).
8 Loraine and Bell, *Hormone Assays and Their Clinical Application*, 2nd ed., Livingstone, Edinburgh, 1966.
9 Riddle et al., *Amer. J. Physiol.*, **105**, 191 (1933); Bates et al., *Endocrinology*, **73**, 217 (1963).
10 Chadwick, A., *J. Endocr.*, **27**, 253 (1963).
11 Scowen and Hadfield, *Cancer*, **8**, 890 (1955).
12 Wolthuis, O.L., *Acta endocr. (Kbh.)*, **42**, 364 and 380 (1963).
13 Browning et al., *J. Arkansas med. Soc.*, **60**, 46 (1963).
14 Hayashida, T., *Ciba Found. Coll. Endocr.*, **14**, 338 (1962).
15 Liebelt and Liebelt, *Cancer Res.*, **21**, 86 (1961); Bardin et al., *Proc. Soc. exp. Biol. (N.Y.)*, **110**, 716 (1962); Dao and Gawlak, *Endocrinology*, **72**, 884 (1963).
16 McCann et al., in *Second International Congress on Hormonal Steroids*, Milan 1966, Excerpta Medica Foundation, Amsterdam, 1966, page 79.
17 Ratner and Meites, *Endocrinology*, **75**, 377 (1964).
18 Ramirez and McCann, *Endocrinology*, **75**, 206 (1964).
19 Nicoll and Meites, *Endocrinology*, **72**, 544 (1963).
20 McGarry and Beck, *Lancet*, **2**, 915 (1962).
21 Peake et al., *J. Lab. clin. Med.*, **72**, 1002 (1968).

Growth hormone[1,2]

(somatotropin, somatotropic hormone = STH;
human growth hormone = HGH)

Chemistry

The growth hormones isolated from the pituitary of various species are long-chain polypeptides of different lengths (see the table below). The growth hormone of monkeys and man consists of a single chain, while those isolated from other species are probably made up of multiple chains. The sequence of the amino-acid residues in human growth hormone has been elucidated[3].

HGH is fairly stable, so that pituitaries removed at autopsy can be kept for months with little loss of activity if stored in acetone or at very low temperature. Hormone isolated by the usual methods is not homogeneous and can be separated into components, for example by gel filtration[4] into two and by electrophoresis[5] into three components.

The growth hormones from different species also differ immunologically. Thus antiserum against HGH reacts also with the hormone from other primates but not, for instance, with that from cattle, sheep, pigs, horses or fish. Unlike the other hormones of the anterior pituitary, growth hormone is species-specific also in its biological activity.

Growth hormone from various species[34]

	Mol. weight	No. of amino acids	N-terminal sequence	C-terminal sequence	Iso-electric point
Sheep..	47800	430	Phe· and Ala·	·Thr·Ala·Phe	6.8
Ox	45000	416	Phe·Ala·Thr· and Ala·Phe·Ala·	·Cys·Ala·Phe	6.8
Pig	41600	–	Phe·Pro·Ala·	·Cys·Ala·Phe	6.3
Whale..	39900	340	Phe·Lys· (?)	·Leu·Ala·Phe	6.2
Monkey	25400	220	Phe·Thr· (?)	·Ala·Gly·Phe	5.5
Man...	21500	188	Phe·Pro·Thr·	·Cys·Gly·Phe	4.9

Units, methods of assay[6]

1 International Unit (IU) of growth hormone is equal to 1 mg of the 1st International Standard (see page 762), prepared from anterior ox pituitary. A Reference Preparation of HGH is also available (see page 762).

The unit of the hormone as determined by Evans' growth test[7] is that daily amount required to be administered over 10 days to hypophysectomized female rats 21–30 days old in order to cause a weight increase of 10 g. In the rat-tibia test the amount of hormone is related to the width of the epiphyseal cartilage in immature hypophysectomized rats[8].

Of the immunological methods of assay, the haemagglutination-inhibition test has proved unreliable in body fluids owing to the presence in the latter of nonspecific inhibitors. The most suitable are the radioimmunological methods, such as those of Hunter and Greenwood[9], Glick et al.[10] and Utiger[11].

Indirectly, growth hormone can be determined by means of the dose-dependent incorporation of tagged sulphur into the rib cartilage of hypophysectomized rats[12]. This method measures the so-called sulphation factor, a component of human serum not identical with HGH but closely related to it.

Biosynthesis, secretion, metabolism

Growth hormone is very probably formed in the acidophile α-cells of the anterior pituitary[13]. The adult human pituitary contains about 3.7–6.0 mg of the hormone[14], and the rate of formation has been estimated at 5 mg per day[15]. Plasma levels of the hormone measured by the radioimmunological technique under basal conditions are shown on page 720. The rate of secretion and plasma level of HGH vary throughout the day and are subject to various physiological and pathological stimuli[16–21]. Glucose administration lowers the plasma HGH level, while any measure lowering the blood glucose level (e.g., insulin or tolbutamide medication) or inhibiting intracellular glucose utilization (e.g., administration of deoxyglucose) stimulates secretion of HGH and thus raises the plasma level. Higher HGH plasma levels are also observed in the neonatal period, in fasting, after protein-rich meals (which increase plasma amino acids), after physical exercise, under mental stress, after 1–4 hours of sleep, after major surgery and as an effect of bacterial pyrogens. The high values sometimes observed in women may be due to an action of the oestrogens[22].

Pathologically high blood HGH levels (hypersomatotropism) can be regarded as those exceeding 10 μg/l that are not depressed below 5 μg/l by oral glucose intake[21]. In most cases of acromegaly the HGH plasma level lies between 20 μg and 100 μg per litre[20,21].

In the plasma the hormone is probably bound to the α_2-macroglobulins[23]. In adults the half-life of the hormone in the circulating blood is about 25 min[15,16], in newborn infants about 13 min[24]. The maternal hormone does not cross the placental barrier[25].

The secretion of growth hormone is to some extent regulated by the hypothalamus, probably via the formation of a 'somatotropin-releasing factor'[26] which stimulates the pituitary. In rats it has been shown that exogenous growth hormone inhibits endogenous hormone secretion, indicating the existence of a feedback mechanism[27].

Plasma levels of growth hormone (μg/l)

	Mean	Range	s	Reference
Cord blood	49.7	–	57.8	36
Children under 12 months.	18.6	–	12.5	36
Children, 1–8 years	8.5	–	7.8	36
Children, 9–10 years	2.8	–	2.8	36
Adolescents, 11–17 years	14.0	–	13.4	36
Adults, hospitalized	0.55	–	0.68	36
Women, lactating	4.5	–	2.1	36
Women	4.91	0.9–10.6	3.32	37
Men	0.27	0.1–0.7	0.14	37

Physiological effects of growth hormone[35]

Protein metabolism	Increased protein synthesis Nitrogen retention* Phosphorus retention* Potassium retention* Diminished urea excretion* Increased intracellular amino-acid transport Increased protein synthesis at ribosomes
Lipid metabolism	Intracellular lipolysis Increased free fatty acid level in plasma* Increased oxidation of fats* Increased ketogenesis in diabetics*
Carbohydrate metabolism	Exacerbation of diabetes* Reduced response to insulin* Diminished conversion of glucose into fat in fatty tissue
Mineral metabolism	Calcium metabolism Increased intestinal absorption* Increased urinary excretion* Sodium retention* Phosphorus retention* Increased blood-phosphate level* Increased serum alkaline phosphatase level*
Organs and tissues	Acromegaly Connective tissue Stimulation of chondroitin sulphate synthesis Stimulation of collagen synthesis Increased excretion of hydroxyproline* Increase in volume of interstitial fluid

* Demonstrable in man after administration of growth hormone.

Biological activity

In man, as in other animal species, the body has a specific requirement for growth hormone. In 6-week-old rats hypophysectomy causes immediate cessation of growth, which recommences immediately when the hormone is administered and continues for as long as the medication is continued. In children with pituitary hypofunction growth is often retarded in even the first year of life[28] and then slows down greatly in the subsequent years. Administration of HGH to individuals with dwarfism due to deficiency of this hormone causes them to grow normally or even faster than normal[29], but animal growth hormone is inactive in this respect. One reason why hypopituitary dwarfism in some cases does not respond to doses of HGH is probably the formation of antibodies against the preparation used[30]. For the therapeutic applications of growth hormone see the literature[2, 31]. Unlike anabolic steroids, growth hormone causes no acceleration of the maturation of bone.

Growth hormone has many other effects on metabolism apart from that on growth, as shown in the table on this page.

Growth hormone has an anabolic effect on protein metabolism, with consequent decrease in urinary nitrogen excretion. The daily nitrogen retention may increase initially to 3–5 g[32], whereas growing children, for instance, require only 0.2 g nitrogen per day. Protein synthesis is probably stimulated via the ribosomes, presumably through promotion of messenger-RNA synthesis[33]. Here insulin acts synergistically.

The modifications of lipid metabolism consist of a reduction in fat synthesis and mobilization of depot fat. The free fatty acid content of the blood increases.

Single doses of the hormone have an effect similar to that of insulin, namely a fall in the blood-sugar level. Over longer periods and at higher dosage, however, growth hormone reduces glucose tolerance and causes hyperglycaemia and ketosis (diabetogenic effect).

Changes in mineral metabolism due to growth hormone comprise retention of sodium, phosphorus, potassium and usually calcium. In the kidneys the rates of glomerular filtration, plasma flow and phosphate reabsorption are increased.

In cartilage, growth hormone stimulates the proliferation of columnar cells, the incorporation of phosphate and the synthesis of collagen.

In experimental animals, human growth hormone has effects similar to those of prolactin.

References

1 Smith et al. (Eds.), *The Hypophyseal Growth Hormone; Nature and Actions*, McGraw-Hill, New York, 1955; Knobil and Hotchkiss, *Ann. Rev. Physiol.*, **26**, 47 (1964); Matsuzaki and Raben, *Ann. Rev. Pharmacol.*, **5**, 137 (1965); Daughaday and Parker, *Ann. Rev. Med.*, **16**, 47 (1965); Root, A., *Pediatrics*, **36**, 940 (1965); Harris and Donovan (Eds.), *The Pituitary Gland*, vols. 1 and 2, Butterworth, London, 1966.
2 Vest, M., *Schweiz. med. Wschr.*, **96**, 405 (1966).
3 Li et al., *J. Amer. chem. Soc.*, **88**, 2050 (1966); Li et al., *Biochim. Biophys. Acta (Amst.)*, **160**, 472 (1968).
4 Peckham, W.D., *J. biol. Chem.*, **242**, 190 (1967).
5 Saxena and Henneman, *Biochem. J.*, **100**, 711 (1966).
6 Loraine and Bell, *Hormone Assays and Their Clinical Application*, 2nd ed., Livingstone, Edinburgh, 1966; Bell, E.T., *Vitam. and Horm.*, **24**, 63 (1966).
7 Evans et al., *Endocrinology*, **22**, 483 (1938); Greenspan et al., in Emmens, C.W. (Ed.), *Hormone Assays*, Academic Press, New York, 1950, page 273.
8 Geschwind and Li, in Smith et al. (Eds.), *The Hypophyseal Growth Hormone; Nature and Actions*, McGraw-Hill, New York, 1955, page 28; Lostroh and Li, *Endocrinology*, **60**, 308 (1957).
9 Hunter and Greenwood, *Biochem. J.*, **85**, 39 P (1962); Hunter and Greenwood, *Biochem. J.*, **91**, 43 (1964).
10 Glick et al., *Nature*, **199**, 784 (1963).
11 Utiger et al., *J. clin. Invest.*, **41**, 254 (1962); Utiger, R.D., *J. clin. Endocr.*, **24**, 60 (1964).
12 Daughaday et al., *J. clin. Endocr.*, **19**, 743 (1959); Collins and Baker, *Metabolism*, **9**, 556 (1960); Kogut et al., *Pediatrics*, **31**, 538 (1963).
13 Ezrin, C., in Netter, P.H. (Ed.), *Endocrine System and Selected Metabolic Diseases*, Ciba Collection of Medical Illustrations, vol. 4, Ciba, New York, 1965, page 10.
14 Gemzell and Heijkenskjöld, *Endocrinology*, **59**, 681 (1956).
15 Parker et al., *J. clin. Invest.*, **41**, 262 (1962).
16 Glick et al., *Recent Progr. Hormone Res.*, **21**, 241 (1965).
17 Greenwood et al., *Brit. med. J.*, **1**, 25 (1964); Hunter et al., *J. Endocr.*, **34**, 139 (1966); Hunter and Rigal, *J. Endocr.*, **34**, 147 (1966); Marks et al., *Nature*, **208**, 686 (1965).
18 Hunter and Greenwood, *Brit. med. J.*, **1**, 804 (1964).
19 Greenwood and Landon, *Nature*, **210**, 540 (1966).
20 Hartog et al., *Brit. med. J.*, **2**, 1229 (1964).
21 Daughaday, W.H., *Med. Clin. N. Amer.*, **52**, 371 (1968).
22 Frantz and Rabkin, *J. clin. Endocr.*, **25**, 1470 (1965).
23 Hadden and Prout, *Nature*, **202**, 1342 (1964).

[24] Cornblath et al., *J.clin.Endocr.*, **25**, 209 (1965).
[25] Gitlin et al., *J.clin.Endocr.*, **25**, 1599 (1965); Laron et al., *Acta endocr. (Kbh.)*, **53**, 687 (1966).
[26] Deuben and Meites, *Endocrinology*, **74**, 408 (1964); Dhariwal et al., *Endocrinology*, **77**, 932 (1965).
[27] Müller and Pecile, *Proc.Soc.exp.Biol.(N.Y.)*, **122**, 1289 (1966).
[28] Brasel et al., *Amer.J.Med.*, **38**, 484 (1965); Seip and Trygstad, *Acta paediat.scand.*, **55**, 287 (1966).
[29] Raben, M.S., *New Engl.J.Med.*, **266**, 82 (1962).
[30] Széky et al., *Helv.paediat.Acta*, **17**, 411 (1962); Prader et al., *Lancet*, **2**, 378 (1964).
[31] Raben, M.S., *Recent Progr.Hormone Res.*, **15**, 71 (1959); Mason and Tanner, in Gardiner-Hill, H. (Ed.), *Modern Trends in Endocrinology*, vol.3, Butterworth, London, 1967, page 1.
[32] Bergenstal and Lipsett, *J.clin.Endocr.*, **20**, 1427 (1960).
[33] Korner, A., *Recent Progr.Hormone Res.*, **21**, 205 (1965).
[34] Li, C.H., *Advanc.Protein Chem.*, **11**, 101 (1956); Root, A., *Pediatrics*, **36**, 940 (1965); Li et al., *J.Amer.chem.Soc.*, **88**, 2050 (1966); Mills, J.B., *Nature*, **213**, 631 (1967).
[35] Daughaday and Parker, *Ann.Rev.Med.*, **16**, 47 (1965); Vest and Girard, *Dtsch.med.Wschr.*, **87**, 1705 (1962).
[36] Hunter and Greenwood, *Biochem.J.*, **91**, 43 (1964).
[37] Unger et al., *Nature*, **205**, 804 (1965).

Human placental lactogen

(HPL, human chorionic growth-hormone prolactin)

HPL is a polypeptide hormone the presence of which in placental extracts[1] and the plasma of pregnant women[2] was demonstrated immunologically by a cross reaction with antiserum against human growth hormone. Since that time preparations with various amounts of activity have been isolated from the placenta. In dilute solution HPL exists as a monomer with a molecular weight of about 20000[14]. The sequence of the first 17 amino acids is very similar to that in human growth hormone[4]. The N-terminal amino acid of the peptide chain is valine, the C-terminal amino acid phenylalanine[3].

HPL can be determined radioimmunologically in tissue extracts and body fluids[5–8]. The site of its production is the placenta[10] and it is contained in the cytoplasm of the syncytiotrophoblast layer of this organ[9]. The hormone can already be detected in the blood and urine in the first trimester of pregnancy; with advancing gestation the plasma level rises and reaches a maximum at term[5–7]. The normal plasma level in the third trimester is 6.8 ± 2.1 mg/l[15]. High levels have been measured in diabetic pregnant women, low levels in women with placental insufficiency. The ratio of HPL to growth hormone in the plasma at term is about 1000:1[6]. A few hours after expulsion of the placenta the hormone has almost completely disappeared from the maternal blood[5–7]. Cord blood contains only very small amounts of HPL[6,7]. In the tissues it is rapidly broken down, the biological half-life being about 20 min[11]. At term the urinary excretion is less than 0.1 mg/24 h[12].

HPL probably combines weak somatotropic activity like that of growth hormone with mammotropic and luteotropic activities like those of prolactin[8]. During pregnancy it possibly acts as a physiological insulin antagonist[11,12] and may play a role in placental steroid metabolism[13].

References

[1] Josimovich and MacLaren, *Endocrinology*, **71**, 209 (1962).
[2] Greenwood et al., *Brit.med.J.*, **1**, 22 (1964).
[3] Catt et al., *Biochem.J.*, **102**, 27c (1967).
[4] Catt et al., *Science*, **157**, 321 (1967).
[5] Kaplan and Grumbach, *Science*, **147**, 751 (1965).
[6] Kaplan and Grumbach, *J.clin.Endocr.*, **25**, 1370 (1965); Beck et al., *J.clin. Endocr.*, **25**, 1457 (1965).
[7] Samaan et al., *J.clin.Endocr.*, **26**, 1303 (1966).
[8] Greenwood, F.C., in Gardiner-Hill, H. (Ed.), *Modern Trends in Endocrinology*, vol.3, Butterworth, London, 1967, page 288.
[9] Sciarra et al., *Nature*, **199**, 1005 (1963).
[10] Grumbach and Kaplan, *Trans.N.Y.Acad.Sci.*, **27**, 167 (1964).
[11] Beck and Daughaday, *J.clin.Invest.*, **46**, 103 (1967).
[12] Samaan et al., quoted by Beck and Daughaday [11].
[13] Tominaga and Troen, *J.clin.Invest.*, **46**, 1124 (1967).
[14] Andrews, P., *Biochem.J.*, **111**, 799 (1969).
[15] Saxena et al., *New Engl.J.Med.*, **281**, 225 (1969).

Melanotropin[1]

(melanocyte-stimulating hormone = MSH, melanophore hormone, chromatophore hormone, pigment hormone, intermedin)

Chemistry[2,3]

The melanocyte-stimulating hormones α-MSH and β-MSH are linear polypeptides in which part of the amino-acid sequence closely resembles the ACTH molecule. α-MSH appears to have the same structure in all species in which it has so far been studied, whereas that of β-MSH is species-specific (see below). The α-MSH chain as well as several β-MSH chains have been synthesized, in-

Structure and biological activity of melanotropins[20]

	Amino-acid sequence	Activity (U/g)*
ACTH.	Ser·Tyr·Ser·Met·Glu·His·Phe·Arg·Trp·Gly·Lys·Pro·Val·Gly·Lys·Lys·Arg·Arg·Pro 1 2 3 4 5 6 7 8 9 10 11 12 13 14 15 16 17 18 19	**
α-MSH (porcine, bovine, equine) . . .	CH_3CO– Ser·Tyr·Ser·Met·Glu·His·Phe·Arg·Trp·Gly·Lys·Pro·Val·NH_2 1 2 3 4 5 6 7 8 9 10 11 12 13	$1.0–2.0 \times 10^{10}$
β-MSH (porcine). .	Asp·Glu·Gly·Pro·Tyr·Lys·Met·Glu·His·Phe·Arg·Trp·Gly·Ser·Pro·Pro·Lys·Asp 1 2 3 4 5 6 7 8 9 10 11 12 13 14 15 16 17 18	$3.0–5.0 \times 10^9$
β-MSH (bovine) . .	Asp·Ser·Gly·Pro·Tyr·Lys·Met·Glu·His·Phe·Arg·Trp·Gly·Ser·Pro·Pro·Lys·Asp 1 2 3 4 5 6 7 8 9 10 11 12 13 14 15 16 17 18	2.0×10^9
β-MSH (equine) . .	Asp·Glu·Gly·Pro·Tyr·Lys·Met·Glu·His·Phe·Arg·Trp·Gly·Ser·Pro·Arg·Lys·Asp 1 2 3 4 5 6 7 8 9 10 11 12 13 14 15 16 17 18	1.2×10^9
β-MSH (human) . .	Ala·Glu·Lys·Lys·Asp·Glu·Gly·Pro·Tyr·Arg·Met·Glu·His·Phe·Arg·Trp·Gly·Ser·Pro·Pro·Lys·Asp 1 2 3 4 5 6 7 8 9 10 11 12 13 14 15 16 17 18 19 20 21 22	3.3×10^9

* Frog-skin test in vitro.   ** On a molar basis naturally occurring ACTH possesses about 1% of the activity of α-MSH, ACTH acetylated at the serine end about 10%.

cluding that of human β-MSH[21]. The α-corticotropin-releasing factors (see page 725) have a structure very similar to that of α-MSH.

Units, methods of assay

Methods of assay depend on the ability of the hormone to cause dispersion of the pigment (mainly melanin) in the melanocytes of amphibia. The test object is the frog[4,5] or, in vitro, its skin[6,7]. The latter reacts to a concentration as low as 10^{-11} mol MSH per litre[8]. The activity of MSH preparations is usually expressed in units based on the test of Shizume et al.[6], 1 unit being that amount with the same activity as 0.04 μg of the standard preparation of these workers.

Biosynthesis and secretion

MSH is probably formed in the polygonal cells of the intermediate lobe of the pituitary, which derives from Rathke's pouch, though it is also present in the anterior and posterior lobes. In view of the structural relationship of MSH to ACTH it is likely that the former is also synthesized in the same type of anterior pituitary cell as the latter[9]. Melanotropic activity has also been detected in plasma extracts, with particularly high values in pregnancy[4,10]. In both tissue and plasma extracts it has been possible to separate melanotropic from corticotropic activity[11]. Using a radioimmunological method, β-MSH concentrations of 20–90 ng/l have been found in human plasma[12]. In frogs and rats there is evidence that MSH secretion is regulated by the blood level of MSH through a feedback mechanism; this mechanism probably causes the hypothalamus to release a factor inhibiting MSH secretion[13]. Melanotropic activity has also been found in urine; in women this varies during the course of the menstrual cycle and rises during pregnancy[10,14].

Biological activity

In cold-blooded animals MSH causes rapid expansion of the melanocytes and dispersion of the pigment (melanin) in these cells, with consequent darkening of the skin. This reversible, physiological process of pigment regulation enables the animal rapidly to adapt itself to the colour of its surroundings. In birds and mammals the pigment content of the melanocytes controls the intensity of skin coloration, a slow process known as morphological pigment regulation in which the role played by MSH is still obscure. Pigment dispersion in frogs takes place in the melanocytes of the epidermis and dermis; this effect is reversible, but only in the dermal melanocytes, by the pineal-gland factor melatonin[15] (see page 730). Morphologically, the epidermal melanocytes of the frog are similar to those of mammals. MSH apparently increases pigment formation; thus the pigment content of frogs rises under long-term treatment with MSH, and in man daily injections of α-MSH result in hyperpigmentation already visible on the second day[16]. Other effects of administering MSH to mammals are hypocalcaemia, hyperlipaemia and increases in thyroid function, pulse rate and the permeability of the blood-aqueous barrier of the eye[3,17], but whether these actions occur at physiological levels of the hormone is not known.

The mode of action of MSH is still obscure. Melanin dispersion is probably only a secondary effect of some direct change in the cell involving sodium and calcium[18]. Melanin is formed in the melanocytes from tyrosine and oxygen (see page 440) in ribosomes containing *o*-diphenol oxidase, whereby these subcellular particles undergo a gradual 'melanization'. It is conceivable that MSH has some action on the enzyme *o*-diphenol oxidase, but this has not been demonstrated[19].

References

1 Gordon, M. (Ed.), *Pigment Cell Biology*, Academic Press, New York, 1959; Lerner and Lee, *Vitam. and Horm.*, **20**, 337 (1962); Barrington, E.J.W., in Pincus and Thimann (Eds.), *The Hormones*, vol. 4, Academic Press, New York, 1964, page 299; Harris and Donovan (Eds.), *The Pituitary Gland*, vol. 3, Butterworth, London, 1966.
2 Lee et al., *Ann. N.Y. Acad. Sci.*, **100**, 658 (1963); Schroeder and Luebke, *The Peptides*, vol. 2, Academic Press, New York, 1966, page 161.
3 Schwyzer, R., *Ann. Rev. Biochem.*, **33**, 259 (1964).
4 McGuinness, B.W., *Ann. N.Y. Acad. Sci.*, **100**, 640 (1963).
5 Teague and Patton, *Ann. N.Y. Acad. Sci.*, **100**, 686 (1963).
6 Shizume et al., *Endocrinology*, **54**, 553 (1954).
7 Lerner and Wright, *Meth. biochem. Anal.*, **8**, 295 (1960); Schuler et al., *Schweiz. med. Wschr.*, **93**, 1027 (1963).
8 Lerner, A.B., *Nature*, **184**, 674 (1959).
9 Pearse and van Noorden, in Benoit and da Lage (Eds.), *Cytologie de l'adénohypophyse*, C.N.R.S., Paris, 1963, page 63.
10 Shizume and Lerner, *J. clin. Endocr.*, **14**, 1491 (1954).
11 Island et al., *J. clin. Endocr.*, **25**, 975 (1965).
12 Abe et al., *J. clin. Invest.*, **46**, 1031 (1967).
13 Kastin and Ross, *Endocrinology*, **77**, 45 (1965); Kastin and Schally, *Nature*, **213**, 1238 (1967).
14 Dahlberg, B., *Ann. N.Y. Acad. Sci.*, **100**, 631 (1963).
15 McGuire and Möller, *Endocrinology*, **78**, 367 (1966).
16 McGuire and Lerner, *Ann. N.Y. Acad. Sci.*, **100**, 622 (1963).
17 Pastan, I., *Ann. Rev. Biochem.*, **35**, 369 (1966).
18 Novales, R.R., *Ann. N.Y. Acad. Sci.*, **100**, 1035 (1963); Novales and Novales, *Gen. comp. Endocr.*, **5**, 568 (1965).
19 Lerner and Takahashi, *Recent Progr. Hormone Res.*, **12**, 303 (1956); Ippen, H., *Dtsch. med. Wschr.*, **89**, 798 (1964).
20 Schroeder and Luebke, *The Peptides*, vol. 2, Academic Press, New York, 1966, page 161.
21 Yajima et al., *Biochim. Biophys. Acta (Amst.)*, **175**, 228 (1969); Rittel, W., in Back et al. (Eds.), *Advances in Experimental Medicine and Biology*, vol. 2, Plenum Press, New York, 1968, page 35.

Oxytocin[1-3]

(pitocin, lactagogin) (for references see page 725)

Vasopressin[1,2]

(pitressin, antidiuretin, antidiuretic hormone = ADH)

Chemistry[4]

As isolated from the posterior pituitary of various species, the hormones oxytocin and vasopressin are cyclic polypeptides made up of 9 amino-acid residues, one disulphide bridge and one terminal amide group; the ring structure is formed from the disulphide form on oxidation of the cysteine residues*. The various oxytocins and vasopressins differ only in the nature of the amino acids at positions 3, 4 and 8. The molecular weight is just over 1000. The structure and biological activity of the naturally occurring hormones are shown in the table on page 724. Arginine vasopressin occurs in most mammals whereas lysine vasopressin is confined to species of swine[5]. The aspartic acid residue in position 5 and the glycinamide residue in position 9 are essential for oxytocin-like activity, while the basic side chain at position 8 is essential for antidiuretic activity[6]. The activity varies with the size of the ring but is not dependent on the existence of the disulphide bridge: activity persists after replacement of the cysteine S of position 1 by a CH_2 group[7].

Units, methods of assay

Synthetic preparations of both these human posterior lobe hormones are available. 1 International Unit (IU) of oxytocic, vasopressor and antidiuretic activity is contained in 0.5 mg of the 3rd International Standard (see page 762).

Various biological methods are available for the assay of the posterior lobe hormones[8], some of which are given in the table on page 724. In interpreting the results it must be borne in mind that most tissues contain other pharmacologically active substances, like histamine, serotonin, acetylcholine and bradykinin, to which the methods of bioassay used for the hormones also respond.

Assay of oxytocic activity is usually carried out by measuring the contractions produced by the preparation in the isolated uterus of rats pretreated with oestrogens (rat uterus test), that of vasopressor activity by determining the rise of blood pressure caused by the preparation in the carotid artery of rats. Radioimmunological techniques may soon be available[9].

Biosynthesis, secretion, metabolism[10]

Oxytocin and vasopressin are formed in the hypothalamus and stored in the posterior lobe of the pituitary. The Golgi apparatus of the hypothalamic neurones, the nucleus supraopticus and nucleus paraventricularis produce a neurosecretory protein material that is deposited as required in nerve endings in the posterior lobe, a process requiring its transport by the axoplasm of the supraopticohypophyseal tract[11]. Both oxytocin and vasopressin have been isolated from this material. The neurosecretion can be demonstrated under the optical microscope by suitable staining (for example Gomori's); under the electron microscope it appears as dense granules 0.1–0.3 μm in diameter. The accumulation of these granules accounts for the specific staining of the nerve endings and for Herring's bodies. When the pituitary stalk is cut the neurosecretion accumulates in the proximal ends of the axons. Physiological stimuli depleting neurohypophyseal activity also deplete stainable neurosecretion in the hypothalamus and posterior pitu-

* If the cysteine residues linked by the disulphide bridge are reckoned as a single amino acid (cystine) oxytocin and vasopressin are octapeptides.

(For references see page 725)

itary. What is stained is probably the protein carrier substance and not the polypeptide hormones themselves. A protein with a molecular weight of about 30000 and possessing oxytocic and vasopressor activity has been isolated from the posterior pituitary (VAN DYKE protein[12], neurophysin[13]).

The hormone content of the hypothalamus and posterior pituitary as well as the ratio of vasopressin to oxytocin in these tissues varies from species to species[14]. The vasopressin content of the human hypothalamus is 4.6%, the oxytocin content 5.9% of that of the posterior pituitary. The proportion of vasopressin to oxytocin in the hypothalamus is 1.9, in the posterior pituitary 1.6. This ratio shows characteristic changes in certain physiological conditions, for example during lactation in dogs and during oestrus in rats[15]. The different distributions of the two hormones may be due to each individual secretory neurone secreting only one hormone and to species differences in the proportion of vasopressin-producing to oxytocin-producing neurones in the nuclei supraopticus and paraventricularis[14].

The neurosecretory cells with thickened nerve endings containing secretion attach themselves to the walls of the posterior lobe capillaries and there give up their hormones; this process is calcium-dependent[16].

The posterior lobe was formerly thought always to release oxytocin and vasopressin together into the circulating blood, regardless of the nature of the stimulus. Several examples of independent release have, however, been described[17,18,34]. Thus vasopressin, but not oxytocin, is secreted following haemorrhage and on stimulation of the sinus nerve by carotid occlusion, while oxytocin, but not vasopressin, is secreted during both suckling and parturition. The neurones of the nuclei supraopticus and paraventricularis are capable not only of elaborating the hormones as required but also of transmitting electrical impulses, so that release of the hormones is associated with electrical activity in the neurones[34].

Owing to their very low concentrations in the blood and other body fluids the posterior lobe hormones cannot be satisfactorily assayed in these media by the methods at present available. The plasma vasopressin level at a normal state of hydration has been estimated at 1–5 mIU/l (1 mIU = ca. 1×10^{-12} mol) (for measured values see the table below); oxytocin appears to be present in plasma at about the same concentration[19]. In women the plasma oxytocin level apparently remains unchanged during lactation[20], but in cows and goats a rise during milking has been observed. In blood the hormones are found only in the plasma and are not bound to the erythrocytes[19]. It is uncertain to what extent the hormones are bound to plasma proteins; under physiological conditions they are probably mainly present in the free form[19].

Vasopressin content of the peripheral plasma (mIU/l)

Normally hydrated		Dehydrated		Reference
Mean	Range	Mean	Range	
1.9	1.0–2.7	6.5	3.4–9.0	36
0.0	–	4.6	2.5–10.0	37
–	0.2–0.4	–	0.9–1.0	38

The hormones disappear rapidly from the circulating blood as a result of inactivation in the tissues and excretion through the kidneys. The biological half-life of vasopressin is 10–20 min, that of oxytocin 10 min or less[19]. At the physiological plasma vasopressin level the total clearance in man is about 150 ml/min, the urinary clearance about 4–10 ml/min[19]; at normal hydration about 5–32 mIU/24 h are excreted in the urine[21]. Enzymes breaking down vasopressin and oxytocin are found mainly in the liver and kidneys but are also present in other tissues such as the mammary glands, the myometrium in pregnancy and the placenta. In pregnant women the enzyme oxytocinase appears in the serum and is capable of breaking down both oxytocin and vasopressin[22].

A syndrome of 'inappropriate secretion of antidiuretic hormone' has been recognized[35], mostly in association with lung carcinoma. Its main features are plasma hypo-osmolality and hyponatraemia, hypertonic urine and natriuresis. In some of the patients the hormone has been identified in the tumour tissue.

Biological activity

The posterior pituitary hormones act on the epithelial membranes – such as the distal renal tubules in mammals and the skin and bladder in tailless amphibians – by increasing their permeability to water, urea and sodium[23]. They also act on the contractile elements, the effect being a stimulatory one on the smooth muscle of the mammalian uterus and oviduct of birds and reptiles, on the myoepithelial cells surrounding the mammary alveoli and on the smooth muscle of mammalian blood vessels, a relaxatory one on the vascular wall in birds. This action on contractile tissue is probably also due to a change in permeability since in such tissues an increase in the latter generally entails an increased depolarization following electrical or chemical stimulation[2]. At the biomolecular level the change in permeability is possibly due to enhanced synthesis of cyclic adenosine 3′,5′-phosphate[24]. Vasopressin-like polypeptides (see page 725) and possibly also vasopressin itself play a part in the regulation of ACTH secretion[25]. The activities of the posterior pituitary hormones in their five most important effects are shown in the table on page 724.

In mammals, *oxytocin* has a powerful action on the uterus and mammary glands. The sensitivity of the uterus to oxytocin rises during the course of pregnancy and is at a maximum shortly before parturition[26]. In animals the sensitivity varies during the oestrous cycle and is at its highest during oestrus. During the luteal phase the uterus is completely insensitive. In the gravid mouse sensitivity to oxytocin is increased by the injection of oestrone. Oxytocin appears to play a role in the initiation of parturition, even though the latter can still proceed after extirpation of the pituitary, probably as a result of regeneration of functional neurosecretory release endings. Disturbances of the birth process have been observed after severe injury to the hypothalamus or destruction of the neurosecretory cells.

The effect of oxytocin on milk ejection is so powerful that injection of as little as 0.01 IU has an action on the mammary glands of lactating women[27]. Release of oxytocin from the posterior pituitary is initiated by the suckling stimulus, but there may be considerable psychic modifications of this reflex activity.

The physiological function of *vasopressin* consists of a role in the production of hypertonic urine[28]. When the hormone is absent from the blood the aqueous permeability of the distal convolution and collecting tubule of the nephron is lowered. In water diuresis the hypotonic fluid flowing out of the ascending part of the loop of HENLE into the distal convolution remains hypotonic up to the mouth of the collecting tubule. Absorption of water in these parts of the tubule almost ceases since the reduced aqueous permeability means that there is no osmotic transfer of water to the isotonic interstice of the cortex and hypertonic interstice of the medulla. In the presence of vasopressin, on the other hand, the aqueous permeability of the distal convolution and collecting tubule is increased. The hypotonic fluid flowing from the ascending loop becomes isotonic in the distal convolution through osmotic water loss and hypertonic during passage through the collecting tubule. The production of hypertonic urine cannot, however, be wholly explained by this increase in aqueous permeability since water has to be pumped against an osmotic gradient, and active transport of water in this way has so far never been observed; in the production of both hyper- and hypotonic urine only solute particles (mainly sodium ions) are actively transported, the subsequent osmotic transfer of water being prevented by the impermeability of the wall of the tubule. The creation of an increased osmotic pressure in the renal medulla is made possible only through the existence of a special system, the 'hairpin' countercurrent system of the HENLE loops, in which there is multiplication of the concentrating effect[29].

The release of vasopressin from the posterior pituitary is thought to be regulated by the total osmotic concentration of electrolytes in the extracellular fluid. Thus when loss of water by the body causes the osmotic concentration to rise, more antidiuretic hormone is released, more water is reabsorbed in the kidneys, and a more concentrated urine is produced. Excessive intake of water has the opposite effect and a very dilute urine is produced (water diuresis). However, the osmotic concentration undergoes only slight variations, so that it is assumed that the hypothalamus contains 'osmoreceptors' which react to the slightest variation[30]. Secretion of vasopressin is also stimulated by any rapid diminution of the volume of the plasma or extracellular fluid such as may occur in severe haemorrhage[31].

Destruction of the hypothalamus results in permanent diabetes insipidus with polyuria averaging 5–10 l/24 h; the clinical symptoms can be suppressed by administration of vasopressin at appropriate dosage[32].

Administration of vasopressin also causes peripheral vasoconstriction, slowing of the heart beat, reduction of the cardiac minute volume and increase in blood pressure. A further effect of the hormone

Structure and biological activity of naturally occurring neuropituitary hormones[33]

	Structure	Oxytocin-like activity (IU/mg)			Vasopressin-like activity (IU/mg)		Occurrence
		Uterus (rat, in vitro)	Blood pressure (chicken)	Mammary glands (rabbit)	Blood pressure (rat)	Anti-diuresis (rat)	
Arginine vasopressin (Arg⁸-vasopressin)	Cys·Tyr·Phe·Glu(NH$_2$)·Asp(NH$_2$)·Cys·Pro·Arg·Gly·NH$_2$ (1 2 3 4 5 6 7 8 9; Cys 1–Cys 6 bridged)	16	60	70	400	400	Man, many mammals
Lysine vasopressin (Lys⁸-vasopressin)	Cys·Tyr·Phe·Glu(NH$_2$)·Asp(NH$_2$)·Cys·Pro·Lys·Gly·NH$_2$ (1 2 3 4 5 6 7 8 9; Cys 1–Cys 6 bridged)	5	40	45	280	250	Pig, hippopotamus
Oxytocin (Ile³–Leu⁸-vasopressin)	Cys·Tyr·Ile·Glu(NH$_2$)·Asp(NH$_2$)·Cys·Pro·Leu·Gly·NH$_2$ (1 2 3 4 5 6 7 8 9; Cys 1–Cys 6 bridged)	450	450	450	5	5	Man, many vertebrates
Arginine vasotocin (Ile³–Arg⁸-vasopressin)	Cys·Tyr·Ile·Glu(NH$_2$)·Asp(NH$_2$)·Cys·Pro·Arg·Gly·NH$_2$ (1 2 3 4 5 6 7 8 9; Cys 1–Cys 6 bridged)	155	285	210	245	250	Birds, reptiles, fish
Isotocin (Ser⁴–Ile⁸-oxytocin, Ile³–Ser⁴–Ile⁸-vasopressin)	Cys·Tyr·Ile·Ser·Asp(NH$_2$)·Cys·Pro·Ile·Gly·NH$_2$ (1 2 3 4 5 6 7 8 9; Cys 1–Cys 6 bridged)	150	320	300	0.06	0.18	Many bony fish
Mesotocin (Ile³–Ile⁸-vasopressin)	Cys·Tyr·Ile·Glu(NH$_2$)·Asp(NH$_2$)·Cys·Pro·Ile·Gly·NH$_2$ (1 2 3 4 5 6 7 8 9; Cys 1–Cys 6 bridged)	289	498	328	6	1.1	Frog, bichir
Glumitocin (Ile³–Ser⁴–Glu⁸–vasopressin)	Cys·Tyr·Ile·Ser·Asp(NH$_2$)·Cys·Pro·Glu(NH$_2$)·Gly·NH$_2$ (1 2 3 4 5 6 7 8 9; Cys 1–Cys 6 bridged)	8					Many elasmobranch fish

is contraction of the smooth muscles of the intestine, gallbladder and urinary bladder. The vasoconstrictive effect is probably of little physiological importance, so that the 'antidiuretic hormone' or 'antidiuretin' is a more appropriate name than 'vasopressin'.

References

[1] SAWYER, W.H., *Pharmac. Rev.*, **13**, 225 (1961); SAWYER, W.H., in NALBANDOV, A.V. (Ed.), *Advances in Neuroendocrinology*, Symposium, Miami 1961, University of Illinois Press, Urbana, 1963, page 68; HARRIS and DONOVAN (Eds.), *The Pituitary Gland*, vol. 3, Butterworth, London, 1966.
[2] KLEEMAN and CUTLER, *Ann. Rev. Physiol.*, **25**, 385 (1963); FARRELL et al., *Ann. Rev. Physiol.*, **30**, 557 (1968).
[3] PINKERTON, J.H.M. (Ed.), *Advances in Oxytocin Research*, Pergamon, London, 1965.
[4] SCHROEDER and LUEBKE, *The Peptides*, vol. 2, Academic Press, New York, 1966; WALTER et al., *Amer. J. Med.*, **42**, 653 (1967).
[5] SAWYER, W.H., *Amer. J. Med.*, **42**, 678 (1967).
[6] WIELAND and DETERMANN, *Ann. Rev. Biochem.*, **35**, 651 (1966).
[7] RUDINGER and JOŠT, *Experientia (Basel)*, **20**, 570 (1964).
[8] SAWYER, W.H., *Meth. med. Res.*, **9**, 210 (1961); SAWYER, W.H., in HARRIS and DONOVAN (Eds.), *The Pituitary Gland*, vol. 3, Butterworth, London, 1966, page 288.
[9] PERMUTT et al., *Endocrinology*, **78**, 809 (1966).
[10] HELLER and CLARK (Eds.), *Neurosecretion*, Proceedings of the 3rd International Symposium of Neurosecretion, Bristol 1961, Academic Press, New York; HELLER and GINSBURG, in HARRIS and DONOVAN (Eds.), *The Pituitary Gland*, vol. 3, Butterworth, London, 1966, page 330.
[11] SCHARRER and SCHARRER, *Recent Progr. Hormone Res.*, **10**, 183 (1954); BARGMANN, W., in HELLER, H. (Ed.), *The Neurohypophysis*, Proceedings of the 8th Symposium, Bristol 1956, Butterworth, London, 1957, page 11; BARGMANN, W., in STUTINSKY, F. (Ed.), *Neurosecretion*, Springer, Berlin, 1967, page 241; SACHS, H., *Amer. J. Med.*, **42**, 687 (1967).
[12] VAN DYKE et al., *J. Pharmacol. exp. Ther.*, **74**, 190 (1942).
[13] ACHER and FROMAGEOT, *Ergebn. Physiol.*, **48**, 286 (1955); ACHER, R., in HARRIS and DONOVAN (Eds.), *The Pituitary Gland*, vol. 3, Butterworth, London, 1966, page 269.
[14] VAN DYKE et al., in HELLER, H. (Ed.), *The Neurohypophysis*, Proceedings of the 8th Symposium, Bristol 1956, Butterworth, London, 1957, page 65; HELLER, H., *Brit. med. Bull.*, **22**, 227 (1966).
[15] VAN DYKE et al., *Recent Progr. Hormone Res.*, **11**, 1 (1955).
[16] DOUGLAS, W.W., in STUTINSKY, F. (Ed.), *Neurosecretion*, Springer, Berlin, 1967, page 178.
[17] GAITAN et al., *J. clin. Invest.*, **43**, 2310 (1964).
[18] ANDERSON, B., in HELLER, H. (Ed.), *The Neurohypophysis*, Proceedings of the 8th Symposium, Bristol 1956, Butterworth, London, 1957, page 131.
[19] LAUSON, H.D., in ANTONIADES, H.N. (Ed.), *Hormones in Human Plasma*, Little, Brown, Boston, 1960, page 225; LAUSON, H.D., *Amer. J. Med.*, **42**, 713 (1967).
[20] HAWKER, R.W., *J. clin. Endocr.*, **18**, 54 (1958).
[21] ALEXANDER and FILBIN, *J. Lab. clin. Med.*, **60**, 855 (1962).
[22] SEMM, K., *Gynaecologia (Basel)*, **159**, 61 (1965); RIAD, A.M., *Acta endocr. (Kbh.)*, **54**, 618 (1967).
[23] LEAF, A., *Amer. J. Med.*, **42**, 745 (1967).
[24] ORLOFF and HANDLER, *Amer. J. Med.*, **42**, 757 (1967).
[25] MARTINI, L., in HARRIS and DONOVAN (Eds.), *The Pituitary Gland*, vol. 3, Butterworth, London, 1966, page 535.
[26] CALDEYRO-BARCIA and HELLER (Eds.), *Oxytocin*, An International Symposium, Uruguay 1959, Pergamon, London, 1961.
[27] BELLER et al., *Acta endocr. (Kbh.)*, **29**, 1 (1958).
[28] BERLINER and BENNETT, *Amer. J. Med.*, **42**, 777 (1967); WIRZ, H., in HELLER, H. (Ed.), *The Neurohypophysis*, Proceedings of the 8th Symposium, Bristol 1956, Butterworth, London, 1957, page 157; SMITH, H.W., *Bull. N.Y. Acad. Med.*, **35**, 293 (1959); WIRZ, H., in *XXII International Congress of Physiological Sciences*, Leiden 1962, vol. 1, part 1, Excerpta Medica Foundation, Amsterdam, 1962, page 359; GOTTSCHALK, C.W., *Amer. J. Med.*, **36**, 670 (1964); ULLRICH and HIERHOLZER, in SARRE, H. (Ed.), *Nierenkrankheiten*, 3rd ed., Thieme, Stuttgart, 1967, page 1.
[29] WIRZ et al., *Helv. physiol. Acta*, **9**, 196 (1951); WIRZ, H., *Helv. physiol. Acta*, **14**, 353 (1956); GOTTSCHALK and MYLLE, *Amer. J. Physiol.*, **196**, 927 (1959).
[30] VERNEY, E.B., *Proc. roy. Soc. B*, **135**, 25 (1947/48).
[31] SHARE, L., *Amer. J. Med.*, **42**, 701 (1967).
[32] COGGINS and LEAF, *Amer. J. Med.*, **42**, 807 (1967).
[33] WALTER et al., *Amer. J. Med.*, **42**, 653 (1967).
[34] LEWIS, G.P., in ROBSON and STACEY (Eds.), *Recent Advances in Pharmacology*, 4th ed., Churchill, London, 1968, page 213.
[35] BARRTER and SCHWARTZ, *Amer. J. Med.*, **42**, 790, (1967); UTIGER, R.D., *Med. Clin. N. A.*, **52**, 381 (1968).
[36] YOSHIDA et al., *J. Lab. clin. Med.*, **62**, 279 (1963).
[37] AHMED et al., *J. clin. Invest.*, **46**, 111 (1967).
[38] HEINTZ et al., *Klin. Wschr.*, **42**, 771 (1964).

Hypothalamic pituitary-regulating factors[1,2]

(hypothalamic releasing and inhibiting factors)

In addition to vasopressin and oxytocin the hypothalamus produces factors that play a role in the synthesis and secretion of the hormones of the middle and anterior lobes of the pituitary. These are released in the primary plexus of the pituitary portal system in the median eminence of the pituitary stalk. Factors identified in the hypothalamus (or neuropituitary) of various animal species are listed in the table below.

Hypothalamic pituitary-regulating factors

	Abbreviation	Reference
Corticotropin-releasing factors	α_1-CRF	5
	α_2-CRF	6
	β-CRF	5, 7
Melanocyte-stimulating-hormone releasing factor	MRF (MSH-RF)	8
Melanocyte-stimulating-hormone inhibiting factor	MIF (MSH-IF)	9
Follicle-stimulating-hormone releasing factor	FRF (FSH-RF)	10
Luteinizing-hormone releasing factor	LRF (LH-RF)	11
Prolactin-releasing factor	PRF (pigeons)	12
Prolactin-inhibiting factor	PIF (mammals)	13
Growth-hormone releasing factor	GRF (GH-RF)	14
Thyroid-stimulating-hormone releasing factor	TRF (TSH-RF)	15

CRF, MIF, FRF, LRF, TRF and GRF are present in the human hypothalamus[3]. FRF and LRF are formed in a closely circumscribed area of this part, TRF apparently in a wider area; the site of CRF synthesis has not yet been identified[4].

The releasing and inhibiting factors are almost certainly polypeptides. α_1-CRF and α_2-CRF have a structure resembling α-MSH, β-CRF appears to be similar to vasopressin, while TRF, LRF and FRF are weakly basic polypeptides containing no cystine and with a molecular weight lying between 1200 and 2500. One TRF preparation has been found to contain only 25–30% of amino acids[2], so that this hormone does not appear to be a simple polypeptide.

References

[1] GUILLEMIN, R., *Recent Progr. Hormone Res.*, **20**, 89 (1964); MARTINI, L., in HARRIS and DONOVAN (Eds.), *The Pituitary Gland*, Butterworth, London, 1966, page 535; HARRIS et al., *Brit. med. Bull.*, **22**, 266 (1966).
[2] GUILLEMIN, R., *Ann. Rev. Physiol.*, **29**, 313 (1967); SCHALLY et al., *Recent Progr. Hormone Res.*, **24**, 497 (1968); MCCANN et al., *Ann. Rev. Physiol.*, **30**, 589 (1968).
[3] SCHALLY et al., *J. clin. Endocr.*, **27**, 755 (1967).
[4] MARTINI et al., *Recent Progr. Hormone Res.*, **24**, 439 (1968); MESS and MARTINI, in JAMES, V.H.T. (Ed.), *Recent Advances in Endocrinology*, 8th ed., Churchill, London, 1968, page 1.
[5] GUILLEMIN et al., *C. R. Acad. Sci. (Paris)*, **250**, 4462 (1960).
[6] SCHALLY et al., *Endocrinology*, **71**, 164 (1962).
[7] SCHALLY et al., *Endocrinology*, **70**, 478 (1962).
[8] TALEISNIK and ORÍAS, *Amer. J. Physiol.*, **208**, 293 (1965).
[9] KASTIN and ROSS, *Endocrinology*, **77**, 45 (1965).
[10] IGARASHI and MCCANN, *Endocrinology*, **74**, 446 (1964).
[11] MCCANN et al., *Proc. Soc. exp. Biol. (N.Y.)*, **104**, 432 (1960).
[12] KRAGT and MEITES, *Endocrinology*, **76**, 1169 (1965).
[13] PASTEELS, J.L., *C. R. Acad. Sci. (Paris)*, **254**, 2664 (1962); MEITES et al., in NALBANDOV, A.V. (Ed.), *Advances in Neuroendocrinology*, University of Illinois Press, Urbana, 1963, page 238.
[14] FRANZ et al., *Acta endocr. (Kbh.)*, **41**, 336 (1962).
[15] SHIBUSAWA et al., *Endocr. jap.*, **6**, 31 (1959).

Thyroid hormones[1–3] (for references see page 728)

Chemistry

The normal human thyroid gland contains about 8 mg of iodine[4]. Over 99% of this iodine is present in the organic form as the iodinated amino acids monoiodotyrosine, di-iodotyrosine, triiodothyronine and thyroxine.

L-3-Monoiodotyrosine

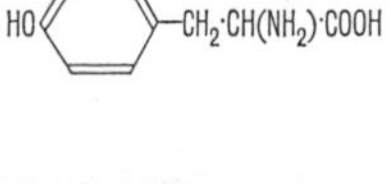

(For references see page 728)

L-3,5-Di-iodotyrosine
(L-iodogorgoic acid)

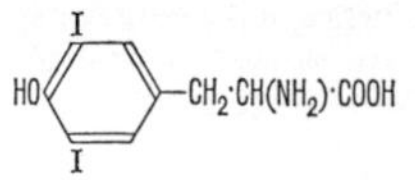

L-3,5,3′-Tri-iodothyronine

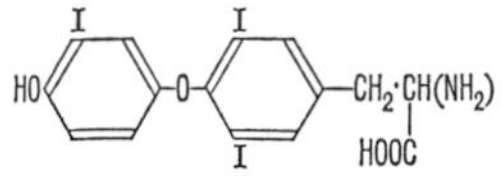

L-Thyroxine

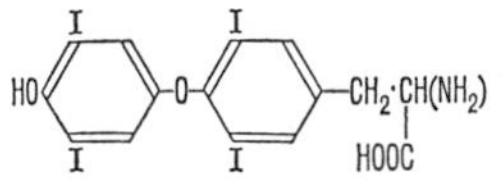

In the thyroid by far the greater part of these iodinated amino acids is bound to high-molecular proteins, the most important of which is thyroglobulin, a glycoprotein with a molecular weight of 660000 and a sedimentation constant of 19 S [5]. Each molecule of thyroglobulin contains roughly 110 tyrosine residues and 26 atoms of iodine [6]; it has also been estimated that each molecule includes 7 monoiodotyrosine residues, 6 di-iodotyrosine residues and 1 thyroxine residue, while every third molecule contains a tri-iodothyronine residue. The proportions of the individual iodinated amino acids present in thyroglobulin depend on the iodine uptake; thus iodine deficiency results in an increase in the proportion of mono-iodotyrosine and tri-iodothyronine.

Biosynthesis, secretion, metabolism

The iodine ingested with food is transported by the blood in the form of iodide, which is then taken up in large amounts by the thyroid. Iodide concentration also occurs in other organs, such as the salivary glands, gastric mucosa, skin, mammary glands and placenta, but only in the thyroid is this process subject to physiological regulation. Iodide concentration by the thyroid is stimulated by thyrotropin, inhibited by hypophysectomy. The iodide is oxidized to iodine or iodinium ions in the epithelial cells of the thyroid follicles under the action of the enzyme peroxidase. It is still not clear whether iodination of the amino acids and coupling of the tyrosines to thyronines takes place in the cells of the thyroid, at the cell-colloid boundary, or even in the colloid itself. It is known, however, that there are variations in the degree of iodination as well as in the structure of the thyroglobulin in the follicular lumina.

The thyroid hormones – thyroxine and tri-iodothyronine – are discharged into the blood only after enzymatic breakdown of the thyroglobulin, a process stimulated by thyrotropin. Thyroglobulin is also present in the lymph of the thyroid, but the physiological significance of the transport of this substance by the lymphatic system is unknown [7]. The mono- and di-iodotyrosines arising from the breakdown of thyroglobulin are deiodinated in the thyroid, the iodine so liberated being again available for the synthesis of thyroid hormones.

Over 90% of the circulating thyroid hormones consists of thyroxine. Mono- and di-iodotyrosines do not appear to be normally present in the blood [8], although there are reports to the contrary [9]. Most of the thyroxine in the serum is bound physicochemically to certain carrier proteins [10], the tri-iodothyronine to a much smaller extent (for normal values of the protein-bound iodine see page 564 and the lower table below). Thyroxine is mainly linked to 'thyroxine-binding globulin', lying electrophoretically between the α_1- and α_2-globulins, and 'thyroxine-binding prealbumin', though some is present in the albumin fraction. Dialysis against a protein-free buffer shows that the proportion of the total thyroxine present in the free state is about 0.05%; the proportion of free tri-iodothyronine is some 10 times greater [11]. Very probably only the free thyroid hor-

*Metabolic data for iodide** [3]

Age (years)	Plasma iodide concentration (µg/l)				Iodide clearance by thyroid (ml/min)				Absolute iodine uptake of thyroid (µg/h)				Renal iodide clearance (ml/min)			
	Men		Women		Men		Women		Men		Women		Men		Women	
	Mean	Range	Mean	Range	Mean	Range	Mean	Range	Mean	Range	Mean	Range	Mean	Range	Mean	Range
0–19 . .	1.4	–	0.8	0.6–1.0	23.0	–	36.2	31.5–40.9	2.0	–	1.6	1.4–1.9	27.0	–	31.5	30.2–32.7
20–39 .	2.3	0.8–3.4	1.6	0.4–2.7	27.5	9.7–57.8	26.4	19.7–38.2	3.2	1.9–8.2	2.2	0.9–3.4	40.6	25.9–61.8	25.0	15.7–41.3
40–59 .	1.7	0.4–3.6	1.6	0.8–2.6	21.8	2.9–38.5	15.6	5.7–37.6	2.5	0.1–6.7	1.3	0.6–2.2	38.8	17.9–53.8	28.4	19.0–37.4
> 60 . .	1.7	0.4–3.5	2.5	1.4–5.7	25.3	13.8–36.0	18.3	5.4–38.6	2.0	0.8–2.9	2.1	0.5–3.1	27.2	21.0–30.8	19.3	11.7–38.5

* Wide deviations from these values may occur in subjects with a high iodine intake.

Thyroid hormones in blood [35]

Age (years)	Endogenous thyroxine distribution (%)						Thyroxine-binding capacity (µg thyroxine/l serum)				Protein-bound iodine (µg/l serum)		Free thyroxine			
	Thyroxine-binding globulin		Thyroxine-binding prealbumin		Albumin		Thyroxine-binding globulin		Thyroxine-binding prealbumin				(ng/l serum)		(% of total serum thyroxine)	
	Mean	s	Mean	s	Mean	s	Mean	s	Mean	s	Mean	s	Mean	s	Mean	s
2–12 . .	55.0	7.0	26.8	5.5	18.2	3.7	27.3	3.6	72	26	61	7	47.0	7.4	0.050	0.007
16–20 . .	43.4	7.2	39.6	6.5	17.0	3.9	–	–	–	–	52	7	36.0	7.7	0.050	0.015
21–30 . .	40.2	4.0	43.1	5.9	16.6	3.3	–	–	–	–	52	11	44.6	14.1	0.057	0.015
31–40 . .	39.5	5.7	44.6	5.8	15.8	1.5	21.5	3.6	183	26	52	7	42.7	9.1	0.055	0.011
41–50 . .	41.7	7.1	42.7	7.9	15.7	2.5	–	–	–	–	53	9	46.0	11.4	0.057	0.008
51–60 . .	44.6	6.3	37.8	6.4	17.7	4.3	–	–	–	–	48	5	35.1	3.8	0.050	0.004
61–70 . .	47.8	9.7	36.5	8.9	15.5	3.1	25.3	5.8	128	60	54	8	47.5	12.3	0.058	0.014
> 70 . . .	50.8	4.7	29.7	5.8	19.5	7.3	–	–	–	–	51	12	42.0	13.4	0.054	0.008

mones are taken up by the tissues, so that only this part is physiologically active[6,10,11]. The concentration of free thyroid hormones in the blood is regulated by a negative feedback mechanism; when the concentration falls, more thyrotropin is secreted and the formation and release of the thyroid hormones are thus stimulated, whereas an increase in the concentration has the opposite effect (see also page 718).

The half-life of thyroxine in the blood is about 6–8 days, that of tri-iodothyronine about 2–3 days[1,12]. Thyroxine is broken down more rapidly in children[13], in adolescents[14] and in hyperthyroid subjects[15], more slowly in aged persons[16] and in hypothyroid subjects[15]. Thyroxine and tri-iodothyronine are present in almost all human tissues[17]. They are taken up rapidly by the liver – about one-third of the extrathyroid thyroxine is contained in this organ[18] – and more slowly by other tissues such as skeletal muscle, intestines and skin. After entry into the cell the thyroid hormones are broken down by a variety of processes including deamination, decarboxylation, and conjugation[10,19]. Deamination and decarboxylation of the alanine side-chain lead to pyruvic and acetic analogues of the hormones, which then undergo deiodination. Rupture of the diphenyl ether bridge to yield di-iodotyrosine and *p*-hydroquinone has also been observed[20]. About 20% of the iodine arising from these deiodination processes is available for the further synthesis of thyroid hormones[21]. Conjugation of the hormones with sulphuric and glucuronic acids occurs in various tissues but mainly in the liver[22]. In the bile, most of the thyroxine is present as the glucuronide[23], part of which is broken down in the gut and reabsorbed. About 15% of the thyroxine formed is excreted in the stools[24]. Only small amounts of thyroxine are present in the urine; that part of the iodine from thyroid-hormone breakdown not taken up by the thyroid is excreted through the kidneys.

Biological activity

The biological activity of the thyroid hormones is extremely diverse. In warm-blooded animals thyroxine and tri-iodothyronine increase oxygen consumption and energy production (calorigenic action); this applies to a varying extent to the heart, muscles, liver, kidneys and leucocytes, but not to the brain. Exogenous thyroid hormones stimulate carbohydrate, fat and protein metabolism and increase the minute volume of the heart and the excitability of the nervous system. They also have an effect on the metabolism of calcium and bone and increase the sensitivity of animals to the cardiovascular, glycogenolytic and lipolytic actions of the catecholamines. Thyroxine deficiency slows growth and has a disturbing effect on foetal differentiation, the latter being especially noticeable in lower animals (metamorphosis test). The thyroid hormones possess the important property of stimulating the maturation of the cerebral cortex in the critical phase of development[25].

Comparative potencies of the thyroid hormones and related compounds[12,36]

		Physiological test		
	Species	Calorigenic action	Growth and differentiation	Thyrotropin depression
L-Thyroxine	All	100	100	100
D-Thyroxine	Rat	5–8	–	–
	Man	8–12	–	–
3,5,3′-Tri-iodo-L-thyronine	Rat	150–350	500	–
	Man	100–250	–	280–540
3,5,3′-Tri-iodo-D-thyronine	Rat	10–15	–	14
3,5-Di-iodo-L-thyronine	Rat	0–5	–	–
3-Iodo-L-thyronine	Rat	0–3	–	–
3,5-Di-iodo-3′-methyl-DL-thyronine	Rat	150	–	–

The action of the thyroid hormones is marked by a so-called 'latent period'; thus in man the basal metabolic rate only begins to rise 2 days after their administration.

The biomolecular effects of the thyroid hormones have also been studied[26]. These include modification of the activity of many enzymes, uncoupling of oxidative phosphorylation in the mitochondria, alteration of the permeability of the mitochondrial membrane, and stimulation of protein synthesis. Some workers regard the last-named action as a primary effect of the hormones to which the calorigenic action is secondary.

The effects of the thyroid hormones and related compounds are closely linked with their chemical structure[27]. In the iodinated thyronines the steric configuration appears to be mainly responsible for biological activity in that the presence of two iodine atoms in the inner ring prevents free rotation of the outer ring. Activity is greatest when the 5′-position (outer ring) is unsubstituted and the 3′-position is occupied by iodine or a group of similar size. This outer ring is the part of the molecule determining biological activity, whereas fixation of the molecule to a binding receptor at the site of action is a function of the inner ring, the oxygen bridge and to a lesser extent the alanine side-chain.

The results of in vivo tests of the biological activity of the various thyroxine analogues should be interpreted with caution since there are wide variations in the strength of their plasma-protein binding which affect their peripheral activity[10]. When given parenterally tri-iodothyronine is twice as active as thyroxine, when given orally four times as active. While thyroxine and tri-iodothyronine have qualitatively the same effects the calorigenic action of the latter is considerably quicker but not so long-lasting.

Evaluation of thyroid function[3,28]

Little can be deduced as to the functional state of the thyroid from its size and shape alone. Except in hyperthyroidism, hyperplasia of the gland merely reflects its increased stimulation by thyrotropin due to increased secretion of this hormone triggered by a reduction in the concentration of thyroxine in the blood (feedback mechanism). This reduction is in turn the result of a substrate deficiency (iodine) or impaired synthesis. Increase in size of the thyroid (goitre) is therefore a compensatory phenomenon which, together with a parallel increase in its secretory capacity, almost always suffices to maintain the patient's euthyroid condition – except in the presence of extreme iodine deficiency or severely impaired synthesis. A severe functional disturbance may, however, be unaccompanied by goitre.

The functional state of the thyroid is best assessed by studying the individual phases of the iodine cycle: iodine uptake, hormone synthesis, hormone release, hormone transport, peripheral hormone uptake, iodine excretion. There is an equilibrium between these various phases that is also maintained in both hypo- and hyperthyroidism. In hyperfunctioning of the thyroid the iodine uptake of the gland is increased along with the rate of hormone synthesis, and the circulating free thyroid hormones are more quickly taken up by the tissues and broken down. In hypofunctioning of the gland all these phases are slowed down. The apparent thyroid hyperfunctioning of pregnancy is the result of increased renal iodide clearance with a compensating increase in thyroid function[37].

Iodine uptake phase. Measurement of the accumulation of a radioactive iodine isotope (^{131}I or ^{132}I): the normal range shows a wide fluctuation according to the amount of iodine ingested (for normal values see pages 287–288). Study of the distribution of radio-iodine in the thyroid parenchyma by means of scintigraphy. Possibly also determination of iodide clearance and absolute iodine uptake (for normal values see the table opposite).

Hormone synthesis phase. Determination of protein-bound iodine (for normal values see page 564 and the table opposite) or, better, butanol-extractable iodine in the serum. Measurement of the rate of secretion by determining radioactive protein-bound iodine after ingestion of a tracer dose. Determination of the conversion rate[29], i.e., the ratio of protein-bound radio-iodine to total radio-iodine in a serum sample (for normal range see page 287). Chromatographic methods for separation of thyroxine from tri-iodothyronine and identification of pathological inactive iodoprotein.

Hormone transport phase. Measurement of the thyroxine-binding capacity of the globulin and prealbumin (for normal values see the table opposite). Determination of free thyroxine in the serum (for normal values see page 288 and the table opposite). Indirect determination of free thyroxine by measuring the free binding capacity of the thyroxine-binding serum proteins (addition of radioactive tri-iodothyronine and measurement of its fixation by erythrocytes[30], ion-exchange resins[31] or haemoglobin-coated charcoal[32]). The normal values vary with the method (see page 288). Newborn infants have higher values[33].

Hormone uptake phase. Measurement of the half-life of intravenously injected radioactive thyroxine (see page 288).

Thyroid activity can also be evaluated indirectly from the activity of the thyroid hormones, for example by measuring the BMR (see page 539), the oxygen consumption of the leucocytes, or the time of the Achilles tendon reflex[34] (slowed in thyroxine deficiency, accelerated in thyroxine excess).

References

1 MEANS et al., *The Thyroid and Its Diseases*, 3rd ed., McGraw-Hill, New York, 1963.
2 INGBAR and GALTON, *Ann. Rev. Physiol.*, **25**, 361 (1963); RALL et al., in PINCUS et al. (Eds.), *The Hormones*, vol. 5, Academic Press, New York, 1964, page 159; ROSENBERG and BASTOMSKY, *Ann. Rev. Physiol.*, **27**, 71 (1965); WERNER and NAUMAN, *Ann. Rev. Physiol.*, **30**, 213 (1968).
3 WAYNE et al., *Clinical Aspects of Iodine Metabolism*, Blackwell, Oxford, 1964.
4 RIGGS, D.S., *Pharmacol. Rev.*, **4**, 284 (1952).
5 EDELHOCH, H., *Recent Progr. Hormone Res.*, **21**, 1 (1965); PASTAN, I., *Ann. Rev. Biochem.*, **35**, 369 (1966).
6 ROBBINS and RALL, *Physiol. Rev.*, **40**, 415 (1960).
7 DANIEL et al., *J. Physiol. (Lond.)*, **188**, 25 (1967).
8 SHALOM, E.S., *J. Endocr.*, **36**, 1 (1966).
9 WERNER and RADICHEVICH, *Nature (Lond.)*, **197**, 877 (1963); DIMITRIADOU et al., *Nature (Lond.)*, **201**, 575 (1964).
10 TATA, J.R., *Recent Progr. Hormone Res.*, **18**, 221 (1962).
11 INGBAR et al., *J. clin. Invest.*, **44**, 1679 (1965).
12 PITT-RIVERS and TATA, *Thyroid Hormones*, Pergamon, Oxford, 1959.
13 HADDAD, H.M., *J. clin. Invest.*, **39**, 1590 (1960).
14 HUNG et al., *Pediatrics*, **35**, 76 (1965).
15 STERLING and CHODOS, *J. clin. Invest.*, **35**, 806 (1956); KLEIN, E., *Klin. Wschr.*, **40**, 3 (1962); THOMSON and WALLACE, *J. clin. Endocr.*, **26**, 875 (1966).
16 GREGERMAN et al., *J. clin. Invest.*, **41**, 2065 (1962); ANBAR et al., *J. clin. Invest.*, **44**, 1986 (1965).
17 TATA, J.R., *Expos. ann. Biochim. méd.*, **25**, 45 (1964).
18 CAVALIERI and SEARLE, *J. clin. Invest.*, **45**, 939 (1966).
19 ROCHE and MICHEL, *Ann. N.Y. Acad. Sci.*, **86**, 454 (1960); GALTON, V.A., in JAMES, V.H.T. (Ed.), *Recent Advances in Endocrinology*, 8th ed., Churchill, London, 1968, page 181.
20 WYNN, J., *Clin. Res.*, **11**, 232 (1963).
21 TATA, J.R., *Biochim. biophys. Acta (Amst.)*, **28**, 95 (1958).
22 CLOSON, J., *Expos. ann. Biochim. méd.*, **25**, 129 (1964).
23 WEST et al., *J. clin. Invest.*, **42**, 1134 (1963).
24 INGBAR and FREINKEL, *Recent Progr. Hormone Res.*, **16**, 353 (1960).
25 EAYRS, J.T., in CAMERON and O'CONNOR (Eds.), *Brain-Thyroid Relationships*, Ciba Foundation Study Group, No. 18, Churchill, London, 1964, page 60.
26 HOCH, F.L., *New Engl. J. Med.*, **266**, 446 (1962); HOCH, F.L., *Physiol. Rev.*, **42**, 605 (1962); TAPLEY and HATFIELD, *Vitam. and Horm.*, **20**, 251 (1962); WOLFF and WOLFF, in PITT-RIVERS and TROTTER (Eds.), *The Thyroid Gland*, vol. 1, Butterworth, London, 1964, page 237; TATA, J.R., *Advanc. metab. Disord.*, **1**, 153 (1964); TATA, J.R., in KARLSON, P. (Ed.), *Mechanisms of Hormone Action*, Academic Press, New York, 1965, page 173.
27 JORGENSEN et al., *J. biol. Chem.*, **237**, 3832 (1962); GREENBERG et al., *Amer. J. Physiol.*, **205**, 821 (1963); JORGENSEN, E.C., *Mayo Clin. Proc.*, **39**, 560 (1964).
28 SCAZZIGA and LEMARCHAND-BÉRAUD, Physiopathology of the Thyroid, *Documenta Geigy, Acta clinica*, No. 5, Basle, 1967.
29 CLARK et al., *Surgery*, **26**, 331 (1949).
30 HAMOLSKY et al., *J. clin. Endocr.*, **17**, 33 (1957); HAMOLSKY et al., *J. clin. Endocr.*, **19**, 103 (1959).
31 MITCHELL et al., *J. clin. Endocr.*, **20**, 1474 (1960).
32 BRAVERMAN et al., *J. Amer. med. Ass.*, **199**, 469 (1967).
33 KUNSTADTER et al., *Pediatrics*, **30**, 27 (1962); FRIDRICH and BÜHLER, *Schweiz. med. Wschr.*, **96**, 1680 (1966).
34 SHERMAN et al., *Lancet*, **1**, 243 (1963); WEISSBECKER et al., *Münch. med. Wschr.*, **109**, 729 (1967).
35 BRAVERMAN et al., *J. clin. Invest.*, **45**, 1273 (1966).
36 TATA, J.R., *Advanc. metab. Disord.*, **1**, 153 (1964).
37 NICOLOFF et al., *J. clin. Invest.*, **43**, 1300 (1964); WILBER, J.F., *Med. Clin. N. Amer.*, **52**, 253 (1968).

Parathyroid hormone[1–3]

(parathormone)

Chemistry

Purified bovine parathyroid hormone has a molecular weight of 8500 and is a single-chain polypeptide with no covalent intra-chain cross linkage[4]. A highly purified preparation with a biological activity of 2500–3000 USP units per milligramme can be obtained by gel filtration. The empirical amino-acid composition of bovine parathyroid hormone is Lys_9, His_4, Arg_5, Asp_8, Thr, Ser_6, Glu_{10}, Pro_3, Gly_4, Ala_7, Val_7, Met_2, Ile_3, Leu_8, Tyr, Phe_2, Trp. Parathyroid hormone is inactivated irreversibly by pepsin, trypsin and chymotrypsin, reversibly by hydrogen peroxide.

Units, methods of assay[5]

1 USP Unit = $^1/_{100}$ of the amount that when administered parenterally to dogs weighing 8–16 kg increases the serum calcium concentration by 1 mg/100 ml within 16–18 hours. The activity of preparations can be determined by making use of this action on the serum calcium level[6] or by measuring their effect on the urinary phosphate excretion of parathyroidectomized rats[7]. The amount of the hormone present in body fluids can be determined by means of its immunological properties, using either the complement-fixation test[8] or radioimmunological methods[9].

Biosynthesis, secretion, metabolism

Parathyroid hormone is formed in the chief cells, the light chief cells and possibly also the oxyphile cells of the parathyroid[10]. Intracytoplasmic droplets seen in GOLGI's apparatus may represent an intracellular form of the hormone[11]. Discharge of the hormone into the blood is regulated by the diminution in the concentration of ionized calcium in the blood flowing into the parathyroid[12]. This does not apply in primary hyperparathyroidism, in which the parathyroid secretes the hormone independently of the blood calcium level. The hypothalamus and pituitary have no detectable effect on the secretion of parathyroid hormone. A substance immunologically similar to parathyroid hormone is produced by some nonendocrine tumours[36].

Published data on the parathyroid hormone content of the blood vary widely. Biological methods give values of 25 μg/l plasma or more, radioimmunoassay values of 0.1 to 1.0 μg/l plasma. The plasma level is increased in adenoma of the parathyroid, some forms of carcinoma (pseudohyperparathyroidism) and chronic kidney disease (secondary hyperparathyroidism)[13]. The circulating hormone is rapidly broken down (half-life in rats 22 min[14]), probably in the liver[7]. Parathyroid hormone is excreted in the urine, the amount decreasing as the level of ionized calcium in the serum rises[15].

Biological activity

Parathyroid hormone maintains the concentration of ionized calcium in the extracellular fluid, a function in which vitamin D (see page 461) and thyrocalcitonin (see page 718) are also involved. The hormone has a direct action on bone[16], in which it causes breakdown of the bone substance reflected in an increase not only of the blood calcium but also of the urinary excretion of mucoproteins[17], hydroxyproline[18] and pyrophosphate[19].

The other site of action of parathyroid hormone is the renal tubules, where it promotes the excretion of inorganic phosphate[20]. 15–40 min after administration of the hormone the latter reaches a maximum lasting several hours, and the consequent fall in the serum phosphate level entails a rapid rise in the serum calcium level. Mobilization of calcium takes place more slowly, however, with a maximum after 6 hours or more, since it is preceded by an increased formation of osteoclasts[3]. There are also indications that the hormone maintains the blood calcium level by stimulating tubular reabsorption of calcium[21] and intestinal calcium absorption[22]. Parathyroid hormone has also been observed to have an effect on lactation[23].

The mode of action of parathyroid hormone has been extensively investigated. The hormone could act on the skeleton by (a) releasing a collagenolytic factor from the bone cells[24], and (b) promoting the formation of citrate and lactate and thus displacing the pH to the acid side, with a consequent increase in dissolution of the hydroxyapatite of bone[25]. The action of the hormone on bone, but not that on renal tubular function, requires the presence of vitamin D[26,27]. At the molecular level parathyroid hormone increases the uptake of phosphate by the mitochondria and, in conjunction with vitamin D, the mobilization of calcium[26,28]. The action on bone is inhibited by actinomycin D, so that this effect, unlike that on the renal tubules, probably has a genetic mechanism[11,29].

Evaluation of parathyroid function[30,31]

Hyperparathyroidism is often accompanied by a rise in serum calcium, increased urinary excretion of phosphate and calcium, and a fall in serum phosphate. The urinary phosphate excretion can be measured by the phosphate clearance[32], by the percentage tubular reabsorption of phosphate[33], or by the phosphate excretion index[34] (see also page 663). Parathyroid suppression tests have been developed for distinguishing primary hyperparathyroidism from other diseases accompanied by disturbance of calcium metabolism[31,35]; these involve measurement of the effect of a calcium infusion on phosphate excretion.

References

1 MUNSON et al., *Ann. Rev. Physiol.*, **25**, 325 (1963); ARNAUD et al., *Ann. Rev. Physiol.*, **29**, 349 (1967).
2 AURBACH and POTTS, *Advanc. metab. Disord.*, **1**, 45 (1964), and *Amer. J. Med.*, **42**, 1 (1967).

3 FISCHER, J.A., *Schweiz.med.Wschr.*, **96**, 273 and 321 (1966).
4 AURBACH, G.D., *J.biol.Chem.*, **234**, 3179 (1959); RASMUSSEN and CRAIG, *Biochim.biophys.Acta (Amst.)*, **56**, 332 (1962); HAWKER et al., *Biochemistry*, **5**, 344 (1966); POTTS et al., *Recent Progr. Hormone Res.*, **22**, 101 (1966).
5 BIERING, A., *Acta pharmacol. (Kbh.)*, **6**, 40 (1950); THORP, R.H., in EMMENS, C.W. (Ed.), *Hormone Assay*, Academic Press, New York, 1950, page 77; THORP, R.H., in DORFMAN, R.I., *Methods in Hormone Research*, vol. 2, Academic Press, New York, 1962, page 477.
6 MUNSON et al., *Fed.Proc.*, **12**, 249 (1953); MUNSON, P.L., *Ann.N.Y.Acad. Sci.*, **60**, 776 (1955); MUNSON, P.L., in GREEP and TALMAGE (Eds.), *The Parathyroids*, Thomas, Springfield, 1961, page 94.
7 KENNY and MUNSON, *Endocrinology*, **64**, 513 (1959); ZIEGLER et al., *Dtsch. med.Wschr.*, **91**, 2114 (1966), and *Germ. med. Mth.*, **12**, 369 (1967).
8 TASHJIAN et al., *Endocrinology*, **74**, 244 (1964); TASHJIAN and MUNSON, *Endocrinology*, **77**, 520 (1965).
9 BERSON et al., *Proc.nat.Acad.Sci. (Wash.)*, **49**, 613 (1963); REISS and CANTERBURY, *Proc. Soc. exp. Biol. (N.Y.)*, **128**, 501 (1968).
10 SELZMAN and FECHNER, *J.Amer.med.Ass.*, **199**, 359 (1967).
11 DAVIS and ENDERS, in GREEP and TALMAGE (Eds.), *The Parathyroids*, Thomas, Springfield, 1961, page 76; MUNGER and ROTH, *J.cell.Biol.*, **16**, 379 (1963); LEVER, J.D., in GAILLARD et al. (Eds.), *The Parathyroid Glands, Ultrastructure, Secretion and Function*, University of Chicago Press, Chicago, 1965, page 11.
12 SHERWOOD et al., *Nature (Lond.)*, **209**, 52 (1966).
13 BERSON and YALOW, *Science*, **154**, 907 (1966); ANDERSON and TOMLINSON, in GRAY and BACHARACH (Eds.), *Hormones in Blood*, 2nd ed., vol. 2, Academic Press, New York, 1967, page 601.
14 MELICK et al., *Endocrinology*, **77**, 198 (1965).
15 ELIEL et al., *J.clin.Endocr.*, **25**, 445 (1965).
16 GAILLARD, P.J., *Exp.Cell Res.*, suppl. 3, 154 (1955); GAILLARD, P.J., in GREEP and TALMAGE (Eds.), *The Parathyroids*, Thomas, Springfield, 1961, page 20; GOLDHABER, P., in GAILLARD et al. (Eds.), *The Parathyroid Glands, Ultrastructure, Secretion and Function*, University of Chicago Press, Chicago, 1965, page 153.
17 ENGEL, M.B., *Arch.Path.*, **53**, 339 (1952).
18 KEISER et al., *J.clin.Invest.*, **43**, 1073 (1964).
19 AVIOLI et al., *J.clin.Invest.*, **45**, 1093 (1966).
20 PULLMAN et al., *Endocrinology*, **67**, 570 (1960).
21 KLEEMAN et al., *Yale J.Biol.Med.*, **34**, 1 (1961).
22 TALMAGE and ELLIOTT, *Fed.Proc.*, **17**, 160 (1958).
23 TOVERUD and MUNSON, *Ann. N.Y.Acad.Sci.*, **64**, 336 (1956).
24 GROSS et al., in LOCKE, M. (Ed.), *Cytodifferentiation and Macromolecular Synthesis*, Academic Press, New York, 1963, page 175; STERN et al., *Biochem. biophys. Res.Commun.*, **13**, 137 (1963).
25 BORLE et al., *J.biol.Chem.*, **235**, 1211 (1960); KENNY, A.D., in GREEP and TALMAGE (Eds.), *The Parathyroids*, Thomas, Springfield, 1961, page 275; NEUMAN and DOWSE, in GREEP and TALMAGE (Eds.), *The Parathyroids*, Thomas, Springfield, 1961, page 310.
26 RASMUSSEN et al., *J.clin.Invest.*, **42**, 1940 (1963).
27 ARNAUD et al., *J.clin.Invest.*, **45**, 1955 (1966).
28 AURBACH et al., *Biochem.biophys. Res.Commun.*, **20**, 592 (1965); DELUCA and SALLIS, in GAILLARD et al. (Eds.), *The Parathyroid Glands, Ultrastructure, Secretion and Function*, University of Chicago Press, Chicago, 1965, page 181.
29 RASMUSSEN et al., *Science*, **144**, 1019 (1964).
30 KYLE et al., *Ann.intern.Med.*, **57**, 957 (1962).
31 HAAS, H.G., *Helv.med.Acta*, **33**, 91 (1966); HAAS, H.G., *Knochenstoffwechsel- und Parathyreoidea-Erkrankungen*, Thieme, Stuttgart, 1966.
32 KYLE et al., *Amer.J.Med.*, **24**, 240 (1958).
33 SCHAAF and KYLE, *Amer.J.med.Sci.*, **228**, 262 (1954).
34 NORDIN and FRASER, *Lancet*, **1**, 947 (1960); NORDIN, B.E.C., *Advanc.clin. Chem.*, **4**, 275 (1961).
35 HOWARD et al., *Trans.Ass.Amer.Phycns*, **65**, 351 (1952); HOWARD et al., *J.clin.Endocr.*, **13**, 1 (1953); PRONOVE and BARTTER, *Metabolism*, **10**, 349 (1961); KYLE et al., *J.clin.Endocr.*, **22**, 52 (1962).
36 SHERWOOD et al., *J. clin. Endocr.*, **27**, 140 (1967).

Calcitonin[1]
(thyrocalcitonin)

During the last few years a factor involved in the homoeostasis of calcium through depression of the blood calcium level has come to light. This effect was first observed during perfusion of the dog parathyroid with hypercalcaemic blood and was ascribed to a substance given the name calcitonin[2]. Later a substance with an identical action was isolated from the thyroid of various species[3], including man[4], to which the name thyrocalcitonin was given. Recently it has been shown that calcitonin is formed in the so-called C cells[5] derived from the last branchial arch and occurring not only in the thyroid but also in other cervical regions, depending on the species and individual[6]. Calcitonin has been demonstrated in the blood of normal persons at rest[7]. In patients with medullary carcinoma of the thyroid an excess of calcitonin has been detected in the blood or tumour[8, 9]. The possibility of calcitonin deficiency states has been suggested after surgical or radiological treatment of thyroid diseases[10]. Hypocalcaemic activity has also been found in the urine of patients with medullary thyroid carcinoma but not in that of normal persons[8].

Chemistry

Calcitonin is a single-chain polypeptide consisting of 32 amino-acid residues and a disulphide bridge. In 1968 the structure of both porcine calcitonin[11] and of calcitonin derived from a human medullary thyroid carcinoma[12] was elucidated, and both hormones have since been synthesized[13]:

Porcine α-calcitonin (mol. wt. 3604)

Cys·Ser·Asp(NH_2)·Leu·Ser·Thr·Cys·Val·Leu·Ser·Ala·Tyr·Trp

Arg·Asp(NH_2)·Leu·Asp(NH_2)·Asp(NH_2)·Phe·His·Arg·Phe·Ser

Gly·Met·Gly·Phe·Gly·Pro·Glu·Thr·Pro(NH_2)

Human calcitonin M (monomer) (mol. wt. 3419)

Cys·Gly·Asp(NH_2)·Leu·Ser·Thr·Cys·Met·Leu·Gly·Thr·Tyr·Thr

Glu(NH_2)·Asp·Phe·Asp(NH_2)·Lys·Phe·His·Thr·Phe·Pro

Glu(NH_2)·Thr·Ala·Ile·Gly·Val·Gly·Ala·Pro(NH_2)

Assay, units

In the rat bioassay method calcitonin is determined by the fall in blood calcium. The unit of the Medical Research Council ('Research Standard B') is defined as the calcium-lowering activity in one standard ampoule. 10 MRC mU will lower the blood calcium roughly 10% in a starved 150 g rat bled 1 hour after intravenous injection[1]. Methods of radioimmunoassay have recently been developed[14]. Human calcitonin does not cross-react significantly in the radioimmunoassay of the porcine hormone[8].

Action

Calcitonin is short-acting, the main site of action being the skeleton[15]. Several animal studies have shown that the hormone is extremely potent; nanogramme quantities lower blood calcium by blocking bone resorption or possibly by stimulation of bone mineralization[16]. Calcitonin has also been reported to resemble parathyroid hormone in promoting renal phosphate excretion[17], but this is of minor importance compared with the action on the skeleton. In a few persons with hypercalcaemia it has been found possible to reduce the blood calcium level by administering calcitonin of human[18] or porcine[19] origin. It has been suggested that excessive secretion of calcitonin is the cause of osteopetrosis[20].

References

1 WEBSTER and FRAZER, *Advanc.clin.Chem.*, **10**, 1 (1967); COPP, D.H., *Advanc. intern. Med.*, **14**, 55 (1968); TENENHOUSE et al., *Ann. Rev. Pharmacol.*, **8**, 319 (1968); FOSTER, G.V., *Postgrad.med.J.*, **44**, 411 (1968); FOSTER, G.V., *New Engl. J. Med.*, **279**, 349 (1968); MUNSON, P.L., in ASTWOOD and CASSIDY (Eds.), *Clinical Endocrinology*, vol. 2, Grune & Stratton, New York, 1968, page 336.
2 COPP et al., *Endocrinology*, **70**, 638 (1962); COPP, D.H., in GAILLARD et al. (Eds.), *The Parathyroid Glands, Ultrastructure, Secretion and Function*, University of Chicago Press, Chicago, 1965, page 73.
3 HIRSCH et al., *Endocrinology*, **73**, 244 (1963); MACINTYRE et al., in GAILLARD et al. (Eds.), *The Parathyroid Glands, Ultrastructure, Secretion and Function*, University of Chicago Press, Chicago, 1965, page 89.
4 ALIAPOULIOS and MUNSON, *Surg.Forum*, **16**, 55 (1965); ALIAPOULIOS et al., *J.clin.Endocr.*, **26**, 897 (1966); BARRETT et al., *J. clin. Endocr.*, **28**, 734 (1968).
5 BUSSOLATI and PEARSE, *J. Endocr.*, **37**, 205 (1967).
6 CARVALHEIRA and PEARSE, in *Calcitonin*, Proceedings of the Symposium on Thyrocalcitonin and the C Cells, London 1967, Heinemann, London, 1968, page 122.
7 STURTRIDGE and KUMAR, *Lancet*, **1**, 725 (1968).
8 TASHJIAN and MELVIN, *New Engl.J.Med.*, **279**, 279 (1968).
9 CUNLIFFE et al., *Lancet*, **2**, 63 (1968).
10 SMITH and LALJEE, in IRVINE, W.J. (Ed.), *Thyrotoxicosis*, Proceedings of an International Symposium, Edinburgh 1967, Livingstone, Edinburgh, 1967, page 186.
11 NEHER et al., *Helv. chim. Acta*, **51**, 917 (1968); POTTS et al., *Proc. Nat. Acad. Sci.*, **59**, 1321 (1968).
12 RINIKER et al., *Helv. chim. Acta*, **51**, 1738 (1968).

[13] RITTEL et al., *Helv. chim. Acta*, **51**, 924 (1968); SIEBER et al., *Helv. chim. Acta*, **51**, 2057 (1968).
[14] DEFTOS et al., *Proc. Nat. Acad. Sci.*, **60**, 293 (1968); ARNAUD et al., *Proc. Mayo Clin.*, **43**, 496 (1968).
[15] ALIAPOULIOS et al., *Fed. Proc.*, **24**, 322 (1965); FRIEDMAN and RAISZ, *Science*, **150**, 1465 (1965); ALIAPOULIOS et al., *Science*, **151**, 330 (1966); KOHLER and PECHET, *J. clin. Invest.*, **45**, 1033 (1966); ANAST et al., *J. clin. Invest.*, **46**, 57 (1967).
[16] DAMBACHER and HAAS, *Med. Klin.*, **64**, 496 (1969); BAUD et al., *Schweiz. med. Wschr.*, **99**, 657 (1969); HAAS et al., *Calcif. Tiss. Res.*, **2**, 21, suppl. (1968).
[17] ROBINSON et al., *Lancet*, **2**, 83 (1966); MILHAUD, G., *Presse méd.*, **75**, 71 (1967); ZIEGLER et al., *Klin. Wschr.*, **45**, 34 (1967).
[18] DAMBACHER et al., *Dtsch. med. Wschr.*, **94**, 798 (1969).
[19] FORSTER et al., *Lancet*, **1**, 107 (1966); MILHAUD and JOB, *Science*, **154**, 794 (1966); HAAS and DAMBACHER, *Helv. med. Acta.*, **34**, 327 (1968); MUNSON et al., *Recent Progr. Hormone Res.*, **24**, 589 (1968).
[20] WHITE and AHMANN, *J. clin. Invest.*, **44**, 1111 (1965).

Thymus hormone

In adult healthy mice thymectomy has virtually no effect except for slight lymphopenia, whereas in newborn animals the operation results in very severe disturbances all of which have their origin in a state of immunological insufficiency[1]. Intraperitoneal reimplantation of the thymus in a diffusion capsule is followed by reversal of these changes to a very large extent. It has been concluded that the thymus produces a humoral factor involved in the development of immunological competence (competence-inducing factor), possibly by furthering the maturation or differentiation of immunologically competent cells from their lymphoid precursors[2]. The formation by the thymus of a humoral factor stimulating the proliferation of lymphatic tissue (lymphocyte-stimulating factor) had been postulated earlier[3]. Such a factor is possibly produced by the medullary epithelioid cells of the thymus in the form of an acid mucopolysaccharide containing sulphate[4]. A lymphopoietic factor active in vitro has been isolated from calf thymus and identified as a heat-stable protein containing carbohydrate[5]. The immunological reactivity of thymectomized mice can be restored by administering an extract of calf thymus[6]. Several humoral factors may contribute to the functioning of the thymus[7].

References

[1] MILLER and OSOBA, *Physiol. Rev.*, **47**, 437 (1967); MILLER and DUKOR, *Die Biologie des Thymus nach dem heutigen Stand der Forschung*, Karger, Basle, 1964.
[2] MILLER and OSOBA, in WOLSTENHOLME and KNIGHT (Eds.), *The Immunologically Competent Cell*, Ciba Foundation Study Group, No. 16, Little, Brown, Boston, 1963, page 62; MILLER, J.F.A.P., *Scand. J. Haemat.*, suppl. *Ser. haemat.*, No. 8, 41 (1965).
[3] METCALF, *Brit. J. Cancer*, **10**, 442 (1956); DEFENDI and METCALF (Eds.), *The Thymus*, Symposium, Wistar Institute Press, Philadelphia, 1964.
[4] CLARK, S.L., in WOLSTENHOLME and PORTER (Eds.), *The Thymus: Experimental and Clinical Studies*, Ciba Foundation Symposium, Churchill, London, 1966, page 3.
[5] GOLDSTEIN et al., *Proc. nat. Acad. Sci.*, **56**, 3 (1966).
[6] TRAININ and LINKER-ISRAELI, *Cancer Res.*, **27**, 309 (1967).
[7] BURNET, F.M., in WOLSTENHOLME and PORTER (Eds.), *The Thymus: Experimental and Clinical Studies*, Ciba Foundation Symposium, Churchill, London, 1966, page 520.

Hormones of the pineal gland

In man the pineal organ is a conical, midline structure about 8 mm long located on the dorsal posterior edge of the epithalamus. It arises embryologically as an evagination of the neuroectoderm of the dorsal diencephalon. It is composed of epithelioid parenchymal cells, and usually contains calcareous deposits in sexually mature individuals. Phylogenetically it is the remnant of midline dorsal light receptors.

Possible pineal hormones. Melatonin (melanocyte-contracting principle, skin-lightening factor) is produced in the vertebrate pineal[1]. Serotonin, as well as its metabolites such as 5-hydroxyindoleacetic acid, occur in the mammalian pineal in high concentrations. Noradrenaline and histamine are found in pineal extracts[2]. Anoestrin, an inhibitor of oestrus, and antigonadotrophic factors have also been alleged to be present in the pineal; they may be identical with melatonin[2]. Glomerulotropin (adrenoglomerulotropin), an accelerator of aldosterone secretion, has been postulated as a pineal hormone[3]; it is reported to be a carboline derivative[4].

Melatonin (*N*-acetyl-5-methoxytryptamine)

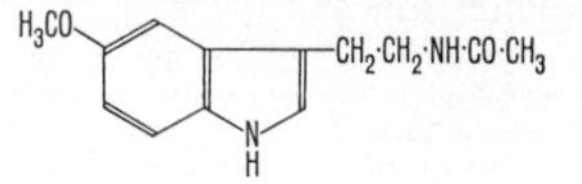

Melatonin is formed in the pineal gland by methylation of *N*-acetyl-5-hydroxytryptamine[1], the reaction being catalysed by hydroxyindole *O*-methyltransferase, a specific enzyme apparently occurring only in the mammalian pineal[5]. The circulating melatonin is rapidly taken up by the tissues, where it is converted mainly into 6-hydroxymelatonin; this substance is excreted in the urine mainly as the sulphate and to a smaller extent as the glucuronate[6].

In rats, the weight, morphology and chemical composition of the pineal gland can be altered by exposing the animals for long periods to continuous light or darkness. Thus light exposure causes the parenchymal cells to contract[7], while dark exposure increases the activity of the enzyme hydroxyindole *O*-methyltransferase and therefore the rate of melatonin synthesis[8]. The serotonin, melatonin and hydroxyindole *O*-methyltransferase contents of the pineal gland are subject to a day-and-night rhythm[8,9] as a result of sympathetic nervous regulation by the amount of light entering the eyes.

In amphibia, melatonin acts as an antagonist to MSH by causing the melanophores to contract (see page 722). In rats, melatonin has been reported to reduce the weight of the ovaries and to inhibit oestrus and sexual development[2,10]; it also inhibits the increased frequency of oestrus observed in pinealectomized rats[11]. In human males, parenchymal-cell pineal tumours are associated with sexual retardation, whereas nonparenchymous tumours which destroy the pineal are associated with sexual precocity[12].

References

[1] LERNER et al., *J. Amer. chem. Soc.*, **80**, 2587 (1958).
[2] ARIËNS KAPPERS and SCHADÉ, *Structure and Function of the Epiphysis Cerebri*, Progress in Brain Research, vol. 10, Elsevier, Amsterdam, 1965.
[3] FARRELL and TAYLOR, *Ann. Rev. Physiol.*, **24**, 471 (1962).
[4] FARRELL and McISAAC, *Arch. Biochem.*, **94**, 543 (1961); FARRELL et al., in MARTINI and PECILE (Eds.), *Hormonal Steroids*, vol. 1, Academic Press, New York, 1964, page 141.
[5] AXELROD and WEISSBACH, *J. biol. Chem.*, **236**, 211 (1961).
[6] KOPIN et al., *J. biol. Chem.*, **236**, 3072 (1961).
[7] ROTH et al., *Endocrinology*, **71**, 888 (1962).
[8] AXELROD et al., *J. biol. Chem.*, **240**, 949 (1965).
[9] FISKE, V.M., *Science*, **146**, 253 (1964); QUAY, W.B., *Proc. Soc. exp. Biol. (N.Y.)*, **115**, 710 (1964).
[10] WURTMAN and AXELROD, *Science*, **141**, 277 (1963).
[11] CHU et al., *Endocrinology*, **75**, 238 (1964).
[12] KITAY and ALTSCHULE, *The Pineal Gland*, Harvard University Press, Cambridge, 1954.

Catecholamines[1–4] (for references see page 734)

Chemistry

The catecholamines are phenylethylamine derivatives in which the benzene ring is *ortho*dihydroxy-substituted, as in catechol. The most important members of this group are dopamine, noradrenaline and adrenaline. The catecholamines occur not only in the vertebrates but also in insects, where *N*-acetyldopamine also plays an important role[5]. The naturally occurring catecholamines are laevorotatory, the dextrorotatory forms being almost devoid of biological activity.

All the catecholamines have very similar chemical properties. Adrenaline and noradrenaline are oxidized spontaneously in alka-

Dopamine (3-hydroxytyramine)

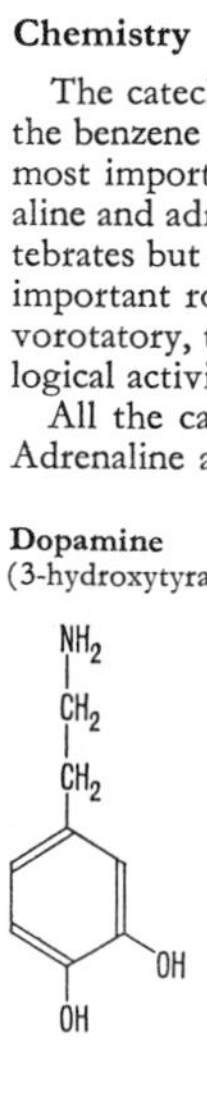

Noradrenaline (norepinephrine)

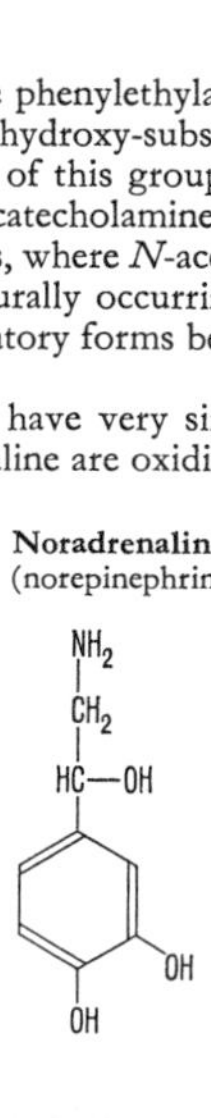

Adrenaline (epinephrine)

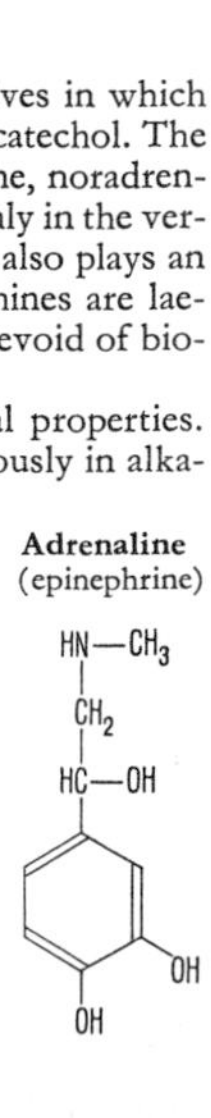

(For references see page 734)

line solution by dissolved oxygen, yielding noradrenochrome and adrenochrome respectively. Alkaline solutions are therefore very unstable. This autoxidation is catalysed by heavy-metal ions, and neutral or acid solutions can be stabilized effectively by addition of EDTA at a concentration of 5×10^{-5} mol/l.

Methods of assay[6,7]

The catecholamines can be determined by a variety of chemical and biological methods, some of which are listed in the table below. When biological methods are used, tissue extracts and body fluids must be treated beforehand to remove other substances like histamine, acetylcholine and serotonin which interfere with the assay. For clinical purposes the chemical methods of assay are preferable. Adrenaline and noradrenaline are best determined by the trihydroxyindole method (as modified for instance by CROUT[8], SOURKES and MURPHY[9] or HÄGGENDAL[49]) or the ethylenediamine method (modification of WEIL-MALHERBE[10] for example). In the former method the catecholamines are oxidized in the presence of weak acid to the adrenochromes, which are in turn converted in the presence of alkali and ascorbic acid into the UV-fluorescent adrenolutins. The basis of the ethylenediamine method is the formation of fluorescent compounds by condensation of catecholamines with ethylenediamine. Adrenaline and noradrenaline can be determined separately after chromatographic separation by oxidation at different pH values or by measuring the fluorescence spectra of the adrenolutins at different wave lengths. Both the trihydroxyindole and ethylenediamine methods can be used to determine dopamine. 3-Methoxy-4-hydroxymandelic acid can be estimated colorimetrically, best after isolation by high-voltage electrophoresis or thin-layer chromatography, or by the isotope dilution technique.

Histological studies on the catecholamines have been immensely helped by the FALCK-HILLARP fluorescence staining technique[55].

Sensitivity of methods of catecholamine assay[44]

Method	Sensitivity (ng)	
	Adrenaline	Noradrenaline
Biological		
Blood pressure, cats	200	100
Blood pressure, rats	50	3
Blood pressure, rats (SHIPLEY and TILDEN)	7	5
Uterus, rat (2 ml)	0.1	15
Ear, rabbit (perfusion)	0.5	1
Ear, rabbit (ARMIN and GRANT)	0.002	–
Intestinal muscle, rabbit (10 ml)	40	40
Intestinal muscle, chicken (2 ml)	2	50
Chemical		
Colorimetrically as adrenochrome	10000	10000
Reduction of arsenomolybdate	50	800
Ethylenediamine method	6	6
Trihydroxyindole method	5	5

Biosynthesis, secretion, metabolism, excretion

The enzymes necessary for the biosynthesis of the catecholamines from tyrosine are found in the cells of the adrenal medulla and the sympathetic neurones. The steps in this synthesis are L-tyrosine → L-dopa → L-dopamine → L-noradrenaline → L-adrenaline, and are discussed in detail on page 440. The *N*-methylation of noradrenaline to adrenaline can take place only in the cells of the adrenal medulla, and not in the neurones. In mammals, only the mature adrenal medulla seems to be capable of synthesizing adrenaline, since in foetal life the prominent catecholamine is noradrenaline[3]. The synthesis of adrenaline in the adrenal medulla appears to be regulated by ACTH and the corticosteroids[11], while its release seems to be additionally regulated by glucagon[12]. The noradrenaline content of the sympathetic nerves is reduced by increased nerve activity[46] and rises when nerve activity is interrupted[47]. Noradrenaline synthesis in the neurones is possibly regulated by a negative feedback mechanism[48]. In the adrenal medulla a small amount of the adrenaline formed is further converted into *N*-methyladrenaline[13].

The catecholamines are stored as a complex with ATP in the form of characteristic chromaffin granules. In the chromaffin cells of the adrenal medulla and in the sympathetic neurones these granules contain catecholamines and ATP in the molar ratio of about 4:1[3,14]. Those present in the chromaffin cells of the adrenal medulla have a diameter up to 100 nm and are located in the endoplasmic reticulum[15]. It is possible that there are two distinct cell types, one storing mainly adrenaline, the other mainly noradrenaline. In the sympathetic neurones, noradrenaline is contained in granules 40–50 nm in diameter located in the myelin-free axons[16]. Dopamine is found in granules in the cytoplasm of the sympathetic nerves and in the chromaffin cells of various organs, including the lungs, liver and gut[17].

The catecholamine content of the adrenals varies from species to species[1], published data ranging from 0.12–14 mg/g (in man 0.27–1 mg/g). The ratio of adrenaline to noradrenaline in the adrenal medulla also varies from species to species; in man it is about 4:1. In young persons the adrenaline content of the medulla, as well as the proportion of adrenaline in the total catecholamines, increases with growth[18]. Dopamine has not been found in the adrenals of all species; its proportion in the total catecholamines does not exceed 2%[3].

The noradrenaline concentration in the peripheral nerves and ganglia is 5–10 μg/g; dopamine is also present in peripheral tissues, almost always in smaller amounts than noradrenaline[50]. Noradrenaline occurs in all sympathetically innervated tissues at a concentration of 0.1–2 μg/g[3]. Adrenaline can also be detected in the peripheral tissues at a concentration of about one-tenth of that of noradrenaline[3]. Noradrenaline occurs in the brain in various species at a concentration of 0.2–0.5 μg/g, the highest values being found in the hypothalamus and limbic system; the adrenaline content of the brain is about 5–10% of the noradrenaline content[3]. Dopamine is present at high concentrations in the carotid body of some species, especially the cat and rabbit (30 μg/g)[51], and in some regions of the brain, particularly the cordate nucleus and putamen (4–8 μg/g)[19].

Tumours of chromaffin tissue sometimes contain large amounts of catecholamines, and values of up to 8.4 mg/g for noradrenaline and 2.3 mg/g for adrenaline have been recorded[20].

Secretion of catecholamines. Release of catecholamines from the adrenal medulla into the blood is actuated by nervous stimuli via the splanchnic nerves. Secretion of the hormones is stimulated by stress and by administration of histamine and other drugs; it is also increased in insulin-induced hypoglycaemia. In general the medulla secretes the catecholamines in proportions that remain constant in a particular species[21]. Some stimuli, such as lowering of the blood glucose level, result in the secretion predominantly of adrenaline[22]. Release of the catecholamines from the secreting cells is believed to proceed by a mechanism of 'exocytosis' in which the soluble contents of the chromaffin granules – catecholamines, ATP and protein ('chromogranin') – but not the particle membrane, are discharged through the cell wall[23]. The process is preceded by the movement of calcium ions into the cell as a result of a change in the permeability of the cell membrane.

The liberation of noradrenaline in the sympathetic nerve endings is actuated by nervous stimuli[14,43] and is likewise preceded by transfer of calcium ions from the extracellular fluid into the cell. The hypothesis that acetylcholine is involved in the liberation of noradrenaline in this way[24] is still a matter of discussion.

Catecholamines in blood. In the plasma of resting subjects the noradrenaline level is less than 1 μg/l, the adrenaline level less than 0.5 μg/l. Higher plasma levels are given by the ethylenediamine method than by the trihydroxyindole method (see the table on page 733). The plasma noradrenaline level rises on changing from the recumbent to the erect posture and during physical exercise, the adrenaline level during insulin hypoglycaemia (for bibliography see LORAINE and BELL[7]). In patients with catecholamine-producing tumours, noradrenaline levels of over 100 times the normal have been observed[25].

From the blood the catecholamines are taken up rapidly by the tissues and in part stored, in part broken down. In the tissues, noradrenaline is more strongly bound to cell components than adrenaline. Two enzymes are involved in degradation of the catecholamines, monoamine oxidase (MAO) and catechol *O*-methyltransferase (COMT). MAO catalyses oxidative deamination and is found mainly in the intestinal tract, liver, kidneys and brain, probably bound to the mitochondria. COMT catalyses the transfer of methyl groups from *S*-adenosylmethionine to the hydroxyl group at C-3

Metabolism of catecholamines

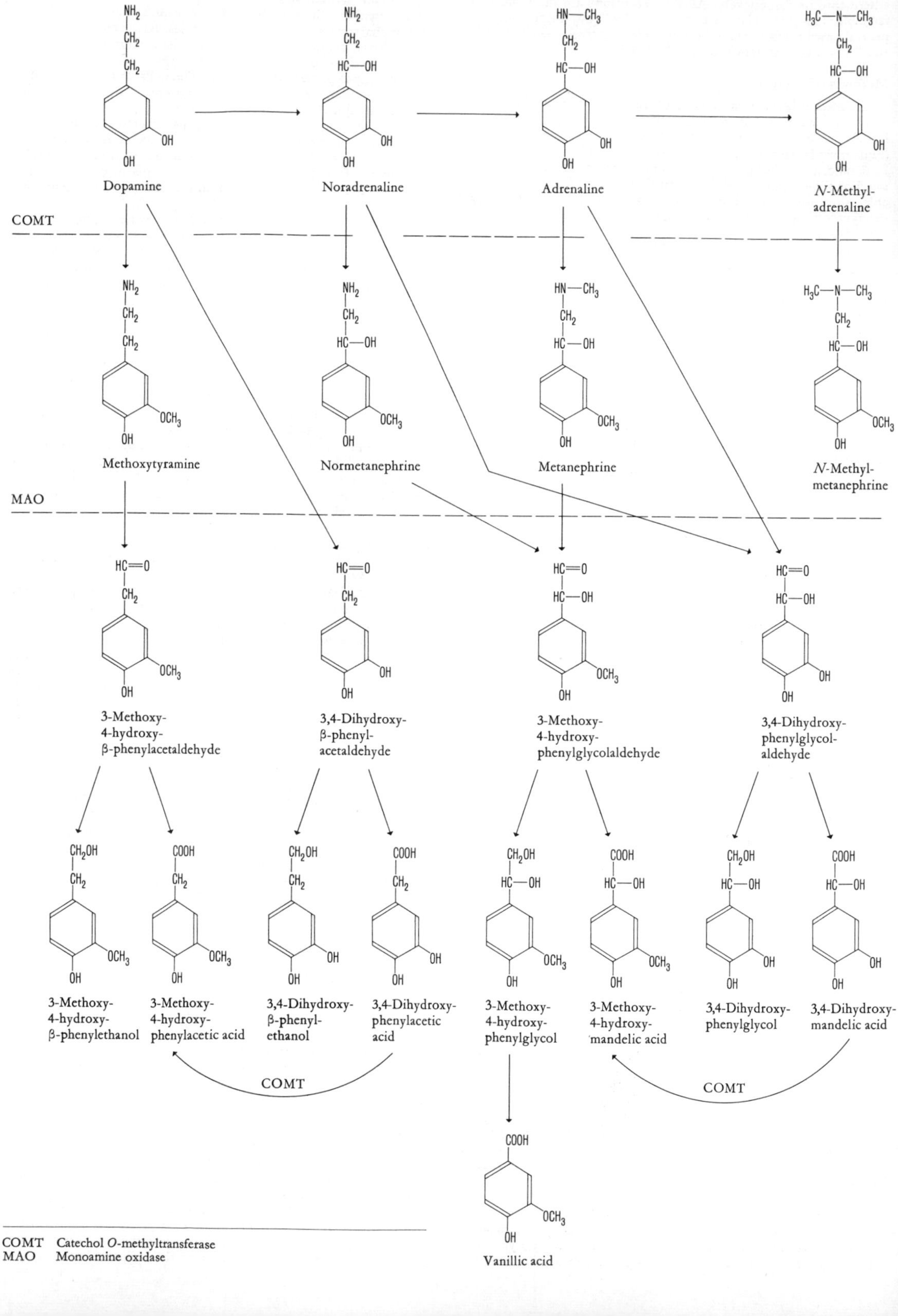

COMT Catechol *O*-methyltransferase
MAO Monoamine oxidase

Plasma levels of adrenaline and noradrenaline (µg/l)

	Adrenaline		Noradrenaline		Reference
	Mean	*s*	Mean	*s*	
Trihydroxyindole method					
Adults	0.06	0.05	0.30	0.07	52
Men	0.07	0.01	0.35	0.01	53
Women	0.06	0.01	0.35	0.01	53
Ethylenediamine method					
Adults	0.22	0.27	0.58	0.66	10
Newborn	0.35	0.64	2.39	2.69	54
Premature	0.86	1.21	3.24	2.03	54

of the catecholamine molecule and occurs mainly in the cytoplasm of the liver and kidneys. The stages of catecholamine degradation are shown on page 732. Noradrenaline is broken down by MAO within the nerves, by COMT outside them[16]. After the release of noradrenaline from nerve endings the principal means of terminating the response of the target organ is by re-uptake of this substance by the nerves[56]. Adrenaline does not appear to be metabolized in the adrenal medulla[26]. The degradation of noradrenaline in the brain closely resembles that in the sympathetic nervous system[27].

Excretion of catecholamines. Only a small part of the endogenous catecholamines appear unchanged in the urine[22]. The catecholamines and their metabolites are to some extent conjugated with glucuronic or sulphuric acid. The proportion of unconjugated to total catecholamines in the urine varies between 1:1.5 and 1:3[3]. Most of the urinary adrenaline appears to come from the adrenal medulla, most of the noradrenaline from the sympathetic nerves, since adrenalectomy reduces the excretion of adrenaline but not that of noradrenaline[28]. Administration of ^{3}H-labelled adrenaline

Catecholamine excretion in nocturnal urine (µg/h)[45]

	Free amines		Total amines	
	Mean	Range	Mean	Range
Adrenaline	0.04	< 1.29	0.06	< 2.35
Noradrenaline	2.36	<11.0	4.69	<21.6
Dopamine	8.22	<23.3	27.2	10.2–56.8
Metanephrine	1.25	< 6.80	3.65	<13.3
Normetanephrine	8.55	<17.8	17.5	4.82–58.0

resulted in the following distribution of tritium in the urine[16]: 6.8% in adrenaline, 0.9% in free and 0.7% in conjugated 3,4-dihydroxymandelic acid, 5.2% in free metanephrine, 6.0% in metanephrine glucuronide, 29.5% in metanephrine sulphate, 41.2% in 3-methoxy-4-hydroxymandelic acid and 7.1% in 3-methoxy-4-hydroxyphenylglycol sulphate.

Normal values for the excretion of catecholamines and their most important metabolites are summarized in the tables on this page. The excretory levels of these compounds are dependent on body weight and surface area and, except in infancy, largely independent of age[29]. The excretion of the catecholamines is affected by posture and bodily activity; it is increased by physical and mental effort. Adrenaline excretion is increased in insulin hypoglycaemia, that of noradrenaline following injection of acetyl-β-methylcholine (for bibliography see LORAINE and BELL[7]). Aggressive states increase the excretion of noradrenaline, anxiety and vaguely threatening situations that of adrenaline[30]. Large amounts of adrenaline, noradrenaline and 3-methoxy-4-hydroxymandelic acid are excreted by persons with tumours of chromaffin tissue, considerable amounts of dopa, dopamine and their metabolite homovanillic acid by those with neuroblastomas (for further details see the literature[20, 31]).

Biological activity

In the animal organism the catecholamines have two important functions, the main physiological function of those secreted by the adrenal medulla being concerned with metabolism, while those released by the adrenergic synapses of the sympathetic nervous system act as transmitters of nervous stimuli.

Metabolic effects. Adrenaline increases oxygen consumption in muscle and adipose tissue and raises the body temperature and BMR[32]. Both adrenaline and noradrenaline have powerful glycogenolytic effects on skeletal muscle, adipose tissue and liver. In muscle, the principal metabolic product is lactate, which is formed by glycolysis. This may lead to a rise in the serum lactate concentration and stimulation of gluconeogenesis in the liver (CORI cycle). In the liver, stimulation of glycogenolysis by the catecholamines leads to an increase of glucose output and a short-lived rise in the blood sugar level. In adipose tissue adrenaline and noradrenaline have a lipolytic action, with an increase in both the release of free fatty acids into the blood and the rate of their re-esterification to triglycerides[33, 34]. Lipolysis is associated with the release of glycerol, and since adipose tissue lacks glycerol kinase, there is an accelerated utilization of α-glycerophosphate formed either from glucose or glycogen for the re-esterification process[34]. To what extent the metabolic effects of adrenaline are responsible for its positive inotropic action is not known[35].

The action of adrenaline on glycogenolysis is mediated by a nucleotide, adenosine cyclic 3′,5′-phosphate (cyclic AMP). Both adrenaline and noradrenaline stimulate the activity of the membrane-bound enzyme adenylate cyclase, which forms cyclic AMP from ATP[36]. Cyclic AMP facilitates phosphorylation of an inactive form of phosphorylase *b* kinase to an active form. Phosphorylase *b* kinase in turn catalyses the phosphorylation and dimerization of phosphorylase *b* to phosphorylase *a*. Unlike phosphorylase *b*, which requires relatively high concentrations of AMP for activity, phosphorylase *a* is the more active form of the enzyme under physio-

Excretion of catecholamines and 3-methoxy-4-hydroxymandelic acid by children and adults

Age (years)	Number	Urinary volume (ml/24 h)	Adrenaline (µg/24 h)		Noradrenaline (µg/24 h)		Dopamine (µg/24 h)		3-Methoxy-4-hydroxy-mandelic acid (mg/24 h)		Reference
			Mean	*s*	Mean	*s*	Mean	*s*	Mean	*s*	
0–1	19	370	1.3	1.2	10.6	3.4	60.9	24.3	0.57	0.31	29
1–5	15	492	3.2	2.7	18.8	7.0	124.1	40.7	1.35	0.44	29
6–15	13	845	4.8	2.4	37.4	16.6	169.3	72.6	2.37	0.70	29
>15	13	1552	7.1	3.3	50.7	15.7	249.1	74.9	3.19	0.67	29
0–10	46	380	9.2	8.6	19	13	–	–	1.0	0.9	57
10–30	28	1010	22	14	52	31	–	–	3.6	1.9	57
30–50	33	1280	26	22	66	34	–	–	4.2	1.7	57
50–70	42	1500	28	21	60	34	–	–	4.1	1.5	57
70–99	8	1010	19	12	43	27	–	–	3.2	1.3	57

logical conditions and produces a rapid breakdown of glycogen to glucose 1-phosphate. Catecholamines appear to activate phosphorylase by a similar mechanism in all tissues. The lipolytic action of adrenaline and noradrenaline appears also to be mediated by cyclic AMP[37], but different forms of a triglyceride lipase have not yet been isolated.

Pharmacological effects. Experimental studies have led to the idea of at least two kinds of adrenaline receptors, α and β[38]; α receptors mediate largely motor effects, β receptors largely the remaining effects. Noradrenaline acts on α receptors, isoprenaline on β receptors, adrenaline on both; adrenaline antagonists act primarily on α receptors. This is an oversimplified picture, and exceptions exist which have led to a further, though somewhat unprofitable, multiplication of postulated receptors.

Effects on blood circulation (see the figure below). In man, continuous intravenous infusion of catecholamines (0.1–0.3 µg/min/kg body weight) can have the following effects[40]: *Noradrenaline.* Prompt increase in the mean blood pressure of systolic and diastolic origin due to an increase in the peripheral resistance (vasoconstriction). Cardiac output unchanged or slightly diminished. *Adrenaline.* Increase in the mean blood pressure due to a fall in the blood pressure in the peripheral circulation (vasodilatation) being overcompensated by an increase in the beat volume and beat frequency. The circulatory effects of adrenaline and noradrenaline are mutually compensatory when the hormones are given at physiological dosage (intravenously up to 0.3 µg/min/kg body weight).

The continuous intravenous infusion of *dopamine* at dosages in the range 5.3–11.6 µg/min/kg body weight may result in an increase in the systolic and mean blood pressures and cardiac output and in a lowering of peripheral resistance[41].

Renal blood flow is diminished by adrenaline[42], large doses of which reduce the glomerular filtration rate. Adrenaline has little effect on the cerebral blood vessels.

Cardiovascular effects of intravenous infusion of noradrenaline, adrenaline and dopamine[39]

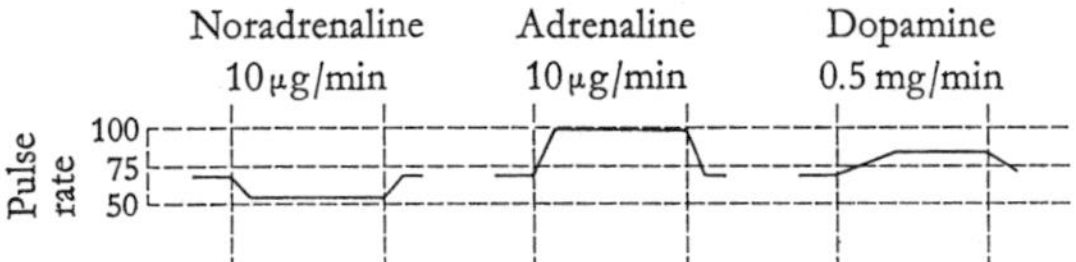

Catecholamines in the central nervous system. Impulses arriving at the efferent ends of the sympathetic nerves cause the release of small amounts of noradrenaline which stimulate or inhibit cellular activity in the target organ (see above). Noradrenaline[27] and dopamine[19] may exercise a similar function in the central nervous system. It has been suggested that in some kinds of depression, particularly the retarded type, there is a noradrenaline deficit at specific receptor sites in certain areas of the central nervous system; conversely, in manic states there would be an excess of noradrenaline in these areas[30].

References

[1] VON EULER, U.S., *Noradrenaline*, Thomas, Springfield, 1956.
[2] First Symposium on Catecholamines, *Pharmacol. Rev.*, **11**, No. 2, part 2 (1959); VANE et al. (Eds.), *Adrenergic Mechanisms*, Ciba Foundation Symposium, Churchill, London, 1960.
[3] WEINER, N., in PINCUS et al. (Eds.), *The Hormones*, vol. 4, Academic Press, New York, 1964, page 403.
[4] Second Symposium on Catecholamines, *Pharmacol. Rev.*, **18**, No. 1, part 1 (1966).
[5] SEKERIS and KARLSON, *Pharmacol. Rev.*, **18**, 89 (1966).
[6] ELMADJIAN, F., in DORFMAN, R.I. (Ed.), *Methods in Hormone Research*, Academic Press, New York, 1962, vol. 1, page 337, vol. 2, page 371.
[7] LORAINE and BELL, *Hormone Assays and Their Clinical Application*, 2nd ed., Livingstone, Edinburgh, 1966.
[8] CROUT, J.R., *Stand. Meth. clin. Chem.*, **3**, 62 (1961).
[9] SOURKES and MURPHY, *Meth. med. Res.*, **9**, 147 (1961).
[10] WEIL-MALHERBE, H., *Meth. med. Res.*, **9**, 130 (1961).
[11] WURTMAN and AXELROD, *First Latin American Symposium on Catecholamines*, Buenos Aires 1966, quoted in *Science*, **154**, 680 (1966).
[12] KUSCHKE et al., *Klin. Wschr.*, **44**, 1297 (1966).
[13] AXELROD, J., *Biochim. biophys. Acta (Amst.)*, **45**, 614 (1960).
[14] IVERSEN, L.L., *Nature*, **214**, 8 (1967).
[15] VANE, J.R., in ROBSON and STACEY (Eds.), *Recent Advances in Pharmacology*, 3rd ed., Churchill, London, 1962, page 95.
[16] AXELROD, J., *Recent Progr. Hormone Res.*, **21**, 597 (1965).
[17] BERTLER et al., *Acta physiol. scand.*, **47**, 251 (1959).
[18] COMLINE and SILVER, *Brit. med. Bull.*, **22**, 16 (1966).
[19] HORNYKIEWICZ, O., *Pharmacol. Rev.*, **18**, 925 (1966).
[20] VON EULER, U.S., *Ciba Found. Coll. Endocr.*, **12**, 268 (1958).
[21] MALMEJAC, J., *Physiol. Rev.*, **44**, 186 (1964).
[22] ELMADJIAN et al., *Recent Progr. Hormone Res.*, **14**, 513 (1958).
[23] DOUGLAS, W.W., *Pharmacol. Rev.*, **18**, 471 (1966); SCHNEIDER et al., *Brit. J. Pharmacol.*, **31**, 94 (1967); DOUGLAS, W.W., *Brit. J. Pharmacol.*, **34**, 451 (1968).
[24] FERRY, C.B., *Physiol. Rev.*, **46**, 420 (1966).
[25] VON EULER, U.S., *Ciba Found. Coll. Endocr.*, **11**, 379 (1957).
[26] KOPIN, I.J., *Pharmacol. Rev.*, **18**, 513 (1966).
[27] GLOWINSKI and BALDESSARINI, *Pharmacol. Rev.*, **18**, 1201 (1966).
[28] VON EULER et al., *Acta physiol. scand.*, **31**, 1 (1954).
[29] VOORHESS, M.L., *Pediatrics*, **39**, 252 (1967).
[30] SCHILDKRAUT and KETY, *Science*, **156**, 21 (1967).
[31] CROUT, J.R., *Pharmacol. Rev.*, **18**, 651 (1966); KÄSER, H., *Pharmacol. Rev.*, **18**, 659 (1966); KÄSER, H., *Schweiz. med. Wschr.*, **96**, 258 (1966); CLOTTEN and MICHAELIS, *Klin. Wschr.*, **44**, 1161 (1966).
[32] LEE, K.S., *J. Pharmacol. exp. Ther.*, **109**, 313 (1953); ELLIS, S., *Pharmacol. Rev.*, **8**, 485 (1956); **11**, 469 (1959).
[33] FRITZ, I.B., *Physiol. Rev.*, **41**, 52 (1961); STEINBERG, D., *Pharmacol. Rev.*, **18**, 217 (1966).
[34] JEANRENAUD, B., *Metabolism*, **10**, 535 (1961); RANDLE, P.J., *Ann. Rev. Physiol.*, **25**, 291 (1963).
[35] HAUGAARD and HESS, *Pharmacol. Rev.*, **18**, 197 (1966); WILLIAMSON, J.R., *Pharmacol. Rev.*, **18**, 205 (1966).
[36] SUTHERLAND and RALL, *Pharmacol. Rev.*, **12**, 265 (1960); SUTHERLAND, E.W., *Harvey Lect.*, **57**, 17 (1962); SUTHERLAND and ROBISON, *Pharmacol. Rev.*, **18**, 145 (1966).
[37] RIZACK, M.A., *J. biol. Chem.*, **239**, 392 (1964); VAUGHAN, M., *Pharmacol. Rev.*, **18**, 215 (1966).
[38] PATON and PAYNE, *Pharmacological Principles and Practice*, Churchill, London, 1968, page 130.
[39] ALLWOOD et al., *Brit. med. Bull.*, **19**, 132 (1963).
[40] GOLDENBERG et al., *Amer. J. Med.*, **5**, 792 (1948); WAKIM and ESSEX, *Circulation*, **5**, 370 (1952).
[41] HORWITZ et al., *Circulat. Res.*, **10**, 237 (1962).
[42] MOYER and HANDLEY, *Circulation*, **5**, 91 (1952).
[43] FERRY, C.B., *Ann. Rev. Pharmacol.*, **7**, 185 (1967).
[44] GADDUM and HOLZBAUER, *Vitam. and Horm.*, **15**, 151 (1957); DEARNALEY, D.P., personal communication.
[45] MATTOK et al., *Clin. chim. Acta*, **14**, 99 (1966).
[46] DEARNALEY and GREFFEN, *Proc. roy. Soc. B*, **166**, 303 (1966).
[47] BROWN et al., *Proc. roy. Soc. B*, **168**, 48 (1967).
[48] STJÄRNE, L., *Acta physiol. scand.*, **67**, 441 (1966).
[49] HÄGGENDAL, J., *Acta physiol. scand.*, **59**, 242 (1963).
[50] ANTON and SAYRE, *J. Pharmacol. exp. Ther.*, **145**, 326 (1964).
[51] BISCARDI and TRAMEZZANI, *Nature (Lond.)*, **212**, 834 (1966); DEARNALEY et al., *Proc. roy. Soc. B*, **170**, 195 (1968).
[52] COHEN and GOLDENBERG, *J. Neurochem.*, **2**, 58 (1957).
[53] VENDSALU, A., *Acta physiol. scand.*, **49**, suppl. 173 (1960).
[54] CHEEK et al., *Pediatrics*, **31**, 374 (1963).
[55] FALCK et al., *J. Histochem. Cytochem.*, **10**, 348 (1962).
[56] BLAKELEY et al., *J. Physiol. (Lond.)*, **173**, 22P (1964); BROWN, G.L., *Proc. roy. Soc. B*, **162**, 1 (1965); GILLESPIE, J.S., *Proc. roy. Soc. B*, **166**, 1 (1966).
[57] RITZEL and HUNZINGER, *Klin. Wschr.*, **41**, 419 (1963).

Insulin[1,2] (for references see page 737)

Chemistry

Up to 1966 the structure of insulins from 20 different animal species had been largely or wholly elucidated[3]. In almost all species the shorter A chain contains 21 amino-acid residues and has an N-terminal glycine residue, at least four free amino groups and an internal disulphide bridge between the cysteine residues at positions 6 and 11. Variations in the amino-acid sequence are mostly in positions 8, 9 and 10. The longer B chain is made up of 28–30 amino-acid residues and contains two or three free amino groups and, in most species, an N-terminal phenylalanine residue. Variations in the amino-acid sequence in this chain are mostly in positions 3, 29

(For references see page 737)

Amino-acid sequence of beef insulin

Phe·Val·Asp(NH$_2$)·Glu(NH$_2$)·His·Leu·Cys·Gly·Ser·His·Leu·Val·Glu·Ala·Leu·Tyr·Leu·Val·Cys·Gly·Glu·Arg·Gly·Phe·Phe·Tyr·Thr·Pro·Lys·Ala
1 2 3 4 5 6 7 8 9 10 11 12 13 14 15 16 17 18 19 20 21 22 23 24 25 26 27 28 29 30

Gly·Ile·Val·Glu·Glu(NH$_2$)·Cys·Cys·Ala·Ser·Val·Cys·Ser·Leu·Tyr·Glu(NH$_2$)·Leu·Glu·Asp(NH$_2$)·Tyr·Cys·Asp(NH$_2$)
1 2 3 4 5 6 7 8 9 10 11 12 13 14 15 16 17 18 19 20 21

and 30. Of the 51 amino-acid positions in the insulin molecule, 29 are known to show variations. Human insulin differs from toadfish insulin for instance in 17 of these positions. At least two species – rats and toadfish – form two structurally different insulins in their pancreas, while identical insulins may be formed by different species, for instance the dog, pig, fin whale and sperm whale.

Differences in the amino-acid sequences of various insulins

Species	A chain position			B chain position
	8	9	10	30
Ox	Ala	Ser	Val	Ala
Pig	Thr	Ser	Ile	Ala
Sheep	Ala	Gly	Val	Ala
Horse	Thr	Gly	Val	Ala
Whale	Thr	Ser	Ile	Ala
Man	Thr	Ser	Ile	Thr

The molecular weight of an insulin naturally depends on its structure; it is 5807 for human, 5733 for beef and 5777 for pig insulin. The absorption maximum is 276 nm. The isoelectric point of beef insulin is 5.4; at pH values above or below this, insulin is soluble and undergoes aggregation to form polymers of at least two molecules (insulin dimer). Whether this occurs in complex solutions like blood is not known. Insulin readily forms complexes with zinc or basic proteins such as histone and protamine. It crystallizes in rhombi or prisms. Heating of insulin solutions at pH<3.5 results in end-to-end aggregation of insulin monomers to form the characteristic insulin fibrils.

The insulins most commonly employed in the treatment of diabetes in man are those of bovine and porcine origin. Pig insulin differs from human insulin in only one amino-acid residue (B chain, position 30), beef insulin in three (A chain, positions 8 and 10; B chain, position 30). This difference in amino-acid structure may explain the greater antigenicity in man of beef insulin compared to pig insulin. In the light of its amino-acid structure, homologous insulin would not be expected to induce the formation of circulating antibodies. It has recently been shown, however, that injection of insulin from beef pancreas into cattle[4] or of pig insulin into pigs[5] does in fact result in the formation of antibodies[6]. Factors other than amino-acid sequence must therefore play a role in determining antigenicity.

Modification of the structure of the insulin molecule has shown that removing the C-terminal alanine residue of the B chain does not lead to any significant loss of activity, whereas removal of the C-terminal asparagine residue of the A chain does[7]. On the other hand, when 8 amino-acid residues at the carboxyl end of the B chain are removed by trypsin the residual molecule still retains about 15% of its initial biological activity[8]. Reductive cleavage of the disulphide bridges results in total loss of activity, indicating that neither the A nor B chain by itself has any insulin activity. Preparations of this kind with residual activity almost certainly contain intact insulin.

The complete synthesis of sheep insulin was achieved by three groups of workers at about the same time[9]; human insulin has also been synthesized[10].

Proinsulin[11,20]. A minor component of pig insulin has been shown to be a single-chain protein of 84 amino acids; this is converted into insulin by proteolytic cleavage. It cross-reacts with insulin in immunoassay.

Synalbumin[12,13]. An insulin-antagonistic factor migrating electrophoretically with albumin has been described (synalbumin insulin antagonist) the physicochemical properties of which suggest that it consists of the B chain of the insulin molecule.

The presence of an artifactual insulin antagonist in albumin preparations has been reported[52].

Unit, methods of assay[14,15]

1 International Unit (IU) corresponds to 0.041 67 mg of the 4th International Standard (see page 763), a mixture consisting of 52% beef insulin and 48% pig insulin. Insulins from different species may show different biological activities in *in vivo* tests. For pharmacological studies various in vivo methods of assay are available, such as measurement of the fall in blood glucose in the rabbit and the mouse convulsion test; paper chromatographic methods are also in use for this purpose[16].

For clinical investigations a variety of techniques can be employed, none of them completely satisfactory. Basically they are of two types: (a) radioimmunological and (b) biological. While the former are reproducible, precise and sensitive they give results that do not necessarily reflect biological activity. Isolation of tagged, antibody-bound insulin can be carried out by paper electrophoresis[17], ion exchange[18] or precipitation of the insulin-antibody complex by a second antibody[19].

The bioassays employ metabolic effects induced in isolated surviving tissues. The preparations commonly used are the rat diaphragm, in which the index of insulin activity is glucose uptake or glycogen synthesis, and rat epididymal adipose tissue, in which the index can be glucose uptake, net gas exchange, oxidation of ^{14}C-labelled glucose to $^{14}CO_2$, or incorporation of the labelled glucose carbon into lipid or adipose tissue glycogen. These methods of assay reflect biological activity in vitro but are not very precise. Moreover, the diaphragm assay technique suffers from a dilution defect in that the total insulin activity increases when the serum is diluted, while the adipose tissue method is probably nonspecific in that it measures 'insulin-like activity' in the sera of untreated patients with diabetic ketosis as well as in pancreatectomized dogs.

Biosynthesis, secretion, metabolism

Insulin is synthesized in the β-cells of the islets of LANGERHANS and stored there in granular form. Insulin is possibly synthesized as a single-chain precursor (proinsulin) which is subsequently enzymatically converted to insulin[20]. In the human foetus, storage granules appear between the 10th and 14th weeks of gestation, the stage at which biologically active insulin is first extractable from the pancreas[21]. In adults the insulin content of the pancreas is 1–4 IU/g[22], the total amount being 100–400 IU with a mean of 250 IU (10 mg). From radioimmunological assays of plasma insulin the daily production of the pancreas has been estimated to be about 50 IU[23]; this corresponds to the daily average replacement dose in patients in whom endogenous production is completely suppressed.

Insulin secretion is stimulated or inhibited by a large number of factors[24–26] (see the table on page 736).

Stimulation of insulin secretion by glucose or tolbutamide causes the secretory granules of the β-cells to migrate to the cell membrane, where their sacs fuse with the latter and rupture, so that the insulin contained in them is released in the extracellular space[27]. The rate of insulin secretion is proportional to the amount of glucose flowing through the pancreas[2], though it is probably not the glucose itself that has the stimulating action but a metabolite from the pentose-phosphate cycle[26]. In man, the insulin level in the peripheral venous blood begins to rise within a few minutes of starting a glucose infusion[28].

The form in which insulin exists in the plasma is not known with certainty, different techniques yielding discrepant information[29]. When the serum is subjected to paper electrophoresis, immunoassay techniques detect insulin in the postalbumin region, while rat adipose tissue methods show it additionally in the region of the α- and β-globulins. This latter insulin-like activity is not inhibited by insulin antibody, whence its description as 'nonsuppressible', 'atypical' or 'bound' insulin[30]. When crystalline insulin is added to the serum it migrates electrophoretically in the postalbumin region.

Factors affecting insulin secretion[24–26]

	In vivo	In vitro
Factors stimulating secretion		
Glucose	+	+
Fructose	+	+
Mannose	+	+
Ribose	+	+
Xylitol	+	+
Ribitol		+
Leucine	+	+
Arginine	+	+
Acetoacetate	+	±
Glucagon	+	+
Growth hormone	+	±
Lactogenic hormone of the placenta	+	
ACTH	+	+
Glucocorticosteroids	+	±
Thyroxine	+	±
Pancreozymin	+	
Secretin	+	+
Insulin antibodies	+	+
Calcium		+
Magnesium		±
Potassium	+	+
Adenosine triphosphate		+
Adenosine cyclic monophosphate		+
Sulphonylureas	+	+
Vagus stimulation	+	
Factors inhibiting secretion		
2-Deoxyglucose	+	+
Glucosamine		+
Mannoheptulose	+	+
Adrenaline	+	+
Noradrenaline	+	
Insulin	+	
Phenethylbiguanides	+	
Diazoxides	+	+
Starvation	+	
Hypoxia		+
Vagotomy	+	

When serum is filtrated on Sephadex G-75, two protein peaks with a protein-free interval are obtained. Insulin-like activity is highest in the first protein fraction; insulin measured by immunoassay is highest in the 'protein-free' interval. This is also the area where labelled crystalline insulin is recovered[31]. When Sephadex G-50 is used for filtration, insulin appears in two peaks, designated 'big' and 'little' insulin, the first of which may be identical with proinsulin[20].

Different methods of assay measure different amounts of insulin and/or insulin activity in the serum. The following mean values have been found in the morning in the serum of persons who have fasted for 12 hours previously: 20 mIU/l by the radioimmunological technique (see the table on this page), 100 mIU/l by the rat diaphragm method[15] and 350 mIU/l by the rat adipose tissue method[31]. The insulin activity of the serum not inhibitable by insulin antibodies has been measured at about 170 mIU/l[32]. Serum insulin levels during the glucose-loading test are shown in the figure on this page. In pregnant women there is a rise in the serum insulin level towards term[34, 35], and under glucose loading the level rises to a greater extent than post partum[34]. In the serum of cord blood the insulin level is low[36]. Small amounts of insulin have been detected in spinal fluid[37].

Plasma insulin determined by immunoassay (mIU/l in fasting subjects)

	Mean	Range	*s*	Reference
Adults	20	0–66	–	17
Adults	20	6–35	–	53
Adults	22	–	10	18
Newborn, 2–8 days	43	–	32	54

Serum insulin after an oral dose of 50 g glucose[33]
(values from 45 subjects, logarithmic scale)

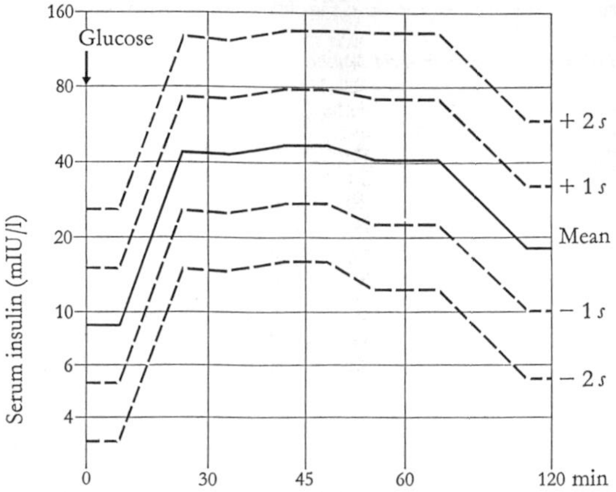

Only part of the insulin secreted by the pancreas reaches the general circulation, nearly a half of it being removed by the liver and degraded. In man the half-life in the circulating blood is about 30 minutes, in animals rather less[2]. Insulin also passes into the tissues, the highest concentrations of labelled insulin having been found in the kidneys, liver and muscle. Small amounts of insulin are found normally in the urine; immunoassay of nocturnal urine has shown an average of 5 mIU/24 h[38, 39]. Insulin clearance in adults is about 0.4 ml/min[38, 39]; in children it is proportional to body weight and amounts to about 0.2 mIU/kg/24 h[40]. The insulin filtered in the glomeruli is almost completely reabsorbed and broken down in the tubules, the daily turnover being about 4 IU at a serum level of 14 mIU/l[38]. Degradation of insulin in the liver – and probably also in the kidneys and other tissues – is initiated by a specific enzyme, protein disulphide reductase, which cleaves the disulphide bonds to free the A and B chains[41], when these in turn are attacked by proteolytic enzymes. During pregnancy the placenta is also involved in the breakdown of insulin[42].

Biological activity

Insulin has a direct or indirect effect on practically all organs and metabolic processes of the body. The most obvious actions, and those most thoroughly studied, are on the fatty tissues[43], muscle[44] and liver[45]. Various theories have been put forward to explain the mode of action, which may well vary from site to site: (a) the insulin-enzyme theory, (b) the insulin-transport theory, (c) the insulin-gene (transcription) theory and (d) the insulin-ribosome (translation) theory. For further details see the literature[46].

The most important role of insulin is in the metabolism of the *fatty tissues*, the principal site of the regulation of energy storage and mobilization. Insulin promotes storage of fat and regulates its release. The hormone stimulates glucose uptake and glucose 6-phosphate metabolism in the fatty tissues as well as glycogenesis, the formation of glyceride glycerol, fatty-acid synthesis from glucose, transamination of glucose into amino acids, and protein synthesis; it inhibits the release of fatty acids by promoting the formation of α-glycerophosphate, with which they form triglycerides.

In *muscle*, insulin activates the transport system responsible for the entry of amino acids and other compounds into the cell. Inside the cell, glucose is converted into glucose 6-phosphate by means of hexokinase and finally into glycogen by activation of UDP-glucose-glycogen glucosyltransferase. Activation of the transport of amino acids proceeds independently of that of glucose. Activation by insulin of protein synthesis in muscle is also independent of these processes and probably occurs by activation of the ribosomes. In addition, insulin promotes synthesis of RNA.

Administration of insulin reduces the amount of glucose released from the *liver*. Unlike the membrane of the cells of fatty tissues and muscle, that of the liver cells is freely permeable to glucose. Insulin acts in the liver by regulating the activity of various enzymes[47]. It stimulates the formation of UDP-glucose-glycogen glucosyltransferase, the glycolytic enzymes glucokinase, phosphofructokinase and pyruvate kinase, and enzymes involved in fatty-acid synthesis. The result is an increase in glucose utilization, glycogenesis, glycolysis and lipogenesis. Enzyme activation is probably preceded by the increase in RNA synthesis[45].

In vivo studies in human subjects have shown that insulin facilitates the transport of glucose to the brain when the serum glucose level is low[48].

Insulin antagonists. This term designates substances that inactivate insulin or inhibit its effects in vitro or in vivo[49,50]. They include the enzyme systems of tissues that break down insulin and the insulin-binding antibodies appearing during treatment with insulin. In vitro antagonists are the free fatty acids inhibiting the uptake and utilization of glucose by muscle[51], and the synalbumin-insulin antagonist inhibiting the action of insulin in the rat diaphragm[12,13,49]. In vivo antagonists include hormones such as growth hormone, corticosteroids, ACTH and adrenaline, all of which promote the release of fatty acids and thus reduce glucose uptake by muscle. The role of all these factors in the pathogenesis of diabetes remains to be elucidated[13].

References

1 RANDLE, P.J., in PINCUS et al. (Eds.), *The Hormones*, vol. 4, Academic Press, New York, 1964, page 481; LEVINE and MAHLER, *Ann. Rev. Med.*, **15**, 413 (1964); RENOLD and CAHILL, in STANBURY et al. (Eds.), *The Metabolic Basis of Inherited Disease*, 2nd ed., McGraw-Hill, New York, 1966, page 69.
2 GRODSKY and FORSHAM, *Ann. Rev. Physiol.*, **28**, 347 (1966).
3 SCHROEDER and LUEBKE, *The Peptides*, vol. 2, Academic Press, New York, 1966; SMITH, L.F., *Amer. J. Med.*, **40**, 662 (1966).
4 RENOLD et al., *Ciba Found. Coll. Endocr.*, **15**, 122 (1964).
5 LOCKWOOD and PROUT, *Metabolism*, **14**, 530 (1965).
6 SCHWICK, H.G., *Behringwerk-Mitteilungen*, No. 46, 87 (1966).
7 CARPENTER, F.H., *Amer. J. Med.*, **40**, 750 (1966).
8 NICOL, D.S., *Biochem. J.*, **75**, 395 (1960).
9 MEIENHOFER et al., *Z. Naturforsch.*, **18 B**, 1120 (1963); KATSOYANNIS et al., *J. Amer. chem. Soc.*, **85**, 2863 (1963), and **86**, 930 (1964); KATSOYANNIS, P.G., *Diabetes*, **13**, 339 (1964); NIU et al., *Sci. Sinica (Peking)*, **13**, 1343 (1964); ZAHN, H., *Naturwissenschaften*, **52**, 99 (1965).
10 KATSOYANNIS, P.G., *Amer. J. Med.*, **40**, 652 (1966).
11 CHANCE et al., *Science*, **161**, 165 (1968).
12 VALLANCE-OWEN, J., *Ciba Found. Coll. Endocr.*, **15**, 217 (1964); VALLANCE-OWEN, J., *Diabetes*, **13**, 241 (1964); JERVELL and VALLANCE-OWEN, *Lancet*, **1**, 21 (1967).
13 VALLANCE-OWEN, J., in GARDINER-HILL, H. (Ed.), *Modern Trends in Endocrinology*, vol. 3, Butterworth, London, 1967, page 152.
14 RENOLD et al., in ANTONIADES, H.N. (Ed.), *Hormones in Human Plasma*, Little, Brown, Boston, 1960, page 49; SMITH, K.L., in DORFMAN, R.I. (Ed.), *Methods in Hormone Research*, vol. 2, Academic Press, New York, 1962, page 413; LORAINE and BELL, *Hormone Assays and their Clinical Application*, 2nd ed., Livingstone, Edinburgh, 1966.
15 VALLANCE-OWEN and WRIGHT, *Physiol. Rev.*, **40**, 219 (1960).
16 FENTON, E.L., *Biochem. J.*, **71**, 507 (1959).
17 YALOW and BERSON, *J. clin. Invest.*, **39**, 1157 (1960); BERSON and YALOW, in PINCUS et al. (Eds.), *The Hormones*, vol. 4, Academic Press, New York, 1964, page 557.
18 MEADE and KLITGAARD, *J. nucl. Med.*, **3**, 407 (1962); MELANI et al., *Klin. Wschr.*, **43**, 1000 (1965).
19 HALES and RANDLE, *Biochem. J.*, **88**, 137 (1963); MORGAN and LAZAROW, *Diabetes*, **12**, 115 (1963).
20 CHANCE and ELLIS, *Arch. intern. Med.*, **123**, 229 (1969); GORDEN and ROTH, *Arch. intern. Med.*, **123**, 237 (1969).
21 STEINKE and DRISCOLL, *Diabetes*, **14**, 573 (1965).
22 STEINKE et al., *J. clin. Invest.*, **42**, 1322 (1963).
23 FIELD, J.B., *Metabolism*, **13**, 407 (1964).
24 WILLIAMS and ENSINCK, *Diabetes*, **15**, 623 (1966); PORTE, D., *Adv. intern. Med.*, **123**, 252 (1969); UNGER and EISENTRAUT, *Adv. intern. Med.*, **123**, 261 (1969).
25 GRODSKY et al., *Amer. J. Physiol.*, **205**, 638 (1963); BROLIN et al. (Eds.), *The Structure and Metabolism of the Pancreatic Islets*, Symposium, Pergamon, New York, 1964; FRERICHS et al., *Klin. Wschr.*, **43**, 136 (1965); FRERICHS et al., *Diabetologia*, **2**, 269 (1966); KARAM et al., *Diabetes*, **15**, 571 (1966).
26 MONTAGUE et al., *Nature*, **215**, 1088 (1967).
27 LACY, P.E., *Ciba Found. Coll. Endocr.*, **15**, 75 (1964).
28 CAHILL, G.F., *Med. Clin. N. Amer.*, **49**, 881 (1965).
29 LYNGSØE, J., *Acta med. scand.*, suppl. 441 (1965); BERSON and YALOW, *Amer. J. Med.*, **40**, 676 (1966).
30 ANTONIADES et al., *Endocrinology*, **76**, 709 (1965); BÜRGI et al., *Biochim. biophys. Acta (Amst.)*, **121**, 360 (1966); POWER, L., *Lancet*, **1**, 1138 (1967).
31 STEINKE and SOELDNER, in LEIBEL and WRENSHALL (Eds.), *On the Nature and Treatment of Diabetes*, Excerpta Medica Foundation, New York, 1965, page 212.
32 JAKOB et al., *Dtsch. med. Wschr.*, **91**, 1314 (1966).
33 WELBORN et al., *Lancet*, **1**, 280 (1966).
34 BLEICHER et al., *New Engl. J. Med.*, **271**, 866 (1964).
35 BURT et al., *Obstet. and Gynec.*, **28**, 836 (1966).
36 THOMAS et al., *Diabetologia*, **2**, 221 (1966).
37 RAFAELSEN et al., *Diabetologia*, **2**, 216 (1966).
38 CHAMBERLAIN and STIMMLER, *J. clin. Invest.*, **46**, 911 (1967).
39 RUBENSTEIN et al., *Metabolism*, **16**, 234 (1967).
40 MCARTHUR and STIMMLER, *Lancet*, **1**, 1236 (1966).
41 MIRSKY, I.A., *Diabetes*, **13**, 225 (1964); TOMIZAWA and VARANDANI, *J. biol. Chem.*, **240**, 3191 (1965).
42 FREINKEL, N., *Diabetes*, **13**, 260 (1964); GITLIN et al., *Pediatrics*, **35**, 65 (1965).
43 RENOLD and CAHILL (Eds.), *American Physiological Society Handbook of Physiology*, Section 5, Williams & Wilkins, Baltimore, 1965; RENOLD et al., *Diabetologia*, **1**, 4 (1965).
44 SOLS, A., in LEIBEL and WRENSHALL (Eds.), *On the Nature and Treatment of Diabetes*, Excerpta Medica Foundation, New York, 1965, page 118; RANDLE et al., *Recent Progr. Hormone Res.*, **22**, 1 (1966).
45 STEINER, D.F., *Vitam. and Horm.*, **24**, 1 (1966); MADISON, L.L., *Adv. intern. Med.*, **123**, 284 (1969).
46 KRAHL, M.E., *The Action of Insulin on Cells*, Academic Press, New York, 1961; Intersociety Symposium: Role of Insulin in Membrane Transport, *Fed. Proc.*, **24**, 1039 (1965); SCHWARTZ and HECHTER, *Amer. J. Med.*, **40**, 765 (1966).
47 WEBER et al., *Fed. Proc.*, **24**, 745 (1965); WEBER et al., *Advanc. Enzyme Reg.*, **4**, 59 (1966).
48 BUTTERFIELD et al., *Lancet*, **1**, 557 (1966).
49 VALLANCE-OWEN, J., *Advanc. metab. Disord.*, **1**, 191 (1964).
50 BERSON and YALOW, *Diabetes*, **13**, 247 (1964); KIPNIS and STEIN, *Ciba Found. Coll. Endocr.*, **15**, 156 (1964).
51 RANDLE et al., *Lancet*, **1**, 785 (1963).
52 ENSINK et al., *Diabetes*, **16**, 289 (1967); HOLCOMB and DULIN, *Proc. Soc. exp. Biol. (N.Y.)*, **128**, 154 (1968).
53 HALES et al., *Lancet*, **1**, 65 (1965).
54 STIMMLER et al., *Lancet*, **1**, 137 (1964).

Glucagon[1,2]

Chemistry

Glucagon from pigs is a straight-chain polypeptide made up of 29 amino-acid residues. It has a molecular weight of 3485 and an absorption maximum at 278 nm. The amino-acid sequence, confirmed by total synthesis[34], is as follows[3]:

His·Ser·Glu(NH_2)·Gly·Thr·Phe·Thr·Ser·Asp·Tyr·Ser·Lys·Tyr

Leu·Asp·Ser·Arg·Arg·Ala·Glu(NH_2)·Asp·Phe·Val·Glu(NH_2)

Try·Leu·Met·Asp(NH_2)·Thr

Glucagon crystallizes in white rhombic dodecahedra. In acid solution it rapidly changes into a filamentous form resembling insulin. Glucagon cannot be a degradation product of insulin since the two molecules have no more than two common amino acids arranged in the same order[4]. Stereochemically, however, the two hormones bear a remarkable similarity[5]. Glucagon differs from other known protein hormones in lacking cystine, proline and isoleucine. The activity of glucagon is destroyed by incubation with pepsin, trypsin, chymotrypsin, subtilopeptidase, leucine aminopeptidase and carboxypeptidase. Glucagon is more resistant to alkali than is insulin, and since it contains no S-S linkages it is unaffected by cysteine. Incubation with cysteine can be used to obtain glucagon preparations free of insulin activity.

Unit, methods of assay

No international unit; amounts are expressed as equivalent weights of existing purified standards of pig and beef glucagon.

Biological methods of assay[6] are based for instance on the hyperglycaemic effect of the hormone in whole animals or its glycogenolytic effect in liver slices or homogenates. A technique of greater specificity and accuracy is radioimmunological assay[7–9]. A system utilizing the ability of glucagon to stimulate adenyl cyclase in subcellular particles of dog liver is more specific than other bioassays[10].

Biosynthesis, secretion, metabolism

Glucagon is probably produced by the α-cells of the islets of LANGERHANS and similar cells located in the upper intestine. Destruction of the pancreatic β-cells by alloxan has no effect on the glucagon content of the pancreas, whereas damage to the α-cells by cobalt chloride or other compounds causes a gradual diminution of glucagon activity. Glucagon can be isolated from those parts of the dog pancreas which contain α-cells but is not found in the uncinate process, where α-cells are lacking. Furthermore, in different species the amount of extractable glucagon in the pancreas correlates well with the relative abundance of α-cells in the organ. Histochemically, tryptophan, a component of glucagon but not of insulin, can be demonstrated in α-cells but not in β-cells[1]. More direct evidence in favour of the α-cell origin of glucagon has been obtained recently with specific immunofluorescence techniques[11].

Both the muscular and mucosal layers of dog and human upper gastrointestinal tract have been found to contain significant amounts of a glucagon-like substance in measurements made by the method of liver adenyl cyclase assay[10]. A glucagon-like substance was also detected in the gastrointestinal tract by radioimmunoassay[12]. This technique reveals a glucagon content in the human pancreas of 4.0–12.4 μg/g and a content of glucagon-like substance in the human colon of 0.006–0.01 μg/g; the glucagon-like immunoreactivity of the whole digestive tract probably does not amount to more than 25–50% of that of the pancreas. Glucagon has also been identified radioimmunochemically in acid alcohol extracts of an undifferentiated bronchogenic carcinoma[13]. There is no evidence to suggest that glucagon is related to hyperglycaemic substances isolated from skin, lymph glands, tongue and spleen.

Published data on the plasma glucagon level in fasting subjects vary from 0.1 μg/l to 5 μg/l; more recent publications indicate that it is below 0.3 μg/l[14]. The glucagon content of the blood increases in starvation, insulin-induced hypoglycaemia, and phlorizin diabetes; administration of glucose to phlorizin-treated animals or persons with hypoglycaemia causes the blood glucagon level to fall[8,15]. Paradoxically, oral glucose loading also causes a rapid rise in the blood glucagon level, an effect that occurs to only a small extent when glucose is given intravenously[16]. This glucagon-like immunoreactivity probably arises from the gut[35]. In the blood, glucagon does not appear to be bound to plasma proteins[17].

Glucagon is degraded by the kidneys, liver and other organs and to some extent in the blood. Following injection of glucagon labelled with ^{131}I, the hormone becomes concentrated in the following organs (in decreasing order of amount stored): kidneys, liver, pituitary, spleen, lungs, salivary glands, adrenals, pancreas, thyroid, heart, duodenum, lymph glands. Hepatectomy and nephrectomy show that the liver and kidneys are the main sites of degradation of glucagon, in which a proteolytic 'glucagonase' of limited specificity is said to take part. This enzyme contains SH groups and is inhibited by insulin, growth hormone, α-ACTH and α-casein. Injected glucagon is thus quickly broken down – in man it has a half-life of less than 10 min[7] – so that it is therefore unlikely to be identical with the glycogenolytic or hyperglycaemia-producing substances found in the urine of normal individuals, diabetics and schizophrenics.

Biological activity

Long-continued administration of neutral red results in degranulation of the pancreatic α-cells and a reduction in their absolute number. Rats treated in this fashion develop fasting hypoglycaemia and subnormal tolerance to insulin and tolbutamide[18].

Glucagon administration to mammals, birds and reptiles causes a rise in the blood glucose concentration. The magnitude of the rise and its duration depend on the dose, the mode of administration, the nutritional state of the subject and the species of animal being tested. This hyperglycaemic effect is maximal in fed animals with plentiful hepatic glycogen reserves, is diminished but not abolished when hepatic glycogen stores are depleted, and is absent in the eviscerated animal. The hyperglycaemia induced by glucagon is accompanied by rapid depletion of hepatic glycogen stores in vivo. In vitro (isolated perfused liver, liver slices, liver homogenates) glucagon is a potent glycogenolytic agent in physiological concentrations[1]. Conversely, glucagon stimulates gluconeogenesis from amino acids and lactate in the perfused rat liver[19,20]. When these substrates are not provided it promotes new glucose formation from endogenous liver protein[21]. Glucagon has an inotropic effect on the heart, where it enhances oxidation of glucose and acetate to CO_2[22].

The manner in which glucagon intervenes in carbohydrate metabolism has been largely elucidated. Like adrenaline (see page 733), glucagon stimulates the formation of adenosine cyclic 3′,5′-phosphate[23] and therefore increases glycogenolysis. This biomolecular action of glucagon has been observed in the liver and heart but – in contrast to adrenaline – not in skeletal muscle[2]. The action of adenosine cyclic 3′,5′-phosphate, and of glucagon, in stimulating gluconeogenesis from lactate in the perfused rat liver probably takes place through activation of phosphopyruvate carboxylase[20]. Glucagon causes a significant release of potassium from the liver. This phenomenon precedes phosphorylase activation, but it is uncertain whether the two effects are related[24].

Glucagon is antagonistic to insulin in that it promotes the release of glucose in the liver in hypoglycaemia[25]; on the other hand it also appears to stimulate insulin secretion in man independently of its hyperglycaemic effect[26]. When added to rabbit pancreatic slices it causes release of insulin into the incubation medium, the reaction rate increasing with the glucose concentration of the medium[27]. In man under physiological conditions it is possible that pancreatic glucagon is primarily insulinogenic and secondarily hyperglycaemic, whereas the glucagon of the digestive tract is primarily hyperglycaemic[12].

When given to animals in large doses over long periods, glucagon produces hyperglycaemia, glycosuria, a markedly negative nitrogen balance, weight loss and increased basal metabolic rate, while in at least one species (rabbit) it may induce permanent diabetes (metaglucagon diabetes)[28]. There is no evidence, however, indicating that hypersecretion of glucagon is a pathogenic factor in diabetes.

Glucagon diminishes gastrointestinal motility[29], inhibits the secretion of gastric juice and hydrochloric acid[2], and abolishes hunger[2]. In the kidneys it has a diuretic action and increases the excretion of sodium, potassium, chloride, bicarbonate, phosphate and uric acid[2,30]. Here glucagon may again act by producing adenosine cyclic 3′,5′-phosphate, which may be capable of changing the permeability of the nephron (see under 'Oxytocin and Vasopressin', page 723).

A further action of glucagon is on lipid metabolism, in that the hormone promotes mobilization of fatty acids from adipose tissue[31]. Once again the underlying mechanism is probably the formation of adenosine cyclic 3′,5′-phosphate (see under 'Catecholamines', page 733).

Clinical significance

Insufficient endogenous glucagon secretion has been postulated as a cause of hypoglycaemia in certain patients in whom histological examination of the pancreas showed it to be deficient in α-cells, but this remains to be confirmed by measurements of pancreatic glucagon content and serum levels of the hormone in this type of patient[32]. A pancreatic islet cell tumour in which immunoassay revealed large amounts of glucagon has been reported, the patient having high serum glucagon and insulin levels and mild diabetes[33]. The full syndrome of glucagon excess as produced experimentally in animals has not yet been shown to occur spontaneously in man.

Diagnostically, glucagon is useful in the evaluation of patients with glycogen storage disease. Depending on the position of the enzymatic block in the glycogenolytic pathway, the hyperglycaemic effect of glucagon may be absent, normal, blunted, or present only shortly after a carbohydrate meal. Atypical results, however, have been reported. The response to glucagon has also been used to evaluate glycogen reserves in ADDISON's disease, diabetes and liver disease. In pharmacological doses glucagon stimulates myocardial contractility and the heart rate, an effect which suggests therapeutic possibilities in congestive heart failure[36].

References

1 FOÀ and GALANSINO, *Glucagon: Chemistry and Function in Health and Disease*, Thomas, Springfield, 1962.
2 FOÀ, P.P., in PINCUS et al. (Eds.), *The Hormones*, vol. 4, Academic Press, New York, 1964, page 531; FOÀ, P.P., *Ergebn. Physiol.*, **60**, 141 (1968).
3 BEHRENS and BROMER, *Vitam. and Horm.*, **16**, 263 (1958).
4 SANGER, F., *Ciba Found. Coll. Endocr.*, **9**, 110 (1956).
5 SCHUSTER, T.M., *Nature*, **209**, 302 (1966).
6 MAKMAN et al., in ANTONIADES, H.N. (Ed.), *Hormones in Human Plasma*, Little, Brown, Boston, 1960, page 119; BROMER and BEHRENS, in DORFMAN, R.I. (Ed.), *Methods in Hormone Research*, vol. 2, Academic Press, New York, 1962, page 459.
7 UNGER et al., *J. clin. Invest.*, **40**, 1280 (1961).
8 UNGER et al., *J. clin. Invest.*, **42**, 1031 (1963).
9 SAMOLS and BILKUS, *Proc. Soc. exp. Biol. (N.Y.)*, **115**, 79 (1964).
10 MAKMAN and SUTHERLAND, *Endocrinology*, **75**, 127 (1964).
11 BAUM et al., *Diabetes*, **11**, 371 (1962).
12 SAMOLS et al., *Lancet*, **2**, 727 (1966).
13 UNGER et al., *J. clin. Endocr.*, **24**, 823 (1964).
14 SOKAL et al., *J. clin. Invest.*, **46**, 778 (1967).
15 FOÀ et al., *Recent Progr. Hormone Res.*, **13**, 473 (1957); UNGER et al., *J. clin. Invest.*, **41**, 682 (1962).

[16] SAMOLS et al., *Lancet*, **2**, 1257 (1965).
[17] MERIMEE and PROUT, *J. Lab. clin. Med.*, **64**, 412 (1964).
[18] OKUDA and GROLLMAN, *Endocrinology*, **78**, 195 (1966).
[19] MILLER, L.L., *Recent Progr. Hormone Res.*, **17**, 539 (1961).
[20] EXTON and PARK, *Pharmacol. Rev.*, **18**, 181 (1966).
[21] GARCIA et al., *Diabetes*, **15**, 188 (1966).
[22] KREISBERG and WILLIAMSON, *Amer. J. Physiol.*, **207**, 721 (1964).
[23] SUTHERLAND and ROBISON, *Pharmacol. Rev.*, **18**, 145 (1966).
[24] FINDER et al., *Amer. J. Physiol.*, **206**, 738 (1964).
[25] UNGER and EISENTRAUT, *Diabetes*, **13**, 563 (1964).
[26] SAMOLS et al., *Lancet*, **2**, 415 (1965); SAMOLS et al., *Diabetes*, **15**, 855 (1966); CROCKFORD et al., *Metabolism*, **15**, 114 (1966).
[27] TURNER and MCINTYRE, *Lancet*, **1**, 351 (1966).
[28] LOGOTHETOPOULOS et al., *Diabetes*, **9**, 278 (1960).
[29] KOCK et al., *Gastroenterology*, **53**, 88 (1967).
[30] PULLMAN et al., *Metabolism*, **16**, 358 (1967).
[31] STEINBERG, D., *Pharmacol. Rev.*, **18**, 217 (1966).
[32] GROLLMAN et al., *Metabolism*, **13**, 686 (1964).
[33] UNGER et al., *Clin. Res.*, **14**, 102 (1966).
[34] WÜNSCH, E., *Z. Naturforsch.*, **22b**, 1269 (1967).
[35] UNGER et al., *J. clin. Invest.*, **47**, 48 (1968).
[36] PARMLEY et al., *New Engl. J. Med.*, **279**, 12 (1968); Editorial, *J. Amer. med. Ass.*, **206**, 1078 (1968); BROGAN et al., *Lancet*, **1**, 482 (1969).

Hormones of the gastrointestinal tract[1]

Gastrin[2,3]

This substance, isolated from the pyloric antrum of the porcine stomach, has been separated into two compounds, gastrin I and gastrin II[4]. Both are single-chain heptadecapeptides with an N-terminal pyroglutamyl group and a C-terminal amide group. The amino-acid sequence of porcine gastrin II is as follows[5]:

```
                                                          SO3H
                                                           |
Glu·Gly·Pro·Try·Met·Glu·Glu·Glu·Glu·Glu·Ala·Tyr
 1   2   3   4   5   6   7   8   9   10  11  12
Gly·Try·Met·Asp·Phe·NH2
 13  14  15  16  17
```

Gastrin I differs from gastrin II in having no sulphate group attached to the tyrosine residue. The human gastrins are distinguished from the porcine compounds by having a leucine instead of methionine residue at position 5[6]. The structure of the canine and ovine gastrins has also largely been elucidated[7]. Both the porcine[8] and human[9] gastrins have been synthesized. The biological activity resides in the C-terminal tetrapeptide, but increases with the length of the amino-acid chain[10]. The sulphate group has no effect on the biological activity. A 'gastrin' made up of 107 amino-acid residues and having a molecular weight of 12500 has been isolated[11]; its relationship to gastrins I and II remains obscure.

Gastrin has been found in the antrum and small intestine of various species[12]. Nothing is known of its mode of formation. It is absent in the normal pancreas but has been isolated from the tumour tissue of patients with the ZOLLINGER-ELLISON syndrome[13]. Gastrin is released on stimulation of the vagus nerve, on contact of food with the pyloric antrum, and on dilation of the antrum. Acetylcholine liberated from the nerves acts as intermediary in gastrin secretion[14]. Vagal stimulation of gastrin secretion is slowed down when the pH value in the pyloric antrum falls below 2. Increased concentrations of gastrin can be demonstrated by radioimmunoassay in the serum of patients with the ZOLLINGER-ELLISON syndrome[17,18].

Gastrin increases the acidity of gastric juice. By the subcutaneous route, the same 'maximum' acid secretion can be achieved with 0.5 µg gastrin/kg body weight as with 40 µg histamine phosphate/kg body weight. With 2 µg gastrin/kg body weight the acid secretion is about 10% higher, but no further increase can be achieved by a higher dose of gastrin[15]. At high dosages, which inhibit acid secretion, gastrin stimulates the secretion of pepsin; it also increases the amount and enzyme content of the exocrine pancreatic secretion, promotes the flow of bile, and has a motor action on the stomach and small intestine. Gastrin also has a stimulating effect on insulin secretion[16].

Secretin[23]

Secretin originates from the mucosa of the upper small intestine. It is a polypeptide consisting of 27 amino-acid residues with the following structure:

```
His·Ser·Asp·Gly·Thr·Phe·Thr·Ser·Glu·Leu·Ser·Arg·Leu·Arg
Asp·Ser·Ala·Arg·Leu·Glu(NH2)·Arg·Leu·Leu·Glu(NH2)·Gly
Leu·Val(NH2)
```

This polypeptide has been synthesized and the synthetic hormone shown to have quantitatively the same physiological properties as highly purified secretin from swine.

Secretin is released on acid stimulation of the duodenum and plays an important part in neutralization of the contents of the small intestine. It increases the blood flow to the pancreas, and in this organ stimulates not only the exocrine secretion of water (see page 651) and bicarbonate (see page 652) but also the endocrine secretion of insulin[16]. Secretin stimulates the flow of bile by favouring the production of a fluid rich in bicarbonate[20].

Secretin has been shown by radioimmunoassay to be present in normal human serum at a concentration of less than 0.4 µg/l in fasting and up to 25 µg/l after oral glucose loading[19].

Cholecystokinin-pancreozymin

Cholecystokinin and pancreozymin were originally thought to be separate hormones, but chemical purification revealed that their two effects on the tract of the small intestine were due to a single molecule containing 33 amino-acid residues[21]. The latter have all been identified but their complete sequence is not known. The molecule has a C-terminal sequence identical with that of gastrin as regards at least two and possibly five residues. Pancreozymin activity has also been detected in the pyloric antrum[22]. Release of this hormone is stimulated by the contact of fatty acids, amino acids and hydrogen ions with the gastrointestinal mucosa.

Cholecystokinin-pancreozymin has the same spectrum of biological activity as gastrin but its effects differ markedly in intensity compared to the latter. It is a very weak stimulant of gastric acid secretion, but unlike gastrin it causes strong contractions of the gall-bladder. The exocrine discharge of enzymes by the pancreas is stimulated (see page 652), but the hormone has no effect on the amount of pancreatic juice secreted or on its bicarbonate content. Cholecystokinin-pancreozymin also stimulates the secretion of insulin and glucagon[16].

Enterogastrone

This hormone is present in the mucosa of the small intestine but has not yet been isolated. Its release is stimulated by contact of fats and sugars with the mucosa of the small intestine. The hormone is thought to inhibit the secretory and motor activity of the stomach.

References

[1] GREGORY, R.A., *Secretory Mechanisms of the Gastro-Intestinal Tract*, Arnold, London, 1962; JORPES and MUTT, in PINCUS et al. (Eds.), *The Hormones*, vol. 4, Academic Press, New York, 1964, page 365; DEMLING, L., *Münch. med. Wschr.*, **108**, 8 (1966).
[2] GROSSMAN, M.I. (Ed.), *Gastrin*, Proceedings of a Conference, Los Angeles 1964, Butterworth, London, 1966.
[3] GROSSMAN, M.I., *Ann. intern. Med.*, **64**, 212 (1966); GROSSMAN, M.I., *Amer. J. dig. Dis.*, **11**, 90 (1966); SEWING, K.-F., *Dtsch. med. Wschr.*, **91**, 1506 (1966); PRESHAW, R.M., in ROBSON and STACEY (Eds.), *Recent Advances in Pharmacology*, 4th ed., Churchill, London, 1968, page 263.
[4] GREGORY and TRACY, *Gut*, **5**, 103 (1964).
[5] GREGORY et al., *Nature*, **204**, 931 (1964).
[6] BENTLEY et al., *Nature*, **209**, 583 (1966).
[7] GREGORY, R.A., *Gastroenterology*, **51**, 953 (1966).
[8] ANDERSON et al., *Nature*, **204**, 933 (1964).
[9] BEACHAM et al., *Nature*, **209**, 585 (1966).
[10] TRACY and GREGORY, *Nature*, **204**, 935 (1964); MORLEY et al., *Nature*, **207**, 1356 (1965).
[11] TAUBER and MADISON, *J. clin. Invest.*, **43**, 1271 (1964); TAUBER, S.D., in GROSSMAN[2], page 27.
[12] LAI, K.S., *Gut*, **5**, 334 (1964); ELWIN and UVNÄS, in GROSSMAN [2], page 69.
[13] GREGORY et al., *Lancet*, **2**, 543 (1967).
[14] FARRAR and BOWER, *Ann. Rev. Physiol.*, **29**, 141 (1967).
[15] MAKHLOUF et al., *Lancet*, **2**, 485 (1964).
[16] DUPRE et al., *Lancet*, **2**, 611 (1967); UNGER et al., *J. clin. Invest.*, **46**, 630 (1967).
[17] ODELL et al., *J. clin. Endocr.*, **28**, 1840 (1968).
[18] MCGUIGAN and TRUDEAU, *New Engl. J. Med.*, **278**, 1306 (1968).
[19] YOUNG et al., *J. Nucl. Med.*, **9**, 641 (1968).
[20] WAITMAN and JANOWITZ, *J. clin. Invest.*, **46**, 1127 (1967).
[21] JORPES and MUTT, *Acta physiol. scand.*, **66**, 196 (1966); JORPES and MUTT, *Nord. Med.*, **77**, 237 (1967); MUTT and JORPES, *Biochem. Biophys. Res. Commun.*, **26**, 392 (1967).
[22] HARPER et al., in DE REUCK and CAMERON (Eds.), *Ciba Foundation Symposium on the Exocrine Pancreas*, Churchill, London, 1962, page 168.
[23] VAGNE et al., *Gastroenterology*, **55**, 260 (1968).

Erythropoietin [1]

Erythropoietin is a factor easily demonstrable in the serum of various animal species under certain circumstances (hypoxia, anaemia, injection of cobalt chloride); it has been shown to stimulate erythropoiesis in a specific fashion. It appears to be a mucopolysaccharide or glycoprotein containing sialic acid and has a reported molecular weight of 10000–62000 [2,3]. Erythropoietin possesses weak antigenic properties [4].

Erythropoietin can be detected in vivo by studying erythropoiesis (^{59}Fe-incorporation in erythrocytes, reticulocytosis) in mice or rats in which this function is suppressed. Its in vitro determination (for instance in bone-marrow cultures) has proved less successful. An immunoassay method has recently been developed [16].

1 International Unit (IU) of erythropoietin is contained in 1.48 mg of the 1st International Reference Preparation (see page 763). This unit is the same as the unit of the Erythropoietin Standard A or B of the National Institute for Medical Research, London [5]. Highly purified preparations from rabbit plasma or human urine have an activity up to 368 IU/mg [3].

The kidneys play a particular role in the formation of erythropoietin, which is either mainly produced in this organ [6] or is the result of the formation by the kidneys of an enzyme (renal erythropoietic factor) that liberates erythropoietin from the plasma proteins [7]. Erythropoietin formation is elicited by oxygen deficiency in the tissues and may be stimulated by the androgens [8], which would account for the higher erythrocyte count in men.

Erythropoietin is barely detectable in normal human plasma by biological methods [9], but immunoassay has revealed a concentration of 7–30 U/l [16]. The hormone disappears fairly rapidly from the circulating blood, the half-life being about 2–3 hours [10]. Normal values for the urinary excretion are given in the table below; discrepancies in reported values can probably be ascribed to differences in methods of measurement. The acceleration of erythropoiesis during pregnancy is associated with increased erythropoietic activity in the plasma and, in the second trimester, in the urine [11]. High levels of erythropoietic activity are found in cord blood [12], and erythropoietin has also been detected in the amniotic fluid [13]. Increased amounts of erythropoietin have been demonstrated in the plasma of many patients with polyglobulism, anaemia, blood loss or haemolysis [9,14].

Urinary excretion of erythropoietin (IU/24 h)

	Mean	Range	s	Reference
Boys	1.0	0.6–1.2	–	17
Men	2.8	1.5–5.2	1.3	17
Women	0.9	0.5–1.8	0.4	17
Men	0.54	0.21–1.2	–	18
Women	0.22	0.16–0.32	–	18
Men in Chacaltaya, Bolivia (5200 m)	9.1	1.1–22.4	–	18

Biological activity

Erythropoietin stimulates proliferation of the erythroblasts in the bone marrow, increases the numbers of reticulocytes and erythrocytes in the peripheral blood and promotes the metabolism of the bone marrow, reticulocytes and erythrocytes (purine synthesis, haem synthesis, DNA synthesis, RNA synthesis) [15].

References

1 GORDON, A.S., *Physiol. Rev.*, **39**, 1 (1959); JACOBSON et al., *Advanc. intern. Med.*, **10**, 297 (1960); LANGE and PAVLOVIC-KENTERA, *Progr. Hemat.*, **4**, 72 (1964); KELLER, H.M., *Schweiz. med. Wschr.*, **94**, 1773 (1964); GURNEY, C.W., *Advanc. metab. Dis.*, **3**, 279 (1968).
2 GOLDWASSER et al., *Biochim. biophys. Acta (Amst.)*, **64**, 487 (1962); ROSSE et al., *J. clin. Invest.*, **42**, 124 (1963); ROSSE and WALDMANN, *Blood*, **24**, 739 (1964); LEWIS et al., *J. Lab. clin. Med.*, **73**, 154 (1969).
3 LOWY and KEIGHLEY, *Clin. chim. Acta*, **13**, 491 (1966).
4 SCHOOLEY and GARCIA, *Proc. Soc. exp. Biol. (N.Y.)*, **109**, 325 (1962).
5 COTES and BANGHAM, *Bull. Wld Hlth Org.*, **35**, 751 (1966).
6 GOLDFARB and TOBIAN, *Proc. Soc. exp. Biol. (N.Y.)*, **111**, 510 (1962); STOHLMAN, F., *New Engl. J. Med.*, **279**, 1437 (1968).
7 CONTRERA et al., *Blood*, **28**, 330 (1966); GORDON et al., *Blood*, **28**, 977 (1966); ZANJANI et al., *Proc. Soc. exp. Biol. (N.Y.)*, **126**, 540 (1967); WONG et al., *Proc. Soc. exp. Biol. (N.Y.)*, **128**, 67 (1968).
8 ALEXANIAN, R., *Blood*, **28**, 1007 (1966); MIRAND et al., *J. Lab. clin. Med.*, **73**, 121 (1969).
9 MIRAND et al., *Proc. Soc. exp. Biol. (N.Y.)*, **118**, 823 (1965).
10 DUKES, P.P., in KARLSON, P. (Ed.), *Wirkungsmechanismen der Hormone*, 18th Colloquium of the Gesellschaft für physiologische Chemie, Mosbach 1967, Springer, Berlin, 1967, page 197.
11 SOLOMON and FRIESEN, *Ann. Rev. Med.*, **19**, 399 (1968).
12 FINNE, P.H., *Acta paediat. scand.*, **55**, 478 (1966).
13 FINNE, P.H., *Brit. med. J.*, **1**, 697 (1965).
14 MOVASSAGHI et al., *Proc. Soc. exp. Biol. (N.Y.)*, **126**, 615 (1967).
15 REMMELE, W., *Die humorale Steuerung der Erythropoiese*, Springer, Berlin, 1963; PIEBER-PERRETTA et al., *Biochim. biophys. Acta (Amst.)*, **95**, 360 (1965); RUDOLPH and PERRETTA, *Proc. Soc. exp. Biol. (N.Y.)*, **124**, 1041 (1967); POWSNER and BERMAN, *Blood*, **30**, 189 (1967).
16 LANGE et al., *J. Lab. clin. Med.*, **73**, 78 (1969).
17 ALEXANIAN, R., *Blood*, **28**, 344 (1966).
18 VAN DYKE et al., *Blood*, **28**, 535 (1966).

Renin–angiotensin system [1,2]

Chemistry

This system consists of a complex enzymatic reaction in which the enzyme renin acts on a plasma protein substrate (angiotensinogen) to liberate the decapeptide angiotensin I (hypertensin I, angiotonin I). This latter substance is broken down to the octapeptide angiotensin II by the action of a plasma enzyme complex (converting enzyme) activated by chloride. Angiotensin II is in turn rapidly converted into inactive peptides by peptide hydrolases ('angiotensinase') present in the tissues (kidneys, liver), erythrocytes and plasma, its half-life in the blood being about 1 min. These reactions are subject to the action of various activators and inhibitors present in the plasma.

Renin is a protein with a molecular weight of about 43000 (in man) [3], angiotensinogen a plasma protein belonging to the α_2-globulin group. The latter is converted by trypsin into a tetradecapeptide, the so-called polypeptide renin substrate, which is split by renin at the Leu·Leu linkage. The structures of this compound and of the angiotensins are shown in the table opposite. The synthetic Val^5-angiotensin-II-Asp^1-β-amide has the same qualitative and quantitative pharmacological properties as naturally occurring angiotensin II [4] and is therefore suitable for use as reference substance.

Units

Renin. 1 GOLDBLATT Unit is the amount of renin that increases the mean arterial blood pressure (measured directly in the femoral artery) by 30 mm Hg when injected intravenously into nonanaesthetized dogs [1]. By using angiotensinogen as substrate, renin concentration can be expressed as enzyme activity, 1 unit corresponding to the formation of 1 ng angiotensin per minute [5,6].

Angiotensin. 1 GOLDBLATT Unit is the amount of angiotensin that increases the mean arterial blood pressure (measured directly in the femoral artery) by 30 mm Hg when injected intravenously into nonanaesthetized dogs [1]. Angiotensin concentration can also be expressed in terms of the reference substance angiotensin II (see above), 1 μg angiotensin II corresponding to about 2.2 GOLDBLATT Units [7].

Methods of assay

Renin

Biological methods. (a) Direct measurement of the hypertensive effect in vivo after intravenous injection of the test solution into nonanaesthetized dogs [1] or in vitro in an aorta preparation [8]. (b) Method of BOCHER et al. [5] for plasma renin (renin-like activity): Incubation of the plasma containing renin and angiotensinogen together with activators and inhibitors at pH 5.5 and 37°C in the presence of Dowex 50W-X2(NH_4), an ion-exchange resin that adsorbs angiotensin and thus prevents its breakdown by angiotensinase; after elution the angiotensin is determined by its hypertensive effect on rats. (c) Method of BROWN et al. for plasma renin [6]: After adsorption of the renin in a DEAE-cellulose column and subsequent elution the angiotensinogen and 'angiotensinase' are eliminated by acidification; the renin so isolated is incubated with bovine angiotensinogen at pH 5.7 and 37 °C and the angiotensin liberated determined by its hypertensive effect on rats.

Chemical methods. Fluorimetric determination of the hydrolysis products in a synthetic substrate acted on by renin [9]. This method is too insensitive for assay of the renin content of plasma.

Structure of angiotensins

	Mol.wt.	Amino-acid sequence	Origin
Ile⁵–polypeptide–renin substrate .	1759	Asp·Arg·Val·Tyr·Ile·His·Pro·Phe·His·Leu·Leu·Val·Tyr·Ser 1 2 3 4 5 6 7 8 9 10 11 12 13 14	Equine plasma after action of trypsin[26]
Ile⁵-angiotensin I	1297	Asp·Arg·Val·Tyr·Ile·His·Pro·Phe·His·Leu 1 2 3 4 5 6 7 8 9 10	Equine[27], porcine[28], human[29] plasma
Val⁵-angiotensin I.............	1283	Asp·Arg·Val·Tyr·Val·His·Pro·Phe·His·Leu 1 2 3 4 5 6 7 8 9 10	Bovine plasma[30]
Ile⁵-angiotensin II..............	1046	Asp·Arg·Val·Tyr·Ile·His·Pro·Phe 1 2 3 4 5 6 7 8	From Ile⁵-angiotensin I
Val⁵-angiotensin II.............	1032	Asp·Arg·Val·Tyr·Val·His·Pro·Phe 1 2 3 4 5 6 7 8	From Val⁵-angiotensin I
Val⁵-angiotensin-II-Asp¹-β-amide	1029	Asp(NH_2)·Arg·Val·Tyr·Val·His·Pro·Phe 1 2 3 4 5 6 7 8	Synthetic[4]

Angiotensin

Biological methods. (a) Direct measurement of the hypertensive effect in vivo after intravenous injection of the test solution into nonanaesthetized dogs[1] or in vitro in an aorta preparation[8]. (b) Adsorption of the angiotensin on Dowex 50W-X2(NH_4), elution followed by paper-chromatographic purification, and determination by hypertensive effect on rats[5]. (c) Radioimmunological methods using angiotensin I or II tagged with ^{125}I or ^{131}I[10].

Biosynthesis, metabolism

Renin is formed in the juxtaglomerular apparatus of the kidneys, possibly also in the uterus[11]. Normal values for the renin activity of fasting, recumbent subjects are given in the table below. The renin activity of the plasma rises on changing from the recumbent to the erect posture[12]; rhythmic fluctuations during the day have also been observed[13]. Plasma renin activity increases on a low-sodium diet, decreases on sodium-loading[12,14,15]. Increases are often seen during pregnancy, especially in the first trimester[16]. Pathological increases of plasma renin activity occur in all conditions accompanied by sodium depletion (diarrhoea, abuse of diuretics, adrenocortical insufficiency, adrenogenital syndrome) or diminution of plasma volume (bleeding, hypoproteinaemia), in renovascular arterial hypertension, in malignant arterial hypertension and often in phaeochromocytoma[15]; in primary aldosteronism it is reduced and may be below the detection threshold[17]. Increased renin activity is not, however, necessarily associated with hypertension.

Normal values for angiotensin in blood are given in the table below; increased values have been observed in pregnant women towards term[18].

Renin and angiotensin contents of blood

	Mean	Range	*s*	Method	Reference
Renin (U/l)					
Plasma...	9.0	0–32	7.6	Biological	14
Plasma...	4	2–10	–	Biological	33
Angiotensin (ng/l)					
Plasma...	60	–	100	Biological	34
Blood ...	95	–	66	Biological	35
Plasma...	–	<8–56	–	Radioimmunological	36
Blood ...	21	–	14	Radioimmunological	37

Biological activity

The active agent in the renin–angiotensin system is free angiotensin II, which has three main effects[19]:

(a) An effect on aldosterone secretion. Angiotensin is the most important stimulant of aldosterone secretion and it apparently acts directly on the zona glomerulosa of the adrenal cortex[20]. In man – in contrast to other species – angiotensin appears to stimulate aldosterone production selectively[31]. The rate of aldosterone secretion is a direct function of the plasma renin activity, which in turn is subject to changes in the sodium balance of the body[14,15].

(b) A contractile action on the smooth muscle of the arterioles. Angiotensin is the most powerful known vasopressor substance. Intravenous injection of angiotensin causes a rapid but brief rise in the arterial blood pressure. Angiotensin has a specific effect on renal haemodynamics; it appears to play a role in the autoregulation of the kidneys[21].

(c) An action on the tubular reabsorption of sodium[22]. Independently of the two actions already mentioned, angiotensin can either increase the tubular reabsorption of sodium (in subjects with normal blood pressure) or decrease it (in hypertensive subjects and patients with cirrhosis)[23].

The renin–angiotensin system appears to be involved in the thirst mechanism since both these substances have been shown to instigate drinking to replace lost fluid[32]. Angiotensin regulates renin secretion through a negative feedback mechanism[24].

Clinical significance

Measurement of plasma renin activity enables a distinction to be made between primary aldosteronism (decreased renin activity) and secondary aldosteronism (increased renin activity). It can also be used to confirm the renovascular origin of arterial hypertension associated with renal arterial stenosis.

Test of KAPLAN and SILAH[25]: Sensitivity to the hypertensive effect of an intravenous infusion of angiotensin is decreased in renovascular arterial hypertension, increased in primary aldosteronism.

References

1 GOLDBLATT, H., *Physiol. Rev.*, **27**, 120 (1947).
2 GROSS, F., *Klin. Wschr.*, **36**, 693 (1958); TOBIAN, L., *Physiol. Rev.*, **40**, 280 (1960); PAGE and BUMPUS, *Physiol. Rev.*, **41**, 331 (1961); PEART, W.S., *Pharmacol. Rev.*, **17**, 143 (1965).
3 WARREN and DOLINSKY, *Proc. Soc. Exp. Biol. (N.Y.)*, **123**, 911 (1966).
4 SCHWYZER and TURRIAN, *Vitam. and Horm.*, **18**, 237 (1960).
5 BOUCHER et al., *Canad. med. Ass. J.*, **90**, 194 (1964).
6 BROWN et al., *Biochem. J.*, **93**, 594 (1964).
7 KHAIRALLAH et al., *Nature*, **196**, 1059 (1962).
8 HELMER, O.M., *Med. Clin. N. Amer.*, **45**, 309 (1961).
9 ROTH and REINHARZ, *Helv. chim. Acta*, **49**, 1903 (1966).
10 VALLOTTON et al., *J. clin. Invest.*, **46**, 1126 (1967); VALLOTTON et al., *Nature*, **215**, 714 (1964); BOYD et al., *Lancet*, **2**, 1002 (1967); CATT et al., *Lancet*, **2**, 1005 (1967); VALLOTTON, M.B., *Lancet*, **1**, 840 (1969); HOLLEMANS et al., *Clin. chim. Acta*, **23**, 7 (1969).
11 CAPELL et al., *J. clin. Invest.*, **46**, 1042 (1967).
12 VEYRAT et al., *Canad. med. Ass. J.*, **90**, 215 (1964); KLAUS et al., *Dtsch. med. Wschr.*, **92**, 2114 (1967).
13 GORDON et al., *J. clin. Invest.*, **45**, 1587 (1966).
14 VEYRAT et al., *Schweiz. med. Wschr.*, **94**, 914 (1964).
15 VEYRAT et al., *Schweiz. med. Wschr.*, **98**, 65 (1968).
16 WINER, B.M., *J. clin. Invest.*, **44**, 1112 (1965); BROWN et al., *Lancet*, **2**, 900 (1963).
17 CONN et al., *J. Amer. med. Ass.*, **190**, 213 (1964).
18 MASSANI et al., *Amer. J. Obstet. Gynec.*, **99**, 313 (1967).
19 GROSS et al., *Recent Progr. Hormone Res.*, **21**, 119 (1965).
20 LARAGH et al., *J. Amer. med. Ass.*, **174**, 234 (1960); GENEST, J., *Canad. med. Ass. J.*, **84**, 403 (1961); GANONG et al., *Recent Progr. Hormone Res.*, **22**, 381 (1966).
21 THURAU, K., *Amer. J. Med.*, **36**, 698 (1964).
22 PETERS, G., *Proc. Soc. exp. Biol. (N.Y.)*, **112**, 771 (1963).

23 AMES et al., *J.clin.Invest.*, **44**, 1171 (1965).
24 VANDER, A.J., *Physiol.Rev.*, **47**, 359 (1967); KLAUS, D., *Dtsch.med.Wschr.*, **92**, 2128 (1967).
25 KAPLAN and SILAH, *J.clin.Invest.*, **43**, 659 (1964).
26 SKEGGS et al., *J.exp.Med.*, **106**, 439 (1957), and **108**, 283 (1958).
27 SKEGGS et al., *J.exp.Med.*, **102**, 435 (1955).
28 BUMPUS et al., *Science*, **125**, 886 (1957).
29 ARAKAWA et al., *Nature*, **214**, 278 (1967); ARAKAWA and NAKAMURA, *Circulat.Res.*, **21**, suppl.2, 101 (1967).
30 ELLIOTT and PEART, *Biochem.J.*, **65**, 246 (1957).
31 BROWN et al., in JAMES, V.H.T. (Ed.), *Recent Advances in Endocrinology*, 8th ed., Churchill, London, 1968, page 271.
32 FITZSIMONS, J.T., *J. Physiol.*, **201**, 349 (1969).
33 KLAUS et al., *Dtsch.med.Wschr.*, **92**, 2114 (1967).
34 GENEST et al., *Canad.med.Ass.J.*, **90**, 263 (1964).
35 ZULEMA et al., *Clin.Sci.*, **30**, 473 (1966).
36 BOYD et al., *Lancet*, **2**, 1002 (1967).
37 CATT et al., *Lancet*, **2**, 1005 (1967).

Plasma kinins [1–3]

Chemistry

The kinins are low-molecular polypeptides of high pharmacological activity arising from the action of proteolytic enzymes on the plasma proteins. Naturally occurring kinins that have also been synthesized are listed in the table below.

The kinins are best detected by means of their contractile action on the isolated guinea-pig ileum or on the isolated uterus of the rat in full oestrus. Bradykinin can be determined by radioimmunoassay by means of its ^{14}C-acetyl derivative [4].

Biosynthesis, metabolism

The inactive precursors of the kinins, the kininogens, are α_2-globulins with a molecular weight of about 50000. These give rise to the plasma kinins through the action of the enzyme kallikrein. A kininogen isolated from bovine serum yielded 20 μg bradykinin/mg [5]. The enzyme kallikrein occurs in urine, sweat, saliva and faeces, its inactive precursor prekallikrein (kallikreinogen) in the pancreas, salivary glands, gut wall, tongue and plasma [2]. In blood, kallikrein is liberated from prekallikrein in the presence of factor XII (HAGEMAN factor). Free kallikrein is inhibited by substances in various tissues, particularly the lungs and salivary glands.

In blood the kinin kallidin is rapidly converted into bradykinin by an aminopeptidase. In the plasma of adults the bradykinin level is less than 2 μg/l [6]; in cord blood the mean level is 12.8 μg/l [6]. Higher values occur in shock, acute pancreatitis and the carcinoid syndrome [3,7]. The plasma kinins are rapidly broken down by peptidases into inactive fragments [7]. Kinin-inactivating enzymes are present in many tissues, for instance in the liver, spleen, kidneys, lungs and lymph glands. When injected intravenously bradykinin is metabolized in the blood with a half-life of 30 s [8]. Urine contains two urokinins with a pharmacological activity resembling that of bradykinin and kallidin, but these probably originate not in the blood but in the epithelium of the renal tubules [9].

Biological activity

The plasma kinins have a contractile effect on smooth muscle, for instance that of the gut, uterus and bronchi, and lower the blood pressure and increase vascular permeability when given intravenously; they cause pain when applied to the base of a cantharides blister. The effect of bradykinin on the isolated rat uterus is about the same as that of oxytocin [3]. The blood pressure-lowering effect is due to dilation of the resistant vessels; the heart rate, minute volume and regional blood flow are all increased.

The physiological function of the kinins is not known, but a role in the regulation of the blood flow to the secretory glands has been suggested [10]. Bradykinin is possibly involved in the transition from foetal to newborn circulation [6].

The plasma kinins play a role in two diseases, hereditary angioneurotic oedema, due to a dominantly inherited, congenital deficiency of plasma kallikrein inhibitors [11], and the carcinoid syndrome, in which the flush-producing principle is identical with bradykinin [12]. The role played by the plasma kinins in inflammatory reactions remains obscure, but it seems that the kinin-forming system is activated wherever tissues are damaged [14]. Kinins have been detected in the synovial fluid of patients with arthritis [2].

Structure and biological activity of naturally occurring plasma kinins [13]

	Mol.wt.	Structure	Relative activity		Occurrence
			in vitro*	in vivo**	
Bradykinin (kallidin I, kallidin-9, kinin-9)	1060	Arg·Pro·Pro·Gly·Phe·Ser·Pro·Phe·Arg	100	100	Bovine plasma, human plasma
Kallidin (kallidin II, lysylbradykinin, kinin-10)	1188	Lys·Arg·Pro·Pro·Gly·Phe·Ser·Pro·Phe·Arg	33	190	Bovine plasma, human plasma
Methionylkallidin (methionyllysylbradykinin, kinin-11)	1329	Met·Lys·Arg·Pro·Pro·Gly·Phe·Ser·Pro·Phe·Arg	25	–	Bovine plasma

* Contraction of the isolated guinea-pig ileum. ** Lowering of blood pressure in rabbits.

References

1 WERLE, E., *Münch.med.Wschr.*, **105**, 2486 (1963); SCHACHTER, M., *Ann. Rev. Pharmacol.*, **4**, 281 (1964); KELLERMEYER and GRAHAM, *New Engl.J.Med.*, **279**, 754, 802, 859 (1968).
2 WEBSTER, M.E., *Arthr.and Rheum.*, **9**, 473 (1966).
3 STÜRMER, E., *Schweiz.med.Wschr.*, **96**, 1667 (1966).
4 RINDERKNECHT et al., *Nature*, **213**, 1130 (1967).
5 HABERMANN, E., *Biochem.Z.*, **337**, 440 (1963).
6 MELMON et al., *J.clin.Invest.*, **46**, 1094 (1967).
7 ERDÖS, E.G., *Gastroenterology*, **51**, 893 (1966).
8 GERSMEYER and SPITZBARTH, *Klin.Wschr.*, **39**, 1227 (1961).
9 YOSHINAGA et al., *Experientia (Basel)*, **20**, 396 (1964).
10 HILTON and LEWIS, *Brit.med.Bull.*, **13**, 189 (1957).
11 LANDERMAN et al., *J.Allergy*, **33**, 330 (1962).
12 OATES et al., *Lancet*, **1**, 514 (1964); OATES et al., *J.clin.Invest.*, **45**, 173 (1966).
13 SCHROEDER and LUEBKE, *The Peptides*, vol.2, Academic Press, New York, 1966.
14 LEWIS, G.P., in ROBSON and STACEY (Eds.), *Recent Advances in Pharmacology*, 4th ed., Churchill, London, 1968, page 213.

Corticosteroids

(adrenocortical hormones) (for references see pages 750–751)

Chemistry

The corticosteroids consist of C_{21}-steroids containing at least three oxygen atoms and are present in the adrenal cortex, blood and urine [1]. The structural formulae of the seven most important biologically active corticosteroids are shown below. Biological activity requires the presence of the Δ^4-3-keto configuration in ring A and of a keto group in the side chain. Characteristic of aldosterone is the aldehyde group (C-18). Other steroids formed in the adrenal cortex are pregnanetriol and the androgens dehydroepiandrosterone, androstenedione and 11β-hydroxyandrostenedione.

Cortisol (hydrocortisone)

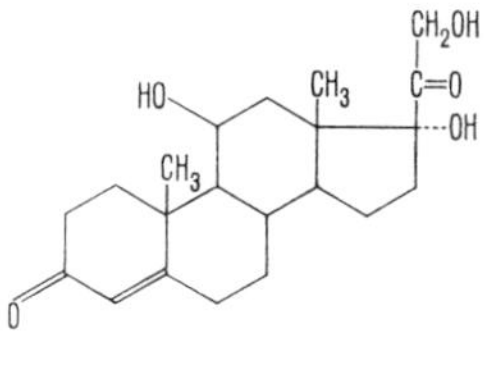

Cortisone

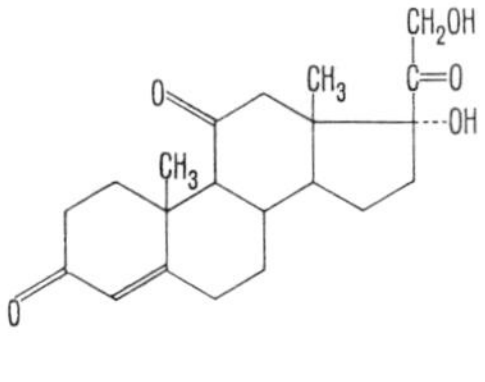

(For references see pages 750–751)

Corticosterone

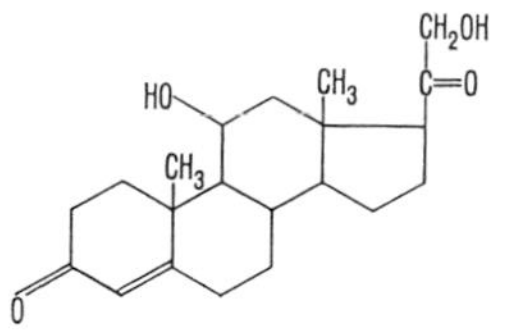

Dehydrocorticosterone
(11-dehydrocorticosterone)

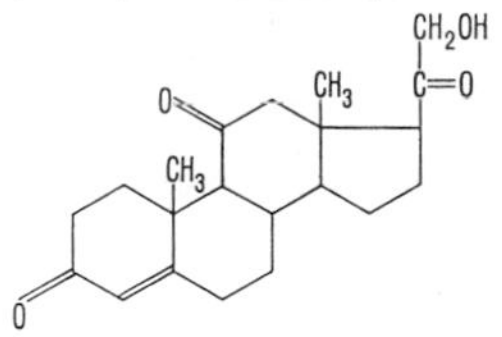

11-Deoxycorticosterone (cortexone)

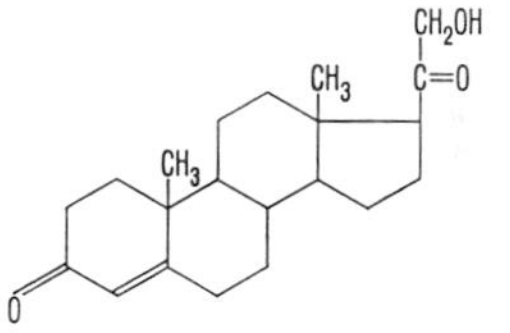

11-Deoxycortisol (cortexolone)

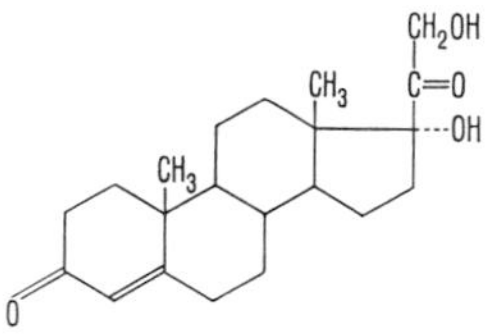

Aldosterone

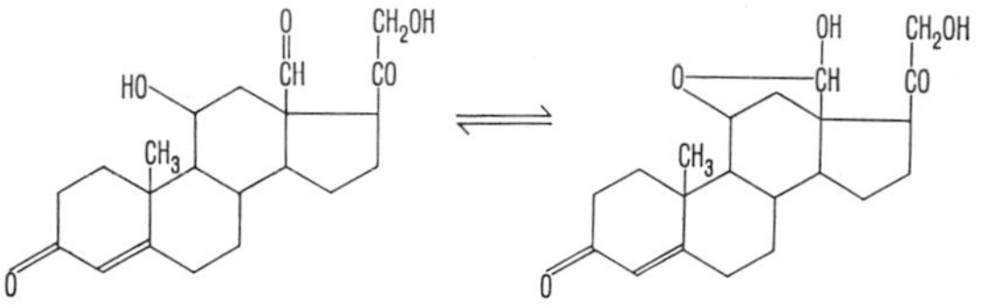

Assay[2]

The hormones must first be extracted from the tissue by means of a suitable solvent. During extraction and subsequent operations care must be taken to avoid the formation of artefacts, either as a result of autoxidation in air or of the techniques employed.

By using group-specific methods, various classes of steroids can be determined (see the table on page 744)[3,4]. If the individual steroids are to be determined, the mixture must first be separated by paper, thin-layer or gas chromatography[5]; occasionally countercurrent distribution may be necessary[3]. Enzymatic methods of assay using specific hydroxysteroid dehydrogenases have been developed[6].

Aldosterone is determined colorimetrically by the method of Neher and Wettstein[7] or by the double isotope dilution technique of Kliman and Peterson[8] (on methods in general see Tait and Tait[9]). The method of Neher and Wettstein[7] can also be used for cortisol and cortisone. Pregnanetriol can be determined by the methods of Bongiovanni and Eberlein[10,96] or Harkness and Love[54], dehydroepiandrosterone by the method of Fotherby[11].

The many biological methods for assay of corticosteroids (for a review see Dorfman[12]), while no longer of clinical interest, are useful for assessing the physiological activity of synthetic compounds. 'Glucocorticoid' activity (see page 748) is best determined by the increase in glycogen synthesis in the liver of fasting, adrenalectomized rats or mice[13,14], 'mineralocorticoid' activity (see page 748) by the decrease in the $^{24}Na/^{42}K$ ratio in the urine of adrenalectomized rats after injection of these isotopes[15].

Biosynthesis, secretion, metabolism

Of the steroids formed in the adrenal cortex, those affecting salt and water balance (aldosterone and, less active in this respect, corticosterone) originate in the outermost layer (zona glomerulosa), those affecting carbohydrate metabolism (cortisol, cortisone and, less active in this respect, corticosterone) in the middle layer (zona fasciculata), and the 17-ketosteroids (mainly dehydroepiandrosterone) in the innermost layer (zona reticularis).

The pattern of corticosteroids secreted differs from one animal species to another. In man, those secreted in the largest amounts are cortisol and corticosterone. The cortisol/corticosterone ratio in the venous blood of the adrenals is 0.5–5, in the peripheral blood 5–30, the difference being due to the more rapid breakdown of corticosterone[16].

After birth the final division of the adrenal cortex into its three zones takes place during the first few months of life, after disappearance of the foetal X-zone. In the newborn the corticosteroid pattern therefore differs from those of older children and adults[17,102].

The biosynthesis of the corticosteroids is discussed on pages 428 to 430. Since the adrenal cortex is incapable of storing large amounts

(continued on page 745)

Corticosteroid content of the normal adrenal gland[55]

	µg/g tissue	
	Mean	Range
Aldosterone	0.06	0.05–0.08
Corticosterone	1.7	0.73–2.9
Cortisol	2.7	0.97–3.9
Cortisone	0.05	0–0.10

Rates of secretion of corticosteroids

	Mean	Range	*s*	Reference
Aldosterone (µg/24 h)				
Newborn	23	9–41	12	75
Infants	72	25–138	29.5	75
Children, 1–15 years	91	57–162	30.4	75
Adults	80	39–138	30.8	75
Adults	135	70–210	–	76
Men, 18–35 years	77	40–110	–	77
Men, 67–88 years	34	20–72	–	77
Women, proliferative phase	139	–	44	78
Women, luteal phase	235	–	101	78
Women, pregnant	–	387–2912	–	79
Corticosterone				
(mg/24 h)				
Adults	2.3	1.5–4.0	–	80
Adults	3.22	2.1–4.2	–	81
(mg/24 h/m² body surface)				
Infants up to 3 months	2.5	–	–	82
Children	0.65	–	–	82
Cortisol				
(mg/24 h)				
Infants up to 3 months	3.8	–	–	83
Children	16	8.5–22.5	–	83
Adults	–	4.9–27.9	–	84
Adults	16.0	10.5–23.5	–	81
Women	17.5	11.4–20.9	1.9	85
Men	21.0	15.9–27.4	3.1	85
Old men	17.7	12.3–23.0	–	86
Pregnant women	15.0	11.3–18.9	–	85
(mg/24 h/m² body surface)				
Newborn, up to 5 days	18.7	–	3.7	87
Infants, 5–20 days	13.9	–	2.9	87
Persons, 4 months–20 years	12.1	–	2.9	87
Dehydroepiandrosterone sulphate				
(mg/24 h)				
Women	12	10–18.5	–	88
Men	17	14–22	–	88
Deoxycorticosterone (µg/24 h)	–	50–160	–	89
11-Deoxycortisol (mg/24 h)	–	0.20–2.0	–	90
18-Hydroxycorticosterone (µg/24h)	305	145–460	–	76

(For references see pages 750–751)

Group-specific methods of corticosteroid assay

Steroid class	Specific chemical structure	Method	Reference
Porter-Silber chromogens.....	17,21-Dihydroxy-20-keto (dihydroxyacetone) side chain (see below)	Colour reaction with phenylhydrazine in ethanolic sulphuric acid	Porter and Silber[61], Peterson et al.[62]
21-Deoxyketols................	17-Hydroxy-20-keto-21-deoxy side chain (see below)	Specific oxidation to 17-ketosteroids followed by Zimmermann's reaction (see under '17-Ketosteroids' below)	Appleby and Norymberski[63]
		Vanillin-phosphoric acid method	McAleer and Kozlowski[64]
17-Ketogenic steroids	Side chain as shown below	Specific oxidation to 17-ketosteroids followed by Zimmermann's reaction (see under '17-Ketosteroids' below)	Norymberski et al.[65]
Total 17-hydroxycorticosteroids .	Side chain as shown below	Specific oxidation to 17-ketosteroids followed by Zimmermann's reaction (see under '17-Ketosteroids' below)	Appleby et al.[66], Few[67]
17-Deoxycorticosteroids	17-Deoxy-20-keto-21-hydroxy side chain (see below)	Specific oxidation to aldehydes and colour reaction of hydroxamic acids	Exley et al.[68]
Reducing corticosteroids........	20-Keto-21-hydroxy side chain (α-ketol group)	Alkaline reduction of blue tetrazolium to a coloured diformazan	Mader and Ruck[69]
11-Hydroxycorticosteroids	Δ^4-11-Hydroxy configuration	Fluorescence in ethanolic sulphuric acid	Mattingly[70], Silber[71]
Δ^5-3β-Hydroxysteroids	Δ^5-3β-Hydroxy configuration (e.g., pregnenolone, but not cholesterol)	Colour reaction in ethanolic sulphuric acid	Oertel and Eik-Nes[72]
Δ^4-3-Ketosteroids.............	α,β-Unsaturated ketones	Colour reaction with isonicotinic hydrazide	Umberger[73]
17-Ketosteroids	Contain $-CO-CH_2-$ group; the 17-keto group is the most reactive	Colour reaction with *m*-dinitrobenzene in alkaline solution	Zimmermann[74]

Structure of steroid side chains

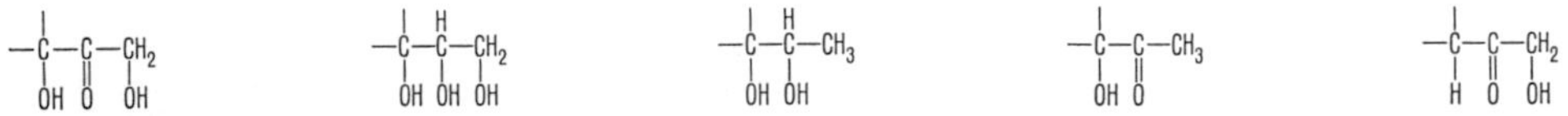

Porter-Silber chromogens

21-Deoxyketols

17-Deoxycorticosteroids

17-Ketogenic steroids

Total 17-hydroxycorticosteroids

(For references see pages 750–751)

of corticosteroids it must be in a position to respond quickly to an increased need with an increase in the rate of biosynthesis. The formation of hormones is stimulated by ACTH; this applies particularly to cortisone, less so to corticosterone and aldosterone (see page 717). An important part in aldosterone secretion is played by angiotensin, a substance whose formation by the catalytic action of renin is increased when the blood volume is diminished or there is sodium deficiency (see page 741).

The rate at which the hormones are secreted can be determined directly or indirectly[18]. The direct methods necessitate a major surgical operation, namely collection of the whole of the venous blood of the adrenals; the indirect methods, for instance urinary analysis, demand precise knowledge of the changes undergone by the secreted steroids as a result not only of metabolic action but also of the analytical procedures. Best results are given by isotope dilution techniques[19, 20].

In health, the normal adult secretes 5–28 mg cortisol per day (see the table on page 743); in CUSHING's syndrome values up to 418 mg cortisol per day have been recorded[21], in ADDISON's disease as little as 0.8 mg per day[20]. The daily cortisol requirement of the adrenalectomized adult is at least 20–30 mg.

The daily aldosterone secretion of the normal adult is 40–200 μg (see the table on page 743); it falls as the sodium intake rises and increases up to 1500 μg per day when the sodium intake is severely limited[17]. Doses of 150–200 μg aldosterone per day are sufficient to suppress the symptoms of ADDISON's disease, in which aldosterone secretion is very low. An increased aldosterone secretion is generally found in CONN's syndrome[20].

Corticosteroids in plasma (μg/l)

	Mean	Range	s	Reference
Aldosterone				
Men	0.06	0.02–0.15	–	91
Adults	0.22	0.06–0.59	–	27
Corticosterone				
Cord blood	58	–	33	92
Children, 3–7 days	63	–	41	92
Children, 3 months–5 years	45	–	22	92
Children, 11–17 years	36	–	24	92
Adults	36	–	18	92
Adults	11	5–20	3	93
Cortisol				
Newborn, up to 12 hours	71	33–198	31.5	94
Infants, 12–24 hours	38	10–107	30.0	94
Infants, 36–48 hours	42	15–66	23.5	94
Infants, 1–5 months	47	38–62	10.4	94
Cord blood	129	–	47	92
Infants, 3–7 days	140	–	48	92
Children, 3 months–5 years	124	–	50	92
Children, 11-17 years	124	–	54	92
Adults	117	–	27	92
Adults	150	–	–	93
Adults	–	21–226	–	95
Cortisone				
Newborn, up to 12 hours	53	24–97	22.4	94
Infants, 12–24 hours	45	24–96	19.0	94
Infants, 36–48 hours	39	20–60	13.5	94
Infants, 1–5 months	6	0–9	4.0	94
11-Deoxycortisol	–	0–14	–	95
Pregnanetriol	–	<50	–	96

The adrenal cortex of both men and women also secretes a conjugated 17-ketosteroid, dehydroepiandrosterone sulphate, at the rate of about 15 mg per day. Free dehydroepiandrosterone is secreted only in small amounts. A further adrenocortical steroid is pregnanetriol, a metabolite of 17α-hydroxyprogesterone.

Corticosteroids in blood. Cortisol and corticosterone are released from the adrenal cortex in unconjugated form and remain so in the circulating blood (for normal values see the table below).

Metabolites of both these steroids are present in the conjugated form in the plasma, as shown by a comparison between the conjugated and unconjugated corticosteroids in the table. Dehydroepiandrosterone is released from the adrenal cortex as sulphate and is found in the blood in this form (see page 752).

Corticosteroid fractions in plasma (μg/l)[56]

	Mean	s
Porter-Silber chromogens		
Unconjugated	129	43
Conjugated	173	56
Δ^4-3-Ketosteroids		
Unconjugated	133	49
Conjugated	118	63
Reducing corticosteroids		
Unconjugated	216	59
Conjugated	750	248

95–97% of the cortisol in the plasma is bound to a protein – probably an α-globulin – known as 'corticosteroid-binding globulin' or 'transcortin'[22]. This protein binds cortisol more strongly than corticosterone; the conjugated cortisol metabolites are not normally bound to protein. A number of studies have shown aldosterone to be only weakly bound to protein[23], mainly albumin. The small proportion of cortisol not bound to protein probably represents the active form of the hormone. The concentration of 'active' corticosteroids in the tissues is only about 10^{-8}-molar. The cortisol and cortisone contents of the parotid saliva are a good measure of the amount of active cortisol in the blood[24]. Like the ACTH content, the corticosteroid content of the blood is subject to a 24-hour rhythm. The fluctuations of the cortisol content during the day are due to the alternation between waking and sleeping, those of the aldosterone content to the alternation between the upright and recumbent postures[25].

17-Hydroxycorticosteroid content of the plasma of 5 adults during the course of the day[25]

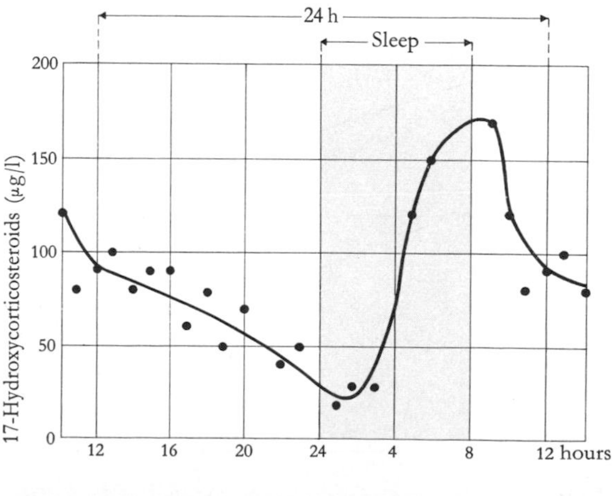

Relationship of important urinary steroid fractions to the steroids of the adrenal cortex and testes

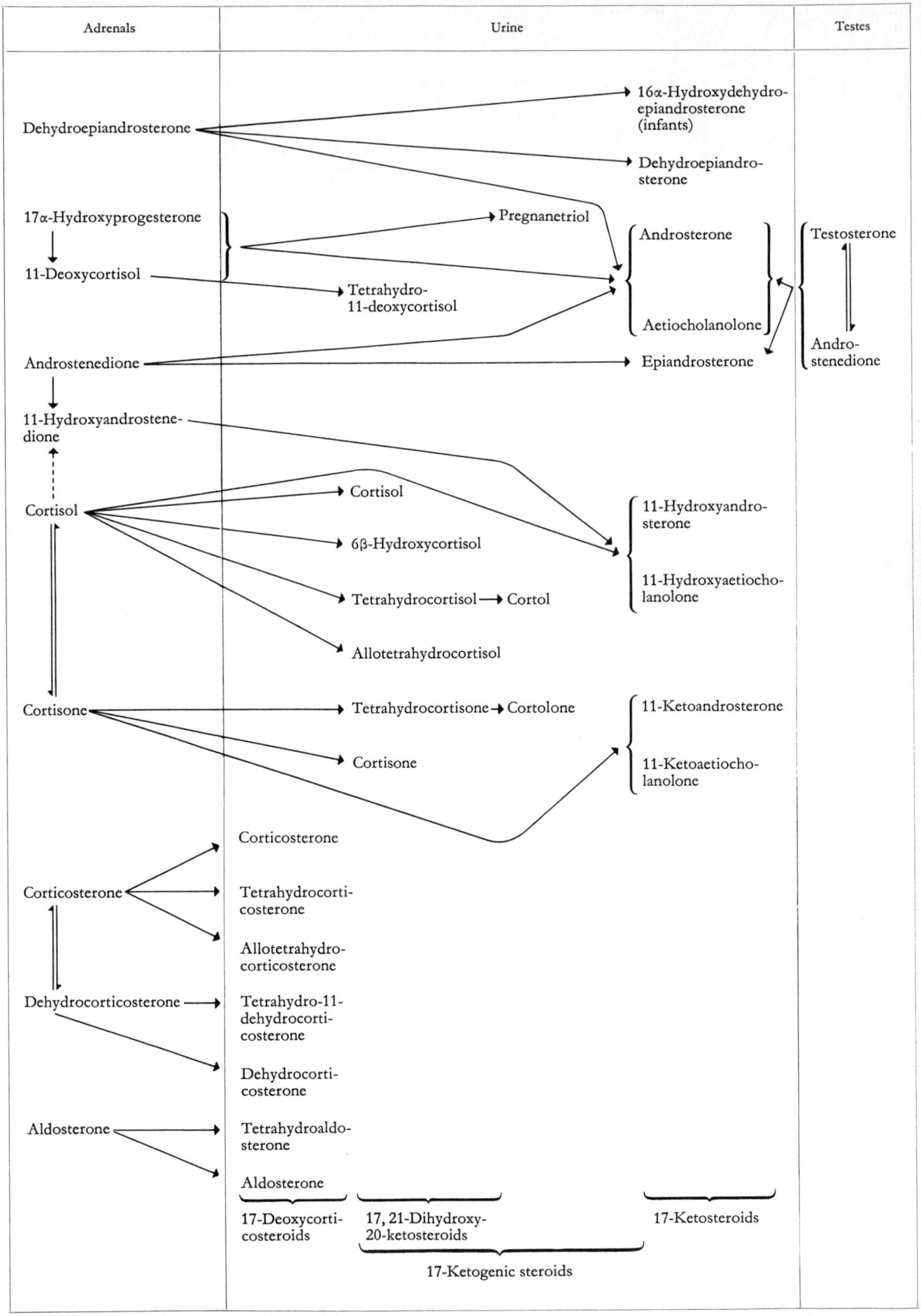

(For references see pages 750–751)

Metabolism of the corticosteroids. The half-life of injected cortisol in the circulating blood is 1.4–3 h, that of corticosterone 0.9–1.6 h, that of cortisone about 30 min[26]; the corresponding value for aldosterone is 33 min[27]. The main site of breakdown of the corticosteroids is the liver, but aldosterone is also metabolized in the kidneys[28]. Reduction of ring A of cortisol and corticosterone gives rise to the corresponding tetrahydro derivatives, reduction of the 20-keto group to α- and β-cortol and α- and β-cortolone. Aldosterone is also reduced to the tetrahydro derivative, but dehydroepiandrosterone is excreted mainly unchanged. Almost all the metabolites appear in the conjugated form as glucuronides or sulphates. For a further discussion of corticosteroid metabolism see pages 428–430.

Corticosteroids in urine. Both corticosteroids and their metabolites are excreted in the urine. Normal values are given in the following tables and figures (pages 747–749). Determination of the individual steroids is too complicated a procedure for the routine laboratory, so that usually only the various steroid groups are determined (see the table on page 744). A difficulty is that to some extent the same metabolites originate from steroids formed in the testes, as shown in the scheme opposite. There are differences of opinion as to which of the usual corticosteroid fractions determined in urine – the

Urinary excretion of cortisol[57], cortisone[57] and aldosterone[58] in children and adults

	Cortisol		Cortisone		Aldosterone	
	μg/24 h	μg/24 h/kg body weight	μg/24 h	μg/24 h/kg body weight	μg/24 h	μg/24 h/kg body weight
Up to 1 year	1.0	0.11	6.9	0.86	2.1	0.24
1–5 years	3.9	0.23	14.4	0.85	3.5	0.23
6–10 years	7.3	0.26	23.9	0.76	4.9	0.17
11–15 years	14.4	0.29	35.2	0.71	6.5	0.13
16–20 years	20.6	0.33	47.2	0.76	6.6	0.10
21–30 years	31.3	0.42	65.7	0.89	7.5	0.10

Urinary corticosteroid excretion during pregnancy[30]

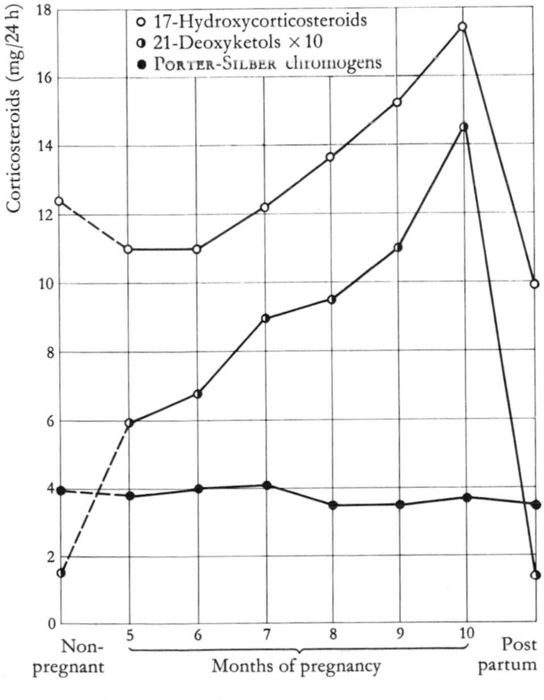

Urinary excretion of corticosteroids
(values for adults unless otherwise stated)

	Mean	Range	Reference
Aldosterone (μg/24 h)	5	2–10	97
Aldosterone, free (μg/24 h)			
Newborn	–	0.03–0.13	98
Adults	–	0.17–0.63	99
18-Aldosterone glucuronide (μg/24 h)			
Newborn	–	0.4–2.5	98
Adults	5.6	3.0–12.0	99
Corticosterone (mg/24 h)	0.02	0–0.04	97
Cortisol (mg/24 h)	0.07	0.03–0.09	97
Cortisol, free (mg/24 h)	0.019	–	100
Cortisol glucuronide (mg/24 h)	0.025	–	100
Cortisone (mg/24 h)	0.09	0.06–0.14	97
Cortisone, free (mg/24 h)	0.057	–	100
Cortisone glucuronide (mg/24 h)	0.063	–	100
Cortolone (mg/24 h)			
Men	1.9	0.3–2.9	99
Women	1.1	0.5–1.6	99
11-Dehydrocorticosterone (mg/24 h)	0.01	0–0.03	97
6β-Hydroxycortisol (mg/24 h)			
Men	0.44	–	99
Women	0.37	–	99
16-Hydroxydehydroepiandrosterone (mg/24 h)			
Newborn, up to 7 days	0.29	0.0–1.1	101
Infants, 4–6 months	0.04	0.0–0.16	101
16-Hydroxypregnenolone (mg/24 h)			
Newborn, up to 7 days	0.98	0.05–3.6	101
Infants, 4–6 months	0.02	0.0–0.08	101
Pregnanetriol (mg/24 h)			
Children before puberty	–	<0.1	102
Men	–	0.11–0.97	103
Women	–	0.11–0.45	103
Tetrahydroaldosterone (μg/24 h)			
Newborn	–	1.9–7.2	98
Adults	–	40–60	99
Tetrahydrocorticosterone (mg/24 h)	0.20	0.10–0.36	97
allo-Tetrahydrocorticosterone (mg/24 h)	0.20	0.08–0.36	97
Tetrahydrocortisol (mg/24 h)	1.0	0.6–1.6	97
Men	2.2	0.8–2.8	99
Women	1.9	0.5–3.7	99
allo-Tetrahydrocortisol (mg/24 h)	0.4	0.1–0.7	97
	1.1	0–2.8	99
Tetrahydrocortisone (mg/24 h)	2.7	1.0–3.8	97
Tetrahydro-11-dehydrocorticosterone (mg/24 h)	0.16	0.06–0.24	97
Tetrahydro-11-deoxycortisol (mg/24)	0.06	0.02–0.10	97

(For references see pages 750–751)

Urinary excretion of 17-ketogenic steroids in women and men[29] (98% confidence limits)

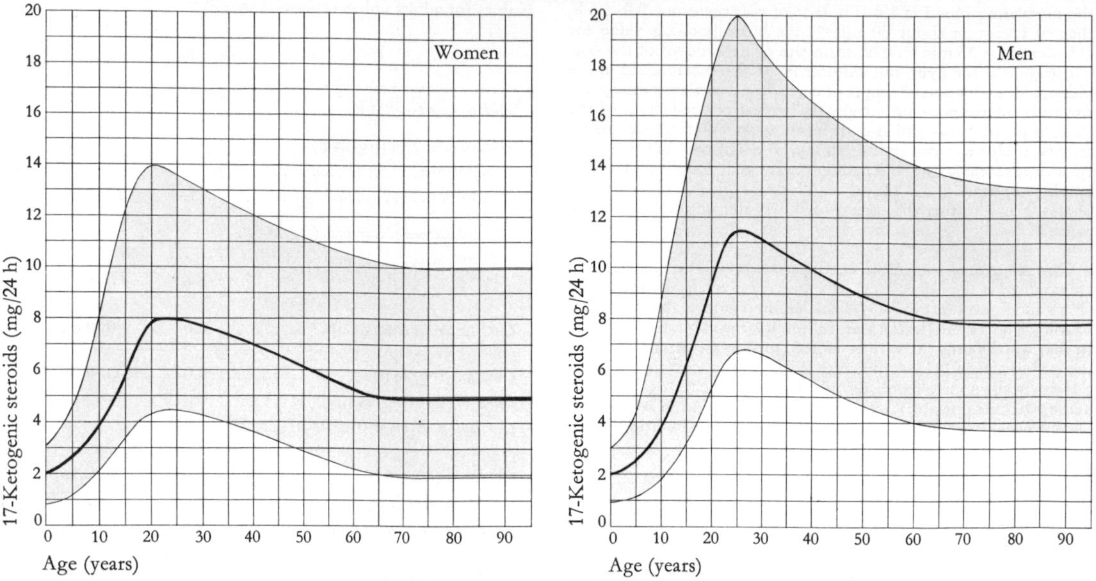

Urinary excretion of 17-ketosteroids in women and men[31] (mean and 98% confidence limits)

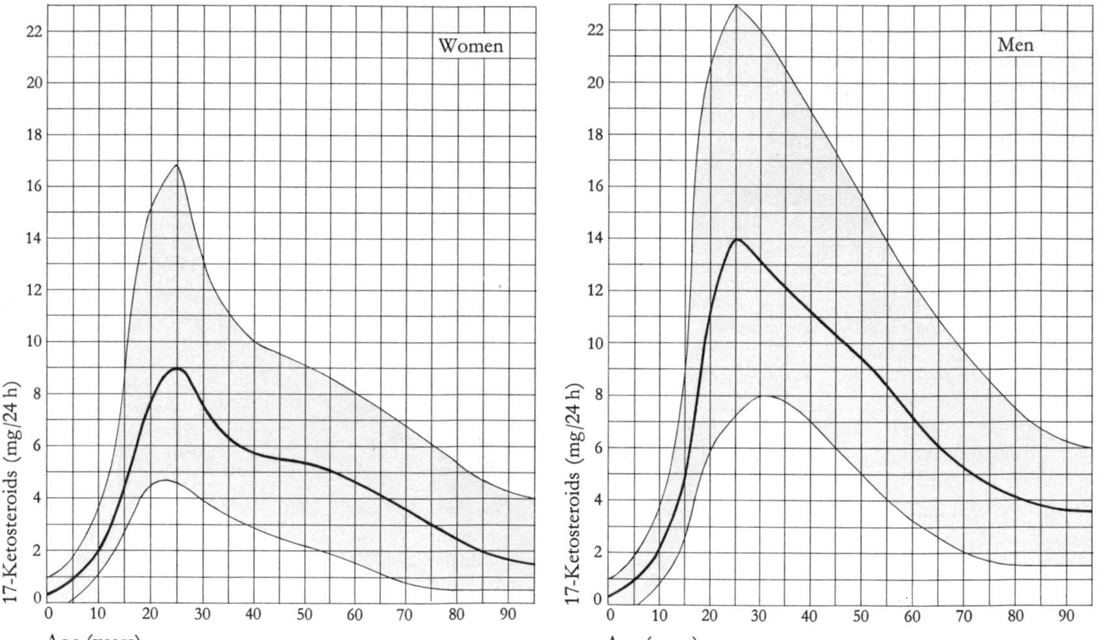

17-ketosteroids, the 17-ketogenic steroids or the 11-hydroxycorticosteroids – best represents the corticosteroid production of the adrenals[32, 33, 99]. In men, about two-thirds of the total 17-ketosteroids are corticosteroid metabolites, one-third testicular steroid metabolites; in women they arise mainly from the corticosteroids, with a small contribution from the ovaries.

In assessing the significance of the urinary aldosterone excretion the state of hydration of the body as well as the potassium and sodium balance must be taken into account. The urinary pregnanetriol level is a valuable indication in patients with congenital adrenocortical hyperplasia. 16α-Hydroxypregnenolone and 16α-hydroxydehydroepiandrosterone – both steroids of adrenal origin – have been found only in the urine of the newborn and infants; they are probably precursors of the oestrogens formed by the placenta.

Functional tests

The functional capacity of the adrenal cortex is determined by assaying the corticosteroids in the blood or urine after an exogenous dose of ACTH, usually 25–50 IU given intravenously[33, 99]. More recently, the synthetic polypeptide tetracosactrin (β^{1-24}-corticotropin) has also been used for this purpose[34]: in 66 subjects given an intramuscular dose of 0.25 mg the plasma level of 11-hydroxycorticosteroids rose from 147 µg/l to 314 µg/l within 30 minutes.

Urinary excretion of 17-ketosteroids in children and adults (mg/24 h)

	Number	11-Hydroxy-aetiocholanolone		11-Hydroxy-androsterone		11-Keto-aetiocholanolone		Dehydroepi-androsterone		Aetiocho-lanolone		Androsterone		Reference
		Mean	Range	Mean	Range	Mean	Range	Mean	Range	Mean	Range	Mean	Range	
Boys, 3–12 years....	9	0.35	0.03–0.88	0.45	0.09–0.92	0.34	0.03–0.62	0.10	<0.01–0.33	0.35	0.04–0.82	0.32	0.07–0.82	104
Girls, 3–11 years....	14	0.25	0.01–0.73	0.64	0.10–1.74	0.33	0.03–0.84	0.08	<0.01–0.34	0.50	0.01–1.56	0.67	0.01–2.28	104
Men, 19–43 years...	10	0.6	0.3–1.1	1.6	1.0–2.1	0.6	0.3–1.4	2.3	0.8–6.4	2.8	1.4–5.1	3.4	1.5–6.0	104
Women, 18–43 years	25	0.6	0.2–1.2	1.4	0.2–2.9	0.7	0.2–1.4	1.1	0.1–2.6	2.7	0.7–4.3	3.1	0.9–4.8	104
Men, 50–71 years...	11	0.8	0.2–2.2	1.7	0.8–3.1	0.7	0.2–1.5	0.7	<0.1–4.0	2.5	1.1–5.0	1.8	1.0–3.8	104
Women, 46–70 years	21	0.6	0.2–1.5	1.0	0.5–1.9	0.7	0.3–1.4	0.3	<0.1–0.7	2.2	0.9–3.7	1.3	0.5–3.8	104
Men	8	0.7	0.3–1.6	0.6	0.3–1.0	0.7	0.2–1.1	0.6	0.1–1.4	2.1	1.0–3.1	2.1	1.1–3.5	105
Women	8	0.9	0.6–1.9	0.5	0.1–0.9	0.5	0.2–0.7	0.4	0.1–1.1	1.9	1.3–3.9	1.6	0.3–3.6	105

Diseases of the adrenal cortex can be identified by means of steroid suppression tests. These depend on the fact that cortisol secretion by the adrenal cortex – so long as it is dependent on the pituitary ACTH – can be suppressed by exogenous doses of corticosteroids. A test of this kind using oral doses of dexamethasone has been standardized by LIDDLE[35]. The metyrapone test is described on page 717.

Unlike the chemical assay of corticosteroids in body fluids, indirect functional tests are not of great diagnostic value. The commonest are the eosinophil test (THORN's test)[36], the diuresis test[37] and tests involving studies of the electrolyte balance.

Biological activity[38]

Broadly speaking, the hormones of the adrenal cortex are responsible for the maintenance of homoeostasis; they enable the body to cope with all the internal and external demands made upon it. The increased corticosteroid activity necessitated by these demands is made possible through the action of corticotropin (ACTH), the secretion of which is in turn controlled by the hypothalamus and other brain centres[39] (see also under 'Corticotropin', page 717). The various corticosteroids differ in the manner and degree of their activity, as shown in the table below. There are also species differences in the activity of the corticosteroids; this is particularly marked between rats and man[40].

On the basis of their activity spectra the corticosteroids are often classified into mineralo- and glucocorticosteroids. A strict classification in this way is, however, impossible since the activity spectra overlap. Corticosteroids with an oxygen atom at C-11 mainly have an effect on carbohydrate and protein metabolism. The action of corticosteroids on mineral metabolism is essential for the maintenance of life, and death ensuing after complete failure of the adrenal cortex is mainly a result of sodium deficiency; absence of the corticosteroids can to some extent be compensated for by a high sodium intake. When the adrenal cortex is functioning normally, ACTH has practically the same effect as glucocorticoids.

Action on carbohydrate and protein metabolism[41]. In animals that have been adrenalectomized, starvation leads to rapid depletion of the carbohydrate reserves, with lowering of the blood sugar level and glycogen content of the liver and muscles. Adrenalectomized animals are also hypersensitive to exogenous insulin. Similar disturbances of carbohydrate metabolism occur in patients with ADDISON's disease. Administration of corticosteroids reverses these changes. Corticosteroids cause a rise in both nitrogen excretion and the amino-acid content of the blood, whence it can be concluded that protein is being converted into carbohydrate (gluconeogenesis). The administration of large doses of cortisol results in symptoms similar to those seen in CUSHING's syndrome, namely an increase in the blood-sugar and liver-glycogen levels together with a reduced response to insulin.

This catabolic action of the corticosteroids is reflected in tissue breakdown, diminution of the muscle mass, osteoporosis and thinning of the epidermis. The mechanism of these processes has been only partially elucidated.

Corticosteroids also have an effect, both in vivo and in vitro, on the activity of many enzymes[42]. Thus in the liver they increase the activity of glucose-6-phosphatase and enzymes, like tryptophan oxygenase and tyrosine aminotransferase, involved in amino-acid metabolism. At the same time corticosteroids promote the formation of messenger-RNA and the de novo synthesis of enzymes[42,43]. Possibly this activity derives from a direct effect of corticosteroids on gene activity[44].

Action on lipid metabolism[45]. The glucocorticoids affect lipid metabolism in all its phases – oxidation, synthesis, mobilization and storage. In failure of the adrenal cortex, mobilization of fat from peripheral depots by adrenaline, noradrenaline, growth hormone or fat-mobilizing peptides of the anterior pituitary is greatly reduced, an effect that is reversed by even small doses of cortisol. However, this effect of the corticosteroids on the action of the hormones mentioned appears to be merely a conditioning one, and this function of the adrenal cortex has been described as 'permissive'. The mechanism by which human lipid metabolism is disturbed during cortisol treatment and in the CUSHING syndrome with resultant changes in body-fat deposition remains obscure.

Action on electrolyte and water balance[46]. Disturbances of adrenocortical function are reflected in changes in electrolyte and water balance. Hypofunctioning of the gland results in loss of sodium in the urine, lowering of serum sodium, increase in serum potassium, diminution of the extracellular fluid volume and increased hydration of the cells. Hyperfunctioning causes an increase in the sodium content of the body, a slight rise in the blood sodium and fall in the blood potassium, and an increase in the extracellular fluid volume. Aldosterone and to a lesser extent deoxycorticosterone have markedly greater effects on mineral metabolism than cortisol. Both aldosterone and deoxycorticosterone augment the reabsorption of sodium in the distal renal tubules and at the same time promote potassium excretion, while the resulting sodium retention results also in water retention. Aldosterone most likely acts by promoting active sodium transport, as has been demonstrated in the urinary bladder of the toad[47]. The first event is possibly a direct involvement of aldosterone in the nuclear synthesis of messenger RNA[60].

Cortisol acts in a different way. Like aldosterone, but to a lesser extent, it promotes sodium reabsorption in the distal tubules, but

Relative activity of corticosteroids in adrenalectomized animals[59]

	Decrease in urinary Na^+/K^+ ratio (rats)	Growth and survival (rats)	Survival (dogs)	Muscle-work test (rats)	Glycogen deposition (rats)
Cortisone	0.6	2.5	0.5	10	10
Cortisol	0.8	0.5	–	19	16
Corticosterone ...	1.4	1.7	–	–	5
11-Dehydro-corticosterone..	–	1.0	–	5	5
11-Deoxycortisol .	0.8	–	–	0.2	–
11-Deoxycortico-sterone........	10	10	10	0.2	0.1
Aldosterone	1000	–	250	–	3

the increased potassium excretion seems more likely to be due to mobilization of tissue potassium than to an effect on renal function. The lowered diuresis occurring in adrenocortical insufficiency can be corrected by giving cortisol but not aldosterone. Cortisol appears to be necessary for maintenance of tubular function and thus of normal diuresis.

Action on blood circulation. This is mainly secondary to the action on water and electrolyte balance (reduction of plasma volume and increase in blood viscosity in adrenocortical insufficiency) but the corticosteroids also have a direct effect on the capillaries, arterioles and myocardium. The stimulating effect of corticosteroids on adrenaline release is also reflected in circulatory changes.

Action on muscles. The impairment of muscular function in adrenocortical insufficiency is primarily a result of the reduced circulation. In primary aldosteronism muscle weakness is due to the lowered blood potassium level, in CUSHING's syndrome to the increased breakdown of muscle.

Action on the central nervous system. The corticosteroids affect the excitability of the brain and the emotions. This is mainly a result of the action of these substances on the cerebral circulation and on the metabolism of γ-aminobutyric acid and electrolytes in the brain[48].

Action on lymphatic tissues. Exogenous corticosteroids give rise to marked involution of the lymphatic organs, with involvement of both the parenchymal and reticular connective-tissue cells[49]. In the initial phase there is characteristic breakdown of the thymocytes in the thymus and of the lymphocytes in the lymph glands and to a lesser extent in the spleen. Following this lymphocytolysis is a second phase marked by inhibition of new cell formation on the one hand (manifested by the absence of mitosis in the thymus, lymph glands and spleen) and by degeneration of the reticular connective tissue on the other.

Corticosteroids cause both an increase and decrease in the numbers of circulating antibodies; the mechanism of these effects is still largely obscure. In man, as in monkeys and guinea-pigs, corticosteroids seem to have little effect on antibody formation, but in rabbits, rats and mice antibodies may be suppressed by these substances under certain conditions.

Action on eosinophils. Administration of corticosteroids or ACTH reduces the number of circulating eosinophils, an effect utilized in THORN's test for adrenocortical insufficiency. The mechanism is unknown[50].

Anti-inflammatory action. Administration of glucocorticoids inhibits or suppresses most inflammatory processes of a toxic, allergic, infectious or traumatic nature. Their effect is, however, merely palliative, and the symptoms reappear when the steroids are withdrawn[51]. This action has been ascribed to a protective effect of corticosteroids on the lysosome membranes[52], the liberation of whose protein-splitting enzymes is thought to cause inflammation.

Action on the pituitary. The circulating corticosteroids exert an inhibitory action on pituitary secretion of ACTH (for further discussion see page 717).

Synthetic steroids. Chemical modification of the steroid skeleton has resulted in synthetic compounds of greater physiological activity and higher specificity than the natural corticosteroids. Over 1200 biologically active steroids, natural and synthetic, are now known. In the table on this page the effects of some synthetic steroids are compared with those of cortisone and cortisol.

Physiological activity of natural and synthetic steroids[53]

	Anti-inflammatory activity	Sodium retention	Potassium excretion	Effect on carbohydrate metabolism
Cortisone	1	1	1	1
Cortisol	1–1.25	1–1.25	1	1.25
Prednisone (1-dehydrocortisone)	3–5	slight	slight	3–5
Prednisolone (1-dehydrocortisol)	3–5	slight	slight	3–5
6α-Methylprednisolone	3–5	none	slight	3–5
9α-Fluorocortisol	10–15	300–900	10–25	10–25
Triamcinolone (9α-fluoro-16α-hydroxy-prednisolone)	3–5	none	slight	3–5
Dexamethasone (9α-fluoro-16α-methyl-prednisolone)	15–28	none	slight	30

References

1 BORTH, R., *Acta endocr. (Kbh.)*, **22**, 125 (1956).
2 LORAINE and BELL, *Hormone Assays and their Clinical Application*, 2nd ed., Livingstone, Edinburgh, 1966.
3 CARSTENSEN, H., *Meth. biochem. Anal.*, **9**, 127 (1962).
4 DORFMAN, R.I., in DORFMAN, R.I. (Ed.), *Methods in Hormone Research*, vol. 1, Academic Press, New York, 1962, page 51; PÉRON, F.G., in DORFMAN, R.I. (Ed.), *Methods in Hormone Research*, vol. 1, Academic Press, New York, 1962, page 199.
5 NEHER, R., *Chromatogr. Rev.*, **1**, 99 (1959); BUSH, I.E., *The Chromatography of Steroids*, Pergamon, Oxford, 1961; HEFTMAN, E., *Chromatogr. Rev.*, **7**, 179 (1965); KUKSIS, A., *Meth. biochem. Anal.*, **14**, 325 (1966).
6 TALALAY, P., *Meth. biochem. Anal.*, **8**, 119 (1960).
7 NEHER and WETTSTEIN, *J. clin. Invest.*, **35**, 800 (1956).
8 KLIMAN and PETERSON, *J. biol. Chem.*, **235**, 1639 (1960).
9 TAIT and TAIT, in DORFMAN, R.I., *Methods in Hormone Research*, vol. 1, Academic Press, New York, 1962, page 265.
10 BONGIOVANNI and EBERLEIN, *Analyt. Chem.*, **30**, 388 (1958).
11 FOTHERBY, K., *Biochem. J.*, **73**, 339 (1959).
12 DORFMAN R.I., in DORFMAN, R.I. (Ed.), *Methods in Hormone Research*, vol. 2, Academic Press, New York, 1962, page 325.
13 VENNING et al., *Endocrinology*, **38**, 79 (1946).
14 PABST et al., *Endocrinology*, **41**, 55 (1947).
15 SIMPSON and TAIT, *Endocrinology*, **50**, 150 (1952).
16 NEHER, R., *Advanc. clin. Chem.*, **1**, 127 (1958).
17 MITCHELL, F.L., *Vitam. and Horm.*, **25**, 191 (1967).
18 DORFMAN and UNGAR, *Metabolism of Steroid Hormones*, Academic Press, New York, 1965; EIK-NES and HALL, *Vitam. and Horm.*, **23**, 153 (1965).
19 PEARLMAN, W.H., *Ciba Found. Coll. Endocr.*, **11**, 233 (1957).
20 COPE, C.L., *Adrenal Steroids and Disease*, Pitman, London, 1965.
21 COPE and PEARSON, *J. clin. Path.*, **18**, 82 (1965).
22 SANDBERG et al., *Recent Progr. Hormone Res.*, **13**, 209 (1957); SLAUNWHITE and SANDBERG, *J. clin. Invest.*, **38**, 384 (1959); SANDBERG and SLAUNWHITE, *J. clin. Invest.*, **38**, 1290 (1959); DE MOOR et al., *J. clin. Endocr.*, **26**, 71 (1966).
23 MILLS, I.H., *Recent Progr. Hormone Res.*, **15**, 261 (1959); SANDBERG et al., *J. clin. Invest.*, **39**, 1914 (1960); DAUGHADAY et al., *J. clin. Endocr.*, **21**, 53 (1961).
24 KATZ and SHANNON, *J. clin. Invest.*, **45**, 1031 (1966).
25 LIDDLE, G.W., *Arch. intern. Med.*, **117**, 739 (1966).
26 AYRES et al., *Ciba Found. Coll. Endocr.*, **11**, 309 (1957); PETERSON, R.E., *Recent Progr. Hormone Res.*, **15**, 231 (1959); GALLAGHER, T.F., *Harvey Lect.*, **52**, 1 (1958); PETERSON, R.E., *Ann. N.Y. Acad. Sci.*, **82**, 846 (1959); PETERSON and PIERCE, *J. clin. Invest.*, **39**, 741 (1960).
27 WOLFF et al., *Schweiz. med. Wschr.*, **95**, 387 (1965).
28 DECK and SIEGENTHALER, *Helv. med. Acta*, **32**, 407 (1965); BLEDSOE et al., *J. clin. Invest.*, **45**, 264 (1966).
29 JØRGENSEN, M., *Acta endocr. (Kbh.)*, **26**, 424 (1957).
30 NORYMBERSKI, J.K., in McGOWAN and SANDLER (Eds.), *The Adrenal Cortex*, Pitman, London, 1961, page 88.
31 HAMBURGER, C., *Acta endocr. (Kbh.)*, **1**, 19 (1948), and personal communication, 1967.
32 COPE, C.L., in McGOWAN and SANDLER (Eds.), *The Adrenal Cortex*, Pitman, London, 1961, page 20; MATTINGLY et al., *Lancet*, **2**, 1046 (1964); MATTINGLY and TYLER, *Brit. med. J.*, **4**, 394 (1967).
33 PRUNTY, F.T.G., in GARDINER-HILL, H. (Ed.), *Modern Trends in Endocrinology*, vol. 3, Butterworth, London, 1967, page 169.
34 WOOD et al., *Lancet*, **1**, 243 (1965).
35 LIDDLE, G.W., *J. clin. Endocr.*, **20**, 1539 (1960).
36 RENOLD et al., *J. clin. Endocr.*, **12**, 763 (1952); RANDOLPH, T.G., *J. Lab. clin. Med.*, **34**, 1696 (1949).
37 ROBINSON et al., *Proc. Mayo Clin.*, **16**, 577 (1941).
38 NOBLE, R.L., in PINCUS and THIMANN (Eds.), *The Hormones*, vol. 3, Academic Press, New York, 1955, page 685; TRAVIS and SAYERS, in GOODMAN and GILMAN (Eds.), *The Pharmacological Basis of Therapeutics*, 3rd ed., Macmillan, New York, 1965, page 1608.
39 YATES and URQUHART, *Physiol. Rev.*, **42**, 359 (1962).
40 RINGLER, I., in DORFMAN, R.I. (Ed.), *Methods in Hormone Research*, vol. 3, Academic Press, New York, 1964, page 227.
41 LONG et al., *Endocrinology*, **26**, 309 (1940); LONG et al., in WOLSTENHOLME and O'CONNOR (Eds.), *Metabolic Effects of Adrenal Hormones*, Ciba Foundation Study Group, No. 6, Churchill, London, 1960, page 4; LANDAU, B.R., *Vitam. and Horm.*, **23**, 1 (1965).
42 ROSEN and NICHOL, *Vitam. and Horm.*, **21**, 135 (1963).
43 GARREN et al., *J. molec. Biol.*, **9**, 100 (1964).
44 KARLSON, P. (Ed.), *Mechanisms of Hormone Action*, NATO Advanced Study Institute, Academic Press, New York, 1965; HECHTER and HALKERSTON, *Ann. Rev. Physiol.*, **27**, 133 (1965).
45 RENOLD et al., in WOLSTENHOLME and O'CONNOR (Eds.), *Metabolic Effects of Adrenal Hormones*, Ciba Foundation Study Group, No. 6, Churchill, London, 1960, page 68; WINEGRAD, A.I., *Vitam. and Horm.*, **20**, 141 (1962).
46 LIPSETT et al., in COMAR and BRONNER (Eds.), *Mineral Metabolism*, vol. 1, part B, Academic Press, New York, 1961, page 473; SLATER, J.D.H., *Postgrad. med. J.*, **40**, 479 (1964); LARAGH and KELLY, *Advanc. metab. Dis.*, **1**, 217 (1964).
47 SHARP and LEAF, *Recent Progr. Hormone Res.*, **22**, 431 (1966).
48 WOODBURY, D.M., *Pharmacol. Rev.*, **10**, 275 (1958).
49 BAKER et al., *Amer. J. Anat.*, **88**, 313 (1951); DOUGHERTY and WHITE, *Amer. J. Anat.*, **77**, 81 (1945); DOUGHERTY et al., *Progr. Hematol.*, **3**, 155 (1962).
50 THORN et al., *New Engl. J. Med.*, **248**, 232, 284, 323, 369, 414, 588, 632 (1953).

51 Mills and Moyer (Eds.), *Inflammation and Diseases of Connective Tissue*, Saunders, Philadelphia, 1961.
52 Weissmann and Thomas, *Recent Progr. Hormone Res.*, **20**, 215 (1964).
53 Liddle, G.W., *Ann. N.Y. Acad. Sci.*, **82**, 854 (1959); Tolksdorf, S., *Ann. N.Y. Acad. Sci.*, **82**, 829 (1959); Frawley et al., *Ann. N.Y. Acad. Sci.*, **82**, 868 (1959); Fried and Borman, *Vitam. and Horm.*, **16**, 303 (1958); Soffer and Orr, *Metabolism*, **7**, 383 (1958).
54 Harkness and Love, *Acta endocr.*, **51**, 526 (1966).
55 Louis and Conn, *Recent Progr. Hormone Res.*, **17**, 415 (1961).
56 Weichselbaum and Margraf, *J. clin. Endocr.*, **17**, 959 (1957).
57 Minick, M.C., *Metabolism*, **15**, 359 (1966).
58 Minick and Conn, *Metabolism*, **13**, 681 (1964).
59 Fruton and Simmonds, *General Biochemistry*, 2nd ed., Wiley, New York, 1958, page 947.
60 Edelman and Fimognari, *Recent Progr. Hormone Res.*, **24**, 1 (1968).
61 Porter and Silber, *J. biol. Chem.*, **185**, 201 (1950).
62 Peterson et al., *Analyt. Chem.*, **29**, 144 (1957).
63 Appleby and Norymberski, *Biochem. J.*, **60**, 460 (1955).
64 McAleer and Kozlowski, *Arch. Biochem.*, **62**, 196 (1956).
65 Norymberski et al., *Lancet*, **1**, 1276 (1953).
66 Appleby et al., *Biochem. J.*, **60**, 453 (1955).
67 Few, J.D., *J. Endocr.*, **22**, 31 (1961).
68 Exley et al., *Biochem. J.*, **81**, 428 (1961).
69 Mader and Buck, *Analyt. Chem.*, **24**, 666 (1952).
70 Mattingly, D., *J. clin. Path.*, **15**, 374 (1962).
71 Silber, R.H., *Meth. biochem. Anal.*, **14**, 63 (1966).
72 Oertel and Eik-Nes, *Analyt. Chem.*, **31**, 98 (1959).
73 Umberger, E.J., *Analyt. Chem.*, **27**, 768 (1955).
74 Zimmermann, W., *Hoppe-Seylers Z. physiol. Chem.*, **233**, 257 (1935), and **300**, 141 (1955).
75 Weldon et al., *Pediatrics*, **39**, 713 (1967).
76 Ulick and Vetter, *J. clin. Endocr.*, **25**, 1015 (1965).
77 Flood et al., *J. clin. Invest.*, **46**, 960 (1967).
78 Gray et al., *J. clin. Endocr.*, **28**, 1269 (1968).
79 Watanabe et al., *J. clin. Invest.*, **42**, 1619 (1963).
80 Peterson and Pierce, *J. clin. Invest.*, **39**, 741 (1960).
81 Karl and Raith, *Klin. Wschr.*, **44**, 303 (1966).
82 Loras et al., in *Second International Congress on Hormonal Steroids*, Milan 1966, Excerpta Medica Foundation, Amsterdam, 1966, page 175.
83 Bertrand et al., *Acta endocr. (Kbh.)*, suppl. 89, 16 (1964).
84 Cope and Black, *Brit. med. J.*, **1**, 1020 (1958).
85 Migeon et al., *Metabolism*, **12**, 718 (1963).
86 Romanoff et al., *J. clin. Endocr.*, **21**, 1413 (1961).
87 Kenny et al., in *Second International Congress on Hormonal Steroids*, Milan 1966, Excerpta Medica Foundation, Amsterdam, 1966, page 175.
88 Baulieu et al., *Recent Progr. Hormone Res.*, **21**, 411 (1965).
89 Biglieri et al., *J. clin. Invest.*, **45**, 1946 (1966).
90 Verdonck et al., in *Second International Congress on Hormonal Steroids*, Milan 1966, Excerpta Medica Foundation, Amsterdam, 1966, page 299.
91 Peterson, R.E., in Baulieu and Robel (Eds.), *Aldosterone*, Blackwell, Oxford, 1964, page 145.
92 Hughes et al., *Amer. J. Dis. Child.*, **104**, 605 (1962).
93 Peterson, R.E., *J. biol. Chem.*, **225**, 25 (1957).
94 Hillman and Giroud, *J. clin. Endocr.*, **25**, 243 (1965).
95 Waxman et al., *J. clin. Endocr.*, **21**, 943 (1961).
96 Bongiovanni et al., *J. clin. Endocr.*, **24**, 1312 (1964).
97 Cost and Vegter, *Acta endocr. (Kbh.)*, **41**, 571 (1962).
98 New et al., *J. clin. Invest.*, **45**, 412 (1966).
99 Tamm, J., in Bartelheimer and Jores (Eds.), *Klinische Funktionsdiagnostik*, 3rd ed., Thieme, Stuttgart, 1967, page 44.
100 Brouillet and Mattox, *J. clin. Endocr.*, **26**, 453 (1966).
101 Reynolds, J.W., *J. clin. Endocr.*, **25**, 416 (1965).
102 Visser, H.K.A., *Arch. Dis. Childh.*, **41**, 2 (1966).
103 Kinoshita et al., *J. clin. Endocr.*, **26**, 1219 (1966).
104 Feher, T., *Clin. chim. Acta*, **14**, 91 (1966).
105 Martin and Hamman, *J. clin. Endocr.*, **26**, 257 (1966).

Androgens [1, 2] (for references see page 753)

Chemistry

The androgens comprise a group of steroids the administration of which compensates for the effects of castration in the adult male animal and promotes the development of the male accessory reproductive glands and secondary sexual characteristics in the sexually immature animal.

Testosterone

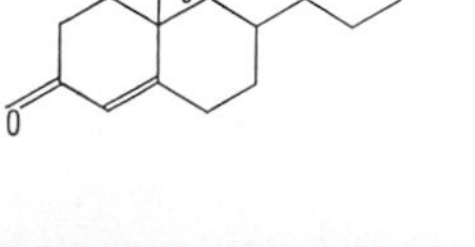

Androsterone
(androstan-3α-ol-17-one)

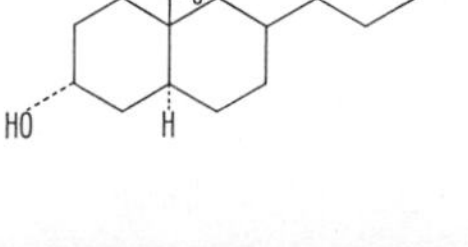

Androstenedione

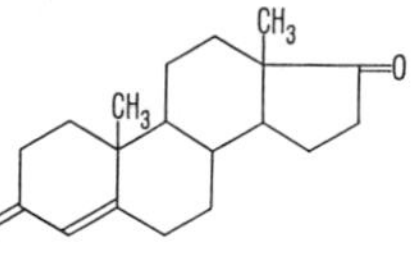

Androstanedione

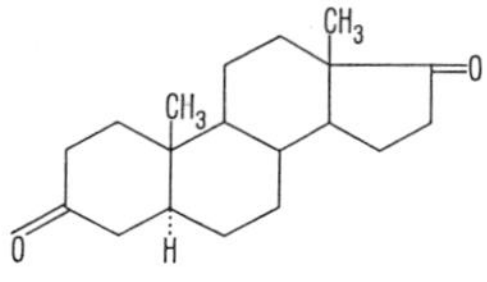

Dehydroepiandrosterone

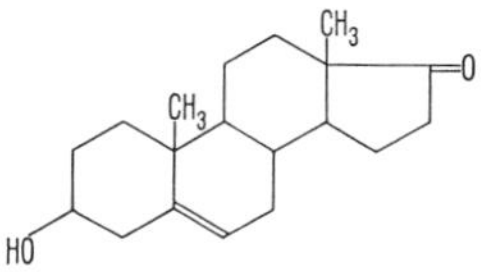

Steroids with androgenic activity have also been synthesized, for example 17-methyltestosterone and fluoxymesterone[3]. Synthetic long-chain esters of testosterone (testosterone cypionate, testosterone enanthate, testosterone phenylacetate) show prolonged androgenic activity. Other testosterone derivatives with an anabolic but less actively virilizing effect have been synthesized, for example methandrostenolone, 19-nortestosterone, norethandrolone[4].

Unit

The use of the international unit of androgenic activity (0.1 mg androsterone) was abandoned in 1950. The biological unit of androgenic activity is the capon unit (CU) and is the minimum amount which given on two successive days causes a 20% enlargement of the capon comb; it corresponds roughly to the activity of 0.1 mg androsterone.

Methods of assay[5]

Androgenic activity can be measured biologically on birds (capon comb test, chick comb test) or rats (seminal vesicle test, prostate test). These tests are suitable for pharmacological studies but in clinical work have been replaced by chemical methods. On account of their chemical structure, some androgens, but not testosterone, appear in the 17-ketosteroid group (see page 744). Dehydroepiandrosterone can be determined by the method of Fotherby[6], testosterone and androstenedione by gas chromatography[7, 29], double isotope dilution[8, 33], or the technique of saturation analysis[23].

Biosynthesis, secretion, metabolism[9]

The biosynthesis of the androgens is described on pages 428–429. The testes produce mainly testosterone and smaller amounts of androstenedione and dehydroepiandrosterone. The last two substances and 11β-hydroxyandrostenedione are also formed in the adrenal cortex. Daily testicular production of androstenedione is 0.4–0.5 mg, of dehydroepiandrosterone 0.6–0.7 mg, the corresponding amounts for the adrenal cortex being 2–3 mg and 9–10 mg respectively[10] (see also page 743). Androstenedione, dehydroepiandrosterone and probably also testosterone are formed in small amounts in the ovaries. In the liver, testosterone is formed from androstenedione and dehydroepiandrosterone, which means that it is almost impossible to calculate the rate of secretion for a particular gland from the androgen levels in the blood and urine; instead, so-called production rates are usually measured (see the table on page 752). Testicular synthesis of androgens by the Leydig cells appears to be stimulated only by the gonadotropins (LH, HCG)[10, 11], whereas adrenocortical synthesis is stimulated by ACTH. The testicular synthesis can be inhibited by giving synthetic androgens or oestrogens. Another steroid secreted along with the androgens is the biologically inactive epitestosterone, but its precise origin is unknown.

The androgen content of the peripheral plasma is shown in the table on page 752. In boys the plasma testosterone level is at first the same as in girls but rises until it reaches the adult male level at puberty[10]. In women it is subject to fluctuations during the course of the menstrual cycle[12]. There are conflicting reports on diurnal variations in the plasma testosterone level in normal males[10, 13]. During pregnancy the plasma testosterone level rises, and at term it is often higher than in men; the normal level is reached again 11 days post partum[14]. The plasma androgens are partly bound to proteins, testosterone probably specifically to a β-globulin[15]. Measurement of the plasma testosterone level provides informa-

Production rates of androgens (mg/24 h)

	Mean	Range	*s*	Reference
Testosterone				
Men	7	–	–	24
Women	0.34	–	–	24
Men	–	3.58–7.56	–	25
Women	–	0.42–0.94	–	25
Men	6.8	–	–	26
Women	0.23	0.13–0.33	0.073	27
Androstenedione				
Men	1.4	–	–	24
Women	3.4	–	–	24
Women	3.3	1.7–6.3	1.86	27
Epitestosterone				
Men	0.22	–	–	26

Androgens in plasma

	Mean	Range	*s*	Reference
Testosterone (μg/l)				
Men	8.0	5–11	2.5	33
Women	0.69	–	–	33
Men	6.4	3.2–13.0	2.0	34
Women	0.36	0.13–0.80	0.09	34
Women	0.37	0.20–0.70	0.09	35
Pregnancy				
20–31 weeks	3.8	3.0–4.6	–	14
39–42 weeks	9.0	5.9–11.7	–	14
Androstenedione (μg/l)				
Adolescents	0.50	–	–	36
Men	0.60	–	0.12	37
Women	1.40	–	0.32	37
Women	1.67	0.9–2.1	0.40	35
Dehydroepiandrosterone sulphate (mg/l)				
Men	1.5	–	–	30
Women	1.0	–	–	30
Androsterone sulphate (mg/l)	0.4	–	–	30

tion on testicular function in men[10] and on virilizing processes and idiopathic hirsutism in women[2].

Testosterone injected into the blood stream is rapidly broken down, the half-life being about 4 min[16]. The most important breakdown products of testosterone and androstenedione are androsterone and aetiocholanolone (see page 746), the excretion of which is discussed in connection with the 17-ketosteroids in the section on 'Corticosteroids', page 749. In urine, testosterone is present mainly as the glucuronide, dehydroepiandrosterone mainly as the sulphate. Published data on the urinary excretion of testosterone are conflicting, but recent values from which the variation with age can be seen are shown in the table and figure on this page. Like the plasma level, the urinary excretion of testosterone in women fluctuates during the course of the menstrual cycle[18,19], with a minimum during and immediately following menstruation and a maximum during the luteal phase of the cycle. The urinary testosterone excretion may fall after the menopause[19].

Urinary testosterone excretion (μg/24 h)

	Mean	Range	Reference
Testosterone, total			
Children, < 10 years	0.4	0.1–0.8	28
Men	37	20–65	28
Women	7.7	3–14	28
Men, 16–20 years	78	60–103	29
Men, 21–63 years	51.7	40–65	29
Women, 20–55 years	6.5	2.1–10.7	29
Testosterone glucuronide			
Men	72	33–120	30
Women	12	7–18	30
Testosterone sulphate			
Men	–	~5–10	31
Testosterone, free			
Men	1.1	–	32
Women	0.7	–	32
Epitestosterone glucuronide			
Men	182	–	30
Women	36	–	30

Testosterone excretion in normal men (mean $\pm 2 \times$ standard deviation in 68 subjects)[17]

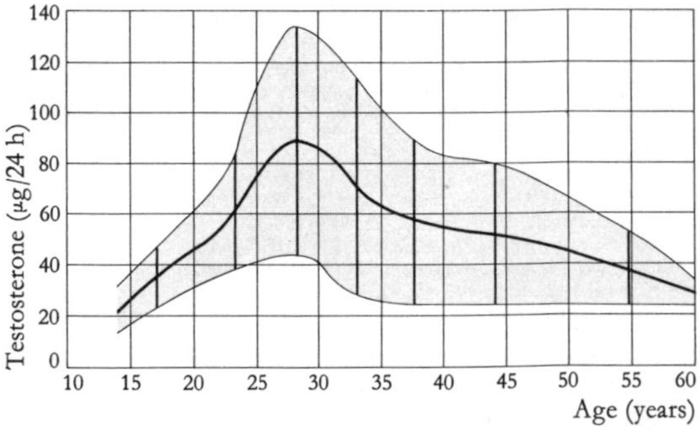

Biological activity

Testosterone has an anabolic effect on protein metabolism[20], and this hormone and its synthetic derivatives have been shown to promote nitrogen retention and accelerate the recovery of persons suffering from nutritional protein deficiency. Testosterone has more marked effects on boys before puberty and on women than on men. The site of action of the hormone in protein synthesis is probably the transfer of the s-RNA/amino acid complex to the ribosomes.

Comparative activities of androgens[1]

	Capon comb test	Seminal vesicle test (rats)	Virilizing effect (women)
Testosterone	100	100	100
Androsterone	10	10	–
Androstenedione	12	20	<5
Androstanedione	12	14	–
Dehydroepiandrosterone	16	3	<5
Methyltestosterone	60	–	–

Testosterone inhibits LH secretion by the pituitary, probably by interfering with the formation of the LH releasing factor in the hypothalamus[21].

The comparative effects of the androgens on some secondary sex characteristics are shown in the table on page 758. In the organs on which it acts testosterone appears to be linked to the cell nucleus, where it probably affects RNA formation[22].

References

1 DORFMAN and SHIPLEY, *Androgens*, Wiley, New York, 1956.
2 SEGRE, E.J., *Androgens, Virilization and the Hirsute Female*, Thomas, Springfield, 1967.
3 DORFMAN, R.I., in DORFMAN, R.I. (Ed.), *Methods in Hormone Research*, vol. 5, Academic Press, New York, 1966, page 235.
4 KINCL, F.A., in DORFMAN, R.I. (Ed.), *Methods in Hormone Research*, vol. 4, Academic Press, New York, 1965, page 21.
5 DORFMAN, R.I., in DORFMAN, R.I. (Ed.), *Methods in Hormone Research*, vol. 2, Academic Press, New York, 1962, page 275; LORAINE and BELL, *Hormone Assays and Their Clinical Application*, 2nd ed., Livingstone, Edinburgh, 1966.
6 FOTHERBY, K., *Biochem. J.*, **73**, 339 (1959).
7 ISMAIL and HARKNESS, *Acta endocr. (Kbh.)*, suppl. 100, 47 (1965); KIRSCHNER and COFFMAN, *J. clin. Endocr.*, **28**, 1347 (1968).
8 HUDSON et al., *Austr. J. exp. Biol.*, **41**, 235 (1963); RIVAROLA and MIGEON, *Steroids*, **7**, 103 (1966).
9 DORFMAN and UNGAR, *Metabolism of Steroid Hormones*, Academic Press, New York, 1965; LIPSETT and KORENMAN, *J. Amer. med. Ass.*, **190**, 757 (1964); PRUNTY, F.T.G., *Brit. med. J.*, **2**, 605 (1966); TAMM, J., in KÜCHMEISTER et al. (Eds.), *Klinische Funktionsdiagnostik*, 3rd ed., Thieme, Stuttgart, 1967, page 95; TAMM, J., *Dtsch. med. Wschr.*, **92**, 1983, 2037, 2080 (1967).
10 HUDSON et al., *Ciba Found. Coll. Endocr.*, **16**, 140 (1967).
11 EIK-NES, K.B., *Physiol. Rev.*, **44**, 609 (1964).
12 LOBOTSKY et al., *J. clin. Endocr.*, **24**, 1261 (1964).
13 RESKO and EIK-NES, *J. clin. Endocr.*, **26**, 573 (1966).
14 MEEKER, C.I., in *Second International Congress on Hormonal Steroids*, Milan 1966, Excerpta Medica Foundation, Amsterdam, 1966, page 174.
15 MERCIER, C., in *Second International Congress on Hormonal Steroids*, Milan 1966, Excerpta Medica Foundation, Amsterdam, 1966, page 269.
16 PEARLMAN, W.H., *Ciba Found. Coll. Endocr.*, **11**, 233 (1957).
17 SCHMIDT and STARCEVIC, *Klin. Wschr.*, **45**, 377 (1967).
18 HORN et al., *Steroids*, **7**, 118 (1966); APOSTOLAKIS et al., *Steroids*, **7**, 146 (1966).
19 GRATTAROLA and JUTISZ, in *Second International Congress on Hormonal Steroids*, Milan 1966, Excerpta Medica Foundation, Amsterdam, 1966, page 304.
20 WYNN, V., in GARDINER-HILL, H. (Ed.), *Modern Trends in Endocrinology*, vol. 3, Butterworth, London, 1967, page 254.
21 MCCANN et al., in *Second International Congress on Hormonal Steroids*, Milan 1966, Excerpta Medica Foundation, Amsterdam, 1966, page 79.
22 WILLIAMS-ASHMAN et al., *Recent Progr. Hormone Res.*, **20**, 247 (1964); KARLSON, P. (Ed.), *Mechanisms of Hormone Action*, NATO Advanced Study Institute, Academic Press, New York, 1965.
23 HORTON et al., *Steroids*, **10**, 245 (1967).
24 HORTON and TAIT, *J. clin. Invest.*, **45**, 301 (1966).
25 CAMACHO and MIGEON, *J. clin. Endocr.*, **26**, 893 (1966).
26 WILSON and LIPSETT, *J. clin. Endocr.*, **26**, 902 (1966).
27 BARDIN and LIPSETT, *J. clin. Invest.*, **46**, 891 (1967).
28 VESTERGAARD et al., *Clin. chim. Acta*, **14**, 540 (1966).
29 ISMAIL and HARKNESS, *Biochem. J.*, **99**, 717 (1966).
30 PRUNTY, F.T.G., *Brit. med. J.*, **2**, 605 (1966).
31 DESSYPRIS et al., *Proc. Soc. exp. Biol. (N.Y.)*, **121**, 1128 (1966).
32 VAN DER MOLEN et al., quoted by PRUNTY [30].
33 RIONDEL et al., *J. clin. Endocr.*, **23**, 620 (1963).
34 LLOYD et al., *J. clin. Endocr.*, **26**, 314 (1966).
35 BARDIN and LIPSETT, *J. clin. Invest.*, **46**, 891 (1967).
36 PRUNTY and LIM, in *Second International Congress on Hormonal Steroids*, Milan 1966, Excerpta Medica Foundation, Amsterdam, 1966, page 133.
37 HORTON, R., *J. clin. Endocr.*, **25**, 1237 (1965).

Progesterone (for references see page 755)

Chemistry

Chemically, progesterone is closely related to the adrenocortical steroids. In man it is the most important progestational hormone. Other, less active, human progestational steroids are 17α-hydroxyprogesterone and the 20α- and 20β-hydroxypregn-4-en-3-ones (20α- and 20β-hydroxyprogesterones). In rabbits the principal progestational hormone appears to be 20α-hydroxypregnenone[1].

Progesterone

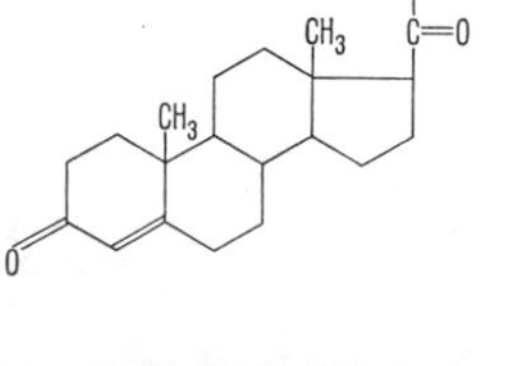

Synthetic progestational steroids are mostly derived from 17α-acetoxyprogesterone[2]. In addition to their progestational effect, derivatives of 19-nortestosterone have a marked androgenic action[2].

Methods of assay

Biological[3]. For clinical purposes biological tests are either not sensitive enough or not specific enough. In CLAUBERG's test, the degree of endometrial development caused by the preparation in immature female rabbits primed with oestrogens is assessed (one rabbit unit corresponds to 0.6 mg progesterone).

Chemical[4]. After chromatographic separation progesterone can be determined spectrophotometrically at 240 nm or as the dithiosemicarbazone at 280 nm[5]. Fluorimetric, colorimetric and more recently gas-chromatographic and double isotope dilution techniques are also available. Pregnanediol is best determined colorimetrically, for instance by the method of KLOPPER et al.[6], or by gas chromatography.

Biosynthesis, secretion, metabolism[7,8]

Progesterone is an intermediary metabolite in the biosynthesis of all other steroid hormones, and is secreted by the adrenal cortex, ovaries, testes and placenta. The corpus luteum of the ovaries and the placenta are the quantitatively most important sources. The amount contained in these organs (corpus luteum ca. 20 µg/g[9], placenta 2–4 µg/g[10]) is small in comparison with the amount secreted during the luteal phase of the menstrual cycle or during pregnancy, so that progesterone must be released as soon as it is formed. Production rates of progesterone are given in the table below. These are so-called urinary production rates obtained from the rate of excretion of pregnanediol, and more recent work indicates that, at least for males, they are too high; thus one study in men yielded a plasma production rate (measured by the double isotope dilution technique) of 0.59 mg per day compared with a urinary production rate of 3.8 mg per day[11]. During pregnancy, progesterone production remains roughly proportional to the weight of the placenta; at term it is about 250 mg per day[12].

*Production rates of progesterone and pregnenolone** (mg/24 h)

	Mean	Range	Reference
Progesterone			
Men	–	1.1–6.5	28
Men, 23–34 years	5.1	3.2–7.4	29
Men, 74–79 years	1.5	0.8–1.9	29
Women, ovariectomized	–	0.9–2.5	28
Women, proliferation phase	–	2.5–5.4	30
Women, luteal phase	–	22–43	30
Pregnenolone			
Men, 23–34 years	15	9–22	29
Men, 74–79 years	3.5	2.6–5.1	29

* Urinary production rates (obtained from urinary excretion of pregnanediol).

Plasma levels of progesterone and some of its metabolites are summarized in the upper table on page 754. During the first trimester of pregnancy the level is below 40 µg/l, after which it rises to reach 80–250 µg/l or more at term[7]. The plasma level of pregnanediol also rises during pregnancy[13,35]. In the blood the major part of the progesterone is bound to plasma proteins, principally to albumin[14].

Metabolism. Injected progesterone disappears rapidly from the circulating blood, the half-life being about 15 min[11]. The causes are diffusion into the tissues, particularly the fatty tissues, from which it is only slowly released[15], and metabolic breakdown in the liver. Well-recognized metabolites are pregnanolone, pregnanediol (5β-pregnanediol) and allopregnanediol (5α-pregnanediol); others present in the urine are hydroxylated at C-6 and C-16[7]. Most of the metabolites formed in the liver are conjugated with glucuronic acid and excreted through the kidneys (normal values are shown in the lower table on page 754), but a small proportion reaches the intestines via the bile and is excreted in the faeces[16]. Probably less than

Plasma levels of progesterone and its metabolites (μg/l)

	Mean	Range	*s*	Reference
Progesterone				
Women, proliferative phase	–	0–5.3	–	31
Women, luteal phase	–	6–21	–	31
Women, proliferative phase	1.13	–	0.49	32
Women, luteal phase	10.4	–	3.2	32
Women, ovariectomized	0.39	–	0.10	32
Men	0.28	–	0.13	32
Men	0.28	<0.15–0.48	–	33
Umbilical vein	372	–	60	34
Umbilical artery	140	–	18	34
17α-Hydroxyprogesterone				
Women, proliferative phase	0.42	–	0.20	27
Women, luteal phase	1.74	–	0.46	27
Men	0.95	–	0.31	27
Umbilical vein	6	–	–	34
Umbilical artery	33	–	–	34
20α-Hydroxypregnenone				
Umbilical vein	10	–	–	34
Umbilical artery	27	–	–	34
20β-Hydroxypregnenone				
Umbilical vein	3	–	–	34
Umbilical artery	14	–	–	34
Pregnanediol				
Women	–	65–129	–	35

Urinary excretion of progesterone metabolites (mg/24 h)

	Mean	Range	*s*	Reference
Pregnanediol				
Boys, 3–15 years	0.76	–	0.32	36
Girls, 3–15 years	0.72	–	0.60	36
Men	0.92	0.38–1.42	–	6
Women, proliferative phase	1.12	0.78–1.50	–	6
Women, luteal phase	3.3	2.1–4.2	–	6
Women, postmenopausal	0.63	0.28–0.86	–	6
Women, proliferative phase	0.48	0.10–1.26	0.31	37
Women, luteal phase	2.68	1.17–9.50	1.68	37
Men, 23–34 years	0.6	–	0.17	29
Men, 74–79 years	0.15	–	0.07	29
Pregnanolone				
Men	–	0.14–0.60	–	38
Women	–	0.06–0.46	–	38

70% of injected progesterone can be recovered from urine and faeces, and less than 40% can be accounted for as known metabolites[7].

During the proliferation phase of the menstrual cycle pregnanediol excretion is usually less than 1 mg/24 h; this pregnanediol probably originates mainly from the steroids formed in the adrenal cortex. After ovulation, pregnanediol excretion increases and in the luteal phase usually reaches 2–6 mg/24 h. In this phase the greater part of the pregnanediol arises from progesterone secreted by the corpus luteum. A few days before menstruation pregnanediol excretion begins to fall, reaching a minimum 2 or 3 days after the start of the period.

The progesterone formed in the placenta passes into the foetus, where it is broken down into less active compounds like 17α-hydroxyprogesterone and the 20α- and 20β-hydroxypregnenones. There is a dynamic exchange of progesterone and its metabolites between foetus and placenta, mother and placenta, and foetus and mother[17]. During pregnancy, the excretion of pregnanediol increases (see the diagram below), as does that of pregnanolone[19]; after parturition it falls again, reaching the proliferation phase value in about a week[20]. Pregnanediol has been isolated from the meconium, where it is present to the extent of 85–95% as sulphate[21].

Urinary pregnanediol excretion during pregnancy[18] (mean and 95% confidence limits)

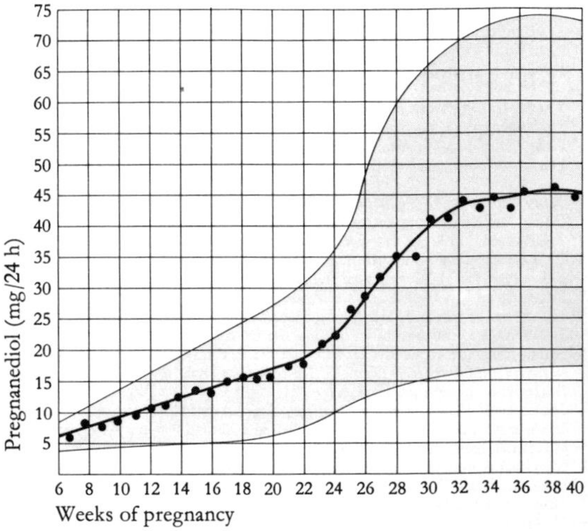

Regulation of progesterone secretion. Little is known of the manner in which progesterone synthesis and secretion is regulated[2,7,22,23]. The formation of the hormone in the ripening follicle is probably stimulated only by LH; whether its secretion during the luteal phase is stimulated by prolactin as well as LH is not known for certain. The manner in which progesterone formation in the placenta is regulated has not been explained, but HCG may play a role in this. Under certain conditions, HCG has been observed to increase progesterone secretion in the corpus luteum.

Biological activity

The main action of progesterone is the maintenance of pregnancy[24], the mechanism of which is poorly understood[25], though it is known that progesterone blocks the spread of the uterine contractile response to oxytocin[24]. The hormone also has other effects on the uterus, notably on its composition and metabolic activity; thus it causes an increase not only of uterine weight but of the collagen, nucleic acid, glycogen and lipid contents of the organ. In many of its uterine effects progesterone acts only in conjunction with oestrogens[7].

The biological activity of progesterone is not confined to the reproductive cycle. The hormone has an inhibitory effect in vitro on enzymes of the respiratory chain and stimulates the metabolism of galactose[7]. It is antagonistic to the sodium-retaining effects of aldosterone and deoxycorticosterone but does not affect potassium excretion; progesterone administration is followed by a compensatory increase in aldosterone secretion. Progesterone has a catabolic effect and causes increased urinary nitrogen excretion; there is some evidence that this is due to inhibition of amino-acid utilization by the liver. In rats and mice, the hormone causes an increase in body weight due to deposition of fat. These general metabolic effects of progesterone probably have little physiological significance except when large amounts of the hormone are secreted.

When administered at high dosage over a long period progesterone inhibits secretion of LH and thereby ovulation. This supports the anti-ovulatory action of oestrogens and is the reason for the inclusion of progestational compounds in the steroid combinations used as oral contraceptives. In these combinations progesterone may also act by rendering the cervical mucus more hostile to sperm penetration[26]. When progesterone is given shortly before an expected ovulation the latter is either induced or its time of onset shortened[22].

References

1 Hilliard et al., *Endocrinology*, **72**, 59 (1963).
2 Miyake and Rooks, in Dorfman, R.I. (Ed.), *Methods in Hormone Research*, vol.5, Academic Press, New York, 1966, page 59; Edgren et al., *Fertil. and Steril.*, **18**, 238 (1967).
3 Miyake, T., in Dorfman R.I. (Ed.), *Methods in Hormone Research*, vol.2, Academic Press, New York, 1962, page 127.
4 Loraine and Bell, *Hormone Assays and Their Clinical Application*, 2nd ed., Livingstone, Edinburgh, 1966, page 309.
5 Pearlman, W.H., *Recent Progr. Hormone Res.*, **9**, 27 (1954).
6 Klopper et al., *J. Endocr.*, **12**, 209 (1955).
7 Fotherby, K., *Vitam. and Horm.*, **22**, 153 (1964).
8 Dorfman and Ungar, *Metabolism of Steroid Hormones*, Academic Press, New York, 1965.
9 Zander et al., *J. clin. Endocr.*, **18**, 337 (1958).
10 Kumar et al., *Amer. J. Obstet. Gynec.*, **87**, 126 (1963).
11 Little et al., *J. clin. Invest.*, **45**, 901 (1966).
12 Zander and von Münstermann, *Klin. Wschr.*, **32**, 894 (1954); Pearlman, W.H., *Ciba Found. Coll. Endocr.*, **11**, 233 (1957).
13 Deshpande and Sommerville, *Lancet*, **2**, 1046 (1958).
14 Westphal et al., *Arch. Biochem.*, **92**, 441 (1961).
15 Kaufmann and Zander, *Klin. Wschr.*, **34**, 7 (1956); Plotz and Davis, *Proc. Soc. exp. Biol. (N.Y.)*, **95**, 92 (1957); Davis and Plotz, *Recent Progr. Hormone Res.*, **13**, 347 (1957).
16 Sandberg and Slaunwhite, *J. clin. Endocr.*, **18**, 253 (1958); Taylor, W., in Taylor, W. (Ed.), *The Biliary System*, NATO Advanced Study Institute, Academic Press, New York, 1965, page 399; Peterson, R.E., in Taylor, W. (Ed.), *The Biliary System*, NATO Advanced Study Institute, Academic Press, New York, 1965, page 385.
17 Diczfalusy and Troen, *Vitam. and Horm.*, **19**, 229 (1961); Diczfalusy, E., *Fed. Proc.*, **23**, 791 (1964).
18 Shearman, R.P., *J. Obstet. Gynaec. Brit. Emp.*, **66**, 1 (1959).
19 van der Molen, H.J., *Acta endocr. (Kbh.)*, **41**, 247 (1962); Lachèse et al., *Clin. chim. Acta*, **8**, 538 (1963).
20 Ehrlich, E.N., *J. Lab. clin. Med.*, **65**, 869 (1965).
21 Francis and Kinsella, *J. clin. Endocr.*, **26**, 128 (1966).
22 Rothchild, I., *Vitam. and Horm.*, **23**, 209 (1965).
23 Savard et al., *Recent Progr. Hormone Res.*, **21**, 285 (1965).
24 Csapo, A., in Wolstenholme and Cameron (Eds.), *Progesterone and the Defence Mechanism of Pregnancy*, Ciba Foundation Study Group, No. 9, Churchill, London, 1961, page 3; Csapo and Wood, in James, V.H.T. (Ed.), *Recent Advances in Endocrinology*, 8th ed., Churchill, London, 1968, page 207.
25 Lloyd and Weisz, *Ann. Rev. Physiol.*, **28**, 267 (1966).
26 Diczfalusy, E., *Brit. med. J.*, **2**, 1394 (1965).
27 Strott and Lipsett, *J. clin. Endocr.*, **28**, 1426 (1968).
28 Little et al., quoted by Fotherby [7].
29 Romanoff et al., *J. clin. Endocr.*, **26**, 1023 (1966).
30 Dominguez et al., quoted by Brooks, R.V., in Gardiner-Hill, H. (Ed.), *Modern Trends in Endocrinology*, vol. 3, Butterworth, London, 1967, page 127.
31 Woolever, C.A., *Amer. J. Obstet. Gynec.*, **85**, 981 (1963).
32 Riondel et al., *J. clin. Endocr.*, **25**, 229 (1965).
33 van der Molen and Groen, *J. clin. Endocr.*, **25**, 1625 (1965).
34 Zander, J., in Wolstenholme and Cameron (Eds.), *Progesterone and the Defence Mechanism of Pregnancy*, Ciba Foundation Study Group, No. 9, Churchill, London, 1961, page 32.
35 Oertel et al., *Arch. Biochem.*, **86**, 148 (1960).
36 Bergstrand and Gemzell, *J. clin. Endocr.*, **17**, 870 (1957).
37 Scommegna et al., *Fertil. and Steril.*, **18**, 257 (1967).
38 van der Molen, H.J., *Acta endocr. (Kbh.)*, **41**, 247 (1962).

Oestrogens (for references see page 757)

Chemistry

All naturally occurring oestrogens are unsaturated phenolic compounds containing either alcoholic or keto groups. They are readily soluble in ether, alcohol, chloroform and acetone, insoluble in water. Their phenolic character means that they can be easily separated by means of aqueous alkalis from the androgens in the same urinary fraction.

Oestrogenic activity is also seen in plant phenols such as genistein and cumoestrol. Synthetic substances with oestrogenic activity include ethinyloestradiol and non-steroid compounds like diethylstilboestrol, hexoestrol, dienoestrol, benzoestrol and chlorotrianisene[1]. Owing to their slower absorption, oestradiol esters have a more protracted action than oestradiol itself.

Oestradiol (17β-oestradiol)

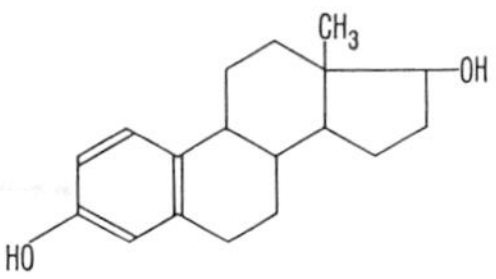

Oestriol

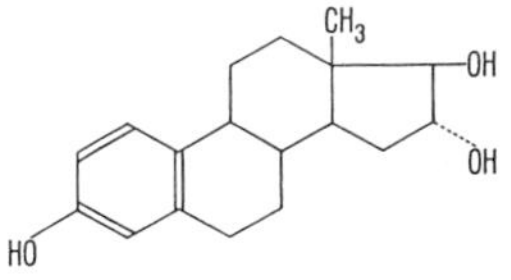

Oestrone

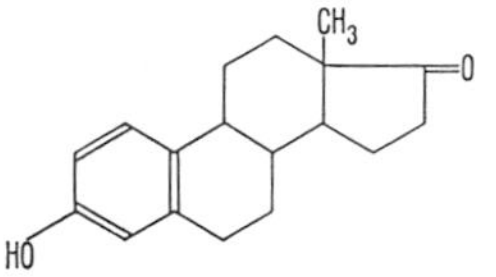

Units

The use of international units for oestrone (1 IU = 0.0001 mg) and oestradiol benzoate (1 IU = 0.0001 mg) has been abandoned and they are now measured by weight.

The mouse unit (MU) and rat unit (RU), also obsolete, are the minimum amounts of these oestrogens that bring about the characteristic change in the vaginal epithelium in the spayed female animal.

Methods of assay

Biological[2]. For example, induction of the characteristic vaginal changes in the spayed female rat or mouse (Allen-Doisy test). Biological tests have the disadvantage, particularly in clinical studies, that they measure only the total activity of the oestrogens present.

Chemical[3]. Oestrogens can be determined colorimetrically (Kober reaction) or fluorimetrically (reaction with sulphuric or phosphoric acid). Individual oestrogens can be determined only after prior chromatographic separation. Oestrogens can be assayed in urine by gas chromatography, in blood by double isotope dilution.

Biosynthesis, secretion, metabolism[4]

The biosynthesis of the oestrogens is described on pages 430–432. The bulk of the oestrogens in man are produced in the ovaries and placenta, smaller amounts in the adrenal cortex and testes. The following concentrations have been found in the ovaries[5]: oestrone 0.10–0.16 μg/g, oestradiol 0.25–0.41 μg/g. The primary products of secretion are oestradiol and oestrone, oestriol being a metabolite of these two. Oestrogens are secreted both by the theca interna and by the stratum granulosum, and are produced by the maturing Graafian follicle and by the corpus luteum after ovulation. During pregnancy, the function of the ovaries as oestrogen producer is taken over by the placenta, the latter becoming the main source from the 2nd or 3rd month. The quantitatively most important placental oestrogen is oestriol. The following concentrations have been found in the placenta[6]: oestrone 0.041 μg/g, oestradiol 0.101 μg/g, oestriol 0.180 μg/g. In men, over two-thirds of the oestrogens may be secreted by the testes[7]. The following concentrations have been found in semen[8]: oestradiol 10 μg/l, oestrone 60 μg/l, oestriol 30 μg/l.

Rates of production of oestradiol are shown in the table below. Reliable data on oestrogen production are obtainable only by the double isotope dilution technique, not by measurements of the urinary excretion. Secretion rates during pregnancy are difficult to

(continued on page 757)

Production rates of oestradiol (μg/24 h)

	Mean	Range	s	Reference
Women.................	–	200–500	–	28
Women.................	–	93–165	–	29
Women, mid-cycle........	–	up to 300	–	30
Women, start of cycle.....	–	35–100	–	30
Men, 21–37 years.........	70	–	29	31

Oestrogens in plasma (μg/l)

	Mean	Range	*s*	Reference
Women				
Proliferative phase				
Oestriol	0.25	–	0.12	32
Oestrone	0.20	–	0.11	32
Oestradiol	0.13	–	0.08	32
Ovulation				
Oestriol	0.37	–	0.23	32
Oestrone	0.70	–	0.25	32
Oestradiol	0.28	–	0.17	32
Men				
Oestrone	0.42	–	0.09	33
Oestradiol	0.15	–	0.12	33
Oestriol	–	trace	–	34
Pregnancy				
36th–38th week				
Oestrone + oestradiol	92	–	32	35
Oestriol	81	–	35	35
39th–42nd week				
Oestrone + oestradiol	108	–	37	35
Oestriol	93	–	39	35
At term				
Oestriol	–	43–175	–	36
Oestrone	–	27–103	–	36
Oestradiol	–	13–29	–	36
Cord blood				
Oestriol	583	–	–	37
Oestrone	13	–	–	37
Oestradiol	6	–	–	37

Urinary oestriol excretion during pregnancy[19] (mean and 95% range)

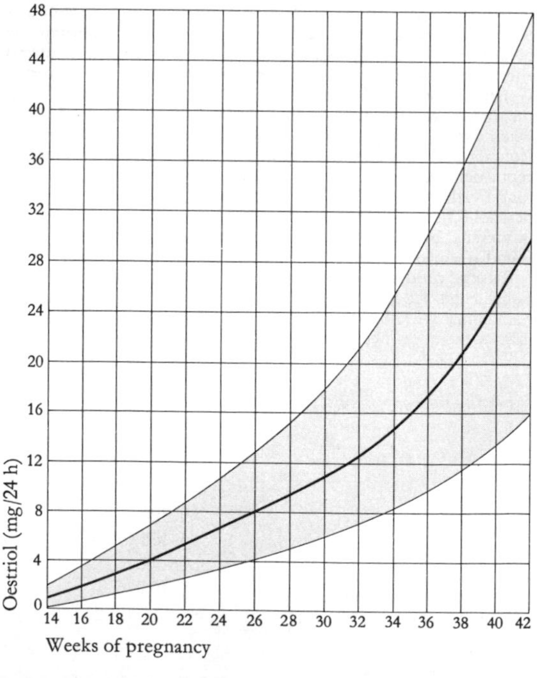

Urinary excretion of oestrogens (μg/24 h)

	Mean	Range	Reference
Children, 9–12 years			
Total oestrogens	–	<1.0	38
Women, postmenopausal			
Total oestrogens	5.5	3.2–9.0	20
Oestriol	3.9	2.2–7.5	20
Oestrone	1.3	0.3–2.4	20
Oestradiol	0.3	0–1.4	20
Men, 20–50 years			
Total oestrogens	10.3	6.0–17.8	39
Oestriol	3.5	0.8–11.0	39
Oestrone	5.4	3.0–8.2	39
Oestradiol	1.5	0–6.3	39
Pregnancy, 1 week ante partum			
Total oestrogens	30800	23200–37200	40
Oestriol	29000	22000–35000	40
Oestrone	1400	930–1600	40
Oestradiol	520	380–630	40

Urinary oestrogen excretion during the menstrual cycle[20] (mean and highest and lowest values in 16 women aged 18 to 41 years)

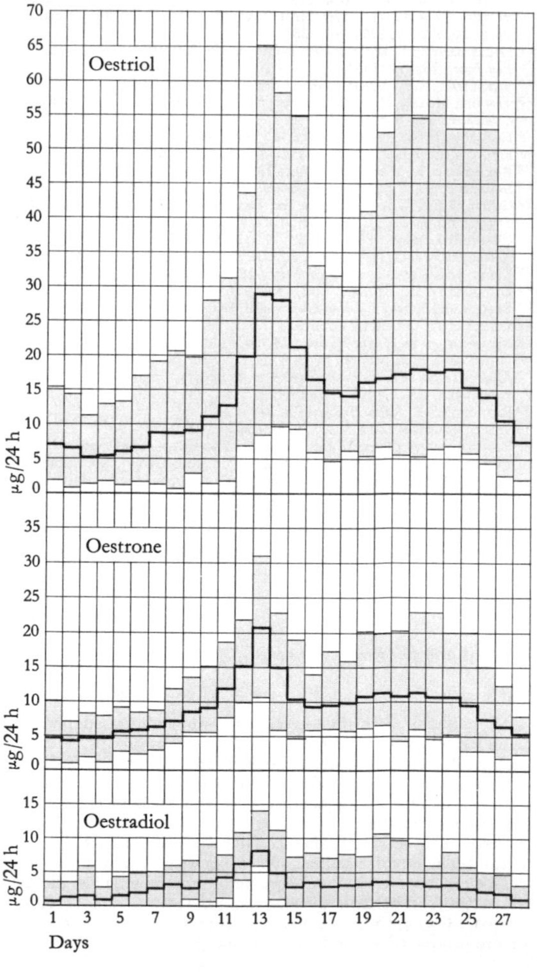

assess. Foetus, placenta and mother appear to be separate compartments in this respect, and not all oestrogens and oestrogen metabolites are free to move from one compartment to another[9]. It has been estimated that there is a daily movement of 1.8 mg oestradiol from placenta to foetus, 4.0 mg from placenta to mother, and 0.7 mg from foetus to mother, while none moves from mother to foetus[10].

Normal plasma oestrogen levels are given in the table opposite. In the course of the menstrual cycle the highest values occur shortly before ovulation[11]. In pregnancy the level rises, the increase being first clearly seen around the 10th week[12], with oestriol showing the greatest rise. In the blood during pregnancy, oestriol is present as glucuronate, sulphate and double conjugate, oestrone mainly as sulphate, while oestradiol is mainly in the free form[13]. Of all the steroid hormones, the oestrogens are the most strongly bound to plasma proteins[14].

Metabolism. The half-life of oestradiol in the circulating blood is about 50 min[11], the breakdown process occurring – except during pregnancy – mainly in the liver. When radioactive 17β-oestradiol is administered, 65% of the activity is found in the urine (23% as oestriol, oestrone and oestradiol) and 10% in the faeces[15]. Other urinary oestrogen metabolites are 16-epioestriol, 16α-hydroxyoestrone, 16-keto-oestradiol, 16β-hydroxyoestrone, 2-methoxyoestrone and 2-methoxyoestriol[16], as well as 15α-hydroxyoestrone, 15β-hydroxyoestrone and 15β-hydroxyoestradiol-17β[17]. The urinary oestrogens are conjugated almost exclusively with glucuronic acid or sulphuric acid. The oestrone and oestradiol excreted in the bile are mostly reabsorbed and excreted in the urine[18].

Normal values for urinary oestrogen excretion and its fluctuation during the menstrual cycle and pregnancy are shown in the table and figures opposite. Oestrogen excretion rises markedly during pregnancy, and at term the urine contains 100 times as much oestrone and oestradiol and about 1000 times as much oestriol as at the time of the luteal maximum[21]. The excretion starts gradually to increase about 7 weeks after the last menstruation[3,21], falls again abruptly a few days after parturition, and remains low during lactation. In the newborn, oestriol excretion falls steeply during the first week; oestrone and oestradiol do not appear to be excreted by the newborn[22]. Oestrogen excretion is lower in children than in adults and starts to rise at puberty[23]. In female children a cyclic pattern of excretion becomes apparent at puberty. 16-Epioestriol has been found in the urine of boys[24] as well as in that of women during both the menstrual cycle[25] and pregnancy[26]; other oestrogens excreted during pregnancy are 2-methoxyoestrone, 16α-hydroxyoestrone and 16-keto-oestradiol[26].

Regulation of oestrogen secretion[27]. Both FSH and LH appear to be necessary for oestrogen formation. The synthesis is also stimulated in men and women by HCG[7].

Biological activity

The effects of the oestrogens on the reproductive functions are summarized in the table on page 758. At the cellular level, oestrogens are bound to specific cell components of the target organ (uterus) and bring about an increased synthesis of nuclear RNA and thus of protein[41].

The oestrogens have a similar but weaker anabolic action on protein metabolism and cause retention of sodium and water.

In the pituitary the oestrogens act by inhibiting secretion of FSH and LH, probably by suppressing the formation of the gonadotropin-releasing factor in the hypothalamus (see under 'Gonadotropins of the Anterior Pituitary', page 714).

References

1 Emmens and Martin, in Dorfman, R.I. (Ed.), *Methods in Hormone Research*, vol. 3, Academic Press, New York, 1964, page 1.
2 Emmens, C.W., in Dorfman, R.I. (Ed.), *Methods in Hormone Research*, vol. 2, Academic Press, New York, 1962, page 59.
3 Loraine and Bell, *Hormone Assays and Their Clinical Application*, 2nd ed., Livingstone, Edinburgh, 1966.
4 Diczfalusy and Lauritzen, *Östrogene beim Menschen*, Springer, Berlin, 1961.
5 Mahesh and Greenblatt, *Recent Progr. Hormone Res.*, **20**, 341 (1964).
6 Schmidt-Elmendorff, H.W., *Acta endocr. (Kbh.)*, **38**, 527 (1961).
7 Fishman et al., *Ciba Found. Coll. Endocr.*, **16**, 156 (1967).
8 Diczfalusy, E., *Acta endocr. (Kbh.)*, **15**, 317 (1954).
9 Diczfalusy and Troen, *Vitam. and Horm.*, **19**, 230 (1961); Diczfalusy, E., *Fed. Proc.*, **23**, 79 (1964); Eik-Nes and Hall, *Vitam. and Horm.*, **23**, 153 (1965); Siiteri and MacDonald, *J. clin. Endocr.*, **26**, 751 (1966).
10 Gurpide et al., in *Second International Congress on Hormonal Steroids*, Milan 1966, Excerpta Medica Foundation, Amsterdam, 1966, page 41.
11 Svendsen and Sørensen, *Acta endocr. (Kbh.)*, **47**, 245 (1964).
12 Roy and Mackay, *J. Obstet. Gynaec. Brit. Cwlth*, **69**, 13 (1962); Keller and Kubli, *Méd. et Hyg. (Genève)*, **20**, 453 (1962).
13 Smith and Hagerman, *J. clin. Endocr.*, **25**, 732 (1965).
14 Sandberg et al., *Recent Progr. Hormone Res.*, **13**, 209 (1957).
15 Brown, J.B., *Advanc. clin. Chem.*, **3**, 157 (1960).
16 Breuer, H., *Vitam. and Horm.*, **20**, 285 (1962); Breuer, H., in Cassano, C. (Ed.), *Research on Steroids*, vol. 1, Il Pensiero Scientifico, Rome, 1964, page 133.
17 Knuppen et al., *Biochem. J.*, **96**, 33C (1965); Knuppen et al., *Steroids*, **8**, 403 (1966).
18 Adlercreutz, H., in Taylor, W. (Ed.), *The Biliary System*, NATO Advanced Study Institute, Academic Press, New York, 1965, page 369; Sandberg et al., in *Second International Congress on Hormonal Steroids*, Milan 1966, Excerpta Medica Foundation, Amsterdam, 1966, page 214.
19 Aasted Frandsen, V., *The Excretion of Oestriol in Normal Human Pregnancy*, Thesis, Copenhagen, 1963.
20 Brown and Matthew, *Recent Progr. Hormone Res.*, **18**, 337 (1962).
21 Merrill, R.C., *Physiol. Rev.*, **38**, 463 (1958).
22 Diczfalusy et al., *Ciba Found. Coll. Endocr.*, **11**, 249 (1957).
23 Nathanson et al., *Endocrinology*, **28**, 851 (1941).
24 Luisi et al., *Clin. chim. Acta*, **14**, 346 (1966).
25 Nocke and Breuer, *Acta endocr. (Kbh.)*, **44**, 47 (1963).
26 Hobkirk and Nilsen, *J. clin. Endocr.*, **22**, 134 (1962).
27 Eik-Nes, K.B., *Physiol. Rev.*, **44**, 609 (1964); Brooks, R.V., in Gardiner-Hill, H. (Ed.), *Modern Trends in Endocrinology*, vol. 3, Butterworth, London, 1967, page 127.
28 Gurpide et al., *J. clin. Endocr.*, **22**, 935 (1962).
29 Morse et al., *J. Endocr.*, **26**, 25 (1963).
30 Goering et al., *Amer. J. Obstet. Gynec.*, **92**, 441 (1965); Goering and Herrmann, *J. clin. Endocr.*, **26**, 65 (1966).
31 Lipsett et al., *Recent Progr. Hormone Res.*, **22**, 245 (1966).
32 Roy et al., *J. Endocr.*, **31**, 177 (1965).
33 Pochi et al., *J. clin. Endocr.*, **25**, 1660 (1965).
34 Kroman et al., *Clin. chim. Acta*, **9**, 73 (1964).
35 Kubli and Keller, *Klin. Wschr.*, **41**, 861 (1963).
36 Aitken and Preedy, *Ciba Found. Coll. Endocr.*, **11**, 331 (1957).
37 Diczfalusy et al., *Recent Progr. Hormone Res.*, **17**, 147 (1961).
38 Persson, B.H., quoted by Loraine and Bell, *Hormone Assays and Their Clinical Application*, 2nd ed., Livingstone, Edinburgh, 1966, page 257.
39 Brown, J.B., *Mem. Soc. Endocr.*, **3**, 1 (1955).
40 Brown, J.B., *Lancet*, **1**, 704 (1956).
41 Hechter and Halkerston, *Ann. Rev. Physiol.*, **27**, 133 (1965); Karlson, P. (Ed.), *Mechanism of Hormone Action*, NATO Advanced Study Institute, Academic Press, New York, 1965.

Functions of the sex hormones

	Androgens	Oestrogens	Progesterone
Male organism			
Development of primary sex organs:			
General, especially testes, prostate, penis	+++	Antagonist	
Muscles and connective tissue of accessory glands	?	+	
Development of secondary sex characteristics	++++	Antagonist	
Emotional behaviour: libido, masculine activity	++++	Antagonist	
Female organism			
Development of primary sex organs	Partial antagonist	+++	0
Development of secondary sex characteristics	Antagonist	++++	?
Emotional behaviour:			
Frigidity	Antagonist	++++	+
Libido	+++	+	Partial antagonist
Menstrual cycle			
Maturation of ovum	?	+++	+
Proliferation phase	?	++++	+
Secretion phase	?	+	++++
Migration of ovum, nidation	?	++	+++
Pregnancy			
Inhibition of maturation of further follicles; quiescence of the uterus; relaxation of the uterine muscles (1); lowering of the Na:K ratio in blood; lowering of the sympathetic tonus (2)	?	Antagonist to (1); synergist to (2)	++++
Indispensable for maintenance of pregnancy	?	++	++
Relaxation of the pelvic girdle; increase of tonus of uterine muscles towards end of pregnancy (3)	?	+++	Antagonist to (3)
Growth of mammary tissue	?	++*	++*
Inhibition of lactation until parturition	?	++	+
Post partum			
Maintenance of lactation	?	++*	++*
Inhibition of lactation at high therapeutic dosage	++	+++++	0
Involution of the uterus and preparation for fresh menstrual cycle	?	+++	0

* See also under 'Prolactin', page 719.

Substance	International Unit (IU) mg	Form in which dispensed	Year of establishment
Antigens I Held by International Laboratory for Biological Standards, Statens Seruminstitut, Copenhagen			
Old tuberculin	(0.011 111 µl)	Ampoules containing 2 ml (90 000 IU per ml)	1965 (3rd Standard)
Mammalian tuberculin (purified protein derivative)	0.000 28	Ampoules containing 10 mg plus 4 mg of salts (500 000 IU per ampoule)	1951 (1st Standard)
Avian tuberculin (purified protein derivative)	0.000 072 6	Ampoules containing 10 mg plus 26.3 mg of salts (500 000 IU per ampoule)	1954 (1st Standard)
Tetanus toxoid (alcohol-purified)	0.03	Ampoules containing 25 mg plus glycine (833 IU per ampoule)	1951 (1st Standard)
Tetanus toxoid (adsorbed)	0.666 7	Ampoules containing 80 mg adsorbed to aluminium hydroxide, plus an equal part of guinea-pig serum, dried (120 IU per ampoule)	1965 (1st Standard)
Diphtheria toxoid (alcohol-purified)	0.50	Ampoules containing 50 mg plus glycine (100 IU per ampoule)	1951 (1st Standard)
Diphtheria toxoid (adsorbed)	0.75	Ampoules containing 80 mg adsorbed to aluminium hydroxide plus an equal part of guinea-pig serum, dried (107 IU per ampoule)	1955 (1st Standard)
Schick test toxin (diphtheria) (purified)	0.004 2	Ampoules containing 0.005 mg plus 1 mg of bovine albumin and 2.74 mg of phosphate buffer salts (900 IU per ampoule)	1954 (1st Standard)
Pertussis vaccine (dried)	1.5	Ampoules containing 52 mg (34.7 IU per ampoule)	1957 (1st Standard)
Cholera vaccine (Inaba) (dried)	–	Ampoules containing 20 mg (1.6×10^{10} organisms per ampoule)	1953 (1st Reference Preparation)
Cholera vaccine (Ogawa) (dried)	–	Ampoules containing 20 mg (1.6×10^{10} organisms per ampoule)	1953 (1st Reference Preparation)
Cardiolipin (purified)	–	Ampoules containing 4, 8 or 16 ml of a solution in ethanol (6.0 mg cardiolipin per ml as calculated from the phosphorus content)	1967 (4th Reference Preparation)
Lecithin (beef heart, purified)	–	Bottles containing 30 ml of a solution in ethanol (30.3 mg lecithin per ml)	1953 (2nd Reference Preparation)
Lecithin (egg, purified)	–	Ampoules containing 4, 8 or 16 ml of a solution in ethanol (26.7 mg of lecithin per ml as calculated from the phosphorus content)	1959 (3rd Reference Preparation)
Rabies vaccine	–	Ampoules containing 121 mg of a UV-inactivated, freeze-dried suspension of rabbit brain infected with fixed rabies virus	1965 (2nd Reference Preparation)
Smallpox vaccine (freeze-dried)	–	Ampoules containing 14 mg	1962 (1st Reference Preparation)
Typhoid vaccine (acetone-inactivated, dried)	–	Ampoules containing 11 mg	1962 (1st Reference Preparation)
Typhoid vaccine (heat-phenol-inactivated, freeze-dried)		Ampoules containing 34 mg	1962 (1st Reference Preparation)
Poliomyelitis vaccine (inactivated, trivalent, frozen)	–	Ampoules containing 10 ml	1962 (1st Reference Preparation)
BCG vaccine (dried)	–	Ampoules containing dried vaccine derived from 2.5 mg (semi-dry weight) of bacillary mass of BCG and 5 mg of sodium glutamate (total weight of dried material 5.72 mg per ampoule)	1965 (1st Reference Preparation)
Influenza virus haemagglutinin (type A) (purified, freeze-dried)	0.093 661	Ampoules containing 18.7322 mg of virus (Type A strain Singapore 1/57 30338), propagated in embryonated hens' eggs, killed by formalin and suspended in phosphate-buffered saline with 1% bovine serum albumin (200 IU per ampoule)	1967 (1st Reference Preparation)
Antigens II Held by International Laboratory for Biological Standards, Central Veterinary Laboratory, Weybridge, England			
Swine erysipelas vaccine (adsorbed, dried)	0.50	Ampoules containing 499 mg, derived from formalin-treated *Erysipelothrix rhusiopathiae (E. insidiosa)* type B, adsorbed to aluminium hydroxide (1000 IU per ampoule)	1959 (1st Standard)
Newcastle disease vaccine (inactivated, freeze-dried)	1.0	Ampoules containing 525 mg of vaccine derived from formaldehyde-treated allantoic fluid of eggs infected with strains of Newcastle disease virus adsorbed to aluminium hydroxide (525 IU per ampoule)	1963 (1st Standard)
Newcastle disease vaccine (live, freeze-dried)	–	Ampoules containing 109.5 mg of allantoic fluid derived from eggs infected with the virus (Hitchner B_1 strain)	1967 (1st Reference Preparation)
Clostridium oedematiens (alpha) toxoid (freeze-dried)	–	Ampoules containing 53.4 mg	1966 (1st Reference Preparation)

[1] From WHO Expert Committee on Biological Standardization, *Wld Hlth Org. techn. Rep. Ser.*, No. 413 (1969).

Substance	International Unit (IU) mg	Form in which dispensed	Year of establishment
Antibodies I Held by International Laboratory for Biological Standards, Statens Seruminstitut, Copenhagen			
Tetanus antitoxin (hyperimmune horse serum, dried)	0.309 4	Bottles containing 10 ml of a solution in saline, containing 66 vol% glycerol (5 IU per ml)	1928 (1st Standard)
Diphtheria antitoxin (hyperimmune horse serum, dried)	0.062 8	Bottles containing 10 ml of a solution in saline, containing 66 vol% glycerol (10 IU per ml)	1922 (1st Standard)
Antidysentery serum (SHIGA) (hyperimmune horse serum, dried)	0.05	Bottles containing 10 ml of a solution in saline, containing 66 vol% glycerol (200 IU per ml)	1928 (1st Standard)
Gas-gangrene antitoxin *(perfringens)* (*Clostridium welchii* type A antitoxin; hyperimmune horse serum, dried)	0.334 6	Bottles containing 90.35 mg (270 IU per ampoule)	1963 (5th Standard)
Gas-gangrene antitoxin *(vibrion septique)* (hyperimmune horse serum, dried)	0.118	Ampoules containing 59 mg of a 1:3 dilution in phosphate-buffered saline (500 IU per ampoule)	1957 (3rd Standard)
Gas-gangrene antitoxin *(oedematiens)* (hyperimmune horse serum, dried)	0.082 8	Ampoules containing 91 mg (1100 IU per ampoule)	1966 (3rd Standard)
Gas-gangrene antitoxin *(histolyticus)* (hyperimmune horse serum, dried)	0.2	Bottles containing 10 ml of a solution in saline, containing 66 vol% glycerol (20 IU per ml)	1951 (2nd Standard)
Gas-gangrene antitoxin *(Sordelli)* (hyperimmune horse serum, dried)	0.133 4	Bottles containing 10 ml of a solution in saline, containing 66 vol% glycerol (20 IU per ml)	1938 (1st Standard)
Staphylococcus α antitoxin (hyperimmune horse serum, dried)	0.237 6	Bottles containing 10 ml of a solution in phosphate-buffered saline, containing 0.01 g thiomersal per 100 ml (20 IU per ml)	1938 (2nd Standard)
Scarlet fever streptococcus antitoxin (hyperimmune horse serum, dried)	0.049	Ampoules containing 490 mg (10 000 IU per ampoule)	1952 (1st Standard)
Anti-streptolysin O (human, dried)	0.021 3	Bottles containing 46 mg (2160 IU per ampoule); distributed as a 10 ml solution containing 10 IU per ml	1959 (1st Standard)
Antipneumococcus serum (type 1) (hyperimmune horse serum, dried)	0.088 6	Bottles containing 10 ml of a solution in saline, containing 66 vol% glycerol (200 IU per ml)	1934 (1st Standard)
Antipneumococcus serum (type 2) (hyperimmune horse serum, dried)	0.089 4	Bottles containing 10 ml of a solution in saline, containing 66 vol% glycerol (200 IU per ml)	1934 (1st Standard)
Anti-Q-fever serum (bovine, dried)	0.101 7	Ampoules containing 101.7 mg (1000 IU per ampoule)	1953 (1st Standard)
Antirabies serum (hyperimmune horse serum, dried)	1.0	Ampoules containing 86.6 mg (86.6 IU per ampoule)	1955 (1st Standard)
Anti-A blood-typing serum (human, dried)	0.346 5	Ampoules containing 88.7 mg (256 IU per ampoule)	1950 (1st Standard)
Anti-B blood-typing serum (human, dried)	0.352 0	Ampoules containing 90.1 mg (256 IU per ampoule)	1950 (1st Standard)
Anti-Rh_0 (anti-D) incomplete blood-typing serum (pooled human serum, dried)	0.95	Ampoules containing 30.4 mg (32 IU per ampoule)	1966 (1st Standard)
Syphilitic human serum (dried)	3.617	Ampoules containing 177.4 mg (49 IU per ampoule)	1958 (1st Standard)
Anti-poliovirus serum (type 1) (hyperimmune monkey serum, dried)	10.78	Ampoules containing 107.8 mg (10 IU per ampoule)	1962 (1st Standard)
Anti-poliovirus serum (type 2) (hyperimmune monkey serum, dried)	10.46	Ampoules containing 104.6 mg (10 IU per ampoule)	1962 (1st Standard)
Anti-poliovirus serum (type 3) (hyperimmune monkey serum, dried)	10.48	Ampoules containing 104.8 mg (10 IU per ampoule)	1962 (1st Standard)
Clostridium botulinum, Type A antitoxin (hyperimmune horse serum, dried)	0.136 0	Ampoules containing 68.0 mg (500 IU per ampoule)	1963 (1st Standard)
Clostridium botulinum, Type B antitoxin (hyperimmune horse serum, dried)	0.174 0	Ampoules containing 87.0 mg (500 IU per ampoule)	1963 (1st Standard)
Clostridium botulinum, Type C antitoxin (hyperimmune horse serum, dried)	0.080 0	Ampoules containing 80.0 mg (1000 IU per ampoule)	1963 (1st Standard)
Clostridium botulinum, Type D antitoxin (hyperimmune horse serum, dried)	0.012 1	Ampoules containing 12.1 mg (1000 IU per ampoule)	1963 (1st Standard)
Clostridium botulinum, Type E antitoxin (hyperimmune horse serum, dried)	0.069 1	Ampoules containing 69.1 mg (1000 IU per ampoule)	1963 (1st Standard)
Clostridium botulinum, Type F antitoxin (hyperimmune rabbit serum, dried)	7.44	Ampoules containing 29.32 mg (4 IU per ampoule)	1965 (1st Standard)
Naja antivenin (horse serum, polyvalent [*Naja* and *Hemachatus* species], purified, dried)	2.69	Ampoules containing 807 mg (300 IU per ampoule)	1964 (1st Standard)
Anti-smallpox serum (pooled human serum, freeze-dried)	0.084 16	Ampoules containing 84.3 mg (1000 IU per ampoule)	1965 (1st Standard)
Anti-toxoplasma serum (pooled human serum, freeze-dried)	0.090 967	Ampoules containing 181.934 mg (2000 IU per ampoule)	1967 (1st Standard)

Substance	International Unit (IU) mg	Form in which dispensed	Year of establishment
Diphtheria antitoxin for flocculation test (hyperimmune horse serum)	–	Bottles containing 10 ml of a dilution in phosphate-buffered saline, containing 0.01 g thiomersal per 100 ml (500 IU per ml)	1956 (4th Reference Preparation)
Antityphoid serum (hyperimmune horse serum, dried)	–	Ampoules containing dried material from 5 ml serum	1952 (1st Reference Preparation)
Anti-yellow-fever serum (monkey serum, dried)	0.5	Ampoules containing 71.5 mg (143 IU per ampoule)	1962 (1st Reference Preparation)
Anti-measles serum (human serum, dried)	9.378	Ampoules containing 93.8 mg (10 IU per ampoule)	1964 (1st Reference Preparation)
Anti-staphylococcal P-V leucocidin serum (horse serum, freeze-dried)	0.356 5	Ampoules containing 53.5 mg (150 IU per ampoule)	1965 (1st Reference Preparation)
Rheumatoid arthritis serum (pooled human serum, freeze-dried)	0.171	Ampoules containing 17.1 mg (100 IU per ampoule)	1965 (1st Reference Preparation)
Anti-rubella serum (pooled human serum, freeze-dried)	–	Ampoules containing 56.28 mg	1966 (1st Reference Preparation) (discontinued 1967)
Antibodies II Held by International Laboratory for Biological Standards, Central Veterinary Laboratory, Weybridge, England			
Anti-*Brucella abortus* serum	0.095 52	Ampoules containing 95.52 mg of freeze-dried bovine serum (1000 IU per ampoule)	1967 (2nd Standard)
Clostridium welchii (perfringens) type B antitoxin (hyperimmune horse serum, dried)	0.013 7	Ampoules containing 68.5 mg (5000 IU per ampoule)	1954 (1st Standard)
Clostridium welchii (perfringens) type D antitoxin (hyperimmune horse serum, dried)	0.065 7	Ampoules containing 65.7 mg (1000 IU per ampoule)	1954 (1st Standard)
Swine erysipelas serum (anti-N) (hyperimmune horse serum, dried)	0.14	Ampoules containing 87.9 mg (628 IU per ampoule)	1954 (1st Standard)
Anti-swine-fever serum (pig serum, freeze-dried)	0.89	Ampoules containing 889.5 mg (1000 IU per ampoule)	1963 (1st Standard)
Anti-canine-distemper serum (hyperimmune horse serum, freeze-dried)	0.089 7	Ampoules containing 89.7 mg (1000 IU per ampoule)	1967 (1st Standard)
Anti-canine-hepatitis serum (hyperimmune horse serum, freeze-dried)	0.079 6	Ampoules containing 79.6 mg (1000 IU per ampoule)	1967 (1st Standard)
Anti-Newcastle-disease serum (chicken serum, freeze-dried)	0.173 4	Ampoules containing 55.5 mg (320 IU per ampoule)	1966 (1st Reference Preparation)
Antibiotics I Held by International Laboratory for Biological Standards, National Institute for Medical Research, London			
Streptomycin (sulphate)	0.001 282	Ampoules containing 175 mg (780 IU per mg)	1958 (2nd Standard)
Dihydrostreptomycin (sulphate)	0.001 219	Ampoules containing 200 mg (820 IU per mg)	1966 (2nd Standard)
Bacitracin (zinc bacitracin)	0.013 51	Ampoules containing 100 mg (74 IU per mg)	1964 (2nd Standard)
Tetracycline (hydrochloride)	0.001 01	Ampoules containing 200 mg (990 IU per mg)	1957 (1st Standard)
Chlortetracycline (hydrochloride)	0.001	Ampoules containing 60 mg (1000 IU per mg)	1953 (1st Standard)
Oxytetracycline (dihydrate)	0.001 136 4	Ampoules containing 100 mg (880 IU per mg)	1966 (2nd Standard)
Erythromycin (dihydrate)	0.001 053	Ampoules containing 200 mg (950 IU per mg)	1957 (1st Standard)
Polymyxin B (sulphate, purified)	0.000 127	Ampoules containing 19 mg (7874 IU per mg)	1955 (1st Standard)
Nystatin	0.000 333	Ampoules containing 75 mg (3000 IU per mg)	1963 (1st Standard)
Amphotericin B	0.001 064	Ampoules containing 100 mg (940 IU per mg)	1963 (1st Standard)
Vancomycin (sulphate)	0.000 993	Ampoules containing 50 mg (1007 IU per mg)	1963 (1st Standard)
Oleandomycin (chloroform adduct)	0.001 176	Ampoules containing 75 mg (850 IU per mg)	1964 (1st Standard)
Novobiocin (acid)	0.001 031	Ampoules containing 100 mg (970 IU per mg)	1965 (1st Standard)
Colistin (sulphate)	0.000 048 78	Ampoules containing 75 mg (20 500 IU per mg)	1968 (1st Standard)
Rolitetracycline	0.001 004	Ampoules containing 100 mg (996 IU per mg)	1968 (1st Standard)
Kanamycin (sulphate)	0.001 232	Ampoules containing 50 mg (812 IU per mg)	1959 (1st Reference Preparation)
Kanamycin B	–	Ampoules containing 5 mg	1964 (1st Reference Preparation)
Viomycin (sulphate)	0.001 37	Ampoules containing 35 mg (730 IU per mg)	1959 (1st Reference Preparation)

Substance	International Unit (IU) mg	Form in which dispensed	Year of establishment
		Antibiotics I (continued)	
Penicillin K (89.9% pure sodium *n*-heptylpenicillin, with 9.6% penicillin dihydro F and 0.5% penicillin F)	–	Ampoules containing 20 mg	1951 (1st Reference Preparation)
Neomycin (sulphate)	0.001 47	Ampoules containing 100 mg (680 IU per mg)	1958 (1st Reference Preparation)
Ristocetin	–	Ampoules containing 45 mg	1960 (1st Reference Preparation)
Ristocetin B	–	Ampoules containing 5 mg	1964 (1st Reference Preparation)
Gramicidin S	0.001 002	Ampoules containing 50 mg (998 IU per mg)	1962 (1st Reference Preparation)
Gramicidin	0.001	Ampoules containing 55 mg (1000 IU per mg)	1966 (1st Reference Preparation)
Spiramycin (base)	0.000 312 5	Ampoules containing 50 mg (3200 IU per mg)	1962 (1st Reference Preparation)
Demethylchlortetracycline	0.001	Ampoules containing 80 mg (1000 IU per mg)	1962 (1st Reference Preparation)
Triacetyloleandomycin	0.001 2	Ampoules containing 100 mg (833 IU per mg)	1962 (1st Reference Preparation)
Procaine benzylpenicillin in oil with aluminium monostearate	–	Vials containing 10 ml	1966 (2nd Reference Preparation)
Paromomycin (sulphate)	0.001 333	Ampoules containing 75 mg (750 IU per mg)	1965 (1st Reference Preparation)
Colistin methane sulphonate	0.000 078 74	Ampoules containing 75 mg (12 700 IU per mg)	1966 (1st Reference Preparation)
Cephalothin (cefalotin) (sodium cephalothin)	0.001 066 1	Ampoules containing 50 mg (938 IU per mg)	1965 (1st Reference Preparation)
Lincomycin (hydrochloride)	0.001 135 1	Ampoules containing 50 mg (881 IU per mg)	1965 (1st Reference Preparation)
Capreomycin (sulphate)	0.001 087	Ampoules containing 80 mg (920 IU per mg)	1967 (1st Reference Preparation)
Rifamycin SV (sodium rifamycin SV)	0.001 127	Ampoules containing 100 mg (887 IU per mg)	1967 (1st Reference Preparation)
Gentamycin (sulphate)	0.001 56	Ampoules containing 50 mg (641 IU per mg)	1968 (1st Reference Preparation)
Lymecycline	0.001 107	Ampoules containing 50 mg (903 IU per mg)	1968 (1st Reference Preparation)
Antibiotics II Held by International Laboratory for Biological Standards, Central Veterinary Laboratory, Weybridge, England			
Tylosin (base)	0.001	Ampoules containing 40 mg (1000 IU per mg)	1966 (1st Standard)
Hygromycin B	0.000 892 8	Ampoules containing 40 mg (1120 IU per mg)	1966 (1st Standard)
Hormones, Vitamins, Enzymes Held by International Laboratory for Biological Standards, National Institute for Medical Research, London			
Oxytocin and vasopressin (antidiuretic hormone) for bioassay (posterior ox pituitary, acetone-dried, powdered)	0.5	Ampoules containing 30 mg (2 oxytocic, 2 vasopressor and 2 antidiuretic IU per mg)	1957 (3rd Standard)
Prolactin for bioassay (active principle from anterior sheep pituitary, dried)	0.045 45	Ampoules containing 10 mg (22 IU per mg)	1962 (2nd Standard)
Corticotropin (ACTH) for bioassay (from anterior pig pituitary, purified)	1.0	Ampoules containing 50 mg with lactose, freeze-dried (1 IU per mg)	1962 (3rd Standard)
Thyrotropin for bioassay (from anterior ox pituitary, purified)	13.5	Ampoules containing ten 20-mg tablets of a blend of 1 part thyrotropin and 19 parts lactose (ca. 1.48 IU per tablet)	1954 (1st Standard)
Growth hormone for bioassay (active principle from anterior ox pituitary, dried)	1.0	Ampoules containing 30 mg (1 IU per mg)	1955 (1st Standard)
Growth hormone for immunoassay (from human anterior pituitary, purified)	24.29	Ampoules containing 8.5 mg with sucrose (0.350 IU per ampoule)	1968 (1st Reference Preparation)

Substance	International Unit (IU) mg	Form in which dispensed	Year of establishment
Human menopausal gonadotropins for bioassay (active principle from urine of post-menopausal women, freeze-dried)	0.229 5	Ampoules containing 9 mg diluted with lactose (40 follicle-stimulating hormone IU and 40 interstitial cell-stimulating hormone IU per ampoule)	1964 (2nd Reference Preparation)
Serum gonadotropin for bioassay (from serum of pregnant mares)	0.003 569	Ampoules containing 5.71 mg with lactose, freeze-dried (1600 IU per ampoule)	1966 (2nd Standard)
Chorionic gonadotropin for bioassay (active principle from human urine of pregnancy)	0.001 279	Ampoules containing 7 mg diluted with lactose, dried (5300 IU per ampoule)	1963 (2nd Standard)
Insulin for bioassay (52% bovine and 48% porcine pancreas, purified)	0.041 67	Ampoules containing 110–125 mg (24 IU per mg)	1958 (4th Standard)
Erythropoietin for bioassay (from human urine)	1.48	Ampoules containing 14.80 mg with lactose (0.675 7 IU per mg)	1965 (1st Reference Preparation)
Heparin (sodium salt of purified active principle from bovine lung tissue)	0.007 7	Ampoules containing 20 mg (130 IU per mg)	1958 (2nd Standard)
Vitamin D_3	0.000 025	Bottles containing 6 g of a solution in vegetable oil (1000 IU per g)	1949 (2nd Standard)
Vitamin B_{12} (cyanocobalamin)	–	Ampoules containing ten 20-mg tablets	1959 (1st Reference Preparation)
Hyaluronidase (from bovine testes, dried)	0.1	Ampoules containing ten 20-mg tablets diluted with lactose (ca. 200 IU per tablet)	1955 (1st Standard)
Streptokinase-streptodornase (active material, dried)		Ampoules containing 1 mg with 5.5 mg of lactose (3100 streptokinase IU and 2400 streptodornase IU per ampoule)	1964 (1st Standard)
Streptokinase	0.002 090		
Streptodornase	0.002 700		
Urokinase (from human urine, purified)	0.001 410	Ampoules containing 6.77 mg with lactose, freeze-dried (4800 IU per ampoule)	1968 (1st Reference Preparation)
Miscellaneous I Held by International Laboratory for Biological Standards, National Institute for Medical Research, London			
Digitalis (dry powdered leaf of *Digitalis purpurea*)	76.0	Ampoules containing 2500 mg (0.013 16 IU per mg)	1949 (3rd Standard)
Neoarsphenamine	–	Ampoules containing 300 mg	1940 (3rd Reference Preparation)
Sulpharsphenamine	–	Ampoules containing 300 mg	1951 (3rd Reference Preparation)
Oxophenarsine (hydrochloride)	–	Sets of 3 ampoules containing: (a) 120 mg oxophenarsine hydrochloride (b) 100 mg anhydrous sodium carbonate (c) 500 mg anhydrous sucrose	1951 (1st Reference Preparation)
Mel B (melaminyl-4-phenylarsenodithioglycerol)	–	Ampoules containing 100 mg	1954 (1st Reference Preparation)
MSb (sodium *p*-melaminylphenylstibonate polymer)	–	Ampoules containing 500 mg	1954 (1st Reference Preparation)
Dimercaprol (BAL; 2,3-dimercaptopropanol)	–	Ampoules containing 2 ml	1952 (1st Reference Preparation)
Protamine	–	Ampoules containing 60 mg	1954 (1st Reference Preparation)
Pyrogen (purified 'O' antigen of *Shigella dysenteriae*, dried)	–	Ampoules containing 2 mg	1958 (1st Reference Preparation)
Miscellaneous II Held by International Laboratory for Biological Standards, Statens Seruminstitut, Copenhagen			
Opacity reference preparation (aqueous suspension of pyrex-glass particles)	–	Ampoules containing 15 ml (10 IU of opacity per ml)	1965 (3rd Reference Preparation)
Miscellaneous III Held by Rijks Instituut voor de Volksgezondheid, Utrecht			
Haemiglobincyanide reference preparation	–	Ampoules containing 10 ml of haemiglobincyanide solution	1967 (1st Reference Preparation)

Substance	Form in which dispensed	Year of establishment
International Biological Reference Reagents **Reference Reagents I** Held by International Laboratory for Biological Standards, Statens Seruminstitut, Copenhagen		
Anti-tick-borne encephalitis sera:		
Anti-tick-borne encephalitis serum (louping ill [Moredun] virus)	Ampoules containing 1 ml of freeze-dried sheep serum	1964 (1st Reference Reagent)
Anti-tick-borne encephalitis serum (Russian spring-summer encephalitis [Sophyn and Absettarov] virus)	Ampoules containing 2 ml of freeze-dried sheep serum	1964 (1st Reference Reagent)
Cholera agglutinating serum (Ogawa)	Ampoules containing 1 ml of monospecific serum	1967 (1st Reference Reagent)
Anti-trichinella human serum	Ampoules containing 1 ml of freeze-dried pooled human serum	1968 (1st Reference Reagent)
Enterovirus antisera:		
Coxsackie virus antisera types A9, B1, B2 and B3	Ampoules containing 0.5 ml of freeze-dried monkey serum	1965 (1st Reference Reagent)
Coxsackie virus antisera types B4 and B5 Echovirus antisera types 1, 2, 3, 4, 5, 6, 6¹, 6¹¹, 7, 8, 9, 11, 12, 13, 14, 15, 16, 17, 18, 19, 20, 21, 22, 23, 24 and 25 Poliovirus antisera types 1, 2 and 3 Reovirus antiserum type 1	Ampoules containing 0.5 ml of freeze-dried monkey serum	1966 (1st Reference Reagent)
Adenovirus antisera:		
Types 1, 2, 3, 5, 6, 7a, 8, 9, 10, 11, 13, 15 and 17	Ampoules containing 0.5 ml of freeze-dried horse serum	1966 (1st Reference Reagent)
Types 12 and 18	Ampoules containing 0.5 ml of freeze-dried horse serum	1967 (1st Reference Reagent)
Parainfluenza virus antisera: Types 1, 2 and 3 Mycoplasma pneumoniae antiserum	Ampoules containing 0.5 ml of freeze-dried horse serum	1968 (1st Reference Reagent)
Reference Reagents II Held by WHO/FAO and WHO Leptospirosis Reference Laboratories		
Anti-*Leptospira* sera:		
Anti-*Leptospira interrogans* serotype *saxkoebing* serum Anti-*Leptospira interrogans* serotype *castellonis* serum Anti-*Leptospira interrogans* serotype *sejroe* serum Anti-*Leptospira interrogans* serotype *mini* serum Anti-*Leptospira interrogans* serotype *australis* serum Anti-*Leptospira interrogans* serotype *copenhageni* serum Anti-*Leptospira interrogans* serotype *tarassovi* serum Anti-*Leptospira interrogans* serotype *autumnalis* serum Anti-*Leptospira interrogans* serotype *rachmati* serum Anti-*Leptospira interrogans* serotype *pomona* serum Anti-*Leptospira interrogans* serotype *bataviae* serum Anti-*Leptospira interrogans* serotype *hebdomadis* serum Anti-*Leptospira interrogans* serotype *andamana* serum Anti-*Leptospira interrogans* serotype *javanica* serum Anti-*Leptospira interrogans* serotype *pyrogenes* serum	Ampoules containing 0.5 ml or 1.0 ml of hyperimmune rabbit serum, dried	1958 (1st Reference Reagent)
Anti-*Leptospira interrogans* serotype *naam* serum Anti-*Leptospira interrogans* serotype *mankarso* serum Anti-*Leptospira interrogans* serotype *sarmin* serum Anti-*Leptospira interrogans* serotype *poi* serum Anti-*Leptospira interrogans* serotype *schueffneri* serum Anti-*Leptospira interrogans* serotype *muenchen* serum Anti-*Leptospira interrogans* serotype *cynopteri* serum Anti-*Leptospira interrogans* serotype *bangkinang* serum Anti-*Leptospira interrogans* serotype *wolffi* serum Anti-*Leptospira interrogans* serotype *hardjo* serum Anti-*Leptospira interrogans* serotype *kremastos* serum Anti-*Leptospira interrogans* serotype *benjamin* serum Anti-*Leptospira interrogans* serotype *zanoni* serum Anti-*Leptospira interrogans* serotype *medanensis* serum Anti-*Leptospira interrogans* serotype *paidjan* serum	Ampoules containing 0.5 ml or 1.0 ml of hyperimmune rabbit serum, dried	1962 (1st Reference Reagent)
Anti-*Leptospira interrogans* serotype *semaranga* serum	Ampoules containing 1.0 ml of hyperimmune rabbit serum, dried	1962 (2nd Reference Reagent)
Anti-*Leptospira interrogans* serotype *canicola* serum Anti-*Leptospira interrogans* serotype *grippotyphosa* serum Anti-*Leptospira interrogans* serotype *icterohaemorrhagiae* serum	Ampoules containing 0.5 ml of hyperimmune rabbit serum, dried	1966 (2nd Reference Reagent)
Anti-*Leptospira interrogans* serotype *atlantae* serum Anti-*Leptospira interrogans* serotype *georgia* serum Anti-*Leptospira interrogans* serotype *bratislava* serum Anti-*Leptospira interrogans* serotype *erinacei-aurati* serum Anti-*Leptospira interrogans* serotype *coxi* serum Anti-*Leptospira interrogans* serotype *fugis* serum Anti-*Leptospira interrogans* serotype *worsfoldi* serum Anti-*Leptospira interrogans* serotype *malaya* serum	Ampoules containing 0.5 ml or 1.0 ml of hyperimmune rabbit serum, dried	1966 (1st Reference Reagent)

A detailed index to the statistical tables (pages 28–131) and chapter on Statistical Methods (pages 146–196) will be found on pages 197–198

A

a (are) 203
a (astronomical year) 206
a (atto-) 9
A. See Adenosine
A (ampere) 215, 216
Å (ångström) 200, 202
A (work of breathing) 546, 552
AB0 blood-group system 626, 627
– clinical significance 633
– secretors and nonsecretors in 631
ABH substances. See Blood-group substances
Absolute zero 208, 209
Absorbed dose of radionuclides 218 sq., 286, 287
Absorptance 224
Abundances of elements and isotopes 234 sq.
Ac. See Actinium
Acceleration, angular, units 211
– due to gravity 211, 230
– linear, units 210, 211
Acetals 308
Acetaldehyde, conversion to acetic acid 402
– from β-alanine 401
– in alcoholic fermentation 390
– in blood 606
– in 2-deoxyribose 5-phosphate degradation 399
– 2-deoxyribose 5-phosphate from 420
– in L-threonine degradation 397
Acetaldehyde-TPP complex in oxidation of sugars 391
Acetal phosphatides. See Plasmalogens
Acetate, formation from acetaldehyde 402
– in amino-sugar formation 424
– in biological materials 366
– in blood 607
– cholesterol synthesis from 426
– in coffee 508
– in faeces 660
– from degradation of foodstuffs 402
– oestrogen synthesis from 431
– in urine 674
– vitamin A synthesis from 457
– in yoghurt 511
Acetate buffer 280 sq.
Acetic acid (*see also Acetate*) 366
– solutions, decinormal 277
– – pH values 279
Acetoacetate, conversion factor into acetone 251
– in blood 608
– in cerebrospinal fluid 639
– in degradation of fats 393
– in leucine degradation 396
– in phenylalanine degradation 398
– accumulation in tissues 393
– in urine 674
Acetoacetyl-CoA-hydrolase in degradation of fats 393
Acetoacetyl-coenzyme A, carnitine transport 491
– in cholesterol synthesis 426, 427
– in degradation of fats 393
– in ketosis 393
– in L-lysine degradation 398
Acetoin in blood 606
Acetone, conversion factor into acetoacetic acid 251
– in blood 608
– conversion factor into β-hydroxybutyrate 251
– accumulation in tissues 393
– in urine 661, 674
Acetone bodies. See Ketone bodies
Acetonitrile in urine 668
N-Acetyl-*S*-arylcysteines, mercapturic acids from 445
Acetylation in detoxication 444
N-Acetyl-*S*-*p*-chlorobenzylcysteine in detoxication of *p*-dichlorobenzene 445
Acetylcholine, in blood 575
– in cerebrospinal fluid 637
– formation and function 434
– enzymatic hydrolysis 414
– in liberation of pancreatic enzymes 651
– in sweat 681
Acetylcholinesterase 414
Acetyl-CoA. See Acetyl-coenzyme A
Acetyl-CoA acyltransferase in degradation of fats 392
Acetyl-CoA carboxylase 487
– in fatty-acid synthesis 424
Acetyl-coenzyme A, in acetylation of amines 444
– in amino-sugar formation 424
– carnitine transport by 491
– in cholesterol degradation 401
– cholesterol synthesis from 426, 427
Acetyl-coenzyme A, in 2-deoxyribose 5-phosphate degradation 399
– in degradation of fats 391, 392
– in fatty acid synthesis 420, 424, 425
– from degradation of foods 402
– in glucosamine formation 423
– in detoxication of halogenobenzenes 445
– in isoleucine degradation 396
– in ketosis 393
– in leucine degradation 396
– in L-lysine degradation 398
– in norleucine degradation 396
– in norvaline degradation 396
– in phenylalanine degradation 398
– in serine degradation 397
– in oxidation of sugars 391
– in L-threonine degradation 397
– in tricarboxylic acid cycle 390, 391
5-*N*-Acetyl, *O*-diacetylneuraminic acid 316
Acetylenic acids 371
Acetylesterase 414
– in milk 689
N-Acetyl-D-galactosamine 315
– in lipids 365
β-Acetylglucosaminase 412, 413
N-Acetyl-D-glucosamine 315
– formation 424
– phosphates 320
– sialic acid from 423
– utilization 424
Acetylglutamate in urea synthesis 442, 443
Acetylhexosamine in serum proteins 581
N-Acetylhistamine in urine 670
N-Acetyl-5-hydroxytryptamine, melatonin from 730
N-Acetylkynurenine, in tryptophan metabolism 475
– in urine 669
S-Acetyl-α-lipoic acid in oxidation of sugars 391
N-Acetyl-D-mannosamine 316
– formation and utilization 424
– 6-phosphate 320
– – formation and utilization 424
– – in *N*-acetylneuraminic acid 9-phosphate formation 423
N-Acetyl-5-methoxytryptamine 730
Acetyl-β-methylcholine, hydrolysis 414
N-Acetylneuraminic acid 316
– formation and utilization 424
– in gangliosides 377
– 9-phosphate 320
– – formation 423, 424
– – utilization 424
– in serum proteins 581
Acetylsulphanilamide 444
Acids, aliphatic, conjugation 442
– aromatic, conjugation 442
– – in urine 675
– – in wine 509
– excess in foods 499 sq.
– organic, in body fluids 523
– – conversion factors 523
– – in faeces 659
– – in urine 674
– phenolic, in coffee 509
– in urine 535
– volatile, in blood 607
– – in urine 674
Acid–amino acid ligases 386
Acid–ammonia ligases 386
Acid–base balance, of blood, nomogram 569
– disturbances, parenteral therapy 530
– – pH of CSF in 635
– pH and 527
Acid–base indicators 283
Acidosis 569
– metabolic 528
– renotubular 449, 452, 453
– – in vitamin D deficiency 461
– respiratory 527
– urinary acidity in 662
Acid phosphatase. See Phosphatase, acid
Acid–thiol ligases 386
Aconitase. See Aconitate hydratase
Aconitate hydratase, in plasma 599
– in tricarboxylic acid cycle 390, 391
cis-Aconitic acid in tricarboxylic acid cycle 390, 391
Acoustical quantities and units 224 sq.
ACP (acyl carrier protein) 425
Acre 203
2-Acroleyl-3-aminofumaric acid in tryptophan degradation 399
Acromegaly 720
Acrylic acid 368
ACTH (adrenocorticotropic hormone). See Corticotropin
Actinides 231, 245–248
Actinium, properties, isotopes, etc. 245
Actinium-228, properties 245
Actinium A (^{215}Po), properties 244
Actinium B (^{211}Pb), properties 243
Actinium C (^{211}Bi), properties 243
Actinium C′ (^{211}Po), properties 244
Actinium C″ (^{207}Tl), properties 242
Actinium K (^{223}Fr), properties 244
Actinium X (^{223}Ra), properties 245
Actinon (^{219}Rn), properties 244
Actinouranium (^{235}U), properties 247
Action, quantum of 228
– units 214
Activators, enzymatic 382, 385
Acyl-adenosine monophosphate. See Acyladenylate
Acyl-adenylate 346
– in degradation of fats 391
Acylcarnitines 491
Acyl carrier protein 425
Acylcholine acyl-hydrolase. See Cholinesterase
Acyl-CoA dehydrogenase in degradation of fats 392
Acyl-CoA synthetase in degradation of fats 391
Acyl-coenzyme A, in degradation of fats 391, 392
– in triglyceride synthesis 426
Acylglucuronide formation in detoxication 442
Acylglycerols (*see also Mono-, Di- and Triglycerides*) 365, 374 sq.
Acylphosphatase 416
Acyltransferases 385
ADDISON's disease, corticosteroid secretion 745
Adenine 338
– degradation 401
– in DNA synthesis 352
– in protein synthesis 353
– in purine degradation 400
– in RNA synthesis 352
– in urine 671
Adeninecyanocobamide 483
Adenine deaminase 401
– in purine degradation 400
Adenine nucleotide. See Adenosine 5′-phosphate
Adenosine (A, Ado) 337, 339
– enzymatic deamination 419
– in purine degradation 400
Adenosine aminohydrolase. See Adenosine deaminase
Adenosine deaminase 401, 419
– in plasma 599
– in purine degradation 400
Adenosine diphosphate (pyrophosphate) (ADP) 337, 343
– conversion to ATP 403, 404
– in biological energy transformations 404
– in biological oxidations 403
– in blood 577
Adenosine 3′,5′-diphosphate in sulphate ester formation 445
Adenosine diphosphate ribose, enzymatic cleavage 416
Adenosine diphosphoflavin ribitol. See Flavin adenine dinucleotide
Adenosine monophosphate (5′-phosphate) (AMP) 337, 343
– in biological energy transformations 404
– biosynthesis 435
– in blood 577
– enzymatic deamination 419
– in purine degradation 400
– in RNA 351
Adenosine 3′,5′-phosphate (cyclic) 345
– biosynthesis, effect of oxytocin and vasopressin 723, 724
– – in adrenals, effect of ACTH 717
– effect of glucagon 738
Adenosine phosphates in saliva 644
Adenosine 3′-phosphate 5′-phosphosulphate 346
– in sulphate ester formation 445
Adenosine 5′-phosphosulphate 346
– in sulphate ester formation 445
Adenosine 5′-pyrophosphate. See Adenosine diphosphate
Adenosine triphosphate (ATP) 337, 343
– in amino-sugar formation and utilization 424
– in bile-acid conjugation 438
– in biological energy transformations 404
– in biological oxidations 403
– biosynthesis 403, 404

A detailed index to the statistical tables (pages 28–131) and chapter on Statistical Methods (pages 146–196) will be found on pages 197–198

Adenosine triphosphate (*contd*), in blood 577
- in carbohydrate synthesis and breakdown. 441
- in carbon-chain extension 424
- catecholamine complexes............... 731
- in cephalin formation.................. 425
- in cholesterol formation 426
- in coenzyme A formation 345, 487
- reaction with creatine 437, 438
- in degradation of fats............. 391, 392
- in fatty acid synthesis from citrate... 424, 425
- in glutathione formation 438
- in formation of glycine conjugates .. 444, 445
- in glycolysis.......................... 389
- in guanylic acid formation 436
- in inosinic acid formation 433, 435
- in isoleucine degradation.............. 396
- in lactic acid fermentation............. 390
- in lecithin formation 425
- in leucine degradation 395, 396
- in L-methionine degradation............ 398
- in NAD and NADP formation 477
- in transfer of one-carbon groups 437
- in pantothenic acid formation 487
- in detoxication of phenylacetic acid...... 445
- in phosphatidic acid formation.......... 375
- in pyrimidine formation 439
- in spermatozoa 684
- in sulphate ester formation............. 445
- in thiamine formation 470
- in urea formation .... 442 sq.
- in vitamin B_{12} formation 484
S-Adenosylhomocysteine, in creatine formation 437
- in L-methionine degradation............ 398
S-Adenosylmethionine, in creatine formation 437
- in L-methionine degradation............ 398
Adenovirus antisera, reference reagents 764
Adenylate cyclase, effect of catecholamines . 733
Adenylate kinase, in synthesis of ATP 404
- in plasma 595
5′-Adenylic acid. See Adenosine monophosphate
Adenylosuccinate lyase in adenylic acid formation 436
Adenylosuccinic acid 342
- in adenylic acid formation.......... 435, 436
Adermine. See Pyridoxine
ADH. See Alcohol dehydrogenase
ADH (antidiuretic hormone). See Vasopressin
Adipic acid in urine 674
Adipohepatic liver, serum enzyme changes . 586
Adipose tissue. See under Tissues
Ado. See Adenosine
Adolescence, basal metabolism............ 539
- blood, acid phosphatase 596
- - alkaline phosphatase................. 596
- - aspartate aminotransferase........... 593
- - calcium............................ 565
- - fructosediphosphate aldolase 599
- - glucose............................ 605
- - growth hormone.................... 720
- - iodine............................. 564
- - lactate dehydrogenase 590
- - magnesium 566
- - inorganic phosphorus 563
- - potassium.......................... 564
- - proteins 583
- - thyroid hormone 726
- - thyroxine breakdown................ 727
- blood pressure 553
- blood volume 554, 555
- body weight 711
- bone marrow cells 621
- erythrocytes, count................. 614, 617
- - diameter........................... 617
- - sedimentation rate 558
- - mean corpuscular volume 617
- haematocrit 617
- haemoglobin 617
- iodide metabolism 726
- leucocyte count.................... 618, 619
- lung values 550
- organ weights 710
- reticulocyte count 613
- development of teeth 709
- urine, corticosteroids .... 747 sq.
- - gonadotropins....................... 714
- - pregnanediol 754
- - testosterone 752
- - volume 661
- vitamin B_6 requirement 475
Adonitol................................. 322
D-Adonose. See D-Ribulose
ADP. See Adenosine diphosphate
Adrenals, ascorbic acid 490
- catecholamines 731
- cholesterol synthesis................... 426
- corticosteroids.................... 743, 746
- hyperplasia........................... 456
- lactic acid fermentation 388
- phenylethanolamine *N*-methyltransferase . 440
- phospholipase A 417
- respiratory rate 387
- weight 710
Adrenal cortex, effect of ACTH....... 430, 717
- androgens 751
- in cardiac infarction 624
- functional tests 747
- hormones. See Corticosteroids
- insufficiency, sodium in sweat 680
- - urinary secretion.................... 661
- oestrogens 755
- pituitary control 430
- progesterone secretion 753
Adrenaline.............................. 730
- in cyclic AMP formation............... 345
- biosynthesis 440, 731
- in blood 731, 733
- breakdown............................ 732
- and haemorrhagic diatheses 623, 624
- release............................... 731
- in urine 668, 733
Adrenal medulla, in cardiac infarction . 623, 624
- catecholamine formation 731
Adrenochrome from adrenaline............ 731
Adrenocortical hormones. See Corticosteroids
Adrenocorticosteroid hormones. See Corticosteroids
Adrenocorticotropic hormone. See Corticotropin
Adrenocorticotropin. See Corticotropin
Adrenogenital syndrome and ossification... 707
Adrenoglomerulotropin 730
Adrenosterone 379
- biosynthesis 428, 429
Aetianedione 379
Aetiocholanedione 379
Aetiocholanolone 379
- in urine 746, 749
3β-Aetiocholanolone 379
Aetiocobalamin......................... 483
Aetioporphyrins 355
Ag. See Silver
Agglomerins in erythrocyte sedimentation.. 559
Agglutinins, cold, in erythrocyte sedimentation 559
Ag groups of serum...................... 634
Aglycons 308
Air (*see also Atmosphere*), molecular weight.. 252
- radiation absorbed by 220
- standard, in spectroscopy 230
- sea level standard values 252
- standard density 230
Al. See Aluminium
Ala. See α-Alanine
Alactasia............................... 451
α-Alanine (L-alanine) (Ala) 330
- in blood 574
- in blood proteins 581
- degradation 394, 402
- in foods 516
- formation from glucose................. 420
- in milk 688
- in saliva 645
- in sweat 680
- in transamination reactions 394
- in tryptophan degradation 399
- in urine 667
β-Alanine.............................. 334
- in blood 574
- in degradation of cytosine and uracil 401
- formation from aspartic acid 394, 434
- function 434
- oxidation 401
- in pantothenic acid synthesis 487
- in saliva 645
- in transamination reactions............. 394
- in urine 667
Alanine aminotransferase, activity, gradients 586
- - temperature correction 585
- in blood 585, 594
- - half-life............................ 586
- - in heart disease 587
- - in liver disease 586, 587
- - effect of muscular work.............. 586
- - in pregnancy 586
- in cerebrospinal fluid 638
Alanine aminotransferase, in gastric juice ... 650
- in milk 689
- in saliva 645
- in seminal plasma 684
- in synovial fluid 641
- in tissues 585
L-Alanine: 2-oxoglutarate aminotransferase. See Alanine aminotransferase
Alanyl-transfer RNA 351
Albinism 448
Albumins 329
Albumin (serum albumin), amino-acid composition 581
- in bile............................... 655
- in blood 580, 582, 583
- in cerebrospinal fluid 637
- characteristics and function............. 580
- in faeces 659
- in gastric juice........................ 650
- glomerular filtration and excretion 536
- in intestinal juice 656
- lipid complex, in erythrocyte sedimentation 559
- metabolism 579
- in milk 688, 689
- osmotic activity 526
- in pancreatic juice..................... 652
- activation of phospholipase A 417
- in saliva 645
- in semen............................. 684
- in synovial fluid 641
- tagged, enteral excretion test 289
- in urine 668
Alcohol. See Ethanol
Alcohols, complex cyclic, as lipid components 365
- conjugation........................... 442
- higher aliphatic, in faeces 659
- - in lipids 365
- polyhydric 312, 322
Alcohol dehydrogenase, in plasma 590
- in isomerization of retinal.............. 460
- in tissues 585
- in vitamin A metabolism............... 457
Alcoholic beverages, composition 509
Alcoholic fermentation 387, 390
Alcohol: NAD oxidoreductase. See Alcohol dehydrogenase
ALD (aldolase). See Fructosediphosphate aldolase
Aldehyde-lyases 386
Aldehyde oxidase, in vitamin A metabolism. 457
- in vitamin B_6 interconversions 473
Aldolase. See Fructosediphosphate aldolase
Aldonic acids 312, 323
Aldoses .... 308 sq.
Aldosterone................ 379, 430, 743 sq.
- in adrenals........................... 743
- biological activity..................... 749
- biosynthesis...................... 428, 429
- in blood 745
- breakdown....................... 746, 747
- secretion, effect of ACTH.............. 717
- - effect of angiotensin................ 741
- - inborn limitation 456
- - effect of progesterone 754
- - rates 743, 745
- in urine 746, 747
Aldo-sugars........................ 308 sq.
Aliesterase 414
Aliphatic acids, conjugation 442
Alizarin yellow indicators 283
Alkaline phosphatase. See Phosphatase, alkaline
Alkalosis 569
- metabolic 528
- respiratory........................... 527
- urinary acidity in 662
Alkaptonuria........................... 448
- homogentisic acid excretion in.......... 675
Alkoxydiglycerides................. 365, 374
Alkylglucuronides, formation in detoxication 442
Alkyl lysophosphatide ethers 365
Alkyloxylysophosphatides................ 376
Allantoic acid in purine degradation....... 401
Allantoin, in plasma..................... 577
- in purine degradation............. 400, 401
- from uric acid 419
- in urine 671
ALLEN-DOISY test 755
Allo-compounds 381
Allocortol 379
β-Allocortol 379
Allocortolone 379
β-Allocortolone 379
α-Allopregnanediol 379

A detailed index to the statistical tables (pages 28–131) and chapter on Statistical Methods (pages 146–196) will be found on pages 197–198

α-Allopregnanediol from progesterone 753
β-Allopregnanediol 379
α-Allopregnanolone 379
D-Allose 310
Allosteric enzymes 382
Allo-steroids 378, 381
Allotetrahydrocorticosterone, breakdown 746
– in urine 747
Allotetrahydrocortisol 379
– breakdown 746
– in urine 747
Allotypy, genetic, of serum proteins 634
D-Allulose 311
Almonds, amino acids 516
– composition 507
Alpha-globulins. See α-Globulins
D-Altroheptulose. See D-Sedoheptulose
D-Altroketoheptose. See D-Sedoheptulose
D-Altrose 310
Aluminium, atomic weight multiples 250
– in blood 567
– in faeces 658
– flame lines 284
– properties, isotopes, etc. 235
– in synovial fluid 641
– in urine 664
Alveolar diffusing capacity 545, 552
– oxygen and carbon dioxide pressures 544
– ventilation 542
Am (americium) 248
Amaurotic familial idiocy 455
AMELUNG-HORN enzyme units 584
Americium, properties and isotopes 248
Amide synthetases 386
Amidine-lyases 386
Amidinotransferases 385
Amines, acetylation 444
– aliphatic, in blood 573
– in urine 668
Aminoacetic acid. See Glycine
Aminoacetone, in erythrocytes 575
– in urine 670
Amino acids 329 sq.
– in bile 654
– in blood 573, 574
– carbohydrate synthesis from 441
– synthesis of cell constituents from 433 sq.
– in cerebrospinal fluid 636
– decarboxylation 394
– determination 329
– essential, dietary requirements 496
– in faeces 659
– in foods 516
– in gastric juice 649
– glomerular filtration and excretion 536
– glucogenic, cell constituents from 434
– in leucocytes 574
– metabolism 393 sq.
– – action of corticosteroids 749
– – inborn errors 448
– in milk 688
– nonessential, formation from glucose 420
– physical and chemical properties 330 sq.
– in protein synthesis 353
– in saliva 645
– in semen 683
– sulphur-containing, in urine 663
– in sweat 680
– in thrombocytes 574
– in transamination reactions 394, 395
– in urine 453, 666, 667
– – in rickets 464
Amino-acid acceptor RNA 351
D-Amino-acid oxidases, in amino-acid degradation 393
– in D-ornithine and D-proline degradation 395
– prosthetic group 345
L-Amino-acid oxidases in amino-acid degradation 393
Amino acid–RNA ligases 386
Aminoaciduria, benign familial 452, 453
– in coproporphyria 455
– in cystinosis 449
– in lactose intolerance 451
α-Aminoacrylic acid, in L-cysteine degradation 397
– in serine degradation 396
Aminoacyl adenosine monophosphates 346
Amino-acyl-dipeptide hydrolase. See Aminopeptidase
α-Amino-acyl-peptide hydrolases 386, 405, 408, 409
Aminoacyl s-RNA in protein synthesis 353
Aminoacyltransferases 385
α-Aminoadipic acid 334
α-Aminoadipic acid, in L-lysine degradation 398
– in urine 667
α-Aminoadipic semialdehyde in L-lysine degradation 398
o-Aminobenzoic acid. See Anthranilic acid
p-Aminobenzoic acid, acetylation 444
– in folic acid synthesis 478
– in urine 668
2-Aminobenzoylpyruvic acid in tryptophan degradation 399
α-Amino-*n*-butyric acid 334
– in blood 574
– degradation 396, 402
– in urine 667
γ-Amino-*n*-butyric acid (GABA) 334
– breakdown in brain, vitamin B_6 in 475
– formation from glutamic acid 394
– in saliva 645
– in transamination reactions 394
– in urine 667
α-Aminocaproic acid. See Norleucine
ε-Aminocaproic acid and haemorrhagic diatheses 623
α-Amino-γ-carbamylbutyric acid. See Glutamine
α-Amino-β-carbamylpropionic acid. See Asparagine
α-Aminocrotonic acid, in homoserine degradation 397
– in L-threonine degradation 397
2-Amino-2-deoxy-D-galactose. See D-Galactosamine
2-Amino-2-deoxy-D-glucose. See D-Glucosamine
2-Aminoethanesulphonic acid. See Taurine
α-Aminoglutaric acid. See Glutamic acid
Aminoglycolipids 365, 377
– accumulation 455
α-Amino-δ-guanidovaleric acid. See Arginine
o-Aminohippuric acid in urine 666, 669
p-Aminohippuric acid (PAH), renal plasma flow 531
– tubular secretion 534
2-Amino-3-hydroxybenzoylpyruvic acid in tryptophan degradation 399
α-Amino-β-hydroxybutyric acid. See Threonine
α-Amino-γ-hydroxybutyric acid. See Homoserine
2-Amino-4-hydroxy-6-hydroxymethyldihydropteridine pyrophosphate in folic acid synthesis 478
α-Amino-β-(*p*-hydroxyphenyl)propionic acid. See Tyrosine
α-Amino-β-hydroxypropionic acid. See Serine
2-Amino-6-hydroxypurine. See Guanine
6-Amino-2-hydroxypyrimidine. See Cytosine
Aminoimidazole carboxamide in urine 671
α-Amino-β-(4-imidazole)propionic acid. See Histidine
α-Amino-β-(3-indolyl)propionic acid. See Tryptophan
β-Aminoisobutyric acid 334
– in blood 574
– oxidation 401
– in thymine degradation 401
– in urine 401, 453, 667
α-Aminoisocaproic acid. See Leucine
α-Aminoisovaleric acid. See Valine
α-Amino-β-ketoadipic acid, in glycine degradation 397
– in haem synthesis 454
– in porphyrin formation 437
δ-Aminolaevulinic acid 334
– biosynthesis, pyridoxal phosphate in 475
– in blood 575
– in glycine degradation 397
– in haem synthesis 454
– in porphyrin formation 437
– in urine 454, 455, 670
δ-Aminolaevulinic acid synthetase in liver 454
2-Amino-2-methylpropane-1,3-diol buffer 280 sq.
α-Amino-γ-methylthiolbutyric acid. See Methionine
α-Amino-β-methylvaleric acid. See Isoleucine
p-[2-Amino-4-oxodihydropteridyl-(6)]-methylaminobenzoyl-L-glutamic acid. See Folic acid
Aminopeptidase 409, 411
– in plasma 598
– in synovial fluid 641
– in urine 672
α-Amino-β-phenylpropionic acid. See Phenylalanine
Aminopropanol in vitamin B_{12} synthesis 484
α-Aminopropionic acid. See α-Alanine
β-Aminopropionic acid. See β-Alanine
Aminopterin 481
4-Aminopteroylglutamic acid 481
6-Aminopurine. See Adenine
Aminosuccinic acid. See Aspartic acid
Amino sugars 311
– formation 423, 424
– utilization 424
α-Amino-β-thiolpropionic acid. See Cysteine
Aminotransferases 386
– cell binding 585
Aminotripeptidase. See Aminopeptidase
α-Amino-δ-ureidovaleric acid. See Citrulline
α-Aminovinylacetic acid in homoserine degradation 397
Ammonia, conversion factors 251
– in blood 449, 450, 573
– in blood proteins 581
– in cerebrospinal fluid 449, 636
– in faeces 659
– in gastric juice 649
– intoxication 449, 450
– in saliva 645
– in semen 683
– solutions, decinormal 277
– – pH values 279
– in sweat 680
– in urine 666
Ammonia-lyases 386
Ammonium (*see also Ammonia*), mol.wt. multiples 250
Ammonium chloride, solutions, conversion factors 274 sq.
– – decinormal 277
– – infusion 529
– – pH values 279
– effect on urinary osmolarity and specific gravity 534
Ammonium dihydrogen phosphate solutions, pH values 279
*di*Ammonium hydrogen phosphate solutions, pH values 279
Ammonium hydroxide, decinormal solutions 277
Ammonium magnesium phosphate in urinary sediments 677, 678
Ammonium nitrite, decinormal solutions 277
Ammonium oxalate solutions, pH values 279
Ammonium phosphate, effect on urinary osmolarity and specific gravity 534
Ammonium sulphate, solutions, decinormal 277
– – pH values 279
– effect on urinary osmolarity and specific gravity 534
Ammonium thiocyanate, decinormal solutions 277
Amniotic fluid, composition 522
– erythropoietic activity 740
– gain in weight 690
Amount of substance 226, 227
AMP. See Adenosine monophosphate
– cyclic. See Adenosine 3′,5′-phosphate
AMP-deaminase 401, 419
– in purine degradation 400
Ampere 215, 216
Amphotericin B, standard 761
amu (atomic mass unit) 227
Amylase 411
– in bile 655
– in blood 597
– – in heart disease 587
– – effect of muscular work 586
– – in pancreatic disease 587
– conversion factors 584
– in intestinal mucosa 413
– isozymes 584
– in milk 689
– in pancreatic juice 652
– in saliva 645, 646
– units 584
– in urine 672
Amylo-1,6-glucosidase. See Dextrin-1,6-glucosidase
Amylopectin 325
– enzymatic hydrolysis 411
Amylopectinosis 450, 451
α-Amylose. See Amylopectin
β-Amylose (amylose) 325
– enzymatic hydrolysis 411
AN factor (biotin sulphoxide) 486
Anaemia 446 sq., 455
– COOLEY's 448
– serum enzyme changes 587

Index

A detailed index to the statistical tables (pages 28–131) and chapter on Statistical Methods (pages 146–196) will be found on pages 197–198

Anaemia (*contd*), erythrocyte coproporphyrin 575
– erythrocyte osmotic resistance 616
– erythrocyte protoporphyrin 576
– haemolytic 454
– – pyruvate kinase in 594
– – serum bilirubin in 577
– macrocytic, in folic acid deficiency 479
– – in vitamin B_{12} deficiency 485
– megaloblastic 453
– – in folic acid deficiency 479, 610
– – serum glucosephosphate isomerase in 600
– – in vitamin B_{12} deficiency 610
– microcytic 448
– pernicious, diagnosis from gastric juice 650
– – gastric acidity and 648
– – gastric juice carbohydrates in 650
– pyridoxine-deficiency 476
– pyridoxine-sensitive 476
– in scurvy, ascorbic acid and 490
– sickle-cell 446, 447
– – blood viscosity in 558
ANDERSEN's disease 450, 451
Androgens 379 sq., 751 sq.
– biological activity 752, 753, 758
– biosynthesis 428, 429
– – inborn excess 456
– in blood 751, 752
– in semen 685
Androstane 381
5α-Androstane-3,17-dione 379, 751 sq.
5β-Androstane-3,17-dione 379
Androstan-3α-ol-17-one. See Androsterone
Δ^4-Androstene-3,17-dione 379, 751 sq.
– biosynthesis 428, 429
– breakdown 746
– in oestrogen synthesis 431
– in testes 746
Androst-4-ene-3,11,17-trione. See Adrenosterone
Androstenolone. See Dehydroepiandrosterone
Androsterone 379, 751 sq.
– in urine 430, 746, 749
Anemia. See Anaemia
Aneosinophilia 620
Aneurin. See Thiamine
Angina pectoris, serum enzyme changes 587
Angioneurotic oedema, plasma kinins 742
Angiotensin 740, 741
Angiotensinase 740
Angiotonin 740, 741
Angles 138, 139
– units 138, 207, 208
Ångström 200, 202
Angular acceleration units 211
– frequency units 208
– momentum, quantum-mechanical unit 228
– velocity units 210
Anhydro-compounds 381
Animal protein factor 482
Anoestrin 730
Anomalistic year 206
ANSBACHER unit for vitamin K 467
Anserine in urine 666
Anteisomargaric acid 371
Anterior pituitary. See under Pituitary
Anthranilic acid, in tryptophan degradation 398, 399, 475
– in urine 669
Antibiotics, standards and reference preparations 761, 762
Antibodies, blood-group specific, clinical importance 632, 633
– action of corticosteroids 750
– formation, pyridoxal phosphate in 475
– carried by immunoglobulins 580
– standards and reference preparations 760, 761
Anticoagulants, use in thrombo-embolism 622
Anticodons 353
Antidiuretic hormone. See Vasopressin
Antidiuretin. See Vasopressin
Antigens, infrequent 632
– private 632
– public 632
– standards and reference preparations 759
– widely distributed 632
Antigen–antibody reaction 626
Anti-inflammatory steroids 379, 380
Antilogarithms, common four-place 11
– explanation 134, 135
Antilogits and logits 56
Antilysokinases 622
Antimony, properties, isotopes, etc. 239
Antimony-124, characteristics 293
Antiplasmin 622
Antirachitic activity 462 sq.
Antisera, standards and reference preparations 760, 761
Antistreptolysin O, standard 760
Antitoxins, standards and reference preparations 760
α_1-Antitrypsin, amino-acid composition 581
– characteristics and function 580
– in serum 580
Anuria 661
Aorta, nomogram for diameter and biological age (inside back cover)
ap (apothecaries' measure) 205
Apocrine sweat. See Sweat
Apo-enzymes 382
Apostilb 223
apoth (apothecaries' measure) 205
Apothecaries' units 204, 205
Apotransaminases in vitamin B_6 interconversions 473
Apples, composition 499
Apple juice, composition 499
– sauce, composition 499
Apricots, composition 499
Aquocobalamin 482, 483
Ar (argon) 235
D-Arabinose 310, 313
– in bile 655
– in saliva 646
– in urine 673
L-Arabitol 322
D-Arabulose. See D-Ribulose
Arachidic acid 367
– in brain gangliosides 377
– in milk 687
Arachidonic acid 370, 492
– in blood lipids 604
– dietary requirements 495
– in foods 498 sq.
– in lecithins 375
– in milk 687
Arc functions 139
Arc measure 138
Arc sine 139
– tables 69
Are 203
Area units 202, 203
Arg. See L-Arginine
Arginase in plasma 598
– in urea cycle 442, 443
L-Arginine (Arg) 330
– in blood 574
– in blood proteins 581
– cell constituents from 434
– creatine from glycine, methionine and 437
– degradation 394, 395, 402
– in foods 516
– in milk 688
– in saliva 645
– in semen 683
– in sweat 680
– in transamination reactions 394
– in urea synthesis 443, 444
– in urine 452, 667
L-Arginine amidinohydrolase. See Arginase
Arginine vasopressin 724
Arginine vasotocin 724
Argininosuccinate, in urea synthesis 442 sq.
– in urine 449
Argininosuccinate lyase, in argininosuccinic aciduria 449
– in urea cycle 442, 443
Argininosuccinate synthetase, in citrullinaemia 449
– in urea cycle 442, 443
Argininosuccinic acid (*see also Argininosuccinate*) 334
Argon, properties, isotopes, etc. 235
Arg^8-vasopressin 724
Ariboflavinosis 473
Aric acids (saccharic acids) 312
Arithmetic mean 137
– series 136, 137
Arms, surface area 528
– circumference during growth 695 sq.
Aromatic acids. See under Acids
Arsenic, atomic weight multiples 250
– in blood 567
– properties, isotopes, etc. 236
– in urine 664
Arsenic-74, characteristics 292
– diagnostic use 289
Arsenic-76, characteristics 292
Arterial blood, carbon dioxide pressure 545
Arterial blood, oxygen pressure and saturation 544
– pH value 545, 560
– viscosity 558
– volume 554
Arterial blood pressure 553
Arthritis. See Rheumatoid arthritis
Artichokes, composition 502
Arylesterase in milk 689
Arylglucuronide formation in detoxication 442
Arylsulphatases in urine 672
As. See Arsenic
asb (apostilb) 223
ASCHHEIM-ZONDEK test 715
Ascorbic acid (L-ascorbic acid) 323, 489, 490
– in blood 490, 611
– in body fluids and tissues 489, 490
– in cerebrospinal fluid 639
– deficiency 490
– dietary requirements 490, 494
– in faeces 660
– in foods 499 sq.
– – losses during cooking 498
– in gastric juice 650
– in milk 689
– redox system 490
– in saliva 646
– in semen 685
– in synovial fluid 642
– in urine 676
Asn. See Asparagine
Asp. See L-Aspartic acid
Asparagine (Asn, Asp[NH_2]) 330
– in blood 574
– in urine 667
Asparagus, composition 502
Aspartate aminotransferase, activity, gradients 586
– – temperature correction 585
– in blood 585, 593
– – half-life 586
– – in heart disease 587
– – in liver disease 586, 587
– – in muscle disease 587
– – effect of muscular work 586
– – in pregnancy 586
– cell binding 585
– in cerebrospinal fluid 638
– in gastric juice 650
– isozymes 584
– in milk 689
– in saliva 645
– in seminal plasma 684
– in synovial fluid 641
– in tissues 585
– in urine 672
Aspartate carbamoyltransferase in pyrimidine synthesis 439
L-Aspartate: 2-oxoglutarate aminotransferase. See Aspartate aminotransferase
L-Aspartic acid (Asp) 330
– in adenylic acid formation 435
– in blood 574
– in blood proteins 581
– cell constituents from 434
– decarboxylation 394
– degradation 394, 402
– in foods 516
– formation from glucose 420
– in inosinic acid formation 435
– in milk 688
– in pyrimidine synthesis 438, 439
– in saliva 645
– in sweat 680
– in transamination reactions 394
– in urea synthesis 442 sq.
– in urine 667
Aspartic acid β-monoamide. See Asparagine
Asp(NH_2). See Asparagine
Associative law 132
Astatine, properties, isotopes, etc. 244
Astronomical unit 200, 201
– year 206
at (technical atmosphere) 212
At (astatine) 244
Atheroma 456
atm (physical atmosphere) 212
Atmosphere (*see also Air*), composition 234 sq.
– ICAO Standard 252 sq.
Atmosphere (pressure unit) 212
Atom, definition 270
Atomic constants 228, 229
– mass constant 229
– mass scale 226, 227
– mass unit 213, 226, 227, 229

A detailed index to the statistical tables (pages 28–131) and chapter on Statistical Methods (pages 146–196) will be found on pages 197–198

Atomic numbers of elements 232, 233
– time 207
– weights of elements 232, 233
– – multiples 250
– – scales 227
ATP. See Adenosine triphosphate
ATP: AMP phosphotransferase. See Adenylate kinase
ATPase in milk 689
ATP: creatine phosphotransferase. See Creatine kinase
ATP: D-fructose 1-phosphotransferase. See Ketohexokinase
ATP: D-hexose 6-phosphotransferase. See Hexokinase
ATP-3-phospho-D-glycerate 1-phosphotransferase. See Phosphoglycerate kinase
ATP: pyruvate phosphotransferase. See Pyruvate kinase
ATPS (ambient temperature and pressure, saturated) 541
atto- (10^{-18}) 9
Au. See Gold
AU (astronomical unit) 200
Auberger blood-group system 632
– clinical significance 633
Autoagglutinins in erythrocyte sedimentation 559
Autoradiography 286
av (avoirdupois) 205
avdp (avoirdupois) 205
Avocados, composition 499
AVOGADRO constant 228
Avoirdupois units 204, 205
Axerophthol 458
8-Azaguanine, enzymatic deamination 419
Azolitmin indicator 283

B

b (barn) 202, 203
B. See Boron
Ba. See Barium
Bacitracin, standard 761
Bacon, composition 511
Bacteria, capsule polysaccharides 325
– cell-wall polysaccharides 325, 349
– in urine 677
Bacteriochlorophyll 363
Bananas, composition 499
Bar 211, 212
Barbital sodium, buffer solution .... 280 sq.
– pH of solutions 279
Barium, in blood 567
– in bone 521
– carbonate, decinormal solutions 277
– chloride, decinormal solutions 277
– flame lines 284
– hydroxide, decinormal solutions 277
– oxide, decinormal solutions 277
– properties, isotopes, etc. 239
Barium–caesium radionuclide, gamma-ray constant 221
Barley, amino acids 516
– composition 507
Barn 203
Barrel 204
Basal metabolism (BMR) 539, 540
– in children 539, 540
– in infants 539, 540
– in menstrual cycle 539
– in pregnancy 539
– standards 539, 540
Base excess, in blood 571
– in foods .... 499 sq.
Basket cells 614
Basophils, blood count 619, 620
– in bone marrow 621
– dimensions 618
bbl (barrel) 204
BCG vaccine, reference preparation 759
Be. See Beryllium
Beans, amino acids 516
– composition 502
Beef, composition 512
Beer, composition 509
Beets, amino acids 516
– composition 503
Beet sugar. See Sucrose
Behenic acid 367
Behenolic acid 371
BENCE-JONES globulin. See under Globulin
Bengal red in hepatic scintigraphy 289
Benzestrol, estrogenic activity 755
Benzimidazolylcyanocobamide 483
Benzoestrol, oestrogenic activity 755
Benzoic acid, conjugation with glycine. 444, 445
– solutions, pH values 279
Benzoyl-coenzyme A in formation of glycine conjugates 445
Benzylorange indicator 283
Beriberi 470, 471
– urinary thiamine in 676
Berkelium, properties and isotopes 248
BERNOULLI numbers 9
BERTHELOT's reagent 572
Beryllium, flame lines 284
– in lungs 519
– properties, isotopes, etc. 234
BESSEY-LOWRY enzyme units 584
Beta-globulins. See β-Globulins
Betaines in urine 668
Betamethasone 379
Betazol, effect on gastric juice acidity 648
Beverages, composition 509
Bi. See Bismuth
Bicarbonate (*see also Carbon dioxide*), in bile . 654
– in blood 562, 571
– – buffer capacity 527
– – determination 568
– in body fluids 523, 525
– in cerebrospinal fluid 636
– conversion factors .... 274 sq., 523
– in erythrocytes 562
– in faeces 658
– in gastric juice 649
– glomerular filtration and excretion 536
– in pancreatic juice 651, 652
– in saliva 643
– in urine 453, 663
Bile .... 653 sq.
– amount 525, 653
– electrolytes 525, 654
– effect of secretin 739
– thyroxine 727
– vitamin B_{12} 484, 655
Bile acids, in bile 655, 656
– in blood 601
– from cholesterol 426
– conjugates, formation 438
– in faeces 659, 660
– action on lipase 414
Bile acyl-coenzyme A in bile-acid conjugation 438
Bile pigments .... 362 sq.
– in bile 654
Bile salts. See Bile acids
Biliary obstruction, serum leucine aminopeptidase in 598
Bilifuscins 364
– in faeces 657
Bilirubin 362, 363
– in bile 654
– in blood 454, 455, 576, 577
– in cerebrospinal fluid 637
– conjugation defects 454
– direct and indirect 576
– in faeces 657, 659
– in urinary sediments 677, 678
– in urine 661, 670
Bilirubinoids .... 362 sq.
Biliverdin 362, 363
– in faeces 657
Binomial coefficients 135, 136
– logarithms .... 70 sq.
– table 25
Binomial distribution .... 183 sq.
– arc-sine transformation 69, 187
– coefficients .... 70 sq.
– confidence limits .... 85 sq., 186, 187
– probabilities .... 78 sq.
Binomial series 137
Biocytin 486
Bioflavonoids 491
Biological oxidation, mechanism .... 402 sq.
Biological standards and reference preparations, international .... 759 sq.
Biotin 486, 487
– in acetyl-CoA carboxylase 424, 487
– antagonists 487
– in blood 611
– deficiency 487
– enzymes 487
– in foods .... 499 sq.
– in milk 689
– requirements 487
– sulphoxide 486
– in urine 676
Biotinsulphone 487
ε-*N*-Biotinyl-L-lysine 486
Bismuth, flame lines 284
– properties, isotopes, etc. 243
– in urine 664
BITÔT's spots 460
Bk (berkelium) 248
Blackberries, composition 499
Black body radiation 222, 223
Bleeding. See Haemorrhagic diatheses
Bleeding time 624
Blindness, night 460
Blood (whole blood) *(see also Plasma, Serum, Erythrocytes, Leucocytes, Thrombocytes)*
– acetaldehyde 606
– acetic acid 607
– acetoacetic acid 608
– acetoin 606
– volatile acids 607
– acid–base balance, nomogram 569
– adenosine diphosphate 577
– adenosine monophosphate 577
– adenosine triphosphate 577
– alkali reserve 571
– aliphatic amines 573
– aluminium 567
– amino acids 573, 574
– ammonia 573
– – in inborn errors of amino-acid metabolism 449, 450
– α-amylase 411
– arsenic 567
– ascorbic acid 611
– barium 567
– base deficit 571
– base excess 571
– bicarbonate 571
– biotin 611
– borate 564
– bromide 563
– buffer bases 571
– – and acid–base balance 569
– buffer capacity 527
– bufotenine 575
– 2,3-butylene glycol 607
– cadmium 567
– carbamino compounds 571
– carbohydrates .... 604 sq.
– carbon dioxide 570, 571
– – in acid–base balance 569
– carbon dioxide combining power 571
– carbon dioxide–bicarbonate system .. 527, 528
– carboxyhaemoglobin 576
– chloride 562
– – in renal acidosis 453
– chromium 567
– circulation. See Circulation
– citric acid 607
– citrulline 449
– coagulation .... 622 sq.
– – vitamin K in 467
– cobalt 566
– colour index 615
– coproporphyrin 575
– mean corpuscular volume 611, 614
– creatine 572
– creatinine 572
– cystamine 575
– dimethylamine 573
– *N*,*N*-dimethyltryptamine 575
– dry substance 561
– electrophoretic mobilities 560
– enzymes .... 584 sq.
– ergothioneine 573
– erythrocyte count 613, 614, 617
– erythrocyte sedimentation rate 558, 559
– ethyl alcohol 606
– flavin adenine dinucleotide 471, 609
– flavin adenine mononucleotide 471, 609
– fluoride 563
– folic acid 610
– formic acid 607
– freezing-point depression 557
– galactose 450
– gases .... 568 sq.
– – respiration and 544, 545
– glucose .... 604 sq.
– glucosidases 412
– glutathione 573
– glycine 449
– glycosidases .... 411 sq.
– gold 567
– guanidine 573
– guanidinoacetic acid 573
– guanosine triphosphate 577

Index

A detailed index to the statistical tables (pages 28–131) and chapter on Statistical Methods (pages 146–196) will be found on pages 197–198

Blood (*contd*), haemiglobin 576
– haemoglobin 576, 579, 615, 617
– histamine 575
– β-hydroxybutyric acid 608
– hydroxyproline 449
– inosine triphosphate 577
– iron 566
– isoleucine 449
– α-ketoglutaric acid 607
– α-ketoisocaproic acid 608
– α-ketoisovaleric acid 607
– α-keto-β-methylvaleric acid 608
– ketone bodies 608
– lactic acid 607
– lead 567
– leucine 449
– lipids 600 sq.
– – excess 374, 456
– malic acid 607
– manganese 567
– mercury 567
– methylguanidine 573
– 5-methyltetrahydropteroylglutamic acid 610
– molybdenum 567
– nicotinamide-adenine dinucleotide 577
– nicotinamide-adenine dinucleotide phosphate 577
– nicotinic acid 477, 610
– nitrite 564
– total nitrogen 572
– nitrogenous substances 572 sq.
– non-nitrogenous metabolites 606 sq.
– nonprotein nitrogen 572
– nucleotides 577
– osmolality 557
– osmotic pressure 557
– oxalic acid 607
– oxaloacetic acid 608
– oxygen values 570
– pantothenic acid 488, 611
– pH value 560
– phenylalanine 448
– phosphoric esters 563
– phosphorus 563
– physicochemical data 557 sq.
– porphyrins 575 sq.
– proline 449, 574
– propionic acid 607
– proteins 579
– protein sulphur 563
– prothrombin deficiency 449, 467, 468
– unconjugated pterins 610
– purines 577
– pyridoxic acid 610
– pyruvic acid 607
– redox potential 560
– reducing substances 604, 605
– riboflavin 471, 609
– rubidium 567
– selenium 567
– serotonin 575
– silicate 564
– specific gravity 557
– specific heat 560
– spermidine 575
– spermine 575
– sulphur 563
– thiamine 470, 609
– tin 567
– tryptamine 575
– tyrosine 449
– urea 572
– uric acid 577
– uridine diphosphate 577
– valine 449
– verdoglobin 576
– viscosity 558
– – and haematocrit 557
– vitamins 609 sq.
– vitamin B_6 475, 609
– vitamin B_{12} 610
– volume 528, 554 sq.
– – nomogram 556
– – gain in pregnancy 691
– – pulmonary and intrapulmonary 544
– – tracer study 289
– water 561
– zinc 567
Blood circulation. See Circulation
Blood-clot retraction 622, 625
– time 625
Blood coagulation. See under Blood
Blood diseases, radiotherapy 291
– serum enzyme changes 587
Blood groups 626 sq.
– clinical significance 632, 633
– mother-and-child incompatibility 611
Blood-group substances, action of β-acetylglucosaminase 413
– biosynthesis 424
– in faeces 659
– in gastric juice 650
– in saliva 645
– secretion 627
– secretor character for 631
Blood platelets. See Thrombocytes
Blood pressure 553, 554
– effect of angiotensin 741
– capillary 526, 554
– effect of oxytocin and vasopressin 723, 724
– pulmonary 544
Blood sugar. See D-Glucose
Blood-typing sera, standards 760
Blood vessels, pressure relationships 544
Blood volume. See under Blood
BMR. See Basal metabolism
Bodansky enzyme units 584
Body, composition 517 sq.
– – approximate 523
– – elementary 234 sq.
– fluids, electrolyte composition 523, 525
– – enzyme activities 585
– – extracellular. See Extracellular fluid
– – interstitial. See Interstitial fluid
– – intracellular. See Intracellular fluid
– – intraluminal, amount and electrolytes 525
– – intravascular, amount and electrolytes 525
– haematocrit. See Haematocrit
– height changes during growth 695 sq.
– length, of embryo 691
– – of foetus 691, 692
– – of infants 693 sq.
– measurements during growth 693 sq.
– metabolic size 473
– organs, weights 710
– parts, surface areas 528
– surface area, age and 528
– – dietary requirements from 524
– – of adults, nomogram 537
– temperature and pressure, saturated (BTPS) 260, 541
– type, blood volume and 528
– – calorie requirement and 495
– water (*see also Water*), balance. See Water balance
– – extracellular. See Extracellular fluid
– – glomerular filtration and excretion 536
– – insensible loss 524
– – intracellular. See Intracellular fluid
– – gain in pregnancy 690
– – total 517, 518, 523
– weight, of adolescents 711
– – of adults, average 711
– – – desirable 712
– – and blood volume 555
– – and calorie requirement 495
– – of children 695 sq.
– – – gastric acidity and 648
– – of embryo 691
– – of foetus 691, 692
– – of infants 693 sq.
– – of newborn 692, 693
– – – loss during first days 692
– – during pregnancy 690
– – proportions of brain, fat and muscle 517
Bohr magneton 229
Bohr radius 228
Boiling point of elements 234 sq.
Boltzmann entropy constant 228
Bombay phenotypes 627
Bone, alkaline phosphatase 415
– barium 521
– composition 521
– cortical, composition 521
– development 706 sq.
– disease, serum alkaline phosphatase in 596
– organic components 522
– parathyroid hormone and 728
– radiation absorbed by 220
– strontium 521
– strontium-90: calcium ratio 521
– tumours, leucocyte mobility 560
– role of vitamin D 461
Bone marrow 621
– lactic acid fermentation 388
– lipid accumulation 455
– respiratory rate 387
Borate, in blood 564
Borate, in whole body 517
– in lungs 519
– in urine 664
Borax, solutions, decinormal 277
– – pH values 279
Boric acid, solutions, decinormal 277
– – pH values 279
Boron, flame lines 284
– properties, isotopes, etc. 234
Br. See Bromide and Bromine
Bradykinin 742
Bragg-Gray conditions 219, 220
Brain, β-acetylglucosaminase 413
– animal, amino acids 516
– – composition 512, 513
– ascorbic acid 489
– biotin 486
– contribution to BMR 539
– catecholamines 731
– cholinesterase 414
– composition 519, 520
– degeneration 455, 456
– gangliosides. See under Gangliosides
– lactic acid fermentation 388
– lipids 369, 372, 377
– phosphatases 416
– phospholipase C 417
– purine nucleoside phosphorylase 418
– radiography 289
– respiratory rate 387
– thiamine 470
– transaminations 394
– vitamin B_6 475
– weight 710
– – proportional 517
Brain sugar. See D-Galactose
Brandy, composition 509
Brassidic acid 369
Brazil nuts, amino acids 516
– composition 507
Bread, amino acids 516
– composition 507, 508
Breasts. See Mammary glands
Breast feeding, effect on urinary amino acids 667
– effect on urinary electrolytes 663, 664
– effect on urinary nitrogen 665, 666
– effect on infants' stools 657
– effect on serum tocopherols 609
Breast milk. See under Milk
Breathing capacity, maximum (MBC) 543
Breddin's method 625
Bremsstrahlung 218
– absorbed dose from 220
British thermal unit 213
Britton-Robinson buffer 280 sq.
Broadbeans, composition 503
Broccoli, amino acids 516
– composition 503
Bromhidrosis 679
Bromide, in blood 563
– in cerebrospinal fluid 636
– in gastric juice 649
– in saliva 644
– decinormal solutions 277
– in sweat 679
– in urine 663
Bromine, atomic weight multiples 250
– properties, isotopes, etc. 237
Bromine-82, characteristics 292
– decay table 299, 300
Bromochlorophenol blue indicator 283
Bromocresol green indicator 283
Bromocresol purple indicator 283
Bromophenol blue indicator 283
Bromothymol blue indicator 283
Brucella abortus antiserum, standard 761
Bruns enzyme units 584
Brussels sprouts, amino acids 516
– composition 503
B substance, secretion 627
BTPS (body temperature and pressure, saturated) 260, 541
Btu (British thermal unit) 213
bu (bushel) 203, 204
Bücher enzyme units 584
Buckwheat flour, composition 508
Buffer solutions 280 sq.
Bufotenine, in blood 575
– in urine 669
Bushel 204
Butanoic acid. See *n*-Butyric acid
Butenoic acids 368
Butter, composition 510
Buttermilk, composition 511

A detailed index to the statistical tables (pages 28–131) and chapter on Statistical Methods (pages 146–196) will be found on pages 197–198

Button unit 200
2,3-Butylene glycol in blood 607
n-Butyric acid 366
– in faeces 660
– in milk 687
– in urine 674
Butyrylcholine, hydrolysis 414

C

c (centesimal minute) 207
c (centi-, 10^{-2}) 9
c (cycle per second) 208
C. See Carbon
C (coulomb) 216
C. See Cytidine
C (clearance). See Renal clearance
C. See Compliance
°C (degree Celsius or Centigrade) 208
Ca. See Calcium
Cabbage, amino acids 516
– composition 503
Cadaverine, formation from lysine 394
Cadmium, inhibition of aminopeptidase 409, 411
– in blood 567
– flame lines 284
– activation of iminodipeptidase 410
– properties, isotopes, etc. 238
– in urine 664
Cadmium-114, vacuum wave lengths 200
Caeruloplasmin, amino-acid composition 581
– in blood 580, 583, 593
– characteristics and function 580
– and serum copper 566
– in erythrocyte sedimentation 559
– in synovial fluid in rheumatoid arthritis 641
Caesium, flame lines 284
– properties, isotopes, etc. 239
Caesium-137, characteristics 293
– decay table 304, 305
– therapeutic use 290
Caesium–barium radionuclide, gamma ray constant 221
Caffeine in coffee 509
cal_{15} (15° calorie) 213
cal_{IT} (Int. Steam Table calorie) 213
$cal_{thermochem}$ (thermochemical calorie) 213
Calcitonin 461, 729
– salmon 809
Calcium, in amniotic fluid 522
– atomic weight multiples 250
– balance, calcitonin and 729
– – vitamin D in 461
– in bile 654
– in blood 565
– – in infants 464
– in whole body 517
– in body fluids 523
– in bone 521
– – ratio of bone strontium-90 to 521
– in catecholamine release 731
– in cerebrospinal fluid 636
– conversion factors 523
– conversion factor into calcium oxide 251
– dietary requirements 493, 494, 496
– in electrolyte balance 525
– in erythrocytes 565
– in faeces 658
– flame lines 284
– in foods 499 sq.
– in gastric juice 649
– glomerular filtration and excretion 536
– in hair and nails 520
– in intestinal juice 656
– ionized, calculation in serum 565
– – parathyroid hormone and 728
– in milk 688
– in muscle 518
– in organs 519
– effect on oxytocin and vasopressin secretion 723
– in pancreatic juice 652
– activation of phospholipases 417
– in placenta 522
– gain in pregnancy 690
– properties, isotopes, etc. 235
– in saliva 644
– in semen 683
– in skin 520
– in sweat 680
– in synovial fluid 641
– in teeth 521
– in urine 453, 664
Calcium-45, specific activity 217
– characteristics 292
– decay table 295, 296
Calcium-47, characteristics 292
– decay table 296
Calcium acetate, conversion factors 274 sq.
Calcium carbonate, decinormal solutions 277
Calcium chloride, conversion factors 274 sq.
– decinormal solutions 277
– hexahydrate, decinormal solutions 277
Calcium citrate solutions, conversion factors 274 sq.
Calcium D-gluconate solutions, conversion factors 274 sq.
Calcium hydroxide, decinormal solutions 277
– pH values 279
Calcium lactate solutions, conversion factors 274 sq.
Calcium laevulinate solutions, conversion factors 274 sq.
Calcium oxalate, accumulation 449
– in urinary sediments 677, 678
Calcium oxide, conversion factors 274 sq.
– conversion factor into calcium 251
– decinormal solutions 277
Calcium phosphate, conversion factors 274 sq.
– in urinary sediments 677
Calcium thiosulphate solutions, conversion factors 274 sq.
Calendar year 206
Calf circumference during growth 695 sq.
Calf, composition 512
Californium, properties and isotopes 248
Calorie 213
Calories, dietary requirements 493 sq., 526, 527
– – of hospital patients 526
– in foods 498 sq., 539
– in milk 688
– turnover, standard 527
– – urinary solutes and 534
Calorific value. See Calories
Camel's milk, composition 511
Cancer (*see also Sarcoma, Tumours*), erythrocyte mobility in 560
– liver. See Liver carcinoma
– serum glucosephosphate isomerase 600
– serum phosphopyruvate hydratase 600
– stomach. See Stomach cancer
Candela 223
Candy, composition 509
Cane sugar. See Sucrose
Cantaloups, composition 499
Capacitance 216
Capillaries, blood volume in 554
– pulmonary, blood volume in 544
Capillary blood, pH value 560
– blood pressure. See Blood pressure
Capon unit 751
Capreomycin, reference preparation 762
Capric acid 366
– in milk 687
Caproic acid 366
– in milk 687
Caprylic acid 366
– in milk 687
Caramel, composition 509
Carat 204
Carbamino compounds in blood and erythrocytes 571
Carbamoylphosphate: L-ornithine carbamoyltransferase. See Ornithine carbamoyltransferase
Carbamoylphosphate synthetase, in hyperammonaemia 450
– in urea cycle 442, 443
Carbamoyltransferases 385
Carbamyl-β-alanine in degradation of cytosine and uracil 401
Carbamyl-β-aminoisobutyric acid in thymine degradation 401
Carbamylaspartic acid 334
– in pyrimidine synthesis 439
Carbamyl phosphate, hydrolysis 416
– in pyrimidine synthesis 438, 439
– in urea synthesis 442, 443
3-*O*-Carbethoxyglucosamine 315
Carbohydrates 308 sq.
– in bile 655
– biosynthesis 441
– in blood 604 sq.
– contribution to BMR 539
– in cerebrospinal fluid 639
– dietary requirements 495
– enzymes attacking 405
Carbohydrates, in foods 498 sq.
– in faeces 659
– in gastric juice 650
– metabolism 389 sq., 405, 441
– – effect of ACTH 717
– – effect of corticosteroids 749
– – effect of glucagon 738
– – effect of growth hormone 720
– – inborn errors 450
– – water from 524
– in milk 689
– oxidation products 323
– in urine 673
Carbon, atomic weight multiples 250
– chains, extension 424
– properties, isotopes, etc. 234
Carbon-12 scale 226, 227
Carbon-14, characteristics 234, 292
– specific activity 217
Carbonates in teeth and bones 521
Carbonate buffer 280 sq.
Carbon–carbon lyases 386
Carbon dioxide (*see also Bicarbonate*), in blood 570, 571
– – determination 568
– in cerebrospinal fluid 636
– conversion factors 276
– standard density 210
– fixation, biotin in 486, 487
– – carbon chain extension by 424
– formation, by erythrocytes 616
– – by nutrients 539
– – by thrombocytes 621
– in intestinal juice 656
– in semen 682
– decinormal solutions 277
– in synovial fluid 640
– in urine 663
Carbon–halide lyases 386
Carbon monoxide, determination in blood 568
– combination with haemoglobin 360
Carbon monoxide hemoglobin. See Carboxyhaemoglobin
Carbon–nitrogen ligases 386
Carbon–nitrogen lyases 386
Carbon–oxygen lyases 386
Carbon–sulphur lyases 386
1′-*N*-Carboxybiotin 486
Carboxyhaemoglobin 359, 360
– in blood 576
Carboxylation, biotin in 486, 487
Carboxylesterase 414
Carboxylic ester hydrolases 386
Carboxyltransferases 385
Carboxy-lyases 386
Carboxypeptidase A 409, 410
– in pancreatic juice 652
Carboxypeptidase B 409
Carcinoid. See Tumours, carcinoid
Carcinoma. See Cancer
Cardiac infarction, blood coagulation 622 sq.
– genesis 623, 624
– serum enzyme changes 587
– serum dehydrogenases 590 sq.
– serum glucosephosphate isomerase 600
– serum phosphopyruvate hydratase 600
– serum transaminases and transferases 593, 594
Cardiac muscle. See under Heart
Cardiolipin 375
– reference preparation 759
Carnitine 491
– in blood 573
– in degradation of fats 392
– in urine 668
Carnosinase 410
Carnosine in urine 666
α-Carotene 458
β-Carotene 458
Carotenes 457 sq.
– in blood 457, 609
– in milk 689
– oxidation, vitamin E in 466
Carotenoids in faeces 659
Carp, composition 514
Carrots, amino acids 516
– composition 503
Cartilage, lactic acid fermentation 388
– respiratory rate 387
Casein 332
– in milk 511, 688
– breakdown by rennin 407
Cashew nuts, composition 507
Cassiopeium 241
cat (catal) 584

Index

A detailed index to the statistical tables (pages 28–131) and chapter on Statistical Methods (pages 146–196) will be found on pages 197–198

Catal ... 584
Catalase ... 361, 362
– in glycine degradation ... 397
– in milk ... 689
Catalysts of biological oxidations ... 402, 403
Cataracts ... 450
Catecholamines (*see also Adrenaline, Dopamine, Noradrenaline*) ... 730 sq.
– assay ... 731
– biosynthesis and release ... 731
– in blood ... 731, 733
– in cardiac infarction ... 623, 624
– metabolism ... 731 sq.
– in urine ... 668, 733
Catechol *O*-methyltransferase in catecholamine breakdown ... 731, 732
Cathepsins ... 410
Cathepsin III. See Leucine aminopeptidase
Cathepsin IV. See Carboxypeptidase A
Cauliflower, amino acids ... 516
– composition ... 503
Caviar, composition ... 514
Cavity ion dose ... 219
Cb (columbium). See Niobium
cc (centesimal second) ... 207
cd (candela) ... 223
Cd. See Cadmium
CDP. See Cytidine diphosphate
Ce. See Cerium
Cefalotin, reference preparation ... 762
Celery, composition ... 503
Celiac disease in vitamin D deficiency ... 461
Cell, metabolism ... 387, 388
– protein, enzyme content ... 584
Cellobiase in intestinal mucosa ... 413
Cellobiose ... 324
Cellulose ... 326
– in faeces ... 657, 659
Celsius temperature scale ... 208, 209
Cental ... 205
Centesimal angle units ... 207, 208
centi- (10^{-2}) ... 9
Centigrade temperature scale ... 208, 209
Centimetre ... 200
– reciprocal ... 213
Centimetre-gramme-second (CGS) electromagnetic and electrostatic units ... 215
Cephalins ... 365, 375
– in bile ... 655
– in blood ... 604
– in brain and spinal cord ... 520
– in cerebrospinal fluid ... 638
– in erythrocytes ... 604
– formation ... 425
– structure and hydrolysis ... 417
Cephalothin, reference preparation ... 762
Ceramide galactosides ... 376
– glucosides in GAUCHER's disease ... 377
– lactoside ... 377
Cereals, amino acids ... 516
– composition ... 507, 508
– vitamin losses in cooking ... 498
Cereal products, composition ... 507, 508
Cerebellar ataxia ... 452
– hemispheres, enzyme activities ... 585
Cerebral cortex, enzyme activities ... 585
Cerebron ... 372, 377
Cerebronic acid ... 372
– in phrenosin ... 377
Cerebrose. See D-Galactose
Cerebrosides ... 365, 376, 377
– in brain and spinal cord ... 520
– – fatty acids of ... 369, 372
– in erythrocyte sedimentation ... 559
Cerebrospinal fluid ... 635 sq.
– ammonia ... 449, 636
– amount ... 525, 635
– electrolytes ... 525, 636
– insulin ... 736
– isoleucine ... 449
– leucine ... 449
– pantothenic acid ... 488, 639
– phenylalanine ... 448
– thiamine ... 470, 639
– valine ... 449
Cerebrum, enzyme activities ... 585
Cerium, flame lines ... 284
– properties, isotopes, etc. ... 239
Ceroid pigment formation, vitamin E in ... 466
Cerotic acid ... 367
– in waxes ... 377
Ceruloplasmin. See Caeruloplasmin
Cesium. See Caesium
Cetoleic acid ... 369
Cetyl alcohol in waxes ... 377
Cf (californium) ... 248
CGS (centimetre-gramme-second) electromagnetic and electrostatic units ... 215
ch (chain) ... 200
ch (metric horsepower) ... 213
Chain ... 200
Chair conformation of steroids ... 378
Chaldron ... 204
Chard, composition ... 503
CHE. See Cholinesterase
Check-valve mechanism ... 542
Cheese, composition ... 510
Chenodeoxycholic acid, in bile ... 655, 656
– in faeces ... 660
– in plasma ... 601
Cherries, composition ... 499
Cherry-red spot ... 455, 456
Chest circumference during growth ... 695 sq.
Chestnuts, composition ... 507
Chick antidermatitis factor. See Pantothenic acid
Chicken, composition ... 512
Chicory, composition ... 503
Children (*see also Infants and Newborn*), ascorbic acid requirement ... 490
– bile, amount ... 653
– – cholesterol ... 655
– bile acids ... 656
– blood, acetoacetic acid ... 608
– – acetone ... 608
– – alanine aminotransferase ... 594
– – amino acids ... 573, 574
– – ammonia ... 573
– – androgens ... 751
– – ascorbic acid ... 611
– – aspartate aminotransferase ... 593
– – borate ... 564
– – caeruloplasmin ... 593
– – carotenes ... 609
– – cholesterol ... 601, 603
– – copper ... 566
– – corticosteroids ... 745
– – creatine ... 572
– – creatinine ... 572
– – ergothioneine ... 573
– – fatty acids ... 601, 603
– – fructosediphosphate aldolase ... 599
– – galactose 1-phosphate ... 605
– – gases ... 570, 571
– – glucose ... 604, 605
– – glycerides ... 601, 603
– – glycerol ... 607
– – glycogen ... 606
– – growth hormone ... 720
– – haemoglobin ... 615, 617
– – β-hydroxybutyric acid ... 608
– – L-iditol dehydrogenase ... 590
– – iodine ... 564
– – iron ... 566
– – α-ketoglutaric acid ... 607
– – ketone bodies ... 608
– – lactate dehydrogenase ... 590
– – lipids ... 601, 603
– – magnesium ... 566
– – nonprotein nitrogen ... 572
– – pepsin ... 598
– – acid phosphatase ... 596
– – alkaline phosphatase ... 596
– – phosphate ... 563
– – inorganic phosphorus ... 563
– – potassium ... 564
– – proteins ... 579, 583
– – protoporphyrin ... 576
– – pyruvic acid ... 607
– – thyroid hormone ... 726
– – thyroxine breakdown ... 727
– – urea ... 572
– – uric acid ... 577
– – viscosity ... 558
– – vitamin A ... 609
– – vitamin D ... 461, 609
– – zinc ... 567
– blood pressure ... 553, 554
– blood volume ... 554, 555
– BMR ... 539, 540
– body surface area ... 528
– – nomogram ... 538
– body weight. See under Body weight
– bone age ... 706, 707
– bone composition ... 521
– bone growth, alkaline phosphatase and ... 585
– – epiphyseal ... 706 sq.
– bone marrow cells ... 621
Children, cerebrospinal fluid, leucocyte count 635
– – protein ... 637
– corticosteroid secretion ... 743
– dietary requirements ... 493 sq.
– erythroblastosis ... 612
– erythrocytes, count ... 614, 617
– – diameter ... 617
– – mean corpuscular haemoglobin ... 615
– – osmotic resistance ... 616
– – sedimentation rate ... 558
– – mean corpuscular volume ... 617
– maximum expiratory flow rate ... 551
– faeces, composition and properties ... 657 sq.
– – vitamin B_6 ... 475
– gastric juice, acidity ... 648
– – pH value ... 647
– – secretion ... 647
– normal measurements during growth ... 695 sq.
– haematocrit ... 617
– iodide metabolism ... 726
– iodine requirements ... 497
– leucocyte count ... 618, 619
– lung values ... 550
– – nomograms ... 547
– mineral requirements ... 496
– nicotinic acid requirement ... 478
– organ weights ... 710
– appearance of ossification centres ... 706 sq.
– pancreatic juice secretion ... 651
– pernicious anaemia ... 485
– pulmonary compliance ... 549, 552
– pulmonary resistances ... 549, 552
– reticulocytes ... 613
– saliva, chloride ... 643
– – pH value ... 643
– – potassium ... 644
– – sodium ... 644
– – volume ... 643
– sweat, acetylcholine ... 681
– – amino acids ... 680
– – electrolytes ... 679, 680
– – glucose ... 681
– – lactic acid ... 681
– – volume ... 679
– teeth, composition ... 521
– – development ... 709
– thiamine requirement ... 471
– thrombocyte count ... 620
– urine, *N*-acetylhistamine ... 670
– – acidity ... 662
– – amino acids ... 666, 667
– – amount ... 661
– – calcium ... 664
– – catecholamines ... 733
– – copper ... 664
– – corticosteroids ... 746 sq.
– – creatine ... 665
– – creatinine ... 665
– – erythropoietin ... 740
– – ethanolamine ... 668
– – fluoride ... 663
– – glucuronic acid ... 673
– – gonadotropins ... 714
– – insulin ... 736
– – nitrogen ... 665
– – oestrogens ... 756
– – organic acids ... 674
– – peptides ... 666
– – porphyrins ... 670
– – pregnanediol ... 754
– – tryptophan metabolites ... 669
– – vitamins ... 676
– vital capacity ... 551
– vitamin A deficiency ... 460
– vitamin A poisoning ... 460
– vitamin A requirement ... 460
– vitamin B_6 requirement ... 475
– vitamin D deficiency ... 461, 464
– vitamin D poisoning ... 464
– vitamin D requirement ... 461
– water requirement ... 524
Chi-squared distribution ... 166 sq.
– significance limits ... 36 sq.
Chitin ... 326
Chitobiase in seminal plasma ... 684
Chitosamine. See D-Glucosamine
Chives, composition ... 504
Chloride, in amniotic fluid ... 522
– in bile ... 654
– in blood ... 453, 562
– in whole body ... 517, 518
– in body fluids ... 523, 525
– in bones ... 521
– in cerebrospinal fluid ... 636

A detailed index to the statistical tables (pages 28–131) and chapter on Statistical Methods (pages 146–196) will be found on pages 197–198

Chloride, conversion factors .... 274 sq., 523
- conversion factor into sodium chloride .. 251
- dietary requirements 496
- in electrolyte balance 525
- in erythrocytes 562
- exchangeable 518
- in faeces 658
- in foods .... 499 sq.
- in gastric juice 648, 649
- glomerular filtration and excretion 536
- in hair and nails 520
- in intestinal juice 656
- in milk 688
- in muscle 518
- in organs 519
- in pancreatic juice 652
- in placenta 522
- in saliva 643
- in semen 682
- in skin 520
- solutions, conversion factors .... 274 sq.
- - decinormal 277
- in sweat 679
- in synovial fluid 640
- in teeth 521
- in urine 662
Chloride shift 562
Chlorine, atomic weight multiples 250
- properties, isotopes, etc. 235
Chlorine-36, characteristics 292
S-(*p*-Chlorobenzyl)cysteine in detoxication of *p*-dichlorobenzene 445
S-(*p*-Chlorobenzyl)glutathione in detoxication of *p*-dichlorobenzene 445
p-Chlorobenzylmercapturic acid in detoxication of *p*-dichlorobenzene 445
Chlorogenic acid in coffee 509
Chlorophenol red indicator 283
Chlorophylls 362, 363
Chloroplastin 363
Chlorotrianisene, oestrogenic activity 755
Chlortetracycline, standard 761
Chocolate, composition 509
Cholane 381
Cholecalciferol. See Vitamin D_3
Cholecystokinin 739
Choleglobin 360, 362
Cholera agglutinating serum, reference reagent 764
- vaccines, reference preparations 759
Cholestane 381
Cholestanol in faeces 660
Cholest-5-en-3β-ol. See Cholesterol
Δ^7-Cholestenol in faeces 660
Cholesterol 374, 379
- accumulation 456
- adrenal steroids and androgens from 428, 429
- in bile 655
- biosynthesis 426, 427
- - inhibition by nicotinic acid 477, 478
- in blood 456, 600, 601, 603, 604
- in brain and spinal cord 520
- in cerebrospinal fluid 638
- degradation 401
- - in liver 426
- in erythrocytes 600, 601
- esters, in cerebrospinal fluid 638
- in faeces 660
- in foods .... 498 sq.
- in leucocytes 601
- in lipoproteins 602
- in milk 689
- oestrogen synthesis from 431
- in saliva 646
- in semen 685
- stereochemistry 378
- in synovial fluid 642
- in thrombocytes 601
- in tissues 522
- in urinary sediments 677, 678
- in urine 675
Cholesterol esterase 414
Cholic acid, in bile 655, 656
- activation of cholesterol esterase 414
- conjugation 438
- in faeces 660
- in plasma 601
Choline 492
- activation 425
- in bile 654
- biosynthesis 434
- - *S*-adenosylmethionine in 398
- in blood 575
- in lecithin synthesis 425
Choline, in lipids 365
- in milk 688, 689
- in phosphatidyl esters 375
- in saliva 645
- in semen 683
- in urine 668
Cholinesterases 414
- in blood 585, 595
- - allotypy 634
- - in liver disease 586, 587
- in cerebrospinal fluid 638
- deficiency, detection 595
- isozymes 584
- in milk 689
- in saliva 645
Chondrocalcinosis, synovial fluid calcium .. 641
Chondroitin sulphate A (4-sulphate) 326
- in urine 668
Chondroitin sulphate B 326
Chondroitin sulphate C (6-sulphate) 326
D-Chondrosamine. See D-Galactosamine
Chorionic gonadotropin 715
- - oestrogens and 757
- growth-hormone prolactin 721
- sac, development 691
- thyrotropin, human 809
Chromaffin granules 731
Chromatophore hormone 721, 722
Chromium, in blood 567
- dietary requirements 497
- flame lines 284
- properties, isotopes, etc 236
- in urine 664
Chromium-51, characteristics 292
- decay table 296
- diagnostic use 289
Chromogranin 731
Chylomicrons 374
- in serum 602
Chymotrypsins 407, 408
- in faeces 659
- in pancreatic juice 653
Chymotrypsinogens 407
- in pancreatic juice 652
Ci (curie) 217
Cinnamic acid, conjugation with glycine ... 444
Circle, geometry 142
Circulation, effect of catecholamines 734
- action of corticosteroids 750
- pulmonary 543, 544
Cirrhosis. See under Liver
Cisternal fluid. See Cerebrospinal fluid
Cis–trans isomerases 386
Cis–trans isomerase in phenylalanine degradation 398
Cis–trans isomerism, of fatty acids 373
- of steroids 378
Citrate, in blood 607
- buffers .... 280 sq.
- in cerebrospinal fluid 639
- cleavage 424
- fatty acid synthesis from 425
- in foods .... 499 sq.
- formation 424
- - from glucose 420
- in milk 689
- poisoning 607
- in saliva 646
- in semen 685
- in tricarboxylic acid cycle 390, 391
- in urine 674
- in yoghurt 511
Citrate (isocitrate) hydrolyase. See Aconitate hydratase
Citrate–phosphate–borate buffer .... 280 sq.
Citric acid (*see also Citrate*) solutions, decinormal 277
- pH values 279
Citric acid cycle. See Tricarboxylic acid cycle
Citrin 491
Citrovorum factor. See 5-Formyltetrahydrofolic acid
Citrullinaemia 449
Citrulline 334
- in blood 449, 574
- degradation 394, 395, 402
- in sweat 680
- in urea synthesis .... 442 sq.
- in urine 449, 667
Cl. See Chloride and Chlorine
Clams, composition 514
CLAUBERG's test 753
Clearance. See Renal clearance
Clostridiopeptidase A in pancreatic juice ... 652
Clostridium botulinum antitoxins, standards .. 760
Clostridium oedematiens toxoid, reference preparation 759
Clostridium welchii antitoxins, standards 761
Clupanodonic acid 370
Cm (curium) 248
cm^{-1} (reciprocal centimetre) 213
CMP. See Cytidine monophosphate
Co. See Cobalt
Co I. See Nicotinamide-adenine dinucleotide
Co II. See Nicotinamide-adenine dinucleotide phosphate
CoA. See Coenzyme A
CoASH. See Coenzyme A
CoA-transferases 386
Cobalamins 482
Cobalt, atomic weight multiples 250
- in blood 566
- in whole body 517
- dietary requirements 497
- in faeces 658
- flame lines 284
- activation of glycyl-glycine dipeptidase .. 410
- in lungs 519
- in milk 688
- properties, isotopes, etc. 236
- in saliva 645
- in urine 664
Cobalt-57, characteristics 292
- decay table 297
- diagnostic use 289
Cobalt-58, characteristics 292
- decay table 297
Cobalt-60, characteristics 292
- decay table 298
- gamma ray constant 221
- therapeutic use 290
Cobamides 482
Cobinamides 482
- in vitamin B_{12} synthesis 484
CO_2-biotin 486
Cobyric acid hexamides 482
Cocarboxylase. See Thiamine diphosphate
Coconuts, amino acids 516
- composition 507
Cod, composition 514
Codecarboxylase. See Pyridoxal phosphate
Codehydrogenase I. See Nicotinamide-adenine dinucleotide
Codehydrogenase II. See Nicotinamide-adenine dinucleotide phosphate
Cod-liver oil, composition 510
Codons 353
Coeliac disease in vitamin D deficiency 461
Coenzymes 382, 385
- nucleotide .... 344 sq.
Coenzyme I. See Nicotinamide-adenine dinucleotide
Coenzyme II. See Nicotinamide-adenine dinucleotide phosphate
Coenzyme A (CoA, CoASH) 345, 488
- in acetylation of amines 444
- in ATP synthesis 404
- in bile-acid conjugation 438
- in cephalin formation 425
- in citrate formation 424
- in detoxication of halogenobenzenes 445
- in detoxication of phenylacetic acid 445
- in degradation of fats .... 391 sq.
- in fatty acid synthesis from citrate ... 424, 425
- in glucosamine formation 423
- in formation of glycine conjugates .. 444, 445
- in glycine degradation 397
- in isoleucine degradation 396
- in lecithin formation 425
- in leucine degradation 395, 396
- in lysine degradation 398
- in norleucine degradation 396
- pantothenic acid incorporation 487
- in phenylalanine degradation 398
- in serine degradation 397
- in oxidation of sugars 391
- in threonine degradation 397
- in tricarboxylic acid cycle 390, 391
- in triglyceride synthesis 426
- in tryptophan degradation 399
- in valine degradation 396
- in vitamin B_{12} synthesis 484
Coenzyme B_{12} 482, 483
Coenzymes Q 403, 466
Coenzyme Q_{10} in urine 676
Coffee, composition 509
COHN fraction in lipoproteins 602
Cola drinks, composition 509

A detailed index to the statistical tables (pages 28–131) and chapter on Statistical Methods (pages 146–196) will be found on pages 197–198

Colistin, reference preparation 762
– standard 761
Collagen, biosynthesis, ascorbic acid in 490
– metabolism, hydroxyproline excretion and 666
– in tissues 522
Collagen diseases, salivary secretion in 643
Collagen hydroxyproline 432
Colloid-osmotic pressure of plasma 526, 558
Colonic mucosa, respiratory rate 387
Colostrum, composition .... 687 sq.
– fatty acids 687
Colour index of blood 615
Colour vision, plates for testing ... (inside back cover)
Columbium. See Niobium
Commutative law 132
Compliance, respiratory 545, 552
– – in children, determination 549
Compound A. See 11-Dehydrocorticosterone
Compound B. See Corticosterone
Compound E. See Cortisone
Compound F. See Cortisol
COMT (catechol *O*-methyltransferase) in catecholamine breakdown 731, 732
Concentration units 226, 227, 271
– conversion of 251
Condensing enzyme in tricarboxylic acid cycle 390, 391
Conductance, pulmonary 546
Conductivity, electric 216
Cone, geometry 142
Cone vision 223
Confectionery, composition 509
Confidence limits .... 150, 152, 154 sq.
– tables .... 43, 63, 85 sq.
Congo red indicator 283
Conjunctival xerosis 460
Connective tissue, effect of growth hormone 720
– respiratory rate 387
CONN's syndrome. See Hyperaldosteronism
Constants, atomic 228, 229
– field 228
– mathematical 9
– physical .... 228 sq.
– thermodynamic 228
Constitution. See Body type
Contact therapy with radionuclides 290
Contractile tissue, effect of oxytocin and vasopressin 723, 724
COOLEY's anaemia 448
– trait 448
COOMBS' test 626
Coordinated Universal Time 207
COP (colloid-osmotic pressure) of blood 526, 558
Copper, in amniotic fluid 522
– atomic weight multiples 250
– in bile 654
– in biological oxidations 403
– in blood 566
– in whole body 517
– in bones 521
– in cerebrospinal fluid 636
– dietary requirements 496
– in erythrocytes 566
– in faeces 658
– flame lines 284
– in foods .... 499 sq.
– in gastric juice 649
– in hair and nails 520
– in milk 688
– in organs 519
– in pancreatic juice 652
– in placenta 522
– properties, isotopes, etc. 236
– in saliva 645
– in semen 683
– in skin 520
– in sweat 680
– in synovial fluid 641
– in teeth 521
– in urate oxidase 419
– in urine 664
Copper-64, characteristics 292
– decay table 298, 299
– gamma ray constant 221
Copper oxide, decinormal solutions 277
Copper sulphate, decinormal solutions 277
Coproporphyria, idiopathic 455
Coproporphyrins 355, 357, 358
– in blood 575
– in faeces 659
– in urine 670
Coproporphyrin I, accumulation 454
– in bile 654
Coproporphyrin I, biosynthesis 454
– in urine 670
Coproporphyrin III, in bile 654
– in haem synthesis 454
– in urine 455, 670
Coproporphyrinogens 356, 357
Coproporphyrinogen I, biosynthesis 454
Coproporphyrinogen III in haem synthesis . 454
Coprosterol in faeces 660
Cord (unit) 203
Cord blood, alanine aminotransferase 594
– amino acids 573
– aspartate aminotransferase 593
– bases 571
– bicarbonate 571
– bilirubin 576, 577
– bradykinin 742
– caeruloplasmin 593
– calcium 565
– carbon dioxide 570, 571
– carotenes 609
– chloride 562
– cholesterol 603
– cholinesterase in 595
– citric acid 607
– copper 566
– coproporphyrin 575
– corticosteroids 745
– creatine kinase 594
– creatinine 572
– ergothioneine 573
– erythroblasts 612
– erythrocyte count 614
– erythrocyte osmotic resistance 616
– erythropoietic activity 740
– fatty acids 601, 603
– folic acid 610
– fructosediphosphate aldolase 599
– galactose 1-phosphate 605
– glucose 604
– glucosephosphate isomerase 600
– growth hormone 720
– haematocrit 614
– haemoglobin 576, 615
– α-hydroxybutyrate dehydrogenase 591
– L-iditol dehydrogenase 590
– insulin 736
– iodine 564
– iron 566
– isocitrate dehydrogenase 591
– α-ketoglutaric acid 607
– lactate dehydrogenase 590
– lactic acid 607
– lecithin 604
– lipids 603
– magnesium 566
– malate dehydrogenase 591
– nonprotein nitrogen 572
– oestrogens 756
– oxygen 570
– alkaline phosphatase 596
– phosphoethanolamine 573
– pH value 560
– placental lactogen 721
– potassium 564
– progesterone and metabolites 754
– proteins 583
– protoporphyrin 576
– pyruvic acid 607
– riboflavin 609
– sodium 565
– thrombocyte count 620
– tocopherols 609
– urea 572
– vitamin A 609
– vitamin B_6 609
– vitamin B_{12} 610
– zinc 567
CORI ester. See D-Glucose 1-phosphate
Corn, sweet (maize), composition 504
Cornflakes, composition 508
Corn flour, composition 508
Corn oil, composition 510
Cornstarch, composition 508
Corn sugar. See D-Glucose
Corpuscular haemoglobin. See under Erythrocytes
– volume. See Erythrocyte volume
Corpus luteum, progesterone secretion 753
Corpus luteum-ripening hormone. See Luteinizing hormone
Correlation coefficient .... 179 sq.
– tables .... 61 sq.
Corrinoids .... 482 sq.
Cortex, adrenal. See Adrenal cortex
– bone, composition 521
Cortexolone. See 11-Deoxycortisol
Cortexone. See Deoxycorticosterone
Corticosteroids .... 381, 742 sq.
– regulation of ACTH secretion 717
– assay 743, 744
– biological activity .... 748 sq.
– biosynthesis .... 426, 428 sq.
– – effect of ACTH 717
– – inborn defects 456
– – rates 743, 745
– in blood 745
– in cardiac infarction 624
– serum dehydroascorbic acid and 611
– 17-deoxy-, structure and assay 744
– – in urine 746
– gluco-. See Glucocorticoids
– 11-hydroxy-, structure and assay 744
– – in urine 747
– 17-hydroxy-, structure and assay 744
– – in plasma 745
– – excretion during pregnancy 749
– 17-ketogenic, structure and assay 744
– – in urine .... 746 sq.
– metabolism .... 428 sq., 430, 746, 747
– – inborn errors 456
– mineralo-. See Mineralocorticoids
– reducing, in plasma 745
– – structure and assay 744
– in urine .... 430, 746 sq.
Corticosteroid-binding globulin 745
Corticosterone .... 379, 743 sq.
– in adrenals 743
– biological activity 749
– biosynthesis 428, 429
– – rates 743
– in blood 745
– – protein binding 428
– breakdown 746, 747
– release, effect of ACTH 717
– in urine 747
Corticotropic hormone. See Corticotropin
Corticotropin (ACTH) 716, 717
– effect on adrenal cortex 430
– testing of adrenocortical function 747
– effect on androgen formation 751
– in cardiac infarction 624
– in catecholamine secretion 731
– and haemorrhagic diatheses 623, 624
– and melanotropins 721
– releasing factors 717, 722, 725
– secretion, effect of vasopressin 723
– standard 762
Cortisol .... 379, 742 sq.
– regulation of ACTH secretion 717
– in adrenals 743
– biological activity 749
– biosynthesis 428, 429
– – rates 743, 745
– in blood 716, 745
– – protein binding 428
– breakdown 746, 747
– and haemorrhagic diatheses 623, 624
– release, effect of ACTH 717
– in urine 430, 747
Cortisone .... 379, 742 sq.
– in adrenals 743
– biological activity 749
– biosynthesis 428, 429
– in blood 745
– breakdown 746, 747
– and haemorrhagic diatheses 623, 624
– in urine 430, 747
α-Cortol 379
β-Cortol 379
α-Cortolone 379
β-Cortolone 379
Cortolones in urine 747
cos (cosine) 139
Cosine 139
cot (cotangent) 138, 139
Cotangent 138, 139
Cottonseed oil, composition 510
Coulomb 216
Cow's milk. See under Milk
Coxsackie virus antisera, reference reagents . 764
Cozymase. See Nicotinamide-adenine dinucleotide
Cp (cassiopeium) 241
CPK (creatine phosphokinase). See Creatine kinase
Cr. See Chromium
Crab, composition 514

A detailed index to the statistical tables (pages 28–131) and chapter on Statistical Methods (pages 146–196) will be found on pages 197–198

Cranberries, composition ... 499
Cream, composition ... 510
Creatine ... 334
– reaction with ATP ... 437, 438
– in blood ... 572
– in cerebrospinal fluid ... 637
– conversion factors ... 251
– formation ... 437
– phosphate, formation and function .. 437, 438
– in semen ... 683
– in urine ... 665
Creatine kinase, in bile ... 655
– in blood ... 585, 594
– – in heart disease ... 587
– – in muscle disease ... 587
– – effect of muscular work ... 586
– – in pregnancy ... 586
– isozymes ... 584
– in milk ... 688
– in seminal plasma ... 684
Creatine phosphokinase. See Creatine kinase
Creatinine ... 334
– in blood ... 531, 572
– in cerebrospinal fluid ... 637
– conversion factors ... 251
– in erythrocytes ... 572
– in gastric juice ... 649
– glomerular filtration and excretion ... 536
– in milk ... 688
– in pancreatic juice ... 652
– in saliva ... 645
– in sweat ... 680
– effect on urinary osmolarity and specific gravity ... 534
– in urine ... 665
p-Cresol in urine ... 675
o-Cresolphthalein indicator ... 283
m-Cresol purple indicator ... 283
Cresol red indicator ... 283
Cress, composition ... 504
Cretinism, goitrous ... 449
CRF (corticotropin-releasing factors) 717, 722, 725
CRIGLER-NAJJAR syndrome ... 454
– serum bilirubin in ... 577
trans-(α-)Crotonic acid ... 368
Crotonyl-coenzyme A in L-lysine degradation 398
Cryoscopic constant ... 270
Cryptoxanthene ... 458
Cs. See Caesium
CSF. See Cerebrospinal fluid
ctg, ctn (cotangent) ... 138, 139
CTP. See Cytidine triphosphate
CU (capon unit) ... 751
Cu. See Copper
Cubes table ... 19
Cubic measures ... 203, 204
Cucumbers, composition ... 504
Cumoestrol, oestrogenic activity ... 755
Curie ... 217
Curium, properties and isotopes ... 248
Currants, composition ... 500
Current, electric, units ... 216
CUSHING's disease, corticosteroid secretion .. 745
cwt (hundredweight) ... 205
Cyanide, decinormal solutions ... 277
– in urine ... 663
Cyanocobinamide ... 483
Cyanocobalamin. See Vitamin B_{12}
Cyanopsin ... 457
Cyanosis, haemiglobin concentration ... 576
Cycle per second ... 208
Cyclo-ligases ... 386
Cyclometric functions ... 139
Cyclopentanoperhydrophenanthrene ring ... 378
Cyd. See Cytidine
Cylinder, geometry ... 142
Cys. See L-Cysteine
Cys-Cys. See Cystine
Cystamine, in blood ... 575
– in urine ... 668
L-Cystathionine ... 335
– in homocysteine degradation ... 397, 398
Cystathionuria ... 476
Cysteic acid ... 335
– decarboxylation ... 394
L-Cysteine (Cys) ... 330
– inhibition of aminopeptidase ... 411
– cell constituents from ... 434
– in coenzyme A formation ... 345, 487
– in cystine degradation ... 397
– degradation ... 397, 402
– formation from glucose ... 420
– glutathione from ... 438
– in L-homocysteine degradation ... 397, 398
L-Cysteine, taurine from ... 438
– in urine ... 667
Cysteinesulphenic acid in L-cysteine degradation ... 397
Cysteinesulphinic acid, in L-cysteine degradation ... 397
– in taurine formation ... 438
Cystine (Cys-Cys) ... 330
– in blood ... 574
– in blood proteins ... 581
– degradation ... 397, 402
– in foods ... 516
– in milk ... 688
– in reticulo-endothelial system ... 449
– in saliva ... 645
– in urinary sediments ... 677, 678
– in urine ... 667
Cystine reductase in cystinosis ... 449
Cystinosis ... 449
Cystinuria ... 452
Cytidine (C, Cyd) ... 339
– in RNA synthesis ... 352
Cytidine diphosphate (CDP) ... 343
Cytidine diphosphate choline ... 350
– in lecithin synthesis ... 425
Cytidine diphosphate ethanolamine ... 350
– in cephalin synthesis ... 425
Cytidine diphosphate glycerol ... 349
Cytidine diphosphate ribitol ... 349
Cytidine monophosphate (CMP) ... 343
– in amino-sugar utilization ... 424
– formation ... 438, 439
– in RNA ... 351
Cytidine monophosphate *N*-acetylneuraminic acid ... 350, 424
Cytidine triphosphate (CTP) ... 343
– in formation of lecithin and cephalin ... 425
– in pyrimidine synthesis ... 439
Cytidine triphosphate synthetase in pyrimidine synthesis ... 439
Cytidylic acid. See Cytidine monophosphate
Cytochromes ... 361, 362
– in biological oxidations ... 403
– in spermatozoa ... 684
Cytochrome c redox potential ... 403
Cytosine ... 338
– degradation ... 401
– in DNA synthesis ... 352
– in protein synthesis ... 353

D

d (day) ... 205
d (deci-, 10^{-1}) ... 9
d- (dextro-) ... 308, 309
D. See Deuterium
da (deca-, 10^{1}) ... 9
dADP (deoxyadenosine diphosphate) ... 343
Dairy products, composition ... 510, 511
DAM unit for vitamin K ... 467
dAMP. See Deoxyadenosine monophosphate
Dandelion greens, composition ... 504
Dates, composition ... 500
dATP (deoxyadenosine triphosphate) ... 343
DAVENPORT pH–bicarbonate diagram ... 528
Day ... 205, 206
db (decibel) ... 225
dCDP (deoxycytidine diphosphate) ... 343
dCMP. See Deoxycytidine monophosphate
dCTP (deoxycytidine triphosphate) ... 343
Dead-space ventilation ... 542
Deamido-NAD (nicotinic acid adenine dinucleotide), in NAD and NADP formation ... 477
Deamination, oxidative, in amino-acid degradation ... 393
DEBRÉ-DE TONI-FANCONI syndrome ... 452, 453
DEBYE-HÜCKEL constant ... 278
deca- (10^{1}) ... 9
Decametre ... 200
Decanoic acid. See Capric acid
Decarboxylases and vitamin B_6 ... 475
Decarboxylation in amino-acid degradation . 394
Decay constant ... 217
Decenoic acids in milk ... 687
Δ^4-Decenoic acid ... 368
Δ^9-Decenoic acid ... 368
deci- (10^{-1}) ... 9
Decibel ... 224
Decimetre ... 200
De-electrification factor ... 216
Degree (angle) ... 138, 207, 208
Degree (temperature) ... 209
Dehydratases and vitamin B_6 ... 475
Dehydration, ketone body excretion ... 674
Dehydroascorbic acid ... 489
– functions ... 490
– redox system ... 490
– in serum ... 490, 611
7-Dehydrocampesterol, vitamin D from ... 461
7-Dehydrocholesterol ... 462
– in faeces ... 660
– vitamin D synthesis from ... 461
Dehydro-compounds ... 381
Dehydrocorticosterone ... 379, 743 sq.
– biological activity ... 749
– biosynthesis ... 428, 429
– breakdown ... 746
– in urine ... 746, 747
1-Dehydrocortisol. See Prednisolone
1-Dehydrocortisone. See Prednisone
Dehydroepiandrosterone ... 379, 751 sq.
– biosynthesis ... 428, 429
– breakdown ... 746, 747
– sulphate, secretion rates ... 743, 745
– in urine ... 430, 746, 749
Dehydrogenases, in blood ... 590 sq.
– NADP-dependent, in oestrogen metabolism ... 431
Dehydroisoandrosterone. See Dehydroepiandrosterone
3-Dehydroretinal. See Vitamin A_2 aldehyde
3-Dehydroretinaldehyde. See Vitamin A_2 aldehyde
3-Dehydroretinol ... 459
7-Dehydrositosterol, vitamin D from ... 461
2-Dehydrostigmasterol, vitamin D from ... 461
Deiodinase in goitrous cretinism ... 449
Demagnetization factor ... 216
Demethylchlortetracycline, reference preparation ... 762
Demyelination ... 454
Density, of elements ... 234 sq.
– standard ... 209
– units ... 209, 210
Dentine, composition ... 521
– organic components ... 522
Deoxyadenosine ... 339
– enzymatic deamination ... 419
– diphosphate (dADP) ... 343
– monophosphate (dAMP) ... 343
– – enzymatic deamination ... 419
– – in DNA ... 351
– triphosphate (dATP) ... 343
5′-Deoxyadenosylcobalamin ... 482, 483, 485
Deoxyadenylic acid. See Deoxyadenosine monophosphate
2-Deoxy-D-*altro*methylose ... 313
Deoxyarabinose. See 2-Deoxy-D-ribose
Deoxycholic acid, in bile ... 655, 656
– conjugation ... 438
– in faeces ... 660
– in plasma ... 601
Deoxy-compounds ... 381
17-Deoxycorticosteroids. See under Corticosteroids
11-Deoxycorticosterone (DOC) ... 379, 743 sq.
– biological activity ... 749
– biosynthesis ... 428, 429
– – increased ... 456
– – rates ... 743
11-Deoxycortisol ... 379, 743 sq.
– biological activity ... 749
– breakdown ... 746
– in plasma ... 745
– secretion rates ... 743
21-Deoxycortisol ... 379
Deoxycytidine ... 340
– diphosphate (dCDP) ... 343
– monophosphate (dCMP) ... 343
– – in DNA ... 351
– triphosphate (dCTP) ... 343
Deoxycytidylic acid. See Deoxycytidine monophosphate
2-Deoxy-D-erythropentose. See 2-Deoxy-D-ribose
6-Deoxy-L-galactose. See L-Fucose
2-Deoxy-D-glucose, effect on gastric juice acidity ... 648
Deoxyguanosine ... 339
– diphosphate (dGDP) ... 343
– monophosphate (dGMP) ... 343
– – in DNA ... 351
– triphosphate (dGTP) ... 343
Deoxyguanylic acid. See Deoxyguanosine monophosphate
Deoxyhaemoglobin. See Haemoglobin

A detailed index to the statistical tables (pages 28–131) and chapter on Statistical Methods (pages 146–196) will be found on pages 197–198

Deoxy-5-hydroxymethylcytidine monophosphate (dHMCMP) 343
Deoxyinosine 341
21-Deoxyketols, structure and assay 744
– excretion during pregnancy 749
6-Deoxy-L-mannose 313
Deoxy-5-methylcytidine monophosphate (dMCMP) 343
Deoxymyoglobin. See Myoglobin
Deoxypentoses, degradation 399
Deoxypyridoxine 474
Deoxyribonucleases in pancreatic juice 652
Deoxyribonuclease I 406, 418
– in plasma 597
Deoxyribonuclease II 406, 418
– in plasma 597
Deoxyribonucleate 3′-nucleotidohydrolase. See Deoxyribonuclease II
Deoxyribonucleate oligonucleotidohydrolase. See Deoxyribonuclease I
Deoxyribonucleic acid (DNA) .... 351 sq.
– biosynthesis 351, 352
– – folic acid in 479
– – vitamin B_{12} in 485
– enzymatic cleavage 406
– depolymerization 418
– in leucocytes 578
– in semen 684
– viral, synthesis 352
Deoxyribonucleoprotein 351
Deoxyribonucleotides, formation, vitamin B_{12} in 485
2-Deoxy-D-ribose 313
– formation from glucose 420
– phosphates 318
– 1-phosphate, formation from nucleosides 339, 340
– 5-phosphate, degradation 399
Deoxyribosyladenine. See Deoxyadenosine
Deoxyribosylcytosine. See Deoxycytidine
Deoxyribosylguanine. See Deoxyguanosine
Deoxyribosylhypoxanthine 341
Deoxyribosylthymine. See Deoxythymidine
Deoxyribosylxanthine 341
21-Deoxysteroids, excessive synthesis 456
Deoxythymidine 340
– diphosphate (dTDP) 343
– monophosphate (dTMP) 343, 438, 439
– – in DNA 351
– – formation 438, 439, 479
– triphosphate (dTTP) 343
Deoxythymidylic acid. See Deoxythymidine monophosphate
Deoxyuridylic acid in pyrimidine synthesis . 439
Deoxyxanthosine 341
Dephospho-coenzyme A in coenzyme A formation 487
Depot fats 374
Dermatan sulphate 326
Dermatitis, photosensitive 452
Dermatomes of primary rami of spinal nerves .... (inside back cover)
Desmosterol in cholesterol synthesis ... 426, 427
Desoxy-. See Deoxy-
Desulphydrases, vitamin B_6 and 475
Detoxication mechanisms .... 442 sq.
Deuterium, properties 234
– oxide, density 230
Deuteroporphyrin 358
– in faeces 659
Dexamethasone 379
– regulation of ACTH secretion 717
– testing of adrenocortical function 747
– relative biological activity 750
Dextrans 327
– as plasma expanders 530
Dextrins, enzymatic hydrolysis 411, 412
– α-limit, from starch 411
Φ-Dextrin 411
Dextrin-1,6-glucosidase 412
– deficiency 450, 451
Dextrinosis, limit 451
Dextro compounds 308, 309
Dextronic acid. See D-Gluconic acid
Dextrose. See D-Glucose
dGDP (deoxyguanosine diphosphate) 343
dGMP. See Deoxyguanosine monophosphate
dGTP (deoxyguanosine triphosphate) 343
DHF. See Dihydrofolic acid
dHMCMP (deoxy-5-hydroxymethylcytidine monophosphate) 343
Diabetes, galactose 450
– gastric juice secretion 647
– from destruction of hypothalamus 723
Diabetes, urinary 1-methyl-2-pyridone 5-carboxylamide 676
– blood thiamine 609
Diabetes insipidus 452, 453
– fluid deprivation test in 535
5-*N*,*O*-Diacetylneuraminic acids 316
Diacylglycerols. See Diglycerides
Diamines in semen 684
Diaminobiotin 487
α,ε-Diamino-*n*-caproic acid. See L-Lysine
α,ε-Diamino-δ-hydroxy-*n*-caproic acid 331
α,ε-Diaminopimelic acid, decarboxylation .. 394
Di-[α-aminopropionic]-β-disulphide. See Cystine
2,5-Diamino-*n*-valeric acid. See L-Ornithine
Diaminoxidase, vitamin B_6 and 475
Diammonium hydrogen phosphate solutions, pH values 279
1,3-Diazine. See Pyrimidine
Dibucaine number 595
p-Dichlorobenzene, mercapturic acids from . 445
Dicumarol, vitamin K and 467
Diego blood-group system 632
– clinical significance 633
Dienoestrol, oestrogenic activity 755
Dietary allowances .... 493 sq.
– tables .... 498 sq.
Diethylstilboestrol, oestrogenic activity 755
Diethyl sulphide in urine 663
Diffusing capacity of lungs 545, 552
Diffusion constants of plasma proteins 580
Digestion 389
Digestive enzymes .... 405 sq.
Digitalis, standard 763
D-Digitoxose 313
Diglycerides 365, 374
– in bile 655
– in faeces 659
– in serum 601
– in triglyceride synthesis 426
Dihydrocholesterol in serum 601
Dihydro-compounds 381
22-Dihydroergosterol 462
– vitamin D from 461
Dihydrofolic acid (DHF), biosynthesis 478
– in pyrimidine synthesis 439
– reduction to tetrahydrofolic acid 437
Dihydro-orotase in pyrimidine synthesis ... 439
Dihydro-orate dehydrogenase in pyrimidine synthesis 439
Dihydro-orotic acid in pyrimidine synthesis . 439
Dihydropteroic acid in folic acid synthesis .. 478
Dihydropteroylglutamic acid. See Dihydrofolic acid
Dihydrosphingosine, in lipids 365
– in sphingolipids 376
Dihydrostreptomycin, standard 761
Dihydrothymine in thymine degradation ... 401
Dihydrouracil in degradation of cytosine and uracil 401
Dihydroxyacetone 311, 313
– phosphate 317
– – in carbohydrate synthesis and breakdown 441
– – in erythrocytes 605
– – in glucose 6-phosphate formation 422
– – glycerophosphates from 420
– – in glycolysis 389
– – in lactic acid fermentation 390
erythro-trans-1,3-Dihydroxy-2-amino-octadec-4-ene. See Sphingosine
Dihydroxycholanic acids in plasma 601
Dihydroxycholesterols in synthesis of adrenal steroids and androgens 428, 429
D-(+)-*N*-(α,γ-Dihydroxy-ββ-dimethylbutyryl)-β-alanine. See Pantothenic acid
5,6-Dihydroxyindole in melanin formation . 440
11α,15-Dihydroxy-9-ketoprosta-5,13-dienoic acid 373
11α,15-Dihydroxy-9-ketoprosta-5,13,17-trienoic acid 373
11α,15-Dihydroxy-9-ketoprost-13-enoic acid 373
17,21-Dihydroxy-20-ketosteroids in urine .. 746
3,4-Dihydroxymandelic acid, from catecholamine breakdown 732
– in urine 675
2,6-Dihydroxy-5-methylpyrimidine. See Thymine
3,4-Dihydroxy-β-phenylacetaldehyde from catecholamine breakdown 732
3,4-Dihydroxyphenylacetic acid, from catecholamine breakdown 732
– in urine 675
3,4-Dihydroxyphenylalanine (dopa), in adrenaline and noradrenaline formation .. 440
3,4-Dihydroxyphenylalanine, decarboxylation 394
– in melanin formation 440
3,4-Dihydroxy-β-phenylethanol from catecholamine breakdown 732
3,4-Dihydroxyphenylethylamine (dopamine) 730
– in adrenaline and noradrenaline formation 440
– breakdown 732
– formation from 3,4-dihydroxyphenylalanine 394
– hydroxylation, ascorbic acid in 490
– in urine 668, 733
3,4-Dihydroxyphenylglycol from catecholamine breakdown 732
3,4-Dihydroxyphenylglycolaldehyde from catecholamine breakdown 732
17α,21-Dihydroxypregna-1,4-diene-3,11,20-trione. See Prednisone
3α,20α-Dihydroxy-5α-pregnane. See α-Allopregnanediol
3β,20α-Dihydroxy-5α-pregnane 379
3α,21-Dihydroxy-5β-pregnane-11,20-dione . 380
11β,21-Dihydroxypregn-4-en-18-al-3,20-dione. See Aldosterone
11β,17α-Dihydroxypregn-4-ene-3,20-dione . 379
11β,21-Dihydroxypregn-4-ene-3,20-dione. See Corticosterone
17α,21-Dihydroxypregn-4-ene-3,20-dione. See 11-Deoxycortisol
17α,21-Dihydroxypregn-4-ene-13,11,20-trione. See Cortisone
2,3-Dihydroxypropanal. See D-Glyceraldehyde
1,3-Dihydroxypropan-2-one. See Dihydroxyacetone
D-α,β-Dihydroxypropionic acid. See D-Glyceric acid
2,6-Dihydroxypurine. See Xanthine
2,6-Dihydroxypyrimidine. See Uracil
2,6-Dihydroxypyrimidine-4-carboxylic acid. See Orotic acid
3,5-Di-iodo-3′-methyl-DL-thyronine, comparative potency 727
3,5-Di-iodo-L-thyronine, comparative potency 727
L-3,5-Di-iodotyrosine 330, 726
– peptide-linked, in thyroid hormone formation 440
Diketohydrindylidenediketohydrindamine .. 329
Dimercaprol, reference preparation 763
N^6,N^6-Dimethyladenosine 354
Dimethylallyl pyrophosphate in cholesterol synthesis 426, 427
Dimethylamine, in blood 573
– in urine 668
p-Dimethylaminoazobenzene indicator 283
Dimethylaminoethylamine buffer .... 280 sq.
N-Dimethylaminoleucylglycine buffer ... 280 sq.
5,6-Dimethylbenzimidazole riboside in vitamin B_{12} synthesis 484
5,6-Dimethylbenzimidazolylaquocobamide 482, 483
5,6-Dimethylbenzimidazolylcyanocobamide. See Vitamin B_{12}
5,6-Dimethylbenzimidazolylhydroxocobamide 482, 483
7,8-Dimethyl-10-(D-dulcityl)isoalloxazine ... 472
Dimethylglutaric acid buffer .... 280 sq.
N^2,N^2-Dimethylguanosine 354
7,8-Dimethyl-10-(D-ribityl)isoalloxazine. See Riboflavin
5,6-Dimethyl-1-(α-ribofuranosyl)benzimidazole 3′-phosphate 363
5,8-Dimethyltocol 465
7,8-Dimethyltocol 465
5,8-Dimethyltocotrienol 465
7,8-Dimethyltocotrienol 465
N,*N*-Dimethyltryptamine, in blood 575
– in urine 669
Dinitrophenol indicators 283
Dipeptidases 408, 409
Dipeptides, enzymatic hydrolysis 408
Dipeptide hydrolases 386
o-Diphenol oxidase, in albinism 448
– caeruloplasmin and 593
1,3-Diphosphoglycerate (D-glyceric acid 1,3-diphosphate) 317
– in carbohydrate synthesis and breakdown . 441
– enzymatic cleavage 416
– in erythrocytes 605
– in glycolysis 389
Diphosphoinositides in brain and spinal cord 520
Diphosphopyridine nucleotide. See Nicotinamide-adenine dinucleotide
Diphtheria antitoxins, standards 760, 761

A detailed index to the statistical tables (pages 28–131) and chapter on Statistical Methods (pages 146–196) will be found on pages 197–198

Diphtheria antitoxins, toxoids, standards.... 759
Dipole moment, electric 216
– magnetic 216
Disaccharides, in faeces 659
– in lipids 365
Distance modulus....................... 201
Distemper antiserum, standard........... 761
Distributive law 132
Diuresis, effect on enzyme excretion....... 672
– osmotic 533
Diuresis test 747
dk (deka-, 10^1) 9
dMCMP (deoxy-5-methylcytidine monophosphate) 343
DNA. See Deoxyribonucleic acid
DNAase. See Deoxyribonuclease
DNA nucleotidyltransferase 351
DNA polymerase 351
DNase. See Deoxyribonuclease
DOC. See Deoxycorticosterone
Docosanoic acid 367
$\Delta^{4,8,12,15,19}$-Docosapentaenoic acid......... 370
Δ^{11}-Docosenoic acid..................... 369
cis-Δ^{13}-Docosenoic acid 369
trans-Δ^{13}-Docosenoic acid 369
13-Docosynoic acid 371
Dodecanoic acid. See Lauric acid
Δ^{4}-Dodecenoic acid 368
Δ^{5}-Dodecenoic acid 368
Δ^{9}-Dodecenoic acid 368
Dodecenoic acids in milk 687
Dombrock blood-group system........... 632
Dopa. See 3,4-Dihydroxyphenylalanine
Dopa decarboxylase in adrenaline and noradrenaline formation 440
Dopamine. See 3,4-Dihydroxyphenylethylamine
Dopamine hydroxylase in adrenaline and noradrenaline formation 440
Dose equivalent of radiation............. 221
Dosimetry of radionuclides.... 217 sq., 286, 287
Dotriacontanoic acid. See Lacceroic acid
dpm (disintegrations per minute).......... 217
DPN (diphosphopyridine nucleotide). See Nicotinamide-adenine dinucleotide
dps (disintegrations per second)........... 217
dr (dram, drachm) 205
Drachm 205
– fluid 204
Dram 205
– apothecaries' 205
– fluid 204
Driving pressure, vascular 544
Drops per minute, nomogram 529
Dry measures 204
dry pt (dry pint)........................ 204
dry qt (dry quart)....................... 204
dTDP (deoxythymidine diphosphate)...... 343
dTMP. See Deoxythymidine monophosphate
dTTP (deoxythymidine triphosphate)...... 343
DUBIN-JOHNSON syndrome 454
– serum bilirubin 577
Duck, composition...................... 512
Duffy blood-group system 632
– clinical significance................... 633
Duodenal ulcer, gastric juice secretion 647
Dwarfism......................... 449, 453
– pituitary 720
– – and ossification 707
– primordial, and ossification............. 707
dwt (pennyweight)...................... 205
Dy. See Dysprosium
dyn (dyne) 211
Dyne................................. 211
Dysentery antiserum, standard........... 760
Dysprosium, flame lines 284
– properties, isotopes, etc. 240

E

e (base of natural logarithms)............ 132
Earth's crust, composition .... 234 sq.
EC numbers of enzymes 385, 386
Eccrine sweat. See Sweat
Echovirus antisera, reference reagents 764
Eel, composition 514
Eggs, amino acids 516
– composition..................... 510, 511
– vitamin losses in cooking 498
Eggplant, composition 504
Egg powder, composition 511
Eicosanoic acid. See Arachidic acid
$\Delta^{4,8,12,15,18}$-Eicosapentaenoic acid.......... 370
$\Delta^{5,8,11,14}$-Eicosatetraenoic acid. See Arachidonic acid
5,8,11-Eicosatrienic acid 492
7,10,13-Eicosatrienic acid 492
Δ^{9}-Eicosenoic acid 369
Δ^{11}-Eicosenoic acid 369
Eicosenoic acids in milk 687
Einsteinium, properties and isotopes 248
Ejaculate (*see also Semen*), volume 682
Elaidic acid 369
Elastance of lungs 545
Elastase. See Pancreatopeptidase E
Elbow, secondary ossification centres .. 706, 708
Elderberries, composition................ 500
Electric field constant 215, 228
Electricity, quantities and units ... 215, 216, 228
Electrolytes (*see also Solutions*) .... 270 sq.
– in body fluids .... 523 sq.
Electrolyte balance.................. 525, 526
– action of corticosteroids 749
– disturbances, parenteral therapy......... 530
– effect of growth hormone 720
– and water balance.................. 523 sq.
Electromagnetic field constants 228
– moment 216
– radiation units........................ 222
– units 215, 216
Electrons, biological removal......... 402, 403
– energy absorbed from .... 218 sq.
– magnetic moment..................... 229
– mass 229
– – reduced, in hydrogen-1 229
– rest mass 229
– mass stopping power.......... 218, 220, 221
– radius 229
Electronic configurations of elements...... 249
Electron transport system................ 403
Electron volt........................... 213
Electrophoretic mobility of plasma proteins. 580
Electrostatic units.................. 215, 216
Elements, alphabetical tables.......... 232, 233
– atomic numbers 232, 233
– atomic weights 232, 233
– – multiples 250
– in human body .... 234 sq., 517 sq.
– electronic configurations 249
– contents in foods .... 498 sq.
– periodic system....................... 231
– properties, isotopes, etc. .... 234 sq.
Elementary charge 228
α-Eleostearic acid....................... 370
Ellipse, geometry 142, 144
Elliptocytosis 614
Em (emanation) 244
Eman 217
Emanation............................ 244
Embryo (*see also Foetus*), haemoglobin 615
– lactic acid fermentation 388
– size and weight.................. 691, 692
emu (electromagnetic units) 215, 216
Enanthic acid 366
Endives, composition 504
Endocrine organs, weights 710
Endopeptidases .... 405 sq.
Energy dose of radionuclides..... 218, 286, 287
– electric 216
– fluence of radiation 218
– flux density of radiation 218, 221
– mechanical, units and symbols 212, 213
– metabolism (*see also Calories*)......... 387 sq.
Energy-supplying reactions .... 389 sq.
ENO (enolase). See Phosphopyruvate hydratase
Enolase. See Phosphopyruvate hydratase
Enoyl-CoA hydratase in degradation of fats. 392
Enteral radiotherapy 290, 291
Enterogastrone 739
Enteropeptidase 408
Enterovirus antisera, reference reagents 764
Entropy constant, BOLTZMANN........... 228
– units 214
Enzymes........................... 382 sq.
– activation 382
– activity gradients 586
– allosteric............................ 382
– in bile.............................. 655
– in biological oxidations 402, 403
– in blood .... 584 sq.
– – elimination......................... 586
– in cell protein 584
– in cerebrospinal fluid.................. 638
– classification and numbering........ 385, 386
– congenital defects .... 446 sq.
– diagnostic use .... 586 sq.
Enzymes, digestive .... 405 sq.
– in faeces 659
– in gastric juice....................... 650
– inhibition .... 382 sq.
– in intestinal juice 656
– kinetics........................... 382 sq.
– in milk 688, 689
– organ-specific 584
– – in diagnosis 586
– in pancreatic juice............... 652, 653
– proteolytic. See Proteolytic enzymes
– in saliva 645
– in semen............................ 684
– in sweat 681
– in synovial fluid 641
– in tissues 585, 586
– tissue-specific........................ 584
– units 584
– in urine .... 672 sq.
Eosinopenia........................... 620
Eosinophils, in blood 619, 620
– in bone marrow 621
– action of corticosteroids 750
– dimensions.......................... 618
Eosinophil test. See THORN's test
Eosinophilia 620
Ephemeris time.................... 206, 207
Epiandrosterone 379
– in urine 746
Epidermis. See Skin
Epididymis, glycosidases................. 412
– weight 710
Epiestr-. See Epioestr-
Epimerases 386
– in uridine diphosphoiduronic acid formation 423
Epinephrine. See Adrenaline
Epioestradiol.......................... 380
16-Epioestriol, biosynthesis and metabolism 431
– in urine 756
16,17-Epioestriol 432
17-Epioestriol 432
Epiphyses, appearance of 706
Episteroids 378, 381
Epitestosterone 380
Epithelial membranes, effect of oxytocin and vasopressin 723, 724
EPS (exophthalmos-producing substance) .. 718
Epsom salts, conversion factors........ 274 sq.
Eq (gramme-equivalent) 226
Equations, solution of.............. 137, 138
Equilenin............................. 380
– in adrenal tumours 432
Equilin 380
Equivalent, amount of.............. 226, 227
Er (erbium)........................... 241
Erbium, properties, isotopes, etc. 241
Erg 212, 213
Ergocalciferol. See Vitamin D_2
Ergostane in steroids 381
Ergosterol 380, 462
– biosynthesis 426
– vitamin D from 461, 463
Ergothioneine 335
– in blood 573
– in leucocytes 573
– in semen............................ 684
Erucic acid 369
ERV (expiratory reserve volume) 541, 550
Erythritol............................. 322
Erythroblasts.......................... 612
– in bone marrow 621
Erythroblastosis 612
Erythrochromia 635
Erythrocuprein, erythrocyte copper as 566
Erythrocytes .... 613 sq.
– *N*-acetylneuraminic acid 316
– adenosine triphosphate 577
– aminoacetone 575
– amino acids 573, 574
– δ-aminolaevulinic acid 575
– bicarbonate 562, 571
– blood grouping and 626
– breakdown, tracer study 289
– buffer systems 527
– calcium............................. 565
– carbamino compounds................. 571
– cations 561
– cephalin 604
– cerebrospinal fluid 635
– chloride 562
– cholesterol 600, 601
– copper 566
– coproporphyrin....................... 575

A detailed index to the statistical tables (pages 28–131) and chapter on Statistical Methods (pages 146–196) will be found on pages 197–198

Erythrocytes (*contd*), count (RBC) ... 613, 614, 617
– creatine ... 572
– creatinine ... 572
– dihydroxyacetone phosphate ... 605
– dimensions ... 613, 614, 617
– diphosphoglyceric acid ... 605
– dry substance ... 561
– surface density of electric charge ... 560
– electrophoretic mobility ... 560
– enzymes ... 585
– – allotypy ... 634
– ergothioneine ... 573
– ethanolamine ... 573
– fatty acids ... 600, 601
– folic acid ... 479, 610
– fructose 1,6-diphosphate ... 605
– fructose 6-phosphate ... 605
– galactose 1-phosphate ... 605
– glucose ... 604
– glucose 6-phosphate ... 605
– glucuronic acid ... 605
– glutathione ... 573
– glyceraldehyde 3-phosphate ... 605
– glycogen ... 606
– glycolipids ... 377
– glycoproteins ... 606
– mean haemoglobin concentration 576, 615, 617
– mean haemoglobin content ... 615, 617
– haemoglobin iron ... 566
– haemolysis. See Haemolysis
– lactic acid ... 607
– lactic acid fermentation ... 388
– lecithin ... 604
– lifetime ... 616
– lipids ... 600, 601
– lipid phosphorus ... 563
– lysolecithin ... 604
– magnesium ... 566
– manganese ... 567
– metabolism ... 616
– 5-methyltetrahydropteroylglutamic acid ... 479
– molybdenum ... 567
– nitrogen ... 572
– nonprotein nitrogen ... 572
– nucleotide pentose ... 605
– octulose 1,8 diphosphate ... 605
– osmotic resistance ... 616
– pentose 5-phosphate ... 605
– pH value ... 560
– phosphatides ... 601, 604
– phosphoenolpyruvic acid ... 605
– phosphoglyceric acids ... 605
– phosphoric esters ... 563
– phosphorus ... 563
– plasmalogens ... 604
– polychromatic. See Reticulocytes
– porphobilinogen ... 575
– porphyrins ... 357, 358
– potassium ... 564
– precursors ... 612
– proteins ... 579
– protein nitrogen ... 572
– protoporphyrin ... 455, 576
– pterins ... 610
– purine nucleoside phosphorylase ... 418
– pyrophosphatase ... 416
– pyruvic acid ... 607
– respiratory rate ... 387
– riboflavin ... 471, 473, 609
– sedimentation mechanism ... 559
– sedimentation rate (ESR) ... 558, 559
– sedoheptulose 1,7 diphosphate ... 605
– sickle-cell ... 614
– – sedimentation ... 559
– sodium ... 565
– specific gravity ... 557
– specific heat ... 560
– sphingomyelin ... 604
– sugar phosphates ... 605
– sulphur ... 563
– in synovial fluid ... 640
– in thalassaemias ... 446
– thiamine ... 470, 609
– triglycerides ... 601
– triosephosphate ... 605
– urea ... 572
– uric acid ... 577
– in urine ... 661, 677
– uroporphyrin ... 576
– vital-granulated. See Reticulocytes
– vitamin B_6 ... 609
– vitamin B_{12} ... 610
– volume ... 554 sq., 613
– – gain in pregnancy ... 691
Erythrocytes, volume, mean (mean corpuscular volume) ... 614, 615, 617
– – nomogram ... 556
– – tracer study ... 289
– water ... 561
– weight gain in pregnancy ... 690
– zinc ... 567
Erythrocyte count (RBC) ... 613, 614, 617
Erythrocyte sedimentation rate (ESR) ... 558, 559
Erythrodontia ... 454
Erythromycin, standard ... 761
D-Erythropentulose. See D-Ribulose
Erythropoiesis, riboflavin and ... 472
Erythropoietin ... 740
– reference preparation ... 763
– riboflavin and ... 472
D-Erythrose ... 310, 313
– 4-phosphate ... 317
– – in pentose phosphate cycle ... 421, 422
D-Erythrulose ... 311
L-Erythrulose ... 313
– 1-phosphate ... 317
Es (einsteinium) ... 248
ESR (erythrocyte sedimentation rate) ... 558, 559
Essential amino acids, dietary requirements ... 496
– fatty acids. See under Fatty acids
Esterases ... 405
– allotypy ... 634
– in bile ... 655
– in cerebrospinal fluid ... 638
– in vitamin A metabolism ... 457
Ester hydrolases. See Esterases
Estr-. See Oestr-
esu (electrostatic units) ... 215, 216
Ethanoic acid. See Acetic acid
Ethanol, in blood ... 606
– calorific value ... 509, 526
– intoxication, serum enzyme changes ... 586
Ethanolamine, in blood ... 573, 574
– in cephalin synthesis ... 425
– in cerebrospinal fluid ... 637
– formation from serine ... 394
– in leucocytes ... 573
– in lipids ... 365
– in phosphatidyl esters ... 375
– in urine ... 668
Ethinyl-. See Ethynyl-
β-Ethylacrylyl-coenzyme A in norleucine degradation ... 396
Ethyl alcohol. See Ethanol
24-Ethyl-5α-cholestane in steroids ... 381
17α-Ethyl-17β-hydroxy-19-norandrost-4-en-3-one ... 380
17α-Ethynyl-17β-hydroxy-19-norandrost-4-en-3-one ... 380
17α-Ethynyl-17β-hydroxyoestr-5(10)-en-3-one ... 380
Ethynyloestradiol ... 380
– oestrogenic activity ... 755
17α-Ethynyloestra-1,3,5(10)-triene-3,17β-diol. See Ethynyloestradiol
Etio-. See Aetio-
Eu. See Europium
Euglobulolysis time ... 625
EULER numbers ... 9
EULER's constant ... 9
Europium, flame lines ... 284
– properties, isotopes, etc. ... 240
eV (electron volt) ... 213
EVANS' growth test ... 719
Exchange transfusions, serum bilirubin as guide to ... 577
Exocytosis ... 731
Exopeptidases ... 405, 408 sq.
Exophthalmos-producing substance ... 718
Expiratory flow rate, maximum (MEFR) ... 543
– – nomograms ... 550
– – values ... 551
– reserve volume ... 541, 550
– volume, forced (FEV) ... 543
– – – determination ... 548, 549
Exponents ... 132
Exponential equations ... 137, 138
– functions ... 16, 17
Extracellular fluid, total volume ... 518, 523
– gain in pregnancy ... 690
Extrinsic system in blood coagulation ... 622, 625

F

f (femto-, 10^{-15}) ... 9
F (farad) ... 216
F. See Fluorine
°F (degree Fahrenheit) ... 209
FA. See Folic acid
Factor A (2-methyladeninecyanocobamide) ... 483
Factor B (aetiocobalamin) ... 483
Factor III (5-hydroxybenzimidazolyl-cyanocobamide) ... 483
Factors I–XIII (blood coagulation) ... 622 sq.
Factorials ... 135, 136
– logarithms ... 26, 27
FAD. See Flavin adenine dinucleotide
Faeces (*see also Stools*) ... 657 sq.
– electrolytes ... 525, 658
– fatty acids ... 371, 660
– glucose and galactose ... 452
– porphyrins ... 358
– porphyrin excess ... 455
– plasma proteins ... 289, 659
– thyroxine ... 727
– vitamin B_6 ... 475, 660
– water loss in ... 524, 657
Fahrenheit temperature scale ... 208, 209
FANCONI syndrome ... 452, 453
– in vitamin D deficiency ... 464
FAO/WHO reference protein ... 516
Farad ... 216
FARADAY constant ... 228
Farnesyl pyrophosphate in cholesterol synthesis ... 426, 427
Fasting, blood, glucose ... 604
– – growth hormone ... 719
– – ketone bodies ... 608
– gastric juice, acidity ... 648
– – volume ... 647
– ketone body excretion ... 674
Fats (*see also Lipids and Triglycerides*) ... 365, 374 sq.
– absorption, transport, storage ... 374
– contribution to BMR ... 539
– in whole body ... 517
– – gain in pregnancy ... 690
– in cerebrospinal fluid ... 638
– depot ... 374, 495
– dietary, composition ... 510
– – effect on blood coagulation ... 622
– – effect on depot fat ... 374
– – in foods ... 498 sq.
– – requirements ... 495
– enzymes attacking ... 405
– in faeces ... 657, 660
– metabolism ... 391 sq.
– – water from ... 524
– in milk ... 687, 689
– neutral. See Triglycerides
fath (fathom) ... 200
Fathom ... 200
Fatty acids ... 366 sq.
– activation ... 425
– in bile ... 655
– biosynthesis ... 420, 424, 425
– – pentose phosphate cycle and ... 422
– in blood ... 600, 601, 603, 604
– breakdown ... 391 sq., 402
– in formation of cephalin ... 425
– in cerebrospinal fluid ... 638
– in erythrocytes ... 600, 601
– essential ... 373, 492
– – dietary requirements ... 495
– in faeces ... 659, 660
– in depot fat ... 374
– in foods ... 498 sq.
– hydroxamic acids from ... 414
– in formation of lecithin ... 425
– in milk ... 687
– in spermatozoa ... 685
– symbols ... 373
– unsaturated, oxidation, vitamin E in ... 466
– in urine ... 675
Fatty acid ester hydrolases ... 404, 414
Fatty acyl-coenzyme A. See Acyl-coenzyme A
Fatty tissues. See under Tissues
Favism, glucose-6-phosphate dehydrogenase 592
F-distribution ... 40, 41, 168, 169
Fe. See Iron
Feces. See Faeces
femto- (10^{-15}) ... 9
Fennel, composition ... 504
Fermentation ... 387 sq.
– alcoholic ... 387, 390
– lactic acid ... 387 sq.
Fermium, properties and isotopes ... 248
Ferricytochromes ... 362
Ferriheme chloride ... 359
– hydroxide. See Haematin
Ferri-hemochromogen ... 359
Ferrihemoglobin ... 359
– hydroxide ... 359

A detailed index to the statistical tables (pages 28–131) and chapter on Statistical Methods (pages 146–196) will be found on pages 197–198

Ferriprotoporphyrin. See Haematin
Ferrocytochromes 361, 362
Ferroheme. See Haem
Ferro-hemochromogen 359
Ferroprotoporphyrin. See Haem
Fertility and spermatozoal properties 686
Fetus. See Foetus
FEV. See Expiratory volume, forced
$FEV_{1.0}$ (one-second volume) 543
FF (renal filtration fraction) 531
Fibre content in foods 498 sq.
Fibrin 622
– in synovial fluid 642
Fibrinogen, characteristics 580
– in erythrocyte sedimentation 559
– function 580, 622
– metabolism 579
– in plasma 579, 580, 582
– in pregnancy and post partum 691
– in synovial fluid 641
– in thrombocytes 579
FICK's principle 544
Field constants, electromagnetic 228
Figs, composition 500
Fine-structure constant, SOMMERFELD 228
FISCHER projection formulae 309, 310
FISCHER-BAER ester. See D-Glyceraldehyde 3-phosphate
Fish, amino acids 516
– composition 514, 515
FK (fructokinase). See Ketohexokinase
Flame photometry lines 284
Flavins in seminal vesical secretion 682
Flavin adenine dinucleotide (FAD) 345, 472
– in blood 609
– enzymatic cleavage 416
– in riboflavin of blood and organs 471
Flavin enzymes, prosthetic group 345
Flavin mononucleotide (FMN) 345, 472
– in blood 609
– in riboflavin of blood and organs 471
– in vitamin B_{12} synthesis 484
Flavin nucleotides, in biological oxidations 402, 403
– redox potential 403
Flavin ribityl phosphate. See Flavin mononucleotide
Flavoproteins 472
– in biological oxidations 403
fl dr (fluid dram, fluid drachm) 204
FLEXNER's carcinoma, lactic acid fermentation 388
– respiratory rate 387
Flounders, composition 514
Flour, amino acids 516
– composition 508
fl oz (fluid ounce) 204
Fluid balance. See Body water balance
– deprivation test 534, 535
– measures 204
Fluoridation of drinking water 497
Fluoride, in blood 563
– in bones and teeth 521
– dietary requirements 497
– in faeces 658
– in gastric juice 649
– in milk 688
– in saliva 644
– in sweat 679
– in urine 663
Fluorine, atomic weight multiples 250
– properties, isotopes, etc. 234
9α-Fluorocortisol 380
– biological activity 750
9α-Fluoro-11β,17β-dihydroxy-17α-methyl-androst-4-en-3-one 380
9α-Fluorohydrocortisone. See 9α-Fluorocortisol
9α-Fluoro-16α-hydroxyprednisolone. See Triamcinolone
Fluorometholone 380
9α-Fluoro-6α-methyl-11β,17α-dihydroxy-pregna-1,4-diene-3,20-dione 380
9α-Fluoro-16α-methylprednisolone. See Dexamethasone
9α-Fluoro-16α-methyl-11β,17α,21-tri-hydroxypregna-1,4-diene-3,20-dione. See Dexamethasone
9α-Fluoro-11β,16α,17α,21-tetrahydroxy-pregna-1,4-diene-3,20-dione. See Triamcinolone
9α-Fluoro-11β,17,21-trihydroxy-16β-methylpregna-1,4-diene-3,20-dione 379
9α-Fluoro-11β,17α,21-trihydroxypregn-4-ene-3,20-dione. See 9α-Fluorocortisol
Fluoxymestrone 380
Fm (fermium) 248
FMN. See Flavin mononucleotide
Foetal haemoglobin. See under Haemoglobin
Foetus, ACTH secretion 716
– bones, composition 521
– role of chorionic gonadotropin 715
– composition 517, 518
– erythrocytes, enzyme activities 585
– haemoglobin. See under Haemoglobin
– muscle, composition 518
– oestradiol 756
– organs, composition 519
– progesterone and metabolites 754
– size and weight 691, 692
– skin, hair and nails, composition 520
– teeth, composition 521
– – development 709
– tissues, organic components 522
– vitamin A deficiency 460
– gain in weight 690
Folacin. See Folic acid
Folic acid 478 sq.
– antagonists 478, 481
– in bile 655
– biosynthesis 478
– in blood 479, 610
– in whole body 479
– in cerebrospinal fluid 639
– deficiency 479
– in erythrocytes 479
– in foods 499 sq.
– hydrogenation, ascorbic acid in 490
– in milk 689
– requirements 479
– in saliva 646
– in urine 479, 676
Folic acid group 478 sq.
Folinic acid. See 5-Formyltetrahydrofolic acid
Follicle-ripening hormone. See Follicle-stimulating hormone
Follicle-stimulating hormone 713, 714
– oestrogens and 757
– releasing factor 725
Follicular hyperkeratosis 460
Foods, amino acids 516
– composition 498 sq.
– effect of cooking 498
– degradation 399 sq.
– – hydrogen ions from 527
– digestion 389, 405 sq.
Foot, secondary ossification centres 706, 708
Foot (unit) 200
– of water 212
Foot poundal 212, 213
FORBES' disease 450, 451
Force units 211
Forced expiratory volume. See under Expiratory volume
Formaldehyde, active. See 5,10-Methylene-tetrahydrofolic acid
Formate, in biological materials 366
– in blood 607
– in coffee 509
– in glycine degradation 397
– in transfer of one-carbon groups 437
– in synthesis of purines and methionine 479
– in urine 674
Formic acid (*see also Formate*) 366
Formiminoglutamic acid, in L-histidine degradation 395
– in synthesis of purines and methionine 479
– in urine 670
5-Formiminotetrahydrofolic acid, in L-histidine degradation 395
– in transfer of one-carbon groups 436, 437
– in synthesis of purines and methionine 479
N-Formylglutamic acid in synthesis of purines and methionine 479
Formylkynurenine in tryptophan degradation 399
Formylmethionyl s-RNA in bacterial protein synthesis 353
5-Formyltetrahydrofolic acid 481
– in transfer of one-carbon groups 436, 437
– in synthesis of purines and methionine 479
– in serum 479
10-Formyltetrahydrofolic acid, in L-histidine degradation 395
– in inosinic acid formation 435
– in transfer of one-carbon groups 436, 437
– in synthesis of purines and methionine 479
Formyltransferases 385
Fourfold table test 109 sq., 191, 195
Fr (francium) 244
Fractions 133
Francium, properties, isotopes, etc. 244
Frankfurters, composition 513
FRC. See Functional residual capacity
Freezing-point depression 270 sq.
– of bile 653
– of cerebrospinal fluid 635
– of gastric juice 647
– of pancreatic juice 651
– of saliva 643
– of semen 682
– of sweat 679
– of urine 662
Frequency 225
– units 208
FRF (follicle-stimulating-hormone releasing factor) 725
FRIEDMAN test 715
Frog legs, composition 514
Fru. See D-Fructose
β-Fructofuranosidase. See Saccharase
Fructokinase. See Ketohexokinase
D-Fructose (Fru) 311, 314
– in cerebrospinal fluid 639
– formation from glucose 420
– intolerance 450
– in lactic acid fermentation 390
– in semen 684
– solutions, calculation 271, 273
– in urine 450, 673
D-Fructose 1,6-diphosphate 319
– in carbohydrate synthesis and breakdown 441
– enzymatic cleavage 415
– in erythrocytes 506
– in glucose 6-phosphate formation from glyceraldehyde 3-phosphate 422
– in glycolysis 389
Fructosediphosphate aldolase, activity gradients 586
– in bile 655
– in blood 599
– – in heart disease 587
– – in muscle disease 587, 599
– – effect of muscular work 586
– – in pregnancy 586
– in cerebrospinal fluid 638
– in 2-deoxyribose 5-phosphate degradation 399
– in gastric juice 650
– in glucose 6-phosphate formation from glyceraldehyde 3-phosphate 422
– in glycolysis 389
– in milk 689
– in synovial fluid 641
– in tissues 585
– units and conversion factors 584
Fructose-1,6-diphosphate D-glyceraldehyde-3-phosphate-lyase. See Fructosediphosphate aldolase
D-Fructose 1-phosphate 318
– in lactic acid fermentation 390
– in urine 450
D-Fructose 6-phosphate 319
– in amino-sugar formation 424
– in carbohydrate synthesis and breakdown 441
– in erythrocytes 605
– fructose from 420
– in L-fucose formation 423
– glucosamine from 423
– in glucose 6-phosphate formation from glyceraldehyde 3-phosphate 422
– in glycolysis 389
– in lactic acid fermentation 390
– in pentose phosphate cycle 421, 422
Fructose-1-phosphate aldolase in fructose intolerance 450
Fructosuria 450
– in tyrosinaemia 449
Fruits, composition 499 sq.
Fruit juices, composition 499 sq.
Fruit sugar. See D-Fructose
Fruit wine, composition 509
FSH. See Follicle-stimulating hormone
FSH-RF (follicle-stimulating-hormone releasing factor) 725
ft (foot) 200
ftH_2O (foot of water) 212
Fucomucins, in gastric juice 650
– in saliva 645
2-(α-L-Fucopyranosido)lactose 324, 423
L-Fucose 313
– in bile 655
– formation 420, 423
– in gastric juice 650
– in milk 689

A detailed index to the statistical tables (pages 28–131) and chapter on Statistical Methods (pages 146–196) will be found on pages 197–198

L-Fucose (*contd*), in plasma ... 606
– in plasma proteins ... 581
– in saliva ... 645
– in urine ... 673
Fucosidolactose ... 324, 423
Fumarase. See Fumarate hydratase
Fumarate, in adenylic acid formation ... 436
– from degradation of foodstuffs ... 402
– in inosinic acid formation ... 435
– in phenylalanine degradation ... 398
– in tricarboxylic acid cycle ... 390, 391
– in urea synthesis ... 443, 444
Fumarate hydratase, in plasma ... 599
– in tricarboxylic acid cycle ... 390, 391
Fumarylacetoacetase in phenylalanine degradation ... 398
Fumarylácetoacetic acid in phenylalanine degradation ... 398
Functions, cyclometric ... 139
– hyperbolic ... 140
– trigonometric ... 138, 139
Functional residual capacity (FRC) 541, 542, 550
– in children nomograms ... 547
fur (furlong) ... 200
Furan ... 308
Furane-2,5-dicarboxylic acid in urine ... 674
Furanoses ... 308 sq.
Furlong ... 200

G

γ (gamma, microgramme) ... 204
^{g} (grade) ... 207
g (gramme) ... 204, 213
G (giga-, 10^9) ... 9
G. See D-Glucose
G. See Guanosine
Ga. See Gallium
GABA. See γ-Amino-*n*-butyric acid
Gadoleic acid ... 369
Gadolinium, flame lines ... 284
– properties, isotopes, etc. ... 240
gal (gallon) ... 203
Gal. See D-Galactose
Gal (galileo) ... 210
Galactocerebrosides ... 376
Galactoflavin ... 472
Galactokinase, in galactose diabetes ... 450
– in lactic acid fermentation ... 390
4′-(β-D-Galactopyranosido)-D-glucopyranose. See Lactose
Galactosaemia ... 450
D-Galactosamine (GalN) ... 314
– in bile ... 655
– in milk ... 689
– 1-phosphate ... 319
– in serum glycoproteins ... 606
– in urine ... 673
D-Galactose (Gal) ... 310, 314
– in bile ... 655
– in blood ... 450
– in blood glycoproteins ... 606
– in faeces ... 452
– formation from glucose ... 420
– glucose formation from ... 347
– in lactic acid fermentation ... 390
– in lipids ... 365
– in urine ... 450, 673
Galactose diabetes ... 450
α-D-Galactose 1-phosphate ... 319
– in erythrocytes ... 605
– in lactic acid fermentation ... 390
– in urine ... 450
Galactose-1-phosphate uridylyltransferase in galactosaemia ... 450
β-Galactosidase ... 412
– in alactasia ... 451
– in lactose intolerance ... 451
– in seminal plasma ... 684
Galactosyl-*N*-acetylgalactosaminylgalactosylglucosylceramide in brain ... 377
Galactosyldiglycerides in chloroplasts ... 375
α-D-Galacturonic acid ... 323
Galaheptulose (D-perseulose) ... 311
Galileo ... 210, 211
Gallbladder, volume of contents ... 653
Gallbladder bile. See Bile
GALLI-MAININI test ... 715
Gallium, flame lines ... 284
– properties, isotopes, etc. ... 236
Gallium-68, diagnostic use ... 289
Gallon ... 204
GalN. See D-Galactosamine
Gametogenesis, gonadotropins in ... 714
Gamma (unit) ... 204
Gammaglobulins. See γ-Globulins
Gamma ray constant ... 221
Gangliosides ... 365, 377
– accumulation ... 455
– brain, components ... 377
– in brain and spinal cord ... 520
– formation ... 424
GAPDH See Glyceraldehydephosphate dehydrogenase
Garlic, composition ... 504
Gases, blood. See under Blood
– ideal, number density of molecules ... 228
– – molar volume ... 228
– ionization ... 285, 286
– standard temperature and pressure ... 541
– volumes, reduction ... 259 sq.
Gas-gangrene antitoxins, standards ... 760
Gastric juice ... 647 sq.
– acidity ... 648
– – effect of gastrin ... 739
– amount ... 525, 647
– electrolytes ... 525, 649
– lipase ... 414, 650
– proteolytic enzymes ... 407, 650
– in stomach cancer. See Stomach cancer
Gastric mucosa, enzyme activities ... 585
Gastric ulcers, gastric acidity and ... 648
Gastricsin ... 407
– in gastric juice ... 650
Gastrin ... 739
– effect on gastric juice acidity ... 648
Gastritis, gastric juice albumin in ... 650
Gastrointestinal tract, enzymes and precursors ... 406 sq.
– effect of glucagon ... 738
– hormones ... 739
GAUCHER's disease ... 377, 455
– spleen cerebrosides in ... 367
Gauss ... 216
Gb (gilbert) ... 216
Gc groups of serum ... 634
Gd. See Gadolinium
GDH. See Glycerophosphate dehydrogenase
GDP. See Guanosine diphosphate
Ge (germanium) ... 236
Geiger counters ... 286
Gelatin, amino acids ... 516
– composition ... 513
Gene mutations ... 446
Genetic code ... 353
Genistein, oestrogenic activity ... 755
Genitals, surface area ... 528
Genotypes, blood-group ... 626 sq.
Gentamycin, reference preparation ... 762
Geodetic units of length ... 200
Geometric mean ... 137
– series ... 136, 137
Geometry ... 140 sq.
Geranyl pyrophosphate in cholesterol synthesis ... 426, 427
Germanium, properties, isotopes, etc. ... 236
gf (gramme-force) ... 211
GH-RF (growth-hormone releasing factor) . 725
gi (gill) ... 204
GIERKE's disease ... 450, 451
giga- (10^9) ... 9
Gigantism, pituitary, and ossification ... 707
Gilbert ... 216
GILBERT's disease ... 454
– serum bilirubin in ... 577
Gill ... 204
GI tract. See Gastrointestinal tract
Gl (glucinium). See Beryllium
Glands, composition ... 519
Glauber's salt. See Sodium sulphate decahydrate
Glc. See D-Glucose
GlcN. See D-Glucosamine
GLDH. See Glutamate dehydrogenase
Gln. See Glutamine
Globoside ... 377
Globulin, BENCE-JONES, structure ... 581
– – in urine ... 668
– thyroxine-binding ... 726
Globulins ... 329
– alpha-. See α-Globulins
– beta-. See β-Globulins
– gamma-. See γ-Globulins
– myeloma, structure ... 581
– osmotic activity ... 526
– in pancreatic juice ... 652
– in plasma and serum ... 582, 583
α-Globulins, metabolism ... 579
– in plasma and serum ... 582
α_1-Globulins in cerebrospinal fluid ... 637
– in plasma and serum ... 582, 583
– in semen ... 684
– in synovial fluid ... 641
– in urine ... 668
α_2-Globulins, allotypy ... 634
– in cerebrospinal fluid ... 637
– in plasma and serum ... 582, 583
– in pregnancy and post partum ... 691
– in semen ... 684
– in synovial fluid ... 641
– in urine ... 668
β-Globulins, in cerebrospinal fluid ... 637
– characteristics and function ... 580
– metabolism ... 579
– in plasma and serum ... 582, 583
– in pregnancy and post partum ... 691
– in synovial fluid ... 641
– in urine ... 668
β_{2a}-Globulin. See γA-Globulin
β_{2M}-Globulin. See γM-Globulin
γ-Globulins, allotypy ... 634
– amino-acid composition ... 581
– in blood ... 582, 583
– in cerebrospinal fluid ... 637
– characteristics and function ... 580
– in gastric juice ... 650
– in intestinal juice ... 656
– metabolism ... 579
– in pregnancy and post partum ... 691
– structure ... 581
– in synovial fluid ... 641
– – in rheumatoid arthritis ... 641
– in urine ... 668
γ_{1a}-Globulin. See γA-Globulin
γ_{1M}-Globulin. See γM-Globulin
γ_2-Globulin. See γG-Globulin
γ_{ss}-Globulin. See γG-Globulin
γA-Globulin, amino-acid composition ... 581
– characteristics and function ... 580
– in gastric juice ... 650
– in milk ... 689
– in saliva ... 645
– in serum ... 580, 583
– structure ... 581
– in urine ... 668
γD-Globulin ... 580
– structure ... 581
γE-Globulin ... 580
– structure ... 581
γG-Globulin, amino-acid composition ... 581
– in bile ... 655
– characteristics and function ... 580
– in faeces ... 659
– in gastric juice ... 650
– in semen ... 684
– in serum ... 580, 583
– structure ... 581
– in urine ... 668
γM-Globulin, amino-acid composition ... 581
– characteristics and function ... 580
– in serum ... 580, 583
– structure ... 581
γU-Globulin, structure ... 581
Glomerular activity ... 535
– filtration rate ... 531, 536
– nephritis, fluid deprivation test in ... 535
Glomerulotropin ... 730
Glu. See L-Glutamate and L-Glutamic acid
Glucagon ... 737, 738
– in cyclic AMP formation ... 345
– in catecholamine secretion ... 731
α-Glucan-branching glycosyltransferase deficiency ... 450, 451
α-1,4-Glucan 4-glucanohydrolase. See Amylase
α-Glucan phosphorylase ... 411
– deficiency ... 450, 451
– in lactic acid fermentation ... 390
– binding of pyridoxal phosphate ... 475
– vitamin B_6 and ... 475
Glucinium. See Beryllium
D-Glucitol. See Sorbitol
Glucocerebrosides, accumulation ... 455
– in GAUCHER's disease ... 377
Glucocorticoids ... 379 sq., 748 sq.
– determination ... 743
– secretion, effect of ACTH ... 717
Glucocorticosteroids. See Glucocorticoids
α-D-Glucofuranose ... 310
Gluconeogenesis ... 441
– action of corticosteroids ... 749

A detailed index to the statistical tables (pages 28–131) and chapter on Statistical Methods (pages 146–196) will be found on pages 197–198

D-Gluconic acid 323
– 6-phosphate 320
α-D-Glucopyranose 310
β-L-Glucopyranose 310
α-D-Glucopyranosido-β-D-fructofuranoside. See Sucrose
4'-(α-D-Glucopyranosido)-β-D-glucopyranose. See Maltose
4'-(β-D-Glucopyranosido)-β-D-glucopyranose 324
D-Glucosamine (GlcN) 315
– in bile 655
– in cerebrospinal fluid 639
– formation 420, 423, 424
– in serum glycoproteins 606
– in milk 689
– 6-phosphate 320
– – formation and utilization 424
– in urine 673
– utilization 424
D-Glucose (G, Glc) 310, 315
– ascorbic acid from 489
– in bile 655
– in blood 604 sq.
– breakdown 402
– cell constituents and metabolites from 420 sq.
– in cerebrospinal fluid 639
– commercial, composition 509
– in erythrocytes 604
– in faeces 452
– formation, from limit-dextrin 412
– – from noncarbohydrates 441
– – from starch 411
– galactose formation from 347
– glomerular filtration and excretion 536
– effect on plasma growth hormone 719
– consumption by leucocytes 618
– in lipids 365
– osmotic activity 526
– oxidation 389 sq.
– – energy yield 387
– in pancreatic juice 652
– reabsorption, in glucosuria 452
– – tubular 534
– in saliva 646
– serine from 432
– solutions, calculation 271, 273
– – infusion, composition 529
– in sweat 681
– in synovial fluid 642
– UDP-glucuronic acid from 423
– effect on urinary osmolarity and specific gravity 534
– in urine 453, 673
– utilization 526
β-D-Glucose 1,6-diphosphate 319
α-D-Glucose-1,6-diphosphate: α-D-glucose-1-phosphate phosphotransferase. See Phosphoglucomutase
Glucose–galactose malabsorption 452
Glucose-6-phosphatase 415
– in carbohydrate synthesis and breakdown 441
– effect of corticosteroids 749
– in plasma 597
D-Glucose 1-phosphate 319
– in carbohydrate synthesis and breakdown 441
– formation, from amylopectin 411
– – from glycogen 411
– – from limit dextrin 412
– glycogen from 420
– in lactic acid fermentation 390
– lactose from UDP-galactose and 347, 420
– UDP-glucuronic acid from 423
D-Glucose 6-phosphate 319
– in carbohydrate synthesis and breakdown 441
– deficiency 450, 451
– in erythrocytes 605
– from glyceraldehyde 3-phosphate 422
– in glycolysis 389
– in lactic acid fermentation 390
– oxidation to 6-phosphogluconate 420, 421
– UDP-glucuronic acid from 423
Glucose-6-phosphate dehydrogenase (G-6-PDH), activity, temperature correction 585
– in bile 655
– in Gierke's disease 450
– isozymes 584
– in milk 689
– in pentose phosphate cycle 422
– in plasma 592
– in tissues 585
Glucosephosphate isomerase, in cerebrospinal fluid 638
Glucosephosphate isomerase, in gastric juice 650
– in glucose 6-phosphate formation from glyceraldehyde 3-phosphate 422
– in glycolysis 389
– in milk 689
– in pentose phosphate cycle 422
– in plasma 600
– – in muscle disease 587
– in synovial fluid 641
D-Glucose-6-phosphate ketol-isomerase. See Glucosephosphate isomerase
D-Glucose-6-phosphate: NADP oxidoreductase. See Glucose-6-phosphate dehydrogenase
D-Glucose-6-phosphate phosphohydrolase. See Glucose-6-phosphatase
Glucose-1-phosphate uridylyltransferase in carbohydrate synthesis and breakdown 441
Glucose phosphomutase. See Phosphoglucomutase
α-Glucosidase 412
– in idiopathic generalized glycogenosis 450, 451
– in intestinal mucosa 413
– in seminal plasma 684
β-Glucosidase 412
Glucosuria, in cystinosis 449
– renal 452
D-Glucuronic acid 323, 423
– in ascorbic acid synthesis 489
– in blood 605
– in erythrocytes 605
– in faeces 659
– formation from glucose 420, 423
– in gastric juice 650
– in urine 673
β-Glucuronidase 412
– in blood 585, 597
– – in pregnancy 586
– in gastric juice 650
– in seminal plasma 684
– in synovial fluid 641
– in urine 672
– in vaginal secretion 597
β-Glucuronides 442
β-D-Glucuronide glucuronohydrolase. See β-Glucuronidase
D-Glucuronolactone in ascorbic acid synthesis 489
Glumitocin 724
Glu(NH_2). See Glutamine
Glutaconyl-coenzyme A in L-lysine degradation 398
L-Glutamate (Glu) 331
– in amino-sugar formation 424
– in blood 574
– in blood proteins 581
– cell constituents from 434
– in cysteinesulphinic acid formation 438
– decarboxylation 394
– degradation 393, 394, 402
– in folic acid synthesis 478
– in foods 516
– formation 420, 432
– glutathione from 438
– in guanylic acid formation 436
– in detoxication of halogenobenzenes 445
– in L-histidine degradation 394, 395
– hydroxyproline from 432
– in inosinic acid formation 433
– in milk 688
– in L-ornithine degradation 385
– in L-proline degradation 395
– proline from 432
– in saliva 645
– in sweat 680
– transamination reactions 394
– – with oxaloacetate 420
– – with pyruvate 420
– in urea synthesis 444
– in urine 667
Glutamate dehydrogenase (GLDH), cell binding 585
– in glutamic acid degradation 393
– isozymes 584
– in plasma 592
– – in heart disease 587
– – in liver disease 586, 587
– in tissues 585
L-Glutamate: NAD(P) oxidoreductase. See Glutamate dehydrogenase
Glutamate–oxalacetate transaminase. See Aspartate aminotransferase
Glutamate–pyruvate transaminase. See Alanine aminotransferase
L-Glutamic acid (Glu) (*see also L-Glutamate*) 331
Glutamic acid β-monoamide. See Glutamine
L-Glutamic γ-semialdehyde, in L-ornithine degradation 395
– in L-proline degradation 395
– in proline and hydroxyproline formation 432
– in transamination reactions 394
Glutamine (Gln, $Glu[NH_2]$) 331
– in amino-sugar formation 424
– in blood 574
– in cerebrospinal fluid 636
– formation and function 434
– in guanylic acid formation 436
– in inosinic acid formation 433
– in detoxication of phenylacetic acid 445
– in urine 667
γ-L-Glutamyl-L-cysteine in glutathione formation 438
Glutarate, in L-lysine degradation 398
– in urine 674
Glutaryl-coenzyme A, in L-lysine degradation 398
– in tryptophan degradation 399
Glutathione (GSH, GSSG), in blood 573
– formation 438
– function 434
– haemolysis and 573
– in detoxication of halogenobenzenes 445
– in semen 684
Glutathione reductase (GR), in plasma 592
– in seminal plasma 684
– in synovial fluid 641
Gly. See Glycine
Glyceraldehyde, stereoisomerism 309
D-Glyceraldehyde 310, 313
– in degradation of fats 392
– in lactic acid fermentation 390
D-Glyceraldehyde 3-phosphate (3-phosphoglyceraldehyde) 317
– in carbohydrate synthesis and breakdown 441
– deoxyribose 5-phosphate from 420
– in 2-deoxyribose 5-phosphate degradation 399
– in erythrocytes 605
– in degradation of fats 392
– in glycolysis 389
– in lactic acid fermentation 390
– oxidation 422
– in pentose phosphate cycle 421, 422
Glyceraldehydephosphate dehydrogenase (GAPDH), in glycolysis 389
– in plasma 592
– in tissues 585
D-Glyceraldehyde-3-phosphate ketolisomerase. See Triosephosphate isomerase
D-Glyceraldehyde-3-phosphate: NAD oxidoreductase. See Glyceraldehydephosphate dehydrogenase
D-Glycerate, in degradation of fats 392
– in serine formation 432
D-Glyceric acid (*see also D-Glycerate*) 323
– 1,3-diphosphate. See 1,3-Diphosphoglycerate
– 2,3-diphosphate 317
– 2-phosphate. See 2-Phosphoglycerate
– 3-phosphate. See 3-Phosphoglycerate
Glyceric 1,2-cyclic phosphoric acid 375
Glycerides. See Diglycerides, Monoglycerides, Triglycerides
Glycerol 322
– degradation 392, 402
– in depot fat 374
– in lipids 365
– in plasma 607
– in wine 509
Glycerol-ester hydrolase. See Lipase
L-Glycerol 1-phosphate. See α-Glycerophosphate
L-Glycerol-3-phosphate: NAD oxidoreductase. See Glycerophosphate dehydrogenase
Glycerol phosphorylcholine, enzymatic cleavage 417
Glycerol teichoic acids, formation 349
α-Glycerophosphate (L-glycerol 1-phosphate) 317
– in degradation of fats 392
– formation from glucose 420
– in formation of lecithin and cephalin 425
– in triglyceride synthesis 426
Glycerophosphate dehydrogenase (GDH), in glycerophosphate formation 420
– isozymes 584
– in plasma 590
– in tissues 585
Glycerophosphatides 365, 375, 376
α-Glycerophosphoric acid (*see also α-Glycerophosphate*) 375

A detailed index to the statistical tables (pages 28–131) and chapter on Statistical Methods (pages 146–196) will be found on pages 197–198

β-Glycerophosphoric acid 375
α-Glycerophosphorylcholine 376
– in semen 683
Glycerophosphorylcholine diesterase 417
α-Glycerophosphorylethanolamine 376
Glycine (Gly) 331
– in bile 654 sq.
– in blood 449, 574
– buffers 280 sq.
– cell constituents from 434
– conjugation, with bile acids 438
– – in detoxication 444, 445
– creatine from arginine, methionine and 437
– degradation 397, 402
– – to oxalic acid 397, 449
– in foods 516
– formation 432
– in glutathione formation 438
– haem synthesis from 454
– in inosinic acid formation 433
– in milk 688
– in porphyrin formation 437
– in saliva 645
– in serum proteins 581
– in sweat 680
– in L-threonine degradation 397
– in transamination reactions 394
– in urine 449, 667
Glycinuria 452
Glycocyamine. See Guanidinoacetic acid
Glycogen 327
– in carbohydrate synthesis and breakdown 441
– degradation 411
– – effect of catecholamines 733
– – effect of glucagon 738
– deposition and utilization, inborn errors 450, 451
– in erythrocytes 606
– formation from glucose 420
– in granulocytes 606
– in lactic acid fermentation 390
– in semen 684
– in tissues 522
Glycogenolysis. See Glycogen degradation
Glycogenosis, idiopathic generalized 450, 451
Glycogen phosphorylase. See α-Glucan phosphorylase
Glycogen storage disease 415
– erythrocyte glycogen in 606
– glucagon in 738
Glycogen synthetase. See UDPglucose–glycogen glycosyltransferase
Glycoglycerides 365, 375
Glycolaldehyde, active, in pentose phosphate cycle 421, 422
Glycolaldehydetransferase. See Transketolase
Glycol dehydrogenase, vitamin B_{12} in 485
Glycolic acid in urine 674
Glycolipids 377
N-Glycolylneuraminic acid 316
Glycolysis 387 sq.
Glycopeptides in urine 668
Glycoproteins 327, 329
– in bile 655
– in blood 606
– formation 347, 348, 350, 424
– in urine 668
$α_1$-Glycoprotein, acid, characteristics and function 580
– – in bile 655
– – composition 581
– – in plasma 580
– – in saliva 645
Glycosidases 309, 386, 405, 411 sq.
Glycosides 308, 309
Glycoside hydrolases 309, 386, 405, 411 sq.
Glycosphingolipids 377
Glycosuria. See Glucosuria
Glycosyltransferases 386, 411 sq.
Glycosyltransferase, α-glucan-branching, deficiency 450, 451
Glycyl-glycine dipeptidase 408, 410
Glycyl-leucine dipeptidase 410
Glyoxalase in glycine degradation 397
Glyoxalate. See Glyoxylate
Glyoxylate, in glycine degradation 397
– in L-hydroxyproline degradation 395
– in plasma 607
– in purine degradation 401
– in transamination reactions 394
Gm serum groups 634
GMP. See Guanosine monophosphate
Goat meat, composition 513
Goat's milk, composition 511
Goitre 727
– cretinism and 449
– diagnosis 289
Gold, in blood 567
– freezing point 209
– properties, isotopes, etc. 242
Gold-198, characteristics 293
– decay table 305
– gamma ray constant 221
– therapeutic use 290
Gold-199, characteristics 293
'Golden section' 133
Gonads, cholesterol synthesis 426
– steroid hormones 428 sq.
Gonadotropins, of anterior pituitary 713, 714
– chorionic. See Chorionic gonadotropin
– reference preparations 713, 763
– releasing factors (GRF) 714
– standards 763
Gonadotropin-inhibiting factor in urine 714
Gonane 381
Gooseberries, composition 500
Goose flesh, composition 513
GOT (glutamate-oxalacetate transferase). See Aspartate aminotransferase
Gout 453
– serum uric acid 577
– synovial fluid uric acid 641
G-6-PDH. See Glucose-6-phosphate dehydrogenase
GPT (glutamate-pyruvate transaminase). See Alanine aminotransferase
gr (grain) 204
GR. See Glutathione reductase
Grade 138, 207, 208
Grain 205
Grain-force 211
Gram. See Gramme
Gramicidins, reference preparations 762
Gramme 204
– as energy unit 213
Gramme-force 211
Granuloblasts in bone marrow 621
Granulocytes, blood count 618, 619
– electrophoretic mobility 560
– enzyme activities 585
– glycogen 606
– half-life 618
Granulopoiesis in bone marrow 621
Grapes, composition 500
Grapefruit, composition 500
Grape juice, composition 500
Grape sugar. See D-Glucose
GRAVES' disease 718
Gravitational constant 201, 228
Gravity, acceleration due to 211, 230
Greek alphabet 9
Gregorian year 206
grf (grain-force) 211
GRF (gonadotropin-releasing factors) 714
GRF (growth-hormone releasing factor) 725
GROTTHUS-DRAPER law 218
Growth, body composition and 517
– growth hormone and 720
– intrauterine 691, 692
– normal measurements during 693 sq.
– thyroxine deficiency and 727
Growth hormone 719, 720
– releasing factor (GRF) 725
– standard and reference preparation 762
Gs (gauss) 216
GSH. See Glutathione
GSSG. See Glutathione
GTP. See Guanosine triphosphate
Guanase. See Guanine deaminase
Guanidine, in blood 573
– in urine 666
Guanidinoacetic acid 335
– in blood 573
– in creatine formation 437
– in urine 666
Guanine 338
– enzymatic deamination 419
– degradation 401
– in DNA synthesis 352
– in protein synthesis 353
– in purine degradation 400
– in RNA synthesis 352
– in urine 671
Guanine aminohydrolase. See Guanine deaminase
Guanine deaminase 401, 419
– in plasma 598
– in purine degradation 400
Guanosine (G, Guo) 339
– in purine degradation 400
Guanosine deaminase 401
– in purine degradation 400
Guanosine diphosphate (GDP) 343
Guanosine diphosphate cobinamide in vitamin B_{12} synthesis 484
Guanosine diphosphate L-fucose 347
– in L-fucose formation 423
– milk oligosaccharides from 423
Guanosine diphosphate 4-keto-6-deoxy-L-galactose in L-fucose formation 423
Guanosine diphosphate 4-keto-6-deoxy-D-mannose in L-fucose formation 423
Guanosine diphosphate mannose 347
– in L-fucose formation 423
Guanosine monophosphate (GMP) 343
– formation 436
– in purine degradation 400, 401
– in RNA 351
Guanosine triphosphate (GTP) 343
– in adenylic acid formation 435
– in ATP synthesis 404
– in blood 577
– in protein synthesis 354
– in tricarboxylic acid cycle 391
– in vitamin B_{12} synthesis 484
Guanylate deaminase 401
– in purine degradation 400
Guanylic acid. See Guanosine monophosphate
D-Guloheptulose 311
L-Gulonolactone in ascorbic acid synthesis 489
L-Gulonolactone oxidase in ascorbic acid synthesis 489
D-Gulose 310
GÜNTHER's disease 454
Guo. See Guanosine

H

h (hecto, 10^2) 9
h (hour) 205
H (henry) 216
H. See Hydrogen
ha (hectare) 203
Haddock, composition 514
Haem 359 sq.
– derivatives 359 sq.
– proteins 329, 360 sq.
– synthesis 454
Haematin 359, 360, 362
– in faeces 657
Haematocrit (Ht) 613, 614, 617
– blood acid–base balance and 569
– blood viscosity and 557
– body 554
– – gain in pregnancy 691
– mean corpuscular volume from 615
– renal blood flow and 531
– venous, gain in pregnancy 691
Haematoidin in urinary sediments 677
Haematoporphyrin 359
Haemiglobin. See Methaemoglobin
Haemiglobincyanide reference preparation 763
Haemin 359
Haemoblastosis, serum adenosine deaminase 599
Haemochromes 362
Haemochromogen 359
Haemodynamics, renal 531 sq.
Haemoglobin (Hb) 359, 360, 362
– in whole blood 576, 579, 615, 617
– – and haematocrit 614, 615
– – gain in pregnancy 691
– and pH of body fluids 527
– breakdown 362
– cyanide, haemoglobin determination as 615
– embryonic 615
– in erythrocytes 576
– foetal 615
– – persistence 448
– haptoglobin binding 576
– iron content 566
– mean corpuscular 615, 617
– – and haematocrit 614, 615
– oxygen binding 570
– in plasma 576
– types 446 sq.
– in urine 661, 671
Haemoglobinopathies 446 sq.
Haemogram, SCHILLING's 620
Haemolysis, erythrocyte thickness and 614
– glutathione stability and 573

A detailed index to the statistical tables (pages 28–131) and chapter on Statistical Methods (pages 146–196) will be found on pages 197–198

Haemolytic anaemia. See under Anaemia
– disease of newborn (HDN) 577, 632
– transfusion reaction 632
Haemopoiesis, vitamin B_{12} in 485
Haemoproteins .... 329, 360 sq.
Haemorrhagic diatheses, blood coagulation in 622, 623
– genesis 623
Haemproteins .... 329, 360 sq.
Hafnium, properties, isotopes, etc. 241
Hair, composition 520
Half-life of nuclides .... 217, 234 sq.
Halibut, composition 514
Halogenobenzenes, mercapturic acids from . 445
Ham, composition 513
Hamburgers, composition 512
HAMOLSKY test 288
Hand (unit) 200
Hand, secondary ossification centres ... 706, 708
Haptoglobin, allotypy 634
– amino-acid composition 581
– in bile 655
– characteristics and function 580
– in erythrocyte sedimentation 559
– binding of haemoglobin 576
– in saliva 645
– in serum 580, 583
– in synovial fluid 641
HARDEN-YOUNG ester. See D-Fructose 1,6-diphosphate
Hare, composition 513
Harmonic mean 137
Hartnup disease 452
HAWORTH ring formulae 310, 311
Hazelnuts, amino acids 516
– composition 507
Hb. See Haemoglobin
Hb_E (erythrocyte mean haemoglobin content) 615, 617
Hb-C disease 447
HBDH. See α-Hydroxybutyrate dehydrogenase
Hb-F. See Haemoglobin, foetal
Hb-S gene and malaria 447
Hb-SC disease 447
HCG (human chorionic gonadotropin). See Chorionic gonadotropin
HDN (haemolytic disease of newborn). 577, 632
He (helium) 234
Head, surface area 528
– circumference, of foetus 692
– – during growth .... 693 sq.
Heart, β-acetylglucosaminase 413
– animal, composition 512, 513
– blood pressure 553
– contribution to BMR 539
– carnitine 491
– composition 518
– disease, serum enzyme changes 587
– failure, myogenic, serum enzyme changes. 587
– infarction. See Cardiac infarction
– minute output, renal fraction 531
– muscle, ascorbic acid 490
– – enzyme activities 585
– – respiration rate 387
– phospholipase A 417
– weight 710
Heat sweat. See Sweat
Heat transfer coefficients 215
Heat units 212, 213
Heavy water, density 230
Hectare 203
hecto- (10^2) 9
Hectometre 200
Height changes during growth .... 695 sq.
Helium, properties, isotopes, etc. 234
Hematin. See Haematin
Heme. See Haem
Hemiacetals 308
Hemicellulose in faeces 659
Hemichrome 359
Hemiglobin (*see also Methaemoglobin*) 359
– hydroxide 359
Hemiketals 308
Hemin 359
Hemo-. See Haemo-
Hemochrome 359
Hendecanoic acid. See Undecylic acid
HENDERSON–HASSELBALCH formula 527, 528
– nomogram 528
Heneicosanoic acid 367
Henry 216
Heparin 327
– in blood 606
Heparin, in blood coagulation 622
– and haemorrhagic diatheses 623, 624
– standard 763
– use in thrombo-embolism 622
β-Heparin 326
Heparinase 413
Heparin tolerance test 625
Hepatic bile. See Bile
– coma, blood ammonia 573
– – serum enzyme changes 586
– disease. See under Liver
Hepatitis, antiserum, standard 761
– bile composition 655
– bilirubin 577
– enzyme changes 586
– fumarate hydratase 599
– glucose-6-phosphatase 597
– glucosephosphate isomerase 600
– hexokinase and ketohexokinase 594
– ketose-1-phosphate aldolase 599
– triosephosphate isomerase 600
Hepatolenticular degeneration. See WILSON's disease
Hepatomegaly .... 449, 451 sq.
Heptacosan in spermatozoa 685
Heptacosanoic acid 367
Heptadecanoic acid 367
Heptanoic acid 366
Heptoses 316
Herring, composition 515
HERS' disease 450, 451
Hertz 208
Δ^7-Hexacosahexaenoic acid 370
Hexacosanoic acid. See Cerotic acid
Δ^{17}-Hexacosenoic acid 369
Hexadecanoic acid. See Palmitic acid
$\Delta^{6,10,14}$-Hexadecatrienoic acid 370
Δ^9-Hexadecenoic acid. See Palmitoleic acid
$\Delta^{2,4}$-Hexadienoic acid 370
Hexaene acids in serum lipids 604
Hexahydrohexahydroxybenzene isomers 309
Hexanoic acid. See Caproic acid
Δ^2-Hexenoic acid 368
Hexoestrol, oestrogenic activity 755
Hexoic acid. See Caproic acid
Hexokinase (HK), in glycolysis 389
– in lactic acid fermentation 390
– in plasma 594
– in saliva 645
– in tissues 585
Hexosamines, in bile 655
– formation and utilization 424
– in gastric juice 650
– in plasma 606
– in saliva 645
– in urine 673
Hexoses .... 314 sq.
– in foods, breakdown 402
– in gastric juice 650
– in lipids 365
– in plasma 606
– in plasma proteins 581
– in saliva 645
– in urine 673
Hexosediphosphatase 415
– in carbohydrate synthesis and breakdown. 441
– in glucose 6-phosphate formation from glyceraldehyde 3-phosphate 422
Hexosephosphate isomerase. See Glucosephosphate isomerase
Hexose 1-phosphate uridylyltransferase in lactic acid fermentation 390
Hexosyltransferases 386
Hf (hafnium) 241
Hg. See Mercury
HGH (human growth hormone). See Growth hormone
Hip, secondary ossification centres 706, 708
Hippuric acid, in formation of glycine conjugates 445
– in urinary sediments 677, 678
– in urine 666
Hiragonic acid 370
Hirsutism 455
His. See L-Histidine
Histaminase, in pregnancy serum 586
– vitamin B_6 and 475
Histamine, in blood 575
– in cerebrospinal fluid 637
– formation from histidine 394
– function 434
– in gastric juice 650
– effect on gastric juice acidity 648
– and haemorrhagic diatheses 623, 624
Histamine, in leucocytes 575
– in lymphocytes 575
– in saliva 645
– in thrombocytes 575
– in urine 670
Histidinaemia 448, 449
L-Histidine (His) 331
– in blood 448, 449, 574
– in blood proteins 581
– cell constituents from 434
– decarboxylation 394
– degradation 394, 395, 402
– dietary requirements 496
– in foods 516
– formation 432
– metabolites, in urine 670
– in milk 688
– in synthesis of purines and methionine ... 479
– in saliva 645
– in sweat 680
– in urine 667
Histidine ammonia-lyase, in histidinaemia .. 449
– in L-histidine degradation 395
HK. See Hexokinase
Ho (holmium) 241
HODGKIN's disease, leucocyte mobility 560
Holmium, properties, isotopes, etc. 241
Holo-enzymes 382
HOLZER-GERLACH enzyme units 584
Homocarnosine in urine 666
Homocitrulline in urine 667
Homo-compounds 381
L-Homocysteine, in creatine formation 437
– degradation 397, 398, 402
– methionine from 437
– in methionine degradation 398
Homocystinuria 449
Homogentisate oxygenase, in alkaptonuria . 448
– in phenylalanine degradation 398
Homogentisic acid, in phenylalanine degradation 398
– in urine 448, 661, 675
Homo-oxybiotin 487
L-Homoserine 335
– degradation 397, 402
– in L-homocysteine degradation 398
Honey, composition 509
Hormones .... 713 sq.
– corticosteroid. See Corticosteroids
– standards and reference preparations. 762, 763
– steroid. See Corticosteroids and Steroid hormones
Horseflesh, composition 513
Horsepower 214
Horsepower-hour 213
Horse-radishes, composition 504
Hour 206
hp (horsepower) 214
HPL (human placental lactogen) 721
H_2PteGlu (dihydropteroylglutamic acid). See Dihydrofolic acid
H_4PteGlu (tetrahydropteroylglutamic acid). See Tetrahydrofolic acid
H substance, secretion 627
Ht. See Haematocrit
HTR (haemolytic transfusion reaction) 632
Hundredweight 205
Hyaline casts in urine 677
Hyaloplasm, enzyme binding 584, 585
Hyaluronate lyase. See Hyaluronidase
Hyaluronic acid 328
– in synovial fluid 642
Hyaluronidase 413
– in spermatozoa 413, 684
– standard 763
Hydrindantin 329
Hydriodic acid, decinormal solutions 277
Hydrobromic acid, decinormal solutions ... 277
Hydrocarbons in faeces 659
Hydrochloric acid (*see also Chloride*), in gastric juice 648
– solutions, conversion factors .... 274 sq.
– – decinormal 277
– – pH values 279
Hydrocortisone. See Cortisol
Hydrocyanic acid (*see also Cyanide*), decinormal solutions 277
Hydrogen, standard atmosphere point 209
– atmospheric, composition 247
– atomic weight multiples 250
– biological removal 402, 403
– boiling point 209
– properties, isotopes, etc. 234
– triple point 209

A detailed index to the statistical tables (pages 28–131) and chapter on Statistical Methods (pages 146–196) will be found on pages 197–198

Hydrogen-1 atom, Bohr radius 228
– mass 229
– Rydberg constant and frequency 229
Hydrogen-3, characteristics 234, 292
Hydrogen electrode, redox potential 403
Hydrogen-ion concentration, definition 278
Hydrogen peroxide in glycine degradation . 397
Hydrolases 386
Hydro-lyases 386
Hydrosphere, composition .... 234 sq.
Hydroxamic acids from fatty acids 414
Hydroxocobalamin 482, 483
3-Hydroxyacyl-CoA dehydrogenase in degradation of fats 392
β-Hydroxyacyl-coenzyme A in degradation of fats 392
11-Hydroxyaetiocholanolone in urine .. 746, 749
3α-Hydroxy-5α-androstan-17-one. See Androsterone
3α-Hydroxy-5β-androstan-17-one. See Aetiocholanolone
3β-Hydroxy-5α-androstan-17-one. See Epiandrosterone
3β-Hydroxy-5β-androstan-17-one. See 3β-Aetiocholanolone
11β-Hydroxy-Δ^4-androstene-3,17-dione, biosynthesis 428, 429
– breakdown 746
19-Hydroxy-Δ^4-androstene-3,17-dione, biosynthesis 428, 429
– in oestrogen synthesis 431
3β-Hydroxyandrost-5-en-17-one. See Dehydroepiandrosterone
17α-Hydroxyandrost-4-en-3-one 380
17β-Hydroxyandrost-4-en-3-one. See Testosterone
11-Hydroxyandrosterone in urine 746, 749
3-Hydroxyanthranilic acid, in tryptophan metabolism 398, 399, 475
– in urine 668
5-Hydroxybenzimidazolylcyanocobamide ... 483
m-Hydroxybenzoic acid in urine 675
β-Hydroxybutyrate, in blood 608
– in cerebrospinal fluid 639
– conversion factor into acetone 251
– in degradation of fats 393
– in urine 674
α-Hydroxybutyrate dehydrogenase (HBDH), in plasma 591
– – in pregnancy 586
3-Hydroxybutyrate dehydrogenase in degradation of fats 393
β-Hydroxy-γ-butyrobetaine. See Carnitine
3-Hydroxy-β-carotene 458
25-Hydroxycholecalciferol 461, 809
Hydroxycorticosteroids. See under Corticosteroids
17α-Hydroxycorticosterone. See Cortisol
18-Hydroxycorticosterone, secretion rates .. 743
2α-Hydroxycortisol 428
6β-Hydroxycortisol, breakdown 746
– in urine 747
16-Hydroxydehydroepiandrosterone in urine 746, 747
17α-Hydroxydeoxycorticosterone, biosynthesis 428, 429
18-Hydroxydeoxycorticosterone, biosynthesis 428, 429
4-Hydroxydihydropteridine in phenylalanine–tyrosine conversion 439
25-Hydroxyergocalciferol 809
Hydroxyestr-. See Hydroxyoestr-
α-Hydroxyethyl-2-thiamine diphosphate 469
β-Hydroxyethyltrimethylammonium hydroxide. See Choline
γ-Hydroxyglutamic acid in L-hydroxyproline degradation 395
α-Hydroxyglutaric acid in glycine degradation 397
γ-Hydroxyglutaric acid in L-hydroxyproline degradation 395
2-Hydroxyhexadecanoic acid 372
m-Hydroxyhippuric acid in urine 666
5-Hydroxyindoleacetaldehyde from 5-hydroxytryptamine 441
5-Hydroxyindoleacetic acid, from 5-hydroxytryptamine 441
– in urine 669
Hydroxyindole *O*-methyltransferase in melatonin formation 730
β-Hydroxyisobutyric acid in valine degradation 396
β-Hydroxyisobutyryl-coenzyme A in valine degradation 396
8-Hydroxykynurenic acid in tryptophan degradation 398, 399
3-Hydroxykynurenine, in tryptophan degradation 398, 399, 475
– in urine 669
Hydroxylases 385
δ-Hydroxylysine 331
6-Hydroxymelatonin 730
Hydroxymethylcytidylic acid synthesis 479
Hydroxymethylglutaryl-coenzyme A, in cholesterol synthesis 426, 427
– in leucine degradation 395
Hydroxymethyltetrahydrofolic acid, in glycine degradation 397
– in glycine formation 432
– in transfer of one-carbon groups 436, 437
Hydroxymethyltransferases 385
α-Hydroxymuconic semialdehyde in tryptophan degradation 399
α-Hydroxymyristic acid 372
Hydroxynervone 372, 377
2-Hydroxynervonic acid 372, 377
2-Hydroxyoctadecanoic acid 372
cis-12-Hydroxy-Δ^9-octadecenoic acid 372
15β-Hydroxyoestradiol-17β in urine 756
3-Hydroxyoestra-1,3,5(10),6,8-penten-17-one. See Equilenin
3-Hydroxyoestra-1,3,5(10),7-tetraen-17-one . 380
3-Hydroxyoestra-1,3,5(10)-trien-17-one. See Oestrone
2-Hydroxyoestrone, biosynthesis and metabolism 431
6α-Hydroxyoestrone, biosynthesis and metabolism 431
6β-Hydroxyoestrone, biosynthesis and metabolism 431
11β-Hydroxyoestrone from oestrone 431
15α-Hydroxyoestrone in urine 756
15β-Hydroxyoestrone in urine 756
16α-Hydroxyoestrone, biosynthesis and metabolism 431
– in urine 756
– – in pregnancy 757
16β-Hydroxyoestrone, biosynthesis and metabolism 431
– in urine 756
18-Hydroxyoestrone, biosynthesis and metabolism 431
– in pregnancy urine 432
α-Hydroxypalmitic acid 372
p-Hydroxyphenylacetic acid in urine 675
p-Hydroxyphenylpyruvic acid in phenylalanine degradation 398
3α-Hydroxy-5α-pregnan-20-one 379
3α-Hydroxy-5β-pregnan-20-one. See Pregnanolone
17α-Hydroxypregn-4-ene-3,20-dione. See 17α-Hydroxyprogesterone
21-Hydroxypregn-4-ene-3,20-dione. See 11-Deoxycorticosterone
21-Hydroxypregn-4-ene-3,11,20-trione. See Dehydrocorticosterone
16-Hydroxypregnenolone in urine 747
21-Hydroxypregnenolone. See 11-Deoxycorticosterone
3β-Hydroxypregn-5-en-20-one. See Pregnenolone
20-Hydroxypregnenones 380, 753
– in plasma 754
17α-Hydroxyprogesterone 380, 753
– biosynthesis 428, 429
– breakdown 746
– in plasma 754
20-Hydroxyprogesterones. See 20-Hydroxypregnenones
Hydroxyprolinaemia 449
L-Hydroxyproline (Hyp) 331
– in blood 449, 574
– degradation 394, 395, 402
– formation 432
– – ascorbic acid in 490
– in proteins 420
– in urine 449, 666, 667
– – parathyroid hormone and 728
6-Hydroxypurine. See Hypoxanthine
γ-Hydroxypyrrolidine-α-carboxylic acid. See Hydroxyproline
3-Hydroxypyrroline-5-carboxylate reductase in hydroxyprolinaemia 449
Hydroxypyruvate, in serine formation 432
– in transamination reactions 394
α-Hydroxystearic acid 372
Δ^5-3β-Hydroxysteroids, structure and assay. 744
21-Hydroxysteroids, deficient synthesis 456
3β-Hydroxysteroid dehydrogenase deficiency 456
2-Hydroxytetracosanoic acid. See Cerebronic acid
2-Hydroxy-Δ^{15}-tetracosenoic acid 372, 377
2-Hydroxytetradecanoic acid 372
18-Hydroxytetrahydrocorticosterone in urine 430
4-Hydroxytetrahydropteridine in phenylalanine–tyrosine conversion 439
2-Hydroxytricosanoic acid 372
5-Hydroxytryptamine. See Serotonin
5-Hydroxytryptophan, decarboxylation 394
– formation, dehydroascorbic acid and 490
– in 5-hydroxytryptamine formation 441
– in tryptophan metabolism 475
3-Hydroxytyramine. See 3,4-Dihydroxyphenylethylamine
β-Hydroxyvaleryl-coenzyme A in norleucine degradation 396
Hygromycin B, standard 762
Hyl (δ-hydroxylysine) 331
Hyp. See L-Hydroxyproline
Hyperaldosteronism, aldosterone secretion .. 745
– sweat sodium and chloride in 680
Hyperammonaemia 450
Hyperbilirubinaemia 454, 455
– posthepatic, serum bilirubin 577
Hyperbolic functions 140
Hypercalcaemia, idiopathic, of infancy 464
Hypercalcinuria 453
Hyperchloraemia 453
Hypercholesterolaemia 456
Hyperchromia 615
Hypergeometric distribution 77, 109 sq., 189 sq.
Hyperglobulinaemia, serum viscosity 558
Hyperglycinaemia 449
Hyperkeratosis, follicular 460
Hyperlipaemia 374
– essential familial 456
Hyperparathyroidism 728
Hyperprolinaemia 449
Hypersomatotropism 719
Hypertensin 740, 741
Hypertension 553
– essential, fluid deprivation test 535
– – urinary concentration 533
Hyperthyroidism 287, 288, 727
– radiotherapy 291
– serum protein-bound iodine 564
Hyperuricaemia. See Gout
Hyperventilation, effect on blood acid–base balance 569
Hypochromia 615
Hypo-γ-globulinaemia 449
Hypoglycaemia, leucine-sensitive 451
Hypophosphataemia 452
Hypophosphatasia 415
Hypoprothrombinaemia 449
– vitamin K and 467, 468
Hypotaurine in taurine formation 438
Hypothalamus, regulation of ACTH secretion by 717
– effect on growth hormone secretion 720
– oxytocin and vasopressin formation . 722, 723
– pituitary-regulating factors 725
– effect on prolactin secretion 718, 719
– releasing and inhibiting factors 725, 809
Hypothyroidism 287, 288, 727
– and ossification 707
– serum protein-bound iodine 564
Hypoventilation, effect on blood acid–base balance 569
Hypoxanthine 338
– enzymatic oxidation 419
– in plasma 577
– in purine degradation 400, 401
– in urine 671
Hypoxanthine oxidase. See Xanthine oxidase
Hz (hertz, cycle per second) 208

I

I. See Inosine
I. See Iodine
IC (inspiratory capacity) 542, 550
ICAO standard atmosphere .... 252 sq.
ICDH. See Isocitrate dehydrogenase
ICSH (interstitial cell-stimulating hormone). See Luteinizing hormone
Icterogenic hepatitis, bile composition 655
Ideal gases. See under Gases
– solutions 270

A detailed index to the statistical tables (pages 28–131) and chapter on Statistical Methods (pages 146–196) will be found on pages 197–198

Idiocy, amaurotic familial ... 455
L-Iditol dehydrogenase, in bile ... 655
– in cerebrospinal fluid ... 638
– in plasma ... 590
– – in heart disease ... 587
– in tissues ... 585
L-Iditol: NAD oxidoreductase. See L-Iditol dehydrogenase
D-Idose ... 310
IDP (inosine diphosphate) in carbohydrate synthesis ... 441
L-Iduronic acid ... 323, 423
– formation from glucose ... 420
IgA. See γA-Globulin
IgD. See γD-Globulin
IgE. See γE-Globulin
IgG. See γG-Globulin
IgM. See γM-Globulin
IHA (*o*-iodohippuric acid) in kidney radiography ... 289
Ii blood-group system ... 632
Il (illinium) ... 240
Ile. See L-Isoleucine
Illinium ... 240
Illuminance ... 223
Imidazoles in urine ... 670
Imidazoleacetic acid, in L-histidine degradation ... 395
– in urine ... 670
Imidazole buffer ... 280 sq.
Imidazolelactic acid in L-histidine degradation 395
Imidazolepyruvic acid, in L-histidine degradation ... 395
– in urine ... 449
Imidazolonepropionic acid in L-histidine degradation ... 395
β-Imidazolylpyruvic acid. See Imidazolepyruvic acid
Imidodipeptidase ... 408, 410
α-Iminobutyric acid, in homoserine degradation ... 397
– in L-threonine degradation ... 397
Iminodipeptidase ... 408, 410
α-Iminopropionic acid, in L-cysteine degradation ... 397
– in serine degradation ... 396
Immunoglobulins, characteristics and function ... 580
– genetic factors ... 634
– in milk ... 688, 689
– structure ... 581
Immunological competence, thymus hormone and ... 730
IMP. See Inosine monophosphate
Impedance of vacuum ... 228
in (inch) ... 200
In. See Indium
Inborn errors of metabolism ... 446 sq.
Inch ... 200
– of mercury ... 212
– of water ... 212
Indican. See 3-Indoxylsulphuric acid
Indicators, acid–base ... 283
Indigotin in urinary sediments ... 677, 678
Indium, flame lines ... 284
– properties, isotopes, etc. ... 238
Indoles in urine ... 452, 669
Indole-3-acetic acid, in plasma ... 575
– in tryptophan degradation ... 398
– in urine ... 670
Indoleacetylglutamine in urine ... 670
Indoleformylglucuronide in urine ... 670
Indole-3-lactic acid, in plasma ... 575
– in urine ... 670
Indolyl-3-acetic acid. See Indole-3-acetic acid
Indolyl-3-lactic acid. See Indole-3-lactic acid
3-Indoxylsulphuric acid, in cerebrospinal fluid ... 637
– in plasma ... 575
– in urine ... 663, 669
Infants (*see also Newborn*), ascorbic acid deficiency ... 490
– ascorbic acid requirement ... 490
– beriberi ... 470
– bile acids ... 656
– blood, alanine aminotransferase ... 594
– – aspartate aminotransferase ... 593
– – bicarbonate and bases ... 571
– – bilirubin ... 576, 577
– – biotin ... 611
– – caeruloplasmin ... 593
– – calcium ... 565
– – carboxyhaemoglobin ... 576
Infants, blood, carotenes ... 609
– – chloride ... 562
– – cholesterol ... 601, 603
– – cholinesterase ... 595
– – copper ... 566
– – corticosteroids ... 745
– – enzymes ... 585
– – ergothioneine ... 573
– – fatty acids ... 604
– – fructosediphosphate aldolase ... 599
– – gases ... 570, 571
– – glycerides ... 601, 603
– – growth hormone ... 720
– – haemoglobin ... 615, 617
– – iron ... 566
– – lactate dehydrogenase ... 590
– – lipids ... 603
– – pepsin ... 598
– – pH value ... 560
– – acid phosphatase ... 596
– – alkaline phosphatase ... 596
– – inorganic phosphorus ... 563
– – potassium ... 564
– – proteins ... 579, 583
– – pyridoxal phosphate ... 610
– – volume ... 554, 555
– blood pressure ... 553
– BMR ... 539, 540
– body composition ... 523
– body surface areas ... 528
– bone composition ... 521
– bone marrow cells ... 621
– breast-milk intake ... 687
– catecholamine excretion ... 733
– cerebrospinal fluid, leucocyte count ... 635
– – potassium ... 636
– – protein ... 637
– corticosteroid secretion ... 743
– body electrolytes ... 518
– erythroblastosis ... 612
– erythrocytes, count ... 614, 617
– – diameter ... 614, 617
– – mean haemoglobin ... 615
– – mean volume ... 617
– faeces, composition and properties ... 657 sq.
– essential fatty acid deficiency ... 492
– essential fatty acid requirement ... 492
– folic acid requirement ... 479
– gastric juice secretion ... 647
– composition of hair and nails ... 520
– idiopathic hypercalcaemia ... 464
– iodide metabolism ... 726
– iodine requirements ... 497
– jaundice ... 576, 577
– leucocyte count ... 618, 619
– lung values ... 550
– normal measurements ... 693 sq.
– mineral requirements ... 496
– composition of muscle ... 518
– nicotinic acid requirement ... 478
– nutritional requirements ... 493 sq.
– organs, composition ... 519
– – weights ... 710
– appearance of ossification centres ... 706 sq.
– premature. See Premature infants
– respiratory quotient ... 539
– reticulocytes ... 612, 613
– saliva, amylase ... 646
– – chloride ... 643
– – volume ... 643
– composition of skin ... 520
– daily number of stools ... 657
– sweat electrolytes ... 679, 680
– teeth, composition ... 521
– – development ... 709
– thiamine requirement ... 471
– thrombocyte count ... 620
– organic components of tissues ... 522
– urine, acidity ... 662
– – amino acids ... 666, 667
– – calcium ... 664
– – chloride ... 662
– – corticosteroids ... 746 sq.
– – creatine ... 665
– – creatinine ... 665
– – magnesium ... 664
– – nitrogen ... 665
– – organic acids ... 674
– – phosphorus ... 663
– – potassium ... 663
– – proteins ... 668
– – specific gravity ... 661
– – sulphur ... 663
– – tryptophan metabolites ... 669
Infants, urine, vitamins ... 676
– – volume ... 661
– vitamin A deficiency ... 460
– vitamin A prophylaxis ... 460
– vitamin A requirement ... 460
– vitamin B$_6$ deficiency ... 476
– vitamin B$_6$ requirement ... 475
– vitamin D poisoning ... 464
– vitamin E deficiency ... 466
– vitamin E requirement ... 466
– body water ... 518
– water requirement ... 524
Infarction. See Cardiac infarction
Inflammation, action of corticosteroids ... 750
– γ-globulin in CSF ... 637
Influenza virus haemagglutinin, reference preparation ... 759
Infusion solutions, composition ... 529
– treatment with ... 528 sq.
inHg (inch of mercury) ... 212
inH$_2$O (inch of water) ... 212
Ino. See Inosine
Inosine (I, Ino) ... 340
– in purine degradation ... 400
Inosine diphosphate (IDP) in carbohydrate synthesis ... 441
Inosine monophosphate (IMP) ... 342, 433
– adenylic acid from ... 435, 436
– formation ... 433, 435
– in purine degradation ... 400, 401
– xanthylic acid from ... 436
Inosine 5′-phosphate. See Inosine monophosphate
Inosine triphosphate (ITP), in blood ... 577
– in carbohydrate synthesis and breakdown. 441
Inosinic acid. See Inosine monophosphate
Inositol, in cerebrospinal fluid ... 639
– isomers ... 309
– in lipids ... 365
– in milk ... 689
– in semen ... 684
– in urine ... 673
Inositol phosphatides ... 365
Inspiratory capacity ... 542, 550
– flow rate, maximum (MIFR) ... 543
– reserve volume ... 541
Insulin ... 734 sq.
– antagonists ... 737
– antibodies, tracer study ... 290
– effect on gastric juice acidity ... 648
– secretion ... 735, 736
– standard ... 763
Integrals ... 28 sq.
Integral absorbed dose ... 218
Intermedin ... 721, 722
International Practical Temperature Scale .. 209
Interstitial cell-stimulating hormone. See Luteinizing hormone
Interstitial fluid, electrolyte composition ... 523
– sodium and potassium exchange ... 526
– total volume ... 523
Interstitial radiotherapy ... 290
Intestinal juice ... 656
– amount ... 525, 656
– electrolytes ... 525, 656
Intestine, adenosine deaminase ... 419
– cholesterol synthesis ... 426
– cholinesterase ... 414
– enteropeptidase ... 408
– enzyme defects ... 451
– glycosidases ... 412, 413
– mucosa, lactic acid fermentation ... 388
– – respiratory rate ... 387
– phosphatases ... 415
– phosphodiesterase ... 418
– proteolytic enzymes ... 407 sq.
– ulcers, gastric acidity and ... 648
Intracavitary radiotherapy ... 290
Intracellular fluid, electrolyte composition .. 523
– gain in pregnancy ... 690
– sodium and potassium exchange ... 526
– total volume ... 523
Intraluminal fluid, amount and electrolyte content ... 525
Intramolecular transferases ... 386
Intrapulmonary blood volumes ... 544
Intravascular fluid, total volume ... 523
Intravenous drip, calculation ... 529
Intravenous radiotherapy ... 290, 291
Intrinsic factor ... 484
– in gastric juice ... 650
Intrinsic system in blood coagulation .. 622, 625
Inulin ... 328
– glomerular filtration rate from ... 531

A detailed index to the statistical tables (pages 28–131) and chapter on Statistical Methods (pages 146–196) will be found on pages 197–198

Involution 132
Iodide. See Iodine
Iodine, absorption and utilization 440
– atomic weight multiples 250
– in cerebrospinal fluid 636
– dietary requirements 494, 497
– in faeces 658
– in milk 688
– in plasma 564, 726
– – butanol-extractable 564
– – protein-bound 564
– properties, isotopes, etc. 239
– renal clearance 726
– in saliva 644
– decinormal solutions 277
– in sweat 679
– in thyroid gland 725
– in thyroid hormone formation 440
– uptake by organs 726
– in urine 663
Iodine-125, characteristics 293
– decay table 303
– diagnostic use 289
Iodine-130, characteristics 293
– gamma ray constant 221
Iodine-131, specific activity 217
– characteristics 293
– decay table 303
– diagnostic use .... 287 sq.
– gamma ray constant 221
– in thyroid function tests .... 287 sq.
– in thyroid scintigraphy 288, 289
Iodine-132, characteristics 293
– decay table 304
Iodinium ions in thyroid hormone formation 440
L-Iodogorgoic acid. See L-3,5-Di-iodotyrosine
o-Iodohippuric acid in kidney radiography .. 289
Iodopsin 457
Ion, definition 270
Ion dose from radionuclides 219
Ionic concentration 227
Ionium (^{230}Th), properties 246
Ionization of gases 285, 286
IPTS-68 (International Practical Temperature Scale) 209
Ir. See Iridium
Iridium, properties, isotopes, etc. 242
Iridium-192, characteristics 293
– decay table 305
– gamma ray constant 221
– therapeutic use 290
Iron, atomic weight multiples 250
– in bile 654
– in blood 566
– in whole body 517
– in bones and teeth 521
– in cerebrospinal fluid 636
– dietary requirements 494, 496
– in faeces 658
– flame lines 284
– in foods .... 499 sq.
– in hair and nails 520
– metabolism, tracer study 289
– in milk 688
– in organs 519
– properties, isotopes, etc. 236
– in skin 520
– in sweat 680
– in synovial fluid 641
– in urine 664
Iron-54, gamma ray constant 221
Iron-55, characteristics 292
Iron-59, characteristics 292
– decay table 296, 297
– diagnostic use 289
Iron porphyrins .... 359 sq.
– in biological oxidations 402, 403
– degradation 401
Irradiance 222
Irrational numbers 132
IRV (inspiratory reserve volume) 541
Isoalloxazine 336
Isoandrosterone. See Epiandrosterone
Isobutyric acid 371
Isobutyryl-coenzyme A in valine degradation 396
Isocaproic acid, in synthesis of adrenal steroids and androgens 428, 429
– in cholesterol breakdown 401
– degradation 401
Isocitrate in tricarboxylic acid cycle ... 390, 391
Isocitrate dehydrogenase (ICDH), cell binding 585
– in cerebrospinal fluid 638
– in gastric juice 650
Isocitrate dehydrogenase (ICDH), isozymes . 584
– in plasma 591
– – in pregnancy 586
– in seminal plasma 684
– in synovial fluid 641
– in tissues 585
– in tricarboxylic acid cycle 390, 391
threo-D$_s$-Isocitrate: NADP oxidoreductase. See Isocitrate dehydrogenase
Iso-(β-)crotonic acid 368
Isodulcitol 313
Isoenzymes. See Isozymes
L-Isoleucine (Ile) 332
– in blood 449, 574
– in blood proteins 581
– in cerebrospinal fluid 449
– degradation 395, 396, 402
– dietary requirements 496
– in foods 516
– in milk 688
– in saliva 645
– in urine 667
Isomaltase. See Oligo-1,6-glucosidase 451
Isomaltose, hydrolysis 412
Isomerases 386
– in vitamin A metabolism 457
cis–trans-Isomerases. See Cis–trans isomerases
Isomeric nuclides 217
cis–trans Isomerism. See Cis–trans isomerism
Isomyristic acid 371
Isopentenyl pyrophosphate, in cholesterol synthesis 426, 427
– in vitamin A synthesis 457
Isosthenuria 534
Isotocin 724
Isotonic solutions 526
– calculation 271
Isotopes. See Nuclides and Radionuclides
Isovaleric acid 371
Isovaleryl-coenzyme A in leucine degradation 395
Isozymes 584
– tissue-specific, in diagnosis 586
ITP. See Inosine triphosphate

J

J (joule) 212, 213, 216
JAFFÉ reaction 572
Jaundice (*see also Kernicterus*) 362, 576, 577
– haemolytic, erythrocyte osmotic resistance 616
– – of newborn 577
– idiopathic, chronic 454
– nonhaemolytic, congenital 454
– obstructive, serum enzyme changes 587
– – serum glucosephosphate isomerase 600
– – serum ketose-1-phosphate aldolase 599
– serum 5′-nucleotidase 597
– simple, of infants 576, 577
JENSEN's sarcoma, lactic acid fermentation .. 388
– respiratory rate 387
Joule 212, 213, 216, 222
Julian year 206

K

k (kilo-, 10^3) 9
K (kelvin) 208, 209, 213
K. See Potassium
Kale, composition 504
Kallidins 742
Kallikrein 742
Kallikreinogen 742
Kanamycins, reference preparations 761
KARMEN-WRÓBLEWSKI enzyme units 584
Kell blood-group system 631
– clinical significance 633
Kelvin 208, 209
– as energy unit 213
KELVIN temperature scale 208, 209
Kerasin 377
– lignoceric acid in 367
Keratan sulphate 328
Keratosulphate 328
Kernicterus 362, 454, 577
– glucose-6-phosphate dehydrogenase 592
Ketals 308
Ketchup, composition 506
Keto acids in urine 449
3-Ketoacid-CoA transferase in degradation of fats 393
Keto acid-lyases 386
3-Ketoacyl-CoA thiolase in degradation of fats 392
β-Ketoacyl-coenzyme A in degradation of fats 392
α-Ketoadipic acid, in L-lysine degradation .. 398
– in tryptophan degradation 399
11-Ketoaetiocholanolone in urine 746, 749
α-Keto-ε-aminocaproic acid in L-lysine degradation 398
α-Keto-δ-aminovaleric acid in D-ornithine and D-proline degradation 395
γ-Keto-δ-aminovaleric acid. See δ-Aminolaevulinic acid
11-Ketoandrosterone in urine 746
2-Keto-D-arabohexose. See D-Fructose
α-Ketobutyric acid, in homoserine degradation 397
– in L-threonine degradation 397
α-Ketocaproic acid in norleucine degradation 396
16-Ketoestradiol. See 16-Keto-oestradiol
17-Ketogenic steroids. See under Corticosteroids
α-Ketoglutarate, reductive amination 432
– in ATP synthesis 404
– in blood 607
– in cerebrospinal fluid 639
– in cysteinesulphinic acid formation 438
– from degradation of foods 402
– in glutamic acid degradation 393, 394
– in glutamic acid formation 432
– in glycine degradation 397
– in L-hydroxyproline degradation 395
– in L-ornithine degradation 395
– in transamination reactions 394, 395
– in tricarboxylic acid cycle 390, 391
– in urea synthesis 444
– in urine 674
α-Ketoglutaric semialdehyde in glycine degradation 397
α-Keto-γ-guanidinovaleric acid in transamination reactions 394
2-Keto-L-gulonic acid 489
– in ascorbic acid synthesis 489
Ketohexokinase, in fructosuria 450
– in lactic acid fermentation 390
– in plasma 594
α-Ketoisocaproic acid, in blood 608
– in leucine degradation 395
– in maple syrup urine disease 449
α-Ketoisovaleric acid, in blood 607
– in maple syrup urine disease 449
– pantothenic acid from 487
– in valine degradation 396
α-Keto-β-methylvaleric acid, in blood 608
– in isoleucine degradation 396
– in maple syrup urine disease 449
Ketone 250 .... 461, 463
Ketone bodies, conversion factors into acetone 251
– in blood 608
– accumulation in tissues 393
– in urine 674
α-Ketonic acids in amino-acid degradation 393, 394
16-Keto-oestradiol, biosynthesis and metabolism 431
– in urine 756
– – in pregnancy 757
6-Keto-oestrone, biosynthesis and metabolism 431
11-Keto-oestrone, biosynthesis and metabolism 431
16-Keto-oestrone, biosynthesis and metabolism 431
α-Ketopantoic acid in pantothenic acid synthesis 487
Ketopentoses in urine 673
3-Keto-6-phosphogluconic acid in pentose phosphate cycle 421, 422
Ketoses .... 308 sq.
Ketose-1-phosphate aldehyde-lyase. See Ketose-1-phosphate aldolase
Ketose-1-phosphate aldolase, in lactic acid fermentation 390
– in plasma 599
– – in heart disease 587
– – in hepatic coma 586, 587
– in tissues 585
Ketosis 393
Δ^4-3-Ketosteroids, assay and structure 744
– in plasma 745
17-Ketosteroids, assay and structure 744
– in urine .... 746 sq.
– – diminished 456

A detailed index to the statistical tables (pages 28–131) and chapter on Statistical Methods (pages 146–196) will be found on pages 197–198

Keto-sugars 308 sq.
β-Ketovaleryl-coenzyme A in norleucine degradation 396
kgf (kilogramme-force) 211
Kidd blood-group system 632
– clinical significance 633
Kidneys (*see also Renal*), animal, amino acids 516
– – composition 512, 514
– ascorbic acid 490
– contribution to BMR 539
– carnitine 491
– composition 519
– glycogen accumulation 451
– glycosidases 412, 413
– lactic acid fermentation 388
– oxidases 419
– peptidases 410, 411
– phosphatases 415, 416
– phospholipase A 417
– thiamine 470
– transaminations 394
– weight 710
KIESSLING ester. See 2-Phosphoglycerate
kilo- (10^3) 9
Kilocycle 208
Kilogramme 204
Kilogramme-force 211
Kilohertz 208
Kilometre 200
Kilopond 211
Kilowatt hour 213
KING-ARMSTRONG enzyme units 584
Kinins in plasma 742
Kininogens 742
KJELDAHL nitrogen determination 572
kn (knot) 200
Knee, secondary ossification centres 706, 708
Knot 200
KOBER reaction 755
Kohlrabi, composition 504
Kr. See Krypton
KREBS cycle. See Tricarboxylic acid cycle
Krypton, properties, isotopes, etc. 237
Krypton-85, characteristics 292
– decay table 300
Krypton-86, vacuum wave lengths 200
KUPPERMAN test 715
Kwashiorkor, serum caeruloplasmin 593
Kynurenic acid, in tryptophan degradation 398, 399
– in tryptophan metabolism 475
– in urine 669
Kynureninase in tryptophan metabolism 475
Kynurenine, in tryptophan degradation 398, 399
– in tryptophan metabolism 475
– in urine 669

L

l (litre) 203
l- (laevo-) 308, 309
L (lambert) 223
La. See Lanthanum
Lacceroic acid 368
Lactacidosis 607
Lactagogin. See Oxytocin
Lactalbumin in milk 511, 688, 689
Lactase in intestinal mucosa 413
Lactate, in bile 655
– in blood 607
– caloric yield 526
– in carbohydrate synthesis and breakdown 441
– in cerebrospinal fluid 639
– formation by erythrocytes 616
– in faeces 659
– in gastric juice 650
– formation by leucocytes 618
– in saliva 646
– in semen 685
– in oxidation of sugars 391
– in sweat 681
– in synovial fluid 642
– formation by thrombocytes 621
– in urine 674
– in wine 509
– in yoghurt 511
Lactate dehydrogenase (LDH), activity gradients 586
– activity, temperature correction 585
– allotypy 634
– in bile 655
– cell binding 585
– in cerebrospinal fluid 638
Lactate dehydrogenase, in gastric juice 650
– in glycolysis 389
– isozyme distribution 584, 590, 591
– in milk 689
– in plasma 590
– – in blood disease 587
– – in carcinoma 587, 588
– – half-life 586
– – in heart disease 587
– – in liver disease 586, 587
– – in muscle disease 587
– – effect of muscular work 586
– – in pregnancy 586
– in seminal plasma 684
– in spermatozoa 684
– in synovial fluid 641
– in tissues 585
– in urine 672
L-Lactate: NAD oxidoreductase. See Lactate dehydrogenase
Lactation, amino-acid requirements 496
– effect of artificial milking 687
– calcium requirement 493, 494
– folic acid requirement 479
– iodine requirement 497
– lactose excretion 673
– nicotinic acid requirement 478
– parathyroid hormone and 728
– plasma growth hormone 720
– plasma oxytocin 723
– effect of prolactin 719
– effects of sex hormones 758
– thiamine requirement 471
– vitamin B_6 requirement 475
– vitamin D requirement 461
Lactic acid (*see also Lactate*), decinormal solutions 277
Lactic acid fermentation 387 sq.
Lactoflavin. See Riboflavin
Lactogen, human placental (HPL) 721
Lactogenic hormone. See Prolactin
Lactoglobulin in milk 688
Lactose 324
– from glucose 1-phosphate and UDP-galactose 347, 420
– intolerance 451
– in milk 689
– milk oligosaccharides from 423
– 1-phosphate 321
– – lactose from 420
– in urine 451, 673
Lactosuria 451
Lactotransferrin in milk 689
Laevo compounds 308, 309
Laevulose. See D-Fructose
Lamb, composition 513
Lambert 223
Lanostane in steroids 381
Lanosterol 380
– in cholesterol synthesis 426, 427
Lanthanides 231, 239–241
Lanthanum, flame lines 284
– properties, isotopes, etc. 239
LAP. See Leucine aminopeptidase
Lard, composition 510
LATS (long-acting thyroid stimulator) 718
Lauric acid 366
– in milk 687
Lauroleic acid 368
Lawrencium, properties and isotopes 248
lb (pound) 204
lbf (pound-force) 211
LDH. See Lactate dehydrogenase
Lead, in blood 567
– in bones and teeth 521
– in brain and nerves 519
– carbonate, decinormal solutions 277
– in faeces 658
– flame lines 284
– oxide, decinormal solutions 277
– poisoning, δ-aminolaevulinic acid excretion 670
– – effect on haem synthesis 454
– – porphyrin excretion 670
– properties, isotopes, etc. 243
– in skin, hair and nails 520
– in urine 664
Leap year 206
Lecithins 365, 375
– in bile 655
– in brain and spinal cord 520
– in cerebrospinal fluid 638
– conversion factor to lipid phosphorus 251
– in erythrocytes 604
Lecithins, formation 425
– in plasma 604
– reference preparations 759
– structure and hydrolysis 417
Leeks, composition 504
Legs, surface area 528
Legumes, vitamin losses during cooking 498
Lemons, composition 500
Lemon juice, composition 500
Length units 200 sq.
Lens of the eye, ascorbic acid 489
– riboflavin in 471
Lentils, amino acids 516
– composition 504
Leptospira antisera, reference reagents 764
Lettuce, composition 504
Leu. See L-Leucine
L-Leucine (Leu) 331
– in blood 449, 574
– in blood proteins 581
– in cerebrospinal fluid 449
– degradation 395, 396, 402
– dietary requirements 496
– in foods 516
– in milk 688
– in saliva 645
– in sweat 680
– in urinary sediments 677
– in urine 667
Leucine aminopeptidase (LAP) 409, 411
– in bile 655
– in cerebrospinal fluid 638
– in gastric juice 650
– isozymes 584
– in plasma 598
– – in obstructive jaundice 587
– – in pregnancy 586
Leucinosis 448, 449
Leucocytes, acylphosphatase 416
– adenosine triphosphate 577
– amino acids 574
– ascorbic acid 490, 611
– in cerebrospinal fluid 635
– cholesterol 601
– count 618, 619
– deoxyribonucleic acid 578
– diameter 618
– ergothioneine 573
– ethanolamine 573
– folic acid 610
– glycoproteins 606
– half-life 618
– histamine 575
– lactic acid fermentation 388
– lipids 455, 601
– metabolism 618
– total nitrogen 572
– nucleic acids 578
– osmotic resistance 618
– packing volume 618
– phosphatides 601
– proteins 572, 579
– unconjugated pterins 610
– pyridoxal phosphate 610
– respiratory rate 387
– riboflavin 471, 609
– ribonucleic acid 578
– sedimentation index (LSI) 558
– specific gravity 557
– in synovial fluid 640, 642
– thiamine 470, 609
– in urine 677
– vitamin B_{12} 610
– volume 618
– zinc 567
Leucocyte count 618, 619
Leucocytocrit 618
Leucocytosis, blood glucose 604
Leucodystrophy, metachromatic 455, 456
– – sulphatides in 377
Leucosis (*see also Leukaemia*), radiotherapy 291
Leucovorin. See 5-Formyltetrahydrofolic acid
L-Leucyl-peptide hydrolase. See Leucine aminopeptidase
Leukaemia, blood, caeruloplasmin 593
– – glucosephosphate isomerase 600
– – glutathione reductase 592
– – histamine 575
– – phosphoglycerate kinase 594
– – viscosity 558
– – vitamin B_{12} 610
– leucocyte zinc 567
– uric acid excretion 671
Leuko-. See Leuco-

A detailed index to the statistical tables (pages 28–131) and chapter on Statistical Methods (pages 146–196) will be found on pages 197–198

Levo compounds 308, 309
Levulose. See D-Fructose
Lewis blood-group system 631, 632
– clinical significance 633
Leydig cells, seminal fructose and 684
LH. See Luteinizing hormone
LH-RF. See Luteinizing-hormone releasing factor
li (link) 200
Li. See Lithium
Life expectation, blood pressure and 553
– body weight and 712
Ligases 386
Light, quantities and units .... 222 sq.
– velocity 215, 216, 228
Light year 201
Lignoceric acid 367
– in kerasin 377
Lime juice, composition 500
Limit-dextrins. See Dextrins
Lincomycin, reference preparation 762
Linderic acid 368
Line (unit) 200
Linear equations, solution 137
Linear velocity units 210
Link 200
Linoleic acid 370, 492
– in bile 655
– in depot fat 374
– dietary requirements 492, 495
– in foods .... 498 sq.
– in serum lipids 604
– in milk 687
Linoleyl alcohol 492
Lipases 405, 414
– in bile 655
– in cerebrospinal fluid 638
– in gastric juice 650
– in milk 689
– in pancreatic juice 652, 653
– in plasma 595
– – in pancreatic disease 587
Lipids (*see also Fats*) .... 365 sq.
– in bile 655
– biosynthesis, inhibition by nicotinic acid 477, 478
– in blood .... 600 sq.
– – excess 374, 456
– in brain and spinal cord 520
– in cerebrospinal fluid 638
– 'compound' 365
– in erythrocytes 600, 601
– in faeces 659, 660
– in gastric juice 650
– in intestinal juice 656
– in leucocytes 601
– metabolism, effect of ACTH 717
– – effect of corticosteroids 749, 750
– – disturbance 455
– – effect of glucagon 738
– – effect of growth hormone 720
– in pancreatic juice 652
– in semen 685
– 'simple' 365
– in sweat 681
– in synovial fluid 642
– in thrombocytes 601
– in urine 675
Lipid phosphorus, in blood 563
– conversion factors to phosphorus 251
– in erythrocytes 563
– in milk 689
– in semen 683
Lipidoses 455, 456
α-Lipoic acid 492
– in plasma 608
– in oxidation of sugars 391
– in tricarboxylic acid cycle 390, 391
Lipoid factor in blood coagulation 622
Lipoproteins 329
– accumulation 456
– allotypy 634
– and cholesterol 374
– in serum 602
– in spermatozoa 685
α-Lipoproteins in serum 580, 602
α_1-Lipoprotein, characteristics and function. 580
– in erythrocyte sedimentation 559
– in serum 580, 583
α_2-Lipoprotein, characteristics and function. 580
– in serum 580
β-Lipoproteins, in cerebrospinal fluid 637
– in serum 602
β_1-Lipoprotein, characteristics and function. 580
β_1-Lipoprotein in serum 580, 583
Lipotropic hormone (LPH) 716
Lipotropin 716
liq.pt (liquid pint) 204
liq.qt (liquid quart) 204
Liquid measures 204
Liter. See Litre
Lithium, flame lines 284
– in plasma 567
– properties, isotopes, etc. 234
Lithocholic acid, in bile 655
– in faeces 660
Lithosphere, composition .... 234 sq.
Litmus indicator 283
Litre 203
Litre atmosphere 213
Liver, adipohepatic, serum enzyme changes. 586
– animal, amino acids 516
– – composition .... 512 sq.
– ascorbic acid 490
– biotin 486
– contribution to BMR 539
– carcinoma, serum enzyme changes 587
– – serum triosephosphate isomerase 600
– carnitine 491
– cholesterol synthesis 426
– cirrhosis 451, 455, 456
– – bile acids 655
– – biliary bilirubin 654
– – gastric juice ammonia 649
– – gastric juice secretion 647
– – leucocyte zinc 567
– – serum, bilirubin 577
– – – enzyme changes 586
– – – pantothenic acid 611
– composition 519
– deaminases 419
– disease, glucuronic acid excretion 673
– – serum, adenosine deaminase 599
– – – arginase 598
– – – cholinesterase 595
– – – dehydrogenases .... 590 sq.
– – – enzyme changes 586
– – – glucose-6-phosphatase 597
– – – glucosephosphate isomerase 600
– – – β-glucuronidase 597
– – – guanine deaminase 598
– – – ketose-1-phosphate aldolase 599
– – – alkaline phosphatase 596
– – – phosphopyruvate hydratase 600
– – – ribosephosphate isomerase 600
– – – transaminases and transferases .. 593, 594
– dysfunction 454
– enlargement .... 449, 451 sq.
– enzyme activities 585
– enzyme activity gradients between serum and 586
– fatty acid esterases 414
– glycogen accumulation 451
– glycosidases .... 411 sq.
– effect of insulin 736, 737
– lactic acid fermentation 388
– lipid accumulation 455
– 5-methyltetrahydropteroylglutamic acid .. 479
– nicotinic acid 477
– oxidases 419
– pantothenic acid 488
– peptidases 410
– phosphatases 415, 416
– phospholipases 417
– porphyrins 454, 455
– purine nucleoside phosphorylase 418
– radiography 289
– respiratory rate 387
– riboflavin 471
– thiamine 470
– thyroid hormones 727
– transaminations 394
– vitamin A 457
– vitamin B_6 475
– vitamin B_{12} 484
– weight 710
Liver starch. See Glycogen
lm (lumen) 222
LMTH (luteomammotropic hormone). See Prolactin
ln. See Logarithms
Lobster, composition 515
log. See Logarithms
$\log_{10}$ e 9
$\log_e$ 10 9
Loganberries, composition 500
Logarithms, common 10
– – of factorials 26, 27
Logarithms, explanation 134, 135
– natural .... 12 sq.
Logistic weights 57
Logits and antilogits 56
Long-acting thyroid stimulator (LATS) 718
Long ton 205
Loschmidt constant 228
Loudness quantities and units 225, 226
Lp groups of serum 634
LPH (lipotropic hormone) 716
Lr (lawrencium) 248
LRF. See Luteinizing-hormone releasing factor
LSI (leucocyte sedimentation index) 558
LTH (luteotropic hormone). See Prolactin
Lu (lutetium) 241
Lumbar fluid. See Cerebrospinal fluid
Lumen 222
Lumiflavin 472
Luminous quantities and units .... 222 sq.
Lumisterol in vitamin D_2 formation ... 461, 463
Lungs, blood pressure 553
– capacity values .... 541 sq., 550, 551
– – in children, nomograms 547
– circulation 543, 544
– compliance. See Compliance
– composition 512, 519
– diffusing capacity 545, 552
– enzyme activities 585
– lactic acid fermentation 388
– peptidases 410
– resistance. See Pulmonary resistance
– values .... 541 sq.
– – calculation from spirometer values . 259 sq.
– – ratios 551
– vital capacity. See Vital capacity
– volumes 541, 542
– water loss from 524
– weight 710
– xanthine oxidase 419
Luteinizing hormone (LH) 713, 714
– oestrogens and 757
– progesterone secretion and 754, 755
– secretion, effect of testosterone 753
Luteinizing-hormone releasing factor (LRF, LH-RF) 714, 725
– effect of testosterone 753
Luteomammotropic hormone. See Prolactin
Luteotropic hormone. See Prolactin
Luteotropin. See Prolactin
Lutetium, properties, isotopes, etc. 241
Lutheran blood-group system 631
– clinical significance 633
Lux 223
lx (lux) 223
l.y. (light year) 201
Lyases 386
Lymecycline, reference preparation 762
Lymphadenosis, leucocyte mobility 560
Lymphatic tissues, action of corticosteroids. 750
Lymph glands, enzyme activities 585
Lymphocytes, blood count .... 618 sq.
– in bone marrow 621
– dimensions 618
– electrophoretic mobility 560
– histamine 575
– in synovial fluid 640
Lymphocyte-stimulating factor 730
Lymphosarcoma, serum ribosephosphate isomerase 600
Lys. See L-Lysine
L-Lysine (Lys) 332
– in blood 574
– in blood proteins 581
– decarboxylation 394
– degradation 398, 402
– dietary requirements 496
– in foods 516
– formation from α,ε-diaminopimelic acid . 394
– in milk 688
– in saliva 645
– in sweat 680
– in urine 452, 667
Lysine vasopressin. See Vasopressin
Lysokinases 622
Lysolecithins, in bile 655
– in cerebrospinal fluid 638
– enzymatic cleavage 417
– in erythrocytes 604
– in erythrocyte sedimentation 559
– formation 375, 376
– in plasma 604
Lysolipids from phospholipids 417
Lysophosphatides 365, 375, 376

A detailed index to the statistical tables (pages 28–131) and chapter on Statistical Methods (pages 146–196) will be found on pages 197–198

Lysophospholipase 417
Lysozyme 413
– in gastric juice 650
– in milk 688
– in saliva 645
D-Lyxoketose. See D-Xylulose
L-Lyxoketose. See L-Xylulose
D-Lyxose 310
D-Lyxulose. See D-Xylulose
L-Lyxulose. See L-Xylulose

M

μ (micro-, 10^{-6}) 9
μ (micron, micrometre) 200
m (metre) 200
m (milli-, 10^{-3}) 9
M (mega-, 10^{6}) 9
Mache unit 217
Mackerel, composition 515
Macrocytic anaemia. See under Anaemia
Macroglobulin, abnormal, structure 581
α_2-Macroglobulin, amino-acid composition . 581
– characteristics and function 580
– in faeces 659
– in serum 580, 583
γ_1-Macroglobulin, structure 581
Macroglobulinaemia, serum viscosity 558
Magnesia. See Magnesium oxide
Magnesium, in amniotic fluid 522
– atomic weight multiples 250
– in bile 654
– in whole body 517
– in body fluids 523
– in bones 521
– in cerebrospinal fluid 636
– conversion factors 523
– – into magnesium oxide 251
– dietary requirements 494, 496
– in electrolyte balance 525
– in erythrocytes 566
– activation of esterases .... 415 sq.
– in faeces 658
– flame lines 284
– in foods .... 499 sq.
– in gastric juice 649
– in hair and nails 520
– in milk 688
– in muscle 518
– in organs 519
– in pancreatic juice 652
– in placenta 522
– in plasma 566
– properties, isotopes, etc. 234
– activation of proteases .... 409 sq.
– in purine formation 433, 435, 436
– in saliva 645
– in semen 683
– in skin 520
– in sweat 680
– in synovial fluid 641
– in teeth 521
– in urine 664
Magnesium carbonate, decinormal solutions 277
Magnesium chloride, conversion factors 274 sq.
– decinormal solutions 277
– hexahydrate, decinormal solutions 277
Magnesium hydroxide, conversion factors 274 sq.
Magnesium oxide, conversion factors 251, 274 sq.
– decinormal solutions 277
Magnesium sulphate, conversion factors. 274 sq.
Magnetic field constant 215, 228
Magnetism, quantities and units .. 215, 216, 228
Magnetons 229
Maize, amino acids 516
– composition 504
– flour, composition 508
Malaria, malignant tertian, and Hb-S gene . 447
L-Malate, in blood 607
– in carbon-chain extension 424
– in foods .... 499 sq.
– in L-hydroxyproline degradation 395
– in phenylalanine degradation 398
– in tricarboxylic acid cycle 390, 391
– in urea synthesis 444
– in urine 674
Malate dehydrogenase (MDH), activity, temperature correction 585
– activity gradients 586
– in bile 655
– cell binding 585
– in cerebrospinal fluid 638
– decarboxylating, in plasma 590
Malate dehydrogenase (MDH), isozymes ... 584
– in milk 689
– in plasma 590, 591
– – effect of muscular work 586
– – in pregnancy 586
– in seminal plasma 684
– in spermatozoa 684
– in synovial fluid 641
– in tissues 585
– in tricarboxylic acid cycle 390, 391
L-Malate hydro-lyase. See Fumarate hydratase
L-Malate:NAD(P) oxidoreductase. See Malate dehydrogenase
Maleylacetoacetic acid in phenylalanine degradation 398
Malic acid (*see also L-Malate*), decinormal solutions 277
Malic enzyme. See Malate dehydrogenase
Malonic semialdehyde, from β-alanine 401
– in transamination reactions 394
Malonyl-coenzyme A in fatty acid synthesis from citrate 420, 424, 425
Maltase. See α-Glucosidase
Maltose 324
– in saliva 646
– from starch 411
Mammary glands, effect of oxytocin 723
– phosphatases 415
– effect of prolactin 719
– weight gain in pregnancy 690
Mammotropin. See Prolactin
Man. See D-Mannose
Manganese, atomic weight multiples 250
– in bile 654
– in blood 567
– in cerebrospinal fluid 636
– dietary requirements 497
– in faeces 658
– flame lines 284
– in foods .... 499 sq.
– activation of hexosediphosphatase 415
– in milk 688
– in organs 519
– properties, isotopes, etc. 236
– activation of proteases .... 409 sq.
– in skin, hair and nails 520
– sulphate, decinormal solutions 277
– in sweat 680
– in tricarboxylic acid cycle 390, 391
– in urine 664
Manganese-52 and -54, characteristics 292
– decay table 296
D-Mannoheptulose 311
Mannosamine, formation 423
D-Mannose (Man) 310, 315
– in serum glycoproteins 606
– 1-phosphate, in L-fucose formation 423
– – guanosine diphosphate mannose from . 347
– 6-phosphate 320
– – in L-fucose formation 423
– in urine 673
Mannosidases in seminal plasma 684
MAO. See Monoamine oxidase
Maple syrup urine disease 448, 449
Mare's milk, composition 511
Margaric acid 367
Margarine, composition 510
Marrow, bone. See Bone marrow
Mass energy transfer coefficient 218, 220
Mass number 217
Mass stopping power 218
Mass units 204, 205
Mastocytosis, urinary histidine metabolites . 670
Mathematical constants 9
– symbols 132
Maxwell 216
Mayonnaise, composition 510
MBC (maximum breathing capacity) 543
McArdle's syndrome 450, 451
MCH (mean corpuscular haemoglobin) 615, 617
MCHC (mean corpuscular haemoglobin concentration) 576, 615, 617
MCV (mean corpuscular volume) . 614, 615, 617
Md (mendelevium) 248
MDH. See Malate dehydrogenase
Means 137
Mean day 207
Measles antiserum, reference preparation ... 761
Meat, amino acids 516
– composition .... 511 sq.
– vitamin losses during cooking 498
Meconium, composition and properties . 657 sq.
– pregnanediol 754
Mediterranean anaemia 448
MEFR. See Expiratory flow rate, maximum
mega- (10^{6}) 9
Megakaryocytes in bone marrow 621
Megaloblastic anaemia. See under Anaemia
Melanin, formation from tyrosine 440, 722
– function 722
– lack 448
– in urine 661
Melanocytes, effect of melanotropin 722
Melanocyte-stimulating hormone 721, 722
Melanocyte-stimulating-hormone releasing factor 725
Melanophore hormone 721, 722
Melanotropin 721, 722
Melatonin 730
Mel B, reference preparation 763
Melissic acid 367
Melons, composition 500
Melting points of elements .... 234 sq.
Menadione 468
Menaquinone 468
Mendelevium, properties and isotopes 248
Ménétrier's disease, gastric juice albumin . 650
Menopause, serum uric acid and 577
Menstrual cycle, blood-cell amino acids 574
– BMR 539
– effect of chorionic gonadotropin 715
– corticosteroid secretion 743
– eosinophil count 620
– erythrocyte sedimentation rate 559
– gonadotropins 714
– iron requirement 496
– oestradiol formation 755
– plasma, amino acids 574
– – androgens 751
– – ascorbic acid 611
– – iron 566
– – oestrogens 756
– – progesterone and metabolites 754
– progesterone secretion 753
– effects of sex hormones 758
– thrombocyte count 620, 621
– urine, amino acids 667
– – citric acid 674
– – creatine 665
– – glucuronic acid 673
– – gonadotropins 714
– – 3-hydroxy-kynurenine 669
– – melanotropin 722
– – 1-methyl-2-pyridone 5-carboxylamide .. 676
– – oestrogens 756, 757
– – pregnanediol 754
– – testosterone 752
Mercaptans in urine 663
Mercapturic acids 330
– in detoxication 445
Mercuric chloride, decinormal solutions ... 277
Mercury, in blood 567
– density 230
– flame lines 284
– inhibition of aminopeptidase 411
– properties, isotopes, etc. 242
– in urine 664
Mercury-197, characteristics 293
– decay table 305, 306
– diagnostic use 289
Mercury-198, vacuum wave lengths 200
Mercury-203, characteristics 293
– decay table 306
Mercury barometer correction 255
Mercury diuretics, effect on thiamine excretion 676
Mesobilane 362, 363
Mesobilene-(b) 364
Mesobilierythrin 364
Mesobilifuscins 364
– in faeces 657
Mesobilirhodin 364
Mesobilirubin 362, 363
Mesobilirubinogen 362, 363
Mesobiliviolin 364
Meso compounds 309
Mesohaems 361
Mesoinositol 322, 491
– in plasma 605
– in urine 673
Mesoporphyrin 358
– in faeces 659
Mesothorium I, properties 245
Mesothorium II, properties 245
Mesotocin 724
Messenger RNA. See under RNA
Met. See L-Methionine

A detailed index to the statistical tables (pages 28–131) and chapter on Statistical Methods (pages 146–196) will be found on pages 197–198

Metabolic acidosis and alkalosis 528
– body size 473
– diseases, congenital 446 sq.
– quotients 387, 388
– rate, basal (BMR). See Basal metabolism
– – resting (RMR) 495
– reactions 389 sq.
Metabolism 387 sq.
– basal. See Basal metabolism
– cell 387, 388
– of erythrocytes 616
– inborn errors 446 sq.
– of leucocytes 618
– of lipids. See under Lipids
– mineral. See Electrolyte balance
– of plasma proteins 579
– of thrombocytes 621
Metamorphosis test 727
Metamyelocytes in bone marrow 621
Metanephrine in urine 668, 733
Metanil yellow indicator 283
Metaphosphatases 405
Meter. See Metre
Methaemoglobin 359, 360
– acid 359
– alkaline 359
– in blood 576
Methaemoglobinaemia 576
– congenital 447
Methanoic acid 366
L-Methionine (Met) 332
– biosynthesis 479
– – from homocysteine 437
– – vitamin B_{12} in 485
– in blood 574
– in blood proteins 581
– cell constituents from 434
– creatine from arginine, glycine and 437
– degradation 398, 402
– dietary requirements 496
– in foods 516
– in milk 688
– in saliva 645
– in urine 667
Methionylkallidin 742
Methionyl-lysylbradykinin 742
Methoxyestr-. See Methoxyoestr-
3-Methoxy-4-hydroxymandelic acid, from catecholamine breakdown 732
– in urine 675, 733
3-Methoxy-4-hydroxy-β-phenylacetaldehyde from catecholamine breakdown 732
3-Methoxy-4-hydroxyphenylacetic acid, from catecholamine breakdown 732
– in urine 675
3-Methoxy-4-hydroxy-β-phenylethanol from catecholamine breakdown 732
3-Methoxy-4-hydroxyphenylglycol, from catecholamine breakdown 732
– in urine 675
3-Methoxy-4-hydroxyphenylglycolaldehyde from catecholamine breakdown 732
2-Methoxyoestriol in urine 756
2-Methoxyoestrone, biosynthesis and metabolism 431
– in urine 756
– – in pregnancy 757
5-Methoxytryptamine in urine 669
Methoxytyramine from catecholamine breakdown 732
α-Methylacetoacetyl-coenzyme A in isoleucine degradation 396
Methylacrylyl-coenzyme A in valine degradation 396
2-Methyladeninecyanocobamide 483
2-Methyladenosine 354
2′-*O*-Methyladenosine 354
N^6-Methyladenosine 354
S-Methyladenosylmethionine in oestrogen metabolism 431
N-Methyladrenaline, breakdown 732
α-Methyl-β-alanine. See β-Aminoisobutyric acid
Methylamine in urine 668
5-Methyl-6-amino-2-hydroxypyrimidine 338
Methylaspartate mutase, vitamin B_{12} 485
Methylation in detoxication 442 sq.
5-Methylbenzimidazolylcyanocobamide 483
2-Methyl-1,2-bis-(3-pyridyl)-1-propanone (metyrapone) test 717
3-Methylbutanoic acid 371
cis-2-Methyl-Δ^2-butenoic acid 371
α-Methylbutyryl-coenzyme A in isoleucine degradation 396
α-Methylcarbamyl-β-alanine in thymine degradation 401
24-Methyl-5α-cholestane in steroids 381
24-Methylcholesta-5,7,22-trien-3β-ol. See Ergosterol
Methylcobalamin 482, 483, 485
– in serum 484, 610
β-Methylcrotonyl-CoA-carboxylase, biotin 487
β-Methylcrotonyl-coenzyme A in leucine degradation 395
2′-*O*-Methylcytidine 354
3-Methylcytidine 354
5-Methylcytidine 354
5-Methylcytosine 338
Methylene group, mol.wt. multiples 250
5,10-Methylenetetrahydrofolic acid, in transfer of one-carbon groups 436, 437
– in synthesis of purines and methionine 479
– in pyrimidine synthesis 439
5,10-Methylenetetrahydropteroylglutamic acid. See 5,10-Methylenetetrahydrofolic acid
N-Methyl-L-glucosamine 315
β-Methylglutaconyl-coenzyme A in leucine degradation 395
1-Methylglycocyamidine. See Creatinine
Methylglycocyamine. See Creatine
Methyl group, mol.wt. multiples 250
Methylguanidine, in blood 573
– in urine 666
1-Methylguanine in urine 671
Methylguanosines 354
1-Methylguanosine 354
14-Methylhexadecanoic acid 371
1-Methylhistidine 335
– in blood 574
– in urine 667
3-Methylhistidine 335
– in blood 574
– in urine 667
α-Methyl-β-hydroxybutyryl-coenzyme A in isoleucine degradation 396
1-Methylhypoxanthine in urine 671
5,10-Methylidynetetrahydrofolic acid, in L-histidine degradation 395
– in inosinic acid formation 433
– in transfer of one-carbon groups 436, 437
– in synthesis of purines and methionine 479
1,4-Methylimidazoleacetic acid in urine 670
1-Methylinosine 354
Methylmalonic acid in urine 449, 674
Methylmalonic semialdehyde, from α-methyl-β-alanine 401
– in valine degradation 396
Methylmalonyl-CoA carboxyltransferase, biotin in 487
Methylmalonyl-CoA mutase, in degradation of fats 392
– vitamin B_{12} 485
Methylmalonyl-CoA racemase in degradation of fats 392
Methylmalonyl-coenzyme A in degradation of fats 392
N-Methylmetanephrine from catecholamine breakdown 732
Methylnaphthoquinone 468
N_1-Methylnicotinamide. See 1-Methylnicotinamide
1-Methylnicotinamide 477
– in plasma 610
– in urine 676
D-[–]-10-Methyloctadecanoic acid 371
Methyl orange indicator 283
6α-Methylprednisolone 380
– biological activity 750
2-Methylpropanoic acid 371
2′-*O*-Methylpseudouridine 354
N_1-Methyl-2-pyridone-5-carboxylamide 477
– in urine 676
1-Methyl-4-pyridone-5-carboxylamide in urine 676
1-Methyl-6-pyridone-3-carboxylamide. See N_1-Methyl-2-pyridone-5-carboxylamide
Methyl red indicator 283
24-Methyl-9,10-secocholesta-5,7,10(19),22-tetraen-3β-ol. See Vitamin D_2
β-Methylserine. See L-Threonine
Methyltestosterone, biological activity 752
5-Methyltetrahydrofolate homocysteine transmethylase, vitamin B_{12} in 485
5-Methyltetrahydrofolic acid 481
– in blood 610
– in whole body 479
– in methionine formation 437
– in transfer of one-carbon groups 436, 437
5-Methyltetrahydrofolic acid, in synthesis of purines and methionine 479
5-Methyltetrahydropteroylglutamic acid. See 5-Methyltetrahydrofolic acid
5-Methyl-THF. See 5-Methyltetrahydrofolic acid
8-Methyltocol 465
8-Methyltocotrienol 465
Methyltransferases 385
O-Methyltransferase in oestrogen metabolism 430
13-Methyltridecanoic acid 371
6α-Methyl-11β,17α,21-trihydroxypregna-1,4-diene-3,20-dione. See 6α-Methylprednisolone
Methyluridines 354
Metre 200
Metre-kilogramme-second-ampere system 215, 216
Metric ton 204
Metyrapone test 717
Mevalonic acid, in cholesterol synthesis 426, 427
– in synthesis of ubiquinones 466
Mevalonyl phosphate in cholesterol synthesis 426, 427
– pyrophosphate in cholesterol synthesis 426, 427
– ribophosphate in cholesterol synthesis 426, 427
Mg. See Magnesium
Mho 216
mi (mile) 200
MICHAELIS constant 382 sq.
micro- (10^{-6}) 9
Microbar 211, 212
Microcytic anaemia 448
Micrometre 200
Micron 200
Mid-expiratory flow, maximum (MMF) 543
– determination 549
MIFR (inspiratory flow rate, maximum) 543
Mil 200
– circular 203
Mile, geographical 200
– nautical 200
– statute 200
Milk, breast (*see also Breast feeding*) 687 sq.
– – amino acids 516, 688
– – fat content variations 687
– – fatty acids 687
– – alkaline phosphatase 415
– – thiamine 470, 689
– – vitamin A 457, 689
– – yield 687
– cow's 687 sq.
– – amino acids 516, 688
– – effect on urinary electrolytes 663, 664
– – fatty acids 687
– – effect on urinary nitrogen 665, 666
– – effect on infants' stools 657
– dietary data 511
– ejection, effect of oxytocin 723
– oligosaccharides 689
– – formation 347, 350, 424
– xanthine oxidase 419
milli- (10^{-3}) 9
Millibar 211, 212
Millimetre 200
– of mercury 212
– of water 212
Millimicron 200
min (minim) 204
min (minute) 205
Mineral metabolism. See Electrolyte balance
Mineralocorticoids 379 sq., 428, 748 sq.
– determination 743
Mineralocorticosteroids. See Mineralocorticoids
Minim 204
Minute 206
Minute (angle) 207, 208
Minute ventilation ($\dot{V}_T$) 542, 550
Minute volume of pulmonary circulation 544
Mitochondria, vitamin B_{12} 485
Mixing time in lung–spirometer system 543
MK (myokinase). See Adenylate kinase
MKSA (metre-kilogramme-second-ampere) units 215, 216
MMF. See Mid-expiratory flow, maximum
mmHg (millimetre of mercury) 212
mmH_2O (millimetre of water) 212
Mn. See Manganese
MNSs blood-group system 627
– clinical significance 633
Mo. See Molybdenum
MOELLER-BARLOW disease 490
mol (mole) 226, 227, 270

A detailed index to the statistical tables (pages 28–131) and chapter on Statistical Methods (pages 146–196) will be found on pages 197–198

Molality ... 227, 271
Molar gas constant ... 228
– number of molecules ... 228
– quantities ... 227
– volume of an ideal gas ... 228
Molarity ... 227, 271
– temperature variation ... 251
Mole ... 226, 227, 270
Molecular concentration ... 227
Molecule, definition ... 270
Molybdenum, in blood ... 567
– dietary requirements ... 497
– in erythrocytes ... 567
– flame lines ... 284
– properties, isotopes, etc. ... 237
– in urine ... 664
Molybdenum-99, characteristics ... 292
– decay table ... 301, 302
Monoamine oxidase (MAO), in cardiac infarction ... 624
– in catecholamine breakdown ... 731, 732
– in 5-hydroxytryptamine formation ... 441
Monocytes, in blood ... 618 sq.
– in bone marrow ... 621
– dimensions ... 618
Monoglycerides ... 365, 374
– in faeces ... 659
– in serum ... 601
L-3-Monoiodotyrosine ... 332, 725
– peptide-linked, in thyroid hormone formation ... 440
Mononucleosis, infectious, glyceraldehyde-phosphate dehydrogenase in ... 592
Monosaccharides ... 308, 313 sq.
– in faeces ... 659
Montanic acid ... 367
Month ... 206
Moroctic acid ... 370
Mortadella, composition ... 514
MRF (melanocyte-stimulating-hormone releasing factor) ... 725
m-RNA. See Ribonucleic acid, messenger
MSb, reference preparation ... 763
MSH (melanocyte-stimulating hormone). 721, 722
MSH-RF (melanocyte-stimulating-hormone releasing factor) ... 725
Mucins, epithelial, formation ... 424
– in gastric juice ... 650
– in saliva ... 645
– in synovial fluid ... 642
Mucolipids ... 377
Mucopeptide glucohydrolase. See Lysozyme
Mucopolysaccharides, in bile ... 655
– biosynthesis ... 348, 349
– of connective tissue, formation ... 424
– in faeces ... 659
– metabolism ... 412, 413
– in saliva ... 645
– in synovial fluid ... 640
– in tissues ... 522
– in urine ... 668
Mucoproteins ... 329
– in cerebrospinal fluid ... 637
– in gastric juice ... 650
– in intestinal juice ... 656
– in pancreatic juice ... 652
– in saliva ... 645
– in semen ... 684
– in sweat ... 681
Mucoproteoses in gastric juice ... 650
Mucous membrane, organic components ... 522
– gastric, enzymes ... 585
– respiratory rate ... 387
Muffins, composition ... 508
Multiples, prefixes and symbols ... 9
Mumps, serum α-amylase ... 597
Muramic acid ... 315
Muramidase ... 413
Mureins ... 325, 349
Muscle, acylphosphatase ... 416
– contribution to BMR ... 539
– buffer capacity ... 527
– cardiac. See under Heart
– carnitine ... 491
– composition ... 518
– action of corticosteroids ... 750
– deaminases ... 419
– disease, serum enzyme changes ... 587
– dystrophy, serum glucosephosphate isomerase ... 600
– – serum triosephosphate isomerase ... 600
– enzyme activities ... 585
– enzyme activity gradients between serum and ... 586
Muscle, fibres, in faeces ... 657
– glycogen accumulation ... 451
– glycosidases ... 411, 412
– heart. See under Heart
– effect of insulin ... 736
– organic components ... 522
– phospholipase A ... 417
– proportion of body weight ... 517
– respiratory rate ... 387
– riboflavin ... 471
– thiamine ... 470
– vitamin B_6 ... 475
Muscular activity. See Physical effort
Mushrooms, composition ... 504
Musical pitch, standard ... 225
Mussels, composition ... 515
Mustard, composition ... 510
Mutton, composition ... 514
MVV. See Ventilation, maximum voluntary
Mx (maxwell) ... 216
Mycobacterium leprae, lipids ... 371, 372
Mycoceranic acid ... 372
Mycolipenic acid ... 372
Mycoplasma pneumoniae antiserum, reference reagent ... 764
Myelin, breakdown, cerebrospinal fluid cephalin and ... 638
– lipids ... 376
Myelin sheath phosphoinositides ... 376
Myeloblasts in bone marrow ... 621
Myelocytes, in bone marrow ... 621
– neutrophile, blood count ... 619, 620
– – dimensions ... 618
Myeloid leukaemia, blood histamine ... 575
Myeloma, structure of globulins ... 581
– multiple, urinary proteins ... 668
Myelosis, leucocyte mobility ... 560
Myoglobin ... 360, 362
– in urine ... 671
Myohaemoglobin. See Myoglobin
Myoinositol. See Mesoinositol.
Myokinase. See Adenylate kinase
Myometrium, composition ... 518
Myristic acid ... 366
– in milk ... 687
– in serum lipids ... 604
Myristoleic acid ... 368
– in milk ... 687

N

n (nano-, 10^{-9}) ... 9
n! (factorial) ... 136
N (newton) ... 211, 216
N. See Nitrogen
Na. See Sodium
NAD, NADH, $NADH_2$. See Nicotinamide-adenine dinucleotide
NAD-cytochrome reductase, prosthetic group ... 345
NAD/NADP-dependent reactions, enzyme units and conversion factors ... 584
NADP, NADPH, $NADPH_2$. See Nicotinamide-adenine dinucleotide phosphate
NADP-cytochrome reductase, prosthetic group ... 345
Nails, composition ... 520
Naja antivenin, standard ... 760
nano- (10^{-9}) ... 9
Nanometre ... 200
Naphthalene, mercapturic acids from ... 445
α-Naphtholphthalein, indicator ... 283
β-Naphthol violet indicator ... 283
Natural numbers ... 132
Nautical length units ... 200
Nb. See Niobium
Nd. See Neodymium
Ne. See Neon
Nectarines, composition ... 500
Neoarsphenamine, reference preparation ... 763
Neodymium, flame lines ... 284
– properties, isotopes, etc. ... 240
Neomycin, reference preparation ... 762
Neon, boiling point ... 209
– properties, isotopes, etc. ... 234
Neoplastic disease, glucuronic acid excretion 673
– serum triosephosphate isomerase ... 600
Nephritis, glomerular, fluid deprivation test ... 535
– serum ribosephosphate isomerase ... 600
– salt-losing ... 662, 663
Nephrocalcinosis ... 449, 453
Nephrogenic diabetes insipidus ... 452, 453
Nephrolithiasis ... 453
Nephrotic syndrome, serum caeruloplasmin ... 593
– serum glucuronic acid ... 605
– urine, glucuronic acid ... 673
– – indoxylsulphuric acid ... 669
– – proteins ... 668
– – sulphur ... 663
Neptunium, properties and isotopes ... 248
Nerves, composition ... 519
– glycerophosphorylcholine diesterase ... 417
– 5′-nucleotidase ... 418
Nervone ... 377
– selacholeic acid in ... 369
Nervonic acid ... 369, 377
Neuberg ester. See D-Fructose 6-phosphate
Neuraminic acids, acylated. See Sialic acids
– in lipids ... 365
Neuritis, peripheral ... 454
Neurokeratin, in brain and spinal cord ... 520
– binding of phosphoinositides ... 376
Neurophysin ... 723
Neutral red indicator ... 283
Neutron, Compton wave length ... 229
– mass ... 229
Neutrophils, blood count ... 619, 620
– dimensions ... 618
Newborn (*see also Infants*), bile acids ... 655, 656
– blood, amino acids ... 574
– – ammonia ... 573
– – α-amylase ... 597
– – ascorbic acid ... 611
– – aspartate aminotransferase ... 593
– – bilirubin ... 576, 577
– – calcium ... 565
– – carboxyhaemoglobin ... 576
– – chloride ... 562
– – cholesterol ... 601, 603
– – chorionic gonadotropin ... 715
– – copper ... 566
– – coproporphyrin ... 575
– – corticosteroids ... 745
– – enzymes ... 585
– – fatty acids ... 601, 603, 604
– – fluoride ... 563
– – fructosediphosphate aldolase ... 599
– – glucose ... 604, 605
– – glycogen ... 606
– – growth hormone ... 719
– – haemoglobin ... 576, 615, 617
– – iodine ... 564
– – – protein-bound ... 564
– – iron ... 566
– – ketone bodies ... 608
– – lactate dehydrogenase ... 590
– – lactic acid ... 607
– – lipids ... 601, 603
– – magnesium ... 566
– – malate dehydrogenase ... 591
– – nonprotein nitrogen ... 572
– – pantothenic acid ... 611
– – pH ... 560
– – acid phosphatase ... 596
– – alkaline phosphatase ... 596
– – phosphatides ... 601, 603
– – inorganic phosphorus ... 563
– – potassium ... 564
– – proteins ... 583
– – prothrombin ... 467, 468
– – protoporphyrin ... 576
– – pyridoxal phosphate ... 610
– – sialic acid ... 606
– – sodium ... 565
– – specific gravity ... 557
– – thiamine ... 609
– – thyrotropin ... 718
– – thyroxine ... 727
– – tocopherols ... 609
– – urea ... 572
– – uric acid ... 577
– – vitamin E ... 466
– blood coagulation ... 622
– blood pressure ... 553
– blood volume ... 554, 555
– body composition ... 517, 518
– body surface area ... 528
– bones, composition ... 521
– – development ... 706
– bone-marrow cells ... 621
– brain weight ... 517
– cerebrospinal fluid, bilirubin ... 637
– – erythrocytes and leucocytes ... 635
– – glucose ... 639
– – protein ... 637
– corticosteroid secretion ... 743
– erythroblastosis ... 612

A detailed index to the statistical tables (pages 28–131) and chapter on Statistical Methods (pages 146–196) will be found on pages 197–198

Newborn (*contd*), erythrocytes, count .. 614, 617
– – diameter 617
– – glutathione 573
– – lifetime 616
– – osmotic resistance 616
– – sedimentation rate 558, 559
– – mean corpuscular volume 615, 617
– faeces, composition and properties ... 657 sq.
– fat weight 517
– functional residual capacity 542
– gastric juice, acidity 648
– – pH 647
– haematocrit 614, 617
– haemolytic jaundice 577, 632
– composition of hair and nails 520
– iodide metabolism 726
– leucocyte count 618, 619
– lung values 550
– normal measurements 692, 693
– muscle, composition 518
– – weight 517
– organs, composition 519
– – weights 710
– pulmonary compliance 545
– respiratory quotient 539
– reticulocytes 612, 613
– saliva, amylase 646
– – volume 643
– skin, composition 521
– daily number of stools 657
– sweat electrolytes 679, 680
– teeth, composition 521
– – development 709
– thiamine 470
– organic components of tissues 522
– under-weight, weight gain 692
– urinary concentration 662
– urine, acidity 662
– – amino acids 666, 667
– – ammonia 666
– – calcium 664
– – carbohydrates 673
– – catecholamines 733
– – chloride 662
– – corticosteroids .... 746 sq.
– – creatine 665
– – creatinine 665
– – erythrocytes 677
– – guanidinoacetic acid 666
– – leucocytes 677
– – magnesium 664
– – nitrogen 665
– – oestriol 756
– – phosphorus 663
– – potassium 663
– – proteins 668
– – specific gravity 661
– – sulphur 663
– – urea 665
– – uric acid 671
– – vitamins 676
– – volume 661
– vital capacity 542
– vitamin A prophylaxis 460
– vitamin A requirement 460
– vitamin E deficiency 466
– vitamin K therapy 468
– water requirement 524
– weight 692, 693
Newcastle disease antiserum, reference preparation 761
– vaccine, standard and reference preparation 759
Newton 211, 216
Ni. See Nickel
Niacin. See Nicotinic acid
Niacinamide 477
Nickel, flame lines 284
– properties, isotopes, etc. 236
– in urine 664
Nicotinamide 477
Nicotinamide mononucleotide (NMN) 344
Nicotinamide-adenine dinucleotide (NAD; in reduced form NADH, $NADH_2$) .. 344, 477
– in alcoholic fermentation 390
– in biological oxidations 403
– in blood 577
– enzymatic cleavage 416
– in L-cysteine degradation 397
– in degradation of fats 392, 393
– formation from nicotinic acid 477
– functions 477
– in glutamic acid formation 432
– in glycolysis 389
– in hydroxyproline formation 432
Nicotinamide-adenine dinucleotide, in isoleucine degradation 396
– in leucine degradation 395
– in methionine formation 479
– in norleucine degradation 396
– in transfer of one-carbon groups 437
– in proline formation 432
– in purine formation 479
– in pyrimidine formation 439
– in serine degradation 397
– in oxidation of sugars 391
– in L-threonine degradation 397
– in tricarboxylic acid cycle 390, 391
– in UDP-glucuronic acid formation 423
– in UDP-iduronic acid formation 423
– in urea synthesis 444
– in valine degradation 396
– in xanthylic acid formation 436
Nicotinamide-adenine dinucleotide phosphate (NADP; in reduced form NADPH, $NADPH_2$) 344, 477
– in blood 577
– in carbon-chain extension 424
– in cholesterol synthesis 426
– enzymatic cleavage 416
– in degradation of fats 392
– in fatty acid synthesis from citrate ... 424, 425
– formation, from nicotinic acid 477
– – in pentose phosphate cycle 422
– functions 477
– in glutamic acid formation 432
– in methionine formation 479
– in transfer of one-carbon groups 437
– in phenylalanine–tyrosine conversion 439
– in purine formation 479
– in tricarboxylic acid cycle 390, 391
Nicotinic acid .... 476 sq.
– in blood 477, 610
– in cerebrospinal fluid 639
– deficiency 478
– dietary requirements 478, 493
– in foods .... 499 sq.
– – losses during cooking 498
– conjugation with glycine 444
– in liver 477
– in milk 689
– NAD formation from 477
– in tryptophan degradation 398, 399, 475
– in urine 477, 676
Nicotinic acid adenine dinucleotide in NAD and NADP formation 477
Nicotinic acid mononucleotide in NAD and NADP formation 477
Nicotinuric acid 477
NIEMANN-PICK disease 455, 456
Ninhydrin 329
Ninhydrin reaction 573
Niobium, flame lines 284
– properties, isotopes, etc. 237
Nisinic acid 370
Niton, properties, isotopes, etc. 244
Nitramine indicator 283
p-Nitraniline, acetylation 444
Nitrate in urine 664
Nitric acid, decinormal solutions 277
Nitrite, in blood 564
– in urine 664
Nitritocobalamin 482
Nitrogen, atomic weight multiples 250
– in blood 572
– – determination 568
– in whole body 517
– in bones and teeth 521
– in foods .... 498 sq.
– in leucocytes 572
– in muscle 518
– nonprotein. See Nonprotein nitrogen
– in organs 519
– in placenta and amniotic fluid 522
– properties, isotopes, etc. 234
– in skin, hair and nails 520
– in thrombocytes 572
Nitrophenol indicators 283
Nitrous acid (*see also Nitrite*), decinormal solutions 277
nmile (nautical mile) 200
NMN (nicotinamide mononucleotide) 344
No (nobelium) 248
Nobelium, properties and isotopes 248
Nodocs 353
Noise levels 225, 226
Nomogram, acid–base balance of blood ... 569
– aortic diameter and biological age .... (inside back cover)
Nomogram, blood, plasma and erythrocyte volumes 556
– body surface area 537, 538
– serum cation concentration 562
– drops per minute 529
– HENDERSON–HASSELBALCH formula 528
– lung values 547, 550
Nonacosanoic acid 367
Nonadecanoic acid 367
Nonanoic acid 366
Nondecylic acid 367
Nonoses 316
Nonprotein nitrogen (NPN), in bile 654
– in blood 572, 683
– in cerebrospinal fluid 636
– in gastric juice 649
– in milk 511, 688
– in pancreatic juice 652
– in saliva 645
– in synovial fluid 641
– in tissues 522
Nonsecretors of ABH substances 631
Noodles, composition 508
Noradrenaline 730
– breakdown 732
– formation from tyrosine 440, 731
– in plasma 731, 733
– release 731
– in urine 668, 733
Noradrenochrome from noradrenaline 731
Nor-compounds 381
Norepinephrine. See Noradrenaline
Norethandrolone 380
Norethindrone 380
Norethisterone 380
Norethynodrel 380
Norleucine 332
– degradation 396, 402
Normal distribution (*see also index, pages 197–198*) .... 161 sq., 169 sq.
'Normal' format 133
Normal solutions of reagents 277
Normal temperature and pressure (NTP) ... 260
Normality, temperature variation 251
Normetanephrine, from catecholamine breakdown 732
– in urine 668, 733
Normoblasts 612
Norvaline degradation 396, 402
Novobiocin, standard 761
Np (neptunium) 248
NPN. See Nonprotein nitrogen
Nt (niton) 244
NTP (normal temperature and pressure) ... 260
Nuclear magneton 229
Nucleases 406, 418, 419
Nucleic acids .... 351 sq.
– biosynthesis from pentose phosphates ... 422
– in leucocytes 578
– minor constituents 354
Nucleoproteins 329
– in semen 684
Nucleosides .... 336, 337, 339 sq.
– enzymatic cleavage 406, 418, 419
– minor 354
Nucleoside diphosphate kinase 336
Nucleoside kinases 339, 340
Nucleoside monophosphate kinase 336
Nucleoside phosphates 343
Nucleosidephosphate kinase in pyrimidine synthesis 439
Nucleotidases 401
5′-Nucleotidase 418
– in plasma 597
– in purine degradation 400
Nucleotides .... 336, 337, 342 sq.
– biosynthesis .... 338 sq.
– in blood 577
– with coenzyme functions .... 344 sq.
– enzymatic cleavage ..... 338 sq., 406, 418, 419
– in erythrocytes 605
Nucleotide pyrophosphatase 416
Nucleotidyltransferases 386
Nuclides 217
– relative atomic masses 226
– natural, properties .... 234 sq.
– radioactive. See Radionuclides
Numbers, definitions 132
– random 131
Nutritional standards .... 493 sq.
– tables .... 498 sq.
Nuts, amino acids 516
– composition 507
Nystatin, standard 761

A detailed index to the statistical tables (pages 28–131) and chapter on Statistical Methods (pages 146–196) will be found on pages 197–198

O

Ω (ohm) 215, 216
$Ω^{-1}$ (mho, reciprocal ohm) 216
O. See Oxygen
Oats, amino acids 516
Oatflakes, composition 508
Obesity, blood volume 528
Obtusilic acid 368
Ochronosis 448
OCT. See Ornithine carbamoyltransferase
Octacosanoic acid 367
cis-cis-$Δ^{9,12}$-Octadecadienoic acid. See Linoleic acid
Octadecanoic acid. See Stearic acid
$Δ^{4,8,12,15}$-Octadecatetraenoic acid 370
cis-$Δ^{9,11,13}$-Octadecatrienoic acid 370
cis-$Δ^{6}$-Octadecenoic acid 369
cis-$Δ^{9}$-Octadecenoic acid. See Oleic acid
trans-$Δ^{9}$-Octadecenoic acid 369
cis-$Δ^{11}$-Octadecenoic acid 369
trans-$Δ^{11}$-Octadecenoic acid 369
$Δ^{12}$-Octadecenoic acid 369
Octadecyl alcohol in waxes 377
6-Octadecynoic acid 371
9-Octadecynoic acid 371
Octanoic acid. See Caprylic acid
cis-2-Octenic acid 492
Octopus, composition 515
Octulose 1,8-diphosphate in erythrocytes 605
Oe (oersted) 216
Oersted 216
Oestradiol (oestradiol-17β) 380, 755 sq.
– biosynthesis and metabolism 431
– in plasma 756
– production rate 755
– in urine 430, 756, 757
Oestradiol-17α 380
Oestrane 381
Oestra-1,3,5(10)-triene-3,17α-diol 380
Oestra-1,3,5(10)-triene-3,17β-diol. See Oestradiol
Oestra-1,3,5(10)-triene-3,16α,17β-triol. See Oestriol
Oestriol 380, 755 sq.
– formation 431, 755
– metabolism 431
– in plasma 756
– in urine 430, 756, 757
Oestrogens 379 sq., 755 sq.
– biological activity 757, 758
– biosynthesis 430 sq., 755, 757
– effect on gonadotropin secretion 714
– metabolism 430 sq.
– interconversion in placenta 430
– in plasma 756
– effect on plasma growth hormone 719
– effect on prolactin secretion 719
Oestrone 380, 755 sq.
– formation 431, 755
– metabolism 431
– in plasma 756
– in urine 430, 756, 757
Oh phenotypes 627
Ohm 216
Oils, dietary, composition 510
– vegetable, fatty acids 374
Old age, blood, calcium 565
– – cholesterol 601, 603
– – glucose 605
– – glycerides 601
– – protein-bound iodine 564
– – phosphatides 601, 603
– – proteins 579
– – pyridoxal phosphate 610
– – thyroid hormone 726
– – thyrotropin 718
– – thyroxine breakdown 727
– – vitamin A 609
– blood coagulation 622
– blood pressure 553
– BMR 539, 540
– cerebrospinal fluid, protein 637
– corticosteroid secretion 743
– erythrocyte sedimentation rate 559
– iodide metabolism 726
– salivary glucose 646
– salivary secretion 643
– urine, corticosteroids 748, 749
– – creatine 665
– – creatinine 665
– – pregnanediol 754
– – volume 661
Oleandomycin, standard 761
Oleate, in bile 655
– in depot fat 374
– in milk 687
– in serum lipids 604
Oleic acid (*see also Oleate*) 369
Oligoglobulinaemia 614
Oligo-1,6-glucosidase 412
– in intestinal mucosa 413
– in sucrose intolerance 451
Oligosaccharides 312, 324
– milk. See under Milk
1,6-α-Oligosaccharides, intolerance to 451
Oliguria 661
Olives, composition 501
Olive oil, composition 510
OMP. See Orotidine monophosphate
Oncotic pressure of plasma 526, 558
One-carbon groups, formation 397
– transfer 436, 437
One-second volume of expired air ($FEV_{1.0}$) 543
Onions, composition 505
Oocyan 363
Opacity reference preparation 763
Ophthalmic acid 334
Opsin, in isomerization of retinal 460
– in visual pigments 457
Oranges, composition 501
Orange I indicator 283
Orange IV indicator 283
Orange juice, composition 501
Organ weights 710
Organic acids. See under Acids
Organ-specific enzymes. See under Enzymes
D-Ornithine, degradation 395
L-Ornithine 335
– in blood 574
– in creatine formation 437
– decarboxylation 394
– degradation 394, 395, 402
– proline and hydroxyproline from 432
– in sweat 680
– in transamination reactions 394, 395
– in urea synthesis 442, 443
– in urine 452, 667
Ornithine carbamoyltransferase (OCT), in cerebrospinal fluid 638
– in hyperammonaemia 450
– in plasma 593
– in urea cycle 442, 443
Ornithine cycle 442, 443
Orosomucoid. See $α_1$-Glycoprotein, acid
Orotic acid 338
– in pyrimidine synthesis 438, 439
– in urine 453, 671
Orotic-aciduria 453
Orotidine monophosphate (OMP) 342
– formation 438, 439
Orotidine-5′-phosphate decarboxylase, lack 453
– in pyrimidine synthesis 439
Orotidine-5′-phosphate pyrophosphorylase, lack 453
Ortho-hydrogen 247
Orthophosphoric monoester phosphohydrolase. See Phosphatase, acid, and Phosphatase, alkaline
Os (osmium) 242
osm (osmole) 271
Osmidrosis 679
Osmium, properties, isotopes, etc. 242
Osmolality 271
Osmolarity 271
Osmole 271
Osmotic coefficient 270
– diuresis 533
– pressure, calculation 270 sq.
– relationships in body water 526
Ossification centres, secondary, appearance 706 sq.
Osteomalacia 453, 461, 464
– with amino-aciduria 452, 453
– serum alkaline phosphatase 596
Osteopetrosis 729
Ounce 205
– fluid 204
– troy 205
Ovaries, androgens 751
– cholinesterase 414
– oestrogens 430, 755
– progesterone secretion 753
– steroid hormone synthesis 428
– weight 710
Ovulation, effect of chorionic gonadotropin 715
– effect of pituitary gonadotropins 714
– effect of progesterone 755, 758
Oxalacetate. See Oxaloacetate
Oxalate, accumulation 449
– in blood 607
– in foods 499 sq.
– metabolism, vitamin B_6 in 475
– in urine 674
Oxalic acid (*see also Oxalate*), solutions, decinormal 277
– – pH values 279
– dihydrate, decinormal solutions 277
Oxaloacetate, in blood 608
– in carbohydrate synthesis and breakdown 441
– in carbon-chain extension 424
– in cerebrospinal fluid 639
– in citrate formation 424
– in fatty acid synthesis from citrate 424, 425
– from degradation of foodstuffs 402
– in ketosis 393
– in phenylalanine degradation 398
– in transamination reactions 394
– transamination with glutamate 420
– in tricarboxylic acid cycle 390, 391
– in urea synthesis 443, 444
γ-Oxalocrotonic acid in tryptophan degradation 399
Oxalosis 449
Oxalosuccinic acid in tricarboxylic acid cycle 390, 391
Oxidation, biological, mechanism 402 sq.
Oxidoreductases 385
– intramolecular 386
Oximinotransferases 386
Oxo-. See also Keto-
Oxobiotin 486
Oxoglutarate dehydrogenase, in gastric juice 650
– in tricarboxylic acid cycle 390, 391
Oxophenarsine, reference preparation 763
Oxy-. See also Hydroxy-
Oxybiotin 486
Oxygen, atomic weight multiples 250
– biological addition 402
– in blood 570
– – determination 568
– boiling point 209
– properties, isotopes, etc. 234
– triple point 209
– uptake, by erythrocytes 616
– – by leucocytes 618
– – by nutrients 539
– – by organs 539
– – by thrombocytes 621
Oxygen-16 scales of atomic weight 227
Oxygen electrode, redox potential 403
Oxygenases 385
Oxyhaemoglobin 359, 360
Oxylone 380
Oxytetracycline, standard 761
Oxythiamine 469
Oxytocin 722 sq.
– activity, action of progesterone 754
– standard 762
Oxytocinase 723
– in plasma 598
– – in pregnancy 586
Oxytocin-cleaving aminoacylpeptidase. See Oxytocinase
Oysters, composition 515
oz (ounce) 205

P

π, value 132
p (pico-, 10^{-12}) 9
p (pond) 211
P. See Phosphorus
P (poise) 214
Pa (protactinium) 246
Packed cell volume. See Haematocrit
PAH. See *p*-Aminohippuric acid
Pair differences, WILCOXON's test for 128
Palladium, flame lines 284
– properties, isotopes, etc. 238
Palm oil, composition 510
Palmitate, in bile 655
– in brain gangliosides 377
– in depot fat 374
– formation from acetyl-coenzyme A 424, 425
– in milk 687
– in serum lipids 604
Palmitic acid (*see also Palmitate*) 367
Palmitoleic acid 368
– in depot fat 374
– in milk 687

A detailed index to the statistical tables (pages 28–131) and chapter on Statistical Methods (pages 146–196) will be found on pages 197–198

Palmitoleic acid (*contd*), in serum lipids 604
Pancakes, composition 508
Pancreas, ascorbic acid 490
– beef, composition 512
– effect of cholecystokinin-pancreozymin 739
– cystic fibrosis, salivary calcium 644
– – salivary chloride 643
– – salivary nitrogen 645
– – salivary sodium 644
– – serum tocopherols 609
– – sweat electrolytes 680
– – sweat iodine 679
– – sweat tonicity 679
– – vitamin E 467
– disease, serum α-amylase 597
– – serum enzyme changes 587
– – serum β-glucuronidase 597
– DNAases 418
– enzyme activities 585
– fatty acid esterases 414
– insulin content 735
– lactic acid fermentation 388
– phospholipases 417
– proteolytic enzymes 408, 409
– proteolytic enzyme precursors 407
– respiratory rate 387
– RNAase 418
– effect of secretin 739
– weight 710
Pancreatic juice 651 sq.
– amount 525, 651
– electrolytes 525, 652
– glycosidases 411, 412
Pancreatitis, faecal trypsin and chymotrypsin 659
– serum enzyme changes 587
– serum lipase 595
Pancreatopeptidase E 408
– in pancreatic juice 652
Pancreozymin 651, 739
Pancreozymin test 652, 653
Panose, hydrolysis 412
Pantethein 488
– in coenzyme A formation 487
Panthenol 488
Pantoic acid in pantothenic acid synthesis 487
Pantothenic acid 487, 488
– in blood 488, 611
– in cerebrospinal fluid 488, 639
– in coenzyme A 345, 487, 488
– deficiency 488
– dietary requirements 488
– in foods 499 sq.
– in liver 488
– in milk 689
– in urine 488, 676
Pantothenyl alcohol 488
N-Pantothenyl-β-aminoethanethiol. See Pantethein
N-Pantoyl-3-propanolamine 488
Para-aminohippuric acid (PAH). See *p*-Aminohippuric acid
Parahaematin 359
Para-hydrogen 247
Parainfluenza virus antisera, reference reagents 764
Parallelepiped, geometry 142
Parallelogram, geometry 142
Parapepsin 407
Paraproteins 581
– in erythrocyte sedimentation 559
Parathormone. See Parathyroid hormone
Parathyroid hormone 728
– vitamin D and 461
Parietal secretion of gastric juice 647
Paromomycin, reference preparation 762
Parotid saliva. See Saliva
Parsec 201
Parsley, composition 505
Parsnips, composition 505
PASTEUR effect 387
Pb. See Lead
P blood-group system 627, 628
– clinical significance 633
pc (parsec) 201
PCV (packed cell volume). See Haematocrit
Pd. See Palladium
pdl (poundal) 211
Peas, amino acids 516
– composition 505
Peaches, composition 501
Peak flow rate. See Expiratory flow rate, maximum
Peanuts, amino acids 516
– composition 507
Peanut butter, composition 510
– oil, composition 510
Pears, composition 501
Pecans, composition 507
Peck 204
Pectic acid 328
Pectins 328
Pelargonic acid 366
Pellagra 478
Pelvic width during growth 695 sq.
Penicillin K, reference preparation 762
Pennyweight 205
Pentacosanoic acid 367
Pentadecanoic acid 367
Pentadecylic acid 367
Pentaene acids in serum lipids 604
Pentanoic acid. See *n*-Valeric acid
Pentoses 308, 313, 314
– degradation 399
– nucleotide, in erythrocytes 605
– in plasma 605
Pentose 5-phosphates in erythrocytes 605
Pentose phosphate cycle 389, 420 sq.
– in degradation of pentoses 399
Pentosuria 451
Pentosyltransferases 386
Peppers, composition 505
Pepsin 407
– formation from pepsinogen 406
– in gastric juice 650
– inhibitor 406
– in plasma 598
Pepsin B 407
Pepsinogen 406
– gastric secretion 647
Peptidases. See Peptide hydrolases
Peptide hydrolases 386, 405 sq.
– in milk 689
Peptides, enzymes hydrolysing 406 sq.
– in urine 666
Peptide nitrogen, in bile 654
– in gastric juice 649
Peptide synthetases 386
Peptidyl-amino-acid hydrolases 386, 405, 408, 409
Peptidyl-peptide hydrolases 386, 405 sq.
Perch (unit) 200
Perch, composition 515
Pericarditis, serum enzyme changes 587
Period (periodic time) 225
Periodic system of the elements 231
Pernicious anaemia. See under Anaemia
Peroxidases 361, 362
– in milk 689
– in thyroid hormone formation 440, 726
Peroxide haemolysis test 466
D-Perseulose 311
Persimmons, composition 501
Pertussis vaccine, standard 759
Petroselinic acid 369
PFA (phosphofructaldolase). See Ketose-1-phosphate aldolase
PGDH. See Phosphogluconate dehydrogenase
PGE, PGF. See Prostaglandins
PGK. See Phosphoglycerate kinase
PGluM. See Phosphoglucomutase
PGM. See Phosphoglycerate phosphomutase
pH value 278
– of bile 654
– of body fluids 527
– of buffers 280 sq.
– of cerebrospinal fluid 635
– and enzyme action 382
– of faeces 657
– of gastric juice 647
– of intestinal juice 656
– of milk 688
– of pancreatic juice 651
– of saliva 643
– of semen 682
– standards 278, 279
– of sweat 679
– of synovial fluid 640
– of urine 662
PH (prolactin hormone). See Prolactin
Phagocytes in synovial fluid 640
Phe. See L-Phenylalanine
Phenacetylglutamine. See Phenylacetylglutamine
Phenol in urine 675
Phenols, conjugation 442
– esterification as sulphate 445
– in faeces 659
– in urine 675
Phenolic acids in coffee 509
Phenolphthalein indicator 283
Phenol red indicator 283
Phenolsulphonphthalein (PSP) test 532, 533
Phenotypes, blood-group 626 sq.
Phenylacetic acid, detoxication 445
Phenylacetyl-coenzyme A in detoxication of phenylacetic acid 445
Phenylacetylglutamine, formation 445
– in urine 666
L-Phenylalanine (Phe) 332
– accumulation 448
– in blood 448, 574
– in blood proteins 581
– in cerebrospinal fluid 448
– decarboxylation 394
– degradation 398, 402
– dietary requirements 496
– in foods 516
– in milk 688
– in saliva 645
– in sweat 680
– conversion to tyrosine 439
– in synthesis of ubiquinones 466
– in urine 667
Phenylalanine 4-hydroxylase, in phenylalanine degradation 398
– in phenylketonuria 448
Phenylethanolamine *N*-methyltransferase in adrenaline and noradrenaline formation 440
Phenylethylamine, formation from phenylalanine 394
Phenylketonuria 448, 449
Phenylpyruvic acid in urine 448
PHI (phosphohexose isomerase). See Glucosephosphate isomerase
Phon 225
Phosphatases 405, 415, 416
Phosphatase, acid 415
– – allotypy 634
– – in bile 655
– – isozymes 584
– – in milk 689
– – in plasma 585, 596
– – – effect of muscular work 586
– – in saliva 645
– – in semen 684
– – in synovial fluid 641
– – units and conversion factors 584
– – in urine 672
– alkaline 415
– – in bile 655
– – and bone growth in children 585
– – in gastric juice 650
– – isozymes 584
– – in milk 689
– – in plasma 415, 596
– – – in heart disease 587
– – – in liver disease 586, 587
– – – effect of muscular work 586
– – – in pregnancy 586
– – in saliva 645
– – in semen 684
– – in synovial fluid 641
– – units and conversion factors 584
– – in urine 672
– in fructose formation 420
– in interconversion of glycogen phosphorylase 411
– in vitamin B_6 interconversions 473
Phosphate (*see also Phosphoric esters and Phosphorus*), in biological energy transformations 404
– in blood, buffer capacity 527
– – inborn disturbance 452
– in body fluids 523
– buffers 280 sq.
– conversion factors 251, 274 sq., 523
– in DNA synthesis 352
– excretion 453, 663
– – calcitonin and 729
– – index 663
– – parathyroid hormone and 728
– in gastric juice 649
– glomerular filtration and excretion 536
– in lipids 365
– in pancreatic juice 652
– in sweat 679
– in synovial fluid 641
– in urinary sediments 677, 678
Phosphatidal ethanolamine 376
Phosphatides 375 sq.
– accumulation 456
– in bile 654, 655

A detailed index to the statistical tables (pages 28–131) and chapter on Statistical Methods (pages 146–196) will be found on pages 197–198

Phosphatides, in brain 520
– – fatty acids 369
– in cerebrospinal fluid 638
– conversion factors to phosphorus 251
– in erythrocytes 601, 604
– in faeces 659
– fatty acids 369, 370
– in leucocytes 601
– in plasma 601, 604
– in saliva 644
– in semen 685
– in spinal cord 520
– structure and hydrolysis 417
– in synovial fluid 642
– in thrombocytes 601
– in urine 675
Phosphatidic acids 365, 375
– in formation of lecithin and cephalin 425
– in triglyceride synthesis 426
Phosphatidopeptides 376
α-Phosphatidylcholines. See Lecithins
Phosphatidyl esters 365, 375
α-Phosphatidylethanolamines. See Cephalins
α-Phosphatidylglycerols 375
Phosphatidylinositides 376
α-Phosphatidylinositols 376
α-Phosphatidylserines 365, 375
Phosphaturia 452
– in cystinosis 449
Phosphocholine in synthesis of lecithin 425
Phosphocozymase. See Nicotinamide-adenine dinucleotide phosphate
Phosphodiesterase 418
Phosphodiesterases (phosphoric diester hydrolases) 386, 405, 416
Phosphoethanolamine, in blood 573
– in synthesis of cephalin 425
– in saliva 644, 645
– in urine 668
Phosphofructaldolase (PFA). See Ketose-1-phosphate aldolase
Phosphofructokinase in glycolysis 389
Phosphoglucoamino-aciduria 452, 453
Phosphoglucomutase (PGluM), allotypy 634
– isozymes 584
– in lactic acid fermentation 390
– in plasma 595
Phosphogluconate dehydrogenase (PGDH), activity, temperature correction 585
– isozymes 584
– in pentose phosphate cycle 422
– in plasma 591
– in tissues 585
– in vaginal fluid 591
6-Phospho-D-gluconate: NADP oxidoreductase. See Phosphogluconate dehydrogenase
6-Phosphogluconic acid in pentose phosphate cycle 420 sq.
6-Phosphogluconolactone in pentose phosphate cycle 421, 422
3-Phosphoglyceraldehyde. See D-Glyceraldehyde 3-phosphate
2-Phosphoglycerate (D-glyceric acid 2-phosphate) 317
– in carbohydrate synthesis and breakdown 441
– in erythrocytes 605
– in degradation of fats 392
– in glycolysis 389
3-Phosphoglycerate (D-glyceric acid 3-phosphate) 317
– in carbohydrate synthesis and breakdown 441
– in erythrocytes 605
– in glycolysis 389
– in saliva 644
– in serine formation 432
2-Phospho-D-glycerate hydro-lyase. See Phosphopyruvate hydratase
Phosphoglycerate kinase (PGK), in glycolysis 389
– in plasma 594
– in tissues 585
Phosphoglycerate phosphomutase (PGM), in glycolysis 389
– in plasma 600
– in tissues 585
D-Phosphoglycerate 2,3-phosphomutase. See Phosphoglycerate phosphomutase
Phosphohexose isomerase (PHI). See Glucosephosphate isomerase
3-Phosphohydroxypyruvic acid in serine formation 432
Phosphoinositides 376
Phosphokinase in interconversion of glycogen phosphorylase 411
Phospholipases 417
– in pancreatic juice 652
Phospholipase A 417
– in bile 655
– in formation of lysolecithins 375, 376
Phospholipase B 417
Phospholipase C 417
Phospholipase D 417
Phospholipids. See Phosphatides
Phosphomonoesterases 386, 405, 415
4′-Phosphopantethein in coenzyme A formation 487
4′-Phosphopantothenic acid in coenzyme A formation 487
4′-Phosphopantothenylcysteine in coenzyme A formation 487
Phosphopyruvate, in amino-sugar utilization 424
– in carbohydrate synthesis and breakdown 441
– in erythrocytes 605
– in glycolysis 389
Phosphopyruvate carboxylase in carbohydrate synthesis 441
Phosphopyruvate hydratase, in glycolysis 389
– isozymes 584
– in plasma 600
– in tissues 585
Phosphopyruvic acid (*see also Phosphopyruvate*) 317
Phosphoriboisomerase. See Ribosephosphate isomerase
5-Phosphoribosylamine. See Ribosylamine 5′-phosphate
5-Phosphoribosyl-1-pyrophosphate. See D-Ribose 5-phosphate-1-pyrophosphate
Phosphoric acid (*see also Phosphate*), decinormal solutions 277
Phosphoric diester hydrolases 386, 405, 416
Phosphoric esters, in blood 563
– in erythrocytes 563
Phosphoric ester hydrolases. See Phosphatases
Phosphoric monoester hydrolases 386, 405, 415
Phosphorus, atomic weight multiples 250
– in bile 654
– in blood 563
– in whole body 517
– in bones and teeth 521
– in cerebrospinal fluid 636
– conversion factors 251
– dietary requirements 494, 496
– in erythrocytes 563
– in faeces 658
– in foods 499 sq.
– in gastric juice 649
– in milk 688
– in muscle 518
– in organs 519
– pentoxide, conversion factor into phosphorus 251
– in placenta and amniotic fluid 522
– properties, isotopes, etc. 235
– in saliva 644
– in semen 683
– in skin, hair and nails 520
– in urine 663
Phosphorus-32, specific activity 217
– characteristics 292
– decay table 295
– therapeutic use 290, 291
Phosphorylase b activation 343
Phosphorylase limit dextrin 411
Phosphorylation, oxidative, in biological energy transformations 403, 404
Phosphorylcholine in semen 683
Phosphoserine in serine formation 432
Phosphotransferases 386
Phot 223
Photon irradiation 219, 220
Photophobia 448, 449
Photopic vision quantities 223
Photosensitization 454, 455
Phrenosin 372, 377
Phrenosinic acid. See Cerebronic acid
Phycocyanins 364
Phycoerythrin 364
Phylloerythrin 359
Phylloquinone 468
Physeteric acid 368
Physical constants 228 sq.
Physical effort, blood, creatine kinase 594
– – enzyme activities 586
– – fructosediphosphate aldolase 599
– – growth hormone 719
– – haemoglobin 576
Physical effort, lactate 607
– – leucocyte count 618
– – pH value 560
– – proteins 579
– – specific gravity 557
– – volume 555
– and calorie requirement 493 sq.
– lung values 550
– urine, haemoglobin and myoglobin 671
– – ketone bodies 674
– – proteins 668
Phytanic acid 371
Phytin 322
Phytoene in vitamin A synthesis 457
Phytol 362
Phytosphingosine in sphingolipids 376
pico- (10^{-12}) 9
Picolinic acid in tryptophan degradation 399
Pie crust, composition 508
PIF (prolactin-inhibiting factor) 719, 725
Pigment hormone 721, 722
Pike, composition 515
Pilocarpine sweat. See Sweat
Pineal gland hormones 730
Pineapples, composition 501
Pine nuts, composition 507
Pint 204
– dry 204
– liquid 204
Pipecolic acid in L-lysine degradation 398
Piperazine buffer 280 sq.
Piperidine in urine 668
Pistachio nuts, composition 507
Pitocin. See Oxytocin
Pitressin. See Vasopressin
Pituitary dwarfism. See under Dwarfism
– gigantism and ossification 707
Pituitary gland, control of adrenal cortex 430
– anterior, ACTH formation 716, 717
– – gonadotropins 713, 714
– – growth hormone 719, 720
– – prolactin formation 718, 719
– – thyrotropin formation 718
– ascorbic acid 489
– in cardiac infarction 624
– effect of corticosteroids 750
– insufficiency, urinary secretion rhythm 661
– intermediate, melanotropin formation 722
– lactic acid fermentation 388
– effect of oestrogens 757
– posterior, 5′-nucleotidase 418
– – oxytocin and vasopressin 722, 723
– respiratory rate 387
– weight 710
pk (peck) 204
PK. See Pyruvate kinase
Placenta, cholinesterase 414
– chorionic gonadotropin 715
– composition 522
– insulin breakdown 736
– oestrogens 755, 756
– oestrogen interconversion 430
– oestrogen synthesis 430
– progesterone and metabolites 753, 754
– steroid hormone synthesis 428
– gain in weight 690
Placental lactogen, human (HPL) 721
Planck constant 228
– radiation constants 228
Plane angles, units 138, 207, 208
Plasma, acetoacetic acid 608
– acetone 608
– acetylcholine 575
– aconitate hydratase 599
– ACTH 716
– adenosine deaminase 599
– adenylate kinase 595
– adrenaline 731, 733
– alanine aminotransferase 594
– albumin 583
– – in pregnancy and post partum 691
– albumin: globulin ratio 582
– alcohol dehydrogenase 590
– aldosterone 745
– allantoin 577
– aluminium 567
– amino acids 573, 574
– δ-aminolaevulinic acid 575
– aminopeptidase 598
– ammonia 573
– α-amylase 597
– androgens 751, 752
– androstenedione 752
– androsterone sulphate 752

A detailed index to the statistical tables (pages 28–131) and chapter on Statistical Methods (pages 146–196) will be found on pages 197–198

Plasma (*contd*), angiotensin ... 741
– arginase ... 598
– ascorbic acid ... 490, 611
– aspartate aminotransferase ... 593
– bicarbonate ... 562, 571
– – blood acid–base balance and ... 569
– bile acids ... 601
– bilirubin ... 362, 576, 577
– – in metabolic disease ... 454
– biotin ... 611
– bradykinin ... 742
– bromide ... 563
– buffer capacity ... 527
– caeruloplasmin ... 583, 593
– calcitonin ... 729
– calcium ... 565
– – calcitonin and ... 729
– carbonic acid, blood acid–base balance and 569
– carnitine ... 573
– carotenes ... 457, 609
– cations ... 561
– – nomogram ... 562
– cephalin ... 604
– chenodeoxycholic acid ... 601
– chloride ... 562
– cholesterol ... 456, 600, 601, 603, 604
– cholesterol esterase ... 414
– choline ... 575
– cholinesterase ... 414, 595
– chorionic gonadotropin ... 715
– chylomicrons ... 602
– citric acid ... 607
– cobalt ... 566
– colloid-osmotic pressure ... 526, 558
– copper ... 566
– coproporphyrin ... 575
– corticosteroids ... 745
– – protein binding ... 428
– corticosterone ... 745
– cortisol ... 716, 745
– cortisone ... 745
– creatine ... 572
– creatine kinase ... 594
– creatinine ... 531, 572
– – and glomerular filtration rate ... 531, 532
– dehydroascorbic acid ... 611
– dehydroepiandrosterone sulphate ... 752
– dehydrogenases ... 590 sq.
– deoxycholic acid ... 601
– 11-deoxycortisol ... 745
– deoxyribonucleases ... 597
– dextran expanders ... 530
– dihydrocholesterol ... 601
– dihydroxycholanic acids ... 601
– dry substance ... 561
– electrolytes ... 523
– – conversion factors ... 523
– enzymes ... 585 sq.
– – allotypy ... 634
– – maintenance ... 585
– enzyme activity gradients between tissue and ... 586
– ergothioneine ... 573
– erythropoietin ... 740
– ethanolamine ... 573
– fats ... 374
– fatty acids ... 600, 601, 603, 604
– fibrinogen ... 579, 582
– flavinadenine dinucleotide ... 609
– flavin mononucleotide ... 609
– flow rate, into small intestine ... 656
– – into stomach ... 650
– fluoride ... 563
– folic acid ... 479, 610
– folinic acid ... 479
– freezing-point depression ... 526, 557
– fructosediphosphate aldolase ... 599
– fucose ... 606
– fumarate hydratase ... 599
– globulin fractions ... 582, 583
– glucose ... 605
– – osmotic activity ... 526
– glucose-6-phosphatase ... 597
– glucose-6-phosphate dehydrogenase ... 592
– glucosephosphate isomerase ... 600
– glucuronic acid ... 605
– β-glucuronidase ... 597
– glutamate dehydrogenase ... 592
– glutathione reductase ... 592
– glyceraldehyde phosphate dehydrogenase. 592
– glycerol ... 607
– glycerophosphate dehydrogenase ... 590
– glycolaldehydetransferase ... 593
– glycoproteins ... 606
Plasma, glyoxalic acid ... 607
– growth hormone ... 719, 720
– guanidinoacetic acid ... 573
– guanine deaminase ... 598
– haemoglobin ... 576
– – haemoglobin excretion and ... 671
– α_2-haptoglobin ... 583
– heparin ... 606
– hexokinase ... 594
– hexosamines ... 606
– hexoses ... 606
– histamine ... 575
– α-hydroxybutyrate dehydrogenase ... 591
– β-hydroxybutyric acid ... 608
– 17-hydroxycorticosteroids ... 745
– hydroxypregnenones ... 754
– 17α-hydroxyprogesterone ... 754
– hypoxanthine ... 577
– L-iditol dehydrogenase ... 590
– indolyl-3-acetic acid ... 575
– indolyl-3-lactic acid ... 575
– 3-indoxylsulphuric acid ... 575
– insulin ... 735, 736
– iodine ... 564, 726
– iron ... 566
– iron-binding capacity ... 566
– isocitrate dehydrogenase ... 591
– ketohexokinase ... 594
– ketose-1-phosphate aldolase ... 599
– Δ^4-3-ketosteroids ... 745
– kinins ... 742
– lactate dehydrogenase ... 590
– lead ... 567
– lecithin ... 604
– leucine aminopeptidase ... 598
– lipase ... 595
– lipids ... 600 sq.
– – fatty acid composition ... 604
– – in pregnancy and post partum ... 691
– lipid phosphorus ... 563
– lipoic acid ... 608
– lipoproteins ... 583, 602
– lithium ... 567
– lysolecithin ... 604
– α_2-macroglobulin ... 583
– magnesium ... 566
– malate dehydrogenase ... 591
– malic acid ... 607
– manganese ... 567
– melanotropins ... 722
– mesoinositol ... 605
– methylcobalamin ... 484, 610
– 1-methylnicotinamide ... 610
– 5-methyltetrahydrofolic acid ... 479
– molarity and molality ... 271
– myoglobin, myoglobin excretion and ... 671
– nicotinic acid ... 477, 610
– nitrogen ... 572
– nonprotein nitrogen ... 572
– – and glomerular filtration rate ... 531, 532
– – and renal inulin clearance ... 532
– noradrenaline ... 731, 733
– 5′-nucleotidase ... 597
– nucleotides ... 577
– oestrogens ... 756
– oncotic pressure ... 526
– ornithine carbamoyltransferase ... 593
– osmolarity ... 271, 526, 557
– – and urinary concentration ... 533
– osmotic pressure ... 526, 557
– oxalic acid ... 607
– oxytocin ... 723
– oxytocinase ... 598, 723
– pantothenic acid ... 611
– parathyroid hormone ... 728
– pentoses ... 605
– pepsin ... 598
– pH value ... 560
– – and blood acid–base balance ... 569
– phosphatases, phosphoethanolamine excretion and ... 668
– acid phosphatase ... 596
– alkaline phosphatase ... 596
– – in bone destruction ... 415
– phosphate ... 563
– – inborn disturbance ... 452
– phosphatides ... 601, 604
– phosphoethanolamine ... 573
– phosphoglucomutase ... 595
– phosphogluconate dehydrogenase ... 591
– phosphoglycerate kinase ... 594
– phosphoglycerate phosphomutase ... 600
– phosphopyruvate hydratase ... 600
– phosphoric esters ... 563
Plasma, phosphorus ... 563
– placental lactogen ... 721
– plasmalogens ... 604
– plasmin ... 410
– PORTER-SILBER chromogens ... 745
– potassium ... 564
– potassium exchange ... 526
– pregnanediol ... 753, 754
– pregnanetriol ... 745
– progesterone ... 753, 754
– proteins ... 579 sq.
– – allotypy ... 634
– – in bile ... 655
– – calculation of ionized calcium from ... 565
– – cation concentration from specific conductivity and ... 562
– – conversion factors ... 276
– – in faeces ... 289, 659
– – in neoplastic disease ... 581
– – osmotic activity ... 526
– – in pregnancy and post partum ... 691
– – in semen ... 684
– protein-bound iodine ... 564, 726
– protein nitrogen ... 572
– protein sulphur ... 563
– protoporphyrin ... 576
– unconjugated pterins ... 610
– purines ... 577
– pyridoxal phosphate ... 610
– pyruvate kinase ... 594
– pyruvic acid ... 607
– renin ... 598, 741
– riboflavin ... 471, 609
– ribosephosphate isomerase ... 600
– secretin ... 739
– serotonin ... 575
– sialic acid ... 606
– β_1-siderophilin ... 583
– sodium ... 565
– sodium exchange ... 526
– specific conductivity ... 560
– – cation concentration from protein content and ... 562
– specific gravity ... 557
– specific heat ... 560
– sphingomyelin ... 604
– succinate dehydrogenase ... 592
– succinic acid ... 607
– sulphate ... 563
– 6-sulphatoxyskatole ... 575
– sulphur ... 563
– testosterone ... 752
– thiamine ... 470, 609
– thiocyanate ... 564
– thyroid hormones ... 726, 727
– thyrotropin ... 718
– thyroxine ... 288, 726, 727
– tocopherols ... 609
– transcobalamins ... 484
– triglycerides ... 601, 604
– trihydroxycholanic acid ... 601
– tri-iodothyronine binding ... 726
– triosephosphate isomerase ... 600
– trypsin-inhibiting capacity ... 598
– ubiquinone-50 ... 609
– urea ... 572
– – osmotic activity ... 526
– – glomerular filtration rate and ... 531, 532
– uric acid ... 577
– – in gout ... 453
– uronic acid ... 606
– vasopressin ... 723
– viscosity ... 558
– vitamin A ... 457, 609
– vitamin B_6 ... 475, 609
– vitamin B_{12} ... 484, 610
– vitamin D ... 461, 609
– vitamin E ... 466
– volume ... 554 sq.
– – nomogram ... 556
– – tracer study ... 289
– water ... 561
– weight gain in pregnancy ... 690, 691
– xanthine ... 577
– xanthine oxidase ... 592
– L-xylulose ... 605
– zinc ... 567
Plasmacytes in bone marrow ... 621
Plasmalogens ... 365, 376
– in cerebrospinal fluid ... 638
– in erythrocytes ... 604
– in plasma ... 604
– in spermatozoa ... 685
Plasmin ... 410, 622

A detailed index to the statistical tables (pages 28–131) and chapter on Statistical Methods (pages 146–196) will be found on pages 197–198

Plasminogen 410
– plasmin from 622
– in synovial fluid 641
Plasmocytes in bone marrow 621
Plasmolysis time 625
Platelets. See Thrombocytes
Platelet thrombus in blood coagulation 622
Platinum, properties, isotopes, etc. 242
Plums, composition 501
Plutonium, properties and isotopes 248
Pm (promethium) 240
Pneumococcus antisera, standards 760
Pneumonia, lobular, serum vitamin A 609
Po (polonium) 244
Poikilocytes 614
Point (printers') 200
Poirrier blue indicator 283
Poise 214
Poisoning, acute, serum enzyme changes ... 586
Poisson distribution .... 187 sq.
– tables 107, 108, 128
Polarization, electric and magnetic 216
Pole 200
Poliomyelitis vaccine, reference preparation. 759
Poliovirus antisera, reference reagents 764
– standards 760
Polonium, properties, isotopes, etc. 244
Polycythaemia vera, blood viscosity 558
– osmotic resistance of erythrocytes 616
– radiotherapy 291
– thrombocyte lifetime 620
– uric acid excretion 671
Polyethenoid acids 373
Polyglobulinaemia 614
Polymyxin B, standard 761
Polynucleotides 336
Polynucleotide phosphorylase 352
Polyolefinic acids 370, 373
Polypeptides 329
Polypeptide s-RNA in protein synthesis 353
Polyribonucleotide nucleotidyltransferase ... 352
Polysaccharides .... 312, 325 sq.
Polyuria 661
Polyvinylpyrrolidone enteral excretion test . 289
Pompe's disease 451
Pond 211
Popcorn, composition 508
Pork, composition 513
Porphin 355
Porphobilinogen 356
– in erythrocytes 575
– in haem synthesis 454
– in porphyrin formation 437
– in urine 454, 455, 670
Porphyria 357, 358, 454, 455
– blood coproporphyrin 575
– cutanea tarda hereditaria 454, 455
– faecal porphyrins 659
– hepatic, porphobilinogen 356
– porphyrin excretion 670
Porphyrins .... 355 sq.
– in bile 654
– in blood .... 575 sq.
– in faeces 455, 659
– formation 437
– – in liver 454
– in liver 454, 455
– in urine 661, 670
– in vitamin B_{12} synthesis 484
Porphyrinogens, oxidation 454
Porphyropsin 457
Port wine, composition 509
Porter-Silber chromogens, in plasma 745
– excretion during pregnancy 749
– structure and assay 744
Positron, charge: mass ratio 229
– Compton wave length 229
Posterior pituitary. See under Pituitary
Potassium, in amniotic fluid 522
– atomic weight multiples 250
– in bile 654
– in whole body 517
– in body fluids 523, 525
– in bones 521
– in cerebrospinal fluid 636
– conversion factors 251, 523
– dietary requirements 496
– in electrolyte balance 525
– in erythrocytes 564
– exchangeable 518, 526
– in faeces 658
– flame lines 284
– in foods .... 499 sq.
– in gastric juice 649
Potassium, glomerular filtration and excretion 536
– in hair and nails 520
– in intestinal juice 656
– in milk 688
– in muscle 518
– in organs 519
– in pancreatic juice 652
– in placenta 522
– in plasma 564
– gain in pregnancy 690
– properties, isotopes, etc. 235
– in purine formation 433, 435, 436
– in saliva 644
– in semen 683
– in skin 520
– in sweat 680
– in synovial fluid 641
– in teeth 521
– in thrombocytes 564
– in urine 663
Potassium-42, characteristics 292
– decay table 295
– gamma ray constant 221
Potassium acetate solutions, conversion factors .... 274 sq.
– pH values 279
Potassium aluminium sulphate solutions, pH values 279
Potassium bicarbonate solutions, conversion factors .... 274 sq.
– decinormal 277
– pH values 279
Potassium biphthalate, buffers .... 280 sq.
– solutions, pH values 279
Potassium bitartrate solutions, decinormal .. 277
– pH values 279
Potassium bromide solutions, conversion factors .... 274 sq.
Potassium carbonate solutions, decinormal . 277
– pH values 279
Potassium chloride, buffer .... 280 sq.
– effect on urinary osmolarity and specific gravity 534
– solutions, conversion factors .... 274 sq.
– – decinormal 277
Potassium citrate solutions, conversion factors .... 274 sq.
Potassium cyanide, decinormal solutions ... 277
Potassium dichromate, decinormal solutions 277
Potassium dihydrogen phosphate solutions, pH values 279
Potassium D-gluconate solutions, conversion factors .... 274 sq.
Potassium hydroxide, decinormal solutions . 277
Potassium oxide, conversion factor into potassium 251
– solutions, conversion factors .... 274 sq.
– – decinormal 277
Potassium permanganate, decinormal solutions 277
Potassium phosphates, solutions, conversion factors .... 274 sq.
– effect on urinary osmolarity and specific gravity 534
Potassium sulphate, effect on urinary osmolarity and specific gravity 534
Potassium tartrate, decinormal solutions ... 277
Potassium tetroxalate solutions, decinormal. 277
– pH values 279
Potatoes, amino acids 516
– composition 505
– vitamin losses during cooking 498
– sweet, composition 506
Potential difference, electric and magnetic .. 216
Poultry, composition .... 512 sq.
Pound 204
– 'apothecaries' 205
– troy 205
Poundal 211
Pound-force 211
Powers 133, 134
Power units 214
Poynting vector 216
Pr. See Praseodymium
Praseodymium, flame lines 284
– properties, isotopes, etc. 240
Prealbumin, amino-acid composition 581
– in cerebrospinal fluid 637
– characteristics and function 580
– in faeces 659
– thyroxine-binding 726
Prednisolone 380
– biological activity 750
Prednisone 380
Prednisone, biological activity 750
Preeclampsia, serum β-glucuronidase 597
Pregnancy, amino-acid requirements 496
– amniotic fluid composition 522
– blood, amino acids 574
– – androgens 751
– – ascorbic acid 611
– – caeruloplasmin 593
– – calcium 565
– – carotenes 609
– – changes 691
– – cholesterol 601, 603
– – coagulation 622
– – copper 566
– – creatine kinase 594
– – enzyme activities 586
– – erythrocyte count 614
– – erythrocyte sedimentation rate 559
– – fatty acids 601, 603
– – folic acid 610
– – glucose 604
– – β-glucuronidase 597
– – glycerides 603
– – glycoproteins 606
– – haematocrit 614
– – haemoglobin 615
– – insulin 736
– – protein-bound iodine 564
– – iron 566
– – lactate 607
– – leucocyte count 618
– – lipids 601, 603
– – nonprotein nitrogen 572
– – oestrogens 756
– – ornithine carbamoyltransferase 593
– – oxytocinase 598, 723
– – pantothenic acid 611
– – pH value 560
– – phosphate 563
– – phosphatides 601, 603
– – phosphoethanolamine 573
– – placental lactogen 721
– – pregnanediol 753
– – proteins 583
– – renin–angiotensin 741
– – riboflavin 609
– – thiamine 609
– – tocopherols 609
– – urea 572
– – vitamin A 609
– – vitamin B_6 609
– – vitamin B_{12} 610
– – volume 555
– – zinc 567
– BMR 539
– calcium requirement 493, 494
– erythrocyte sodium 565
– erythropoiesis 740
– folic acid deficiency and requirement 479
– iodine requirement 497
– iron requirement 496
– muscle composition 518
– nicotinic acid requirement 478
– oestrogen formation 755
– placenta, chorionic gonadotropin 715
– – composition 522
– effect of progesterone 754, 758
– progesterone production 753
– salivary pH value 643
– effects of sex hormones 758
– thiamine requirement 471
– thyroid hyperfunction 727
– organic components of tissues 522
– urine, amino acids 667
– – calcium 664
– – chorionic gonadotropin 715
– – corticosteroids 749
– – creatine 665
– – erythrocytes 677
– – fluoride 663
– – follicle-stimulating hormone 713
– – lactose 673
– – leucocytes 677
– – melanotropin 722
– – 1-methyl-2-pyridone 5-carboxylamide .. 676
– – oestrogens 756, 757
– – oestrogen metabolites 432
– – pregnanediol 754
– – pregnanolone 754
– – urea 665
– uterine oxytocin sensitivity 723
– vitamin A deficiency 460
– vitamin B_6 requirement 475
– vitamin B_{12} requirement 485

Index

A detailed index to the statistical tables (pages 28–131) and chapter on Statistical Methods (pages 146–196) will be found on pages 197–198

Pregnancy (*contd*), vitamin D 464
– – poisoning 464
– – requirement 461
– weight gain 690
Pregnane 381
5α-Pregnanediol. See α-Allopregnanediol
5β-Pregnanediol 380
– in meconium 754
– in plasma 753, 754
– from progesterone 753
– in urine 754
5α-Pregnane-3α,11β,17α,20β,21-pentol 379
5β-Pregnane-3α,11β,17α,20α,21-pentol 379
5β-Pregnane-3α,11β,17α,20α,21-pentol 379
5β-Pregnane-3α,11β,17α,20β,21-pentol 379
Pregnanetriol 380
– breakdown 746
– in plasma 745
– secretion 745
– in urine 747
5β-Pregnane-3α,17α,20α-triol. See Pregnanetriol
Pregnanolone 380
– from progesterone 753
– in urine 754
Pregn-4-ene-3,20-dione. See Progesterone
Pregnenolone 380
– biosynthesis 401, 428, 429
– production rate 753
Prekallikrein 742
Premature infants, blood, amino acids 574
– – ammonia 573
– – aspartate aminotransferase 593
– – bilirubin 576
– – cations 561
– – fructosediphosphate aldolase 599
– – glucose 605
– – lactate dehydrogenase 590
– blood pressure 553
– cerebrospinal fluid, leucocyte count 635
– – protein 637
– erythroblastosis 612
– erythrocytes, lifetime 616
– – mean corpuscular haemoglobin 615
– treatment of rickets 464
– urinary concentration 662
– urine, amino acids 666, 667
– – creatine 665
– – creatinine 665
– – proteins 668
– – volume 661
– vitamin E deficiency 466
– vitamin K therapy 468
– weight gain 692
Pressure, standard atmospheric 212
– units 211
– values, correction 255
Pretzels, composition 508
PRF (prolactin-releasing factor) 725
Primaquine sensivity, enzymes in 592
Prime numbers 9
Pro. See L-Proline
Probit transformation 54, 55, 163, 164
Procaine benzylpenicillin, reference preparation 762
Procarboxypeptidases in pancreatic juice ... 652
Procarboxypeptidase A 409
Pro-erythroblasts 612
Pro-erythrocytes. See Reticulocytes
Progestagens. See Progestational hormones
Progestational hormones ...... 379, 380, 753 sq.
– accumulation 456
Progesterone .... 380, 753 sq.
– biological activity 754, 755, 758
– biosynthesis 428, 429
– effect on gonadotropin secretion 714
– in plasma 753, 754
– production rate 753
Proinsulin 735
Prolactin 718, 719
– chorionic growth-hormone 721
– standard 762
Prolactin-inhibiting factor 719, 725
Prolactin-releasing factor (PRF) 725
Prolamines 329
Prolidase 408, 410
Prolinase 408, 410
D-Proline degradation 395
L-Proline (Pro) 332
– in blood 449, 574
– in blood proteins 581
– degradation 394, 395, 402
– in foods 516
– formation 432
L-Proline, hydroxylation, ascorbic acid in... 490
– in milk 688
– in saliva 645
– in sweat 680
– in urine 449, 667
Promethium, properties, isotopes, etc. 240
Promyelocytes in bone marrow 621
1,3-Propanediamine in semen 684
Propanoic acid. See Propionic acid
Propenoic acid 368
Propentdyopents 364
Propionaldehyde from α-methyl-β-alanine .. 401
Propionic acid 366
– in blood 607
– in cholesterol degradation 401
– in faeces 660
– in valine degradation 396
Propionic aldehyde in valine degradation... 396
Propionylcholine, hydrolysis 414
Propionyl-CoA-carboxylase, biotin in 487
Propionyl-coenzyme A, in α-aminobutyric acid degradation 396
– in degradation of fats 392
– in isoleucine degradation 396
– in α-methyl-β-alanine degradation 401
– in norleucine degradation 396
– in L-threonine degradation 397
– in valine degradation 396
Propyl red indicator 283
Prostaglandins 373, 492
– in semen 685
Prostate, carcinoma, serum acid phosphatase 596
– 5′-nucleotidase 418
– secretion .... 682 sq.
– weight 710
Prosthetic groups 382, 385
Protactinium, properties, isotopes, etc. 246
Protamine, reference preparation 763
– sulphate, haemorrhagic diatheses and 623
Proteases. See Proteolytic enzymes
Proteins 329
– in bile 655
– biosynthesis 353, 354
– in whole blood 579
– in whole body, gain in pregnancy 690
– in body fluids 523
– in brain and spinal cord 520
– calorific value and respiratory quotient for 539
– in cerebrospinal fluid 637
– conversion factors 523
– dietary requirements .... 493 sq.
– enzymes attacking. See Proteolytic enzymes
– in erythrocytes 579
– in faeces 659
– in foods .... 498 sq.
– in gastric juice 650
– – urinary concentration and 534
– intake, blood urea and 572
– in intestinal juice 656
– ionized, buffer capacity in blood 527
– in leucocytes 579
– metabolism, effect of corticosteroids 749
– – effect of growth hormone 720
– – effect of oestrogens 757
– – effect of testosterone 752
– – water from 524
– in milk 511, 688
– nitrogen, in blood 572
– – conversion factors 251
– in pancreatic juice 652
– para-. See Paraproteins
– in plasma. See Plasma proteins
– in saliva 645
– in semen 684
– in serum (*see also Plasma proteins*) 579, 582
– sulphur, in blood 563
– in synovial fluid 641
– in thrombocytes 579
– in tissues 522
– in urine 453, 668
Protein-bound carbohydrates. See Glycoproteins
Protein disulphide reductase, insulin degradation by 736
Proteinuria in cystinosis 449
Proteolipidprotein in brain and spinal cord . 520
Proteolytic enzymes .... 405 sq.
– in gastric juice 650
– in pancreatic juice 652
– precursors 406, 407
Prothrombin 622
– deficiency 449
– – vitamin K and 467, 468
– thrombin from 410
Prothrombin time 625
Protocollagen 432
Protohaem. See Haem
Proton, charge: mass ratio 229
– COMPTON wave length 229
– gyromagnetic ratio 229
– magnetic moment 229
– mass 229
– rest mass 229
Protoporphyria, erythropoietic 455, 576
Protoporphyrin 355, 358
– in erythrocytes 455, 576
– in faeces 659
– in haem synthesis 454
– in serum 576
Protoporphyrinogen in haem synthesis 454
Provitamins 461, 462
Provitamin, animal. See 7-Dehydrocholesterol
Prunes, composition 501
PS (metric horsepower) 214
Pseudohyperparathyroidism 728
Pseudouridine 354
– in s-RNA 351
– in urine 671
Pseudovitamin B_{12} 483
Psicose (D-allulose) 311
Psoriasis, uric acid excretion 671
PSP (phenolsulphonphthalein) test 532, 533
pt (pint) 204
Pt. See Platinum
$PteGlu_3$ (pteroyltriglutamic acid) 480
$PteGlu_7$ (pteroylheptaglutamic acid) 480
Pteridines, folic acid synthesis from 478
Pterins, unconjugated, in blood 610
Pteroylglutamic acid. See Folic acid
Pteroylheptaglutamic acid ($PteGlu_7$) 480
Pteroyltriglutamic acid ($PteGlu_3$) 480
Ptyalin in saliva 646
Pu (plutonium) 248
Puberty, bone development and 706, 707
– pseudo-precocious, and ossification 707
Puerperium, urinary creatine 665
Pulmonary circulation 543, 544
– embolism, serum enzyme changes 587
– resistance 546
– – in children, determination 549
– – values 552
Pulsatance units 208
Pumpkins, composition 505
Purine 336
Purines 338
– biosynthesis .... 433 sq., 479
– in blood 577
– in faeces 659
– folic acid synthesis from 478
– metabolism .... 399 sq.
– – inborn errors 453
– in urine 671
Purine deaminases 401
Purine nucleoside phosphorylase 418
– in purine degradation 400, 401
Purine oxidases 401
Purpura 455
Purslane, composition 505
Putrescine, formation from ornithine 394
– in semen 684
PVI. See Polyvinylpyrrolidone
Pyelonephritis, chronic, fluid deprivation test in 535
Pyramid, geometry 142
Pyran 308
Pyranoses .... 308 sq.
Pyridine 336
Pyridine-3-carboxylamide 477
Pyridine-3-carboxylic acid. See Nicotinic acid
Pyridine nucleotides, in biological oxidations 402, 404
– redox potential 403
Pyridoxal 473, 474
– phosphate 473, 474
– – in blood 610
– – in enzymatic reactions 475
– – in glycogen phosphorylase 411
Pyridoxal kinase in vitamin B_6 interconversions 473, 475
Pyridoxamine 474
– phosphate 473, 474
– – in enzymatic reactions 475
Pyridoxamine phosphate oxidase in vitamin B_6 interconversions 473
Pyridoxic acid 473, 474
– in blood 610
– in urine 676

A detailed index to the statistical tables (pages 28–131) and chapter on Statistical Methods (pages 146–196) will be found on pages 197–198

Pyridoxine 473, 474
– phosphate in vitamin B_6 interconversions. 473
Pyridoxine dehydrogenase in vitamin B_6 interconversions 473
Pyridoxol. See Pyridoxine
Pyrimidine 336
– in thiamine 469, 470
Pyrimidines 338
– formation 438, 439
– metabolism 399, 401
– – inborn errors 453
– in urine 671
Pyrimidine nucleoside phosphorylase 418
Pyrocatechol in urine 675
Pyrogen, reference preparation 763
L-Pyroglutamyl-L-histidyl-L-prolinamide ... 809
Pyrophosphatases 405
Pyrophosphatase, inorganic 416
– – in milk 689
– – in urea cycle 442, 443
Pyrophosphate, energy storage by 336, 404
– in urine 663
Pyrophosphotransferases 386
Pyrrole 355
– derivatives, metabolic errors 454, 455
Pyrrolidine-α-carboxylic acid. See Proline
Pyrroline-5-carboxylate dehydrogenase in hyperprolinaemia 449
Pyrroline-5-carboxylate reductase, in hyperprolinaemia 449
– in proline and hydroxyproline formation . 432
L-Δ^1-Pyrroline-5-carboxylic acid, in L-proline degradation 395
– in proline and hydroxyproline formation . 432
Pyruvate, in alcoholic fermentation 390
– in amino-sugar utilization 424
– in blood 607
– in carbohydrate synthesis and breakdown. 441
– addition of carbon dioxide 424
– in cerebrospinal fluid 639
– in L-cysteine degradation 397
– cysteinesulphinic acid from 438
– formation, by erythrocytes 616
– – by thrombocytes 621
– in glycolysis 389
– in L-hydroxyproline degradation 395
– in semen 685
– in serine degradation 397
– in oxidation of sugars 391
– in sweat 681
– in transamination reactions 394, 420
– in urine 674
Pyruvate carboxylase, biotin in 487
– in carbohydrate synthesis 441
– molecular weight 382
Pyruvate kinase (PK), activity gradients 586
– in glycolysis 389
– isozymes 584
– in plasma 594
– – effect of muscular work 586
– tissue activities 585
Pyruvic acid. See Pyruvate
– enol phosphate (*see also Phosphopyruvate*) .. 317

Q

Q-fever antiserum, standard 760
qr (quarter) 205
qt (quart) 205
Quadratic equations, solution 137
Quadrilateral, geometry 141, 142
Quality factor, radiation 221
Quantum of action 228
Quantum-mechanical unit of angular momentum 228
Quart 204
– dry 204
– liquid 204
Quarter 204, 205
QUECKENSTEDT test 635
Quinces, composition 501
Quinolinic acid in tryptophan degradation . 399

R

r (revolution) 208
r (roentgen) 218
r (correlation coefficient) .... 178 sq.
R (roentgen) 218
°R (degree Rankine) 208
Ra. See Radium
Rabbit, composition 513
Rabies antiserum, standard 760
– vaccine, reference preparation 759
Racemases 386
– vitamin B_6 and 475
Racemates 309
rad (radian) 207, 208
Rad 218
Radian 207, 208
Radiance 222
Radiant quantities and units 222
Radiation constants, PLANCK 228
– dosimetry .... 217 sq., 286, 287
– protection 221
– units .... 217 sq.
Radioactinium (^{227}Th), properties 245
Radioactive disintegration 217, 285, 286
– labelling 285
Radioactivity units .... 217 sq.
Radioimmunological methods 290
Radio-iodine. See Iodine-131
Radioisotopes. See Radionuclides
Radionuclides .... 217, 285 sq.
– decay tables .... 294 sq.
– diagnostic use 287
– dosimetry .... 217 sq., 286, 287
– half-life .... 217, 234 sq.
– therapeutic use 290, 291
Radiotherapy 290, 291
Radiothorium (^{228}Th), properties 245
Radishes, composition 505
Radium, properties, isotopes, etc. 245
Radium-226, therapeutic use 290
Radium-228, properties 245
Radium A (^{218}Po), properties 244
Radium B (^{214}Pb), properties 243
Radium C (^{214}Bi), properties 243
Radium C′ (^{214}Po), properties 244
Radium C″ (^{210}Tl), properties 243
Radium D (^{210}Pb), properties 243
Radium E (^{210}Bi), properties 243
Radium E″ (^{206}Tl), properties 242
Radium F (^{210}Po), properties 244
Radium G (^{206}Pb), properties 243
Radon, properties, isotopes, etc. 244
Raisins, composition 502
Random numbers 131
Rankine temperature scale 208, 209
Rank tests 192, 193
– tables .... 124 sq.
Rare-earth elements 231
Raspberries, composition 502
Rational numbers 132
Rat uterus test 722
Rb. See Rubidium
RBC (red blood count) 613, 614, 617
RBE (relative biological effectiveness) 221
RBF (renal blood flow) 531
RBP (retinol binding protein) 809
rd (rad) 218
rd (rod) 200
Re (rhenium) 241
Real numbers 132
Recalcification time 625
Reciprocals of factorials 27
– of integers 18
– of square roots 23
Reciprocal centimetre 213
– ohm 216
– second 208, 213, 217
Rectangular coordinates 138, 143, 144
Red blood count (RBC) 613, 614, 617
Reduced-NAD(P): oxidized-glutathione oxidoreductase. See Glutathione reductase
Reducing substances, in bile 655
– in blood 604, 605
– in cerebrospinal fluid 639
– in pancreatic juice 652
– in saliva 646
– in sweat 681
– in synovial fluid 642
– in urine 673
Reduction of gas volumes 269
Reference preparations, international biological .... 759 sq.
– protein, FAO/WHO 516
– subject in nutrition 493, 494
REFSUM's syndrome, phytanic acid 371
Regressions .... 174 sq.
Relative atomic masses of nuclides 226
– biological effectiveness (RBE) 221
– density 210
Rem 221
Renal (*see also Kidneys*) acidosis 449, 452, 453
– – in vitamin D deficiency 461
Renal blood flow (RBF) 531
– concentrating capacity 534
– cortex, enzyme activities 585
– extraction 531
– failure, acute, fluid deprivation test 535
– – blood, α-amylase 597
– – – lactate 607
– – – nonprotein nitrogen 532
– – chronic, excretion of organic acids 674
– filtration fraction 531
– free-water clearance, maximum 533
– function, effect of growth hormone 720
– – parathyroid hormone and 728
– – values .... 531 sq.
– glomeruli. See under Glomerular
– glucosuria 452
– haemodynamics .... 531 sq.
– inulin clearance 531
– – plasma creatinine and nonprotein nitrogen and 532
– iodide clearance 726
– medulla, enzyme activities 585
– PAH clearance 531
– – and PSP test 533
– plasma clearances 531
– plasma flow 531, 535
– radiography 289
– respiratory rate 387
– transport maxima 534, 535
– transport mechanisms, inborn errors 452
– tubules. See Tubules
Renin 740, 741
– in plasma 598
Renin–angiotensin system 740, 741
Rennin 407
Reovirus antiserum, reference reagent 764
Reproductive organs, weights 710
Residual volume of air in lungs (RV) 541, 542, 550, 551
Resistance, electric 216
Resistivity, electric 216
Resorcin yellow indicator 283
Respiration .... 541 sq.
– blood gases and 544, 545
Respiratory acidosis and alkalosis 527
– chain 403
– loop 546
– mechanics 545, 546
– quotient (RQ) 539
– rate 550
– – of animal tissues 387
– time quotient 543, 550
Resting metabolic rate 495
Reticular cells in bone marrow 621
Reticulocytes 612, 613
Reticulocyte count 612, 613
– mean corpuscular volume and 615
– erythrocyte coproporphyrin content and . 575
– erythrocyte protoporphyrin content and . 576
Reticulo-endothelial system, cystine deposition in 449
Reticulosis, serum adenosine deaminase 599
Retina, lactic acid fermentation 388
– 5′-nucleotidase 418
– respiratory rate 387
Retinal 459
– isomerization 460
– in visual pigments 457
11-*cis*-Retinal 459
– in isomerization of retinal 460
Retinaldehyde. See Retinal
Retinal isomerase in isomerization of retinal 460
Retinene$_1$. See Retinal
Retinene$_2$. See Vitamin A_2 aldehyde
α-Retinene. See Vitamin A_2 aldehyde
β-Retinene. See Retinal
all-trans-Retinol 458
– isomerization 460
11-*cis*-Retinol 458
– isomerization 460
Retinol binding protein (RBP) 809
Retraction. See Blood-clot retraction
Rh. See Rhesus
Rh. See Rhodium
L-Rhamnose 313
Rhenium, properties, isotopes, etc. 241
Rhesus blood-group system .... 628 sq.
– clinical significance 633
Rhesus genotypes of English people 630
Rheumatic fever, indoxylsulphuric acid excretion 669
Rheumatoid arthritis, reference antiserum .. 761
– serum pantothenic acid in 611
– synovial fluid in 641

A detailed index to the statistical tables (pages 28–131) and chapter on Statistical Methods (pages 146–196) will be found on pages 197–198

Rheumatoid factor, serum viscosity and.... 558
Rh-Hr phenomena and genotypes......... 629
Rhizopterin.......................... 480
Rhodium, flame lines.................. 284
– properties, isotopes, etc............ 238
Rhodopsin........................... 457
– in isomerization of retinal........... 460
Rhubarb, composition................. 505
Ribitol.............................. 322
Ribitol teichoic acids, formation........ 349
Riboflavin........................ 471 sq.
– antagonists........................ 472
– in blood...................... 471, 609
– deficiency......................... 472
– dietary requirements............ 472, 493
– in erythrocytes................. 471, 473
– in foods...................... 499 sq.
– – losses during cooking............. 498
– in leucocytes...................... 471
– in milk............................ 689
– 5′-phosphate. See Flavin mononucleotide
– in tryptophan metabolism............ 475
– in urine................... 471, 473, 676
D-Ribofuranose. See D-Ribose
Ribonuclease (RNAase).............. 406, 418
– in cerebrospinal fluid............... 638
– in gastric juice..................... 650
– isozymes.......................... 584
– pancreatic, reactions catalysed by...... 406
– in pancreatic juice.................. 652
– structure and synthesis.............. 382
– in urine........................... 672
Ribonucleic acid (RNA)............. 351 sq.
– amino-acid acceptor................ 351
– biosynthesis....................... 352
– – effect of testosterone............. 753
– enzymatic cleavage.................. 406
– depolymerization................... 418
– in leucocytes...................... 578
– messenger.................... 351, 353
– – formation, effect of corticosteroids.... 749
– ribosomal......................... 351
– soluble....................... 351, 353
– transfer...................... 351, 353
– viral, synthesis..................... 352
Ribonucleosides...................... 337
Ribonucleotides...................... 337
5′-Ribonucleotide phosphohydrolase. See 5′-Nucleotidase
Ribonucleotide reductase, vitamin B_{12} in... 485
D-Ribose...................... 310, 314
– in bile............................ 655
– in saliva.......................... 646
D-Ribose 1,5-diphosphate.............. 318
D-Ribose 1-phosphate................. 317
– formation from nucleosides...... 339, 340
– in purine degradation............... 400
D-Ribose 5-phosphate................. 318
– formation from glucose.............. 420
– in inosinic acid formation........... 433
– in degradation of pentoses........... 399
– in pentose phosphate cycle...... 421, 422
Ribosephosphate isomerase, in cerebrospinal fluid.............................. 638
– in pentose phosphate cycle........... 422
– in plasma......................... 600
D-Ribose-5-phosphate ketol-isomerase. See Ribosephosphate isomerase
D-Ribose 5-phosphate-1-pyrophosphate.... 318
– in inosinic acid formation........... 433
– in pyrimidine synthesis.............. 439
'Ribosides'.......................... 337
Ribosomes................ 351, 353, 354
Ribosyladenine. See Adenosine
Ribosyladenine 5′-phosphate. See Adenosine monophosphate
Ribosylamine 5′-phosphate............. 342
– biosynthesis....................... 453
– in inosinic acid formation........... 433
Ribosyl-5-amino-4-carboxyimidazole 5′-phosphate in inosinic acid formation.. 435
1-Ribosyl-5-aminoimidazole-4-carboxamide 5′-phosphate........................ 342
– in inosinic acid formation........... 435
1-Ribosyl-5-aminoimidazole 5′-phosphate.. 342
– in inosinic acid formation....... 433, 435
Ribosyl-5-amino-4-succinocarboxamidoimidazole 5′-phosphate in inosinic acid formation 435
Ribosylbases......................... 337
– phosphates........................ 337
Ribosylcytosine. See Cytidine
Ribosyl-5-formamido-4-carboxamidoimidazole 5′-phosphate in inosinic acid formation 435
Ribosylformylglycinamide 5′-phosphate.... 342
Ribosylformylglycinamide 5′-phosphate in inosinic acid formation.............. 433
Ribosylformylglycinamidine 5′-phosphate.. 342
– in inosinic acid formation........... 433
Ribosylglycinamide 5′-phosphate......... 342
– in inosinic acid formation........... 433
Ribosylguanine. See Guanosine
N^2-Ribosylguanine.................. 354
Ribosylhypoxanthine. See Inosine
Ribosylorotic acid 5′-phosphate. See Orotidine monophosphate
Ribosyluracil........................ 340
5-Ribosyluracil. See Pseudouridine
Ribosyluric acid..................... 341
Ribosylxanthine. See Xanthosine
'Ribotides'.......................... 337
D-Ribulose.................... 311, 314
– 5-phosphate........................ 318
– – in pentose phosphate cycle...... 421, 422
– in urine........................... 673
Ribulosephosphate 3-epimerase in pentose phosphate cycle...................... 422
Rice, amino acids.................... 516
– composition........................ 508
Ricinoleic acid...................... 372
Rickets................... 453, 461, 464
– serum alkaline phosphatase........... 596
– vitamin D-resistant.......... 449, 452, 453
Rifamycin SV, reference preparation...... 762
Right angle.................... 207, 208
RINGER infusion solutions............. 529
Ristocetins, reference preparations....... 762
RMR (resting metabolic rate)........... 495
Rn (radon).......................... 244
RNA. See Ribonucleic acid
RNAase. See Ribonuclease
RNA nucleotidyl transferase....... 352, 353
RNA polymerase.............. 352, 353
ROBISON ester. See D-Glucose 6-phosphate
ROBISON-TANKO ester. See D-Fructose 1-phosphate
Rod (unit).......................... 200
Rod vision quantities................. 223
Roentgen........................... 219
Rolitetracycline, standard.............. 761
Rood............................... 203
Roots (arithmetic)................. 132 sq.
– square, tables..................... 20 sq.
Rosolic acid indicator................. 283
Rotational frequency units............. 208
ROTOR syndrome..................... 454
– serum bilirubin..................... 577
Round cells......................... 614
ROUS sarcoma, lactic acid fermentation..... 388
– respiratory rate.................... 387
RQ (respiratory quotient).............. 539
RSH. See Coenzyme A
Ru. See Ruthenium
Rubella antiserum, reference preparation... 761
Rubidium, in blood................... 567
– flame lines........................ 284
– properties, isotopes, etc............ 237
– in synovial fluid.................... 641
Rubidium-86, characteristics............ 292
Rum, composition.................... 509
Runs.......................... 194, 195
– tables........................ 129, 130
Rutabagas, composition............... 506
Ruthenium, flame lines................ 284
– properties, isotopes, etc............ 238
RV (residual volume of air in lungs)................ 541, 542, 550, 551
Ry (rydberg)........................ 213
Rydberg............................ 213
RYDBERG constants................... 229
Rye, amino acids..................... 516
Rye bread, composition................ 508
Rye flour, composition................ 508

S

σ (standard deviation)................. 158
σ^2 (variance)........................ 158
s (scruple)......................... 205
s (second).......................... 205
s^{-1} (reciprocal second)............ 208, 213
s (estimate of standard deviation)........ 159
s^2 (estimate of variance)............... 159
S. See Sulphur
Saccharase in intestinal mucosa.......... 413
– in sucrose intolerance............... 451
Saccharic acids...................... 312
Saccharides...................... 308 sq.
Saccharose. See Sucrose
Safflower oil, composition.............. 510
SAHLI percentages.................... 615
Salami, composition.................. 514
Salicylic acid solutions, pH values........ 279
Saliva.......................... 643 sq.
– amount...................... 525, 643
– α-amylase................. 411, 645, 646
– corticosteroids in plasma and.......... 745
– electrolytes................. 525, 643 sq.
– lipase............................ 414
– lysozyme...................... 413, 645
Salmon, composition.................. 515
Salsify, composition.................. 506
Salt, table, iodination................. 497
Salts............................... 270
Salt-losing nephritis.............. 662, 663
Samarium, flame lines................ 284
– properties, isotopes, etc............ 240
Sarcoma, lactic acid fermentation........ 388
– respiratory rate.................... 387
Sardines, composition................. 515
SAT (Stepped Atomic Time)............ 207
Sauerkraut, composition............... 506
Sausages, composition............. 513, 514
sb (stilb)........................... 223
Sb. See Antimony
Sc. See Scandium
Scallops, composition................. 515
Scandium, flame lines................. 284
– properties, isotopes, etc............ 235
Scarlet fever streptococcus antitoxin, standard........................... 760
SCHAPIRA enzyme units................ 584
SCHICK test toxin, standard............ 759
SCHILLING's haemogram............... 620
SCHILLING's test................. 289, 485
Scintigraphy, thyroid.............. 288, 289
Scintillation counters................. 286
Sclerosis, multiple, cerebrospinal fluid γ-globulin.......................... 637
Scotopic vision quantities.............. 223
Scruple............................ 205
Scurvy............................. 490
Scyllitol in urine..................... 673
SDH (sorbitol dehydrogenase). See L-Iditol dehydrogenase
Se. See Selenium
Sea foods, composition............ 514, 515
9,10-Secocholesta-5,7,10(19)-trien-3β-ol. See Vitamin D_3
Seco-compounds..................... 381
Second......................... 205 sq.
– reciprocal.................... 208, 213
Second (angle).................. 207, 208
Secretin........................ 651, 739
Secretin test.................... 651, 652
Secretors of ABH substances........... 631
Sedimentation constants of plasma proteins. 580
Sedimentation rate, erythrocyte...... 558, 559
D-Sedoheptulose................. 311, 316
– 1,7-diphosphate.................... 321
– – in erythrocytes................... 605
– 7-phosphate....................... 321
– – in pentose phosphate cycle...... 421, 422
– in urine........................... 673
Sedoheptulose-7-phosphate: D-glyceraldehyde-3-phosphate glycolaldehydetransferase in plasma...................... 593
Segmented cells, in blood.......... 619, 620
– in bone marrow.................... 621
Selacholeic acid................. 369, 377
Selenium, in blood................... 567
– dietary requirements................ 497
– in milk........................... 688
– properties, isotopes, etc............ 237
Selenium-75, characteristics............ 292
– decay table....................... 299
Semen.......................... 682 sq.
– 5′-nucleotidase.................... 418
– oestrogens........................ 755
Semidehydroascorbic acid.............. 490
Seminal vesicles, secretion.......... 682 sq.
– weight........................... 710
Seminose. See D-Mannose
Semolina, composition................ 508
Sequential analysis charts.... (inside back cover)
Ser. See L-Serine
L-Serine (Ser)....................... 332
– in blood.......................... 574
– in blood proteins................... 581
– cell constituents from............... 434
– decarboxylation.................... 394
– degradation................ 396, 397, 402

A detailed index to the statistical tables (pages 28–131) and chapter on Statistical Methods (pages 146–196) will be found on pages 197–198

L-Serine, in foods 516
– formation from glucose 420, 432
– glycine from 432
– in glycine degradation 397
– in L-homocysteine degradation 398
– as lipid component 365
– in milk 688
– in phosphatidyl esters 375
– in synthesis of purines and methionine 479
– in saliva 645
– in sweat 680
– in thyroid hormone formation 440
– in transamination reactions 394
– in urine 667
L-Serine dehydratase, in homocystinuria 449
– in serine degradation 396
Serine hydroxymethyltransferase, in glycine formation 432
– vitamin B_6 and 475
α_1-Seromucoid. See α_1-Glycoprotein, acid
Serotonin, in blood 575
– in cerebrospinal fluid 637
– degradation 441
– formation 394, 441
– function 434
– and haemorrhagic diatheses 623, 624
– in pineal gland 730
– in thrombocytes 575
– in urine 669
Serum (*see also Plasma*), albumin-globulin ratio 582
– α-amino acids in plasma and 573
– enzyme activities in plasma and 586
– proteins 579, 582
– – fractions 582
– specific gravity 557
– surface tension 559
– thrombin 410
– viscosity 558
Serum groups 634, 809
Serum water, electrolyte composition 523
SGOT (serum glutamate-oxalacetate transaminase). See Aspartate aminotransferase
SGPT (serum glutamate-pyruvate transaminase). See Alanine aminotransferase
sh cwt (short hundredweight) 205
Sheep's milk, composition 511
SHINOWARA enzyme units 584
Short ton 205
Shoulder, secondary ossification centres 706, 708
– width during growth 695 sq.
Shrimps, composition 515
sh tn (short ton) 205
Shunt volume, intrapulmonary 544
Si. See Silicon
SI (International System of Units) 200 sq.
Sialic acids 311, 316
– effect on electrophoretic mobility of blood cells 560
– in brain and spinal cord 520
– in cerebrospinal fluid 637
– formation 423
– in gangliosides 377
– in gastric juice 650
– in plasma 606
– in saliva 645
– in semen 684
– in synovial fluid 642
– in urine 673
Sialomucins, in gastric juice 650
– in saliva 645
SIBLEY-LEHNINGER enzyme units 584
Sickle cells. See Erythrocytes, sickle-cell
Sickle-cell anaemia. See under Anaemia
Sickle-cell trait 448
Sidereal year 206
β_1-Siderophilin. See Transferrin
Siemens 216
Significance tests 156 sq.
Silicate, in blood 564
– in pancreatic juice 652
– in skin, hair and nails 520
– in urine 664
Silicon, atomic weight multiples 250
– properties, isotopes, etc. 235
Silver, flame lines 284
– freezing point 209
– nitrate, decinormal solutions 277
– properties, isotopes, etc. 238
– in urine 664
Silver-111, characteristics 293
$\sin^{-1}$ (arc sine) 139
Sine 138, 139
β-Sitosterol, synthesis 426
Sitting height during growth 693 sq.
SI units 200 sq.
SJÖGREN's syndrome, salivary secretion 643
Skeletal development 706 sq.
Skin, composition 520, 522
– lactic acid fermentation 388
– pigmentation 455
– respiratory rate 387
– vitamin D 461
– water loss from 524
SLR factor (rhizopterin) 480
Sm. See Samarium
Smallpox antiserum, standard 760
– vaccine, reference preparation 759
Sn. See Tin
Snails, composition 515
Soaps 365
Sodium, in amniotic fluid 522
– atomic weight multiples 250
– in bile 654
– in whole body 517, 518
– in body fluids 523, 525
– in bones 521
– in cerebrospinal fluid 636
– conversion factors 251, 523
– dietary requirements 496
– in electrolyte balance 525
– in erythrocytes 565
– exchangeable 518, 526
– in faeces 658
– flame lines 284
– in foods 499 sq.
– in gastric juice 649
– glomerular filtration and excretion 536
– in hair and nails 520
– in intestinal juice 656
– in milk 688
– in muscle 518
– in organs 519
– in pancreatic juice 652
– in placenta 522
– in plasma 565
– gain in pregnancy 690
– properties, isotopes, etc. 234
– in saliva 644
– in semen 683
– in skin 520
– in sweat 680
– in synovial fluid 641
– in teeth 521
– in urine 663
Sodium-22, characteristics 292
– decay table 294
– gamma ray constant 221
Sodium-24, specific activity 217
– characteristics 292
– decay table 294
– gamma ray constant 221
Sodium acetate, buffer 280 sq.
– solutions, conversion factors 274 sq.
– – pH values 279
Sodium aminosalicylate, solutions, conversion factors 274 sq.
Sodium benzoate solutions, pH values 279
Sodium bicarbonate, solutions, conversion factors 274 sq.
– – decinormal 277
– – for infusion 529
– – pH values 279
– effect on urinary osmolarity and specific gravity 534
Sodium bisulphate solutions, pH values 279
Sodium borate buffer 280 sq.
Sodium bromide solutions, conversion factors 274 sq.
Sodium carbonate, buffer 280 sq.
– solutions, decinormal 277
– – pH values 279
Sodium chloride, conversion factor, into chlorine 251
– – into sodium 251
– solutions, calculation 271, 273
– – conversion factors 274 sq.
– – decinormal 277
– – for infusion 529
– effect on urinary osmolarity and specific gravity 534
Sodium citrate, buffers 280 sq.
– solutions, conversion factors 274 sq.
Sodium dihydrogen phosphate, effect on urinary osmolarity and specific gravity 534
Sodium hydroxide, solutions, decinormal 277
– – pH values 279
Sodium lactate solutions, conversion factors 274 sq.
Sodium oxide, conversion factor into sodium 251
– solutions, conversion factors 274 sq.
– – decinormal 277
Sodium phosphates, solutions, conversion factors 274 sq.
– – decinormal 277
– – pH values 279
Sodium salicylate solutions, conversion factors 274 sq.
Sodium sulphate solutions, conversion factors 274 sq.
Sodium sulphide, decinormal solutions 277
Sodium tetraborate, decinormal solutions 277
– decahydrate. See Borax
Sodium thiosulphate solutions, conversion factors 274 sq.
Soft drinks, carbonated, composition 509
Solar time units 205, 206
Solid angles, units 207, 208
Soluble RNA 351, 353
Solutions (*see also Electrolytes*) 270 sq.
– buffer 280 sq.
– concentration, measures 271
– – temperature variation 251
– decinormal, of reagents 277
– dissociation 278, 279
– ideal and real 270
– infusion. See Infusion solutions
– isotonic. See Isotonic solutions
– osmotic properties 270, 271
– viscosity 214
Somatotropic hormone. See Growth hormone
Somatotropin. See Growth hormone
Somatotropin-releasing factor 720
SOMMERFELD fine-structure constant 228
SOMOGYI enzyme units 584
Sone 225
Sorbic acid 370
Sorbitol 322
– in semen 685
Sorbitol dehydrogenase (SDH). See L-Iditol dehydrogenase
D-Sorbose 311
Sound levels 225, 226
– quantities and units 224 sq.
– velocity 225
– – at various altitudes 252 sq.
Soybeans, amino acids 516
– composition 506
Soybean flour, amino acids 516
– composition 508
Spaghetti, composition 508
Span 200
SPEARMAN correlation coefficient 181, 182
– tables 66 sq.
Specific activity of nuclides 217
– gamma ray constant 221
– gravity 210
– weight 210
Spectral quantities 224
Spectrometric units 201
Sperm. See Semen and Spermatozoa
Spermatocrit 686
Spermatozoa, composition 682 sq.
– role of hyaluronidase 413, 684
– maturation, vitamin B_{12} in 485
– number and structure 686
– properties 682, 686
Spermidine, in blood 575
– in semen 684
Spermine, in blood 575
– in semen 684
Sphere, geometry 143
Spherocytes 614
– osmotic resistance 616
Sphingolipids 365, 376, 377
Sphingomyelins 365, 376
– accumulation 456
– in brain and spinal cord 520
– in cerebrospinal fluid 638
– enzymatic cleavage 417
– in erythrocytes 604
– lignoceric acid in 367
– in plasma 604
– selacholeic acid in 369
Sphingosine 376
– in lipids 365
Spinach, amino acids 516
– composition 506
Spinal cord, composition 519, 520
– fluid. See Cerebrospinal fluid
Spiramycin, reference preparation 762
Spirometer values, conversion 259 sq.

A detailed index to the statistical tables (pages 28–131) and chapter on Statistical Methods (pages 146–196) will be found on pages 197–198

Spleen, animal, composition 512
– cathepsins 410
– composition 519
– enlargement 455, 456
– glycosidases 412, 413
– lactic acid fermentation 388
– lipid accumulation 455
– nucleases 418, 419
– acid phosphatase 415
– respiratory rate 387
– weight 710
– xanthine oxidase 419
Sprue, serum caeruloplasmin 593
Squalene 374
– in cholesterol synthesis 426, 427
Squares, tables 20 sq.
Square degree and grade 207, 208
– measures 202, 203
– roots, extraction with calculators 24, 25
– – reciprocals 23
– – tables 20 sq.
Squash, composition 506
sr (steradian) 207
Sr. See Strontium
s-RNA (soluble RNA) 351, 353
st (stere) 203
St (stokes) 214
Stab cells, in blood 619, 620
– in bone marrow 621
Standard BMR values 540
– density 209
– deviation 47, 48, 158
– substances 230
– temperature and pressure, dry (STPD) 260, 541
Standards and reference preparations, international biological 759 sq.
Staphylococcal P-V leucocidin antiserum, reference preparation 761
Staphylococcus α antitoxin, standard 760
Starch, enzymatic digestion 411, 412
– A-fraction. See Amylose
– B-fraction. See Amylopectin
– liver. See Glycogen
Statistical methods 145 sq.
– tables 28 sq.
Stearic acid 367
– in brain gangliosides 377
– in depot fat 374
– in milk 687
– in serum lipids 604
Stearidonic acid 370
Stearolic acid 371
6-Stearolic acid 371
Steatorrhoea, faecal fats 660
– idiopathic, faecal porphyrins 659
– – in vitamin D deficiency 461
Stefan-Boltzmann constant 228
Stellar time 205, 206
Stepped Atomic Time 207
Steradian 207, 208
Stercobilin 362, 364
– in faeces 657
Stercobilinogen 362, 364
Stere 203
Stereochemistry of steroids 378
– of sugars 308 sq.
Steroids 378 sq.
– hydroxy-. See Hydroxysteroids
– keto-. See Ketosteroids
Steroid hormones (*see also Corticosteroids*) 381
– of adrenal cortex. See Corticosteroids
– of gonads, synthesis and metabolism 428 sq.
– progestational 379, 380, 753 sq.
– synthetic 750
Steroid hydroxylases, deficiency 456
Sterols 377
– biosynthesis 426
– in faeces 659, 660
– in foods 498 sq.
– in spermatozoa 685
Steryl esters 365, 377
– in faeces 659
STH (somatotropic hormone). See Growth hormone
Stigmastane in steroids 381
Stilb 223
Stokes 214
Stomach cancer, gastric juice 647
– – albumin 650
– – carbohydrates 650
– – pepsin 650
Stomach muscle, enzyme activities 585
Stomach ulcers, gastric acidity and 648
Stone 205
Stools, daily number 657
STPD (standard temperature and pressure, dry) 260, 541
Strawberries, composition 502
Streptidine 322
Streptokinase-streptodornase, standard 763
Streptomycin, standard 761
Stress, effect on ACTH secretion 716, 717
– and haemorrhagic diatheses 623, 624
Strontium, in bone 521
– in faeces 658
– flame lines 284
– properties, isotopes, etc. 237
– in urine 664
Strontium-89, characteristics 292
– decay table 300
Strontium-90, in bone 521
– characteristics 292
– decay table 300, 301
– therapeutic use 290
Student distribution 166
– tables 32–35, 42
Submandibular saliva. See Saliva
Submaxillary gland, lactic acid fermentation 388
– respiratory rate 387
Submultiples, prefixes and symbols 9
Substance, amount of 226, 227
Substance S. See 11-Deoxycortisol
Succinate, in α-aminobutyric acid degradation 396
– in biological oxidations 403
– in cerebrospinal fluid 639
– in degradation of fats 392, 393
– from degradation of foods 402
– in isoleucine degradation 396
– from α-methyl-β-alanine 401
– in plasma 607
– in tricarboxylic acid cycle 390, 391
– in urine 674
– in wine 509
Succinate dehydrogenase, in cerebrospinal fluid 638
– in plasma 592
– prosthetic group 345
– in spermatozoa 684
– in tricarboxylic acid cycle 390, 391
Succinate:(acceptor) oxidoreductase. See Succinate dehydrogenase
Succinic acid (*see also Succinate*), solutions, decinormal 277
– – pH values 279
Succinic semialdehyde in transamination reactions 394
Succinyladenosine 5′-phosphate. See Adenylosuccinic acid
Succinyladenylic acid. See Adenylosuccinic acid
Succinyl-coenzyme A, in ATP synthesis 404
– in degradation of fats 392, 393
– in glycine degradation 397
– haem synthesis from 454
– in porphyrin formation 437
– in tricarboxylic acid cycle 390, 391
Suckling stimulus 719
– effect on oxytocin release 723
Sucrose 324
– composition 509
– intolerance 451
– in urine 673
Sugars (*see also Carbohydrates*) 308 sq.
Sugar phosphates 312, 317 sq.
– in erythrocytes 605
– in saliva 644
Sulf-. See Sulph-
Sulphaemoglobin 361
Sulphanilamide, acetylation 444
Sulpharsphenamine, reference preparation 763
Sulphatases 386, 405
Sulphate, active 445
– in blood 563
– in body fluids 523
– conversion factors 251, 274 sq., 523
– in faeces 658
– inorganic, glomerular filtration and excretion 536
– in lipids 365
– in sweat 679
– in synovial fluid 641
– in urine 663
Sulphate ester formation in detoxication 445
Sulphatides 365, 377
– accumulation 456
6-Sulphatoxyskatole, in plasma 575
– in urine 669
β-Sulphinylpyruvic acid, in cysteinesulphinic acid formation 438
– in L-cysteine degradation 397
Sulphonamides in urinary sediments 677, 678
Sulphotransferases 386
Sulphur, atomic weight multiples 250
– in blood 563
– in cerebrospinal fluid 636
– conversion factors 251
– in erythrocytes 563
– in foods 499 sq.
– in milk 688
– in pancreatic juice 652
– properties, isotopes, etc. 235
– in saliva 644
– trioxide, conversion factor into sulphur 251
– – decinormal solutions 277
– in urine 663
Sulphur-35, characteristics 292
– decay table 295
Sulphuric acid (*see also Sulphate*), decinormal solutions 277
Sulphuric ester hydrolases 386, 405
Sulphurtransferases 386
Surface tension units 215
Susceptibility, electric and magnetic 216
Sutter blood-group system 631
Sweat 679 sq.
– amount 525, 679
– electrolytes 525, 679, 680
– glands, number of 679
– and water loss 496, 679
Sweetbreads, composition 512
Swine erysipelas serum, standard 761
– vaccine, standard 759
Swine-fever antiserum, standard 761
Symbols, of amino acids 330 sq.
– of elements 232, 233
– of hexoses 314, 315
– mathematical 132 sq.
– of nucleotides 343 sq.
– of units 199
Synalbumin 735
Synovial cells in synovial fluid 640
Synovial fluid 640 sq.
Synthases, vitamin B$_6$ and 475
Syphilitic human serum, standard 760

T

t (metric ton) 204
t (troy measure) 205
T (tera-, 10^{12}) 9
T (tesla) 216
T (renal function) 533 sq.
T$_3$. See L-3,5,3′-Tri-iodothyronine
T$_4$. See L-Thyroxine
Ta. See Tantalum
Table salt, iodination 497
Tachycardia, serum enzyme changes 587
Tachysterol in vitamin D$_2$ formation 461, 463
D-Tagatose 311
D-Talose 310
tan (tangent) 138, 139
Tangent 138, 139
Tangerines, composition 502
tanh, tanh^{-1} 140
Tantalum, properties, isotopes, etc. 241
Tantalum-182, characteristics 293
– therapeutic use 290
Tapioca, composition 508
Target cells 614
Tariric acid 371
Tartaric acid, isomers 309
– solutions, decinormal 277
– – pH values 279
– in wine 509
Taurine 335
– in bile 655, 656
– conjugation with bile acids 438
– in blood 574
– formation in liver 394, 438
– in saliva 645
– in sweat 680
– in urine 667
Tay-Sachs' disease 377, 455
Tb. See Terbium
Tc. See Technetium
TDP (thiamine diphosphate). See Thiamine pyrophosphate
Te. See Tellurium
Tea, composition 509
Technetium, properties, isotopes, etc. 237

A detailed index to the statistical tables (pages 28–131) and chapter on Statistical Methods (pages 146–196) will be found on pages 197–198

Technetium-99m, characteristics 293
– decay table 302
– diagnostic use 289
– in thyroid scintigraphy 288, 289
Teeth, composition 521
– development 709
– organic components 522
Teichoic acids 328
– formation 349
Teletherapy with radionuclides 290
Tellurium, flame lines 284
– properties, isotopes, etc. 239
Tellurium-121, characteristics 293
Tellurium-132, characteristics 293
– decay table 302, 303
Temperature scales and units 208, 209
tera- (10^{12}) 9
Terbium, flame lines 284
– properties, isotopes, etc. 240
Teropterin 480
Terpenol pyrophosphate in vitamin A synthesis 457
Tesla 216
Testes, androgens 751
– corticosteroids 746
– glycosidases 413
– lactic acid fermentation 388
– 5′-nucleotidase 418
– oestrogens 755
– progesterone secretion 753
– respiration rate 387
– steroid hormone synthesis 428
– weight 710
Testosterone 380, 751 sq.
– biosynthesis 428, 429
– effect on gonadotropin secretion 714
– in testes 746
Tetanus antitoxin, standard 760
– toxoid, standard 759
Tetany, serum calcium and 565
Tetracosactrin, testing of adrenocortical function 747
$\Delta^{4,8,12,15,18,21}$-Tetracosahexaenoic acid 370
Tetracosanoic acid. See Lignoceric acid
cis-Δ^{15}-Tetracosenoic acid 369, 377
Tetracycline, standard 761
Tetradecanoic acid. See Myristic acid
Δ^4-Tetradecenoic acid 368
Δ^5-Tetradecenoic acid 368
Δ^9-Tetradecenoic acid. See Myristoleic acid
Tetraethylethylenediamine buffer 280 sq.
Tetrahydro-A 380
Tetrahydroaldosterone in urine 746, 747
Tetrahydroaldosterone glucuronide from aldosterone 430
Tetrahydro-B 380
Tetrahydrocorticosterone, breakdown 746
– in urine 747
Tetrahydrocortisol, breakdown 746
– in urine 747
Tetrahydrocortisone, breakdown 746
– in urine 747
Tetrahydro-11-dehydrocorticosterone, breakdown 746
– in urine 747
Tetrahydro-11-deoxycortisol, breakdown 746
– in urine 747
Tetrahydro-E 380
Tetrahydro-F 380
Tetrahydrofolate dehydrogenase, in phenylalanine–tyrosine conversion 439
– in tetrahydrofolic acid synthesis 478
Tetrahydrofolic acid (THF) 481
– dietary requirements 494
– formation 478
– – ascorbic acid in 490
– – from dihydrofolic acid 437
– in glycine formation 432
– in L-histidine degradation 394, 395
– in inosinic acid formation 433, 435
– in transfer of one-carbon groups 436, 437
– in synthesis of purines and methionine 479
(–)-Tetrahydromesobilane 362, 364
(–)-Tetrahydromesobilene-(b). See Stercobilin
Tetrahydropteroylglutamic acid. See Tetrahydrofolic acid
Tetrahydropyridinecarboxylic acids in L-lysine degradation 398
Tetrahydro-S 380
3α,11β,17α,21-Tetrahydroxy-5α-pregnan-20-one. See Allotetrahydrocortisol
3α,11β,17α,21-Tetrahydroxy-5β-pregnan-20-one 380
3α,17α,20α,21-Tetrahydroxy-5α-pregnan-11-one 379
3α,17α,20α,21-Tetrahydroxy-5β-pregnan-11-one 379
3α,17α,20β,21-Tetrahydroxy-5α-pregnan-11-one 379
3α,17α,20β,21-Tetrahydroxy-5β-pregnan-11-one 379
3,5,3′,5′-Tetraiodothyronine. See Thyroxine
3,7,11,15-Tetramethylhexadecanoic acid 371
Tetroses 308, 313
tg (tangent) 138, 139
Th (thorium) 245, 246
Thalassaemias 446 sq.
Thalassaemia major, erythrocyte osmotic resistance 616
Thallium, flame lines 284
– properties, isotopes, etc. 242
Thallium-204, characteristics 293
Thermal conductivity units 215
Thermodynamic constants 228
– temperature scales 208
THF. See Tetrahydrofolic acid
Thiaminase 470
Thiamine 469 sq.
– biosynthesis 469, 470
– in blood 470, 609
– in cerebrospinal fluid 639
– deficiency 470, 471
– dietary requirements 470, 471, 493
– diphosphate. See Thiamine pyrophosphate
– in foods 499 sq.
– – losses during cooking 498
– in leucocytes 470
– in milk 689
– pyrophosphate (TPP) 469, 470
– – coenzyme functions 470
– – in oxidation of sugars 391
– – in transketolase 421
– – in tricarboxylic acid cycle 390, 391
– in spinal fluid 470
– triphosphate, formation 470
– in tryptophan metabolism 475
– in urine 470, 471, 676
Thiazole as component of thiamine 469, 470
Thiochrome 469
Thioctic acid 492
Thiocyanate, in cerebrospinal fluid 636
– in gastric juice 649
– in plasma 564
– in saliva 644
– in urine 663
Thioether hydrolases 386
Thiol compounds, activation of cathepsins 410
– oxidation, vitamin E in 466
– – vitamin B_{12} in 485
Thiolester hydrolases 386
Thiolhistidine betaine. See Ergothioneine
THOMSON cross-sections 229
Thoracic compliance and elastance 545
– tissue resistance 546, 552
Thorium, properties, isotopes, etc. 245, 246
Thorium A (^{216}Po), properties 244
Thorium B (^{212}Pb), properties 243
Thorium C (^{212}Bi), properties 243
Thorium C′ (^{212}Po), properties 244
Thorium C″ (^{208}Tl), properties 242
Thorium X (^{224}Ra), properties 245
THORN's test 747
– action of corticosteroids 750
Thoron (^{220}Rn), properties 244
Thr. See L-Threonine
L-Threonine (Thr) 333
– in blood 574
– in blood proteins 581
– degradation 397, 402
– dietary requirements 496
– in foods 516
– in milk 688
– in saliva 645
– in sweat 680
– in urine 667
– in vitamin B_{12} synthesis 484
Threonine aldolase, vitamin B_6 and 475
D-Threopentulose. See D-Xylulose
L-Threopentulose. See L-Xylulose
D-Threose 310
Thrombin 410, 622
Thrombo-asthenia, effect on blood coagulation 623
Thrombocytes 620, 621
– adenosine triphosphate 577
– amino acids 574
– cholesterol 601
Thrombocytes, count 620, 621
– diameter 620
– electrophoretic mobility 560
– enzyme activities 585
– fibrinogen 579
– glycoproteins 606
– histamine 575
– lactic acid fermentation 388
– lifetime 620
– lipids 601
– metabolism 621
– nitrogen 573
– osmotic resistance 620
– packing volume 620
– phosphatides 601
– potassium 564
– proteins 579
– protein nitrogen 572
– respiratory rate 387
– serotonin 575
– sodium 565
– specific gravity 557
– stability, effect on blood coagulation 623
– viscous metamorphosis, in blood coagulation 622
– volume 620
Thrombocyte aggregometer 625
Thrombocyte count 620, 621
Thrombocyte thrombus in blood coagulation 622
Thrombocytocrit 620
Thrombocytopenia, effect on blood coagulation 623
– thrombocyte osmotic resistance 620
Thrombo-elastograph 625
Thrombo-embolism, blood coagulation 622
Thrombopathy, thrombocyte osmotic resistance 620
Thrombopenic purpura, thrombocyte volume 620
Thromboplastins 622
Thrombosis, blood coagulation 622
– genesis 623
Thulium, properties, isotopes, etc. 241
Thulium-170, characteristics 293
Thymidylic acid. See Deoxythymidine monophosphate
Thymine 338
– degradation 401
– in DNA synthesis 352
– in protein synthesis 353
Thyminose. See 2-Deoxy-D-ribose
Thymol blue indicator 283
Thymolphthalein indicator 283
Thymus, lactic acid fermentation 388
– purine nucleoside phosphorylase 418
– respiratory rate 387
– weight 710
Thymus hormone 730
Thynnic acid 370
Thyrocalcitonin. See Calcitonin
Thyroglobulin, binding of thyroid hormones 440, 726
Thyroid, calcitonin from 729
– disease, diagnosis 289
– function, evaluation 727, 728
– – salivary iodide and 644
– – tests 287 sq.
– iodine 725
– iodine uptake 726
– effects of LATS 718
– respiratory rate 387
– scintigraphy 288, 289
– effect of thyrotropin 718
– weight 710
Thyroid hormones 287, 725 sq.
– biosynthesis 440, 726
– deficiency 449
– in plasma 726, 727
– effect on prolactin secretion 719
– effect on thyrotropin secretion 718
Thyroid-stimulating globulin (TSG) 718
Thyroid-stimulating hormone. See Thyrotropin
Thyroid-stimulating-hormone releasing factor 718, 725, 809
Thyrotoxicosis, serum glucosephosphate isomerase 600
Thyrotropic hormone. See Thyrotropin
Thyrotropin 718
– standard 762
Thyrotropin-releasing factor 718, 725
D-Thyroxine, biological activity 727
L-Thyroxine (T_4) 333, 726
– in bile 727

A detailed index to the statistical tables (pages 28–131) and chapter on Statistical Methods (pages 146–196) will be found on pages 197–198

L-Thyroxine (*contd*), binding capacity of plasma for ... 726
– biological activity ... 727
– in blood ... 288, 726, 727
– in cerebrospinal fluid ... 636
– in faeces ... 727
– in liver ... 727
– metabolism ... 288
– effect on thyrotropin secretion ... 718
Thyroxine-binding globulin ... 726
Ti. See Titanium
Tick-borne encephalitis antisera, reference reagents ... 764
Tidal volume, respiratory (V_T) ... 541, 550
Tiglic acid ... 371
Tiglyl-coenzyme A in isoleucine degradation 396
TIM. See Triosephosphate isomerase
Time units ... 205 sq.
Timnodonic acid ... 370
Tin, in blood ... 567
– in faeces ... 658
– flame lines ... 284
– properties, isotopes, etc. ... 238
– in urine ... 664
Tin-113, characteristics ... 293
Tissues, active mass, and BMR ... 539
– adipose, enzyme activities ... 585
– – effect of insulin ... 736
– – lactic acid fermentation ... 388
– – respiratory rate ... 387
– buffer capacity ... 527
– composition ... 517
– enzymes ... 584 sq.
– nonfatty, metabolic water ... 524
– organic components ... 522
– respiratory rates ... 387
– soft, radiation absorption ... 220
Tissue-specific enzymes ... 584
Titanium, flame lines ... 284
– properties, isotopes, etc. ... 235
– in urine ... 664
Tl. See Thallium
TLC (total lung capacity) ... 542
Tm. See Thulium
Tm (renal function) ... 533 sq.
Tocochromanol-3 ... 465
Tocol ... 465
Tocols ... 465
Tocopherols. See Vitamin E
α-Tocopherol ... 465
– in foods ... 499 sq.
Tocopherol-like compounds ... 466
Tocopheronic acid ... 466
Tocopheronolactone ... 466
α-Tocopherylquinone ... 466
Tocotrienols ... 465
Tolerance limits ... 150, 152, 154 sq.
– tables ... 128
Tomatoes, composition ... 506
– vitamin losses during cooking ... 498
Tomato juice, composition ... 506
Ton ... 205
Ton, metric ... 204
tonf (ton-force) ... 211
Ton-force ... 211
Tongue, composition ... 512, 513
Torr ... 212
Toxoplasma antiserum, standard ... 760
TPN (triphosphopyridine nucleotide). See Nicotinamide-adenine dinucleotide phosphate
TPP. See Thiamine pyrophosphate
tr (troy measure) ... 205
Transaldolase in pentose phosphate cycle 421, 422
Transaminases ... 394
– in bile ... 655
– in plasma ... 593, 594
– vitamin B_6 and ... 475
Transaminations, in amino-acid degradation ... 393, 397–399
– vitamin B_6 in ... 475
Transcarboxylation, biotin in ... 486, 487
Transcobalamins in serum ... 484
Transcortin ... 745
Transcription of DNA code ... 352, 353
Transferases ... 385, 386
Transferrin ... 289
– allotypy ... 634, 809
– amino-acid composition ... 581
– in bile ... 655
– characteristics and function ... 580
– in faeces ... 659
– in saliva ... 645
– in semen ... 684
Transferrin, in serum ... 580, 583
– and serum iron ... 566
– in urine ... 668
Transferring enzyme in tricarboxylic acid cycle ... 390, 391
Transfer RNA ... 351, 353
z-Transformation ... 62, 64, 65, 180
Transfusion, exchange, serum bilirubin as guide ... 577
Transfusion reaction, haemolytic ... 632
Transketolase, in pentose phosphate cycle ... 421, 422
– in plasma ... 593
Transketolase test in thiamine deficiency 470, 471
Transmural pressure, vascular ... 544
Transudates, electrolyte content ... 525
Transuranic elements, properties and isotopes ... 248
Trapezoid, geometry ... 142
TRF (thyrotropin-releasing factor) 718, 725, 809
Triacetyloleandomycin, reference preparation 762
Triacontanoic acid ... 367
Triacylglycerols. See Triglycerides
Triamcinolone ... 380
– biological activity ... 750
Triangle, geometry ... 140, 141
Tricarboxylic acid cycle ... 390, 391
– and amino-acid degradation ... 393
– in degradation of foods ... 402
Trichinella antiserum, reference reagent ... 764
Trichloracetic acid solutions, pH values ... 279
Tricosanoic acid ... 367
Tridecanoic acid ... 366
Tridecylic acid ... 366
Triene acids in serum lipids ... 604
Triethanolamine buffer ... 280 sq.
Triglycerides (*see also Fats*) ... 365, 374
– accumulation ... 456
– in bile ... 655
– in cerebrospinal fluid ... 638
– in erythrocytes ... 601
– in faeces ... 659
– formation ... 426
– enzymatic hydrolysis ... 414
– in plasma ... 601, 604
– in spermatozoa ... 685
– in synovial fluid ... 642
Trigonelline in coffee ... 509
Trigonometric functions ... 138, 139
Trihydroxycholanic acid. See Cholic acid
Trihydroxycoprostanic acid in bile ... 655
3α,11β,21-Trihydroxy-20-oxo-5β-pregnan-18-al ... 380
11β,17α,21-Trihydroxypregna-14-diene-3,20-dione. See Prednisolone
3α,17α,21-Trihydroxy-5β-pregnane-11,20-dione ... 380
3α,11β,21-Trihydroxy-5β-pregnan-20-one ... 380
3α,17α,21-Trihydroxy-5β-pregnan-20-one ... 380
11β,17α,21-Trihydroxypregn-4-ene-3,20-dione. See Cortisol
9α,11α,15-Trihydroxyprosta-5,13-dienoic acid ... 373
9α,11α,15-Trihydroxyprosta-5,13,17-trienoic acid ... 373
9α,11α,15-Trihydroxyprost-13-enoic acid ... 373
2,6,8-Trihydroxypurine. See Uric acid
D-3,5,3′-Tri-iodothyronine, biological activity ... 727
L-3,5,3′-Tri-iodothyronine (T_3) ... 333, 726
– biological activity ... 727
– in liver ... 727
– plasma binding ... 726
– test for thyroid function ... 288
Triketohydrindene ... 329
– hydrate. See Ninhydrin
4,4,14α-Trimethylcholesta-8,24-dien-3β-ol. See Lanosterol
4,4,14α-Trimethyl-5α-cholestane in steroids. 381
7,8,10-Trimethylisoalloxazine ... 472
[+]-2,4,6-Trimethyltetracos-2-enoic acid ... 372
5,7,8-Trimethyltocol. See α-Tocopherol
5,7,8-Trimethyltocotrienol ... 465
Triokinase in lactic acid fermentation ... 390
Trioses ... 308, 313
Triosephosphate in erythrocytes ... 605
Triosephosphate dehydrogenase. See Glyceraldehydephosphate dehydrogenase
Triosephosphate isomerase (TIM), in glucose 6-phosphate formation from glyceraldehyde 3-phosphate ... 422
– in glycolysis ... 389
– in plasma ... 600
Triparanol and cholesterol synthesis ... 426
Tripe, composition ... 512
Tripeptides, enzymatic hydrolysis ... 409
Triphosphopyridine nucleotide. See Nicotinamide-adenine dinucleotide phosphate
Triphosphoric monoester hydrolases ... 386
Triple point of water ... 208, 209
Trisaccharides as lipid component ... 365
Tris buffer ... 280 sq.
Trismaleate buffer ... 280 sq.
Tritium, characteristics ... 234, 292
t-RNA (transfer RNA) ... 351, 353
Tropaeolin indicators ... 283
Tropical year ... 206
Troposphere, composition ... 234 sq.
Trout, composition ... 515
Troy units ... 204, 205
Trp. See L-Tryptophan
Trunk, surface area ... 528
Trypsin ... 407
– in faeces ... 659
– inhibition, in pancreatic juice ... 652
– – in serum ... 598
– in pancreatic juice ... 653
Trypsinogen ... 407
– in pancreatic juice ... 652
Tryptamine, in blood ... 575
– in urine ... 669
L-Tryptophan (Trp) ... 333
– delayed absorption ... 452
– in blood ... 574
– in blood proteins ... 581
– cell constituents from ... 434
– dietary requirements ... 496
– in foods ... 516
– hydroxylation, dehydroascorbic acid and . 490
– 5-hydroxytryptamine from ... 441
– loading test ... 668
– metabolism ... 398, 399, 402
– – B vitamins in ... 475
– metabolites in urine ... 668
– in milk ... 688
– nicotinic acid from ... 476, 477
– in saliva ... 645
– in sweat ... 680
– in urine ... 667
Tryptophan oxygenase, effect of corticosteroids ... 749
TSG (thyroid-stimulating globulin) ... 718
TSH (thyroid-stimulating hormone). See Thyrotropin
TSH-RF (thyroid-stimulating-hormone releasing factor) ... 718, 725
Tsuzuic acid ... 368
Tubercle bacilli, lipids ... 371, 372
Tuberculins, standards ... 759
Tuberculostearic acid ... 371
Tubules, transport functions ... 534, 535
– – inborn defects ... 452
– effect of oxytocin and vasopressin ... 723, 724
Tumours, blood, enzyme changes ... 587, 588
– – glyceraldehydephosphate dehydrogenase 592
– – pyruvate kinase ... 594
– bone, leucocyte mobility ... 560
– carcinoid, blood histamine ... 575
– – blood tryptamine ... 575
– – 5-hydroxyindoleacetic acid excretion ... 669
– – plasma kinins ... 742
– – thrombocyte serotonin ... 575
Tungsten, properties, isotopes, etc. ... 241
Tunny, composition ... 515
Turkey, composition ... 514
Turnips, composition ... 506
Tylosin, standard ... 762
Typhoid antiserum, reference preparation ... 761
– vaccine, reference preparation ... 759
Tyr. See Tyrosine
Tyramine, formation from tyrosine ... 394
– in urine ... 668
Tyrosinaemia, familial ... 449
Tyrosinase. See *o*-Diphenol oxidase
Tyrosine (Tyr) ... 333
– adrenaline and noradrenaline from ... 440
– in blood ... 449, 574
– in blood proteins ... 581
– cell constituents from ... 434
– decarboxylation ... 394
– degradation ... 398, 402
– in foods ... 516
– melanin from ... 440
– in milk ... 688
– peptide-linked, in thyroid hormone formation ... 440
– from phenylalanine ... 398, 439
– in saliva ... 645

A detailed index to the statistical tables (pages 28–131) and chapter on Statistical Methods (pages 146–196) will be found on pages 197–198

Tyrosine, in sweat 680
– in urinary sediments 677
– in urine 449, 667
Tyrosine aminotransferase, effect of corticosteroids 749
Tyrosine hydroxylase in adrenaline and noradrenaline formation 440
Tyrosine iodinase in goitrous cretinism 449

U

u (atomic mass unit) 213, 226
U. See Uranium
U. See Uridine
Ubichromenols 466
Ubiquinones 403, 404, 466
Ubiquinone-50 in plasma 609
UDP. See Uridine diphosphate
UDPG. See Uridine diphosphate glucose
UDPglucose. See Uridine diphosphate glucose
UDPglucose epimerase in lactic acid fermentation 390
UDPglucose–glycogen glycosyltransferase, in carbohydrate synthesis and breakdown. 441
– deficiency 451
– in glycogen formation from glucose 420
UDPglucose pyrophosphorylase, in glycogen formation from glucose 420
– in lactic acid fermentation 390
UDPglucuronyl transferase in infantile jaundice 576
Umbilical blood. See Cord blood
UMP. See Uridine monophosphate
Undecylic acid 366
Units of measurement 200 sq.
– symbols 199
Universal time 205 sq.
Uracil 338
– degradation 401
– in RNA synthesis 352
Uraemia, gastric juice, ammonia 649
– – urea 649
Uranium, flame lines 284
– properties, isotopes, etc. 247
Uranium I (^{238}U), properties 247
Uranium II (^{234}U), properties 247
Uranium X_1 (^{234}Th), properties 246
Uranium X_2 (^{234}Pa), properties 246
Uranium Y (^{231}Th), properties 246
Uranium Z (^{234}Pa), properties 246
Urate, accumulation 453
– in blood 577
– in cerebrospinal fluid 637
– enzymatic oxidation 419
– in faeces 659
– in gastric juice 649
– glomerular filtration and excretion 536
– in milk 688
– in pancreatic juice 652
– in purine degradation 400, 401
– in saliva 645
– in semen 684
– in sweat 680
– in synovial fluid 641
– in urinary calculi 453
– in urinary sediments 677, 678
– in urine 665, 671
Urate oxidase 419
– in purine degradation 400, 401
Urd. See Uridine
Urea, in bile 654
– biosynthesis 442 sq.
– in blood 572
– in cerebrospinal fluid 637
– conversion factors 251
– in gastric juice 649
– glomerular filtration and excretion 536
– in milk 688
– osmotic activity 526
– in pancreatic juice 652
– in purine degradation 401
– in saliva 645
– in semen 683
– in sweat 680
– effect on urinary osmolarity and specific gravity 534
– in urine 665
Urea cycle 442, 443
Ureides, poisoning, porphobilinogen in 356
Ureidosuccinic acid. See Carbamylaspartic acid
Uric acid (*see also Urate*) 338
Uric acid, conversion factors 251
– in urinary sediments 677, 678
Uridine (U, Urd) 340
– pseudo-. See Pseudouridine
Uridine diphosphate (UDP) 343
– in blood 577
– in glucuronide formation 442
Uridine diphosphate *N*-acetylgalactosamine. 349
– formation and utilization 424
– sulphate 349
Uridine diphosphate *N*-acetylglucosamine 348
– formation and utilization 424
– phosphate 348
Uridine diphosphate galactose 347
– in lactic acid fermentation 390
– lactose from 420
Uridine diphosphate glucosamine 348
Uridine diphosphate glucose (UDPG) 347
– in carbohydrate synthesis and breakdown. 441
– glycogen from 420
– in lactic acid fermentation 390
– UDPglucuronic acid from 423
Uridine diphosphate glucuronic acid 348, 423
– in glucuronide formation 442
– and conjugation of oestrogens 432
– and conjugation of steroids 430
Uridine diphosphate iduronic acid from UDPglucuronic acid 423
Uridine monophosphate (UMP) 343
– biosynthesis 438, 439
– – failure of 453
– in RNA 351
Uridine triphosphate (UTP) 343
– in amino-sugar utilization 424
– in carbohydrate synthesis and breakdown. 441
– in lactic acid fermentation 390
– UDPglucuronic acid from 423
Uridylic acid. See Uridine monophosphate
Urine 661 sq.
– acetone 661, 674
– acetonitrile 668
– *N*-acetylhistamine 670
– acetylkynurenine 669
– acids 535, 536
– acidity 662
– adenine 671
– adipic acid 674
– adrenaline 668, 733
– alanine 667
– β-alanine 667
– allantoin 671
– amines 668
– aminoacetone 670
– amino acids 666, 667
– – in rickets 464
– α-aminoadipic acid 667
– *o*-aminobenzoic acid 669
– *p*-aminobenzoic acid 668
– α-aminobutyric acid 667
– γ-aminobutyric acid 667
– *o*-aminohippuric acid 666, 669
– aminoimidazole carboxamide 671
– β-aminoisobutyric acid 453, 667
– δ-aminolaevulinic acid 670
– ammonia 666
– amylase 672
– androsterone 430
– anserine 666
– arabinose 673
– arginine 667
– argininosuccinic acid 449
– aromatic acids 675
– arsenic 664
– ascorbic acid 676
– asparagine 667
– aspartic acid 667
– bacteria 677
– betaines 668
– bicarbonate 663
– bilirubin 661, 670
– biotin 676
– borate 664
– bromide 663
– bufotenine 669
– calcium 453, 664
– calculi 453
– carbohydrates 673
– carbon dioxide 663
– carnitine 668
– carnosine 666
– catecholamines 668, 733
– cells 677
– chloride 662
– cholesterol 675
Urine, choline 668
– chondroitin sulphate A 668
– chorionic gonadotropin 715
– citric acid 674
– citrulline 449, 667
– coenzyme Q_{10} 676
– colour 661
– concentration and dilution 533
– copper 664
– coproporphyrin 670
– corticosteroids 430, 746, 747
– cortisol 430
– cortisone 430
– creatine 665
– creatinine 665
– *p*-cresol 675
– cyanide 663
– cystamine 668
– cysteine 667
– cystine 667
– dehydroepiandrosterone 430
– diethyl sulphide 633
– dihydroxymandelic acid 675
– dihydroxyphenylacetic acid 675
– dimethylamine 668
– *N,N*-dimethyltryptamine 669
– dopamine 668
– electrolytes 525, 536
– enzymes 672 sq.
– 16-epioestriol 756
– epitestosterone glucuronide 752
– erythrocytes 661, 677
– erythropoietin 740
– ethanolamine 668
– fluoride 663
– folic acid 479, 676
– formic acid 674
– formiminoglutamic acid 670
– freezing-point depression 662
– fructose 450, 673
– fructose-1-phosphate 450
– furane-2,5-dicarboxylic acid 674
– galactose 450, 673
– galactose-1-phosphate 450
– glucose 673
– glucuronic acid 673
– glutamic acid 667
– glutamine 667
– glutaric acid 674
– glycine 449, 667
– glycolic acid 674
– gonadotropins 713, 714
– gonadotropin-inhibiting factor 714
– guanidine 666
– guanidinoacetic acid 666
– guanine 671
– haemoglobin 661, 671
– hexosamines 673
– hexoses 673
– hippuric acid 666
– histamine 670
– histidine 667
– histidine metabolites 670
– homocarnosine 666
– homocitrulline 667
– homocystine 449
– homogentisic acid 448, 661, 675
– hyaline casts 677
– 3-hydroxyanthranilic acid 668
– *m*-hydroxybenzoic acid 675
– *m*-hydroxyhippuric acid 666
– 5-hydroxyindoleacetic acid 669
– 3-hydroxykynurenine 669
– *p*-hydroxyphenylacetic acid 675
– hydroxyproline 449, 666, 667
– 18-hydroxytetrahydrocorticosterone 430
– hypoxanthine 671
– imidazoles 670
– imidazoleacetic acid 670
– β-imidazolylpyruvic acid 449
– indoles 669
– indole-3-acetic acid 670
– indoleacetylglutamine 670
– indoleformylglucuronide 670
– indole-3-lactic acid 670
– indoxylsulphuric acid 663, 669
– inorganic constituents 662 sq.
– inositol 673
– insulin 736
– iodide 663
– iron 664
– isoleucine 667
– keto acids 449
– α-ketoglutaric acid 674

A detailed index to the statistical tables (pages 28–131) and chapter on Statistical Methods (pages 146–196) will be found on pages 197–198

Urine (*contd*), ketone bodies ... 674
– ketopentoses ... 673
– kynurenic acid ... 669
– kynurenine ... 669
– lactic acid ... 674
– lactose ... 451, 673
– lead ... 664
– leucine ... 667
– leucocytes ... 677
– lipids ... 675
– lysine ... 667
– magnesium ... 664
– malic acid ... 674
– manganese ... 664
– maple syrup ... 448, 449
– melanin ... 661
– melanotropins ... 722
– mercaptans ... 663
– mercury ... 664
– metanephrine ... 668
– methionine ... 667
– 3-methoxy-4-hydroxymandelic acid .. 675, 733
– 3-methoxy-4-hydroxyphenylacetic acid ... 675
– 3-methoxy-4-hydroxyphenylglycol ... 675
– 5-methoxytryptamine ... 669
– α-methyl-β-alanine ... 401
– methylamine ... 668
– methylguanidine ... 666
– 1-methylguanine ... 671
– 1-methylhistidine ... 667
– 3-methylhistidine ... 667
– 1-methylhypoxanthine ... 671
– 1,4-methylimidazoleacetic acid ... 670
– methylmalonic acid ... 449, 674
– 1-methylnicotinamide ... 477, 676
– 1-methyl-2-pyridone-5-carboxylamide 477, 676
– 5-methyltetrahydrofolic acid ... 479
– molybdenum ... 664
– mucopolysaccharides ... 668
– myoglobin ... 671
– nicotinic acid ... 477, 676
– nitrate ... 664
– nitrite ... 664
– nitrogen ... 665
– – contribution to BMR ... 539
– nitrogenous substances ... 665 sq.
– non-nitrogenous metabolites ... 674, 675
– noradrenaline ... 668, 733
– normetanephrine ... 668
– odour ... 661
– oestradiol-17β ... 430
– oestriol ... 430
– oestrogens and metabolites ... 756
– oestrone ... 430
– organic acids ... 674
– ornithine ... 667
– orotic acid ... 453, 671
– osmolarity ... 533 sq., 662
– oxalic acid ... 674
– pantothenic acid ... 488, 676
– parathyroid hormone ... 728
– peptides ... 666
– pH value ... 536, 662
– phenol ... 675
– phenols ... 675
– phenylacetylglutamine ... 666
– phenylalanine ... 667
– phenylpyruvic acid ... 448
– phosphate ... 663
– phospholipids ... 675
– phosphorus ... 663
– physical properties ... 661, 662
– piperidine ... 668
– placental lactogen ... 721
– porphobilinogen ... 670
– porphyrins ... 357, 358, 454, 455, 661, 670
– potassium ... 663
– pregnancy. See under Pregnancy
– pregnanediol ... 754
– pregnanolone ... 754
– pregnenolone ... 753
– progesterone ... 753
– progesterone metabolites ... 753, 754
– proline ... 449, 667
– proteins ... 668
– purines ... 671
– pyridoxic acid ... 676
– pyrimidines ... 671
– pyrocatechol ... 675
– pyrophosphate ... 663
– pyruvic acid ... 674
– reducing substances ... 673
– riboflavin ... 471, 473, 676
– 5-ribosyluracil ... 671
Urine, sediments ... 677, 678
– serine ... 667
– serotonin ... 669
– sialic acid ... 673
– silicate ... 664
– sodium ... 663
– solutes, calorie turnover and ... 534
– – protein intake and ... 534
– specific gravity ... 661
– – osmolarity and ... 534, 535
– steroid hormones ... 430
– succinic acid ... 674
– sucrose ... 673
– 'sugar' ... 673
– sulphate ... 663
– 6-sulphatoxyskatole ... 669
– sulphur ... 663
– sulphur amino acids ... 663
– surface tension ... 661
– taurine ... 667
– testosterone ... 752
– thiamine ... 470, 471, 676
– thiocyanate ... 663
– threonine ... 667
– trace elements ... 664
– tryptamine ... 669
– tryptophan ... 667
– tryptophan metabolites ... 668
– turbidity ... 661
– tyramine ... 668
– tyrosine ... 449, 667
– urea ... 665
– uric acid ... 665, 671
– urobilinogen ... 661, 670
– urocanic acid ... 670
– uromucoids ... 668
– uropepsinogen ... 672
– uroporphyrin ... 670
– valine ... 667
– vanillic acid ... 675
– vasopressin ... 723
– viscosity ... 661
– vitamins ... 676
– vitamin B_6 ... 676
– vitamin B_{12} ... 676
– volatile acids ... 674
– volume ... 661
– – osmolarity and ... 535
– water turnover ... 524
– xanthine ... 671
– xanthurenic acid ... 669
– xylose ... 673
– L-xylulose ... 451
– zinc ... 664
Uroaldosterone ... 380
Urobilins ... 362
(+)-Urobilin ... 364
Urobilin IX-α ... 364
Urobilinogen, in faeces ... 659
– in urine ... 661, 670
(+)-Urobilinogen ... 362, 364
Urobilinogen IX-α ... 362, 363
Urocanic acid, in L-histidine degradation ... 395
– in sweat ... 680
– in urine ... 670
Urocortisol ... 380
Urocortisone ... 380
Urokinase, reference preparation ... 763
Uromucoids in urine ... 668
Uronic acids ... 312, 323
– degradation ... 401
– in plasma ... 606
Uropepsinogen in urine ... 672
Uroporphyrins ... 355, 357
– in erythrocytes ... 576
– in urine ... 670
Uroporphyrin I, accumulation ... 454
– synthesis ... 454
Uroporphyrin III in haem synthesis ... 454
Uroporphyrinogens ... 356
Uroporphyrinogen I, synthesis ... 454
Uroporphyrinogen III in haem synthesis ... 454
Uroporphyrinogen isomerase in erythropoietic porphyria ... 454
Ursodeoxycholic acid in bile ... 655
UT (Universal Time) ... 205 sq.
UTC (Coordinated Universal Time) ... 207
Uteroverdin ... 363
Uterus, enzyme activities ... 585
– effect of oestrogens ... 757, 758
– organic components ... 522
– effect of oxytocin and vasopressin ... 723, 724
– effect of plasma kinins ... 742
– effect of progesterone ... 754, 758
Uterus, proteolytic enzymes ... 410
– weight ... 710
– – gain in pregnancy ... 690
UTP. See Uridine triphosphate

V

V. See Vanadium
V (volt) ... 215, 216
$\dot{V}_A$ (alveolar ventilation) ... 542
$\dot{V}_T$ (minute ventilation) ... 542, 550
$\dot{V}_T$ (tidal volume) ... 541, 550
cis-Vaccenic acid ... 369
trans-Vaccenic acid ... 369
Vaccines, standards and reference preparations for ... 759
Vaginal secretion, β-glucuronidase ... 597
– phosphogluconate dehydrogenase ... 591
Val. See L-Valine
Valency of elements ... 234 sq.
n-Valeric acid ... 366
– in faeces ... 660
Valeryl-coenzyme A in norleucine degradation ... 396
L-Valine (Val) ... 333
– in blood ... 449, 574
– in blood proteins ... 581
– in cerebrospinal fluid ... 449
– degradation ... 395, 396, 402
– dietary requirements ... 496
– in foods ... 516
– in milk ... 688
– in saliva ... 645
– in sweat ... 680
– in urine ... 667
Vanadium, dietary requirements ... 497
– properties, isotopes, etc. ... 235
– in urine ... 664
Vancomycin, standard ... 761
VAN DEN BERGH reaction ... 576
VAN DYKE protein ... 723
Vanillic acid, from catecholamine breakdown 732
– in urine ... 675
VAN SLYKE's determination of amino acids . 329
Variance ... 158
Vascular driving and transmural pressures .. 544
– resistance ... 544
Vasopressin ... 722 sq.
– standard ... 762
– and urinary concentration ... 533
VC. See Vital capacity
Veal, composition ... 514
Vegetables, amino acids ... 516
– composition ... 502 sq.
– vitamin losses during cooking ... 498
Vegetable fat, composition ... 510
– oils, fatty acids ... 374
Velocity, angular, units ... 210
– of light ... 228
– linear, units ... 210
Venison, composition ... 514
Venous blood, pH value ... 560
– viscosity ... 558
– volume ... 554
Venous blood pressure ... 554
Ventilation (respiratory) ... 542, 543, 550
– function tests ... 543
– maximum voluntary (MVV) ... 543
– – determination from respiratory rate ... 548
Ventilation/perfusion ratio ... 544
Ventricular fluid. See Cerebrospinal fluid
Verdoglobin in blood ... 576
Verdoglobin A ... 360, 362
Verdoglobin S ... 361
Verdohaemoglobin ... 360, 362
Viomycin, reference preparation ... 761
Viral DNA and RNA, synthesis ... 352
Viscosity units ... 214
Vision, colour, plates for testing (inside back cover)
Visual acuity, plate for testing (inside back cover)
– pigments, vitamin A and ... 457
Vital capacity (VC) ... 541, 542
– nomograms ... 547
– values ... 550, 551
Vitamins ... 457 sq.
– in blood ... 609 sq.
– in cerebrospinal fluid ... 639
– dietary requirements ... 493, 494
– in faeces ... 660
– in foods ... 498 sq.
– – losses during cooking ... 498
– in gastric juice ... 650
– in milk ... 689

A detailed index to the statistical tables (pages 28–131) and chapter on Statistical Methods (pages 146–196) will be found on pages 197–198

Vitamins, in saliva 646
– in semen 685
– in urine 676
Vitamin A .... 457 sq.
– in blood 457, 609
– deficiency 460
– dietary requirements 460, 493
– in foods .... 499 sq.
– in liver 457
– in milk 457, 689
– oxidation, vitamin E in 466
– toxicity 460
Vitamin A_1. See *all-trans*-Retinol
9-*cis*-Vitamin A_1 458
11-*cis*-Vitamin A_1. See 11-*cis*-Retinol
13-*cis*-Vitamin A_1 459
Vitamin A_2 459
Vitamin A acid 457
Vitamin A alcohol 457
– transport by serum proteins 809
Vitamin A aldehyde 457
Vitamin A_1 aldehyde (*all-trans*). See Retinal
11-*cis*-Vitamin A_1 aldehyde. See 11-*cis*-Retinal
Vitamin A_2 aldehyde 459
– in visual pigments 457
Vitamin B_1. See Thiamine
Vitamin B_2. See Riboflavin
Vitamin B_6 .... 473 sq.
– antagonists 474, 475
– in blood 475, 609
– in whole body 475
– in cerebrospinal fluid 639
– deficiency 475, 476
– – xanthurenic acid excretion and 668
– dietary requirements 475, 476, 494
– in faeces 475, 660
– in foods .... 499 sq.
– in milk 689
– in organs 475
– in tryptophan metabolism 475
– in urine 676
Vitamin B_{12} .... 363, 482 sq.
– absorption 484
– in bile 484, 655
– in blood 484, 610
– in whole body 484
– in cerebrospinal fluid 639
– coenzyme functions 485
– deficiency 485
– dietary requirements 485, 494
– in faeces 660
– in foods .... 510 sq.
– in gastric juice 650
– in intestine 484
– in liver 484
– in milk 689
– pseudo- 483
– in synthesis of purines and methionine ... 479
reference preparation 763
– in semen 685
– urinary excretion test 289
– in urine 484, 676
Vitamin B_{12a} 482, 483
Vitamin B_{12b} 482, 483
Vitamin B_c. See Folic acid
Vitamin B_c conjugate. See Pteroylheptaglutamic acid
Vitamin B_T. See Carnitine
Vitamin C. See Ascorbic acid
Vitamin D .... 461 sq.
– in blood 461, 609
– calcitonin and 461
– in calcium balance 461
– deficiency 461, 464
– dietary requirements 461, 464, 494
– in foods .... 504, 510 sq.
– in milk 689
– parathyroid hormone and 461, 728
– toxicity 464
Vitamin D_2 .... 380, 462
– formation 461
– active metabolite 809
Vitamin D_3 .... 380, 462
– active metabolite 809
– standard 763
Vitamin D_4 463
Vitamin E .... 464 sq.
– in biological oxidations 404
– in blood 466, 609
– deficiency 466, 467
– dietary requirements 466, 467, 494
– in foods .... 499 sq.
– in milk 689
– in semen 685
Vitamin F. See Fatty acids, essential
Vitamin K 467, 468
– in biological oxidations 404
– in foods 502, 503, 505, 506, 510, 512
Vitamin K_1 and haemorrhagic diatheses 623
Vitamin K_2 468
Vitamin K_3 468
Vitamin $K_{(20)}$ 468
Vitamin-like substances 491, 492
Vitaminoids 491, 492
Vitamin P group 491
Vitamin PP. See Nicotinamide and Nicotinic acid
Vitellin 332
Volatile acids. See under Acids
Volemose 311
Volt 216
Volume units 203, 204

W

W (watt) 214, 216
W (wolfram) 241
Walnuts, amino acids 516
– composition 507
Water, in amniotic fluid 522
– body. See Body water
– boiling point 209
– – at various altitudes .... 252 sq.
– – tables 257, 258
– in bones and teeth 521
– density 230
– – maximum 210
– dietary requirements 496, 524
– dissociation 278, 279
– drinking, fluoridation 497
– in faeces 657
– in foods .... 498 sq.
– in gastric juice 647
– in hair and nails 520
– heavy, density 230
– ion product constant 278
– molecular weight, multiples 250
– in muscle 518
– in organs 519
– in pancreatic juice 651
– in placenta 522
– radiation absorption 220
– in saliva 643
– in semen 682
– in skin 520
– specific heat capacity 230
– in sweat 679
– in synovial fluid 640
– triple point 208, 209
– vapour, saturation pressure 256
– vapour pressure tables 257, 258
– viscosity 230
Water balance. See under Body water
Watercress, composition 506
Water-drive phenomenon 719
Watt 214, 216, 222
Waxes 365, 377
Wb (weber) 216
WBC (white blood count) 618, 619
Weber 216
Weight. See Body weight
Weight units 204, 205
Wernicke's disease 470
Whale meat, composition 514
Wheat flour, composition 508
Wheat germ, amino acids 516
– composition 508
Whey, composition 511
– protein, in milk 688
Whisky, composition 509
White blood count (WBC) 618, 619
Whole circular angle 207, 208
Whortleberries, composition 502
Wien's displacement law constant 228
Wilcoxon test .... 124 sq., 158, 192
Wilson's disease (hepatolenticular degeneration) 452
– serum, caeruloplasmin 593
– – copper 566
– – uric acid 577
– urine, copper 664
– – uric acid 671
Wine, composition 509
Wohlgemuth enzyme units 584
Wolfram 241
Work, of breathing 546, 552
– physical. See Physical effort
Work sweat. See Sweat
Work units 212, 213
Wrist, circumference during growth .... 695 sq.
– secondary ossification centres 706, 708

X

X. See Xanthosine
Xanthine 338
– calculi 453
– enzymatic oxidation 419
– in plasma 577
– in purine degradation 400, 401
– in urine 453, 671
Xanthine oxidase 419
– deficiency 453
– in milk 689
– in plasma 592
– prosthetic group 345
– in purine degradation 400
Xanthine:oxygen oxidoreductase. See Xanthine oxidase
Xanthinuria 453
Xanthochromia 635
Xanthomata 456
Xanthosine (X, Xao) 341
– in purine degradation 400
Xanthosine monophosphate (XMP) 342
– formation 436
– guanylic acid from 436
– in purine degradation 400, 401
Xanthurenic acid, in tryptophan degradation 398, 399, 475
– in urine 668, 669
Xanthylic acid. See Xanthosine monophosphate
Xao. See Xanthosine
Xe (xenon) 239
Xenon, properties, isotopes, etc. 239
Xerophthalmia 460
Xg blood-group system 632
Ximenic acid 369
XMP. See Xanthosine monophosphate
XU (X-unit) 201
X-unit 201
L-Xyloascorbic acid. See Ascorbic acid
D-Xyloketose. See D-Xylulose
L-Xyloketose. See L-Xylulose
D-Xylose 310
– in urine 673
D-Xylulose 311, 314
– 5-phosphate 318
– – in pentose phosphate cycle 421, 422
L-Xylulose 314
– in plasma 605
– in urine 451, 673
L-Xylulose reductase in pentosuria 451

Y

Y. See Yttrium
Yard 200
Yb (ytterbium) 241
yd (yard) 200
Year 206, 207
Yeast, composition 507
– nucleic acids 354
Yellow-fever antiserum, reference preparation 761
Yoghurt, composition 511
Yt blood-group system 632
Ytterbium, properties, isotopes, etc. 241
Yttrium, flame lines 284
– properties, isotopes, etc. 237
Yttrium-90, characteristics 292
– decay table 301
– therapeutic use 290

Z

Zeeman splitting constant 229
ZF (Zwischenferment). See Glucose-6-phosphate dehydrogenase
Zimmermann reaction 744
Zinc, atomic weight multiples 250
– in bile 654
– in blood 567
– in whole body 517
– in carboxypeptidase A 409
– dietary requirements 497
– in faeces 658

Index

A detailed index to the statistical tables (pages 28–131) and chapter on Statistical Methods (pages 146–196) will be found on pages 197–198

Zinc (*contd*), flame lines 284
– freezing point 209
– in leucocytes 567
– in milk 688
– in organs 519
– in pancreatic juice 652
– in placenta and amniotic fluid 522
– properties, isotopes, etc. 236
– activation of proteases 410
– in semen 683
– sulphate, decinormal solutions 277
Zinc, in sweat 680
– in synovial fluid 641
– in urine 664
Zinc-65, characteristics 292
– decay table 299
Zirconium, properties, isotopes, etc. 237
Zn. See Zinc
ZOLLINGER-ELLISON syndrome, gastric acidity 648
– gastric juice secretion 647
– gastrin 739
Zr (zirconium) 237
z-transformation 62, 64, 65, 180
Zwieback, composition 508
Zwischenferment. See Glucose-6-phosphate dehydrogenase
Zwitterions 329
Zymohexase. See Fructosediphosphate aldolase
Zymosterol in cholesterol synthesis 426, 427

Addenda

Vitamin A (page 457): The protein transporting vitamin A alcohol in human serum has been identified and given the name 'retinol binding protein' (RBP). It is present in serum as a complex with another protein of prealbumin mobility (KANAI et al., *J. clin. Invest.*, **47**, 2025 [1968]; GOODMAN, D. S., *Amer. J. clin. Nutr.*, **22**, 911 [1969]).

Vitamin D (page 461): The biologically active metabolite of vitamin D_2 (ergocalciferol) has been identified as 25-hydroxyergocalciferol (SUDA et al., *Biochem. biophys. Res. Commun.*, **35**, 182 [1969]).

25-Hydroxycholecalciferol, the metabolite of cholecalciferol, is 1.4 times as biologically active in curing rickets in rats as the parent vitamin D_3; it is also much more active than the latter in promoting bone mobilization and intestinal calcium transport (DeLUCA, H. F., *Arch. intern. Med.*, **124**, 442 [1969]). The 25-hydroxylation of cholecalciferol takes place in the liver (PONCHON et al., *J. clin. Invest.*, **48**, 2032 [1969]).

Serum transferrin groups (page 634): The number of transferrin variants identified up to 1964 was fifteen (BEARN and PARKER, in GROSS, F. [Ed.], *Iron Metabolism*, Springer, Berlin, 1964, page 60).

Thyrotropin (page 718): A polypeptide with thyrotropic activity has been extracted from the human placenta. It has some chemical similarity to thyrotropin and has been named 'human chorionic thyrotropin' (HENNEN et al., *J. clin. Endocr.*, **29**, 581 [1969]; HERSHMAN and STARNES, *J. clin. Invest.*, **48**, 923 [1969]).

Hypothalamic pituitary-regulating factors (page 725): The thyroid-stimulating-hormone releasing factor (TRF) has been isolated from the hypothalamus of sheep and pigs (Medical News, *J. Amer. med. Ass.*, **210**, 2347 [1969]). It is a peptide with the unusual structure L-pyroglutamyl-L-histidyl-L-prolinamide and has been synthesized (GILLESSEN et al., *Helv. chim. Acta*, **53**, 63 (1970).

Calcitonin (page 729): A calcitonin has been isolated from salmon and has been found to have the same basic structure as human and porcine calcitonin; with a potency of 5000 U/mg compared to 200 U/mg for porcine and 120 U/mg for human calcitonin it is one of the most potent biological substances known (COPP, D. H., *Ann. Rev. Physiol.*, **32**, 61 [1970]).

Errata

Logits and antilogits (page 56): In the table entered at 0.800, for '1.38269' read '1.38629'.

Porphyrins (page 355): In the formula of aetioporphyrin IV, pyrrole rings 2 and 4 should each contain one methyl and one ethyl group.

Gastric juice (page 650): In Remarks under 'Enzymes', for 'oxyglutarate dehydrogenase' read 'oxoglutarate dehydrogenase'.

Users of the Scientific Tables are requested to address correspondence to J. R. Geigy S.A., CH-4000 Basle 18, Switzerland

Notes